S0-CJQ-059

American Book Publishing Record Cumulative 1950–1977

An American National Bibliography

This edition of the AMERICAN BOOK PUBLISHING RECORD CUMULATIVE 1950-1977 was prepared by the R. R. Bowker Company's Department of Bibliography in collaboration with its Product Development and Marketing Department and its Publication Systems Department.

Senior Staff of the Department of Bibliography working on this project include:
Evelyn Russell, Manager, Department of Bibliography,
Beverley Lamar, Project Manager.

Senior Staff of the Systems Group includes:
Michael B. Howell, Business Systems Manager,
Leonard Levine and Daniel Wu, Senior Systems Analysts,
Harendra K. Sinha, Programmer/Analyst.

Andrew H. Uszak, Vice President and Publisher, Data Services Division.
Gertrude Jennings, Manager, Product Development and Marketing.
Debra K. Brown, Project Manager, Product Development.
Scott D. MacFarland, Research Coordinator, Product Development.

American Book Publishing Record Cumulative 1950–1977

An American National Bibliography

A cumulation of American book production for the years 1950-1977, in 15 volumes, as cataloged by the Library of Congress and recorded in the American Book Publishing Record and the National Union Catalog. Arranged by Subject according to Dewey Decimal Classification and indexed by Author and Title with a separate Subject Guide including Library of Congress Subject Tracings, Dewey Decimal Classification Numbers and Library of Congress Classification Numbers.

R.R. BOWKER COMPANY
New York, 1978

Published by the R. R. Bowker Company (a Xerox Publishing Company)
1180 Avenue of the Americas, New York, N.Y. 10036

International Standard Book Number: 0-8352-1094-4
International Standard Serial Number: 0002-7707
Library of Congress Catalog Card Number: 66-19741
Printed and bound in the United States of America

Contents

Preface

Since 1876 the R. R. Bowker Company has published a *Weekly Record* of publishing. In 1960 the first monthly cumulations of the *Weekly Record*, titled the *American Book Publishing Record*, were published. Each year, since 1960, monthly editions have been cumulated into an annual. There are three five-year cumulations: 1960-1964, 1965-1969 and 1970-1974.

The AMERICAN BOOK PUBLISHING RECORD CUMULATIVE 1950-1977 goes beyond the traditional *American Book Publishing Record* cumulation both in the increased number of years cumulated and the additional data included. It provides, in a single interfiled cumulation, some 900,000 entries, virtually every title in every field published and distributed in the United States during this 28 year span. It is essentially an *American National Bibliography*.

We chose the years 1950-1977 for our first cumulation to exceed five years because these years represent the greatest explosion of new titles in the history of publishing—one of the most significant eras in U.S. publishing.

The entries for the AMERICAN BOOK PUBLISHING RECORD CUMULATIVE 1950-1977 were compiled from books submitted to the R. R. Bowker Company by U.S. publishers and by authorized American distributors of works published in foreign countries, as well as information from the Library of Congress on MARC* II tapes already published in the *American Book Publishing Record* for the period 1960 to 1977. Thousands of titles from the *National Union Catalog* for the years 1950 to 1968 and from the Library of Congress MARC tapes for the years 1968 to 1977 that have not appeared in previous cumulations of the *American Book Publishing Record* are included.

The Dewey Decimal Classification arrangement follows the style used in monthly and annual issues of the *American Book Publishing Record*.

These 15 volumes were produced from records stored on magnetic tape, edited by computer programs and set in type by computer-controlled photo-composition. In addition to data for the years 1968-1977 already in automated form some 500,000 entries were converted to magnetic tape from the *National Union Catalog* and earlier editions of the *American Book Publishing Record* which had not been automated.

The AMERICAN BOOK PUBLISHING RECORD CUMULATIVE 1950-1977 provides optimum efficiency of access. Titles can be found by Dewey Decimal Classification, by author, by title, and by Library of Congress Subject Tracings. It is not necessary to know the exact year of publication to find a title. These and other features of the AMERICAN BOOK PUBLISHING RECORD CUMULATIVE 1950-1977 are described more fully below.

Not included in these listings are federal and other governmental publications (with the exception of some city and state government reports), subscription books, dissertations, new printings (as distinct from reprints, reissues, and revised or new editions), quarterlies and other periodicals, pamphlets under forty-nine pages, and specialized publications of a transitory nature or intended as advertising. Although the UNESCO definition of a book as a non-periodical publication of forty-nine pages or more (not including covers) is strictly observed in the statistical count of books published, books and pamphlets with fewer pages are listed when the subject is deemed to be of sufficient interest or value to merit public attention.

Certain titles appearing in the *National Union Catalog* have not had Dewey Decimal Classification numbers assigned. Since the main section of the AMERICAN BOOK PUBLISHING RECORD CUMULATIVE 1950-1977 is in Dewey Decimal Classification sequence, these unclassified titles have not been included in the first 11 volumes of this bibliography. All titles without Dewey Decimal Classification numbers are listed in Volume 12 and are accessible through the Author and Title Indexes and the Subject Guide.

Entries represent cataloging prepared by the Library of Congress, except those marked with an asterisk (*) which were prepared by the R. R. Bowker Staff. Entries without collation are Cataloging in Publication (C.I.P.) data from recent editions of the *American Book Publishing Record* for which completed L.C. cataloging was not received before this edition went to press. Preliminary C.I.P. entries and Bowker-cataloged entries have been replaced by full L.C. cataloging where possible. Entries

*Machine Readable Cataloging (MARC).

dated from 1974 on reflect the new ISBD (M) † cataloging which introduces a new system of formal punctuation as well as a number of other changes. A full explanation is supplied in the Revised Chapter Six of the Anglo-American Cataloging Rules (AACR) as well as in other professional publications. Briefly, the ISBD format divides the monographic bibliographic description into seven areas: (1) title and statement of authorship, (2) edition, (3) imprint, (4) collation, (5) series, (6) notes, and (7) ISBN, binding, and price. On the Library of Congress printed cards, each of these areas is divided from the following by a period-space-dash-space (. —) unless the paragraphing and/or topography clearly delineate them. In the AMERICAN BOOK PUBLISHING RECORD CUMULATIVE 1950-1977 entry, this period-space-dash-space convention will not be used. Additionally, the ISBN-binding-price area has been positioned after the Library of Congress call number(s), secondary Dewey number (if present), and card number.

Entry information includes: main entry, title (in italics), subtitle, author statement, publication place, publisher, publication date, collation, series statement, general note or contents note, L.C. Classification number (in brackets), Dewey Decimal Classification number (except entries in Volume 12), L.C. card number, price when available, and tracings. New or obscure publishers' addresses were added to entries originally published in the *American Book Publishing Record*. Entries originally published in the *American Book Publishing Record* include prices that were current when they were originally published. *National Union Catalog* and MARC entries added to the AMERICAN BOOK PUBLISHING RECORD CUMULATIVE 1950-1977 database which have not been published in the *American Book Publishing Record* before may not have prices. The ISBN (International Standard Book Number) is recorded for each volume (where one is assigned), and in multivolume works and variant editions the volume, edition, or part to which each number applies is identified. All ISBN numbers have been validated by a special computer program. A small percentage of ISBNs from MARC or the *National Union Catalog* which could not be validated as accurate numbers have not been included in this publication for the benefit of all users of this important book information system. When not specified, the binding is cloth.

ARRANGEMENT

The fifteen volumes of the AMERICAN BOOK PUBLISHING RECORD CUMULATIVE 1950-1977 are arranged as follows: the main section consists of non-fiction titles filed in numerical sequence by Dewey Decimal Classification numbers. Volume 1 contains GENERALITIES (000-099), 26,214 entries, and PHILOSOPHY AND RELATED SUBJECTS (100-199), 25,076 entries; Volume 2 contains RELIGION (200-299), 50,832 entries; Volumes 3 and 4 contain THE SOCIAL SCIENCES (300-399), 97,526 and 97,766 entries respectively; Volume 5 contains LANGUAGE (400-499), 11,517 entries and PURE SCIENCES (500-599), 68,678 entries; Volumes 6 and 7 contain TECHNOLOGY (APPLIED SCIENCES) (600-699), 60,998 and 60,523 entries respectively; Volume 8 contains THE ARTS (700-799), 63,488 entries; Volume 9 contains LITERATURE (BELLES-LETTRES) (800-899), 73,902 entries; Volume 10 contains GENERAL GEOGRAPHY AND HISTORY (900-999), 102,711 entries; Volume 11 contains adult FICTION and JUVENILE FICTION sections, 72,557 and 40,395 entries respectively, arranged by author. Volume 12 consists of entries which do not have Dewey Decimal Classification numbers and, therefore, could not be listed in the other volumes. It was decided that, although these entries represent a small proportion of the total number of entries, they should be included in a separate volume in the interest of making this bibliography as complete as possible. The entries in Volume 12 are arranged in main entry sequence and are fully accessible through the Author and Title Indexes and the Subject Guide. The Author Index refers the user to Volume 12 as well as giving the appropriate Dewey Decimal Classification number citations for titles in the numerically sequenced volumes. The Title Index gives a reference to Volume 12 with the author's name in parentheses. The Subject Guide gives the subject tracing, the author's last name in parentheses and the Library of Congress Classification number, where applicable. Volume 13 is the AUTHOR INDEX; Volume 14 is the TITLE INDEX; Volume 15 is the SUBJECT GUIDE, which includes Library of Congress Subject Tracings, Dewey Decimal Classification Numbers and Library of Congress Classification Numbers. In volumes containing two Dewey Decimal Classification sequences the second sequence also begins on page 1, following a page identifying the beginning of the sequence.

In both the Author and Title Indexes reference to the main section is given by the first nine digits of the Dewey Decimal Classification number except entries listed in Volume 12. The prime marks within the Dewey Decimal Classification numbers divide those numbers into segments. An example would be as follows: 796.3576'-4'0924. This service was initiated by the Library of Congress to enable libraries that find some Dewey Decimal numbers too long for their purposes to cut the numbers logically without having to assign the task to professional persons. Entries in the FICTION and JUVENILE FICTION sections are referenced in the author and title indexes by a section code, i.e. FIC and JUV respectively, with the author's last name in parentheses in the title index.

THE SUBJECT GUIDE—VOLUME 15

The Subject Guide represents the correlation between the subject tracings, Dewey Decimal Classification and Library of Congress Classification numbers. The Subject Guide is arranged alphabetically by the traced subjects, author names and uniform titles represented in the AMERICAN BOOK PUBLISHING RECORD CUMULATIVE 1950-1977. In response to requests from users personal names used as subject tracings and traced uniform titles, which were not included in the Subject Indexes to the 1976 and 1977 annual editions of the *American Book Publishing Record,* have been added

†International Standard Bibliographic Description for Monographic Publications

to the Subject Guide of the AMERICAN BOOK PUBLISHING RECORD CUMULATIVE 1950-1977.

The Subject Guide entry is designed to show the corresponding Dewey Decimal Classification and Library of Congress Classification numbers for each traced subject. The related Dewey Decimal Classification numbers are listed in numerical sequence following the tracing, when more than one is present. This listing provides access to all Dewey Decimal Classification numbers as originally classified and can therefore serve as a survey of the retrospective numbers used (see 'Provisions for Dewey Decimal Classification Number Changes' for further information). Similarly, the Library of Congress Classification numbers are listed in alpha-numeric sequence enclosed in brackets following the Dewey Decimal Classification numbers. Sample entries are given below:

Abdomen—Radiography. 617.550757 [RD540]
Abdomen—Surgery. 617.55 [RD540]
Abdominal pain. 616; 616.026; 617.55; 618.1075; 618.923 [RC944; RG103; RJ446]
Abel, Rudolf. 327.1 [UB271]
Abelian groups. 512.86 [QA3; QA171]
Aberconway abbey. 255.12094292 [BX2596]

A total of 233,830 tracings are represented in this volume. Of that total 185,877 are traced subjects, 46,458 traced author names and 1,486 traced uniform titles.

PROVISIONS FOR DEWEY DECIMAL CLASSIFICATION NUMBER CHANGES

In compiling the AMERICAN BOOK PUBLISHING RECORD CUMULATIVE 1950-1977, a major factor taken into consideration was how to accommodate the 3,760 relocations in the Dewey Decimal Classification schemes that spanned the 28 years of publishing covered. A relocation is defined as an adjustment in the tables resulting in the shifting of a topic from the number provided in the previous edition to a number in the present edition that differs.

The 15th Edition, published in 1952, contained 1,015 such relocations from the 14th Edition. The 15th Edition was used concurrently with the 14th Edition through November, 1958. Two divisions were revised, 300-309, Social Sciences, and 920-929, Biography. Upon publication of the 16th Edition in 1958, 1,603 relocations were made from both the 14th and 15th Editions. The 16th Edition restored 528 numbers as they were in the 14th Edition, initiated 498 additional revisions from the 14th, reaffirmed 487 and added 90 new relocations from the 15th Edition. Schedules 546 and 547 were remodeled for inorganic and organic chemistry in this edition. The 17th Edition, published in 1965, reflected 746 relocations from Edition 16, approximately half as many changes as from the 15th to the 16th Edition. Schedule 150, Psychology, reused 65 numbers and relocated 27 topics. The currently used 18th Edition reflects only 396 relocations, again approximately half the total of changes from the 16th to the 17th Edition. Schedules 340 and 510, Law and Mathematics respectively, were remodeled. Again, 14 numbers were reused with new meanings.

These conditions made it necessary to pose the question of whether to change the retrospective titles to conform to the current 18th Edition or to retain the original classifications of the Library of Congress. The first consideration was to reclassify but upon further examination it was decided to retain the integrity of the original cataloging. Without the publications in hand it would not have been possible to assign Dewey Decimal Classification numbers as precise as the original assignments. Computer-assignment was considered, but this would have resulted in the assignment of a general Dewey Decimal Classification number as opposed to the specific cataloging that the Library of Congress originally assigned.

To facilitate the use of original cataloging retained in the AMERICAN BOOK PUBLISHING RECORD CUMULATIVE 1950-1977, a Table of Relocations for Dewey Decimal Classification Numbers has been provided. This Table should be consulted to survey the changes between the past editions and the present. Only numbers appear in this table, for details of the topics consult the general tables of the 15th, 16th, 17th or 18th editions of the *Dewey Decimal Classification and Relative Index*.

The following are examples of relocation from the 17th to the 18th Edition: 001.42 relocated to 001.433; 001.425 was discontinued and relocated to 001.434; all of 246.3 was relocated, some to 246.53 and some to 247.3; 001.555 has been discontinued and its contents moved to the broader number 001.55. Similar conditions obtain in changes between other editions.

Numbers enclosed in brackets, beginning with relocations from the 16th to the 17th Edition, denote complete relocations, these numbers being no longer in use. Numbers not in brackets have lost part of their meaning through relocation but still retain some of their original meaning. Numbers followed by an asterisk have been discontinued as a result of schedule reduction.

A Table of Obsolescent Dewey Decimal Classification Numbers is also provided listing 70 three-digit numbers not in use and designating the edition in which they were last used.

Also note that the Subject Guide to the AMERICAN BOOK PUBLISHING RECORD CUMULATIVE 1950-1977, Volume 15, can be used as an access to all Dewey Decimal Classification numbers represented in this work.

The *Weekly Record* ($15.00 per year U.S.A.) formerly a section of *Publishers Weekly* and now a separate publication is published in 51 weekly issues a year. The *American Book Publishing Record*, published monthly ($23.75 per year U.S.A.), cumulates the *Weekly Record*. Annual cumulatives of the *American Book Publishing Record* for the years 1965 through 1969 and 1974 through 1978 are available at $45.00 per volume. Three five-year cumulatives are available at $110.00 per set. They cover the years 1960-1964, 1965-1969 and 1970-1974. The prices given are those in effect at the date of this publication.

The R. R. Bowker Company has used its best efforts in collecting and preparing material for inclusion in the AMERICAN BOOK PUBLISHING RECORD

CUMULATIVE 1950-1977 but does not assume, and hereby disclaims any liability to any party for any loss or damage caused by errors or omissions in the AMERICAN BOOK PUBLISHING RECORD CUMULATIVE 1950-1977 whether such errors or omissions result from negligence, accident or any other cause.

In one way or another almost every member of Bowker's Data Services Division has contributed to this project. Gertrude Jennings, Manager of Product Development and Marketing for the Data Services Division was responsible for the concept and design of the AMERICAN BOOK PUBLISHING RECORD 1950-1977. Debra Brown, Senior Project Manager, was responsible for technical liaison with the Publication Systems Group and direction of computer processing. Scott MacFarland, Research Coordinator, handled production of the front matter. Beverley Lamar made a major contribution in the role of Project Manager with responsibility for management and quality control of hundreds of thousands of entries and the staff editing them.

It is not possible to mention all the individuals whose contributions to this project were indispensable. Among them are: Evelyn Russell, Manager, Department of Bibliography, Enea Bacci, Senior Database Production Manager, Susan Olson, Senior Database Production Manager, Lewis Borress, Editorial Coordinator, Angela Barrett and Constance Pierce, Assistant Editors of *Weekly Record,* and Michael Goodman and Richard Wininger, editorial assistants and other members of the staff of the Department of Bibliography; Gary Ink, Database Production Manager, and members of the Serials Bibliography Department; Michael B. Howell, Business Systems Manager, Leonard Levine and Daniel Wu, Senior Systems Analysts, and Harendra K. Sinha, Programmer/Analyst of the Publication Systems Department; Susan J. Brown, Systems Consultant; Francis J. McWade, Data Processing Operations Manager, and his staff.

Our special appreciation to Robert F. Asleson, President of the R. R. Bowker Company and Andrew H. Uszak, Vice-President and Publisher of the Data Services Division, for their guidance and encouragement in completing this project.

Gertrude Jennings, *Manager, Product Development and Marketing*

Debra K. Brown, *Senior Project Manager, Product Development*

Table of Relocations of Dewey Decimal Classifications Numbers

From Edition 15	To Edition 16
546.1	546.2
546.12	546.731
546.12	546.732
546.12	546.733
546.12	546.734
546.12	546.735
546.17	546.711
546.17	546.712
546.17	546.715
546.17	546.716
546.17	546.718
546.2	546.721
546.2	546.723
546.2	546.724
546.2	546.726
546.2	546.728
546.28	546.512
546.28	546.513
546.28	546.514
546.28	546.681
546.28	546.683
546.29	546.751
546.29	546.752
546.29	546.753
546.29	546.754
546.29	546.755
546.29	546.756
546.3	546.381
546.3	546.382
546.3	546.383
546.3	546.384
546.3	546.385
546.3	546.386
546.4	546.391
546.4	546.392
546.4	546.393
546.4	546.394
546.4	546.395
546.4	546.396
546.5	546.684
546.5	546.686
546.5	546.688
546.56	546.652
546.56	546.654
546.56	546.656
546.58	546.661
546.58	546.662
546.58	546.663
546.6	546.401
546.6	546.403
546.6	546.411
546.6	546.412
546.6	546.413
546.6	546.413 5
546.6	546.414
546.6	546.415
546.6	546.415 5
546.6	546.416
546.6	546.416 5
546.6	546.417
546.6	546.417 5
546.6	546.418
546.6	546.418 5
546.6	546.419
546.6	546.419 5
546.6	546.421
546.6	546.422
546.6	546.424
546.6	546.43
546.6	546.432
546.6	546.434
546.6	546.44
546.6	546.442
546.6	546.444
546.6	546.448
546.6	546.449
546.66	546.671
546.66	546.673
546.66	546.675
546.66	546.677
546.66	546.678
546.7	546.621
546.7	546.623
546.7	546.625
546.71	546.541
546.71	546.543
546.71	546.545
546.75	546.332
546.75	546.534
546.75	546.536
546.8	546.522
546.8	546.524
546.8	546.526
546.9	546.632
546.9	546.634
546.9	546.636
546.9	546.641
546.9	546.643
546.9	546.645

From Edition 16	To Edition 17
[002]	001.552
[002]	655
[006]	001.51
[006]	001.53
[007]	001.4
010	020.75
010	029.7
016	011
019	017.5-.8
020.6	021.7
[020.713]	023.5
021.62	027.4
[021.65]	027.4
021.85	025.26
[021.89]	340
[021.93]	025.26
[022.2]	022.3
[022.2]	368
022.3	727.8
[023.3]	021.82
[023.8]	658.322 2
[023.8]	658.325
025.11	657.834
[025.175]	025.172
025.35	021.64
025.52	027.424
027.574 71	027.68
027.7	027.68
028.8	025.54
[029.1]	371.302 81
[029.3]	025.172
[029.3]	651.53
[029.6]	808.02
[040]	080
069.09	069.2
[069.6]	651
[069.6]	657.834
[070.13]	340
[070.3]	658
070.43	808.066
081	082
081	083-089
082	081
082	083-089
094	093
099	001.552 3
111.1	142.7
131	152
131.3	614.58
[131.34]	150.195
[131.34]	616.891 7
[132]	157
[134]	154.7
135	154.6
[135.37]	154.3
[136]	155
137	155.2
[144.2]	146.4
[150.13]	158
[150.192 4]	150.198 2
150.72	152
[151]	153.9
[151.3]	156
[152.2]	152.15
152.3	152.166
152.4	152.167
152.5	152.182
[152.6]	152.188
[152.7]	153.7
153.1	153.23
153.3	153.24
[153.5]	153.46
[153.6]	153.43
153.8	154
154	153.1
155	153.3
156	153.44
157	152.4
158.1	152.44
158.3	152.3
158.4	152.32-.33
158.5	152.35
[158.8]	152.38
[159.1]	153.83
[159.2]	153.8
[159.3]	155.24
[159.4]	152.5
[178.5]	340
179.9	177.7
220.47	220.5
220.6	220.013
[220.88]	809.935 22
[223.3]	223.2
[223.4]	223.2
[223.5]	223.2
[223.5]	264
[223.6]	223.2
232.93	232.92
[232.931]	232.91
[232.931 7]	246.9
[232.931 8]	242.74
[232.931 8]	245
[232.931 8]	248
232.932	246.9
232.932	248
232.933	246.9

From Edition 16	To Edition 17
232.933	248
232.958	232.963 5
235.2	246.9
235.2	248
[237]	236.2
242	248.3
242	252
243	252
[248.37]	242
254	651
254.8	331.2
[261.6]	261.87
[261.75]	261.5
[262.6]	262.91-.93
[262.82]	262.91
[263.8]	340
264.022	264.024
264.023	264.024
[264.026]	264.023
[264.029]	264.020 09
[264.039]	264.030 09
[266.021]	266.09
271	248.894
[271.96]	271.901
274-279	266
[280.1]	262.001
284	280.4
[284.7]	284.1
[285.3]	285.1
[285.4]	285.1
[285.5]	285.1
[285.6]	285.1
[291.12]	200.19
291.61	291.63
291.64	291.63
[294.300 2-.300 8]	294.34-.38
[294.31]	294.34-.38
[294.31]	294.391
[294.32]	294.34-.38
[294.32]	294.392
[294.552]	294.556
[294.554]	294.551 2
[294.598]	294.548
297.89	297.88
[301.158]	301.18
[301.424]	301.41
[301.424 3]	350.764
[301.425]	301.414
301.426	301.414
301.426	362.82
301.43	301.186
[321.025-.028]	321.08
[321.2]	321.12
321.6	321.14
321.6	321.9
321.9	321.07
[323.34]	301.452 2
[323.41]	323.5
[323.61]	340
323.64	323.632
323.67	323.631
324.25	324.24
324.273	329.025
325.1	301.32
326	301.452 2
326	323.3
[326.1]	380.144
[326.92]	s.s. 092
[326.92]	920
328.37	328.1
328.4-.9(08)	328.4-.9(05)
329.01	329.1-.8
[330.19]	000-999
[331.16]	347.9
[331.26]	340
[331.284 7]	331.281 647
[331.68]	331.63
[331.82]	613.62
[331.823]	614.85
[331.83]	362.85
[331.833]	301.54
[331.85]	374
331.86	331.55
[331.880 8]	364.143
[332.14]	332.178
[332.27]	332.178
332.423	332.424
[332.43]	332.152
[332.43]	332.42
332.56	332.42
332.64	350.825
333.33	658
[333.34]	340
[333.34]	350.825
[333.35]	340
333.5	333.012
335.3	335.2
336.2	350.724
336.25	336.23
[337]	350.827
[337]	382
338	350.82
338	380.1
338.12	338.762-.769
338.17	338.13
338.45	338.06
338.45	338.1-.3
338.526	340
338.542	338.49
338.76	338.64
338.76	338.65
[339.420 7]	640.73
[340.9]	800
341.11-.18	336.091 6
341.11	060
[348]	262.9
[348]	290
351.1	351.001
351.3	s.s. 076
351.3	352.005
351.4	351.167
[351.54]	355.115 1
[351.744]	658
[351.79]	351.74
[351.792]	359.97
[351.94-.95]	340
[351.98]	351.992
352.008	352.007
352.008	352.009
352.03-.09	352.000 9
352.1	336
352.7	352.5
352.9	352.4
355.13	174.9
[355.232]	350.755
[355.232]	363.35
[356.182]	356.184
358.18	358.12
358.4	353.63
358.4	354
362.15	362.83
362.19	362.781 9
362.61	362.62
[362.72]	362.73
363	329.006
[364.123]	364.127 9
364.13-.17	364.3
364.13	364.14
[364.5]	340
364.76	350.84
365.6	350.84
368	340
368	350.825
368	658.8
368.23	368.24
368.364	368.384
368.572	368.092
368.576	368.093
368.576	368.24
368.576	368.384
[370.75]	370.71
371.1	371.201-.202
371.103	370.193 1
[371.16]	331.2
[371.17]	331.252
[371.211-.212]	372.11-.18
[371.213]	373.12-.18
[371.214]	378.105
371.26	371.281
[371.291 3]	371.282
371.33	371.396
[371.365]	371.895
[371.393]	371.381
371.425	331.115
371.425	331.702
[371.426]	373.246
[371.426]	374.013
[371.427]	371.425 2
371.5	371.102
371.53	371.891
[371.55-.56]	371.54
[371.622]	022
[371.622]	069.2
[371.66]	371.623
371.67	371.624
[371.72]	371.712
[371.73]	613.7
[371.732 2]	372.86
[371.74]	371.892
[371.74]	796
[371.75]	371.893
[371.75]	796
[371.76]	372.37
[371.76]	613.07
371.805	371.897
[371.857]	373.12-.18
371.86	371.625
371.895	791.62
371.895	792.022-.028
371.895	800
[371.927]	371.914
371.97	370.193 42
371.97	370.193 44
372.2	372.11-.18
[372.214]	372.64
[372.215]	372.87
[372.415]	372.62
[372.42]	372.63
372.5	372.66
[372.51]	372.6
[374.24]	374.22
374.8	374.29
376	372
376.8	378.4-.9
[377.2]	370.114
[377.4]	377.8
[377.5]	377.8
[378.13]	378.155 4
378.242	808.02
[378.32]	001.44
[378.99]	378.013
[379.14]	340
379.15	350.85
[379.16]	378.05
[379.17]	379.2
[379.175]	371.872
[379.175]	379.153 5
380	341.57
380	347.7
380	350.87
380	363.6
380	658
382	380.1
[383.148]	383.143 8
[383.22]	769.56
384	001.5
384	301.16
385	380.5
[385.9]	388.5
386.45	386.46
[387.129]	387.109
388.33	388.34-.35
391	746.9
[396]	301.412
[396.2]	340
398.3	391-395
398.32	398.23
[408.7]	417.2
[408.9]	401.3
[408.9]	499.99
410	418.02
411	414
[419.25]	411
[421.4]	421.52
[421.8]	423.1
[424]	422-423
[424]	428
[434]	432-433
[434]	438
439	430
439.2	439.1
439.4	439.1
[444]	442-443
[444]	448
[454]	452-453
[454]	458
[464]	462-463
[464]	468
[469.9]	469.794
[474]	472-473
[474]	478
[479.3]	471-476
[479.3]	478
[484]	482-483
[484]	488
[489.1]	480
491	411-418
491.49	491.45
[491.54]	491.992
[491.83]	491.82
[492.5]	492.29
[494.813]	494.827
[494.821]	494.81
[494.822]	494.81
[494.826]	494.81
[495.5]	495.49
[495.5]	495.87
[496.2]	496.1
496.3	496.92
[496.4]	493.7
[496.4]	496.3
[499.6]	499.15
520.1	520.9
520.78	522.1-.6
521.6	523.98
[523.14]	523.12
[526.88]	912.014 8
[526.89]	655.383
[530.101]	530.01
530.8	530.15
530.8	530.16
[531.017]	531.015 17
[531.26]	531.162
[531.36]	531.163
[532.3]	532.2
532.56	532.517
533.13	533.28
[534.16]	534.52
534.2	534.47
[534.59]	534.47
[534.6]	534.46
[541.25]	541.222
[541.25]	541.242
[541.383]	541.28
[541.396]	541.224
[541.396]	541.244
[541.396]	541.246
[541.6]	541.223
541.7	541.225
[541.901 5]	541.26

From Edition 16	To Edition 17
544.6	545.83
544.8	545.84
544.83	544.85
[544.84]	544.834
[544.84]	544.925
546	544
548.84	548.86
548.85	548.86
549.53	549.525
549.74	549.528
550.1	551.701
551.313	551.315
[551.32]	551.314
[551.33]	551.314
551.4	910
551.46	551.470 8
551.518	551.517
551.559	551.553
551.565	551.566
551.565	551.567
551.572	551.574
[551.572 4]	551.575
[551.572 4]	551.576
[551.572 8]	551.577 3
[551.573]	551.577
[551.573 3]	551.578 1
[551.573 5]	551.578 4
[551.573 5]	551.578 7
[551.573 5]	551.579
[551.573 8]	551.68
[551.59]	551.6
[551.726]	551.731
553.3	553.1
553.46	553.499
553.499	553.465
553.499	553.492
553.64	553.636
[571]	913
572	390
[572.4]	398.23
573.3	573.2
[574.167]	574.166 7
[574.193]	574.192 5
[574.194]	574.192 6
[574.194]	574.192 7
[574.196]	574.192 9
575.1	573.21
575.2	573.22
577.8	575.5
[581.193-.196]	581.192
[581.462]	586.046
[581.463-.467]	582.046
583.53	583.38
[591.193-.196]	591.192
[598.139]	598.119
[600.74]	607.34
[600.78]	602.8
[606.4]	607.34
[606.4]	607.39
611.67	611.62
612.115	612.117
[612.648]	612.652
614	340
614	350.77
[614.25]	331.2
[614.25]	338.47
[614.25]	658.883
[614.548]	614.547 8
614.772	614.599 6
615.2	615.19
615.406 5	338.47
[615.845 3]	615.832 3
615.89	615.882
[615.923-.924]	615.925
[615.926-.929]	615.925
[615.93]	615.952
615.94	615.952
616.132	616.136
[616.843]	616.852 8
[616.952]	616.951 5
[616.952 3]	616.951 8
617.53	617.523
[617.554 8]	617.554 7
618.45	617.96
[618.895]	617.96
[620.03]	620.002 12
[620.04]	620.002 22
[620.07]	340
[620.08]	620.002 72
[620.09]	620.008
[620.101]	620.3
[620.102]	620.2
620.112 3	620.112 9
[621.01]	621.402 1
[621.22-.23]	621.21
[621.300 4]	621.319 2
[621.300 7]	340
[621.300 7]	352.923
[621.300 8]	621.302 72
[621.300 9]	621.308
621.313 6	621.316
[621.381 8]	621.389
[621.384 154]	621.384 133
621.922	621.914
[622.001]	622.021
[622.007]	340
[622.009]	622.08
[622.41]	622.81
[623.32]	623.271
623.38	623.371
623.38	623.375
623.38	623.737
623.38	623.77
623.43	623.633
623.43	623.747 5
[623.454 4]	623.731 3
[623.53]	623.513
[623.54]	623.514
[623.56]	623.516
623.732-.733	623.734-.735
623.823	623.820 4
[623.831]	623.819
623.852	623.850 3
623.864	623.856
623.88	340
[624.27]	624.37
625.81-.86	625.881-.886
[625.892]	625.147
[625.892]	625.792
627.12	627.14
[627.6]	627.24
[628.28]	628.742
628.39	628.168 2
[628.41-.43]	628.742
[628.49]	628.445
[628.52]	628.53
628.54	628.168 3
629.133 2	629.132 52
629.133 2	629.134
629.133 3	629.132 52
629.133 3	629.134
629.135 1	629.135 2
[629.138 8]	629.4
[629.213]	336.2
[629.213]	340
[629.213]	350.875-.878
[629.213]	629.282 6
630	657.863
630	658
630.717	630.715
631.42	631.407 2
[631.75]	338.22-25
632.58	581.65
633.82	633.83
[634.12]	634.11
[634.24]	634.23
[634.26]	634.25
634.32	634.31
[634.324]	634.34
[634.722-.724]	634.721
[634.922]	581.5
[634.925]	333.75
[634.927]	333.75
634.928	658.3
[634.94]	581.5
[634.94]	582.160 5
634.985	634.972 1
[634.986 2]	634.975 186
[634.986 5]	633.895 2
[634.986 5]	634.973
634.987	634.973
635.4	635.51
635.4	635.56
[635.966 3–.966 4]	745.92
[636.081 3]	636.01
636.088 2	636.088 6
636.088 2	636.088 8
636.088 3	636.088 4
[636.108 13]	636.101
[636.208 13]	636.201
[636.235]	636.234
[636.237]	636.236
[636.308 13]	636.301
[636.390 813]	636.390 1
[636.408 13]	636.401
[636.508 13]	636.501
[636.708 13]	636.701
[636.74]	636.73
[636.808 13]	636.801
[636.92]	636.088 4
637.141	637.142 2
[638.51]	639.75
639.27	639.13
[639.279 9]	639.14
[639.379 9]	639.39
[639.6]	639.73
641.1	641.33–.39
641.3	338.19
641.3	390
641.563	641.562 7
641.563	641.579
641.6	641.865 2
646.01	391
[646.73]	646.72
[647.969 8]	647.98
[647.969 9]	647.99
[647.97]	647.94
[651.1]	658.2
651.26	651.8
[651.34]	658.3
[651.38]	658.32
[651.42]	658.312 1—.312 2
[651.71]	651.29
651.74	808.066
[652.4]	655.2–.3
655.325	655.315
655.4–.5	658.8
[655.6]	340
[657.64]	657.45
[658.14]	658.15
[658.156]	658.155
[658.157]	658.155
658.16	658.152
[658.17]	658.153
658.3	658.407
658.311	658.312 5–.312 8
658.312 4	658.302
[658.381]	658.312 1–.312 2
658.386	658.312 43
[658.39]	658.402
[658.58]	658.202
[658.77]	658.72
658.873	658.870 2–.870 3
658.874	658.870 1
[658.877]	658.870 6
658.9	658.022
659.101 15	659.101 9
[661.7]	661.894
[662.3]	662.26
[663.8]	641.874
[664.729]	664.722 73
[664.729]	664.756
[664.802 8]	664.028
[664.83]	664.152
[665.32]	664.36
665.822	665.73
[665.825]	665.89
[666.159]	661.43
666.72	662.92
[668.47]	668.372
668.62	668.64
[668.7]	661.8
[671.9]	669.04
[676.29]	676.280 27
[676.44]	661.802
677.4	667.39
681.14	621.381 95
[681.84]	621.389 3
[684.2]	684.16
[684.8]	684.08–.09
[685.37]	685.367
687.11–.13	687.14
687.11–.13	687.16
687.2	687.16
692.1–.2	720.223
692.8	331.2
[692.9]	340
[692.9]	352.922
693.522	693.544
[694.7]	694.67
[694.8]	694.68
[696.9]	340
[696.9]	352.926
697.3	697.03
697.507 8	697.07
[706.9]	702.3
[706.9]	704.01–.89
[706.9]	706.5
708	745.1
708.9	708.29
709.03	709.024
709.3–.9	709.011
[711.17]	340
[711.17]	711.061
[711.51]	340
726.8	725.597
[729.36]	729.35
730.9	732.2
[736.3]	737.6
[738.88]	738.027 8
[739.21]	739.202 78
[739.228 8]	739.220 278
[741.591]	741.593–.599
759.1–.9	759.011
759.9	759.29
[769.41]	760.277–.278
[770.281]	661.808
[770.69]	770.23
780.071	174.9
780.071	780.23
[780.85]	780.29
781.3	786.3
781.3	786.7
781.61	784.028
781.62	784.015
[781.632]	785.028 4
781.633	781.634
781.973	781.972
[781.98]	655
782.07	782.107
782.08	782.13
782.08	782.813
782.08	792.84
782.12	782.107 3
782.95	792.84
[783.66]	783.65
[784.106 8]	784.106 1–.106
784.4	781.7
[784.5]	784.079
784.61	784.96

From Edition 16	To Edition 17
784.95	782.07
785	780.01—781.97
785	781.91
785.1	785.066–.068
[785.107]	785.066–.068
785.12	785.13
[785.132–.134]	785.135
785.41	785.066 6
785.42	785.066 7
785.42	785.067 2
785.43	785.067 5
[785.46]	785.066 2
[785.46]	785.11
[785.46]	785.3
[785.46]	785.5
[785.46]	785.8
[785.47]	785.066 3
[785.47]	785.11
[785.47]	785.3
]785.47]	785.5
[785.47]	785.8
787.1	787.01
[787.108 1]	787.109 2
787.5	787.05
788.1	788.01
788.5	788.05
788.6	788.056
789.1	789.01
789.69	788.9
791.4	790.2
791.43	384.8
[791.432]	808.066
719.44	384.54
[791.442]	806.066
791.45	384.554
[791.452]	808.066
791.53	745.592 2
792.2	792.7
[793.1]	792.022–.028
793.9	736.98
794.7	796.346
797.14	797.124
797.14	797.125
797.23	797.24
798.2	636.108 88
[798.48]	798.401
799	639.9
799.21	799.202 83
799.24	799.25
799.27	799.255–.259
799.31	799.202 83
[804]	809
[808.9]	899
[809.94–.99]	809.893–.899
810.8	818.1–.5
[869.9]	869.01–.84
[870.81]	878.01–.04
879	870.1–878.04
[880.81]	888.01–.03
889	880.1–888.03
901.9	913.03
910.4	904
911	913
[912.2]	912.198 12
913	914–919
914–919	390.09
[920.002]	808.066
[940.318]	000—999
[940.49]	940.302 2
[940.531 8]	000–999
[940.549]	940.530 22
941.949	940.27
[941.605]	941.609
[943.056]	943.055
[970.2]	s.s. 092
[970.2]	920
970.5	000–999
970.6	000–999
[972.01]	970.4
[972.014]	970.3

From Edition 16	To Edition 17
[972.015]	970.3
[972.801]	970.4
[972.810 1]	970.4
[972.820 1]	970.4
[972.830 1]	970.4
[972.840 1]	970.4
[972.850 1]	970.4
[972.860 1]	970.4
[972.901]	970.4
[972.910 1]	970.4
[972.920 1]	970.4
[972.930 1]	970.4
[972.940 1]	970.4
[972.950 1]	970.4
[973.39]	973.302 2
[973.529]	973.520 22
[973.629]	973.620 22
973.784	917.503 7
[973.79]	973.702 2
[973.899]	973.890 22
[980.2]	s.s. 092
[980.2]	920
980.5	000–999
980.6	000–999
[982.01]	980.4
[983.01]	980.4
[984.01]	980.4
[985.01]	980.3
[985.01]	980.4
986.201	980.4
[987.01]	980.4
[989.201]	980.4
[989.501]	980.4
[s.s. 04]	s.s. 08
[s.s. 058]	s.s. 025
[s.s. 069]	174
[s.s. 071 4]	s.s. 071 54
[s.s. 081]	s.s. 092
[s.s. 083]	s.s. 021 2
[s.s. 083]	s.s. 021 6
[s.s. 084]	s.s. 022
[s.s. 085]	s.s. 029
[s.s. 088 7]	s.s. 027 5
area 3–9	area 171 2
area 36	area 174
[area 394 5]	area 33
area 4	area 182 2
[area 431 1]	area 438 3
[area 431 1]	area 474 7
[area 431 1]	area 475
[area 431 2]	area 438 2
[area 431 3]	area 438 4
[area 431 4]	area 438 5
[area 431 6]	area 431 7
[area 431 6]	area 438 1
[area 431 6]	area 438 2
[area 431 75]	area 435 1
[area 432 3–432 8]	area 432 2
[area 434 23]	area 435 5
[area 434 25]	area 434 3
[area 435 7]	area 434 1
[area 435 8]	area 434 1
[area 435 8]	area 434 3
[area 436 55]	area 497 3
[area 436 7]	area 497 3
[area 436 8]	area 453 92
[area 436 8]	area 453 93
[area 436 8]	area 497 2
[area 436 8]	area 497 3
[area 436 9]	area 497 2
area 437 3	area 437 2
[area 437 4]	area 438 6
[area 437 4]	area 477 1
[area 437 5]	area 477 1
[area 437 5]	area 498 4
[area 439 15]	area 497 1
[area 439 15]	area 498 4
[area 439 2]	area 498 4
[area 439 3]	area 497 2
[area 439 4]	area 497 2

From Edition 16	To Edition 17
[area 439 5–439 6]	area 497 42
[area 497 5]	area 497 45
[area 498 5]	area 477
[area 513 7]	area 513 8
[area 517 1]	area 575
[area 517 6]	area 517 7
[area 518 85]	area 518 4
[area 526]	area 577
[area 527]	area 577
area 53	area 174
[area 532]	area 538
[area 533 4]	area 533 5
[area 534]	area 533 5
area 536	area 538
[area 538 3]	area 536 3
[area 538 5]	area 536 5
[area 538 7]	area 536 7
[area 541 45]	area 549 2
[area 541 9]	area 549 8
[area 542 3]	area 549 12
[area 542 6]	area 549 6
[area 542 7]	area 549 7
[area 544 5]	area 543
[area 544 6]	area 547 5
[area 544 7]	area 547 5
[area 545 3]	area 545 2
[area 545 4]	area 545 5
[area 545 8]	area 549 14
[area 545 9]	area 549 16
area 547	area 549 1—549 2
area 548 2	area 548 1
[area 548 5]	area 548 7
[area 548 9]	area 549 3
[area 548 9]	area 549 5
area 549	area 548 4
[area 561 7]	area 563
[area 566 4]	area 479 2
[area 568]	area 569 1
[area 569 3]	area 174
[area 582–583]	area 581
[area 588]	area 549 15
[area 588]	area 558
[area 592]	area 591
[area 598—599]	area 597
[area 619]	area 612
[area 624 1]	area 625
area 67	area 174
[area 676 8]	area 677 3
[area 677 2]	area 677 3
[area 683]	area 684
[area 689 2]	area 689 1
[area 689 3]	area 689 1
area 698	area 699
[area 712 8]	area 714 17
[area 714 19]	area 719
[area 729 71]	area 729 73
[area729 71]	area 729 74
[area 729 71]	area 729 75
[area 729 71]	area 729 76
[area 729 71]	area 729 77
[area 755 415]	area 755 416
[area 761 28]	area 761 29
area 763 355	area 763 36
area 764 87	area 764 9
area 783 4	area 783 5
area 784 3	area 784 5
area 786 5	area 786 8
area 9	area 142
[area 969 32]	area 969 9
[area 971 2]	area 973
area 98	area 701

From Edition 17	To Edition 18
001.42	001.433
[001.425]	001.434
[001.426]	001.432
[001.429]	001.433
[001.555]*	001.55
[001.92]*	001.9
026–027	021.7
[070.11]	174.909 7
[164]	511.3
245	264.2
[246.3]	246.53
[246.3]	247.3
246.6	247.11
[247.6]	246.56
[247.9]	246.55
[258]	361.75
[265.65]	262.935
[273.23]*	273.2
[273.25]	meaningless
[287.84–.86]	meaningless
[287.88–.89]	meaningless
[289.522–.523]*	289.52
[294.553]	294.6
[301.152 2]	301.157
[301.152 3]	301.154
[301.153]	301.242
[301.186]	322.43
301.2	301.63
[301.245–.246]*	301.24
[301.37]	309.1
[301.402]	301.185
[301.403]	meaningless
[301.404]	meaningless
[301.405]	301.183 2
[301.406]	meaningless
[301.412 1–.412 9]*	301.412
[301.413]	301.417
301.422	301.429
301.426	301.418
301.426	301.427
[301.428 5]	301.427
[301.446]	301.452
[301.447]	301.451
[301.448]	301.451
[301.452 1]*	301.45
[301.452 2]	301.449 3
[301.452 3]	301.441
[301.453]	301.451
[301.47]	362.1–.4
[311.2]	001.422
[311.2]	519.5
[311.3–.4]	310.6
[320.13]	320.157
[320.155]	320.17
[320.158]	320.54
[320.159]	320.54
[320.18]	meaningless
[321.7]	321.8
[323.111]	322.1
[323.111]	323.3
[323.12]	323.11
[323.2]	322.42
[323.35]	meaningless
[324.23]	329.022
[325.22]*	325
328.1	060.42
[328.368]	328.38
[329.022 4]*	329.022
[329.04]*	329
[329.05]	301.154 332 9
330.153	330.155
[330.161]*	330.16
[330.162]	338.521
[330.163]	339.201
[331.112]	331.12
[331.113]	331.133
[331.115]	331.128
[331.116]	331.89
[331.122]	331.259 6
[331.134]	331.891 5
[331.138]*	331.13
[331.15]	331.891 4
[331.18]	331.04
[331.19]	331.09
[331.218]*	331.21
331.255	331.257 6

From Edition 17	To Edition 18
[331.57]	331.117 32
[331.582]	331.117 34
[331.584]	331.51
[331.66]	333.563
[331.67]	331.544
[331.81]	331.257
[331.86]	331.259 2
331.893	331.892 6
[332.13]	332.123
[332.172]*	332.1
[332.24]	332.12
332.41	332.420 42
[332.428]	332.427
332.46	332.404 3
[332.52]	332.427
[332.53]	332.404 4
[332.61]	332.642
[332.633 2]	332.632 3
[332.633 3]	332.632–.632 7
[332.754]*	332.75
[332.78]	332.1–.3
[333.334]	333.5
[333.55]	333.335
[333.6]	333.337
333.7–.9	333.1–.5
333.78	333.95
335.411	335.412
335.413	320.532
335.42	329.072
[335.432]	329.078
[335.44]	329.07
[336.202–.204]*	336.2
[336.21]	336.294
[336.271]	336.294
[336.271 1–.271 3]*	336.271
[336.273]	336.16
[336.274]	336.16
[336.294 2–.294 4]*	336.294
[336.295]	339.52
[338.012]*	338.01
[338.013]	338.51
[338.016]	338.512
[338.016]	338.521
[338.016]	338.521 2
[338.016]	338.604 6
[338.018 2]	338.604 6
[338.018 3]	338.09
[338.018 5]	338.604 8
[338.018 6]	338.6
[338.019]	338.009
[338.064]*	338.06
338.1–.4	338.6
[338.12]*	338.1
[338.22]*	338.2
[338.25]*	338.2
[338.32–.36]*	338.3
338.4	380.3
338.4	380.5
[338.42]*	338.4
[338.49]*	338.4
338.64	338.632
338.65	338.644
338.7	338.04
339.42	339.47
339.46	339.43
340.1	171.2
340.3	340–348
340.4	347.052
340.4	345.056
340.5	340.2
[340.6]	614.19
341	341
341.12	341.22
341.13	341.23
341.18	341.24
341.2	341.026
341.2	341.1
341.2	341.37
341.2	341.66
341.3	341.6

From Edition 17	To Edition 18
341.31	341.58
341.31	341.6
341.31	341.63
341.31	341.67
341.32	341.66
341.33	341.65
341.35	341.64
341.36	341.63
341.36	343.01
341.37	341.63
341.39	341.68
341.4	341.488
341.4	341.77–.78
341.41	341.69
341.49	341.488
341.52	341.47
341.52	341.63
341.57	341.44
341.57	341.75
341.59	340.9
341.6	341.52
341.63	341.52
341.65	341.58
341.67	341.73
341.672	341.73
341.674	341.73
341.675	341.73
341.7	341.33
341.8	341.33
342–349	342–348
342	342
342.01	342.023
342.02	342.024–.029
343	345
343	345.05
343	345.05–.08
343.1	345.05
343.1	345.06
343.1	345.064
343.1	345.066
343.1	345.07
343.1	345.072–.075
343.1	345.072
343.1	345.075
343.2	345.077
343.3–.7	345.02
343.3–.7	345.07
344	342.062
345	348
345.1	348.022
345.2	348.023
345.3	348.026
345.4	348.04
345.5	348.046
346	348
346.1	348.022
346.2	348.023
346.3	348.026
346.4	348.04
346.5	348.046
347	340.57
347	346
347.1	346.012
347.2	346.043
347.3	346.047
347.4	346.02
347.4	346.029
347.42	346.072
347.5	346.03
347.5	346.032
347.6	346.015
347.65	346.052–.057
347.65	346.052
347.7	346.029
347.7	346.07
347.75	343.096
347.8	340.57
347.8	347
347.9	347.01
347.9	347.05–.08

From Edition 17	To Edition 18
347.91	347.07
347.91	347.075
347.92	347.072
347.93	347.055
347.94	347.06
347.94	347.064
347.94	347.066
347.94	347.072–.075
347.95	347.077
347.95	347.08
347.96	347.016
347.98	347.012
347.99	347.05
347.99	347.07
349.37	348.370 23
349.371	348.370 2
349.372	348.370 23
349	348
349	348.022
349	348.023
349	348.026
349	348.04
349	348.046
[350.007]	350.995
[350.009 12–.009 14]*	350.009 1
[350.122]	350.103
[350.162 6]	350.15
[350.167]	350.147
[350.175]	350.147
[350.4]	350.1–.3
350.85	379
[350.870 2–.870 6]*	350.87
[350.871 02–.871 06]*	350.871
[350.872 202–.872 206]*	350.872 2
[350.872 302–.872 306]*	350.872 3
[350.92]*	350
[352.000 93–.000 99]*	352.03–.09
[352.004]	324.2
355.022	301.593
355.022	301.633 4
355.133 2	343.014
[355.225 5]*	355.225
[355.611]*	355.6
[355.613]*	355.61
[355.614]*	355.6
[355.622 3]	657.835
[356.2]*	356
362.1	651.5
[362.15]	362.198 2
[362.62]	362.5
[362.62]	362.7
[362.731]*	362.73
[363.236]*	363.2
[363.243]	365.3
[363.245]*	363.2
[363.248]	363.232
[363.36]*	363.3
[363.612–.613]*	363.61
[364.127 9]	364.128
[364.140 6]	364.106
364.143	364.106 7
364.155	364.185
364.163	364.162
364.163	364.165
[364.178]	364.187
364.3	364.13–.18
364.61	364.68
[364.64]*	364.6
[364.682–.684]*	364.68
[364.7]	365
[366.9]	366.009
[368.014 5]*	368.014
[370.193 32]	370.116
[370.193 34]	370.115
[371.104 2–.104 6]	371.104
[371.13]	379.157
[371.142]	370.196 3
[371.235]*	371.23

From Edition 17	To Edition 18
[371.255]*	371.25
[371.264 2–.264 4]*	371.264
[371.281–.282]*	371.28
[371.307 81–.307 82]*	371.307 8
[371.371–.373]*	371.37
[371.381–.383]*	371.38
[371.391]	370.196 2
[371.425 1–.425 3]*	371.425
[371.48]	371.404 4
[371.626–.628]	690.7
[371.871–.872]*	371.87
[371.891–.895]*	371.89
[371.98]	371.97
[372.413]	372.43
[373.231]*	373.23
373.243	373.222
[374.291–.292]*	374.29
[376.7]*	376
[378.102]	658.159 32
[378.123]	370.196.3
[379.121 22]*	379.121 2
[379.121 24]	379.322
[379.121 42]*	379.121 4
[379.121 44]	379.324
[379.132–.134]*	379.13
379.15	379.34
379.152	379.151
[379.152 1]	379.158
[379.152 2]*	379.15
382.3	382.17
[383.143 5–.143 8]*	383.143
[383.144 7–.144 8]*	383.144
[385.29]*	385.2
[387.122–.125]*	387.12
[387.549]*	387.54
[387.749]*	387.74
388.322	388.321
[388.329]*	388.32
[388.349]*	388.34
388.46	388.413 22
390	301.2
391.7	391.65
[392.32]	301.421
[392.33]	301.421
392.37	394.1
395.3	395.54
[398.323]	398.47
[398.324]	398.356
398.362	398.363
[398.37]	398.41
399	394.9
[418.022]*	418.02
[418.028]	029.756
419	001.56
[479.1]	440
[492.49]	437.947
[496.91]	493.72
[496.92]	496.392
510	511.5
511	513
511.1	513.5
511.2	513.2
511.2	513.25
511.2	513.4
511.207 8	513.028
511.3	513.23
511.7	513.22
511.8	513.93
512	512.92
512	512.923
512.21	512.942
512.22	512.924
512.22	513.24
512.5	512.925
512.6	512.93
512.7	512.922
512.8	512.02
512.8	519.3
512.81	512.7
512.81	512.73

From Edition 17	To Edition 18
512.81	512.74
512.812	515.783
512.815	512.3
512.815	512.4
512.817	511.3
512.817	512.7
512.82	512.94
512.83	512.943
512.86	512.2
512.865	512.7
512.87	512.944
512.88	512.944
512.89	511.32
512.89	512.55
512.89	512.57
512.893	512.53
512.895	512.5
512.896	512.57
512.896	512.943
512.897	512.5
513	516
513	516.2
513.1	516.2
513.8	516.9
513.8	516.93
513.83	514
513.83	514.2
513.83	514.23
513.83	514.24
513.83	514.7
513.84	516.9
514	516.24
514	516.34
515	604.201 516
515	516.6
516	516.3
516.5	516.35
516.5	516.352
516.57	516.5
516.7	516.36
516.7	516.373
516.7	516.377
516.74	516.36
516.83	515.63
517	515
517	515.242
517	515.42
517.2	515.33
517.21	515.243
517.28	515.37
517.3	515.43
517.32	515.43
517.32	515.52
517.35	515.53
517.35	515.785
517.352	515.55
517.355	515.243 3
517.36	515.983
517.37	515.45
517.38	515.35
517.382	515.352
517.383	515.353
517.4	515.64
517.5	515.7
517.5	515.73
517.52	515.8
517.6	511.7
517.6	515.62
517.6	515.623
517.6	515.624
517.6	515.625
517.6	519.4
517.7	515.722 3
517.8	515.9
517.8	515.98
517.81	515.223
517.85	515.9
519	519.5
519	519.82
519.1	519
519.1	519.2
519.1	519.233
519.1	519.287
519.6	519.5
519.7	001.539
519.7	519.54
519.8	519.535
519.8	519.536
519.92	519.7
519.92	519.703
519.92	519.72
519.93	519.52
519.93	519.86
[521.11–.16]*	521.1
[522.21–.27]*	522.2
[522.41–.46]*	522.4
[522.51–.58]*	522.5
[522.71–.78]	522.7
[522.91–.98]*	522.9
[523.016–.017]	522.68
[523.13]	574.999
[523.24]*	523.2
[523.28]	523.007 4
[523.28]	523.207 8
[523.29]*	523
[523.34]	919.91
[523.35]*	523.3
523.63	523.64
523.66	523.64
523.67	523.64
523.81–.83	523.84–.85
523.86	523.84–.85
523.87	523.84–.85
[530.123]*	530.12
[531.23–.25]*	531.2
[531.52]*	531.5
[532.8]*	532
[533.14]*	533.1
[533.8]*	533
[534.12–.15]*	534.1
[534.8]*	534
[536.8]*	536
[537.11]	530.141
537.12	530.141
[537.16]	530.44
[537.64]*	537.6
[537.8]*	537
[538.8]*	538
539.72	539.754
539.721 6	539.721 14
[539.721 9]*	539.721
541	546
[541.345 4]*	541.345
[542.9]*	542
543–545	546
[543.1–6]	Scatter
[544.08]*	544
[545.085]	545.81
[545.086]	545.4
[545.087]	545.3
[545.088]	545.82
[546.1]	541.39
[546.11]*	546
[546.440 1–.440 2]*	546.44
[547.09]*	547
[547.33]	Scatter
[547.49]*	547.4
[547.868]*	547.86
[548.812–.814]*	548.81
[549.118]*	549.11
[552.01–.02]*	552
[553.69]*	553.6
[572.7]	301.2
[574.192 99]*	574.192 9
[574.55]	574.524
[576.164]	660.62
[576.2]	574.29
[576.2[	581.29
[576.2]	591.29
[576.4]	574.2
[576.4]	581.2
[576.4]	591.2
[577.011–.013]*	*577*
[577.2–.6]*	577
[577.7]	574.2
[577.7]	581.2
[577.7]	591.2
[577.8]	574.36
578	502.8
[578.1]	535.332
[578.46]*	578.4
[578.7–.8]	069.53
581.12	581.133
[581.134]	581.31
[581.135]	581.3
[581.139]	581.374
[581.17]	581.31
[581.172]*	581.17
[581.27]*	581.2
[581.28]	632
[581.522 5–.522 6]	581.522
[581.524 2–.524 5]	581.524
[581.533]*	581.53
[581.55]	581.524
583.135	583.124
583.216	583.214
583.48	583.687
583.57	583.58
583.8	583.54
583.87	583.88
[583.89]	583.87
[583.899]*	583.89
[584.37]	584.38
[589.26]	589.256
[589.28]	589.258
[589.62]	589.4
[589.62]	589.481
[589.8]	589.46
[591.34]*	591.3
[591.51]*	591.5
[591.55]	591.524
[595.13]	595.182
[595.131]	595.184
[595.133]*	595.13
[595.135]	595.186
[595.135]	595.188
[595.15]	595.145
[595.16]	595.146
[595.17]	595.147
[595.174–.176]	595.17
[595.178]*	595.148
598.201 3	639.978 2
610.695 2	617.023 2
[611.012]	616.043
[612.018]	612.028
[612.215]*	612.21
612.26	612.39
[612.5]	612.014 26
[612.57]	612.39
[612.59]	612.014 46
[612.811 5–.811 6]*	612.811
[613.119]*	613.1
[613.18]	613.5
[613.92–.93]*	613
[613.97]	613.043
[614.2]	350.824 3
[614.351–.354]*	614.35
[614.37]*	614.3
[614.82]*	614.8
[614.843–.846]	628.925 2–.925 4
[615.369]*	615.36
[615.49]*	615.4
[615.831 9]*	615.831
[616.075 5]*	616.075
[616.092]*	616.09
[616.159]*	616.15
616.49	618.19
[616.699]*	616.69
[616.858 39]*	616.858 3
[616.927 9]*	616.927
617.549	618.19
[617.601 8]	617.601
[617.951–.959]	617.4–.5
[618.78]*	618.7
[620.112 8]	621.8
[620.112 8]	624.177 2–.177 9
[620.39]*	620.3
[621.11]*	621.1
[621.13]	625.261
[621.14]	629.229 2
[621.165 1–.165 3]*	621.165
[621.183 6–.183 8]*	621.183
[621.184 1–.184 7]*	621.184
[621.194 1–.194 3]*	621.194
[621.197 2–.197 7]*	621.197
[621.28]	681.2
[621.312 2–.312 3]	621.312 1
[621.313 1]*	621.313
[621.317 2–.317 8]*	621.317
[621.319 223–.319 225]*	621.319 22
[621.319 8]*	621.319
[621.328]	621.319 24
[621.329]	621.366
[621.381 76]*	621.381 7
[621.384 121–.384 128]*	621.384 12
[621.386 2–.386 3]*	621.386
[621.386 92]*	621.386 9
[621.386 93]*	621.386
[621.387 9]*	621.387
[621.41]*	621.4
[621.438]*	621.43
[621.489]*	621.48
[621.49]*	621.4
[621.68]	628.925 2
[622.81–.86]*	622.8
[623.34]*	623.3
[623.59]*	623.5
[623.864]*	623.86
[624.199]*	624.19
[624.9]	690.15
[625.71]*	625.7
[625.78]*	625.7
[625.89]*	625.8
[627.135 9]*	627.135
[627.79]*	627.7
[628.93]	628.95
[629.133 39]*	629.133 3
[629.135 9]*	629.135
[629.136 14–.136 15]*	629.136 1
[629.138]*	629.13
[629.233]	629.232
[629.42]	629.475
[629.49]*	629.4
[630.11]	301.35
[630.11]	901.9
[630.208]	631
[631.459]*	631.45
[621.88]	631.810 72
[634.989]*	634.98
[641.11]*	641.1
[641.15]*	641.1
641.3	641.2
[647.1]	640.42
647.2–.6	640.46
[651.263–.269]	Scatter
[651.372]	651.371
[651.41]	651.32
[651.44]*	651.4
[651.85–.89]*	651.8
[652.322–.324]*	652.32
[655]	686
[655.1–.3]	686.2
[655.328]	686.44
[655.4–.5]	070.5
[655.7]	686.3
657.2	657.1
[657.422–.424]*	657.42
657.6	657.45

From Edition 17	To Edition 18
[658.023 2–.0235]*	658.023
[658.023 6]	658.18
658.153	658.152
658.154	658.155 2
658.154	658.787
[658.311 22–.311 23]*	658.311 2
[658.312 3]	658.306
[658.312 9]	658.314
[658.386]	658.312 4
[658.501]	658.403
[658.502]	658.403 2
[658.503 2–.503 5]*	658.503
[658.505]	658.054 044
[658.506]	658.054 25
[658.507]	658.054 042
[658.511–.513]*	658.51
658.516	658.562
[658.561]	658.53–.54
[658.788 3]	658.155 3
[659.112 7]*	659.112
[659.132 5]*	659.132
[659.137–.138]*	659.13
[659.153]*	659.15
[661.29]*	661.2
[661.36]*	661.3
[664.24]*	664.2
[664.33]*	664.3
[671.739]*	671.73
[674.282–.287]*	674.28
[677.399]*	677.3
[679.9]	604.6

From Edition 17	To Edition 18
[681.12]	681.2
[681.13]	681.418
[684.088]*	684.08
[684.7]	688.6
[687.101]	746.92
688.765 4	658.53
[694.28]	694.202 8
[696.8]	696.1
[697.32]*	697.3
[697.507 3–.507 8]*	697.507
[697.51]*	697.5
[698.124]*	698.12
[698.128]	667.9
701.8	702.8
[708.01–.07]	069
[725.99]	meaningless
[726.779 9]	726.78
[728.2]	728.31
[728.34]	728.31
[731.1]	730.18
[740.1–.9]	741.01–.09
741	745.61
[741.4]	741.018
[741.4]	741.2
[744]	604.2
[744.424]	720.28
[744.428]	526.86
[746.445]	746.3
[769.3]*	769
[771.534]	661.808
[772.2]	686.42

From Edition 17	To Edition 18
[778.1]	686.4
[778.311]*	778.31
[778.315]	686.43
[778.33]	621.367 3
778.34	621.367 2
[778.352–.353]*	778.35
[780.071–.074]*	780.07
[780.075]	350.854
785.062 3–.062 9	785.073
[790.019]	790.19
790.023	790.13
[791.430 22]	791.433
[791.440 22]	791.443
[791.450 22]	791.453
796.48	796.98
879.9	840
[892.49]	839.09
[909.097 4]	909.04
[910.001]	910.01
[910.002–.008]	910.2–.8
[910.093–.099]	910.9
914–919	914–919
[0974]	06
930–990	930–990
[00974]	004
[943.910 2–.910 5]	943.902–.905
[966.201–.205]	966.230 1–.230 5
[966.601–.603]	966.620 1–.620 3
[966.801–.805]	966.830 1–.830 5
[967.501–.503]	967.510 1–.510 3
[s.s. 010 9]	s.s. 09

From Edition 17	To Edition 18
s.s. 018	s.s. 072 3
[s.s. 018 5]	s.s. 072 4
[s.s. 018 6]	s.s. 072 2
[area 166]	area 162–167
[area 416 3]	area 416 93
[area 416 7]	area 416 97
area 421 2	area 421 42
area 421 2	area 421 43
area 421 4	area 421 32
area 421 5	area 421 44
[area 421 9]	area 421 8
area 422 1	area 421 79
area 422 3	area 421 77–421 78
area 425 5	area 425 62
area 426 7	area 421 72–421 76
[area 434 27]*	area 434 2
[area 477 6]	area 477 17
[area 612 2]*	area 612
[area 613]	area 612
[area 614]	area 612
area 648	area 646
[area 763 355]*	area 763 35
area 796 32	area 796 59
[area 91]	area 598
[area 911 5]	area 595 3
[area 914]	area 599
[area 92]	are 598
[area 99]	area 989
lang. sub. 802 8	029.756

Table of Obsolescent Dewey Decimal Classification Numbers

Three-Figure Numbers not in Use

Number	*Last Used in Edition*	*Number*	*Last Used in Edition*
002	16	307	16
004	never	308	16
005	never	311	17
006	16	313	14
007	16	337	16
008	never	396	16
009	never	397	16
040	16	404	16
041	16	424	16
042	16	434	16
043	16	444	16
044	16	454	16
045	16	464	16
046	16	474	16
047	16	484	16
048	16	504	16
049	16	517	17
104	16	518	15
132	16	524	14
134	16	571	16
136	16	626	14
151	16	654	14
163	16	655	17
164	17	656	14
237	16	689	14
244	15	699	14
256	14	744	17
257	14	762	14
258	17	768	14
298	11	775	14
302	16	776	14
303	16	777	14
304	16	804	16
305	16	991	17
306	16	992	17

American Book Publishing Record Cumulative 1950–1977

An American National Bibliography

VOLUME 2

200-299

Religion

200-299
Religion

200 RELIGION

ABRAVANEL, Isaac, 1437-1508. 200
Maimonides and Abrabanel on prophecy, by Alvin Jay Reines. Cincinnati, Hebrew Union College Press, 1970. lxxxi, 239 p. 24 cm. Translation of selections from Perush 'al Sefer Moreh nevukhim (romanized form) Includes bibliographical references. [BS1198.A2713] 73-119106
1. Moses ben Maimon, 1135-1204. Dalalat al-ha'irin. 2. Prophets. I. Reines, Alvin Jay, 1926- ed. II. Title.

ADLER, Felix, 1851-1933. 200
Creed and deed: a series of discourses. New York, Arno Press, 1972 [c1877] iv, 243 p. 22 cm. (Religion in America, series II) Contents.Contents.—Immortality.—Religion.—The new ideal.—The priest of the ideal.—The form of the new ideal.—The religious conservatism of women.—Our consolations.—Spinoza.—The founder of Christianity.—The anniversary discourse. Appendix: The evolution of Hebrew religion.—Reformed Judaism, I, II, III. [BL50.A33 1972] 76-38430 ISBN 0-405-04051-2
1. Religion—Addresses, essays, lectures. 2. Ethics—Addresses, essays, lectures. 3. Ethical culture movement—Addresses, essays, lectures. I. Title.

ADLER, Mortimer Jerome, 1902- 200
Religion and theology, by Mortimer J. Adler and Seymour Cain. Prefaces by John Cogley [and others] Chicago, Encyclopaedia Britannica, 1961. 278 p. 21 cm. (The Great ideas program) Bibliography: p. 271-278. [BT77.3.A3] A 63
1. Theology—Study and teaching. 2. Religion—Study and teaching. I. Cain, Seymour, 1914- joint author. II. Title. III. Series: The Great ideas program, 4

AGINES, Charles S. 200
God doesn't live here any more, by Charles S. Agines. Boston, Branden Press [1970, c1969] 148 p. 23 cm. Autobiographical. [BL2790.A35A3] 76-76469 4.00
1. Christianity—Controversial literature. I. Title.

ALLEGRO, John Marco, 1923- 200
The end of a road [by] John M. Allegro. New York, Dial Press, 1971. 184 p. 22 cm. [BL2775.2.A44 1971] 77-145179 5.95
1. Christianity—Controversial literature. I. Title.

ALLEGRO, John Marco, 1923- 200
The sacred mushroom and the cross; a study of the nature and origins of Christianity within the fertility cults of the ancient Near East, by John M. Allegro. [1st ed. in U.S.] Garden City, N.Y., Doubleday [1970] xxii, 349 p. illus. (part col.), maps. 24 cm. Includes bibliographical references. [BL444.A44 1970b] 73-111140 7.95
1. Mushrooms (in religion, folk-lore, etc.) 2. Fertility cults—Near East. 3. Christianity—Origin. I. Title.

AMBERLEY, John Russell, viscount, 1842-1876. 200
An analysis of religious belief. New York, Arno Press, 1972. iv, 745 p. 23 cm. (The Atheist viewpoint) Reprint of the 1877 ed. [BL80.A6 1972] 76-161318 ISBN 0-405-03621-3
1. Religions. I. Title. II. Series.

BALLOU, Robert Oleson, 1892- 200
The nature of religion [by] Robert O. Ballou. New York, Basic Books [1968] vi, 246 p. 22 cm. (Culture & discovery) Bibliography: p. 229-236. [BL48.B36] 68-22858
1. Religion. I. Title.

BARTLETT, Frederic Charles, Sir, 1887- 200
Religion as experience, belief, action, by Sir Frederic Bartlett. London, New York, G. Cumberlege, 1950. 38 p. 24 cm. (Riddell memorial lectures, 22d ser.) Includes bibliographical references. [BL50.B346] 73-172237
1. Religion. 2. Experience (Religion) I. Title. II. Series.

BARTON, George Aaron, 1859-1942. 200
The religions of the world. New York, Greenwood Press [1969, c1919] xiii, 414 p. 23 cm. Includes bibliographies. [BL80.B3 1969] 74-90469 ISBN 8-371-22163-
1. Religions. I. Title.

BERRIGAN, Daniel. 200
The raft is not the shore : conversations toward a Buddhist/Christian awareness / Daniel Berrigan, Thich Nhat Hanh. Boston : Beacon Press, [1975] 139 p., [3] leaf of plates : ill. ; 21 cm. (Beacon paperback ; 523) [BL50.B46] 75-5287 ISBN 0-8070-1124-X : 7.95. ISBN 0-8070-1125-8 pbk. : 3.45
1. Religion—Addresses, essays, lectures. I. Nhat Hanh, Thich, joint author. II. Title.

BIERSTED, Sonja. 200
A humanist's view of religion; the sword of the spirit. New York, Philosophical Library [1966] 151 p. 22 cm. [BR124.B5] 65-27460
1. Christianity—Miscellanea. I. Title.

BLAIKLOCK, E. M. 200
Why I am still a Christian. Compiled and edited by E. M. Blaiklock. Grand Rapids, Mich., Zondervan Pub. House [1971] 176 p. 21 cm. (A Zondervan horizon book) Includes bibliographical references. [BT1105.B5] 79-143799
1. Apologetics—20th century—Addresses, essays, lectures. I. Title.

BLISS, Kathleen. 200
The future of religion [Baltimore] Penguin [1972, c.1969] x, 193 p. 18 cm. (Pelican book) Bibl.: p. 182-186 [BL48.B56] ISBN 0-14-021366-X pap., 2.25
1. Religion. 2. Religions. I. Title.

BRANDEIS, Donald, 1928- 200
A faith for modern man. Grand Rapids, Baker Book House, 1961. 129p. 23cm. [BT77.B75] 61-18798
1. Theology, Doctrinal—Popular works. I. Title.

BROWN, Opal Hartsell. 200
The cross, the cow, or the prayer rug. Philadelphia, Dorrance [1970] viii, 194 p. 22 cm. Bibliography: p. 193-194. [BL80.2.B76] 71-116752 4.95
1. Religions. 2. Voyages around the world. I. Title.

BULTMANN, Rudolf Karl, 1884- 200
Essays, philosophical and theological. New York, Macmillan [1955] xi, 337p. 22cm. (The Library of philosophy and theology) Translation by J. C. G. Greig of the author's Glauben und Verstehen: gesammelte Aufsatze, II. [BT15.B] A56
1. Theology—Addresses, essays, lectures. 2. Philosophy, Modern—Addresses, essays, lectures. I. Title. II. Series.

CHATEAUBRIAND, Francois August Rene, vicomte de, 1768-1848. 200
The genius of Christianity : or, The spirit and beauty of the Christian religion / by Viscount de Chateaubriand ; a new and complete translation from the French, with a pref., biographical notice of the author, and critical and explanatory notes by Charles I. White. New York : H. Fertig, 1975. p. cm. Translation of Genie du christianisme. Reprint of the 1856 ed. published by J. Murphy, Baltimore. Includes bibliographical references. [BR121.C472 1975] 75-25532 26.00
1. Christianity. 2. Theology, Doctrinal. 3. Art and religion. 4. Worship. I. White, Charles Ignatius, 1807-1878. II. Title. III. Title: The spirit and beauty of the Christian religion.

CLEAGE, Albert B. 200
The black Messiah [by] Albert B. Cleage, Jr. New York, Sheed and Ward [1968] 278 p. 22 cm. [E185.7.C59] 68-9370 6.50
1. Jesus Christ—Negro interpretations. 2. Negroes—Race identity. I. Title.

COBBE, Frances Power, 1822-1904. 200
Darwinism in morals, and other essays. Freeport, N.Y., Books for Libraries Press [1972] 399 p. 22 cm. (Essay index reprint series) Reprint of the 1872 ed. Contents.Contents.—Darwinism in morals.—Hereditary piety.—The religion of childhood.—An English Broad churchman.—A French theist.—The devil.—A pre-historic religion.—The religions of the world.—The religions of the East.—The religion and literature of India.—Unconscious cerebration.—Dreams, as illustrations of involuntary cerebration.—Auricular confession in the Church of England.—The evolution of morals and religion. Includes bibliographical references. [BR85.C544 1972] 72-3306 ISBN 0-8369-2895-4
1. Theology—Addresses, essays, lectures. 2. Religions—Addresses, essays, lectures. I. Title.

COLLOQUIUM on Religious Studies, Auckland, N.Z., 1975. 200
The religious dimension : a selection of essays presented at a Colloquium on Religious Studies held at the University of Auckland, New Zealand in August, 1975 / edited by John C. Hinchcliff. Auckland : Rep Prep, 1976. 103 p. ; 29 cm. Errata slip inserted. Includes bibliographies. [BL21.C64 1975] 77-351054
1. Religion—Congresses. I. Hinchcliff, John C. II. Title.

CONE, James H. 200
A Black theology of liberation [by] James H. Cone. [1st ed.] Philadelphia, Lippincott [1970] 254 p. 21 cm. (C. Eric Lincoln series in Black religion) [BT78.C59 1970] 74-120333 5.50
1. Theology, Doctrinal. 2. Freedom (Theology) 3. Negroes—Religion. I. Title. II. Series.

COUGHTRY, Frank W. 200
The mingled people, by Frank W. Coughtry. [1st ed. Lakeland, Fla., Barma Books, 1969] 197 p. 22 cm. [BR124.C65] 71-83161
1. Bible—Criticism, interpretation, etc. 2. Christianity—Controversial literature. 3. Segregation—Religious aspects. I. Title.

COULT, Allan D. 200
Psychedelic anthropology : the study of man through the manifestation of the mind / Allan D. Coult. Philadelphia : Dorrance, c1977. xxix, 296 p. : ill. ; 22 cm. Bibliography: p. 287-296. [BL50.C68] 77-151025 ISBN 0-8059-2270-9 : 10.95
1. Religion—Miscellanea. 2. Anthropology—Miscellanea. I. Title.

COURTENAY, William J., comp. 200
The Judeo-Christian heritage, edited by William J. Courtenay. New York, Holt, Rinehart and Winston [1970] xii, 251 p. illus., maps. 24 cm. (Western man) Bibliography: p. 249-251. [BS1192.5.A1C68 1970] 70-113826
1. Bible. O.T.—Theology—Addresses, essays, lectures. 2. Bible—Ethics—Addresses, essays, lectures. I. Title.

CRANSTON, Ruth. 200
World faith; the story of the religions of the United Nations. Freeport, N.Y., Books for Libraries Press [1968, c1949] xi, 193 p. 23 cm. (Essay index reprint series) [BL80.C8 1968] 68-58782
1. Religions. I. Title.

CURTIS, Charles J. 200
Contemporary Protestant thought [by] C. J. Curtis. New York, Bruce Pub. Co. [1970] xiv, 225 p. 23 cm. (Contemporary theology series) Includes bibliographical references. [BT28.C87] 72-87991
1. Theology, Protestant—History—20th century. 2. Theology, Doctrinal—History—20th century. I. Title.

DARA. 200
Now God has to advertise — and this is good. North Quincy, Mass., Christopher Pub. House [1969] 108 p. 21 cm. [BL2775.2.D35] 72-91803 2.95
1. Christianity—Controversial literature. 2. Religion—Controversial literature. I. Title.

DAVIS, Charles, 1923- 200
Temptations of religion. [1st U.S. ed.] New York, Harper & Row [1974, c1973] 89 p. 21 cm. Includes bibliographical references. [BL48.D3725 1974] 73-6341 ISBN 0-06-061701-2 4.95
1. Religion. I. Title.

DAVIS, Charles, S. T. L. 200
The study of theology. London, New York, Sheed and Ward [1962] 348 p. 23 cm. Essays. [BT77.D3] 63-4548
1. Theology, Doctrinal — Popular works. I. Title.

DAWSON, Christopher Henry, 1889- 200
Enquiries into religion and culture, by Christopher Dawson. Freeport, N.Y., Books for Libraries Press [1968] xi, 347 p. 22 cm. (Essay index reprint series) Reprint of the 1933 ed. Bibliographical footnotes. [BL55.D27 1968] 68-29200
1. Religion—Addresses, essays, lectures. 2. Civilization—Addresses, essays, lectures. I. Title.

DAWSON, Christopher Henry, 1889- 200
Progress and religion; an historical enquiry [by] Christopher Dawson. Westport, Conn., Greenwood Press [1970] xvii, 254 p. 23 cm. Reprint of the 1929 ed. Bibliography: p. 251-254. [BL55.D3 1970] 79-104266
1. Progress. 2. Religion. 3. Civilization, Christian. 4. History—Philosophy. I. Title.

DEMERATH, Nicholas Jay. 200
Religion in social context; tradition and transition [by] N. J. Demerath III and Phillip E. Hammond. New York, Random House [1968, c1969] ix, 246 p. 21 cm. Bibliography: p. [233]-238. [BL60.D45] 68-20032 5.95
1. Religion and sociology. I. Hammond, Phillip E., joint author. II. Title.

DEMERSCHMAN, Lucille. 200
New light upon old tradition, with spiritual guidelines for the new age. Los Angeles, DeVorss [1969] 279 p. 24 cm. [BL48.D385] 79-101300
1. Jesus Christ—Biography. 2. Religion. 3. Christianity. I. Title.

DIMICK, John M. 200
Some formulas, old and new, affecting man's past conduct and future survival, by John Dimick. Philadelphia, Dorrance [1970] 63 p. 22 cm. Bibliography: p. 63. [AC8.D653] 75-128141 3.95
I. Title.

DIXON, Jeane. 200
Reincarnation and prayers to live by. New York, W. Morrow, 1970 [c1969] 62 p. 18 cm. [BL515.D57 1970] 77-115439
1. Reincarnation. 2. Prayers. I. Title.

DRAKE, Durant, 1878-1933. 200
Problems of religion; an introductory survey. New York, Greenwood Press, 1968 [c1916] xiii, 425 p. 20 cm. Includes bibliographies. [BL48.D7 1968] 68-19268
1. Religion. 2. Christianity. 3. Religion—Philosophy. I. Title.

DUCASSE, Curt John, 1881- 200
A philosophical scrutiny of religion. New York, Ronald Press Co. [1953] x, 441 p. illus. 22 cm. Biographical footnotes. [BL48.D78] 53-5700
1. Religion. I. Title.

DUDLEY, Guilford, 1932- 200
The recovery of Christian myth, by Guilford Dudley III. Philadelphia, Westminster Press [1967] 127 p. 21 cm. Bibliographical references included in "Notes" (p. 119-123) [BL65.L2D8] 67-15869
1. Religion and language. 2. Myth. 3. Bible. N.T. Revelation — Criticism, interpretation, etc. I. Title.

DURKHEIM, Emile, 1858-1917. 200
Durkheim on religion : a selection of readings with bibliographies / [compiled by] W. S. F. Pickering ; new translations by Jacqueline Redding and W. S. F. Pickering. London ; Boston : Routledge & K. Paul, 1975. x, 376 p. ; 23 cm. Includes bibliographies and indexes. [BL50.D85 1975] 75-325445 ISBN 0-7100-8108-1 : 21.75
1. Religion—Addresses, essays, lectures. I. Pickering, W. S. F. II. Title.

DURKHEIM, Emile, 1858-1917. 200
Durkheim on religion : a selection of readings with bibliographies / [compiled by] W. S. F. Pickering ; new translations by Jacqueline Redding and W. S. F. Pickering. London ; Boston : Routledge & K. Paul, 1975. x, 376 p. ; 23 cm. Includes bibliographies and indexes. [BL50.D85 1975] 75-325445 ISBN 0-7100-8108-1 : £6.95
1. Religion—Addresses, essays, lectures. I. Pickering, W. S. F. II. Title.

DUTCH, Andrew K. 200
The God within : brotherhood nyet / by Andrew K. Dutch. Boca Raton, Fla. : Dutch Treat Syndicate, [1975] xxix, 277 p. ; 23 cm. [BL48.D87] 74-24542
1. Religion. I. Title.

ELERT, Werner, 1885-1954. 200
An outline of Christian doctrine. Translated by Charles M. Jacobs ... Philadelphia, Pa., The United Lutheran Publication House [1927] 112 p. 20 cm. Translation of Die Lehre des Luthertums im Abriss. [BX8065.E55] 27-3208
1. Lutheran Church—Doctrinal and controversial works. I. Jacobs, Charles Michael, 1875-1938, tr. II. Title.

EVANS, Allan Stewart, 1939- 200
What man believes: a study of the world's great faiths, by Allan S. Evans, Riley E. Moynes [and] Larry Martinello. Toronto, New York, McGraw-Hill Ryerson [1973] xvi, 421 p. illus. 24 cm. Bibliography: p. 410-418. [BL80.2.E82 1973] 73-7047 ISBN 0-07-077440-4
1. Religions. 2. Religion. I. Moynes, Riley E., joint author. II. Martinello, Larry, joint author. III. Title.

EXPLORING religious meaning 200
[by] Robert Monk [and others] Englewood Cliffs, N.J., Prentice-Hall [1974, c1973] xviii, 395 p. illus. 24 cm. Includes bibliographical references. [BL48.E95] 73-4888 ISBN 0-13-297499-1 9.95
1. Religion. 2. Religious literature (Selections: Extracts, etc.) I. Monk, Robert C.
Pbk. 5.95; ISBN 0-13-297481-9.

FOOTE, Henry Wilder, 1875- 200
The religion of an inquiring mind. Boston, Starr King Press distributed by Beacon Press [1955] 260p. 22cm. [BR121.F6516] 55-7800
1. Christianity—Essence, genius, nature. I. Title.

FOOTE, Henry Wilder, 1875- 200
The religion of an inquiring mind. [Gloucester, Mass., Peter Smith, 1962, c.1955] 265p. (Beacon paperback rebound) Bibl. 4.00
1. Christianity—Essence, genius, nature. I. Title.

FRIEDMAN, Maurice S. 200
Searching in the syntax of things; experiments in the study of religion. Essays by Maurice Friedman, T. Patrick Burke [and] Samuel Laeuchli. With an introd. by Franklin H. Littell. Philadelphia, Fortress Press [1972] xv, 144 p. 23 cm. [BL50.F75] 70-171494 ISBN 0-8006-0103-3 3.75
1. Religion—Addresses, essays, lectures. I. Burke, Thomas Patrick, 1934- II. Laeuchli, Samuel. III. Title.

GARDAVSKY, Vitezslav. 200
God is not yet dead; translated from the German by Vivienne Menkes. Harmondsworth, Penguin, 1973. 224 p. 18 cm. (Pelican books) The German ed. Gott ist nicht ganz tot was translated from the original Czech entitled Buh neni zcela mrtev. Includes bibliographical references and index. [BL2775.2.G313] 73-168508 ISBN 0-14-021322-8 £0.45
1. Religion—Controversial literature. 2. Atheism. I. Title.

GARDAVSKY, Vitezslav. 200
God is not yet dead; translated from the German by Vivienne Menkes. Harmondsworth, Penguin, 1973. 224 p. 18 cm. (Pelican books) The German ed. Gott ist nicht ganz tot was translated from the original Czech entitled Buh neni zcela mrtev. Includes bibliographical references and index. [BL2775.2.G313] 73-168508 ISBN 0-14-021322-8
1. Religion—Controversial literature. 2. Atheism. I. Title.
Distributed by Penguin, Baltimore, Md. 2.25 (pbk.)

GAVIN, Frank Stanton Burns, 1890-1938. 200
Some aspects of contemporary Greek Orthodox thought. New York, AMS Press [1970] xxxiv, 430 p. 23 cm. Reprint of the 1923 ed. Originally presented as lectures at the Western Theological Seminary, Chicago, on the invitation of the Committee of the Hale Lectureship Foundation. Bibliography: p. [xxix]-xxxiv. [BX320.G3 1970] 73-133818
1. Orthodox Eastern Church—Doctrinal and controversial works. I. Title.

GERBER, John A. 200
The psychoneurosis called Christianity [by] John A. Gerber. [1st ed. Roslyn Heights, N.Y.] Libra Publishers [1969] 110 p. 22 cm. [BL2775.2.G4] 70-79733 4.95
1. Christianity—Controversial literature. 2. Philosophical anthropology. I. Title.

GLOCK, Charles Y., comp. 200
Religion in sociological perspective; essays in the empirical study of religion. Edited by Charles Y. Glock. With contributions by Earl R. Babbie [and others] Belmont, Calif., Wadsworth Pub. Co. [1973] ix, 315 p. 23 cm. (The Wadsworth series in sociology) "From the Research Program in Religion and Society, Survey Research Center, University of California, Berkeley." Includes bibliographical references. [BL60.G553] 72-87021 ISBN 0-534-00216-1
1. Religion and sociology—Addressses, essays, lectures. I. Title.

GLOCK, Charles Y., comp. 200
Religion in sociological perspective; essays in the empirical study of religion. Edited by Charles Y. Glock. With contributions by Earl R. Babbie [and others] Belmont, Calif., Wadsworth Pub. Co. [1973] ix, 315 p. 23 cm. (The Wadsworth series in sociology) "From the Research Program in Religion and Society, Survey Research Center, University of California, Berkeley." Includes bibliographical references. [BL60.G553] 72-87021 ISBN 0-534-00216-1 4.95
1. Religion and sociology—Addressses, essays, lectures. I. Title.

GOLDBERG, Ben Zion, 1895- 200
Sex in religion [by] B. Z. Goldberg. New York, Liveright [1970, c1930] xv, 386 p. illus. 21 cm. Originally published under title: The sacred fire. Bibliography: p. 371-376. [BL65.S4G6 1970] 78-131281 2.95
1. Sex and religion. I. Title.

GORDH, George Rudolph, 1912- 200
Christian faith and its cultural expression. Englewood Cliffs, N.J., Prentice [c.]1962. 354p. illus. 24cm. Bibl. 62-13195 7.35
1. Christianity. 2. Religion and literature. 3. Sociology, Christian. I. Title.

GORDIS, Robert, 1908- 200
A faith for moderns. New York, Bloch Pub. Co., [c.]1960. xii, 316p. 24cm. 60-15012 5.00 bds.,
1. Religion. I. Title.

GORDIS, Robert, 1908- 200
A faith for moderns. Rev. and augm. ed. New York, Bloch Pub. Co. [1971] xviii, 340 p. 23 cm. [BL48.G64 1971] 76-136424 ISBN 0-8197-0001-0 3.95
1. Religion. I. Title.

GRAHAM, Aelred, 1907- 200
Contemplative Christianity : an approach to the realities of religion / Aelred Graham. New York : Seabury Press, [1975] c1974. x, 131 p. ; 22 cm. "A Crossroad book." Includes index. [BV4501.2.G724 1975] 74-26989 ISBN 0-8164-0269-8 : 6.95
1. Spiritual life. 2. Christianity—20th century. 3. Christianity and other religions. I. Title.

GRAHAM, Aelred, 1907- 200
The end of religion; autobiographical explorations. New York, Harcourt [1973, c.1971] xii, 292 p. 21 cm. (Harvest Book, HB249) Includes bibliographical references. [BL48.G68] 77-139461 ISBN 0-15-628790-0 pap., 2.85
1. Religion. 2. Religions. I. Title.

GRAY, Henry David, 1908- 200
The theology for Christian youth. Hartford, Independent Press [1970] 144 p. 19 cm. Bibliography: p. 140-142. [BT77.G82 1970] 70-16620
1. Theology, Doctrinal—Popular works. I. Title.

GREENALL, Raphael. 200
The second fall. Liverpool, Keys Pub. Co. [1963] 112 p. 22 cm. Bibliographical footnotes. [BR307.G7] 64-1769
1. Reformation—Addresses, essays, lectures. 2. Civilization, Modern—Addresses, essays, lectures. I. Title.

GRIFFITH, Arthur Leonard, 1920- 200
Barriers to Christian belief. [London] Hodder and Stoughton [1962] 191 p. 22 cm. [BR121.2.G7 1962] 63-32291
1. Christianity — 20th cent. I. Title.

HACKMAN, George Gottlob. 200
Religion in modern life [by] George G Hackman, Charles W. Kegley [and] Viljo K. Nikander. New York, Macmillan [1957] 480 p. 22 cm. Includes bibliography. [BL48.H23] 57-5545
1. Religion. 2. Christianity—20th century.

HACKWOOD, Frederick William, 1851- 200
Christ lore; being the legends, traditions, myths, symbols, customs & superstitions of the Christian church. London, E. Stock, 1902. Detroit, Gale Research Co., 1969. xvi, 290 p. illus. 22 cm. Includes bibliographical references. [BR135.H3 1969] 69-16064
1. Christian art and symbolism. 2. Legends, Christian. I. Title.

HALL, Samuel H 200
Sixty years in the pulpit; or, Compound interest in religion. [Ann Arbor! Mich., 1956, c1955] 230p. illus. 24cm. [BX7094.C95H26] 57-19383
1. Churches of Christ—Clergy—Correspondence, reminiscences, etc. I. Title.

HALL, Samuel H 200
Sixty years in the pulpit; or, Compound interest in religion. [Ann Arbor? Mich., 1956, c1955] 230p. illus. 24cm. [BX7094.C95H26] 57-19383
1. Churches of Christ—Clergy—Correspondence, reminiscences, etc. I. Title.

HAPPOLD, Frederick Crossfield, 1893- 200
Prayer and meditation: their nature and practice [by] F. C. Happold. Harmondsworth, Penguin, 1971. 381 p. music. 19 cm. (Pelican books, A1257) Includes bibliographical references. [BV210.2.H36] 72-176065 ISBN 0-14-021257-4 £0.50
1. Prayer. 2. Prayers. 3. Devotional literature. I. Title.

HARDON, John A. 200
Religions of the Orient; a Christian view [by] John A. Hardon. Chicago, Loyola University Press [1970] viii, 212 p. 23 cm. Bibliography: p. 189-194. [BL80.2.H297] 71-108377 ISBN 8-294-01857-
1. Religions. 2. Christianity and other religions. I. Title.

HARTMAN, Charles. 200
The life of Mary, mother of Jesus; 91 masterworks of art. Text selection and introd. by Charles Hartman. Pref. by Walter M. Abbott. New York, Guild Press [c1963] 191 p. col. plates. 28 cm. Text selections in poetry and prose. [N8070.H33] 63-25570
1. Mary, Virgin — Art. 2. Mary, Virgin — Poetry. I. Title.

HEDGES, Sidney George, 1897- 200
Prayers and thoughts from world religions [by] Sid G. Hedges. Richmond, Va., John Knox Press [1972, c1970] 181 p. 21 cm. First published in 1970 under title: With one voice. [BL560.H4 1972] 72-1875 ISBN 0-8042-2500-1 4.95
1. Prayers. 2. Meditations. I. Title.

HEILIG, Matthias R. 200
Discussions on the Styx [by] Matthias R. Heilig. New York, Philosophical Library [1969] 118 p. 23 cm. [BL50.H46] 69-20333 4.50
1. Religion—Addresses, essays, lectures. I. Title.

HELLWIG, Monika. 200
What are the theologians saying? Dayton, Ohio, Pflaum Press, 1970. xiv, 98 p. 21 cm. Bibliography: p. 97-98. [BT77.H413] 78-114694 1.50
1. Theology, Doctrinal—Popular works. I. Title.

HERBERT, Arthur Gabriel, 1886- 200
Scripture and the faith. New York, Morehouse-Barlow Co. [1962] 94p. 19cm. [BS480.H36 1962] 62-5699
1. Bible—Evidence, authority, etc. 2. Bible—Use. I. Title.

HOLMER, Paul L. 200
Theology and the scientific study of religion. Minneapolis, T. S. Denison [1961] 233 p. 22 cm. (The Lutheran studies series, v. 2) [BL48.H53] 61-18613
1. Religion. 2. Faith. I. Title.

HOOD, Frederic. 200
God's plan. With a foreword by the Bishop of London. London, New York, Longmans, Green [1955] 93p. 17cm. [BT77.H595] 55-4297
1. Theology, Doctrinal—Popular works. I. Title.

HROMADKA, Josef Lukl, 1889-1969. 200 B
Impact of history on theology; thoughts of a Czech pastor [by] Josef L. Hromadka. [Translated from the Czech by Monika and Benjamin Page] Notre Dame, Ind., Fides [1970] vi, 117 p. 22 cm. Published originally in French under the title: Pour quoi je vis. Bibliography: p. 116-117. [BX4827.H7A3513 1970] 78-108029 1.95
I. Title.

HUNTER, Howard. 200
Humanities, religion, and the arts tomorrow. Edited by Howard Hunter. New York, Holt, Rinehart and Winston [1972] vii, 247 p. illus. 24 cm. Includes bibliographical references. [BL65.H8H85] 77-186568 ISBN 0-03-085391-5
1. Religion and the humanities—Addresses, essays, lectures. I. Title.

IMITATIO Christi. English. 200
The imitation of Christ, by Thomas a Kempis. Edited by Paul Simpson McElroy. Illus. by Stanley Clough. Mount Vernon, N. Y., Peter Pauper Press [c1965] 61 p. col. illus. 19 cm. [BV4821.A1] 67-121940
I. McElroy, Paul Simpson, 1902- comp. II. Peter Pauper Press, Mount Vernon, N. Y. III. Title.

IMITATIO Christi. English. 200
The imitation of Chrsit, by Thomas a Kempis. Translated from the Latin into Modern English [by] Aloysius Croft and Harry F. Bolton] Milwaukee, Bruce Pub. Co. [1962] xiii, 257p. 18cm. [BV4821.A1 1962a] 62-51531
I. Croft, Aloysius, tr. II. Bolton, Harry F., tr. III. Title.

ISHERWOOD, Margaret. 200
Searching for meaning; a religion of inner growth for agnostics and believers. Philadelphia, Macrae Smith Co. [1971, c1970] 175 p. illus. 24 cm. [BJ1470.I83 1971] 73-150681 ISBN 0-8255-4700-8 5.95
1. Self-realization. 2. Religion. I. Title.

JACQUES, John Herbert. 200
The mushroom and the bride: a believer's examination and refutation of J. M. Allegro's book 'The Sacred mushroom and the cross', by John H. Jacques. Derby, Citadel Press, 1970. [11], 126 p. 23 cm. [BL444.A45J3 1970] 70-864149 ISBN 0-902791-00-1 £1.50
1. Allegro, John Marco, 1923- The sacred mushroom and the cross. I. Title.

JENKINS, Daniel Thomas, 1914- 200
Christian maturity and the theology of success / [by] Daniel Jenkins. London : S.C.M. Press, 1976. [7], 84 p. ; 20 cm. Revised version of the Warfield Lectures given at Princeton Theological Seminary from 31 March to 4 April 1975. Includes bibliographical references. [BV4501.2.J43] 76-375641 ISBN 0-334-00152-8 : £0.90
1. Christian life—1960- —Addresses, essays, lectures. I. Title.

JENKINS, David E. 200
The contradiction of Christianity / [by] David E. Jenkins. London : S.C.M. Press, 1976. viii, 162 p. ; 23 cm. (Edward Cadbury lectures ; 1974) Includes bibliographical references and index. [BR85.J44] 76-375639 ISBN 0-334-00289-3 : £4.50
1. Theology—Addresses, essays, lectures. I. Title. II. Series.

JENSON, Robert W. 200
A religion against itself [by] Robert W. Jenson. Richmond, John Knox Press [1967] 127 p. 21 cm. [BR121.2.J4] 67-12427
1. Christianity—20th century. I. Title.

JOLLY, David E 200
Knowledge beyond understanding; a topic essay book of enlightenment, by David E. Jolly. [Seattle, 1967] 153 p. 24 cm. [BL50.J55] 67-9692
1. Religion. I. Title.

JOLLY, David E. 200
Knowledge beyond understanding; a topic essay book of enlightenment, by David E. Jolly. [Seattle, 1967] 153 p. 24 cm. [BL50.J55] 67-9692
1. Religion. I. Title.

JOYCE, Donovan. 200
The Jesus scroll. [New York] Dial Press, 1973 [c1972] 216 p. 22 cm. Bibliography: p. [215]-216. [BT303.J68 1973] 73-10454 5.95
1. Jesus Christ—Biography—History and criticism. I. Title.

JOYCE, Donovan. 200
The Jesus scroll: a timebomb for Christianity? Melbourne, Ferret Books, 1972. 216 p. plates. 22 cm. Bibliography: p. [215]-216. [BT303.J68] 73-168019 ISBN 0-909660-00-X 4.95
1. Jesus Christ—Biography—History and criticism. 2. Christianity—Origin. I. Title.

JOYCE, Donovan. 200
The Jesus scroll. [New York] New American Library [1974, c1973] 194 p. 18 cm. (A Signet book) Bibliography: p. 193-194. [BT303.J68 1974] 1.50 (pbk.)
1. Jesus Christ—Biography—History and criticism. I. Title.
L.C. card number for original ed.: 73-10454.

KAHL, Joachim, 1941- 200
The misery of Christianity: or, A plea for a humanity without God; with a preface by Gerhard Szczesny, translated [from the German] by N. D. Smith. Harmondsworth, Penguin, 1971. 215 p. 19 cm. (Pelican books) Translation of Das Elend des Christentums. Bibliography: p. 200-[213] [BL2775.2.K2213 1971] 72-193970 ISBN 0-14-021324-4 £0.35
1. Christianity—Controversial literature. I. Title. II. Title: A plea for a humanity without God.

KAHL, Joachim, 1941- 200
The misery of Christianity: or, A plea for a humanity without God; with a preface by Gerhard Szczesny, translated [from the German] by N. D. Smith. Harmondsworth, Penguin, 1971. 215 p. 19 cm. (Pelican books) Translation of Das Elend des Christentums. Bibliography: p. 200-[213] [BL2775.2.K2213 1971] 72-193970 ISBN 0-14-021324-4 Pap. 1.25
1. Christianity—Controversial literature. I. Title. II. Title: A plea for a humanity without God.
Available from Penguin Books, Baltimore.

KALT, William J 200
The religions of man [by] William J. Kalt and Ronald J. Wilkins. Chicago, Regnery [1967] v, 122 p. illus. 23 cm. (To live is Christ. Discussion booklet 2) Bibliographical footnotes. [BL80.2.K34] 67-29305
1. Religions. I. Wilkins, Ronald J., joint author. II. Title.

KALT, William J. 200
The religions of man [by] William J. Kalt and Ronald J. Wilkins. Chicago, Regnery [1967] v, 122 p. illus. 23 cm. (To live is Christ. Discussion booklet 2) Bibliographical footnotes. [BL80.2.K34] 67-29305
1. Religions. I. Wilkins, Ronald J., joint author. II. Title.

KAUFMANN, Walter Arnold. 200
Religions in four dimensions : existential and aesthetic, historical and comparative / text and photos. by Walter Kaufmann. 1st ed. New York : Reader's Digest Press : distributed by Crowell, 1976. 490 p. : ill. ; 27 cm. Includes index. Bibliography: p. [475]-482. [BL80.2.K38 1976] 76-15367 30.00
1. Religions. 2. Arts and religion. I. Title.

KEGLEY, Charles W., 1912- 200
The philosophy and theology of Anders Nygren. Edited by Charles W. Kegley. Carbondale, Southern Illinois University Press [1970] xiv, 434 p. 25 cm. "Bibliography of the publications of Anders Nygren to 1970 [by] Ulrich E. Mack": p. [379]-397. [BX8080.N8K4] 76-83670 ISBN 0-8093-0427-9 12.95
1. Nygren, Anders, Bp., 1890- —Addresses, essays, lectures. I. Title.

KING, Winston Lee, 1907- 200
Introduction to religion. [1st ed.] New York, Harper [c1954] 563p. 24cm. Includes bibliography. [BL48.K48] 53-10970
1. Religion. I. Title.

KING, Winston Lee, 1907- 200
Introduction to religion; a phenomenological approach [by] Winston L. King. New York, Harper & Row [1968] vii, 391 p. illus. 24 cm. Includes bibliographies. [BL48.K48 1968] 68-11455
1. Religion. I. Title.

KRAEMER, Hendrik, 1888- 200
Why Christianity of all religions? Translated by Hubert Hoskins. Philadelphia, Westminster Press [1962] 125p. 21cm. Translation of Waarom nu juist het Christendom? [BR121.K813] 62-14048
1. Christianity—Essence, genius, nature. 2. Christianity and other religions. I. Title.

KUPPERS, Leonhard, 1903- 200
Mary. [Translated from the German by Hans Hermann Rosenwald] Recklinghausen [Ger.] A. Oongers; distributed by Taplinger Pub. Co. [New York, 1967, c1965] 64 p. col. illus. 18 cm. (The Saints in legend and art, v. 14) [N8070.K7913] 67-4425
1. Mary, Virgin — Art. I. Title.

LA BARRE, Weston, 1911- 200
The ghost dance; origins of religion. [1st ed.] Garden City, N.Y., Doubleday, 1970. xvi, 677 p. 24 cm. Includes bibliographical references. [BL48.L25] 71-89094 12.50
1. Religion. 2. Psychology, Religious. I. Title.

LIFE (Chicago) 200
The world's great religions, by the editorial staff of Life. Specially adapted for this edition. New York, Golden Press [1967] 224 p. illus. (part col.) 21 cm. [BL80.2.L5 1967] 67-4288
1. Religions. I. Title.

LINCOLN, Charles Eric, comp. 200
The Black experience in religion, edited by C. Eric Lincoln. Garden City, N.Y., Anchor Press, 1974. xii, 369 p. 21 cm. (C. Eric Lincoln series on Black religion) Includes bibliographical references. [BR563.N4L56] 73-16508 ISBN 0-385-01884-3 3.95 (pbk.).
1. Negroes—Religion. I. Title. II. Series.

LOCKRIDGE, S. M. 200
The challenge of the church; provocative discussions of vital modern issues, by S. M. Lockridge. Grand Rapids, Zondervan Pub. House [1969] 64 p. 21 cm. [BR125.L757] 77-81041
1. Christianity—Addresses, essays, lectures. I. Title.

LOOMIS, William Farnsworth, 200
1914-
The God within; an up-to-date sketch of the genesis of man and of the personal God within him, by W. Farnsworth Loomis. Foreword by James A. Pike. [1st ed.] New York, October House [1968,c.1967] ix, 117p. illus. 27cm. [BL430.L6] 67-14086 5.95
1. Religion—Hist. I. Title.

LORTZ, Joseph, 1887- 200
How the Reformation came. [Translated by Otto M. Knab. New York] Herder and Herder [1964] 115 p. 21 cm. [BR307.L613] 63-18152
1. Reformation — Causes. I. Title.

LORTZ, Joseph, 1887- 200
How the Reformation came. [Translated by Otto M. Knab. New York] Herder and Herder [1964] 115 p. 21 cm. [BR307.L613] 63-18152
1. Reformation — Causes. I. Title.

MCINTOSH, William Alexander, 200
1884-
The story, a book for those who care to think. Springfield, Vt. [1950] 79 p. 18 cm. [BR126.M3554] 50-29217
I. Title.

MACLENNAN, David Alexander, 200
1903-
Let's take another look; basic beliefs reinterpreted, by David A. MacLennan. Waco, Tex., Word Books [1970] 125 p. 21 cm. Originally published in The Link as a series of articles entitled Faith reinterpreted. Includes bibliographical references. [BT77.M163] 75-122495 2.95
1. Theology, Doctrinal—Popular works. I. Title.

MCLOUGHLIN, William Gerald. 200
The meaning of Henry Ward Beecher; an essay on the shifting values of mid-Victorian America, 1840-1870 [by] William G. McLoughlin. [1st ed.] New York, Knopf, 1970. xiii, 275 p. 22 cm. Includes bibliographical references. [BX7260.B3M33 1970] 77-111239 7.95
1. Beecher, Henry Ward, 1813-1887. 2. U.S.—Religion—19th century. 3. U.S.—Civilization—19th century. I. Title.

MAGEE, John Benjamin, 1917- 200
Religion and modern man; a study of the religious meaning of being human [by] John B. Magee. New York, Harper [1967] xiv, 510.p. 24cm. Bibl. [BL41.M28] 67-15791 8.00
1. Religion. I. Title.

MALACHI, Martin. 200
The new castle; reaching for the ultimate. [1st ed.] New York, Dutton, 1974. x, 209 p. 22 cm. [BL80.2.M283 1974] 74-9663 ISBN 0-525-16553-3 7.95; 3.95 (pbk.).
1. Religions. 2. Civilization, Modern—1950- I. Title.

MALACHI, Martin. 200
The new castle; reaching for the ultimate. [by] Malachi Martin. [New York, Dell, 1975, c1974] 204 p. 18 cm. (A Laurel edition) [BL80.2M283 1975] 1.25 (pbk.)
1. Religions. 2. Civilization, Modern—1950- I. Title.
L.C. card number for original ed.: 74-9663.

MARTINDALE, Cyril Charlie, 200
1879-1963.
The faith of the Roman Church. New York, Greenwood Press [1969, c1950] x, 134 p. 23 cm. [BX1751.M37 1969] 70-94589
1. Catholic Church—Doctrinal and controversial works—Catholic authors. I. Title.

MASON, Philip. 200
The dove in harness / Philip Mason. London : Cape, 1976. 189 p. ; 23 cm. Bibliography: p. [186]-189. [BT1105.M37 1976] 77-354312 ISBN 0-224-01313-0 : £3.95
1. Apologetics—20th century—Addresses, essays, lectures. I. Title.

MICKLEM, Nathaniel, 1888- 200
Religion. Westport, Conn., Greenwood Press [1973] 224 p. 17 cm. Reprint of the 1948 ed., which was issued as no. 201 of The Home university library of modern knowledge. Bibliography: p. 216-220. [BL48.M48 1973] 73-168964 ISBN 0-8371-6234-3 10.00
1. Religion. 2. Religions.

MOBERG, David O. 200
International directory of religious information systems. David O. Moberg, editor. Milwaukee, Wis., Dept. of Sociology and Anthropology, Marquette University [1971] 88 p. 23 cm. [BL35.M62] 75-156952
1. Religion—Information services. I. Marquette University, Milwaukee. Dept. of Sociology and Anthropology. II. Title.

NASH, Arnold Samuel, ed. 200
Protestant thought in the twentieth century: whence & whither? New York, Macmillan, 1951. xii, 296 p. 21 cm. Contents.Contents.—America at the end of the Protestant era, by A. S. Nash. —The study of the Old Testament, by G. E. Wright.—The study of the New Testament, by F. V. Filson.—The philosophy of religion, by G. F. Thomas.—Systematic theology, by W. M. Horton.—Christian ethics by W. Beach and J. C. Bennett.—Church history, by G. H. Williams.—Pastoral theology and psychology, by S. Hiltner.—Preaching, by C. W. Gilkey.—Christian education, by H. S. Smith.—Reunion and the ecumenical movement, by H. S. Leiper.—Christianity and other religions, by J. A. Mackay. Includes bibliographies. [BR479.N3] 51-11218
1. Theology—20th century. 2. Protestantism. 3. Religious thought—20th century. I. Title.

NEVISON, R. L. B. 200
The last problem / [by] R. L. B. Nevison. [Harrogate] : [The author], 1976. [3], ii, 97 p. ; 21 cm. Includes bibliographical references. [BL51.N447] 76-380959 ISBN 0-9505166-0-0 : £1.00
1. Religion—Philosophy. I. Title.

NOBILE, Philip, comp. 200
Catholic nonsense. Drawings by Kieran Quinn. [1st ed.] Garden City, N.Y., Doubleday, 1970. 155 p. illus. 18 cm. [BX1755.N55] 76-116240 3.95
1. Theology, Catholic—Quotations, maxims, etc. I. Title.

NORBECK, Edward, 1915- 200
Religion in human life: anthropological views. New York, Holt, Rinehart and Winston [1974] p. (Basic anthropology units) Bibliography: p. [BL48.N67] 73-7862 ISBN 0-03-091284-9
1. Religion. I. Title.

OCCHIO, Joseph M 200
Perspectives in Christian humanism [by]Joseph M. Occhio. [1st ed.] New York, Exposition Press [1966] 146 p. 21 cm. (An Exposition-university book) Includes bibliographical references. [BR123.O27] 66-14084
1. Christianity — Addresses, essays, lectures. I. Title.

OURSLER, Will [William 200
Charles Oursler]
The road to faith. New York, Rinehart [c.1960] 223p. 21cm. 60-5227 3.50
1. Religion. I. Title.

OURSLER, William Charles, 200
1913-
The road to faith. New York, Rinehart [1960] 223p. 21cm. [BL48.O86] 60-5227
1. Religion. I. Title.

PARRINDER, Edward Geoffrey. 200
Religions of the world, from primitive beliefs to modern faiths. General editor: Geoffrey Parrinder. [1st U.S. ed.] New York, Madison Square Press [1971] 440 p. illus. (part col.) 30 cm. Bibliography: p. 432-433. [BL80.2.P346 1971] 73-149816 ISBN 0-448-02128-5 14.95
1. Religions. I. Title.

PATHWAY Press. 200
Is Christianity the only way? Cleveland, Tenn. : Pathway Press, [1975] 164 p. : ill. ; 18 cm. (Making life count new life series) Bibliography: p. 163-164. [BT60.P29] 74-22530 ISBN 0-87148-429-3 pbk. : 1.15
1. Christianity—Essence, genius, nature. 2. Religions. 3. Occult sciences. I. Title.

PATTERSON, Robert Leet. 200
The role of history in religion. [1st ed.] New York, Exposition Press [1971] 176 p. 21 cm. (An Exposition-university book) Includes bibliographical references. [BL65.H5P36] 77-159495 ISBN 0-682-47296-4 6.50
1. History (Theology) I. Title.

PEASE, Eugene Moody. 200
Religion can be amazing, how religion can and will evolve. [1st ed.] New York, Pageant Press [1957] 83p. 21cm. [BL50.P43] 57-8309
1. Religion. I. Title.

PENNSYLVANIA. State 200
University. Center for Continuing Liberal Education.
Exploring religious ideas: the great Western faiths. [study-discussion course] by Luther H. Harshbarger, Benjamin M. Kahn, John A. Mourant. Edited by Ralph W. Condee. University Park [c1959] vi, 158p. 28cm. On the cover, Kahn's name appears first. Includes bibliographies. [BT77.P44] 59-63350
1. Theology—Outlines, syllabi, etc. I. Harshbarger, Luther H. II. Kahn, Benjamin M. III. Title.

PENNSYLVANIA. University. 200
Bicentennial Conference.
Religion and the modern world, by Jacques Maritain [and others] Port Washington, N.Y., Kennikat Press [1969, c1941] 192 p. 25 cm. (Essay and general literature index reprint series) [BR41.P4 1969] 68-26204
1. Theology—20th century. I. Maritain, Jacques, 1882- II. Title.

PHILLIPS Brooks House Association, Harvard University. 200
Religion and modern life; lectures given for the Phillips Brooks House Association, Harvard University. Freeport, N.Y., Books for Libraries Press [1972] x, 370 p. 23 cm. (Essay index reprint series) Reprint of the 1927 ed. [BL50.P5 1972] 75-39104 ISBN 0-8369-2713-3
1. Religion—Addresses, essays, lectures. I. Title.

PITTENGER, William Norman, 1905- 200
The pathway to believing. Indianapolis, Bobbs-Merrill [1960] 192 p. 22 cm. Includes bibliography. [BT60.P5] 60-13599
1. Christianity—Essence, genius, nature. I. Title.

POTTER, Bernard. 200
Mortals and gods. [1st ed.] New York, Vantage Press [1955] 200p. illus. 23cm. [BL50.P6] 54-13132
1. Religion. I. Title.

PYNE, Mable Mandeville, 1903- 200
The story of religion, written and illustrated by Mable Mandeville Pyne. Boston, Houghton Miffin, 1954. 54 p. illus. 29 cm. [BL50.P85] 54-12232
1. Religion.

RADHAKRISHNAN, Sarvepalli, Pres. India, 1888- 200
Religion in a changing world [by] S. Radhakrishnan. London, Allen & Unwin; New York, Humanities, 1967. 3-187 p. 21cm. Bibl. [BL55.R33] 67-85914 5.00
1. Religion. 2. Civilization. I. Title.

RANDALL, John Herman, 1899- 200
The meaning of religion for man. New York, Harper & Row [1968] 125 p. 21 cm. (Harper torchbooks, TB1379) "Originally published in 1946 ... as part IV of Preface to philosophy: textbook ... The author has made revisions [with a new introduction] for the Torchbook edition." [BL48.R27] 70-3431 1.60
1. Religion. I. Title.

REGAMEY, Raymond, 1900- 200
Religious art in the twentieth century. [New York] Herder and Herder [1963] 256 p. 21 cm. Bibliographical footnotes. [N7831.R413] 63-18157
1. Christian art and symbolism. 2. Art, Modern — 20th cent. I. Title.

RIESENFELD, Harald. 200
The Gospel tradition; essays. Foreword by W. D. Davies. Philadelphia, Fortress Press [1970] x, 214 p. 23 cm. "The translation of eight chapters of this book, from Swedish and French, was made by E. Margaret Rowley; the translation of one chapter, from German, was made by Robert A. Kraft." Includes bibliographical references. [BS2395.R53] 77-101427 8.50
1. Bible. N.T.—Addresses, essays, lectures. I. Title.

ROBINS, Sidney Swaim. 200
Religion and common sense. New York, Philosophical Library [1966] vii, 204 p. 22 cm. [BR124.R6] 65-28764
1. Christianity—Miscellanea. I. Title.

ROSZAK, Theodore, 1933- 200
Unfinished animal : the aquarian frontier and the evolution of consciousness / Theodore Roszak. 1st ed. New York : Harper & Row, [1975] ix, 271 p. : ill. ; 22 cm. Includes bibliographical references and index. [BL48.R56 1975] 75-9333 ISBN 0-06-067016-9 : 10.00
1. Religion. 2. Evolution. I. Title.

ROSZAK, Theodore, 1933- 200
Unfinished animal : the acquarian frontier and the evolution of consciousness / Theodore Roszak. New York : Harper & Row [1977] c1975. ix, 271p. : ill. ; 20 cm. (Harper Colophon Books) Includes bibliographical references and index. [BL48.R56] ISBN 0-06-090537-9 pbk. : 3.45
1. Religion. 2. Evolution. I. Title.
L.C. card no. for original ed.: 75-9333.

SANDERSON, John W. 200
Encounter in the non-Christian era [by] John W. Sanderson, Jr. Grand Rapids, Mich., Zondervan Pub. House [1970] 95 p. 21 cm. (Ontario Bible College. The Elmore Harris series, 2) (A Zondervan horizon book.) [BT1102.S25] 79-120030
1. Apologetics—20th century. I. Title. II. Series: The Elmore Harris series, 2

SCHLEIERMACHER, Friedrich Ernst Daniel, 1768-1834. 200
On religion: addresses in response to its cultured critics. Translated, with introd. and notes, by Terrence N. Tice. Richmond, John Knox Press [1969] 383 p. 21 cm. (Research in theology) Translation of Uber die Religion. Bibliographical references included in "Notes" (p. [348]-373) [BL48.S33 1969] 72-82936
1. Religion. I. Tice, Terrence N., ed. II. Title.

SCHWENCKFELD, Caspar, 1490?-1561. 200
Passional and prayer book. In modern translation by John Joseph Stoudt. [1st ed.] Pennsburg, Pa., Schwenkfelder Library, 1961. 139p. illus. 23cm. 'First appeared in Nurnberg in 1539 with the title, Deutsch Passional vnsers Herren Jesu Christi, mit schonen trostilchen Gebetlein.' [BV262.S313] 61-18289
1. Schwenkfelder Church—Prayer-books and devotions. I. Title.

SEEBERG, Reinhold, 1859-1935. 200
Text-book of the history of doctrines. Translated by Charles E. Hay. Grand Rapids, Baker Book House, 1952. 2v. in 1. 23cm. Contents.v. 1. History of doctrines in the ancient church.--v. 2. History of doctrines in the middle and early modern ages. Bibliographical footnotes. [BT21.S] A53
1. Theology, Doctrinal—Hist. I. Title.

SEZNEC, Jean. 200
The survival of the pagan gods : the mythological tradition and its place in Renaissance humanism and art / by Jean Seznec ; translated from the French by Barbara F. Sessions. New York : Harper, 1961, c1953. xiv, 376 p. : 108 ill. ; 21 cm. (The Bollingen library) (Harper torchbooks ; TB 2004) "Originally published in French as La survivance des dieux antiques, Studies of the Warburg Institute, vol. XI, London, 1940." Reprint of the ed. published by Pantheon Books, New York, which was issued as no. 38 of the Bollingen series. Includes index. Bibliography: p. 327-345. [BR135.S483 1961] 76-350680
1. Humanism. 2. Art, Renaissance. 3. Mythology, Classical. 4. Gods in art. I. Title. II. Series: Bollingen series ; 38.

SHINN, Larry D., 1942- 200
Two sacred worlds : experience and structure in the world's religions / Larry D. Shinn. Nashville : Abingdon, [1977] p. cm. [BL48.S516] 76-45645 ISBN 0-687-42781-9 pbk. : 6.95
1. Religion. 2. Religions. I. Title.

SILVERMAN, William B 200
God help me! From kindergarten religion to the radical faith. New York, Macmillan, 1961. 294 p. 22 cm. [BL50.S55] 61-8111
1. Religion. I. Title. II. Title: From kindergarten religion to the radical faith.

SIMPSON, William John Sparrow, 1859- 200
Our Lord's resurrection. Grand Rapids, Mich., Zondervan [1964] xxxii, 320p. 23cm. [232.5] 4.95
1. Jesus Christ—Resurrection. I. Title.

SINCLAIR, Upton Beall, 1878-1968. 200
The profits of religion; an essay in economic interpretation. New York, AMS Press [1970] 315 p. 23 cm. Reprint of the 1918 ed. [BL2775.S54 1970] 73-120566
1. Christianity—Controversial literature. I. Title.

SMITH, Rockwell Carter, 1908- 200
The role of rural social science in theological education; with particular application to the town and country ministry of the Methodist Church [by] Rockwell C. Smith. [Evanston, Ill., 1969] 88 p. 23 cm. Bibliography: p. 82-85. [BX8219.S6] 70-17001
1. Theology—Study and teaching—Methodist church. 2. Sociology, Rural. 3. Sociology, Christian. I. Title.

SMITH, Wilfred Cantwell, 1916- 200
Questions of religious truth. New York, Scribner [1967] 127 p. 21 cm. "The material ... was delivered first as the Taylor lectures for 1963 at Yale Divinity School, except the opening chapter." Contents.Contents.—The "Death of God"?—Is the Qur'an the word of God?—Can religions be true or false?—Christian—noun, or adjective? Bibliographical footnotes. [BL27.S45] 67-14494
1. Religion—Addresses, essays, lectures. 2. Truth—Addresses, essays, lectures. I. Title.

SMITH, Wilfred Cantwell, 1916- 200
Religious diversity : essays / by Wilfred Cantwell Smith ; edited by Willard B. Oxtoby. 1st ed. New York : Harper & Row, c1976. p. cm. (A Harper forum book) Includes index. Bibliography: p. [BL50.S58 1976] 76-9968 ISBN 0-06-067463-6 : 10.00. ISBN 0-06-067464-4 pbk. : 4.95
1. Religion—Addresses, essays, lectures. 2. Religions—Addresses, essays, lectures. I. Title.

STARR, Irina. 200
The sound of light; experiencing the transcendental. New York, Philosophical Library [1969] xiii, 131 p. 22 cm. [BT769.S7] 69-20335 4.95
1. Mystical union. 2. Experience (Religion) I. Title.

STEDMAN, Ray C. 200
Body life, by Ray C. Stedman. [2d ed.] Glendale, Calif., G/L Regal Books [1972] 149 p. illus. 18 cm. [BV600.2.S75 1972] 74-181764 ISBN 0-8307-0143-5 0.95
1. Peninsula Bible Church. 2. Church. I. Title.

STEINHAUSER, Gerard R. 200
Jesus Christ, heir to the astronauts / by Gerhard R. Steinhauser. New York : Pocket Books, 1976c1974. 176p. : ill. ; 18 cm. Includes bibliographic references. [BR126.S7913] ISBN 0-671-80548-7
1. Jesus Christ-Miscellanea. 2. Christianity — Miscellanea. I. Title.
L.C. card no. of 1975 Abelard-Schuman edition:75-614698.

STEINHAUSER, Gerhard R. 200
Jesus Christ, heir to the astronauts / Gerhard R. Steinhauser ; translated [from the German] by Susanne Flatauer. London ; New York : Abelard-Schuman, 1974 [i.e.,1975] [4], 139 p., [8] p. of plates : ill., plans ; 23 cm. Translation of Jesus Christus-Erbe der Astronauten. Incudes bibliographical references. [BR126.S7913 1974] 75-314698 ISBN 0-200-04026-X : 6.95
1. Jesus Christ—Miscellanea. 2. Christianity—Miscellanea. I. Title.

STIRRINGS : 200
essays Christian and radical / edited by John J. Vincent. London : Epworth Press, 1976. 128 p. ; 22 cm. (City soundings) [BT28.S69] 76-381620 ISBN 0-7162-0265-4 : £1.00
1. Theology—20th century—Addresses, essays, lectures. I. Vincent, John J.

STOKES, Mack B. 200
The Bible and modern doubt [by] Mack B. Stokes. Old Tappan, N.J., F. H. Revell Co. [1970] 286 p. 21 cm. Bibliography: p. 281-282. [BS543.S73] 79-123059 5.95
1. Bible—Theology. 2. Belief and doubt. 3. Apologetics—20th century. I. Title.

STOTT, John R. W. 200
Christ the controversialist; a study in some essentials of evangelical religion [by] John R. W. Stott. [1st ed.] Downers Grove, Ill., Inter-Varsity Press [1970] 214 p. 20 cm. Includes bibliographical references. [BR1640.S7 1970] 73-127934
1. Evangelicalism—Addresses, essays, lectures. I. Title.

STREIKER, Lowell D. 200
The gospel of irreligious religion; insights for uprooted man from major world faiths [by] Lowell D. Streiker. New York, Sheed and Ward [1969] xix, 169 p. 21 cm. Includes bibliographical references. [BL85.S73] 75-82603 4.95
1. Religions. 2. Religion. I. Title.

STREIKER, Lowell D., comp. 200
Who am I? Second thoughts on man, his loves, his gods, edited by Lowell D. Streiker. New York, Sheed & Ward [1970] xxxii, 216 p. illus. 22 cm. [BV4801.S77] 76-101546 ISBN 0-8362-1208-8 4.50
1. Devotional literature. I. Title.

STRENG, Frederick J. 200
Understanding religious life / Frederick J. Streng. 2d ed. Encino, Calif. : Dickenson Pub. Co., c1976. 207 p. : ill. ; 23 cm. (The Religious life of man) First ed. published in 1969 under title: Understanding religious man. Includes bibliographies and index. [BL48.S77 1976] 75-26540 ISBN 0-8221-0168-8 pbk. : 4.95
1. Religion. I. Title.

TEMPLE, William, Abp. of Canterbury, 1881-1944. 200
What Christians stand for in the secular world. With a pref. by J. H. Oldham. Philadelphia, Fortress Press [1965] ix, 35 p. 19 cm. (Facet books. Social ethics series, 7) Contents.What Christians stand for in the secular world. -- The problem of power. Bibliography: p. 32-33. [BR121.T415] 65-21081
1. Christianity — Essence, genius, nature. I. Title. II. Series.

THEOLOGY and modern life; 200
essays in honor of Harris Franklin Rall. Edited by Paul Arthur Schilpp. Freeport, N.Y., Books for Libraries Press [1970] x, 297 p. port. 23 cm. (Essay index reprint series) Reprint of the 1940 ed. Contents.Contents.—Harris Franklin Rall, by I. G. Whitchurch.—Our immortality, by S. S. Cohon.—The significance of critical study of the Gospels for religious thought today, by F. C. Grant.—The Christian doctrine of man, by A. C. Knudson.—Facing the problem of evil, by F. J. McConnell.—The realistic movement in religious philosophy, by E. W. Lyman.—The meaning of rational faith, by P. A. Schilpp.—Interpreting the religious situation, by I. G. Whitchurch.—The kingdom of God and the life of today, by C. C. McCown.—The church and social optimism, by S. Mathews.—The church, the truth, and society, by E. S. Brightman.—Let the church be the church! By E. F. Tittle.—Bibliography of the writings of Harris Franklin Rall (p. 285-297) [BT10.T53 1970] 70-117852
1. Theology—Addresses, essays, lectures. I. Rall, Harris Franklin, 1860-1964. II. Schilpp, Paul Arthur, 1897- ed.

THILS, Gustave, 1909- 200
A "non-religious" Christianity? [Translated by John A. Otto.] Staten Island, N.Y., Alba House [1970] xiii, 168 p. 22 cm. Translation of Christianisme sans religion? Includes bibliographical references. [BT83.7.T4813] 78-129171 4.95
1. Secularization (Theology) I. Title.

TOPPING, Coral Wesley, 1889- 200
The Jesus revolution : for daggers and handcuffs, a torch / C. W. Topping. [Vancouver : College Printers and Publishers, c1976] [iv], 75 p. ; 21 cm. "By the same author": p. [iii] [BT202.T66] 76-373000 3.95
1. Jesus Christ—Person and offices. 2. Christianity. I. Title.

TRAPP, Jacob, 1899- 200
The light of a thousand suns; mystery, awe, and renewal in religion. Photos. by Bruce Roberts. [1st ed.] New York, Harper & Row [1973] ix, 149 p. illus. 14 x 21 cm. Includes bibliographical references. [BL80.2.T7 1973] 72-78061 ISBN 0-06-068431-3 3.50
1. Religions. 2. Religion. I. Title.

TRUEBLOOD, David Elton, 1900- 200
Signs of hope in a century of despair. [1st ed.] New York, Harper [1950] 125 p. 20 cm. [BR481.T76] 50-5309
1. Christianity—20th century. I. Title.

VAIL, Albert Ross, 1880- 200
Transforming light; the living heritage of world religions [by] Albert Vail and Emily McClellan Vail. [1st ed.] New York, Harper & Row [1970] xvii, 451 p. 24 cm. [BL80.2.V3 1970] 70-85065 12.50
1. Religions. 2. Religion. I. Vail, Emily McClellan, joint author. II. Title.

WATSON, David C. K., 1933- 200
My God is real [by] David C. K. Watson. New York, Seabury Press [1970] 95 p. 21 cm. (A Seabury paperback SP 68) Includes bibliographical references. [BT1102.W37] 70-122630 1.65
1. Apologetics—20th century. I. Title.

*WEST, Virginia. 200
The Message. New York, Vanatage [1968] 77p. 21cm. 2.75
I. Title.

WETZEL, Willard W 200
The decision maker. Boston, United Church Press [c1963] 124 p. illus. 21 cm. (An Adult resource book) "Part of the United Church curriculum, prepared and published by the Division of Christian Education and the Division of Publication of the United Church Board for Homeland Ministries." Bibliographical references included in "Acknowledgments" (p. 123-124) [BR125.W4673] 63-19206
1. Christianity — 20th cent. 2. Christian life — Study and teaching. I. United Church of Christ. II. Title.

WILMORE, Gayraud S. 200
Black religion and Black radicalism. Garden City, N.Y., Anchor Pr./Doubleday, 1973 [c.1972] xiii, 344 p. 21 cm. (Anchor Books, AO-91) (C. Eric Lincoln series on Black religion) Bibliography: p. [307]-329. [BR563.N4W53] 75-180116 ISBN 0-385-09125-7 3.50 (pbk.)
1. Negroes—Religion. I. Title. II. Series.

WILSON, John, 1928- 200
Religion. London, Heinemann Educational, [1972, i.e 1973] viii, 119 p. 20 cm. (Concept books, 14) Imprint covered by label: Distributed in the USA by Humanities Press, New York. Bibliography: p. 117. [BL48.W49] 73-161650 ISBN 0-435-46194-X 2.00 (pbk.)
1. Religion.

WINKWORTH, Douglas Eric. 200
A critical look at religion / D. E. Winkworth. London ; New York : Regency Press, 1974. 58 p. ; 20 cm. [BR125.W7544] 74-196192 ISBN 0-7212-0349-3 : £1.20
1. Christianity. 2. Religion. 3. Revelation. 4. Reincarnation. I. Title.

WOLCOTT, Leonard T. 200
Religions around the world, by Leonard and Carolyn Wolcott. Nashville, Abingdon Press [1967] 191 p. col. illus. 25 cm. [BL92.W6] 67-17382
1. Religions — Juvenile literature. I. Wolcott, Carolyn Muller, joint author. II. Title.

WOLCOTT, Leonard T. 200
Religions around the world, by Leonard and Carolyn Wolcott. Nashville, Abingdon Press [1967] 191 p. col. illus. 25 cm. [BL92.W6] 67-17382
1. Religions—Juvenile literature. I. Wolcott, Carolyn Muller, joint author. II. Title.

YINGER, John Milton. 200
The scientific study of religion [by] J. Milton Yinger. [New York] Macmillan [1970] x, 593 p. illus. 24 cm. Bibliography: p. 536-576. [BL48.Y46 1970] 75-95188
1. Religion. I. Title.

ALDRIDGE, Alfred Owen, 200.1
1915-
Benjamin Franklin and nature's God. Durham, N. C., Duke, 1967. 279p. 23cm. Bibl. [E302.6.F8A45] 67-13409 7.50
1. Franklin, Benjamn, 1706-1790—Religion. 2. Religious thought. I. Title.

ARNETT, Willard Eugene, 200.1
1921- ed.
A modern reader in the philosophy of religion [edited by] Willard E. Arnett. New York, Appleton-Century-Crofts [1966] x, 563 p. 22 cm. (The Century philosophy series) Includes bibliographical references. [BL51.A68] 66-20470
1. Religion—Philosophy—Collections. I. Title.

BAGGS, Ralph L. 200.1
International brotherhood through service clubs; a practical path to peace, by Ralph L. Baggs. [1st ed.] New York, Exposition Press [1967] 80 p. 21 cm. [BL390.B27] 67-8439
1. Religions (Proposed, universal, etc.) 2. Associations, institutions, etc. I. Title.

BAILLIE, John, 1886-1960. 200'.1
The interpretation of religion : an introductory study of the theological principles / by John Baillie. Westport, Conn. : Greenwood Press, [1977] c1928. xv, 477 p. ; 23 cm. Reprint of the ed. published by Scribner, New York. Includes bibliographical references and index. [BL48.B2 1977] 76-49990 ISBN 0-8371-9038-X lib. bdg. : 25.00
1. Religion. 2. Religion—Philosophy. 3. Theology, Doctrinal. I. Title.

BARBOUR, Ian G. 200'.1
Myths, models, and paradigms; a comparative study in science and religion [by] Ian G. Barbour. [1st ed.] New York, Harper & Row [1974] vi, 198 p. 21 cm. Includes bibliographical references. [BL240.2.B36 1974] 73-18698 6.95
1. Religion and science—1946- I. Title.

BELLAH, Robert Neelly, 200'.1
1927-
Beyond belief; essays on religion in a post-traditional world [by] Robert N. Bellah. [1st ed.] New York, Harper & Row [1970] xxi, 298 p. 22 cm. Includes bibliographical references. [BL60.B37] 77-109058 7.95
1. Religion and sociology—Addresses, essays, lectures. I. Title.

BELLAH, Robert Neelly, 200.1
1927-
Beyond belief essays on religion in a post-traditional world /Robert N. Bellah New York Harper and Row [1976 c1970] xxii, 298 p.; 20 cm. Includes bibliographical references and index [BL60.B37] ISBN 0-06-060775-0 pbk.: 4.95
1. Religion and sociology—Addresses, essays, lectures. I. Title.
L.C. card no. for original edition: 77-109058.

BENNETT, Charles Andrew 200'.1
Armstrong, 1885-1930.
The dilemma of religious knowledge. Edited, with a pref., by William Ernest Hocking. Port Washington, N.Y., Kennikat Press [1969] xv, 126 p. 22 cm. (Lowell lectures, 1930) (Essay and general literature index reprint series.) Reprint of the 1931 ed. Bibliographical references included in "Notes" (p. [121]-123) [BL48.B4 1969] 71-85986
1. Religion. 2. Religion—Philosophy. 3. Supernatural. I. Title. II. Series: Lowell Institute lectures, 1930

BETTIS, Joseph Dabney, 200'.1
comp.
Phenomenology of religion; eight modern descriptions of the essence of religion. [1st U.S. ed.] New York, Harper & Row [1969] viii, 245 p. 21 cm. (Harper forum books) Contents.Contents.—Introduction, by J. D. Bettis.—An introduction to phenomenology: What is phenomenology? by M. Merleau-Ponty.—The phenomenology of religion: The meaning of religion, by W. B. Kristensen.—A naturalistic description: Religion in essence and manifestation, by G. van der Leeuw.—A supernaturalistic description: Approaches to God, by J. Maritain.—A projective description: The essence of Christianity, by L. Feuerbach.—Religion as a faculty: On religion, by F. Schleiermacher. The Christian faith, by F. Schleiermacher.—Religion as a dimension: Religion as a dimension in man's spiritual life, by P. Tillich.—Religion as a social function: Magic, science, and religion, by B. Malinowski.—Religion as structure and archetype: The sacred and the profane, by M. Eliade.—Religion as encounter: I and thou, by M. Buber. Bibliographical footnotes. [BL51.B547 1969] 69-17005 3.50
1. Religion—Philosophy. 2. Phenomenology. I. Title.

BIANCHI, Eugene C. 200'.1
The religious experience of revolutionaries [by] Eugene C. Bianchi. [1st ed.] Garden City, N.Y., Doubleday, 1972. 223 p. 22 cm. Includes bibliographies. [BL60.B45] 72-76122 ISBN 0-385-05412-2 6.95
1. Religion and sociology. I. Title.

BIANCHI, Joseph Salvatore, 200'.1
1915-
Philosophy of the unknown [by] Joseph S. Bianchi. Santa Monica, Calif., DeVorss [1973] 325 p. illus. 23 cm. On spine: The unknown. [BL240.2.B54] 73-77352
1. Religion and science—1946- I. Title. II. Title: The unknown.

BIANCHI, Joseph Salvatore, 200'.1
1915-
Philosophy of the unknown / Joseph S. Bianchi. Los Alamitos, CA. : Hwong Pub. Co., c1976. vii, 174 p. : ill. ; 18 cm. Cover title: The unknown. [BD511.B5 1976] 76-28144 ISBN 0-89260-066-7 lib.bdg. : 4.95 ISBN 0-89260-067-5 pbk. : 1.95
1. Cosmology. 2. Man. 3. Evolution. 4. Religion and science—1946- I. Title. II. Title: The unknown.

BIEBERMAN, Lisa. 200'.1
Phanerothyme; a western approach to the religious use of psychochemicals. Cambridge, Mass., Psychedelic Information Center [1968] 32 p. 19 cm. [BL65.D7B5] 68-3701
1. Hallucinogenic drugs and religious experience. I. Title.

BLOCH, Ernst, 1885- 200'.1
Man on his own; essays in the philosophy of religion. Translated by E. B. Ashton. [New York] Herder and Herder [1970] 240 p. 22 cm. Translation of Religion im Erbe. Contents.Contents.—Foreword, by H. Cox.—Introduction, by J. Moltmann.—Karl Marx; death and apocalypse.—Incipit vita nova.—Biblical resurrection and apocalypse.—Christ, or The uncovered countenance.—Religious truth.—Christian social utopias.—The nationalized God and the right to community.—Man's increasing entry into religious mystery. [BL51.B584513] 79-87749 5.50
1. Religion—Philosophy—Addresses, essays, lectures. I. Title.

BOCHENSKI, Innocentius M. 200.1
1902-
The logic of religion, by Joseph M. Bochenski. [New York] New York University Press, 1965. x, 179 p. 22 cm. "A re-elaboration of a series of lectures ... [delivered] in March, 1963, at New York University" and sponsored by the Deems Fund. [BL65.L2B6] 65-11762
1. Religion and language. 2. Semantics (Philosophy) I. Title.

BOCHENSKI, Innocentius M., 200.1
1902-
The logic of religion, by Joseph M. Bochenski [New York] N.Y.U. [c.1965] x, 179p. 22cm. A re-elaboration of a ser. of lects. delivered in March, 1963, at N.Y.U. and sponsored by the Deems Fund. [BL65.L2B6] 65-11762 5.00
1. Religion and language. 2. Semantics (Philosophy) I. Title.

BRADEN, William. 200.1
The private sea; LSD and the search for God. Chicago, Quadrangle Books [1967] 255 p. 22 cm. [BL65.D7B7] 67-12353
1. Hallucinogenic drugs and religious experience. I. Title.

BRADEN, William. 200.1
The private sea, LSD & the search for God. New York, Bantam [1968,c.1967] 212p. 18cm. (N3733) [BL65.D7B7] .95 pap.,
1. Hallucinogenic drugs and religious experience. I. Title.

BRIGHTMAN, Edgar 200'.1
Sheffield, 1884-1953.
A philosophy of religion. New York, Greenwood Press [1969, c1940] xvii, 539 p. 23 cm. Bibliography: p. 490-522. [BL51.B689 1969] 72-95112
1. Religion—Philosophy. I. Title.

BROD, Max, 1884-1968. 200'.1
Paganism, Christianity, Judaism; a confession of faith. Translated from the German by William Wolf. University, University of Alabama Press [1970] x, 276 p. 24 cm. Translation of Heidentum, Christentum, Judentum. [BL51.B75713] 78-104937 10.00
1. Religion—Philosophy. I. Title.

BRODY, Boruch A., comp. 200'.1
Readings in the philosophy of religion; an analytic approach. Edited by Baruch A. Brody. Englewood Cliffs, N.J., Prentice-Hall [1974] xii, 667 p. 24 cm. Bibliography: p. 664-667. [BL51.B758] 73-20485 ISBN 0-13-759340-6 11.95
1. Religion—Philosophy—Collected works. I. Title.

BRONSTEIN, Daniel J., 200'.1
1908- ed.
Approaches to the philosophy of religion; a book of readings, edited by Daniel Jay Bronstein and Harold M. Schulweis. Freeport, N.Y., Books for Libraries Press [1969, c1954] ix, 532 p. 22 cm. (Essay index reprint series) Bibliography: p. 519-522. [BL51.B76 1969] 77-93320
1. Religion—Philosophy. I. Schulweis, Harold M. II. Title.

BROWN, Colin. 200'.1
Karl Barth and the Christian message. [1st ed.] Chicago, Inter-varsity Press [1967] 163 p. 20 cm. (A Tyndale paperback) "A note on books": p. [154]-159. Bibliographical footnotes. [BX4827.B3B69] 66-30696
1. Barth, Karl, 1886-

BROWN, Stuart C. 200'.1
Do religious claims make sense? [By] Stuart C. Brown. New York, Macmillan [1969] xx, 188 p. 23 cm. Includes bibliographical references. [BL51.B777 1969b] 71-93568 5.95
1. Religion—Philosophy. I. Title.

BURCH, George Bosworth, 200'.1
1902-
Alternative goals in religion; love, freedom, truth. With a foreword by W. Norris Clarke. Montreal, McGill-Queen's University Press, [1973 c1972] 118 p. 22 cm. Includes bibliographical references. [BL51.B84] 72-82248 ISBN 0-7735-0122-3 6.50
1. Religion—Philosophy. 2. Absolute, The. 3. Christianity. 4. Buddha and Buddhism. 5. Vedanta. I. Title.
Publisher's Address: 136 South Broadway N.Y. 10533. pap 2.50; ISBN 0-7735-0163-0.

BURKE, Thomas Patrick, 200'.1
1934-
The reluctant vision; an essay in the philosophy of religion [by] T. Patrick Burke. Philadelphia, Fortress Press [1974] 136 p. 19 cm. Includes bibliographic references. [BL51.B854] 73-88354 ISBN 0-8006-1068-7 3.00
1. Religion—Philosophy. I. Title.

BURRELL, David B. 200'.1
Exercises in religious understanding [by] David B. Burrell. Notre Dame, University of Notre Dame Press [1974] x, 243 p. 22 cm. Includes bibliographical references. [BL51.B858] 74-12566 ISBN 0-268-00548-6 9.95
1. Religion—Philosophy. I. Title.

BUSSELL, Frederick 200'.1
William, 1862-1944.
Religious thought and heresy in the Middle Ages. Port Washington, N.Y., Kennikat Press [1971] 3 v. (xiii, 873 p.) 22 cm. Reprint of the 1918 ed. Includes bibliographical references. [BR252.B87 1971] 72-118516 ISBN 0-8046-1138-6
1. Church history—Middle Ages, 600-1500. 2. Religions—History. 3. Sects, Medieval. 4. Middle Ages—History. I. Title.

CAHN, Steven M., comp. 200'.1
Philosophy of religion, edited by Steven M. Cahn. New York, Harper & Row [1970] vi, 397 p. 21 cm. (Sources in contemporary philosophy) Bibliography: p. [395]-397. [BL51.C23] 75-108414
1. Religion—Philosophy—Collections. I. Title.

CAIRD, John, 1820-1898. 200'.1
An introduction to the philosophy of religion. New ed. New York, AMS Press [1970] xi, 343 p. 23 cm. Reprint of the 1901 ed. [BL51.C25 1970] 75-113569
1. Religion—Philosophy. I. Title.

CAMPBELL, James Ian, 1935- 200'.1
The language of religion [by] James I. Campbell. New York, Bruce Pub. Co. [1971] 183 p. 22 cm. (Horizons in philosophy) Bibliography: p. 164-176. [BL65.L2C33] 76-121005
1. Religion and language. I. Title.

CAPITAN, William H. 200'.1
Philosophy of religion; an introduction [by] William H. Capitan. Indianapolis, Pegasus [1972] viii, 214 p. 21 cm. (Traditions in philosophy) Bibliography: p. 207-209. [BL51.C324] 70-128669
1. Religion—Philosophy. I. Title.

CERMINARA, Gina. 200'.1
Insights for the age of aquarius. Englewood Cliffs, N.J., Prentice-Hall [1973] 314 p. 24 cm. Includes bibliographical references. [BL51.C44 1973] 72-8449 ISBN 0-13-467589-4 7.95
1. Religion—Philosophy. 2. General semantics. I. Title.

CERMINARA, Gina. 200'.1
Insights for the age of aquarius : a guide to religious realism / by Gina Cerminara. Wheaton, Ill. : Theosophical Pub. House, 1976, c1973. p. cm. (A Quest book) Includes bibliographical references and index. [BL51.C44 1976] 76-6173 ISBN 0-8356-0483-7
1. Religion—Philosophy. 2. General semantics. I. Title.

THE Challenge of religion 200'.1
today : essays on the philosophy of religion / John King-Farlow, editor. New York : Science History Publications, 1976. p. cm. (Canadian contemporary philosophy series) Bibliography: p. [BL51.C48] 76-13492 ISBN 0-88202-157-5 pbk. : 3.95
1. Religion—Philosophy—Addresses, essays, lectures. I. King-Farlow, John.

CHARLESWORTH, Maxwell 200'.1
John.
Philosophy of religion: the historic approaches [by] M. J. Charlesworth. [New York] Herder and Herder [1972] xiv, 216 p. 22 cm. (Philosophy of religion series) Includes bibliographical references. [BL51.C49 1972b] 75-176367 8.95
1. Religion—Philosophy. I. Title.

CHARLESWORTH, Maxwell 200'.1
John, comp.
The problem of religious language [compiled by] M. J. Charlesworth. Englewood Cliffs, N.J., Prentice-Hall [1974] viii, 253 p. 21 cm. (Contemporary problems in philosophy) Contents.Contents.—Charlesworth, M. J. Introduction.—Marshall, G. D. Religious language must be descriptive.—Otto, R. Religious language describes religious experiences I.—Horsburgh, H. J. N. Religious language describes religious experiences II.—Joyce, G. H. Religious language is analogously descriptive.—Carnap, R. Religious language is meaningless.—Randall, J. H., Jr. Religious language is symbolic and "impressive."—Ramsey, I. T. Religious language is paradoxically evocative.—Le Roy E. Religious language is "practical."—Arnold, M. Religious language is moral-emotive.—Santayana, G. Religious language is poetic-ethnic.—Hare, R. M. Religious language expresses quasi-metaphysical "attitudes."—Hudson, W. D. Religious language has its own proper meaning. Includes bibliographical references. [BL65.L2C48] 73-17263 ISBN 0-13-720011-0 7.95
1. Religion and language. I. Title.
Contents omitted.

CHARTIER, Emile, 1868- 200'.1
1951.
The gods [by] Alain. Translated by Richard Pevear. [New York, New Directions Pub. Corp., 1974] 186 p. 21 cm. (A New Directions book) Translation of Les dieux. Contents.Contents.—Aladdin.—Pan.—Jupiter.—Christophorous.—Selected bibliography (p. 185-186.) [BL51.C513 1974] 74-8291 ISBN 0-8112-0547-9 8.95
1. Religion—Philosophy. 2. Truth. 3. Gods. I. Title.
Pbk. 3.95, ISBN 0-8112-0548-7

COLISH, Marcia L. 200'.1
The mirror of language; a study in the medieval theory of knowledge, by Marcia L. Colish. New Haven, Yale University Press, 1968. xxiii, 404 p. 24 cm. (Yale historical publications. Miscellany, 88) Bibliography: p. 349-393. [BL51.C59] 68-13901
1. Knowledge, Theory of (Religion) 2. Semantics (Philosophy) 3. Philosophy, Medieval. I. Title. II. Series.

COLLINGWOOD, Robin George, 200'.1
1889-1943.
Faith & reason; essays in the philosophy of religion. Edited with an introd. by Lionel Rubinoff. Chicago, Quadrangle Books, 1968. 317 p. 22 cm. Bibliography: p. [305]-311. [BL51.C595] 67-21641
1. Religion—Philosophy. I. Rubinoff, Lionel, ed. II. Title.

COLLINS, James Daniel. 200.1
The emergence of philosophy of religion, by James Collins. New Haven, Yale University Press, 1967. xv. 517 p. 25 cm. (St. Thomas More lectures, 1963) Bibliography: p. [492]-506. [BL51.C62] 67-13432
1. Religion — Philosophy — Hist. I. Title. II. Series. III. Series: The St. Thomas More lectures, 1963

COLLINS, James Daniel 200.1
The emergence of philosophy of religion, by James Collins. New Haven, Yale, 1967. xv, 517p. 25cm. (St. Thomas More lects., 1963) Bibl. [BL51.C62] 67-13432 12.50
1. Religion—Philosophy—Hist. I. Title. II. Series: The St. Thomas More lectures, 1963

CONGER, George Perrigo, 200'.1
1884-
The ideologies of religion. Freeport, N.Y., Books for Libraries Press [1969] viii, 271 p. 23 cm. (Essay index reprint series) Reprint of the 1940 ed. Includes bibliographical reference. [BL51.C636 1969] 70-93329
1. Religion—Philosophy. I. Title.

CORNELL, George W. 200'.1
The untamed God / George W. Cornell. 1st ed. New York : Harper & Row, [1975] 152 p. ; 21 cm. Includes index. Bibliography: p. [143] -146. [BR85.C783 1975] 74-25690 ISBN 0-06-061582-6 : 7.95
1. Theology—Addresses, essays, lectures. I. Title.

CRITES, Stephen. 200'.1
In the twilight of Christendom; Hegel vs. Kierkegaard on faith and history. Chambersberg, Pa., American Academy of Religion, 1972. 109 p. 24 cm. (AAR studies in religion, no. 2) Revised and expanded from a paper presented at the Symposium on Hegel's Philosophy of Religion, held at Wofford College, Spartanburg, S.C., November, 1968. Bibliography: p. 108-109. [B2949.R3C74 1972] 77-188905 2.75
1. Hegel, Georg Wilhelm Friedrich, 1770-1831—Religion. 2. Kierkegaard, Soren Aabye, 1813-1855. I. Title. II. Series: American Academy of Religion. AAR studies in religion, no. 2.

CUPITT, Don. 200'.1
The leap of reason / [by] Don Cupitt. London : Sheldon Press, 1976. xi, 145 p. ; 23 cm. (Studies in philosophy and religion) Includes bibliographical references and index. [BL51.C84 1976b] 76-374287 ISBN 0-85969-084-9 : £4.50
1. Knowledge, Theory of (Religion) 2. Pluralism. 3. Ethical relativism. 4. Revelation. I. Title. II. Series.

DAVIS, William Hatcher. 200'.1
Philosophy of religion, by William H. Davis. Abilene, Tex., Biblical Research Press [1969] 78 p. 22 cm. (The Way of life series, no. 114. Adult class series) [BL51.D365] 75-92048
1. Religion—Philosophy. I. Title.

DEUTSCH, Eliot. 200'.1
Humanity and divinity; an essay in comparative metaphysics. Honolulu, University of Hawaii Press, 1970. x, 151 p. illus. 24 cm. Includes bibliographical references. [BD111.D45] 76-128081 ISBN 0-87022-190-6 8.00
1. Metaphysics. 2. Man. 3. Absolute, The. I. Title.

DIAMOND, Malcolm Luria. 200'.1
Contemporary philosophy and religious thought: an introduction to the philosophy of religion [by] Malcolm L. Diamond. New York, McGraw-Hill [1974] xiii, 450 p. 23 cm. Includes bibliographical references. [BL51.D48] 73-17084 ISBN 0-07-016721-4
1. Religion—Philosophy. 2. God. I. Title.

DIAMOND, Malcolm Luria, 200'.1
comp.
The logic of God; theology and verification, edited by Malcolm L. Diamond and Thomas V. Litzenburg, Jr. Introd., The challenge of contemporary empiricism, by Malcolm L. Diamond. [1st ed.] Indianapolis, Bobbs-Merrill [1975] x, 552 p. 24 cm. Bibliography: p. [525]-552. [BL51.D49] 74-32235 ISBN 0-672-60792-1 9.95
1. Religion—Philosophy. I. Litzenburg, Thomas V., joint comp. II. Title.

DRANE, James F. 200'.1
The possibility of God / by James F. Drane. Totowa, N.J. : Littlefield, Adams, c1976. p. cm. (A Littlefield, Adams quality paperback ; no. 321) [BD450.D67] 75-45124 ISBN 0-8226-0321-7
1. Man. 2. Alienation (Social psychology) 3. Religion and culture. 4. God. 5. United States—Civilization. I. Title.

DRANE, James F. 200'.1
The possibility of God : a reconsideration of religion in a technological society / by James Drane. Totowa, N.J. : Littlefield, Adams, 1976. xix, 194 p. ; 21 cm. (A Littlefield, Adams quality paperback ; no. 321) Includes bibliographical references and index. [BD450.D67] 75-45124 ISBN 0-8226-0321-7 pbk. : 3.50
1. Man. 2. Alienation (Social psychology) 3. Religion and culture. 4. God. 5. United States—Civilization. I. Title.

*DRURY, John. 200.1
Angels and dirt; an inquiry into theology and prayer. New York, Macmillan. [1974, c1972]. 104 p. 18 cm. [BL51] 1.95 (pbk.)
1. Religion—Philosophy. I. Title.
L.C. card number for original ed.: 73-14427.

DUNNE, John S., 1929- 200'.1
The way of all the earth; experiments in truth and religion [by] John S. Dunne. New York, Macmillan [1972] xiii, 240 p. 22 cm. [BL85.D87] 78-167928 6.95
1. Religions. 2. Spiritual life. I. Title.

THE Dynamic in Christian thought. 200'.1
Edited by Joseph Papin. [Villanova, Pa.] Villanova University Press [1970] vii, 291 p. 23 cm. (The Villanova University symposium, v. 1, 1968) Includes bibliographical references. [BR50.D9] 70-107942 ISBN 0-87723-008-0
1. Theology—Addresses, essays, lectures. I. Papin, Joseph, 1914- ed. II. Title. III. Series.

EASTMAN, Roger, comp. 200'.1
The ways of religion / edited by Roger Eastman. San Francisco : Canfield Press, [1975] viii, 597 p. : ill. ; 23 cm. Includes bibliographies and indexes. [BL74.E18] 74-30211 ISBN 0-06-382595-3 pbk. : 8.95
1. Religions—Collected works. I. Title.

EDWARDS, Rem B. 200'.1
Reason and religion; an introduction to the philosophy of religion [by] Rem B. Edwards. New York, Harcourt Brace Jovanovich [1972] xiv, 386 p. 21 cm. Includes bibliographies. [BL51.E42] 72-80882 ISBN 0-15-576002-5
1. Religion—Philosophy. I. Title.

FARRER, Austin Marsden 200.1
Finite and infinite; a philosophical essay. Westminster [London] Dacre pr. [New York, Humanities, c.1966] xii, 300p. 24cm. First pub. March 1943. 6.50
1. Religion — Philosophy. 2. Substance (Philosophy) 3. God. I. Title.

FEAVER, J. Clayton 200.1
Religion in philosophical and cultural perspective; a new approach to the philosophy of religion through cross-disciplinary studies, ed. by J. Clayton Feaver, William Horosz. Princeton, N. J., Van Nostrand [1967] xiv. 504p. 24cm. Bibl. [BL51.F39] 67-3112 3.95
1. Religion—Philosophy— Addresses, essays lectures. I. Horosz, William, joint author. II. Title.

FEAVER, J. Clayton. 200.1
Religion in philosophical and cultural perspective; a new approach to the philosophy of religion through cross-disciplinary studies, edited by J. Clayton Feavor and William Horosz. Princeton, N.J., Van Nostrand [1967] xiv, 504 p. 24 cm. Includes bibliographies. [BL51.F39] 67-3112
1. Religion-Philosophy—Addresses, essays, lectures. I. Horosz, William, joint author. II. Title.

FEIBLEMAN, James Kern, 200'.1
1904-
Religious Platonism; the influence of religion on Plato and the influence of Plato on religion [by] James K. Feibleman. Westport, Conn., Greenwood Press [1971, c1959] 236 p. 22 cm. Includes bibliographical references. [B398.R4F4 1971] 78-161628 ISBN 0-8371-6184-3
1. Plato—Religion. 2. Plato—Influence. I. Title.

FERRE, Frederick. 200'.1
Basic modern philosophy of religion. New York, viii, 465 p. 24 cm. Includes bibliographies. [BL51.F48] 67-15490
1. cribner 2. Religion—Philosophy. I. Title.

FERRE, Frederick. 200'.1
Basic modern philosophy of religion. New York, Scribner [1967] viii, 465 p. 24 cm. Includes bibliographies. [BL51.F48] 67-15490
1. Religion—Philosophy. I. Title.

FERRE, Nels Fredrick 200'.1
Solomon, 1908-
The universal word; a theology for a universal faith, by Nels F. S. Ferre. Philadelphia, Westminster Press [1969] 282 p. 24 cm. [BL51.F494] 69-12907 9.00
1. Religion—Philosophy. I. Title.

FEUERBACH, Ludwig Andreas, 200'.1
1804-1872.
Lectures on the essence of religion. Translated by Ralph Manheim. [1st ed.] New York, Harper & Row [1967] xv, 359 p. 22 cm. Translation of Vorlesungen uber das Wesen der Religion. Bibliography: p. 357-359. [B2971.W62E5 1967] 67-21548
I. Title.

*FLEW, Antony. 200.'1
The presumption of atheism and other philosophical essays on God, freedom and immortality / Antony Flew. New York : Barnes & Noble Books, 1976. 183p. ; 23 cm. Includes index. Bibliography: p. [176]-180. [BL2747.3] 75-43411 ISBN 0-06-492119-0 : 20.00
1. Religion-Philosophy-Addresses, essays, lectures. 2. Atheism. 3. Rationalism. 4. Immortality. I. Title.

FOSDICK, Harry Emerson, 200'.1
1878-1969.
As I see religion / by Harry Emerson Fosdick. Westport, Conn. : Greenwood Press, 1975, c1932. v, 201 p. ; 20 cm. Reprint of the ed. published by Harper, New York. Includes bibliographical references and index. [BL48.F6 1975] 75-11835 ISBN 0-8371-8142-9
1. Religion. I. Title.

FOSDICK, Harry Emerson, 200'.1
1878-1969.
As I see religion / by Harry Emerson Fosdick. Westport, Conn. : Greenwood Press, 1975, c1932. v, 201 p. ; 20 cm. Reprint of the ed. published by Harper, New York. Includes bibliographical references and index. [BL48.F6 1975] 75-11835 ISBN 0-8371-8142-9 lib.bdg. : 12.00
1. Religion. I. Title.

*GANDHI, Ramchandra. 200.1
The availability of religious ideas / Ramchandra Gandhi. New York : Barnes & Noble, c1976. 109p. ; 23 cm. (Library of philosophy and religion) Includes index. [BL51] 75-46318 ISBN 0-06-492324-X : 22.50
1. Religion-Philosophy. I. Title.

GANDHI, Ramchandra, 1937- 200'.1
The availability of religious ideas / Ramchandra Gandhi. New York : Barnes & Noble Books, 1976. 109 p. ; 23 cm. (Library of philosophy and religion) Includes index. [BL51.G325 1976] 76-371912 ISBN 0-06-492324-X : 22.50
1. Religion—Philosophy. I. Title.

GANDHI, Ramchandra, 1937- 200'.1
The availability of religious ideas / Ramchandra Gandhi. London : Macmillan, 1976. 109 p. ; 23 cm. (Library of philosophy and religion) Includes index. [BL51.G325 1976b] 76-378093 ISBN 0-333-13757-4 : £7.95
1. Religion—Philosophy—Addresses, essays, lectures. I. Title.

GILL, Jerry H., comp. 200'.1
Philosophy and religion; some contemporary perspectives, edited by Jerry H. Gill. Minneapolis, Burgess Pub. Co. [1968] vii, 372 p. 23 cm. Contents.Contents.—Reason and quest for revelation, by P. Tillich.—On the ontological mystery, by G. Marcel.—The problem of non-objectifying thinking and speaking, by M. Heidegger.—The problem of natural theology, by J. Macquarrie.—Metaphysical rebellion, by A. Camus.—Psychoanalysis and religion by E. Fromm.—Why I am not a Christian, by B. Russell.—The quest for being, by S. Hook.—The sacred and the profane; a dialectical understanding of Christianity, by T. J. J. Altizer. Three strata of meaning in religious discourse by C. Hartshorne.—The theological task, by J. B. Cobb.—Theology and objectivity, by S. A. Ogden.—Can faith validate God-talk? by K. Nielsen.—The logic of God, by J. Wisdom.—Mapping the logic of models in science and theology, by F. Ferre.—On understanding mystery, by I. T. Ramsey.—Teilhard de Chardin; a philosophy of precession, by E. R. Baltazar.—The nature of apologetics, by H. Bouillard.—Metaphysics as horizon, by B. Lonergan.—Deciding whether to believe, by M. Novak. Includes bibliographical references. [B56.G5] 68-54894
1. Philosophy and religion—Addresses, essays, lectures. I. Title.

GILL, Jerry H. 200'.1
The possibility of religious knowledge, by Jerry H. Gill. Grand Rapids, Eerdmans [1971] 238 p. 21 cm. Bibliography: p. 224-227. [BL51.G626] 74-78023
1. Knowledge, Theory of (Religion) I. Title.

GLADSTONE, William Ewart, 200'.1
1809-1898.
Later gleanings. A new series of Gleanings of past years: theological and ecclesiastical. Freeport, N.Y., Books for Libraries Press [1972] 426 p. 23 cm. (Essay index reprint series) Reprint of the 1897 ed. Includes bibliographical references. [BR85.G53 1972] 72-8478 ISBN 0-8369-7314-3
1. Theology—Addresses, essays, lectures. I. Title.

GLANVILL, Joseph, 1636- 200'.1
1680.
Collected works of Joseph Glanvill; facsimile editions prepared by Bernhard Fabian. Hildesheim, New York, G. Olms, 1970- v. 23 cm. Contents.Contents.— —v. 5. Philosophia pia. Logou threskeia. (romanized form) [BL51.G665] 77-560142
1. Religion—Philosophy. 2. Faith and reason. I. Fabian, Bernhard, ed.

GROSS, Mark, 1918- 200'.1
Quattlebaum's truth. [1st ed.] New York, Harper & Row [1970] 145 p. 22 cm. Includes bibliographical references. [BL51.G76] 70-124706 4.95
1. Religion—Philosophy. I. Title.

HALL, James, 1933- 200'.1
Knowledge, belief, and transcendence : philosophical problems in religion / James Hall. Boston : Houghton Mifflin, [1975] xiii, 237 p. ; 24 cm. Includes bibliographical references and index. [BL51.H255] 74-11952 ISBN 0-395-19502-0 pbk. : 5.95
1. Religion—Philosophy. 2. Knowledge, Theory of (Religion) 3. Theism. 4. Religion and language. I. Title.

HARNED, David Baily. 200'.1
The ambiguity of religion. Philadelphia, Westminster Press [1968] 158 p. 21 cm. Bibliographical references included in "Notes" (p.[153]-158) [BL51.H326] 68-11584
1. Religion—Philosophy. 2. Secularization (Theology) 3. Church and the world. I. Title.

HARRINGTON, John B. 200'.1
Issues in Christian thought [by] John B. Harrington. New York, McGraw-Hill [1968] x, 452 p. 23 cm. Bibliography: p. 439-452. [BL51.H328] 68-13515
1. Religion—Philosophy. 2. Religious thought—20th century. I. Title.

HAUGHT, John F. 200'.1
Religion and self-acceptance / by John F. Haught. New York : Paulist Press, c1976. vii, 189 p. ; 21 cm. (An exploration book) Includes bibliographical references. [BL51.H36] 75-44805 ISBN 0-8091-1940-4 pbk. : 4.95
1. Religion—Philosophy. 2. Self-acceptance. I. Title.

HERBERG, Will, ed. 200'.1
Four existentialist theologians : a reader from the works of Jacques Maritain, Nicolas Berdyaev, Martin Buber, and Paul Tillich / selected and with an introd. and biographical notes by Will Herberg. Westport, Conn. : Greenwood Press, 1975, c1958. p. cm. Reprint of the ed. published by Doubleday, Garden City, N.Y. [BL51.H469 1975] 75-17472 ISBN 0-8371-8303-0 lib.bdg. : 17.25
1. Religion—Philosophy. 2. Existentialism. I. Title.

HESCHEL, Abraham Joshua, 200'.1
1907-
Man is not alone; a philosophy of religion. New York, Octagon Books, 1972 [c1951] 305 p. 23 cm. [BL51.H476 1972] 74-169258 ISBN 0-374-93879-2
1. Religion—Philosophy. 2. Judaism. I. Title.

HICK, John, ed. 200'.1
Classical and contemporary readings in the philosophy of religion. 2d ed. Englewood Cliffs, N.J., Prentice-Hall [1970] xviii, 558 p. 24 cm. Includes bibliographical references. [BL51.H487 1970] 75-98092 11.95
1. Religion—Philosophy—Collections. 2. Theology—Collections. I. Title. II. Title: Philosophy of religion.

HICK, John. 200'.1
God and the universe of faiths; essays in the philosophy of religion. New York, St. Martin's Press [1974, c1973] xii, 201 p. 23 cm. Includes bibliographical references. [BL51.H493 1974] 73-88027 12.95
1. Religion—Philosophy—Addresses, essays, lectures. I. Title.

HICK, John. 200'.1
Philosophy of religion. 2d ed. Englewood Cliffs, N.J., Prentice-Hall [1973] ix, 133 p. 23 cm. (Foundations of philosophy series) Bibliography: p. 130. [BL51.H494 1973] 72-5429 ISBN 0-13-663948-8 2.95
1. Religion—Philosophy. I. Title.

HILTNER, Seward, 1909- 200'.1
Theological dynamics. Nashville, Abingdon Press [1972] 224 p. 24 cm. Includes bibliographical references. [BR118.H53] 76-186829 ISBN 0-687-41465-2 5.75

1. Theology. 2. Psychology, Religious. I. Title.

HINKLE, Gerald H. 200'.1
Faith amid the Amorites; the case for critical religious humanism, by Gerald H. Hinkle. North Quincy, Mass., Christopher Pub. House [1970] 203 p. 21 cm. Bibliography: p. 191-198. [BL2747.6.H55] 73-116033 6.50
1. Humanism, Religious. 2. Religion—Philosophy. I. Title.

HoFFDING, Harald, 1843- 200'.1
1931.
The philosophy of religion. Translated from the German ed. by B. E. Meyer. Freeport, N.Y., Books for Libraries Press [1971] viii, 410 p. 22 cm. Translation of Religionsfilosofi. Reprint of the 1906 ed. Includes bibliographical references. [BL51.H67 1971] 71-152987 ISBN 0-8369-5739-3
1. Religion—Philosophy. I. Title.

INSTITUTE for Religious 200'.1
and Social Studies. Jewish Theological Seminary of America.
Moments of personal discovery. Edited by R. M. MacIver. Port Washington, N.Y., Kennikat Press [1969, c1952] ix, 170 p. 23 cm. (Essay and general literature index reprint series.) (Religion and civilization series) "Based on lectures given at the Institute for Religious and Social Studies of the Jewish Theological Seminary of America during the winter of 1951-1952." Contents.Contents.—What a poem did to me, by D. Moore.—Ants, galaxies, and men, by H. Shapley.—The neurosis wears a mask, by L. S. Kubie.—Out of the things I read, by M. Mead.—Persons, places, and things, by P. Weiss.—The road to understanding, by L. Bryson.—The sum of it all, by J. M. Proskauer.—There really is a God, by H. E. Fosdick.—How to live creatively as a Jew, by M. M. Kaplan.—A philosopher meditates on discovery, by R. McKeon.—Thinkers who influenced me, by H. Taylor.—Arnold Toynbee kindles a light, by D. Auchincloss.—Sometimes a miracle happens, by W. G. Constable. [BL50.I5 1969] 68-26194
1. Religion—Addresses, essays, lectures. I. MacIver, Robert Morrison, 1882- ed. II. Title. III. Series.

ISHERWOOD, Margaret. 200'.1
The root of the matter; a study in the connections between religion, psychology, and education. With a foreword by Gerald Heard. Westport, Conn., Greenwood Press [1970, c1954] 236 p. 23 cm. Includes bibliographical references. [BL48.I8 1970] 72-90534 ISBN 0-8371-3962-7
1. Religion. I. Title.

JOHNSON, Roger A., 1930- 200'.1
Critical issues in modern religion [by] Roger A. Johnson and Ernest Wallwork, with Clifford Green, H. Paul Santmire [and] Harold Y. Vanderpool. Englewood Cliffs, N.J., Prentice-Hall [1973] viii, 472 p. 23 cm. Includes bibliographies. [BL240.2.J55] 72-10829 ISBN 0-13-193987-4 6.50
1. Religion and science—1946- 2. Religion—Addresses, essays, lectures. I. Wallwork, Ernest, joint author. II. Title.

KEIGHTLEY, Alan, 1944- 200'.1
Wittgenstein, grammar and God / [by] Alan Keightley. London : Epworth Press, 1976. 176 p. ; 22 cm. Includes index. Bibliography: p. 163-172. [B3376.W564K38] 76-374827 ISBN 0-7162-0264-6 : £1.75
1. Wittgenstein, Ludwig, 1889-1951. 2. Faith. 3. Grammar, Comparative and general. I. Title.

KELLY, Cardinal Lyle. 200'.1
The role of the mind in the universe, by C. Lyle Kelly. Philadelphia, Dorrance [1969] 32 p. 22 cm. Bibliographical footnotes. [BL95.K43] 68-57733 3.00
1. Religions—Addresses, essays, lectures. I. Title.

KING-FARLOW, John. 200'.1
Faith and the life of reason. By John King-Farlow and William Niels Christensen. Dordrecht, Reidel, [1973] xiii, 253 p. 23 cm. Bibliography: p. [244]-248. [BL51.K498] 72-83376 ISBN 9-02-770275-6
1. Religion—Philosophy. I. Christensen, William Niels, joint author. II. Title.
Distributed by Reidel, Boston; 22.00 (lib. bdg.).

KING, Thomas Mulvihill, 200'.1
1929-
Sartre and the sacred / Thomas M. King. Chicago : University of Chicago Press, 1974. xii, 200 p. ; 22 cm. Includes index. Bibliography: p. 193-196. [B2430.S34K44] 73-87304 ISBN 0-226-43612-8
1. Sartre, Jean Paul, 1905- 2. Holy, The. I. Title.

KOLENDA, Konstantin. 200'.1
Religion without God / by Konstantin Kolenda. Buffalo : Prometheus Books, 1976. 125 p. ; 23 cm. Includes bibliographical references. [BL51.K65] 76-19349 ISBN 0-87975-073-1 : 8.95
1. Religion—Philosophy. I. Title.

LANG, Andrew, 1844-1912. 200'.1
The making of religion. New York, AMS Press [1968] 380 p. 23 cm. Reprint of the 1898 ed. Includes bibliographical references. [BL430.L3 1968] 68-59286
1. Religion—History. 2. Religion, Primitive. 3. Spiritualism. I. Title.

LING, Trevor Oswald. 200.1
Buddha, Marx, and God: some aspects of religion in the modern world, by Trevor Ling. London, Melbourne [etc.] Macmillan New York, St. Martin's P., 1966. xii, 228 p. 22 1/2 cm. (B 66-21487) Bibliography: p. 218-222. [BL51.L52] 67-10332
1. Religion — Philosophy. 2. Buddha and Buddhism — 20th cent. I. Title.

LUIJPEN, Wilhelmus 200'.1
Antonius Maria, 1922-
Myth and metaphysics / William A. Luijpen ; translated by Henry J. Koren. The Hague : Nijhoff, 1976. viii, 186 p. ; 24 cm. Translation of Theologie is anthropologie. Includes bibliographical references. [BL51.L7213] 76-369438 ISBN 9-02-471750-7 : 18.00
1. Religion—Philosophy. I. Title.

LUIJPEN, Wilhelmus 200'.1
Antonius Maria, 1922-
Theology as anthropology; philosophical reflections on religion, by William A. Luijpen. Pittsburgh, Duquesne University Press; distributed by Humanities Press, New York [1973] 148 p. 21 cm. (Duquesne studies. Theological series, 12) Translation of De erwtensoep is klaar! Includes bibliographical references. [BL51.L713] 72-90638 ISBN 0-391-00324-0 6.50 (pbk.)
1. Religion—Philosophy. I. Title. II. Series.

LUNDEEN, Lyman T. 200'.1
Risk and rhetoric in religion; Whitehead's theory of language and the discourse of faith [by] Lyman T. Lundeen. Philadelphia, Fortress Press [1972] xii, 276 p. 23 cm. Includes bibliographical references. [BL65.L2L85] 71-171501 9.50
1. Whitehead, Alfred North, 1861-1947. 2. Religion and language. I. Title.

MCCLENDON, James William. 200'.1
Understanding religious convictions / James Wm. McClendon, Jr., and James M. Smith. Notre Dame [Ind.] : University of Notre Dame Press, [1975] viii, 230 p. ; 24 cm. Includes bibliographical references and index. [BL51.M17] 74-34519 ISBN 0-268-01903-7 : 14.95
1. Religion—Philosophy. 2. Religion and language. I. Smith, James Marvin, 1933- joint author. II. Title.

MACGREGOR, Geddes. 200'.1
Philosophical issues in religious thought. Boston, Houghton Mifflin [1972, c1973] xii, 500 p. 25 cm. Includes bibliographical references. [BL51.M2148] 72-5247 ISBN 0-395-14045-5
1. Religion—Philosophy. I. Title.

MACKEY, James Patrick. 200'.1
The problems of religious faith, by James P. Mackey. Chicago, Franciscan Herald Press [1973] p. Includes bibliographical references. [BL51.M225] 73-6670 ISBN 0-8199-0454-6 12.95
1. Religion—Philosophy. 2. Faith. I. Title.

MCLEAN, George F. 200'.1
Religion in contemporary thought. [by] George F. McLean. Staten Island, N.Y., Alba House [1973] xiv, 326 p. 21 cm. Includes bibliographical references. [BL51.M236] 72-6837 ISBN 0-8189-0256-6 4.95
1. Religion—Philosophy—Addresses, essays, lectures. 2. Death of God theology—Addresses, essays, lectures. I. Title.

MACMURRAY, John, 1891- 200'.1
The structure of religious experience. [Hamden, Conn.] Archon Books, 1971 [c1936] xi, 77 p. 21 cm. [BL53.M36 1971] 73-122406 ISBN 0-208-00958-2 4.00
1. Experience (Religion) 2. Religion—Philosophy. I. Title.

MARTI, Fritz, 1894- 200'.1
Religion, reason, and man / by Fritz Marti. St. Louis : W. H. Green, c1974. xi, 127 p. : port. ; 24 cm. Includes index. [BL51.M352] 74-9353 ISBN 0-87527-141-3 : 7.75
1. Religion—Philosophy. I. Title.

MARTIN, James Alfred, 200'.1
1917-
Empirical philosophies of religion, with special reference to Boodin, Brightman, Hocking, Macintosh and Wieman. Freeport, N.Y., Books for Libraries Press [1970, c1945] xii, 146 p. 23 cm. (Essay index reprint series) Bibliography: p. [138]-146. [BL51.M355 1970] 78-111850 ISBN 8-369-16182-
1. Religion—Philosophy. I. Title.

MASARYK, Tomas Garrigue, 200'.1
Pres. Czechoslovak Republic, 1850-1937.
Modern man and religion. Translated by Ann Bibza and Vaclar Benes. Translation rev. by H. E. Kennedy. With a pref. by Vasil K. Skrach. Westport, Conn., Greenwood Press [1970] viii, 320 p. 23 cm. Translations of Moderni clovek a nabozenstvi, Jak pracovat, and Idealy humanitni. Includes bibliographical references. [BL51.M47 1970b] 78-109783 ISBN 0-8371-4273-3
1. Philosophy and religion. I. Title.

MASARYK, Tomas Garrigue, 200'.1
Pres. Czechoslovak Republic, 1850-1937.
Modern man and religion [by] Thomas Garrigue Masaryk. Translated by Ann Bibza and Vacla[v] Benes. Translation rev. by H. E. Kennedy. With a pref. by Vasil K. Skrach. Freeport, N.Y., Books for Libraries Press [1970] viii, 320 p. 23 cm. Translations of Moderni clovek a nabozenstvi, Jak pracovat, and Idealy humanitni. Reprint of the 1938 ed. [BL51.M47 1970] 74-107816
1. Philosophy and religion. I. Title.

MAVRODES, George I. 200'.1
Belief in God; a study in the epistemology of religion [by] George I. Mavrodes. New York, Random House [1970] ix, 117 p. 21 cm. (Studies in philosophy) Includes bibliographies. [BL51.M4757] 78-92831
1. Knowledge, Theory of (Religion) 2. God—Knowableness. I. Title.

MAVRODES, George I., comp. 200'1
Problems and perspectives in the philosophy of religion, ed. by George I. Mavrodes. Stuart C. Hackett. Boston, Allyn [1967] viii, 492p. illus. 22cm. Bibl. [BL51.M476] 67-17758 7.95
1. Religion—Philosophy— Collections. I. Hackett, Stuart Cornelius, joint comp. II. Title.

MILL, John Stuart, 1806- 200'.1
1873.
Three essays on religion. New York, Greenwood Press [1969] xi, 302 p. 23 cm. Reprint of the 1874 ed. Contents.Contents.—Nature.—Utility of religion.—Theism.—Berkeley's life and writings. [BL51.M62 1969] 69-13997
1. Berkeley, George, Bp. of Cloyne, 1685-1753. 2. Religion—Philosophy. 3. Nature. 4. Theism. I. Title.

MILL, John Stuart, 1806- 200'.1
1873.
Three essays on religion. [1st AMS ed.] New York, AMS Press [1970] xi, 302 p. 23 cm. Reprint of the New York 1874 ed. Contents.Contents.—Nature.—Utility of religion.—Theism.—Berkeley's life and writings. [BL51.M62 1970] 76-130995 ISBN 0-404-04325-9
1. Berkeley, George, Bp. of Cloyne, 1685-1753. 2. Religion—Philosophy. 3. Nature. 4. Theism. I. Title.

MILLER, David LeRoy. 200.1
Gods and games; toward a theology of play [by] David L. Miller. New York, World Pub. Co. [1970] xiii, 209 p. 22 cm. Bibliography: p. [197]-206. [BF717.M53 1970] 74-90923 5.95
1. Play. 2. Psycology, Religious. I. Title.

MILLER, Eddie L., 1937- 200'.1
comp.
Philosophical and religious issues: classical and contemporary statements [by] Ed L. Miller. Encino, Calif., Dickenson Pub. Co. [1971] xii, 448 p. 24 cm. Includes bibliographical references. [BL51.M626] 75-162678
1. Religion—Philosophy—Collections. I. Title.

MITCHELL, Basil. 200'.1
The justification of religious belief. [London, New York] Macmillan [1973] 180 p. 23 cm. (Philosophy of religion series) Bibliography: p. 170-176. [BL51.M654 1973] 74-154832 ISBN 0-333-09942-7 £3.95
1. Religion—Philosophy. I. Title.

MITCHELL, Basil. 200'.1
The justification of religious belief. New York, Seabury Press [1974] v, 180 p. 22 cm. (Philosophy of religion series) "A Crossroad book." Bibliography: p. 170-176. [BL51.M654 1974] 73-17904 ISBN 0-8164-1152-2 8.95
1. Religion—Philosophy. I. Title.

MITCHELL, Basil. 200'.1
Neutrality and commitment: an inaugural lecture delivered before the University of Oxford on 13 May 1968. Oxford, Clarendon P., 1968. 22 p. 22 cm. [BL51.M655] 79-362880 5/-

1. Philosophy and religion—Addresses, essays, lectures. I. Title.

MONTAGUE, William 200'.1
Pepperell, 1873-1953.
Belief unbound; a Promethean religion for the modern world. Freeport, N.Y., Books for Libraries PRess [1970] 98 p. 23 cm. Reprint of the 1930 ed. [BL51.M67 1970] 72-109630
1. Religion—Philosophy. I. Title.

MUNSON, Thomas N. 200'.1
Reflective theology; philosophical orientations in religion, by Thomas N. Munson. New Haven, Yale University Press, 1968. xi, 211 p. 22 cm. Bibliography: p. [189]-202. [BL51.M87] 68-27763 6.00
1. Religion—Philosophy. I. Title.

MUNSON, Thomas N. 200'.1
Reflective theology : philosophical orientations in religion / by Thomas N. Munson. Westport, Conn. : Greenwood Press, 1976, c1968. xi, 211 p. ; 23 cm. Reprint of the ed. published by Yale University Press, New Haven. Includes index. Bibliography: p. [189]-202. [BL51.M87 1976] 75-36099 ISBN 0-8371-8624-2 lib.bdg. : 13.00
1. Religion—Philosophy. I. Title.

NIELSEN, Kai. 200'.1
Contemporary critiques of religion. [New York] Herder and Herder [1971] vii, 163 p. 22 cm. Bibliography: p. 150-160. [BL51.N496 1971b] 72-170200 6.95
1. Religion—Philosophy. I. Title.

NOVAK, Michael. 200.1
Ascent of the mountain, flight of the dove; an invitation to religious studies. [1st ed.] New York, Harper & Row [1971] xvi, 240 p. front. 22 cm. Includes bibliographical references. [BL48.N68] 70-128050 ISBN 0-06-066320-0 5.95
1. Religion. 2. Religion and sociology. I. Title.

NYGREN, Anders, Bp., 1890- 200'.1
Meaning and method; prolegomena to a scientific philosophy of religion and a scientific theology. Authorized translation by Philip S. Watson. [1st American ed.] Philadelphia, Fortress Press [1972] xv, 412 p. 26 cm. Bibliography: p. 387-401. [BL51.N88 1972] 72-157541 ISBN 0-8006-0038-X 12.95
1. Religion—Philosophy. 2. Meaning (Philosophy) I. Title.

OATES, Wayne Edward, 1917- 200'.1
The psychology of religion, by Wayne E. Oates. Waco, Tex., Word Books [1973] 291 p. 24 cm. Includes bibliographical references. [BL53.O29] 73-77951 7.95
1. Psychology, Religious. I. Title.

O'DEA, Thomas F. 200.1
The sociology of religion. Englewood Cliffs. N.J., Prentice [c.1966] viii, 120p. 24cm. (Founds. of mod. soc. ser.) Bibl. [BL60.O3] 66-10807 3.95; 1.50 pap.,
1. Religion and sociology. I. Title.

OMAN, John Wood, 1860-1939. 200.1
The natural & the supernatural. Freeport, N.Y., Books for Libraries Press [1972] xiii, 506 p. 23 cm. Reprint of the 1931 ed. [BL48.O6 1972] 79-39696 ISBN 0-8369-9941-X
1. Religion. 2. Philosophy and religion. 3. Reality. 4. Supernatural. 5. Knowledge, Theory of. 6. Religions—Classification. I. Title.

OUTKA, Gene H. 200'.1
Religion and morality; a collection of essays. Edited by Gene Outka and John P. Reeder, Jr. [1st ed.] Garden City, N.Y., Anchor Press [1973] viii, 448 p. 21 cm. Bibliography: p. [389]-392. [BL25.O9] 72-84966 ISBN 0-385-03992-1 4.95 (pbk.)
1. Religion—Collected works. 2. Ethics—Collected works. I. Reeder, John P., ed. II. Title.

OWENS, Gene, 1930- 200'.1
Confessions of a religionless Christian / Gene Owens. Nashville : Abingdon Press, [1975] 112 p. ; 20 cm. Includes bibliographical references. [BR121.2.O94] 75-14317 ISBN 0-687-09386-4 : 4.95
1. Religion. 2. Christianity—Essence, genius, nature. I. Title.

PATTERSON, Robert Leet. 200'.1
Adventures in the philosophy of religion / Robert Leet Patterson. 1st ed. Hicksville, N.Y. : Exposition Press, c1977. 87 p. ; 21 cm. (An Exposition-university book) Includes bibliographical references. [BL51.P318] 77-74567 ISBN 0-682-48827-5 : 5.50
1. Religion—Philosophy—Addresses, essays, lectures. I. Title.

PATTERSON, Robert Leet. 200'.1
A philosophy of religion. Durham, N.C., Duke University Press, 1970. 571 p. 25 cm. Includes

bibliographical references. [BL51.P324] 74-101130
1. Religion—Philosophy. I. Title.

PENELHUM, Terence, 1929- 200'.1
Religion and rationality; an introduction to the philosophy of religion. [1st ed.] New York, Random House [1971] xvi, 392 p. 22 cm. Includes bibliographical references. [BL51.P345] 75-135893 ISBN 0-394-31022-5
1. Religion—Philosophy. I. Title.

THE Persistence of 200'.1
religion. Edited by Andrew Greeley and Gregory Baum. [New York] Herder and Herder [1973] 160 p. 23 cm. (Concilium, 81) Series statement also appears as: The New concilium. Includes bibliographical references. [BL50.P474] 72-3947 ISBN 0-8164-2537-X 3.95
1. Religion—Addresses, essays, lectures. I. Greeley, Andrew M., 1928- ed. II. Baum, Gregory, 1923- ed. III. Series: Concilium (New York) 81.

PFLEIDERER, Otto, 1839- 200'.1
1908.
The philosophy of religion on the basis of its history / by Otto Pfleiderer ; translated from the German of the 2d and greatly enl. ed., by Alexander Stewart and Allan Menzies. Millwood, N.Y. : Kraus Reprint Co., 1975. 4 v. in 2 ; 24 cm. Translation of Religionsphilosophie auf geschichtlicher Grundlage. Vols. 2-4: translated by A. Menzies. Reprint of the 1886-88 ed. published by Williams and Norgate, London. Includes index. Contents.Contents.—1. History of the philosophy of religion from Spinoza to the present day. 2 v.—2. Genetic-speculative philosophy of religion. 2 v. [BL51.P4713 1975] 75-23050 ISBN 0-527-03238-7 (v. 1/2) : 42.00
1. Religion—Philosophy. 2. Religion—History. 3. Religions. 4. Cultus. I. Title.

PHILLIPS, D Z comp. 200'.1
Religion and understanding, edited by D. Z. Phillips. New York, Macmillan [1967] vii, 216 p. 23 cm. Bibliographical footnotes. [BL51.P52] 67-22156
1. Religion—Philosophy—Addresses, essays, lectures. I. Title.

PHILLIPS, Dewi Zephaniah. 200'.1
Faith and philosophical enquiry [by] D. Z. Phillips. New York, Schocken Books [1971, c1970] viii, 277 p. 20 cm. Bibliography: p. 273-277. [B56.P48 1971] 79-135520 ISBN 0-8052-3366-0
1. Philosophy and religion. 2. Belief and doubt. I. Title.

PHILLIPS, Dewi Zephaniah, 200'.1
comp.
Religion and understanding, edited by D. Z. Phillips. New York, Macmillan [1967] vii, 216 p. 23 cm. Bibliographical footnotes. [BL51.P52 1967] 67-22156
1. Religion—Philosophy—Addresses, essays, lectures. I. Title.

PHILLIPS, Dewi Zephaniah. 200'.1
Religion without explanation / D. Z. Phillips. Oxford : Blackwell, c1976. xi, 200 p. ; 23 cm. Includes indexes. Bibliography: p. [192]-195. [BL51.P523] 77-356891 ISBN 0-631-17100-2 : £7.00
1. Religion—Philosophy—Addresses, essays, lectures. I. Title.

PHILOSOPHY of religion and 200'.1
theology : 1976 proceedings / compiled by Peter Slater. Missoula, Mont. : Published by Scholars Press for the American Academy of Religion, c1976. p. cm. Papers prepared for the 1976 annual meeting of the American Academy of Religion. Includes bibliographies. [BL51.P54] 76-29664 ISBN 0-89130-089-9 pbk. : 3.50
1. Religion—Philosophy—Congresses. 2. Theology—Congresses. I. Slater, Peter, 1934- II. American Academy of Religion.

PHILOSOPHY of religion and 200'.1
theology: 1971. Edited by David Griffin. Chambersburg, Pa., American Academy of Religion, 1971. 240 p. 23 cm. Proceedings of the Philosophy of Religion and Theology Section of the 1971 American Academy of Religion annual meeting. Includes bibliographical references. [BL51.P53] 72-192659
1. Religion—Philosophy—Addresses, essays, lectures. 2. Nature (Theology)—Addresses, essays, lectures. I. Griffin, David, 1939- ed. II. American Academy of Religion.

PLOTKIN, Frederick. 200'.1
Faith and reason; essays in the religious and scientific imagination. New York, Philosophical Library [1970] 192 p. 23 cm. Includes bibliographical references. [BL50.P55] 72-97937 4.95
1. Religion—Addresses, essays, lectures. I. Title.

PORTER, Burton Frederick. 200'.1
Deity and morality, with regard to the naturalistic fallacy [by] Burton F. Porter. New York, Humanities Press, 1968. 176 p. 23 cm. Includes bibliographical references. [BJ47.P62 1968] 68-16017
1. Religion and ethics. I. Title.

PRICE, Henry Habberley, 200'.1
1899-
Essays in the philosophy of religion: based on the Sarum lectures, 1971 [by] H. H. Price. Oxford, Clarendon Press, 1972. [7], 125 p. 21 cm. (The Sarum lectures, 1971) Includes bibliographical references. [BL51.P73] 72-195626 ISBN 0-19-824376-6
1. Religion—Philosophy—Addresses, essays, lectures. 2. Psychical research—Addresses, essays, lectures. 3. Experience (Religion)—Addresses, essays, lectures. I. Title. II. Series.
Available from Oxford Univ. Pr., 7.25.

THE Process of religion; 200'.1
essays in honor of Dean Shailer Mathews. Edited by Miles H. Krumbine. Freeport, N.Y., Books for Libraries Press [1972] viii, 266 p. port. 23 cm. (Essay index reprint series) Reprint of the 1933 ed. Contents.Contents.—Shailer Mathews, a biographical note, by R. E. Mathews.—Theology and the social process, by E. E. Aubrey.—Whither historicism in theology, by S. J. Case.—Confused Protestantism, by J. W. Nixon.—Some reflections on the progress and decline of religion in New England, by D. C. Macintosh.—The philosophy of Protestantism in its relation to industry, by C. A. Ellwood.—The social and the individual in religion, by D. A. McGregor.—Truth and paradox, by L. H. Hough.—The validity of the concept of revelation in an empirical age, by W. M. Horton.—Theological contexts and patterns, by J. W. Buckham.—The plight of mechanism, by R. M. Vaughan.—The New Testament and the origin of Jesus (a study in social interpretation) by E. W. Parsons.—The renaissance of religion, by A. E. Haydon. [BR50.P75 1972] 71-38776 ISBN 0-8369-2667-6
1. Theology—Addresses, essays, lectures. 2. Religion—Addresses, essays, lectures. I. Mathews, Shailer, 1863-1941. II. Krumbine, Miles Henry, 1891- ed.

†PROUDFOOT, Wayne, 1939- 200'.1
God and the self : three types of philosophy of religion / Wayne Proudfoot. Lewisburg [Pa.] : Bucknell University Press, c1976. 241 p. ; 22 cm. Includes index. Bibliography: p. 233-237. [BL51.P74] 75-28983 ISBN 0-8387-1769-1 : 13.00
1. Religion—Philosophy. I. Title.

REISCHAUER, August Karl, 200.1
1879-
The nature and truth of the great religions; toward a philosphy of religion. Tokyo, Rutland, Vt., C.E. Tuttle Co. [1966] xvii, 340 p. 22 cm. Bibliography: p. [333]-354. [BL51.R34] 65-20612
1. Religion — Philosophy. I. Title.

REISCHAUER, August Karl, 200.1
1879-
The nature and truth of the great religions; toward a philosophy of religion. Rutland, Vt., Tuttle [c.1966] xvii, 340p. 22cm. Bibl. [BL51.R34] 65-20612 7.50
1. Religion — Philosophy. I. Title.

RELIGIOUS language and 200'.1
knowledge. Edited by Robert H. Ayers and William T. Blackstone. Athens, University of Georgia Press [1972] x, 149 p. 22 cm. Essays originally presented in the 1965 Great Thinkers Forum sponsored by the Dept. of Philosophy and Religion at the University of Georgia, the 1st of a series of meetings; papers of the 2d are entered under the title: Education and ethics. Includes bibliographical references. [BL65.L2R43] 72-169950 ISBN 0-8203-0269-4 4.00
1. Religion and language—Addresses, essays, lectures. I. Ayers, Robert Hyman, ed. II. Blackstone, William T., ed.

RICHMOND, James, 1931- 200.1
Faith and philosophy. Philadelphia, Lippincott [1966] 224 p. 21 cm. (Knowing Christianity) Bibliographical footnotes. [BL51.R47 1966a] 66-25411
1. Religion—Philosophy. I. Title.

ROHEIM, Geza, 1891-1953. 200'.1
The panic of the gods and other essays. Edited with an introd. by Werner Muensterberger. [1st Harper torchbook ed.] New York, Harper & Row [1972] xxiii, 227 p. 21 cm. (Harper torchbooks, TB1674) Contents.Contents.—Primitive high gods.—Animism and religion.—Aphrodite, or the woman with a penis.—The panic of the gods. [BL50.R55 1972] 72-80870 ISBN 0-06-131674-1 3.95
1. Religion—Addresses, essays, lectures. 2. Mythology—Addresses, essays, lectures. I. Title.

THE Role of reason in 200'.1
belief / edited by George F. McLean. Lancaster, Pa. : Concorde Pub. Co., c1974. vi, 148 p. ; 23 cm. Includes bibliographical references. [BL51.R596] 74-84465
1. Religion—Philosophy—Addresses, essays, lectures. I. McLean, George F.

ROTH, John K. 200.1
Problems of the philosophy of religion [by] John K. Roth. Scranton, Chandler Pub. Co. [1971] x, 203 p. 21 cm. (Chandler publications in philosophy.) (Problems of philosophy: a Chandler series) Bibliography: p. 195-196. [BL51.R5976] 74-126546 ISBN 0-8102-0396-0 2.95
1. Religion—Philosophy—History. I. Title.

ROTH, Robert J. 200'.1
American religious philosophy [by] Robert J. Roth. New York, Harcourt, Brace & World [1967] vi, 211 p. 21 cm. Bibliography: p. 191-199. [BL51.R598] 67-18540
1. Religion—Philosophy. 2. Philosophy, American. 3. Religious thought—United States. I. Title.

ROWE, William L., comp. 200'.1
Philosophy of religion; selected readings. Edited by William L. Rowe [and] William J. Wainwright. Under the general editorship of Robert Ferm. New York, Harcourt Brace Jovanovich [1972, c1973] xv, 489 p. 24 cm. Includes bibliographical references. [BL51.R599] 72-93725 ISBN 0-15-570580-6 pap. 6.95
1. Religion—Philosophy—Collections. I. Wainwright, William J., joint comp. II. Title.

RUST, Eric Charles. 200.1
Evolutionary philosophies and contemporary theology, by Eric C. Rust. Philadelphia, Westminster Press [1969] 256 p. 21 cm. Bibliographical references included in "Notes" (p. [231]-248) [BT83.6.R8] 69-10419 6.50
1. Process theology. 2. Philosophy, Modern. I. Title.

SAHER, P. J. 200'.1
Eastern wisdom and Western thought; a comparative study in the modern philosophy of religion, by P. J. Saher. New York, N.Y., Barnes and Noble [1970] 292 p. 23 cm. Includes bibliographical references. [B799.S32 1970] 73-16605
1. Philosophy, Comparative. 2. Religion—Philosophy. I. Title.

SANDMEL, Samuel. 200'.1
A little book on religion (for people who are not religious) / Samuel Sandmel. Chambersburg, Pa. : Wilson Books, c1975. xi, 146 p. ; 21 cm. [BL48.S274] 75-1831 ISBN 0-89012-002-1 : 4.95
1. Religion. 2. God. I. Title.

SANDMEL, Samuel. 200'.1
Two living traditions; essays on religion and the Bible. Detroit, Wayne State University Press, 1972. 366 p. 24 cm. Includes bibliographical references. [BM535.S217 1972] 72-173919 ISBN 0-8143-1460-0 16.95
1. Judaism—Relations—Christianity—Addresses, essays, lectures. 2. Christianity and other religions—Judaism—Addresses, essays, lectures. 3. Theology—Addresses, essays, lectures. I. Title.

SCHEDLER, Norbert O., 200'.1
comp.
Philosophy of religion: contemporary perspectives [by] Norbert O. Schedler. New York, Macmillan [1974] xiv, 564 p. 24 cm. Includes bibliographies. [BL51.S419] 73-1959 ISBN 0-02-406720-2 8.95
1. Religion—Philosophy—Collected works. I. Title.

SCHNEIDER, Herbert 200'.1
Wallace, 1892-
Civilized religion; an historical and philosophical analysis. [1st ed.] New York, Exposition Press [1972] 112 p. 22 cm. (An Exposition-university book) [BL48.S373] 79-186484 ISBN 0-682-47426-6 5.00
1. Religion. I. Title.

SCHUON, Frithjof, 1907- 200'.1
The transcendent unity of religions / Frithjof Schuon ; translated by Peter Townsend ; introd. by Huston Smith. Rev. ed. New York : Harper & Row, 1975. xxxii, 156 p. ; 21 cm. (Harper torchbooks ; TB 1818) Translation of De l'unite transcendante des religions. Includes bibliographical references and index. [BL51.S4643 1975] 74-9137 ISBN 0-06-139415-7 : 3.95
1. Religion—Philosophy. 2. Christianity and other religions. 3. Religions. I. Title.

SHERRY, Patrick. 200'.1
Religion, truth, and language-games / Patrick Sherry. New York : Barnes & Noble Books, 1977. p. cm. (Library of philosophy and religion) Includes index. Bibliography: p. [BL51.S5226 1977] 75-41579 ISBN 0-06-496236-9 : 18.50
1. Wittgenstein, Ludwig, 1889-1951. 2. Religion—Philosophy. 3. Religion and language. I. Title.

SHESTOV, Lev, 1866-1938 200.1
Athens and Jerusalem [by] Lev Shestov. Tr., introd. by Bernard Martin. New York, S. & S. [1968,c.1966] 447p. 21cm. (CL 017) Bibl. [BL51.S52273] 2.45 pap.,
1. Religion—Philosophy. 2. Philosophy and religion. I. Title.

SHESTOV, Lev, 1866-1938. 200.1
Athens and Jerusalem [by] Lev Shestov. Translated, with an introd., by Bernard Martin. Athens, Ohio University Press [1966] 447 p. 22 cm. Bibliographical footnotes. [BL51.S52273] 66-18480
1. Religion—Philosophy. 2. Philosophy and religion. I. Title.

SMART, Ninian, 1927- 200'.1
The phenomenon of religion [by] Ninian Smart. [New York] Herder and Herder [1973] v, 157 p. 22 cm. (Philosophy of religion series) Bibliography: p. 153-156. [BL48.S592 1973b] 72-8067 ISBN 0-07-073793-2 6.95
1. Religion. I. Title.

SMART, Ninian, 1927- 200'.1
Philosophers and religious truth. [2d ed. 1st American ed. New York] Macmillan [1970, c1969] xii, 211 p. 18 cm. Includes bibliographical references. [BL51.S569 1970] 74-102974 1.95
1. Philosophy and religion. I. Title.

SMART, Ninian, 1927- 200'.1
The science of religion & the sociology of knowledge: some methodological questions. [Princeton, N.J.] Princeton University Press [1973] vii, 164 p. 21 cm. (The Virginia and Richard Stewart memorial lectures, 1971) Bibliography: p. 161-164. [BL48.S5923] 72-12115 ISBN 0-691-07191-8 8.50
1. Religion. I. Title. II. Series.

SMITH, Ethel (Sabin) 1887- 200'.1
God and other gods; essays in perspective on persisting religious problems. [1st ed.] New York, Exposition Press [1973] xiii, 185 p. 22 cm. (An Exposition-university Book) [BL48.S594] 73-154811 ISBN 0-682-47619-6 7.50
1. Religion. 2. Religions. I. Title.

SMITH, Huston. 200'.1
Forgotten truth : the primordial tradition / Huston Smith. 1st ed. New York : Harper & Row, c1976. x, 182 p. : ill. ; 22 cm. Includes bibliographical references and index. [BL51.S572 1976] 74-15850 ISBN 0-06-013902-1 : 7.95
1. Religion—Philosophy. I. Title.

SMITH, John Edwin. 200'.1
Experience and God [by] John E. Smith. New York, Oxford University Press, 1968. viii, 209 p. 21 cm. Bibliographical footnotes. [BL51.S573] 68-18566
1. Religion—Philosophy. I. Title.

SMITH, John Edwin. 200'.1
Experience and God / John Edwin Smith. London ; New York : Oxford University Press, 1974. ix, 209 p. ; 21 cm. (A Galaxy book) Includes bibliographical references and index. [BL51.S573 1974] 75-323360 ISBN 0-19-501847-8 pbk. : 2.95
1. Religion—Philosophy. I. Title.

SMITH, John Edwin. 200'.1
Religion and empiricism, by John E. Smith. Milwaukee, Marquette University Press, 1967. 68 p. 19 cm. (The Aquinas lecture 1967) "Under the auspices of the Wisconsin-Alpha Chapter of Phi Sigma Tau." Bibliographical references included in "Notes" (p. [67]-68) [BL51.S579] 67-20684
1. Religion—Philosophy. 2. Empiricism. I. Title. II. Series.

SONTAG, Frederick. 200'.1
How philosophy shapes theology; problems in the philosophy of religion. New York, Harper & Row [1971] xv, 495 p. 21 cm. Includes bibliographical references. [BL51.S622 1971] 71-170618 ISBN 0-06-046349-X
1. Religion—Philosophy. I. Title.

STACE, Walter Terence, 200'.1
1886-
Time and eternity; an essay in the philosophy of religion, by W. T. Stace. Princeton, N.J., Princeton University Press, 1952. New York, Greenwood Press [1969] vii, 169 p. 23 cm. Bibliographical footnotes. [BL51.S6257 1969] 69-14094
1. Religion—Philosophy. I. Title.

STEPHEN. 200'.1
The caravan. [New York] Random House [1972] 1 v. (unpaged) 25 cm. [BP605.S66A43] 71-39580 ISBN 0-394-48039-2 7.95
I. Title.

THEOLOGICAL crossings 200'.1
[by] Robert McAfee Brown [and others] Edited by Alan Geyer and Dean Peerman. Grand Rapids, Eerdmans [1971] 155 p. ports. 21 cm. Essays, originally published in the Christian century as the 4th of a decennial series of articles entitled How my mind has changed. [BR50.T422] 79-168439 2.95
1. Theology—20th century—Addresses, essays, lectures. I. Brown, Robert McAfee, 1920- II. Geyer, Alan F., ed. III. Peerman, Dean G., ed. IV. The Christian century.

THOMAS, George Finger, 200'.1
1899-
Philosophy and religious belief [by] George F. Thomas. New York, Scribner [1970] xii, 372 p. 24 cm. Includes bibliographical references. [BL51.T438] 76-106534 10.00
1. Religion—Philosophy. I. Title.

TILLICH, Paul, 1886-1965. 200.1
What is religion? Edited and with an introduction by James Luther Adams. New York, Harper [1973, c.1969] 191 p. 20 cm. (Harper torchbooks, TB1732) [BL51.T58] 67-17014 ISBN 0-06-131732-2 2.25 (pbk.)
1. Religion—Philosophy. I. Title.

TOULMIN, Stephen Edelston. 200'.1
Metaphysical beliefs; three essays by Stephen Toulmin, Ronald W. Hepburn [and] Alasdair Macintyre. With a pref. by Alasdair MacIntyre. New York, Schocken Books [1970] xii, 206 p. 23 cm. Includes bibliographical references. [BD573.T6 1970b] 75-13956 5.95
1. Philosophy and religion. I. Hepburn, Ronald W. II. MacIntyre, Alasdair C. III. Title.

TRANSCENDENCE and 200'.1
immanence: reconstruction in the light of process thinking; festschrift in honour of Joseph Papin. Edited by Joseph Armenti. [Saint Meinrad, Ind.] Abbey Press [1972- v. port. 23 cm. Contents.Contents.—v. 1. Curran, C. E. The present state of Catholic moral theology. Baltazar, E. R. Process thinking in theology. Gustafson, J. M. Toward ecumenical Christian ethics: some brief suggestions. Swidler, L. Aufklarung Catholicism's mass reforms. Tavard, G. H. Can the ministry be reconstructed? Bonniwell, B. L. Transmaterial time in psychology. Schmemann, A. Crisis in theology and liturgy: orthodox insight. Katsh, A. I. Hebraic studies in early America. Peter, C. J. Christian eschatology and a theology of exceptions, part I. Blake, E. C. Ecumenism, structured and unstructured. Schoonenberg, P. The transcendence of God, part I. Beniak, V. Umriet' doma. Allen-Shore, L. From the garden of Slovakia ... Includes bibliographical references. [BR50.T715] 72-83737
1. Theology—Addresses, essays, lectures. I. Papin, Joseph, 1914- II. Armenti, Joseph, ed.

TREMMEL, William C. 200'.1
Religion : what is it? / William Calloley Tremmel. New York : Holt, Rinehart and Winston, c1976. x, 277 p. ; 21 cm. Includes index. Bibliography: p. 251-264. [BL48.T7] 75-38955 ISBN 0-03-015551-7 pbk. : 4.95
1. Religion. I. Title.

TRUEBLOOD, David Elton, 200'.1
1900-
The essence of spiritual religion / D. Elton Trueblood. New York : Harper & Row, 1975, c1936. xii, 156 p. ; 21 cm. Includes index. [BR100.T75 1975] 74-7684 pbk. : 1.95
1. Religion—Philosophy. 2. Mysticism. 3. Spiritual life. I. Title.

TRUEBLOOD, David Elton, 200'.1
1900-
Philosophy of religion / David Elton Trueblood. Westport, Conn. : Greenwood Press, 1975 [i.e.1976] c1957 xv, 324 p. ; 22 cm. Reprint of the ed. published by Harper, New York. Includes bibliographical references and indexes. [BL51.T683 1975] 75-31446 ISBN 0-8371-8514-9 : 16.00
1. Religion—Philosophy.

TUCKWELL, James Henry. 200'.1
Religion and reality; a study in the philosophy of mysticism. Port Washington, N.Y., Kennikat Press [1971] ix, 318 p. 22 cm. Reprint of the 1915 ed. Includes bibliographical references. [BL53.T77 1971] 77-118552
1. Religion. 2. Experience (Religion) 3. Mysticism. I. Title.

TURNER, John Evan. 200'.1
Essentials in the development of religion; a philosophic and psychological study, by J. E. Turner. Port Washington, N.Y., Kennikat Press [1970] 308 p. 22 cm. Reprint of the 1934 ed. Bibliographical footnotes. [BL53.T8 1970] 70-102587 ISBN 8-04-607478-
1. Experience (Religion) 2. Psychology, Religious. 3. Philosophy and religion. I. Title.

VAN BUREN, Paul Matthews, 200'.1
1924-
The edges of language; an essay in the logic of a religion [by] Paul M. van Buren. New York, Macmillan [1972] 178 p. 22 cm. Includes bibliographical references. [BL65.L2V35] 70-187077 7.95
1. Religion and language. I. Title.

VON HILDEBRAND, Alice M. 200'.1
(Jourdain)
Introduction to a philosophy of religion, by Alice von Hildebrand. Chicago, Franciscan Herald Press [1970] ix, 178 p. 22 cm. Includes bibliographical references. [BL51.V58] 79-139972 6.95
1. Religion—Philosophy. I. Title.

WATTS, Alan Wilson, 1915- 200'.1
Cloud-hidden, whereabouts unknown; a mountain journal [by] Alan Watts. New York, Vintage Books [1974, c1973] xi, 208 p. 18 cm. [BL50.W32 1974] 73-13747 ISBN 0-394-71999-9 1.95 (pbk.)
1. Religion—Addresses, essays, lectures. I. Title.

WATTS, Alan Wilson, 1915- 200'.1
Cloud-hidden, whereabouts unknown; a mountain journal [by] Alan Watts. [1st ed.] New York, Pantheon Books [1973] xi, 179 p. illus. 25 cm. [BL50.W32 1973] 72-12384 ISBN 0-394-48253-0 6.95
1. Religion—Addresses, essays, lectures. I. Title.

WEISS, Miriam Strauss. 200'.1
A lively corpse. South Brunswick [N.J.] A. S. Barnes [1969] 385 p. 25 cm. Bibliography: p. 369-374. [HX807.W4] 68-23068 10.00
1. Utopias—Religious aspects. I. Title.

WEISS, Paul, 1901- 200'.1
The God we seek. Carbondale, Southern Illinois University Press [1973, c1964] 258 p. 20 cm. (Arcturus paperbacks, AB106) [B945.W396G6 1973] 72-11838 ISBN 0-8093-0628-X 2.95
1. Religion—Philosophy. 2. Experience (Religion) I. Title.

WESTERHOFF, John H. 200'.1
Generation to generation; conversations on religious education and culture, by John H. Westerhoff, III and Gwen Kennedy Neville. Philadelphia, United Church Press [1974] 192 p. 22 cm. "A Pilgrim Press book." Includes bibliographical references. [BV1473.W47] 74-508 ISBN 0-8298-0274-6
1. Christian education—Addresses, essays, lectures. 2. Religion and culture—Addresses, essays, lectures. I. Neville, Gwen Kennedy, 1938- joint author. II. Title.

WIEMAN, Henry Nelson, 200'.1
1884-
Seeking a faith for a new age ; essays on the interdependence of religion, science, and philosophy / by Henry Nelson Wieman ; edited and introduced by Cedric L. Hepler. Metuchen, N.J. : Scarecrow Press, 1975. ix, 313 p. ; 22 cm. Includes index. Bibliography: p. 295-304. [BL51.W585] 74-34052 ISBN 0-8108-0795-5 : 12.50
1. Religion—Philosophy—Addresses, essays, lectures. 2. Worth—Addresses, essays, lectures. 3. Religion and science—1946- — Addresses, essays, lectures. I. Title.

WILLIAMSON, William 200'.1
Bedford, 1918-
Decisions in philosophy of religion / William B. Williamson. Columbus, Ohio : Merrill, c1976. viii, 407 p. ; 26 cm. Includes bibliographical references and indexes. [BL51.W59] 75-32716 ISBN 0-675-08629-9 : 11.95
1. Religion—Philosophy—Addresses, essays, lectures. I. Title.

WOLF, William J 200'.1
Man's knowledge of God. [1st ed.] Garden City, N. Y., Doubleday, 1955. 189p. 22cm. (Christian faith series) [BT101.W580i31] 55-5261
1. God (Theory of knowledge) I. Title.

WOLFSON, Harry Austryn, 200'.1
1887-1974.
From Philo to Spinoza : two studies in religious philosophy / by Harry Austryn Wolfson ; introd. by Isadore Twersky. New York : Behrman House, c1977. p. cm. Contents.Contents.—What is new in Philo?—Spinoza and the religion of the past. Includes bibliographical references. [B689.Z7W685 1977] 77-1909 ISBN 0-87441-265-5 pbk. : 3.95
1. Philo Judaus. 2. Spinoza, Benedictus de, 1632-1677. 3. Religion—Philosophy—History. I. Wolfson, Harry Austryn, 1887-1974. Spinoza and the religion of the past. 1977. II. Title.

WOOD, Allen W. 200'.1
Kant's moral religion [by] Allen W. Wood. Ithaca, Cornell University Press [1970] xii, 283 p. 22 cm. Bibliography: p. [273]-279. [B2799.E8W6] 71-99100 ISBN 8-01-405483-9.00
1. Kant, Immanuel, 1724-1804—Ethics. 2. Religion—Philosophy. I. Title.

YANDELL, Keith E., 1938- 200'.1
Basic issues in the philosophy of religion [by] Keith E. Yandell. Boston, Allyn and Bacon [1971] ix, 238 p. 24 cm. Includes bibliographical references. [BL51.Y27] 72-107427
1. Religion—Philosophy. I. Title.

YANDELL, Keith E., 1938- 200'.1
God, man, and religion; readings in the philosophy of religion [by] Keith E. Yandell. New York, McGraw-Hill [1973] xii, 541 p. 23 cm. Includes bibliographical references. [BL51.Y272] 72-1978 ISBN 0-07-072247-1 6.95
1. Religion—Philosophy—Collections. 2. Experience (Religion)—Collections. 3. Ethics—Collections. I. Title.

ZAEHNER, Robert Charles. 200'.1
Evolution in religion: a study in Sri Aurobindo and Pierre Teilhard de Chardin, by R. C. Zaehner. Oxford, Clarendon Press, 1971. xi, 121 p. 21 cm. [BL1270.G4Z3] 79-585013 ISBN 0-19-826628-6 £1.90
1. Ghose, Aurobindo, 1872-1950. 2. Teilhard de Chardin, Pierre. I. Title.

ZUURDEEG, Willem 200'.1
Frederick.
Man before chaos. Prepared for publication by Esther Cornelius Swenson. Nashville, Abingdon Press [1968] 160 p. 20 cm. Bibliographical footnotes. [BD450.Z85] 68-11714
1. Nietzsche, Friedrich Wilhelm, 1844-1900. 2. Man. 3. Religion—Philosophy. 4. Civilization—Philosophy. I. Swenson, Esther Cornelius. II. Title.

BOLDUAN, Miriam F. 200'.1'4
Words to see by, by Miriam F. Bolduan. Philadelphia, Fortress Press [1970] vi, 122 p. 22 cm. [BL65.L2B63] 73-94816 2.95
1. Religion and language. 2. Meditations. I. Title.

DEWART, Leslie. 200'.1'4
Religion, language, and truth. [New York] Herder and Herder [1970] 174 p. 21 cm. Includes bibliographical references. [BL65.L2D44] 70-127870 5.95
1. Religion and language. 2. Christianity—Philosophy. I. Title.

DONOVAN, Peter, 1940- 200'.1'4
Religious language / Peter Donovan. New York : Hawthorn Books, 1976. 113 p. ; 21 cm. Includes index. Bibliography: p. 111-112. [BL65.L2D66 1976] 75-31372 ISBN 0-8015-6278-3 : 3.50
1. Religion and language. I. Title.

DONOVAN, Peter, 1940- 200'.1'4
Religious language / [by] Peter Donovan. London : Sheldon Press, 1976. ix, 114 p. : 20 cm. (Issues in religious studies) Includes index. Bibliography: p. 111-112. [BL65.L2D66 1976b] 76-373614 ISBN 0-85969-054-7 : £1.60
1. Religion and language. I. Title.

FAWCETT, Thomas. 200'.14
The symbolic language of religion. Minneapolis, Augsburg Pub. House [1971] 288 p. 23 cm. Includes bibliographical references. [BL65.L2F37 1971] 79-140423 ISBN 0-8066-1117-0
1. Religion and language. 2. Symbolism. I. Title.

HEIMBECK, Raeburne 200'.1'4
Seeley.
Theology and meaning: a critique of metatheological scepticism [by] Raeburne S. Heimbeck. Stanford, Stanford University Press, 1969. 276 p. 23 cm. Bibliography: p. [261]-269. [BL65.L2H4 1969b] 68-13146 7.50
1. Religion and language. 2. Semantics (Philosophy) I. Title.

HIGH, Dallas M., comp. 200'.1'4
New essays on religious language. Edited by Dallas M. High. New York, Oxford University Press, 1969. xv, 240 p. 21 cm. Contents.Contents.—Introduction, by D. M. High.—Ludwig Wittgenstein: unphilosophical notes, by E. Heller.—Wittgenstein and theology, by P. L. Holmer.—Religion and science: a philosopher's approach, by I. T. Ramsey.—Mapping the logic of models in science and theology, by F. Ferre.—Metaphysics and the limits of language, by C. B. Daly.—God and the "private I", by W. H. Poteat.—Paradox in religion, by I. T. Ramsey.—Birth, suicide, and the doctrine of creation, by W. H. Poteat.—The justification of religious belief, by B. Mitchell.—Assertion and analogy, by T. McPherson.—A neglected use of theological language, by R. C. Coburn. Bibliographical footnotes. [BL65.L2H53] 73-75116 5.00
1. Religion and language—Addresses, essays, lectures. I. Title.

LANGUAGE in religious 200'.1'4
practice / edited by William J. Samarin. Rowley, Mass. : Newbury House Publishers, c1976. xi, 177 p. ; 23 cm. (Series in sociolinguistics) Includes bibliographies and index. [BL65.L2L37] 76-17553 ISBN 0-88377-059-8 pbk. : 7.95
1. Religion and language—Addresses, essays, lectures. I. Samarin, William J.

MACCORMAC, Earl R. 200'.1'4
Metaphor and myth in science and religion / Earl R. MacCormac. Durham, N.C. : Duke University Press, 1976. xviii, 167 p. ; 23 cm. Includes bibliographical references and indexes. [BL65.L2M26] 75-23941 ISBN 0-8223-0347-7 : 7.95
1. Religion and language. 2. Science—Language. 3. Metaphor. 4. Religion and science—1946- I. Title.

SANTONI, Ronald E., 200'.1'4
comp.
Religious language and the problem of religious knowledge, edited with an introd. by Ronald E. Santoni. Bloomington, Indiana University Press [1968] 382 p. 22 cm. Includes bibliographies. [BL65.L2S2] 68-27352 8.50
1. Religion and language. 2. Knowledge, Theory of (Religion) I. Title.

STAHMER, Harold. 200'.1'4
"Speak that I may see Thee!" The religious significance of language. New York, Macmillan [1968] xi, 304 p. 21 cm. Bibliography: p. 287-293. [BL65.L2S7] 68-21305
1. Religion and language. I. Title.

TAYLOR, John Thomas, 200'.1'48
1947-
An illustrated guide to abbreviations, for use in religious studies / prepared by John T. Taylor ; edited by John L. Sayre. Enid, Okla. : Seminary Press, 1976. iii, 70 p. ; 28 cm. Includes index. [BR96.5.T39] 76-14705 ISBN 0-912832-13-4 pbk. : 5.00
1. Theology—Abbreviations. 2. Religion—Abbreviations. I. Title.

HARTT, Julian Norris. 200'.1'8
Theological method and imagination / Julian N. Hartt. New York : Seabury Press, c1977. p. cm. "A Crossroad book." [BR118.H37] 76-49901 ISBN 0-8164-0335-X : 12.95
1. Theology—Methodology. I. Title.

LONERGAN, Bernard J. F. 200'.1'8
Method in theology [by] Bernard J. F. Lonergan. [New York] Herder and Herder [1972] xii, 405 p. 22 cm. Includes bibliographical references. [BR118.L65] 78-181008 10.00
1. Theology—Methodology. I. Title.

SZYMANSKI, Ladislas. 200'.1'8
The translation procedure of Epiphanius-Cassiodorus in the Historia tripartia, books I and II. Washington, Catholic University of America Press, 1963. xxv, 273 p. 23 cm. (Catholic University of America. Studies in medieval and renaissance Latin language and literature, v. 24) Thesis -- Catholic University of America. Bibliography: p. xxi-xxv. [PA6271.C4H58] 63-23704
1. Cassiodorus Senator, Falvius Magnus Aurelius, ca. 487-ca. 580. Historia ecclesiastica tripartia. I. Title. II. Series.

ANDERSON, George 200'.19
Christian.
Your religion: neurotic or healthy? [1st ed.] Garden City, N.Y., Doubleday, 1970. 191 p. 22 cm. [BL53.A573] 74-123682 5.95
1. Psychology, Religious. I. Title.

BAKAN, David. 200.19
The duality of human existence; an essay on psychology and religion. Chicago, Rand McNally [1966] 242 p. 23 cm. Bibliographical footnotes. [BL53.B29] 66-13438
1. Psychology, Religious. I. Title.

BARCLAY, Robert, 1648- 200'.1'9
1690.
A catechism and confession of faith, approved of and agreed unto by the general assembly of the patriarchs, prophets. and apostles, Christ Himself chief speaker in and among them. Philadelphia, Friends' Book Store [n. d.] 103 p. 19 cm. [BX7730.B35] 50-43675

1. Friends. Society of—Catechisms and creeds—English. I. Title.

BARNHART, Joe E., 1931- 200'.19
Religion and the challenge of philosophy / by J. E. Barnhart. Totowa, N.J. : Littlefield, Adams, 1975. x, 312 p. ; 21 cm. (A Littlefield, Adams quality paperback ; no. 291) Includes bibliographical references and indexes. [BL51.B245] 75-16364 ISBN 0-8226-0291-1 pbk. : 4.95
1. Religion—Philosophy. I. Title.

BEIT-HALLAHMI, Benjamin, comp. 200'.19
Research in religious behavior: selected readings. Edited by Benjamin Beit-Hallahmi. Monterey, Calif., Brooks/Cole Pub. Co. [1973] x, 404 p. 23 cm. (Core books in psychology series) Contents.Contents.—Elkind, D. Piaget's semi-clinical interview and the study of spontaneous religion.—Nunn, C. Z. Child-control through a "coalition with God."—Crandall, V. C. and Gozali, J. The social desirability responses of children of four religious-cultural groups.—Ezer, M. The effect of religion upon children's responses to questions involving physical causality.—Allport, G. W. The religious context of prejudice.—Allport, G. W. and Ross, J. M. Personal religious orientation and prejudice.—Rokeach, M. Religion, values, and social compassion.—Stark, R. Age and faith: a changing outlook or an old process.—Shaw, B. W. Religion and conceptual models of behavior.—Nunn, C. Z., Kosa, J., and Alpert, J. J. Causal locus of illness and adaptation to family disruptions.—Lindenthal, J. J., Myers, J. K., Pepper, M. P., and Stern, M. S. Mental status and religious behavior.—Alland, A., Jr. "Possession" in a revivalistic Negro church.—Hine, V. H. Pentecostal glossolalia—toward a functional interpretation.—Allison, J. Adaptive regression and intense religious experiences.—Anderson, C. H. Religious communality and party preference.—Johnson, B. Ascetic Protestantism and political preference.—Marx, G. T. Religion: opiate or inspiration of civil rights militancy among Negroes. Includes bibliographies. [BL53.B38] 72-95822 ISBN 0-8185-0091-3
1. Psychology, Religious—Addresses, essays, lectures. I. Title.

BEIT-HALLAHMI, Benjamin, comp. 200'.19
Research in religious behavior: selected readings. Edited by Benjamin Beit-Hallahmi. Monterey, Calif., Brooks/Cole Pub. Co. [1973] x, 404 p. 23 cm. (Core books in psychology series) Includes bibliographies. [BL53.B38] 72-95822 ISBN 0-8185-0091-3 4.50
1. Psychology, Religious—Addresses, essays, lectures. I. Title.
Contents Omitted. Contents Omitted.

BOURGUIGNON, Erika, 1924- 200'.19
Religion, altered states of consciousness, and social change. Edited by Erika Bourguignon. Columbus, Ohio State University Press, 1973. x, 389 p. illus. 22 cm. Includes bibliographies. [BL53.B643] 72-8448 ISBN 0-8142-0167-9 12.50
1. Psychology, Religious. 2. Trance. 3. Sects. 4. Religion and sociology. I. Title.

*BROWN, L. B., ed. 200.19
Psychology and religion; selected readings, edited by L. B. Brown. [Harmondsworth, Eng., Penguin, 1973] 400 p. 20 cm. (Penguin Modern Psychology Readings) Includes bibliographical references. [BL53] ISBN 0-14-080538-9
1. Psychology, Religious. I. Title.
Available from Penguin, Baltimore for 4.95 (pbk)

BROWN, Laurence Binet, 1927- comp. 200'.19
Psychology and religion: selected readings, edited by L. B. Brown. Harmondsworth, Penguin Education, 1973. 400 p. 20 cm. (Penguin modern psychology readings) (Penguin education) Includes index. Bibliography: p. 383-389. [BL53.B68] 74-158980 ISBN 0-14-080538-9
1. Psychology, Religious—Collected works. I. Title.
Distributed by Penguin, Baltimore, Md., 4.95 (pbk.).

BURR, Anna Robeson Brown, 1873-1941. 200'.1'9
Religious confessions and confessants. With a chapter on the history of introspection. [Folcroft, Pa.] Folcroft Library Editions, 1974 [c1914] p. cm. Reprint of the ed. published by Houghton Mifflin, Boston. Bibliography: p. [BR1690.B8 1974] 74-18010 45.00
1. Psychology, Religious. 2. Mysticism. 3. Autobiography. I. Title.

CAPPS, Donald, comp. 200'.19
The religious personality, edited by Donald Capps and Walter H. Capps. Belmont, Calif., Wadsworth Pub. Co. [1970]. 381 p. 23 cm. Includes bibliographies. [BL53.C27] 76-125185
1. Psychology, Religious—Collections. I. Capps, Walter H., joint comp. II. Title.

CLARK, Walter Houston, 1902- 200'.19
Chemical ecstasy; psychedelic drugs and religion. New York, Sheed and Ward [1969] ix, 179 p. 22 cm. Includes bibliographical references. [BL65.D7C57] 74-82600 5.00
1. Hallucinogenic drugs and religious experience. I. Title.

COX, Richard H. 200'.19
Religious systems and psychotherapy, edited by Richard H. Cox. With a foreword by E. Mansell Pattison. Springfield, Ill., Thomas [1973] xxiv, 519 p. 26 cm. Includes bibliographies. [BL53.C66] 72-93207 ISBN 0-398-02753-6
1. Psychology, Religious. 2. Psychotherapy. I. Title.

COX, Richard H. 200'.19
Religious systems and psychotherapy, edited by Richard H. Cox. With a foreword by E. Mansell Pattison. Springfield, Ill., Thomas [1973] xxiv, 519 p. 26 cm. Includes bibliographies. [BL53.C66] 72-93207 ISBN 0-398-02753-6
1. Psychology, Religious. 2. Psychotherapy. I. Title.

CREEL, Richard E., 1940- 200'.1'9
Religion and doubt : toward a faith of your own / Richard E. Creel. Englewood Cliffs, N.J. : Prentice-Hall, 1976c1977 p. cm. Bibliography: p. [BL48.C725] 76-23102 ISBN 0-13-771949-3 : 8.95
1. Religion. I. Title.

CURRENT perspectives in the psychology of religion / edited by H. Newton Malony. Grand Rapids : Eerdmans, c1976. p. cm. Includes indexes. Bibliography: p. [BL53.C79] 76-44493 ISBN 0-8028-1660-6 pbk. : 4.95 200'.1'9
1. Psychology, Religious—Addresses, essays, lectures. I. Malony, H. Newton.

DE LUCA, Anthony J. 200'.1'9
Freud and future religious experience / Anthony J. De Luca. New York : Philosophical Library, c1976. 263 p. ; 22 cm. Includes index. Bibliography: p. 251-261. [BF173.F85D4] 75-3782 ISBN 0-8022-2173-4 : 12.50
1. Freud, Sigmund, 1856-1939. 2. Psychoanalysis and religion. I. Title.

DE LUCA, Anthony J. 200'.1'9
Freud and future religious experience / Anthony J. De Luca. Totowa, N.J. : Littlefield, Adams, 1977, c1976. 263 p. ; 21 cm. (Littlefield, Adams quality paperback ; 330) Includes index. Bibliography: p. 251-261. [BF173.F85D4 1977] 77-6798 ISBN 0-8226-0330-6 : 4.95
1. Freud, Sigmund, 1856-1939. 2. Psychoanalysis and religion. I. Title.

DE LUCA, Anthony J. 200'.1'9
Freud and future religious experience / Anthony J. De Luca. Totowa, N.J. : Littlefield, Adams, 1977, c1976. 263 p. ; 21 cm. (Littlefield, Adams quality paperback ; 330) Includes index. Bibliography: p. 251-261. [BF173.F85D4 1977] 77-6798 ISBN 0-8226-0330-6 : 4.95
1. Freud, Sigmund, 1856-1939. 2. Psychoanalysis and religion. I. Title.

THE Dialogue between theology and psychology, by LeRoy Aden [and others] Edited by Peter Homans. Chicago, University of Chicago Press [1968] x, 295 p. 24 cm. (Essays in divinity, v. 3) Many of the papers were first presented at the Alumni Conference of the Religion and Personality Field, Jan. 27-29, 1969, celebrating the 75th anniversary of the University of Chicago and the 100th anniversary of its Divinity School. Bibliographical footnotes. [BL53.D47] 68-16698 200'.19
1. Psychology, Religious. I. Homans, Peter, ed. II. Aden, LeRoy. III. Chicago. University. Divinity School. IV. Title. V. Series.

DU PREEZ, J. P. 200'.1'9
Psychology and religion : an inaugural lecture given in the University of Fort Hare on the 18th March 1976 / by J. P. du Preez. [Fort Hare, South Africa] : Fort Hare University Press, 1976. 24 p. ; 22 cm. (Fort Hare inaugural lectures ; C. 33) Bibliography: p. 24. [BL53.D86] 77-371609 ISBN 0-949974-32-3
1. Psychology, Religious—Addresses, essays, lectures. I. Title. II. Series.

FABER, Heije, 1907- 200'.1'9
Psychology of religion / by Heije Faber ; [translated by Margaret Kohl]. Philadelphia : Westminster Press, c1975. p. cm. Translation of Cirkelen om een geheim. Includes index. Bibliography: p. [BF175.F1513] 75-43721 ISBN 0-664-20748-0 : 12.50
1. Psychoanalysis and religion. I. Title.

FABER, Heije, 1907- 200'.1'9
Psychology of religion / Heije Faber ; [translated from the Dutch by Margaret Kohl]. London : S.C.M. Press, 1976. ix, 338 p. ; 23 cm. Translation of Cirkelen om een geheim. Includes indexes. Bibliography: p. 326-331. [BF175.F1513 1976] 77-366213 ISBN 0-334-01354-2 : £6.50
1. Psychoanalysis and religion. I. Title.

FERM, Vergilius Ture Anselm, 1896- ed. 200'.19
Religion in transition [by] S. Radhakrishnan [and others] Edited by Vergilius Ferm. Freeport, N.Y., Books for Libraries Press [1969] 266 p. facsims. 21 cm. (Essay index reprint series) Reprint of the 1937 ed. Contents.Contents.—My search for truth, by S. Radhakrishnan.—A pilgrim's progress, by C. F. Andrews.—My own little theatre, by G. A. Coe.—From credence to faith, by A. Loisy.—The making of a psychologist of religion, by J. H. Leuba.—Religion's use of me, by E. D. Starbuck. Includes bibliographies. [BL53.F4 1969] 68-29204
1. Psychology, Religious. I. Radhakrishnan, Sarvepalli, Pres. India, 1888- II. Title.

FREUD, Sigmund, 1856-1939. 200'.1'9
The future of an illusion / Sigmund Freud ; newly translated from the German and edited by James Strachey. New York : Norton, [1975] c1961. 63 p. ; 20 cm. Translation of Die Zukunft einer Illusion. Includes indexes. Bibliography: p. 57-59. [BL53.F67 1975] 75-15645 ISBN 0-393-01120-8 : 5.95
1. Psychology, Religious. 2. Religion. 3. Psychoanalysis. I. Strachey, James. II. Title.

FURST, Peter T. 200'.19
Flesh of the gods; the ritual use of hallucinogens. Edited by Peter T. Furst. New York, Praeger Publishers [1972] xvi, 304 p. illus. 25 cm. Bibliography: p. 279-294. [BL65.D7F87] 78-143970 10.00
1. Hallucinogenic drugs and religious experience—Addresses, essays, lectures. 2. Indians—Rites and ceremonies—Addresses, essays, lectures. I. Title.

GLEASON, John J., 1934- 200'.19
Growing up to God; eight steps in religious development [by] John J. Gleason, Jr. Nashville, Abingdon Press [1975] 141 p. 19 cm. Includes bibliographical references. [BL53.G58] 74-17093 ISBN 0-687-15972-5 3.50 (pbk.)
1. Erikson, Erik Homburger, 1902- 2. Psychology, Religious. I. Title.

GODIN, Andre, ed. 200.19
Child and adult before God, edited by A. Godin. Chicago, Loyola University Press, 1965. 160 p. illus. 24 cm. (Loyola pastoral series: Lumen vitae studies) Includes bibliographies. [BL53.G6] 65-16549
1. Psychology, Religious — Addresses, essays, lectures. I. Title.

GODIN, Andre, ed. 200.19
Child and adult before God. Chicago, Loyola [c.]1965. 160p. illus. 24cm. (Loyola pastoral ser.: Lumen vitae studies) Bibl. [BL53.G6] 65-16549 3.50
1. Psychology, Religious—Addresses, essays, lectures. I. Title.

GOTZ, Ignacio L. 200'.19
The psychedelic teacher; drugs, mysticism, and schools, by Ignacio L. Gotz. Philadelphia, Westminster Press [1972] 154 p. 19 cm. Bibliography: p. [147]-154. [BL65.D7G64] 75-183118 ISBN 0-664-20923-8 2.95 (pbk)
1. Hallucinogenic drugs and religious experience. I. Title.

HARNER, Michael J. 200'.19
Hallucinogens and shamanism. Edited by Michael J. Harner. New York, Oxford University Press, 1973. xv, 200 p. illus. 22 cm. Bibliography: p. [191]-194. [BL65.D7H37] 72-92292 8.50
1. Hallucinogenic drugs and religious experience. 2. Shamanism. I. Title.

HARPER, Ralph, 1915- 200.19
Human love, existential and mystical. Baltimore, Hopkins [1966] 178p. 22cm. Bibl. [BD436.H3] 66-24410 5.50
1. Love. I. Title.

HARPER, Ralph, 1915- 200.19
Human love, existential and mystical. Baltimore, Johns Hopkins Press [1966] 178 p. 22 cm. Bibliographical footnotes. [BD436.H3] 66-24410
1. Love. I. Title.

HAUGHTON, Rosemary. 200'.19
The liberated heart; transactional analysis in religious experience. New York, Seabury Press [1974] xxi, 192 p. 21 cm. "A Crossroad book." Bibliography: p. 191-192. [BL53.H35] 74-18271 ISBN 0-8164-1167-0 7.95
1. Psychology, Religious. 2. Transactional analysis. I. Title.

HAVENS, Joseph, 1919- 200.19
Psychology and religion; a contemporary dialogue [by] Joseph Havens, with the collaboration of David Bakan [and others] Princeton, N.J., Van Nostrand [1968] vii, 151 p. 19 cm. (An Insight book, 42) Bibliography: p. 140-147. [BL53.H36] 68-4750
1. Psychology, Religious. I. Bakan, David. II. Title.

HEANEY, John J., comp. 200'.19
Psyche and spirit; readings in psychology and religion, edited by John J. Heaney. New York, Paulist Press [1973] ix, 310 p. 23 cm. Bibliography: p. 305-310. [BL53.H37] 73-83810 ISBN 0-8091-1786-X 5.95 (pbk.)
1. Psychology, Religious—Addresses, essays, lectures. I. Title.

HOWLAND, Elihu S. 200'.1'9
Speak through the earthquake: religious faith and emotional crisis [by] Elihu S. Howland. Philadelphia, Pilgrim Press [1972] 125 p. 22 cm. Includes bibliographical references. [BL53.H65] 79-185180 ISBN 0-8298-0229-0 4.95
1. Psychology, Religious. I. Title.

JAMES, Muriel. 200'.1'9
The power at the bottom of the well : transactional analysis and religious experience / Muriel James, Louis M. Savary. Study guide ed. New York : Harper & Row, 1976. p. cm. "A Collins Associates book." Includes bibliographical references. [BL53.J35 1976] 76-13204 ISBN 0-06-064114-2 pbk. : 4.95
1. Experience (Religion) 2. Transactional analysis. I. Savary, Louis M., joint author. II. Title.

JAMES, Muriel. 200'.19
The power at the bottom of the well; transactional analysis and religious experience [by] Muriel James [and] Louis M. Savary. [1st ed.] New York, Harper & Row [1974] x, 150 p. 21 cm. "A Collins Associates book." Includes bibliographical references. [BL53.J35 1974] 74-4639 ISBN 0-06-064115-0 6.95
1. Experience (Religion) 2. Transactional analysis. I. Savary, Louis M., joint author. II. Title.

JUNG, Carl Gustav, 1875-1961. 200'.19
Psychology and religion: West and East. Translated by R. F. C. Hull. 2d ed. [Princeton, N.J.] Princeton University Press [1969] xiii, 699 p. illus. 24 cm. (His Collected works, v. 11) (Bollingen series, 20.) Translation of Zur Psychologie westlicher und ostlicher Religion. Bibliography: p. [609]-640. [BL53.J8413 1969] 74-13858 12.50
1. Psychology, Religious. I. Title. II. Series.

KELLY, Linda, 1936- 200.19
The young romantics : Paris, 1827-37 / [by] Linda Kelly. London : Bodley Head, 1976. [11], 146 p., [16] p. of plates : ill., ports. ; 23 cm. Includes index. Bibliography: p. 139-141. [PQ287.K4 1976b] 76-359699 ISBN 0-370-10264-9 : £3.75
1. Romanticism—France. 2. Authors, French—Biography. 3. Paris—Intellectual life. I. Title.

KLEPS, Art. 200'.19
The Boo Hoo bible; the Neo-American Church catechism. With a review by Timothy Leary. [San Cristobal, N.M., Toad Books, 1971] 211 p. illus. 23 cm. Cover title. [BL65.D7K57] 73-29356 ISBN 0-9600388-1-7
1. Hallucinogenic drugs and religious experience. I. Neo-American Church. II. Title.

LEARY, Timothy Francis, 1920- 200'.19
High priest, by Timothy Leary. Original art by Allen Atwell and Michael Green. New York, World Pub. Co. [1968] 353 p. illus. 24 cm. (An NAL book) Bibliography: p. 349-353 [BL65.D7L4] 68-9031 7.95
1. Hallucinogenic drugs and religious experience. 2. Hallucinations and illusions. 3. Hallucinogenic drugs. I. Title.

LEUBA, James Henry, 1868-1946. 200'.19
A psychological study of religion, its origin, function, and future. New York, AMS Press [1969] xiv, 371 p. 23 cm. Reprint of the 1912 ed. "The author's publications on the psychology of religion": p. 361-362. [BL53.L4 1969] 75-98628
1. Psychology, Religious. 2. Religion—Philosophy. I. Title.

MCCOMAS, Henry Clay, 1875 200'.19
The psychology of religious sects; a

comparison of types, by Henry C. McComas. New York, F. H. Revell Co. [New York, AMS Press, 1973] 235 p. 23 cm. Reprint of the 1912 ed. [BL53.M3 1973] 70-172763 ISBN 0-404-04107-8 10.00
1. Psychology, Religious. 2. Sects. I. Title.

MORE, Henry, 1614-1687 200.19
Enthusiasmus triumphatus (1662) Introd. by M. V. DePorte. Los Angeles, William Andrews Clark Memorial Lib., Univ. of Calif., 1966. x, 48p. 22cm. (Augustan Reprint Soc. Pubn. no. 118) (Augustan Reprint Soc. Pubn. no. 118) Original t. p. reads: Enthusiasmus triumphatus: or, A brief discourse of the nature, causes, kinds, and cure of enthusiasm ... [BR112.M6 1966] 66-6699 .90 pap.,
1. Enthusiasm. I. Title. II. Series.

MORENO, Antonio, 1918- 200'.19
Jung, gods, & modern man. Notre Dame [Ind.] University of Notre Dame Press [1970] xiii, 274 p. 24 cm. Bibliography: p. 265-269. [BL53.M64] 73-122047 7.95
1. Jung, Carl Gustav, 1875-1961. 2. Nietzsche, Friedrich Wilhelm, 1844-1900. 3. Psychology, Religious. I. Title.

ODEN, Thomas C. 200'.19
The structure of awareness [by] Thomas C. Oden. Nashville, Abingdon Press [1969] 283 p. 24 cm. Bibliographical footnotes. [BL53.O35] 75-84711 6.50
1. Psychology, Religious. 2. Phenomenology. 3. Philosophical anthropology. I. Title.

PANZARELLA, Andrew. 200'.1'9
Religion and human experience / by Andrew Panzarella. Winona, Minn. : St. Mary's College Press, [1974] 109, [1] p. : ill. ; 21 cm. Bibliography: p. 109-[110] [BL53.P2] 73-87024 ISBN 0-88489-058-9 : 3.00
1. Psychology, Religious. I. Title.

PARRINDER, Edward 200'.1'9
Geoffrey.
West African psychology : a comparative study of psycholgical and religious thought / by G. Parrinder. New York : AMS Press, 1976. p. cm. Reprint of the 1951 ed. published by Lutterworth Press, London, which was issued as v. 37 of Lutterworth library, Missionary research series no. 17. Includes indexes. [BL2465.P297 1976] 74-15076 15.00
1. Africa, West—Religion. I. Title.

PATRICK, Ted. 200'.1'9 B
Let our children go! / By Ted Patrick, with Tom Dulack. 1st ed. New York : Dutton, 1976. 285 p. : ill. ; 22 cm. "Thomas Congdon books." [BP603.P37 1976] 75-45298 ISBN 0-525-14450-1 : 7.95
1. Patrick, Ted. 2. Sects—Controversial literature. 3. Youth—Religious life. I. Dulack, Tom, 1935- joint author. II. Title.

PATRICK, Ted. 200'.1'9
Let our children go! / by Ted Patrick, with Tom Dulack. New York : Ballantine Books, 1977c1976. vii, 176p. : ill. ; 18 cm. [BP603.P37 1976] ISBN 0-345-25663-8 pbk. : 1.95
1. Patrick, Ted. 2. Sects-Controversial literature. 3. Youth-Religious life. I. Dulack, Tom., joint author. II. Title.
L.C. card no. for 1976 E.P. Dutton ed.: 75-45298.

PRATT, James Bissett, 200.1'9
1875-1944.
The religious consciousness; a psychological study. New York, Hafner Pub. Co., 1971 [c1920] viii, 488 p. 22 cm. "Facsimile of the 1920 edition." Includes bibliographical references. [BL53.P8 1920a] 72-153585
1. Psychology, Religious. 2. Religion. I. Title.

PRUYSER, Paul W. 200.'19
A dynamic psychology of religion / Paul W. Pruyser. New York : Harper & Row, 1976c1968. x, 367 ; 24 cm. Includes bibliographical references and index. [BL53.P82] pbk. : 5.95
I. Title.
L.C. card no. for 1968 ed. 68-17589.

PRUYSER, Paul W. 200'.19
A dynamic psychology of religion [by] Paul W. Pruyser. [1st ed.] New York, Harper & Row [1968] x, 367 p. 25 cm. Bibliographical references included in "Notes" (p. 341-355) [BL53.P82] 68-17589
1. Psychology, Religious. I. Title.

REDDING, David A. 200'.19
The couch and the altar [by] David A. Redding. [1st ed.] Philadelphia, Lippincott [1968] 125 p. 21 cm. Bibliographical references included in "Notes" (p. [123]-125) [BL53.R35] 68-29729 3.95
1. Psychology, Religious. I. Title.

REGARDIE, Israel. 200'.19
Roll away the stone; an introduction to Aleister Crowley's essays on the psychology of hashish. St. Paul, Llewellyn Publications, 1968. 241 p. 25 cm. "The herb dangerous" (p. 67-241) was first published in Equinox, 1909-10. Contents.Contents.—Roll away the stone, by I. Regardie.—The herb dangerous: A pharmaceutical study, by E. Whineray. The psychology of hashish, by O. Haddo [i.e. A. Crowley] The poem of hashish, by C. Baudelaire; translated by A. Crowley. [Selections from] The hashish eater, by H. G. Ludlow. Includes bibliographies. [BL65.D7R4 1968] 68-7264 7.50
1. Hallucinogenic drugs and religious experience. I. Crowley, Aleister, 1875-1947. II. Equinox. III. Title.

RUDIN, Josef. 200'.19
Psychotherapy and religion. Translated by Elisabeth Reinecke and Paul C. Bailey. Notre Dame [Ind.] University of Notre Dame Press [1968] xiii, 244 p. 22 cm. Bibliographical footnotes. [BL53.R813] 68-12291 5.95
1. Psychology, Religious. 2. Psychotherapy. I. Title.

SADLER, William Alan, 200'.19
comp.
Personality and religion; the role of religion in personality development. Edited by William A. Sadler, Jr. [1st U.S. ed.] New York, Harper & Row [1970] 245 p. 21 cm. (Harper forum books, RD 12) Contents.Contents.—Introduction. The scientific study of religion and personality, by W. A. Sadler, Jr.—Religion and the formation of a personal world: The religious dimension of human experience, by D. Lee. Obsessive actions and religious practices, by S. Freud. Thought organization in religion, by P. Pruyser. The religious context of prejudice, by G. W. Allport. The prophet, by M. Weber. Formation of the need to achieve, by D. C. McClelland. Individual and social narcissism, by E. Fromm. Christ, a symbol of the self, by C. G. Jung. Father and son in Christianity and Confucianism, by R. N. Bellah. Religious aspects of peak-experiences, by A. H. Maslow.—The role of religion in existential crises: Religion in times of social distress, by T. F. O'Dea. Crises in personality development, by A. Boisen. Coming to terms with death, by D. Bakan.—Re-evaluating religion in relation to personality development and the personality sciences: Paradoxes of religious belief, by M. Rokeach. The common enemy, by K. Menninger. Includes bibliographical references. [BL53.S23 1970] 74-109076 3.95
1. Psychology, Religious—Addresses, essays, lectures. I. Title.

SCOBIE, Geoffrey E. W. 200'.1'9
Psychology of religion / Geoffrey E. W. Scobie. New York : Wiley, 1975. 189 p. ; 23 cm. "A Halsted Press book." Includes index. Bibliography: p. [170]-179. [BL53.S35] 74-21832 ISBN 0-470-76712-X : 8.95
1. Psychology, Religious. I. Title.

SIEGMUND, Georg, 1903- 200.19
Belief in God and mental health. Tr. by Isabel and Florence McHugh. Pref. by James H. Van der Veldt. New York, Desclee, 1965[c.1962] 210p. 22cm. [RC455.S5313] 65-20315 4.50
1. Psychiatry and religion. I. Title.

SPINKS, George Stephens 200.19
Psychology and religion; an introduction to contemporary voews. by G. Stephens Spinks. Boston. Beacon [1967. c.1963] xv, 221p. 21cm. (BP273) [BL53.S63 1965] 65-23471 2.45 pap.,
1. Psychology, Religious. I. Title.

STEPHEN. 200'.19
Monday night class [by] Stephen. [Santa Rosa, Calif., Book Farm, 1970] 1 v. (unpaged) illus. 21 cm. Recorded and transcribed by William Myers. [BP610.S8] 74-135168 1.95
I. Myers, William. II. Title.

STORY, Thomas, 1662- 200'.1'9
1742.
The doctrines of the Society of Friends as set forth in the life and writings of Thomas Story. Philadelphia, Book Assn. of Friends [n.d.] 195 p. 17 cm. [BX7730.S8] 48-41865
1. Friends, Society of — Doctrinal and controversial works. I. Title.

STRUNK, Orlo, comp. 200'.19
The psychology of religion; historical and interpretative readings. Nashville, Abingdon Press [1971] 152 p. 23 cm. (Apex books) "A revision and enlargement of part I of [the editor's] Readings in the psychology of religion." Bibliography: p. 135-144. [BL53.S763] 77-158672 ISBN 0-687-34862-5
1. Psychology, Religious. I. Title.

THOULESS, Robert Henry, 200'.19
1894-
An introduction to the psychology of religion [by] Robert H. Thouless. 3rd ed. London, Cambridge University Press, 1971. viii, 152 p. 23 cm. Includes bibliographical references. [BL53.T5 1971] 76-184142 ISBN 0-521-08149-1 £2.40 ($7.50 U.S.)
1. Psychology, Religious. I. Title.

TRANSPERSONAL 200'.1'9
psychologies / edited by Charles T. Tart. 1st ed. New York : Harper & Row, [1975] 502 p. : ill. ; 24 cm. Includes indexes. Bibliography: p. [473]-485. [BL53.T67 1975] 73-18672 ISBN 0-06-067823-2 : 12.50
1. Psychology, Religious. I. Tart, Charles T., 1937-

TRANSPERSONAL 200'.1'9
psychologies / edited by Charles T. Tart. New York : Harper & Row, 1977c1975. 504p. : ill. ; 21 cm. (Harper Colophon Books) Includes index. Bibliography: p. [480]-490. [BL53R67] ISBN 0-06-090486-0 pbk. : 6.95
1. Psychology, Religious. I. Tart, Charles T., 1937-
L.C. card no. for original ed.: 73-18672.

ULANOV, Ann Belford. 200'.19
Religion and the unconscious / by Ann and Barry Ulanov. Philadelphia : Westminster Press, [1975] 287 p. ; 24 cm. Includes bibliographical references and index. [BL53.U45] 75-16302 ISBN 0-664-20799-5 : 10.00
1. Psychology, Religious. 2. Subconsciousness. 3. Ethics. I. Ulanov, Barry, joint author. II. Title.

VERGOTE, Antoine. 200'.19
The religious man; a psychological study of religious attitudes. Translated by Marie-Bernard Said. Dayton, Ohio, Pflaum Press, 1969. vii, 306 p. 21 cm. Translation of Psychologie religieuse. Bibliographical footnotes. Bibliography: p. 305-306. [BL53.V3813] 70-93006 6.95
1. Psychology, Religious. I. Title.

YUNGBLUT, John R. 200'.1'9
Seeking light in the darkness of the unconscious / John Yungblut. [Wallingford, Pa. : Pendle Hill Publications], 1977. 24 p. ; 19 cm. (Pendle Hill pamphlet ; 211 ISSN 0031-4250s) "Presented March 19, 1976, at Ben Lomond, California, at the first Conference on Psychology and Religion held by Friends on the West Coast." Includes bibliographical references. [BL53.Y86] 77-71933 ISBN 0-87574-211-4 : 0.95
1. Psychology, Religious—Addresses, essays, lectures. I. Title.

ZAEHNER, Robert Charles. 200'.19
Zen, drugs, and mysticism [by] R. C. Zaehner. New York, Vintage Books [1974, c1972] 223 p. 18 cm. Reprint of the 1973 ed. published by Pantheon Books, New York. Includes bibliographical references. [BL65.D7Z3 1974] 73-15523 1.95 (pbk.)
1. Hallucinogenic drugs and religious experience. 2. Mysticism. I. Title.

ZAEHNER, Robert Charles. 200'.19
Zen, drugs, and mysticism, by R. C. Zaehner. [1st American ed.] New York, Pantheon Books [1973, c1972] 223 p. 22 cm. British ed. published under title: Drugs, mysticism and make-believe. Includes bibliographical references. [BL65.D7Z3 1973] 72-11871 ISBN 0-394-48540-8 6.95
1. Hallucinogenic drugs and religious experience. 2. Mysticism. I. Title.

ZIELINSKI, Stanislaw A. 200'.1'9
Psychology & silence / by Stanislaw Zielinski ; edited by Daniel Bassuk. Wallingford, Pa. : Pendle Hill Publications, 1975. 32 p. : port. ; 19 cm. (Pendle Hill pamphlet ; 201) Contents.Contents.—The role of psychology in religious mysticism.—Silent meeting. [BL53.Z48] 75-7413 ISBN 0-87574-201-7 : 0.95
1. Friends, Society of—Doctrinal and controversial works. 2. Psychology, Religious. 3. Silence. I. Title.

WAGONER, Walter D., 200'.2'07
comp.
Bittersweet grace; a treasury of twentieth-century religious satire, edited by Walter D. Wagoner. Cleveland, World Pub. Co. [1967] x, 181 p. 22 cm. Bibliography: p. 179-181. [BL50.W2] 67-11437
1. Religion—Anecdotes, facetiae, satire, etc. I. Title.

WAGONER, Walter D., 200'.2'07
comp.
Bittersweet grace; a treasury of twentieth-century religious satire, edited by Walter D. Wagoner. Cleveland, World Pub. Co. [1967] x, 181 p. 22 cm. Bibliography: p. 179-181. [BL50.W2] 67-11437
1. Religion—Anecdotes, facetiae, satire, etc. I. Title.

RIPLEY, Robert Le Roy, 200'.22'2
1893-1949.
Believe it or not; the world of religion. Westwood, N.J., F. H. Revell Co. [1967] 1 v. (unpaged) illus., ports. 18 cm. [AG243.R4 1967] 67-66352
1. Curiosities. I. Title.

RIPLEY, Robert Le Roy, 200'.22'2
1893-1949.
Believe it or not; the world of religion. Westwood, N.J., F. H. Revell Co. [1967] 1 v. (unpaged) illus., ports. 18 cm. [AG243.R4 1967] 67-66352
1. Curiosities and wonders. I. Title.

RIPLEY'S Believe it or 200'22'2
not! the world of religion. Westwood, N.J., Revell [1967] liv. (unpaged) chiefly illus. 18cm. .95 pap.,

THATCHER, Joan. 200'.23
Church vocations / Joan Thatcher. Minneapolis : Dillon Press, c1976. 106 p. : ill. ; 24 cm. (Looking forward to a career) Includes index. Bibliography: p. [104]-106. Describes the range of careers available within church and synagogue, including those of rabbi, priest, missionary, chaplain, teacher, and others. Includes a discussion of church careers for women. [BV4740.T45] 75-33177 ISBN 0-87518-100-7 : 5.95 pbk. : 2.76
1. Vocation, Ecclesiastical—Juvenile literature. I. Title.

SPIRITUAL community 200'.25'7
guide. [San Rafael, Calif.] 1972- v. illus. 21 cm. annual. [BP602.S66] 72-621784
1. Cults—United States—Directories. 2. Cults—Canada—Directories.
Vol. 1 of this new series is available from the Spiritual Community, Box 1080, San Rafael, CA 94902 for 2.95

FRIEDLANDER, Ira. 200'.25'73
Year one catalog; a spiritual directory for the new age. Edited by Ira Friedlander. Introd. by Pir Vilayat Inayat Khan. [1st ed.] New York, Harper & Row [1972] 152 p. ports. 21 cm. [BP602.F74 1972] 73-150151 ISBN 0-06-063018-3 1.95
1. Religions—Directories. 2. Sects—Directories. I. Title.

MELTON, J. Gordon. 200'.25'73
A directory of religious bodies in the United States / compiled from the files of the Institute for the Study of American Religion [by] J. Gordon Melton with James V. Geisendorfer. New York : Garland Pub., 1977. p. cm. (Garland reference library of the humanities ; v. 91) Bibliography: p. [BL2530.U6M44] 76-52700 lib.bdg. : 21.00
1. United States—Religion—Directories. I. Geisendorfer, James V., joint author. II. Institute for the Study of American Religion. III. Title.

BLUNT, John Henry, 1823- 200'.3
1884.
Dictionary of sects, heresies, ecclesiastical parties, and schools of religious thought. London, Rivingtons, 1874. Detroit, Gale Research Co., 1974. viii, 648 p. 23 cm. [BR95.B6 1974] 74-9653 ISBN 0-8103-3751-7 28.50
1. Theology—Dictionaries. 2. Sects—Dictionaries. I. Title.

BLUNT, John Henry, 1823- 200'.3
1884.
Dictionary of sects, heresies, ecclesiastical parties, and schools of religious thought. Edited by John Henry Blunt. Ann Arbor, Mich., Gryphon Books, 1971. viii, 648 p. 22 cm. Reprint of the 1874 ed. [BR95.B6 1971] 71-107136
1. Theology—Dictionaries. 2. Sects—Dictionaries. I. Title.

CANNEY, Maurice Arthur, 200'.3
1872-1942.
An encyclopaedia of religions. Detroit, Gale Research Co., 1970. ix, 397 p. 28 cm. Reprint of the 1921 ed. Bibliography: p. [vii]-ix. [BL31.C3 1970] 75-123370
1. Religion—Dictionaries. I. Title.

CATTELL, Ann, 1893- 200.3
A dictionary of esoteric words. [1st ed.] New York, Citadel Press [1967] 128 p. 21 cm. [BL31.C35] 67-25648
1. Religion—Dictionaries. I. Title.

FERM, Vergilius Ture 200'.3
Anselm, 1896-1974, ed.
An encyclopedia of religion / edited by Vergilius Ferm. Westport, Conn. : Greenwood Press, 1976, c1945. xix, 844 p. ; 24 cm. Reprint of the ed. published by Philosophical Library, New York. Includes bibliographies. [BL31.F4 1976] 75-36508 ISBN 0-8371-8638-2 lib.bdg. : 40.00
1. Religion—Dictionaries. I. Title.

KAUFFMAN, Donald T. ed. 200'.3
Baker's pocket dictionary of religious terms, [edited by] Donald T. Kauffman. Grand Rapids, Baker Book House, [1975 c1967] 445 p. 18 cm. Formerly published under the title, the dictionary of religious terms. [BL31.K34] ISBN 0-8010-5361-7 2.95 (pbk.)
1. Religion—Dictionaries. I. Title.
L.C. card no. for original ed.: 67-22570.

KAUFFMAN, Donald T. 200'.3
The dictionary of religious terms, by Donald T. Kauffman. Westwood, N.J., Revell [1967] 445 p. 24 cm. [BL31.K34] 67-22570
1. Religion—Dictionaries. I. Title.

LEE, Frederick George, 1832-1902. 200'.3
A glossary of liturgical and ecclesiastical terms. London, B. Quaritch, 1877. Detroit, Tower Books, 1971. xxxix, 452 p. illus. 23 cm. Bibliography: p. [xxxi]-xxxix. [BR95.L4 1971] 76-174069
1. Theology—Dictionaries. 2. Liturgical objects—Dictionaries. I. Title.

MATHEWS, Shailer, 1863-1941, ed. 200'.3
A dictionary of religion and ethics. Edited by Shailer Mathews and Gerald Birney Smith. London, Waverly Book Co. Detroit, Gale Research Co., 1973 [c1921] vii, 513 p. 23 cm. Bibliography: p. 485-513. [BL31.M3 1973] 70-145713 17.50
1. Religion—Dictionaries. 2. Ethics—Dictionaries. I. Smith, Gerald Birney, 1868-1929, joint ed. II. Title.

SEMINAR on Research Perspectives and Problems, Chicago, 1961. 2003
Agrarian reform & economic growth in developing countries; papers. Sponsored by the North Central Land Tenure Research Committee; the Farm Foundation; and the Farm Economics Division, Economic Research Service. Washington, Farm Economics Division, Economic Research Service, U. S. Dept. of Agriculture, 1962. 74 p. illus. 27 cm. Includes bibliography. [HD1251.S4 1961] 63-61338
1. Land tenure. 2. Economic development. I. North Central Land Tenure Research Committee. II. Title.

SHARPE, Eric J., 1933- 200'.3
Fifty key words: comparative religion, by Eric J. Sharpe. Richmond, John Knox Press [1971] 85 p. 20 cm. [BL31.S47 1971] 70-161840 ISBN 0-8042-3897-9 1.95
1. Religion—Dictionaries. I. Title. II. Title: Comparative religion.

UNITED Nations. Secretary-General, 1946-(Lie) 2003
Economic development of under-developed countries: Land reform, defects in agrarian structure as obstacles to economic development; report under General Assembly Resolution 401 (V) [New York, 1951] 119 p. 28 cm. (United Nations. [Document] E/2003. 14 June 1951) At head of title: United Nations Economic and Social Council. 13th sess. [JX1977.A2 E] 333 52-1219
1. Land tenure. I. United Nations. Economic and Social Council. II. Title. III. Title: Land reform. IV. Title: Defects in agrarian structure as obstacles to economic development. V. Series.

DAIGLE, Richard J. 200'.4
The Mentor dictionary of mythology and the Bible, by Richard J. Daigle and Frederick R. Lapides. New York, New American Library [1973] vi, 202 p. 18 cm. (A Mentor book) [BL715.D24] 73-76392 1.95 (pbk.)
1. Bible—Dictionaries. 2. Mythology—Dictionaries. I. Lapides, Frederick R., joint author. II. Title.

DE SANTILLANA, Giorgio, 1902- 200.4
Hamlet's mill; an essay on myth and the frame of time [by] Giorgio de Santillana and Hertha von Dechend. Boston, Gambit, 1969. xxv, 505 p. illus. 24 cm. Bibliography: p. [453]-484. [BL304.D43] 69-13267 10.00
1. Myth. 2. Knowledge, Theory of. I. Dechend, Hertha von, 1915- joint author. II. Title.

ENCYCLOPAEDIA of religion and ethics, edited by James Hastings, with the assistance of John A. Selbie, and other scholars. New York, Scribner, 1951. 13v. in 7. illus., plates, facsims., taples. 27cm. [BL31.E] A53 200'.4
1. Religion—Dictionaries 2. Ethics—Dictionaries. 3. Theology—Dictionaries. I. Hastings, James, 1852-1922, ed.

HAIGH, Madelon. 200.4
Myths are somebody's religion. Los Angeles, Tinnon-Brown [1968] v, 64 p. 23 cm. [BL311.H34] 68-57775
1. Mythology. I. Title.

HARTLAND, Edwin Sidney, 1848-1927. 200'.4
The legend of Perseus; a study of tradition in story, custom, and belief. [Folcroft, Pa.] Folcroft Library Editions, 1973. p. Reprint of the 1894-96 ed. published by D. Nutt, London, which was issued as no. 2, 3, and 5 of Grimm library. Contents.Contents.—v. 1. The supernatural birth.—v. 2. The life-token.—v. 3. Andromeda. Medusa. Bibliography: v. 1, p. xiii-xxxiv; v. 3, p. [xiii]-xxxvii. [GR75.P53H37 1973] 73-11485 45.00
1. Perseus. 2. Folk-lore—Classification. 3. Rites and ceremonies. I. Title.

JACKSON, Samuel Macauley, 1851-1912, ed. 200'.4
Schaff-Herzog encyclopedia. Grand Rapids, Mich, Baker, 1949-50. 13 v. 25 cm. Vols. 2-12 have abbreviated title which varies slightly; v. 13; Index by George William Gilmore. "Editor-in-chief of supplementary volumes, Lefferts A. Loetscher." [[BR95.S]] A51
1. Theology — Dictionaries. I. Title. II. Title: The new Schaff-Herzog encyclopedia of religious knowledge, embracing Biblical, historical, doctrinal, and practical theology, and Biblical, theological, and ecclesiastical biography from the earliest times to the present day; based on the 3d ed. of the Realencyklopadic founded by J. J. Herzog, and edited by Albert Hauke, prepared by more than six hundred scholars and specialists under the supervision of Samuel Macauley Jackson (editor-in-chief) with the assistance of Charles Colebrook Sherman and George William Gilmore (associate editors) and [others]

*JAMES, E. O. 200.4
Christian myth and ritual; a historical study. Gloucester, Mass., Peter Smith, 1973. 341 p. 21 cm. First published in London by John Murray, 1933. Bibliography: p. 328-340. [BL304] ISBN 0-8446-2307-5 6.00
1. Myth. 2. Folk-lore. 3. Religion, Primitive. I. Title.

LANG, Andrew, 1844-1912. 200'.4
Custom and myth. New York, AMS Press [1968] 312 p. illus. 23 cm. Reprint of the 1885 ed. Includes bibliographical references. [BL310.L3 1968] 68-59267
1. Folk-lore. 2. Religion, Primitive. 3. Mythology. I. Title.

LEEMING, David Adams, 1937- 200'.4
Mythology; the voyage of the hero. Philadelphia, Lippincott [1973] vii, 338 p. 23 cm. Bibliography: p. 322-326. [BL311.L326] 73-913 ISBN 0-397-47276-5 4.95
1. Mythology—Collections. I. Title.

MULLER, Friedrich Max, 1823-1900. 200.4
Selected essays on language, mythology and religion / by F. Max Muller. New York : AMS Press, 1976. p. cm. Reprint of the 1881 ed. published by Longmans, Green, London. Includes index. [P27.M8 1976] 73-18814 ISBN 0-404-11456-3 : 67.50
1. Language and languages—Collected works. 2. Mythology—Collected works. 3. Religion—Collected works. I. Title.

MYTHS and symbols; studies in honor of Mircea Eliade. Edited by Joseph M. Kitagawa and Charles H. Long. With the collaboration of Gerald C. Brauer and Marshall G. S. Hodgson. Chicago, University of Chicago Press [1969] 438 p. port. 23 cm. [BL25.M85] 69-12132 200.4
1. Mythology. 2. Symbolism. I. Eliade, Mircea, 1907- II. Kitagawa, Joseph Mitsuo, 1915- ed. III. Long, Charles H., ed.

NORMAN, Dorothy, 1905- 200.4
The hero: myth, image, symbol. New York, World Pub. Co. [1969] xvii, 238 p. illus. 26 cm. "An NAL book." Bibliographical footnotes. [BL304.N6] 68-57956 10.00
1. Myth. 2. Symbolism. 3. Art and mythology. I. Title.

A Quest anthology / with an introd. by James Webb. New York : Arno Press, 1976. p. cm. (The Occult) Reprint of articles originally published in the Quest, London, 1909-1927. Includes bibliographical references. [BL50.Q47 1976] 75-36916 ISBN 0-405-07971-0 : 35.00 200'.4
1. Grail—History and criticism—Addresses, essays, lectures. 2. Religion—Addresses, essays, lectures. 3. Mysticism—Addresses, essays,lectures. I. Webb, James, 1946- II. The Quest (London, 1909-1930) III. Series: The Occult (New York, 1976-)

NEW Larousse encyclopedia of mythology. Introd. by Robert Graves. [Translated by Richard Aldington and Delano Ames, and rev. by a panel of editorial advisers from the Larousse mythologie generale edited by Felix Guirand. New ed. New York] Putnam [1968, c1959] xi, 500 p. illus., col. plates. 30 cm. Bibliography: p. [486]-487. [BL311.N43 1968] 68-57758 17.95 200.4'03
1. Mythology. 2. Folk-lore. I. Guirand, Felix, ed. Mythologie generale. II. Title: Larousse encyclopedia of mythology.

SEDGWICK, Paulita. 200'.4'03
Mythological creatures; a pictorial dictionary. [1st ed.] New York, Holt, Rinehart and Winston [1974] 1 v. (unpaged) illus. 24 cm. Includes bibliography. Brief alphabetically arranged entries identify creatures of myth and folklore from various countries including goblins, sylphs, werewolves, Punch and Judy, Ravana, and others. [GR825.S42] 74-8004
1. Animals, Mythical—Dictionaries—Juvenile literature. 2. Mythology—Dictionaries—Juvenile literature. I. Title.

BROOMALL, Wick, 1902- 200.6
Biblical criticism. Grand Rapids, Zondervan Pub. House [1957] 320 p. 23 cm. Includes bibliography. [BS476.B67] 57-2368
1. Bible—Hermeneutics. I. Title.

PETERSEN, William J. 200.6
Those curious new cults [by] William J. Petersen. New Canaan, Conn., Keats [1973] vii, 214 p. 22 cm. Bibliography: p. 213-214. [BF1411.P47] 72-93700 ISBN 0-87983-031-X 4.95
1. Occult sciences. 2. Psychical research. 3. Sects. 4. Religions. I. Title.

PETERSEN, William J. 200'.6
Those curious new cults / William J. Petersen. New Canaan, Conn. : Keats Pub., 1975. 272 p. ; 18 cm. (A Pivot family reader) Bibliography: p. 271-272. [BF1411.P47 1975] 75-328425 pbk. : 1.95
1. Occult sciences. 2. Psychical research. 3. Sects. 4. Religions. I. Title.

SLEETH, Ronald Eugene. 200.6
Proclaiming the Word. New York, Abingdon Press [1964] 142 p. 20 cm. Bibliographical footnotes. [BV4211.2.S56] 64-10605
1. Preaching. I. Title.

SMITH, Robert Tighe, 1926- 200'.6
Cult & occult [by] Robert T. Smith. Minneapolis, Winston Press [1973] 142 p. 24 cm. [BF1411.S658] 72-93590 ISBN 0-03-007536-X 2.95
1. Occult sciences. 2. Psychical research. 3. Sects. I. Title.
Publisher's address: 25 Groveland Terrace.

TURNBULL, Ralph G. 200.6
The preacher's heritage, task, and resources, by Ralph G. Turnbull. Grand Rapids, Baker Book House [1968] 178 p. 20 cm. Bibliography: p. 169-178. [BV4211.2.T87] 68-19215 2.95
1. Preaching. I. Title.

BRAYBROOKE, Marcus. 200'.6'21
Faiths in fellowship : a short history of the World Congress of Faiths and its work / [by] Marcus Braybrooke ; with a foreword by George Appleton. London : World Congress of Faiths, [1976] [8], 39 p., [4] p. of plates : ports. ; 21 cm. Includes bibliographical references. [BL21.W55B92] 77-351239 ISBN 0-905468-00-7 : £0.50
1. World Congress of Faiths—History. I. Title.

AMERICAN Academy of Religion. Academic Study of Religion Section. 200'.7
The academic study of religion : 1975 proceedings and Public schools religion-studies : 1975 proceedings / American Academy of Religion annual meeting, 1975. Missoula, Mont. : Distributed by Scholars Press, University of Montana, c1975. p. cm. "Preprinted papers for the Academic Study of Religion Section, compiled by Anne Carr, and the Public Schools Religion-Studies Group, compiled by Nicholas Piediscalzi." Includes bibliographical references. [BL41.A47 1975] 75-26653 ISBN 0-89130-023-6 : 2.00
1. Religion—Study and teaching—Congresses. 2. Religion in the public schools—Congresses. I. Carr, Anne. II. Piediscalzi, Nicholas. III. American Academy of Religion. Public Schools Religion-Studies Group. IV. Title. V. Title: Public schools religion studies.

BRADFORD, Ann. 200'.7
Working with primaries through the Sunday school. Nashville, Convention Press [1961] 149p. illus. 19cm. [BV1545.B587] 61-11413
1. Religious education of children. 2. Religious education— Teacher training. 3. Sunday-schools. I. Title.

BURKS, Thompson. 200'.7
Religions of the world; a study course for adults. Cincinnati, Standard Pub. [1972] [16], 112 p. 22 cm. The main work, also issued separately, is preceded by the author's "Instructor" with special t.p. Bibliography: p. 112 (2d group) [BL80.2.B78 1972] 72-188037
1. Religions—Study and teaching. I. Title.

COMSTOCK, W. Richard. 200'.7
The study of religion and primitive religions [by] W. Richard Comstock. New York, Harper & Row [1972] 117 p. illus. 24 cm. (Religion and man) Bibliography: p. 107-112. [BL50.C67] 76-185899 ISBN 0-06-041338-7
1. Religion. 2. Religion, Primitive. I. Title. II. Series.

EISTER, Allan W. 200'.7
Changing perspectives in the scientific study of religion, edited by Allan W. Eister. New York, Wiley [1974] xxii, 370 p. illus. 23 cm. (Contemporary religious movements) "A Wiley-Interscience publication." Includes bibliographies. [BL41.E37] 74-2092 ISBN 0-471-23476-1 14.50
1. Religion—Study and teaching. 2. Religion and sociology. I. Title.

GLOCK, Charles Y. 200'.7
Beyond the classics? Essays in the scientific study of religion, edited by Charles Y. Glock and Phillip E. Hammond, with contributions by Norman Birnbaum [and others] New York, Harper & Row [1973] xvii, 422 p. 21 cm. (Harper torchbooks, HR 1751) Includes bibliographies. [BL41.G55 1973] 72-13909 ISBN 0-06-136105-4 12.00
1. Religion—Study and teaching—History. I. Hammond, Phillip E., joint author. II. Birnbaum, Norman. III. Title.

GUNDRY, D. W. 200'.7
The teacher and the world religions, by D. W. Gundry. Cambridge, James Clarke, 1968. 160 p. 21 cm. (The Education and religion series) Includes bibliographical references. [BL41.G85] 75-538622 18/6
1. Religions—Study and teaching. 2. Religions—Historiography. I. Title.

KEITH, Noel Leonard. 200'.7
Religion; an introduction and guide to study [by] Noel Keith. [2d ed.] Dubuque, Iowa, W. C. Brown Book Co. [1967] xii, 467 p. illus., port. 24 cm. Includes bibliographies. [BL41.K4] 67-23296
1. Religion—Study and teaching. I. Title.

O'DOHERTY, Eamonn Feichin. 200'.7
The religious formation of the elementary school child [by] E. F. O'Doherty. New York, Alba House [1973] viii, 151 p. 22 cm. [BV1475.2.O33] 72-11911 ISBN 0-8189-0261-2 3.95
1. Religious education of children. I. Title.

SUMMERS, Jester. 200'.7
God loves everybody; leadership material. A unit to use with primary children. Nashville, Convention Press [1963] 84 p. illus. 19 cm. Hymns, with music (p. 77-84) [BV1545] 63-8380
1. Religious education of children. I. Title.

VRIES, Jan de, 1890-1964. 200'.7
Perspectives in the history of religions / Jan de Vries ; translated with an introd. by Kees W. Bolle. Berkeley : University of California Press, 1977, c1967. xxiii, 231 p. ; 21 cm. Translation of Godsdienstgeschiedenis in vogelvlucht. Includes bibliographical references and indexes. [BL41.V713 1977] 76-20154 ISBN 0-520-03300-0 pbk. : 3.95
1. Religion—Study and teaching. 2. Religion—Historiography. I. Title.

WAARDENBURG, Jean Jacques. 200'.7
Classical approaches to the study of religion. Aims, methods and theories of research, by Jacques Waardenburg. The Hague, Paris, Mouton, [1973- v. 23 cm. (Religion and reason, v. 3) Contents.Contents.—1. Introduction and anthology. Bibliography: v. 1, p. [667]-672. [BL41.W28] 70-152082
1. Religion—Study and teaching—Collected works. I. Title.
Distributed by Humanities; 20.00

EVANS, J. J., comp. 200'.71
Guard our unbelief: passages for discussion; selected by J. J. Evans. London, Oxford University Press, 1971. xii, 180 p. 21 cm. [BV1561.E83] 78-591485 ISBN 0-19-913035-3 £0.75
1. Religious education—Text-books. 2. Readers—Religion. I. Title.

WHAT future for the Agreed Syllabus? : report of a working party to the Religious Education Council of England and Wales. Farnham : The Council, 1976. 19 p. ; 21 cm. [LC314.G7W47] 77-356631 ISBN 0-905437-00-4 : £0.30 200'.7'1041
1. Moral education—Great Britain—Curricula. 2. Religious education—Great Britain—Curricula. I. Religious Education Council of England and Wales.

KING, Noel Quinton. 200'.71'1
The queen of the sciences as a modern African professional woman; reflections on the place of religious studies in the tropical African university scene, by Noel King. [Nairobi]

Published for Makerere University College by Oxford University Press [1967] 46 p. 25 cm. "An inaugural lecture delivered at Makerere University College (University of East Africa) Kampala, Uganda, on 14th July, 1966." Bibliography: p. 43-46. [BL41.K5] 68-89360
1. Religion—Study and teaching—Africa. 2. Universities and colleges—Africa. 3. Universities and colleges—Religion. I. Title.

WELCH, Claude. 200'.7'1173
Religion in the undergraduate curriculum; an analysis and interpretation. With essays contributed by Beverly A. Asbury [and others] Washington, Association of American Colleges, 1972. v, 129 p. 23 cm. Bibliography: p. 127-129. [BL41.W43] 72-182245
1. Religion—Study and teaching—United States. I. Asbury, Beverly A. II. Title.

INTERNATIONAL 200'.7'1178961
Correspondence Schools, Scranton, Pa.
How to get your share of industrial business; field staff training course. Serial 2807A-1-Ed. Scranton, c1962- v. illus. 19cm. [LC6001.I5772] 62-5179
1. Correspondence schools and courses. I. Title.

ST. JOHN, Martinus 200'.7'1178961
The tragedy of the Jews, of the Protestants, and of the Catholics in our contemporary civilization. [1st ed. Albuquerque, N.M.] American Classical College Press [1973] 30 l. illus. 28 cm. [LC6001.A364S25] 73-85331 ISBN 0-913314-17-X
1. American Classical College. 2. Catholic Church—Addresses, essays, lectures. 3. Judaism—Addresses, essays, lectures. 4. Protestantism—Addresses, essays, lectures. I. Title.

KENNEDY, James R. 200'.7'2
Library research guide to religion and theology : illustrated search strategy and sources / by James R. Kennedy, Jr. Ann Arbor, Mich. : Pierian Press, 1974. x, 53 p. : ill. ; 29 cm. (Library research guides series ; no. 1) Includes index. Bibliography: p. 43-51. [BL41.K45] 73-90317 ISBN 0-87650-038-6
1. Religion—Research—Handbooks, manuals, etc. 2. Reference books—Theology. 3. Libraries—Handbooks, manuals, etc. I. Title.

METHODOLOGICAL issues in 200'.7'2
religious studies / edited by Robert D. Baird ; contributions from Wilfred Cantwell Smtih [sic], Jacob Neusner, Hans Penner. [Chico, Ca.] : New Horizons Press, c1975. vi, 129 p. ; 22 cm. Proceedings of a symposium held Apr. 15-17, 1974, at the School of Religion of the University of Iowa. Includes bibliographical references. [BL41.M43] 75-44170 ISBN 0-914914-08-1 : 8.50. ISBN 0-914914-07-3 pbk. : 4.50
1. Religion—Historiography—Congresses. 2. Religions—Historiography—Congresses. I. Baird, Robert D., 1933- II. Smith, Wilfred Cantwell, 1916-

APPEL, Georg. 200'.8 s
De Romanorum precationibus / Georgius Appel. New York : Arno Press, 1975. 222 p. ; 23 cm. (Ancient religion and mythology) Reprint of the 1909 ed. (Gissae, Impensis A. Toepelmanni), which was issued as vol. 7, part 2 of Religionsgeschichtliche Versuche und Vorarbeiten. Includes bibliographical references and index. [BL25.R37 Bd. 7, Heft 2] [BL815.P68] 292'.3'8 75-10628 ISBN 0-405-07004-7
1. Prayer (Roman religion) I. Title. II. Series. III. Series: Religionsgeschichliche Versuche und Vorarbeiten ; 7 Bd., 2 Heft.

*BACH, T. J. 200.8
710 pointed quotations and illustrations. Grand Rapids, Mich., Baker Bk. 1965[c.1951] 104p. 20cm. (Preaching helps ser.) Previously printed under title Pearls from many seas. 1.00 pap.,
I. Title.

BUXTON, Richard F. 200'.8 s
Eucharist and institution narrative : a study in the Roman and Anglican traditions of the consecration of the Eucharist from the eighth to the twentieth centuries / Richard F. Buxton. Great Wakering, Eng. : Published for the Alcuin Club [by] Mayhew-McCrimmon, 1976. 276 p. ; 21 cm. (Alcuin Club collections ; no. 58) Includes index. Bibliography: p. 258-269. [BX5141.A1A6 no. 58] [BV825.5] 265'.3 77-357546 £5.00
1. Lord's Supper (Liturgy)—History. 2. Lord's Supper—History. I. Title. II. Series: Alcuin Club. Collections ; no. 58.

CAPPS, Walter H., comp. 200'.8
Ways of understanding religion [by] Walter H. Capps. New York, Macmillan [1971, c1972] xvi, 399 p. 24 cm. Includes bibliographies. [BL25.C3 1972] 77-151166 4.95
1. Religion—Collections. I. Title.

CARD, Claudia F., comp. 200'.8
Religious commitment and salvation; readings in secular and theistic religion. Edited by Claudia F. Card [and] Robert R. Ammerman. Columbus, Ohio, Merrill [1974] xiv, 370 p. 23 cm. Bibliography: p. 357-370. [BL25.C33] 73-87527 ISBN 0-675-08871-2 6.95
1. Religion—Collected works. 2. Theology—Collected works. I. Ammerman, Robert R., joint author. II. Title.

FRAZIER, Allie M., comp. 200'.8
Issues in religion; a book of readings [by] Allie M. Frazier. [New York] American Book Co. [1969] viii, 373 p. illus. 24 cm. Includes bibliographical references. [BL51.F68127] 70-2733
1. Religion—Philosophy—Collections. I. Title.

FRAZIER, Allie M., comp. 200'.8
Issues in religion : a book of readings / Allie M. Frazier. 2d ed. New York : Van Nostrand, [1975] viii, 435 p. ; 24 cm. Includes bibliographies and index. [BL25.F65 1975] 74-21155 ISBN 0-442-21680-7 : 7.25
1. Religion—Collected works. 2. Religion—Philosophy—Collected works. I. Title.

THE Great harmony : 200'.8
teachings and observations of the way of the universe / edited, with an introd., by S. Negrin. New York : Times Change Press, c1977. p. cm. Includes index. Bibliography: p. [PN6084.R3G7] 77-77387 ISBN 0-87810-533-6 : 8.00 ISBN 0-87810-033-4 pbk. : 3.00
1. Religion—Quotations, maxims, etc. I. Negrin, Su.

THE Great harmony : 200'.8
teachings and observations of the way of the universe / edited, with an introd., by S. Negrin. New York : Times Change Press, c1977. p. cm. Includes index. Bibliography: p. [PN6084.R3G7] 77-77387 ISBN 0-87810-533-6 : 8.00 ISBN 0-87810-033-4 pbk. : 3.00
1. Religion—Quotations, maxims, etc. I. Negrin, Su.

KENNEDY, John Fitzgerald, 200.8
1917-1963
Religious views of President John F. Kennedy in his own words. Comp. by Nicholas A. Schneider. St. Louis, B. Herder [c.]1965. xv, 125p. 23cm. [E842.1.A6S3] 65-26875 price unreported
1. Kennedy, John Fitzgerald, Pres. U.S., 1917-1963—Religion. I. Schneider, Nicholas A., comp. II. Title.

KENNEDY, John Fitzgerald, 200.8
Pres. U.S., 1917-1963.
Religious views of President John F. Kennedy in his own words. Compiled by Nicholas A. Schneider. St. Louis, Herder, 1965. xv, 125 p. 23 cm. [E842.1.A6S3] 65-26875
1. Kennedy, John Fitzgerald, Pres. U.S., 1917-1963 — Religion. I. Schneider, Nicholas A., comp. II. Title.

LESSA, William Armand, ed. 200'.8
Reader in comparative religion; an anthropological approach. [Edited by] William A. Lessa [and] Evon Z. Vogt. 3d ed. New York, Harper & Row [1972] xii, 572 p. illus. 26 cm. Bibliography: p. [559]-570. [BL80.2.L44 1972] 76-164691 ISBN 0-06-043992-0
1. Religions—Collections. I. Vogt, Evon Zartman, 1918- joint ed. II. Title.

LIN, Timothy Tian-min, 200'.8
comp.
Readings in the world's living religions. Dubuque, Iowa, Kendall/Hunt Pub. Co. [1974] vii, 253 p. 23 cm. [BL29.L56] 74-76460 ISBN 0-8403-0913-9 6.50 (pbk.)
1. Religious literature—Collected works. I. Title.

MURPHY, Carol R. 200.8
Many religions, one God; toward a deeper dialogue, by Carol R. Murphy. [Wallingford, Pa., 1966] 31 p. 19 cm. (Pendle Hill pamphlet 150) Bibliography: p. 31. [BL50.M88] 66-30689
1. Religion—Addresses, essays, lectures. 2. Christianity and other religions—Addresses, essays, lectures. I. Title.

NEEDLEMAN, Jacob, comp. 200'.8
Religion for a new generation. [Edited by] Jacob Needleman, A. K. Bierman [and] James A. Gould. New York, Macmillan [1973] xiv, 592 p. 24 cm. Includes bibliographies. [BL25.N43] 72-77149 9.95
1. Religion—Collections. I. Bierman, Arthur Kalmer, 1923- joint comp. II. Gould, James A., 1922- joint comp. III. Title.

NEEDLEMAN, Jacob, comp. 200'.8
Religion for a new generation / edited by Jacob Needleman, Arthur K. Bierman, James A. Gould. 2d ed. New York : Macmillan, c1977. xiii, 572 p. ; 24 cm. Includes bibliographical references. [BL50.N39 1977] 76-10540 ISBN 0-02-385990-3 : 7.95
1. Religion—Addresses, essays, lectures. I. Bierman, Arthur Kalmer, 1923- joint comp. II. Gould, James A., 1922- joint comp. III. Title.

NEEDLEMAN, Jacob, comp. 200'.8
The sword of gnosis: metaphysics, cosmology, tradition, symbolism; essays by Frithjof Schuon [and others] Baltimore, Penguin Books [1974] 464 p. illus. 18 cm. (The Penguin metaphysical library) Includes bibliographical references. [BL50.N4] 73-81717 ISBN 0-14-003768-3 4.95 (pbk.)
1. Religion—Addresses, essays, lectures. I. Schuon, Frithjof, 1907- II. Title.

NOCK, Arthur Darby, 1902- 200'.8
1963.
Essays on religion and the ancient world. Selected and edited, with an introd., bibliography of Nock's writings, and indexes, by Zeph Stewart. Cambridge, Mass., Harvard University Press, 1972. 2 v. (xvii, 1029 p.) port. 25 cm. Includes bibliographical references. [BL50.N562] 74-135192 ISBN 0-674-26725-7 35.00 (set)
1. Religion—Addresses, essays, lectures. I. Stewart, Zeph, 1921- ed. II. Title.

PAUL Carus Memorial 200'.8
Symposium, Peru, Ill., 1957.
Modern trends in world religions. Edited by Joseph M. Kitagawa. Freeport, N.Y., Books for Libraries Press [1972, c1959] xiv, 286 p. 22 cm. (Essay index reprint series) Bibliography: p. [283]-286. [BL87.P28 1957b] 72-5676 ISBN 0-8369-7294-5
1. Religions—Addresses, essays, lectures. I. Kitagawa, Joseph Mitsuo, 1915- ed. II. Title.

SIMONSON, Harold Peter, 200'.8
1926- comp.
Dimensions of man [compiled by] Harold P. Simonson [and] John B. Magee. New York, Harper & Row [1973] xxviii, 368 p. 24 cm. [BL25.S5] 73-1037 ISBN 0-06-046177-2 4.95 (pbk.)
1. Religion—Collections. I. Magee, John Benjamin, 1917- joint comp. II. Title.

TOURNIER, Paul. 200'.8
A Tournier companion. London : S.C.M. Press, 1976. xii, 177, [1] p. ; 23 cm. Contains extracts from the author's works. [BL53.T666] 77-359978 ISBN 0-334-01664-9 : £2.80
1. Psychology, Religious—Miscellanea. 2. Conduct of life—Miscellanea. I. Title.

WATTS, Alan Wilson, 1915- 200'.8
1973.
Three / by Alan Watts. New York : Pantheon Books, [1977] p. cm. Includes bibliographies. [BQ9265.4.W37 1977] 77-76500 ISBN 0-394-41904-9 : 15.00
1. Zen Buddhism. 2. Religion—Philosophy. 3. Sex and religion. 4. Psychotherapy. 5. East and West. I. Title.
Contents omitted

BACH, Marcus, 1906- 200'.9
Strange sects and curious cults / by Marcus Bach. Westport, Conn. : Greenwood Press, 1977, c1961. viii, 277 p. ; 23 cm. Reprint of the 1962 ed. published by Dodd, Mead, New York. Includes index. [BL85.B3 1977] 76-52474 ISBN 0-8371-9457-1 lib.bdg. : 17.00
1. Religions. 2. Sects. I. Title.

CLEMEN, Carl Christian, 200'.9
1865-1940, ed.
Religions of the world; their nature and their history, by Carl Clemen, in collaboration with Franz Babinger [and others] Translated by A. K. Dallas. Freeport, N.Y., Books for Libraries Press [1969, c1931] xiv, 482 p. illus., ports. 24 cm. (Essay index reprint series) Translation of Die Religionen der Erde. Includes bibliographies. [BL80.C66 1969] 69-17570
1. Religions. 2. Religions—History. I. Babinger, Franz Carl Heinrich, 1891- II. Title.

DAWSON, Christopher Henry, 200'.9
1889-1970.
Religion and world history : a selection from the works of Christopher Dawson / edited by James Oliver and Christina Scott ; foreword by R. C. Zaehner. 1st ed. Garden City, N.Y. : Image Books, 1975. 351 p. ; 18 cm. (An Image book original) Includes bibliographical references and index. [BL80.2.D35 1975] 74-33612 ISBN 0-385-09551-1 pbk. : 2.45
1. Religions. 2. Church history. 3. Civilization, Modern. I. Title.

ELIADE, Mircea, 1907- 200'.9
The quest; history and meaning in religion. Chicago, University of Chicago Press [1969] 180 p. 23 cm. Bibliographical footnotes. [BL50.E46] 69-19059
1. Religion. I. Title.

THE Future of our religious 200.9
past; essays in honour of Rudolf Bultmann. Edited by James M. Robinson. Translated by Charles E. Carlston and Robert P. Scharlemann. New York, Harper & Row [1971] xi, 372 p. port. 22 cm. Translation of selected papers from Zeit und Geschichte. Contents.Contents.—Exegesis: Eschatology and history in the light of the Dead Sea scrolls, by N. A. Dahl. Eschatological expectation in the proclamation of Jesus, by W. G. Kummel. Some thoughts on the theme 'The doctrine of reconciliation in the New Testament,' by E. Kasemann. The theological aspects of primitive Christian heresy, by H. Koester. Logoi sophon: on the Gattung of Q, by J. M. Robinson. [Baptisma metanoias eis aphesin amarteion (romanized form)], by H. Thyen. Peter's confession and the Satan saying: the problem of Jesus' messiahship, by E. Dinkler. The risen Lord and the earthly Jesus: Matthew 28.16-20, by G. Bornkamm. The mother of wisdom, by H. Conzelmann.—Theology and philosophy: Time and word, by G. Ebeling. The hermeneutical problem, by E. Fuchs. Dietrich Bonhoeffer and Rudolf Bultmann, by G. Krause. The debt and responsibility of theology, by F. Gogarten. From the last Marburg lecture course, by M. Heidegger. Philosophical meditation on the seventh chapter of Paul's Epistle to the Romans, by H. Jonas.—List of English works and translations (p. [351]-357) [BR50.B849132 1971] 70-148440 18.95
1. Theology—Addresses, essays, lectures. I. Bultmann, Rudolf Karl, 1884- II. Robinson, James McConkey, 1924- ed.

HALL, Angus. 200'.9
Strange cults / by Angus Hall. Garden City, N.Y. : Doubleday, 1976. 144 p. : ill. ; 27 cm. (A New library of the supernatural) [BP603.H34] 76-5344 ISBN 0-385-11324-2 : 8.95
1. Sects. I. Title. II. Series.

THE History of religions; 200.9
essays on the problem of understanding, by Joachim Wach [and others] Edited by Joseph M. Kitagawa with the collaboration of Mircea Eliade and Charles H. Long. Chicago, University of Chicago Press [1967] xii, 264 p. 24 cm. (Essays in divinity v. 1) Most of the papers were presented at the Alumni Conference of the Field of History of Religions, Oct. 11-13, 1965, celebrating the 75th anniversary of the University of Chicago and the 100th anniversary of its Divinity School. Bibliographical footnotes. [BL41.H5] 67-20574
1. Religion—Study and teaching—Addresses, essays, lectures. 2. Religion—Historiography—Addresses, essays, lectures. I. Kitagawa, Joseph Mitsuo, 1915- ed. II. Wach, Joachim, 1898-1955. III. Chicago. University. Divinity School. IV. Title. V. Series.

HUTCHISON, John Alexander, 200'.9
1912-
Paths of faith [by] John A. Hutchison. New York, McGraw-Hill [1969] xv, 656 p. illus., ports. 24 cm. Includes bibliographies. [BL80.2.H78] 68-11930
1. Religion—History. 2. Religions. I. Title.

HUTCHISON, John Alexander, 200'.9
1912-
Paths of faith [by] John A. Hutchison. 2d ed. New York, McGraw-Hill [1975] xvii, 667 p. illus. 24 cm. Includes bibliographies. [BL80.2.H78 1975] 74-2432 ISBN 0-07-031531-0 10.95
1. Religion—History. 2. Religions. I. Title.

KETTELKAMP, Larry. 200'.9
Religions, East and West. New York, Morrow, 1972. 128 p. illus. 23 cm. Discusses the similarities and differences of ten of the world's major religions. [BL92.K45] 72-75805 ISBN 0-688-20030-3 3.95
1. Religions—Juvenile literature. I. Title.

LEWIS, John, 1889- 200'.9
The religions of the world made simple. Rev. ed. Garden City, N.Y., Doubleday [1968] 191 p. 26 cm. (Made simple books) Includes bibliographies. [BL82.L4 1968] 68-14221
1. Religion—History. I. Title.

LING, Trevor Oswald. 200'.9
A history of religion East and West; an introduction and interpretation [by] Trevor Ling. New York, Harper & Row [1970, c1968] xxix, 464 p. maps. 21 cm. (Harper colophon books, CN 155) Bibliography: p. [431]-439. [BL80.2.L53 1970] 71-102219 3.45
1. Religions—History. I. Title.

MCCASLAND, Selby Vernon, 200'.9
1896-
Religions of the world [by] S. Vernon McCasland, Grace E. Cairns [and] David C. Yu. New York, Random House [1969] xviii, 760 p. illus., maps. 25 cm. Includes bibliographies. [BL80.2.M27] 69-10524 8.50
1. Religions. I. Cairns, Grace Edith, 1908- joint author. II. Yu, Chien-shen, 1918- joint author. III. Title.

MARETT, Robert Ranulph, 1866-1943. 200'.9
Faith, hope, and charity in primitive religion. New York, B. Blom, 1972. 181 p. 21 cm. Reprint of the 1932 ed. "These lectures were originally given in Boston in the Fall of 1930 under the auspices of the Lowell Institution. They were then amplified and, as Gifford Lectures, were delivered before the University of St. Andrews during the academic year 1931-2." [GN470.M23 1972] 72-80150
1. Religion, Primitive—Addresses, essays, lectures. 2. Ethics, Primitive—Addresses, essays, lectures. I. Title.

NOSS, John Boyer. 200'.9
Man's religions [by] John B. Noss. 4th ed. [New York] Macmillan [1969] xx, 598 p. illus. 24 cm. Includes bibliographical references. [BL80.2.N6 1969] 69-11587
1. Religions. I. Title.

NOSS, John Boyer. 200'.9
Man's religions [by] John B. Noss. 5th ed. New York, Macmillan [1974] xviii, 589 p. illus. 24 cm. Includes bibliographies. [BL80.2.N6 1974] 72-13972 ISBN 0-02-388440-1 9.95
1. Religions. I. Title.

PARRISH, Fred Louis. 200.9
History of religion; the destiny-determining factor in the world's cultures. [1st ed.] New York, Pageant Press [1965] 279 p. 21 cm. [BL96.P3] 65-19181
1. Religion—Hist. I. Title.

PARRISH, Fred Louis 200.9
History of religion: the destiny-determining factor in the world's cultures. New York, Pageant [c.1965] 279p. 21cm. [BL96.P3] 65-19181 5.00
1. Religion—Hist. I. Title.

RINGGREN, Helmer, 1917- 200'.9
Religions of mankind today & yesterday, by Helmer Ringgren and Ake V. Strom. Edited by J. C. G. Greig; translated by Niels L. Jensen. [1st American ed.] Philadelphia, Fortress Press [1967] xiii, 426 p. 24 cm. Translation of Religionera l historia och nutid. Includes bibliographies. [BL80.2.R5513] 67-11252
1. Religions — Hist. I. Strom, Ake V., joint author. II. Title.

RINGGREN, Helmer, 1917- 200'.9
Religions of mankind today & yesterday, by Helmer Ringgren and Ake V. Strom. Edited by J. C. G. Greig; translated by Niels L. Jenson. [1st American ed.] Philadelphia, Fortress Press [1967] xiii, 426 p. 24 cm. Translation of Religionerna i historia och nutid. Includes bibliographies. [BL80.2.R5513 1967b] 67-11252
1. Religions—History. I. Strom, Ake V., joint author. II. Title.

ROYCE, Josiah, 1855-1916. 200'.9
The religious philosophy of Josiah Royce / edited, with an introductory essay, by Stuart Gerry Brown. Westport, Conn. : Greenwood Press, 1976, c1952. 239 p. ; 23 cm. Reprint of the ed. published by Syracuse University Press, Syracuse, N.Y. Contents.Contents.—The possibility of error.—Individuality and freedom.—The temporal and the eternal.—The conception of immortality.—Loyalty and religion.—The idea of the universal community.—The moral burden of the individual.—The realm of grace.—Time and guilt.—Atonement. [B945.R61B7 1976] 76-4496 ISBN 0-8371-8810-5 lib.bdg. : 14.00
1. Religion—Philosophy—Addresses, essays, lectures. I. Title.
Contents omitted.

RUST, Eric Charles. 200'.9
Positive religion in a revolutionary time, by Eric C. Rust. Philadelphia, Westminster Press [1970] 233 p. 21 cm. Includes bibliographical references. [BL48.R84] 78-90782 3.65
1. Religion—History. 2. Secularism. 3. Christianity—20th century. I. Title.

SCHMIDT, Wilhelm, 1868-1954. 200'.9
The origin and growth of religion; facts and theories. Translated from the original German by H. J. Rose. New York, Cooper Square Publishers, 1972. xvi, 302 p. 24 cm. Translation of Ursprung und Werden der Religion; Theorien und Tatsachen. Reprint of the 1931 ed. Includes bibliographical references. [BL430.S43 1972] 78-184909 ISBN 0-8154-0408-5 9.00
1. Religion, Primitive. 2. Religion—History. 3. Religion—Historiography. I. Title.

SCHOEPS, Hans Joachim. 200'.9
The religions of mankind. Translated from the German by Richard and Clara Winston. [1st ed. in the U.S.A.] Garden City, N.Y., Doubleday, 1966. xiii, 320 p. illus., col. maps (on lining-papers) 24 cm. Translation of Religionen: Wesen und Geschichte. [BL80.2.S353] 66-14927
1. Religions—History. I. Title.

SEIFERT, Harvey. 200'.9
Reality and ecstasy; a religion for the 21st century. Philadelphia, Westminster Press [1974] 173 p. 19 cm. Includes bibliographical references. [BL48.S43] 74-9713 ISBN 0-664-24990-6 3.25 (pbk.).
1. Religion. I. Title.

SMART, Ninian, 1927- 200'.9
The religious experience of mankind. New York, Scribner [1969] xii, 576 p. illus., maps, port. 25 cm. Bibliography: p. [545]-550. [BL80.2.S6] 68-12508 10.00
1. Religions—History. 2. Religion. 3. Experience (Religion) I. Title.

TOY, Crawford Howell, 1836-1919. 200'.9
Introduction to the history of religions. [1st AMS ed.] New York, AMS Press [1970] xix, 639 p. 23 cm. Reprint of the 1913 ed. Bibliography: p. 585-623. [BL80.T7 1970] 76-126655 ISBN 0-404-06498-1
1. Religions—History. 2. Religion—History. 3. Rites and ceremonies. 4. Mythology. I. Title.

VRIES, Jan de, 1890-1964. 200'.9
The study of religion; a historical approach. Translated with an introd. by Kees W. Bolle. New York, Harcourt, Brace & World [1967] xxiii, 231 p. 21 cm. Bibliographical references included in "Notes" (p. 223-228) [BL41.V713] 67-19964
1. Religion—Study and teaching. 2. Religion—Historiography. I. Title.

HAHN, Theophilus. 200'.9011
Tsuni-llGoam: the supreme being of the Khoi-khoi. Freeport, N.Y., Books for Libraries Press, 1971. xi, 154 p. 22 cm. (The Black heritage library collection) Reprint of the 1880 ed. Bound with Trubner, firm, publishers, London. (1880. Trubner & Co.) Trubner's oriental & linguistic publications. London, 1880. [BL2480.H6H34 1971] 70-164388 ISBN 0-8369-8847-7
1. Hottentots—Religion. I. Title. II. Series.

ANGUS, Samuel, 1881-1943. 200'.9'015
The mystery-religions : a study in the religious background of early Christianity / by S. Angus. New York : Dover Publications, 1975. xvi, 359 p. ; 22 cm. Reprint of the 2d ed. published in 1928 by Scribner, New York under title: The mystery-religions and Christianity. Includes indexes. Bibliography: p. 315-352. [BL610.A6 1975] 74-12657 ISBN 0-486-23124-0 pbk. : 3.95
1. Mysteries, Religious. 2. Christianity and other religions. I. Title.

CAHIERS d'histoire mondiale 200.904
Religions and the promise of the twentieth century; readings in the history of mankind. Edited for the International Commisssion for a History of the Scientific and Cultural Development of Mankind, by Guy S. Metraux and Francois Crouzet. New York, New American Library [1965] 277 p. 18 cm. (A Mentor book. Readings in the history of mankind) "These materials were used in the preparation of volume vI of the History of mankind: cultural and scientific development" and were originally published in the Journal of world history. Includes bibliographies. [BL80.2.C3] 65-22037
1. Religions. Theology—20th cent. I. Metraux, Guy S., ed. Crouzet, Francois, 1922- ed. International Commission for a History of the Scientific and Cultural Development of Mankind. IIistory of mankind. cultural and scientific development. Title. II. Title. III. Series: Readings in the history of mankind

CAHIERS D'HISTOIRE MONDIALE 200.904
Religions and the promise of the twentieth century; readings in the history of mankind. Ed. for the Intl. Commn. for a Hist. of the Scientific and Cultural Development of Mankind, by Guy S. Metraux, Francois Crouzet. New York, New Amer. Lib. (c.1965] 277p. 18cm. (Mentor bk., MQ651; Readings in the hist. of mankind) Title. (Series: Readings in the history of mankind) These materials were used in the prep. of v.6 of the History of mankind: cultural and scientific development, and were orig. pub. in the Journal of World history. Bibl. [BL80.2C3] 65-22037 .95 pap.,
1. Religions. 2. Theology—20th cent. I. Metraux, Guy S., ed. II. Crouzet, Francois, 1922- ed. III. International Commission for a History of the Scientific and Cultural Development of Mankind. IV. Title. V. Series.

COGLEY, John. 200'.9'04
Religion in a secular age; the search for final meaning. Pref. by Arnold Toynbee. New York, Praeger [1968] xxi, 147 p. 24 cm. (Britannica perspective) Bibliographical footnotes. [BL48.C556] 68-28156 5.95
I. Title.

MEAD, Margaret, 1901- 200'.9'04
Twentieth century faith: hope and survival. [1st ed.] New York, Harper & Row [1972] xviii, 172 p. 22 cm. (Religious perspectives, v. 25) [BL50.M35 1972] 72-78081 ISBN 0-06-065549-6 6.95
1. Religion—Addresses, essays, lectures. I. Title. II. Series.

JOHNSTONE, Patrick J. St. G. 200'.9'047
World handbook for the world Christian / by Patrick J. St. G. Johnstone. South Pasadena, Calif. : World Christian Book Shelf, [1976] p. cm. [BL82.J64 1976] 76-15187 ISBN 0-87808-727-3
1. Religions—Handbooks, manuals, etc. 2. Geography—Handbooks, manuals, etc. I. Title.

†JOHNSTONE, Patrick J. St. G. 200'.9'047
World handbook for the world Christian / by Patrick J. St. G. Johnstone. South Pasadena, Calif. : World Christian Book Shelf, c1976. 208 p. 15 p. ; 22 cm. [BL82.J64 1976] 76-15187 ISBN 0-87808-727-3 pbk. : 4.95
1. Religions—Handbooks, manuals, etc. 2. Geography—Handbooks, manuals, etc. I. Title.

SOPHER, David Edward 200'.91
Geography of religion [by] David E. Sopher. Englewood Cliffs, N.J., Prentice [1967] x, 118p. illus., maps. 23cm. (Founds. of cultural geog. ser.) Bibl. [BL65.G4S6] 67-13357 4.50; 1.95 pap.,
1. Religion and geography. I. Title.

THE Biographical process 200'.92
: studies in the history and psychology of religion / edited by Frank E. Reynolds and Donald Capps. The Hague : Mouton, 1977 xi, 436 p. ; 23 cm. (Religion and reason ; 11) Based on seminars held at the Divinity School, University of Chicago, 1972 and 1973. Includes indexes. Bibliography: p. 413-426. [BL72.B56] 77-352279 ISBN 9-02-797522-1 : 31.25
1. Religion—Biography—Addresses, essays, lectures. 2. Biography (as a literary form)—Addresses, essays, lectures. I. Reynolds, Frank, 1930- II. Capps, Donald. III. Chicago. University. Divinity School.
Distributed by Humanities Press

*DILES, David L. 200.92
Twelfth man in the huddle / David L. Diles. Waco, Tx. : Word Books, c1976. 187p. : ill. ; 23 cm. [BV4596.A8] 76-19529 ISBN 0-87680-442-3 : 6.95
1. Athletes-Religions life 2. Football. I. Title.

MERKLEY, Paul. 200.92
Reinhold Niebuhr : a political account / Paul Merkley. Montreal : McGill-Queen's University Press, 1975. xii, 289 p. ; 24 cm. Includes index. Bibliography: p. [273]-277. [BX4827.N5M47] 76-351874 ISBN 0-7735-0216-5 : 13.50
1. Niebuhr, Reinhold, 1892-1971.
Distributed by McGill-Queen's University Press, Irvington, N.Y.

BANCROFT, Anne, 1923- 200'.92'2 B
Twentieth century mystics and sages / Anne Bancroft. Chicago : Regnery, 1976. p. cm. Includes bibliographical references and index. [BL72.B36] 76-153 ISBN 0-8092-8148-1. ISBN 0-8092-8237-2 pbk.
1. Religions—Biography. I. Title.

BURROWS, Millar, 1889- 200'.92'2 B
Founders of great religions, being personal sketches of famous leaders. Freeport, N.Y., Books for Libraries Press [1973] p. (Essay index reprint series) Reprint of the 1931 ed. [BL72.B8 1973] 72-13272 ISBN 0-8369-8148-0
1. Religions—Biography. I. Title.

EASTMAN, Max, 1883-1969. 200'.922
Seven kinds of goodness. New York, Horizon Press [1967] 156 p. 22 cm. [BL72.E15] 67-17781
1. Religions—Biography. I. Title.

ENCOUNTER with 200'.92'2 B
Erikson : historical interpretation and religious biography / edited by Donald Capps, Walter H. Capps, M. Gerald Bradford. Missoula, Mont. : Published by Scholars Press for the American Academy of Religion and the Institute of Religious Studies, University of California, Santa Barbara, c1977. xvi, 429 p. ; 24 cm. (Series on formative contemporary thinkers ; no. 2) Paper presented at a symposium to honor E. H. Erikson on the occasion of his seventieth birthday, held at La Casa de Maria Retreat Center near Santa Barbara, Calif., Feb. 17-19, 1972. "Erik Homburger Erikson: a bibliography of his books and articles": p. 421-429. [BL72.E5] 76-44434
1. Erikson, Erik Homburger, 1902- — Congresses. 2. Religions—Biography—Congresses. 3. Psychohistory—Congresses. 4. Psychology, Religious—Congresses. I. Erikson, Erik Homburger, 1902- II. Capps, Donald. III. Capps, Walter H. IV. Bradford, Miles Gerald, 1938- V. American Academy of Religion. VI. California. University, Santa Barbara. Institute of Religious Studies. VII. Title. VIII. Series.

FREMANTLE, Anne (Jackson) 1909- 200'.922
Pilgrimage to people, by Anne Fremantle. New York, McKay [1968] viii, 231 p. 21 cm. [BL72.F73] 68-10539
1. Religions—Biography. I. Title.

LANDAU, Rom, 1899- 200'.92'2 B
God is my adventure; a book on modern mystics, masters, and teachers. Freeport, N.Y., Books for Libraries Press [1972] viii, 407, iv p. ports. 22 cm. (Essay index reprint series) Reprint of the 1936 ed. Bibliography: p. 397-407. [BL72.L3 1972] 72-1265 ISBN 0-8369-2848-2
1. Religions—Biography. I. Title.

MODERN theologians: 200'.922
Christians and Jews; introduction to the works of Martin Buber [and others] Editor: Thomas E. Bird. Notre Dame [Ind.[University of Notre Dame Press [1967] xii, 224 p. 21 cm. (Theology today, v.2) [BT28.M6] 68-696
1. Theologians. 2. Theology, Doctrinal—Hist.—20th cent. I. Series.
contents omitted

MODERN theologians: 200'.922
Christians and Jews; introduction to the works of Martin Buber [and others] Editor: Thomas E. Bird. Notre Dame [Ind.] University of Notre Dame Press [1967] xii, 224 p. 21 cm. (Theology today, v. 2) Contents.Contents.—Theologians of dialogue: Martin Buber, by L. D. Streiker. John Courtney Murray, by T. T. Love. Josef Hromadka, by C. C. West.—Theologians of the life of the church: Bernard Haring, by S. O. Weselowsky. Edward Schillebeeckx, by M. J. Houdijk. John A. T. Robinson, by L. D. Streiker.—Theologians of intellectual renewal: Bernard Lonergan, by F. E. Crowe. John Hick, by L. D. Streiker.—Theologians of mystical experience: Abraham Josua Heschel, by F. A. Rothschild. Henri de Lubac, by W. C. Russell.—Bibliography (p. 201-224) [BT28.M6] 68-696
1. Theologians. 2. Theology, Doctrinal—History—20th century.

MOYER, Elgin Sylvester, 1890- ed. 200'.922
Who was who in church history, by Elgin S. Moyer. Rev. ed. Chicago, Moody Press [1968] vi, 466 p. 24 cm. [BR1700.M64 1968] 67-14391
1. Christian biography. I. Title.

STROUP, Herbert Hewitt, 1916- 200'.92'2 B
Founders of living religions, by Herbert Stroup. Philadelphia, Westminster Press [1974] 256 p. 21 cm. Bibliography: p. [241]-244. [BL72.S8] 74-10934 ISBN 0-664-24994-9 4.25
1. Religions—Biography. 2. Religions. I. Title.

BEIDELMAN, Thomas O. 200'.92'4 B
W. Robertson Smith and the sociological study of religion / T. O. Beidelman ; with a foreword by E. E. Evans-Pritchard. Chicago : University of Chicago Press, 1975. xiv, 92 p. ; 23 cm. Bibliography: p. 69-92. [BX9225.S55B46] 74-7568 ISBN 0-226-04158-1 : 8.95 pbk. : 1.95
1. Smith, William Robertson, 1846-1894. 2. Religion and sociology—History. I. Title.

FRANKFORT, Henri, 1897-1954. 200'.932
Ancient Egyptian religion; an interpretation. New York, Harper, 1961. x, 172 p. plates. 21 cm. (Harper torchbooks: The Cloister library) Wyoming. Univ. Libr. [[BL2441.F]] A63
1. Egypt — Religion. I. Title.

FRANKFORT, Henri, 1897-1954. 200'.932
Ancient Egyptian religion; an interpretation. New York, Harper, 1961. x, 172 p. plates. 21 cm. (Harper torchbooks: The Cloister library) Wyoming. Univ. Libr. [[BL2441.F]] A63
1. Egypt — Religion. I. Title.

PETRIE, William Matthew Flinders, Sir, 1853-1942. 200'.932
Religion and conscience in ancient Egypt; lectures delivered at University College, London. New York, B. Blom, 1972. 179 p. illus. 18 cm. Reprint of the 1898 ed. [BL2441.P38 1972] 72-83176 11.50
1. Egypt—Religion. 2. Conscience—History of doctrines. I. Title.

PETRIE, William Matthew Flinders, Sir, 1853-1942. 200'.932
Religious life in ancient Egypt, by Sir Flinders Petrie. New York, Cooper Square Publishers, 1972. x, 221 p. front. 22 cm. Reprint of the 1924 ed. [BL2421.P4 1972] 72-78238 ISBN 0-8154-0422-0
1. Egypt—Religion. I. Title.

FERGUSON, John, 1921- 200'.937
The religions of the Roman Empire. Ithaca, N.Y., Cornell University Press [1970] 296 p. illus. 23 cm. (Aspects of Greek and Roman life) Bibliography: p. [244]-274. [BL802.F45 1970] 71-110992 8.50
1. Rome—Religion. I. Title. II. Series.

GLOVER, Terrot Reaveley, 1869-1943. 200'.937
The conflict of religions in the early Roman Empire / by T. R. Glover. Washington : Cannon Press, 1974. vii, 359 p. ; 22 cm. Reprint of the 1909 ed. published by Methuen, London. Includes bibliographical references and index. [BR170.G6 1974] 75-312221 ISBN 0-913686-18-2 : 8.95
1. Church history—Primitive and early church, ca. 30-600. 2. Christianity and other religions. 3. Rome—Religion. I. Title.

GLOVER, Terrot Reaveley, 1869-1943. 200'.937
The conflict of religions in the early Roman Empire / by T. R. Glover. New York : Cooper Square Publishers, 1975. vii, 359 p. ; 22 cm. Reprint of the 1932 ed. published by Methuen, London. Includes bibliographical references and indexes. [BR170.G6 1975] 74-20182 ISBN 0-8154-0510-3 lib.bdg. : 10.95
1. Church history—Primitive and early church, ca. 30-600. 2. Christianity and other religions. 3. Rome—Religion. I. Title.

DAVIES, Charles Maurice, 1828-1910. 200'.9421
Heterodox London; or, Phases of free thought in the metropolis. New York, A. M. Kelley, 1969. 2 v. in 1. 22 cm. (Reprints of economic classics) Reprint of the 1874 ed. [BR764.D3 1969] 69-17494
1. London—Religion. I. Title.

DAVIES, Charles Maurice, 1828-1910. 200'.9421
Unorthodox London; or, Phases of religious life in the metropolis. New York, A. M. Kelley, 1969. viii, 448 p. 22 cm. (Reprints of economic classics) Reprint of the 1875 ed. [BR764.D5 1969] 69-17495
1. London—Religion. I. Title.

SMITH, Warren Sylvester, 1912- 200'.9421
The London heretics, 1870-1914 New York, Dodd, Mead [1968] xvii, 319 p. illus., ports. 22 cm. Bibliography: p. 299-307. [BR764.S6 1968] 68-2791
1. Religious thought—England—London. 2. Religious thought—19th century. 3. London—Religion. I. Title.

HAINES, Charles Reginald. 200'.946
Christianity and Islam in Spain, A.D. 756-1031, by C. R. Haines. London, K. Paul, Trench, 1889. [New York, AMS Press, 1972] viii, 182 p. 19 cm. Bibliography: p. [175]-182. [BR1024.H3 1972] 76-144625 ISBN 0-404-03024-6 9.00
1. Christianity—Spain. 2. Christian martyrs—Spain. 3. Islam—Spain. I. Title.

ASPECTS of religion in the Soviet Union, 1917-1967. 200'.947 Edited by Richard H. Marshall, Jr. Associate editors: Thomas E. Bird and Andrew Q. Blane. Chicago, University of Chicago Press [1971] xv, 489 p. port. 24 cm. Bibliography: p. [465]-470. [BL980.R8A9] 70-115874 ISBN 0-226-50700-9
1. Russia—Religion—Addresses, essays, lectures. I. Marshall, Richard H., 1897- ed.

BAKER, Alonzo Lafayette, 1894- 200.9'47
Religion in Russia today, by Alonzo L. Baker. Nashville, Southern Pub. Association [1967] 141 p. illus. (part col.), ports (part col.) 24 cm. Bibliography: p. 139-141. [BR936.B2] 67-28907
1. Russia—Religion—1917- I. Title.

GORODETZKY, Nadejda, 1904- 200'.947
The humiliated Christ in modern Russian thought, by Nadejda Gorodetzky. London, Society for Promoting Christian Knowledge, 1938. [New York, AMS Press, 1973] xiii, 185 p. 23 cm. Includes bibliographical references. [BR936.G57 1973] 79-168159 ISBN 0-404-02883-7 10.00
1. Religious thought—Russia. 2. Incarnation—History of doctrines. I. Title.

RELIGION and the search for new ideals in the USSR, 200'.9'47 edited by William C. Fletcher and Anthony J. Strover. New York, Published for the Institute for the Study of the USSR [by] Praeger [1967] vi, 135 p. 25 cm. (Praeger publications in Russian history and world communism, no. 187) Papers presented at an international symposium, Munich, Germany, April 25-27, 1966, sponsored by the Institute for the Study of the USSR. Contents.Contents.—Communism and the problem of intellectual freedom, by G. Wetter.—The problem of alienation; life without spiritual or religious ideals, by P. B. Anderson.—Orthodoxy and the younger generation in the USSR, by D. Konstantinov.—The rejuvenation of the Russian Orthodox clergy, by N. Teodorovich.—Pseudo-religious rites introduced by the party authorities, by N. Struve.—Changes in Soviet medical ethics as an example of efforts to find stable moral values, by H. Schulz.—Protestant influences on the outlook of the Soviet citizen today, by W. C. Fletcher.—The search for new ideals in the USSR: some first-hand impressions, by P. B. Reddaway.—The tenacity of Islam in Soviet central Asia, by G. von Stackelberg.—Jews and Judaism in the Soviet Union, by H. Lamm.—The significance of religious themes in Soviet literature, by Z. Shakhovskaya.—Summary, by M. Hayward. Bibliographical footnotes. [BR932.R38] 67-16683
1. Russia—Religion. 2. Russia—Social life and customs. I. Fletcher, William C., ed. II. Strover, Anthony J., ed. III. Institut zur Erforschung der UdSSR. IV. Title.

RELIGION and the Soviet State: 200'.947 a dilemma of power, edited by Max Hayward and William C. Fletcher. New York, Published for the centre de recherches et d'etude des institutions religieuses by Praeger [1969] x, 200 p. 22 cm. Papers of a conference sponsored by the Centre de recherches et d'etude des institutions religieuses in Geneva, in Sept. 1967. Bibliographical footnotes. [BR936.R43] 73-85539 6.50
1. Russia—Religion—1917- —Addresses, essays, lectures. I. Hayward, Max, ed. II. Fletcher, William C., ed. III. Centre de recherches et d'etude des institutions religieuses.

THE Faith of the Finns: 200'.9471 *historical perspectives on the Finnish Lutheran church in America.* Edited by Ralph J. Jalkanen. [East Lansing] Michigan State University Press, 1972. xvi, 360 p. 24 cm. Includes bibliographical references. [BX8060.F5F35] 72-85879 ISBN 0-87013-174-5 12.50
1. Finnish Evangelical Lutheran Church of America. 2. Finland—Religion. I. Jalkanen, Ralph J., ed.

STROUP, Herbert Hewitt, 1916- 200'.95
Four religions of Asia; a primer, by Herbert Stroup. [1st ed.] New York, Harper & Row [1968] x, 212 p. 22 cm. Includes bibliographies. [BL1032.S7] 68-17587
1. Asia—Religion. I. Title.

BUSH, Richard Clarence, 1923- 200.9'51
Religion in Communist China [by] Richard C. Bush, Jr. Nashville, Abingdon Press [1970] 432 p. 25 cm. Includes bibliographical references. [BL1802.B87] 70-109678 ISBN 0-687-36015-3 9.50
1. China—Religion. I. Title.

CHAN, Wing-tsit, 1901- 200'.951
Religious trends in modern China. New York, Octagon Books, 1969 [c1953] xiii, 327 p. 24 cm. (The Haskell lectures at the University of Chicago, 1950.) (Lectures on the history of religions, new ser., no. 3) Bibliography: p. [265]-281. [BL1802.C48] 71-96176
1. China—Religion. 2. Religious thought—China. I. Title. II. Series. III. Series: Haskell lectures in comparative religion, University of Chicago, 1950

MACINNIS, Donald E., comp. 200'.951
Religious policy and practice in Communist China; a documentary history [compiled] by Donald E. MacInnis. New York, Macmillan [1972] xxiv, 392 p. 23 cm. Includes bibliographical references. [BL1802.M3] 74-182020
1. China—Religion—History—1949- —Sources. I. Title.

PLOPPER, Clifford Henry 1885- 200'.951
Chinese religion seen through the proverb, by Clifford H. Plopper. New York, Paragon Book Reprint Corp., 1969. xi, 381 p. illus. 24 cm. Reprint of the 1935 ed. Includes bibliographical references. [BL1801.P6 1969] 79-77385
1. China—Religion. 2. Proverbs, Chinese. 3. Folk-lore, Chinese. I. Title.

SMITH, David Howard. 200'.951
Chinese religions [by] D. Howard Smith. [1st ed.] New York, Holt, Rinehart and Winston [1968] xiii, 221 p. illus. 25 cm. (History of religion series) $7.95 Bibliography: p. 195-203. [BL1802.S6] 68-12215
1. China—Religion. I. Title.

SMITH, David Howard. 200'.951
Chinese religions [by] D. Howard Smith. [1st ed.] New York, Holt, Rinehart and Winston [1968] xiii, 221 p. illus. 25 cm. (History of religion series) Bibliography: p. 195-203. [BL1802.S6 1968b] 68-12215 7.95
1. China—Religion. I. Title.

THOMPSON, Laurence G., comp. 200'.9'51
The Chinese way in religion [by] Laurence G. Thompson. Encino, Calif., Dickenson Pub. Co. [1973] ix, 241 p. 23 cm. (The Religious life of man) Includes bibliographical references. [BL1802.T52] 72-90753 ISBN 0-8221-0109-2 pap. 3.95
1. China—Religion—Collections. I. Title.

YANG, Yung-ch'ing, 1892-1956. 200'.951
China's religious heritage. Freeport, N.Y., Books for Libraries Press [1972] 196 p. 22 cm. (Essay index reprint series) Based upon a series of lectures on the Quillian Foundation, given at Emory University, Jan., 1942. Reprint of the 1943 ed. Includes bibliographical references. [BL1801.Y3 1972] 72-4542 ISBN 0-8369-2981-0
1. China—Religion. I. Title.

BASABE, Fernando M. 200'.952
Japanese religious attitudes [by] Fernando M. Basabe. Maryknoll, N.Y., Orbis Books [1972] vii, 94 p. illus. 20 cm. (Maryknoll documentation series) [BL2209.B37] 70-188666 2.95
1. Japan—Religion—20th century. I. Title.

EARHART, H. Byron. 200'.9'52
Japanese religion; unity and diversity [by] H. Byron Earhart. Belmont, Calif., Dickenson Pub. Co. [1969] 115 p. 23 cm. (The Religious life of man.) Bibliography: p. 102-111. [BL2202.E17] 69-13761
1. Japan—Religion. I. Title.

EARHART, H. Byron. 200'.9'52
Japanese religion: unity and diversity [by] H. Byron Earhart. 2d ed. Encino, Calif., Dickenson Pub. Co. [1974] viii, 148 p. map. 23 cm. (The Religious life of man series) Bibliography: p. 131-144. [BL2202.E17 1974] 73-93288 ISBN 0-8221-0123-8 3.95 (pbk.)
1. Japan—Religion. I. Title.

EARHART, H. Byron, comp. 200'.952
Religion in the Japanese experience: sources and interpretations [by] H. Byron Earhart. Encino, Calif., Dickenson Pub. Co. [1973, c1974] xv, 270 p. illus. 23 cm. (The Religious life of man) Includes bibliographies. [BL2202.E18] 73-81295 ISBN 0-8221-0104-1
1. Japan—Religion. I. Title.

JAPAN. Bunkacho. 200'.952
Japanese religion; a survey, by the Agency for Cultural Affairs. [1st ed.] Tokyo, Palo Alto [Calif.] Kodansha International [1972] 272 p. illus. 22 cm. [BL2202.A43] 72-77795 ISBN 0-87011-183-3 Y2400 ($10.00 U.S.)
1. Japan—Religion. I. Title.

KITAGAWA. JOSEPH MITSUO, 1915- 200.952
Religion in Japanese history [by] Joseph M. Kitagawa. New York, Columbia. 1966. x, 475p. 22cm. (Lect. on the hist. of religions sponsored by the Amer. Council of Learned Socs. New series, no. 7) Bibl. [BL2202.K5] 65-23669 10.00
1. Japan — Religion. I. Title. II. Series.

CHETHIMATTAM, John B. 200'.954
Patterns of Indian thought [by] John B. Chethimattam. Maryknoll, N.Y., Orbis Books [1971] viii, 172 p. 23 cm. (Indian religions and philosophies) Bibliography: p. 155-157. [B131.C5824 1971b] 77-164418 4.95
1. Philosophy, Indic. I. Title. II. Series.

LYALL, Alfred Comyn, Sir, 1835-1911. 200'.954
Asiatic studies, religious and social. New ed. New York, Books for Libraries Press [1973] p. (Essay index reprint series) Reprint of the 1899 ed., published by J. Murray, London. [BL1031.L8 1973] 73-4528 ISBN 0-518-10089-8
1. India—Religion. 2. China—Religion. 3. India—Civilization. 4. Religion, Primitive. I. Title.

ARBERRY, Arthur John, 1905- 200'.956
Religion in the Middle East: three religions in concord and conflict; general editor A. J. Arberry. London, Cambridge U.P., 1969. 2 v. 32 plates, 41 illus., facsim., 25 maps. 24 cm. Contents.Contents.—v. 1. Juduism and Christianity.—v. 2. Islam. Bibliography: v. 2, p. 659-690. [BL1600.A7] 68-21187 7/-/- ($22.50)
1. Near East—Religion. I. Title.

FRANKFORT, Henri, 1897- 200'.956
Before philosophy, the intellectual adventure of ancient man; an essay on speculative thought in the ancient Near East, by H. and H. A. Frankfort [and others] Harmonds-worth, Middlesex, Penguin Books [1951] 275p. 18cm. (Pelican books, A 198) 'An Oriental Institute essay.' Originally published under title: The intellectual adventure of ancient man. [BL96.F] A54
1. Religious thought—Ancient period. 2. Civilization, Ancient. 3. Philosophy, Ancient. I. Frankfort, Henriette Antonia (Groenewegen) 1806- joint author. II. Title.
Contents omitted.

FRANKFORT, Henri, 1897- 200'.956
Before philosophy, the intellectual adventure of ancient man; an essay on speculative thought in the ancient Near East, by B. and B. A. Frankfort [and others] Harmondsworth, Middlesex, Penguin Books [1951] 275 p. 18 cm. (Pelican books, A 198) "An Oriental Institute essay." Originally published under title: The intellectual adventure of ancient man. Contents.CONTENTS.—Introduction: Myth and reality, by H. and B. A. Frankfort.—Egypt: The nature of the universe. The function of the state. The values of life. By J. A. Wilson.—Mesopotamia: The cosmos of the state. The function of the state. The good life. By T. Jacobsen. Conclusion: The emancipation of thought from myth, by H. and H. A. Frankfort. [BL96.F] A54
1. Religious thought—Ancient period. 2. Civilization, Ancient. 3. Philosophy, Ancient. I. Frankfort, Henriette Antonia Groenewegen, 1896- joint author. II. Title.

JURJI, Edward Jabra, 1907- 200'.956
The Middle East; its religion and culture, by Edward J. Jurji. Westport, Conn., Greenwood Press [1973, c1956] 159 p. 22 cm. Bibliography: p. 156-159. [BL1060.J8 1973] 72-9809 ISBN 0-8371-6597-0
1. Near East—Religion. 2. Near East—Civilization.

JURJI, Edward Jabra, 1907- 200'.956
The Middle East; its religion and culture, by Edward J. Jurji. Westport, Conn., Greenwood Press [1973, c1956] 159 p. 22 cm. Bibliography: p. 156-159. [BL1060.J8 1973] 72-9809 ISBN 0-8371-6597-0 8.50
1. Near East—Religion. 2. Near East—Civilization.

TEIXIDOR, Javier. 200'.956
The pagan god : popular religion in the Greco-Roman Near East / by Javier Teixidor. Princeton, N.J. : Princeton University Press, c1977. xii, 192 p. ; 23 cm. Includes index. Bibliography: p. 165-174. [BL1060.T44] 76-24300 ISBN 0-691-07220-5 : 10.00
1. Near East—Religion. I. Title.

HASLUCK, Frederick William, 1878-1920. 200'.9561
Christianity and Islam under the sultans. Edited by Margaret M. Hasluck. New York, Octagon Books, 1973. 2 v. (lxiv, 877 p.) front. 23 cm. Reprint of the 1929 ed. Bibliography: v. 1, p. [xxi]-lxiv. [BP63.T8H3 1973] 72-13668 ISBN 0-374-93747-8 37.50 (Lib. binding)
1. Islam—Turkey. 2. Folk-lore—Turkey. 3. Christianity—Turkey. 4. Christianity and other religions—Islam. 5. Islam—Relations—Christianity. I. Title.

BLISS, Frederick Jones, 1859-1937. 200'.9569
The religions of modern Syria and Palestine; lectures delivered before Lake Forest College on the foundation of the late William Bross. New York, Scribner, 1912. [New York, AMS Press, 1972] xiv, 354 p. front. 23 cm. Original ed. issued as v. 5 of the Bross library. [BL2340.B6 1972] 76-39454 ISBN 0-404-00897-6 20.00
1. Syria—Religion. 2. Palestine—Religion. I. Title. II. Series: The Bross library, v. 5.

ROSENBERG, Stuart E. 200'.95694
Great religions of the Holy Land; an historical guide to sacred places and sites [by] Stuart E. Rosenberg. South Brunswick, A. S. Barnes [1971] 192 p. illus. 29 cm. [DS108.5.R68 1971] 70-159839 ISBN 0-498-07994-5 15.00
1. Palestine—Description and travel—Views. 2. Shrines—Palestine. I. Title.

U.S. Bureau of Naval Personnel. 200'.9597
The religions of South Vietnam in faith and fact. [Washington] 1967. vii, 97 p. illus., maps. 26 cm. Cover title. "NAVPERS 15991." Includes bibliographies. [BL2055.U5] 67-62247
1. Vietnam—Religion. I. Title.

MBITI, John S. 200'.96
African religions & philosophy [by] John S. Mbiti. New York, Praeger [1969] xiii, 290 p. map (on lining papers) 23 cm. Bibliography: p. 278-282. [BL2400.M38] 70-76092 8.00
1. Africa—Religion. I. Title.

PARRINDER, Edward Geoffrey. 200'.96
Africa's three religions / [by] Geoffrey Parrinder. 2nd ed. London : Sheldon Press, 1976. 253 p. : map ; 19 cm. First ed. published in 1969 under title: Religion in Africa. Includes index. Bibliography: p. 239-242. [BL2400.P374 1976] 77-351032 ISBN 0-85969-096-2 : £1.75
1. Africa—Religion. I. Title.

PARRINDER, Edward Geoffrey. 200'.96
Religion in Africa [by] Geoffrey Parrinder. New York, Praeger Publishers [1969] 253 p., map. 22 cm. Bibliography: p. 239-[242] [BL2400.P374 1969c] 74-95587 6.50
1. Africa—Religion. I. Title.

*MCVEIGH, Malcolm J. 200.960
God in Africa conceptions of God in African traditional Religion and Christianity [by] Malcolm J. McVeigh Cape Cod, Mass. C. Stark [1974] 235 p. illus. 23 cm. Bibliography: p. 189-204. [BL2400] 74-76005 ISBN 0-89007-003-2 8.00
1. Africa—Religion. I. Title.

PARRINDER, Edward Geoffrey. 200'.9669'2
Religion in an African city, by Geoffrey Parrinder. Westport, Conn., Negro Universities Press [1972] 211 p. illus. 22 cm. Reprint of the 1953 ed. [BL2470.N5P37 1972] 74-142921 ISBN 0-8371-5947-4
1. Ibadan, Nigeria—Religion. I. Title.
Available from Greenwood, 10.75.

THE Historical study of African religion. 200'.967 Edited by T. O. Ranger and I. N. Kimambo. Berkeley, University of California Press, 1972. ix, 307 p. maps. 26 cm. Papers presented at a conference sponsored by the University of Dar es Salaam and the African Studies Center of the University of California, Los Angeles, and held in Dar es Salaam in June 1970. Includes bibliographical references. [BL2400.H53 1972] 76-186104 ISBN 0-520-02206-8 12.95
1. Africa—Religion—Congresses. I. Ranger, Terence O., ed. II. Kimambo, Isaria N., ed. III. Dar es Salaam. University. IV. California. University. University at Los Angeles. African Studies Center.

DALE, Godfrey. 200'.9678'1
The peoples of Zanzibar: their customs and religious beliefs. New York, Negro Universities Press [1969] 124 p. 23 cm. Reprint of the 1920 ed. [BL2470.Z35D3 1969] 78-90112
1. Zanzibar—Religious life and customs. I. Title.

CALLAWAY, Godfrey, 1865or6-1942. 200'.968
The fellowship of the veld; sketches of native life in South Africa. With pref. by the Bishop of Zululand. New York, Negro Universities Press [1969] ix, 114 p. illus. 23 cm. Reprint of the 1926 ed. [BR1450.C3 1969] 71-89027
1. Africa, South—Religious life and customs. I. Title.

BASTIDE, Roger, 1898- 200'.97
African civilisations in the New World. Translated from the French by Peter Green, with a foreword by Geoffrey Parrinder. New York, Harper & Row [1971] vi, 232 p. 23 cm. (A Torchbook library edition) Translation of Les Ameriques noires, les civilisations africaines dans le Nouveau monde. Includes bibliographies. [E29.N3B4213 1971] 75-158981 ISBN 0-06-136057-0 12.50
1. Negroes in America—Religion. 2. Negroes in America. 3. Africa—Religion. I. Title.

HEDRICK, Basil Calvin, 1932- 200'.972
Religious syncretism in Spanish America, by B. C. Hedrick. Greeley, Colorado State College, Museum of Anthropology, 1967. 18, [3] l. illus. 28 cm. (Museum of Anthropology miscellaneous series, no. 2) Cover title. Bibliography: leaf [21] [GN4.U53 no. 2] 68-66854
1. Latin America—Religion. 2. Christianity and other religions. I. Title. II. Series: Colorado. State College, Greeley. Museum of Anthropology. Miscellaneous series, no. 2.

ELKINS, W. F. 200'.97292
Street preachers, faith healers, and herb doctors in Jamaica, 1890-1925 / by W. F. Elkins. New York : Revisionist Press, 1976. p. cm. (Studies in the Caribbean series) Bibliography: p. [BR645.J3E44] 76-14484 ISBN 0-87700-241-X lib.bdg. : 29.95
1. Jamaica—Religion. 2. Sects—Jamaica. 3. Revivals—Jamaica. I. Title.

ABBEY, Merrill R. 200'.973
Day dawns in fire : America's quest for meaning / Merrill R. Abbey. Philadelphia : Fortress Press, c1976. vi, 122 p. ; 20 cm. Includes bibliographical references. [BR515.A22] 75-36439 ISBN 0-8006-1218-3 pbk. : 3.25
1. United States—Religion. 2. United States—Civilization. I. Title.

AHLSTROM, Sydney E. 200'.973
A religious history of the American people [by] Sydney E. Ahlstrom. New Haven, Yale University Press, 1972. xvi, 1158 p. 26 cm. Bibliography: p. 1097-1128. [BR515.A4 1972] 72-151564 ISBN 0-300-01475-9 19.50
1. United States—Religion. I. Title.

AHLSTROM, Sydney E. 200'.973
A religious history of the American people / Sydney E. Ahlstrom. Garden City, N.Y. : Image Books, 1975, c1972. 2 v. ; 18 cm. Reprint of the ed. published by Yale University Press, New Haven, with a new pref. Includes index. Bibliography: p. [621]-666. [BR515.A4 1975] 75-22362 ISBN 0-385-11164-9 (v. 1) : 3.50 ISBN 0-385-11165-7(v.2)
1. United States—Religion. I. Title.

BEDELL, George C. 200'.973
Religion in America / George C. Bedell, Leo Sandon, Jr., Charles T. Wellborn. New York : Macmillan, [1975] xv, 538 p. ; 24 cm. Includes bibliographical references and index. [BR515.B48] 74-2867 ISBN 0-02-307920-7 : 10.95.
1. United States—Religion. I. Sandon, Leo, joint author. II. Wellborn, Charles, joint author. III. Title.

BIERSDORF, John E., 1930- 200'.973
Hunger for experience : vital religious communities in America / John E. Biersdorf. New York : Seabury Press, [1975] p. cm. "A Crossroad book." [BL632.5.U5B53] 75-28079 ISBN 0-8164-1198-0 : 7.95
1. Religious communities—United States. 2. Religious and ecclesiastical institutions—United States. I. Title.

*CLEBSCH, William A. 200.9'73
American religious thought: a history, [by] William A. Clebsch. Chicago, University of Chicago Press [1973] xxi, 212 p. 21 cm. (Chicago history of American religion.) Bibliography: p. 197-205. [BR515] 73-82911 ISBN 0-226-10960-7 6.95
1. United States—Religion. I. Title.

COLLEGE Theology Society. 200'.973
America in theological perspective : proceedings of the College Theology Society / edited by Thomas M. McFadden. New York : Seabury Press, c1976. p. cm. "A Crossroad book." "All essays ... were, with two exceptions, delivered at the 1975 convention of the College Theology Society at Boston College." [BR515.C64 1976] 75-45201 ISBN 0-8164-0294-9 : 7.95
1. United States—Religion—Congresses. I. McFadden, Thomas M. II. Title.

COX, Harvey Gallagher. 200'.973
Turning east : the promise and peril of the new orientalism / Harvey Cox. New York : Simon and Schuster, c1977. 192 p. ; 22 cm. Includes index. Bibliography: p. 177-180. [BL2530.U6C69] 77-8600 ISBN 0-671-22851-X : 8.95
1. Cox, Harvey Gallagher. 2. Cults—United States. 3. United States—Religion. 4. Christianity and other religions. 5. Spiritual life—Baptist authors. I. Title.

CROWLEY, Dale. 200'.973
Can America survive??? : Our God-given freedoms threatened by deadly enemies within and without / by Dale Crowley. Washington : National Bible Knowledge Association, c1975. xi, 156 p. ; 22 cm. "Bi-centennial special." [BR515.C93] 75-29986
1. United States—Religion. 2. United States—Moral conditions. I. Title.

DIRKS, Lee E. 200.973
Religion in action; how America's faiths are meeting new challenges. The National observer dist. New York, Dow Jones, 1965 211p. illus., facsim., col. map, ports. 28cm. (National observer [Silver Spring, Md.] Newsbk.) [BR526.D5] 65-15132 2.00
1. U.S.—Religion. I. Title. II. Series.

FAUSET, Arthur Huff, 1899- 200'.973
Black gods of the metropolis; Negro religious cults of the urban North. [Philadelphia] University of Pennsylvania Press [1971] xi, 128 p. illus., group ports. 21 cm. "Originally published in 1944 as volume 111 of the Brinton memorial series, Publications of the Philadelphia Anthropological Society." Bibliography: p. 123-126. [BR563.N4F3 1971] 75-133446 ISBN 0-8122-1001-8
1. Negroes—Religion. 2. Negroes—Philadelphia. 3. Sects—U.S. I. Title.

FAUSET, Arthur Huff, 1899- 200'.973
Black gods of the metropolis; Negro religious cults of the urban North. New York, Octagon Books, 1970 [c1944] ix, 126 p. illus., ports. 24 cm. (Publications of the Philadelphia Anthropological Society, v. 3) (Brinton memorial series, [no. 2]) "A study of five Negro religious cults in the Philadelphia of today." Issued also as the author's thesis, University of Pennsylvania. [BR563.N4F3 1970] 73-120251
1. Negroes—Religion. 2. Negroes—Philadelphia. 3. Sects—U.S. I. Title. II. Series. III. Series: Philadelphia Anthropological Society. Publications, v. 3.

FOX, Matthew, 1940- 200'.973
Religion USA; an inquiry into religion and culture by way of Time magazine. [Dubuque, Iowa] Listening Press, 1971. 451 p. 22 cm. Includes bibliographical references. [BR517.F64] 76-151967 3.65
1. Time, the weekly news-magazine. 2. U.S.—Religion. 3. Religion and culture. I. Title.

*GAUSTAD, Edwin Scott. 200.9'73
Dissent in American religion. Chicago, University of Chicago Press [1973] xii, 184 p. 21 cm. (Chicago history of American religion.) Bibliography: p. 161-176. [BR515] 73-77131 ISBN 0-226-28436-0 6.95
1. Religious thought—U.S. 2. U.S.—Religion. I. Title.

GREELEY, Andrew M., 1928- 200'.973
The denominational society; a sociological approach to religion in America [by] Andrew M. Greeley. Academic advisor in sociology: Peter H. Rossi. Glenview, Ill., Scott, Foresman [1972] 266 p. 23 cm. Bibliography: p. 255-258. [BR515.G74] 70-173239
1. United States—Religion. 2. Religion and sociology. I. Title.

GREENFIELD, Robert. 200'.973
The spiritual supermarket / Robert Greenfield. 1st ed. New York : Saturday Review Press, [1975] 277 p. ; 22 cm. [BL2520.G73 1975] 74-23291 ISBN 0-8415-0367-2 : 8.95 pbk. : 3.95
1. United States—Religion. 2. East (Far East)—Religion. 3. Sects—United States. I. Title.

HANDY, Robert T., comp. 200'.973
Religion in the American experience: the pluralistic style. Edited by Robert T. Handy. Columbia, University of South Carolina Press [1972] xxii, 246 p. 24 cm. [BR514.H35] 72-5338 ISBN 0-87249-275-3 9.95
1. United States—Religion—History—Sources. I. Title.

HANDY, Robert T., comp. 200'.973
Religion in the American experience: the pluralistic style. Edited by Robert T. Handy. New York, Harper & Row [1972] xxii, 246 p. 21 cm. (Documentary history of the United States) "HR 1648." Includes bibliographical references. [BR514.H35 1972b] 70-186140 ISBN 0 06 138790-8
1. United States—Religion—History—Sources. I. Title.

HEENAN, Edward F., comp. 200'.973
Mystery, magic & miracle; religion in a post-Aquarian age, edited by Edward F. Heenan. Englewood Cliffs, N.J., Prentice-Hall [1973] vii, 180 p. 21 cm. (A Spectrum book) Includes bibliographical references. [BR526.H35] 73-932 ISBN 0-13-609032-X 5.95
1. United States—Religion. I. Title.
pap 2.45

HUDSON, Winthrop Still, 1911- 200'.973
Religion in America; an historical account of the development of American religious life [by] Winthrop S. Hudson. 2d ed. New York, Scribner [1973] xiii, 463 p. 23 cm. (Scribners university library, SUL 1015) Bibliography: p. 442-444. [BR515.H79 1973] 72-9415 pap 5.95
1. United States—Religion. I. Title.
Hard Cover 12.50.

KINCHELOE, Samuel Clarence, 1890- 200'.973
Research memorandum on religion in the depression, by Samuel C. Kincheloe. Westport, Conn., Greenwood Press [1970] ix, 158 p. illus., maps. 23 cm. Reprint of the 1937 ed. Includes bibliographical references. [BR525.K5 1970] 76-109761 ISBN 0-8371-4251-2
1. United States—Religion—1901-1945. 2. United States—Economic conditions—1918-1945. I. Title.

KINCHELOE, Samuel Clarence, 1890- 200'.973
Research memorandum on religion in the depression, by Samuel C. Kincheloe. [New York] Arno Press [1972] ix, 158 p. illus. 23 cm. On spine: Religion in the depression. Reprint of the 1937 ed., which was issued as Bulletin 33 of the Social Science Research Council and also as no. 7 of the series: Studies in the social aspects of the depression. [BR525.K5 1972] 71-162843 ISBN 0-405-00846-5
1. United States—Religion—1901-1945. 2. United States—Economic conditions—1918-1945. I. Title. II. Title: Religion in the depression. III. Series: Social Science Research Council. Bulletin 33. IV. Series: Studies in the social aspects of the depression, no. 7.

LINDSEY, Jonathan A., 1937- 200'.973
Change and challenge / Jonathan A. Lindsey. [Wilmington, N.C.] : Consortium Books, [1977] p. cm. (Faith of our fathers ; 8) [BL2530.U6L56] 77-9551 ISBN 0-8434-0627-5 : 9.50
1. United States—Religion—1945- I. Title. II. Series.

MCCREADY, William C., 1941- 200'.973
The ultimate values of the American population / William C. McCready, Andrew M. Greeley. Beverly Hills : Sage Publications, c1976. p. cm. (Sage library of social research ; v. 23) Includes bibliographical references and index. [BR526.M28] 75-40337 ISBN 0-8039-0502-5 : 12.00. ISBN 0-8039-0503-3 pbk. : 7.00
1. United States—Religion—1945- —Case studies. 2. Religion and sociology—Case studies. 3. Worth—Case studies. I. Greeley, Andrew M., 1928- joint author. II. Title.

MARANELL, Gary Michael, 1932- 200'.973
Responses to religion; studies in the social psychology of religious belief, by Gary M. Maranell. Lawrence, University Press of Kansas [1974] xvii, 313 p. illus. 25 cm. Bibliography: p. 295-304. [BR517.M37] 73-19860 ISBN 0-7006-0114-7 10.00
1. United States—Religious life and customs—Statistics. 2. Sociology, Christian—United States. 3. Christianity—Psychology. I. Title.

MARTY, Martin E., 1928- 200'.973
A nation of behavers / Martin E. Marty. Chicago : University of Chicago Press, c1976. xi, 239 p. ; 21 cm. Includes bibliographical references and index. [BR515.M32] 76-7997 ISBN 0-226-50891-9 : 8.95
1. United States—Religion—1945- 2. Sociology, Christian—United States. I. Title.

MEAD, Frank Spencer, 1898- 200'.973
Handbook of denominations in the United States / Frank S. Mead. New 6th ed. Nashville : Abingdon Press, [1975] 320 p. ; 23 cm. Includes index. Bibliography: p. 291-305. [BR516.5.M38 1975] 75-2363 ISBN 0-687-16569-5 : 5.95
1. Sects—United States. I. Title.

MEAD, Sidney Earl, 1904- 200'.973
The nation with the soul of a church / Sidney E. Mead. 1st ed. New York : Harper & Row, [1975] x, 158 p. ; 21 cm. (A Harper forum book) Includes bibliographical references and indexes. [BR515.M45 1975] 75-9332 ISBN 0-06-065546-1 : 7.95 ISBN 0-06-065547-X pbk. : 3.95
1. United States—Religion—Addresses, essays, lectures. I. Title.

MONTGOMERY, John Warwick. 200'.973
The shaping of America : a true description of the American character, both good and bad, and the possibilities of recovering a national vision before the people perish / John Warwick Montgomery. Minneapolis : Bethany Fellowship, c1976. 255 p. : ill. ; 23 cm. Bibliography: p. [241]-255. [BR515.M57] 76-15682 ISBN 0-87123-227-8 : 5.95
1. United States—Religion. 2. United States—Moral conditions. I. Title.

NEUHAUS, Richard John. 200'.973
Time toward home : the American experiment as revelation / Richard John Neuhaus. New York : Seabury Press, [1975] viii, 231 p. ; 24 cm. "A Crossroad book." Includes bibliographical references and index. [BR526.N42] 75-5714 ISBN 0-8164-0272-8 : 9.50

1. United States—Religion—1945- 2. United States—Civilization—1945- I. Title.

PIEPKORN, Arthur Carl, 1907-1973. 200'.973
Profiles in belief : the religious bodies of the United States and Canada / by Arthur Carl Piepkorn. 1st ed. New York : Harper & Row, c1977- v. ; 24 cm. Contents.Contents.—v. 1. Roman Catholic, Old Catholic, Eastern Orthodox. Includes bibliographies and index. [BR510.P53 1977] 76-9971 ISBN 0-06-066580-7 : 15.95
1. Sects—North America. I. Title.

RELIGION in American 200'.973
history : interpretive essays / edited by John M. Mulder, John F. Wilson. Englewood Cliffs, N.J. : Prentice-Hall, [1978,i.e.1977] p. cm. Bibliography: p. [BR515.R435] 77-2883 ISBN 0-13-771998-1 : 11.95 ISBN 0-13-771980-9 pbk. : 7.95
1. United States—Religion—Addresses, essays, lectures. I. Mulder, John M., 1946- II. Wilson, John Frederick.

THE Religion of the 200'.973
Republic. Edited by Elwyn A. Smith. Philadelphia, Fortress Press [1971] viii, 296 p. 22 cm. Includes bibliographical references. [BR515.R44] 70-130326 8.95
1. U.S.—Religion—Addresses, essays, lectures. I. Smith, Elwyn Allen, 1919- ed.

RICHEY, Russell E. 200'.973
American civil religion. Edited by Russell E. Richey and Donald G. Jones. [1st ed.] New York, Harper & Row [1974] viii, 278 p. 21 cm. (A Harper forum book) Bibliography: p. 273-278. [BR515.R5 1974] 73-18702 ISBN 0-06-066856-3 3.95
1. United States—Religion. I. Jones, Donald G., joint author. II. Title.

RUPP, Israel Daniel, 1803-1878, ed. 200'.973
He pasa ekklesia; an original history of the religious denominations at present existing in the United States, containing authentic accounts of their rise, progress, statistics and doctrines. Written expressly for the work by eminent theological professors, ministers, and lay-members of the respective denominations. Freeport, N.Y., Books for Libraries Press [1973] p. Reprint of the 1844 ed. [BR516.5.R86 1973] 72-12769 ISBN 0-8369-7149-3
1. Sects—United States. I. Title.

THE Sixties: radical 200'.973
change in American religion. Special editor of this volume: James M. Gustafson. Philadelphia [American Academy of Political and Social Science] 1970. x, 250 p. 24 cm. (The Annals of the American Academy of Political and Social Science, v. 387) Includes bibliographical references. [H1.A4 vol. 387] 74-112786 3.00 (pbk.)
1. U.S.—Religion—1945- I. Gustafson, James M., ed. II. Series: American Academy of Political and Social Science, Philadelphia. Annals, v. 387

SNOOK, John B. 200'.973
Going further; life-and-death religion in America [by] John B. Snook. Englewood Cliffs, N.J., Prentice-Hall [1973] viii, 184 p. 21 cm. (A Spectrum book) Includes bibliographical references. [BR515.S63] 73-14532 ISBN 0-13-357814-3 6.95
1. United States—Religion. 2. Sects—United States. I. Title.
Pbk. 2.45; ISBN 0-13-357806-2.

SNYDER, Gerald S. 200'.973
The religious reawakening in America [by Gerald S. Snyder] Washington, Books by U.S. News & World Report [1972] 191 p. illus. 23 cm. [BR145.2.S66] 72-88685 2.95
1. United States—Religion. I. Title.

SOCIOLOGICAL Resources for the Social Studies (Project) 200'.973
Religion in the United States. Boston, Allyn and Bacon [1971] v, 38 p. illus. 23 cm. (Episodes in social inquiry series) Bibliography: p. 38. [BR515.S64] 77-153562 6.36
1. United States—Religion. 2. Sociology, Christian—United States. I. Title.

STEVENS, Edward, 1928- 200'.973
The religion game, American style / by Edward Stevens. New York : Paulist Press, c1976. 152 p. ; 23 cm. Includes bibliographical references. [BL51.S657] 76-9367 ISBN 0-8091-1951-X pbk. : 5.95
1. Religion—Philosophy. 2. Religion and sociology. 3. Religious thought—United States. I. Title.

STROUT, Cushing. 200'.973
The new heavens and new earth; political religion in America. [1st ed.] New York, Harper & Row [1973, c1974] xv, 400 p. 24 cm. Includes bibliographical references. [BR515.S77 1973] 73-4128 ISBN 0-06-014171-9 12.50
1. United States—Religion. I. Title.

WARD, Hiley H. 200'.973
Religion 2101 A.D. / by Hiley H. Ward. 1st ed. Garden City, N.Y. : Doubleday, 1975. xiii, 247 p. ; 22 cm. Includes bibliographical references and index. [BR124.W37] 73-10864 ISBN 0-385-00981-X : 7.95
1. Christianity—20th century. 2. Twenty-second century—Forecasts. I. Title.

WILLIAMS, John Paul, 1900- 200'.973
What Americans believe and how they worship, by J. Paul Williams. 3d ed. New York, Harper & Row [1969] x, 530 p. 22 cm. Bibliographical references included in "Notes" (p. 493-520) [BR516.5.W5 1969] 79-4791 6.00
1. U.S.—Religion—1945- 2. Sects—U.S. I. Title.

ZARETSKY, Irving I. 200'.973
Religious movements in contemporary America, edited by Irving I. Zaretsky and Mark P. Leone. Princeton, N.J., Princeton University Press [1974] p. cm. Bibliography: p. [BR516.5.Z37] 73-39054 ISBN 0-691-07186-1 25.00
1. United States—Religious life and customs. 2. United States—Religion—1965- I. Leone, Mark P., joint author. II. Title.

RELIGIONS in St. 200'.9778'66
Louis : a strong heritage / edited by Robert P. Jacobs. Saint Louis, Mo. : Interfaith Clergy Council, c1976. 152 p. : ill. ; 23 cm. [BR560.S2R44] 76-50368 3.95
1. St. Louis—Church history. 2. St. Louis—Religion. I. Jacobs, Robert P.

FAITH on the frontier 200'.9788
: religion in Colorado before August 1876 / edited by Louisa Ward Arps. Religion in Colorado : a bibliography / compiled by Harold M. Parker, Jr. Denver : Colorado Council of Churches, 1976. xiii, 155 p. : ill. ; 22 cm. [BR555.C6F34] 77-152426
1. Colorado—Church history. 2. Colorado—Religion—History. I. Arps, Louisa Atkinson Ward, 1901- II. Parker, Harold M. Religion in Colorado. 1976.

THE Religious 200'.9794'9
heritage of southern California : a Bicentennial survey / edited by Francis J. Weber. Los Angeles : Interreligious Council of Southern California, c1976. 119 p. ; 21 cm. [BL2530.U6R44] 76-370716 3.00
1. California, Southern—Religion. I. Weber, Francis J. II. Interreligious Council of Southern California.

MOL, J. J. 200'.994
Religion in Australia; a sociological investigation [by] Hans Mol. [Melbourne, Thomas] Nelson [(Australia) 1971] xviii, 380 p. tables. 22 cm. Bibliography: p. 351-362. [BR1480.M64] 71-865350 ISBN 0-17-001904-7 9.95
1. Australia—Religious life and customs. I. Title.

GALLAGHER, Charles F. 200'.9969
Hawaii and its gods : text / by Charles F. Gallagher ; photos. by Dana Levy ; with a foreword by O. A. Bushnell. 1st ed. New York : Weatherhill, 1975. 150 p. : ill. ; 27 cm. [BL2620.H3G34] 74-28153 ISBN 0-8348-2501-5 : 20.00
1. Hawaii—Religion. I. Levy, Dana, ill. II. Title.

MULHOLLAND, John Field. 200'.9969
Hawaii's religions, by John F. Mulholland. Rutland, Vt., C. E. Tuttle Co. [1970] 344 p. illus., port. 19 cm. Includes bibliographies. [BR555.H3M8 1970] 76-104197 5.00
1. Hawaii—Religion. I. Title.

201 Philosophy Of Christianity

ABBEY, Merrill R. 201
Man, media, and the message [by] Merrill R. Abbey. New York, Friendship Press [1970, c1960] 159 p. 18 cm. Bibliography: p. 157-159. [BV4319.A24] 70-102946 1.75 (pbk)
1. Communication (Theology) I. Title.

ABBOTT, Lyman, 1835-1922. 201
The evolution of Christianity. New York, Johnson Reprint Corp., 1969. xxx, vi, 258 p. 18 cm. (Lowell Institute lectures) Reprint of the 1892 ed. with a new introd. by J. A. De Jong. Includes bibliographical references. [BR121.A25 1969] 72-80040
1. Christianity—Essence, genius, nature. I. Title. II. Series. III. Series in American studies.

ABERNETHY, George L., ed. 201
Philosophy of religion, a book of readings, edited by George L. Abernethy and Thomas A. Langford. New York, Macmillan [1962] 542 p. 24 cm. Includes bibliography. [BL51.A32] 62-7056
1. Religion—Philosophy. I. Langford, Thomas A., joint ed. II. Title.

ABERNETHY, George L. 201
Philosophy of religion; a book of readings, edited by George L. Abernethy and Thomas A. Langford. 2d ed. New York, Macmillan [1968] xvii, 586 p. 24 cm. Includes bibliographies. [BL51.A32 1968] 68-10237
1. Religion—Philosophy. I. Langford, Thomas A., joint ed. II. Title.

ALLPORT, Gordon Willard 201
The individual and his religion, a psychological interpretation. New York, Macmillan, 1960 [c.1950] xi, 147p. (Bibl. footnotes) 21cm. (Macmillan paperback 1) 1.25 pap.,
1. Psychology, Religious. I. Title.

ALLPORT, Gordon Willard, 1897-1967. 201
The individual and his religion, a psychological interpretation. New York, Macmillan, 1950. xi, 147 p. 21 cm. Bibliographical footnotes. [BL53.A428] 50-5982
1. Psychology, Religious. I. Title.

ALSTON, William P., ed. 201
Religious belief and philosophical thought; readings in the philosophy of religion. New York, Harcourt [1963] 626p. 24cm. 63-13110 7.50
1. Natural theology—Collections. 2. Religion—Philosophy—Collections. I. Title.

ALTIZER, Thomas J. J. 201
Mircea Eliade and the dialectic of the sacred. Philadelphia, Westminster, [1964, c.1963] 219p. 21cm. Bibl. 63-14639 6.00
1. Eliade, Mircea, 1907- I. Title.

ANSTRUTHER, William, Sir, d.1711. 201
Essays, moral and divine. With a pref. for the Garland ed. by Arthur Freeman. New York, Garland Pub., 1973. 5, 238 p. 23 cm. (The English stage: attack and defense, 1577-1730) Reprint of the 1701 ed. printed by G. Mosman, Edinburgh. [BL50.A697 1973] 74-170474 ISBN 0-8240-0623-2 22.00 ea.
1. Religion—Addresses, essays, lectures. I. Title. II. Series.
Part of a 50 volume series selling for 1050.00 set.

*ARNELLOS, Gabriel J. 201
Arising call for every man and every nation. Tr. from Greek by George S. Vournas [Chicago, Adams Pr.] 1966. 100p. ports. 23cm. 3.75 pap.,
I. Title.

ARNETT, Willard Eugene, 1921- 201
Religion and judgment; an essay on the method and meaning of religion. New York, Appleton-Century-Crofts [1966] xi, 835 p. 22 cm. (The Century philosophy series) Bibliography: p. 323-327. [BL51.A7] 66-11680
1. Religion — Philosophy. I. Title.

ARNETT, Willard Eugene, 1921- 201
Religion and judgment; an essay on the method and meaning of religion. New York, Appleton [c.1966] xi, 335p. 22cm. (Century phil. ser.) Bibl. [BL51.A7] 66-11680 4.50
1. Religion — Philosophy. I. Title.

ARNOLD, Matthew, 1822-1888. 201
Literature and dogma. Edited, abridged, and with an introd. by James C. Livingston. New York, Ungar [1970] xxix, 162 p. 20 cm. (Milestones of thought in the history of ideas) Bibliography: p. xxvi-xxvii. [BS511.A7 1970] 79-107032 2.45
1. Bible—Criticism, interpretation, etc. I. Livingston, James C., 1930- ed. II. Title. III. Series.

AURICCHIO, John. 201
The future of theology. Staten Island, N.Y., Alba House [1970] 486 p. 22 cm. Bibliography: p. [441]-486. [BX1747.A8] 69-15853 6.95
1. Theology, Catholic—History. I. Title.

BAILEY, Page. 201
Commitments and consequences; a Christian account of human experience. [1st ed.] Philadelphia, Lippincott [1968] xii, 302 p. 22 cm. Bibliographical footnotes. [BR100.B33] 68-19827 5.95
1. Christianity—Philosophy. I. Title.

BAILLIE, John, 1886- 201
The interpretation of religion; an introductory study of theological principles. Nashville, Abingdon [1965, c.1928] xv, 477p. 21cm. (Apex bk., V1) [BL48B2] 2.45 pap.,
1. Religion. 2. Religion—Philosophy. 3. Theology, Doctrinal. I. Title.

BALTAZAR, Eulalio R. 201
Teilhard and the supernatural, by Eulalio R. Baltazar. Baltimore, Helicon [1966] 336 p. 22 cm. Bibliographical footnotes. [B2430.T374B27] 66-26481
1. Teilhard de Chardin, Pierre. 2. Supernatural. I. Title.

BALTHASAR, Hans Urs von, 1905- 201
A theology of history. New York, Sheed and Ward [1963] 149p. 21 cm. [BR115.H5B313] 62-11100
1. History—Philosophy. I. Title.

BAMBROUGH, Renford. 201
Reason, truth and God. London, Methuen [1973, c.1969] 164 p. 21 cm. (University paperbacks, UP490) Bibliography: p. [159]-160. [BL51.B23] 73-390962 ISBN 0-416-70240-6 3.50 (pbk.)
1. Religion—Philosophy—Addresses, essays, lectures. I. Title.
Available from Barnes & Noble, New York, for 5.35.

BELANGER, Merlyn. 201
On religious maturity. New York, Philosophical Library [1962] 82p. 23cm. [BL2775.2.B4] 61-15238
1. Religion. I. Title.

BELONGING and alienation : 201
religious foundations for the human future / edited by Philip Hefner and W. Widick Schroeder. Chicago : Center for the Scientific Study of Religion, c1976. vii, 248 p. ; 23 cm. (Studies in religion and society) Includes bibliographical references. [BL50.B39] 75-30254 ISBN 0-913348-07-4 : 10.95 ISBN 0-913348-08-2 pbk. :
1. Religion—Addresses, essays, lectures. 2. Sociology, Christian—United States—Addresses, essays, lectures. I. Hefner, Philip J. II. Schroeder, W. Widick. III. Series.

BERDIAEV, Nikolai Aleksandrovich, 1874-1948. 201
Freedom and the spirit. [by] Nicolas Berdyaev. Translated by Oliver Fielding Clarke. Freeport, N.Y., Books for Libraries Press [1972] xix, 361 p. 22 cm. Translation of Filosofiia svobodnago dukha. [BL51.B5244 1972] 72-2567 ISBN 0-8369-6848-4
1. Religion—Philosophy. 2. Apologetics—20th century. I. Title.

BERTOCCI, Peter Anthony. 201
Introduction to the philosophy of religion. New York, Prentice-Hall, 1951. 565 p. 22 cm. (Prentice-Hall philosophy series) [BL51.B54] 51-14584
1. Religion—Philosophy. I. Title.

BERTOCCI, Peter Anthony. 201
Religion as creative insecurity. New York, Association Press [1958] 128 p. 20 cm. Includes bibliography. [BL51.B543] 58-6471
1. Religion—Philosophy. 2. Security (Psychology) I. Title.

BERTOCCI, Peter Anthony. 201
Religion as creative insecurity [by] Peter A. Bertocci. Westport, Conn., Greenwood Press [1973, c1958] 128 p. 22 cm. Reprint of the ed. published by Association Press, New York. Bibliography: p. 127-128. [BL51.B543 1973] 73-1836 ISBN 0-8371-6803-1 8.00
1. Religion—Philosophy. 2. Security (Psychology) I. Title.

BEWKES, Eugene Garrett, 1895- 201
The Western heritage of faith and reason [by] Eugene G. Bewkes [and others. Rev. ed. by] J. Calvin Keene. New York, Harper & Row [1963] 703 p. illus. 25 cm. First ed. published in 1940 under title: Experience, reason and faith: a survey in philosophy and religion. [BL51.B55] 63-9052
1. Philosophy and religion. 2. Religious thought — Hist. 3. Judaism. I. Keene, James Calvin. II. Title.

BEWKES, Eugene Garrett, 1895- 201
The Western heritage of faith and reason [by] Eugene G. Bewkes [others. Rev. ed. by] J. Calvin Keene. New York, Harper [c.1963] 703p. illus. 25cm. First ed. pub. in 1940 under title: Experience, reason and faith: a survey in philosophy and religion. 63-9052 8.00
1. Philosophy and religion. 2. Religious thought—Hist. 3. Judaism. I. Keene, James Calvin. II. Title.

BIGG, Charles, 1840-1908. 201
The Christian Platonists of Alexandria; the 1886 Bampton lectures. Oxford, Clarendon P., 1968. 386 p. 23 cm. "First published 1913." Bibliographical footnotes. [BR1705.B5 1968] 76-370393 unpriced
1. Philo Judaus. 2. Clemens, Titus Flavius, Alexandrinus. 3. Origenes. 4. Platonists. I. Title.

BIGG, Charles, 1840-1908. 201
The Christian Platonists of Alexandria; eight lectures preached before the University of Oxford in the year 1886 of the foundation of the late Rev. John Bampton. New York, AMS Press [1970] xxvii, 304 p. 23 cm. Reprint of the 1886 ed. Includes bibliographical references. [BR1705.B5 1970] 75-123764
1. Philo Judaus. 2. Clemens, Titus Flavius, Alexandrinus. 3. Origenes. 4. Platonists. I. Title.

BIRNBAUM, Norman, comp. 201
Sociology and religion; a book of readings [by] Norman Birnbaum [and] Gertrud Lenzer. Englewood Cliffs, N.J., Prentice-Hall [1969] x, 452 p. 24 cm. Includes bibliographical references. [BL60.B48] 68-28878 7.95
1. Religion and sociology—Collections. I. Lenzer, Gertrud, joint comp. II. Title.

BIXLER, Julius Seelye, 1894- 201
Conversations with an unrepentant liberal. Port Washington, N.Y., Kennikat Press [1973, c1946] x, 113 p. 21 cm. "Based upon the twenty-second series of lectures delivered at Yale University on the foundation established by the late Dwight H. Terry." [BR1615.B48 1973] 72-85298 ISBN 0-8046-1713-9 7.50
1. Liberalism. I. Title.

BLACKSTONE, William T. 201
The problem of religious knowledge; the impact of philosophical analysis on the question of religious knowledge. Neglewood Cliffs, N. J., Prentice-Hall [1963] 175 p. 21 cm. (A Spectrum book) Includes bibliography. [BL51.B584] 63-11783
1. Knowledge, Theory of (Religion) I. Title.

BLACKSTONE, William T. 201
The problem of religious knowledge; the impact of philosophical analysis on the question of religious knowledge. Englewood Cliffs, N.J., Prentice [c.1963] 175p. 21cm. (Spectrum bk. S-58) Bibl. 63-11783 3.95; 1.95 pap.,
1. Knowledge, Theory of (Religion) I. Title.

BLAKE, Clinton Hamlin, 1920- 201
An elementary introduction to religion and Christianity. Boston, Christopher Pub. House [1954] 63p. 21cm. [BL50.B26] 54-12019
1. Religion. 2. Christianity—Essence, genius, nature. I. Title.

BLANTON, Smiley, 1882- 201
Faith is the answer; a pastor and a psychiatrist discuss your problems. By Norman Vincent Peale and Smiley Blanton. [New and rev. ed.] New York, Prentice-Hall, 1950. vi, 243 p. 21 cm. In the earlier edition Blanton's name appeared on the title page. [BV4012.B53 1950] 50-8115
1. Psychology, Pastoral. I. Peale, Norman Vincent, 1898- II. Title.

BODKIN, Maud. 201
Studies of type-images in poetry, religion, and philosophy. London, New York, Oxford University Press, 1951. xii, 184 p. 21 cm. [BL51.B62] 51-14429
1. Religion—Philosophy. I. Title.

BODKIN, Maud. 201
Studies of type-images in poetry, religion, and philosophy. [Folcroft, Pa.] Folcroft Library Editions, 1974. p. cm. Reprint of the 1951 ed. published by the Oxford University Press, London. [BL51.B62 1974] 74-14665 15.00 (lib. bdg.).
1. Religion—Philosophy. I. Title.

BOSTROM, Christopher Jacob, 1797-1866. 201
Philosophy of religion. Translation with introd. [by] Victor E. Beck [and] Robert N. Beck. New Haven, Yale University Press, 1962. lvi, 187p. 23cm. 'The original research and translation ... were done by [Victor E. Beck] ... and submitted to Boston University ... as a dissertation, 'A translation of C. J. Bostrom's Philosophy of religion with a critical commentary,' 1947.' 'The translation is the third part of Bostrom's lectures on religion ... recorded from class notes and edited by Sigurd Ribbing ... in the volume Chr. Jac. Bostrom's forelisningar 1 religionsfilosofi.' Bibliography: p.177-181. [BL51.B642] 62-8236
1. Religion— Philosophy. I. Beck, Victor Emanuel, 1894- ed. and tr. II. Title.

BOYNTON, Richard Wilson, 1870- 201
Beyond mythology; a challenge to dogmatism in religion. [1st ed.] Garden City, N. Y., Doubleday, 1951. xiv, 257 p. 21 cm. [BL48.B644] 51-9244
1. Religion. 2. Humanism, Religious. 3. Religions (Proposed, universal, etc.) I. Title.

BRADSHAW, Marion John, 1886- 201
Philosophical foundations of faith, a contribution toward a philosophy of religion. New York, AMS Press [1969, c1941] x, 254 p. 23 cm. Includes bibliographical references. [BL51.B6485 1969] 78-99248
1. Religion—Philosophy. 2. Philosophy and religion. I. Title.

BROADHURST, Allan R. 201
He speaks the word of God; a study of the sermons of Norman Vincent Peale. Englewood Cliffs, N.J., Prentice-Hall [1963] 106 p. 24 cm. Includes bibliography. [BX9543.P4B7] 63-8280
1. Peale, Norman Vincent, 1898- I. Title.

BRONSTEIN, Daniel J 1908- ed. 201
Approaches to the philosophy of religion; a book of readings, edited by Daniel J. Bronstein and Harold M. Schulweis. New York, Prentice- Hall, 1954. 532p. 22cm. Includes bibliography. [BL51.B76] 54-11638
1. Religion—Philosophy. I. Schulweis, Harold M., joint ed. II. Title.

BROWN, Colin. 201
Philosophy and the Christian faith; a historical sketch from the Middle Ages to the present day. [1st ed.] Chicago, Inter-varsity Press [1969] 319 p. 20 cm. (A Tyndale paperback) "A note on books": p. [291]-309. [BR100.B65] 68-58083 12/-
1. Philosophy and religion. 2. Christianity—Philosophy. I. Title.

BROWN, Delwin, 1935- comp. 201
Process philosophy and Christian thought. Edited by Delwin Brown, Ralph E. James, Jr. [and] Gene Reeves. Indianapolis, Bobbs-Merrill [1971] xiv, 495 p. 23 cm. Bibliography: p. 475-489. [BT83.6.B76] 74-127586 6.95
1. Process theology—Collections. I. James, Ralph E., joint comp. II. Reeves, Gene, joint comp. III. Title.

BRUNNER, Heinrich Emil, 1889- 201
Truth as encounter. A new ed., much enl., of The divine-human encounter. Philadelphia, Westminster Press [1964] xii, 210 p. 21 cm. Bibliographical footnotes. [BT78.B874] 64-11192
1. Dialectical theology. 2. Revelation. I. Title.

BRUNNER, Heinrich Emil, 1889- 201
Truth as encounter. New ed., much enl., of The divine-human encounter [Tr. from German by Amandus W. Loos, David Cairns] Philadelphia, Westminster [c.1943, 1964] xii, 210p. 21cm. Bibl. 64-11192 5.00
1. Dialectical theology. 2. Revelation. I. Title.

BRYAN, William Jennings, 1860-1925. 201
In His image. Freeport, N.Y., Books for Libraries Press [1971] 266 p. 23 cm. (Essay index reprint series) Reprint of the 1922 ed. [BR123.B74 1971] 73-156618 ISBN 0-8369-2270-0
1. Christianity—Addresses, essays, lectures. I. Title.

BUBER, Martin, 1878- 201
Eclipse of God; studies in the relation between religion and philosophy. [1st ed.] New York, Harper [1952] 192 p. 20 cm. [BL51.B82] 52-8464
1. Religion—Philosophy. 2. Religion and philosophy. I. Title.

BUBER, Martin, 1878- 201
Eclipse of God; studies in the relation between religion and philosophy. New York, Harper [1957, c1952] 152p. 21cm. (Harper torchbooks, TB12) Includes bibliography. [BL51.B82 1957] 61-678
1. Religion—Philosophy. 2. Philosophy and religion. I. Title.

BUBER, Martin, 1878-1965. 201
Eclipse of God; studies in the relation between religion and philosophy. New York, Harper [1957, c1952] 152 p. 21 cm. (Harper torchbooks, TB12) Includes bibliography. [BL51.B82 1957] 61-678
1. Religion—Philosophy. 2. Philosophy and religion. I. Title.

BUBER, Martin, 1878-1965. 201
Eclipse of God : studies in the relation between religion and philosophy / Martin Buber. Westport, Conn. : Greenwood Press, 1977. p. cm. Translation of Gottesfinsternis. Reprint of the 1952 ed. published by Harper, New York, which was issued as TB12 of Harper torchbooks. Includes index. Bibliography: p. [BL51.B8213 1977] 77-10030 ISBN 0-8371-9718-X lib.bdg. : 14.00
1. Religion—Philosophy. 2. Philosophy and religion. I. Title.

*BUEHNE, Willis G. 201
Why is religion? New York, Exposition Pr. [1973] 42 p. 21 cm. [BR121.2] ISBN 0-682-47674-9 3.00
1. Religion—Philosophy—Addresses, essays, lectures. 2. Christianity—20th century. I. Title.

BURROUGHS, James H 201
In praise of zero; thoughts on revealed religion and nature, by James H. Burroughs. Philadelphia, Dorrance [1964] 84 p. illus 20 cm. [BL51.B86] 63-22254
1. Religion — Philosophy. I. Title.

BURROUGHS, James H. 201
In praise of zero; thoughts on revealed religion and nature, by James H. Burroughs. Philadelphia, Dorrance [c.1964] 84p. illus. 20cm. 63-22254 2.50
1. Religion—Philosophy. I. Title.

BURTT, Edwin Arthur, 1892- 201
Types of religious philosophy. Rev. ed. New York, Harper [1951] xi, 468 p. 22 cm. Includes bibliographies. [BL51.B87 1951] 51-11521
1. Religion—Philosophy. 2. Religion—Philosophy—History. I. Title.

CAILLIET, Emile, 1894- 201
The clue to Pascal. Foreword by John A. Mackay. [Folcroft, Pa.] Folcroft Library Editions, 1973. 128 p. 20 cm. Reprint of the 1944 ed. published by S. C. M. Press, London. Includes bibliographical references. [BX4735.P26C3 1973] 73-15921 ISBN 0-8414-3504-9 (lib. bdg.)
1. Pascal, Blaise, 1623-1662. I. Title.

CALHOUN, Robert Lowry, 1896- 201
God and the common life. Hamden, Conn., Shoe String Press [1954, c1935] 303p. 23cm. Includes bibliography. [BL51.C32 1954] 59-40376
1. Religion—Philosophy. 2. God. 3. Vocation. I. Title.

CAMPBELL, Ernest T. 201
Christian manifesto [by] Ernest T. Campbell. [1st ed.] New York, Harper & Row [1970] x, 114 p. 22 cm. Includes bibliographical references. [BR121.2.C24 1970] 78-109069 3.95
1. Christianity—20th century. I. Title.

CATHOLIC University of America. 201
Christian philosophy and religious renewal. Ed. by George F. McLean. Washington, Catholic Univ. [1966] x, 174p. 23cm. Part of the Catholic Univ. of Amer. 75th anniversary philosophy workshop on Christian phil. and religious renewal. Bibl. [BR100.C38 1964] [orkshop on Christian Philosophy and Religious Renewal, 1964.] 66-25649 4.95 pap.,
1. Christianity — Philosophy — Addresses, essays, lectures. I. McLean, George F., ed. II. Title. III. Title: Renewal.

CATHOLIC University of America. Workshop on Christian Philosophy and Religious Renewal, 1964. 201
Christian philosophy and religious renewal. Edited by George F. McLean. Washington, Catholic University of America Press [1966] x. 174 p. 23 cm. "Part of the Catholic University of America 75th anniversary philosophy workshop on 'Christian philosophy and religious renewal.'" Bibliography: p. 72-73. Bibliographical footnotes. [BR100.C38] 66-25649
1. Christianity — Philosophy — Addresses, essays, lectures. I. McLean, George F., ed. II. Title.

CATHOLIC University of America. Workshop on Christian Philosophy and Religious Renewal, 1964. 201
Christian philosophy in the college and seminary; [proceedings] Edited by George F. McLean. Washington, Catholic University of America Press, 1966. vii, 193 p. 23 cm. Bibliographical footnotes. [B52.C34] 66-9148
1. Philosophy and religion. 2. Philosophy — Study and teaching. I. McLean, George F., ed. II. Title.

CATHOLIC University of America. Workshop on Christian Philosophy and Religious Renewal, 1964. 201
Christian philosophy in the college and seminary; [proceedings] Ed. by George F. McLean. Washington, Catholic Univ. of Amer. Pr., 1966. vii, 193p. 23cm. Bibl. [B52.C34 1964] 66-9148 5.50 pap.,
1. Philosophy and religion. 2. Philosophy — Study and teaching. I. McLean, George F., ed. II. Title.

CAUTHEN, Wilfred Kenneth. 201
Christian biopolitics; a credo & strategy for the future [by] Kenneth Cauthen. Nashville, Abingdon Press [1971] 159 p. 21 cm. Includes bibliographical references. [BR121.2.C343] 78-162459 ISBN 0-687-07046-5 4.00
1. Christianity—20th century. I. Title.

CHENU, Marie Dominique, 1895- 201
Is theology a science? Translated from the French by A. H. N. Green-Armytage. [1st ed.] New York, Hawthorn Books [1959] 126p. 21cm. (The Twentieth century encyclopedia of Catholicism, v. 2. Section I: Knowledge and faith) Includes bibliography. [BR118.C433] 59-6732
1. Theology. I. Title.

CHRISTIAN, William A 201
Meaning and truth in religion. Princeton, N.J., Princeton University Press, 1964. ix, 273 p. 23 cm. Bibliographical footnotes. [BL65.L2C5] 64-12180
1. Semantics (Philosophy) 2. Religion and language. I. Title.

CHRISTIAN, William A. 201
Meaning and truth in religion. Princeton, N.J., Princeton [c.]1964. ix, 273p. 23cm. Bibl. 64-12180 6.00
1. Semantics (Philosophy) 2. Religion and language. I. Title.

CHURCH and the world. (The) 201
New York, Paulist [c.1965] viii, 184p. 24cm. (Concilium theology in the age of renewal: Fundamental theology, v.6) Bibl. [BV603.C45] 65-24899 4.50
1. Church—Addresses, essays, lectures. I. Metz, Johannes B., 1928- II. Series: Concilium theology in the age of renewal, v.6

THE Church faces 201
liberalism; a confrontation between Bible truth and some liberalistic views of the latter half of the twentieth century. Editor: Thomas B. Warren. Nashville, Gospel Advocate Co. [1970] 407 p. illus., ports. 24 cm. (Freed-Hardeman College. Lectures, 1970) Includes bibliographical references. [BR1616.C48] 79-15943
1. Liberalism (Religion)—Addresses, essays, lectures. 2. Apologetics—20th century—Addresses, essays, lectures. I. Warren, Thomas B., ed. II. Title. III. Series.

CLARK, Gordon Haddon. 201
Religion, reason, and revelation. Philadelphia, Presbyterian and Reformed Pub. Co., 1961. 241 p. 22 cm. (International library of philosophy and theology. Philosophical and historical studies series) [BL51.C544] 61-11012
1. Religion—Philosophy. 2. Ethics. 3. Free will and determinism. I. Title.

CLARKE, John Henry, 1852-1931. 201
William Blake, 1757-1827, on the Lord's prayer New York, Haskell House, 1971. [14], 174 p. 23 cm. Reprint of the 1927 ed. Bibliography: 10th-12th prelim. pages. [PR4147.C6 1971] 70-95421 ISBN 0-8383-0967-4
1. Blake, William, 1757-1827—Criticism and interpretation. 2. Thornton, Robert John, 1768?-1837. 3. Lord's prayer.

CLINCHY, Russell James, 1893- 201
An answer for agnostics, by Russell J. Clinchy. Boston, Christopher Pub. House [1966] 173p. 21cm. Bibl. [BR121.2.C55] 66-25048 3.95
1. Christianity — Essence, genius, nature. I. Title.

CLINCHY, Russell James, 1893- 201
An answer for agnostics. by Russell J. Clinchy. Boston, Christopher Pub. House [1966] 173 p. 21 cm. Bibliographical footnotes. [BR121.2.C55] 66-25048
1. Christianity—Essence, genius, nature. I. Title.

COFFIN, Henry Sloane, 1877-1954. 201
Religion yesterday and today. Freeport, N.Y., Books for Libraries Press [1970, c1940] 183 p. 23 cm. (Essay index reprint series) Contents.Contents.—Evolutionary science.—The divine immanence. Biblical criticism. Religious experience.—The social conscience.—The church. Includes bibliographical references. [BR525.C58 1970] 75-117769 ISBN 8-369-17901-
1. Religious thought—U.S. I. Title.

COLLEGE Theology Society. 201
Theology in revolution; [proceedings] George Devine, editor. Staten Island, N.Y., Alba House [1970] xi, 286 p. 21 cm. "Based on the Society's last annual convention in Chicago, April 6-8, 1969." Includes bibliographical references. [BR50.C59] 71-110590 ISBN 8-18-901764- 3.95
1. Theology—Addresses, essays, lectures. I. Devine, George, 1941- ed. II. Title.

COMBES, Gustave, 1880- 201
Revival of paganism. Translated by Augustine Stock. St. Louis, Herder, 1950. v, 360 p. 25 cm. Translation of Le retour offensif du paganisme. Bibliographical footnotes. [BR127.C583] 50-3484
1. Paganism. 2. Religion—Philosophy. I. Title.

CONSULTATION on the Future of Philosophical Theology, McCormick Theological Seminary, 1970. 201
The future of philosophical theology. Edited

by Robert A. Evans. Philadelphia, Westminster Press [1971] 190 p. 21 cm. [BT40.C65 1970] 77-141196 ISBN 0-664-20902-5 6.95
1. Philosophical theology—Addresses, essays, lectures. I. Evans, Robert A., 1937- ed. II. Title.

CULLITON, Joseph T. 201
A processive world view for pragmatic Christians / by Joseph T. Culliton. New York : Philosophical Library, c1975. 302 p. ; 22 cm. Includes bibliographical references. [BD331.C84] 75-3781 ISBN 0-8022-2170-X : 12.50
1. Teilhard de Chardin, Pierre. 2. Dewey, John, 1859-1952. 3. Reality. 4. Evolution. 5. Christianity—Philosophy. 6. Pragmatism. I. Title.

DAVIES, William David, 1911- 201
The setting of the Sermon on the Mount. Cambridge [Eng.] University Press, 1964. xiii, 546 p. 24 cm. Bibliography: p. 481-504. [BT380.D37] 64-630
1. Sermon on the Mount. I. Title.

DAVIS, Charles, 1923- 201
Body as spirit : the nature of religious feeling / by Charles Davis. New York : Seabury Press, c1976. 181 p. ; 22 cm. "A Crossroad book." Includes bibliographical references and index. [BR110.D29] 75-42023 ISBN 0-8164-0288-4 : 7.95
1. Christianity—Psychology. 2. Perception. 3. Experience (Religion) 4. Man (Theology) I. Title.

DENBEAUX, Fred J. 201
The art of Christian doubt. New York, Association Press [c.1960] x, 181p. (bibl. footnotes) 20cm. (A Haddam House book) 60-6557 3.50 bds.,
1. Christianity—Philosophy. I. Title.

DEVAUX, Andre A. 201
Teilhard and womanhood, by Andre A. Devaux. Translated by Paul Joseph Oligny and Michael D. Meilach. New York, Paulist Press [1968] vii, 83 p. 19 cm. (Deus books) Translation of Teilhard et la vocation de la femme. [B2430.T374D483] 68-31259 0.95
1. Teilhard de Chardin, Pierre. 2. Woman. I. Title.

DEWART, Leslie. 201
The foundations of belief. [New York] Herder and Herder [1969] 526 p. 21 cm. Bibliographical footnotes. [BL51.D417] 69-17777 9.50
1. Religion—Philosophy. I. Title.

DEWEY, John 201
A common faith. New Haven, [Conn.], Yale University Press [1960, c.1934] 87p. 21cm. (Yale paperbound Y-18) .95 pap.,
1. Religion. I. Title.

DE WOLF, Lotan Harold, 1905- 201
The religious revolt against reason, by L. Harold DeWolf. [1st ed.] New York, Greenwood Press, 1968 [c1949] 217 p. 22 cm. Bibliographical footnotes. [BL51.D42] 68-23282
1. Religion— Philosophy. 2. Reason. I. Title.

DE WOLF, Lotan Harold, 1905- 201
The religious revolt against reason, by L. Harold DeWolf. [1st ed.] New York, Greenwood Press, 1968 [c1949] 217 p. 22 cm. Bibliographical footnotes. [BL51.D42 1968] 68-23282
1. Religion—Philosophy. 2. Reason. I. Title.

DI GIACOMO, James. 201
The longest step : searching for God / James Di Giacomo and John Walsh. [Minneapolis] : Winston Press, c1977. 94 p. : ill. ; 22 cm. (The Encounter series) Discusses various ways of coming to terms with God. [BX2350.2D5] 77-72547 ISBN 0-03-021276-6 pbk. : 2.95
1. Spiritual life—Catholic authors. I. Walsh, John J., 1913- joint author. II. Title.

DORNER, Isaak August, 1809-1884. 201
History of Protestant theology; particularly in Germany, viewed according to its fundamental movement and in connection with the religious, moral, and intellectual life, by J. A. Dorner. Translated by George Robson and Sophia Taylor. With a pref. to the translation by the author. New York, AMS Press [1970] 2 v. 24 cm. Author's pref. in German and English. Reprint of the 1871 ed. Translation of Geschichte der protestantischen Theologie. Includes bibliographical references. [BX4811.D6713 1970] 72-133823 ISBN 0-404-02147-6
1. Theology, Protestant—History. 2. Germany—Church history. 3. Theology, Protestant—Germany. I. Title.

DUMERY, Henry. 201
Faith and reflection. Edited and with an introd. by Louis Dupre. Translated by Stephen McNierney and Mother M. Benedict Murphy. [New York] Herder and Herder [1968] xxxiii, 220 p. 22 cm. Includes bibliographical references. [BL51.D83] 68-54078 7.50
1. Religion—Philosophy. I. Dupre, Louis K., 1925- ed. II. Title.

DUMERY, Henry. 201
Phenomenology and religion : structures of the Christian institution / Henry Dumery. Berkeley : University of California Press, 1975. ix, 114 p. ; 23 cm. (Hermeneutics, studies in the history of religions ; v. 5) Translation of Phenomenologie et religion, structures de l'institution chretienne. Bibliography: p. 111-114. [BR100.D7913] 73-94443 ISBN 0-520-02714-0 : 7.95
1. Christianity—Philosophy. 2. Religion—Philosophy. I. Title. II. Series.

ENCYCLOPEDIC dictionary of 201
Christian doctrine. Edited by John P. Bradley. Gastonia, N.C., Good Will Publishers [1970] 3 v. (xi, 1304, iii p.) illus. (part col.), facsims., ports. (part col.) 25 cm. (The Catholic layman's library, v. 7-9) Includes bibliographies. [BR95.E49] 78-92779
1. Theology—Dictionaries. I. Bradley, John P., ed. II. Title. III. Series.

EVANS, William Glyn 201
The road to power. Chicago, Moody Press [c.1961] 160p. Bibl. 61-3049 2.75
1. Christianity—Essence, genius, nature. I. Title.

FACKRE, Gabriel J. 201
Humiliation and celebration; post-radical themes in doctrine, morals, and mission, by Gabriel Fackre. New York, Sheed and Ward [1969] viii, 307 p. 22 cm. Includes bibliographical references. [BT28.F3] 72-82605 6.95
1. Theology—20th century. I. Title.

FEE, Zephyrus Roy, 1890- 201
The Christian's philosophy of religion. Part I. Fundamental considerations. Part II. Christian experience and revelation in the light of philosophy. [Dallas? 1951] 128 p. 20 cm. [BL51.F42] 52-17001
1. Religion—Philosophy. I. Title.

FEIBLEMAN, James Kern, 1904- 201
Religious Platonism; the influence of religion on Plato and the influence of Plato on religion. New York, Barnes & Noble [1962, c.1959] 236p. 23cm. Bibl. 60-1560 5.00
1. Plato. 2. Plato—Influence. I. Title.

FEUERBACH, Ludwig Andreas, 1804-1872. 201
The essence of Christianity; edited and abridged by E. Graham Waring and F. W. Strothmann. New York, F. Ungar Pub. Co. [1957] 65 p. 21 cm. (Milestones of thought in the history of ideas) [B2971.W4E52] 57-8650
1. Religion—Philosophy. 2. Christianity—Controversial literature. I. Title.

FITCH, Robert Elliot, 1902- 201
The kingdom without end; a prophetic interpretation of history and civilization. New York, Scribner, 1950. xiv, 137 p. 21 cm. [BR100.F53] 50-14972
1. Christianity—Philosophy. 2. History—Philosophy. I. Title.

FONTINELL, Eugene. 201
Toward a reconstruction of religion; a philosophical probe. [1st ed.] Garden City, N.Y., Doubleday, 1970. 261 p. 22 cm. Includes bibliographical references. [BR100.F65] 78-97661 5.95
1. Christianity—Philosophy. 2. Pragmatism. I. Title.

FRANK, Erich, 1883- 201
Philosophical understanding and religious truth [by] Erich Frank. New York, Oxford, 1966[c.1945] xii, 209p. 21cm. (Galaxy bk. GB174) Bibl. Rev. of the Mary E. Flexner lects. delivered at Bryn Mawr in 1943. [BL51.F68] 45-1882 1.50 pap.,
1. Philosophy and religion. I. Title.

FRANTZ, Ezra, 1895- 201
Preface to a religious philosophy of living. [1st ed.] New York, Pageant Press [1952] 246p. 24cm. [BL51.F6812] 53-856
1. Religion—Philosophy. I. Title.

FREEMAN, David Hugh. 201
A philosophical study of religion [by] David Hugh Freeman in collaboration with David Freeman. Nutley, N.J., Craig Press, 1964. vii, 270 p. 23 cm. Includes bibliographical references. [BL51.F6813] 63-21699
1. Religion — Philosophy. I. Title.

FREEMAN, David Hugh 201
A philosophical study of religion [by] David Hugh Freeman, with David Freeman. Nutley, N.J., Craig Pr. [c.]1964. vii, 270p. 23cm. Bibl. 63-21699 5.00; 3.75 pap.,
1. Religion—Philosophy. I. Title.

FREUD, Sigmund, 1856-1939. 201
The future of an illusion. Translated by W. D. Robson-Scott. Garden City, N. Y., Doubleday, 1957. 102p. 18cm. (Doubleday anchor books, A99) [BL53] 57-1077
1. Psychology, Religious. 2. Religion. 3. Psychoanalysis. I. Title.

*FREUD, Sigmund, 1856-1939 201
The future of an illusion. Tr. [from German] by W. D. Robson-Scott. Rev., newly ed. by James Strachey. Garden City, N. Y., Doubleday [1964, c.1961] 105p. 18cm. (Anchor bk., A381) Bibl. .95 pap.,
I. Title.

FUHRMANN, Paul Traugott, 1903- 201
Extraordinary Christianity, the life and thought of Alexander Vinet. With a pref. by John T. McNeill. Philadelphia Westminster Press [1964] 125 p. 21 cm. Bibliography: p. 123-125. [BX4827.V5F8] 64-10520
1. Vinet, Alexander Rodolphe, 1797-1847. I. Title.

FUHRMANN, Paul Traugott, 1903- 201
Extraordinary Christianity; the life and thought of Alexander Vinet. Pref. by John T. McNeil. Philadelphia. Westminster [c.1964] 125p. 21cm. Bibl. 64-10520 3.00
1. Vinet, Alexandre Rodolphe, 1797-1847. I. Title.

GARELICK, Herbert M. 201
The anti-Christianity of Kierkegaard; a study of Concluding unscientific postscript. The Hague, M. Nijhoff [New York, Humanities, 1966, 1813-1885. Afsluttende uvidenskabelig efterskrift. [BR100.K48G3] 66-2257
I. Title.

GARRONE, Gabriel Marie, 1901- 201
This we believe. Foreword by John J. Wright. Translated by M. Angeline Bouchard. New York, Desclee Co. [1969] viii, 258 p. 22 cm. Translation of Que faut-il croire? Includes bibliographical references. [BX1751.2.G3413] 69-20371 4.95
1. Catholic Church—Doctrinal and controversial works—Catholic authors. I. Title.

GILL, Jerry H. 201
Ian Ramsey : to speak responsibly of God / by Jerry H. Gill. London : Allen and Unwin, 1976. 13-166 p. ; 22 cm. (Contemporary religious thinkers series) Includes index. Bibliography: p. 159-164. [BR100.G478] 76-363853 ISBN 0-04-230014-2 : 12.25
1. Ramsey, Ian T. 2. Experience (Religion) 3. Religion and language. 4. Knowledge, Theory of (Religion)
Distributed by Allen and Unwin Inc. 198 Ash St. Reading, Mass. 01867

GOODALL, J. L. 201
An introduction to the philosophy of religion [by] J. L. Goodall. London, Longmans, 1966. viii, 182p. 21cm. (Educ. today) Bibl. [BL51.G712] 66-78165 2.25 pap.,
1. Religion—Philosophy. I. Title.
American distributor: Humanities, New York.

GOODRICH, Frances C. 201
The third Adam, by Frances C. Goodrich. New York, Philosophical Library [1967] ix, 108 p. 22 cm. [BR124.G6] 66-22003
1. Christianity—Essence, genius, nature. I. Title.

GREENE, Eli B. 201
God's many houses; the religions we use and abuse. New York, Vantage [c.1963] 119p. 21cm. 2.50 bds.,
I. Title.

GRIMSLEY, Ronald. 201
Rousseau and the religious quest. Oxford, Clarendon P., 1968. xiv, 148 p. 23 cm. Bibliography: p. [143]-144. [B2138.R4G7] 68-124344 ISBN 0-19-815380-5 25/-
1. Rousseau, Jean Jacques, 1712-1778. I. Title.

GRONBECH, Vilhelm Peter, 1873-1948. 201
Religious currents in the nineteenth century, by Vilhelm Gronbech. Translated from the Danish by P. M. Mitchell and W. D. Paden. Lawrence, University of Kansas Press, 1964. 201 p. port. 24 cm. Bibliographical references included in "Notes" (p. 195-198) [BR477.G713] 64-20567
1. Religion. 2. Evolution. 3. Nineteenth century. I. Title.

GRONBECH, Vilhelm Peter, 1873-1948 201
Religious currents in the nineteenth century. Tr. from Danish by P. M. Mitchell, W. D. Paden. Lawrence, Univ. of Kan. Pr. [c.]1964. 201p. port. 24cm. Bibl. [BR477.G713] 64-20567 4.50
1. Religion. 2. Evolution. 3. Nineteenth century. I. Title.

GRoNBECH, Vilhelm Peter, 1873-1948. 201
Religious currents in the nineteenth century. Translated from the Danish by P. M. Mitchell and W. D. Paden. Carbondale, Ill., Arcturus Books [1973, c1964] p. Translation of Religiose stromninger i det nittende aarhundrede. Includes bibliographical references. [BR477.G713 1973b] 72-11830 ISBN 0-8093-0630-1 (pbk)
1. Religion. 2. Religion and evolution. 3. Nineteenth century. I. Title.

GRoNBECH, Vilhelm Peter, 1873-1948. 201
Religious currents in the nineteenth century. Translated from the Danish by P. M. Mitchell and W. D. Paden. Carbondale, Southern Illinois University Press [1973, c1964] 201 p. port. 20 cm. (Arcturus books, AB110) Translation of Religiose stromninger i det nittende aarhundrede. Includes bibliographical references. [BR477.G713 1973] 72-11829 ISBN 0-8093-0629-8 2.45 (pbk.)
1. Religion. 2. Religion and evolution. 3. Nineteenth century. I. Title.

GROSS, Leonard. 201
God and Freud. New York, D. McKay Co. [1959] 215 p. 21 cm. [BL53.G78] 59-6696
1. Freud, Sigmund, 1856-1939. 2. Psychology, Religious. 3. Pastoral psychology. I. Title.

HALL, Robert William, comp. 201
Studies in religious philosophy [compiled by] Robert W. Hall. [New York] American Book Co. [1968, c1969] viii, 408 p. 23 cm. Includes bibliographies. [BL51.H26] 78-1746
1. Religion—Philosophy. I. Title.

HAMILTON, Kenneth. 201
Words and the word. Grand Rapids, Mich., Eerdmans [1971] 120 p. 21 cm. "A slightly expanded version of the Payton lectures delivered at Fuller Theological Seminary during spring quarter of 1970." Bibliography: p. 111-115. [BL65.L2H3] 76-132031 2.95
1. Bible—Criticism, interpretation, etc. 2. Religion and language. 3. Myth. I. Title.

HANSEN, Matthew, 1873- 201
Mr. Jones and his Maker. San Anselmo, Calif., 1951. 108 p. 24 cm. [BL51.H34] 52-29136
1. Religion—Philosophy. I. Title.

HARRISON, Frederic, 1831-1923. 201
The positive evolution of religion, its moral and social reaction. Freeport, N.Y., Books for Libraries Press [1971] xx, 267 p. 23 cm. (Essay index reprint series) Reprint of the 1913 ed. [B831.H5 1971] 74-142641 ISBN 0-8369-2053-8
1. Positivism. 2. Religion. I. Title.

HARTSHORNE, Charles, 1897- 201
Aquinas to Whitehead : seven centuries of metaphysics of religion / by Charles E. Hartshorne. Milwaukee : Marquette University Publications, 1976. 54 p. ; 19 cm. (The Aquinas lecture ; 1976) Includes bibliographical references. [BL200.H32] 76-5156 ISBN 0-87462-141-0 : 4.00
1. Theism—History—Addresses, essays, lectures. I. Title. II. Series.

HARTSHORNE, Charles, 1897- ed. 201
Philosophers speak of God, by Charles Hartshorne, William L. Reese [Chicago] Univ. of Chic. Pr. [1963, c.1953] 535p. 23cm. (Phoenix bk., P142) 2.95 pap.,
1. God. I. Reese, William L., joint ed. II. Title.

HARTSHORNE, Charles, 1897- ed. 201
Philosophers speak of God, by Charles Hartshorne and William L. Reese. [Chicago] University of Chicago Press [1953] 535 p. 25 cm. [BD573.H3] 53-10041
1. God. I. Reese, William L., joint ed. II. Title.

*HATCH, P. C. 201
The kingdom at hand. New York, Vantage [1967] 75p. 21cm. 2.50 bds.,
I. Title.

HAUGHTON, Rosemary. 201
Why be a Christian? [1st ed.] Philadelphia, Lippincott [1968] 140 p. 23 cm. [BT60.H38] 68-24192 3.95
1. Christianity—Essence, genius, nature. 2. Apologetics—20th century. I. Title.

HAZELTON, Roger 201
New accents in contemporary theology. New York, Harper [c.1960] 144p. Bibl.: p.141-142. 22cm. 60-11777 3.00 half cloth
1. Christianity—Philosophy. I. Title.

HAZELTON, Roger, 1909- 201
New accents in contemporary theology. New

York, Harper [1965, c.1960] 144p. 21cm. (Harper Chapel Bk., CB18F) Bibl. [BT40.H35] .95 pap.,
1. Christianity—Philosophy. I. Title.

HAZELTON, Roger, 1909- 201
New accents in contemporary theology. [1st ed.] New York, Harper [1960] 144 p. 22 cm. Includes bibliography. [BT40.H35] 60-11777
1. Christianity—Philosophy. I. Title.

HEARD, Gerald, 1889- 201
The human venture. [1st ed.] New York, Harper [1955] 310p. 22cm. [BL51.H3816] 55-8532
1. Religion— Philosophy. 2. Civilization—Hist. I. Title.

HEFNER, Philip J. 201
The promise of Teilhard; the meaning of the twentieth century in Christian perspective, by Philip Hefner. [1st ed.] Philadelphia, Lippincott [1970] 127 p. 21 cm. (The Promise of theology) Bibliography: p. 125-127. [B2430.T374H37] 79-118976 3.95
1. Teilhard de Chardin, Pierre. I. Title.

HEPBURN, Ronald W. 201
Christianity and paradox; critical studies in twentieth-century theology [by] Ronald W. Hepburn. New York, Pegasus [1968, c1958] ix, 210 p. 21 cm. "A Pegasus original." [BD573.H4 1968] 68-17550
1. Philosophy and religion. 2. Theology, Doctrinal—History—20th century. I. Title.

HERBERG, Will, ed. 201
Four existentialist theologians; a reader from the works of Jacques Maritain, Nicolas Berdyaev, Martin Buber, and Paul Tillich. Selected, and with an introd. and biographical notes, by Will Herberg. [1st ed.] Garden City, N. Y., Doubleday, 1958. 346p. 22cm. (Doubleday anchor books) [BL51.H469 1958a] 58-7578
1. Religion—Philosophy. 2. Existentialism. I. Title.

HESCHEL, Abraham Joshua, 201
1907-
Man is not alone; a philosophy of religion. New York, Farrar, Straus & Young, 1951. 305 p. 22 cm. [BL51.H476] 51-9992
1. Religion—Philosophy. 2. Judaism. I. Title.

HESCHEL, Abraham Joshua, 201
1907-
Man is not alone; a philosophy of religion. New York, Harper [1966, c.1951] 303p. 21cm. (Torchbk., TB838. Temple lib.) [BL51.H476] 2.95 pap.,
1. Religion — Philosophy. 2. Judaism. I. Title.

HICK, John, ed. 201
Classical and contemporary readings in the philosophy of religion. Englewood Cliffs, N. J., Prentice-Hall [1964] xv, 494 p. 24 cm. "Introductory notes and bibliographies": p. 465-485. [BL51.H487] 64-16056
1. Religion—Philosophy—Collections. 2. Theology—Collections. I. Title.

HICK, John. 201
Faith and knowledge; a modern introduction to the problem of religious knowledge. Ithaca, N. Y., Cornell University Press [1957] 221p. 23cm. [BL51.H49] 57-13858
1. Knowledge, Theory of (Religion) 2. Faith. I. Title.

HICK, John. 201
Faith and knowledge. 2d ed. Ithaca, N.Y., Cornell University Press [1966] x, 268 p. 23 cm. [BL51.H49 1966] 66-28018
1. Knowledge, Theory of (Religion) 2. Faith. I. Title.

HICK, John, ed. 201
Faith and the philosophers. New York, St. Martin's press, 1964. viii, 255 p. 23 cm. "Product of a two day conference...held at the Princeton Theological Seminary, Princeton, New Jersey, in December 1962." Bibliographical footnotes. [BR110.H5] 64-16778
1. Psychology, Religious — Congress. 2. Faith — Psychology. I. Princeton Theological Seminary. II. Title.

HICK, John. 201
Philosophy of religion. Englewood Cliffs, N.J., Prentice-Hall [1963] 111 p. 23 cm. (Prentice-Hall foundations of philosophy series) [BL51.H494] 63-10528
1. Religion—Philosophy. I. Title.

HOCKING, William Ernest, 201
1873-
The meaning of God in human experience; a philosophic study of religion. New Haven, Conn., Yale [1963, c.1912] 586p. 21cm. (Y-98) 2.95 pap.,
1. Religion—Philosophy. 2. God. I. Title.

HODGSON, Leonard, 1889- 201
Essays in Christian philosophy. Freeport, N.Y., Books for Libraries Press [1969] vi, 175 p. 23 cm. (Essay index reprint series) Reprint of the 1930 ed. Bibliographical footnotes. [BR100.H58 1969] 69-17577
1. Christianity—Philosophy. I. Title.

HODGSON, Leonard, 1889- 201
For faith and freedom. New York, Scribner, 1956-57. 2v: 23cm. (Gifford lectures, 1955-1957) [BR100.H582] 57-13540
1. Christianity—Philosophy. 2. Theology, Doctrinal. I. Title.

HOULT, Thomas Ford. 201
The sociology of religion. New York, Dryden Press [1958] 436p. 22cm. (The Dryden Press sociology publications) Includes bibliography. [BL60.H64] 58-7384
1. Religion and sociology. I. Title.

HOUSELANDER, Frances Caryll. 201
Guilt. New York, Sheed & Ward, 1951. 279 p. illus. 22 cm. [BL53.H63] 51-13263
1. Guilt. 2. Psychology, Pathological. 3. Psychology, Religious. I. Title.

HOWARD, Thomas. 201
An antique drum; the world as image. [1st ed.] Philadelphia, Lippincott [1969] 157 p. 22 cm. [BR1725.H69A298] 72-86079 5.95
I. Title.

HUME, David, 1711-1776. 201
Hume on religion. Ed., introd. by Richard Wollheim. Cleveland, World [1964, c.1963] 287p. 18cm. (Meridian bks., M172) 64-10002 1.95 pap.,
1. Religion—Philosophy—Collected works. I. Title. II. Title: On religion.

HUME, David, 1711-1776. 201
The natural history of religion. Edited with an introd. by H. E. Root. Stanford, Calif., Stanford University Press [1957] 76p. 23cm. (A Library of modern religious thought) 'The text followed ... is that established by T. H. Green and T. H. Grose and printed in their critical edition of Hume's Essays, moral, political, and literary (London: Longmans, 1875)' [BL51] 57-9373
1. Religion—Philosophy. I. Title. II. Series.

HUME, David, 1711-1776. 201
The natural history of religion. Edited with an introd. by H. E. Root. Stanford, Calif., Stanford University Press [1957] 76p. 23cm. (A Library of modern religious thought) 'The text followed ... is that established by T. H. Green and T. H. Grose and printed in their critical edition of Hume's Essays. moral. political, and literary (London: Longmans, 1875)' [BL51] 57-9373
1. Religion—Philosophy. I. Title. II. Series.

HUTCHISON, John Alexander, 201
1912-
Faith, reason, and existence; an introduction to contemporary philosophy of religion. New York, Oxford University Press, 1956. 306 p. 21 cm. [BL51.H974] 56-5670
1. Religion—Philosophy. 2. Faith and reason. I. Title.

HUXLEY, Aldous Leonard, 1894- 201
The perennial philosophy. Cleveland, World [1962, c.1944, 1945] 311p. 19cm. (Meridian bks., M144) 62-18675 1.55 pap.,
1. Religion—Philosophy. 2. Philosophy and religion. I. Title.

HUXLEY, Aldous Leonard, 1894- 201
1963.
The perennial philosophy. Freeport, N.Y., Books for Libraries Press [1972, c1945] xi, 312 p. 23 cm. (Essay index reprint series) Bibliography: p. 303-306. [BL51.H98 1972] 76-167362 ISBN 0-8369-2773-7
1. Religion—Philosophy. 2. Philosophy and religion. I. Title.

IINO, Norimoto, 1908- 201
A seven-hued rainbow. New York, Philosophical Library [1967] 127 p. 22 cm. Bibliography: p. 126-127. [BL51.I58] 66-26966
1. Philosophy and religion. 2. Philosophy, Japanese. 3. Christianity—Japan. I. Title.

INGE, William Ralph, 1860- 201
1954.
The church in the world; collected essays. Freeport, N.Y., Books for Libraries Press [1969] xi, 275 p. 23 cm. (Essay index reprint series) Reprint of the 1927 ed. Contents.Contents.—The condition of the Church of England.—The crisis of Roman Catholicism.—The Quakers.—Hellenism in Christianity.—Science and theology.—Science and ultimate truth.—Faith and reason.—The training of the reason. Bibliographical footnotes. [BR85.I6 1969] 68-57324
1. Religion—Addresses, essays, lectures. I. Title.

INGRAM, Kenneth, 1882- 201
Christianity, communism and society. London, New York, Rider [1951] 216p. 19cm. [BL48.I5] 53-20
1. Religion. 2. Christianity—Essence, genius, nature. 3. Sociology, Christian. I. Title.

INTELLECTUAL honesty and 201
religious commitment [by] Henry D. Aiken [and others] Edited and with an introd. by Arthur J. Bellinzoni, Jr. and Thomas V. Litzenburg, Jr. Philadelphia, Fortress Press [1969] xii, 84 p. 20 cm. "This volume has grown out of a symposium ... sponsored by the Departments of Philosophy and Religion at Wells College, February 21-22, 1964." [BL237.I5] 71-83677 1.95
1. Religion. 2. Faith. I. Aiken, Henry David, 1912- II. Bellinzoni, Arthur J., ed. III. Litzenburg, Thomas V., ed.

ISHERWOOD, Margaret. 201
The root of the matter; a study in the connections between religion, psychology, and education. With a foreword by Gerald Heard. New York, Harper [1954] 238p. illus. 21cm. [BL48] 54-8957
1. Religion. I. Title.

JACKSON, Alvin R., 1889- 201
Religious sanity, the philosophy of individual life; an abridgment by A. R. Jackson of the literature of the Great School of Natural Science, addressed to the progressive intelligenceof the age. With a foreword by J. W. Norwood. New York, Exposition Press [1951] 94 p. 22 cm. "A condensation of the Harmonic series of books (eight in all), andother literature of natural science and the philosophy of individual life." [BL50.J3] 51-10212
1. Religion. I. Great School of Natural Science, Hollywood, Calif. II. Title.

JAMES, Henry, 1811-1882. 201
The literary remains of Henry James. With an introd. by William James. Upper Saddle River, N.J., Literature House [1970] 471 p. port. 23 cm. Reprint of the 1884 ed. Contents.Contents.—Introduction.—Immortal life: an autobiographical sketch.—Spiritual creation.—Some personal recollections of Carlyle.—Bibliography (p. [469]-471) [B921.J2 1970] 73-104495
I. James, William, 1842-1910, ed.

JAMES, William, 1842-1910. 201
The varieties of religious experience; a study in human nature. Foreword by Jacques Barzun. [New York] New American Library [1958] 406p. 19cm. (Gifford lectures, 1901-02) A Mentor book, MD221. 'Delivered at Edinburgh.' Bibliographical footnotes. [BR110.J3 1958] 58-1697
1. Religion. 2. Philosophy and religion. 3. Conversion. 4. Psychology. Religious. I. Title. II. Series.

JAMES, William, 1842-1910. 201
The varieties of religious experience; a study in human nature. Enl. ed., with appendices and introd. by Joseph Ratner. New Hyde Park, N. Y., University Books [1963] xiii, 626 p. 24 cm. (Gifford lectures on natural religion, 1901-02) Bibliographical footnotes. [BR110.J3 1963] 63-14505
1. Religion. 2. Philosophy and religion. 3. Conversion. 4. Psychology, Religious. I. Title. II. Series: Gifford lectures, 1901-02

JASPERS, Karl, 1883- 201
Myth and Christianity; an inquiry into the possibility of religion without myth, by Karl Jaspers and Rudolf Bultmann. New York, Noonday Press [1958] 116 p. 21 cm. Translation of Die Frage der Entmythologisierung. [BL51.J353] 58-8951
1. Bultmann, Rudolf Karl, 1884- 2. Demythologization. I. Bultmann, Rudolf Karl, 1884- II. Title.

JOAD, Cyril Edwin Mitchinson, 201
1891-1953.
The recovery of belief : a restatement of Christian philosophy / by C. E. M. Joad. Westport, Conn. : Greenwood Press, 1976. p. cm. Reprint of the 1952 ed. published by Faber and Faber, London. Includes index. [BR100.J6 1976] 76-26097 ISBN 0-8371-9022-3 lib.bdg. : 16.00
1. Christianity—Philosophy. I. Title.

JOHNSON, William Alexander 201
On religion: a study of theological method in Schleiermacher and Nygren. Leiden, E. J. Brill [New York, Humanities, 1966, c.1964] x, 167p. 25cm. Bibl. [BR118.J6] 65-4258 5.00
1. Schleiermacher, Friedrich Ernst Daniel, 1768-1834. 2. Nygren, Anders, Bp., 1890- 3. Theology — Methodology. I. Title.

JONES, David Gareth. 201
Teilhard de Chardin: an analysis and assessment [by] D. Gareth Jones. Grand Rapids, Eerdmans [1970, c1969] 72 p. 21 cm. Includes bibliographical references. [B2430.T374J6 1970] 70-127933 1.25
1. Teilhard de Chardin, Pierre.

JONES, Rufus Matthew, 1863- 201
1948, ed.
Religious foundations, by A. Clutton-Brock [and others] Edited by Rufus M. Jones. Freeport, N.Y., Books for Libraries Press [1973] p. (Essay index reprint series) Reprint of the 1923 ed. [BR50.J6 1973] 73-1195 ISBN 0-518-10057-X
1. Theology—Addresses, essays, lectures. I. Clutton-Brock, Arthur, 1868-1924. II. Title.

JORDAN, Rudolf, 1905- 201
Bridges to the unknown, an essay on religion. New York, F. Fell [1957] 109p. 23cm. [BL51.J82 1957] 57-7883
1. Religion—Philosophy. I. Title.

JORDAN, Rudolf, 1905- 201
Bridges to the unknown, an essay on religion. New York, Fell [1966, c.1957] 109p. 21cm. (Concept bk. 101) [BL51.J82] 57-7883 1.95 pap.,
1. Religion — Philosophy. I. Title.

JUNG, Carl Gustav 201
Psychology and religion. New Haven, [Conn.,] Yale University Press [1960, c.1938] 131 p. Bibl. notes: p.[115]-131. 21 cm. (Yale paperbound Y-14) pap., .90
1. Psychology, Religious. 2. Symbolism. I. Title.

JUNG, Carl Gustav, 1875- 201
Answer to Job. Translated by R. F. C. Hull. New York, Meridian Books [1960, c1954] 223p. 19cm. (Meridian books, M86) Includes bibliography. [BL51.J853 1960] 60-6738
1. Religion—Philosophy. 2. Bible. O. T. Job—Criticism, interpretation, etc. I. Title.

JUNG, Carl Gustav, 1875-1961. 201
Answer to Job [by] C. G. Jung [2d ed.] [Princeton] Princeton Univ. Pr. [1973, c.1969] xv, 121 p. 22 cm. (Bollingen paperbacks; Bollingen series, XX) Includes bibliography. [BL51.J853 1969] ISBN 0-691-01785-9 pap., 2.95
1. Bible. O.T. Job—Criticism, interpretation, etc. 2. Religion—Philosophy. I. Title.
L.C. card no. for the 1960 ed.: 60-6738.

KAUFMANN, Walter 201
Critique of religion and philosophy. Garden City, N.Y., Doubleday 453p. (Anchor bk. A252) Bibl. 1.45 pap.,
1. Religion. 2. Philosophy and religion. I. Title.

KAUFMANN, Walter Arnold. 201
Critique of religion and philosophy. [1st ed.] New York, Harper [1958] 325 p. 22 cm. Includes bibliography. [BL48.K38] 58-7097
1. Religion. 2. Philosophy and religion. I. Title.

KAUFMANN, Walter Arnold 201
The faith of a heretic. Garden City, N.Y., Doubleday, 1961 [c.1959-1961] 432p. Bibl. 61-9523 4.95
1. Philosophy and religion. I. Title.

KAUFMANN, Walter Arnold 201
The faith of a heretic. Garden City, N.Y., Doubleday [1963, c.1959-1961] 414p. 18cm. (Anchor bk., A336) Bibl. 1.45 pap.,
1. Philosophy and religion. I. Title.

KIERKEGAARD, Soren Aabye, 201
1813-1855.
Armed neutrality, and An open letter; with relevant selections from his journals and papers. Edited and translated with an introd. by Howard V. Hong and Edna H. Hong. Background essay and commentary by Gregor Malantschuk. Bloomington, Indiana University Press [1968] 179 p. 22 cm. $6.95 Armed neutrality is a translation of his Den bevaebnede neutralitet. An open letter is a transiation of his Foranledigt ved en yttring af Dr. Rudelbach mig betraeffend, published in Faedrelandet, Jan. 31, 1851. Includes bibliographical references. "Kierkegaard's works in English translation": p. 155-158. [BR125.K483] 68-14606
1. Christianity—19th cent.—Addresses, essays, lectures. I. Kierkegaard, Soren Aabye. 1813-1855. An open letter. II. Hong, Howard Vincent, 1912- ed. III. Hong, Edna (Hatlestad) 1913- ed. IV. Malantschuk, Gregor. V. Title. VI. Title: An open letter.

KIERKEGAARD, Soren Aabye, 201
1813-1855.
Armed neutrality, and An open letter; with relevant selections from his journals and papers. Edited and translated with an introd. by Howard V. Hong and Edna H. Hong. Background essay and commentary by Gregor Malantschuk. Bloomington, Indiana University Press [1968] 179 p. 22 cm. Armed neutrality is a translation of his Den bevaebnede neutralitet. An open letter is a translation of his Foranledigt ved en yttring af Dr.

Rudelbach mig betraeffend, published in Faedrelandet, Jan. 31, 1851. Includes bibliographical references. [BR125.K483] 68-14606 6.95
1. Christianity—19th century—Addresses, essays, lectures. I. Hong, Howard Vincent, 1912- ed. II. Hong, Edna (Hatlestad) 1913- ed. III. Malantschuk, Gregor. IV. Kierkegaard, Soren Aabye, 1813-1855. An open letter. 1968. V. Title. VI. Title: An open letter.

KIERKEGAARD, Soren Aabye, 1813-1855. 201
The difficulty of being Christian. Texts edited and introduced by Jacques Colette. English version by Ralph M. McInerny and Leo Turcotte. Notre Dame, University of Notre Dame Press [1968] xx, 311 p. 21 cm. Translation of La difficulte d'etre chretien. Bibliography: p. 5-9. [BX4827.K5A253] 68-17063
1. Kierkegaard, Soren Aabye, 1813-1855. I. Colette, Jacques, ed. II. Title.

KIERKEGAARD, Soren Aabye, 1813-1855. 201
The difficulty of being Christian. Texts edited and introduced by Jacques Colette. English version by Ralph M. McInerny and Leo Turcotte. Notre Dame, University of Notre Dame Press [1968] xx, 311 p. 21 cm. Translation of La difficulte d'etre chretien. Bibliography: p. 5-9. [BX4827.K5A253] 68-17063
1. Kierkegaard, Soren Aabye, 1813-1855. I. Colette, Jacques, ed. II. Title.

KIERKEGAARD, Soren Aabye, 1813-1855 201
Philosophical fragments; or. A fragment of philosophy, by Johannes Climacus [pseud.] . . . Responsible for publication: S. Kierkegaard. Orig. tr. introd. by David F. Swenson. New introd. and commentary by Niels Thulstrup. Tr. rev. and commentary tr. by Howard V. Hong. [2d ed.] Princeton, N. J., Princeton [1967,c.1962] xcvii, 260p. 21cm. [BL51.K487 1962] 62-7408 2.95 pap.,
1. Religion—Philosophy. I. Title.

KIERKEGAARD, Soren Aabye 1813-1855. 201
Philosophical fragments; or, A fragment of philosophy, by Johannes Climacus [pseud.] ... Responsible for publication: S. Kierkegaard. Originally translated and introduced by David F. Swenson. New introd. and commentary by Niels Thulstrup. Translation rev. and commentary translated by Howard V. Hong. [2d ed.] Princeton, N.J., Princeton University Press, 1962. xcvii, 260 p. 23 cm. [BL51.K487 1962] 62-7408
1. Religion—Philosophy.

KIERKEGAARD, Soren Aabye, 1813-1855. 201
The witness of Kierkegaard, selected writings on how to become a Christian. Edited by Carl Michalson. New York, Association Press [c.1960] 127p. Bibl.: p.[15]-17. 16cm. (An Association Press reflection book) 60-12724 .50 pap.,
1. Christianity—Philosophy. I. Title.

KIMPEL, Benjamin Franklin. 201
Language and religion; a semantic preface to a philosophy of religion. New York, Philosophical Library [1957] 153p. 22cm. [BL51.K497] 57-2538
1. Religion—Philosophy. 2. Semantics (Philosophy) I. Title.

KIMPEL, Benjamin Franklin. 201
Religious faith, language, and knowledge; a philosophical preface to theology. New York, Philosophical Library [1952] 162 p. 22 cm. [BT50.K5] 52-11098
1. Christianity—Philosophy. 2. Apologetics—20th cent. I. Title.

KNOX, John, 1900- 201
Myth and truth; an essay on the language of faith. Charlottesville, Univ. Pr. of Va. [1964] vii, 87p. 21cm. (Richard lects., Univ. of Va., 1963-64] Bibl. 64-25858 2.50
1. Myth. I. Title. II. Series.

KNUDSEN, Harold F. 201
To know or not to be; an arraignment of the religiously oriented attitude, by Harold F. Knudsen. New York, William-Frederick Pr., 1966. 120p. 22cm. [BV4509.5.K58] 65-28153 2.50 pap.,
1. Religiousness. I. Title.

KOENKER, Ernest Benjamin. 201
Great dialecticians in modern Christian thought [by] Ernest B. Koenker. Minneapolis, Minn., Augsburg Pub. House [1971] 158 p. 23 cm. Contents.Contents.—Ancient and medieval dialecticians: the lengthening shadow of Plato.—Traveller on the royal way: Martin Luther on simul justus et peccator.—Musician in the concert of God's joy: Jacob Boehme on ground and unground.—Prodigy between finite and infinite: Pascal's dialectic of grandeur and misery.—Thinker of the thoughts of God: Hegel and the dialectic of movement.—Venturer at the brinks: Kierkegaard and the dialectic of the suffering self.—Walker on the narrow ridge: Karl Barth and the dialectic of the human and divine.—Bridge-builder beyond the boundaries: Tillich's dialectic of estrangement and reconciliation.—Wanderer in the forest: Heidegger on the being of beings.—Man suspended in mid-air: Rudolph Bultmann on the believer as free for the future.—Struggler under the twofold verdict of God: Werner Elert and the dialectic of law and gospel.—Epilog.—Selected bibliography (p. 159) [B809.7.K56] 76-135234 ISBN 0-8066-1115-4 5.95
1. Dialectic—History. 2. Christianity—Philosophy. I. Title.

KRING, Walter Donald. 201
Religion is the search for meaning. Boston, Starr King Press [1955] 63p. 24cm. [BL50.K7] 55-4547
1. Religion. I. Title.

KRONER, Richard 201
Speculation and revelation in the age of Christian philosophy. Philadelphia, Westminster Press [c.1959] 269p. Includes bibliography. 24cm. (His Speculation and revelation in the history of philosophy) 59-9947 6.00
1. Theology, Doctrinal—Hist. 2. Philosophy—Hist. I. Title.

KRONER, Richard, 1884- 201
Speculation and revelation in the age of Christian philosophy. Philadelphia, Westminster Press [1959] 269p. 24cm. (His Speculation and revelation in the history of philosophy) Includes bibliography. [BT23.K7] 59-9947
1. Theology, Doctrinal— Hist. 2. Philosophy—Hist. I. Title.

KUITERT, Harminus Martinus. 201
The reality of faith; a way between Protestant orthodoxy and existentialist theology, by H. M. Kuitert. Translated by Lewis B. Smedes. Grand Rapids, Mich., W. B. Eerdmans Pub. Co. [1968] 213 p. 23 cm. Translation of De realiteit van het geloof. Bibliographical footnotes. [BT40.K813] 68-12788
1. Christianity—Philosophy. 2. Theology, Doctrinal—History—20th century. 3. History (Theology) 4. Existentialism. I. Title.

LATOURELLE, Rene. 201
Theology: science of salvation. Translated by Mary Dominic. Staten Island, N.Y., Alba House [1969] xii, 276 p. 22 cm. Translation of Theologie, science du salut. Includes bibliographies. [BR118.L313] 79-94697 5.95
1. Theology. I. Title.

LAWLER, Justus George. 201
The range of commitment; essays of a conservative liberal. Milwaukee, Bruce Pub. Co. [1969] xi, 202 p. 22 cm. Contents.Contents.—Theology and the uses of history.—The bishops as teachers.—Priests in the world.—Charles Davis: the glamour of dissent.—Contraception and the natural law.—Antisemitism and theological arrogance.—Marxism as propaedeutic.—In defense of the Catholic university.—Aid to Catholic schools.—Toward a theology of animals.—The future of belief debate.—Diction as morality.—Matter ecclesia. Bibliographical footnotes. [BX891.L3] 68-55280 6.50
1. Catholic Church—Addresses, essays, lectures. I. Title.

LEEUW, Gerardus van der, 1890- 201
Religion in essense and manifestation, 2. v. Tr. [from German] by J. E. Turner. With appendices to the Torch-bk. ed. incorporating the additions of the 2d German ed. by Hans H. Penner. New York, Harper [c.1963] 2v. 714p. 21cm. (Harper torchbks., Cloister lib., TB100-101) Bibl. 1.95 pap., ea.,
1. Religion—Philosophy. 2. Phenomenology. I. Turner, John Evans, tr. II. Title.

LEEUW, Gerardus van der, 1890-1950. 201
Religion in essence and manifestation. Translated by J. E. Turner, with appendices to the Torchbook ed. incorporating the additions of the 2d German ed. by Hans H. Penner. New York, Harper & Row [1963] 2 v. 21 cm. (Harper torchbooks. The Cloister library) Translation of Phanomenologie der Religion. [BL51.L456] 63-1870
1. Religion — Philosophy. 2. Phenomenology. I. Title.

LEVI, Anthony. 201
Religion in practice, an outline of Christian religious teaching in the light of the religious relevance of humane standards of conduct. London, Toronto [etc.] Oxford U. P., 1966. xii, 206 p. 20 1/2 cm. 30/- (B 66-18643) [BR121.2.L4 1966a] 66-76546
1. Christianity — Essence, genius, nature. I. Title.

LEWIS, Clive Staples. 201
C.S. Lewis : five best books in one volume. Grand Rapids : Baker Book House, 1976c1969. vii, 520p. ; 18 cm. First published 1969 by Iverson Associates. Title on spine: The best of C.S. Lewis. [BR83.L48] ISBN 0-913686-02-6 pbk. : 3.95
I. Title.
Contents omitted. L.C. card no. for original ed.72-93142

LEWIS, Clive Staples, 1898-1963. 201
C. S. Lewis; five best books in one volume. [Christianity today ed.] New York, Iversen Associates, 1969. vii, 520 p. 22 cm. On spine: The best of C. S. Lewis. Contents.Contents.—The Screwtape letters.—The great divorce.—Miracles.—The case for Christianity.—Christian behaviour. [BR83.L48] 72-93142
1. Church of England—Collected works. 2. Theology—Collected works—20th century. I. Title: The best of C. S. Lewis.

LEWIS, Clive Staples, 1898-1963. 201
God in the dock; essays on theology and ethics, by C. S. Lewis. Edited by Walter Hooper. Grand Rapids, Eerdmans [1970] 346 p. 23 cm. Includes bibliographical references. [BR85.L484] 70-129851 6.95
1. Theology—Addresses, essays, lectures. I. Title.

LEWIS, Hywel David 201
Our experience of God. New York, Macmillan [1960] 301p. (bibl. footnotes) 23cm. (The Muir head library of philosophy) 60-600 5.25
1. Christianity—Philosophy. 2. Apologetics—20th cent. I. Title.

LEWIS, Hywel David 201
Philosophy of religion, by H. D. Lewis. London, English Univ. Pr. Imprint covered by label: New York, Barnes ; Noble [1965] x, 338p. 19cm. (Teach yourself bks.) Bibl. [BL51.L468] 66-8804 2.50 bds.,
1. Religion — Philosophy. I. Title.
Available from Barnes & Noble, New York.

LIGON, Ernest M., 1897- 201
The psychology of Christian personality. New York, Macmillan, 1961 [c.1935] 393p. (Macmillan paper. back, 76) Bibl. 1.95 pap.,
1. Sermon on the Mount. 2. Personality. 3. Psychology, Religious. I. Title. II. Title: Christian personality

LILJE, Hanns, 1899- 201
Atheism, humanism, and Christianity; today's struggle for the mind of man. Tr. [from German] by Clifford Davis. Minneapolis, Augsburg [c.1964] 77p. 20cm. Bibl. 64-21510 1.75 pap.,
1. Atheism—Addresses, essays, lectures. 2. Humanism—Addreses, essays, lectures. 3. Christianity—20th cent.—Addresses, essays, lectures. I. Title.

LILJE, Hanns, Bp., 1899- 201
Atheism, humanism, and Christianity; today's struggle for the mind of man. Translated by Clifford Davis. Minneapolis, Augsbury Pub. House [1964] 77 p. 20 cm. "Notes, citations, documentations": p. 57-77. [BR100.L513] 64-21510
1. Atheism — Addresses, essays, lectures. 2. Humanism — Addresses, essays, lectures. 3. Christianity — 20th cent. — Addresses, essays, lectures. I. Title.

LING, Trevor Oswald. 201
Prophetic religion [by] Trevor Ling. London, Medlbourne [etc.] Macmillan New York, St. Martin's P., 1966. xii, 179 p. 19 1/2 cm. (B 66-15896) Bibliography: p. 172-174. [BT60.L5] 66-19251
1. Christianity-Essence, genius, nature. I. Title.

LING, Trevor Oswald 201
Prophetic religion [by] Trevor Ling London, Melbourne [etc.] Macmillan; New York, St. Martin's Pr., 1966. xii, 179p. 20cm. Bibl. [BT60.L5 1966] 66-19251 5.00 bds.,
1. Christianity — Essence, genius, nature. I. Title.

LIVINGSTON, James C., 1930- 201
Modern Christian thought: from the Enlightenment to Vatican II [by] James C. Livingston. New York, Macmillan [1971] xvi, 523 p. ports. 24 cm. Includes bibliographies. [BT28.L55] 76-121675
1. Theology, Doctrinal—History—Modern period, 1500- I. Title.

LONERGAN, Bernard J. F. 201
Doctrinal pluralism, by Bernard Lonergan. Milwaukee, Marquette University Press, 1971. 75 p. 19 cm. (The Pere Marquette theology lectures, 1971) Includes bibliographical references. [BT75.2.L58] 70-155364 ISBN 0-87462-220-4
1. Theology, Doctrinal. 2. Pluralism. I. Title. II. Series.

LUBAC, Henri de, 1896- 201
The mystery of the supernatural. Translated by Rosemary Sheed. [New York] Herder and Herder [1967] xiii, 321 p. 23 cm. Bibliographical footnotes. [BT745.L813] 68-1423
1. Supernatural (Theology) I. Title.

LUBAC, Henri de, 1896- 201
The mystery of the supernatural. Translated by Rosemary Sheed. [New York] Herder and Herder [1967] xiii, 321 p. 23 cm. Bibliographical footnotes. [BT745.L813 1967] 68-1423
1. Supernatural (Theology) I. Title.

LUBAC, Henri de, 1896- 201
Teilhard explained. Translated by Anthony Buono. New York, Paulist Press [1968] xi, 115 p. 19 cm. (Deus books) Translation of Teilhard, missionaire et apologiste. "List of Teilhard's works": p. 91-94. Bibliographical references included in "Notes" (p. 95-115) [B2430.T374L833] 68-16677
1. Teilhard de Chardin, Pierre. I. Title.

LUTHERAN Church in America. Task Group for Long-Range Planning. 201
Theology; an assessment of current trends; report. Edward W. Uthe, director. Philadelphia, Fortress Press [1968] ix, 164 p. 21 cm. Bibliography: p. 159-164. [BT28.L88] 68-55757 2.25
1. Theology, Doctrinal—History—20th century. I. Uthe, Edward W. II. Title.

LYNCH, Lawrence E., 1915- 201
A Christian philosophy [by] Lawrence E. Lynch. New York, Scribners [1968] xi, 277p. 23cm. Based on radio lects, given by the author in 1962 as pt. of the Canadian Broadcasting Corp. ser., Univ. of the Air, and pub. in 1963 under title: Christian philosophy. Bibl. refs. [BR100.L93 1968] 67-21341 3.95
1. Thomas Aquinas, Saint, 1225?- 1274—Philosophy. 2. Christianity—Philosophy. I. Title.

MCCLENDON, James William 201
Pacemakers of Christian thought. Nashville, Broadman [c.1962] 68p. 20cm. (Broadman starbk.) Bibl. 62-9198 1.00 pap.,
1. Theology—20th cent. 2. Theologians. I. Title.

MACGREGOR, Geddes. 201
Introduction to religious philosophy. Boston, Houghton Mifflin [1959] 366p. 22cm. Includes bibliography. [BL51.M214] 59-3231
1. Religion—Philosophy. I. Title.

MACGREGOR, Geddes [John Geddes MacGregor] 201
Introduction to religious philosophy. Boston, Houghton Mifflin [c.1959] 366 p. (Includes bibliography) 22 cm. 59-3231 6.75
1. Religion—Philosophy. I. Title.

MCINTYRE, John, 1916- 201
The Christian doctrine of history. Grand Rapids, W. B. Eerdmans Pub. Co. [1957] 119p. 21cm. Includes bibliography. [BR115.H5M22] 59-16166
1. History—Philosophy. 2. Christianity—Philosophy. I. Title.

MCPHERSON, Thomas 201
The philosophy of religion. Princeton, N. J., Van Nostrand [c.1965] ix, 207p. 20cm. Bibl. [BL51.M246] 65-20160 5.95; 2.95 pap.,
1. Religion — Philosophy. I. Title.

MACQUARRIE, John, comp. 201
Contemporary religious thinkers from idealist metaphysicians to existential theologians, selected and introduced by John Macquarrie. [1st ed.] New York, Harper & Row [1968] xii, 285 p. 21 cm. (Harper forum books) [BR50.M2] 68-11747
1. Theology—Collections. 2. Religion—Philosophy—Collections. I. Title.

MAERTENS, Thierry, 1921- 201
Bible themes; a source book. Notre Dame, Ind., Fides [1970? c1964] 2 v. 21 cm. Includes bibliographical references. [BS543.A1M232] 71-111267
1. Bible—Theology—Handbooks, manuals, etc. I. Title.

MARNEY, Carlyle, 1916- 201
Faith in conflict. New York, Abingdon Press [1957] 158p. illus. 21cm. [BR100.M28] 57-6119
1. Christianity—Philosophy. I. Title.

MARTIN, Charles Burton. 201
Religious belief. Ithaca, N. Y., Cornell University Press [1959] 168p. 23cm.

(Contemporary philosophy) Includes bibliography. [BL51.M353] 59-4815
1. Religion—Philosophy. I. Title.

MARX, Karl, 1818-1883. 201
On religion [by] Karl Marx and Friedrich Engels. Introd. by Reinhold Niebuhr. New York, Schocken Books [1964] 382 p. 21 cm. (Schocken paperbacks) "SB67." Bibliographical references included in "Notes" (p. [348]-359) [BL2775.M3983 1964] 64-15219
1. Religion. I. Engels, Friedrich, 1820-1895. II. Title.

MAURER, Herrymon, 1914- 201
What can I know? The prophetic answer. [1st ed.] New York, Harper [1953] 253p. 22cm. [BL51.M475] 53-5442
1. Religion—Philosophy. I. Title.

MEHL, Roger. 201
The condition of the Christian philosopher. Translated by Eva Kushner. Philadelphia, Fortress Press [1963] 221 p. 23 cm. Bibliography: p.[213]-217 [BT40.M423] 64-12991
1. Christianity — Philosophy. I. Title.

MEHL, Roger 201
The condition of the Christian philosopher. Tr. by Eva Kushner. Philadelphia, Fortress [c.1963] 221p. 23cm. Bibl. 64-12991 4.50
1. Christianity—Philosophy. I. Title.

MEILACH, Michael D., comp. 201
There shall be one Christ, edited by Michael D. Meilach. Saint Bonaventure, N.Y., Franciscan Institute, Saint Bonaventure University, 1968. viii, 85 p. 23 cm. Cover has subtitle: A collection of essays on Teilhard de Chardin. Bibliographical footnotes. [B2430.T374M38] 68-7926 1.50
1. Teilhard de Chardin, Pierre. I. Title.

METZ, Johannes B., 1928- 201
The Church and the world. New York, Paulist Press [1965] viii, 184 p. 24 cm. (Concilium theology in the age of renewal: Fundamental theology, v. 6) Contents.Preface, by J. B. Metz. -- Articles: The church in the modern world, by G. Philips; translated by A. Bourneuf. Meeting God in today's world, by H. Urs von Balthasar; translated by J. F. McCue. Christianity and ideology, by K. Rahner; translated by B. E. Scott. Unbelief as a theological problem, by J. B. Metz; translated by T. Rattler. Human experience as the starting point of fundamental theology, by H. Bouillard; translated by E. O'Gorman. Philosophy, handmaid of theology? by M. Nedoncelle; translated by R. Dowd. -- Bibliographical survey: The problem of ideology and Christian belief, by H. R. Schlette; translated by T. Rattler. -- DO-C: Documentation belief, by H. R. Schlette; Translated by T. Rattler. -- DO-C: Documentation concilium: The Reformed churches, by J. F. Lescrauwaet; translated by T. L. Westow. -- Chronicle of the living church: The World Council of Churches; report of the General Secretary to the Central Committee (Enugu, Nigeria, January 1965) The "New situation" between Rome and the Reformed churches, translated by T. L. Westow. The international foundation of Pro Mundi Vita, translated by T. L. Westow. Bibliographical footnotes. [BV603.C45] 65-24899
1. Church — Addresses, essays, lectures. I. Title. II. Series. III. Series: Concilium theology in the age of renewal, v. 6

MICHALSON, Carl. 201
The hinge of history; an existential approach to the Christian faith. New York, Scribner [1959] 256p. 22cm. Includes bibliography. [BR115.H5M48] 59-11659
1. History—Philosophy. 2. Christianity—Philosophy. 3. Existentialism. I. Title.

MILLER, Oscar W 201
Thunder on the left: some religio-philosophical essays. New York, Philosophical Library [1959] 95p. 23cm. Includes bibliography. [BL51.M63] 59-16366
1. Religion—Philosophy—Addresses, essays, lectures. I. Title.

MILLER, Samuel Howard, 1900- 201
The great realities. [1st ed.] New York, Harper [1955] 181p. 22cm. [BR100.M57] 55-9687
1. Christianity—Philosophy. I. Title.

MOORE, Edward Le Roy. 201
The Robinson from Mars papers; dialogues and lectures on truth and reality. [1st ed.] New York, Exposition Press [1956- v. 21cm. [BL50.M6] 56-12375
1. Religion. I. Title.

MORGAN, Everett J., comp. 201
Christian witness in the secular city. Compiled and edited by Everett J. Morgan. Chicago, Loyola University Press [1970] 12, 352 p. 23 cm. Includes bibliographical references. [BR50.M64] 75-133951
1. Theology—Addresses, essays, lectures. I. Title.

MORGAN, Thomas, d.1743. 201
The moral philosopher, 1737 / Thomas Morgan. New York : Garland Pub., 1977. xii, 450 p. ; 19 cm. (British philosophers and theologians of the 17th & 18th centuries) Includes index. Reprint of the 1737 ed. printed for the author, London. [BR100.M683 1977] 75-11239 ISBN 0-8240-1791-9 : 25.00
1. Christianity—Philosophy. 2. Christian ethics. 3. Deism. I. Title. II. Series.

MORGAN, William Sacheus, 201
1865-
The philosphy of religion; a consideration of the more profound aspects of religious thought. New York, Philosophical Library [1950] xv, 413 p. 23 cm. Bibliographical references included in "Notes" (p. 399-408) [BL51.M74] 50-9827
1. Religion — Philosophy. I. Title.

MORRIS, Colin M. 201
Include me out! Confessions of an ecclesiastical coward [by] Colin Morris. Nashville, Abingdon Press [1968] 99 p. 19 cm. [BR121.2.M65] 69-12012
1. Christianity—20th century. I. Title.

MORRIS, George Sylvester, 201
1840-1889.
Philosophy and Christianity : a series of lectures delivered in New York, in 1883, on the Ely Foundation of the Union Theological Seminary / George S. Morris. Reprint ed., with a new introd. Hicksville, N.Y. : Regina Press, 1975 [c1883] 4, xiv, 315 p. ; 23 cm. (The Rise of modern religious ideas in America) (Reprint of the ed. published by R. Carter, New York, in series: The Elias P. Ely lectures on the evidences of Christianity.) Contents.Contents.—Religion and intelligence.—The philosophic theory of knowledge.—The absolute object of intelligence.—The Biblical theory of knowledge.—Biblical ontology: the absolute.—Biblical ontology: the world.—Biblical ontology: man.—Comparative philosophic content of Christianity. Includes bibliographical references. [BR100.M7 1975] 74-78379 ISBN 0-88271-016-8
1. Christianity—Philosophy—Addresses, essays, lectures. 2. Knowledge, Theory of—Addresses, essays, lectures. 3. Ontology—Addresses, essays, lectures. I. Title. II. Series: The Elias P. Ely lectures on the evidences of Christianity.

MORRIS, Leon. 201
The abolition of religion; a study in religionless Christianity. [1st ed.] Chicago, Inter-varsity Press [1964] iii p. 18 cm. (Christian books for the modern world) Bibliographical footnotes. [BT55.R63M6] 64-54622
1. Christianity — 20th cent. I. Robinson, John Arthur Thomas, Bp., 1919- Honest to God. II. Title.

MORRIS, Leon 201
The abolition of religion; a study in religionless Christianity. Chicago, Inter-Varsity [c.1964] 111p. 18cm. (Christian bks. for the mod. world) Bibl. 64-54622 1.25 pap.,
1. Robinson, John Arthur Thomas, Bp., 1919- Honest to God. 2. Christianity—20th cent. I. Title.

MOURANT, John Arthur, 1903- 201
ed.
Readings in the philosophy of religion. New York, Crowell, 1954. 500p. 22cm. [BL51.M75] 54-7581
1. Religion—Philosophy. I. Title.

MURRAY, Albert Victor, 1890- 201
Personal experience and the historic faith; an essay. [New ed.] New York, Harper [1955] 303p. 22cm. [BR110.M8 1955] 55-4124
1. Experience (Religion) I. Title.

MYERS, Ernest R 201
Modern problems and creation; an analysis of the Bible philosophy of the cycles of life. [1st ed.] New York, Exposition Press [1959] 211p. 21cm. [BS652.M9] 59-16416
1. Creation. I. Title.

THE Nature of religious 201
experience; essays in honor of Douglas Clyde Macintosh, by Eugene Garrett Bewkes [and others] Freeport, N.Y., Books for Libraries Press [1971, c1937] xiv, 244 p. port. 23 cm. (Essay index reprint series) Contents.Contents.—Common sense realism, by E. G. Bewkes.—Theology and religious experience, by V. Ferm.—A reasoned faith, by G. F. Thomas.—Can religion become empirical? By J. S. Bixler.—Value theory and theology, by H. R. Niebuhr.—The truth in myths, by R. Niebuhr.—Is subjectivism in value theory compatible with realism and meliorism? By C. Kruse.—The semi-detached knower: a note on radical empiricism, by R. L. Calhoun.—The new scientific and metaphysical basis for epistemological theory, by F. S. C. Northrop.—A psychological approach to reality, by H. Hartshorne.—A definition of religious liberalism, by D. S. Robinson. Includes bibliographical references. [BL51.N32 1971] 78-152202 ISBN 0-8369-2286-7
1. Knowledge, Theory of (Religion) 2. Experience (Religion) 3. Religion—Philosophy. I. Macintosh, Douglas Clyde, 1877-1948. II. Bewkes, Eugene Garrett, 1895-

NEDONCELLE, Maurice [Gustave] 201
Is there a Christian philosophy? Translated from the French by Illtyd Trethowan. New York, Hawthorn Books [c.1960] 154p. (2p. bibl.: bibl. footnotes) 21cm. (The Twentieth century encyclopedia of Catholicism, v. 10, Section 1: Knowledge and faith) 60-8784 2.95 half cloth,
1. Christianity—Philosophy. I. Title.

NEW York University Institute 201
of Philosophy, 4th, 1960.
Religious experience and truth; a symposium, edited by Sidney Hook. [New York] New York University Press, 1961. xiii, 333 p. 21 cm. "Proceedings of the fourth annual New York University Institute of Philosophy ... New York, October 21-22, 1960." Includes bibliographical references. [BL51.N47 1960] 61-15886
1. Philosophy and religion. 2. Symbolism. 3. Faith. 4. Knowledge, Theory of (Religion) I. Hook, Sidney, 1902- ed. II. New York University. III. Title.

NICHOLSON, John Angus. 201
Philosophy of religion. New York, Ronald Press Co. [1950] viii, 419 p. 22 cm. Bibliography: p. 411-413. [BL51.N8] 50-7613
1. Religion — Philosophy. I. Title.

NIEBUHR, Reinhold, 1892- 201
Beyond tragedy; essays on the Christian interpretation of history. New York, Scribners [1961, c.1937] 306p. (Scribner lib., SL38) 1.45 pap.,
1. Christianity—Philosophy. 2. History—Philosophy. I. Title.

NIEBUHR, Reinhold, 1892-1971. 201
Beyond tragedy; essays on the Christian interpretation of history. Freeport, N.Y., Books for Libraries Press [1971, c1937] xi, 306 p. 23 cm. (Essay index reprint series) [BR100.N55 1971] 76-167397 ISBN 0-8369-2437-1
1. Christianity—Philosophy. 2. History—Philosophy. I. Title.

NYGREN, Anders, Bp., 1890- 201
Essence of Christianity; two essays. Translated by Philip S. Watson. Grand Rapids, Mich., Eerdmans [1973, c1960] 128 p. 18 cm. "The two essays ... were originally published in Swedish in 1922 and 1932 under the titles of Det bestaende i kristendomen and Forsoningen en Gudsgarning, respectively." Reprint of the ed. published by the Epworth Press, London. Contents.Contents.—The permanent element in Christianity.—The atonement as a work of God. [BR121.2.N9 1973] 73-10272 1.95 (pbk.)
1. Christianity—Essence, genius, nature. 2. Atonement. 3. God—Love. I. Nygren, Anders, Bp., 1890- Forsoningen en Gudsgarning. English. 1973. II. Title.

OTTO, Rudolf, 1869-1937. 201
The idea of the holy; an inquiry into the non-rational factor in the idea of the divine and its relation to the rational. Translated by John W. Harvey. New York, Oxford University Press, 1958. xix, 232p. 21cm. (A Galaxy book, GB14) Translation of Das Heilige. Bibliographical footnotes. [BL48.O82 1958] 58-776
1. Religion. I. Title.

OTTO, Rudolf, 1869-1937. 201
The idea of the holy : an inquiry into the non-rational factor in the idea of the divine and its relation to the rational / by Rudolf Otto ; translated by John W. Harvey. 2d ed. New York : Oxford University Press, 1950, 1970 printing. xix, 232 p. ; 22 cm. Translation of Das Heilige. Includes bibliographical references and index. [BL48.O82 1970] 75-329632
1. Holy, The. I. Title.

PARSONS, Talcott, 1902- 201
Religious perspectives of college teaching in sociology and social psychology. New Haven, Edward W. Hazen Foundation [1951?] 47 p. 23 cm. [BL60.P3] 52-4258
1. Religion and sociology. I. Title.

PATON, Herbert James, 1887- 201
The modern predicament; a study in the philosophy of religion. Based on Gifford lectures delivered in the University of St. Andrews. London, Allen & Unwin; New York, Macmillan [1955] 405p. 23cm. (The Muirhead library of philosophy) [BL51.P316 1955] 55-4627
1. Religion—Philosophy. I. Title.

PATON, Herbert James, 1887- 201
The modern predicament; a study in the philosophy of religion. New York, Collier [1962, c.1955] 414p. 18cm. (BS146V) 1.50 pap.,
1. Religion—Philosophy. I. Title.

PATTERSON, Robert Leet. 201
An introduction to the philosophy of religion. New York, Holt [1958] 342p. 22cm. Includes bibliography. [BL51.P319] 58-6325
1. Religion—Philosophy. I. Title.

PATTERSON, Robert Leet. 201
Irrationalism and rationalism in religion. Westport, Conn., Greenwood Press [1973, c1954] 155 p. 22 cm. Reprint of the ed. published by Duke University Press, Durham, N.C. [BL51.P32 1973] 73-436 ISBN 0-8371-6769-8 8.75
1. Religion—Philosophy. I. Title.

PATTON, Kenneth Leo, 1911- 201
A religion for one world: art and symbols for a universal religion. Charles R. McCormick, photographer. Boston, Beacon [c.1964] xii, 484p. illus. 24cm. 63-18732 7.50
1. Religions (Proposed, universal, etc.) I. Title.

PAUL, Leslie Allen, 1905- 201
The meaning of human existence. Philadelphia, Lippincott, 1950 [c1949] 258 p. 21 cm. [BR100.P33 1950] 50-5579
1. Christianity—Philosophy. I. Title.

PAUL, Leslie Allen, 1905- 201
The meaning of human existence, by Leslie Paul. Westport, Conn., Greenwood Press [1971, c1949] 258 p. 23 cm. [BR100.P33 1971] 73-148642 ISBN 0-8371-6008-1
1. Christianity—Philosophy. I. Title.

PEGIS, Anton Charles, 1905- 201
Christian philosophy and intellectual freedom. Milwaukee, Bruce Pub. Co. [1960] 89p. 19cm. (The Gabriel Richard lecture, 1955) Includes bibliography. [BR100.P38] 60-15483
1. Christianity—Philosophy. 2. Liberty. I. Title.

PETERS, Eugene Herbert, 1929- 201
The creative advance; an introduction to process philosophy as a context for Christian faith, by Eugene H. Peters. With a comment by Charles Hartshorne. St. Louis, Bethany Press, 1966. 151 p. 20 cm. (The library of contemporary theology) Includes bibliographical references. [BR100.P386] 66-19812
1. Whitehead, Alfred North, 1861-1947. 2. Christianity—Philosophy. I. Title.

PHENIX, Philip Henry, 1915- 201
Intelligible religion. New York, Harper [1954?] 189p. 21cm. [BL48] 54-13475
1. Religion. I. Title.

PHILOSOPHICAL resources for 201
Christian thought, edited and with an introductory essay by Perry LeFevre. Nashville, Abingdon Press [1968] 142 p. 20 cm. "Material was presented originally as the [1966] Alden -Tuthill lectures at Chicago Theological Seminary." Contents.Contents.—Theology and philosophy in the recent past; an introductory essay, by P. LeFevre.—Process philosophy as a resource for Christian thought, by C. Hartshorne.—Phenomenology as resource for Christian thinking, by Q. Lauer.—The two faces of Socrates; language analysis as resource for Christian thought, by F. Ferre.—Existentialism and Christian thought, by J. Macquarrie. Bibliographical footnotes. [BR100.P5] 68-11465
1. Christianity—Philosophy—Addresses, essays, lectures. I. LeFevre, Perry D., ed.

PICARD, Max, 1888- 201
The flight from God. [Translated from the German by Marianne Kuschnitzky and J. M. Cameron] With a note on Max Picard by Gabriel Marcel and an introd. by J. M. Cameron. Chicago, H. Regnery Co., 1951. 185 p. 18 cm. (The Humanist library) [BT165.P513] 52-6245
1. God. 2. Religion — Philosophy. I. Title.

PIET, John H. 201
The road ahead; a theology for the church in mission, by John H. Piet. [Grand Rapids, Mich.] W. B. Eerdmans [1970] 103 p. 22 cm. [BV600.2.P53] 79-107619 1.95
1. Church. I. Title.

POTEAT, Edwin McNeill, 1892- 201
God makes the difference; studies in the faith of nature and the nature of faith. [1st ed.]

New York, Harper [1951] ix, 242 p. 21 cm. [BL51.P62] 51-10343
1. Religion — Philosophy. 2. God. I. Title.

PRATT, Charles Edgar 201
Paganism in Christianity; a new testament for rational believers. New York, Exposition Press [c.1961] 258p. (Exposition-Banner bk.) 5.00
1. Religion—Philosophy and theories. I. Title.

PYLE, Eric H 1918- 201
Introducing Christianity [by] E. H. Pyle [and] S. G. Williamson. [Harmondsworth, Middlesex] Penguin Books [1961] 157p. 18cm. (African series, WA11) Includes bibliography. [BR121.2.P9 1961] 61-66599
1. Christianity—Essence, genius, nature. I. Williamson, Sydney George, 1906- joint author. II. Title.

PYLE, Eric H. 1918- 201
Introducing Christianity [by] E. H. Pyle, S. G. Williamson. PenguinBks. [dist. New York, Atheneum, c.1961] 157p. (African ser., WA11) Bibl. 61-66599 .95 pap.,
1. Christianity—Essence, genius, nature. I. Williamson, Sidney George, 1906- joint author. II. Title.

RADHAKRISHNAN, Sarvepalli, Sir 1888- 201
Recovery of faith. [1st ed.] New York, Harper [1955] 205 p. 20 cm. (World perspectives, v. 4) [BL48.R23] 55-7219
1. Religion. 2. Belief and doubt. I. Title.

*RADHAKRISHNAN, Sarvepalli, Pres. India, 1888- 201
An idealist view of life; being the Hibbert lectures for 1929. New York, Barnes & Noble [1963, c.1932] 352p. 22cm. 4.00
I. Title.

RAHNER, Karl, 1904- 201
Hearers of the word. Translated by Michael Richards. [New York] Herder and Herder [1969] x, 180 p. 22 cm. Translation of Horer des Wortes. Bibliographical footnotes. [BL51.R2413] 69-14389 6.50
1. Religion—Philosophy. 2. Knowledge, Theory of (Religion) I. Title.

RAMSEY, Ian T. 201
Christian empiricism / Ian Ramsey ; edited by Jerry H. Gill. Grand Rapids : Eerdmans, [1974] 260 p. ; 21 cm. (Studies in philosophy and religion) Bibliography: p. [258]-260. [BR100.R34 1974] 74-182340 pbk. : 4.95
1. Philosophy and religion—Addresses, essays, lectures. I. Title.

RANDALL, John Herman, 1899- 201
The role of knowledge in Western religion. Boston, Starr King Press [1958] x, 147p. 21cm. (Mead-Swing lectures, 1955-1956) [BT50.R2] 58-8396
1. Knowledge, Theory of (Religion) I. Title. II. Series.

RASHDALL, Hastings, 1858-1924. 201
Philosophy and religion; six lectures delivered at Cambridge. Westport, Conn., Greenwood Press [1970] xvi, 189 p. 23 cm. Reprint of the 1910 ed. Contents.Contents.—Mind and matter.—The universal cause.—God and the moral consciousness.—Difficulties and objections.—Revelation.—Christianity. Includes bibliographical references. [B56.R3 1970] 79-98791
1. Philosophy and religion. 2. Christianity.

REARDON, Bernard M. G. 201
Hegel's philosophy of religion / Bernard M. G. Reardon. New York : Barnes & Noble Books, 1977. xvii, 147 p. ; 23 cm. (Library of philosophy and religion) Includes index. Bibliography: p. [142]-143. [B2949.R3R4 1977b] 77-375415 ISBN 0-06-495806-X : 20.00
1. Hegel, Georg Wilhelm Friedrich, 1770-1831—Religion. I. Title.

REIK, Theodor, 1888- 201
Dogma and compulsion psychoanalytic studies of religion and myths. [Translated by Bernard Miall] New York, International Universities Press [1951] 332 p. 23 cm. Bibliographical footnotes. [BL53.R37] 51-10993
1. Psychology, Religious. 2. Dogma. 3. Authority (Religion) 4. Bible — Psychology. I. Title.

REYNOLDS, Ferris E 201
Thinking about religion; an introduction to the problems of interpreting religion, by Ferris E. Reynolds. [1st ed.] New York, American Press [c1965] 233 p. 23 cm. Includes bibliographies. [BL51.R39] 65-26017
1. Religion — Philosophy. I. Title.

REYNOLDS, Ferris E. 201
Thinking about religion; an introduction to the problems of interpreting religion, by Ferris E. Reynolds. [1st ed.] New York, American Pr. [c.1965] 233p. 23cm. [BL51.R39] 65-26017 5.00
1. Religion — Philosophy. I. Title.

RICHARDS, Alun. 201
God—alive! [By] Alun Richards, Edna Lambert, and Les George. Philadelphia, Westminster Press [1973] 182 p. illus. 23 cm. [BR96.R48] 73-9980 ISBN 0-664-24978-7
1. Theology—Caricatures and cartoons. I. Lambert, Edna, joint author. II. George, Les, joint author. III. Title.

ROBERTS, David Everett 201
Psychotherapy and a christian view of man. New York, Scriber [1960, c.1950] xiv, 161 p. (Bibl.: p. 155-156) 21 cm. (Scriber Library, SL 29) pap., 1.25
1. Psychology Pastoral. 2. Christianity—Psychology. 3. Psychotherapy. I. Title.

ROBERTS, David Everett, 1911- 201
Psychotherapy and a Christian view of man. New York, Scribner, 1950. xiv, 161 p. 21 cm. Bibliography: p. 155-156. [BV4012.R59] 50-6770
1. Psychology, Pastoral. 2. Christianity — Psychology. 3. Psychotherapy. I. Title.

ROBERTS, Louis. 201
The achievement of Karl Rahner. [New York] Herder and Herder [1967] viii, 312 p. 22 cm. Includes bibliographical references. [BX4705.R287R6] 67-25883
1. Rahner, Karl, 1904- I. Title.

ROBERTS, Louis. 201
The achievement of Karl Rahner. [New York] Herder and Herder [1967] viii, 312 p. 22 cm. Includes bibliographical references. [BX4705.R287R6] 67-25883
1. Rahner, Karl, 1904- I. Title.

ROGERS, Lewis M., 1918- comp. 201
And more about God. Lewis M. Rogers [and] Charles H. Monson, Jr., editors. Salt Lake City, University of Utah Press [1969] 363 p. 21 cm. Includes bibliographical references. [BL51.R592] 72-80722
1. Religion—Philosophy—Collections. I. Monson, Charles H., joint comp. II. Title.

ROMAN Catholic/Presbyterian and Reformed Conversation Group. 201
Reconsiderations; Roman Catholic/Presbyterian and Reformed theological conversations, 1966-67. Papers presented by John L. McKenzie [and others. New York, World Horizons, c1967] 157 p. 21 cm. Includes bibliographical references. [BT90.R6] 74-3313 1.25
1. Tradition (Theology)—Addresses, essays, lectures. 2. Dogma, Development of—Addresses, essays, lectures. 3. Church polity—Addresses, essays, lectures. I. McKenzie, John L. II. Title.

ROSE, Mary Carman. 201
Essays in Christian philosophy. Boston, Christopher Pub. House [1963] 200 p. 21 cm. [BR100.R65] 63-11504
1. Philosophy and religion — Addresses, essays, lectures. I. Title.

ROSE, Mary Carman 201
Essays in Christian philosophy. Boston, Christopher [c.1963] 200p. 21cm. Bibl. 63-11504 3.75
1. Philosophy and religion—Addresses, essays, lectures. I. Title.

ROSS, James F., 1931- 201
Introduction to the philosophy of religion, by James F. Ross. [New York] Macmillan [1969] 185 p. 20 cm. Bibliography: p. [177]-178. [BL51.R597] 74-80298
1. Religion—Philosophy. I. Title.

*ROUSH, Lester L. 201
A free man's legacy. New York, Vantage [1968] 159p. 21cm. 3.50 bds.,
I. Title.

ROUSSEAU, Jean Jacques, 1712-1778. 201
The creed of a priest of Savoy. Translated, with an introd., by Arthur H. Beattie. 2d, enl. ed. New York, F. Ungar Pub. Co. [c1957] 84p. 21cm. (Mill)0estones of thought in the history of ideas) [PQ2040.P6E5 1957] 57-13345
I. Title. II. Series.

ROUSSEAU, Jean Jacques, 1712-1778. 201
The creed of a priest of Savoy. Translated with an introd. by Arthur H. Beattie. New York, F. Ungar Pub. Co. [1956] xii, 50p. 20cm. (Milestones of thought in the history of ideas) Bibliography: p. xii. [PQ2040.P6E5 1956] 56-7501
I. Title. II. Series.

ROYCE, Josiah, 1855-1916 201
The sources of religious insight. New York, Scribners [1963, c.1912, 1940] 297p. 21cm. (Scribner lib., SL88) 1.65 pap.,
1. Religion—Philosophy. I. Title. II. Title: Religious insight, the sources of.

ROYCE, Josiah, 1855-1916. 201
The sources of religious insight : lectures delivered before Lake Forest College on the foundation of the late William Bross / by Josiah Royce. New York : Octagon Books, 1977, c1912. xv, 297 p. ; 19 cm. Reprint of the ed. published by Scribner, New York, as v. 6 in series: The Bross library. [BL51.R6 1977] 76-56454 ISBN 0-374-96989-2 lib.bdg. : 14.50
1. Religion—Philosophy—Addresses, essays, lectures. I. Title. II. Series: The Bross library ; v. 6.

RUMMERFIELD, Walter Glen. 201
Psychology of religion applied to everyday living. San Gabriel, Calif., Willing Pub. Co. [1960] 178p. 20cm. [BF639.R78] 60-1043
1. New Thought. I. Title.

RUSHDOONY, Rousas John. 201
The Biblical philosophy of history, by Rousas J. Rushdoony. Nutley, N.J., Presbyterian and Reformed Pub. Co., 1969. 148 p. 21 cm. (International library. Philosophical and historical studies) Includes bibliographical references. [BS680.H47R87] 77-94222
1. History (Theology)—Biblical teaching. I. Title. II. Series: International library of philosophy and theology. Philosophical and historical studies series

RUSHDOONY, Rousas John. 201
By what standard? An analysis of the philosophy of Cornelius Van Til. Philadelphia, Presbyterian and Reformed Pub. Co., 1959. 209p. 22cm. Includes bibliography. [BX9225.V37R8] 58-59921
1. Van Til, Cornelius, 1895- I. Title.

SABATIER, Auguste, 1839-1901. 201
Outlines of a philosophy of religion based on psychology and history. New York, Harper [1957] 337p. 21cm. (Harper torchbooks, TB 28) The Library of religion and culture. [BL51.S3 1957] 57-10121
1. Religion—Philosophy. 2. Christianity—Philosophy. 3. Dogma. I. Title.

SALL, Millard J. 201
Faith, psychology & Christian maturity / Millard J. Sall. Grand Rapids : Zondervan Pub. House, c1975. 181 p. ; 23 cm. Includes index. Bibliography: p. 173-176. [BR110.S27] 74-25354 5.95
1. Christianity—Psychology. I. Title.

SAYERS, Dorothy Leigh, 1893-1957. 201
The mind of the Maker. Westport, Conn., Greenwood Press [1970, c1941] xiv, 229 p. 23 cm. [BR100.S3 1970] 72-106698 ISBN 0-8371-3372-6
1. Christianity—Philosophy. I. Title.

SCHAEFFER, Francis August. 201
He is there and He is not silent [by] Francis A. Schaeffer. Wheaton, Ill., Tyndale House Publishers [1972] xi, 100 p. 22 cm. [BR100.S34] 72-79830 ISBN 0-8423-1412-1 3.95
1. Christianity—Philosophy. 2. Knowledge, Theory of. I. Title.

SCHELER, Max Ferdinand, 1874-1928. 201
On the eternal in man; translated by Bernard Noble. New York, Harper [1961, c1960] 480 p. 23 cm. "Bibliography of Scheler's published works": p. [457]-461. Bibliographical footnotes. [BL51.S423 1961] 61-7349
1. Philosophy and religion. 2. Religion—Philosophy. I. Title.

SCHMAHL, Philipp J R 201
The logic of faith; an invitation to pause and reflect, by Philipp Schmahl. New York, Philosophical Library [1965] 111 p. 22 cm. Bibliography: p. 110-111. [B945.S283L6] 65-20327
I. Title.

SCHMAHL, Philipp J R. M.D. 201
The logic of faith; an invitation to pause and reflect. New York, Philosophical [c.1965] 111p. 22cm. Bibl. [B945.S283L6] 65-20327 3.50
I. Title.

SCHMEMANN, Alexander, 1921- ed. 201
Ultimate questions; an anthology of modern Russian religious thought. [1st ed.] New York, Holt, Rinehart and Winston [1965] vii, 310 p. 22 cm. Includes bibliographies. [BX478.S3] 65-10132
1. Orthodox Eastern Church, Russian—Collected works. 2. Theology—Collected works. 3. Religious literature, Russian—Translations into English. I. Title.

SCHNEIDER, Louis, 1915- ed. 201
Religion, culture, and society; a reader in the sociology of religion. New York, Wiley [1964] xvii, 663 p. fold. map. 25 cm. Includes bibliographical references. [BL60.S3] 64-23859
1. Religion and sociology—Collections. I. Title.

SCHNEIDER, Louis, 1915- ed. 201
Religion, culture, and society; a reader in the sociology of religion. New York, Wiley [c.1964] xvii, 663p. fold. map. 25cm. Bibl. 64-23859 9.95
1. Religion and sociology—Collections. I. Title.

SCHUON, Frithjof, 1907- 201
Stations of wisdom. Tr. from French by G. E. H. Palmer [Hollywood-by-the-Sea, Fla., Transatlantic 1962, c.1961] 157p. Bibl. 62-2622 5.25
1. Religion—Philosophy. I. Title.

SCHUON, Frithjof, 1907- 201
The transcendent unity of religions; translated by Peter Townsend. [New York] Pantheon [1953] 199p. 22cm. [BL51.S4643] 53-9950
1. Religion—Philosophy. 2. Christianity and other religions. 3. Religions. I. Title.

SCHWEITZER, Albert, 1875-1965. 201
The essence of faith; philosophy of religion. Translated and edited, with a foreword, by Kurt F. Leidecker. New York, Philosophical Library; [distributed to the trade by Book Sales, inc., 1966] 124 p. 20 cm. [B2799.R4S313] 66-23987
1. "Study...based on Kantian metaphysics, from The critique of pure reason to Religion within the limits of reason alone." 2. Kant, Immanuel, 1724-1804. 3. Religion—Philosophy. I. Leidecker, Kurt Friedrich, 1902- ed. and tr. II. Title.

SCOTT, William A., 1920- 201
Historical Protestantism; an historical introduction to Protestant theology [by] William A. Scott. Englewood Cliffs, N.J., Prentice-Hall [1970, c1971] ix, 229 p. 23 cm. Bibliography: p. 217-224. [BT27.S35] 76-123085
1. Theology, Protestant—History. I. Title.

*SHEEN, Fulton John, Bp 1895- 201
The Fulton J. Sheen treasury. New York, Popular Lib. [1967] 512p. 18cm. (Eagle bks., 125-5 1.25 pap.,
I. Title.
Contents omitted.

SHEEN, Fulton John, Bp., 1895- 201
Moods and truths, by Fulton J. Sheen. Port Washington, N.Y., Kennikat Press [1970, c1932] ix, 238 p. 21 cm. (Essay and general literature index reprint series) A continuation of the author's Old errors and new labels. [BX1395.S5 1970] 77-91054
1. Religious thought—20th century. I. Title.

SHEEN, Fulton John, Bp., 1895- 201
Religion without God. 368p. 22cm. arden City, N. Y., [BL51] 54-4711
1. Religion—Philosophy. sPhilosophy and religion. 2. God. I. Title.

SHIEL, James. 201
Greek thought and the rise of Christianity. New York, Barnes & Noble [1968] xi, 161 p. illus. 22 cm. (Problems and perspectives in history) "Sources quoted": p. 146-154. Bibliography: p. 155. [BR128.G8S5 1968b] 74-6279 2.50
1. Christianity and other religions—Greek. 2. Hellenism. I. Title.

SIMMEL, Georg 201
Sociology of religion. Translated from the German by Curt Rosenthal. New York, Philosophical Library [c.1959] x, 76p. 20cm. 60-2684 3.75 bds.,
1. Religion. I. Title.

SIMMEL, Georg, 1858-1918. 201
Sociology of religion. Translated from the German by Curt Rosenthal. New York, Philosophical Library [c1959] 76 p. 20 cm. Translation of Die Religion. [BL48.S573] 60-2684
1. Religion. I. Title.

SKINNER, Tom, 1942- 201
How black is the Gospel? Philadelphia, Lippincott [1970] 128 p. 22 cm. (Evangelical perspectives) Bibliography: p. 126-128. [BT60.S56] 75-124544 4.95
1. Christianity—Essence, genius, nature. 2. Church and race problems—U.S. I. Title.

SKRADE, Carl. 201
God and the grotesque. Philadelphia, Westminster Press [1974] 176 p. 20 cm. Includes bibliographical references.

[BV4638.S56] 74-10972 ISBN 0-664-20710-3 7.50
1. Hope. 2. Theology—20th century. 3. Rationalism. 4. Grotesque. I. Title.
Pbk. 3.50, ISBN 0-664-20710-3

SMART, Ninian, 1927- ed. 201
Historical selections in the philosophy of religion. [1st ed.] New York, Harper & Row [1962] 510 p. 22 cm. [BL51.S568] 62-14582
1. Religion — Philosophy. I. Title.

SMART, Ninian, 1927- ed. 201
Historical selections in the philosophy of religion. New York, Harper [c.1962] 510p. 22cm. Bibl. 62-14582 7.00
1. Religion—Philosophy. I. Title.

SMEDAL, Gottfried Athanasius, 1861- 201
The historic reality of Christianity its origin, its essence, its blessing. Boston, Christopher Pub. House [c1956] 59p. 21cm. [BR121.S646] 56-20602
1. Christiarity—Essence, genius, nature. I. Title.

SMEDAL, Gottfried Athanasius, 1861- 201
The historic reality of Christianity; its origin, its essence, its blessing. Boston, Christopher Pub. House [c1956] 59 p. 21 cm. [BR121.S646] 56-20602
1. Christianity — Essence, genius, nature. I. Title.

SMITH, John Edwin. 201
The analogy of experience: an approach to understanding religious truth [by] John E. Smith. [1st ed.] New York, Harper & Row [1973] xx, 140 p. 21 cm. ([The Annie Kinkead Warfield lectures, 1970]) Includes bibliographical references. [BR100.S54 1973] 72-77820 ISBN 0-06-067420-2 6.95
1. Christianity—Philosophy. 2. Experience. I. Title. II. Series.

SMITH, John Edwin, ed. 201
Philosophy of religion [by] John E. Smith. New York, Macmillan [1965] 124 p. 23 cm. (Sources in philosophy) Bibliography: p. 123-124. [BL51.S575] 65-11875
1. Religion — Philosophy — Collections. I. Title. II. Series.

SMITH, John Edwin, ed. 201
Philosophy of religion. New York, Macmillan [c.1965] 124p. 23cm. (Sources in philos.) Bibl. [BL51.S575] 65-11875 1.50 pap.,
1. Religion—Philosophy—Collection. I. Title. II. Series.

SMITH, Joseph Fielding, 1876- 201
Seek ye earnestly ... Salt Lake City, Utah, Deseret Book Co., 1970. viii, 459 p. col. port. 24 cm. [BX8639.S57S4] 77-136242 ISBN 0-87747-367-6 5.95
1. Mormons and Mormonism—Sermons. 2. Sermons, American. 3. Mormons and Mormonism—Addresses, essays, lectures. I. Title.

SMITH, Wilfred Cantwell 201
The meaning and end of religion; a new approach to the religious traditions of mankind [New York] New Amer. Lib. [1964, c.1962, 1963] 352p. 18cm. (Mentor bk., MT575) Bibl. .75 pap.,
1. Religion—Philosophy. 2. Religions. I. Title.

SMITH, Wilfred Cantwell, 1916- 201
The meaning and end of religion; a new approach to the religious traditions of mankind. New York, Macmillan [1963] 340 p. illus. 22 cm. [BL51.S587] 62-21207
1. Religion — Philosophy. 2. Religions. I. Title.

SMITH, Wilfred Cantwell, 1916- 201
The meaning and end of religion; a new approach to the religious traditions of mankind. New York, Macmillan [c.1962, 1963] 340p. illus. 22cm. 62-21207 7.00
1. Religion—Philosophy. 2. Religions. I. Title.

SONTAG, Frederick. 201
The future of theology; a philosophical basis for contemporary Protestant thought. Philadelphia, Westminster Press [1968, c1969] 155 p. 21 cm. Bibliography: p. [153]-155. [BR100.S58] 68-21039 ISBN 0-664-20848-7 4.95
1. Christianity—Philosophy. 2. Theology, Protestant—United States. I. Title.

STACE, Walter Terence 201
Time and eternity: an essay in the philosophy of religion. Princeton, N. J., Princeton University Press [1959, c.1952] vii, 169p. 22cm. 1.45 pap.,
1. Religion—Philosophy. I. Title.

STACE, Walter Terence, 1886- 201
Time and eternity: an essay in the philosophy of religion. Princeton, Princeton University Press, 1952. vii, 169 p. 23 cm. [BL51.S6257] 52-5835
1. Religion — Philosophy. I. Title.

STACE, Wlater Terence, 1886- 201
Religion and the modern mind. [1st ed.] Philadelphia, Lippincott [1952] 285 p. 22 cm. [BL51.S6256] 52-7471
1. Religion—Philosophy. 2. Skepticism—Controversial literature. I. Title.

STENSON, Sten H. 201
Sense and nonsense in religion; an essay on the language and phenomenology of religion [by] Sten H. Stenson. Nashville, Abingdon Press [1969] 255 p. 24 cm. Bibliography: p. 237-246. [BL51.S655] 69-19737 5.95
1. Religion. 2. Philosophy and religion. I. Title.

STOB, Ralph. 201
Christianity and classical civilization. Grand Rapids, Eerdmans, 1950. 198 p. 23 cm. Bibliography: p. 193-198. [BR115.C5S67] 50-11237
1. Civilization, Christian. I. Title.

TEILHARD de Chardin, Pierre. 201
Writings in time of war. Translated by Rene Hague. [1st U.S. ed.] New York, Harper & Row [1968] 315 p. 22 cm. Essays translated from Ecrits du temps de la guerre. Bibliographical footnotes. [B2430.T372E5 1968] 68-17597
1. Philosophy—Collected works. I. Title.

TEILHARD DE CHARDIN, Pierre. 201
The divine milieu; an essay on the interior life. [1st ed.] New York, Harper [1960] 144 p. 22 cm. [BR100.T373 1960] 60-11787
1. Christianity — Philosophy. I. Title.

TEILHARD DE CHARDIN, Pierre. 201
The divine milieu; an essay on the interior life. [1st ed.] New York, Harper [1960] 144 p. 22 cm. [BR100.T373 1960] 60-11787
1. Christianity—Philosophy. I. Title.

TEILHARD DE CHARDIN, Pierre 201
The divine milieu; an essay on the interior life [Tr. from French] New York, Harper [1965, c.1957, 1960] 160p. 21cm. (Harper Torchbk., Cathedral lib. TB384G) [BR100.T373] 60-11787 1.25 pap.,
1. Christianity—Philosophy. I. Title.

THEOLOGY and church in times of change. 201 [Essays in honor of John Coleman Bennett] Edited by Edward Le Roy Long, Jr. and Robert T. Handy. Philadelphia, Westminster Press [1970] 304 p. 24 cm. Contents.Contents.—Theology and the Gospel: Reflections on theological method, by R. M. Brown.—Deossification of theological obstacles in view of ecumenism, by B. Haring.—God, Torah, and Israel, by A. J. Heschel.—Theology, the churches, and the ministry, by G. W. Webber.—Theological ethics: Retrospect and prospect, by R. L. Shinn.—Aspects of the interpenetration of religion and politics, by D. E. Sturm.—Theology and international relations, by K. W. Thompson.—The eclipse of a public: Protestant reflections on religion and public education, 1940-1968, by R. W. Lynn.—Jerusalem and Athens in transition, by J. A. Martin, Jr.—John Coleman Bennett: Theologian, churchman, and educator, by R. Niebuhr.—The theology of John Coleman Bennett, by D. D. Williams.—A select bibliography of the writings of John Coleman Bennett, by R. F. Beach (p. [267]-304) Includes bibliographical references. [BR50.T429] 78-96699 ISBN 6-642-08819-10.00
1. Bennett, John Coleman, 1902- — Bibliography. 2. Theology—Addresses, essays, lectures. I. Bennett, John Coleman, 1902- II. Long, Edward Le Roy, ed. III. Handy, Robert T., ed.

THOMAS, George Finger, 1899- 201
Religious philosophies of the West [by] George F. Thomas. New York, Scribner [1965] xviii, 454 p. 24 cm. Bibliography: p. 439-444. [BL51.T44] 65-13662
1. Religion — Philosophy — Hist. 2. Religious thought — Hist. I. Title.

THOMAS, George Finger, 1899- 201
Religious philosophies of the West. New York, Scribners [c.1965] xviii 454p. 25cm. Bibl. [BL51.T44] 65-13662 7.95
1. Religion—Philosophy—Hist. 2. Religious thought—Hist. I. Title.

THOMAS, George Finger, 1899- ed. 201
The vitality of the Christian tradition. Edited by George F. Thomas. Freeport, N.Y., Books for Libraries Press [1971, c1944] xi, 367 p. 24 cm. (Essay index reprint series) Contents.Contents.—The faith of ancient Israel, by J. Muilenburg.—The beginnings of Christianity, by J. Knox.—The early centuries of the church, by V. Corwin.—The significance of medieval Christianity, by L. D. [i.e. T.] White.—The Reformation and classical Protestantism, by A. C. Outler.—The nineteenth century and today, by H. P. Van Dusen.—The devotional literature of Christianity, by D. V. Steere.—The Christian tradition in modern culture, by A. N. Wilder.—Christianity and modern philosophy, by G. F. Thomas.—The Christian tradition and physical science, by H. B. Jefferson.—Christianity and contemporary psychology, by E. R. Hilgard.—Christian ethics and Western thought, by J. Moore.—Christianity and democracy, by G. F. Thomas. [BR121.T49 1971] 70-134143 ISBN 0-8369-2378-2
1. Christianity—Essence, genius, nature. 2. Christianity—Philosophy. 3. Civilization, Christian. I. Title.

THOMPSON, Samuel Martin. 201
A modern philosophy of religion. Chicago, H. Regnery Co., 1955. 601 p. 22 cm. [BL51.T53] 55-1237
1. Religion—Philosophy. I. Title.

THOMTE, Reidar. 201
Kierkegaard's philosophy of religion. New York, Greenwood Press [1969, c1948] viii, 228 p. 23 cm. Bibliographical footnotes. [BX4827.K5T5 1969] 69-14116
1. Kierkegaard, Soren Aabye, 1813-1855. I. Title.

THORNTON, Martin. 201
The function of theology. [New York] Seabury Press [1968] 184 p. 23 cm. (The Library of practical theology) [BR118.T5 1968b] 68-25318 3.95
1. Theology. I. Title.

THOULESS, Robert Henry, 1894- 201
Authority and freedom; some psychological problems of religious belief. Greenwich, Conn., Seabury Press [1954] 124p. 19cm. (The Hulsean lectures delivered at the University of Cambridge, 1952) [BL53] 55-14293
1. Psychology, Religious. 2. Authority (Religion) 3. Religious though—Gt. Brit. I. Title.

TILLICH, Paul, 1886- 201
Theology of culture, edited by Robert C. Kimball. New York, Oxford University Press, 1959. ix, 213 p. 20 cm. [BT40.T5] 59-9814
1. Christianity—Philosophy. 2. Culture. I. Title.

TILLICH, Paul, 1886-1965. 201
Biblical religion and the search for ultimate reality. [Chicago] University of Chicago Press [1955] 84 p. 20 cm. (The James W. Richard lectures in the Christian religion, University of Virginia, 1951-52) [BR100.T53] 55-5149
1. Christianity—Philosophy. I. Title.

TILLICH, Paul, 1886-1965. 201
Theology of culture, edited by Robert C. Kimball. New York, Oxford University Press, 1959. ix, 213 p. 20 cm. [BT40.T5] 59-9814
1. Christianity—Philosophy. 2. Culture. I. Title.

TILLICH, Paul Johannes Oskar, 1886- 201
Biblical religion and the search for ultimate reality. [Chicago] Univ. of Chic. Pr. [1964, c.1955] 84p. 20cm. (James W. Richard lectures in the Christian religion, Univ. of Va. 1951-52, Phoenix bk. P154) 1.00 pap.,
1. Christianity—Philosophy. I. Title.

TILLICH, Paul Johannes Oskar, 1886- 201
Theology of culture, ed. by Robert C. Kimball. New York, Oxford [1964, c.1959] ix, 213p. 20cm. (Galaxy bk., GB124) 1.45 pap.,
1. Christianity—Philosophy. 2. Culture. I. Title.

TOURNIER, Paul. 201
The strong and the weak. Translated by Edwin Hudson. Philadelphia, Westminster Press [1963] 254 p. 23 cm. [BL53.T653] 63-8898
1. Psychology, Religious. I. Title.

TOYNBEE, Philip. 201
The age of the spirit : religion as experience / Philip Toynbee. 1st U.S. ed. New York : Harper & Row, c1973. 79 p. ; 16 cm. [BR100.T65 1973] 73-18676 ISBN 0-06-068405-4 : 4.95
1. Christianity—Philosophy. 2. Experience (Religion) I. Title.

TRANTER, Gerald. 201
The mystery teachings and Christianity. Wheaton, Ill., Theosophical Pub. House [1969] 208 p. 19 cm. (A Quest book) [BR115.P85T7] 75-8450 1.75
1. Christianity and psychical research. I. Title.

TRETHOWAN, Illtyd, 1907- 201
The basis of belief. [1st ed.] New York, Hawthorn Books [1961] 142 p. 21 cm. (Twentieth century encyclopedia of Catholicism, v. 13. Section 1: Knowledge and faith) Includes bibliography. [BL51.T64] 61-9457
1. Religion — Philosophy. I. Title.

TRETHOWAN, Illtyd, 1907- 201
The basis of belief. New York, Hawthorn Books [c.1961] 142p. (Twentieth century encyclopedia of Catholicism, v.13. Section 1: Knowledge and faith) Bibl. 61-9457 3.50 bds.,
1. Religion—Philosophy. I. Title.

TROELTSCH, Ernst, 1865-1923. 201
The absoluteness of Christianity and the history of religions. Introd. by James Luther Adams. Translated by David Reid. Richmond, John Knox Press [1971] 173 p. 21 cm. (Research in theology) Translation of Die Absolutheit des Christentums und die Religionsgeschichte, 3d ed. Includes bibliographical references. [BT60.T7613 1971] 74-133242 ISBN 0-8042-0462-4
1. Christianity—Essence, genius, nature. I. Title.

TRUEBLOOD, David Elton, 1900- 201
Philosophy of religion. [1st ed.] New York, Harper [1957] 324 p. 22 cm. Includes bibliography. [BL51.T683] 57-7342
1. Religion — Philosophy. I. Title.

TRUEBLOOD, David Elton, 1900- 201
Philosophy of religion. [1st ed.] New York, Harper [1957] 324 p. 22 cm. Includes bibliography. [BL51.T683] 57-7342
1. Religion—Philosophy.

TRUEBLOOD, David Elton, 1900- 201
Philosophy of religion. Grand Rapids, Mich., Baker Book, [1973, c1957] xv, 324, 22 cm. [BL51.T683] 3.95 (pbk.)
1. Religion—Philosophy. I. Title.
L.C. card no. for hardbound ed.: 57-7342

VAN TIL, Cornelius, 1895- 201
Christianity and idealism. Philadelphia, Presbyterian and Reformed Pub. Co., 1955. 139p. 23cm. [BR100.V3] 55-9041
1. Philosophy and religion. 2. Idealism. I. Title.

VERNON, Glenn M 201
Sociology of religion. New York, McGraw-Hill, 1962. 413 p. 24 cm. (McGraw-Hill series in sociology) Includes bibliography. [BL60.V4] 61-18136
1. Religion and sociology. I. Title.

VERNON, Glenn M. 201
Sociology of religion. New York, McGraw [c.] 1962. 413p. 24cm. (McGraw ser. in soc.) Bibl. 61-18136 7.95
1. Religion and sociology. I. Title.

VETTER, George B 201
Magic and religion, their psychological nature, origin, and function. New York, Philosophical Library [1958] 555 p. illus. 22 cm. [BL53.V4] 58-59410
1. Religion — Psychology. 2. Magic. I. Title.

VETTER, George B. 201
Magic and religion, their psychological nature, origin, and function. New York, Philosophical Library [1958] 555 p. illus. 22 cm. [BL53.V4] 58-59410
1. Psychology, Religious. 2. Magic.

VIEUJEAN, Jean. 201
The living religion. Translated from the French by David Heimann. Westminster, Md., Newman Press, 1964. xii, 261 p. 22 cm. Bibliographical references included in "Notes" (p. 241-255) [BT60.V513] 63-23492
1. Christianity — Essence, genius, nature. 2. Religion — Philosophy. I. Title.

VIEUJEAN, Jean 201
The living religion. Tr. from French by David Heimann. Westminster, Md., Newman [c.] 1964. xii, 261p. 22cm. Bibl. 63-23492 4.50
1. Christianity—Essence, genius, nature. 2. Religion—Philosophy. I. Title.

WACH, Joachim, 1898- 201
Sociology of religion. [Chicago] University of Chicago Press [1958, c1944] xii, 418 p. 21 cm. (Phoenix books, P25) Bibliography: p. 391-395. [BL60.W3 1958] 58-14679
1. Religion and sociology. 2. Sociology. I. Title.

WACH, Joachim, 1898-1955. 201
Sociology of religion. [Chicago] Univ. of Chic. Pr. [1962, c.1944] 418p. 21cm. (Phoenix bks., P92) Bibl. 1.95 pap.,
1. Religion and sociology. 2. Sociology. I. Title.

WAGNER, C. Peter. 201
Latin American theology: radical or

evangelical? The struggle for the faith in a young church, by C. Peter Wagner. Grand Rapids, Eerdmans [1970] 118 p. 21 cm. Bibliography: p. 110-118. [BX4811.W3] 73-88076 2.45
1. Theology, Protestant—Latin America. I. Title.

WALLACE, Anthony F. C., 1923- 201
Religion; an anthropological view, by Anthony F. C. Wallace. New York, Random House [1966] xv, 300 p. map. 22 cm. Bibliography: p. 271-290. [BL48.W185] 66-15811
1. Religion. I. Title.

WATTS, Alan Wilson 201
Nature, man, and woman. [New York] New American Library [1960, c.1958] 176p. (bibl. p. [174]-176) illus. 18cm. (Mentor bk. MD282) .50 pap.,
1. Religion—Philosophy. 2. Philosophy, Chinese. 3. Sex and religion. I. Title.

WATTS, Alan Wilson, 1915- 201
Nature, man, and woman. [New York] Pantheon [1958] 209 p. illus. 22 cm. Includes bibliography. [BL51.W3713] 58-8266
1. Religion—Philosophy. 2. Philosophy, Chinese. 3. Sex and religion. I. Title.

WATTS, Alan Wilson, 1915- 201
The supreme identity; an essay on Oriental metaphysic and the Christian religion. [1st ed. New York] Pantheon Books [1950] 204 p. diagrs. 23 cm. Bibliography: p. 195-199. [BR127.W3] 50-9499
1. Christianity and other religions. 2. Religion — Philosophy. 3. Philosophy, Oriental. I. Title.

WATTS, Alan Wilson, 1915- 201
The supreme identity; an essay on Oriental metaphysic and the Christian religion. New York, Vintage Books [1972] 204 p. 19 cm. Reprint of the 1950 ed. Bibliography: p. 195-199. [BR127.W3 1972] 72-3410 1.95
1. Christianity and other religions. 2. Religion—Philosophy. 3. Philosophy, Oriental. I. Title.

WELLS, Donald A. 201
God, man, and the thinker: philosophies ofreligion. [New York, Dell, 1967, c. 1962] 507p. 21cm. (Delta bk., 9697) [BL51.W379] 2.45 pap.,
1. Religion—Philosophy. 2. Theology. I. Title.

WELLS, Donald A. 201
God, man, and the thinker: philosophies of religion. New York, Random House [1962] 507 p. 24 cm. [BL51.W379] 62-10778
1. Religion—Philosophy. 2. Theology. I. Title.

WHITEHEAD, Alfred North, 201
1861-1947.
Religion in the making. New York, Meridian Books [1960, c1954] 154 p. 19 cm. (Living age books, LA 28) "Four lectures ... delivered in King's Chapel, Boston ... February, 1926." [BL48.W35 1960] 60-6736
1. Religion. I. Title.

WHITLEY, Olive: Read 201
Religious behavior: where sociology and religion meet. Englewood Cliffs, N.J., Prentice [c.1964] xiii, 177p. 22cm. Bibl. 64-8062 7.95 bds.,
1. Religion and sociology. I. Title.

WHITLEY, Oliver Read. 201
Religious behavior; where sociology and religion meet [by] Oliver R. Whitley. Englewood Cliffs, N.J., Prentice-Hall [1964] xiii, 177 p. 22 cm. Bibliographical footnotes. [BL60.W5] 64-8062
1. Religion and sociology. I. Title.

WIEMAN, Henry Nelson, 1884- 201
Intellectual foundation of faith. New York, Philosophical Library [1961] 212 p. 22 cm. Includes bibliography. [BL51.W565] 60-13665
1. Religion — Philosophy. I. Title.

WIEMAN, Henry Nelson, 1884- 201
Intellectual foundation of faith. New York, Philosophical Library [c.1961] 212p. Bibl. 60-13665 3.75
1. Religion—Philosophy. I. Title.

WIEMAN, Henry Nelson, 1884- 201
Man's ultimate commitment. Carbondale, Southern Illinois University Press, 1958. 318 p. 24 cm. Includes bibliography. [BL51.W376] 58-5488
1. Religion — Philosophy. 2. Creative ability. I. Title.

WIEMAN, Henry Nelson, 1884- 201
Man's ultimate commitment. Carbondale, Southern Ill. Univ. Pr. [1963, c.1958] 318p. 21cm. (ARCTURUS bk., ABI) Bibl. 6.00; 1.95 pap.,
1. Religion—Philosophy. 2. Creative ability. I. Title.

WIEMAN, Henry Nelson, 1884- 201
Religious experience and scientific method. Westport, Conn., Greenwood Press [1970] 387 p. 23 cm. Reprint of the 1926 ed. [BL51.W58 1970] 73-109877 ISBN 0-8371-4368-3
1. Religion—Philosophy. 2. Religion and science—1926-1945. I. Title.

WILD, John Daniel, 1902- 201
Human freedom and social order; an essay in Christian philosophy. Durham, N.C., Published for the Lilly Endowment Research Program in Christianity and Politics by the Duke University Press, 1959. 250 p. 22 cm. [BR100.W49] 59-14243
1. Christianity — Philosophy. I. Title.

WILDER, Amos Niven, 1895- 201
Theopoetic : theology and the religious imagination / by Amos Niven Wilder. Philadelphia : Fortress Press, c1976. vi, 106 p. ; 20 cm. Includes bibliographical references. [BR85.W5657] 75-36458 ISBN 0-8006-0435-0 : 4.95
1. Theology—Addresses, essays, lectures. 2. Imagination—Addresses, essays, lectures. I. Title. II. Title: Theology and the religious imagination.

WILSON, James Maurice, 1836- 201
1931.
Essays and addresses; an attempt to treat some religious questions in a scientific spirit. Freeport, N.Y., Books for Libraries Press [1973] p. (Essay index reprint series) [BR85.W585 1973] 73-1193 ISBN 0-518-10070-7
1. Theology—Addresses, essays, lectures. I. Title.

WILSON, John, 1928- 201
Language and Christian belief. London, Macmillan; New York, St. Martin's Press, 1958. 135 p. 20 cm. Includes bibliography. [BR100.W5] 58-2871
1. Christianity — Philosophy. I. Title.

WILSON, John, 1928- 201
Philosophy and religion; the logic of religious belief. London, New York, Oxford University Press, 1961. 119 p. 19 cm. Includes bibliography. [BL51.W62 1961] 61-19355
1. Philosophy and religion. I. Title.

WILSON, John Boyd, 1928- 201
Philosophy and religion; the logic of religious belief. New York, Oxford [c.]1961. 119p. Bibl. 61-19355 2.00 bds.,
1. Philosophy and religion. I. Title.

WOLFSON, Harry Austryn 201
Religious philosophy; a group of essays. New York, Atheneum, 1965 [c.1947-1961] xii, 278p. 18cm. (Atheneum 75) Bibl. 1.95 pap.,
1. Philosophy and religion. I. Title.

WOLFSON, Harry Austryn, 1887- 201
Religious philosophy, a group of essays. Cambridge, Belknap Press of Harvard University Press, 1961. 278 p. 23 cm. [BL51.W757 1961] 61-16696
1. Philosophy and religion. I. Title.

WOLFSON, Harry Austryn, 1887- 201
Religious philosophy, a group of essays. Cambridge, Mass., Belknap Pr. of Harvard [c.1947-1961] 278p. 61-16696 6.00
1. Philosophy and religion. I. Title.

YEAXLEE, Basil Alfred, 1883- 201
Religion and the growing mind. [3d ed.] Greenwich, Conn., seabury Press, 1952. 220 p. 23 cm. [BL53.Y4 1952] 52-12151
1. Psychology, Religious. 2. Child study. 3. Religious education. I. Title.

YINGER, John Milton. 201
Religion, society, and the individual; an introduction to the sociology of religion. New York, Macmillan [1957] 655 p. 24 cm. Includes bibliography. [BL60.Y52] 57-8266
1. Religion and sociology. I. Title.

YINGER, John Milton. 201
Religion, society, and the individual; an introduction to the sociology of religion. New York, Macmillan [1957] 655 p. 24 cm. Includes bibliography. [BL60.Y52] 57-8266
1. Religion and sociology. I. Title.

ZUURDEEG, Willem Frederik. 201
An analytical philosophy of religion. New York, Abingdon Press [1958] 320 p. illus. 24 cm. [BL51.Z8] 58-9527
1. Religion—Philosophy. I. Title.

ALLISON, Henry E 201.0924
Lessing and the Enlightenment; his philosophy of religion and its relation to eighteenth-century thought, by Henry E. Allison. Ann Arbor, University of Michigan Press [1966] ix. 216 p. 24 cm. Bibliographical references included in "Notes" (p. 167-206) [PT2418.R4A7] 66-11080
1. Lessing, Gotthold Ephraim, 1729-1781 — Religion and ethics. 2. Enlightenment. I. Title.

ALLISON, Henry E. 201.0924
Lessing and the Enlightenment; his philosophy of religion andits relation to eighteenth-century thought. Ann Arbor, Univ. of Mich. Pr. [c.1966] ix, 216p. 24cm. Bibl. [PT2418.R4A7] 66-11080 7.50
1. Lessing, Gotthold Ephraim, 2. Enlightenment. I. Title.

ALVES, Rubem A., 1933- 201'.1
A theology of human hope [by] Rubem A. Alves. New York, Corpus Books [1971, c1969] xv, 199 p. 21 cm. Bibliography: p. 185-192. [BT810.2.A55] 76-82271 5.95
1. Freedom (Theology) 2. Humanism. 3. Messianism. 4. Hope. I. Title.

AMBROSIUS, Saint, Bp. of 201'.1
Milan.
Seven exegetical works. Translated by Michael P. McHugh. Washington, Catholic University of America Press in association with Consortium Press [1972] viii, 486 p. 22 cm. (The Fathers of the church, a new translation, v. 65) Contents.Contents.—Isaac, or the soul.—Death as a good.—Jacob and the happy life.—Joseph.—The patriarchs.—Flight from the world.—The prayer of Job and David. Bibliography: p. vi-vii. [BR65.A313E55 1972] 71-157660 ISBN 0-8132-0065-2 15.85
1. Theology—Collected works—Early church, ca. 30-600. I. Title. II. Series.

BALTHASAR, Hans Urs von, 201'.1
1905-
The theology of Karl Barth. Translated by John Drury. [1st ed.] New York, Holt, Rinehart and Winston [1971] x, 323 p. 22 cm. Translation of Karl Barth: Darstellung und Deutung seiner Theologie. Bibliography: p. 313-317. [BX4827.B3B2613] 69-10237 ISBN 0-03-068450-1 8.95
1. Barth, Karl, 1886-1968. I. Title.

BARCLAY, William, lecturer 201.1
in the University of Glasgow.
By what authority? / William Barclay. Valley Forge : Judson Press, [1975, c1974] 221 p. ; 22 cm. [BT88.B35 1975] 75-4532 ISBN 0-8170-0675-3 pbk. : 3.95
1. Authority (Religion)—History of doctrines. I. Title.

BATSON, Charles Daniel, 201'.1
1943-
Commitment without ideology; the experience of Christian growth, by C. Daniel Batson, J. Christiaan Beker [and] W. Malcolm Clark. Philadelphia United Church Press [1973] 207 p. 22 cm. "A Pilgrim Press book." Includes bibliographical references. [BV4916.B33] 72-13000 ISBN 0-8298-0245-2 6.95
1. Experience (Religion) I. Beker, Johan Christiaan, 1924- II. Clark, Warren Malcolm, 1936- III. Title.

BERRIGAN, Daniel. 201.1
The geography of faith; conversations between Daniel Berrigan, when underground, and Robert Coles. Boston, Beacon Press [1971] 179 p. ports. 22 cm. [BX4705.B3845A294 1971] 70-159844 ISBN 0-8070-0538-X 7.50
I. Coles, Robert. II. Title.

BESANT, Annie (Wood) 1847- 201'.1
1933.
Esoteric Christianity; or, The lesser mysteries. Wheaton, Ill., Theosophical Pub. House [1970, c1953] viii, 277 p. 18 cm. (A Quest book. Theosophical classics series) Includes bibliographical references. [BP567.B47 1970] 71-113470 ISBN 0-8356-0028-9 1.95
1. Christianity—Miscellanea. 2. Theosophy. I. Title.

BILDSTEIN, Walter J. 201'.1
Radical response / Walter J. Bildstein. 2d ed. Hicksville, N.Y. : Exposition Press, [1974] xvi, 144 p. ; 21 cm. (An Exposition-testament book) First ed. published in 1972 under title: Secularization: the theology of John A. T. Robinson, a radical response. Bibliography: p. [131]-144. [BX5199.R722B54 1974] 74-186984 ISBN 0-682-47931-4 : 6.50
1. Robinson, John Arthur Thomas, Bp., 1919- 2. Secularization (Theology) I. Title.

BLANSHARD, Brand, 1892- 201'.1
Reason and belief / Brand Blanshard. New Haven : Yale University Press, [1975, c1974. 620 p. ; 23 cm. Includes bibliographical references and index. [BT50.B53 1975] 74-13253 ISBN 0-300-01825-8 : 30.00
1. Faith and reason. 2. Revelation. 3. Christian ethics—Controversial literature. 4. Rationalism. I. Title.

*BROOKS, Robert E. 201.1
Utopian universe. Detroit R. J. R. Press [1973] 103 p. 22 cm. [HX807.B74]
1. Christian life—Addresses, essays, lectures. 2. Faith—Addresses, essays, lectures. I. Title.

Publisher's address: P.O. Box 308, College Park Sta., Detroit, Mich. 48221.

BROWN, Robert McAfee, 201'.1
1920-
The pseudonyms of God. Philadelphia, Westminster Press [1972] 234 p. 21 cm. Includes bibliographical references. [BR85.B839] 77-178813 ISBN 0-664-20930-0
1. Theology—Addresses, essays, lectures. 2. Church and the world—Addresses, essays, lectures. I. Title.

BROWNSON, Orestes 201'.1
Augustus, 1803-1876.
Essays and reviews, chiefly on theology, politics, and socialism. New York, Arno Press, 1972 [c1852] xii, 521 p. 23 cm. (The Romantic tradition in American literature) [AC8.B724 1972] 72-4954 ISBN 0-405-04626-X 24.00
I. Title. II. Series.

CALVIN, Jean, 1509-1564. 201'.1
John Calvin: selections from his writings. Edited and with an introd. by John Dillenberger. Garden City, N.Y., Anchor Books, 1971. viii, 590 p. 18 cm. Bibliography: p. [574]-575. [BX9420.A32D54] 72-123715 2.45
1. Reformed Church—Collected works. 2. Theology—Collected works—16th century. I. Dillenberger, John, ed.

*CASSELS, Louis. 201'.1
Forbid them not. New York, Family library, 1973 94 p., illus, 18 cm. [BT77] ISBN 0-515-03207-7. 0.95 (pbk.)
1. Religion—Philosophy. I. Title.

CHANNING, William Ellery, 201'.1
1780-1842.
The works of William E. Channing. New York, B. Franklin [1970] iv, 931 p. 24 cm. (Burt Franklin research & source works series 626. American classics in history and social science 163) Reprint of the 1882 ed. [BX9815.C4 1970] 70-114815 ISBN 0-8337-0530-X
1. Unitarian churches—Collected works. 2. Theology—Collected works—19th century.

CLEVELAND, Edward Earl. 201'.1
Ask the prophets [by] E. E. Cleveland. [Takoma Park, Washington D.C., Review and Herald Pub. Association, c1970] 192 p. illus. 21 cm. [BR96.C57] 72-113039
1. Theology—Miscellanea. I. Title.

CLUTTON-BROCK, Arthur, 201'.1
1868-1924.
More essays on religion. With an introd. by B. H. Streeter. Freeport, N.Y., Books for Libraries Press, [1971] vii, 215 p. 23 cm. (Essay index reprint series) Reprint of the 1928 ed. Contents.Contents.—Crashaw's Christmas poems.—Christina Rossetti.—The Rev. Robert Herrick.—Ecclesiastical art.—"Restoration and renovation."—The problem of evil.—Creative religion.—An unborn Catholicism.—The pursuit of happiness.—The problem of Martha.—On Jonahs.—The remedy.—Sheep without a shepherd.—The kingdom of heaven. [BR85.C54 1971] 76-156632 ISBN 0-8369-2349-9
1. Theology—Addresses, essays, lectures. I. Title.

COBB, John B. 201'.1
Liberal Christianity at the crossroads, by John B. Cobb, Jr. Philadelphia, Westminster Press [1973] 125 p. 22 cm. [BR1615.C57] 73-9738 ISBN 0-664-20977-7 4.95
1. Liberalism (Religion) I. Title.

COLLEGE Theology Society. 201'.1
That they may live: theological reflections on the quality of life; [proceedings] George Devine, editor. Staten Island, N.Y., Alba House [1972] viii, 306 p. 21 cm. Proceedings of the national convention of the College Theology Society, held in St. Paul, Minn., Apr. 12-14, 1971. Includes bibliographical references. [BR50.C588] 72-3488 ISBN 0-8189-0243-4 3.95
1. Theology—Addresses, essays, lectures. I. Devine, George, 1941- ed. II. Title.

COX, Harvey Gallagher. 201'.1
The seduction of the spirit; the use and misuse of people's religion [by] Harvey Cox. New York, Simon and Schuster [1973] 350 p. 22 cm. Bibliography: p. 331-334. [BX4827.C68A37] 73-2314 ISBN 0-671-21525-6 8.95
1. Cox, Harvey Gallagher. 2. Religion. I. Title. Pbk. 2.95.

THE Crisis of religious 201'.1
language. Edited by Johann Baptist Metz and Jean-Pierre Jossua. [New York] Herder and Herder [1973] 139 p. 23 cm. (Concilium: religion in the seventies, 85) On cover: the New concilium: religion in the seventies. Includes bibliographical references.

[BV4319.C7] 72-12423 ISBN 0-8164-2541-8 3.95
1. Communication (Theology)—Addresses, essays, lectures. I. Metz, Johannes Baptist, 1928- ed. II. Jossua, Jean Pierre, ed. III. Series: Concilium (New York) v. 85.

CUPITT, Don. 201'.1
Crisis of moral authority. Philadelphia, Westminster Press [1972] 159 p. 22 cm. "Based on Stanton lectures delivered at Cambridge in the Lent term of 1971 under the general title 'Moral criticisms of Christian theology and ethics.'" [BT1102.C8] 72-2443 ISBN 0-664-20950-5
1. Apologetics—20th century. I. Title.

DANTE ALIGHIERI, 1262- 201'.1
1321.
Onarchy, and Three political letters. Sith an introd. by Donald Nicholl, and a note on the chronology of Dante's political works by Colin Hardie. New York, Noonday Press [1955?] xxi, 121p. 19cm. (Library of ideas) Monarchy translated by D. Nicholl: Three political letters, translated by C. Hardie. Bibliography: p. [xx]-xxi. [PQ4315.62.N] A56
1. Church and state. 2. Italy-Pol. & govt.-476-1268. I. Dante Alighleri. Three political letters. II. Nicholl, Donald, 1923- tr. III. Title.

DAUGHTERS of St. Paul. 201'.1
Religion for people of today. [Boston] St. Paul Editions [1971] 109 p. illus. 18 cm. [BR96.D27] 78-160576 0.95
1. Theology—Miscellanea. I. Title.

DUNN, James D. G., 1939- 201'.1
Unity and diversity in the New Testament : an inquiry into the character of earliest Christianity / by James D. G. Dunn. Philadelphia : Westminster Press, c1977. p. cm. Includes index. Bibliography: p. [BS2397.D85] 77-22598 ISBN 0-664-21342-1 : 19.50
1. Bible. N.T.—Theology. 2. Theology, Doctrinal—History—Early church, ca. 30-600. I. Title.

DUNN, James D. G., 1939- 201'.1
Unity and diversity in the New Testament : an inquiry into the character of earliest Christianity / by James D. G. Dunn. Philadelphia : Westminster Press, c1977. p. cm. Includes index. Bibliography: p. [BS2397.D85] 77-22598 ISBN 0-664-21342-1 : 19.50
1. Bible. N.T.—Theology. 2. Theology, Doctrinal—History—Early church, ca. 30-600. I. Title.

DYNAMICS of the faith; 201'.1
evangelical Christian foundations, edited by Gene Miller, Max Gaulke [and] Donald Smith. [Houston, Gulf-Coast Bible College, 1972] 304 p. ports. 23 cm. Includes bibliographies. [BR50.D93] 72-193745 4.95
1. Theology—Addresses, essays, lectures. I. Miller, Gene, 1929- ed. II. Gaulke, Max R., ed. III. Smith, Donald, June 15, 1935- ed.

ENCYCLOPEDIA of theology 201'.1
: the concise Sacramentum mundi / edited by Karl Rahner. New York : Seabury Press, [1975] xiv, 1841 p. ; 24 cm. "A Crossroad book." Contains revised articles from Sacramentum mundi, together with articles from Lexikon fur Theologie und Kirche and Theologisches Taschenlexikon, and new articles. [BR95.E48] 74-33145 ISBN 0-8164-1182-4 : 32.50
1. Theology—Dictionaries. I. Rahner, Karl, 1904- ed.

FERM, Vergilius Ture 201'.1
Anselm, 1896-1974.
Philosophy beyond the classroom / by Vergilius Ferm. North Quincy, Mass. : Christopher Pub. House, [1974] 407 p. ; 25 cm. Includes bibliographies. [BR85.F415] 74-75159 ISBN 0-8158-0314-1 : 12.95
1. Theology—Addresses, essays, lectures. I. Title.

FEY, Harold Edward, 1898- 201'.1
comp.
The Christian century reader; representative articles, editorials, and poems selected from more than fifty years of the Christian century, by Harold E. Fey and Margaret Frakes. Freeport, N.Y., Books for Libraries Press [1972, c1962] 447 p. 23 cm. (Essay index reprint series) [BR53.F48 1972] 72-331 ISBN 0-8369-2786-9
1. Christianity—20th century—Addresses, essays, lectures. 2. Church and social problems—Addresses, essays, lectures. I. Frakes, Margaret, joint comp. II. The Christian century. III. Title.

FORSYTH, Peter Taylor, 201'.1
1848-1921.
The Gospel and authority; a P. T. Forsyth reader. Edited by Marvin W. Anderson. Minneapolis, Augsburg Pub. House [1971] 199 p. 22 cm. Contents.Contents.—The evangelical churches and the higher criticism.—The distinctive thing in Christian experience.—Revelation and the Bible.—A rallying ground for the free churches.—The church's one foundation.—Authority and theology.—The cross as the final seat of authority.—The soul of Christ and the cross of Christ. [BX7117.F62] 72-159014 ISBN 0-8066-1136-7 5.59
1. Theology—Collected works—20th century. 2. Congregational churches—Collected works. I. Title.

FOX, Douglas A., 1927- 201'.1
Mystery and meaning : personal logic and the language of religion / Douglas A. Fox. Philadelphia : Westminster Press, [1975] 189 p. ; 21 cm. Includes bibliographical references. [BR118.F74] 75-15738 ISBN 0-664-24768-7 pbk. : 4.95
1. Theology. I. Title.

GABRIEL, Ralph Henry, 201'.1
1890- ed.
Christianity and modern thought, by Charles R. Brown [and others] Edited with a foreword by Ralph H. Gabriel. Freeport, N.Y., Books for Libraries Press [1973] p. (Essay index reprint series) Reprint of the 1924 ed. [BR50.G2 1973] 72-10705 ISBN 0-8369-7217-1
1. Theology—Addresses, essays, lectures. I. Brown, Charles Reynolds, 1862-1950. II. Title.

GOD, secularization, and 201'.1
history; essays in memory of Ronald Gregor Smith. Edited by Eugene Thomas Long. [1st ed.] Columbia, University of South Carolina Press [1974] xii, 161 p. 22 cm. [BR50.G545] 73-15712 ISBN 0-87249-293-1 7.95
1. Smith, Ronald Gregor. 2. Smith, Ronald Gregor—Bibliography. 3. Theology. I. Smith, Ronald Gregor. II. Long, Eugene Thomas, ed. Contents omitted.

GRISEZ, Germain Gabriel, 201'.1
1929-
Beyond the new theism : a philosophy of religion / Germain Grisez. Notre Dame [Ind.] : University of Notre Dame Press, [1975] xiii, 418 p. ; 24 cm. Includes bibliographical references and index. [BL51.G743] 74-27885 ISBN 0-268-00567-2 : 16.95 ISBN 0-268-00568-0 pbk. : 6.95
1. Religion—Philosophy. 2. God—Proof. 3. Religion and language. 4. Apologetics—20th century. I. Title.

GUILLAUME de Saint- 201'.1 s
Thierry, 1085(ca.)-1148?
The enigma of faith. Translated, with an introd. and notes, by John D. Anderson. Washington, Cistercian Publications, 1974 [c1973] vii, 122 p. ; 23 cm. (The Works of William St. Thierry, v. 3) (Cistercian Fathers series, no. 9) "Based on the reading of the only twelfth-century manuscript of the Enigma extant, Charleville MS. 114, and an examination of the fifteenth-century manuscript Uppsala C. 79." Revision of the editor's thesis, Catholic University of America, 1971, presented under title: The enigma fidei of William of Saint Thierry, a translation and commentary. Bibliography: p. 119-120. [BX890.G848 1971 vol. 3] [BT100] 234'.2 74-4465 ISBN 0-87907-309-8
1. God—Knowableness. 2. Faith—Early works to 1800. 3. God—Name. 4. Trinity—Early works to 1800. I. Anderson, John Douglas, 1943- ed. II. Title.

GUILLAUME de Saint- 201.1 s
Thierry, 1085(ca.)-1148?
The golden epistle: a letter to the brethren at Mont Dieu. Translated by Theodore Berkeley. Introd. by J. M. Dechanet. Spencer, Mass., Cistercian Publications, 1971. xxxiii, 117 p. 23 cm. (His The works of William of St Thierry, v. 4) (Cistercian Fathers series, no. 12) Translation of De vita solitaria. Bibliography: p. 107-109. [BX890.G848 1971 vol. 4] [BX2349] 248'.48'2 72-152482 ISBN 0-87907-312-8 7.50
1. Spiritual life—Catholic authors. I. Title.

GUILLAUME de Saint- 201'.1 s
Thierry, 1085(ca.)-1148?
On contemplating God. Prayer. Meditations. Translated by Sister Penelope. Spencer, Mass., Cistercian Publications, 1971 [c1970] v, 199 p. 23 cm. (The works of William of St. Thierry, v. 1) (Cistercian Fathers series, no. 3) Bibliography: p. 191-192. [BX890.G848 1971, vol. 1] [BX2181] 242'.1 77-152478
1. Meditations. 2. God—Worship and love. I. Title.

GUILLAUME de Saint- 201'.1 s
Thierry, 1085(ca.)-1148?
The works of William of St. Thierry. Spencer, Mass., Cistercian Publications, 1971- [c1970- v. 23 cm. (Cistercian Fathers series, no. 3, 12,) Vol. distributed by Consortium Press, Washington. Contents.Contents.—v. 1. On contemplating God. Prayer. Meditations. —v. 3. The enigma of faith.—v. 4. The golden epistle. [BX890.G848 1971] 72-181841 ISBN 0-87907-300-4
1. Catholic Church—Collected works. 2. Theology—Collected works—Middle Ages, 600-1500. I. Title.

GUTIERREZ, Gustavo, 1928- 201'.1
A theology of liberation: history, politics, and salvation. Translated and edited by Sister Caridad Inda and John Eagleson. Maryknoll, N.Y., Orbis Books, 1973. xi, 323 p. 22 cm. Includes bibliographical references. [BT738.G8613] 72-85790 4.95
1. Sociology, Christian. 2. Theology—20th century. 3. Christianity—Latin America. I. Title.

HEALEY, Francis G. 201.1
What theologians do [by] P. R. Ackroyd [and others] Edited by F. G. Healey. Grand Rapids, Eerdmans [1971, c1970] 354 p. 22 cm. First published in London in 1971 under title: Preface to Christian studies. Includes bibliographies. [BR118.H42 1971b] 75-162040
1. Theology—Addresses, essays, lectures. I. Ackroyd, Peter R. II. Title.

HOEDEMAKER, Libertus 201'.1
Arend, 1935-
The theology of H. Richard Niebuhr, by Libertus A. Hoedemaker. Philadelphia, Pilgrim Press [1970] xix, 204 p. 22 cm. A revision of the author's thesis entitled: Faith in total life, Utrecht, 1966. "Bibliography of the writings of H. Richard Niebuhr, compiled by Jane E. McFarland": p. 196-204. [BX4827.N47H6 1970] 78-139271 ISBN 0-8298-0186-3 10.00
1. Niebuhr, Helmut Richard, 1894-1962. I. Title.

HOLMES, Arthur Frank, 201'.1
1924-
All truth is God's truth / by Arthur F. Holmes. Grand Rapids : Eerdmans, c1977. ix, 145 p. ; 21 cm. Includes bibliographical references and indexes. [BT50.H6] 77-3567 ISBN 0-8028-1701-7 pbk. : 3.95
1. Faith and reason. 2. Truth. 3. Christianity—Philosophy. I. Title.

HUGEL, Friedrich, 201'.1
Freiherr von, 1852-1925.
Essays & addresses on the philosophy of religion. Westport, Conn., Greenwood Press [1974] xix, 308 p. 22 cm. Reprint of the 1921 ed. published by J. M. Dent, London. Contents.Contents.—Responsibility in religious belief.—Religion and illusion; and religion and reality.—Progress in religion.—Preliminaries to religious belief.—The apocalyptic element in the teaching of Jesus.—The specific genius of Christianity.—What do we mean by heaven? and what do we mean by hell?—The essentials of Catholicism.—The convictions common to Catholicism and Protestantism.—Institutional Christianity.—Christianity and the supernatural. Includes bibliographical references. [BL51.H9 1974] 72-9828 ISBN 0-8371-6219-X
1. Jesus Christ—Messiahship. 2. Troeltsch, Ernst, 1865-1923. 3. Catholic Church—Doctrinal and controversial works—Catholic authors. 4. Religion—Philosophy. 5. Theism. 6. Heaven. 7. Hell. I. Title.

HUSAIN, Itrat. 201'.1
The dogmatic and mystical theology of John Donne. With a pref. by Sir Herbert J. C. Grierson. Westport, Conn., Greenwood Press [1970] xv, 149 p. port. 23 cm. "Originally published in 1938 ... for the Church Historical Society." Bibliography: p. 148-149. [BX5199.D66H8 1970] 76-109753 ISBN 0-8371-4243-1
1. Donne, John, 1572-1631. I. Church Historical Society (Gt. Brit.) II. Title.

ICE, Jackson Lee. 201'.1
Schweitzer: prophet of radical theology. Philadelphia, Westminster Press [1971] 208 p. 21 cm. Includes bibliographical references. [BX4827.S35I3] 74-141991 ISBN 0-664-20906-8 7.50
1. Schweitzer, Albert, 1875-1965—Theology. I. Title. II. Title: Prophet of radical theology.

JENNINGS, Theodore W. 201'.1
Introduction to theology : an invitation to reflection upon the Christian mythos / Theodore W. Jennings, Jr. Philadelphia : Fortress Press, c1976. viii, 184 p. ; 22 cm. Includes bibliographical references and index. [BR118.J44] 76-7867 ISBN 0-8006-1234-5 : 5.95
1. Theology—Methodology. I. Title.

JERUSALEM and Athens; 201'.1
critical discussions on the theology and apologetics of Cornelius Van Til. Edited by E. R. Geehan. [Nutley, N.J.] Presbyterian and Reformed Pub. Co., 1971. xv, 498 p. 23 cm. Includes bibliographical references. [BR50.J4] 78-155779 9.95
1. Van Til, Cornelius, 1895- 2. Van Til, Cornelius, 1895- —Bibliography. 3. Theology—Addresses, essays, lectures. I. Geehan, E. R., ed.

JOHNSON, H. Eugene. 201'.1
The Declaration and address for today, by H. Eugene Johnson. Nashville, Reed [1971] 68 p. 23 cm. Includes bibliographical references. [BX7321.J56] 77-30522 2.95
1. Campbell, Thomas, 1763-1854. Declaration and address of the Christian Association of Washington. I. Title.

JOHNSON, Tom, 1923- 201'.1
No tall buildings in Nazareth; parent-child conversations on religion. Drawings by Dan Marshall. [1st ed.] New York, Harper & Row [1973] viii, 101 p. illus. 21 cm. [BV1475.2.J56] 72-160640 ISBN 0-06-064193-2 4.95
1. Religious education of children. I. Title.

JONES, Eli Stanley, 1884- 201'.1
Selections from E. Stanley Jones; Christ and human need. Compiled by Eunice Jones Mathews and James K. Mathews. Nashville, Abingdon Press [1972] 255 p. 23 cm. [BR85.J63] 76-173952 ISBN 0-687-37426-X 4.95
1. Methodist Church—Collected works. 2. Theology—Collected works—20th century. I. Title.

KLAUDER, Francis J. 201'.1
Aspects of the thought of Teilhard de Chardin, by Francis J. Klauder. North Quincy, Mass., Christopher Pub. House [1971] 151 p. 21 cm. Includes bibliographical references. [B2430.T374K57] 70-155359 ISBN 0-8158-0259-5 4.95
1. Teilhard de Chardin, Pierre. I. Title.

KLOPPENBURG, Boaventura, 201'.1
1919-
Temptations for the theology of liberation. Translated by Matthew J. O'Connell. Chicago, Franciscan Herald Press [1974] p. cm. (Synthesis series of booklets, no. 27) [BT83.57.K5513] 74-17089 ISBN 0-8199-0362-0
1. Liberation theology. I. Title.

KNUTSON, Kent S. 201'.1
The shape of the question; the mission of the church in a secular age [by] Kent S. Knutson. Minneapolis, Augsburg Pub. House [1972] 128 p. 20 cm. [BT75.2.K58] 72-78558 ISBN 0-8066-1225-8 2.50
1. Theology, Doctrinal. 2. Christianity—20th century. I. Title.

KOlAKOWSKI, Leszek. 201'.1
The key to heaven: edifing tales from Holy Scripture to serve as teaching and warning [by] Leszek Kolakowski. Translated by Salvator Attanasio and Conversations with the devil translated by Celina Wieniewska. New York, Grove Press [distributed by Random House, c1972] vi, 168 p. 21 cm. [BJ1012.K6] 72-3710 ISBN 0-394-48273-5 6.95
1. Ethics. 2. Devil. 3. God. I. KoLakowski, Leszek. Conversations with the devil. 1972. II. Title. III. Title: Conversations with the devil.

LANDEEN, William M. 201'.1
Martin Luther's religious thought, by William M. Landeen. Mountain View, Calif., Pacific Press Pub. Association [1971] 218 p. 22 cm. Bibliography: p. 215-218. [BR333.2.L35] 70-146044
1. Luther, Martin, 1483-1546—Theology. I. Title.

LAWSON, John. 201'.1
An evangelical faith for today. Nashville, Abingdon Press [1972] 95 p. 19 cm. Bibliography: p. 93-95. [BT77.L325] 75-186826 ISBN 0-687-12180-9
1. Theology, Doctrinal—Popular works. 2. Evangelicalism. I. Title.

LEE, Bernard. 201'.1
The becoming of the Church; a process theology of the structures of Christian experience. New York, Paulist Press [1974] vii, 304 p. 23 cm. Bibliography: p. 299-304. [BT83.6.L43] 73-90718 ISBN 0-8091-1816-5 5.95 (pbk.)
1. Process theology. 2. Church. 3. Sacraments. I. Title.

LE FEVRE, Jacques, 201'.1
d'Etaples, d.1537.
The prefatory epistles of Jacques Lefevre d'Etaples and related texts. Edited by Eugene F. Rice, Jr. New York, Columbia University Press, 1972. xl, 629 p. 24 cm. Texts chiefly in Latin, some in French; editorial matter in English. Bibliography: p. 535-568. [BR1725.L28A4 1972] 77-123577 ISBN 0-231-03163-7 15.00
1. Prefaces. I. Rice, Eugene F., ed. II. Title.

LESTER, W. Sybel. 201'.1
The Black church gang, by W. Sybel Lester.

Philadelphia, House of Gemini [1972] ix, 83 p. illus. 17 cm. (A Gemini book) [BL2776.L47] 72-197912 2.00
1. Christianity—Controversial literature. 2. Negroes—Religion. 3. Negro clergy. I. Title.

LEWIS, Clive Staples, 1898-1963. 201'.1
The world's last night, and other essays. New York, Harcourt Brace Jovanovich [1973, c1960] 113 p. 21 cm. (A Harvest book, HB 260) Contents.Contents.—The efficacy of prayer.—On obstinacy in belief.—Lilies that fester.—Screwtape proposes a toast.—Good work and good works.—Religion and rocketry.—The world's last night. [BR123.L487 1973] 73-4887 ISBN 0-15-698360-5 1.75 (pbk.)
1. Christianity—Addresses, essays, lectures. I. Title.

LYNN, Mary Loyola. 201.1
Index to the writings of Saint Francis de Sales; including in one alphabet seven titles translated from the French into English. Compiled by Mary Loyola Lynn and Mary Grace Flynn. Foreword by John J. Conmy. [Wilmington, Del.] First and Second Federations, Visitation Monasteries in the United States; [distributed by Sisters of the Visitation] 1968. viii, 136 p. 26 cm. Appendices (p. 131-136):—1. List of books indexed.—2. List of letters indexed.—3. Parallel references to The controversies in the English and the French editions. [BX4700.F85L94] 73-264247
1. Francois de Sales, Saint, Bp. of Geneva, 1567-1622—Concordances. I. Flynn, Mary Grace, joint author. II. Title.

MCGINN, John T., comp. 201'.1
Doctrines do grow; a challenge to believers, edited by John T. McGinn. New York, Paulist Press [1972] v, 118 p. 19 cm. (Deus books) Includes bibliographical references. [BX1751.2.M254] 75-180542 1.45
1. Theology, Catholic—Addresses, essays, lectures. I. Title.

MCLACHLAN, Herbert, 1876- 201'.1
The religious opinions of Milton, Locke, and Newton / by H. McLachlan. Folcroft, Pa. : Folcroft Library Editions, 1974. vii, 221 p. ; 23 cm. Reprint of the 1941 ed. published by Manchester University Press, Manchester, Eng., which was issued as Publications no. 276, theological series no. 6, of the University of Manchester. Includes index. [BR756.M32 1974] 74-20740 ISBN 0-8414-5930-4 lib. bdg. : 11.95.
1. Milton, John, 1608-1674—Religion and ethics. 2. Locke, John, 1632-1704. 3. Newton, Isaac, Sir, 1642-1727. 4. Religious thought—England. I. Title. II. Series: Victoria University of Manchester. Publications. Theological series ; no. 6.

MCLACHLAN, Herbert, 1876- 201'.1
The religious opinions of Milton, Locke, and Newton / by H. McLachlan. Norwood, Pa. : Norwood Editions, 1976. vii, 221 p. ; 23 cm. Reprint of the 1941 ed. published by the Manchester University Press, Manchester, which was issued as no. 276 of Publications of the University of Manchester and as no. 6 of Publications of the University of Manchester Theological series. Includes bibliographical references and index. [BR756.M32 1976] 76-2350 ISBN 0-88305-532-5 : 15.00
1. Milton, John, 1608-1674—Religion and ethics. 2. Locke, John, 1632-1704. 3. Newton, Isaac, Sir, 1642-1727. 4. Religious thought—England. I. Title. II. Series: Victoria University of Manchester. Publications ; no. 276. III. Series: Victoria University of Manchester. Publications : Theological series ; no. 6.

MCLACHLAN, Herbert, 1876- 201'.1
The religious opinions of Milton, Locke, and Newton / by H. McLachlan. Folcroft, Pa. : Folcroft Library Editions, 1974. vii, 221 p. ; 23 cm. Reprint of the 1941 ed. published by Manchester University Press, Manchester, Eng., which was issued as Publications no. 276, theological series no. 6, of the University of Manchester. Includes index. [BR756.M32 1974] 74-20740 ISBN 0-8414-5930-4 lib. bdg.
1. Milton, John, 1608-1674—Religion and ethics. 2. Locke, John, 1632-1704. 3. Newton, Isaac, Sir, 1642-1727. 4. Religious thought—England. I. Title. II. Series: Victoria University of Manchester. Publications. Theological series ; no. 6.

MCNEILL, John Thomas, 1885- 201'.1
Books of faith and power, by John T. McNeill. Freeport, N.Y., Books for Libraries Press [1971, c1947] ix, 183 p. 23 cm. (Essay index reprint series) Includes bibliographical references. [BR117.M2 1971] 75-134112 ISBN 0-8369-1996-3
1. Christian literature—History and criticism. I. Title.

MALET, Andre. 201'.1
The thought of Rudolf Bultmann. Translated from the French by Richard Strachan. Pref. by Rudolf Bultmann. Garden City, N.Y., Doubleday, 1971, [c1969] vii, 440 p. 24 cm. Translation of Mythos et logos. Includes bibliographical references. [BX4827.B78M313] 79-139065 8.95
1. Bultmann, Rudolf Karl, 1884- I. Title.

MALLOCK, William Hurrell, 1849-1923. 201'.1
Studies of contemporary superstition. Freeport, N.Y., Books for Libraries Press [1972] xii, 302 p. 23 cm. (Essay index reprint series) Reprint of the 1895 ed. [BR85.M25 1972] 72-333 ISBN 0-8369-2804-0
1. Fabian Society, London. 2. Christianity—Addresses, essays, lectures. 3. Socialism. I. Title.

MANDEVILLE, Bernard, 1670-1733. 201'.1
Free thoughts on religion, the church, and national happiness / by Bernard Mandeville. Delmar, N.Y. : Scholars' Facsimiles & Reprints, [1977] p. cm. Photoreprint of the 1720 ed. printed by T. Jauncy, London. [BR75.M28 1977] 77-17171 ISBN 0-8201-1300-X lib.bdg. : 35.00
1. Theology—Addresses, essays, lectures. 2. Political science—Addresses, essays, lectues. I. Title.

MANSEL, Henry Longueville, 1820-1871. 201'.1
The limits of religious thought examined in eight lectures delivered before the University of Oxford, in the year MDCCCLVIII, on the Bampton Foundation. 1st American, from the 3d London ed., with the notes translated. Boston, Gould and Lincoln, 1859. [New York, AMS Press, 1973] 364 p. 19 cm. Includes bibliographical references. [BL51.M3 1973] 72-172840 ISBN 0-404-04182-5 15.00
1. Religion—Philosophy. 2. Rationalism. I. Title.

MARLER, Don C. 201'.1
Imprisoned in the brotherhood [by] Don C. Marler. [1st ed.] New York, Exposition Press [1973] 62 p. 21 cm. Bibliography: p. 62. [BR110.M37 1973] 73-91098 ISBN 0-682-47877-6 3.50
1. Christianity—Psychology. 2. Fundamentalism. I. Title.

MEAGHER, John C. 201'.1
The way of the Word : the beginning and the establishing of Christian understanding / John C. Meagher. New York : Seabury Press, [1975] v, 234 p. ; 24 cm. "A Crossroad book." Includes bibliographical references and index. [BT60.M4] 75-4881 ISBN 0-8164-0270-1 : 9.50
1. Christianity—Essence, genius, nature. 2. Theology—Methodology. I. Title.

MELAND, Bernard Eugene, 1899- 201'.1
The reawakening of Christian faith. Freeport, N.Y., Books for Libraries Press [1972, c1949] xiii, 125 p. 23 cm. (Essay index reprint series) Original ed. issued as The Clark lectures, Pomona College, Claremont, Calif., 1947. [BR121.M46 1972] 72-142670 ISBN 0-8369-2663-3
1. Christianity—Essence, genius, nature. I. Title. II. Series: The Clark lectures, Pomona College, Claremont, Calif., 1947

MILLER, Eddie L., 1937- 201'.1
God and reason; a historical approach to philosophical theology [by] Ed. L. Miller. New York, Macmillan [1972] xi, 244 p. 21 cm. Includes bibliographical references. [BL51.M624] 70-176059
1. Religion—Philosophy. I. Title.

MOLTMANN, Jurgen. 201'.1
Hope and planning. [1st U.S. ed.] New York, Harper & Row [1971] viii, 228 p. 22 cm. "Translated by Margaret Clarkson from selections from the German Perspektiven der Theologie; gesammelte Aufsatze." Includes bibliographical references. [BT15.M6132 1971] 79-124703 6.50
1. Theology—Addresses, essays, lectures. I. Title.

MOONEY, Christopher F., 1925- 201'.1
The making of man; essays in the Christian spirit, by Christopher F. Mooney. New York, Paulist Press [1971] vii, 181 p. 21 cm. Includes bibliographical references. [BR85.M62] 72-147906 2.95
1. Theology—Addresses, essays, lectures. I. Title.

OLFORD, Stephen F. 201.1
The tabernacle: camping with God, by Stephen F. Olford. Neptune, N.J., Loizeaux Bros. [1971] 187 p. illus. 21 cm. Bibliography: p. 185-187. [BT225.O4] 78-173686 ISBN 0-87213-675-2 3.95
1. Typology (Theology) 2. Tabernacle.

OSTERHAVEN, Maurice Eugene, 1915- 201'.1
The spirit of the Reformed tradition, by M. Eugene Osterhaven. Grand Rapids, Eerdmans [1970, c1971] 190 p. 22 cm. Bibliography: p. 179-187. [BX9422.2.O8] 75-127625 3.45
1. Theology, Reformed Church. I. Title.

PANNENBERG, Wolfhart, 1928- 201'.1
Basic questions in theology; collected essays. Translated by George H. Kehm. Philadelphia, Fortress Press [1970-71] 2 v. 23 cm. Translation of Grundfragen systematischer Theologie. Includes bibliographical references. [BT80.P3413] 79-123505 9.75 per vol.
1. Theology, Doctrinal—Addresses, essays, lectures. I. Title.

PANNENBERG, Wolfhart, 1928- 201'.1
The idea of God and human freedom. Philadelphia, Westminster Press [1973] ix, 213 p. 22 cm. Translation of 1 essay by the author from Terror und Spiel and 5 essays from his Gottesgedanke und menschliche Freiheit. Also published as v. 3 of his Basic questions in theology. Includes bibliographical references. [BT80.P34133] 73-3165 ISBN 0-664-20971-8 6.95
1. Theology, Doctrinal—Addresses, essays, lectures. 2. Christianity—Philosophy—Addresses, essays, lectures. I. Title.

PORTEOUS, Alvin C., 1922- 201'.1
The search for Christian credibility; explorations in contemporary belief [by] Alvin C. Porteous. Nashville, Abingdon Press [1971] 207 p. 20 cm. Includes bibliographical references. [BT75.2.P67] 74-148069 ISBN 0-687-37121-X
1. Theology, Doctrinal. I. Title.

QUEST for a Black theology. Edited by James J. Gardiner, and J. Deotis Roberts. Philadelphia [Pilgrim Press, 1971] xiii, 111 p. 22 cm. Five of six essays originally presented at an interdenominational conference held in Washington, D.C., May 2-3, 1969, and jointly sponsored by the Graymoor Ecumenical Institute and the Georgetown University Dept. of Theology. Includes bibliographical references. [BR563.N4Q4] 76-151250 ISBN 0-8298-0196-0 5.95 201'.1
1. Negroes—Religion—Addresses, essays, lectures. 2. Negroes—Race identity. I. Gardiner, James J., ed. II. Roberts, James Deotis, ed. III. Graymoor Ecumenical Institute. IV. Georgetown University, Washington, D.C. Dept. of Theology.

REIK, Theodor, 1888-1969. 201'.1
Dogma and compulsion; psychoanalytic studies of religion and myths. Westport, Conn., Greenwood Press [1973, c1951] 332 p. 22 cm. Includes bibliographical references. [BL53.R37 1973] 72-9369 ISBN 0-8371-6577-6
1. Bible—Psychology. 2. Psychology, Religious. 3. Dogma. 4. Sphinxes. I. Title.

REIK, Theodor, 1888-1970. 201'.1
Dogma and compulsion; psychoanalytic studies of religion and myths. Westport, Conn., Greenwood Press [1973, c1951] 332 p. 22 cm. Includes bibliographical references. [BL53.R37 1973] 72-9369 ISBN 0-8371-6577-6 13.25
1. Bible—Psychology. 2. Psychology, Religious. 3. Dogma. 4. Sphinxes. I. Title.

REST, Friedrich, 1913- 201'.1
You've got a point there. Philadelphia, United Church Press [1974] 128 p. 22 cm. "A Pilgrim Press book." [BR96.R45] 74-900 ISBN 0-8298-0271-1 4.95
1. Christianity—Miscellanea. I. Title.

RICHARDS, James McDowell, 1902- 201'.1
Change and the changeless; articles, essays, and sermons. Decatur, Ga., Columbia Theological Seminary, 1972. 90 p. 23 cm. Contents.Contents.—Chronology of J. McDowell Richards.—Reflections on Armistice Day.—Brothers in black.—Christian church in a world at war.—A condemnation of mob violence.—Woodrow Wilson—the Christian and the churchman.—God's commandment for His people.—A call to civil obedience and racial good will.—A prayer of invocation.—The strange story of our times.—The relevance of the Gospel.—The Holy Spirit and the church.—The church and its ministry.—World missions—a Christian imperative.—The theological seminary as a graduate professional school.—Change, and the changeless. [BR85.R53] 72-87843
1. Theology—Addresses, essays, lectures. I. Title.

ROTH, Robert P. 201'.1
Story and reality; an essay on truth, by Robert P. Roth. Grand Rapids, Eerdmans [1973] 197 p. 21 cm. [BT50.R65] 72-93621 ISBN 0-8028-1496-4 3.45
1. Truth (Theology) 2. Philosophical theology. I. Title.

ROYCE, Josiah, 1855-1916. 201'.1
The problem of Christianity; lectures delivered at the Lowell Institute in Boston and at Manchester College, Oxford. Chicago, Regnery Co. [1968] 2 v. 18 cm. "Gateway edition." Contents.Contents.—v. 1. The christian doctrine of life.—v. 2. The real world and the Christian ideas. Includes bibliographical references. [BR121.R67 1968b] 68-14366 2.45 per vol.
1. Christianity—Essence, genius, nature. 2. Christianity—Philosophy. I. Title.

RUETHER, Rosemary Radford. 201'.1
Radical social movement and the radical church tradition [by] Rosemary R. Ruether. Power and violence: a Biblical study [by] Graydon F. Snyder. Oak Brook, Ill., Bethany Theological Seminary [1971] 59, [1] p. 23 cm. (Bethany Theological Seminary. Colloquium no. 1) The first item was originally presented as the Hoff lectures at the seminary in Nov. 1970; the second was originally 4 lectures presented at the Burkhart Institute, held at La Verne College, Calif., in Apr. 1970. Bibliography: p. [60] [BV631.R8] 72-31175
1. Church and state. 2. Socialism. 3. Christianity and culture. 4. Power (Theology)—Biblical teaching. I. Snyder, Graydon F. Power and violence: a Biblical study. 1971. II. Title. III. Series: Bethany Theological Seminary, Oak Brook, Ill. Colloquium no. 1

SABRAMES, Demosthenes S. 201'.1
The satanizing of woman; religion versus sexuality [by] Demosthenes Savramis. Translated from the German by Martin Ebon. [1st ed. in the U.S.A.] Garden City, N.Y., Doubleday, 1974. ix, 226 p. 22 cm.. Translation of Religion und Sexualitat. Includes bibliographical references. [BL65.S4S2313] 72-96232 ISBN 0-385-04485-2 6.95
1. Sex and religion. I. Title.

SCHILLEBEECKX, Edward Cornelis Florentius Alfons, 1914- 201'.1
The understanding of faith: interpretation and criticism [by] Edward Schillebeeckx. Translated by N. D. Smith. New York, Seabury Press [1974] p. cm. "A Crossroad book." Translation of Geloofsverstaan. Includes bibliographical references. [BR85.S274313] 74-12465 ISBN 0-8164-1185-9 6.95
1. Theology—Addresses, essays, lectures. 2. Hermeneutics—Addresses, essays, lectures. I. Title.

SCHILLEBEECKX, Edward Cornelis Florentius Alfons, 1914- 201'.1
World and church [by] Edward Schillebeeckx. Translated by N. D. Smith. New York, Sheed and Ward [1971] vii, 306 p. 22 cm. Translation of Wereld en kerk. Includes bibliographical references. [BR115.W6S273] 78-103361 ISBN 0-8362-1351-3 7.50
1. Church and the world—Addresses, essays, lectures. I. Title.

SCHOOF, T. Mark, 1933- 201'.1
A survey of Catholic theology, 1800-1970 [by] Mark Schoof. With an introd. by E. Schillebeeckx. Translated by N. D. Smith. Glen Rock, N.J., Paulist Newman Press [1970] 275 p. 21 cm. Translation of Aggiornamento. Includes bibliographical references. [BX1747.S313] 79-133569 4.95
1. Catholic Church—Doctrinal and controversial works—Catholic authors. 2. Theology, Catholic—History. I. Title.

SELWYN, Edward Gordon, 1885- ed. 201'.1
Essays Catholic & critical, by members of the Anglican communion. 3d ed. Freeport, N.Y., Books for Libraries Press [1971] xxxii, 456 p. 23 cm. (Essay index reprint series) "First published 1926." Contents.Contents.—The emergence of religion, by E. O. James.—The vindication of religion, by A. E. Taylor.—Authority: Authority as a ground of belief, by A. E. J. Rawlinson. The authority of the church, by W. L. Knox.—The Christian conception of God, by L. S. Thornton.—The Christ of the synoptic Gospels, by Sir E. C. Hoskyns.—The incarnation, by J. K. Mozley.—Aspects of man's condition: Sin and the fall, by E. J. Bicknell. Grace and freedom, by J. K. Mozley.—The atonement, by K. E. Kirk.—The resurrection, by E. G. Selwyn.—The spirit and the church in history, by E. Milner-White.—The Reformation, by A. H. Thompson.—The origins of the sacraments, by N. P. Williams.—The Eucharist, by W. Spens.

Includes bibliographical references. [BR50.S43] 75-142695 ISBN 0-8369-2075-9
1. Theology—Addresses, essays, lectures. I. Title.

SLAATTE, Howard Alexander. 201'.1
The paradox of existentialist theology; the dialectics of a faith-subsumed reason-in-existence [by] Howard A. Slaatte. New York, Humanities Press, 1971 [i.e. 1972] xv, 254 p. 24 cm. Bibliography: p. 233-245. [BT84.S57] 75-172936 ISBN 0-391-00161-2 7.50
1. Theology, Doctrinal. 2. Existentialism. I. Title.

SMITH, Gerard. 201'.1
Christian philosophy and its future; six essays. [Milwaukee] Marquette University Press, 1971. xvi, 130 p. 24 cm. Contents.Contents.—What is philosophy about?—Mr. Adler and the Order of learning.—The position of philosophy in a Catholic college.—Philosophy and the unity of man's ultimate end.—A note on the future of Catholic philosophy.—An appraisal of scholastic philosophy. Includes bibliographical references. [BR100.S53] 75-140071 ISBN 0-87462-439-8
1. Christianity—Philosophy. I. Title.

SPERRY, Willard Learoyd, 1882-1954. 201'.1
What we mean by religion. Freeport, N.Y., Books for Libraries Press [1971, c1940] 177 p. 23 cm. (Essay index reprint series) (Florida Southern College lectures) Includes bibliographical references. [BR121.S73 1971] 78-128316 ISBN 0-8369-2370-7
1. Christianity—Essence, genius, nature. I. Title. II. Series.

TEEPLE, Howard Merle, 1911- 201'.1
The Mosaic eschtological prophet. Philadelphia, Society of Biblical Literature, 1957. 122 p. 23 cm. (Journal of Biblical literature. Monograph series, v. 10) "Revision and expansion of the writer's doctoral dissertation ... University of Chicago." [BM615.T4] 58-15404
1. Messiah. 2. Moses. I. Title.

TEILHARD de Chardin, Pierre. 201'.1
Christianity and evolution. Translated by Rene Hague. [1st American ed.] New York, Harcourt Brace Jovanovich [1971] 255 p. 21 cm. "A Helen and Kurt Wolff book." Translation of Comment je crois. Includes bibliographical references. [BR85.T3313 1971] 78-162798 ISBN 0-15-117850-X
1. Theology—Addresses, essays, lectures. I. Title.

TEILHARD de Chardin, Pierre. 201'.1
Christianity and evolution. Translated by Rene Hague. New York, Harcourt Brace Jovanovich [1974, c1971] 255 p. illus. 21 cm. (A Harvest book, HB 276) "A Helen and Kurt Wolff book." Translation of Comment je crois. Includes bibliographical references. [BR85.T3313 1974] 73-12926 ISBN 0-15-617740-4 2.95 (pbk.)
1. Theology—Addresses, essays, lectures. I. Title.

TERESA, Saint, 1515-1582. 201'.1
The prison of love; selections from St. Teresa of Avila. Edited by Catharine Hughes. New York, Sheed & Ward [1972] [80] p. chiefly illus. 28 cm. (Mysticism and modern man) [BX890.T39 1972] 72-6606 ISBN 0-8362-0503-0 2.95
1. Catholic Church—Collected works. 2. Theology—Collected works—16th century. 3. Mysticism—Collected works. I. Hughes, Catharine, 1935- ed. II. Title.

UNDERDOWN, Emily. 201'.1
Stories from Dante, by Norley Chester. London, New York, F. Warne, 1898. x, 227 p. 8 plates, port. 19 cm. [PQ4315.9.U5] 2-23538
1. Dante Alighier, 1265-1821. divina Comedia. I. Title.

VON HILDEBRAND, Dietrich, 1889- 201'.1
The devastated vineyard. Chicago, Franciscan Herald Press [1973] p. Translation of Der verwustete Weinberg. [BX1751.2.V6613] 73-18117 ISBN 0-8199-0462-7 5.95
1. Catholic Church—Doctrinal and controversial works—Catholic authors. I. Title.

WANSBROUGH, Henry, 1934- 201'.1
Theology in St. Paul. Notre Dame, Ind., Fides Publishers [1970] 96 p. 18 cm. (Theology today, no. 16) Bibliography: p. 94. [BS2651.W35] 76-22057 0.95
1. Bible. N.T. Epistles of Paul—Theology. I. Title.

WATTS, Isaac, 1674-1748. 201.1
Miscellaneous thoughts. New York, Garland Pub., 1971. xx, 350 p. 21 cm. Facsimile reprint. Original t.p. reads: Reliqviae juveniles: miscellaneous thoughts in prose and verse on natural, moral, and divine subjects; written chiefly in younger years, by I. Watts, D.D. London: Printed for Richard Ford at the Angel, and Richard Hett at the Bible and Crown, both in the Poultry, 1734. [BX5200.W36 1734a] 72-112259
I. Title.

*WILES, Maurice, comp. 201.'1
Documents in early Christian thought / Edited by Maurice Wiles [and] Mark Sainter. London ; New York : Cambridge University Press [1976]c1975. x, 268p. ; 23 cm. Includes bibliographical references. [B631] 74-3180 ISBN 0-521-09915-3 : 22.50
1. Christian literature, Early (Collections) 2. Fathers of the Church. I. Santer, Mark, joint comp. II. Title.

WILES, Maurice F. 201'.1
What is theology? / Maurice Wiles. London ; New York : Oxford University Press, 1976. viii, 117 p. ; 21 cm. "Based on lectures ... given ... at King's College, London ... and in the University of Oxford." Includes index. Bibliography: p. [112]-114. [BR118.W58] 77-360493 ISBN 0-19-213525-2 : 5.25 ISBN 0-19-289066-2 pbk. : 2.50
1. Theology—Methodology—Addresses, essays, lectures. I. Title.

WINQUIST, Charles E., 1944- 201'.1
The communion of possibility / Charles E. Winquist. Chico, Calif. : New Horizons Press, [1975] 155 p. ; 22 cm. (The religious quest ; v. 2) Includes bibliographical references and index. [BL65.L2W52] 75-2420 ISBN 0-914914-05-7 lib.bdg. : 8.95 ISBN 0-914914-04-9 pbk. : 4.95
1. Religion and language. 2. Hermeneutics. 3. Church. I. Title. II. Series.

WOELFEL, James W. 201'.1
Borderland Christianity; critical reason and the Christian vision of love [by] James W. Woelfel. Nashville, Abingdon Press [1973] 207 p. 21 cm. Includes bibliographical references. [BR100.W6] 73-4004 ISBN 0-687-03849-9 4.95
1. Christianity—Philosophy. I. Title.

THE Word in the world; 201'.1
essays in honor of Frederick L. Moriarty, S.J. Edited by Richard J. Clifford & George W. MacRae. [Cambridge, Mass.] Weston College Press, 1973. x, 282 p. port. 23 cm. [BR50.W63] 72-97356 3.50 (pbk.)
1. Moriarty, Frederick L. 2. Moriarty, Frederick L.—Bibliography. 3. Theology—Addresses, essays, lectures. I. Moriarty, Frederick L. II. Clifford, Richard J., ed. III. MacRae, George W., ed.
Publisher's Address: 3 Phillips Place Cambridge, Mass. 02138.

A World more human, a 201'.1
church more Christian. George Devine, editor-in-chief. New York, Alba House [1973] vi, 195 p. 22 cm. "Annual publication of the College Theology Society," i.e. based in part on the proceedings of the Society's annual convention, held in Los Angeles in 1972. Includes bibliographical references. [BR50.W634] 73-9512 ISBN 0-8189-0265-5 3.95
1. Theology—Addresses, essays, lectures. I. Devine, George, 1941- ed. II. College Theology Society.

AMERICAN Tract Society. 201'.1'06573
The American Tract Society documents, 1824-1925. New York, Arno Press, 1972. 1 v. (various pagings) illus. 23 cm. (Religion in America, series II) Contents.Contents.—The address of the Executive Committee of the American Tract Society to the Christian public [first published 1825]—The American Colporteur system [first published 1836]—The centennial report of the American Tract Society [first published 1925]—Instructions of the Executive Committee of the American Tract Society to colporteurs and agents [first published 1868]—Proceedings of the first ten years of the American Tract Society [of Boston, first published 1824]—Sketch of the origin and character of the principal series of tracts [first published 1859] [BV2375.A489 1972] 70-38434 ISBN 0-405-04055-5
1. American Tract Society. I. Title.

NEW England Tract Society. 201'.1'06573
Report. [Andover, Mass.] Printed by Flagg and Gould. v. 21 cm. annual. Report year ends Apr. 30. [BV2375.N44] 64-58581
I. Title.

THE Carey memorial 201'.1'08
lectures. Delivered at the annual sessions of Baltimore Yearly Meeting, 1947-1971. [Compiled by Benjamin H. Branch, Jr. Lincoln? Va., 1972] viii, 103 p. 24 cm. [BR50.C37] 72-192655
1. Theology—Addresses, essays, lectures. I. Branch, Benjamin Harrison, 1919- comp. II. Friends, Society of. Baltimore Yearly Meeting.

HERZOG, Frederick, comp. 201'.1'08
Theology of the liberating word. Nashville, Abingdon Press [1971] 123 p. 23 cm. Translation of articles selected from Evangelische Theologie, with an introd. by the compiler. Contents.Contents.—Introduction: A new church conflict? By F. Herzog.—God, as a word of our language; for Helmut Gollwitzer on his sixtieth birthday, by E. Jungel.—From the Word to the words; Karl Barth and the tasks of practical theology, by H.-D. Bastian.—The living God; a chapter of Biblical theology, by H.-J. Kraus.—Paul's doctrine of justification: theology or anthropology? By H. Conzelmann. Includes bibliographical references. [BR50.H425] 78-141148 ISBN 0-687-41534-9 2.75
1. Theology—Addresses, essays, lectures. I. Evangelische Theologie. II. Title.

SMITH, Goldwin, 1823-1910. 201'.1'08
Guesses at the riddle of existence, and other essays on kindred subjects. Freeport, N.Y., Books for Libraries Press [1972] ix, 244 p. 23 cm. (Essay index reprint series) Reprint of the 1897 ed. Contents.Contents.—Guesses at the riddle of existence.—The church and the Old Testament.—Is there another life?—The miraculous element in Christianity.—Morality and theism. [BR85.S488 1972] 72-8529 ISBN 0-8369-7326-7
1. Theology—Addresses, essays, lectures. I. Title. II. Title: The riddle of existence, and other essays on kindred subjects.

WIRT, Sherwood Eliot, comp. 201'.1'08
Great reading from Decision: selections from the first ten years of publication. Edited by Sherwood E. Wirt and Mavis R. Sanders. Minneapolis, World Wide Publications [1970] 432 p. illus. (part col.) 23 cm. [BR50.W56] 75-141316 4.95
1. Theology—Collections. I. Sanders, Mavis R., joint comp. II. Decision. III. Title.

BURKILL, T. Alec. 201'.1'09
The evolution of Christian thought, by T. A. Burkill. Ithaca [N.Y.] Cornell University Press [1971] x, 504 p. 24 cm. Bibliography: p. 487-488. [BT21.2.B86] 76-127601 ISBN 0-8014-0581-5 12.50
1. Theology, Doctrinal—History. I. Title.

MCCONNELL, Francis John, Bp., 1871-1953. 201'.1'0922 B
Evangelicals, revolutionists, and idealists; six English contributors to American thought and action. Port Washington, N.Y., Kennikat Press [1972, c1942] 184 p. 21 cm. (Essay and general literature index reprint series) Contents.Contents.—James Edward Oglethorpe.—John Wesley.—George Whitefield.—Thomas Paine.—George Berkeley.—William Wilberforce. [BR758.M3 1972] 75-153252 ISBN 0-8046-1505-5
1. Oglethorpe, James Edward, 1696-1785. 2. Wesley, John, 1706-1791. 3. Whitefield, George, 1714-1770. 4. Paine, Thomas, 1737-1809. 5. Berkeley, George, Bp. of Cloyne, 1685-1753. 6. Wilberforce, William, 1759-1833. 7. Religious thought—Gt. Brit. 8. Religious thought—U.S. I. Title.

SCHMIEL, David. 201'.1'0924
Via propria and via mystica in the theology of Jean le Charlier de Gerson. [St. Louis, Mo., O. Slave, ltd., 1969] vii, 107 p. 22 cm. (Concordia Seminary. School of Graduate Studies. Graduate study, no. 10) Originally presented as the author's thesis, Concordia Theological Seminary, St. Louis. Bibliography: p. [104]-107. [BX4705.G45S27 1969] 75-19933
1. Gerson, Joannes, 1363-1429. 2. Spiritual life—Middle Ages, 600-1500. 3. Mysticism—Middle Ages, 600-1500. I. Title. II. Series: Concordia Theological Seminary, St. Louis. School of Graduate Studies. Graduate study, no. 10

ELLIOTT-BINNS, Leonard Elliott, 1885- 201'.1'0942
The development of English theology in the later nineteenth century, by L. E. Elliott-Binns. [Hamden, Conn.] Archon Books, 1971. ix, 137 p. 19 cm. (The Burroughs memorial lectures for 1950) Reprint of the 1952 ed. Includes bibliographical references. [BR759.E49 1971] 72-122411 ISBN 0-208-01045-9
1. Gt. Brit.—Church history—19th century. 2. Theology—19th century. 3. Theology, Doctrinal—History—Gt. Brit. I. Title: English theology in the later nineteenth century. II. Series: The Burroughs memorial lectures, Leeds University, 1950

WACKERBARTH, Marjorie. 201.W17
Games for all ages, and how to use them, by Marjorie Wackerbarth and Lillian S. Graham. Minneapolis, Denison [1959] 256 p. illus 22 cm. [GV] 703 59-13578
1. Games I. Title.

VACCA, Roberto, 1927- 201.24'3
The coming Dark Age. Translated from the Italian by J. S. Whale. [1st ed.] Garden City, N.Y., Doubleday, 1973. 221 p. 22 cm. Translation of Il Medioevo prossimo venturo. Includes bibliographical references. [CB478.V2313] 73-81118 ISBN 0-385-06340-7 6.95
1. Technology and civilization. 2. Civilization, Modern—1950- I. Title.

ALTIZER, Thomas J. J. 201'.4
The self-embodiment of God / Thomas J. J. Altizer. 1st ed. New York : Harper & Row, c1977. 96 p. ; 21 cm. [BL65.L2A45 1977] 76-62952 ISBN 0-06-060160-4 : 6.95
1. Religion and language. I. Title.

BOYLE, Marjorie O'Rourke, 1943- 201'.4
Erasmus on language and method in theology / Marjorie O'Rourke Boyle. Toronto ; Buffalo : University of Toronto Press, c1977. p. cm. (Erasmus studies ; 2) Includes index. Bibliography: p. [B785.E64B69] 77-2606 ISBN 0-8020-5363-7 : 17.50
1. Erasmus, Desiderius, d. 1536. 2. Religion and language—History. 3. Theology—Methodology—History. I. Title. II. Series.

BURKE, Kenneth, 1897- 201.4
The rhetoric of religion; studies in logology. Boston, Beacon Press [1961] vi, 327p. 21cm. [BL65.L2B8] 61-7249
1. Religion and language. 2. Semantics (Philosophy) 3. Augustinns, Aurellus, Saint, Bp. of Hippo. Confessiones. 4. Bible. O. T. Genesis—Language, style. I. Title.

BURKE, Kenneth, 1897- 201'.4
The rhetoric of religion; studies in logology. Berkeley, University of California Press, 1970. vi, 327 p. 21 cm. "Cal 188." Includes bibliographical references. [BL65.L2B8 1970] 70-89892 2.95
1. Augustinus, Aurelius, Saint, Bp. of Hippo. Confessiones. 2. Bible. O.T. Genesis—Language, style. 3. Religion and language. 4. Semantics (Philosophy) I. Title.

BURKE, Kenneth, [Kenneth Duva Burke] 1897- 201.4
The rhetoric of religion; studies in logology. Boston, Beacon [c.1961] vi, 327p. 61-7249 6.95
1. Augustinus, Aurelius, Saint, Bp: of Hippo. Confessiones. 2. Religion and language. 3. Semantics (Philosophy) 4. Bible. O. T. Genesis—Language, style. I. Title.

COLLE, Beau. 201'.4
CB for Christians / Beau Colle, with Jo Colle ; foreword by Landrum P. Leavell. Nashville : Broadman Press, c1976. 159 p. : ill. ; 18 cm. Bibliography: p. 158-159. [BV656.2.C64] 76-45554 ISBN 0-8054-5576-0 pbk. : 2.25
1. Citizens band radio in religion. I. Colle, Jo, joint author. II. Title.

JENSON, Robert W. 201'.4
The knowledge of things hoped for; the sense of theological discourse [by] Robert W. Jenson. New York, Oxford University Press, 1969. viii, 243 p. 21 cm. Bibliographical footnotes. [BR96.5.J4] 79-75601 5.75
1. Religion and language. 2. Theology—Terminology. I. Title.

MOREAU, Jules Laurence. 201.4
Language and religious language; a study in the dynamics of translation. Philadelphia, Westminster Press [c1961] 207p. 21cm. (Westminster studies in Christian communication) Includes bibliography. [BR115.L25M6] 60-10170
1. Languages—Religious aspects. 2. Language question in the church. I. Title.

PRELLER, Victor. 201'.4
Divine science and the science of God; a reformulation of Thomas Aquinas. Princeton, N.J., Princeton University Press, 1967. ix, 281 p. 23 cm. "Original version ... was submitted as a doctoral dissertation to the Department of Religion at Princeton University." Bibliography: p. 273-278. [BX1749.T7P7] 66-21838
1. Thomas Aquinas, Saint, 1225?-1274—Theology. 2. Religion and language. I. Title.

PRELLER, Victor. 201'.4
Divine science and the science of God; a reformulation of Thomas Aquinas. Princeton, N.J., Princeton University Press, 1967. ix, 281 p. 23 cm. "Original version ... was submitted as a doctoral dissertation to the Department of Religion at Princeton University."

Bibliography: p. 273-278. [BX1749.T7P7] 66-21838
1. Thomas Aquinas, Saint, 1225?-1274—Theology. 2. Religion and language. I. Title.

GRIFFIN, Emory A. 201'.41
The mind changers : the art of Christian persuasion / Emory A. Griffin. Wheaton, Ill. : Tyndale House, c1976. 228 p. : ill. ; 21 cm. Includes bibliographical references. [BV4319.G73] 76-44649 ISBN 0-8423-4290-7 : 4.95
1. Communication (Theology) I. Title.

NIDA, Eugene Albert, 1914- 201'.41
Message and mission : the communication of the Christian faith / Eugene A. Nida. [2d ed.]. South Pasadena, Calif. : William Carey Library, 1975, c1960. xviii, 253 p. : ill. ; 22 cm. Includes index. Bibliography: p. 239-248. [BV4319.N52 1975] 75-332490 ISBN 0-87808-711-7 pbk. : 3.95
1. Communication (Theology) I. Title.

ANDERSON, George Christian. 201.6
Man's right to be human; to have emotions without fear. New York, Morrow, 1959. 191 p. 21 cm. [BL53.A57] 59-8188
1. Psychology, Religious. I. Title.

ANDERSON, George Christian. 201.6
Man's right to be human to have emotions withour fear. New York, Morrow, 1959. 191p. 21cm. [BL53.A57] 59-8188
1. Psychology, Religious. I. Title.

ARGYLE, Michael. 201.6
Religious behavior. Glencoe, Ill., Free Press [1959] 196p. illus. 23cm. Includes bibliography. [BL53.A7 1959] 59-16264
1. Psychology, Religious. I. Title.

BAKER, Oren Huling, 1894- 201.6
Human nature under God; or, Adventure of personality. New York. Association Press [1958] 316p. 20cm. [BL53.B3] 58-11524
1. Psychology, Religious. 2. Bible—Psychology. 3. Personality. I. Title.

BARKER, Charles Edward, 1908- 201.6
Psychology's impact on the Christian faith. London, Allen & Unwin [dist. Hollywood-by-the-Sea, Fla., Transatlantic, c.1964] 220p. 23cm. Bibl. 64-56250 7.50 bds.,
1. Psychology, Religious. I. Title.

BIDDLE, William Earl, 1906- 201.6
Integration of religion and psychiatry. New York, Macmillan, 1955. 171p. 22cm. [BL53.B45] 55-14123
1. Psychology, Religious. I. Title.

BIDDLE, William Earl, 1906- 201.6
Integration of religion and psychiatry. New York, Collier [1962, c.1955] 188p. (AS139) Bibl. .95 pap.,
1. Psychology, Religious. I. Title.

BOISEN, Anton Theophilus, 1876- 201.6
Religion in crisis and custom; a sociological and psychological study. [1st ed.] New York, Harper [1955] 271p. 22cm. [BL53.B62] 55-8519
1. Psychology, Religious. 2. Religion and sociology. 3. U. S.—Religion. I. Title.

CARRIER, Herve, 1921-. 201.6
The sociology of religious belonging. [Translated by Arthur J. Arrieri. New York] Herder and Herder [1965] 335 p. 22 cm. Bibliography: p. 302-318. [BL60.C37] 64-13684
1. Religion and sociology. 2. Psychology, religious. I. Title.

CARRIER, Herve, 1921- 201.6
The sociology of religious belonging. [Tr. from French by Arthur J. Arrieri. New York] Herder & Herder [c.1965] 335p. 22cm. Bibl. [BL60.C37] 64-13684 6.50
1. Religion and sociology. 2. Psychology, Religious. I. Title.

CATES, Wayne Edward, 1917- 201.6
The religious dimensions of personality. New York, Association Press [1957] 320p. 21cm. [BL53.O3] 57-11600
1. Psychology, Religious. 2. Personality. I. Title.

CLARK, Walter Houston, 1902- 201.6*
The psychology of religion; an introduction to religious experience and behavior. New York, Macmillan [1958] 485 p. illus. 22 cm. Includes bibliography. [BL53.C57] 58-5210
I. Title.

DRAKEFORD, John W 201.6
Psychology in search of a soul [by] John W. Drakeford. Nashville, Broadman Press [1964] 301 p. illus. 22 cm. Bibliography: p. 287-298. [BL53.D66 1964] 64-15096
1. Psychology, Religious. 2. Soul. I. Title.

DRAKEFORD, John W. 201.6
Psychology in search of a soul. Nashville, Broadman *c.1964] 301p illus. 22cm. Bibl. 64-150963 5.75
1. Psychology, Religious. 2. Soul. I. Title.

FEINSILVER, Alexander, 201.6
In search of religious maturity. [Yellow Springs, Ohio] Antioch Press [c.]1960. 124p. 22cm. 60-15084 3.50
1. Psychology, Religious. I. Title.

GODIN, Andre, ed. 201.6
From religious experience to a religious attitude. Ed. by A. Godin. Chicago, Loyola [c.]1965. viii, 210p. illus. 24cm. (Loyola pastoral ser.: Lumen vitae studies) Bibl. [BX926.G6] 65-12553 4.00
1. Religious education—Psychology. 2. Psychology, Religious. I. Title.

GOODENOUGH, Erwin Ramsdell, 1893- 201.6
The psychology of religous experiences. New York, Basic Books [1965] xii, 192 p. 22 cm. Bibliographical footnotes. [BR110.G63] 65-15280
1. Psychology, Religious. I. Title.

GRENSTED, Laurence William, 1884- 201.6
The psychology of religion. London, New York, Oxford University Press, 1952. 181 p. 18 cm. (The Home university library of modern knowledge, 221) [BL53.G75 1952a] 52-4100
1. Psychology, Religious. I. Title.

GRENSTED, Laurence William, 1884- 201.6
The psychology of religion. New York, Oxford University Press, 1952. 181 p. 19 cm. [BL53.G75] 52-12536
1. Psychology, Religious. I. Title.

GUIRDHAM, Arthur 201.6
Christ and Freud; a study of religious experience and observance. Pref. by Lawrence Durrell. New York, Collier [1962, c.1959] 224p. 18cm. (AS 336V) .95 pap.,
1. Freud, Sigmund, 1856-1939. 2. Experience (Religion) 3. Psychology, Religious. I. Title.

HERR, Vincent V 201.6
Religious psychology [by] Vincent V. Herr. Staten Island, N. Y., Alba House [c1965] 277 p. 22 cm. (Mental health series, 5) Bibliography: p. [265]-267. [BR110.H4] 64-20109
1. Psychology, Religious. I. Title.

HERR, Vincent V. 201.6
Religious psychology. Staten Island, N. Y., Alba House [c.1965] 277p. 22cm. (Mental health ser., 5) Bibl. [BR110.H4] 64-20109 4.95
1. Psychology, Religious. I. Title.

HOPKINS, Pryns, 1885- 201.6
The social psychology of religious experience. New York, Paine-Whitman, 1962. 135 p. illus. 24 cm. [BL53.H569] 62-18494
1. Psychology, Religious. I. Title.

HOSTIE, Raymond, 1920- 201.6
Religion and the psychology of Jung. Translated by G. R. Lamb. New York, Sheed & Ward [1957] 249p. 21cm. Translation of Analytische psychologie en godsdienst. Includes bibliography. [BL53.H583] 57-6049
1. Jung, Carl Gustav, 1875- 2. Psychology, Religious. I. Title.

JAMES, William, 1842-1910. 201.6
The varieties of religious experience; a study in human nature. With a new introd. by Reinhold Niebuhr. New York, Collier Books [1961] 416p. 18cm. (Collier books, AS39) Bibliographical footnotes. [BR110.J3 1961] 61-17497
1. Religion. 2. Philosophy and religion. 3. Conversion. 4. Psychology. Religious. I. Title.

JOHNSON, Paul Emanuel, 1898- 201.6
Psychology of religion. Rev. and enl. New York, Abingdon Press [1959] 304p. 24cm. Includes bibliography. [BL53.J56 1959] 59-8198
1. Psychology, Religious. I. Title.

JUNG, Carl Gustav 201.6
Answer to Job; translated from the German by R. F. C. Hull. New York, Meridian Books [1960, c.1954] 223p. 19cm. (M86) 1.35 pap.,
1. Religion—Philosophy. 2. Bible O.T. Job—Criticism, interpretation, etc. I. Title.

JUNG, Carl Gustav, 1875-1961. 201.6
Psychology and religion. New Haven, Yale University Press [1962, c1938] 131 p. 21 cm. "Based on the Terry lectures delivered [in 1937] at Yale University." Bibliographical references included in "Notes" (p. [115]-131) [[BL53]] A 63
1. Psychology, Religious. 2. Symbolism. I. Title.

LEE, Roy Stuart. 201.6
Your growing child and religion, a psychological account. New York, Macmillan [1963] 224 p. 18 cm. (Macmillan paperbacks, 140) [BR110.L37] 63-15687
1. Children—Religious life. 2. Psychology, Religious. I. Title.

MASLOW, Abraham Harold. 201.6
Religions, values, and peak-experiences, by Abraham H. Maslow. Columbus, Ohio State University Press [1964] xx, 123 p. 21 cm. ([The Kappa Delta Pi lecture series]) Bibliography: p. 117-123. [BL53.M38] 64-23886
1. Psychology, Religious. 2. Experience (Religion) I. Title. II. Series.

NEILL, Stephen Charles, Bp. 201.6
A genuinely human existence, towards a Christian psychology. [1st ed.] Garden City, N. Y., Doubleday, 1959. 312p. 22cm. [BR110.N37] 59-8315
1. Christianity— Psychology. I. Title.

NOCK, Arthur Darby, 1902- 201.6
Conversion; the old and the new in religion from Alexander the Great to Augustine of Hippo. [London] Oxford University Press [1961] 309p. 20cm. (Oxford paperbacks, no.30) Includes bibliography. [BL85.N65 1961] 61-65952
1. Conversion—Hist. 2. Psychology, Religious. 3. Christianity and other religions. I. Title.

OATES, Wayne Edward, 1917- 201.6
The religious dimensions of personality. New York, Association Press [1957] 320 p. 21 cm. [BL53.O3] 57-11600
1. Psychology, Religious. 2. Personality. I. Title.

OATES, Wayne Edward, 1917- 201.6
What psychology says about religion. New York, Association Press [1958] 128p. 16cm. (An Association Press reflection book) Includes bibliography. [BL53.O33] 58-11533
1. Psychology, Religious. I. Title.

OLT, Russell, 1895- 201.6
An approach to the psychology of religion. Boston, Christopher Pub. House [c1956] 183p. 21cm. [BL53.O44] 56-13760
1. Psychology, Religious. I. Title.

OSTOW, Mortimer. 201.6
The need to believe; the psychology of religion, by Mortimer Ostow and Ben-Ami Scharfstein. New York, International Universities Press [1954] 162p. 23cm. [BL53.O8] 54-8070
1. Psychology, Religious. I. Scharfstein, Ben-Ami, 1919- joint author. II. Title.

STRUNK, Orlo. 201.6
Mature religion; a psychological study [by] Orlo Strunk, Jr. New York, Abingdon Press [1965] 160 p. 20 cm. Includes bibliographical references. [BR110.S77] 65-15235
1. Psychology, Religious. I. Title.

STRUNK, Orlo. 201.6
Mature religion; a psychological study [by] Orlo Strunk, Jr. New York, Abingdon Press [1965] 160 p. 20 cm. Includes bibliographical references. [BR110.S77] 65-15235
1. Psychology, Religious. I. Title.

STRUNK, Orlo, ed. 201.6
Readings in the psychology of religion. Nashville, Abingdon Press [1959] 288 p. 24 cm. Includes bibliography. [BL53.S76] 59-12787
1. Psychology, Religious. I. Title. II. Title: Psychology of religion.

STRUNK, Orlo. 201.6
Religion, a psychological interpretation. New York, Abingdon Press [1962] 128 p. 20 cm Includes bibliography. [BL53.S77] 62-9386
1. Psychology, Religious. I. Title.

STRUNK, Orlo 201.6
Religion, a psychological interpretation. Nashville, Abingdon [c.1962] 128p. 20cm. Bibl. 62-9386 2.50
1. Psychology, Religious. I. Title.

THOULESS, Robert Henry, 1894- 201.6
An introduction to the psychology of religion. [1st paperback ed.] Cambridge [Eng.] University Press, 1961. 286 p. 19 cm. [BL53.T5 1961] 61-16140
1. Psychology, Religious. I. Title.

THOULESS, Robert Henry, 1894- 201.6
An introduction to the psychology of religion. [New York] Cambridge [c.]1961. 286p. 61-16140 1.75 pap.,
1. Psychology, Religious. I. Title.

TOURNIER, Paul. 201.6
The seasons of life Translated by John S. Gilmour. Richmond, John Knox Press [1963] 63 p. 21 cm. [BR110.T613] 63-8709
1. Psychology, Religious. 2. Christian life. I. Title.

WELLS, George Ross, 1884- 201.6
Sense and nonsense in religion [1st ed.] New York, Vantage Press [1962, c1961] 182 p. 21 cm. [BL53.W4] 62-16028
1. Psychology, Religious. 2. Christianity — Essence, genius, nature. I. Title.

WHITE, Victor. 201.6
God and the unconscious. With a foreword by C. G. Jung. and an appendix by Gebhard Frei. Chicago, H. Regnery Co., 1953. xxv. 277p. 22cm. Bibliography p. 269-273. [BL53.W52 1953] 53-5779
1. Jung, Carl Gustav, 1875- 2. Psychology, Religions. I. Title.

WHITE, Victor 201.6
Soul and psyche; and enquiry into the relationship of psychotherapy and religion. New York, Harper [1960] 312p. Bibl. notes: p.262-308. 22cm. (Edward Cadbury lectures, 1958-1959) 60-11790 5.00
1. Psychology, Religious. 2. Soul. 3. Psychotherapy. 4. Psychoanalysis. I. Title.

WHITE, Victor, 1902-1960. *201.6
God and the unconscious. With a foreword by C. G. Jung, and an appendix by Gebhard Frei. Chicago, H. Regnery Co., 1953. xxv, 277 p. 22 cm. Bibliography: p. 269-273. [[BL53]] 53-5779
1. Jung, Carl Gustav, 1875-1961. 2. Psychology, Religious. I. Title.

WHITE, Victor, 1902-1960 201.6
God and the unconscious. Foreword by C. G. Jung. Cleveland, World Pub. Co. [1961, c.1952] 287p. (Meridian bks., M120) Bibl. 61-15741 1.35 pap.,
1. Jung, Carl Gustav, 1875-1961. 2. Psychology, Religious. I. Title.

WITHERINGTON, Henry Carl. 201.6
Psychology of religion; a Christian interpretation. Grand Rapids, W. B. Eerdmans Pub. Co., 1955. 344p. 22cm. [BL53.W58] 55-13911
1. Psychology, Religious. 2. Christianity—Psychology. I. Title.

JOURNET, Charles. 201.8
The wisdom of faith, an introduction to theology; translated by R. F. Smith. Westminster, Md., Newman Press, 1952. 225 p. 23 cm. Translation of Introduction a la theologie. [BR118.J67] 52-7508
1. Theology—Methodology. 2. Catholic Church—Doctrinal and controversial works. I. Title.

MELAND, Bernard Eugene, 1899- 201'.8
Fallible forms and symbols : discourses on method in a theology of culture / Bernard E. Meland. Philadelphia : Fortress Press, c1976. xvi, 206 p. ; 24 cm. Includes bibliographical references and index. [BR118.M44] 76-7868 ISBN 0-8006-0453-9 : 11.95
1. Theology—Methodology—Addresses, essays, lectures. I. Title.

CALABRESE, Alphonse. 201'.9
[Prescription symbol], the Christian love treatment / Alphonse Calabrese and William Proctor. 1st ed. Garden City, N.Y. : Doubleday, c1976. p. cm. [BR110.C33] 75-40716 ISBN 0-385-04851-3 : 5.95
1. Calabrese, Alphonse. 2. Christianity—Psychology. 3. Psychoanalysis and religion. 4. Christian life—1960- I. Proctor, William, joint author. II. Title.

CLUFF, Charles E. 201'.9
Parapsychology and the Christian faith / Charles E. Cluff. Valley Forge, Pa. : Judson Press, [1976] p. cm. Bibliography: p. [BR115.P85C58] 76-25015 ISBN 0-8170-0715-6 pbk. : 3.95
1. Christianity and psychical research. I. Title.

COLLINS, Gary R. 201'.9
The rebuilding of psychology : an integration of psychology and Christianity / by Gary R. Collins. Eastbourne, Eng. : Coverdale House ; Wheaton, Ill. : Tyndale House, 1977. 211 p. ; 21 cm. Includes index. Bibliography: p. 203-206. [BR110.C625] 76-47299 ISBN 0-8423-5315-1 : 4.95
1. Christianity—Psychology. I. Title.

COLLINS, Gary R. 201'.9
Search for reality; psychology and the Christian. Wheaton, Ill., Key Publishers [1969] 207 p. illus. 21 cm. Bibliographical footnotes. [BR110.C626] 73-95261
1. Christianity—Psychology. I. Title.

CURRAN, Charles Arthur. 201'.9
Psychological dynamics in religious living [by] Charles A. Curran. [New York] Herder and Herder [1971] 228 p. 22 cm. [BL53.C78] 72-170968 6.95
1. Psychology, Religious. I. Title.

DARLING, Harold W. 201'.9
Man in triumph; an integration of psychology and biblical faith [by] Harold W. Darling. Introd. by David L. McKenna. Pref. by E. Stanley Jones. Grand Rapids, Zondervan Pub. House [1969] 158 p. illus. 21 cm. Bibliography: p. [148]-153. [BR110.D27] 75-81046 3.95
1. Christianity—Psychology. I. Title.

DOLBY, James R., 1934- 201'.9
I, too, am man; a psychologist's reflections on Christian experience [by] James R. Dolby. Waco, Tex., Word Books [1969] 143 p. 22 cm. Includes bibliographies. [BR110.D6] 69-12815 3.95
1. Christianity—Psychology. I. Title.

DRIVER, Tom Faw, 1925- 201'.9
Patterns of grace : human experience as word of God / Tom F. Driver. San Francisco : Harper & Row, c1977. p. cm. Includes index. [BR110.D74] 77-14520 ISBN 0-06-062089-7 : 10.00
1. Christianity—Psychology. 2. Experience. 3. Word of God (Theology) 4. Creation. 5. Storytelling (Christian theology) 6. Gestalt therapy. I. Title.

DRIVER, Tom Faw, 1925- 201'.9
Patterns of grace : human experience as word of God / Tom F. Driver. San Francisco : Harper & Row, c1977. p. cm. Includes index. [BR110.D74] 77-14520 ISBN 0-06-062089-7 : 10.00
1. Christianity—Psychology. 2. Experience. 3. Word of God (Theology) 4. Creation. 5. Storytelling (Christian theology) 6. Gestalt therapy. I. Title.

GROUNDS, Vernon C. 201'.9
Emotional problems and the Gospel / by Vernon Grounds. Grand Rapids : Zondervan Pub. House, c1976. 111 p. ; 21 cm. (Contemporary evangelical perspectives) (Elmore Harris series ; no. 5) Includes bibliographical references. [BR110.G77] 75-38590 pbk. : 2.95
1. Bible—Psychology. 2. Christianity—Psychology. I. Title. II. Series.

HOOKER, Douglas. 201'.9
The healthy personality and the Christian life / by Douglas Hooker. North Quincy, Mass. : Christopher Pub. House, c1977. 141 p. ; 24 cm. Includes index. Bibliography: p. 133-138. [BR110.H58] 77-78029 ISBN 0-8158-0351-6 : 8.95
1. Barth, Karl, 1886-1968. 2. Christianity—Psychology. 3. Mental health. 4. Humanistic psychology. I. Title.

HOUSELANDER, Frances Caryll. 201.9
Guilt. New York, Gordian Press, 1971 [c1952] xiii, 268 p. ports. 23 cm. [BL53.H63 1971] 76-131251 ISBN 0-87752-053-4
1. Guilt. 2. Psychology, Pathological. 3. Psychology, Religious. I. Title.

JEEVES, Malcolm A., 1926- 201'.9
Psychology & Christianity : the view both ways / Malcolm A. Jeeves. Downers Grove, Ill. : InterVarsity Press, 1976. 177 p. : ill. ; 21 cm. Includes bibliographical references and indexes. [BR110.J37 1976] 76-12299 ISBN 0-87784-778-9 : 3.95
1. Christianity—Psychology. I. Title.

LODER, James Edwin. 201.9
Religious pathology and Christian faith, by James E. Loder. Philadelphia, Westminster Press [1966] 255 p. 21 cm. Bibliographical references included in "Notes" (p. 231-247) [BR110.L62] 66-11918
1. Psychology, Religious. I. Title.

LODER, James Edwin 201.9
Religious pathology and Christian faith. Philadelphia, Westminster [c.1966] 255p. 21cm. Bibl. [BR110.L62] 66-11918 5.00
1. Psychology, Religious. I. Title.

MACGREGOR, Geddes 201.9
God beyond doubt; an essay in the philosophy of religion. Philadelphia, Lippincott [c.1966] 240p. 21cm. Bibl. [BR110.M2] 66-16660 3.95
1. Psychology, Religious. I. Title.

MADDEN, Myron C. 201'.9
The power to bless [by] Myron C. Madden. Nashville, Abingdon Press [1970] 159 p. illus. 20 cm. Includes bibliographical references. [BR110.M26] 75-97576 3.50
1. Christianity—Psychology. 2. Pastoral counseling. I. Title.

SKOGLUND, Elizabeth. 201'.9
The whole Christian / Elizabeth R. Skoglund. 1st ed. New York : Harper & Row, c1976. xii, 113 p. ; 20 cm. Includes bibliographical references. [BR110.S54 1976] 75-12288 ISBN 0-06-067389-3 pbk. : 2.95
1. Christianity—Psychology. I. Title.

STERN, E. Mark, 1929- 201'.9
Psychotheology, by E. Mark Stern and Bert G. Marino. Paramus [N.J.] Newman Press [1970] 146 p. 22 cm. [BR110.S725] 79-128142 5.25
1. Christianity—Philosophy. I. Marino, Bert G., joint author. II. Title.

STERN, E. Mark, 1929- 201'.9
Psychotheology, by E. Mark Stern & Bert G. Marino. Paramus [N.J.] Paulist Pr. [1973, c.1970] vii, 146 p. 18 cm. (Deus Books) [BR110.S725] ISBN 0-8091-1782-7 1.45 (pbk.)
1. Christianity—Philosophy. I. Marino, Bert G., joint author. II. Title.

TOURNIER, Paul. 201'.9
A place for you; psychology and religion. [1st U.S. ed.] New York, Harper & Row [1968] 224 p. 22 cm. Translation of L'homme et son lieu. Bibliographical footnotes. [BL53.T6563] 68-29559
1. Psychology, Religious. 2. Self. I. Title.

WIEMAN, Henry Nelson, 1884- 201'.9
Normative psychology of religion, by Henry Nelson Wieman and Regina Westcott-Wieman. Westport, Conn., Greenwood Press [1971] x, 564 p. 23 cm. Reprint of the 1935 ed. Includes bibliographies. [BL53.W55 1971] 70-109876 ISBN 0-8371-4367-5
1. Psychology, Religious. I. Westcott, Regina (Hanson) 1886- joint author. II. Title.

202 Miscellany Of Christianity

CLERGYMAN'S fact book (The) 202
1964-65 New York, M. Evans; dist. in assn. with Lippincott, Philadelphia [1964, c.1963] v. 22cm. Ed.: 1964/65- B. Y. Landis. 63-19658 4.95
1. Handbooks, vade-mecums, etc. I. Landis, Benson Young, 1897- ed.

KUNG, Hans, 1928- 202
Structures of the church. Translated from the German by Salvator Attanasio. New York, T. Nelson [1964] xviii, 394 p. 22 cm. [BV600.2.K813] 63-19353
1. Church. 2. Councils and synods, Ecumenical. I. Title.

YEARBOOK of American 202
churches; information on all faiths in the U.S.A. 29th issue, 1961. Ed. by Benson Y. Landis. New York 27,475 Riverside Drive. Office of Publication and Distribution. National Council of the Churches of Christ in the U.S.A., [c.1960] 314p. Title varies 16-5726 5.95 bds.,
1. Sects—U. S. I. Federal Council of the Churches of Christ in America.

BAKER'S dictionary of 202'.02
practical theology. Edited by Ralph G. Turnbull. Grand Rapids, Baker Book House [1967] xxii, 469 p. 25 cm. Includes bibliographies. [BV3.B3] 67-18199
1. Theology, Practical—Handbooks, manuals, etc. I. Turnbull, Ralph G., ed. II. Title: Dictionary of practical theology.

TURNBULL, Ralph G., ed. 202'.02
Title: Dictionary of practical theology.
Baker's dictionary of practical theology Edited by Ralph G. Turnbull. Grand Rapids, Baker Book House [1967] xxii, 469 p. 25 cm. Includes bibliographies. [BV3.B3] 67-18199
1. Theology, Practical—Handbooks, manuals, etc. I. Title.

ANDERSON, Kenneth, 1917- 202'.07
People of the steeple. Written by Ken Anderson. Drawings by Noelle. Waco, Tex., Word Books [1971] [48] p. illus. 15 cm. [BV4.A49] 72-170909
1. Theology, Practical—Anecdotes, facetiae, satire, etc. I. Title.

ARNOLD, Oren. 202'.07
More steeple stories. Compiled by Oren Arnold. Grand Rapids, Kregel [1969] 80 p. 19 cm. [PN6231.C5A65] 77-76437
1. Clergy—Anecdotes, facetiae, satire, etc. I. Title.

HYERS, M. Conrad, comp. 202'.07
Holy laughter; essays on religion in the comic perspective, edited by M. Conrad Hyers. New York, Seabury Press [1969] vi, 264 p. 22 cm. Contents.Contents.—The comic profanation of the sacred, by M. C. Hyers.—The humanity of comedy, by W. F. Lynch.—The bias of comedy and the narrow escape into faith, by N. A. Scott, Jr.—The clown as the lord of disorder, by W. M. Zucker.—The clown in contemporary art, by S. H. Miller.—The rhetoric of Christian comedy, by B. Ulanov.—Christian faith and the social comedy, by P. L. Berger.—Humour and faith, by R. Niebuhr.—The traditional roots of Jewish humour, by I. Knox.—The humour of Christ, by E. Trueblood.—Eutrapelia: A forgotten virtue, by H. Rahner.—Zen humour, by R. H. Blyth.—The dialectic of the sacred and the comic, by M. C. Hyers.—On being with it: An afterword, by C. Walsh.—Appendix: Christian sobriety, by R. Barclay. Includes bibliographical references. [PN6149.M6H9] 70-84978 6.95
1. Wit and humor—Moral and religious aspects. I. Title.

MANOS, Charley. 202'.07
Where's God, Daddy? Illus. by Edith Corbett. Valley Forge [Pa.] Judson Press [1969] [63] p. illus. 16 cm. [PN6328.C5M35] 79-79730 1.00
1. Children—Anecdotes and sayings. 2. Children—Religious life—Anecdotes, facetiae, satire, etc. I. Corbett, Edith, illus. II. Title.

PINTAURO, Joseph. 202'.07
The earth mass. Words by Joe Pintauro. Drawn & lettered by Alicia Bay Laurel. [1st ed.] New York, Harper & Row [1973] [64] p. illus. (part col.) 29 cm. [BL2777.R5P56 1973] 72-78062 ISBN 0-06-066649-8 4.95 (pbk.)
1. Collective settlements—Religious life. I. Laurel, Alicia Bay, illus. II. Title.

SHAW, Jean. 202'.07
Please don't stand up in my canoe! / By Jean Shaw ; cartoons by Sam Butcher. Grand Rapids, Mich. : Zondervan Pub. House, [1975] 126 p. : ill. ; 18 cm. [PN6231.C35S48] 74-11860 pbk. : 1.25
1. Christianity—Anecdotes, facetiae, satire, etc. I. Title.

VAN DYKE, Dick. 202'.07
Altar egos. Westwood, N.J., Revell [1967] 1v. (in paged ports. 16x220 cm. [PN6231.R4V3] 67-28866 1.00 pap.,
1. Religion—Anecdotes, facetiae, satire, etc. I. Title.

WHITE, Floyd Edward. 202'.07
Nuggets of gold and a barrelful of chuckles. Kennewick, Wash., 1973. 64 p. 21 cm. [BV4515.2.W46] 73-81335
1. Christian life—Stories. I. Title.

SCRIPTURE sourcebook 202.2
(The); a topical text-book of Bible persons, places and subjects for Christian workers, students and teachers. Introd. on 'How to study the Bible' by D. L. Moody. Grand Rapids, Mich., Zondervan [c.1962] 192, 22p. 21cm. Previous eds. pub. by the Amer. Tract Soc. under title: The Bible textbook. 62-53034 2.50
1. Bible—Indexes, Topical.

AMERICAN Library Association. Public Libraries Dicision. Coordinating Committee on Recision of Public Library Standards. 2027.4
Public library service; a guide to evaluation, with minimum standards. Chicago, American Library Association, 1956. xxi, 71p. 21cm. Prelim ed. has title: Public library service to America. [Z731.A5285] 56-12393
1. Libraries—Standards. I. Title.

203 Dictionaries Of Christianity

BAKER'S dictionary of 203
theology. Everett F. Harrison, editor-in-chief; Geoffrey W. Bromiley, associate editor; Carl F. H. Henry, consulting editor. Grand Rapids, Baker Book House, 1960. 566 p. 25 cm. Includes bibliography. [BR95.B25] 60-7333
1. Theology—Dictionaries. I. Harrison, Everett Falconer, 1902- ed. II. Title: Dictionary of theology.

BUECHNER, Frederick, 1926- 203
Wishful thinking; a theological ABC. [1st ed.] New York, Harper & Row [1973] xii, 100 p. 22 cm. [BR95.B785 1973] 72-9872 ISBN 0-06-061155-3 4.95
1. Theology—Dictionaries. I. Title.

BUMPUS, John Skelton, 1861-1913. 203
A dictionary of ecclesiastical terms; being a history and explanation of certain terms used in architecture, ecclesiology, music, ritual, cathedral constitution, etc. London, T. W. Laurie [1910] Detroit, Gale Research Co., 1969. 323 p. 23 cm. [BR95.B8 1969] 68-30653
1. Religion—Dictionaries. 2. Encyclopedias and dictionaries. I. Title.

CHRISTIAN periodical index. 203
1958- [Buffalo, N. Y.] Christian Librarians' Fellowship. v. 25cm. annual. A subject index to periodical literature.' [Z7753.C5] 60-36226
1. Theology—Period.—Indexes. I. Christian Librarians' Fellowship.

CORPUS dictionary of Western 203
churches. Edited by T. C. O'Brien. Washington, Corpus Publications [1970] xviii, 820 p. 25 cm. Includes bibliographical references. [BR95.C67] 78-99501 25.00
1. Theology—Dictionaries. I. O'Brien, Thomas C., ed.

CULLY, Iris V 203
An introductory theological wordbook, by Iris V. and Kendig Brubaker Cully. Philadelphia, Westminster Press [1963] 204 p. 21 cm. [BR95.C8] 64-10033
1. Theology — Dictionaries. I. Cully, Kendig Brubaker, joint author. II. Title. III. Title: An introductory theological wordbook,

CULLY, Iris V. 203
An introductory theological wordbook, by Iris V. and Kendig Brubaker Cully. Philadelphia, Westminster Press [1963] 204 p. 21 cm. [BR95.C8] 64-10033
1. Theology—Dictionaries. I. Cully, Kendig Brubaker, joint author. II. Title. III. Title: Theological wordbook.

DICTIONARY of church terms 203
and symbols. Comp. by Loice Gouker. Ed. by Carl F. Weidmann. Designed by Tyyne Hakola. Norwalk, Conn., C. R. Gibson [1964] 69p. illus. 18cm. 64-18545 price unreported
1. Theology—Dictionaries. I. Gouker, Loice, comp. II. Title: Church terms and symbols.

DOUGLAS, James Dixon. 203
The new international dictionary of the Christian church. J. D. Douglas, general editor. Earle E. Cairns, consulting editor. Grand Rapids, Zondervan Pub. Co. [1974] xii, 1074 p. 25 cm. Includes bibliographical references. [BR95.D68] 74-8999 24.95
1. Theology—Dictionaries. I. Title.

FERM, Vergilius Ture Anselm, 1896- 203
Concise dictionary of religion; a lexicon of Protestant interpretation, by Vergilius Ferm. New York, Philosophical Library [1964? c1951] ix, 283 p. 22 cm. First published in 1951 under title: A Protestant dictionary. "Revised edition."--Dust jacket. [BR95.F37] 64-4055
1. Theology—Dictionaries. 2. Protestants—Dictionaries. I. Title.

FERM, Vergilius Ture Anselm, 1896- 203
A Protestant dictionary. New York, Philosophical Library [1951] 283 p. 22 cm. [BR95.F37] 51-14412
1. Theology—Dictionaries. 2. Protestantism—Dictionaries. I. Title.

FORLONG, James George Roche, d. 1904. 203
Faiths of man; encyclopedia of religions. Introd. by Margery Silver. New Hyde Park, N.Y., University Books [1964] 3 v. port. 24 cm. Republished verbatim from the London 1906 ed. [BL31.F7 1964] 64-19387
1. Religion—Dictionaries. I. Title.

FORLONG JAMES GEORGE ROCHE 1904 203
Faiths of man; encyclopedia of religions [3v.] Introd. by Margery Silver. New Hyde Park, N. Y., Univ. Bks. [c.1964] 3v. (569;582;527p.) port. 24cm. Repub. verbatim from the London 1906 ed. 64-19387 25.50 set,
1. Religion—Dictionaries. I. Title.

HEALEY, Frances G. 203
Fifty key words in theology, by F. G. Healey. Richmond, John Knox [1967] 84p. 20cm. (Fifty key word bks.) [BR96.5.H4] 67-16692 1.65 pap.,
1. Theology—Terminology. I. Title.

HERMANN, Fritz, writer on the Catholic Church. 203
Ein Schwarzbuch des xx, Jahrhunderts; Beitrage zur Rom-Frage.' Hamburg, Eekboom-Verlag [1955] 82p. illus. 21cm. [BX1775.G4H47] 55-59613
1. Catholic Church—Doctrinal and controversial works—Miscelaneous authors. I. Title.

KELLETT, Arnold. 203
Isms and ologies; a guide to unorthodox and non -- Christian beliefs. New York, Philosophical Library [1965] 156 p. 19 cm. Bibliography: p. 149-156. [(BR157)] 65-28943
1. Sects. I. Title.

KERR, James S. 203
A Christian's dictionary; 1,600 names, words and phrases [by] James S. Kerr and Charles

Lutz. Philadelphia, Fortress Press [1969] viii, 178 p. 22 cm. Bibliographical references included in "Acknowledgments" (p. vii-viii) [BR95.K4] 74-84542 2.95
1. Theology—Dictionaries. I. Lutz, Charles, joint author. II. Title.

MCCLINTOCK, John, 1814-1870. 203
Cyclopaedia of Biblical, theological, and ecclesiastical literature, prepared by John M'Clintock and James Strong. Grand Rapids, Baker Book House [1968- c1895- v. illus. 26 cm. [BR95.M35] 68-56007 12.95 per vol.
1. Bible—Dictionaries. 2. Church history—Dictionaries. 3. Theology—Dictionaries. I. Strong, James, 1822-1894, joint author. II. Title.

MCCLINTOCK, John, 1814-1870. 203
Cyclopaedia of Biblical, theological, and ecclesiastical literature, by John M'Clintock and James Strong. New York, Arno Press [1969] 10 v. in 5. illus. 32 cm. Title on spine: Cyclopaedia of Biblical literature. Reprint of the 1871-1881 ed. [BR95.M352] 68-56048
1. Bible—Dictionaries. 2. Church history—Dictionaries. 3. Theology—Dictionaries. I. Strong, James, 1822-1894, joint author. II. Title. III. Title: Cyclopaedia of Biblical literature.

MALLOCH, James M., D.D. comp. 203
A practical church dictionary. Ed. by Kay Smallzried. New York, Morehouse [c.1964] xiv, 520p. 25cm. Bibl. 64-23976 13.95
1. Theology—Dictionaries. 2. Anglican Communion—Dictionaries. I. Title.

MOSSE, Walter M. 203
A theological German vocabulary; German theological key words illustrated in quotations from Martin Luther's Bible and the Revised standard version, by Walter M. Mosse. New York, Octagon Books, 1968 [c1955] viii, 148 p. 21 cm. [BR95.M6 1968] 68-15887
1. Theology—Dictionaries—German. 2. German language—Dictionaries—English. I. Title.

THE New Catholic Peoples' encyclopedia. 203 Editor: Edward G. Finnegan. [New and rev. ed.] Chicago, Catholic Press, 1973. 3 v. (880 p.) illus. 25 cm. First published in 1965 under title: Virtue's Catholic encyclopedia. [BX841.V5 1973] 73-10485 ISBN 0-8326-2001-7
1. Catholic Church—Dictionaries. I. Finnegan, Edward G., ed. II. Virtue's Catholic encyclopedia. III. Title: Catholic encyclopedia.

THE Oxford dictionary of the Christian Church, 203 edited by F. L. Cross. London, New York, Oxford University Press, 1957. xix, 1492p. 25cm. Includes bibliographical references. [BR95.O8] 57-4541
1. Theology— Dictionaries. I. Cross, Frank Leslie, 1900- ed.

THE Oxford dictionary of the Christian Church, 203 edited by F. L. Cross. London, New York, Oxford University Press, 1957. xix, 1492 p. 25 cm. Includes bibliographical references. [BR95.O8] 57-4541
1. Theology—Dictionaries. I. Cross, Frank Leslie, 1900- ed.

THE Oxford dictionary of the Christian Church, 203 edited by F. L. Cross. London, New York, Oxford University Press [1966] xix, 1492 p. 25 cm. Includes bibliographical references. [BR95.O8 1966] 72-443015 unpriced
1. Theology—Dictionaries. I. Cross, Frank Leslie, 1900- ed.

PIKE, Edgar Royston, 1896- 203
Encyclopaedia of religion and religions. New York, Meridian Books [1958] 406p. 21cm. (Meridian library, ML9) [BL31.P5 1958] 58-8530
1. Religion—Dictionaries. 2. Religions—Dictionaries. I. Title.

PROTESTANT Episcopal Church 203
in the U. S. A. National Council. Dept. of Christian Education.
More than words; a resource book for church school teachers and for students in junior high school classes. Rev. ed. Greenwich, Conn., Seabury Press [1958] 216p. 22cm. (The Seabury series, R-7B) [BX5007.P7 1958] 58-9264
1. Protestant Episcopal Church in the U. S. A.—Dictionaries. I. Title.

PURVIS, John Stanley, 1890- 203
Dictionary of ecclesiastical terms. London, New York, T. Nelson [1962] vii, 204p. 22cm. [BR95.P8] 62-51845
1. Theology—Dictionaries. I. Title. II. Title: Ecclesiastical terms.

SACRAMENTUM mundi; 203
an encyclopedia of theology. [Edited by Karl Rahner and others. New York] Herder and Herder [1968- v. 27 cm. Includes bibliographies. [BR95] 68-25987
1. Theology—Dictionaries. I. Rahner, Karl, 1904- ed.

SCHAFF-HERZOG encyclopedia. 203
The new Schaff-Herzog encyclopedia of religious knowledge, embracing Biblical, historical, doctrinal, and practical theology, and Biblical, theological, and ecclesiastical biography from the earliest times to the present day; based on the 3d ed. of the Real encyklopadie founded by J.J. Herzog, and edited by Albert Hauck, prepared by more than six hundred scholars and specialists under the supervision of Samuel Macauley Jackson (editor-in-chief) with the assistance of Charles Colebrook Sherman and George William Gilmore (associate editors) and others. Grand Rapids, Mich., Baker, 1949-50. Grand Rapids, Mich., Baker, 1955. 13v. 23cm. 2 v .(xx, 1205p.) 25cm. Vols. 2-12 have abbreviated title which varies slightly; v. 13: Index by George William Gilmore.--Twentieth century encyclopedia of religious knowledge. An extension of The new Schaff-Herzog encyclopedia of religious knowledge. Editor-in-chief: Uefferts A. Loetscher. Includes bibliographies. A51
1. Theology—Dictionaries. I. Jackson, Samuel Macauley, 1851-1912. bd. II. Udetscher, Leffert Augustine, 1904- ed. III. Title.

SHANNON, Ellen C. 203
A layman's guide to Christian terms, by Ellen C. Shannon. South Brunswick [N.J.] A. S. Barnes [1969] 347 p. 22 cm. Bibliography: p. 347. [BR95.S45] 69-15776 10.00
1. Theology—Dictionaries. I. Title.

STUBER, Stanley Irving, 1903- 203
ed.
The illustrated Bible and church handbook, edited by Stanley I. Stuber. New York, Association Press [1966] 532 p. illus., ports. 24 cm. [BR95.S79] 66-11794
1. Theology — Dictionaries. I. Title.

STUBER, Stanley Irving, 1903- 203
ed.
The illustrated Bible and church handbook / edited by Stanley I. Stuber. New York : Galahad Books, [197-] c1966. 532 p. : ill. ; 24 cm. Originally published by Association Press. Includes index. [BR95.S79 1970z] 73-79814 ISBN 0-88365-024-X : 7.95
1. Theology—Dictionaries. I. Title.

STUBER, Stanley Irving, 1903- 203
ed.
The illustrated Bible and church handbook. New York, Association [c.1966] 532p. illus., ports. 24cm. [BR95.S79] 66-11794 5.95
1. Theology — Dictionaries. I. Title.

WHITE, Richard Clark, 1926- 203
The vocabulary of the church: a pronunciation guide. New York, Macmillan, 1960. xiv, 178 p. 22 cm. [BR95.W53] 60-11810
1. Theology — Dictionaries. I. Title.

WHITE, Richard Clark, 1926- 203
The vocabulary of the church: a pronunciation guide. New York, Macmillan [c.]1960. xiv, 178p. 22cm. 60-11810 3.50
1. Theology—Dictionaries. I. Title.

WRIGHT, Charles Henry 203
Hamilton, 1836-1909, ed.
A Protestant dictionary, containing articles on the history, doctrines, and practices of the Christian Church, edited by Charles H. H. Wright and Charles Neil. London, Hodder and Stoughton, 1904. Detroit, Gale Research Co., 1972. xv, 832 p. illus. 23 cm. Includes bibliographical references. [BR95.W7 1972] 73-155436 27.50
1. Catholic Church—Doctrinal and controversial works—Protestant authors. 2. Theology—Dictionaries. 3. Protestantism—Dictionaries. I. Neil, Charles, 1841- joint ed. II. Title.

204 General Special

BAGGS, Ralph L 204
Religion could be wonderful, if! [1st ed.] New York, Greenwich Book Publishers, 1955. 87p. 22cm. [BL50.B25] 55-11467
1. Religion. I. Title.

BASILIUS, Harold A ed. 204
Contemporary problems in religion. Detroit, Wayne University Press, 1956. viii, 128p. port. 21cm. (The Leo M. Franklin lectures in human relations, 1953-54) 'References': p. 123-126. [BL25.B3] 56-7842
1. Religion—Addresses, essays, lectures. I. Title. II. Series.

BELL, Hermon Fiske, 1880- 204
Talks on religion. New York, Philosophical Library [1958] 73p. 21cm. [BL50.B38] 58-59400
1. Religion. I. Title.

BENTZ VAN DEN BERG, John 204
Cato, 1903-
Themes to ponder; religious essays. [1st ed.] New York, Vantage Press [1957] 135p. 21cm. [BR126.B38] 57-9294
I. Title.

BOOTH, Edwin Prince, 1898- 204
The greater church of the future. Foreword by Lyman V. Rutledge. Boston, Beacon Press [1951] 51 p. 22 cm. [BL390.B65] 52-6156
1. Religions (Proposed, universal, etc.) 2. Liberalism (Religion) 3. religions (Proposed, universal, etc.) 4. Liberalism (Religion) I. Title.

BOWMAN, Archibald Allan, 204
1883-1936.
The absurdity of Christianity, and other essays. Edited, with an introd., by Charles W. Hendel. New York, Liberal Arts Press [1958] xxxiii, 62p. 21cm. (The Library of liberal arts, no. 56) [BR100.B58 1958] 57-14625
1. Christianity—Philosophy. I. Title.

BURNABY, John. 204
Christian words and Christian meanings. New York, Harper [c1955] 160p. 20cm. [BR96.5.B8 1955a] 55-11477
1. Theology- Terminology. I. Title.

CALHOUN, Arthur Wallace, 204
1885-
The cultural concept of Christianity. Grand Rapids, Eerdmans, 1950. 155 p. 23 cm. [BR115.C8C3] 50-10591
1. Culture. 2. Civilization, Christian. I. Title.

CARRUTHERS, Thomas Neely, 204
Bp., 1900-
Sparks of fire, and other thoughts about things that matter. New York, Morehouse-Gorham Co., 1953. 166p. 21cm. [BR123.C35] 53-13149
1. Christianity—Addresses, essays, lectures. I. Title.

CICOGNANI, Anteto Giovanni, 204
Abp., 1883-
Addresses and sermons. New York, Benziger Bros., 1938-55. 4 v. ports. 21 cm. Subtitle, v. 2: 1938-1942; v. 3: 1942-1951; v. 4: 1951-1955. Vols. 2-4 have imprint: Paterson, N. J., St. Anthony Guild Press. [BX1756.C53A3] 38-10315
1. Catholic Church—Addresses, essays, lectures. I. Title.

COLE, Stewart Grant, 1892- 204
ed.
This is my faith the convictions of representative Americans today. [1st ed.] New York, Harper [1956] 291p. 22cm. [BL48.C56] 55-11403
1. Religion. I. Title.

COLLINS, Willard. 204
Collins-Craig auditorium meeting; a series of sermons delivered in the municipal auditorium in Nashville, Tennessee, October 7-14, 1962. [Mack Wayne Craig, song leader] Nashville, Gospel Advocate Co. [c1962] xxiii, 97 p. illus., ports. 20 cm. [BV3797.C64] 63-23813
1. Evangelistic sermons. 2. Sermons, American. I. Craig, Mack Wayne. II. Title.

CONWELL, Russell Herman 204
Acres of diamonds. With an introductory statement by Millard E. Gladfelter. Philadelphia, Winston [c.1905-1959] viii, 38p. 24cm. 59-15577, not for sale
1. Success. I. Title.

CONWELL, Russell Herman, 204
1843-1925
Acres of diamonds. [Westwood, N.J.] Revell [1960] 64p. 17cm. (Revell inspirational classic) [BX6333.C6A3 1960] 61-318 3.95
1. Success. I. Title.

CONWELL, Russell Herman, 204
1843-1925.
Acres of diamonds. [Westwood, N.J.] Fleming H. Revell [c.1960] 64p. (Revell inspirational classic) 1.00 bds.,
1. Success. I. Title.

CONWELL, Russell Herman, 204
1843-1925
Acres of diamonds. New York, Pyramid [1966, c.1960] 64p. 17cm. (Little inspiration classic, LP8) [BX6333C6A3 1960] .35 pap.,
1. Success. I. Title.

FREEMAN, John Davis, 1884- 204
Death loses the game. Chicago, Moody Press [1954] 188p. 22cm. [BX6495.F7A3] 54-1084
1. Baptists—Clergy—Correspondence, reminiscences, etc. I. Title.

GILLIS, James Martin, 1876- 204
This mysterious human nature. New York, Scribner [1956] 244p. 21cm. [BX890.G515] 56-11869
1. Catholic Church—Addresses, essays, lectures. 2. Christian ethics— Catholic authors. I. Title.

GRAHAM, Lorah Harris. 204
Inspirations: radio talks and travel sketches. Ringgold, Ga., Ringgold Bible Club [1950] 270 p. port. 21 cm. [BR123.G65] 50-34889
1. Christianity—Addresses, essays, lectures. I. Title.

HIGH, Stanley, 1895- 204
... Faith for today, by Stanley High, Frank Kingdon, Gerald Groveland Walsh, S. J., Louis Finkelstein, PH. D., Swami Nikhilananda, with an introduction and postscript by George V. Denny, jr. Garden City, N.Y., Town hall press and Doubleday, Doran and company, inc., 1941. x, 266 p. 19 1/2 cm. At head of title: Five faiths look at the world. "Enlarged and amplified versions of ... [the authors'] Town hall lectures." -- Introd. "First edition." [BR516.F3] 41-18045
1. U.S. — Religion. I. Kingdon, Frank, 1894- II. Walsh, Gerald Groveland, 1892-1952. III. Finkelstein, Louis, 1895- IV. Nikhiiananda, Swami. V. Denny, George Vernon, 1899- VI. Town hall, inc., New York. VII. Title.

HOBBS, Herschel H. 204
Welcome speeches, and emergency addresses for all occasions. Grand Rapids, Michigan, Zondervan [c.1960] 64p. 20cm. 1.00 pap.,
I. Title.

LEBRET, Louis Joseph, 1897- 204
Human ascent; translated by Robert and Martha Faulhaber. Illustrated by Clarence E. Giese. Chicago, Fides Publishers Association [1955] 122p. illus. 20cm. [BR121.L375] 55-7392
1. Christianity—Essence, genius, nature. 2. Religion—Philosophy. I. Title.

LEWIS, Clive Staples 204
The world's last night, and other essays. New York, Harcourt, Brace [c.1952-1960] 113p. 21cm. 60-5439 3.00

1. Christianity—Addresses, essays, lectures. I. Title.

LEWIS, Clive Staples, 1898- 204
The world's last night, and other essays. [1st ed.] New York, Harcourt, Brace [1960] 113p. 21cm. [BR123.L487] 60-5439
1. Christianity—Addresses, essays, lectures. I. Title.

LEWIS, Clive Staples, 1898- 204
1963.
Mere Christianity; a revised and enlarged edition, with a new introduction of the three books, The case for christianity, Christian behaviour, and Beyond personality. New York, Macmillan, 1952. 175 p. 21 cm. [BR123.L484 1952] 52-14321
1. Christianity—Addresses, essays, lectures. I. Title.

LEWIS, Norman, 1903- 204
Light from God; essays on the true religious principles. [1st ed.] New York, Exposition Press [1956] 65p. illus. 21cm. [BL50.L43] 56-9560
1. Religion. I. Title.

LONG, Valentine, Father. 204
Not on bread alone. [2d ed., 7th print.] Paterson, N. J., St. Anthony Guild Press [1954] 213p. 20cm. [BX890.L6 1954] 54-42582
1. Catholic Church—Addresses, essays, lectures. 2. Literature—Addresses, essays, lectures. 3. Religion in literature. I. Title.

LUCCOCK, Halford Edward, 204
1885-
Like a mighty army; selected letters of Simeon Stylites [pseud.] New York, Oxford University Press, 1954. 182 p. 20 cm. [BR125.L87] 54-12003
1. Christianity—Addresses, essays, lectures. I. Title.

MACHEN, John Gresham, 1881- 204
1937.
What is Christianity? and other addresses; edited by Ned Bernard Stonehouse. Grand Rapids, Eerdmans, 1951. 317 p. 21 cm. [BR121.M3222] 51-1399
1. Christianity—Addresses, essays, lectures. I. Title.

MARCHANT, James, Sir 1867- 204
ed.
The coming-of- age of Christianity [by] John Foster [and others] Edited by Sir James Marchant. Chicago, H. Regnery, 1951. xvii, 190p. 22cm. [BR155.M] A53
1. Church history—Addresses, essays, lectures. I. Foster, John. II. Title.

MAURIAC, Francois, 1885- 204
Words of faith. [Translated from the original French, Paroles catholiques, by Edward H. Flannery] New York, Philosophical Library [1955] 118p. 21cm. [BR123.M435] 55-13769
1. Christianity—Addresses, essays, lectures. I. Title.

MOODY, Dwight Lyman, 1837- 204
1899.
Moody's child stories as related by Dwight Lyman Moody in his revival work in Europe and America. Copiously illustrated from Gustave Dorc and by J. Stuart Littlejohn. It also contains story of Moody's life. Chicago, Rhodes & McClure Pub. Co., 1900. 293 p. illus., port. 20 cm. [BV3797.M7C5] 1-29942
1. Homiletical illustrations. 2. Christian life — Stories. I. Title.

MURRAY, Gilbert, 1866- 204
Stoic, Christian, and humanist. Essays] Boston, Beacon Press, 1950. 180 p. 19 cm. Bibliography: p. 17-18. [BL87.M8] 51-4096
1. Religion — Addresses, essays, lectures. I. Title.

NEWELL, William Reed, 1868- 204
Famous messages, mostly hitherto unpublished. Chicago, Moody Press, 1951. 251 p. 20 cm. [BR123.N35] 52-20825
1. Christianity — Addresses, essays, lectures. I. Title.

NIEBUHR, Reinhold, 1892-1971. 204
Essays in applied Christianity. Selected and edited by D. B. Robertson. New York, Meridian Books [1959] 348 p. 19 cm. (Living age books, LA26) Bibliography: p. 345-348. [BR123.N5] 59-7189
1. Christianity—Addresses, essays, lectures. I. Title: Applied Christianity.

PIUS XII, Pope, 1876- 204
The mind of Pius XII. Edited by Robert C. Pollock New York, Crown Publishers [1955] xix, 234p. port. 22cm. Excerpts from communications of His Holiness. Bibliography: p. 231-234. [BX890.P5818] 55-7235
1. Pius XII, Pope, 1876- —Dictionaries, indexes, etc. I. Title.

PRATT, James Bissett, 1875- 204
1944.
Eternal values in religion. New York, Macmillan, 1950. viii, 162 p. 20 cm. Essays. [BR123.P65] 50-5728
1. Christianity—Addresses, essays, lectures. I. Title.

SCHLEIERMACHER, Friedrich 204
Ernst Daniel, 1768-1834.
On religion: speeches to its cultured despisers. Translated by John Oman. With an introd. by Rudolf Otto. New York, Harper [1958] 287p. 21cm. (The Library of religion and culture) Harper torchbooks, TB36. [BL48.S33 1958] 58-7108
1. Religion. I. Title.

SHEEN, Fulton John, 1895- 204
Moods and truths. Garden City, N.Y., Garden City Pub. Co. [1950, c1932] ix, 237 p. 21 cm. A continuation of the author's Old errors and new labels. [BX1395.S5 1950] 51-1975
1. Religious thought—20th cent. I. Title.

SHEEN, Fulton John, 1895- 204
Old errors and new labels. Garden City, N.Y., Garden City Pub. Co. [1950, c1931] ix, 336 p. 21 cm. [B804.S5 1950] 51-2078
1. Philosophy, Modern. 2. Philosophy and religion. I. Title.

SKINNER, Clarence Russell, 204
1881-1949.
Worship and the well ordered life. Boston, Universalist Historical Society [1955] 183p. 22cm. [BR85.S47] 56-19966
1. Church. 2. Worship. 3. Christian life. I. Title.

UNAMUNO Y JUGO, Miguel de, 204
1864-1936.
The agony of Christianity. Translated with an introd. by Kurt F. Reinhardt. New York, F. Ungar Pub. Co. [1960] 155 p. 19 cm. (Selected books on religion and philosophy) [BR121.U48] 60-13989
1. Christianity — 20th cent. I. Title.

UNAMUNO Y JUGO, Miguel de, 204
1864-1936.
The agony of Christianity. Translated [from the Spanish] with an introd. by Kurt F. Reinhardt. New York, F. Ungar Pub. Co. [c.1960] 155p. (Atlantic paperback 510) 60-13989 4.00; 1.45 pap.,
1. Christianity—20th cent. I. Title.

WALMSLEY, Arthur E., ed. 204
The church in a society of abundance. New York, Seabury [c.]1963. viii, 178p. 22cm. Bibl. 63-9058 3.95
1. Christianity—20th cent.—Addresses, essays, lectures. I. Title.

WHITESELL, Jack R 204
Sermon outlines for soul winning. [Westwood, N.J.] Revell [1962] 64 p. 21 cm. (Revell's sermon outline series) [BV3797.W433] 62-10742
1. Evangelistic sermons — Outlines. I. Title.

BADARAYANA. 204.1
The Vedanta Sutras. With the commentary by Sankara. Translated by George Thibaut. New York, Dover Publications [1962] 2 v. 22 cm. (The Sacred books of the East v. 34, 38) The Sacred books of the East, v. 34, 38) Contents.CONTENTS.--pt. 1 Adhyaya I-II (Pada I-II)--pt. 2, Adhyaya II (Pada III-IV)-IV. [BL1115.B23] 62-53242
1. Brahmanism. I. Sankaracarya. II. Thibaut, George Frederick William, 1848-1914, ed. and tr. III. Title. IV. Series.

*BALSIGER, Dave. 204.5
In search of Noah's ark / by Dave Balsiger & Charles E. Sellier Jr. Los Angeles : Sun Classic Books, 1976. 218, [32]p. : ill. ; 18 cm. (A Schick-Sun classic book) Includes bibliographical references. [BL325.D4] ISBN 0-917214-01-3 pbk. : 1.95
1. Noah's ark. I. Sellier, Charles E. joint author. II. Title.

DUGGAN, William J. 204.5
Myth and Christian belief [by] William J. Duggan. Notre Dame, Ind., Fides [1971] viii, 141 p. illus. 20 cm. Bibliography: p. 141. [BL304.D84] 76-140145 ISBN 0-8190-0431-6 2.95
1. Myth. 2. Religion and language. I. Title.

EVERY, George. 204'.5
Christian mythology. Feltham, Hamlyn, 1970. 5-141 p. illus. (some col.) 29 cm. Illus. on lining papers. Bibliography: p. 138. [BR135.E9] 72-595863 ISBN 0-600-31601-7 £1.25
1. Legends, Christian. I. Title.

SEZNEC, Jean. 204.5
The survival of the pagan gods; the mythological tradition and its place in Renaissance humanism and art. Translated from the French by Barbara F. Sessions. [New York] Pantheon Books [1953] xvi, 376 p. illus. 27 cm. (Bollingen series, 38) "Originally published ... as La survivance des dieux antiques ... The present edition has been revised by the author." Bibliography: p. 327-345. [BR135.S483] 52-10520
1. Humanism. 2. Art, Renaissance. 3. Mythology, Classical. 4. Gods in art. I. Title.

205 Serials On Christianity

CORPUS Scriptorum 205
Ecclesiasticorum Latinorum: v.33. 40 (2 pts.) 60, 63. New York, Johnson Reprint [1963] 5v. (various p.) 23cm. Contents.v.33, pt. 1, 1896.--v.40, pts. 1-2, 1900--v.60, pt.1, 1913--v.63. pt.3, 1922. v.33, pap., 15.00; v.40, pts. 1-2, pap., ea., 20.00; v.60, pt. 1, pap., 20.00; v. 63, pt.3, 15.00

JOURNAL for the theology and 205
the church. 3- Tubingen, J. C. B. Mohr; New York, Harper, 1967- v. 20cm. (Harper torchbks. TB253) Intial numbers are limited to trs. of articles from Zeitschrift fur Theologie und Kirche. [BR1.J58] 65-8933 2.95 pap.,
1. Theology—Period. I. Zeitschrift fur Theologie und Kirche. II. as distinctive title: Distinctive Protestant and Catholic thekem reconsidered. v. 3 ed. by R. W. Funk others.

JOURNAL for theology and the 205
church. 4- Tubingen, J. C. B. Mohr; New York, Harper 1967- v.21cm. (Harper torchbks. TB254) Initial numbers are limit ed to trs. of articles from Zeitschrift fur Theologie und Kirche. [BR1.J58] 65-8933 2.25 pap.,
1. Theology—Period. I. Zeitschrift fur Theologie und Kirche.

**JOURNAL of Biblical* 205
literature; v.49-69. New York, Johnson Reprint [1964] 21v. (various p.) Contents.v.49-69. 1939-1950. With index to v.41-60 for 1922-1941. set, pap., 420.00; ea., pap., 20.00. index, pap., 5.00

PERSPECTIVE; 205
a Princeton journal of Christian opinion. Princeton, N. J., Student Christian Association of Princeton University] v. in 26cm. 8 no. (during the school year) Began publication with Apr. 1949 issue. Cf. Union list of serials. [BR1.P38] 59-54651
1. Theology—Period. 2. Students—Period. I. Princeton University. Student Christian Association.

**REVUE de theologie et de* 205
philosophie; ser. 1, v. 1-44, 1868-1911. Geneve, H. Georg. 1868-1911, New York, Johnson Reprint, 1966. 44v. (various p.) 21cm. 1,230.00; 1.100.000; 25.00 set, set, pap., ea., pap.,

ZEITSCHRIFT fur Theologie and 205
Kirche.
Journal for theology and the church. 1- Tubingen, J. C. B. Mohr; New York, Harper & Row, 1965- v. 20 cm. (Harper torchbooks) Initial numbers are limited to translations of articles from Zeitschrift fur Theologie and Kirche. [BR1.J58] 65-8933
1. Theology — Period. I. Title.

206 Organizations Of Christianity

BAND, Benjamin. 206
Portland Jewry, its growth and development. Portland, Me., Jewish Historical Society [1955] 117p. 24cm. [F29.P9B2] 56-17715
1. Jews in Portland, Me. I. Title.

DEFENDERS of the 206'.2'73
Christian Faith.
Fire by night and cloud by day; a history of Defenders of the Christian Faith. Compiled and written by Defenders editorial staff. Wichita, Kan., Mertmont Pub. Co. [1966] 128 p. illus., facsims., ports. 21 cm. Cover title: Amazing history of Defenders of the Christian Faith. [BR21.D4] 68-3108
1. Defenders of the Christian Faith—Hist. I. Title. II. Title: Amazing history of Defenders of the Christian Faith.

DEFENDERS of the 206'.2'73
Christian Faith.
Fire by night and cloud by day; a history of Defenders of the Christian Faith. Compiled and written by Defenders editorial staff. Wichita, Kan., Mertmont Pub. Co. [1966] 128 p. illus., facsims., ports. 21 cm. Cover title: Amazing history of Defenders of the Christian Faith. [BR21.D4] 68-3108
1. Defenders of the Christian Faith—History. I. Title. II. Title: Amazing history of Defenders of the Christian Faith.

VITRANO, Steven P. 206'.2773'11
An hour of good news; the Chicago Sunday Evening Club, a unique preaching ministry [by] Steven P. Vitrano. Chicago, Chicago Sunday Evening Club, 1974. x, 177 p. illus. 22 cm. Includes bibliographical references. [BV4208.U6V57] 74-182341
1. Chicago Sunday Evening Club. 2. Hour of good news. 3. Preaching—History—United States. I. Title.

HERTZ, Richard C. 206.3
What can a man believe? By Richard C. Hertz. New York, Bloch Pub. Co. [1967] 95 p. 21 cm. Bibliographical footnotes. [BM601.H38] 66-20832
1. Jewish theology. I. Title.

LANDIS, Benson Young, 1897- 206.9
Careers of service in the church, a description of many interesting and satisfying vocations [by] Benson Y. Landis. New York, M. Evans; distributed in association with Lippincott, Philadelphia [1964] 256 p. 22 cm. [BV683.L3] 64-207811
1. Church work as a profession. I. Title.

RAND, Willard J 206.9
Call and response; an enlistment guide for church occapations. New York, Abingdon Press [1964] 160 p. 20 cm. Bibliography: p. 154-157. [BV4740.R3] 64-14620
1. Vocation. 2. Church work as a profession. 3. Christian leadership. I. Title.

RAND, Willard J., Jr. 206.9
Call and response; an enlistment guide for church occupations. Nashville, Abingdon [c.1964] 160p. 20cm. Bibl. 64-14620 1.75 pap.,
1. Vocation. 2. Church work as a profession. 3. Christian leadership. I. Title.

WINN, Albert Curry, 1921- 206.9
You and your lifework; a Christian choice for youth, written by Albert Curry Winn in collaboration with the Dept. of the Ministry of the Commission on Higher Education, National Council of the Churches of Christ in the U.S.A. Illustrated by Nita Engle. Chicago. Science Research Associates [1963] 90 p. illus. 28 cm. [BV4740.W5] 63-11011
1. Vocational guidance. 2. Vocation. I. Title.

WINN, Alert Curry, 1921- 206.9
You and your lifework; a Christian choice for youth, written by Albert Curry Winn in collaboration with the Dept. of Ministry of the Commission on Higher Educ., Natl. Council of the Churches of Christ in the U.S.A. Illus. by Nita Engle. Chicago, Science Res. Assocs. [c.1963] 90p. illus. 28cm. 63-11001 1.25 pap.,
1. Vocational guidance 2. Vocation. I. Title.

207 Study & Teaching Of Christianity

ALLEN, Yorke. 207
A seminary survey; a listing and review of the activities of the theological schools and major seminaries located in Africa, Asia, and Latin America which are training men to serve as ordained ministers and priests in the Protestant, Roman Catholic, and Eastern churches. New York, Harper [1960] xxvi, 640 p. maps (part fold.) tables. 24 cm. Bibliography: p. 604-628. [BV4020.A6] 60-5325
1. Theology—Study and teaching. 2. Theological seminaries. I. Title.

ARMSTRONG, Wesley Earl, 1899- 207
A manual on certification requirements for school personnel in the United States, including requirements in the forty-eight States, Alaska, District of Columbia, Hawaii, and Puerto Rico. 1953 ed. Prepared jointly by W. Earl Armstrong and T. M. Stinnett. Washington, National Education Association of the United States, 1953. v, 172p. tables. 26cm. First published in 1951 under title: Certification requirements for school personnel. [LB1771.A] A54
1. Teachers—Certification—U. S. I. Stinnett, Timothy M., 1901- joint author. II. Title. III. Title: Certification requirements for school personnel in the United States.

AUGUSTINIAN Educational 207
Association.
Proceedings. [n. p.] v. 23cm. annual. [LC461.A82] 61-46628
1. Catholic Church in the U. S.—Education—Societies, etc. I. Title.

BABIN, Pierre 207
Options: approaches for the religious education of adolescents. Tr. & adapted by John F. Murphy. [New York] Herder & Herder [1967] Tr. of Options pour une education de la foi des jeuses. Bibl. [BX926.B313] 67-14140 3.95
1. Religious education of children. 2. Catechetics—Catholic Church. I.)0c173p. 21cm. II. Title.

BABIN, Pierre. 207
Options: approaches for the religious education of adolescents. Translated and adapted by

John F. Murphy. [New York] Herder and Herder [1967] 173 p. 21 cm. Translation of Options pour une education de la foi des jeunes. Bibliographical footnotes. [BX926.B313] 67-14140
1. Religious education of children. 2. Cateschetics—Catholic Church. I. Title.

BLUEM, A. William. 207
Religious television programs; a study of relevance, by A. William Bluem. New York, Hastings House [1969] viii, 220 p. illus. 22 cm. (Communication arts books) Includes bibliographical references. [BV656.3.B55] 68-31687 4.95
1. Television in religion. I. Title.

CATECHETICS for the future. 207
Edited by Alois Muller. [New York] Herder and Herder [1970] 159 p. 23 cm. (Concilium: theology in the age of renewal: Pastoral theology, v. 53) Includes bibliographical references. [BV1473.C3] 76-110787 2.95
1. Christian education—Addresses, essays, lectures. I. Muller, Alois, 1924- ed. II. Series: Concilium (New York) v. 53

CATHOLIC Church. Pope, 1939- 207
(Pius XII) Sedes sapientiae (31 May 1956) English.
The Apostolic constitution, Sedes sapientiae and the General statutes annexed to it, on the religious, clerical, and apostolic training to be imparted to clerics in the states of perfection to be acquired. Washington, Priv. print., Provinceof Washington, Society of Mary, 1957. v, 75p. 22cm. At head of title: The Sacred Congregation of Religious. [BX900.A55 1957] 57-47820
1. Monasticism and religious orders—Education. 2. Theology—Study and teaching—Catholic Church. I. Catholic Church. Congregatio de Religiosis. II. Title.

CATHOLIC Church. Pope, 1939- 207
(Pius XII) Sedes sapientiae (31 May 1956) English.
The Apostolic constitution, Sedes sapientiae and the General statutes annexed to it, on the religious, clerical, and apostolic training to be imparted to clerics in the states of perfection to be acquired. 2d ed. Washington, Sacred Congregation of Religious; distributor: Catholic University of America Press, 1957. v, 97p. 23cm. At head of title: The Sacred Congregation of Religious. [BX900.A55 1957a] 57-4522
1. Monasticism and religious orders—Education. 2. Theology— Study and teaching—Catholic Church. I. Catholic Church. Congregatio de Religiosis. II. Title.

CATHOLIC University of 207
America. Conference on the Curriculum of the Minor Seminary, 1955.
Curriculum of the minor seminary: social studies, Greek, and the general curriculum; the proceedings of the Sixth Annual Conference on the Curriculum of the Minor Seminary, conducted at the Catholic University of America, May 13, 14, 15, 1955. Edited by Roy J. Deferrari. Washington, Catholic University of America Press, 1956. iv, 81p. 22cm. Includes bibliographies. [BX905.C3 1955] 56-1552
1. Theologic seminaries, Catholic. 2. Greek language—Study and teaching. 3. Social science—Study and teaching (Secondary) I. Deferrari, Roy Joseph, 1890- ed. II. Title.

CATHOLIC University of 207
America. Workshop on Integration in the Catholic Secondary School Curriculum, 1950.
The integration of the Catholic secondary school curriculum; the proceedings of the Workshop on the Integration of the Catholic Secondary School Curriculum, conducted at Catholic University of America from June 9 to June 20, 1950. Edited by Sister Mary Janet, s.c. Washington, Catholic University of America Press, 1951. v, 154p. 23cm. 'General bibliography':p. 139-149. [LC485.C33 1950] A51
1. High schools—Curricula. 2. Articulation (Education) 3. Catholic Church in the U. S.—Education. I. Miller, Mary Janet, Sister, 1897- II. Title.

COVELL, Ralph R. 207
An extension seminary primer [by] Ralph R. Covell [and] C. Peter Wagner. South Pasadena, Calif., William Carey Library [1971] xi, 140 p. illus. 23 cm. Bibliography: p. 134-138. [BV4020.C635] 72-168665 ISBN 0-87808-106-2 2.45
1. Theology—Study and teaching. I. Wagner, C. Peter. II. Title.

CULLY, Kendig Brubaker. 207
Does the church know how to teach? An ecumenical inquiry. Edited by Kendig Brubaker Cully. [New York] Macmillan [1970] viii, 387 p. 21 cm. Includes bibliographical references. [BV1473.C8 1970] 79-90872
1. Christian education—Addresses, essays, lectures. I. Title.

CULLY, Kendig Brubaker. 207
The search for a Christian education since 1940. Philadelphia, Westminster Press [1965] 205 p. 21 cm. Bibliographical references included in "Notes" (p. [183]-197) [BV1471.2.C79] 65-15290
1. Religious education—Addresses, essays, lectures. I. Title.

DITTES, James E. 207
Vocational guidance of theological students; a manual for the use of the Theological school inventory [by] James E. Dittes. [Dayton, Ohio, Ministry Studies Board, 1964] 1 v. (various pagings) illus. 28 cm. "The Theological school inventory was developed in research conducted by Educational Testing Service, directed by Frederick R. Kling, supported by Lilly Endowment, inc." [BV4011.4.D5] 254 68-2363
1. Theological school inventory. I. Title.

DONLAN, Thomas C 207
Theology and education. Dubuque, W. C. Brown Co., 1952. 134p. 24cm. (Dominican Fathers, Province of St. Albert the Great. The Aquinas library. Doctrinal studies, 2) [BV1610.D65] 53-1515
1. Universities and colleges—Religion. 2. Religious education. 3. Catholic Church—Education. 4. Theology—Study and teaching. I. Title.

DONNELLAN, Michael. 207
What to believe; changing patterns in religious education. Dublin, Gill [1968] vii, 132 p. 20 cm. (Logos books) Includes bibliographical references. [BV1471.D63] 78-261387 13/6
1. Christian education. I. Title.

DRESSELHAUS, Richard L. 207
Teaching for decision [by] Richard L. Dresselhaus. Springfield, Mo., Gospel Pub. House [1973] 123, [1] p. 19 cm. Bibliography: p. [124] [BV1471.2.D73] 73-75502
1. Religious education. 2. Evangelistic work. I. Title.

DRESSELHAUS, Richard L. 207
Teaching for decision [by] Richard L. Dresselhaus. Springfield, Mo., Gospel Pub. House [1973] 123, [1] p. 19 cm. Bibliography: p. [124] [BV1471.2.D73] 73-75502 1.25 (pbk.)
1. Religious education. 2. Evangelistic work. I. Title.

EDWARDS, Paul M. 207
Inquiring faith; an exploration in religious education, by Paul M. Edwards. [Independence, Mo., Herald, 1967] 112p. 21cm. Bibl. [BV1471.2.E3] 67-4880 2.25; 1.50 pap.,
1. Religious education. I. Title.

FERRE, Nels Fredrick 207
Solomon, 1908-
A theology for Christian education by Nels F. S. Ferre. Philadelphia, Westminster Press [1967] 224 p. 21 cm. [BT78.F42] 67-10510
1. Christian education. 2. Theology, Doctrinal. I. Title.

FOUNDATIONS for Christian 207
education in an era of change / edited by Marvin J. Taylor. Nashville : Abingdon, c1976. 288 p. ; 22 cm. Supplement to An introduction to Christian education, edited by M. J. Taylor. Includes index. Bibliography: p. 271-283. [BV1473.F677] 75-44185 ISBN 0-687-13329-7 pbk. : 6.50
1. Christian education—Addresses, essays, lectures. I. Taylor, Marvin J., 1921- II. Taylor, Marvin J., 1921- An introduction to Christian education.

HALL, Brian P. 207
Value clarification as learning process; a handbook for Christian educators, by Brian P. Hall [and] Maury Smith. Consultant authors: Gerald Conway, Michael J. Kenney [and] Joseph Osburn. [New York, Paulist Press, 1973] 270 p. illus. 26 cm. (Educator formation books) Bibliography: p. 258-265. [BV1464.H3] 73-81108 ISBN 0-8091-1797-5 7.95
1. Religious education. 2. Worth. I. Smith, Maury, joint author. II. Title.

HAUGHTON, Rosemary. 207
Beginning life in Christ; Gospel bearings on Christian education. Westminster, Md., Newman Press [1966] 192 p. 21 cm. Bibliography: p. 191-192. [BV1475.2.H38] 66-8856
1. Religious education of children. I. Title.

*HENDRICKS, William C. 207
Object lessons from sports and games, [by] William C. Hendricks and Merle Den Bleyker. Grand Rapids, Baker Book House, [1975] 106 p. 20 cm. [BV1471] [BV4227] ISBN 0-8010-4134-1 1.95 (pbk.)
1. Religious education. I. Bleyker, Merle Den. joint author. II. Title.

HOFINGER, Johannes. 207
Imparting the Christian message. [Notre Dame, Ind.] University of Notre Dame Press 1961. 119 p. 21 cm. "NDP 9." "Part I ... is a reprint of an interview with Father Hofinger, made at the historic Eichstatt Conference ... The interview is followed by a summary of the Eichstaff program. Part II [p. 21-119] ... is taken verbatim from his larger work. The art of teaching Christian doctrine." [BX921.H6 1961] 64-54537
1. Religious education. I. Title.

HOLBROOK, Clyde A. 207
Religion, a humanistic field. Englewood Cliffs, N.J., Prentice-Hall [1963] xvi, 299 p. 22 cm. (The Princeton studies: humanistic scholarship in America) Bibliographical footnotes. [BL41.H6] 63-12269
1. Religion—Study and teaching. I. Title. II. Series.

HOOLE, Daryl (Van Dam) 207
The art of teaching children, by Daryl V. Hoole. Illus. [by] Dick and Mary Scopes. Salt Lake City, Deseret Book Co., 1964. xix, 230 p. illus. 24 cm. "Oh! hang up the baby's stocking, author of words unknown, music arranged [for voice and piano] by Ellen F. Bentley": (p. 64) [BX8610.H6] 64-4289
1. Mormons and Mormonism — Education. 2. Religious education of children. I. Bentley, Ellen F., arr. Hang up the baby's stocking. II. Title.

HOWARD, Philip Eugene, 1898- 207
Answers for inquiring Christians; notes on open letters to the Sunday school times. [Westwood, N. J.] F. H. Revell Co. [1954] 172p. 22cm. [BR96.H6] 54-8001
1. Questions and answers—Theology. I. Title.

*HUTCHCROFT, Vera 207
Object lessons for church groups. Grand Rapids, Baker Book House, [1975] 95 p. 20 cm. (Object lesson series) [BV1471] [BV4227] ISBN 0-8010-4107-4 1.95 (pbk.)
1. Religious education. I. Title.

KANE, J. Herbert. 207
Missionary candidates: how to breed the best, by J. Herbert Kane. Prepared for the joint EFMA/IFMA executives's [sic] retreat, Winona Lake, Ind., Oct. 4, 1968. [Monrovia, Calif., Missions Advanced Research & Communication Center, 1968?] 12 p. 28 cm. [BV2091.K35] 73-172378 0.50
1. Missionaries, Training of. I. Title.

KELSEY, Morton, 1917- 207
Can Christians be educated? : A proposal for effective communication of our Christian religion / Morton Kelsey ; compiled and edited by Harold William Burgess. Mishawaka, Ind. : Religious Education Press, c1977. 154 p. ; 23 cm. Bibliography: p. 151-153. [BV1471.2.K44] 77-3691 ISBN 0-89135-008-X pbk. : 5.95
1. Christian education. I. Title.

KELSEY, Morton, 1917- 207
Can Christians be educated? : A proposal for effective communication of our Christian religion / Morton Kelsey ; compiled and edited by Harold William Burgess. Mishawaka, Ind. : Religious Education Press, c1977. 154 p. ; 23 cm. Bibliography: p. 151-153. [BV1471.2.K44] 77-3691 ISBN 0-89135-008-X pbk. : 5.95
1. Christian education. I. Title.

LARSEN, Earnest. 207
Will religion make sense to your child? [By] Earnest Larsen [and] Patricia Galvin. Liguori, Mo., Liguorian Books [1970] 144 p. col. illus. 19 cm. Includes bibliographies. [BV1475.2.L3] 76-133946 1.25
1. Christian education of children. 2. Theology, Doctrinal—Popular works. I. Galvin, Patricia, joint author. II. Title.

LEE, James Michael, ed. 207
Seminary education in a time of change, edited by James Michael Lee and Louis J. Putz. Contributors: John Tracy Ellis [and others] Foreword by Joseph Cardinal Ritter. Introd. by Frank Norris. [Notre Dame, Ind.] Fides Publishers, 1965. xii, 590 p. 24 cm. Bibliographical footnotes. [BX900.L4] 65-13797
1. Theological seminaries, Catholic. I. Putz, Louis J., joint ed. II. Ellis, John Tracy, 1905- III. Title.

LEE, James Michael, ed. 207
Seminary education in a time of change, ed. by James Michael Lee, Louis J. Putz. Contributors: John Tracy Ellis [others] Foreword by Joseph Cardinal Ritter. Introd. by Frank Norris [Notre Dame, Ind.] Fides [c.] 1965. xii, 590p. 24cm. Bibl. [BX900.L4] 65-13797 7.95
1. Theological seminaries, Catholic. I. Putz, Louis J., joint ed. II. Ellis, John Tracy, 1905- III. Title.

LINK, Mark J. 207
Faith and commitment; aim of religious education [by] Tilmann [and others. Mark J. Link, editor] Chicago, Loyola University Press, 1964. vii, 309 p. 24 cm. (Loyola pastoral studies) "Selected readings for busy teachers": p. 305-309. Bibliographical references included in footnotes. [BX926.L5] 64-20940
1. Religious education. I. Title.

LINK, Mark J., ed. 207
Faith and commitment; aim of religious education [by] Tilmann [others. Mark J. Link, ed.] Chicago, Loyola Univ. Pr. [c.]1964. vii, 309p. 24cm. (Loyola pastoral studies) Bibl. 64-20940 3.50
1. Religious education. I. Title.

MILLER, Randolph Crump, 1910- 207
The language gap and God; religious language and Christian education. Philadelphia, Pilgrim Press [1970] xvii, 199 p. 22 cm. Bibliography: p. 179-184. [BV1464.M5] 72-126863 ISBN 0-8298-0180-4 4.95
1. Christian education. 2. Religion and language. 3. Analysis (Philosophy) I. Title.

MINOR Seminary Conference. 207
11th, Catholic University of America, 1960.
Self-evaluation in the minorseminary; the proceedings of the Eleventh Minor Seminary Conference, conducted at the Catholic University of America, May 13, 14, 15, 1960. Ed. by Cornelius M. Cuyler. Washington, D.C., Catholic Univ. of America Press [c.] 1961. v, 70p. Bibl. 61-1077 1.50 pap.,
1. Theological seminaries—Accreditation. I. Cuyler, Cornelius M., ed. II. Title.

MINOR Seminary Conference. 207
12th, Catholic University America, 1961.
Minor Seminary Conference on outcomes the proceedings of the twelfth Minor Seminary Conference, conducted at the Catholic University of America, May 12, 13, and 14, 1961. Ed. by Cornelius M. Cuyler. Washington, D.C., Catholic Univ. of Amer. Pr. [c.]1961. v, 90p. 61-66767 1.50 pap.,
1. Seminarians. 2. Prediction of scholastic success. I. Cuyler, Cornelius M., ed. II. Title.

MINOR Seminary Conference. 207
11th, Catholic University of America, 1960.
Self-evaluation in the minor seminary; the proceedings of the Eleventh Minor Seminary Conference, conducted at the Catholic University of America, May 13, 14, 15, 1960. Edited by Cornelius M. Cuyler. Washington, Catholic University of America Press, 1961. v. 70p. 22cm. Includes bibliographical references. [BX903.M425 1960] 61-1077
1. Theological seminaries—Accreditation. I. Cuyler, Cornelius M., ed. II. Title.

MORAN, Gabriel. 207
Design for religion; toward ecumenical education. [New York] Herder and Herder [1970] 168 p. 22 cm. Includes bibliographical references. [BV1471.2.M56] 78-130860 4.95
1. Catholic Church—Education. 2. Christian education. I. Title.

*MORRIS, Colin. 207
The hammer of the Lord; signs of hope. Nashville, Abingdon [1974, c1973] 159 p. 20 cm. [BV1471.2] ISBN 0-687-16547-4 4.75
1. Religious education. 2. Evangelistic work. I. Title.
L.C. card number for original edition: 73-12234.

MYLLER, Rolf. 207
The Bible puzzle book / Rolf Myller. 1st ed. San Francisco : Harper & Row, c1977. p. cm. [GV1507.B5M94 1977] 77-7836 ISBN 0-06-066060-0 : pbk. : 3.95
1. Bible games and puzzles. I. Title.

NATIONAL Catholic Educational 207
Association.
NCEA papers no. 1- Dayton, Ohio [1967]- v. illus., ports. 22 cm. [LC461.N432] 67-6805
1. Catholic Church in the U.S. — Education — Societies, etc. I. Title.

NELSON, Carl Ellis, 1916- 207
Using evaluation in theological education / C. Ellis Nelson. Nashville : Discipleship Resources, c1975. 121 p. ; 22 cm. Bibliography: p. [117]-121. [BV4020.N4] 75-16640
1. Theology—Study and teaching—Evaluation. I. Title.

NIEBUHR, Helmut Richard, 207
1894-
The advancement of theological education, by H. Richard Niebuhr, Daniel Day Williams [and] James M. Gustafson. [1st ed.] New York, Harper [1957] 239p. 22cm. [BV4030.N5] 56-120716

1. Theology—Study and teaching—U. S. I. Title.

NIEBUHR, Helmut Richard, 1894- 207
The purpose of the church and its ministry; reflections on the aims of theological education. In collaboration with Daniel Day Williams and James M. Gustafson. [1st ed.] New York, Harper [1956] 134p. 20cm. [BV4020.N5] 56-7026
1. Theology—Study and teaching. 2. Church. 3. Clergy. 4. Theological seminaries —U. S. I. Title.

ON the other side 207
[ed. by] Katherine T. Hargrove. Englewood Cliffs, N.J., Prentice ,531967] vi, 104p. 22cm. Rev. of paps., orig. delivered at the 1966 annual meeting of the Soc. of Catholic Coll. Teachers of Sacred Doctrine, held at Denver. Bibl. [BX905.O5] 67-16386 2.75 pap.,
1. Catholic Church—Education. 2. Religious education. I. Hargrove, Katharine T., ed. II. Society of Catholic College Teachers ofSacfed Doctrine.

PROCTOR, Robert A. 207
Too old to learn? [By] Robert A. Proctor. Nashville, Broadman Press [1967] 126 p. 21 cm. Includes bibliographical references. [BV1488.P7] 67-10307
1. Religious education of adults. I. Title.

PROTESTANT theological 207
seminaries and Bible schools in Asia, Africa, the Middle East, Latin America, the Caribbean and Pacific areas; a directory. 1960- New York, Missionary Research Library. v. 27cm. (MRL directory series) [BV2030.N43] 61-1632
1. Theological seminaries, Protestant. I. New York, Missionary Research Library. II. Series: New York, Missionary Research Library, MRL directory series

RICHARDS, Lawrence O. 207
A theology of Christian education / Lawrence O. Richards. Grand Rapids : Zondervan Pub. House, c1975. 324 p. : ill. ; 24 cm. [BV1464.R48] 74-25353 8.95
1. Christian education (Theology) I. Title.

RIMMER, Harry, 1890- 207
'That's a good question!' Grand Rapids, W. B. Eerdmans Pub. Co., 1954. 137p. 20cm. [BR96.R5] 54-6233
1. Questions and answers—Theology. I. Title.

*RUNK, Wesley T. 207
Challenging object lessons. Grand Rapids, Baker Book House [1974, c1971] 83 p., 20 cm. Formerly published under the title, Let's go to God's Party. [BV1471] ISBN 0-8010-7630-7 1.95 (pbk.)
1. Religious education. I. Title.

*RUNK, Wesley T. 207
Object lessons for christian growth. Grand Rapids, Baker Book House [1974, c1973] 104 p., 20 cm. Formerly published under the title, Growing up in God. [BV1471] ISBN 0-8010-7629-3 1.95 (pbk.)
1. Religious education. I. Title.

*RUNK, Wesley T. 207
Timely object lessons. Grand Rapids, Mich. Baker Book House. [1974, c1971] 95 p., 20 cm. [BV1471] ISBN 0-8010-7628-5 1.95 (pbk.)
1. Religious education. I. Title.

RUSSELL, Letty M. 207
Christian education in mission, by Letty M. Russell. Philadelphia, Westminster Press [1967] 159 p. 19 cm. (Studies on the church for others) Bibliographical references included in "Notes" (p. [147]-159) [BV1471.2.R8] 67-10926
1. Religious education. I. Title.

SANGSTER, William Edwin, 1900- 207
Questions people ask about religion. New York, Abingdon Press [1959] 142p. 21cm. London ed. (Epworth) has title: Give God a chance. [BR96.S22 1959] 60-5235
1. Questions and answers—Theology. I. Title.

SANGSTER, William Edwin [Robert] 207
Questions people ask about religion. Nashville, Abingdon Press [c.1959] 142p. 21cm. 60-5235 2.25 bds.,
1. Questions and answers—Theology. I. Title.

SANGSTER, William Edwin Robert, 1900- 207
Questions people ask about religion. Nashville, Abingdon [1965, c.1959] 142p. 21cm. (Apex bk. T6) London ed. (Epworth) has title: Give God a chance. [BR96.S22] 1.00 pap.,
1. Questions and answers—Theology. I. Title.

*SULLIVAN, Jessie P. 207
Object lessons and stories for children's church. Grand Rapids, Baker Book House [1974, c1973] 162 p., 20 cm. Formerly published under the title, Children's church programs. [BV1471] ISBN 0-8010-8037-1 2.50 (pbk.)
1. Religious education. I. Title.

THEOLOGICAL education as 207
professional education; the report of a convocation sponsored by the Episcopal Theological School during its centennial year observance. Edited by Olga Craven, Alden L. Todd [and] Jesse H. Ziegler. Dayton, Ohio, American Association of Theological Schools [1969] xi, 167 p. 26 cm. Bibliographical references included in "Footnotes" (p. 155-164) [BV4030.T48] 72-9346
1. Theology—Study and teaching—U.S. 2. Professional education—U.S. I. Craven, Olga, ed. II. Todd, Alden, ed. III. Ziegler, Jesse H., ed. IV. Cambridge, Mass. Episcopal Theological School.

TOWARD a future for religious 207
education. Contributors: Bernard Cooke [and others] Edited by James Michael Lee and Patrick C. Rooney. Dayton, Ohio, Pflaum Press, 1970. viii, 252 p. 21 cm. Includes bibliographical references. [BV1473.T68] 77-93008 2.95
1. Christian education—Addresses, essays, lectures. I. Cooke, Bernard J. II. Lee, James Michael, ed. III. Rooney, Patrick C., ed.

UNITARIAN Universalist 207
Association. Committee to Study Theological Education.
R comprehensive plan of education for the Unitarian Universalist ministry; complete report. Boston, Unitarian Universalist Association [c1962] 137 p. 22 cm. [BX9817.U6] 63-45295
1. Theology — Study and teaching — Unitarian churches 2. Theological seminaries, Unitarian. I. Title.

WELLS, Harold Philmore. 207
You can be a magician! / Harold Philmore Wells. Chicago : Moody Press, c1976. 126 p. : ill. ; 19 cm. [BV4227W44] 75-35535 ISBN 0-8024-9823-X : 2.25
1. Christian education—Audio-visual aids. 2. Preaching. I. Title.

WILSON, J Christy, 1891- ed. 207
Ministers in training; a review of field work procedures in theological education, by the directors of field work in the seminaries of the Presbyterian Church, U. S. A., representatives of the boards of the church and other specialists. [Princeton, N. J.] Directors of field work in the theological seminaries of the Presbyterian Church, U. S. A., 1957. xii, 177p. 24cm. Bibliography: p. 171-172. [BV4020.W5] 57-3054
1. Theological seminaries— U. S. 2. Theology—Study and teaching—Presbyterian Church. I. Title. II. Title: Field work procedures in theological education.

WORKSHOP on the Integration 207
of the Catholic Secondary School Curriculum, Catholic University of America, 1950.
The integration of the Catholic secondary school curriculum; the proceedings of the Workshop on the Integration of the Catholic Secondary School Curriculum, conducted at the Catholic University of America from June 9 to June 20, 1950. Edited by Sister Mary Janet, s.c. Washington, Catholic University of America Press, 1951. v, 154 p. 23 cm. "General bibliography": p. 139-149. [LC485.W64 1950] A51
1. High schools [Catholic] 2. Articulation (Education) 3. Catholic Church in the U.S. — Education. I. Miller, Mary Janet, Sister, 1897- ed. II. Title.

WORKSHOP on Vatican Council 207
II: its Challenge to Education, Catholic University of America, 1966
Vatican Council II, its challenge to education; proceedings Ed. by George F. Donovan. Washington, Catholic Univ. [1967] x, 182p. 22cm. Conducted under the general auspices of the director of workshops of the Catholic Univ. of America. Bibl. [BX895.W6 1966] 67-28294 2.95 pap.,
1. Catholic Church — Education. 2. Vatican Council. 2d. 1962-1965. I. Donovan, George Francis, 1901- ed. II. Catholic University of American. III. Title.

WORKSHOP on Vatican Council 207
II: its Challenge to Education, Catholic University of America, 1966.
Vatican Council II, its challenge to education; proceedings. Edited by George F. Donovan. Washington, Catholic University of America Press [1967] x, 182 p. 22 cm. "Conducted under the general auspices of the director of workshops of the Catholic University of America." Includes bibliographicsl references. [BX895.W6] 67-28294
1. Catholic Church—Education. 2. Vatican Council. 2d, 1962-1965. I. Donovan, George Francis, 1901- ed. II. Catholic University of America. III. Title.

BRIDSTON, Keith R. ed. 207.082
The making of ministers; essays on clergy training today. Edited by Keith R. Bridston [and] Dwight W. Culver. Minneapolis, Augsburg Pub. House [1964] xx, 275 p. 22 cm. "Written from material gathered by the Lilly Endowment study of pre-seminary education."—Dust jacket. [BV4020.B7] 64-13435
1. Theology—Study and teaching. 2. Theological seminaries. I. Culver, Dwight W., joint ed. II. Title.

ACCREDITING Association of 207.1
Bible Colleges.
Manual. Rev. [Fort Wayne?] 1960. 71 p. 21 cm. [BV4030.A6] 63-38053
1. Bible colleges — Accreditation. I. Title.

*HOLM, Jean L. 207.1
Teaching religion in school; a practical approach, [by] Jean L. Holm. [London, New York] Oxford University Press 1975 200 p. 21 cm. (Oxford studies in education) Includes index. Bibliography: p. 178-197. [BV1534] ISBN 0-19-913224-0 3.50 (pbk.)
1. Religion—Study and teaching. 2. Theology—Study and teaching. 3. Religious—Education. I. Title.

MOHLER, James A. 207'.1
The school of Jesus; an overview of Christian education yesterday and today [by] James Mohler. New York, Alba House [1973] xii, 279 p. illus. 22 cm. Bibliography: p. [267]-274. [BV1465.M6] 72-11835 ISBN 0-8189-0262-0 5.95
1. Religious education—History. I. Title.

PROTESTANT Episcopal 207'.1
Church in the U.S.A. Massachusetts (Diocese) Commission on the Ministry.
Continuing education for ministry; a catalog of resources. Boston, Protestant Episcopal Diocese of Massachusetts, 1973. 86 p. 22 x 29 cm. [BV4165.P76 1973] 73-84421 10.00
1. Clergy—Post-ordination training—Directories. I. Title.

ROUCH, Mark A., 1925- 207'.1
Competent ministry; a guide to effective continuing education [by] Mark A. Rouch. Nashville, Abingdon Press [1974] 190 p. 22 cm. Bibliography: p. 173-176. [BV4165.R66] 73-22309 ISBN 0-687-09318-X 3.75 (pbk.)
1. Clergy—Post-ordination training. I. Title.

WESTERHOFF, John H. 207'.1
A colloquy on Christian education, edited by John H. Westerhoff, III. Philadelphia, United Church Press [1972] 254 p. 22 cm. "A Pilgrim Press book." [BV1525.W45] 72-4258 ISBN 0-8298-0238-X
1. Christian education—Addresses, essays, lectures. I. Title.

WITMER, Safara Austin, 1899- 207.1
The Bible college story: education with dimension. Pref. by Merrill C. Tenney. Manhasset, N.Y., Channel Press [1962] 253 p. 21 cm. [BV4030.W5] 62-13413
1. Bible colleges. I. Title.

AMERICAN Association of 207'.11
Theological Schools. Task Force on Spiritual Development.
Voyage, vision, venture; a report [by the] Task Force on Spiritual Development, David E. Babin [and others] Dayton, Ohio, American Association of Theological Schools, 1972. 45 p. 23 cm. [BV4011.6.A45] 72-190320
1. Seminarians—Religious life. 2. Spiritual life. I. Babin, David E. II. Title.

AMERICAN Congress of 207'.11
Churches.
Proceedings. 1885- Hartford. Case, Lockwood & Brainard Co. v. 23cm. [BX6.A5A5] 59-58358
1. Christian union—Congresses. I. Title.

BOSLEY, Harold Augustus, 1907- 207'.11
What did the World Council say to you? New York, Abingdon Press [1955] 127p. 20cm. [BX6.W78B6] 280
1. World Council of Churches. 2d Assembly, Evanston, Ill. I. Title.

BRIDSTON, Keith R. 207.11
Pre-seminary education; report of the Lilly Endowment study, by Keith R. Bridston, Dwight W. Culver. Minneapolis. Augsburg [c.1965] xi, 257p. 23cm. Bibl. [BV4163.B7] 65-12141 4.75
1. Pretheological education. I. Culver, Dwight W., joint author. II. Lilly Endowment, inc., Indianapolis. III. Title.

BRIDSTON, Keith R. 207.11
Pre-seminary education; report of the Lilly Endowment study, by Keith R. Bridston and Dwight W. Culver. Minneapolis, Augsburg Pub. House [1965] xi, 257 p. 23 cm. Includes bibliographical references. [BV4163.B7] 65-12141
1. Pretheological education. I. Culver, Dwight W., joint author. II. Lilly Endowment, Inc., Indianapolis.

DANIEL, William Andrew, 1895- 207'.11
The education of Negro ministers, by W. A. Daniel. Based upon a survey of theological schools for Negroes in the United States made by Robert L. Kelly and W. A. Daniel. New York, Negro Universities Press [1969] 187 p. 23 cm. Reprint of the 1925 ed. "The Institute of Social and Religious Research ... is responsible for this publication." [BV4080.D3 1969] 71-78581 ISBN 0-8371-1410-1
1. Negro theological seminaries. 2. Theology—Study and teaching. 3. Negroes—Education. I. Institute of Social and Religious Research. II. Title.

DOBBINS, Gaines Stanley, 1886- 207.11
Great teachers make a difference [by] Gaines S. Dobbins. Nashville, Broadman Press [1965] 123 p. 20 cm. [LA2303.D6] 65-21199
1. Educators, American. I. Title.

DOBBINS, Gaines Stanley, 1886- 207.11
Great teachers make a difference. Nashville, Broadman [c.1965] 123p. 20cm. [LA2303.D6] 65-21199 1.50 bds.,
1. Educators, American. I. Title.

GRUBB, Norman Percy, 1895- 207'.11
Modern viking; the story of Abraham Vereide, pioneer in Christian leadership. Grand Rapids, Zondervan Pub. House [1961] 205p. illus. 23cm. [BX6.8.V4G7] 61-16751
1. Vereide, Abraham, 1886- I. Title.

OLSON, Arnold Theodore. 207'.11
Believers only an outline of the history and principles of the Free Evangelical movement in Europe and North America affiliated with the International Federation of Free Evangelical Churches. Minneapolis, Free Church Publications [1964] 367 p. group port. 22 cm. Bibliography: p. 359-363. [BX6.I65O4] 64-22145
1. Internationaler Bund Freier Evangelischer Gemeinden. I. Title.

POOLE, Stafford. 207.11
Seminary in crisis. [New York] Herder and Herder [1965] 190 p. 21 cm. Bibliographical references included in "Footnotes" (p. [170]-190) [BX900.P6] 65-20558
1. Theological seminaries, Catholic. 2. Theology—Study and teaching—Catholic Church. I. Title.

POOLE, Stafford 207.11
Seminary in crisis. [New York] Herder & Herder [c.1965] 190p. 21cm. Bibl. [BX900.P6] 65-20558 3.95
1. Theological seminaries. Catholic. 2. Theology—Study and teaching—Catholic Church. I. Title.

ROMAN Catholic-Protestant 207'.11
Colloquium, Harvard University, 1963.
Ecumenical dialogue at Harvard; the Roman Catholic-Protestant Colloquium. Edited by Samuel H. Miller and G. Ernest Wright. Cambridge, Mass., Belknap Press of Harvard University Press, 1964. xi, 385 p. 22 cm. Sponsored by Harvard Divinity School. Bibliographical footnotes. [BX6.R6A5] 64-19583
1. Christian union—Congresses. I. Miller, Samuel Howard, 1900- ed. II. Wright, George Ernest, 1909- ed. III. Harvard University. Divinity School. IV. Title.

SKOGLUND, John E 207'.11
Fifty years of Faith and Order; an interpretation of the Faith and Order movement, by John E. Skoglund and J. Robert Nelson. [New York, Committee for the Inter-seminary Movement of the National Student Christian Federation, 1963] v. 113 p. 19 cm. Bibliography: p. 111-113. [BX6.W7S5] 64-28489
1. World Conference on Faith and Order. I. Nelson, John Robert. 1920- II. Title.

SMITH, Charles Stanley, 1890?-1959. 207'.11
Protestant theological seminaries and Bible schools in Asia, Africa, the Middle East, Latin America, the Caribbean and Pacific areas; a directory. Compiled by C. Stanley Smith and Herbert F. Thomson. Edited by Frank W. Price. New York, Missionary Research Library, 1960. viii, 50 p. 28 cm. (MRL

directory series, no. 12) [BV2030.N43 no. 12] 77-234260 2.00
1. Theological seminaries, Protestant—Directories. 2. Bible colleges—Directories. I. Thomson, Herbert F., joint author. II. Title. III. Series: New York. Missionary Research Library. MRL directory and survey series, no. 12

WAGONER, Walter D 207'.11
The seminary: Protestant and Catholic, by Walter D. Wagoner. New York, Sheed and Ward [1966] xxiii, 256 p. 22 cm. Includes bibliographical references. [BV4020.W3] 66-22029
1. Theological seminaries. 2. Catholic Church—Relations—Protestant churches. 3. Protestant churches—Relations—Catholic Church. I. Title.

WAGONER, Walter D. 207'.11
The seminary: Protestant and Catholic, by Walter D. Wagoner. New York, Sheed and Ward [1966] xxiii, 256 p. 22 cm. Includes bibliographical references. [BV4020.W3] 66-22029
1. Catholic Church—Relations—Protestant churches. 2. Theological seminaries. 3. Protestant churches—Relations—Catholic Church. I. Title.

WORLD Conference on Faith 207'.11
and Order. Continuation Committee.
Meeting [proceedings] Oxford [etc.] Eng., New York. v. 22cm. annual. (Its [Pamphlets]) [BX6.W7A42] 57-52871
I. Title.

WORLD Conference on Faith 207'.11
and Order. Continuation Committee.
Meeting [proceedings] Oxford [etc.] Eng., New York. v. 22cm. annual.a [BX6.W7A42] 57-52871
I. Title.

WORLD Conference on Faith 207'.11
and Order. Continuation Committee.
Meeting [proceedings] Oxford [etc.] Eng., New York. v. 22 cm. (Its [Pamphlets] annual. [BX6.W7A42] 57-52871
I. Title. II. Series.

CHRISTOPHER Study Week. 207.112
2d, New York, 1964.
Apostolic renewal in the seminary in the light of Vatican Council II; the papers of the 2nd Christopher Study Week, July 20-24, 1964 with the conclusions of the 1st and 2nd Christopher Study Weeks. Edited by James Keller [and] Richard Armstrong. New York, Christophers [1965] 305 p. 17 cm. [BX900.C48 1964] 65-5585
1. Theological seminaries, Catholic — Congresses. I. Keller, James Gregory, 1900- ed. II. Armstrong, Richard G., ed. III. Title.

ELLIS, John Tracy, 207'.11'2
1905-
Essays in seminary education. Notre Dame, Ind., Fides Publishers [1967] x. 278 p. 22 cm. Bibliographical footnotes. [BX900.E47] 67-24811
1. Theological seminaries, Catholic. 2. Theology—Study and teaching—Catholic Church. I. Title. II. Title: Seminary education.

ELLIS, John Tracy, 207'.11'2
1905-
Essays in seminary education. Notre Dame, Ind., Fides Publishers [1967] x, 278 p. 22 cm. Bibliographical footnotes. [BX900.E47] 67-24811
1. Theological seminaries, Catholic. 2. Theology—Study and teaching—Catholic Church. I. Title. II. Title: Seminary education.

HUGHES, Thomas 207'.11'2
Aloysius, 1849-1939.
Loyola and the educational system of the Jesuits. New York, Scribner, 1892. Grosse Pointe, Mich., Scholarly Press [1969?] ix, 302 p. 23 cm. (The Great educators) Bibliography: p. 297-298. Bibliographical footnotes. [LB375.L6H8 1969] 74-7860
1. Jesuits. 2. Loyola, Ignacio de, Saint, 1491-1556. 3. Education—History. I. Title. II. Series.

LONSWAY, Francis A. 207'.11'2
Ministers for tomorrow; a longitudinal study of Catholic seminarians in theology, by Francis A. Lonsway. Washington, Center for Applied Research in the Apostolate, 1972. ix, 119 p. illus. 29 cm. (CARA information service) Bibliography: p. 117-119. [BX905.L65] 72-181297
1. Seminarians—Statistics. 2. Theology—Study and teaching—United States—Statistics. I. Title.

POLLARD, Hugh M 207'.11'2
Pioneers of popular education, 1760-1850. Cambridge, Harvard University Press, 1957. xii, 297p. 22cm. Bibliography: p. 281-293. [LA123.P] A 58
1. Education—Hist. I. Title.

PROTESTANT Episcopal 207'.11'3
Church in the U. S. A. Special Committee on Theological Education.
Ministry for tomorrow; report. Nathan M. Pusey, chairman. Charles L. Taylor, director of the study. New York, Seabury Press [1967] xi, 147 p. 22 cm. "Presented to the general convention of the Episcopal Church in Seattle in September, 1967." Bibliography: p. [143]-147. [BX5850.A35] 67-28443
1. Theology—Study and teaching—Anglican communion. 2. Theology—Study and teaching—U. S. I. Taylor, Charles Lincoln, 1901- II. Protestant Episcopal Church in the U. S. A. General Convention, Seattle, 1967. III. Title.

PROTESTANT Episcopal 207/.11/3
Church in the U.S.A. Special Committee on Theological Education.
Ministry for tomorrow; report. Nathan M. Pusey, chairman. Charles L. Taylor, director of the study. New York. Seabury [1967] xi, 147p. 22cm. Presented to the gen. convention of the Episcopal Church in Seattle in Sept., 1967. Bibl. [BX5850.A35] 67-28443 3.95; 2.50 pap.,
1. Theology—Study and teaching—Anglican communion. 2. Theology—Study and teaching—U.S. I. Taylor Charles Lincoln, 1901- II. Protestant Episcopal Church in the U.S.A. General Convention. Seattle, 1967. III. Title.

BLACKMAN, George L. 207'.11'33
Faith and freedom; a study of theological education and the Episcopal Theological School [by] George L. Blackman. New York, Seabury [1967] xvi, 400p. 22cm. Bibl. [BV4070.C36B55] 67-13311 7.50
1. Cambridge, Mass. Episcopal Theological School. 2. Protesant Episcopl)0al Church in the U.S.A.—Education. I. Title.

BLACKMAN, George L. 207'.11'33
Faith and freedom; a study of theological education and the Episcopal Theological School [by] George L. Blackman. New York, Seabury Press [1967] xvi, 400 p. 22 cm. Bibliography: p. 381-394. [BV4070.C36B55] 67-13311
1. Cambridge, Mass. Episcopal Theological School. 2. Protestant Episcopal Church in the U.S.A.—Education. I. Title.

STRIVING for 207'.11'41312
ministry : centennial essays interpreting the heritage of Luther Theological Seminary / edited by Warren A. Quanbeck, Eugene L. Fevold, and Gerhard E. Frost. Minneapolis : Augsburg Pub. House, c1977. 200 p. ; 20 cm. Includes bibliographical references. [BV4070.L87S8] 77-72466 ISBN 0-8066-1580-X : 4.95
1. Luther Theological Seminary, St. Paul—Addresses, essays, lectures. I. Quanbeck, Warren A. II. Fevold, Eugene L. III. Frost, Gerhard E. IV. Luther Theological Seminary, St. Paul.
Contents omitted

FUKUYAMA, Yoshio, 207'.11'5834
1921-
The ministry in transition; a case study of theological education. University Park, Pennsylvania State University Press [1972] xx, 167 p. 24 cm. Includes bibliographical references. [BX9884.A3F83] 72-1395 ISBN 0-271-01129-7 9.50
1. United Church of Christ—Clergy, Training of. 2. Theology—Study and teaching—United States. I. Title.

FUKUYAMA, Yoshio, 207'.11'5834
1921-
The ministry in transition; a case study of theological education. University Park, Pennsylvania State University Press [1972] xx, 167 p. 24 cm. Includes bibliographical references. [BX9884.A3F83] 72-1395 ISBN 0-271-01129-7 9.50
1. United Church of Christ—Clergy, Training of. 2. Theology—Study and teaching—United States. I. Title.

TEACHING with Witness 207'.12'2
junior high handbook for use in 1970-1971. [Dayton, Ohio, G. A. Pflaum, 1970] 32 p. 21 cm. Cover title. Bibliography: p. 25-32. [BV1475.9.T4] 77-131309
1. Christian education of adolescents. I. Title: Witness junior high handbook for use in 1970-1971.

DOHERTY, Reginald, 207'.12'79777
ed.
The Christian in the world. General editor: Reginald Doherty. [Authors: Francis Kelly and others] Dubuque, Iowa, Priory Press [1963] viii, 527 p. maps. 24 cm. (The Challenge of Christ, no. 4) [BV1549.94.C5] 63-21761
1. Religious education — Text-books for young people — Catholic. I. Title. II. Series.

FARLEY, Claude J. 207'.12'79777
"Be-attitudes"; an involvement approach to teaching Christian values [by] Claude J. Farley. Staten Island, N.Y., Alba House [1973] xx, 130 p. illus. 19 cm. [BV1485.F37] 72-6753 ISBN 0-8189-0260-4 pap. 1.35
1. Religious education of young people. I. Title.

KEVANE, Eugene, ed. 207'.12'79777
Divine providence and human progress series. General editor: Eugene Kevane. Washington, Christian Culture Press [c1963- v. 25 cm. Contents.-- v. 4. Christian social living in the modern world, by J. P. Ashton. [BV1549.9D5] 64-28475
1. Religious education — Text-books for adolescents — Catholic. I. Title.

RAMSEY, Paul, ed. 207.2
Religion [Essays by] Philip H. Ashby [others] Englewood Cliffs, N.J., Prentice [c.1965] x, 468p. 22cm. (Princeton studies: humanistic scholarship in Amer.) Bibl. [BL41.R3] 64-23553 8.95
1. Religion—Study and teaching—U. S. 2. Theology—Study and teaching—U.S. I. Title. II. Series.

RAMSEY, Paul, ed. 207.2
Religion. [Essays] [by] Philip H. Ashby [and others] Englewood Cliffs, N. J., Prentice-Hall [1965] x, 468 p. 22 cm. (The Princeton studies: humanistic scholarship in America) "Bibliographical note": p. 449-450. Bibliographical footnotes. [BL41.R3] 64-23553
1. Religion—Study and teaching—U.S. 2. Theology—Study and teaching—U.S. I. Title. II. Series.

RUPP, Ernest Gordon. 207.2'024
Hort and the Cambridge tradition: an inaugural lecture, by E. G. Rupp. London, Cambridge U.P., 1970. [1], 22 p. 19 cm. Cover title. "This inaugural lecture was delivered in the University of Cambridge on 14 November 1969." Includes bibliographical references. [BX5199.H85R8] 75-116840 6/- (<0.95)
1. Hort, Fenton John Anthony, 1828-1892. I. Title.

DOWNING, Francis Gerald. 207'.2'2
The church and Jesus; a study in history, philosophy, and theology [by] F. Gerald Downing. Naperville, Ill., A. R. Allenson [1968] vi, 199 p. 22 cm. (Studies in Biblical theology, 2d ser., 10) Bibliographical footnotes. [BR138.D73] 78-3050 3.75 (pbk)
1. Jesus Christ—Biography—Sources. 2. Church history—Historiography. 3. Church history—Sources. I. Title. II. Series.

BULLOCK, Frederick 207'.41
William Bagshawe.
A history of training for the ministry of the Church of England in England and Wales from 1875 to 1974 / by F. W. B. Bullock. London : Home Words Printing and Publishing Co. Ltd, 1976. xxvi, 177 p. ; 23 cm. Continues A history of training for the ministry of the Church of England in England and Wales from 1800 to 1874. Includes bibliographical references and indexes. [BX5175.B843] 77-350371 ISBN 0-905629-00-0 : £9.50
1. Church of England—Clergy, Training of—History. I. Title: A history of training for the ministry of the Church of England ...

THEOLOGICAL training and 207'.42
the future of theological colleges / [by] John Broadhurst ... [et al.]. London : Church Literature Association, 1976. [2], 5 p. ; 21 cm. (Dolphin papers ; 2) Cover title. [BX5175.T48] 76-383982 ISBN 0-85191-081-5 : £0.15
1. Church of England—Clergy, Training of. I. Broadhurst, John.

MCNAMARA, Robert Francis, 207.45
1910-
The American College in Rome. 1855-1955. Foreword by Edward Cardinal Mooney. Rochester, N. Y., Christopher Press, 1956. xxiii, 838p. illus., ports., maps (on lining papers) 24cm. Bibliographical references included in 'Notes' (p.689-789) Bibliographical note: p.791-792. [BX920.R66M35] 56-7591
1. Rome (City) Collegio americano degil Stati Uniti. I. Title.

MCNAMARA, Robert Francis, 207.45
1910-
Student register, North American College, Rome, Italy: undergraduate department, 1859-1959; graduate department, 1933-1959. Rev. and augm. [Rochester, N. Y., 1961] 56p. 23cm. Revision of an apendix to the author's The American College in Rome, first published in 1956. [BX920.R646M3 1961] 62-1936
1. Rome (City) Collegio americano degil Stati Uniti—Registers. I. Title.

VAITKUS, Mykolas, 1883- 207.45
Mistiniame sode; Kunigu seminarija Kaune, 1903-1906. Atsiminimai. [Putnam, Conn,] Immaculata [1957] 207 p. 22 cm. [BX920.K3V3] 61-28799
1. Kaunas, Kunigu seminarijn. I. Title.

ARNOLD, Charles 207.476855
Harvey.
Near the edge of battle; a short history of the Divinity School and the Chicago school of theology, 1866-1966. [Chicago, Divinity School Association, University of Chicago, c1966] viii, 131 p. 21 cm. Bibliography: p. 119-131. [BV4070.C525A8] 68-407
1. Chicago. University. Divinity School—Hist I. Title.

CHICAGO. Evangelistic 207.476855
Institute.
Year book. [Chicago] v. ports. 24 cm. [BV4070.C395] 51-26078
I. Title.

CHICAGO Theological 207.476855
Seminary.
Report. Chicago. v. 24cm. annual. [BV4070.C43] 55-33814
I. Title.

GORDON College of 207.476855
Theology and Missions
Gordon 75th anniversary war Gordon seventy-fifth anniversary war [Wenham, Mass., Gordon College and Gordon Divinity School, 1964] 1 v. (unpaged) illus., ports. 28 cm. Cover title. [BV4070.G7565 1964] 66-53513
I. Gordon College of Theology and Missions. Divinity School. II. Title.

KUHN, Harold B ed. 207.476855
The distinctive emphases of Asbury Theological Seminary, Cover title: The doctrinal distinctives of Asbury Theological Seminary. Imprint on mounted label. Includes bibliographical references. [BV4070.A5758K8] 64-1034
1. Asbury Theological Seminary, Wilmore, Ky. 2. Theology, Doctrinal — Addresses, essays, lectures. I. Title. II. Title: The doctrinal distinctives of Asbury Theological Seminary.

KUHN, Harold B ed. 207.476855
The distinctive emphases of Asbury Theological Seminary, [Berne, Ind., Herald Press, 1963] 100 p. 21 cm. Cover title: The doctrinal distinctives of Asbury Theological Seminary. Imprint on mounted label. Includes bibliographical references. [BV4070.A5758K8] 64-1034
1. Asbury Theological Seminary, Wilmore, Ky. 2. Theology, Doctrinal — Addresses, essays, lectures. I. Title. II. Title: The doctrinal distinctives of Asbury Theological Seminary.

POWELL, Ruth Marie. 207.476855
Lights and shadows; the story of the American Baptist Theological Seminary, 1924-64. [Nashville? 1965] 176 p. illus., ports. 21 cm. Bibliography: p. 105-106. [BV4070.A493P6] 66-2695
1. American Baptist Theological Seminary, Nashville. I. Title.

RICHMOND. Union 207.476855
Theological Seminary.
The days of our years, 1812-1962; the historical conuocations held April 24-27, 1962 as a feature of the celebration of the sessuicentennial of Union Theological Seminary in Virginia Richmond [1962?] 91 p. 26 cm. Contents.The first years, by E. T. Thompson. -- Times of crisis, by F. B. Lewis. -- Rebuilding, by J. Appleby. -- The twentieth century, by E. T. Thompson. [BV4070.R665] 66-39503
I. Title.

SHIPPS, Howard 207.476855
Fenimore.
A short history of Asbury Theological Seminary. [Berne, Ind., Herald Press, 1963] 96 p. 21 cm. Imprint on mounted label. [BV4070.A5756S5] 64-1035
1. Asbury Theological Seminary, Wilmore, Ky.—Hist. I. Title.

TAPPERT, Theodore 207.4811
Gerhardt, 1904-
History of the Lutheran Theological Seminary at Philadelphia, 1864-1964. Philadelphia, Lutheran Theological Seminary. 1964. 168p. illus., facsims., ports. 24cm. Bibl. 64-22501 2.25
1. Philadelphia. Lutheran Theological Seminary. I. Title.

WEBSTER, Douglas, 1920- 207'.56
Survey of the training of the ministry in the Middle East; report of a survey of theological education in Iran, the Arabian-Persian Gulf, Jordan, Lebanon and Syria, and Egypt, undertaken in September to November, 1961, by Douglas Webster [and] K. L. Nasir. Geneva, New York, Commission on World Mission and Evangelism, World Council of

Churches, 1962. 63 p. 22 cm. [BV4140.N4W4] 71-265080
1. Theology—Study and teaching—Near East. I. Nasir, K. L., joint author. II. World Council of Churches. Commission on World Mission and Evangelism. III. Title.

HILL, David Leslie, 207'.599
1932-
Designing a theological education by extension program; a Philippine case study [by] D. Leslie Hill. South Pasadena, Calif., William Carey Library [1973] p. Bibliography: p. [BV4164.H54] 73-12788 ISBN 0-87808-312-X
1. Seminary extension—Philippine Islands. I. Title.

HILL, David Leslie, 207'.599
1932-
Designing a theological education by extension program; a Philippine case study [by] D. Leslie Hill. South Pasadena, Calif., William Carey Library [1974] x, 197 p. illus. 23 cm. Bibliography: p. 193-197. [BV4164.H54] 73-12788 ISBN 0-87808-312-X 3.95 (pbk.)
1. Seminar, extension—Philippine Islands. I. Title.

GRAHAM, William Franklin, 207.6
1918-
My answer. New York, Pocket Bks. [1967. c.1960] 243p. 18cm. (50550) [BR96.G7] .50 pap.,
1. Questions and answers—Theology. I. Title.

GRAHAM, William Franklin, 207.6
1918-
My answer. [1st ed.] Garden City, N.Y., Doubleday, 1960. 259 p. 22 cm. [BR96.G7] 60-15942
1. Questions and answers—Theology. I. Title.

THIELICKE, Helmut, 1908- 207.6

Between heaven and earth; conversations with American Christians. Translated and edited by John W. Doberstein. [1st ed.] New York, Harper & Row [1965] xvii, 192 p. 22 cm. Translation of Gesprache Uber Himmel und Erde. Bibliographical footnotes. [BR123.T453] 65-10703
1. Theology — Addresses, essays, lectures. I. Title.

THIELICKE, Helmut, 1908- 207.6
Between heaven and earth; conversations with American Christians. Tr. [from German] ed. by John W. Doberstein. New York, Harper [c.1965] xvii, 192p. 22cm. Bibl. [BR123.T453] 65-10703 3.75
1. Theology—Addresses, essays, lectures. I. Title.

MULHOLLAND, Kenneth B. 207'.7283
Adventures in training the ministry : a Honduran case study in theological education by extension / by Kenneth Mulholland ; with foreword by F. Ross Kinsler. [Nutley, N.J.] : Presbyterian and Reformed Pub. Co., 1976. xvi, 219 p. : diagrs. ; 21 cm. (Studies in the world church and missions) "Grew out of an S.T.M. thesis presented to the faculty of the Lancaster Theological Seminary in 1971 ..." Bibliography: p. 209-219. [BV4140.L3M84] 76-5151 5.95
1. Seminary extension—Latin America. 2. Seminary extension—Honduras—Case studies. 3. Theology—Study and teaching—Latin America. I. Title. II. Series.

THEOLOGICAL EDUCATION 207'.7283
CONSULTATION, Suva, Fiji Islands, 1961.
Theological education in the Pacific. Report prepared and published by the Theological Education Fund Committee of the International Missionary Council. New York [1961] 82 p. 22 cm. "Sponsored by the Theological Education Fund." [BV4140.P3T5] 63-44891
1. Theology — Study and teaching — Islands of the Pacific. I. International Missionary Council. Theological Education Fund. II. Title.

AMERICAN Baptist 207.73
convention. Board of education.
Theological education in the Northern Baptist convention, a survey; prepared by Hugh Hartshorne and Milton C. Froyd for the Commission on a survey of theological education of the Board of education of the Northern Baptist convention. 1944-1945. [Philadelphia, The Judson press, 1954] 242p. 24cm. [BX6219.A65] 46-1218
1. Theology—Study and teaching—Baptists. 2. Theological seminaries, Baptist. 3. Baptists—Education. I. Hartshorne, Hugh, 1885- II. Froyd, Milton C. III. Title.

CATHOLIC University of 207.73
America. Conference on the Organization and Administration of the Minor Seminary, 1950.
The organization and administration of the minor seminary; the proceedings of a Conference on the Organization and Administration of the Minor Seminary, conducted at the Catholic University of America on May 19, 20, 21, 1950. Edited by Roy J. Deferrari. Washington, Catholic University of America Press, 1951. iv, 91 p. 23 cm. Includes bibliographies. [BX905.C33 1950] A51
1. Theological seminaries, Catholic. I. Deferrari, Roy Joseph, 1890- ed. II. Title.

CENTER for Applied 207'.73
Research in the Apostolate, Washington, D.C.
U.S. Catholic institutions for the training of candidates for the priesthood; a sourcebook for seminary reweval, 1971. Washington [1971?] xviii, 156 p. 28 cm. [BX905.C44] 72-182405
1. Theology—Study and teaching—Catholic Church—Directories. 2. Theological seminaries, Catholic—Directories. 3. Theological seminaries—United States.—Directories. I. Title.

DANIEL, William Andrew, 207'.73
1895-
The education of Negro ministers, by W. A. Daniel. Based upon a survey of theological schools for Negroes in the United States made by Robert L. Kelly and W. A. Daniel. New York, J. & J. Harper Editions [1969] vii, 187 p. 22 cm. Bibliography footnotes. [BV4080.D3 1969b] 70-98002
1. Theological seminaries. 2. Theology—Study and teaching. 3. Negroes—Education. I. Title.

JOINT Survey Commission of 207.73
the Baptist Inter-convention Committee.
The Negro Baptist ministry; an analysis of its profession, preparation, and practices, by Ira De A. Reid. Report of a survey conducted by the Joint Survey Commission of the Baptist Inter-convention Committee: the American Baptist Convention, the National Baptist Convention [and] the Southern Baptist Convention. [Philadelphia, H. and L. Advertising Co.] 1951[i.e. 1952] 145p. 28cm. [BV4080.J6] 52-67070
1. Theological seminaries, Baptist. 2. Baptists, Negro— Education. I. Reid, Ira De Augustine, 1901- II. Title.

LINDBECK, George A. 207'.73
University divinity schools : a report on ecclesiastically independent theological education / by George Lindbeck, in consultation with Karl Deutsch and Nathan Glazer. [New York] : Rockefeller Foundation, 1976. vii, 107 p. ; 28 cm. (Working papers - the Rockefeller Foundation) Includes bibliographical references. [BV4030.L53] 76-3506
1. Theological seminaries—United States. 2. Theology—Study and teaching—United States. I. Deutsch, Karl Wolfgang, 1912- II. Glazer, Nathan. III. Title. IV. Series: Rockefeller Foundation. Working papers — the Rockefeller Foundation

LOVE, Julian Price, 1894- 207'.73
In quest of a ministry. Richmond, John Knox Press [1969] 136 p. 21 cm. [BV4030.L6] 69-12369 2.45
1. Theology—Study and teaching—U.S. 2. Seminarians. I. Title.

MICHAELSEN, Robert. 207.73
The study of religion in American universities; ten case studies with special reference to State universities. New Haven, Society for Religion in Higher Education, 1965. x, 164 p. 23 cm. [BL41.M5] 65-5231
1. Religion — Study and teaching — U.S. I. Title.

MINOR Seminary Conference, 207.73
Catholic University of America.
Proceedings. 1st-1950- Washington, Catholic University Press. v. 23 cm. annual. Each vol. has also a distinctive title. Issued by the conference under earlier names: 1950, Conference on the Organization and Administration of the Minor Seminary; 1951-55, Conference on the Curriculum of the Minor Seminary; 1956-57, Minor Seminary Conference on the Curriculum of the Minor Seminary. [BX903.M425] 61-66767
1. Theological seminiaries, Catholic—Congresses. I. Title. II. Title: Catholic University of America.

MINOR Seminary Conference. 207.73
1st, Catholic University of America, 1950.
The organization and administration of the minor seminary; the proceedings of a Conference on the Organization and Administration of the Minor Seminary, conducted at the Catholic University of America on May 19, 20, 21, 1950. Edited by Roy J.Deferrari. Washington, Catholic University of America Press, 1951. iv, 91p. 23cm. Includes bibliographies. [BX905.M5 1950] A51
1. Theological seminaries, Catholic. I. Deferrari, Roy Joseph, 1890- ed. II. Title.

MINOR Seminary Conference. 207.73
2d, Catholic University of America. 1951.
The curriculum of the minor seminary; the proceedings of a Conference on the Curriculum of the Minor Seminary, conducted at the Catholic University of America, May 4, 5, 6, 1951. Edited by Michael J. McKeough. Washington, Catholic University of America Press, 1952. iv, 99p. tables. 23cm. Bibliographical footnotes. [BX905.M5 1951] A52
1. Theological seminaries, Catholic. 2. Theology—Study and teaching— Catholic Church. I. McKeough, Michael John, 1891- ed. II. Title.

MINOR Seminary Conference. 207.73
3d, Catholic University of America. 1952.
Latin and English syllabi in the minor seminary; the proceedings of a Conference on the Curriculum of the Minor Seminary, conducted at the Catholic University of America, May 9, 10, 11, 1952. Edited by Roy J. Deferrari. Washington, CatholicUniversity of America Press, 1953. iv, 94p. 28cm. [BX905.M5 1952] A53
1. Theological seminaries, Catholic. 2. Latin language—Study and teaching. 3. English language—Study and teaching. I. Deferrari, Roy Joseph, 1890- ed. II. Title.

MINOR Seminary Conference. 207.73
4th, Catholic University of America. 1953.
Latin and religion syllabi in the minor seminary; the proceedings of a Conference on the Curriculum of the Minor Seminary, conducted at the Catholic University of America, May 8, 9, 10, 1953. Edited by Roy J. Deferrari. Washington, Catholic University of America Press, 1954. v. 77p. 23cm. [BX905.M5 1953] A54
1. Theological seminaries, Catholic. 2. Latin language—Study and teaching. 3. Theology—Study and teaching. I. Deferrari, Roy Joseph, 1890- ed. II. Title.

MINOR Seminary Conference. 207.73
5th, Catholic University of America. 1954.
Curriculum of the minor seminary: religion, Greek, and remedial reading; the proceedings of the Fifth Annual Conference on the Curriculum of the Minor Seminary, conducted at the Catholic University of America, May 14, 15, 16, 1954. Edited by Roy J. Deferrari. Washington, Catholic University of America Press, 1955. iii, 59p. 23cm. Includes bibliographies. [BX905.M5 1954] A55
1. Theological seminaries, Catholic. 2. Religious education [of young people] 3. Greek language—Study and teaching. 4. Reading—Remedial teaching. I. Deferrari, Roy Joseph, 1890- ed. II. Title.

MINOR Seminary Conference. 207.73
6th, Catholic University of America, 1955.
Curriculum of the minor seminary: social studies, Greek, and the general curriculum; the proceedings of the Sixth Annual Conference on the Curriculum of the Minor Seminary, conducted at the Catholic University of America, May 13, 14, 15, 1955. Edited by Roy J. Deferrari. Washington, Catholic University of America Press, 1956. iv, 81p. 22cm. Includes bibliographies. [BX905.M5 1955] 56-1552
1. Theological seminaries, Catholic. 2. Greek language—Study an teaching. 3. Social sciences—Study and teaching (Secondary) I. Deferrari, Roy Joseph, 1890- ed. II. Title.

MINOR Seminary Conference. 207.73
7th, Catholic University of America, 1956.
Curriculum of the minor seminary: natural sciences and curriculum review; the proceedings of the Seventh Annual Minor Seminary Conference on the Curriculum of the Minor Seminary, conducted at the Catholic University of America, May 11, 12, 13, 1956. Edited by Cornelius M. Cuyler. Washington, Catholic University of America Press, 1957. iv, 97p. 22cm. Includes bibliographical references. [BX905.M5 1956] 57-793
1. Theological seminaries, Catholic. 2. Science—Study and teaching (Secondary) I. Cuyler, Cornellus M., ed. II. Title.

MINOR Seminary Conference, 207.73
8th, Catholic University of America, 1957.
Curriculum of the minor seminary: natural sciences and modern languages; the proceedings of the Eighth Annual Minor Seminary Conference on the Curriculum of the Minor Seminary, conducted at the Catholic University of America, May 17, 18, 19, 1957. Edited by Cornelius M. Cuyler. Washington, Catholic University of America Press, 1958. v. 87p. 22cm. Includes bibliographies. [BX905.M5 1957] 57-59522
1. Theological seminaries, Catholic. 2. Science—Study and teaching (Secondary) 3. Languages, Modern—Study and teaching. I. Cuyler, Cornelius M., ed. II. Title.

MINOR Seminary Conference. 207.73
9th, Catholic University of America, 1958.
Curriculum of the minor seminary: mathematics and speech training; the proceedings of the Ninth Annual Minor Seminary Conference on mathematics and speech training, conducted at the Catholic University of America, May 9, 10, 11, 1958. Ed. by Cornelius M. Cuyler. Washington, Catholic University of America Press, 1959. vi, 103p. 22cm. Includes bibliographical references. [BX905.C3 1958] 59-2837
1. Theological seminaries, Catholic. 2. Mathematics—Study and teaching. 3. Languages, Modern—Study and teaching. I. Cuyler, Cornelius M., ed. II. Title.

MINOR Seminary Conference, 207.73
Catholic University of America
Proceedings. 18th-1967 Washington. Catholic Univ. Pr. v. 22cm. annual. Each v. has also a distinctive title. Issued by the conf. under earlier names: 1950, Conference on the Organization and Administration of the Minor Seminary- 1951-55, Conference on the Curriculum of the Minor Seminary; 1956-57, Minor Seminary Conference on the Curriculum of the Minor Seminary. Ed. 1967: C. M. Cuyler [BX903.M425] 61-66767 3.95 pap.,
1. Theological seminaries, Catholic—Congresses. I. Catholic University of America. II. Title.

MINOR Seminary Conference, 207.73
Catholic University of America.
Proceedings. 17th. Washington, Catholic Univ. of Amer. Pr. [1967] v. 22cm. annual. Each vol. has also a distinctive title. 1966. Some answers to current criticism of the Minor Seminary Issued by the cont. under earher names: 1950, Conf. on the Org. and Admin. of the Minor Seminary; 1951-55, Cont. on the Curriculum of the Minor Seminary 1956-57, Minor Seminary Cont. on the Curriculum of the Minor Seminary. 1966. Minor Seminary Cont. [BX903.M425] 61-66767 3.50 pap.,
1. Theological seminaries, Catholic—Congresses. I. Catholic University of America. II. Title.

MINOR Seminary Conference, 207.73
Catholic University of America
Proceedings. 16th, May 14-16, 1965. Ed. by Rev. Cornclius M. Cuyler. Washington, D.C., Catholic Univ. [c.1965] 101p. 22cm. annual. Ea. vol. has a distinctive title: 1965: Programs and procedures of the Minor Seminary [BX903.M425] 61-66767 2.75 pap.,
1. Theological seminaries, Catholic—Congresses. I. Catholic University of America. II. Title.

NATIONAL Council of the 207'.73
Churches of Christ in the United States of America. Committee on Theological Study and Teaching.
The study of religion in college and university and its implications for church and seminary; a report on a consultation held in New York City, January 26-27, 1967. Foreword by Claude Welch. [New York?] Dept. of Higher Education, National Council of Churches [1967] xii, 100 p. 26 cm. Includes bibliographies. [BV4030.N3] 68-5492
1. Theology—Study and teaching—United States. 2. Universities and colleges—Religion. I. Title.

THE Study of religion in 207'.73
colleges and universities. Edited by Paul Ramsey and John F. Wilson. With chapters by William A. Clebach [and others. Princeton, N.J.] Princeton University Press, 1970. ix, 353 p. port. 23 cm. Revised papers from a conference, held at Princeton University in 1968, in honor of G. F. Thomas. Bibliography: p. 347-352. [BL41.S78] 70-90957 10.00
1. Religion—Study and teaching—Addresses, essays, lectures. I. Ramsey, Paul, ed. II. Wilson, John Frederick, ed. III. Thomas, George Finger, 1899-

WHITE, Alex Sandri 207.73025
Guide to religious education: the directory of seminaries, Bible colleges, and theological schools covering the USA and Canada. 1965-1966 ed. Allenhurst, N. J., Aurea Pubns., c.1965. 82.1 30cm. [BV4030.W46] 65-5823 4.95 pap.,
1. Theological seminaries—U.S.—Direct. I. Title.

FLEMING, Sandford, 1888- 207'.74
Children & Puritanism. New York, Arno Press, 1969 [c1933] xii, 236 p. 24 cm. (American education: its men, ideas and institutions) Bibliography: p. [209]-220. [BV1467.F5 1969] 70-89178
1. Christian education—New England. 2. Puritans—New England. 3. New England—Church history. 4. Congregational churches in New England. 5. Children in New England. 6. New England theology. I. Title. II. Series.

GAMBRELL, Mary Latimer. 207'.74
Ministerial training in eighteenth-century New England. New York, AMS Press, 1967 [c1937] 169 p. 24 cm. (Studies in history, economics, and public law, no. 428) Originally presented as the author's thesis, Columbia University. Bibliography: p. 148-159. [BV4033.G3 1967] 71-168094
1. Theology—Study and teaching—History. 2. Theological seminaries—New England. I. Title. II. Series: Columbia studies in the social sciences, 428.

WILLIAMS, George 207.744
Huntston, 1914- ed.
The Harvard Divinity School: its place in Harvard University and in American culture. Boston, Beacon Press [1954] xvi, 366p. illus., ports. 22cm. Bibliographical footnotes. [BV4070.H46W5] 54-8425
1. Harvard University. Divinity School. I. Title.

WILLIAMS, Daniel Day, 207'.744'5
1910-
The Andover liberals; a study in American theology. New York, Octagon Books, 1970 [c1941] viii, 203 p. 24 cm. Thesis—Columbia University, 1941. Bibliography: p. [193]-199. [BV4070.A56W5 1970] 79-111636
1. Andover Theological Seminary. 2. Theology, Doctrinal—History—U.S. I. Title.

BAINTON, Roland Herbert, 207.746
1894-
Yale and the ministry; a history of education for the Christian ministry at Yale from the founding in 1701. Line drawings by the author. [1st ed.] New York, Harper [1957] xiii, 297p. illus., ports. 22cm. Bibliographical references included in 'Notes' (p. 269-290) [BV4070.Y36B3] 57-7344
1. Yale University. Divinity School. I. Title.

COFFIN, Henry Sloane, 207.747
1877-
A half century of Union Theological Seminary, 1896-1945 an informal history. New York, Scribner, 1954. 261p. 21cm. [BV4070.U66C6] 54-6526
1. New York, Union Theological Seminary. I. Title.

DAWLEY, Powel Mills, 207'.7471
1907-
The story of the General Theological Seminary; a sesquicentennial history, 1817-1967. New York, Oxford University Press, 1969. xvii, 390 p. illus., ports. 24 cm. Bibliographical footnotes. [BV4070.G46D3] 69-17760 7.50
1. New York. General Theological Seminary of the Protestant Episcopal Church in the United States—History. I. Title.

RICHARDS, George Warren, 207.748
1869-
History of the Theological Seminary fo the Reformed Church in the United States, 1825-1934, Evangelical and Reformed Church, 1934-1952. Lancaster, Pa., 1952. xix, 660 p. illus., ports. 24 cm. Bibliography: p. 632-648 [BV4070.L26R5] 52-40071
1. Lancaster, Pa. Theological Seminary of the Evangelical and Reformed Church. I. Title.

SHILLING, Henry, 1902- 207.748
The second seven years of faith, 1945-1952. Freeport, Pa., Fountain Press [195 --] 332 p. illus. 24 cm. [BV4070.T7S5] 58-26847
1. Transylvania Bible School. I. Title. II. Title: Seven years of faith.

GUFFIN, Gilbert Lee, 207.74811
ed.
What God hath wrought; Eastern's first thirty-five years. Chicago, Judson Press [1960] 179p. 24cm. [BV4070.P546G8] 60-9653
1. Philadelphia. Eastern Baptist Theological Seminary. I. Title.

PHILADELPHIA. Lutheran 207.74811
Theological Seminary.
Biographical record of the Lutheran Theological Seminary at Philadelphia, 1864-1962, by John A. Kaufmann. Philadelphia, Author, 1964. v, 275p. 24cm. 64-22820 2.25
I. Kaufmann, John Augustus, 1920- ed. II. Title.

ALEXANDRIA, Va. 207.755
Protestant Episcopal Theological Seminary in Virginia.
Alumni directory, Virginia Theological Seminary. [Alexandria?] v. 21cm. Issues for 1958-'published as a supplement to the Seminary journal.' [BV4070.A417] 58-27119
I. Title.

MUELLER, William A. 207'.763'355
The school of providence and prayer; a history of the New Orleans Baptist Theological Seminary, by William A. Mueller. [New Orleans, Printed by the Print. Dept. of the New Orleans Baptist Theological Seminary, 1969] 143 p. illus., ports. 22 cm. Bibliographical references included in "Notes" (p. 140-143) [BV4070.N4356M8] 69-20321
1. New Orleans. Baptist Theological Seminary. I. Title.

BLANDY, Gray M. 207'.764'31
The story of the first twenty-five years of the Episcopal Theological Seminary of the Southwest / by Gray M. Blandy and Lawrence L. Brown. [Austin, Tex.] : Episcopal Theological Seminary of the Southwest, c1976. v, 94 p. ; 22 cm. Cover title. Includes bibliographical references. [BV4070.E736B55] 76-383091
1. Austin, Tex. Episcopal Theological Seminary of the Southwest. I. Brown, Lawrence L., joint author. II. Title.

ST. John's and 207.764'35
Assumption Seminaries Alumni Association.
Priest forever; history of St. John's Seminary, San Antonio, Texas, 1915-1965. San Antonio, 1966. 129 p. illus., ports. 24 cm. [BX915.S476] 67-3890
1. St. John's Seminary of San Antonio, Tex. 2. Seminary of the Assumption of the Blessed Virgin Mary of SanAntonio, Tex. I. Title.

ST. John's and 207.764'35
Assumption Seminaries Alumni Association.
Priest forever; history of St. John's Seminary, San Antonia, Texas, 1915-1965. San Antonio, 1966. 129 p. illus., ports. 24 cm. [BX915.S476] 67-3890
1. St. John's Seminary of San Antonio, Tex. 2. Seminary of the Assumption of the Blessed Virgin Mary of San Antonio, Tex. I. Title.

LEXINGTON, Ky. College of 207.769
the Bible.
That there may be more ministers; a report of the centennial development convocation held by the College of the Bible, Wednesday, Thursday, and Friday, October 31-November 2, 1956, including the installation addresses of Professors William R. Baird, Jr., Charles C. Manker, Jr. [and] William L. Reed. Lexington, Ky., 1957. 72p. 23cm. [BV4070.L48A4] 58-27489
1. Disciples of Christ—Addresses, essays, lectures. 2. Theology—Study and teaching—Disciples of Christ. I. Title.

SANDERS, Robert Stuart. 207.769
History of Louisville Presbyterian Theological Seminary, 1853-1953. [Louisville] Louisville Presbyterian Theological Seminary, 1953. 100p. illus. 24cm. [BV4070.L6956S3] 54-1802
1. Louisville Presbyterian Theological Seminary (1901-) I. Title.

JOHNSON, Inman. 207.76944
Of parsons and profs. Nashville, Broadman Press [1959] 114p. 22cm. The author's experiences and observations as a student, professor, and alumni secretary at Southern Baptist Theological Seminary, Louisville, Ky. [BV4070.L759J6] 59-9698
1. Louisville, Ky. Southern Baptist Theological Seminary. I. Title.

MUELLER, William A 207.76944
A history of Southern Baptist Theological Seminary. Nashville, Broadman Press [1959] 256p. illus. 22cm. [BV4070.L76M8] 59-9687
1. Louisville, Ky. Southern Baptist Theological Seminary. I. Title.

MOORE, George Voiers, 207'.769'47
1897-
Centennial directory of the College of the Bible (Lexington Theological Seminary); alumni and former students, 1865 to 1965. Compiled and edited by George Voiers Moore. Lexington, Ky., [Printed as a private ed. by the Keystone Printery] 1965. ii, 485 p. 19 cm. [BV4070.L46M6] 78-258079
1. Lexington, Ky. College of the Bible—Directories. I. Lexington, Ky. College of the Bible. II. Title.

STEVENSON, Dwight 207.76947
Eshelman, 1906-
Lexington Theological Seminary, 1865-1965; the College of the Bible century [by] Dwight E. Stevenson. St. Louis, Bethany Press [1964] 495 p. 23 cm. Bibliography: p. 463-481. [BV4070.L46S8] 65-1137
1. Lexington, Ky. College of the Bible. I. Title.

SCHAUFFLER, Grace 207.771
Leavitt, 1894-
Fields of the Lord; the story of Schauffler College, 1886-1957. [Oberlin? Ohio, 1957] 99p. illus., ports. 24cm. [BV4176.S45S4] 57-41481
1. Schauffler College of Religious and Social Work, Cleveland. 2. Oberlin College. Schauffler Division of Christian Education. I. Title.

SPIELMANN, Richard M. 207'.771'52
Bexley Hall, 150 years : a brief history / by Richard M. Spielmann. [Rochester, N.Y.] : Colgate Rochester Divinity School/Bexley Hall/Crozer Theological Seminary, [1974] 112 p. ; 23 cm. [BV4070.K48S68] 75-301797
1. Kenyon College, Gambier, Ohio. Divinity School (Bexley Hall) I. Title.

SELLERS, Ovid Rogers, 207.773
1884-
The Fifth quarter century of McCormick., the story of the years 1929-1954 at McCormick Theological Seminary. Chicago, Mccormick Theological Seminary, 1955- 139p. illus. 23 cm. [BV4070.M366S4] 56-2441
1. McCormick Theological Seminary, Chicago. I. Title.

GETZ, Gene A. 207'.773'11
MBI; the story of Moody Bible Institute [by] Gene A. Getz. Chicago, Moody Press [1969] 393 p. illus., maps, ports. 24 cm. Bibliography: p. 356-369. [BV4070.M76G4] 69-13110 5.95
1. Moody Bible Institute of Chicago.

SKILLRUD, Harold 207'.773'11
Clayton.
LSTC: decade of decision; a history of the merger of the Lutheran School of Theology at Chicago with special emphasis on the decade 1958-1968. Chicago, Lutheran School of Theology at Chicago, 1969. xii, 327 p. illus., facsims., maps, plans. 23 cm. Bibliography: p. 170-173. [BV4070.6.S55] 78-94887
1. Lutheran School of Theology at Chicago. I. Title.

*TURNBULL, Ralph G. 207'.773.11
A treasury of W. Graham Scroggie compiled by Ralph G. Turnbull. Grand Rapids, Baker Book House [1974] 220 p. 20 cm. Bibliography: p. 218-220. [BX6093] ISBN 0-8010-8822-4 3.95 (pbk.)
I. Title.

WIERSBE, Warren W. 207'.773'11 B
William Culbertson: a man of God, by Warren W. Wiersbe. Chicago, Moody Press [1974] 176 p. illus. 22 cm. [BX6093.C77W53] 74-162937 ISBN 0-8024-9559-1 4.95
1. Culbertson, William.

JOHNSON, Peter Leo. 207.775
Halcyon days; story of St. Francis Seminary, Milwaukee, 1856-1956. Foreword by Albert G. Meyer. Milwaukee, Bruce Pub. Co. [1956] 416p. illus. 23cm. [BX915.Si6J6] 56-59133
1. St. Francis Seminary, St. Francis, Wis. I. Title.

BACH, Marcus, 1906- 207.777
Of faith and learning; the story of the School of Religion at the State University of Iowa. Iowa City, School of Religion, SUI [1952] 261p. 22cm. [BV1612.I 6B2] 52-12127
1. Iowa. University. School of Religion. I. Title.

CUP. 207.778
Springfield, Mo. v. illus. 28 cm. "By the sentors of Central Bible Institute." [BV4070.C39313] 52-41388
1. Springfield, Mo. Central Bible Institute.

CAEMMERER, Richard 207.77866
Rudolph, 1904- ed.
Toward a more excellent ministry. Eds.: Richard R. Caemmerer, Alfred O. Fuerbringer. St. Louis, Concordia [1964] xi, 153p. 24cm. Essays in honor of the 125th anniversary of the founding of Concordia Theological Seminary, St. Louis. [BV4070.C8C3] 64-24267 3.00
1. Concordia Theological Seminary, St. Louis. 2. Theology—Study and teaching—Lutheran Church. 3. Pastoral theology—Lutheran Church—Addresses, essays, lectures. I. Fuerbringer, Alfred Ottomar, 1903- joint ed. II. Concordia Theological Seminary, St. Louis. III. Title.

CONCORDIA Theological 207'.778'66
Seminary, St. Louis. Board of Control.
Exodus from Concordia : a report on the 1974 walkout / by the Board of Control, Concordia Seminary, St. Louis, Missouri. St. Louis : The Board, c1977. 186 p. : ill. ; 23 cm. Includes bibliographical references. [BV4070.C8A54] 77-152169
1. Concordia Theological Seminary, St. Louis. 2. Lutheran Church-Missouri Synod—History. I. Title.

MEYER, Carl Stamm, 207.77866
1907-
Log cabin to Luther Tower; Concordia Seminary during one hundred and hundred and twenty-five years toward a more excellent ministry, 1839-1964. St. Louis, Concordia [1966, c.1965] xi, 322p. 24cm. Bible. [BV4070.X8M4] 65-28163 7.95
1. Concordia Theological Seminary, St. Louis. 2. Lutheran Church — Missouri Synod. I. Title.

POWERS, James Michael, 207.789
1907- ed.
Memoirs: the Seminary of Montezuma; documents and writings of Most Reverend John Mark Gannon, chairman of the Bishops' Committee for Montezuma Seminary, and his episcopal associates. Erie, Pa., 1953. 225p. illus. 24cm. [BX915.M76P6] 53-38810
1. Montezuma Seminary, Montezuma, N.M. I. Gannon, John Mark, Bp., 1877?- II. Title.

BAIRD, Jesse Hays, 207.79462
1889-
The San Anselmo story; a personalized history of San Francisco Theological Seminary. Stockton, California Lantern Press, 1963. 124 p. 21 cm. [[BV4070.S26B3]] 63-5403
1. San Francisco Theological Seminary, San Anselmo, Calif. I. Title.

FLEMING, Sandford, 207.79467
1888-
For the making of ministers,: a history of Berkeley Baptist Divinity School, 1871-1961. Valley Forge, Judson [c.1963] 167p. 25cm. Bibl. 62-20951 3.50
1. Berkeley Baptist Divinity School, Berkeley, Calif. I. Title.

THE Graduate 207'.794'67
Theological Union; its participants and their ecclesiastical heritage. Edited by Elizabeth Kelley Bauer and Florence Noyce Wertz. [Berkeley, Calif.] Graduate Theological Union Guild, 1970. 50 p. illus. 24 cm. [BV4070.G7664] 75-21850
1. Graduate Theological Union. 2. Theological seminaries—California—Berkeley. I. Bauer, Elizabeth (Kelley), ed. II. Wertz, Florence Noyce, ed. III. Graduate Theological Union Guild.

WEBER, Francis J. 207.79492
A guide to Saint John's Seminary, Camarillo, California, by Francis J. Weber. [Los Angeles] Westernlore Pr., 1966. 32p. illus., col. port. 21cm. Issued to commemorate the silver episcopal jubilee of James Francis Cardinal McIntyre. [BX915.C342W44] 66-23590 3.00
1. St. John's Seminary, Carmarillo, Calif. I. McIntyre, James Francis, Cardinal. II. Title.

GRIFFETH, Ross John, 207'.795'31
1896-
Crusaders for Christ. Eugene, Or., Northwest Christian College [1971] 144 p. illus., ports. 28 cm. [BV4070.E9G73] 73-26827
1. Eugene, Or. Northwest Christian College. I. Title.

THEOLOGICAL education by 207'.8
extension. Edited by Ralph D. Winter. South Pasadena, Calif., William Carey Library [1969] xxvi, 589, 28 p. illus. 23 cm. Bibliography: p. 1-28 (3d group) [BV4140.L3T48] 78-96751 5.25
1. Theology—Study and teaching—Latin America. I. Winter, Ralph D., ed.

WELD, Wayne. 207'.8
The world directory of theological education by extension [by] Wayne C. Weld. South Pasadena, Calif., William Carey Library [1973] xiii, 374 p. 23 cm. Bibliography: p. 359-374. [BV4164.W44] 73-8894 ISBN 0-87808-134-8 5.95 (pbk.)
1. Seminary extension—Directories. I. Title. II. Title: Theological education by extension.

208 Collections Of Christianity

AQUINAS Institute of 208
Philosophy and Theology. School of Theology. Dubuque, Iowa.
Lagrange lectures. Dubuque, Iowa. 1963 v. 19 cm. Published by the Aquinas Institute of Philosophy and Theology, School of Theology. [BS413.L3] 64-36013
1. Lagrange, Marie Joseph, 1855-1938. 2. Bible — Collected works. I. Title.

AQUINAS Institute of 208
Philosophy and Theology. School of Theology. Dubuque, Iowa.
Lagrange lectures. Dubuque, Iowa. 1963 v. 19 cm. Published by the Aquinas Institute of Philosophy and Theology, School of Theology. [BS413.L3] 64-36013
1. Lagrange, Marie Joseph, 1855-1938. 2. Bible — Collected works. I. Title.

BARCLAY, William, lecturer 208
in the University of Glasgow.
In the hands of God. Selected by Rita F. Snowden. New York, Harper & Row [1967] 157 p. 21 cm. (Harper chapel books, CB38) 1966 ed. has title: Seen in the passing. [BR85.B4 1967] 67-22765
1. Christianity—Addresses, essays, lectures. I. Title.

BARNHOUSE, Donald Grey, 1895- 208
1960.
Words fitly spoken. Wheaton, Ill., Tyndale

House Publishers [1969] x, 242 p. 22 cm. [BR85.B4175] 74-79465
1. Christianity—20th century—Addresses, essays, lectures. I. Title.

BELL, Hermon Fiske, 1880- comp. 208
Religion through the ages; an anthology, assembled by Hermon F. Bell. Edited and interpreted by Charles S. MacFarland. New York, Greenwood Press, 1968 [c1948] xlvi, 445 p. 23 cm. [BL29.B4 1968] 68-23275
1. Religious literature. I. Title.

BONHOEFFER, Dietrich, 1906-1945. 208
I loved this people. Testimonies of responsibility with an introd. by Hans Rothfels. Translated by Keith R. Crim. Richmond, John Knox Press [1965] 62 p. 19 cm. (Chime paperbacks) [BX8080.B645A53] 65-15715
I. Title.

BONHOEFFER, Dietrich, 1906-1945 208
I loved this people. Testimonies of responsibility. Introd. by Hans Rothfels. Tr. [from German] by Keith R. Crim. Richmond, Va., Knox [c.1965] 62p. 19cm. (Chime paperbacks) [BX8080.B645A53] 65-15715 1.00 pap.,
I. Title.

BRIDGES, Horace James, 1880- 208
Criticisms of life; studies in faith, hope, and despair. Freeport, N.Y., Books for Libraries Press [1969] xvii, 295 p. 22 cm. (Essay index reprint series) Reprint of the 1915 ed. Contents.Contents.—Francis Thompson's "The hound of heaven": a study in religious experience.—Mr. G. K. Chesterton as theologian.—Professor Ernst Haeckel's new Calvinism.—Sir Oliver Lodge and the evidence for immortality.—Mr. Winston Churchill and clerical "heresy."—Ellen Key and the "new morality" of free love.—The right to die: Maeterlinck and Ingersoll versus humanity.—The victorious death of Captain Scott.—Epilogue: in the time of war and tumults. Bibliographical footnotes. [BR123.B69 1969] 75-99684
1. Christianity—Addresses, essays, lectures. I. Title.

CAIRNS, William Thomas, d.1944. 208
The religion of Dr. Johnson, and other essays. Freeport, N.Y., Books for Libraries Press [1969, c1946] xiii, 137 p. 23 cm. (Essay index reprint series) Contents.Contents.—The religion of Doctor Johnson.—John Newton: a vindication.—The constituents of a good hymn.—Jupiter Carlyle and the Scottish moderates.—A reformation diarist and his times. Bibliographical footnotes. [BR783.C3 1969] 71-93324
1. Johnson, Samuel, 1709-1784—Religion and ethics. 2. Scotland—Church history. I. Title.

CAPONIGRI, Aloysius Robert, 1913- 208
Modern Catholic thinkers. Edited by A. Robert Caponigri. New York Harper & Row [1965- v. 21 cm. (The Cathedral library) Harper torchbooks, TB 306II. Bibliographical footnotes. [BX885.C26] 65-9086
1. Catholic literature. I. Title.

CAPONIGRI, Aloysius Robert, 1913- ed. 208
Modern Catholic thinkers; an anthology. Edited, with a pref., by Aloysius Robert Caponigri. Introd. by Martin Cyril D'Arcy. Freeport, N.Y., Books for Libraries Press [1970, c1960] xvi, 636 p. 24 cm. (Essay index reprint series) Includes bibliographical references. [BX880.C26 1970] 78-117775
1. Catholic literature—Addresses, essays, lectures. I. Title.

CLEMENS, E Bryan. 208
Sermon outlines you can preach. Natick, Mass., W. A. Wilde Co. [1963] 79 p. 22 cm. [BV4223.C56] 63-22171
1. Sermons — Outlines. I. Title.

COLQUHOUN, Frank 208
Total Christianity. Chicago, Moody [1965, c.1962] 91p. 19cm. (Christian forum bks.) [BT60] 65-8371 .95 pap.,
1. Christianity — Essence, genius, nature. I. Title.

CONGAR, Yves Marie Joseph, 1904- 208
A gospel priesthood [by] Yves Congar. Tr. by P. F. Hepburne-Scott. [New York] Herder & Herder [1967] 250p. 22cm. Tr. of Sacerdoce et laicat. Bibl. [BX891.C5813 1967b] 67-14143 5.95
1. Theology—Collected works—20th cent. 2. Catholic Church—Collected works. I. Title.

CONGAR, Yves Marie Joseph, 1904- 208
A gospel priesthood [by] Yves Congar. Translated by P. F. Hepburne-Scott. [New York] Herder and Herder [1967] 250 p. 22 cm. Translation of Sacerdoce et laicat. Bibliography: p. 237-241. [BX891.C5813] 67-14143
1. Theology—Collected works—20th cent. 2. Catholic Church—Collected works. I. Title.

CONTEMPORARY problems in religion. Harold Albert Basilius, editor. Freeport, N.Y., Books for Libraries Press [1970, c1956] viii, 128 p. port. 23 cm. (Essay index reprint series) Includes bibliographical references. [BL25.C6 1970] 78-93315 ISBN 8-369-15453- 208
1. Religion—Addresses, essays, lectures. I. Basilius, Harold Albert, ed.

FICKER, Victor B., comp. 208
The revolution in religion. Edited by Victor B. Ficker [and] Herbert S. Graves. Columbus, Ohio, Merrill [1973] vi, 169 p. 23 cm. Contents.Contents.—Leary, J. P. The revolution in religion.—Harrington, M. Religion and revolution.—Gelpi, D. Religion in the age of Aquarius.—Berrigan, D. Conscience, the law, and civil disobedience.—Rose, S. C. The coming confrontation on the church's war investments.—Hadden, J. K. Clergy involvement in civil rights.—Groppi, J. E. The church and civil rights.—Newsweek. Verdict at First Baptist.—Bloy, M. B., Jr. The counter-culture: it just won't go away.—Forman, J. The Black manifesto.—McIntire, C. Christian manifesto.—Sandeen, E. R. Fundamentalism and American identity.—Kuhn, H. B. Obstacles to Evangelism in the world.—Zahn, G. C. A religious pacifist looks at abortion.—The Lutheran Church-Missouri Synod. Abortion: theological, legal, and medical aspects.—Bayer, C. H. Confessions of an abortion counselor.—Osborn, R. T. Religion on the campus.—Ficker, V. B. The search for meaning. Includes bibliographical references. [BR50.F46] 73-75682 ISBN 0-675-08932-8
1. Theology—Collections. 2. Church and social problems—Collections. 3. Christianity—20th century—Collections. I. Graves, Herbert S., 1914- joint comp. II. Title.

FORELL, George Wolfgang. 208
The proclamation of the Gospel in a pluralistic world; essays on Christianity and culture [by] George W. Forell. Philadelphia, Fortress Press [1973] vi, 138 p. 19 cm. Includes bibliographical references. [BR115.C8F6] 73-79354 ISBN 0-8006-1035-0 3.50
1. Christianity and culture—Addresses, essays, lectures. I. Title.
Contents omitted.

FULLERTON, Kemper, 1865-1940. 208
Essays & sketches, Oberlin, 1904-1934. Freeport, N.Y., Books for Libraries Press [1971, c1938] x, 284 p. 23 cm. (Essay index reprint series) [BV4310.F8 1971] 70-156644 ISBN 0-8369-2361-8
1. Oberlin College. 2. Theology—Addresses, essays, lectures. I. Title.

*FUNK, Robert W., ed. 208
Journal for theology and the church; 1 [Magnolia, Mass., P. Smith, 1966, c.] 1965. xi, 183p. 21cm. (Harper torchbk., Cloister lib. rebound) Orig. pub. in Tubingen by J. C. B. Mohr (Paul Siebeck) 4.00
I. Title.
Contents omitted.

*FUNK, Robert W., ed. 208
Journal for theology and the church, v.2: translating theology into the modern age, ed. [by] Robert W. Funk [others. Tr. from German by Charles E. Carleston, others] New York, Harper [c.]1965. 179p. 21cm. (Harper torchbks., Cloister lib., TB252L) 1.95 pap.,
I. Title.

*FUNK, Robert W., ed. 208
Journal for theology and the church; v.2. Edit. bd.: Robert W. Funk [others] [Magnolia, Mass., P. Smith, 1966, c.1965] (Torchbks., Cloister lib., TB252L rebound) Tr. from German by Charles E. Carlston, others Contents.contents—v. 2 Translating theology into the modern age Bibl. 4.00
I. Title.

GAEBELEIN, Frank Ely, 1899- 208
A varied harvest; out of a teacher's life and thought; a collection of essays by Frank E. Gaebelein. Grand Rapids, [1967] 198 p. 23 cm. [BR123.G18] 66-18732
1. Christianity-20th cent.-Addresses, essays, lectures. I. Title.

GAEBELEIN, Frank Ely, 1899- 208
A varied harvest; out of a teacher's life and thought; a collection of essays by Frank E. Gaebelein. Grand Rapids, Eerdmans [1967] 198 p. 23 cm. [BR123.G18] 66-18732
1. Christianity—20th century—Addresses, essays, lectures. I. Title.

GARRISON, Winfred Ernest, 1874- 208
Variations on a theme: "God saw that it was good." St. Louis, Bethany Press [1964] 208 p. 23 cm. Bibliographical references included in footnotes. [BT80.G37] 64-12009
1. Theology — Addresses, essays, lectures. I. Title.

GARRISON, Winfred Ernest, 1874- 208
Variations on a theme: 'God saw that it was good.' St. Louis, Bethany [c.1964] 208p. 23cm. Bibl. 64-12009 3.50
1. Theology—Addresses, essays, lectures. I. Title.

GASQUET, Francis Aidan, Cardinal, 1846-1929. 208
The old English Bible, and other essays. Port Washington, N.Y., Kennikat Press [1968] vii, 399 p. 22 cm. Reprint of the 1897 ed. Contents.Contents.—Notes on mediaevel monastic libraries.—The monastic scriptorium.—A forgotten English preacher.—The pre-Reformation English Bible.—Religious instruction in England during the fourteenth and fifteenth centuries.—A royal Christmas in the fifteenth century.—The Canterbury claustral school in the fifteenth century.—The note books of William Worcester, a fifteenth century antiquary.—Hampshire recusants, a story of their troubles in the time of Queen Elizabeth. Bibliographical footnotes. [BR744.G33 1969] 68-26209
1. Bible. English—Versions. 2. Education—England—History. 3. Libraries—History—400-1400. I. Title.

GEACH, Peter Thomas. 208
God and the soul, by Peter Geach. New York, Schocken Books [1969] xxi, 138 p. 23 cm. (Studies in ethics and the philosophy of religion) [BL50.G36] 69-17835 4.50
1. Religion—Addresses, essays, lectures. I. Title.

GLEN, John Stanley, 1907- 208
Erich Fromm; a Protestant critique, by J. Stanley Glen. Philadelphia, Westminster Press [1966] 224 p. 21 cm. Bibliography: p. [213]-224. [BX4817.G5] 66-21807
1. Fromm, Erich, 1900- 2. Protestantism.

GRAHAM, William Franklin, 1918- 208
The faith of Billy Graham. Compiled and edited by T. S. Settel. Introd. by Cort R. Flint. [1st ed.] Anderson, S.C., Droke House [1968] 127 p. 24 cm. [BV3785.G69A25 1968] 68-28781 3.95
1. Graham, William Franklin, 1918- 2. Bible—Homiletical use. I. Settel, Trudy S., ed. II. Title.

GUITTON, Jean. 208
The Pope speaks: dialogues of Paul VI with Jean Guitton. English tr. by Anne and Christopher Fremantle. [1st U. S. ed.] New York, Meredith [1968] xiv, 306p. 24cm. Tr. of dialogues avec Paul VI. [BX1378.3.G813] 68-15204 5.95
1. Paulus VI, Pope 1897- I. Title.

HALES, John, 1584-1656. 208
The works of John Hales. New York, AMS Press [1971] 3 v. in 2. 18 cm. Reprint of the 1765 ed., originally published under title: The works of the ever memorable John Hales of Eaton. Includes bibliographical references. [BR75.H32 1971] 77-131037 ISBN 0-404-03050-5
1. Theology—Collected works—17th century.

HALL, Joseph, Bp. of Norwich, 1574-1656. 208
The works of the Right Reverend Joseph Hall. A new ed., rev. and corrected with some additions, by Philip Wynter. New York, AMS Press [1969] 10 v. 23 cm. Reprint of the 1863 ed. Includes bibliographical references. [BX5037.H26 1969] 76-86830
1. Church of England—Collected works. 2. Theology—Collected works—17th century. I. Wynter, Philip, 1793-1871, ed. II. Title.

HENRY, Carl Ferdinand Howard, 1913- 208
Faith at the frontiers, by Carl F. H. Henry. Chicago, Moody Press [1969] 204 p. 22 cm. Bibliography: p. 197-198. [BR85.H55] 78-5729 3.95
1. Christianity—20th century—Addresses, essays, lectures. I. Title.

HOLMES, John Haynes, 1879-1964. 208
A summons unto men; an anthology of the writings of John Haynes Holmes. Edited, with foreword by Carl Hermann Voss. Pref. by James Luther Adams, Dana MacLean Greeley [and] Donald Szantho Harrington. New York, Simon and Schuster [1971] 255 p. 21 cm. Bibliography: p. 241-243. [BX9869.H535A2 1971] 74-139664 ISBN 0-671-20995-7 7.95
I. Title.

HORNE, Herman Harrell, 1874-1946. 208
The essentials of leadership; and other papers in moral and religious education. Freeport, N.Y., Books for Libraries Press [1970] 136 p. 23 cm. (Essay index reprint series) Reprint of the 1931 ed. Includes bibliographical references. [LC283.H6 1970] 76-117808
1. Moral education—Addresses, essays, lectures. 2. Religious education—Addresses, essays, lectures. 3. Leadership. I. Title.

KNOX, Thomas Malcolm, Sir, 1900- 208
A heretic's religion / by Sir Malcolm Knox. Dundee : University of Dundee, 1976. 93 p. ; 21 cm. [BL50.K56] 77-354224 ISBN 0-901396-11-7
1. Religion—Addresses, essays, lectures. I. Title.

LAI, Chaman, ed. 208
Mysteries of life and death. [Fort Lauderdale, Fla.] 1965. xvi, 237 p. 21 cm. [BL29.L3] 66-54962
1. Religious literature (Selections: Extracts, etc.) I. Title.

LEICESTERSHIRE Education Committee. 208
Gathered together: readings on religious themes [by Leicestershire Education Authority] London, Oxford University Press, 1971. v, 91 p. 19 cm. First published as a section of Gathered together: a service book for senior schools. [BL29.L44] 73-28821 ISBN 0-19-233414-X £0.62
1. Religious literature. I. Title.

LEWIS, Clive Staples, 1898-1963. 208
Christian reflections, by C. S. Lewis. Edited by Walter Hooper. Grand Rapids, W. B. Eerdmans Pub. Co. [1967] xiv, 176 p. 23 cm. Bibliographical references included in "Preface" (p. viii-xiv) [BR123.L4824 1967a] 67-2003
1. Christianity—20th century—Addresses, essays, lectures. I. Hooper, Walter, ed. II. Title.

LONNING, Per. 208
Off the beaten path [by] Per Lonning. [Translated by J. M. Moe and H. George Anderson. 1st ed.] New York, Harper & Row [1966] ix, 176 p. 22 cm. "Portions...have appeared in Norwegian in two volumes, Kan kirken moderniseres? ...and Utenfor allfarvel." [BR85.L83] 66-20780
1. Theology — Addresses, essays, lectures. I. Title.

LONNING, Per 208
Off the beaten path [by] Per Lonning. [Tr. by J. M. Moe, H. George Anderson. 1st ed.] New York, Harper [1966] ix, 176p. 22cm. Portions have appeared in Norwegian in two volumes, Kan kirken moderniseres? and Utenfor allfarvei. [BR85.L83] 66-20780 4.50
1. Theology — Addresses, essays, lectures. I. Title.

LUTHER, Martin, 1483-1546. 208
D. Martin Luther's Werke; kritische Gesammtausgabe. Weimar, H. Bohlau, 1883- 19 v. in illus., facsims., music, ports. 27 cm. Section 1, v.: sections 2-4 have special titles. Section 1, v. 7. 10-11, 15- ; sections 2-4 published by H. Bohlaus Nachf. -- -- Revisionsnachtrag. Weimar, H. Bohlaus Nachf., 19 v. 28 cm. Contents. -- [1. Abt. Schriften] Bd. Contents.Contents. -- [1, Abt. Schriften] [2. Abt.] Tischreden. 6 v. -- [3. Abt.] Die deutsche Bibel. [4. Abt.] Briefwechsel. Bibliographical footnotes. [BR330.A2 1883] 5-33483
1. Theology — Collected works — 16th cent. 2. Luthern Church — Collected works. I. Title.

LUTHER, Martin, 1483-1546 208
Works. Philadelphia, Fortress [1967] v. 24cm. General ed.: v. 1-30, Jaroslav Pelikan; v. 31-55 Helmut T. Lehmann. Vs. 31- have imprint: Philadelphia, Muhlenberg. Contents.v. 54. Table talk, ed. by. te)0r. by Theodore G. Tappert. Companion v. Luther, the exposition. Introduction to the Reformer's exegetical writings, by Jaroslav Pelican, St. Louis, Concordia, 1959 [BR330. E51955] 208 55-9893 6.50
1. Theology — Collected works — 16th cent. 2. Lutheran Church — Collected works. 3. Bible— Criticism, interpretation, etc. — Hist. I. Pelikan, Jaroslav, 1923- ed. II. Lehmann, Helmut T., ed. III. Title. IV. Title: Ed. by Jaroslav Polikan [St. Louis, Concordia] V. Title: Luther, the expositor.

LUTHER, Martin, 1483-1546 208
Works. Ed. by Jaroslav Pelikan. [St. Louis, Concordia] Philadelphia, Fortres [1967] v. 24cm. ontents. kv.46. The Christians in Society. III, ed. by Robert C. Schultz. Bibl. Companion vol. Luther the Exposititor introduction to the Reformer's exegetical writings, by Jaroslav Pelikan. St. Louis, Concordia [1959] xiii, 286p. 24cm. Vs. 31- ed. by Harold J. Grimm [others] General ed.: Helmut T. Lehmann v. 46: General ed. H. T. Lehmann. Vs. 31- have imprint: Philadelphia, Muhlenberg. [BR330.E5 1955] 208 55-9893 5.00
1. Theology—Collected works—16th cent. 2. Lutheran Church—Collected works. 3. Bible—Criticism, interpretation, etc.—Hist. I. Pelikan, Jaroslav, 1923- ed. II. Lehmann, Helmut T., ed. III. Title. IV. Title: Luther the expositor.

MADELEINE, M. Sister 208
Nun-sense [by] Sister M. Madelain Milwaukee, Bruce Pub. Co. [1964] x, 147 p. 21 cm. [BX891.M3] 64-22618
1. Catholic Church—Addresses, essays, lectures. I. Title.

MASSEY, Gerald, 1828-1907. 208
Gerald Massey's Lectures / with foreword by John G. Jackson ; introd. by Sibyl Ferguson. New York : S. Weiser, 1974. vii, 287 p. ; 24 cm. "Originally published in a private edition c. 1900." [BL50.M327 1974] 73-92165 ISBN 0-87728-249-8 : 12.50
1. Religion—Addresses, essays, lectures.

MAST, Daniel E 1848-1930. 208
Salvation full and free. Edited by John B. Mast. [Inman kan., 1958] 528p. 24cm. Translation of Anweisungen zur Seligkeit. [BX8109.M253] 58-35734
1. Mennonites— Addresses, essays, lectures. I. Title.

METZGER, Bruce Manning. 208
Historical and literary studies; pagan, Jewish, and Christian, by Bruce M. Metzger. Grand Rapids, Mich., W. B. Eerdmans, 1968. x, 170 p. illus. 25 cm. (New Testament tools and studies, v. 8) [BR85.M475] 70-3860
1. Bible—Addresses, essays, lectures. 2. Christianity—Early Church ca. 30-600. 3. Mysteries, Religious. I. Title. II. Series.

MONTGOMERY, John Warwick. 208
Where is history going? Essays in support of the historical truth of the Christian revelation. With a commendatory letter by C. S. Lewis. [1st ed.] Grand Rapids, Mich., Zondervan Pub. House [1969] 250 p. 23 cm. Bibliographical footnotes. [BR115.H5M6] 69-11659 5.95
1. History (Theology)—Addresses, essays, lectures. 2. History—Philosophy—Addresses, essays, lectures. I. Title.

MURRAY, Gilbert, 1866-1957. 208
Stoic, Christian, and humanist. Freeport, N.Y., Books for Libraries Press [1969] 189 p. 23 cm. (Essay index reprint series) Reprint of the 1940 ed. Bibliography: 17-18. [BL87.M8 1969] 75-99712
1. Religion—Addresses, essays, lectures. I. Title.

NEWMAN, John Henry, 208
Cardinal, 1801-1890.
Essays and sketches. [Edited by Charles Frederick Harrold] Westport, Conn., Greenwood Press [1970, c1948] 3 v. 23 cm. Contents.Contents.—v. 1. Personal and literary character of Cicero, 1824. Poetry, with reference to Aristotle's Poetics, 1829. Primitive Christianity, 1833-36. The rationalistic and the Catholic tempers contrasted, 1835. Holy Scripture in its relation to the Catholic Creed, 1838. Prospects of the Anglican Church, 1839.—v. 2. The theology of St. Ignatius, 1839. Catholicity of the Anglican Church, 1840. Private judgement, 1841. The Tamworth Reading Room, 1841. Milman's view of Christianity, 1841. Rise and progress of universities (Selections from the original discourses) 1856.—v. 3. The church of the Fathers, 1833. The last years of St. Chrysostom, 1859-60. Benedictine schools, 1858-59. An internal arguement for Christianity, 1866. Includes bibliographical references. [BX890.N415 1970] 76-98785
1. Catholic Church—Collected works. 2. Theology—Collected works—19th century. I. Harrold, Charles Frederick, 1897-1948, ed.

NORDEN, Rudolph F 208
The voice of the prophets; sixteen timely pulpit meditations based on texts from the sixteen Old Testament prophets. Saint Louis, Concordia Pub. House [1963] xi, 161 p. 23 cm. [BX8066.N6V6] 63-20177
1. Sermons, American. 2. Lutheran Church — Sermons. I. Title.

PHELPS, William Lyon, 1865- 208
1943.
Adventures and confessions. Freeport, N.Y., Books for Libraries Press [1970] 206 p. 23 cm. (Essay index reprint series) Reprint of the 1926 ed. [PS3531.H4A66 1970] 71-121497
I. Title.

PRIDEAUX, Sherburne Povah 208
Tregelles, 1880-
More outline sermons on general subjects. London, A. R. Mowbray; New York, Morehouse-Gorham Co. [1952] 96p. 19cm. [BV4223.P7] 57-17917
1. Sermons— Outlines. I. Title.

RAMSEY, Arthur Michael, Abp. 208
of Canterbury, 1904-
Sacred and secular; a study in the otherwordly and thisworldly aspects of Christianity. New York, Harper [c.1965] x, 83p. 22cm. (Holland lects.,1964] Bibl. [BR115.W6R3] 66-10232 3.00
1. Christianity—Addresses, essays, lectures. I. Title. II. Series.

RAYMOND, Father, 1903- 208
The silent spire speaks [by] M. Raymond. Milwaukee, Bruce Pub. Co. [1966] vii, 194 p. 23 cm. [BX4705.R3744A3] 66-28857
1. Trappists—Correspondence, reminiscence, etc. I. Title.

RAYMOND, Father, 1903- 208
The silent spire speaks [by] M. Raymond. Milwaukee, Bruce [1966] vii, 194p. 23cm. [BX4705.R3744A3] 66-28857 4.95
1. Frappists — Correspondence, reminiscences, etc. I. Title.

ROLLE, Richard, of Hampole, 208
1290?-1349.
English writings of Richard Rolle, hermit of Hampole. Edited by Hope Emily Allen. Oxford, Clarendon Press, 1931. St. Clair Shores, Mich., Scholarly Press, 1971. lxiv, 180 p. illus. 22 cm. Includes bibliographical references. [PR2135.A2A6 1971] 74-161958 ISBN 0-403-01328-3
I. Allen, Hope Emily, ed. II. Title.

SARTORY, Thomas A. 208
A new interpretation of faith, by Thomas Sartory. Translated by Martha Schmidt. Westminster, Md., Newman Press [1968] 94 p. 21 cm. Translation of Eine neue Interpretation des Glaubens. Bibliographical footnotes. [BR123.S2613] 68-16672
1. Christianity—20th century—Addresses, essays, lectures. I. Title.

SAYERS, Dorothy Leigh, 1893- 208
1957.
Christian letters to a post-Christian world; a selection of essays. Selected and introduced by Roderick Jellema. Grand Rapids, Eerdmans [1969] xiii, 236 p. illus. (part col.), port. 23 cm. Contents.Contents.—Selections from The Pantheon papers.—The greatest drama ever staged.—Strong meat.—The dogma is the drama.—What do we believe?—Creed or chaos?—A vote of thanks to Cyrus.—The dates in The Red-Headed League.—Towards a Christian aesthetic.—Creative mind.—The image of God.—Problem picture.—Christian morality.—The other six deadly sins.—Dante and Charles Williams.—The writing and reading of allegory.—Oedipus simplex.—The Faust legend and the idea of the devil. Bibliographical footnotes. [BT15.S27 1969] 67-19331 6.95
1. Theology, Doctrinal—Addresses, essays, lectures. I. Jellema, Roderick, ed. II. Title.

SCHOFIELD, Alfred Taylor, 208
1846-1929.
Plain papers for young believers. [2d ed.] New York, Loizeaux Bros., 1945. 160p. 20cm. [BR85.S277 1945] 55-24902
1. Christianity—Addresses, essays, lectures. I. Title.

SIMPSON, Robert L. ed. 208
One faith: its Biblical, historical, and ecumenical dimensions; a series of essays in honor of Stephen J. England on the occasion of his seventieth birthday. Robert L. Simpson, editor. Enid, Okla., Phillips Univ. Pr., 1966. ix, 135p. port. 24cm. Bibl. [BR50.S53] 66-27821 2.50
1. England, Stephen Jackson, 1895- 2. Theology — Addresses, essays, lectures. I. England, Stephen Jackson, 1895- II. Title. Contents omitted.

SMITH, Gerald Birney, 1868- 208
1929, ed.
Religious thought in the last quarter-century, by J. M. Powis Smith [and others] Freeport, N.Y., Books for Libraries Press [1970] vii, 239 p. 23 cm. (Essay index reprint series) Reprint of the 1927 ed. Contents.—Old Testament interpretation, by J. M. P. Smith.—The life of Jesus, by S. J. Case.—The study of early Christianity, by H. R. Willoughby.—The interpretation of Protestantism, by J. T. McNeill.—Theological thinking in America, by G. B. Smith.—The psychology of religion in America, by E. L. Schaub.—History of religions, by A. E. Haydon.—Religious education, by T. G. Soares.—American preaching, by O. S. Davis.—Thought concerning Protestant foreign missions, by A. G. Baker.—The development of social Christianity in America, by S. Mathews. Includes bibliographical references. [BR479.S66 1970] 71-107739
1. Christianity—Addresses, essays, lectures. I. Smith, John Merlin Powis, 1866-1932. II. Title.

STRENG, Frederick J., comp. 208
Ways of being religious; readings for a new approach to religion [compiled by] Frederick J. Streng, Charles L. Lloyd, Jr. [and] Jay T. Allen. Englewood Cliffs, N.J., Prentice-Hall [1973] xii, 627 p. illus. 24 cm. Includes bibliographical references. [BL25.S65] 72-7388 ISBN 0-13-946277-5 9.95
1. Religion—Collections. I. Lloyd, Charles L., 1935- joint comp. II. Allen, Jay T., 1934- joint comp. III. Title.

TILLOTSON, John, Abp. of 208
Canterbury, 1630-1694.
The golden book of Tillotson; selections from the writings of the Rev. John Tillotson. Edited, with a sketch of his life, by James Moffatt. Westport, Conn., Greenwood Press [1971] vii, 238 p. 23 cm. Reprint of the 1926 ed. [BX5037.T6 1971] 72-109866 ISBN 0-8371-4357-8
I. Moffatt, James, 1870-1944, ed. II. Title.

VOLTAIRE, Francois Marie 208
Arouet de, 1694-1778.
Voltaire on religion: selected writings. Translated and introduced by Kenneth W. Appelgate. New York, F. Ungar Pub. Co. [1974] xiii, 222 p. 22 cm. Includes bibliographical references. [BL27.V64213 1974] 74-127204 ISBN 0-8044-5975-4 7.50
1. Religion—Collected works. I. Appelgate, Kenneth W., tr. II. Title.

WALLIS, J. L. 208
A newspaper man reports—the good news is true, by J. L. Wallis. [Talladega? Ala., 1967] xii, 287 p. 24 cm. Selections from the author's newspaper column, Passing scene, published in the Talladega daily home. [BR123.W32] 68-2256
1. Christianity—20th century—Addresses, essays, lectures. I. Title.

WAR, poverty, freedom; 208
the Christian response. New York, Paulist [1966] x, 163p. 24cm. Concilium theol. in the age of renewal: Moral theol, v. 15) Bibl. [BR121.2.W3] 66-24233 4.50
1. Christianity—20th cent.—Addresses, essays, lectures. I. Series.

WESLEY, John, 1703-1791. 208
John Wesley; [a representative collection of his writings] Edited by Albert C. Outler. New York, Oxford University Press, 1964. xvi, 516 p. 24 cm. (A Library of Protestant thought) Bibliography: p. 500-506. [BX8217.W54O8] 64-15525
1. Theology—Collected works—18th century. 2. Methodist Church—Collected works. I. Outler, Albert Cook, 1908- ed. II. Title. III. Series.

WHITESELL, Faris Daniel, 208
1895-
Sermon outlines on favorite Bible chapters. [Westwood, N.J.] Revell [1962] 64 p. 21 cm. (Revell's sermon outline series) [BV4223.W4462] 62-10740
1. Sermons — Outlines. I. Title.

WILKINSON, Rupert. 208
The prefects: British leadership and the public school tradition; a comparative study in the making of rulers. London, New York, Oxford University Press, 1964. xv, 243 p. 23 cm. "An undergraduate honours thesis presented to the Government Department, Harvard University, in the spring of 1961." Bibliography: p. 231-237. [LA634.W52] 64-3140
1. Public schools (Endowed) — England. 2. Gt. Brit. — Officials and employees. I. Title.

WOODS, Ralph Louis, 1904- ed. 208
The world treasury of religious quotations; diverse beliefs, convictions, comments, dissents, and opinions from ancient and modern sources, compiled and edited by Ralph L. Woods. [1st ed.] New York, Hawthorn Books [1966] xiv, 1106 p. 25 cm. [BL29.W6] 66-15355
1. Religion—Quotations, maxims, etc. I. Title.

WYCLIFFE, John., d.1384 208
Latin works; v. 1-34. [London, Pub. for the Wyclif Soc. by Trubner, 1883-1922] New York, Johnson Reprint, 1967. 22v. in 34 illus. 24cm. Cover title. Vs. 20-22 have imprint: Pub. for the Vyclif Soc. by C. K. Paul. [BR75.W8] 53-57104 560.00 set,; 17.00 ea.,
1. Theology—Collected works—Middle Ages. I. Wyclif Society, London. II. Title.

ARMINIUS, Jacobus, 1560- 208.1
1609.
Writings. Translated from the Latin, in three volumes, the first and second by James Nichols, the third by W. R. Bagnall; with a sketch of the life of the author. Grand Rapids, Baker Book House, 1956. 3v. 24cm. Photolithoprinted from the author's Works, published in 1853. [BX6195.A65 1956] 56-7575
1. Theology—Collected works—16th cent. I. Title.

BANNERMAN, James, 1807- 208.1
1868.
The church of Christ; a treatise on the nature, powers, ordinances, discipline, and government of the Christian church. Swengel, Pa., [dist. Bible Truth Depot, 1960] 2 y. 480; 468p. illus. (Student's reformed theological library) Bibl. 60-36391 7.50
1. Church. 2. Sacraments. 3. Church polity. I. Title.

BARTH, Karl, 1886- 208.1
Against the stream; shorter post-war writings, 1946-52. [Edited by Ronald Gregor Smith] New York, Philosophical Library [1954] 252p. port. 23cm. 'Bibliography of Karl Barth's writings in English': p. [247]-248. [BX9410.B3] 54-2880
1. Theology—20th cent.—Addresses, essays, lectures. 2. Reformed Church—Addresses, essays, lectures. I. Title.

BENSON, Purnell Handy, 208.1
1913-
Religion in contemporary culture; a study of religion through social science. New York, Harper, 1960. 839 p. 25 cm. (Harper's social science series) Includes bibliography. [BL48.B43] 60-7021
1. Religion. I. Title.

BLISS, Marion Louise 208.1
The way of wonder. New York, Vantage Press [1960, c.1959] 160p. (bibl. p. 159-160) 22cm. 60-753 3.00 bds.,
I. Title. II. Title: Wonder.

BONAVENTURA Saint, Cardinal 208.1
The works of Bonaventure: cardinal, serc)0aphic doctor, and saint, v. 4. Tr. from Latin by Jose de Vinck. Paterson, N.J., St. Anthony Guild Pr. [1966] 312p. illus. 24cm. ontents. kv.4. Defense of the mendicants Bibl. [BX890.B673123] 60-53110 6.75
1. Catholic Church— Collected works. 2. Theology—Collected work—Middle Ages. I. Vinck, Jose de, tr. II. Title.

BONAVENTURA, Saint, 208.1
Cardinal, 1221-1274.
The works of Bonaventure: cardinal, seraphic doctor, and saint. Translated from the Latin by Jose de Vinck. Paterson, N. J., St. Anthony Guild Press [c1960- v. illus. 24cm. Contents.1. Mystical opuscula. Includes bibliographical references. [BX890.B673123] 60-53110
1. Catholic Church—Collected works. 2. Theology—Collected works—Middle Ages. I. Vinck, Jose de, tr. II. Title.

BONAVENTURA, Saint, 208.1
Cardinal, 1221-1274.
The works of Bonaventure: cardinal, seraphic doctor, and saint. Tr. from Latin by Jose de Vinck. Paterson, N. J., St. Anthony Guild Press [c.1960] xiii, 266p. illus. Contents.1. Mystical opuscula. Bibl. 60-53110 4.00
1. Catholic Church—Collected works. 2. Theology—Collected works—Middle Ages. I. Vinck, Jose de, tr. II. Title.

BONHOEFFER, Dietrich, 1906- 208.1
1945.
No rusty swords; letters, lectures and notes, 1928-1936, from the Collected works of Dietrich Bonhoeffer, volume 1. Edited and introduced by Edwin H. Robertson. Translated by Edwin H. Robertson and John Bowden. New York, Harper & Row [1965] 384 p. 22 cm. [BX8080.B645A253] 65-15398
I. Title.

BROWNE, Benjamin P 208.1
Signal flares; or, Convictions of a Christian editor. [Philadelphia] Priv. print. by the Judson Press [c1960] 122p. 20cm. 500 copies printed. 123. Editorials which first appeared in Baptist leader.' [BR123.B73] 61-3340
1. Christianity— Addresses, essays, lectures. I. Title.

BUNYAN, John, 1628-1688. 208.1
God's knotty log; selected writings. Edited and introduced by Henri A. Talon. Cleveland, World Pub. Co. [1961] 313p. 18cm. (Living age books, LA31) Meridian books. [BR75.B73 1961] 61-12373
I. Title.

CASEL, Odo, 1886-1948. 208.1
The mystery of Christian worship, and other writings. Edited by Burkhard Neunheuser; with a pref. by Charles Davis. Westminster, Md., Newman Press [1962] 212p. 22cm. 'Translation of the fourth German edition of Das christliche kuttmysterium and of the other writings ... which appeared with it in 1960. [BV5082.2.C313] 62-5084
1. Mysticism—Catholic Church. I. Title.

CASEL, Odo [Secular name: Johannes Casel] 1886-1948. 208.1
The mystery of Christian worship, and other writings. Ed. by Burkhard Neunheuser; Pref. by Charles Davis. Westminster, Md., Newman [c.1962] 212p. 22cm. Tr. of the 4th German ed. of Das christliche Kultmysterium and of the other writings which appeared with it in 1960. 62-5084 5.75
1. Mysticism—Catholic Church. I. Title.

CATHOLIC Church. Pope, 1903-1914(Piusx) 208.1
All things in Christ; encyclical letters and selected documents of Blessed Pius x, edited by Vincent A. Yzermans. Introd. by Peter W. Bartholome. [Saint Paul?] '1952. xxviii, 231 p. 28 cm. Bibliography: p. 229-231. [BX870 1903] 52-4099
I. Title.

CATHOLIC Church. Pope, 1903-1914 (Pius x) 208.1
All things in Christ; encyclicals and selected documents of Saint Pius x. Edited by Vincent A. Yzermans. Westminster, Md., Newman Press, 1954. xviii, 275p. 24cm. Bibliography: p. 261-269. [BX870 1903a] 54-7544
I. Yzermans, Vincent Arthur, 1925- ed. II. Title.

CHEN, Richard M. J. 208.1
A letter to American Christians. New York, Exposition Press [c.1961] 55p. 61-3499 2.50
1. U. S.—Religion. I. Title.

DIMOCK, Marshall Edward, 1903- 208.1
Creative religion, as seen by a social scientist. Boston, Beacon Press [1963] viii, 133 p. 21 cm. Bibliography: p. 125-133. [BL50.D47] 63-18731
1. Religion—Addresses, essays, lectures. I. Title.

DRUMMOND, Henry, 1851-1897. 208.1
Henry Drummond: an anthology, edited, and with the story of his life by James W. Kennedy. Introd. by Samuel M. Shoemaker. [1st ed.] New York, Harper [c1953] 253p. illus. 22cm. [BR85.D696] 52-10673
1. Theology—Collected works—19th cent. I. Kennedy, James William, 1905- ed. II. Title.

•DUDDE, John H. 208.1
Truth is the word of God; theological realism. St. Petersburg, Fla., Great Outdoors [c.1964] 199p. 22cm. 1.50 pap.,
I. Title.

EDWARDS, Jonathan, 1703-1758. 208.1
Puritan sage; collected writings of Jonathan Edwards, edited by Vergilius Ferm. New York, Library Publishers [1953] xxvii, 640p. illus., facsims. 23cm. [BX7117.E3 1953] 53-3143
I. Title.

EDWARDS, Jonathan, 1703-1758 208.1
Representative selections, introd., bibl., notes by Clarence H. Faust, Thomas H. Johnson. Rev. ed. [Gloucester, Mass., Peter Smith, c.1935, 1962] 434p. 18cm. (Hill & Wang bk. rebound) Bibl. 4.25
1. Congregational churches — Collected works. 2. Theology—Collected works—18th cent. I. Title.

EDWARDS, Jonathan, 1703-1758. 208.1
Representative selections, with introduction, bibliography, and notes by Clarence H. Faust and Thomas H. Johnson. Rev. ed. New York, Hill and Wang [1962] cxlii, 434 p. 19 cm. (American writers, ACW47) (American century series.) Bibliography: p. cxix-cxlii. [BX7117.E33F3 1962] 62-9490
1. Congregational churches—Collected works. 2. Theology—Collected works—18th century.

ERASMUS, Desiderius, d.1536. 208.1
Christian humanism and the Reformation; selected writings. With The life of Erasmus, by Beatus Rhenanus. Edited by John C. Olin. New York, Harper & Row [1965] ix, 201 p. facsims., ports. 21 cm. (Harper torchbooks; the Academy library, TB1166) Contents.Contents.—The Compendium vitae of Erasmus of Rotterdam.—The life of Erasmus, by B. Rhenanus.—Letter to Martin Dorp, May 1515.—The Paraclesis.—Letter to Paul Volz, August 14, 1518.—Letter to Albert of Brandenburg, October 19, 1519.—The Axiomata.—Letter to Jodocus Jonas on Luther, May 1), 1521.—Letter to Jodocus Jonas on Vitrier and Colet, June 13, 1521.—Appendix; Letter to Guy Morillon, August 30, 1534.—Bibliography (p. 195-199) [BR75.E743 1965] 65-10218
I. Olin, John C., ed. II. Title.

ERASMUS, Desiderius, d. 1536 208.1
Christian humanism and the Reformation; selected writings. With The life of Erasmus, by Beatus Rhenanus. Ed. by John C. Olin. New York, Harper [c.1965] ix, 201p. facsims., ports. 21cm. (Harper torchbks.; Acad. lib., TB1166) Bibl. [BR75.E743] 65-10218 1.95 pap.,
I. Olin, John C., ed. II. Title.

ERASMUS, Desiderius, d. 1536 208.1
Christian humanism and the Reformation; selected writings. With the life of Erasmus, by Beatus Rhenanus. Ed. by John C. Olin [Gloucester, Mass., P. Smith, c.1965] ix, 201p. facsims., ports. 21cm. (Harper torchbks., Acad. lib., TB1166 rebound) Bibl. [BR75.E743] 4.00
I. Olin, John C., ed. II. Title.

FELIX, Reynold Reynold, 1890- 208.1
The sixth sense. [2d ed.] Brooklyn, Impel Creative Utopia, inc., 1950] 160 p. 23 cm. [BR125.F37 1950] 50-39468
I. Title.

FERRE, Gustave Adolph 208.1
The layman examines his faith. St. Louis, Bethany Press [c.1960] 96p. (bibl. and bibl. footnotes) 21cm. 60-7385 1.95 bds.,
1. Christianity—Essence, genius, nature. I. Title.

FOSBROKE, Hughell E. W. 208.1
God in the heart of things. Introductory memoir by Stephen F. Bayne, Jr. Edward French, ed. Greenwich, Conn., Seabury [c.] 1962. 152p. 62-9615 3.75 bds.,
1. Theology—Addresses, essays, lectures. I. Title.

FRANCESCO D'ASSISI, Saint, 1182-1226. 208.1
The words of Saint Francis, an anthology, compiled and arr, by James Meyer. Chicago, Franciscan Herald Press [1952] viii, 345 p. 16 cm. [BX890.F669] 52-3547
1. Catholic Church—Collected works. 2. Theology—Collected works—13th cent. I. Title.

FRANCESCO D'ASSISI, Saint, 1182-1226. 208.1
Writings. Translated by Benen Fahy. With introd. and notes, by Placid Hermann. Chicago, Franciscan Herald Press [1964] 200 p. 23 cm. Bibliography: 177-181. [BX890.F665] 64-7149
I. Hermann, Placid, ed. II. Title.

FRANCESCO D'ASSISI, Saint 1182-1226 208.1
Writings. Tr. [from Latin] by Benen Fahy. Introd., notes, by Placid Hermann. Chicago, Franciscan Herald [1964] 200p. 23cm. Bibl. 64-7149 4.95
I. Hermann, Placid, ed. II. Title.

FRANCESCO D'ASSISI, Saint, 1182-1226 208.1
The words of Saint Francis, an anthology, comp., arr. by James Meyer Chicago, Franciscan Herald [1966, c.1952] viii, 359p. 18cm. [BX890.F669] 52-3547 1.95 pap.,
1. Catholic Church — Collected works. 2. Theology — Collected works — Middle Ages. I. Title.

GLENN, Paul Joseph, 1893-1957. 208.1
A tour of the Summa. St. Louis, Mo., B. Herder Book Co. [c.1960] 466p. 60-16942 5.00
1. Thomas Aquinas, Saint. Summa theologica. I. Title.

GORRES, Ida Friederike (Coudenhove) 1901- 208.1
Broken lights; diaries and letters, 1951-1959. Tr. [from German] by Barbara Waldstein-Wartenberg. Pref. by Alan Pryce-Jones. Westminster, Md., Newman [c.1960, 1964] ix, 30 80p. 23cm. Bibl. 64-7148 5.95
I. Title.

GRAFTON, Warren 208.1
A Saturday night talk with God, and other editorials. Introd. by Ralph W. Sockman. St. Louis, Bethany [c.1961] 160p. 61-15531 2.95
1. Disciples of Christ—Addresses, essays, lectures. I. Title.

HAMILTON, William Hughes, 1924- 208.1
The new essence of Christianity. New York, Association [c.1961] 159p. Bibl. 61-14172 3.00 bds.,
1. Theology—20th cent. 2. Christianity—20th cent. I. Title.

HUDSON, Virginia Cary. 208.1
Credos & quips. Illustrated by Karla Kuskin. New York, Macmillan [1964] vii, 65 p. illus. 20 cm. [BV4515.H78] 64-22161
I. Kuskin, Karla, illus. II. Title.

JONES, Rufus Matthew, 1863-1948 208.1
Rufus Jones speaks to our time, an anthology; ed. by Harry Mrson Fosdick. New York, Macmillan, 1961[c.1951] xvii, 289p. (Macmillan paperback, 81) 1.95 pap.,
1. Friends, Society of—Collected work. 2. Spiritual life. 3. Mysticism. I. Title.

JONES, Rufus Matthew, 1863-1948. 208.1
Rufus Jones speaks to our time, an anthology; edited by Harry Emerson Fosdick. New York, Macmillan, 1951. xvii, 289 p. port. 25 cm. "Books written by Rufus Jones": p. 287-289. "Books edited by Rufus Jones": p. 289. [BX7617.J6] 51-13983
1. Friends, Society of—Collected works. 2. Spiritual life. 3. Mysticism. I. Title.

JUAN de la Cruz, Saint, 1542-1591. 208.1
The complete works of Saint John of the Cross, doctor of the Church. Translated and edited by E. Allison Peers from the critical edition of P. Silverio de Santa Teresa. 3 v. in 1. Westminster, Md., Newman Press [1964] lxxiv, 457, vi, 448, vi, 463 p. plan. 23 cm. Contents.Contents.—v. 1. Ascent of Mount Carmel. Dark night of the soul.—v. 2. Spiritual canticles. Poems.—v. 3. Living flame of love. Cautions and counsels. Spiritual sentences and maxims. Letters and documents. Bibliography (p. 405-439) Indices. [BX890.J617 1964] 64-2595
1. Catholic Church—Collected works. 2. Theology—Collected works—16th cent. 3. Mysticism—Collected works. I. Silverio de Santa Teresa, Father 1878-1954 ed. II. Peers, Edgar Allison, ed. and tr.

JUAN DE LA CRUZ, Saint, 1542-1591. 208.1
Collected works. Translated by Kieran Kavanaugh and Otilio Rodriguez. With introduction by Kieran Kavanaugh. [1st ed.] Garden City, N.Y., Doubleday, 1964. 740 p. illus., facsim. 25 cm. [BX890.J6233] 64-11725
1. Mysticism — Collected works. 2. Theology — Collected works — 16th cent. 3. Catholic Church — Collected works — 16th cent. 4. Catholic Church — Collected works. I. Title.

JUAN DE LA CRUZ, Saint 1542-1591 208.1
Collected works. Tr. by Kieran Kavanaugh, Otilio Rodriguez, Introds. by Kieran Kavanaugh. Garden City, N.Y., Doubleday [c.] 1964. 740p. illus., facsim. 25cm. 64-11725 11.95
1. Mysticism—Collected works. 2. Theology—Collected works—16th cent. 3. Catholic Church—Collected works. I. Title.

KEAN, Charles Duell, 1910- 208.1
That hearing they shall perceive. New York, Seabury Press, 1963. 92 p. 20 cm. [BR155.K4] 63-16288
1. Christianity — 20th cent. — Addresses, essays, lectures. I. Title.

KEAN, Charles Duell, 1910- 208.1
That hearing they shall perceive. New York, Seabury [c.]1963. 92p. 20cm. 63-16288 2.50
1. Christianity—20th cent.—Addresses, essays, lectures. I. Title.

KEGLEY, Charles W ed. 208.1
The theology of Emil Brunner. New York, Macmillan [1962] xiv, 395 p. illus. 22 cm. (The Library of living theology, v. 3) Essays by seventeen contemporary scholars. "Bibliography of writings of Emil Brunner": p. 355-384. [BX4827.B67K4] 62-16886
1. Brunner, Heinrich Emil, 1889- I. Title.

KEGLEY, Charles W., ed. 208.1
The theology of Emil Brunner. Edited by Charles W. Kegley. New York, Macmillan [1962] xiv, 395 p. illus. 22 cm. (The Library of living theology, v. 3) Essays by seventeen contemporary scholars. "Bibliography of writings of Emil Brunner": p. 355-384. [BX4827.B67T5] 62-16886
1. Brunner, Heinrich Emil, 1889- . I. Title. II. Series.

KIERKEGAARD, Soren Aabye, 1813-1855. 208.1
Christian discourses & The lilies of the field and the birds of the air & Three discourses at the Communion on Fridays. Tr. [from Danish] with introd. by Walter Lowrie. New York, Oxford Univ. Press, [1961] 389p. (Galaxy bk. GB49) 1.85 pap.,
1. Christianity—Addresses, essays, lectures. I. Lowrie, Walter, tr. II. Title.

KIERKEGAARD, Soren Aabye, 1813-1855 208.1
The present age, and Of the difference between a genius and an apostle. Tr. by Alexander Dru. Introd. by Walter Kaufmann. [Gloucester, Mass., Peter Smith, 1963, c.1962] 108p. 21cm. (Harper torchbks. Cloister lib., TB94 rebound) Orig. pub. with a third essay under the title The present age and two minor ethico-religious treaties in 1940. 3.25
I. Title.

KIERKEGAARD, Soren Aabye, 1813-1855. 208.1
The present age, and Of the difference between a genius and apostle. Translated by Alexander Dru. Introd. by Walter Kaufmann. New York, Harper & Row [1962] 108 p. 21 cm. (Harper torchbooks. The Cloister library, TB94) "Originally published ... with a third essay ... under the title The present age and two minor ethico-religious treaties in 1940." [B85.K4578] 62-51867
I. Title.

KNOX, Ronald Arbuthnott, 1888- 208.1
The belief of Catholics. 4th ed. London, New York, Sheed and Ward [1953] ix, 214p. 21cm. [BX1751.K] A55
1. Catholic Church—Doctrinal and controversial works—Catholic authors. I. Title.

LAW, William, 1686-1761. 208.1
The pocket William Law. With a foreword by the Archbishop of York. Edited by Arthur W. Hopkinson. Philadelphia, Westminster Press [1950] 160p. 20cm. [BR75.L344] 52-6520
1. Theology—Collected works—18th cent. I. Title.

LEWIS, Clive Staples, 1898- 208.1
Mere Christianity. A revised and enlarged edition, with a new introduction, of the three books The case for Christianity, Christian behaviour, and Beyond personality, by C. S. Lewis. New York, Macmillan, 1960 [c.1943-1952] vii, 175p. 21cm. (Macmillan paperbacks 32) 1.25 pap.,
1. Christianity—Address, essays, lectures. I. Title.

LUTHER, Martin 208.1
Luther's works. v. 34, Career of the reformer IV. Edited by Lewis W. Spitz. Philadelphia, Muhlenberg Press [c.1960] xvii, 387p. 24cm. 55-9893 5.00
1. Theology—Collected works—16th cent. 2. Lutheran Church—Collected works. I. Pelikan, Jaroslav, ed. II. Lehmann, Helmut T., ed. III. Title.

LUTHER, Martin 208.1
Luther's works. v. 9, Lectures on Deuteronomy [edited by] Jaroslav Pelikan and Daniel Poellot. Saint Louis, Concordia Pub. House [c.1960] x, 334p. 24cm. 55-9893 6.00
1. Theology—Collected works—16th cent. 2. Lutheran Church—Collected works. I. Pelikan, Jaroslav, ed. II. Lehmann, Helmut., ed. III. Title.

LUTHER, Martin 208.1
Luther's works. Companion volume. Luther the expositor, introduction to the Reformer's exegetical writings [edited] by Jaroslav Pelikan. Saint Louis, Concordia Pub. House [c.1959] xiii, 286p. 24cm. 55-9893 4.00
1. Theology—Collected works—16th cent. 2. Lutheran Church—Collected works. I. Pelikan, Jaroslav, ed. II. Lehmann, Helmut T., ed. III. Title.

LUTHER, Martin, 1483-1546 208.1
Luther's works, v.48. Ed. by Helmut T. Lehmann. Philadelphia, Fortress [c.1963] 426p. 24cm. Contents.v.48: Letters, 1. Ed., tr. by Gottfried G. Krodel. Bibl. 55-9893 6.00
1. Theology—Collected works—16th cent. 2. Lutheran Church—Collected works. 3. Bible—Criticism, interpretation, etc.—Hist. I. Krodel, Gottfried G., ed., tr. II. Lehmann, Helmut T., ed. III. Title.

LUTHER, Martin, 1483-1546 208.1
Luther's works; v.53. Ed. by Ulrich S. Leupold. General ed.: Helmut T. Lehmann. Philadelphia, Fortress [c.1965] xx, 356p. 24cm. Contents.v.53. Liturgy and hymns. Amer. ed., tr. based on the Weimar ed. of 1883. Bibl. 55-9893 6.00
1. Theology—Collected works—16th cent. 2. Lutheran Church—Collected works. 3. Bible—Criticism, interpretation, etc.—Hist. I. Leupold, Ulrich S., ed. II. Title.

LUTHER, Martin, 1483-1546 208.1
Martin Luther, selections from his writings.

Ed., introd. by John Dillenberger. Chicago, Quadrangle [c.1961] 526p. 8.00
1. Theology—Collected works—16th cent. 2. Lutheran Church—Collected works. I. Dillenberger, John, ed. II. Title.

LUTHER, Martin, 1483-1546. 208.1
Martin Luther, selections from his writings. Edited and with an introd. by John Dillenberger. [1st ed.] Garden City, N.Y., Doubleday, 1961. xxxiii, 526 p. 19 cm. (Anchor books, A271) [BR331.E5D5] 61-9503
1. Lutheran Church—Collected works. 2. Theology—Collected works—16th century. I. Dillenberger, John, ed.

LUTHER, Martin, 1483-1546. 208.1
Reformation writings. Translated with introd. and notes from the definitive Weimar ed. by Bertram Lee Woolf. New York, Philosophical Library [1953- v. port. 23 cm. "A chronological table of Luther's writings...and of contemporary events": v. 1, p. [381]-387. Contents.Contents.—v. 1. The basis of the Protestant Reformation.— [BR331.E5W6] 53-8176
1. Reformation. I. Title.

LUTHER, Martin, 1483-1546 208.1
Works
I. Title.
Volume 29, "Lectures on Titus, Philemon, and Hebrews" is now available from Concordia, St. Louis. for $6.00. L. C. card order no.: 55-9893 rev3.

LUTHER, Martin, 1483-1546. 208.1
Works. Edited by Jaroslav Pelikan. Saint Louis, Concordia Pub. House [1955- v. 24cm. Contents.v. 12. Selected Psalms, I. [BR330.E5 1955] 55-9893
1. Theology— Collected works—16th cent. 2. Lutheran Church—Collected works. I. Pellkan, Jaroslav, 1923- ed. II. Title.

LUTHER, Martin, 1483-1546 208.1
Works. Ed. by Jaroslav Pelikan, Walter A. Hansen. St. Louis, Concordia [1968- v. 24cm. Contents.v. 5. Lectures on Genesis, chapters 26-30. [BR330.E5 1955] 55-9893 6.00
1. Theology—Collected works—16th cent. 2. Lutheran Church—Collected works. 3. Bible—Criticism, interpretation, etc.—Hist. I. Pelikan, Jaroslav, 1923- ed. II. Hansen, Walter A. ed. III. Title.

LUTHER, Martin, 1483-1546 208.1
Works. Ed.: Jaroslav Pelikan, Walter A. Hansen. St. Louis, Concordia [1967] v. 24cm. Contents.v. 30. The Catholic epistles. Pub. jointly by Concordia Pub. House & Fortress Pr. Bibl. 55-9893 6.00
1. Theology—Collected works—16th cent. 2. Lutheran Church—Collected works. 3. Bible—Criticism, interpretation, etc.—Hist. I. Leupold, Uirich S., ed. II. Pelikan, Jaroslav, ed. III. Hane)0sen, Walter A., ed. IV. Title.

LUTHER, Martin, 1483-1546. 208.1
Works. Edited by Jaroslav Pelikan. Saint Louis, Concordia Pub. House [1955- v. 1, 1958] Saint Louis, Concordia Pub. House [1959] v. 24cm. xiii, 286p. 24cm. Vols. 31- edited by Harold J. Grimn. [and others] General editor: Helmut T. Lehmann. Vols. 31- have imprint: Philadelphia, Muhlenberg Press. Bibliographical footnotes. [BR330.E5 1955] 55-9893
1. Theology—Collected works—16th cent. 2. Lutheran Church—Collected works. 3. Bible—Criticism, interpretation, etc.—Hist. I. Pelikan, Jaroslav, 1923- ed. II. Lehmann, Helmut T., ed. III. Title. IV. Title: —Companion volume. V. Title: Luther the expositor.

LUTHER, Martin, 1483-1546 208.1
Works, v.37. General ed.: Holmut T. Lehmann. Philadelphia, Muhlenberg [c.1961] 406p. Contents.v.37. Word and sacrament, ed. by Robert H. Fischer. 55-9893 5.00
1. Theology—Collected works—16th cent. 2. Lutheran Church—Collected works. I. Title.

LUTHER, Martin, 1483-1546. 208.1.
Works. v. 2, lectures on Genesis, chapts 6-14. Jaroslav Pelikan, ed.; Daniel E. Poellot, ass't. ed. St. Louis, Concordia [c.1960] 433p. Bibl. 55-9893 6.00
1. Theology—Collected works—16th cent. 2. Lutheran Church—Collected works. I. Pelikan, Jaroslav, 1923- ed. II. Title.

LUTHER, Martin, 1483-1546 208.1
Works: v.4. St. Louis, Concordia [c.1964] 443p. 24cm. Contents.v.4. Lectures on Genesis, chapters 21-25. Bibl. 55-9893 6.00
1. Theology—Collected works. 2. Bible—Criticism. interpretation, etc.—Hist. I. Pelikan. Jaroslav. 1923- ed. II. Hansen, Walter A., ed. III. Title. IV. Title: Lectures on Genesis.

LUTHER, Martin, 1483-1546 208.1
Works; v.45. Ed. by Walther I. Brandt. General ed.: Helmut T. Lehmann. Philadelphia, Muhlenberg [c.1962] 424p. 24cm. Contents.v.45. The Christian in society, 2. Bibl. 55-9893 6.00
1. Theology—Collected works—16th cent. 2. Lutheran Church—Collected works. 3. Bible—Criticism, interpretation, etc.—Hist. I. Brandt, Walther I., ed. II. Lehmann, Helmut T., ed. III. Title.

LUTHER, Martin, 1483-1546 208.1
Works; v.7. Jaroslav Pelikan, ed. Walter A. Hansen, assoc. ed. St. Louis, Concordia [c.1965] x, 406p. 24cm. Contents.v.7. Lectures on Genesis, chapters 38-44, tr. by Paul D. Pahl. Bibl. 55-9893 6.00
1. Theology—Collected works—16th cent. 2. Lutheran Church—Collected works. 3. Bible—Criticism. interpretation, etc.—Hist. I. Pelikan, Jaroslav, 1923-ed. II. Hansen, Walter A., ed. III. Title. IV. Title: Lectures on Genesis.

LUTHER, Martin, 1483-1546 208.1
Works; v.8. Jaroslav Pelikan ed. Walter A. Hansen, assoc. ed. St. Louis, Concordia [c.1966] viii, 360p. 24cm. Contents.v.8. Lectures on Genesis chapters 45-50, tr. by Paul D. Pahl. Bibl. 55-9893 6.00
1. Theology — Collected works — 16th cent. 2. Lutheran Church — Collected works. 3. Bible — Criticism. Interpretation, etc. — Hist. I. Pelikan, Jaroslay, 1923- ed. II. Hansen, Walter A., ed. III. Title. IV. Title: Lectures on Genesis.

LUTHER, Martin, 1483-1546 208.1
Works; v.26. Ed.: Jaroslav Pelikan; assoc. ed.: Walter A. Hansen [Tr. from German by Jaroslav Pelikan] St. Louis, Concordia [c.1963] 492p. 24cm. Contents.v.26, Lectures on Galatians 1535, chapters 1-4. Bibl. 55-9893 6.00
1. Theology—Collected works—16th cent. 2. Lutheran Church—Collected works. 3. Bible—Cricism, interpretation, etc.—Hist. I. Pelikan, Jaroslav, 1923- ed. II. Hansen, Walter A., ed. III. Title. IV. Title: Lectures on Galatians.

MCKAY, Arthur R 208.1
God's people in God's world. Philadelphia, Westminster Press [1961] 64p. 19cm. Addresses delivered at the National Meeting of United Presbyterian Women held at Purdue University from June 26 to July 1, 1961. [BR123.M344] 61-10991
1. Christianity—20th cent. I. Title.

MACKINTOSH, Charles Henry, 208.1
1820-1896.
Miscellaneous writings. New York, Loizeaux Bros. [1951] 6 v. 17cm. Contents.v. 1. The all sufficiency of Christ.--v. 2. The Lord's coming.--v. 3. The assembly of God.--v. 4. The great commission.--v. 5. Elijah the Tiahbite.--v. 6. Life and times of David. [BR85.M18] 55-16561
1. Theology—Collected works—19th century. I. Title.

MCNABB, Vincent Joseph, 208.1
1868-1943.
Father McNabb reader; selections from the writings of Vincent McNabb, o. p. Edited by Francis Edward Nugent. New York, P. J. Kenedy [1954] 227p. 21cm. [BX890.M227] 54-10068
1. Catholic Church—Collected works. 2. Theology—Collected works—20th cent. I. Title.

MENNO SIMONS, 1496-1561. 208.1
Complete writings; translated from the Dutch by Leonard Verduin and edited by John Christian Wenger, with a biography by Harold S. Bender. Scottdale, Pa., Herald Press [1956] xi, 1092p. illus., ports., facsims. 25cm. [BX8109.M32 1956] 55-9815
1. Mennonites—Collected works. 2. Theology—Collected works—16th cent. I. Title.

*METCALFE, John J. 208.1
Christ at work. New York, Vantage [c.1964] 148p. 21cm. 3.00 bds.,
I. Title.

MILLER, William A 208.1
Some boast of chariots. Tahlequah, Okla, Pan Press [1960] 89p. 22cm. [BR124.M5] 60-6383
1. Christianity —Essence, genius, nature. I. Title.

MUDGE, Lewis Seymour. 208.1
Is God alive? Philadelphia, United Church Press [1963] 95 p. 19 cm. [BR123.M85] 63-17158
1. Christianity — 20th cent. — Addresses, essays, lectures. I. Title.

MUDGE, Lewis Seymour 208.1
Is God alive? Philadelphia, United Church [c.1963] 95p. 19cm. 63-17158 1.45 pap.,
1. Christianity—20th cent.—Adcressex, essays, lectures. I. Title.

MULLER, Eberhard Johannes 208.1
Conversation on faith; tr. [from German] by John W. Doberstein. Philadelphia, Muhlenberg Press [1961] 196p. 61-6747 3.50 bds.,
1. Christianity—Essence, genius, nature. I. Title.

MYERS, Jacob Martin, 1904- 208.1
ed.
Theological and missionary studies in memory of John Aberly. Edited by J. M. Myers, O. Reimherr [and] H. N. Bream. Gettysburg, Pa., Printed by Times and News Pub. Co., 1965. vii, 152 p. port. 24 cm. (Gettysburg theological studies,2) Contents.Contents omitted. Bibliographical footnotes. [BR50.M84] 65-16692
1. Theology — Addresses, essays, lectures. 2. Missions — Addresses, essays, lectures. 3. Aberly, John, 1867-1963. I. Reimherr, Otto, 1917- joint ed. II. Bream, H. N., joint ed. III. Aberly, John, 1867-1963. IV. Title. V. Series.

NEWMAN, John Henry, 208.1
Cardinal, 1801-1890.
The living thoughts of Cardinal Newman, presented by Henry Tristram. New York, McKay [1953] 167 p. illus. 20 cm. (The Living thoughts library, 24) Includes bibliography. [BX890.N44] 53-7608
1. Catholic Church—Collected works. 2. Theology—Collected works—19th century. I. Tristram, Henry. II. Title.

NYGREN, Anders Theodor 208.1
Samuel Bp., 1890-
Essence of Christianity. Tr. [from Swedish] by Philip S. Watson. Philadelphia, Muhlenberg [1961, c.1960] 128p. 61-14756 2.00
1. Christianity—Essence, genius, nature. 2. Atonement. 3. God—Love. I. Title.

NYMEYER, Frederick, 1897- 208.1
Minimal religion. South Holland, Ill., Libertarian Pr. [1964] xiv, 384p. 25cm. Bibl. [BR123.N9] 63-18098 3.00
1. Christianity—Addresses, essays, lectures. I. Title.

OLDS, Charles Burnell 208.1
Love: the issue. Boston, Christopher Pub. House [c.1960] 227p. (bibl. footnotes) 21cm. 60-9024 3.00
1. Christianity—Essence, genius, nature. 2. Love (Theology) I. Title.

OLDS, Charles Burnell. 208.1
Love, the issue. Boston, Christopher Pub. House [1960] 227p. 21cm. Includes bibliography. [BR124.O4] 60-9024
1. Christianity—Essence, genius, nature. 2. Love (Theology) I. Title.

PAULUS VI, Pope, 1897- 208.1
Dialogues: reflections on God and man, by Paul VI. Tr., arranged by John G. Clancy. New York, S & S [1968c.1964] xxix, 254p. 21cm. (Credo perspectives) [BX891.P323] 1.95 pap.,
1. Catholic Church—Addresses, essays, lectures. I. Clancy, John G. ed. and tr. II. Title.

PAULUS VI, Pope, 1897- 208.1
Dialogues: reflections on God and man. Tr., arr. by John G. Clancy. New York, Pocket Bks. [1965, c.1964] xxxi, 254p. 17cm. (Cardinal ed., credo ser.) [BX891.P323] .75 pap.,
1. Catholic Church—Addresses, essays, lectures. I. Clancy, John G., ed. and tr. II. Title.

PAULUS VI, Pope, 1897- 208.1
Dialogues: reflections on God and man, by Paul VI. Tr., arr. by John G. Clancy. New York [Trident] 1965 [c.1964] xxxi, 254p. 21cm. (Credo ser.) Sequence of Pope Paul's reflections on specific subjects, culled from his speeches and writings. [BX891.P323] 65-13107 4.95
1. Catholic Church—Addresses, essays, lectures. I. Clancy, John G., ed. and tr. II. Title.

PHILLIPS, John Bertram, 208.1
1906-
Good news; thoughts on God and man. Westwood, N.J., Revell [1967, c.1963] 142p. 18cm. (Spire bk.) .60 rap.,
1. Christianity—Addresses, Essays, lectures. 2. Theological virtues. I. Title.

PHILLIPS, John Bertram, 208.1
1906-
Good news; thoughts on God and man. [1st American ed.] New York, Macmillan [1963] 209 p. 18 cm. [BR85.P575] 63-13326
1. Christianity—Addresses, essays, lectures. 2. Theological virtues. I. Title.

PHILLIPS, John Bertram, 208.1
1906-
Good news; thoughts on God and man. New York, Macmillan [c.1963] 209p. 18cm. 63-13326 2.95 bds.,
1. Christianity—Addresses, essays, lectures. 2. Theological virtues. I. Title.

PITTS, Mildred. 208.1
In my Father's house are many mansions. New York, Carlton Press, 1961. 195p. 21cm. (A Reflection book) [BR123.P54] 61-65674
1. Christianity—Addresses, essays, lectures. I. Title.

PITTS, Miled 208.1
In my Father'as house are many mansions. New York, Carlton Pr. [dist. Comet, c.]1961. 195p. (Reflection bk.) 61-65674 3.00
1. Christianity—Addresses, essays, lectures. I. Title.

RAHNER, Karl, 1904- 208.1
Inquiries [New York] Herder & Herder [c.1964] viii, 462p. 22cm. Studies which appeared separately in the series Quaestiones disputatae as nos. 1. 10, 9, 4, 11. [BX891.R3] 64-20435 8.00
1. Theology—Collected works—20th cent. 2. Catholic Church—Collected works. I. Title.
Contents omitted

RAUSCHENBUSCH, Walter, 208.1
1861-1918.
A gospel for the social awakening; selections from the writings of Walter Rauschenbusch, compiled by Benjamin E. Mays, with an introd. by C. Howard Hopkins. New York, Association Press, 1950. 187 p. 20 cm. (A Haddam House book) Bibliography: p. [6] [BR115.S6R38] 51-1462
1. Sociology, Christian. I. Title.

REDMAN, Edward H 208.1
Religion's new frontiers. Chicago, Curtis Reese Press [1961] 115p. 22cm. Includes bibliography. [BR1616.R4] 61-18171
1. Liberalism (Religion) I. Title.

REID, Albert Clayton, 1894- 208.1
Christ and human values. Nashville, Broadman Press [1961] 109p. 21cm. Includes bibliographies. [BR123.R4] 61-7550
1. Christianity—Addresses, essays, lectures. I. Title.

ROLFE, Eugene 208.1
The intelligent agnostic's introduction to Christianity. [dist. New York, Macmillan, 1961] 248p. Bibl. 61-2249 5.00 bds.,
1. Apologetics—20th cent. 2. Lord's Supper. I. Title.

ROSENGRANT, John. 208.1
Assignment: overseas, by John Rosengrant and others. New York, Crowell [1960] 152p. 22cm. Includes bibliography. [BV4520.R65] 60-11546
1. Christians. 2. Americans in foreign countries. I. Title.

ROSENGRANT, John [ed.] 208.1
Assignment: overseas, by John Rosengrant and others. New York, Crowell [c.1960] viii, 152p. Includes bibliography 22cm. 60-11546 3.50; 1.95 pap.,
1. Christians. 2. Americans in foreign countries. I. Title.

ROUGEMONT, Denis de, 1906- 208.1
The Christian opportunity. Translated by Donald Lehmkuhl. [1st ed.] New York, Holt, Rinehart and Winston [1963] 185 p. 22 cm. Includes bibliography. [BR121.2.R6] 63-11869
1. Christianity—20th century—Addresses, essays, lectures. I. Title.

SCHWEITZER, Albert, 1875- 208.1
Albert Schweitzer: an anthology. Enlarged ed., ed. by Charles R. Joy. [Gloucester, Mass., Peter Smith, 1961, c.1947] 355p. (Beacon Press bk. rebound in cloth) Bibl. 3.75
I. Joy, Charles Rhind, 1885- ed. II. Title.

SHEPPARD, Hugh Richard 208.1
Lawrie, 1880-1937.
The best of Dick Sheppard (H. R. L. Sheppard) Edited, with an introd., by Halford E. Luccock. [1st ed.] New York, Harper [1951] xx, 162 p. 21 cm. Bibliography: p. [v] [BX5037.S45] 51-9056
1. Theology—Collected works—20th cent. 2. Church of England—Collected works. I. Title.

SIEGEL, Meyer D 1883- 208.1
Religion is here to stay whether you like it or not; a new concept of what religion is and what it is not. "Christian Science" debunked. [2d ed.] Scarsdale, N. Y., Author's Book Distributors [1963] vii, 184 p. port. 22 cm. Bibliography: p. 113. [BL87.S5] 63-25558
1. Religion—Addresses, essays, lectures. 2. Christian Science—Legal aspects. I. Title.

SIEGEL, Meyer D., 1883- 208.1
Religion is here to stay, whether you like it or not; a new concept of what religion is and what it is not. 'Christian Science' debuked [2d ed.] Scarsdale, N. Y., 30 E. 42nd St., New York 17, Author's Bk. Distributors [dist.

Author, c.1963] vii, 184p. port. 22cm. Bibl. 63-25558 1.95 pap.,
1. Religion—Addresses, essays, lectures. 2. Christian Science—Legal aspects. I. Title.

STEIN, Edith, 1891-1942. 208.1
Writings. Selected, translated and introduced by Hilda Graef. Westminster, Md., Newman Press, 1956. 206p. illus. 22cm. [BX890.S656] 56-9323
1. Catholic Church—Collected works. 2. Theology—Collected works—20th cent. I. Title.

STEIN, Edith, 1891-1942. 208.1
Writings. Selected, translated and introduced by Hilda Graef. Westminster, Md., Newman Press, 1956. 206 p. illus. 22 cm. [BX890.S656] 56-9323
1. Catholic Church — Collected works. 2. Theology — Collected works — 20th cent. I. Title.

STEINBERG, Milton, 1903-1950. 208.1
Anatomy of faith. Edited, with an introd., by Arthur A. Cohen. [1st ed.] New York, Harcourt, Brace [1960] 304 p. 21 cm. [BM45.S794] 60-5442
1. Judaism — Addresses, essays, lectures. I. Title.

STEINBERG, Milton, 1903-1950. 208.1
Anatomy of faith. Edited, with an introd., by Arthur A. Cohen. [1st ed.] New York, Harcourt, Brace [1960] 304 p. 21 cm. [BM45.S794] 60-5442
1. Judaism—Addresses, essays, lectures. I. Title.

TAGORE, Rabindranath, Sir 208.1
The religion of man, being the Hibbert lectures for 1930. Beacon Baeacon [1961, c.1931] 239p. (BP125) 1.65 pap.,
I. Title.

TAYLOR, Jeremy, Bp. of Down and Connor, 1613-1667. 208.1
The house of understanding; selections from the writings of Jeremy Taylor by Margaret Gest. Philadelphia, University of Pennsylvania Press, 1954. x, 118p. port. 24cm. Bibliography: p. 116-118. [BR75.T28] 54-5011
1. Theology— Collected works—17th cent. 2. Church of England—Collected works. I. Title.

TEMPLE, William, Atp. of Canterbury, 1881-1944. 208.1
William Temple's teaching, edited by A. E. Baker. Philadelphia, Westminster Press [1951] 202 p. 21 cm. [BX5037.T43] 51-9316
1. Church of England — Collected works. 2. Theology — Collected works — 20th cent. I. Baker, Albert Edward, 1884- ed. II. Title.

TERESA, Saint, 1515-1582. 208.1
Selected writings of St. Teresa of Avila, a synthesis of her writings. Compiled and arr. by William J. Doheny; with a pref. by Timothy Manning. Milwuakee, Bruce [1950] xxxv. 443 p. col. map. 23 cm. Bibliographical footnotes. [BX890.T39] 50-13439
1. Catholic Church — Collected works. 2. Theology — Collected works — 16th cent. I. Title.

THEOLOGY of Emil Brunner (The) 208.1
Ed. by Charles W. Kegley. New York, Macmillan [c.1962] xiv, 395p. illus. 22cm. (Lib. of living theology, v. 3) Bibl. 62-16886 7.50
1. Brunner, Heinrich Eil, 1890- I. Kegley, Charles W., ed.

THOMAS Aquinas, Saint, 1225?-1274. 208.1
Selected writings. Edited by M. C. D'Arcy. New York, Dutton, 1950. xiv, 283 p. 19 cm. (Everyman's library, 953 A. Philosophy and theology) Includes bibliographies. [AC1.E8] 50-11232
1. Theology — Collected works — Middle Ages. 2. Catholic Church — Collected works. I. Title.

THOMAS AQUINAS, Saint, 1225?-1274. 208.1
The pocket Aquinas; selections from the writings of St. Thomas. Edited, with some passages newly translated, and a general introd., by Vernon J. Bourke. New York, Washington Square Press [1960] 372 p. 17 cm. (A Washington Square Press book, W575) [B765.T52E474] 61-923
I. Bourke, Vernon Joseph, 1907- ed. II. Title.

THOMAS AQUINAS, Saint, 1225?-1274. 208.1
Theological texts. Selected and translated with notes and an introd. by Thomas Gilby. London, New York, Oxford University Press, 1955. xvii, 423p. 19cm. 'Biographical and bibliographical note': p. [xv]-xvii. Bibliographical footnotes. [BX890.T62E6 1955] 55-14254
1. Theology—Collected works— Middle Ages. I. Title.

TROWBRIDGE, Buel 208.1
Religion for our times. Foreword by Kirtly F. Mather. Washington, D.C., Public Affairs Pr. [c.1963] 175p. 24cm. Bibl. 63-10818 4.50
1. Christianity—20th cent. I. Title.

TROWBRIDGE, Buel. 208.1
Religion for our times. Foreword by Kirtley F. Mather. Washington, Public Affairs Press [1963] 175 p. 24 cm. Includes bibliography. [BR121.2.T7] 63-10818
1. Christanity — 20th cent. I. Title.

TYNDALE, William, d. 1536. 208.1
The work of William Tyndale. Ed., introd. by G. E. Duffield. Pref. by F. F. Bruce. Philadelphia, Fortress [c.1965] x1, 406p. facsim., port. 23cm. (Courtenay lib. of Reformation classics) Bibl. [BR75.T77] 65-3003 6.25
1. Theology—Collected works—16th cent. I. Duffield, Gervase E., ed. II. Title.

WARNER, William Lloyd, 1898- 208.1
The family of God; a symbolic study of Christian life in America. New Haven, Conn., Yale Univ. Pr. 1961 [c.1959, 1961] 451p. illus. 'Consists of sections of [the author's] The living and the dead . . . revised and supplementedr' (Yale paperbound Y-45) Bibl. 61-11400 1.75 pap.,
1. U. S.—Religion. 2. U. S.—Soc. life & cust. 3. Symbolism. I. Title.

WEIGEL, Gustave, 1906- 208.1
The modern God; faith in a secular culture. New York, Macmillan [1963] 168 p. 22 cm. [BR123.W4] 63-12138
1. Christianity—20th century—Addresses, essays, lectures. I. Title.

WYLIE, Samuel J 208.1
Precede the dawn; the church in an age of change. New York, Morehouse-Barlow Co., 1963. 126 p. 19 cm. Bibliographical references included in "Acknowledgments and notes" (p. 124-126) [BR121.2.W9] 63-20377
1. Christianity — 20th cent. — Addresses, essays, lectures. I. Title.

WYLIE, Smanel J. 208.1
Precede the dawn; the church in an age of change. New York, Morehouse [c.]1963. 126p. 19cm. Bibl. 63-20377 3.50 bds.,
1. Christnity—20th cent.—Addresses, essays, lectures. I. Title.

AMERICA 208.2
Between two cities; God and man in America; a commentary on our times. Ed. by Thurston N. Davis, Donald N. Campion, L. C. McHugh. Chicago, Loyola Univ. Pr. [c.]1962. 496p. illus. 62-10907 5.00
1. Civilization, Christian. 2. Church and social problems—Catholic Church. I. Davis, Thurston, N., ed. II. Title.

AMERICA (New York, 1909-) 208.2
Between two cities: God and man in America a commentary on our times. Edited by Thurston N. Davis, Donald R. Campion [and] L. C. McHugh. Chicago, Loyola University Press, 1962. 406p. illus. 24cm. [BR115.C5A6] 62-10907
1. Civilization, Christian. 2. Church and social problems—Catholic Church. I. Davis, Thurston N., ed. II. Title.

BARTH, Karl, 1886- 208.2
Karl Barth's table talk, recorded and edited by John D. Godsey. Richmond, John Knox Press [1963] ix, 99 p. 22 cm. Notes taken at a series of discussions held by Barth for English speaking students between 1953 and 1956, with an introductory paper by Godsey read before the Nov. 8, 1955 meeting. [BX4827.B3A25 1963] 63-20140
1. Barth, Karl, 1886- I. Godsey, John D., ed. II. Title.

BELL, Hermon Fiske, 1880- 208.2
Current problems in religion. New York, Philosophical Library [1956] viii, 648p. 22cm. Includes bibliographical references. [BL27.B44] 56-14029
1. Religion—Addresses, essays, lectures. 2. Religious literature (Selections: Extracts, etc.) I. Title.

A Benedictine of Stanbrook Abbey, ed. 208.2
Letters from the saints, arr. and selected by a Benedictine of Stanbrook Abbey. With illus. by Vivian Berger. New York, Hawthorne Books [1964] ix, 302 p. illus., facsims. 22 cm. Bibliography: p. 300-301. [BX4654.L4 1964] 64-19205
1. Saints — Correspondence, reminiscences, etc. I. Title.

BERTHOLD, Fred, 1922- ed. 208.2
Basic sources of the Judaeo-Christian tradition. Editors: Fred Berthold, Jr. [and others] Englewood Cliffs, N. J., Prentice-Hall, 1962. xi, 444 p. illus. 26 cm. Includes bibliographies. [BR53.B4] 62-9946
1. Religious literature (Selections: Extracts, etc.) 2. Judaism—Collections. I. Title.

BRANTL, George, ed. 208.2
The religious experience. New York, G. Braziller [1964] 2 v. (1144 p.) 24 cm. Contents.CONTENTS. -- v. 1. The image and the idol: the God of immanence. -- v. 1. Beyond the gods: the God of transcendence. In place of God: from nihllism to affirmation. A gift of presence: the God of dialogue. Includes bibliographical references. [PN6071.R4B7] 64-23163
1. Religious literature (Selections: Extracts, etc.) 2. Theology — Collections. I. Title.

BRETALL, Robert Walter, 1913- ed. 208.2
The empirical theology of Henry Nelson Wieman. New York, Macmillan [1963] 423 p. illus. 22 cm. (The Library of living theology, v. 4) [BX4827.W45B7] 62-21217
1. Wieman, Henry Nelson, 1884- I. Title.
Contents omitted.

BURTNESS, James H ed. 208.2
The new community in Christ; essays on the corporate Christian life. Edited by James H. Burtness and John P. Kildahl. Minneapolis, Augsburg Pub. House [1963] 207 p. 22 cm. [BR121.2.B8] 62-20841
1. Christianity — 20th cent. — Addresses, essays, lectures. I. Kildahl, John P., joint ed. II. Title.

BURTNESS, James H., ed. 208.2
The new community in Christ; essays on the corporate Christian life. Ed. by James H. Burtness, John P. Kildahl. Minneapolis, Augsburg [c.1963] 207p. 22cm. Bibl. 62-20841 4.50
1. Christianity—20th cent.—Addresses, essays, lectures. I. Kildahl, John P., joint ed. II. Title.

CAPONIGRI, Aloysius Robert, ed. 208.2
Modern Catholic thinkers, an anthology introd. by Martin CyrilD Arcy. New York, Harper [c.1960] xvi, 636p. Sources and acknowledgement': p. ix-xii. 25cm. 60-9135 15.00
1. Catholic liture. I. Title.

CAPONIGRI, Aloysius Robert, 1913- ed. 208.2
Modern Catholic thinkers, an anthology. Introd. by Martin Cyril D'Arcy. New York, Harper [1960] xvi, 636p. 25cm. 'Sources and acknowledgements': p. ix-xii. Includes bibliography. [BX885.C26 1960a] 60-9135
1. Catholic literature. I. Title.

CHAMPION, Selwyn Gurney, comp. 208.2
Readings form world religions, complied by Selwyn Gurney Champion and Dorothy Short. Greenwich, Conn., Fawcett Pubns. [1959, c.1951] 319p. (bibl. p. 317-319) 19cm. (Premier bk. d85) .50 pap.,
1. Sacred books (Selections: Extracts, etc.) 2. Religions. I. Short, Dorothy (Field) joint comp. II. Title.

THE Christian century. 208.2
The Christian century reader; representative articles, editorials,and poems selected from more than fifty years of the Christian century, by Harold E. Fey and Margaret Frakes. New York, Association Press [1962] 447p. 21cm. [DR53.C38] 62-9390
1. Christianity—20th cent.—Addresses, essays, lectures. 2. Church and social problems—Addresses, essays, lectures. I. Fey, Harold Edward, 1808- ed. II. Frakes, Margaret, ed. III. Title.

THE Christian century. 208.2
How my mind has changed [by] John C. Bennet [and others] Edited and introduced by Harold E. Fey. Cleveland, Meridian Books [1961] 191p. 18cm. (A Living age book, LA33) 'The contributions ... were first published as articles [in the Christian century] during the 1959-60 publishing year.' [BR481.C48] 61-15600
1. Religious thought—20th cent. 2. Theology—20th cent. I. Fey, Harold Edward, 1898- ed. II. Title.

CHRISTIAN perspectives. 208.2
1960- [Toronto, Association for Reformed Scientific Studies] v. ports. 28cm. annual. Includes bibliography. [BX9409.C5] 60-9912
1. Reformed Church—Addresses, essays, lectures. I. Association for Reformed Scientific Studies.

CHRISTIAN CENTURY 208.2
The Christian century reader; representative articles, editorials, and poems selected from more than fifty years of the Christian century, by Harold E. Fey, Margaret Frakes. New York, Association [c.1962] 447p. 62-9390 7.50 bds.,
1. Christianity—20th cent.—Addresses, essays, lectures. 2. Church and social problems—Addresses, essays, lectures. I. Fey, Harold Edward, 1898- ed. II. Frakes, Margaret. ed. III. Title.

CLANCY, William 208.2
Religion and American society; a statement of principles, by William Clancy [others] Introd. by Henry P. Van Dusen. Santa Barbara, Calif., Center for the Study of Democratic Insts. [c.1961] 79p. gratis pap.,
I. Title.

EMPIRICAL theology of Henry Nelson Wieman (The) 208.2
Ed. by Robert W. Bretall. New York, Macmillan [1963] 423p. illus. 22cm. (Lib. of living theology, v.4) 62-21217 8.50
1. Wieman, Henry Nelson, 1884- I. Bretall, Robert Walter, 1913- ed.
Contents omitted.

FEY, Harold E., ed. 208.2
How my mind has changed. Cleveland, Meridian Bks. [dist.] World Pub. Co. [c.1960, 1961] 191p. (Living age bk., LA33) 61-15600 1.25 pap.,
1. Religious thought—20th cent. 2. Theology—20th cent. I. Fey, Harold Edward, 1898- ed. II. Title.

GOLLANCZ, Victor, 1893-1967, comp. 208.2
Man and God; passages chosen and arranged to express a mood about the human and divine. Boston, Houghton Mifflin, 1951 [c1950] 576 p. music. 21 cm. First published in London in 1950 under title: A year of grace; passages chosen & arranged to express a mood about God and man. Bibliography: p. 560-572. [PN6071.R4G6 1951] 51-11493
1. Religious literature. I. Title.

HEFNER, Philip J., ed. 208.2
The scope of grace; essays on nature and grace in honor of Joseph Sittler, Philadelphia, Fortress [1964] x, 310p. port. 22cm. Bibl. 64-23065 4.95
1. Theology—Addresses, essays, lectures. 2. Sittler, Jooseph. I. Sittler, Joseph. II. Title.

KAUFMANN, Walter, ed. 208.2
Religion from Tolstoy to Camus [Selected, introd., prefaces by Walter Kaufmann] New York, Harper [c.1961, 1964] 450p. 21cm. (CL/TB-123) 2.95 pap.,
1. Religious thought—Modern period. I. Title.

KAUFMANN, Walter Arnold, ed. ed. 208.2
Religion from Tolstoy to Camus. New York, Harper [1961] 450 p. 25 cm. Bibliographical footnotes. [BL25.K35] 61-12838
1. Religious thought—Modern period, 1500- I. Title.

KRANZ, Gisbert. 208.2
Modern Christian literature. Translated from the French by J. R. Foster. [1st ed.] New York, Hawthron Books [1961] 174p. 21cm. (Twentieth century encyclopedia of Catholicism, v. 119. Section 11. Catholicism and literature) Includes bibliography. [BR117.K713] 61-9460
1. Religious literature—Hist. & crit. I. Title.

LERHINAN, John Patrick, 1915- ed. 208.2
Background to morality [Contributors:] Thomas J. Harte [others] New York, Desclee [c.1964] vii, 216p. 21cm. Presented a tribute to Father Francis Connell on the occasion of his golden jubilee as a priest. Bibl. [BX885.L4] 64-24533 4.75
1. Catholic Church—Addresses, essays, lectures. I. Connell, Francis Jeremiah, 1888- II. Title.

LETTERS from the saints., 208.2
arr., selected by a Benedictine of Stanbrook Abbev. Illus. by Vivian Berger. New York, Hawthorn [c.1964] ix, 302p. illus., facsims. 22cm. Bibl. 64-19205 4.95
1. Saints—Correspondence, reminiscences, etc. I. A Benedictine of Stanbrook Abbey, ed.

LIFE of the spirit. 208.2
The Christian vision; readings from the first ten years of the Life of the spirit. Arr. and edited by Mary Ellen Evans. With a foreword by the editor of the Life of the spirit. Westminster, Md., Newman Press [1956] 311p. 22cm. [BX885.L5] 56-14065
1. Catholic Church—Addresses, essays, lectures. I. Evans, Mary, Ellen, 1912- II. Title.

MACGREGOR, Geddes, comp. 208.2
Readings in religious philosophy [by] Geddes MacGregor [and] J. Wesley Robb. [Under the

editorship of Lucius Garvin] Boston, Houghton Mifflin [1962] 424p. 24cm. [BL51.M215] 62-4425
1. Philosophy and religion—Addresses, essays, lectures. I. Robb, John Wesley, joint comp. II. Title.

MACGREGOR, Geddes [John Geddes MacGregor] comp. 208.2
Readings in religious philosophy [by] Geddes MacGregor, Boston, Houghton [c.1962] 424p. 24cm. Bibl. 62-4425 3.95 pap.,
1. Philosophy and religion—Addresses, essays, lectures. I. Robb, John Wesley, joint comp. II. Title.

MAGILL, Frank Northen, 1907- ed. 208.2
Masterpieces of Catholic literature in summary form, edited by Frank N. Magill with associate editors A. Robert Caponigri [and] Thomas P. Neill. New York, Harper & Row [1965] xxvi, 1134, v p. 24 cm. "Acknowledgments" (biographical): p. [v]-xii. [BX885.M2] 63-20740
1. Theology—Abstracts. 2. Catholic literature—Abstracts. I. Title.

METHODIST Publishing House, Nashville. 208.2
Training series A. [Nashville] Personnel and Public Relations Division, Methodist Publishing House, 1953- v. 28cm. Contents.Course 1. An outline and bibliographical guide for the study of the living non-Christian religions of the world, by J. M. Batten.--Course 2. An outline and bibliographical guide for the study of the history of the Christian church. by J. M. Batten.-- Course 7. The Methodist Publishing House, Its organisation and function. Includes bibliography. [BR45.M36] 54-19592
1. Theology—Collections. I. Title.

MURPHY, Joseph Stanley, ed. 208.2
Christianity and culture. With an introd. by Donald McDonald. Baltimore, Helicon Press, 1960 [i. e. 1961] 198p. 23cm. Includes bibliography. [BR115.C8M8] 60-15488
1. Christianity—Addresses, essays, lectures. 2. Culture. I. Title.

PEGIS, Anton Charles, 1905- ed. 208.2
The wisdom of Catholicism. [1st Modern Library giant ed.] New York, Modern Library [1955] 988 p. 21 cm. (The modern library of the world's best books [G56]) [BX880] 55-6396
1. Theology—Collections—Catholic authors. 2. Catholic literature. I. Title.

PHILLIPS, Dorothy Berkley, 1906- ed. 208.2
The choice is always ours; an anthology on the religious way, chosen from psychological, religious, philosophical, poetical, and biographical sources, edited by Dorothy Berkley Phillips, co-edited by Elizabeth Boyden Howes [and] Lucille M. Nixon. Rev. and enl. ed. New York, Harper [1960] 430 p. 24 c,. [BL48.P5 1960] 59-5222
1. Religion. 2. Mysticism. I. Title.

RIAN, Edwin Harold, 1900- ed. 208.2
Christianity and world revolution. New York, Harper [c.1963] 237p. 22cm. 63-7600 4.00 bds.,
1. Christianity—20th cent.—Addresses, essays, lectures. I. New York. Biblical Seminary. II. Title.

VOSS, Carl Hermann, ed. 208.2
The universal God, the eternal quest in which all men are brothers; an interfaith anthology of man's search for God. Boston, Beacon [1961, c.1953] 326p. (Beacon LR 14) Bibl. 1.75 pap.,
1. Religious literature (Selections: Extracts, etc.) 2. God. I. Title.

VOSS, Carl Hermann, ed. 208.2
The universal God, the eternal quest in which all men are brothers; an interfaith anthology of man's search for God. [1st ed.] Cleveland, World Pub. Co. [1953] 306p. 22cm. [BL29.V6] 53-6645
1. Religious literature (Selections: Extracts, etc.) 2. God. I. Title.

WALHOUT, Donald 208.2
Interpreting religion. Englewood Cliffs, N.J., Prentice [c.]1963. 481p. 24cm. Bibl. 63-9965 9.00
1. Religion—Philosophy. 2. Theology—Collections. I. Title.

WHITE, Hugh C ed. 208.2
Christians in a technological era. [Contributors: Margaret Mead [and others] New York, Seabury Press, 1964. 143 p. 22 cm. Papers delivered at a consultation held at Louvain, Belgium, April 1961, under the sponsorship of the World Student Christian Federation and Pax Romana, plus introductory and concluding chapters. "The papers were first published in the Student world, LIV: 3 (1961) ... Translations from French ... by Margaret House." Bibliographical footnotes. [BR123.W48] 64-12943
1. Christianity — 20th cent. — Addresses, essays, lectures. 2. Religion and science — 1946- — Addresses, essays, lectures. I. World Student Christian Federation. II. Pax Romana, International Catholic Movement for Intellectual and Cultural Affairs. III. Title.

WHITE, Hugh C., ed. 208.2
Christians in a technological era. [Contributors]: Margaret Mead [others] New York, Seabury [c.]1964. 143p. 22cm. Papers delivered at a consultation held at Louvan, Belguim, April 1961, under the sponsorship of the World Student Christian Federation and and Pax Romana, plus introductory and concluding chapters. The papers were first pub. in the Student world, LIV:3(1961) . . . Tr. from French . . . by Margaret House. Bibl. 64-12943 3.50
1. Christianity—20th cent.—Addresses, essays, lectures. I. World Student Christian Federation. II. Pax Romana, International Catholic Movement for Intellectual and Cultural Affairs. III. Title.

WIKGREN, Allen Paul, 1906- ed. 208.2
Early Christian origins; studies in honor of Harold R. Willoughby. Chicago, Quadrangle Books, 1961. 160 p. illus. 22 cm. Includes bibliography. [BR129.W5] 61-7933
1. Willoughby, Harold Rideout, 1890- 2. Christianity — Origin. 3. Jesus Christ — Historicity. 4. Church history — Primitive and early church. I. Title.

WIKGREN, Allen Paul, 1906- ed. 208.2
Early Christian origins; studns in honor of Harold R. Willoughby. Chicago, Quadrangle [c.]1961. 160p. illus. Bibl. 61-7933 5.00
1. Willoughby, Harold Rideout, 1890- 2. Christianity—Origin. 3. Jesus Christ—Historicity. 4. Church history—Primitive and early church. I. Title.

WYLAND, Fred Bloom, 1890- ed. 208.2
Religion and the church tomorrow. Fred B. Wyand, editor, Albert W. Beaven, Francis J. McConnell [and others] ... Nashville, Cokesbury press [c1936] 222 p. 21 cm. [BR479.W9] 36-5078
1. Christianity — 20th cent. I. Title.

MAGILL, Frank Northen, 1907- ed. 208.22
Masterpieces of Christian literature in summary form, ed. by Frank N. Magill with Ian P. McGreal. New York, Harper [c.1963] xxix, 1193, v p. 24cm. 63-10622 3.95
1. Theology—Abstracts. 2. Protestantism—Collections. I. Title.

NAISMITH, A. 208.22
1200 notes, quotes and anecdotes. Chicago, Moody [1963. c.1962] 237p. 24cm. 3.95
I. Title.

VOSS, Carl Hermann, ed. 208.22
The universal God, the eternal quest in which all men are brothers; an interfaith anthology of man's search for God. [Gloucester, Mass., Peter Smith, 1962, c..1953] 326p. (Beacon paperback rebound) Bibl. 3.75
1. Religious literature (Selections: Extracts, etc.) 2. God. I. Title.

CARTER, W H 1909- 208.8
The philosopher's stone, by the Inkhorn. Boston, Meador Pub. Co. [1955] 69p. 22cm. [BR126.C28] 55-28915
I. Title.

FLYNN, Leslie B. 208.8
Serve Him with mirth: the place of humor in the Christian life. Grand Rapids, Mich., Zondervan Pub. House [c.1960] 191p. 60-51823 2.95
1. Wit and humor—Hist. & crit. 2. Christian life. I. Title.

JAMESON, Vic. 208.8
Bull at a new gate, by Vic Jameson and Don C. Westfall. Illustrated by Johanna Sperl. Philadelphia, Fortress Press [1965] x, 54 p. illus. 20 cm. [PN6231.C35J3] 65-13404
1. Christianity—Anecdotes, facetiae, satire, etc. I. Westfall, Don C., joint author. II. Title.

JAMESON, Vic 208.8
Bull at a new gate, by Vic Jameson, Don C. Westfall. Illus. by Johanna Sperl. Philadelphia, Fortress [c.1965] x, 54p. illus. 20cm. [PN6231.C35J3] 65-13404 2.00 bds.,
1. Christianity—Anecdotes, facetiae, satire, etc. I. Westfall, Don C., joint author. II. Title.

MARTY, Martin E., 1928- 208.8
Pen-ultimates: comment on the folk religions of America, by Martin E. Marty, Dean G. Peerman. New York, Holt [c.1960-1963] 110p. 20cm. 63-11876 2.95 bds.,
1. Religion—Anecdotes, facetiae, satire, etc. I. Peerman, Dean G., joint author. II. Title.

SCHEEL, Theodor, 1905- 208.8
Religious remarkables. [1st ed.] New York, Rockport Press [1950] 1 v. of illus. 24 cm. [BR96.S26] 51-18543
1. Curiosities. I. Title.

209 History & Geography Of Christianity

BACH, Marcus, 1906- 209
Strange sects and curious cults. New York, Dodd, Mead [c.] 1961. 277p. 61-7167 4.50
1. Religions. 2. Sects. I. Title.

BACH, Marcus, 1906- 209
Strange sects and curious cults. New York, Apollo [1962, c.1961] 277p. (A38) 1.75 pap.,
1. Religions. 2. Sects. I. Title.

BACH, Marcus, 1906- 209
Strange sects and curious cults. New York, Dodd, Mead, 1961. 277p. 22cm. [BL85.B3] 61-7167
1. Religions, 2. Sects. I. Title.

BASS, Reginald Howard 209
The story of natural religion. New York, Lyle Stuart [1964, c.1963] 192p. 21cm. Bibl. 62-7779 4.95 bds.,
1. Religion—Hist. I. Title.

BROW, Robert. 209
Religion: origins and ideas. [1st ed. Chicago, Inter-varsity Press [1966] 128 p. 21 cm. Includes bibliographical footnotes. [BL48.B73 1966a] 66-30594
1. Religion—History. I. Title.

CATHOLIC Students' Mission Crusade, United States of America National Center 209
Ecumenism and universalism; a collection of readings on world outlooks for the 'sixties. Pref., Karl J. Alter. Contributors, Paul Broadhurst [and others] Edited by J. Paul Spaeth. Cincinnati, CSMS Press [1963] xi. 89 p. illus., ports. 22 cm. (World cultures and religion series) Bibliographical footnotes. [BX8.2.A1C35] 64-247
1. Christian union. 2. Christianity — 20th cent. 3. Missions — Theory. I. Spaeth, J. Paul, ed. II. Title.

*CHESLOV, Esak 209
Thou shalt not bow: a thought-provoking dialogue, giving the reader a greater insight and understanding into the relationship of religion and humanism. New York, Vantage [c.1966] 100p. 21cm. 2.75
I. Title.

COPPA, Frank J. 209
Religion in the making of Western man [by] Frank J. Coppa. [Jamaica, N.Y., St. John's University Press, 1974] p. [BR115.C5C63] 74-2431 ISBN 0-87075-072-0
1. Christianity—Influence. 2. Religion. 3. Civilization, Occidental. I. Title.

COPPA, Frank J. 209
Religion in the making of Western man. Edited with an introd. by Frank J. Coppa. [Jamaica, N.Y., St. John's University Press, 1974] ix, 179 p. 23 cm. Includes bibliographies. [BR115.C5C63] 74-2431 ISBN 0-87075-072-0 6.95
1. Christianity—Influence. 2. Religion. 3. Civilization, Occidental. I. Title.

CROOK, Margaret Brackenbury 209
Women and religion. Boston, Beacon [1965, c.1964] x, 272p. 24cm. Bibl. [BV639.W7C7] 64-20496 5.95
1. Women in Christianity. I. Title.

DANIELOU, Jean. 209
Historical theology [by] J. Danielou, A. H. Couratin & John Kent. Harmondsworth, Penguin, 1969. 383 p. 18 cm. (Pelican books, A 1049.) (The Pelican guide to modern theology, v. 2) Bibliographical footnotes. [BR67.D33] 73-446793 10/-
1. Fathers of the church. 2. Liturgies—History. 3. Church history—20th century. I. Couratin, Arthur Hubert, 1902- II. Kent, John, 1923- III. Title. IV. Series.

DAVIES, Horton 209
The challenge of the sects. [Rev., enl. ed.] Philadelphia, Westminster [1962,c.1961] 176p. 19cm. First pub. in 1954 under title: Christian deviations. Bibl. 62-1216 1.45 pap.,
1. Religions, Modern. I. Title.

DAVIES, Horton. 209
Christian deviations: the challenge of the new spiritual movements. 3d rev. ed. Philadelphia, Westminster Press [1973, c1972] viii, 133 p. 22 cm. [BL98.D3 1973] 72-7365 ISBN 0-664-24966-3
1. Religions, Modern. I. Title.

DOUGLAS, James Dixon, ed. 209
Evangelicals and unity; six essays. Edited by J. D. Douglas. [Contributors] M. H. Cressey [and others] Appleford, Marcham Manor Press [1964] 96 p. 19 cm. [BX8.2A1D6] 66-92625
1. Christian union — Addresses, essays, lectures. 2. Evangelicalism. I. Cressey, M. H. II. Title.

DOUGLAS, James Dixon, ed. 209
Evangelicals and unity; six essays. Edited by J. D. Douglas. [Contributors] M. H. Cressey [and others] Appleford, Marcham Manor Press [1964] 96 p. 19 cm. [BX8.2A1D6] 66-92625
1. Christian union — Addresses, essays, lectures. 2. Evangelicalism. I. Cressey, M. H. II. Title.

EASTWOOD, Charles Cyril, 1916- 209
Life and thought in the ancient world. Philadelphia, Westminster [1965, c.1964] 187p. 22cm. Bibl. [BL96.E25] 65-21055 2.25 pap.,
1. Religion Hist— 2. Religions—Hist. I. Title.

ENVIRONMENTAL factors in Christian history. Edited by John Thomas McNeill, Matthew Spinka [and] Harold R. Willoughby. Port Washington, N.Y., Kennikat Press [1970, c1939] x, 417 p. port. 23 cm. (Essay and general literature index reprint series) "Presented to Dr. Shirley Jackson Case." Includes bibliographical references. [BR141.E6 1970] 70-91047 209
1. Case, Shirley Jackson, 1872-1947—Bibliography. 2. Church history—Addresses, essays, lectures. 3. Christianity and other religions. I. Case, Shirley Jackson, 1872-1947. II. McNeill, John Thomas, 1885- ed. III. Spinka, Matthew, 1890- ed. IV. Willoughby, Harold Rideout, 1890-1962, ed.

GASCOIGNE, Bamber. 209
The Christians / Bamber Gascoigne ; with photos. by Christina Gascoigne. New York : Morrow, 1977. 304 p., [24] leaves of plates : ill. ; 26 cm. Includes bibliographical references and index. [BR150.G33 1977b] 77-73590 ISBN 0-688-03220-6 : 17.50
1. Church history—Popular works. I. Title.

GASCOIGNE, Bamber. 209
The Christians / Bamber Gascoigne ; with photos. by Christina Gascoigne. New York : Morrow, 1977. 304 p., [24] leaves of plates : ill. ; 26 cm. Includes bibliographical references and index. [BR150.G33 1977b] 77-73590 ISBN 0-688-03220-6 : 17.50
1. Church history—Popular works. I. Title.

GIFFORD, William Alva, 1877- 209
The seekers; why Christian orthodoxy is obsolete. Boston, Beacon Press [1954] 306p. 22cm. [BL2775.G47] 54-6166
1. Christianity—Controversial literature. I. Title.

GRANT, Robert McQueen, 1917- 209
After the New Testament [by] Robert M. Grant. Philadelphia, Fortress Press [1967] xxiii, 228 p. 23 cm. "Editions cited": p. 215-217. Bibliographical footnotes. [BR67.G68] 67-17402
1. Christian literature, Early—Hist. & crit. 2. Church history—Prmitive and early church. I. Title.

HOLMES, Chauncey D. 209
Christian spirituality in geologic perspective / Chauncey Holmes. Philadelphia : Dorrance, [1975] 116 p. ; 22 cm. Includes bibliographical references. [BV4490.H6] 75-313613 ISBN 0-8059-2136-2 : 4.95
1. Spirituality—History. 2. Theology. I. Title.

JOHNSON, Paul. 209
A history of Christianity / Paul Johnson 1st American ed. New York : Atheneum, 1976. viii, 556 p. : 24 cm. Includes index Bibliography: p. 519-533. [BR145.2.J63 1976] 76-9002 ISBN 0-689-10728-5 : 13.95
1. Church history. I. Title.

JOHNSON, Paul, 1928- 209
A history of Christianity / Paul Johnson. London : Weidenfeld & Nicolson, c1976. viii, 556 p. ; 24 cm. Includes index. Bibliography: p. [519]-533. [BR145.2.J63 1976b] 76-372932 ISBN 0-297-77080-2 : £7.00
1. Church history. I. Title.

KILLINGER, John. 209
The second coming of the church. Nashville, Abingdon [1974] 112 p. 19 cm. [BR121.2.K49] 73-22118 ISBN 0-687-37280-1 3.95
1. Christianity—20th century. I. Title.

LARSON, Martin Alfred, 1897- 209
The religion of the Occident; or, The origin and development of the Essene-Christian faith.

Patterson, N. J., Littlefield, Adams & Co., 1961. 711 p. 23 cm. Includes bibliography. [BR129.L36] 59-16449
1. Christianity—Origin. I. Title.

LATOURETTE, Kenneth Scott, 1884-1968. 209
A history of the expansion of Christianity. Grand Rapids, Zondervan Pub. House [1970] 7 v. illus., maps. 22 cm. (Contemporary evangelical perspectives) Contents.Contents.—V. 1. The first five centuries.—V. 2. The thousand years of uncertainty.—V. 3. Three centuries of advance.—V. 4. The great century: Europe and the United States.—V. 5. The great century: the Americas, Australasia and Africa.—V. 6. The great century: North Africa and Asia.—V. 7. Advance through storm. Includes bibliographies. [BR145.L33] 73-120050 22.95 (set)
1. Church history. I. Title.

LEHMANN, Johannes, 1929- 209
The Jesus establishment. Translated by Martin Ebon. [1st ed.] Garden City, N.Y., Doubleday, 1974. 212 p. 22 cm. Translation of Die Jesus G.m.b.H. Bibliography: p. [211]-212. [BR129.L39313] 73-81440 ISBN 0-385-08291-6 5.95
1. Christianity—Origin. 2. Christianity—Essence, genius, nature. I. Title.

LIETZMANN, Hans, 1875-1942. 209
From Constantine to Julian. Translated by Bertram Lee Woolf. New York, Scribner, 1950. 340p. 23cm. (His A history of the early church, v. 3) Translation of Die Relchskirche bis zum Tode Julius. 'Corrigenda et emendanda slip inserted. Bibliography: p.[329]-333. [BR205.L] A53
1. Church history— Primitive and early church. I. Title.

LOPER, William Campbell. 209
The Lord of history. Philadelphia, Westminster Press [1965] 192 p. 21 cm. Bibliographical references included in "Notes" (p. [184]-186) [BR115.H5L6] 65-10320
1. History — Philosophy. I. Title.

LOPER, William Campbell 209
The Lord of history. Philadelphia, Westminster [c.1965] 192p. 21cm. Bibl. [BR115.H5L6] 65-10320 4.50
1. History—Philosophy. I. Title.

*MCNEILL, John Thomas, 1885- 209
Makers of the Christian tradition. New York, Harper [1964, c.1935] viii, 277p. 21cm. (CL/TB-121) 1.85 pap.,
I. Title.

*MCNEILL, John Thomas, 1885- 209
Makers of the Christian tradition from Alfred the Great to Schleiermacher [Gloucester, Mass., P. Smith, 1965, c.1935, 1964] xiv, 274p. 21cm. (Harper torchbk., Cloister lib., TB121 rebound) Bibl. 3.85
I. Title.

PAUL JAMES FRANCIS, Father, 1863-1940. 209
Father Paul and Christian unity; an anthology on Christian reunion prepared from the writings, sermons and addresses of Father Paul James Francis, S. A., 1863-1940. Compiled and edited by Titus Cranny. Foreword by Gregory Peter Cardinal Agagianian. Garrison, N. Y., Chair of Unity Apostolate [c1963] xv, 334 p. port. 22 cm. [BX8.P36] 63-21981
1. Christian union—Collected works. I. Cranny, Titus F., 1921- ed. II. Title.

PAYNE, Pierre Stephen Robert, 1911- 209
The Christian centuries from Christ to Dante [by] Robert Payne. [1st ed.] New York, Norton [1966] 438p. illus. 24cm. Bibl. [BR162.2.P38] 65-20240 8.95
1. Church history — Primitive and early church. 2. Church history — Middle Ages. I. Title.

PURINTON, Carl Everett. 209
Christianity and its Judaic heritage; an introduction with selected sources. New York, Ronald Press Co. [1961] 534p. illus. 22cm. Includes bibliography. [BR145.2.P8] 61-7734
1. Church history. 2. Christianity and other religions—Judaism. 3. Judaism—Hist. I. Title.

RIEPEN, Harry O 209
Mankind and religion: past, present, future. Kendall, Fla., Kendall Pub. Co. [c1959] 454p. 21cm. [BL80.2.R5] 60-20387
1. Religions. 2. Religion. I. Title.

*ROSS, Floyd H. 209
The great religions by which men live [Reissue] (Title orig.: Questions that matter most asked by the world's religions) By Floyd H. Ross, Tynette Hills. Greenwich, Conn., Fawcett [1965, c.1956] 192p. 18cm. (Premier bk., R199) .60 pap.,
I. Title.

SAHULA-DYCKE, Ignatz, 1900- 209
The God fixation : polenic [sic] essays about religious fixations that impede educational progress / Ignatz Sahula-Dycke. 1st ed. New York : Exposition Press, c1976. 79 p. ; 22 cm. (An Exposition-university book) [BL2775.2.S27] 76-2891 ISBN 0-682-48504-7 : 4.50
1. Christianity—Controversial literature. I. Title.

SAVAGE, Katharine. 209
The history of world religions. [Maps by Richard Natkiel] New York, Walck [1973? c.1966] 283 p. plates, maps. 21 cm. Bibl.: p. 275-278. [BL82.S35] 66-18534 ISBN 0-8098-3401-4 pap., 1.95
1. Religions—History—Juvenile literature. I. Title.

SAVAGE, Katharine. 209
The story of world religions. New York, H. Z. Walck, 1967 [c1966] 283 p. illus., maps. 21 cm. First published in 1966 under title: The history of world religions. [BL82.S35 1967] 66-18534
1. Religions—Hist.—Juvenile literature. I. Title.

SAVAGE, Katharine. 209
The story of world religions. New York, H. Z. Walck, 1967 [c1966] 283 p. illus., maps. 21 cm. First published in 1966 under title: The history of world religions. A survey of the basic beliefs and historical background of man's diverse religions, from the nature worship of Early Sumeria and Egypt to the major religions and religious cultures active today. [BL82.S35 1967] AC 67
1. Religions—History. I. Title.

SCHOEPS, Hans-Joachim. 209
The religions of mankind. Tr. from German by Richard and Clara Winston. Garden City, N.Y., Doubleday [1968,c.1966] xiii, 343p. 18cm. (Anchor. A621) [BL80.2.S353] 66-14927 1.75 pap.,
1. Religions—Hist. I. Title.

SCHONFIELD, Hugh Joseph, 1901- 209
The Jesus party [by] Hugh J. Schonfield. [First American ed.] New York, Macmillan [1974] 320 p. maps. 24 cm. British ed. published under title: The Pentecost revolution. Includes bibliographical references. [BR129.S36 1974] 74-9666 6.95
1. Christianity—Origin. 2. Christianity and other religions—Judaism. 3. Judaism—Relations—Christianity. I. Title.

*STOWMAN, Knud 209
Lord of history. New York, Vantage [c.1964] 254p. 21cm. 4.50 bds.,
I. Title.

*SZEKELY, Edmond Bordeaux 209
The Essene gospel of peace: book two: The unknown books of the Essenes. Translated and edited by Edmond Bordeaux Szekely. San Diego, Calif., Academy Books, 1974 144 p. illus. 23 cm. [BL2775.2] 3.95 (pbk.)
1. Christianity—Controversial Literature. I. Title.

*SZEKELY, Edmond Bordeaux 209
The Essene gospel of peace: book three: Lost scrolls of the Essene brotherhood. Translated and edited by Edmond Bordeaux Szekely. San Diego, Calif., Academy Books, 1974. 148 p. illus. 23 cm. [BL2775.2] 4.50 (pbk.)
1. Christianity—Controversial literature. I. Title.

TRUEBLOOD, David Elton, 1900- 209
The company of the committed. [1st ed.] New York, Harper [1961] 113 p. 21 cm. [BR481.T75] 61-12834
1. Christianity — 20th cent. I. Title.

TRUEBLOOD, David Elton, 1900- 209
The company of the committed. [1st ed.] New York, Harper [1961] 113 p. 21 cm. [BR481.T75] 61-12834
1. Christianity—20th cent. I. Title.

WEIGALL, Arthur Edward Pearse Brome, 1880-1934. 209
The paganism in our Christianity. New York, Gordon Press, 1974. vi, 277 p. 24 cm. Reprint of the 1928 ed. published by Putnam, New York. Includes bibliographical references. [BR135.W4 1974] 74-9710 ISBN 0-87968-149-7 29.75 (lib. bdg.)
1. Christianity. I. Title.

WHALE, John Seldon, 1896- 209
Christian reunion: historic divisions reconsidered, by J. S. Whale. Grand Rapids, Mich., W. B. Eerdmans Pub. Co. [1971] 141 p. 21 cm. Includes bibliographies. [BX8.2.W45] 73-168440 2.95
1. Jesus Christ—History of doctrines. 2. Christian union. 3. Church—History of doctrines. 4. Lord's Supper—History. I. Title.

WHELESS, Joseph, 1868- 209
Forgery in Christianity : a documented record of the foundations of the Christian religion / by Joseph Wheless. New York : Gordon Press, 1976, c1930. p. cm. Reprint of the ed. published by Knopf, New York. Includes index. [BL2775.W465 1976] 76-997 ISBN 0-87968-358-9 lib.bdg. : 49.95
1. Christianity—Controversial literature. I. Title.

WILKEN, Robert Louis, 1936- 209
The myth of Christian beginnings; history's impact on belief [by] Robert L. Wilken. [1st ed.] Garden City, N.Y., Doubleday, 1971. x, 218 p. 22 cm. Includes bibliographical references. [BR145.2.W5] 71-123712 5.95
1. Church history. 2. Christianity—Essence, genius, nature. I. Title.

HALLIDAY, William Reginald, Sir, 1886-1966. 209'.015
The pagan background of early Christianity. New York, Cooper Square Publishers, 1970. xvi, 334 p. 22 cm. Reprint of the 1925 ed. Bibliography: p. 324-328. [BR170.H25 1970] 70-118640 ISBN 0-8154-0331-3
1. Church history—Primitive and early church, 30-600. 2. Rome—Civilization. 3. Civilization, Christian. 4. Christianity and other religions. I. Title.

UMEN, Samuel. 209'.015
Links between Judaism and Christianity. New York, Philosophical Library [1966] xi, 153 p. 22 cm. Bibliography:p. 151-153. [BR129.U4] 66-18489
1. Christianity—Origin. 2. Christianity and other religions—Judaism. 3. Judaism—Relations—Christianity. I. Title.

CONTEMPORARY reflections 209'.02
on the medieval Christian tradition; essays in honor of Ray C. Petry. Edited by George H. Shriver. Durham, N.C., Duke University Press, 1974. xv, 279 p. 25 cm. Includes bibliographical references. [BR252.C58] 73-77639 ISBN 0-8223-0304-3 9.75
1. Petry, Ray C. 2. Petry, Ray C.—Bibliography. 3. Christianity—Middle Ages, 600-1500—Addresses, essays, lectures. I. Petry, Ray C., 1903- II. Shriver, George H., ed.
Contents omitted.

CONTEMPORARY reflections 209'.02
on the medieval Christian tradition; essays in honor of Ray C. Petry. Edited by George H. Shriver. Durham, N.C., Duke University Press, 1974. xv, 279 p. 25 cm. Contents.Contents.—Henry, S. C. Ray C. Petry: an appreciation.—Ritchie, B. M. Preaching and pastoral care in John Tauler.—Mallard, W. Clarity and dilemma: the Forty sermons of John Wyclif.—White, J. F. Durandus and the interpretation of Christian worship.—Shinn, G. H. The eschatological function of the iconography in the Dresden manuscript of the Sachsenspiegel.—Shriver, G. H. Images of catharism and the historian's task.—Bond, H. L. Nicholas of Cusa and the reconstruction of theology.—Jordan, J. Jacques Lefevre d'Etaples: principles and practice of reform at Meaux.—Ray, R. D. Orderic vitalis on Henry I.—Zinn, G. A., Jr. Historia fundamentum est: the role of history in the contemplative life according to Hugh of St. Victor.—McNeill, J. T. Perspectives on Celtic church history.—Burr, D. Olivi and the limits of intellectual freedom.—Cannon, W. R. The genesis of the university.—Farris, J. L. and D. M. Ray C. Petry: a bibliography (p. [223]-225)—Three addresses by Ray C. Petry selected and introduced by George H. Shriver: The church and church history, in classroom and parish. Christ and the Gospels in worship and the arts. The historic university and the divinity school. Includes bibliographical references. [BR252.C58] 73-77639 ISBN 0-8223-0304-3 9.75
1. Petry, Ray C. 2. Petry, Ray C.—Bibliography. 3. Christianity—Middle Ages, 600-1500—Addresses, essays, lectures. I. Petry, Ray C., 1903- II. Shriver, George H., ed.

MONKS, bishops, and 209'.021
pagans : Christian culture in Gaul and Italy, 500-700 : sources in translation, including the World of Gregory of Tours / edited and translated by William G. McDermott ; edited with an introd. by Edward Peters. Philadelphia : University of Pennsylvania Press, [1975] xiii, 238 p. ; 21 cm. (Sources of medieval history) Bibliography: p. 229-238. [BR251.M66] 74-33702 ISBN 0-8122-7687-6 : 12.50. ISBN 0-8122-1069-7 pbk. : 3.95
1. Christianity—Middle Ages, 600-1500—Collected works. I. McDermott, William Coffman, 1907- II. Peters, Edward M.

PAWSON, Geoffrey Philip Henry. 209'.032
The Cambridge Platonists and their place in religious thought, by G. P. H. Pawson. With a foreword by Alexander Nairne. New York, B. Franklin Reprints [1974] 95 p. 22 cm. (Burt Franklin research and source works series. Philosophy and religious history monographs, 142) Reprint of the 1930 ed. published by Society for Promoting Christian Knowledge, London. [B1133.C2P3 1974] 72-82363 ISBN 0-8337-4313-9 10.00
1. Cambridge Platonists. I. Title. II. Series.

KIERKEGAARD, Soren Aabye, 1813-1855. 209'.034
Kierkegaard's attack upon "Christendom," 1854-1855. Translated, with an introd., by Walter Lowrie. Princeton, N.J., Princeton University Press [1968] xxxiii, 303 p. 21 cm. Contents.Contents.—Kierkegaard and the Church, a supplement to the translator's introd. by H. A. Johnson.—Articles in the Fatherland, I-XX.—This has to be said—so be it now said.—Last article in the Fatherland, XXI.—The instant, nos. I and II.—What Christ's judgement is about official Christianity—The instant, nos. III-VII.—The instant, nos. VIII-X. Includes bibliographical references. [BR121.K4313 1968] 68-5956 2.95
1. Christianity—19th century. I. Lowrie, Walter, 1868-1959, ed. and tr.

WELCH, Claude. 209'.034
Protestant thought in the nineteenth century. New Haven, Yale University Press, 1972- v. 24 cm. Contents.Contents.—v. 1. 1799-1870. Includes bibliographical references. [BT28.W394] 72-75211 ISBN 0-300-01535-6 12.50
1. Theology, Doctrinal—History—19th century. 2. Theology, Protestant—History. I. Title.

*BANOWSKY, William Slater. 209'.04
It's a Playboy world [by] William S. Banowsky. New York, Family Library [1973, c.1969] 127 p. 18 cm. [BR121.2] ISBN 0-515-02979-3 0.95 (pbk.)
1. Christianity—20th century—Churches of Christ authors. I. Title.

BLACKHAM, Harold John, 1903- 209.04
Religion in a modern society [by] H. J. Blackham. New York, F. Ungar Pub. Co. [1967, c1966] xii, 229 p. 21 cm. "Notes and references": p. [217]-229. [BR123.B57 1967] 66-26508
1. Christianity—20th century—Addresses, essays, lectures. I. Title.

BLACKIE, Bruce L., 1936- 209'.04
Gods of goodness; the sophisticated idolatry of the main line churches [by] Bruce L. Blackie. Philadelphia, Westminster Press [1975] 170 p. 21 cm. Includes bibliographical references. [BR121.2.B468] 74-19096 ISBN 0-664-20719-7 5.95
1. Christianity—20th century. 2. Church renewal. I. Title.

*CHESTERTON, Gilbert Keith, 1874-1936. 209'.04
Orthodoxy, by Gilbert K. Chesterton. Garden City, N.Y., Doubleday [1973] 160 p. 18 cm. (Image Books, D84) First published in 1908; reissue of the Image Book edition of 1959. [BR121.2] ISBN 0-385-01536-4 pap., 1.25
1. Christianity—Evidences—20th century. I. Title.

COFFIN, Henry Sloane, 1877-1954. 209'.04
What men are asking; some current questions in religion. Freeport, N.Y., Books for Libraries Press [1970, c1961] 196 p. 23 cm. (The Cole lectures for 1933, delivered at Vanderbilt University) (Essay index reprint series.) Contents.—Where can we start?—Of what use is religion?—Can we know God?—Is Jesus authoritative?—What is spirituality?—What do you mean by "God"?—References (p. 189-196) [BR123.C638 1970] 70-117770
1. Christianity—20th century—Addresses, essays, lectures. I. Title. II. Series: The Cole lectures. Vanderbilt University, 1933

DE WOLF, Lotan Harold, 209.04
The enduring message of the Bible. New York, Harper [c.1960] 128p. 22cm. 60-7961 2.75 half cloth,
1. Christianity—20th cent. I. Title.

EDWARDS, K. Morgan 209.04
More than survival; the need for a moral and spiritual revolution. Nashville, Abingdon [c.1961] 128p. 61-10811 2.25 bds.,
1. Christianity—20th cent. I. Title.

FORD, Leighton. 209'.04
One way to change the world. New York, Harper [1973, c.1970] viii, 119 p. 21 cm. [BR121.2.F63 1970] 71-124701 ISBN 0-06-062682-8 pap., 1.95
1. Christianity—20th century. I. Title.

GREELEY, Andrew M., 1928- 209'.04
Religion in the year 2000, by Andrew M. Greeley. New York, Sheed and Ward [1969] 175 p. 21 cm. [BR124.G7] 79-82604 4.95
1. Christianity—20th century. I. Title.

HADDEN, Jeffrey K. 209'.04
The gathering storm in the churches [by] Jeffrey K. Hadden. [1st ed.] Garden City, N.Y., Doubleday, 1969. xxix, 257 p. 22 cm. Bibliographical references included in "Notes" (p. [237]-248) [BR115.W6H28] 68-22613 5.95
1. Church and the world. 2. Church and race problems. 3. Clergy. 4. Laity. 5. U.S.—Religion—1945- I. Title.

HALVORSON, Loren E., 209'.04
1927-
Grace at point zero [by] Loren E. Halvorson. New York, Friendship Press [1972] 96 p. 20 cm. Includes bibliographical references. [BR121.2.H324] 73-182978 ISBN 0-377-02111-3 1.75
1. Christianity—20th century. I. Title.

HARDON, John A. 209'.04
Christianity in the twentieth century [by] John A. Hardon. [1st ed.] Garden City, N.Y., Doubleday, 1971. 527 p. 22 cm. Includes bibliographical references. [BR121.2.H333] 74-139029 9.95
1. Christianity—20th century. I. Title.

HARKNESS, Georgia Elma, 209'.04
1891-
Stability amid change, by Georgia Harkness. Nashville, Abingdon Press [1969] 160 p. 20 cm. The first six chapters were originally written and presented in two series of lectures: the Annual fall lectureship of the Central Church, San Antonio, Texas, Oct. 1967, and the Barton lectures, Boston Avenue Methodist Church, Tulsa, Okla., Jan. 1968. Bibliographical footnotes. [BR121.2.H334] 69-12019 3.00
1. Christianity—20th century. I. Title.

JOAD, Cyril Edwin 209'.04
Mitchinson, 1891-1953.
The present and future of religion. Westport, Conn., Greenwood Press [1974, c1930] 310 p. 22 cm. Reprint of the ed. published by Macmillan, New York. [BR479.J6 1974] 77-109756 ISBN 0-8371-4246-6 12.75
1. Christianity—20th century. 2. Religion. I. Title.

KENNEDY, Eugene C. 209'.04
The return to man [by] Eugene C. Kennedy. [1st ed.] Garden City, N.Y., Doubleday, 1973. 192 p. 22 cm. [BR121.2.K44] 72-88705 ISBN 0-385-06502-7 5.95
1. Christianity—20th century. I. Title.

KEYES, Charles Don. 209'.04
God or Ichabod? A non-violent Christian nihilism [by] C. D. Keyes. [Cincinnati, Forward Movement Publications, 1973?] 128 p. 17 cm. (A Forward Movement miniature book) Includes bibliographical references. [BR121.2.K474] 73-157523
1. Christianity—20th century. I. Title.
Publishers address: 412 Sycamore St., Cincinnati, Ohio 45202.

KONIJN, Seef, 1935- 209'.04
The bridge; from old to new in Christian belief. [Translated into English by Hubert Hoskins] St. Meinrad, Ind., Abbey Press, 1973. 123 p. 21 cm. (A Priority edition) Translation of Ter overbrugging. [BR121.2.K6613] 73-86288 ISBN 0-225-65975-1 2.95
1. Christianity—20th century. I. Title.

KUHN, Margaret E. 209'.04
Get out there and do something about injustice, by Margaret E. Kuhn. New York, Friendship Press [1972] 143 p. 18 cm. Bibliography: p. 140-143. [BR121.2.K83] 77-182979 ISBN 0-377-02121-0 1.95
1. Christianity—20th century. 2. Faith. 3. Justice. I. Title.

MEREDITH, Lawrence, 1928- 209'.04
The Sensuous Christian; a celebration of freedom and love. New York, Association Press [1972] 192 p. 21 cm. Includes bibliographical references. [BR121.2.M42] 72-8225 ISBN 0-8096-1852-4 6.95
1. Christianity—20th century. 2. Theology—20th century. I. Title.

MILLER, Samuel Howard, 209'.04
1900-
Religion in a technical age [by] Samuel H. Miller. Cambridge, Harvard University Press, 1968. ix, 146 p. 22 cm. [BR123.M535] 68-17628
1. Christianity—20th century—Addresses, essays, lectures. I. Title.

MILLER, William Robert. 209'.04
Goodbye, Jehovah; a survey of the new directions in Christianity. New York, Walker [1969] 206 p. 22 cm. Includes bibliographical references. [BT28.M53] 69-11834 5.95
1. Theology, Doctrinal—History—20th century. 2. Christianity—20th century. I. Title.

MULLEN, Thomas James, 209'.04
1934-
The dialogue gap [by] Thomas J. Mullen. Nashville, Abingdon Press [1969] 126 p. 19 cm. (An Original Abingdon paperback) Includes bibliographies. [BR121.2.M83] 69-18444
1. Christianity—20th century. 2. Church renewal. I. Title.

PAUL, Robert S. 209'.04
The church in search of itself, by Robert S. Paul. Grand Rapids, Eerdmans [1972] 384 p. 23 cm. [BV600.2.P39] 72-75573 ISBN 0-8028-3422-1 7.95
1. Church. 2. Christianity—20th century. I. Title.

PAUL, Robert S. 209'.04
Kingdom come! By Robert S. Paul. Grand Rapids, Mich., Eerdmans [1974] 88 p. 18 cm. Includes bibliographical references. [BR121.2.P33] 74-607 ISBN 0-8028-1564-2 2.25 (pbk.).
1. Christianity—20th century. I. Title.

RIDEOUT, Gus. 209'.04
The smug theology. Philadelphia, Dorrance [1971] ix, 84 p. 22 cm. [BR121.2.R49] 76-163075 ISBN 0-8059-1588-5 3.95
1. Christianity—20th century. I. Title.

SCHAEFFER, Francis 209'.04
August.
Death in the city [by] Francis A. Schaeffer. Chicago, Inter-varsity Press [1969] 143 p. 21 cm. [BT1102.S28] 74-78922
1. Christianity—20th century. 2. Apologetics—20th century. I. Title.

SOPER, David Wesley, 1910- 209.04
ed.
Exploring the Christian world mind, personal interviews, the United Nations community. New York, Philosophical Library [1964] x, 193 p. 21 cm. [BR123.S72] 63-20081
1. Christianity—20th cent.—Addresses, essays, lectures. I. Title.

SOPER, David Wesley, 1910- 209.04
ed.
Exploring the Christian world mind; personal interviews, the United Nations community. New York, Philosophical [c.1964] x, 193p. 21cm. 63-20081 5.00
1. Christianity—20th cent.—Addresses, essays, lectures. I. Title.

SPERRY, Willard Learoyd, 209'.04
1882-1954.
Signs of these times. Freeport, N.Y., Books for Libraries Press [1968] viii, 179 p. 22 cm. (Essay index reprint series.) (The Ayer lectures, 1929) Reprint of the 1929 ed. [BR85.S635 1968] 68-29247
1. Christianity—20th century. I. Title. II. Series.

STRENG, William D. 209'.04
In search of ultimates, by William D. Streng. Minneapolis, Augsburg Pub. House [1969] xi, 156 p. illus. 22 cm. Includes bibliographies. [BT77.3.S7] 69-14182 2.50
1. Theology, Doctrinal—Outlines, syllabi, etc. 2. Discussion in religious education. I. Title.

TRUEBLOOD, David Elton, 209'.04
1900-
The future of the Christian [by] Elton Trueblood. [1st ed.] New York, Harper & Row [1971] x, 102 p. 22 cm. Includes bibliographical references. [BR121.2.T74 1971] 70-126281 2.95
1. Christianity—20th century. I. Title.

WALLIS, Jim. 209'.04
Agenda for Biblical people / Jim Wallis. 1st ed. New York : Harper & Row, c1976. xi, 145 p. ; 21 cm. Bibliography: p. 141-142. [BR121.2.W25 1976] 75-36745 ISBN 0-06-069236-7 pbk. : 3.95
1. Christianity—20th century. 2. Church and the world. I. Title.

WALSH, Chad, 1914- 209'.04
God at large. New York, Seabury Press [1971] 134 p. illus. 22 cm. [BR121.2.W27] 77-129207 3.95
1. Christianity—20th century. 2. Religion and language. 3. Resurrection. I. Title.

WILSON, Bryan. 209'.04
Contemporary transformations of religion / by Bryan Wilson. London ; New York : Oxford University Press, 1976. ix, 116 p. ; 19 cm. (Riddell memorial lectures ; 45th ser.) "The Riddell memorial lectures, forty-fifth series, delivered at the University of Newcastle upon Tyne on 2, 3, 4 December 1974." Includes bibliographical references. [BR123.W58] 76-378405 ISBN 0-19-713914-0 : 6.50
1. Christianity—20th century—Addresses, essays, lectures. 2. Sects—Addresses, essays, lectures. 3. Religion and sociology—Addresses, essays, lectures. I. Title. II. Series.

WOODYARD, David O. 209'.04
Living without God, before God, by David O. Woodyard. Philadelphia, Westminster Press [1968] 156 p. 19 cm. Bibliography: p. [153]-156. [BR121.2.W6] 68-14145
1. Christianity—20th century. I. Title.

DAVID : 209.04'074'0147277
hommage a Michelangelo : Galerie Levy [Ausstellung vom 26. Mai - 26. Juli : Katalog / Text, Peter Grimm]. Hamburg : die Galerie, [1975?] [28] p. : chiefly ill. ; 21 x 30 cm. Limited ed. of 500 copies. [N6488.G3H283] 75-515163
1. Buonarroti, Michel Angelo, 1475-1564. David. 2. David, King of Israel—Art. 3. Art, Modern—20th century—Exhibitions. I. Grimm, Peter. II. Galerie Levy.

NEW York 209.04'074'0147277
University. Art Collection.
20th-century painting & sculpture from the New York University Art Collection [New York] New York University [1971] 24 p. illus. 18 x 21 cm. Catalogue of an exhibition held at the Hudson River Museum, Yonkers, N.Y., Oct. 2-Nov. 14, 1971. [N6487.Y6H86] 78-173887
1. Art, Modern—20th century—Exhibitions. I. Hudson River Museum. II. Title.

ARSEN'EV, Nikolai 209'.042
Sergeevich, 1888-
We beheld His glory; the primitive Christian message and present-day religious trends, by Nicholas Arseniev. Translated from the German by Mary Anita Ewer. New York, Morehouse Pub. Co., 1936. [New York, AMS Press, 1971] xx, 219 p. 19 cm. Translation of Der urchristliche Realismus und die Gegenwart. Includes bibliographical references. [BR121.A8413 1971] 76-113545 ISBN 0-404-00407-5
1. Christianity—20th century. 2. Theology—20th century. I. Title.

QUOIST, Michel. 209'.046
Christ is alive! Translated by J. F. Bernard. Garden City, N.Y., Doubleday, 1971. 168 p. 22 cm. Translation of Le Christ est vivant. [BT60.Q613] 71-131101 4.95
1. Christianity—Essence, genius, nature. 2. Christian life—1960- I. Title.

FORMAN, Charles W., ed. 209.18'11
Christianity in the non-western world, edited by Charles W. Forman. Englewood Cliffs, N. J., Prentice-Hall [1967] viii, 146 p. maps. 21 cm. (The Global history series) A Spectrum book. Bibliography: p. 143-146. [BR1065.F6] 67-14851
1. Christianity—Asia. 2. Christianity—Africa. I. Title.

BARSTAD, Glenna. 209.22
They dared for God. Illustrated by Dick Cole. Mountain View, Calif., Pacific Press Pub. Association [1958] 128p. illus. 21cm. [BR1704.B3] 58-10579
1. Christian biography. I. Title.

ANTHONY, Ole. 209'.2'2
Cross fire / Ole Anthony. Plainfield, N.J. : Logos International, c1976. ix, 210 p. ; 20 cm. Selections from interviews originally broadcast on radio program One Trinity Place, KDTX, Dallas, Tex. [BV4501.2.A57] 75-38198 ISBN 0-88270-157-6 pbk. : 2.95
1. Christian life—1960- 2. Christian biography. 3. Conversion. I. Title.

BARKER, William Pierson. 209'.22
Who's who in church history [by] William P. Barker. Old Tappan, N.J., F. H. Revell Co. [1969] 319 p. 24 cm. [BR1700.2.B37] 74-85306 6.95
1. Christian biography. I. Title.

BERGEY, Alyce. 209'.22
The world God made; the story of creation: Genesis 1 and 2 for children. Illustrated by Obata Studio. St. Louis, Concordia Pub. House [1965] 1 v. (unpaged) col. illus. 21 cm. (Arch books) [BS551.2.B46] 63-23145
1. Bible stories, English — O.T. Genesis I-II. I. Title.

BOWDEN, Henry Warner. 209'.2'2 B
Dictionary of American religious biography / Henry Warner Bowden ; Edwin S. Gaustad, advisory editor. Westport, Conn. : Greenwood Press, 1976. p. cm. Includes bibliographies and index. [BL72.B68] 76-5258 ISBN 0-8371-8906-3 lib.bdg. : 29.95
1. Religions—Biography. 2. United States—Biography. I. Title.

BROWN, LeRoy C. 209.22
Champions all, by LeRoy Brown. Cover painting by Thomas Dunbebin. Washington, Review and Herald Pub. Association [1966] 96 p. ports. 22 cm. [BR1704.B7] 66-19421
1. Christian biography—Juvenile literature. I. Title.

[CALKINS, Frances 209'.22
Manwaring] 1795-1869.
The Bible primer. New York. Boston, American Tract Society [c1854-] v. illus., map. 17 cm. Contents.CONTENTS.--pt. 1. Primer of the Pentateuch.--pt. 2. Primer of the historical books. [BS605.C24] 65-79418
1. Bible—Study—Text-books. I. Title.

[CALKINS, Frances 209'.22
Manwaring] 1795-1869.
Youth's Bible studies. New York, American Tract Society [c1854-] v. illus. 17 cm. Preface signed: F.M.C. Also published under title: Bible primer. Contents.CONTENTS.--pt. 1. Pentateuch.--pt. 1. Historical books.--pt. 3. Prophets.-- pt. 5. The Gospels. [BS605.C242] 65-78432
1. Bible—Study—Textbooks. I. C., F.M. II. Title.

DAUGHTERS of St. Paul. 209'.2'2 B
Every man's challenge; profiles of great men and women. [Boston] St. Paul Editions [1974] 345 p. illus. 22 cm. [BR1700.2.D345 1974] 73-89938 5.00
1. Christian biography. I. Title.

DAVEY, Cyril James. 209'.22 B
Fifty lives for God [by] Cyril Davey. Valley Forge [Pa.] Judson Press [1974, c1973] 167 p. 23 cm. Bibliography: p. 166-167. [BR1700.2.D35 1974] 73-13450 ISBN 0-8170-0629-X 4.95
1. Christian biography. I. Title.

DAVIDSON, Henry Martin 209'.22 B
Perkins, 1901-
Good Christian men [by] Henry Martin P. Davidson. Freeport, N.Y., Books for Libraries Press [1971, c1940] x, 260 p. 23 cm. (Essay index reprint series) Bibliography: p. 251-256. [BR150.D3 1971] 70-142616 ISBN 0-8369-2390-1
1. Church history. 2. Christian biography. I. Title.

DAVIES, Horton. 209'.22 B
Great South African Christians. Westport, Conn., Greenwood Press [1970] vii, 190 p. 23 cm. Reprint of the 1951 ed. Bibliography: p. 181-182. [BR1450.D3 1970] 70-104242
1. Africa, South—Biography. 2. Christians in Africa, South. I. Title.

DAY, Richard Ellsworth, 209'.22 B
1884-
Beacon lights of grace. Freeport, N.Y., Books for Libraries Press [1971, c1947] 169 p. illus., ports. 23 cm. (Biography index reprint series) "Twelve biographical vignettes: Amos of Tekoa [and others]" [BR1700.D4 1971] 71-148210 ISBN 0-8369-8057-3
1. Christian biography. I. Title.

EINSPRUCH, Henry, 1892- 209'.22
comp.
Raisins and almonds. Baltimore, Lewis and Harriet Lederer Foundation [1967] 86 p. illus. 19 cm. Text in English, Hebrew, or Yiddish. Includes music. [BR158.E4] 67-19843
1. Jewish Christians. I. Title.

ELLINGBOE, Betty. 209'.22
The little man from Jericho. Written and illustrated by Betty Ellingboe. Minneapolis, Augsburg Pub. House [1963] unpaged. illus. 22 x 28 cm. [BS2520.Z3E4] 63-16596
1. Zacchaeus (Biblical character) — Juvenile literature. I. Title.

ENLOW, David R. 209'.2'2 B
Saved from bankruptcy : the story of the boatbuilding Meloons / by David and Dorothy Enlow. Chicago : Moody Press, [1975] p. cm. [BR1725.M36E54] 75-23223 ISBN 0-8024-7540-X : 4.95
1. Meloon, Wilfred C. 2. The Meloon family. 3. Success. I. Enlow, Dorothy, joint author. II. Title.

FOSTER, Warren Dunham, 209'.22 B
1886- ed.
Heroines of modern religion. Freeport, N.Y., Books for Libraries Press [1970]. iv, 275 p. ports. 23 cm. (Essay index reprint series) Reprint of the 1913 ed. Contents.Contents.—Anne Hutchinson, by A. E. Jenkins.—Susannah Wesley, by W. H. Foster.—Elizabeth Ann Seton, by R. V. Trevel.—Lucretia Mott, by A. E. Jenkins.—Fanny Crosby, by W. Bradbury—Sister Dora, by G. L. Mumford.—Hannah Whitall Smith, by W. H. Foster.—Frances Ridley Havergal, by W. Bradbury.—Ramabai Dongre Medhavi, by J. C. Minot.—Maud Ballington Booth, by R. V. Trevel.

Bibliography: p. 258-261. [CT3203.F75 1970] 77-107700
1. Woman—Biography. I. Title.

GIBBARD, Mark. 209'.2'2 B
Twelve who prayed : 20th century models of prayer / Mark Gibbard. 1st U.S. ed. Minneapolis : Augsburg Pub. House, 1977, c1974. vii, 120 p. ; 20 cm. Originally published under title: Twentieth-century men of prayer. Includes index. Bibliography: p. 115-119. [BR1702.G44 1977] 77-72459 ISBN 0-8066-1595-8 pbk. : 3.50
1. Christian biography. 2. Prayer—Case studies. I. Title.

GIBBARD, Mark. 209'.2'2 B
Twelve who prayed : 20th century models of prayer / Mark Gibbard. 1st U.S. ed. Minneapolis : Augsburg Pub. House, 1977, c1974. vii, 120 p. ; 20 cm. Originally published under title: Twentieth-century men of prayer. Includes index. Bibliography: p. 115-119. [BR1702.G44 1977] 77-72459 ISBN 0-8066-1595-8 pbk. : 3.50
1. Christian biography. 2. Prayer—Case studies. I. Title.

GOD lives! : 209'.2'2 B
True stories of God's work in the lives of famous people such as Helen Hayes, Pat O'Brien, Anita Bryant, Pat Boone, and many others / edited by Shifra Stein ; illustrated by James Hamil. [Kansas City, Mo. : Hallmark Cards, 1975] 45 p. : ill. ; 20 cm. (Hallmark editions) [BV4510.2.G63] 74-76162 ISBN 0-87529-391-3 : 3.50
1. Christian life—1960- 2. Christian biography. I. Stein, Shifra.

GOODWIN, Frank Judson, 1862- 209'.22
A harmony and commentary on the life of St. Paul according to the Acts of the Apostles and the Pauline Epistles. Grand Rapids, Baker Book House, 1951. 240p. 20cm. 'In issuing this third edition ... the original edition has been reprinted without change.' First ed. published in 1895 under title: A harmony of the life of St. Paul. [BS2505.G] A53
1. Paul, Saint, apostle. I. Title.

HAMMOND, Laurence. 209'.2'2 B
Beyond love / Laurence Hammond. Carol Stream, Ill. : Creation House, c1976. 287 p. ; 21 cm. Autobiographical. [BX5995.H285A32] 76-14542 ISBN 0-88419-000-5 : 6.95
1. Hammond, Laurence. 2. Hammond, Merikay. 3. Christian biography. 4. Conversion. I. Title.

HILLERBRAND, Hans Joachim. 209'.22
A fellowship of discontent, [by] Hans J. Hillerbrand. [1st ed.] New York., Harper & Row [1967] xiv, 176 p. 22 cm. [BR1702.H5] 67-11509
1. Christian biography. I. Title.

A History of religious educators / Elmer L. Towns, editor. Grand Rapids : Baker Book House, c1975. 330 p. ; 23 cm. Includes bibliographies and index. [BV1470.2.H57] 75-16794 ISBN 0-8010-8829-1 : 8.95 209'.2'2 B
1. Educators, Christian—Biography. 2. Christian biography. 3. Christian education—History. I. Towns, Elmer L.

HODGES, George, 1856-1919. 209'.22 B
Saints and heroes since the Middle Ages. Freeport, N.Y., Books for Libraries Press [1970] 318 p. illus., ports. 23 cm. (Essay index reprint series) Reprint of the 1912 ed. Contents.Contents.— Luther, 1483-1546.—More, 1478-1535.—Loyola, 1491-1556.—Cranmer, 1489-1556.—Calvin, 1509-1564.—Knox, 1505-1572.—Coligny, 1519-1572.—William the Silent, 1533-1584.—Brewster, 1560-1644.—Laud, 1573-1645.—Cromwell, 1599-1658.—Bunyan, 1628-1688.—Fox, 1624-1691.—Wesley, 1703-1791. [BR1700.H58 1970] 75-107713
1. Christian biography. I. Title.

HODGES, Turner, ed. 209'.22
The Bible story library; the Holy Scriptures retold in story form for the young and as an explanation and commentary for all, based on traditional texts and illustrated with the most famous Biblical art. Edited by Turner Hodges with the assistance of Elizabeth MacLean. Designed and produced by Donald D. Wolf with the assistance of Margot L. Wolf. Indianapolis, T. Audel [1963] 2 v. (xiv, 726 p.) illus. (part col.) col. maps. 25 cm. Contents.CONTENTS.--v. 1. From creation to David.--v. 2. From Solomon to the Apocalypse. [BS551.2.B5] 65-4278
1. Bible stories, English. 2. Bible—History of Biblical events. I. Title.

HOSIER, Helen Kooiman. 209'.2'2 B
Profiles : people who are helping to change the world / Helen Kooiman Hosier. New York : Hawthorn Books, c1977. viii, 184 p. : ports ; 22 cm. [BR1700.2.H67 1977] 75-2566 ISBN 0-8015-6082-9 : 6.95
1. Christian biography. I. Title.

HULL, Eleanor (Means) 209'.22
The sling and the swallow. Illustrated by Arthur Polonsky. Boston, United Church Press [c1963] 96 p. col. illus. 23 cm. [BS551.2.H8] 63-11064
1. Bible stories. English. I. Title.

HUNT, Gladys M. 209'.22
Does anyone here know God? Stories of women who do [by] Gladys M. Hunt. Grand Rapids, Zondervan Pub. House [1967] 224 p. ports. 23 cm. Bibliographical footnotes. [BR1713.H78] 67-11622
1. Christian biography. 2. Woman—Biography. I. Title.

HURLBUT, Jesse Lyman, 1843-1930. 209'.22
Hurlbut's story of the Bible for young and old; a continuous narrative of the Scriptures told in one hundred sixty-eight stories. Illus. in full color by Ralph Pallen Coleman. Text drawings in two colors by Steel Savage New and exapnded ed.] New York, Holt, Rinehart and Winston [1963?, c1957] xvi, 655, 64, 62 p. col. illus., 18 col. maps. 25 cm. Includes Hurlbut's Bible lessons for young and old, and History of the books of the Bible, by Joseph Howard Gray. [BS551.H8] 63-7320
1. Bible — History of Biblical events. I. Gray, Joseph Howard. History of the books of the Bible. II. Coleman, Ralph Pallen, illustrator. III. Title.

JOHNSON, Paul Emanuel, 1898- 209.2'2 B
Healer of the mind; a psychiatrist's search for faith. Paul E. Johnson, editor. Nashville, Abingdon Press [1972] 270 p. 23 cm. Includes bibliographical references. [BR1702.J58] 78-186824 ISBN 0-687-16738-8 6.95
1. Christian biography. I. Title.

JOHNSON, Ruth I. 209'.22
Christians with courage, by Ruth I. Johnson. Lincoln, Neb., Back to the Bible Broadcast [1968] 128 p. 18 cm. [BR1703.J58] 78-40 0.50
1. Christian biography. I. Title.

JONES, Mary Alice, 1898- 209'.22
Bible stories for little children. Illustrated by Janet Robson Kennedy. Chicago, Rand McNally, 1964, c1949. 1 v. (unpaged) col. illus. 26 cm. [BS551.2.J73 1964] 64-15252
1. Bible stores, English I. Title.

KATZENBERG, Julius. 209'.22
Biblical history for school and home. Methodically arr., with appended observations. New York, Industrial School of the Hebrew Orphan Asylum, 1978- v. 18cm. Contents.Pt. 1. From the creation to the death of Joseph. [BS551.K34] 58-50327
1. Bible stories, English—O. T. I. Title.

KELLNER, Esther. 209'.22
Moses and the liberation from Egypt. Garden City, N. Y., 1962. 64 p. 21 cm. (Know your Bible program) [BS551.2.K43] 62-53412
1. Bible stories, English — O. T. Exodus. 2. Moses — Juvenile literature. I. Title. II. Series.

KENNETH, Brother, C. G. A. 209'.2'2 B
Saints of the twentieth century / by Brother Kenneth. London : Mowbrays, 1976. xvii, 206 p. ; 21 cm. Includes index. Bibliography: p. 190-195. [BR1700.2.K38] 76-383579 ISBN 0-264 66285 7 : £3.75
1. Christian biography. I. Title.

KEPLER, Thomas Samuel, 1897- 209'.22 B
A journey with the saints, by Thomas S. Kepler. Freeport, N.Y., Books for Libraries Press [1971, c1951] 150 p. 23 cm. (Biography index reprint series) Includes bibliographical references. [BR1700.2.K4 1971] 70-148223 ISBN 0-8369-8070-0
1. Christian biography. I. Title.

KOOIMAN, Helen W. 209'.22
Cameos, women fashioned by God [by] Helen W. Kooiman. Wheaton, Ill., Tyndale House [1969, c1968] 163 p. ports. 22 cm. [BR1713.K66] 68-56393 3.50
1. Woman—Biography. 2. Christian biography. I. Title.

LIND, Marie. 209'.22 B
Dramatic stories for missionary programs; accounts of witnessing Christians in West Africa. Photos. by Marilyn Birch. Grand Rapids, Mich., Baker Book House [1972] 175 p. illus. 22 cm. [BR1700.2.L54] 72-93075 ISBN 0-8010-5525-3 2.95
1. Christian biography. 2. Sierra Leone—Biography.

LOCKYEAR, Herbert 209'.22
The man who changed the world; or, conquests of Christ through the centuries. Grand Rapids. Zondervan [1966] 2v. 24cm. Bibl. [BR1700.2.L6] 66-13696 9.95
1. Christian biography. I. Title.

LOCKYER, Herbert. 209'.22
The man who changed the world; or, Conquests of Christ, through the centuries. Grand Rapids, Zondervan Publ. House [1966] 2 v. 24 cm. Bibliography: v. 2, p. 427-428. [BR1700.2.L6] 66-13696
1. Christian biography. I. Title.

LUDWIG, Charles, 1918- 209'.2'2 B
Their finest hour / Charles Ludwig Elgin, Ill. : D. C. Cook Pub. Co., c1974. 108 p., [8] leaves of plates : ill. ; 18 cm. [BR1600.2.L8] 74-82112 ISBN 0-912692-45-6 : 1.95
1. Christian biography. I. Title.

MCCLENDON, James William. 209'.2'2 B
Biography as theology; how life stories can remake today's theology [by] James Wm. McClendon, Jr. Nashville, Abingdon Press [1974] 224 p. 22 cm. Includes bibliographical references. [BR118.M28] 74-9715 ISBN 0-687-03540-6 13.95; 4.95 (pbk.).
1. Theology—Methodology. 2. Christian biography. 3. Christian ethics. I. Title.

MCPHERSON, Anna Talbott. 209'.22
They dared to be different. Chicago, Moody Press [1967] 192 p. 18 cm. (Moody pocket books, 99) Contents.--Fire kindled in his soul: D. L. Moody.--Through portals of song: Ira D. Sankey.--Prince among preachers: Charles Haddon Spurgeon.--Born to suffer: Henry Martyn.--Because they knew she loved them: Capt. Catherine Booth.--Out of a gypsy camp: Gypsy Smith.--A desperate Scotsman in a desperate day: John Knox.--Neither persecution nor peril: Hester Ann (Roe) Rogers.--Sweet singer of Methodism: Charles Wesley.--In prison and she visited them: Elizabeth Gurney Fry.--To the heart: William Bramwell.--Great things for God: William Carey.--The shepherd-heart: Andrew Murray.--So valuable a life: Richard Watson.--She walked in white: Mary Bosanquet.--Beloved friend of little waifs: George Mueller.--The seeing heart: Fanny Crosby. [BR1700.2.M3] 68-3068
1. Christian biography. I. Title.

MCPHERSON, Anna Talbott. 209'.22
They dared to be different. Chicago, Moody Press [1967] 192 p. 18 cm. (Moody pocket books, 99) Contents.Contents.—Fire kindled in his soul: D. L. Moody.—Through portals of song: Ira D. Sankey.—Prince among preachers: Charles Haddon Spurgeon.—Born to suffer: Henry Martyn.—Because they knew she loved them: Capt. Catherine Booth.—Out of a gypsy camp: Gypsy Smith.—A desperate Scotsman in a desperate day: John Knox.—Neither persecution nor peril: Hester Ann (Roe) Rogers.—Sweet singer of Methodism: Charles Wesley.—In prison and she visited them: Elizabeth Gurney Fry.—To the heart: William Bramwell.—Great things for God: William Carey.—The shepherd-heart: Andrew Murray.—So valuable a life: Richard Watson.—She walked in white: Mary Bosanquet.—Beloved friend of little waifs: George Mueller.—The seeing heart: Fanny Crosby. [BR1700.2.M3] 68-3068
1. Christian biography. I. Title.

THE man who changed the world; or, Conquests of Christ, through the centuries. Grand Rapids, Zondervan Publ. House [1966] 2 v. 24 cm. Bibliography: v. 2, p. 427-428. [BR1700.2.L6] 66-13696 209'.22
1. Christian biography.

MARY ELEANOR, Mother, 1903- 209'.22
The last apostle. Illustrated by George Pollard. Milwaukee, Bruce Pub. Co. [1956] 150p. illus. 22cm. (Catholic treasury books) [BS2505.M318] 56-11154
1. Paul, Saint, apostle—Juvenile literature. I. Title.

MATTHEWS, Ronald, 1903- 209'.22 B
English messiahs; studies of six English religious pretenders, 1656-1927. New York, B. Blom, 1971. xvi, 230 p. illus., ports. 21 cm. Reprint of the 1936 ed. Contents.Contents.—James Nayler, "the Quakers' Jesus."—Joanna Southcott, "the bride of the Lamb."—Richard Brothers, "God Almighty's nephew."—John Nichols Tom, "the peasants' saviour."—Henry James Prince, John Hugh Smyth-Pigott and the "abode of love." [BR1718.A1M3 1971] 76-172553
1. Imposters and imposture—Great Britain. 2. Fanaticism. I. Title.

MODERN stories of inspiration / Bill Stephens, compiler. Nashville : Broadman Press, [1975] 127 p. ; 21 cm. [BR1700.2.M58] 74-77355 ISBN 0-8054-8418-3 : 1.95 209'.2'2 B
1. Christian biography. 2. Christian life—1960- I. Stephens, Bill.
Contents omitted.

MUGGERIDGE, Malcolm, 1903- 209'.2'2 B
A third testament / Malcolm Muggeridge. 1st ed. Boston : Little, Brown, c1976. 207 p. : ill. ; 25 cm. "A Time-Life Television book." A collection of 6 scripts of the television series: A third testament. [BR1700.2.M83] 76-1304 12.95
1. Augustinus, Aurelius, Saint, Bp of Hippo. 2. Pascal, Blaise, 1623-1662. 3. Blake, William, 1757-1827. 4. Kierkegaard, Soren Aabye, 1813-1855. 5. Tolstoi, Lev Nikolaevich, Graf, 1826-1910. 6. Bonhoeffer, Dietrich, 1906-1945. I. Title.
Contents omitted

PEABODY, Francis Greenwood, 1847-1936. 209'.22
Reminiscences of present-day saints. Freeport, N.Y., Books for Libraries Press [1972] vii, 307 p. illus. 23 cm. (Essay index reprint series) Reprint of the 1927 ed. Contents.Contents.—Ephraim Peabody.—Andrew Preston Peabody.—James Freeman Clarke.—Friedrich August Gottreu Tholuck.—Edward Everett Hale.—Charles Carroll Everett.—Alfred Tredway White.—Phillips Brooks.—Samuel Chapman Armstrong.—Henry Drummond.—Carl Hilty.—Louisa and Georgina Schuyler.—Frederic Illsley Phillips.—Charles William Eliot. [BR1700.P4 1972] 74-37525 ISBN 0-8369-2576-9
1. Christian biography. I. Title.

POLLOCK, John Charles. 209'.22 B
Victims of the long march, and other stories [by] John Pollock. Waco, Tex., Word Books [1970] 115 p. 21 cm. "These sketches first appeared either in World vision or Crusade magazines." Contents.Contents.—All my friends are but one.—Judson's darkest hour.—Friend of the slaves.—Young man with a pigtail.—He tamed the tribes.—Lord Apostol.—Stroke oar.—Cannibal Easter.—Left in Lagos.—Santa Claus of the north.—Victims of the long march.—Tuan change. [BR1700.2.P64] 79-125270 2.95
1. Christian biography. I. Title.

PRAETORIUS, Elmer Wesley, Bp. 209'.2'2
The potter and the clay. [Harrisburg, Pa., 1958] 76p. illus. 17cm. [BV4510.P68] 58-47866
1. Christian life. I. Title.

PROPHETS in the church. 209'.22
Edited by Roger Aubert. New York, Paulist Press [1968] viii, 152 p. 24 cm. (Concilium: theology in the age of renewal. Church history, v. 37) Includes articles translated from several languages by various persons. Bibliographical footnotes. [BR1702.P7] 68-57877 4.50
1. Christian biography. 2. Reformers—Biography. I. Aubert, Roger, ed. II. Series: Concilium: theology in the age of renewal, v. 37

REDDING, David A. 209'.22 B
What is the man? [By] David A. Redding. Waco, Tex., Word Books [1970] 169 p. 23 cm. Includes bibliographical references. [BS571.R37] 71-128447 4.50
1. Bible—Biography. 2. Christian biography. I. Title.

REED, Frank A., 1895- 209'.2'2 B
Lumberjack sky pilot / by Frank A. Reed. Rev. ed. Lakemont, N.Y. : North Country Books, c1976. ix, 221 p., [24] leaves of plates : ill. ; 24 cm. [BV4470.R43 1976] 77-357002 7.95
1. Church work with loggers—United States. 2. Lumbering—United States. 3. Clergy—United States—Biography. I. Title.

ROBERTSON, Edwin Hanton. 209'.2'2 B
Breakthrough / by Edwin Robertson. Belfast : Christian Journals Ltd, 1976. 141 p. ; 18 cm. Bibliography: p. 139-141. [BR1700.2.R56] 76-380407 ISBN 0-904302-20-2 : £0.90
1. Christian biography. I. Title.

ROWE, Henry Kalloch, 1869-1941. 209'.22
Modern pathfinders of Christianity; the lives and deeds of seven centuries of Christian leaders. Freeport, N.Y., Books for Libraries Press [1968] 253 p. 23 cm. (Essay index reprint series) Reprint of the 1928 ed. [BR1700.R65 1968] 68-16973
1. Christian biography. I. Title.

ROWLAND, Benjamin Jr. 209.22
Men for others. New York, Friendship [c.1965] 175p. 21cm. [BR1700.2.R6] 65-11439 1.95 pap.,

1. Christian biography. I. Title.

RUSSELL, Arthur James. 209'.22 B
Their religion, by Arthur J. Russell. Freeport, N.Y., Books for Libraries Press [1971, c1935] ix, 352 p. 23 cm. (Essay index reprint series) The religious belief of Abraham Lincoln, Robert Burns, Marshal Foch, Gladstone, Napoleon, Disraeli, Nelson, Dickens, Washington, Livingstone, Cromwell, Darwin, Shakespeare and Jesus of Nazareth. [BR1700.R8 1971] 78-128308 ISBN 0-8369-2131-3
1. Christian biography. I. Title.

SMART, William James, 1895- 209.22
Profiles in Christian commitment, by W. J. Smart. Cleveland, World Pub. Co. [1965, c1961] 196 p. 21 cm. First published in London in 1961 under title: Miracles of achievement. [BR1702.S6 1965] 65-5072
1. Christian biography. I. Title.

SNYDER, Richard L 209'.22
Reuel makes a decision. Illustrated by Shirley Hirsch. Boston, United Church Press [c1963] 96 p. col. illus. 23 cm. [BS551.2.S6] 64-1709
1. Bible stories, English — N.T. I. Title.

SPALDING, Arthur Whitefield, 1877-1954. 209'.22
Wonder tales of the Bible. Illustrated by Herbert Rudeen. Washington, Review and Herald Pub. Association, 1963- v. col. illus. 30 cm. [BS551.S692] 63-17758
1. Bible stories, English. I. Title.

SPEER, Robert Elliott, 1867-1947. 209'.22
Some great leaders in the world movement. Freeport, N.Y., Books for Libraries Press [1967] 295 p. 22 cm. (The Cole lectures, 1911) "First published 1911." Essay index reprint series. [BR1703.S7 1967] 67-26786
1. Christian biography. I. Title. II. Series: The Cole lectures. Vanderbilt University, 1911
:Contents omitted

SPEER, Robert Elliott, 1867-1947. 209'.22
Some great leaders in the world movement. Freeport, N.Y., Books for Libraries Press [1967] 295 p. 22 cm. (The Cole lectures, 1911) (Essay index reprint series) "First published 1911." Contents.Contents.—Raymond Lull, the Christian crusader and his conquest.—William Carey, the Christian pioneer and his problems.—Alexander Duff, the Christian student and the world's education. —George Bowen, the Christian mystic and the ascetic ideal.—John Lawrence, the Christian statesman and the problem of religion and politics.—Charles George Gordon, the Christian knight errant and the power of pure devotion. [BR1703.S7 1967] 67-26786
1. Christian biography. I. Title. II. Series: The Cole lectures. Vanderbilt University, 1911.

STRAHAN, Thomas W. 209'.2'2 B
Retainer from the Lord / by Thomas W. Strahan. Lake Mills, Iowa : Graphic Pub. Co., c1976. viii, 126 p. : ports. ; 21 cm. Bibliography: p. 123-126. [BR569.S87] 76-42134 ISBN 0-89279-003-2 pbk. : 2.95
1. Christian biography—United States. 2. Lawyers—United States—Biography. I. Title.

TALLACH, John. 209'.2'2 B
God made them great / John Tallach ; illustrated by Lawrence Littleton Evans. Edinburgh ; Carlisle, Pa. : Banner of Truth Trust, 1974. viii, 135 p. : ill. ; 22 cm. [BR1700.2.T34] 74-185858 ISBN 0-85151-190-2 : £1.25
1. Annan, Robert, 1834-1867. 2. Brainerd, David, 1718-1747. 3. Bray, William, 1794-1868. 4. Kuhn, Isobel. 5. Muller, George, 1805-1898. I. Title.

THOMAS, Reuen, 1840-1907. 209'.2'2 B
Leaders of thought in the modern church. Freeport, N.Y., Books for Libraries Press [1972] 191 p. 23 cm. (Essay index reprint series) Reprint of the 1892 ed. Contents.Contents.—Jonathan Edwards.—William Ellery Channing.—John Henry Newman.—Thomas Chalmers.—Frederick W. Robertson.—Emanuel Swedenborg.—Horace Bushnell.—Frederick Denison Maurice. [BR1700.T5 1972] 72-8559 ISBN 0-8369-7333-X
1. Christian biography. I. Title.

TILLEY, Ethel. 209'.22
Book of the ages; a course for junior high groups in the vacation church school. Teacher's book. Rev. ed. New York, Published for the Cooperative Publication Association by Abingdon Press [1962] 110 p. illus. 23 cm. (The Cooperative series: vacation church school texts) [BS605.T55 1962] 62-10417
1. Bible—Study—Text-books. 2. Vacation schools, Religious—Text-books. I. Title.

TILTMAN, Marjorie (Hand) Hessell. 209'.22
God's adventures, by Marjorie H. Tiltman. Freeport, N.Y., Books for Libraries Press [1968] 317 p. illus., ports. 23 cm. (Essay index reprint series) Reprint of the 1933 ed. [BV3700.T53 1968] 68-16979
1. Christian biography. 2. Missionaries. I. Title.

TOWNS, Elmer L. 209'.2'2 B
The Christian Hall of Fame / Elmer L. Towns ; [introd. by Harold Henniger]. Rev. ed. Grand Rapids : Baker Book House, c1975. 247 p. : ports. ; 22 cm. [BR1700.2.T68 1975] 76-353728 pbk. : 3.95
1. Christian biography. I. Title.

VOS, Catherine Frances (Smith) 209'.22
The child's story Bible, by Catherine F. Vos. Rev. by Marianne Catherine Vos Radius. Illus. and maps by Betty Beeby. [4th ed. Grand Rapids] Eerdmans [1966] xx, 436 p. col. illus., col. maps. 27 cm. [BS551.V72 1966] 66-30329
1. Bible stories, English. I. Radius, Marianne Catherine (Vos) ed. II. Beeby, Betty, illus. III. Title.

WALKER, Williston, 1860-1922. 209'.22
Great men of the Christian church. Freeport, N.Y., Books for Libraries Press [1968] 378 p. 23 cm. (Essay index reprint series) Reprint of the 1908 ed. Contents.Contents.—Justin Martyr.—Tertullian.—Athanasius.—Augustine.—Patrick.—Benedict.—Hildebrand.—Godfrey.—Francis.— Thomas Aquinas.—John Wiclif.—Martin Luther.—John Calvin.—John Knox.—Ignatius Loyola.—George Fox.—Nicolaus Ludwig von Zinzendorf.—John Wesley.—Jonathan Edwards.—Horace Bushnell. Includes bibliographies. [BR1700.W3 1968] 68-8502
1. Christian biography. I. Title.

WALLACE, Archer, 1884- 209'.22
The religious faith of great men. Freeport, N.Y., Books for Libraries Press [1967] 217 p. 22 cm. (Essay index reprint series) Reprint of the 1934 ed. Bibliography: p. [v]-[vii] [BR1702.W3] 67-26792
1. Christian biography. I. Title.

WALLACE, Archer, 1884- 209'.22
The religious faith of great men. Freeport, N.Y., Books for Libraries Press [1967] 217 p. 22 cm. (Essay index reprint series) Reprint of the 1934 ed. Bibliography: p. [v]-[vii] [BR1702.W3 1967] 67-26792
1. Christian biography. I. Title.

WARNER, Gary. 209'.22
The home team wears white; unsung All-Americans on the number one team. Grand Rapids, Mich., Zondervan Pub. House [1969] 152 p. ports. 21 cm. (A Zondervan paperback) [BR1702.W34] 70-82800 0.95 (pbk)
1. Christian biography. 2. Athletes, American—Biography. I. Title.

YONGE, Charlotte Mary, 1823-1901. 209'.22
Child's Bible reader; stories from the Old and New Testaments told for 52 Sabbaths of the year. Rev. ed. Nashville, Southwestern Co., 1957. 260p. illus. 24cm. Published in 1898 under title: Aunt Charlotte's stories of Bible history for young disciples. [BS551.Y6 1957] 57-10196
1. Bible stories, English. I. Title.

CLARK, Miles Morton, 1920- 209'.2'4 B
Glenn Clark : his life and writings / Miles Clark. Nashville : Abingdon Press, [1975] 160 p. ; 19 cm. "Writings of Glenn Clark": p. 158-160. [BX9225.C549C5] 75-6877 ISBN 0-687-14810-3 pbk. : 3.95
1. Clark, Glenn, 1882-1956. 2. Meditations. I. Clark, Glenn, 1882-1956.

COOK, David C., 1912- 209'.2'4 B
Invisible halos / David C. Cook. Elgin, Il. : D. C. Cook Pub. Co., [1975] 159 p. ; 18 cm. [BR1725.C59A33] 74-17732 ISBN 0-912692-40-5 : 1.50
1. Cook, David C., 1912- I. Title.

COOK, David C., 1912- 209'.2'4 B
Invisible halos / David C. Cook. Elgin, Il. : D. C. Cook Pub. Co., [1975] 159 p. ; 18 cm. [BR1725.C59A33] 74-17732 ISBN 0-912692-40-5 pbk. : 1.50
1. Cook, David C., 1912- I. Title.

GREEN, Henry Gordon, 1912- 209.24
The faith of our father, by H. Gordon Green. [1st ed.] New York., Dutton, 1966. 218p. 21cm. [BR1725.G84G7] 66-25129 4.50 bds.,
1. Green, Henry, 1883- I. Title.

HIEBERT, Paul Gerhardt, 1892- 209'.2'4 B
Doubting castle / Paul Hiebert. Winnipeg : Queenston House, c1976. 120 p. ; 24 cm. [BR1725.H456A33] 77-366899 ISBN 0-919866-15-8
1. Hiebert, Paul Gerhardt, 1892- 2. Christian biography—Manitoba. I. Title.

HILL, Harold, 1905- 209'.2'4 B
How to live like a king's kid / by Harold Hill ; as told to Irene Burk Harrell. Plainfield, N.J. : Logos International, c1974. xvi, 213 p. ; 22 cm. [BR1725.H47A33] 73-93002 ISBN 0-88270-086-3 : 5.95. ISBN 0-88270-083-9 pbk. : 2.95
1. Hill, Harold, 1905- 2. Christian life—1960- I. Harrell, Irene Burk. II. Title.

KOONTZ, Bessie B., 1893- 209'.24 B
Trails through God's back pastures, by Bessie B. Koontz. Philadelphia, Dorrance [1968] 171 p. 22 cm. Autobiographical. [BR1725.K66A3] 68-22807 4.00
I. Title.

MACGREGOR, William Malcolm, 1861-1944. 209'.2'4 B
Persons and ideals; addresses to my students and others. Freeport, N.Y., Books for Libraries Press [1973] p. (Essay index reprint series) Reprint of the 1939 ed. published by T. & T. Clark, Edinburgh. [BR1700.M254 1973] 73-5626 ISBN 0-518-10116-9
1. Christian biography. 2. Theology—Addresses, essays, lectures. I. Title.

MULLINGS, Gwendolyn Lydia, 1928- 209'.2'4 B
My pilgrim journey : the making of an evangelist / by Gwendolyn Lydia Mullings. New York : William-Frederick Press, 1976. 91 p. ; 22 cm. [BX8809.M84A35] 76-47764 ISBN 0-87164-035-X : 3.50
1. Mullings, Gwedolyn Lydia, 1928- 2. Plymouth Brethren in New York (City)—Biography. 3. New York (City)—Biography. I. Title.

ROGERS, Dale Evans. 209'.2'4 B
Trials, tears, and triumph / Dale Evans Rogers. Old Tappan, N.J. : F. H. Revell Co., c1977. 128 p., [4] leaves of plates : ill. ; 21 cm. [BR1725.R63A324] 76-51293 ISBN 0-8007-0847-4 : 4.95
1. Rogers, Dale Evans. 2. Christian biography—California. I. Title.

STAGAARD, George Hansen. 209'.2'4 B
Pursuer or pursued [incidents from my life, by George Hansen Stagaard as told through P. P. W. New York, Loizeaux Bros., 1954?] 31 p. 17 cm. (Treasury of truth, no. 200) Cover title. [BR1725.S73A33] 75-304115
1. Stagaard, George Hansen. I. P. P. W. II. W., P. P. III. Title. IV. Series.

JAEGER, Werner Wilhelm, 1888-1961. 209.38
Early Christianity and Greek paideia. Cambridge, Belknap Press of Harvard University Press, 1961. 154 p. 22 cm. Includes bibliography. [BR128.G8J3] 61-15275
1. Christianity and other religions—Greek. 2. Hellenism. 3. Education, Greek. 4. Greece—Religion. I. Title.

WESTCOTT, Brooke Foss, Bp. of Durham, 1825-1901. 209'.4
Essays in the history of religious thought in the West. Freeport, N.Y., Books for Libraries Press [1972] p. (Essay index reprint series) Reprint of the 1891 ed. [BL690.W5 1972] 72-8480 ISBN 0-8369-7338-0
1. Whichcote, Benjamin, 1609-1683. 2. Europe—Religion. 3. Philosophy and religion. I. Title.

BRADLEY, Ian C. 209'.41
The call to seriousness : the evangelical impact on the Victorians / Ian Bradley. London : Cape, 1976. 224 p., [4] leaves of plates : ports. ; 23 cm. Includes index. Bibliography: p. 215-218. [BX5125.B68 1976b] 76-370418 ISBN 0-224-01162-6 : £4.95
1. Evangelicalism—Church of England. 2. England—Civilization—19th century. I. Title.

BRADLEY, Ian C. 209'.41
The call to seriousness : the Evangelical impact on the Victorians / Ian Bradley. 1st American ed. New York : Macmillan, 1976. 224 p., [4] leaves of plates : ill. ; 23 cm. Includes bibliographical references and index. [BX5125.B68 1976] 75-44282 ISBN 0-02-514420-0 : 9.95
1. Evangelicalism—Church of England. 2. England—Civilization—19th century. I. Title.

WILSON, Ron, 1932- 209'.416
A flower grows in Ireland / Ron Wilson. Elgin, Ill. : D. C. Cook Pub. Co., c1976. xiv, 144 p., [2] leaves of plates : ill. ; 22 cm. Bibliography: p. 144. [BX4839.W54] 75-18646 ISBN 0-912692-78-2 : 3.95
1. Protestants in Northern Ireland. 2. Catholics in Northern Ireland. 3. Northern Ireland—History—1969- I. Title.

COCKSHUT, A. O. J. 209.42
The unbelievers; English agnostic thought, 1840-1890 [by] A. O. J. Cockshut. [New York] New York University Press, 1966 [c1964] 191 p. 22 cm. [BR759.C603] 66-13549
1. Religious thought—England. 2. Religious thought—19th cent. I. Title.

CRAGG, Gerald Robertson. 209'.42
Freedom and authority : a study of English thought in the early seventeenth century / by Gerald R. Cragg. Philadelphia : Westminster Press, [1975] 334 p. ; 23 cm. Includes index. Bibliography: p. 303-323. [BR757.C85] 75-4946 ISBN 0-664-20738-3 : 12.50
1. Authority (Religion)—History. 2. Liberty—History. 3. England—Intellectual life—17th century. 4. Catholics in England. 5. Religious thought—England. I. Title.

PRISM (LONDON) 209.42
Prismatics; edited by Christopher Martin. London, Hodder & Stoughton [1966] 123 p. 18 cm. 6/- (B 66-1046) Articles reprinted from Prism, 1958-1965. [BR743.2.P7] 66-70566
1. Gt. Brit.—Religion—Addresses, essays, lectures. I. Martin, Christopher, ed. II. Title.

CHRISTLICH-DEMOKRATISCHE Union (Germany (Democratic Republic)). 209.431
Christians and the Church in the German Democratic Republic. Dresden, Verlag Zeit im Bild [1969?] 38 p. illus. 20 cm. Published by the Secretariat of the Central Executive Committee of the Christian Democratic Union of Germany. Translation of: Christen und Kirchen in der Deutschen Demokratischen Republik. [BR856.35.C4713] 79-585738 2.75M
1. Church and state in Germany (Democratic Republic, 1949-) 2. Christianity—Germany (Democratic Republic, 1949-) I. Title.

LOCHMAN, Jan Milic. 209'.437
Church in a Marxist society; a Czechoslovak view. [1st ed.] New York, Harper & Row [1970] 198 p. 22 cm. [BX4854.C9L6 1970b] 77-85067 5.95
1. Protestant churches—Czechoslovak Republic. 2. Communism and Christianity—Czechoslovak Republic. I. Title.

CHARLTON, Donald Geoffrey. 209.44
Secular religions in France, 1815-1870. London, New York, Published for the University of Hull by the Oxford University Press, 1963. 249 p. 23 cm. (University of Hull publications) [BR843.C48 1963] 63-5127
1. Sects — France. 2. France — Religion. 3. Philosophy, French. I. Title.

CHARLTON, Donald Geoffrey 209.44
Secular religions in France, 1815-1870. New York, Pub. for the Univ. of Hull v)by Oxford [c.1963] 249p. 23cm. (Univ. of Hull pubns.) Bibl. 63-5127 5.60
1. Sects—France. 2. France—Religion. 3. Philosophy, French. I. Title.

GARRETT, Clarke, 1935- 209'.44
Respectable folly : millenarians and the French Revolution in France and England / Clarke Garrett. Baltimore : Johns Hopkins University Press, [1975] x, 237 p. ; 23 cm. Includes bibliographical references and index. [BR845.G36] 74-24378 ISBN 0-8018-1618-1 : 10.00
1. Millennialism—France. 2. Millennialism—England. 3. France—History—Revolution. I. Title.

GOLDSTEIN, Doris S. 209'.44
Trial of faith : religion and politics in Tocqueville's thought / Doris S. Goldstein. New York : Elsevier, [1975] xi, 144 p. ; 24 cm. Includes index. Bibliography: p. 133-139. [BR115.P7G59] 75-4753 ISBN 0-444-99001-1 : 10.00
1. Tocqueville, Alexis Charles Henri Maurice Clerel de, 1805-1859. 2. Christianity and politics—History. 3. France—Religion. 4. France—Politics and government. 5. United States—Religion. 6. Religions. I. Title.

CHRISTIAN, William A., 1944- 209'.46'1
Person and God in a Spanish valley [by] William A. Christian, Jr. New York, Seminar Press, 1972. xiii, 215 p. illus. 24 cm. (Studies in social discontinuity) Bibliography: p. 195-198. [BR1027.N36C56 1972] 72-7697 ISBN 0-12-816150-7 8.95
1. Nansa Valley, Spain—Religious life and customs. I. Title. II. Series.

ARMSTRONG, O. K. 209.47
Religion can conquer communism, by O. K. Armstrong and Marjorie Moore Armstrong. London, New York, Nelson [1964] 258 p. 21 cm. Bibliography: p. 246-250. [HX536.A72] 64-25280

1. Communism and religion. I. Armstrong, Marjorie Moore, joint author. II. Title.

ARMSTRONG, O. K. 209.47
Religion can conquer communism, by O. K. Armstrong, Marjorie Moore Armstrong. New York, Nelson [c.1964] 258p. 21cm. Bibl. 64-25280 4.95
1. Communism and religion. I. Armstrong, Marjorie Moore, joint author. II. Title.

BERDIAEV, Nikolai 209.47
Aleksandrovich, 1874-1948.
The Russian revolution. [Ann Arbor] University of Michigan Press [1961] 91 p. 21 cm. (Ann Arbor paperbacks for the study of communism and Marxism. AA55) [BR936.B44 1961] 61-42468
1. Church and state in Russia—1917- 2. Russia—Religion—1917- 3. Communism—Russia. I. Title.

BRAUN, Leopold L S 209.47
Religion in Russia, from Lenin to Khrushchev; an uncensored account. Paterson, N. J., St. Anthony Guild Press [1959] 88p. 18cm. [BR936.B67] 59-35890
1. Russia—Religion—1917- I. Title.

DEYNEKA, Anita. 209'.47
Christians in the shadow of the Kremlin / Anita and Peter Deyneka, Jr. Elgin, Il. : D. C. Cook Pub. Co., c1974. 96 p., [8] leaves of plates : ill. ; 18 cm. [BR936.D38] 74-17730 ISBN 0-912692-48-0 : 1.50
1. Russia—Religious life and customs. I. Deyneka, Peter, 1931- joint author. II. Title.

GOULD, Alfred Ernest. 209.47
Changed men of our time; the Damascus Road in the twentieth century, by A. E. Gould. Derby, P. Smith, 1964. xii, 102 p. 19 cm. [BV4930.G64] 67-8481
1. Converts. I. Title.

KLINE, George Louis, 209'.47
1921-
Religious and anti-religious thought in Russia [by] George L. Kline Chicago, University of Chicago Press [1968] 179 p. 21 cm. (The Weil lectures) Bibliographical footnotes. [BR936.K55] 68-54484
1. Religious thought—Russia—19th century. 2. Religious thought—Russia—20th century. 3. Atheism—Russia. I. Title. II. Series.

KOLARZ, Walter. 209.47
Religion in the Soviet Union. [New York] St. Martin's Press, 1961 [i. e. 1962] xii, 518 p. illus., ports., maps, facsims. 23 cm. Bibliographical footnotes. [BR936.K58 1962] 62-323
1. Russia—Religion—1917- 2. Russia—Church history—1917- I. Title.

KORCHMARYK, Franko 209'.47
Bohdan.
Christianization of the European East and messianic aspirations of Moscow as the "Third Rome" [by] Frank B. Kortschmaryk. Toronto, New York, Studium Research Institute, 1971. 56 p. maps. 22 cm. "Shevchenko Scientific Society, no. 10." Bibliography: p. 42-44. [BR738.6.K66] 72-193577
1. Europe, Eastern—Church history. 2. Monasticism and religious orders—Europe, Eastern. 3. Moscow—History. I. Title.

NOBLE, John H 209.47
I found God in Soviet Russia, by John Noble and Glenn D. Everett. With an introd. by Billy Graham. New York, St. Martin's Press [1959] 192p. 22cm. [BV4935.N56A3] 58-13054
1. Converts. 2. Vorkuta, Russia. 3. Christians in Russia. I. Everett, Glenn. II. Title.

NOBLE, John H. 209'.47
I found God in Soviet Russia, by John Noble and Glenn D. Everett. With an introd. by Billy Graham. Grand Rapids, Zondervan Pub. House [1972, c1959] 192 p. 18 cm. (Zondervan books) [BV4935.N56A3 1972] 70-156258 0.95 (pbk)
1. Converts, Protestant. 2. Vorkuta, Russia. 3. Christians in Russia. I. Everett, Glenn D. II. Title.

PARSONS, Howard L. 209'.47
Christianity in the Soviet Union, by Howard L. Parsons. [New York, American Institute for Marxist Studies, 1972] 72 p. 21 cm. (American Institute for Marxist Studies. Occasional paper no. 11) Cover title. Includes bibliographical references. [BR936.P35] 72-195211 2.00
1. Christianity—Russia. I. Title. II. Series.

PASCAL, Pierre, 1890- 209'.47
The religion of the Russian people / P. Pascal ; translated by Rowan Williams. London : Mowbrays, 1976. ix, 130 p. ; 22 cm. Translation of La religion du peuple russe, being v. 2 of the author's Civilisation paysanne en Russie. Includes bibliographical references. [BR932.P37213 1976b] 76-374983 £2.95
1. Russia—Religion. 2. Persecution—Russia. I. Title.

SCHEFFBUCH, Winrich. 209'.47
Christians under the hammer & sickle. Translated from the German by Mark A. Noll. Grand Rapids, Zondervan Pub. House [1974] 214 p. illus. 21 cm. [BR1608.R85S3413] 73-13077 2.95 (pbk.).
1. Persecution—Russia—History—Sources. 2. Sects—Russia—History—Sources. I. Title.

ZERNOV, Nicolas. 209'.47
Three Russian prophets: Khomiakov, Dostoevsky, Soloviev. 3d ed., with a pref. by the author. [Gulf Breeze, Fla.] Academic International Press, 1973. xiii, 8-171 p. ports. 24 cm. (Russian series, v. 23) "The basis of a course of lectures ... delivered at the School of Slavonic Studies in Oxford and London in 1942." Bibliography: p. [169]-171. [BX595.Z4 1973] 72-97040 ISBN 0-87569-050-5
1. Khomiakov, Aleksei Stepanovich, 1804-1860. 2. Dostoevskii, Fedor Mikhailovich, 1821-1881. 3. Solov'ev, Vladimir Sergeevich, 1853-1900. 4. Religious thought—Russia. I. Title.

SPINKA, Matthew, 1890- 209'.496
A history of Christianity in the Balkans; a study in the spread of Byzantine culture among the Slavs. [Hamden, Conn.] Archon Books, 1968 [c1933] 202 p. 23 cm. Bibliography: p. 189-191. [BR737.S6S6 1968] 68-20379
1. Orthodox Eastern Church—History. 2. Slavs, Southern—Church history. I. Title. II. Title: Christianity in the Balkans.

CLARKE, James Franklin, 209'.4977
1906-
Bible societies, American missionaries, and the national revival of Bulgaria [by] James F. Clarke. New York, Arno Press, 1971. 358 p. 24 cm. (The Eastern Europe collection) Reprint of the author's thesis, Harvard, 1937. Bibliography: p. 309-358. [DR83.C57 1971] 71-135841 ISBN 0-405-02783-4
1. Bible—Publication and distribution—Societies, etc. 2. Bulgaria—History—1393-1878. 3. Missions—Bulgaria. I. Title.

THE Church in Asia / 209'.5
edited by Donald E. Hoke. Chicago : Moody Press, [1975, i.e.1976] p. cm. Includes bibliographies and index. [BR1065.C45] 75-11879 ISBN 0-8024-1543-1 : 12.95
1. Christianity—Asia. 2. Asia—History. 3. Asia—Religion. I. Hoke, Donald E.

FORMAN, Charles W., ed. 209'.5
Christianity in the non-Western world. Edited by Charles W. Forman. Freeport, N.Y., Books for Libraries Press [1970, c1967] viii, 146 p. map. 23 cm. (Essay index reprint series) Bibliography: p. 143-146. [BR1065.F6 1970] 71-117792
1. Christianity—Asia. 2. Christianity—Africa. I. Title.

CRAWFORD, Don, 1929- 209'.51
Inside the wall. Wheaton, Ill., Tyndale House Publishers [1973] 86 p. illus. 18 cm. Short stories. [BV3415.2.C7] 72-97650 ISBN 0-8423-1650-7 1.25 (pbk.)
1. Christians in China. 2. China—Politics and government—1949- I. Title.

LIU, Kwang-Ching, 1921- 209'.51
ed.
American missionaries in China; papers from Harvard seminars. Edited and with an introd. by Kwang-Ching Liu. [Cambridge] East Asian Research Center, Harvard University, distributed by Harvard University Press, 1966. Seven articles by Harvard seminar students previously published in the annual volumes of Papers on China, 1955-1964. Includes bibliographical references. [BV3415.L55] 66-31226
1. Missions, American — Addresses, essays, lectures. 2. Missions — China — Addresses, essays, lectures. I. Title.

MOULE, Arthur 209'.51
Christopher, 1873-1957.
Christians in China before the year 1550 / by A. C. Moule. New York : Octagon Books, 1977. xvi, 293 p., [11] leaves of plates : ill. (5 fold.) ; 23 cm. Reprint of the 1930 ed. published by the Society for Promoting Christian Knowledge, London. Includes bibliographical references and index. [BR1285.M6 1977] 77-21996 ISBN 0-374-95972-2 lib.bdg. : 14.50
1. Christians in China. 2. China—Church history. 3. Missions—China. I. Title.

YANG, Ch'ing-k'un, 1910- 209.51
Religion in Chinese society; a study of contemporary social functions of religion and some of their historical factors. Berkeley, University of California Press, 1961. viii, 473 p. 24 cm. Bibliography: p. 423-434. [BL1802.Y3 1961] 61-7520
1. China—Religious life and customs. 2. China—Social conditions.

*DRESSMAN, Robert C. 209.52
Japan in five hours; a study on the land, the people, traditional religions, new religions, the church, and current events [2d ed.] Cincinnati, CSMS Pr., 5100 Shattuc Ave. [c.1965] 54p. illus., map. 22cm. (Catholic student's mission crusade 5 hr. ser.) .90 pap.,
I. Title.

DRUMMOND, Richard Henry. 209'.52
A history of Christianity in Japan. Grand Rapids, Mich., W. B. Eerdmans Pub. Co. [1971] 397 p. map. 20 cm. (Christian world mission books) Bibliography: p. 367-375. [BV3445.2.D75] 70-78022 4.95
1. Missions—Japan. 2. Japan—Church history. I. Title.

HAMMER, Raymond 209.52
Japan's religious ferment; Christian presence amid faiths old and new. New York, Oxford, 1962 [c.1961] 207p. (Christian presence ser.) Bibl. 62-662 2.95 bds.,
1. Japan—Religion. 2. Christianity and other religions. I. Title.

MCFARLAND, Horace Neill, 209.52
1923-
The rush hour of the gods; a study of new religious movements in Japan [by] H. Neill McFarland. New York, Macmillan [c. 1967] xvi. 267p. 21cm. Bibl. [BL2202.M25] 67-10576 5.95
1. Japan—Religion—20th cent. I. Title.

SCHEINER, Irwin. 209'.52
Christian converts and social protest in Meiji Japan. Berkeley, University of California Press, 1970. x, 268 p. 23 cm. Bibliography: p. 256-262. [BR1307.S34 1970] 74-94981 6.50
1. Christianity—Japan. 2. Japan—Social conditions.

CONFERENCE on Religion in 209.54
South Asia, University of California, Berkeley, 1961.
Religion in South Asia; [papers] Edited by Edward B. Harper. Seattle, University of Washington Press, 1964. 199 p. illus. 26 cm. Previously published in a special supplementary issue of the Journal of Asian Studies. Includes bibliographies. [BL1055.C6 1961aa] 64-23197
1. South Asia—Religious life and customs. I. Harper, Edward B., ed. II. California. University. III. Title.

STEWART, William 209.54
India's religious frontier; Christian presence amid modern Hinduism. Introd. by M.A.C. Warren. Philadelphia, Fortress [1965, c.1964] 183p. 19cm. [BR128.H5S7] 65-19196 2.50 bds.,
1. Christianity and other religions—Hinduism. 2. Hinduism—Relations—Christianity. 3. Missions—India. I. Title.

WEBSTER, John C. B., 209'.54'2
1935-
The Christian Community and change in nineteenth century north India / John C. B. Webster. Delhi : Macmillan Co. of India, 1976. xii, 293 p. : maps ; 22 cm. Revision of the author's thesis, University of Pennsylvania, 1971. Includes index. Bibliography: p. [275]-286. [BR1170.P86W42 1976] 76-900837 Rs65.00
1. Christianity—Punjab—History. 2. Christianity—Uttar Pradesh—History. I. Title.

WEINER, Herbert Abraham, 209.5694
1919-
The wild goats of Ein Gedi; a journal of religious encounters in the Holy Land. Garden City, N. Y., Doubleday, 1961 [c.1954-1961] 312p. 61-12601 4.50
1. Israel—Religion. I. Title.

WEINER, Herbert Abraham, 209.5694
1919
The wild goats of Ein Gedi; a journal of religious encounters in the Holy Land. Cleveland, World [1963] 312p. 21cm. (Meridian bks., JP31; Jewish Pubn. Soc. of Amer.) 1.95 pap.,
1. Israel—Religion. I. Title.

ANDERSON, Gerald H. 209'.59
Christ and crisis in Southeast Asia, edited by Gerald H. Anderson. New York, Friendship Press [1968] 176 p. map. 19 cm. Includes bibliographical references. [BR1178.A5] 68-14057
1. Christianity—Asia, Southeastern. I. Title.

COOLEY, Frank L. 209'.598
Indonesia: church & society, by Frank L. Cooley. New York, Friendship Press [1968] 128 p. 23 cm. Bibliography: p. 128. [BR1220.C66] 68-54899
1. Christianity—Indonesia. 2. Indonesia. I. Title.

BARRETT, David B. 209'.6
Schism and renewal in Africa; an analysis of six thousand contemporary religious movements [by] David B. Barrett. Nairobi, Oxford Univ. Pr., 1968. xx, 363p. illus., fold. col. map (in pocket), ports. 22cm. Bibl. [BR1360.B37] 68-133480 5.50 pap.,
1. Christianity—Africa. 2. Nativistic movements—Africa. I. Title.
Order from the publisher's New York office

HASTINGS, Adrian. 209'.6
African Christianity / Adrian Hastings. New York : Seabury Press, [1977] p. cm. "A Crossroad book." Includes index. Bibliography: p. [BR1360.H3] 77-1890 ISBN 0-8164-0336-8 : 6.95
1. Christianity—Africa. I. Title.

INTERNATIONAL African 209.6
Seminar. 3d, Salisbury, Southern Rhodesia, 1960.
African systems of thought; studies presented and discussed at the third International African Seminar in Salisbury, December, 1960. Pref. by M. Fortes and G. Dieterlen. London, New York, Published for the International African Institute by the Oxford University Press, 1965. viii, 392 p. 23 cm. Includes bibliographies. [BL2400.I5 1960] 65-2218
1. Africa — Religion — Congresses. I. Title.

INTERNATIONAL African 209.6
Seminar. 3d, Salisbury, Southern Rhodesia, 1960
African systems of thought; studies presented and discussed at the 3d Intl. African Seminar in Salisbury, December, 1960. Pref. by M. Fortes, G. Dieterlen. New York, Pub. for the Intl. African Inst. by Oxford [c.]1965. viii, 392p. 23cm. Bibl. [BL2400.I5] 65-2218 8.00
1. Africa—Religion—Congresses. I. Title.

INTERNATIONAL African 209'.6
Seminar, 7th University of Ghana 1965
Christianity in tropical Africa: studies presented and discussed at the seventh International African Seminar, University of Ghana, April 1965; ed., introd. by C. G. Baeta. Foreword by Daryll Forde. London, published for the Intl. African Inst. by the Oxford Univ. Pr. 1968. xiii, 449p. 23cm. Resumes in French. Bibl. [BR1360.I5 1965] 68-115427 8.80
1. Christianity—Africa. Sub-Saharan. I. Baeta, C. G. ed. II. Ghana. University, Legon. III. International African Institute. IV. Title.
Available from the publisher's New York office.

PAYNE, Denis, ed. 209.6
African independence and Christian freedom; addresses delivered at Makerere University College, Uganda, in 1962. London, Oxford University Press, 1965. 89 p. 19 cm. (A Three crowns book) Includes bibliographical references. [BR1360.P3] 66-5878
1. Religion and state—Africa. 2. Christianity—Africa. I. Title.

TAYLOR, John Vernon, 1914- 209.6
The primal vision; Christian presence amid African religion. Introd. by M. A. C. Warren. Philadelphia, Fortress [1964, c.1963] 212p. 20cm. On cover: Christian presence amid African religion. Bibl. 64-11228 3.25 bds.,
1. Missions—Africa, Sub-Saharan. 2. Africa, Sub-Saharan—Religious life and customs. I. Title. II. Title: Christian presence amid African religion.

COOLEY, John K., 1927- 209.61
Baal, Christ, and Mohammed; religion and revolution in North Africa [by] John K. Cooley. With maps by Charles McDonnell. [1st ed.] New York, Holt, Rinehart and Winston [1965] xiv, 369 p. maps. 22 cm. Bibliography: p. 348-353. [BL2462.C6] 64-21922
1. Africa, North—Religion. 2. Missions—Africa, North. 3. Islam—Africa, North—History. I. Title.

THEMES in the Christian 209'.67
history of Central Africa / edited by T. O. Ranger and John Weller. Berkeley : University of California Press, 1975. xvi, 285 p., [4] leaves of plates : ill. ; 25 cm. Includes bibliographical references and indexes. [BR1450.T46] 73-83051 ISBN 0-520-02536-9 : 16.50
1. Christianity—Africa, Southern. 2. Africa, Southern—Religion. I. Ranger, Terence O. II. Weller, John C.

WELBOURN, Frederick 209'.67
Burkewood.
East African Christian [by] F. B. Welbourn. London, Oxford University Press, 1965. vi, 226 p. illus. 19 cm. (The Students' library 4) Bibliography: p. 214-218. [BR1440.W44] 75-303856

1. Christianity—Africa, Eastern. I. Title.

HAGEMAN, Alice L., comp. 209.7291
Religion in Cuba today; a new church in a new society. Edited by Alice L. Hageman and Philip E. Wheaton. New York, Association Press [1971] 317 p. 21 cm. Includes bibliographical references. [BL2530.C9H3] 73-152895 ISBN 0-8096-1823-0 7.95
1. Cuba—Religion. I. Wheaton, Philip E., joint comp. II. Title.

AGAINST the world for the 209'.73
world : the Hartford appeal and the future of American religion / edited by Peter L. Berger and Richard John Neuhaus. New York : Seabury Press, c1976. ix, 164 p. ; 22 cm. "A Crossroad book." Includes bibliographical references. [BR526.A33] 75-42142 ISBN 0-8164-0286-8 : 7.95. ISBN 0-8164-2121-8 pbk. : 3.95
1. Appeal for theological affirmation. 2. United States—Religion—1945- —Congresses. 3. Christianity—20th century—Congresses. I. Berger, Peter L. II. Neuhaus, Richard John. III. An Appeal for theological affirmation. 1976.

ALBANESE, Catherine L. 209'.73
Sons of the fathers : the civil religion of the American Revolution / Catherine L. Albanese. Philadelphia : Temple University Press, 1976. xiv, 274 p. ; 23 cm. Includes bibliographical references and index. [E209.A4] 76-17712 ISBN 0-87722-073-5 : 12.50
1. United States—History—Revolution, 1775-1783—Religious aspects. I. Title.

AMERICAN Academy of 209.73
Political and Social Science, Philadelphia.
Religion in American society. Special editor: Richard D. Lambert. Philadelphia, 1960. viii, 220p. illus. 24cm. (Its Annals, v. 332) Bibliographical footnotes. [H1.A4 vol. 332] 60-51981
1. U. S.—Religion. I. Lambert, Richard D., ed. II. Title. III. Series.

AMERICAN Academy of 209.73
Political and Social Science, Philadelphia. Annals.
Not many wise, a reader on religion in American society. Pilgrim Pr. [dist. Philadelphia, United Church, c.1962] 169p. 21cm. (Pilgrimbk.) Bibl. 62-13706 2.25 pap.,
1. U.S.—Religion. 2. U.S.—Church history—20th cent. I. Title.

AMERICAN Academy of 209.73
Political and Social Science, Philadelphia. Annals.
Not many wise, a reader on religion in American society. Boston, Pilgrim Press [1962] 169p. 21cm. (A Pilgrim book) 'Essays ...selected from the November 1960 issue of the Annals of the American Academy of Political and Social Science.' Includes bibliography. [BR526.A62] 62-13706
1. U. S.—Religion. 2. U. S.—Church history—20th cent. I. Title.

AMERICAN Academy of 209.73
Political and Social Science, Philadelphia. Annals, v. 332
Not many wise, a reader on religion in American society. Boston, Pilgrim Press [1962] 169 p. 21 cm. (A Pilgrim book) "Essays ... selected from the November 1960 issue of the Annals of the American Academy of Political and Social Science." Includes bibliography. [BR526.N6] 62-13706
1. U.S. — Religion. 2. U.S. Church history — 20th cent. I. Title.

THE American religious 209'.73
experiment : piety and practicality / edited by Clyde L. Manschreck and Barbara Brown Zikmund. Chicago : Exploration Press, c1976. xiii, 145 p. ; 24 cm. (Studies in ministry and parish life) Includes bibliographies. [BR515.A54] 76-7199 ISBN 0-913552-06-2 : 8.00 ISBN 0-913552-07-0 pbk. :
1. United States—Religion—Addresses, essays, lectures. I. Manschreck, Clyde Leonard, 1917- II. Zikmund, Barbara Brown. III. Series.

BAIRD, Robert, 1798-1863. 209'.73
Religion in America. A critical abridgement with introd. by Henry Warner Bowden. New York, Harper & Row [1970] xxxvii, 314 p. 21 cm. (Harper torchbooks, TB 1509) First published in 1844 under title: Religion in the United States of America. Bibliography: p. 304-305. [BR515.B322B3] 75-114093 2.95
1. U.S.—Church history. I. Bowden, Henry Warner, ed. II. Title.

BANKS, William L. 209'.73
The Black church in the U.S.; its origin, growth, contributions, and outlook, by William L. Banks. Chicago, Moody Press [1972] 160 p. 22 cm. Bibliography: p. 154-156. [E185.7.B3] 76-175492 ISBN 0-8024-0870-2 2.25
1. Negroes—Religion. I. Title.

BERGER, Peter L. 209.73
The noise of solemn assemblies; Christian commitment and the religious establishment in America. [1st ed.] Garden City, Doubleday, 1961. 189 p. 21 cm. Includes bibliography. [BR526.B45] 61-14587
1. United States—Religious life and customs. 2. United States—Church history. I. Title.

BERGER, Peter L. 209'.73
Religion in a revolutionary society; delivered at Christ Church, Alexandria, Virginia, on February 4, 1974 [by] Peter L. Berger. Washington, American Enterprise Institute for Public Policy Research [1974] 16 p. illus. 25 cm. (Distinguished lecture series on the Bicentennial) Includes bibliographical references. [BR515.B53] 74-79895 ISBN 0-8447-1306-6 1.00
1. United States—Religion. I. Title. II. Series.

BICENTENNIAL Congress on 209'.73
Prophecy, Philadelphia, 1976.
America in history and Bible prophecy / edited by Thomas McCall. Chicago : Moody Press, c1976. 143 p. : 22 cm. Includes bibliographical references. [BR515.B55 1976] 76-43049 ISBN 0-8024-0209-7 : 2.95
1. Bible—Prophecies—Congresses. 2. United States—Religion—Congresses. 3. Jews in the United States—Congresses. I. McCall, Thomas S. II. Title.

BISHOP, Isabella Lucy 209'.73
(Bird) 1831-1904.
The aspects of religion in the United States of America. New York, Arno Press, 1972. 189 p. 23 cm. (Religion in America, series II) Reprint of the 1859 ed. [BR515.B57 1972] 75-38438 ISBN 0-405-04059-8
1. United States—Religion. I. Title.

BOUMAN, Walter R., 1929- 209'.73
Christianity American style, by Walter R. Bouman. Dayton, G. A. Pflaum, 1970. 128 p. illus. 18 cm. (Christian identity series) (Witness book, CI 10.) [BR515.B66] 75-114724 .95
1. U.S.—Religion. I. Title.

BOYD, Malcolm, 1923- 209'.73
Christian : its meanings in an age of future shock / Malcolm Boyd. New York : Hawthorn Books, c1975. xvi, 181 p. : ill. ; 22 cm. [BR121.2.B63 1975] 74-31633 ISBN 0-8015-1270-0 : 7.95
1. Boyd, Malcolm, 1923- 2. Christianity—20th century. 3. Christian life—Anglican authors. I. Title.

BRAUER, Jerald C. 209'.73
Images of religion in America, by Jerald C. Brauer. Philadelphia, Fortress Press [1967] x, 35 p. 19 cm. (Facet books. Historical series, 8) First published in Church history, v. 30, Mar. 1961, p. 3-18. Bibliographical footnotes. [BR515.B68] 67-22984
1. U.S. — Religion. I. Title.

BRAUER, Jerald C. 209'.73
Reinterpretation in American church history, by R. Pierce Beaver [and others] Edited by Jerald C. Brauer. Chicago, University of Chicago Press [1968] xi, 227 p. 24 cm. (Essays in divinity, v. 5) Bibliographical footnotes. [BR515.B72] 68-20186
1. United States—Church history—Addresses, essays, lectures. I. Beaver, Robert Pierce, 1906- II. Title. III. Series.

BRILL, Earl H. 209'.73
The future of the American past; a study course on American values, by Earl H. Brill. New York, Seabury Press [1974] 96 p. 21 cm. "A Crossroad book." Includes bibliographies. [BR515.B74] 73-17890 ISBN 0-8164-2086-6 2.95 (pbk.)
1. United States—Religion. 2. United States—Civilization. I. Title.

BROWN, Harold O. J., 209'.73
1933-
The reconstruction of the Republic Harold O. J. Brown. New Rochelle, N.Y. : Arlington House Publishers, c1977. 207 p. ; 24 cm. Includes index. [BR515.B76] 76-57954 ISBN 0-87000-230-9 : 8.95
1. Christianity—United States. 2. Christianity and politics. I. Title.

BUCHER, Glenn Richard. 209'.73
Confusion and hope; clergy, laity, and the church in transition, edited by Glenn Richard Bucher and Patricia Ruth Hill. Philadelphia, Fortress Press [1974] xi, 128 p. 21 cm. Includes bibliographical references. [BR123.B76] 74-76923 ISBN 0-8006-1303-1 3.50 (pbk.).
1. Christianity—20th century—Addresses, essays, lectures. I. Hill, Paricia Ruth, joint author. II. Title.

BUNDY, Edgar C. 209.73
Aposles of deceit, by Edgar C. Bundy. Wheaton, Ill., Church League of America [1966] xii, 528 p. 22 cm. [BR517.B87] 66-24178
1. U.S. — Religion. 2. Communism — U.S. I. Title.

BUSHMAN, Richard L., 209'.73
comp.
The Great Awakening; documents on the revival of religion, 1740-1745. Edited by Richard L. Bushman. [1st ed.] New York, Published for the Institute of Early American History and Culture at Williamsburg, Va. [by] Atheneum, 1970 [c1969] xiv, 174 p. 25 cm. (Documentary problems in early American history) Bibliography: p. 173-174. [BR520.B94 1970] 74-108821 8.95
1. Great Awakening. I. Institute of Early American History and Culture, Williamsburg, Va. II. Title. III. Series.

CALIFORNIA. University. 209.73
University Extension.
Religion and the face of America; papers of the conference, presented at Asilomar, Pacific Grove, California, November 28, 29, and 3d. 1958. Edited by Jane C. Zahn. Berkeley [1959] 87p. 23cm. [BR526.C3] 59-63690
1. U. S.—Religion. I. Zahn, Jane C., ed. II. Title.

CAMPBELL, Timothy James, 209.73
1883-
Central themes of American life. Grand Rapids, Mich., Eerdmans [1959] 188p. 21cm. Includes bibliography. [BR517.C3] 59-8751
1. U. S.—Religion. I. Title.

CARTER, Paul Allen, 1926- 209'.73
The spiritual crisis of the gilded age [by] Paul A. Carter. DeKalb, Northern Illinois University Press, 1971. xiii, 295 p. illus. 25 cm. Bibliography: p. 269-285. [BR525.C37] 72-156938 ISBN 0-87580-026-2 (hbd) 8.50
1. United States—Religion—19th century. I. Title.

CLEBSCH, William A. 209.73
From sacred to profane America; the role of religion in American history, by William A. Clebsch. New York, Harper & Row [1968] xi, 242 p. 22 cm. Bibliographical references included in "Notes" (p. 219-232) [BR515.C55] 68-11730
1. U.S.—Religion. 2. U.S.—Church history. I. Title.

COVEY, Cyclone 209.73
The American pilgrimage; the roots of American history, religion, and culture. [Gloucester, Mass., Peter Smith, 1962, c.1961] 122p. 18cm. (Collier bks. original, AS29 rebound) Bibl. 3.00
1. Death. 2. Religious thought—U.S. I. Title.

DRUMMOND, Andrew Landale. 209'.73
Story of American Protestantism. 2d ed. Boston, Beacon Press, 1951. xii, 418 p. 23 cm. Bibliography: p. 407-413. [BR515.D] A52
1. Protestant churches—U. S. 2. U. S.—Church history. I. Title.

ERNST, Eldon G. 209'.73
Without help or hindrance : religious identity in American culture / by Eldon G. Ernst. Philadelphia : Westminster Press, c1977. 240 p. ; 21 cm. Includes index. Bibliography: p. 225-231. [BR515.E76] 76-27742 ISBN 0-664-24128X : 6.95
1. Christianity—United States. I. Title.

ERNST, Eldon G. 209'.73
Without help or hindrance : religious identity in American culture / by Eldon G. Ernst. Philadelphia : Westminster Press, c1977. 240 p. ; 21 cm. Includes index. Bibliography: p. 225-231. [BR515.E76] 76-27742 ISBN 0-664-24128X : 6.95
1. Christianity—United States. I. Title.

FORDHAM, Monroe, 1939- 209'.73
Major themes in Northern Black religious thought, 1800-1860 / Monroe Fordham. 1st ed. Hicksville, N.Y. : Exposition Press, [1975] xii, 172 p. ; 22 cm. (An Exposition-university book) Includes index. Bibliography: p. 159-167. [BR563.N4F65] 75-10618 ISBN 0-682-48256-0 : 8.50
1. Negroes—Religion. 2. Negro churches—United States. 3. Religious thought—19th century. I. Title.

THE Future of the 209'.73
American church. Philip J. Hefner, editor. Contributors: Sidney E. Mead [and others] Philadelphia, Fortress Press [1968] vi, 90 p. 19 cm. The 1966 Zimmerman lectures given to commemorate the 140th anniversary of the Lutheran Theological Seminary at Gettysburg. Contents.Contents.—Preface, by P. J. Hefner.—Prospects for the church in America, by S. E. Mead.—Two requisites for the American church: moral discourse and institutional power, by J. M. Gustafson.—Freedom and the churches, by J. Haroutunian.—Schmucker and Walther: a study of Christian response to American culture, by L. D. Jordahl. Bibliographical footnotes. [BR526.F6] 68-12328
1. United States—Religion—1946- I. Hefner, Philip J., ed. II. Mead, Sidney Earl, 1904- III. Gettysburg. Theological Seminary of the United Lutheran Church in America.

GARVIN, Philip, 1947- 209'.73
Religious America. Photos. by Philip Garvin. Text by Philip Garvin and Julia Welch. [New York] McGraw-Hill [1974] 189 p. illus. 23 x 29 cm. [BR515.G27] 74-11049 ISBN 0-07-022918-X 15.00
1. United States—Religious life and customs. I. Welch, Julia. II. Title.

GAUSTAD, Edwin Scott, 209'.73
comp.
Religious issues in American history. [1st ed.] New York, Harper & Row [1968] xxii, 294 p. 21 cm. (Harper forum books RD6) [BR515.G32] 68-17601 3.50
1. United States—Religion—Collections. I. Title.

HANDY, Robert T. 209'.73
The American religious depression, 1925-1935; by Robert T. Handy. Philadelphia, Fortress Press [1968] vii, 27 p. 19 cm. (Facet books. Historical series, 9) Reprint from Church history, v. 29, 1960. Bibliography: p. 23. [BR515.H35] 68-31338 0.85
1. United States—Religion—1901-1945. 2. Protestant churches—United States. 3. Protestantism—20th century. I. Title.

HANDY, Robert T 209.'73
The American religious depression, 1925-1935: by Robert T. Handy. Philadelphia, Fortress Press [1968] vii, 27 p. 19 cm. (Facet books. Historical series, 9) $0.85 Reprint from Church history, v. 29, 1960. Bibliography: p. 23 [BR515.H33] 68-31338
1. U.S.—Religion—1901-1945. 2. Protestant churches—U. S. 3. Protestantism—20th cent. I. Title.

HART, Roderick P. 209'.73
The political pulpit / by Roderick P. Hart. West Lafayette, Ind. : Purdue University Press, 1977. ix, 141 p. ; 23 cm. Includes index. Bibliography: p. 127-133. [BR517.H37] 76-12290 ISBN 0-911198-44-X : 8.95 ISBN 0-911198-45-8 pbk. : 3.50
1. United States—Religion—1945- 2. Church and state in the United States. I. Title.

HEFLEY, James C. 209'.73
America, one nation under God / James C. Hefley. Wheaton, Ill. : Victor Books, c1975. 144 p. ; 21 cm. (An Input book) [BR515.H43] 75-12194 ISBN 0-88207-721-X pbk. : 1.95
1. United States—Religion. 2. United States—Moral conditions. I. Title.

HEIMERT, Alan E., comp. 209'.73
The Great Awakening: documents illustrating the crisis and its consequences, edited by Alan Heimert and Perry Miller. Indianapolis, Bobbs-Merrill [1967] lxx, 663 p. 21 cm. (The American heritage series, 34) Bibliography: lxiii-lxv. [BR520.H39] 66-23537
1. Great Awakening. 2. United States—Church history—Colonial period, ca. 1600-1775—Sources. I. Miller, Perry, joint comp. II. Title.

HOWLETT, Duncan. 209.73
The fourth American faith. [1st ed.] New York, Harper & Row [1964] xv, 239 p. 21 cm. Bibliographical references included in "Notes" (p. [217]-232) [BR517.H6] 64-14372
1. U.S.—Religion. I. Title.

HUDSON, Winthrop Still, 209.73
1911-
Religion in America [by] Winthrop S. Hudson. New York, Scribner [1965] xii, 447 p. 25 cm. Bibliographical footnotes. [BR515.H79] 65-28188
1. U.S.—Religion I. Title.

HUDSON, Winthrop Still, 209.73
1911-
Religion in America. New York, Scribners [c.1965] xii, 447p. 25cm. Bibl. [BR515.H79] 65-28188 7.95
1. U.S. — Religion. I. Title.

JONG, Pieter de. 209'.73
Evangelism and contemporary theology; a study of the implications for evangelism in the thoughts of six modern theologians. Nashville, Tidings [1962] 116p. 22cm. Includes bibliography. [BT28.J6] 62-13349
1. Theology, Doctrinal—Hist.—20th cent. 2. Evangelistic work. I. Title.

KENDALL, R. T. 209'.73
The influence of Calvin and Calvinism upon the American heritage / by R. T. Kendall. London : Evangelical Library, 1976. 24 p. ; 22 cm. (Annual lecture of the Evangelical Library ; 1976) Includes bibliographical references.

[BX9418.K43] 77-367633 ISBN 0-901891-04-5 : £0.40
1. Calvin, Jean, 1509-1564. 2. Calvinism. 3. United States—Religion. I. Title. II. Series: Evangelical Library. Annual lecture ; 1976.

*KOLKE, Daniel. 209'.73
The church and her walls; twentieth-century parallels from the Book of Revelation. New York, Exposition Pr. [1973] 166 p. 21 cm. (Exposition-Testament Book) Bibliography: p. 163-166. [BR515] ISBN 0-682-47720-6 6.00
1. U.S.—Church history. 2. Christianity—20th century. I. Title.

KURFMAN, Dana G. 209.73
Teacher-made test items in American history: emphasis junior high school, edited by Dana Kurfman. [1st ed.] Washington, National Council for the Social Studies [1968] xi, 98 p. (p. 97-98 advertisements) 23 cm. (National Council for the Social Studies. Bulletin no. 40) [E178.25.K8] 68-23443 2.00
1. United States—History—Examinations, questions, etc. I. Title. II. Series.

LITTELL, Franklin Hamlin 209.73
From state church to pluralism: a Protestant interpretation of religion in American history. Chicago, Aldine [c.1962] 174p. 22cm. (Aldine lib. ed.) Bibl. 62-15090 5.00
1. U. S.—Church history. 2. U. S.—Religion. 3. Sects—U. S. I. Title.

LITTELL, Franklin Hamlin. 209.73
From state church to pluralism; a Protestant interpretation of religion in American history. [1st ed.] Garden City, N. Y., Anchor Books, 1962. 174 p. 18 cm. (Anchor books, A294) [BR515.L55] 61-9530
1. U.S.—Church history. 2. U.S.—Religion. 3. Sects—U.S. I. Title.

MCDONALD, Donald John, 1920- 209.73
Religion; one of a series of interviews on the American character. Interviews by Donald McDonald with Robert E. Fitch, John J. Wright, Louis Finkelstein. [Santa Barbara, Calif.] Ctr. for the Study of Dem. Insts. [1963, c.1962] 78p. 21cm. 63-1610 gratis pap.,
1. U.S.—Religion. I. Title.

MCLOUGHLIN, William Gerald. 209.73
Religion in America, edited by William G. McLoughlin and Robert N. Bellah. Boston, Houghton Mifflin, 1968. xxiv, 433 p. illus. 24 cm. (The Daedalus library [v. 12]) Papers, by contributors chosen by the editors, based on preparatory conferences held at the American Academy of Arts and Sciences, Boston. Includes bibliographical references. [BR526.M32] 68-17174 6.50
1. United States—Religion—1945- I. Bellah, Robert Neeley, 1927- joint author. II. American Academy of Arts and Sciences, Boston. III. Title. IV. Series.

MARSH, Spencer. 209'.73
God, man, and Archie Bunker / Spencer Marsh ; foreword by Carroll O'Connor. 1st ed. New York : Harper & Row, [1975] xiv, 104 p., [1] leaf of plates : ill. ; 21 cm. [BT28.M279 1975b] 74-25694 ISBN 0-06-065423-6 : 5.95 ISBN 0-06-065422-8 pbk. : 2.95
1. All in the family. 2. Theology—20th century. I. Title.

MARSHALL, Peter, 1940- 209'.73
The light and the glory / Peter Marshall, David Manuel. Old Tappan, N.J. : Revell, c1977. 384 p. ; 24 cm. Includes index. Bibliography: p. 371-378. [E189.M36] 77-23352 ISBN 0-8007-0886-5 : 9.95
1. United States—History—Colonial period, ca. 1600-1775. 2. United States—History—Revolution, 1775-1783. 3. United States—Church history—Colonial period, ca. 1600-1775. 4. History (Theology) 5. Providence and government of God. I. Manuel, David, joint author. II. Title.

MARTY, Martin E., 1928- 209.73
The new shape of American religion. New York, Harper [1959] 180 p. 22 cm. Includes bibliography. [BR526.M35] 59-10336
1. United States—Religion—1945- I. Title.

MARTY, Martin E., 1928- 209'.73
The pro & con book of religious America : a bicentennial argument / Martin E. Marty. Waco, Tex. : Word Books, [1975] 143, 149 p. ; 23 cm. [BR515.M325] 74-27478 6.95
1. United States—Religion. I. Title.

MARTY, Martin E., 1928- 209'.73
Religion, awakening & revolution / Martin E. Marty. Wilmington, N.C. : Consortium Books, [1977] p. cm. (Faith of our fathers ; v. 4) [BR520.M38] 77-9558 ISBN 0-8434-0623-2 : 9.50
1. Christianity—United States. 2. United States—Religion—To 1800. I. Title. II. Series.

MARTY, Martin E., 1928- 209'.73
What do we believe? The stance of religion in America, by Martin E. Marty, Stuart E. Rosenberg, and Andrew M. Greeley. [1st ed.] New York, Meredith Press [1968] vi, 346 p. 24 cm. Includes bibliographical references. [BR526.M355] 68-26326 6.95
1. United States—Religion—1945- 2. Public opinion—United States. I. Rosenberg, Stuart E., joint author. II. Greeley, Andrew M., 1928- joint author. III. Title.

MARTY, Martin E., 1928- 209.73
Youth considers 'do-it-yourself' religion. New York, Nelson [c.1965] 93, [2]p. 21cm. (Youth forum ser.) Bibl. [BR526.M36] 65-15404 1.50 pap.,
1. U. S.—Religion. I. Title. II. Series.

MATHISON, Richard R. 209.73
Faiths, cults, and sects of America: from atheism to Zen. Indianapolis, Bobbs-Merrill [c.1960] 384p. 22cm. 60-13589 5.00 bds.,
1. Sects—U. S. 2. U. S.—Religion. I. Title.

MATHISON, Richard R 209.73
Faiths, cults, and sects of America: from atheism to Zen. [1st ed.] Indianapolis, Bobbs-Merrill [1960] 384p. 22cm. [BR516.5.M29] 60-13589
1. Sects—U. S. 2. U. S.—Religion. I. Title.

MATHISON, Richard R. 209.73
God is a millionaire [Bobbs, dist. New York, Macfadden, 1962, c.1960] 384p. 21cm. (Charter bks. 106) Orig. pub. under title: Faiths, cults and sects of America. Bibl. 1.85 pap.,
1. Sects—U.S. 2. U.S.—Religion. I. Title.

MEAD, Sidney Earl, 1904- 209'.73
The old religion in the brave new world : reflections on the relation between Christendom and the Republic / Sidney E. Mead. Berkeley : University of California Press, c1977. xii, 189 p. ; 21 cm. (The Jefferson memorial lectures) Includes bibliographical references. [BR515.M453] 76-24588 ISBN 0-520-03322-1 : 12.95
1. Christianity—United States—Addresses, essays, lectures. I. Title. II. Series.

MICHAELSEN, Robert. 209'.73
The American search for soul / Robert S. Michaelsen. Baton Rouge : Louisiana State University Press, [1975] xii, 131 p. ; 23 cm. (Rockwell lectures) "Revised and augmented version of lectures delivered under the title The crisis in American faith and learning, at Rice University in February, 1973." Includes index. Bibliography: p. 119-128. [BR515.M5] 74-82005 ISBN 0-8071-0097-8 : 7.95
1. United States—Religion—Addresses, essays, lectures. 2. National characteristics, American—Addresses, essays, lectures. I. Title. II. Series.

A Nation under God? / 209'.73
Edited by C. E. Gallivan. Waco, Tex. : Word Books, c1976. 136 p. ; 21 cm. (Discovery books) [BR515.N37] 75-38048 ISBN 0-87680-875-5 pbk. : 3.50
1. United States—Religion—Addresses, essays, lectures. I. Gallivan, C. E.

NATIONAL Council of the Churches of Christ in the United States of America. Bureau of Research and Survey. 209'.73
Churches and church membership in the United States; an enumeration and analysis by counties, states and regions, ser. A-E. New York, 1956-58. 80 no. diagrs. 28cm. Ser. A: Major faiths by regions, divisions and states. 4 no. --Ser. B: Denominational statistics by regions, divisions and states. 8 no.-- Ser. C: Denominational statisties by states and counties. 59 no.--Ser. d: Denominational statistics by metropolitan areas. 6 no.--Ser. E: Socioeconomic characteristics. 3 no. [BR526.N3] 56-12497
1. Church statistics—U. S. 2. U. S.— Religion. I. Title.

NATIONAL Council of the Churches of Christ in the United States of America. Bureau of Research and Survey. 209'.73
Churches and church membership in the United States; an enumeration and analysis by counties, states and regions. ser. A-E. New York, 1956-58. 80 no. diagrs. 28 cm. Ser. A: Major faiths by regions, divisions and states. 4 no.—Ser. B: Denominational statistics by regions, divisions and states. 8 no.—Ser. C: Denominational statistics by states and counties. 59 no.—Ser. D: Denominational statistics by metropolitan areas. 6 no.—Ser. E: Socioeconomic characteristics. 3 no. [BR526.N3] 56-12497
1. Church statistics—United States. 2. United States—Religion—1945-

OLMSTEAD, Clifton E. 209.73
History of religion in the United States. Englewood Cliffs, N. J., Prentice-Hall, 1960. 628 p. 24 cm. [BR515.O4] 60-10355
1. U.S.—Religion. 2. U.S.—Church history.

OLMSTEAD, Clifton E. 209.73
Religion in America, past and present. Englewood Cliffs, N. J., Prentice-Hall [1961] 172 p. 21 cm. (A Spectrum book, S-20) Includes bibliography. [BR515.O43] 61-16978
1. U.S.—Religion. 2. U.S.—Church history. I. Title.

PHARES, Ross. 209.73
Bible in pocket, gun in hand; the story of frontier religion. [1st ed.] Garden City, N. Y., Doubleday, 1964. 182 p. 22 cm. Bibliographical references included in "Notes" (p. [167]-182) [BR517.P5] 64-11375
1. U.S.—Religious life and customs. 2. Frontier and pioneer life—U.S. I. Title.

PITTENGER, William Norman, 1905- 209'.73
The historic faith and a changing world, by W. Norman Pittenger. Westport, Conn., Greenwood Press [1971, c1950] viii, 181 p. 23 cm. [BR481.P5 1971] 79-112329 ISBN 0-8371-4717-4
1. Christianity—20th century. I. Title.

RAAB, Earl, ed. 209.73
Religious conflict in America; studies of the problems beyond bigotry. [1st ed.] Garden City, N. Y., Anchor Books, 1964. viii, 231 p. 18 cm. "A392." Bibliographical footnotes. [BR516.5.R3] 64-11733
1. U. S.—Religion. I. Title.

RAAB, Earl, ed. 209.73
Religious conflict in America; studies of the problems beyond bigotry. Garden City, N.Y., Doubleday [c.]1964. viii, 231p. 18cm. (Anchor bk., A392) Bibl. 64-11733 1.25 pap.,
1. U.S.—Religion. I. Title.

RELIGION and the American revolution / edited by Jerald C. Brauer ; with contributions by Jerald C. Brauer, Sidney E. Mead, Robert N. Bellah. Philadelphia : Fortress Press, c1976. xi, 73 p. ; 22 cm. Contents.Contents.—Brauer, J. C. Puritanism, revivalism, and the Revolution.—Mead, S. E. Christendom, enlightenment, and the Revolution.—Bellah, R. N. The Revolution and the civil religion. Includes bibliographical references. [BR520.R44] 76-9718 pbk. : 2.95 209'.73
1. United States—Religion—To 1800—Addresses, essays, lectures. 2. United States—History—Revolution, 1775-1783—Addresses, essays, lectures. I. Brauer, Jerald C. II. Brauer, Jerald C. Puritanism, revivalism, and the Revolution. III. Mead, Sidney Earl, 1904- Christendom, enlightenment, and the Revolution. IV. Bellah, Robert Neely, 1927- The Revolution and the civil religion.

ROWE, H. Edward. 209'.73
Save America! / H. Edward Rowe. Old Tappan, N.J. : F. H. Revell Co., c1976. 159 p. ; 20 cm. [BR526.R68] 76-3517 ISBN 0-8007-0798-2 pbk. : 3.95
1. Christianity—United States. 2. United States—Moral conditions. 3. Church and social problems—United States. I. Title.

RUPP, Israel Daniel. 1803-1878, ed. 209'.73
He pasa ekklesia; an orginal history of the religious denominations at present existing in the United States ... Written expressly for the work by eminent theological professors, ministers, and lay-members... Projected, compiled, and arr. by I. Daniel Rupp. Philadelphia, J. Y. Humphreys, 1844. 734 p. 25 cm. Microfilm. Ann Arbor, Mich., University Microfilms, 1964. 1 reel. 35 mm. (American culture series, 258:4) Microfilm 01291 reel 258, no. 4 E [BR515.R9 1844] 67-117443
1. Sects—U.S. 2. Sects. 3. Religions. I. Title. II. Title: An original history of the religious denominations at present existing in the United States.

SALISBURY, William Seward. 209.73
Religion in American culture, a sociologicalinterpretation, by W. Seward Salisbury. Homewood, Ill., Dorsey Press, 1964. ix, 538 p. maps. 24 cm. (The Dorsey series in anthropology and sociology) Bibliography: p. 491-515. [BR515.S23] 64-22110
1. U.S.—Religion. I. Title.

SALISBURY, William Seward 209.73
Religion in American culture, a sociological interpretation. Homewood, Ill., Dorsey [c.] 1964. ix, 538p. maps. 24cm. (Dorsey ser. in anthropology and soc.) Bibl. 64-22110 10.60
1. U.S.—Religion. I. Title.

SHEA, Daniel B. 209'.73
Spiritual autobiography in early America, by Daniel B. Shea, Jr. Princeton, N.J., Princeton University Press, 1968. xvi, 280 p. 23 cm. Includes bibliographical references. [BR520.S5] 68-11447 7.50
1. United States—Church history—Colonial period. 2. Spiritual life—History of doctrines. 3. Autobiography. I. Title.

SMART, James D. 209'.73
The cultural subversion of the Biblical faith : life in the 20th century under the sign of the cross / by James D. Smart. 1st ed. Philadelphia : Westminster Press, c1977. p. cm. [BL2530.U6S63] 77-22063 ISBN 0-664-24148-4 pbk. : 4.95
1. United States—Religion—1945- 2. Christianity—United States. 3. United States—Civilization—1945- I. Title.

SPENCE, Hartzell, 1908- 209.73
The story of America's religions. Published in co-operation with the editors of Look magazine. [1st ed] New York, Holt, Rinehart and Winston [1960] 86 p. illus. 35 cm. Deluxe ed. with illustrations. [BR516.5S7 1960] 60-12319
1. Sects — U.S. 2. U.S. — Religion. I. Title.

SPENCE, Hartzell, 1908- 209.73
The story of America's religions. Nashville, Abingdon [1962, c.1957-1960] 258p. 21cm. (Apex Bks. K 3) 1.50 pap.,
1. Sects—U.S. 2. U.S.—Religion. I. Title. II. Title: America's religions.

SPENCE, Hartzell, 1908- 209.73
The story of America's religions. Published in cooperation with the editors of Look magazine. New York, Holt, Rinehart and Winston [1960, c.1957-1960] ix, 86p. illus., col. plates, 35cm. 60-12319 14.95; regular ed. (no illus.) 4.00
1. Sects—U. S. 2. U. S.—Religion. I. Title. II. Title: America's religions.

TONKS, A. Ronald. 209'.73
Faith, stars, and stripes : the impact of Christianity on the life history of America / A. Ronald Tonks and Charles W. Deweese. Nashville : Broadman Press, c1976. 124 p. ; 21 cm. Includes bibliographical references. [BR515.T66] 75-36888 ISBN 0-8054-6522-7 : 3.95
1. United States—Religion. I. Deweese, Charles W., joint author. II. Title.

WAMBLE, G Hugh, 1923- 209'.73
The shape of faith. Nashville, Broadman Press [1962] 88 p. 20 cm. (A Broadman starbook) [BR526.W27] 62-9201
1. Protestant churches — U.S. I. Title.

WARNER, William Lloyd, 1898-1970. 209'.73
The family of God : a symbolic study of Christian life in America / by W. Lloyd Warner. Westport, Conn. : Greenwood Press, 1975, c1961. x, 451 p. : diagrs. ; 22 cm. Reprint of the ed. published by Yale University Press, New Haven, which was issued as A Yale paperbound, Y-45. Revised selections from the author's The living and the dead. Includes index. Bibliography: p. 431-442. [BR526.W3 1975] 75-11494 ISBN 0-8371-8206-9 lib.bdg. : 20.00
1. United States—Religion—1945- 2. United States—Social life and customs—1945- 3. Symbolism. I. Title.

WEISS, Benjamin. 209.73
God in American history; a documentation of America's religious heritage. Foreword by Walter H. Judd. Grand Rapids, Zondervan Pub. House [1966] 256 p. illus., ports. 23 cm. Bibliography: p. 251-253. [BR515.W42] 66-13692
1. U.S. — Religion. I. Title.

WEISS, Benjamin 209.73
God in American history; a documentation of America's religious heritage. Foreword by Walter H. Judd. Grand Rapids, Mich., Zondervan [c.1966] 256p. illus., ports 23cm. Bibl. [BR515.W42] 66-13692 4.95
1. U.S. — Religion. I. Title.

WOLF, William J. 209'.73
Freedom's holy light : American identity and the future of theology / by William J. Wolf. Wakefield, Mass. : Parameter Press, [1977] p. cm. Includes index. Bibliography: p. [BR515.W64] 77-75711 ISBN 0-88203-007-8 pbk. : 5.35
1. Christianity—United States. 2. United States—Religion. I. Title.

WOOD, James Edward. 209'.73
Nationhood and the kingdom / James E. Wood, Jr. Nashville : Broadman Press, c1977. 127 p. ; 20 cm. Bibliography: p. 126-127. [BR516.W65] 76-48576 ISBN 0-8054-8805-7 pbk. : 2.50
1. Church and state in the United States. 2. Church and state. 3. Nationalism and religion—United States. I. Title.

GAUSTAD, Edwin Scott. 209.73084
Historical atlas of religion in America. [1st ed.] New York, Harper & Row [1962] 179 p. maps (1 fold. col. in pocket) diagrs. 31 cm.

Includes bibliographies. [G1201.E4G3 1962] Map
1. Ecclesiastical geography—United States—Maps. 2. United States—Church history. I. Title: Religion in America.

WARREN, Austin, 1899- 209'.74
New England saints / Austin Warren. Westport, Conn. : Greenwood Press, 1976. p. cm. Reprint of the 1956 ed. published by University of Michigan Press, Ann Arbor. Bibliography: p. [F4.W36 1976] 76-28302 ISBN 0-8371-9086-X lib.bdg. : 13.25
1. New England—Intellectual life. 2. Religious thought—New England. I. Title.

JAMISON, Wallace N. 209.749
Religion in New Jersey: a brief history. Princeton, N.J., Van Nostrand [c.]1964. xiii, 183p. illus., fold maps. (on lining papers) 22cm. (N.J. hist. ser., v.13) Bibl. 64-23966 3.95 bds.,
1. New Jersey—Church history. I. Title. II. Series.

PHOTIADIS, John D. 209'.754
Religion in an Appalachian state / by John Photiadis and B. B. Maurer. [Morgantown] : Division of Personal and Family Development, Appalachian Center, West Virginia University, [1974] 27 p. ; 28 cm. (Research report - Appalachian Center, West Virginia University ; 6) Caption title. Includes bibliographical references. [BR555.W4P47] 74-624112
1. West Virginia—Religion. I. Maurer, Beryl Blake, 1920- joint author. II. Title. III. Series: West Virginia. University. West Virginia Center for Appalachian Studies and Development. Research report ; 6.

BOLES, John B. 209'.769
Religion in antebellum Kentucky / John B. Boles. Lexington : University Press of Kentucky, c1976. ix, 147, [1] p. ; 21 cm. (The Kentucky bicentennial bookshelf) Bibliography: p. 146-[148] [BR555.K4B66] 76-4434 ISBN 0-8131-0227-8 : 3.95
1. Kentucky—Church history. I. Title. II. Series.

SCHROEDER, W. Widick 209.77
Religion in American culture; unity and diversity in a midwestern county [by] W. Widick Schroeder, Victor Obenhaus [New York] Free Pr. [c.1964] xxiii, 254p. illus. 2icm. Bibl. 64-16966 8.50
1. U.S.—Religion. 2. Religion and sociology—Case studies. 3. Middle West—Religion. I. Obenhaus, Victor, joint author. II. Title.

SCHROEDER, W Widick. 209.77
Religion in American culture; unity and diversity in a midwestern county [by] W. Widick Schroeder and Victor Obenhaus. [New York] Free Press of Glencoe [1964] xxiii, 254 p. illus. 22 cm. Bibliographical footnotes. [BR526.S3] 64-16966
1. U. S.—Religion. 2. Religion and sociology—Case studies. 3. Middle West—Religion. I. Obenhaus, Victor, joint author. II. Title.

DUSSEL, Enrique D. 209'.8
History and the theology of liberation : a Latin American perspective / Enrique Dussel ; translated by John Drury. Maryknoll, N.Y. : Orbis Books, c1976. xvi, 189 p. : ill. ; 22 cm. Translation of Caminos de liberacion latinoamericana I. Bibliography: p. 183-189. [BR600.D8613] 75-21773 ISBN 0-88344-179-9 : 8.95. ISBN 0-88344-180-2 pbk. : 4.95
1. Latin America—Church history. 2. Liberation theology. 3. Theology, Doctrinal—History—Latin America. I. Title.

GEERTZ, Clifford 209.9222
The religion of Java. New York, Free Pr. [1964, c.1960] xv, 392p. maps. 22cm. Pt. of the material issued in 1958 under title: Modjokuto, religion in Java. 7.95; 2.45 bds., pap.,
1. Modjokerto, Java—Religion. I. Title.

FIRTH, Raymond William, 1901- 209'.93'5
Rank and religion in Tikopia; a study in Polynesian paganism and conversion to Christianity, by Raymond Firth. Boston, Beacon Press [1970] 424 p. illus., ports. 24 cm. Includes bibliographical references. [GN473.F47 1970b] 71-112710 10.00
1. Tikopians. 2. Rites and ceremonies—Polynesia. I. Title.

210 NATURAL RELIGION

ANDERSON, James Francis, 1910- 210
Natural theology; the metaphysics of God. Milwaukee, Bruce [c.1962] 179p. 24cm. (Christian culture and philosophy ser.) Bibl. 62-10339 3.50
1. Natural theology. 2. Thomas Aquinas, Saint—Theology. I. Title.

ANDERSON, James Francis, 1910- 210
Natural theology; the metaphysics of God. Milwaukee, Bruce Pub. Co. [1962] 179p. 24cm. (Christian culture and philosophy series) Includes bibliography. [BL182.A5] 62-10339
1. Natural theology. 2. Thomas Aquinas, Saint—Theology. I. Title.

BABBAGE, Charles, 1792-1871 210
The ninth Bridgewater treatise: a fragment. 2nd ed., reprinted. London, Cass, 1967. viii, xxi, 23-273p. tables, diagrs. 23cm. (Cass Lib. of sci. classics, no. 6) New impression, with index, of the Second (London) ed. [BL175.B89 1838a] 67-110707 14.50
1. Natural theology. I. Title. II. Series.
Distributed by Barnes & Noble, New York.

BAELZ, Peter R. 210
Christian theology and metaphysics [by] Peter R. Baelz. American ed. Philadelphia, Fortress Press [1968] vi, 152 p. 20 cm. Bibliographical references included in "Notes" (p. 147-149) [BR100.B3 1968] 68-19076
1. Christianity—Philosophy. 2. Philosophical theology. I. Title.

BENEDETTO, Arnold J. 210
Fundamentals in the philosophy of God. New York, Macmillan [c.1963] 330p. illus. 22cm. Bibl. 63-7394 5.00
1. Natural theology. I. Title. II. Title: Philosophy of God.

BLAKE, Michael P., 1919- 210
The grand analogy [by] Michael P. Blake. [South Haven, Mich., MPB Associates, 1972- v. 22 cm. Contents.Contents.—v. 1. Of devolution and destiny. [BP610.B613] 74-170446
I. Title.

BLAKE, Michael P., 1919- 210 s
Of devolution and destiny [by] Michael P. Blake. [1st ed.] South Haven, Mich., MPB Associates [1972] v, 296 p. 22 cm. (His The grand analogy, v. 1) Also has title: The first analogy. Sequel to From maya to the grand analogy. Bibliography: p. 287-289. [BP610.B613 vol. 1] 210 72-94216
I. Title.

BONIFAZI. CONRAD, 1912- 210
A theology of things; a study of man in his physical environment [1st ed.] Philadelphia, Lippincott [1967] 237 p. 21 cm. Bibliographical footnotes. [BD581.B587] 67-20168
1. Philosophy of nature. 2. Christian ethics. I. Title.

BONIFAZI, Conrad, 1912- 210
A theology of things; a study of man in his physical environment. [1st ed.] Philadelphia, Lippincott [1967] 237 p. 21 cm. Bibliographical footnotes. [BD581.B587] 67-20168
1. Philosophy of nature. 2. Christian ethics. I. Title.

BONIFAZI, Conrad, 1912- 210
A theology of things : a study of man in his physical environment / Conrad Bonifazi. Westport, Conn. : Greenwood Press, 1976, c1967. 237 p. ; 23 cm. Reprint of the ed. published by Lippincott, Philadelphia. Includes bibliographical references and index. [BD581.B587 1976] 76-7549 ISBN 0-8371-8838-5 lib.bdg. : 14.00
1. Philosophy of nature. 2. Nature (Theology) I. Title.

BRENTANO, Mary Bernarda. 210
Nature in the works of Fray Juis [i.e. Luis] de Granada. New York, AMS Press [1969, c1936] xix, 160 p. 22 cm. (The Catholic University of America. Studies in Romance languages and literatures, v. 15) Originally presented as the author's thesis, Catholic University of America, 1936. Bibliography: p. 154-156. [PQ6412.L8Z57 1969] 75-94164
1. Luis de Granada, 1504-1588. 2. Nature in literature. I. Title. II. Series.

BURNS, Paul P., 1890- 210
The knowledge of God, by Paul P. Burns. Philadelphia, Dorrance [1972] ix, 73 p. 22 cm. [BT102.B84] 72-79872 ISBN 0-8059-1707-1 3.95
1. God—Knowableness. I. Title.

CARNELL, Edward John, 1919- 210
The burden of Soren Kierkegaard. Grand Rapids, Mich. Eerdmans [c.1965] 174p. 22cm. Bibl. [BX4827.K5C3] 65-18088 3.50
1. Kierkegaard, Soren Aabye, 1813-1855. I. Title.

CAROTHERS, J. Edward. 210
The pusher and puller; a concept of God [by] J. Edward Carothers. Nashville, Abingdon Press [1968] 223 p. 23 cm. Bibliography: p. 213-216. [BL182.C26] 68-17435
1. Natural theology. I. Title.

CASSERLEY, Julian Victor Langmead, 1909- 210
Graceful reason; the contribution of reason to theology. Foreword by John Heuss. Greenwich, Conn., Seabury Press, 1954. 163p. 22cm. [BL181.C28] 54-9008
1. Natural theology. I. Title.

CASSERLEY, Julian Victor Langmead, 1909- 210
Graceful reason; the contribution of reason to theology. Foreword by John Heuss. London, New York, Longmans, Green [1955] 163p. 23cm. [BL181.C28 1955] 55-2014
1. Natural theology. I. Title.

CIORAN, Emile M., 1911- 210
The new gods [by] E. M. Cioran. Translated from the French by Richard Howard. [New York] Quadrangle [1974] 120 p. 22 cm. Translation of Le Mauvais demiurge. [BL226.C5613 1974] 74-77939 ISBN 0-8129-0475-3 5.95
1. Creation. 2. Good and evil. 3. Man (Theology) 4. Suicide. I. Title.

CLUTTON-BROCK, Arthur, 1868-1924. 210
Essays on religion. With an introd. by Canon B. H. Streeter. Freeport, N.Y., Books for Libraries Press [1969] xxvi, 171 p. 23 cm. (Essay index reprint series) Reprint of the 1926 ed. [BR85.C536 1969] 79-84302
1. Theology—Addresses, essays, lectures. I. Title.

COBB, John B. 210
A Christian natural theology, based on the thought of Alfred North Whitehead, by John B. Cobb, Jr. Philadelphia, Westminster Press [1965] 288 p. 21 cm. Bibliographical footnotes. [B1674.W354C6] 65-11612
1. Whitehead, Alfred North, 1861-1947. 2. Natural theology. I. Title.

COBB, John B., Jr. 210
A Christian natural theology, based on the thought of Alfred North Whitehead. Philadelphia, Westminster [c.1965] 288p. 21cm. Bibl. [B1674.W354C6] 65-11612 6.50
1. Whitehead, Alfred North, 1861-1947. 2. Natural theology. I. Title.

CUPITT, Don. 210
Christ and the hiddenness of God. Philadelphia, Westminster Press [1971] 219 p. 21 cm. "Based on the Stanton Lectures delivered at Cambridge in the Lent Terms of 1969 and 1970." Includes bibliographical references. [BT40.C78] 75-144038 ISBN 0-664-20905-X 6.00
1. Philosophical theology. I. Title.

CURREY, Cecil B. 210
Reason and revelation : John Duns Scotus on natural theology / Cecil B. Currey. Chicago : Franciscan Herald Press, [1977] p. cm. (Synthesis series) Includes bibliographical references. [BL182.C87] 77-9614 ISBN 0-8199-0717-0 pbk. : 0.65
1. Duns, Joannes Scotus, 1265?-1308?—Addresses, essays, lectures. 2. Natural theology—History of doctrines—Addresses, essays, lectures. I. Title.

CURREY, Cecil B. 210
Reason and revelation : John Duns Scotus on natural theology / Cecil B. Currey. Chicago : Franciscan Herald Press, [1977] p. cm. (Synthesis series) Includes bibliographical references. [BL182.C87] 77-9614 ISBN 0-8199-0717-0 pbk. : 0.65
1. Duns, Joannes Scotus, 1265?-1308?—Addresses, essays, lectures. 2. Natural theology—History of doctrines—Addresses, essays, lectures. I. Title.

DONCEEL, Joseph F., 1906- 210
Natural theology. New York, Sheed [1962] 178p. 21cm. 62-9106 3.00
1. Natural theology. I. Title.

FLEW, Antony Garrard Newton, 1923- 210
God & philosophy [by] Antony Flew. [1st American ed.] New York, Harcourt, Brace & World [1966] 208 p. 21 cm. Bibliography: p. [195]-204. [BL182.F55 1966] 66-23807
1. Natural theology. I. Title.

FLEW, Antony Garrard Newton, 1923- 210
The presumption of atheism and other philosophical essays on God, freedom, and immortality / Antony Flew. New York : Barnes & Noble, 1976. 183 p. ; 23 cm. Includes index. Bibliography: p. [176]-180. [BR85.F54 1976b] 76-361131 ISBN 0-06-492119-0 : 20.00
1. Theology—Addresses, essays, lectures. 2. Immortality—Addresses, essays, lectures. I. Title: The presumption of atheism ...

GORDON, William Clark, 1865-1936. 210
The social ideals of Alfred Tennyson as related to his time. New York, Haskell House, 1966. vi, 256 p. 24 cm. Reprint of the 1906 ed. Thesis—University of Chicago, 1899. Bibliography: p. 251-252. [PR5592.S5G6 1966] 68-812
1. Tennyson, Alfred Tennyson, Baron, 1809-1892. 2. Social problems in literature. I. Title.

HARDY, Alister Clavering, Sir. 210
The biology of God : a scientist's study of man the religious animal / Alister Hardy. New York : Taplinger Pub. Co., 1976, c1975. 238 p. ; 23 cm. Errata slip inserted. Includes bibliographical references and index. [BL263.H334 1976] 75-35473 ISBN 0-8008-0740-5 : 9.95
1. Evolution and religion. I. Title.

HARTSHORNE, Charles, 1897- 210
A natural theology for our time. La Salle, Ill., Open Court [1967] xi, 145 p. 22 cm. (The Open Court library of philosophy.) (Morse lectures, 1964) "Somewhat extended and revised versions of ... [the] lectures." [BL182.H34] 66-14722
1. Natural theology. I. Title. II. Series.

HEARD, Gerald, 1889- 210
Is God in history? An inquiry into human and prehuman history, in terms of the doctrine of creation, fall and redemption. [1st ed.] New York, Harper [1950] xii, 269 p. 22 cm. Bibliographical references included in "Notes" (p. 245-262) [BL51.H382] 50-8535
1. Religion—Philosophy. 2. History—Philosophy. 3. Creation. 4. Fall of man. 5. Redemption. I. Title.

HEZMALL, Everett F. 210
God speaks through nature / by Everett F. Hezmall. Lincoln, Neb. : Venture Pub., 1975. 102 p. ; 18 cm. [BT695.5.H49] 75-29556 1.25
1. Presbyterian Church—Sermons. 2. Nature (Theology)—Sermons. 3. Sermons, American. I. Title.

HOLLOWAY, Maurice R 210
An introduction to natural theology. New York, Appleton-Century-Crofts [1959] 492p. 22cm. [BL181.H63] 59-6522
1. Natural theology. I. Title.

HUME, David, 1711-1776 210
Dialogues concerning natural religion, 2d. ed. Ed., introd. by Norman Kemp Smith. Indianapolis, Bobbs [1963, c.1947] 249p. 21cm. (Lib. of liberal arts 174) 1.45 pap.,
1. Natural theology. I. Title.

HUME, David, 1711-1776. 210
Dialogues concerning natural religion. Edited and with commentary by Nelson Pike. Indianapolis, Bobbs-Merrill [1970] xxiii, 238 p. 21 cm. (The Bobbs-Merrill text and commentary series, TC6) Bibliography: p. xxi-xxii. [BL180.H8 1970] 77-132933 2.95
1. Natural theology—Early works to 1900. I. Pike, Nelson, ed. II. Title.

HUME, David, 1711-1776. 210
The natural history of religion / by David Hume; edited by A. Wayne Colver, and Dialogues concerning natural religion / by David Hume ; edited by John Valdimir Price. Oxford [Eng.] : Clarendon Press, 1976. 299 p. ; 22 cm. The natural history of religion is from the text of the 1st ed. of 1757; Dialogues concerning natural religion is edited from the author's original manuscript. Includes index. Bibliography: p. [287]-295. [BL51.H963 1976] 77-354407 ISBN 0-19-824379-0 : 21.00
1. Religion—Philosophy. 2. Natural theology—Early works to 1900. I. Colver, Anthony Wayne. II. Price, John Valdimir. III. Hume, David, 1711-1776. Dialogues concerning natural religion. 1976. IV. Title: The natural history of religion.
Dist. by Oxford University Press NY NY

THE Idea of God; 210
philosophical perspectives. Compiled and edited by Edward H. Madden, Rollo Handy, and Marvin Farber. Springfield, Ill., Thomas [1968] x, 181 p. 24 cm. (American lecture series, publication no. 731. A monograph in American lectures in philosophy) The major addresses and commentaries presented at the symposium held at the State University of New York at Buffalo, October 5-6, 1967. Includes bibliographical references. [BL51.I3] 68-25976
1. God—Addresses, essays, lectures. 2. Religion—Philosophy—Addresses, essays, lectures. I. Madden, Edward H., ed. II. Handy, Rollo, ed. III. Farber, Marvin, 1901- ed. IV. New York. State University, Buffalo.

JOHNSON, Raynor Carey 210
A religious outlook for modern man. Foreword by Leslie D. Weatherhead. New York,

McGraw [1964, c.1963] 220p. 23cm. Bibl. 64-19695 4.95
I. Title.

JOYCE, George Hayward, 1864-1943. 210
Principles of natural theology. London, Longmans, Green, 1923. [New York, AMS Press, 1972] xxviii, 612 p. 19 cm. Original ed. issued in series: Stonyhurst philosophical series. [BL181.J6 1972] 79-170829 ISBN 0-404-03609-0
1. Natural theology. 2. God. I. Title. II. Series: Stonyhurst philosophical series.

KUENZLI, Alfred E., ed. 210
Reconstruction in religion; a symposium. Contributors: Ernest E. Bayles [others] Boston, Beacon [c.1961] xvi, 253p. Bibl. 61-13121 3.95
1. Religions (Proposed, universal, etc.) I. Bayles, Ernest Edward, 1897- II. Title.

MCTAGGART, John McTaggart Ellis, 1866-1925. 210
Some dogmas of religion. New York, Greenwood Press [1968] xx, 299 p. 24 cm. Reprint of the 1906 ed. Bibliographical footnotes. [BT78.M35 1968] 68-57622
1. Dogma. 2. Immortality. 3. Free will and determinism. 4. God. I. Title.

MARTY, Martin E., 1928- 210
Varieties of unbelief. Garden City, N.Y., Doubleday [1966, c.1964] vii, 222p. 18cm. (Anchor bk., A491) Bibl. [BL2747.M3] 1.25 pap.,
1. Irreligion. I. Title.

MASCALL, Eric Lionel, 1905- 210
The openness of being; natural theology today [by] E. L. Mascall. Philadelphia, Westminster Press [1972, c1971] xiii, 278 p. 23 cm. (The Gifford lectures, 1970-71) Bibliography: p. [267]-274. [BL182.M35 1972] 72-75839 ISBN 0-664-20944-0 9.75
1. Natural theology. 2. Theism. I. Title. II. Series.

MATHER, Cotton, 1663-1728. 210
The Christian philosopher: a collection of the best discoveries in nature, with religious improvements. Gainesville, Fla., Scholars' Facsimiles & Reprints, 1968. xiii, vii, 304 p. 23 cm. Reprint of the 1721 ed., with an introd. by Josephine K. Piercy. [BL180.M4 1968] 68-29082
1. Natural theology—Early works to 1900. I. Title.

MAX, Peter, 1937- 210
Love. [With the words of Swami Sivananda, Himalayas]. Editorial assistance by Arjuna (Victor Zurbel). New York, Morrow, 1970. [31] p. col. illus. 15 cm. [BV4639.M34] 79-118294 1.95
1. Love (Theology) I. Sivananda, Swami. II. Title.

MAX, Peter, 1937- 210
Peace. [With the words of Swami Sivananda, Himalayas]. Editorial assistance by Arjuna (Victor Zurbel). New York, Morrow, 1970. [31] p. col., illus., 15 cm. [BV4908.5.M34] 75-118293 1.95
1. Peace of mind. 2. Peace (Theology) I. Sivananda, Swami. II. Title.

MAX, Peter, 1937- 210
Thought. [With the words of Swami Sivananda, Himalayas]. Editorial assistance by Arjuna (Victor Zurbel). New York, Morrow, 1970. [31] p. col. illus. 15 cm. [BF637.P3S55] 78-118291 1.95
1. Peace of mind. I. Sivananda, Swami. II. Title.

MESLIER, Jean, 1664-1729. 210
Le Testament / Jean Meslier. Hildesheim ; New York : G. Olms, 1974. 3 v. in 1 ; 20 cm. Reprint of the ed. published in 1864 in Amsterdam by R. C. Meijer. [BL2773.M45 1974] 74-194533 ISBN 3-487-05278-4
1. Religion—Controversial literature. 2. Christianity—Controversial literature. I. Title.

MORRISS, Frank. 210
The forgotten revelation; essays on God and nature. Chicago, Franciscan Herald Press [1964] 91 p. 22 cm. [BL182.M6] 64-24286
1. Natural theology — Addresses, essays, lectures. I. Title.

MORRISS, Frank 210
The forgotten revelation; essays on God and nature. Chicago, FranciscanHerald [c.1964] 91p. 22cm. [BL182.M6] 64-24286 2.95
1. Natural theology—Addresses, essays, lectures. I. Title.

MULLER, Friedrich Max, 1823-1900. 210
Natural religion : the Gifford lectures delivered before the University of Glasgow in 1888 / by F. Max Muller. New York : AMS Press, [1975] xix, 608 p. ; 19 cm. Reprint of the 1889 ed. published by Longmans, Green, London, in series: Gifford lectures, 1888. Includes bibliographical references and index. [BL181.M8 1975] 73-18810 ISBN 0-404-11450-4 : 31.00
1. Natural theology—Early works to 1900. 2. Religion. 3. Mythology. I. Title. II. Series: Gifford lectures, 1888.

NICHOLLS, William. 210
Systematic and philosophical theology. Harmondsworth, Penguin, 1969. 363 p. 18 cm. (Pelican books, A1048.) (The Pelican guide to modern theology, v. 1) Bibliography: p. 349-352. [BT28.N5] 70-446866 ISBN 1-402-10482- 10/-
1. Theology, Doctrinal—History—20th century. I. Title. II. Series.

*NICHOLS, Brougham 210
Eternity is now. New York, Vantage [c.1964] 134p. 21cm. 3.50
I. Title.

PARKER, Francis H. 210
Reason and faith revisited, by Francis H. Parker. Milwaukee, Marquette University Press, 1971. 45 p. 19 cm. (The Aquinas lecture, 1971) Bibliography: p. 45. [BT50.P37] 79-154285
1. Faith and reason. I. Title. II. Series.

PURTILL, Richard L., 1931- 210
Reason to believe [by] Richard L. Purtill. Grand Rapids, Eerdmans [1974] 166 p. 21 cm. Bibliography: p. 163-164. [BL51.P87] 73-21905 ISBN 0-8028-1567-7 2.95 (pbk.)
1. Religion—Philosophy. I. Title.

RAY, John, 1627-1705. 210
The wisdom of God manifested in the works of the creation / John Ray. Nachdr. d. Ausg. London 1691. Hildesheim ; New York : Olms, 1974. 249 p. ; 17 cm. (Anglistica & Americana ; 122) Reprint of the 1691 ed. printed for S. Smith, at the Princes Arms in S. Pauls Church Yard, London. [BL180.R3 1974] 75-329441 ISBN 3-487-05403-5 : DM39.80
1. Natural theology—Early works to 1900. 2. Science—Early works to 1800. I. Title. II. Series.

RICHMOND, James, 1931- 210
Theology and metaphysics. New York, Schocken Books [1971, c1970] xii, 156 p. 23 cm. Includes bibliographical references. [BR100.R5 1971] 72-159483 ISBN 0-8052-3411-X 6.50
1. Christianity—Philosophy. 2. Natural theology. 3. Theism. I. Title.

SCHARLEMANN, Robert P. 210
Reflection and doubt in the thought of Paul Tillich [by] Robert P. Scharlemann. New Haven, Yale University Press, 1969. xx, 220 p. 23 cm. Bibliography: p. [203]-209. [BX4827.T53S28] 79-81430 6.75
1. Tillich, Paul, 1886-1965. I. Title.

SMITH, Gerard. 210
Natural theology: Metaphysics II New York, Macmillan [1951] 297 p. 22 cm. (Christian wisdom series) [BL205.S56] 51-6955
1. God (Theory of knowledge) I. Title.

STEINER, Rudolf, 1861-1925. 210
Life between death and rebirth; sixteen lectures. [Translated by R. M. Querido] New York, Anthroposophic Press [1968] viii, 308 p. 22 cm. Translation of: Okkulte Untersuchungen uber das Leben zwischen Tod und neuer Geburt. [BP595.S895A543] 68-57429
1. Intermediate state. I. Title.

STRAUSS, Leo. 210
Spinoza's critique of religion. [Translated by E. M. Sinclair] New York, Schocken Books [1965] 351 p. 24 cm. Bibliographical references included in "Notes" (p. [271]-304) [B3985.Z7S73] 65-10948
1. Spinoza, Benedictus de, 1632-1677. Tractatus theologico-politicus. I. Title.

STRAUSS, Leo 210
Spinoza's critique of religion [Tr. from German by E. M. Sinclair] New York, Schocken [c.1965] 351p. 24cm. Bibl. [B3985.Z7S73] 65-10948 8.50
1. Spinoza, Benedictus de, 1632-1677. Tractatus theologico-politicus. I. Title.

TAYLOR, Alfred, 1896- 210
A human heritage; the wisdom in science and experience. Wheaton, Ill., Theosophical Pub. House [1975] 146 p. 22 cm. (A Quest book) [BP565.T35] 74-18360 ISBN 0-8356-0455-1 2.50 (pbk.)
1. Theosophy. I. Title.

WALKER, Raymond B., 1888-1974. 210
Beside still waters / by Raymond B. Walker. 1st ed. Portland, Or. : Binford & Mort, [1976] c1975. 165 p. : ill. ; 28 cm. Includes bibliographical references. [BT695.5.W34] 75-32601 ISBN 0-8323-0264-3 : 12.50
1. Nature (Theology)—Meditations. I. Title.

WALLACE, Robert, 1697-1771. 210
Various prospects of mankind, nature and providence. 1761. To which is added Ignorance and superstition, a source of violence and cruelty, a sermon preached in the High Church of Edinburgh, January 6, 1746. New York, A. M. Kelley, 1969. viii, 406, 39 p. 22 cm. (Reprints of economic classics) Reprint of the 1761 ed. and 1746 ed., respectively. [BL180.W3 1969] 69-19550 ISBN 0-678-00491-9
1. Natural theology—Early works to 1900. I. Wallace, Robert, 1697-1771. Ignorance and superstition. II. Title.

*WARREN, Glenn B. 210
A Christian faith for today, an attempt at understanding. New York, Vantage [c.1964] 99p. 21cm. Bibl. 2.50 bds.,
I. Title.

WHEELER, Herschel 210
My Father's world. by Herschel & Ruth Wheeler. Mountain View, Calif., Pacific Pr. Pub [1966. c.1965] 119p. illus. 26cm. Bibl. [BL182.W5] 65-23811 4.50 bds.,
1. Natural theology. I. Wheeler, Ruth Lellah (Carr) 1899- joint author. II. Title.

WILKINS, John, Bp. of Chester, 1614-1672. 210
Of the principles and duties of natural religion. With a new introd. by Henry G. Van Leeuwen. New York, Johnson Reprint Corp., 1969. xxxvii, 410 p. 19 cm. (Texts in early modern philosophy) Reprint of the 1693 ed. Bibliography: p. xxxvi-xxxvii. [BL180.W5 1969] 68-58291
1. Natural theology—Early works to 1900. I. Title.

CAIRD, Edward, 1835-1908. 210'.38
The evolution of theology in the Greek philosophers. Glasgow, J. MacLahose, 1904. Grosse Pointe, Mich., Scholarly Press, 1968. 2 v. 22 cm. (Gifford lectures, 1900-1902) "Delivered in the University of Glasgow in sessions 1900-1 and 1901-2." [B187.T5C3 1968] 72-3480
1. Philosophy, Ancient. 2. Theology. 3. God (Greek religion) I. Title. II. Series.

GARRARD, Lancelot Austin, 1904- 210.8
Athens or Jerusalem? A study in Christian comprehension London, Allen & Unwin [dist. Mystic, Conn., Verry, c.1965] 183p. 21cm. (Minns lects., 1963) Bibl. [BR1616.G3] 65-6314 4.58 bds.,
1. Liberalism (Religion)—Addresses, essays, lectures. I. Title.

MILLER, Eddie L., 1937- comp. 210'.8
Classical statements on faith and reason. Edited, with an introd., by Ed. L. Miller. New York, Random House [1970] xv, 235 p. 21 cm. (Studies in philosophy) Contents.Contents.—Athens or Jerusalem? By Tertullian.—Philosophy the handmaid of theology, by Clement of Alexandria.—Faith in search of understanding, by St. Augustine.—Revelation and analogy, by St. Thomas Aquinas.—The mystic way, by M. Eckhart.—The darkened intellect, by J. Calvin.—The reasons of the heart, by B. Pascal.—Faith, reason, and enthusiasm, by J. Locke.—Miracles and the skeptic, by D. Hume.—The limits of reason, by I. Kant.—Truth and subjectivity, by S. Kierkegaard.—In justification of faith, by W. James.—Religion as poetry, by G. Santayana.—Faith and symbols, by P. Tillich.—Three parables on falsification, by A. Flew, R. M. Hare, and B. Mitchell.—For further reading (p. 233-235) [BT50.M54] 78-81166
1. Faith and reason—Addresses, essays, lectures. I. Title.

SAHAKIAN, William S ed. 210.8
Philosophies of religion [by] William S. Sahakian. Cambridge, Mass., Schenkman Pub. Co. [1965] xi, 476 p. 24 cm. Bibliographical footnotes. [BL51.S347] 65-20304
1. Religion—Philosophy—Collections. I. Title.

SAHAKIAN, William S., ed. 210.8
Philosophies of religion. Cambridge, Mass., Schenkman [c.1965] xi, 476p. 24cm. Bibl. [BL51.S347] 65-20304 6.95
1. Religion—Philosophy—Collections. I. Title.

TALAFOUS, Camillus D., ed. 210.8
Readings in science and spirit Englewood Cliffs, N.J. Prentice c.1966 xi, 271p. 22cm. Bibl. xi, 271p. 22cm. Bibl. [BL51.T34] 66-10611
1. Religion — sReligion— Philosophy — Addresses, essays, lectures. 2. Science — Philosophy — Addresses, essays, lectures. 3. Philosophical anthropology — Addresses, essays, lectures. I. Title.

LONNING, Per 210.81
The dilemma of contemporary theology prefigured in Luther, Pascal, Kierkegaard, Nietzsche. [Oslo] Universitetsforlaget; New York, Humanities, 1964, c.1962] 139p. illus. 23cm. (Scandinavian univ. bks.) 64-5569 3.00 bds.,
1. Theology—Addresses, essays, lectures. I. Title.

LONNING, Per. 210.81
The dilemma of contemporary theology prefigured in Luther, Pascal, Kierkegaard, Nietzsche. [Olso] Universitetsforlaget; New York, Humanities Press, 1962 [i.e. 1964] 139 p. illus. 23 cm. (Scandinavian university books) [BT15.L6] 64-5569
1. Theology — Addresses, essays, lectures. I. Title.

TEILHARD de Chardin, Pierre. 210.81
Hymn of the universe. [Translated by Simon Bartholomew] New York, Harper & Row [1965] 157 p. 22 cm. [B2430.T373H93] 65-10375
1. Mysticism—Catholic Church. 2. Cosmology. 3. Creation. I. Title.

TEILHARD DE CHARDIN, Pierre 210.81
Hymn of the universe [Tr. by Simon Bartholomew] New York, Harper [c.1961, 1965] 157p. 22cm. [B2430.T373H93] 65-10375 3.00
1. Mysticism—Catholic Church. 2. Cosmology. 3. Creation. I. Title.

TOLSTOI, Lev Nikolaevich, graf 210.81
Lift up your eyes; the religious writings of Leo Tolstoy. Introd. by Stanley R. Hopper. New York, Julian Press, [c.] 1960. 581p. port. 21cm. 59-15567 5.95
1. Theology—Collected works—19th cent. I. Title.

BAISNEE, Jules Albert, 1879- ed. 210.82
Readings in natural theology. Westminster, Md., Newman Press, 1962. 321 p. 22 cm. (The College readings series, no. 7) [BL175.B3] 62-16556
1. Natural theology—Collections. I. Title.

BAISNEE, Jules Albert, 1879- ed. 210.82
Readings in natural theology. Westminster, Md., Newman [c.]1962. 321p. 22cm. (Coll. readings ser., no. 7) Bibl. 62-16556 2.50 pap.,
1. Natural theology—Collections. I. Title.

BAYNE, Stephen Fielding, Bp., 1908- ed. 210.82
Space age Christianity. Foreword by William Fisher Lewis. New York, Morehouse [c.1963] 191p. 21cm. Bibl. 63-12112 4.50
1. Christianity—20th cent. Addresses, essays, lectures. 2. Religion and science—1946- — Addresses, essays, lectures. I. Title.

IN search of God and immortality [by] Julius Seelye Bixler [and others] Boston, Beacon Press [1961] 168p. 21cm. (The Garvin lectures) Includes bibliography. [BT102.A1 I 5] 61-7251 210.82
1. God. 2. Immortality. 3. Religion and science—1946- I. Bixler, Julius Seelye, 1894-

BAYNE, Stephen Fielding. Bp., 1908- ed. 210.83
Space age Christianity. Foreword by William Fisher Lewis. New York, Morehouse-Barlow [1963] 191 p. 21 cm. "An edited account of the lectures and discussions on Space age Christianity which took place in August 1962 at the Seattle World's Fair." Bibliography: p. 189-191. [BL241.B35] 63-12112
1. Christianity — 20t cent. — Addresses, essays, lectures. 2. Religion and science — 1946- — Addresses, essays, lectures. I. Title.

REDWOOD, John. 210'.942
Reason, ridicule, and religion : the Age of Enlightenment in England, 1660-1750 / John Redwood. Cambridge, Mass. : Harvard University Press, 1976. 287 p. ; 24 cm. Includes index. Bibliography: p. 269-272. [B1302.E65R4 1976b] 75-46350 12.00
1. Enlightenment. 2. Philosophy, English—18th century. I. Title.

REDWOOD, John. 210'.942
Reason, ridicule, and religion : the age of enlightenment in England, 1660-1750 / John Redwood. London : Thames & Hudson, c1976. 287 p. ; 24 cm. Errata slip inserted. Includes index. Bibliography: p. 269-272. [B1302.E65R4] 76-357176 ISBN 0-500-25043-X : £7.00

1. Enlightenment. 2. Philosophy, English—18th century. I. Title.

211 God

AGEE, James, 1909- 211
Religion and the intellectuals; a symposium with James Agee [and others. New York, 1950] 139 p. 23 cm. (PR series, no. 3) First published in Partisan review, v. 17, no. 2-5, Feb.-May/June, 1950. [BL237.R4] 51-620
1. Religion. 2. Intellectuals. I. Partisan review. II. Title.

ANDERSON, Ray Sherman. 211
Historical transcendence and the reality of God : A Christological critique / Ray Sherman Anderson ; with a foreword by D. M. MacKinnon. 1st American ed. Grand Rapids [Mich.] : Eerdmans, 1975. xxii, 328 p. ; 22 cm. Includes indexes. Bibliography: p. [307]-317. [BT102.A49 1975] 75-33737 ISBN 0-8028-3473-6 pbk. : 3.95
1. God. 2. Incarnation. I. Title.

ANSTON, Oscar, 1904- 211
Jesus, the Son of nobody. New York, Sagittarius Press [1949, '1950] 270 p. 20 cm. [BL2775.A54 1950] 50-1641
1. Free thought. 2. Jesus Christ—Miscellanes. I. Title.

AUBREY, Edwin Ewart, 1896- 211
Secularism a myth; an examination of the current attack on secularism. [1st ed.] New York, Harper [1954] 191p. 22cm. (The Ayer lectures for 1953) [BL2750.A8] 54-6900
1. Secularism. I. Title.

BAILLIE, John, 1886-1960. 211
The sense of the presence of God. New York, Scribner [1962] 269 p. 22 cm. (Gifford lectures, 1961-2) [BT102.B3] 62-9638
1. God (Theory of knowledge) I. Title.

BARTH, Karl, 1886- 211
Anselm: Fides quaerens intellectum; Anselm's proof of the existence of God in the context of his theological scheme. [Translated by Ian W. Robertson from the German. 1st English ed.] Richmond, Va., John Knox Press [1960] 173p. 23cm. Bibliographical footnotes. [B765.A83P833] 61-5569
1. God—Proof, Ontological. I. Anselm, Saint, Abp. of Canterbury, 1033-1100. II. Title. III. Title: Fides quaerens intellectum.

BARTH, Karl, 1886- 211
Anselm: Fides quaerens intellectum; faith in search of understanding. Tr. from German by Ian W. Robertson. Cleveland, World [1962, c.1960] 173p. 18cm. (Living age bks.: Meridian bks., LA39) Bibl. 1.35 pap.,
1. Anselm, Saint, Abp. of Canterbury, 1033-1109. Prosologium. 2. God—Proof, Ontological. I. Title. II. Title: Fides quaerens intellectum.

BARTH, Karl, 1886- 211
Anselm: Fides quaerens intellectum; Anselm's proof of the existence of God in the context of his theological scheme. [Tr. by Ian W. Robertson from German.] Richmond, Va., John Knox Press [c.1960, i.e., 1961] 173p. Bibl. 61-5569 3.00 bds.,
1. Anselm, Saint, Abp. of Canterbury. 1033-1109. Prosologium. 2. God—Proof, Ontological. I. Title. II. Title: Fides quaerens intellectum.

BARTH, Karl, 1886-1968. 211
Anselm, fides quaerens intellectum : Anselm's proof of the existence of God in the context of his theological scheme / Karl Barth ; [translated by Ian W. Robertson from the German Fides quaerens intellectum 2d ed., 1958] 1st English ed. Pittsburgh : Pickwick Press, [1976] c1960. p. cm. (Pittsburgh reprint series ; no. 2) Reprint of the ed. published by SCM Press, London, in series: The Library of philosophy and theology; with new pref. Includes bibliographical references and index. [B765.A83P833 1976] 76-10795 ISBN 0-915138-09-3 : 3.75
1. Anselm, Saint, Abp. of Cantebury, 1033-1109. Prosologium. 2. God—Proof, Ontological. I. Title. II. Title: Fides quaerens intellectum.

BERTOCCI, Peter Anthony. 211
Is God for real, by Peter A. Bertocci. New York, T. Nelson [1971] viii, 76 p. 21 cm. (Youth forum series, YF19) Includes bibliographical references. [BT102.B4] 75-169033 ISBN 0-8407-5317-9 1.95
1. God. I. Title. II. Series.

BOUILLARD, Henri. 211
The knowledge of God. Translated by Samuel D. Femiano. [New York] Herder and Herder [1968] 127 p. 22 cm. First published in 1967 under title: Connaissance de Dieu, foi cretienne et theologie naturelle. Bibliographical footnotes. [BT102.B613] 68-9494 3.95
1. Barth, Karl, 1886-1968. 2. God—Knowableness. 3. Natural theology. I. Title.

BOWKER, John. 211
The sense of God; sociological, anthropological and psychological approaches to the origin of the sense of God. Oxford, Clarendon P., 1973. xiii, 237 p. 23 cm. "Based on the Wilde Lectures, given in Oxford in 1972." Includes index. Bibliography: p. 219-229. [BL48.B63] 73-180543 ISBN 0-19-826632-4 16.00
1. Religion. 2. God. I. Title.
Distributed by Oxford University Press, New York; Library edition 12.64

BUCKLEY, Michael J. 211
Motion and motion's God; thematic variations in Aristotle, Cicero, Newton, and Hegel, by Michael J. Buckley. [Princeton, N.J.] Princeton University Press, 1971. 287 p. 22 cm. Includes bibliographical references. [BD620.B8] 73-132234 ISBN 0-691-07124-1 10.00
1. Motion. 2. God—Proof. 3. Dialectic. I. Title.

BUDD, Susan. 211
Varieties of unbelief : atheists and agnostics in English society, 1850-1960 / Susan Budd. London : Heinemann Educational Books, 1977. vii, 307 p. ; 22 cm. Imprint covered by label which reads: Holmes & Meier Publishers, New York. Bibliogrpahy: p. [282]-299. Includes index. [BL2765.G7B83] 77-363322 ISBN 0-435-82100-8 : £9.50 ($20.00 U.S.)
1. Rationalism—History. 2. Religious thought—England. I. Title.

BURY, John Bagnell, 1861-1927. 211
A history of freedom of thought. With an epilogue by H. J. Blackham. 2d ed. London, New York, Oxford University Press, 1952. 246 p. 17 cm. (The Home university library of modern knowledge, 74) [BL2750.B8 1952] 52-11971
1. Free thought—Hist. 2. Rationalism—Hist. I. Title. II. Title: Freedom of thought.

CARDIFF, Ira Detrich, ed. 211
What great men think of religion, by Ira D. Cardiff. New York, Arno Press, 1972 [c1945] 503 p. 23 cm. (The Atheist viewpoint) [BL2710.C3 1972] 71-161322 ISBN 0-405-03625-6
1. Free thought. 2. Religion. I. Title. II. Series.

CELL, Edward. 211
Language, existence & God; interpretations of Moore, Russell, Ayer, Wittgenstein, Wisdom, Oxford philosophy, and Tillich. Nashville, Abingdon Press [1971] 400 p. 25 cm. Bibliography: p. 383-388. [B808.5.C43] 71-148079 ISBN 0-687-21063-1 8.95
1. Analysis (Philosophy) 2. God—Knowableness—History of doctrines. 3. Religion and language. I. Title.

CICERO, Marcus Tullius. 211
The nature of the gods. Translated [from the Latin] by Horace C. P. McGregor; with an introduction by J. M. Ross. Harmondsworth, Penguin, 1972. 278 p. 18 cm. (The Penguin classics, L265) Translation of De natura deorum. Includes index. Bibliography: p. 253-255. [PA6308.D4M3] 73-166072 ISBN 0-14-044265-0
I. Ross, John MacDonald. II. Title.
Distributed by Penguin, Baltimore; 2.25 (pbk.).

COLLINS, James Daniel. 211
God in modern philosophy. Chicago, H. Regnery Co., 1959. 476 p. 25 cm. Includes bibliography. [BD573.C6] 59-10545
1. God. 2. Philosophy, Modern. I. Title.

CRITIQUES of God / 211
edited by Peter Angeles. Buffalo, N.Y. : Prometheus Books, 1976. xvii, 371 p. ; 23 cm. Bibliography: p. 369-371. [BT102.C74] 76-43520 ISBN 0-87975-078-2
1. God—Addresses, essays, lectures. 2. Atheism—Addresses, essays, lectures. 3. Religion—Philosophy—Addresses, essays, lectures. I. Angeles, Peter Adam, 1931-

DUMERY, Henry 211
The problem of God in philosophy of religion; a critical examination of the category of the Absolute and the scheme of transcendance. Tr. [from French] introd. by Charles Courtney [c.] 1964. [Evanston, Ill.] Northwestern Univ. Pr. [c.]1964. 1v. 135p. 20cm. (Northwestern Univ. studies in phenomenology & existential philosophy) 64-19454 4.95
1. God. 2. Religion—Philosophy. I. Title. II. Series.

DUMERY, Henry. 211
The problem of God is philosophy of religion; a critical examination of the category of the Absolute and the scheme of trancendence. Translated, with an introd. by Charles Courtney. [Evanston, Ill.] Northwestern University Press, 1964. iv, 135 p. 20 cm. (Northwestern University studies is phenomenology & existential philosophy) Bibliographical footnoes. [BL182.D813] 64-19454
1. God. 2. Religion — Philosophy. I. Title. II. Series.

DUNS, Joannes, Scotus, 1265?-1308? 211
A treatise on God as first principle; a revised Latin text of the De primo principio translated into English along with two related questions from an early commentary on the Sentences, by Allan B. Wolter. [Chicago?] Forum Books [1966] xxiii, 189 p. 21 cm. (A Quincy College publication) English and Latin on opposite pages. Includes bibliographical references. [B765.D73D43 1966] 65-28880
1. Natural theology. 2. God—Proof, Ontological. I. Wolter, Allan Bernard, 1913- ed. II. Title. III. Series: Quincy, Ill. College. Publications

EVANS, William Arthur, 1898- 211
The realization of God in daily living. Dallas, Institute Press ['1950] 255 p. illus. 21 cm. [BL2775.E88] 51-32290
1. Christianity—Controversial literature. 2. Pantheism. I. Title.

FLOOD, Edmund. 211
Evidence for God. New York, Paulist Press [1972] v, 55 p. 17 cm. Includes bibliographical references. [BT102.F56] 72-91455 ISBN 0-8091-1741-X 0.75 (pbk.)
1. God. I. Title.

GEISLER, Norman L. 211
Philosophy of religion / Norman L. Geisler. Grand Rapids : Zondervan Pub. House, [1974] 416 p. ; 23 cm. Includes index. Bibliography: p. 404-412. [BT102.G384] 73-22703 7.95
1. God—Proof. 2. Experience (Religion) 3. Religion and language. 4. Good and evil. I. Title.

THE God experience: essays in hope. 211
Edited by Joseph P. Whelan. New York, Newman Press [1971] vi, 263 p. 23 cm. (The Cardinal Bea lectures, v. 2) Series of lectures delivered during the years 1968-70, in the Cardinal Bea Institute of Spirituality, Woodstock College, New York. Includes bibliographical references. [BT102.G594] 78-163649 4.95
1. God—Addresses, essays, lectures. 2. Hope—Addresses, essays, lectures. I. Whelan, Joseph P., ed. II. Title. III. Series.

GORNALL, Thomas 211
A philosophy of God. the elements of Thomist natural theology New York, Sheed [1963, c.1962] 250p. 20cm. Bibl. 63-17140 3.95
1. Thomas Aquinas, Saint—Theology. 2. Natural theology. I. Title.

GUYAU, Jean Marie, 1854-1888. 211
The non-religion of the future; a sociological study. Introd. by Nahum N. Glatzer New York, Schocken Books [1962] 538 p. 21 cm. (Schocken paperbacks, SB39) [BL2747.G83 1962] 62-19393
1. Religion. 2. Social sciences. I. Title.

HACKETT, Stuart Cornelius. 211
The resurrection of theism; prolegomena to Christian apology. Chicago, Moody Press [1957] 381p. 24cm. Includes bibliography. [BL200.H2] 57-3368
1. Theism. I. Title.

HARKNESS, Georgia Elma, 1891- 211
The modern rival of Christian faith; an analysis of secularism. New York, Abingdon-Cokesbury Press [1952] 223 p. 23 cm. [BT1210.H335] 52-7073
1. Secularism—Controversial literature. 2. Apologetics—20th cent. I. Title.

HARTSHORNE, Charles, 1897- 211
Anselm's discovery: a re-examination of the ontological proof for God's existence. La Salle, Ill., Open Court [1965] xvi, 333p. 21cm. (Open Court lib. of phil.) Bibl. [BT102.H36] 65-20278 6.00
1. Anselm, Abp. of Canterbury, 1033-1109. 2. God—Proof, Ontological. I. Title.

HARTSHORNE, Charles, 1897- 211
Man's vision of God and the logic of theism. Hamden, Conn., Archon [dist. Shoe String] 1964[c.1941] xxi, 360p. 21cm. Bibl. 64-24714 10.00
1. Theism. 2. God—Proof. I. Title.

HERBSTER, Ben M., 1904- 211
God still makes sense, by Ben M. Herbster. Philadelphia, Pilgrim Press [1972] 126 p. 21 cm. [BT102.H47] 75-184454 ISBN 0-8298-0228-2 1.95
1. God. I. Title.

HICK, John. 211
Arguments for the existence of God. [New York] Herder and Herder [1971] xiii, 148 p. 22 cm. (Philosophy of religion series [v. 1]) Bibliography: p. 136-146. [BT102.H5 1971] 75-150305 6.95
1. God—Proof. I. Title.

HILL, William J., 1924- 211
Knowing the unknown God, by William J. Hill. New York, Philosophical Library [1971] iii, 304 p. 22 cm. Bibliography: p. 219-273. [BT102.H53] 70-145465 ISBN 0-8022-2049-5 12.00
1. God—Knowableness. I. Title.

HUXLEY, Julian Sorell, 1887- 211
Religion without revelation. New and rev. ed. New York, Harper [1957] 252p. 22cm. Includes bibliography. [BL48.H8 1957] 57-8170
1. Religion. I. Title.

HUXLEY, Julian Sorell, Sir, 1887- 211
Religion without revelation. [New and rev. ed.] New York, Harper [1957] 252 p. 22 cm. Includes bibliography. [BL48.H8 1957] 57-8170
1. Religion. I. Title.

KALLEN, Horace Meyer, 1882- 211
Secularism is the will of God; an essay in the social philosophy of democracy and religion. New York, Twayne Publishers [c1954] 233p. 23cm. [BL2775.K315] 55-14050
1. Secularism. 2. Religious liberty. 3. U. S.—Religion. I. Title.

KAUFMAN, Gordon D. 211
God the problem [by] Gordon D. Kaufman. Cambridge, Mass., Harvard University Press, 1972. xx, 276 p. 22 cm. Includes bibliographical references. [BT102.K34] 70-174543 ISBN 0-674-35525-3
1. God—Addresses, essays, lectures. I. Title.

KELLENBERGER, James. 211
Religious discovery, faith, and knowledge. Englewood Cliffs, N.J., Prentice-Hall [1972] xi, 207 p. 23 cm. Bibliography: p. 194-204. [BL51.K416] 76-37362 ISBN 0-13-773283-X (pbk) 4.95 (pbk)
1. Knowledge, Theory of (Religion) I. Title.

KREYCHE, Robert J 1920- 211
God and reality; an introduction to the philosophy of God [by] Robert J. Kreyche. New York, Holt, Rinehart and Winston [1965] xiv, 124 p. 21 cm. Bibliography: p. 119-120. [BL182.K7] 65-21065
1. Natural theology. I. Title.

KREYCHE, Robert J., 1920- 211
God and reality; an introduction to the philosophy of God. New York, Holt [c.1965] xiv, 124p. 21cm. Bibl. [BL182.K7] 65-21065 2.00 pap.,
1. Natural theology. I. Title.

LAW, Edmund, Bp. of Carlisle, 1703-1787. 211
An enquiry into the ideas of space, time, immensity, and eternity : 1734 / Edmund Law. New York : Garland Pub., 1976. 196 p. ; 23 cm. (British philosophers and theologians of the 17th & 18th centuries) Original t.p. has subtitle: In answer to a book lately publish'd by Mr. Jackson, entitled, The existence and unity of God proved from His nature and attributes. Reprint of the 1734 ed. printed by W. Fenner and R. Beresford, for W. Thurlbourn, Cambridge, Eng. "A dissertation upon the argument a priori," by D. Waterland: p. 98 [BL51.L45 1976] 75-11230 ISBN 0-8240-1783-8 lib.bdg. : 25.00
1. Jackson, John, 1686-1763. The existence and unity of God proved from His nature and attributes. 2. Religion—Philosophy. I. Waterland, Daniel, 1683-1740. II. Title. III. Series.

LECKY, William Edward Hartpole, 1838-1903. 211
History of the rise and influence of the spirit of rationalism in Europe. Introd. by C. Wright Mills. New York, G. Braziller, 1955. 405, 386p. 21cm. Bibliographical footnotes. [BL2750.L4 1955] 55-37386
1. Rationalism—Hist. I. Title.

LEWIS, Joseph, 1889- 211
An atheist manifesto. New York, Freethought Press Association [1954] 64p. 20cm. [BL2775.L39] 55-15707
1. Atheism. I. Title.

LILLY, John Cunningham, 1915- 211
Simulations of God : the science of belief / by John C. Lilly. New York : Simon and Schuster, [1975] 288 p. ; 22 cm. Bibliography: p. 277-279. [BT102.L55] 75-1039 ISBN 0-671-21981-2 lib.bdg. : 8.95
1. God—Miscellanea. 2. Experience (Religion) I. Title.

LILLY, John Cunningham, 1915- 211
Simulations of God; the science of belief by

John C. Lilly. New York, Bantam [1976 c1975] 284 p. 18 cm. Bibliography: p. 273-275. [BT102.L55] pbk. : 2.25
1. God—Miscellanea. 2. Experience (Religion) I. Title.
L.C. card no. 1975 Simon & Schuster edition: 75-1039.

LINDSAY, John, 1923- 211
Man's spiritual quest; a survey of man's search for ultimate truth, meaning, and security in the universe which is his home, his school, his house of worship. [1st ed.] New York, Greenwich Book Publishers, 1957. 76p. 21cm. [BL2780.L63] 57-9792
I. Title.

LUIJPEN, Wilhelmus Antonius Maria, 1922- 211
What can you say about God? (Except "God.") By William A. Luijpen. Translated by Henry J. Koren. New York, Paulist Press [1971] vii, 88 p. 18 cm. (Deus books) Bibliography: p. 84-88. [BT175.L76] 76-171103 0.95
1. God. I. Title.

LYON, Thoburn Cassady, 1896- 211
Witness in the sky. Chicago, Moody Press [1961] 128p. illus. 20cm. Includes bibliography. [BT175.L9] 61-66179
1. God—Miscellanea. I. Title.

MCCLENDON, Gene. 211
Secularism and salvation. [1st ed.] New York, Vantage Press [1958, c1957] 76p. 21cm. [BL2775.M225] 58-14528
1. Secularism. I. Title.

MCLEAN, George F. 211
Traces of God in a secular culture [edited by] George F. McLean. Staten Island, N.Y., Alba House [1973] xvi, 407 p. 21 cm. Includes bibliographical references. [BT102.M25] 73-3141 ISBN 0-8189-0268-X 5.95 (pbk.)
1. God. 2. Religion—Philosophy. I. Title.

MATHEWS, Shailer, 1863-1941. 211
The growth of the idea of God. Freeport, N.Y., Books for Libraries Press [1973] p. Reprint of the 1931 ed. published by Macmillan, New York. [BT98.M33 1973] 73-4477 ISBN 0-518-19035-8
1. God. I. Title.

MILL, John Stuart, 1806-1873. 211
Theism. Edited with an introd. by Richard Taylor. New York, Liberal Arts Press [1957] xx, 95p. 21cm. (The Library of liberal arts, no. 64) 'Reprinted from the fourth edition of [the author's] Three essays on religion (London, 1875).' Bibliography: p. xx. [BL200.M56 1957] 57-2053
1. Theism. I. Title.

MOLER, Charles Clyde. 211
A bit of reasoning and believing. Chambersburg, Pa., Printed for the author by the Craft Press, c1954. 150p. 24cm. [BL2780.M58] 54-26090
I. Title.

MUELLER, Gustav Emil, 1898- 211
Discourse on religion. New York, Bookman Associates [c1951] 203 p. 23 cm. [BL51.M78] 52-6474
1. Religion — Philosophy. I. Title.

MULLER, Olga (Erbsloh) 1894- 211
Let there be God: an approach to Deity for thinking man. New York, Philosophical Library [1967, c1966] 57 p. 22 cm. [BL2775.2.M8] 66-23436
1. God. I. Title.

MULLER, Olga (Erbsloh) 1894- 211
Let there be God: an approach to Deity for thinking man. New York, Philosophical Library [1967, c1966] 57 p. 22 cm. [BL2775.2.M8] 66-23436
1. God. I. Title.

NEW questions on God. 211
Edited by Johannes B. Metz. [New York] Herder and Herder [1972] 156 p. 23 cm. (Concilium: religion in the seventies. Church and world, v. 76) On cover: The New concilium: religion in the seventies. Includes bibliographical references. [BT102.N48] 73-185752 2.95
1. God—Addresses, essays, lectures. I. Metz, Johannes Baptist, 1928- ed. II. Series: Concilium (New York), v. 76.

*OBERFIELD, William J., 1921- 211
The conflict within; a heretic's views. New York. Exposition [1968] 106p. 21cm. (EP 46802) 4.00
1. Philosophy and religion. I. Title.

OTT, Heinrich. 211
God. Translated by Iain and Ute Nicol. Richmond, John Knox Press [1974] 124 p. 19 cm. Bibliography: p. 124. [BT102.O8613] 73-5350 ISBN 0-8042-0590-6 3.95
1. God.

OWEN, Huw Parri. 211
Concepts of deity [by] H. P. Owen. [New York] Herder and Herder [1971] xi, 174 p. 22 cm. (Philosophy of religion series) Bibliography: p. 166-172. [BL200.O9] 72-150307 7.95
1. Theism. 2. God—History of doctrines. I. Title.

PAINE, Thomas, 1737-1809. 211
Inspiration and wisdom from the writings of Thomas Paine. With three addresses on Thomas Paine by Joseph Lewis. New York, Freethought Press Association, 1954. 303p. illus. 20cm. [BL2735.A1 1954] 54-429
1. Rationalism. I. Lewis, Joseph, 1889- comp. II. Title.

PAINE, Thomas, 1787-1809. 211
Age of reason; being an investigation of true and fabulous theology. Baltimore, Ottenheimer [1956] 2pts. in 1. 22cm. [BL2740] 57-2505
1. Rationalism. I. Title.

PERSONS, Stow, 1913- 211
Free religion, an American faith [Gloucester, Mass., P. Smith, 1964, c.1947] 162p. 21cm. (Beacon paperback LR20 rebound) Bibl. 3.75
1. Free throught—Hist. 2. Free Religious Association. Boston. 3. Unitarianism—Hist. 4. Humanism, Religious. I. Title.

PERSONS, Stow, 1913- 211
Free religion, an American faith. Boston, Beacon [1963. c.1947] 162p. 18cm. (LR 20) 1.75 pap.,
1. Free thought—Hist. 2. Free Religious Association, Boston. 3. Unitarianism—Hist. 4. Humanism, Religious. I. Title.

PLANTINGA, Alvin, ed. 211
The ontological argument, from St. Anselm to contemporary philosophers. Introd. by Richard Taylor. Garden City, N.Y., Doubleday [c.] 1965. xviii, 180p. 19cm. (Anchor bk. A435) Bibl. [BT101.A1P55] 65-10634 .95 pap.,
1. God—Proof, Ontological—Collections. I. Title.

PLANTINGA, Alvin, ed. 211
The ontological argument, from St. Anselm to contemporary philosophers. With an introd. by Richard Taylor. Garden City, N.Y., Anchor Books, 1965. xviii, 180 p. 19 cm. "A435." Bibliographical footnotes. [BT101.A1P55] 65-10634
1. God—Proof, Ontological—Collections. I. Title.

ROBERTSON, John Mackinnon, 1856-1933. 211
A short history of freethought, ancient and modern. New York, Russell & Russell [1957] 447p. 22cm. [BL2750.R7 1957] 57-8672
1. Free thought —Hist. I. Title.

ROTH, Robert J. 211
God knowable and unknowable. Edited by Robert J. Roth. New York, Fordham University Press, 1973. xi, 269 p. 24 cm. Includes bibliographies. [BT102.R675] 77-188274 ISBN 0-8232-0920-2 10.00
1. God—Knowableness—Addresses, essays, lectures. I. Title.

ROYCE, Josiah, 1855-1916. 211
The conception of God; a philosophical discussion concerning the nature of the divine idea as a demonstrable reality, by Josiah Royce [and others] New York, Macmillan Co., 1898. St. Clair Shores, Mich., Scholarly Press, 1971 [c1897] xxxviii, 354 p. 22 cm. Includes bibliographical references. [BT101.R8 1971] 79-107189 ISBN 0-403-00309-1
1. God. I. Title.

RUSSELL, Bertrand Russell, 3d earl, 1872- 211
Why I am not a Christian, and other essays on religion and related subjects. Edited, with an appendix on the 'Bertrand Russell case,' by Paul Edwards. New York, Simon and Schuster, 1957. 266p. 21cm. [BL2780.R87 1957] 57-10982
1. Free thought. I. Title.

RUSSELL, Bertrand Russell, 3d earl, 1872-1970. 211
Why I am not a Christian, and other essays on religion and related subjects. Edited, with an appendix on the "Bertrand Russell case," by Paul Edwards. New York, Simon and Schuster, 1957. 266 p. 21 cm. [BL2780.R87 1957] 57-10982
1. Free thought. I. Title.

SCHILLING, Sylvester Paul, 1904- 211
God incognito [by] S. Paul Schilling. Nashville, Abingdon Press [1974] 207 p. 21 cm. Includes bibliographical references. [BT102.S33] 73-12756 ISBN 0-687-15133-3 5.95
1. God. 2. Experience (Religion) I. Title.

SHRAKE, Henry L 211
Let's worship God alone. New York, Philosophical Library [1954] 274p. 23cm. [BL2775.S467] 55-667
1. Christianity—Controversial literature. I. Title.

SHUTE, John Raymond. 211
The golden dawn. Monroe, N.C., Nocalore Press, 1950. 78 p. 24 cm. [BL2775.S47] 50-19917
1. Free thought. I. Title.

SMITH, John Edwin 211
Reason and God; encounters of philosophy and religion. New Haven, Yale Univ. Pr. [1967, c.1961] xv, 274p. 21cm. (Y181) 1.75 pap.,
1. Philosophy and religion. I. Title.

SMITH, John Edwin. 211
Reason and God; encounters of philosophy with religion. New Haven, Yale University Press, 1961. 274 p. 23 cm. [BL51.S577] 61-15002
1. Philosophy and religion. I. Title.

SMITH, John Edwin 211
Reason and God; encounters of philosophy with religion. New Haven, Conn., Yale [c.] 1961. 274p. 61-15002 5.00
1. Philosophy and religion. I. Title.

SONTAG, Frederick. 211
The God of evil: an argument from the existence of the Devil. [1st ed.] New York, Harper & Row [1970] x, 173 p. illus. 22 cm. Includes bibliographical references. [BT102.S58 1970] 70-109887 5.95
1. God—Proof. 2. Atheism. 3. Good and evil. I. Title.

SZCZESNY, Gerhard 211
The future of unbelief. Tr. from German by Edward B. Garside. New York, Braziller, 1961 [c.1958, 1961] 221 p. 60-11665 4.00
1. Secularism. I. Title.

TCHURMIN, Avrhum Yuhzov. 211
Meditations from an exploration of the ultimate mysteries. North Quincy, Mass., Christopher Pub. House [1972] 110 p. 21 cm. [BT102.T34] 72-85932 4.95
1. God. 2. Man. 3. Ontology. I. Title.

TYRRELL, Bernard, 1933- 211
Bernard Lonergan's philosophy of God [by] Bernard Tyrrell. [American ed.] [Notre Dame, Ind.] University of Notre Dame Press [1974] xiv, 202 p. 23 cm. Based on the author's thesis, Fordham University, 1972. Includes bibliographical references. [BT102.T9 1974] 73-22205 ISBN 0-268-00540-0 12.95
1. Lonergan, Bernard J. F. 2. God—History of doctrines—20th century. I. Title.

WARNE, Floyd Lawrence. 211
Christianity: a critique of religious doctrine. [1st ed.] New York, Vantage Press [c1956] 114p. 21cm. Includes bibliography. [BL2775.W27] 55-10841
1. Christianity—Controversial literature. I. Title.

WARNE, Floyd Lawrence. 211
Christianity: a critique of religious doctrine. [1st ed.] New York, Vantage Press [c1956] 114 p. 21 cm. Includes bibliography. [BL2775.W27] 55-10841
1. Christianity — Controversial literature. I. Title.

WEBB, Clement Charles Julian, 1865-1954. 211
Divine personality and human life. Freeport, N.Y., Books for Libraries Press [1972] 291 p. 23 cm. Reprint of the 1920 ed., issued in series: Gifford lectures, 1918-19 and Library of philosophy. Includes bibliographical references. [BT101.W18 1972] 77-37917 ISBN 0-8369-6754-2
1. Philosophy and religion. 2. God. 3. Personality. I. Title. II. Series: Gifford lectures, 1918-1919. III. Series: Library of philosophy.

WEIGEL, Gustave, 1906- 211
Religion and the knowledge of God [by] Gustave Weigel [and] Arthur G. Madden. Englewood Cliffs, N.J., Prentice-Hall [1961] 181 p. 21 cm. (A Spectrum book, S-21) Includes bibliography. [BT102.W4] 62-7448
1. God (Theory of knowledge) 2. Philosophy and religion. I. Madden, Arthur G., joint author. II. Title.

WEIGEL, Gustave, 1906- 211
Religion and the knowledge of God [by] Gustave Weigel, Arthur G. Madden. Englewood Cliffs, N.J., Prentice-Hall [c.1961] 181p. (Spectrum bk., S-21) Bibl. 62-7448 3.75; 1.75 pap.,
1. God(Theory of knowledge) 2. Philosophy and religion. I. Madden, Arthur G., joint author. II. Title.

WEISS, Paul, 1901- 211
The God we seek. Carbondale, Southern Illinois University Press [1964] 258 p. 22 cm. [B945.W396G6] 64-13476
1. Religion—Philosophy. 2. Experience (Religion) I. Title.

ZAHRNT, Heinz, 1915- 211
What kind of God? A question of faith. [1st U.S. ed.] Minneapolis, Augsburg Pub. House [1972, c1970] 279 p. 23 cm. Translation of Gott kann nicht sterben. Includes bibliographical references. [BT28.Z2813 1972] 77-176102 ISBN 0-8066-1209-6
1. Theology—20th century. 2. God. I. Title.

MAVRODES, George I., comp. 211'.08
The rationality of belief in God. Edited by George I. Mavrodes. Englewood Cliffs, N.J., Prentice-Hall [1970] x, 208 p. 22 cm. (Central issues in philosophy series) Contents.Contents.—Is the nonexistence of God conceivable? By St. Anselm.—Five proofs of God's existence, by St. Thomas Aquinas.—Comments on St. Thomas' Five ways, by F. C. Copleston.—Two proofs of God's existence, by A. E. Taylor.—God's existence as a postulate of morality, by I. Kant.—The existence of God, by J. J. C. Smart.—The problem of evil, by D. Hume.—The experience of God, by J. Baille.—Instinct, experience, and theistic belief, by C. S. Pierce.—The ethics of belief, by W. K. Clifford.—The will to believe, by W. James.—Faith as passionate commitment, by S. Kierkegaard.—God as projection, by L. A. Feuerbach.—Bibliographical essay (p. 205-208) [BT102.A1M35] 79-117010 ISBN 0-13-753194-X 5.95
1. God—Proof—Collections. 2. Faith—Collections. I. Title.

HICK, John, ed. 211.082
The existence of God; readings selected, edited, and furnished with an introductory essay, by John Hick. New York, Macmillan [1964] xiv, 305 p. 18 cm. (Problems of philosophy series) "164." Bibliography: p. 299-305. [BT98.H5] 64-15840
1. God—Proof—Collections. 2. God—History of doctrines. I. Title. II. Series.

HACK, Roy Kenneth. 211'.0922
God in Greek philosophy to the time of Socrates. New York, B. Franklin [1970] vii, 157 p. 23 cm. (Burt Franklin research & source works series, 455) (Philosophy monograph series, 28.) Reprint of the 1931 ed. Bibliography: p. 155-157. [B188.H17 1970] 76-118174
1. Philosophy, Ancient. 2. Greece—Religion. 3. Gods. 4. Monotheism. 5. Religious thought—To 600. 6. Religious thought—Greece. I. Title.

O'MEARA, Thomas F., 1935- 211'.092'4
Paul Tillich's theology of God [by] Thomas Franklin O'Meara. [Dubuque, Iowa] Listening Press [1970] ix, 165 p. 23 cm. A revision of the author's thesis, Ludwig-Maximilian University, Munich, which had the title: Theologie und Ontologie dargestellt an der Gotteslehre von Paul Tillich. Bibliography: p. 154-162. [BT102.O46 1970] 75-304374
1. Tillich, Paul, 1886-1965. 2. God—History of doctrines—20th century. I. Title.

ANSELM, Saint, Abp. of Canterbury, 1033-1109. 211.3
St. Anselm's Proslogion. With, A reply on behalf of the fool, by Gaunilo, and the author's reply to Gaunilo. Translated with an introd. and philosophical commentary, by M. J. Charlesworth. Oxford, Clarendon Press, 1965. vi, 196 p. 23 cm. The three texts are in English and Latin. Includes bibliographical references. [B765.A83P7] 65-5321
1. God — Proof, Ontological. I. Charlesworth, Maxwell John, ed. II. Gaunilo, 11th cent. A reply on behalf of the fool. III. Title.

ANSELM, Saint Abp. of Canterbury 1033-1109 211.3
St. Anselm's Proslogion: With, A reply on behalf of the fool, by gaunilo, and the author's reply to Gaunilo. Tr., intor., philosophical commentary, by M. J. Charlesworth. [New York] Oxford [c.]1965. vi, 196p. 23cm. The three texts are in English and Latin. Bibl. [B765.A83P7] 65-5321 5.60
1. God—Proof, Ontological. I. Charlesworth, Maxwell John, ed. II. Gaunilo, 11th cent. A reply on behalf of the fool. III. Title.

BURKLE, Howard R. 211'.3
The non-existence of God; antitheism from Hegel to Dumery [by] Howard R. Burkle. [New York] Herder and Herder [1969] 220 p. 22 cm. Includes bibliographical references. [BT98.B87] 77-80052 5.95

1. God—History of doctrines—20th century. I. Title.

DONNELLY, John, comp. 211'.3
Logical analysis and contemporary theism. New York, Fordham University Press, 1972. xi, 337 p. 23 cm. Contents.Contents.—On proofs for the existence of God, by J. F. Ross.—Two criticisms of the cosmological argument, by W. L. Rowe.—The argument from design, by R. G. Swinburne.—The claims of religious experience, by H. J. N. Horsburgh.—Ineffability, by W. P. Alston.—The divine simplicity, by D. C. Bennett.—Necessary being, by J. H. Hick.—A new theory of analogy, by J. F. Ross.—Hume on evil, by N. Pike.—The perfect goodness of God, by A. Plantinga.—C. B. Martin's contradiction in theology, by W. L. Rowe.—Divine foreknowledge and human freedom, by A. Kenny.—Some puzzles concerning omnipotence, by G. I. Mavrodes.—The paradox of the stone, by C. W. Savage.—Creation ex nihilo, by J. Donnelly.—The miraculous, by R. F. Holland.—On miracles, by P. J. Dietl.—The tacit structure of religious knowing, by J. H. Gill.—On the observability of the self, by R. M. Chisholm.—Re-examining Kierkegaard's "Teleological suspension of the ethical," by J. Donnelly. Includes bibliographical references. [BL200.D6] 77-168693 ISBN 0-8232-0940-7 12.50
1. Theism—Addresses, essays, lectures. I. Title.

FENN, William Wallace, 1862-1932. 211'.3
Theism; the implication of experience. Edited by Dan Huntington Fenn. Peterborough, N.H., Noone House, 1969. xv, 198 p. 24 cm. Bibliographical references included in "Notes" (p. 193-196) [BT102.F37] 68-57276 5.00
1. Theism. 2. God—Proof. I. Title.

GIBSON, Alexander Boyce, 1900- 211'.3
Theism and empiricism, by A. Boyce Gibson. New York, Schocken Books [1970] vii, 280 p. 23 cm. Includes bibliographical references. [BL51.G57 1970b] 70-111210 8.00
1. Religion—Philosophy. 2. Empiricism. 3. God—Proof. 4. Faith. I. Title.

HAWKINS, Denis John Bernard, 1906-1964. 211'.3
The essentials of theism. Westport, Conn., Greenwood Press [1973, c1949] v, 151 p. 20 cm. [BL200.H38 1973] 72-9373 ISBN 0-8371-6579-2 8.50
1. Theism. I. Title.

HURLBUTT, Robert H. 211.3
Hume, Newton, and the design argument, by Robert H. Hurlbutt, III. Lincoln, University of Nebraska Press [1965] xiv, 221 p. 24 cm. Bibliographical footnotes. [BD541.H8] 65-10047
1. Newton, Isaac, 1642-1727. 2. Hume, David, 1711-1776. 3. Teleology — Hist. I. Title. II. Title: The design argument.

HURLBUTT, Robert H., III 211.3
Hume, Newton, and the design argument. Lincoln, Univ. of Neb. Pr, [c.1965] xiv, 221p. 24cm. Bibl. [BD541.H8] 65-10047 5.00
1. Newton, Isaac, 1642-1727. 2. Hume, David, 1711-1776. 3. Teleology—Hist. I. Title. II. Title: The design argument.

LAIRD, John, 1887-1946. 211'.3
Mind and deity; being the second series of a course of Gifford lectures on the general subject of metaphysics and theism given in the University of Glasgow in 1940. [Hamden, Conn.] Archon Books, 1970. 322 p. 22 cm. ([Gifford lectures, 1940]) Reprint of the 1941 ed. Includes bibliographical references. [BL200.L27 1970] 70-114424
1. Theism. 2. Idealism. 3. God—Proof. I. Title. II. Series.

LAIRD, John, 1887-1946. 211'.3
Theism and cosmology, being the first series of a course of Gifford lectures on the general subject of metaphysics and theism given in the University of Glasgow in 1939. Freeport, N.Y., Books for Libraries Press [1969] 325 p. 23 cm. (Essay index reprint series.) (Gifford lectures, 1939) Reprint of the 1940 ed. Bibliographical footnotes. [BL200.L3 1969] 74-84317
1. Theism. 2. God—Proof. 3. Cosmology. I. Title. II. Series.

MASCALL, Eric Lionel, 1905- 211'.3
Existence and analogy; a sequel to 'He who is', by E. L. Mascall. [Hamden, Conn.] Archon, 1967. xix, 188p. 22cm. Reprint of the 1949 ed. Bibl. [BL200.M318 1967] 67-14497 5.00
1. Theism. 2. Existentialism. 3. Analogy (Religion) I. Title.

MASCALL, Eric Lionel, 1905- 211'.3
He who is; a study in traditional theism, by E. L. Mascall. [Hamden, Conn.] Archon Books, 1970 [c1966] xviii, 238 p. 20 cm. Bibliography: p. 227-234. [BL200.M32 1970] 76-95026
1. Theism. I. Title.

MONSON, Charles H ed. 211.3
Great issues concerning theism, edited and with an introd. by Charles H. Monson, Jr. Salt Lake City, University of Utah Press [1965] 164 p. 20 cm. (Utah. University. The great issues forum, 1964-1965- Errata slip inserted. Bibliographical footnotes. [BT102.A1M6] 65-26132
1. Theism — Congresses. I. Title. II. Series.

NIEBUHR, Helmut Richard 211.3
Radical monotheism and Western culture, with supplementary essays. New York, Harper [c.1960] 144p. (Bibl. footnotes) 22cm. 60-11784 2.75 half cloth,
1. Monotheism. 2. Civilization, Occidental. I. Title.

NIEBUHR, Helmut Richard, 1894- 211.3
Radical monotheism and Western civilization. Lincoln, University of Nebraska, 1960. 101p. 21cm. (Montgomery lectureship on contemporary civilization, 1857) Includes bibliography. [BL221.N5] 60-11341
1. Monotheism. 2. Religion—Philosophy. 3. Civilization, Occidental. I. Title.

NIEBUHR. HELMUT RICHARD, 1894- 211.3
Radical monotheism and Western culture, with supplementary essays. New York, Harper [1960] 144p. 22cm. [BL221.N52] 60-11784
1. Monotheism. 2. Civilization, Occidental. I. Title.

OWEN, Huw Parri 211.3
The moral argument for Christian theism, by H. P. Owen. London, Allen & Unwin [1965] 127p. 21cm. Bibl. [BT102.O9] 65-29351 3.00 bds.,
1. God — Proof, Moral. I. Title.
Now available from Humanities, New York.

PLANTINGA, Alvin. 211'.3
God and other minds; a study of the rational justification of belief in God. Ithaca, N. Y., Cornell University Press [1967] xi, 277 p. 23 cm. (Contemporary philosophy) Bibliographical footnotes. [BT102.P55] 67-20519
1. God—Proof. 2. Theism. I. Title. II. Series.

PLANTINGA, Alvin. 211'.3
God and other minds; a study of the rational justification of belief in God. Ithaca, N.Y., Cornell University Press [1967] xi, 277 p. 23 cm. (Contemporary philosophy) Bibliographical footnotes. [BT102.P55] 67-20519
1. God—Proof. 2. Theism. I. Title. II. Series: Contemporary philosophy series

SHEPHERD, John J. 211'.3
Experience, inference, and God / John J. Shepherd. New York : Barnes & Noble, 1975. 190 p. ; 23 cm. (Library of philosophy and religion) Based on a doctoral thesis prepared at the University of Lancaster. Includes index. Bibliography: p. [185]-187. [BT102.S49 1975] 75-317435 ISBN 0-06-496235-0 : 16.50
1. Theism. 2. God. 3. Natural theology. I. Title.

BRIDGES, Horace James, 1880- 211'.4
The God of fundamentalism, and other studies. Freeport, N.Y., Books for Libraries Press [1969] xviii, 319 p. 23 cm. (Essay index reprint series) Reprint of the 1925 ed. Contents.Contents.—Epistle dedicatory to Edwin Stanton Fetcher.—The God of fundamentalism.—Thomas Henry Huxley; a centenary tribute.—Mr. Clarence Darrow on mechanism and irresponsibility.—Mr. Hilaire Belloc on the Jewish problem.—Erasmus and the Reformation.—Mr. Ludwig Lewisohn versus America.—Joseph Conrad; a memorial tribute. [PS3503.R526G6 1969] 79-86733
I. Title.

BURY, John Bagnell, 1861-1927. 211'.4
A history of freedom of thought / J. B. Bury ; with an epilogue by H. J. Blackham. 2d ed. Westport, Conn. : Greenwood Press, [1975] 246 p. ; 19 cm. Reprint of the 1952 ed. published by G. Cumberlege at the Oxford University Press, London, New York, which was issued as no. 74 of the Home university library of modern knowledge. Includes index. Bibliography: p. [240]-241. [BL2750.B8 1975] 74-30844 ISBN 0-8371-7935-1 lib.bdg. : 13.25
1. Free thought—History. 2. Rationalism—History. I. Title.

COHEN, Chapman, 1868- 211'.4
Primitive survivals in modern thought. New York, Arno Press, 1972. 141 p. 22 cm. (The Atheist viewpoint) Reprint of the 1935 ed. [BL2747.C57 1972] 74-169207 ISBN 0-405-03807-0
1. Free thought. I. Title. II. Series.

ELDER, Frederick Stanton, 1868- 211.4
Morals and religion. New York, Philosophical Library [1963] 179 p. 22 cm. [BL2775.2.E4] 62-18534
1. Religion — Controversial literature. I. Title.

ELDER, Frederick Stanton, 1868- 211.4
Morals and religion. New York, Philosophical [c.1963] 179p. 22cm. 62-18534 3.75
1. Religion—Controversial literature. I. Title.

GREENE, Eli B. 211'.4
The umbilical cord, by Eli B. Greene. Philadelphia, Dorrance [1968] 159 p. 21 cm. [BL2775.2.G7] 68-14372
1. Christianity—Controversial literature. I. Title.

THE Infidel tradition from 211'.4
Paine to Bradlaugh / edited by Edward Royle. London : Macmillan, 1976. xvii, 228 p. ; 23 cm. (History in depth) Includes index. Bibliography: p. [221]-224. [BL2751.I53] 77-353219 ISBN 0-333-17434-8 : £10.00
1. Rationalism—History—Sources. 2. Radicalism—History—Sources. I. Royle, Edward.

JOHNSTONE, Parker Lochiel. 211'.4
Life, death, and hereafter / by Parker Lochiel Johnstone. Philadelphia : Theoscience Foundation, c1976. 170 p. ; 23 cm. Includes index. [BL2747.5.J63] 76-21518 5.95
1. Free thought. I. Title.

LEWIS, Joseph, 1889- 211'.4
Atheism and other addresses. New York, Arno Press, 1972 [c1941] 1 v. (unpaged) 23 cm. (The Atheist viewpoint) [BL2730.L4A52] 72-161333 ISBN 0-405-03800-3
1. Free thought. I. Title. II. Series.

MCCARTHY, William, 1876- 211'.4
Bible, church, and God. New York, Arno Press, 1972 [c1946] 736 p. illus. 24 cm. (The Atheist viewpoint) [BL2775.M22 1972] 70-169211 ISBN 0-405-03805-4
1. Free thought. I. Title. II. Series.

OGILVIE, John, 1733-1813. 211'.4
An inquiry into the causes of the infidelity and scepticism of the times, 1783 by John Ogilvie. New York : Garland Pub., 1975. xvi, 462, 2 p. ; 19 cm. (The Life & times of seven major British writers) (Gibboniana ; 12) Reprint of the ed. printed for Richardson and Urquhart, London, and W. Gordon, W. Creech, and J. Dickson, Edinburgh. [DG206.G5G52 vol. 12] [BL2758] 75-31549 ISBN 0-8240-1348-4 lib.bdg. : 28.00
1. Rationalism—History. 2. Deism—History. 3. Skepticism—History. I. Title. II. Series.

POST, Albert, 1915- 211'.4
Popular freethought in America, 1825-1850. New York, Octagon Books, 1974 [c1943] 258 p. 24 cm. Reprint of the ed. published by Columbia University Press, New York, which was issued as no. 497 of Studies in history, economics and public law. Originally presented as the author's thesis, Columbia University. Bibliography: p. 235-249. [BL2760.P6 1974] 73-20002 ISBN 0-374-96531-5 11.00
1. Free thought—History. I. Title. II. Series: Columbia studies in social science, no. 497.

POTTER, Charles Francis, 1885-1962 211.4
The lost years of Jesus. [Greenwich, Conn.,] Fawcett [1968,c.1962] 160p. 18cm. (d1930) [BM487.P7 1963] .50 pap.,
1. Dead Sea scrolls. 2. Essenes. 3. Christianity and other religions—Judaism. I. Title.

TRIBE, David H. 211'.4
100 years of freethought [by] David Tribe. London, Elek, [1967] 259p. 23cm. Bibl. [BL2759.T7] 67-105789 6.50
1. Free thought—Hist. 2. Rationalism—Hist. I. Title.
Distributed by Humanities, New York.

WARREN, Sidney, 1916- 211.4
American free thought, 1860-1914. New York, Gordian Press, 1966. 257 p. 23 cm. First published in 1943. Bibliography: p. 233-252. [BL2760.W3] 66-20711
1. Free thought — Hist. I. Title.

WARREN, Sidney, 1916- 211.4
American freethought, 1860-1914. New York, Gordian Pr. [c.]1966. 257p. 23cm. First pub. in 1943 by Columbia Univ. Pr. Bibl. [BL2760.W3] 66-20711 7.00

1. Free thought — Hist. I. Title.

CLASSICS of free 211'.4'08
thought / edited by Paul Blanshard. Buffalo : Prometheus Books, [pref. 1977] xi, 190 p. ; 23 cm. [BL2710.C55] 77-73846 ISBN 0-87975-071-5 : 12.95
1. Free thought—Addresses, essays, lectures. I. Blanshard, Paul, 1892-

FARRAR, Adam Storey, 1826-1905. 211'.4'09
A critical history of free thought in reference to the Christian religion. New York, B. Franklin [1974] p. "Eight lectures preached before the University of Oxford, in the year M.DCCC.LXII., on the foundation of the late Rev. John Bampton." Reprint of the 1896 ed. published by D. Appleton, New York. [BL2750.F3 1974] 74-8137 ISBN 0-8337-4095-4 22.50
1. Free thought—History. I. Title.

MACDONALD, George Everett Hussey, 1857-1944. 211'.4'09
Fifty years of freethought. New York, Arno Press, 1972. 544, xviii, 657 p. illus. 21 cm. (The Atheist viewpoint) Reprint of the 1929-31 ed., which was issued in 2 v. [BL2790.M3A32] 76-161334 ISBN 0-405-03793-7
1. The truth seeker. 2. Free thought—History. 3. Rationalism—History. I. Title. II. Series.

ROBERTSON, John Mackinnon, 1856-1933. 211'.4'09
A short history of freethought, ancient and modern. New York, Arno Press, 1972 [c1957] xv, 447 p. 23 cm. (The Atheist viewpoint) Includes bibliographical references. [BL2750.R7 1972] 74-169215 ISBN 0-405-03804-6
1. Free thought—History. I. Title. II. Series.

BUSHELL, Thomas L 211.4'0924
The sage of Salisbury: Thomas Chubb, 1679-1747, by T. L. Bushell. New York, Philosophical Library [1967] 159 p. port. 22 cm. Bibliography: p. 151-156. [BL2790.C5B8] 67-17633
1. Chubb, Thomas, 1679-1747. I. Title.

GROSSMANN, Walter, 1918- 211'.4'0924 B
Johann Christian Edelmann : from orthodoxy to enlightenment / by Walter Grossman. The Hague : Mouton, [1976] ix, 209 p. ; 24 cm. (Religion and society ; 3) Includes index. Bibliography: p. [199]-203. [BL2790.E33G76] 76-377412 ISBN 9-02-797691-0 : 14.00
1. Edelmann, Johann Christian, 1698-1767. 2. Rationalists—Germany—Biography. I. Title. II. Series: Religion and society (The Hague) ; 3.
Distributed by Humanities

URIEL Acosta: 211'.4'0924
A specimen of human life. New York, Bargman [1967] 127 p. illus. 22 cm. Contents.Contents.—Uriel Acosta's Account of his own life.—Uriel Acosta's Eleven theses against the tradition.—Excommunication of Uriel Acosta.—Limborch's defense of Christianity in answer to Acosta's objections.—Bibliography (p. 126—27) [BL2790.A2U7] 66-28486
1. Judaism—Controversial literature. I. Acosta, Uriel, 1585 (ca.)-1640. Account of his own life. II. Acosta, Uriel, 1585 (ca.)-1640. Eleven theses against the tradition. III. Limborch, Philippus van, 1663-1712. The remarkable life of Uriel Acosta. IV. Title: A specimen of human life.

SPINK, John Stephenson. 211'.4'0944
French free-thought from Gassendi to Voltaire, by J. S. Spink. New York, Greenwood Press [1969, c1960] ix, 345 p. 23 cm. Bibliography: p. [329]-330. [B1815.S68 1969] 69-14089
1. Philosophy, French. 2. Philosophy—History—France. 3. Free thought—History. I. Title.

MORE, W Robert. 211.44
Christianity never survived; Christ of the church: a present-day problem. [1st ed.] New York, Exposition Press [1960] 118p. 21cm. [BL2775.2.M6] 60-50185
I. Title.

GILDON, Charles, 1665-1724. 211'.5
The Deist's manual, 1705 / Charles Gildon. New York : Garland Pub., 1977. p. cm. (British philosophers and theologians of the 17th & 18th centuries ; no. 23) Reprint of the 1705 ed. printed for A. Roper, London. [BT1180.G54 1977] 75-11220 ISBN 0-8240-1774-9 lib.bdg. : 25.00
1. Deism—Controversial literature. I. Title. II. Series.

GAY, Peter, 1923- comp. 211'.5'08
Deism; an anthology. Princeton, N.J., Van

Nostrand [1968] 191 p. 19 cm. (An Anvil original, 93) Bibliography: p. 190-191. [BL2710.G34] 68-2432
1. Deism—Collections.

PIKE, Edgar Royston, 1896- 211'.5'0922
Slayers of superstition; a popular account of some of the leading personalities of the deist movement, by E. Royston Pike. Port Washington, N.Y., Kennikat Press [1970] vi, 106 p. ports. 19 cm. Reprint of the 1931 ed. Contents.Contents.—The origins of European scepticism.—The pioneers of deism.—Toland and Collins.—Wollaston and Tindal.—Woolston and Chubb.—Hume.—Gibbon.—French scepticism, from Descartes to the Revolution. [BL2785.P5 1970] 78-102581
1. Deism—Biography. I. Title.

KOCH, Gustav Adolf, 1900- 211'.5'0973
Religion of the American enlightenment, by G. Adolf Koch. New York, Crowell [1968] xviii, 334 p. 20 cm. Originally published in 1933 under title: Republican religion. Reprint with a new foreword. Bibliography: p. 299-328. [BL2760.K6 1968] 68-29621 2.45
1. United States—Religion—To 1800. 2. United States—Church history. 3. Deism—History. I. Title.

KOCH, Gustav Adolf, 1900- 211.50973
Republican religion; the American Revolution and the cult of reason. Gloucester, Mass., P. Smith [1965, c.1933] xvi, 334p. illus. 21cm. (Studies in religion and culture. Amer. rel. ser. vii) Bibl. [BL2760.K6] 65-2746 5.00
1. U.S.—Religion. 2. U.S.—Church history. 3. Deism—Hist. I. Title. II. Title: The American Revolution and the cult of reason. (Series) III. Series.

MORAIS, Herbert Montfort 211.50973
Deism in eighteenth century America. New York, Russell & Russell, 1960[c.1934] 203p. (bibl.) 22cm. 60-8198 4.50
1. Deism—Hist. 2. U.S.—Religion. 3. U.S.—Church history—Colonial period. I. Title.

CAPEL, Evelyn Francis. 211'.53
The tenth hierarchy / by Evelyn Francis Capel. London : Christian Community, 1976. [6], 95 p. ; 22 cm. [BP595.C36] 77-361316 ISBN 0-904693-01-5 : £1.00
1. Anthroposophy. I. Title.

BLACKHAM, Harold John, 1903- 211'.6
Humanism / H. J. Blackham. 2nd revised ed. Hassocks : Harvester Press, 1976. [6], 225 p. ; 23 cm. Includes index. Bibliography: p. 213-219. [B105.H8B6 1976b] 77-354487 ISBN 0-85527-209-0 : £5.95
1. Humanism. I. Title.

BLACKHAM, Harold John, 1903- 211'.6
Humanism / H. J. Blackham. 2d rev. ed. New York : International Publications Service, 1976. 224 p. ; 22 cm. Includes index. Bibliography: p. 213-219. [B105.H8B6 1976] 75-30604 ISBN 0-8002-0162-0 : 11.25
1. Humanism.

BLACKHAM, Harold John, 1903- 211'.6
Objections to humanism [by] H. J. Blackham [and others] Edited by H. J. Blackham. Westport, Conn., Greenwood Press [1974] 128 p. 22 cm. Reprint of the 1963 ed. published by Constable, London. [BL2747.6.B55 1974] 73-16796 ISBN 0-8371-7235-7 8.00
1. Humanism. I. Title.

BLAMIRES, Harry. 211.6
The Christian mind. New York, Seabury Press, 1963. 181 p. 22 cm. [BR121.1.B5] 63-15452
1. Secularism. 2. Christianity — 20th cent. I. Title.

BLAMIRES, Harry 211.6
The Christian mind. New York, Seabury [c.] 1963. 181p. 22cm. 63-15452 3.50
1. Secularism. 2. Christianity—20th cent. I. Title.

BREEN, Quirinus, 1896- 211'.6
Christianity and humanism; studies in the history of ideas. With a foreword by Paul Oskar Kristeller and a pref. by Heiko A. Oberman. Edited by Nelson Peter Ross. Grand Rapids, W. B. Eerdmans Pub. Co. [1968] xviii, 283 p. 22 cm. Includes bibliographical references. [BR115.H8B7] 65-28566
1. Humanism—History. 2. Christianity—Influence. 3. Roman law—History. I. Ross, Nelson Peter, ed. II. Title.

CHILDRESS, James F., comp. 211'.6
Secularization and the Protestant prospect. Edited, with an introd. by James F. Childress and David B. Harned. Philadelphia, Westminister Press [1970] 220 p. 19 cm. Includes bibliographical references. [BL2747.8.C47] 77-98118 3.50
1. Secularism. 2. Secularization (Theology) I. Harned, David Baily, joint comp. II. Title.

CHRISTIAN hope and the secular. 211'.6 Edited by Daniel F. Martensen. Minneapolis, Augsburg Pub. House [1969] ix, 115 p. 22 cm. (Christian hope series) Contents.Contents.—Dialogical theology: an introductory essay, by D. F. Martensen.—A Biblical view of the secular, by V. R. Gold.—The dialectic of the secular, by W. H. Capps.—Eastern Orthodoxy and the secular, by D. F. Martensen.—Marxism and the secular; by R. L. Moellering.—Church worship and the secular, by R. Johnson. Includes bibliographical references. [BL2747.8.C49] 73-84811 2.50
1. Secularism—Addresses, essays, lectures. 2. Theology—20th century—Addresses, essays, lectures. I. Martensen, Daniel F., ed.

EGGENSCHWILER, David, 1936- 211'.6
The Christian humanism of Flannery O'Connor. Detroit, Wayne State University Press, 1972. 148 p. 24 cm. Bibliography: p. 141-148. [PS3565.C57Z665] 79-179560 ISBN 0-8143-1463-5 8.95
1. O'Connor, Flannery. 2. Humanism, Religious. I. Title.

ELLUL, Jacques. 211'.6
The new demons / Jacques Ellul ; translated by C. Edward Hopkin. New York : Seabury Press, [1975] viii, 228 p. ; 22 cm. "A Crossroad book." Translation of Les nouveaux possedes. Includes bibliographical references. [BL2747.8.E4313] 75-6969 ISBN 0-8164-0266-3 : 9.95
1. Secularism. 2. Christianity—20th century. 3. Mythology. I. Title.

HEWITT, Emily C. 211'.6
Models of secularization in contemporary sociological theory [by] Emily C. Hewitt, Lawrence H. Mamiya [and] Michael C. Mason. [New York, Auburn Theological Seminary] 1972. i, 44 p. 28 cm. (Auburn Studies in Education, publication #1) Bibliography: p. 43-44. [BL2747.8.H47] 72-184966 1.00
1. Secularism. 2. Religion and sociology. I. Mamiya, Lawrence H., joint author. II. Mason, Michael C., joint author. III. Title. IV. Series.

HUMANISM and Christianity. 211'.6 Edited by Claude Geffre. [New York] Herder and Herder [1973] 137 p. 23 cm. (Concilium, 86) Series statement also appears as: The New concilium: religion in the seventies. Includes bibliographical references. [BR128.H8H84] 72-12424 ISBN 0-8164-2542-6 3.95
1. Christianity and religious humanism. 2. Christianity—20th century. I. Geffre, Claude, ed. II. Series: Concilium (New York), 86.

IRION, Mary Jean. 211'.6
From the ashes of Christianity; a post-Christian view. [1st ed.] Philadelphia, Lippincott [1968] 191 p. 20 cm. Bibliography: p. 189-191. [BL2775.2I7] 68-12484
1. Christianity—Controversial literature. I. Title.

JARRETT-KERR, Martin, 1912- 211.6
The secular promise; Christian presence amid contemporary humanism. Introd. by M. A. C. Warren. Philadelphia, Fortress [1965, c.1964] 224p. 20cm. Bibl. [PR121.2.J3] 65-13406 3.25 bds.,
1. Christianity—20th cent. 2. Humanism. I. Title.

LOEN, Arnoldus Ewout, 1896- 211'.6
Secularization; science without God? [By] Arnold E. Loen. Translated by Margaret Kohl. Philadelphia, Westminster Press [1967] 213 p. 23 cm. [BL2747.8.L613 1967a] 67-21794
1. Secularism. I. Title.

MARTIN, David A. 211'.6
The religious and the secular; studies in secularization [by] David Martin. New York, Schocken Books [1969] xi, 164 p. 23 cm. Bibliography: p. 157-161. [BL2747.8.M35] 69-17729 5.00
1. Secularism. I. Title.

MILLER, Samuel Howard, 1900- 211.6
The dilemma of modern belief. [1st ed.] New York, Harper & Row [1963] 113 p. 22 cm. (The Lyman Beecher lectures, Yale Divinity School) [BL2747.8.M5] 63-11893
1. Secularism. 2. Christianity — 20th cent. — Addresses, essays, lectures. I. Title.

MILLER, Samuel Howard, 1900- 211.6
The dilemma of modern belief. New York, Harper [c.1963] 113p. 22cm. (Lyman Beecher lects., Yale Divinity Sch.) 63-11893 3.00 bds.,
1. Secularism. 2. Christianity—20th cent.—Addresses, essays, lectures. I. Title.

NEWBIGIN, James Edward Lesslie, Bp. 211.6
Honest religion for secular man, by Lesslie Newbigin. Philadelphia, Westminster Press [1966] 159 p. 19 cm. (Adventures in faith) Based on the Firth lectures, University of Nottingham, 1964. [BL2747.8.N4] 66-16552
1. Secularism. I. Title.

NEWBIGIN, James Edward Lesslie, Bp. 211.6
Honest religion for secular man. Philadelphia, Westnminster [c.1966] 159p. 19cm. (Adventures in faith) Based on the Firth lects., Univ. of Nottingham, 1964. [BL2747.8.N4 1966] 66-16552 1.45 pap.,
1. Secularism. I. Title.

SACRALIZATION and secularization. 211'.6 Edited by Roger Aubert. New York, Paulist Press [1969] viii, 182 p. 24 cm. (Concilium: theology in the age of renewal. Church history, v. 47) Includes articles translated from several languages by various persons. Bibliographical footnotes. [BL2747.8.S23] 76-96949 4.50
1. Secularism—History—Addresses, essays, lectures. I. Aubert, Roger, ed. II. Series: Concilium (New York) v. 47

SPANN, John Richard, 1891- ed. 211'.6
The Christian faith and secularism. Edited by J. Richard Spann. Port Washington, N.Y., Kennikat Press [1969, c1948] 296 p. 24 cm. (Essay and general literature index reprint series) Bibliographical footnotes. [BT1210.S68 1969] 70-86062
1. Apologetics—20th century. 2. Secularism—Controversial literature. I. Title.

SPEER, James P 211.6
For what purpose? An angry American's appeal to reason. Washington, Public Affairs Ress (1960) 86 p. 24 cm. [BT736.2.S6] 59-15845
1. War and religion. I. Title.

THOMAS, Madathilparampil M. 211'.6
The secular ideologies of India and the secular meaning of Christ / M. M. Thomas. Bangalore : Published for The Christian Institute for the Study of Religion and Society by The Christian Literature Society, Madras, 1976. viii, 207 p. ; 22 cm. (Confessing the faith in India series ; no. 12) Includes bibliographical references and index. [BL2765.I5T46] 76-904071 Rs14.00
1. Secularism—India. 2. Christianity—India. I. Title. II. Series.

VAHANIAN, Gabriel, 1927- 211.6
The death of God; the culture of our post-Christian era. New York, Braziller [1966, c.1957-1961] xxxiii, 253p. 21cm. Bibl. [BL2759.V3] 1.95 pap.,
1. Secularism. 2. Civilization, Modern. I. Title.

VAHANIAN, Gabriel, 1927- 211.6
The death of God; the culture of our post-Christian era. New York, G. Braziller, 1961. 253 p. 21 cm. Includes bibliography. [BL2759.V3] 61-9962
1. Secularism. 2. Civilization, Modern. I. Title.

VERHALEN, Philip A. 211'.6
Faith in a secularized world : [an investigation into the survival of transcendence] / by Philip A. Verhalen. New York : Paulist Press, c1976. vii, 172 p. ; 21 cm. Bibliography: p. 166-172. [BT124.5.V47] 76-360434 ISBN 0-8091-1937-4 pbk. : 3.95
1. Transcendence of God. 2. Secularism. 3. Theology—20th century. I. Title.

WEST, Charles C. 211'.6
The power to be human; toward a secular theology, by Charles C. West. New York, Macmillan [1970, c1971] 270 p. 21 cm. Includes bibliographical references. [BR100.W46] 75-109454
1. Christianity—Philosophy. 2. Humanism. I. Title.

WILLIAMS, David Rhys, 1890- 211.6
Faith belond humanism. Introd. by Philip S. Bernstein. New York, Philosophical [c.1963] 223p. 22cm. Bibl. 62-20877 5.00
1. Humanism, Religious. I. Title.

WILLIAMS, David Rhys, 1890- 211.6
Faith beyond humanism. Introd. by Philip S. Bernstein. New York, Philosophical Library [c1963] 223 p. 22 cm. [B821.W5] 62-20877
1. Humanism, Religious. I. Title.

BUSHELL, Thomas L. 211'.6'0924
The sage of Salisbury: Thomas Chubb, 1679-1747, by T. L. Bushell. New York, Philosophical Lib. [1967] 159p. port. 22cm. Bibl. [BL2790.C5B8] 50211 67-17633 5.00
1. Chubb, Thomas, 1679-1747. I. Title.

CLAMPETT, Frederick William. 211'.6'0924
Luther Burbank, "our beloved infidel"; his religion of humanity, by Frederick W. Clampett. Westport, Conn., Greenwood Press [1970] 144 p. facsim., port. 23 cm. Reprint of the 1926 ed. [BL2790.B8C5 1970] 73-109720
1. Burbank, Luther, 1849-1926.

HOWLETT, Duncan. 211'.6'0973
The fourth American faith. Boston, Beacon Press [1968] xvi, 239 p. 21 cm. (Beacon paperback no. 296) Bibliographical references included in "Notes" (p. 218-232) [BR517.H6 1968] 74-5405 1.95
1. U.S.—Religion. I. Title.

*ASHTON, John. 211'.7
Why were the gospels written? Notre Dame, Ind., Fides Publishers [1973] 91 p. 18 cm. (Theology today series, no. 15) Bibliography: p. 90-91. [BL51.] ISBN 0-85342-261-3 0.95 (pbk.)
1. Religion—Philosophy. I. Title.

DARROW, Clarence Seward, 1857-1938, comp. 211'.7
Infidels and heretics : an agnostic's anthology / by Clarence Darrow and Wallace Rice. New York : Gordon Press, [1975] c1929. p. cm. Reprint of the ed. published by Stratford Co., Boston. [BL2710.D25 1975] 75-20289 ISBN 0-87968-240-X lib.bdg. : 34.95
1. Agnosticism—Addresses, essays, lectures. I. Rice, Wallace de Groot Cecil, 1859-1939, joint comp. II. Title.

SYMPOSIUM on the Culture of Unbelief, Rome, 1969. 211'.7
The culture of unbelief; studies and proceedings from the First International Symposium on Belief held at Rome, March 22-27, 1969. Symposium sponsors: the Agnelli Foundation, the University of California at Berkeley, the Vatican Secretariat for Non-Believers. Edited by Rocco Caporale and Antonio Grumelli. Berkeley, University of California Press, 1971. xx, 303 p. 24 cm. The Symposium on the Culture of Unbelief was held as part of the First International Symposium on Belief. [BD215.S88 1969] 75-138513 ISBN 0-520-01856-7 10.00
1. Belief and doubt—Congresses. 2. Skepticism—Congresses. I. Caporale, Rocco, 1927- ed. II. Grumelli, Antonio, ed. III. International Symposium on Belief, 1st, Rome, 1969. IV. Fondazione Giovanni Agnelli. V. California. University. VI. Catholic Church. Secretariatus pro Non Credentibus. VII. Title.

WARING, Edward Graham, comp. 211'.7
Deism and natural religion: a source book, ed., introd., by E. Graham Waring. New York, Ungar [1967] xxiv, 276p. 20cm. (Milestones of thought) [BL2710.W3] 211 66-28139 6.00; 1.95 pap.,
1. Deism—Collections. I. Title. II. Series: Milestones of thought in the history of ideas.)
Contents omitted.

INGERSOLL, Robert Green, 1833-1899. 211.7081
Ingersoll's greatest lectures, containing speeches and addresses never before printed outside of the complete works. Authorized ed. Hackensack, N.J., Wehman Bros. [1964] 1 v. (various pagings) 22 cm. "Printed from the plates of the original Dresden edition." [[BL2720.A2]] 64-9963
1. Free thought — Addresses, essays, lectures. I. Title.

STRATHMANN, Ernest Albert, 1906- 211.7'092'4
Sir Walter Ralegh; a study in Elizabethan skepticism, by Ernest A. Strathmann. New York, Octagon Books, 1973 [c1951] ix, 292 p. 23 cm. Reprint of the ed. published by Columbia University Press, New York. Includes bibliographical references. [DA86.22.R2S86 1973] 73-8897 ISBN 0-374-97640-6 11.50
1. Raleigh, Walter, Sir, 1552?-1618. 2. Skepticism.

BENTLEY, Richard, 1662-1742. 211'.8
Eight Boyle lectures on atheism / Richard Bentley. New York : Garland Pub., 1976. 300 p. in various pagings ; 23 cm. (British philosophers and theologians of the 17th & 18th centuries) Reprint of 8 sermons published 1692-1693 by T. Parkhurst and H. Mortlock, London. Contents.Contents.—The folly of atheism.—Matter and motion cannot think.—A confutation of atheism from the structure and origin of humane bodies, pts. 1-3.—A

confutation of atheism from the origin and frame of the world, pts. 1-3. [BL2747.3.B46 1976] 75-11196 ISBN 0-8240-1752-8 lib.bdg. : 25.00
1. Catholic Church—Sermons. 2. Atheism—Sermons. 3. Sermons, English. I. Title. II. Series.

BLOCH, Ernst, 1885- 211'.8
Atheism in Christianity; the religion of the Exodus and the Kingdom. Translated by J. T. Swann. [New York] Herder and Herder [1972] 273 p. 22 cm. [BR128.A8B5513] 72-165497 ISBN 0-665-00012-X 9.50
1. Christianity and atheism. I. Title.

BORNE, Etienne. 211.8
Atheism. Translated from the French by S. J. Tester. [1st ed.] New York, Hawthorn Books [1961] 156p. 21cm. (The Twentieth century encyclopedia of Catholicism, v. 91. Section 9: The church and the modern world) Translation of Dieu n'est pas mort. Includes bibliography. [BT1211.B653] 61-15607
1. Atheism —Controversial literature. I. Title.

BULTMANN, Rudolf Karl, 1884- 211.8
Primitive Christianity in its contemporary setting. Translated by R. H. Fuller. London, New York, Thames and Hudson [1956] 240p. 22cm. 'Bibliography and notes': p. [209]-231. [BR128.A2B] A57
1. Christianity and other religions. I. Title. II. Title: Translation of Das Urchristentum im Rahmen der antiken Religionen.

BULTMANN, Rudolf Karl, 1884- 211.8
Primitive Christianity in its contemporary setting. Translated by R. H. Fuller. London, New York, Thames and Hudson [1956] 240p. 22cm. Translation of Das Urchristentum im Rahmen der antiken Religionen. 'Bibliography and notes': p. [200]-231. [BR128.A2B] A 57
1. Christianity and other religions. I. Title.

COFFY, Robert. 211'.8
Dieu des athees, Marx, Sartre, Camus. [2 edition] Lyon, Chronique sociale de France, 1966. 176 p. 18 cm. (Le Fond du probleme, 8) 9.50 F. Illustrated cover. Bibliographical footnotes. [BL2759.C6] 67-95066
1. Atheism — Hist. — Modern period. 2. Christianity and atheism. I. Title.

DE BONA, Maurice. 211'.8
God rejected : a summary of atheistic thought / Maurice De Bona, Jr. 1st ed. Culver City, Calif. : Desserco Pub. Co., 1976. 128 p. (p. 125-128 blank for "Thoughts") ; 22 cm. Bibliography: p. 123-124. [BL2747.3.D42] 75-46088 ISBN 0-916698-00-9 : 4.95. pbk. : 2.95
1. Atheism. I. Title.

GIBSON, Arthur, 1922- 211'.8
The faith of the atheist. [1st ed.] New York, Harper & Row [1968] 218 p. 22 cm. Bibliographical references included in "Notes" (p. 213-218) [BL2747.3.G5] 68-29563 5.95
1. Atheism. I. Title.

HANVILLE, Merrill F 211.8
Straw gods, by Merrill F. Hanville. [Portland, Or.] 1965. 132 p. illus. port. 21 cm. [BL2775.2.H3] 66-869
I. Title.

[HOLBACH, Paul Henri Thiry, baron d'] 1723-1789. 211'.8
Superstition in all ages: by Jean Meslier, a Roman Catholic priest, who, after a pastoral service of thirty years at Etrepigny and But in Champagne, France, wholly abjured religious dogmas, and left as his last will and testament to his parishioners, and to the world, to be published after his death, the following pages, entitled, Common sense. Translated from the French original by Miss Anna Knoop. New York, Arno Press, 1972. vi, 339 p. port. 23 cm. (The Atheist viewpoint) Running title: Common sense. The first part is a translation of Le bon sens du cure Meslier, by Baron d'Holbach. The second part is Abstract of testament of John Meslier, by Voltaire (p. 283-339) Reprint of the 1950 ed. [BL2773.H63 1972] 77-161337 ISBN 0-405-03795-3
1. Atheism. I. Meslier, Jean, 1664-1729. II. Voltaire, Francois Marie Arouet de, 1694-1778. Extrait du testament de Jean Meslier. English. 1972. III. Title. IV. Title: Common sense. V. Series.

KOCH, Hans Gerhard. 211.8
The abolition of God; materialistic atheism and Christian religion. [Translated by Robert W. Fenn] Philadelphia, Fortress Press [1963] 191 p. 22 cm. Bibliographical references included in footnotes. [BT1215.K613] 63-13877
1. Apologetics—20th century. 2. Communism and religion. I. Title.

KOCH, Hans-Gerhard, 1913- 211.8
The abolition of God; materialistic atheism and Christian religion. [Translated by Robert W. Fenn] Philadelphia, Fortress Press [1963] 191 p. 22 cm. Bibliographical references included in footnotes. [BT1215.K613] 63-13877
1. Apologetics—20th cent. 2. Communism and religion. I. Title.

LACROIX, Jean, 1900- 211.8
The meaning of modern atheism. Translated and introduced by Garret Barden. New York, Macmillan, 1965. 115 p. 20 cm. Bibliographical footnotes. [BL2747.3.L313] 65-22610
1. Atheism. I. Title.

LACROIX, Jean, 1900- 211.8
The meaning of modern atheism. Tr. [from French] introd. by Garret Barden. New York, Macmillan [c.]1965. 115p. 20cm. Bibl. [BL2747.3.L313] 65-22610 2.95
I. Title.

LEPP, Ignace, 1909- 211.8
Atheism in our time. Translated by Bernard Murchland. New York, Macmillan [1963] 195 p. 22 cm. Translation of Psychanalyse de l'atheisme moderne. [BT1211.L413] 63-9597
1. Atheism — Controversial literature. I. Title.

LEPP, Ignace, 1909-1966. 211.8
Atheism in our time. Translated by Bernard Murchland. New York, Macmillan [1963] 195 p. 22 cm. Translation of Psychanalyse de l'atheisme moderne. [BT1211.L413] 63-9597
1. Atheism—Controversial literature. I. Title.

LUIJPEN, Wilhelmus Antonius Maria, 1922- 211.8
Phenomenology and atheism, by William A. Luijpen. [tr. from Dutch by Walter van de Putte] Pittsburgh, Duquesne Univ. Pr. [1965, c.]1964. xv, 344p. 27cm. (Duquesne studies, Philosophical series, 17) Bibl. [BL2747.3.L753] 64-17127 6.50
1. Atheism. 2. Atheism—Controversial literature. 3. Phenomenology. I. Title. II. Series.

LUIJPEN, Wilhelmus Antonius Maria, 1922- 211'.8
Religion and atheism, by William A. Luijpen and Henry J. Koren. Pittsburgh, Duquesne University Press [1971] 199 p. 22 cm. Includes bibliographies. [BL2747.3.L765] 73-143295 ISBN 0-8207-0133-5 6.95
1. Atheism. I. Koren, Henry J., joint author. II. Title.

MAGNO, Joseph. 211'.8
Atheism & Christianity [by] Joseph Magno [and] Victor LaMotte. [Dubuque, Iowa] Listening Press, 1972. 116 p. 16 cm. Bibliography: p. [115]-116. [BL2747.3.M27] 72-90433 1.95
1. Atheism. I. LaMotte, Victor, joint author. II. Title.

MAYLONE, W. Edgar. 211'.8
Thrown at the atheist's head, by W. Edgar Maylone. Philadelphia, Dorrance [1973] 816 p. 24 cm. Includes bibliographical references. [BL2747.3.M35] 76-188586 ISBN 0-8059-1688-1 12.50
1. Atheism. I. Title.

MICELI, Vincent P., 1915- 211'.8
The gods of atheism [by] Vincent P. Miceli. New Rochelle, N.Y., Arlington House [1971] xvii, 490 p. 24 cm. Bibliography: p. [478]-485. [BL2747.3.M52] 76-115349 ISBN 0-87000-099-3 12.50
1. Atheism. I. Title.

NOCK, Arthur Darby, 1902- 211.8
Early gentile Christianity and its Hellenistic background. With an introd. by the author, 1962, and two additional essays, A note on the resurrection and Hellenistic mysteries and Christian sacraments. New York, Harper & Row [1964] xxi, 155 p. 21 cm. (Harper torchbooks. The Cloister library) "TB 111." Bibliography: p. xviii,-xxi. [BR128.G8N6] 64-330
1. Christianity and other religions — Greek. 2. Church history — Primitive and early church. I. Title.

REID, John, 1927- 211'.8
Man without God; an introduction to unbelief. New York, Corpus [1971] xix, 306 p. 24 cm. (Theological resources) Bibliography: p. 293-298. [BL2747.3.R4 1971] 72-110420 ISBN 0-664-20910-6 9.95
1. Atheism. I. Title.

ROBINSON, Richard. 211.8
An atheist's values. Oxford, Clarendon Press, 1964. 256 p. 23 cm. [BL.2747.3.R56] 64-1501
1. Atheism—Addresses, essays, lectures. I. Title.

ROBINSON, Richard 211.8
An atheist's values. [New York] Oxford [c.] 1964. 256p. 23cm. 64-1501 4.50
1. Atheism—Addresses, essays, lectures. I. Title.

RUSSELL, Bertrand Russell, 3d Earl, 1872-1970. 211'.8
Atheism; collected essays, 1943-1949. New York, Arno Press, 1972. 1 v. (various pagings) port. 24 cm. (The Atheist viewpoint) Contents.Contents.—Am I an atheist or an agnostic? [First published 1949].—An outline of intellectual rubbish [first published 1943].—Can men be rational? [First published 1947].—The faith of a rationalist [first published 1947] .—Ideas that have harmed mankind [first published 1946].—Ideas that have helped mankind [first published 1946].—On the value of scepticism [first published 1947].—The value of free thought [first published 1944].—What can a free man worship? [First published 1944] [BL2747.3.R84] 71-169217 ISBN 0-405-03808-9
1. Atheism—Addresses, essays, lectures. I. Title. II. Series.

SCHILLING, Sylvester Paul, 1904- 211'.8
God in an age of atheism [by] S. Paul Schilling. Nashville, Abingdon Press [1969] 239 p. 23 cm. Bibliography: p. 217-232. [BL2747.3.S37] 72-84713 5.50
1. Atheism. 2. God. I. Title.

SHELLEY, Percy Bysshe, 1792-1822. 211'.8
Selected essays on atheism. New York, Arno Press, 1972. 32, 32, 32 p. 22 cm. (The Atheist viewpoint) Reprint of A logical objection to Christianity, first published 19—; of The necessity of atheism, first published 19—; and of A refutation of deism, first published 19—; which were issued as no. 935-937 of Little blue book. [BL2745.S48] 72-161341 ISBN 0-405-03794-5
1. Free thought—Collected works. I. Title. II. Series. III. Series: Little blue book, no. 935-937.

STRUNK, Orlo. 211'.8
The choice called atheism [by] Orlo Strunk, Jr. Nashville, Abingdon Press [1968] 160 p. 19 cm. [BR128.A8S8] 68-25364
1. Atheism—Controversial literature. 2. Christianity and atheism. I. Title.

ATHEIST magazines: 211'.8'08
a sampling, 1927-1970. New introd. by Madalyn Murray O'Hair. New York, Arno Press, 1972. 1 v. (various pagings) illus. 29 cm. (The Atheist viewpoint) [BL2747.3.A83] 72-171441 ISBN 0-405-03812-7
1. Atheism—Collections. I. O'Hair, Madalyn Murray. II. Title. III. Series.

O'HAIR, Madalyn Murray. 211'.8'08
What on earth is an atheist! Austin, Tex., American Atheist Press, 1969. v, 282 p. 24 cm. Bibliography: p. 276-282. [BL2747.3.O36] 71-88701
1. Atheism. I. Title.

O'HAIR, Madalyn Murray. 211'.8'08
What on earth is an atheist! New York, Arno Press, 1972 [c1969] v, 282 p. 23 cm. (The Atheist viewpoint) Bibliography: p. 276-282. [BL2747.3.O36 1972] 74-161339 ISBN 0-405-03802-X
1. Atheism. I. Title. II. Series.

BUCKLEY, George Truett, 1898- 211.809
Atheism in the English Renaissance [Reissue] New York, Russell & Russell, 1965 [c.1932] xi, 163p. 23cm.Bibl. [BL2765.G7B8] 65-13936 6.50
1. Atheism—Hist. 2. Renaissance—England. 3. Religion in literature. 4. English literature—Early modern (to 1700)—Hist. & crit. 5. Gt. Brit.—Religion. I. Title.

SIEGMUND, Georg, 1903- 211'.8'09
God on trial; a brief history of atheism. Translated by Elinor Castendyk Briefs. New York, Desclee Co. [1967, c1957] x, 457 p. 22 cm. Translation of Der Kampf um Gott. Bibliography: p. [447]-452. Bibliographical footnotes. [BL2751.S513] 68-26913 6.95
1. Atheism—History. I. Title.

FABRO, Cornelio. 211'.8'0903
God in exile: modern atheism; a study of the internal dynamic of modern atheism, from its roots in the Cartesian cogito to the present day. Translated and edited by Arthur Gibson. Westminster, Md., Newman Press [1968] xlii, 1230 p. 24 cm. Translation of Introduzione all'ateismo moderno. Bibliography: p. 1155-1202. [BL2757.F213] 68-20846
1. Atheism—History—Modern period, 1500- I. Title.

MACINTYRE, Alasdair C. 211'.8'0904
The religious significance of atheism [by] Alasdair MacIntyre and Paul Ricoeur. New York, Columbia University Press, 1969. 98 p. 21 cm. (Bampton lectures in America, no. 18) [BL2747.3.M26] 68-28398 4.75
1. Atheism. I. Ricoeur, Paul, joint author. II. Title. III. Series.

DOLAN, William M 211.9
Moses and the liberation from Egypt. Garden City, N.Y. [Coubleday, 1962] 64 p.illus. 21 cm. (The Catholic know-your-Bible-program) [BS580.M6D59] 63-3128
1. Moses — Juvenile literature. 2. Bible stories, English — O.T. — Exodus. I. Title.

212 Nature Of God

AIKEN. ALFRED. 212
Now, a book on the Absolute. New York, Hillier Press [1956] 256p. 21cm. [BL220.A33] 57-17931
1. Pantheism. I. Title.

AIKEN, Alfred. 212
Now, a book on the Absolute. New York, Hillier Press [1956] 256p. 21cm. [BL220.A33] 57-17391
1. Pantheism. I. Title.

AIKEN, Alfred. 212
That which is, a book on the Absolute. New York, Hillier Press [1955] 249 p. 21 cm. [BL220.A35] 55-42628
1. Pantheism. I. Title.

ANDREWES, Lancelot, Bp. of Winchester, 1555-1626. 212
The private devotions of Lancelot Andrewes. Proces private. Translated. with an introd. and notes. by F. E. Brightman, and including 'Lancelot Andrewes' (1926) by T. S. Eliot. New York, Meridian Books [1961] ixii, 392p. 19cm. (Living age books, LA32) In English. [BV4830.A652 1961] 61-16150
1. Devotional exercises. I. Brightman, Frank Edward 1856-1932. tr. II. Title.

BAILEY, Alice Anne (La Trobe-Bateman), 1880- 212
A treatise on the seven rays. 2d ed. London, Lucis Press; New York, Lucis Pub. Co. [19 v. 22 cm. Contents.v. 2. Esoteric psychology. [BP565.B312] 50-2141
1. Theosophy. I. Title. II. Title: Seven rays.

BENNETT, John Godolphin, 1897- 212
Approaching Subud; ten talks. And a discussion with Steve Allen. New York, dharma Book Co. [1962] 274p. 18cm. [BP605.B36] 62-5123
I. Title. II. Title: Subud.

BLAVATSKY, Helene Petrovna (Hahn-Hahn) 1831-1891. 212
Collected writings . [Boris De Zirkoff, compiler] 1st [American] e d. Los Angeles, Philosophical Research Society [1950- v. ports. 24 cm. Contents.[1] 1883. Bibliography: v. 1. p. 361-38 6. [BP561.A1 1950] 51-16462
1. Theosophy—Collected works. I. Title.

CARRINGTON, Ulrich Steindorff, 1888- tr. 212
Of Gods and miracles; wondrous tales of the ancient Egyptians. [1st ed.] San Jose, Calif., Supreme Grand Lodge of AMORC [1954] 189p. illus: 20cm. (Rosicrusion library, v. 24) [BF1623.R7C28] 53-9733
1. Rosichucians. I. Title.

DRAGONA-MONACHOU, Myrto. 212
The stoic arguments for the existence and the providence of the gods / by Myrto Dragona-Monachou. Athens : National and Capodistrian University of Athens, Faculty of Arts, 1976. 321 p. ; 24 cm. (S. Saripolos' library ; 32) Added t.p.: Ta epicheiremata ton stoikon gia ten hyparxe kai ten pronoia ton theon. Summary in Greek. Originally presented as the author's thesis, London. Includes indexes. Bibliography: p. [291]-303. [BL473.D68 1976] 77-365933
1. Gods—History of doctrines. 2. Stoics. I. Title. II. Series: Vivliotheke Sophias N. Saripolou ; 32.

GOETHE, Johann Wolfgang von, 1749-1832. 212
Iphigenia in Tauris [by] Goethe; translated from the German by John Prudhoe, Manchester, Manchester U.P.; New York, Barnes & Noble, 1966. xxx, 71 p. 18 1/2 ch. 10/6 (B66-21863) Bibliography: p. xxx. [PT2026.I4P7] 67-76493
I. Prudhoe, John, tr. II. Title.

GOETHE, Johann Wolfgang von, 1749-1832. 212
The parable. Translated by Alice Raphael. [1st ed.] New York, Harcourt, Brace & World [1963] xiii, 73 p. 21 cm. Translation of Das Marchen. Bibliographical references included in "Notes" (p. 67-70) Bibliography: p. 71-73. [PT1971.M2E57] 63-17776
I. Raphael, Alice Pearl, 1887- tr. II. Title.

GOETHE, Johann Wolfgang von, 1749-1832. 212
The story of Reynard the Fox. Translated by Thomas James Arnold from the original German poem Reineke Fuchs; with a new introd. by Edward Lazare and with illus. engraved on wood by Fritz Eichenberg. New York, Herit-age Press [1954] x, 247p. illus. 23cm. [PT2026.R3A] A55
I. Arnold, Thomas James, 1804?-1877, tr. II. Title. III. Title: Raynard the Fox.

HEINDEL, Max, 1865-1919. 212
The desire body. 1st ed. Oceanside, Calif., Rosicrucian Fellowship [1953] 160p. illus. 20cm. [BF1623.R7H28] 53-36888
1. Rosicrucians. 2. Desire. I. Title.

HEINDEL, Max, 1865-1919. 212
The vital body. 1st ed. Oceanside, Calif., Rosicrucian Fellowship [1951, '1950] 198 p. port. 20 cm. [BF1623.R7H57] 51-20324
1. Rosicrucians. I. Title.

LEHRS, Ernst. 212
Man or matter; introduction to a spiritual understanding of nature on the basis of Goethe's method of training observation and thought. 2d ed., rev. and enl. New York, Harper [1958] 456p. illus. 22cm. [BP595.L44 1958a] 58-10377
1. Goethe, Johann Wolfgang von, 1749-1832. 2. Anthroposophy. 3. Comology. I. Title.

LEWIS, Harve Spencer, 1883-1939. 212
Self mastery and fate, with the cycles of life. [14th ed.] San Jose, Calif., Supreme Grand Lodge of AMORC [1954] 271p. illus. 20cm. (Rosicrucian library, v. 7) [BF1623.R7R65 vol.7 1954] 55-16785
1. Rosicrucians. 2. Success. I. Title.

LEWIS, Ralph Maxwell, 1904- 212
The conscious interlude. [1st ed.] San Jose, Calif., Supreme Grand Lodge of AMORC [1957] 390p. illus. 20cm. (Rosicrucian library, v. 26) [BF1623.R7R65 vol.26] 57-8541
1. Rosicrucians. I. Title. II. Series.

LUTYENS, Lady Emily (Lytton) 1874- 212
Candles in the sun. Philadelphia, Lippincott [1957] 196p. plate, ports. 21cm. [BP585.L85A3 1957a] 57-12383
1. Krishnamurti, Jiddu, 1895- 2. Theosophists—Correspondence, reminiscences, etc. 3. Theosophical Society. I. Title.

LUTYENS, Emily (Lytton) Lady 1874- 212
Candles in the sun. Philadelphia, Lippincott [1957] 196p. plate, ports. 21cm. [BP585.L85A3 1957a] 57-12383
1. Krishnamurti, Jiddu, 1895- 2. Theosophists—Correspondence, reminiscences, etc. 3. Theosophical Society. I. Title.

MAX, Peter, 1937- 212
God. [With the words of Swami Sivananda, Himalayas]. Editorial assistance by Arjuna (Victor Zurbel). New York, Morrow, 1970. [31] p. col. illus. 15 cm. [BT175.M38] 71-118292 1.95
1. God. I. Sivananda, Swami.

MOZART, Johann Chrysostom Wolfgang Amadeus, 1756-1791. 212
Symphony in G minor, K. 550. The score of the new Mozart ed., historical note, analysis, views, and comments. Edited by Nathan Broder. [1st ed.] New York, W. W. Norton [1967] miniature score (114 p.) 21 cm. (Norton critical scores) Analysis, etc.: p. 69-114 [M1001.M92K.550.B75] 67-17011
1. Symphonies—To 1800—Scores. 2. Symphonies—To 1800—Analysis, appreciation. I. Broder, Nathan, ed. II. [Symphony, K. 550, G minor]

NEWHOUSE, Flower Arlene (Sechler) 1909- 212
Disciplines of the holy quest, from the wise and the strong. Escondido, Calif., Christward Publications [1959] 196p. illus. 25cm. [BP605.C5N4] 59-15553
1. Christward Ministry. I. Title.

NEWHOUSE, Mildred (Sechler) 1909- 212
Disciplines of the holy quest from the wise and the strong, edited by Flower A. Newhouse. Escondido, Calif., Christward Publications [1959] 196p. illus. 25cm. [BP605.C5N4] 59-15553
I. Title.

NEWHOUSE, Mildred (Sechler) 1909- 212
The kingdom of the shining ones, by Flower A. Newhouse. [1st ed.] Vista, Calif., Christward Publications [1955] 94p. illus. 25cm. [BP573.A5N37] 56-21064
1. Angels. I. Title.

NEWHOUSE, Mildred (Sechler) 1909- 212
Natives of eternity; an authentic record of experiences in realms of super-physical consciousness, by Flower A. Newhouse. [4th ed.] Vista, Calif., L. G. Newhouse [1950] 96 p. illus. 25 cm. [BP573.A5N4] 50-29278
1. Theosophy. 2. Angels. I. Title.

NEWHOUSE, Mildred (Sechler) 1909- 212
Rediscovering the angels, by Flower A. Newhouse. Illus. by Valorie Fechter and Donald Burson. [1st ed.] Vista, Calif., L. G. Newhouse [1950] 94 p. illus. 25 cm. Sequel to Natives of eternity. [BP573.A5N42] 50-13810
1. Theosophy. 2. Angels. I. Title.

PALMER, Humphrey. 212
Analogy; a study of qualification and argument in theology. New York, St. Martin's Press [1973, i.e.1974] xvi, 186 p. 23 cm. (New studies in the philosophy of religion) Includes bibliographical references. [BT102.P3] 73-75112 5.95
1. God. 2. Analogy (Religion) I. Title.

PERCIVAL, Harold Waldwin, 1868- 212
Man and woman, and child. [1st ed.] New York, The Word Pub. Co. [c1951] 235 p. 21 cm. [BP605.P38] 52-6126
1. Theosophy. I. Title.

PURUCKER, Gottfried de, 1874-1942. 212
Occult glossary; a compendium of oriental and theosophical terms. Pasadena, Calif., Theosophical University Press [1953] 193p. 22cm. [BP527.P8 1953] 53-37086
1. Theosophy—Dictionaries. I. Title.

REICHENBACH, Bruce R. 212
The cosmological argument: a reassessment, by Bruce R. Reichenbach. Springfield, Ill., Thomas [1972] xiv, 150 p. 24 cm. Includes bibliographical references. [BT102.R36] 74-165894
1. God—Proof, Teleological. I. Title.

ROGERS, Louis William, 1859- 212
Elementary theosophy. 5th ed. Wheaton, Ill., Theosophical Press [1950] 269p. 20cm. [BP565.R7 1950] A51
1. Theosophy. I. Title.

ROGERS, Louis William, 1859- 212
Man; an embryo god, and other lectures. [Rev. ed.] Wheaton, Ill., Theosophical Press [1950] 197 p. 19 cm. Published in 1925 under title: Gods in the making. [BP565.R74 1950] 51-334
1. Theosophy. I. Title.

ROSICRUCIAN FELLOWSHIP, Oceanside, Calif. 212
Complete index of books by Max Heindel. 1st ed. Oceanside, 1950. 278 p. port. 20 cm. [BF1623.R7H63] 50-37394
1. Heindel, Max, I. Title.

STEINER, Rudolf, 1861-1925 212
The arts and their mission. Eight lectures delivered in Dornach. Switzerland. May 27-June 3, 1923. and in Kristiana (Oslo), Norway, May 18 and 20, 1923. Tr. [from German] by Lisa D. Monges, Virginia Moore. New York, Anthroposophic Pr., 1964. xi, 116p. 22cm. 64-55553 4.00
1. Anthroposophy. I. Title.

STEINER, Rudolf, 1861-1925. 212
The Gospel of St. Mark; ten lectures delivered in Basel, September 15-24, 1912. Translated from the original by Erna McArthur. New York, Anthroposophic Press, 1950. xxvi, 195 p. 24 cm. [BP595.S8536] 50-33159
1. Anthroposophy. 2. Bible. N. T. Mark — Addresses, essays, lectures. I. Title.

STEINER, Rudolf, 1861-1925 212
Man as a being of spirit and soul [Authorized tr. from German] Blauvelt, N.Y. [Rudolf Steiner Pubns., 151 N. Moison Rd., 1965, c.1964] 93p. 23cm. (Free deeds bks.) [BP595.S854733] 64-8533 3.06
1. Anthroposophy. I. Title.

STEINER, Rudolf, 1861-1925. 212
Man's being, his destiny, and world-evolution; six lectures, Kristiania (Oslo), May 16-21, 1923. Translated from the original by Erna McArthur. New York, Anthroposophic Press, 1952. 114 p. 23 cm. Cover title: The human being, his destiny, and world evolution. [BP595.S8554] 52-1796
1. Anthroposophy. I. Title.

STEINER, Rudolf, 1861-1925 212
The nature of anthroposophy [Authorized tr. from German] Blauvelt, N.Y. [Rudolf Steiner Pubns., 151 N. Moison Rd., 1965, c.1964] 116p. 23cm. (Free deeds bks.) [BP595.S86463] 64-8532 3.00
1. Anthroposophy. I. Title.

STEINER, Rudolf, 1861-1925. 212
Reincarnation and karma. How karma works, Translated by Lisa D. Monges. New York, Anthroposophic Press, 1962. 57 p. 20 cm. [BP573.R5S83] 62-5124
1. Theosophy. I. Title.

STEINER, Rudolf, 1861-1925 212
The science of spirit [Authorized tr. from German] Blauvelt, N.Y. [Rudolf Steiner Pubns., 151 N. Moison Rd., 1965, c.1964] 96p. 23cm. (Free deeds bks.) [BP595.S88123] 64-8531 3.00
1. Anthroposophy. I. Title.

STEINER, Rudolf, 1861-1925. 212
Spiritual guidance of man and humanity three lectures. [Authorized English translation] New York, Anthroposophic Press, 1950. 85 p. 20 cm. [BP595.S85167] 51-3951
1. Anthroposophy. I. Title.

STEINER, Rudolf, 1861-1925 212
Spiritual guidance of man and humanity; results of the science of spirit concerning the evolution of humanity [in Russian] Blauvelt, N.Y., Rudolf Steiner [c.]1964. 64p. 28cm. 64-55179 2.00 pap.,
1. Anthroposophy. I. Title.

STEINER, Rudolf, 1861-1925 212
Supersensible in man and world [Authorized tr. from German] Blauvelt, N.Y. [Rudolf Steiner Pubns., 151 N. Moison Rd., 1965, c.1964] 92p. 23cm. (Free deeds bks.) [BP595.S88143] 64-8529 3.00
1. Anthroposophy. I. Title.

STEVENS, Robert Meredith. 212
Paradise plantation. [Visalia, Calif., McBee and Black Pub. Co., 1958] 136 p. illus. 24 cm. (Yoke publications) [BV4832.2.S8] 59-11571
1. Devotional literature.) I. Title.

THE Theosophical movement, 1875-1950. 212
Los Angeles, Cunningham Press [1951] xiii, 351 p. 24 cm. A continuation of The theosophical movement, 1875-1925, a history and a survey, with a "consolidation of the treatment of earlier events." Bibliography included in "notes" (p. [333]-343) [BP530.T52] 51-25094
1. Theosophy — Hist.

VIETOR, Karl, 1892- 212
Goethe, the thinker. [Translated from the German by Bayard Q. Morgan] Cambridge, Mass., Harvard University Press, 1950. x, 212 p. 24 cm. Translation of the second and third parts of "Goethe; Dichtung, Wissenschaft, Weltbild." Contents.CONTENTS. -- Universal genius. -- The student of nature -- The thinker. [PT2177.V53.928.3] 50-10644
1. Goethe, Johann Wolfgang von, 1749-1832. 2. Goethe, Johann Wolfgang von — Knowlege — Science. 3. Goethe, Johann Wolfgang von — Philosophy. I. Title.

*WHITE, Joseph L. 212
The creation of a God. By Joseph L. White Madison, Tenn., White Publications [1975] 119 p. 22 cm. [BT98] 6.50
1. Religion and Science. 2. God-Proof. 3. Creation. I. Title.
Available from author 221 Neely's Bend Road Madison, Tenn. 37115

MILLER, David LeRoy. 212'.2
The new polytheism; rebirth of the gods and goddesses [by] David L. Miller. [1st ed.] New York, Harper & Row [1974] x, 86 p. 21 cm. Includes bibliographical references. [BL355.M54 1974] 73-6345 ISBN 0-06-065751-0 4.95
1. Polytheism. 2. Gods, Greek. I. Title.

ARUNDALE, George Sydney, 1878-1945. 212.5
Personal memories of G. S. Arundale, third President of the Theosophical Society. by some of his numerous friends and admirers; [ed. by Herbert Staggs, Catharine Mayes]. London, Wheaton, Ill., Theosophical Pub. House. 1967. xiv, 152p. 12 plates (ports.). 23cm. [BP585.A7P.4] (B) 67-93908 5.00
1. Arundale. George Sydney. 1878-1945. I. Title.

BAILEY, Alice Anne (La Trobe Bateman) 1880-1949. 212.5
A treatise on the seven rays. 4th ed. New York, Lucius Pub. Co. 1962- v. 24 cm. Contents.Contents.—v.1-2. Esoteric psychology.—v.3. Esoteric astrology.—v.4. Esoteric healing.—v.5. The rays and the initiations. [BP565.B314] 62-6365
1. Theosophy. I. Title: Seven rays.

BENDIT, Laurence John, 1898- 212'.5
The mirror of life and death, by Laurence J. Bendit. Wheaton, Ill., Theosophical Pub. House [1967, c1965] ix, 199 p. 18 cm. (A Quest book) [BP573.D4B4] 67-4423
1. Death. 2. Future life. 3. Theosophy. I. Title.

BENDIT, Laurence John, 1898- 212'.5
Self knowledge; a yoga for the West, by Laurence J. Bendit. Wheaton, Ill., Theosophical Pub. House [1967] 100 p. 19 cm. (A Quest book) [BP565.B42] 67-7871
1. Theosophy. I. Title.

BENNETT, John Godolphin, 1897- 212.5
Concerning Subud. New York, University Books [1959] 191p. 22cm. [P605.B37] 59-9899
I. Title. II. Title: Subud.

BENNETT, John Godolphin, 1897- 212'.5
A spiritual psychology / J. G. Bennett. 1st American ed., rev. Lakemont, Ga. : CSA Press, 1974. 268 p. : ill. ; 22 cm. Includes bibliographical references and index. [BP605.S7B4 1974] 73-81620 ISBN 0-87707-128-4 : 6.95
1. Psychology, Religious. 2. Subud. I. Title.

BENNETT, John Godolphin, 1897- 212.5
Towards the true self, in the practice of Subud. New York, Dharma Book Co. [1963] xii, 229 p. 18 cm. [BP605.B377] 63-24380
I. Title.

BENNETT, John Godolphin, 1897- 212.5
Towards the true self, in the practice of Subud. New York, Dharma [c.1963] xii, 229p. 18cm. 63-24380 3.50
I. Title. II. Title: Subud.

BLAVATSKY, Helene Petrovna (Hahn-Hahn) 1831-1891. 212'.5
An abridgement of The secret doctrine, [by] H. P. Blavatsky. Edited by Elizabeth Preston and Christmas Humphreys. Wheaton, Ill., Theosophical Pub. House [1968, c1966] xxxii, 260 p. illus., port. 21 cm. (Theosophical classics series) (A Quest book.) Bibliography: p. [253] [BP561] 79-5835 2.25
1. Theosophy. I. Preston, Elizabeth, ed. II. Humphreys, Christmas, 1901- ed. III. Title. IV. Title: The secret doctrine.

BLAVATSKY, Helene Petrovna (Hahn-Hahn) 1831-1891. 212'.5 B
Personal memoirs. Compiled by Mary K. Neff. Wheaton, Ill., Theosophical Pub. House [1967] 323 p. illus., port. 21 cm. (A Quest book) Bibliography: p. 312. [BP585.B6A32 1967] 67-3800
I. Neff, Mary Katherine, 1877- comp. II. Title.

CODD, Clara M. 212.'5
The ageless wisdom of life, by Clara M. Codd. [4th ed.] Wheaton, Ill., Theosophical Pub. House [1967, c1957] viii, 269 p. 18 cm. (A Quest book) [BP565.C62 1967] 67-8630
1. Theosophy. I. Title.

EMMONS, Viva. 212'.5
The roots of peace; a study of human potential in relation to peace. Wheaton, Ill., Theosophical Pub. House [1969] xv, 111 p. 21 cm. (A Quest book original) Bibliography: p. 97-100. [BP573.P3E45] 73-78911 1.75
1. Theosophy. 2. Peace. I. Title.

FARTHING, Geoffrey A. 212'.5
Theosophy: what's it all about? A brief summary of a wonderfully exciting and vitally important subject, by Geoffrey A. Farthing. London, Wheaton, Ill. [etc.] Theosophical Publishing House, 1967. x, 92 p. 18 112 cm. 10/6 Bibliography: p. 92. [BP565.F33] 67-94094
1. Theosophy. I. Title.

FARTHING, Geoffrey A. 212'.5
Theosophy: what's it all about? A brief summary of a wonderfully exciting and vitally important subject, by Geoffrey A. Farthing. London, Wheaton, Ill., Theosophical Pub House, 1967. x. 92p. 19cm. Bibl. [BP565.F33] 67-94094 1.75 pap.,
1. Theosophy. I. Title.

GARBER, Bernard J 212.5
Shards from the heart; a spiritual odyssey in 20th century America, by Bernard J. Garber, [1st ed. Blauvelt, N.Y.] Free Deeds Books [1965] [BP595.G3] 64-13358
1. Anthroposphy. I. Title.

GARBER, Bernard J. 212.5
Shards from the heart; a spiritual odyssey in 20th century America.Free Deeds Bks. [dist. Blauvelt, N.Y., Rudolf Steiner, 151 North Moison Rd., c.1965] 159p. 23cm. [BP595.G3] 64-13358 3.00
1. Anthroposophy. I. Title.

*HARDING, Charles E. 212.5
Speculations on the universe: physical--life--spiritual. New York, Vantage [1968] 151p. 21cm. 3.50
I. Title.

HODSON, Geoffrey. 212.5
Man's supersensory and spiritual powers. Madras, Theosophical Pub. House; [Label: sold by Theosophical Press, Wheaton, Ill.] 1957. 199p. 19cm. Includes bibliography. [BP573.E9H6] 59-1641
1. Theosophy. 2. Extrasensory preception. I. Title.

HODSON, Geoffrey. 212.5
Theosophy answers some problems of life. [2d ed.] madras. Theosophical Pub. House; [label: sold by Theosophical Press, Wheaton, Ill.] 1955. 228p. illus. 19cm. [BP570.H6 1955] 59-1536
1. Theosophy—Addresses, essays, lectures. I. Title.

JINARAJADASA, 212.5
Curuppumullage, 1875-
First principles of theosophy. 10th ed. Madras, Theosophical Pub. House; [label: sold by Theosophical Press, Wheaton, Ill.] 1956. 43p. illus. 19cm. [BP565.J516 1956] 59-1558
1. Theosophy. I. Title.

JUDGE, William Quan, 1851- 212.5
1896.
The scope of reincarnation. Alhambra, Calif., Cunningham Press [1960] 98p. 21cm. 'Passages taken from [the author's] . . . Ocean of theosophy, which first appeared in 1893.' [BP573.R5J8] 60-52058
1. Reicearnation. 2. Theosophy. I. Title.

KINGSLAND, William, 1855- 212'.5
1936.
The gnosis or ancient wisdom in the Christian Scriptures; or, The wisdom in a mystery. Wheaton, Ill., Theosophical Pub. House [1970, c1937] 230 p. 21 cm. (Theosophical classics series) (A Quest book.) Bibliography: p. [219]-222. [BP567.K52 1970] 71-98268 1.95
1. Bible and theosophy. I. Title.

KUHN, Alvin Boyd, 1880- 212'.5
1963.
A rebirth for Christianity. Wheaton, Ill., Theosophical Pub. House [1970] xi, 218 p. 23 cm. Bibliography: p. 217-218. [BP567.K8 1970] 76-104032
1. Theosophy. 2. Christianity. I. Title.

LAYTON, Eunice S. 212'.5
Theosophy, key to understanding, by Eunice S. Layton and Felix Layton. Wheaton, Ill., Theosophical Pub. House [1967] xi, 170 p. 18 cm. (A Quest book) [BP565.L24] 67-6516
1. Theosophy. I. Layton, Felix, joint author. II. Title.

LAYTON, Eunice S. 212'.5
Theosophy, key to understanding, by Eunice S. Layton and Felix Layton. Wheaton, Ill., Theosophical Pub. House [1967] xi, 170 p. 18 cm. (A Quest book) [BP565.L24] 67-6516
1. Theosophy. I. Layton, Felix, joint author. II. Title.

MEAD, George Robert Stow, 212'.5
1863-1933.
The doctrine of the subtle body in Western tradition; an outline of what the philosophers thought and Christians taught on the subject. Wheaton, Ill., Theosophical Pub. House [1967] 109 p. 18 cm. (A Quest book) On spine: The subtle body. [BP573.H8M4 1967] 68-148
1. Body, Human (in religion, folk-lore, etc.) I. Title. II. Title: The subtle body.

NEWHOUSE, Flower Arlene 212'.5
(Sechler) 1909-
Here are more answers; containing inspired spiritual answers to over 500 contemporary questions, by Flower A. Newhouse. [1st ed.] Escondido, Calif., Christward Publications [1969] 227 p. 23 cm. [BP605.C5N417] 76-103410 5.00
1. Christward Ministry. 2. Theosophy—Miscellanea.

NEWHOUSE, Flower Arlene 212.5
(Sechler) 1909-
The kingdom of the shining ones. [1st ed.] Vista, Calif., Christward Publications [1955] 94p. illus. 25cm. [BP605.C5N43] 56-21064
1. Christward Ministry. 2. Angels. I. Title.

NEWHOUSE, Flower Arlene 212.5
(Sechler) 1909-
Natives of eternity; an authentic record of experiences in realms of super-physical consciousness. [4th ed.] Vista, Calif., L. G. Newhouse [1950] 96p. illus. 25cm. Sequel: Rediscovering the angels. [BP605.C5N44 1950] 50-29278
1. Christward Ministry. 2. Angeles I. Title.

NEWHOUSE, Flower Arlene 212.5
(Sechler) 1909-
Rediscovering the angels. Illus. by Valorie Fechter and Donald Burson. [1st ed.] Vista, Calif., L. G. Newhouse [1950] 94p. illus. 25cm. Sequel to Natives of eternity. [BP605.C5N45] 50-13810
1. Christward Ministry. 2. Angels. I. Title.

OSBORN, Arthur Walter, 212'.5
1891-
The cosmic womb; an interpretation of man's relationship to the infinite, by Arthur W. Osborn. Wheaton, Ill., Theosophical Pub. House [1969] xiv, 233 p. 21 cm. (A Quest book original) Bibliography: p. [217]-226. [BP573.G6O8] 69-17714 2.25
1. God (Theosophy) I. Title.

PEARSON, E. Norman 212.5
Space, time and self, by E. Norman Pearson. Wheaton, Ill, Theosophical Pub. [1967, c.1957] xi, 288p. illus. 20cm. (Quest bk.) [BP565.P33 1964] 65-7294 1.75 pap.,
1. Theosophy. I. Title.

PEARSON, E Norman. 212.5
Space, time, sTheosophy. [BP565.P33] 59-1534
I. Title.

PICTON, James Allanson, 212'.5
1832-1910.
Pantheism; its story and significance. Freeport, N.Y., Books for Libraries Press [1973] p. Reprint of the 1905 ed. published by A. Constable, London, issued in series: Religions ancient and modern. Bibliography: p. [BL220.P5 1973] 73-4495 ISBN 0-518-19038-2
1. Pantheism. I. Title. II. Series: Religions ancient and modern.

ROGERS, Louis William, 212.5
1859-
Elementary theosophy, by L. W. Rogers. 6th ed. Wheaton, Ill., Theosophical Press [1956] 269 p. 20 cm. [BP565.R7] 65-81168
1. Theosophy. I. Title.

SAWREY-COOKSON, Roseanna. 212'.5
A first introduction to Subud / [by] Roseanna Sawrey-Cookson. Didcot : Subud Publications International, [1976] [8] p. ; 21 cm. [BP605.S7S28] 77-373874
1. Subud. I. Title.

*SCHOTT, Agnes Treick 212.5
The teen-ager's ultimate; the love beyond self. Foreword by Marie S. Watts. New York, Exposition [c.1965] 118p. 21cm. (EP 43027) 3.50
I. Title.

STEINER, Rudolf 212.5
Cosmic memory; prehistory of earth and man, Translated from the German by Karl E. Zimmer. Englewood, N.J., [25 Pershing Rd] Rudolf Steiner Publications [c.1959] 273p. 22cm. 4.75
I. Title.

WA SAID, Dibinga. 212'.5
Theosophies of Plato, Aristotle and Plotinus. New York, Philosophical Library [1970] 205 p. 22 cm. Bibliography: p. 199-205. [B398.G6W2] 72-81817 6.25
1. Plato. 2. Aristoteles. 3. Plotinus. 4. God (Greek religion) 5. Theosophy—History. I. Title.

LONG, James A 212.508
Expanding horizons [by] James A. Long. Pasadena, Calif. Theosophical University Press [1965] 246 p. 20 cm. (A Sunrise library book) [BP570.L6] 65-24093
1. Theosophy — Addresses, essays, lectures. I. Title.

BARBORKA, Geoffrey A. 212'.52
The peopling of the Earth : a commentary on archaic records in The secret doctrine / by Geoffrey Barborka. Wheaton, Ill. : Theosophical Pub. House, 1975. xiv, 233 p. : ill. ; 23 cm. (Quest books) Includes bibliographical references and index. [BP561.S43B37] 75-4243 ISBN 0-8356-0221-4 : 10.00
1. Blavatsky, Helene Petrovna Hahn-Hahn, 1831-1891. The secret doctrine. 2. Theosophy. I. Title.

BESANT, Annie (Wood) 1847- 212.52
1933.
Thought power, its control and culture. Wheaton, Ill., Theosophical Pub. House [1966] vi, 128 p. 18 cm. (A Quest book) [BP565] 70-1591 0.95
1. Theosophy. 2. Thought and thinking. I. Title.

BLAVATSKY, Helene 212'.52 s
Petrovna Hahn-Hahn, 1831-1891.
From the caves and jungles of Hindostan, 1883-1886 / by Radda-Bai (H. P. Blavatsky) ; translated from the Russian. 1st ed. Wheaton, Ill. : Theosophical Pub. House, 1975. p. cm. (Her Collected writings) [BP561.A1 1950, suppl.] [DS413] 915.4'04'35 74-26605 ISBN 0-8356-0219-2 : 12.50
1. Blavatsky, Helene Petrovna Hahn-Hahn, 1831-1891. 2. India—Description and travel—1859-1900. 3. India—Religion. 4. Tibet—Description and travel. 5. Tibet—Religion. I. Title. II. Series.

BLAVATSKY, Helene 212'.52 s
Petrovna Hahn-Hahn, 1831-1891.
From the caves and jungles of Hindostan, 1883-1886 / by Radda-Bai (H. P. Blavatsky); translated from the Russian 1st ed. Wheaton, Ill. : Theosophical Pub. House, 1975. p. cm. (Her Collected writings) [BP561.A1 1950, suppl.] [DS413] 915.4'04'35 74-26605 ISBN 0-8356-0219-2 : 12.50
1. Blavatsky, Helene Petrovna Hahn-Hahn, 1831-1891. 2. India—Description and travel—1859-1900. 3. India—Religion. 4. Tibet—Description and travel. 5. Tibet—Religion. I. Title. II. Series.

BLAVATSKY, Helene 212'.52
Petrovna Hahn-Hahn, 1831-1891.
Isis unveiled: a master-key to the mysteries of ancient and modern science and theology. Pasadena, Calif., Theosophical University Press [1972] 2 v. 23 cm. Reprint of the 1877 ed. Contents.Contents.—v. 1. Science.—v. 2. Theology. Includes bibliographical references. [BP561.I7 1972b] 72-186521 12.50
1. Theosophy. I. Title.

BLAVATSKY, Helene 212'.52
Petrovna (Hahn-Hahn) 1831-1891.
Isis unveiled: collected writings, 1877. [New ed., rev. and corr., and with additional material] Wheaton, Ill., Theosophical Pub. House [1972] 2 v. illus. 24 cm. Contents.Contents.—v. 1. Science.—v. 2. Theology. Includes bibliographical references. [BP561.I7 1972] 78-130982 ISBN 0-8356-0193-5
1. Theosophy—Collected works. I. Title.

BLAVATSKY, Helene 212'.52
Petrovna (Hahn-Hahn) 1831-1891.
The key to theosophy. An abridgement, edited by Joy Mills. Wheaton, Ill., Theosophical Pub. House [1972] xv, 176 p. 21 cm. (A Quest book) (Theosophical classics series) [BP561.K4 1972] 75-181716 ISBN 0-8356-0427-6 1.95
1. Theosophy. I. Mills, Joy, ed. II. Title.

BLAVATSKY, Helene 212'.52
Petrovna (Hahn-Hahn) 1831-1891.
The key to theosophy; being a clear exposition, in the form of question and answer, of the ethics, science, and philosophy for the study of which the Theosophical Society has been founded. Pasadena, Calif., Theosophical University Press [1972] xii, 373, 53 p. 20 cm. Reprint of the 1889 ed. published by Theosophical Pub. Co., London, with the addition of the glossary from the 2d ed. and a new index. [BP561.K4 1972b] 72-95701 3.50
1. Theosophy. I. Title.

BLAVATSKY, Helene 212'.52
Petrovna Hahn-Hahn, 1831-1891.
The voice of the silence being chosen fragments from the "Book of the golden precepts." For the daily use of lanoos (disciples). Translated and annotated by "H.P.B." [2d. Quest book miniature ed., from original ed. of 1889] Wheaton, Ill., Theosophical Pub. House [1973] 110 p. 15 cm. (A Quest miniature.) Contents.Contents.—The voice of the silence.—The two paths.—The seven portals. [BP561.V7 1973] 73-7619 ISBN 0-8356-0380-6 1.25 (pbk.)
1. Theosophy. I. Title.

CODD, Clara M. 212'.52
Trust yourself to life / by Clara Codd. Wheaton, Ill. : Theosophical Pub. House, 1975, c1968. x, 116 p. ; 16 cm. (A Quest book miniature) Includes bibliographical references. [BP565.C643 1975] 75-4245 ISBN 0-8356-0464-0 pbk. : 1.75
1. Theosophy. I. Title.

CONGER, Margaret Guild. 212'.52
Combined chronology for use with The Mahatma letters to A. P. Sinnett and The letters of H. P. Blavatsky to A. P. Sinnett [arranged by] Margaret Conger. Also, First letter of K. H. to A. O. Hume [and] View of the Chohan on the T. S. Pasadena, Calif., Theosophical University Press [1973] xiii, 47 p. 23 cm. Bibliography: p. 26. [BP565.M33C6 1973] 73-92461 ISBN 0-911500-17-0 2.00 (pbk.)
1. Blavatsky, Helene Petrovna Hahn-Hahn, 1831-1891. The letters of H. P. Blavatsky to A. P. Sinnett. 2. The Mahatma letters to A. P. Sinnett. I. Blavatsky, Helene Petrovna Hahn-Hahn, 1831-1891. The letters of H. P. Blavatsky to A. P. Sinnett. II. The Mahatma letters to A. P. Sinnett. III. Title.

FIVE years of theosophy 212'.52
: mystical, philosophical, theosophical, historical, and scientific essays selected from "The Theosophist" / edited by G. R. S. Mead. New York : Arno Press, 1976. p. cm. (The Occult) Reprint of the 1894 ed. published by Theosophical Publishing Society, London. [BP570.F57 1976] 75-36850 ISBN 0-405-07966-4 : 22.00
1. Theosophy—Addresses, essays, lectures. I. Mead, George Robert Stow, 1863-1933. II. The Theosophist. III. Series: The Occult (New York, 1976-)

GRANT, Terry. 212'.52
Your precious heritage; do you care? Philadelphia, Dorrance [1972] 32 p. 22 cm. [BP565.G695] 72-84849 ISBN 0-8059-1732-2 2.50
1. Theosophy. I. Title.

JINARAJADASA, 212'.52
Curuppumullage, 1875-1953.
The divine vision; three lectures delivered at the Queen's Hall, London, and one lecture delivered at Palermo, Italy. Wheaton, Ill., Theosophical Pub. House [1973, c1928] 109 p. 18 cm. (A Quest book) [BP565.J54D58 1973] 72-10072 ISBN 0-8356-0433-0 1.45 (pbk.)
1. Theosophy. I. Title.

KRISHNAMURTI, Jiddu, 212'.52
1895-
The first and last freedom / by J. Krishnamurti ; with a foreword by Aldous Huxley. New York : Harper & Row, 1975, c1954. 288 p. ; 20 cm. Reprint of the ed. published by the Theosophical Pub. Co., Wheaton, Ill., in series: A Quest book. [BP565.K7F5 1975] 74-25687 ISBN 0-06-064831-7 pbk. : 2.95
1. Theosophy. I. Title.

KRISHNAMURTI, Jiddu, 212'.52
1895-
The flight of the eagle: authentic report of talks and discussions in London, Amsterdam, Paris, and Saanen, Switzerland [by] J. Krishnamurti. New York. Harper [1973, c.1971] 154 p. 18 cm. (Perennial Library, P302) [BP585.K7A3] ISBN 0-06-080302-9 1.25 (pbk)
I. Title.
L.C. card no. for hardbound edition: 70-862073

LEEUW, Jacobus Johannes 212'.52
van der, 1893-
The fire of creation / by J. J. van der Leeuw. Wheaton, Ill. : Theosophical Pub. House, 1976. xiv, 130 p. ; 21 cm. (Theosophical classics series) Reprint of the 1926 ed. published by the Theosophical Press, Chicago. "A Quest book." Includes index. [BP565.L63F57 1976] 75-26823 ISBN 0-8356-0470-5 pbk. : 2.95
1. Theosophy. I. Title.

PEARSON, E. Norman. 212*.52
Space, time, and self, by E. Norman Pearson. [Rev. ed.] Wheaton, Ill., Theosophical Pub. House [1967] xi, 288 p. illus. 21 cm. (A Quest book) [BP565] 71-1546 1.75
1. Theosophy. I. Title.

PURUCKER, Gottfried de, 212'.52
1874-1942.
Fountain-source of occultism : a modern presentation of the ancient universal wisdom based on The secret doctrine by H. P. Blavatsky / G. de Purucker ; edited by Grace F. Knoche. Pasadena, Calif. : Theosophical University Press, 1974. xv, 744 p. : ill. ; 24 cm. Includes bibliographical references and index. [BP565.P8F68 1974] 72-92155 ISBN 0-911500-70-7 : 12.00
1. Theosophy. I. Blavatsky, Helene Petrovna Hahn-Hahn, 1831-1891. The secret doctrine. II. Title.

RYAN, Charles James. 212'.52
What is theosophy? : A general view of occult doctrine / by Charles J. Ryan. San Diego, Calif. : Point Loma Publications, c1975. viii, 85 p. ; 18 cm. (Theosophical manual ; no. 1) [BP565.R88W46 1975] 75-321702 ISBN pbk. : 2.25
1. Theosophy. I. Title. II. Series.

WOOD, Ernest, 1883-1965. 212'.52
The seven rays / by Ernest Wood. Wheaton, Ill. : Theosophical Pub. House, [1976] c1925. xiv, 190 p. : ill. ; 21 cm. (A Quest book) [BP565.W67 1976] 76-4909 ISBN 0-8356-0481-0 pbk. : 2.95
1. Theosophy. I. Title.

BLAVATSKY, Helene 212'.52'03
Petrovna Hahn-Hahn, 1831-1891.
The theosophical glossary. London, Theosophical Pub. Society. Detroit, Gale Research Co., 1974. 389 p. 18 cm. Reprint of the 1892 ed. [BP561.T5 1974] 73-12778 15.00
1. Theosophy—Dictionaries. I. Title.

BLAVATSKY, Helen 212'.52'0924 B
Petrovna Hahn-Hahn, 1831-1891.
The letters of H. P. Blavatsky to A. P. Sinnett, and other miscellaneous letters. Transcribed, compiled, and with an introd. by A. T. Barker. Facsim. ed. Pasadena, Calif., Theosophical University Press [1973] xv, 404 p. facsim.,

port. 23 cm. [BP585.B6A47 1973] 73-84138 10.00
1. Blavatsky, Helen Petrovna Hahn-Hahn, 1831-1891. 2. Theosophy. I. Sinnett, Alfred Parcy, 1840-1921. II. Barker, Alfred Trevor, 1893-1941, ed.

INCIDENTS in the 212'.52'0924 B
life of Madame Blavatsky / edited by A. P. Sinnett. New York : Arno Press, 1976. p. cm. (The Occult) Reprint of the 1886 ed. published by G. Redway, London. [BP585.B6I5 1976] 75-36919 ISBN 0-405-07974-5 : 19.00
1. Blavatsky, Helen Petrovna Hahn-Hahn, 1831-1891. I. Sinnett, Alfred Percy, 1840-1921. II. Series: The Occult (New York, 1976-)

LEONARD, Maurice. 212'.52'0924 B
Madame Blavatsky : medium, mystic and magician / by Maurice Leonard. London ; New York : Regency Press, 1977. 115 p. ; 23 cm. [BP585.B6L43] 77-373898 £2.00
1. Blavatsky, Helene Petrovna Hahn-Hahn, 1831-1891. 2. Theosophists—Biography. I. Title.

MURPHET, Howard. 212'.52'0924 B
Hammer on the mountain: life of Henry Steel Olcott (1832-1907) Wheaton, Ill., Theosophical Pub. House [1972] xii, 339 p. illus. 23 cm. "H. S. Olcott's works": p. [326]-327. [BP585.O4M8] 72-76427 ISBN 0-8356-0210-9 7.95
1. Olcott, Henry Steel, 1832-1907. I. Title.

MURPHET, Howard. 212'.52'0924 B
When daylight comes : a biography of Helena Petrovna Blavatsky / by Howard Murphet. Wheaton, Ill. : Theosophical Pub. House, 1975. xxxi, 277 p., [8] leaves of plates : ill. ; 21 cm. (A Quest book) Includes index. Bibliography: p. [266]-274. [BP585.B6M87] 74-18958 ISBN 0-8356-0461-6 : 8.95 ISBN 0-8356-0459-4 pbk. : 3.50
1. Blavatsky, Helene Petrovna Hahn-Hahn, 1831-1891. I. Title.

PURUCKER, Gottfried 212'.52'0924
de, 1874-1942.
H. P. Blavatsky : the mystery / by Gottfried de Purucker, in collaboration with Katherine Tingley. San Diego, Calif. : Point Loma Publications, [1974] xvi, 242 p. : port. ; 23 cm. Chapters of this book first appeared serially 40 years ago in The Theosophical path. [BP585.B6P87] 74-189478 pbk. : 4.95
1. Blavatsky, Helene Petrovna Hahn-Hahn, 1831-1891. 2. Theosophy. I. Tingley, Katherine Augusta Westcott, 1847-1929, joint author. II. The Theosophical path. III. Title.

RYAN, Charles 212'.52'0924 B
James.
H. P. Blavatsky and the theosophical movement : a brief historical sketch / by Charles J. Ryan. [2d ed]. San Diego, Calif. : Point Loma Publications, [1975] xxii, 441 p., [5] leaves of plates ; 22 cm. Includes index. [BP585.B6R8 1975] 75-319620 ISBN pbk. : 7.00
1. Blavatsky, Helene Petrovna Hahn-Hahn, 1831-1891. 2. Theosophical Society. 3. Theosophy. I. Title.

RYAN, Charles 212'.52'0924 B
James.
H. P. Blavatsky and the theosophical movement : a brief historical sketch / Charles J. Ryan. 2d and rev. ed. / edited by Grace F. Knoche. Pasadena, Calif. : Theosophical University Press, c1975. xviii, 358 p. : ill. ; 22 cm. Includes index. Bibliography: p. 325-335. [BP585.B6R8 1975b] 75-4433 ISBN 0-911500-79-0 : 8.50
1. Blavatsky, Helene Petrovna Hahn-Hahn, 1831-1891. 2. Theosophical Society. 3. Theosophy. I. Title.

SOLOV'EV, Vsevolod 212'.52'0924 B
Sergeevich, 1849-1903.
A modern priestess of Isis / Vsevolod Sergyeevich Solovyoff ; abridged and translated by Walter Leaf. New York : Arno Press, 1976. p. cm. (The Occult) Translation of Sovremennaia zhritsa Izidy. Translated on behalf of the Society for Psychical Research. Reprint of the 1895 ed. published by Longmans, Green, London. Appendices (p.): A. Abstract of pamphlet entitled: "H. P. Blavatsky and a modern priest of truth. Reply of Madame Y to Mr. Vs. Solovyoff, "by V. Jelihovsky.—B. Reply to Madame Jelihovsky's pamphlet, by V. S. Solvyoff.—C. The sources of Madame Blavatsky's writings, by W. E. Coleman. [BP585.B6S6 1976] 75-36921 ISBN 0-405-07976-1 : 20.00
1. Blavatsky, Helene Petrovna Hahn-Hahn, 1831-1891. I. Society for Psychical Research, London. II. Title. III. Series: The Occult (New York, 1976-)

WACHTMEISTER, 212'.52'0924 B
Constance.
Reminiscences of H. P. Blavatsky and The secret doctrine / by Countess Constance Wachtmeister et al. Wheaton, Ill. : Theosophical Pub. House, c1976. xiv, 141 p. : map ; 21 cm. (Theosophical classics series) (A Quest book) [BP585.B6W3 1976] 76-44810 ISBN 0-8356-0488-8 pbk. : 3.75
1. Blavatsky, Helene Petrova Hahn-Hahn, 1831-1891. 2. Blavatsky, Helene Petrova Hahn-Hahn, 1831-1891. The secret doctrine. 3. Theosophists—Biography. 4. Theosophy. I. Title.

EASTON, Stewart Copinger, 212'.53
1907-
Man and world in the light of anthroposophy / by Stewart C. Easton. Spring Valley, N.Y. : Anthroposophic Press, c1975. vi, 536 p. ; 21 cm. Includes bibliographical references and index. [BP595.E17] 74-33879 pbk. : 6.95
1. Anthroposophy. I. Title.

STEINER, Rudolf, 1861- 212'.53
1925.
Awakening to community : ten lectures given in Stuttgart and Dornacht, January 23rd to March 4, 1923 / by Rudolf Steiner ; [translated by Marjorie Spock]. Spring Valley, N.Y. : Anthroposophic Press, [1975,] c1974 vi, 178 p. ; 22 cm. "Translated from shorthand reports unrevised by the lecturer, from the German edition published with the title, Anthroposophische Gemeinschaftsbildung (vol. 257 in the Bibliographical survey, 1961)" [BP595.S82513] 75-311795 6.50
1. Anthroposophy. I. Title.

STEINER, Rudolf, 1861- 212'.53
1925.
The Christ impulse and the development of ego consciousness / by Rudolf Steiner. Valley, N.Y. : Anthroposophic Press, c1976. 156 p. ; 21 cm. Translation of Der Christus-Impuls und die Entwickelung des Ich-Bewusstseins. [BP595.S84513] 76-11907 ISBN 0-910142-71-8 pbk. : 3.95
1. Anthroposophy—Addresses, essays, lectures. I. Title.

STEINER, Rudolf, 1861- 212'.53
1925.
From symptom to reality in modern history : nine lectures given in Dornach from 18th October to 3rd November 1918 / Rudolf Steiner ; translated [from the German] by A. H. Parker. London : Rudolf Steiner Press, 1976. 245 p. : ill. ; 23 cm. "Translated from shorthand reports unrevised by the lecturer. In the Complete Edition of the works of Rudolf Steiner the volume containing the original German text is entitled 'Geschichtliche Symptomatologie'." Includes bibliographical references. [BP595.S852613 1976] 77-350218 ISBN 0-85440-298-5 : £3.75
1. Anthroposophy—Addresses, essays, lectures. I. Title.

UNGER, Carl, 1878-1929. 212'.53
Principles of spiritual science / by Carl Unger. Spring Valley, N.Y. : Anthroposophic Press, c1976. vi, 80 p. ; 19 cm. [BP595.U55 1976] 76-362759 pbk : 2.95
1. Anthroposophy. I. Title.

WITZENMANN, Herbert. 212'.53
The virtues : contemplations / Herbert Witzenmann ; translated from German by Daisy Aldan. New York : Folder Editions, c1975. 35 p. ; 22 cm. Translation of Die Tugenden. [BP595.W5713] 75-326522 ISBN 0-913152-09-9
1. Anthroposophy. 2. Meditations. I. Title.

213 Creation

BAERG, Harry J. 213
Creation and catastrophe; the story of Our Father's world. Written and illustrated by Harry J. Baerg. Washington, Review and Herald Pub. Association [1972] 159 p. illus. 25 cm. Includes bibliographies. [BS651.B22] 71-182511 5.95
1. Creation. 2. Deluge. I. Title.

BARCLAY, Vera Charlesworth, 213
1893-
Challenge to the Darwinians. Newport, Mon., R. H. Johns [1951] 296p. 19cm. [BL263.B32] 53-610
1. Evolution. 2. Man—Origin. 3. Religion and science—1900- I. Title.

BURNET, Thomas, 1635?-1715. 213
The sacred theory of the earth. With an introd. by Basil Wiley. Carbondale, Southern Illinois University Press [1965] 412 p. illus., facsims, map, port. 26 cm. (Centaur classics) First published in Latin, 1681-89, under title: Telluris theoria sacra. Includes bibliographical references. [BL224.B82] 65-10027
1. Creation — Early works to 1800. 2. Cosmogony — Early works to 1800. I. Title.

BURNET, Thomas, 1635?-1715 213
The sacred theory of the earth. Introd. by Basil Willey. Carbondale, Southern Ill. Univ. Pres. [c.1965] 412p. illus., facsims, maps, port. 26cm. (Centaur classics) First pub. in Latin, 1681-89, under title: Telluris theoria sacra, Bibl. [BL224.B82] 65-10027 22.50
1. Creation—Early works to 1800. 2. Cosmogony—Earl) works to 1800. I. Title.

CHILD, John, 1922-. 213
Australian rocks and minerals; an introduction to geology. [Gladesville, Australia] Periwinkle Press [1963] vi, 74 p. illus. (part col.) 19 cm. Bibliography: p. 71. [QE31.C56] 66-41705
1. Geology. I. Title.

CLARK, Adrian V. 213
Cosmic mysteries of the universe [by] Adrian V. Clark. West Nyack, N.Y., Parker Pub. Co. [1968] 214 p. 24 cm. Bibliographical footnotes. [BS651.C53] 68-20502
1. Cosmology. 2. Creation. I. Title.

CLARK, Harold Willard, 1891- 213
Genesis and science, by Harold W. Clark. Nashville, Southern Pub. Association [1967] 124 p. illus. 20 cm. [BS651.C552] 67-28546
1. Origin of species. 2. Bible and science. 3. Evolution. 4. Creation. 5. Bible. O.T. Genesis—Criticism, interpretation, etc. I. Title.

CLARK, Harold Willard, 1891- 213
Genesis and science, by Harold W. Clark. Nashville, Southern Pub. Association [1967] 124 p. illus. 20 cm. [BS651.C552 1967] 67-28546
1. Bible. O.T. Genesis—Criticism, interpretation, etc. 2. Origin of species. 3. Bible and science. 4. Bible and evolution. 5. Creation. I. Title.

COFFIN, Harold G. 213
Creation; accident or design? [by] Harold G. Coffin. Washington, Review and Herald Pub. Association [1969] 512 p. illus., maps. 24 cm. Includes bibliographies. [BS650.C63] 68-18744
1. Bible and science. 2. Religion and science—1946- I. Title.

CRISWELL, Wallie A. 213
Did man just happen? By W. A. Criswell. Foreword by John N. Moore. [Rev.] Grand Rapids, Mich., Zondervan Pub. House [1972] 120 p. 18 cm. [BS659.C74 1972] 73-189577 0.95
1. Bible and evolution. I. Title.

DANKENBRING, William F. 213
The first genesis : a new case for creation / William F. Dankenbring. Altadena, Calif. : Triumph Pub. Co., [1975] xxii, 359 p. : ill. ; 22 cm. Bibliography: p. [355]-359. [BL240.2.D27] 75-10841 8.95
1. Religion and science—1946- 2. Creation. 3. Evolution. I. Title.

DAVIDHEISER, Bolton. 213
Evolution and Christian faith. Grand Rapids, Mich., Baker Book House [1969] 372 p. 23 cm. Includes bibliographies. [BS659.D3] 70-76782 6.50
1. Bible and evolution. 2. Evolution. I. Title.

DEVINE, Bob. 213
Born a snake fighter / by Bob Devine ; [Pictures by Carolyn Bowser]. Chicago : Moody Press, c1977. 32 p. : ill. (some col.) ; 21 cm. (God in creation series) Brief tales demonstrate God's creative activity in relation to five animals. [BS651.D488] 77-10022 ISBN 0-8024-0888-5 pbk. : 1.50
1. Creation—Juvenile literature. I. Bowser, Carolyn Ewing. II. Title. III. Series.

DEVINE, Bob. 213
Born a snake fighter / by Bob Devine ; [Pictures by Carolyn Bowser]. Chicago : Moody Press, c1977. 32 p. : ill. (some col.) ; 21 cm. (God in creation series) Brief tales demonstrate God's creative activity in relation to five animals. [BS651.D488] 77-10022 ISBN 0-8024-0888-5 pbk. : 1.50
1. Creation—Juvenile literature. I. Bowser, Carolyn Ewing. II. Title. III. Series.

DEVINE, Bob. 213
The shape of the stars / by Bob Devine ; [pictures by Carolyn Bowser]. Chicago : Moody Press, c1977. 32 p. : ill. (some col.) ; 21 cm. (God in creation series) Explanation of five scientific phenomena which demonstrate God's involvement in the creation of the universe. [BS651.D49] 77-9982 ISBN 0-8024-7896-4 pbk. : 1.50
1. Creation—Juvenile literature. I. Bowser, Carolyn Ewing. II. Title. III. Series.

DEVINE, Bob. 213
The shape of the stars / by Bob Devine ; [pictures by Carolyn Bowser]. Chicago : Moody Press, c1977. 32 p. : ill. (some col.) ; 21 cm. (God in creation series) Explanation of five scientific phenomena which demonstrate God's involvement in the creation of the universe. [BS651.D49] 77-9982 ISBN 0-8024-7896-4 pbk. : 1.50
1. Creation—Juvenile literature. I. Bowser, Carolyn Ewing. II. Title. III. Series.

EVERS, Alf. 213
In the beginning; with pictures by Helen Sewell. New York, Macmillan, c1954. unpaged. illus. 24cm. [BS651.E85] 54-4622
1. Creation—Juvenile literature. I. Title.

EVOLVING world and theology 213
(The) Ed. by Johannes Metz. New York, Paulist [1967] viii, 184p. 24cm. (e(Concilium, theology in the age of renewial: fundamental theology, v. 26) Bibl. [BL263.E9] 67-25695 4.50
1. Evolution—Addresses, essays, lectures. 2. Religion and science—1946- —Addresses, essays, lecture. I. Metz, Johnes Baptist, 1928- ed. II. Series: Concilum: theology in the age of renewal, v. 26
Contents omitted.

FECHTENBURG, Jorgen F H 213
History's greatest prince! Eddington, Pa., c1954. 82p. illus. 20cm. [BS652.F4] 55-18732
1. Bible and science. I. Title.

FISHER, Aileen Lucia, 1906- 213
I stood upon a mountain, by Aileen Fisher. Illustrated by Blair Lent. New York, T. Y. Crowell [1973] p. Standing on top of a mountain, a young boy wonders about the creation of the world. [BL226.F57] 78-187935 ISBN 0-690-43345-X
1. Creation—Juvenile literature. I. Lent, Blair, illus. II. Title.

FITTI, Charles J. 213
A philosophy of creation. New York, Philosophical [c.1963] viii, 101p. 22cm. 63-15601 3.75
1. Truth. 2. God. 3. Sacraments. I. Title.

FOTHERGILL, Philip Gilbert 213
Evolution and Christians. [New York] Longmans [c.1961] 395p. illus. Bibl. 61-65665 9.50
1. Evolution. 2. Religion and science—1946- I. Title.

FRAIR, Wayne 213
The case for creation, by Wayne Frair, P. William Davis. Chicago, Moody [1967] 96p. illus. 18cm. (Christian Forum bks.) Bibl. [BS651.F74] 67-14381 .95 pap.,
1. Creation. 2. Bible and science. I. Davis, P. William, joint author. II. Title.

GATEWOOD, Willard B 213
Preachers, pedagogues & politicians; the evolution controversy in North Carolina, 1920-1927, by Willard B. Gatewood, Jr. Chapel Hill, University of North Carolina Press [1966] viii, 268 p. illus. 24 cm. Errata slip inserted. Bibliography: p. [251]-259 [BL263.G34] 66-15504
1. Religion and science — 1900-1925. 2. Evolution. I. Title.

GATEWOOD, Willard B., Jr. 213
Preachers, pedagogues & politicians; the evolution controversy in North Carolina. 1920-1927. Chapel Hill, Univ. of N. C. Pr. [c.1965, 1966] viii, 268p. illus. 24cm. Bibl. [BL263.G34] 66-15504 5.95
1. Religion and science — 1900-1925. 2. Evolution. I. Title.

GILKEY, Langdon Brown, 1919- 213
Maker of heaven and earth; a study of the Christian doctrine of creation. Garden City, N.Y., Doubleday [1965, c.1959] xi, 378p. 18cm. (Anchor bk., A442) [BT695.G5] 1.45 pap.,
1. Creation. I. Title.

GILKEY, Langdon Brown, 1919- 213
Maker of heaven and earth; a study of the Christian doctrine of creation. [1st ed.] Garden City, N. Y., Doubleday, 1959. 311 p. 22 cm. (Christian faith series) [BT695.G5] 59-6992
1. Creation. I. Title.

GILLISPIE, Charles Coulston. 213
Genesis and geology, a study in the relations of scientific thought, natural theology, and social opinion in Great Britain, 1790-1850. Cambridge, Harvard University Press, 1951. xiii, 315 p. 22 cm. (Harvard historical studies, v. 58) "Bibliographical essay": p. [229]-258. Bibliographical referencesincluded in "Notes" (p. [259]-302) [BS657.G55] 51-10449
1. Religion and science—History of controversy. 2. Geology. I. Title. II. Series.

GILLISPIE, Charles Coulston. 213
Genesis and geology; a study in the relations of scientific thought, natural theology, and social opinion in Great Britain, 1790-1850. New York, Harper [1959, c1951] 306 p. 21 cm. (Harper torchbooks, TB51) Includes bibliography. [BS657.G55 1959] 59-6649

1. Religion and science—History of controversy. 2. Geology. I. Title.

*GRITTON, George R. 213
The sum and the substance; a new total concept of creation based on energy levels. New York, Exposition [c.1966] 46p. 21cm. 3.00
I. Title.

HAMARNEH, Sami Khalaf, 1925- 213
A brief study of customs and civilization in Bible lands. Washington, 1960. 60 p. illus., maps. 22 cm. Includes bibliographies. [BS1235.5.H3] 63-525
1. Bible. O. T. Genesis—History of contemporary events. I. Title. II. Title: Customs and civilization in Bible lands.

HASELDEN, Kyle, comp. 213
Changing man: the threat and the promise; five scientists and five theologians on Christian faith and evolutionary thought. Edited by Kyle Haselden and Philip Hefner. [1st ed.] Garden City, N.Y., Doubleday, 1968. vi, 184 p. 22 cm. Collection of articles which originally appeared in the Christian century, 1967. Bibliography: p. [169]-173. [BL263.H336] 68-17787
1. Human evolution. 2. Religion and science—1946- I. Hefner, Philip J., joint comp. II. Title.

HEIM, Karl, 1874- 213
The world: its creation and consummation; the end of the present age and the future of the world in the light of the Resurrection. Tr. [from German] by Robert Smith. Philadelphia, Muhlenberg [c.]1962. 159p. 23cm. illus. 62-9748 3.00
1. Religion and science—1946- 2. Cosmogony. 3. Creation. 4. Resurrection. I. Title.

HEIM, Karl, 1874- 213
The world: its creation and consummation; the end of the present age and the future of the world in the light of the Resurrection. Translated by Robert Smith. Philadelphia, Muhlenberg Press, 1962. 159p. 23cm. 'A translation of the second German edition of Weltschopfung und Weltende, published in 1958 ... as Bd. VI of Der evangellsche Glaube und das Denken der Gegenwart: Grundzilge einer christichen Lebensanschanung [sic]' [BL245.H413 1962] 62-9748
1. Religion and science—1946- 2. Cosmogony. 3. Creation 4. Resurrection. I. Title.

HOBHOUSE, Leonard Trelawney, 1864-1929. 213
Development and purpose; an essay towards a philosophy of evolution. New ed., rev. and in part re-written. London, Macmillan, 1927. Grosse Pointe, Mich., Scholarly Press, 1969. xxxix, 494 p. 23 cm. [B818.H6 1969] 78-3941
1. Evolution. I. Title.

HULSBOSCH, A., 1912- 213
God in creation and evolution. Tr. by Martin Versfeld. New York. Sheed [1966, c.1965] xv, 240p. 21cm. [BL263H8313] 66-12268 4.95
1. Evolution. 2. Religion and science — 1946- I. Title.

HULSBOSCH, A 1912- 213
God's creation; creation, sin, and redemption in an evolving world [by] A. Hulsbosch. Translated by Martin Versfeld. London, New York, Sheed and Ward [1965] xvi, 270 p. 18 cm. (Sheed & Ward stagbooks) [BT695.H813] 66-6844
1. Creation. I. Title.

HULSBOSCH, Ansfridus, 1912- 213
God in creation and evolution [by] A. Hulsbosch. Translated by Martin Versfeld. New York, Sheed and Ward [1966, c1965] xv, 240 p. 21 cm. Translation of De schepping Gods. [BL263.H8313 1966] 66-12268
1. Evolution. 2. Religion and science—1946- I. Title.

INSTITUTE for Creation Research. 213
Scientific creationism / prepared by the technical staff and consultants of the Institute for Creation Research ; edited by Henry M. Morris. San Diego, Calif. : Creation-Life Publishers, c1974. v, 277 p. ; 24 cm. Includes indexes. Bibliography: p. 257-260. [BS651.I57 1974] 74-14160 ISBN 0-89051-004-0. ISBN 0-89051-003-2 pbk.
1. Creation. 2. Bible and evolution. I. Morris, Henry Madison, 1918- II. Title.

JAUNCEY, James H 213
Science returns to God. Grand Rapids, Zondervan Pub. House [1961] 120p. 22cm. Includes bibliography. [BS650.J3] 61-14869
1. Bible and science. 2. Religion and science—1946- I. Title.

JOHNSON, James Weldon, 1871-1938. 213
"I'll make a world"; James Weldon Johnson's story of the creation. Designed by Jay Johnson. [Kansas City, Mo., Hallmark, c1972] 45 p. illus. 25 cm. (Hallmark crown editions) The author's sermon The creation, previously published in a collection, God's trombones, in 1927 by Viking Press. [PS3519.O2625C7 1972] 72-77476 ISBN 0-87529-313-1
I. Title.

KATTER, Reuben Luther. 213
The history of creation and origin of the species. [Minneapolis, Theotes Logos Research, c1967] xxii, 433 p. 22 cm. Bibliographical footnotes. [BS651.K3] 68-4036
1. Creation. 2. Bible and science. I. Title.

KLOTZ, John William. 213
Genes, Genesis, and evolution. Saint Louis, Concordia Pub. House [1955] 575 p. illus. 24 cm. Includes bibliography. [BL263.K57] 55-6434
1. Evolution. 2. Religion and science—1900- I. Title.

KLOTZ, John William. 213
Genes, genesis, and evolution, by John W. Klotz. 2d rev. ed. Saint Louis, Concordia Pub. House [1970] vii, 544 p. illus. 24 cm. Includes bibliographical references. [BL263.K57 1970] 73-17696
1. Bible and evolution. 2. Religion and science—1946- I. Title.

KOFAHL, Robert E. 213
The creation explanation : a scientific alternative to evolution / Robert E. Kofahl, Kelly L. Segraves. Wheaton, Ill. : H. Shaw Publishers, c1975. xiv, 255 p. : ill. ; 24 cm. Includes index. Bibliography: p. [247]-250. [BS651.K63] 76-358226 ISBN 0-87788-141-3 : 7.95
1. Creation. 2. Evolution. I. Segraves, Kelly L., joint author. II. Title.

LARSON, Muriel. 213
God's fantastic creation / Muriel Larson. Chicago : Moody Press, [1975] 188 p. ; 19 cm. Bibliography: p. 187-188. [BT695.L39] 75-12511 ISBN 0-8024-3033-3 pbk. : 1.25
1. Creation. I. Title.

LONG, Edward Le Roy. 213
Religious beliefs of American scientists. Philadelphia, Westminster Press [1952] 108 p. 21 cm. Revision of thesis, Columbia University, published in microfilm form in 1951 under title: Religious philosophies of natural scientists. [BL240.L66 1952] 52-9193
1. Religion and science—1900- I. Title.

*MCGOWEN, C. H. 213
In six days / C. H. McGowen. Van Nuys, Calif. : Bible Voice, 1976. 108, [1]p. ; 21 cm. Bibliography: p. [109] [BS650] pbk. : 2.95
1. Religion and science-1946- 2. Creation. 3. Evolution. I. Title.
Pub. address P.O. Box 7491 91409.

MCNAUGHTON, Ruth L 213
Tiny words about the beginning; illustrated by Faith McNaughton Lowell. Wheaton, Ill., Van Kampen Press, c1953. unpaged. illus. 21cm. [BS651.M2] 53-24290
1. Creation—Juvenile literature. I. Title.

MAURER, Arthur James 213
Unveiling the mystery of creation; the wording of Scripture proves that our universe and all life is controlled by electronic energy. [Rev. ed. Chicago, Adams, c.1963] 417p. 24cm. 63-8706 5.95
1. Bible and science. 2. Creation—Miscellanea. I. Title.

MELTON, David. 213
And God created ... / written and illustrated by David Melton. Independence, Mo. : Independence Press, [1975] p. cm. [BS651.M43] 75-8945 ISBN 0-8309-0144-2
1. Creation. I. Title.

MESSENGER, Ernest Charles, 1888- ed. 213
Theology and evolution; a sequel to Evolution and theology. By various writers. Westminster, Md., Newman Press [195-?] 337 p. 23 cm. [BL263.M472] 52-8011
1. Evolution. 2. Religion and science — 1900- 3. Man — Origin. 4. Man(Theology) I. Title.

MORRIS, Henry Madison, 1918- 213
The remarkable birth of planet earth [by] Henry M. Morris. Minneapolis, Dimension Books [1972, i.e. 1973] viii, 111 p. 18 cm. Bibliography: p. 101-105. [BS652.M62] 73-166083 ISBN 0-87123-485-8 0.95 (pbk.)
1. Creation. I. Title.

MOUIREN, Trophime, 1921- 213
The creation. Translated from the French by S. J. Tester. [1st ed.] New York, Hawthorn Books [1962] 126 p. 21 cm. (The Twentieth century encyclopedia of Catholicism, v. 19. Section 2: The basic truths) [BT695.M613] 62-21733
1. Creation. I. Title.

MOUIREN, Trophime, 1921- 213
The creation. Tr. from French by S. J. Tester. New York, Hawthorn [c.1962] 126p. 21cm. (Twentieth century encyclopedia of Catholicism, v.19. Sect. 2: The basic truths) Bibl. 62-21733 3.50
I. Title.

NOGAR, Raymond J 213
The wisdom of evolution. [1st ed.] Garden City, N.Y., Doubleday, 1963. 408 p. illus. 22 cm. Bibliographical references included in "Notes." [BL263.N6] 63-18212
1. Evolution. 2. Religion and science — 1946- I. Title.

NOGAR, Raymond J. 213
The wisdom of evolution. Garden City, N.Y., Doubleday [c.]1963. 408p. illus. 22cm. Bibl. 63-18212 5.75
1. Evolution. 2. Religion and science—1946- I. Title.

NOGAR, Raymond J. 213
The wisdom of evolution. New York, New Amer. Lib. [1966, c.1963] 368p. 18cm. (Mentor-Omega bk., MO701) Bibl. .95 pap.,
1. Evolution. 2. Religion and science — 1946- I. Title.

O'CONNOR, Daniel, comp. 213
Creation: the impact of an idea. Edited by Daniel O'Connor and Francis Oakley. New York, Scribner [1969] ix, 262 p. 24 cm. (Scribner source books in religion) Contents.Contents.—Nature. Introduction: two philosophies of nature, by D. O'Connor. The Christian doctrine of creation and the rise of modern natural science, by M. Foster. Christian theology and the Newtonian science: the rise of the concept of the laws of nature, by F. Oakley. What accelerated technological progress in the Western Middle Ages? By L. White, Jr.—Man. Introduction: the human and the divine, by D. O'Connor. The problem of time, by E. Brunner. Letter and spirit, by E. Frank. Christian optimism, by E. Gilson.—Society. Introduction: the sacral norm, by F. Oakley. Kingship in Israel and in Babylon, by A. T. van Leeuwen. Christianity changes the conditions of government, by N. Fustel de Coulanges. The Western church and the post-Roman world, by T. M. Parker. Medieval canon law and Western constitutionalism, by B. Tierney. Epilogue. Jewish and Christian elements in the Western philosophical tradition, by H. Jonas. An introductory bibliography: p. 259-262. Bibliographical footnotes. [BT695.O25] 69-11958
1. Creation—Addresses, essays, lectures. 2. Theology—Addresses, essays, lectures. I. Oakley, Francis, joint comp. II. Title.

PADOVANO, Anthony T. 213
Eden and Easter, by Anthony T. Padovano. New York, Paulist Press [1974] v, 87 p. 19 cm. [BT695.P3] 73-91370 ISBN 0-8091-1810-6 1.25 (pbk.)
1. Jesus Christ—Passion. 2. Jesus Christ—Resurrection. 3. Creation. I. Title.

PILKINGTON, Roger. 213
In the beginning; the story of creation. Drawings by Piet Klaasse. New York, St. Martin's Press [1957] 59p. illus. 23cm. [BS651.P53] 57-12099
1. Creation. 2. Bible and science. I. Title.

PILKINGTON, Roger 213
In the beginning; the story of creation. Drawings by Piet Klaasse. Nashville, Abingdon [1966, c.1957] 59p. col. illus. 22cm. [BS651.P53] 66-2678 2.50 bds.,
1. Creation. 2. Bible and science. I. Title.

REHWINKEL, Alfred Martin, 1887- 213
The wonders of creation; an exploration of the origin & splendors of the universe, by Alfred M. Rehwinkel. Minneapolis, Bethany Fellowship [1974] 288 p. 22 cm. Includes bibliographical references. [BS651.R39] 74-8416 ISBN 0-87123-649-4 3.95 (pbk.)
1. Bible. O.T. Genesis I-II—Criticism, interpretation, etc. 2. Creation. I. Title.

RENEKENS, Henricus. 213
Israel's concept of the beginning: the theology of Genesis 1-3. [New York] Herder and Herder [1964] 320 p. 22 cm. "A series of articles which originally appeared in four successive volumes of Verbum (1950-1953)" "Translated from Israels visie op het verleden." [BS1235.2.R453] 64-13690
1. Bible. O.T. Genesis I-III — =criticism, interpretation, etc. I. Title.

REUMANN, John Henry Paul. 213
Creation & new creation; the past, present, and future of God's creative activity [by] John Reumann. Minneapolis, Augsburg Pub. House [1973] 128 p. 22 cm. Includes bibliographical references. [BT695.R48] 73-78271 ISBN 0-8066-1335-1 3.95
1. Creation. I. Title.

RIDDERBOS, Nicolaas Herman. 213
Is there a conflict between Genesis 1 and natural science? [Translated by John Vriend] Grand Rapids, Eerdmans [1957] 88p. 19cm. (Pathway books) Translation of Beschouwingen over Genesis I. [BS651.R532] 57-9774
1. Bible and science. 2. Religion and science—1900- 3. Creation. 4. Barth, Karl, 1886- I. Title.

RIEGLE, David D. 213
Creation or evolution? Grand Rapids, Mich., Zondervan [c.1962] 64p. 21cm. Bibl. 1.00 pap.,
I. Title.

ROOTS of spring : 213
a narrative anthology / edited by Avery Brooke ; drawings by Robert Pinart. Noroton, Conn. : Vineyard Books, c1975. 96 p. : ill. ; 23 cm. Includes bibliographical references. [BL226.R63] 75-325045 ISBN 0-913886-03-3 : 4.95
1. Creation—Meditations. I. Brooke, Avery. II. Pinart, Robert.

RUFFINI, Ernesto, Cardinal. 213
The theory of evolution judged by reason and faith; translated by Francis O'Hanlon. Foreword by Thomas A. Boland; introd. by John E. Steinmueller. New York, J. F. Wagner [1959] 205p. 21cm. Includes bibliography. [BL263.R813] 59-16903
1. Religion and science—1900- 2. Evolution. I. Title.

SALISBURY, Frank B. 213
The creation / Frank B. Salisbury. Salt Lake City : Deseret Book Co., 1977 xv, 314 p. : ill. ; 24 cm. Includes index. Bibliography: p. [300] -302. [BS651.S316] 76-47071 ISBN 0-87747-627-6 : 3.95
1. Creation. 2. Religion and science—1946- 3. Evolution. I. Title.

SPANNER, D. C. 213
Creation and evolution; some preliminary considerations [by] D. C. Spanner. Grand Rapids, Zondervan Pub. House [1968, c1965] 61 p. 21 cm. (A Zondervan paperback) [BS659.S6] 68-22834
1. Bible and evolution. 2. Creation. I. Title.

A Symposium on creation, 213
by Henry M. Morris and others. Grand Rapids, Baker Book House [1968] 156 p. illus., maps. 22 cm. "Papers presented ... at the annual conference on Christian schooling in Houston, Texas, under the auspices of the Association for Christian Schools." Includes bibliographies. [BS651.S9] 68-19213
1. Creation. I. Morris, Henry Madison, 1918- II. Association for Christian schools.

SYMPOSIUM on creation II, 213
by Donald W. Patten and others. Grand Rapids, Mich., Baker Book House [1970] 151 p. illus. 22 cm. Bibliographical footnotes. [BS651.S92] 73-13812 1.95
1. Creation. I. Patten, Donald Wesley, 1929-

SYMPOSIUM on creation III. 213
Edited by Donald W. Patten. Grand Rapids, Baker Book House [1971] 150 p. illus. 22 cm. Includes bibliographical references. [BS651.S93] 70-30843 ISBN 0-8010-6892-4 2.95
1. Creation. I. Patten, Donald Wesley, 1929- ed.

THROCKMORTON, Burton Hamilton, 1921- 213
Creation by the word; a study of the idea of creation in Second Isaiah and the Gospel according to John [by] Burton H. Throckmorton, Jr. Boston, United Church Press [1968] 156 p. illus. 21 cm. [BS651.T49] 68-20569
1. Bible. O.T. Isaiah XL-LV—Study—Outlines, syllabi, etc. 2. Bible. N.T. John—Study—Outlines, syllabi, etc. 3. Creation—Biblical teaching. I. Title.

TRESMONTANT, Claude. 213
The origins of Christian philosophy. Translated from the French by Mark Pontifex. [1st ed.] New York, Hawthorn Books [1963] 126 p. 21 cm. (The Twentieth century encyclopedia of Catholicism, v. 11. Section 1: Knowledge and faith) [B631.T713] 63-10985
1. Fathers of the church. 2. Creation — History of doctrines. 3. Man (Theology) — History of doctrine. I. Title.

TRESMONTANT, Claude 213
The origins of Christian philosophy. Tr. from French by Mark Pontifex. NewYork, Hawthorn [c.1963] 126p. 21cm. (Twentieth century encyclopedia of Catholicism, v. 11. Sect. 1: Knowledge and faith) 63-10985 3.50 bds.,
1. Fathers of the church. 2. Creation—History of doctrines. 3. Man (Theology)—History of doctrine. I. Title.

WESTERMANN, Claus. 213
Beginning and end in the Bible. Translated by Keith Crim. Philadelphia, Fortress Press [1972] xvii, 46 p. 20 cm. (Facet books. Biblical series, 31) Translation of Anfang und Ende in der Bibel. Bibliography: p. 40-44. [BS652.W4313] 72-75659 ISBN 0-8006-3071-8 1.00
1. Creation—Biblical teaching. 2. Eschatology—Biblical teaching. I. Title.

WHEELER, Gerald W. 213
The two-taled dinosaur : why science and religion conflict over the origin of life / by Gerald W. Wheeler. Nashville : Southern Pub. Association, c1975. 224 p. ; 22 cm. Includes index. Bibliography: p. 211-217. [BL245.W47] 75-28530 ISBN 0-8127-0090-2
1. Religion and science—History of controversy. 2. Evolution. 3. Creation. I. Title.

WHITNEY, Dudley J. 213
Genesis versus evolution; the problem of creation and atheistic science. New York, Exposition Press [c.1961] 61p. (Exposition-Banner bk.) 2.50
1. Universe, Creation of. 2. Atheism. I. Title.

WHITNEY, Dudley Joseph. 213
The face of the deep; a defense of divine creation. [1st ed.] New York, Vantage Press [1955] 102p. illus. 21cm. [BS651.W425] 54-12637
1. Creation. 2. Religion and science—1900- I. Title.

WILDER-SMITH, A. E. 213
Man's origin, man's destiny : a critical survey of the principles of evolution and Christianity / A. E. Wilder Smith. Minneapolis : Bethany Fellowship, 1975, c1968. 320 p. ; 21 cm. Reprint of the ed. published by H. Shaw, Wheaton, Ill. Translation of Herkunft und Zukunft des Menschen. Includes index. Bibliography: p. 319-320. [BS659.W5413 1975] 74-28508 ISBN 0-87123-356-8 pbk. : 3.95
1. Bible and evolution. 2. Man—Origin. 3. Human evolution. I. Title.

WOODS, Andrew J. 213
The center of the earth, by Andrew J. Woods. Discussion by Henry M. Morris. San Diego, Calif., Institute for Creation Research [1973] 18 l. illus. 28 cm. (ICR technical monograph no. 3) [GA23.W66] 73-79064 1.50
1. Earth. I. Title. II. Series: Institute for Creation Research. ICR technical monograph no. 3.

YOUNG, Norman James. 213
Creator, creation, and faith / by Norman Young. Philadelphia : Westminster Press, c1976. p. cm. Includes bibliographical references and index. [BT695.Y68] 76-10324 ISBN 0-664-21334-0 : 8.50
1. Creation. I. Title.

ZIEGLER, John Sherman, 1873- 213
'In the beginning'; a six thousand year old secret has come to light. Mohawk, N. Y. [1954] 126p. illus. 20cm. [BS652.Z5] 55-21994
1. Creation—Miscellanea. I. Title.

LAMMERTS, Walter Edward, 1904- comp. 213'.08
Why not creation? Selected articles from the Creation Research Society Quarterly, volumes I through V (1964-1968). Walter E. Lammerts, editor. [Nutley, N.J.] Presbyterian and Reformed Pub. Co., 1970. 388 p. illus. 23 cm. Includes bibliographical references. [BS651.L25] 78-133085 7.50
1. Creation—Addresses, essays, lectures. 2. Bible and science—Addresses, essays, lectures. I. Creation Research Society. Quarterly. II. Title.

ALLEN, Leslie Henri, 1887- ed. 213'.0922
Bryan and Darrow at Dayton; the record and documents of the "Bible-evolution trial," edited and compiled by Leslie H. Allen. New York, Russell & Russell [1967] viii, 218 p. ports. 23 cm. Reprint of the 1925 ed. [BL263.A5 1967] 67-18289
1. Bryan, William Jennings, 1860-1925. 2. Darrow, Clarence Seward, 1857-1938. 3. Bible and evolution. 4. Modernist-fundamentalist controversy. I. Scopes, John Thomas, Tennessee, plantiff. II. Title. III. Title: "Bible-evolution trial."

CLARK, Harold Willard, 1891- 213'.0924
Crusader for creation; the life and writings of George McCready Price, by Harold W. Clark. Incorporating biog. materials prepd. by R. Lyle James. Mountain View, Calif., Ppacific Pr. Pub. [c.1966] 102p. 22cm. (Destiny bk., D-110) Bibl. [BX6193.P7C5] 66-28531 1.50 pap.,
1. Price, George McCready, 1870- I. Title. II. Title: The life and writings of George McGready Price.

CLARK, Harold Willard, 1891- 213'.0924
Crusader for creation; the life and writings of Geroge McCrendy Price, by Harold W. Clark. Incorporating biographical materials prepared by R. Lyle James. Mountain View, Calif., Pacific Press Pub. Association [c1966] 102 p. 22 cm. (A Destiny book, D-110) "Books by George McCready Price": p. 101-102. [BX6193.P7C5] 66-28531
1. Price, George McCready, 1870- I. Title. II. Title: The life and writings of George McCready Price.

ALLEN, Harold W. G. 213.5
Ye shall know the truth. New York, Vantage Press [1961, c.1960] 241p. 3.95 bds.,
1. Creation of life. I. Title.

*CULP, G. Richard. 213.5
Remember thy creator [by] G. Richard Culp. Grand Rapids, Baker Book House [1975] 207 p. ill. 22 cm. Includes bibliographical references and index. [BL263] ISBN 0-8010-2365-3 3.95 (pbk.)
1. Evolution. 2. Creation. I. Title.

GRUBER, Jacob W 213.5
A conscience in conflict: the life of St. George Jackson Mivart. New York, Published for Temple University Publications by Columbia University Press, 1960. 266p. illus. 24cm. [BL263.G68 1960] 60-10645
1. Mivart. St. George Jackson, 1827-1900. 2. Religion and science—1860-1899. 3. Evolution. I. Title.

HEINZE, Thomas F. 213'.5
The creation vs. evolution handbook, by Thomas F. Heinze. Grand Rapids, Baker Book House [1970] 79 p. 20 cm. Includes bibliographical references. [BS659.H4] 70-129055 ISBN 8-01-040027- 1.50
1. Bible and evolution. I. Title.

HEINZE, Thomas F. 213'.5
The creation vs. evolution handbook [by] Thomas F. Heinze. Rev. ed. Grand Rapids, Baker Book House [1972] 96 p. 20 cm. Includes bibliographical references. [BS659.H4 1972] 72-196018 ISBN 0-8010-4002-7 1.50
1. Bible and evolution. I. Title.

HILL, Harold, 1905- 213'.5
From goo to you by way of the zoo : how did it all begin? / Harold Hill, with Irene Harrell ; illustrated by John Lawing. Plainfield, N.J. : Logos International, c1976. xvi, 104 p. : ill. ; 18 cm. Bibliography: p. 93-99. [BS651.H49] 75-20898 ISBN 0-88270-140-1 pbk. : 1.45
1. Creation. 2. Evolution. 3. Conversion. I. Harrell, Irene Burk. II. Title.

KOPP, Josef Vitalis. 213.5
Teilhard de Chardin; a new synthesis of evolution [by] Joseph V. Kopp. Glen Rock, N.J., Paulist Press [1964] 72 p. 18 cm. (Deus books) Translation of Entstehung and Zukunft des Menschen; Pierre Tellhard de Chardin and sein Weltbild. [QE707.T4K63] 65-3171
1. Tellhard de Chardin, Pierre. I. Title.

KOPP, Josef Vitalis 213.5
Teilhard de Chardin; a new synthesis of evolution [Tr. from German] Glen Rock, N.J., Paulist [1965, c.1964] 72p. 18cm. (Deus bks.) [QE707.T4K63] 65-3171 .75 pap.,
1. Teilhard de Chardin, Pierre. I. Title.

LAMMERTS, Walter Edward, 1904- comp. 213'.5
Scientific studies in special creation. Walter E. Lammerts, editor. [Nutley, N.J.] Presbyterian and Reformed Pub. Co., 1971. xi, 343 p. illus. 23 cm. "Selected articles from the Creation Research Society Quarterly, volume I through V (1964-1968)." Includes bibliographical references. [BS651.L24] 70-150955 6.95
1. Creation—Addresses, essays, lectures. 2. Bible and science—Addresses, essays, lectures. I. Creation Research Society. Quarterly. II. Title.

LAMMERTS, Walter Edward, 1904- comp. 213'.5
Scientific studies in special creation. Walter E. Lammerts, editor. Grand Rapids, Mich., Baker Book House [1973, c.1971] xi, 343 p. illus. 22 cm. "Selected articles from the Creation Research Society Quarlerly, vol. I through V (1964-1968)." Includes bibliographical references. [BS651.L24] ISBN 0-8010-5526-1 3.95 (pbk.)
1. Creation—Addresses, essays, lectures. 2. Bible and science—Addresses, essays, lectures. I. Title. II. Title: Creation Research Society. Quarterly.

LEVER, Jan. 213.5
Creation and evolution. Translated from the Dutch by Peter G. Berkhout. Grand Rapids, Grand Rapids International Publications; distributed by Kregel, 1958. 244p. illus. 23cm. Includes bibliography. [BL263.L443] 57-13247
1. Religion and science—1900- 2. Evolution. I. Title.

LONG, Charles H. 213.5
Alpha: the myths of creation. New York, Braziller [c.]1963. xxii, 264p. 32 plates, diagrs. 22cm. (Patterns of myth. I: Myth and experience) Bibl. 63-18188 6.00
1. Creation. I. Title. II. Series.

LONG, Charles H. 213.5
Alpha the myths of creation. New York, G. Braziller, 1963. xxii, 264 p. 32 plates, diagrs. 22 cm. (Patterns of myth. I: Myth and experience) Bibliography: p. 248-251. [BL325.C7L6] 63-18188
1. Creation. I. Title.

O'BRIEN, John Anthony, 1893- 213.5
God and evolution; the bearing of evolution upon the Christian faith. With supplementary chapters by Achille Cardinal Lienart and J. Franklin Ewing, and an introd by Gustave Weigel. [2d rev. and enl. ed. Notre Dame, Ind.] University of Notre Dame Press, 1961. cci, 313 p. illus., diagrs. 23 cm. First published in 1932 under title: Evolution and religion. Bibliographical footnotes. [BL263.O3 1961] 61-10851
1. Evolution. 2. Philosophy and religion. 3. Religion and science — 1926-1045. I. Title.

ONG, Walter J., ed. 213.5
Darwin's vision and Christian perspectives; [papers] Foreword by JohnWright. New York, Macmillan, [c:]1960. 154p. Bibl. 22cm. 60-14486 4.00
1. Darwin, Charles Robert, 1809-1882. 2. Religion and science—1946- 3. Evolution. I. Title.

TAYLOR, Kenneth Nathaniel. 213'.5
Evolution and the high school student. Compiled and edited by Kenneth N. Taylor. Wheaton, Ill., Tyndale House Publishers [1970, c1969] 56 p. illus., ports. 21 cm. [BS659.T37] 70-75248 ISBN 8-423-08008-
1. Bible and evolution. I. Title.

TRESMONTANT, Claude. 213.5
Pierre Teilhard de Chardin; his thought. With a pref. by Gustave Weigel. [Translation by Salvator Attansio] Baltimore, Helicon Press, 1959. 128 p. 23 cm. Translation of Introduction a la pensee de Teilhard de Chardin. Includes bibliography. [QE707.T4T73] 59-14334
1. Teilhard de Chardin, Pierre. 2. Evolution. 3. Religion and science — 1900- I. Title.

ZIMMERMAN, Paul Albert, 1918- ed. 213.5
Darwin, evolution, and creation [by] Paul A. Zimmerman, editor [and others] Saint Louis, Concordia Pub. House, 1959. xii, 231 p. 24 cm. Bibliography: p. 205-214. [BL263.Z58] 59-11471
1. Darwin, Charles Robert, 1809-1882. 2. Evolution. 3. Religion and science—1900- I. Title.

ZIMMERMANN, Paul Albert, 1918- ed. 213.5
Darwin, evolution, and creation [ed. by] Paul A. Zimmermann [others] Saint Louis, Concordia [1962, c.1961] xii, 231p. (12-2203) Bibl. 1.95 pap.,
1. Darwin, Charles Robert, 1809-1882. 2. Evolution. 3. Religion and science—1900- I. Title.

214 Theodicy

AHERN, M. B. 214
The problem of evil [by] M. B. Ahern. New York, Schocken Books [1971] xiv, 85 p. 23 cm. (Studies in ethics and the philosophy of religion) Bibliography: p. 80-82. [BJ1401.A48 1971b] 72-150985 ISBN 0-8052-3407-1 4.50
1. Good and evil. I. Title.

PIKE, Nelson, ed. 214
God and evil; readings on the theological problem of evil. Englewood Cliffs, N. J., Prentice-Hall [1964] viii, 114 p. 22 cm. (Contemporary perspectives in philosophy series) Bibliography: p. 113-114. [BJ1401.P5] 64-11869
1. Good and evil. I. Title.

PIKE, Nelson, ed. 214
God and evil; readings on the theological problem of evil. Englewood Cliffs, N. J., Prentice [c.1964] viii, 114p. 22cm. (Contemporary perspectives in philosophy ser.) Bibl. 64-11869 2.25 pap.,
1. Good and evil. I. Title.

215 Science & Religion

ABELE, Jean, 1886- 215
Christianity and science. Translated from the French by R. F. Trevett. [1st ed.] New York, Hawthorn Books [1961] 140p. 21cm. (The Twentieth century encyclopedia of Catholicism, v. 14. Section 1: Knowledge and faith) Translation of Le christianisme se desinteresse-t-ii de la science? Includes bibliography. [BL240.2.A213] 61-17755
1. Religion and science—History of controversy. I. Title.

ABELE, Jean Marie Joseph Edouard, 1886- 215
Christianity and science. Tr. from French by R. F. Trevett. New York, Hawthorn [c.1961] 140p. (Twentieth cent. ency. of Catholicism, v. 14. Section 1: Knowledge and faith) Bibl. 61-17755 3.50 bds.,
1. Religion and science—History of controversy. I. Title.

ALLER, Catherine 215
The challenge of Pierre Teilhard de Chardin. New York, Exposition [c.1964] 56p. 21cm. 64-1039 3.00
1. Teilhard de Chardin, Pierre. Le phenomene humain. I. Title.

ALLER, Catherine. 215
The challenge of Pierre Teilhard de Chardin. 2d ed. New York, Exposition Press [1967] 62 p. 21 cm. [B2430.T373P57 1967] 67-3843
1. Teilhard de Chardin, Pierre. Le phenomene humain. I. Title.

AMERICAN Scientific Affiliation. 215
Modern science and Christian faith; a symposium on the relationship of the Bible to modern science, by members of the American Scientific Affiliation. 2d ed., enl. Wheaton, Ill., Van Kampen Press [1950] xii, 316 p. illus. 22 cm. Bibliographical footnotes. [BL240.A64 1950] 50-54737
1. Religion and science—1900- I. Title.

THE American weekly (New York) 215
The faith of great scientists; a collection of "My faith" articles from the American weekly. [New York, Hearst Pub. Co., 1950] 63 p. ports. 23 cm. Cover title. [BL240.A643] 50-3271
1. Religion and science—1900- I. Title.

AOUSSAT, Claude A. 215
The march of God on earth. New York, Pageant [c.1963] 46p. 21cm. 2.50
I. Title.

APPLING, Phillip Holden, 1910- 215
Gospel in the twentieth century; essays on science and religion. Illustrated by Frances Elois Appling. [1st ed.] New York, Exposition Press [1973] 127 p. illus. 21 cm. Bibliography: p. 125-127. [BL240.2.A66] 72-90060 ISBN 0-682-47594-7 5.00
1. Religion and science—1946- I. Title.

AUBERT, Jean Marie. 215
A God for science? Translated by Paul Barrett. Westminster, Md., Newman Press [1967] vi, 154 p. 21 cm. Translation of Recherche scientifique et foi chretienne. Bibliographical footnotes. [BL240.2.A813] 67-23605
1. Religion and science—1946- I. Title.

AUSTIN, William H. 215
The relevance of natural science to theology / [by] William H. Austin. London : Macmillan, 1976. ix, 132 p. ; 23 cm. (Library of philosophy and religion) Includes bibliographical references and index. [BL240.2.A87 1976] 76-368460 ISBN 0-333-18660-5 : £7.95
1. Religion and science—1946- I. Title.

AUSTIN, William H. 215
The relevance of natural science to theology / William H. Austin. New York : Barnes & Noble Books, 1976. 132 p. ; 23 cm. (Library of philosophy and religion) Includes bibliographical references and index. [BL240.2.A87 1976b] 75-43222 ISBN 0-06-490240-4 : 22.50
1. Religion and science—1946- I. Title.

AYRES, Clarence Edwin, 1891- 215
Science: the false messiah & Holier than thou; the way of the righteous [by] Clarence E. Ayres. [1st ed.] Clifton [N.J.] A. M. Kelley [1973] xii, 240 p. 22 cm. (Reprints of economic classics) Reprints of the 1927 and 1929 editions, both published by Bobbs-Merrill Co., Indianapolis, with a new introd. [B67.A79] 71-130660 ISBN 0-678-00774-8
1. Science—Philosophy. 2. Inventions. 3. Religion and science—1926-1945. 4. Ethics. 5. Social ethics. I. Ayres, Clarence Edwin, 1891- Holier than thou. 1973. II. Title. III. Title: Holier than thou.

BARBOUR, Ian G 215
Christianity and the scientist. New York, Association Press [1960] 128p. 20cm. (The

Haddam House series on the Christian in his vocation) A Haddam House book. Includes bibliography. [BL240.2.B35] 60-12715
1. Religion and science—1946- I. Title.

BARBOUR, Ian G 215
Issues in science and religion [by] Ian G. Barbour. Englewood Cliffs, N.J., Prentice-Hall [1966] x, 470 p. 22 cm. Bibliographical footnotes. [BL245.B3] 66-16387
1. Religion and science — History of controversy. I. Title.

BARBOUR, Ian G. 215
Issues in science and religion [by] Ian G. Barbour. Englewood Cliffs, N.J., Prentice-Hall [1966] x, 470 p. 22 cm. Bibliographical footnotes. [BL245.B3] 66-16387
1. Religion and science—History of controversy. I. Title.

BARBOUR, Ian G., comp. 215
Science and religion; new perspectives on the dialogue, edited by Ian G. Barbour. [1st ed.] New York, Harper & Row [1968] xi, 323 p. 21 cm. (Harper forum books) Bibliographical footnotes. [BL240.2.B37 1968] 68-11744
1. Religion and science—1946- I. Title.

BEARD, Clarence M 215
The only true God. Boston, Christopher Pub. House [1956] 237p. illus. 21cm. [BS650.B37] 56-43425
1. Bible and science. I. Title.

BECK, Stanley D. 215
Modern science and Christian life [by] Stanley D. Beck. Minneapolis, Augsburg Pub. House [1970] 157 p. illus. 22 cm. Includes bibliographies. [Q125.B36] 73-121965 2.95
1. Religion and science—1946- I. Title.

BENEDICT, Robert P. 215
Journey away from God [by] Robert P. Benedict. Old Tappan, N.J., F. H. Revell Co. [1972] 189 p. 21 cm. Includes bibliographical references. [BS650.B39] 77-186533 ISBN 0-8007-0519-X 4.95
1. Bible and science. I. Title.

BENSON, Clarence Herbert, 1879- 215
The greatness and grace of God, conclusive evidence that refutes evolution; arranged to be used as a textbook in Christian evidences. Chicago, Scripture Press [1953] 224p. illus. 21cm. [BL253.B38] 54-652
1. Religion and science—1900- 2. Astronomy. I. Title.

BIRCH, L. Charles, 1918- 215
Nature and God [by] L. Charles Birch. Philadelphia, Westminster Press [1965] 128 p. 29 cm. (Adventures in faith) Bibliography: p. [118]-125. [BL240.2.B58] 66-10066
1. Religion and science—1946- I. Title.

BIRCH, L. Charles, 1918- 215
Nature and God. Philadelphia, Westminster [1966, c.1965] 128p. 19cm. (Adventures in faith) Bibl. [BL240.2.B58] 66-10066 1.45 pap.,
1. Religion and science — 1946- I. Title.

BIVORT DE LA SAUDEE, Jacques de, 1900- ed. 215
God, man and the universe; a Christian answer to modern materialism. New York, Kenedy [1953?] 421p. illus. 22cm. Translation of Essai sur Dieu, I homme et I univers, with additional material. [BX1751.B5733] 53-11513
1. Catholic Church—Apologetic works. 2. Religion and science—1900- 3. Communism. I. Title.

BOOTH, Edwin Prince, 1898- ed. 215
Religion ponders science. [1st ed.] New York, Appleton-Century [1964] xii, 302 p. diagrs. 22 cm. Bibliographical footnotes. [BL240.2B66] 64-12457
1. Religion and science — 1946- — Addresses, essays, lectures. I. Title.

BOUTROUX, Emile, 1845-1921. 215
Science & religion in contemporary philosophy. Translated by Jonathan Nield. Port Washington, N.Y., Kennikat Press [1970] xi, 400 p. 22 cm. Reprint of the 1909 ed. Bibliographical footnotes. [B56.B72 1970] 70-102563
1. Religion and science—1900-1925. 2. Philosophy, Modern. I. Title.

BRAIN, Walter Russell Brain, baron, 1895- 215
Science, philosophy, and religion. Cambridge [eng.] University Press, 1959. 30 p. 19 cm. (Arthur Stanley Eddington memorial lecture, 12) [BL240.2.B7] 59-1912
1. Religion and science — 1946- 2. Science — Philosophy. 3. Philosophy — Addresses, essays, lectures. I. Title. II. Series.

BRINTON, Howard Haines, 1884- 215
Evolution and the inward light; where science and religion meet [by] Howard H. Brinton. [Wallingford, Pa., Pendle Hill [1970] 47 p. 19 cm. (Pendle Hill pamphlet 173) [BX7732.B7225] 77-137101 0.55
1. Friends, Society of—Doctrinal and controversial works. 2. Logos. I. Title.

BROCK, Fred R., comp. 215
The Biblical perspective of science; readings in physical and biological science, edited by Fred R. Brock, III [and] Michael J. Bardon. New York, MSS Information Corp. [1972] 242 p. illus. 23 cm. Includes bibliographical references. [BS650.B76] 72-5880 ISBN 0-8422-5038-7 6.25
1. Bible and science—Addresses, essays, lectures. I. Bardon, Michael J., joint comp. II. Title.

BROPHY, Donald, comp. 215
Science and faith in the 21st century. New York, Paulist Press [1968] ix, 118 p. 18 cm. (Deus books) Contents.-Breaking the genetic code, by V. G. Dethler.--Experiment: man, by K. Rahner.--Reflections on biological engineering, by G. M. Schurr.--Birth control: time for a second look, by R. Tobias.--Life in a test tube, by P. R. Gastonguay.--Terrestrial and cosmic polygenism, by R. J. Pendergast.--Teilhard de Chardin, by B. Towers.--Cybernetics and the knowledge of God, by S. Beer.--The God of contradiction, by R. B. McLaren. [BL240.2.B76] 67-31105
1. Religion and science—1945- I. Title.

BROPHY, Donald, comp. 215
Science and faith in the 21st century. New York, Paulist Press [1968] ix, 118 p. 18 cm. (Deus books) Contents.Contents.—Breaking the genetic code, by V. G. Dethier.—Experiment: man, by K. Rahner.—Reflections on biological engineering, by G. M. Schurr.—Birth control: time for a second look, by R. Tobias.—Life in a test tube, by P. R. Gastonguay.—Terrestrial and cosmic polygenism, by R. J. Pendergast.—Teilhard de Chardin, by B. Towers.—Cybernetics and the knowledge of God, by S. Beer.—The God of contradiction, by R. B. McLaren. [BL240.2.B76] 67-31105
1. Religion and science—1946- I. Title.

BROWNE, Laurence Edward, 1887- 215
Where science and religion meet. Wallington, Surrey, Religious Education Press, 1950. 128 p. 20 cm. (Gateway handbooks of religious knowledge, 3) Bibliography: p. 126. [BL240.B74] 51-27683
1. Religion and science—1900- I. Title. II. Series.

BUBE, Richard H., 1927- 215
The encounter between Christianity and science, edited by Richard H. Bube. Grand Rapids, W. B. Eerdmans Pub. Co. [1968] 318 p. 21 cm. Includes bibliographical references. [BL240.2.B8] 67-13987
1. Religion and science—1946- I. Title.

BUBE, Richard H., 1927- 215
The human quest; a new look at science and the Christian faith [by] Richard H. Bube. Waco, Tex., Word Books [1971] 262 p. illus. 23 cm. Bibliography: p. 254-257. [BL240.2.B82] 70-160294 5.95
1. Religion and science—1946- I. Title.

BURNABY, John. 215
Darwin and the human situation. Cambridge, W. Heffer [1959] iii, 30 p. 19 cm. Bibliographical footnotes. [BL263.B87] 68-32238
1. Religion and science—1945- 2. Evolution. I. Title.

CATHOLIC Church. Pope, 1939- (Pius XII) Le prove della esistenza di Dio (22 Nov. 1951) English. 215
Modern science and God. [Edited and translated] by P. J. McLaughlin. New York, Philosophical Library [1954] 89p. 19cm. Address delivered to the members of the Pontificial Academy of Science. [BL240] 54-13051
1. Religion and science—1900- 2. God—Proof. I. McLaughlin, P. J., ed. and tr. II. Title.

CAUTHEN, Wilfred Kenneth. 215
Science, secularization & God; toward a theology of the future [by] Kenneth Cauthen. Nashville, Abingdon Press [1968, c1969] 237 p. 24 cm. Bibliographical footnotes. [BL240.2.C3] 69-12010 5.50
1. Religion and science—1946- 2. Church and the world. 3. Theology, Doctrinal. I. Title.

CHAUCHARD, Paul, 1912- 215
Science and religion. Translated from the French by S. J. Tester. [1st ed.] New York, Hawthorn Books [1962] 156p. 21cm. (The Twentieth century encyclopedia of Catholicism, v. 130. Section 13: Catholicism and science) Translation of La science detruit-elle la religion? Includes bibliographies. [BL240.2.C473] 62-16132
1. Religion and science—1946- I. Title.

CHAUCHARD, Paul Albert, 1912- 215
Science and religion. Tr. from French by S. J. Tester. New York, Hawthorn [c.1962] 156p. 21cm. (Twentieth cent. encyclopedia of Catholicism, v.130. Section 13: Catholicism and sci.) Bibl. 62-16132 3.50
1. Religion and science—1946- I. Title.

CHAUVIN, Remy 215
God of the scientists. God of the experiment. Translated by Salvator Attanasio. Baltimore. Helicon Press [c.]1960. 152p. Bibl.:p.149-152. 60-15633 3.95
1. Religion and science—1946- 2. God—Proof. I. Title.

CHAUVIN, Remy. 215
God of the scientists, God of the experiment. Translated by Salvator Attanasio. Baltimore, Helicon Press, 1960. 152p. 23cm. Includes bibliography. [BL240.2.C513] 60-15633
1. Religion and science—1946- 2. God—Proof. I. Title.

CHEN, Philip Stanley, 1903- 215
A new look at God / by Philip S. Chen. 2d ed. Camarillo, Calif. : Chemical Elements Pub. Co., [1975] 228 p. ; 23 cm. Includes bibliographical references. [BL240.2.C52 1975] 75-5419 5.95
1. Religion and science—1946- I. Title.

CLARK, John Ruskin, 1911- 215
The great living system : new answers from the sciences to old religious questions / by John Ruskin Clark. Pacific Grove, CA : Boxwood Press, [1977] p. cm. Includes index. Bibliography: p. [BL240.2.C548] 76-53812 pbk. : 4.95
1. Religion and science—1946- 2. Religion—Philosophy. I. Title.

CLARK, Robert E. D. 215
Darwin: before and after; an evangelical assessment. Chicago, Moody [1967, c.1966] 192p. 17cm. (Moody giants, no. 52) Bibl. .89 pap.,
I. Title.

CLARK, Robert Edward David 215
Christian belief and science; a reconciliation and a partnership. Philadelphia, Muhlenberg [1961, c.1960] 160p. Bibl. 61-19759 2.25 pap.,
1. Religion and science—1946- I. Title.

CLARK, Robert Edward David. 215
The Christian stake in science, by Robert E. D. Clark. Chicago, Moody Press [1967] 160 p. 22 cm. Bibliographical footnotes. [BL240.2] 68-1816
1. Religion and science—1946- I. Title.

CLARK, Robert Edward David. 215
The Christian stake in science, by Robert E. D. Clark. Chicago, Moody Press [1967] 160 p. 22 cm. Bibliographical footnotes. [BL240.2] 68-1816
1. Religion and science—1946- I. Title.

CLARK, Robert Edward David. 215
Science and Christianity—a partnership, by Robert E. D. Clark. Mountain View, Calif., Pacific Press Pub. Association [1972] 192 p. 22 cm. (Dimension 114) Bibliography: p. 177-183. [BL240.2.C577] 72-80665
1. Religion and science—1946- I. Title.

CLARK, Robert Edward David. 215
The universe: plan or accident? The religious implications of modern science, by Robert E. D. Clark. Grand Rapids, Zondervan Pub. House [1972, c1961] 236 p. illus. 21 cm. (Contemporary evangelical perspectives) "First published 1949. Third ed. (rev. and enl.) 1961." Includes bibliographical references. [BL240.C5673 1972] 78-171204 2.95
1. Religion and science—1946- I. Title.

COTTON, Edward Howe, 1881-1942, ed. 215
Has science discovered God? A symposium of modern scientific opinion. Freeport, N.Y., Books for Libraries Press [1968] lviii, 308 p. ports. 23 cm. (Essay index reprint series) Reprint of the 1931 ed. [BL240.C68 1968] 68-8452
1. Religion and science—1926-1945—Addresses, essays, lectures. I. Title.

COULSON, Charles Alfred. 215
Science and Christian belief. Chapel Hill, University of North Carolina Press, 1955. 127p. 20cm. (The John Calvin McNair lectures) [BL240] 55-12908
1. Religion and science—1900- I. Title.

COULSON, Charles Alfred 215
Science, technology, and the Christian. Nashville, Abingdon Press [1961, c.1960] 111p. 19cm. 61-826 2.50 bds.,
1. Religion and science—1946- 2. Technology. I. Title.

CRISWELL, Wallie A 215
Did man just happen? Grand Rapids, Zondervan Pub. House [1957] 121 p. 21 cm. [BL240.C73] 57-38983
1. Religion and science—1900- 2. Evolution. I. Title.

CUPITT, Don. 215
The worlds of science & religion / Don Cupitt. New York : Hawthorn Books, 1976. 115 p. ; 21 cm. (Issues in religious studies) Includes index. Bibliography: p. 110-112. [BL240.2.C86 1976] 75-41795 ISBN 0-8015-8924-X pbk. : 3.50
1. Religion and science—1946- I. Title.

CURTIS, Winterton Conway, 1875-- 215
Fundamentalism vs. evolution at Dayton, Tennessee; abstracts from the autobiographical notes of Winterton C. Curtis. [n. p.] c1956. 64p. illus. 23cm. 'Reprinted in part from the Falmouth enterprise, July 20 to August 31, 1956.' [BL245.C78] 57-1913
1. Religion and science—History of controversy. 2. Scopes, John Thomas, defendant. I. Title.

DAVIDHEISER, Bolton. 215
Science and the Bible. Grand Rapids, Mich., Baker Book House [1971] 121 p. 20 cm. [BS650.D265] 73-146116 ISBN 0-8010-2807-8 3.95
1. Bible and science. I. Title.

DILLENBERGER, John 215
Protestant thought and natural science; a historical interpretation. Nashville, Abingdon [1967, c.1960] 320p. 21cm. (Apex bks., Z-1p Bibl. [BL240.2.D5] 2.25 pap.,
1. Religion and science—History of controversy. 2. Religious thought— Modern period. I. Title.

DILLENBERGER, John. 215
Protestant thought and natural science; a historical interpretation. [1st ed.] Garden City, N.Y., Doubleday, 1960. 310 p. 22 cm. Includes bibliography. [BL240.2.D5] 60-13517
1. Religion and science—History of controversy. 2. Religious thought—Modern period. I. Title.

DILLENBERGER, John. 215
Protestant thought and natural science : a historical interpretation / by John Dillenberger. Westport, Conn. : Greenwood Press, 1977 [c1960] p. cm. Reprint of the 1st ed., published by Doubleday, Garden City, N.Y. Includes index. Bibliography: p. [BL240.2.D5 1977] 77-7200 ISBN 0-8371-9670-1 lib.bdg. : 18.50
1. Religion and science—History of controversy. 2. Religious thought—Modern period, 1500- I. Title.

EARTH might be fair; 215
reflections on ethics, religion, and ecology. Edited by Ian G. Barbour. Englewood Cliffs, N.J., Prentice-Hall [1972] vii, 168 p. 23 cm. [GF80.E15] 73-167916 ISBN 0-13-222687-1
1. Human ecology—Moral and religious aspects. 2. Nature (Theology) I. Barbour, Ian G., ed.

ESTERER, Arnulf K 215
Towards a unified faith. New York, Philosophical Library [1963] 102 p. illus. 22 cm. [BL240.2.E8] 62-20870
1. Religion and science — 1946- I. Title.

ESTERER, Arnulf K. 215
Towards a unified faith. New York, Philosophical Library [c.1963] 102p. illus. 22cm. Bibl. 62-20870 3.75
1. Religion and science—1946- I. Title.

EYRING, Henry, 1901- 215
The faith of a scientist. Salt Lake City, Bookcraft [1967] 196 p. illus., ports. 24 cm. Essays. Includes bibliographical references. [BL240.2.E9] 67-25432
1. Religion and science—1946- —Addresses, essays, lectures. I. Title.

FERBER, Adolph C 215
Where is heaven? [1st ed.] New York, Pageant Press [1955] 243p. 24cm. [BL240.F45] 55-7358
1. Swedenborg, Emanuel. 1688-1772. 2. Religion and science—1900- 3. Heaven. 4. Extrasensory perception. I. Title.

GARRISON, Webb B 215
Wonders of science; mysteries that point to God, by Gary Webster [pseud.] New York, Sheed & Ward [1956] 135p. 21cm. [BL243.G3] 56-6132
1. Religion and science—1900- I. Title.

GASPAR, Geza. 215
Science, conscience and God. Should the

scientist believe New York, Helicon Books [1950] 64 p. 24 cm. [BL240.G29] 50-9312
1. Religion and science—1900- I. Title.

GILKES, A. N. 215
Faith for modern man. New York, Roy [1961, c.1960] 160p. 61-12673 3.00
1. Religion andscience—1946- 2. Christianity—20th cent. I. Title.

GILKEY, Langdon Brown, 1919- 215
Religion and the scientific future; reflections on myth, science, and theology, by Langdon Gilkey. [1st ed.] New York, Harper & Row [1970] x, 193 p. 22 cm. (The Deems lectures, 1967) Includes bibliographical references. [BL240.2.G54 1970] 72-109070 5.95
1. Religion and science—1946- I. Title. II. Series.

GITTELSOHN, Roland Bertram, 1910- 215
Man's best hope. New York, Random House [1961] 200 p. 21 cm. [BL48.G57] 61-14892
1. Religion. I. Title.

GOSLING, David L., 1939- 215
Science and religion in India / by David L. Gosling. Madras : Published for Christian Institute for the Study of Religion and Society, Bangalore, by Christian Literature Society, 1976. 176 p. ; 23 cm. (Series on religion ; no. 21) A portion of the author's thesis, University of Lancaster. Includes bibliographical references. [BL245.G67] 76-904188 Rs12.50
1. Religion and science—History of controversy—India. I. Title.

GREENE, John C 215
Darwin and the modern world view. Baton Rouge, Louisiana State University Press [1961] 141p. 21cm. (Rockwell lectures, Rice University) Includes bibliography. [BL263.G66] 61-154896
1. Religion and science—History of controversy. 2. Natural theology. 3. Ethics, Evolutionary. I. Title.

GREENE, John C. 215
Darwin and the modern world view, the Rockwell lectures, Rice University. New York, New Amer. Lib. [c.1961, 1963] 126p. 18cm. (Mentor Bk. MP485) Bibl. .60 pap.,
1. Religion and science—History of controversy. 2. Natural theology. 3. Ethics, Evolutionary. I. Title.

GUTKIND, Eric, 1877-1965. 215
The body of God; first steps toward an anti-theology; the collected papers of Eric Gutkind. Edited by Lucie B. Gutkind and Henry Le Roy Finch. Introd. by Henry Le Roy Finch. New York, Horizon Press [1969] 237 p. 25 cm. [B56.G8] 70-92718 6.95
1. Philosophy and religion—Addresses, essays, lectures. 2. Judaism—Addresses, essays, lectures. I. Title.

HABER, Francis C 215
The age of the world: Moses to Darwin. Baltimore, Johns Hopkins Press, 1959. xi, 303p. 23cm. 'An extension of ... [the author's] dissertation, Revolution in the concept of historical time: a study in the relationship between Biblical chronology and the rise of modern science ... Johns Hopkins University, 1957. Bibliographical footnotes. Includes bibliography. [BL245.H3] 59-14893
1. Religion and science—History of controversy. 2. Earth—Age. I. Title.

HABGOOD, John Stapyiton. 215
Religion and science, by J. S. Habgood. With a forword by Bryan Matthews. London, Mills & Boon [1964] 159 p. illus. 23 cm. (Science in society, no. 8) Bibliography: p. 152-153. [BL240.2.H3 1964] 65-89076
1. Religion and science — 1946- I. Title.

HABGOOD, John Stapylton. 215
Truths in tension; new perspectives on religion and science by John Habgood. Foreword by Sir Bryan Matthews. [1st ed.] New York, Holt, Rinehart and Winston [1965, c1964] 157 p. illus., maps. 22 cm. First published in London in 1964 under title: Religion and science. Bibliography: p. 152-153. [BL240.2.H3 1965] 65-13820
1. Religion and science—1946- I. Title.

HANDRICH, Theodore Lewis, 1906- 215
The creation: facts, theories, and faith. Chicago, Moody Press [1953] 311p. 22cm. [BL240.H258] 53-3667
1. Religion and science—1900- I. Title.

HARPER, Samuel Alain, 1875- 215
Man's high adventure; with an introd. by A. J. Carlson. Chicago, R. F. Seymour [1955] 185p. 23cm. [BL240.H28] 56-4377
1. Religions and science—1900- I. Title.

HARRIS, Errol E 215
Revelation through reason; religion in the light of science and philosophy. New Haven, Yale University Press, 1958. 158p. 21cm. (The Terry lectures) [BL240.H29] 58-11253
1. Religion and science—1900- 2. Revelation. I. Title.

HARTSHORNE, Marion Holmes. 215
The promise of science and the power of faith. Philadelphia, Westminster Press [1958] 143p. 21cm. [BL240.H35] 58-8940
1. Religion and science—1900- I. Title.

HEDLEY, George Percy, 1899- 215
Religion and the natural world. Seattle, Dist. by the Univ. of Wash.Pr. [1963] 49p. 22cm. Three lects. given in the med. student res. training program at the Univ. of Wash. Sch. of Med. 63-4038 1.50
1. Religion and science—History of controversy. 2. Washington (State) University. School of Medicine. I. Title.

HEIM, Karl, 1874- 215
Christian faith and natural science. [Translation by N. Horton Smith] New York, Harper [1953] 256p. 22cm. Translation of Der chfistliche Gottesglaube und die Naturwissenschaft, i, Grundlegung. [BT75.H536 1953a] 53-8371
1. Religion and science—1900- I. Title.

HEIM, Karl, 1874- 215
Christian faith and natural science. [1st Harper torchbook ed.] New York, Harper [1957] 256p. 21cm. (Harper torchbooks, TB 16) Translation by N. Horton Smith of Der christliche Gottesglaube und die Naturwissenschaft, I, Grundiegung. [BT75] 57-7536
1. Religion and science—1900- I. Title.

HEIM, Karl, 1874- 215
The transformation of the scientific world view. New York, Harper [c1953] 262p. 22cm. Translation of Der christliche Gottesglaube und die Naturwissenschaft, ii, Die Wandlung im naturwissenschaftlichen Weltbild. [BT75.H537 1953a] 53-10966
1. Religion and science—1900- I. Title.

HEIM, Karl, 1874-1958. 215
Christian faith and natural science. [1st Harper torchbook ed.] New York, Harper [1957] 256 p. 21 cm. (Harper torchbooks, TB16) Translation by N. Horton Smith of Der christliche Gottenglaube und die Naturwissenschaft, I. Grundiegung. [BT75.H536 1957] 57-7536
1. Religion and science—1946- I. Title.

HEINECKEN, Martin J. 215
God in the space age. [1st ed.] Philadelphia, Winston [1959] 216 p. 22 cm. Includes bibliography. [BL254.H4] 59-5327
1. God. 2. Religion and astronautics. I. Title.

HUXLEY, Thomas Henry, 1825-1895. 215
Essays upon some controverted questions. Freeport, N.Y., Books for Libraries Press [1973] p. (Essay index reprint series) Reprint of the 1892 ed. Contents.Contents.—Prologue.—The rise and progress of palaeontology.—The interpreters of Genesis and the interpreters of nature.—Mr. Gladstone and Genesis.—The evolution of theology: an anthropological study.—Science and morals.—Scientific and pseudo-scientific realism.—Science and pseudo-science.—An Episcopal trilogy.—Agnosticism.—The value of witness to the miraculous.—Agnosticism: a rejoinder.—Agnosticism and Christianity.—The lights of the church and the light of science.—The keepers of the herd of swine.—Illustrations of Mr. Gladstone's controversial methods.—Hasisadra's adventure. [Q171.H916 1973] 73-1231 ISBN 0-518-10048-0
1. Science—Addresses, essays, lectures. 2. Religion and science—1860-1899—Addresses, essays, lectures. I. Title.

HUXLEY, Thomas Henry, 1825-1895. 215
Science and Christian tradition; essays. New York, Greenwood Press [1968] xxxiv, 419 p. 23 cm. (His Collected essays, v. 5) "Originally published in 1897." Contents.Contents.—Prologue (controverted questions, 1892).—Scientific and pseudo-scientific realism (1887).—Science and pseudo-science (1887).—An Episcopal trilogy (1887).—The value of witness to the miraculous (1889).—Possibilities and impossibilities (1891).—Agnosticism (1889).—Agnosticism: a rejoinder (1889).—Agnosticism and Christianity (1889).—The keepers of the herd of swine (1890).—Illustrations of Mr. Gladstone's controversial methods (1891) [Q171.H902 vol. 5] [BL240] 79-29963
1. Religion and science—1860-1899. 2. Agnosticism. 3. Miracles—Controversial literature. I. Title.

HUXLEY, Thomas Henry, 1825-1895. 215
Science and Hebrew tradition; essays. New York, Greenwood Press [1968] xvi, 372 p. 23 cm. (His Collected essays, v. 4) "Originally published in 1896." Contents.Contents.—On the method of Zadig (1880).—The rise and progress of palaeontology (1881).—Lectures on evolution (New York, 1876).—The interpreters of Genesis and the interpreters of nature (1885).—Mr. Gladstone and Genesis (1886).—The lights of the church and the light of science (1890).—Hasisadra's adventure (1891).—The evolution of theology: an anthropological study (1886) [Q171.H902 vol. 4] 71-29961
1. Science—Addresses, essays, lectures. 2. Bible and science—Addresses, essays, lectures. 3. Evolution—Addresses, essays, lectures. 4. Paleontology—Addresses, essays, lectures. I. Title.

INGE, William Ralph, 1860-1954. 215
Science and ultimate truth. [Folcroft, Pa.] Folcroft Library Editions, 1973. 32 p. 24 cm. "Delivered at Guy's Hospital Medical School, March 25, 1926." Reprint of the 1926 ed. published by Longmans, Green, New York and issued as the Fison memorial lecture, 1926. [BL51.I6 1973] 73-7513 ISBN 0-8414-2109-9 (lib. bdg.)
1. Religion—Philosophy—Addresses, essays, lectures, 2. Religion and science—1926-1945—Addresses, essays, lectures. I. Title. II. Series: The Fison memorial lecture, 1926.

INGE, William Ralph, 1860-1954. 215
Science and ultimate truth / by W. R. Inge. Norwood, Pa. : Norwood Editions, 1976. 32 p. ; 23 cm. "Delivered at Guy's Hospital Medical School, March 25, 1926." Reprint of the 1926 ed. published by Longmans, Green, New York, which was issued as the Fison memorial lecture, 1926. [BL51.I6 1976] 76-8218 ISBN 0-8482-1154-5 lib. bdg. : 6.50
1. Religion—Philosophy—Addresses, essays, lectures. 2. Religion and science—1926-1945—Addresses, essays, lectures. I. Title. II. Series: The Fison memorial lecture, 1926.

ISAACS, Alan, 1925- 215
The survival of God in the scientific age. Harmondsworth, Penguin, 1966. 224 p. diagrs. 18 cm. (Pelican book A843) Bibliography: p. 216-218. [BL240.2.I8] 67-70936
1. Religion and science—1946- I. Title.

*ISHERWOOD, Margaret 215
Faith without dogma. New York, Harper [1964] 1v. 24cm. 3.00
I. Title.

JACOBS, Thornwell, 1877- 215
For heretics only. Atlanta, Westminster Publishers [1954] 293p. 24cm. [BL2775.J28] 55-22576
1. Christianity —Controversial literature. I. Title.

JAUNCEY, James H. 215
Science returns to God. Grand Rapids, Mich., Zondervan [c.1961] 120p. Bibl. 61-14869 1.95; 1.00 bds., pap.,
1. Bible and science. 2. Religion and science—1946- I. Title.

JEEVES, Malcolm A. 215
The scientific enterprise & Christian faith [by] Malcolm A. Jeeves. Downers Grove, Ill., Inter-varsity Press [1969] 168 p. 22 cm. Based on papers and discussions prepared for the International Conference of Science and Faith, held at Oxford, 1965. Bibliographical footnotes. [BL240.2.J4 1969] 74-93034 4.50
1. Religion and science—1946- I. International Conference of Science and Faith, Oxford, 1965. II. Title.

KENNEY, W. Henry, 1918- 215
A path through Teilhard's Phenomenon [by] W. Henry Kenney. Dayton, Ohio, Pflaum Press, 1970. xii, 284 p. 21 cm. (Themes for today) Bibliography: p. 267-279. [B2430.T373P65] 69-20172 2.95
1. Teilhard de Chardin, Pierre. Le phenomene humain. I. Title.

KING, Rachel Hadley, 1904- 215
The creation of death and life, by Rachel H. King. New York, Philosophical Library [1970] x, 444 p. 22 cm. Bibliography: p. 431-432. [BS650.K55] 75-97935 8.95
1. Bible and science. 2. Theism. I. Title.

KIPPER, Herman Brunswick, 1882- 215
Christianity and the gamut of evolution; the final goal: immortal life, by H. B. Kipper. Boston, Christopher Pub. House [1967] 254 p. 21 cm. [Q173.K57] 67-23753
1. Science—Miscellanea. 2. Evolution. 3. Religion and science—1946- I. Title.

KLOTZ, John William 215
The challenge of the space age. St. Louis, Concordia [c.1961] 112p. (Concord bks.) 61-13456 1.00 pap.,
1. Religion and astronautics. 2. Atomic energy. I. Title.

KLOTZ, John William. 215
Modern science in the Christian life. Saint Louis, Concordia Pub. House [1961] 191p. 21cm. Includes bibliography. [BL210.2.K53] 60-15575
1. Religion and science—1946- I. Title.

KOCHER, Paul Harold, 1907- 215
Science and religion in Elizabethan England. San Marino, Calif., Huntington Library, 1953. xii, 340p. 24cm. (Huntington Library publications) Bibliographical footnotes. [BL245.K6] 53-9115
1. Religion and science—History of controversy. I. Title. II. Series: Henry E. Huntington Library and Art Gallery, San Marino, Calif. Huntington Library publications

KOCHER, Paul Harold, 1907- 215
Science and religion in Elizabethan England, by Paul H. Kocher. New York, Octagon Books, 1969 [c1953] xii, 340 p. 24 cm. Bibliographical footnotes. [BL245.K6 1969] 73-96198
1. Religion and science—History of controversy—England. I. Title.

KOESTLER, Arthur, 1905- 215
The sleep walkers; a history of man's changing vision of the universe. With an introd. b Herbert Butterfield. New York, Macmillan, 1959. 624p. illus. 22cm. Includes bibliography. [BL245.K63 1959a] 59-7218
1. Religion and science—History of controversy. I. Title.

KOESTLER, Arthur, 1905- 215
The sleep walkers; a history of man's changing vision of the universe. Introd. by Herbert Butterfield. New York, Grosset [1963, c.1959] 624p. diagrs. 21cm. (Universal lib., 0159) Bibl. 2.65 pap.,
1. Religion and science—History of controversy. I. Title.

KOESTLER, Arthur, 1905- 215
The sleepwalkers. With an introd. by Herbert Butterfield and with a new pref. by the author. [1st American ed.] New York, Macmillan [1968] 624 p. illus. 21 cm. (Danube edition) Bibliography: p. 611-613. [BL245.K63 1968b] 68-27603 8.95
1. Astronomy—History. 2. Religion and science—History of controversy. I. Title.

KRIMSKY, Joseph Hayyim. 215
A doctor's soliloquy. New York, Philosophical Library [1953] 116p. 20cm. [BL241.K7] 53-6244
1. Religion and science—1900- 2. Religion—Philosophy. I. Title.

LANGFORD, Jerome J 215
Galileo, science, and the church, by Jerome J. Langford. Foreword by Stillman Drake. New York, Desclee Co. [1966] xv, 237 p. 21 cm. Bibliography: p. [223]-232. [BL245.L27] 66-17861
1. Galilei, Galileo, 1564-1642. 2. Religion and science — History of controversy. I. Title.

LANGFORD, Jerome J. 215
Galileo, science, and the church. Foreword by Stillman Drake. New York. Desclee. [c.1966] xv, 237p. 21cm. Bibl. [BL245.L27] 66-17861 5.95
1. Galilci Galilco, 1564-1642. 2. Rcligion and science — History of controversy. I. Title.

LANGMACK, Holger Christian. 215
God and the universe; unity of science and religion. New York, Philosophical Library [1953] 173p. illus. 22cm. [BL240.L28] 53-13071
1. Religion and science—1900- I. Title.

LEVER, Jan. 215
Where are we headed? A biologist talks about origins, evolution, and the future. Translated by Walter Lagerwey. Grand Rapids, Mich., W. B. Eerdmans [1970] 59 p. 22 cm. Cover title: Where are we headed? A Christian perspective on evolution. Translation of Waar blijven we? Een bioloog over de wording van deze aardse werkelijkheid. [BL240.2.L4713] 78-127631 1.65
1. Religion and science—1946- 2. Philosophical anthropology. I. Title.

LONG, Edward Le Roy. 215
Religious beliefs of American scientists [by] Edward LeRoy Long, Jr. Westport, Conn., Greenwood Press [1971, c1952] 168 p. 23 cm. [BL240.2.L65 1971] 70-141415 ISBN 0-8371-4693-3
1. Religion and science—1946- I. Title.

LONG, Edward Le Roy. 215
Science & Christian faith; a study in partnership. New York, Association Press, 1950. 125 p. 20 cm. (A Haddam House book) [BL240.L67] 50-6377
1. Religion and science—1900- I. Title.

LOPER, W. Harold. 215
The curious layman : science, belief, and the common man / W. Harold Loper. 1st ed. Hicksville, N.Y. : Exposition Press, [1975] xii, 96 p. ; 22 cm. (An Exposition-university book) Bibliography: p. 93-96. [BL55.L56] 74-21444 ISBN 0-682-48170-X : 5.50
1. Religion and civilization. 2. Cosmology. I. Title.

LUNN, Arnold Henry Moore, 1888- 215
The revolt against reason. New York, Sheed & Ward, 1951. 273 p. 22 cm. [BL240.L825 1951] 51-12845
1. Religion and science—1900- 2. Science—Philosophy. I. Title.

LUNN, Arnold Henry Moore, 1888- 215
The revolt against reason. London, Eyre & Spottiswoode [1950] 252p. 23cm. Bibl. [BL240.L825] 51-546 2.50 bds.,
1. Religion and science — 1900- 2. Science — Philosophy. I. Title.
Now available from Hillary House, New York.

LUNN, Arnold Henry Moore, Sir, 1888- 215
The revolt against reason, by Arnold Lunn. Westport, Conn., Greenwood Press [1971, c1951] xiv, 273 p. 23 cm. Includes bibliographical references. [BL240.L825 1971] 72-108396 ISBN 0-8371-3819-1
1. Religion and science—1946- 2. Science—Philosophy. I. Title.

MCCUTCHEN, Duval Talmadge, 1908- 215
The creation story and modern man. [1st ed.] Arlington, Va., 1954. 56p. 20cm. [BL941.M17] 55-32976
1. Religion and science—1900- 2. Creation. I. Title.

MCLAUGHLIN, P. J. 215
The church and modern science. New York, Philosophical Library [1957] 374p. 22cm. 'The second part . . . consists almost entirely of addresses delivered by H. H. Pope Plus xii to scientific and other professional bodies.' 'Acts of Pius xii relating to science and technology':p. 351-359. 'Acts of Pius xii relating to atomic energy':p. 360. Bibliography: p. 361-366. [BL240.M318] 57-59054
1. Religion and science—1900- I. Pius XII, Pope, 1876- II. Title.

MCNEUR, Ronald W. 215
Space, time, God. Philadelphia, Westminster Press [1961] 157 p. 21 cm. Includes bibliography. [BT102.M26] 61-9888
1. God (Theory of knowledge) 2. Religion and science—1946- I. Title.

MARSH, Frank Lewis, 1899- 215
Life, man, and time. Mountain View, Calif., Pacific Press Pub. Association [1957] 200p. 21cm. [BL240.M3447] 57-11332
1. Religion and science—1900- I. Title.

MASCALL, Eric Lionel, 1905- 215
Christian theology and natural science: some questions on their relations. London, New York, Longmans, Green [1956] 328p. 23cm. (The Bampton lectures, 1956) [BR45.B3 1956] 56-58533
1. Religion and science—1900- I. Title.

MATHEWS, Shailer, 1863-1941. 215
Contributions of science to religion, by Shailer Mathews, with the cooperation of William E. Ritter [and others] Freeport, N.Y., Books for Libraries Press [1970, c1924] vii, 427 p. illus. 23 cm. (Essay index reprint series) [BL240.M37 1970] 79-117822
1. Science—Addresses, essays, lectures. 2. Religion and science—1926-1945—Addresses, essays, lectures. I. Ritter, William Emerson, 1856-1944. II. Title.

MILL, John Stuart, 1806-1873. 215
Nature, and Utility of religion. [Essays] Edited with an introd. by George Nakhnikian. New York, Liberal Arts Press [1958] xxx, 80p. 21cm. (The Library of liberal arts, no. 81) Bibliography: p. xxix. [BL51.M58] 58-59889
1. Nature. 2. Religion. I. Title. II. Title: Utility of religion.

MORRIS, Daniel Luzon. 215
Possibilities unlimited; a scientist's approach to Christianity. With a foreword by Kirtley F. Mather. [1st ed.] New York, Harper [1952] 191 p. illus. 20 cm. [BL240.M736] 52-5465
1. Religion and science — 1900- I. Title.

MORRIS, Henry M 1918- 215
The Bible and modern science. Chicago, Moody Press [c1951] 191 p. 20 cm. [BS650.M56] 51-14999
1. Bible and science. 2. Religion and science — 1900- I. Title.

MORRIS, Henry Madison, 1918- 215
The Bible and modern science. Chicago, Moody Press [1951] 191 p. 20 cm. [BS650.M56] 51-14999
1. Bible and science. I. Title.

MORRIS, Henry Madison, 1918- 215
Studies in the Bible and science; or, Christ and creation, by Henry M. Morris. Grand Rapids, Baker Book House, 1966. 186 p. 23 cm. [BS650.M57] 66-16684
1. Bible and science. I. Title. II. Title: Christ and creation.

MORRIS, Henry Madison, 1918- 215
Studies in the Bible and science; or, Christ and creation. Grand Rapids, Mich., Baker Bk. [c.] 1966. 186p. 23cm. [BS650.M57] 66-16684 3.50
1. Bible and science. I. Title. II. Title: Christ and creation.

MORRIS, Henry Madison, 1918- 215
The twilight of evolution. Grand Rapids. Mich., Baker Bk., 1963. 103p. 20cm. Bibl. 63-21471 price unreported
1. Evolution. I. Title.

MORRISON, Abraham Cressy, 1864-1951. 215
Seven reasons why a scientist believes in God. [Westwood, N. J.,] Revell [1962] 61p. 17cm. (A Revell inspirational classic) [BL240.M7383] 62-17109
1. Religion and science—1926-1945. 2. God—Proof. I. Title.

NEEDHAM, Joseph, 1900- ed. 215
Science, religion & reality. Introductory essay by George Sarton. New York, G. Braziller, 1955. 355p. 21cm. [BL240.N4 1955] 55-13670
1. Religion and science—1900- I. Title.

NEEDHAM, Joseph, 1900- ed. 215
Science, religion, and reality [by] Arthur James, Earl of Balfour [and others] Edited by Joseph Needham. Port Washington, N.Y., Kennikat Press [1970] 396 p. 22 cm. (Essay and general literature index reprint series) Reprint of the 1925 ed. [BL240.N4 1970] 70-108706
1. Religion and science—1946- I. Balfour, Arthur James Balfour, 1st Earl of, 1848-1930. II. Title.

NYE, Ernest J 215
Secret power of life. New York, Vantage Press [1953] 115p. 22cm. [BL240.N9] 53-12147
1. Religion and science— 1900- I. Title.

OSTLIN, Melvin T 215
Thinking out loud about the space age. Is the Christian faith adequate for a space age? Philadelphia, Dorrance [1962] 144p. 20cm. Includes bibliographies. [BL254.O8] 62-11977
1. Religion and astronautics. I. Title.

OVERMAN, Ralph T. 215
Who am I? The faith of [a] scientist [by] Ralph T. Overman. Waco, Tex., Word Books [1971] 94 p. 21 cm. [BL240.2.O88] 79-170908 1.95
1. Religion and science—1946- I. Title.

OWEN, Derwyn Randolph Grier. 215
Scientism, man, and religion. Philadelphia, Westminster Press [1952] 208 p. 21 cm. [BL240.O85] 52-8226
1. Religion and science — 1900- I. Title.

PAYNE, Harriet Chaffey. 215
Eternal crucible : a new cosmology / Harriet Chaffey Payne. 1st ed. Hicksville, N.Y. : Exposition Press, [1974] viii, 344 p. ; 24 cm. Includes index. [BD511.P34] 74-76032 ISBN 0-682-47966-7 : 10.00
1. Cosmology. 2. Religion and science—1946- I. Title.

PEACOCKE, Arthur Robert. 215
Science and the Christian experiment, [by] A. R. Peacocke. London, New York, Oxford University Press, 1971. xiii, 214 p. 23 cm. Bibliography: p. 206-207. [BL240.2.P34 1971] 76-881338 ISBN 0-19-213953-3 £4.00
1. Religion and science—1946- I. Title.

PILKINGTON, Roger. 215
Heavens alive; the impact of science on the image of God. London, Macmillan; New York, St. Martin's Press, 1964. x, 149 p. 21 cm. [BL240.2P515 1964] 64-4435
1. Religion and science—1946- I. Title.

PILKINGTON, Roger 215
Heavens alive; the impact of science on the image of God. London, Macmillan; New York, St. Martin's [c.]1964. x, 149p. 21cm. 64-4435 3.50 bds.,
1. Religion and science—1946- I. Title.

PILKINGTON, Roger. 215
World without end. London, Macmillan; New York, St. Martin's Press, 1960. 165p. 21cm. [BL210.2.P52] 60-2762
1. Religion and science—1900- I. Title.

PIRONE, Frank John, 1912- 215
Science and the love of God. New York, Philosophical Library [1957] 233p. 22cm. [BL240.P57] 57-2753
1. Religion and science—1900- I. Title.

POLLARD, William Grosvenor, 1911- 215
Physicist and Christian, a dialogue between the communities. Greenwich, Conn., Seabury Pr. [c.]1961. 178p. Bibl. 61-14381 4.25 bds.,
1. Religion and science—1946- I. Title.

POLLARD, William Grosvenor, 1911- 215
Physicist and Christian, a dialogue between the communities. New York, Seabury [1964, c.1961] 178p. 21cm. Orig. given as the Bishop Paddock lects. (1959) at the General Theological Seminary, New York City. (SP11) Bibl. 1.65 pap.,
1. Religion and science—1946- I. Title.

POLLARD, William Grosvenor, 1911- 215
Science and faith: twin mysteries, by William G. Pollard. New York, T. Nelson [1970] xiv, 116 p. illus. 21 cm. (A Youth forum book, YF 11) Examines the relationship of religion and science and maintains that the two fields are not necessarily in opposition. [BL240.2.P58] 76-127076 1.95
1. Religion and science—1946- I. Title. II. Series: Youth forum series, YF 11

POWELL, Arthur Edward, 1882- 215
The nature of man; a synthesis of science and religion. [1st ed.] New York, Vantage Press [1957] 295p. 21cm. Includes bibliography. [BL240.P726] 56-12925
1. Religion and science—1900- I. Title.

QUEFFELEC, Henri, 1910- 215
Technology and religion. Translated from the French by S. J. Tester. [1st ed.] New York, Hawthorn Books [1964] 110, [1] p. 21 cm. (The Twentieth century encyclopedia of Catholocism, v. 94. Section 9: The church and the modern world) Translation of La technique contre is fol? Bibliography: p. [111] [BL240.2.Q413] 64-13009
1. Religion and science—1946- I. Title. II. Series: The Twentieth century encyclopedia of Catholicism, v. 94

QUEFFELEC, Henri, 1910- 215
Technology and religion. Tr. from French by S. J. Tester. New York, Hawthorn [c.1964] 110 [1]p. 21cm. (Twentieth cent. ency. of Catholicism, v.94. Section 9: The church and the modern world) Bibl. 64-13009 3.50 bds.,
1. Religion and science—1946- I. Title. II. Series. III. Series: The Twentieth century encyclopedia of Catholicism, v.94

RABUT, Olivier A. 215
God in an evolving universe [by] Olivier A. Rabut. Translated by William Springer. [New York] Herder and Herder [1966] 154 p. 22 cm. "The French edition of this work contains four 'Notes justificatives' which have been omitted from this translation." Originally published in 1962 under title: "Le probleme de Dieu inscrit dans l'evolution." Bibliographical references included in footnotes. [BL240.2.R283] 66-13069
1. Religion and science—1946- 2. Natural theology. 3. Cosmology. I. Title.

RAMM, Bernard, 1916- 215
The Christian view of science and Scripture. [1st ed.] Grand Rapids, W. B. Eerdmans Pub. Co., 1954. 368 p. 23 cm. [BS650.R28] 54-12335
1. Bible and science. 2. Religion and science—1900- I. Title.

RANSOM, John Crowe, 1888- 215
God without thunder; an unorthodox defense of orthodoxy [Reissue] Hamden, Conn., Archon [dist. Shoe String, 1965, c.1930] x, 334p. 21cm. [BL240.R25] 65-17410 9.00
1. Religion and science—1926-1945. I. Title.

RAVEN, Charles Earle, 1885- 215
Christianity and science. New York, Association Press [1955] 96p. 20cm. (World Christian books) [BL240.R314] 55-7566
1. Religion and science—1900- I. Title.

RAVEN, Charles Earle, 1885- 215
Natural religion and Christian theology. Cambridge [Eng.] University Press, 1953. 2v. 23cm. (Gifford lectures, 1951-52) Contents.1st ser. Science and religion.--2d ser. Experience and Interpretation. [BL245.R28] 53-8684
1. Religion and science—History of controversy. 2. Theology, Doctrinal—Addresses, essays, lectures. I. Title.

REEDER, Aaron 215
The Wabash philosopher; letters to a small-town editor. New York, Exposition. [1962, c.1963] 65p. 21cm. 2.50
I. Title.

REID, James, 1912- 215
God, the atom, and the universe. Grand Rapids, Zondervan Pub. House [1968] 240 p. illus. 23 cm. Includes bibliographies. [BS651.R4] 68-12949
1. Bible and science. 2. Creation. I. Title.

REID, William Stanford, 1913- 215
Christianity and scholarship [by] W. Stanford Reid. Nutley, N.J. Craig Press, 1966. viii, 110 p. 26 cm. (University series: philosophical studies) Bibliographical footnotes. [BL240.2.R4] 66-21725
1. Religion and science—1946- 2. Learning and scholarship. 3. Philosophy and religion. I. Title.

REID, William Stanford, 1913- 215
Christianity and scholarship [by] W. Stanford Reid. Nutley, N.J., Craig Press, 1966. viii, 110 p. 20 cm. (University series: philosophical studies) Bibliographical footnotes. [BL240.2.R4] 66-21725
1. Religion and science—1946- 2. Learning and scholarship. 3. Philosophy and religion. I. Title.

RICH, James Walter, 1870- 215
The message of the stars. Nashville, Southern Pub. Association [c1950] 128p. illus. 20cm. [BL253.R5] 54-22105
1. Religion and science—1900- 2. Astronomy. 3. Seventh-Day Adventists—Doctrinal and controversial works. I. Title.

RIMMER, Harry, 1890-1952. 215
The harmony of science and Scripture. New York, Books, inc. [1960] 238p. 22cm. (John Lawrence Frost memorial library, v. 1) [BS650.R5 1960] 61-662
1. Bible and science. 2. Religion and science—1926-1945. I. Title.

RITLAND, Richard M., 1925- 215
A search for meaning in nature; a new look at creation and evolution [by] Richard M. Ritland. Mountain View, Calif., Pacific Press Pub. Association [1970] 320 p. illus., map, ports. 22 cm. Includes bibliographies. [BL240.2.R55] 71-115432
1. Religion and science—1946- I. Title.

ROBERTS, Alpheus J 215
Final Christian understanding of science, religion, and survival of mankind. Boston, Christopher Pub. House [1957] 61p. illus. 21cm. [BD701.R652] 57-34939
I. Title.

ROCK strata and the Bible record. 215 Edited by Paul A. Zimmerman. Saint Louis, Concordia Pub. House [1970] 209 p. illus. 22 cm. Position papers of a study project carried out under the auspices of the Lutheran Church—Missouri Synod. [BS657.R6 1970] 78-111692
1. Bible and geology—Addresses, essays, lectures. I. Zimmerman, Paul Albert, 1918- ed. II. Lutheran Church—Missouri Synod.

RUSHDOONY, Rousas John. 215
The mythology of science. Nutley, N.J., Craig Press, 1967. 134 p. 20 cm. (University series: historical studies) Bibliographical footnotes. [BL240.2.R78] 67-28460
1. Religion and science—1946- I. Title.

RUSHDOONY, Rousas John. 215
The mythology of science. Nutley, N.J., Craig Press, 1967. 134 p. 20 cm. (University series: historical studies) Bibliographical footnotes. [BL240.2.R78] 67-28460
1. Religion and science—1946- I. Title.

RUSSELL, Bertrand Arthur Russell, 3rd earl 1872- 215
Religion & science. New York, Oxford, 1961 255p. (Galaxy bk. gb50) 1.25 pap.,
1. Religion and science—1900- 2. Religion and science—History of controversy. I. Title.

RUST, Eric Charles 215
Science and faith; towards a theological understanding of nature, by Eric C. Rust. New York, Oxford Univ. Pr., 1967. xiii, 330p. 21cm. Bibl. [BL240.2.R8] 67-28130 6.50
1. Religion and science—1946- I. Title.

RUST, Eric Charles. 215
Science and faith; towards a theological understanding of nature, by Eric C. Rust. New York, Oxford University Press, 1967. xiii, 330

p. 21 cm. Bibliographical footnotes. [BL240.2.R8] 67-28130
1. Religion and science—1946- I. Title.

SABINE, Paul Earls, 1879- 215
Atoms, men, and God. New York, Philosophical Library [1953] 226p. 23cm. [BL240.S2] 53-7918
1. Religion and science—1900- I. Title.

SALISBURY, Frank B. 215
Truth by reason and by revelation. Salt Lake City, Deseret, 1965. x, 362p. illus. 24cm. Bibl. [BL240.2.S25] 65-18576 price unreported
1. Religion and science—1946- I. Title.

SANDEN, Oscar Emanuel, 1901- 215
Does science support the Scriptures? Foreword by "Billy" Graham. Grand Rapids, Zondervan [1951] 175 p. 20 cm. Bibliography: p. 173-175. [BS650.S33] 51-2865
1. Bible and science. 2. Religion and science — 1900- I. Title.

SCHILLING, Harold Kistler, 1899- 215
The new consciousness in science and religion [by] Harold K. Schilling. Philadelphia, United Church Press [1973] 288 p. 21 cm. "A Pilgrim Press book." Bibliography: p. 287-288. [BL240.2.S28] 72-13792 ISBN 0-8298-0247-9 7.95
1. Religion and science—1946- I. Title.

SCHILLING, Harold Kistler, 1899- 215
Science and religion, an interpretation of two communities. New York, Scribner [1962] 272 p. illus. 22 cm. [BL240.2.S3] 62-17732
1. Religion and science—1946- I. Title.

SCHMIDT, Karl Otto, 1904- 215
Applied cybernetics; atomic energies of the mind [by] K. O. Schmidt. Translated by Leone Muller. Lakemont, Ga., CSA Press [1973] 205 p. 22 cm. [BJ1581.2.S37713] 73-77609 ISBN 0-87707-124-1 5.95
1. Conduct of life. I. Title.

SCHNABEL, A. O. 215
Has God spoken? By A. O. Schnabel. Rev. and enl. San Diego, Ca., Creation-Life Publishers [1974] iv, 118 p. illus. 19 cm. Includes bibliographical references. [BS480.S335] 74-81483 ISBN 0-89051-009-1 1.95 (pbk.)
1. Bible—Evidences, authority, etc. 2. Religion and science—1946- I. Title.
Publisher's address: Box 15666, San Diego, Calif. 92115.

SCIENCE & religion; 215
a symposium. With a foreword by Michael Pupin. Freeport, N.Y., Books for Libraries Press [1969] xi, 175 p. 23 cm. (Essay index reprint series) Reprint of the 1931 ed. Twelve talks, by Julian Huxley, J. Arthur Thomson, J. S. Haldane and others, broadcast between September and December 1930 by the British Broadcasting Corporation. [BL240.S367 1969] 75-84336
1. Religion and science—1926-1945. I. British Broadcasting Corporation.

**SCIENTISTS who believe;* 215
ten interviews with Christian men of science. Elgin, Ill., David C. Cook Pub. Co. [1964, c.1963] 63p. 22cm. price unreported. pap.,

SEARS, Jack Wood, 1918- 215
Conflict and harmony in science and the Bible. Grand Rapids, Baker Book House [1969] 97 p. illus. 22 cm. (University Christian Student Center. Annual lectureship) Includes bibliographical references. [BS650.S37] 71-94695 1.95
1. Bible and science—Addresses, essays, lectures. I. Title. II. Series: Mississippi. University. University Christian Student Center. Annual lectureship

SEMINAR on Science and the Spiritual Nature of Man. 2d, Rye, N. Y., 1958. 215
Second Seminar on Science and the Spiritual Nature of Man. [Rye? N. Y.] c1959. ii, 113p. 28cm. [BL240.2.S4 1958] 60-29872
1. Religion and science—1946- I. Title.

SEMINAR on Science and the Total Nature of Man. 2d, Rye, N. Y., 1958. 215
Second Seminar on Science and the Spiritual Nature of Man; [papers. Rye? N. Y.] c1959. ii, 113p. 28cm. 'Sponsored by the Laymen's Movement for a Christian World.' [BL240.2.S4 1958] 60-29872
1. Religion and science—1946- I. Laymen's Movement for a Christian World. II. Title.

SEMINAR on Science and the Total Nature of Man. 3d, Rye, N. Y., 1960. 215
Seminar on Science and the Total Nature of Man; [papers. Rye] c1962. 70p. diagrs. 30cm. 'Sponsored by the Laymen's Movement.' [BL240.2.S4 1960] 62-43477
1. Religion and science—1946- I. Laymen's Movement for a Christian World. II. Title.

SHAFER, Robert, 1889-1956. 215
Christianity and naturalism; essays in criticism, second series. Port Washington, N.Y., Kennikat Press [1969] viii, 307 p. 22 cm. Reprint of the 1926 ed. Contents.Contents.—Religious thought in England in the XVIIth and XVIIIth centuries.—Coleridge.—Cardinal Newman.—Huxley.—Matthew Arnold.—Samuel Butler.—Thomas Hardy.—Naturalism and Christianity. Bibliographical footnotes. [BL240.S42 1969] 68-26206
1. Coleridge, Samuel Taylor, 1772-1834—Religion and ethics. 2. Newman, John Henry, Cardinal, 1801-1890. 3. Huxley, Thomas Henry, 1825-1895. 4. Arnold, Matthew, 1822-1888—Religion and ethics. 5. Butler, Samuel, 1835-1902. 6. Hardy, Thomas, 1840-1928. 7. Religion and science—1900-1925. 8. Religious thought—Great Britain. I. Title.

SHAPLEY, Harlow, ed. 215
Science ponders religion. New York, Appleton-Century-Crofts [c.1960] x, 308p. Bibl. footnotes 22cm. 60-15840 5.00
1. Religion and science—1946- I. Title.

SHAPLEY, Harlow, 1885- ed. 215
Science ponders religion. New York, Appleton-Century-Crofts [1960] 308 p. 22 cm. Includes bibliography. [BL240.2.S53] 60-15840
1. Religion and science — 1946- I. Title.

SHIDELER, Emerson W 215
Believing and knowing: the meaning of truth in Biblical religion and in science [by] Emerson W. Shideler. [1st ed.] Ames, Iowa State University Press, 1966. xvii, 196 p. 24 cm. Bibliography: p. 185-188. [BL240.2.S56] 66-14588
1. Science and religion—1945- I. Title.

SHIDELER, Emerson W. 215
Believing and knowing: the meaning of truth in Biblical religion and in science [by] Emerson W. Shideler. [1st ed.] Ames, Iowa State University Press, 1966. xvii, 196 p. 24 cm. Bibliography: p. 185-188. [BL240.2.S56] 66-14588
1. Religion and science—1946- I. Title.

THE single reality. 215
Preston Harold, author of The shining stranger. Winifred Babcock, author of The Palestinian mystery play. Introduction and summary by Oliver L. Reiser. Preface for the Physical scientist by Robert M. L. Baker, Jr. [Winston-Salem, N.C., Harold Institute]; distributed by Dodd, Mead, New York [1971] 386 p. illus. 24 cm. Contents.Contents.—The Palestinian mystery play, by W. Babcock.—If thine eye be single, by W. Babcock.—On the nature of universal cross-action, by P. Harold.—Bibliography (p. 375-376) [BL240.2.S58] 78-121985 ISBN 0-396-06206-7 7.95
1. Jesus Christ—Miscellanea. 2. Religion and science—1946- 3. Occult sciences. I. Harold, Preston. On the nature of universal cross-action. 1971. II. Babcock, Winifred. The Palestinian mystery play. 1971.

SINNOTT, Edmund Ware, 1888- 215
Two roads to truth; a basis for unity under the great tradition. New York, Viking Press, 1953. 241 p. 22 cm. [BL240.S54] 52-12885
1. Religion and science—1900- I. Title.

SMETHURST, Arthur F 215
Modern science and Christian beliefs. Nashville, Abingdon Press [1957, c1955] 300p. 23cm. [BL240.S58 1957] 57-13655
1. Religion and science—1900- 2. Philosophy, Modern. I. Title.

SMETHURST, Arthur F 215
Modern science and Christian beliefs. Nashville, Abingdon Press [1957, c1955) 300 p. 23 cm. [BL240.S58 1957] 57-13655
1. Religion and science — 1900-0000 2. Philosophy, Modern. I. Title.

SONTAG, Peter J 215
A course in moral law, for high school students; character training on an ethical basis. Patna, Catholic Book Crusuade, 1950. 185 p. 19 cm. [BJ1249.S58] 62-26022
1. Christian ethics — Catholic authors. 2. Youth — Conduct of life. I. Title.

SPILMAN, John M 215
My universe and my faith; a Catholic layman's views on science and his religion. [1st ed.] New York, Exposition Press [1959] 179 p. 21 cm. [BL240.2.S68] 59-4163
1. Religion and science — 1900- I. Title.

STEVENS, Clifford J. 215
Astrotheology for the cosmic adventure [by] Clifford J. Stevens. Techny, Ill., Divine Word Publications [1969] 87 p. illus. 18 cm. Includes bibliographical references. [BL254.S7] 75-94093 1.95
1. Space theology. I. Title.

STONER, Peter Winebrenner. 215
Science speaks; an evaluation of certain Christian evidences. Wheaton, Ill., Van Kampen Press [1953, c1952] 91p. illus. 20cm. [BS651.S85] 53-24289
1. Bible and science. 2. Bible—Prophecies. 3. Bible—Evidences, authority, etc. I. Title.

TEILHARD de Chardin, Pierre. 215
Science and Christ. Translated from the French by Rene Hague. [1st U.S. ed.] New York, Harper & Row [1968] 230 p. 22 cm. [B2430.T373S313] 69-10470 5.00
1. Religion and science—1946- I. Title.

THORPE, William Homan, 1902- 215
Science, man, and morals. Ithaca, N. Y., Cornell Univ. Pr. [1966, c.1965] xii, 176p. illus. 23cm. Based upon the Fremantle lects. delivered in Balliol Coll., Oxford, Trinity term, 1963. Bibl. [BL240.2.T47] 66-17580 4.95
1. Religion and science — 1946- 2. Science and ethics. I. Title.

THORPE, William Homan, 1902- 215
Science, man, and morals : based upon the Fremantle lectures delivered in Balliol College, Oxford, Trinity term, 1963 / W. H. Thorpe. Westport, Conn. : Greenwood Press, 1976, c1965. p. cm. Reprint of the ed. published by Scientific Book Club, London. Includes bibliographical references and index. [BL240.2.T47 1976] 76-14962 ISBN 0-8371-8143-7 lib.bdg. : 13.25
1. Religion and science—1946- 2. Science and ethics. I. Title.

*TINER, John Hudson. 215
When science fails. Grand Rapids, Baker Book House [1974] 136 p. 18 cm. (Direction books.) [BL245] ISBN 0-8010-8823-2 1.25 (pbk.)
1. Religion and science. I. Title.

TODD, Charles Mack, 1893- 215
Atomic energy plus. Daytona Beach, Fla., College Pub. Co. [c1955] 115p. 24cm. [BS652.T6] 57-3149
1. Bible and science. 2. Bible—History of Biblical events. I. Title.

TORRANCE, Thomas Forsyth, 1913- 215
God and rationality [by] Thomas F. Torrance. London, New York, Oxford University Press, 1971. xi, 216 p. 23 cm. Includes bibliographical references. [BR100.T63] 76-21679 ISBN 0-19-213948-7 £2.75
1. Christianity—Philosophy. 2. Religion and science—1946- I. Title.

TRESMONTANT, Claude. 215
Toward the knowledge of God. Translated by Robert J. Olsen. Baltimore, Helicon Press [1961] 120 p. 29 cm. Translation on Essal sur la connaissance de Dieu. [BT102.T713] 61-14674
1. God (Theory of knowledge) I. Title.

TRESMONTANT, Claude 215
Toward the knowledge of God. Tr. [from French] by Robert J. Olsen. Baltimore, Helicon Pr. [c.1961] 120p. 61-14674 3.50
1. God (Theory of knowledge) I. Title.

TRINKLEIN, Frederick E. 215
The God of science; personal interviews with 38 leading American and European scientists on the nature of truth, the existence of God, and the role of the church [by] Frederick E. Trinklein. Grand Rapids, Eerdmans [1971] xxii, 192 p. 22 cm. [BL241.T74] 72-162034 3.45
1. Religion and science—1946- I. Title.

TUTE, Richard Clifford, Sir, 1874- 215
After materialism—what? Freeport, N.Y., Books for Libraries Press [1973, c1945] 222 p. 23 cm. (Essay index reprint series) Reprint of the 1945 ed. [BL240.T78 1973] 72-13176 ISBN 0-8369-8175-8
1. Religion and science—1926-1945. 2. Philosophy and religion. I. Title.

VAN DER ZIEL, Aldert 215
The natural sciences and the Christian message. Minneapolis, T. S. Denison [c.1960] 259p. (bibl. notes) diagrs. 23cm. (The Lutheran studies series, v. 1) 'This book is the result of a series of lectures on the natural sciences given for Lutheran pastors in the Lutheran Student Hall of the St. Paul Campus of the University of Minnesota.' 60-9802 4.50
1. Religion and science—1946- I. Title. II. Title: The Christian message III. Series.

VAN DER ZIEL, Aldert, 1910- 215
The natural sciences and the Christian message. Minneapolis, T. S. Denison [1960] 259 p. diagrs. 23 cm. (The Lutheran studies series, v. 1) "This book is the result of a series of lectures on the natural sciences given for Lutheran pastors in the Lutheran Student Hall of the St. Paul campus of the University of Minnesota." Includes bibliographies. [BL240.2.V3] 60-9802
1. Religion and science — 1946- I. Title. II. Title: The Christian message. III. Series.

WALTER, R. Kenneth. 215
Science, saints, & sense, by R. Kenneth Walter. Salt Lake City, Bookcraft [1973] ix, 140 p. 24 cm. Includes bibliographical references. [BL240.2.W29] 73-84592 3.50
1. Religion and science—1946- I. Title.

WARD, Duren James Henderson, 1851-1942. 215
The modern God. With an introd. by Claude W. Blake. [Denver? 1956] 62p. illus. 23cm. [BL241.W25] 56-33038
1. Religion and science—1900- 2. God. I. Title.

WARD, Duren James Henderson, 1851-1942. 215
The modern God. With an introd. by Claude W. Blake. [Denver? 1956] 62 p. illus. 23 cm. [BL241.W25] 56-33038
1. God. 2. Religion and science — 1900- I. Title.

WATERS, F. William, 1889- 215
The way in and the way out; science and religion reconciled [by] F. W. Waters. Toronto, Oxford University Press, 1967. x, 269 p. 19 cm. Bibliography: p. [260]-266. [BL240.2.W32] 68-78081 4.75
1. Religion and science—1946- I. Title.

WESTFALL, Richard S. 215
Science and religion in seventeenth-century England. New Haven, Yale University Press, 1958. ix, 235 p. 25 cm. (Yale historical publications. Miscellany 67) "Bibliographical essay": p. 221-228. Bibliographical footnotes. [BL245.W4] 58-6548
1. Religion and science — History of doctrines. 2. Gt. Brit. — Church history — 17th cent. I. Title. II. Series.

WESTFALL, Richard S. 215
Science and religion in seventeenth-century England. [Ann Arbor] Univ. of Michigan Pr. [1973, c.1958] x, 239 p. 21 cm. (Ann Arbor paperbacks, AA190) (Yale historical publications. Miscellany, 67) "Bibliographical essay": p. 221-228. [BL245.W4] ISBN 0-472-06190-9 2.95 (pbk.)
1. Religion and science—History of doctrines. 2. Gt. Brit.—Church history—17th cent. I. Title. II. Series.
L.C. card no. for the hardbound edition: 58-6548.

WHITE, Andrew Dickson, 1832-1918 215
A history of the warfare of science and theology in Christendom, Abridged. New York, Free Pr. [c.1965] 538p. 22cm. (93507) Bibl. [BL245.W5] 2.95 pap.,
1. Religion and science—History of controversy. 2. Science—Hist. I. Title.

WHITE, Andrew Dickson, 1832-1918. 215
A history of the warfare of science with theology in Christendom. New York, Dover Publications [1960] 2 v. 21 cm. "Unabridged and unaltered republication of the first edition that appeared in 1896." Includes bibliography. [BL245.W5 1960] 60-2524
1. Religion and science — History of controversy. 2. Science — Hist. I. Title.

WHITE, Andrew Dickson, 1832-1918. 215
A history of the warfare of science with theology in Christendom. Abridged for the modern reader, with a pref. and epilogue by Bruce Mazlish. New York, Free Press [1965] 538 p. 21 cm. (A Free Press paperback) Bibliographical footnotes. [BL245.W5 1965] 63-7311
1. Religion and science — History of controversy. 2. Science — Hist. I. Mazlish, Bruce, 1923- ed. II. Title.

WHITE, Andrew Dickson, 1832-1918 215
A history of the warfare of science with theology in Christendom; 2 v. [Gloucester, Mass., P. Smith, 1965] 2 v. (various p.) 21cm. [Dover bk. rebound] Unabridged, unaltered repubn. of the first ed. of 1896. Bibl. [BL245.W5] 8.00 set.,
1. Religion and science—History of controversy. 2. Science—Hist. I. Title.

WHITE, Edward Arthur, 1907- 215
Science and religion in American thought; the impact of naturalism. Stanford, Stanford University Press, 1952. viii, 117 p. 24 cm. (Stanford University publications. University series. History, economics, and political science,v. 8) [BL245.W63] AS36.L54 vol. 8 52-5982
I. Title.

WHITE, Edward Arthur, 1907- 215
Science and religion in American thought; the impact of naturalism [by] Edward A. White. New York, AMS Press [1968] viii, 117 p. 22 cm. (Stanford University publications. University series. History, economics, and political science, v. 8) Reprint of the 1952 ed. Bibliographical footnotes. [BL245.W63 1968] 68-54307
1. Religion and science—History of controversy—United States. I. Title. II. Series: Stanford studies in history, economics, and political science, v. 8

WHITEHOUSE, Walter Alexander 215
Order, goodness, glory. New York, Oxford University Press, 1960[ ] 83 p. (bibl. notes: p. 81-83) 19 cm. (The Riddell memorial lectures, 31st series) 60-1974 1.55
1. Religion and science—1946- I. Title.

WIDTSOE, John Andreas, 1872- 215
1952.
Joseph Smith as scientist; a contribution to Mormon philosophy. Salt Lake City, Bookcraft [c1964] 162 p. 24 cm. Bibliographical footnotes. [BX8695.S6W5] 65-1772
1. Smith, Joseph, 1805-1844. I. Title.

WIER, Frank E., 1930- 215
The Christian views science [by] Frank E. Wier. Nashville, Published for the Cooperative Publication Association by Abingdon Press [1969] 192 p. illus. 22 cm. (The Cooperative through-the-week series) Bibliography: p. 189-192. [BL240.2.W52] 71-10212
1. Religion and science—1946- I. Title.

WILLIAMS, John Gordon. 215
Christian faith and the space age, by John G. Williams. [1st American ed.] Cleveland, World Pub. Co. [1968] 123 p. 20 cm. First published in 1964 under title: The faith and the space age. [BL240.2.W55] 67-24756
1. Religion and science—1946— 2. Chrisianity—20th cent. I. Title.

WOLTERSTORFF, Nicholas. 215
Reason within the bounds of religion / by Nicholas Wolterstorff. Grand Rapids, Mich. : W. B. Eerdmans Pub. Co., c1976. 115 p. ; 18 cm. Includes bibliographical references. [BD215.W65] 76-7514 ISBN 0-8028-1643-6 pbk. : 2.95
1. Belief and doubt—Addresses, essays, lectures. 2. Theory (Philosophy)—Addresses, essays, lectures. 3. Philosophy and religion—Addresses, essays, lectures. 4. Thought and thinking—Addresses, essays, lectures. I. Title.

WOLTHUIS, Enno, 1911- 215
Science, God, and you. Grand Rapids, Baker Book House, 1963. 121 p. 20 cm. [BL240.2.W6] 63-21464
1. Religion and science — 1946- I. Title.

WOLTHUIS, Enno, 1911- 215
Science, God, and you. Grand Rapids, Mich., Baker Bk. [c.]1963. 121p. 20cm. 63-21464 2.50 bds.,
1. Religion and science—1946- I. Title.

LANGMACK, Holger 215.0151
Christian.
Science, faith and logic; scientific faith substantiated by a logical science. New York, Philosophical Library [1965] xviii, 146 p. illus., port. 22cm. [BL240.2.L34] 64-13325
1. Religion and science — 1946- I. Title.

LANGMACK, Holger 215.0151
Christian.
Science, faith and logic; scientific faith substantiated by a logical science. New York, Philosophical [c.1965] xviii, 146p. illus., port. 22cm. [BL240.2.L34] 64-13325 6.00
1. Religion and science—1946- I. Title.

WARD, James, 1843-1925. 215'.08
Naturalism and agnosticism. 4th ed. London, A. & C. Black, 1915. New York, Kraus Reprint Co., 1971. xvi, 623 p. 23 cm. (Gifford lectures, 1896-1898) Includes bibliographical references. [BD541.W3 1971] 78-149170
1. Religion and science—1860-1899. 2. Natural theology. 3. Agnosticism. 4. Monism. I. Title. II. Series.

BOOTH, Edwin Prince, 215.082
1898- ed.
Religion ponders science. New York, Appleton-Century [dist. Meredith, c.1964] xii, 302p. diagrs. 22cm. Bibl. 64-12457 5.95
1. Religion and science—1946- —Addresses, essays, lectures. I. Title.

KENNEDY, Gail, 1900- ed. 215.082
Evolution and religion; the conflict between science and theology in modern America. Boston, Heath [1957] 114 p. 24 cm. (Problems in American civilization; readings selected by the Dept. of American Studies, Amherst College) [BL245.K4] 57-1698
1. Religion and science—History of controversy—United States. I. Title.

MONSMA, John Clover, ed. 215.082
The evidence of God in an expanding universe; forty American scientists declare their affirmative views on religion. New York, Putnam [1958] 250 p. 21 cm. [BL240.M715] 58-8903
1. God—Proof. 2. Religion and science—1900- I. Title.

MONSMA, John Clover, ed. 215.082
Science and religion; twenty-three prominent churchmen express their opinions. New York, Putnam [1962] 253 p. 21 cm. [BL240.2.M6] 62-7350
1. Religion and science—1946- I. Title.

SCIENCE and your faith in 215.082
God; a selected compilation of writings and talks by prominent Latter-Day Saints scientists on the subjects of science and religion: Henry Eyring [and others] Salt Lake City, Bookcraft, 1958. 317p. 24cm. [BL240.2.S35] 59-902
1. Religion and science—1900- I. Eyring, Henry, 1901-

HOOYKAAS, Reijer, 1906- 215'.09
Religion and the rise of modern science, by R. Hooykaas. [1st American ed.] Grand Rapids, Mich., Eerdmans Pub. Co. [1972] xiii, 162 p. 21 cm. Based on the Gunning lectures which were delivered under the auspices of the Faculty of Divinity in the University of Edinburgh, Feb. 1969. Includes bibliographical references. [BL245.H63 1972] 72-75568 ISBN 0-8028-1474-3 2.65
1. Religion and science—History of controversy. I. Title. II. Series: The Gunning lectures, 1969.

SIMPSON, James Young, 215'.09
1873-1934.
Landmarks in the struggle between science and religion. Port Washington, N.Y., Kennikat Press [1971] xiii, 288 p. 22 cm. "First published in 1925." Includes bibliographical references. [BL245.S5 1971] 75-118549 ISBN 8-04-611742-
1. Religion and science—History of controversy. I. Title.

SCIENCE and human 215'.09'05
values in the 21st century. Edited by Ralph Wendell Burhoe Philadelphia, Westminster Press [1971] 203 p. 22 cm. Includes bibliographical references. [BL241.S317] 74-146667 ISBN 0-664-20907-6 6.95
1. Religion and science—1946- —Addresses, essays, lectures. 2. Technology and ethics—Addresses, essays, lectures. I. Burhoe, Ralph Wendell, 1911- ed.

JACOB, Margaret C., 215.0942
1943-
The Newtonians and the English Revolution, 1689-1720 / Margaret C. Jacob. Ithaca, N.Y. : Cornell University Press, 1976. p. cm. Includes bibliographical references and index. [BL245.J3 1976] 75-36995 ISBN 0-8014-0981-0 : 14.50
1. Religion and science—History of controversy—England. 2. Physics—History. 3. England—Intellectual life—17th century. 4. Great Britain—History—Revolution of 1688. I. Title.

WESTFALL, Richard S. 215'.0942
Science and religion in seventeenth-century England [by] Richard S. Westfall. [Hamden, Conn.] Archon Books, 1970 [c1958] vii, 235 p. 23 cm. Includes bibliographical references. [BL245.W4 1970] 72-103992 ISBN 2-08-008438-
1. Religion and science—History of controversy—England. 2. Gt. Brit.—Church history—17th century. I. Title.

ALIGARH, India. Muslim 215'.2
University. Directorate of General Education Reading Material Project.
The changing concept of the universe. New York, Asis Pub. House [1963] xii, 108 p. illus. 22 cm. (Aligarh Muslim University. General Education reading material series, 15) [QB51.A37] 63-24989
1. Astronomy — Addresses, essays, lectures. I. Title. II. Series: Aligarh, India. Muslim University. General education reading material series, 15

ALIGARH, India. Muslim 215'.2
University. Directorate of General Education Reading Material Project.
The changing concept of the universe. Bombay, New York, Asia Pub. House [1963] xii, 108 p. diagrs. 22 cm. (Aligarh Muslim University. General education readings material series, 15) [[QB51]] S A
1. Astronomy — Addresses, essays, lectures. 2. (Series: Aligarh, India. Muslim University. General education reading material series, 15) I. Title.

BURNHAM, Robert, 215'.2
Burnham's celestial handbook; an observer's guide to the universe beyond the solar system. A descriptive catalog and reference handbook of deep-sky wonders for the observer, student, research worker, amateur or professional astonomer. Flagstaff, Ariz, Celestial Handbook Publications [1966] 218 p. illus, 23 cm. [QB63.B898] 68-73
1. Astronomy—Observers' manuals. I. Title. II. Title: Celestial handbook.

CAMPANELLA, Tommaso, 1568- 215'.2
1639.
The defense of Galileo / Thomas Campanella ; [translated and edited, with introd. and notes by Grant McColley]. New York : Arno Press, 1975. xliv, 93 p. ; 23 cm. (History, philosophy and sociology of science) Translation of Apologia pro Galileo. Reprint of the 1937 ed. published by the Dept. of History of Smith College, Northampton, Mass., which was issued as v. 22, no. 3-4 of Smith College studies in history. Includes bibliographical references and index. [QB36.G2C32 1975] 74-26254 ISBN 0-405-06582-5 : 8.00
1. Galilei, Galileo, 1564-1642. 2. Copernicus, Nicolaus, 1473-1543. 3. Religion and science—Early works to 1800. I. Title. II. Series. III. Series: Smith College studies in history ; v. 22, no. 3-4.

CAMPANELLA, Tommaso, 1568- 215'.2
1639.
The defense to Galileo of Thomas Campanella : for the first time translated and edited, with introd. and notes / by Grant McColley. Merrick, N.Y. : Richwood Pub. Co., 1976. p. cm. Translation of Apologia pro Galileo. Reprint of the 1937 ed. published by the Dept. of History of Smith College, Northampton, Mass., which was issued as v. 22, no. 3-4 of Smith College studies in history. Includes bibliographical references and index. [QB36.G2C32 1976] 76-1114 ISBN 0-915172-20-8 : 12.50 lib.bdg. : 14.50
1. Galilei, Galileo, 1564-1642. 2. Copernicus, Nicolaus, 1473-1543. 3. Religion and science—Early works to 1800. I. McColley, Grant. II. Title. III. Series: Smith College studies in history ; v. 22, no. 3-4.

CARVER, Harry Clyde, 1890- 215'.2
To my dear children; a synopsis of scientific facts that children in their teens should know, by Harry C. Carver. [Ann Arbor? Mich., 1966] 65 p. illus. 24 cm. [QB44.C28] 66-31209
1. Astronomy—Popular works. 2. Civilization—History. I. Title.

DOLPHIN, Lambert. 215'.2
Lord of time and space. Westchester, Ill., Good News Publishers [1974] 79 p. 18 cm. (One evening book) Includes bibliographical references. [BL254.D64] 73-92178 0.95 (pbk.)
1. Space theology. 2. Time (Theology) 3. Religion and science—1946- I. Title.

GJUROVICH, Yovo. 215'.2
Two different keys. [1st ed.] New York, Greenwich Book Publishers [1965] 496 p. 23 cm. [BL2775.2.G5] 65-12849
1. Christianity — Controversial literature. 2. Free thought. 3. U.S. — Civilization. I. Title.

HALF hours with modern 215'.2
scientists. New Haven, Conn., C. C. Chatfield, 1871-77. 2v. illus. 19cm. (University series, no. 1-10) Half title: University scientific series. Each no. has special t. p. [Q171.H16] 5-22041
1. Science—Addresses, essays, lectures. I. Series: University series (New Haven, Conn.) no. 1-10

LOVELL, Alfred Charles 215'.2
Bernard, 1913- Sir
The exploration of outer space. London, Oxford University Press, 1962. 87 p. illus. 22 cm. [QB51.L6 1962a] 63-1887
1. Astronomy — Addresses, essays, lectures. I. Title.

LOVELL, Alfred Charles 215'.2
Bernard, 1913- Sir
The exploration of outer space. London, Oxford University Press, 1962. 87 p. illus. 22 cm. [QB51.L6 1962a] 63-1887
1. Astronomy — Addresses, essays, lectures. 2. Cosmology. 3. Astronautics and ethics. I. Title.

MORRISON, Paul G. 21.52
Old covered bridge days Philadelphia, Dorrance [c.1962] 58p. 20cm. (Contemporary Poets of Dorrance 543) 2.50
I. Title.

NEELY, Henry Milton, 1877- 215'.2
The stars by clock & fist. New York, Viking Press, 1956. 192p. charts, diagrs. 28cm. [QB63.N440223.89] 56-5607
1. Constellations. 2. Stars—Atlases. I. Title.

PARROTT, Bob W. 215'.2
Earth, moon, and beyond [by] Bob W. Parrott. Waco, Tex., Word Books [1969] 176 p. illus. (part col.) 23 cm. [BL254.P37] 77-85828 4.95
1. Religion and astronautics. 2. Astronautics—U.S. I. Title.

ROYAL Society of London. 215'.2
Space research in the United Kingdom: reports. London, Royal Society. v. 22 cm. annula. Began publication in 1961 under title: Space research in United Kingdom universities. Cf. New serial titles, 1964. At head of title: British National Committee on Space Research. [QB500.S6] 66-40167
1. Space sciences. 2. Research — Gt. Brit. I. Royal Society of London. British National Committee on Space Research. II. Title.

SEAGRAM (Joseph E.) and 215'.2
Sons, inc.
Proceedings of 'The next hundred years'; a scientific symposium [sponsored by Joseph E. Seagram & Sons, inc. on the occasion of its centennial] New York, 1957. 72p. illus., ports. 22cm. [Q171.S44] 58-24126
1. Science— Addresses, essays, lectures. I. Title. II. Title: The next hundred years.

TELLER, Woolsey. 215'.2
The atheism of astronomy; a refutation of the theory that the universe is governed by intelligence. New York, Arno Press, 1972 [c1938] 126 p. 23 cm. (The Atheist viewpoint) Includes bibliographical references. [BL2775.T4 1972] 79-169219 ISBN 0-405-03806-2
1. Astronomy. 2. Atheism. I. Title. II. Series.

YOUNG, Louise B ed. 215'.2
The exploration of the universe. Chicago, American Foundation for Continuing Education [1961] 228 p. illus., plates. 28 cm. (The Citizen and the new age of science, v. 1) Bibliographical footnotes. [Q171.Y68] 62-2272
1. Science — Addresses, essays, lectures. 2. Science — Philosophy. I. Title. II. Series.

SNIPES, A M 215.24
This holy thing, by A.M. Snipes. [1st ed.] Sparta, N.C., Cosmic Press [1965] iv, 145 p. 21 cm. Bibliography: p. 141-145. [BF1999.S56] 65-25325
I. Title.

SNIPES, A. M. 215.24
This holy thing. Sparta, N. C., Cosmic Pr. P. O. Box 6, c.1965. iv, 145p. 21cm. Bibl. [BF1999.S56] 65-25325 2.50 pap.,
I. Title.

DRAKE, Walter Raymond. 215'.25
Gods and spacemen in the ancient East, by W. Raymond Drake. [New York] New American Library [1973, c.1968] 247 p. 18 cm. (Signet Book, W5737) First published in 1930 in London under title: Spacemen in the ancient East. Bibliography: p. 230-242. [BL254.D7] 1.50 (pbk.)
1. Religion and astronautics. 2. Flying saucers. I. Title.
L.C. card no. for the hardbound (London) edition: 71-353952.

SCHAAFFS, Werner. 215'.3
Theology, physics, and miracles / Werner Schaaffs ; translated by Richard L. Renfield. Washington : Canon Press, c1974. v, 100 p. ; 22 cm. Translation of Theologie und Physik vor dem Wunder. Includes index. Bibliography: p. 97-98. [BT97.2.S2513] 75-312391 ISBN 0-913686-22-0
1. Miracles. 2. Bible and science. I. Title.

HITCHCOCK, Edward, 1793- 215'.5
1864.
The religion of geology and its connected sciences / Edward Hitchcock. Reprint ed. with a new introd. Hicksville, N.Y. : Regina Press, 1975. xvi, 511 p. : ill. ; 23 cm. (The Rise of modern religious ideas in America) Reprint of the 1852 ed. published by Phillips, Sampson, Boston. Includes bibliographical references. [BS657.H53 1975] 74-78277 ISBN 0-88271-014-1
1. Bible and geology. 2. Religion and science—1800-1859. I. Title.

NELSON, Byron Christopher, 215'.5
1893-
The deluge story in stone; a history of the flood theory of geology, by Byron C. Nelson. Minneapolis, Bethany Fellowship [1968] xvi, 190 p. illus. 22 cm. [BS658.N4 1968] 79-173 3.50
1. Deluge. 2. Bible and geology. I. Title.

CLARK, Robert Edward 215-62-1412
David
The universe: plan or accident? The religious implications of modern science. Philadelphia, Muhlenberg [1962, c.1961] 240p. illus. 3.50
1. Religion and science—1946- I. Title.

GOPI Krishna, 1903- 215'.7
The biological basis of religion and genius. With an introd. by Carl Friedrich Freiherr von Weizsacker. [1st ed.] New York, Harper & Row [1972] xvi, 118 p. 22 cm. (Religious

perspectives, v. 22) [BL263.G63 1972] 71-178013 ISBN 0-06-064789-2 5.95
1. Religion. 2. Evolution. I. Title. II. Series.

SHALER, Nathaniel Southgate, 1841-1906. 215'.7
The interpretation of nature. Freeport, N.Y., Books for Libraries Press [1973] p. (Essay index reprint series) "Lectures on the Winkley Foundation ... delivered before the students of Andover Theological Seminary in 1891." Reprint of the 1893 ed. [BL240.S435 1973] 72-14095 ISBN 0-518-10023-5
1. Religion and science—1860-1899. I. Title.

WATSON, David Charles Cuningham. 215'.7
The great brain robbery / by David C. C. Watson. Chicago : Moody Press, c1976. 128 p. ; 19 cm. Bibliography: p. 126-128. [BS659.W37 1976] 76-41909 ISBN 0-8024-3303-0 pbk. : 1.50
1. Bible and evolution. 2. Creation—Biblical teaching. 3. Life—Origin. I. Title.

HARDY, Alister Clavering, Sir. 215'.74
The biology of God : a scientist's study of man, the religious animal / Alister Hardy. [Pittsburgh] : University of Pittsburgh Press, [1976] p. cm. Includes index. [BL262.H27] 75-30984
1. Religion and science—1946- 2. Evolution and religion. 3. Biology. I. Title.

HICK, John. 215'.74
Biology and the soul: the twenty-fifth Arthur Stanley Eddington memorial lecture delivered at Cambridge University, 1 February 1972. London, Cambridge University Press, 1972. [6], 29 p. 19 cm. (Arthur Stanley Eddington memorial lectures, 25) Includes bibliographical references. [QH438.7.H5] 72-304970 ISBN 0-521-09716-9 £0.30
1. Human genetics—Moral and religious aspects—Addresses, essays, lectures. 2. Soul—Addresses, essays, lectures. I. Title. II. Series.

LOUISIANA. State University and Agricultural and Mechanical College. Laboratory School. B2157.U5L6 1964
Handbook for student teachers, by the Faculty, University Laboratory School, in cooperation with W. A. Lawrence, W. R. Eglin [and] W. M. Smith. [Rev.] Baton Rouge, Louisiana State University and Agricultural and Mechanical College, 1955 [i.e. 1964] 93 p. forms. 28 cm. Bibliography: p. 83-84. [L] 65-65419
1. Student teaching. I. Title.

CONVOCATION on Medicine and Theology, Mayo Clinic and Rochester Methodist Hospital, 1967. 215'.9
Dialogue in medicine and theology. Edited by Dale White. Nashville, Abingdon Press [1968] 176 p. 20 cm. Sponsored by the Board of Hospitals and Homes, and other boards, of the Methodist Church. Includes bibliographical references. [BL65.M4C6 1967] 68-17450 1.95
1. Medicine and religion. I. White, Dale, 1925- ed. II. Methodist Church (United States) Board of Hospitals and Homes. III. Title.

216 Good & Evil

BOUWMAN, Gijs, 1918- 216
The truth will liberate you; Biblical reflections on freedom and law, by Gilbert Bouwman. Translated by Roger and Johanna Geffen. De Pere, Wis., St. Norbert Abbey Press, 1968. 116 p. 20 cm. Translation of De waarheid zal u vrijmaken. Includes bibliographical references. [BS2545.F7B6813] 68-58122 ISBN 0-8316-1027-1 2.95
1. Freedom (Theology)—Biblical teaching. 2. Law (theology)—Biblical teaching. I. Title.

CAPON, Robert Farrar. 216
The third peacock; the goodness of God and the badness of the world. [1st ed.] Garden City, N.Y., Doubleday, 1971. 119 p. 22 cm. [BJ1401.C28] 73-147357 4.95
1. Good and evil. 2. Theology, Doctrinal—Popular works. I. Title.

CONNELLAN, Colm, 1921- 216
Why does evil exist? : A philosophical study of the contemporary presentation of the question / Colm Connellan. 1st ed. Hicksville, N.Y. : Exposition Press, [1974] vii, 211 p. ; 21 cm. (Exposition-testament book) Bibliography: p. 203-211. [BJ1401.C6] 74-76020 ISBN 0-682-47940-3 : 10.00
1. Good and evil. I. Title.

ERLICK, A. C. LA216
Evaluation of educational attitudes [by] A. C. Erlick] [West Lafayette, Ind.] Measurement and Research Center, Purdue University, 1972. 25, 1a-20a p. 28 cm. (Report of poll of the Purdue Opinion Panel, 95) Bibliography: p. 21-22. [HQ796.P83 no. 95] 373.1'8'10973 301 72-171257 2.50
1. Students—United States—Attitudes. 2. Education—United States. I. Title. II. Series: Purdue Opinion Panel Report of poll 95.)

FROMM, Erich, 1900- 216
The heart of man, its genius for good and evil. New York, Harper [1968,c.1964] 160p. illus. 21cm. (Religious perspectives, v. 12; Colophon bks., CN 119) Bibl. [BJ45.F68] 64-18053 1.45 pap.,
1. Ethics. 2. Psychology. I. Title. II. Series.

FROMM, Erich, 1900- 216
The heart of man, its genius for good and evil. [1st ed.] New York, Harper & Row [1964] 156 p. illus. 22 cm. (Religious perspectives, v. 12) Bibiographical footnotes. [BJ45.F68] 64-18053
1. Ethics. 2. Psychology. I. Title. II. Series.

FROMM, Erich, 1900- 216
The heart of man, its genius for good and evil. [1st ed.] New York, Harper & Row [1964] 156 p. illus. 22 cm. (Religious perspectives, v. 12) Bibliographical footnotes. [BJ45.F68] 64-18053
1. Ethics. 2. Psychology. I. Title. II. Series.

JAMES, John rel 216
Why evil? A Biblical approch. [Harmondsworth, Middlesex; Baltimore] Penguin Books [1960] 122p. (Bibl. footnotes) 18cm. (Pelican books, A460) 60-4405 .95 pap.,
1. Good and evil. 2. Redemption. I. Title.

JOURNET, Charles. 216
The meaning of evil. Translated by Michael Barry. New York, P. J. Kenedy [1963] 299 p. 23 cm. Translation of Le mal. [BJ1401.J673] 63-10457
1. Good and evil. I. Title.

JOURNET, Charles 216
The meaning of evil. Tr. [from French] by Michael Barry. New York, Kenedy [c.1963] 299p. 23cm. Bibl. 63-10457 5.95 bds.,
1. Good and evil. I. Title.

KIERKEGAARD, Soren Aabye, 1813-1855 216
The concept of dread. Tr., introd., notes by Walter Lowrie. [2d ed.] Princeton, N.J., Princeton [1967,c.1957] xiii, 154p. 21cm. (90) Bibl. [BT720.K52 1957] 57-13241 1.95 pap.,
1. Sin, Original. 2. Psychology, Religious. 3. Fear. I. Title.

KIERKEGAARD, Soren Aabye, 1813-1855. 216
The concept of dread. Translated with introd. and notes by Walter Lowrie. [2d ed.] Princeton, Princeton University Press, 1957. xiii, 154p. 23cm. Bibliographical references included in 'Notes' (p. [147]-152) [BT720.K52 1957] 57-13241
1. Sin, Original. 2. Psychology, Religious. 3. Fear. I. Title.

PHILP, Howard Littleton. 216
Jung and the problem of evil. New York, R. M. McBride Co. [1959, c1958] 271p. 23cm. Includes bibliography. [BF173.J85P5 1959] 59-8874
1. Jung, Carl Gustav, 1875- 2. Good and evil. I. Title.

PLANTINGA, Alvin. 216
God, freedom, and evil / Alvin Plantinga. New York : Harper & Row, 1974. viii, 112 p. ; 21 cm. (Basic conditions of life) (Harper torchbooks ; TB 1811) Includes bibliographical references. [BT102.P56 1974] 73-17603 ISBN 0-06-136140-2. ISBN 0-06-131811-6 pbk. : 3.45
1. God—Proof. 2. Good and evil. 3. Theodicy. I. Title.

SILVESTER, Hugh. 216
Arguing with God; a Christian examination of the problem of evil. Downers Grove, Ill., InterVarsity Press [1972, c1971] 128 p. 18 cm. [BJ1401.S53 1972] 76-186348 ISBN 0-87784-350-3
1. Good and evil. 2. Providence and government of God. I. Title.

STUERMANN, Walter Earl, 1919- 216
The divine destroyer; a theology of good and evil, by Walter E. Stuermann. Philadelphia, Westminster Press [1967] 187 p. 21 cm. [BJ1401.S84] 67-13205
1. Good and evil. 2. Vocation. I. Title.

SMITH, Roy Lemon, 1887- 216.6
The future is upon us. New York, Abingdon Press [1962] 252 p. 24 cm. [BR115.I7S5] 62-16812
1. Christianity and international affairs. I. Title.

STURZO, Luigi, 1871- 216.7
Church and state. With an introd. by A. Robert Caponigri. [Translated by Barbara Barclay Carter. Notre Dame, Ind.] University of Notre Dame Press 1962. 2 v (584 p.) 21 cm. (Notre Dame paperbooks, NDP13n-b) Bibliography: p. 565-569. [BX1790.S78 1962] 62-12467
1. Church and state—Catholic Church. 2. Church and social problems—Catholic Church. I. Title.

SWANCARA, Frank. 216.7
The separation of religion and government: the first amendment, Madison's intent, and the McCollum decision; a study of separationism in America. New York, Truth Seeker Co. [1950] viii, 246 p. ports. 21 cm. Bibliographical footnotes. [JK361.S9] 50-4903
1. Church and state in the U.S. I. Title.

STRINGFELLOW, William 216.83
Dissenter in a great society; a Christian view of America in crisis. [1st ed.] New York Holt, [1966] x, 164p. 22cm. [HN57.S86] 65-22472 4.95
1. U.S.—Soc. condit. 2. U.S. — Moral conditions. I. Title.

217 Worship & Prayer

BAILEY, Charles James Nice. 217
Two contemporary theologies of worship: Masure and Barth; a study in comparative dogmatics. Nashville, 1963. vii, 136 l. 28 cm. Bibliography: leaves 131-136. [BV8.B3] 63-25852
1. Worship—Hist. I. Masure, Eugene, 1882- II. Barth, Karl, 1886- III. Title.

BAILEY, Charles James Nice. 217
Two contemporary theologies of worship: Masure and Barth; an ecumenical study in comparative dogmatics [by Charles-James N. Bailey] Rev. ed. Ann Arbor, Mich., University Microfilms, 1965. xi, 165 p. (on double leaves) 22 cm. Bibliography: p. [155]-165. [BV8.B3] 65-2237
1. Worship—Hist. I. Masure, Eugene, 1882- II. Barth, Karl, 1886- III. Title.

CHRISTIANS worship, 217
edited by Oscar E. Feucht. Saint Louis, Concordia Pub. House [1971] 146 p. illus. 21 cm. (The Discipleship series) Includes bibliographies. [BV10.2.C45] 76-161192 ISBN 0-570-06308-6
1. Worship—Addresses, essays, lectures. I. Feucht, Oscar E., ed.

PANIKKAR, Raymond, 1918- 217
Worship and secular man; an essay on the liturgical nature of man, considering secularization as a major phenomenon of our time and worship as an apparent fact of all times. A study towards an integral anthropology, by Raimundo Pannikkar. Maryknoll, N.Y., Orbis Books [1973] 109 p. 20 cm. Bibliography: p. 94-109. [BL550.P27] 72-93339 3.95
1. Worship. 2. Secularism. I. Title.

218 Man

ALLEN, Charles Livingstone, 1913- 218
The miracle of love [by] Charles L. Allen. Old Tappan, N.J., F. H. Revell Co. [1972] 126 p. 21 cm. "First book of Corinthians, chapter thirteen": p. 89-126. [BV4639.A38] 72-5430 ISBN 0-8007-0543-2 3.95
1. Love (Theology) I. Bible. N.T. 1 Corinthians XIII. English. 1972. II. Title.

ALLEN, Charles Livingstone, 1913- 218
The miracle of love [by] Charles L. Allen. Boston, G. K. Hall, 1973 [c1972] 202 p. 25 cm. Large print ed. "First book of Corinthians, chapter thirteen": p. [141]-202. [BV4639.A38 1973] 73-9910 7.95 (lib. bdg.)
1. Love (Theology) I. Bible. N.T. 1 Corinthians XIII. English. 1973. II. Title.

BARRETT, J. Edward, 1932- 218
How are you programmed? [By] J. Edward Barrett. Richmond, John Knox Press [1971] 122 p. 21 cm. [BT701.2.B3] 70-155782 ISBN 0-8042-0604-X 2.45
1. Man (Theology) I. Title.

BRABAKER, J. Omar. 218
Understanding people: children, youth, adults, by J. Omar Brabaker [and] Robert E. Clark. [1st ed.] Wheaton, Ill., Evangelical Teacher Training Association [1972] 95 p. 23 cm. Includes bibliographies. [BR110.B77] 75-172116 ISBN 0-910566-15-1
1. Christianity—Psychology. I. Clark, Robert E., joint author. II. Evangelical Teacher Training Association. III. Title.

CHERESO, Cajetan. 218
The virtue of honor and beaty according to St. Thomas Aquinas; an analysis of moral beauty. River Forest, Ill., 1960. xviii, 89 p. 23 cm. (The Aquinas library) Bibliography: p. 86-89. [BV4647.T4C5] 64-56370
1. Thomas Aquinas, Saint — Ethics. 2. Temperance (Virtue) I. Title.

CHESEN, Eli S. 218
Religion may be hazardous to your health. New York, Collier Books [1973, c.1972] ix, 145 p. 18 cm. Bibliography: p. 137-139. [BL53.C45] 1.50 (pbk.)
1. Psychology, Religious. 2. Religious education of children. I. Title.
L.C. card no. for the hardbound edition: 76-189524.

*COKER, Marie. 218
So tomorrow. New York, Vantage Press [1974] 57 p. 21 cm. [BL53] ISBN 0-533-01123-X 3.95
1. Religion—Philosophy. 2. Conduct of life. I. Title.

COOPER, Irving Steiger, Bp., 1882-1935. 218
The secret of happiness / by Irving S. Cooper. Wheaton, Ill. : Theosophical Pub. House, 1976. 75 p. ; 15 cm. (A Quest book miniature) [BJ1481.C75 1976] 75-26815 ISBN 0-8356-0469-1 pbk. : 1.75
1. Happiness. 2. Theosophy. I. Title.

DUCASSE, Curt John, 1881- 218
A critical examination of the belief in a life after death. Springfield, Ill., Thomas [1961] 318 p. 24 cm. (American lecture series, publication no. 423. A monograph in the Bannerstone Division of American lectures in philosophy.) Includes bibliography. [BD421.D76] 60-12660
1. Immortality (Philosophy) 2. Reincarnation. 3. Mind and body. I. Title.

GOLDSMITH, Joel S., 1892-1964. 218
The gift of love / Joel S. Goldsmith ; edited by Lorraine Sinkler. 1st ed. New York : Harper & Row, [1975] 83 p. ; 15 cm. [BV4639.G65 1975] 75-9330 ISBN 0-06-063172-4 : 3.95
1. Love (Theology) I. Title.

GOWAN, Donald E. 218
When man becomes God : humanism and hybris in the Old Testament / by Donald E. Gowan. Pittsburgh : Pickwick Press, 1975. p. cm. (Pittsburgh theological monograph series ; no. 6) Includes bibliographical references and index. [BS661.G68] 75-17582 ISBN 0-915138-06-9 : 6.95
1. Man (Theology)—Biblical teaching. 2. Pride and vanity—Biblical teaching. 3. Myth in the Old Testament. I. Title. II. Series.

HAMMES, John A. 218
Humanistic psychology: a Christian interpretation [by] John A. Hammes. New York, Grune & Stratton [1971] xv, 203 p. illus. 24 cm. Bibliography: p. 189-196. [BR110.H25] 76-110448 ISBN 0-8089-0650-X
1. Christianity—Psychology. 2. Philosophical anthropology. I. Title.

HART, Ray L. 218
Unfinished man and the imagination; toward an ontology and a rhetoric of revelation [by] Ray L. Hart. [New York] Herder and Herder [1968] 418 p. 22 cm. Includes bibliographical references. [BT127.2.H285] 68-8354
1. Revelation. 2. Imagination. I. Title.

HOWES, Elizabeth Boyden, 1907- 218
The choicemaker / Elizabeth B. Howes and Sheila Moon. Wheaton, Ill. : Theosophical Publishing House, 1977, c1973. 221 p. ; 21 cm. (A Quest book) "Formerly published under the title Man the choicemaker." Includes bibliographical references and index. [BD431.H672 1977] 76-55374 ISBN 0-8356-0492-6 pbk. : 3.95
1. Life. 2. Man. 3. Man (Theology) 4. Choice (Psychology) I. Moon, Sheila, joint author. II. Title.

HOWES, Elizabeth Boyden, 1907- 218
Man the choicemaker, by Elizabeth Boyden Howes and Sheila Moon. Philadelphia, Westminster Press [1973] 218 p. 21 cm. Includes bibliographical references. [BD431.H672] 73-10016 ISBN 0-664-20982-3 9.00
1. Man. 2. Man (Theology) 3. Choice (Psychology) 4. Life. I. Moon, Sheila, joint author. II. Title.

JEREMIAS, Joachim, 1900- 218
The problem of the historical Jesus. Translated by Norman Perrin. Philadelphia, Fortress Press [1964] xviii, 28 p. 20 cm. (Facet books. Biblical series, 13) Bibliographical footnotes. Bibliography: p. 25-27. [BT303.2.J413] 64-23064
1. Jesus Christ — Historicity. I. Title. II. Series.

LEUTY, Joseph D 1909- 218
In God we trust; everyday essays on life and philosophy. [1st ed.] New York, Exposition Press [1956] 84p. 21cm. [BV4637.L46] 56-12680
1. Trust in God. I. Title.

LEWIS, Samuel L., 1896- 218
This is the new age, in person, by Samuel L. Lewis. Tucson, Ariz., Omen Press, 1972, [i.e. 1973] xii, 158 p. 21 cm. [BT702.L48] 72-83264 ISBN 0-912358-13-0 2.95 (pbk.)
1. Bible. N.T. 1 Corinthians—Criticism, interpretation, etc. 2. Man (Theology) I. Title.

LINDSEY, Hal. 218
The liberation of planet earth / Hal Lindsey. Grand Rapids : Zondervan Pub. House, c1974. 236 p. : ill. ; 21 cm. [BT751.2.L49] 73-13075 5.95
1. Lindsey, Hal. 2. Salvation. I. Title.

LOCKERBIE, D. Bruce. 218
The liberating word: art and the mystery of the Gospel, by D. Bruce Lockerbie. Grand Rapids, Eerdmans [1974] 125 p. 21 cm. [BS652.L6] 74-8928 ISBN 0-8028-1586-3 2.95 (pbk.)
1. Creation. 2. Creation (Literary, artistic, etc.) 3. Christian literature—History and criticism. I. Title.

MOLTMANN, Jurgen. 218
Theology of play. Translated by Reinhard Ulrich. [1st ed.] New York, Harper & Row [1972] vii, 113 p. 22 cm. The first liberated men in creation was originally published in German under title: Die ersten Freigelassenen der Schopfung. Contents.Contents.—Moltmann, J. The first liberated men in Creation.—Responses: Neale, R. E. The Crucifixion as play.—Keen, S. godsong.—Miller, D. L. Playing the game to lose.—Moltmann, J. Are there no rules of the game? Includes bibliographical references. [BJ1483.M65] 73-160635 ISBN 0-06-065902-5 4.95
1. Pleasure. 2. Freedom (Theology) I. Neale, Robert E. II. Keen, Sam. III. Miller, David LeRoy. IV. Moltmann, Jurgen. Die ersten Freigelassenen der Schopfung. English. 1972. V. Title.

MONTAGU, Ashley, 1905- 218
Immortality. New York, Grove Press [c1955] 72p. 21cm. [BD421.M58] 55-5109
1. Immortality. I. Title.

PALMER, Earl F. 218
Love has its reasons : an inquiry into New Testament love / Earl F. Palmer. Waco, Tex. : Word Books, c1977. 126 p. ; 23 cm. Includes bibliographical references. [BS2545.L6P34] 76-19539 ISBN 0-87680-481-4 : 5.95
1. Bible. N.T.—Criticism, interpretation, etc. 2. Love (Theology)—Biblical teaching. I. Title.

PERKINS, James Scudday. 218
Through death to rebirth. [1st ed.] Wheaton, Ill., Theosophical Press [1961] 124 p. illus. 20 cm. [BP573.D4P4] 61-13301
1. Death. 2. Theosophy. I. Title.

PIUS XII, Pope, 1876-1958. 218
The problem of teen-age purity; the teachings of Pope Pius XII. Compiler: Nazareno Camilleri; translator: Marion Barrows. New Rochelle, N. Y., Salesiana Publishers and Distributors [1961] 82p. 23cm. [BV4647.C5P513] 61-19848
1. Chastity—Papal documents. I. Title. II. Title: Teen-age purity.

RAVITCH, Norman, comp. 218
Christian man. Belmont, Calif., Wadsworth Pub. Co. [1973] x, 266 p. 23 cm. (Images of Western man, 2) [BR53.R37] 72-89431 ISBN 0-534-00228-5 3.95
1. Christian literature (Selections: Extracts, etc.) I. Title.

ROSIN, Jacob. 218
In God's image. New York, Philosophical Library [1969] 81 p. 23 cm. [BT925.R65] 75-86507 4.00
1. Immortality. I. Title.

RUDHYAR, Dane, 1895- 218
Culture, crisis, and creativity / Dane Rudhyar. 1st Quest book ed. Wheaton, Ill. : Theosophical Pub. House, 1977. 227 p. ; 21 cm. (A Quest book) Includes bibliographical references and index. [BP570.R82] 76-43008 ISBN 0-8356-0487-X pbk. : 4.25
1. Theosophy—Addresses, essays, lectures. 2. Culture—Addresses, essays, lectures. I. Title.

SEYMOUR, Peter S. 218
I am my brother. Writen by Peter Seymour. Illustrated by Donni Giambrone [and others. Kansas City, Mo., Hallmark Cards, c1972] [53] p. illus. 25 cm. (Hallmark crown editions) [BV4647.B7S48] 76-187755 ISBN 0-87529-279-8
1. Brotherliness. I. Title.

STEWART, Ora (Pate) 1910- 218
A letter to my daughter. Salt Lake City, Bookcraft [c1956] 160 p. 17 cm. [BV4451.S8] 57-31081
1. Young women — Religious life. I. Title.

SYMINGTON, Thomas Alexander, 1883- 218
Religious liberals and conservatives; a comparison of those who are liberal in their religious thinking and those who are conservative, by Thomas A. Symington. New York, Bureau of Publications, Teachers College, Columbia University, 1935. [New York, AMS Press, 1972, ie 1973] v, 104 p. 22 cm. Reprint of the 1935 ed., issued in series: Teachers College, Columbia University. Contributions to education, no. 640. Originally presented as the author's thesis, Columbia. Bibliography: p. 76-77. [BR1615.S9 1972] 70-177727 ISBN 0-404-55640-X 10.00
1. Psychology, Religious. 2. Attitude (Psychology) 3. Liberalism (Religion) 4. Religious education. I. Title. II. Series: Columbia University. Teachers College. Contributions to education, no. 640.

VALENTINE, Ferdinand. 218
The apostolate of chastity; a treatise for religious sisters. Westminster, Md., Newman Press [1954] 245p. 22cm. [BV4647.C5V3] 54-12606
1. Chastity. I. Title.

WOODWARD, Luther Ellis, 1897- 218
Relations of religious training and life patterns to the adult religious life; a study of the relative significance of religious training and influence and of certain emotional and behavior patterns for the adult religious life. New York, Bureau of Publications, Teachers College, Columbia University, 1932. [New York, AMS Press, 1973, c1972] v, 75 p. 22 cm. Reprint of the 1932 ed., issued in series: Teachers College, Columbia University. Contributions to education, no. 527. Originally presented as the author's thesis, Columbia. Includes bibliographical references. [BL53.W65 1972] 71-177627 ISBN 0-404-55527-6 10.00
1. Psychology, Religious. 2. Religious education. I. Title. II. Series: Columbia University. Teachers College. Contributions to education, no. 527.

MORGAN, Edwin P., 1914- 2*.18*41
Gold finding secrets, by Edwin P. Morgan. 1st ed. [Sacramento? Calif., 1966] 80 p. illus., map, port. 23 cm. Bibliography: p. 75. [TN410.M66] 73-10774
1. Gold mines and mining. I. Title.

219 Analogy

BROWNE, Peter, Bp. of Cork and Ross, d.1735. 219
Things divine and supernatural / Peter Browne. New York : Garland Pub., 1976. p. cm. (British philosophers and theologians of the 17th & 18th centuries ; no. 9) Reprint of the 1733 ed. published by W. Innys and R. Manby, London. [BL210.B7 1976] 75-11203 ISBN 0-8240-1758-7 lib.bdg. : 25.00
1. Analogy (Religion) 2. Knowledge, Theory of (Religion) 3. Apologetics—18th century. I. Title. II. Series.

BUTLER, Joseph, Bp. of Durham, 1692-1752. 219
The analogy of religion. Introd. by Ernest C. Mossner. New York, F. Unfar Pub. Co. [1961] xii, 259p. 21cm. (Milestones of thought in the history of ideas) [BT1100.B9 1961] 60-53362
1. Analogy (Religion) 2. Natural theology. 3. Apologetics—18th cent. 4. Revelation—Early works to 1800. 5. Eschatology—Early works to 1800. I. Title. II. Series.

220 BIBLE

ABILENE Christian College. 220
Our Bible. Edited by Frank Pack. [Abilene, Tex., 1953] 192p. illus. 21cm. Essays honoring six retiring members of the faculty. [BS475.A2] 53-23421
1. Bible — Inspiration. 2. Bible — Canon. 3. Bible —Versions. 4. Churches of Christ—Biog. I. Pack, Frank, 1916- ed. II. Title.

AKIN, Johnnye. 220
Helping the Bible speak; how to read the Bible aloud more effectively, by Johnnye Akin [and others] New York, Association Press [1956] 117p. 21cm. [BS617.A36] 56-6446
1. Bible—Reading. 2. Bible as literature. I. Title.

ANDERSON, Bernhard W 220
The unfolding drama of the Bible; eight studies introducing the Bible as a whole. New York, Association Press [1957] 124p. 16cm. (An Association Press reflection book) 'A Haddam House publication now reprinted as a Reflection book' Includes bibliography. [BS605.A6 1957] 57-11608
1. Bible—Study—Text-books. I. Title.

ANDERSON, Bernhard W 220
The unfolding drama of the Bible; eight studies introducing the bible as a whole. New York, Association Press [1957] 124p. 16cm. (An Association Press reflection book) 'A Haddam House publication now reprinted as a Reflection book.' Includes bibliography. [BS605.A6 1957] 57-11608
1. Bible—Study—Text-books. I. Title.

ANDERSON, Bernhard W. 220
The unfolding drama of the Bible; eight studies introducing the Bible as a whole [by] Bernhard W. Anderson. [Rev., enl., updated] New York, Association Press [1971] 128 p. 18 cm. Bibliography: p. [125]-128. [BS605.2.A5 1971] 78-141870 ISBN 0-8096-1815-X 1.75
1. Bible—Study—Text-books. I. Title.

ASHBY, La Verne j220
The Bible is a special book. Illus. by Anne R. Kasey. Nashville, Broadman [1966] 46p. illus. 23cm. [BS539.A7] 66-7014 1.35 bds.,
1. Bible — Juvenile literature. I. Title.

BAXTER, James Sidlow. 220
Explore the Book, a basic and brodly interpretative course of Bible study from Genesis to Revelation. Grand Rapids, Zondervan Pub. House [1960] 6v. illus. 22cm. Contents.v. 1. Geneisi to Jochua.--v. 2. Judges to Eather.--v. 3. Job to Lamentations.--v. 4. Ezekiel to Malachi.--v. 5. Inter-Testament and the Goapels.--v. 6. Acts to Revelation. [BS600.2.B35] 60-50187
1. Bible—Study Text-books. I. Title.

BAXTER, James Sidlow. 220
The strategic grasp of the Bible; a series of studies in the structural and dispensational characteristics of the Bible [by] J. Sidlow Baxter. Grand Rapids, Zondervan Pub. House [1970, c1968] 405 p. 23 cm. [BS475.2.B34 1970] 71-95049 6.95
1. Bible—Introductions. I. Title.

BECK, Harrell Frederick, 1922- 220
Our Biblical heritage [student's bk.] Boston, United Church [1964] 114p. illus. 21cm. 64-14497 1.50; 2.25 teacher's bk.,
1. Bible—Study—Text-books. I. Title.

BECK, Harrell Frederick, 1922- 220
Our Biblical heritage, by Harrell F. Beck. [Rev. ed.] Philadelphia, United Church Press [1972] 114 p. illus. 21 cm. Includes bibliographical references. [BS605.2.B4 1972] 77-77907
1. Bible—Study—Text-books. I. Title.

BEEBE, H. Keith, 1921- 220
The Old Testament [by] H. Keith Beebe. Belmont, Calif., Dickenson Pub. Co. [1970] xvii, 505 p. illus., maps. 24 cm. Bibliography: p. 479-496. [BS1140.2.B4] 77-121024
1. Bible. O.T.—Introductions. I. Title.

BIBLE. English. 1963. Holy Name version. 220
The Holy Name Bible, containing the Holy Name version of the Old and New Testaments, critically compared with ancient authorities, and various manuscripts. Rev. by A.B. Traina. Irvington, N. J.,1125 Stuyvesant Ave. Scripture Research Assoc., [c.1963] xi, 1102, 346p. col. maps. 22cm. New Testament has special t. p. 63-2798 10.00; 20.00 leather,
I. Traina, A. B. II. Scripture Research Association, Irvington, N. J. III. Title.

BIBLE. English. 1964. Authorized. 220
The Holy Bible. Containing the Old and New Testaments in the King James version. The living word; the family library. San Antonio, J. W. Cain [1964] 1 v. (various pagings) illus., plates (part col.) maps, forms. 31 cm. [BS1851964.S3] 64-2563
I. Title.
Contents Omitted

BIBLE. English. 1964. Authorized. 220
The new chain-reference Bible: containing Thompson's original and complete system of Bible study, including a complete numerical system of chain references, analyses of books, outline studies of characters, and unique charts. To which has been added a new and valuable series of pictorial maps, archaeological discoveries, together with many other features. Self-prounouncing test. Compiled and edited by Frank Charles Thompson 4th improved ed. Indianapolis, B. B. Kirbridge Bible Co. [c1964] 1 v. (various pagings) illus., facsims., maps (part col.) 23 cm. Added to.p.: The marginal chain-reference New Testament. [BS1851964.I5] 65-1443
1. Bible — Study. I. Thompson, Frank Charles, 1958-ed. II. Title. III. Title: Chain-reference Bible. IV. Title: The marginal chain-reference New Testament.

BIBLE. English. Authorized. Selections. 1968. 220
Wings of the morning; verses from the Bible. Selected by Robin Palmer. Illustrated by Tony Palazzo. New York, H. Z. Walck, 1968. [29] p. illus. (part col.) 20 cm. Bible verses whose content and accompanying illustrations stress elements of nature. [BS391.2.P3] AC 68
1. Bible—Selections. I. Palmer, Robin, 1911- II. Palazzo, Tony, 1905- illus. III. Title.

BIBLE. English. Authorized. Selections. 1974. 220
A little book of faith. Illustrated by Betsey Clark. [Kansas City, Mo., Hallmark Cards, 1974] [34] p. illus. 11 cm. (Hallmark editions) [BS391.2.C52] 73-83385 ISBN 0-87529-366-2 1.95
I. Clark, Betsey, illus. II. Title.

BIBLE, English, Selections, 1965. 220
A book of good tidings from the Bible [Comp., illus. by] Joan Walsh Anglund. New York, Harcourt [c.1965] lv. (unpaged) illus. (pt. col.) 11x8cm. [BS391.2.A5] 65-17986 1.95, bxd.
1. Anglund, Joan (Walsh) comp. and illus. II. Title.

BIBLE. English. Selections. 1970. 220
The wonderful promises of God as expressed in the Twenty-third psalm, together with other choice portions of Holy Scripture. Compiled and illustrated by Royal V. Carley. Norwalk, Conn., C. R. Gibson Co. [1970] 1 v. (unpaged) illus. (part col.) 19 cm. Cover title: The Twenty-third psalm for today. [BS1430.5.C3] 73-101450 2.50
1. Bible. O.T. Pslams XXIII. I. Carley, Royal V. II. Title. III. Title: The Twenty-third psalm for today.

BIBLE. English. Today's English. Selections. 1972. 220
Dimensions of love; as set forth in selected portions of Holy Scripture. Compiled and illustrated by Royal V. Carley. Norwalk, Conn., C. R. Gibson Co. [1972] [28] p. illus. (part col.) 19 cm. [BS391.2.C37] 72-78466 ISBN 0-8378-2003-0 2.50
I. Carley, Royal V., comp. II. Bible. English. Authorized. Selections. 1972. III. Title.

BLAIR, Edward Payson, 1910- 220
The Bible and you; a guide for reading the Bible in the Revised standard version. Nashville, Published for the Co-operative Publication Association by Abingdon-Cokesbury Press [1953] 154p. 20cm. (The Cooperative series leadership training texts) Includes bibliography. [BS617.B57] 53-6348
1. Bible—Reading. 2. Bible—Study. I. Title.

*BONEY, Mary L. 220
God calls. Illus. by Edgar Mallory. Richmond, Va., CLC Pr. [dist. Knox, c.1964] 191p. 24cm. (Covenant Life Curriculum bk.) 2.95 pap.,
I. Title.

BOOSE, Rose E. 220
Let's study the Bible; the message of the Bible co-ordinating facts and events for a clearer understanding of the Book of Books. Mountain View, Calif., Pacific Press Pub. Association [1950] 176 p. 21 cm. [BS605.B62] 50-35722
1. Bible—Study—Text-books. I. Title.

BOWER, William Clayton, 1878- 220
The living Bible. Rev. ed. Freeport, N.Y., Books for Libraries Press [1969, c1936] ix, 229 p. 23 cm. (Essay index reprint series) Bibliography: p. 217-219. [BS511.B63 1969] 79-99618
1. Bible—Use. 2. Bible—Criticsm, interpretation, etc. I. Title.

BRANNON, T. Leo. 220
The Bible and evangelism, by T. Leo Brannon. Nashville, Methodist Evangelistic Materials [1964] 72 p. 19 cm. Bibliographical footnotes. [BS600.2.B7] 64-23186
1. Bible — Study. I. Title.

BRANNON, T. Leo 220
The Bible and evangelism. Nashville, Methodist Evangelistic Materials [c.1964] 72p. 19cm. Bibl. 64-23186 .60 pap.,
1. Bible—Study. I. Title.

BRATTON, Fred Gladstone, 1896- 220
A history of the Bible; an introduction to the historical method. Boston, Beacon Press, 1959. 382p. 21cm. Includes bibliography. [BS445.B65] 59-10660
1. Bible—Hist. I. Title.

BRATTON, Fred Gladstone, 1896- 220
A history of the Bible; an introduction to the

historical method. Boston, Beacon [1967, c.1959] 382p. 20cm. (BP239) Bibl. [BS445.B65] 59-10660 2.45 pap.,
1. Bible—Hist. I. Title.

BROKHOFF, John R 220
Read and live; a study dealing with how to use the Bible. Arthur H. Getz, editor. Philadelphia, Muhlenberg Press [1953] 96p. illus. 18cm. [BS600.B836] 53-3714
1. Bible—Study. I. Title.

BURNETT, Ulala Howard, 1880- 220
Bible study made easy. [Cisco? Tex.] c1953. 206p. 22cm. [BS600.B86] 53-39477
1. Bible-Study. I. Title.

CAN I trust my Bible? 220
Important questions often asked about the Bible, with some answers by eight evangelical scholars. Chicago, Moody Press [1963] 190 p. 22 cm. Bibliographical footnotes. [BS612.C33] 64-105
1. Bible—Examinations, questions, etc.

CAN I trust my Bible? 220
Important questions often asked about the Bible, with some answers by eight evangelical scholars. Chicago, Moody [1968,c.1963] 190p. 18cm. Bibl. footnotes. [BS612.C33] 64-105 .60 pap.,
1. Bible—Examinations, questions, etc.

CARLYON, J T 220
Interpreting the Bible to youth. New York, Abingdon Press [1954] 155p. 19cm. Includes bibliographies. [BS600.C3] 54-14576
1. Bible—Study. I. Title.

CASSELS, Louis. 220
Your Bible. [1st ed.] Garden City, N.Y., Doubleday, 1967. xvii, 267 p. maps. 22 cm. Bibliography: p. [245]-246. [BS617.C3] 67-11197
1. Bible—Reading. I. Title.

CASSELS, Louis. 220
Your Bible. [New York] Funk & Wagnalls [1969, c1967] xvii, 267 p. maps. 18 cm. (A Funk & Wagnalls paperbook, F66) Bibliography: p. [245]-246. [BS617.C3 1969] 74-3652 1.50
1. Bible—Reading. I. Title.

CATHOLIC University of America. Conferences on the Curciculum of the Minor Seminary, 1953. 220
Latin and religion syllabi in the minor seminary; the proceedings of a Conference on the Curriculum of the Minor Seminary, conducted at the Catholic University of America, May 8, 9, 10, 1953. Edited by Roy J. Deferrari. Washington, Catholic University of America Press, 1954. v, 77p. 23cm. [BX904.C3 1953] A 54
1. Theological seminaries, Catholic. 2. Latin language—Study and teaching. 3. Theology — Study and teaching. I. Deferrari, Roy Joseph, 1890- ed. II. Title.

CAWOOD, John W. 220
Let's know the Bible [by] John W. Cawood. Old Tappan, N.J., Revell [1971] 152 p. illus., maps. 21 cm. [BS475.2.C35] 70-137441 ISBN 0-8007-0431-2 3.95
1. Bible—Introductions. I. Title.

CLAUDEL, Paul, 1868-1955. 220
The essence of the Bible. [Translated from the French by Wade Baskin] New York, Philosophical Library [c1957] 120p. 22cm. Translation of J'aime la Bible. [BS538.C553] 58-14654
1. Bible—Appreciation. I. Title.

CLINTON, Kenneth. 220
Let's read the Bible. New York, Macmillan, 1950. ix, 149 p. 21 cm. Bibliography: p. 142-145. [BS617.C56] 50-5691
1. Bible—Reading. I. Title.

COCHRAN, Sue Eleanor, 1869- 220
The thread of Bible narrative. San Antonio, Press of the Naylor Co. [1950] xi, 116 p. 21 cm. [BS591.C58] 50-13527
1. Bible—Study—Outlines, syllabi, etc. I. Title.

COLWELL, Ernest Cadman, 1901- 220
The study of the Bible. Rev. ed. Chicago, University of Chicago Press [1964] xv, 202 p. 21 cm. Includes bibliographies. [BS475.C46 1964] 64-23411
1. Bible—Introductions. I. Title.

COMSTOCK, Edna Elizabeth, 1904- 220
Teen-age Bible. New York, Millington Co. [1954] 84p. 16cm. [BS613.C58] 54-30267
1. Bible—Study—Text-books. I. Title.

CONNICK, C. Milo. 220
The message and meaning of the Bible. Belmont, Calif., Dickenson [dist. Wadsworth, c.1965] xiii, 225p. illus., maps. 23cm. Bibl. [BS600.2.C64] 65-21116 5.95 pap.,
1. Bible—Study. I. Title.

CROWE, Charles M 220
Getting help from the Bible. [1st ed.] New York, Harper [1957] 211p. 22cm. [BS538.C7] 57-7348
1. Bible—Use. 2. Christian life. I. Title.

DAY, Gwynn McLendon. 220
The wonder of the Word. [Westwood, N. J.] Revell [1957] 222p. 22cm. [BS480.D33] 57-6973
1. Bible—Exidences, authority, etc. 2. Bible—Influence. I. Title.

DAY, Gwynn McLendon 220
The wonder of the Word. Chicago, Moody [1963, c.1957] 255p. 17cm. .89 pap.,
1. Bible—Evidences, authority, etc. 2. Bible—Influence. I. Title.

DEAL, William S. 220
Baker's pictorial introduction to the Bible / William S. Deal. Grand Rapids, Mich. : Baker Book House, [1975] 431 [4] p. : ill. ; 18 cm. (Direction books) Bibliography: p. [433]-[435]. [BS475.2.D4 1975] 75-315625 ISBN 0-8010-2826-4 pbk. : 2.95
1. Bible—Introductions. I. Title. II. Title: Pictorial introduction to the Bible.

DEAN, James Elmer. 220
Keys that unlock the Scriptures. [1st ed.] New York, Dutton, 1953. 214p. 21cm. Includes bibliography. [BS417.D4] 52-12946
1. Bible—Handbooks, manuals, etc. I. Title.

DENBEAUX, Fred J. 220
Understanding the Bible. Philadelphia, Westminster Press [1958] 94 p. 20 cm. (Layman's theological library) [BS538.D45] 58-10218
1. Bible—Criticism, interpretation, etc. I. Title.

DONNE, John, 1573-1631. 220
Sermons on the Psalms and Gospels, with a selection of prayers and meditations. Edited, with an introd. by Evelyn M. Simpson. Berkeley, University of California Press, 1963. 244 p. 22 cm. [BX5133.D6S44 1963] 63-16249
1. Church of England — Sermons. 2. Sermons, English. I. Simpson, Evelyn Mary (Spearing) 1885- ed. II. Title.

DONNE, John, 1573-1631 220
Sermons on the Psalms and Gospels. with a selection of prayers and meditations. Ed., introd. by Evelyn M. Simpson. Berkeley, Univ. of Calif. Pr. [c.]1963. 244p. 22cm. (Cal 84) 63-16249 1.95 pap.,
1. Church of England—Sermons. 2. Sermons, English. I. Simpson, Evelyn Mary (Spearing) 1885- ed. II. Title.

ERICKSON, Melvin E 220
Bible quizzes. Washington, Review and Herald Pub. Association [1963] 128 p. 22 cm. [BS612.E7] 63-10404
1. Bible — Examinations, questions, etc. 2. Bible games and puzzles. I. Title.

FELDMAN, Abraham Jehiel, 1893- 220
A companion to the Bible, by Abraham J. Feldman. New York, Bloch Pub. Co. [1964] xiii, 174 p. 22 cm. Bibliographical references included in "Notes" (p. 163-167) [BX1194.F4] 64-20096
1. Bible. O.T.—Study. I. Title.

FELDMAN, Abraham Jehiel, 1893- 220
A companion to the Bible [Reissue] New York, Bloch [c.1964] xiii, 174p. 22cm. Bibl. 64-20096 2.75
1. Bible. O.T.—Study. I. Title.

FENIMORE, George. 220
Alice in Bibleland. [A playlet, by] George Wills [pseud.] New York, Philosophical Library [1953] 54p. 22cm. [BS530.F4] 53-9166
1. Bible Criticism, interpretation, etc. I. Title.

FOWLER, George P., 1909- 220
Our religious heritage; a guide to the study of the Bible [by] George P. Fowler. Dubuque, Iowa, W. C. Brown Book Co. [1969] x, 454 p. 23 cm. Bibliography: p. 434-443. [BS475.2.F6] 75-85806
1. Bible—Introductions. I. Title.

FOWLER, George P., 1909- 220
Our religious heritage; a guide to the study of the Bible [by] George P. Fowler. Dubuque, Iowa, Kendall/Hunt Pub. Co. [1972] x, 454 p. 23 cm. Bibliography: p. 434-443. [BS475.2.F6 1972] 72-190674 ISBN 0-8403-0581-8
1. Bible—Introductions. I. Title.

FRASER, James, 1896- 220
A Bible study. [1st ed.] Boston, Delta Press [1953] xix, 618p. illus., maps. 23cm. Edition statement from label mounted on fly leaf. Bibliography: p. 591-600. [BS475.F53] 53-10996
1. Bible—Introductions. 2. Bible—History of Biblical events. I. Title.

FRAZIER, Claude Albee, 1920- 220
Through the Bible with a physician, by Claude A. Frazier. With forewords by Mrs. Billy Graham, Woodrow Clark and Cecil E. Sherman. Springfield, Ill., Thomas [1971] xvii, 282 p. 24 cm. [BS540.F7] 76-149183
1. Bible—Addresses, essays, lectures. I. Title.

GEISLER, Norman L. 220
A general introduction to the Bible [by] Norman L. Geisler and William E. Nix. Foreword by Samuel J. Schultz. Chicago, Moody Press [1968] 480 p. illus. 24 cm. Bibliography: p. 457-469. [BS475.2.G39] 68-18890 6.95
1. Bible—Introductions. I. Nix, William E., joint author. II. Title.

GETTYS, Joseph Miller, 1907- 220
How to enjoy studying the Bible, with worksheets. [Rev. ed., enl.] Richmond, John Knox Press [1956] 72p. illus. 23cm. [BS600.G39 1956] 56-14439
1. Bible— Study. I. Title.

GRAY, James Martin, 1851-1935. 220
How to master the English Bible, an experience, a method, a result, an illustration. Chicago, Moody Press ['1951] 127 p. 17 cm. (Colportage library, 211) [BS600.G7 1951] 52-803
1. Bible—Study. I. Title.

HALL, Richard Walter. 220
How to read the Bible [by] Richard Hall and Eugene P. Beitler, in association with Francis Carr Stifler. [1st ed.] Philadelphia, Lippincott [1957] 255p. illus. 21cm. [BS617.H3] 57-8944
1. Bible—Reading. I. Beitler, Eugene P., joint author. II. Title.

*HANDFORD, Elizabeth Rice 220
Scripture crossword puzzles, no.3. Chicago, Moody [1966] 64p. (chiefly illus.) 21cm. (Bible IQ ser.) .50 pap.,
1. Bible — Crossword puzzles. I. Title.

*HARDIE, Katherine Johnson j220
The book of God's people [by] Katherine Johnson Hardie, Pauline Palmer Meek. Illus. by David K. Stone. Richmond, Va., CLC Pr., 1966 32p. col. illus. 22cm. 1.45 bds.,
1. Bible — Juvenile literature. I. Meek, Pauline Palmer joint author. II. Title.
Available from Knox.

HARKNESS, Georgia Elma, 1891- 220
Toward understanding the Bible. [Cincinnati] Woman's Division of Christian Service, Board of Missions and Church Extension, Methodist Church [1952] 134 p. 19 cm. Includes bibliography. [BS538.H3] 52-31041
1. Bible—Criticism, interpretation, etc. I. Title.

HARKNESS, Georgia Elma, 1891- 220
Toward understanding the Bible. New York, Scribner, 1954. 138 p. 20 cm. [BS538.H3 1954] 54-6327
1. Bible—Criticism, interpretation, etc. I. Title.

HARRINGTON, Wilfrid J. 220
Key to the Bible / Wilfrid J. Harrington. Garden City, N.Y. : Image Books, 1976. 3 v. ; 18 cm. Contents.Contents.—v. 1. Record of revelation.—v. 2. The Old Testament: record of the promise.—v. 3. The New Testament: record of the fulfillment. Includes bibliographies. [BS475.2.H29 1976] 76-375421 ISBN 0-385-12205-5 (v.1) pbk. : 1.95 ISBN 0-385-12207-1 (v.3) pbk. : 1.95 ISBN 0-385-12206-3 (v.2) pbk. : 19.5
1. Bible—Introductions. I. Title.

HARRINGTON, Wilfrid J 220
Record of revelation; the Bible [by] Wilfrid J. Harrington. Foreword by Roland de Vaux. Chicago, Priory Press [1965] xiv, 143 p. 24 cm. "The Bible text ... is from the Revised standard version." [BS475.2.H3] 65-19356 3.95
1. Bible — Introductions. I. Title.

HARRINGTON, Wilfrid J. 220
Record of revelation: the Bible. Foreword by Roland de Vaux. Chicago, Priory Pr. [c.1965] xiv, 143p. 24cm. The Bible text is from the Revised standard version. Bibl. [BS475.2.H3] 65-19356 3.95
1. Bible—Introductions. I. Title.

HARRISON, Everett Falconer, 1902- 220
Introduction to the New Testament, by Everett F. Harrison. Grand Rapids, Eerdmans [1964] xiv, 481 p. 24 cm. Includes bibliographies. [BS2330.2.H33] 64-16589
1. Bible. N. T.—Introductions. I. Title.

HASTINGS, Cecily. 220
Pattern of Scripture, by Cecily Hastings, Vincent Rochford [and] Alexander Jones. New York, Sheed and Ward [1959] 96p. 18cm. (Canterbury books) [BS617.H37] 59-6397
1. Mary, Virgin. 2. Bible—Reading. 3. Church. I. Title.

HAYES, John Haralson, 1934- 220
Introduction to the Bible, by John H. Hayes. Philadelphia, Westminster Press [1971] xvi, 515, 4, xvi p. illus., col. maps. 25 cm. Bibliography: p. 467-478. [BS475.2.H36] 76-105395 ISBN 0-664-20885-1 9.95
1. Bible—Introductions. I. Title.

HAYNES, Carlyle Boynton, 1882- 220
The Book of all nations. Rev. Nashville, Southern Pub. Association [1950] 420 p. 18 cm. First ed. published in 1935 under title: God's Book. [BS475.H36 1950] 50-7157
1. Bible—Criticism, interpretation, etc. I. Title.

HEIM, Ralph Daniel, 1895- 220
Reader's companion to the Bible / by Ralph D. Heim. Philadelphia : Fortress Press, [1975] viii, 135 p. ; 22 cm. Includes index. [BS605.2.H43] 74-26329 ISBN 0-8006-1090-3 pbk. : 3.50
1. Bible—Study—Text-books. I. Title.

HESTER, Hubert Inman, 1895- 220
The Book of Books. Nashville, Convention Press [1959] 138p. illus. 20cm. [BS600.2.H46] 59-10927
1. Bible—Study—Text-books. I. Title.

*HILL, Dave 220
The big Bible puzzle book. St. Louis, Mo., Bethany, c.1965. 64p. illus. 23cm. (10B643) 1.49 pap.,
I. Title.

HOOPER, John Stirling Morley, 1882- 220
Bible translation in India, Pakistan and Ceylon. 2d ed. rev by W.J. Culshaw. [Bombay] Indian Branch, Oxford University Press, 1963. xi, 226 p. illus., fold. map, facsim. 19 cm. First ed. published in 1938 under title: The Bible in India, with a chapter on Cylon. [BV2369.5.S6H6] SA64
1. Bible — Publication and distribution — South Asia. 2. Bible — Versions, Asian. 3. Missions — South Asia. I. Title.

HUGHES, Mary Dawson. 220
The Lord is my shepherd; new inspiration from favorite Bible verses. Illustrated by Betsey Clark. Selected by Mary Dawson Hughes. [Kansas City, Mo.] Hallmark Editions [1969] [47] p. col. illus. 16 cm. [BS483.5.H8] 70-81846 2.00
1. Bible—Meditations. I. Clark, Betsey, illus. II. Title.

HYATT, James Philip, 1909- 220
The heritage of Biblical faith, an aid to reading the Bible. Saint Louis, Bethany Press [1964] 367 p. 23 cm. Pages 363-367 blank for "Notes." Bibliographical footnotes. [BS475.2.H9] 64-13404
1. Bible—Introductions. 2. Bible—Study. I. Title.

INTERPRETATION. 220
Tools for Bible study, edited by Balmer H. Kelly [and] Donald G. Miller. Richmond, John Knox Press [1956] 159p. 26cm. Bibliographical footnotes. [BS417.I5] 56-11774
1. Bible—Handbooks, manuals. etc. 2. Bible—Study. I. Kelly, Balmer H., ed. II. Miller, Donald G., ed. III. Title.
Contents omitted.

JONES, Clifford Merton. 220
The Bible today for those who teach it. by Clifford M. Jones. With a pref. by Randolph Crump Miller. Philadelphia, Fortress Press [1964] 240 p. illus., maps. 21 cm. Includes bibliographies. [BS600.2.J6] 64-14659
1. Bible—Study. I. Title.

JONES, Clifford Merton 220
The Bible today for those who teach it. Pref. by Randolph Crump Miller. Philadelphia, Fortress [1964] 240p. illus., maps. 21cm. Bibl. 64-14659 3.85
1. Bible—Study. I. Title.

JONES, Mary Alice, 1898- j220
Know your Bible. Illustrated by Seymour Fleishman. Chicago, Rand McNally [1965] 71 p. illus. (part col.) maps. 29 cm. [BS539.J6] 64-17447
1. Bible—Juvenile literature. I. Fleishman, Seymour, illus. II. Title.

JONES, Mary Alice, 1898- 220
Know your Bible. Illus. by Seymour Fleishman. Chicago, Rand McNally [c.1965] 71p. illus. (pt. col.) maps. 29cm. [BS539.J6] 64-17447 1.95 bds.,
1. Bible—Juvenile literature. I. Fleishman, Seymour, illus. II. Title.

JONES, Russell Bradley 1894- 220
The story of God's redeeming love; a survey of the Bible. [Jefferson City Tenn.] 1953. 315p. 23cm. [BS591.J63] 53-33645
1. Bible—Study—Outlines, syllabi, etc. 2. Bible—History of Biblical events. I. Title.

JONES, Russell Bradley, 1894- 220
A survey of the Old and New Testaments; the Bible story of redeeming love. Grand Rapids, Baker Book House, 1957. 372 p. illus. 23 cm. Includes bibliography. [BS591.J64] 57-12191
1. Bible—Study—Outlines, syllabi, etc. I. Title.

KHOOBYAR, Helen. 220
Facing adult problems in Christian education. Philadelphia, Westminster Press [c1963] 140 p. 21 cm. Bibliographical references included in "Notes" (p. 139-140) [BV1471.2.K5] 63-15467
1. Religious education. I. Title.

KUITERT, Harminus Martinus. 220
Signals from the Bible, by Harry M. Kuitert. Translated by Lewis B. Smedes. Grand Rapids, Eerdmans [1972] 95 p. 21 cm. Translation of De spelers en het spel. [BS440.K8513] 79-184700 ISBN 0-8028-1439-5 1.95
1. Bible—Dictionaries. I. Title.

LANTZ, John Edward. 220
Reading the Bible aloud. New York, Macmillan, 1959. 144p. 22cm. Includes bibliography. [BS617.L25] 59-10991
1. Bible—Reading. I. Title.

LARSON, Mildred. 220
A manual for problem solving in Bible translation / Mildred Larson. Grand Rapids : Zondervan Pub. House, c1975. 245 p. ; 24 cm. Includes bibliographies. [BS449.L37] 74-11863
1. Bible—Translating—Handbooks, manuals, etc. I. Title.

LAYMON, Charles M. 220
The message of the Bible. Nashville, Abingdon Press [c.1960] 127p. bibl.illus. 20cm. 60-1254 1.00
1. Bible—Criticism, interpretation, etc. I. Title.

LEONARD, Maria, 1880- 220
Bible truth for today's youth. New York, Carlton Press [1964] 327 p. illus., maps. 21 cm. (A Reflection book) Bibliography: p. 319. [BS1194.L4] 64-56970
1. Bible — Study. I. Title.

LEONARD, Maria, 1880- 220
Bible truth for today's youth. New York, Carlton [c.1964] 327p. illus., maps. 21cm. (Reflection bk.) Bibl. 64-569709 5.00
1. Bible—Study. I. Title.

LEVY, Jerome, ed. 220
A clinical approach to the problems of pastoral care, edited by Jerome Levy [and] Roma K. McNickle. Boulder, Colo., Western Interstate Commission for Higher Education, 1964. vii, 106 p. 28 cm. "Report to two institutes on mental health, Anchorage, Alaska. September 9-10, 1963, and Fairbanks, Alaska, Septemper 12-13, 1963." Sponsored by the Western Interstate Commission for Higher Education. [BV4012.L48] 64-63497
1. Pastoral psychology — Congresses. 2. Psychiatry and religion. I. McNickle, Roma K., joint ed. II. Western Interstate Commission for Higher Education. III. Title.

LONGFELLOW, Albert Edward. 220
A guide to the study of the Bible. New York, Comet Press Books [1957] 125p. 21cm. (A Reflection book) [BS591.L6] 57-7148
1. Bible—Study—Outlines, syllabi, etc. I. Title.

LOOSE, Alice Larkin (Wilson) 220
1866-
The battle of the ages, by Israel Wilson [pseud.] New York. Vantage Press [1952] 76p. 23cm. [BR121.L62] 52-11905
1. Christianity—20th cent. I. Title.

LOVE, Julian Price, 1894- 220
How to read the Bible. Rev. ed. New York, Macmillan, 1959. 180p. 22cm. Includes bibliography. [BS617.L6 1959] 58-13177
1. Bible—Reading. I. Title.

LYNCH WILLIAM E 220
The word dwells among us; a foreword to the Biblical books, by William E. Lynch. Milwaukee, Bruce Pub. Co. [1965] x, 171 p. 22 cm. (Impact books) Bibliography: p. 155-158. [BS475.2.L9] 65-26692
1. Bible — Introductions. I. Title.

*MCCARTER, Neely Dixon 220
Hear the word of the Lord. Illus. by Dudley Cook, Richard Loader. CLC Pr. [dist.] Richmond, Va. [Knox, c.1964] 223p. 24cm. (Covenant life curriculum) 2.95 pap.,
I. Title.

MCGAVRAN, Grace Winifred. 220
Stories of the Book of books. Rev. ed. New York, Friendship Press [1960] 183p. 20cm. [BS445.M27 1960] 60-10797
1. Bible—Hist. 2. Bible—Versions. I. Title.

MARSH, John, 1904- 220
A year with the Bible. New York, Harper [1957] 191p. 22cm. [BS617.M28 1957a] 57-2529
1. Bible—Reading. I. Title.

MEETING God in Scripture; 220
meditations on some outstanding books of the Bible. Nashville, Upper Room [1964] 172 p. 18 cm. Each chapter originally published separately in the "Meeting God" series. Bibliographical footnotes. [BS483.5.M4] 64-8090
1. Bible — Meditations.
Contents omitted

MEETING God in Scripture; 220
meditations on some outstanding books of the Bible. Nashville, Upper Room [c.1964] 172p. 18cm. Bibl. [BS483.5.M4] 64-8090 1.00
1. Bible—Meditations.

MORGAN, Charles Herbert, 220
1852-
A year's Bible course; based on the Scofield reference Bible, by Charles H. Morgan. Grand Rapids, Baker Book House [1966] 144 p. illus., maps. 23 cm. First published in 1925 under title: Busy peoples Bible course. [BS605] 67-2183
1. Bible—Study—Text-books. I. Title.

*MULLIN, Richard J. 220
Down you go! Chicago, Moody [c.1966] 64p. 19cm. (Bible IQ ser., 30-2265 MP50) .50 pap.,
I. Title.

MURRAY, Albert Victor, 1890- 220
How to know your Bible; a guide to Biblical study. Boston, Beacon Press [1952] 185p. illus. 22cm. [BS475.M85] 53-6308
1. Bible—Introductions. I. Title.

NETTLES, Kenneth James, 1922- 220
The supernatural origi of the Bible; a study of ten points in evidence for divine authority. Foreword by Eugene T. Pratt. [1st ed.] New York, Exposition Press [1957] 179p. 21cm. (An Exposition-Testament book) Includes bibliography. [BS480.N37] 57-7661
1. Bible—Evidences, authority, etc. I. Title.

NETTLES, Kenneth James, 1922- 220
The supernatural origin of the Bible; a study of ten points in evidence for divine authority. Foreword by Eugene T. Pratt. [1st ed.] New York, Exposition Press [1957] 179p. 21cm. (An Exposition-Testament book) Includes bibliography. [BS480.N37] 57-7661
1. Bible—Evidences, authority, etc. I. Title.

NILES, Daniel Thambyrajah. 220
Reading the Bible today. New York, Association Press [1956, c1955] 88 p. 20 cm. (World Christian books [7]) [BS617.N5] 55-9117
1. Bible—Reading. I. Title.

OATES, Wayne Edward, 1917- 220
The Bible in pastoral care. Philadelphia, Westminster Press [1953] 127p. 20cm. [BV4012.O2] 52-11246
1. Bible—Use. 2. Theology, Pastoral. I. Title.

OLSSON, Karl A. 220
Meet me on the patio : new relational Bible studies for individuals and groups / Karl A. Olsson. Minneapolis : Augsburg Pub. House, c1977. 127 p. ; 21 cm. [BS605.2.O44] 77-72453 ISBN 0-8066-1550-8 : 6.95. ISBN 0-8066-1590-7 pbk. : 3.50
1. Bible—Study—Text-books. I. Title.

OREGON. State Board of 220
Health.
The Pastoral function and mental health. April 30-May 3, 1962, Menucha Retreat House, Corbett, Oregon. [n. p., 1962?] 62 l. 28 cm. Cover title. "Sponsored by: Oregon State Board of Health, Mental Health Association of Oregon [and] Oregon Council of Churches." Bibliographical footnotes. [BV4012.P32] 65-64271
1. Pastoral psychology—Congresses. I. Title.

PADGETT, Chester John, 1915- 220
Handbook of Christian truth. Placentia, Calif., Printed by Placentia Courier Pub. Co., c1951. ix, 193 p. 23 cm. "Basic books for the Christian's library": p. 61-80. [BS605.P26] 51-26522
1. Bible — Study — Text-books. I. Title.

PARMELEE, Alice 220
A guidebook to the Bible. New York, Harper [1965, c.1948] xi, 331p. map(on lining-papers) 21cm. (Chapel bks., CB15L) Bibl. [BS475.P317] 1.95 pap.,
1. Bible—Introductions. I. Title.

[PASSELECQ, Paul] 220
Guide to the Bible, by the Monks of Maredsous. Translated from the French by Gerda R. Blumenthal, with pref.by John M. T. Barton. London, Sands [1953; label: distributed by W. S. Heinman, New York] 92p. illus. 19cm. Bible--Study--Text-books. [BS606.P383] 53-3189
I. Maredsous (Benedictine abbey) II. Title.

PERRY, Lloyd M 220
How to study your Bible [by] Lloyd M. Perry and Walden Howard. Introd. by Billy Graham. [Westwood, N. J.] Revell [1957] 218p. 21cm. Includes bibliography. [BS600.P45] 57-5408
1. Bible—Study. I. Howard, Walden, joint author. II. Title.

PERRY, Lloyd Merle. 220
How to study your Bible [by] Lloyd M. Perry and Walden Howard. Introd. by Billy Graham. [Wastwood, N. J.] Revell [1957] 218p. 21cm. Includes bibliography. [BS600.P45] 57-5408
1. Bible—Study. I. Howard, Walden, joint author. II. Title.

PERRY, Lloyd Merle. 220
How to study your Bible [by] Lloyd M. Perry and Walden Howard. Introd. by Billy Graham. [Westwood, N. J.] Revell [1957] 218 p. 21 cm. Includes bibliography. [BS600.2.P47] 57-5408
1. Bible—Study. I. Howard, Walden, joint author. II. Title.

POELMAN, Roger, Abbe 1911- 220
How to read the Bible; tr. by a nun of Regina Laudis. New York, All Saints [dist.] Guild [1966, c.1953] 128p. 17cm. (AS247) [BS617.P614] .50 pap.,
1. Bible. — Reading. 2. Bible — Study — Outlines, syllabi, etc. I. Title.

PORLAS, Mary Eve. 220
A manifesto. [1st ed.] New York, Vantage Press [1957] 85p. 21cm. [BS605.P6] 57-59567
1. Bible—Study— Text-books. I. Title.

*PRIME, Derek 220
Tell me about the Bible. Chicago, Moody [1967, c.1965] 62p. illus. 19cm. (Moody arrows: devotional, no. 17) .50 pap.,
1. Bible—Juvenile literature. I. Title.

RECE, Ellis Heber. 220
Reading the Bible, a guide [by] E. H. Rece [and] William A. Beardslee. Englewood Cliffs, N. J., Prentice-Hall, 1956. 188p. illus. 22cm. Previous editions published under title: A handbook for the study of the English Bible. [BS605.R32 1956] 56-8142
1. Bible—Study—Text-books. I. Beardslee, William A., joint author. II. Title.

RECE, Ellis Heber. 220
Reading the Bible, a guide [by] E. H. Rece [and] William A. Beardslee. Englewood Cliffs, N. J., Prentice-Hall, 1956. 188p. illus. 22cm. Previous editions published under title: A handbook for the study of the English Bible. [BS605.R32 1956] 56-8142
1. Bible—Study—Text- books. I. Beardslee, William A., joint author. II. Title.

REID, John Kelman Sutherland. 220
The authority of Scripture; a study of the Reformation and post-Reformation understanding of the Bible. New York, Harper [1957] 286p. 22cm. [BT89.R4 1957] 58-5196
1. Bible—Evidences, authority, etc. I. Title.

RICE, John R., 1895- 220
Dr. Rice, here is my question: Bible answers to 294 important questions in forty years' ministry. Wheaton, Ill., Sword of the Lord Publishers [c1962] 367 p. 21 cm. [BR96.R47] 63-23940
1. Questions and answers — Theology. I. Title.

RINGEL, Erwin. 220
The priest and the unconscious, by Erwin Ringel and Wenzel van Lun. Edigted and translated from the German by Meyrick Booth. Westminster, Md., Newman Press, 1954. 118p. 19cm. Translation of Die Tiefenpsychologie hilft dem Seelsorger. [BV4012.R543] 55-14201
1. Psychology. Pastoral. 2. Psychotherapy. I. Lun, Wenzel van, joint author. II. Title.

ROBERTSON, Edwin Hanton 220
The Bible in the local church. New York, Association [c.1963] 107p. 19cm. (Bible in our time) 63-3782 1.50 pap.,
1. Bible—Use. I. Title.

ROBERTSON, Edwin Hanton. 220
Bible weeks. New York, Association Press [1961] 80p. 19cm. (The Bible in our time) [BS600.2.R58 1961] 61-7466
1. Bible—Study. I. Title.

SCHAFF-HERZOG encyclopedia. 220
The text canon. and principal versions of the Bible. by Elmer E. Flack. Bruce M. Metzger and others. A brief survey of recent research extracted from the Twentieth century encyclopedia of religious knowledge [an extension of The new Schafl-Herzog encyclopedia of religious knowledge] Grand Rapids, Baker Book House, 1956. 63p. 25cm. Includes bibliographies. [BS175.S33] 56-7580
1. Bible—Criticism. Textual. 2. Bible—Canon. 3. Bible—Versions. I. Flack, Elmer Ellsworth, 1894- II. Title.

SCHAFF-HERZOG encyclopedia. 220
The text. canon, and principal versions of the Bible, by Elmer E. Flack, Bruce M. Metzger and others. A brief survey of recent research extracted from the Twentieth century encyclopedia of religious knowledge [an extension of The new Schaff-Herzog encyclopedia of religious kndwledge] Grand Rapids, Baker Book House, 1956. 63p. 25cm. Includes bibliographies. [BS475.S33] 56-7580
1. Bible—Criticism. Textual. 2. Bible—Canon. 3. Bible—Versions. I. Flack, Elmer Ellsworth, 1894- II. Title.

SCHONFIELD, Hugh Joseph, 220
1901-
Readers' A to Z Bible companion [by] Hugh J. Schonfield. New York, New American Library [1967] 191 p. 18 cm. (A Signet reference book) [BS417.S34] 68-1654
1. Bible—Handbooks, manuals, etc. I. Title.

SEMINARS for Clergymen, 220
Cleveland, 1962.
Mental health problems confronting clergymen; proceedings of Seminars for Clergymen presented by the Cleveland Mental Health Association in cooperation with the Academy of Religion and Mental Health, Cleveland Metropolitan Group. Edward N. Hinko, editor. Gwen Converse, editorial assistant. Cleveland, Cleveland Mental Health Association, 1963. viii, 74 p. 28 cm. Organized by the Committee on Assistance to the Clergy, Cleveland Mental Health Association. Includes bibliographies. [BV4012.S4 1962] 63-25376
1. Pastoral psychology. I. Hinko, Edward N., ed. II. Cleveland Mental Health Association. Committee on Assistance to the Clergy. III. Title.

SHARP, Roland Hall. 220
On wings of the Word. [1st ed.] New York, Duell, Sloan and Pearce [1955] 297p. illus. 21cm. [BV2369.S45] 55-6539
1. Bible—Publication and distribution. 2. Missions. I. Title.

SHOTWELL, B. M. 220
Getting better acquainted with your Bible [by] Berenice Myers Shotwell. Kennebunkport, Me., Shadwold Press [1972] x, 566 p. illus. 29 cm. Includes bibliographical references. [BS475.2.S5] 75-173349
1. Bible—Introductions. I. Title.

SMITH, John Holland. 220
Understand the Bible; a guide for Catholics [by] J. Holland Smith. Garden City, N.Y., Doubleday [1968,c.1965] 280p. 18cm. (Image bk., D238) Bibl. [BS587.S56] 1.25 pap.,
1. Bible—Study—Catholic Church. I. Title.

SUGGS, M Jack. 220
The layman reads his Bible. St. Louis, Bethany Press [1957] 96p. illus. 21cm. [BS617.S85] 57-8363
1. Bible—Reading. 2. Bible—Study. I. Title.

SUGGS, M Jack. 220
The layman reads his Bible. St. Louis, Bethany Press [1957] 96 p. illus. 21 cm. [BS617.S85] 57-8363
1. Bible—Reading. 2. Bible—Study. I. Title.

SWAIM, Joseph Carter, 1904- 220
Right and wrong ways to use the Bible. Philadelphia, Westminster Press [1953] 176 p. 21 cm. [BS538.S9] 53-5959
1. Bible—Use. I. Title.

SWIHART, Stephen D. 220
The Victor Bible sourcebook / Stephen D. Swihart. Wheaton, Ill. : Victor Books, c1977. 239 p. : ill. ; 21 cm. [BS417.S86] 76-62741 ISBN 0-88207-802-X pbk. : 3.50
1. Bible—Handbooks, manuals, etc. I. Title.

TAMISIER, Robert, 1907- 220
Discovering the Bible, book by book. Illustrated by Birte Dietz. Translated by K. White. Staten Island, N.Y., Alba House [1970?] 72 p. col. illus. 30 cm. Translation of La Bible au fil de ses livres. [BS475.2.T3413] 72-18658
1. Bible—Introductions. I. Title.

TAYLOR, Charles L. 220
The marked Bible. Mountain View, Calif., Pacific Pr. Pub. [1967, c.1966] 111p. illus. 18cm. Text and t.p. (except pub.'s imprint) in Ukranian in Cyrillic alphabet. .50 pap.,
I. Title.

THEOLOGY, a course for college students. [Syracuse? N.Y., 1952- v. 24 cm. Contents. -- v. 1. Christ as Prophet and King [by] J. J. Fernan. [BX904.T45] 52-4093 220
1. Theology. 2. Catholic Church — Doctrinal and controversial works.

TRENT, Robbie, 1894- 220
How the Bible came to us. Illus. by Don Fields. Nashville, Broadman [1964] 167p. illus., maps. 21cm. 64-20238 2.95
1. Bible—Hist. Juvenile literature. I. Title.

UNGER, Merrill Frederick, 1909- 220
Unger's guide to the Bible [by] Merrill F. Unger. Wheaton, Ill., Tyndale House Publishers [1974] xi, 777 p. illus. 24 cm. "Bible dictionary": p. [423]-620. "Bible concordance": p. [621]-777. [BS475.2.U5] 74-79606 ISBN 0-8423-7790-5 12.95
1. Bible—Introductions. 2. Bible—Dictionaries. 3. Bible—Concordances, English. I. Title. II. Title: Guide to the Bible.

VAWTER, Bruce. 220
The Bible in the church. New York, Sheed and Ward [1959] 95 p. 18 cm. (Caterbury books) [BS587.V35] 59-6396
1. Bible — Study — Catholic Church. I. Title.

WATON, Harry. 220
The key to the Bible. [New York] Spinoza Institute of America [c1952] 96p. 24cm. [BS534.W37] 53-9518
1. Bible—Miscellanea. 2. Symbolism of numbers. I. Title.

WAYNER, Walter. 220
You better know God! [Chicago, 1964] 158 p. illus. 23 cm. [BS612.W3] 64-13087
1. Bible — Examinations, questions, etc. I. Title.

WEED, Michael R. 220
Bible handbook for young learners / Michael and Libby Weed. Austin, Tex. : Sweet Pub. Co., [1974] xiii, 236 p. : col. ill. ; 24 cm. [BS539.W43] 73-91023 ISBN 0-8344-0082-0 : 7.95 pbk. : 5.95
1. Bible—Juvenile literature. I. Weed, Libby, joint author. II. Title.

WELLS, Amos Russel, 1862-1933. 220
The Bible quiz and cross word puzzle book, by Amos R. Wells [and] S.K. Davis. Boston, W.A. Wilde Co. [1951] 142 p. 19 cm. (Blue book series) "The cross word puzzles are taken from The Bible cross word puzzle book; #2, by S. K. Davis, and the quizzes are from the books by Amos R. Wells, Bible sayings, Go till you guess, and Know your Bible." [BS612.W38] 51-7759
1. Bible — Catechisms, question-books. 2. Games. I. Title.

WILLIAMS, Albert Nathaniel, 1914- 220
The book by my side; the story of the sixty-six books of the Bible: their authorship, their historical setting, how they were collected, their content, and their religious meaning. With an introd. by Henry Sloane Coffin. New York, Duell, Sloan and Pearce [1951] 368 p. illus. 22 cm. [BS475.W47] 51-10419
1. Bible—Introductions. I. Title.

WILLIAMS, Ronald Ralph, Bp. of Leicester, 1906- 220
The Bible in worship and ministry; the McMath lectures, with other essays on Biblical themes. London, A. R. Mowbray [dist. Westminister, Md., Canterbury, c.1962] vii, 136p. 19cm. 63-596 2.50
1. Bible—Use. I. Title.

WOLFF, Werner, 1901- 220
Changing concepts of the Bible; a psychological analysis of its words, symbols, and beliefs. [1st ed.] New York, Hermitage House [1951] 463 p. illus. 22 cm. Bibliography: p. 413-434. [BS651.W63] 51-11013
1. Creation. 2. Symbolism. 3. Bible. O.T. — Language, style. I. Title.

YARRINGTON, Roger. j220
The auditorium; world headquarters building of the Reorganized Church of Jesus Christ of Latter Day Saints. Independence, Mo., Herald House [1962] 90 p. illus. 26 cm. [BX8674.Y3] 62-9963
1. Reorganized Church of Jesus Christ of Latter-Day Saints. 2. Independence, Mo. Auditorium. I. Title.

LUCE, Alice Eveline. 220.0
Pictures of Pentecost in the Old Testament. [Springfield, Mo., Gospel Pub. House, c1950] 238 p. 20 cm. [BS478.L82] 52-20934
1. Typology (Theology) I. Title.

KUIST, Howard Tillman, 1895- 220.013
Scripture and the Christian response. Richmond, John Know Press [1964, c1947] 189 p. illus. 21 cm. (ALETHEIA paperbacks) First published in 1947 under title: These words upon thy heart. "Ruskin's Essay on composition (abridged)": p. 161-181. Includes bibliographical references. [BS538.7.K8 1964] 64-16281
1. Bible — Influence. I. Title.

KUIST, Howard Tillman, 1895- 220.013
Scriptures and the Christian response. Richmond, Va., Knox [1964, c.1947] 189p. illus. 21cm. (Aletheia paperaabacks) First pub in 1947 under title: These words upon thy heart. Bibl. 64-16281 1.95 pap.,
1. Bible—Influence. I. Title.

STAUDACHER, Joseph M. 220'.01'4
Lector's guide to Biblical pronunciations / Joseph M. Staudacher. Huntington, Ind. : Our Sunday Visitor, c1975. 72 p. ; 14 cm. [BS435.S7] 75-14609 ISBN 0-87973-773-5
1. Bible—Names—Pronunciation. 2. English language—Pronunciation. I. Title.

ALVES, Colin 220.02
The Scriptures. [New York] Cambridge [c.] 1962. 194p. maps. 20cm. 62-51432 1.75 bds.,
1. Bible—Study—Outlines, syllabi, etc. I. Title.

ALVES, Colin. 220.02
The Scriptures. Cambridge [Eng.] University Press, 1962. 194p. illus. 20cm. [BS591.A4] 62-51432
1. Bible—Study—Outlines, syllabl, etc. I. Title.

DARBY, John Nelson, 1800-1882. 220.02
Synopsis of the books of the Bible. [2d ed.] New York, Loizeaux Bros. [1950] 5 v. 18 cm. Contents.v. 1. Genesis-2 Chronicles. -- v. 2. Extra-Malachi. -- v. 3. Matthew-John. -- v. 4. Acts-Philippians. -- v. 5. Colossians-The Revelation. [BS418.D3 1950] 62-46577
1. Bible — Study — Outlines, syllabi, etc. I. Title.

DEHOFF, George Washington, 1913- 220.02
DeHoff's Bible handbook. Murfreesboro, Tenn., DeHoff Pubns. [1964] 331p. illus., maps. 21cm. 64-6347 price unreported
1. Bibl—Study—Outlines, syllabi, etc. I. Title. II. Title: Bible handbook.

DEMARAY, Donald E 220.02
Cowman handbook of the Bible, by Donald E. Demaray. Los Angeles, Cowman Pub. Co [1964] xvii, 400 p. illus., col. maps. 25 cm. [BS417.D44] 64-8717
1. Bible — Handbooks, manuals, etc. I. Title. II. Title: Handbook of the Bible.

DEMARAY, Donald E. 220.02
Cowman handbook of the Bible. Los Angeles, Cowman Pub. Co., 747 N. Seward St. [c.1964] xvii, 400p. illus., col. maps. 25cm. (Cowan adult educ. ser.) [BS417.D44] 64-8717 8.95 bds.,
1. Bible—Handbooks, manuals, etc. I. Title. II. Title: Handbook of the Bible.

GARRISON, Webb B. 220'.02
Strange facts about the Bible [by] Webb Garrison. Nashville, Abingdon Press [1968] 304 p. 24 cm. Bibliography: p. 289-290. [BS538.G3] 68-17446
1. Bible—Miscellanea. I. Title.

HOYT, Edyth Viola (Sage) Armstrong, 1888- 220.02
Studies in the Bible; a practical collateral volume for the modern reader, to be used in connection with the English Bible. [8th ed. Columbus? Ohio, 1950] 207 p. illus., maps, facsims. 28 cm. "Presented as a workbook in syllabus form ... [with] articles of general interest and special value to the reader, student or teacher of today." Includes bibliographies. [BS591.H7 1950] 51-1231
1. Bible—Study—Outlines, syllabi, etc. I. Title.

LEISHMAN, Thomas Linton, 1900- 220.02
The Bible handbook, by Thomas L. Leishman and Arthur T. Lewis [2d ed.] New York, T. Nelson [1965] 285 p. maps. 23 cm. Bibliography: p. 265-272. [BS417.L4] 65-15403
1. Bible — Handbooks, manuals, etc. I. Lewis, Arthur Thomas, 1891- joint author. II. Title.

LEISHMAN, Thomas Linton, 1900- 220.02
The Bible handbook, by Thomas L. Leishman, Arthur T. Lewis [2d. ed.] New York, Nelson [c.1965] 283p. maps. 23cm. Bibl. [BS417.L4] 65-15403 4.95 bds.,
1. Bible—Handbooks, manuals, etc. I. Lewis, Arthur Thomas, 1891- joint author. II. Title.

NEIL, William, ed. 220.02
The Bible companion; a complete pictorial and reference guide to the people,places, events, background, and faith of the Bible. Contributors: William Barclay [and others] New York, McGraw-Hill, 1960[ ] xii, 468p. Bibl.: p.433-436. illus. (part col.) maps, facsims. 28cm. 59-12350 9.95 half cloth,
1. Bible—Handbooks, manuals, etc. I. Title.

SLEMMING, Charles William 220.02
Bible digest [3v.] London, Bible Testimony Fellowship [dist. Grand Rapids, Mich., Kregel, 1964, c.1960] 3v. (286; 303; 359p.) port. 23cm. Contents.--v.1. Genesis to Job.--v.2. Psalms to Malachi.--v.3. Matthew to Revelation. 64-4476 12.95 set,
1. Bible—Study—Outlines, syllabi, etc. I. Title.

*SLEMMING, Charles William 220.02
Bible digest charts; 62 Bible charts presenting a pictorial outline of each book of the Bible. Grand Rapids, Mich., Kregel [c.1965] lv (unpaged) chiefly illus. 28cm. [BS418.S5] 3.95 pap.,
1. Bible—Study—Outlines, syllabi, etc. I. Title.

SMITH, Wilbur M.. 220.02
The incomparable book: to guide you as you read it through. Grand Rapids, Mich., Baker Bk. [1962, c.1961] 64p. 21cm. .75 pap.,
I. Title.

BELL, Alvin Eugene, 1882- 220'.02'02
The gist of the Bible book by book, by Alvin E. Bell, d. D. New York, George H. Doran company [c1926] xip., i 1., 15-169p. 20cm. [BS418.B4] 27-2263
I. Title.

BLAIR, Edward Payson, 1910- 220'.02'02
Abingdon Bible handbook / Edward P. Blair. Nashville : Abingdon Press, [1975] 511 p., [8] leaves of plates : ill. ; 24 cm. Includes index. Includes bibliographies. [BS475.2.B5] 75-6774 ISBN 0-687-00169-2 : 13.95
1. Bible—Introductions. I. Title.

BROOKS, Keith Leroy, 1888- 220.0202
The summarized Bible; a guide to daily devotional Bible study. Grand Rapids, Mich., Baker Bk., 1965. 297p. 24cm. Reprinted from the orig. printing made in 1919. [BS418.B77] 66-821 3.95
1. Bible — Study — Outlines, syllabi. etc. I. Title.

EERDMANS' handbook to the Bible. Edited by David Alexander [and] Pat Alexander. Consulting editors: David Field [and others] [1st ed.] Grand Rapids, Mich., Eerdmans [1973] 680 p. illus. 23 cm. [BS417.E35 1973] 73-7638 ISBN 0-8028-3436-1 12.95 220'.02'02
1. Bible—Handbooks, manuals, etc. I. Alexander, David, 1937- ed. II. Alexander, Pat, 1937- ed. III. Title: Handbook to the Bible.

JENSEN, Irving Lester. 220'.02'02
Jensen Bible study charts / by Irving L. Jensen. Chicago : Moody Press, c1976. 3 v. : ill. ; 28 cm. Contents.Contents.—v. 1. General survey.—v. 2. Old. Testament.—v. 3. New Testament. [BS592.J44] 75-42138 ISBN 0-8024-4298-6 (v. 2) : 9.95
1. Bible.—Study—Outlines, syllabi, etc. I. Title. II. Title: Bible study charts.

*JONES, Irene 220.0202
Know your scriptures; a reading program. Independence, Mo., Herald [1966] 107p. 20cm. 1.50 pap.,
I. Title.

MCBRIDE, Alfred. 220'.02'02
A short course on the Bible. Milwaukee, Bruce Pub. Co. [1968] xi, 140 p. 22 cm. [BS592.M26] 68-20896
1. Bible—Study—Outlines, syllabi, etc. I. Title.

MARSH, Frederick Edward, 1858-1919. 220'.02'02
1000 Bible study outlines. Foreword by F. B. Meyer. [1st American ed.] Grand Rapids, Kregel Publications [1970] xx, 473 p. 23 cm. [BS592.M37 1970] 75-125115 5.95
1. Bible—Study—Outlines, syllabi, etc. I. Title.

SCHAEFFER, Francis August. 220'.02'02
Basic Bible studies, by Francis A. Schaeffer. Wheaton, Ill., Tyndale House Publishers [1972] 86 p. 19 cm. [BS605.2.S3] 72-81228 ISBN 0-8423-0103-8 (pbk)
1. Bible—Study—Text-books. I. Title.

SLEMMING, Charles William. 220'.02'02
The Bible digest, by Charles W. Slemming. [1st American ed.] Grand Rapids, Kregel Publications [1968, c1960] 905 p. 22 cm. [BS418.S5 1968] 68-27671 9.95
1. Bible—Study—Outlines, syllabi, etc. I. Title.

WOOD, Fred M. 220'.02'02
The instant Bible; an easy-to-read summary in layman's language of the greatest book ever written. by Fred M. Wood. Grand Rapids. Zondervan [1967, c.1966] 128p. 18cm. [BS418.W6] 67-17243 1.00 pap.,
1. Bible—Study—Outlines, syllabi;tct. I. Bible. English. Paraphrases. 1967. II. Title.

SLEMMING, Charles William. 220.0222
Bible digest charts; 62 Bible charts presenting a pictorial outline of each book of the Bible, by Charles W. Slemming. Grand Rapids, Kregel Publications [1965] 1 v. (unpaged) illus. 28 cm. [BS418] 64-17168
1. Bible — Study — Outlines, syllabi, etc. I. Title.

†CONN, Charles Paul. 220'.02'455
The relevant record / Charles Paul Conn, Charles W. Conn. Cleveland, Tenn. : Pathway Press, c1976. 143 p. : ill. ; 18 cm. (Making life count new life series) Discusses the Bible and its importance in our daily lives. Bibliography: p. 143. [BS539.C66] 76-2969 ISBN 0-87148-732-2 pbk. : 1.19
1. Bible—Juvenile literature. I. Conn, Charles W., joint author. II. Title.

ENCYCLOPEDIC dictionary of the Bible. A translation and adaptation of A. van den Born's Bijbels woordenboek. by Louis F. Hartmen. 2d rev. ed., 1954-1957. New York, McGraw-Hill, 1963. xv p. 2634 colummns illus., plates, maps (1 fold.) facsims 25 cm. Includes bibliographical references. [BS440.B523] 63-9699 220.03
1. Bible—Dictionaries. I. Born, Adrianus van den, 1904- II. Hartman, Louis Francis, 1901- ed. and tr.

MCARTHUR, Harvey K., ed. 220.04
New Testament sidelight. essays in honor of Alexander Converse Purdy. . . Hartford 5, Conn., 55 Elizabeth St. Hartford Seminary Foundation, [c.]1960 vii, 135p. bibl. p.129-35 and bibl. notes. port. 21cm. 60-2687 4.25
1. Purdy, Alexander Converse, 1890- 2. Bible. N. T.—Addresses, essays, lectures. I. Title.

MCARTHUR, Harvey K ed. 220.04
New Testament sidelights; essays in honor of Alexander Converse Purdy ... Hartford, Hartford Seminary Foundation Press, 1960. vii, 135p. port. 21cm. Includes bibliographies. [BS2280.M3] 60-2687
1. Purdy, Alexander Converse, 1890- 2. Bible. N. T.—Addresses, essays, lectures. I. Title.
Contents omitted.

MYERS, Jacob Martin, ed. 220.04
Biblical studies in memory of H. C. Alleman. Edited by J. M. Myers, O. Reimherr, H. N. Bream. Locust Valley, N.Y., J. J. Augustin, 1960[ ] 224p. (Gettysburg theological studies) Bibl. footnotes port. 60-13573 6.00
1. Alleman, Herbert Christian, 1868-1953. 2. Bible-Addresses, essays, lectures. I. Title. II. Series.

ST. John's University, Collegeville, Minn. 220'.05
Library index to Biblical journals. Edited by Thomas Peter Wahl. Established by Raymond Breun. Collegeville, Minn., St. John's University Press, 1971. 1 v. (unpaged) 24 cm. "July 1970. Fifth edition." [Z7770.S33] 73-27544
1. Bible—Periodicals—Indexes. I. Wahl, Thomas Peter, ed. II. Title.

GUY, Harold A. 220.06
The Synoptic Gospels [dist.] New York, St. Martin's Press [c.] 1960 [i.e., 1961] 183 p. illus. Bibl. 61-870 3.50
1. Bible. N.T. Gospels—Criticism, interpretation, etc. I. Title.

ADENEY, Carol, comp. 220'.07
This morning with God; a daily devotional guide for your quiet time. Chicago, Inter-varsity Press [1968- v. 21 cm. Studies originally published in His magazine. Vols. 2- have imprint: Downers Grove, Ill., Inter-Varsity Press. [BS592.A3] 68-28080 ISBN 0-87784-675-8 (v. 4) 2.50 (v. 4)
1. Bible—Study—Outlines, syllabi, etc. I. His. II. Title.

*ALVES, Colin 220.07
The Scriptures; a supplement for teachers [New York] Cambridge [c.1964] 77p. 19cm. cover title. 1.50 pap.,
I. Title.

ASHCROFT, J Robert. 220.07
Ways of understanding God's Word. Springfield, Mo., Gospel Pub. House [c1960] 103p. 20cm. [BS600.2.A8] 61-22599
1. Bible—Study. I. Title.

†BAKER, Wesley C. 220'.07
You belong in the Bible! : Introducing the Wayne Biblical experience / by Wesley C. Baker. Corte Madera, Calif. : Omega Books, c1976. 96 p. ; 22 cm. [BS600.2.B25] 76-42600 ISBN 0-89353-020-4 pbk. : 3.95
1. Bible—Study. I. Title.

BAUGHMAN, Ray E. 220'.07
Creative Bible study methods : visualized for personal and group study / by Ray E. Baughman ; illustrated by Larinda Skaggs. Chicago : Moody Press, c1976. 128 p. : ill. ; 22 cm. Bibliography: p. 127-128. [BS600.B34] 76-46625 ISBN 0-8024-1635-7 pbk. : 2.50
1. Bible—Study. I. Title.

BEERS, Victor Gilbert, 220*.07
1928-
The ABQ book, by V. Gilbert Beers. Illustrated by Alla Skuba. Chicago, Moody Press [1972] [44] p. col. illus. 20 x 26 cm. An alphabetically arranged Bible quiz with more than one hundred questions about such topics as Abraham, bulrushes, Calvary, and vineyards. Answers are at the back. [BS539.B44] 72-88039 ISBN 0-8024-0134-1
1. Bible—Juvenile literature. I. Skuba, Alla, illus. II. Title.

BEERS, Victor Gilbert, 220'.07
1928-
The book of life / written and edited by V. Gilbert Beers ; illustrated by David Chenoweth. [Grand Rapids : Zondervan Corp.] , c1973. 384 p. : ill. ; 24 cm. (Bible for daily living ; v. 10) [BS605.2.B43] 75-319614
1. Bible—Study—Text-books. I. Title.

BEERS, Victor Gilbert, 220'.07
1928-
God is my helper, by V. Gilbert Beers. Illustrated by Robert Boehmer. Grand Rapids, Zondervan Pub. House [1973] [96] p. col. illus. 23 cm. (His Learning to read from the Bible series) Includes twelve Bible stories and study questions and suggested activities emphasizing their application to modern life. [BS551.2.B435] 72-85561 3.95
1. Bible stories, English. I. Boehmer, Robert, illus. II. Title.

BEGUIN, Olivier, comp. 220.07
Roman Catholicism and the Bible. New York, Association Press [1963] 95 p. 20 cm. [BS587.B4] 63-20198
1. Bible—Study—Catholic Church. 2. Bible—Publication and distribution. I. Title.

BIBLE characters and 220'.07
doctrines. [1st U.S.A. ed.] Grand*1Rapids, [Eerdmans [1972- v. 18 cm. [BS605.2B47] 72-189855 ISBN 0-8028-1460-3 1.50 (pbk.)
1. Bible—study—Text-books. I. Blaiklock, E. M. II. Wright, John Stafford. III. Grogan, Geoffrey.

**BIBLE (The): book of* 220.07
faith, by Theological professors of the American Lutheran Church. Minneapolis, Agsburg [c.1964] 175p. diagr. 22cm. Bibl. pap., 1.75; 2pt. instructor's gd., pap., set, 1.50

BINKLEY, Olin Trivette, 220'.07
1908-
How to study the Bible [by] Olin T. Binkley. Mavis Allen, editor. Nashville, Convention Press [1969] x, 178 p. illus. 21 cm. (Bible survey series, v. 2) "Text for course 3202 of subject area Biblical revelation of the Christian development series, New church study course." Includes bibliographies. [BS600.2.B5] 69-18733
1. Bible—Study. I. Title. II. Series.

BISHOP, Robert L. 220.07
A book study of the Bible: student's book. Nashville, Broadman [1964] 96p. illus. (pt. col.) 22cm. (Weekday Bible study ser.) 64-22299 1.00; 2.75 teacher's bk.,
1. Bible—Study—Text-books. I. Title.

BJERKE, Ward. 220'.07
Through the Bible day by day; a simplified method for reading and understanding the Scriptures. Old Tappan, N.J., Revell [1973] 127 p. 18 cm. [BS617.B53] 73-1700 ISBN 0-8007-0586-6 Pbk.0.95
1. Bible—Reading. I. Title.

BROOKS, D. P. 220'.07
The Bible; how to understand and teach it [by] D. P. Brooks. Nashville, Broadman Press [1969] 128 p. 20 cm. [BS600.2.B74] 69-14365
1. Bible—Study. I. Title.

BROWN, Velma Darbo. 220'.07
Preparing for effective Bible teaching [by] Velma Darbo Brown & H. C. Brown, Jr. Nashville, Broadman Press [1971] 77 p. 20 cm. [BS600.2.B753] 76-157404 ISBN 0-8054-3417-8
1. Bible—Study. I. Brown, Henry Clifton, joint author. II. Title.

BROWN, William John, 220'.07
1924-
Practical help for teaching the Bible [by] William J. Brown. Nashville, Broadman Press [1971] 55 p. 19 cm. [BS600.2.B755] 71-146275 ISBN 0-8054-3416-X
1. Bible—Study. I. Title.

BRUEGGEMANN, Walter. 220'.07
Confronting the Bible; a resource and discussion book for youth. Boston, United Church Press [1968] 75 p. illus. 22 cm. (Confirmation education series) "Part of the United Church curriculum, prepared and published by the Division of Christian Education and the Division of Publication of the United Church Board for Homeland Ministries." Bibliography: p. 73-75. [BS600.2.B77] 68-10037
1. Bible—Study—Text-books. 2. Christian education—Text-books for young people—United Church of Christ. I. United Church Board for Homeland Ministries. Division of Christian Education. II. United Church Board for Homeland Ministries. Division of Publication. III. Title.

CALDWELL, Irene Catherine 220'.07
(Smith) 1919-
Teaching that makes a difference. [Rev. ed.] Anderson, Ind., Warner Press [1962] 95p. illus. 21cm. [BV1534.C24 1962] 62-13334
1. Religious education—Teaching methods. I. Title.

CARLSON, G. Raymond. 220'.07
Preparing to teach God's word / G. Raymond Carlson. Springfield, Mo. : Gospel Pub. House, [1975] 128 p. ; 19 cm. [BS600.2.C36] 75-5221 pbk. : 1.25
1. Bible—Study. I. Title.

CHIFFLOT, Th. G. 220'.07
Water in the wilderness, understanding the Bible [by] T. G. Chifflot. Tr. by Luke O'Neill. [New York] Herder & Herder [1967] 141p. [BS617.C5313] 67-13298
I. Title.

CHIFFLOT, Th. G. 220'.07
Water in the wilderness: understanding the Bible [by]T. G. Chifflot. Translated by Luke O'Neill. [New York] Herder and Herder [1967] 141 p. 21 cm. Translation of Comprendre in Bible. [BS617.C5313] 67-13298
1. Bible — Reading. I. Title.

CHRISTENSEN, Winnie. 220'.07
Caught with my mouth open. Wheaton, Ill., H. Shaw [1969] 143 p. illus. 18 cm. Bibliographical footnotes. [BS603.C47] 77-86529
1. Bible—Study. I. Title.

CULLEY, Iris V 220.07
Imparting the Word; the Bible in Christian education. Philadelphia, Westminister Press [1962] 174 p. 21 cm. Includes bibliographies. [BS600.2.C8] 62-16759
1. Bible — Study. I. Title.

CULLY, Iris V. 220.07
Imparting the Word; the Bible in Christian education. Philadelphia, Westminster [1963, c.1962] 174p. 21cm. Bibl. 62-16759 3.95
1. Bible—Study. I. Title.

CULLY, Kendig Brubaker. 220.07
Exploring the Bible; a survey of the Holy Scriptures. [1st ed.] New York, Morehouse-Barlow [1963, c1960] 189 p. col. maps. 21 cm. (Episcopal Church fellowship series, course 9 reader) [BS600.2.C78] 60-10850
1. Bible — Study. I. Title. II. Series.

DALPADADO, J. Kingsley, 220'.07
1922-
Reading the Bible; a guide to the word of God for everyone [by] J. Kingsley Dalpadado. [Boston] St. Paul Editions [1973] 330 p. 22 cm. Bibliography: p. 285-298. [BS592.D33] 73-86208 6.00
1. Bible—Study—Outlines, syllabi, etc. I. Title.

DANKER, Frederick W. 220.07
Multipurpose tools for Bible study. St. Louis, Concordia Pub. House, [c.] 1960. xviii, 289p. (bibl. notes and bibl. footnotes) 22cm. 59-15554 3.75
1. Bible—Handbooks, manuals, etc. 2. Bible—Study—Bibl. I. Title.

DANNEMILLER, Lawrence 220.07
Reading the Word of God. Baltimore, Helicon Press, [c.]1960. xiv, 201p. 23cm. 60-9792 4.50
1. Bible—Study—Text-books. I. Title.

DERHAM, Arthur Morgan 220.07
A Christian's guide to Bible study [Westwood, N.J.] Revell [1964, c.1963] 63p. 18cm. Bibl. 64-643 .75 pap.,
1. Bible—Study. I. Title.

DRAKEFORD, John W. 220'.07
Experiential Bible study [by] John W. Drakeford. Nashville, Broadman Press [1974] 138 p. 20 cm. [BS600.2.D7] 74-80338 ISBN 0-8054-1930-6 1.95 (pbk.)
1. Bible—Study. I. Title.

EASTMAN, Frances W. 220.07
God speaks through the Bible. Philadelphia, United Church [1964] 124p. illus. 26cm. Bibl. 64-14495 2.25
1. Bible—Study—Text-books. I. Title.

*EVANS, B. Hoyt 220.07
Youth programs from the Bible. Grand Rapids, Mich., Baker Bk. [1966] 119p. 20cm. (Paperback program ser.) Cover title: 37 youth programs from the Bible. 1.50 pap.,
I. Title.

EYNON, Dana. 220'.07
Through the Bible in a year / prepared by Dana Eynon. Teacher [ed.]. Cincinnati : Standard Pub. Co., [1975] 112, 64 p. : ill. ; 28 cm. "Pupil's workbook" (64 p. at end) has special t.p. [BS592.E93 1975] 74-27239 ISBN 0-87239-028-4 teacher's manual : 4.95 ISBN 0-87239-011-X work book : 1.50
1. Bible—Study—Outlines, syllabi, etc. 2. Bible—Study—Text-books. I. Title.

THE Family Bible study 220'.07
book / Betsey Scanlan, editor. Old Tappan, N.J. : F. H. Revell Co., [1975] 255 p. ; 24 cm. Includes indexes. Bibliography: p. 241-242. [BS605.2.F35] 75-5680 ISBN 0-8007-0730-3 : 6.95
1. Bible—Study—Text-books. I. Scanlan, Betsey.

FEUCHT, Oscar E. 220'.07
Learning to use your Bible [by] Oscar E. Feucht. Saint Louis, Concordia Pub. House [1969] 170 p. 21 cm. (A Basic Christian library) Includes bibliographies. [BS417.F48] 77-76228
1. Bible—Handbooks, manuals, etc. 2. Bible—Study. I. Title.

*FISCHER, Howard A. 220.07
Bible basketball; Bible questions and answers graded for basketball competition. Chicago, Moody [1966] 64p. 22cm. .60 pap.,
I. Title.

*FISCHER, Howard A. 220.07
Bible hockey; Bible questions and answers graded for hockey competition. Chicago, Moody [1968] 64p. 22cm. .60 pap.,
I. Title.

FITGERALD, Robert David, 220'.07
1902-
Of some country; 27 poems. With drawings by Sister Mary Corita. [Austin] University of Texas [c1963] 46 p. illus. 23 cm. (Tower series, no. 4) [PR6011.I85O4] 63-63491
I. Title. II. Series.

FORD, Josephine 220'.07
Massyngberde.
Wellsprings of Scripture, by J. Massingberd Ford. New York, Sheed and Ward [1968] xiii, 238 p. 22 cm. Includes bibliographical references. [BS592.F6] 68-13854
1. Bible—Study—Outlines, syllabi, etc. I. Title.

FOSDICK, Harry Emerson, 220.07
1878-
The modern use of the Bible. New York, Macmillan, 1961 [c.1924, 1952] 291p. (Macmillan paperback, 56) Bibl. 1.95 pap.,
1. Bible—Criticism, interpretation, etc. I. Title.

FURNISH, Dorothy Jean, 220'.07
1921-
Exploring the Bible with children / Dorothy Jean Furnish. Nashville : Abingdon Press, [1975] 174 p. ; 20 cm. Bibliography: p. 172-174. [BS600.2.F87] 74-34486 ISBN 0-687-12426-3 pbk. : 3.95
1. Bible—Study. 2. Children—Religious life. I. Title.

GARRISON, Webb B. 220.07
A guide to reading the entire Bible in one year. Indianapolis, Bobbs-Merrill [1963] 320 p. 22 cm. [BS617.G35] 63-18990
1. Bible — Reading. I. Title.

GARRISON, Webb B. 220.07
A guide to reading the entire Bible in one year. Indianapolis, Bobbs [c.1961-1963] 320p. 22cm. 63-18990 3.95 bds.,
1. Bible—Reading. I. Title.

†GARVIN, Mary H. 220'.07
Bible study can be exciting! : A handbook for small-group Bible study / by Mary H. Garvin ; foreword by Rosalind Rinker. Grand Rapids : Zondervan Pub. House, c1976. 141, [2] p. ; 20 cm. Bibliography: p. 141-[143] [BS600.2.G37] 75-43816 pbk. : 2.95
1. Bible—Study. I. Title.

GETTYS, Joseph Miller, 220.07
1907-
How to teach the Bible. [Rev. ed.] Richmond, Va., John Knox Press [c.1949, 1961] 112p. Bibl. 61-13517 2.00 pap.,
1. Bible—Study. I. Title.

**GIST of the lesson* 220.07
(The); a concise exposition of the International sunday school lessons for 1966. Originated by R. A. Torrey. Ed. by Donald T. Kaufman. Westwood, N.J., Revell [c.1965] 127p. 18cm. .95 pap.,

GRAYUM, H. Frank. 220'.07
The Bible: God's word to man. H. Frank Grayum, editor. Nashville, Convention Press [1970] 73 p. 21 cm. Includes bibliographies. [BS605.2.G73] 74-120191
1. Bible—Study—Text-books. I. Title.

*GUTZKE, Manford George. 220'.07
A look at The Book a discussion guide to understanding the Bible [by] Manford G. Gutzke. Grand Rapids, Baker Book House [1975 c1969] 148 p. 18 cm. (Contemporary Discussion Series) [BS600.2] 69-16632 ISBN 0-8010-3693-3 1.65 (pbk.)
1. Bible—Study. I. Title.

HALDEMAN, Isaac Massey, 220.07
1845-1933
How to study the Bible, the Second Coming, and other expositions. Grand Rapids, Mich., Baker Bk., 1963. 502p. 20cm. 63-13804 3.95
1. Bible—Study. 2. Bible—Criticism, interpretation, etc. 3. Second Advent. I. Title.

HATCH, Mildred M 220.07
The Bible and your child, by Mildred M. Hatch. Anderson, Ind., Warner Press [1964] 64 p. 21 cm. Bibliography: p. vi. [BS600.2.H36] 64-22159
1. Bible — Study. 2. Religious eduction of children. I. Title.

HATCH, Mildred M. 220.07
The Bible and your child. Anderson, Ind., Warner [c.1964] 64p. 21cm. Bibl. 64-22159 1.00 pap.,
1. Bible—Study. 2. Religious education of children. I. Title.

HEIKKINEN, Jacob W. 220.07
Helping children know the Bible, by JacOb W. New York, Scholastic Bk. Servs. [c.1955, 1962] Philadelphia, Lutheran Church Pr. [c.1962] 80p. 176p. illus. (pt. col.) 21cm. (Leadership educ. ser.) Heikkinen, Barbara M. Luebbe. John Gretzer, artist. Philip R. Hoh, ed. 62-3296 1.50
1. Bible—Study. I. Luebbe, Barbara M., joint author. II. Title.

HEIKKINEN, Jacob W. 220.07
Helping youth and adults know the Bible [Pupil's bk.] by Jacob W. Heikkinen, N. Leroy Norquist. Philip R. Hoh, ed. Philadelphia, Lutheran Church Pr. [c.1962] 176p. illus. 21cm. (Leadership educ. ser.) Bibl. 62-2671 1.50
1. Bible—Study—Text-books. I. Norquist, N. Leroy. II. Title.

HEIKKINEN, Jacob W 220.07
Helping youth and edults know the Bible, by Jacob W. Heikkinen and N. Leroy Norquist. Philip R. Hoh, editor. Philadelphia, Lutheran Church Press [1962] Philadelphia, Lutheran Church Press [1962] 176p. illus. 21cm. 48p. 21cm. (Leadership education series) Includesbibliography. [BS605.2.H4] 62-2671
1. Bible—Study—Text-books. I. Norquist, N. Leroy. II. Title. III. Title: Teacher's guide.

*HENDRIKSEN, William. 220.'07
Survey of the Bible : a treasury of Bible information / William Hendriksen. 4th rev. ed. Grand Rapids : Baker Book House, 1976. 497p. : ill. ; 24 cm. Includes bibliographical references and index. [BS600.2] 76-507 ISBN 0-8010-4119-8 : 11.95
1. Bible-Study. I. Title.

HOW to understand the 220'.07
Bible. [By] Ralph Herring, Frank Stagg, and others. Nashville, Broadman Press [1974] 194 p. 21 cm. Bibliography: p. 189-192. [BS475.2.H68] 74-75674 ISBN 0-8054-1127-5 5.95
1. Bible—Introductions. I. Herring, Ralph A.

HUNT, Gladys M. 220'.07
It's alive; the dynamics of small group Bible study, by Gladys Hunt. Wheaton, Ill., H. Shaw [1971] 118 p. illus. 18 cm. [BS600.2.H85] 73-169168
1. Bible—Study. I. Title.

INTRODUCTION to college 220.07
theology through sacred Scripture, a course designed for college students. Notre Dame, Ind., Univ. of Notre Dame Pr. [c.1963] 158p. 23cm. Fruit of discussions by a comm. invited by Rev. Robert S. Pelton, C. S. C., head of the

Dept. of Theology at the Univ. of Notre Dame. Bibl. 63-22222 1.75 pap.,
1. Bible—Study—Outlines, syllabi, etc. 2. Bible—Theology—Study and teaching. I. Notre Dame, Ind. University. Dept. of Theology.

JENSEN, Irving Lester. 220.07
Independent Bible study; using the analytical chart and the inductive method. Chicago, Moody Press [1963] 188 p. illus. 22 cm. [BS600.2.J4] 63-12114
1. Bible — Study. I. Title.

JENSEN IRVING LESTER 220.07
Independent Bible study; using the analytical chart and the inductive method. Chicago, Moody [c.1963] 188p. illus. 22cm. Bibl. 63-12114 3.50
1. Bible—Study. I. Title.

JOB, John B. 220'.07
How to study the Bible; an introduction to methods of Bible study. Edited by John B. Job. Foreword by Paul E. Little. Downers Grove, Ill., InterVarsity Press [1973, c1972] 110 p. 21 cm. [BS600.2.J55 1973] 73-75895 ISBN 0-87784-480-1 1.95 (pbk.)
1. Bible—Study. I. Title.

*KRUTZA, William J. 220'.07
The second coming Bible, study guide no. 1 [by] William J. Krutza. Grand Rapids, Mich., Baker Book House [1973] 96 p. 18 cm. (Contemporary discussion series.) [BS600.2] ISBN 0-8010-5329-3 0.95 (pbk.)
1. Bible—Study. I. Title.

LAHAYE, Tim F. 220'.07
How to study the Bible for yourself / Tim LaHaye. Irvine, Calif. : Harvest House Publishers, c1976. 145 p. : ill. ; 21 cm. [BS600.2.L33] 76-5568 ISBN 0-89081-021-4 pbk. : 2.95
1. Bible—Study.

LAYMON, Charles M. 220.07
The use of the Bible in teaching youth. Nashville, Abingdon [1963, c.1962] 175p. maps. 19cm. 1.50 pap.,
I. Title.

LINCOLN, William C., 220'.07
1926-
Personal Bible study / William C. Lincoln. Minneapolis : Bethany Fellowship, [1975] 153 p. ; 21 cm. Bibliography: p. [151]-153. [BS600.2.L44] 75-2345 ISBN 0-87123-458-0 : 2.95
1. Bible—Study. I. Title.

LINK, John R. 220'.07
Help in understanding the Bible [by] John R. Link. Valley Forge [Pa.] Judson Press [1974] 125 p. 22 cm. Bibliography: p. 119-124. [BS600.2.L45] 74-2953 ISBN 0-8170-0644-3
1. Bible—Study. I. Title.

LINK, John R 220.07
You can understand the Bible [by] John R. Link. Valley Forge [Pa.] Judson Press [1966] 224 p. 21 cm. Bibliography: p. 215-219. [BS600.2.L47] 66-12541
1. Bible — Study. I. Title.

LINK, John R. 220.07
You can understand the Bible. Valley Forge [Pa.] Judson [c.1966] 224p. 21cm. Bibl. [BS600.2.L47] 66-12541 4.75
1. Bible — Study. I. Title.

LITTLE, Sara. 220.07
The role of the Bible in contemporary Christian education. Richmond, John Knox Press [1961] 190 p. 21 cm. Based on thesis, Yale University. [BS600.2L5] 61-7497
1. Bible—Study. 2. Religious education. I. Title.

LOCKYER, Herbert. 220'.07
All about Bible study / Herbert Lockyer. Grand Rapids : Zondervan Pub. House, c1977. 150 p. ; 25 cm. Includes indexes. [BS600.2.L56] 77-24019 ISBN 0-310-28160-1 : 6.95
1. Bible—Study. I. Title.

LUCAS, Jerry. 220'.07
Remember the word / Jerry Lucas. Los Angeles : Acton House, c1975- v. ; 24 cm. Contents.Contents.—v. 1. The Gospels. [BS617.7.L8] 75-24967
1. Bible—Memorizing. I. Title.

MCELRATH, William N. 220'.07
Bible guidebook [by] William N. McElrath. Illustrated by Don Fields. Nashville, Broadman Press [1972] 144 p. illus. 24 cm. [BS475.2.M24] 72-79174 ISBN 0-8054-4410-6 4.50
1. Bible—Introductions. I. Fields, Don, illus. II. Title.

*MARTIN, Alfred. 220'.07
Not my own; total commitment in stewardship. Chicago, Moody [1968] 126p. 18 cm. (MP33-528) .50 pap.,
I. Title.

MIDWESTERN Institute of 220'.07
Pastoral Theology, 6th, Sacred Heart Seminary, Detroit, 1966.
The church teaching through Scripture. [Proceedings of the] sixth annual institute, August 22-25, 1966. Detroit, 1966 [c1967] 146 p. 22 cm. [BS587.M5 1966] 67-22800
1. Bible—Study—Catholic Church. I. Detroit. Sacred Heart Seminary. II. Title.

MILLER, Donald Eugene. 220'.07
Using Biblical simulations [by] Donald E. Miller, Graydon F. Snyder [and] Robert W. Neff. Valley Forge [Pa.] Judson Press [1973] 224 p. 27 cm. Instructions for the re-enactment of events from the Bible with a guide for subsequent discussion by the participants. [BV1534.4.M55] 72-9569 ISBN 0-8170-0580-3 4.95
1. Bible plays. 2. Drama in religious education. I. Snyder, Graydon F., joint author. II. Neff, Robert W., joint author. III. Title.

*MORTON, Mildred B. 220'.07
A lamp to our feet. New York, Vantage [1968] 86p. 21cm. 2.95 bds.,
1. Bible—Study and teaching—Methodist authors. I. Title.

MURCH, James DeForest, 220'.07
1892-
The sword and the trowel; exile and restoration. Glendale, Calif., Regal Books [1968] 141, [3] p. map. 18 cm. Bibliography: p. [143]-[144] [BS592.M8] 68-21025
1. Bible—Study—Outlines, syllabi, etc. I. Title.

MURRAY, Albert Victor, 220.07
1890-
Teaching the Bible, especially in secondary schools. Cambridge [Eng.] University Press, 1955. 231p. illus. 22cm. [BS600.M8] 55-13765
1. Bible—Study. I. Title.

*NORWOOD, H. Dorothy. 220'07
The Bible tells it like it is; the imminent fifth universal empire. [First ed.] New York, Vantage [1972] 153 p. 21 cm. [BS600] ISBN 0-533-00369-5 4.95
1. Bible—Study. I. Title.

NURSES Christian 220'.07
Fellowship.
Standing orders; Bible studies prepared by staff members. [Rev. ed.] Chicago, Inter-varsity Press [1969] 51 p. 18 cm. [BS605.2.N8 1969] 74-76881
1. Bible—Study—Text-books. I. Title.

OAKES, John P. 220.07
Exploring your Bible; a comprehensive and useful handbook, a complete study-method manual. Grand Rapids, Mich., Zondervan Pub. House [c.1960] 155p. Includes bibliography. illus. 23cm. 60-1441 2.95
1. Bible—Study. I. Title.

OAKES, John P 220.07
Exploring your Bible; a comprehensive and useful handbook, a complete study-method manual. Grand Rapids, Zondervan Pub. House [1960] 155p. illus. 23cm. Includes bibliography. [BS600.2.O2] 60-1441
1. Bible—Study. I. Title.

OLSSON, Karl A. 220'.07
Find your self in the Bible; a guide to relational Bible study for small groups [by] Karl A. Olsson. Minneapolis, Augsburg Pub. House [1974] 127 p. 20 cm. [BS605.2.O43] 73-88605 ISBN 0-8066-1408-0 2.95 (pbk.)
1. Bible Study Text books. I. Title.

*PALMER, W. Robert 220.07
How to understand the Bible; study course for youth and adults. Cincinnati, Ohio, 45231, Standard Pub., 8121 Hamilton Av. [c.1965] 112p. 22cm. (2592) 1.25 pap.,
1. Bible — Study and teaching. I. Title.

PERRY, Lloyd Merle. 220'.07
How to search the scriptures, by Lloyd M. Perry and Robert D. Culver. Foreword by Harry L. Evans. Grand Rapids, Baker Book House [1967] 276 p. 20 cm. Bibliography: p. 272-276. [BS600.2.P46] 67-18190
1. Bible—Study. I. Culver, Robert D., joint author. II. Title.

PUTNAM, Robert C. 220.07
Ten Bible lessons. New York, Pageant [c.1963] 131p. 23cm. 3.00, plastic bdg. pap.,
I. Title.

RAHTJEN, Bruce D. 220'.07
Biblical truth and modern man [by] Bruce D. Rahtjen. Nashville, Abingdon Press [1968] 143 p. 19 cm. Bibliography: p. 133-140. [BS600.2.R3] 68-27625 1.75
1. Bible—Study. I. Title.

RAMSEY, George Henry, 220'.07
1922-
Tools for Bible study (and how to use them) by George H. Ramsey, Sr. Anderson, Ind., Warner Press [1971] 112 p. 19 cm. [BS600.2.R34] 71-150371 ISBN 0-87162-120-7
1. Bible—Study. I. Title.

RECE, Ellis Heber. 220.07
Reading the Bible, a guide [by] E. H. Race [and] William A. Beardslee. 2d ed. Englewood Cliffs, N.J., Prentice-Hall [1964] ix, 198 p. maps. 22 cm. First published in 1941 under title: A handbook for the study of the English Bible. Bibliography: p. 190-196. [BS605.R32] 64-10253
1. Bible — Study — Text-books. I. Beardslee, William A., joint author. II. Title.

RECE, Ellis Heber 220.07
Reading the Bible, a guide [by] E. H. Rece, William A. Beardslee. 2d ed. Englewood Cliffs, N. J., Prentice [c.1964] ix, 198p. maps. 22cm. First pub. in 1941 under title: A handbook for the study of the English Bible. Bibl. 64-10253 3.75 pap.,
1. Bible—Study—Text-books. I. Beardslee, William A., jointauthor. II. Title.

RICHARDS, Lawrence O. 220'.07
Creative Bible study; a handbook for small group, family, and personal Bible study with adventure questions for discussion, by Lawrence O. Richards. Grand Rapids, Zondervan Pub. House [1971] 215 p. illus. 22 cm. Includes bibliographical references. [BS600.2.R52] 78-156244 4.95
1. Bible—Study. I. Title.

RICHARDS, Lawrence O. 220'.07
Creative Bible teaching / Lawrence O. Richards. Chicago : Moody Press, 1973, c1970. 288 p. : ill. ; 24 cm. Bibliography: p. 286-288. [BS600.2.R53 1973] 74-104830 ISBN 0-8024-1640-3 : 4.95
1. Bible—Study. I. Title.

ROBERTSON, Edwin Hanton 220.07
Take and read; a guide to group Bible study. Richmond, Va., John Knox Press [1961] 128p. Bibl. 61-6688 1.75 bds.,
1. Bible—Study. I. Title. II. Title: Group Bible study.

ROBINSON, Russell D. 220'.07
Teaching the Scriptures; a syllabus for Bible study for Sunday school teachers and Bible students, by Russell D. Robinson. [2d ed., rev.] Milwaukee, Bible Study Press [1968] xii, 143 p. illus., maps. 26 cm. Bibliography: p. 120-129. [BS592.R6 1968] 68-7868
1. Bible—Study—Outlines, syllabi, etc. I. Title.

*SALISBURY, Hugh M. 220.07
A guide to effective Bible events, historical value, sources, and contents of each book of the Holy Bible, by Max G. Plowman. [New York?] 1966 x, 114p. 24cm. Based on the 1611, Authorized (King James) version of the Bible. Bibl. 5.25
1. Bible— Introductions. I. Title.
Available from Rare Bk. Co., 99 Nassau St. N.Y. N.Y. 10038.

*SALISBURY, Hugh M. 220.07
A guide to effective Bible teaching. by Hugh M. Salisbury, Larry D. Peabody. Grand Rapids, Michigan, Baker Bk. [1966] 108p. 20cm. 1.50 pap.,
I. Title.

SAMLLEY, Beryl. 220.07
The study of the Bible in the Middle Ages. [2d ed.] New York, Philosophical Library [1952] xxii, 406p. 2 facsims. 23cm. Bibliographical footnotes. [BS500.S] A53
1. Bible—Criticism. interpretation, etc.—Hist. I. Title.

SCHEIDT, David L. 220'.07
Getting to know your Bible. Philadelphia : Fortress Press, c1976. 58 p. : ill. ; 18 cm. "Freely adapted translation by David L. Scheidt of the book by Hans-Georg Lubkoll and Eugene Wiesnet entitled Wie liest man die Bibel? Eine Gebrauchsanweisung fur Neugierige, Anfanger und Fortgeschrittene." [BS475.2.S33] 75-34527 ISBN 0-8006-1217-5 pbk. : 1.95
1. Bible—Introductions. 2. Bible—Reading. I. Lubkoll, Hans-Georg. Wie liest man die Bibel? II. Title.

SCHROEDER, David. 220.07
Learning to know the Bible. Newton, Kan., Faith and Life Press [1966] 112 p. 20 cm. (Christian service training series) [BS600.2.S3] 66-29106
1. Bible—Study. I. Title.

SCHROEDER, David. 220.07
Learning to know the Bible. Newton, Kan., Faith and Life Press [1966] 112 p. 20 cm. (Christian service training series) [BS600.2.S3] 66-29106
1. Bible—Study. I. Title.

SEVENTH-DAY Adventists. 220'.07
General Conference. Sabbath School Dept.
Teaching teachers to teach; especially prepared for teachers of the primary, junior, earliteen, and youth divisions of our Sabbath schools, by the General Conference, Sabbath School Department. Rev. ed. Nashville, Southern Pub. Association [c1964] 406 p. illus. 22 cm. [BV1534.S42 1964] 63-21240
1. Seventh-Day Adventists—Education. 2. Religious education—Teaching methods. I. Title.

SHEDD, Charlie W. 220'.07
The exciting church : where they really use the Bible / Charlie W. Shedd. Waco, Tex. : Word Books, [1975] 122 p. ; 21 cm. [BS600.2.S5] 74-22714 3.95
1. Bible—Study. I. Title: The exciting church : where they relly use the Bible.

SIMON, Martin P. 220.07
How to know and use your Bible. Grand Rapids, Mich., Zondervan [c.1963] 285p. 21cm. 1.00 pap.,
I. Title.

SMALLEY, Beryl 220.07
The study of the Bible in the Middle Ages. [Notre Dame, Ind.] Univ. of Notre Dame Pr. [c.]1964. 406p. 21cm. (ndp39) Bibl. 2.25 pap.,
1. Bible—Criticism, interpretation, etc.—Hist. I. Title.

SMITH, Wilbur Moorehead, 220.07
1894-
Profitable Bible study; seven simple methods, with an annotated list of over one hundred basic books for the Bible student's library, by Wilbur M. Smith. 2d rev. ed. Natick, Mass., W.A. Wilde, 1963. 166 p. 20 cm. [BS600.S617 1963] 62-20932
1. Bible — Study. 2. Bible — Study — Bibl. 3. Bibliography — Best books — Theology. I. Title.

SMITHER, Ethel Lisle. 220.07
Children and the Bible. Henry M. Bullock, general editor. New York, Abingdon Press [1960] 183 p. 19 cm. Includes bibliography. [BS600.2.S6] 60-2608
1. Bible — Study. 2. Religious education. I. Title.

SOCIETY of Biblical 220'.07
Literature.
One hundred seventh annual meeting seminar papers 28-31 October 1971, Regency Hyatt House, Atlanta, Ga. [Atlanta? c1971] 2 v. (iv, 600 p.) 22 cm. [BS411.S6 1971] 73-176529
1. Bible—Congresses.

A Source book of the 220'.07
Bible for teachers. Edited by Robert C. Walton. Camden, N.J., T. Nelson [1970] xxi, 394 p. illus., maps. 26 cm. "Replaces the Teachers' commentary." Bibliography: p. 355-356. [BS600.2.S65 1970b] 79-125333 7.95
1. Bible—Study—Addresses, essays, lectures. 2. Bible—Introductions—Addresses, essays, lectures. I. Walton, Robert Clifford, ed. II. The Teachers' commentary.

SURGY, Paul de. 220.07
The mystery of salvation. Translated by Rosemary Sheed. [1st American ed. Notre Dame, Ind.] University of Notre Dame Press [1966] xi, 242 p. maps. 20 cm. Translation of Les grandes etapes du mystere du salut. Bibliography: p. 241-242. [BS592.S8513 1966] 66-21167
1. Bible—Study—Outlines, syllabi, etc. I. Title.

SWAIM, Joseph Carter, 220.07
1904-
New insights into Scripture; studying the Revised standard version. Philadelphia, Published for the Cooperative Publication Association by Westminster Press [1962] 206 p. 24 cm. (The Cooperative series) [BX191.S9] 62-12646
1. Bible—Study. 2. Bible. English. 1952. Revised standard. I. Title.

SWAIM, Joseph Carter, 220.07
1904-
New insights into Scripture; studying the Revised standard version. Philadelphia, Published for the Cooperative Publication Association by Westminster Press [1962] 206 p. 21 cm. (The Cooperative series) [BS191.S9] 62-12646
1. Bible—Study. 2. Bible. English. Revised Standard. 1952. I. Title.

TODD, J. H. 220.07
Vital teachings of God's word. Chicago, Moody [1963] 79p. 18cm. (Compact bks., 36) .29 pap.,
I. Title.

TORREY, Reuben Archer, 220'.07
1856-1928.
How to study the Bible for the greatest profit. Old Tappan, N.J., F. H. Revell Co. [1972?] 121 p. 20 cm. [BS600.T58 1972] 79-181524 ISBN 0-8007-0499-1 3.50
1. Bible—Study. I. Title.

VANHOOSE, Raymond H., 220'.07
1905-
Revelation's wonderland; from the Alpha to the Omega, by Raymond H. VanHoose. Philadelphia, Dorrance [1973] 117 p. 22 cm. [BS475.2.V36] 73-77373 ISBN 0-8059-1853-1 4.95
1. Bible—Introductions. 2. Bible—Study and teaching. I. Title.

VEDRAL, Joyce L. 220'.07
A literary survey of the Bible, by Joyce L. Vedral. Edited by Dennis Baker. Plainfield, N.J., Logos International [1973] xxii, 243 p. 21 cm. Bibliography: p. 169-172. [BS475.2.V42] 72-94184 ISBN 0-88270-024-3 2.50
1. Bible—Introductions. I. Title.

VIGEVENO, H. S. 220'.07
Wisdom, by H. S. Vigeveno. Glendale, Calif., Regal Books [1968] 131 p. 18 cm. Bibliography: p. 131. [BS592.V48] 68-16265
1. Bible—Study—Outlines, syllabi, etc. 2. Bible—Study—Outlines, syllabi, etc. I. Title.

WALD, Oletta. 220'.07
The joy of discovery in Bible study / Oletta Wald. Rev. ed. Minneapolis : Augsburg Pub. House, c1975. 96 p. ; 22 cm. [BS600.2.W28 1975] 75-22710 ISBN 0-8066-1513-3 pbk. : 2.50
1. Bible—Study. I. Title.

*WALSH, Charles ed. 220.07
God lives! [Alexandria, Ind.] 1967. 60p. 22cm. 1.25 pap.,
1. Bible—Study and teaching. I. Title.
Order from the author, Box 94, Alexandria, Ind., 46001.

WATCH Tower Bible and 220.07
Tract Society of Pennsylvania.
"All Scripture is inspired of God and beneficial." [1st ed. New York. Watchtower Bible and Tract Society of New York, 1963] 352 p. maps (on lining papers) 24 cm. [BS592.W3] 63-25975
1. Bible — Study — Outlines, syllabi, etc. I. Title.

WATCH Tower Bible and 220.07
Tract Society of Pennsylvania
'All Scripture is inspired of God and beneficial.' [Brooklyn, N.Y., Watchtower Bible & Tract Soc. of N.Y., c.1963] 352p. maps (on lining papers) 24cm. 63-25975 1.00
1. Bible—Study—Outlines, syllabi, etc. I. Title.

WEAVER, Horace R. 220'.07
Getting straight about the Bible / Horace R. Weaver. Nashville : Abingdon Press, [1975] 157 p. : ill. ; 20 cm. Includes bibliographical references. [BS511.2.W4] 75-2342 ISBN 0-687-14138-9 pbk. : 3.95
1. Bible—Study. 2. Bible and science. 3. Eschatology—Biblical teaching. 4. Religion and astronautics. I. Title.

WINK, Walter. 220'.07
The Bible in human transformation; toward a new paradigm for biblical study. Philadelphia, Fortress Press [1973] v, 90 p. 18 cm. Includes bibliographical references. [BS600.2.W57] 73-79037 ISBN 0-8006-1034-2 2.95 (pbk.)
1. Bible—Study. 2. Bible—Criticism, interpretation, etc.—History. I. Title.

SCHONEVELD, J. 220'.07'105694
The Bible in Israeli education : a study of approaches to the Hebrew Bible and its teaching in Israeli educational literature / J. Schoneveld. Assen : Van Gorcum, 1976. ix, 296 p. ; 23 cm. Errata slip inserted. Includes indexes. Bibliography: p. 272-277. [BS585.S36] 76-378102 ISBN 9-02-321368-8 : fl 49.50
1. Bible. O.T.—Study—Israel. 2. Education—Israel. I. Title.

BARRETT, Charles 220.072
Kingsley.
Biblical problems and Biblical preaching. Philadelphia, Fortress Press [1964] xii 52 p. 19 cm. (Facet books. Biblical series, 6) Includes 2 addresses by the author: Yesterday, today, and for ever: the New Testament problem. Biblical preaching and Biblical scholarship. [BS538.3.B3] 64-11857
1. Bible — Homiletical use. I. Title. II. Series.

BARRETT, Charles Kingsley 220.072
Biblical problems and Biblical preaching. Philadelphia, Fortress [c.1964] xii, 52p. 19cm. (Facet bks. Biblical ser., 6) Includes 2 addresses by the author: Yesterday, today, and for ever: the New Testament problem. Biblical preaching and Biblical scholarship. 64-11857 .85 pap.,
1. Bible—Homiletical use. I. Title. II. Series.

ALBRIGHT, William 220.0722
Foxwell, 1891-
New horizons in Biblical research [by] W. F. Albright. London, New York, Oxford 1966. ix, 51p. 20cm. (Whidden lects., 1961) Bibl. [BS540.A56] 66-73912 1.70 bds.,
1. Bible — Addresses, essays, lectures. I. Title.
Available from publisher's New York office.

HOUSTON, Tex. 220'.074'016414
University.
University of Houston exhibition of Bibles and related materials, Christmas 1970. Houston, 1970. [24] p. illus., facsims. (2 col.) 32 cm. "Notes prepared by Mrs. Marian Orgain, curator of special collections." [Z7770.H85] 73-634912
1. Bible—Bibliography—Catalogs. I. Orgain, Marian. II. Title.

**5500 Questions and* 220'076
answers on the Holy Bible, comprising all the books of the New Testament. Grand Rapids, Mich., Zondervan [1967, c.1946] 92p. 22cm. .95 pap.,

ALWARD, Benjamin B comp. 220.076
Know the Bible. 6th ed., rev. and enl. Salt Lake City, Deseret Book Co., 1954. 337p. 24cm. [BS612.A5 1954] 55-20572
1. Bible—Examinations, questions, etc. I. Title.

BIBLE. English. 220.076
Selections. 1933
Is that in the Bible? By Charles Francis Potter. Greenwich, Conn., Fawcett [1965, c.1933] 272p. 18cm. (Crest bk. R 791) [BS432.P6] .60 pap.,
1. Bible—Indexes, Topical. I. Potter, Charles Francis, 1885- ed. II. Title.

DE HAAN, Martin Ralph, 220.076
1891-
508 answers to Bible questions, with answers to seeming Bible contradictions. Grand Rapids, Zondervan Pub. House [1952] 254p. 21cm. [BS612.D4] 53-21575
1. Bible—Examinations, questions, etc. I. Title.

DOOR, Peter. 220.076
Teaching Bible doctrine from the Bible; a textbook for young people and adults. Grand Rapids, W. B. Erdmans Pub. Co. [1964] 96 p. 26 cm. [BS600.2.D66] 64-8576
1. Bible — Study. I. Title.

DOOT, Peter 220.076
Teaching Bible doctrine from the Bible; a textbook for young people and adults. Grand Rapids, Mich., Eerdmans [c.1964] 96p. 26cm. [BS600.2.D66] 64-8576 1.65 pap.,
1. Bible—Study. I. Title.

ERICKSON, Melvin E. 220.076
Bible quizzes. Washington, D.C., Review & Herald [c.1963] 128p. diagrs. 22cm. 63-10404 3.00 bds.,
1. Bible—Examinations, questions, etc. 2. Bible games and puzz9les. I. Title.

*FISCHER, Howard A. 220.076
Bible football; Bible questions and answers graded for football competition. Chicago, Moody [c.1965] 64p. 22cm. (MP60) .60 pap.,
I. Title.

4000 questions and 220'.076
answer on the Bible. Westwood, N.J., Revell [1967] 143 p. 18 cm. (Spire books) [BS612.F58] 67-9669
1. Bible—Examinations, questions, etc.

HARDINGE, Miriam. 220.076
Happy Sabbaths. Washington, Review and Herald Pub. Association [1950] 192 p. illus. (part col.) 24 cm. [BS613.H29] 50-13815
1. Games. I. Title.

KARRAKER, William 220.076
Archibald, 1888-
The Bible in questions and answers; a guide to the study of the Holy Scriptures based on the King James version, with annotations from the American and Revised standard versions. Introd. by William A. Irwin. New York, D. McKay Co. [1953- v. 22cm. [BS605.K25] 53-11371
1. Bible—Study—Text-books. 2. Bible—Examinations, questions, etc. I. Title.

MCBRIDE, Leda P 220.076
Fun from the Bible; Bible puzzles and quizzes. Grand Rapids, Zondervan Pub. House [1958] 61p. 20cm. [BS613.M3] 59-23965
1. Bible games and puzzles. I. Title.

MCDONALD, Christina, 220.076
1890-
Young folks Bible quiz book. [1st ed.] Cleveland, World Pub. Co. [1953] 223p. 22cm. [BS612.M262] 52-8443
1. Bible—Examinations, questions, etc. I. Title.

MOEHLMANN, F Herbert, 220.076
1893-
Bible challenges: quiz book no. 1- Saint Louis, Concordia Pub. House [1958, c1957- v. 20cm. [BS612.M54] 58-64
1. Bible—Examinations, questions, etc. I. Title.

NANCE, Mabel H. 220.076
Who holds the answer. New York, Vantage [c.1961] 82p. 2.50 bds.,
1. Bible—Quizzes. I. Title.

NEWMAN, Margaret M 220.076
Bible quiz and answers; a guide through the Old and New Testaments, [1st ed.] New York, Exposition Press [1959] 64p. 21cm. [BS612.M47] 59-3749
1. Bible—Examinations, questions, etc. I. Title.

*NIXON, Leroy 220.076
What does the Bible say? New York, Carlton [c.1964] 61p. 21cm. (Reflection bk.) 2.00
I. Title.

*SANDISON, Goerge H. 220.'07'6
1,000 difficult Bible questions answered / By George H. Sandison and staff. Grand Rapids : Baker Book House, 1976. 555, [11]p. ; 18cm. (Direction books) Includes index. [BS612] ISBN 0-8010-8071-1 pbk. : 2.95.
1. Bible-Examinations, questions, etc. I. Title.

SCHWARTZ, Frederick L.B. 220.076
A Biblical diary and quiz book. New York, Vantage [c.1961] 155p. 2.95 bds.,
I. Title.

SEGAL, Elizabeth. 220'.07'6
The Bible quizbook / by Elizabeth Segal. New York : Drake Publishers, [1975] p. cm. [BS612.S39] 75-10778 ISBN 0-8473-1114-7 pbk. : 4.95 4.95
1. Bible—Examinations, questions, etc. I. Title.

SHOUP, Carl Sumner, 220'.076
1902-
Test your Bible knowledge; multiple-choice questions and answers keyed to Scripture verses [by] Carl S. Shoup, with Carolyn S. Scott. Old Tappan, N.J., F. H. Revell Co. [1971] 221 p. 18 cm. Includes bibliographical references. [BS612.S53] 70-149369 ISBN 0-8007-0452-5
1. Bible—Examinations, questions, etc. I. Scott, Carolyn S., joint author. II. Title.

SMITH, May 220.076
Search the Bible quizzes. Cincinnati, Standard Publishing Company [c.1960] 48p. 22cm. .50 pap.,
I. Title.

SMITH, May 220.076
Sixty-eight Bible quizzes Cincinnati. Standard Publishing Company [c.1960] 48p. 21cm. .50 pap.,
I. Title.

SMITH, May C. 220'.076
Who? why? what? A Bible quiz book, by May C. Smith. Grand Rapids, Zondervan Pub. House [1971, c1969] 64 p. 21 cm. Includes bibliographical references. [BS612.S64 1971] 71-146563
1. Bible—Examinations, questions, etc. 2. Bible games and puzzles. I. Title.

STILSON, Max. 220.076
Bible number quiz. Boston, W. A. Wilde Co. [c1957] 2 v. 19 cm. No. 2 has title: Bible number quizbook. [BS612.S74] 58-75
1. Bible — Examinations, questions, etc. I. Title.

STIMPSON, George 220'.076
William, 1896-
Questions and answers about the Bible [by] George Stimpson. New York, Funk & Wagnalls [1968, c1945] x, 509 p. 18 cm. (A Funk & Wagnalls paperbook, F36) 1945 ed. published under title: A book about the Bible. [BS612.S75 1968] 68-18155
1. Bible—Examinations, questions, etc. I. Title.

STRAUGHN, Harold. 220'.076
Through the Bible with those who were there : a guide to the Scriptures / by Harold and Carole Straughn. Wheaton, Ill. : Tyndale House Publishers, 1975. xi, 270 p. : ill. ; 23 cm. [BS605.2.S83] 74-19646 ISBN 0-8423-7150-8 pbk. : 3.95
1. Bible—Study—Text-books. I. Straughn, Carole, joint author. II. Title.

SWAIM, Joseph Carter, 220.076
1904-
Answers to your questions about the Bible [by] J. Carter Swaim. New York, Vanguard Press [1965] 441 p. 24 cm. "An Edward Ernest book." [BS612.S753] 65-20649
1. Bible—Examinations, questions, etc. I. Title.

WAYNER, Walter 220.076
You better know God. [Thmopsonville, Conn.,44 Sharren Lane, Author. c.1964] 158p. illus. 23cm. 64-13087 4.95
1. Bible—Examinations, questions, etc. I. Title.

BENOIT, Pierre, 220.08
Aug.3,1906- ed.
The Dynamism of Biblical tradition. New York, Paulist Press [1967] ix ,213 p. 24 cm. [Concillum theology in the age of renewal: Scripture v. 20) Contents.--Preface, by P. Renoit, R.E. Murphy, and B. van Iersel.--Tradition as source and environment of scripture, by P. Grelot.--The development of the Israelite credo, by J. Schreiner.--Scope and depth of exodus tradition in Deutero-Isaiah 40-55, by J. Blenkinsopp.--Proverbs 1-9, a first theological synthesis of the tradition of the sages, by R. Tournay.--The tradiiton of the sayings of Jesus: Mark 9, 33-50, by F. Neirynck.--The son of David tradition and Matthew 22, 41-46 and parallels, by J. Fitzmyer.--The primitive preaching: the traditional schems. by D. Stanley.--Paul and tradition, by J. Cambier.--French literature on the homily, by T. Maertens.--English literature on the homily, by G.S. Sloyan.--German literature on the homily, by L. Bertsch.--Spanish literature on the homily, by C. Floristan.--Italian literature on the homily, by S. Zedda.--Dutch literature on the homily, by G. Hoogbergen.--"This same Jesus", by M.C. Vanhengel.--Biographical notes.--Subject index to Concilium, vol. 11-vol. 20. [BS540.D9] 67-15983
1. Bible—Addresses, essays, lectures. 2. Tradition (Theology) I. Title. II. Series. III. Series: Concillum theology in the age of renewal, v. 20

DYNAMISM of Biblical 220.08
tradition (The) New York, Paulist [c.1967] ix, 213p. 24cm. (Concilium theol. in the age of renewal: Scripture, v.20) [BS540.D9] 67-15983 4.50
1. Bible — Addresses, essays, lectures. 2. Tradition (Theology) I. Benoit, Pierre, Aug. 3, 1906- ed. II. Series: Concilium theology in the age of renewal, v. 20
Contents. omitted.

HOOKE, Samuel Henry, 220'.08
1874-1968.
The Siege Perilous; essays in Biblical anthropology and kindred subjects. Freeport, N.Y., Books for Libraries Press [1970, c1956] 264 p. illus. 23 cm. [BS531.H66 1970] 73-130552
1. Bible—Addresses, essays, lectures. I. Title.

JOURNAL for Theology and 220.08
the Church; v. 1. [Tr. from German] Edit. bd.: Robert W. Funk, chm.; Frank M. Cross [others] Ed.: Robert W. Funk. Tubingen, J. C. B. Mohr; New York, Harper [c.1965] 183p. 21cm. (Harper torchbks.; the cloister lib./TB251L) Contents.v. 1. The Bultmann school of biblical interpretation: new directions. Bibl. 1.95 pap.,

MCCARTHY, Dennis J. comp. 220.08
Modern Biblical studies; an anthology from Theology digest, ed., introd., by Dennis J. McCarthy, William B. Callen. Milwaukee, Bruce [1967] xvi, 186p. 22cm. [BS540.M23] 67-29590 5.95
1. Bible—Addresses, essays, lectures. I. Callen, William B. joint comp. II. Theology digest. III. Title.

*RICE, William B., 1904- 220'.08
Challenge; the sayings of Jesus in a modern setting [by] A. Siecker. New York, Vantage [1968] 61p. 21cm. 2.50 bds.,
1. Bible—Addresses, essays, lectures. I. Title.

TRANSITIONS in Biblical 220'.08
scholarship, by G. W. Ahlstrom [and others] Edited by J. Coert Rylaarsdam. Chicago, University of Chicago Press [1968] x, 317 p. 24 cm. (Essays in divinity, v. 6) Papers from one of the seven alumni conferences held to celebrate the 75th anniversary of the University of Chicago and 100th anniversary of its Divinity School. Bibliographical footnotes. [BS413.T7] 68-9135
1. Bible—Addresses, essays, lectures. I. Ahlstrom, Gosta Werner, 1918- II. Rylaarsdam, John Coert, 1907- ed. III. Chicago. University. Divinity School. IV. Title. V. Series.

THE Truest story / 220'.08
edited by Kenneth Ryan. New York : Pillar Books, 1976. 383 p. ; 18 cm. Includes index. [BS540.T78] 76-16463 ISBN 0-89129-160-1 pbk. : 1.95
1. Bible—Addresses, essays, lectures. I. Ryan, Kenneth.

WENGER, John Christian, 220.08
1910-
God's word written; essays on the nature of Biblical revelation, inspiration, and authority

[by] J. C. Wenger, Scottdale, Pa., Herald Pr. [1966] 150p. 20cm. (Conrad Grebel lect. bks.) Bibl. Title (Series: The Conrad Grebel lectures, 1966) [BS540.W4] 66-24292 3.50
1. Bible — Addresses, essays, lectures. I. Title. II. Series.

WOODS, Ralph Louis, 1904- ed. 220.08
The Catholic companion to the Bible. Foreword by John J. Wright, Bishop of Worcester, Mass. [1st ed.] Philadelphia, Lippincott [1956] 313p. 22cm. [BS538.W57] 56-6416
1. Bible—Appreciation. 2. Catholic literature (Selections: Extracts, etc.) I. Title.

WOODS, Ralph Louis, 1904- ed. 220.08
The Catholic companion to the Bible. Foreword by John J. Wright, Bishop of Worcester, Mass. [1st ed.] Philadelphia, Lippincott [1956] 313 p. 22 cm. [BS538.W57] 56-6416
1. Bible — Appreciation. 2. Catholic literature (Selections: Extracts, etc.) I. Title.

CRISWELL, Wallie A 220.081
The Bible for today's world, by W. A. Criswell. Grand Rapids, Zondervan Pub. House [1965] 128 p. 21 cm. [BS491.5.C7] 65-4153
1. Bible—Sermons. 2. Baptists—Sermons. 3. Sermons, American. I. Title.

CRISWELL, Wallie A. 220.081
The Bible for today's world. Grand Rapids, Mich. Zondervan [c.1965] 128p. 21cm. [BS491.5.C7] 65-4153 2.50 bds.,
1. Bible—Sermons. 2. Baptists—Sermons. 3. Sermons, American. I. Title.

HERTZ, Solange Strong, 1920- 220.081
Come down, Zacchaeus; adventures in Scripture. Westminster, Md., Newman Press, 1961. 319p. 23cm. [BS540.H4] 61-16568
1. Bible—Addresses, essays, lectures. I. Title.

SWAIM, Joseph Carter, 1904- 220.081
Why read the Bible? New York, Friendship [1965] 64p. 16cm. (Questions for Christians, no. 1) [BS592.S9] 65-11429 .65 pap,
1. Bible—Study—Outlines, syllabi, etc. I. Title. II. Series.

TORREY, Reuben Archer, 1856-1928. 220.081
You and your Bible; an anthology of R. A. Torrey. [Westwood, N.J.] Revell [1958] 220 p. 22 cm. Bible -- Collected works. [BS415.T6] 58-5344
I. Title.

AHERN, Barnabas M. 220.082
New horizons; studies in biblical theology. Ed. by Carroll Stuhlmueller. Foreword by Kathryn Sullivan. Notre Dame, Ind., Fides [1964, c.1963] 218p. 21cm. 63-20807 3.95
1. Bible—Theology. I. Title.

AMERICAN Council of Learned Societies Devoted to Humanistic Studies. 220.082
Five essays on the Bible; papers read at the 1960 annual meeting, by Erwin R. Goodenough [and others] New York, [Author] [1961, c.1960] 80p. 60-53166 1.00 bds.,
1. Bible—Addresses, essays, lectures. I. Goodenough, Erwin Ramsdell, 1893- II. Title.

FURROW, (The). 220.082
The Word of Life; essays on the Bible. Foreword by E. J. Kissane. Westminster, Md., Newman Press, 1960 [c.1959] 123p. Bibl. 61-360 1.75 pap.,
1. Bible—Addresses, elsays, lectures. I. Title.

SALM, Celestine Luke, ed. 220.082
Studies in salvation history. Englewood Cliffs, N. J., Prentice-Hall [1964] xvii, 236 p. 22 cm. Includes bibliographies. [BS543.S34] 64-18184
1. Bible—Theology. 2. Bible—History of Biblical events. I. Title.

SALM, Celestine Luke, ed. 220.082
Studies in salvation history. Englewood Cliffs, N.J., Prentice [c.1964] xvii, 236p. 22cm. Bibl. 64-18184 2.95 pap.,
1. Bible—Theology. 2. Bible—History of Biblical events. I. Title.

DORE, Gustave, 1832-1883. 220.084
The Holy Bible, illustrated. Edited by the Daughters of Saint Paul. [Boston] St. Paul Editions [1963] 191 p. (chiefly illus. (part col.)) col maps (on lining paper 23 cm. [BS560.D6] 63-17308
1. Bible — Picture Bibles. I. Daughters of St. Paul. II. Title.

DORE, Gustave [Louis Auguste Gustave Dore] 1832-1883 220.084
The Holy Bible, illustrated. Ed. by the Daughters of Saint Paul. [Boston] St. Paul Eds. [dist. Daughters of St. Paul, c.1963] 191p. chiefly illus. (pt. col.) col. maps (on lining paper) 22cm. 63-17308 4.00 bds.,
1. Bible—Picture Bibles. I. Daughters of St. Paul. II. Title.

MURRAY, Jane Marie, 1896- 220.084
The story of salvation [by] Jane Marie Murray and Eugene S. Geissler. Notre Dame, Ind., Fides Publishers Association [1961] 166p. illus. 24cm. [BS560.M85] 61-9866
1. Bible—Pictures, illustrations, etc. I. Geissler, Eguene S. joint author. II. Title.

MURRAY, Jane Marie 1896- 220.084
The story of salvation [by] Jane Marie Murray, Eugene S. Geissler. Notre Dame, Ind., Fides [c.1961] 166p. illus. 61-9866 4.95
1. Bible—Pictures, illustrations, etc. I. Geissler, Eugene S., joint author. II. Title.

*STRACHAN, James 220.084
Pictures from a mediaeval Bible. London, Finlayson [dist. Chester Springs, Pa., Dufour, 1965, c.]1959. 127p. illus. 23cm. 3.50
I. Title.

DUFFY, Joseph A 220.088
Catholic Bible play book [by] Joseph A. Duffy, Marguerite R. Duffy [and] Frances W. Keene. Pelham, N. Y., Seahorse Press [1954] 128p. illus. 29cm. (Seahorse fun books, 110) [BS613.D8] 54-8168
I. Title.

MOUNT, Ralph H., jr. 220.088
God's tabernacle in Israel's wilderness journey [2d. ed.] 2d. ed. Mansfield, Ohio, Author [1963]c.1960, 1962. 93p. illus. 28cm. 2.00 pap.,
I. Title.

MOUNT, Richard H., jr. 220.088
The law prophesied. Mansfield, Ohio, Author [1963, c.1962] 57p. illus. 28cm. 2.00 pap.,
I. Title.

THE Cambridge history of the Bible. 220'.09
Cambridge; New York: Cambridge University Press, [1975] 3 v. illus.; 23 cm. Contents.Contents.— v. 1. From the beginnings to Jerome, ed. by P. R. Ackroyd and C. F. Evans.— v. 2. The West from the Fathers to the Reformation, ed. by G. W. H. Lampe.— v. 3. The West from the Reformation to the present day, ed. by S. L. Greenslade. Bibliographies. [BS445.C26] 63-24435 ISBN 0-521-29018-X(set) 24.50 (pbk.) set
1. Bible—History. 2. Bible—Versions. I. Ackroyd, Peter R., ed. II. Evans, Christopher Francis, ed. III. Lampe, Geoffrey William Hugo, ed. IV. Greenslade, Stanley Lawrence, ed.
V. 1, ISBN 0-521-09973-0; v. 2, ISBN 0-521-29017-1; v. 3, ISBN 0-521-29016-3. 9.95 each.

EARLE, Ralph. 220'.09
How we got our Bible / by Ralph Earle. Grand Rapids : Baker Book House, 1973. 119 p. : facsims. ; 20 cm. Reprint of the 1971 ed. published by Beacon Hill Press, Kansas City, Mo. Includes bibliographical references. [BS445.E2 1973] 75-321705 ISBN 0-8010-3271-7 : 1.50
1. Bible—History. 2. Bible—Versions. I. Title.

FRANK, Harry Thomas. 220'.09
The Bible through the ages [by] Harry Thomas Frank, Charles William Swain [and] Courtlandt Canby, assisted by Michael Harwood. Cleveland, World Pub. Co., [1967] 246 p. illus. (part col.), col. maps. 29 cm. [BS445.F8 1967] 67-29087
1. Bible—Hist. I. Swain, Charles William, joint author. II. Canby, Courtlandt, joint author. III. Title.

FRANK, Harry Thomas. 220'.09
The Bible through the ages [by] Harry Thomas Frank, Charles William Swain [and] Courtlandt Canby, assisted by Michael Harwood. Cleveland, World Pub. Co. [1967] 246 p. illus. (part col.), col. maps. 29 cm. [BS445.F8 1967] 67-29087
1. Bible—History. I. Swain, Charles William, joint author. II. Canby, Courtlandt, joint author. III. Title.

HOWKINS, Kenneth Gordon. 220'.09
The challenge of religious studies [by] Kenneth G. Howkins. Foreword by John W. Alexander. Downers Grove, Ill., InterVarsity Press [1973, c1972] 150 p. 22 cm. Includes bibliographical references. [BS600.2H68 1973] 73-75896 ISBN 0-87784-714-2 2.50
1. Bible—Study. I. Title.

KENYON, Frederic George, Sir 1863-1952. 220'.09
The story of the Bible; a popular account of how it came to us, by Sir Frederic Kenyon. New ed. with supplementary material by F. F. Bruce. [Special U.S. ed.] Grand Rapids, Eerdmans [1967] 150 p. facsims. 19 cm. "The principal manuscripts and versions of the Greek Bible": p. [139]-144. Bibliography: p. [145]-146. [BS445.K48 1967] 67-19311
1. Bible — Hist. I. Bruce, Frederick Fyvie, 1910- II. Title.

KENYON, Frederic George,Sir 1863-1952. 220'.09
The story of the Bible; a popular account of how it came to us, by Sir Frederic Kenyon. New ed. with supplementary material by F. F. Bruce. [Special U. S. ed.] Grand rapids, Eerdmans [1967] 150p. facsims, 19cm. The principalmanuscripts and versions of the Greek Bible: p. [139]-144.bBibl. [BS445.K48 1967] 67-19311 1.95 pap.,
1. Bible—Hist. I. Bruce, Frederick Fyvie, 1910. II. Title.

KOCH, Klaus. 220'.09
The book of books; the growth of the Bible. [Translated by Margaret Kohl from the German] Philadelphia, Westminster Press [1968] 192 p. 19 cm. Translation of Das Buch der Bucher. [BS445.K613] 69-12299 2.65
1. Bible—History. I. Title.

TRENT, Robbie, 1894- 220'.09
The story of your very own Bible / Robbie Trent. Waco, Tex. : Word Books, c1977. 164 p. : ill. ; 23 cm. Relates the history of the Bible and describes its various translations. [BS445.T73] 76-19544 ISBN 0-87680-488-1 : 5.95
1. Bible—History—Juvenile literature. I. Title.

WEGENER, Gunther S 220.09
6000 years of the Bible. [Translated by Margaret Shenfield] New York, Harper & Row [c1963] 352 p. illus., ports., facsims. 24 cm. Translation of 6000 Jahre und ein Buch. [BS445.W373] 63-16406
1. Bible — Hist. I. Title.

HARRISVILLE, Roy A. 220'.092'4 B
Benjamin Wisner Bacon, pioneer in American Biblical criticism / Roy A. Harrisville. Missoula, Mont. : Scholars Press for the Society of Biblical Literature, [1976] p. cm. (SBL studies in American Biblical scholarship ; 2) Bibliography: p. [BS501.B3H37] 76-16178 ISBN 0-89130-110-0
1. Bacon, Benjamin Wisner, 1860-1932. I. Title. II. Series: Society of Biblical Literature. SBL studies in American Biblical scholarship ; 2.

ROBERTSON, Edwin Hanton. 220.0942
The Bible in the British scene. New York, Association Press [1961] 70p. 19cm. (The Bible in our time) [BS538.3.R63 1961] 61-14164
1. Bible—Use. 2. Gt. Brit.— Religion. I. Title.

ROBERTSON, Edwin Hanton 220.09431
The Bible in East Germany. New York, Association [c.1961] 93p. (Bible in our time) Bibl. 61-14165 1.25 pap.,
1. Bible—Use. 2. Germany (Democratic Republic, 1949)—Religion. I. Title.

ABBA, Raymond. 220.1
The nature and authority of the Bible. Philadelphia, Muhlenberg Press [1959, c1958] 333p. 23cm. Includes bibliography. [BS538.A25 1959] 59-3813
1. Bible—Criticism, Interpretation, etc. 2. Bible—Evidences, authority, etc. I. Title.

ALEXANDER, Archibald, 1772-1851. 220.1
Evidences of the authenticity, inspiration, and canonical authority of the Holy Scriptures. New York, Arno Press, 1972. 308 p. port. 23 cm. (Religion in America, series II) Reprint of the 1836 ed. [BT1101.A56 1972] 70-38431 ISBN 0-405-04052-0
1. Bible—Evidences, authority, etc. 2. Apologetics—19th century. I. Title.

ANDERSON, Stanley Edwin. 220.1
Our inerrant Bible / by S. E. Anderson. Texarkana, Tex. : Bogard Press, c1977. 180 p. ; 22 cm. Bibliography: p. 177-180. [BS480.A66] 77-76981
1. Bible—Evidences, authority, etc. I. Title.

BIBLICAL authority / 220.1
edited by Jack Rogers. Waco, Tex. : Word Books, c1977. 196 p. ; 22 cm. Includes bibliographical references. [BS480.B475] 76-56482 ISBN 0-87680-800-3 : 4.50
1. Bible—Inspiration—History of Doctrines—Addresses, essays, lectures. 2. Bible—Evidences, authority, etc.—Addresses, essays, lectures. I. Rogers, Jack Bartlett.

BLUNT, John James, 1794-1855. 220.1
Undesigned coincidences in the writings both of the Old and New Testament: an argument of their veracity, with an appendix, containing undesigned coincidences between the Gospels and Acts, and Josephus, by J. J. Blunt. 18th ed. Birmingham, Christadelphian, 1965. xi, 365 p. 19 1/2 cm. (B 66-6288) [BS480.B55] 66-73960
1. Bible — Evidences, authority, etc. I. Title.

BOOTH, Abraham, 1734-1806. 220.1
An essay on the kingdom of Christ, by Abraham Booth; to which is added The doctrine of the covenants, wherein is shewn that there never was a covenant of works made with Adam, nor any other covenant ever made with man, respecting things purely of a spiritual nature, by Samuel Jones. Norwich, Printed and sold by J. Sterry, 1801. 188p. 18cm. [BT94.B65 1801] 57-51062
1. Jesus Christ—Kingdom. 2. Covenants (Theology) I. Jones Samuel, 1735-1814. The doctrine of the covenants. II. Title.

BOWMAN, Allen 220.1
Is the Bible true? Westwood, N. J., Revell [c.1965] 189p. 21cm. [BS480.B63] 65-23620 3.95 bds.,
1. Bible — Evidences, authority, etc. I. Title.

BREVICK, Harald. 220.1
Books were opened. Rev. ed. Minneapolis, Thule Pub. Co., 1951. 291 p. 21 cm. First published in 1946 under title: It is happening. [BS647.B67 1951] 51-40206
1. Bible—Prophecies. I. Title.

BRIGGS, Charles Augustus, 1841-1913. 220.1
Inaugural address and defense, 1891/1893. New York, Arno Press, 1972. iii, xx, 193 p. 23 cm. (Religion in America, series II) Reprint of the author's The authority of Holy Scripture, first published 1891; and of his The defence of Professor Briggs before the Presbytery of New York, first published 1893. [BS480.B64 1972] 70-38442 ISBN 0-405-04062-8 16.00
1. Presbyterian Church in the U.S.A.—Doctrinal and controversial works. 2. Presbyterian Church in the U.S.A. Presbyteries. New York. 3. Bible—Evidences, authority, etc. I. Briggs, Charles Augustus, 1841-1913. The defence of Professor Briggs before the Presbytery of New York. 1972. II. Title.

CAN I trust my Bible? 220.1
Important questions often asked about the Bible, with some answers by eight evangelical scholars. Chicago, Moody [c.1963] 190p. 22cm. Bibl. 64-105 3.50
1. Bible—Examinations, questions, etc.

CONFERENCE on the Inspiration and Authority of Scripture, Ligonier, Pa., 1973. 220.1
God's inerrant Word; an international symposium on the trustworthiness of Scripture, edited by John Warwick Montgomery. Minneapolis, Bethany Fellowship, inc. [1974] 288 p. 23 cm. Sponsored by the Ligonier Valley Study Center. Includes bibliographical references. [BS480.C623 1973] 74-4100 ISBN 0-87123-179-4 6.95
1. Bible—Evidences, authority, etc.—Congresses. 2. Bible—Inspiration—Congresses. I. Montgomery, John Warwick, ed. II. Ligonier Valley Study Center. III. Title.

CONN, Charles W. 220.1
The Bible: book of books. Cleveland, Tenn., Pathway [1962, c.1961] 111p. 20cm. (Workers' Training Course 201) 62-4375 1.50
I. Title.

CRISWELL, Wallie A. 220.1
Why I preach that the Bible is literally true [by] W. A. Criswell. Nashville, Broadman Press [1969] 160 p. 21 cm. [BS480.C7] 69-13142 3.50
1. Bible—Evidences, authority, etc. I. Title.

DAVIS, Stephen T., 1940- 220.1
The debate about the Bible : inerrancy versus infallibility / by Stephen T. Davis. Philadelphia : Westminster Press, c1977. p. cm. Bibliography: p. [BS480.D32] 77-3457 ISBN 0-664-24119-0 pbk. : 5.45
1. Bible—Evidences, authority, etc. I. Title.

DE HAAN, Martin Ralph, 1891- 220.1
The Jew and Palestine in prophecy. Grand Rapids, Zon dervan Pub. House [1950] 183 p. 20 cm. [BS649J5D4] 50-8662
1. Bible—Prophecies—Jews. I. Title.

FRIEDMAN, Bob. 220.1
So that's how we got the Bible [by] Bob Friedman and Mal Couch. Wheaton, Ill., Tyndale House Publishers [1973] 106 p. illus. 18 cm. "Under the auspices of the Evangelical Communications Research Foundation." [BS455.F73] 73-81013 ISBN 0-8423-6090-5 1.25
1. Bible. English—Versions. I. Couch, Mal, joint author. II. Title.

FRIEDMAN, Bob. 220.1
So that's how we got the Bible [by] Bob Friedman and Mal Couch. Wheaton, Ill., Tyndale House Publishers [1973] 106 p. illus. 18 cm. "Under the auspices of the Evangelical Communications Research Foundation." [BS455.F73] 73-81013 ISBN 0-8423-6090-5 1.25 (pbk.)
1. Bible. English—Versions. I. Couch, Mal, joint author. II. Title.

FROOM, Le Roy Edwin, 1890- 220.1
The prophetic faith of our fathers; the historical development of prophetic interpretation. Washington, Review and Herald [1946-54; v.1, 1950] 4v. illus., ports. 24cm. Contents.v.1. Early church exposition, subsequent deflections, and medieval revival.--v.2. Pre-Reformation and Reformation; restoration, and second departure.--v.3. pt. 1, Colonial and early national American exposition. pt.2, Old World nineteenth century advent awakening.--v.4. New World recovery and consummation of prophetic interpretation. Includes bibliographies. [BS647.F72] 47-1131
1. Bible—Prophecies. 2. Eschatology—History of doctrines. I. Title.

*GERSTNER, John H. 220.1
A Bible inerrancy primer. Grand Rapids, Mich., Baker Bk. [c.] 1965. 63p. 22cm. Bibl. .85 pap.,
I. Title.

GRELOT, Pierre, 1917- 220.1
The Bible, word of God; a theological introduction to the study of scripture. Translated from the 2d French ed. by Peter Nickels. New York, Desclee Co. [1968] xx, 408 p. 24 cm. Translation of La Bible, parole de Dieu. Includes bibliographical references. [BS513.2.G713] 68-31196
1. Bible—Criticism, interpretation, etc. I. Title.

HENGSTENBERG, Hans Eduard, 220.1
1904-
Der Leib und die letzten Dinge. [2.] wesentlich erweiterte und umgearb. Aufl. Regensburg, F. Pustet [1955] 301p. 20cm. First ed. published in 1938 under title: Tod und Vollendung. [BT821.H] A55
1. Eschatology. I. Title.

HENRY, Carl Ferdinand 220.1
Howard, 1913- ed.
Revelation and the Bible; contemporary evangelical thought [by] G. C. Berkouwer [and others] Grand Rapids, Baker Book House [1958] 413 p. 24 cm. ([Contemporary evangelical thought]) Includes bibliography. [BS413.H45] 58-59822
1. Bible—Addresses, essays, lectures. 2. Bible—Evidences, authority, etc. 3. Revelation. 4. Evangelicalism. I. Title.

HUBBARD, David Allan. 220.1
Does the Bible really work? Waco, Tex., Word Books [1971] 75 p. 21 cm. "Offered originally as a series of talks on the national radio broadcast 'The joyful sound.'" Bibliography: p. 73. [BS480.H76] 70-136286 2.95
1. Bible—Evidences, authority, etc.—Addresses, essays, lectures. I. The joyful sound (Radio program) II. Title.

HUXTABLE, William John 220.1
Fairchild
The Bible says. Richmond, Va. Knox [c.1962] 125p. 20cm. Bibl. 62-12081 1.75
1. Bible—Evidences, authority, etc. I. Title.

INFIDEL testimony 220.1
concerning the truth of the Bible : exhibiting in parallel columns passages of Scripture verified by the ancient inscriptions of Sennacherib and Nebuchadnezzar, also more than one hundred and seventy quotations from the writings of the prophets, which are shown to have been fulfilled by seventy quotations from the writings of sceptics like Volney and Gibbon, confirmed by one hundred and fifty extracts from the writings of other historians and travelers, selected from Alexander Keith's Demonstration of the truth of the Christian religion, with arguments and remarks by H. L. Hastings. 1st twentieth century ed. Malverne, N.Y. : Christian Evidence League, 1973. 38 p. ; 22 cm. [BS480.I43] 75-330951 0.50
1. Bible—Evidences, authority, etc. I. Hastings, Horace Lorenzo, 1833?-1899. II. Keith, Alexander, 1791-1880. Demonstration of the truth of the Christian religion.

JOHNSON, L. D., 1916- 220.1
An introduction to the Bible [by] L. D. Johnson. Nashville, Convention Press [1969] xiii, 165 p. 21 cm. (Bible survey series, v. 1) "Text for course 3201 of subject area Biblical revelation of the Christian development series, New church study course." Includes bibliographical references. [BS475.2.J6] 68-57027
1. Bible—Introductions. I. Title. II. Series.

LAMPE, Geoffrey William j220.1
Hugo
Discovering the Bible [by] G. W. H. Lampe, David Scott Daniell. Illus. by Steele Savage. Nashville, Abingdon [1966] 160p. illus., facsims., map. 22cm. Bibl. [BS539.L3] 66-10570 3.25
1. Bible — Juvenile literature. I. Daniell, Albert Scott, 1906- joint author. II. Savage, Steele, illus. III. Title.

LAVIK, John Rasmus, 1881- 220.1
The Bible is the Word of God: a basic issue briefly reviewed. With an introd. by Alvin N. Rogness. Minneapolis, Augsburg Pub. House [1959] 62p. 20cm. [BT89.L3] 59-10758
1. Bible—Evidences, authority, etc. I. Title.

LORETZ, Oswald. 220.1
The truth of the Bible; tr. [from German] by David J. Bourke. Revised version of orig. German ed. London, Burns & Oates; New York, Herder & Herder, 1968. x, 182p. 21cm. Tr. of: Die Wahrheit der Bibel. [BS480.L633 1968] 68-13560 4.95
1. Bible—Evidences, authority, etc. I. Title.

MACARTHUR, John, 1936- 220.1
Focus on fact : why you can trust the Bible / John F. MacArthur, Jr. Old Tappan, N.J. : Revell, c1977. p. cm. [BS480.M2] 77-21755 ISBN 0-8007-0885-7 pbk. : 3.95
1. Bible—Evidences, authority, etc. 2. Bible—Inspiration. I. Title.

MARKLEY, Mary Mauger. 220.1
America and the story of the prophets. New York, Bookman Associates [1950] 292 p. 23 cm. [BS649.U6M3] 50-11148
1. Bible—Prophecies—U. S. I. Title.

MAXWELL, Arthur Graham, 220.1
1921-
You can trust the Bible; why, after many translations, it is still the word of God, by A. Graham Maxwell. Mountain View, Calif., Pacific Press Pub. Association [c1967] 96 p. 18 cm. [BS480.M38] 67-31071
1. Bible—Evidences, authority, etc. I. Title.

MILLER, Donald G. 220.1
The authority of the Bible [by] Donald G. Miller. Grand Rapids, Eerdmans [1972] 139 p. 21 cm. First given as the Carson Memorial Lectures, May, 1971, at the First Presbyterian Church, Richmond, Va. Includes bibliographical references. [BT89.M53] 70-184694 ISBN 0-8028-1440-9 2.25
1. Bible—Evidences, authority, etc. I. Title.

MORAN, Gabriel. 220.1
Scripture and tradition; a survey of the controversy. [New York] Herder and Herder [1963] 127 p. 21 cm. Bibliography: p. 89-98. [BT89.M63] 63-9555
1. Bible — Evidences, authority, etc. 2. Tradition (Theology) I. Title.

MORAN, Gabriel 220.1
Scripture and tradition; a survey of the controversy. [New York] Herder & Herder [c.1963] 127p. 21cm. Bibl. 63-9555 3.50
1. Bible—Evidences, authority, etc. 2. Tradition (Theology) I. Title.

NEDERLANDSE Hervormde Kerk. 220.1
Generale Synode.
The Bible speaks again; a guide from Holland, commissioned by the Netherlands Reformed Church. With a foreword by William Barclay. [Translated from the Dutch by Annebeth Mackie] Minneapolis, Augsburg Pub. House [1972, c1969] 224 p. 22 cm. Translation of Klare Wijn: Rekenschap over geschiedenis, geheim en gezag van de Bijbel. Bibliography: p. [219] [BS475.2.N413 1972] 79-75400 3.75
1. Bible—Introductions. 2. Bible—Evidences, authority, etc. 3. Bible—Use. I. Title.

NETTLETON, David, 1918- 220.1
Our infallible Bible / David Nettleton. Schaumburg, Ill. : Regular Baptist Press, [1977] p. cm. [BS480.N38] 77-15540 ISBN 0-87227-055-6 pbk. : 0.95
1. Bible—Evidences, authority, etc. I. Title.

NEWMAN, John Henry, 220.1
Cardinal, 1801-1890.
John Henry Newman and the Abbe Jager : a controversy on scripture and tradition (1834-1836) / edited from the original manuscripts and the French version by Louis Allen. London ; New York : Oxford University Press, 1975. 202 p. ; 23 cm. (University of Durham publications) Includes index. Bibliography: p. [189]-195. [BT89.N48 1975] 76-358303 ISBN 0-19-713138-7 : 18.75
1. Bible and tradition. I. Jager, Jean-Nicolas, 1790-1868. II. Allen, Louis. III. Title. IV. Series: Durham, Eng. University. Publications.

NEWMAN, John Henry, 220.1
Cardinal, 1801-1890.
John Henry Newman and the Abbe Jager : a controversy on scripture and tradition (1834-1836) / edited from the original manuscripts and the French version by Louis Allen. London ; New York : Oxford University Press, 1975. 202 p. ; 23 cm. (University of Durham publications) Includes index. Bibliography: p. [189]-195. [BT89.N48 1975] 76-358303 ISBN 0-19-713138-7 : £7.50
1. Bible and tradition. I. Jager, Jean-Nicolas, 1790-1868. II. Allen, Louis. III. Title. IV. Series: Durham, Eng. University. Publications.

PIETERS, Albertus, 1869- 220.1
Can we trust Bible history? Grand Rapids, Society for Reformed Publications, 1954. 119p. 21cm. [BS480.P55] 54-10171
1. Bible—Evidences, authority. etc. I. Title.

PINNOCK, Clark H., 1937- 220.1
Biblical revelation, the foundation of Christian theology, by Clark H. Pinnock. Chicago, Moody Press [1971] 256 p. 22 cm. Bibliography: p. 231-250. [BS480.P618] 70-143479 4.95
1. Bible—Inspiration. I. Title.

PLOWMAN, Max G. 220.1
Bible facts and precis, regarding the dates of writing, authorship, dates of [BS475.2.P56] 66-31773
I. Title.

PLOWMAN, Max G 220.1
Bible facts and precis, regarding the dates of writing, authorship, dates of events, historical value, sources, and contents of each book of the Holy Bible, by Max G. Plowman [New York?] 1966. x. 114 p. 24 cm. "Based on the 1611. Authorized (King James) version of the Bible." Bibliography: p. 99-106. [BS475.2.P56] 66-31773
1. Bible—Introductions I. Title.

RAND, Howard B 1889- 220.1
Documentary studies. Haverhill, Mass., Destiny Publishers [1947-54] 3v. illus., maps. 23cm. 'Originally published as articles in Destiny magazine during the jears from 1941 to [1954]' [BS647.R3] 48-18135
1. Bible—Prophecies. I. Title.

RIDENOUR, Fritz. 220.1
Who says? A discussion of basic questions of the Christian faith; including the existence of God, the trustworthiness of the Bible, the conflict between science and Scripture. Editor: Frtiz Ridenour. Writing and research consultants: David Harvey [and others] Illustrator: Joyce Thimsen. Glendale, Calif. [Regal Books Division, G/L Publications, c1967] 186 p. illus. 18 cm. Includes bibliograpies. [BS480.R52] 68-16268
1. Bible—Evidences, authority, etc. 2. Bible and science. I. Title.

RIDENOUR, Fritz. 220.1
Who says? A discussion of basic questions of the Christian faith; including the existence of God, the trustworthiness of the Bible, the conflict between science and Scripture. Editor: Fritz Ridenour. Writing and research consultants: David Harvey [and others] Illustrator: Joyce Thimsen. Glendale, Calif. [Regal Books Division, G/L Publications, c1967] 186 p. illus. 18 cm. Includes bibliographies. [BS480.R52] 68-16268
1. Bible—Evidences, authority, etc. 2. Bible and science. I. Title.

ROLSTON, Holmes, 1900- 220.1
The Bible in Christian teaching. Richmond, Va., John Knox [c.1962] 104p. 62-10238 1.50 pap.,
1. Bible—Evidences, authority, etc. I. Title.

ROLSTON, Holmes, 1900- 220.1
The Bible in Christian teaching. Richmond, Va., Knox [1966, c.1962] 104p. 21cm. (Aletheia ed.) [BT89.R6] 62-10238 1.45 pap.,
1. Bible — Evidences, authority, etc. I. Title.

RUNIA, Klaas. 220.1
Karl Barth's doctrine of Holy Scripture. Grand Rapids, Erdmans [1962] ix, 225p. 23cm. Bibliographical footnotes. [BS480.R77] 61-10866
1. Barth, Karl, 1886- 2. Bible—Evidences, authority, etc.—History of doctrines. I. Title.

SIZOO, Joseph Richard, 220.1
1884-
I believe in the Bible. New York, Abingdon Press [1958] 80 p. 20 cm. [BS480.S55] 58-9525
1. Bible — Evidences, authority, etc. I. Title.

SKUPINSKA-LoVSET, Ilona, 220.1
1945-
The Ustinov collection : the Palestinian pottery / Ilona Skupinska-Lovset. Oslo : Universitetsforl., c1976. 177 p., [20] leaves of plates : ill. ; 25 cm. Bibliography: p. 7-11. [DS111.9.S55] 77-462122 ISBN 8-200-01564-5 : kr80.00
1. Ustinow, Plato, Baron von—Archaeological collections. 2. Palestine—Antiquities—Catalogs. 3. Pottery—Palestine—Catalogs. I. Title.

SURBURG, Raymond F., 1909- 220.1
How dependable is the Bible? [By] Raymond F. Surburg. [1st ed.] Philadelphia, Lippincott [1972] 204 p. 21 cm. (Evangelical perspectives) "A Holman book." Bibliography: p. 196-204. [BS480.S77] 75-39707 ISBN 0-87981-003-3 5.95
1. Bible—Evidences, authority, etc. 2. Bible—Criticism, interpretation, etc. I. Title.

SYME, George S. 220.1
The closer you look, the greater the book : Bible proofs / George S. Syme, Charlotte U. Syme. Denver : Accent Books, c1976. 160 p. ; 21 cm. Published in 1968 under title: The Scriptures cannot be broken. Includes indexes. Bibliography: p. 155-156. [BS480.S88 1976] 76-8731 ISBN 0-916406-20-2 pbk. : 2.95
1. Bible—Evidences, authority, etc. I. Syme, Charlotte U., joint author. II. Title.

TENNEY, Merrill Chapin, 220.1
1904-
The Bible; the living word of revelation, edited by Merrill C. Tenney. With essays by John H. Gerstner [and others] Grand Rapids, Zondervan Pub. House [1968] 228 p. ports. 23 cm. (An Evangelical Theological Society publication. Monograph no. 6) Includes bibliographical references. [BS480.T4] 69-11632 5.95
1. Bible—Sources, authority, etc. 2. Revelation. I. Gerstner, John H. II. Title. III. Series: Evangelical Theological Society. Monograph no. 6

THOMAS, James David, 1910- 220.1
Heaven's window : sequel to We be brethren / by J. D. Thomas. Abilene, Tex. : Biblical Research Press, c1974. viii, 151 p. ; 23 cm. Includes bibliographical references. [BS480.T48] 74-28950 6.95
1. Bible—Evidences, authority, etc. 2. Knowledge, Theory of (Religion) 3. Churches of Christ—Doctrinal and controversial works. I. Title.

*VOS, Howard F 220.1
Can I trust the Bible? Important questions often asked about the Bible ... with some answers by eight evangelical scholars. Edited by Howard F. Vos. Chicago, Moody Press [1973, c.1963] 190 p. 21 cm. (Moody evangelical focus) [BT89] ISBN 0-8024-1161-4 2.50 (pbk.)
1. Bible—Evidence, authority, etc. I. Title.

WARD, Wayne E. 220.1
Is the Bible a human book? Edited by Wayne E. Ward [and] Joseph F. Green. Nashville, Tenn., Broadman Press [1970] 159 p. 21 cm. [BS480.W29] 79-95418 3.50
1. Bible—Evidences, authority, etc.—Addresses, essays, lectures. I. Green, Joseph Franklin, 1924- joint author. II. Title.

WATCH Tower Bible and Tract 220.1
Society of Pennsylvania.
Is the Bible really the word of God? [1st ed. Brooklyn, Watchtower Bible and Tract Society of New York, 1969] 190 p. illus. (part col.) 17 cm. Includes bibliographical references. [BS480.W36] 78-11105
1. Bible—Evidences, authority, etc. I. Title.

WENHAM, John William. 220.1
Christ & the Bible [by] John W. Wenham. Downers Grove, Ill., InterVarsity Press [1973, c1972] 206 p. 21 cm. Includes bibliographical references. [BS511.2.W46 1973] 72-97950 ISBN 0-87784-760-6 2.95
1. Jesus Christ—Attitude towards the Old Testament. 2. Jesus Christ—Person and offices. 3. Bible—Criticism, interpretation, etc. I. Title.

WILLIAMS, Herbert Lee. 220.1
No room for doubt / Herbert Lee Williams ; foreword by Ramsey Pollard. Nashville : Broadman Press, c1976. 163 p. ; 19 cm. Includes bibliographical references. [BS480.W524] 75-39574 ISBN 0-8054-5236-2 pbk. : 2.95
1. Bible—Evidences, authority, etc. 2. Apologetics—20th century. I. Title.

WILSON, Clifford A. 220.1
Rocks, relics, and Biblical reliability : a study based on archaeological evidence / Clifford Wilson ; with a response by R. K. Harrison. Grand Rapids : Zondervan Pub. House, [1977] p. cm. (Christian free university curriculum) Bibliography: p. [BS621.W466] 77-9415 ISBN 0-310-35701-2 : 3.95
1. Bible—Antiquities. I. Title. II. Series.

WOLSELEY, Charles, Sir, 2d 220.1
bart., 1630?-1714.
The reasonableness of Scripture-belief (1672) A facsim. reproduction with an introd. by Robert W. McHenry, Jr. Delmar, N.Y., Scholars' Facsimiles & Reprints, 1973. xii, [12]

, 447 p. 23 cm. Original t.p. reads: The reasonablenes of Scripture-belief. A discourse giving some account of those rational grounds upon which the Bible is received as the word of God. Written by Sir Charles Wolseley, bart. London, Printed by T. R. & N. T. for Nathaniel Ponder at the Peacock in Chancery Lane near Fleet-Street, 1672. Wing W3313. [BS480.W67 1973] 73-2618 ISBN 0-8201-1113-9 25.00
1. Bible—Evidences, authority, etc. I. Title.

BARCLAY, William 220.12
The making of the Bible. Nashville, Abingdon Press [1961] 95, [1]p. (Bible guides, no. 1) Bibl. 61-2734 1.00 pap.,
1. Bible—Canon. I. Title.

CAMPENHAUSEN, Hans, Freiherr von, 1903- 220.1'2
The formation of the Christian Bible, by Hans von Campenhausen. Translated by J. A. Baker. Philadelphia, Fortress Press [1972] xiv, 342 p. 23 cm. Translation of Die Entstehung der christlichen Bibel. Includes bibliographical references. [BS465.C313 1972] 73-171495 ISBN 0-8006-0223-4 10.95
1. Bible—Canon. I. Title.

FILSON, Floyd Vivian, 1896- 220.12
Which books belong in the Bible? A study of the canon. Philadelphia, Westminster Press [1957] 174 p. 21 cm. Includes bibliography. [BS465.F5] 57-6289
1. Bible—Canon. I. Title.

HARRIS, Robert Laird. 220.12
Inspiration and canonicity of the Bible; an historical and exegetical study. Grand Rapids, Zondervan Pub. House [1957] 304p. 23cm. Includes bibliography. [BS480.H27] 57-27076
1. Bible—Inspiration. 2. Bible—Canon. I. Title.

HARRIS, Robert Laird. 220.1'2
Inspiration and canonicity of the Bible; an historical and exegetical study, by R. Laird Harris. Grand Rapids, Zondervan Pub. House [1971, c1969] 316 p. 21 cm. (Contemporary evangelical perspectives) Includes bibliographical references. [BS480.H27 1971] 78-81044
1. Bible—Inspiration. 2. Bible—Canon. I. Title.

KLINE, Meredith G. 220.1'2
The structure of Biblical authority, by Meredith G. Kline. Grand Rapids, Mich., Eerdmans [1972] 183 p. 21 cm. Includes bibliographical references. [BS465.K57] 72-75576 ISBN 0-8028-1475-1 2.95
1. Bible—Canon. 2. Covenants (Theology)—Biblical teaching. I. Title.

SWAIM, Joseph Carter, 1904- 220.12
Where our Bible came from; how the Old Testament canon and the New Testament cannon came into being. New York, Association Press [1960] 128 p. 16 cm. (An Association Press reflection book) Includes bibliography. [BX465.S9] 60-6571
1. Bible—Cannon. I. Title.

SWAIM, Joseph Carter, 1904- 220.12
Where our Bible came from; how the Old Testament canon and the New Testament canon came into being. New York, Association Press [1960] 128 p. 16 cm. (An Association Press reflection book) Includes bibliography. [BS465.S9] 60-6571
1. Bible—Canon. I. Title.

ALONSO Schokel, Luis, 1920- 220.1'3
The inspired word: Scripture in the light of language and literature. Translated by Francis Martin. [New York] Herder and Herder [1972, c1965] 418 p. 21 cm. Translation of La palabra inspirada. Includes bibliographies. [BS540.A5813 1972] 72-178995 ISBN 0-665-00016-2 5.95
1. Bible—Addresses, essays, lectures. 2. Bible—Inspiration—Addresses, essays, lectures. I. Title.

ALONSO SCHOKEL, Luis, 1920- 220.13
The inspired word; Scripture in the light of language and literature. Translated by Francis Martin. [New York] Herder and Herder [1965] 418 p. 22 cm. Includes bibliographies. [BS540.A5813] 65-21943
1. Bible — Addresses, essays, lectures. 2. Bible — Inspiration — Addresses, essays, lectures. I. Title.

ALONSO SCHOKEL, Luis, 1920- 220.13
The inspired word; Scripture in the light of language and literature. Tr. by Francis Martin [New York] Herder & Herder [c.1965] 418p. 22cm. Bibl. [BS540.A5813] 65-21943 8.50
1. Bible — Addresses, essays, lectures. 2. Bible — Inspiration — Addresses, essays, lectures. I. Title.

ANDERSON, Stanely Edwin. 220.13
Our dependable Bible. Grand Rapids, Baker Book House, 1960. 248p. 23cm. Includes bibliography. [BS480.A65] 60-15501
1. Bible—Evidences, authority, etc. I. Title.

BEEGLE, Dewey M. 220.13
The inspiration of Scripture. Philadelphia, Westminster [c.1963] 223p. 21cm. Bibl. 63-7342 4.50
1. Bible—Inspiration. I. Title.

BEEGLE, Dewey M. 220.1'3
Scripture, tradition, and infallibility [by] Dewey M. Beegle. Grand Rapids, Eerdmans [1973] 332 p. 21 cm. Published in 1963 under title: The inspiration of Scripture. Bibliography: p. 313-320. [BS480.B363 1973] 73-78218 ISBN 0-8028-1549-9 4.95 (pbk.)
1. Bible—Inspiration. 2. Revelation. 3. Bible and tradition. I. Title.

BENOIT, Pierre, Aug. 3, 1906- 220.13
Aspects of Biblical inspiration. Tr. by J. Murphy-O'Connor, S. K. Ashe. Chicago, Prior Pr. 2005 S. Ashland Ave [1965] 127p. 19cm. (Probe bks.) [BS480.B38] 65-19359 2.45
1. Bible—Inspiration. 2. Revelation. I. Title. II. Title: The analogies of inspiration. III. Title: Revelation and inspiration.
Contents omitted.

BRYANT, Robert H. 220.1'3
The Bible's authority today, by Robert H. Bryant. Minneapolis, Augsburg Pub. House [1968] 235 p. 22 cm. Bibliography: p. 215-223. [BT89.B7] 68-13429
1. Bible—Evidences, authority, etc. 2. Authority (Religion) I. Title.

COLERIDGE, Samuel Taylor, 1772-1834. 220.13
Confessions of an inquiring spirit. Edited with an introductory note by H. StJ. Hart. Stanford, Calif., Stanford University Press [1957] 120p. 23cm. (A Library of modern religious thought) 'Reprinted from the third edition 1853, with the introduction by Joseph Henry Green and the note by Sara Coleridge.' [BS480.C6 1957] 57-9372
1. Bible—Inspiration. 2. Lessing. Gotthold Ephraim, 1729-1781. 3. 1802-1852. I. Celeridge, Sara (Coleridge) II. Title. III. Series.

CUSTER, Stewart, 1931- 220.1'3
Does inspiration demand inerrancy? A study of the Biblical doctrine of inspiration in the light of inerrancy. Nutley, N.J., Craig Press [1968] 120 p. 22 cm. Includes bibliographical references. [BS480.C83] 71-1057 3.50
1. Bible—Inspiration—History of doctrines. I. Title.

EDWARDS, David Lawrence. 220.1'3
This Church of England. With a pref. by the Bishop of London. Westminster, Church Information Office [1962] 196 p. 19 cm. [BX5131.2.E3] 64-36037
1. Church of England. I. Title.

*HARLESS, Dan 220'.13
Fireside chats a treasury of inspiration Grand Rapids, Baker Book, [1974] 91 p. illus., 21 cm. [BT125] 74-20201 ISBN 0-8010-4103-1 4.95
1. Bible—Inspiration. I. Title.

*HUMBER, Thomas. 220.13
The fifth gospel; the miracle of the holy shroud. New York, Pocket Books [1974] 176 p. 18 cm. Bibliography: p. 171-175 [BS480] ISBN 0-671-78467-6 1.50 (pbk.)
1. Bible—Inspiration. I. Title.

JEREMIAH, James T. 220.1'3
The importance of inspiration, by James T. Jeremiah. Des Plaines, Ill., Regular Baptist Press [1972] 93 p. 22 cm. Bibliography: p. 91-93. [BS480.J47] 76-187282 2.95
1. Bible—Inspiration. I. Title.

KELSEY, David H. 220.1'3
The uses of Scripture in recent theology / by David H. Kelsey. Philadelphia : Fortress Press, [1975] ix, 227 p. ; 24 cm. Includes index. Bibliography: 218-224. [BT89.K44] 74-26344 ISBN 0-8006-0401-6 : 11.95
1. Bible—Evidences, authority, etc.—History of doctrines. 2. Theology, Doctrinal—History—20th century. 3. Theology, Protestant. I. Title.

LEWIS, Edwin, 1881- 220.13
The Biblical faith and Christian freedom. Philadelphia, Westminster Press [1953] 224p. 22cm. (The Southwestern lectures, 1952) [BS480.LA93] 52-13516
1. Bible—Evidences, authority, etc. 2. Bevelation. 3. Bible—Criticism, interpretation, etc. I. Title.

LINDSELL, Harold, 1913- 220.1'3
The battle for the Bible / Harold Lindsell. Grand Rapids : Zondervan Pub. House, c1976. 218 p. ; 22 cm. Includes bibliographical references and index. [BS480.L55] 75-38794 6.95
1. Bible—Inspiration. 2. Bible—Evidences, authority, etc. I. Title.

LOHFINK, Gerhard, 1934- 220.1'3
The Gospels; God's word in human words. Translated by William R. Poehlmann. Chicago, Franciscan Herald Press [1972] 68 p. 18 cm. (Herald Biblical booklets) Translation of Die Bibel. [BS480.L5813] 72-77453 ISBN 0-8199-0212-8 pap. 0.95
1. Bible—Inspiration. I. Title.

NEWMAN, John Henry, Cardinal, 1801-1890 220.1'3
On the inspiration of Scripture. Ed. by J. Derek Holmes, Robert Murray. [1st ed.] Washington, Corpus Bks. [c1967] 153p. 23 cm. Bibl. [BS480.N42 1967] 68-8315 6.50
1. Bible—Inspiration. I. Holmes, J. Derek. ed. II. Murray, Robert, 1925- ed. III. Title.
Publisher's address: 1330 Massachusetts Ave., N.W., Washington, D.C. 20005.

PACHE, Rene. 220.1'3
The inspriation and authority of Scripture. Translated by Helen I. Needham. Chicago, Moody Press [1969] 349 p. 24 cm. Translation of L'inspiration et l'autorite de la Bible. Bibliography: p. 334-338. [BS480.P2313] 72-13505 5.95
1. Bible—Inspiration. 2. Bible—Evidences, authority, etc. I. Title.

PACKER, James Innell. 220.13
God speaks to man; revelation and the Bible, by J. L. Packer. Philadelphia, Westminster Press [1965] 95 p. 19 cm. (Christian foundations) Bibliography: p. 94-95. [BS480.P24] 66-11607
1. Bible — Inspiration. I. Title.

PACKER, James Innell 220.13
God speaks to man; revelation and the Bible. Philadelphia, Westminster [c.1965] 95p. 19cm. (Christian founds.) Bibl. [BS480.P24] 66-11607 1.25 pap.,
1. Bible — Inspiration. I. Title.

PINNOCK, Clark H., 1937- 220.1'3
A defense of Biblical infallibility [by] Clark H. Pinnock. Philadelphia, Presbyterian and Reformed Pub. Co., 1967. 32 p. 23 cm. (The Tyndale lecture in Biblical theology, 1966) (International library of philosophy and theology: Biblical and theological studies.) (International library of philosophy and theology: Biblical and theological studies) Bibliographical footnotes. [BS480.P62] 66-30703
1. Bible—Evidences, authority, etc. 2. Bible—Inspiration. I. Title. II. Series. III. Series: The Tyndale Biblical theology lecture, 1966.

RAHNER, Karl, 1904- 220.13
Inspiration in the Bible. [New York] Herder and Herder [1961] 79p. 22cm. (Quaestiones disputatae, 1) [BS480.R253] 61-11442
1. Bible—Inspiration. I. Title.

RAHNER, Karl, 1904- 220.13
Inspiration in the Bible. [Translated by Charles H. Henkey] Friburh, Herder [1961] 79p. 22cm. (Quaestiones disputatae, 1) Includes bibliography. [BS480.R253 1961a] 61-10179
1. Bible—Inspiration. I. Title.

RICE, John R., 1895- 220.1'3
Our God-breathed book, the Bible, by John R. Rice. Murfreesboro, Tenn., Sword of the Lord Publishers [1969] 416 p. 24 cm. Includes bibliographical references. [BS480.R48] 70-107027 5.95
1. Bible—Inspiration. I. Title.

RIDDERBOS, Herman N. 220.1'3
Studies in Scripture and its authority / by Herman Ridderbos. Grand Rapids : Eerdmans, c1977. p. cm. Revised versions of lectures given under the sponsorship of the Calvin Foundation. [BS480.R517] 77-13206 ISBN 0-8028-1707-6 pbk. : 3.95
1. Bible—Inspiration—Addresses, essays, lectures. 2. Bible—Evidences, authority, etc.—Addresses, essays, lectures. 3. Bible. N.T. Gospels—Criticism, interpretation, etc.—Addresses, essays, lectures. I. Title.

SCHOKEL, Luis, 1920- 220.1'3
The inspired word: Scripture in the light of language and literature; translated [from the Spanish] by Francis Martin. London, Burns & Oates; New York, Herder, 1967. 3-418 p. 22 1/2 cm. 63/- (B 67-22249) Translation of La Palabra inspirada. Includes bibliographies. [BS540.A5813 1967] 68-124841
1. Bible—Addresses, essays, lectures. 2. Bible—Inspiration—Addresses, essays, lectures. I. Title.

SCULLION, John. 220.1'3
The theology of inspiration. Notre Dame, Ind., Fides Publishers [1971, c1970] 96 p. 19 cm. (Theology today, no. 10) Bibliography: p. 92-93. [BS480.S644] 73-27745 ISBN 0-85342-229-X 0.95
1. Bible—Inspiration. I. Title.

VAWTER, Bruce. 220.1'3
Biblical inspiration. Philadelphia, Westminster [Press] [1972] xii, 194 p. 24 cm. (Theological resources) Bibliography: p. 179-184. [BS480.V3 1972] 77-137396 ISBN 0-664-20914-9 9.95
1. Bible—Inspiration. I. Title.

WALVOORD, John F ed. *220.13
Inspiration and interpretation. Grand Rapids, Eerdmans [1957] 280 p. 23 cm. "An Evangelical Theological Society publication." Bibliographical footnotes. [BS500.W3] 57-7392
1. Bible — Criticism, interpretation, etc. — Hist. I. Title.

WALVOORD, John F ed. 220.13
Inspiration and interpretation. Grand Rapids, Eerdmans [1957] 280p. 23cm. (An Evangelical Theological Society publication) Bibliographical footnotes. [BS500.W3] 57-7392
1. Bible—Criticism, interpretation, etc. —Hist. I. Title. II. Series: Evangelical Theological Society. Publication

WARFIELD, Benjamin Breckinridge, 1851-1921 220.13
Limited inspiration. Grand Rapids, Mich., Baker Bk. [1962] 54p. 23cm. (Intl. lib. of philosophy and theology; Biblical and theological studies) Appeared orig. in the January 1894 issue of the Presbyterian and Reformed review, under the title: Professor Henry Preserved Smith on inspiration. 61-11747 1.25 pap.,
1. Smith, Henry Preserved, 1874-1927. 2. Bible—Inspiration—History of doctrines. I. Title.

WORLD Council of Churches. *220.13
The Biblical authority for today; a World Council of Churches symposium on "The Biblical authority for the churches' social and political message today," edited by Alan Richardson [and] W. Schweitzer. Philadelphia, Westminster Press [1951] 347 p. 22 cm. [BS480.W785] 52-7065
1. Bible — Evidences, authority, etc. 2. Bible — Hermeneuties. I. Richardson, Alan, 1905- ed. II. Schweitzer, Wolfgang, joint ed. III. Title.

YOUNG, Edward Joseph. *220.13
Thy word is truth; some thoughts on the Biblical doctrine of inspiration. Grand Rapids, Eerdmans [1957] 287 p. 23 cm. [BS480.Y6] 57-11585
1. Bible — Inspiration. I. Title.

YOUNG, Edward Joseph. 220.13
Thy word is truth; some thoughts on the Biblical doctrine of inspiration. Grand Rapids, Eerdmans [1957] 287 p. 23 cm. [BS480.Y6] 57-11585
I. Title.

BURTCHAELL, James Tunstead. 220.1'3'09
Catholic theories of Biblical inspiration since 1810: a review and critique. London, Cambridge U.P., 1969. viii, 342 p. 23 cm. Bibliography: p. 306-335. [BS480.B79] 77-77284 ISBN 5-210-74851- 70/- ($9.50)
1. Bible—Inspiration—History of doctrines. I. Title.

GLADDEN, Washington, 1836-1918. 220.1'4
Who wrote the Bible? A book for the people. Freeport, N.Y., Books for Libraries Press [1972] 381 p. 22 cm. Reprint of the 1891 ed. [BS511.G525 1972] 72-5435 ISBN 0-8369-6909-X
1. Bible—Criticism, interpretation, etc. I. Title.

ALDERMAN, Paul Repton, 1911- 220.15
The unfolding of the ages: prophecy fulfilled, prophecy being fulfilled, prophecy to be fulfilled. Introd. by Jacob Gartenhaus Foreword by E. Schuyler English. Grand Rapids, Zondervan Pub. House [1954] 148p. 20cm. [BT875.A63] 54-3697
1. Bible—Prophecies. I. Title.

ALDERMAN, Paul Repton, Jr., 1911- 220.15
The unfolding of the ages: prophecy fulfilled, prophecy being fulfilled, prophecy to be fulfilled. Introd. by Jacob Gartenhaus; foreword by E. Schuyler English. Neptune, N. J., Loizeaux [1965, c.1954] 148p. 19cm. [BT875.A63] 1.00 pap.,
1. Bible—Prophecies. I. Title.

ARMSTRONG, Herbert W 220.1'5
The United States and British Commonwealth in prophecy [by] Herbert W. Armstrong. [Passadena, Calif., Ambassador College Press, 1967] xii, 226 p. illus. (part col.) col. maps. 22 cm. [BS649.G7A83] 68-802
1. Bible—Prophecies—Gt. Brit. 2. Anglo-Israelism. I. Title.

ARMSTRONG, Herbert W. 220.1'5
The United States and British Commonwealth in prophecy [by] Herbert W. Armstrong. [Pasadena, Calif., Ambassador College Press, 1967] xii, 226 p. illus. (part col.) col. maps, 22 cm. [BS649.G7A83] 68-802
1. Bible—Prophecies—Gt. Brit. 2. Anglo-Israelism. I. Title.

ATKINS, Mary (Sayles), 1879- 220.15
The conquest of chaos, by Mary Sayles Moore [pseud.] Biddeford, Me., A. A. Beauchamp Co. [1952]- v. illus. 20 cm. [BS647.A75] 52-64331
1. Bible—Prophecies. I. Title.

BENSON, Carmen. 220.1'5
Supernatural dreams and visions; Bible prophecy for the future revealed. With foreword by Ray Charles Jarman. Plainfield, N.J., Logos International [1970] xiii, 322 p. 21 cm. [BF1099.B5B4] 71-110460
1. Bible—Prophecies. 2. Dreams in the Bible. 3. Visions in the Bible. I. Title.

BERCOVICI, Myrna, comp. 220.1'5
Prophecy; an interpretation. Text and photos. selected by Myrna Bercovici. Los Angeles, J. P. Tarcher; distributed by Hawthorn Books, New York [1973] 93 p. illus. 23 cm. Selected from the Old Testament, King James version. [BS1091.B43] 73-83282 ISBN 0-87477-011-4 3.95 ($4.50 Can)
I. Bible. O.T. English. Authorized. Selections. 1973. II. Title.

BERG, Orley. 220.1'5
The restless land : Israel, its place in history and prophecy / Orley M. Berg. Washington : Review and Herald Pub. Association, c1974. 111 p. ; 22 cm. [BS649.J5B44] 74-81129
1. Bible—Prophecies—Jews. 2. Israel. I. Title.

BOICE, James Montgomery, 1938- 220.1'5
The last and future world. Grand Rapids, Zondervan Pub. House [1974] xi, 148 p. 21 cm. [BS647.2.B64] 73-22702 3.95; 1.95 (pbk.)
1. Bible—Prophecies. I. Title.

BOOTS, Ra 220.15
Prophetic time marches on. [1st ed.] New York, Vantage Press [1957] 86p. 21cm. Includes bibliography. [BS647.B58] 56-12924
1. Bible—Prophecies. I. Title.

BOTTS, R A 220.15
Prophetic time marches on. [1st ed.] New York, Vantage Press [1957] 86p. 21cm. Includes bibliography. [BS647.B58] 56-12924
1. Bible—Prophecies. I. Title.

BRITT, George L 220.15
When dust shall sing; the world crisis in the light of Bible prophecy. [1st ed.] Cleveland, Tenn., Pathway Press [1958] 203p. 21cm. [BT875.B753] 58-13663
1. End of the world. 2. Bible—Prophecies. I. Title.

*BURLING, Donald O. 220.1'5
From Tekoa to Tarsus. New York, Vantage [1967] 250p. 21cm. 4.50 bds.,
I. Title.

BUXTON, Clyne W. 220.1'5
The Bible says you can expect these things [by] Clyne W. Buxton. Old Tappan, N.J., F. H. Revell Co. [1973] 160 p. 21 cm. Half title: Expect these things. Bibliography: p. 152-156. [BS647.2.B8] 72-10330 ISBN 0-8007-0572-6 2.95 (pbk.)
1. Bible—Prophecies. I. Title. II. Title: Expect these things.

CLEMENT, George H. 220.1'5
The ABC's of the prophetical scriptures [by] George H. Clement. Nashville, Tenn., Broadman Press [1970] 64 p. 19 cm. [BS647.2.C55] 78-117306
1. Bible—Prophecies. I. Title.

CONGRESS on Prophecy. 3d, Chicago, 1963 220.15
Focus on prophecy; message delivered at the Congress on Prophecy convened by the American Board of Missions to the Jews at the Moody Memorial Church in Chicago. Ed. by Charles L. Feinberg Westwood, N.J. Revell [c.1964] 254p. 21cm. 64-16602 3.95 bds.,
1. Bible—Prophecies—Congresses. I. Feinberg, Charles Lee, ed. II. American Board of Missions to the Jews. III. Title.

CONGRESS on Prophecy, 5th, New York, 1967. 220.1'5
Prophetic truth unfolding today; messages delivered at the Congress on Prophecy convened by the American Board of Mission[s] to the Jews, inc., in the metropolitan New York area. Edited by Charles Lee Feinberg. Westwood, N.J., F. H. Revell Co. [1968] 160 p. 21 cm. [BS647.2.C63 1967a] 68-11364
1. Bible—Prophecies. I. Feinberg, Charles Lee, ed. II. American Board of Missions to the Jews. III. Title.

CONGRESS on Prophecy, 7th, New York, 1973. 220.1'5
Jesus the King is coming / Charles Lee Feinberg, editor. Chicago : Moody Press, [1975] 190 p. ; 22 cm. Messages presented at the Congress on Prophecy sponsored by the American Board of Missions to the Jews. [BS647.2.C63 1973] 74-15351 ISBN 0-8024-4331-1 : 4.95
1. Bible—Prophecies—Congresses. I. Feinberg, Charles Lee. II. American Board of Missions to the Jews. III. Title.

CONGRESS on Prophecy, 6th, New York, 1970. 220.1'5
Prophecy and the seventies. Charles Lee Feinberg, editor. Chicago, Moody Press [1971] 255 p. 22 cm. Messages delivered at the Congress on Prophecy sponsored by the American Board of Missions to the Jews, inc. Includes bibliographical references. [BS647.2.C63 1970] 77-143470 4.95
1. Bible—Prophecies—Congresses. I. Feinberg, Charles Lee, ed. II. American Board of Missions to the Jews. III. Title.

COOKE, A. Ernest 220.15
Fulfilled prophecy; the evidence of the truth of the Bible record. Chicago, Moody [c.1963] 64p. 18cm. (Compact bks., 32) .29 pap.,
I. Title.

DAVIS, George Thompson Brown, 1873- 220.15
Bible prophecies fulfilled today. Philadelphia, Million Testaments Campaigns [1955] 106p. illus. 19cm. [BS619.J5D33] 55-11677
1. Jews—Restoration. I. Title.

DAY, Bertram, 1871- 220.15
The Prophets' dawn; the Prophets speak. Boston, Christopher Pub. House [1957] 294p. 21cm. [BS647.D35] 57-11961
1. Bible—Prophecies. I. Title.

DEHAAN, Richard W. 220.1'5
Israel and the nations in prophecy, by Richard W. DeHaan. Foreword by Lehman Strauss. Grand Rapids, Zondervan Pub. House [1968] 146 p. 22 cm. [BS647.2.D4] 68-22171
1. Bible—Prophecies. I. Title.

DEHAAN, Richard W. 220.1'5
Israel and the nations in prophecy / Richard W. DeHaan. Newly rev. condensed ed. Grand Rapids, Mich. : Zondervan Pub. House, 1977. 95 p. ; 18 cm. [BS649.J5D42 1977] 77-371293 ISBN 0-310-23512-X : 1.50
1. Bible—Prophecies—Jews. 2. Bible—Prophecies—Russia. I. Title.

DREAMS, visions, and oracles : the layman's guide to Biblical prophecy / edited by Carl Edwin Armerding and W. Ward Gasque. Grand Rapids, Mich. : Baker Book House, c1977. 262 p. ; 23 cm. Bibliography: p. 249-254. [BS647.2.D7] 77-151250 ISBN 0-8010-0088-2 : 9.95 220.1'5
1. Bible—Prophecies—Addresses, essays, lectures. I. Amerding, Carl Edwin. II. Gasque, W. Ward.

DREAMS, visions, and oracles : the layman's guide to Biblical prophecy / edited by Carl Edwin Armerding and W. Ward Gasque. Grand Rapids, Mich. : Baker Book House, c1977. 262 p. ; 23 cm. Bibliography: p. 249-254. [BS647.2.D7] 77-151250 ISBN 0-8010-0088-2 : 9.95 220.1'5
1. Bible—Prophecies—Addresses, essays, lectures. I. Amerding, Carl Edwin. II. Gasque, W. Ward.

DUKES, T. F. 220.1'5
Adam, Abraham and the Apocalypse, by T. F. Dukes. Philadelphia, Dorrance [1970] 161 p. 22 cm. [BS647.2.D8] 74-113984 4.00
1. Bible—Prophecies. 2. Apocalyptic literature. I. Title.

ELLISEN, Stanley A. 220.1'5
Biography of a great planet / Stanley A. Ellisen. Wheaton, Ill. : Tyndale House Publishers, 1975. 272 p. : ill. ; 21 cm. Includes indexes. [BS647.2.E43] 75-7223 ISBN 0-8423-0111-9 pbk. : 3.95
1. Bible—Prophecies. I. Title.

FEINBERG, Charles Lee. 220.1'5
Israel in the spotlight / Charles Lee Feinberg. Rev. ed. Chicago : Moody Press, c1975,i.e.1976 190 p. ; 22 cm. Includes bibliographical references. [BS649.J5F37 1975] 76-361423 ISBN 0-8024-4178-5 : 4.95
1. Bible—Prophecies—Jews. I. Title.

FOWLER, Daniel Keener, 1926- 220.1'5
Understanding the last days / author, Daniel Keener Fowler. Montgomery, Ala. : Fowler, c1975. vi, 114 p. ; 22 cm. [BS647.2.F65] 75-29651
1. Fowler, Daniel Keener, 1926- 2. Bible—Prophecies. I. Title.

GIRDLESTONE, Robert Baker, 1836-1923. 220.15
The grammar of prophecy; a systematic guide to Biblical prophecy. Grand Rapids, Kregel Publications, 1955. 192p. 20cm. [BS647.G5] 55-9466
1. Bible—Prophecies. I. Title.

HAGEE, John C. 220.1'5
Like a cleansing fire [by] John C. Hagee. Old Tappan, N.J., Revell [1974] p. cm. [BS649.U6H33] 74-13523 ISBN 0-8007-0685-4 1.25 (pbk.)
1. Bible—Prophecies—United States. I. Title.

HANSON, Richard S. 220.1'5
The future of the great planet earth; what does Biblical prophecy mean for you? [By] Richard S. Hanson. Minneapolis, Augsburg Pub. House [1972] 123 p. 20 cm. [BS647.2.H34] 72-78554 ISBN 0-8066-1222-3 2.95
1. Bible—Prophecies. I. Title.

HORTON, Stanley M. 220.1'5
What you should know about prophecy / C. M. Ward ; adapted from Bible prophecy by Stanley M. Horton. Springfield, Mo. : Gospel Pub. House, c1975. 127 p. ; 18 cm. (Radiant books) [BS647.2.H67] 75-22610 ISBN 0-88243-890-5 : 1.25
1. Bible—Prophecies. I. Horton, Stanley M. Bible prophecy. II. Title.

HUGHES, Philip Edgcumbe. 220.1'5
Interpreting prophecy : an essay in Biblical perspectives / by Philip Edgcumbe Hughes. Grand Rapids : Eerdmans, c1976. 135 p. ; 21 cm. [BS647.2.H78] 75-41484 ISBN 0-8028-1630-4 pbk. : 2.95
1. Bible—Prophecies. I. Title.

HUGHES, Ray H 220.1'5
The order of future events. [Cleveland? Tenn., 1962] 80p. illus. 19cm. [BS647.2.H8] 62-20851
1. Bible—Prophecies. 2. Pentecostal churches—Sermons. 3. Sermons, American. I. Title.

HUGHES, Ray H. 220.15
The order of future events. [Cleveland, Tenn., Pathway, c.1962] 80p. illus. 19cm. 62-20851 1.00 pap.,
1. Bible—Prophecies. 2. Pentecostal churches—Sermons. 3. Sermons, American. I. Title.

INCH, Morris A., 1925- 220.1'5
Understanding Bible prophecy / Morris A. Inch. 1st ed. New York : Harper & Row, c1977. vii, 151 p. ; 21 cm. [BS647.2.I5 1977] 77-2608 ISBN 0-06-064087-1 pbk. : 3.95
1. Bible—Prophecies. I. Title.

JENNINGS, Frederick Charles, 1847- 220.1'5
Studies in Isaiah. New York, Loizeaux Bros. [1950] 784p. 23cm. [BS1515.J44] 55-41748
1. Bible. O. T. Isaiah-Commentaries. I. Title.

JERUSALEM Conference on Biblical Prophecy, 1971. 220.1'5
Prophecy in the making; messages prepared for Jerusalem Conference on Biblical Prophecy [by] W. A. Criswell [and others] edited by Carl F. H. Henry. Carol Stream, Ill., Creation House [1971] 394 p. 23 cm. Includes bibliographical references. [BS647.2.J47 1971] 77-182857
1. Bible—Prophecies—Addresses, essays, lectures. I. Criswell, Wallie A. II. Henry, Carl Ferdinand Howard, 1913- ed. III. Title.

JONES, Milton H., 1911- 220.1'5
Let's take a walk with Jesus through the Bible / by Milton H. Jones. Philadelphia : Dorrance, [1974] 207 p. ; 22 cm. [BS647.2.J66] 74-75254 ISBN 0-8059-2000-5 : 6.95
1. Bible—Prophecies. I. Title.

JONES, Russell Bradley, 1894- 220.15
The latter days. [Rev. ed.] Grand Rapids, Mich., Baker Bk. House, 1961[c.1947] 196p. A revision of the author's The things which shall be hereafter. 61-17553 2.95
1. Bible—Prophecies. I. Title.

KIRBAN, Salem. 220.1'5
Kirban's book of charts on prophecy. Huntingdon Valley, Pa., S. Kirban, inc. [1969] 131 p. illus. (part col.), facsims., col. maps, ports. 29 x 44 cm. [BS647.2.K5] 77-103141 10.00
1. Bible—Prophecies. I. Title. II. Title: Book of charts on prophecy.

KIRBAN, Salem. 220.1'5
Questions frequently asked me on prophecy. [Huntingdon Valley, Pa., 1972] 63 p. illus. 22 cm. Cover title. [BS647.2.K52] 72-78025 ISBN 0-912582-01-4 1.95
1. Bible—Prophecies. I. Title.

KNOPF, Eugene. 220.15
When God comes down. [1st ed.] New York, Pageant Press [1959] 64p. 21cm. [BS647.K58] 59-13332
1. Bible—Prophecies. I. Title.

KOCH, Kurt E. 220.1'5
The coming one; Israel in the last days, by Kurt E. Koch. [1st ed.] Grand Rapids, Kregel Publications [1972] 94 p. illus. 18 cm. Translation of Der Kommende. [BS649.J5K5413] 72-85597 ISBN 0-8254-3011-9 pap. 1.00
1. Bible—Prophecies—Jews. 2. Israel—Description and travel. I. Title.

KURTZ, Edward Cuyler. 220.15
Headlines. Cleveland, Union Gospel Press [1952] 288p. 20cm. [BS647.K85] 52-67064
1. Bible—Prophecies. 2. Religion and science—1900- I. Title.

LEA, Charles 220.15
World events in the light of God's Word. New York, Comet Press Books [c.]1959. 47p. 21cm. (A Reflection book) 60-226 2.00
1. End of the world. 2. Bible—Prophecies. I. Title.

LEVITT, Zola. 220.1'5
Israel in agony : the beginning of the end? / By Zola Levitt. Irvine, Ca. : Harvest House Publishers, c1975. 100 p. ; 18 cm. [BM625.5.L48] 75-4222 ISBN 0-89081-012-5 pbk. : 1.45
1. Bible—Prophecies—Israel. 2. Israel-Arab War, 1973. I. Title.

LEWIS, Nettie Edell. 220.15
Lord of the harvest; gather the wheat into my barn. [1st ed.] New York, Exposition Press [1959] 315p. 21cm. [BS649.J5L43] 59-4503
1. Jews—Restoration. I. Title.

LIGHTNER, Robert Paul. 220.1'5
Prophecy in the ring / Robert P. Lightner. Denver : Accent Books, c1976. 127 p. : ill. ; 21 cm. Bibliography: p. 123-126. [BS647.2.L47] 76-8736 ISBN 0-916406-21-0 pbk. : 2.75
1. Bible—Prophecies. I. Title.

LIMBURG, James, 1935- 220.1'5
The prophets and the powerless / James Limburg. Atlanta : John Knox Press, c1977. vi, 104 p. ; 20 cm. Bibliography: p. [103]-104. [BS1198.L5] 76-12397 ISBN 0-8042-0156-0 pbk. : 3.45
1. Prophets. 2. Prophecy. I. Title.

LINDSEY, Hal. 220.1'5
The late great planet earth, by Hal Lindsey, with C. C. Carlson. Grand Rapids, Zondervan [1970] 192 p. maps. 22 cm. Includes bibliographical references. [BS647.2.L5] 71-122967 3.95
1. Bible—Prophecies. I. Carlson, Carole C., joint author. II. Title.

LOCKYER, Herbert. 220.1'5
All the messianic prophecies of the Bible. Grand Rapids, Zondervan Pub. House [1973] 528 p. 25 cm. [BT235.L82] 72-95526 7.95
1. Messiah—Prophecies. I. Title.

LOGSDON, S. Franklin. 220.1'5
Profiles of prophecy, by S. Franklin Logsdon. Grand Rapids, Mich., Zondervan Pub. House [1970] 128 p. 21 cm. (A Zondervan paperback) [BS647.2.L6] 74-95039 0.95
1. Bible—Prophecies. I. Title.

LUDWIGSON, R. 220.1'5
A survey of Bible prophecy [by] R. Ludwigson. Grand Rapids, Zondervan [1973] 187 p. illus. 21 cm. (Contemporary evangelical perspectives) A revision of the author's Bible prophecy notes, first published in 1951. Includes bibliographies. [BS647.2.L8 1973] 73-161643 2.95
1. Bible—Prophecies. I. Title.

*LUDWIGSON, Raymond. 220.1'5
A survey of Bible prophecy [by] R. Ludwigson. [Rev. & updated] Grand Rapids, Mich. Zondervan Pub. House [1973] 187 p. 20 cm. (Contemporary evangelical perspectives) First published in 1951 as Bible prophecy notes. [BS647.2] 2.95 (pbk.)
1. Bible—Prophecies. I. Title.

MCCALL, Thomas S. 220.1'5
Satan in the sanctuary, by Thomas S. McCall

and Zola Levitt. New York, Bantam Books [1975, c1974] 112 p. 18 cm. Includes bibliographical references. [BS649.J4M3] 1.50 (pbk.)
1. Bible-Prophecies—Jerusalem Temple. I. Levitt, Zola, joint author. II. Title.
L.C. card number for original ed.: 73-7327.

MCCALL, Thomas S. 220.1'5
Satan in the sanctuary, by Thomas S. McCall and Zola Levitt. Chicago, Moody Press [1973] 120 p. 22 cm. Includes bibliographical references. [BS649.J4M3] 73-7327 ISBN 0-8024-8799-8 3.95
1. Bible—Prophecies—Jerusalem Temple. I. Levitt, Zola, joint author. II. Title.

MCELENEY, Neil J. 220.1'5
The oracle of the Lord; introduction to the prophets, by Neil J. McEleney. New York, Paulist Press [1973] 55 p. illus. 23 cm. (Pamphlet Bible series, v. 24) [BS491.2.P3 vol. 24] [BS1198] 74-155418 1.00
1. Prophets. I. Title. II. Series.

MCMILLEN, Sim I., 1898- 220.1'5
Discern these times [by] S. I. McMillen. Old Tappan, N.J., Revell [1971] 192 p. 21 cm. Bibliography: p. 187-192. [BS647.2.M2] 74-149370 ISBN 0-8007-0455-X 4.95
1. Bible—Prophecies. I. Title.

*MCNEILUS, James A. 220.1'5
The unveiling of the great whore and the diverse beast [by] James A. McNeilus. 1st ed. New York, Vantage, 1974 301 p. 21 cm. [BS647] ISBN 0-533-01110-8 6.95
1. Bible—Prophecies. I. Title.

MAILS, Thomas E. 220.1'5
The vultures gather, the fig tree blooms; a study concerning the fulfillment of prophecy in our time [by Thomas E. Mails. Hayfield, Minn., Hayfield Pub. Co., 1972] 100 p. illus. 28 cm. Bibliography: p. 99-100. [BS647.2.M24] 72-197279 2.95
1. Bible—Prophecies. I. Title.

MARTENS, C. G. 220.1'5
The warm light on history, by C. G. Martens. Philadelphia, Dorrance [1970] vii, 123 p. 22 cm. [BS647.2.M28] 79-124151 4.00
1. Bible—Prophecies. I. Title.

MASON, Clarence E. 220.1'5
Prophetic problems with alternate solutions [by] Clarence E. Mason, Jr. Chicago, Moody Press [1973] 254 p. illus. 22 cm. [BS647.2.M34] 73-7335 ISBN 0-8024-6907-8 4.95
1. Bible—Prophecies. I. Title.

MILLER, C. Leslie. 220.1'5
Goodbye, World, by C. Leslie Miller. Glendale, Calif., Regal Books [1972] 150 p. 18 cm. [BS647.2.M48] 72-85642 ISBN 0-8307-0192-3
1. Bible—Prophecies. I. Title.

MILLS, Newt V. 220.1'5
This is the last message : the end time—the Lord's return / by Newt V. Mills. [Monroe? La.] : Newt V. Mills Crusade, c1975. viii, 145 p. ; 22 cm. [BT821.2.M5] 75-18799
1. Bible—Prophecies. 2. Eschatology. I. Title.

MORROW, Charles Malone. 220.15
The great warfare. [1st ed.] New York, Pageant Press [1953] 239p. 22cm. [BS647.M675] 53-10073
1. Bible—Prophecies. I. Title.

MYER, J. Richard, 1932- 220.1'5
Israel: God's peculiar treasure, by J. Richard Myer. [Manheim, Pa., Truth and Times, 1969] 302, [9] p. illus., maps, ports. 23 cm. [BS649.J5M9] 75-93175 6.75
1. Bible—Prophecies—Jews. I. Title.

NICKLIN, J. Bernard. 220.15
Signposts of history. Merrimac, Mass., Destiny Publishers [c1956] 203p. illus. 21cm. [BS647.N5] 56-13463
1. Bible—Prophecies. I. Title.

NYQUIST, John G 1874- 220.15
The kingdom of the world in prophecy. [1st ed.] New York, Pageant Press [1956] 87p. 21cm. [BS647.N9] 56-13130
1. Bible—Prophecies. I. Title.

OXTOBY, Gurdon C. 220.15
Prediction and fulfillment in the Bible, by Gurdon C. Oxtoby. Philadelphia, Westminster Press [1966] 159 p. 21 cm. [BS647.2.O9] 66-20094
1. Bible—Prophecies. 2. Bible. N.T.—Relation to O.T. I. Title.

PALESTINE and the 220.1'5
Bible. M. T. Mehdi, editor. [New York, New World Press, 1970] 60 p. 22 cm. [BS649.J5P26] 71-114557 2.00
1. Jews—Restoration. I. Mehdi, Mohammad Taki, ed.

PENTECOST, J Dwight. 220.15
Prophecy for today; a discussion of major themes of prophecy. Grand Rapids, Zondervan Pub. House [1961] 191p. 22cm. [BS647.2.P44] 61-31892
1. Bible—Prophecies. I. Title.

PENTECOST, J. Dwight. 220.1'5
Will man survive? Prophecy you can understand, by J. Dwight Pentecost. Chicago, Moody Press [1971] 208 p. 22 cm. [BS647.2.P45] 70-155687 4.95
1. Bible—Prophecies. I. Title.

PHILLIPS, John, 1927- 220.1'5
Only God can prophesy! / John Phillips. Wheaton, Ill. : H. Shaw Publishers, c1975. 147 p. : ill. ; 21 cm. Bibliography: p. [145]-147. [BS647.2.P48] 75-24996 ISBN 0-87788-627-X
1. Bible—Prophecies. I. Title.

PONT, Charles Ernest, 220.15
1898-
The world's collision. With an introd. by E. Schuyler English. Boston, W. A. Wilde Co., 1956. 298p. illus. 22cm. Includes bibliography. [BS647.P59] 56-7049
1. Bible— Prophecies. I. Title.

PRICE, Walter K. 220.1'5
[Le-shanah ha-ba 'ah bi-Yerushalayim (romanized form)] = Next year in Jerusalem / Walter K. Price. Chicago : Moody Press, [1975] 199 p. ; 22 cm. In English. Includes index. Bibliography: p. 187-196. [BS649.J5P67] 74-15341 ISBN 0-8024-5928-5 : 4.95
1. Bible—Prophecies—Jews. 2. Messiah—Prophecies. 3. Jewish-Arab relations. I. Title: Next year in Jerusalem.

RAND, Howard B 1889- 220.15
Marvels of prophecy. Merrimac, Mass., Destiny Publishers [1959] 120p. 20cm. [BS647.R32] 59-13355
1. Bible—Prophecies. I. Title.

EL Reino de Dios y 220.15
America Latina / C. Rene Padilla, editor. 1. ed. [El Paso, Tex.] : Casa Bautista de Publicaciones, 1975. 160 p. ; 22 cm. Papers presented at the 2d meeting of the Fraternidad Teologica Latinoamericana, held in Lima, Peru, Dec. 11-18, 1972. [BT94.R34] 75-321271
1. Kingdom of God—Congresses. I. Rene Padilla, C. II. Fraternidad Teologica Latinoamericana.

RICHARDS, Le Grand, Bp., 220.15
1886-
Israel! Do you know? Salt Lake City, Deseret Book Co., 1954. 254p. illus. 23cm. [BS649.J5R5] 54-41455
1. Jews—Restoration. 2. Mormons and Mormonism —Doctrinal and controversial works. I. Title.

RIGGS, Ralph M 1895- 220.1'5
The story of the future, by Ralph M. Riggs. Springfield, Mo. Gospel Pub. House [1968] 174 p. map 20 cm. [BS647.2.R5] 67-31330
1. Bible—Prophecies. I. Title.

RIGGS, Ralph M., 1895- 220.1'5
The story of the future, by Ralph M. Riggs. Springfield, Mo., Gospel Pub. [1968] 174p. map. 20cm. [BS647.2.R5] 67-31330 2.95
1. Bible—Prophecies. I. Title.
Publisher's address: 1445 Boonville Ave., Springfield, Mo. 65802.

RITCHIE, Jacob Marion, *220.15
1878-
Messiah, the Prince; a study in Biblical prophecy. New York, Exposition Press [1952] 137 p. 23 cm. [BT235.R54] 52-7659
1. Messiah — Prophecies. 2. Jesus Christ — Messiahship. I. Title.

ROGERS, E. W. 220.15
Concerning the future. Chicago, Moody [1963, c.1962] 122p. 22cm. 2.50
I. Title.

*ROGERS, E. W. 220.15
Concerning the future. Chicago, Moody [1966, c.1962] 122p. 17cm. (Colportage lib., MCL 516) .39 pap.,
I. Title.

RYRIE, Charles Caldwell, 220.1'5
1925-
The Bible and tomorrow's news; a new look at prophecy [by Charles C. Ryrie. Wheaton, Ill., Scripture Press Publications, 1969] 190 p. illus. 18 cm. [BS647.2.R9] 69-17068
1. Bible—Prophecies. I. Title.

SMITH, Wilbur Moorehead, 220.1'5
1894-
Egypt in biblical prophecy [by] Wilbur M. Smith. Grand Rapids, Mich., Baker Book House [1973, c.1957] 256 p. maps. 20 cm. [BS649.E5S5] ISBN 0-8010-7986-1 2.95 (pbk.)
1. Bible—Prophecies—Egypt. I. Title.
L.C. card no. for the hardbound edition: 57-13418.

SMITH, Wilbur Moorehead, 220.1'5
1894-
Israeli/Arab conflict, and the Bible, by Wilbur M. Smith. Glendale, Calif., Regal Books [1967] 162 p. illus., maps, ports. 18 cm. "Notes and bibliographies": p. [143]-162. [BS647.2.S6] 67-29634
1. Bible—Prophecies. I. Title.

SMITH, William Martin, 220.15
1872-
Bible history of world government and a forecast of its future from Bible prophecy. [5th ed.] Westfield, Ind., Union Bible Seminary [1955] 208p. illus. 20cm. [BS647.S6 1955] 55-4288
1. Bible—Prophecies. 2. Providence and government of God. I. Title.

*STOYKOFF, Todor Philip, 220.1'5
1912-
Sermon of God. Translated from Bulgarian. New York, Vantage [1973] 141 p. illus. 21 cm. [BS647.2] ISBN 0-533-00473-X 4.95
1. Bible—Prophecies. I. Title.

STRAUSS, Lehman. 220.15
God's plan for the future. Grand Rapids, Zondervan Pub. House [1965] 198 p. 23 cm. Bibliography: p. [191]-194. [BS647.2.S7] 64-8837
1. Bible — Prophecies. I. Title.

STRAUSS, Lehman 220.15
God's plan for the future. Grand Rapids, Mich., Zondervan [c.1965] 198p. 23cm. Bibl. [BS647.2.S7] 64-8837 3.95 bds.,
1. Bible—Prophecies. I. Title.

SUNDERWIRTH. Wilbert W 220.15
What time is it,
World? A
time table of prophecy. New York, Vantage Press [1953] 231p. 23cm. [BS647.S785] 52-13306
1. Bible—Prophecies. I. Title.

TATFORD, Frederick A., 220.1'5
1901-
God's program of the ages, by Frederick A. Tatford. Grand Rapids, Kregel Pubns. [1967] 160p. 22cm. Bibl. [BS647.2.T3] 67-26075 3.50; 1.95 pap.,
1. Bible—Prophecies. I. Title.

TAYLOR, Charles R. 220.1'5
World war III and the destiny of America / by Charles R. Taylor] Redondo Beach, Calif. : Today in Bible Prophecy, inc., c1971. xxvi, 358 p., [1] fold. leaf of plates : ill. ; 21 cm. Includes index. [BS649.U6T38] 75-308793 4.95
1. Bible—Prophecies—United States. 2. Bible—Prophecies—World War III. I. Title.

TAYLOR, Oral E 220.1'5
Christianity vs. communistic atheism. [Bebee? W.Va.] 1963. 72 p. illus. 23 cm. Imprint on cover: Chicago, Adams Press. [BS647.2.T36] 63-22174
1. Bible—Prophecies—Addresses, essays, lectures. I. Title.

*THOMPSON, Fred P., Jr. 220.15
Bible prophecies; study course for youth and adult. Cincinnati, Standard Pub. [c.1964] 127p. 22cm. Bibl. 1.25 pap.,
I. Title.

UNGER, Merrill Frederick, 220.15
1909-
Great neglected Bible prophecies. Chicago, Scripture Press [1955] 167p. 21cm. [BS647.U55] 55-12747
1. Bible—Prophecies. I. Title.

†WALKER, Paul L. 220.1'5
Knowing the future / Paul L. Walker. Cleveland, Tenn. : Pathway Press, c1976. 144 p. ; 18 cm. (Making life count new life series) Bibliography: p. 144. [BS647.2.W25] 76-710 ISBN 0-87148-477-3 pbk. : 1.19
1. Bible—Prophecies. I. Title.

WALKER, William H. 220.15
Will Russia conquer the world? 2d ed. 2d ed. New York, Loizeaux [1963] 87p. 22cm. 62-21065 .75 pap.,
1. Bible—Prophecies—Russia. I. Title.

WALKER, William Henry, 220.15
1913-
Will Russia conquer the world? [2d ed.] New York, Loizeaux Bros. [1962] 87 p. 22 cm. [BS649.R9W3 1962] 62-21065
1. Bible — Prophecies — Russia. I. Title.

WALTERS, Arthur L 1878- 220.15
And it came to pass, by Moses I I. [Los Angeles; 1955] 247p. illus. 22cm. [BS647.W33] 56-32390
1. Bible—Prophecies. 2. Church of England. Book of Common Prayer. I. Title.

WALVOORD, John F 220.1'5
Israel in prophecy. Grand Rapids, Zondervan Pub. House [1962] 138 p. 21 cm. Includes bibliography. [BS649.J5W3] 62-4367
1. Bible — Prophecies — Jews. 2. Israel. I. Title.

WALVOORD, John F. 220.1'5
The nations in prophecy, by John F. Walvoord. [1st ed.] Grand Rapids, Zondervan [1967] 176p. 21cm. [BS647.2.W3] 67-17241 4.95 bds.,
1. Bible—Prophecies. I. Title.

WALVOORD, John F. 220.1'5
The nations in prophecy, by John F. Walvoord. [1st ed.] Grand Rapids, Zondervan Pub. House [1967] 176 p. 21 cm. [BS647.2.W3] 67-17241
1. Bible — Prophecies. I. Title.

WHITESIDE, Robertson 220.15
Lafayette, 1869-1951.
The kingdom of promise and prophecy. Denton, Tex., I. Whiteside, 1956. 199p. 20cm. [BS647.W43] 57-31080
1. Bible—Prophecies. I. Title.

WHITESIDE, Robertson *220.15
Lafayette, 1869-1951.
The kingdom of promise and prophecy. Denton, Tex., I. Whiteside, 1956. 190 p. 20 cm. [BS647.W43] 57-31080
1. Bible — Prophecies. I. Title.

WOOD, Arthur Skevington. 220.15
Prophecy in the space age; studies in prophetic themes. Grand Rapids, Zondervan Pub. House [1963] 159 p. 21 cm. [BS647.2.W6] 63-15739
1. Bible — Prophecies. I. Title.

WOOD, Arthur Skevington 220.15
Prophecy in the space age; studies in prophetic themes. Grand Rapids, Mich., Zondervan [c.1963] 159p. 21cm. 63-15739 2.50
1. Bible—Prophecues. I. Title.

WOODSON, Leslie H., 1929- 220.1'5
Population, pollution, and prophecy [by] Leslie H. Woodson. Old Tappan, N.J., Revell [1973] 159 p. 21 cm. Bibliography: p. 158-159. [BS647.2.W63] 73-7967 ISBN 0-8007-0621-8 4.95
1. Bible—Prophecies. I. Title.

WRIGHT, Eula Lena (Ryan) 220.15
1903-
The spiritual interpretation of God's word. New York, Greenwich [c.1961] 28p. 61-9420 2.00
I. Title.

WUEST, Kenneth Samuel, 220.15
1893-
Prophetic light in the present darkness. [1st ed.] Grand Rapids W. B. Eerdmans Pub. Co., 1955. 135p. 20cm. (His Word studies in the Greek New Testament, 15) [BT885.W8] 55-22579
1. Second Advent. I. Title.

WYNGAARDEN, Martin J 220.15
The future of the kingdom in prophecy and fulfillment; a study of the scope of 'sprititualization' in Scripture. Grand Rapids, Baker Book House, 1955. 211p. 23cm. [BS647.W78] 55-7586
1. Bible—Prophecies. 2. Bible—Hermeneutics. I. Title.

YDUR, Rudy. 220.1'5
The Hasmonean hoax / Rudy Ydur. San Carlos, Calif. : Lumeli Press, c1977. 195 p. ; 22 cm. Includes index. Bibliography: p. [177]-181. [BS647.2.Y39] 76-53428 ISBN 0-930592-01-8: 7.95 ISBN 0-930592-02-6 pbk. : 4.95
1. Bible—Prophecies. I. Title.

PAYNE, John Barton, 220.1'5'03
1922-
Encyclopedia of Biblical prophecy; the complete guide to scriptural predictions and their fulfillment [by] J. Barton Payne. [1st ed.] New York, Harper & Row [1973] xxiv, 754 p. 25 cm. Bibliography: p. 685-692. [BS647.2.P38] 72-11362 ISBN 0-06-066476-2 19.95
1. Bible—Prophecies. I. Title.

BEEGLE, Dewey M 220.18
The inspiration of Scripture. Philadelphia, Westminster Press [1963] 233 p. 21 cm. Includes bibliography. [BS480.B363] 63-7342
1. Bible — Inspiration. I. Title.

KUENNE, Robert E. 220.182
The theory of general economic equilibrium. Princeton, N. J., Princeton University Press, 1963. xv. 590 p. illus. 24 cm. Bibliography: p. 571-580. [HB171.K73] 62-21105

1. Economics. I. Title.

ADISON, Jacob Myer, 1885- comp. 220.2
Wisdom of life from the Bible, with a complete topical index. Introd. by Robert H. Pfeiffer. Boston, House of Edinboro [1954] 123p. 21cm. [BS432.A3] 54-21453
1. Bible—Indexes, Topical. I. Title.

AMERICAN Bible Society. 220.2
A new concordance to the Holy Bible, King James version. New York, 1960. iv, 182p. 21cm. [BS425.A53] 61-4258
1. Bible—Concordances, English. 2. Bible. English—Versions —Authorized. I. Title.

AMERICAN Bible Society 220.2
A new concordance to the Holy Bible, King James version. Grand Rapids, Mich., Baker Bk., 1965[c.1960] iv, 482p. 21cm. [BS425.A53] 61-4258 3.95
1. Bible—Concordances, English. 2. Bible. English—Versions—Authorized. I. Title.

AMERICAN Bible Society. 220.2
World's concordance to the Holy Bible, King James version. New York, World Pub. Co. [1969, c1960] iv, 482 p. 22 cm. "Originally published by the American Bible Society under the title: A new concordance to the Holy Bible. [BS425.A53 1969] 78-96794 5.95
1. Bible—Concordances, English. 2. Bible. English—Versions—Authorized. I. Title. II. Title: Concordance to the Holy Bible.

**BAKER'S pocket bible* 220.2
concordance. Grand Rapids, Baker Book House [1974] 576 p. 18 cm. [BS425] ISBN 0-8010-0616-3 2.45 (pbk.)
1. Bible—Concordances. 2. Bible—Dictionaries.

BERREY, Lester V., 1907- ed. 220.2
A treasury of Biblical quotations. Garden City, N.Y., Doubleday [1964, c.1948] 264p. 22cm. 64-608 3.95 bds.,
1. Bible—Indexes—Topical. I. Title.

BIBLE. ENGLISH. SELECTIONS. 1933 220.2
Is that in the Bible? By Charles Francis Potter. [A classified collection of the odd, amusing, unusual, and surprising items of human interest in the Bible, many of which have escaped the attention of average reader.] Greenwich, Conn., Fawcett [1967, c.1933] ix, 272p. 18cm. (Crest bk., R1032) [BS432.P6] .60 pap.,
1. Bible—Indexes, Topicals. I. Potter, Charles Francis, 1885- ed. II. Title.

BIBLE. ENGLISH. SELECTIONS. 1933 220.2
Is that in the Bible? Greenwich, Conn., Fawcett [1962, c.1933] 272p. 18cm. (Crest bk., R580) .60 pap.,
1. Bible—Indexes, Topical. I. Potter, Charles Francis, 1885- ed. II. Title.

BUTTERWORTH, John, 1727-1803. 220.2
The comprehensive Bible concordance, edited by Adam Clarke. Grand Rapids, Kregel Publications [1960] 284p. illus. 26cm. 'Based on ... [A new concordance to the Holy Scriptures] by John Butterworth ... Reprinted from the Supplement to The comprehensive Bible commentary, edited by William Jenks ... published ... 1846.' [BS425.B8 1960] 60-15404
1. Bible—Concordances, English. 2. Bible—Dictionaries. I. Clarke, Adam, 1760?-1832, ed. II. Title.

CHURCH, John Edward. 220.2
Every man a Bible student : a handbook of basic Bible doctrines / by J. E. Church. Grand Rapids : Zondervan, [1977] c1976. 127 p. ; 22 cm. [BS432.C553 1977] 77-4326 ISBN 0-310-35651-2 pbk. : 2.95
1. Bible—Indexes, Topical. I. Title.

CLARKE, Samuel, 1684-1750, comp. 220.2
Precious Bible promises / compiled by Samuel Clarke. Rev. ed. Chappaqua, N.Y. : Christian Herald Books, c1976. viii, 320 p. ; 16 cm. (A Christian Herald classic) [BS432.C57 1976] 76-16722 ISBN 0-915684-07-1 : 5.95
1. Bible—Indexes, Topical. 2. God—Promises. I. Title.

COMPREHENSIVE concordance 220.2
of the New World translation of the Holy Scriptures. [Brooklyn, Watchtower Bible and Tract Society of New York, 1973] 1275 p. 25 cm. [BS425.C66] 73-168200 5.00
1. Bible—Concordances, English—New World. I. Watch Tower Bible and Tract Society.
Publishers Address: 124 Columbia Heights, Brooklyn, N.Y. 11201

CRUDEN, Alexander, 1701-1770. 220.2
Compact concordance. Grand Rapids, Zondervan Pub. House [1968] 563 p. 19 cm. ([The Bible handbook series]) "Based on the ... work of Alexander Cruden, as edited by John Eadie." First published in 1738 under title: A complete concordance to the Holy Scriptures of the Old and New Testament. [BS425.C85 1968] 68-22839 3.95
1. Bible—Concordances, English. I. Eadie, John, 1810-1876, ed. II. Title.

CRUDEN, Alexander, 1701-1770. 220.2
Complete concordance to the Old and New Testaments. Edited by A. D. Adams, C. H. Irwin [and] S. A. Waters. Grand Rapids, Zondervan Pub. House [1955, c1949] vii, 800p. 22cm. [BS425.C8 1955] 56-1384
1. Bible—Concordances, English. I. Title.

CRUDEN, Alexander, 1701-1770. 220.2
Concordance to the Holy Scriptures. Edited by John Eadie. [Handy reference ed.] Grand Rapids, Baker Books) House, 1954 c342p. 26cm. [BS425.C85 1954] 54-11084
1. Bible—Concordances, English. I. Eadle, John, 1810-1876, ed. II. Title.

CRUDEN, Alexander, 1701-1770. 220.2
Cruden's Complete concordance of the Old and New Testaments. Edited by A. D. Adams, C. H. Irwin, [and] S. A. waters. New York, Holt, Rinehart and Winston [c1949] vii, 783 p. 22 cm. First published under title: A complete concordance to the Holy Scriptures of the Old and New Testaments. [BS425.C85 1949] 64-55083
1. Bible — Concordances, English. I. Title.

CRUDEN, Alexander, 1701-1770. 220.2
Cruden's complete concordance to the Old and New Testamants. Edited by A. D. Adams, C. H. Irwin [and] S. A. Waters. Notes and Biblical proper names under one alphabetical arrangement, plus a list of proper names. With a foreword by Walter L. Wilson. Grand Rapids, Zondervan Pub. House [1968] 803 p. 23 cm. First published under title: A complete concordance to the Holy Scriptures of the Old and New Testaments. [BS425.C85 1968b] 76-14641 4.95
1. Bible—Concordances, English. I. Title.

CRUDEN, Alexander, 1701-1770. 220.2
Cruden's useful concordance of the Holy Scriptures comprising most of the references which are really needed. New York, Pyramid Books [1970] 352 p. 18 cm. First published under title: A complete concordance to the Holy Scriptures of the Old and New Testament. [BS425.C8 1970] 70-16020 1.25
1. Bible—Concordances, English. I. Title: Useful concordance of the Holy Scriptures.

CRUDEN, Alexander, 1701-1770. 220.2
Handy concordance; to which is added an index to the Holy Bible of persons, places and subjects mentioned in Scripture. Edited and adapted by Charles H. H. Wright. [American ed.] UN Grand Rapids, Zondervan Pub. House [1963] 235 p. 18 cm. Based on the work first published under title: A complete concordance to the Holy Scriptures of the Old and New Testaments. [BS425.C85 1963] 63-24671
1. Bible — Concordances, English. I. Wright, Charles Henry Hamilton, 1836-1909, ed. II. Title.

CRUDEN, Alexander, 1701-1770 220.2
Handy concordance Ed., adapted by Charls H. H. Wright, D. D., to which is added an Index to the Holy Bible of persons, places and subjects mentioned in Scripture. Grand Rapids, Mich., Zondervan [1963] 235p. 18cm. 1.95 pap.,
1. Bible—Concordances, English. 2. Bible—Index. I. Wright, Charles H. H., ed. II. Title.

CRUDEN, Alexander, 1701-1770.Concordance 220.2
in Hitchcock, Roswell Dwight, 1817-1887. Hitchcock's Topical Bible and Cruden's Concordance. Grand Rapids, Baker Book House, 1952. [BS432.H5 1952] 52-13315
I. Title.

CRUDEN, Alexander, 1701-1770. 220.2
Popular concordance. Clear type reference ed. Grand Rapids, Mich., Zondervan Pub. House [1960] 563p. 'Based on the . . . work of Alexander Cruden, as edited by John Eadie.' First published in 1738 under title: A complete concordance to the Holy Scriptures of the Old and New Testament. 60-51199 2.95
1. Bible—Concordances, English. I. Eadie, John, 1810-1876, ed. II. Title.

CRUDEN, Alexander, 1701-1770. 220.2
Unabridged concordance to the Old and New Testaments and the Apocrypha. Grand Rapids, Baker Book House, 1953. 719p. 26cm. First published under title: A complete concordance to the Holy Scriptures of the Old and New Testament. [BS425.C8 1953] 54-2609
1. Bible—Concordances, English. I. Title.

EBERHARDT, Ernest Godlove, 1864-1953, comp. 220.2
Eberhardt's Bible thesaurus; choice Scriptural texts alphabetically arranged under more than 100 essential topics to show what the Bible teaches, as an aid for study and devotional reading. Foreword by Herbert E. Eberhardt. [1st ed.] New York, Exposition Press [1953] xvii, 715p. port. 22cm. [BS432.E25] 51-11843
1. Bible—Indexes, Topical. I. Title. II. Title: Bible theasurus.

ELLISON, John William, 1920- 220.2
Nelson's complete concordance of the Revised standard version of the Bible. Compiled under the supervision of John W. Ellison. New York. Nelson [c1957] 2157p. 28cm. [BS425.E4 1957] 57-7122
1. Bible—Concordances, English. 2. Bible, English—Versions—Revised standard. I. Nelson (Thomas) and Sons, inc. II. Title.

GANT, William John. 220.2
The Moffatt Bible concordance; a complete concordance to: The Bible, a new translation by James Moffatt. New York, Harper [1950] 550 p. 25 cm. London ed. (Hodder and Stoughton) has title: Concordance of the Bible in the Moffatt translation. [BS425.G3 1950a] 50-12690
1. Moffatt, James, 1870-1944. 2. Bible—Concordances, English. 3. Bible. English—Versions—Moffatt. I. Title.

GARLAND, George Frederick. 220.2
Subject guide to Bible stories. Compiled by George Frederick Garland. New York, Greenwood Pub. Corp. [1969] x, 365 p. 24 cm. [BS432.G258 1969] 69-19012 12.00
1. Bible—Indexes, Topical. I. Title.

GLASHEEN, P. 220.2
A preacher's concordance. Westminster, Md., Newman [1964, c.]1963. 284p. 22c8m 64-1904 3.95
1. Bible—Indexes, Topical. I. Title.

HOLMAN (A. J.) Company, Philadelphia. 220.2
A new practical comparative concordance to the Old and New Testaments. Philadelphia [1955] 176p. 19cm. Cover title: Bible concordance. [BS425.H6] 56-27712
1. Bible—Concordances, English. I. Title.

HOLMAN topical 220.2
concordance. An index to the Bible, arranged by subjects, in alphabetical order. [1st ed.] Philadelphia, A. J. Holman Co. [1973] 279 p. 24 cm. [BS432.H63] 73-7656 ISBN 0-87981-019-X 5.95
1. Bible—Indexes, Topical. I. Holman (A. J.) Company, Philadelphia.

THE Holy Bible index 220.2
book; compiled from the Authorized version of King James, A.D. 1611, revised A.D. 1881. [Edited by J. J. Court Ashton] 1st ed. [New York, 1973] 401 p. illus. 28 cm. A reprint of reference material appearing in various editions of the Bible. "Number 21 of a limited first printing." [BS475.2.H63] 73-181344 20.00
1. Bible—Introductions. 2. Bible—Dictionaries. 3. Bible—Concordances, English. I. Ashton, Joseph J. Court, comp.

INGLIS, James, fl.1859-1885. 220.2
A topical dictionary of Bible texts; a complete classification of Scripture texts in the form of an alphabetical list of subjects. Introd. by Wilbur M. Smith. Grand Rapids, Baker Book House [1968] iv, 524 p. 22 cm. "Originally published [1859] under the title: The Bible text cyclopedia." [BS432.I5 1968] 70-3371 4.95
1. Bible—Indexes, Topical. I. Title.

JOY, Charles Rhind, 1885- 220.2
A concordance of Bible readings, comp. by Charles R. Joy. Cleveland, World [c.1965] 112p. 24cm. [BS432.J618] 65-25778 3.95
1. Bible — Indexes, Topical. I. Title.

JOY, Charles Rhind, 1885- 220.2
A concordance of Bible readings, compiled by Charles R. Joy. [1st ed.] Cleveland, World Pub. Co. [1965] 112 p. 24 cm. [BS432.J618 1965] 65-25778
1. Bible—Indexes, Topical. I. Title.

JOY, Charles Rhind, 1885- 220.2
Harper's topical concordance. Rev. and enl. ed. New York, Harper [1962] ix, 628 p. 25 cm. [BS432.J63 1962] 62-11129
1. Bible—Indexes, Topical. I. Title.

JOY, Charles Rhind, 1885- 220.2
Harper's topical concordance /compiled by Charles R. Joy Revised and enlarged edition. New York: Harper and Row [1976 c1940] ix, 628 p.; 23 cm. [BS432.J63] ISBN 0-06-064229-7 pbk.: 8.95
1. Bible—Indexes, topical. I. Title.
L.C. card no. for original edition: 62-17129.

KIEFER, William J 220.2
Biblical subject index. Westminster, Md., Newman Press, 1958. 197p. 21cm. [BS432.K45] 58-8757
1. Bible—Indexes, Topical. I. Title.

KOPPLIN, Dorothea (Simons) 220.2
Scripture to live by. Garden City, N.Y., Hanover House 1960[c.1955] 222p. 22cm. 2.50
1. Bible—Indexes, Topical. I. Title.

LEARY, Lewis Gaston, 1877- comp. 220.2
The Bible when you want it. New York, Association Press, 1951. unpaged. 15cm. [BS432] 52-6597
1. Bible—Indexes, Topical. I. Title.

MALLETTE, Myrtle, comp. 220.2
A treasury of Bible highlights; a scriptural guide for religious leaders, teachers, students, and laymen, containing 2,000 King James excerpts applicable for daily living, selected and arranged under 75 topics. [1st ed.] New York, Exposition Press [1955] 181p. 21cm. [BS432.M35] 55-11125
1. Bible—Indexes, Topical. I. Title.

MEAD, Frank Spencer, 1898- 220.2
What the Bible says. [Westwood, N. J.] Revell [1958] 128p. 21cm. [BS432.M38] 58-5346
1. Bible—Indexes, Topical. I. Title.

METZGER, Bruce Manning. 220.2
The Oxford concise concordance to the Revised standard version of the Holy Bible. Compiled by Bruce M. Metzger and Isobel M. Metzger. New York, Oxford University Press, 1962. 158p. 23cm. [BS425.M4] 62-52472
1. Bible—Concordances, English—Revised standard. I. Metzger, Isobel M. II. Title.

MILLER, D. M., ed. 220.2
Topical concordance of vital doctrines. [Westwood, N. J.] Revell [1959] 32p. 17cm. 59-16755 .50 bds.,
1. Bible—Indexes, Topical. 2. Theology, Doctrinal. I. Title.

MILLER, Daniel Morrison 220.2
The topical Bible concordance for the use of ministers, missionaries, teachers, and Christian workers, ed. with additional material by D. M. Miller. Westwood, N.J., Revell [1965] 128p. 20cm. [BS432.M49] 65-1174 1.50
1. Bible—Indexes, Topical. I. Title.

MILLER, Daniel Morrison. 220.2
Topical concordance of vital doctrines. [Westwood, N.J.] Revell [1959?] 32 p. 17 cm. [BS432.M5] 59-16755
1. Bible — Indexes, Topical. 2. Theology, Doctrinal. I. Title.

MONSER, Harold E 1868-1918, ed. 220.2
Topical index and digest of the Bible. Harold E. Monser, editor-in-chief; associate editors: Charles Reign Scoville [and others] Grand Rapids, Baker Book House, 1960. 681p. 22cm. 'Contains all the topical analyses or footnotes of The cross-reference Bible.' First published in 1914 under title: Cross-reference digest of Bible references. [BS432.M6 1960] 60-15538
1. Bible—Indexes, Topical. 2. Bible—Study—Outlines, syllabi, etc. I. Title.

MOODY Bible Institute of Chicago. 220.2
Pocket Bible concordance. Chicago, Moody Press [c1959] 160p. 18cm. (Moody pocket books, 40) [BS425.M6] 60-1912
1. Bible—Concordances, English. I. Title.

NAVE, Orville James, 1841-1917 220.2
Topical Bible. Condensed ed. Chicago, Moody [1962] 1615p. 25cm. .89 pap.,
1. Bible—Indexes, Topical. I. Title.

NAVE, Orville James, 1841-1917 220.2
Topical Bible; a digest of the Holy Scriptures: more than twenty thousand topics and subtopics, and one hundred thousand references to the Scriptures. Nashville, Southwestern [1962] 1615p. 24cm. 62-51199 18.95
1. Bible—Indexes, Topical. I. Title.

NEW American standard Bible 220.2
concordance to the Old and New Testaments. La Habra, Calif., Foundation Press

Publications, publisher for the Lockman Foundation [1972] 115 p. 20 cm. [BS425.N38] 72-179124 0.95 (pbk.)
1. Bible—Concordances, English—New American standard. I. Lockman Foundation, La Habra, Calif. II. Title.

NEW combined Bible 220.2
dictionary and concordance (The). Introd. on how to study the Bible, by Charles F. Pfeiffer. Grand Rapids, Mich., Baker Bk., 1965[c.1961] 454p. 23cm. [BS440.N43] 65-16376 4.50; before Aug. 31, 1965, 3.95
1. Bible—Dictionaries. 2. Bible—Concordances, English. I. Pfeiffer, Charles F. II. Title: Combined Bible dictionary and concordance.

THE New World idea index to 220.2
the Holy Bible. Edited by Harvey K. Griffith. New York, World Pub. [1972] xxv, 907 p. 24 cm. [BS432.N43] 72-77416 14.95
1. Bible—Indexes, Topical. I. Griffith, Harvey K., ed. II. World Publishing Company, Cleveland.

THE Scripture sourcebook; 220.2
a topical text-book of Bible persons, places and subjects for Christian workers, students and teachers. With an introd. on 'How to study the Bible' by D.L. Moody. Grand Rapids, Zondervan Pub. House [1962] 192, 22p. 21cm. Previous editions published by the American Tract Society under title: The Bible textbook. 'Index to the four Gospels, by T.B. Bishop': p. 186-192. 'The Bible student's manual' (22p.) at end. [BS432.B53 1962] 62-53034
1. Bible—Indexes, Topical.

SCRIPTURE sourcebook 220.2
(The); a topical text-book of Bible persons, places and subjects for Christian workers, students and teachers. Introd. on "How to study the Bible" by D. L. Moody. Grand Rapids, Mich., Zondervan [c.1962] 192, 22 p. 21 cm. Previous eds. pub. by the Amer. Tract Soc. under title: The Bible textbook. 62-53034 2.50
1. Bible—Indexes, Topical.

SIMMONS, Charles, d. 1856. 220.2
Topical text-finder. Grand Rapids, Baker Book House, 1954. 528p. 21cm. [Co-operative reprint library] 'Formerly published as Scripture manual.' [BS432.S5 1954] 54-2610
1. Bible—Indexes, Topical. I. Title.

SMITH, Jay J., 1930- 220.2
Concise Bible concordance. Compiled and edited by Jay J. Smith and Mary Smith. New York, World Pub. Co. [1970] xv, 198 p. 14 cm. (Bible study guides) [BS425.S6] 74-96793
1. Bible—Concordances, English. I. Smith, Mary, 1936- joint author. II. Title.

SMITH, Miles Woodward 220.2
Invitation to Bible study; an original, newly prepared set of helps. Philadelphia 1, National Pub. Co. [dist. National Bible Press, 24th and Losust Sts.] [c.1960] 112, 96p. col. maps 25cm. 60-4267 3.95; deluxe ed., lea. cl., 5.95, bxd.
1. Bible—Handbooks, manuals, etc. I. Title.

SMITH, Miles Woodward, 220.2
1889-
Invitation to Bible study; an original, newly prepared set of helps ... Philadelphia, National Pub. Co. [1960] 112, 96 p. illus. 25 cm. [BS417.S53] 60-4267
1. Bible — Handbooks, manuals, etc. I. Title.

SPEER, Jack Atkeson. 220.2
The living Bible concordance, edited and compiled under the supervision of Jack Atkeson Speer. [2d ed.] Poolesville, Md., Poolesville Presbyterian Church [1974] p. cm. "Based on a paraphrased text by Dr. Kenneth N. Taylor." [BS425.S67 1974] 74-16081 ISBN 0-9600694-2-9
1. Bible—Concordances, English—Living Bible. I. Taylor, Kenneth Nathaniel. The living Bible, paraphrased. II. Title.

SPEER, Jack Atkeson. 220.2
The living Bible concordance complete, edited and compiled under the supervision of Jack Atkeson Speer. Poolesville, Md., Poolesville Presbyterian Church [1973] xi, 1209 p. 29 cm. "Based on a paraphrased text by Dr. Kenneth N. Taylor." [BS425.S67] 73-10013 ISBN 0-9600694-1-0
1. Bible—Concordances, English—Living Bible. I. Taylor, Kenneth Nathaniel. The living Bible, paraphrased. II. Title.

STARKS, Arthur E., 1911- 220.2
Concordance supplement for the inspired version of the Holy Scriptures. Independence, Mo., Herald Pub. House [c.]1962. 231p. 23cm. 62-8399 3.50
1. Bible—Concordances, English. 2. Bible. English—Versions—Smith. I. Title.

STRONG, James, 1822-1894. 220.2
Strong's Exhaustive concordance : handy edition / James Strong. Rev. and abridged ed. Grand Rapids : Guardian Press, 1976. 1216 p. ; 23 cm. Earlier editions published under title: The exhaustive concordance of the Bible. [BS425.S8 1976] 76-370721 ISBN 0-89086-027-0 : 9.95
1. Bible—Concordances, English. I. Title. II. Title: Exhaustive concordance.

UBER, Guy Lloyd, comp. 220.2
Words or wisdom from the Bible. New York, Vantage Press [c1954] 215p. 23cm. [BS432.U2] 53-11624
1. Bible—Indexes, Topical. I. Title.

VIENING, Edward. 220.2
The Zondervan topical Bible. Edited by Edward Viening. Grand Rapids, Zondervan Pub. House [1969] 1114 p. 25 cm. [BS432.V5] 71-95274 9.95
1. Bible—Indexes, Topical. 2. Bible—Dictionaries. I. Title.

WALKER, James Bradford 220.2
Richmond, 1821-1885.
Walker's Comprehensive Bible concordance / by J. B. R. Walker. Grand Rapids, Mich. : Kregel Publications, 1976. 968 p. ; 25 cm. Previous editions published under title: The comprehensive concordance to the Holy Scriptures. [BS425.W3 1976] 76-15841 ISBN 0-8254-4010-6 : 12.95
1. Bible—Concordances, English. I. Title. II. Title: Comprehensive Bible concordance.

WHARTON, Gary. 220.2
The new compact topical Bible. Compiled by Gary Wharton. Grand Rapids, Mich., Zondervan Pub. House [1972] 536 p. 19 cm. (The Bible handbook series) "A compact edition of The Zondervan topical Bible ... edited by Edward Viening." [BS432.W48] 72-83885 4.95
1. Bible—Indexes, Topical. 2. Bible—Dictionaries. I. Viening, Edward. The Zondervan topical Bible. II. Title.

WHITESELL, Faris Daniel, 220.2
1895-
Evangelistic illustrations from the Bible. Grand Rapids, Zondervan Pub. House [1955] 121p. 20cm. [BS432.W53] 55-1346
1. Bible—Indexes, Topical. I. Title.

WIGRAM, George V. 220.2
The Englishman's Hebrew and Chaldee concordance of the Old Testament: being an attempt at a verbal connection between the original and the English translation; with indexes, a list of the proper names, and their occurances, etc. [by George V. Wigram] 5th ed. Grand Rapids, Mich., Zondervan Pub. House [1972] xvi, 1682, 78 p. 25 cm. Fifth ed. first published in 1963. [BS1125.W5 1972] 75-106436
1. Bible. O.T.—Concordances, Hebrew. 2. Hebrew language—Dictionaries—English. I. Title.

WOLFF, Christian M 1886- 220.2
Easy finding Bible index. [Denver? 1952] 149 p. 18 cm. [BS432.W6] 52-41865
1. Bible — Indexes, Topical. I. Title.

YOUNG, Robert, 1822-1888. 220.2
Analytical concordance to the Bible on an entirely new plan containing about 311,000 references, subdivided under the Hebrew and Greek originals, with the literal meaning and pronunciation of each; designed for the simplest reader of the English Bible. Also index lexicons to the Old and New Testaments, being a guide to parallel passages and a complete list of Scripture proper names showing their modern pronunciation. 22d American ed., rev. by Wm. B. Stevenson. To which is added a supplement entitled Recent discoveries in Bible lands, by William F. Albright. New York, Funk & Wagnalls [1955] ix, 1090, 93, 23, 51p. 29cm. 'Recent discoveries in Bible lands' has special t. p. On cover: Authorized edition. [BS425.Y7 1955] 55-5338
1. Bible—Concordances, English. 2. Hebrew language—Dictionaries—English. 3. Greek languages, Biblical—Dictionaries—English. 4. Bible—Antiq. 5. Palestine— Antiq. I. Albright, William Faxwell, 1891- II. Title. III. Title: Recent discoveries in Bible lands.

YOUNG, Robert, 1822-1888. 220.2
Analytical concordance to the Bible on an entirely new plan containing about 311,000 references, subdivided under the Hebrew and Greek originals, with the literal meaning and pronunciation of each; designed for the simplest reader of the English Bible. Also index lexicons to the Old and New Testaments, being a guide to parallel passages and a complete list of Scripture proper names showing their modern pronunciation. 2d American ed., rev. by Wm. B. Stevenson. To which is added a supplement entitled Recent discoveries in Bible lands, by William F. Albright. Grand Rapids, W. B. Eerdmans Pub. Co. [1955] ix, 1090, 93, 23, 51 p. 29 cm. "Recent discoveries in Bible lands" has special t. p. On cover: Authorized edition. [BS425.Y7] 65-33821
1. Bible. — Concordances, English. 2. Hebrew language — Dictionaries — English. 3. Greek language, Biblical — Dictionaries — English. 4. Bible — Antiq. 5. Palestine — Antiq. I. Albright, William Foxwell, 1891- II. Title. III. Title: Recent discoveries in Bible lands.

THE Zondervan expanded 220.2
concordance. Grand Rapids, Zondervan Pub. House [1968] 1848 p. 25 cm. [BS425.Z6] 68-27466 14.95
1. Bible—Concordances, English.

UNGER, Merrill Frederick, 220.202
1909-
Unger's Bible handbook; an essential guide to understanding the Bible, by Merrill F. Unger. Chicago, Moody, 1966. xxii, 930p. illus., facsims., maps. 18cm. [BS417.U5] 66-16224 4.95
1. Bible — Handbooks, manuals, etc. I. Title. II. Title: Bible handbook.

THE Computer Bible / 220.2'08
edited by J. Arthur Baird and David Noel Freedman. Missoula, Mont. : Published by Scholars Press for Biblical Research Associates, c197 v. : graphs ; 28 cm. Vol. in Hebrew; introd. in English. [BS421.C64 1975] 75-34503 ISBN 0-89130-038-4 (v. 2) : 10.00
1. Bible. O.T.—Concordances, Hebrew. I. Baird, Joseph Arthur. II. Freedman, David Noel, 1922-

MORRIS, Peter M. K. 220.2'08 s
A critical word book of Leviticus, Numbers, Deuteronomy / by Peter M. K. Morris and Edward James. Missoula, Mont. : Scholars Press, 1975. p. cm. (The Computer Bible ; v. 8) [BS421.C64 vol.8] [BS1225.2] 222'.13'02 75-15550
1. Bible. O.T. Leviticus—Concordances, Hebrew. 2. Bible. O.T. Numbers—Concordances, Hebrew. 3. Bible. O.T. Deuteronomy—Concordances, Hebrew. 4. Bible. O.T. Leviticus—Language, style—Statistics. 5. Bible. O.T. Numbers—Language, style—Statistics. 6. Bible. O.T. Deuteronomy—Language, style—Statistics. I. James, Edward B., joint author. II. Title. III. Series.

MORTON, Andrew Queen. 220.2'08 s
A critical concordance to the Acts of the Apostles / concordance editors A. Q. Morton and S. Michaelson. [Wooster, Ohio] : Biblical Research Associates, c1976. ix, 210 p. ; 28 cm. (The Computer Bible ; v. 7) [BS421.C64 no. 7] [BS2625.2] 226'.6'02 75-31552 ISBN 0-89130-045-7
1. Bible. N.T. Acts—Concordances, Greek. I. Michaelson, S., joint author. II. Title. III. Series.

RADDAY, Yehuda Thomas. 220.2'08 s
An analytical linguistic key-word-in-context concordance to the books of Haggai, Zechariah, and Malachi / by Yehuda T. Radday. Missoula, Mont. : Published by Scholars Press for Biblical Research Associates, [1975] c1974. p. cm. (The Computer Bible ; no. 4) In Hebrew, introd. in English. [BS421.C64 1975 no. 4] [BS1560] 224'.9 75-33803 ISBN 0-89130-054-6
1. Bible. O.T. Haggai—Concordances, Hebrew. 2. Bible. O.T. Zechariah—Concordances, Hebrew. 3. Bible. O.T. Malachi—Concordances, Hebrew. I. Title. II. Series.

RADDAY, Yehuda Thomas. 220.2'08 s
An analytical lingustic concordance to the book of Isaiah / by Yehuda T. Radday. Missoula, Mont. : Scholars Press for Biblical Research Associates, c1975. p. cm. (The Computer Bible ; v. 2) [BS421.C64 vol. 2] [BS1515.2] 224'.1'2 75-30628 ISBN 0-89130-038-4 : 10.00
1. Bible. O.T. Isaiah—Concordances, Hebrew. I. Title. II. Series.

ALLMEN, Jean Jacques von, 220.3
ed.
A companion to the Bible. Introd. by H. H. Rowley. [Translated from the 2d French ed., by P. J. Allcock and others] New York, Oxford University Press, 1958. 479p. 23cm. Translation of Vocabulaire biblique. [BS440.A473] 57-11558
1. Bible—Dictionaries. I. Title.

ARNOLD, A. Stuart. 220.3
ABC of Bible lands : an alphabetic handbook for travelers / A. Stuart Arnold. Nashville : Broadman Press, c1977. 142 p. : ill. ; 18 cm. [BS622.A76] 76-47757 ISBN 0-8054-5702-X pbk. : 4.95
1. Bible—Dictionaries. I. Title.

BAUER, Johannes Baptist, 220.3
1927-
Sacramentum verbi; an encyclopedia of Biblical theology. Edited by Johannes B. Bauer. [New York] Herder and Herder [1970] 3 v. (xxxiii, 1141 p.) 27 cm. Translation of 3d enl. and rev. ed. (1967) of Bibeltheologisches Worterbuch. Bibliography: v. 3, p. 1015-1025. [BS440.B4313] 74-114764 49.50
1. Bible—Dictionaries. 2. Bible—Theology—Dictionaries. I. Title.

BEERS, Gil, 1928- 220'.3
The children's illustrated Bible dictionary / by Gil Beers. Nashville : T. Nelson, [1977] p. cm. Includes index. Short definitions, scripture references, and a topical guide identifies personal names, cities, and other terms in the Bible. [BS440.B46] 77-12650 7.95
1. Bible—Dictionaries, Juvenile. I. Title.

BRYANT, Al, 1926- 220.3
The new compact Bible dictionary, edited by T. Alton Bryant. Grand Rapids, Zondervan Pub. House [1967] 621 p. illus., maps. 19 cm. (The Bible handbook series) [BS440.B78] 67-22682
1. Bible—Dictionaries. I. Title.

CATHOLIC Biblical 220.3
encyclopedia [by] John E. Steinmueller and Kathryn Sullivan. Introd. by James-M. Voste. New York, J. F. Wagner [1950- v. illus., col. maps (1 fold.) 26 cm. Contents.[1] New Testament. "Bibliographies": v. 1, p. [681]-702. [BS2312.C3] 50-4611
1. Bible. N. T.—Dictionaries. I. Steinmueller, John E., 1899- II. Sullivan, Kathryn, 1905-

CATHOLIC Biblical 220.3
encyclopedia [by] John E. Steinmueller and Kathryn Sullivan. Introd. by Athanasius Miller. New York, J. F. Wagner [1956, v. 2, c1950] 2 v. in 1. illus., maps (part col.) 26cm. Introd., v. 2, by James-M. Voste. Contents.[1] Old Testament.--[2] New Testament. [BS440.C36] 58-33655
1. Bible—Dictionaries. I. Steinmueller, John E., 1899- II. Sulliavan, Kathryn, 1905-

CHARLEY, Julian. 220.3
50 key words, the Bible Richmond, John Knox Press [1971] 69 p. 20 cm. [BS440.C48 1971] 76-143419 1.65
1. Bible—Dictionaries. I. Title.

COLLINS gem dictionary of 220.3
the Bible [by] Rev. James L. Dow [New York] Collins [c.1964] 639p. 12cm. 64-8855 1.25
1. Bible—Dictionaries. I. Dow, James L. II. Title: Gem dictionary of the bibl: III. Title: Bible dictionary.

THE Combined Biblical 220.3
dictionary & concordance [for the New American Bible. Charlotte, N.C., C. D. Stampley Enterprises, 1971] 252 p. 29 cm. [BS440.C594] 77-27265
1. Bible—Dictionaries. 2. Bible—Concordances, English—New American Bible.

CONCISE Bible dictionary. 220.3
New York, World Pub. Co. [1970, c1969] xii, 163 p. 14 cm. (Bible study guides) [BS440.C598] 70-96792
1. Bible—Dictionaries.

CORNFELD, Gaalyahu, 1902- 220.3
ed.
Pictorial Biblical encyclopedia; a visual guide to the Old and New Testaments. Ed. by Gaalyahu Cornfeld assisted by Bible scholars, historians, and archaeologists. New York, Macmillan [1965, c.]1964. 712p. illus., maps. 28cm. [BS440.C63] 65-12852 17.50
1. Bible—Dictionaries. I. Title.

*CRUDEN, Alexander. 220.'3
Cruden's pocket dictionary of Bible terms / Alexander Cruden. Grand Rapids : Baker Book House, 1976. 383p. ; 18 cm. Formerly, published under the title, Cruden's Dictionary of Bible Terms. [BS440] ISBN 0-8010-2380-7 : 2.95
1. Bible-Dictionaries. I. Title.

DAVIS, John D 1854-1926. 220.3
A dictionary of the Bible. 4th rev. ed. Grand Rapids, Baker Book House, 1954 [c1924] v, 840p. illus., ports., maps. 24cm. [BS440.D3 1954] 54-2652
1. Bible—Dictionaries. I. Title.

DEURSEN, Arie van. 220.3
Illustrated dictionary of Bible manners and customs, by A. van Deursen. Illustrated by J. de Vries. [New York] Philosophical Library [*67] 142 p. illus. 20 cm. Translation of Bijbels beeldwoordenboek. Bibliography: p. 126-128. [BS622.D413] 68-1284
1. Bible—Antiq.—Dictionaries. I. Vries, J. de, illus. II. Title.

DEURSEN, Arie van. 220.3
Illustrated dictionary of Bible manners and

customs, by A. van Deursen. Illustrated by J. de Vries. [New York] Philosophical Library [1967] 142 p. illus. 20 cm. Translation of Bijbels beeldwoordenboek. Bibliography: p. 126-128. [BS622.D413] 68-1284
1. Bible—Antiquities—Dictionaries. I. Vries, J. de, illus. II. Title.

DOUGLAS, James Dixon, ed. 220.3
The new Bible dictionary. Consulting eds.: F. F. Bruce [others]. Grand Rapids, Mich., Eerdmans [c. 1962] xvi, 1375p. illus., maps (pt. fold., pt. col.) 25cm. 62-6077 12.95
1. Bible—Dictionaries. I. Title.

ENCYCLOPEDIA of the Bible 220.3
(The) [General ed.: P. A. Marijnen. Tr. from Dutch by D. R. Welsh, with emendations by Claire Jones] Englewood Cliffs, N. J., Prentice [c.1965] vi, 248p. illus., geneal. table, maps, plans. 21cm. (Spectrum book) [BS440.E453] 64-23557 5.50
1. Bible—Dictionaries. I. Marijnen, P. A., ed.

THE Family Bible 220.3
encyclopedia. [Created and produced by Copylab Pub. Counsel. New York, Curtis Books, 1972] 22 v. illus. 25 cm. More than five thousand alphabetical, cross-referenced entries covering biblical history, literature, and interpretation for the whole family, with special large-type entries for younger readers. [BS440.F42] 79-187552
1. Bible—Dictionaries, Juvenile.

FAY, Frederic Leighton, 220.3
1890-
A student's Bible dictionary. Drawings by William Duncan. Boston, Whittemore Associates [1956] 64p. illus. 19cm. [BS440.F47] 56-32389
1. Bible—Dictionaries. I. Title.

FURNESS, John Marshall. 220.3
Vital words of the Bible, by J. M. Furness. Grand Rapids, Eerdmans [1967, c1966] 127 p. 20 cm. [BS440.F88] 67-1707
1. Bible—Dictionaries. 2. Theology—Terminology. I. Title.

GAERTNER, George W. 220.3
Which is being interpreted: a dictionary of words in the King James Bible by George W. Gaertner, Theodore Delaney. St. Louis, Concordia [c.1963] unpaged. 21 cm. pap., 1.50
I. Title.

GEHMAN, Henry Snyder, 220'.3
1888-
The new Westminster dictionary of the Bible. Edited by Henry Snyder Gehman. Philadelphia, Westminster Press [1970] xi, 1027, 4 p. illus., maps (incl. 6 col.) 25 cm. (Westminster aids to the study of the Scriptures) Based on A dictionary of the Bible, by J. D. Davis. [BS440.G4] 69-10000 10.95
1. Bible—Dictionaries. I. Davis, John D., 1854-1926. A dictionary of the Bible. II. Title. III. Series.

GRAYDON, H 220.3
Bible meanings; a short theological word-book of the Bible by H. Graydon, D. E. Jenkins [and] E. C. D. Stanford. [London] Oxford University Press, 1963. 80 p. 19 cm. [BS530.G77] 63-24168
1. Bible—Dictionaries. 2. Bible—Theology. I. Title.

GRAYDON, H. 220.3
Bible meanings: a short theological word-book of the Bible, by H. Graydon. D. E. Jankins, E. C. D. Stanford. [New York] Oxford [c.]1963. 80p. 19cm. 63-24168 1.40 bds.,
1. Bible—Dictionaries. 2. Bible—Theology. I. Title.

HANDY dictionary of the 220.3
Bible. Gen. ed., Merrill C. Tenney. Grand Rapids, Mich., Zondervan [c.1965] 167p. illus., map. 18cm. [BS440.H234] 65-24407 1.00 pap.,
1. Bible—Dictionaries. I. Tenney, Merrill Chapin, 1904- ed.

HASTINGS, James, 1852- 220.3
1922, ed.
Dictionary of the Bible. Rev. ed. by Frederick C. Grant and H. H. Rowley. New York, Scribner [1963] xxi, 1059 p. illus., col. maps. 25 cm. Includes bibliography. [BS440.H5 1963] 62-21697
1. Bible—Dictionaries. I. Grant, Frederick Clifton, 1891- II. Rowley, Harold Henry, 1890-1969, ed.

HORN, Siegfried H 1908- 220.3
Seventh-Day Adventist Bible dictionary. With contributions by other writers. With atlas. Washington, Review and Herald Pub. Association, 1960. xxxii, 1199p. illus., maps (part col.) 25cm. (Commentary reference series, v.8) Includes bibliographical references. [BS440.H73] 60-12204
1. Bible—Dictionaries. I. Title.

THE Interpreter's 220.3
dictionary of the Bible : an illustrated encyclopedia identifying and explaining all proper names and significant terms and subjects in the Holy Scriptures, including the Apocrypha, with attention to archaeological discoveries and researches into the life and faith of ancient times : supplementary volume / Keith Crim, general editor ... [et al.]. Nashville : Abingdon, c1976. xxv, 998 p., [8] leaves of plates : ill. ; 27 cm. [BS440.I63 Suppl.] 76-379986 ISBN 0-687-19269-2 : 17.95
1. Bible—Dictionaries. I. Crim, Keith R.

THE Interpreter's 220.3
dictionary of the Bible; an illustrated encyclopedia identifying and explaining all proper names and significant terms and subjects in the Holy Scriptures, including the Aprocrypha, with attention to archaeological discoveries and researches into the life and faith of ancient times. [Editorial board: George Arthur Buttrick, dictionary editor, and others] New York, Abingdon Press [1962] 4 v. illus (part col.) maps (part col.) 27 cm. Includes bibliographies. [BS440.I63] 62-9387
1. Bible—Dictionaries. I. Buttrick, George Arthur, 1892- ed.

JENKINS, Horace Carroll. 220.3
A modern dictionary of the Holy Bible, King James version. [2d ed.] Gwynedd, Pa., Locllyn Publishers [1958] 233p. 22cm. Includes bibliography. [BS440.J4 1958] 58-14425
1. Bible—Dictionaries. I. Title.

JOHNSON, Frend Irwin. 220.3
What does the Bible say? [1st ed.] New York, Vantage Press [1956] 364p. 21cm. [BS440.J57] 55-10853
1. Bible—Dictionaries. I. Title.

JOHNSON, Frend Irwin. 220.3
What does the Bible say? [1st ed.] New York, Vantage Press [1956] 364p. 21cm. [BS440.J57] 55-10853
1. Bible—Dictionaries. I. Title.

KOMROFF, Manuel, 1890- 220.3
Bible dictionary for boys and girls, by Manuel and Odette Kemroff. Illustrated by Steele Savage. [1st ed.] Philadelphia, Winston [1957] 84p. illus. 25cm. [BS440.K6] 56-5094
1. Bible—Dictionaries. I. Komroff, Odette, joint author. II. Title.

KOMROFF, Manuel, 1890- 220.3
Bible dictionary for boys and girls, by Manuel and Odette Komroff. Illustrated by Steele Savage. [1st ed.] Philadelphia, Winston [1957] 84p. illus. 25cm. [BS440.K6] 56-5094
I. Komroff, Odette, joint author. II. Title.

LEON-DUFOUR, Xavier, comp. 220.3
Dictionary of Biblical theology. Translated from the French under the direction of Joseph Cahill. New York, Desclee Co., 1967. xxix, 617 p. 25 cm. Translation of Vocabulaire de theologie biblique. [BS543.A1L43] 67-30761
1. Bible—Dictionaries. 2. Bible—Theology. 3. Theology—Dictionaries. I. Title.

LEON-DUFOUR, Xavier. 220.3
Dictionary of Biblical theology. Edited under the direction of Xavier Leon-Dufour, translated under the direction of P. Joseph Cahill. 2d ed. rev. and enl. Revisions and new articles translated by E. M. Stewart. New York, Seabury Press [1973] xxxii, 711 p. 24 cm. "A Crossroad book." Translation of Vocabulaire de theologie biblique. [BS543.A1L413 1973] 73-6437 ISBN 0-8164-1146-8 17.50
1. Bible—Dictionaries. 2. Bible—Theology. 3. Theology—Dictionaries. I. Title.

LUEKER, Erwin Louis, 1914- 220.3
The Concordia Bible Dictionary. St. Louis, Concordia, 1963. vi, 146p. col. maps. 22cm. 63-2622 1.95 pap.,
1. Bible—Dictionaries. I. Title.

MCELRATH, William N. 220.3
A Bible dictionary for young readers, Illus. by Don Fields. Nashville, Broadman [c.1965] 126p. illus. 24cm. [BS440.M34] 65-15604 2.95
1. Bible—Dictionaries, Juvenile. I. Title.

MCFARLAN, Donald Maitland. 220.3
Who & what & where in the Bible [by] Donald M. McFarlan. Foreword by William Barclay. Atlanta, John Knox Press [1974, c1973] 199 p. maps. 22 cm. First published in 1973 under title: Bible readers' reference book. [BS440.M348 1974] 74-3709 ISBN 0-8042-0001-7 3.45 (pbk.)
1. Bible—Dictionaries. I. Title.

MCKENZIE, John L. 220.3
Dictionary of the Bible [by] John L. McKenzie. Milwaukee, Bruce Pub. Co. [1965] xviii, 954 p. illus., geneal. table, col. maps. 25 cm. Bibliography: p. xi-xiv. [BS440.M36 1965a] 65-26691
1. Bible—Dictionaries. I. Title.

MARIJNEN, P. A., ed. 220.3
The Encyclopedia of the Bible. [General editor: P. A. Marijnen. Translated from the Dutch by D. R. Welsh, with emendations by Claire Jones] Englewood Cliffs, N.J., Prentice-Hall [1965] vi, 248 p. illus., geneal. table, maps, plans. 21 cm. (A Spectrum book) Translation of Elseviers encyclopedie van de Bijbel. [BS440.E453] 64-23557
1. Bible — Dictionaries. I. Title.

MARTIN, William Clyde, 1893- 220.3
The Layman's Bible encyclopedia . . . by William C. Martin. Nashville, Southwestern Co. [1964] x, 999 p. 27 cm. [BS440.L3] 64-15419
1. Bible — Dictionaries. I. Title.

MARTIN, William Curtis, 220.3
1937-
The layman's Bible encyclopedia ... by William C. Martin. Nashville, Southwestern Co. [1964] x, 999 p. 27 cm. APPENDIX (p. 901-974): The history of the books of the Bible.—The history of the formation and translation of the English Bible.—The kings of Israel and Judah.—Alphabetical table of the first lines of the Psalms.—Miracles recorded in the Scriptures. [BS440.M415] 64-15419
1. Bible—Dictionaries. I. Title.

MILLER, Madeleine (Sweeney) 220.3
1890-
Harper's Bible dictionary, by Madeleine S. Miller and J. Lane Miller, in consultation with eminent authorities. Drawings by Claire Valentine [6th ed.] New York, Harper [1959] x, 850, 4 p. illus., maps (part col.) 24 cm. [BS440.M52 1959] 59-7622
1. Bible—Dictionaries. I. Miller, John Lane, 1884-1954, joint author. II. Title.

MILLER, Madeleine (Sweeny) 220.3
1890-
Encyclopedia of Bible life, by Madeleine S. Miller and J. Lane Miller. [Rev. ed.] New York, Harper [1955] xvi, 493p. illus., col. maps. 24cm. Includes bibliographies. [BS440.M5 1955] 55-3515
1. Bible—Dictionaries. I. Miller, John Lane, 1884-1954, joint author. II. Title.

MILLER, Madeleine (Sweeny) 220.3
1890-
Harper's Bible dictionary, by Madeleine S.Miller and J. Lane Miller. Drawings by Claire Valentine. New York, Harper [c1958] x, 850p. illus., maps (part col.) 24cm. [BS440.M52 1958] 58-5786
1. Bible—Dictionaries. I. Miller, John Lane, 1884-1954, joint author. II. Title.

MILLER, Madeleine (Sweeney) 220.3
1890-
Harper's Bible dictionary, by Madeleine S. Miller and J. Lane Miller. Drawings by Claire Valentice [7th ed.* New York, Harper [c1961] x, 854p. illus., maps (part. col.) 25cm. [BS440.M52 1961] 61-14623
1. Bible—Dictionaries. I. Miller, John Lane, 1884-1954, joint author. II. Title.

MILLER, Madeleine (Sweeny) 220.3
1890-
Harper's Bible dictionary, by Madeleine S. Miller and J. Lane Miller in consultation with eminent authorities. Drawings by Claire Valentine. New York, Harper [1954] x, 850p. illus., maps (part col.) 25cm. [BS440.M52 1954a] 54-9936
1. Bible—Dictionaries. I. Miller, John Lane, 1884-1954, joint author. II. Title.

MILLER, Madeleine (Sweeny) 220.3
1890-
Harper's Bible dictionary, by Madeleine S. Miller and J. Lane Miller in consultation with eminent authorities. Drawings by Claire Valentine. [4th ed.] New York, Harper [1956] x, 850p. illus., maps (part col.) 24cm. [BS440.M52 1956] 56-8498
1. Bible—Dictionaries. I. Miller, John Lane, 1884-1954. joint author. II. Title.

MILLER, Madeleine Sweeny, 220.3
1890-
Harper's Bible dictionary, by Madeleine S. Miller and J. Lane Miller, in consultation with eminent authorities. Drawings by Claire Valentine. New York, Harper [1952] x, 851 p. illus., maps (part col.) 25 cm. [BS440.M52] 52-7292
1. Bible—Dictionaries. I. Miller, John Lane, 1884-1954, joint author. II. Title.

MILLER, Madeleine (Sweeny) 220.3
1890-
Harper's Bible dictionary, by Madeleine S. Miller and J. Lane Miller. Rev. by eminent authorities. Drawings by Claire Valentine. [8th ed.] New York, Harper & Row [1973] ix, 853 p. illus. 25 cm. [BS440.M52 1973] 73-6327 ISBN 0-06-065673-5 12.50
1. Bible—Dictionaries. I. Miller, John Lane, 1884-1954, joint author. II. Title.

NEILL, Stephen Charles, 220.3
Bp., ed.
The modern reader's dictionary of the Bible, edited by Stephen Neill, John Goodwin [and] Arthur Dowle. New York, Association Press [1966] vi, 339 p. 23 cm. [BS440.N34] 65-25153
1. Bible — Dictionaries. I. Goodwin, John, joint ed. II. Dowle, Arthur, joint ed. III. Title.

NEILL, Stephen Charles, 220.3
Bp., ed.
The modern reader's dictionary of the Bible, ed. by Stephen Neill, John Goodwin. Arthur Dowle. New York, Association [c.1966] vi, 339p. 23cm. [BS440.N34] 65-25153 5.95
1. Bible — Dictionaries. I. Goodwin, John, joint ed. II. Dowle, Arthur, joint ed. III. Title.

NORTHCOTT, William Cecil, j 220.3
1902-
Bible encyclopedia for children, by Cecil Northcott. Designed and illustrated by Denis Wrigley. Philadelphia, Westministe Press [1964] 174 p. illus. (part col.) 27 cm. [BS440.N57] 64-10800
1. Bible — Dictionaries, Juvenile. I. Title.

NORTHCOTT, William Cecil, 220.3
1902-
Bible encyclopedia for children. Designed, illus. by Denis Wrigley. Philadelphia, Westminster [c.1964] 174p. illus. (pt. col.) 27cm. 64-10800 3.95
1. Bible—Dictionaries, Juvenile. I. Title.

PALMER, Geoffrey. 220.3
The junior Bible encyclopedia. [Cleveland] Shepherd [1965] 140 p. illus., facsims., maps, ports. 20 cm. [BS440.P33] 65-15122
1. Bible — Dictionaries, Juvenile. I. Title.

RICHARDS, Hubert J 1921- 220.3
ABC of the Bible [by] Hubert J. Richards. Milwaukee, Bruce Pub. Co. [1967] 216 p. 25 cm. [BS440.R52 1967] 67-30413
1. Bible—Dictionaries. I. Title.

RICHARDS, Hubert J., 1921- 220.3
ABC of the Bible [by] Hubert J. Richards. Milwaukee, Bruce Pub. Co. [1967] 216 p. 25 cm. [BS440.R52 1967] 67-30413
1. Bible—Dictionaries. I. Title.

RICHARDSON, Alan, 1905- ed. 220.3
A theological word book of of the Bible. New York, Macmillan [1962, c.1950] 290p. 24cm. (111) 1.95 pap.,
1. Bible—Dictionaries. I. Title.

RICHARDSON, Alan, 1905- ed. 220.3
A theological word book of the Bible. New York, Macmillan, 1951 [c1950] 290 p. 24 cm. [BS440.R53 1951] 51-9970
1. Bible—Dictionaries. I. Title.

ROGERS, Isaac Wallace, 220.3
1887-
Great Bible words; with a sermon on the world's greatest event, by I. W. Rogers. San Antonio, Faith Book House [1969] vi, 143 p. 22 cm. Bibliography: p. 143. [BS440.R66] 78-105094 1.75
1. Bible—Dictionaries. I. Title.

ROWLEY, Harold Henry, 1890- 220.3
Short dictionary of Bible themes [by] H. H. Rowley. New York, Basic Books [1968] 114 p. 22 cm. [BS440.R74] 68-54156 3.95
1. Bible—Dictionaries. I. Title.

SMITH, Barbara, 1922- 220.3
Young people's Bible dictionary; for use with the Revised standard version of the Bible. Philadelphia, Westminster Press [1965] 161, [24] p. illus., col. maps. 25 cm. "Westminster historical maps of Bible lands, edited by G. Earnest Wright and Floyd V. Filson": [24] p. (2d group) Bibliography: p. 161. [BS440.S59] 65-10003
1. Bible — Dictionaries, Juvenile. I. Wright, George Ernest, 1909- ed. II. Title. III. Title: Westminster historical maps of Bible lands.

SMITH, Barbara, 1922- 220.3
Young people's Bible dictionary; for use with the Revised standard version of the Bible. Philadelphia, Westminster [c.1965] 162, [24]p. illus., col. maps. 25cm. Westminster hist. maps of Bible lands, ed. by G. Ernest Wright, Floyd V. Filson. Bibl. [BS440.S59] 65-10003 4.50
1. Bible—Dictionaries, Juvenile. I. Wright, George Ernest, 1909- ed. Westminster historical maps of Bible lands. II. Title.

SMITH, William, Sir, 1813- 220.3
1893.
A dictionary of the Bible, comprising its antiquities, biography, geography, and natural history. Edited by William Smith. New York,

N. Tibbals. St. Clair Shores, Mich., Scholarly Press, 1972. p. At head of title: Columbian edition. [BS440.S64 1972] 72-11711 ISBN 0-403-02354-8
1. Bible—Dictionaries. I. Title.

SMITH, William, Sir, 1813-1893. 220.3
The new Smith's Bible dictionary. Completely rev. by Reuel G. Lemmons in association with Virtus Gideon, Robert F. Gribble [and] J. W. Roberts. Garden City, N.Y., Doubleday, 1966. xi, 441 p. maps (on lining papers) 25 cm. Revision of the author's A dictionary of the Bible. [BS440.S67 1966] 66-20927
1. Bible—Dictionaries. I. Lemmons, Reuel G., ed. II. Title. III. Title: Bible dictionary.

SMITH, William, Sir 1813-1893 220.3
Smith's Bible dictionary. Westwood, N.J., Revell [1967] 768p. 18cm. Complete and unabridged [Spire Bks.] [BS440.S67] .95 pap.,
1. Bible—Dictionaries. I. Lemmons, Reuel G., ed. II. Title. III. Title: Bible dictionary.
Also published by Pyramid Pr. as Pyramid Inspiration Bk., N1595.

UNGER, Merrill Frederick, 1909- 220.3
Bible dictionary. Drawings by Robert F. Ramey. Chicago, Moody Press [1957] vii, 1192 p. illus., ports., maps (part col.) facsims, geneal. tables, tables. 25 cm. Based on The people's Bible encyclopedia, edited by C. R. Barnes. [BS440.U5] 58-181
1. Bible — Dictionaries. I. Barnes, Charles Randall, 1836- ed. The people's Bible encyclopedia. II. Title.

UNGER, Merrill Frederick, 1909- 220.3
Bible dictionary. Drawings by Robert F. Ramey. Chicago, Moody Press [1957] vii, 1192 p. illus., ports., maps (part col.) facsims., geneal. tables, tables. 25 cm. Based on The people's Bible encyclopedia, edited by C. R. Barnes. [BS440.U5] 58-181
1. Bible—Dictionaries. I. Barnes, Charles Randall, 1836- ed. The people's Bible encyclopedia.

UNGER, Merrill Frederick, 1909- 220.3
Unger's Bible dictionary, by Merrill F. Unger. Drawings by Robert F. Ramey. [3d ed., rev.] Chicago, Moody Press [c1966] vii, 1192 p. illus., facsims., geneal. tables, maps (part col.) ports. 25 cm. [BS440.U5 1966] 67-1754
1. Bible — Dictionaries. I. Title.

WATCH Tower Bible and Tract Society of Pennsylvania. 220.3
Aid to Bible understanding, containing historical, geographical, religious, and social facts concerning Bible persons, peoples, places, plant and animal life, activities, and so forth. [1st ed. Brooklyn, Watchtower Bible and Tract Society of New York, 1969] 544 p. illus. (part col.) 24 cm. Contains articles arranged alphabetically by subject, Aaron-Exodus only. The entire work is projected to be published in 1 v. in 1970. [BS440.W36] 79-8601
1. Bible—Dictionaries. I. Title.

WEIGLE, Luther Allan, 1880- 220.3
The living word; some Bible words explained. New York, T. Nelson [1956] 72p. 23cm. [BS186.W42] 57-2669
1. Bible. English—Versions—Authorised. 2. Bible. English—Versions—Revised standard. 3. English language—Words— Hist. I. Title.

WEIGLE, Luther Allan, 1880- 220.3
The living word; some Bible words explained. New York, T. Nelson [1956] 72 p. 23 cm. [BS186.W42] 57-2669
1. Bible. English — Versions — Authorized. 2. Bible. English — Versions — Revised standard. 3. English language — Words — Hist. I. Title.

WILLIAMS, Albert Nathaniel, 1914- 220.3
Key words of the Bible; a new guide to better understanding of the Scriptures. [1st ed.] New York, Duell, Sloan and Pearce [and] Little Brown, Boston [1956] 268 p. 21 cm. [BS440.W43] 56-6772
1. Bible — Dictionaries. I. Title.

WILLIAMS, Albert Nathaniel, 1914- 220.3
Key words of the Bible; a new guide to better understanding of the Scriptures. [1st ed.] New York, Duell, Sloan and Pearce [and] Little, Brown, Boston [1956] 268 p. 21 cm. [BS440.W43] 56-6772
1. Bible—Dictionaries. I. Title.

THE Wycliffe Bible encyclopedia / editors, Charles F. Pfeiffer, Howard F. Vos, John Rea. Chicago : Moody Press, [1975] 2 v. (xix, 1851 p., [8] leaves of plates : ill. ; 24 cm. Includes bibliographies. [BS440.W92] 74-15360 ISBN 0-8024-9697-0 : 29.95 220.3
1. Bible—Dictionaries. I. Pfeiffer, Charles F., ed. II. Vos, Howard Frederic, 1925- ed. III. Rea, John, 1925- ed.

YOUNG readers dictionary of the Bible, for use with the Revised standard version of the Bible. Nashville, Abingdon Press [1969] 321 p. illus. (part col.), maps (part col.) 30 cm. An alphabetically arranged dictionary of Biblical persons, places, events, ideas, and terms. Includes scriptural references, pronunciation guides, maps, a table of kings, and a time scale of Biblical history. [BS440.Y68] 69-10618 5.95 220.3
1. Bible—Dictionaries, Juvenile.

THE Zondervan pictorial Bible dictionary. General editor: Merrill C. Tenney. Associate editor: Steven Barabas. Picture and layout editor: Peter deVisser. With the assistance of 65 contributors, scholars and experts in various fields. Grand Rapids, Zondervan Pub. House, 1963. xiv, 927 p. illus., maps (part col.) 25 cm. Includes bibliographies. [BS440.Z6] 62-16808 220.3
1. Bible—Dictionaries. I. Tenney, Merrill Chapin, 1904- ed. II. Title: Pictorial Bible dictionary.

ZONDERVAN pictorial Bible dictionary (The). General ed.: Merrill C. Tenney. Assoc. ed.: Steven Barabas. Picture and layout ed.: Peter de Visser. With 65 contributors, scholars, experts in various fields Grand Rapids, Mich., Zondervan [c.] 1963. xiv, 927p. illus., maps (pt. col.) 25cm. Bibl. 63-9310 9.95 220.3
1. Bible—Dictionaries. I. Tenney, Merrill Chapin, 1904- ed. II. Title: Pictorial Bible dictionary.

THE Zondervan pictorial encyclopedia of the Bible. General editor: Merrill C. Tenney. Associate editor: Steven Barabas. Consulting editors—Old Testament: Gleason L. Archer [and] R. Laird Harris. Consulting editors—New Testament: Harold B. Kuhn, [and] Addison H. Leitch. Archeology editor: E. M. Blaiklock. Manuscript editor—Edward Viening. Photo and layout editor, T. Alton Bryant. Grand Rapids, Zondervan Pub. House [1975- v. illus. 25 cm. Contents.Contents.— —v. 5. Q-Z. [BS440.Z63] 74-6313 220.3
1. Bible—Dictionaries. I. Tenney, Merrill Chapin, 1904- ed.

*JOHNSON, Gladys Cordray 220.'3'076
What the scriptures say. New York, Pageant [1967] 134p. 21cm. 2.75
1. Bible—Addresses, essays, lectures. I. Title.

*PINK, Arthur W. 220.3'6
The divine inspiration of the Bible / Arthur W. Pink. Rev. ed. Grand Rapids : Baker Book House, 1976. 108p. ; 21 cm. [BS 5387] ISBN 0-8010-7005-8 pbk. : 2.95.
1. Bible-criticism, interpretation, etc. I. Title.

AUZOU, Georges. 220.4
The formation of the Bible; history of the sacred writings of the people of God. [The English version of Josefa Thornton] Saint Louis, Herder [1963] x, 386 p. 24 cm. Translation of La tradition biblique. Bibliographical footnotes. [BS445.A853] 63-22743
1. Bible — Hist. I. Title.

AUZOU, Georges 220.4
The formation of the Bible; history of the sacred writings of the people of God [Eng. version by Josefa Thornton tr. from French] St. Louis, B. Herder [c.1963] x, 386p. 24cm. Bibl. 63-22743 6.00
1. Bible—Hist. I. Title.

BEEKMAN, John. 220.4
Translating the Word of God, with scripture and topical indexes / John Beekman and John Callow. Grand Rapids : Zondervan Pub. House, [1974] 399 p. ; 24 cm. Accompanied by a companion vol., Discourse considerations in Translating the Word of God, by Kathleen Callow. Bibliography: p. 368-381. [BS449.B43] 74-4950 pbk. : 5.95
1. Bible—Versions. I. Callow, John, fl. 1965- joint author. II. Title.

BRUCE, Frederick Fyvie, 1910- 220.4
The books and the parchments; some chapters on the transmission of the Bible, [3rd and] rev. ed. [Westwood, N.J.] Revell [1963] 286 p. illus. 22 cm. [BS445.B68] 63-5128
1. Bible — Hist. 2. Bible — Versions. I. Title.

BRUCE, Frederick Fyvie, 1910- 220.4
The books and the parchments; some chapters on the transmission of the Bible. [3d and] rev. ed. [Westwood, N.J.] Revell [c.1963] 286p. illus. 22cm. 63-5128 4.00
1. Bible—Hist. 2. Bible—Versions. I. Title.

CALLOW, Kathleen. 220.4
Discourse considerations in Translating the Word of God / Kathleen Callow. Grand Rapids : Zondervan Pub. House, [1974] 101 p. ; 24 cm. Companion vol. to Translating the Word of God, by John Beekman. Includes index. Bibliography: p. 95-96. [BS449.B433C34] 75-301314
1. Beekman, John. Translating the Word of God. 2. Bible—Versions. I. Title. II. Title: Translating the Word of God.

FULLER, David Otis, 1903- comp. 220'.4
True or false? The Westcott-Hort textual theory examined. Grand Rapids, Grand Rapids International Publications [1973] 295 p. 21 cm. Continuation of the compiler's Which Bible? Contents.Contents.—Fuller, D. O. Introduction.—Philpot, J. C. The authorized version.—Brown, T. H. God was manifest in the flesh.—Gaussen, L. The divine inspiration of the Holy Scriptures.—Gardiner, G. P. The story of Philip Mauro.—Mauro, P. Which version?—Burgon, J. W. The revision revised.—Pickering, W. N. Contribution of John William Burgon to New Testament textual criticism. Includes bibliographical references. [BS471.F84] 72-93355 ISBN 0-8254-2614-6
1. Bible—Criticism, Textual—History. 2. Bible—Versions. I. Title.

HERKLOTS, Hugh Gerard Gibson, 1903- 220.4
How our Bible came to us, its texts and versions. New York, Oxford University Press, 1954. 174 p. illus. 23 cm. London ed. (Benn) has title: Back to the Bible. [BS455.H43 1954a] 54-12217
1. Bible—History. I. Title.

KENYON, Frederic George, Sir 1863-1952. 220.4
Our Bible and the ancient manuscripts. Rev. by A. W. Adams. Introd. by G. R. Driver. New York, Harper [1958] 352p. illus., facsims. 23cm. [BS445.K46 1958a] 58-7098
1. Bible—Hist. 2. Bible—Versions. 3. Bible. Manuscripts. I. Title.

LEISHMAN, Thomas Linton 220.4
Our ageless Bible, from early manuscripts to modern versions. New York, Nelson [c.1939, 1960] 158p. (2p. bibl.) 21cm. 60-7293 2.75
1. Bible—Hist. 2. Bible—Versions. I. Title.

LEISHMAN, Thomas Linton, 1900- 220.4
Our ageless Bible, from early manuscripts to modern versions. New York, Nelson [1960] 158p. 21cm. Includes bibliography. [BS445.L37 1960] 60-7293
1. Bible— Hist. 2. Bible—Versions. I. Title.

PETERSEN, Mark E. 220.4
As translated correctly [by] Mark E. Petersen. Salt Lake City. Desert, 1966. 150p. illus. 23cm [BS455.P4] 66-20706 2.50
1. Bible — Versions. I. Title.

PRICE, Ira Maurice, 1856-1939. 220.4
The ancestry of our English Bible; an account of manuscripts, texts, and versions of the Bible. 3d rev. ed. by William A. Irwin [and] Allen P. Wikgren. New York, Harper [1956] xx, 363p. illus., ports., facsims. 22cm. Bibliography:p. 331-344. [BS445.P7 1956] 55-11644
1. Bible Hist. 2. Bible Versions. 3. Bible. English—Versions. I. Irwin, William Andrew, 1884- ed. II. Title.

ROBINSON, Henry Wheeler, 1872-1945, ed. 220.4
The Bible in its ancient and English versions. Edited by H. Wheeler Robinson. Westport, Conn., Greenwood Press [1970] vii, 337 p. 23 cm. Reprint of the 1940 ed. Contents.Contents.—Introduction, by the editor.—The Hebrew Bible, by the editor.—The Greek Bible, by W. F. Howard.—The Syriac Bible, by T. H. Robinson.—The Latin Bible, by H. F. D. Sparks.—The English versions (to Wyclif) by W. A. Craigie.—The Sixteenth-century English versions, by J. Isaacs.—The Authorized version and after, by J. Isaacs.—The Revised version and after, by C. J. Cadoux.—The Bible as the word of God, by the editor.—Bibliography (p. [303]-316) [BS445.R66 1970] 76-109832
1. Bible—History. 2. Bible—Versions. 3. Bible. English—Versions. I. Title.

SMYTH, John Paterson, d.1932. 220'.4
How we got our Bible / by J. Paterson Smyth. Folcroft, Pa. : Folcroft Library Editions, 1977. p. cm. Reprint of the 1912 ed. published by S. Low, Marston, London. [BS445.S65 1977] 77-24190 ISBN 0-8414-7793-0 lib. bdg. : 20.00
1. Bible—History. 2. Bible. English—Versions. I. Title.

TORREY, Reuben Archer, 1956-1928 220.4
Difficulties and alleged errors and contradictions in the Bible. Grand Rapids, Mich., Baker Bk., 1964. 127p. 21cm. 2.50
I. Title.

REUMANN, John Henry Paul. 220.409
The romance of Bible scripts and scholars; chapters in the history of Bible transmission and translation [by] John H. P. Reumann. Englewood Cliffs, N.J., Prentice-Hall [1965] viii, 248 p. 24 cm. Bibliographical references included in "Notes" (p. 223.234) [BS445.R4] 65-21174
1. Bible — Hist. 2. Bible — Versions. I. Title.

REUMANN, John Henry Paul. 220.409
The romance of Bible scripts and scholars: chapters in the history of Bible transmission and translation. Englewood Cliffs, N. J. Prentice [c.1965] viii, 248p. 24cm. Bibl. [BS445.R4] 65-21174 5.95
1. Bible—Hist. 2. Bible—Versions. I. Title.

*MULLAN, Carol. 220.42
Bible picture stories from the old and new testaments by Carol Mullan. Illustrated by Gordon Laite. New York, Golden Press 1974 1 v. (unpaged) illus. 32 cm. (Golden Books) [BS551] 0-307 1.25
1. Bible—Juvenile literature. I. Title.

BIBLE. English. 1957. Lamsa. 220.43
The Holy Bible from ancient Eastern manuscripts. Containing the Old and New Testaments, translated from the Peshitta, the authorized Bible of the church of the East, by George M. Lamsa. Philadelphia, A. J. Holman Co., 1957. xix, 1243p. facsims. 22cm. Syriac word and symbol for the triune God at head of title. [BS12 1957.L3] 57-12183
1. Bible. Syriac—Translations into English. I. Lamsa, George Mamishisho, 1893- tr. II. Title.

*BROCKINGTON, L. H. 220.44
The Hebrew text of the Old Testament. The readings adopted by the translators of the New English Bible [by]L. H. Brockington. New York, Oxford University Press [1974 c1973] 269 p. 24 cm. [BS715] 72-164449 ISBN 0-19-826169-1 14.50
1. Bible O. T. Hebrew I. Title.

BURROWS, Millar, 1889- 220.44
The Dead Sea scrolls. With translations by the author. New York, Viking Press, 1955. xv, 435 p. illus., maps, facsim. 24 cm. Translations (p. [347]-415): The Damascus document. The Habakkuk commentary. The Manual of discipline. Selections from the War of the Sons of Light with the Sons of Darkness. Selections from the Thanksgiving psalms. Bibliography: p. 419-435. [BM487.A3B8] 55-9645
1. Dead Sea scrolls. I. Dead Sea scrolls. English.

GINSBURG, Christian David, 1831-1914. 220.44
Introduction to the Massoretico-critical edition of the Hebrew Bible, by Christian D. Ginsburg. With a prolegomenon by Harry M. Orlinsky: The Masoretic text; a critical evaluation. [New York] Ktav Pub. House [1966] ii, 1028 p. 24 cm. Erratum slip inserted. "Appendix iii. Tables of Masorah, Magna and Parva" and "Tables ... of manuscripts ... [and] of printed editions" (6 fold. leaves in pocket) Bibliographical footnotes. [BS718.G5] 65-21744
1. Bible. O. T. Hebrew. 1894. I. Title. II. Title: The Massoretico-critical edition of the Hebrew Bible.

GINSBURG, Christian David, 1831-1914 220.44
Introduction to the Massoretico-critical edition of the Hebrew Bible. With a prolegomenon by Harry M. Orlinsky: Th Masoretic text; a critical evaluation. [New York] KTAV [c.1966] li, 1028p. 24cm. Appendix III. Tables of Massorah, Magna and Parva and Tables of manuscripts [and] of printed editions (6 fold. leaves in pocket) Bibl. [BS718.G5] 65-21744 22.50
1. Bible. O. T. Hebrew. 1894. I. Title. II. Title: The Massortico-critical edition of the Hebrew Bible.

WILSON, Edmund, 1895- 220.44
The scrolls from the Dead Sea. New York, Oxford University Press, 1955. vi, 121 p. 20 cm. Title in Hebrew on cover. [BM40.D4W5] 55-11322
1. Dead Sea scrolls. I. Title.

NORMAN, Don Cleveland. 220.47
The 500th anniversary pictorial census of the Gutenberg Bible. With introd. on the life and

work of Johannes Gutenberg by Aloys Ruppel. Chicago, Coverdale Press, 1961. xvi, 263p. illus. (part col.) ports. (part col.) col. maps, facsims. 43cm. Issued in a case. [Z241.B58N6] 60-53456
1. Bible. Latin. ca. 1454-55. Mainz. Gutenberg (42 lines)—Bibl. I. Ruppel, Aloys Leonhard, 1882- II. Title.

THE Pamplona Bibles; 220.4'7
a facsimile compiled from two picture Bibles with martyrologies commissioned by King Sancho el Fuerte of Navarra (1194-1234): Amiens manuscript Latin 108 and Harburg MS. 1, 2, Lat. 4 , 15. By Francois Bucher. New Haven, Yale University Press, 1970 [i.e. 1971] 2 v. illus., geneal. table, 4 maps, 570 plates (part col.) 32 cm. Contents.Contents.—v. 1. Text.—v. 2. Facsimile. Bibliography: v. 1, p. 153-161. [ND3355.P3] 73-99820
1. Sancho VII, King of Navarre, 1160 (ca.)-1234. 2. Bible—Pictures, illustrations, etc. 3. Illumination of books and manuscripts, Medieval. I. Bucher, Francois. II. Amiens. Bibliotheque municipale. MSS. (Lat. 108) III. Furstlich Oettingen-Wallerstein'sche Bibliothek. MSS. (1, 2, Lat. 4 , 15 IV. Bible. Latin. King Sancho's Bible. V. Bible. Latin. Harburg Bible.

THORPE, James Ernest, 1915- 220'.47
The Gutenberg Bible, landmark in learning / by James Thorpe. San Marino, Calif. : Huntington Library, 1975. 23 p. : facsims. ; 24 cm. [Z241.B58T47] 75-324777
1. Gutenberg, Johann, 1397?-1468. 2. Bible. Latin. ca.1454-55. Mainz. Gutenberg (42 lines) I. Title.

ARISTEAS' epistle. 220.48
Aristeas to Philocrates; letter of Aristeas, edited and translated by Moses Hadas. New York, Published for the Dropsie College for Hebrew and Cognate Learning by Harper [1951] vii, 233 p. 21 cm. (Jewish apocryphal literature) Greek and English. Bibliographical footnotes. [BS744.H3] 51-9329
1. Bible. O. T. Greek—Versions—Septuagint. I. Hadas, Moses, 1900- ed. and tr. II. Title. III. Series.

BIBLE. N.T. Greek. 1964. 220.48
The Greek New Testament being a text translated in the New English Bible 1961 Edited with introd., textual notes, and appendix by R. V. G. Tasker. [London] Oxford University Press, 1964. xiii, 445 p. 24 cm. [BS1965] 64-3131
I. Bible. English. 1961. New English. The New English Bible. II. Tasker, Randolph Vincent Greenwood, 1895- III. Title.

BIBLE. N. T. GREEK. 1964. 220.48
The Greek New Testament: being the text translated in The New English Bible, 1961. Ed. with introd., textual notes, appendix by R. V. G. Tasker. New York, Cambridge [and] Oxford [c.1964] xiii, 445p. 24cm. 64-3131 4.50
I. Bible. English. 1961. New English. The New English Bible. II. Tasker, Randolph Vincent Greenwood, 1895- III. Title.

WORRELL, William Hoyt, 1879- 220'.49
The Coptic manuscripts in the Freer collection. Edited by William H. Worrell, New York, Macmillan, 1923. [New York, Johnson Reprint Corp. 1972] xxvi, 396 p. illus. 23 cm. Original ed. issued in series: University of Michigan studies. Humanistic series, v. 10. Includes a translation of the 2 homilies and magical text. Part 1 was first published in 1916. Both parts of the present ed. also issued separately. Contents.Contents.—The Psalter and two fragments: The Coptic Psalter. Psalter fragment. Job fragment.—Two homilies and a magical text: A homily on the Archangel Gabriel, by Celestinus, Abp. of Rome. A homily on the Virgin, by Theophilus, Abp. of Alexandria. A magical text. [BS100.3.W67 1972] 70-39135
1. Gabriel, Archangel. 2. Mary, Virgin. 3. Bible. Manuscripts, Coptic. O.T. Psalms. 4. Manuscripts, Coptic. I. Freer Gallery of Art, Washington, D.C. MSS. (Coptic) II. Theophilus, patriarch, Abp. of Alexandria. III. Coelestinus I, Saint, Pope, d. 1432. IV. Bible. O.T. Psalms. Coptic (Sahidic). Selections. 1972. V. Title. VI. Series: Michigan. University. University of Michigan studies. Humanistic series, v. 10.

BIBLE. English. Selections. 1968. 220.5
God who saves us; a Bible for students. [Translated by J. Brennan. 1st ed. New York, Herder and Herder [1968] xxvii, 435 p. 21 cm. Translation of Gott unser Heil. [BS391.2.B7] 68-19354 2.95
I. Title.

CHILDREN'S Bible (The): 220.5
the Old Testament, the New Testament. Edit. Advisory Bd.: Joseph E. Krause, Samuel Terrien, David H. Wice. New York, Golden [c.1965] 510p. col. illus. 27cm. [BS551.2.C46] 65-15748 4.95 bds.,
1. Bible stories, English.

THE Children's Bible: the Old Testament, the New Testament. 220.5
Editorial Advisory Board: Joseph E. Krause, Samuel Terrien [and] David H. Wice. New York, Golden Press [1965] 510 p. col. illus. 27 cm. [BS551.2.C46] 65-15748
1. Bible stories, English.

EVANS, Owen E. 220.5
On translating the Bible / [by] Owen E. Evans. London : Epworth Press, 1976. 31 p. ; 20 cm. (The A. S. Peake memorial lecture ; 1975) Cover title. Includes bibliographical references. [BS449.E9] 76-378887 ISBN 0-7162-0271-9 : £0.40
1. Bible—Versions—Addresses, essays, lectures. I. Title. II. Series.

GULSTON, Charles 220.5
No greater heritage: our English Bible, the drama of the birth of the English Bible. Grand Rapids, Mich., Eerdmans [c.1960. 1961] 233p. Bibl. 1.95 pap.,
1. Bible—Hist. 2. Bible. English—Hist. 3. Bible. Afrikaans—Hist. I. Title.

HEIDERSTADT, Dorothy. 220.5
To all nations; how the Bible came to the people. New York, Nelson [1959] 192p. illus. 21cm. [BS450.H4] 59-5340
1. Bible—Hist. I. Title.

MACGREGOR, Geddes. 220.5
The Bible in the making. [1st ed.] Philadelphia, Lippincott [1959] 447p. 22cm. 'List of the principal Biblical manuscripts': p.328-330. 'Modern languages into which the Bible has been translated': p.331-383. [BS445.M28] 59-13071
1. Bible— Hist. 2. Bible, Manuscripts. 3. Bible—Versions. I. Title.

MORRELL, Minnie Cate 220.5
A manual of Old English Biblical materials. Knoxville, Univ. of Tenn. Pr. [1965] xi, 220p. 25cm. [BS132.M6] 65-17346 7.50
1. Bible. Manuscripts, Anglo-Saxon. 2. Bible. Anglosaxon—Versions. I. Title. II. Title: Old English Biblical materials.

NIDA, Eugene Albert, 1914- 220.5
God's Word in man's language. [1st ed.] New York, Harper, [1952] 191 p. 21 cm. [BS450.N52] 52-5466
1. Bible — Hist. 2. Bible — Versions. I. Title.

NORTH, Eric McCoy, 1888- 220.5
The Book of a thousand tongues; being some account of the translation and publication of all or part of the Holy Scriptures into more than a thousand languages and dialects with over 1100 examples from the text, edited by Eric M. North. New York, Published for the American Bible Society [by] Harper, 1938 [c1939] Detroit, Tower Books, 1971. 386 p. ports. 29 cm. [P352.A2N6 1971] 73-174087
1. Bible—Versions. 2. Polyglot texts, selections, quotations, etc. 3. Printing—Specimens. I. American Bible Society. II. Title.

WHEELER, Ruth Lellah (Carr) 1899- 220.5
The miracle of the Book, by Ruth Wheeler and Eugene W. Erickson. Illustrated by Don Muth. Mountain View, Calif., Pacific Press Pub. Association [c1960] 147 p. illus. 21 cm. [BS445.W45] 61-6482
1. Bible — Hist. I. Erickson, Eugene W., joint author. II. Title.

WHEELER, Ruth Lellah (Carr) 1899- 220.5
The miracle of the Book, by Ruth Wheeler, Eugene W. Erickson. Illus. by Don Muth. Mountain View, Calif., Pacific Press [1961, c.1960] 147p. 147p. 61-6482 3.00
1. Bible—Hist. I. Erickson, Eugene W., joint author. II. Title.

WOOD, Violet. 220.5
Great is the company. Illus. by Rafael Palacios. Rev. ed. New York, Friendship Press, 1953. 167p. illus. 22cm. [BS450.W6 1953] 53-9344
1. Bible—Versions. I. Title.

MACGREGOR, Geddes. 220.5'09
A literary history of the Bible; from the Middle Ages to the present day. Nashville, Abingdon Press [1968] 400 p. 25 cm. Bibliographical footnotes. [BS455.M32] 68-11477
1. Bible. English—History. I. Title.

WESTCOTT, Brooke Foss, Bp. of Durham, 1825-1901. 220.5'09
A general view of the history of the English Bible. 3d ed. rev. by William Aldis Wright. New York, Lemma Pub. Corp., 1972. xx, 356 p. 23 cm. Reprint of the 1905 ed. [BS455.W5 1972] 77-180773 ISBN 0-87696-037-9
1. Bible. English—History. I. Wright, William Aldis, 1831-1914, ed. II. Title.

AARON, David, 1909- 220.5'2
Aaron's riming Bible. Philadelphia, Dorrance [1971- v. 22 cm. Contents.Contents.—[1] Genesis.—v. 2. Exodus.—v. 3. Leviticus.—v. 4. Numbers.—v. 5. Deuteronomy.—v. 6. Joshua.—v. 7. Job. [BS559.A27] 78-162022 ISBN 0-8059-1582-6 (v. 1) 4.00 per vol.
1. Bible. O.T.—Paraphrases, English. I. Title.

ALEXANDER, Wade, comp. 220.52
God's greatest hits. Selected by Wade Alexander with drawings by Sister Morgan. [Los Angeles] Stanyan Books [1970] [55] p. col. illus. 20 cm. (A Stanyan book, 6) [BS391.2.A495] 78-15313 3.00
I. Bible. English. Selections. 1970. II. Title.

BEEGLE, Dewey M. 220.52
God's word into English. [1st ed.] New York, Harper [1960] 178 p. illus. 22 cm. [BS455.B44] 60-11770
1. Bible. English—Versions. I. Title.

BEEGLE, Dewey M. 220.52
God's word into English. Grand Rapids, Mich., Eerdmans [1965, c.1960] x, 230p. illus. 21cm. Bibl. [BS455.B44] 2.25 pap.,
1. Bible. English—Versions. I. Title.

BIBLE. English. 1962 Revised standard. 220.52
The Holy Bible, Revised standard version, containing the Old and New Testaments. Translated from the original tongues, being the version set forth A.D. 1611, revised A.D. 1881-1885 and A.D. 1901; compared with the most ancient authorities and revised A.D. 1946-1952. Reference ed. New York, Nelson [1962] xiii, 1296, 32 [32], 94 p. col. illus., plates (part col.) col. maps, tables. 26 cm. Issued in a box. "Bible study helps" (32 p. (2d group)), "The story of Jesus Christ for young Christians" ([32] p. (3d group)) and "Reader's concordance to the Revised standard version of the Holy Bible and index to Nelson's Bible atlas" (94 p. (4th group)) have special title pages. [BS191.A11962.N42] 62-53315
I. Title.

BIBLE. Anglo-Saxon. Selections. 1974. 220.5'2
Biblical quotations in Old English prose writers. Edited with the Vulgate and other Latin originals, introduction on Old English Biblical versions, Index of Biblical passages, and Index of principal words by Albert S. Cook. [Folcroft, Pa.] Folcroft Library Editions, 1974. p. cm. Reprint of the 1898 ed. published by Macmillan, London and New York. [BS131.C58 1974] 74-7275 ISBN 0-8414-3552-9 (lib. bdg.)
I. Cook, Albert Stanburrough, 1853-1927, ed. II. Bible. Anglo-Saxon. Selections. 1898. III. Title.

†THE Bible as/in literature / 220.5'2
James S. Ackerman, Thayer S. Warshaw, [editors] ; John Sweet, editorial consultant. Glenview, Ill. : Scott, Foresman, c1976. viii, 439 p. : ill. ; 23 cm. Includes index. [BS535.B496] 77-670031 ISBN 0-673-03423-2 pbk. : 2.40
1. Bible as literature. 2. Bible in literature. I. Ackerman, James Stokes. II. Warshaw, Thayer S., 1915- III. Sweet, John, 1916-

THE Bible companion; 220.52
with illus. by James Joseph Jacques Tissot. Includes A dictionary, concordance, and collation of the Scriptures [Gilbert James Brett, editor] encompassing references in the Old and New Testaments, The parables of Jesus, and other features. [Good Saviour ed.] Chicago, Consolidated Book Publishers [1950] xiv, 302 p. col. illus., 4 col. maps on fold. 1. 27 cm. [BS417.B45 1950] 50-11308
1. Bible—Handbooks, manuals, etc. I. Brett, Gilbert James. ed. II. Tissot, James Joseph Jacques, 1836-1902, illus. III. Title: Dictionary, concordance, and collation of Scriptures.

BIBLE. English. 1901 Authorized. 220.52
The Holy Bible containing the Old and New Testaments, translated out of the original tongues and with the former translations diligently compared and revised, by His Majesty's special command. Appointed to be read in churches. Glasgow, D. Bryce [1901] 1 v. (various pagings) facsim., plate. 49 mm. On cover: Illustrated miniature Bible. [BS185 1901.G55] 65-59534
I. Title. II. Title: Illustrated miniature Bible.

BIBLE. English. 1948. Catholic Biblical Association. 220.52
The Holy Bible, tr. from the original languages with critical use of all the ancient sources by members of the Catholic Biblical Assn. of America. Sponsored by the Episcopal Committee of the Confraternity of Christian Doctrine. Vol. 4, The Prophetic bks., Isaia to Malachia. Paterson, N. J., St. Anthony Guild Press [c.1961] 776p. 48-8688 7.00
I. Catholic Biblical Association of America. II. Confraternity of Christian Doctrine. III. Title.

BIBLE. English. 1950. Authorised. 220.52
The Holy Bible. Authorized King James version, with the words of Jesus in red and all proper names self-pronounced; comprising the complete text of the Bible supplemented by full color paintings, illuminations, and illustrations to beautify and clarify; plus The Bible in alphabet [Gilbert James Brett, editor] Golden Book ed. Chicago, Consolidated Book Publishers; distributed by L. B. Price Mercantile Co. [1950] 1 v. (various pagings) illus. (part col.) 4 col. maps on feld. 1. 27 cm. "Text ... previously published as the New indexed Bible." [BS185 1950.C53] 50-4480
I. Brett, Gilbert James. ed. II. Title.

BIBLE. English. 1950. Authorized. 220.52
The Holy Bible. Authorized King James version comprising the Old and New Testaments, a comprehensive encyclopedic guide to Biblical knowledge, and other features. with the words of Jesus printed in red, and self-pronunciation of all proper names. With illus. by celebrated old masters. [Heritage ed.] Chicago, Consolidated Book Publishers [1950] xv. 894, 304 p. col. illus., 4 col. maps on fold. 1. 30 cm. Gilbert James Brett, editor of dictionary, concordance and other helps. Cf. Copyright application. [BS185 1950.C535] 50-14035
I. Brett, Gilbert James. ed. II. Title.

BIBLE. English. 1950. Authorized. 220.52
The Holy Bible. Authorized King James version comprising the Old and New Testaments, a comprehensive encyclopedic guide to Biblical knowledge, and other features, with the words of Jesus printed in red and self-pronunciation of all proper names. With illus. by James Joseph Jacques Tissot. [Good Saviour ed.] Chicago, Consolidated Book Publishers [1950] xv, 894, 302 p. col. illus., 4 col. maps on fold. 1. 30 cm. "Dictionary, concordance. and collation of the Scriptures, GilbertJames Brett, editor": p. 1-286 (2d group) [BS185 1950.C52] 50-4481
I. Brett, Gilbert James. ed. II. Tissot, James Joseph Jacques, 1836-1902, illus. III. Title.

BIBLE. English. 1950. Authorized. 220.52
The new analytical Bible and Dictionary of the Bible. Authorized King James version with the addition, in brackets, of renderings from the American revised version. Comprehensive subject index ed. Chicago, J. A. Dickson Pub. Co. [1950] xiii, 204, 1702 p. maps (4 col. on fold. 1.) 23 cm. Old and New Testaments have special title pages. [BS185 1950.C54] 50-3971
I. Title. II. Title: Analytical Bible.

BIBLE. English 1950 (Basic English) 220.52
The Basic Bible, containing the Old and New Testaments in Basic English. [1st ed.] New York, Dutton, 1950. 910 p. 21 cm. [BS196.A1 1950.N4] 50-5865
I. Title.

BIBLE. English. 1950. Douai. 220.52
The Holy Bible. Old Testament in the Douay-Challoner text, New Testament and Psalms in the Confraternity text. Edited by John P. O'Connell, with illus. by James Joseph Jacques Tissot. Published with the approbation of Samuel Cardinal Stritch. Chicago, Catholic Press [1950] 1 v. (various pagings) illus. (part col.) col. maps. 30 cm. On spine: Holy Family edition of the Catholic Bible. "A practical dictionary of Biblical and general Catholic information" and "A collation of texts from the New Testament": 288 p. at end. [BS180 1950a] 51-1178
I. Challoner, Richard, Bp., 1691-1781. II. Confraternity of Christian Doctrine. III. Title.

BIBLE. English. 1950. Moffatt. 220.52
A new translation of the Bible, containing the Old and New Testaments [by] James Moffatt. [Concordance ed.] New York, Harper ['1950] 2 v. in 1. col. maps. 19 cm. Cover title: The Bible, a new translation. Vol. 2 has special t. p. with title: A new translation of the New Testament. [BS195.M5 1950] 51-14851
I. Moffatt, James, 1870-1944. tr. II. Title.

BIBLE. English; 1950; Moffatt. 220.52
A new translation of the Bible, containing the Old and New Testaments /James Moffatt. New York: Harper and Row [1976 c1954]

xlvii, 1531 p.; 22 cm. Includes concordance. [BS195.M5] ISBN 0-06-065778-2: 14.95
I. Moffatt, James, 1870-1944, tr. II. Title.

BIBLE. English. 1951. 220.52
Authorized.
The devotional family Bible, containing the Old and New Testaments (Authorized or King James version) Selfpronouncing ... Red letter ed. (words spoken by Christ printed in red) ... Dictionary-concordance and many other important and useful aids to the studies of the Holy Scriptures ... Wichita, Kan., Dixie Bibles [1951] 1088 p. illus. (part col.) col. maps. 30 cm. [BS185 1951.W5] 52-312
I. Dixie Bibles. Wichita, Kan. II. Title.

BIBLE. English. 1951. 220.52
Authorized.
Holy Bible; the new standard alphabetical indexed Bible (Authorized or King James version) School and library reference ed. Containing the Old and New Testaments translated out of the original tongues and with all former translations diligently compared and revised; to which are added many unique features of the Bible. Pictorial pronouncing dictionary ... Red letter ed. Chicago, J. A. Hertel Co. [1951] 1 v. (various pagings) illus. (part col.) col. maps. facsim. 30 cm. On spine: Masonic edition. New Testament has special t. p. [BS198.F8H4 1951] 51-2863
I. Title. II. Title: New stand. ard alphabetical indexed Bible.

BIBLE. English. 1951. 220.52
Authorized.
The reader's Bible, being the Authorized version of the Holy Bible, containing the Old and New Testaments and the Apocrypha translated out of the original tongues. Designed for general reading. New York, Oxford University Press [1951] xivii, 1267, 304, 367 p. maps. 25 cm. [BS185 1951.N4] 51-6651
I. Title.

BIBLE. English. 1951. 220.52
Douai.
The Holy Bible; edited by John P. O'Connell. Holy Trinity ed. Chicago, Catholic Press [1951] 1 v. illus. 27 cm. [BS180 1951] 51-6648
I. Title.

BIBLE. English. 1952. 220.52
Authorized.
The Holy Bible. Authorized King James version, with illus. by celebrated old masters, easy-to-use references, complete indexes and charts ... and other features ... Chicago, Consolidated Book Publishers [1952] xxvii, [268]. 921 p. illus. (part col.) 4 col. maps on fold. 1. 30 cm. On spine: The Good Leader Bible. "Encyclopedic index, concordance, and dictionary, Gilbert James Brett, editor": p. [xxv]-xxvii, [1]-[268] [BS185 1952.C52] 52-4754
I. Brett, Gilbert James. ed. II. Title. III. Title: The Good Leader Bible.

BIBLE. English. 1952. 220.52
Catholic Biblical Association.
The Holy Bible, translated from the original languages with critical use of all the ancient sources by members of the Catholic Biblical Association of America. Paterson, N. J., St. Anthony Guild Press, 1952- v. 20 cm. "Sponsored by the Episcopal Committee of the Confraternity of Christian Doctrine." Contents.v. 1. Genesis to Ruth.-- [BS195.C36] 52-13526
I. Catholic Biblical Association of America. II. Confraternity of Christian Doctrine. III. Title.

BIBLE. English. 1952. 220.52
Douai.
The Holy Bible. Old Testament in the Douay-Challoner text, New Testament and Psalms in the Confraternity text. Edited by John P. O'Connell, with illus. by celebrated old masters. Published with the approbation of Samuel Cardinal Stritch. [Papal ed.] Chicago, Catholic Press [1952] 1 v. (various pagings) illus. (part col.) ports. (part col.) maps (part col.) 27 cm. "A Catholic home encyclopedia": 288 p. at end. [BS180 1952] 52-4402
I. Challoner, Richard, Bp., 1691-1781. II. Confraternity of ChristianDoctrine. III. Title.

BIBLE. English. 1952. 220.52
Douai.
The Holy Bible. Old Testament in the Douay-Challoner text, New Testament and Psalms in the Confraternity text. Edited by John P. O'Connell, with illus. by celebrated old masters. [Papal ed.] Published with the approbation of Samuel Cardinal Stritch. Chicago, Catholic Press [1952] 1 v. (various pagings) illus. (part col.) ports. (part col.) maps. coats of arms. 27 cm. "A Catholic home encyclopedia": 288 p. at end. [BS180 1952a] 52-4985
I. Challoner, Richard, Bp., 1691-1781. II. Confraternity of ChristianDoctrine. III. Title.

BIBLE. English. 1952. 220.52
Revised standard.
The Holy Bible. Revised standard version containing the Old and New Testaments, translated from the original tongues; being the version set forth A.D. 1611, revised A.D. 1881-1885 and A.D. 1901; compared with the most ancient authorities and revised A.D. 1952. New York, T. Nelson, 1952. xii, 997, iii, 294 p. 22 cm. New Testament has special t.p.: The New Covenant, commonly called the New Testament of Our Lord and Savior Jesus Christ; revised standard version translated from the Greek ... compared with the most ancient authorities and revised A.D. 1946. [BS191.A1 1952.N4] 52-2922

BIBLE. English. 1953. 220.52
Authorized.
The Holy Bible, containing the Old and New Testaments (Authorized or King James version); self-pronouncing, words spoken by Christ printed in red. To which is added an alphabetical and cyclopedic index, a unique set of charts from Adam to Christ, leading doctrines, harmony of the Gospels, parables and miracles, Bible dictionary; all alphabetically arranged for practical and everyday use . . . Chicago, J. A. Hertel Co. [c1953] 317, 1504p. illus. (part col.) col. maps. 26cm. [BS185 1953.C5] 54-21462
1. Hertel (John A.) Company, Chicago. I. Title.

BIBLE. English. 1953. 220.52
Confraternity version.
Catholic family edition of the Holy Bible. New York, J. J. Crawley [1953] xiii, 1186, 381p. col. illus., col. maps. 22cm. 'The first eight books and the book of Psalms from the Old Testament and the entire New Testament are in the Confraternity of Christian Doctrine text; the remaining books are in the Challoner-Douay text.' [BS180 1953a] 53-13414
1. Confraternity of Christian Doctrine. I. Title.

BIBLE. English. 1953. 220.52
Confraternity version.
The Holy Bible. Catholic action ed. Confraternity text: Genesis to Ruth, Psalms, New Testament; Douay-Challoner text: remaining books of Old Testament. Edited by Paul John Bradley. Published with the approbation of Vincent George Taylor. Gastonia, N. C., Good will Publishers [c1953] 1v. (various pagings) illus. (part col.) 26cm. [BS180 1953c] 54-1449
I. Bradley, Paul John, ed. II. Title.

BIBLE. English. 1953. 220.52
Confraternity version.
New Catholic edition of the Holy Bible; the Old Testament, Confraternity-Douay version, with the new Confraternity of Christian Doctrine translation of the first eight books, and a new translation of the Book of Psalms from the new Latin version approved by Pope Pius XII; and the New Testament, Confraternity edition, a revision of the Challoner-Rheims version, edited by Catholic scholars under the patronage of the Episcopal Committee of the Confraternity of Christian Doctrine. [New ed.] New York, Catholic Book Pub. Co. [1953] 1118, 383p. illus., col. maps. 21cm. The New Testament has special t. p. [BS180 1953] 53-37779
1. Confraternity of Christian Doctrine. I. Title.

BIBLE. English. 1953. 220.52
Douai.
The family Rosary edition of the Holy Bible; edited by John P. O'Connell. Chicago, Catholic Press [1953] ixii, 909, 304, 288p. illus. (part col.) col. port., col. maps. 26cm. 'A Catholic home encyclopedia':288p. at end. [BS180 1953a] 54-16101
1. Catholic Church— Dictionaries. I. O'Connell, John P., ed. II. Title.

BIBLE. English. 1954. 220.52
Authorized.
The devotional, alphabetical indexed family Bible, containing the Old and New Testaments (Authorized or King James version) Self-pronouncing . . . Dictionary-concordance and many other important and useful aids to the studies of the Holy Scriptures . . . Wichita, Kan., Dixie Bibles [1954] 1088p. illus. (part col.) col. maps. 30cm. [BS185 1954.W5] 54-17882
I. Dixle Bibles, Wichita, Kan. II. Title.

BIBLE. English. 1954. 220.52
Authorized.
The Holy Bible. Authorized King James version. Comprising the Old and New Testaments, a comprehensive encyclopedic guide to Biblical knowledge, and other features, with the words of Jesus printed in red, and self-pronunciation of all proper names. With illus. by celebrated old masters. [Good Samaritan ed.] Chicago, Consolidated Book Publishers [1954] xv, 894, 304p. illus. (part col.) maps (4 col. on fold. 1.) 30cm. 'Dictionary. concordance. and collation of Scriptures. Gilbert James Brett, editor':p. 1-286 (2d group) [BS185 1954.C52] 54-2418
I. Brett, Gilbert James., ed. II. Title.

BIBLE, English. 1954. 220.52
Douai.
The Holy Bible; Old Testament in the Douay-Challoner text, New Testament and Psalms in the Confraternity text. Edited by John P. O'Connell. With illus. by celebrated old masters. Published with the approbation of Samuel Cardinal Stritch. Chicago, Catholic Press [c1954] 1v. (various pagings) illus. (part col.) ports. (part col.) maps (part col.) coats of arms. 30cm. 'A Catholic home encyclopedia': 288 p. at end. [BS180 1954] 55-304
I. Chaloner, Richard Bp., 1691-1781. II. Confraternity of Christian Doctrine. III. Title.

BIBLE. English. 1955. 220.52
Authorized.
The Holy Bible. Authorized King James version. Comprising the Old and New Testaments, a comprehensive encyclopedic guide to Biblical knowledge, and other features, with the words of Jesus printed in red, and self-pronunciation of all proper names. With illus. by James Joseph Jacques Tissot. [Good Saviour ed.] Chicago, Consolidated Book Publishers [c1955] xv, 894, 302p. col. illus., 4 col. maps on fold. l. 30cm. 'Dictionary concordance, and collation of Scriptures [by] Gilbert James Brett, editor':p. 1-286 (2d group) [BS185 1955.C5] 55-449
I. Brett, Gilbert James, ed. II. Tissot, James Joseph Jacques. 1836-1902, illus. III. Title.

BIBLE. English. 1955. 220.52
Authorized.
Holy Bible. Authorized King James version with illus. by celebrated old masters; comprising the Old and New Testaments, a comprehensive encyclopedic guide to Biblical knowledge, and other features, with the words of Jesus printed in red, and self-pronunciation of all proper names. Masonic ed., with articles on the history and philosophy of Masonry and an alphabetical dictionary of Masonic Knowledge, prepared especially for this Bible, by Curt A. Mundstock. Chicago, Consolidated Book Publishers [1955] iv, 894, 302p. illus. (part col.) maps (4 col. on fold. 1.) 30cm. 'Dictionary concordance and collation of Scriptures. Gilbert James Brett, editor': p. 1-286 (last group) [BS198.F8C6] 55-4180
I. Mundstock, Curt A. II. Brett. Gilbert James. ed. III. Title.

BIBLE. English. 1955. 220.52
Authorized.
Holy Bible (Authorized or King James version) The new standard alphabetical indexed Bible. School and library reference ed. Containing the Old and New Testaments translated out of the original tongues and with all former translations diligently compared and revised; to which are added many unique features of the Bible. Pictorial pronouncing dictionary and other interesting instructive features . . . Red letter ed. Chicago, J. A. Hertel Co. for International Sunday School League [1955] 294, 954p. illus. (part col.) col. maps, facsim. 30cm. On spine: New standard reference Bible. Blue ribbon. New Testament has special t. p. [BS185 1955.C52] 55-1442
I. International Sunday School League. II. Title. III. Title: The new standard alphabetical indexed Bible. IV. Title: New standard reference Bible.

BIBLE. English. 1955. 220.52
Confraternity version.
The Holy Bible, translated from the Latin Vulgate. The Old Testament: Douay version; Genesis to Ruth and the book of Psalms translated from the original languages with critical use of all the ancient sources by members of the Catholic Biblical Association of America, and the New Testament: Confraternity edition, a revision of the Challoner-Rheims version edited by Catholic scholars under the patronage of the Episcopal Committee of the Confraternity of Christian Doctrine. Alexandria [La.] Apostolate of the Press [c1955] 1280, 382p. illus. (part col.) col. maps (1 fold.) 21cm. On spine: Daughters of St. Paul. [BS180 1955a] 59-23941
I. Challoner, Richard, Bp., 1691-1781. II. Catholic Biblical Association of America. III. Confraternity of Christian Doctrine. IV. Title.

BIBLE. English. 1955. 220.52
Douai.
The Holy Bible; Old Testament in the Douay-Challoner text, New Testament and Psalms in the Confraternity text Edited by John P. O'Connell. With illus. by James Joseph Jacques Tissot. Published with the approbation of Samuel Cardinal Stritch. Chicago, Catholic Press [c1955] 1v. (various pagings) illus. (part col.) ports. (part col.) col. maps. coats of arms. 30cm. On cover: The Martin de Porres edition of the Catholic Bible. 'A practical dictionary of Biblical and general Catholic information':p. 288 at end. [BS180 1955] 56-964
I. Challoner, Richard. Bp., 1691-1781. II. Confraternity of Christian Doctrine. III. Title.

BIBLE. English. 1955. 220.52
Douai.
The Holy Bible, translated from the Latin Vulgate. The Old Testament: Douay version; Genesis to Ruth and the book of Psalms translated from the original languages with critical use of all the ancient sources by members of the Catholic Biblical Association of America, and the New Testament: Confraternity edition, a revision of the Challoner-Rheims version edited by Catholic scholars under patronage of the Episcopal Committee of the Confraternity of Christian Doctrine. Alexandria [La.] Apostolate of the Press [c1955] 1280, 382p. illus. (part col.) col. maps (1 fold.) 21cm. On spine: Daughters of St. Paul. [BS180 1955a] 59-23941
I. Challoner, Richard, 1691-1781. II. Catholic Biblical Association of America. III. Confraternity of Bp., Christian Doctrine. IV. Title.

BIBLE. English. 1955. 220.52
Revised standard.
The Holy Bible, containing the Old and New Testaments. Revised standard version, translated from the original tongues; being the version set forth A.D. 1611, revised A.D. 1881-1885 and A.D. 1901; compared with the most ancient authorities and revised A.D. 1952. New York, T. Nelson, 1953 i.e. 1955, c1946-55 vii 981, 63 p. col. illus., col. maps. 20 cm. New Testament has special t.p.: The New Covenant, commonly called the New Testament ... revised A.D.1946. "Helps to the study of the Revised standard version Bible": 63 p. at end. [BS191.A1 1955.N4] 55-1522

BIBLE. English. 1956. 220.52
Authorized.
The Holy Bible, containing the Old and New Testaments and the Apocrypha in the authorized King James version. New York, Hawthorn Books [1956] x, 818, 196, 258, 135p. illus., 56 col. plates. 28cm. [BS185 1956.N4] 56-5386
I. Title.

BIBLE, English. 1956. 220.52
Authorized.
The Holy Bible. Authorized or King James version. Family circle ed. [Philadelphia, Universal Book and Bible House, 1956] 1v. (various pagings) illus. (part col.) col. maps. 26cm. On cover: 500th anniversary. Includes various Bible helps. [BS185 1956.P5] 56-33590
I. Universal Book and Bible House, Philadelphia. II. Title.

BIBLE. English. 1956. 220.52
Authorized.
The Holy Bible, containing the Old and New Testaments in the Authorized (King James) version. Chicago, Good Counsel Pub. Co. [1956] 96, 958, 292, 94, 96p. illus. (part col.) 30cm. On spine: Good Book edition. 'Illustrated story of the Bible for young and old': 94p. (4th group) 'The Scriptural directory': 96p. (last group) [BS185 1956.C5] 56-27709
I. Title.

BIBLE. English. 1956. 220.52
Authorized.
The Holy Bible, containing the Old and New Testaments translated out of the original tongues, and with the former translations diligently compared and revised, by His Majesty's special command. Authorized King James version. New York, Harper [1956] viii, 1053. 322, [186]p. col. maps. 19cm. The New Testament has special t. p. 'Concordance to the Old and New Testaments': p. [1]-[160] (4th group) 'An index to the wome of the Bible, based on All of the women of the Bible, by Edith R. Deen': p. [161]-[174] (4th group) [BS185 1956.N42] 56-3453
I. Title.

BIBLE. English. 1956. 220.52
Authorized.
The Holy Bible; the complete text of the Authorized King James version, to which are added approximately 9,000 informative parallel renderings from the American standard version and the Revised standard version. Comprising the Old and New Testaments, with the words of Jesus printed in red, and including a comprehensive encyclopedic guide to Biblical knowledge, together with many other features. Clarified ed. Chicago, Consolidated Book Publishers [c1956] xviii, 1328p. col. illus., fold. col. maps. 31cm. On spine: Good Samaritan edition. 'Encyclopedic index, concordance and dictionary. Gilbert James Brett, editor': p. [1009]-[1280] [BS185 1956.C48] 57-1205
I. Brett, Gilbert II. Title.

BIBLE. English. 1956? 220.52
Authorized.
The interlinear Bible; the Authorised version

and the Revised version, together with the marginal notes of both versions and central references. London, Oxford University Press [1956?] xx, 1202, xv, 349p. col. maps. 23cm. Added t. p.: The Holy Bible containing the Old and New Testaments translated out of the original tongues ... New Testament has special t. p.: The New Testament of Our Lord and Saviour Jesus Christ ... 'Bible paper edition.'--Dust jacket. [BS188.A3 1956.L6] 56-2217
I. Bible. English. 1956? Revised. II. Title.

BIBLE. English. 1956. 220.52
Confraternity version.
Catholic family edition of the Holy Bible. New York, J. J. Crawley [1956] xiii, 1186, 381p. col. illus., col. maps. 23cm. 'The first eight books, the book of Psalms, and the sapiental books, Job to Sirach, from the Old Testament and the entire New Testament are in the Confraternity of Christian Doctrine text; the remaining books are in the Challoner-Douay text.' [BS180 1956a] 57-435
I. Confraternity of Christian Doctrine. II. Title.

BIBLE. English. 1956. 220.52
Confraternity version.
The Holy Bible. Confraternity text: Genesis to Ruth, Psalms, New Testament; Douay-Challoner text: remaining books of Old Testament. Published with the approbation of Vincent George Taylor. New York, C. Wildermann Co. [c1956] xviii, 912, 302p. illus. (part col.) 27cm. [BS180 1956b] 57-22422
I. Confraternity of Christian Doctrine. II. Title.

BIBLE. English. 1956. 220.52
Confraternity version.
The Holy Bible. Sacred Heart ed. Confraternity text: Genesis to Ruth, Psalms, New Testament; Douay-Challoner text: remaining books of Old Testament. Published with the approbation of John George Bennett, Bishop of the Diocese of Lafayette in Indiana. Chicago, Good Counsel Pub. Co. [1956] xxxii, 912, 302, 96p. illus. (part col.) 26cm. [BS180 1956] 56-1187
I. Good Counsel Publishing Company, inc., Chicago. II. Title.

BIBLE. English. 1956. 220.52
Knox.
The Holy Bible; a translation from the Latin Vulgate in the light of the Hebrew and Greek originals. Authorized by the Hierarchy of England and Wales and the Hierarchy of Scotland. [Translated by Monsignor Knox] New York, Sheed & Ward, 1956 [c1950] vii, 913, 285p. maps. 22cm. [BS195] 57-459
I. Knox, Ronald Arbuthnott, 1888- tr. II. Title.

BIBLE. English. 1956. 220.52
Revised standard
The Holy Bible, containing the Old and New Testaments. Revised standard version, translated from the original tongues; being the version set forth A. D. 1611, revised A. D. 1881-1885 and A. D. 1901; compared with the most ancient authorities and revised A. D. 1952. Boston, Massachusetts Bible Society [1956] 981, 63p. col. illus., col. maps. 20cm. New Testament has special t. p.: The New Covenant, commonly called the New Testament of Our Lord and Savior Jesus Christ: Revised standard version ... revised A. D. 1946. 'Helps to the study of the Revised standard version Bible, edited by Sidney A. Weston' (63 p. at end) has special t. p. [BS191.A1 1956.B6] 56-30628
I. Title.

BIBLE. English. 1956. 220.52
Revised standard.
The Holy Bible. Revised standard version containing the Old and New Testaments, translated from the original tongues; being the version set forth A. D. 1611, revised A. D. 1881-1885 and A. D. 1901; compared with the most ancient authorities and revised A. D. 1952. Rock Island [Ill., Published for] Augustana Book Concern [by T. Nelson, 1956] viii, 981, 64p. col. illus., col. maps. 21cm. New Testament has special t. p.: The New Covenant, commonly called the New Testament of Our Lord and Savior Jesus Christ; revised standard version translated from the Greek ... compared with the most ancient authorities and revised A. D. 1946. 'Helps to the study of the Revised standard version Bible' (64 p. at end) has special t. p. [BS191.A1 1956.R6] 56-1163
I. Title.

BIBLE. ENGLISH. 1956. 220.52
REVISED STANDARD.
The Holy Bible, containing the Oldand New Testaments. Revised standard version, translated from the original tongues; being the version set forth A. D. 1881-1885 and A. D. 1901; compared with the most ancient authorities and revised A. D. 1952. Boston, Massachusetts Bible Society [1956] 981, 63p. col. illus., col. maps. 20cm. New Testament has special t. p.: The New Covenant, commonly called the New Testament of Our Lord and Savior Jesus Christ; Revised standard version . . . revised A. D. 1946. 'Helps to the study of the Revised standard version Bible, edited by Sidney A. Weston' (63 p. at end) has special t. p. [BS191.A1 1956.B6] 56-30628
I. Title.

BIBLE. English. 1956. 220.52
Young.
Young's literal translation of the Holy Bible. Rev. ed. Grand Rapids, Baker Book House, 1956. 586, 178p. 23cm. The text is a photolithoprint of the rev. ed. published in 1898 under title: The Holy Bible. [BS195.Y6 1956] 56-7589
I. Young, Robert, 1822-1888, tr. II. Bible. English. 1898. Young. III. Title.

BIBLE. English. 1957. 220.52
Authorized.
Holy Bible. Authorized King James version. Comprising the Old and New Testaments, with the words of Jesus printed in red and all proper names self-pronounced. The divine healing ed., with helps on healing, salvation, miracles. Dallas, Barrett [1957] xii, 1270, 156p. col. illus*5cm. [BS185 1957.D3] 57-3268
I. Title.

BIBLE. English. 1957. 220.52
Authorized.
The Holy Bible, containing the Old and New Testaments and the Apocrypha. Translated out of the original tongues: and with the former translations diligently compared and revised, by His Majesty's special command. Appointed to be read in churches. Cambridge [Eng.] University Press distributed by Dryden Press. New York, [1957] xxii, 870p. maps. 20cm. [BS185] 57-2582
I. Title.

BIBLE. English. 1957. 220.52
Confraternity version.
New Catholic edition of the Holy Bible: the Old Testament, Confraternity-Douay version, with the new Confraternity of Christian Doctrine translation of the first eight books, and the seven sapiential books of the Old Testament, and the New Testament, Confraternity edition, a revision of the Challoner-Rheims version, edited by Catholic scholars under the patronage of the Episcopal Committee of the Confraternity of Christian Doctrine. [New ed.] New York, Catholic Book Pub. Co. [1957] 1150, 383p. illus., col. maps. 21cm. The New Testament has special t. p. [BS180 1957] 57-4788
I. Confraternity of Christian Doctrine. II. Title.

BIBLE. English. 1958. 220.52
Authorized.
The Holy Bible, containing the Old and New Testaments in the Authorized (King James) version. Chicago, Good Counsel Pub. Co. [c1958] 958, 292, 140p. col. illus. 20cm. On spine: Good Book ed. 'Concordance': p. [1]-124 (3d group) 'The Bible renders' aids': p. [125]-149 (3d group) [BS185 1958.C52] 60-21504
I. Title.

BIBLE. English. 1958. 220.52
Authorized.
The Holy Bible, Authorized or King James version, containing the Old and New Testaments translated out of the original tongues and with the former translations diligently compared and revised. Philadelphia, Universal Book and Bible House [1958] 1v. (various pagings) illus., col.plates, col. maps, facsim. 26cm. (International series. Self-pronouncing) Each section has special t. p. On cover: Salvation ed. On spine: Illustrated red letter ed. [BS185 1958.P5] 59-21540
I. Title.
Contents omited.

BIBLE. English. 1958. 220.52
Authorized.
Holy Bible (Authorized or King James version) The new standard alphabetical indexed Bible. School and library reference ed., containing the Old and New Testaments translated out of the original tongues and with all former translations diligently compared and revised; to which are added many unique features of the Bible: pictorial pronouncing dictionary and other intersting instructive features. Red letter ed. Chicago, J. A. Hertel Co. for International Sunday School League [1958] viii, 294, 954p. illus. (part col.) maps (part col.) facsims. 30cm. On spine: New standard reference Bible. Blue ribbon. New Testament has special t. p. 'A guide for the use of The new standard alphabetical indexed Bible' (6p.) in pocket. [BS185 1958.C5] 58-22712
I. International Sunday School League. II. Title. III. Title: The new standard alphabetical indexed Bible. IV. Title: New standard reference Bible.

BIBLE. English. 1958. 220.52
Confraternity version.
The Holy Bible. Confraternity text; Genesis to Ruth, Psalms, New Testament; Douay-Challoner text: remaining books of the Old Testament. Chicago, Good Counsel Pub. Co. [c1958] xxxi, 912, 302p. illus. (part col.) 29cm. [BS180 1958a] 60-24943
I. Confraternity of Christian Doctrine. II. Title.

BIBLE. English. 1958. 220.52
Confraternity version.
The Holy Bible. New American Catholic ed. With the pronouncements of Pope Leo XIII and Pope Pius XII on the study of the Scriptures, historical and chronological index, a table of references, and maps. New York, Benziger Bros [1958] xxx, 992, 32, 288p. illus., col. maps. 21cm. 'The Old Testament is the new Confraternity of Christian Doctrine translation for the Books of Genesis to Ruth and the Books of Job to Sirach; the remaining books are the Douay version. The New Testament is the Confraternity of Christian Doctrine translation.' [BS180 1958c] 60-42654
I. Confraternity of Christian Doctrine. II. Title.

BIBLE. English. 1958. 220.52
Confraternity version.
The Holy Bible, translated from the Latin Vulgate, with annotations, references, and an historical and chronological table. The Douay version of the Old Testament. The Confraternity edition of the New Testament, a revision of the Challoner-Rheims version edited by Catholic scholars under the patronage of the Episcopal Committee of the Confraternity of Christian Doctrine. [Memorial ed.] Nashville, Memorial Bibles [c1958] vi, 1086, 359p. illus. (part col.) col. maps. 21cm. On spine: New Catholic version. [BS180 1958b] 60-42658
I. Challoner, Richard, Bp., 1691-1781. II. Confraternity of Christian Doctrine. III. Title.

BIBLE. English. 1958. 220.52
Confraternity version.
The Holy Bible. Illustrated in color with paintings from the world's museums, churches, and private collections. Prepared under under the direction of John P. O'Connell. Introductions to each book of the Bible [by] Alexander Jones. Chicago, Catholic Press [c1958] 4v. in 3. col. illus., maps (part col.) 27cm. Each vol. has special t. p. Contents.[1] The Old Testament [Confraternity-Douay version]--[2-3] The New Testament [Confraternity version] An encyclopedia of the Bible & church; a practical work of reference for the Catholic layman, edited by J. P. O'Connell. 2v. in 1.--[4] The family record: a book for recording the history of a Catholic family: its sacramental life, its important activities and events, and its growth through five generations, prepared by M. P. Ryan. [BS180 1958] 59-3099
I. Catholic Church—Dictionaries. I. Confraternity of Christian Doctrine. II. O'Connell, John P., ed. An encyclopedia of the Bible church. III. Ryan, Mary Perkins 1915- IV. Title. V. Title: An encyclopedia of the Bible & church.

BIBLE. English. 1958. 220.52
Westminster version.
The Holy Bible. [The Old Testament in the Douay text, the New Testament the Psalms in the Westminster text. Prepared and produced under the editorial direction of Philip Caraman and John J. Dougherty] New York, Hawthorn Books [1958] xviii, 980, 367p. illus. (part col.) col. port., col. maps. 28cm. 'Published in the British Commonwealth (excluding Canada) ... as The Holy Bible for the family.' [BS195.W46] 58-8556
I. Caraman, Philip. 1911- ed. II. Dougherty, John J., ed. III. Title.

BIBLE. English. 1959. 220.52
American revised.
The cross-reference Bible. American standard version. With topical analysis and cross references, with variorum readings and renderings. Harold E. Monser, editor-in-chief. Grand Rapids, Baker Book House, 1959. xx, 2405p. 24cm. 'Originally printed in 1910.' [BS190.A1 1959.G7] 59-8342
I. Monser, Harold E., 1868-1918, ed. II. Title.

BIBLE. English. 1959. 220.52
Authorized.
Holy Bible. King James version. New York, Sanns Pub. Co., c1959- v. col. illus. 27cm. [BS185 1959.N4] 59-15819
I. Title.

BIBLE. English. 1959. 220.52
Authorized.
The Holy Bible, containing the Old and New Testaments in the Authorized King James version. [Masterpiece ed.] New York, Abradale Press [c1959] 856, 276, 225p. col. plates, 18col. maps. 30cm. [BS185 1959.N38] 59-54423
I. Title.

BIBLE. English. 1959. 220.52
Authorized.
The Holy Bible; containing the Old and New Testaments translated out of the original tongues and with the former translations diligently compared and revised. The authorized King James version. [Rembrandt ed.] New York, Abradale Press [1959] 856, 276, 229p. illus., plates (part col.) col. maps. 30cm. [BS185] 59-5444
I. Title.

BIBLE. English. 1959. 220.52
Berkeley version.
The Holy Bible, the Berkeley version in modern English containing the Old and New Testaments. Translated afresh from the original languages and diligently compared with previous translations, with numerous helpful non-doctrinal notes to aid the understanding of the reader. Gerrit Verkuyl, editor-in-chief and translator of New Testament section. Grand Rapids, Zondervan Pub. House, 1959. Grand Rapids, Zondervan Pub. House [c1945] viii, 944, 289p. 22cm. New Testament has special t. p.: The Berkeley version of the New Testament in modern English. Translated from the original Greek, with notes, by Gerrit Verkuyl. [BS195.B38] 59-16253
I. Verkuyl, Gerrit, 1872- ed. and tr. II. Title. III. Title: The Berkeley version in modern English containing the Old and New Testaments.

BIBLE. English. 1959. 220.52
Confraternity version.
The Holy Bible, containing the Old and New Testaments in Confraternity and Douay texts. [Masterpiece ed.] New York, Abradale Press [c1959] xxvii, 1078, 326p. col. plates, 18 col. maps. 30cm. [BS180 1959] 59-5443
I. Title.

BIBLE. English. 1959. 220.52
Confraternity version.
The Holy Bible; containing the Old Testament in the Confraternity-Douay texts and the entire New Testament in the Confraternity translation. [Rembrandt ed.] New York, Abradale Press [c1959] xxvii, 1078, 330p. plates (part col.) col. maps. 30cm. [BS180] 59-5445
I. Title.

BIBLE. English. 1959. 220.52
Revised standard.
The Holy Bible, containing the Old and New Testaments. Revised standard version. Translated from the original tongues, being the version set forth A. D. 1611; revised A. D. 1881-1885 and A. D. 1901; compared with the most ancient authorities and revised A. D. 1946-1952. Reference ed., with Concise concordance. New York, T. Nelson [1959] xiii, 1296, 191p. col. maps. 22cm. [BS191.A1 1959.N4] 59-4505
I. Title.

BIBLE. English. 1959. 220.52
Rotherham.
The emphasized Bible; a translation designed to set forth the exact meaning, the proper terminology and the graphic style of the sacred original, by Joseph Bryant Rotherham. Grand Rapids, Mich., Kregel Publications [1959] v, 920, 272 p. 25 cm. 59-7560
I. Rotherham, Joseph Bryant, 1828-1910, tr. II. Title.

BIBLE. English. 1960. 220.52
Authorized.
The Holy Bible, containing the Old and New Testaments in the Authorized King James version. [De luxe ed.] Chicago, Good Counsel Pub. Co. [1960] 1v. (various pagings) col. illus. 29cm. [BS185 1960.C5] 60-4777
I. Title.

BIBLE. English. 1960. 220.52
Authorized.
Holy Bible (Authorized or King James version) The new standard alphabetical indexed Bible. School and library reference ed., containing the Old and New Testaments translated out of the original tongues and with all former translations diligently compared and revised; to which are added many unique features of the Bible: pictorial pronuncing dictionary and other interesting instructive features. Red letter ed. Chicago, U. A. Hertel Co. for International Sunday School League [1960] 64, 294, 954p. illus. (part col.) ports., maps (part col.) 30cm. On spine: New standard reference Bible. Blue ribbon. Odd Fellows edition. New Testament has special t. p. 'Comprehensive Bible dictionary, by ... William Smith': p. 763-858. 'Cruden's Complete concordance to the Old and New

Testaments': p. 859-950. [BS198.O3H4 1960] 60-36289
I. International Sunday School League. II. Title. III. Title: The new standard alphabetical indexed Bible. IV. Title: New standard reference Bible.

BIBLE. English. 1960. 220.52
Authorized.
The Newberry study Bible, edited by Thomas Newberry. With a foreword by F. F. Bruce. Large-type reference ed., complete with supplements. [1st American ed.] Grand Rapids, Kregel Publications [1960] xxiii, 1189, xxiv, 394, 115p. map, diagr., plans. 27cm. 'Reproduced ... from the 1886 edition ... published by Hodder and Stoughton under the title, The Engleshman's Bible. [BS185 1960.G7] 60-10575
I. Newberry, Thomas, 1810-1901, ed. II. Title.

BIBLE. English. 1960. 220.52
Confraternity version.
The Holy Bible. Confraternity text: Genesis to Ruth, Psalms, New Testament; Douay-Challoner text: remaining books of Old Testament. Published with the approbation of Vincent George Taylor. [Catholic life ed.] Chicago, Good Counsel Pub. Co. [1960] 1v. (various pagings) col. illus., col. port. 29cm. [BS180 1960] 60-37444
I. Confraternity of Christian Doctrine. II. Title.

BIBLE. English. 1961. New 220.52
English.
The New English Bible. [New York] Oxford University Press, 1961- v. 24 cm. Translated under the supervision of the Joint Committee on the New Translation of the Bible. [BS192.A11961.N4] 61-16025
I. Joint Committee on the New Transalation of the Bible. II. Title.
Contents Omitted

BIBLE. English. 1961 220.52
The new English Bible. [New York] Pub. jointly by Cambridge and Oxford [1962, g.1961] 446p. Tr. under the supervision of the Joint Committee on the New Translation of the Bible. 1.45 pap.,
I. Joint Committee on the New Translation of the Bible. I. Title.

BIBLE. English. 1961. 220.52
Confraternity version.
The Holy Bible. With the Confraternity text. [Immaculate conception ed.] Charlotte, N. C., Catholic Bible House [1961] xxxii, 834, 236, 203p. col. plates. 33cm. [BS180 1961c] 62-739
I. Confraternity of Christian Doctrine. II. Title.

BIBLE. English. 1961. 220.52
Confraternity version.
The Holy Bible, illustrated with masterpieces of religious art and containing numerous Bible study helps. The Confraternity of Christian Doctrine translation of the text is used in the Old Testament books Genesis through Ruth and Job through Sirach and in the New Testament The remaining books are from the Douay-Challoner text. This ed. prepared by religious and biblical scholars under the editorial direction of Howard E. Reichardt. With a foreword by John A. O'Brien. [1961 ed.] Chicago, Catholic Bible Publishers [c1960] xxii, 1228, 254p. illus., col. plates, col. ports., col. maps. 27cm. [BS180 1960a] 61-660
I. Title.

BIBLE. English. 1961. 220.52
Confraternity version.
The Holy Bible. New American Catholic ed. With the pronouncements of Pope Leo XIII and Pope Pius XIII on the study of the Scriptures. historical and chronological index, a table of references, and maps. New York, Benziger Bros. [1961] xxx, 1016, 32, 288p. illus., col. maps. 21cm. 'The Old Testament is the new Confraternity of Christian Doctrine translation for the books of Genesis to Ruth, Job to Sirach and the Prophetical books; the remaining books are the Douay version. The New Testament is the new Confraternity of Christian Doctrine translation.' [BS180 1961] 61-65883
I. Confraternity of Christian Doctrine. II. Title.

BIBLE. English. 1961. New 220.52
World.
New World translation of the Holy Scriptures, rendered from the original languages by the New World Bible Translation Committee. Rev. ed.] Brooklyn, Watchtower Bible and Tract Society of New York] 1961. 1460 p. maps, plans. 19 cm. [BS195.N4] 61-36018
I. New World Bible Translation Committee. II. Title.

BIBLE. English. 1961. 220.52
Revised standard
The Holy Bible, containing the Old and New Testaments. Rev. standard version. Tr. from orig. tongues, being the version set forth A. D. 1611; rev. A.D. 1881-1885 and A.D. 1901; compared with the most ancient authorities and rev. A. D. 1952. New York, Harper [1962, c.1946, 1952] various p. col. illus. col. maps. 20cm. New Testament has special t.p.: The New Covenant, commonly called the New Testament of Our Lord and Savior, Jesus Christ. Brevier text Bible, black letter, 3.75, red letter, 4.00; Brevier ref. Bible, 13.95, bxd.
I. Title.

BIBLE. English. 1961. 220.52
Revised standard.
The Holy Bible, containing the Old and New Testaments. Revised standard version. Translated from the original tongues, being the version set forth A. D. 1611; rev. A. D. 1881-1885 and A. D. 1901; compared with the most ancient authorities and rev. A. D. 1952. Minneapolis, Augsburg Pub. House [1961] viii, 981, 64p. col. illus., col. maps. 20cm. New Testament has special t. p.: The New Covenant, commonly called the New Testament of Our Lord and Savior, Jesus Christ. 'Helps to the study of the Bible, by Gerhard E. Frost' (64 p. at end) has special t. p. [BS191.A1 1961.M5] 61-3344
I. Title.

BIBLE. English. 1962. 220.52
Children's version.
The children's version of the Holy Bible [1st ed.] New York, McGraw-Hill [1962] 1175, 352 p. col. illus. 23 cm. [BS197.M3] 62-17636
I. Title.

BIBLE. English. 1962. 220.52
Revised standard.
The Holy Bible, containing the Old and New Testaments. Revised standard version. Translated from the original tongues, being the version set forth A.D. 1611; rev. A.D. 1881-1885 and A.D. 1901; compared with the most ancient authorities and rev. A.D. 1952. Philadelphia, Westminster Book Stores [1962] xiv, 843, 242, 80 p. col. illus., col. maps. 20 cm. "Bible study helps, based on Westminster aids to the study of the Scriptures" (30 p. at end) has special t.p. [BS191.A11962.P54] 63-2131
I. Title.

BIBLE. English. 1962. 220.52
Revised standard.
The Holy Bible. Revised standard version containing the Old and New Testaments. Translated from the original tongues; being the version set forth A.D. 1611, revised A.D. 1881-1885 and A.D. 1901; compared with the most ancient authorities and revised A.D. 1946-1952. Self-pronouncing ed. Teaneck, N.J., Cokesbury [1962] 843, 243, 14, 30 p. illus. 19 cm. "A summary of the books of the Bible": 14 p. (3d group); "Study helps to the understanding of the Bible, prepared and edited by Henry M. Bullock": 30 p. (4th group) [BS191.A11962.T4] 63-4230
I. Title.

*BIBLE. English. 1962. 220.52
Authorized.
The holy Bible. Rev. standard version, containing the Old and New Testaments. Self-pronouncing ed. Cleveland, World [1964, c.1946, 1962] various p. 18cm. (Merdian living age bk., LA42) 1.95 pap.,
I. Title.

BIBLE. English. 1962. 220.52
Authorized.
The Holy Bible, containing the Old and New Testament, commonly known as the Authorized or King James version. Nashville, Southwestern [1962] 1v. (various p.) illus. (pt. col.) col. maps. 32cm. New Testament has special t. p. 62-5298 29.95
I. Title.

BIBLE. English. 1962. 220.52
Authorized
The Holy Bible. containing the Old and New Testaments. Tr. out of the original tongues and with the former translations diligently compared and rev. King James version, 1611. Reference ed., with concordance. New York, American Bible [1963] 1414p. col. maps. 22cm. A63 2.05
1. American Bible Society. I. Title.

BIBLE. English. 1962. 220.52
Authorized.
Modern King James version of the Holy Bible. [1st ed. New York, McGraw-Hill, 1962] 1175, 352p. col. illus. 23cm. [BS185 1962.N37] 62-17637
I. Title.

BIBLE. English. 1962. 220.52
Authorized.
Modern King James version oi the Holy Bible. New York, McGraw [c.1962] 1175, 352p. col. illus. 23cm. 62-17637 7.95
I. Title.

BIBLE. English. 1962. 220.52
Authorized.
The teen-age version of the Holy Bible. [1st ed.] New York, McGraw-Hill, 1962] 1175, 352p. col. plates 23cm. [BS185 1962.N4] 62-17635
I. Title.

BIBLE. English. 1962. 220.52
Children's version
The children's version of the Holy Bible. New York, McGraw [c.1962] 1175, 352p. col. illus. 23cm. 62-17636 7.95
I. Title.

BIBLE. English. 1962. 220.52
Revised standard.
The Holy Bible. Revised standard version, containing the Old and New Testaments. Translated from the original tongues, being the version set forth A. D. 1611, rev. A. D. 1881-1885, and A. D. 1901, compared with the most ancient authorities and rev. A. D. 1952. Verse reference ed.--Holman study Bible. Philadelphia, A.J. Holman Co. [1962] xii, 1a-1b, 1224, 191p. col. maps. 22cm. Cover title: Holman study Bible. 'Concise concordance to the Revised standard version of the Holy Bible' (191p. at end) has special t. p. [BS191.A1 1962.P5] 62-17986
I. Title. II. Title: Holman study Bible.

BIBLE. English. 1962. 220.52
Revised standard.
The Holy Bible. Rev. standard version, containing the Old and New Testaments. Tr. from orig. tongues, being the version set forth A. D. 1611, rev. A. D. i881-1885, and A. D. 1901, compared with the most ancient authorities and rev. A. D. 1952. Philadelphia, Holman [1963, c.1946, 1952] vi, 1240p. 34cm. (Pulpit Bible, RSV74). Persian morocco, 65.00, bxd.
I. Title.

BIBLE. English. 1962. 220.52
Revised standard.
The Holy Bible. Rev. standard version containing the Old and New Testaments. Tr. from orig. tongues, being the version set forth A.D. 1611, rev. A.D. 1881-1885 and A.D. 1901 compared with the most ancient authorities and rev. A.D. 1962. Introds., comments, cross references, general articles, tables of chronology and of measures and weights, and index. Ed. by Herbert G. May. Bruce M. Metzger. New York, Oxford 1962 [c.1946-1962] xxiv, 1544p. col. maps. 23cm. At head of title: The Oxford annotated Bible. 62-6807 7.95
I. May, Herbert Gordon, 1904- ed. II. Metzger, Bruce Manning, ed. III. Title. IV. Title: The Oxford annotated Bible.

BIBLE. English. 1962. 220.52
Revised standard.
The Holy Bible, Revised standard version, containing the Old and New Testaments. Tr. from the orig. tongues, being the version set forth A.D. 1611, rev. A.D. 1881-1885 and A.D. 1901; compared with the most ancient authorities and rev. A.D. 1946-1952. Reference ed. New York, Nelson [1962] xiii, 1296, 32, [32], 94p. col. illus., plates (pt. col.) col. maps, tables. 26cm. 'Bible study helps' (32p. [2d group]), 'The story of Jesus Christ for young Christians' ([32]p. [3d group]) and 'Reader's concordance to the Revised standard version of the Holy Bible and index to Nelson's Bible atlas' (94p. [4th group]) have special title pages. 62-53315 3.75 bxd.,
I. Title.

BIBLE. English. 1962. 220.52
Revised standard.
The Holy Bible. Revised standard version containing the Old and New Testaments. Translated from the original tongues, being the version set forth A. D. 1611, rev. A. D. 1881-1885 and A. D. 1901, compared with the most ancient authorities and rev. A. D. 1952. Holman peerless text ed. Philadelphia, A. J. Holman Co., [1962] vii, 1172, 32p. col. illus., col. maps. 19cm. 'Biblical backgrounds': 32 p. (3d group) [BS191.A1 1962a.P5] 62-52744
I. Title.

BIBLE.ENGLISH. 1963. 220.52
Confraternity version.
The Holy Bible, with the Confraternity text. Chicago, Good Counsel Pub. Co. [c1963] xxix, 834, 11, 236 p. col. plates, col. port. 29 cm. On cover: Catholic version. Includes forms for "Family records." [BS180] 63-25769
I. Confraternity of Christian Doctrine. II. Title.

BIBLE. English. 1963. 220.52
Authorized.
The Holy Bible. The Authorized or King James version of 1611 now reprinted with the Apocrypha. With reproductions of 105 of the sixteenth-century woodcuts of Bernard Salomon. London, Nonesuch Press; New York, Random House, 1963. 3 v. illus. 25 cm. Contents.CONTENTS. -- v. 1. The Old Testament, Genesis to Kings. -- v. 2. The Old Testament, Chronicles to Malachi. -- v. 3. The New Tesatment, followed by the Apocrypha of the Old Testament. [BS1851963.L6] 63-24703
I. Salomon, Bernard, 16th cent., illus. II. Title.

BIBLE. English. 1963. 220.52
Confraternity version.
Saint Joseph edition of the Holy Bible; The Old Testament, Confraternity-Douay, with the new Confraternity of Christian Doctrine translation of the first eight books, the seven sapiential books, and the eighteen prophetic books of the Old Testament, and the New Testament, Confraternity version, a revision of the Challoner-Rheims version edited by Catholic scholars under the patronage of the Episcopal Committee of the Confraternity of Christian Doctrine. New York, Catholic Book Pub. Co. [c1963] 42, 1014, 334 p. illus., maps. 22 cm. [BS180] 64-56879
I. Confraternity of Christian Doctrine. II. Title.

BIBLE. English. 1963. 220.52
Authorized.
The Holy Bible. [3v.] The Authorized or King James version of 1611 now reprinted with the Apocrypha. Reproductions of 105 of the sixteenth-century woodcuts of Bernard Salomon. London, Nonesuch Pr.; New York, Random, 1963. 3v. (700; 806; 778p.) illus. 25cm. Contents.v.1. The Old Testament, Genesis to Kings.--v.2. The Old Testament, Chronicles to Malachi.--v.3. The New Testament, followed by the Apocrypha of the Old Testament. 63-24703 45.00 set,
I. Salomon, Bernard, 16th cent., illus. II. Title.

BIBLE. English. 1963. 220.52
Authorized
The marked chain-reference Bible, being the King James or Authorized version of the Old and New Testaments. Marked by the best methods of Bible marking on all subjects connected with the themes of salvation, the Holy Spirit, temporal blessings, prophetic subjects . . . Marked, ed. by J. Gilchrist Lawson. [Tr. from Greek] Grand Rapids, Mich., Zondervan [1963, c.1928] 995, 47, 92, 16, 390p. illus., 17 col. maps, facsims. 22cm. 63-22889 14.95, bxd.; leather, 19.95 bxd.
I. Lawson, James Gilchrist, 1874-1946, ed. II. Gray, Joseph Howard, comp. Parallel quotations from the Old Testament and the New Testament. III. Hurlbut, Jesse Lyman, 1843-1930, ed. The International teachers' handy Bible encyclopedia and concordance. IV. Title.

BIBLE. English. 1963. 220.52
Confraternity version.
The Holy Bible, with the Confranternity text. Chicago, Good Counsel Pub. Co. [c1963] xxix, 834, ii, 236p. col. plates, col. port. 29cm. On cover: Catholic version. Includes forms for Family record. 63-25769 price unreported
I. Confraternity of Christian Doctrine. II. Title.

BIBLE. English. 1963. 220.5'2
Holy Name version.
The Holy Bible, containing the Holy Name version of the Old and New Testaments, critically compared with ancient authorities, and various manuscripts. Rev. by A. B. Traina. Irvington, N.J., Scripture Research Association, 1963. xi, 1102, 346 p. col. maps. 22 cm. New Testment has special t. p. [BS195.H6] 63-2798
I. Traina, A. B. II. Scripture Research Association, Irvington, N.J. III. Title.

BIBLE. English. 1964. 220.52
Revised standard.
Harper study Bible: The Holy Bible. Rev. standard version. Translated from the original tongues, being the version set forth A.D. 1611, rev. A.D. 1881-1885 and A.D. 1901, compared with the most ancient authorities and rev. A.D. 1952. Reference ed. with concordance and maps. Introductions, annotations, topical headings, marginal references, and index prepared and edited by Harold Lindsell. New York, Harper & Row [1964] xiv, 1902, 191 p. col. maps. 22 cm. "Concordance to the Holy Bible, revised standard version": 191 p. (3d group) [BS191.A11964.N4] 64-17541
I. Lindsell, Harold, 1913- ed. II. Title.

BIBLE. English. 1964. 220.52
Authorized.
Holy Bible, Authorized or King James version; Old and New Testaments translated out of the original tongues and with all former translations diligently compared and revised. Red letter ed. Pictorial pronouncing dictionary and other interesting instructive features, a family Bible beautifully illustrated with masterpieces of religious art. Wichita, Kan., Heirloom Bible Publishers [1964] 762, 128 p. illus. (part col.) col. maps. 30 cm. On Spine:

Master reference edition. New Testment has special t.p. [BS1851964.W5] 64-5567
I. Title.

BIBLE. English. 1964. 220.52
Authorized.
Holy Bible, containing both the Old and New Testaments. King James version. Red letter ed. New clarified reference Bible. Family and library reference ed. Johnson City, Tenn., Royal Publishers [1964] 1200 p. col. illus., forms. col. maps. 29 cm. New Testament has special t.p. "Published under auspices of the National Sunday School League, Nashville, Tennessee." [BS1851964.J6] 64-56197
I. Title.

BIBLE. English. 1964. 220.52
Authorized.
The Holy Bible, illustrated from the works of Michelangelo Buonarroti, 1475-1564. Conceived by Vincent Price expressly for Sears, Roebuck and Co. and Simpsons-Sears, ltd. Designed by Jack Carter, Mary Grant Price and Curtis S. Ruddle. Illustrated reproduced by Skira, art publishers, Geneva. Philadelphia, National Bible Press, [1964] viii, 1462, 96, 96 p. illus. (part col.) col. maps, ports. 25 cm. "The national concordance to the Holy Scriptures": 96 p. (3d group) Bible study helps, by M. W. Smith, with t.p., 96 p. (4th group) [BS1851964.P5] 64-57121
I. Buonarroti, Michel Angelo, 1475-1564. II. Title.

BIBLE. English. 1964. 220.52
Authorized.
Self-pronouncing King James Authorized version of the Holy Bible, containing the Old and New Testaments translated out of the original tongues and with the former translations diligently compared and revised. Wtih self-pronouncing reference dictionary index. Rev. and newly edited, by W. C. Sanderson. Philadelphia, A. J. Holman Co., 1964 [c1937] 1 v. (various pagings) illus., maps, plates (part col.) 30 cm. On cover: Holy Bible. Reference dictionary. New Testament has separate t.p. Includes masonic material and aids to Bibical study. Includes "Complete and practical household dictionary of the Bible ... by ... William Smith" (112 p.) [BS198.F8S3] 64-5723
1. Freemasons. I. Sanderson, William Charles, 1878- ed. II. Smith, Sir William, 1813-1893. Complete and practical household dictionary of the Bible. III. Title. IV. Title: Complete and practical household dictionary of the Bible.

*BIBLE. English. 1964. 220.52
Authorized.
The Holy Bible, containing the Old and New Testaments tr. out of the orig. tongues and with th former trs. diligently compared and rev. Authorized King James version. Self-pronouncing ed., with all proper names divided into syllables, accented and marked with the vowel sounds showing how they should be pronounced. Cleveland. World [1964] 1v. (various p.) 19cm. (Living age Meridian bk., LA41) 1.95 pap.,
I. Title.

BIBLE. English. 1964. 220.52
Authorized.
Self-pronouncing King James Authorized version of the Holy Bible, containing the Old and New Testaments translated out of the original tongues and with the former translations diligently compared and revised. With self-pronouncing reference dictionary index. Rev., newly ed., by W. C. Sanderson. Philadelphia, A. J. Holman [dist. Lippincott] 1964 [c.1937] 1v. (various p.) illus., maps, plates (pt. col.) 30cm. On cover: Holy Bible. Reference dictionary. New Testament has separate t.p. 64-5723 price unreoorted
1. Freemasons. I. Sanderson, William Charles. 1878- ed. II. Smith, William, Sir 1813-1893. Complete and practical household dictionary of the Bible. III. Title. IV. Title: Complete and practical household dictionary of the Bible.

BIBLE. English. 1964. 220.52
Revised standard
Harper study Bible: The Holy Bible. Rev. Standard version. Tr. from the original tongues, being the version set forth A.D. 1611, rev. A.D. 1881-1885 and A.D. 1901, compared with the most ancient authorities and rev. A.D. 1952. Ref. ed. with concordance and maps. Introd., annotations, topical headings, marginal ref., index prep., ed. by Harold Lindsell. New York, Harper [1964] xiv, 1902, 191p. col. maps.22cm. Includes concordance to the Holy Bible, rev. standard version. 64-17541 price unreported
I. Lindsell, Harold, 1913- ed. II. Title.

BIBLE. English. 1965. 220.52
Siewert.
The amplified Bible, containing the amplified Old Testament and the amplified New Testament. Grand Rapids, Zondervan Pub. House [1965] 1076, 409 p. 22 cm. Translation by Frances E. Siewert. [BS198.S5Z6] 65-19500
I. Seiwert, Frances E., ed. and tr. II. Title.

BIBLE. English. 1965. 220.52
Confraternity version.
The Holy Bible, with the Confraternity text. Chicago, Good Counsel Pub. Co. [1965] xxxii, 834, ii, 236, 70, 72 p. illus. (part col.) col. ports. 29 cm. On cover: Catholic life edition. Includes forms for "Family record." "A record of the more important events of the Old and New Testaments": 70 p. (5th group) "Catholic doctrinal guide": 72 p. 6th group) [BS180] 65-3948
1. Confraternity of Christian Doctrine. I. Title.

BIBLE. English. 1966. 220.52
Confraternity version.
Holy Bible containing both the Old and New Testaments. The entire Sacrifice of the Mass in pictures and explanatory text in accord with the Constitution on Sacred Liturgy of Vatican Council II; the Way of the Cross; and a complete Catholic dictionary keyed to the Bible and its use. Family and library references ed. Nashville, Catholic Publishers [1966] 1417 p. col. illus., col. maps., col. port. 30 cm. "The Old Testament, the new Confraternity translation of the first eight books, the seven Sapiential books, and the eighteen Prophetic books. The balance is in the Douay version. The New Testament, all books in the Confraternity of Christian Doctrine version in current usage. New Catholic liturgical Bible." [BS195.C6] 66-6063
I. Confraternity of Christian Doctrine. II. Title.

BIBLE. English. 1972. 220.5'2
The Holy Bible, in four translations: King James version, New American Standard Bible, the New English Bible, the Jerusalem Bible. [Parallel ed. New York] World-Wide Publications [1972] xxvii, 2899 p. maps. 29 cm. [BS125.W6 1972] 72-89778

BIBLE. English. 220.52
Authorized. Selections. 1952.
Readings from the Bible; selected and edited by Mary Ellen Chase. New York, Macmillan, 1952. ix, 422 p. 22 cm. [BS391.C46] 52-12884
I. Chase, Mary Ellen, 1887-1962, ed. II. Title.

BIBLE. English. 220.52
Authorized. Selections. 1964.
The Bible for students of literature and art. Selected, with an introd., by G. B. Harrison. Garden City, N.Y., Doubleday, 1964. xxxi, 563 p. maps (1 fold.) 22 cm. "The present text is based on The reader's Bible [1951]" [BS391.2.H3] 64-13820
I. Harrison, George Bagshawe, 1894- ed. II. Bible. English. The Reader's Bible. Authorized. 1951. III. Title.

BIBLE. English. 220.5'2
Authorized. Selections. 1974.
A concise treasury of Bible quotations / [edited] by Robert Garvey. Middle Village, N.Y. : Jonathan David Publishers, 1974, c1975. 175 p. ; 22 cm. [BS391.2.G37] 74-1966 8.95
I. Garvey, Robert, ed. II. Title.

BIBLE. English. Beck. 220.5'2
1976.
The Holy Bible in the language of today : an American translation / by William F. Beck. Philadelphia : A. J. Holman Co., c1976. vi, 1106, 337 p. ; 22 cm. Includes index. [BS195.B33 1976] 77-3429 ISBN 0-87981-082-3
I. Beck, William F. II. Title.

BIBLE. English. Byington. 220.5'2
1972.
The Bible in living English. Translated by Steven T. Byington. [Brooklyn, Watchtower Bible and Tract Society of New York, 1972] 1592 p. maps. 24 cm. [BS195.B9] 72-190031 6.00
I. Byington, Steven Tracy, 1868-1957, tr.

BIBLE. English. 220.52
Confraternity version. 1961.
The Holy Bible, with annotations, references, maps, and a historical and chronological table. The Old Testament, Douay version and the New Testament, Confraternity version. New York, Kenedy [1961] vi, 1086, 360 p. col. maps. 21 cm. On spine: New Catholic version. "First published by the English college at Douay, 1609; New Testament revised and edited by Catholic scholars under the patronage of the Episcopal Committee of the Confraternity of Christian Doctrine." [BS180 1961b] 62-232
I. Confraternity of Christian Doctrine.

BIBLE. English. New 220.52
English. 1970.
The New English Bible with the Apocrypha. London, Oxford U.P., 1970. xxi, 336 p. 21 cm. Includes the 2nd ed. of the New English Bible New Testament. "A completely new translation [by] the Joint Committee on the New Translation of the Bible." [BS192.A1 1970.L6] 75-498997 35/- ($9.95)
I. Joint Committee on the New Translation of the Bible. II. Title.

BIBLE. English. Revised 220.52
standard. 1962.
The Holy Bible, containing the Old and New Testaments. Revised standard version. Translated from the original tongues, being the version set forth A. D. 1611; rev. A. D. 1881-1885 and A. D. 1901; compared with the most ancient authorities and rev. A. D. 1952. Philadelphia, Westminster Book Stores [1962] xiv, 843, 242, 30 p. col. illus., col. maps. 20 cm. "Bible study helps, based on Westminster aids to the study of the Scriptures" (30 p. at end) has special t. p. [BS191.A1 1962.P54] 63-2131

BIBLE. English. Revised 220.52
standard. Selections. 1959.
Bible readings for boys and girls; selected passages from the Revised standard version of the Holy Bible. Illustrated by Lynd Ward. New York, T. Nelson [1959] 256 p. illus. 24 cm. [BS197.N4] 59-13757
I. Title.

BIBLE. English. Selection. 220.52
1962
The kingdom of God; a short Bible. Trs., explanations, paraphrases under the direction of Louis J. Putz. Notre Dame, Ind., Fides [1964, c.1962] 383p. illus., maps. Orig. pub. in German. 22cm. 2.45 pap.,
I. Putz, Louis J., ed. II. Title.

BIBLE. English. 220.52
Selections. 1836.
A new hieroglyphical Bible, with four hundred embellishments on wood. 11th ed. Chiswick [Eng.] Printed by C. Whittingham for W. Jackson, New York, 1836. New York, American Heritage Press [1970] 100 p. illus. 16 cm. (An American heritage attic reprint) [BS560.A3 1836b] 74-121897
1. Hieroglyphic Bibles. I. Bible. English. Selections. 1970. II. Title.

BIBLE. English. 220.52
Selections. 1950. Authorized.
The Dartmouth Bible; an abridgment of the King James version, with aids to its understanding as history and literature, and as a source of religious experience. The Old Testament, the Apocrypha, and the New Testament, with introductions, prefaces, notes, and annotated maps. [By] Roy B. Chamberlin [and] Herman Feldman, with the counsel of an advisory board of Biblical scholars. Boston, Houghton Mifflin, 1950. xxxviii, 1257 p. maps. 23 cm. Bibliography: p. 1205-1213. [BS391.C45] 50-13249
I. Chamberlin, Roy Bullard, 1887- II. Feldman, Herman, 1894-1947. III. Title.

BIBLE. English. 220.52
Selections. 1950. Authorized.
The Dartmouth Bible; an abridgment of the King James version, with aids to its understanding as history and literature, and as a source of religious experience. The Old Testament, the Apocrypha, and the New Testament, with introds., prefs., notes, annotated maps. [By] Roy B. Chamberlin, Herman Feldman, with the counsel of an advisory board of Biblical scholars [2d ed., rev., enlarged] Boston, Houghton, 1965[c.1950, 1961] xxxviii, 1257p. maps. 23cm. (Sentry 45) Bibl. [BS391.C45] 50-13249 3.95 pap.,
I. Chamberlin, Roy Bullard, 1887- II. Feldman, Herman, 1894-1947. III. Title.

BIBLE. English. 220.52
Selections. 1950. Authorized.
The home Bible, arranged for family reading from the King James version by Ruth Hornblower Greenough; with illus. from designs by William Blake, decorations by Rudolph Ruzicka. New York, Harper ['1950] xv, 339, 393 p. illus. (part col.) maps. 27 cm. Originally published in 2 v. under title: The Bible for my grandchildren. [BS197.G7 1950a] 51-12410
I. Greenough. Ruth Hornblower. ed. II. Blake, William, 1757-1827, illus. III. Title.

BIBLE. English. 220.52
Selections. 1951.
The shorter Oxford Bible, abridged and edited by G. W. Briggs, G. B. Caird [and] N. Micklem. London, Oxford University Press, 1951. xxiii, 476 p. col. maps. 19 cm. [BS391.B7215] 51-3309
I. Briggs, George Wallace, 1875- ed. II. Caird, George B. ed. III. Title.

BIBLE. English. 220.52
Selections. 1951. Authorized.
The bedside Bible; an anthology for the quiet hours, selected and arr. with introductions and notes by Arthur Stanley [pseud.] New York, Scribner [1951?] 369 p. 18 cm. [BS391.M44] 51-14915
I. Megaw. Arthur Stanley, 1872- ed. II. Title.

BIBLE. English. 220.52
Selections. 1951. Authorized.
The condensed Bible; all Bible gems, Genesis through Revelation. A guide for inspirational reading, selected with commentary, by William A. Cocke. New York, Exposition Press [1951] 517 p. illus. 23 cm. [BS391.C6] 51-13199
I. Cocke, William Alexander, 1874- ed. II. Title.

BIBLE. English. 220.52
Selections. 1951. Authorized.
The pocket Bible; the Old and New Testaments in the King James version. An abridgment with pref. by Cyril C. Richardson of The Bible designed to be read as living literature as edited and arranged by Ernest Sutherland Bates. New York, Pocket Books [1951] xviii. 461 p. 17 cm. (A Cardinal edition. C-9) [BS391.R53] 51-40200
I. Richardson, Cyril Charles, 1909- II. Bible. English. Selections.1936 Authorized. III. Title. IV. Title: The Bible designed to be read as living literature.

BIBLE. English. 220.52
Selections. 1951. Authorized.
The shorter Bible for Bible game contestants; selected passages from both the King James and Douay versions of the Holy Bible. Chicago, Times Sales Co. [1951] 124 p. illus. 15 cm. [BS391.T55] 51-26519
I. Bible. English. Selections. 1951. Doual. II. Title.

BIBLE. English. 220.52
Selections. 1952. Authorized.
Best Bible verses, compiled by Henry H. Halley. 2d ed. Chicago, H. H. Halley [1952] 648 p. 15 cm. [BS391.H29 1952] 52-36172
1. Bible—Indexes, Topical. I. Halley, Henry Hampton, 1874- comp. II. Title.

BIBLE. English. 220.52
Selections. 1952. Authorized.
The Bible; selections from the Old and New Testaments, edited with an introd. and notes by Allan G. Chester. New York, Rinehart [1952] xxxi, 415 p. 19 cm. (Rinehart editions, 56) [BS391.C47] 52-5606
I. Chester, Allan Griffith, 1900- ed. II. Title.

BIBLE. English. 220.52
Selections. 1952. Authorized.
The golden treasury of the Bible. compiled by Emily V. Hammond. 4th ed. New York, William Sloane Associates [1952] 372p. 15cm. [BS391.H3 1952] 52-14803
I. Hammond. Emily Vanderbilt (Sloane) 1874- comp. II. Title.

BIBLE. English. 220.52
Selections. 1952. Authorized.
The living Bible; a shortened version for modern readers based on the King James translation, edited by Robert O. Ballou. New York, Viking Press, 1952. xviii, 729 p. 22 cm. [BS391.B32] 52-7103
I. Ballou, Robert Oleson, 1892- ed. II. Title.

BIBLE. English. 220.52
Selections. 1952. Authorized.
Olive Pell Bible. condensed from the King James version. New York, Crown Publishers [c1952] 381p. illus. 18cm. [BS391] 52-6097
I. Pell, Olive, ed. II. Title.

BIBLE. English. 220.52
Selections. 1953. Authorized.
The Bible for boys and girls. Selections from the text of the authorized version of the Bible. New York, Philosophical Library [1953] 576p. col. illus.,col. maps. 16cm. [BS197.P47] 53-1196
I. Title.

BIBLE. English. 220.52
Selections. 1953. Authorized.
The companion Bible; the authorized or King James version of the Scriptures from Genesis to Revelation in shortened form, compiled by William A. Cocke. Philadelphia, Winston [1953] xii, 496p. 22cm. First published in 1951 under title: The condensed Bible. [BS391.C6 1953] 52-12902
I. Cocke, William Alexander. 1874- ed. II. Title.

BIBLE. English. 220.52
Selections. 1953. Authorized.
Daily light on the daily path, morning and evening hour; a devotional text book for every day in the year in the very words of Scripture. With additional readings for special occasions. New York, Harper [1953, c1950] unpaged. 15cm. [BS390.B2 1953] 53-1498
1. ,devotional calendars. I. Title.

BIBLE. English. 220.52
Selections. 1953. Authorized.
Every man's Bible; selected and arr. from the King James version by Manuel Komroff. New York [Lion Books] by arrangement with Cornell Pub. Corp. [1953] 192p. 17cm. (A Lion book, 167) [BS391.K6] 54-339
I. Komroff, Manuel. 1890- ed. II. Title.

BIBLE. English. 220.52
Selections. 1954-
The book of Bible prayer; prayers from the Bible, selected and arranged by Paul G. Koch. Milwaukee, Northwestern Pub. House [1954] 108p. 20cm. [BV228.K6] 54-43126
1. Bible—Prayers. I. Koch, Paul George, 1918- ed. II. Title.

BIBLE. English. 220.52
Selections. 1954-
The kingdom and the golden calves, by Mary J. Tschirhart. New York, Philosophical Library [1954] 68p. 24cm. [BS391.T84] 54-9012
I. Tschirhart. Mary J., ed. II. Title.

BIBLE. English. 220.52
Selections. 1954. Authorized.
A Bible for the humanities; edited by John C. Thirlwall and Arthur Waldhorn. New York, Harper [1954] xxiv, 471p. maps (on lining papers) 21cm. [BS391.T42] 54-7332
I. Thirlwall, John Connop, 1904- ed. II. Waldhorn, Arthur, ed. III. Title.

BIBLE. English. 220.52
Selections. 1954. Authorized.
The glory and the wonder of the Bible; edited and interpreted by Daniel A. Poling and Henry Thomas. New York, Crowell [1954] xix, 344p. 22cm. [BS391.P56] 54-9160
I. Poling. Daniel Alfred, 1884- ed. II. Thomas, Henry, 1886- ed. III. Title.

BIBLE. English. 220.52
Selections. 1954. Authorized.
The Holy Bible in brief, the King James text; edited and arr. by James Reeves. With a foreword by Angus Dunn. New York, J. Messner [1954] xi, 302p. maps. 22cm. London ed. (Wingate) has title: The Bible in brief. [BS391.R42 1954a] 54-10593
I. Reeves, James, 1909- ed. II. Title.

BIBLE. English. 220.52
Selections. 1954. Authorized.
The inspirational reader; selections from the Bible for everyday use, compiled by William Oliver Stevens and an editorial panel: Phillips P. Elliott [and others. 1st ed.] Garden City, N. Y., Doubleday, 1954. 253p. 22cm. [BS391.S672] 54-5166
I. Stevens. William Oliver, 1878- ed. II. Title.

BIBLE. English.Selections. 220.52
1955. Authorized.
The compact Bible; the Old andNew Testaments in the King James version, edited for easy reading by Margaret Nicholson. New York, Hawthorn Books [c1955] vi, 504p. 20cm. [BS391.N5] 55-6440
I. Nicholson, Margaret, ed. II. Title.

BIBLE. English. 220.52
Selections. 1956.
The main channel; a digest of the continuous stream of Bible history from Genesis to Revelation [by] Leona Willingham Parsons. Liberty, Mo., W. Jewell Press [1956] 264p. illus. 24cm. [BS391.P32] 56-43820
I. Parsons, Leona Willingham, 1894- II. Title.

BIBLE. English. 220.52
Selections. 1956. Authorized.
The Bible for family reading, with introductions and notes. The Old Testament prepared by Joseph Gaer. The New Testament prepared by Joseph Gaer and Chester C. McCown. [1st ed.] Boston, Little, Brown [1956] xxv, 752p. 25cm. [BS391.G27] 56-10647
I. Gaer, Joseph, 1897- ed. II. McCown, Chester Charlton, 1877- ed. III. Title.

BIBLE. English. 220.52
Selections. 1956. Revised standard.
Nearer to Thee; meditations from the RSV Bible, compiled by Harriet Ann Daffron & Betty Jean Clark. New York, T. Nelson [1956] 160p. 24cm. [BS391.D23] 56-10856
I. Daffron, Harriet Ann, ed. II. Clark, Betty Jean, ed. III. Title.

BIBLE. ENGLISH. 220.52
SELECTIONS. 1956. REVISED STANDARD.
Nearer to Thee; meditations from the RSV Bible, compiled by Harriet Ann Daffron & Betty Jean Clark. New York, T. Nelson [1956] 160p. 24cm. [BS391.D23] 56-10856
I. Daffron, Harriet Ann, ed. II. Clark, Betty Jean, ed. III. Title.

BIBLE. English. 220.52
Selections. 1957. Authorized.
The Almighty God's prescription for peace and everlasting life, by Thomas Spence Herron. [1st ed.] New York, Vantage Press [1957] 238p. 22cm. [BS391.H45] 55-11652
I. Herron, Thomas Spence, comp. II. Title.

BIBLE. English. 220.52
Selections. 1957. Authorized.
The core of the Bible. Arranged by Austin Farrer from the Authorized King James version. [1st Harper torchbook ed.] New York, Harper [1957, c1956] 156p. 21cm. (Harper torchbooks, TB7) First published in London in 1956 under title: A short Bible. [BS391.F3 1957] 57-13604
I. Farrer, Austin Marsden, ed. II. Title.

BIBLE. English. 220.52
Selections. 1957. Revised standard.
Daily Bible readings from the Revised standard version Selected and arranged by Harold Lindsell New York, Harper [1957] unpaged. 13cm. [BS390.L55] 57-9264
I. Devotional calendars. II. Lindsell, Harold, 1913- ed. III. Title.

BIBLE. English. 220.52
Selections. 1957. Revised standard.
Daily Bible readings from the Revised standard version. Selected and arranged by Harold Lindsell. New York, Harper [1957] unpaged. 13cm. [BS390.L55] 57-9264
1. Devotional calendars. I. Lindsell, Harold, 1913- ed. II. Title.

BIBLE. English, 220.52
Selections. 1961. Authorized.
The bedside Bible; an anthology for the quiet hours, selected and arr. with introd. and notes by Arthur Stanley [pseud.] New York, Scribners [1961] xvi, 368p.. 61-66431 2.95
I. Megaw, Arthur Stanley, 1872- II. Title.

BIBLE. English. 220.52
Selections, 1961. Authorized.
The Dartmouth Bible; an abridgment of the King James version, with aids to its understanding as history and literature, and as a source of religious experience. The Old Testament, the Apocrypha, and the New Testament, with introductions, prefaces, notes, and annotated maps. [By] Roy B. Chamberlin, Herman Feldman, with the counsel of an advisory board of Biblical scholars. 2d ed. rev. and enl. Boston, Houghton, 1961 [c.1950, 1961] 1ii, 1257p. maps Bibl. 61-7609 10.00
I. Chamberlin, Roy Bullard, 1887- II. Feldman, Herman, 1894-1947. III. Title.

BIBLE. English. 220.52
Selections. 1961. Authorized.
The pocket Bible, the Old and New Testaments in the King James version. An abridgment with pref. by Cyril C. Richardson of The Bible designed to be read as living literature, as edited and arranged by Ernest Sutherland Bates. New York, Washington Square Press [1961, c1951] xviii, 461p. 16cm. (Washington Square Press classics, W584) [BS391.R53 1961] 61-38464
I. Richardson, Cyril Charles, 1909- II. Bible. English. Selections. 1936. Authorized The Bible designed to be read as living literature. III. Title.

BIBLE. English. 220.52
Selections. 1962.
The kingdom of God; a short Bible. Translations, explanations, and paraphrases under the direction of Louis J. Putz. Notre Dame, Ind., Fides Publishers [1962] 383p. illus., maps. 23cm. 'Originally published in German, under the title of 'Reich Gotes." [BS390.P8] 62-16337
I. Putx, Louis J., ed. II. Title.

BIBLE. English. 220.52
Selections. 1962. Authorised.
The concise Bible; synopses of all sixty-six books with the full text of the most famous quotations from the King James version. A condensation by Frances Kanes Hazlitt. Chicago, H. Regnery Co., 1962. viii, 213p. 21cm. Bibliography: p. 265-206. [BS391.H39] 62-19387
I. Hazlitt, Frances Kanes. II. Title.

BIBLE. English. 220.52
Selections. 1962. Authorized.
The concise Bible; synopses of all sixty-six books with the full text of the most famous quotations from the King James version. A condensation by Frances Kanes Hazlitt. Chicago, Regnery [c.]1962. viii, 213p. 21cm. Bibl. 62-19387 4.00
I. Hazlitt, Frances Kanes. II. Title.

BIBLE. English. 220.52
Selections. 1963. Confraternity version.
The new Saint Joseph simplified Bible, 'the heart of the Bible'; the most important texts of each book of the Holy Bible, in the official Confraternity version, modern format and with short helpful notes. Ed. by John E. Steinmueller, Kathryn Sullivan. New York 11. 257 W. 17 St. Catholic Bk. Pub. Co., [1964, c.1963] 704p. illus., maps. 21cm. 64-1751 4.50
I. Steinmueller, John E., 1899- ed. II. Sullivan, Kathryn, 1905- ed. III. Confraternity of Christian Doctrine. IV. Title.

BIBLE. English. 220.52
Selections. 1964. Authorized.
The Bible for students of literature and art. Selected with an introd., by G. B. Harrison. Garden City, N.Y., Doubleday, 1964. xxxi, 563 p. maps (1 fold.) 22 cm. "The present text is based on 'the reader's Bible [1951]" [BS391.2.H3] 64-13820
I. Harrision, George Bagshawe, 1894- ed. II. Bible. English. 1951. Authorized. The reader's Bible. III. Title.

BIBLE. English. 220.52
Selections. 1964. Revised standard.
A shortened arrangement of the Holy Bible. Revised standard version. Edited by Robert O. Ballou. [1st ed.] Philadelphia, Published by A. J. Holman Co. for Lippincott [1964] xxxii, 773 p. 22 cm. [BS391.2.B3] 64-14460
1. Ballous, Robert Oleson, 1892- ed. I. Title.

BIBLE. English. Selections 220.52
1964 Authorized.
Christian's Bible. Condensed from the Authorized King James version (1611) by Stephen Condit. New York, Exposition [1964] 281p. 22cm. The King James text has been reduced ten to one without changing a verse. 64-6452 4.00
I. Condit, Stephen, 1909- ed. II. Title.

BIBLE. English. 220.52
Selections. 1965.
A book of good tidings from the Bible. [Compiled and illustrated by] Joan Walsh Anglund. [1st ed.] New York, Harcourt, Brace & World [1965] 1 v. (unpaged) illus. (part col.) 11 cm. [BS391.2.A5] 65-17986
I. Anglund, Joan (Walsh) comp. and illus. II. Title.

BIBLE. English. 220.52
Selections. 1967.
Consider the lilies; great inspirational verses from the Bible. Edited by Mary Jo Heller and Dorothy Price. Illustrated by Ron Dubuque. [Kansas City, Mo.] Hallmark Editions [1967] 60 p. col. illus. 20 cm. [BS391.2.H4] 67-20440
I. Heller, Mary Jo, ed. II. Price, Dorothy, ed. III. Title.

BIBLE. English. 220.5'2
Selections. 1973.
Hear now the word of the Lord, by Theodore Maakestad. Philadelphia, Dorrance [1973] 134 p. 22 cm. Bible passages selected and arranged according to content. [BS391.2.M27] 72-93915 ISBN 0-8059-1798-5 3.95
1. Bible—Devotional literature. I. Maakestad, Theodore, comp. II. Title.

BIBLE. English. 220.5'2
Selections. 1973.
Heavy bread. Arranged by Elizabeth J. Kauffman and Nancy J. Kauffman. New Canaan, Conn., Keats [1973] ix, 210 p. 18 cm. (A Pivot original) [BS391.2.K38] 73-75087 1.25
I. Kauffman, Elizabeth J., comp. II. Kauffman, Nancy J., comp. III. Title.

*BIBLE. English. 220.5'2
Selections. 1973.
A little child shall lead them; familiar Bible verses [selected by] Caroline Bentley. [Valley Forge, Pa., Judson Pr., 1973] 1 v. (unpaged) col. illus. 18 cm. [BS391]
I. Bentley, Caroline, ed. II. Title.

BIBLE. English. 220.5'2
Selections. 1973.
Presence and absence : versions from the Bible / by Reynolds Price. Bloomfield Hills, Mich. : Bruccoli Clark, 1973, c1974. 44 p. ; 25 cm. "A Bruccoli-Clark collector's edition." Three hundred copies printed. Issued in a case. [BS391.2.P7] 75-306767
I. Price, Reynolds, 1933- II. Title.

*BIBLE. English. 220.52
Selections. 1973.
Quotations from the Bible for modern man. Edited by James Z. Nettinga. New York, Pocket Books [1973] 236 p. illus. 18 cm. [BS391] ISBN 0-671-77694-0 0.95 (pbk.)
I. Nettinga, James Z., ed. II. Title.

BIBLE. English. 220.5'2
Selections. 1974.
The English Bible, 1534-1859 [compiled by] Peter Levi. Grand Rapids, Eerdmans [1974] 222 p. 22 cm. Includes bibliographical references. [BS391.2.L48 1974] 73-23038 ISBN 0-8028-3446-9 6.95
1. Bible. English—Versions. I. Levi, Peter, comp. II. Title.

BIBLE. English. 220.5'2
Selections. 1974.
The Lord's prayer for today, together with other choice portions of Holy Scriptures. Compiled and illustrated by Royal V. Carley. Norwalk, Conn., C. R. Gibson Co. [1974] [27] p. illus. 19 cm. [BS391.2.C374] 73-86686 ISBN 0-8378-2005-7 2.50
I. Carley, Royal V., comp. II. Title.

BIBLE. English. 220.5'2
Selections. 1975.
The beatitudes for today : with other selected scriptures / compiled and illustrated by Royal V. Carley. Norwalk, Conn. : C. R. Gibson Co., [1975] [27] p. : ill. ; 20 cm. [BS391.2.C3695] 74-21142 ISBN 0-8378-2010-3
I. Carley, Royal V. II. Title.

BIBLE. English. 220.5'2
Selections. 1975.
The bridled tongue : Bible words about words / selected by Florence M. Taylor. New Canaan, Conn. : Keats Pub., c1975. xvi, 152 p. ; 22 cm. Includes index. [BS391.2.T39 1975] 75-19545 ISBN 0-87983-115-4 : 5.95
I. Taylor, Florence Marian Tompkins, 1892- II. Title.

BIBLE. English. 220.52
Selections. Authorized.
The pocket Bible; the Old and New Testaments in the King James version. Abridgment, with pref. by Cyril C. Richardson, of The Bible designed to be read as living literature as ed. and arranged by Ernest Sutherland Bates. New York, Washington Sq. Pr. [dist. Affiliated Pubs. 1961, c.1936, 1951] xviii, 461p. (W-584) .60 pap.,
I. Richardson, Cyril Charles, 1909- II. Bible English. Selections. 1936. Authorized. The Bible designed to be read as living literature. III. Title.

BIBLE. English. Smith. 220.52
1970.
Joseph Smith's new translation of the Bible; a complete parallel comparison of the inspired version of the Holy Scriptures and the King James authorized version. Introd. by F. Henry Edwards. Independence, Mo., Herald Pub. House, 1970. 523 p. 23 cm. [BX8630.A2 1970] 74-127097
I. Smith, Joseph, 1805-1844. II. Bible. English. Authorized. 1970. III. Title.

BIBLE. English. Smith. 220.5'2
1974.
The Holy Scriptures. Inspired version: containing the Old and New Testaments, an inspired revision of the Authorized version, by Joseph Smith, Jr. Independence, Mo., Herald Pub. House [1974] 1201, 88 p. 21 cm. A publication of the Reorganized Church of Jesus Christ of Latter Day Saints. "Concordance, especially prepared for use with the Inspired version of the Holy Scriptures": p. 1-80 (2d group) [BX8630.A2 1974] 73-87524 9.00; 25.00 (deluxe ed.)
I. Smith, Joseph, 1805-1844. II. Reorganized Church of Jesus Christ of Latter-Day Saints. III. Bible. English. Authorized. 1974.

BIBLE. English. Today's 220.5'2
English. 1976.
Good news Bible : the Bible in Today's English version. New York : American Bible Society, 1976. 1041, 408 p. : ill. ; 20 cm. "The basic text for the Old Testament is the Masoretic text printed in Biblia Hebraica (3rd edition, 1937) ... for the New Testament is the Greek New Testament published by the United Bible Societies (3rd edition, 1975)." [BS195.T63 1976] 76-150947
I. American Bible Society. II. Title.

BIBLE. N.T. English. 1961. 220.52
New English.
The New English Bible; New Testament. [New York] Oxford University Press, 1961. xiii, 446 p. 24 cm. Translated under the supervision of the Joint Committee on the New Translation of the Bible. [BS192.A1 1961.N4] 61-16025
I. Joint Committee on the New Translation of the Bible.

BIBLE. N.T. English. 1963. 220.52
Norlie.
The New Testament. New tr. in mod. Eng. for today's reader. With The Psalms for today; a new tr. from Hebrew into current Eng., by R. K. Harrison. 3d ed. Grand Rapids, Mich., Zondervan [1963, c.1961] 601; 160p. 18cm. The Psalms for today has separate t.p. 2.95
I. Norlie, Olaf Morgan, 1876- tr. II. Harrison, Roland Kenneth, tr. III. Bible. O.T. Psalms. English. IV. Title. V. Title: The Psalms for today.

*BIBLE, N.T. English. King 220.52
James
The New Testament of Our Lord and Saviour Jesus Christ, translated out of the original

Greek: and with the former translations diligently compared and revised. King James version appointed to be read in churches. Large type ed. New York, Watts [1967] 457p. 29cm. (Keith Jennison bk.) 7.95
I. Title.

BRETT, Gilbert James. ed. 220.52
Dictionary, concordance, and collation of Scriptures in The Bible companion [Good Saviour ed.] Chicago, Consolidated Book Publishers [1950] [BS417.B45 1950] 50-11308
I. Title.

BRIDGES, Ronald. 220.52
The Bible word book, concerning obsolete or archaic words in the King James version of the Bible, New York, Nelson [c.1960] vii, 422p. 22cm. 'Bibliography and abbreviations': p. vii. [BS186.B7] 60-6749
1. Bible. English—Versions—Authorized. 2. Bible. English—Versions—Revised standard. 3. Bible. English—Glossaries, vocabularies, etc. 4. English language—Words—Hist. I. Weigle, Luther Allan, 1880- joint author. II. Title.

BRIDGES, Ronald 220.52
The Bible word book, concerning obsolete or archaic words in the King James version of the Bible, by Ronald Bridges and Luther A. Weigle. New York, Nelson [c.1960] vii, 422p. 'Bibliography and abbreviations': p. vii, 22cm. 60-6749 5.00
1. Bible, English—Versions—Authorized. 2. Bible. English—Versions—Revised standard. 3. Bible. English—Glossaries, vocabularies, etc. 4. English language—Words—Hist. I. Weigle, Luther Allan, joint author. II. Title.

BROWN, John, 1830-1922. 220.5'2
The history of the English Bible / by John Brown. Folcroft, Pa. : Folcroft Library Editions, 1977. p. cm. Reprint of the 1911 1st ed. published by University Press, Cambridge, Eng., in series: The Cambridge manuals of science and literature. Includes index. Bibliography: p. [BS455.B7 1977] 77-13187 ISBN 0-8414-9929-2 lib. bdg. : 15.00
1. Bible. English—Versions. I. Title.

BRUCE, Frederick Fyvie, 220.52
1910-
The English Bible: a history of translations. New York, Oxford University Press, 1961. xiv, 233 p. illus., ports., facsims. 23 cm. Bibliographical footnotes. [BS455.B74] 61-960
1. Bible. English—Versions. I. Title.

BRUCE, Frederick Fyvie, 220.52
1910-
The English Bible; a history of translations from the earliest English versions to the New English Bible, by F. F. Bruce. [New and rev. ed.] New York, Oxford University Press, 1970. xiv, 262 p. illus., facsims., ports. 23 cm. Includes bibliographical references. [BS455.B74 1970] 74-15923 6.95
1. Bible. English—Versions. I. Title.

BRUCE, Frederick Fyvie, 220.52
1910-
The King James version: the first 350 years, 1611-1961. New York, Oxford University Press [c.]1960. 42p. port., facsims. 16cm. 'With some slight changes . . . one chapter of . . . [the author's] The English Bible: a history of translations from the earliest English versions to the New English Bible.' 'Of this first edition, 360 copies have been set aside by the publisher as Monograph no. 62 for distribution by the Typophiles.' 61-118 not for sale pap.,
1. Bible. English—Versions—Authorized. I. Title.

BUCKLEW, Henry, 1925- 220.5'2
Your daily dozen spiritual vitamins, With a foreword by W. A. Criswell. [1st ed.] New York, American Press [1963] 272 p. 22 cm. Full name: William Henry Bucklew. [BV4811.B8] 62-19875
1. Devotional calendars — Baptists. I. Title.

BURROWS, Millar, 1889- 220.52
Diligently compared; the Revised standard versions and the King James version of the Old Testament. London, New York, Nelson [1964] vi, 278 p. 22 cm. [BS891.B8] 64-25281
1. Bible. O. T. English — Versions — Revised standard. 2. Bible. O. T. English — Versions — Authorized. I. Title.

BURROWS, Millar, 1889- 220.52
Diligently compared; the Revised standard version and the King James version of the Old Testament. New York, Nelson [c.1964] vi, 278p. 22cm. 64-25281 6.50
1. Bible. O. T. English—Versions—Revised standard. 2. Bible. O. T. English—Versions—Authorized. I. Title.

CLARK, Joshua Reuben, 220.52
1871-
Why the King James version; a series of study notes, neither treatises nor essays, dealing with certain elementary problems and specific Scriptural passages, involved in considering the preferential English translations of the Greek New Testament text, whether the King James version (the Authorized verison), 1611-Britisn or the British revised version, 1880's or the American standard version, 1900-1901; or the American revised standard version, 1946-1952. Salt Lake City, Deseret Book Co., 1956. 473p. illus. 24cm. Includes bibliography. [BS186.C57] 56-3478
1. Bible. English- Versions-Authorized. 2. Bible. N.T.-Criticism, Textual. I. Title.

DEL FIORENTINO, Dante, ed. 220.52
The Catholic Bible in pictures. New York, Greystone Press [1956] 320p. illus. 25cm. The text is based on the Confraternity of Christian Doctrine version. [BS560.D4] 55-10779
1. Bible—Pictures, illustrations, etc. I. Bible. English. Selections. 1956. Confraternity version. II. Title.

DES BARRES, Frederick W W. 220.52
Story of the English Bible. New York, R. F. Moore [1950] ix, 92 p. 17 cm. Bibliographical footnotes. [BS455.D47] 50-9948
1. Bible. English—Hist. I. Title.

GRANT, Frederick Clifton, 220.52
1891-
Translating the Bible. Greenwich, Conn., Seabury Press, [c.]1961. 183p. illus. Bibl.: p.165-173 and bibl. footnotes. 61-5794 4.25
1. Bible—Hist. 2. Bible. English—Versions. 3. Bible—Criticism, Textual. I. Title.

*HAMMOND, Emily V. comp. 220.52
The golden treasury of the Bible. New York, Pyramid [1968,c.1952] 224p. 18cm. (Inspiration bk., T1777) .75 pap.,
1. Bible. English—Selections. I. Title.

HEFLIN, Jimmie H 220.52
Men and motives; the story behind the making of our English Bible. Boston, Christopher Pub. House [1964] 63 p. 21 cm. "The result of a manuscript prepared ... to meet the requirements for ... a master of arts degree." [BS455.H35] 64-15610
1. Bible. English — Hist. — Addresses, essays, lectures. I. Title.

HEFLIN, Jimmie H. 220.52
Men and motives; the story behind the making of our English Bible. Boston, Christopher Pub. House [c.1964] 63p. 21cm. Bibl. 64-15610 2.00 bds.,
1. Bibl. English—Hist.—Addresses, essays, lectures. I. Title.

HEUMAN, Fred S. 220.5'2
The uses of Hebraisms in recent Bible translations / by Fred S. Heuman. New York : Philosophical Library, c1977. 154 p. ; 22 cm. Includes index. Bibliography: p. 136-140. [BS1421.H48] 76-16238 ISBN 0-8022-2190-4 : 8.50
1. Bible. O.T. Psalms. English—Versions. 2. Bible—Translating. 3. English language—Foreign words and phrases—Hebrew. I. Title.

HUNT, Geoffrey. 220.52
About the New English Bible; compiled by Geoffrey Hunt. London, Oxford U.P., 1970. viii, 83 p., 5 plates. illus., ports. 19 cm. [BS192.H84] 71-485930 ISBN 0-19-180015-5 6/-
1. Bible. English—Versions—New English. I. Title.

JEFFERY, Graham. 220.5'2
The Barnabas bible. [1st U.S. ed.] New York, Harper & Row, Publishers [1973] 256 p. illus. 25 cm. [BS560.J43] 73-6318 ISBN 0-06-064128-2 4.95
1. Bible—Cartoons, satire, etc. 2. Australian wit and humor, Pictorial. I. Title.

KEHL, D. G., comp. 220.52
Literary style of the old Bible and the new, edited by D. G. Kehl. New York, Bobbs-Merrill [1970] 64 p. 28 cm. (The Bobbs-Merrill series in composition and rhetoric, 21) Contents.Contents.—The noblest monument of English prose, by J. L. Lowes.—The English Bible and the grand style, by J. M. Murry.—A sermon on style, by H. S. Canby.—Biblical English, by B. Evans and C. Evans.—The summing up, by W. Somerset Maugham.—The Bible in modern undress, by D. MacDonald.—The old Bible and the new, by D. Thompson.—The Greek "word" was different, by F. L. Lucas.—A scholar finds the beauty wrung out of new English Bible's verses.—"Understanded of the people", by S. E. Hyman.—The finalised version, by V. S. Pritchett.—Bibliography (p. 64) [BS537.K43] 72-117334 1.00
1. Bible—Language, style—Addresses, essays, lectures. I. Title.

THE kingdom of God; 220.52
a short Bible. Trs., explanations, and paraphrases under the direction of Louis J. Putz. Notre Dame, Ind., Fides [c.1962] 383p. illus., maps. 23cm. ible. English. Selections. 1962. 62-16337 4.95
I. Putz, Louis J., ed.

KUBO, Sakae, 1926- 220.5'2
So many versions? : Twentieth century English versions of the Bible / Sakae Kubo & Walter Specht. Grand Rapids : Zondervan Pub. House, c1975. 244 p. ; 21 cm. Bibliography: p. 233-244. [BS455.K8] 74-25351 5.95 pbk. : 2.95
1. Bible. English—Versions. I. Specht, Walter Frederick. II. Title.

LET the living Bible help 220.5'2
you / [edited by] Alice Zillman Chapin. 1st ed. New York : Harper & Row, [1975] vi, 185 p. ; 22 cm. Readings assembled from The living Bible. [BS550.2.L3 1975] 74-25689 ISBN 0-06-061582-6 : 6.95
1. Bible—Paraphrases, English. 2. Consolation. I. Chapin, Alice Zillman. II. Taylor, Kenneth Nathaniel. The living Bible, paraphrased. Selections.

MCCARY, James Leslie. 220.52
The abbreviated Bible [with the Apocrypha, by] James Leslie McCary and Mark McElhaney. New York, Van Nostrand Reinhold [1971] xxiii, 695 p. 22 cm. [BS405.M25 1971] 76-173420
1. Bible—Abridgments. I. McElhaney, Mark, joint author. II. Title.

MANN, Christopher Stephen 220.52
The new English New Testament, an introduction. [New York, Morehouse-Barlow, c.1961] 203p. Bibl. 61-4436 3.00 bds.,
1. Bible. English—Versions—New English Bible. I. Title.

MATTHEWS, Robert J. 220.5'2
"A plainer translation" : Joseph Smith's translation of the Bible, a history and commentary / Robert J. Matthews. Provo : Brigham Young University Press, [1975] xxxii, 468 p. : facsims. ; 24 cm. Includes indexes. Bibliography: p. 441-443. [BX8630.M37] 75-5937 ISBN 0-8425-1411-2 : 12.95
1. Bible. English—Versions—Smith. I. Title: Joseph Smith's translation of the Bible.

MAY, Herbert Gordon, 1904- 220.52
Our English Bible in the making; the Word of Life in living language. Philadelphia, Published for the Cooperative Pub. Association by Westminster Press [1952] 154 p. 21 cm. [BS455.M34] 52-8858
1. Bible. English—Hist. I. Title.

MAY, Herbert Gordon, 1904- 220.52
Our English Bible in the making; the Word of Life in living language. Rev. ed. Philadelphia, Pub. for the Cooperative Pubn. Assn. by the Westminster Pr. [c.1962, 1965] 163p. 21cm. [BS455.M34] 65-4479 3.95
1. Bible. English—Hist. I. Title.

MYERS, A. J. William 220.52
God's world and God's people; stories for boys and girls. Nashville, The Upper Room [c.1963] 56p. 16cm. .35 pap.,
1. Bible stories, English—Juvenile literature. I. Title.

THE new English Bible. 220.52
[New York] Oxford Univ. Press [c.]1961- xiii, 446p. Tr. under the supervision of the Joint Committee on the New Translation of the Contents.[1] New Testament. ible. English. 1961. 61-16025 4.95
I. Joint Committee on the New Translation of the Bible.

NIDA, Eugene Albert, 220.5'2
1914-
Good news for everyone : how to use the Good news Bible (Today's English version) / Eugene A. Nida. Waco, Tex. : Word Books, c1977. 119 p. : ill. ; 22 cm. [BS195.T632N5] 76-48552 ISBN 0-87680-792-9 : 3.25
1. Bible. English—Versions—Today's English. I. Title.

PAINE, Gustavus Swift. 220.52
The learned men. New York, Crowell [1959] 212 p. illus. 22 cm. Includes bibliography. [BS186.P3] 59-12495
1. Bible. English—Versions—Authorized. I. Title.

POPE, Hugh, 1869-1946. 220.52
English versions of the Bible. Revised and amplified by Sebastian Bullough. St. Louis, Herder, 1952. ix, 787 p. 24 cm. Bibliography: p. 686-718. [BS455.P74] 52-10395
1. Bible. English — Versions. 2. Bible. English — Hist. 3. Bible. English — Versions, Catholic. I. Bullough, Sebastian. II. Title.

POPE, Hugh, Father, 1869- 220.52
1946.
English versions of the Bible. Revised and amplified by Sebastian Bullough. St. Louis, Herder, 1952. ix, 787p. 24cm. Bibliography: p. 686-718. [BS455.P74] 52-10359
1. Bible. English—Versions. 2. Bible. English—Hist. 3. Bible. English—Versions, Catholic. I. Bullough, Sebastian. II. Title.

POPE, Hugh, 1869-1946. 220.5'2
English versions of the Bible. Rev. and amplified by Sebastian Bullough. Westport, Conn., Greenwood Press [1972, c1952] ix, 787 p. 23 cm. Bibliography: p. 686-718. [BS455.P74 1972] 73-152600 ISBN 0-8371-6035-9 30.25
1. Bible. English—Versions. 2. Bible. English—History. 3. Bible. English—Versions, Catholic. I. Bullough, Sebastian. II. Title.

REUMANN, John Henry Paul 220.52
Four centuries of the English Bible. Philadelphia, Muhlenberg Press [c.1961] 63p. (Fortress book) Bibl. 61-6753 1.00 bds.,
1. Bible. English—Versions. I. Title.

ROBERTSON, Edwin Hanton 220.52
The new translations of the Bible. Naperville, Ill., A. R. Allenson [1959] 190p. Bibliography: p.185-188. 22cm. (Studies in ministry and worship, 12) 59-65051 2.50 pap.,
1. Bible. English—Versions. I. Title. II. Series.

SCHWARTZ, Frederick L B 220.5'2
A Biblical diary and quiz book. [1st ed.] New York, Vantage Press [c1960] 155p. 21cm. [BS617.S27] 61-66579
1. Bible—Reading. 2. Bible—Examinations, questions, etc. I. Title.

SCHWARTZ, Werner, 1905- 220.52
Principles and problems of Biblical translation; some Reformation controversies and their background. Cambridge [Eng.] University Press, 1955. xiv, 224 p. 23 cm. Bibliography: p. 213-214. Bibliographical footnotes. [BS450.S3] 55-3878
1. Bible—Versions. 2. Bible—Hermeneutics. 3. Bible—History. 4. Reformation. I. Title.

[TAYLOR, Kenneth 220.5'2
Nathaniel]
Light from The living Bible. [Edited by] Perry Tanksley. Old Tappan, N.J., F. H. Revell Co. [1973] 126 p. illus. 22 cm. [BS550.2.T38 1973b] 73-5859 ISBN 0-8007-0597-1 4.95
1. Bible—Paraphrases, English. I. Tanksley, Perry, ed. II. Title.

[TAYLOR, Kenneth 220.5'2
Nathaniel]
The living Bible, paraphrased. Wheaton, Ill., Tyndale House; distributed by Doubleday [New York, 1971] 1020 p. plans. 23 cm. "A compilation of the Scripture paraphrases previously published ... under the following titles: Living letters, 1962; Living prophecies, 1965; Living Gospels, 1966; Living Psalms and Proverbs, 1967; Living lessons of life and love, 1968; Living books of Moses, 1969; Living history of Israel, 1970." [BS550.2.T38] 78-156898 ISBN 0-8423-2250-7
1. Bible—Paraphrases, English. I. Title.

[TAYLOR, Kenneth 220.5'2
Nathaniel]
The living Bible, paraphrased. Holman illustrated ed. Philadelphia, A. J. Holman Co., 1973 [c1971] xiii, 1226 p. col. illus. 26 cm. "A compilation of the Scripture paraphrases previously published ... under the following titles: Living letters, 1962; Living prophecies, 1965; Living Gospels, 1966; Living Psalms and Proverbs, 1967; Living lessons of life and love, 1968; Living books of Moses, 1969; Living history of Israel, 1970." [BS550.2.T38 1973] 73-3323 ISBN 0-87981-023-8 14.95
1. Bible—Paraphrases, English. I. Title.

[TAYLOR, Kenneth 220.5'2
Nathaniel]
The living Bible, paraphrased. All photos. in this book by Erich Lessing. Deluxe illustrated ed. Wheaton, Ill., Tyndale House [1973] xviii, 915, [296] p. col. illus. 28 cm. "A compilation of the Scripture paraphrases previously published ... under the following titles: Living letters, 1962; Living prophecies, 1965; Living Gospels, 1966; Living Psalms and Proverbs, 1967; Living lessons of life and love, 1968; Living books of Moses, 1969; Living history of Israel, 1970." On spine: Family treasure edition. [BS550.2.T38 1973c] 73-2058 ISBN 0-8326-1415-7
1. Bible—Paraphrases, English. I. Lessing, Erich. II. Title.

[TAYLOR, Kenneth 220.5'2
Nathaniel]
The way. An illustrated ed. of the Living Bible, as developed by the editors of Campus life magazine, Youth for Christ International. Wheaton, Ill., Tyndale House [1972] 1116 p. illus. 23 cm. [BS550.2.T38 1973d] 72-84415 ISBN 0-8423-7820-0 5.95
1. Bible—Paraphrases, English. I. Campus life. II. Title.

[TAYLOR, Kenneth Nathaniel] 220.5'2
The way. Complete Catholic ed., including the Deuterocanonical books / foreword to the Catholic ed. by Keith Clark. An illustrated ed. of the Living Bible / as developed by the editors of Campus life magazine, Youth for Christ International. Wheaton, Ill. : Tyndale House, 1976. 1284 p. : ill. ; 23 cm. [BS550.2.T38 1976] 76-3289 ISBN 0-87973-831-6 : 6.95
1. Bible—Paraphrases, English. I. Campus life. II. Title.

TAYLOR, Millicent J 1892- 220.52
Treasure of free men; highlights of the history of the Bible. [1st ed.] Kansas City, Mo., Allan Publications. [1959? c1953] 88 p. 22 cm. Includes bibliography. [BS445.T3 1959] 59-4574
1. Bible — Hist. 2. Bible. English — Hist. I. Title.

TAYLOR, Millicent J., 1892- 220.52
Treasure of free men, highlights of the history of the Bible. [1st ed.] New York, Harper [1953] 88 p. 22 cm. [BS445.T3] 53-10930
1. Bible—History. 2. Bible. English—History. I. Title.

TAYLOR, William Carey, 1886- 220.52
The new Bible, pro and con. New York, Vantage Press [1955] 351p. 22cm. [BS191.T39] 54-9140
1. Bible. English—Versions—Revised standard. I. Title.

WATSON, Jane (Werner) 1915- ed. 220.52
The Holy Bible, selected and arr. by Elsa Jane Werner and Charles Hartman. The Old Testament illus. by Feodor Rojankovsky; the New Testament illus. by Alice and Martin Provensen. [Catholic ed.] New York, Guild Pr., dist. by Golden Pr. [1961, c.1946-1960] 251p. col. illus. 28cm. Previous ed. published in 1958 under title: A Catholic child's Bible. 60-50302 4.95
1. Bible stories, English. I. Hartman, Charles, joint ed. II. Title.

WEIGLE, Luther, Allan, 1880- 220.52
Bible words in living language. London, New York, T. Nelson [c1957] 100 p. 23 cm. [BS186.W38 1957] 58-3428
1. Bible. English — Versions — Authorized. 2. Bible. English — Versions — Revised standard. 3. English language — Words — Hist. I. Title.

WHAT Bible can you trust? 220.5'2
Nashville : Broadman Press, [1974] 116 p. ; 19 cm. [BS125.W45] 73-83828 ISBN 0-8054-1126-7 pbk. : 2.50
1. Bible. English—Versions.

WILSON, James I 220.5'2
The principles of war, by James I. Wilson. Annapolis, Christian Books in Annapolis [1964] 62 p. 18 cm. Bibliographical footnotes. [BV4509.5.W5] 65-9382
1. Christian life. I. Title.

YONGE, Charlotte Mary, 1823-1901. 220.52
Aunt Charlotte's stories of Bible history, told for the 52 Sabboths of the year; containing over one hundred stories from the Old and New Testaments. With over 100 fine engravings, color plates, half-tones, woodcuts, and pen drawings made especially for this volume. [Rev. ed.] Philadelphia, Winston, 1951. 296 p. illus 24 cm. Published in 1898 under title. Aunt Charlotte's stories of Bible history for young disciples. [BS551.Y6] 51-7384
1. Bible stories, English. I. Title.

YONGE, Charlotte Mary, 1823-1901. 220.52
Child's Bible reader; stories from the Old and New Testaments told for 52 Sabbaths of the year. Rev. ed. Nashville, Southwestern Co., 1957. 260 p. illus. 24 cm. Published in 1898 under title: Aunt Charlotte's stories of Bible history for young disciples. [BS551.Y6 1957] 57-10196
1. Bible stories, English. I. Title.

BUTTERWORTH, Charles C., 1894-1957. 220.52'009
The literary lineage of the King James Bible, 1340-1611. New York, Octagon Books, 1971 [c1941] xi, 394 p. facsim. 24 cm. Bibliography: p. 359-383. [BS455.B8 1971] 76-120241
1. Bible. English—History. I. Title.

SPARKS, Hedley Frederick Davis. 220.5'2'009
On translations of the Bible, the Ethel M. Wood lecture delivered before the University of London on 6 March 1972, by H. F. D. Sparks. London, Athlone Press, 1973. 20 p. 22 cm. (Ethel M. Wood lecture) Distributed in the U.S.A. and Canada by Humanities Press, New York. Includes bibliographical references. [BS455.S55] 74-159208 ISBN 0-485-14316-X 1.50 (pbk.)
1. Bible. English—Versions. 2. Bible—Versions. I. Title. II. Series: The Ethel M. Wood lecture, 1972.

BIBLE. English. 1560. Geneva version. 220.52'01
The Geneva Bible, a facsimile of the 1560 edition. With an introd. by Lloyd E. Berry. Madison, University of Wisconsin Press, 1969. vi, 28 p., iv, 474, 122, [14] l. illus., maps. 28 cm. Leaves printed on both sides. The facsim. was produced primarily from the copy in the Scheide Library, Princeton University, with reproduction of some pages from the copy in the Chapin Library, Williams College. Original t.p. reads: The Bible and Holy Scriptvres conteyned in the Olde and Newe Testament. Translated according to the Ebrue and Greke, and conferred with the best translations in diuers langages. With moste profitable annotations vpon all the hard places, and other things of great importance as may appeare in the Epistle to the reader. At Geneva. Printed by Rovland Hall. M.D.LX. "The translators do not identify themselves anywhere in the Bible ... William Whittingham has always been considered to have been the general editor."—Introd., p. 7-8 (2d group) Bibliography: p. 25-28 (2d group) [BS170 1560a] 75-81318
I. Berry, Lloyd Eason, 1935- II. Whittingham, William, d. 1579. III. Bible. English. Geneva version. 1969. IV. Title.

DEANESLY, Margaret 220.5201
The Lollard Bible and other medieval Biblical versions, by Margaret Deanesly. Cambridge, Univ. Pr. 1920. xx, 483p. 24cm. (Half-title: Cambridge studies in medieval life & thought) Bibl. [BS455.D4] 20-16787 11.00
1. Bible. English—Hist. 2. Bible. English Reading. 3. Lollards. I. Title.

RYRIE, Charles Caldwell, 1925- 220.52'01
The Bible of the middle way [by] Charles C. Ryrie. Fort Worth, Brite Divinity School, Texas Christian University [1969] [6] p. illus. 26 cm. Cover title. An address given Oct. 3, 1968, at Brite Divinity School at the opening of an exhibition sponsored jointly with the Mary Couts Burnett Library commemorating the 400th anniversary of the publication of the first Bishops' Bible. [BS176.R9] 76-22491
1. Bible. English—Versions—Bishops'. I. Brite Divinity School. II. Mary Couts Burnett Library. III. Title.

WIKGREN, Allen Paul, 1906- 220.5'201
A leaf from the first edition of the first complete Bible in English, the Coverdale Bible, 1535 : with an historical introd. / by Allen P. Wikgren and a census of copies recorded in the British Isles and North America [compiled by John Howell]. San Francisco : Book Club of California, 1974. 45 p., 1 fold. leaf of plates : ill., fold. map, port. ; 36 cm. (Publication of the Book Club of California ; no. 145) "425 copies." L. C. copyright deposit copies contain a facsim. instead of an original leaf. "Selected bibliography": p. 39-40. [BS146.W47] 74-194407
1. Bible. English—Versions—Coverdale. I. Bible. English. 1535. Coverdale. II. Title. III. Series: Book Club of California, San Francisco. Publication ; no. 145.

BIBLE. English. (1611) 1965. Authorized. 220.52'03
The Holy Bible, conteyning the Old Testament, and the New; newly translated out of the originall tongues & with the former translations diligently compared and reuised. London, Imprinted by Robert Barker, printer to the Kings, 1611. [Cleveland, World Pub. Co., 1965] [38], 34, [1430] p. illus., coat of arms, map. 40 cm. "Facsimile of the first impression." [BS185 1611a.L6] 73-2845
I. Bible. English. 1965. Authorized.

BIBLE. English. 1782. Authorized. 220.52'03
The Holy Bible. As printed by Robert Aitken and approved & recommended by the Congress of the United States of America in 1782. American Bible Society ed. New York, Arno Press, 1968. 2 v. in 1. 19 cm. Facsimile reprint, with a new foreword and an historical pref. Originally published in Philadelphia by R. Aitken, the Old Testament in 1782 and the New Testament in 1781. Bibliography: v. 1, 15th prelim. page. [BS185 1782.P512] 68-20448
I. Aitken, Robert, 1734-1802. II. American Bible Society. III. Bible. English. Authorized. 1968.

BIBLE. English. 1903. Authorized. 220.5'203
The English Bible, translated out of the original tongues by the commandment of King James the First, anno 1611. New York, AMS Press, 1967. 6 v. 23 cm. Reprint of the 1903-04 ed., which was issued as v. 33-38 of the Tudor translations. Contents.Contents.—v. 1. Genesis to Joshua.—v. 2. Judges to Esther.—v. 3. Job to Song of Solomon.—v. 4. Isaiah to Malachi.—v. 5. Apocrypha.—v. 6. The New Testament. [BS185 1903.L62] 73-153238
I. Bible. English. 1967. Authorized. II. Title. III. Series: The Tudor translations, 1st ser., v. 33-38.

BIBLE. English. 1963. Authorized. 220.52'03
Holy Bible (Authorized or King James version) The new standard alphabetical indexed Bible. Scholl and library reference ed., containing the Old and New Testaments translated out of the original tongues and with all former translations diligently compared and revised; to which are added many unique features of the Bible: pictorial pronouncing dictionary and other interesting instructive features. Red letter ed. Chicago, J. A. Hertel Co. for International Sunday School League [c1963] 294, 954, B32 p. illus. (part col.) col. maps, ports. (part col.) 30 cm. On spine: New standard reference Bible; special blue ribbon edition. New Testament has special t.p. [BS1851963.C52] 67-8732
I. International Sunday School League. II. Title. III. Title: New standard alphabetical indexed Bible. IV. Title: New standard reference Bible.

BIBLE. English. 1965. Authorized. 220.5203
The Holy Bible, containing the Old and New Testaments (Authorized or King James version). To which is added an alphabetical and cyclopedic index, a unique set of charts from Adam to Christ, leading doctrines, harmony of the gospels, parables and miracles, Bible dictionary, all alphabetically arranged for practical and everyday use. Chicago, J. A. Hertel Co. [c1965] 317, 1504 p. illus., col. maps. 23 cm. On spine: Cyclopedic indexed Bible: good shepherd edition. [BS1851965.C52] 67-5571
I. Title. II. Title: Cyclopedic indexed Bible.

BIBLE. English. 1965? Authorized. 220.5203
The Holy Bible, containing the Old and New Testaments. Translated out of the original tongues, and with the former translations diligently compared and revised, by His Majesty's special command. Appointed to be read in churches. Cambridge, University Press [1965?] vi, 1109, 339, 160, 151 p. 8 col. mpas. 19 cm. New Testament has special t. p. "a concise Biblical encyclopedia based on the Cambridge companion to the Bible": 160 p. (4th group) has special t.p. "Concordance to the Old and New Testaments": 151 p. (5th group) has special t.p. [BS1851965.C3] 65-6349
I. Title.

BIBLE. English. 1965. Authorized 220.5203
The Holy Bible, containing the Old and New Testaments in the authorized King James version. Chicago, Good Counsel Pubs., 6 North Michigan [1965] 1v. (various p.) illus. (pt. col.) forms, col. plates. 29cm. On spine: Peace of mind edition. New Testament has special t.p. [BS1851965.C5] 65-5890 price unreported
1. Illustrated story of the Bible for young and old. I. Title.

BIBLE. English. 1966. Authorized. 220.52'03
Heirloom edition of the Holy Bible, containing the Old and New Testaments(Authorized on King James version) Chicago, J. A. Hertel Co.[c1966] xvi, 1504 p. illus. (part col.) col. maps. 23 cm. [BS1851966.C5] 67-5698
I. Title.

BIBLE. English. 1966. Authorized. 220.5203
The Holy Bible, containing the Old and New Testaments; translated out of the original tongues: and with the former translations diligently compared and revised, by His Majesty's special command. Appointed to be read in churches. [Cambridge cameo Bible, red letter, with concordance] London, Cambridge U.P. [1966] vi, 1109, 339, 100 p. 8 col. plates (maps) 19 cm. 75/- [BS1851966.C3] 66-69086
I. Title.

BIBLE. English. 1967. Authorized. 220.52'03
The Holy Bible, containing the Old and New Testaments. King James version, 1611. Translated out of the original tongues and with the former translations diligently compared and rev. A reference ed. New York, American Bible Society [1967] 1094 p. col. maps (on lining papers) 19 cm. [BS185 1967.N38] 77-265079
I. American Bible Society.

BIBLE. English. 1967. Authorized. 220.52'03
The new Scofield reference Bible; Holy Bible, authorized King James version, with introductions, annotations, subject chain references, and such word changes in the text as will help the reader. Editor, C. I. Scofield. Editorial Committee of the new ed.: E. Schuyler English, chairman. New York, Oxford University Press, 1967. xvi, 1392, 192 p. col. maps. 23 cm. [BS185 1967.N4] 67-1356
I. Scofield, Cyrus Ingerson, 1843-1921, ed. II. Title.

BIBLE. English. Authorized. 1968. 220.52'03
The Holy Bible containing the Old and the New Testaments. Translated out of the original tongues and with the former translations diligently compared and rev., the text conformable to that of the ed. of 1611 commonly known as the Authorized or King James' Version. Verse reference ed. Philadelphia, A. J. Holman [1968] 1280, 159, 176, 48 p. maps (part col.), forms. 26 cm. Contents.Contents.—Helps to Bible study: Outline-surveys of each Bible book. A thematic approach to Bible study, by J. W. Ingles. New light from the dead sea scrolls, by F. F. Bruce. The Bible and modern science, by C. F. H. Henry. The archaeology of the Bible, by J. L. Kelso. Between the testaments, by D. H. Wallace. The chronology of the Bible, by D. J. Wiseman.—Concordance.—Bible atlas. [BS185 1966.P5] 77-20875

BIBLE. English. Authorized. 1969. 220.52'03
The Holy Bible, containing the Old and New Testaments in the authorized King James version. [Michelangelo ed.] New York, Abradale Press [1969] 856, 276 p. illus. (part col.), forms, col. maps. 27 cm. [BS185 1969.N4] 65-21825
I. Buonarroti, Michel Angelo, 1475-1564, illus.

BIBLE. English. Authorized. 1970. 220.52'03
The Holy Bible, containing the Old and New Testaments in the King James version. The Crusade analytical ed. Nashville, Crusade Bible Publishers [1970] 1000, 608, 40, 96 p. illus. (part col.) 30 cm. [BS185 1970.N3] 74-19370
I. Title.

BIBLE. English. Authorized. 1970. 220.52'03
The Holy Bible. Containing the Old and New Testaments translated out of the original tongues and with the former translations diligently compared. Authorized (King James) version. Self-pronouncing ed. [Philadelphia, Pa.] National Bible Press [1970] 794, 16, 96, p. illus. (part col.), col. map (on lining paper) 21 cm. "Red letter concordance edition." [BS185 1970.P5] 73-21540

BIBLE. English. Authorized. 1970. 220.52'03
Holy Bible; Authorized or King James version. Old and New Testaments translated out of the original tongues and with all former translations diligently compared and revised. Pictorial pronouncing dictionary and other interesting instructive features. Red letter ed. Wichita, Kan. Hertel Bible Publishers [1970] xxvi, 762, 128 p. illus. (part col.), col. maps, col. plates, col. ports. 30 cm. [BS185 1970.W5] 78-19485

BIBLE. English. Authorized. 1970. 220.52'03
The Holy Bible containing the Old and New Testaments. Translated out of the original tongues, and with the former translations diligently compared and rev. The text conformable to that of the ed. of 1611, commonly known as the authorized King James' version. Philadelphia, A. J. Holman Co. [1970] 1246, [437] p. col. illus., forms. 29 cm. [BS185 1970.P52] 78-22718

BIBLE. English. Authorized. 1971. 220.52'03
The Holy Bible, containing the Old and New Testaments translated out of the original tongues and with the former translations diligently compared and revised. King James version, 1611. Pleasantville, N.Y., Reader's Digest Association [1971] xx, 951 p. col. illus., col. maps. 32 cm. [BS185 1971.P6] 79-79828
I. Title.

BIBLE. English. Authorized. 1971. 220.5'203
The Holy Bible, containing the Old and New Testaments translated out of the original tongues: and with the former translations diligently compared and revised, by His

Majesty's special command. Appointed to be read in churches. Grand Rapids, Mich., Zondervan Pub. House [1971] xiii, 1133, 352, [156] p. 10 col. maps. 18 cm. On spine: Red letter edition. "A concordance to the Old and New Testaments": [156] p. at end. [BS185 1971.G72] 73-166093

BIBLE. English. 220.5'203
Authorized. 1971.
The new analytical Bible anu Dictionary of the Bible. Authorized King James version with the addition in many instances, within brackets, of the more correct renderings of the American standard version (1901). Comprehensive general index ed. [Rev. ed.] Chicago, J. A. Dickson Pub. Co. [1971] xi, 204, 1724 p. maps (part col.) 23 cm. Old and New Testaments have special title pages. [BS185 1971.C482] 78-112500 ISBN 0-8326-1404-1
I. Title. II. Title: Analytical Bible.

BIBLE. English. 220.5'203
Authorized. 1973.
The Holy Bible, with marginal notes and analytical references in the King James version. Nashville, Dove Publishers [1973] 1000, 862 p. illus. 29 cm. "Red letter edition." "Contains A complete analysis of the Holy Bible; or, The whole Bible arranged in subjects, and Comprehensive Bible helps arranged in alphabetical order." [BS185 1973.N372] 73-175587 49.95
I. Dove Publishers.
Pbk. 39.95

BIBLE. English. 220.5'203
Authorized. 1973.
The Holy Bible in giant print : containing the Old and New Testaments in the King James version. Red letter ed. Nashville : Crusade Bible Publishers, c1973. 1854 p., [8] leaves of plates : col. ill. ; 25 cm. [BS185 1973.N368] 74-189521
I. Title.

BIBLE. English. 220.5'203
Authorized. 1973.
Holy Bible: the Old and New Testaments. King James version, authorized in 1611. With an appendix of Bible study aids. Nashville, Broadman Press [1973] 1078, 29 p. illus. 21 cm. [BS185 1973.N37] 73-159485 ISBN 0-8054-1050-3 3.95 (white binding)

BIBLE. English. 220.5'203
Authorized. 1973.
The new analytical Bible and dictionary of the Bible. [Rev. ed.] Chicago, J. A. Dickson Pub. Co. [1973] xi, 204, 1692 p. maps. 24 cm. "Authorized King James version with the addition in many instances, within brackets, of the more correct renderings of the American standard version (1901). Comprehensive general index edition." On spine: Holy Bible. Old and New Testaments have special title pages. [BS185 1973.C482] 73-166390 ISBN 0-8326-1411-4
I. Title. II. Title: Analytical Bible.

BIBLE. English. 220.5'203
Authorized. 1974.
The Holy Bible : authorized King James version / all photos. by Erich Lessing. New York : Tabor House, [1974] 806, [196] p., [32] leaves of plates : ill. ; 27 cm. Includes index. [BS185 1974.N48] 72-11780 ISBN 0-8326-1418-1
I. Title.

BIBLE. English. 220.5'203
Authorized. 1974.
The Holy Bible, containing the Old and New Testaments, translated out of the original tongues and diligently compared with former translations : authorized King James version, with chain center references. Dallas, Tex. : International Bible Association, c1974. 1260, 240 p., [4] leaves of plates : col. maps ; 23 cm. Includes index. [BS185 1974.D33] 75-331065
I. Title.

BIBLE. English. 220.5'203
Authorized. 1975.
The Holy Bible in giant print : containing the Old and New Testaments in the King James version. Red letter ed. and concordance. Nashville, Tenn. : Regal, c1975. 1826 p., [9] leaves of plates : col. ill. ; 25 cm. [BS185 1975.N37] 76-350495
I. Title.

BIBLE. English. 220.5'203
Authorized. 1976.
The Holy Bible : King James version. Black heritage ed. Nashville : Today, c1976. 90, 879, 92 p., [26] leaves of plates : ill. ; 31 cm. [BS185 1976.N38] 77-151393
I. Title.

BIBLE. English. 220.52'03
Authorized. Selections. 1969.
The literature of the Bible; selections and comments, by Robert G. Jacobs. Dubuque, Iowa, W. C. Brown Co. [1969] xiv, 441 p. map. 23 cm. Bibliography: p. 438-441. [BS391.2.J3] 70-77570
I. Jacobs, Robert G. II. Title.

BIBLE. English. 220.52'03
Authorized. Selections. 1969.
A time for peace; verses from the Bible. Selected, edited, and with an introd. by Louis Untermeyer. Illustrated by Joan Berg Victor. New York, World Pub. Co. [1969] [64] p. illus. 22 cm. [BS391.2.U5 1969] 70-82780 3.86
I. Untermeyer, Louis, 1885- ed. II. Victor, Joan (Berg) illus. III. Title.

BIBLE. English. 220.5'203
Authorized. Selections. 1972.
The Bible designed to be read as living literature; the Old and the New Testaments in the King James version. Arranged and edited by Ernest Sutherland Bates. [New York] Simon and Schuster [1972, c1936] xxvi, 1285 p. 21 cm. (A Touchstone book) "In the case of Proverbs, Job, Ecclesiastes, and the Song of songs ... the Revised version is used ... Genealogies and repetitions are omitted, as well as the whole of Chronicles, the minor Epistles, and similar unimportant passages." [BS391.2.B34 1972] 72-171279 ISBN 0-671-21407-1 4.95
I. Bates, Ernest Sutherland, 1879-1939, ed. II. Title.

BIBLE. English. 220.5'203
Authorized. Selections. 1973.
God's love letters. Edited and interpreted by Daniel A. Poling and Henry Thomas. [West Palm Beach? Fla., E. W. Smith, 1973] 333, xix p. 23 cm. First published in 1954 under title: The glory and the wonder of the Bible. [BS391.2.P6 1973] 73-174137
I. Poling, Daniel Alfred, 1884-1968, ed. II. Thomas, Henry, 1886- ed. III. Title.

BIBLE. English. 220.5'203
Authorized. Selections. 1973.
The Mentor Bible: a literary abridgment; the King James version of the Old and New Testaments, edited and with commentary by Michael Fixler. New York, New American Library [1973] xxx, 418 p. 18 cm. (A Mentor book, 451) Bibliography: p. 414-418. [BS391.2.F58 1973] 73-79859 1.95 (pbk.)
I. Fixler, Michael, ed. II. Title.

BIBLE. English. 220.5'203
Authorized. Selections. 1974.
Favorite Bible verses; words of wisdom, strength, and praise. Selected by Kitty McDonald Clevenger. Calligraphy by Hermann Zapf. [Kansas City, Mo., Hallmark Cards, 1974] 45 p. illus. 21 cm. (Hallmark editions) [BS391.2.C53] 73-80096 ISBN 0-87529-352-2 3.00
I. Clevenger, Kitty McDonald, comp. II. Title.

BIBLE. English. 220.5'203
Authorized. Selections. 1974.
Hid in my heart: the word of God in times of need, by Florence M. Taylor. New York, Seabury Press [1974] xiv, 113 p. 21 cm. "A Crossroad book." [BS391.2.T39 1974] 74-9828 ISBN 0-8164-1186-7 5.95
I. Taylor, Florence Marian Tompkins, 1892- comp. II. Title.

BIBLE. English. 220.5'2'03
Authorized. Selections. 1975.
God's love letters / edited and interpreted by Daniel A. Poling and Henry Thomas. West Palm Beach, Fla. : Key Publishers, c1975. 333, [17] p. ; 23 cm. Published in 1954 under title: The glory and the wonder of the Bible. [BS391.2.P6 1975] 75-326572
I. Poling, Daniel Alfred, 1884-1968. II. Thomas, Henry, 1886- III. Title.

BIBLE. English. 220.5'203
Authorized. Selections. 1975.
What God has promised / Geoffery E. Garne. Washington : Review and Herald Pub. Association, [1975] 112 p. ; 18 cm. [BS391.2.G35] 74-81648 2.50
I. Garne, Geoffery E. II. Title.

BIBLE. English. 220.5'203
Authorized. Selections. 1976.
The concise Bible : a condensation / by Frances Kanes Hazlitt. Indianapolis : Liberty Press, c1976. 257 p. ; 22 cm. Reprint of the ed. published by H. Regnery Co., Chicago. Includes index. Bibliography: p. [249]-251. [BS391.2.H35 1976] 76-26330 ISBN 0-913966-17-7 : 7.95. ISBN 0-913966-18-5 pbk. : 1.95
I. Hazlitt, Frances Kanes. II. Title.

BIBLE. English. 220.5'203
Authorized. Selections. 1976.
My lamp and my light / Jo Petty, compiler. Old Tappan, N.J. : F. H. Revell, c1976. p. cm. "Scripture quotations in this volume are from the King James version of the Bible." [BS391.2.P46] 76-2047 ISBN 0-8007-0797-4 : 4.95
I. Petty, Jo. II. Title.

BIBLE. English. 220.5'203
Authorized. Selections. 1977.
Lift up thine eyes : 36 inspirational Biblical masterpieces : text from the Holy Bible, authorized King James version / with an introd. by Boyce M. Bennett, Jr. ; compiled by Pamela Riddle ; designed by Ken Sansone. New York : Harmony Books, 1977. p. cm. [BS391.2.B34 1977] 77-10179 ISBN 0-517-53184-4 : 10.95 ISBN 0-517-53120-8 pbk : 5.95
1. Bible—Pictures, illustrations, etc. I. Riddle, Pamela, 1946- II. Title.

BIBLE. English. 220.5203
Selections. 1965. Authorized.
The Bible; selections from the King James version for study as literature. Edited with an introd. and notes by Roland Mushat Frye. Boston, Houghton Mifflin [1965] xiv, 591 p. maps. 21 cm. (Riverside editions, C91) "Suggestions for further reading": p. xi-xiiv. [BS1091.F7] 65-9648
1. Bible as literature. I. Frye, Roland Mushat, ed. II. Title.

BIBLE, English 220.5203
Selections, 1965 Authorized.
The Bible; selections from the King James version for study as literature. Ed., introd., notes by Roland Mushat Frye. Boston, Houghton [c.1965] xiv, 591p. maps. 21cm. (Riverside ed. C91) Bibl. [BS1091.F7] 65-9648 3.00; 2.15 pap.,
1. Bible as literature. I. Frye, Roland Mushat, ed. II. Title.

BIBLE. English. 220.5203
Selections. 1966. Authorized.
Bible parts to learn by heart; summary of God's words, by Arthur Pickens. San Antonio, Naylor Co. [1966] xiii, 220 p. 22 cm. [BS391.2.P5] 65-28291
I. Pickens, Arthur, ed. II. Title.

BIBLE, English. 220.5203
Selections. 1966. Authorized.
Bible parts to learn by heart; summary of God's word. San Antonio, Tex., Naylor c.1966 xiii, 220p. 22cm. [BS391.2.P5] 65-28291 4.95
I. Pickens. Arthur, ed. II. Title.

BIBLE. English. 220.5'203
Selections. 1970 Authorized.
The Bible designed to be read as living literature. The Old and the New Testaments in the King James version. This edition arranged and edited by Ernest Sutherland Bates. New York, Simon and Schuster [1970, c1936] xxvi, 1285 p. col. maps (on lining papers) 25 cm. "In the case of Proverbs, Job, Ecclesiastes, and the Song of songs ... the Revised version is used ... Genealogies and repetitions are omitted, as well as the whole of Chronicles, the minor Epistles, and similar unimportant passages." [BS391.2.B34 1970] 74-11581 12.50
I. Bates, Ernest Sutherland, 1879-1939, ed. II. Title.

BIBLE. English. Today's 220.5'203
English. Selections. 1977.
Illustrated study Bible : with Today's English version / selection from material compiled by Frank H. Meade and Arnold W. Zimmerman ; illustrated by Shirley Smith and H. H. Turner. Valley Forge, Pa. : Judson Press, c1977. 191 p. : ill. ; 25 cm. "Material in this book has been selected from The school study Bible." Old and New Testament selections from the Today's English Version Bible are accompanied by illustrations and brief text explaining the way of life in Biblical times and countries. [BS391.2.M4 1977] 76-48540 ISBN 0-8170-0740-7 pbk. : 5.95
I. Meade, Frank H. II. Zimmermann, Arnold Walter. III. Smith, Shirley. IV. Turner, H. H. V. Bible. English. Selections. 1960. Authorized. The school study Bible. VI. Title.

BIBLE. N.T. English. 220.5'203
Authorized. 1976.
The Ryrie study Bible : the New Testament / Charles Caldwell Ryrie. New York : Pillar Books, 1976. ix, 769 p. ; 18 cm. [BS2085 1976.N5] 76-17518 ISBN 0-89129-102-4 : 2.25
I. Ryrie, Charles Caldwell, 1925- II. Title.

BIBLE. N.T. English. 220.5'203
Authorized. 1976.
The Ryrie study Bible : Authorized King James version : with introductions, annotations, outlines, marginal references, subject index, harmony of the Gospels, and maps / Charles Caldwell Ryrie. Chicago : Moody Press, c1976. p. cm. [BS2085 1976.C48] 76-20695 ISBN 0-8024-7431-4 : 9.95
I. Ryrie, Charles Caldwell, 1925- II. Title.

BOIS, John, 1560-1644. 220.52'03
Translating for King James; being a true copy of the only notes made by a translator of King James's Bible, the Authorized version, as the Final Committee of Review revised the translation of Romans through Revelation at Stationers' Hall in London in 1610-1611. Taken by John Bois ... these notes were for three centuries lost, and only now are come to light, through a copy made by the hand of William Fulman. Here translated and edited by Ward Allen. [Nashville] Vanderbilt University Press, 1969. xi, 155 p. facsims. 27 cm. "The life of that famous Grecian, Mr. John Bois ... by Anthony Walker:" p. 127-152. Facsimile reproduction, and transcription with additions, of f. 61-80 of MS. CCC312, Corpus Christi College Library, Oxford University. [BS186.B6] 69-17535 10.00
1. Bois, John, 1560-1644. 2. Bible. English—Versions—Authorized. I. Allen, Ward, 1922- ed. II. Oxford. University. Corpus Christi College. Library. MSS. (CCC312) III. Walker, Anthony, d. 1692. The life of that famous Grecian, Mr. John Bois. IV. Title.

DAICHES, David, 1912- 220.52'03
The King James version of the English Bible; an account of the development and sources of the English Bible of 1611 with special reference to the Hebrew tradition. [Hamden, Conn.] Archon Books, 1968 [c1941] vii, 228 p. 20 cm. Bibliographical footnotes. [BS186.D3 1968] 68-16338
1. Bible. English—Versions—Authorized. 2. Bible. English—History. I. Title.

ELLIOTT, Melvin E. 220.52'03
The language of the King James Bible; a glossary explaining its words and expressions [by] Melvin E. Elliott. [1st ed.] Garden City, N.Y., Doubleday, 1967. x, 227 p. 24 cm. Bibliography: p. 226-227. [BS186.E4] 67-11169
1. Bible. English—Versions—Authorized. 2. Bible. English—Glossaries, vocabularies, etc. 3. English language—Etymology. I. Title.

ENGLISH, Eugene 220.5'203
Schuyler, 1899-
A companion to The new Scofield reference Bible [by] E. Schuyler English. New York, Oxford University Press, 1972. xi, 165 p. 23 cm. [BS511.2.E5] 70-190298 4.50
1. Bible—Criticism, interpretation, etc. I. Bible. English. 1967. Authorized. The new Scofield reference Bible. II. Title.

FULLER, David Otis, 220.5'203
1903- comp.
Which Bible? 3d ed., rev. and enl. Grand Rapids, Mich., Grand Rapids International Publications [1972] viii, 318 p. 21 cm. Contents.Contents.—Fuller, D. O. Why this book?—Brown, T. H. The learned men.—Hodges, Z. C. The Greek text of the King James version.—Coray, H. W. The incomparable Wilson: the man who mastered forty-five languages and dialects.—Wilson, R. D. Is the higher criticism scholarly?—Hills, E. F. The magnificent Burgon, doughty champion and defender of the Byzantine text.—Bishop, G. S. The principle and tendency of the revision examined.—Anderson, Sir R. The Bible and modern criticism.—Fuller, D. O. In defense of the textus receptus.—Hoskier, H. C. The Codex Vaticanus and its allies.—Martin, A. A critical examination of the Westcott-Hort textual theory.—Fuller, D. O. About the author of Our authorized Bible vindicated.—Wilkinson, B. G. Our authorized Bible vindicated (p. 176-318) Includes bibliographical references. [BS186.F8 1972] 73-152728 ISBN 0-8254-2612-X 2.95
1. Bible. English—Versions—Authorized. 2. Bible—Versions. 3. Bible—Criticism, Textual. I. Wilkinson, Benjamin George, 1872- Our authorized Bible vindicated. 1972. II. Title.

NEIL, William, 1909- 220.5'203
Harper's bible commentary. New York, Harper & Row [1975, c1962] 544 p. 19 cm. Original title: One volume Bible commentary. [BS491.2.N4] 63-7607 ISBN 0-06-066091-0 3.95 (pbk.)
1. Bible—Commentaries. I. Title.

ROSENAU, William, 1865- 220.5'203
1943.
Hebraisms in the Authorized version of the Bible / William Rosenau. Folcroft, Pa. : Folcroft Library Editions, 1976, c1902. p. cm. Reprint of the 1903 ed. published by Friedenwald Co., Baltimore. Originally presented as the author's thesis, Johns Hopkins University, 1900. [BS186.R67 1976] 76-9047 ISBN 0-8414-7247-5 lib. bdg. : 25.00
1. Bible. English—Versions—Authorized. 2. Bible. O.T. English—Glossaries, vocabularies, etc. 3. English language—Foreign words and phrases—Hebrew. I. Title.

BIBLE. English. 1962. 220.52'04
Revised standard.
The Holy Bible, containing the Old and New Testaments. Revised standard version. Translated from the original tongues;being the version set forth A. D. 1611, revised A. D. 1881-1885 and A. D. 1901;compared with the most ancient authorities, and revised A. D.

1952. New York, American Bible Society [1962, c1946-52] xiv, 843, 242 p. 8 col. maps. 20 cm. [BS191.A1 1962.N35] 70-265881
I. American Bible Society.

BIBLE. English. 1964? 220.52'04
Revised standard.
The Old and the New Testaments of the Holy Bible. Rev. standard version. Translated from the original tongues. being the version set forth A. D. 1611, revised 1611, revised A. D. 1881-1885 and A. D. 1901;compared with the most ancient authorities and evised A. D. 1952. Toronto, Camden, N.J., T. Nelson [1964? c1952-64] 1 v. (various pagings) illus. (part col.), col. maps. 21 cm. New Testament has special t.p.: The New Covenant, commonly called the New Testament ... revised A.D. 1946. Includes Bible study helps, the Holy Land, and A Concise and practical dictionary of the Bible, at end. [BS191.A1 1964.T6] 71-13328
I. Title.

BIBLE. English. 1965. 220.5204
Revised standard.
The Holy Bible, revised standard version containing the Old and New Testaments. Translated from the original tongues being the version set forth A.D. 1611, rev. A.D. 1881-1885 and A.D. 1901, compared with the most ancient authorities and rev. A.D. 1952. With introductory articles and prefaces, explanatory footnotes and maps. New York, Collins' Clear-Type Press [1965] xxvi, 1283, x, 434 p. col. maps. 24 cm. At head of title: Westminster study bible. [BS191.A11965.N394] 66-3258
I. Title: Westminster study Bible. II. Title.

BIBLE. English. 1965. 220.5204
Revised standard.
Westminster study Bible: the Holy Bible, Revised standard version. Containing the Old and New Testaments. Translated from the original tongues; being the version set forth A.D. 1611, rev. A.D. 1881-1885 and A.D. 1901, compared with the most ancient authorities and rev. A.D. 1962. New York, Collins' Clear-Type Press [1965] 1 v. (various pagings) col. maps. 24 cm. First ed. based on the Authorized version and published under title: The Westminster study edition of the Holy Bible. [BS191.A11965.N42] 65-6956
I. Bible. English. 1948. Authorized. The Westminster study edition of the Holy Bible. II. Title.

BIBLE. English. 1965. 220.5204
Revised standard.
Young readers Bible; the Holy Bible. Revised standard version, translated from the original tongues; being the version set forth A.D. 1611, revised A.D. 1881-1885 and A.D. 1901; compared with the most ancient authorities and revised A.D. 1952. Study helps for each book of the Bible and additional materials prepared by Henry M. Bullock and Edward C. Peterson. Philadelphia, Published by the A. J. Holman Co. for Cokesbury [1965] 18, 871 p. illus., col. maps. 29 cm. [BS191.A11965.P5] 66-5021
I. Bullock, Henry Morton. II. Peterson, Edward C. III. Title.

BIBLE. English. 1965. 220.5204
Revised Standard
The Oxford annotated Bible, with the Apocrypha. Rev. standard version. Introductory article, The number, order, and names of the books of the Bible. Ed. by Herbert G. May, Bruce M. Metzger. New York, Oxford 1965]c.1946-1965] 1v. (various p.) fold. col. maps, plans. 23cm. [BS191.A1 1965.N4] 65-23646 10.50; 7.95 coll. ed.,
I. May, Herbert Gordon, 1904- II. Metzger, Bruce Manning. III. Title.

BIBLE. English. 1965. 220.5204
Revised Standard
Westminster study Bible: the Holy Bible, Rev. standard version. Containing the Old and New Testaments. Tr. from the orig. tongues; being the version set forth A.D. 1611, rev. A. D. 1881-1885 and A. D. 1901, compared with the most ancient authorities and rev. A. D. 1962. New York, Collins' [c.1946-1965] 1v. (various ps.) col. maps. 24cm. First ed. based on the Authorized version and pub. under title: The Westminster study edition of the Holy Bible [BS191.A1 1965 N42] 65-6956 8.95; 12.50 deluxe ed.,
1. Bible. English. 1948. Authorized. The Westminster study edition of the Holy Bible. I. Title.

BIBLE. English. 1966. 220.5204
Jerusalem Bible.
The Jerusalem Bible. general editor Alexander Jones. London, Darton, Longman & Todd, 1966. xvi, 1547; 499 p. 8 plates (maps) tables, diagr. 24 1/2 cm. 84/- (B66-20244) [BS195.J4] 66-69681
I. Jones, Alexander, 1905- ed. II. Title.

BIBLE. English. 1966. 220.5204
Jerusalem Bible.
The Jerusalem Bible. General editor: Alexander Jones. Garden City, N.Y., Doubleday, 1966. xvi, 1547, 498 p. maps (part col.) 25 cm. "The principal collaborators in translation and literary revision were: Joseph Leo Alston [and others]" [BS195.J4 1966] 66-24278
I. Jones, Alexander, 1906- ed. II. Title.

BIBLE, English. 1966. 220.5204
Revised standard.
The Holy Bible, containing the Old and New Testaments. Rev. standard version. Catholic ed. Tr. from the original tongues, being the version set forth A.D. 1611; Old and New Testaments rev. A. D. 1881-1885 and A. D. 1901, Apocrypha rev. A. D. 1894; compared with the most ancient authorities and rev. A. D. 1952, Apocrypha rev. A. D. 1957. Prepd. by the Catholic Biblical Assn. of Great Britain. Foreword by Richard Cardinal Cushing. Toronto, Camden, N.J. 08103, Nelson [c.1966] xvi, 250p. 22cm. [BS191.A1 1966.T6] 66-6323 6.50; 12.50, de luxe ed.,
I. Title.

BIBLE. English. 1967. 220.52'04
Revised standard.
The Holy Bible. Revised standard version containing the Old and New Testaments, translated from the original tongues; being the version set forth A.D. 1611, revised A.D. 1881-1885 and A.D. 1901; compared with the most ancient authorities and revised A.D. 1952. Minneapolis, Augsburg Pub. House [1967] xii, 842, 250, 75, 127 p. col. illus., col. maps. 20 cm. New Testament has special t.p.: The New Covenant, commonly called the New Testament of Our Lord and Savior Jesus Christ; revised standard version translated from the Greek ... compared with the most ancient authorities and revised A.D. 1946. Includes study materials and concordance at end. [BS191.A1 1967.M5] 67-66319

BIBLE. English. 1967. 220.52'04
Revised standard.
The Holy Bible, containing the Old and New Testaments. Rev. standard version. Translated from the original tongues; being the version set forth A.D. 1611, rev. A.D. 1881-1885, and A.D. 1901, compared with the most ancient authorities and rev. A.D. 1952. New York, American Bible Society [1967] x, 1087 p. col. maps (on lining papers) 21 cm. [BS191.A1 1967.N4] 70-264754
I. American Bible Society.

BIBLE. English. 220.5'204
Jerusalem Bible. 1971.
The Jerusalem Bible. [General editor Alexander Jones] Reader's ed. Garden City, N.Y., Doubleday, 1971 [c1968] xi, 1340, 358 p. maps (part col.) 24 cm. [BS195.J4 1971] 74-153643 5.95
I. Jones, Alexander, 1906- ed. II. Title.

BIBLE. English. New 220.5'204
American Standard. 1971.
New American standard Bible. [1st ed.] La Habra, Calif., Foundation Press Publications, publisher for the Lockman Foundation [1971] x, 1334, 396 p. 24 cm. On spine: Reference edition. [BS195.N35] 70-26152 10.95
I. Lockman Foundation, La Habra, Calif. II. Title.

BIBLE. English. New 220.5'204
American Standard. 1973.
New American standard Bible. La Habra, Calif., Foundation Press Publications, publisher for the Lockman Foundation [1973] x, 1334, 396 p. 24 cm. On spine: Reference edition. [BS195.N35 1973] 73-177592 10.95
I. Lockman Foundation, La Habra, Calif. II. Title.

BIBLE. English. New 220.5'204
American Standard. 1975.
New American standard Bible. Reference ed. [New York] : Collins-World, c1975. x, 1181, 96 p., [4] leaves of plates : col. maps ; 22 cm. [BS195.N35 1975] 75-332342
I. Title.

BIBLE. English. Revised 220.52'04
standard. 1971.
The Holy Bible, containing the Old and New Testaments. Revised standard version. Translated from the original tongues, being the version set forth A.D. 1611, rev. A.D. 1881-1885 and A.D. 1901, compared with the most ancient authorities and rev. A.D. 1952. [New York] Published by W. Collins for Board of Publication of the Lutheran Church in America, Philadelphia [1971] xiv, 843, 242, 32, 96 p. col. illus., col. maps. 20 cm. "Helps to the study of the Revised standard version Bible": 32 p. (4th group) "Concise concordance to the Revised standard version of the Holy Bible": 96 p. (5th group) [BS191.A1 1971.N4] 72-30222

BIBLE. English. Revised 220.5'204
Standard. 1973.
The Holy Bible; revised standard version containing the Old and New Testaments, with the Apocrypha/Deuterocanonical books. An ecumenical ed. [New York] Collins [1973] xvi, 843, 223, 242 p. 20 cm. (Fontana religious) (Fontana books) On cover: Common Bible. [BS191.A1 1973.N38] 73-162038 7.95
I. Title: Common Bible.
Pbk. 4.95

BIBLE. English. Revised 220.5'204
standard. 1973.
The new Oxford annotated Bible with the Apocrypha. Rev. standard version, containing the 2d ed. of the New Testament. Edited by Herbert G. May [and] Bruce M. Metzger. New York, Oxford University Press, 1973. xxviii, 1564, xxii, 298 p. illus. 23 cm. At head of title: An ecumenical study Bible. [BS191.A1 1973.N43] 72-96564 11.95
I. May, Herbert Gordon, 1904- ed. II. Metzger, Bruce Manning, ed. III. Title.

BIBLE. English. 220.52'04
Selections. 1969.
The Bible reader; an interfaith interpretation. With notes from Catholic, Protestant, and Jewish traditions and references to art, literature, history, and the social problems of modern man, prepared by Walter M. Abbott, Arthur Gilbert, Rolfe Lanier Hunt [and] J. Carter Swaim. New York, Bruce Pub. Co. [1969] xxiv, 995 p. 22 cm. "The Revised standard version is the text of the Bible generally used ... Exceptional samples from other translations, old and new, Protestant, Catholic, and Jewish, are also used."—Jacket. "Index to introductions, essays, and notes": p. [983]-995. [BS391.2.A48 1969] 76-93545 7.95
I. Abbott, Walter M. II. Gilbert, Arthur. III. Hunt, Rolfe Lanier, 1903- IV. Swaim, Joseph Carter, 1904- V. Title.

BIBLE. N.T. English. 220.52'04
1967. Today's English
Good news for modern man; the New Testament in Today's English version, with easy-to-use, marked references to guide you to a new life of peace and happiness through Jesus Christ. Nashville, Broadman Press [1967] iv, 597 p. illus. 18 cm. [BS2095.T56] 67-8142
I. Title. II. Title.

BIBLE. O.T. English. 220.52'04
Jerusalem Bible. 1969.
The Old Testament of the Jerusalem Bible. [General editor: Alexander Jones] Reader's edition. [Garden City, N.Y.] [Doubleday] [1973, c.1968] 4 v. maps. 18 cm. (Image Books, D311-D314) "The principal collaborators in translation and literary revision were: Joseph Leo Alston [others]" Reprint of the 1-volume edition. Contents.Contents.—v. 1. Genesis—Ruth.—v. 2. I Samuel—II#Maccabees.—v. 3. Job—Ecclesiasticus.—v. 4. The Prophets—Malachi. [BS895.J38 1969] 73-12890 ISBN 0-385-07036-5 (v. 3); each 1.95 (pbk.)
I. Jones, Alexander, 1906- ed. II. Title.

ECKER, Jakob, 1851- 220.52'04
1912.
Beginner's Bible. Translated from the German edition; edited under the direction of the Fulda Conference of Bishops. Collegeville, Minn., Liturgical Press [1966] 350 p. col. illus. 19 cm. Translation of Katholische Schulbibel. [BS551.2.E313] 67-8607
1. Bible stories, English. I. Title.

BIBLE. 220.52'04
English. 1967. Minneapolis, Augsburg Pub. House [1967] xii, 842, 250, 75, 127 p. col. illus., col. maps. 20 cm. New Testament has special t. p.: The New Covenant, commonly called the New Testament of Our Lord and Savior Jesus Christ; revised standard version translated from the Greek ... compared with the most ancient authorities and revised A. D. 1946. Includes study materials and concordance at end. [BS191.A1 1967.M5] 67-66319
I. Title: The Holy Bible.

BIBLE. English. 1966. 220.5205
Confraternity version.
The Holy Bible, with the Confraternity text. Chicago, Good Counsel Publishers [1966] 1 v. (various pagings) col. illus., col. plates, col. ports. 29 cm. Includes approved texts of the Ordinary of the Mass in English with musical settings, a Catholic doctrinal guide, The Bible story for young and old, and other material. [BS180] 66-8184
I. Confraternity of Christian Doctrine. II. Title.

BIBLE. English. 1967. 220.52'05
Confraternity version.
Holy Bible containing the Old and New Testaments. The entire Sacrifice of the Mass in pictures and explanatory text in accord with the Constitution on Sacred Liturgy of Vatican Council II; the Way of the Cross; and a complete Catholic dictionary keyed to the Bible and its use. Catholic family ed. Philadelphia, Family and Home Press [1967] 1417 p. col. illus., col. maps., col. port. 30 cm. "The Old Testament, the new Confraternity translation of the first eight books, the seven Sapiential books, and the eighteen Prophetic books. The balance is in the Douay version. The New Testament, all books in the Confraternity of Christian Doctrine version in current usage." [BS195.C6 1967] 67-9343
1. Confraternity of Christian Doctrine. Episcopal Committee. I. Title.

BIBLE. English. 220.5'205
Catholic Biblical Association of America. Selections. 1973.
The Spirit Bible. Compiled by Eugene S. Geissler. Notre Dame, Ind., Ave Maria Press [1973] 272 p. 17 cm. [BS192.3.A1 1973.N67] 73-88004 ISBN 0-87793-062-7 2.25 (pbk.)
1. Spirit—Biblical teaching. 2. Holy Spirit—Biblical teaching. I. Geissler, Eugene S., comp. II. Title.

BIBLE. English. New 220.52'05
American. 1970.
The new American Bible. Translated from the original languages, with critical use of all the ancient sources by members of the Catholic Biblical Association of America. New York, P. J. Kenedy [1970] xvi, 1347, 401, 47 p. maps. 21 cm. "Sponsored by the Bishops' Committee of the Confraternity of Christian Doctrine." [BS192.3.A1 1970.N48] 78-20066 4.95 (pbk.)
I. Catholic Biblical Association of America. II. Confraternity of Christian Doctrine. Bishops' Committee. III. Title.

BIBLE. English. New 220.52'05
American. 1970.
The new American Bible. Translated from the original languages, with critical use of all the ancient sources by members of the Catholic Biblical Association of America. With textual notes on Old Testament readings. Paterson, N.J., St. Anthony Guild Press [1970] 21, 1103, 462 p. illus., maps. 24 cm. "Sponsored by the Bishops' Committee of the Confraternity of Christian Doctrine." [BS192.3.A1 1970P3] 71-141768
I. Catholic Biblical Association of America. II. Confraternity of Christian Doctrine. Bishops' Committee. III. Title.

BIBLE. English. New 220.52'05
American. 1970.
The new American Bible. Translated from the original languages with critical use of all the ancient sources by members of the Catholic Biblical Association of America. [1971-1972 ed.] Wichita, Kan., Catholic Bible Publishers [1970] 44, 1250, 251 p. illus. (part col.) 30 cm. On spine: Holy Bible. Deluxe parish edition. "Sponsored by the Bishops' Committee of the Confraternity of Christian Doctrine." [BS192.3.A1 1970.W5] 74-21945
I. Catholic Biblical Association of America. II. Confraternity of Christian Doctrine. Bishops' Committee. III. Title.

BIBLE. English. New 220.52'05
American. 1971.
The new American Bible. Translated from the original languages with critical use of all the ancient sources by members of the Catholic Biblical Association of America. Pleasantville, N.Y., Reader's Digest Association [1971] xvii, 1162 p. illus. (part col.), col. maps. 32 cm. Sponsored by the Bishops' Committee of the Confraternity of Christian Doctrine. [BS192.3.A1 1971.P6] 73-138384
I. Catholic Biblical Association of America. II. Confraternity of Christian Doctrine. Bishops' Committee. III. Title.

BIBLE. English. New 220.52'05
American. 1971.
The new American Bible. Translated from the original languages, with critical use of all the ancient sources by members of the Catholic Biblical Association of America. [Living word ed. Charlotte, N.C.] Catholic Educational Guild [1971] [54], 968, 300, [16], 252 p. col. illus., forms. 29 cm. Cover title: Holy Bible. "Sponsored by the Bishops' Committee of the Confraternity of Christian Doctrine." "The combined Biblical dictionary & concordance": 252 p. (5th group) [BS192.3.A1 1971.C47] 70-24962
I. Catholic Biblical Association of America. II. Confraternity of Christian Doctrine. Bishops' Committee. III. Title.

BIBLE. English. New 220.5'205
American. 1971.
The new American Bible. Translated from the original languages, with critical use of all the ancient sources by members of the Catholic Biblical Association of America. [1st ed.] Chicago, Catholic Press [1971, c1970] lii, 828, 254, 219 p. col. illus., forms, maps (part col.), col. ports. 27 cm. Cover title: Holy Bible. On

spine: The Christian life edition. "Sponsored by the Bishops' Committee of the Confraternity of Christian Doctrine." "An encyclopedic dictionary of Biblical and general Catholic information": 219 p. at end. [BS192.3.A1 1971.C482] 77-132629 ISBN 0-8326-1205-7
I. Catholic Biblical Association of America. II. Confraternity of Christian Doctrine. Bishops' Committee. III. Title.

BIBLE. English. New American. 1971. 220.52'05
The new American Bible. Translated from the original languages, with critical use of all the ancient sources by members of the Catholic Biblical Association of America. [Catholic de luxe ed.] Chicago, Good Counsel Publishers [1971] xxxii, [6], 968, 300, 62, 96 p. col. illus., forms, ports. 29 cm. Cover title: Holy Bible. "Sponsored by the Bishops' Committee of the Confraternity of Christian Doctrine." "The Bible story for young and old; a record of the more important events of the Old and New Testaments": 62 p. (5th group) "Bible dictionary": 96 p. (6th group) [BS192.3.A1 1971.C48] 70-24202
I. Catholic Biblical Association of America. II. Confraternity of Christian Doctrine. Bishops' Committee. III. Title.

BIBLE. English. New English. 1971. 220.52'06
The New English Bible. New York, Cambridge University Press, 1971 [c1970] xxi, 1166, ix, 336 p. 21 cm. Includes the 2nd ed. of the New English Bible New Testament. Prepared under the authority of the Joint Committee on the New Translation of the Bible. [BS192.A1 1971.N4] 76-23089 4.45
I. Joint Committee on the New Translation of the Bible. II. Title.

BIBLE. English. New English. 1971. 220.52'06
The New English Bible with the Apocrypha. New York, Cambridge University Press, 1971 [c1970] xxi, 1166, viii, 275, ix, 336 p. 21 cm. Includes the 2nd ed. of the New Enlgish Bible New Testament. Prepared under the authority of the Joint Committee on the New Translation of the Bible. [BS192.A1 1971.N42] 75-23043 4.95
I. Joint Committee on the New Translation of the Bible. II. Title.

BIBLE. English. New English. 1976. 220.5'206
The New English Bible, with the Apocrypha / Samuel Sandmel, general editor, M. Jack Suggs, New Testament editor, Arnold J. Tkacik, Apocrypha editor. Oxford Study ed. New York : Oxford University Press, 1976. 1036, 257, 333, [100] p. : 9 maps ; 25 cm. Prepared under the authority of the Joint Committee on the New Translation of the Bible. [BS192.A1 1976.N48] 75-32364 14.95
I. Sandmel, Samuel. II. Suggs, M. Jack. III. Tkacik, Arnold J. IV. Joint Committee on the New Translation of the Bible. V. Title.

GRIERSON, Herbert John Clifford, Sir, 1866-1960. 220.5'2'09
The English Bible / Sir Herbert Grierson. Folcroft, Pa. : Folcroft Library Editions, 1977. p. cm. Reprint of the 1943 ed. published by Collins, London, in the 2 series: Britain in pictures and the British people in pictures. [BS455.G7 1977] 77-6836 ISBN 0-8414-4453-6 lib. bdg. : 10.00
1. Bible. English—History. 2. Bible. English—Versions. 3. Bible as literature. 4. Bible in literature. I. Title. II. Series: Britain in pictures. III. Series: The British people in pictures.

GRIERSON, Herbert John Clifford, Sir, 1866-1960. 220.5'2'09
The English Bible / Sir Herbert Grierson. Folcroft, Pa. : Folcroft Library Editions, 1977. p. cm. Reprint of the 1943 ed. published by Collins, London, in the 2 series: Britain in pictures and the British people in pictures. [BS455.G7 1977] 77-6836 ISBN 0-8414-4453-6 lib. bdg. : 10.00
1. Bible. English—History. 2. Bible. English—Versions. 3. Bible as literature. 4. Bible in literature. I. Title. II. Series: Britain in pictures. III. Series: The British people in pictures.

BIBLE. Anglo-Saxon. Selections. 1974. 220.5'29
Biblical quotations in Old English prose writers. 2d series, edited with the Latin originals, index of Biblical passages, and index of principal words by Albert S. Cook. [Folcroft, Pa.] Folcroft Library Editions, 1974 [c1903] x, 396 p. 23 cm. Reprint of the ed. published by Scribner, New York, in series: Yale bicentennial publications. [BS131.C6 1974] 74-2465 ISBN 0-8414-3552-9 (lib. bdg.)
I. Cook, Albert Stanburrough, 1853-1927, ed. II. Bible. Latin. Selections. 1974. III. Title. IV. Series: Yale bicentennial publications.

BIBLE. Anglo-Saxon. Selections. 1976. 220.5'29
Biblical quotations in old English prose writers / edited with the Vulgate and other Latin originals, introd. on old English Biblical versions, index of Biblical passages, and index of principal words by Albert S. Cook. Norwood, Pa. : Norwood Editions, 1976. p. cm. Reprint of the 1898 ed. published by Macmillan, London and New York. Includes bibliographical references and indexes. [BS131.C58 1976] 76-15291 ISBN 0-8482-0362-3 lib. bdg. : 35.00
I. Cook, Albert Stanburrough, 1853-1927. II. Title.

BLUHM, Heinz Siegfried 220.53
Martin Luther, creative translator. St. Louis, Concordia [1966, c.1965] xv, 236p. facism., port. 24cm. Bibl. [BS240.B5] 65-28162 8.00
1. Bible. German — Versions — Luther. 2. Bible — Translating. I. Title.

KOOIMAN, Willem Jan, 1903- 220.53
Luther and the Bible. Translated by John Schmidt. Philadelphia, Muhlenberg Press [1961] 243p. 22cm. Includes bibliography. [BS240.K613] 61-10280
1. Luther, Martin, 1483-1546. 2. Bible, German— Versions—Luther. I. Title.

STRAND, Kenneth Albert, 1927- 220.5'3
Early Low-German Bibles; the story of four pre-Lutheran editions, by Kenneth A. Strand. Grand Rapids, Erdmans [1967] 48p. 14facsims. 28cm. In celebration of the earliest vernacular printed Bible, 1466. A campanion vol. to the author's German Bibles before Luther: the story of 14 High German editions. Bibl. [BS236.5.S68] 67-19316 4.00
1. Bible. German (Middle Low German)—Versions. I. Title.

STRAND, Kenneth Albert, 1927- 220.5'3
Early Low-German Bibles; the story of four pre-Lutheran editions, by Kenneth A. Strand. Grand Rapids, W. B. Eerdmans Pub. Co. [1967] 48 p. 14 facsims, 28 cm. "In celebration of the earliest vernacular printed Bible, 1466." A companion volume to the author's German Bibles before Luther: the story of 14 High-German editions. Bibliographical footnotes. [BS236.5.S68] 67-19316
1. Bible. German (Middle Low German) — Versions. I. Title.

STRAND, Kenneth Albert, 1927- 220.53
German Bibles before Luther; the story of 14 High-German editions, by Kenneth A. Strand. Grand Rapids, W. B. Eerdmans Pub. Co. [1966] 64 p. illus., facsims. 29 cm. "In celebration of the earliest vernacular printed Bible, 1466." Includes bibliographical references. [BS236.5.S7] 66-2040
1. Bible. German (Middle High German) — Versions. I. Title.

STRAND, Kenneth Albert, 1927- 220.53
German Bibles before Luther; the story of 14 High-German editions. Grand Rapids, Mich., Eerdmans [c.1966] 64p. illus., facsims. 29cm. In celebration of the earliest vernacular printed Bible, 1466. Bibl. [BS236.5.S7] 66-2040 4.00
1. Bible. German (Middle High German) — Versions. I. Title.

VAPORIS, Nomikos Michael. 220.58'9
The controversy on the translation of the Scriptures into modern Greek and its effects, 1818-1843. [New York] 1970. 272 l. 29 cm. Thesis—Columbia University. Bibliography: leaves 242-272. [BS243.V36] 70-287692
1. Bible. Greek—Versions. I. Title.

AASENG, Rolf E. 220.6
The sacred sixty-six; introducing the books of the Bible, by Rolf E. Aaseng. Minneapolis, Augsburg Pub. House [1967] 200 p. 22 cm. [BS475.2.A2] 67-11721
1. Bible—Introductions. I. Title.

*AHRESEN, Bertha Fidjeland 220.6
Bible topics, pro and con. New York, Pageant [c.1963] 83p. 21cm. 2.50
I. Title.

ALLEY, Robert S., 1932- 220.6
Revolt against the faithful; a Biblical case for inspiration as encounter [by] Robert S. Alley. [1st ed.] Philadelphia, Lippincott [1970] 192 p. 21 cm. Bibliography: p. 187-188. [BS480.A53] 73-120330 4.95
1. Bible—Inspiration. 2. Bible—Criticism, interpretation, etc. I. Title.

ALONSO SCHOKEL, Luis, 1920- 220.6
Understanding Biblical research. Translated by Peter J. McCord. [New York] Herder and Herder [1963] 130 p. 24 cm. Translation of El hombre de hoy ante la Bibilia. [BS500.S313] 63-14308
1. Bible — Criticism, Interpretation, etc. — Hist. 2. Bible — Study — Catholic Church. I. Title.

ARNOLD, Matthew, 1822-1888. 220.6
Literature & dogma, an essay towards a better apprehension of the Bible. London, Murray, 1924. xxi, 232 p. 20 cm. [[BS511]] 63-6750
1. Bible — Criticism, interpretation, etc. I. Title.

AUZOU, Georges 220.6
The Word of God; approaches to the mystery of the Sacred Scriptures. Translated by Josefa Thorton. St. Louis, Mo., Herder [c.1960] 255p. 60-16941 4.75
1. Bible—Introductions. I. Title.

AUZOU, Georges. 220.6
The Word of God; approaches to the mystery of the Sacred Scriptures. Translated by Josefa Thornton. St. Louis, Herder [1960] 255p. 21cm. [BS475.2.A853] 60-16941
1. Bible—Introductions. I. Title.

BAKER, D. L. 220.6
Two Testaments, one Bible : a study of some modern solutions to the theological problem of the relationship between the Old and New Testaments / by D. L. Baker. Downers Grove, Ill. : InterVarsity Press, c1976. 554 p. ; 22 cm. Originally presented as the author's thesis, University of Sheffield, 1975, under title: The theological problem of the relationship between the Old Testament and the New Testament. Includes indexes. Bibliography: p. [391]-535. [BS2387.B33 1976] 77-359566 ISBN 0-87784-872-6 : pbk. : 7.95
1. Bible. N.T.—Relation to O.T. I. Title.

BALCOMB, Raymond E. 220.6
Try reading the Bible this way, by Raymond E. Balcomb. Philadelphia, Westminster Press [1971] 208 p. 19 cm. Bibliography: p. [203]-206. [BS617.B28] 76-153866 2.95
1. Bible—Reading. I. Title.

BARCLAY, William, lecturer in the University of Glasgow. 220.6
The King and the Kingdom. Philadelphia, Westminster Press [1968] 211 p. 19 cm. Rev. and amended ed. of a Bible class handbook originally prepared for the Boys' Brigade. [BS605.2.B34 1968] 69-12836 2.45
1. Bible—Study—Text-books. I. Title.

BARNDOLLAR, W. W. 220.6
The validity of dispensationalism, by W. W. Barndollar. Des Plaines, Ill., Regular Baptist Pr. [1967, c.1964] 70p. 22cm. Bibl. [BT157.B33 1967] 67-23370 1.50 pap.,
1. Dispensationalism. I. Title.

BARNDOLLAR, W W 220.6
The validity of dispensationalism, four chapel messages by W. W. Barndollar. Johnson City, N.Y., Baptist Bible Seminary, 1964. ix. 47 p. illus., port. 23 cm. Bibliographical references included in "Footnotes" (p. 45-46) [BT157.B33] 64-23719
1. Dispensationalism. I. Title.

BARR, James. 220.6
The Bible in the modern world. [1st U.S. ed.] New York, Harper & Row [1973] xii, 193 p. 22 cm. Bibliography: p. [185]-188. [BS511.2.B37 1973b] 73-6336 ISBN 0-06-060547-2 5.95
1. Bible—Criticism, interpretation, etc. I. Title.

BARR, James, 1924- 220.6
Old and new in interpretation; a study of the two Testaments. [1st ed.] New York, Harper [1966] 215p. 22cm. (Currie lects. 1964) Bibl. [BS540.B3 1966a] 66-20773 5.50
1. Bible — Addresses, essays, lectures. 2. Bible. N. T. — Relation to O. T. I. Title. II. Series.

BARTH, Markus. 220.6
Conversation with the Bible. [1st ed.] New York, Holt, Rinehart and Winston [1964] xiii, 338 p. 22 cm. Bibliographical references included in "Notes" (p. 313-330) [BS475.2.B3] 64-14366
1. Bible—Introductions. I. Title.

BARTHELEMY, Dominique. 220.6
God and His image; an outline of Biblical theology. Translated by Aldhelm Dean. New York, Sheed and Ward [1966] xix, 199 p. 22 cm. Originally published as articles in La vie spirituelle, from Nov. 1961 to April 1963. [BS543.B3713 1966a] 66-22008
1. Bible—Theology. I. Title.

BARTON, Bruce, 1886- 220.6
The Book nobody knows. New York, Bobbs-Merrill Co. [1967, 1959] 189 p. 21 cm. [BS530.B35] 67-23035
1. Bible — Criticism, interpretation, etc. I. Title.

BARTON, Bruce, 1886- 220.6
The Book nobody knows. New York, Bobbs [1967, c.1959] 189p. 21cm. [BS530.B35 1967] 67-23035 1.35 pap.,
1. Bible—Criticism, interpretation, etc. I. Title.

BELL, Alvin Eugene, 1882- 220.6
The gist of the Bible book by book. Grand Rapids, Mich., Zondervan [1961, c.1926] 169p. 1.50 pap.,
I. Title.

BENNION, Lowell Lindsay, 1908- 220.6
Teachings of the New Testament. Salt Lake City, Deseret Book Co. [c1956] 376p. 24cm. 'Second edition.'--Pref. [BS2397.B4 1956] 57-20289
1. Bible. N. T.—Theology. 2. Mormons and Mormonism—Doctrinal and controversial works. I. Title.

BERKHOF, Louis, 1873- 220.6
Principles of Biblical interpretation; sacred hermeneutics. Grand Rapids, Baker Book House, 1950. 169 p. 23 cm. Includes bibliographies. [BS476.B45] 50-13488
1. Bible—Hermeneutics. I. Title.

BERKOUWER, Gerrit Cornelis, 1903- 220.6
Holy Scripture / by G. C. Berkouwer ; [translated and edited by Jack B. Rogers]. Grand Rapids : W. B. Eerdmans Pub. Co., [1975] 377 p. ; 23 cm. (His Studies in dogmatics) Translation of De Heilige Schrift. Includes bibliographical references and index. [BS518.D8B4713] 74-32237 ISBN 0-8028-3394-2 : 8.95
1. Bible—Criticism, interpretation, etc. 2. Bible—Evidences, authority, etc. I. Rogers, Jack Bartlett, ed. II. Title.

BIBLE, English, Selections 1960. Authorized. 220.6
Literature from the Bible, Selected by Joseph Frank. Boston, Little [c.1963] ix, 404p. 21cm. Bibl. 63-11138 4.95
1. Bible—Introductions. I. Frank, Joseph, 1916- comp. II. Title.

BIBLE. Enlgish. Selections. 1963. Authorized. 220.6
Literature from the Bible. Selected by Joseph Frank Boston, Little, Brown [1963] ix, 404 p. 21 cm. Includes bibliography. [BS391.2F7] 63-11138
1. Bible—Introductions. I. Frank, Joseph, 1916- comp. II. Title.

BIBLICAL studies : 220.6
essays in honor of William Barclay / edited by Johnston R. McKay and James F. Miller. Philadelphia : Westminster Press, c1976. 223 p. ; 21 cm. Contents.Contents.—McKay, J. R. A personal appreciation.—Falconer, R. Barclay the broadcaster.—Barbour, R. S. The Bible, Word of God?—Davidson, R. The Old Testament, a question of theological relevance.—Anderson, H. A future for apocalyptic?—Caird, G. B. Eschatology and politics.—Scobie, C. H. H. North and South.—Alexander, N. The epistle for today.—Best, E. Mark 10:13-16.—Black, M. Some Greek words with "Hebrew" meanings in the Epistles and Apocalypse.—Hunter, A. M. Apollos the Alexandrian.—Neil, W. Five hard sayings of Jesus.—O'Neill, J. C. Glory to God in the highest.—Johnston, G. New Testament Christology in a pluralistic age.—McHardy, W. D. Cambridge Syriac fragment XXVI. "Books by William Barclay": p. [221]-223. [BS540.B446] 76-6943 ISBN 0-664-20760-X 12.50
1. Barclay, William, lecturer in the University of Glasgow. 2. Bible—Criticism, interpretation, etc.—Addresses, essays, lectures. I. Barclay, William, lecturer in the University of Glasgow. II. McKay, Johnston R. III. Miller, James F.
Contents omitted

BISCHOFF, Louis V. 220.6
A new look at the Bible tradition. New York, Philosophical Library [1963] 380 p. 24 cm. [BS533.B57] 62-21556
1. Bible—Critism, interpretation, etc. 2. Religion—Controversial literature. I. Title.

BISCHOFF, Louis V. 220.6
A new look at the Bible tradition. New York, Philosophical [c.1963] 380p. 24cm. 62-21556 7.50
1. Bible—Criticism, interpretation, etc. 2. Religion—Controversial literature. I. Title.

BLACKMAN, Edwin Cyril. 220.6
Biblical interpretation. Philadelphia, Westminster Press. [1957] 212p. 21cm. Includes bibliography. [BS476.B53] 59-5040
1. Bible —Hermeneutics. 2. Bible—Criticism, interpretation, etc.—Hist. I. Title.

BOER, Harry R. 220.6
Above the battle? : The Bible and its critics / by Harry R. Boer. Grand Rapids : Eerdmans,

c1977. 109 p. ; 18 cm. [BS511.2.B63] 76-57225 ISBN 0-8028-1693-2 pbk. : 2.95
1. Bible—Criticism, interpretation, etc. 2. Bible—Inspiration. I. Title.

BOHLMANN, Ralph A. 220.6
Principles of Biblical interpretation in the Lutheran confessions [by] Ralph A. Bohlmann. Saint Louis, Concordia Pub. House [1968] 144 p. 21 cm. Bibliography: p. 141-144. [BS500.B6] 68-13312
1. Lutheran Church—Catechisms and creeds—History and criticism. 2. Bible—Criticism, interpretation, etc.—History. I. Title.

BRANNON, Clarence Ham, 1900- 220.6
An introduction to the Bible. [Raleigh? N. C., [1951, '1950] xi, 292 p. 24 cm. Bibliography: p. 238-248. [BS175.B65] 51-18545
1. Bible—Introductions. I. Title.

*BRASINGTON, Virginia F. 220.6
Flying saucers in the Bible. Clarksburg, W. Va., [Bx. 2228, Saucerian Bks. 1964, c.1963] 78 1. illus. 28cm. 3.00 pap.,
I. Title.

BROOMALL, Wick, 1902- 220.6
Biblical criticism. Grand Rapids, Zondervan Pub. House [1957] 320p. 23cm. Includes bibliography. [BS476.B67] 57-2368
1. Bible—Hermeneutics. I. Title.

BROWN, Robert McAfee, 1920- 220.6
The Bible speaks to you. Philadelphia, Westminster Press [1955] 320 p. 22 cm. [BS538.B74] 55-7089
1. Bible—Criticism, interpretation, etc. 2. Theology, Doctrinal—Popular works. I. Title.

BROWNLEE, Frederick Leslie, 1883- 220.6
Contemporary antiquities; a study of the social and personal problems which confront our world today--in the light of a humane wisdom as old as the prophets. New York, American Press [c1958] 136p. 22cm. [BS533.B74] 58-10431
1. Bible— Criticism, Interpretation, etc. I. Title.

BRUCE, Frederick Fyvie, 1910- 220.6
The New Testament development of Old Testament themes, by F. F. Bruce. Grand Rapids, Mich., W. B. Eerdmans Pub. Co. [1969, c1968] 122 p. 23 cm. Based on the Payton lectures for 1968. Bibliographical footnotes. [BS2387.B78] 78-5579 3.95
1. Bible. N.T.—Relation to O.T. 2. Bible—Criticism, interpretation, etc. I. Title.

BRUEGGEMANN, Walter. 220.6
The Bible makes sense / by Walter Brueggemann. Winona, Minn. : St. Mary's College Press, c1977. 155 p. ; 21 cm. [BS511.2.B78] 76-29883 ISBN 0-88489-087-2 pbk. : 3.95
1. Bible—Criticism, interpretation, etc. I. Title.

BRUNS, J Edgar, 1923- 220.6
Hear His voice today; a guide to the content and comprehension of the Bible. New York, P. J. Kenedy [1963] 207 p. 22 cm. Includes bibliography. [BS475.2.B7] 63-11353
1. Bible — Introductions. I. Title.

BRUNS, J. Edgar, 1923- 220.6
Hear His voice today; a guide to the content and comprehension of the Bible. New York, Kenedy [c.1963] 207p. 22cm. Bibl. 63-11353 4.50
1. Bible—Introductions. I. Title.

BUNCH, Taylor Grant. 220.6
Bible paradoxes. Mountain View, Calif., Pacific Press Pub. Association [1953] 120p. 21cm. [BS537.B84] 53-6431
1. Bible—Language, style. 2. Paradoxes. I. Title.

BUTLER, Basil Christopher 220.6
The church and the Bible. Baltimore, Helicon Press [c.1960] 111p. Bibl. 60-11477 2.95 bds.,
1. Bible—Study—Catholic Church. I. Title.

CARTHEDGE, Samuel Antoine, 1903- 220.6
The Bible: God's word to man. Nashville, Broadman [1967, c.1961] 142p. 19cm. [BS475.2.C27] 1.50 pap.,
1. Bible—Introduction. I. Title.

CARTLEDGE, Samuel Antoine, 1903.- 220.6
The Bible: God's word to man. Philadelphia, Westminster Pr. [c.1961] 143p. 61-10286 3.00
I. Title.

CASTELOT, John J 220.6
Meet the Bible. Baltimore, Helicon Pres, 1960-63. 3 v. illus., maps. 23 cm. Includes bibliography. [BS475.2.c3] 60-15634
1. Bible — Introductions. I. Title.

CASTELOT, John J. 220.6
Meet the Bible! Baltimore, Helicon [c.]1961. 140p. illus. Bibl. 60-15634 3.95
1. Bible—Introductions. I. Title.

CASTELOT, John J. 220.6
Meet the Bible! The New Testament [v.3] Baltimore, Helicon [dist. New York, Taplinger, c.]1963. 240p. maps. 22cm. 4.95
1. Bible—Introduction. I. Title.

CENTRE de pastorale liturgique, Strasbourg. 220.6
The liturgy and the Word of God. [Papers given at the Third National Congress] Collegeville, Minn., Liturgical Press [c1959] xv, 183p. 24cm. 'First published under the title: Parole de dieu et liturgie, Lex orandl series, Ed. du Cerf.' Bibliographical footnotes. [BS538.3.C413] 60-4880
1. Bible—Liturgical use. 2. Catholic Church. Liturgy and ritual. I. Title.

CEVETELLO, Joseph F X 220.6
Getting to know the Bible. New York, Society of St. Paul [1957] 224p. 21cm. Includes bibliography. [BS475.C35] 57-12244
1. Bible—Introductions. I. Title.

THE Channel : 220.6
communication for Biblical, theological, and related studies. Washington : [General Conference of Seventh-Day Adventists], 1976. 56 p. ; 28 cm. Contents.Contents.—Abstracts : Ford, D. A rhetorical study of certain Pauline addresses. Maxwell, D. M. The significance of the Parousia in the theology of Paul. Butler, J. Adventism and the American experience. Ford, D. The abomination of eschatology in Biblical eschatology.—Papers: Baldwin, D. D. SDA presuppositions to Bibliocal studies, a call for presupposition research. Johnsson, W. G. SDA presuppositions to Biblical studies. Edwards, R. D. Tithing in the Middle Ages. Includes bibliographical references. [BS540.C52] 77-356447
1. Seventh-Day Adventists—Doctrinal and controversial works—Address, essays, lectures. 2. Bible—Criticism, interpretation, etc.—Addresses, essays, lectures. I. Seventh-Day Adventists. General Conference.

CHARLIER, Celestin. 220.6
The Christian approach to the Bible (La lecture Chretienne de la Bible) Translated from the French by Hubert J. Richards and Brendan Peters. Pref. by John M. T. Barton. New York, Paulist Press [1967] 298 p. 19 cm. (Deus books) [[BS475.2]] 67-7384
1. Bible — Introductions. Title I. Title.

CHARLIER, Celestin. 220.6
The Christian approach to the Bible (La lecture chretienne de la Bible) Translated from the French by Hubert J. Richards and Brendan Peters. Pref. by John M. T. Barton. Westminster, Md., Newman Press [1958] 298p. 22cm. [BS475.C383] 58-2674
1. Bible—Introductions. I. Title.

CHARLIER, Celestin. 220.6
The Christian approach to the Bible (La lecture Chretienne de la Bible) Translated from the French by Hubert J. Richards and Brendan Peters. Pref. by John M. T. Barton. New York, Paulist Press [1967] 298 p. 19 cm. (Deus books) [BS475.2] 67-7384
1. Bible—Introductions. I. Title.

CHARLIER, Celestin Dom 220.6
The Christian approach to the Bible (La Lecture chretienne de la Bible) Tr. from French by Hubert J. Richards, Brendan Peters. Pref. by John M. T. Barton. Glen Rock, N.J. Paulist [1967] 298p. 18cm. (Deus bks.) [BS475.C383] 1.45 pap.,
1. Bible—Introductions. I. Title.

CHICHESTER, James, 1918- 220.6
Thread of history; a nondenominational interpretation of the Bible. [1st ed.] New York, Exposition Press [1969] 156 p. 22 cm. [BS511.2.C48] 73-98953
1. Bible—Criticism, interpretation, etc. I. Title.

CHILDS, Brevard S. 220.6
Myth and reality in the Old Testament. Naperville, Ill., A. R. Allenson [1960] 112p. (bibl. footnotes) 22cm. (Studies in Biblical theology, no. 27) 60-1911 2.00 pap.,
1. Demythologization. 2. Bible. O. T.—Criticism, interpretation, etc. I. Title.

CLARK, Georgia T. 220.6
The quest. New York, Vantage Press [c.1960] 140p. 22cm. 3.00 bds.,
I. Title.

COLSON, Howard P., 1910- 220.6
I recommend the Bible / Howard P. Colson. Nashville, Tenn. : Broadman Press, c1976. iv, 156 p. ; 21 cm. [BS511.2.C64] 76-39714 ISBN 0-8054-1942-X : 4.95
1. Bible—Criticism, interpretation, etc. I. Title.

CORBON, Jean, 1924- 220.6
Path to freedom; Christian experiences and the Bible. Translated by Violet Nevile. New York, Sheed and Ward [1969] viii, 246 p. 22 cm. Translation of L'experience Chretienne dans la Bible. [BX2350.2.C6313] 69-16993 5.00
1. Bible—Devotional literature. 2. Christian life—Catholic authors. I. Title.

CREAGER, Alfred L. 220.6
Old Testament heritage. Philadelphia, United Church [c.1955, 1962] 111p. 19cm. (Pilgrim bk.) 62-19784 1.45 pap.,
1. Bible, O. T.—Introductions. I. Title.

CROWELL, Norton B 220.6
The triple soul; Browning's theory of knowledge. [1st ed. Albuquerque] University of New Mexico Press [1963] xiv, 235 p. 24 cm. Bibliography: p. 230-232. [PR4242.P4C7] 63-21031
1. Browning, Robert, 1812-1889. I. Title.

DANIEL-ROPS, Henri, 1901- 220.6
[Realname:HenryJulesCharlesPetlot]
What is the Bible? Tr. from French by J. R. Foster. Garden City, N.Y., Doubleday [1968,c.1958] c.1958] 153p. 18cm. (Image bks., D250) Bibl. .95 pap.,
1. Bible—Introduction. I. Title.

DAUGHERTY, Kathryn 220.6
The time of the end; the story of mankind and his destiny. New York, Exposition [c.1962] 82p. 21cm. 3.00
I. Title.

DAVIDSON, Robert 220.6
The Bible speaks. New York, Crowell [1959] 258p. 21cm. 60-6244 3.95 bds.,
1. Bible—Theology. I. Title.

DAVIES, William David, 1911- ed. 220.6
The background of the New Testament and its eschatology, ed. by W. D. Davies, D. Daube in honour of Charles Harold Dodd [New York] Cambridge, 1964. xviii, 554p. port. 24cm. Most of the essays are in English, some in German, some in French. Bibl. 11.50
1. Dodd, Charles Harold, 1884- 2. Bible. N.T.—Addresses, essays, lectures. 3. Eschatology—Biblical teaching. I. Daube, David, joint ed. II. Title.

DEFEHR, J Jennings. 220.6
Do both Bible Testaments harmonize Nashville, Southern Pub. Association [1964] 160 p. front. 18 cm. [BS2387.D44] 63-17058
1. Bible. N.T. — Relation to O.T. I. Title.

DEITZ, Reginald W. 220.6
What the Bible can mean for you. Philadelphia, Muhlenberg [c.1962] 52p. (Fortress bk.) 62-8206 1.00 bds.,
1. Bible—Criticism, interpretation, etc.—Hist. 2. Bible—Appreciation. I. Title.

*DEKOSTER, Lester. 220.6
How to read the Bible. Grand Rapids, Baker Book House, [1975] 83 p. 18 cm. (Direction books) [BS617] ISBN 0-8010-2836-1 1.25 (pbk.)
1. Bible—Reading. I. Title.

DENTAN, Robert Claude, 1907- 220.6
The design of the Scriptures; a first reader in Biblical theology. New York, Seabury [1965, c.1961] 276p. 21cm. (SP20) Bibl. [BS543.D43] 1.95 pap.,
1. Bible—Theology. I. Title.

DENTAN, Robert Claude, 1907- 220.6
The design of the Scriptures; a first reader in Biblical theology. [1st ed.] New York, McGraw-Hill [1961] 276 p. 21 cm. Includes bibliography. [BS543.D43] 60-15254
1. Bible—Theology. I. Title.

DEWOLF, Lotan Harold, 1905- 220.6
The enduring message of the Bible, by L. Harold DeWolf. Rev. ed. Richmond, John Knox Press [1965] 128 p. 21 cm. (Aletheia paperbacks) [BR121.2.D4] 65-11500
I. Title.

DE WOLF, Lotan Harold, 1905- 220.6
The enduring message of the Bible. Rev. ed. Richmond, Va., Knox [c.1965] 128p. 21cm. Orig. pub. in 1960 by Harper. (Aletheia paperbacks) [BR121.2.D4] 65-11500 1.45 pap.,
1. Christianity—20th cent. I. Title.

DODSON, Samuel Kendrick 220.6
From darkness to light; a study of the spiritual meanings of light and darkness as revealed in God's Word to mankind. New York, Greenwich Book Publishers [1960, c.1959] 110p. (bibl. notes) 22cm. 59-15649 2.75
1. Light and darkness (in religion, folk-lore, etc.) 2. Bible—Theology. I. Title.

DOUGHERTY, John J. 220.6
Searching the Scriptures [rev. ed.] Garden City, N.Y., Doubleday [c.1959, 1963] 159p. 18cm. (Image bk. D151) Bibl. .75 pap.,
1. Bible—Introductions. I. Title.

DOWNING, Barry H., 1938- 220.6
The Bible and flying saucers, by Barry H. Downing [1st ed.] Philadelphia, Lippincott [1968] 221 p. 21 cm. Includes bibliographical references. [TL789.D68] 68-14129
1. Bible—Criticism, interpretation, etc. 2. Flying saucers. I. Title.

DRAKE, Walter Raymond. 220.6
Gods and spacemen of the ancient past / by W. Raymond Drake. New York : New American Library, 1974. 266 p. ; 18 cm. (A Signet book) Includes bibliographical references and index. [CB156.D7] 74-193285 pbk. : 1.50
1. Bible—Miscellanea. 2. Interplanetary voyages. 3. History, Ancient. I. Title.

DRINKWATER, Francis Harold, 1886- 220.6
Talks to teen-agers. Westminster, Md., Newman Press, 1954. 109p. 19cm. [BX2355.D7] 54-39029
1. Conduct of life. 2. Youth-Religious life. 3. Christian life—Catholic authors. I. Title.

EASON, Joshua Lawrence, 1887- 220.6
The new Bible survey, an introduction to the reading and study of the Bible. Grand Rapids, Zondervan Pub. House [1963] 544 p. illus., maps, facsims. 23 cm. Bibliography: p. 520-538. [BS475.2E2] 63-9314
1. Bible—Introductions. I. Title.

ELLER, Meredith Freeman, 1912- 220.6
The beginnings of the Christian religion; a guide to the history and literature of Judaism and Christianity. College & Univ. Pr. [dist. New York, Twayne, 1962, c.1958] 518p. 21cm. (P1) Bibl. 3.45 pap.,
1. Bible—Introductions. 2. Jews—Hist.—To 70 A.D. 3. Bible. N.T.—History of Biblical events. I. Title.

ERDMAN, Charles Rosenbury, 1866- 220.6
Your Bible and you. [1st ed.] Philadelphia, Winston [1950] vii, 180 p. 22 cm. [BS475.E7] 50-10629
1. Bible—Introductions. I. Title.

ESSAYS on typology 220.6
[by] G.W. H. Lampe [and] K.J.Woollcombe. Naperville, Ill., A. R. Allenson [1957] 80p. 22cm. (Studies in Biblical theology, no.22) Bibliographical footnotes. [BS478.E75] 57-3248
1. Typology (Theology) I. Lampe, Geoffrey William Hugo. II. Woollcombe, K. J. III. Series.
Contents omitted.

FARRAR, Frederic William, 1831-1903. 220.6
History of interpretation. Grand Rapids, Mich., Baker Bk. House, 1961 553p. (Bampton lectures, 1885) Bibl. 61-10004 6.95
1. Bible—Criticism, interpretation, etc.—Hist. I. Title.

FAW, Chalmer Ernest, 1910- 220.6
A guide to Biblical preaching. Nashville, Broadman [c.1962] 198p. 22cm. 62-11389 3.50 bds.,
1. Bible—Homiletical use. I. Title. II. Title: Biblical preaching.

FIELD, Margaret Joyce. 220.6
Angels and ministers of grace; an ethno-psychiatrist's contribution to Biblical criticism [by] M. J. Field. [1st American ed.] New York, Hill and Wang [1972, c1971] xv, 135 p. 22 cm. Includes bibliographical references. [BS1199.A5F5 1972] 71-185426 ISBN 0-8090-2664-3 5.95
1. Bible. O.T.—Psychology. 2. Angels—Biblical teaching. 3. Prophets. I. Title.

FISHER, Clay C. 220.6
New concept of Bible mysteries and eschatologies, by Clay C. Fisher. [Chicago, Adams Press, 1969] vii, 122 p. 22 cm. [BS511.2.F57] 76-96074 2.50
1. Bible—Criticism, interpretation, etc. 2. Eschatology—Biblical teaching. I. Title.

FLANAGAN, Neal M 220.6
Salvation history; an introduction to Biblical theology [by] Neal M. Flanagan. New York,

Sheed and Ward [1964] viii, 245 p. illus., maps. 22 cm. [BS543.F55] 64-19902
1. Bible — Theology. I. Title.

FLANAGAN, Neal M. 220.6
Salvation history; an introduction to Biblical theology. New York, Sheed [c.1964] viii, 245p. illus., maps. 22cm. 64-19902 5.00
1. Bible—Theology. I. Title.

FLANERY, E. B. 220.6
The crack in the Bible, by E. B. Flanery. [1st ed.] Port Washington, N.Y., Ashley Books [1973] vii, 97 p. 22 cm. [BS533.F54] 73-76536 ISBN 0-87949-011-X 5.95
1. Bible—Criticism, interpretation, etc. 2. Christianity—Controversial literature. I. Title.

FOREMAN, Lawton Durant, 1913- 220.6
The Bible in eight ages. 3d ed., rev. Little Rock, Ark.,Seminary Press [1952] 174p. illus. 23cm. [BT155.F58 1952] 52-67718
1. Covenants (Theology) I. Title.

FOWLER, David C., 1921- 220.6
The Bible in early English literature / by David C. Fowler. Seattle : University of Washington Press, c1976. p. cm. Includes index. Bibliography: p. [BS538.7.F68] 76-7786 ISBN 0-295-95438-8 : 14.95
1. Higden, Ranulph, d. 1364. Polychronicon. 2. Bible—Influence—History. 3. Bible—Criticism, interpretation, etc.—History—Middle Ages, 600-1500. 4. Bible. English—Versions. 5. Cursor mundi. 6. Bible in literature. I. Title.

FOX, Emmet. 220.6
Diagrams for living; the Bible unveiled. [1st ed.] New York, Harper & Row [1968] 192 p. 22 cm. [BS511.2.F68] 69-10475 4.95
1. Bible—Criticism, interpretation, etc. 2. Conduct of life. I. Title.

FRENCH, Holland 220.6
Concerning the Book with the greatest plan: guide and information to enable the reader better to comprehend the wonder of God's Word to the individual man. [New York, Salvation Army Supplies, Print. and Pub. Dept., 1963] 158p. 23cm. (Salvation Army. Instructional ser., no. 1) Cover title: The greatest plan. Bibl. 63-18573 2.50
1. Bible—Introductions. I. Title. II. Title: The greatest plan.

FRIEDER, Emma. 220.6
Altar fires; essays in sacred literature. [1st ed.] New York, Exposition Press [1957] 232p. 21cm. (A Testament book) Includes bibliography. [BS475.F65] 56-12674
1. Bible—Introductions. I. Title.

FRIEDER, Emma. 220.6
Altar fires; essays in sacred literature. 3d rev. ed. New York, Hurst Pub. Co. [1971] 232 p. 22 cm. Bibliography: p. [229]-232. [BS475.2.F74 1971] 75-26309 5.00
1. Bible—Introductions. I. Title.

FRIEDER, Emma. 220.6
Altar fires; essays in sacred literature. 2d, rev. ed. New York, Exposition Press [1969] 232 p. 22 cm. (An Exposition-testament book) Bibliography: p. [229]-232. [BS475.2.F74 1969] 68-24887 5.00
1. Bible—Introductions. I. Title.

GEORGE, Augustin 220.6
Scripture study series [v.2&5] Notre Dame, Ind., Fides [c.1964] 125;195p. 19cm. Bibl. [BS475.2G4] 64-23514 v.2, pap., 1.25; v.5, pap., 1.95
1. Bible—Introductions. 2. Bible—Study. I. Title.
Contents omitted.

GEORGE, Augustin 220.6
Scripture study series [no.3] Notre Dame, Ind., Fides, c.1964] 1v. (122p.) 19cm. Contents.3. The gospel of Paul; study guide for the letters of St. Paul. Tr. [from French] by Edward Harper. Bibl. 64-23514 1.25 pap.,
1. Bible—Introductions. 2. Bible—Study. I. Title.

GOD'S wisdom and the Holy 220.6
Bible / [Leon Gutterman, editor and publisher ; Betty-Jane Lang, editorial director]. Beverly Hills, Calif. : Gutterman, c1976. 159 p. : ill. ; 34 cm. Cover title. [BS511.2.G62] 77-351276
1. Bible—Criticism, interpretation, etc. I. Gutterman, Leon. II. Lang, Betty-Jane.

**GOD'S word and my faith;* 220.6
students bk. Prepd. for the Bd. of Parish *educ., and the Bd. of Pubn. of the Amer. Lutheran Church. Minneapolis, Augsburg [1966] 176p. illus. (pt. col.) 22cm. (Core curriculum, adult educ.) 2.00; 2.00 pap., teacher's guide, pap.,
1. Bible — Introduction. 2. Bible study.

GORDIS, Robert, 1908- 220.6
The Biblical text in the making; a study of the kethib-qere. Augm. ed., with a prolegomenon. [New York] Ktav Pub. House, 1971 [i.e. 1972] lvi, 219 p. 24 cm. Includes bibliographical references. [BS718.G6 1972] 70-149606 ISBN 0-87068-157-5 14.95
1. Bible. O.T.—Criticism, Textual. 2. Bible. Manuscripts, Hebrew. O.T. 3. Masorah. I. Title.

GRAHAM, Lloyd. 220.6
Deceptions and myths of the Bible / by Lloyd Graham. Secaucus, N.J. : University Books, c1975. vii, 484 p. ; 24 cm. Includes index. [BS533.G68 1975] 74-28543 ISBN 0-8216-0251-9 : 14.95
1. Bible—Criticism, interpretation, etc. 2. Christianity—Controversial literature. I. Title.

GRAHAM, Lloyd. 220.6
Deceptions and myths of the Bible / by Lloyd Graham. Secaucus, N.J. : University Books, c1975. vii, 484 p. ; 24 cm. Includes index. [BS533.G68 1975] 74-28543 ISBN 0-8216-0251-9 : 14.95
1. Bible—Criticism, interpretation, etc. 2. Christianity—Controversial literature. I. Title.

GRANT, Robert McQueen, 1917- 220.6
Perspectives on Scripture and tradition : essays / by Robert M. Grant, Robert E. McNally, George H. Tavard ; edited by Joseph F. Kelly. Notre Dame, Ind. : Fides Publishers, c1976. xi, 129 p. ; 20 cm. Contents.Contents.—Grant, R. M. The creation of the Christian tradition. From tradition to Scripture and back.—McNally, R. E. Christian tradition and the early Middle Ages. Tradition at the beginning of the Reformation.—Tavard, G. H. Tradition in theology: A problematic approach. A methodological approach. Includes bibliographical references and index. [BT89.G68] 76-2497 ISBN 0-8190-0617-3 pbk. : 3.95
1. Bible and tradition—Addresses, essays, lectures. I. McNally, Robert E. II. Tavard, Georges Henri, 1922- III. Title.
Contents omitted

*GREGG, Darrell L., 1903- 220.6
The miracle of the Bible, [by] Darrell L. Gregg [1st ed.] New York, Vantage Press [1973] 227 p. 21 cm. [BS538] ISBN 0-533-00541-8 6.95
1. Bible—History and criticism. I. Title.

GREGORY, Dick. 220.6
Dick Gregory's Bible tales, with commentary / by Dick Gregory ; edited by James R. McGraw. New York : Stein and Day, [1974] 187 p. ; 22 cm. [BS483.5.G7 1974] 73-91859 ISBN 0-8128-1682-X : 6.95
1. Bible—Meditations. I. Title. II. Title: Bible tales.

GRELOT, Pierre, 1917- 220.6
Introduction to the Bible. Translated by G. Patrick Campbell. [New York] Herder and Herder [1967] 436 p. maps. 22 cm. A revision of the 2d French ed., published under title: Introduction aux Livres saints. Includes bibliographies. [BS635.2.G713] 66-22603
1. Bible—History of Biblical events. 2. Bible—Introductions. I. Title.

GROLLENBERG, Lucas Hendricus, 1916- 220.6
Bible study for the 21st century / Lucas Grollenberg ; translated from the 3d rev. ed. by John E. Steely. [Wilmington, N.C.] : Consortium, 1977,c1976. 179 p. ; 23 cm. Translation of Modern Bijbellezen. Includes bibliographical references. [BS500.G7613] 76-19773 ISBN 0-8434-0605-4 : 12.00
1. Bible—Criticism, interpretation, etc.—History. I. Title.

GROLLENBERG, Lucas Hendricus, 1916- 220.6
Bible study for the 21st century / Lucas Grollenberg ; translated from the 3d rev. ed. by John E. Steely. [Wilmington, N.C.] : Consortium, 1977,c1976. 179 p. ; 23 cm. Translation of Modern Bijbellezen. Includes bibliographical references. [BS500.G7613] 76-19773 ISBN 0-8434-0605-4 : 12.00
1. Bible—Criticism, interpretation, etc.—History. I. Title.

GROLLENBERG, Lucas Hendricus, 1916- 220.6
A new look at an old book, by Luke H. Grollenberg. Translated by Richard Rutherford. Paramus, N.J., Newman Press [1969] viii, 408 p. illus. 22 cm. Translation of Nieuwe kijk op het oude boek. [BS512.2.G713] 73-92042 f16.95
1. Bible—Criticism, interpretation, etc. I. Title.

GROLLENBERG, Lucas Henricus, 1916- 220.6
Interpreting the Bible, by Luke H. Grollenberg. Translated by Jeanne C. Schoffelen Nooijne and Richard Rutherford. New York, Paulist Press [1968] v, 138 p. 18 cm. (Deus books) Translation of Inleiding tot de Bijbel. [BS475.2.G713] 68-20849
1. Bible—Introductions. 2. Bible—Use. I. Title.

GUILLET, Jacques. 220.6
Themes of the Bible. Translated by Albert J. LaMothe, Jr. Notre Dame, Ind., Fides Publishers Association [c1960] 279p. 23cm. Includes bibliography. [BS2387.G813] 61-9867
1. Bible, N. T.—Relation to O. T. 2. Bible—Criticism, interpretation, etc. I. Title.

*GULAS, William, ed. 220.6
Exploring the Bible. Discussion questions and Scriptural readings by Evan Netzel. Pulaski. Wis., Franciscan Pubs. [c.1966] 64p. 19cm. .35 pap.,
I. Title.

HALDEMAN, Isaac Massey, 1845-1933 220.6
Bible expositions: v.1. Complete, unabridged ed. Grand Rapids, Mich., Baker Bk. 1964. 652p. 21cm. 64-5281 4.50
1. Bible, O. T.—Sermons. 2. Sermons, American. 3. Baptists—Sermons. I. Title.

HAMMER, Paul L. 220.6
Biblical witness and the world; guide for adult group study [by] Paul L. Hammer [and] Arthur L. Merrill. Boston, United Church Press [1967] xv, 141 p. illus. 21 cm. Includes bibliographical references. [BS592.H3] 67-19498
1. Bible—Study—Outlines, syllabi, etc. I. Merrill, Arthur L., joint author. II. Title.

HANSON, Richard Patrick Crosland. 220.6
Allegory and event; a study of the sources and significance of Origen's interpretation of scripture. Richmond, John Knox Press [1959] 400p. 23cm. Bibliography: p. 376-381. [BS501.O7H3] 58-11492
1. Bible—Criticism. interpretation, etc.— Hist. 2. Origenes. 3. Bible—Hermeneutics. 4. Allegory. I. Title.

HARRISVILLE, Roy A 220.6
His hidden grace; an essay on Biblical criticism [by] Roy A. Harrisville. New York, Abingdon Press [1965] 95 p. 20 cm. Bibliographical references included in "Notes" (p. 93-95) [BS476.H28] 65-14719
1. Bible — Hermeneutics. I. Title.

HARRISVILLE, Roy A. 220.6
His hidden grace; an essay on Biblical criticism. Nashville, Abingdon [c.]1965. 95p. 20cm. Bibl. [BS476.H28] 65-14719 2.00 bds.,
1. Bible—Hermeneutics. I. Title.

HAURET, Charles. 220.6
Introduction to Sacred Scripture. Translated by Dennis Pardee. De Pere, Wis., St. Norbert Abbey Press, 1969. 226 p. 20 cm. Translation of Initiation a l'Ecriture Sainte. Bibliography: p. [207]-212. [BS475.2.H3313] 76-87811 3.95
1. Bible—Introductions. I. Title.

HAYDEN, Eric W. 220.6
Preaching through the Bible: v.2. Pref by Wilbur M. Smith. Grand Rapids, Mich., Zondervan [1967] v. 23cm. 64-11946 5.95 bds.,
1. Bible—SRmons. 2. Baptists—Sermons. 3. Sermons—English. I. Title.

HAYDEN, Eric W. 220.6
Preaching through the Bible. Foreword by J. Sidlow Baxter. Grand Rapids, Mich., Zondervan [c.1964] 283p. 23cm. 64-11946 3.95
1. Bible—Sermons. 2. Baptists—Sermons. 3. Sermons. English. I. Title.

HEFFERNAN, Virginia Mary. 220.6
The Bible for everyone. Milwaukee, Bruce Pub. Co. [1968, c1969] xii, 180 p. 24 cm. [BS475.2.H4] 68-54986 4.95
1. Bible—Introductions. I. Title.

HEFLEY, James C. 220.6
What's so great about the Bible [by] James C. Hefley. Rev. and expanded ed. Elgin, Ill., D. C. Cook Pub. Co. [1973] 128 p. illus. 18 cm. Bibliography: p. 126-127. [BS530.H44 1973] 73-168132 ISBN 0-912692-06-5 1.25 (pbk.)
1. Bible—Criticism, interpretation, etc. I. Title.

HOBBY, Alvin 220.6
Cycle of the ages. New York, Vantage Press [c.1961] 176p. 3.00 bds.,
1. Bible—Study& interpretation. I. Title.

HOFMANN, Johann Christian Konrad von, 1810-1877. 220.6
Interpreting the Bible. Translated from the German by Christian Preus. Minneapolis, Augsburg Pub. House [1959] xviii, 236p. 22cm. [BS476.H613] 59-12029
1. Bible—Hermeneutics. I. Title.

THE Human reality of Sacred 220.6
Scripture. New York, Paulist Press [c1965] viii, 212 p. 24 cm. (Concilium theology in the age of renewal: Scripture, v. 10) Bibliographical footnotes. [BS540.H8] 65-28869
1. Bible—Addresses, essays, lectures. I. Series: Concilium theology in the age of renewal, v. 10

HUMAN reality of Sacred 220.6
Scripture (The) New York, Paulist Pr. [c.1965] viii, 121p. 24cm. (Concilium theology in the age of renewal: Scripture, v. 10) Bibl. [BS540.H8] 65-28869 4.50
1. Bible—Addresses, essays, lectures. I. Series: Concillum theology in the age of renewal, v. 10

HUNT, Ignatius, 1920- 220.6
Understanding the Bible. New York, Sheed and Ward [1962] 207p. 21cm. [BS511.2.H8] 62-919
1. Bible— Criticism, interpretation, etc. I. Title.

INTERPRETING God's word 220.6
today [by] Marinus J. Arntzen [and others] Edited by Simon Kistemaker. Grand Rapids, Baker Book House [1970] 313 p. 23 cm. Bibliography: p. 291-301. [BS540.I65] 78-101612 6.95
1. Bible—Criticism, interpretation, etc.—Addresses, essays, lectures. I. Arntzen, Marinus J. II. Kistemaker, Simon, ed.

*JANSEN, John F. 220.'6
Biblical images : windows to God's way in our world / John F. Jansen. New York : Hawthorn Books, Inc., 1976c1974. xiii, 110o, ; 21 cm. [BS511.2] 75-31370 ISBN 0-8015-0613-1 pbk. : 3.50
1. Bible-Criticism, interpretation, etc. I. Title.

JARVIS, Frank Washington, 1939- 220.6
Prophets, poets, priests, and kings; the Old Testament story [by] F. Washington Jarvis. New York, Seabury Press [1974] x, 292 p. maps. 22 cm. "A Crossroad book." Bibliography: p. [291]-292. [BS1171.2.J37] 73-17900 ISBN 0-8164-2089-0 6.95 3.95 (pbk.)
1. Bible. O.T.—Criticism, interpretation, etc. I. Title.

JOCZ, Jakob 220.6
The spiritual history of Israel. London, Eyre & Spottiswoode, [dist. Mystic, Conn., Verry, 1965, c.1961] 260p. 23cm. Bibl. [BS635.2.J57] 63-352 5.00
1. Bible—Criticism, interpretation, etc. 2. Christianty and other religious—Judaism I. Title.

*JOHANSSON, Catherine 220.6
Concepts of freedom in the Old Testament. New York, Vantage [c.1965] 92p. 21cm. 2.50 bds.,
I. Title.

JOHNSON, Douglas 220.6
The Christian and his Bible. [2d ed.] Grand Rapids, Mich., Eerdmans [1960] 158p. 18cm. (Eerdmans pocket editions) Bibl. 61-1355 1.25 pap.,
1. Bible—Criticism, interpretation, etc. I. Title.

KEACH, Benjamin, 1640-1704. 220.6
Preaching from the types and metaphors of the Bible. Foreword by Herbert Lockyer. Grand Rapids, Mich., Kregel Publications [1972] xxviii, 1007 p. 25 cm. (Kregel reprint library) Reprint of the 1855 ed., published under title: Tropologia; a key to open Scripture metaphors, together with types of the Old Testament. [BS537.K4 1972] 78-165059 ISBN 0-8254-3008-9 12.95
1. Bible—Language, style. 2. Bible—Homiletical use. 3. Metaphor. I. Title.

KECK, Leander E. 220.6
Taking the Bible seriously; an invitation to think theologically. New York, Association [c.1962] 185p. 20cm. (Haddam house bk.) Bibl. 62-16872 3.75
1. Bible—Study. I. Title.

KEMPIN, Albert J 1900- 220.6
Twelve great chapters from the Book of Life. Anderson, Ind., Warner Press [1955] 144p. 20cm. [BS538.K38] 55-36414
1. Bible—Appreciation. I. Title.

KERNS, H. J. 220.6
Secrets of wisdom; the mystery of His sacred name revealed. New York, Exposition [c.1963] 105p. 21cm. 3.00
I. Title.

KIRVAN, John J. 220.6
The restless believers, by John J. Kirvan. Glen Rock, N.J., Paulist Press [1966] ix, 109 p. 18 cm. (Deus books) [BX2373.S8K5] 66-29818
1. Students—Religious life. 2. Pastoral theology—Catholic Church. I. Title.

KNOCH, Adolf E. 220.6
The mystery of the Gospel [by] A. E. Knoch. Saugus, Ca[lif.] Concordant Pub. Concern [1969] 301 p. 20 cm. [BS534.K63] 78-6087
1. Bible—Criticism, interpretation, etc. I. Title.

KOENIG, Robert E 220.6
The use of the Bible with adults. Philadelphia, Published for the Cooperative Publication Association [by] Christian Education Press [1959] 183p. 20cm. Includes bibliography. [BS600.20K6] 59-13115
1. Bible—Study. 2. Bible.—Use. I. Title.

KUITERT, Harminus Martinus. 220.6
Do you understand what you read? On understanding and interpreting the Bible [by] H. M. Kuitert. Translated by Lewis B. Smedes. Grand Rapids, Eerdmans [1970] 111 p. 22 cm. Translation of Verstaat gij wat gij leest? [BS511.2.K813] 77-103448 1.95
1. Bible—Criticism, interpretation, etc. I. Title.

LAMBERT, Herbert H., 1929- 220.6
Getting inside the Bible / by Herbert H. Lambert. Saint Louis : Bethany Press, c1976. 144 p. : ill. ; 22 cm. Includes bibliographical references. [BS475.2.L27] 76-10325 ISBN 0-8272-1218-6 pbk. : 4.95
1. Bible—Introductions. I. Title.

LANDIS, Benson Young, 1897- 220.6
An outline of the Bible, book by book. New York, Barnes & Noble [1963] 186p. illus. 21cm. ,)(Everday handbks. 263) 63-18448 2.95; 1.25 pap.,
1. Bible—Introductions. I. Title.

LEARY, William. 220.6
The hidden Bible. New York, Publications [1952] 112p. 26cm. [BS534.L4] 53-16278
1. Bible—Miscellanea. I. Title.

*LESLIE, John 220.6
The Bible comes alive. New York, Exposition [c.1965] 167p. 21cm. 3.50
I. Title.

LEVIE, Jean 220.6
The Bible, word of God in words of men. [English version by S. H. Treman] New York, Kenedy [1962] 323p. Bibl. 61-14295 7.50
1. Bible—Criticism, interpretation, etc.—Hist. I. Title.

THE Liberating word : 220.6
a guide to nonsexist interpretation of the Bible / edited by Letty M. Russell, in cooperation with the Task Force on Sexism in the Bible, Division of Education and Ministry, National Council of the Churches of Christ in the U.S.A. Philadelphia : Westminster Press, c1976. p. cm. Bibliography: p. [BS680.S5L5] 76-18689 ISBN 0-664-24751-2 pbk. : 3.95
1. Bible—Criticism, interpretation, etc.—Addresses, essays, lectures. 2. Sex (Theology)—Biblical teaching—Addresses, essays, lectures. 3. Woman (Theology)—Biblical teaching—Addresses, essays, lectures. I. Russell, Letty M. II. National Council of the Churches of Christ in the United States of America. Task Force on Sexism in the Bible.

*LIEVSAY, R. J. 220.6
The higher Biblical criticism: an analysis and a critique; a brief anthology presenting the weaknesses in the criteria of the literary critics and presenting evidences supporting the orthodox Judeo-Christian position. [Arnold, Mo., Shield Pr., 1973] 25 p. 22 cm. Cover title. Includes bibliography. 0.25 (pbk.)
1. Bible—Criticism, interpretation, etc. I. Title.
Publisher's address: 2806 Rosewood Drive, Arnold, MO 63010.

LIMENTANI, Uberto, ed. 220.6
The mind of Dante, Edited by U. Limentani. Cambrige Eng., University Press, 1965. vii, 199 p. 21 cm. Lectures delivered at the University of Cambridge in 1965 in observance of the seventh centenary of Dante's birth. Bibliographical footnotes. [PQ4390.L65] 65-21790
1. Dante Alighieri, 1265-1321. I. Cambridge. University. II. Title.
Contents omitted

LINDARS, Barnabas 220.6
[Frederick Chevallier Lindars]
New Testament apologetic; the doctrinal significance of the Old Testament quotations. Philadelphia, Westminster Pr. [1962, c.1961] 303p. Bibl. 62-7262 6.00
1. Bible, O. T.—Quotations in the N. T. 2. Apologetics—Early church. I. Title.

LINK, Mark J 220.6
Christ teaches us today. Chicago, Loyola University Press [1964] xi, 277 p. illus. 24 cm. [BX930.L485] 64-2920
1. Religious education — Text-books for young people — Catholic. I. Title.

LINK, Mark J. 220.6
Christ teaches us today. Chicago, Loyola Univ. Pr. [c.1964] xi, 277p. illus. 24cm. 64-2920 3.00
1. Religious education—Text books for young people Catholic. I. Title.

*LOCKYER, Herbert. 220.6
Selected scripture summaries. Grand Rapids, Baker Book House, [1975] v. 21 cm. Contents: v. 1 "From the whole Bible"; v. 2 "From the new testament". [BV194.R5] ISBN 0-8010-5546-6(vol.1) 3.95 (pbk. ea.)
1. Bible—Criticism, interpretation, etc. I. Title.

LONGSTRETH, Lee 220.6
The seventieth week. New York, Carlton [dist. Comet, c.]1961. 191p. (Reflection bk.) 3.50
I. Title.

LUCAS, Jerry. 220.6
Theomatics : God's best kept secret revealed / Jerry Lucas, Del Washburn. Briarcliff Manor, N.Y. : Stein and Day, c1977. 347 p. ; 24 cm. [BS534.L84] 76-49958 ISBN 0-8128-2181-5 : 8.95
1. Bible—Miscellanea. 2. Numbers in the Bible. I. Washburn, Del, joint author. II. Title.

LUKE, James 220.6
The master's creation. New York, Vantage [c.1962] 119p. Bibl. 2.75
I. Title.

LYNIP, Ryllis (Alexander) 220.6
Goslin, 1901-
Great ideas of the Bible outlined for moderns. With selected passages from The Bible: a new translation by James Moffatt. [1st ed.] New York, Harper [1954-55] 2v. 22cm. [BS543.L9] 53-10929
1. Bible—Theology. I. Bible. English. Selections. 1954. Moffatt. II. Title.

MCCARTY, Doran. 220.6
Rightly dividing the word. Nashville, Broadman Press [1973] 126 p. 20 cm. Includes bibliographical references. [BS511.2.M23] 73-78217 ISBN 0-8054-8120-6
1. Bible—Criticism, interpretation, etc. I. Title.

MCCASHLAND, Selby Vernon, 220.6
1896-
The religion of the Bible. New York, [Apollo Eds. 1968, c.1960] 346p. 22cm. (A172) Bibl. [BS511.2.M25] 2.25 pap.,
1. Bible—Criticism, interpretation, etc. 2. Bible—Theology. I. Title.

MCCASLAND, Selby Vernon, 220.6
1896-
The religion of the Bible. New York, T. Y. Crowell [1968] 346p. 22cm. Bibl. [BS511.2.M25] 60-9158 2.25 pap.,
1. Bible—Criticism, interpretation, etc. 2. Bible—Theology. I. Title.

*MCCLAIN, Alva J. 220.6
Law and grace. Chicago, Moody [1967. c.1954] 80p. 18cm. (Compact bks., no. 60) .29 pap.,
I. Title.

MCCLELLAN, Albert 220.6
Share the word now. Nashville, Broadman Press [1973] 128 p. 21 cm. [BS511.2.M253] 72-94402 ISBN 0-8054-8415-9 1.50 (pbk.)
1. Bible—Criticism, interpretation, etc. 2. Evangelistic work. 3. Church renewal. I. Title.

MCGOWAN, H. C. 220.6
God's garden of segregation. New York, Vantage Press [c.1961] 94p. illus. 2.50 bds.,
1. Bible—Study and interpretation. I. Title.

MCKENZIE, John L., ed. 220.6
The Bible in current Catholic thought. [New York] Herder & Herder [1963, c.1962] xiii, 247p. illus. 23cm. (Saint Mary's theology studies, 1) Pub. in honor of Michael J. Gruenthaner. Bibl. 62-21949 6.50
1. Gruenthaner, Michael J., 1887-1962. 2. Bible.—Addresses, essays, lectures. I. Title. II. Series.

MCKENZIE, John L. 220.6
Mastering the meaning of the Bible. Wilkes-Barre, Barre, Dimension Bks. [1968,c.1966] 138p. 19cm. [BS540.M37 1966] 66-27469 1.25 pap.,
1. Bible—Addresses, essays, lectures. I. Title.

MCKENZIE, John L. 220.6
Myths and realities: studies in Biblical theology. Milwaukee, Bruce [c.1963] xvi, 285p. 23cm. Bibl. 63-21345 4.75
1. Bible—Theology—Addresses, essays, lectures. I. Title.

MCKENZIE, John L. 220.6
Vital concepts of the Bible, by John L. McKenzie. [1st American ed.] Wilkes-Barre, Pa., Dimension Books [1967] 167 p. 20 cm. Bibliographical footnotes. [BS540.M27] 67-19969
1. Bible—Addresses, essays, lectures. I. Title.

MCKNIGHT, Edgar V. 220.6
Opening the Bible [by] Edgar V. McKnight. Nashville, Broadman [1967] 127p. 20cm. Bibl. [BS475.2.M3] 67-17430 1.50 bds.,
1. Bible—Introductions. I. Title.

MACKY, Peter W. 220.6
The Bible in dialogue with modern man, by Peter W. Macky. [1st ed.] Waco, Tex., Word Books [1970] 219 p. 23 cm. [BS511.2.M28] 74-96288 4.95
1. Bible—Criticism, interpretation, etc. I. Title.

MACPHAIL, James Russell. 220.6
The bright cloud; the Bible in the light of the transfiguration. London, New York, Oxford University Press, 1956 [i. e. 1957] 190p. 19cm. [BS543.M3] 57-475
1. Bible—Theology. I. Title.

MARSH, John, 1904- 220.6
The fulness of time. New York, Harper [c1952] 189p. 23cm. [BR115] 53-12809
1. History—Philosophy. I. Title.

MARTRIT, Minna Louise. 220.6
Bible highpoints: a comprehensive synopsis; things to be remembered in every book of the Bible. King James versin. [Tomball, Tex., J. Randolph, 1956] 170p. 20cm. [BS475.M42] 56-7642
1. Bible—Introductions. I. Title.

MARTY, Martin E ed. 220.6
New directions in Biblical thought. New York, Association Press [1960] 128p. (Bibl. notes) 16cm. (An Association Press reflection book) 60-12721 .50 pap.,
1. Bible—Criticism, interpretation, etc. I. Title.

MATTHEWS, John L. 220.6
A layman looks at the Gods of the Bible [by] John L. Matthews. Philadelphia, Dorrance [1970] x, 193 p. 22 cm. [BS511.2.M36] 75-94251
1. Bible—Criticism, interpretation, etc. 2. Bible—Prophecies. I. Title.

*MEARS, Henrietta C. 220.6
What the Bible is all about. Glendale, Calif., 91205, Gospel Light Pubns. [725 E. Colorado, Box 1591. 1966, c.1953] 675p. map, charts. 20cm. (Regal bks., GL295-1) 2.95 pap.,
I. Title.

MEVES, Christa. 220.6
The Bible answers us with pictures / Christa Meves ; translated by Hal Taussig ; photos. by Hal and Verena Taussig. Philadelphia : Westminster Press, c1977. 171 p. : ill. ; 21 cm. Translation of the 5th ed. of Die Bibel antwortet uns in Bildern. [BS645.M4813] 76-49909 ISBN 0-664-24130-1 pbk. : 5.95
1. Bible—Psychology. I. Title.

MICKELSEN, A. Berkeley 220.6
Interpreting the Bible. Grand Rapids, Mich., Eerdmans [c.1963] xiv, 425p. 24cm. Bibl. 63-17785 5.95
1. Bible—Hermeneutics. I. Title.

MICKELSON, A. Berkeley. 220.6
Interpreting the Bible. Grand Rapids, Eerdmans [1963] xiv, 425 p. 24 cm. Bibliography: p. 383-392. [BS476.M37] 63-17785
1. Bible — Hermeneutics. I. Title.

MILLER, C. Leslie. 220.6
They talked with God / C. Leslie Miller. Burbank, Calif. : Manna Books, c1975. 110 p. ; 18 cm. Includes bibliographical references. [BV228.M54] 74-33130
1. Prayer—Biblical teaching. I. Title.

MILTON, John, 1608-1674. 220.6
Paradise lost; a poem, in twelve books. Philadelphia, B. Warner; Griggs & Co., printers, 1819. 356p. port. 14cm. Added t. p., engr. [PR3560 1819] 55-52985
I. Title.

MINEAR, Paul Sevier, 1906- 220.6
Eyes of faith, a study in the Biblical point of view. [Red. ed.] St. Louis, Bethany [1966, c.1946, 1965] 368p. 22cm. [BS511.M513] 3.45 pap.,
1. Bible — Theology. I. Title.

MORGAN, George Campbell, 220.6
1863-1945.
The unfolding message of the Bible; the harmony and unity of the Scriptures. [Westwood, N.J.] Revell [1961] 416p. 22cm. [BS481.M65] 61-9842
1. Bible—Criticism, interpretation, etc. I. Title.

†MORRIS, Henry Madison, 220.6
1918-
The Bible has the answer / Henry M. Morris and Martin E. Clark. Rev. & enl. San Diego : Creation-Life Publishers, c1976. xi, 380 p. ; 21 cm. Includes indexes. [BR96.M67 1976] 76-20206 ISBN 0-89051-018-0 pbk. : 4.95
1. Bible.—Examinations, questions, etc. 2. Theology—Miscellanea. I. Clark, Martin E., joint author. II. Title.

*MUMFORD, Bessie Carpenter 220.6
Let there be light. New York, Vantage [1967] 180p. 21cm. 3.50 bds.,
1. Bible— Criticism, interpretation, etc. I. Title.

MURPHY, Richard Thomas 220.6
Aquinas, 1908- ed.
Lagrange and Biblical renewal. Richard Murphy, editor. Chicago, Priory Press [1966] 169 p. 19 cm. (Aquinas Institute studies, no. 1) Contents.The Dominican School in Jerusalem and Old Testament studies, by J. M. T. Barton. -- History in the Bible, by P. W. Skehan. -- The Pentateuch; an appraisal, by E. H. Maly. -- The prophets, by B. Vawter. -- Paul and the indwelling Christ, by G. T. Montague. -- From Wrede to the new quest, by S. Bullough. Bibliographical footnotes. [BS413.M85] 66-17484
1. Bible — Addresses, essays, lectures. 2. Lagrange, Marie Joseph, 1855-1938. I. Lagrange, Mare Joseph 1855-1938. II. Title. III. Series.

MURPHY, Richard Thomas 220.6
Aquinas, 1908, ed.
Lagrange and Biblical renewal. Richard Murphy, ed. Chicago, Priory Pr. [c.1966] 169p. 20cm. (Aquinas Inst. studies, no. 1) Bibl. [BS413.M85] 66-17484 2.95
1. Lagrange, Marie Joseph, 1855-1938. 2. Bible — Addresses, essays, lectures. I. Lagrange, Marie Joseph, 1855-1938. II. Title. III. Series.
Contents omitted

NEIL, William, 1909- 220.6
Modern man looks at the Bible. New York, Association Press [1958] 128p. 16cm. (An Association Press reflection book) A revision of the author's The plain man looks at the Bible, published in 1956. [BS538.N36] 58-6476
1. Bible—Criticism, interpetation, etc. I. Title.

NEIL, William, 1909- 220.6
The rediscovery of the Bible. New York, Harper [1955, c1954] 255 p. 22 cm. [BS511.2.N4 1955] 55-7084
1. Bible—Criticism, interpretation, etc. I. Title.

NINEHAM, Dennis Eric, 1921- 220.6
The use and abuse of the Bible : a study of the Bible in an age of rapid cultural change / [by] Dennis Nineham. London : Macmillan, 1976. xi, 295 p. : ill. ; 23 cm. (Library of philosophy and religion) Includes bibliographical references and indexes. [BS540.N56 1976b] 77-360729 ISBN 0-333-10489-7 : £10.00
1. Bible—Criticism, interpretation, etc.—Addresses essays, lectures. I. Title.

NINEHAM, Dennis Eric, 1921- 220.6
The use and abuse of the Bible : a study of the Bible in an age of rapid cultural change / Dennis Nineham. New York : Barnes & Noble Books, 1976. xi, 295 p. : ill. ; 23 cm. (Library of philosophy and religion) A revision and expansion of the author's Edward Cadbury lectures delivered at Birmingham University, 1971. [BS540.N56 1976] 76-15690 ISBN 0-06-495178-2 : 17.00
1. Bible—Criticism, interpretation, etc.—Addresses, essays, lectures. I. Title. II. Series: Edward Cadbury lectures ; 1971.

ORLINSKY, Harry Meyer, 220.6
1908-
Essays in Biblical culture and Bible translation [by] Harry M. Orlinsky. New York, Ktav Pub. House [1974] xv, 462 p. port. 24 cm. Includes bibliographies. [BS1192.O74] 72-14069 ISBN 0-87068-218-0 15.00
1. Bible. O.T.—Addresses, essays, lectures. 2. Bible. O.T.—Versions, Jewish—Addresses, essays, lectures. I. Title.

PETERSON, Mrs. Fred. 220.6
Prepare to meet thy God: the 'silent missionary' book. New York, Greenwich Book Publishers [1960, c.1959] 99p. 21cm. 59-12075 2.50
1. Christianity—20th cent. I. Title.

PHILLIPS, John, 1927- 220.6
Exploring the Scriptures. Foreword by Stephen F. Olford. Chicago, Moody Press [1967, c1965] 288 p. illus., maps. 22 cm. [BS475.2.P48] 68-3631
1. Bible—Introductions. I. Title.

PHILLIPS, John, 1927- 220.6
Exploring the Scriptures. Foreword by Stephen F. Olford. Chicago, Moody Press [1967, c1965] 288 p. illus., maps. 22 cm. [BS475.2.P48] 68-3631
1. Bible—Introductions. I. Title.

PILLAI, K. C. 220.6
Light through an eastern window. New York, Speller [c.1963] 129p. 17cm. 63-14701 2.50
1. Bible—Criticism, interpretation, etc.—Addresses, essays, lectures. 2. Near East—Soc. life & cust. I. Title.

PINK, Arthur Walkington, 1886-1952. 220.6
The divine inspiration of the Bible [by] Arthur W. Pink. [dist. Grand Rapids, Mich., Baker Bk., 1962, c.1917] 144p. 20cm. 1.50 pap.,
1. Bible—Inspiration. I. Title.

POELMAN, Roger, 1911- 220.6
Times of grace; the sign of forty in the Bible. [Translated from the French by D. P. Farina. New York,] Herder and Herder[1964] 189 p. 21 cm. Translation of Le signe biblique des quarante jours. Bibliographical footnotes. [BV85.P575] 64-13689
1. Lent 2. Bible—Meditations. 3. Forty (The number) I. Title.

POELMAN, Roger, 1911- 220.6
Times of grace; the sign of forty in the Bible. [Tr. from French by D. P. Farina. New York] Herder & Herder [c.1964] 189p. 21cm. Bibl. 64-13689 3.95
1. Lent. 2. Bible—Meditations. 3. Forty (The number) I. Title.

POTTS, George C. 220.6
Background to the Bible; an introduction. New York, Harper [1966, c.1964] 162p. maps. 21cm. (Harper chapel bks., CB22G) First pub. in Gt. Brit. in 1964 under title: A beginner's modern Bible background. Bibl. [BS475.2.P67] 66-1119 1.25 pap.,
1. Bible — Introductions. I. Title.

*PRESTON, Burman H. 220.6
The Bible --a personal epitome and commentary. New York, Carlton [1968] 192p. 21cm. (Hearthstone bk.) 3.50
I. Title.

RAMM, Bernard, 1916- 220.6
Protestant Biblical interpretation; a textbook of hermeneutics for conservative Protestants. Complete rev. ed. Boston, Wilde [1956] 274p. 20cm. [BS476.R35 1956] 56-11809
1. Bible—Hermeneutics. I. Title.

RAMM, Bernard, 1916- 220.6
Protestant Biblical interpretation; a textbook of hermeneutics for conservative Protestants. Boston, Wilde [1950] xv, 197 p. 21 cm. Vivliogrpahical footnotes. [BS476.R35] 50-12737
1. Bible — Hermeneutics. I. Title.

REAVES, Laurie 220.6
Lo! the poor innocents. New York, Carlton [c.1963] 85p. 21cm. (Reflection bk.) 1.95
I. Title.

RICE, John R., 1895- comp. 220.6
A coffer of jewels about our infallible, eternal Word of God, the Bible; sermons, addresses, scholarly studies assessing, describing, praising, defending the Bible, by Charles H. Spurgeon [and others] Murfreesboro, Tenn., Sword of the Lord Publishers [1963] 318 p. 21 cm. [BS540.R5] 64-1991
1. Bible — Addresses, essays, lectures. I. Title.

ROBERT, Andre, 1883- ed. 220.6
Guide to the Bible; an introduction to the study of Holy Scripture. Published under the direction of A. Robert and A. Tricot. 2d ed., rev. and enl. Translated from the recast and enl. 3d French ed. by Edward P. Arbez and Martin R. P. McGuire. Paris, New York, Desclee Co., 1960- v. 22cm. Translation of Initiation biblique. Includes bibliographies. [BS475.R6132] 60-50336
1. Bible— Introductions. I. Tricot, Alphonse Elle, 1884- joint ed. II. Title.

ROBERT, Andre, 1883- ed. 220.6
Guide to the Bible; an introduction to the study of Holy Scripture, published under the direction of A. Robert and A. Tricot New ed., rev. and enl. English translation prepared under the direction of Edward P. Arbez and Martin R. P. McGuire. Westminster, Md., Newman Press, 1951- v. front. 23 cm. Translation of Initiation Biblique. Full name: Andre Marie Edmond Robert. Includes bibliographies. [BS475.R613] 52-4101
1. Bible — Introductions. I. Tricot, Alphonse Elle, 1884- joint ed. II. Title.

ROBERT, Andre, 1883-1955. 220.6
Interpreting the scriptures [edited by] A. Robert [and] A. Feuillet. Translated from the French by Patrick W. Skehan [and others] With an appendix on the Dogmatic constitution on divine revelation, by Wilfrid Harrington and Liam Walsh. New York, Desclee Co., 1969. xiii, 247 p. 23 cm. "The original French ... was published as a General introduction to the Bible in Introduction a la Bible, Vol. I." Includes bibliographical references. [BS475.2.R6214 1969] 69-20372 6.75
1. Bible—Introductions. I. Feuillet, Andre, joint author. II. Vatican Council, 2d, 1962-1965. Constitutio dogmatica de divina revelatione. III. Title.

ROBERT, Andre [Marie Edmond] ed. 220.6
Guide to the Bible; an introduction to the study of Holy Scripture, published under the direction of A. Robert and A. Tricot. 2nd ed., rev. and enl. Translated from the recast and enlarged 3rd French edition by Edward P. Arbez and Martin R. P. McGuire. Vol. 1. New York, Desclee Co., 1960[ ] xxvi, 812p. (Bibl. footnotes) 22cm. 52-4101 8.00
1. Bible—Introductions. I. Tricot, Alphonse Elie, joint ed. II. Title.

ROBERTSON, Edwin Hanton 220.6
Methods of Bible study. New York, Association [1962] 62p. 19cm. (Bible in our time) Bibl. 62-51118 1.25 pap.,
1. Bible—Study. I. Title.

ROBERTSON, Edwin Hanton. 220.6
The recovery of confidence. New York, Association Press [1961] 63p. 19cm. (The Bible in our time) Includes bibliography. [BS445.R48 1961] 61-7107
1. Bible—Hist. 2. Bible— Influence. I. Title.

ROLLINS, Marion Josephine (Benedict) 1898- 220.6
The God of the Old Testament in relation to war, by Marion J. Benedict ... New York city, Teachers college, Columbia university, 1927. viii, 185p. 24cm. (Teachers college, Columbia university. Contributions to education, no. 263) Published also as thesis (PH. D.) Columbia university, 1927. Bibliography: p. 185. [BS1199.W2R6 1927a] 27-23552
1. God. 2. Bible. O. T.—Criticism, interpretation, etc. 3. War. 4. War and religion. I. Title.

RUTENBORN, Guenter, 1912- 220.6
The Word was God; book by book through the Book of Books. Translated from the German by Elmer E. Foelber. New York, Nelson [1959] 228 p. 22 cm. [BS475.2.R85] 59-14153
1. Bible—Introductions. I. Title.

RYPINS, Stanley. 220.6
The Book of Thirty Centuries; an introduction to modern study of the Bible. New York, Macmillan, 1951. xvii, 420 p. facsim. 22 cm. Bibliography: p. 347-350. [BS475.R84] 51-6810
1. Bible—Criticism, Textural. 2. Bible—Canon. 3. Bible—Criticism, interpretation, etc. I. Title.

SAGEBEER, Joseph Evans, 1861- 220.6
The Bible in court; the method of legal inquiry applied to the study of the Scriptures. Philadelphia, Lippincott, 1900 [c1899] xiv, 201p.19cm. [BS511.S25] 99-5541
1. Bible—Criticism. interpretation, etc. 2. Evidence. I. Title.

SCHNEIDAU, Herbert N. 220.6
Sacred discontent : the Bible and Western tradition / Herbert N. Schneidau. Baton Rouge : Louisiana State University Press, c1976. p. cm. Includes index. Bibliography: p. [BS511.2.S36] 75-18044 ISBN 0-8071-0181-8 : 15.00
1. Bible—Criticism, interpretation, etc. 2. Bible—Influence—Civilization, Occidental. 3. Bible in literature. I. Title.

SCHNEIDAU, Herbert N. 220.6
Sacred discontent : the Bible and Western tradition / Herbert N. Schneidau. Berkeley, Calif. : University of California Press, 1977. 331p. : ill. ; 23 cm. Includes index Bibliography:p.307-320. [BS511.2S36] ISBN 0-520-03165-2 pbk. : 5.95
1. Bible-Criticism, interpretation, etc. 2. Bible-Influence-Civilization, Occidental. 3. Bible in literature. I. Title.
L.C. card no. for 1976 Louisiana State University Press ed.:75-18044.

SCHOKEL, Luis Alonso 220.6
Understanding Biblical research. Tr. [from Spanish] by Peter J. McCord. [New York] Herder & Herder [c.1963] 130p. 21cm. Bibl. 63-11308 3.50
1. Bible—Criticism, interpretation, etc.—Hist. 2. Bible—Study—Catholic Church. I. Title.

*SEASHORE, Gladys. 220.6.
Jesus and me. Minneapolis, His International Service [1975] 63 p. ill. 21 cm. [BS530.] ISBN 0-911802-37-1. 1.50 (pbk.)
1. Bible—Criticism, interpretation. I. Title.

SEE, Ruth Douglas, 1910- 220.6
Make the Bible your own. Richmond, Pub. for the Cooperative Pubn. Asson. by John Knox [c.1961] 94p. (Faith for life ser.)) Bibl. 61-16520 1.00 pap.,
1. Bible—Introductions. I. Title.

SELBY, Donald Joseph. 220.6
Introduction to the Bible [by] Donald J. Selby [and] James King West. New York, Macmillan [1971] xxi, 544, 530 p. illus. 25 cm. "The two parts of this volume are available separately as Introduction to the Old Testament: 'Hear O Israel,' by James King West, and Introduction to the New Testament: 'The word became flesh,' by Donald J. Selby." Includes bibliographies. [BS475.2.S43 1971] 78-152821
1. Bible—Introductions. I. West, James King. Introduction to the Old Testament: "Hear O Israel." 1970. II. Selby, Donald Joseph. Introduction to the New Testament: "The word became flesh." 1970. III. Title.

SENDY, Jean, 1910- 220.6
The moon: outposts of the Gods. Trans. by Lowell Bair. New York, Berkley Pub. Co. [1975, c1968] ix, 147 p. 18 cm. (A Berkley medallion book) Translation of La lune cle de la Bible [BS534.S4] ISBN 0-425-02798-8 1.50 (pbk.)
1. Bible—Criticism, interpretation, etc. I. Title.
L.C. card number for original ed.: 68-132406

SEVENTH-DAY Adventists. General Conference. Committee on Problems in Bible Translation. 220.6
Problems in Bible translation; a study of certain principles of Bible translation and interpretation, together with an examination of several Bible texts in the light of these principles. Washington, Printed by the Review and Herald Pub. Association [1954] 316p. 22cm. Bibliography: p. 300-312. [BS476.S43] 54-3394
1. Bible—Hermeneutics. 2. Bible—Versions. 3. Seventh-Day Adventists—Doctrinal and controversial works. I. Title.

*SHARROW, Clarence E. 220.6
God hath spoken at sundry times and in divers manners. New York, Pageant [c.1964] 142p. 21cm. 2.75
I. Title.

SMART, James D. 220.6
The interpretation of Scripture. Philadelphia, Westminster Press [1961] 317 p. 24 cm. Includes bibliography. [BS511.2.S6] 61-5624
1. Bible—Criticism, interpretation, etc. 2. Bible—Theology. I. Title.

*SMITH, Paul Dewey 220.6
Man's relationship and duty to God. New York, Carlton [c.1964] 546p. 24cm. 10.00
I. Title.

SNYDER, Russell Dewey, 1898- 220.6
The Book of Life. Arthur H. Getz, editor. Philadelphia, Muhlenberg Press [1950] 96 p. illus. 18 cm. Bibliography: p. 96. [BS475.S717] 50-36843
1. Bible — Introductions. I. Title.

SOCIETY of Biblical Literature. 220'.6
1975 seminar papers : one hundred eleventh annual meeting, 30 October-2 November 1975, Palmer House, Chicago, Illinois / Society of Biblical Literature; George MacRae, editor Missoula, Mont. : Distributed by Scholars Press, University of Montana, c1975. p. cm. Includes bibliographical references. [BS411.S625 1975] 75-28349 ISBN 0-89130-033-3 (v. 1) : 2.50. ISBN 0-89130-032-5 (v. 2) : 2.50
1. Bible—Congresses. I. MacRae, George W.

SOCIETY of Biblical Literature. 220.6
1974 seminar papers : one hundred tenth annual meeting, 24-27 October, 1974, Washington Hilton, Washington, D.C. / George MacRae, editor. Cambridge, Mass. : Society of Biblical Literature, 1974. 2 v. ; 22 cm. Includes bibliographical references. [BS411.S623] 74-14210 ISBN 0-88414-046-6 (v. 2)
1. Bible—Congresses. I. MacRae, George W., ed.

SOCIETY of Biblical Literature. 220.6
One hundred eighth annual meeting, Friday-Tuesday, 1-5 September, 1972; book of seminar papers. Lane C. McGaughy, editor. [Los Angeles? c1972] 2 v. (iv, 607 p.) 22 cm. Includes bibliographical references. [BS411.S625 1972] 74-166404
1. Bible—Congresses. I. McGaughy, Lane C., ed.

SOULEN, Richard N., 1933- 220.6
Handbook of Biblical criticism / by Richard N. Soulen. Atlanta : John Knox Press, c1976. 191 p. ; 23 cm. Bibliography: p. 191. [BS417.S6] 76-12398 ISBN 0-8042-0044-0 : 6.95
1. Bible—Handbooks, manuals, etc. I. Title.

SOWERS, Sidney G 220.6
The hermeneutics of Philo and Hebrews; a comparison of the interpretation of the Old Testament in Philo Judaeus and the Epistle to the Hebrews, by Sidney G. Sowers. Richmond, John Knox Press [1965] 154 p. 21 cm. (Basel studies of theology, no. 1) Issued also as thesis--Basel. Bibliography: p. 141-146. [BS1160.S64 1965] 65-10146
1. Bible. O. T.—Criticism, interpretation, etc.—Hist. 2. Bible N. T. Hebrews—Relation to O. T. 3. Philo Judeus. 4. Allegory. I. Title. II. Series.

SOWERS, Sidney G. 220.6
The hermeneutics of Philo and Hebrews; a comparison of the interpretation of the Old Testament in Philo Judaeus and the Epistle to the Hebrews. Richmond, Va., Knox [c.1965] 154p. 21cm. (Basel studies of theology, no.1) Bibl. [BS1160.S64] 65-10146 2.75 pap.,
1. Philo Judaeus 2. Bible. O. T.—Criticism, interpretation, etc.—Hist. 3. Bible. N. T. Hebrews—Relation to O. T. 4. Allegory. I. Title. II. Series.

SPEAKER'S Bible (The). 220.6
Ed. by James Hastings, asst. by B. A. Clark. Grand Rapids, Mich., Baker Bk. House, 1961 . various p. 25cm. Contents.[1] Hebrews.--[2]--[3] Luke. v. 1-2.--[4] Deuteronomy. Joshua. Judges. Ruth.--[5] I and II Peter. Jude.--[6] Job. Psalms I. Bibl. 61-16755 3.95 ea.,
1. Bible—Sermons. I. Hastings, James, 1852-1922, ed.

STACEY, Walter David. 220.6
Interpreting the Bible / David Stacey. New York : Hawthorn Books, 1977. v, 120 p. ; 21 cm. (Issues in religious studies) Includes index. Bibliography: p. 117-118. [BS511.2.S72 1977] 75-41796 ISBN 0-8015-4077-1 pbk. : 3.50
1. Bible—Criticism, interpretation, etc. I. Title.

STATON, Knofel. 220.6
Don't divorce the Holy Spirit. Cincinnati, New Life Books [1974] 112 p. 18 cm. [BS511.2.S8] 73-87496
1. Bible—Criticism, interpretation, etc. I. Title.

STEINMANN, Jean. 220.6
Biblical criticism. Translated from the French by J. R. Foster. [1st ed.] New York, Hawthorn Books [1958] 124 p. 21 cm. (The Twentieth century encyclopedia of Catholicism, v. 63. Section 6: The word of God) Translation of La critique devant la Bible. Bibliography: p. [122]-124. [BS475.S7233] 58-14108
1. Bible — Introductions. I. Title. II. Series: The Twentieth century encyclopedia of Catholocism, v. 63

STEPHENS, George T 1884?-1956. 220.6
True revival; six messages With a message on revival and the home and a biographical sketch of the author by his wife. [Abington, Pa.] Bible Evangelism [1961] 134 p. 21 cm. [BV3790.S766] 61-17479
1. Revivals. I. Title.

STERRETT, T. Norton. 220.6
How to understand your Bible / T. Norton Sterrett. Rev. ed. Downers Grove, Ill. : InterVarsity Press, [1974] 179 p. ; 21 cm. [BS511.2.S83 1974] 74-78674 ISBN 0-87784-638-3 : 2.50
1. Bible—Criticism, interpretation, etc. I. Title.

STRUCTURAL analysis and Biblical exegesis : interpretational essays / by R. Barthes ... [et al.] ; translated by Alfred M. Johnson, Jr. Pittsburgh : Pickwick Press, 1974. p. cm. (Pittsburgh theological monograph series ; no. 3) Translation of Analyse structurale et exegese biblique. Bibliography: p. [BS531.A513] 74-31334 ISBN 0-915138-02-6 : 6.95 220.6
1. Bible. O.T. Genesis XXXII, 23-33—Criticism, interpretation, etc. 2. Bible. N.T. Mark V, 1-20—Criticism, interpretation, etc. 3. Structuralism. I. Barthes, Roland. II. Title. III. Series.

STUHLMUELLER, Carroll 220.6
The Bible and college theology. Washington, D.C., 487 Michigan Ave., N.E., Thomist Pr., c.1962. 52p. 18cm. (Compact studies theology ser.) .35 pap.,
I. Title.

SWAIM, Joseph Carter, 1904- 220.6
Do you understand the Bible? Philadelphia, Westminster Press [1954] 173p. 21cm. [BS538.S8] 54-9282
1. Bible—Hermeneutics. 2. Bible—Criticism, interpretation, etc. I. Title.

SWANSTON, Hamish F. G., 1933- 220.6
The community witness; an exploration of some of the influences at work in the New Testament community and its writings [by]

Hamish F. G. Swanston. New York, Sheed and Ward [1967] viii, 230 p. 22 cm. [BS538.S93] 67-20751
1. Bible—Criticism, interpretation, etc. I. Title.

TERRIEN, Samuel 220.6
The Bible and the church; an approach to Scripture. Philadelphia, Westminster [1963, c.1962] 95p. 20cm. (Westminster guides to the Bible) 63-7261 1.50
1. Bible—Introductions. I. Title.

THOMAS, Latta R. 220.6
Biblical faith and the Black American / Latta R. Thomas. Valley Forge, Pa. : Judson Press, c1976. 160 p. ; 22 cm. Includes index. Bibliography: p. 153-158. [BS511.2.T48] 76-13640 ISBN 0-8170-0718-0 pbk. : 4.95
1. Bible—Criticism, interpretation, etc. 2. Afro-Americans—Religion. 3. Freedom (Theology)—Biblical teaching. I. Title.

THURSTON, Joseph Smith. 220.6
The mystery of creation, a study of what Jesus taught. [1st ed.] New York, Exposition Press [1952] 161 p. 21 cm. [BR126.T458] 52-9825
I. Title.

THE Times, London. 220.6
The Bible today; historical, social, and literary aspects of the Old and New Testaments, described by Christian scholars. New York, Harper [c1955] 208p. illus. 22cm. Originally published as a special supplement to the London times. [BS475.T48] 55-11479
1. Bible—Introductions. I. Christian scholars. II. Title.

TRAINA, Robert Angelo, 1921- 220.6

Methodical Bible study; a new approach to hermeneutics. [Ridgefield Park, N.J., 1952] 269 p. illus. 24 cm. [BX476.T7] 52-44401
1. Bible — Hermeneutics. 2. Bible — Study. I. Title.

USHERWOOD, Stephen. 220.6
The Bible, book by book. Illustrated by Anthony & Geoffrey Harper. New York, Norton [1962] 93 p. illus. 29 cm. [BS475.2.U8] 62-12290
1. Bible — Introductions. I. Title.

USHERWOOD, Stephen 220.6
The Bible, book by book. Illus. by Anthony & Geoffrey Harper. New York, Norton [c.1962] 93p. col. illus. 29cm. 62-12290 5.95
1. Bible—Introductions. I. Title.

VANARSDALL, David B 220.6
The word of life. [1st ed.] New York, Greenwich Book Publishers [c1961] 159 p. 21 cm. [BS538.5.V3] 61-18676
1. Bible — Appreciation. I. Title.

†WALKER, Paul L. 220.6
Understanding the Bible and science / Paul L. Walker. Cleveland, Tenn. : Pathway Press, c1976. 144 p. : ill. ; 18 cm. (Making life count new life series) Bibliography: p. 144. [BS650.W34] 75-25343 ISBN 0-87148-878-7 pbk. : 1.19
1. Bible and science. 2. Creation. I. Title.

WATTS, Harold Holliday, 220.6
1906-
The modern reader's guide to the Bible. Rev. ed. New York, Harper [1959] 544 p. 25 cm. Includes bibliography. [BS475.W319 1959] 58-11586
1. Bible — Introductions. I. Title.

WEBER, Otto [Heinrich 220.6
Ground plan of the Bible; translated [From the German] by Harold Knight. Philadelphia, Westminster Press [1959] 221p. 23cm. 59-9195 3.95
1. Bible—Introductions. I. Title.

WESTERMANN, Claus. 220.6
Our controversial Bible. Translated and edited by Darold H. Beekmann. Minneapolis, Augsburg Pub. House [1969] vi, 136 p. 22 cm. Translation of Umstrittene Bibel. Bibliography: p. 121-130. [BS514.2.W413] 70-84813 3.95
1. Bible—Criticism, interpretation, etc. I. Title.

WESTMINSTER introduction to 220.6
the books of the Bible. Prepared by the editors of the Westminster study edition of the Holy Bible. Philadelphia, Westminster Press [1958] 224 p. 24 cm. (Westminster aids to the study of the Scriptures) "Presents in a separate volume those articles and introductions contained originally in the Westminster study edition of the Holy Bible." [BS475.W44] 58-9739
1. Bible — Introductions.

WIERWILLE, Victor Paul. 220.6
Power for abundant living; the accuracy of the Bible. New Knoxville, Ohio, American Christian Press [1971] x, 368 p. 20 cm. [BV4501.2.W519] 72-164674 ISBN 0-910068-01-1
1. Bible—Evidences, authority, etc. 2. Christian life—1960- I. Title.

WILD, Laura Hulda, 1870- 220.6
A literary guide to the Bible : a study of the types of literature present in the Old and New Testaments / by Laura H. Wild. Norwood, Pa. : Norwood Editions, 1976 [c1922] p. cm. Reprint of the ed. published by Allen & Unwin, London. Includes bibliographies and index. [BS535.W5 1976] 76-7625 ISBN 0-8482-2852-9 lib. bdg. : 17.50
1. Bible—Criticism, interpretation, etc. 2. Bible as literature. 3. Literary form. I. Title.

WILKINSON, John Donald. 220.6
Interpretation and community. London, Macmillan; New York, St. Martin's Press, 1963. 243 p. 23 cm. Includes bibliography. [BS476.W5] 63-3813
1. Bible — Hermeneutics. 2. Bible — Evidences, authority, etc. I. Title.

WILKINSON, John Donald 220.6
Interpretation and community. London, Macmillan [dist.] New York, St. Martin's [c.] 1963. 243p. 23cm. Bibl. 63-3813 6.75
1. Bible—Hermeneutics. 2. Bible—Evidences, authority, etc. I. Title.

WILLMINGTON, H. L. 220.6
That manuscript from outer space / H. L. Willmington. 1st updated ed. Nashville : T. Nelson, 1977, c1974. 154 p. ; 21 cm. Includes bibliographical references. [BS480.W525 1977] 77-23596 ISBN 0-8407-9503-3 pbk. : 3.95
1. Bible—Evidences, authority, etc. 2. Bible—Criticism, interpretation, etc. I. Title.

*WILMOT, John 220.6
Inspired principles of prophetic interpretation: God means what He says and says what He means. Foreword by D. M. Lloyd-Jones. Swengel, Pa., Reiner Pubns., 1967. 290p. port. 20cm. 3.95
1. Bible—Criticism, interpretation. I. Title.

WILSON, Clifford A. 220.6
A greater than Adam is here, by Clifford Wilson. [Melbourne, Australian Institute of Archaeology in association with Word of Truth Productions, 1969?] 50 p. 23 cm. (A Word of Truth production) [BS620.W63] 71-466249 unpriced
1. Jesus Christ—Person and offices. 2. Bible. O.T.—Antiquities. I. Australian Institute of Archaeology. II. Title.

WILSON, Wlater Lewis, 1881- 220.6
Wilson's dictionary of Bible types. Grand Rapids, Eerdmans [c1957] 519 p. 23 cm. [BS477.W53] 57-14495
1. Symbolism. 2. Bible — Dictionaries. 3. Typology (Theology) I. Title. II. Title: Dictionary of Bible types.

*WOSSILEK, Joseph. 220.6
Gifts for men. New York, Vantage [1968] 139p. 21cm. 3.50 bds.,
1. Bible—Introduction. I. Title.

WOYCHUK, N. A. 220.6
The infallible word. Chicago, Moody [c.1963] 77p. 18cm. (Compact bks., 38) .29 pap.,
I. Title.

WRIGHT, George Ernest 220.6
The rule of God; essays in Biblical theology. Garden City, N.Y., Doubleday, [c.]1960. viii, 133p. (bibl. footnotes) 22cm. 60-6921 2.95 bds.,
1. Bible—Theology. I. Title.

WRIGHT, George Ernest, 220.6
1909-
The Book of the acts of God; Christian scholarship interprets the Bible, by G. Ernest Wright and Reginald H. Fuller. [1st ed.] Garden City, N.Y., Doubleday, 1957. 372 p. 22 cm. (Christian faith series) [BS475.W75] 57-7291
1. Bible — Introductions. I. Fuller, Reginald Horace, joint author. II. Title.

WRIGHT, George Ernest, 220.6
1909-
The Book of the acts of God; Christian scholarship interprets the Bible, by G. Ernest Wright and Reginald H. Fuller. [1st ed.] Garden City, N.Y., Doubleday, 1957. 372 p. 22 cm. (Christian faith series) [BS475.W75] 57-7291
1. Bible—Introductions. I. Fuller, Reginald Horace, joint author. II. Title.

WRIGHT, George Ernest, 220.6
1909-
The Book of the acts of God; contemporary scholarship interprets the Bible, by G. Ernest Wright and Reginald H. Fuller. Garden City, N.Y., Doubleday, 1960. 420 p. 19 cm. (A Doubleday anchor book, A222) [BS475.2.W74 1960] 60-13563
1. Bible—Introductions. I. Fuller, Reginald Horace, joint author. II. Title.

WRIGHT, George Ernest, 220.6
1909-
The rule of God; essays in Biblical theology. [1st ed.] Garden City, N.Y., Doubleday, 1960. 133 p. 22 cm. Includes bibliography. [BS543.W7] 60-6921
1. Bible—Theology. I. Title.

WURTHWEIN, Ernst, 1909- 220.6
The text of the Old Testament; an introduction to Kittel-Kahle's Biblia Hebraica. Translated by Peter R. Ackroyd. New York, Macmillan, 1957. x, 173p. illus., facsims, 24cm. 'This translation has been made from the author's revision of his Der Text des Alten Testaments (1952)' Bibliography: p.[169]-173. [BS1185.W] A57
1. Bible. O. T.—Criticism, Textual. 2. Bible. Manuscripts, Hebrew. I. Bible. O. T. Hebrew. 1937. II. Title.

WURTHWEIN, Ernst, 1909- 220.6
The text of the Old Testament; an introduction to Kittel-Kahle's Biblia Hebraica. Translated by Peter R. Ackroyd. New York, Macmillan, 1957. x, 173 p. illus., facsims. 24 cm. Bibliography: p. [169]-173. [[BS1185.W]] A57
1. Bible. O.T. — Criticism, Textual. 2. Bible. Manuscripts, Hebrew. I. Bible. O.T. Hebrew. 1937. II. Title. III. Title: "This translation has been made from the author's revision of his Der Text des Alten Testaments (1952)"

YATES, Kyle Monroe, 1895- 220.6
Preaching from great Bible chapters. Nashville, Broad-man Press [1957] 209p. 21cm. [BS511.Y3] 57-6326
1. Bible—Homiletical use. I. Title.

YATES, Kyle Monroe, 1895- 220.6
Preaching from great Bible chapters. Nashville, Broadman Press [1957] 209 p. 21 cm. [BS511.Y3] 57-6326
1. Bible — Homiletical use. I. Title.

ROBINSON, James McConkey, 220.601
1924- ed.
The new hermeneutic, edited by James M. Robinson [and] John B. Cobb, Jr. [1st ed.] New York, Harper & Row [1964] xii, 243 p. 22 cm. (New frontiers in theology: discussions among continental and American theologians, v. 2) [BS476.R6] 64-14380
1. Bible — Hermeneutics. 2. Theology — Methodology. 3. Theology, Doctrinal — Hist. — 20th Cent. I. Cobb, John B., joint ed. II. Title. III. Series. IV. Series: New frontiers in theology, v. 2

ROBINSON, James McConkey, 220.601
1924- ed.
The new hermeneutic, by James M. Robinson, John B. Cobb, Jr. New York, Harper [c.1964] xii, 243p. 22cm. (New frontiers in theology; discussions among continental and Amer. theologians, v.2) 64-14380 5.00
1. Bible—Hermeneutics. 2. Theology—Methodology. 3. Theology, Doctrinal—Hist. 20th cent. I. Cobb, John B., joint ed. II. Title. III. Series: New frontiers in theology, v.2

MAIER, Gerhard. 220.6'07
The end of the historical-critical method / Gerhard Maier ; translated by Edwin W. Leverenz and Rudolf F. Norden. St. Louis : Concordia Pub. House, c1977. 108 p. ; 20 cm. Translation of Das Ende der historisch-kritischen Methode. Bibliography: p. 103-105. [BS500.M2413] 76-56222 ISBN 0-570-03752-2 pbk. : 4.50
1. Bible—Criticism, interpretation, etc.—History. 2. Bible—Evidences, authority, etc. I. Title.

SOCIETY of Biblical 220.609
Literature.
The Bible in modern scholarship; papers read at the 100th meeting of the Society of Biblical Literature, December 28-30, 1964. Edited by J. Philip Hyatt. Nashville, Abingdon Press [1965] 400 p. 25 cm. Bibliographical footnotes. [BS411.S635] 66-11059
1. Bible—Congresses. 2. Bible—Criticism, interpretation—History. I. Hyatt, James Philip, 1909- ed. II. Title.

KRENTZ, Edgar. 220.60904
Biblical studies today; a guide to current issues and trends. St. Louis, Concordia Pub. House [1966] 80 p. 19 cm. (Biblical monographs) Includes bibliographies. [BS500.K7] 66-29455
1. Bible — Criticism, interpretation, etc. — Hist. — 20th cent. I. Title. II. Series.

KRENTZ, Edgar. 220.60904
Biblical studies today; a guide to current issues and trends. St. Louis, Concordia Pub. House [1966] 80 p. 19 cm. (Biblical monographs) Includes bibliographies. [BS500.K7] 66-29455
1. Bible—Criticism, interpretation, etc.—Hist.—20th cent. I. Title. II. Series.

HARRISVILLE, Roy A. 220.6'092'4 B
Frank C. Porter, pioneer in American Biblical interpretation / Roy A. Harrisville. [Missoula, Mont.] : Scholars Press for the Society of Biblical Literature, [1976] p. cm. (SBL studies in American Biblical scholarship ; 1) "Part one." Bibliography: p. [BS501.P67H37] 76-4498 ISBN 0-89130-104-6
1. Porter, Frank Chamberlin, 1859-1946. I. Title. II. Series: Society of Biblical Literature. SBL studies in American Biblical scholarship ; 1.

INNES, Kathleen Elizabeth 220.6'1
Royds.
The Bible as literature, by Kathleen E. Innes. With a foreword by F. W. Norwood. [Folcroft, Pa.] Folcroft Library Editions, 1974. 255 p. 26 cm. Reprint of the 1930 ed. published by J. Cape, London. [BS535.I5 1974] 74-3080 ISBN 0-8414-5058-7 (lib. bdg.)
1. Bible—Criticism, interpretation, etc. 2. Bible as literature. I. Title.

INNES, Kathleen Elizabeth 220.6'1
Royds.
The Bible as literature, by Kathleen E. Innes. With a foreword by F. W. Norwood. [Folcroft, Pa.] Folcroft Library Editions, 1974. p. Reprint of the 1930 ed. published by J. Cape, London. [BS535.I5 1974] 74-3080 17.50
1. Bible—Criticism, interpretation, etc. 2. Bible as literature. I. Title.

STRATON, George Douglas, 220.61
1916-
Introduction to the literature and thought of the Bible: a study guide for college students. [Corvallis? 1966] 1 v. (various pagings) 30 cm. Bibliographical footnotes. [BS475.2.S8] 220.6 68-969
1. Bible—Introductions. I. Title.

AUGSBURGER, Myron S. 220.6'3
Principles of Biblical interpretation, by Myron S. Augsburger. Scottdale, Pa., Herald Press [1967] 39 p. 20 cm. Bibliographical references included in "Footnotes" (p. 35-37) [BS476.A9] 67-1706
1. Bible—Hermeneutics. 2. Mennonites—Doctrinal and controversial works. I. Title.

CORBON, Jean, 1924- 220.6'3
God's Word to men [by] Michael Bouttier, Jean Corbon [and] George Khodre. Translated by Agnes Cunningham. Techny, Ill., Divine Word Publications [1969] ix, 142 p. 18 cm. (Churches in dialogue, DWP 111) Translation of La Parole de Dieu. Bibliographical footnotes. [BS476.C613] 69-20419 1.95
1. Bible—Hermeneutics. 2. Revelation. I. Bouttier, Michel, 1921- II. Khodre, Georges, 1923- III. Title.

*DIONE, R. L. 220.6'3
Is God supernatural? The 4,000-year misunderstanding. An exegesis by R. L. Dione. New York, Bantam [1976] 162 p. 18 cm. Includes index. Bibliography: p. [153] [BS476] 1.50 (pbk.)
1. Bible—Hermencutics. I. Title.

FREI, Hans W. 220.6'3
The eclipse of Biblical narrative; a study in eighteenth and nineteenth century hermeneutics [by] Hans W. Frei. New Haven, Yale University Press, 1974. ix, 355 p. 22 cm. Includes bibliographical references. [BS500.F73 1974] 73-86893 ISBN 0-300-01623-9 15.00
1. Bible—Criticism, interpretation, etc.—History—19th century. 2. Bible—Criticism, interpretation, etc.—History—20th century. I. Title.

GEISLER, Norman L. 220.6'3
Christ: the key to interpreting the Bible [by] Norman L. Geisler. Chicago, Moody Press [1975, c1968] 128 p. 22 cm. [BS476.G37] ISBN 0-8024-1394-3 2.25 (pbk.)
1. Bible—Hermeneutics. 2. Messiah—Prophecies. 3. Jesus Christ—History of doctrines—Early church. 4. Typology (Theology) I. Title.
L.C. card number for original ed.: 68-2644.

HERMENEUTICS, 220.6'3
by Bernard L. Ramm and others. Grand Rapids, Mich., Baker Book House [1971?] 152 p. 18 cm. (Practical theology series) The essays in this book originally appeared as section 3 of Baker's dictionary of practical theology. Includes bibliographies. [BS476.H47] 73-155862 ISBN 0-8010-7605-6 1.45
1. Bible—Hermeneutics—Addresses, essays, lectures. I. Ramm, Bernard L., 1916-

HIRSCH, Eric Donald. 220.6'3
The aims of interpretation / E. D. Hirsch, Jr. Chicago : University of Chicago Press, c1976. vi, 177 p. ; 24 cm. Includes bibliographical references and index. [PN81.H49] 75-21269 ISBN 0-226-34240-9 lib.bdg. : 10.00
1. Hermeneutics. I. Title.

INTERPRETING the word of God : festschrift in honor of Steven Barabas / edited by Samuel J. Schultz and Morris A. Inch. Chicago : Moody Press, c1976. 281 p. ; 24 cm. Bibliography: p. 238-272. [BS476.I65] 75-43659 ISBN 0-8024-4092-4 : 8.95 220.6'3
1. Bible—Hermeneutics—Addresses, essays, lectures. I. Barabas, Steven. II. Schultz, Samuel J. III. Inch, Morris A., 1925-

JANSEN, John Frederick. 220.6'3
Exercises in interpreting Scripture. Philadelphia, Geneva Press [c1968] 128 p. 21 cm. (Decade books) Bibliography: p. 119-126. [BS476.J33] 68-10044
1. Bible—Hermeneutics. I. Title.

KAISER, Otto, 1924- 220.6'3
Exegetical method; a student's handbook [by] Otto Kaiser and Werner George Kummel. Tr., introd., by E. V. N. Goetchius New York, Seabury [1967] 95p. 21cm. Orig. pub., with a third essay by G. Adam, in 1963 under title: Einfuhrung in die exegetischen Methoden. bibl. [BS476.K313] 67-15734 245 pap.,
1. Bible—Hermeneutics. I. Kummel, Werner Georg, 1905- II. Title.
Contents omitted.

KRENTZ, Edgar. 220.6'3
The historical-critical method / by Edgar Krentz. Philadelphia : Fortress Press, c1975. vi, 88 p. ; 22 cm. (Guides to Biblical scholarship) Includes bibliographical references. [BS476.K73] 74-26345 ISBN 0-8006-0460-1 pbk. : 2.75
1. Bible—Hermeneutics. I. Title.

MARLE, Rene. 220.6'3
Introduction to hermeneutics. [Translated by E. Froment and R. Albrecht. New York, Herder and Herder [1967] 128 p. 21 cm. [BS4.76.M2813] 66-13071
1. Bible—Hermeneutics. 2. Theology, Doctrinal—History—20 century. I. Title.

MARSH, Frederick Edward, 1858-1919. 220.6'3
The structural principles of the Bible; or, How to study the word of God. Grand Rapids, Kregel Publications [1969] xvi, 442 p. illus. 23 cm. With an index; published in London in 1960 without an index. [BS476.M3 1969] 68-58842 5.95
1. Bible—Hermeneutics. I. Title.

PINK, Arthur Walkington, 1886-1952. 220.6'3
Interpretation of the scriptures. Grand Rapids, Mich., Baker Book House [1972] 137 p. 23 cm. [BS476.P55 1972] 75-183682 ISBN 0-8010-6909-2 4.95
1. Bible—Hermeneutics. I. Title.

QUANBECK, Philip A. 220.6'3
When God speaks; understanding the Bible, by Philip A. Quanbeck. Minneapolis, Augsburg Pub. House [1968] 124, [3] p. 20 cm. (A Tower book) Bibliography: p. [125] [BS476.Q25] 68-13428
1. Bible—Hermeneutics. 2. Bible—Use. I. Title.

RAMM, Bernard L., 1916- 220.6'3
Protestant Biblical interpretation; a textbook of hermeneutics. 3d rev. ed. Grand Rapids, Baker Book House [1970] xvii, 298 p. 20 cm. Includes bibliographical references. [BS476.R35 1970] 75-19026 ISBN 0-8010-7600-5 4.50
1. Bible—Hermeneutics. I. Title.

SEVENTH-DAY Adventists. General Conference. Biblical Research Committee. 220.6'3
A symposium on Biblical hermeneutics. Edited by Gordon M. Hyde. [Washington, Printed by Review and Herald Pub. Association, 1974] ix, 273 p. 23 cm. Includes bibliographies. [BS476.S432 1974] 74-176165
1. Bible—Hermeneutics—Addresses, essays, lectures. I. Hyde, Gordon M., ed. II. Title.

SMART, James D. 220.6'3
The strange silence of the Bible in the church; a study in hermeneutics, by James D. Smart. Philadelphia, Westminster Press [1970] 186 p. 19 cm. Bibliography: p. [175]-186. [BS476.S63] 72-118323 2.95
1. Bible—Hermeneutics. I. Title.

TAN, Paul Lee. 220.6'3
The interpretation of prophecy. Foreword by John C. Whitcomb, Jr. Winona Lake, Ind., BMH Books [1974] 435 p. 23 cm. Originally presented as the author's thesis, Grace Theological Seminary, Winona Lake, Ind. Bibliography: p. [371]-390. [BS647.2.T27 1974] 73-85613 ISBN 0-88469-000-8 6.95
1. Bible—Prophecies. I. Title.

TERRY, Milton Spenser, 1840-1914. 220.6'3
Biblical hermeneutics: a treatise on the interpretation of the Old and New Testaments / Milton S. Terry. Grand Rapids, Mich. : Zondervan Pub. House, 1974. 782 p. ; 22 cm. Reprint of the 2d ed. Includes indexes. Bibliography: p. [739]-752. [BS476.T4 1974] 74-195129 pbk. : 6.95
1. Bible—Hermeneutics. I. Title.

WARD, Wayne E. 220.6'3
The word comes alive [by] Wayne E. Ward. Nashville, Broadman Press [1969] 112 p. 21 cm. [BS476.W35] 69-14370 2.95
1. Bible—Hermeneutics. I. Title.

WOOD, Arthur Skevington. 220.6'3'09
The principles of Biblical interpretation as enunciated by Irenaeus, Origen, Augustine, Luther, and Calvin, by A. Skevington Wood. Grand Rapids, Zondervan [1967] 103 p. 21 cm. Bibliography: p. 97-99. [BS500.W6] 66-30570
1. Bible—Criticism, interpretation, etc.—History. 2. Bible—Hermeneutics. I. Title.

BROWN, Jerry Wayne. 220.6'3'0974
The rise of Biblical criticism in America, 1800-1870; the New England scholars. [1st ed.] Middletown, Conn., Wesleyan University Press [1969] vi, 212 p. 22 cm. Includes bibliographical references. [BS500.B7] 69-17793 10.00
1. Bible—Criticism, interpretation, etc.—History—19th century. 2. New England—Intellectual life. I. Title.

ADDINGTON, Jack Ensign. 220.6'4
The hidden mystery of the Bible. New York, Dodd, Mead [1969] ix, 276 p. 21 cm. Bibliography: p. 275-276. [BS534.A28] 70-93549 5.00
1. Bible—Criticism, interpretation, etc. 2. Symbolism. I. Title.

BLAIKLOCK, E. M. 220.6'4
Word pictures from the Bible [by] E. M. Blaiklock. Grand Rapids, Mich., Zondervan Pub. House [1971, c1969] 95 p. illus. 22 cm. [BS537.B56 1971] 73-133361 2.95
1. Bible—Language, style. I. Title.

CHARITY, Alan Clifford. 220.64
Events and their afterlife: the dialectics of Christian typology in the Bible and Dante, by A. C. Charity. Cambridge, Cambridge U.P., 1966. xi, 288 p. 22 1/2 cm. 60/- Bibliography; p. 262-272. (B 66-21454) [BS478.C5] 66-18116
1. Dante Alighieri, 1265-1321 — Knowledge — Bible. 2. Typology (Theology) I. Title.

CHARITY, Alan Clifford 220.64
Events and their afterlife: the dialectics of Christian typology in the Bible and Dante, by A. C. Charity. Cambridge. Cambridge Univ. Pr. 1966. xi, 288p. 23cm. Bibl. [BS478.C5] 66-18116 9.50
1. Dante Alighieri, 1265-1321—Knowledge—Bible. 2. Typology (Theology) I. Title.
Available from publisher's New York office.

HODSON, Geoffrey. 220.6'4
The hidden wisdom in the Holy Bible. Wheaton, Ill., Theosophical Pub. House [1967- v. illus. 21 cm. (A Quest book) Vol. 1: revised. Contents.Contents.—[1] An examination of the idea that the contents of the Bible are partly allegorical.—v. 2-3. The golden grain of wisdom in the Book of Genesis. Includes bibliographies. [BS534.H67 1967] 67-8724 ISBN 0-8356-0005-X (v. 2) 2.75 (v. 3)
1. Bible. O.T. Genesis—Miscellanea. 2. Symbolism in the Bible. I. Title.

MACKY, Peter W. 220.6'4
The pursuit of the divine snowman / Peter Macky. Waco, Tex. : Word Books, c1977. 240 p. ; 23 cm. Includes bibliographies. [BS477.M33] 76-19540 ISBN 0-87680-484-9 : 6.95
1. Symbolism in the Bible. 2. Symbolism. I. Title.

ANDERSON, Bernhard W. 220.6'6
Understanding the Old Testament / Bernhard W. Anderson. 3d ed. Englewood Cliffs, N.J. : Prentice-Hall, [1975] xxi, 649 p., [4] leaves of plates : ill. ; 23 cm. Includes indexes. Bibliography: p. 607-633. [BS1197.A63 1975] 74-34245 ISBN 0-13-936153-7 : 11.95
1. Jews—History—To 70 A.D. 2. Bible. O.T.—History of Biblical events. I. Title.

ARNDT, William, 1880-1957. 220.6'6
Does the Bible contradict itself? : A discussion of alleged contradictions in the Bible / by W. Arndt. 5th ed., rev. St. Louis : Concordia Pub. House, 1976. p. cm. Reprint of the 1955 ed. [BS511.A66 1976] 75-31712 ISBN 0-570-03721-2 pbk. : 2.50
1. Bible—Criticism, interpretation, etc. I. Title.

ARNOLD, Matthew, 1822-1888. 220.6'6
God & the Bible; a review of objections to 'Literature & dogma.' New York, Macmillan, 1875. [New York, AMS Press, 1970] L, 394 p. 18 cm. Includes bibliographical references. [BS511.A75 1970] 75-129382 ISBN 0-404-00386-9
1. Arnold, Matthew, 1822-1888. Literature and dogma. 2. Bible—Criticism, interpretations, etc. I. Title.

ARNOLD, Matthew, 1822-1888. 220.6'6
Literature & dogma; an essay towards a better apprehension of the Bible. New York, AMS Press [1970] xxviii, 351 p. 23 cm. Reprint of the 1883 ed. [BS511.A7 1970b] 78-126650 ISBN 4-04-003877-
1. Bible—Criticism, interpretation, etc. I. Title.

BAKER, Nelson B. 220.6'6
You can understand the Bible by its unifying themes [by] Nelson B. Baker. [1st ed.] Philadelphia, A. J. Holman [1973] 143 p. 21 cm. Bibliography: p. [144] [BS543.B33 1973] 72-8399 2.95
1. Bible—Theology. I. Title.

BIBLE. N.T. 1 Corinthians. English. Orr-Walther. 1976. 220.6'6 s
I Corinthians : a new translation / introd., with a study of the life of Paul, notes, and commentary by William F. Orr and James Arthur Walther. 1st ed. Garden City, N.Y. : Doubleday, 1976. xv, 391 p. ; 24 cm. (The Anchor Bible ; 32) Includes indexes. Bibliography: p. [133]-138. [BS192.2.A1 1964.G3 vol. 32] [BS2673] 227'.2'07 75-42441 ISBN 0-385-02853-9 : 9.00
1. Paul, Saint, Apostle. 2. Bible. N.T. 1 Corinthians—Commentaries. I. Orr, William Fridell, 1907- II. Walther, James Arthur, 1918- III. Title. IV. Series.

BIBLE. N.T. Apocryphal books. Gospels. Syrian. 1899. 220.6'6 s
The history of the Blessed Virgin Mary and The history of the likeness of Christ which the Jews of Tiberias made to mock at : the Syriac texts / edited with English translations by E. A. Wallis Budge. New York : AMS Press, 1976. 2 v. ; 23 cm. "The history of the likeness of Christ" purports to be written by "Philotheus, the deacon of the country of the East." Reprint of the 1899 ed. published by Luzac, London, which was issued as v. 4-5 of Luzac's Semitic text and translation series. Contents.Contents.—v. 1. The Syriac texts.—v. 2. English translations. [BS2850.S8B8 1976] 229'.8 73-18848 ISBN 0-404-11341-9 : 32.50 (2 vols)
I. Budge, Ernest Alfred Thompson Wallis, 1857-1934. II. Philotheus, deacon of the country of the East, fl. 5th cent.? III. Title: The history of the Blessed Virgin Mary ... IV. Title: The history of the likeness of Christ. V. Series: Luzac's Semitic text and translation series.

BIBLE. N.T. Ephesians. English. Barth. 1974. 220.6'6 s
Ephesians. Introd., translation, and commentary by Markus Barth. [1st ed.] Garden City, N.Y., Doubleday, 1974. 2 v. (xxxiv, 849 p.) 25 cm. (The Anchor Bible, v. 34-34A) Includes bibliographies. [BS192.2.A1 1964.G3 vol. 34-34A] [BS2693] 227'.5'077 72-79373 ISBN 0-385-04412-7 16.00
1. Bible. N.T. Ephesians—Commentaries. I. Barth, Markus, ed. II. Title. III. Series.

BIBLE. N.T. Revelation. English. Ford. 1975. 220.6'6 s
Revelation / introduction, translation, and commentary by J. Massyngberde Ford. 1st ed. Garden City, N.Y.: Doubleday, 1975. xlviii, 455 p. ; 24 cm. (The Anchor Bible ; 38) Includes index. Bibliography: p. [58]-66. [BS192.2.A1 1964.G3 vol. 38] [BS2823] 228'.07'7 74-18796 ISBN 0-385-00895-3 : 9.00
1. Bible. N.T. Revelation—Commentaries. I. Ford, Josephine Massyngberde. II. Title. III. Series.

BIBLE. O.T. Apocrapha. English. Selections. 1977. 220.6'6 s
Daniel, Esther, and Jeremiah : the auditions / a new translation with introd. and commentary by Carey A. Moore. 1st ed. Garden City, N.Y. : Doubleday, 1977. p. cm. (The Anchor Bible ; 44) Includes bibliographies and index. [BS192.2.A1 1964.G3 vol. 44] [BS1695] 229 76-42376 ISBN 0-385-04702-9 : 12.95
1. Bible. O.T. Apocrypha—Commentaries. I. Moore, Carey A., 1930- II. Title. III. Series.

BIBLE. O.T. Apocrypha. 1 Maccabees. English. Goldstein. 1976. 220.6'6 s
I Maccabees : a new translation, with introduction and commentary / by Jonathan A. Goldstein. 1st ed. Garden City, N.Y. : Doubleday, 1976. xxiii, 592 p. : maps ; 24 cm. (The Anchor Bible ; 41) Includes indexes. Bibliography: p. [180]-186. [BS192.2.A1 1964.G3 vol. 41] [BS1823] 229'.73'07 75-32719 ISBN 0-385-08533-8 : 9.00
1. Bible. O.T. Apocrypha. 1 Maccabees—Commentaries. I. Goldstein, Jonathan A., 1929- II. Title. III. Series.

BIBLE. O.T. Job. English. Pope. 1973. 220.6'6 s
Job. Introd., translation, and notes by Marvin H. Pope. [3d ed.] Garden City, N.Y., Doubleday [1973] lxxxix, 405 p. 24 cm. (The Anchor Bible, v. 15) Bibliography: p. [lxxxv]-lxxxix. [BS192.2.A1 1964.G3 vol. 15, 1973] [BS1415.3] 223'.1'077 73-181325 8.00
1. Bible. O.T. Job—Commentaries. I. Pope, Marvin H., ed. II. Title. III. Series.

BIBLE. O.T. Judges. English. Boling. 1975. 220.6'6 s
Judges / introd., translation, and commentary by Robert G. Boling. 1st ed. Garden City, N.Y. : Doubleday, [1975] xxi, 338 p., [6] leaves of plates : ill. ; 24 cm. (The Anchor Bible ; 6A) Includes bibliographical references and indexes. [BS192.2.A1 1964.G3, vol. 6A] [BS1305.3] 222'32'077 72-96229 ISBN 0-385-01029-X : 8.00
1. Bible. O.T. Judges—Commentaries. I. Boling, Robert G., ed. II. Title. III. Series.

BIBLE. O.T. Ruth. English. Campbell. 1975. 220.6'6 s
Ruth : a new translation with introduction, notes, and commentary / by Edward F. Campbell, Jr. 1st ed. Garden City, N.Y. : Doubleday, 1975. xx, 188 p., [4] leaves of plates : ill. ; 24 cm. (The Anchor Bible ; 7) Includes index. Bibliography: p. [42]-45. [BS192.2.A1 1964.G3 vol. 7] [BS1313] 222'.35'077 74-18785 ISBN 0-385-05316-9 : 8.00
1. Bible. O.T. Ruth—Commentaries. I. Campbell, Edward Fay. II. Title. III. Series.

BIBLE. O.T. Song of Solomon. English. Pope. 1977. 220.6'6
Song of songs / a new translation with introduction and commentary by Marvin H. Pope. 1st ed. Garden City, N.Y. : Doubleday, 1977. p. cm. (The Anchor Bible ; 7C) Includes bibliographies and indexes. [BS192.2.A1 1964.G3 vol. 7c] [BS1485.3] 223'.9'066 72-79417 ISBN 0-385-00569-5 : 12.00
1. Bible. O.T. Song of Solomon—Commentaries. I. Pope, Marvin H. II. Title. III. Series.

BIBLE. O. T. Apocrypha. 1 Esdras. English. Myers. 1974 220.6'6 s
I and II Esdras. Introd., translation and commentary by Jacob M. Myers. [1st ed.] Garden City, N.Y., Doubleday, 1974. xxiv, 383 p. illus. 25 cm. (The Anchor Bible, 42) Bibliography: p. 20-22. [BS192.2.A1 1964.G3 vol. 42] [BS1713] 222'.7'066 72-84935 ISBN 0-385-00426-5 8.00
I. Myers, Jacob Martin, 1904- ed. II. Bible. O.T. Apocrypha. 2 Esdras. English. Myers. 1974. III. Title. IV. Series.

BRUCE, Frederick Fyvie, 1910- 220.6'6
Answers to questions [by] F. F. Bruce. Grand Rapids, Mich., Zondervan [1973, c1972] 264 p. 25 cm. Questions and answers previously printed in the Harvester. [BS612.B78] 72-95520 ISBN 0-85364-101-3 6.95
1. Bible—Examinations, questions, etc. 2. Questions and answers—Theology. I. Title.

BUCHANAN, George Wesley. 220.6'6 s
To the Hebrews. Translation, comment, and conclusions by George Wesley Buchanan. [1st ed.] Garden City, N.Y., Doubleday, 1972. xxx, 271 p. illus. 24 cm. (The Anchor Bible, 36) "Abbreviations and references": p. [xiii]-xvi. [BS192.2.A1 1964.G3 vol. 36] [BS2775.3] 227'.87'077 72-76127 ISBN 0-385-02995-0 7.00
1. Bible. N.T. Hebrews—Commentaries. I. Bible. N.T. Hebrews. English. Buchanan. 1972. II. Title. III. Series.

COOK, Albert Stanburrough, 1853-1927, comp. 220.6'6
The Bible and English prose style; selections and comments. Edited with an introd. by Albert S. Cook. [Folcroft, Pa.] Folcroft Library Editions, 1971 [c1892] lxx, 61 p. 23 cm. "Limited to 150 copies." [BS535.C6 1971] 72-192049
1. Bible as literature. I. Bible. English. Authorized. Selections. 1971. II. Title.

CURRENT issues in Biblical and patristic interpretation; studies in honor of Merrill C. Tenney presented by his former students. Edited by Gerald F. Hawthorne. Grand Rapids, Eerdmans [1975] 377 p. port. 25 cm. "Select bibliography of the writings of Merrill C. Tenney": p. 19-20. [BS413.C8] 74-19326 ISBN 0-8028-3442-6 9.95 220.6'6

1. Tenney, Merrill C. 2. Bible—Addresses, essays, lectures. 3. Theology—Early church, ca. 30-600—Addresses, essays, lectures. I. Tenney, Merrill Chapin, 1904- II. Hawthorne, Gerald F., 1925- ed.

DODS, Marcus, 1834-1909. 220.6'6
The Bible, its origin, and nature; seven lectures delivered before Lake Forest College on the foundation of the late William Bross. Freeport, N.Y., Books for Libraries Press [1972] xiii, 245 p. 22 cm. "The Bross lectures, 1904." Reprint of the 1905 ed., which was issued as v. 2 of the Bross library. Includes bibliographical references. [BS511.D58 1972] 72-4255 ISBN 0-8369-6876-X
1. Bible—Criticism, interpretation, etc. I. Title. II. Series: The Bross library, v. 2.

FLANDERS, Henry Jackson. 220.6'6
Introduction to the Bible [by] Henry Jackson Flanders, Jr. [and] Bruce C. Cresson. New York, Ronald Press Co. [1973] xv, 558 p. illus. 24 cm. Bibliography: p. 537-547. [BS475.2.F5] 72-97147 8.50
1. Bible—Introductions. I. Cresson, Bruce C., joint author. II. Title.

FOOTE, George William, 220.6'6
1850-1915.
The Bible handbook for freethinkers and inquiring Christians. Edited by G. W. Foote and W. P. Ball. 11th ed. New York, Arno Press, 1972. 175 p. 21 cm. (The Atheist viewpoint) Originally published in 1961. [BS533.F66 1972] 71-161330 ISBN 0-405-03797-X
1. Bible—Criticism, interpretation, etc. I. Ball, William Platt, joint author. II. Title. III. Series.

FRAZIER, Claude Albee, 220.6'6
1920- comp.
What did the Bible mean? Claude A. Frazier, compiler. Nashville, Broadman Press [1971] 144 p. ports. 19 cm. [BS612.F7] 70-178061 ISBN 0-8054-5127-7
1. Bible—Examinations, questions, etc. I. Title.

GRACE upon grace : 220.6'6
essays in honor of Lester J. Kuyper / edited by James I. Cook. Grand Rapids : Eerdmans, [1975] 154 p. : port. ; 24 cm. Contents.Contents.—Hesselink, I. J. Lester J. Kuyper: faith and fidelity.—Berkhof, H. The (Un)changeability of God.—Mullenburg, J. The Biblical view of time.—Gehman, H. S. The oath in the Old Testament: its vocabulary, idiom, and syntax; its semantics and theology in the Masoretic text and the Septuagint.—Wright, G. E. Women and masculine theological vocabulary in the Old Testament.—Rylaarsdam, J. C. Jewish-Christian relationships: the two convenants and the dilemmas of Christology.—Cook, J. I. The Old Testament concept of the image of God.—De Vries, S. J. Deuteronomy: an exemplar of a non-sacerdotal appropriation of sacred history.—Kooy, V. H. The fear and love of God in Deuteronomy.—Woudstra, M. H. The ark of the covenant in Jeremiah 3:16-18.—Vriezen, T. C. How to understand Malachi 1:11.—Ellis, E. E. Exegetical patterns in 1 Corinthians and Romans.—Oudersluys, R. C. Exodus in the letter to the Hebrews. "A bibliography of the writings of Lester J. Kuyper": p. 153-154. [BS543.G7] 75-12903 ISBN 0-8028-3463-9
1. Kuyper, Lester Jacob, 1904- 2. Kuyper, Lester Jacob, 1904- —Bibliography. 3. Bible—Theology—Addresses, essays, lectures. I. Cook, James I., 1925- II. Kuyper, Lester Jacob, 1904-

HILLERS, Delbert R. 220.6'6 s
Lamentations. Introd., translation, and notes by Delbert R. Hillers. [1st ed.] Garden City, N.Y., Doubleday, 1972. xlviii, 116 p. 24 cm. (The Anchor Bible, 7A) Bibliography: p. [xliii]-xlviii. [BS192.2.A1 1964.G3 vol. 7A] [BS1535.3] 224'.3'07 70-176347 6.00
1. Bible. O.T. Lamentations—Commentaries. I. Bible. O.T. Lamentations. English. Hillers. 1972. II. Title. III. Series.

HORNE, Thomas Hartwell, 220.6'6
1780-1862.
An introduction to the critical study and knowledge of the Holy Scriptures. 8th ed., corr. and enl. Grand Rapids, Baker Book House [1970] 4 v. in 5. illus. 23 cm. Title on spine: Introduction to the Scriptures. Reprint of the 1839 ed. "Bibliographical appendix": v. 2, pt. 2, p. [1]-404. [BS475.H65 1970] 76-132693 ISBN 0-8010-4003-5 29.95
1. Bible—Introductions. 2. Bible—Bibliography. I. Title. II. Title: Introduction to the Scriptures.

KLUG, Eugene F. 220.6'6
From Luther to Chemnitz; on Scripture and the Word [by] E. F. Klug. Grand Rapids, Eerdmans [1971] x, 261 p. 25 cm. Bibliography: p. 249-261. [BS500.K58] 72-183104
1. Luther, Martin, 1483-1546—Theology. 2. Chemnitz, Martin, 1522-1586. 3. Bible—Criticism, interpretation, etc.—History—16th century. I. Title.

KOCH, Klaus. 220.6'6
The growth of the Biblical tradition; the form-critical method. Translated from the 2d German ed. by S. M. Cupitt. New York, Scribner [1969] xv, 233 p. 23 cm. (Scribner studies in biblical interpretation) Translation of Was ist Formgeschichte? Bibliographical footnotes. [BS511.2.K613] 68-17350
1. Bible—Criticism, Form. I. Title.

LAYMON, Charles M. 220.6'6
They dared to speak for God [by] Charles M. Laymon. Nashville, Abingdon Press [1974] 176 p. 22 cm. Includes bibliographical references. [BS511.2.L4] 73-17196 ISBN 0-687-41649-3 5.95
1. Bible—Criticism, interpretation, etc. 2. Bible—Biography. 3. Preaching—Biblical teaching. I. Title.

LEABO, John. 220.6'6
The harmonizing of science and the Bible to reveal secrets of life and creation for humanitarian utopian promotion. Port Angeles, Wash., Christian Zion Advocate [1971] iv, 148 p. illus. 23 cm. [BS650.L4] 78-172051 3.89
1. Bible—Prophecies. 2. Bible and science. I. Title.

LEHMAN, Chester Kindig, 220.6'6
1895-
Biblical theology, by Chester K. Lehman. Scottdale, Pa., Herald Press [1971-74] 2 v. 23 cm. Contents.Contents.—v. 1. Old Testament.—v. 2. New Testament. Includes bibliographies. [BS543.L43] 74-141829 ISBN 0-8361-1633-X (vol. 1) 15.95 (v. 1) 18.95 (v. 2)
1. Bible—Theology. I. Title.

LINDBLOM, Johannes, 1882- 220.6'6
The Bible: a modern understanding, by J. Lindblom. Translated by Eric H. Wahlstrom. Philadelphia, Fortress Press [1973] viii, 197 p. 19 cm. Translation of the first eight chapters in Tio kapitel om Bibeln. Bibliography: p. 187-197. [BS516.2.L5413] 72-91525 ISBN 0-8006-0125-4 3.95
1. Bible—Criticism, interpretation, etc. I. Title.

*LITTLE, Robert J. 220.6'6
Here's your answer. Chicago, Moody Pr. [1973, c.1967] 220 p. 17 cm. [BS612] ISBN 0-8024-3526-2 0.95 (pbk)
1. Bible—Examinations, questions, etc. I. Title.

LOCKYER, Herbert. 220.6'6
All the divine names and titles in the Bible : a unique classification of all scriptural designations of the three persons of the Trinity / by Herbert Lockyer. Grand Rapids : Zondervan Pub. House, c1975. 360 p. ; 25 cm. Includes indexes. Bibliography: p. 343-344. [BT99.L57] 74-25338 8.95
1. Jesus Christ—Person and offices—Biblical teaching. 2. God—Biblical teaching. 3. Holy Spirit—Biblical teaching. I. Title.

LONGENECKER, Richard N. 220.6'6
Biblical exegesis in the apostolic period [by] Richard N. Longenecker. [Grand Rapids] Eerdmans [1974, c1975] 246 p. 21 cm. Bibliography: p. [221]-230. [BS500.L66] 74-13757 ISBN 0-8028-1569-3
1. Bible—Criticism, interpretation, etc.—History—Early church, ca. 30-600. 2. Bible. N.T.—Relation to O.T. I. Title.

MACKINTOSH, Charles 220.6'6
Henry, 1820-1896.
The Mackintosh treasury : miscellaneous writings / by C. H. Mackintosh. Neptune, N.J. : Loizeaux Bros., [1976] p. cm. First published in 1898 under title: The miscellaneous writings of C. H. Mackintosh. [BR85.M18 1976] 75-44323 ISBN 0-87213-609-4 : 12.95
1. Theology—Collected works—19th century. I. Title.

MANNING, Francis V. 220.6'6
The Bible: dogma, myth, or mystery? By Francis V. Manning. Staten Island, N.Y., Alba House [1968] 315 p. 22 cm. Bibliography: p. [289]-308. [BS587.M35] 68-15382 5.50
1. Bible—Study—Catholic Church. I. Title.

MONTEFIORE, Claude Joseph 220.6'6
Goldsmid, 1858-1938.
The Old Testament and after. Freeport, N.Y., Books for Libraries Press [1972] xi, 601 p. 22 cm. Reprint of the 1923 ed. [BM565.M62 1972] 72-2566 ISBN 0-8369-6862-X 18.75
1. Bible. O.T.—Criticism, interpretation, etc. 2. Bible. N.T.—Criticism, interpretation, etc. 3. Rabbinical literature—History and criticism. 4. Hellenism. 5. Reform Judaism. I. Title.

MORGAN, Richard. 220.6'6
God's Biblical sacrificial blueprints and specifications for reconciling the world into Himself. Nashville, Tenn., Parthenon Press [1972] 248 p. 24 cm. On spine: God's blueprints and specifications. [BS511.2.M66] 78-186552 8.00
1. Bible—Criticism, interpretation, etc. 2. Christian life—1960- I. Title.

MORRIS, Henry Madison, 220.6'6
1918-
The Bible has the answer; practical Biblical discussions of 100 frequent questions, by Henry M. Morris. Grand Rapids, Mich., Baker Book House [1971] x, 256 p. 22 cm. [BR96.M67] 71-165506 3.25 (pbk)
1. Bible—Examinations, questions, etc. 2. Theology—Miscellanea. I. Title.

MURPHY, Roland Edmund, 220.6'6
1917-
Theology, exegesis, and proclamation. Edited by Roland Murphy. [New York] Herder and Herder [1971] 143 p. 23 cm. (Concilium: religion in the seventies, v. 70: Scripture) On cover: The New concilium: religion in the seventies. Includes bibliographical references. [BS531.M87] 74-168652 2.95
1. Bible—Criticism, interpretation, etc.—Addresses, essays, lectures. I. Title. II. Series: Concilium (New York), v. 70.

NEWPORT, John P., 1917- 220.6'6
Why Christians fight over the Bible, by John P. Newport and William Cannon. Nashville, T. Nelson [1974] 165 p. 21 cm. Bibliography: p. 151-156. [BS480.N43] 74-4288 ISBN 0-8407-5067-6 2.95 (pbk.)
1. Bible—Evidences, authority, etc. 2. Bible—Criticism, interpretation, etc. I. Cannon, William, 1918- joint author. II. Title.

SANDS, Percy Cooper. 220.6'6
Literary genius of the Old Testament / by P. C. Sands. Folcroft, Pa. : Folcroft Editions, 1975. 123 p. ; 23 cm. Reprint of the 1924 ed. published at the Clarendon Press, Oxford. Includes bibliographical references and index. [BS535.S25 1975] 75-35756 ISBN 0-8414-7646-2 lib. bdg. : 12.50
1. Bible. O.T.—Criticism, interpretation, etc. 2. Bible. O.T.—Language, style. 3. Bible as literature. I. Title.

SCHAEFFER, Edith. 220.6'6
Christianity is Jewish / Edith Schaeffer. Wheaton, Ill. : Tyndale House Publishers, 1975. 224 p. ; 22 cm. [BS635.2.S28] 75-7224 ISBN 0-8423-0243-3 : 5.95
1. Bible—History of Biblical events. 2. Christianity and other religions—Judaism. 3. Judaism—Relations—Christianity. I. Title.

SHIRES, Henry M. 220.6'6
Finding the Old Testament in the New, by Henry M. Shires. Philadelphia, Westminster Press [1974] 251 p. 21 cm. Bibliography: p. [207]-209. [BS2387.S54] 73-19600 ISBN 0-664-20993-9 7.50
1. Bible. N.T.—Relation to O.T. I. Title.

SIMON, Ulrich E. 220.6'6
Story and faith in the Biblical narrative / [by] Ulrich Simon. London : S.P.C.K., 1975. x, 126 p. ; 20 cm. Bibliography: p. [122]-126. [BS535.S53] 75-328588 ISBN 0-281-02793-5 : 15.00 ISBN 0-281-02843-5 pbk. : 7.50
1. Bible as literature. 2. Prose literature—History and criticism. I. Title.
Distributed by Allenson.

UNDERSTANDING the Sacred 220.6'6
Text; essays in honor of Morton S. Enslin on the Hebrew Bible and Christian beginnings. Edited by John Reumann. Advisory editorial committee: F. W. Beare [and others] Valley Forge [Pa.] Judson Press [1972] 256 p. port. 23 cm. Contents.Contents.—The sum of many parts, by T. V. Enslin.—A select bibliography of the writings of Morton Scott Enslin. (p. 21-26)—The ancient mind and ours, by S. Sandmel.—Midrash and the Old Testament, by B. S. Childs.—Nationalism; universalism in the book of Jeremiah, by H. M. Orlinsky.—Some remarks on the New English Bible, by W. F. Stinespring.—Sarepta in history and tradition, by J. B. Pritchard.—The synoptic apocalypse: Matthean version, by F. W. Beare.—The transfiguration in Mark: Epiphany or apocalyptic vision? By H. C. Kee.—Forms, motives, and omissions in Mark's account of the teaching of Jesus, by M. Smith.—The ending of the Gospel according to Mark in Ethiopic manuscripts, by B. M. Metzger.—The quest for the historical Baptist, by J. Reumann.—When Acts sides with John, by P. Parker.—The resurrection of Jesus Christ in the Book of Acts and in early Christian literature, by E. F. Harrison.—Eusebius and his Church history, by R. M. Grant.—Tabula gratulatoria. Includes bibliographical references. [BS413.U5] 72-165592 ISBN 0-8170-0487-4 15.00
1. Bible—Addresses, essays, lectures. I. Enslin, Morton Scott, 1897- II. Reumann, John Henry Paul, ed.

DEMAREST, Bruce A. 220.6'6'08 s
A history of interpretation of Hebrews 7, 1-10 [seven, one to ten] from the reformation to the present / by Bruce Demarest. 1. Aufl. Tubingen : Mohr, 1976. viii, 146 p. ; 24 cm. (Beitrage zur Geschichte der biblischen Exegese ; 19) ISSN 0408-8298) A revision of the author's thesis, University of Manchester, 1973. Bibliography: p. [137]-146. [BS500.B4 no. 19] [BS2775.2] 227'.87'06 76-377634 ISBN 3-16-138531-4 : DM32.00
1. Bible. N.T. Hebrews VII, 1-10—Criticism, interpretation, etc.—History. I. Title. II. Series.

BULLINGER, Ethelbert 220.6'8
William, 1837-1913.
Number in Scripture; its supernatural design and spiritual significance. Grand Rapids, Kregel Publications [1967] viii, 303 p. illus. 23 cm. Reprint of the 1894 ed. Bibliographical footnotes. [BS534.B83] 67-26498
1. Symbolism of numbers. 2. Symbolism in the Bible. 3. Bible—Criticism, interpretation, etc. I. Title.

BULLINGER, Ethelbert 220.6'8
William, 1837-1913.
Number in Scripture; its supernatural design and spiritual significance. Grand Rapids, Kregel Publications [1967] viii, 303 p. illus. 23 cm. Reprint of the 1894 ed. Bibliographical footnotes. [BS534.B83 1967] 67-26498
1. Bible—Criticism, interpretation, etc. 2. Symbolism of numbers. 3. Symbolism in the Bible. I. Title.

DAVIS, John James, 1936- 220.6'8
Biblical numerology, by John J. Davis. Grand Rapids, Baker Book House [1968] 174 p. 20 cm. Bibliography: p. 157-167. [BS680.N8D3] 68-19207 3.95
1. Numbers in the Bible. I. Title.

PIRKLE, Estus W. 220.6'8
Preachers in space, by Estus W. Pirkle. Greenville, S.C., Hiott Press, 1969. 263 p. illus. 23 cm. Bibliography: p. 261. [BS655.P52] 70-2741
1. Bible—Astronomy. I. Title.

ROLT-WHEELER, Francis 220.6'8
William, 1876-1960.
The manifestations of Christ universal. [Translated by Robert Whipple Wilson. Tampa? Fla., c1968- v. (various pagings) 23 cm. Translation of Le christianisme esoterique. Includes bibliographies. [BS534.R613] 75-3028
1. Jesus Christ—Miscellanea. 2. Bible—Miscellanea. I. Title.

SHEALY, Julian Belton, 220.6'8
1902-
The key to our God given heritage. Columbia, S. C., State Print. Co. [1967] ix, 618 p. illus. 24 cm. [BS534.S45] 68-281
1. Bible—Criticism, interpretation, etc. 2. Numbers in the Bible. 3. Pyramids—Curiosa and miscellany. I. Title.

SHEALY, Julian Belton, 220.6'8
1902-
The key to our God given heritage. Columbia, S.C., State Print. Co. [1967] ix, 618 p. illus. 24 cm. [BS534.S45] 68-281
1. Bible—Criticism, interpretation, etc. 2. Numbers in the Bible. 3. Pyramids—Miscellanea. I. Title.

SWAIM, Joseph Carter, 220.6'8
1904-
Unlocking the treasures in Biblical imagery, by J. Carter Swaim. New York, Association Press [1966] 128 p. 16 cm. (A Reflection book) [BS476.S9] 66-20478
1. Bible—Hermeneutics. I. Title.

WUELLNER, Wilhelm H., 220.6'8
1927-
The meaning of 'Fishers of men' [by] Wilhelm H. Wuellner. Philadelphia, Westminster [1967] 256p. 23cm. (New Testament lib. Bibl. [BS2545.F5W8] 67-12012 6.95
1. Fishing in the Bible. 2. Fishing (in religion, folk-lore, etc.) I. Title.

ALL the books and chapters 220.7
of the Bible; combination of Bible study and daily meditation plan. Grand Rapids, Zondervan Pub. House [1966] 313 p. 24 cm. [BS491.2.L6] 65-25952
1. Bible — Commentaries.

ANDERSON, Bernhard W. 220.7
Rediscovering the Bible. New York, Association Press, 1951. 272 p. 23 cm. (A Haddam House book) [BS511.A53] 51-12127
1. Bible—Criticism, interpretation, etc. I. Title.

ARNDT, William, 1880-1957. 220.7
Bible difficulties; an examination of passages of the Bible alleged to be irreconcilable with its inspiration. St. Louis. Concordia Pub. House [1957, c1932] 176p. 19cm. [BS511.A65 1957] 58-488
1. Bible—Criticism, interpretation, etc. I. Title.

ARNDT, William, 1880-1957. 220.7
Does the Bible contradict itself A discussion of alleged contradictions in the Bible. 5th ed., rev. St. Louis, Concordia Pub. House, 1955. 173p. 19cm. [BS511.A66 1955] 58-481
1. Bible—Criticism, interpretation, etc. I. Title.

AVERY, Margaret, 1890- 220.7
Teaching Scripture; a book on method. Wallington, Surrey, Religious Education Press [1951] 192p. illus. 19cm. (Gateway handbooks of religious knowledge, 4) [BS600.A85] 53-611
1. Bible—Study. I. Title.

BAUER, Charles George. 220.7
The eternal triumphant Christ; the Lord Jesus Christ from Genesis to Revelation. [Philadelphia? c1957] 304p. 21cm. [BS538.B33] 58-28346
1. Bible— Criticism, Interpretation, etc. I. Title.

BEACON Bible commentary. 220.7
Kansas City, Mo., Beacon Hill Press [1964-] v. illus. map. 24 cm. Includes bibliography. [BS491.2.B4] 64-22906
1. Bible — Commentaries.

BIBLE. English. 1957. 220.7
American standard.
The Evangelical commentary on the Bible. [Grand Rapids, Mich., Zondervan Pub. House, 1957- v. maps. 25 cm. Each vol. has special t.p. Various publishers. Includes bibliographies. [BS491.E8] 57-34945
1. Bible — Commentaries. I. Title.

BIBLE. English. 1957. 220.7
Authorized.
The Evangelical commentary on the Bible. [Grand Rapids, Zondervan Pub. House, 1957- v. map. 25cm. Each vol. has also special t.p. [BS491.E8] 57-34945
1. Bible— Commentaries. I. Title.

BIBLE. English. 1960. 220.7
Authorized.
Commentary on the Holy Bible, by Matthew Henry and Thomas Scott. With explanatory notes from other writers. Grand Rapids, Baker Book House, 1960. 6v. map, plan. 25cm. Contents.v. 1. Genesis-Deuteronomy.--v. 2. Joshua-Esther.--v. 3. Job-Song of Solomon.--v. 4. Isaiah-Malachi.--v. 5. Matthew-Acts.--v. 6. Romans-Revelation. [BS491.H4 1960] 60-10188
1. Bible—Commentaries. I. Henry, Matthew, 1662-1714. II. Scott, Thomas, 1747-1821. III. Title.

BIBLE. English. 1964. 220.7
The Anchor Bible. Introd., translation, and notes. [1st ed.] Garden City, N. Y., Doubleday, 1964- v. 24 cm. Includes bibliographical references. [BS192.2.A1 1964.G3] 64-55388
1. Bible—Commentaries. I. Title.

BIBLE. English. Selections. 220.7
1965. Authorized.
The everlasting light; the King James version of the Bible chronologically condensed, by Erma Wood Carlson. [Boston, T. Todd Co., c1965] xi, 1353 p. 24 cm. [BS391.2.W6] 66-6322
1. Carlson, Erma Wood. I. Title. II. Title: The King James version of the Bible chronologically condensed.

BIBLE, English. Selections. 220.7
1965. Authorized.
The everlasting light; the King James version of the Bible chronologically condensed, by Erma Wood Carlson. [Boston, T. Todd Co., c.1965] xi, 1353p. 24cm. [BS391.2.W6] 66-6322 15.00
I. Carson, Erma Wood. II. Title. III. Title: The King James version of the Bible chronologically condensed.
Available from Mrs. Elizabeth O. Rockwell, Carlson Books, P.O Box 66735, Houston, Texas 7706.

BIBLE handbook 220.7
[24th rev. ed.] Grand Rapids, Mich., Zondervan [c.1927-1965] 860p. illus., maps. 19cm. First ed. pub. in 1924. Title varies: 24th ed.: Halley's Bible handbook; an abbreviated Bible commentary. Comp., ed.: H. H. Halley. [BS417.B48] 32-8057 3.95
1. Bible—Handbooks, manuals, etc. 2. Church history—Outlines, syllabi, etc. I. Halley, Henry Hampton, 1874- comp.

THE Biblical expositor; 220.7
the living theme of the Great Book, with general and introductory essays and exposition for each book of the Bible. Consulting editor: Carl F. H. Henry. [1st ed.] Philadelphia, A. J. Holman Co. [1960] 3v. 24cm. Contents.v. 1. The Old Testament: Genesis-- --Esther.--v. 2. The Old Testament: Job--Malachi.--v. 3. The New Testament. [BS491.2.B5] 60-5198
1. Bible—Commentaries. I. Henry, Carl Ferdinand Howard, 1913- ed.

THE Biblical expositor; 220.7
the living theme of the Great Book, with general and introductory essays and exposition for each book of the Bible. Introd. by Billy Graham. Consulting editor: Carl F. H. Henry. Philadelphia, A. J. Holman Co. [1973] xxviii, 1282 p. 24 cm. [BS491.2.B5 1973] 73-599 ISBN 0-87981-020-3 9.95
1. Bible—Commentaries. I. Henry, Carl Ferdinand Howard, 1913- ed.

BIBLICAL expositor (The); 220.7
the living theme of the Great Book, with general and introductory essays and exposition for each book of the Bible; v. 2. Consulting editor: Carl F. H. Henry, Philadelphia, A. J. Holman Co. [c.1960] viii, 402p. 24cm. 60-5198 6.95
1. Bible—Commentaries. I. Henry, Carl Ferdinand Howard, ed.

BIBLICAL expositor (The); 220.7
the living theme of the Great Book, with general and introductory essays and exposition for each book of the Bible. Consulting editor: Carl F. H. Henry. Philadelphia, A. J. Holman Co. [c.1960] xii, 402p.; viii, 500p. 24cm. Contents.v. 1. The Old Testament: Genesis-Esther. v. 3. The New Testament. 60-5189 6.95 ea.,
1. Bible—Commentaries. I. Henry, Carl Ferdinand Howard, ed.

BLACK, Mattew, ed. 220.7
Peake's commentary on the Bible. General editor and New Testament editor: Mattew Black. Old Testament editor: H. H. Rowley. London, New York, T. Nelson, 1962. xv, 1126, 4p. 16col. maps. 27cm. 'An entirely new work. Based on the text of the Revised standard version.' Includes bibliographies. [BS491.B57] 62-6297
1. Bible—Commentaries. I. Rowley, Harold Henry, 1890- ed. II. Peake, Arthur Samuel, 1865-1929. ed. A commentary on the Bible. III. Title.

BLACK, Matthew, ed 220.7
Peake's commentary on the Bible. Gen. ed., New Testament ed.: Matthew Black. Old Testament ed.: H. H. Rowley. New York, Nelson [c.]1962. xv, 1126, 4 p. 16 col. maps. 27cm. 62-6297 15.00
1. Bible—Commentaries. I. Rowley, Harold Henry, 1890- ed. II. Peake, Arthur Samuel, 1865-1929, ed. A commentary on the Bible. III. Title.

BOOTH, James Scripps. 220.7
Adventure in analysis; a searching Biblical commentary, by Edmund Wood Gagnier [pseud.] New York, Philosophical Library [1954] 696p. 24cm. [BS533.B65] 54-4864
1. Bible—Criticism, interpretation, etc. I. Title.

BOUYER, Louis, 1913- 220.7
The meaning of Sacred Scripture. Translated by Mary Perkins Ryan. [Notre Dame, Ind.] University of Notre Dame Press, 1958. 258p. 24cm. (Notre Dame [Ind.] University. Liturgical studies, v. 5) Translation of La Bible et l'Evangile. [BS531.B653] 57-11376
1. Bible—Criticism, interpretation, etc. 2. Bible—Evidences, authority, etc. I. Title.

THE Broadman Bible 220.7
commentary. General Editor: Clifton J. Allen. Rev. Nashville, Broadman Press [1973- v. 24 cm. Contents.Contents.—v. 1. General articles, Genesis-Exodus. [BS491.2.B672] 74-150427 ISBN 0-8054-1125-9 7.50
1. Bible—Commentaries. I. Allen, Clifton J., 1901- ed. II. Broadman Press. III. Bible. English. Revised standard. 1973.

BROWN, Raymond Edward, 220.7
comp.
The Jerome Biblical commentary, edited by Raymond E. Brown, Joseph A. Fitzmyer [and] Roland E. Murphy. With a foreword by Augustin Cardinal Bea. Englewood Cliffs, N.J., Prentice-Hall [1968] 2 v. in 1. illus., geneal. table, maps (1 fold.) 28 cm. Contents.Contents.—v. 1. The Old Testament, edited by R. E. Murphy.—v. 2. The New Testament, and topical articles, edited by J. A. Fitzmyer and R. E. Brown. Includes bibliographies. [BS491.2.B7] 68-9140
1. Bible—Commentaries. I. Fitzmyer, Joseph A., joint comp. II. Murphy, Roland Edmund, 1917- joint comp. III. Title.

BRUDNO, Ezra Selig, 1877- 220.7
A guide for the misguided. New York, Philosophical Library [1951] xix, 103 p. 23 cm. [BS533.B76] 51-10048
1. Bible—Criticism, interpretation, etc. I. Title.

CALVIN, Jean, 1509-1564. 220.7
Calvin: commentaries. Newly translated and edited by Joseph Haroutunian, in collaboration with Louise Pettibone Smith. Philadelphia, Westminster Press [1958] 414p. 24cm. (The Library of Christian classics. v. 23) Cover title: Calvin: commentaries and letters. [BS485.C333 1958] 58-5060
1. Bible—Commentaries. I. Haroutunian, Joseph, 1904- ed. and tr. II. Title.

CALVIN, Jean, 1509-1564 220.7
Commentaries [11] Eds.: David W. Torrance, Thomas F. Torrance. Grand Rapids, Mich., Eerdmans [1966, c.1965] v, 369p. 23cm. 60-3628 6.50
1. Bible — Commentaries. I. Torrance, David Wishart, ed. II. Torrance, Thomas Forsythe, 1913- ed. III. Title. IV. Title: New Testament commentaries.
Contents omitted.

CALVIN, Jean, 1509-1564 220.7
Commentaries [10] Eds.: David W. .Torrance, Thomas F. Torrance. Grand Rapids, Mich., Eerdmans [c.1964] 410p. 23cm. On spine: Calvin's New Testament commentaries. 60-3628 6.00
1. Bible—Commentaries. I. Torrance, David Wishart, ed. II. Torrance, Thomas Forsythe, 1913- ed. III. Title. IV. Title: New Testament commentaries.
Contents omitted.

CALVIN, Jean. 1509-1564 220.7
Commentaries [7] Eds.: David W. Torrance, Thomas F. Torrance. Grand Rapids, Mich., Eerdmans [c.1966] v, 329p. 23cm. On spine: New Testament commentaries. [BS485.C24] 60-3621 6.00
1. Bible — Commentaries. I. Torrance, David Wishart, ed. II. Torrance, Thomas Forsyth, 1913- ed. III. Title. IV. Title: New Testament commentaries.
Contents omitted.

CALVIN, Jean, 1509-1564. 220.7
Commentaries. Eds: David W. Torrance, Thomas F. Torrance. Grand Rapids, Mich., Eerdmans, c.1961 327p. Contents.v.5. The Gospel according to St. John, 11-21 and the First Epistle of John. Translator: T. H. L. Parker. 4.50
1. Bible—Commentaries. I. Torrance, David Wishart, ed. II. Torrance, Thomas Forsyth, 1913- ed. III. Title. IV. Title: New Testament commentaries.

CALVIN, Jean, 1509-1564 220.7
Commentaries [v.4] Editors: David W. Torrance [and] Thomas F. Torrance. Grand Rapids, Mich. Eerdmans [1959] vi, 278p. On spine: New Testament commentaries. Contents.4. The Gospel according to St. John, 1-10. Translator T. H. L. Parker. 60-3628 4.50
1. Bible—Commentaries. I. Torrance, David Wishart, ed. II. Torrance, Thomas Forsyth, ed. III. Title. IV. Title: New Testament commentaries.

CALVIN, Jean, 1509-1564 220.7
Commentaries [6] Eds.: David W. Torrance, Thomas F. Torrance. Grand Rapids, Mich., Eerdmans [1966, c.1965] vi, 410p. 23cm. On spine: New Testament commentaries. Trs.: John W. Fraser, W. J. G. McDonald. [BS485.C24] 60-3628 6.00
1. Bible — Commentaries. I. Torrance, David Wishart, ed. II. Torrance, Thomas Forsyth, 1913- ed. III. Title. IV. Title: New Testament commentaries.
Contents omitted.

CALVIN, Jean, 1509-1564 220.7
Commentaries. Eds.: David W. Torrance, Thomas F. Torrance. Grand Rapids, Mich., Eerdmans [1961] 433p. On spine: New Testament commentaries. Contents.8. The Epistles of Paul the Apostle to the Romans and to the Thessalonians. Tr.: John W. Fraser. 60-3628 6.00
1. Bible—Commentaries. I. Torrance, David Wishart, ed. II. Torrance, Thomas Forsyth, 1913- ed. III. Title. IV. Title: New Testament commentaries.

CALVIN, Jean, 1509-1564. 220.7
Commentaries [v.9] Editors: David W. Torrance [and] Thomas F. Torrance. Grand Rapids, Mich., Eerdmans [1960] v, 370p. p. v. On spine: New Testament commentaries. Contents.9. The First Epistle of Paul to the Corinthians. Translator: John W. Fraser. Bibl.: 60-3628 5.00
1. Bible—Commentaries. I. Torrance, David Wishart, ed. II. Torrance, Thomas Forsyth, ed. III. Title. IV. Title: New Testament commentaries.

CALVIN, Jean, 1509-1564 220.7
Commentaries [v.12] Eds. [by] David W. and Thomas F. Torrance. Tr. [by] William B. Johnston. Grand Rapids, Mich.. Eerdmans [c.1963] 378p. 23cm. On spine: New Testament commentaries. Contents.v.12, The Epistle of Paul to the Hebrews, The first and second Epistles of St. Peter. 60-3628 6.00
1. Bible—Commentaries. I. Torrence, David Wishart, ed. II. Torrence, Thomas Forsyth, ed. III. Johnston, William B., tr. IV. Title. V. Title: New Testament commentaries.

CALVIN, John, 1509-1564 220.7
Corpus Reformatorum. Ioannis Calvini: Opera quae supersunt omnia; v.1-59, ser. no. 29-87. New York, Johnson Reprint, 1965. 58v. (various p.) 26cm. 1,225.00; 30.00 set; ea.,
I. Title.

CASTELOT, John J 220.7
God so loved the world... A commentary on the Bible. With a foreword by Leo J. Trese. Notre Dame, Ind., Fides Publishers [1962] 150p. 21cm. [BS635.2.C3] 62-20573
1. Bible—History of Biblical events. I. Title.

CASTELOT, John J. 220.7
God so loved the world . . . A commentary on the Bible. Foreword by Rev. Leo J. Trese. Notre Dame, Ind., Fides [c.1962] 150p. 21cm. 62-20573 3.95
1. Bible—History of Biblical events. I. Title.

CLARK, George Luther, 1877- 220.7
A lawyer looks at the Bible. 1st ed. New York, Vantage Press [1956] 336p. 21cm. [BS538.C5] 56-9029
1. Bible—Criticism, interpretation, etc. I. Title.

CUMMINS, Betty Jane, 1909-- 220.7
Toward a new concept of the Bible. Boston, Meador Pub. Co. [1952] 121p. 24cm. [BS533.C84] 53-5984
1. Bible—Criticism, interpretation. etc. I. Title.

DAVIES, Arthur Powell. 220.7
Religion in the Bible. Boston, Beacon Press [1952] 30 p. 21 cm. (Beacon reference series) Includes bibliography. [BS531.D27] 52-10167
1. Bible—Criticism, interpretation, etc. I. Title.

DEAL, William S 220.7
Baker's pictorial introduction to the Bible, by William S. Deal. Grand Rapids, Baker Book House [1967] 431, [4] p. illus., ports. 25 cm. Bibliography: p. [433]-[435] [BS475.2.D4] 67-20517
1. Bible—Introductions. I. Title. II. Title: Pictorial Introduction to the Bible.

DEAL, William S. 220.7
Baker's pictorial introduction to the Bible, by William S. Deal. Grand Rapids, Baker Book House [1967] 431, [4] p. illus., ports. 25 cm. Bibliography: p. [433]-[435] [BS475.2.D4] 67-20517
1. Bible—Introductions. I. Title. II. Title: Pictorial introduction to the Bible.

DE HOFF, George Washington, 220.7
1913-
Alleged Bible contradictions explained. Murfreesboro, Tenn., De Hoff Publications, 1950. 303 p. port. 20 cm. [BS511.D36] 50-14567
1. Bible—Criticism, interpretation, etc. I. Title.

DODD, Charles Harold 220.7
The Bible today. [New York] Cambridge University Press, 1960 ix, 168p. 19cm. 'Open lectures given under the auspices of the Divinity faculty of the University of Cambridge.' 1.45 pap.,
1. Bible—Criticism, interpretation, etc. I. Title.

EXELL, Joseph Samuel, 1849- 220.7
ed.
The Biblical illustrator. Grand Rapids, Baker Pub. House, 1954- v. 24cm. [BS491] 54-11086
1. Bible—Commentaries. I. Title.

GAEBELEIN, Arno Clemens, 220.7
1861-1945.
The annotated Bible; the Holy Scriptures analyzed and annotated. [Neptune, N.J.] Moody Press, Loizeaux Brothers [1970] 4 v. 21 cm. Contents.Contents.—v. 1. Genesis to Second Chronicles.—v. 2. Ezra to Malachi.—v. 3. Matthew to Ephesians.—v. 4. Philippians to Revelation. [BS491.G32] 78-119745 24.95
I. Title.

GAEBELEIN, Frank Ely, 1899- 220.7
Exploring the Bible; a study of background and principles. 3d rev. ed. Wheaton, Ill., Van Kampen Press [1950] xiv, 150 p. 20 cm. "An Our Hope Press book." Bibliographical footnotes. [BS511.G25 1950] 51-311
1. Bible—Criticism, Interpretation, etc. I. Title.

GRANT, Frederick Clifton, 220.7
1891-
How to read the Bible. Foreword by Horace W. B. Donegan. New York, Morehouse-Gorham, 1956. 168p. 20cm. (The Annual Bishop of New York books, 1956) [BS600.G67] 56-5285
1. Bible—Study. 2. Bible—Reading. I. Title.

GRANT, Frederick Clifton, 220.7
1891-
How to read the Bible. [Foreword by Horace W. B. Donegan] New York, Collier Bks. [1962, c.1956] 122p. e(AS32) Bibl. .95 pap.,
1. Bible—Study. 2. Bible—Reading. I. Title.

GRANT, Frederick Clifton, 1891- ed. 220.7
Nelson's Bible commentary. Based on the Revised standard version. New York, T. Nelson [c1962- v. 22 cm. Contents.CONTENTS.--v. 6. New Testament: Matthew--Acts.--v. 7. New Testament: Romans--Revelation. Includes bibliographies. [BS491.2.G7] 62-20244
1. Bible—Commentaries. I. Title.

GRANT, Frederick Clifton, 1891- ed. 220.7
Nelson's Bible commentary [v. 6 & 7] Based on the Revised standard version. New York, Nelson [c.1962] 2v., 518; 425p. 22cm. Contents.v.6. New Testament: Matthew-Acts.--v.7. New Testament: Romans-Revelation. Bibl. 62-20244 5.00 ea.,
1. Bible—Commentaries. I. Title.

GRANT, Robert McQueen, 1917- 220.7
The Bible in the church, a short history of interpretation. rev. ed. New York, Macmillan [c.1948, 1963] 224p. 18cm. (137) Bibl. 1.45 pap.,
1. Bible—Criticism, interpretation, etc.—Hist. I. Title.

GRANT, Robert McQueen, 1917- 220.7
A short history of the interpretation of the Bible. Rev. ed. New York, Macmillan [1963] 224p. 18cm. (MP137) First ed. pub. in 1948 under title: The Bible in the church. Bibl. 63-25042 1.45 pap.,
1. Bible—Criticism, interpretation, etc.—Hist. I. Title.

GUTHRIE, Donald, 1916- 220.7
The new Bible commentary, revised, edited by D. Guthrie [and] J. A. Motyer. Consulting editors: A. M. Stibbs [and] D. J. Wiseman. [3d ed., completely rev. and reset] Grand Rapids, Mich., Eerdmans [1970] xv, 1310 p. 24 cm. Earlier editions edited by F. Davidson. Based on the text of the Revised standard version. [BS491.2.G8 1970] 71-111346 12.95
1. Bible—Commentaries. I. Motyer, J. A., joint author. II. Davidson, Francis. The new Bible commentary. III. Title.

HASTINGS, James, 1852-1922, ed. 220.7
The great texts of the Bible. Grand Rapids, Eerdmans [1958- v. 23cm. Contents.v. 1. Genesis--Numbers.--v.8. St. Matthew.--v. 9. St. Mark.--v. 10. St. Luke. Includes bibliographies. [BS491.H32] 58-13517
1. Bible— Commentaries. I. Title.

HEIM, Ralph Daniel, 1895- 220.7
Youth's companion to the Bible. Philadelphia, Muhlenberg Press [1959] 245p. illus. 22cm. [BS605.H38] 59-8741
1. Bible—Study—Text-books. I. Title.

HEIM, Ralph Daniel, 1895- 220.7
Youth's companion to the Bible. Philadelphia, Fortress [1965, c.1959] 245p. illus. 19cm. [BS605.H38] 1.95 pap.,
1. Bible—Study—Text-books. I. Title.

[HELINE, Corinne (Smith) Dunklee], 1882- 220.7
The New Age Bible interpretation; an exposition of the inner significance of the Holy Scriptures in the light of the ancient wisdom. [Rev. and enl.] Los Angeles, New Age Press [1950- v. 24 cm. Contents.v. 4. The New Testament, pt. 1. [BS530.H48] 50-58197
1. Bible—Miscellanea. I. Title.

HENRY, Matthew, 1662-1714. 220.7
Commentary on the whole Bible, Genesis to Revelation. Ed. by Rev. Leslie F. Church. Grand Rapids, Mich., Zondervan Pub. House [1961, c.1960] xi, 1204, 784p. 25cm. 61-1491 9.95
1. Bible—Commentaries. I. Title.

HENRY, Matthew, 1662-1714. 220.7
Commentary on the whole Bible, Genesis to Revelation. Edited by Leslie F. Church. Grand Rapids, Zondervan Pub. House [1961] ix, 1986p. 25cm. [BS490.H4 1961a] 61-40016
1. Bible—Commentaries. I. Title.

HENRY, Matthew, 1662-1714 220.7
Concise commentary on the whole Bible [by] Matthew Henry, Thomas Scott [others] Chicago, Moody [1963] 1024p. 24cm. 5.95 bds.,
1. Bible commentaries. I. Scott, Thomas, joint author. II. Title.

HUDSON, Roland Vernon, 1913- 220.7
Bible survey outlines; the Bible in setting, summary, and significance, its historical background, spiritual analysis and contemporary application. Grand Rapids, Eerdmans, 1954. 426p. 23cm. Includes bibliographies. 'General bibliography and commentaries': p.[421]-426. [BS591.H8] 54-4590
1. Bible—Study —Outlines, syllabi, etc. I. Title.

THE Interpreter's Bible: 220.7
the Holy Scriptures in the King James and Revised standard versions with general articles and introduction, exegesis, exposition for each book of the Bible. [Editorial board: George Arthur buttrick, commentary editor, and others] New York, Abingdon-Cokesbury Press [1951- v. maps. 27 cm. Contents.v. 7. General articles on the New Testament. Matthew. Mark. Includes bibliographies. [BS491.I 65] 51-12276
1. Bible—Commentaries. I. Bible. English. 1951. Authorized. II. Bible. English. 1951. Revised standard. III. Buttrick, George Arthur, 1892- ed.

THE Interpreter's one 220.7
volume commentary on the Bible: introd. and commentary for each book of the Bible including the Apocrypha, with general articles. Edited by Charles M. Laymon. Nashville, Abingdon Press [1971] xiv, 1386 p. illus., maps (16 col.) 27 cm. [BS491.2.I57] 71-144392 ISBN 0-687-19299-4 17.50
1. Bible—Commentaries. I. Laymon, Charles M., ed.

IRONSIDE, Henry Allan, 1876-1951. 220.7
Dr. Ironside's Bible: notes and quotes from the margins. Introd. by Herbert J. Pugmire. [1st ed.] New York, Loizeaux Bros. [1955] 187p. port., facsims. 20cm. [BS491.I68] 55-14761
1. Bible—Commentaries. I. Title.

JAMIESON, Robert, 1802-1880. 220.7
A commentary, critical, experimental, and practical, on the Old and New Testaments, by Robert Jamieson, A. R. Fausset, and David Brown. Grand Rapids, Mich., Eerdmans [1973] p. Contents.Contents.—v. 1. pt. 1. Jamieson, R. Genesis-Deuteronomy. pt. 2. Jamieson, R. Joshua-Esther.—v. 2. pt. 1. Fausset, A. R. Job-Isaiah. pt. 2. Fausset, A. R. Jeremiah-Malachi.—v. 3. pt. 1. Brown, D. Matthew-John. pt. 2. Brown, D. Acts-Romans. pt. 3. Fausset, A. R. 1 Corinthians-Revelation. [BS491.J3 1973] 73-14988 ISBN 0-8028-2158-8
1. Bible—Commentaries. I. Fausset, Andrew Robert, 1821-1910. II. Brown, David, 1803-1897. III. Title.

JAMIESON, Robert, 1802-1880. 220.7
Commentary, practical and explanatory, on the whole Bible [by] Robert Jamieson, A. R. Fausset [and] David Brown. [New ed.] Grand Rapids, Zondervan Pub. House, 1961. 1591 p. 25 cm. [BS491.J33] 61-16236
1. Bible—Commentaries.

JENNEY, Ray Freeman, 1891- 220.7
Bible primer. Foreword by Ralph W. Sockman. [1st ed.] New York, Harper [1955] 190p. 22cm. [BS475.J4] 55-8524
1. Bible-Introductions. I. Title.

JOHNSON, Douglas. 220.7
The Christian and his Bible. [1st ed.] Grand Rapids, Eerdmans, 1953. 144p. 19cm. [BS538] 55-380
1. Bible—Criticism, interpretation, etc. I. Title.

KELLY, Balmer H., ed. 220.7
The Layman's Bible commentary. Balmer H. Kelly, editor; Donald G. Miller [and] Arnold B. Rhodes, associate editors. Richmond, John Knox Press [1959-64] 25 v. 19 cm. v. 19 cm. A leader's guide, by Leslie Bullock. Richmond. John Knox Press, 1959- Includes bibliographies. [BS491.2.L3] 59-10454
1. Bible — Commentaries. I. Bullock, Leslie. II. Title.

KNOX, John, 1900- 220.7
Criticism and faith. New York, Abingdon-Cokesbury Press [1952] 128 p. 20 cm. [BS520.K6] 52-8843
1. Bible—Criticism, Interpretation, etc. 2. Bible—Evidences, authority. etc. I. Title.

THE Layman's Bible 220.7
commentary. Balmer H. Kelly, editor; Donald G. Miller [and] Arnold B. Rhodes, associate editors. Richmond, John Knox Press [1959-64] 25 v. 19 cm. v. 19 cm. A leader's guide, by Leslie Bullock. Richmond. John Knox Press, 1959- Includes bibliographies. [BS491.2.L3] 59-10454
1. Bible — Commentaries.

THE Layman's Bible 220.7
commentary. Balmer H. Kelly, editor; Donald G. Miller [and] Arnold B. Rhodes, associate editors. Richmond, John Knox Press [1959-Richmond, John Knox Press [1959- v. 19cm. v. 19cm. Includes bibliography. [BS491.2.L3] 59-10454
1. Bible—Commentaries. I. Kelly, Balmer H., ed. II. Bullock, Leslie. III. Title: —A leader's guide, by Leslie Bullock.

LAYMAN'S Bible commentary 220.7
(The); v. 11. Balmer H. Kelley, ed; Donald G. Miller [others] assoc. eds. Richmond, Va. Knox [c.1964] 159 p. 19 cm. Contents.Contents—v.11, the book of Isaiah, by G. Ernest Wright. 59-10454 bds. 2.00
1. Bible—Commentaries. I. Wright, G. Ernest.

LAYMAN'S Bible commentary 220.7
(The) Balmer H. Kelly, ed.; Donald G. Miller, Arnold B. Rhodes, assoc. eds. Large type ed. Richmond, Knox [1967,c.1959-1963] v. 28cm. Bibl. [BS491.2.L3] 50-10454 3.95 ea.,
1. Bible—Commentaries. I. Kelly, Balmer H. ed. II. Bullock, Leslie.

LAYMAN'S Bible commentary 220.7
(The) v. 8, 15, 17, 24. Balmer H. Kelly, ed.; Donald G. Miller, Arnold B. Rhodes, assoc. eds. Richmond, Va., Knox [c.1962] (4 v.) various p. 19cm. 59-10454 2.00 bds., ea.,
1. Bible—Commentaries. I. Kelly, Balmer H., ed.

LAYMAN'S Bible commentary 220.7
(The); v.3. Balmer H. Kelly, ed.; Donald G. Miller, Arnold B. Rhodes, assoc. eds. Richmond, Va., Knox [c.1963] 125p. 19cm. Contents.v.3. The book of Exodus [by] B. Davie Napier. 59-10454 2.00 bds.,
1. Bible—Commentaries. I. Kelly, Balmer H., ed.

LAYMAN'S Bible commentary 220.7
(The). Balmer H. Kenny, ed.; Donald G. Miller, Arnold B. Rhodes, assoc. eds. Richmond, Va., John Knox Press [c.1960] 4v. various pages Contents.v.9, Psalms; v.12, Jeremiah, Lamentations; v.20, Acts; v.25, 1,2,3 John, Jude, Revelation. Bibl. 59-10454 2.00, 7.00 bds., ea., bxd. set,
1. Bible—Commentaries. I. Kelly, Balmer H., ed.

LAYMAN'S Bible commentary 220.7
(The): v.5, 7.10. Balmer H. Kelly, ed.: Donald G. Miller, Arnold B. Rhodes, assoc. eds. Richmond, Va., Knox [c.1964] 3v. (various p.) 19cm. Contents.v.5. The Book of Deuteronomy, The Book of Joshua, by Edward P. Blair.--v.7. First and Second Books of Kings, First and Second Books of the Chronicles. by Robert C. Dentan.--v.10. The Proverbs. Ecclesiastes. Song of Solomon, by J. Coert Rylaarsdam. 59-10454 2.00 bds., ea.,
1. Bible—Commentaries. I. Kelly, Balmer H., ed.

LAYMAN'S Bible commentary 220.7
(The); v.4, 19, 23. Balmer H. Kelly, ed., Donald G. Miller, Arnold B. Rhodes, assoc. eds. Richmond, Va., Knox [c.1963] 143; 155; 131p. 19cm. Contents.v.4. The Book of Leviticus, the Book of Numbers, by James L. Mays.--v.19. The Gospel according to John, by Floyd V. Filson.--v.23. The 1st & 2d Letters of Paul to the Thessalonians; the 1st & 2d Letters of Paul to Timothy; the Letter of Paul to Titus; the Letter of Paul to Philemon, by Holmes Rolston. 59-10454 2.00 bds., ea.,
1. Bible—Commentaries. I. Kelly, Balmer, H., ed.

LAYMAN'S Bible commentary 220.7
(The) [vs. 6, 13, 16, 21.] Balmer H. Kelly, ed.; Donald G. Miller, Arnold B. Rhodes, assoc. eds. Richmond, Va. John Knox [c.1961] various p. Contents.v.6. The Book of Judges, The Book of Ruth, The First and Second Books of Samuel, by Eric C. Rust. v.13. The Book of Ezekiel, The Book of Daniel, by Carl G. Howie. v.16. The Gospel according to Matthew, by Suzanne de Dietrich, v.21. The Letter of Paul to the Romans, The First Letter of Paul to the Corinthians, The Second Letter of Paul to the Corinthians, by Kenneth J. Foreman. 59-10454 7.00; ea., 2.00 bds., set, ea.,

LOCKYER, Herbert. 220.7
All the books and chapters of the Bible; combination of Bible study and daily meditation plan. Grand Rapids, Zondervan Pub. House [1966] 313 p. 24 cm. [BS491.2.L6] 65-25952
1. Bible — Commentaries. I. Title.

LOCKYER, Herbert 220.7
All the books and chapters of the Bible; combination of Bible study and daily meditation plan. Grand Rapids, Mich., Zondervan [c.1966] 313p. 24cm. [BS491.2.L6] 65-25952 4.95
1. Bible — Commentaries. I. Title.

MCNALLY, Robert E 220.7
The Bible in the early Middle Ages. Westminster, Md., Newman Press, 1959. 121p. 22cm. (Woodstock papers; occasional essays for theology, no. 4) A Newman paperback. Includes bibliography. [BS482.M2] 59-10289
1. Bible—Criticism, interpretation, etc.—Hist. I. Title.

*MALONE, Dolores Mathis. 220.7
God's covenent; the one story of the Bible. Illus. by Shannon Stirnweis. Richmond, Va., John Knox Press [1973] 159 p. illus. (pt. col.) 21 cm. (Covenant life curriculum) 3.45 (pbk.)
1. Bible—Study and teaching. I. Title. II. Series.

*MARTIN, Alfred 220.7
Teacher's manual [for] Learning from God, no. 2, a doctrine course, by Alfred Martin, Dorothy Martin. Chicago, Moody [1965, c.1964] 64p. 22cm. pap., .75; student's manual, pap., .29
I. Title.

MEYER, Frederick Brotherton, 1847-1929 220.7
Our daily homily; chapter by chapter through the Bible. [Westwood, N.J.] Revell [1966] 469p. 24cm. [BS491.M45 1966] 66-9626 8.95
1. Bible — Commentaries. I. Title.

MORGAN, George Campbell, 1863-1945. 220.7
The analyzed Bible [by] G. Campbell Morgan. Westwood, N. J., F. H. Revell [1964] viii, 600 p.22 cm. [BS511.M532] 64-16600
1. Bible — Commentaries. I. Title.

MORGAN, George Campbell, 1863-1945 220.7
The analyzed Bible. Westwood, N.J., Revell [c.1964] viii, 600p. 22cm. 64-16600 8.95
1. Bible—Commentaries. I. Title.

MORGAN, George Campbell, 1863-1945. 220.7
An exposition of the Bible, chapter by chapter in one volume. [Westwood, N.J.] Revell [1959] 542p. 22cm. [BS491.M62 1959] 59-8719
1. Bible— Commentaries. I. Title.

MOYLE, Frank W 220.7
About the Bible. New York, Scribner [1957, c1956] 182p. 22cm. [BS538.M67 1957] 57-7581
1. Bible— Criticism, interpretation, etc. I. Title.

NEIL, William, 1909- 220.7
Harper's Bible commentary. New York, Harper & Row [c1962] 544 p. 22 cm. First published in England in 1962 under title: One volume Bible commentary. [BS491.2.N4 1964] 63-7607
1. Bible — Commentaries. I. Title.

NEIL, William, 1909- 220.7
Harper's Bible commentary / William Neil. New York : Harper & Row, 1975, c1962. 544 p. ; 19 cm. First published in London under title: One volume Bible commentary. [BS491.2.N4 1975] 75-311132 ISBN 0-06-066091-0 : 3.95
1. Bible—Commentaries. I. Title.

NICHOL, Francis David, 1897- ed. 220.7
The Seventh-Day Adventist Bible commentary; the Holy Bible with exegetical and expository comment. [Editor: Francis D. Nichol; associate editors: Raymond F. Cottrell and Don F. Neufeld; assistant editor: Julia Neuffer] Washington, Review and Herald Pub. Association [1953-57] 7 v. illus., maps (part col.) 25cm. Contents.v. 1. Genesis to Deuteronomy.--v. 2. Joshua to 2 Kings.--v. 3. 1 Chronicles to Song of Solomon.--v. 4. Isaiah to Malachi.--v. 5. Matthew to John.--v. 6. Acts to Ephesians.--v. 7. Philippons to Revelation. [BS491.N48] 53-37093
1. Bible—Commentaries. I. Bible, English, 1953. Authorized. II. Title.

ORCHARD, Bernard, Father, 1910- ed. 220.7
A Catholic commentary on Holy Scripture. Editorial Committee: Bernard Orchard [and others] With a foreword by the Cardinal Archbishop of Westminster. London, New York, Nelson [1953] xvi, 1312p. col. maps. 27cm. [BS491.O7 1953] 53-1573
1. Bible—Commentaries. I. Title.

PAMPHLET bible series; 220.7
a commentary and complete text of the Old and New Testaments. [Neil J. McEleney, general editor.] New York, Paulist Press [c.1960- 96 p. illus. "The scriptual translation...prepared by scholars of the Catholic Bible Association of America. Contents.Contents—v.11. The book of Josue, with a commentary by Joseph J. Devault. 60 pap., .75
1. Bible—Commentaries. I. Bible. English. 1960. Catholic Bible Association. II. McEleney, Neil J., ed.

PAMPHLET Bible series; 220.7
a commentary and complete text of the Old

and New Testaments. [Neil J. McEleney, general editor] New York 19, Paulist Press, 401 W. 59th st. [c.1960] 2v. (96 p.; p6p.) "The scriptural translation...prepared by scholars of the catholic Biblical Association of America." Contents.Contents—The Book of Exodus, part 1; part 2, with a commentary by Roland E. Murphy. 60-9284 .75 each
1. Bible—Commentaries. I. Bible, English. 1960. Catholic Biblical Association. II. McEleney, Neil J., ed.

PAMPHLET Bible series: 220.7
45. pt. 3, with a commentary by Robert North. New York, Paulist Pr. [c.1963] 96p. 23cm. 60-9284 .50 pap.,
1. Bible—Commentaries. I. Bible. English. 1960. Catholic Biblical Association.

PAMPHLET Bible series: 220.7
a commentary and complete text of the Old and New Testaments. v.36. [Neil J. McEleney, general ed., Scriptural tr., prepared by scholars of the Catholic Biblical Assn. of America] New York, Paulist [c.1963] 94p. illus. 23cm. 60-9284 .50 pap.,
1. Bible—Commentaries. I. Bible. English. 1960. Catholic Biblical Association. II. McEleney, Neil, J., ed.
Contents omitted.

PARKER, Joseph, 1830-1902. 220.7
Preaching through the Bible. Grand Rapids, Baker Book House, 1959- v. 23cm. 'Originally printed under the title, The people's Bible.' [BS491.P32] 59-10860
1. Bible— Sermons. I. Title.

PASCHALL, Henry Franklin. 220.7
The teacher's Bible commentary. Edited by H. Franklin Paschall, Old Testament [and] Herschel H. Hobbs, New Testament. Nashville, Broadman Press [1972] 817 p. illus. 24 cm. [BS491.2.P34] 75-189505 ISBN 0-8054-1116-X
1. Bible—Commentaries. I. Hobbs, Herschel H. II. Title.

PETRUS RIGA, d.1209 220.7
Aurora: Petri Rigae Biblia versificata; a verse commentary on the Bible; 2 pts. Paul E. Beichner, ed. [Notre Dame, Ind.] Univ. of Notre Dame Pr. [c.]1965. 2v. (various p.) 24cm. (Pubs. in medieval studies, Univ. of Notre Dame, 19) Bibl. Title. (Series: Notre Dame, Ind. University. Publications in mediaeval studies, 19) [BS485.P4] 65-15986 15.00, set bxd.,
1. Bible—Commentaries. I. Beichner, Paul E., ed. II. Title. III. Series.

PFEIFFER, Charles F. 220.7
The Wycliffe Bible commentary. Edited by Charles F. Pfeiffer, Old Testament [and] Everett F. Harrison, New Testament. Chicago, Moody Press [1962] xv, 1525 p. 24 cm. Includes bibliographies. [BS491.2.P4] 62-20893
1. Bible—Commentaries. I. Harrison, Everett Falconer, 1902- II. Title.

ROWLEY, Harold Henry, 1890- 220.7
The unity of the Bible. Philadelphia, Westminster Press [1953] 201p. 23cm. [BS480] 55-6000
1. Bible—Evidences, authority, etc. 2. Bible—Criticism, interpretation, etc. I. Title.

ROWLEY, Harold Henry, 1890- 220.7
The unity of the Bible. New York, Meridian Books, 1957. 232p. 19cm. (Living age books, LA16) Includes bibliography. [BS480.R68 1957] 57-10849
1. Bible—Evidences, authority, etc. 2. Bible—Criticism, interpretation, etc. I. Title.

SHERGOLD, William J 220.7
A devotional commentary on the Bible, with special reference to The shorter Oxford Bible. New York, Oxford University Press, 1955. 284p. 20cm. Includes bibliography. [BS491.2.S5] 55-13546
1. Bible—Commentaries. I. Title.

SMITHER, Ethel Lisle 220.7
Children and the Bible. Henry M. Bullock, general editor. Nashville, Abingdon Press [c.1960] 183p. (bibls.) 19cm. 60-2608 1.50 pap.,
1. Bible—Study. 2. Religious education. I. Title.

SOMMARIPA, George. 220.7
Meditations of a young man on the Bible. [1st ed.] New York, Exposition Press [1955] 49p. 21cm. [BS530.S65] 55-12284
1. Bible—Criticism, interpretation, etc. I. Title.

STEELE, Algernon Odell, 220.7
1900-
The Bible and the human quest. New York, Philosophical Library [c1956] 240p. 21cm. [BR121.S82] 57-1204
1. Christianity—20th cent. I. Title.

STEELE, Algernon Odell, 220.7
1900-
The Bible and the human quest. New York, Philosophical Library [c1956] 240 p. 21 cm. [BR121.S82] 57-1204
1. Christianity — 20th cent. I. Title.

SWAIM, Joseph Carter, 1904- 220.7
The Book God made. [1st ed.] New York. Hawthorn Books [1959] 95 p. 21 cm. [BS538.S78] 59-5615
1. Bible—Criticism, interpretation, etc. I. Title.

SWAIM, Joseph Carter, 1904- 220.7
The Book God made. [1st ed.] New York, Hawthorn Books [1959] 95 p. 21 cm. [BS538.S78] 59-5615
1. Bible—Criticism, interpretation, etc. I. Title.

THOMAS AQUINAS, Saint 220.7
1225?-1274
Aquinas Scripture series; v.2. Albany, Magi Bks. [c.1966] 313p. illus. 24cm. Bibl. Contents.v.2. Commentary on Saint Paul's Epistle to the Ephesians; tr., introd. by M. L. Lamb. [BS491.2.T5] 66-19306 5.95 bds.,
1. Bible — Commentaries. I. Title.

TILLEY, Ethel. 220.7
Book of the ages; a course for junior high groups in the vacation church school. Teacher's book. Nashville, Published for the Cooperative Publication Association by Abingdon Press [1956] 144p. 20cm. (The Cooperative series: vacation church school texts) [BS605.T55] 56-6357
1. Bible—Study—Text-books. 2. Vacation schools, Religious—Text-books. I. Title.

TILLEY, Ethel. 220.7
Book of the ages; a course for junior high groups in the vacation church school. Teacher's book. Nashville, Published for the Cooperative Publication Association by Abingdon Press [1956] 144 p. 20 cm. (The Cooperative series: vacation church school texts) [BS605.T55] 56-6357
1. Bible—Study—Text-books. 2. Vacation schools, Religious—Text-books. I. Title.

TOWNSEND, Edgar Jerome, 220.7
1864-
A layman's view of the Bible. [Ann Arbor? c1953] 135p. 19cm. [BS538.T6] 54-31762
1. Bible —Criticism, interpretation, etc. I. Title.

THE Twentieth century Bible 220.7
commentary, edited by G. Henton Davies, Alan Richardson and Charles L. Wallis. Rev. ed. New York, Harper [c1955] xvi, 571p. illus., col. maps. 24cm. 'First edition...was published in 1932 under the title The Teachers' commentary and edited by Hugh Martin.' Includes bibliographies. [BS491.T4 1955a] 55-11488
1. Bible—Commentaries. I. Davies, Gwynne Henton, ed.

VOS, Howard Frederic, 1925- 220.7
Effective Bible study. Grand Rapids, Zondervan Pub. House [1956] 224p. 22cm. [BS600.V6] 56-25035
1. Bible—Study. I. Title.

VOS, Howard Frederic, 1925- 220.7
Effective Bible study. Grand Rapids, Zondervan Pub. House [1956] 224 p. 22 cm. [BS600.V6] 56-25035
1. Bible — Study. I. Title.

WESLEYAN Bible commentary 220.7
(The)
Volume 2, "Job," "Psalms, 1-150" and "Proverbs" is now available from Eerdmans, Grand Rapids, Mich. for $8.95. L.C. card order no.: 64-23335.1

WESLEYAN Bible commentary 220.7
(The) [Edit. bd.: Chairman and gen. ed.: Charles W. Carter. New Testament ed.: Ralph Earle. Old Testament ed.: W. Ralph Thompson. Assoc. ed.: Lee Haines] Grand Rapids, Eerdmans [1967] v. maps (on lining papers) 25cm. Contents.V. 1, pt. 1. Genesis and Exodus [by] Lee Haines.--Leviticus [by] Armour D. Peisker.--Numbers and Deuteronomy [by] Howard A. Hanke.--v. 1, pt. 2. Joshua--Esther [by] Charles R. Wilson Bibl. [BS491.2.W4] 64-23335 8.95 ea.,
1. Bible—Commentaries. I. Carter, Charles Webb, 1905- II. Earle, Ralph. ed. III. Thompson, W. Ralph. ed.

WESLEYAN Bible commentary 220.7
(The) v.4. [Ed. Board: Chairman, general ed.: Charles W. Carter. N. T. ed.: Ralph Earle. O. T. ed.: W. Ralph Thompson. Assoc. ed.: Lee Haines] Grand Rapids, Mich., Eerdmans [c.1964] vii, 749p. maps (on lining papers) 25cm. Contents.v.4. Matthew, Mark, Luke, john, Acts, by R. Earle, H. J. S. Blaney, and C. W. Carter. Bibl. 64-23335 8.95
1. Bible—Commentaries. I. Carter, Charles Webb, 1905- ed. II. Earle, Ralph, ed. III. Thompson, W. Ralph, ed.

WESLEYAN Bible commentary 220.7
(The); v.6. Edit. bd.: Chairman, gen. ed., Charles W. Carter.er. New Testament ed.: Ralph Earle. Old Testament ed.: W. Ralph Thompson. Assoc. ed.: Lee Haines. Grand Rapids, Mich., Eerdmans [c.1966] viii, 523p. maps (on lining paps.) 25cm. Contents.v.6. Hebrews, by Charles W. Carter. -- James and Jude, by R. Duane Thompson. -- I & II Peter, by Charles S. Ball. -- I, II, III John, by Leo G. Cox. -- Revelation, by Harvey J. S. Blaney [BS491.2.W4] 64-23335 8.95
1. Bible — Commentaries. I. Carter, Charles Webb, 1905- ed. II. Earle, Ralph, ed. III. Thompson, W. Ralph, ed.

WESLEYAN Bible commentary 220.7
(The); v.5. Edit. Bd.: Chairman, gen. ed.: Charles W. Carter. New Testament ed.: Ralph Earle. Old Testament ed.: W. Ralph Thompson. Assoc. ed.: Lee Haines. Grand Rapids, Mich., Eerdmans [c.1965] viii, 675p. maps (on lining paps.) 25cm. Contents.v.5. Romans and Galatians, by Wilber T. Dayton.--I Corinthians, and Ephesians, by Clarence W. Carter.--II Corinthians, by Clarence H. Zahniser.--Philippians and Colossians, by George A. Turner.--I & II Thessalonians, by W. O. Klopfenstein.--I & II Timothy and Titus, by Roy S. Nicholson.--Philemon, by George E. Failing [BS491.2W4] 64-23335 8.95
1. Bible—Commentaries. I. Carter, Charles Webb, 1905- ed. II. Earle, Ralph, ed. III. Thompson, W. Ralph, ed.

WILLIAMS, George, 1850- 220.7
1928.
The student's commentary on the Holy Scriptures; analytical, synoptical, and synthetical. New improved [6th] ed. Grand Rapids, Kregel Publications [1971] vii, 1058 p. 25 cm. [BS491.2.W53 1971] 72-180043 ISBN 0-8254-4001-7 11.95
1. Bible—Commentaries. I. Title.

ZERR, Edward Michael, 1877- 220.7
Bible commentary. University City, Mo., Missouri Mission Messenger [1947-55] 6 v. 24cm. Vols. 3--6 have imprint: St. Louis, Mission Messenger. Contents.v. 1. Genesis to Ruth.--v. 2. 1 Samuel to Job.--v. 3. Psalms to Isaiah.--v. 4. Jeremiah to Malachi.--v. 5. Matthew to Romans. --v. 6. First Corinthians to Revelation. [BS491.Z4] 47-23931
1. Bible—Commentaries. I. Title.

MCCREARY, William Burgess, 220.76
1894-
Bible quizzes and questions. Anderson, Ind., Warner Press [1956] 96p. 19cm. [BS612.M259] 56-4175
1. Bible—Examinations, questions, etc. I. Title.

BEACON Bible 220.7'7
expositions. Editors: William M. Greathouse [and] Willard H. Taylor. Kansas City, Mo., Beacon Hill Press [1974- v. 20 cm. [BS491.2.B42] 74-176138
1. Bible—Commentaries. I. Greathouse, William M., ed. II. Taylor, Willard H., ed.

BIBLE. English. 220.7'7
Authorized. 1977.
The Holy Bible, containing the Old and New Testaments, the text carefully printed from the most correct copies of the present authorized translation, including the marginal readings and parallel texts : with a commentary and critical notes designed as a help to a better understanding of the sacred writings / by Adam Clarke. New ed., with the author's final corrections. Nashville : Abingdon, [1977] 6 v. in 3 ; 27 cm. On spine: Clarke's commentary. Vol. 5-6 has title: The New Testament of our Lord and Saviour Jesus Christ. A reprint of the 6 v. ed. of 1851, which was originally published as an 8 v. ed., 1810-1825, by Butterworth, London. [BS185 1977.N37] 77-151643 ISBN 0-687-09119-5 (v. 1-2) : 19.50 per vol.
1. Bible—Commentaries. I. Clarke, Adam, 1760?-1832. II. Title: The Holy Bible ... III. Title: Clarke's commentary.

BIBLE. English. Jerusalem 220.7'7
Bible. 1975.
The Bible in order : all the writings which make up the Bible, arranged in their chronological order according to the dates at which they were written, or edited into the form in which we know them, seen against the history of the times as the Bible provides it : with introd. and notes / edited by Joseph Rhymer. Garden City, N.Y. : Doubleday, 1975. xxxii, 1917 p. ; 24 cm. Chart, "Guidelines to the Old Testament", inserted inside back cover. [BS195.J4 1975] 75-11363 ISBN 0-385-11062-6
I. Rhymer, Joseph, 1927- II. Title.

THE Broadman Bible 220.7'7
commentary. General editor: Clifton J. Allen. Old Testament consulting editors: John I. Durham and Roy L. Honeycutt, Jr. New Testament consulting editors: John William MacGorman and Frank Stagg. Nashville, Broadman Press [1969-72] 12 v. 25 cm. Contents.Contents.—v. 1. Genesis. Exodus.—v. 2. Leviticus. Numbers. Deuteronomy. Joshua. Judges. Ruth.—v. 3. 1-2 Samuel. 1 Kings. 2 Kings. 1-2 Chronicles. Ezra. Nehemiah.—v. 4. Esther. Job. Psalms.—v. 5. Proverbs. Ecclesiastes. Song of Solomon. Isaiah.—v. 6. Jeremiah. Lamentations. Ezekiel. Daniel.—v. 7. Hosea. Joel. Amos. Obadiah. Jonah. Micah. Nahum. Habakkuk. Zephaniah. Haggai. Zechariah. Malachi.—v. 8. Matthew. Mark.—v. 9. Luke. John.—v. 10. Acts. Romans. 1 Corinthians.—v. 11. 2 Corinthians. Galatians. Ephesians. Philippians. Colossians. 1-2 Thessalonians. 1-2 Timothy. Titus. Philemon.—v. 12. Hebrews. James. 1-2 Peter. 1-2-3 John. Jude. Revelation. [BS491.2.B67] 78-93918 7.50 per vol.
1. Bible—Commentaries. I. Allen, Clifton J., 1901- ed.

CLARKE, Adam, 1760?-1832. 220.7'7
Commentary on the Holy Bible. Abridged from the original six-volume work, by Ralph Earle. Kansas City, Mo., Beacon Hill Press of Kansas City [1967] 1356 p. 25 cm. "One-volume edition." Originally published 1810-1825 in 8 vol. under title: the Holy Bible ... with a commentary and critical notes. Printed in the standard 6 v. ed. in 1851. Cf. BM, v. 17, col. 147 and DNB, v. 10, p. 414. [BS491.C613] 67-13093
1. Bible—Commentaries. I. Earle, Ralph, ed. II. Title.

NICHOL, Francis David, 220.7'7
1897-1966, ed.
The Seventh-Day Adventist Bible commentary : the Holy Bible with exegetical and expository comment / [editor, Francis D. Nichol, associate editors, Raymond F. Cottrell, Don F. Neufeld, assistant editor, Julia Neuffer ; contributors, Milian L. Andreasen ... et al.]. Rev. Washington : Review and Herald Pub. Association, 1976- v. : ill. ; 25 cm. Contents.Contents.—v. 1. Genesis to Deuteronomy.—v. 2. Joshua to 2 Kings.—v. 3. 1 Chronicles to Song of Solomon. [BS491.2.A52 1976] 77-153833
1. Bible—Commentaries. I. Andreasen, Milian Lauritz, 1876- II. Bible. English. 1953. Authorized. III. Title.

BIBLE. O.T. 1 220.7'7'08 s
Chronicles. English. New American. 1973.
The first book of Chronicles. With a commentary by John A. Grindel. New York, Paulist Press [1973] 117 p. illus. 23 cm. (Pamphlet Bible series, v. 17) [BS491.2.P3 vol. 17] [BS1343] 222'.63'077 74-156898 1.00 (pbk.).
I. Grindel, John A. II. Title. III. Series.

BIBLE. O.T. 1 Kings. 220.7'7'08 s
English. New American. 1973.
The first book of Kings. With a commentary by Geoffrey Wood. New York, Paulist Press [1973] 111 p. illus. 23 cm. (Pamphlet Bible series, v. 15) [BS491.2.P3 vol. 15] [BS1333] 222'.53'077 74-156894 1.00 (pbk.)
I. Wood, Geoffrey, 1928- II. Title. III. Series.

BIBLE. O.T. 1 220.7'7'08 s
Samuel. English. 1971.
The first book of Samuel, with a commentary by Frederick Moriarty. New York, Paulist Press [1971] 128 p. illus. 23 cm. (Pamphlet Bible series, 13) [BS491.2.P3 vol. 13] [BS1323] 70-25522 1.00
I. Moriarty, Frederick L. II. Title. III. Series.

BIBLE. O.T. 2 220.7'7'08 s
Chronicles. English. New American. 1973.
The second book of Chronicles. With a commentary by John A. Grindel. New York, Paulist Press [1973] 125 p. illus. 23 cm. (Pamphlet Bible series, v. 18) [BS491.2.P3 vol. 18] [BS1343] 222'.64'077 74-156896 1.00 (pbk.)
I. Grindel, John A. II. Title. III. Series.

BIBLE. O.T. 2 Kings. 220.7'7'08 s
English. New American. 1973.
The second book of Kings. With a commentary by Geoffrey Wood. New York, Paulist Press [1973] 102 p. illus. 23 cm. (Pamphlet Bible series, v. 16) [BS491.2.P3 vol. 16] [BS1333] 222'.54'077 74-156893 1.00 (pbk.)
I. Wood, Geoffrey, 1928- II. Title. III. Series.

BIBLE. O.T. 2 220.7'7'08 s
Samuel. English. New American. 1971.
The second book of Samuel, with a commentary by Frederick Moriarty. New York, Paulist Press [1971] 103 p. illus. 23 cm. (Pamphlet Bible series, 14) [BS491.2.P3 vol. 14] [BS1323] 73-25523 1.00
I. Moriarty, Frederick L. II. Title. III. Series.

BIBLE. O.T. 220.7'7'08 s
Apocrypha. 1 Maccabees. English. New American. 1973.
The first book of Maccabees. With a commentary by Neil J. McEleney. New York, Paulist Press [1973] 120 p. 23 cm. (Pamphlet Bible series, F22) [BS491.2.P3 vol. 22] [BS1823] 229'.73 74-156900 1.00 (pbk.)
I. McEleney, Neil J. II. Title. III. Series.

BIBLE. O.T. 220.7'7'08 s
Apocrypha. 2 Maccabees. English. New American. 1973.
The second book of Maccabees. With a commentary by Neil J. McEleney. New York, Paulist Press [1973] 101 p. illus. 23 cm. (Pamphlet Bible series, v. 23) [BS491.2.P3 vol. 23] [BS1823] 229'.73 74-156899 1.00 (pbk.)
I. McEleney, Neil J. II. Title. III. Series.

BIBLE. O.T. Esther. 220.7'7'08 s
English. New American. 1973.
The books of Esther & Judith. With a commentary by George T. Montague. New York, Paulist Press [1973] 110 p. illus. 23 cm. (Pamphlet Bible series, 21) [BS491.2.P3 vol. 21] [BS1373] 222'.9'077 74-156895 1.00 (pbk.)
I. Montague, George T. II. Bible. O.T. Apocrypha. Judith. English. New American. 1973. III. Title. IV. Series.

BIBLE. O.T. Ruth. 220.7'7'08 s
English. New American. 1973.
The books of Ruth & Tobit. With a commentary by George T. Montague. New York, Paulist Press [1973] 87 p. illus. 23 cm. (Pamphlet Bible series, v. 20) [BS491.2.P3 vol. 20] [BS1313] 222'.35'077 74-156892 1.00 (pbk.)
I. Montague, George T. II. Bible. O.T. Apocrypha. Tobit. English. New American. 1973. III. Title. IV. Series.

BERTRANGS, A. 220.8
The Bible on suffering, by A. Bertrangs. Translated by F. Vander Heijden. De Pere, Wis., St. Norbert Abbey Press, 1966. 62 p. 17 cm. Bibliographical references included in "Notes" (p. [57]-62) [BT732.7.B413] 66-16990
1. Suffering — Biblical teaching. I. Title.

BERTRANGS, A. 220.8
The Bible on suffering. Tr. by F. Vander Heijden. De Pere, Wis., St. Norbert Abbey Pr. [c.]1966. 62p. 17cm. Bibl. [BT732.7.B413] 66-16990 .95 pap.,
1. Suffering — Biblical teaching. I. Title.

BIBLE. English. Selections. 220.8
196-? Authorized.
Animals of the Bible; a picture book, by Dorothy P. Lathrop. With text selected by Helen Dean Fish from the King James Bible. Philadelphia, Lippincott [196-? c1937] vi, 66 p. illus. 26 cm. [BS663.F5] 65-6688
1. Bible — Natural history — Juvenile literature. I. Fish, Helen Dean, comp. Lathrop, Dorothy Pulis, 1891—— illus. II. Title.

BIBLE. English. Selections. 220.8
1965. Authorized.
My Bible book. Verses selected by Janie Walker. Pictures by Dean Bryant. Chicago, Rand McNally, 1965, c.1946. 1v. (unpaged) col. illus. 32cm. [BS560.W3] 65-15345 1.00 pap.,
1. Bible — Pictures, illustrations, etc. I. Walker, Janie, comp. II. Everr, Helen illus. III. Title.

*BULLINGER, Ethelbert W. 220.8
Figures of speech used in the Bible explained and illustrated. Grand Rapids, Baker Bk. [1968] xlviii, 1104p. 23cm. Reprint of the 1898 ed. pub. by Eyre & Spottiswoode, London 14.95.
1. Bible—Interpretation. 2. Bible—Figures of speech. I. Title.

CALLIES, Fritz A. j220.8
God's animals; a book about Biblical beasts, by Fritz A. Callies. Milwaukee, Northwestern Pub. House [c1966] 62 p. col. illus. 24 cm. [BS663.C3] 63-14674
1. Bible—Natural history—Juvenile literature. I. Title.

DOANE, Pelagie 220.8
Animals in the Bible. New York, Guild [dist. Golden, c.1963] 29p. col. illus. 20cm. (Catholic child's readwith-me bk.) 1.00 bds.,
I. Title.

FARB, Peter. 220.8
The land, wildlife, and peoples of the Bible. Illus. by Harry McNaught. New York, Harper & Row [1967] 171 p. illus., maps. 24 cm. Bibliography: p. 161-162. Discusses the geography, geology, animals, plants, and peoples of the Bible, in light of present knowledge, following the order of the Biblical references and explaining their background. [BS660.F3] AC 67
1. Bible—Natural history. I. McNaught, Harry, illus. II. Title.

KERR, James S. j220.8
Whose zoo? Pictures by Ollie Jensen. Minneapolis, Augsburg Pub. House [1963] unpaged. illus. 22 cm. [BS663.K4] 63-16599
1. Bible — Natural history — Juvenile literature. I. Title.

KERR, James S. 220.8
Whose zoo? Pictures by Ollie Jensen. Minneapolis, Augsburg [c.1963] unpaged. col. illus. 22cm. 63-16599 1.75
1. Bible—Natural history—Juvenile literature. I. Title.

*KITTEL, Gerhard, ed. 220.8
Bible key words; v.4. New York, Harper [c.1962, 1964] 1v. 24cm. 4.50
I. Title.

MOSLEY, Jean (Bell) 1913- 220.8
Animals of the Bible. Garden City, N. Y. [N. Doubleday, 1962] 64p. illus. 21cm. (Know your Bible program) [BS663.M65] 62-2719
1. Bible—Natural history. I. Title.

*PICKERING, Hy, comp. 220.8
One thousand subjects for speakers and students, compiled by Hy Pickering. Grand Rapids, Baker Book House [1974]. 215 p. 20 cm. [BS587] ISBN 0-8010-6971-8 2.95 (pbk.)
1. Bible—Study. I. Title.

REINER, Edwin W. 220.8
The covenants, by Edwin W. Reiner. Nashville. Southern Pub. [c1967] 128p. 20cm. [BS680.C67R4] 67-31341 2.95
1. Covenants (Theology)—Biblical teaching. I. Title.

ROBINSON, William Wilcox, 220.8
1891-
The book of Bible animals, by W. W. Robinson. Drawings by Irene B. Robinson. Los Angeles, Ritchie [1966] 58p. illus. 29cm. [BS551.R62 1966] 66-26521 2.95; 2.92 bds., lib. ed.,
1. Bible—Natural history. 2. Bible stories, English. I. Robinson, Irene Bowen, 1891- illus. II. Title.
Available from Golden Gate in San Carlos, Calif.

SIBUM, L 220.8
The Bible on light, by L. Sibum. Translated by F. Vander Heijden. De Pere, Wis., St. Norbert Abbey Press, 1966 104 p. 17 cm. Revision of a paper read at the third general meeting of the World Council of Churches in 1961, and first published in Het Christelijk oosten en hereniging, v. 14, no. 1-2. Bibliographical footnotes. [BS680.L53S513] 66-16992
1. Light and darkness in the Bible. I. Title.

SIBUM, L. 220.8
The Bible on light. Tr. by F. Vander Heijden. De Pere, Wis., St. Norbert Abbey Pr. [c.] 1966. 104p. 17cm. Rev. of a paper read at the third general meeting of the World Council of Churches in 1961, and first pub. in Het Christelijk oosten en hereniging, v. 14, no. 1-2. Bibl. [BS680.L53S513] 66-16992 .95 pap.,
1. Light and darkness in the Bible. I. Title.

*WARREN, Mary 220.8
The lame man who walked again: Matthew 9:2-8 for children. Illus. by Betty Wind. St. Louis, Concordia, c.1966. 1v. (unpaged) col. illus. 21cm. (Arch bks., set 3, no. 59-1129) .35 pap.,
1. Healing. 2. Bible stories, English — N.T. — Juvenile literature. I. Title.

WILLS, Garry, 1934- 220.8
Animals of the Bible Sponsored by the Benedictine monks of Belmont Abbey. Garden City, N. Y. [N. Doubleday, 1962] 64 p. illus. 21 cm. (The Catholic know-your Bible program) [BS663.W53] 62-2759
1. Bible — Natural history. I. Title.

BRASINGTON, Virginia 220.8'001'94
F.
Flying saucers in the Bible, by Virginia F. Brasington. Clarksburg, W. Va. [Saucerian Press, c1963] 78 p. illus., port. 28 cm. [TL789.B68] 71-262500
1. Flying saucers (in religion, folk-lore, etc.) I. Title.

THE Gift of joy. 220.8'1118'4
Edited by Christian Duquoc. New York, Paulist Press [1968] viii, 164 p. 24 cm. (Concilium: theology in the age of renewal. Spirituality, v. 39) Translated by Theodore L. Westow and others. Includes bibliographical references. [BV4905.2.G5] 68-59156 4.50
1. Joy—Addresses, essays, lectures. 2. Eschatology—Addresses, essays, lectures. I. Duquoc, Christian, ed. II. Series: Concilium (New York) v. 39

DELITZSCH, Franz Julius, 220.813
1813-1890
A system of Biblical psychology. 2d ed., rev. and enl. Tr. from German by the Rev. Robert Ernest Wallis. Grand Rapids, Mich., Baker Bk., 1966. xvi, 585p. 23cm. (Limited eds. lib.) Reprinted from 1899 ed. printed in Edinburgh by T. & T. Clark [BS645.D45] 8.95
1. Bible — Psychology. I. Wallis, Robert Ernest, 1870-1900, tr. II. Title. III. Title: Biblical psychology.

WESTMAN, Heinz, 1902- 220.8131341
The springs of creativity. With an introd. to pt. 3 by Herbert Read. [1st ed.] New York, Atheneum, 1961. xiv, 269 p. illus. (part col.) 24 cm. Erratum slip inserted. Bibliographical references included in "Notes" (p. 265-269) [BS645.W45] 61-6375
1. Bible—Psychology. 2. Psychoanalysis—Cases, clinical reports, statistics. I. Title.

BASHAM, Don, 1926- 220.8'133
The most dangerous game : a Biblical expose of occultism / Don Basham and Dick Leggatt. Greensburg, Pa. : Manna Christian Outreach, c1974. 128 p. ; 21 cm. Bibliography: p. 127-128. [BS680.O26B37] 74-23010 ISBN 0-8007-0726-5 pbk. : 1.95
1. Occult sciences—Biblical teaching. I. Leggatt, Dick, joint author. II. Title.

STAINAKER, Leo, 1897- 220.8133335
Mystic symbolism in Bible numerals. Philadelphia, Dorrance [1952] 148 p. 20 cm. [BS680.C2S8] 52-13775
1. Symbolism of numbers. 2. Bible — Criticism, interpretation, etc. I. Title.

ROSS, Alexander Cephas, 220.81335
1885-
Star lore and the Bible: astronomical, astrological, interpretation. [Detroit, Mantis Pub. Co., 1956] 217p. illus. 22cm. [BF1721.R6] 56-23118
1. Astrology. I. Title.

ROSS, Alexander Cephas, 220.81335
1885-
Star lore and the Bible: astronomical, astrological, interpretation. [Detroit, Mantis Pub. Co., 1956] 217p. illus. 22cm. [BF1721.R6] 56-23118
1. Astrology. I. Title.

WOMACK, David A. 220.8'1335
12 signs, 12 sons : astrology in the Bible / David Womack. 1st ed. San Francisco : Harper & Row, c1977. p. cm. Bibliography: p. [BF1721.W65 1977] 77-10163 pbk. : 3.95
1. Bible and astrology. I. Title.

HERON, Laurence 220.8'1338
Tunstall.
ESP in the Bible. [1st ed.] Garden City, N.Y., Doubleday, 1974. 212 p. 21 cm. Includes bibliographical references. [BS534.H45] 73-14050 ISBN 0-385-09603-8 5.95
1. Bible—Miscellanea. 2. Religion and parapsychology. I. Title.

KIMPEL, Benjamin 220.817
Franklin.
Moral principles in the Bible; a study of the contribution of the Bible to a moral philosophy. New York, Philosophical Library [1956] 172p. 23cm. [BS680.E84K5] 56-13604
1. Bible—Ethics. I. Title.

MURRAY, John, 1898- 220.817
Principles of conduct; aspects of Biblical ethics. Grand Rapids, W. B. Eerdmans Pub. Co. [1957] 272p. 28cm. [BS2545.E8m8] 57-13943
1. Bible. N. T.—Ethics. I. Title.

SLEEPER, Charles 220.8'17
Freeman.
Black power and Christian responsibility; some Biblical foundations for social ethics [by] C. Freeman Sleeper. Nashville, Abingdon Press [1968, c1969] 221 p. 23 cm. Bibliography: p. 205-217. [BS680.E84S5] 69-12769 4.50
1. Bible—Ethics. 2. Social ethics. 3. Negroes—History—1964- I. Title.

FISHER-HUNTER, William, 220.81731
1899-
The divorce problem fully discussed, and a Scriptural solution. 1st ed. Waynesboro, Pa., MacNeish Publishers, 1952. 173 p. 20 cm. On cover: Marriage and divorce. [HQ821.F5] 52-24904
1. Divorce. I. Title.

HEFLEY, James C. 220.8'176
Sex, sense, and nonsense; what the Bible does and doesn't say about sex [by] James C. Hefley. Elgin, Ill., D. C. Cook Pub. Co. [1971] 96 p. 19 cm. Bibliography: p. 95-96. [BS680.S5H4] 71-147213 0.95
1. Sex in the Bible. I. Title.

SCORER, Charles Gordon 220.8176
The Bible and sex ethics today [by] C. G. Scorer. [1st ed. London, Tyndale P., 1966.] 124p. 20cm. (A Tyndale paperback) [BS680.S5S35] 66-72628 1.50 pap.,
1. Sex in the Bible. I. Title.
Available from Inter-Varsity, Chicago.

LOCKYER, Herbert 220.823
All the doctrines of the Bible; a study and analysis of major Bible doctrines. Grand Rapids, Mich., Zondervan [c.1964] 310p. 24cm. Bibl. [BS543.L6] 64-15558 4.95
1. Bible—Theology. I. Title.

IERSEL, Bastiaan 220.8231
Martinus Franciscus van.
The Bible on the living God, by B. van Iersel. Translated by H. J. Vaughan. De Pere, Wis., St. Norbert Abbey Press, 1965. 102 p. 17 cm. [BT99.I 313] 65-18140
1. God — Biblical teaching. I. Title.

IERSEL, Bastiaan 220.8231
Martinus Franciscus van
The Bible on the living God. Tr. [from German] by H. J. Vaughan. De Pere, Wis., St. Norbert Abbey Pr. [c.]1965. 102p. 17cm. [BT99.I313] 65-18140 .95 pap.,
1. God—Biblical teaching. I. Title.

POWELL, Cyril H. 220.82314
The Biblical concept of power. London, Epworth Pr. [dist. Mystic, Conn., Verry, 1964, c.1963] vii, 222p. 23cm. Bibl. 64-5207 6.00
1. Power (Theology) I. Title.

LOCKYER, Herbert. 220.823173
All the miracles of the Bible; the supernatural in Scripture, its scope and significance. Grand Rapids, Zondervan Pub. House [1961] 480p. 24cm. Includes bibliography. [BT97.2.L6] 61-16752
1. Miracles. I. Title.

LOCKYER, Herbert Henry 220.823173
John
All the miracles of the Bible; the supernatural in Scripture, its scope and significance. Grand Rapids, Mich., Zondervan [c.1961] 480p. Bibl. 61-16752 5.95
1. Miracles. I. Title.

RINGGREN, Helmer [Karl 220.82324
Vilhelm Helmer Ringgren] 1917-
Sacrifice in the Bible. New York, Association [1963] 80p. 19cm. (World Christian bks., no. 42, 2d ser.) 63-3228 1.00 pap.,
1. Sacrifice—Biblical teaching. I. Title.

BIEDERWOLF, William 220.8'232'6
Edward, 1867-1939.
The millennium Bible, being a help to the study of the Holy Scriptures in their testimony to the second coming of our Lord and Saviour Jesus Christ. Grand Rapids, Baker Book House [1966] 728 p. 24 cm. Reprint of the 1924 ed. [BT885.B49 1966] 64-8345
1. Bible—Criticism, interpretation, etc. 2. Second Advent. I. Title.

GELIN, Albert 220.82332
Sin in the Bible. Old Testament [by] Albert Gelin. New Testament [by] Albert Descamps. Tr. by Charles Schaldenbrand. New York, Desclee [1965] 140p. 22cm. Orig. appeared in French as part of Theologie du peche.' Bibl. [BT715.G47] 65-15629 3.75
1. Sin—Biblical teaching. I. Descamps, Albert. II. Title.

SMITH, Wilbur 220.8'236'24
Moorehead, 1894-
The Biblical doctrine of heaven, by Wilbur M. Smith. [1st ed.] Chicago, Moody Press [1968] 317 p. 22 cm. Bibliography: p. 289-301. [BT846.2.S6] 68-18883
1. Heaven—Biblical teaching. I. Title.

SCHEP, J A 220.82368
The nature of the resurrection body, a study of the Biblical data, by J. A. Schep. Grand Rapids, W. B. Eerdmans Pub. Co. [1964] 252 p. 23 cm. Bibliography: p. 230-241. [BT872.S3] 64-16586
1. Resurrection—Biblical teaching. I. Title.

SCHEP, J. A. 220.82368
The nature of the resurrection body, a study of the Biblical data. Grand Rapids, Mich., Eerdmans [c.1964] 252p. 23cm. Bibl. 4.95
1. Resurrection—Biblical teaching. I. Title.

GRISPINO, Joseph A tr. 220.824
Foundations of Biblical spirituality, translated by Joseph A. Grispino. Staten Island, N.Y., Alba House [1965] 142 p. 22 cm. [BS680.S7G7] 65-15726
1. Spiritual life — Biblical teaching. Bible — Theology. I. Title.

GRISPINO, Joseph A. tr. 220.824
Foundations of Biblical spirituality. Staten Island, N. Y., Alba [c.1965] 142p. 22cm. [BS680.S7G7] 65-15726 3.95
1. Spiritual life—Biblical teaching. 2. Bible—Theology. I. Title.

BARROSSE, Thomas. 220.8241
Christianity: mystery of love; an essay in

biblical theology. Notre Dame, Ind., Fides Publishers [1964] 99 p. 21 cm. [BV4639.B36] 64-23518
1. Love (Theology) — Biblical teaching. I. Title.

BARROSSE, Thomas 220.8241
Christianity: mystery of love; an essay in biblical meology. Notre Dame, Ind., Fides [c.1964] 99p. 21cm. 64-23518 2.95
1. Love (Theology)—Biblical teaching. I. Title.

GELIN, Albert. 220.8241
The poor of Yahweh. Translated by Mother Kathryn Sullivan. Collegeville, Minn., Liturgical Press [1964] 125 p. 20 cm. Bibliographical footnotes. [BS680.P47G4] 65-547
1. Poverty (Virtue)—Biblical teaching. I. Title.

LEGRAND, Lucien, 1927- 220.8241
The Biblical doctrine of virginity. New York, Sheed & Ward [1963] 167 p. 21 cm. Includes bibliography. [BV4647.C5L4] 63-174130
1. Virginity — Biblical teaching. I. Title.

LEGRAND, Luicin, 1927- 220.8241
The Biblical doctrine of virginity. New York, Sheed [c.1963] 167p. 21cm. Bibl. 63-17413 3.50 bds.,
1. Virginity—Biblical teaching. I. Title.

MASTON, Thomas Bufford, 220.8'241
1897-
Biblical ethics; a survey [by] T. B. Maston. [1st ed.] Cleveland, World Pub. Co. [1967] xi, 300 p. 22 cm. Bibliographical footnotes. [BS680.E84M3] 66-24994
1. Bible—Ethics. I. Title.

BARKER, William 220.82483
Pierson.
Kings in shirtsleeves men who ruled Israel. [Westwood, N. J.] Revell [1961] 119p. 21cm. [BS579.K5B3] 61-13620
1. Bible. O. T.—Biog. 2. Jews—Kings and rulers. I. Title.

BOUNDS, Edward 220.82483
McKendree, 1835-1913
Bible men of prayer. Foreword by Frank C. Laubach. Grand Rapids. Mich., Zondervan [1964] 116p. 21cm. [BS571.B56] 65-612 2.50 bds.,
1. Bible—Biog. 2. Prayer—Biblical teaching. I. Title.

HEIL, L E 220.82483
... But I must decrease, by L. E. Heil. [Cleveland, Tenn., Pathway Press, c1963] 173 p. port. 20 cm. [BS572.H37] 63-19209
1. Bible — Biog. I. Title.

RICHARDS, Alberta Rae 220.82483
(Sune)
Women of the Bible ... [Gastonia, N. C., Geographical Pub. Co., 1962] unpaged. illus. 26cm. [BS575.R48] 62-3988
1. Women in the Bible. 2. Bible—Biog. I. Title.

WHITESELL, Faris 220.82483
Daniel, 1895-
Sermon outlines on women of the Bible. [Westwood, N.J.] Revell [1962] 64 p. 21 cm. (Revell's sermon outline series) [BS575.W53] 62-10739
1. Women in the Bible. 2. Sermons — Outlines. I. Title.

STEVENSON, Dwight 1906- 220.8'251
In the Biblical preacher's workshop [by] Dwight E. Stevenson. Nashville. Abingdon [1967] 223p. 23cm. Bibl. [BV4211.2.S745] 67-14988 3.95
1. Bible— Homiletical use. 2. Preaching. I. Title.

STEVENSON, Dwight 220.8'251
Eshelman, 1906-
In the Biblical preacher's workshop [by] Dwight E. Stevenson. Nashville, Abingdon Press [1967] 223 p. 23 cm. Bibliographical footnotes. [BV4211.2.S745] 67-14988
1. Bible — Homiletical use. 2. Preaching. I. Title.

LESCRAUWAET, Josephus 220.826201
Franciscus
The Bible on Christian unity, by J. S. [i. e. F.] Lescrauwaet, Tr. by N. D. Smith. De Pere, Wis., St. Norbert Abbey Pr. [c.]1965. 159 [1]p. 17cm. Bibl. [BV601.5.L413] 65-22863 .95 pap.,
1. Church — Unity — Biblical teaching. I. Title.

BIBLE. English. 220.82641
Selections. 1959. Authorized.
The prayers of the Bible. Compiled by Philip Watters. Grand Rapids, Baker Book House, 1959. 334p. 23cm. 'Reprinted ... from the original edition first issued in 1883.' [BV235.W3 1959] 58-59776
1. Bible—Prayers. I. Watters, Philip, comp. II. Title.

KILMARTIN, Edward J. 220.82653
The Eucharist in the primitive church [by] Edward J. Kilmartin. Englewood Cliffs, N. J., Prentice-Hall [1965] x, 181 p. 21 cm. Bibliography: p. 166-173. [BV823.K48] 65-17533
1. Lord's Supper — Biblical teaching. I. Title.

KILMARTIN, Edward J. 220.82653
The Eucharist in the primitive church. Englewood Cliffs, N. J., Prentice [c.1965] x, 181p. 21cm. Bibl. [BV823.K48] 65-17533 5.50 bds.,
1. Lord's Supper—Biblical teaching. I. Title.

HARRINGTON, Wilfrid 220.8'265'5
J.
The promise to love; a scriptural view of marriage [by] Wilfrid J. Harrington. Staten Island, N.Y., Alba House [1968] 141 p. 19 cm. Bibliographical footnotes. [BS680.M35H3] 68-15381
1. Marriage—Biblical teaching. I. Title.

KLEMME, Huber F 220.83
The Bible and our common life. Philadelphia, Christian Education Press [1953] 123p. 21cm. [BS670.K55] 53-9921
1. Sociology, Biblical. I. Title.

STEVENS, Rene. 220.83
The Bible and today's headlines. [1st ed.] New York, Greenwich Book Publishers [c1961] 56 p. 22 cm. [BS670.S7] 61-17973
1. Sociology, Biblical. I. Title.

STEVENS, Rene 220.83
The Bible and today's headlines. New York, Greenwich [1962, c.1961] 56p. 22cm. 61-17973 2.50
1. Sociology, Biblical. I. Title.

OSTROM, Karl A., 220.8'301'363
1939-
Is there hope for the city? / Karl A. Ostrom and Donald W. Shriver, Jr. 1st ed. Philadelphia : Westminster Press, c1977. p. cm. (Biblical perspectives on current issues) Includes bibliographical references and index. [BS680.C5O84] 77-22187 ISBN 0-664-24147-6 pbk. : 5.95
1. Cities and towns—Biblical teaching. I. Shriver, Donald W., joint author. II. Title. III. Series.

SKLBA, Richard J. 220.8'30136
The faithful city / by Richard J. Sklba. Chicago : Franciscan Herald Press, 1976. p. cm. (Herald Biblical booklets) [BS680.C5S54] 75-44467 ISBN 0-8199-0725-1 pbk. : 0.95
1. Cities and towns—Biblical teaching. I. Title.

ADAMS, Queenie 220.8'30141'2
Muriel.
Neither male nor female; a study of the Scriptures, [by] Q. M. Adams. Ilfracombe, Stockwell, 1973. 255 p. 22 cm. Includes index. Bibliography: p. [237]-[239] [BS575.A24 1973] 74-158259 ISBN 0-7223-0394-7
1. Women in the Bible. I. Title.
Distributed by Verry, 7.50.

BRISCOE, Jill. 220.8'30141'2
Prime Rib and Apple / by Jill Briscoe. Grand Rapids : Zondervan Pub. House, c1976. p. cm. [BS575.B67] 76-25054 5.95
1. Women in the Bible. I. Title.

DEEN, Edith. 220.8'30141'2
The Bible's legacy for womanhood. [1st ed.] Garden City, N.Y., Doubleday, 1969 [i.e. 1970] xviii, 340 p. 22 cm. Bibliography: p. [321]-326. [BS575.D42] 75-93203 5.95
1. Women in the Bible. 2. Woman—Religious life. I. Title.

DRIMMER, Frederick. 220.8'30141'2
Daughters of Eve : women in the Bible / by Frederick Drimmer ; ill. by Hal Frenck. Norwalk, Conn. : C. R. Gibson Co., [1975] 88 p. : ill. ; 21 cm. [BS575.D7] 74-83776 ISBN 0-8378-1765-X
1. Women in the Bible. I. Frenck, Hal. II. Title.

DRIMMER, Frederick. 220.8'30141'2
Daughters of Eve : women in the Bible / by Frederick Drimmer ; ill. by Hal Frenck. Norwalk, Conn. : C. R. Gibson Co., [1975] 88 p. : ill. ; 21 cm. [BS575.D7] 74-83776 ISBN 0-8378-1765-X : 3.95
1. Women in the Bible. I. Frenck, Hal. II. Title.

DUBARLE, Andre 220.8'30141
Marie, 1910-
Love and fruitfulness in the Bible, by A. M. Dubarle. Translated by Religious Book Consultants. De Pere, Wis., St. Norbert Abbey Press, 1968. 82, [1] p. 20 cm. Translation of Amour et fecondite dans la Bible. Bibliography: p. [83] [BS680.S5D813] 68-58124 ISBN 0-8316-1028-X 2.95
1. Sex in the Bible. 2. Marriage—Biblical teaching. I. Title.

HORNER, Thomas 220.8'30141'7
Marland, 1927-
Sex in the Bible [by] Tom Horner. Rutland, Vt., C. E. Tuttle Co. [1974] 188 p. 20 cm. [BS680.S5H6] 73-87676 ISBN 0-8048-1124-5 7.50
1. Sex in the Bible.

JEWETT, Paul King. 220.8'30141'2
Man as male and female : a study in sexual relationships from a theological point of view / by Paul K. Jewett. Grand Rapids : Eerdmans, [1975] 200 p. ; 21 cm. Includes indexes. Bibliography: p. 189-190. [BT708.J48] 74-32471 ISBN 0-8028-1597-9
1. Sex (Theology) 2. Woman (Theology)—Biblical teaching. I. Title.

K*UIJF, T. C. de 220.830141
The Bible on sexuality Tr. by F. Vander Heijden. DePere, Wis., St. Norbert Abbey Pr. [c.]1966 103 p. 17 cm [BS680S5K713] 66-16989 pap., .95
1. sex in the bible. I. Title.

KRUIJF, Th C de. 220.830141
The Bible on sexuality, by T. C. De Kruijf. Translated by F. Vander Heijden. DePere, Wis., St. Norbert Abbey Press, 1966. 103 p. 17 cm. [BS680.S5K713] 66-16989
1. Sex in the Bible. I. Title.

MAERTENS, Thierry, 220.8'30141'2
1921-
The advancing dignity of woman in the Bible. [Edited by Lisa McGaw] Translated by Sandra Dibbs. De Pere, Wisc., St. Norbert Abbey Press, 1969. 241 p. 19 cm. Translation of La promotion de la femme dans la Bible. Includes bibliographies. [BT704.M313] 70-87815 4.95
1. Woman (Theology)—Biblical teaching. 2. Ordination of women. I. McGaw, Lisa, ed. II. Title.

PRICE, Eugenia. 220.8'30141'2
The unique world of women, in Bible times and now. Grand Rapids, Zondervan Pub. House [1969] 245 p. 25 cm. Bibliography: p. 245. [BS575.P7] 79-91644 3.95
1. Women in the Bible. I. Title.

PRICE, Eugenia. 220.8'30141'2
The unique world of women ... in Bible times and now. Boston, G. K. Hall, 1974 [c1969] 287 p. 25 cm. Large print ed. Bibliography: p. 287. [BS575.P7 1974] 74-5126 ISBN 0-8161-6218-2 9.95 (lib. bdg.)
1. Women in the Bible. 2. Sight-saving books. I. Title.

PRICE, Eugenia. 220.8'30141'2
The unique world of women . . . in Bible times and now. Grand Rapids, Mich., Zondervan Pub. Co. [1973, c.1969] 175 p. 18 cm. Bibliography: p. 175. [BS575.P7] 79-91644 1.25 (pbk.)
1. Women in the Bible. I. Title.

STANTON, Elizabeth 220.8'30141'2
Cady, 1815-1902.
The original feminist attack on the Bible (The woman's Bible). Introd. by Barbara Welter. New York, Arno Press, 1974 [c1895-98] xlii, 217 p. 22 cm. Reprint of the ed. published by the European Pub. Co., New York. Contents.Contents.—pt. 1. Comments on Genesis, Exodus, Leviticus, Numbers, and Deuteronomy.—pt. 2. Comments on the Old and New Testaments from Joshua to Revelation. [HQ1395.S72 1974] 74-9343 ISBN 0-405-05997-3 6.95 (lib. bdg.)
1. Bible—Commentaries. 2. Women in the Bible. I. Title. II. Title: The woman's Bible.

STANTON, Elizabeth 220.8'30141'2
(Cady) 1815-1902.
The woman's Bible. New York, Arno Press, 1972 [c1895-98] 2 v. in 1. 24 cm. (American women: images and realities) Contents.Contents.—pt. 1. Comments on Genesis, Exodus, Leviticus, Numbers, and Deuteronomy.—pt. 2. Comments on the Old and New Testaments from Joshua to Revelation. [HQ1395.S72] 72-2626 ISBN 0-405-04481-X 16.00
1. Bible—Commentaries. 2. Women in the Bible. I. Bible. English. Selections. 1972. II. Title. III. Series.

STANTON, Elizabeth 220.8'30141'2
Cady, 1815-1902.
The woman's Bible [by] Elizabeth Cady Stanton and the Revising Committee. Seattle, Coalition Task Force on Women and Religion [1974, c1895-98] xvii, 152, 217 p. 21 cm. Reprint of the ed. published by European Pub. Co., New York. Contents.Contents.—Comments on Genesis, Exodus, Leviticus, Numbers, and Deuteronomy.—Comments on the Old and New Testaments from Joshua to Revelation. [HQ1395.S72 1974b] 74-182269
1. Bible—Commentaries. 2. Women in the Bible. I. Bible. English. Selections. 1974. II. Title.

STENDAHL, Krister 220.830141
The Bible and the role of women; a case study in hermeneutics. Tr. by Emilie T. Sander. Philadelphia, Fortress [1966] xiv, 48 p. 20 cm. (Facet bks. Biblical ser., 15) Tr. of Bibelsynen och kvinnan, which was orig. pub. in Kvinnan, Samballet, Kyrkan (Stockholm, Svenska Kyrkans Diakonistyreleses Bokforlag, 1958) p. 138-167. Bibl. [BV676.S713] 66-25262 pap., .85
1. Ordination of woman. 2. Women in the Bible. I. Title. II. Series.

STENDAHL, Krister. 220.830141
The Bible and the role of women; a case study in hermeneutics. Translated by Emilie T. Sander. Philadelphia, Fortress Press [1966] xiv, 48 p. 20 cm. (Facet books. Biblical series, 15) Translation of Bibelaynen och kvinnan, which was originally published in Kvinnan, Samballet, Kyrkan (Stockholm, Svenska Kyrkans Diakonistyrelses Bokforiag, 1958) p. 138-167. Bibliography: p. 44-47. [BV676.S713] 66-25262
1. Ordination of women. 2. Women in the Bible. I. Title. II. Series.

GARRISON, Webb B. 220.830142
The Biblical image of the family. Nashville, Tenn., Tidings, 1908 Grand Ave. [1965] 64p. 19cm. [BS680.F3G3] 65-17327 price unreported
1. Family—Biblical teaching. I. Title.

GRELOT, Pierre, 1917- 220.8301426
Man and wife in Scripture. [Translated by Rosaleen Brennan. New York] Herder and Herder [1964] 126 p. 21 cm. Translation of Le couple humain dans l'Ecriture. Bibliographical footnotes. [BS680.M35G73 1964a] 64-11975
1. Marriage — Biblical teaching. I. Title.

GRELOT, Pierre, 1917- 220.8301426
Man and wife in Scripture. [Tr. from French by Rosaleen Brennan. New York] Herder & Herder [c.1964] 126p. 21cm. Bibl. 64-11975 2.95
1. Marriage—Biblical teaching. I. Title.

LEE, Mark W., 1923- 220.8'30142
Our children are our best friends; marriage is a family affair [by] Mark W. Lee. Grand Rapids, Zondervan Pub. House [1970] 221 p. 23 cm. Includes bibliographical references. [BS680.M35L42] 70-106448 4.95
1. Marriage—Biblical teaching. I. Title.

MCKIRACHAN, John 220.830142
Charles, 1907-
Older than Eden; great homes of the Bible, by J. Charles McKirachan. Minneapolis, Augsburg Pub. House [1966] vi, 168 p. 22 cm. Includes bibliographical references. [BS680.F3M3] 66-22564
1. Family—Biblical teaching. I. Title.

PATAI, Raphael, 1910- 220.830142
Sex and family in the Bible and the Middle East. [1st ed.] Garden City, N. Y., Doubleday. 1959. 282p. 22cm. Includes bibliography. [BS680.S5P3] 59-8268
1. Sex and religion. 2. Near East—Soc. life & cust. I. Title.

STRANGE, Marcaia 220.8301426
Couples of the Bible. Notre Dame, Ind., Fides [c.1963] 192p. illus. 21cm. First appeared as a series in Marriage magazine, St. Meinrad, Indiana. 63-20805 3.50
1. Bible—Biog. 2. Marriage—Biblical teaching. I. Title.

VOLLEBREGT, G. N. 220.8301426
The Bible on marriage. Tr. by R. A. Downie. DePere, Wis., St. Norbert Abbey Pr., 1965. 115p. 17cm. Bibl. [BS680.M35V613] 65-18141 .95 pap.,
1. Marriage—Biblical teaching. I. Title.

WHITE, Henry E. 220.830142
Marriage, the family, and the Bible. Boston, Christopher Pub. House [c.1961] 84p. 61-15198 2.50
1. Marriage—Biblical teaching. 2. Family—Biblical teaching. I. Title.

LOCKYER, Herbert. 220.8'30143'1
All the children of the Bible. Grand Rapids, Zondervan Pub. House [1970] 287 p. 24 cm. [BS576.L6] 70-120052 5.95
1. Children in the Bible. 2. Children—Biblical teaching. I. Title.

MCGOWAN, Herman 220.8301451
Craig.
God's garden of segregation. [1st ed.] New York, Vantage Press [1961] 94p. illus. 21cm. [BT734.3.M24] 61-3448
1. Segregation—Religious aspects. I. Title.

SUNDERLAND, La 220.8'30145'22
Roy, 1802-1885.
The testimony of God against slavery, or A collection of passages from the Bible, which show the sin of holding property in man; with

notes. Boston, Webster & Southard, 1835. St. Clair Shores, Mich., Scholarly Press, 1970. 104 p. 21 cm. [E449.S958 1970] 73-92444
1. Slavery in the United States—Controversial literature—1835. I. Title.

MCLAIN, C. E. 220.8'32
Place of government, by C. E. McLain. [1st ed.] Oklahoma City, Classics Pub. Trust [1968] 52 p. 22 cm. Bibliographical footnotes. [BS680.P45M3] 68-7400
1. Bible—Political science. I. Title.

TILSON, Charles Everett. 220.832341
Segregation and the Bible. New York, Abingdon Press [1958] 176 p. 21 cm. Includes bibliography. [BT734.3.T5] 58-7437
1. Segregation—Religious aspects. I. Title.

COLEMAN, Arthur D. 220.8'331'7
Occupations: contemporary and Biblical; a review of job titles mentioned in the Bible and a comparison with their present day American counterparts. Complied by Arthur D. Coleman. Salt Lake City, Utah, 1969. ix, 164 l. 22 cm. [BS680.O3C6] 74-89853
1. Bible—Antiquities. 2. Occupations—History. 3. Occupations—Classification. I. Title.

DUCKAT, Walter B. 220.8'3317
Beggar to king; all the occupations of Biblical times, by Walter Duckat. [1st ed.] Garden City, N.Y., Doubleday, 1968. xxvii, 327 p. 22 cm. Bibliography: p. [325]-327. [BS680.O3D8] 67-19112
1. Bible—Antiquities. 2. Occupations—History. I. Title.

BRUEGGEMANN, Walter. 220.8'333
The land : place as gift, promise, and challenge in Biblical faith / Walter Brueggemann. Philadelphia : Fortress Press, c1977. xviii, 203 p. ; 22 cm. (Overtures to biblical theology) Includes bibliographical references and indexes. [BS543.B68] 76-15883 ISBN 0-8006-1526-3 pbk. : 5.50
1. Bible—Theology. 2. Land—Biblical teaching. I. Title. II. Series.

EHRLICH, Jacob W., 1900- 220.834
The Holy Bible and the law. New York, Oceana [c.1962] 240p. 61-14004 7.95
1. Bible and law. 2. Jewish law. I. Title.

*UYS, Sue. 220.837
Successful Bible teaching: a creative approach. Grand Rapids, Mich., Baker Book House [1973] 139, [2] p. illus., 28 cm. Bibliography: p. [141] [BS603] ISBN 0-8010-9200-0 3.95 (pbk.)
1. Bible—Study and teaching. I. Title.

PATAI, Raphael, 1910- 220.8392
Family, love, and the Bible. London, Macgibbon & Kee, Imprint covered by label. New York, Humanities [1966, 1959] 255p. 23cm. Bibl. [BS680.F3P3] 66-7738 4.50
1. Family — Biblical teaching. 2. Sex in the Bible. I. Title.

KERR, Edith A. 220.8'394'1
Alcohol and the scriptures by Edith A. Kerr. With introduction by A. T. Stevens. 2d. ed. rev. and enl. Melbourne, Temperance Committee of the Presbyterian Church of Victoria, 1968. 44 p. 21 cm. Bibliography: p. 42. [HV5182.K43 1968] 77-359108 0.35
1. Temperance—Biblical arguments. I. Presbyterian Church of Victoria. Temperance Committee. II. Title.

GARRISON, Webb B. 220.8396
Women in the life of Jesus. Indianapolis, Bobbs [c.1962] 192p. 22cm. 62 20683 3.95
1. Women in the Bible. I. Title.

CODER, Samuel Maxwell, 1902- 220.85
The Bible, science, and creation, by S. Maxwell Coder, George F. Howe. Chicago, Moody [1966, c.1965] 128p. illus. 22cm. [BS650.C6] 66-3190 2.95
1. Bible and science. I. Howe, George F., joint author. II. Title.

DOWKONTT, George H, 1869- 220.85
Wisdom, world, foolishness, by George H. Dowkontt. Boston, Meador Pub. Co. [1951] 199 p. illus. 21 cm. [BS480.D66] 51-14088
1. Bible—Evidenees, authority, etc. 2. Bible and science. I. Title.
Contents Omitted.

*MOLINARE, Nicholas 220.85
DNA, RNA and the atom: what does God say about them? New York, Vantage [1964, c.1963] 134p. 21cm. 2.95 bds.,
I. Title.

MORRIS, Henry Madison, 1918- 220.8'5
Biblical cosmology and modern science, by Henry M. Morris. Grand Rapids, Baker Book House [1970] 146 p. 19 cm. Includes bibliographical references. [BS650.M563] 75-115634 2.50
1. Bible science—Addresses, essays, lectures. I. Title.

ODENWALD, Robert P 1899- 220.85
How God made you. Pictures by Mary Reed Newland. New York, P J. Kenedy [1960] 32p. illus. 26cm. [BS652.O3] 60-14644
1. Creation—Juvenile literature. I. Title.

ODENWALD, Robert P., M.D. 1899- 220.85
How God made you. Pictures by Mary Reed Newland. New York, P. J. Kenedy [c.1960] 32p. illus. (col.) 26cm. 60-14644 2.50
1. Creation—Juvenile literature. I. Title.

REID, James, 1912- 220.8'5
Does science confront the Bible? Grand Rapids, Zondervan Pub. House [1971] 160 p. illus. 22 cm. Includes bibliographical references. [BS650.R43] 77-146551 3.95
1. Bible and science. I. Title.

RICHARDSON, Alan, 1905- 220.85
The Bible in the age of science. Philadelphia, Westminster Press [1961] 192p. 19cm. (The Cadbury lectures, 1961) Includes bibliography. [BS650.R48 1961] 61-9908
1. Bible and science. 2. Religion and science—History of controversy. I. Title.

TAYLOR, Eustace Lovatt Hebden, 1925- 220.8'5
Evolution and the reformation of biology; a study of the biological thought of Herman Dooyeweerd of Amsterdam and J. J. Duyvene de Wit. Nutley, N.J., Craig Press, 1967. xii, 92 p. 21 cm. (University series: historical studies) Includes bibliographies. [B4051.D64T3] 67-31164
1. Dooyeweerd, Herman, 1894- 2. Duyvene de Wit, Johannes Jacobus, 1909- 3. Bible and evolution. I. Title.

TAYLOR, Hebden, 1925- 220.8'5
Evolution and the reformation of biology; a study of the biological thought of Herman Dooyeweerd of Amsterdam and J. J. Duyvene de Wit. Nutley, N. J., Craig Press, 1967. xii, 92 p. 21 cm. (University series: historical studies) Includes bibliographies. [B4051.D64T3] 67-31164
1. Dooyeweerd, Herman, 1894- 2. Duyvene de Wit, Johannes Jacobus, 1909- 3. Bible and evolution. I. Title.

FARB, Peter. 220.8'5009
The land, wildlife, and peoples of the Bible. Illus. by Harry McNaught. New York, Harper & Row [1967] 171 p. illus., maps. 24 cm. Bibliography: p. 161-162. [BS660.F3] 67-17105
1. Bible—Natural history. I. Title.

BRACKBILL, Maurice Thaddeus, 1891- 220.852
The heavens declare. Chicago, Moody Press [1959] 128p. illus. 22cm. [BS655.B7] 59-48896
1. Bible and science. 2. Astronomy. I. Title.

BULLINGER, Ethelbert William, 1837-1913. 220.8'52
The witness of the stars. Grand Rapids, Kregel Publications [1967] viii, 204 p. illus., charts. 23 cm. Reprint of the 1893 ed. Bibliographical footnotes. [BS655.B76] 68-16762
1. Bible—Astronomy. 2. Astronomy. 3. Constellations. 4. Bible and science. I. Title.

BULLINGER, Ethelbert William, 1837-1913. 220.8'52
The witness of the stars. Grand Rapids, Kregel Publications [1967] viii, 204 p. illus., charts. 23 cm. Reprint of the 1893 ed. Bibliographical footnotes. [BS655.B76 1967] 68-16762
1. Bible—Astronomy. 2. Astronomy. 3. Constellations. 4. Bible and science. I. Title.

CALLIES, Fritz A. 220.852
God's stars. Minneapolis, Augsburg Pub. House [c.1960] 48p. diagrs. 29cm. 60-8897 1.95 bds.,
1. Bible—Astronomy—Juvenile literature. I. Title.

BARR, James. 220.8529
Biblical words for time. Naperville, Ill., A. R. Allenson [1962] 174p. 22cm. (Studies in Biblical theology, no. 33) [BS680.T54B3] 62-51602
1. Time. 2. Bible— Language, style. I. Title.

WRIGHT, Ruth V. 220.8'549
Gems and minerals of the Bible [by] Ruth V. Wright [and] Robert L. Chadbourne. [1st ed.] New York, Harper & Row [1970] xii, 148 p. col. illus. 25 cm. [BS667.W7 1970] 70-109067 4.95
1. Bible—Mineralogy. I. Chadbourne, Robert L., joint author. II. Title.

RICH, James Walter 220.855
After the storm, the restoring fire. Boston, Christopher Pub. House [c.1960] 254p. 21cm. 60-9030 3.00
1. Deluge. 2. End of the world. I. Title.

RICH, James Walter, 1870- 220.855
After the storm, the restoring fire. Boston, Christopher Pub. House [1960] 254p. 21cm. [BS658.R5] 60-9030
1. Deluge. 2. End of the world. I. Title.

CALIGAN, James Henley. 220.8574
The shadow of heaven; a guide to the creative spiritual appreciation of nature. [1st ed.] New York, Vantage Press [1956] 143p. illus. 21cm. [BS660.C3] 56-7521
1. Bible— Natural history. 2. Nature in the Bible. I. Title.

SMITH, Willard S. 220.8'574
Animals, birds, and plants of the Bible, by Willard S. Smith. Drawings by William Duncan. [1st ed.] Needham Heights, Mass., Church Art [1971] 63 p. illus. 19 cm. Bibliography: p. 63. [BS660.S63] 73-26145 0.95
1. Bible—Natural history. I. Title.

ZIMMERMAN, Paul Albert, 1918- comp. 220.8'575
Creation, evolution, and God's word. Paul A. Zimmerman, editor. St. Louis, Concordia Pub. House [1972] 176 p. 18 cm. Revision and updating of Essays from the creationist viewpoint, first printed in limited ed. in 1966. Contents.Contents.—An evaluation of the evidence for evolution, by J. W. Klotz.—Analysis of so-called evidences of evolution, by W. H. Rusch.—The word of God today, by P. A. Zimmerman.—There was evening—and there was morning, by R. G. Korthals.—Critique of evolution theory, by W. E. Lammerts. Includes bibliographical references. [BS659.Z55 1972] 70-182220 ISBN 0-570-03122-2
1. Bible and evolution—Addresses, essays, lectures. I. Title.

ANDERSON, Alexander Walter, 1901- 220.858
Plants of the Bible. New York, Philosophical Library [1957] 72p. illus. (part col.) 26cm. [BS665] 57-3020
1. Bible—Natural history. I. Title.

MOLDENKE, Harold Norman, 1909- 220.858
Plants of the Bible, by Harold N. Moldenke and Alma L. Moldenke. Waltham, Mass., Chronica Botanica Co., 1952. xix, 328 p. illus., facsims. 27 cm. (A New series of plant science books, v. 28) Bibliography: p. 250-274. [BS665.M6] 52-12737
1. Bible — Natural history. I. Moldenke, Alma Lance (Ericson) 1908- joint author. II. Title. III. Series.

MOLDENKE, Harold Norman, 1909- 220.858
Plants of the Bible, by Harold N. Moldenke and Alma L. Moldenke. Waltham, Mass., Chronica Botanica Co., 1952. xix, 328 p. illus., facsims. 27 cm. (A New series of plant science books, v. 28) Bibliography: p. 259-274. [BS665.M6] 52-12737
1. Bible—Natural history. I. Moldenke, Alma Lance (Ericson) 1908- joint author. II. Title. III. Series: Chronica botanica; new series of plant science books, v. 28

UNTERMEYER, Louis, 1885- 220.8'58
Plants of the Bible. Paintings by Anne Ophelia Dowden. New York, Golden Press [1970] 1 v. (unpaged) col. illus. 18 cm. [BS665.U57] 77-127308 1.95
1. Bible—Natural history. 2. Botany—Palestine. I. Dowden, Anne Ophelia (Todd) 1907- illus. II. Title.

WALKER, Winifred. 220.858
All the plants of the Bible. Text and illus. by Winifred Walker. New York, Harper [1957] 244 p. illus. 25 cm. [BS665.W3] 57-9886
1. Bible — Natural history. I. Title.

PEELMAN, Nancy. 220.8'581
The plants of the Bible / by Nancy Peelman ; illustrated by Ben F. Kocian. New York : Morehouse-Barlow Co., [1975] 40 p. : ill. ; 29 cm. Bibliography: p. 40. [BS665.P43] 75-14607 ISBN 0-8192-1196-6 pbk. : 3.25
1. Bible—Natural history.

THRAPP, Grace R., 1886-1971. 220.8'582'13
Flowers of the Bible, written and illustrated by Grace R. Thrapp. [Independence, Mo., Independence Press, c1972] 63 p. illus. 21 cm. [BS665.T47] 74-156560 ISBN 0-8309-0072-1
1. Bible—Natural history. I. Title.

CANSDALE, George Soper. 220.8'59
All the animals of the Bible lands, by George Cansdale. Foreword by John R. W. Stott. [1st ed.] Grand Rapids, Zondervan Pub. House [1970] 272 p. illus., maps, plates (part col.) 24 cm. Bibliography: p. 255-256. [BS663.C34 1970] 76-120040 6.95
1. Bible—Natural history. 2. Zoology—Palestine. I. Title.

FERGUSON, Walter. 220.8'59
Living animals of the Bible. Text and illus. by Walter W. Ferguson. New York, Scribner [1974] 95 p. col. illus. 29 cm. Bibliography: p. 93. Gives color illustrations and Hebrew, English, and scientific names of animals mentioned in the Bible that still exist. Includes Biblical references and brief information on habits and habitats. [BS663.F4] 72-11112 ISBN 0-684-13346-6 9.95
1. Bible—Natural history—Juvenile literature. I. Title.

HUBARTT, Paul 220.859
Animals of the Bible, stories and drawings by Paul Hubartt. Grand Rapids, Mich. Zondervan, c.1960. unpaged illus. 28cm. .50 pap.,
I. Title.

MOLLER-CHRISTENSEN, Vilhelm. 220.859
Encyclopedia of Bible creatures, by V. Moller-Christensen and K. E. Jordt Jorgensen. M. Theodore Heinecken, editor. Arne Unhjem, translator. Carol Wilde, illustrator. Philadelphia, Fortress Press [1965] xviii, 302 p. illus. 24 cm. Translation of Bibelens dyreliv. [BS663.M613] 65-21082
1. Bible—Natural history. I. Jorgensen, Kai Eduard Jordt, joint author. II. Heinecken, M. Theodore, ed. III. Title.

NEFF, Ethel Maxine. 220.859
The Bible zoo. Mountain View, Calif., Pacific Press Pub. Association [1958] 83p. illus. 24cm. [BS663.N4] 58-10581
1. Bible Natural history. I. Title.

NEVIL, Susan R. 220.859
The Biblical zoo; the story of a very special zoo in he land of the Bible. Written and illustrated by Susan R. Nevil. [New York] McKay [c.1960] 44p. illus. (part col.) 20x26cm. 59-5382 3.75
1. Bible—Natural history. I. Title.

PINNEY, Roy. 220.859
The animals in the Bible; the identity and natural history of all the animals mentioned in the Bible. With a collection of photos, of living species taken in the Holy Land by the author. 1st ed., Philadelphia, Chilton Books, [1964] x, 227 p. illus. 24 cm (Frontiers of knowledge series) Bibliography: p. 223. [BS663.P5] 64-11481
1. Bible—Natural history 2. Zoology—Palestine. I. Title.

PINNEY, Roy 220.859
The animals in the Bible; the identity and natural history of all the animals mentioned in the Bible. With a collection of photos. of living species taken in the Holy Land by the author. Philadelphia, Chilton [c.1964] x, 227p. illus. 24cm. (Frontiers of knowledge ser.) Bibl. 64-11481 6.95
1. Bible—Natural history. 2. Zoology—Palestine. I. Title.

POTTEBAUM, Gerard A. 220.859
How the animals got their names. Illus. by Robert Strobridge. Dayton, Ohio, 38 W. 5th St., Geo. A. Pflaum, c.1963. unpaged. col. illus. 18cm. (Little people's paperbacks, LPP2) .35 pap.,
I. Title.

WILEY, Lulu Rumsey, 220.859
Bible animals; mammals of the Bible. [1st ed.] New York, Vantage Press [1958, c1957] 479 p. illus. 21 cm. [BS663.W5] 58-59428
1. Bible — Natural history. I. Title.

PEELMAN, Nancy. 220.8'591
The beasts, birds, and fish of the Bible / by Nancy Peelman ; illustrated by Ben F. Kocian. New York : Morehouse-Barlow Co., [1975] 40 p. : ill. ; 29 cm. Bibliography: p. 40. [BS663.P4] 75-14605 ISBN 0-8192-1197-4 pbk. : 3.25
1. Bible—Natural history. I. Title.

HOLMGREN, Virginia C. 220.8'5982
Bird walk through the Bible [by] Virginia C. Holmgren. New York, Seabury Press [1972] viii, 216 p. 22 cm. Bibliography: p. 213-216. [BS664.H64] 70-179555 ISBN 0-8164-0233-7 6.95
1. Bible—Natural history. I. Title.

PARMELEE, Alice. 220.85982
All the birds of the Bible; their stories, identification and meaning. New York, Harper [1959] 279 p. illus. 25 cm. [BS664.P3] 59-14533
1. Bible—Natural history. I. Title.

BIBLE. English. 220.861
Selections. 1958. Authorised.
The healings of the Bible. Compiled by Nellie B. Woods. New York, Hawthorn Books [1958] 94p. 19cm. [BS680.H4W6] 58-5622
1. Bible—Medicine, hygiene, etc. 2. Faith-cure. I. Woods, Nellie Belfre, 1891- comp. II. Title.

EBSTEIN, Wilhelm, 1836- 220.861
1912
Die Medizin im Neuen Testament und im Talmud. Miinchen, W. Fritsch [New York, Hafner] 1965. vii, 338p. 21cm. Photomechanischer Neudruck der Ausgabe Stuttgart, Ferd. Enke Verlag, 1903. [R135.5.E22] 65-26955 13.25
1. Bible — Medicine, hygiene, etc. 2. Talmud — Medicine, hygiene, etc. I. Title.

GREENBLATT, Robert 220.861
Benjamin, M.D., 1906-
Search the Scriptures; a physician examines medicine in the Bible. Foreword by Ralph McGill. Philadelphia, Lippincott [c.1963] 127p. 24cm. 63-21906 4.00 bds.,
1. Bible—Medicine, hygiene, etc. I. Title.

GREENBLATT, Robert 220.8'61
Benjamin, 1906-
Search the Scriptures; modern medicine and Biblical personages [by] Robert B. Greenblatt. With an introd. by Walter C. Alvarez and a foreword by Ralph McGill. 2d and enl. ed. Philadelphia, Lippincott [1968] 168 p. 24 cm. [R135.5.G72 1968] 68-28869 4.50
1. Bible—Medicine, hygiene, etc. I. Title.

GREENBLATT, Robert 220.8'61
Benjamin, 1906-
Search the Scriptures : modern medicine and Biblical personages / Robert B. Greenblatt ; foreword by Henry King Stanford. 3d and enl. ed. Philadelphia : Lippincott, 1977,c1976 p. cm. Includes index. [R135.5.G72 1976] 76-50054 ISBN 0-397-59060-1 : 8.95
1. Bible—Medicine, hygiene, etc. I. Title.

GREENBLATT, Robert 220.8'61
Benjamin, 1906-
Search the Scriptures : modern medicine and Biblical personages / Robert B. Greenblatt ; foreword by Henry King Stanford. 3d and enl. ed. Philadelphia : Lippincott, 1977,c1976 p. cm. Includes index. [R135.5.G72 1976] 76-50054 ISBN 0-397-59060-1 : 8.95
1. Bible—Medicine, hygiene, etc. I. Title.

LEVIN, Simon S. 220.8'61
Adam's rib; essays on Biblical medicine [by] Simon S. Levin. Los Altos, Calif., Geron-X [1970] 180 p. 22 cm. Includes bibliographical references. [R135.5.L48] 78-111609 ISBN 8-7672-0068- 6.95
1. Bible—Medicine, hygiene, etc. I. Title.

SHORT, Arthur Rendle 220.8'61
The Bible and modern medicine; a survey of health and healing in the Old and New Testaments. Chicago, Moody [1967, c.1953] 160p. 18cm. (Moody pocket bks., 98) Orig. pub. in England in 1953. [R135.5.S46] .59 pap.,
1. Bible—Medicine, hygienc, etc. I. Title.

SMITH, Charles Raimer, 220.861
1892-
The physician examines the Bible. New York, Philosophical Library [1950] vii, 394 p. 22 cm. [BS640.S5] 50-12990
1. Bible—Medicine, hygiene, etc. 2. Religion and science—1900- 3. Temperance—Biblical arguments. I. Title.

THOMSEN, Russel J. 220.8'61
The Bible book of medical wisdom [by] Russel J. Thomsen. Old Tappan, N.J., F. H. Revell Co. [1974] 160 p. 21 cm. Includes bibliographical references. [R135.5.T47] 74-11162 ISBN 0-8007-0682-X 4.95
1. Bible—Medicine, hygiene, etc. I. Title.

TOURNIER, Paul. 220.861
A doctor's casebook in the light of the Bible. Translated by Edwin Hudson. [1st American ed.] New York, Harper [1960] 256 p. 22 cm. Translation of Bible et medecine. Includes bibliography. [BT732.T653 1960] 60-8140
1. Medicine and religion. 2. Bible — Medicine, Hygiene, etc. I. Title.

TOURNIER, Paul. 220.861
A doctor's casebook in the light of the Bible. Translated by Edwin Hudson. [1st American ed.] New York, Harper [1960] 256 p. 22 cm. Translation of Bible et medecine. Includes bibliography. [BT732.T653 1960] 60-8140
1. Medicine and religion. 2. Bible—Medicine, hygiene, etc. I. Title.

MACKAY, Alastair I 220.863
Farming and gardening in the Bible. [1st ed.] Emmaus, Pa., Rodale Press, [1950] 280 p. front. 24 cm. [BS665.M2] 51-9556
1. Bible—Natural history. I. Title.

KING, Eleanor Anthony, 220.8'635
1901-
Bible plants for American gardens / by Eleanor Anthony King. New York : Dover Publications, 1975. xii, 204 p., [4] leaves of plates : ill. ; 21 cm. Reprint of the 1941 ed. published by Macmillan, New York. Includes index. [SB454.K5 1975] 75-3646 ISBN 0-486-23188-7 pbk. : 3.00
1. Bible—Natural history. 2. Gardening. 3. Plants, Cultivated. I. Title.

WEISS, Francis Joseph, 220.8'6413
1898-
The food in the Bible. Paper presented at the SOS/70 (Science of Survival), the Third International Congress of Food Science and Technology, Washington, D.C., August 13th, 1970. [Washington? 1970] [7] p. 23 cm. Caption title. In English with a summary in French. Bibliography: p. [6] [BS680.F6W43] 78-18130
1. Food in the Bible. I. International Congress of Food Science and Technology, 3rd, Washington, 1970. II. Title.

CALVERT, Ian. 220.8'68
Crafts in the Bible / by Ian Calvert ; illustrations by Joan Martin May. Oxford : Blackwell, 1976. [1], 59 p., [4] leaves of plates : ill. (some col.) ; 21 cm. (Blackwell's learning library ; no. 92) Includes index. [BS680.H35C34] 77-358538 ISBN 0-631-13340-2 : £0.85
1. Handicraft in the Bible—Juvenile literature. I. Title.

GRAHAM, Jonathan. 220.872596
The office of a wall. Foreword by the Archbishop of Canterbury. London, Faith Press; New York, Morehouse-Barlow Co. [1966] 93 p. 19 cm. (The Archbishop of Canterbury's Lent book [1966]) [BS680.W17G7] 66-2271
1. Walls in the Bible. I. Title. II. Series.

GRAHAM, Jonathan 220.872596
The office of a wall. Foreword by the Abp. of Canterbury. London, Faith Pr.; New York, Morehouse [c.1966] 93p. 19cm. (Abp. of Canterbury's Lent bk., 1966) [BS680.W17G7] 66-2271 1.75 pap.,
1. Walls in the Bible. I. Title. II. Series.

GRAUMAN, Helen G 220.878
Music in my Bible. Illus. by Joseph Maniscalco. Mountain View, Calif., Pacific Press Pub. Association [1956] 182p. illus. 23cm. [ML166.G74] 56-9488
1. Bible—Music. I. Title.

SMITH, William Sheppard. 220.878
Musical aspects of the New Testament. Amsterdam, W. ten Have, 1962. xiii, 187 p. 24 cm. Proefschrift -- Amsterdam. "Propositions" ([5] p.) inserted. Includes bibliographical footnotes. [ML166.S6] 62-52898
1. Bible — Music. 2. Music — Jews. 3. Music in churches. I. Title.

WARREN, Betsy. 220.878
Make a joyful noise; music of the Bible in instrument and song. Text and illus. by Betsy Warren. Minneapolis, Augsburg Pub. House [1962] 64 p. illus. 20 cm. [ML166.W26] 62-20845
1. Bible — Music. I. Title.

WARREN, Betsy 220.878
Make a joyful noise; music of the Bible in instrument and song. Text, illus. by Betsy Warren. Minneapolis, Augsburg [1963] 64p. illus. 20cm. 62-20845 1.75 pap.,
1. Bible—Music. I. Title.

CASMAN, Frances White 220.87937
(Coppage) 1908-
Bible play book, for grade school boys and girls . . . by Frances W. Keene [pseud.] Pelham, N. Y., Seahorse Press [1951] 128p. illus. 29cm. (A Seahorse fun book) [BS613.C28] 51-6703
1. Games. I. Title.

KEENE, Frances W. 220.87937
Bible play book, for grade school boys and girls ... Pelham, N. Y., Seahorse Press [1951] 128 p. illus. 29 cm. (A Seahorse fun book) [BS613.K4] 51-6703
1. Games. I. Title.

HARRIS, Roy 220.8793735
Bible riddles in rhyme. Grand Rapids, Mich., Zondervan [c.1960] 29p. 20cm. .50 pap.,
I. Title.

CHASE, Mary Ellen, 1887- 220.88
The Bible and the common reader. Rev. ed. New York, Macmillan [1962, c.1944, 1952] 381p. 18cm. (117) Bibl. 1.45 pap.,
1. Bible as literature. 2. Bible—Introductions. I. Title.

FOWLER, David C 1921- 220.88
Outlines for the study of the Bible as literature. Seattle, Distributed by University of Washington Press, 1956. 82p. 22cm. [BS591] 57-4325
1. Bible—Study— Outlines, syllabi, etc. I. Title. II. Title: Bible as literature.

REID, Mary Esson, ed. 220.88
The Bible read as literature, an anthology. [1st 54*Cleveland] H. Allen [1959] Cleveland* H. Allen *1959* 375p. 24cm. Includes bibliography. [BS535.R4] 58-11714
1. Bible as literature. I. Title.

JOURNAL of Biblical 220.8805
literature; v.49-69. New York, Johnson Reprint [1963] 21v. (various p.) 22cm. Contents.v.49-69, 1930-1950, including index to v.41-60. pap., set, 420.00; pap., ea., 20.00

GARRISON, Webb B. 220.880887
Laughter in the Bible [by] Gary Webster [pseud.] St. Louis, Bethany Press [c.1960] 160p. 21cm. 60-14650 2.95
1. Laughter. 2. Wit and humor, Ancient. 3. Bible—Language, style. I. Title.

JOHNSON, Marshall D. 220.8'9292
The purpose of the Biblical genealogies, with special reference to the setting of the genealogies of Jesus [by] Marshall D. Johnson. London, Cambridge U.P., 1969. x, 310 p. 23 cm. (Society for New Testament Studies. Monograph series, 8) Bibliography: p. 276-288. [BS569.J6] 69-10429 80/- ($12.50)
1. Bible—Genealogy. I. Title. II. Series: Studiorum Novi Testamenti Societas. Monograph series, 8

AHARONI, Jochanan. 220.9
The Macmillan Bible atlas, by Yohanan Aharoni, Michael Avi-Yonah. Prepd. by Carta, Jerusalem. New York, Macmillan [1968] 184p. illus., col. maps. 30cm. [G2230.A2 1968] Map 14.95
1. Bible—Geography—Maps. I. Avi-Yonah, Michael, 1904- joint author. II. Carta, Jerusalem. III. Title.

ALONSO SCHOKEL, Luis, 1920- 220.9
Journey through the Bible lands. Translated by John Drury. Milwaukee, Bruce Pub. Co. [1964] xii. 346 p. illus., maps. 22 cm. Translation of Viaje al pais del Antiquo Testamento. Bibliography: p. 329-333. [BS1180.A453] 64-22617
1. Bible. O. T. — History of contemporary events. etc. 2. Bible. O. T. — Antiq. I. Title.

ALONSO SCHOKEL, Luis, 1920- 220.9
Journey through the Bible lands. Tr. [from Spanish] by John Drury. Milwaukee, Bruce [c.1964] xii, 346p. illus., maps. 22cm. Bibl. 64-22617 4.95
1. Bible. O. T.—History of contemporary events, etc. 2. Bible. O. T.—Antiq. I. Title.

ARCHAEOLOGY and Bible 220.9
history, by Joseph P. Free. [8th ed.] Wheaton, Ill., Scripture Press Publications [1964, c1962] xviii, 398 p. illus., ports., maps. 22 cm. Bibliography: p. 360-371. [BS621.F7 1964] 62-17742
1. Bible — Antiq. I. Title.

THE Bible and history, 220.9
by William Barclay [and others] Nashville, Abingdon Press [1969, c1968] 370 p. maps. 23 cm. Includes bibliographies. [BS635.2.B5 1969] 71-2937 6.50
1. Bible—History of contemporary events, etc. I. Barclay, William, lecturer in the University of Glasgow.

BROWN, George E 220.9
Our living Bible for Young People. San Antonio, Naylor Co. [1962] 284p. illus. 22cm. [BS635.2.B7] 62-18030
1. Bible—History of Biblical events. I. Title.

BROWN, George E. 220.9
Our living Bible for young people. San Antonio, Tex., Naylor [c.1962] 284p. illus., map 22cm. 62-18030 5.95
1. Bible—History of Biblical events. I. Title.

CULVER, Douglas J 220.9
Bible people and places; a historical, geographical survey of the Bible, by Douglas J. Culver. Chicago, Harvest Publications [c1965] 94 p. 20 cm. (A Harvest learning-for-serving book) [BS635.2.C8] 65-28720
1. Bible — History of Biblical events. 2. Bible — Geography. I. Title.

DEGERING, Etta B. 220.9
My Bible friends [bks. 1-5] Washington, D. C., Review & Herald, c.1963. 5v. (various p.) col. illus. 25cm. Contents.bk. 1. Baby Moses, Baby Jesus.--bk. 2. Joseph's new coat, Joseph and his brothers.--bk. 3. Jesus and the storm, Jesus and the children.--bk. 4. Samuel, the little priest; David the youngest boy.--bk. 5. 'Go wash in the river,' Barley loaves and fishes. 3.75 19.75 ea., set,
I. Title.

DILLARD, Pauline (Hargis) 220.9
1916-
Bible stories for me. Pictures by Dorothy Handsaker Scott. Nashville Broadman c.1961. unpaged. illus (pt. col.) 25cm. (Little treasure ser., 13) 61-7553 .65 bds.,
1. Bible stories, English. I. Title.

EDWARDS, Arthur, 1917- 220.9
The number of years, as the great week of time. New York, William-Frederick [c.]1963. 85p. 22cm. 63-13404 2.50 pap.,
1. Bible—Chronology. I. Title.

EDWARDS, Arthur, 1917- 220.9
The number of years, as the great week of time. New York, William-Frederick Press, 1963. 85 p. 22 cm. [BS637.2.E3] 63-13404
1. Bible — Chronology. I. Title.

EGERMEIER, Elsie Emilie, 220.9
1890-
Egermeier's favorite Bible stories; selected stories for young children. Story adaptations by Dorothy Nicholson. Illus. by Clive Uptton. Anderson, Ind., warner [c.1965] 127p. col. illus. 25cm. Based on Egermeier's Bible story book, rev. ed., copyright 1963 and 1955. [BS551.E4] 65-11354 2.95
1. Bible stories, English. I. Nicholson, Dorothy. II. Title. III. Title: Favorite Bible stories.

EICHHOLZ, Georg. 220.9
Landscapes of the Bible. Translated by John W. Doberstein. New York, Harper & Row [1963] 151 p. col. illus. 29 cm. [DS108.5.E413] 63-16402
1. Bible—Geography. 2. Levant—Description and travel—Views. I. Title.

FIDES Trumpet books 220.9
[T3 &T4] Notre Dame, Ind., Fides [c.1964] 2v. (unpaged) col. illus. 22cm. .75 pap.,
1. Bible stories (Catholic authors)—Juvenile literature. I. Bak, Hedi.
Contents omitted.

FINEGAN, Jack, 1908- 220.9
Handbook of Biblical chronology; principles of time reckoning in the ancient world and problems of chronology in the Bible. Princeton, N. J., Princeton University Press, 1964. xxvi, 338 p. 24 cm. Includes bibliographical references. [BS637.2.F5] 63-18642
1. Bible—Chronology. I. Title.

FRASER, Edith, 1903- 220.9
The Bible tells me so; thirty-two stories from the Old and New Testaments. Color plates by John Turner. Line drawings by J. Pander. Cleveland, World [1965, c.1960] 1v. (unpaged) illus. (pt. col.) 25cm. (Shepherd bks.) [BS551.2.F7] 65-15120 2.95
1. Bible stories, English. I. Title.

FREE, Joseph P 220.9
Archaeology and Bible history, by Joseph P. Free. [8th ed.] Wheaton, Ill., Scripture Press Publications [1964, c1962] xviii, 398 p. illus., ports., maps. 22 cm. Bibliography: p. 360-371. [BS621.F7 1964] 62-17742
1. Bible — Antiq. I. Title. I. Title.

GOUKER, Loice 220.9
New Testament stories: with pictures to color. Drawings by Roelof Klein. Philadelphia, Muhlenberg, c.1962. 63p. 19x27cm. .75 pap.,
I. Title.

HALL, Arlene Stevens 220.9
Picture story Bible ABC book. Favorite stories by Elsie Egermeier, adapted for young children by Arlene Hall. Anderson, Ind., Warner, c.1963. unpaged. col. illus. 29cm. 'Adapted from Egermeier's Bible story book.' 63-10214 2.95 bds.,
1. Bible stories, English. I. Egermeier, Elsie Emilie, 1890- Bible story book. II. Title.

HALL, Arlene Stevens. j 220.9
Picture story Bible ABC book. Favorite stories by Elsie Egermeier, adapted for young children by Arlene Hall. Anderson, Ind., Warner Press c1963. unpaged. illus. 29 cm. "Adapted from Egermeier's Bible story book." [BS551.2.H3] 63-10214
1. Bible stories, English. I. Egermeier, Elsie Emilie, 1890- Bible story book. II. Title.

*HAYES, Wanda 220.9
My book of Bible stories. Illus. by Frances Hook. Cincinnati, Ohio, Standard Pub. Co., c.1964. unpaged. col. illus. 31cm. cover title. (3047) 1.50 bds.,
I. Title.

HENDERSON, Robert J. 220.9 (j)
Life in Bible times, by Robert Henderson and Ian Gould. Consultant editor, Mary Alice Jones. [Chicago] Rand McNally [1967] 48 p. illus. (part col.) 28 cm. [BS621.H44 1967] 67-18286
1. Bible—Antiquities. 2. Palestine—Social life

and customs. I. Gould, Ian, joint author. II. Title.

HODGES, Bert. 220.9
Short stories on the Bible. Boston, Christopher Pub. House [1962] 117p. 21cm. [BS550.2.H6] 62-9714
1. Bible—History of Biblical events. I. Title.

HOLMAN (A. J.) Company, Philadelphia. 220.9
A pictorial pilgrimage through Bible lands, consisting of a series of full-page photographic repordictions of the most notable places mentioned in the Scripture narrative from Genesis to Revelation; a historical sketch accompanies each illustration. Philadelphia, c1898. [82]p. (chiefly illus.) 22cm. [DS108.5.H7] 56-52587
1. Palestine—Descr. & trav.—Views. 2. Levant—Descr. & rav.—Views. I. Title.

ILLUSTRATED world of the 220.9
Bible library. [Editorial board: Chairman, Benjamin Mazar; editors, Michael Avi-Yonah and others. English ed.: translator, Merton Dagut] New York, McGraw-Hill [1961, c1958-61] 5v. illus. (part col.) col. maps, 30cm. The first four volumes were published in Jerusalem under the title, Views of the Biblical world, and are a translation of (transliterated: Pene 'olam ha-Mikra) Contents.1. The Law.--2. The former prophets.--3. The latter prophets.--4. The writings.--5. New Testament. [BS621] 61-66624
1. Bible—Antiq. 2. Near East—Antiq. 3. Bible—Pictures, illustrations, etc. I. Maisler, Benjamin, 1906- ed. II. Title: World of the Bible library.

**IN God's care;* 220.9
the way of salvation in the Old and New Testaments, for religious instruction in the junior school [Illus. by Albert Burkart. New York, Herder & Herder, 1965, c.1964] 166p. 19cm. 1.50 pap.,

IRONSIDE, Henry Allan, 1876-1951. 220.9
Things seen and heard in Bible lands; a series of gospel addresses based upon a visit to Syria, Palestine, and Egypt. [3d ed.] New York, Loizeaux Bros. [1941] 172p. 19cm. [BS630.I7 1941] 55-47067
1. Bible—Geography. I. Title.

JIRKU, Anton, 1885- 220.9
The world of the Bible. Tr. by Ann E. Keep. Cleveland, World [c.1967] 166p. illus., map. 25cm. (Ancient cultures) World ancient cultures ser. Bibl. [BS621.J513 1967b] 67-22273 10.00
1. Bible—Antiq. 2. Bible—History of contemporary events, etc. 3. Palestine—Hist.—To 70 A D. 4. Syria—Hist. I. Title.

JONES, Harold, 1904- 220.9
Noah and the ark, by Harold Jones, Kathleen Lines. New York, Watts [c.]1961. 1v. (chiefly col. illus.) 30x22cm. 61-12879 3.95
1. Noah's ark—Juvenile literature. I. Lines, Kathleen, joint author. II. Title.

KEYES, Nelson Beecher, 1894- 220.9
Reader's digest story of the Bible world, in map, word and picture: Pleasantville. N. Y., Reader's Digest Association [1962] 208p. illus. 26cm. First ed. published in 1959 under title: Story of the Bible world. [BS635.2.K4 1962] 62-17861
1. Bible—History of Biblical events. 2. Bible—History of contemporary events, etc. I. Title. II. Title: Story of the Bible world.

KEYES, Nelson Beecher, 1894- 220.9
Reader's digest story of the Bible world, in map, word and picture. Pleasantville, N.Y., Reader's Digest [1962] 208p. illus. 26cm. First ed. pub. in 1959 under title: Story of the Bible world. 62-17861 7.95; 31, 5.95 before Dec.
1. Bible—History of Biblical events. 2. Bible—History of contemporary events, etc. I. Title. II. Title: Story of the Bible world.

KEYES, Nelson Beecher, 1894- 220.9
Story of the Bible world, in map, word, and picture. Maplewood, N.J., Hammond [1959] 192 p. illus. 26 cm. [BS635.K48] 59-16136
1. Bible—History of Biblical events. 2. Bible—History of contemporary events, etc. I. Title.

KRAELING, Emil Gottliee Heinrich, 1892- 220.9
Rand McNally historical atlas of the Holy Land. Chicago, Rand McNally, c1959. 88p. illus., maps (part col.) 26cm. [G2230.K72 1959] Map
1. Bible— Geography—Maps. I. Title. II. Title: Historical atlas of the Holy Land.

MCDONALD, Mary Reynolds 220.9
Little stories about God. Illus. by the Daughters of St. Paul [Boston, Daughters of St. Paul, 1964] 132p. col. illus. 25cm. 64-22430 4.00; 3.00 pap.,
1. Bible stories, English. I. Title.

*MARSHALL, Robert J. 220.9
The mighty acts of God: a survey of Bible thought and history [Philadelphia, Lutheran Church Pr., c.1964] 232p. 21cm. (LCA Sunday church sch. ser.) pap., 1.50; teacher's gd., pap., 2.00
I. Title.

MASTER library (The) 220.9
[10v. Rev. ed.] Chicago, Good Counsel Pub. Co. 6 No. Michigan [1963] 10v. (various p.) illus. (pt. col.) maps. 25cm. Contents.v.1. Leaders of olden days.--v.2. The book of the kingdom.--v.3. Heroes and heroines.--v.4. The living wisdom.--v.5. Songs and the seers.--v.6. Everyday life in old Judea.--v.7. The perfect life.--v.8. Pioneers of the faith.--v.9. Using and teaching the Bible.--v.10. My best book. 63-24092 price unreported
1. Bible stories—Collections.

*MATHEWS, Eleanor Muth 220.9
God's way in the Old Testament; gr. 5 Illus. by Davis Meltzer. Joseph W. Inslee, ed. Philadelphia, Lutheran Church Pr. [c.1964] 176p. 22cm. 1.50; 2.50 teacher's guide,
I. Title.

MAY, Herbert Gordon, 1904- ed. 220.9
Oxford Bible atlas. Edited by Herbert G. May, with the assistance of R. W. Hamilton and G. N. S. Hunt. London, New York, Oxford University Press, 1962. 144 p. illus., col. maps, facsims. 26 cm. [BS630.M35 1962] 62-6531
1. Bible—Geography. I. Title.

MAY, Herbert Gordon, 1904- 220.9
Oxford Bible atlas. 2nd ed. / edited by Herbert G. May with the assistance of G. N. S. Hunt in consultation with R. W. Hamilton. London ; New York : Oxford University Press, 1974. 144 p. : ill., col. maps, col. plans, ports. ; 26 cm. Includes index. [BS630.M35 1974] 74-184843 ISBN 0-19-211557-X pbk. : 3.95
1. Bible—Geography. 2. Bible—Geography—Maps. I. Hunt, Geoffrey N. S., joint author. II. Hamilton, R. W. III. Title.

MEILACH, Dona Z j220.9
First book of Bible heroes. Illus. by Ezekiel Schloss, assisted by Uri Shulevitz. [New York] Ktav Pub. House, [1963- v. illus. 26 cm. Workbook. [New York] Ktav Pub. House, 1963-v. illus. 26 cm. [BM107.M4] 63-12714
1. Bible stories. English — O. T. I. Title.

MEILACH, Dona Z. 220.9
First book of Bible heroes [2 pts.] Illus. by Ezekiel Schloss, asst. by Uri Shulevitz [New York] Ktav [c.1963] 2v. (64;68p.) illus. (pt. col.) 26cm. 63-12714 2.00, ea., bxd.
1. Bible stories, English—O.T. I. Title.

MOORE, Doraine. j220.9
A dream and a promise. Saint Louis, Concordia Pub. House [1964] 151 p. 21 cm. [BS580.J6M6] 63-23490
1. Joseph, the patriarch — Juvenile literature. I. Title.

MOORE, Doraine 220.9
A dream and a promise. St. Louis, Concordia [c.1964] 151p. 21cm. 63-23490 2.95 bds.,
1. Joseph, the patriarch—Juvenile literature. I. Title.

MOSES, Montefiore J 220.9
Bible stories for Jewish children. New York, Holt Brothers, printers, 1958. 143p. 18cm. [BM107.M6] 58-51937
1. Bible stories, English—O. T. I. Title.

NEGENMAN, Jan H. 220.9
New atlas of the Bible [by] Jan H. Negenman. Edited by Harold H. Rowley. Translated by Hubert Hoskins and Richard Beckley. With a foreword by Harold H. Rowley and an epilogue by Lucas H. Grollenberg. Garden City, N.Y., Doubleday, 1969. 208 p. illus. (part col.), facsims., maps (part col.), plans. 36 cm. Translation of De bakermat van de Bijbel. [BS621.N4413 1969b] 69-11566 19.95
1. Bible—Antiquities. 2. Bible—History of contemporary events, etc. I. Rowley, Harold Henry, 1890-1969, ed. II. Title.

NOBLITT, Loren W 220.9
Basic elements of Biblical history [by] Loren W. Noblitt. Columbus, Ohio, Center for Biblical Research [1967] xv, 478 p. illus., maps. 23 cm. Includes bibliographical references. [BS635.2.N6] 67-31356
1. Bible—History of Biblical events. I. Title.

NOBLITT, Loren W. 220.9
Basic elements of Biblical history [by] Loren W. Noblitt. Columbus, Ohio, Center for Biblical Research [1967] xv, 478 p. illus., maps. 23 cm. Includes bibliographical references. [BS635.2.N6] 67-31356
1. Bible—History of Biblical events. I. Title.

OZANNE, C. G. 220.9
The first 7000 years; a study in Bible chronology [by] C. G. Ozanne. [1st ed. New York, Exposition Press [1970] 229 p. 22 cm. (An Exposition-testament book) Includes bibliographical references. [BS637.2.O9] 73-114063 5.00
1. Bible—Chronology. I. Title.

PFEIFFER, Charles F 220.9
The Wycliffe historical geography of Bible lands [by] Charles F. Pfeiffer [and] Howard F. Vos. Chicago, Moody Press [1967] xix, 588 p. illus., maps (part col.), plans. 26 cm. Includes bibliographies. [BS630.P47] 67-14382
1. Bible—Geography. I. Vos, Howard Frederic, 1925- joint author. II. Title.

PFEIFFER, Charles F. 220.9
The Wycliffe historical geography of Bible lands [by] Charles F. Pfeiffer [and] Howard F. Vos. Chicago, Moody Press [1967] xix, 588 p. illus., maps (part col.), plans. 26 cm. Includes bibliographies. [BS630.P47] 67-14382
1. Bible—Geography. I. Vos, Howard Frederic, 1925- joint author. II. Title.

RAMSAY, DeVere Maxwell. 220.9
God's promises; a book of Bible stories for young children. Illustrated by Rita Endhoven. Grand Rapids, Eerdmans [1964] 48 p. illus., music. 27 cm. [BS551.2.R3] 63-20685
1. Bible stories, English. I. Title.

RAMSAY, DeVere Maxwell 220.9
God's promises; a book of Bible stories for young children. Illus. by Rita Endhoven. Grand Rapids, Mich., Eerdmans [c.1964] 48p. illus., music. 27cm. 63-20685 1.95 bds.,
1. Bible stories, English. I. Title.

ROBINSON, Charles Alexander, 1900- 220.9
The first book of ancient Bible lands. New York, F. Watts [1962] 66 p. illus. 23 cm. [The First books, 158] [BS633.R6] 62-8621
1. Bible—Geography—Juvenile literature. I. Title.

[ROTHSCHILD, Robert L.] comp. 220.9
The young people's book of Bible stories. New York, Grosset [c.1963] 256p. illus. (pt. col.) col. maps. 26cm. 63-24145 2.95
1. Bible stories, English. I. Title.

SILVERMAN, Althea Osber. 220.9
The harp of David; legends of Mount Zion. Adapted from legends and tales related by S. Z. Kahana. Illustrated by Ezekiel Schloss. Hartford, Hartmore House [1964] 199 p. col. illus. 21 cm. [BM107.S53] 64-1650
1. Legends, Jewish. 2. David, King of Israel—Juvenile literature. I. Title.

STACHEN, Lee Garland. j220.9
Abraham the patriarch. Garden City, N.Y., [N. Doubleday 1963] 64 p. illus. 21 cm. (Know your Bible program) [BS580.A3S7] 63-1779
1. Abraham, the patriarch — Juvenile literature. 2. Bible stories, English — O.T. — Genesis. I. Title.

STEIN, Jack. 220.9
Great events in the Bible recorded on maps, by J. Stein. Dayton, Ohio, 1963. [1] 1., 141. of fold. maps. 29 cm. Reproduced photographically. [G2230.S835 1963] Map
1. Bible. O. T.—Geography—Maps. I. Title.

TERRIEN, Samuel. 220.9
The golden Bible atlas. Illustrated by William Bolin. New York, Golden Press [1963, c1957] 96 p. illus. (part col.) col. maps. 34 cm. Half title: Lands of the Bible. First published under title: Lands of the Bible. [BS635] 63-6990
1. Bible — History of Biblical events. 2. Bible — Geography — Maps. I. Title. II. Title: Lands of the Bible.

TERRIEN, Samuel L 1911- j 220.9
The golden Bible atlas. Illustrated by William Bolin. New York, Golden Press [1963, c1957] 96 p. illus. (part col.) col. maps. 34 cm. Half title: Lands of the Bible. First published under title: Lands of the Bible. [[BS635]] 63-6990
1. Bible—History of Biblical events. 2. Bible—Geography—Maps. I. Title. II. Title: Lands of the Bible.

UNWIN, Nora Spicer, 1907- 220.9
The way of the Shepherd; a story of the twenty-third Pslam, written and illustrated by Nora S. Unwin. New York, McGraw-Hill [1963] 32 p. illus. 26 cm. [BS551.2.U5] 63-12133
1. Bible stories, English — O.T. Psalms. I. Title.

UNWIN, Nora Spicer, 1907- 220.9
The way of the Shepherd; a story of the twenty-third Pslam, written, illus. by Nora S. Unwin. New York, McGraw [c.1963] 32p. illus. (pt. col.) 26cm. 63-12133 2.50
1. Bible stories, English—O.T. Psalms. I. Title.

VAN Ness, Bethann Beal (Faris) 1902- j 220.9
The Bible story book. Illustrated by Harold Minton. Nashville, Broadman Press [1963] 672 p. illus. (part col.) maps (on lining papers) 23 cm. [BS551.2.V3] 63-9758
1. Bible stories, English. I. Title.

VAN NESS, Bethann Beal (Faris) 1902- 220.9
The Bible story book. Illus. by Harold Minton. Nashville, Broadman [c.1963] 672p. illus. (pt. col.) maps (on lining papers) 23cm. 63-9758 4.95
1. Bible stories. English. I. Title.

VAUGHT, Bonny 220.9
Chosen to serve. Illus. by William K. Plummer. Ed.: Joseph W. Inslee. Philadelphia, Lutheran Church [c.1964] 143p. 22cm. (LCA weekday church sch. ser.) 1.50; 2.50 teacher's guide,
I. Title.

WARD, Elaine M. 220.9
A big book; stories from the Bible. Illus. by Howard Simon Nashville, Abingdon [1965] 38p. illus. (pt. col.) 23cm. [BS551.2.W25] 65-10725 .75 pap.,
1. Bible stories, English. I. Simon, Howard, 1903- illus II. Title.

WILSON, Robert R., 1942- 220.9
Genealogy and history in the Biblical world / Robert R. Wilson. New Haven : Yale University Press, 1977. xv, 222 p. ; 24 cm. (Yale Near Eastern researches ; 7) A revision of the author's thesis, Yale, 1972, entitled: Genealogy and history in the Old Testament. Includes indexes. Bibliography: p. [207]-215. [BS569.W54 1977] 76-40056 ISBN 0-300-02038-4 : 17.50
1. Bible—Genealogy. 2. Bible. O.T.—Historiography. I. Title. II. Series.

WINN, Laura Rocke 220.9
Margie asks why. Illus. by Jim R. Padgett. Nashville. Southern Pub. Assn. [1963] 284p. illus. 21cm. 63-12807 apply.
1. Children's stories. I. Title.

YOUNGMAN, Bernard R 220.9
The lands and peoples of the living Bible; a narrative history of the Old and New Testaments. Edited by Walter Russell Bowie. [1st ed.] New York, Hawthorn Books [1959] 382 p. illus., maps (2 col.) 26 cm. [BS551.2.Y65] 59-12174
1. Bible — History of Biblical events. I. Title.

THE Zondervan pictorial 220.9
Bible atlas. Edited by E. M. Blaiklock. Grand Rapids, Zondervan Pub. House [1969] xix, 491 p. illus., maps (part col.) 25 cm. Includes bibliographies. [BS630.Z64] 78-95273 9.95
1. Bible—Geography. 2. Bible—History of contemporary events. I. Blaiklock, E. M., ed. II. Title: Pictorial Bible atlas.

ADAMS, James McKee, 1886-1945. 220.91
Biblical backgrounds [by] J. Mckee Adams. Rev. by Joseph Callaway. Nashville, Broadman Press [1965] xvi, 231 p. illus., maps (part col.) 25 cm. [BS630.A35 1965] 66-10023
1. Bible — Geography. 2. Bible — History of contemporary events, etc. I. Callaway, Joseph A., ed. II. Title.

ADAMS, James McKee, 1886-1945 220.91
Biblical backgrounds. Rev. by Joseph Callaway. Nashville, Broadman [c.1965] xvi, 231p. illus., maps (pt. col.) 25cm. [BS630.A35] 66-10023 6.50
1. Bible — Geography. 2. Bible — History of contemporary events, etc. I. Callaway, Joseph A., ed. II. Title.

AHARONI, Jochanan. 220.91
The land of the Bible; a historical geography, by Yohanan Aharoni. Translated from the Hebrew by A. F. Rainey. Philadelphia, Westminster Press [1967] xiv, 409 p. maps. 25 cm. Translation of Erets-Yisreal bi-tekufat ha-Mikra. Bibliographical footnotes. [DS118.A3313] 67-11273
1. Bible—Geography. 2. Palestine—History—To 70 A. D. I. Title.

AHARONI, Yohanan, 1919 220.91
The Macmillan Bible atlas, by Yohanan Aharoni and Michael Avi-Yonah. New York, Macmillan Co. [1968] 184 p. illus., col. maps. 30 cm. [G2230.A2 1968] Map
1. Bible—Geography—Maps. I. Avi-Yonah, Michael, 1904- joint author. II. Carta, Jerusalem. III. Title.

BALY, Denis. 220.91
Atlas of the Biblical world [by] Denis Baly and A. D. Tushingham. Consultants: R. P. Roland de Vaux [and others] New York, World Pub. Co. [1971] xiii, 208 p. illus. (part col.), maps (part col.), plans. 29 cm. Bibliography: p. 177-185. [BS630.B337 1971] 71-107641 12.95
1. Bible—Geography. 2. Bible—History of contemporary events, etc. 3. Near East—Description and travel. I. Tushingham, A. Douglas, 1914- joint author. II. Title.

BALY, Denis. 220.91
Geographical companion to the Bible. New York, McGraw-Hill, 1963. 196 p. plates, maps (part fold., part col.) diagrs. 24 cm. Bibliographical references included in "Notes" (p. 134-137) [BS630.B338] 63-14214
1. Bible—Geography. I. Title.

BALY, Denis. 220.91
The geography of the Bible; a study in historical geography. New York, Harper [1957] 303 p. illus. 25 cm. [BS630.B34] 56-12061
1. Bible—Geography. I. Title.

BALY, Denis. 220.9'1
The geography of the Bible. New and rev. ed. New York, Harper & Row [1974] xv, 288 p. illus. 24 cm. Bibliography: p. 257-262. [BS630.B34 1974] 73-6340 ISBN 0-06-060371-2 10.95
1. Bible—Geography. I. Title.

BEN-HAR, Bezalel 220.91
The concealed map of the land of Israel. Tr. from Hebrew by Gerald J. Blidstein. [Jerusalem] Concealed Biblical Maps Pubn. Project [dist. Brooklyn 25, N.Y., P.O. Box 83, Lefferts Stn., Author, 1964] 32p. col. maps. 26cm. 64-2074 3.00 bds.,
1. Bible—Geography—Maps. I. Title.

BERRETT, LaMar C. 220.9'1
Discovering the world of the Bible [by] LaMar C. Berrett. Provo, Utah, Young House [1973] xxi, 701 p. illus. 23 cm. Bibliography: p. 662-665. [DS43.B43] 72-80275 ISBN 0-8425-0598-9 14.95
1. Near East—Description and travel—Guide-books. I. Title.
Pbk; 10.95, ISBN 0-8425-0599-7.

DUFFIELD, Guy P., 1909- 220.91
Handbook of Bible lands, by Guy P. Duffield. Glendale, Calif., G/L Regal Books [1969] 186 p. illus., maps. 18 cm. Bibliography: p. 181-182. [BS630.D8] 77-80446 1.65
1. Bible—Geography. 2. Near East—Description and travel—Guide-books. I. Title. II. Title: Bible lands.

FAY, Frederic Leighton, 220.91
1890-
A map book for Bible students, by Frederic L. Fay. Drawings by William Duncan. Needham Heights, Mass., Whittemore Associates [1966] 64 p. illus., maps. 19 cm. [G2230.F3 1966] Map
1. Bible—Geography—Maps. I. Duncan, William, cartographer. II. Title.

GILBERTSON, Merrill T 220.91
Where it happened in Bible times. Edited by Harriet L. Oberholt. Cartography by Bert Bauman. Minneapolis, Augsburg Pub. House [1963] viii, 168 p. maps. 20 cm. Sequel to The way it was in Bible times. Bibliography: p. 153-154. [BS630.G47] 63-16597
1. Bible — Geography. I. Title.

GILBERTSON, Merrill T. 220.91
Where it happened in Bible times. Ed. by Harriet L. Oberholt. Cartography by Bert Baumann. Minneapolis Augsburg [c.1963] viii, 168p. maps. 20cm. Sequel to The way it was in Bible times. Bibl. 63-16597 1.75 pap.,
1. Bible—Geography. I. Title.

GLUECK, Nelson, 1900- 220.91
The River Jordan. New York, McGraw-Hill [1968] xvi, 235 p. illus., map, port. 23 cm. Bibliography: p. [215] [DS110.J6G55 1968] 66-22910
1. Bible—Geography. 2. Jordan River. 3. Palestine—Description and travel. I. Title.

KRAELING, Emil Gottlieb 220.91
Heinrich, 1892-
Rand McNally Bible atlas. [2d ed.] New York, Rand McNally [1962] 487 p. illus., maps (part col.) 27 cm. [BS630.K7] 62-21843
1. Bible — Geography. I. Title. II. Title: Bible atlas.

KRAELING, Emil Gottlieb 220.91
Heinrich, 1892-
Rand McNally Bible atlas [by] Emil G. Kraeling. [3d ed.] Chicago, Rand McNally [c1966] 487 p. illus., facsims., maps (part col.), plans. 26 cm. [BS630.K7 1966] 66-20881
1. Bible-Geography. I. Title. II. Title: Bible atlas.

KRAELING, Emil Gottlieb 220.91
Heinrich, 1892-
Rand McNally Bible atlas. Chicago, Rand McNally [1956] 487 p. illus., maps (part col.) facsims. 26 cm. [BS630.K7] 56-12823
1. Bible—Geography. I. Title. II. Title: Bible atlas.

KRAELING, Emil Gottlieb 220.91
Heinrich, 1892-
Rand McNally Bible atlas. [2d ed.] New York, Rand McNally [1962] 487 p. illus., maps (part col.) 27 cm. [BS630.K7 1962] 62-21843
1. Bible—Geography. I. Title. II. Title: Bible atlas.

LAMBIE, Thomas Alexander, 220.91
1885-
A bruised reed; light from Bible lands on Bible illustrations. [1st ed.] New York, Loizeaux Bros. [1952] 192 p. illus. 20 cm. [BS620.L27] 52-41519
1. Bible—Antiq. I. Title.

MESSER, Thomas Stockton, 220.91
1923-
Walking where Jesus walked; a journey in Bible lands. Cape Girardeau, Mo. [1955] 117p. illus. 23cm. [DS107.4.M4] 55-37357
1. Bible—Geography. 2. Levant—Descr. & trav. I. Title.

MITCHELL, Antoinette. 220.91
Bible places: historic and geographic highlights. Designed by Tyyne Hakola. Norwalk, Conn., C. R. Gibson Co. [c1966] 71 p. illus., maps, plan. 19 cm. [BS630.M57] 66-27871
1. Bible—Geography—Dictionaries. I. Title.

NATIONAL Geographic 220.91
Society, Washington, D. C. Book Service.
Everyday life in Bible times. [Washington] National Geographic Society [1967] 448 p. illus. (part col.), col. maps (1 fold. in pocket) 26 cm. (Story of man library) [BS620.N37] 67-23392
1. Bible—Antiq. 2. Civilization, Ancient. I. Title.

NATIONAL Geographic 220.91
Society, Washington, D.C. Book Service.
Everyday life in Bible times. [Washington] National Geographic Society [1967] 448 p. illus. (part col.), col. maps (1 fold. in pocket) 26 cm. (Story of man library) [BS620.N37] 67-23392
1. Bible—Antiquities. 2. Civilization, Ancient. I. Title.

PFEIFFER, Charles F. 220.91
Baker's Bible atlas. Consulting eds.: E. Leslie Carlson, Martin H. Scharlemann. Grand Rapids, Mich., Baker Bk. House, 1961. 333p. illus., maps (pt. col.) 25cm. 60-15536 7.95
1. Bible—Geography. I. Title. II. Title: Bible atlas.

*PFEIFFER, Charles F. 220.91
Baker's pocket atlas of the Bible. Grand Rapids, Mich., Baker Book House [1973] 108 p. illus., col. plates, maps (15 full-page col.) 18 cm. (Direction Books) Bibliography: p. 103. [BS630] ISBN 0-8010-6946-7 1.95 (pbk.)
1. Bible—Geography. I. Title. II. Title: Pocket atlas of the Bible.

PIKE, Edgar Royston, 1896- 220.91
Lands of the Bible, by E. Royston Pike. Drawings by Sally Mellersh. London, Weidenfeld & Nicolson [dist. New Rochelle, N.Y., SportShelf, 1965, c.1962] 144p. illus., maps. 20cm. (Young historian ser. 8; Young enthusiast lib.) [BS630.P54] 65-29538 3.25 bds.,
1. Bible — Geography. I. Title. II. Series.

RICE, Lillian (Moore) 220.91
In the land where Jesus lived. Illustrated by Don Fields. [Teacher's ed.] Nashville, Convention Press [1967] 104, [17] p. illus., forms. 20 cm. Map on p. [4] of cover. "Church study course [of the Sunday School Board of the Southern Baptist Convention] This book is number 95 in category 2, section for juniors." "Helps for the teacher": [17] p. (2d group) [BS621.R5] 67-27898
1. Bible—Antiq.—Study and teaching. 2. Palestine—Soc. life & cust.—Study and teaching. I. Southern Baptist Convention. Sunday School Board. II. Title.

RICE, Lillian (Moore) 220.91
In the land where Jesus lived. Illustrated by Don Fields. [Teacher's ed.] Nashville, Convention Press [1967] 104, [17] p. illus., forms. 20 cm. Map on p. [4] of cover. "Church study course [of the Sunday School Board of the Southern Baptist Convention] This book is number 95 in category 2, section for juniors." "Helps for the teacher": [17] p. (2d group) [BS621.R5] 67-27898
1. Bible—Antiquities—Study and teaching. 2. Palestine—Social life and customs—Study and teaching. I. Southern Baptist Convention. Sunday School Board. II. Title.

RICE, Lillian (Moore) 220.91
In the land where Jesus lived. Illustrated by Don Fields. [Teacher's ed.] Nashville, Convention Press [1967] 104, [17] p. illus., forms. 20 cm. Map on p. [4] of cover. "Church study course [of the Sunday School Board of the Southern Baptist Convention] This book is number 95 in category 2, section for juniors." "Helps for the teacher": [17] p. (2d group) A teacher's supplement to Sunday School teaching, which describes the social customs, geography, and climate of Palestine in Biblical times. [BS621.R5] AC 67
1. Bible—Antiquities—Study and teaching. 2. Palestine—Social life and customs—Study and teaching. I. Southern Baptist Convention. Sunday School Board. II. Fields, Don, illus. III. Title.

ROBINSON, Edward, 1794- 220.9'1
1863.
Biblical researches in Palestine, Mount Sinai, and Arabia Petraea / Edward Robinson. New York : Arno Press, 1977. p. cm. (America and the Holy Land) Also authored by E. Smith. Reprint of the 1841 ed. published by Crocker & Brewster, Boston. Includes bibliographical references. [DS107.R664 1977] 77-70738 ISBN 0-405-10281-Xlib.bdg. : 120.00
1. Robinson, Edward, 1794-1863. 2. Smith, Eli, 1801-1857. 3. Bible—Geography. 4. Palestine—Description and travel. 5. Sinaitic Peninsula—Description and travel. 6. Palestine—Antiquities. 7. Sinaitic Peninsula—Antiquities. I. Smith, Eli, 1801-1857, joint author. II. Title. III. Series.

ROWLEY, Harold Henry, 220.91
1890-
The modern reader's Bible atlas. [New York] Association [1961, c.1960] viii, 88p. illus., col. maps. (Reflection bk giant, 700) First published in 1960 under title: The teach yourself Bible atlas. 61-14177 1.75 pap.,
1. Bible—Geography. I. Title.

STEVE, M. J. 220.91
The living world of the Bible. Tr. [from French] by Daphne Woodward. Cleveland, World Pub. Co. [c.1961] 231p. illus., maps. 61-13874 12.50
1. Bible—Geography. 2. Near East—Antiq. I. Bible. O.T. English. Selections. 1961. Authorized. II. Title.

STEVE, Marie Joseph, 1911- 220.91
The living world of the Bible. [Translated by Daphne Woodward. 1st ed.] Cleveland, World Pub. Co. [1961] 231 p. illus., maps. 24 cm. "Passages detached from the Bible are placed side by side with photographs illustrating them ... Each group ... is preceded by a few pages of commentary." Translation of Sur les chemins de in Bible. [BS621.S813] 61-13874
1. Bible — Geography. 2. Near East — Antiq. I. Bible. O. T. English. Selections. 1961. Authorized II. Title.

WRIGHT, George Ernest, 220.91
1909-
The Westminster historical atlas to the Bible, edited by George Ernest Wright and Floyd Vivian Filson. With an introductory article by William Foxwell Albright. Rev. ed. Philadelphia, Westminster Press [1956] 130 p. illus., maps. 37 cm. (Westminster aids to the study of the Scriptures) [BS630.W7 1956] 56-9123
1. Bible — Geography. 2. Bib-e — Geography — Maps. I. Filson, Floyd Vivian, 1896- joint author. II. Title. III. Series.

WRIGHT, George Ernest, 220.91
1909-
The Westminster historical atlas to the Bible, edited by George Ernest Wright and Floyd Vivian Filson. With an introductory article by William Foxwell Albright. Rev. ed. Philadelphia, Westminster Press [1956] 130 p. illus., maps. 37 cm. (Westminster aids to the study of the Scriptures) [BS630.W7 1956] 56-9123
1. Bible—Geography. 2. Bible—Geography—Maps. I. Filson, Floyd Vivian, 1896- joint author. II. Title. III. Series.

ALEXANDER, George M. 220.92
The handbook of Biblical personalities. Greenwich, Conn., Seabury [c.1962] xv, 299p. 22cm. Bibl. 62-9613 5.75
1. Bible—Biog.—Dictionaries. I. Title. II. Title: Biblical personalities.

ALEXANDER, George M 220.92
The handbook of Biblical personalities. Greenwich, Conn., Seabury Press, 1962. xv, 299p. 22cm. Bibliography: p. 295-299. [BS570.A55] 62-9613
1. Bible—Biog.— Dictionaries. I. Title. II. Title: Biblical personalities.

ANDREASEN, Milian Lauritz, 220.92
1876-
Saints and sinners. Washington, Review and Herald Pub. Association [1951] 192 p. 20 cm. [BS571.A6] 51-35224
1. Bible—Biog. 2. Seventh-Day Adventists—Sermons. I. Title.

BARKER, William Pierson. 220.92
Everyone in the Bible [by] William P. Barker. Westwood, N.J., F. H. Revell Co. [1966] 370 p. 24 cm. [BS570.B3] 66-21894
1. Bible—Biography—Dictionaries. I. Title.

BARKER, William Pierson. 220.92 B
Saints and swingers; the under-thirties in the Bible [by] William P. Barker. Old Tappan, N.J., F. H. Revell Co. [1971] 160 p. 22 cm. [BS571.B34] 72-149375 ISBN 0-8007-0446-0 3.95
1. Bible—Biography. I. Title.

BARKER, William 220.9'2 B
Pierson.
When God says no [by] William P. Barker. Old Tappan, N.J., F. H. Revell Co. [1974] 160 p. 20 cm. [BS571.B344] 73-18148 ISBN 0-8007-0643-9 4.95
1. Bible—Biography. 2. Providence and government of God. I. Title.

BARKER, William 220.9'2 B
Pierson.
Women and the Liberator [by] William P. Barker. Old Tappan, N.J., F. H. Revell Co. [1972] 128 p. 22 cm. [BS2445.B37] 73-186532 ISBN 0-8007-0518-1 3.95
1. Jesus Christ—Attitude towards women. 2. Women in the Bible. I. Title.

BARR, George, 1916- 220.9'2
Who's who in the Bible. Middle Village, N.Y., Jonathan David Publishers [1975] 177 p. 22 cm. [BS570.B33] 74-1965
1. Bible—Biography—Dictionaries. I. Title.

BAXTER, James Sidlow. 220.92
Mark these men; practical studies in striking aspects of certain Bible. characters. Grand Rapids, Zondervan Pub. House [1960] 192p. 20cm. [BS571.5.B3] 60-50186
1. Bible—Biog. 2. Baptists—Sermons. 3. Sermons, English—Scotland. I. Title.

BOWIE, Walter Russell, 220'.92
1882-1969.
See yourself in the Bible. [1st ed.] New York, Harper & Row [1967] xi, 176 p. 22 cm. Bibliographical footnotes. [BS571.B58] 67-11500
1. Bible—Biography. I. Title.

BURKE, Carl F. 220.9'2 B
The boy who stayed cool, and other stories of young people in the Bible [by] Carl F. Burke. New York, Association Press [1973] 125 p. 19 cm. Retells in slang forty Biblical tales describing the lives of various people in the Old and New Testament. [BS551.2.B87] 73-15685 ISBN 0-8096-1877-X 4.95
1. Bible—Biography. 2. Bible stories, English. I. Title.
Pbk. 2.95.

CHAPPELL, Clovis Gillham, 220.92
1882-
Feminine faces. Nashville, Abingdon [1966, c.1942] 219p. 20cm. (Apex bks., X3-125) [BS575.C53] 42-5030 1.25 pap.,
1. Women in the Bible. 2. Bible — Biog. I. Title.

CHAPPELL, Clovis Gillham, 220.92
1882-
Meet these men. New York, Abingdon Press [1956] 156p. 20cm. [BS571.C42] 56-6354
1. Bible—Biog. I. Title.

CHAPPELL, Clovis Gillham, 220.92
1882-1972.
Meet these men: sermons on Bible characters. Grand Rapids, Baker Book House [1974, c1956] 156 p. 20 cm. [BS571.C42] ISBN 0-8010-2354-8 2.50 (pbk.)
1. Bible—Biography. I. Title.
L.C. card no. for original edition: 56-6354.

CHEVILLE, Roy Arthur, 220.92
1897-
Meet them in the Scriptures; a guide to

character appreciation through family reading. Independence, Mo., Herald House [c.1960] 224p. 60-51797 2.50
1. Bible—Biog. 2. Reorganized Church of Jesus Christ of Latter-Day Saints—Doctrinal and controversial works. I. Title.

CHUPP, Tommy. 220.9'2 B
Bible characters : sinners, saints and servants / Tommy Chupp. Nashville : T. Nelson, [1975] x, 149 p. : ill. ; 21 cm. Title on spine: Sinners, saints and servants. [BS572.C47] 74-23285 ISBN 0-8407-5589-9 pbk. : 3.50.
1. Bible—Biography. I. Title. II. Title: Sinners, Saints, and servants.

CROWELL, Grace (Noll) 220.92
1877-
God's masterpieces. New York, Abingdon Press [1963] 96 p. 18 cm. [BS572.C7] 63-7479
1. Bible — Biog. I. Title.

CROWELL, Grace (Noll) 220.92
1877-
God's masterpieces. Nashville, Abingdon [c.1963] 96p. 18cm. 63-7479 1.75 bds.,
1. Bible—Biog. I. Title.

CULLY, Iris V. 220.9'2 B
From Aaron to Zerubbabel : profiles of Bible people / Iris V. Cully and Kendig Brubaker Cully. New York : Hawthorn Books, c1976. vi, 149 p. ; 21 cm. [BS570.C84 1976] 76-7830 ISBN 0-8015-6084-5 : 2.95
1. Bible—Biography. I. Cully, Kendig Brubaker, joint author. II. Title.

DAUGHTERS of St. Paul. 220.9'2 B
Women of the Gospel / written by the Daughters of St. Paul ; ill. by Gregori. Boston : St. Paul Editions, 1975. 134 p. : ill. ; 25 cm. [BS2445.D38] 74-32122
1. Bible. N.T.—Biography. 2. Women in the Bible. I. Title.

DEEN, Edith. 220.92
All of the women of the Bible. [1st ed.] New York, Harper [1955] xxii, 410p. 25cm. Bibliography: p.381-385. [BS575.D4] 55-8521
1. Women in the Bible. 2. Bible—Biog. I. Title.

DEEN, Edith. 220.9'2 B
All the Bible's men of hope. [1st ed.] Garden City, N.Y., Doubleday, 1974. xxiv, 310 p. 22 cm. Bibliography: p. [297]-299. [BS571.D4] 73-22786 ISBN 0-385-05100-X 7.95
1. Bible—Biography. 2. Hope—Biblical teaching. I. Title.

DOWLEY Bible atlas; 220.9'2
an historical chronological outline of events from the formation of Adam to the building of Solomon's temple; the divided kingdoms of Judah and Israel, and the prophets after the division ... A biography of more than three thousand persons mentioned in the Bible; one hundred and twelve subjects of the positive and negative powers of life; a list of 3132 Bible names, alphabetically and numerically arranged with key for locating same on the accompanying chart; the Adam family tree with cross keyed index and Bible references. Jackson, Mich., Dowley Bible Atlas Co. [1972] 330 p. illus. 29 cm. [BS570.D68] 78-186595
1. Bible—Biography—Dictionaries. I. Title: Bible atlas.

EDMAN, David. 220.9'2
Of wise men and fools; realism in the Bible. Introd. by Kenneth L. Wilson. [1st ed.] Garden City, N.Y., Doubleday, 1972. viii, 229 p. 22 cm. [BS571.E33] 76-180072 5.95
1. Bible—Biography. I. Title.

EIKAMP, Arthur R 220.9'2
Jesus Christ; a study of the Gospels. Anderson, Ind., Warner Press [c1963] 176 p. 22 cm. [BT301.2.E5] 63-20427
1. Jesus Christ — Biog. I. Title.

*EVANS, B. Hoyt 220.92
Youth programs about Bible people. Grand Rapids, Mich., Baker Bk. [c.]1964. 107p. 20cm. 1.50 pap.,
I. Title.

FAULKNER, James, 1876- 220.92
Romances and intrigues of the women of the Bible. [1st ed.] New York, Vantage Press [1957] 162p. 21cm. [BS575.F33] 56-12197
1. Women in the Bible. I. Title.

FICKETT, Harold L 220.92
Profiles in clay. [1st ed.] Los Angeles, Cowman Pub. Co. [1963] 147 p. 21 cm. [BS571.F43] 63-12081
1. Bible — Biog. I. Title.

FICKETT, Harold L. 220.92
Profiles in clay. Los Angeles, 747 Seward St., Cowman, 1963 147p. 21cm. 63-12081 2.95
1. Bibl.—Biog. I. Title.

FLETCHER, William C. 220.92
Unlikely saints of the Bible, surprising and dramatic character sketches of familiar and unfamiliar personalities in Scripture. Illus. by Dirk Gringhuis. Grand Rapids, Mich., Zondervan Pub. House [c.1961] 144p. 25cm. 61-3397 2.95
1. Bible—Biog. I. Title.

FOSTER, Rupert Clinton, 220.9'2
1888-
Studies in life of Christ [2v. in 1. 3d. ed] Grand Rapids, mich, Baker [1966] (2v.in1) 505 p. illus. 23 cm Contents.An introduction to the life of christ and studies in the life of Christ. [bt301.f6] 232 5.95
1. 1. Jesus-biog. title I. Title.

GIBBS, Paul T 220.92
Men such as we. Washington, Review and Herald Pub. Association [1963] 192 p. illus. 22 cm. [BS571.G5] 63-10403
1. Bible — Biog. I. Title.

GIBBS, Paul T. 220.92
Men such as we. Washington, D.C., Review & Herald [c.1963] 192p. illus. 22cm. 63-10403 3.50
1. Bible—Biog. I. Title.

GOUKER, Loice. 220.92
Bible people; highlights from their lives. Designed by Tyyne Hakola. Norwalk, Conn., C. R. Gibson Co. [c1965] 68 p. illus. 19 cm. [BS539.G6] 65-16437
1. Bible — Biog. — Dictionaries, Juvenile. I. Title.

GOUKER, Loice 220.92
Bible people: highlights from their lives. Designed by Tyyne Hakola. Norwalk, Conn., C. R. Gibson Co. [c.1965] 68p. illus. 19cm. [BS539.G6] 65-16437 1.35
1. Bible — Biog. — Dictionaries, Juvenile. I. Title.

GREAT people of the Bible 220.9'2
and how they lived. Pleasantville, N.Y., Reader's Digest Association [1974] 432 p. illus. (part col.) 29 cm. On spine: Readers digest. [BS571.G73] 73-86027 14.95
1. Bible—Biography. 2. Bible—History of Biblical events. I. The Reader's digest.

HAVENS, Joseph, 1919- 220.9'2
The journal of a college student. [Wallingford, Pa, Pendle Hill Publications, 1965] 32 p. 20 cm. (Pendle Hill pamphlet 141) [BV4531.2.H36] 65-19208
1. Students — Religious life I. Title.

HENDRICKS, Jeanne W. 220.9'2 B
A woman for all seasons / by Jeanne W. Hendricks. Nashville : T. Nelson, [1977] c1971. p. cm. [HQ759.H5 1977] 77-23045 ISBN 0-8407-5630-5 pbk. : 2.95
1. Wives. 2. Wives—Conduct of life. 3. Women in the Bible. I. Title.

HEWITT, Charles Edward. 220.92
'Songs in the night' for birds with broken wing. New York, Loizeaux Bros. [1938] 124p. 20cm. [BS572.H48] 55-46598
1. Bible—Biog. I. Title.

HUGHES, Edna Beougher. 220.92
Voices from eternity. [1st ed.]. New York, Pageant Press [1957, c1956] 96). 21cm. [BS571.H76] 56-13121
1. Bible—Biog. I. Title.

*HUGHES, Elmer R. 220.92
Famous mothers from the Bible and history: the stories of great men and the women behind them. New York, Exposition [c.1963] 156p. 21cm. 3.00
I. Title.

JENKINS, Sara Lucile, 220.92
1905-
The young people of the Bible. New York, Appleton Century-Crofts [1958] 210p. 21cm. [BS576.J4] 58-6919
1. Children in the Bible. 2. Bible—Biog. I. Title.

KULOW, Nelle Wahler. 220.92
Even as you and I; sketches of human women from the Divine Book. Columbus, Ohio, Wartburg Press [1955] 72p. 20cm. [BS575.K76] 55-4428
1. Women in the Bible. 2. Bible—Biog. I. Title.

LA SOR, William Sanford. 220.92
Great personalities of the Bible. Westwood, N.J., F.H. Revell Co. [1965] 192 p. 21 cm. "Most of the material in this book was originally published in the two volumes entitled Great personalities of the Old Testament and Great personalities of the New Testament." Bibliography: p. 185-189. [BS571.L318 1965] 65-10560
1. Bible — Bbiog. I. Title.

LA SOR, William Sanford 220.92
Great personalities of the Bible. Westwood, N. J., Revell [1965, c.1964] 192p. 21cm. Most of the mat. in this bk. was orig. pub. in the two vols. entitled Great personalities of the Old Testament and Great personalities of the New Testament. Bibl. [BS571.L318] 65-10560 5.95 bds.,
1. Bible—Biog. I. Title.

LEBRETON, Jules, 1873- 220.9'2
1956.
The life & teachings of Jesus Christ Our Lord. Translated from the French New York, Macmillan, 1957. 2v. in 1. 21cm. [BT301.1.] A60
1. Jesus Christ—Biog. 2. Jesus Christ — Teachings. I. Title.

LEHMAN, Louis Paul. 220.92
Tears of the Bible. Grand Rapids, Zondervan Pub. House [1958] 93p. 20cm. [BS571.L45] 58-2477
1. Bible—Biog. I. Title.

LEHMBERG, Ben F. 220.92
Seven tall men. Grand Rapids, Mich., Eerdmans [c.1961] 73p. 60-53089 2.00 bds.,
1. Bible—Biog. I. Title.

LEWIS, Ethel (Clark) 220.92
Portraits of Bible women. [1st ed.] New York, Vantage Press [1956] 252p. 21cm. [BS575.L43] 55-11659
1. Women in the Bible. I. Title.

LOCKYER, Herbert. 220.92
All the kings and queens of the Bible; tragedies and triumps of royalty in past ages. Grand Rapids, Zondervan Pub. House [1961] 253p. maps. 24cm. Bibliography: p. 249-250. [BS579.K5L6] 61-1477
1. Bible—Biog. I. Title.

LOCKYER, Herbert. 220.92
All the men of the library of more than 3000 Biblical characters. Grand Bible; a portrait gallery and reference Rapids, Zondervan Pub. House [1958] 381p. 24cm. Bibliography: p. 373-374. [BS570.L6] 58-4616
1. Bible—Biog.— Dictionaries. I. Title.

*LOCKYER, Herbert 220.92.
Ancient portraits in modern frames Grand Rapids, Baker Book House [1975] 135p. 20 cm. Contents.Contents: vol. 1: bible biographies [BS571] ISBN 0-8010-5545-8. 2.95 (pbk)
I. Bible-Biography. I. Title.

LOCKYER, Herbert. 220.92
The women of the Bible. [1st ed.] Grand Rapids, Zondervan Pub. House [1967] 321 p. 24 cm. Bibliography: p. 307-308. [BS575.L56] 67-22687
1. Women in the Bible. I. Title.

LOCKYER, Herbert. 220.92
The women of the Bible. [1st ed.] Grand Rapids, Zondervan Pub. House [1967] 321 p. 24 cm. Bibliography: p. 307-308. [BS575.L56] 67-22687
1. Women in the Bible. I. Title.

LOCKYER, Herbert [Henry 220.92
John]
All the kings and queens of the Bible; tragedies and triumphs of royalty in past ages. Grand Rapids, Mich., Zondervan Pub. House [c.1961] 253p. maps. Bibl. 61-1477 3.95 bds.,
1. Bible—Biog. I. Title.

MACARTNEY, Clarence Edward 220.92
Noble, 1879-
Chariots of fire, and other sermons on Bible characters. New York, Abingdon-Cokesbury Press [1951] 192 p. 20 cm. [BS571.M222] 51-13256
1. Bible—Biog. 2. Presbyterian Church—Sermons. 3. Sermons, American. I. Title.

MACARTNEY, Clarence Edward 220.92
Noble, 1879-
The man who forgot, and other sermons on Bible characters. New York, Abingdon Press [1956] 140p. 20cm. [BS571.M228] 56-5125
1. Bible—Biog. 2. Presbyterian Church—Sermons. 3. Sermons, American. I. Title.

MACARTNEY, Clarence Edward 220.92
Noble, 1879-
The man who forgot, and other sermons on Bible characters. New York, Abington Press [1956] 140p. 20cm. [BS571.M228] 56-5125
1. Bible—Biog. 2. Presbyterian Church—Sermons. 3. Sermons, American. I. Title.

MACARTNEY, Clarence Edward 220.92
Noble, 1879-
The woman of Tekoah, and other sermons on Bible characters. Nashville, Abingdon Press [c1955] 160p. 20cm. [BS571.M243] 55-5397
1. Bible—Biog. 2. Presbyterian Church—Sermons. 3. Sermons, American. I. Title.

MCGEE, John Vernon, 220.9'2 B
1904-
Vessels, vehicles, and victory : unforgettable men of the Bible / J. Vernon McGee. Chicago : Moody Press, c1976. 128 p. ; 18 cm. [BS571.M253] 76-9042 ISBN 0-8024-9157-X pbk. : 0.95
1. Bible—Biography. I. Title.

MARSHALL, Zona Bays. 220.92
Certain women; a study of Biblical women. With a foreword by James Gordon Lott, and an introd. by Robert G. Lee. [1st ed.] New York, Exposition Press [1960] 141p. 21cm. (An Exposition-Testament Book) [BS575.M337] 60-2131
1. Women in the Bible. I. Title.

MEAD, Frank Spencer, 1898- 220.92
Who's who in the Bible; 25o Bible biographies. New York, Harper [1966, c.1934] xi p., 1 1., 250p. 21cm. (Chapel bks., CB25H) Formerly pub. under the title, 250 Bible biographies. [BS571.M376] 38-27349 1.45 pap.,
1. Bible — Biog. I. Title.

MILHOUSE, Paul William, 220.92
1910-
At life's crossroads. Anderson, Ind, Warner Press [1959] 112p. 20cm. [BS572.M5] 59-8790
1. Bible— Biog. 2. Decision-making. I. Title.

MORTON, Henry Canova 220.92
Vollam, 1892-
Women of the Bible. Illustrated with a full-color front. and 18 ports. by famous old masters. [Illustrated ed.] New York, Dodd, Mead, 1956 [c1941] 204p. illus. 21cm. [BS575] 57-817
1. Women in the Bible. 2. Bible—Biog. I. Title.

NEAL, Hazel G 220.92
Bible women of faith. Anderson, Ind., Warner Press [1955] 158p. 20cm. [BS575.N4] 55-3206
1. Women in the Bible. 2. Bible—Biog. I. Title.

NEWSHAM, Harold Goad. 220.92
The man who feared a bargain, and other sermons on Bible characters. New York, Abingdon Press [1958] 125p. 20cm. [BS571.N58] 58-5391
1. Bible—Biog. 2. Congregational churches—Sermons. 3. Sermons, American. I. Title.

OCKENGA, Harold John, 220.92
1905-
Women who made Bible history; messages and character sketches dealing with familiar Bible women. Grand Rapids, Zondervan Pub. House [1962] 239 p. illus. 23 cm. [BS575.O27] 62-7373
1. Women in the Bible. 2. Congregational churches—Sermons. 3. Sermons, American. I. Title.

OGDEN, R. James. 220.9'2 B
Going public with one's faith / R. James Ogden, editor. Valley Forge, Pa. : Judson Press, [1975] 128 p. : ill. ; 22 cm. Includes bibliographical references. [BS605.2.O35] 74-31462 ISBN 0-8170-0673-7 pbk. : 2.50
1. Bible—Biography. 2. Bible—Study—Text-books. I. Title.

PATRICK, Sam. 220.92
The children of Bible times, by Sam Patrick and Omar Garrison. Englewood Cliffs, N. J., Prentice-Hall [1958] 127p. illus. 28cm. [BS576.P37] 58-13103
1. Children in the Bible. I. Garrison, Omar, joint author. II. Title.

PINK, Arthur Walkington, 220.9'2
1886-1952.
The sovereignty of God. Grand Rapids, Baker Book House, 1965 [c1930] 320 p. 21 cm. [BT135.P5. 1965] 63-18713
1. Providence and government of God. I. Title.

POWELL, Ivor 220.92
Bible cameos. Grand Rapids, Mich., Zondervan Pub. House [1960, 1951] 173p. 21cm. 60-4695 2.50
1. Bible—Biog. I. Title.

POWELL, Ivor 220.92
Bible pinnacles. With a foreword by F. W. Boreham. Grand Rapids, Mich., Zondervan Pub. House [1960] [viii], 174p. 21cm. 60-4694 2.50
1. Bible—Biog. I. Title.

POWELL, Ivor 220.92
Bible treasures. With a foreword by Lionel B. Fletcher. Grand Rapids, Mich., Zondervan Pub. House [1960] 182p. 21cm. 60-4697 2.50
1. Bible—Biog. I. Title.

REDHEAD, John A 220.92
Sermons on Bible characters. New York, Abingdon Press [1963] 144 p. 21 cm. [BS571.5.R4] 63-11380
1. Bible — Biog. — Sermons. 2. Presbyterian Church — Sermons. 3. Sermons, American. I. Title.

REDHEAD, John A. 220.92
Sermons on Bible characters. Nashville, Abingdon [c.1963] 144p. 21cm. 63-11380 2.75
1. Bible—Biog.—Sermons. 2. Presbyterian Church—Sermons. 3. Sermons, American. I. Title.

ROBINSON, Ruth (Grace) 220.9'2
Seventeen come Sunday; a birthday letter, by Ruth Robinson. Philadelphia, Westminster [c.1966] 78p. illus. 20cm. [BV4531.2.R57] 248 2.50
1. Youth—Religious life. I. Title.

RUSCHE, Helga. 220.92
They lived by faith; women in the Bible. Translated by Elizabeth Williams. Baltimore, Helicon [1963] vi, 124 p. 22 cm. [BS575.R813] 63-19402
1. Women in the Bible. I. Title.

RUSCHE, Helga 220.92
They lived by faith: women in the Bible. Tr. by Elizabeth Williams. Helicon[dist. New York, Taplinger, c.1963] vi, 124p. 22cm. 63-19402 2.95
1. Women in the Bible. I. Title.

SANDERS, John Oswald, 220.92
1902-
Robust in faith: men from God's school, by J. Oswald Sanders. Chicago, Moody Press [1965] 219 p. 22 cm. "An Overseas Missionary Fellowship book." [BS571.S23] 65-4898
1. Bible—Blog. I. Title.

SANDERS, John Oswald, 220.92
1902-
Robust in faith: men from God's school. Chicago, Moody [c.1965] 219p. 22cm. (Overseas Missionary Fellowship bk.) [BS571.S23] 65-4898 3.50
1. Bible—Biog. I. Title.

SAXON, Kurt. 220.9'2 B
The instant who's who in the Bible / Kurt Saxon. [Eureka, Calif. : Atlan Formularies, 1974] 302 p. ; 28 cm. Cover title. [BS570.S38] 74-11874
1. Bible—Biography—Dictionaries. 2. Bible—Geneaology. I. Title.

SCHOFIELD, Joseph 220.92
Anderson, 1897-1955.
Sunday talks about children of the Bible. Natick, Mass., W. A. Wilde Co. [1959] 189p. 21cm. [BS576.S37] 59-14835
1. Children in the Bible. 2. Children's sermons. I. Title.

SEAGREN, Daniel. 220.9'2 B
Couples in the Bible; a discussion guide [by] Daniel R. Seagren. Grand Rapids, Baker Book House [1972] 162 p. 18 cm. (Contemporary discussion series) Includes bibliographical references. [BS579.H8S4] 72-90330 ISBN 0-8010-7971-3 1.25
1. Bible—Biography. 2. Marriage—Biblical teaching. I. Title.

SESSIONS, Will. 220.92
Greater men and women of the Bible. St. Louis, Bethany Press [1958] 208 p. 23 cm. [BX571.S44] 58-7478
1. Bible — Biog. I. Title.

SIMS, Albert E ed. 220.92
Who's who in the Bible; an ABC cross reference of names of people in the Bible, compiled and edited by Albert E. Sims and George Dent. London, New York, W. Foulsham [1958] 96 p. 20 cm. [BS570.S5] 58-35740
1. Bible — Biog. — Dictionaries. I. Dent, George, joint ed. II. Title.

SIMS, Albert E ed. 220.92
Who's who in the Bible; an ABC cross reference of names of people in the Bible, compiled and edited by Albert E. Sims and George Dent. New York, Philosophical Library [1960] 96 p. 20 cm. [BS570.S5 1960] 60-16209
1. Bible — Biog. — Dictionaries. I. Dent, George, joint ed. II. Title.

SIMS, Albert E., ed. 220.92
Who's who in the Bible: an ABC cross reference of names of people in the Bible, compiled and edited by Albert E. Sims and George Dent. New York, Philosophical Library [c.1960] 96p. 20cm. 60-16209 3.75
1. Bible—Biog.—Dictionaries. I. Dent, George, joint ed. II. Title.

SMEAD, Elizabeth. 220.92
Women of the Scriptures, by Elizabeth Smead and Elizabeth Stone. [1st ed.] New York, Vantage Press [c1956] 67p. 21cm. [BS575.S17] 56-11199
1. Bible— Biog. 2. Women in the Bible. I. Stone, Elizabeth Blinn, joint author. II. Title.

SMEAD, Elizabeth. 220.92
Women of the Scriptures, by Elizabeth Smead and Elizabeth Stone. [1st ed] New York, Vantage Press [c1956] 67 p. 21 cm. [BS575.S47] 56-11199
1. Bible — Biog. 2. Women in the Bible. I. Stone, Elizabeth Blinn, joint author. II. Title.

SMITH, Betty 220.92
Friends of Jesus. Illus. by Cicely Steed. Philadelphia, Westminster [1963, c.1962] 32p. illus. (pt. col.) 21cm. (Stories of Jesus, bk. 4) .75 bds.,
1. Bible—Biog.—Juvenile literature. I. Title.

SMITH, Joyce Marie. 220.9'2 B
A woman's priorities / Joyce Marie Smith. Wheaton, Ill. : Tyndale House Publishers, 1976. 63 p. ; 19 cm. (New life Bible studies) Bibliography: p. 63. [BS575.S49 1976] 76-9372 ISBN 0-8423-8380-8 pbk. : 1.25
1. Bible—Biography—Study and teaching. 2. Women in the Bible—Study and teaching. I. Title. II. Series.

SMITH, Tom A 220.9'2
Be! A guide for personal growth, by Tom A. Smith and Don Knipschield. Anderson, Ind., Warner Press [1962] 64 p. 19 cm. [BV4531.2.S6] 62-11102
1. Youth — Religious life. I. Knipschield, Don, joint author. II. Title.

STEVENSON, Herbert F 220.92
A galaxy of saints; lesser known Bible men and women. Foreword by Paul S. Rees. [Westwood, N.J.] Revell [1958] 158 p. 21 cm. [BS571.S83] 58-8650
1. Bible — Biog. I. Title.

SUDLOW, Elizabeth 220.92
(Williams) 1878-
Career women of the Bible. [1st ed] New York, Pageant Press [1951] 79 p. 21 cm. [BS575.S8] 51-14985
1. Women in the Bible. 2. Bible — Biog. I. Title.

THOMAS, Metta Newman. 220.92
Women of the Bible; a study in their life and character. Nashville, 20th Century Christian, 1956. 131p. 21cm. [BS575.T48] 57-20949
1. Women in the Bible. 2. Bible—Biog. I. Title.

THOMAS, Metta Newman. 220.92
Women of the Bible; a study in their life and character. Nashville, 20th Century Christian, 1956. 131 p. 21 cm. [BS575.T48] 57-20949
1. Women in the Bible. 2. Bible — Giog. I. Title.

THOMSON, Lucy Gertsch. 220.92
Women of the Bible; a book telling the life stories of twenty prominent women of the Old and New Testament. Salt Lake City, Deseret Book Co. [1957] 96p. 16cm. [BS575.T53] 57-59113
1. Women in the Bible. I. Title.

THOMSON, Lucy Gertsch. 220.92
Women of the Bible: a book telling the life stories of twenty prominent women of the Old and New Testament. Salt Lake City, Deseret Book Co. [1957] 96 p. 16 cm. [BS575.T53] 57-59113
1. Women in the Bible. 2. Women in the Bible. I. Title.

TINNEY, Ethel. 220.92
Women of the Bible, in verse. [1st ed.] New York, Pageant Press [1953] 50p. 24cm. [BS575.T55] 53-12703
1. Women in the Bible. I. Title.

TO be a person of 220.9'2 B
integrity / R. James Ogden, editor. Valley Forge, Pa. : Judson Press, [1975] 111 p. : ill. ; 22 cm. Includes bibliographical references. [BS605.2.T6] 75-4901 ISBN 0-8170-0678-8 pbk. : 2.50
1. Bible—Biography. 2. Bible—Study—Text-books. 3. Christian life—Baptist authors. I. Ogden, R. James.

VAJDA, Jaroslav 220.92
They followed the King. St. Louis, Concordia [c.1964] 140p. 19cm. 64-16983 1.50 pap.,
1. Bible—Biog. I. Title.

VANDER VELDE, Frances. 220.92
She shall be called woman; a gallery of character sketches. With illus. by Dick Gringhuis. Grand Rapids, Grand Rapids International Publications; distributed by Kregel's [1957] 258 p. illus. 23 cm. (Women of the Bible) Includes bibliography. [BS575.V3] 57-13178
1. Women in the Bible. 2. Bible — Biog. I. Title.

WHITESELL, Faris Daniel 220.92
Sermon outlines on Bible characters. [Westwood, N. J.] Revell [c.1960] 64p. 21cm. (Revell's sermon outline series) 60-8460 1.00 pap.,
1. Bible—Biog. I. Title.

WHITESELL, Faris Daniel, 220.92
1895-
Sermon outlines on Bible characters. [Westwood, N.J.] Revell [1960] 64 p. 21 cm. (Revell's sermon outline series) [BS571.W52] 60-8460
1. Bible — Biog. I. Title.

WOLCOTT, Carolyn Muller. 220.9'2
God planned it that way, by Carolyn Edna Muller. Pictures by Lloyd Dotterer. New York, Abingdon-Cokesbury Press, c1952. unpaged. illus. 19 x 23 cm. [BT135.W6] 52-11653
1. Providence and government of God — Juvenile literature. I. Title.

WOOD, Fred M 220.92
Bible truth in person [by] Fred M. Wood. Nashville, Broadman Press [1965] 126 p. 20 cm. Bibliographical footnotes. [BX571.W58] 65-11767
1. Bible — Biog. I. Title.

WOOD, Fred M. 220.92
Bible truth in person. Nashville, Broadman [c.1965] 126p. 20cm. Bibl. [BS571.W58] 65-11767 1.50 bds.,
1. Bible—Biog. I. Title.

YATES, Elizabeth, 1905- j220.92
Children of the Bible. Illustrated by Nora S. Unwin. New York, Dutton [1963, c1950] 92 p. illus. 20 cm. [BS576.Y3 1963] 66-2842
1. Children in the Bible. I. Title.

YATES, Elizabeth McGreal, 220.92
1905-
Children of the Bible; illustrated by Nora S. Unwin. [1st ed.] New York, Aladdin Books, 1950. 92 p. illus. 20 cm. [BS576.Y3] 50-12529
1. Children in the Bible. I. Title.

FREMANTLE, Anne 220'.922
(Jackson), 1909-
Pilgrimage to people, by Anne Fremantle. New York., McKay [1968] viii, 231p. 21cm. [BL72.F73] 68-10539 5.50
1. Religions—Biog. I. Title.

LEE, G. Avery. 220.92'2
Great men of the Bible and the women in their lives by G. Avery Lee. Waco, Tex., Word Books [1968] 107 p. 21 cm. Bibliographical footnotes. [BS572.L4] 68-22236
1. Bible—Biography. 2. Women in the Bible. I. Title.

ROWLEY, Harold Henry, 220.92'2
1890-
Short dictionary of Bible personal names [by] H. H. Rowley. New York, Basic Books [1968] 168 p. 22 cm. [BS570.R63] 68-54157 4.50
1. Bible—Biography—Dictionaries. I. Title.

SCHREINER, Samuel 220.92'2
Jonathan.
Faces of God; daily devotionals based on Biblical personalities [by] Samuel J. Schreiner. Nashville, Broadman Press [1969] 128 p. 20 cm. (A Broadman inner circle book) [BS572.S37] 69-18143
1. Bible—Biography—Devotional literature. I. Title.

BANEY, Ralph E 1909- 220.9'3
Search for Sodom and Gomorrah. Condensed version. Kansas City, Mo., CAM Press, 1962. 320p. illus. 18cm. [DS110.D38B3] 61-18476
1. Dead Sea-Antiq. 2. Sodom. I. Title.

BEEBE, Catherine, 1898- 220.93
The Bible story: the promised Lord and His coming. Illustrated by Robb Beebe. New York, Vision Books [1957] 192p. illus. 20cm. (Vision books, 20) [BS551.2.B4] 57-5289
1. Bible stories, English. I. Title.

THE Biblical 220.93
archaeologist.
The Biblical archaeologist reader. Edited by David Noel Freedman and G. Ernest Wright. [1st ed.] Garden City, N. Y., Doubleday, 1961. 342p. illus. 19cm. (Anchor books, A250) [BS621.B5] 61-7649
1. Bible —Antiq. I. Freedman, David Noel, 1922- ed. II. Title.

THE Biblical 220.93
archaeologist.
The Biblical archaeologist reader. Edited by David Noel Freedman and G. Ernest Wright. [1st ed.] Garden City, N. Y., Anchor Books, 1961-64. 2 v. illus., maps, plans. 19 cm. Vol. 2 edited by Edward F. Campbell, Jr., and David Noel Freedman. Bibliographical footnotes. [BS621.B5] 61-7649
1. Bible—Antiq. I. Freedman, David Noel, 1922- ed. II. Wright, George Ernest, 1900- ed. III. Campbell, Edward Fay, ed. IV. Title.

BOYD, Robert T 220.93
Dead stones with living messages, by Bob Boyd. Binghamton, N. Y., Printed by Hall Print. Co., c1960. 182p. illus. 23cm. Includes bibliography. [BS621.B66] 61-21266
1. Bible—Antiq. 2. Bible—Evidences, authority, etc. I. Title.

BOYD, Robert T. 220.93
Tells, tombs, and treasure; a pictorial guide to Biblical archaeology [by] Robert T. Boyd. Grand Rapids, Baker Book House [1969] 222 p. illus., maps. 25 cm. Bibliography: p. 211-212. [BS621.B67] 75-94696
1. Bible—Antiquities. I. Title.

BURROWS, Millar, 1889- 220.93
What mean these stones? The significance of archeology for Biblical studies. New York, Meridian Books, 1957 [c1956] 306 p. illus. 19 cm. (Living age books, LA7) [BS620.B75 1957] 57-6676
1. Bible—Antiquities. I. Title.

CHAVEZ, Moises. 220.9'3
Enfoque arqueologico del mundo de la Biblia / Moises Chavez. Miami, Fla. : Editorial Caribe, c1976. 138 p. : 21 cm. "Tabla arqueologica del mundo de la Biblia": fold. sheet inserted in pocket. Includes index. [DS111.C46] 76-25325
1. Bible. O.T.—Antiquities. 2. Palestine—Antiquities. 3. Man, Prehistoric—Palestine. I. Title.

CORNFELD, Gaalyahu, 1902- 220.9'3
Archaeology of the Bible : book by book / Gaalyah Cornfeld ; David Noel Freedman, consulting editor. 1st U.S. ed. New York : Harper & Row, c1976. 334 p. : ill. ; 25 cm. Includes indexes. [BS621.C6415 1976] 76-9979 ISBN 0-06-061584-2 : 16.95
1. Bible—Antiquities. I. Title.

CORSWANT, Willy, 1883- 220.93
1954.
A dictionary of life in Bible times. Completed and illustrated by Edouard Urech. Translated from the French by Arthur Heathcote. Foreword by Andre Parrot. New York, Oxford University Press, 1960[ ] xix, 308, [1]p. (Bibl. footnotes) illus. 26cm. 60-4719 6.50 half cloth,
1. Bible—Antiq.—Dictionaries. I. Urech, Edouard, ed. II. Title.

COTTRELL, Roy Franklin, 220.93
1878-
The triumphs of archaeology in Bible lands. Mountain View, Calif., Pacific Press Pub. Association [1953] 94p. illus. 20cm. [BS620.C57] 53-11061
1. Bible—Antiq. 2. Bible—Evidences, authority, etc. I. Title.

DEVER, William G. 220.9'3
Archaeology and Biblical studies: retrospects and prospects [by] William G. Dever. Evanston, Ill., Seabury-Western Theological Seminary, 1974. 46 p. 23 cm. (The William C. Winslow lectures, 1972) Includes bibliographical references. [BS621.D48] 74-171042
1. Bible—Antiquities. I. Title. II. Series.

DU BUIT, Michel 220.93
Biblical archaeology; tr. from French by Kathleen Pond. New York, HawthornBooks [c.1960] 110p. (Twentieth century encyclopedia of Catholicism, v.62. Section 6: The word of God) Bibl. 60-53119 3.50 bds.,
1. Bible—Antiq. 2. Palestine—Antiq. I. Title.

EISENBERG, Azriel Louis, 220.93
1903-
Voices from the past; stories of great Biblical discoveries. Illustrated by Laszlo Matulay. London, New York, Abelard-Schuman [1959] 160 p. illus. 21 cm. [BS621.E4] 59-5395
1. Bible—Antiquities. I. Title.

EISENBERG, Azriel Louis, 220.93
1903-
Worlds lost and found; discoveries in Biblical archeology, by Azriel Eisenberg and Dov Peretz Elkins. Illustrated by Charles Pickard. London, New York, Abelard-Schuman [1964] 208 p. illus. 21 cm. [BS620.E4] 64-12118
1. Bible—Antiquities. I. Elkins, Dov Peretz, joint author. II. Title. III. Title: Discoveries in Biblical archeology.

ELDER, John. 220.93
Prophets, idols, and diggers; scientific proof of Bible history. [1st ed.] Indianapolis, Bobbs-Merrill [1960] 240 p. illus. 24 cm. Includes bibliography. [BS621.E44] 60-7160
1. Bible—Antiquities. 2. Bible—Evidences, authority, etc. I. Title.

THE Encyclopedia of 220.9'3
archaeological excavations in the Holy Land. Michael Avi-Yonah, general editor. English-language ed. Englewood Cliffs, N.J., Prentice-Hall [1973- p. [DS111.A2E5] 73-14997 25.00
1. Bible—Antiquities—Dictionaries. 2. Palestine—Antiquities—Dictionaries. I. Avi-Yonah, Michael, 1904- ed.

FINEGAN, Jack, 1908- 220.93
Light from the ancient past; the archeological background of Judaism and Christianity. [2d ed.] Princeton, N.J., Princeton University Press, 1959. xxxvii, 638 p. illus., ports., maps, facsims. 25 cm. Bibliographical footnotes. [BS635.F5 1959] 59-11072
1. Bible—History of contemporary events, etc. 2. Bible—Antiquities. 3. History, Ancient. 4. Christian antiquities. 5. Judaism—History—Ancient period. I. Title.

FRANK, Harry Thomas. 220.93
Bible, archaeology, and faith. Nashville, Abingdon Press [1971] 352 p. illus. 22 cm. Includes bibliographical references. [BS621.F68] 75-158677 ISBN 0-687-03111-7 12.50
1. Bible—Antiquities. I. Title.

FREE, Joseph P. 220.93
Archaeology and Bible history. Wheaton, Ill., Van Kampen Press [1950] xviii, 398 p. illus., ports., maps. 22 cm. Bibliography: p. 360-371. [BS620.F74] 50-2101
1. Bible—Antiquities. I. Title.

FREEDMAN, David Noel, 1922- comp. 220.93
The Biblical archaeologist reader. Edited by David Noel Freedman and G. Ernest Wright. [1st ed.] Garden City, N.Y., Anchor Books, 1961-70. 3 v. illus., maps, plans. 19 cm. Vols. 2-3 edited by E. F. Campbell, Jr., and D. N. Freedman. Bibliographical footnotes. [BS621.F73] 61-7649
1. Bible—Antiquities—Addresses, essays, lectures. I. Wright, George Ernest, 1900- joint comp. II. Campbell, Edward Fay, joint comp. III. The Biblical archaeologist. IV. Title.

FREEDMAN, David Noel, 1922- comp. 220.9'3
The Biblical archaeologist reader / edited by G. Ernest Wright and David Noel Freedman. [Missoula, Mont.] : American Schools of Oriental Research : distributed by Scholars Press, [1975] 2 v. : ill. ; 21 cm. Vol. 2 edited by E. F. Campbell and D. N. Freedman. Reprint of vols. 1 and 2 published in 1961 and 1964 respectively by Anchor Books, Garden City, N.Y. Includes bibliographical references. [BS621.F732] 75-9592 ISBN 0-89130-001-5 (v. 1) : 7.00
1. Bible—Antiquities—Addresses, essays, lectures. I. Wright, George Ernest, 1909- joint comp. II. Campbell, Edward Fay, joint comp. III. The Biblical archaeologist. IV. Title.

GILBERTSON, Merrill T. 220.93
Uncovering Bible times; a study of Biblical archeology, by Merrill T. Gilbertson. Minneapolis, Augsburg Pub. House [1968] 137 p. illus. 20 cm. Bibliography: p. 129-130. [BS621.G49] 68-25799 1.95
1. Bible—Antiquities. I. Title.

GROLLENBERG, Luc. H. 220.93
Shorter atlas of the Bible. Translated [from the Dutch] by Mary F. Hedlund: [New York, T. Nelson] 1959 [i.e., 1960] 196p. illus., maps (part col., part fold.) 21cm. 60-1540 3.95
1. Bible—Antiq. 2. Jews—Hist.—To 70 A.D. 3. Bible—Geography—Maps. I. Title.

HARKER, Ronald. 220.9'3
Digging up the Bible lands. Illustrated with photos. and maps, with drawings by Martin Simmons. New York, H. Z. Walck [1973, c1972] 127 p. illus. (part col.) 27 cm. (A Walck archaeology) Bibliography: p. 124. Examines eight historical sites in the Middle East showing how archaeology has expanded man's knowledge of Biblical times. [BS621.H37 1973] 72-6954 ISBN 0-8098-3111-2 8.95
1. Bible—Antiquities—Juvenile literature. 2. Excavations (Archaeology)—Palestine—Juvenile literature. I. Simmons, Martin, illus. II. Title.
pap 4.95.

HINDSON, Edward E. 220.9'3
The Philistines and the Old Testament, by Edward E. Hindson. Grand Rapids, Baker Book House [1972, c1971] 184 p. illus. 22 cm. (Baker studies in Biblical archaeology) Bibliography: p. 175-181. [DS90.H56] 72-182084 ISBN 0-8010-4034-5 3.95
1. Bible. O.T.—History of Biblical events. 2. Philistines. I. Title.

HOEH, Herman L 220.93
Compendium of world history, by Herman L. Hoeh. [Pasadena, Calif., 1963] 504 p. 24 cm. Thesis -- Ambassador College. Bibliography: p. [494]-504. [D59.H58] 65-51567
1. History, Ancient. I. Title.

HORN, Siegfried H 1908- 220.93
The spade confirms the Book. Washington, Review and Herald Pub. Association [1957] 256p. illus. 23cm. [BS620.H6] 58-1766
1. Bible—Antiq. 2. Excavations (Archaeology) I. Title.

JEWISH Theological Seminary of America. Jewish Museum. 220.9'3
Beer-sheba: the excavation of a Biblical city. New York [1973] 16 p. illus. 25 cm. An exhibition, held at the Jewish Museum Oct. 2, 1973-Jan. 4, 1974, of the results of excavations conducted by Tel-Aviv University. Bibliography: p. 16. [DS110.B35J48 1973] 73-87736
1. Beersheba, Israel—Antiquities. I. Tel-Aviv. University. II. Title.

KOHLER, Ludwig Hugo, 1880- 220.93
Hebrew man. Translated by Peter R. Ackroyd. Nashville, Abingdon Press [1957, c1956] 160p. 21cm. [BS620.K573 1957] 57-5077
1. Jews. 2. Bible. O. T.—Criticism, interpretation, etc. I. Title.

LAMBIE, Thomas Alexander, 1885-1954. 220.93
A bride for His Son; more light from Bible lands on Bible illustrations. [1st ed.] New York, Loizeaux Bros. [1957] 188p. 20cm. [BS620.L268] 57-45929
1. Bible—Antiq. I. Title.

LANDAY, Jerry M. 220.9'3
Silent cities, sacred stones: archaeological discovery in the land of the Bible [by] Jerry M. Landay. London, Weidenfeld and Nicolson, 1971. 272 p. illus. (some col.), maps, ports. 25 cm. Illus. on lining papers. American ed. (New York, McCalls) has title: Silent cities, sacred stones: archaeological discovery in Israel. [DS111.L35 1971b] 72-185212 ISBN 0-297-00426-3
1. Palestine—Antiquities. I. Title.
14.95, ISBN 0-8415-0112-2. Available from Saturday Review Press

LAPP, Paul W. 220.93
Biblical archaeology and history, by Paul W. Lapp. New York, World Pub. Co. [1969] ix, 129 p. illus. 21 cm. Originally delivered as the Haskell lectures at Oberlin College, Oct. 3 and 6, 1966. Bibliographical references included in "Notes" (p. 121-129) [BS621.L35] 75-80440 5.95
1. Bible—Antiquities. 2. Bible—Historiography. 3. Historiography. I. Title.

LAPP, Paul W. 220.9'3
The tale of the Tell : archaeological studies / by Paul W. Lapp ; edited by Nancy L. Lapp. Pittsburgh : Pickwick Press, 1975. xii, 148 p., [12] leaves of plates : ill. ; 22 cm. (Pittsburgh theological monograph series ; no. 5) Includes bibliographies and index. [DS108.9.L3] 75-5861 ISBN 0-915138-05-0 : 6.50
1. Excavations (Archaeology)—Palestine. 2. Palestine—Antiquities. I. Title. II. Series.

LAWLOR, John Irving. 220.9'3
The Nabataeans in historical perspective. Grand Rapids, Baker Book House [1974] 159 p. illus. 22 cm. (Baker studies in Biblical archaeology) Bibliography: p. 144-150. [DS154.2.L38] 74-156928 ISBN 0-8010-5536-9 3.95 (pbk.).
1. Nabataeans. I. Title.

MAZAR, Amihay, 1942- 220.93
Voices from the past, by Amihay Mazar and Alexandra Trone. Illustrated by Milka Cizik. Irvington-on-Hudson, N.Y., Harvey House [1968, c1967] 191 p. illus. (part col.), facsims., maps, plans. 26 cm. (A Story of science series book) Bibliography: p. 185-186. Presents, in chronological order from the earliest period from which there are artifacts, the discoveries of archeologists working in the Biblical land of Palestine and what they have contributed to our knowledge of history and life in this time and place. [DS111.M33] AC 68
1. Palestine—Antiquities. I. Trone, Alexandra, 1933- joint author. II. Cizik, Milka, illus. III. Title.

MORSLEY, Harold Victor 220.93
Junior Bible archaeology [5th rev. ed.] New York, Roy [1964, c.1963] xiii, 183p. illus., 8 plates, map (on lining papers) 19cm. Bibl. 64-12132 3.50 bds.,
1. Bible—Antiq.—Juvenile literature. I. Title.

NEW directions in Biblical archaeology. 220.93
Edited by David Noel Freedman and Jonas C. Greenfield. [1st ed.] Garden City, N.Y., Doubleday, 1969. xix, 191 p. illus. 22 cm. Based on papers originally presented at a symposium on Biblical archaeology, held in the San Francisco Bay area, Mar. 14-16, 1966. Includes bibliographies. [BS621.N46] 69-15185 6.95
1. Bible—Antiquities. 2. Dead Sea scrolls. 3. Qumran community. I. Freedman, David Noel, 1922- ed. II. Greenfield, Jonas C., 1926- ed.

OUR Living Bible. 220.93
Old Testament text by Michael Avi-Yonah. New Testament text by Emil G. Kraeling. New York, McGraw [c.1962] 384p. illus. (pt. col.) col. maps. 29cm. Condensed ed. of: Illustrated world of the Bible library. 62-16134 15.00
1. Bible—Antiq. 2. Near East—Antiq. 3. Bible—Pictures, illustrations, etc. I. Avi-Yonah, Michael, 1904- II. Kraeling, Emil Gottlieb Heinrich, 1892-

OWEN, George Frederick, 1897- 220.93
Archaeology and the Bible. [Westwood, N. J.] Revell [1961] 384p. illus. 22cm. Includes bibliography. [BS621.O8] 61-9237
1. Bible—Antiq. I. Title.

OWEN, George Frederick, 1897- 220.93
Archaeology and the Bible. [Westwood, N.J.] Revell [c.1961] 384p. illus., maps Bibl. 61-9237 4.95 bds.,
1. Bible—Antiq. I. Title.

PFEIFFER, Charles F. 220.93
Ras Shamra and the Bible. Grand Rapids, Mich., Baker Bk. [c.]1962. 73p. illus. 22cm. (Baker studies in Biblical archaeology) Bibl. 62-15162 1.50 pap.,
1. Ras Shamra. 2. Bible. O.T.—Antiq. I. Title.

SMICK, Elmer B. 220.9'3
Archaeology of the Jordan Valley [by] Elmer B. Smick. Grand Rapids, Mich., Baker Book House [1973] 193 p. illus. 22 cm. (Baker studies in biblical archaeology, 3) Bibliography: p. 173-179. [DS153.3.S64] 72-85713 ISBN 0-8010-7951-9 4.95
1. Bible—Antiquities. 2. Jordan Valley—Antiquities. I. Title.

THOMPSON, John Arthur, 1913- 220.93
The Bible and archaeology. Grand Rapids, Eerdmans [1962] 468 p. illus. 24 cm. "Contains the material which formerly appeared in the three smaller Pathway Books: Archaeology and the Old Testament ... Archaeology and the pre-Chiristian centuries ... and Archaeology and the New Testament." [BS621.T52] 62-11246
1. Bible — Antiq. 2. Bible — History of contemporary events, etc. I. Title.

THOMPSON, John Arthur, 1913- 220.93
The Bible and archaeology. Grand Rapids, Mich., Eerdmans [1962] 468p. illus., maps. 24cm. Bibl. 62-11246 5.95
1. Bible—Antiq. 2. Bible—History of contemporary events, etc. I. Title.

THOMPSON, John Arthur, 1913- 220.9'3
The Bible and archaeology, by J. A. Thompson. [Rev. ed.] Grand Rapids, Mich., Eerdmans [1972] xxiv, 474 p. illus. 24 cm. "Contains the material which formerly appeared in the three smaller Pathway books: Archaeology and the Old Testament (1957, 2nd ed., 1959), Archaeology and the pre-Christian centuries (1958, 2nd ed., 1959), and Archaeology and the New Testament (1960)." Bibliography: p. 453-460. [BS621.T52 1972] 73-154197 ISBN 0-8028-3268-7 7.95
1. Bible—Antiquities. 2. Bible—History of contemporary events, etc. I. Title.

VARDAMAN, E Jerry. 220.93
Archaeology and the living word [by] Jerry Vardaman. Nashville, Broadman Press [1965] 128 p. illus., maps. 20 cm. Bibliography: p. 128. [BS621.V3] 65-15599
1. Bible — Antiq. I. Title.

VARDAMAN, E. Jerry 220.93
Archaeology and the living word Nashville, Broadman [c.1965] 128p. illus., maps. 20cm. Bibl. [BS621.V3] 65-15599 1.50 bds.,
1. Bible—Antiq. I. Title.

VOS, Howard Frederic, 1925- 220.9'3
Archaeology in Bible lands / by Howard F. Vos. Chicago : Moody Press, c1977. p. cm. Includes bibliographies and index. [BS621.V59] 77-2981 ISBN 0-8024-0293-3 : 7.95
1. Bible—Antiquities. 2. Excavations (Archaeology)—Near East. I. Title.

VOS, Howard Frederic, 1925- 220.9'3
Beginnings in Bible archaeology / by Howard F. Vos. Rev. ed. Chicago : Moody Press, [1973] 112 p. ; 22 cm. Published in 1956 and 1959 under title: An introduction to Bible archaeology. Bibliography: p. 110-112. [BS621.V6 1973] 73-7332 ISBN 0-8024-0601-7 : 1.50
1. Bible—Antiquities. I. Title.

*VOS, Howard Frederic, 1925- 220.93
Beginnings of Bible archaeology, by Howard F. Vos. Chicago, Moody Pr. [1973] 112 p. 21 cm. First published in 1956 under title: An introduction to Bible archaeology. Bibliography: p. 110-112. [BS621] ISBN 0-8024-0601-7 1.50 (pbk.)
1. Bible—Antiquities. I. Title.

VOS HOWARD FREDERIC, 1926- 220.93
An introduction to Bible archaeology. [Rev. ed.] Chicago, Moody Press [1959, c1956] 127 p. 18 cm. (Colportage library, 316) Includes bibliography. [BS621.V6 1959] 60-786
1. Bible — Antiq. I. Title.

WIGHT, Fred Hartley, 1899- 220.93
Highlights of archaeology in Bible lands. Chicago, Moody Press [1955] 243p. illus. 22cm. [BS620.W54] 55-2644
1. Bible—Antiq. I. Title.

WIGHT, Fred Hartley, 1899- 220.93
Manners and customs of Bible lands. Chicago, Moody Press [1953] 336p. illus. 22cm. An outgrowth of the author's thesis (M. A.) submitted to Passadena College, under title: A study of manners and customs of domestic life in Palestine as related to the Scriptures. Includes bibliography. [BS620.W55] 53-13455
1. Bible—Antiq. I. Title.

WILLIAMS, Albert Nathaniel, 1914- 220.93
What archaelogy says about the Bible. New York, Association Press [1957] 125 p. 16 cm. (An Association Press reflection book) Includes bibliography. [BS620.W57] 57-11609
1. Bible — Antiq. I. Title.

WILLIAMS, Albert Nathaniel, 1914- 220.93
What archaeology says about the Bible. New York, Association Press [1957] 125p. 16cm. (An Association Press reflection book) Includes bibliography. [BS620.W57] 57-11609
1. Bible—Antiq. I. Title.

WILLIAMS, Walter George, 1903- 220.93
Archaeology in Biblical research. Nashville, Abingdon [c.1965] 223p. illus., maps. 24cm. Bibl. [BS620.W59] 65-10813 4.75
1. Bible—Antiq. I. Title.

WILLIAMS, Walter George, 1903- 220.93
Archaeology in Biblical research, [by] Walter G. Williams. New York, Abingdon Press [1965] 223 p. illus., maps. 24 cm. Bibliography: p. 209-214. [BS620.W59] 65-10813
1. Bible—Antiquities. I. Title.

WILSON, Clifford A. 220.9'3
That incredible book ... the Bible, by Clifford A. Wilson. Melbourne, Hill of Content, 1973. 199 p. ill. 22 cm. Index. Bibliography: p. 183-189. [BS621.W47] 74-169004 ISBN 0-85572-051-4 1.50
1. Bible—Antiquities. I. Title.

WILSON, Clifford A. 220.9'3
That incredible book, the Bible / Clifford A. Wilson. New York : Family Library, 1975, c1973. 239 p. ; 18 cm. Includes indexes. Bibliography: p. 223-231. [BS621.W47 1975] 75-4397 ISBN 0-515-03730-3 pbk. : 1.75
1. Bible—Antiquities. I. Title.

WISEMAN, Donald John. 220.93
Illustrations from biblical archaeology. [1st ed.] Grand Rapids, Mich., Eerdmans [1958] 112 p. illus. 16 x 23 cm. [BS621.W5 1958] 59-6954
1. Bible—Antiquities. I. Title.

WRIGHT, George Ernest, 1909- 220.93
Biblical archaeology. [New and rev. ed.] Philadelphia, Westminster Press [1962] 291 p. illus. 29 cm. [BS621.W72 1962] 63-906
1. Bible — Antiq. I. Title.

WRIGHT, George Ernest, 1909- 220.93
Biblical archaeology. [New and rev. ed.] Philadelphia, Westminster Press [1962] 291 p. illus. 29 cm. [BS621.W72 1962] 63-906
1. Bible—Antiquities. I. Title.

WRIGHT, George Ernest, 1909- 220.93
Biblical archaeology. Abridged ed. Philadelphia, Westminster Press [c.1960] 198p. Bibl. footnotes. Index of Biblical refs.: p.189-191. 60-9709 1.65 pap.,
1. Bible—Antiq. I. Title.

WRIGHT, George Ernest, 1909- 220.93
Biblical archaeology. Philadelphia, Westminster Press [1957] 288 p. illus., maps. 29 cm. Includes bibliographies. Bibliographical footnotes. [BS620.W7] 57-5020
1. Bible—Antiquities.

WRIGHT, George Ernest, 1909- 220.93
Biblical archaeology. Philadelphia, Westminister Press [1957] 288 p. illus., maps.

29 cm. Includes bibliographies. Bibliographical footnotes. [BS620.W7] 57-5020
1. Bible — Antiq. I. Title.

YADIN, Yigael, 1917- 220.9'3
Hazor; the rediscovery of a great citadel of the Bible. [1st American ed.] New York, Random House [1975] 280 p. illus. 26 cm. [DS110.H38Y28 1975] 74-5406 ISBN 0-394-49454-7 20.00
1. Hazor—Antiquities. 2. Gezer, Israel—Antiquities. 3. Megiddo. I. Title.

YAMAUCHI, Edwin M. 220.9'3
The stones and the Scriptures [by] Edwin M. Yamauchi. [1st ed.] Philadelphia, Lippincott [1972] 207 p. illus. 21 cm. (Evangelical perspectives) Bibliography: p. 167-173. [BS621.Y35] 74-39483 ISBN 0-87981-002-5
1. Bible—Antiquities. I. Title.

PFEIFFER, Charles F. ed. 220.9303
The Biblical world; a dictionary of Biblical archaeology, edited by Charles F. Pfeiffer. Consulting editors: E. Leslie Carlson, Claude F. A. Schaeffer, and J. A. Thompson. Grand Rapids, Baker Book House [1966] 612 p. illus., maps. 25 cm. Includes bibliographies. [BS622.P4] 66-19312
1. Bible—Antiquities—Dictionaries. 2. Near East—Antiquities—Dictionaries. I. Title.

CARLYLE, H B 220.94
Simplified key to the Bible. Dallas, Booth Pub. Co. [c1950-] v. illus. 22cm. Contents.v. 1. The life and times of the Old Testament as illustrated by the chrono-chart. [BS637.C3] 52-67016
1. Bible—Chronology. I. Title.

ROBERTSON, Edwin Hanton. 220.9431
The Bible in East Germany. New York, Association Press [1961] 93p. 19cm. (The Bible in our time) Includes bibliography. [BS538.3.R6 1961] 61-14165
1. Bible—Use. 2. Germany (Democratic Republic, 1949-)—Religion. I. Title.

ARMSTRONG. APRIL (OURSLER) 220.95
Bible stories for young readers. Adapted by April Oursler Armstrong from 'The greatest story ever told' and 'The greatest book ever written'by Fulton Oursler. Illustrated by Jules Gotlieb. Garden City, N. Y., Junior Deluxe Edjtions [1956] 350p. illus. 22cm. [BS551.2.A7] 57-642
1. Bible stories, English. I. Title.

ARMSTRONG, April (Oursler) 220.95
Bible stories for young readers. Adapted by April Oursler Armstrong grom "The greater story ever told" and "The greatest book ever written" by Fulton Oursler. Illustrated by Jules Gotlieb. Garden City, N. Y., Junior Deluxe Editions [1956] 350p. illus. 22cm. [BS551.2.A7] 57-642
1. Bible stories. English. I. Title.

ASIMOV, Isaac, 1920- 220.95
Asimov's guide to the Bible. Maps by Rafael Palacios. [1st ed.] Garden City, N.Y., Doubleday, 1968-69. 2 v. maps (part col.) 24 cm. Contents.Contents.—v. 1. The Old Testament.—v. 2. The New Testament. [BS635.2.A8] 68-23566 9.95
1. Bible—History of Biblical events. 2. Bible—Criticism, interpretation, etc. I. Title. II. Title: Guide to the Bible.

AYRES, Webb Wilford. 220.95
The Bible story; the lives and events from Adam to Paul, retold. [1st ed.] New York, Exposition Press [1964] 145 p. 22 cm. [BS551.2.A9] 65-548
1. Bible stories, English. I. Title.

*AYRES, Webb Wilford 220.95
The Bible story; the lives and events from Adam to Paul. New York, Exposition [c.1964] 145p. 21cm. (EP 42108) 3.00
I. Title.

BARRETT, Ethel. 220.95 (j)
It didn't just happen, and other talk-about Bible stories. Glendale, Calif., Regal Books Div., G/L Publications [1967] 200 p. illus. 24 cm. [BS551.2.B3] 67-30248
1. Bible stories, English. I. Title.

BEDDOE, Everett E. 220.95
Let's talk about giants, by Everett E. Beddoe, as told to Frances Sorensen. Mountain View, Calif. Pacific Press Pub. Association [1966] 78 p. illus. 28 cm. Tells about giants in the Bible and explains how children, though small in stature, can become spiritual giants for God. Publisher prints exclusively for Seventh-day Adventists. [BS1199.G5B4] AC 67
1. Giants in the Bible. I. Sorensen, Frances. II. Title.

BEEBE, Catherine, 1898- 220.95
The Bible story; the promised Lord and His coming. Illustrated by RobbBeebe. New York, Vision Books [1957] 192p. illus. 20cm. (Vision books, 20) [BS551.2.B4] 57-5289
1. Bible stories, English. I. Title.

BEGBIE, Harold, 1871-1929. 220.95
The Bible in story and pictures; revised from the original edition of 'The children's story Bible' by Harold Begbie. Illustrated by Cyrus LeRoy Baldridge [and others] New York, H. S. Stuttman Co. distributed by Garden City Books,Garden City, N. Y., [1956] 2v. (508p.) illus. (part col.) 23cm. [BS551.B377 1956] 56-1033
1. Bible stories, English. I. Title.

BERON, Richard, 1903- ed. 220.95
The Bible story, simply told by Richard Beron. [Translated by Isabel and Florence McHugh] With applications to daily living by Alexander Jones. Chicago, Catholic Press [c1959] 2v. illus. 18cm. (Library of Catholic devotion) Translation, in part, of Kinder-und Hausbibel. [BS551.B3913 1959] 60-52328
1. Bible stories. English. I. Title.

BIBLE. English.Selections. 220.95
1953.
The Book of Life, arr. and edited by Newton Marshall Hall and Irving Francis Wood. 21st ed. Chicago. J. Rudin. c1953. 8v. illus. (part col.) maps. 24cm. Contents.v. 1. Bible treasures.--v. 2. Bible heroes. pioneers.--v. 3. Bible kings. captains.--v. 4. Bible prophets. statesmen.--v. 5. Bible poetry.--v. 6. Life of the Master.-- v. 7. Paul. life. letters.--v.8. Bible educator. Indexes. [BS197.H3 1953] 53-1996
1. Bible—History of Biblical events. 2. Bible stories. English. I. Hall, Newton Marshall, 1865-1926. ed. II. Wood,Irving Francis. 1861-1934, ed. III. Title.

BIBLE. English. 220.95
Selections. 1954. Authorized.
God's Book for me, by Hattie Bell Allen. Illustrated by Mariel Wilhoite Turner. Nashville, Broadman Press, c1954. unpaged. illus. 25cm. (Little treasure series, 8) [BS551.A47] 54-42580
1. Bible stories, English. I. Allen, Hattie Bell (McCracken) 1896- comp. II. Title.

BIBLE. English. 220.95
Selections. 1958.
A first Bible. Illustrated by Helen Sewell. [New York?] H. Z. Walck [1958, c1934] 109p. illus. 29cm. [BS391.2.F5 1958] 58-12904
1. Bible stories, English. I. Title.

BIBLE. English. 220.95
Selections. 1962.
The Book of life. Arranged and edited by Newton M. Hall [and] Irving F. Wood. [27th ed.] Chicago, J. Rudin [1962] 9v. illus. 24cm. [BS197.H3 1962] 62-3497
1. Bible—History of Biblical events. 2. Bible stories, English. I. Hall, Newton Marshall, 1865-1926, ed. II. Wood, Irving Francis, 1861-1934, ed. III. Title.

BIBLE. English. 220.95 (j)
Selections. 1966. Authorized.
One hundred Bible stories in the words of Holy Scripture (King James version). With colored illus., maps, scripture passages, prayers, and explanatory notes. St. Louis, Concordia Pub. House [1966] 214 p. col. illus., col. maps. 23 cm. [BS551.C6863 1966] 66-31714
1. Bible stories, English. I. Title. II. Title: Bible stories in the words of Holy Scripture.

BIBLE stories. 220.95
Illus. by Lajos Segner. Racine, Wis, Whitman Pub. Co., '1952. unpaged. illus. 21 cm. (A Cozy-corner book) [BS551.B44] 52-4344
1. Bible stories, English—O. T. I. Segner, Lajos. illus.

THE Bible story library; 220.95
the Holy Scriptures retold in story form for the young and as an explanation and commentary for all, based on traditional texts and illustrated with the most famous Biblical art. Edited by Turner Hodges with the assistance of Elizabeth MacLean. With many new illus. in full color by Rafaello Busoni. New York, Educational Book Guild, 1956. 4v. illus. 24cm. [BS551.2.B5] 57-25841
1. Bible—History of Biblical events. I. Hodges, Turner, ed.

BIBLE story library 220.95
(The); the Holy scriptures retold in story form for the young and as an explanation and commentary for all, based on traditional texts and illustrated with the most famous Biblical art. Ed. by Turner Hodges, with Elizabeth MacLean. Designed, produced by Donald B. Wold, with Margot L. Wolf. Introd. by Webb Garrison. Indianapolis, Bobbs [1965, c.1956-1963] xiv, 726p. col. illus., col. maps. 25cm. [BS551.2.B5] 65-2002 5.95
1. Bible stories, English. 2. Bible—History of Biblical events. I. Hodges, Turner, ed.

THE Big golden book of 220.95
Bible stories from the Old and New Testaments. Pictures by Schnorr von Carolsfeld, colored by Fritz Kredel. New York, Simon and Schuster [1958] 70p. illus. 28cm. ([A Big golden book] 584) [BS551.2.B53] 58-1515
1. Bible stories, English.

BLYTON, Enid. 220.95
Before I go to sleep; a book of Bible stories and prayers for children; illustrated by Catherine Scholz. [1st ed.] Boston, Little, Brown [1953] 118p. illus. 22cm. [BS551.B544] 52-5504
1. Bible stories, English. 2. Children—Prayer-books and devotions—English. I. Title.

BOWIE, Walter Russell, 220.95
1882-1969.
The Bible story for boys and girls. New York, Abingdon-Cokesbury Press [1951-52] 2 v. illus. 24 cm. Contents.Contents.—[1] New Testament.—[2] Old Testament. [BS551.B624] 51-9920
1. Bible stories, English. I. Title.

BRENNEMAN, Charles Gage, 220.95
1893-
A guide to Bible study. [San Diego? Calif., 1954] 424p. illus. 24cm. [BS636.B7] 54-25070
1. Bible—History of Biblical events. I. Title.

BRIGHT, John, 1908- 220.95
Early Israel in recent history writing; a study in method. Chicago, A. R. Allenson [1956] 128p. 22cm. (Studies in Biblical theology, no. 19) [BS1171.B67] 56-14328
1. Bible. O. T.—Criticism, interpretation, etc. 2. Jews—Hist.—Historiography. I. Title.

*BUCHANAN, Elizabeth 220.95
The voice; Bible stories retold. New York, Exposition [c.1964] 138p. 22cm. 3.00
I. Title.

BULL, Norman J 220.95
Children of the Bible, by Norman J. Bull. Illus. by Charles Mozley. Celveland, yworld Pub. Co. [c1966] 92 p. illus. 23 cm. "Shepherd books." [BS576.B75-] 66-24990
1. Children in the Bible. I. Title.

*BUYS, J. 220.95
Christ our light, Notre Dame, Fides [1967] 190p. illus. maps. 22cm. (Young Christians today. v. 2. Fides PBT24) Orig. pub. as Jesus-Christ Lumiere du Monde, v. 1 in the ser. Temoins du Christ, 4th French ed., pub. by Les Editions de Lumen Vitae, Brussels. 1962. Tr. by Geoffrey Chapman. 1.95 pap.,
1. Bible—Study I. Title. II. Series.

CAMPBELL, Alexander. 220.95
The covenant story of the Bible. Philadelphia, United Church Press [1963] 205 p. illus. 23 cm. [Bible--History of Biblical events.] [BX635.2.C27] 63-12580
I. Title.

CAMPBELL, Alexander 220.95
The covenant story of the Bible. Philadelphia, United Church Pr. [c.1963] 205p. illus. 23cm. 63-12580 3.50
1. Bible—History of Biblical events. I. Title.

CARNEY, H. Stanton 220.95
From Adam to me. Grand Rapids, Mich., Eerdmans 1965[c.1964] ix, 300p. 23cm. [BS635.2.C29] 64-22034 4.50
1. Bible—History of Biblical events. 2. Church history—Outlines, syllabi, etc. I. Title.

CHOURAQUI, Andre, 1917- 220.9'5
The people and the faith of the Bible / Andre Chouraqui ; translated by William V. Gugli. Amherst : University of Massachusetts Press, 1975. 211 p. ; 25 cm. Translation of La vie quotidienne des Hebreux au temps de la Bible. Bibliography: p. 209-211. [DS112.C4813] 74-21237 ISBN 0-87023-172-3 : 12.50
1. Jews—Civilization. I. Title.

CHRISTIANSON, Nora D 220.95
The scarlet cord. [1st ed.] New York, Vantage Press [1955] 235p. 21cm. [BS550.C42] 55-8620
1. Bible—History of Biblical events. I. Title.

CULWELL, Kitty Jones 220.95
Abraham's children. Murfreesboro, Tenn., DeHoff Pubns., 749 N.W. Broad St. [c.1965] 159p. 24cm. [BS600.2.C83] 65-20420 3.50
1. Bible—Study. I. Title.

DAUGHTERS of St. Paul. 220.95
Bible stories for everyone; Old and New Testament, with catechetical comments from the revised Baltimore catechism no. 3. [Boston] St. Paul Editions [c1959] 431 p. illus. 22 cm. [BS550.2.D3 1959] 62-21989
1. Bible stories, English. I. Title.

DIETRICH, Suzanne de. 220.95
God's unfolding purpose; a guide to the study of the Bible. Translated by Robert McAfee Brown from the French, Le dessein de Dieu. Philadelphia, Westminster Press [1960] 287 p. 21 cm. Includes bibliography. [BS635.D513] 60-6169
1. Bible—History of Biblical events. I. Title.

DREANY, E Joseph. 220.95
Bible stories from the Old Testament in pop-up action pictures. New York, Maxton Publishers, c1953. unpaged. illus. 27cm. Bible stories, English--O. T. [BS551.D73] 53-37094
I. Title.

DUEWEL, W. Michael. 220.9'5
Earth : theater of the universe / [written by W. Michael Duewel ; art panels by Lorenzo Ghiglieri ; studies compiled by Richard E. Lange]. Portland, Or. : Theater of the Universe, 1974. 96 p. : ill. ; 29 x 37 cm. Includes index. Bibliography: p. 89. [BS635.2.D8 1974] 74-79815
1. Bible—History of Biblical events. I. Ghiglieri, Lorenzo, ill. II. Lange, Richard E. III. Title.

EASTMAN, Frances W. 220.95
Good news. Philadelphia, United Church [1964] 122p. illus., maps. 21cm. Included hymns with music. 64-14496 1.50
1. Bible stories, English. 2. Hymns, English. I. Title.

EGERMEIER, Elsie Emilie, 220.95
1890-
Bible story book; a complete narration from Genesis to Revelation for young and old. Story rev. by Arlene S. Hall. [Rev. Standard ed.] Anderson, Ind., Warner [c.1955, 1963] 576p. col. illus. 25cm. 63-1371 4.95; 6.50, deluxe ed., bxd.
1. Bible stories, English. I. Title.

EYNON, Dana 220.95
Bible 1, 2, 3's [teaches Bible story recognition as well as numbers] Cincinnati, O., Standard Publishing Co., 1960] unpaged illus. (part col.) .50 pap.,
I. Title.

FANCHIOTTI, Margherita. 220.95
Stories from the Bible. Illustrated by Joan Kiddell-Monroe. [London] Oxford University Press, 1955. 239p. illus. 23cm. [Oxford books for boys and girls] [BS551.2.F3] 57-13703
1. Bible stories, English. I. Title.

FORREST, Katharine A. ed. 220.95
King James Bible stories. Front. by Patricia Fudger. New York, Exposition Press [1952] 198 p. illus. 22 cm. [BS551.F58] 51-11845
1. Bible stories, English. I. Title.

FRANK, Harry Thomas. 220.9'5
Discovering the Biblical world. Maplewood, N.J., Hammond; distributed by Harper & Row, New York [1974, c1975] 277 p. illus. 29 cm. Bibliography: p. 277. [BS635.2.F7] 74-7044 ISBN 0-06-063014-0
1. Bible—History of Biblical events. 2. Bible—History of contemporary events, etc. I. Title.

FRANK, Harry Thomas. 220.9'5
Discovering the Biblical world. Maplewood, N.J., Hammond; distributed by Harper & Row, New York [1974, c1975] 277 p. illus. 29 cm. Bibliography: p. 277. [BS635.2.F7] 74-7044 ISBN 0-8437-3624-0 16.95
1. Bible—History of Biblical events. 2. Bible—History of contemporary events, etc. I. Title.

FROST, S. E., 1899- ed. 220.95
Favorite stories from the Bible. Garden City, N. Y., Permabooks [1950, '1945] 189 p. 17 cm. (Permabooks. p. 92) "Previously published as part of [the editor's] Great religious stories." [BS571.F7] 51-33043
1. Bible stories, English. I. Title.

GALE, Richard Nelson, 220.95
Sir, 1896-
Great battles of Biblical history [by] Sir Richard Gale. [1st American ed.] New York, John Day Co. [1970, c1968] xii, 156 p. illus., maps (1 fold.) 22 cm. [DS119.2.G3 1970] 70-105562 5.95
1. Bible. O.T.—Military history. I. Title.

GANT, Sophia 220.95
Poor Mr. Job. New York, Vantage [c.1965] 83p. 21cm. 2.50 bds.,
I. Title.

GAUBERT, Henri, 1895- 220.95
The destruction of the kingdom. Translated by Lancelot Sheppard. New York, Hastings House [1970] 212 p. illus., maps, plans. 20 cm. (The Bible in history, v. 6) "A Giniger book." Translation of L'Exil a Babylone. Bibliography: p. 208-209. [DS121.6.G3713] 69-15816 ISBN 0-8038-0720-1 5.95
1. Jews—History—953-586 B.C. 2. Jews—History—586 B.C.-70 A.D. I. Title. II. Series.

GIBSON, Katharine, 1893- 220.95
The tall book of Bible stories, retold by Katharine Gibson. Illustrated by Ted Chaiko. [New York] Harper [1957] 124 p. illus. 32 x 14 cm. [BS551.2.G5] 57-10952
1. Bible stories, English. I. Title.

GOODMAN, George, 1866- 220.95
Seventy best Bible stories. Grand Rapids, Mich., Kregel [1966] 269p. 19cm. [BS550.G6] 66-4927 3.95
1. Bible stories, English. I. Title.

GOODMAN, George, 1866- 220.95
Seventy familiar Bible stories. Grand Rapids, Mich., Kregel [1966] 278p. 19cm. [BS550.G62] 66-4928 3.95
1. Bible stories, English. I. Title.

GOODMAN, George, 1866- 220.95
Seventy less-known Bible stories. Grand Rapids, Kregel Publications [1966] 331 p. 19 cm. [BS550.G63 1966] 66-4926
1. Bible stories, English. I. Title.

GOODMAN, George 1866- 220.95
Seventy less-known Bible stories. Grand Rapids, Mich., Kregel [1966] 331p. 19cm. [BS550.G63] 66-4926 3.95
1. Bible stories, English. I. Title.

GORDON, Cyrus H. 220.95
New horizons in Old Testament literature. Ventnor, N.J., [P.O.B. 2098] Ventnor Publishers [c.]1960. 32p. Bibl. 1.00 pap.,
I. Title.

GREEN, Ronald 220.95
The great news. Illus. by Treyer Evans. [dist. Grand Rapids, Mich., Zondervan, 1960c.1959] 72p. illus. (part col.) 19cm. (The Blandford keystone series, 1) 61-711 1.00 bds.,
1. Bible—History of Biblical events. I. Title.

GWYNNE, John Harold, 1899- 220.95
The rainbow book of Bible stories. Illustrated by Steele Savage. [1st ed.] Cleveland, World Pub. Co. [1956] 319p. illus. 29cm. [BS551.2.G87] 56-9264
1. Bible stories, English. I. Title.

GWYNNE, John Harold, 1899- 220.95
The rainbow book of Bible stories. Illustrated by Steele Savage. [1st ed.] Cleveland, World Pub. Co. [1956] 319p. illus. 29cm. [BS551.2.G87] 56-9264
1. Bible stories, English. I. Title.

*HAAN, Sheri Dunham. 220.9'5
Bible stories in rhyme and rhythm. Grand Rapids, Baker Book House [1974] 63 p. 22 cm. [BS539] ISBN 0-8010-4105-8 1.95 (pbk.)
1. Bible stories—Juvenille literature. 2. Stories in rhyme—Juvenile literature. I. Title.

HARKNESS, Georgia Elma, 220.9'5
1891-1974.
Biblical backgrounds of the Middle East conflict / Georgia Harkness, Charles F. Kraft. Nashville : Abingdon, c1976. 208 p. : maps ; 21 cm.650/2(d Includes bibliographical references. [BS1197.H26 1976] 76-22644 ISBN 0-687-03435-3 : 7.95
1. Bible. O.T.—History of Biblical events. 2. Jewish-Arab relations—History. I. Kraft, Charles Franklin, 1911- joint author. II. Title.

HARRISON, Roland Kenneth. 220.95
Old Testament times, by R. K. Harrison. Grand Rapids, Mich., Eerdmans [1970] xvi, 357 p. illus., maps. 24 cm. Bibliography: p. 341-342. [BS1197.H27] 69-12314 6.95
1. Bible. O.T.—History of Biblical events. 2. Near East—History—To 622. I. Title.

HILLMANN, Willibrord, 220.95
1912-
Children's Bible. [Translation by Lawrence Atkinson. Illus. by Johannes Gruger] Baltimore, Helicon Press [1959] 92p. illus. 21cm. Translation of Bilderbibel. [BS551.2.H513] 59-14335
1. Bible stories, English. I. Title.

HODGES, Turner, ed. 220.95
The Bible story library; the Holy scriptures retold in story form for the young and as an explanation and commentary for all, based on teaditional texts and illustrated with the most famous Biblical art. Edited by Turner Hodges with the assistance of Elizabeth MacLean. Designed and produced by Donald D. Wolf with the assistance of Margot L. Wolf. Introd. by Webb Garrison. Indianapolis, Bobbs-Merrill Co. [1965, c1963] xiv, 726 p. col. illus., col. maps. 25 cm. [BS551.2.B5] 65-2002
1. Bible stories, English. 2. Bible-History of Biblical events. I. Title.

*HOOPER, Roberta Anderson 220.95
The Bible story in verse; the great narratives of the Old and New Testaments. Adapted from the Authorized version 1611. Illus. by Lili Rethi. New York, Exposition [c.1963] 191p. illus. 3.00
I. Title.

HOST, Mabel M (Browning) 220.95
1891-
Pathway to the fold; the basic teachings of the Old and New Testaments for young people today. [1st ed.] New York, Greenwich Book Publishers [1958] 82p. 22cm. [BS551.2.H67] 58-59916
1. Bible stories, English. I. Title.

HURIBUT, Jesse Lyman, 220.95
1843-1930.
Bible stories everyone should know; wonder books) of Bible stories. Illus. in full color by Robert Leinweber. Text drawings by Bruno Frost. New York, Grosset & Dunlap [1958] 253p. illus 24cm. [BS551.H78 1958] 58-59639
1. Bible stories, English. I. Title. II. Title: Wonder book of Bible stories.

HURLBUT, Jesse Lyman, 220.95
1843-1930.
Hurlbut's Story of the Bible for young and old; a continuous narrative of the Scriptures told in one hundred sixty-eight stories. Text drawings in two colors by Steele Savage. Grand Rapids, Zondervan Pub. House [1967] xvi, 655, 64, 62 p. col. illus., 18 col. maps. 24 cm. "New and expanded ed." Includes Hurlbut's Bible lessons for young and old, and History of the books of the Bible, by Joseph Howard Gray. [BS551.H8 1967] 68-1225
1. Bible—History of Biblical events. I. Gray, Joseph Howard. History of the books of the Bible. 1967. II. Title. III. Title: Story of the Bible for young and old.

HURLBUT, Jesse Lyman, 220.95
1843-1930.
Story of the Bible for young and old; a continuous narrative of the Scriptures told in one hundred sixty-eight stories. Illus. in full color by Ralph Pallen Coleman. Text drawings in two colors by Steele Savage. [5th ed.] Philadelphia [1957] 655 p. illus. 25 cm. [BS551.H8 1957] 57-12775
1. Bible—History of Biblical events.

JACKSON, Mildred L 220.95
Once-upon-a-time Bible stories. Illustrated by Stina Nagel. [1st ed.] New York, Exposition Press [1959] 233p. illus. 21cm. [BS551.2.J3] 59-3889
1. Bible stories, English. I. Title.

JOHNSON, George, 1889- 220.95
1944.
The Bible story; [a textbook for use in the lower grades. By] George Johnson, Jerome D. Hannan [and] Sister M. Dominica. [New rev. ed. with suggestions for study by Sister M. Gabriel and Sister Louis Mary] New York, Benziger Bros. [1960] 276p. illus. 23cm. [BS551.J67 1960] 60-11628
1. Bible stories, English. I. Title.

JOHNSTON, Leonard. 220.95
Witnesses to God. New York, Sheed and Ward [1961, c1960] 174p. 21cm. [BS635.J6] 61-7284
1. Bible—History of Biblical events. 2. Revelation. I. Title.

JOHNSTON, Leonard. 220.95
Witnesses to God. Glen Rock, N. J., Paulist Press [1964] c1960] 176 p. 19 cm. (Deus books) [BS635.2.J6] 64-14153
1. Bible — History of Biblical events. 2. Revelation. I. Title.

JONES, Mary Alice, 1898- 220.95
Bible stories; illustrated by Manning de V. Lee. Chicago, Rand McNally [1952] 113 p. illus. 29 cm. [BS551.J72] 52-10415
1. Bible stories, English.

JUERGENS, Mary. 220.95
The big book of favorite Bible stories; selected by Mary Juergens. Illustrated by Felix Palm. New York, Grosset & Dunlap, cunpaged. illus. 34cm. (Big treasure books) [BS551.J797] 53-2291
1. Bible stories, English. I. Title.

KEE, Howard Clark. 220.95
Understanding the New Testament [by] Howard Clark Kee [and] Franklin W. Young. Englewood Cliffs, N. J., Prentice-Hall, 1957. 492p. illus. 24cm. Includes bibliography. [BS2407.K37] 57-8714
1. Bible. N. T.—History of Biblical events. 2. Bible. N. T.—Introductions. I. Young, Franklin W., joint author. II. Title.

KELLER, Werner, 1909- 220.95
The Bible as history; a confirmation of the Book of Books. Translated by William Neil. New York, W. Morrow [1956] xxv, 452 p. illus., maps. 22 cm. Translation of Und die Bibel hat doch recht. Bibliography: p. 431-436. [BS635.K43] 56-11301
1. Bible—History of contemporary events, etc. I. Title.

KELLER, Werner, 1909- 220'.95
The Bible as history; a confirmation of the Books of Books. Translated by William Neil. New York, Bantam Books [1974, c1964] xii, 515 p. illus. 18 cm. Translation of Und die Bibel hat doch recht. Bibliography: p. 495-500. [BS635.K43] 1.95 (pbk.)
1. Bible—History of comptempory events. I. Title.
L.C. card no. for original ed.: 56-11301

KELLER, Werner, 1909- 220.95
The Bible as history; a confirmation of the Book of Books. Translated by William Neil. New York, W. Morrow [1969, c1956] xviii, 458 p. illus. 21 cm. (Apollo editions, A-237) "Fully revised by the author, 1964." Translation of Und die Bibel hat doch recht. Bibliography: p. 441-445. [BS635.K43 1969] 78-8416 3.50
1. Bible—History of contemporary events, etc. I. Title.

KELLER, Werner, 1909- 220.95
The Bible as history in pictures. [English translation by William Neil] New York, Morrow [1964] 360 p. illus., facsims., col. maps (on lining papers) 8 col. plates, ports. 23 cm. Translation of Und die Bibel hat doch recht in Bildern. Bibliography: p. 337. [BS635.K43 1964] 64-22312
1. Bible—History of contemporary events, etc. I. Title.

KIRBY, Ralph. ed. 220.95
The Bible in pictures. Editorial consultants: E. O. James, C. C. Martindale [and] S. H. Hooke. New York, Greystone Press [1952] 320 p. illus. (part col.) 26 cm. [BS560.K5 1952] 52-14920
1. Bible—Pictures, illustrations, etc. I. Title.

KIRBY, Ralph, ed. 220.95
The Bible story with living pictures. Editorial consultants: E. O. James, Harold Roberts, Sebastian Bullough. New York, Harper [1961, c.1960] 320p. illus. (part col.) 26cm. Previous eds. published under title: The Bible in pictures. 61-9647 5.95
1. Bible—Pictures, illustrations, etc. I. Title.

KLINK, Johanna Louise. 220.95
Bible for children [by] J. L. Klink. Illustrated by Piet Klaase. Translated by Patricia Crampton. Philadelphia, Westminster Press [1967- v. illus. 26 cm. Translation of Bijbel voor de Kinderen. Contents.Contents.—v. 1. The Old Testament with songs and plays. A simplification of the Bible for young readers, combining prose, verse, songs, drama and illustrations to present a complete impression of the times and forces that inspired or influenced its writing. [BS551.2.K5713] AC 68
1. Bible stories. I. Klaase, Piet, illus. II. Title.

KORFKER, Dena 220.95
My picture story Bible. With full-color pictures by C. P. Robison and Ben Wood, and additional illus. in the text by Dirk Gringhuis. Grand Rapids, Mich., Zondervan Pub. House [c.1960] 512p. illus. (part col.), col. endpaper map. 24cm. 60-4673 3.95
1. Bible stories, English. I. Title.

KORFKER, Dena, 1908- 220.95
My picture story Bible. With full-color pictures by C. P. Robison and Ben Wood, and additional illus. in the text by Dirk Gringhuis. Grand Rapids, Zondervan Pub. House [1960] 512p. illus. 24cm. [BS551.2.K65] 60-4673
1. Bible stories, English. I. Title.

LAMB, Philip J 22095
The drama of the Bible. London, New York, Oxford University Press, 1964. xii, 206 p. 22 cm. [BS635.2.L3] 64-2690
1. Bible — History of Biblical events. I. Title.

LAMB, Philip J. 220.95
The drama of the Bible. New York, Oxford [c.]1964. xii, 206p. 22cm. 64-2690 4.80
1. Bible—History of Biblical events. I. Title.

*LEE, Robert G. 220.9'5
Talks on the miracles of the Bible. [By] Robert G. Lee. Grand Rapids, Mich., Baker Book House, [1973, c1927] 102 p., 20 cm. [BS550] ISBN 0-8010-5537-7 1.95 (pbk.)
1. Bible stories. I. Title.

LE SOURD, Leonard Earle. 220.95
The Bible quizzle book for boys and girls from 6 to 12; illustrated by Kay and Mitchell Hooks. New York, S. Gabriel Sons [1951] 62 p. illus. 30 cm. Hieroglyphic Bibles. [BS560.L4] 51-7429
I. Title.

LEWIS, Jack Pearl, 1919- 220.95
Historical backgrounds of Bible history, by Jack P. Lewis. Grand Rapids, Mich., Baker Book House [1971] 199 p. illus. 22 cm. (University Christian Student Center. Annual lectureship, 1969) Includes bibliographical references. [BS635.2.L49] 79-156594 ISBN 0-8010-5507-5 3.95
1. Bible—History of contemporary events. 2. Bible—Antiquities. 3. Bible—Biography. I. Title. II. Series.

LIGHTFOOD, Neil R 220.95
How we got the Bible. Grand Rapids, Baker Book House, 1963. 126 p. illus. 20 cm. [BS445.L47] 62-22230
1. Bible — Hist. I. Title.

LIGHTFOOT, Neil R. 220.95
How we got the Bible. Grand Rapids, Mich., Baker Bk. [c.]1963. 126p. illus. 20cm. Bibl. 62-22230 2.50 bds.,
1. Bible—Hist. I. Title.

LONGSTRETH, Edward, 1894- 220.95
The hill of the Lord. [1st ed.] Philadelphia, Lippincott [1964] 125 p. 21 cm. [BS550.2.L6] 64-7508
1. Bible stories, English. I. Title.

LOVASIK, Lawrence George, 220.95
1913-
New Catholic picture Bible; popular stories from the Old and New Testaments. New York, Catholic Book Pub. Co. [1960] 208p. illus. 24cm. First ed. published in 1955 under title: Catholic picture Bible. [BS551.2.L57 1960] 61-317
1. Bible stories, English. 2. Bible—Pictures, Illustrations, etc. I. Title.

[LOWE, Edith May (Kovar)] 220.95
1905-
Well known Bible stories from the Old and New Testaments. Kenosha, Wis., S. Lowe [1955] unpaged. illus. 20cm. (A Bonnie book, 4071) [BS551.2.L6] 55-58686
1. Bible stories, English. I. Title.

LOYASIK, Lawrence George, 220.95
1913-
Catholic picture Bible; popular stories from the Old and New Testaments. New York, Catholic Book Pub. Co. [1955] 208p. illus. 24cm. [BS551.2.L57] 56-424
1. Bible stories, English. 2. Bible—Pictures, illustrations, etc. I. Title.

LYNCH, James Charles. 220.95
God, His Son Jesus, and man. Narrative by James Charles Lynch. Dodge City, Kan., Religious Publications [1955] 283p. illus. 19cm. [BS550.L85] 56-23733
1. Bible stories, English. 2. Bible—Pictures, illustrations, etc. I. Title.

MCGINNIS, Howard Justus, 220.95
1882-
Know your Bible better; a layman studies the Old Testament history and literature. Durham, N.C., Seeman [c.]1962. 208p. illus. 24cm. Bibl. 62-2866 3.50
1. Bible. O.T.—History of Biblical events 2. Bible. O.T.—Language, style. I. Title.

MAND, Evald. 220.95
Men of tomorrow; stories from the Bible for youth of today, by Ewald Mand. Illustrated by John Lear. Philadelphia, Westminster Press [1958] 224p. illus. 24cm. [BS551.2.M33] 58-5118
1. Bible—History of Biblical events. I. Title.

MARTIN, William Clyde, 220.95
1893-
These were God's people; a Bible history: the story of Israel and early Christianity, based on the Holy Scriptures, ancient historical and religious documents, and the findings of archaeology, by William C. Martin. Nashville, Southwestern Co. [1966] iv, 506p. col. illus., col. maps. 27cm. Bibl. [BS635.2.M3] 66-20336 7.95
1. Bible — History of Biblical events. I. Title.

MAXWELL, Arthur Stanley, 220.95
1896-
The Bible story; two hundred and fifty stories in seven volumes covering the entire Bible from Genesis to Revelation. Washington, Review and Herald Pub. Association [1953- v. illus. 26cm. [BS551.M379] 54-16316
1. Bible stories, English. I. Title.

MAXWELL, Arthur Stanley, 220.95
1896-
The Bible story ... Stories ... covering the entire Bible from Genesis to Revelation. Washington, Review and Herald Pub. Association [1953-57] 10 v. illus. 26cm. [BS551.M379] 54-16316
1. Bible stories, English. I. Title.

MEYER, Edith Patterson. 220.95
Bible stories for young readers. Illustrated by Howard Simon. New York, Abingdon Press [1958] 288p. illus. 24cm. [BS551.2.M4] 58-1002
1. Bible stories, English. I. Title.

MOULD, Elmer Wallace King, 1886- 220.95
Bible history digest. New York, Exposition Press [1950] x, 201 p. maps. 23 cm. [BS635.M648] 50-9049
1. Bible — History of Biblical events. 2. Jews — Hist. — To A.D. 70. I. Title.

MOULD, Elmer Wallace King, 1886-1950. 220.95
Essentials of Bible history. Rev. ed. New York, Ronald Press Co., [1951] xxxii, 687. 8 p. illus., 12 col. maps. 22 cm. Bibliography: p. 621-623. [BS635.M64] 51-10708
1. Bible — History of Biblical events. I. Title.

MOULD, Elmer Wallace King, 1886-1950. 220.95
Essentials of Bible history. 3d ed. rev. by H. Neil Richardson [and] Robert F. Berkey. New York, Ronald Press Co. [1966] xx, 842 p. illus., facsims., col. maps. 22 cm. Bibliography: p. 747-751. Bibliographical footnotes. [BS635.M64 1966] 66-17907
1. Bible—History of Biblical events. I. Richardson, Henry Neil, 1916- II. Berkey, Robert F. III. Title.

MOULD, Elmer Wallace King, 1886-1950 220.95
Essentials of Bible history. 3d ed. rev. by N. Neil Richardson, Robert F. Berkey. New York, Ronald [c.1939-1966] xx, 842p, illus., facsims., col. maps. 22cm. Bibl. [BS635.M64] 66-17907 7.75
1. Bible — History of Biblical events. I. Richardson Henury Neil, 1916- II. Berkey Robert F. III. Title.

NEFF, Merlin L. 220.95
Our heritage of faith. [3v.] Mountain View, Calif., Pacific Pr. Pub. Assn. [c.1962 3v.] 370; 382; 472p. illus. (pt. col.) col. maps. 62-7021 49.50, set, bxd.
1. Bible—History of Biblical events. 2. Seventh-Day Adventists—Doctrinal and controversial works. 3. U. S.—Religion. I. Title.

NEIL, William, 1909- 220.9'5
The Bible story. Drawings by Gyula Hincz. Nashville, Abingdon Press, 1971. 272 p. illus. 24 cm. [BS635.2.N4 1971] 72-175325 ISBN 0-687-03394-2 6.95
1. Bible—History of Biblical events. 2. Bible—Biography. I. Title.

NEILSON, Francis 220.95
From Ur to Nazareth; an economic inquiry into the religious and political history of Israel. New York, 50 E. 69 St. Robert Schalkenbach Foundation, [1960, c.1959] x, 461p. Bibl. p. 441-446 25cm. 60-1483 6.00
1. Bible—History of Biblical events. 2. Bible—History of contemporary events, etc. 3. Jews—Hist.—To 70 A.D. I. Title.

NEWLAND, Mary (Reed) 220.95
The family and the Bible. New York, Random House [1963] xiv, 272 p. 22 cm. [BS1197.N46] 63-11624
1. Bible — History of Biblical events. 2. Bible — Reading. I. Title.

NEWLAND, Mary (Reed) 220.95
The family and the Bible. Foreword by Carroll Stuhlmueller. Garden City. New York, Doubleday [1967.c.1963] 315p. 18cm. (Image bk., D228) [BS1197.N46] 1.25 pap.,
1. Bible—Hist. of biblical events. 2. Bible—Reading. I. Title.

NEWLAND, Mary (Reed) 220.95
The family and the Bible. New York, Random [c.1963] xiv, 272p. 22cm. 63-11624 5.95
1. Bible—History of Biblical events. 2. Bible—Reading. I. Title.

NEWMAN, Margaret M. 220.95
Bible vignettes. New York, Vantage Press [c.1960] 172p. 22cm. 3.00 bds.,
I. Title.

NOLAND, Cora Mabel (Shaw) 1882- 220.95
It happened at night. Mountain View, Calif., Pacific Press Pub. Association [1952] 192 p. illus. 23 cm. [BS551.N55] 52-13416
1. Bible stories, English. I. Title.

*NORFLEET, Mary Crockett 220.95
God and his people; a Bible story book for young children. Illus. by Phero Thomas. Richmond, Va., CLC Pr. [dist. Knox, 1966] 64p. 21cm. 1.95 bds.,
I. Title.

NORTHCOTT, William Cecil, 1902- 220.95 (j)
People of the Bible, by Cecil Northcott. Designed and illustrated by Denis Wrigley. Philadelphia, Westminster Press [1967] 157 p. illus. (part col.) 26 cm. [BS551.2.N6] 67-12336
1. Bible stories, English. I. Title.

NORTHCOTT, William Cecil, 1902- 220.95
People of the Bible, by Cecil Northcott. Designed and illustrated by Denis Wrigley. Philadelphia, Westminster Press [1967] 157 p. illus. (part col.) 26 cm. Bible stories retold as portraits of human life, emphasizing the major characters of the Old and New Testaments. [BS551.2.N6] AC 67
1. Bible stories. I. Wrigley, Denis, illus. II. Title.

OTEY, William Wesley, 1867- 220.95
The tree of life lost and regained. Bellaire, Tex., Bible Bulwarks [1956] 141p. illus. 23cm. [BS635.O75] 58-35744
1. Bible—History of Biblical events. I. Title.

PADDOCK, Charles Lee, 1891- 220.95
Bible ABC's; illustrated by Joseph Maniscalco, decorative drawings by Harold Munson. Mountain View, Calif., Pacific Press Pub. Association [1956, c1955] unpaged. illus. 24cm. (Tiny tots library) [BS551.2.P32] 55-12372
1. Bible stories, English. I. Title.

PADDOCK, Charles Lee, 1891- 220.95
Bible firsts; illustrated by Earl Thollander. Mountain View, Calif., Pacific Press Pub. Association [1956] unpaged. illus. 24cm. (Tiny tots library) [BS551.2.P33] 56-25347
1. Bible stories, English. I. Title.

PADDOCK, Charles Lee, 1891- 220.95
Boys and girls of the Bible; illustrated by Don Muth, Jr. Mountain View, Calif., Pacific Press Pub. Association [1956] unpaged. illus. 24cm. (Tiny tots library) [BS576.P32] 56-25348
1. Children in the Bible. I. Title.

PAUL, Louis, 1901- 220.95
Heroes, kings, and men. New York, Dial Press, 1955. 409 p. 22 cm. [BS550.P3] 55-11200
1. Bible—History of Biblical events. I. Title.

PAYNE, John Barton, 1922- 220.95
An outline of Hebrew history. Grand Rapids, Baker Book House, 1954. 257p. 21cm. [DS117.P3] 54-11075
1. News—Hist.—To 70 A. P. 2. Bible—History of Biblical events. I. Title. II. Title: Hebrew history.

PETERSEN, Emma Marr. 220.95
Bible stories for young Latter-Day saints, illustrated by Milton E. Swensen. Salt Lake City, Bookcraft Pub. Co., 1950. 310 p. illus. 24 cm. [BX8630.A28P4] 52-27057
1. Bible stories, English. I. Title.

PFLEIDERER, Otto, 1839-1908. 220.95
Primitive Christianity, its writings and teachings in their historical connections. Translated by W. Montgomery, and edited by W. D. Morrison. Clifton, N. J., Reference Book Publishers, 1965. 4 v. 23 cm (Library of religious and philosophic thought) Translation of Das Urchristenthum. Bibliographical footnotes. [BS2410.P62] 65-22085
1. Church history—Primitive and early church. 2. Bible. N. T.—Introductions. 3. Christian literature, Early—Hist. & crit. I. Title.

PIHL, Herman Gottfrid, 1894- 220.95
Follow me; stories from the Bible for children, by H. G. Pihl, K. Beckman. [Tr. by Edward Carney] New York, Association [1967, c.1966] 95p. col. illus. 20cm. [BS551.2.P513] 67-1574 2.50 bds.,
1. Bible stories, English. 2. Children—Prayer-books and devotions. I. Beckman, Karin, 1904- joint author. II. Title.

PIPER, David Roy, 1887- 220.95
Youth explores the Bible; a new story of the world's most popular book. Illustrated by Beatrice Stevens. Rev. ed. Boston, W. A. Wilde Co., 1953 [c1941] 354p. illus. 21cm. [BS635.P55 1953] 53-9055
1. Bible—History of Biblical events. I. Title.

PRICE, Eugenia. 220.9'5
Beloved world; the story of God and people as told from the Bible. Grand Rapids, Zondervan Pub. House [1972, c1961] 474 p. 20 cm. Bibliography: p. 468. [BS550.2.P7 1972] 68-12948
1. Bible—History of Biblical events. I. Title.

PRICE, Eugenia. 220.95
Beloved world; the story of God and people as told from the Bible. Illustrated by Kirk Gringhuis. Grand Rapids, Zondervan Pub. House, 1961. 512 p. illus. 25 cm. Includes bibliography. [BS550.2.P7] 61-14867
1. Bible—History of Biblical events. I. Title.

PURCELL, William Ernest, 1909- 220.95
Behold my glory; great stories from the Bible and the masterpieces they have inspired. New York, Hawthorn Books [1957?] 160 p. illus. 28 cm. [BS635.P8] 57-6367
1. Bible—History of Biblical events. 2. Bible—Pictures, illustrations, etc. I. Title.

REID, Lizzie Murdock, 1866- 220.95
Story of the Bible also, A series of devotionals. [Cedarville? Ohio, 1951] 105 p. illus. 19 cm. [BS539.R4] 51-38566
1. Bible — History of Biblical events. 2. Devotional literature. I. Title.

REYNOLDS, Ruth (Sutton) 220.95
The Bible & people who lived and wrote it; a layman's discovery of the fascination of the Old Testament and of its influence on the New. [1st ed.] New York, Exposition Press [1955] 231p. illus. 21cm. (A Banner book) Includes bibliography. [BS635.R46] 55-11132
1. Bible. O. T.—History of Biblical events. 2. Bible. O. T.—Biog. I. Title.

*RHODES, Arnold B. 220.95
The mighty acts of God. CLC Pr. [dist.] Richmond, Va. Knox, c.1964 446p. 21cm. (Covenant life curriculum) 2.95 pap.,
I. Title.

RINGENBERG, Loyal R. 220.9'5
The Living Word in history / Loyal R. Ringenberg. 1974 revision. Broadview, Ill. : Gibbs Pub. Co., 1974. xviii, 520 p. : ill. ; 25 cm. Published in 1953 under title: The Word of God in history. Includes bibliographies and index. [BS605.2.R56 1974] 73-86015 8.95.
1. Bible—Study—Text-books. I. Title.

RINGENBERG, Loyal R 220.95
The word of God in history; a course in basic Bible study. Butler, Ind., Higley Press [1953] 518p. illus. 24cm. [BS635.R53] 54-653
1. Bible—History of Biblical events. I. Title.

ROBINSON, George Livingstone,1864- 220.95
Leaders of Israel; a brief history of the Hebrew people from the earliest times to the fall of Jerusalem, A. D. 70. Grand Rapids, Baker Book House, 1955 [c1906] 246p. illus. 20cm. Includes bibliography. [BS571.R45 1955] 55-9474
1. Bible—Biog. 2. Jews—Hist.—To 70 A. D. I. Title.

*RUDOLPH, Mary Baine 220.95
God and His covenant people [Gr. 1] Illus. by Shannon Stirnweis. Richmond,Va., CLC Pr. [dist. Knox 1966, c.1964] 160p. col. illus. 20cm. 2.25 pap.,
I. Title.

*RUDOLPH, Mary Baine 220.95
Living in covenant with God. Richmond, Va. Covenant Life Curriculum Pr. [dist. Knox, 1966, c.1965] 95p. 20cm. 1.45 pap.,
I. Title.

RUTH, Dallas. 220.95
The road to paradise. New York, Vantage Press [1954] 168p. illus. 23cm. [BS550.R8] 54-9932
1. Bible stories, English. I. Title.

SALISBURY, Helen Wright, 1895- 220.95
Bible stories then and now. Los Angeles, Cowman Pub. Co., c1961. 1 v. unpaged. col. illus. 29 cm. [BS551.2.S3] 61-17433
1. Bible stories, English. I. Title.

SCHONFIELD, Hugh Joseph, 1901- 220.95
A history of Biblical literature. [New York] New American Library [1962] 223p. illus. 18cm. (A Mentor book, MT376) Includes bibliography. [BS445.S3] 62-9701
1. Bible—Hist. I. Title. II. Title: Biblical literature.

SCHOOLLAND, Marian M 1902- 220.95
The Bible story. Grand Rapids, Eerdmans, 1951. 119 p. illus. 24 cm. [BS551.S37] 51=8159
1. Bible stories, English. I. Title.

SCROGGIE, William Graham, 1877-1958. 220.9'5
The unfolding drama of redemption; the Bible as a whole. Grand Rapids, Zondervan Pub. House [1972, c1953-70] 505, 493, 443 p. maps. 23 cm. [BS635.2.S362 1972] 74-163555 16.95
1. Bible—History and Biblical events. 2. Bible—Study—Outlines, syllabi, etc. 3. Redemption—Biblical teaching. I. Title.

SCROGGIE, William Graham, 1877-1958. 220.9'5
The unfolding drama of redemption; the Bible as a whole. Old Tappan, N.J., F. H. Revell Co. [1970] 3 v. illus. 22 cm. (His The unfolding drama of redemption; the Bible as a whole) At head of title: Know your Bible. Vol. 1 first published in 1953; v. 2 in 1957. Contents.Contents.—v. 1. The prologue and act I of the drama, embracing the Old Testament.—v. 2. The interlude and act II of the drama embracing the inter-Testament period, the gospels and acts.—v. 3. Act II and the epilogue of the drama embracing the Epistles and the Book of Revelation. [BS635.2.S362] 72-152551 ISBN 0-7208-0192-3 (v. 1) 34.95
1. Bible—History of Biblical events. 2. Bible—Study—Outlines, syllabi, etc. 3. Redemption—Biblical teaching. I. Title. II. Title: Know your Bible. III. Series.

SIGSTEDT, Cyriel Sigrid (Ljungberg Odhner) 220.95
Stories from the Word; a selection of suitable readings for small children [by] Sigrid O. Sigstedt. [Philadelphia, Printed by Blaetz bros., inc.] 19535. viii, 58p. incl. front. 22cm. Song (with music) :p. 13.Blank page for 'Other notes' (58) [BS551.S48] 36-2184
1. Bible stories, English. I. Title.

SIMON, Martin Paul William, 1903- 220.95
Bible readings for the family hour. Chicago, Moody Press [1954] 368p. 24cm. [BS551.S5] 54-10844
1. Bible stories, English. I. Title.

SLAUGHTER, Frank Gill, 1908- 220.95
The land and the promise; the greatest stories from the Bible, retold by Frank G. Slaughter. [1st ed.] Cleveland, World Pub. Co. [1960] 341 p. 22 cm. [BS550.2.S53] 60-11455
1. Bible stories. I. Title.

SMITH, Horace Greeley. 220.95
The world's greatest story, in its cosmic and timeless setting. Chicago, Rand McNally [1965] 46, [1] p. 21 cm. Bibliography: p. [47] [BS550.2.S57] 65-11816
1. Bible stories, English. I. Title.

SMITH, James Walter Dickson, 1899- 220.95
Bible background. New York, Roy Publishers [1959] 73 p. illus. 22 cm. Includes bibliography. [BMI65.S63] 60-7755
1. Jews — Hist. — To 70 A.D. I. Title.

SPALDING, Arthur Whitefield, 1877--1954. 220.95
Golden treasury of Bible stories; two hundred and three Bible stories from Genesis to Revelation. Paintings by Clyde N. Provonsha and Robert Temple Ayres. Nashville Southern Pub. Association 1954 492p. illus. 27cm. [BS551.S67] 54-9398
1. Bible stories, English. I. Title.

STOB, George 220.95
Handbook of Bible history. Grand Rapids, Mich., Eerdmans [c.1963] 178p. 22cm. Contents.bk. 3. The Gospels, the story of Jesus the Savior. 62-21369 1.50 pap.,
1. Bible—History of Biblical events. I. Title.

TAYLOR, Kenneth Nathaniel. 220.95
The Bible in pictures for little eyes. Chicago, Moody Press [1956] unpaged. illus. 17 x 26cm. [BS551.2.T37] 56-14484
1. Bible stories, English. 2. Bible—Pictures, Illustrations, etc. I. Title.

TAYLOR, Kenneth Nathaniel. 220.95
The Bible in pictures for little eyes. Chicago, Moody Press [1956] unpaged. illus. 17 x 26 cm. [BX551.2.T37] 56-14484
1. Bible stories, English. 2. Bible — Pictures, illustrations, etc. I. Title.

TERRIEN, Samuel. 220.95
Lands of the Bible. Illustrated by William Bolin. New York, Simon and Schuster [1957] 97p. illus. (part col.) col. maps. 34cm. (A Golden historical atlas) [BS635.T4] 57-13756
1. Bible—History of Biblical events. 2. Bible—Geography—Maps. I. Title.

TERRIEN, Samuel. 220.95
Lands of the Bible. Illustrated by William Bolin. New York, Simon and Schuster [1957] 97 p. illus. (part col.) col. maps. 34 cm. (A Golden historical atlas) [BS635.T4] 57-13756
1. Bible — History of Biblical events. 2. Bible — Geography — Maps. I. Title.

TERRIEN, Samuel L 1911- 220.95
Lands of the Bible. Illustrated by William Bolin. New York, Simon and Schuster [1957] 97 p. illus. (part col.) col. maps. 34 cm. (A Golden historical atlas) [BS635.2.T4] 57-13756
1. Bible—History of Biblical events. 2. Bible—Geography—Maps. I. Title.

THAT wonderful night, 220.95
the story of the very first Christmas, by the Daughters of St. Paul. Illus. by C. Venzi.

Boston, St. Paul Eds. [dist.] Daughters of St. Paul, c.1965. 28p. col. illus. 22cm. (Bedtime stories) .50; .35 pap.,

TIGNER, Marcy. 220.95
Little Marcy's favorite Bible stories. Waco, Tex., Word Books [1968] 35 p. illus. (part col.) 22 cm. Five Bible stories: Baby Moses, the First Christmas, Jesus in the Temple, The Little Lost Lamb, Five Loaves and Two Fishes. [BS551.2.T5] AC 68
1. Bible stories. I. Title. II. Title: Favorite Bible stories.

TILLMAN, Bonnie. 220.95
Bible babies. Front cover painting and inside illus. by Georgette Delattre. Nashville, Southern Pub. Association [1955, c1954] 90p. illus. 24cm. [BS551.T53] 55-25498
1. Bible stories, English. I. Title.

TURNBULL, Ralph G 220.95
Later Hebrew history and prophets. Grand Rapids, Baker Book House, 1962. 78 p. 22 cm. (His Bible companion series for lesson and sermon preparation) [BS1197.T8] 62-3493
1. Bible, O.T. — History of Biblical events. 2. Bible, O. T. — Homiletical use. I. Title.

TURNBULL, Ralph G. 220.95
Later Hebrew history and prophets. Grand Rapids, Mich., Baker [c.]1962. 78p. 22cm. (His Bible companion ser. for lesson and sermon preparation) 62-3493 1.00 pap.,
1. Bible. O. T.—History of Biblical events. 2. Bible. O. T.—Homiletical use. I. Title.

VAN LOON, Hendrik 220.95 (j)
Willem, 1882-1944.
The story of the Bible, written and drawn by Hendrik Willem van Loon. New York, Grosset & Dunlap [1966, c1951] xxv, 452 p. illus. 21 cm. "A Biblical reading list for children, selected by Leonore St. John Power": p. 440-446. [BS551] 66-9344
1. Bible stories, English. I. Title.

VOS, Catherine Frances 220.95
(Smith)
The child's story Bible, by Catherine F. Vos. Rev. by Marianne Catherine Vos Radius. Illus. and maps by Betty Beeby. [4th ed. Grand Rapids] Eerdmans [1966] xx, 436 p. col. illus., col. maps. 27 cm. Tales of the Bible rewritten for young children. [BS551.V72 1966] AC 67
1. Bible stories. I. Radius, Marianne Catherine (Vos) ed. II. Beeby, Betty, illus. III. Title.

VOS, Catherine Frances 220.95
(Smith)
The child's story Bible. Illustrators; Dirk Gringhuis [and] Norman Mathesis. Grand Rapids, Eerdmans [1958] 732 p. illus 24 cm. [BS551.V72] 60-916
1. Bible stories, English. I. Title.

VRIES, Anne de, 1904- 220.95
The children's Bible; the Holy Scripture as retold for children by Anne de Vries. Saint Louis, Concordia [1963] 255p. illus. (pt. col.) 23cm. Tr. into English by Baukje Gray and David Rudston from the Dutch original 'Kleuter vertelboek voor bijbelse geschiedenis.' 62-53280 3.50 bds.,
1. Bible stories, English. I. Title.

VRIES, Anne de, 1904-1964. 220.95
Children in the Bible. Translated by Marian Schoolland. St. Louis, Concordia Pub. House, 1966. 187 p. col. illus. 24 cm. Stories retold about a few of the children in the Bible—Cain and Abel, Benjamin, Miriam, Samuel, and Paul's nephew. [BS551.2.V6813] AC 67
1. Bible stories. I. Title.

WADDELL, Helen Jane, 1889- 220.95
Stories from Holy Writ. New York, Macmillan, 1950. xi, 244 p. 21 cm. [BS551.W2] 50-9430
1. Bible stories, English. I. Title.

WARREN, Mary. 220.95
The little boat that almost sank ... Illustrated by Kveta Rada. [St. Louis] Concordia Pub. House [1965] [32] p. col. illus. 21 cm. (Arch books) On cover: How Jesus stopped the storm. [BS2401.W3] 64-23371
1. Stilling of the storm (Miracle) — Juvenile literature. I. Title. II. Title: How Jesus stopped the storm.

WATSON, Jane (Werner) 220.95
1915-
Bible stories of boys and girls, retold by Jane Werner. Pictures by Rachel Taft Dixon and Marjorie Hartwell. New York, Simon and Schuster [1953] unpaged. illus. 21cm. (A Little golden book, 174) [BS576.W36] 53-3747
1. Children in the Bible. I. Title.

WATSON, Jane (Werner) 220.95
1915- ed.
A Catholic child's Bible, selected and arr. by Elsa Jane Werner and Charles Hartman. New York, Simon and Schuster; Catholic distribution by Catechetical Guild Educational Society, St. Paul [1958] 2 v. illus. (part col.) 33 cm. (A Giant golden book, 665-666) Contents.[1] Stories from the Old Testament. -- [2] The New Testament. [BS551.2.W28] 58-59604
1. Bible stories, English. I. Hartman, Charles, joint ed. II. Title.

WEGENER, Gunther S. 220.95
6000 years of the Bible. New York, Harper [c.1963] 1 v. illus. 63-16406 6.95; after dec. 31, 7.95
I. Title.

WEIDENSCHILLING, John 220.95
Martin, 1893-
The history of Israel from Moses to Christ. St. Louis, Concordia Pub. House [1952, 1951] 164 p. illus. 19 cm. Teacher's guide. St. Louis, Concordia Pub. House [1952] 172 p.20 cm. Jews -- Hist. -- To 70 A.D. [DS118.W37] 52-2006
I. Title.

WHITE, Freda Dunlop. 220.95
The torch of faith; a living account of Bible times and people. [1st ed.] Philadelphia, Winston [1958] 212 p. illus. 22 cm. [BS551.2.W45] 58-7147
1. Bible—History of Biblical events. I. Title.

WILLIAMS, Jane, 1891- 220.95
More Bible friends to know. Pictures by Griffith Foxley. Nashville, Broadman Press, c1957. unpaged. illus. 25cm. (Little treasure series, 12) [BS551.2.W49] 57-13969
1. Bible stories, English. I. Title.

WILLIAMS, Jane, 1891- 220.95
More Bible friends to know. Pictures by Griffith Foxley. Nashville, Broadman Press, c1957. unpaged. illus. 25 cm. (Little treasure series, 12) [BS551.2.W49] 57-13969
1. Bible stories, English. I. Title.

WIND, Gerhard Lewis, 1896- 220.95
My Bible story book; an outline of the Bible for small children. Pictures by Bette Hollis [and others] Saint Louis, Mo., Concordia Pub. House [1956] 95 p. illus. 28 cm. [BS551.2.W5] 56-44102
1. Bible stories, English. I. Title.

WINDER, Blanche 220.95
Stories from the Bible, retold by Blanche Winder. London, Ward, Lock; [stamped: distributed by SportShelf, New Rochelle, N.Y., 1960] 256p. illus. (front.) 18cm. (Royal ser.) 60-878 2.00 bds.,
1. Bible stories, English. I. Title.

WRIGHT, Sara Margaret. 220.95
A brief survey of the Bible. [1st ed.] New York, Loizeaux Bros. [1958] 241 p. 20 cm. [BS635.W7] 58-2032
1. Bible — History of Biblical events. I. Title.

WRIGLEY, Louise Scott. 220.95
God is love. Illustrated by Vivian Robbins. Independence, Mo., Herald House [1955] unpaged. illus. 19cm. [BS551.2.W75] 55-8012
1. Bible stories, English. I. Title.

MALY, Eugene H. 220.9500901
The world of David and Solomon. Englewood Cliffs, N.J., Prentice [c.1966] ix, 182 p. maps (on lining papers) 22 cm. (Prentice backgrounds to the Bible ser.) Bibl. [BS1286.5.M3] 66-13646 17.35
1. David, King of Israel. 2. Solomon, King of Israel. 3. Jews—Hist.—From entrance into Canaan to 953 B.C. I. Title. II. Series.

FARGUES, Marie. 220.95'00939'47
Sacred history. Translated by Patrick Hepburne Scott. Notre Dame, Inc., Fides Publishers [c1960-] v. illus. maps. 22 cm. (A Fides paperback textbook PBT-8 Translation of Histoire sainte d'apres les textes bibliques. Contents.v. 1. The Old Testament. [BS635.2.F313] 65-13804
1. Bible — History of Biblical events. I. Title.

MONTGOMERY, James 220.95'00939'47
Alan, 1866-1949.
Arabia and the Bible. Prolegomenon by Gus W. Van Beek. [New York] Ktav Pub. House, 1969. xxxv, 207 p. 23 cm. (The Library of Biblical studies) Reprint of the 1934 ed. Bibliographical footnotes. [BS635.M6 1969] 68-25721
1. Bible—History of contemporary events, etc. 2. Bible—Geography. 3. Arabia—Description and travel. 4. Civilization, Arab. I. Title. II. Series.

ALLEN, J. S. 220.9'505
Nelson's Picture bible. Text by J. S. Allen. Elmer Towns, Bernice Rich, Lane Easterly, editors. Nashville, Tenn., T. Nelson [1973] p. An illustrated, non-denominational Bible in simplified form. [BS560.A79] 73-7648 9.95
1. Bible—Picture Bibles. I. Title.

ANDRES, Stefan Paul, 220.9505
1906-
The Bible story, retold by Stefan Andres. Illus. by Gerhard Oberlander. Tr. from German by Michael Bullock. New York, McGraw [c.1966] 445 p. col. illus., fold. col. map. 24 cm. [BS551.2A513] 66-10321 7.95
1. Bible stories, English. I. Oberlander, Gerhard, illus. II. Title.

*ARNOLD, Charlotte E. 220.950'5
Group readings for the church, by Charlotte E. Arnold. Grand Rapids, Baker Book House, [1975] 74 p. ill. 20 cm. Bibliography: p. 18. [BS617] ISBN 0-8010-0065-3 1.95 (pbk.)
1. Bible—Reading. 2. Bible stories, English. 3. Group reading. I. Title.

BEERS, Victor Gilbert, 220.95'05
1928-
A child's treasury of Bible stories [by] V. Gilbert Beers. Chicago, Parent and Child Institute, c1970. 4 v. illus. (part col.) 27 cm. Four volumes of Bible stories from the Old Testaments with scriptural notation of the passages on which they are based. [BS551.2.B43] 78-31399
1. Bible stories, English. I. Title.

BEERS, Victor Gilbert, 220.9'505
1928-
God is my friend, by V. Gilbert Beers. Illustrated by Robert Boehmer. Grand Rapids, Zondervan Pub. House [1973] [96] p. col. illus. 24 cm. (His Learning to read from the Bible series) Includes twelve Bible stories and study questions and suggested activities emphasizing their application to modern life. [BS551.2.B434] 72-85562 3.95
1. Bible stories, English. I. Boehmer, Robert, illus. II. Title.

BEERS, Victor Gilbert, 220.9'505
1928-
Jesus is my guide, by V. Gilbert Beers. Illustrated by Robert Boehmer. Grand Rapids, Zondervan Pub. House [1973] [96] p. col. illus. 23 cm. (His Learning to read from the Bible series) Includes twelve Bible stories and study questions and suggested activities emphasizing their application to modern life. [BS551.2.B437] 72-95536 3.95
1. Bible stories, English. I. Boehmer, Robert, illus. II. Title.

BEERS, Victor Gilbert, 220.9'505
1928-
Jesus is my teacher, by V. Gilbert Beers. Illustrated by Robert Boehmer. Grand Rapids, Zondervan Pub. House [1973] [96] p. col. illus. 24 cm. (His Learning to read from the Bible series) Includes twelve Bible stories and study questions and suggested activities emphasizing their application to modern life. [BS551.2.B438] 72-95535 3.95
1. Bible stories, English. I. Boehmer, Robert, illus. II. Title.

BEERS, Victor Gilbert, 220.9'505
1928-
Through golden windows / by V. Gilbert Beers ; illustrated by Helen Endres. Chicago : Moody Press, [1975] 144 p. : col. ill. ; 26 cm. (The Muffin family picture Bible) Each Bible story is followed by a tale involving the Muffin family which illustrates the contemporary application of Biblical principles. [BS551.2.B44] 75-25535 ISBN 0-8024-8753-X : 6.95
1. Bible stories, English. I. Endres, Helen. II. Title.

BEERS, Victor Gilbert, 220.9'505
1928-
Under the tagalong tree / by V. Gilbert Beers ; illustrated by Helen Endres. Chicago : Moody Press, c1976. p. cm. A number of Bible stories that are followed by tales involving the Muffin family which illustrate the contemporary application of Biblical principles. [BS551.2.B45] 76-22173 ISBN 0-8024-9021-2 : 6.95
1. Bible stories, English. 2. Christian life. I. Endres, Helen. II. Title.

BEERS, Victor Gilbert, 220.9'505
1928-
With sails to the wind / by V. Gilbert Beers. Chicago : Moody Press, c1977. p. cm. A collection of illustrated Bible stories with parallel stories of contemporary application of Biblical truths and principles. [BS551.2.B453] 77-24955 ISBN 0-8024-9570-2 : 6.95
1. Bible stories, English. I. Title.

BIBLE. N. T. Gospels. 220.9'505
English. Harmonies. 1958. Meissner.
New Testament Gospels, a modern translation by Lawrence Meissner. All the verses in 40 Fewer words .. Portland, Or., c1958. 88p. 22cm. [BT299.M43] 58-48843
1. Jesus Christ—Biog.— Sources, Biblical. I. Meissner, Lawrence, tr. II. Title.

BIBLE. N.T. Gospels. 220.9'505
English. Harmonies. 1962. Shank.
Jesus, His story; the four Gospels as one narrative in language for today. Translation by Robert Shank. Illus. by Paul Shank. Springfield, Mo., Westcott Publishers [1962] 256 p. illus. 23 cm. [BT299.2.S4] 62-17864
1. Jesus Christ—Biog.—Sources, Biblical. I. Shank, Robert, 1918- tr. II. Title.

BIBLE. Selections. 220.9'505
English. Jahsmann. 1977.
The Holy Bible for children : a simplified version of the Old and New Testaments / edited by Allan Hart Jahsmann ; ill. and maps by Don Kueker. St. Louis : Concordia, c1977. 415 p., [8] leaves of plates : col. ill. 25 cm. A simplified retelling including maps and pictures, of selected portions of each of the books of the Bible. [BS197.J27] 77-3226 ISBN 0-570-03465-5 : 8.95
I. Jahsmann, Allan Hart. II. Kueker, Don. III. Title.

BRITTON, Louisa. 220.9'505
The Bible story picture book : stories from the Old and New Testaments / retold by Louisa Britton ; illustrated by Victor Ramon Mojica. New York : Platt & Munk, c1975. 69 p. : col. ill. ; 32 cm. (A Child guidance book) [BS551.2.B75] 74-24952 ISBN 0-8228-7101-7 lib.bdg. : 3.95
1. Bible stories, English. I. Mojica, Victor Ramon. II. Title.

BUCK, Pearl 220.95'05
(Sydenstricker) 1892-
The story Bible, by Pearl S. Buck. [New York] Bartholomew House [1971] xi, 526 p. 27 cm. "The complete Old and New Testaments retold in seventy-two 'story-sections.'"—Jacket. [BS550.2.B76] 71-141871 ISBN 0-87794-025-8 7.95
1. Bible stories, English. I. Title.

BURKE, Carl F. 220.95'05
God is beautiful, man; interpretations of Bible passages and stories, as told by some of God's bad-tempered angels with busted halos to Carl F. Burke. New York, Association Press [1969] 127 p. 19 cm. [BS550.2.B79] 69-18841 3.50
1. Bible stories, English. I. Title.

BURKE, Carl F. 220.9505
God is for real, man; interpretations of Bible passages and stories as told by some of God's bad-tempered angels with busted halos to Carl F. Burke. New York, Association Press [1966] 128 p. 18 cm. [BS550.2.B8] 66-15746
1. Bible stories, English. I. Title.

DALE, Alan T. 220.9'505
New world; the heart of the New Testament in plain English, by Alan T. Dale. New York, Morehouse-Barlow Co. [1973, c1967] xvii, 365 p. illus. 23 cm. [BS2095.D3 1973] 73-180310 4.95 (pbk.)
1. Bible. N.T.—Paraphrases, English. I. Title.

DALE, Alan T. 220.9'505
Winding quest: the heart of the Old Testament in plain English, by Alan T. Dale [colour illustrations by Geoffrey Crabbe] London, Oxford University Press, 1972. 432, [24] p. illus. (some col.), maps. 24 cm. Based on selections from the Old Testament. Includes bibliographical references. [BS1197.D28] 73-152185 ISBN 0-19-833826-0 £4.00
1. Bible. O.T.—History of Biblical events. 2. Bible stories, English—O.T. I. Title.

DAUGHTERS of St. Paul. 220.95'05
Bible stories for young readers. Written and illustrated by the Daughters of St. Paul. [1st ed. Boston] St. Paul Editions [1969] 99 p. col. illus. 25 cm. A retelling of Bible stories from the creation through the Resurrection. [BS550.2.D35] 68-59067
1. Bible stories, English. I. Title.

DOAN, Eleanor Lloyd, 220.9'505
1914-
The Bible story picture book, compiled by Eleanor L. Doan. Glendale, Calif., G/L Regal Books [1972] 195 p. illus. 24 cm. [BS551.2.D57] 73-152801 ISBN 0-8307-0093-5 4.95
1. Bible stories, English. I. Title.

DOSS, Helen (Grigsby) 220.95'05
Young readers' book of Bible stories [by] Helen Doss. Illustrated by Tom Armstrong. Nashville, Abingdon Press [1970] 384 p. col. illus., col. maps. 29 cm. Summaries of various eras in Biblical history accompany chronologically arranged stories from the Old and New Testaments. [BS551.2.D64 1970] 76-95199 ISBN 6-87468-221- 7.95
1. Bible stories. I. Armstrong, Tom, illus. II. Title.

EFRON, Marshall. 220.9'505
Bible stories you can't forget, no matter how hard you try / Marshall Efron & Alfa-Betty Olsen ; illustrated by Ron Barrett. 1st ed. New

York : Dutton, c1976. xi, 79 p. : ill. ; 24 cm. Retelling of eight familiar Bible stories in contemporary language. [BS551.2.E36 1976] 76-9853 ISBN 0-525-26500-7 : 6.95
1. Bible stories, English. I. Olsen, Alfa-Betty, joint author. II. Barrett, Ron. III. Title.

EGERMEIER, Elsie Emilie, 1890- 220.95'05
Bible story book; a complete narration from Genesis to Revelation for young and old. Stories by Elsie E. Egermeier. Story revision by Arlene S. Hall. [Illus. by Clive Uptton. New ed.] Anderson, Ind., Warner Press [1969] 576 p. col. illus., col. ports. 25 cm. "Standard edition." Three hundred and twelve stories from the Old and New Testaments with color illustrations by the British artist Clive Uptton. [BS551.E4 1969] 68-23397 5.95
1. Bible stories, English. I. Hall, Arlene Stevens. II. Uptton, Clive, illus. III. Title.

EGERMEIER, Elsie Emilie, 1890- 220.95'05
Bible story book; a complete narration from Genesis to Revelation for young and old. Stories by Elsie E. Egermeier. Story revision by Arlene S. Hall. [Deluxe ed.] Anderson, Ind., Warner Press [1969] 576, 64, 16 p. illus. (part col.) 24 cm. Illustrated by Clive Uptton. Bible stories from the Old and New Testaments are accompanied by full-page color illustrations, photographs of Biblical lands today, study questions and answers, maps, and a brief history of the Bible. [BS551.E4 1969b] 71-9004
1. Bible stories, English. I. Hall, Arlene Stevens. II. Uptton, Clive, illus. III. Title.

FLETCHER, Sarah. 220.9'505
My Bible story book : Bible stories for small children / written by Sarah Fletcher ; art by Don Kueker. St. Louis : Concordia Pub. House, [1974] 71 p. : col. ill. ; 28 cm. Retells thirty-four stories from the Old and New Testaments. [BS551.2.F55] 73-91810 ISBN 0-570-03423-X : 2.95
1. Bible stories, English. I. Kueker, Don, ill. II. Title.

FRIENDS in the Bible. 220.9'505
Valley Forge, Pa. : Judson Press, c1976. 47 p. : col. ill. ; 22 cm. Retells twenty Bible stories that demonstrate the meaning of friendship and brotherhood. [BS551.2.F75] 75-43660 ISBN 0-8170-0714-8 : 1.50
1. Bible stories, English.

GRANGER, Muriel. 220.9'505
365 Bible stories and verses, retold by Muriel Granger New York, Golden Press [1973] 237 p. col. illus. 29 cm. Both the Old and New Testaments are retold in 365 stories interspersed with appropriate verse. [BS551.2.G72] 72-94289 4.95
1. Bible stories, English. I. Title.

GROSS, Arthur William, 1896- 220.95'05
Concordia Bible story book [by] Arthur W. Gross. Saint Louis, Concordia Pub. House [1971] 511 p. col. illus. 27 cm. Retellings of 148 stories from the Old Testament and 125 from the New Testament, arranged chronologically with references to the Biblical passages on which each story is based. [BS551.2.G76] 72-139512 ISBN 0-570-03401-9
1. Bible stories, English. I. Title.

HAAN, Sheri Dunham. 220.9'505
A child's storybook of Bible people. Martha Bentley, illustrator. Grand Rapids, Mich., Baker Book House [1973] 239 p. illus., music. and phonodisc (1 s. 7 in. 33 1/3 rpm.) in pocket. 24 cm. Includes hymns with music. Old and New Testament stories about Biblical characters are arranged in three sections: Children of the Bible, Women of the Bible, and Men of the Bible. Includes related songs, plays, and rhythm poems. [BS551.2.H24] 73-76202 ISBN 0-8010-4077-9 5.95
1. Bible stories, English. I. Bentley, Martha, illus. II. Title.

HAAN, Sheri Dunham. 220.95'05
Good news for children, written and illustrated by Sheri Dunham Haan. Grand Rapids, Baker Book House [1974, c1969] 240 p. col. illus. 24 cm. A simplified retelling of stories from the Bible. [BS551.2.H25] 78-97507 ISBN 0-8010-4073-6 4.95 (pbk.)
1. Bible stories, English. I. Title.

HOOK, Martha. 220.9'505
Little ones listen to God. Text by Martha Hook. Illustrated by Tinka Boren. Grand Rapids, Zondervan Pub. House [1971] [127] p. col. illus. 22 cm. Sixteen Old and New Testament stories retold for young children. Includes scriptural references and discussion questions. [BS551.2.H64] 72-156256
1. Bible stories, English. I. Boren, Tinka, illus. II. Title.

HUDSON, Virginia Cary. 220.95'05
Close your eyes when praying. Edited by Charles L. Wallis. Illustrated by Susan Perl. [1st ed.] New York, Harper & Row [1968] 127 p. illus. 22 cm. [BS550.2.H8] 68-29565 3.95
1. Bible stories, English. I. Title.

HURLBUT, Jesse Lyman, 1843-1930 220.9505
Hurlbut's story of the Bible; the complete Bible story, running from Genesis to Revelation, told in the simple language of today for young and old. One hundred and sixty-eight stories each complete in itself and together forming a connected narrative of the Holy scripture. New York, Pyramid [1966] 623p. 18cm. (N1385) [BS551.H8] .95 pap.,
1. Bible — History of Biblical events. I. Title.

JAHSMANN, Allan Hart 220.95'05
My favorite Bible stories, originally written by Allan Jahsmann for Concordia Bible lessons. Selected, arranged by Lillian Brune. St. Louis, Concordia [1967] 95p. col. illus. 27cm. [BS551.2.J33] 67-15957 1.50 pap.,
1. Bible stories, English. I. Brune, Lillian, comp. II. Title.

JOHNSTON, Louisa Mae. 220.9'505
The Bible story hour, by Louisa M. Johnston. Illustrated by Anna Marie Magagna. Managing editor: Anne Neigoff. [Chicago] Standard Educational Corp., 1974 [c1975] p. cm. A retelling of forty-six Bible stories from the Old and New Testaments. [BS551.2.J6] 74-9831 8.95
1. Bible stories, English. I. Magagna, Anna Marie, illus. II. Title.

JONES, Mary Alice, 1898- 220.9'505
Bible stories for children / by Mary Alice Jones ; illustrated by Manning de V. Lee. Chicago : Rand McNally, c1952, 1974 printing. 113 p. : ill. (some col.) ; 29 cm. Originally published under title: Bible stories. Nineteen retellings of Bible stories featuring Abraham, Gideon, Elijah, Esther, Mary, Peter, Jesus, and others. [BS551.2.J618 1974] 74-1245 4.95
1. Bible stories, English. I. Lee, Manning de Villeneuve, 1894- ill. II. Title.

JONES, Mary Alice, 1898- 220.9'505
Bible stories: God at work with man. Illustrated by Tom Armstrong. Nashville, Abingdon Press [1973] 77 p. illus. (part col.) 27 cm. Included among these retold Bible stories are accounts of Abraham, Amos, Joseph, Moses, David, Peter, and Paul. [BS551.2.J62] 72-13486 3.95
1. Bible stories, English. I. Armstrong, Tom, illus. II. Title.

KLINK, Johanna Louise. 220.95'05
Bible for children [by] J. L. Klink. Illustrated by Piet Klaase. Translated by Patricia Crampton. Philadelphia, Westminster Press [1967- v. illus. 26 cm. Translation of Bijbel voor de Kinderen. Contents.Contents.--v. 1. The Old Testament with songs and plays. [BS551.2.K5713] 68-10178
1. Bible stories, English. I. Title.

KLINK, Johanna Louise. 220.95'05
Bible for children [by] J. L. Klink. Illustrated by Piet Klaase. Translated by Patricia Crampton. Philadelphia, Westminster Press [1967- v. illus. 26 cm. Translation of Bijbel voor de Kinderen. Contents.Contents.—v. 1. The Old Testament with songs and plays. [BS551.2.K5713] 68-10178
1. Bible stories, English. I. Title.

LEHN, Cornelia. 220.95'05
God keeps His promise; a Bible story for kindergarten children. Illustrated by Beatrice Darwin. Newton, Kan., Faith and Life Press [1970] 192 p. illus. (part col.) 27 cm. Seventy stories retold from the Old and New Testaments for use at home and in Sunday School. [BS551.2.L4] 76-90377
1. Bible stories, English. I. Darwin, Beatrice, illus. II. Title.

MCBRIDE, Alfred. 220.95'05
Growing in grace. Gastonia, N.C., Good Will Publishers [1970] 363 p. col. illus. 25 cm. (The Catholic layman's library, v. 10) [BS635.2.M24] 72-92780
1. Bible—History of Biblical events. I. Title. II. Series.

MARTIN, Patricia Summerlin 220.9505
Bible stories that live. Nashville, Southwestern Co. [1966] xii, 366p. col. illus. 27cm. [BS550.2.M3] 66-23204 8.95
1. Bible stories, English. I. Title.

MOORE, Jessie Eleanor. 220.9505
Songs in our Bible. Illus. by James A. Woodend. Valley Forge [Pa.] Judson Press [1966] 127 p. col. illus. 23 cm. [BS551.2.M65] 66-12540
1. Bible stories, English. I. Title.

MOORE, Jessie Eleanor 220.9505
Songs in our Bible. Illus. by James A. Woodend. Valley Forge, Pa., Judson [c.1966] 127p. col. illus. 23cm. [BS551.2.M65] 66-12540 2.95
1. Bible stories, English. I. Title.

MUELLER, Arnold Carl, 1891- 220.95'05
My Good Shepherd; Bible story book. Originally written by A. C. Mueller. Artwork by Richard Hook. Selected and arr. by Lillian Brune. St. Louis, Concordia Pub. House [1969] 175 p. col. illus. 29 cm. Simplified retellings of eighty-six Bible stories. [BS551.2.M8] 70-89876 4.95
1. Bible stories, English. I. Hook, Richard, illus. II. Brune, Lillian, comp. III. Title.

MULLAN, Carol. 220.9'505
Bible picture stories from the Old and New Testaments / as told by Carol Mullan ; illustrated by Gordon Laite. Racine, Wis. : Golden Press, [1974] [20] p. : col. ill. ; 32 cm. Well-known Old and New Testament stories are represented by a full-page illustration, brief summary, and scriptural reference for each. [BS551.2.M83] 74-187764 ISBN 0-307-10496-6 : 1.25
1. Bible stories, English. I. Laite, Gordon, ill. II. Title.

PEALE, Norman Vincent, 1898- 220.9'505
Bible stories, told by Norman Vincent Peale. With illus. by Grabianski. New York, F. Watts, 1973. 247 p. col. illus. 25 cm. [BS550.2.P4] 73-4481 ISBN 0-531-02634-5 7.95
1. Bible stories, English. I. Title.

RACHLEFF, Owen S. 220.95'05
Great Bible stories and master paintings; a complete narration of the Old and New Testaments, by Owen S. Rachleff. Illustrated with one hundred and four works of art from Giotto to Corot. New York, Abradale Press [1968] 399 p. col. illus. 31 cm. [BS550.2.R3] 68-29485
1. Bible—Pictures, illustrations, etc. 2. Bible stories, English. I. Title.

RACHLEFF, Owen S. 220.9'505
An illustrated treasury of Bible stories, retold by Owen S. Rachleff. New York, Abradale Press [1970] 2 v. (487 p.) col. illus. 31 cm. Retellings accompanied by illustrations of Old and New Testament stories. [BS551.2.R25 1970] 71-82034 ISBN 0-8109-0192-7
1. Bible stories, English. 2. Bible stories. I. Title.

RICHARDS, Jean Hosking. 220.95'05
The Richards Bible story book. Illus. by Dorothy Teichman. Grand Rapids, Zondervan Pub. House [1968] 512 p. illus. (part col.) 27 cm. Retells twenty-five stories from the Old Testament and eighty-four from the New Testament. [BS551.2.R48] 68-27465 7.95
1. Bible stories, English. I. Teichman, Dorothy, illus. II. Title. III. Title: Bible story book.

ROBERTSON, Jenny. 220.9'505
The encyclopedia of Bible stories. Stories retold by Jenny Robertson. Illustrated by Gordon King. [1st ed.] Philadelphia, Holman [1974] 268 p. illus. 32 cm. "Fifty-one Old Testament narratives, from the Creation through the Prophets, and sixty-eight New Testament selections, from the Birth of Jesus through Revelation." [BS550.2.R6 1974] 74-1081 ISBN 0-87981-036-X 7.95
1. Bible stories, English. I. Title.

RUTLEDGE, Archibald Hamilton, 1883- 220.9'505
Voices of the long ago; Bible stories retold, by Archibald Rutledge. [Columbia, S.C., R. L. Bryan Co., c1973] vi, 96 p. 24 cm. [BS550.2.R87] 73-90805 5.95
1. Bible stories, English. I. Title.

SEGAL, Elizabeth. 220.95'05
Great stories from the Bible. Greenwich, Conn., Fawcett Publications [1966] 191 p. 18 cm. (A Fawcett crest book, R953) [BS550.2.S4] 66-22776
1. Bible stories, English. I. Title.

THE Taize picture 220.95'05
Bible: stories from the Scriptures, adapted from the text of the Jerusalem Bible. With illus. by Brother Eric de Saussure of the Taize Community. Philadelphia, Fortress Press [1969, c1968] 277 p. illus. (part col.), map (on lining paper) 24 cm. "The text on the Jerusalem translation has been altered for younger readers or listeners."—Jacket. London ed. (Darton, Longman & Todd) has title: Bible stories for children. A selection of 143 Old and New Testament stories from the creation of earth to the conversion of Saul. [BS551.2.B48 1969] 69-11860 4.95
1. Bible stories, English. I. Saussure, Eric de, illus. II. Title: Bible stories for children.

TAYLOR, Kenneth Nathaniel. 220.95'05
Taylor's Bible story book [by] Kenneth N. Taylor. Wheaton, Ill., Tyndale House Publishers [1971, c1970] 476 p. illus. 27 cm. One hundred ninety-eight stories retold from the Old and New Testaments. [BS551.2.T38] 76-123034 ISBN 0-8423-6700-4 6.95
1. Bible stories, English. I. Title. II. Title: Bible story book.

TURNER, Philip. 220.95'05
Brian Wildsmith's illustrated Bible stories, as told by Philip Turner. New York, F. Watts [1969] c1968. 134 p. col. illus. 28 cm. [BS551.2.T8 1969] 68-14250
1. Bible stories, English. I. Wildsmith, Brian, illus. II. Title. III. Title: Illustrated Bible stories.

VREUGDENHIL, John. 220.95'05
The Bible history; told to our children. With a pref. by A. Verhagen. Translated from the Holland language ... by John Van Grouw. [Grand Rapids? Mich.] Distributed by the Netherland Reformed Congregations of America [1971- v. 27 cm. Translation of De Bijbelse geschiedenis verteld aan onze kinderen. [BS551.2.V6613] 74-26487
1. Bible stories, English. I. Title.

WADDELL, Helen Jane, 1889-1965. 220.9'505
Stories from Holy writ / Helen Waddell. Westport, Conn. : Greenwood Press, 1975. xv, 280 p. ; 21 cm. Reprint of the 1949 ed. published by Constable, London. Retellings of fifteen Old and New Testament Bible stories originally written for publication in "Daybreak," a missionary magazine. [BS551.W2 1975] 74-25538 ISBN 0-8371-7872-X : 14.25
1. Bible stories, English. I. Title.

WESTPHAL, Barbara (Osborne) 220.95'05
Crazy pigs and other Bible stories, by Barbara Westphal. Washington, Review and Herald Pub. Association [1968] 95 p. illus. 24 cm. Ten stories about animals that appear in the Bible. Includes the dove from Noah's Ark, Jonah's whale, the Lion and Daniel, and others. [BS551.2.W4] 68-25112
1. Bible stories, English. I. Title.

WHITEHOUSE, Elizabeth Scott, 1893- 220.95'05
Bible stories to tell [by] Elizabeth S. Whitehouse. Valley Forge, Judson Press [1967] 221 p. 23 cm. [BS550.2.W4] 67-25892
1. Bible stories, English. I. Title.

221 Old Testament

ANDERSON, Bernard W., ed. 221
The Old Testament and Christian faith. New York, Harper [c.1963] 1v. 22cm. 63-15952 5.00
I. Title.

ARCHER, Gleason Leonard, Jr., 1916- 221
A survey of Old Testament introduction. Chicago, Moody [1964] 507p. illus., port. 25cm. Bibl. [BS1140.2.A7] 64-20988 6.95
1. Bible. O. T.-Introductions. I. Title. II. Title: Old Testament introduction.

ARCHER, Gleason Leonard, 1916- 221
A survey of Old Testament introduction, by Gleason L. Archer, Jr. Chicago, Moody Press [1964] 507 p. illus., port. 25 cm. Bibliographical footnotes. Bibliography: p. 479-481. [BS1140.2.A7] 64-20988
1. Bible. O. T.—Introductions. I. Title. II. Title: Old Testament introduction.

ARCHER, Gleason Leonard, 1916- 221
A survey of Old Testament introduction, by Gleason L. Archer, Jr. [Rev. ed.] Chicago, Moody Press [1974] 528 p. illus. 24 cm. Bibliography: p. 510-512. [BS1140.2.A7 1974] 74-176038 ISBN 0-8024-8446-8 7.95
1. Bible. O.T.—Introductions. I. Title. II. Title: Old Testament introduction.

BAMBERGER, Bernard Jacob, 1904- 221
The Bible: a modern Jewish approach. New York, B'nai B'rith Hillel Foundations, 1955. 96p. 18cm. (Hillel little books, v.2) Bibliography: p.94-96. [BS1140.B23] 55-10877
1. Bible. O.T.—Introductions. I. Title. II. Series.

BERGEY, Alyce 221
The world God made; the story of creation: Genesis 1 and 2 for children. Illus. by Obata Studio. St. Louis, Concordia c.1965. iv. (unpaged) col. illus. 21cm. (Arch bks., set 2, no. 59-1114) [BS551.2.B46] 63-23145 .35 pap.,
1. Bible stories, English—O. T. Genesis i-ii. I. Title.

BERKOVITS, Eliezer, 1908- 221
Man and God; studies in Biblical theology. Detroit, Wayne State University Press, 1969. 376 p. 24 cm. Bibliographical references included in "Notes" (p. 349-368) [BS1192.5.B46] 69-10735 12.50
1. Bible. O.T.—Theology. I. Title.

BIBLE. O.T. Aramaic. 221
Selections. 1971.
Interlinear Aramaic-English Old Testament. Translated by James S. Wallace [and] Frederick J. Schwartz. Illustrated by Daniel Fernandez. Berrien Springs, Mich., Andrews University, 1971. v, 135 l. illus. 28 cm. [BS1099.A3W3] 75-187578
I. Wallace, James S., tr. II. Schwartz, Frederick J., tr. III. Bible. O.T. English. Selections. 1971. IV. Title.

BIBLE. O. T. ENGLISH. 1962. 221
SIEWERT.
The amplified Old Testament [2d ed.] Grand Rapids, Mich., Zondervan [c.]1962. 1213p. 17cm. Ed., tr. by Frances E. Siewert. Contents.pt. 2. Job-Malachi. 62-1064 4.95
I. Siewert, Frances E., ed. and tr. II. Title.

BIBLE. O.T. English. 221
Selections. 1972.
The Book of Genesis, for the use of divinity students; history, prophecy and wisdom, samples of the divine word, translated and transliterated from the Hebrew, by Edward J. Tubbs. [Newport, Eng., Starling Press; distributed by Miles Bullivant Associates] 1973. 286 p. 13 cm. Cover title: History, prophecy and wisdom. Includes the Book of Genesis, Isaiah and Proverbs. [BS1091.T78] 74-176955
I. Tubbs, Edward J., tr. II. Title: History, prophecy and wisdom.

BIBLE. O.T. Five Scrolls. 221
English. New English. 1975.
The books of Ruth, Esther, Ecclesiastes, the Song of Songs, Lamentations : the Five Scrolls / commentary by Wesley J. Feurst. Cambridge, [Eng.] : Cambridge University Press, 1975. p. cm. (The Cambridge Bible commentary : New English Bible) Includes index. Bibliography: p. [BS1309.A3F48] 74-82589 ISBN 0-521-20651-0. ISBN 0-521-09920-X pbk.
1. Bible. O.T. Five Scrolls—Commentaries. I. Feurst, Wesley J. II. Title. III. Series.

BICKERMAN, Elias Joseph, 221
1897-
Four strange books of the Bible: Jonah, Daniel, Koheleth, Esther [by] Elias Bickerman. New York, Schocken Books [1968, c1967] vii, 240 p. illus. 22 cm. Includes bibliographical references. [BS1200.B5] 67-15748
1. Bible. O. T. Jonah—Criticism interpretation, etc. 2. Bible. O. T. Daniel—Criticism, interpretation, etc. 3. Bible. O. T. Ecclesiastes—Criticism, interpretation, etc. 4. Bible. O. T. Esther—Criticism, interpretation, etc. I. Title.

BOX, George Herbert, 1869- 221
1933.
Judaism in the Greek period, from the rise of Alexander the Great to the intervention of Rome (333 to 63 B.C.). Westport, Conn., Greenwood Press [1971] xiv, 239, [17] p. illus. 23 cm. (The Clarendon Bible, Old Testament, v. 5) "The Old Testament, chronologically arranged, by Evelyn W. Hippisley": p. [2]-[16] (3d group) Reprint of the 1932 ed. [BS1200.B69 1971] 73-109712 ISBN 0-8371-4288-1
1. Bible. O.T. Hagiographa—Commentaries. 2. Bible. O.T. Prophets—Commentaries. 3. Bible. O.T. Apocrypha—Commentaries. I. Title. II. Series.

BREISCH, Francis. 221
The kingdom of God; a guide for Old Testament study. Grand Rapids, National Union of Christian Schools, 1958. 243 p. illus. 23 cm. Includes bibliography. [BS1194.B7] 58-9442
1. Bible. O. T.—Study—Text-books. 2. Kingdom of God—Biblical teaching.

BRYANT, Verda Evelyn (Bilger) 221
Between the covers of the Old Testament, by Verda E. Bryant. Illustrated by Stele A. Bryant. Independence, Mo., Herald House [1965] 400 p. illus., maps. 21 cm. Bibliography: p. 400. [BS1193.B78] 65-28008
1. Bible. O. T. — Study. I. Title.

BRYANT, Verda Evelyn (Bilger) 221
Between the covers of the Old Testament. Illus. by Stele A. Bryant. Independence, Mo., Herald House [c.1965] 400p. illus., maps. 21cm. Bibl. [BS1193.B78] 65-28008 4.75
1. Bible. O.T. — Study. I. Title.

BUBER, Martin, 1878-1965. 221
On the Bible; eighteen studies. Edited by Nahum N. Glatzer. New York, Schocken Books [1968] vi, 247 p. 22 cm. Includes bibliographical references. [DS1192.B8] 68-16653 5.95
1. Bible. O.T.—Addresses, essays, lectures. I. Title.

CHASE, Mary Ellen, 1887- 221
Life and language in the Old Testament. New York, Norton [1962, c.1955] 197p. 20cm. (Norton lib., N109) Bibl. 1.45 pap.,
1. Bible, O. T.—Language, style. 2. Bible O. T.—Criticism, interpretation, etc. 3. Bible as literature. I. Title.

CHASE, Mary Ellen, 1887- 221
Life and language in the Old Testament. [1st ed.] New York, Norton [1955] 201 p. 22 cm. Includes bibliography. [BS535.C48] 55-13627
1. Bible. O.T.—Language, style. 2. Bible. O.T.—Criticism, interpretation, etc. 3. Bible as literature. I. Title.

EISSFELDT, Otto, 1887- 221
The Old Testament; an introduction, including the Apocrypha and Pseudepigrapha, and also the works of similar type from Qumran; the history of the formation of the Old Testament. Translated by Peter R. Ackroyd. New York, Harper and Row [1965] xxiv, 861 p. 26 cm. Translated from the 3d German ed. of a work first published in Tubingen in 1934 under title: Einleitung in das Alte Testament. Includes bibliographical references. [BS1140.E583] 65-15399
1. Bible. O.T. — Introductions. 2. Bible. O.T. — Apocrypha and Apocryphal books — Introductions. I. Title.

EISSFELDT, Otto, 1887- 221
The Old Testament; an introduction, including the Apocrypha and Pseudepigrapha, and also the works of similar type from Qumran; the history of the formation of the Old Testament. Tr. [from German]by Peter R. Ackroyd. New York, Harper [c.1965] xxiv, 861p. 26cm. From the 3d German ed. of a work first pub. in Tubingen in 1934. Bibl. [BS1140.E583] 65-15399 9.50
1. Bible. O. T.—Introductions. 2. Bible. O. T.—Apocrypha and Apocryphal books—Intoructions. I. Title.

EUDY, Susan Olyve. 221
A light that shines in dark places. Boston, Christopher Pub. House [1955] 68p. 21cm. [BS534.E9] 55-14539
I. Title.

EVANGELICAL Theological 221
Society.
New perspectives on the Old Testament. J. Barton Payne, editor. Waco, Tex., Word Books [1970] x, 305 p. 25 cm. (Its Symposium series, #3) Papers presented at the 20th annual meeting of the Evangelical Theological Society, Dec. 26-28, 1968. Includes bibliographical references. [BS1192.E9] 75-111958 6.95
1. Bible. O.T.—Addresses, essays, lectures. I. Payne, John Barton, 1922- ed. II. Title. III. Series.

GLUECK, Nelson, 1900- 221
Hesed in the Bible. Translated by Alfred Gottschalk, with an introd. by Gerald A. Larue. Edited by Elias L. Epstein. Cincinnati, Hebrew Union College Press, 1967. ix, 107 p. 24 cm. Translation of the author's dissertation, Jena, 1927, with title: Das Wort hesed im alttestamentlichen Sprachgebrauche als menschliche und gottliche gemeinschaftsgemasse Verhaltungsweise. [BS525.G653] 68-3695
1. Hesed (The word) 2. Bible. O. T.—Theology. I. Title.

GLUECK, Nelson, 1900- 221
Hesed in the Bible. Translated by Alfred Gottschalk, with an introd. by Gerald A. Larue. Edited by Elias L. Epstein. Cincinnati, Hebrew Union College Press, 1967. ix, 107 p. 24 cm. Translation of the author's dissertation, Jena, 1927, with title: Das Wort hesed im alttestamentlichen Sprachgebrauche als menschliche und gottliche gemeinschaftsgemasse Verhaltungsweise. Bibliography: p. 103-105. [BS525.G653] 68-3695
1. Bible. O.T.—Theology. 2. Hesed (The word) I. Title.

GORDIS, Robert, 1908- 221
Poets, prophets, and sages; essays in Biblical interpretation. Bloomington, Indiana University Press [1971] x, 436 p. 24 cm. Contents.Contents.—The Bible: its origin, growth, and meaning.—Primitive democracy in ancient Israel.—The structure of Biblical poetry.—The heptad as an element of Biblical and rabbinic style.—Quotations in Biblical, oriental, and rabbinic literature.—The social background of wisdom literature.—The knowledge of good and evil in the Old Testament and the Dead Sea scrolls.—The composition and structure of Amos.—Hosea's marriage and message.—Isaiah: prophet, thinker, world statesman.—Micah's vision of the end-time.—All men's book: the book of Job.—The temptation of Job.—The wisdom of Koheleth.—The Song of songs. Includes bibliographical references. [BS1192.G65 1971] 79-98984 ISBN 0-253-16655-1 15.00
1. Bible. O.T.—Addresses, essays, lectures. I. Title.

GROSS, Heinrich, 1916- 221
A Biblical introduction to the Old Testament. Notre Dame, University of Notre Dame Press [1968] vii, 142 p. 18 cm. (Contemporary catechetics series) Translation of Kleine Bibelkunde zum Alten Testament. Bibliographical references included in "Notes" (p. 137-142) [BS1140.2.G713] 68-25930 1.95
1. Bible. O.T.—Introductions. I. Title.

HAHN, Herbert Ferdinand, 221
1905-
Old Testament in modern research. Philadelphia, Muhlenberg Press [1954] 267p. 22cm. [BS1160.H3] 54-9179
1. Bible. O. T.—Criticism, interpretation, etc.—Hist. I. Title.

HARRINGTON, Wilfrid J 221
Record of the promise; the Old Testament [by] Wilfrid J. Harrington. Chicago, Priory Press [1965] xviii, 433 p. maps. 24 cm. "The Bible text ... is from the Revised standard version." Bibliography: p. 397-401. [BS1140.2.H32] 65-19357
1. Bible. O.T. — Introductions. I. Title.

HARRINGTON, Wilfrid J. 221
Record of the promise: the Old Testament [v.2] Chicago, Priory Pr. [c.1965] xviii, 433p. maps. 24cm. The Bible text is from the Revised standard version. Bibl. [BS1140.2.H32] 65-19357 7.50
1. Bible. O.T.—Introductions. I. Title.

HARRISON, Roland Kenneth 221
Archaeology of the Old Testament. New York, Harper, [1966.c.1963] xiii, 162p. illus., maps, port. 21cm. (Chapel Bks., CB24G) Bibl. [BS620.H35] 1.25 pap.,
1. Bible. O. T. — Antiq. I. Title.

HARRISON, Roland Kenneth. 221
Introduction to the Old Testament; with a comprehensive review of Old Testament studies and a special supplement on the Apocrypha, by R. K. Harrison. Grand Rapids, Eerdmans [1969] xvi, 1325 p. 24 cm. Bibliographical footnotes. [BS1140.2.H35] 64-22030 12.50
1. Bible. O.T.—Introductions. 2. Bible. O.T. Apocrypha—Introductions. I. Title.

HEINISCH, Paul, 1878- 221
Theology of the Old Testament. English ed. by William Heidt. Collegeville, Minn., Liturgical Press [1950] 386 p. 24 cm. A translation from the ms. of rev. ed. of Theologie des Alten Testamentes. Bibliography: p. 336-358. [BM605.H413] 50-4198
1. Bible. O. T.—Theology. I. Title.

HENSHAW, Thomas 221
The Writings; the third division of the Old Testament canon. London, Allen & Unwin [dist. New York, Humanities, c.1963] 397 p. 23 cm. Bibl. 63-4469 8.50
1. Bible. O.T. Hagiographa—Introductions. I. Title.

HORTON, Naomi. 221
The story of Esther. [Milwaukee, Northwestern Pub. House, c1960] 61 p. illus. 18 cm. [BS551.2.H65] 60-12504
1. Esther, Queen of Persia — Juvenile literature. 2. Bible stories. English — O. T. Esther. I. Title.

JONES, Alexander, 1906- 221
Unless some man show me. New York, Sheed and Ward, 1951. 162 p. 20 cm. [BS1171.J57] 51-12715
1. Bible. O. T.—Criticism, interpretation, etc. I. Title.

*JOWETT, J. H. 1864-1923 221
The eagle life and other studies in the Old Testament. / K. H. Jowett. Grand Rapids : Baker Book House, 1976c1922. vii, 164p. ; 20 cm. (His Library) [BS600.] ISBN 0-8010-5066-9 pbk. : 2.95.
1. Bible-Sermons-O. T. I. Title.

KLAPERMAN, Gilbert 221
The how and why wonder book of the Old Testament. Illus. by John Hull. Ed. production: Donald D. Wolf. Ed. under the supervision of Paul E. Blackwood. Text, illus. approved by Oakes A. White [Deluxe ed.] New York, Grosset [c.1964] 47p. illus. (pt. col.) 29cm. (How and why wonder bks., 4049) 64-14937 bds., 1.00; lib. ed., 2.08; pap., .50
1. Bible. O. T.—Juvenile literature I. Title.

LAURIN, Robert B., 1927- 221
The layman's introduction to the Old Testament [by] Robert B. Laurin. Valley Forge [Pa.] Judson Press [1970] 160 p. 22 cm. Includes bibliographies. [BS1140.2.L37] 70-88114 2.95
1. Bible. O.T.—Introductions. I. Title.

THE Law and the prophets : 221
Old Testament studies prepared in honor of Oswald Thompson Allis / John H. Skilton, general editor ; Milton C. Fisher, Leslie W. Sloat, associate editors. [Nutley, N.J.] : Presbyterian and Reformed Pub. Co., 1974. xxv, 499 p., [1] leaf of plates : port. ; 23 cm. Bibliography: p. 20-28. [BS1192.L35] 73-84667 12.50
1. Allis, Oswald Thompson, 1880-1973. 2. Allis, Oswald Thompson, 1880-1973—Bibliography. 3. Bible. O.T.—Addresses, essays, lectures. I. Allis, Oswald Thompson, 1880-1973. II. Skilton, John H. III. Fisher, Milton C. IV. Sloat, Leslie W.

LEISHMAN, Thomas Linton, 221
1900-
The interrelation of the Old and New Testaments. [1st ed.] New York, Vantage Press [1968] 299 p. 21 cm. Bibliographical footnotes. [BS2387.L4] 78-355 4.95
1. Bible. N.T.—Relation to O.T. 2. Bible—Criticism, interpretation, etc. I. Title.

LESSING, Erich. 221
The Bible: history and culture of a people; a pictorial narration by Erich Lessing. Foreword by David Ben-Gurion. [Translation by Kevin Smyth. New York] Herder and Herder [1970] 307 p. illus. (part col.), maps. 31 cm. Translation of Verite et poesie de la Bible. [BS540.L4513] 70-111020 33.00
1. Bible—Addresses, essays, lectures. 2. Bible—Antiquities. I. Title.

LOHFINK, Norbert. 221
The Christian meaning of the Old Testament. Translated by R. A. Wilson. Milwaukee, Bruce Pub. Co. [1968] ix, 169 p. 22 cm. Translation of Das Siegeslied am Schilfmeer. [BS1192.L613] 68-28444
1. Bible. O.T.—Addresses, essays, lectures. I. Title.

LYON, Thoburn Cassady, 1896- 221
Witness in the sky. Chicago, Moody [c.1961] 128p. illus. Bibl. 61-66179 2.50
1. God—Miscellanea. I. Title.

MACARTNEY, Clarence Edward 221
Noble, 1879-
The parables of the Old Testament. Grand Rapids, Baker Book House, 1955. 122p. 21cm. [BS1199] 55-10432
1. Bible. O.T.—Parables. I. Title.

MAISLER, Benjamin, 1906- ed. 221
Views of the Biblical world. [Editorial board: chariman, Benjamin Mazar: editors, Michael Avi-Yonah and Abraham Amlamat] 1st international ed. Chicago, Jordan Publications, 1959- v. illus. 30 cm. [BS621.P414] 9084 59-7767
1. Bible. O.T. — Antiq. 2. Near East — Antiq. 3. Bible. O.T. — Pictures, illustrations, etc. I. Title.

*MEARS, Henrietta C. 221
A look at the Old Testament; an abridge survey, Genesis-Malachi. Glendale, Calif. [Gospel Lignt Pubns., 1966] 263p. 18cm. (Regal bks., G195-1) .95 pap.,
I. Title.

MURPHY, John, 1876-1949. 221
The origins and history of religions. [New York] Philosophical Library [1952] 453p. 22cm. Bibliographical footnotes. [BL80.M] A 53
1. Religions. I. Title.

NEAR Eastern studies in honor 221
of William Foxwell Albright. Edited by Hans Goedicke. Baltimore, Johns Hopkins Press [1971] xxvi, 474 p. illus., facsims. 23 cm. English, French or German. Includes bibliographical references. [BS1192.N4] 70-142817 ISBN 0-8018-1235-6 15.00
1. Bible. O.T.—Addresses, essays, lectures. I. Albright, William Foxwell, 1891- II. Goedicke, Hans, ed.

NICOLL, William Robertson, 221
Sir 1851-1923, ed.
139 sermon outlines on the Old Testament. Grand Rapids, Baker Book House, 1957. 292p.

20cm. 'Reprint of the 1887 printing by Hodder and Stoughton.' [BS1151.N45] 57-8564
1. Bible. O. T.—Sermons—Outlines. I. Title.

NOTRE Dame, Ind. University. 221
Dept. of Theology.
Introduction to college theology through sacred Scripture, a course designed for college students. Notre Dame, Ind., University of Notre Dame Press [1963] 158 p. 23 cm. "Presented as the fruit of discussions by a committee invited by Reverend Robert S. Pelton, C.S.C., head of the Department of Theology at the University of Notre Dame ... The meetings were held there during the 1963 summer session." Includes bibliographies. [BS592.I5] 63-22222
1. Bible — Study — Outlines, syllabi, etc. 2. Bible — Theology — Study and teaching. I. Title.

PROCLAMATION and presence; 221
Old Testament essays in honour of Gwynne Henton Davies. Edited by John I. Durham & J. R. Porter. Richmond, John Knox Press [1970] xx, 315 p. port. 23 cm. Contents.Contents.—Gwynne Henton Davies; a biographical appreciation.—A bibliography of the writings of Gwynne Henton Davies.—Old Testament hermeneutics. The limits of Old Testament interpretation, by N. W. Porteous.—The Hexateuch. What do we know about Moses? By G. Widengren.—The revelation of the divine name YHWH, by R. de Vaux.—The Deuteronomic legislator; a proto-Rabbinic type, by J. Weingreen.—Gilgal or Shechem? By O. Eissfeldt.—The succession of Joshua, by J. R. Porter.—The former prophets and the latter prophets. All the King's horses? By D. R. Ap-Thomas.—Elijah at Horeb; reflections on I Kings 19.9-18, by E. Wurthwein.—Prophet and covenant: observations on the exegesis of Isaiah, by W. Eichrodt.—Jeremiah's complaints: liturgy or expressions of personal distress? By J. Bright.—Baruch the scribe, by J. Muilenberg.—Shiloh, the customary laws and the return of the ancient kings, by H. Cazelles.—The Psalms. Psalm 23 and the household of faith, by A. R. Johnson.—Shalom and the presence of God, by J. I. Durham. Includes bibliographical references. [BS1192.P75 1970] 71-85517 9.95
1. Bible. O.T.—Addresses, essays, lectures. I. Davies, Gwynne Henton. II. Durham, John I., 1933- ed. III. Porter, Joshua Roy, ed.

RAD, Gerhard von, 1901- 221
Old Testament theology. Translated by D. M. G. Stalker. Edinburgh, Oliver and Boyd, 1962- v. 25cm. Contents.v. 1. The theology of Israel's historical traditions. [BS1192.5.R313] 62-51431
1. Bible. O. T.—Theology. I. Title.

RHYMER, Joseph, 1927- 221
Companion to the Good news Old Testament / [by] Joseph Rhymer and Anthony Bullen. [London] : Fontana, 1976. 223 p. : maps, plan ; 18 cm. (Fontana theology and philosophy series) [BS1140.2.R45] 77-373914 ISBN 0-00-623354-6 : £0.95
1. Bible. O.T.—Introductions. I. Bullen, Anthony Francis, joint author. II. Title.

ROBERT, Andre, 1883-1955, 221
ed.
Introduction to the Old Testament [by] A. Robert [and] A. Feuillet. Translated from the second French ed. by Patrick W. Skehan [and others] New York, Desclee Co. [1968] xxv, 650 p. maps. (part col.) 23 cm. Translation of Introduction a la Bible, vol. I, Ancien Testament. Includes bibliographies. [BS2330.2.R612] 68-25351 9.95
1. Bible—Introductions. I. Feuillet, Andre, joint ed. II. Title.

ROSNER, Joseph, 1922- 221
The story of the writings. Edited by Eugene B. Borowitz. Illus. by Stephen Kraft. New York, Behrman House [1970] 159 p. illus. 24 cm. [BS1308.R67] 78-116680 ISBN 0-87441-038-X
1. Bible. O.T. Hagiographa—Criticism, interpretation, etc. I. Title.

ROWLEY, Harold Henry, 1890- 221
The growth of the Old Testament. London, New York, Hutchinson's University Library, 1950. 192 p. 19 cm. (Hutchinson's university library: Christian religion, no. 45) Bibliography: p. 175-179. [BS1140.R66] 51-3831
1. Bible. O.T. — Introductions. I. Title.

SANDMEL, Samuel, comp. 221
Old Testament issues. [1st ed.] New York, Harper & Row [1968] xiv, 267 p. 21 cm. (Harper forum books, RD7) Includes bibliographical references. [BS1192.S2] 68-17600 3.50
1. Bible. O.T.—Addresses, essays, lectures. I. Title.

SANFORD, Agnes Mary (White) 221
The healing power of the Bible [by] Agnes Sanford. [1st ed.] Philadelphia, Lippincott [1970, c1969] 221 p. 21 cm. [BS571.S25] 75-88737 4.95
1. Bible. O.T.—Biography. 2. Miracles. I. Title.

SEVENTH-DAY Adventists. 221
General Conference. Dept. of Education.
Life and times of the Old Testament. Rev. ed. Mountain View, Calif., Pacific Press Pub. Association [1957] 568p. illus. 24cm. Includes bibliography. [BS1194.S4 1957] 57-44920
1. Bible. O.T.—Study—Text-books. I. Title.

SEVENTH-DAY ADVENTISTS. 221
GENERAL CONFERENCE. DEPT. OF EDUCATION.
Life and times of the Old Testament. Rev. ed. Mountain View, Calif., Pacific Press Pub. Association [1957] 568 p. illus. 24 cm. Includes bibliography. [BS1194.S4 1957] 57-44920
1. Bible. O.T. — Study — Text books. I. Title.

SIMPSON, Cuthbert Aikman, 221
1892-1969.
Revelation and response in the Old Testament, by Cuthbert A. Simpson. New York, Columbia University Press. New York, AMS Press [1972] viii, 197 p. 19 cm. Reprint of the 1947 ed., issued in the series: The Bishop Paddock lectures. [BM165.S55 1972] 73-176022 ISBN 0-404-06056-0 5.00
1. Judaism—History—To 70 A.D. I. Series: The Paddock lectures.

STILSON, Max. 221
Major religions of the world. Grand Rapids, Zondervan Pub. House [1964] 123 p. 21 cm. Bibliography: p. 113-123. [BL80.2.S74] 64-11951
1. Religions. I. Title.

THOMSON, James G S S 221
The Old Testament view of revelation. Grand Rapids, Eerdmans [1960] 107 p. 21 cm. Includes bibliography. [BS1199.R4T48] 60-10095
1. Revelation—Biblical teaching. 2. Bible. O. T.—Theology. I. Title.

THOMSON, James G. S. S. 221
The Old Testament view of revelation. Grand Rapids, Mich., Eerdmans [c.1960] 107p. Bibl. 60-10095 2.50
1. Revelation—Biblical teaching. 2. Bible. O. T.—Theology. I. Title.

VOS, Howard Frederick, 1925- 221
Beginnings in the Old Testament : [an introductory guide to the Old Testament] / by Howard F. Vos. Chicago : Moody Press, [1975] 191 p. ; 22 cm. Bibliography: p. 190-191. [BS1140.2.V65] 74-15345 ISBN 0-8024-0610-6 : 2.95
1. Bible. O.T.—Introductions. I. Title.

*WEAVER, Horace R. 221
The everlasting covenant; content and value of the Old Testament. Nashville, Graded Pr. [dist. Abingdon [c.1965] 231p. 19cm. 2.50 pap.,
I. Title.

WEST, James King, 1930- 221
Introduction to the Old Testament: "Hear, O Israel." New York, Macmillan [1971] xxiv, 546 p. illus., maps. 24 cm. "This book and its companion, 'Introduction to the New Testament: 'The word became flesh,' by Donald J. Selby are available in a one-volume edition entitled 'Introduction to the Bible,' by Donald J. Selby and James King West." Includes bibliographies. [BS1140.2.W478] 74-152820
1. Bible. O.T.—Introductions. I. Selby, Donald Joseph. Introduction to the New Testament: "The word became flesh." II. Selby, Donald Joseph. Introduction to the Bible. III. Title.

WESTON, Sidney A. 221
The prophets and the problems of life. [rev. ed.] Boston, Whittemore [c.1963] 96p. illus. 19cm. .75 pap.,
I. Title.

WILLIAMS, Jay G. 221
Understanding the Old Testament [by] Jay G. Williams. New York, Barron's Educational Series, inc. [1972] ix, 340 p. 22 cm. "Gloria M. Barron editions." Bibliography: p. 331-340. [BS1140.2.W54] 74-162825 ISBN 0-8120-0424-8 2.95
1. Bible. O.T.—Introductions. I. Title.

WOOD, Jean H 1907- 221
Masterpieces of Old Testament literature. Pupil's book. Chicago, Published for the Cooperative Publication Association by the Judson Press [1954] Chicago, Published for the Cooperative Publication Association by the Judson Press [1954] 110p. illus. 23cm. 144p. 20cm. [BS1194.W63] 54-4620
1. Bible. O.T.—Study—Text-books. 2. Week-day church schools—Text-books. I. Title. II. Title: —Teacher's book.

WRIGHT, George Ernest, 1909- 221
The Old Testament and theology, by G. Ernest Wright. [1st ed.] New York, Harper & Row [1969] 190 p. 21 cm. Bibliographical footnotes. [BS1192.5.W7] 69-17022 6.00
1. Bible. O.T.—Theology. I. Title.

YOHN, David Waite. 221
The Christian reader's guide to the Old Testament. Grand Rapids, Eerdmans [1972] 200 p. 22 cm. [BS1199.C6Y64] 70-151984 ISBN 0-8028-1368-2 3.45
1. Bible. O.T.—Criticism, interpretation, etc. 2. Covenants (Theology)—Sermons. 3. Sermons, American. I. Title.

YOUNGBLOOD, Ronald F. 221
Great themes of the Old Testament, by Ronald F. Youngblood. Chicago, Harvest Publications [1968] 133 p. port. 20 cm. (A Harvest learning-for-serving book) Bibliography: p. 130. [BS1192.5.Y65] 68-17861
1. Bible. O.T.—Theology. I. Title.

ZIMMERMANN, Frank. 221
Biblical books translated from the Aramaic / by Frank Zimmermann. New York : Ktav Pub. House, [1975] viii, 183 p. ; 24 cm. Includes indexes. Bibliography: p. 169-170. [BS1308.A4A78] 74-34107 ISBN 0-87068-252-0 : 12.50
1. Bible. O.T. Hagiographa. Aramaic—Versions. 2. Bible. O.T. Hagiographa—Language, style. I. Title.

SCHULTZ, Samuel J. 221.002
Old Testament survey; law and history. Wheaton, Ill., Box 327, Evangelical Teacher Training Assn. c.1964. 94p. map. 28cm. (Evangelical Teacher Training Assn., Certificate ser., unit 1) Bibl. 64-10037 1.35 pap., plastic bds.
1. Bible. O. T.—Study—Outlines, syllabi, etc. I. Title.

ADAM, Ben 221.007
The origin of heathendom. Minneapolis 31, 6820 Auto Club Rd. Bethany Fellowship, [c.1963] 128p. 19cm. 1.50 pap.,
I. Title.

*SCHULTZ, Samuel J. 221.007
Enriching your teaching of the E.T.T.A. course. Wheaton, Ill., Evangelical Teacher Training Assn., Bx. 327, c.1964. unpaged. 29cm. .85, pap., plastic bdg.
I. Title.
Contents omitted.

ROWLEY, Harold Henry, 221.0081
1890-
From Moses to Qumran; studies in the Old Testament. New York, Association Press [1963] xiv, 293 p. 22 cm. Bibliographical footnotes. [BS1192.R64] 63-16046
1. Bible. O. T. — Addresses, essays, lectures. I. Title.

ROWLEY, Harold Henry, 221.0081
1890-
From Moses to Qumran; studies in the Old Testament. New York, Association [c.1963] xiv, 93p. 22cm. Bibl. 63-16046 7.50
1. Bible. O.T.—Addresses, essays, lectures. I. Title.

JOHNSON, Aubrey Rodway 221.019
The vitality of the individual in the thought of ancient Israel [2d ed.] Cardiff, Univ. of Wales Pr. [dist. Mystic, Conn., Verry, 1965] xi, 154p. 23cm. Bibl. [BS1199.P9J6] 65-29536 4.00
1. Soul. 2. Bible. O.T. — Psychology. I. Title.

ACKERMAN, Robert William, 221.02
1910-
Review notes and study guide to the Old Testament, by Robert Ackerman, Ruth H. Blackburn, Unicio J. Violi. New York, Monarch Pr. [1966, c.1964] 169p. 21cm. (Monarch review notes and study guides, 626) Bibl. [BS1193] 65-7167 2.50
1. Bible. O.T. — Study — Outlines, syllabi, etc. I. Blackburn, Ruth Harriett, 1915- joint author. II. Violi, Unicio Jack, joint author. III. Title.

ZWEMER, Samuel Marinus, 221.02
1867-
Sons of Adam; studies of Old Testament characters in New Testament light. Pref. by Emile Cailliet. Grand Rapids, Baker Book House, 1951. 164 p. 20 cm. [BS571.Z9] 51-2736
1. Bible. O. T. — Biog. I. Title.

*BIBLE. O.T. English 221.0202
The Old Testament; notes, including introduction, outline of Old Testament history, order of the writings, summaries and commentaries, chronology, selected bibliography, by Charles H. Patterson. Lincoln, Neb., Cliff's Notes [c.1965] 96p. 22cm. Bibl. 1.00 pap.,
1. Bible. O.T. Commentaries. I. Patterson, Charles H. II. Title.

MYERS, Franklin G. 221'.02'02
The Old Testament. Prepared by Franklin G. Myers. New York, Barnes & Noble [1968] 94 p. 22 cm. (Barnes & Noble book notes) "This guide uses as its source the Authorized, or King James, translation." Bibliography: p. 94. [BS1193.M885] 68-21337 1.00 (1.10 Can)
1. Bible. O.T.—Study—Outlines, syllabi, etc. I. Title.

VAN DOOREN, L. A. T. 221'.02'02
Introducing the Old Testament, by L. A. T. Van Dooren. [1st ed.] Grand Rapids, Zondervan [1967] 192p. 23cm. Bibl. [BS1140.2.V3] 67-17237 4.95 bds.,
1. Bible. O. T.—Introducions. I. Title.

WESTERMANN, Claus. 221'.02'02
Handbook to the Old Testament. Translated and edited by Robert H. Boyd. Minneapolis, Augsburg Pub. House [1967] xvi, 285 p. illus., col. maps (on lining papers) 22 cm. Based on the introduction and Old Testament sections of the author's Abriss der Bibelkunde. Includes bibliographical references. [BS1193.W4] 67-25362
1. Bible. O.T.—Study—Outlines, syllabi, etc. I. Westerman, Claus. Abriss der Bibelkunde. II. Boyd, Robert Henry, ed. and tr. III. Title.

HOBBS, Edward C ed. 221.04
A stubborn faith; papers on Old Testament and related subjects presented to honor William Andrew Irwin. Dallas, Southern Methodist University Press, 1956. xii, 170p. 21cm. Bibliographical footnotes. [BS413.H6] 56-12567
1. Irwin, William Andrew, 1884- 2. Bible. O. T.—Addresses, essays, lectures. I. Title.
Contents omitted.

ENGNELL, Ivan, 1906-1964. 221'.06
A rigid scrutiny; critical essays on the Old Testament. Translated from the Swedish and edited by John T. Willis, with the Collaboration of Helmer Ringgren. Nashville, Vanderbilt University Press, 1969. xiv, 303 p. port. 25 cm. Translation of essays published originally in Svenskt bibliskt uppslagsverk, 2d ed., 1962. Bibliographical footnotes. [BS1171.2.E5 1969] 70-76166 10.00
1. Bible. O.T.—Criticism, interpretation, etc. I. Title.

FISKE, Arland O. 221.06
Search: Old Testament survey 2. Minneapolis, Augsburg, c.1962. 52p. 22cm. pap., .75; instructor's guide, pap., .75
I. Title.

NORDEN, Rudolph F 221.06
Parables of the Old Testament, by Rudolph F. Norden. Grand Rapids, Baker Book House, 1964. 101 p. 21 cm. [BS1199.P3N6] 64-16939
1. Bible. O.T. — Parables. 2. Bible. O.T. — Homiletical use. I. Title.

NORDEN, Rudolph F. 221.06
Parables of the Old Testament. Grand Rapids. Mich., Baker Bk. [c.]1964. 101p. 21cm. 64-16939 1.95
1. Bible. O. T.—Parables. 2. Bible. O. T.—Homiletical use. I. Title.

ROTH, Wolfgang M W 221.06
Numerical sayings in the Old Testament. A form-critical study, by W. M.Roth. Leiden, E. J. Brill, 1965 [1966] 116 p. 25 cm. (Supplements to Vetus testamentum, v. 13) fl 24.- (Ne66-1) [BS410.V452 vol. 13] 67-110481
1. Bible. O. T.—Criticism, Form. 2. Numbers in the Bible. I. Title. II. Series: Vetus testamentum. Supplements, v. 13

ROWLEY, Harold Henry, 221.06
1890-
The faith of Israel; aspects of Old Testament thought. Philadelphia, Westminster Press [1957] 220p. 23cm. [BS1192.5.R65 1957] 57-5060
1. Bible. O.T.—Theology. I. Title.

TOS, Aldo J 221.06
Approaches to the Bible; the Old Testament. Englewood Cliffs, N. J., Prentice-Hall, 1963. 286 p. illus. 25 cm. "Quotations from the first eight books, the sapietnial books, the prophetic books of the Old Testament, and the books of the New Testament are from Confraternity of Christian Doctrine translation... Oter Biblical quotations are from the Dousy version." Includes bibliography. [BS1140.2.T6] 63-9966
1. Bible. O. T. — Introductions. I. Title.

TOS, Aldo J., Rev. 221.06
Approaches to the Bible: the Old Testament. Englewood Cliffs, N.J., Prentice [c.]1963. 286p. illus. 25cm. Bibl. 63-9966 5.25, pap., plastic bds.
1. Bible. O. T.—Introductions. I. Title.

WESTERMANN, Claus, ed. 221.06
Essays on Old Testament hermeneutics. English translation edited by James Luther Mays. Richmond, John Knox Press [1963] 363 p. 21 cm. Translation of Probleme alttestamentlicher Hermeneutik. Includes bibliography. [BS476.W473 1963] 63-10637
1. Bible. O.T.—Hermeneutics—Addresses, essays, lectures. I. Title.

ADAR, Zvi. 221'.07
Humanistic values in the Bible. [Tr. from Hebrew by Mrs. Victor Tcherikover] New York, Reconstructionist Pr., 1967. 429p. 22cm. Tr. (romanized): ha-'Arakhim ha-hinukhiyim shel ha-Tanakh. [BS1193.A313] 67-24730 6.50
1. Bible. O. T.—Study. I. Title.

ADAR, Zvi. 221'.07
Humanistic values in the Bible. [Translated from the Hebrew by Mrs. Victor Tcherikover] New York, Reconstructionist Press, 1967. 429 p. 22 cm. Translation (romanized: ha-Arakhim ha-hinukhiyim shel ha-Tanakh) [BS1193.A313] 67-24730
1. Bible. O. T.—Study I. Title.

GINN, D Perry. 221.07
A study of the Old Testament [by] D. Perry Ginn [and] Eugene Chamberlain. James C. Barry, editor. Nashville, Broadman Press [1963] 192 p. 21 cm. (The Weekday Bible study series) "Teacher's book for use with 14 year olds." Includes bibliographical references. [BS1193.G45] 63-19070
1. Bible. O. T. — Study. I. Chamberlain, Eugene, joint author. II. Title.

GINN, D. Perry 221.07
A study of the Old Testament [by] D. Perry Ginn, Eugene Chamberlain. student's bk., for use with 14 year olds. James C. Barry, ed. Nashville, Broadman [c.1963] 192p. 21cm. (Weekday Bible study ser.) Bibl. 63-19070 pap., 1.00; Teacher's bk., pap., 2.75
1. Bible. O.T.—Study. I. Chamberlain, Eugene, joint author. II. Title.

LACE, O. Jessie 221.07
Teaching the Old Testament. Foreword by Cuthbert A. Simpson. Greenwich, Conn., Seabury Press [c.]1960. 79p. (bibl.) 21cm. 60-5361 1.65 pap.,
1. Bible. O. T.—Study I. Title.

MYERS, Jacob Martin, 1904- 221.07
Invitation to the Old Testament [by] Jacob M. Myers. [1st ed.] Garden City, N. Y., Doubleday, 1966. x, 252 p. 25 cm. Bibliography: p. [231]-238. [BS1193.M9] 66-12216
1. Bible. O. T.—Study. I. Title.

POWER, John, 1927- 221'.07
History of salvation; introducing the Old Testament. Staten Island, N.Y., Alba House [1967] 199 p. 21 cm. Dublin ed. (Gill) has title: Set my exiles free. [BS1193.P6] 67-6847
1. Bible. O.T.—Study—Outlines, syllabi, etc. 2. Bible. O.T.—Introductions. I. Title.

POWER, John, 1927- 221'.07
Set my exiles free; introducing the Old Testament. Dublin, Gill [1967] 199 p. 20 cm. (Logos books) American ed. (Staten Island, N.Y., Alba House) has title: History of salvation. [BS1193.P6 1967b] 74-238533 18s/-
1. Bible. O.T.—Study—Outlines, syllabi, etc. 2. Bible. O.T.—Introductions. I. Title.

TUCK, William C 221.07
Step by step introduction to the Old Testament; a programed study of the Biblical story for junior highs and up, for home or class use preparatory to discussion of the relevance and meaning for today of these Old Testament personalities and events. New York, Association Press [1963] 144 p. 23 cm. [BS592.T8] 63-160489
1. Bible. O.T. — Study — Text-books. I. Title.

TUCK, William C. 221.07
Step by step introduction to the Old Testament; a programed study of the Biblical story for junior highs and up, for home or class use preparatory to discussion of the relevance and meaning for today of these Old Testament personalities and events. New York, Association [c.1963] 144p. 23cm. 63-16048 3.00 pap.,
1. Bible. O. T. — Study—Text-books. I. Title.

TURNBULL, Ralph G 221.07
Early Hebrew history. Grand Rapids, Baker Book House, 1964. 99 p. 22 cm. (Bible companion series for lesson and sermon preparation) [BS1193.T8] 64-3866
1. Bible. O. T. — Study — Outlines, syllabi, etc. I. Title.

TURNBULL, Ralph G. 221.07
Early Hebrew history. Grand Rapids, Mich., Baker Bk. [c.]1964. 99p. 22cm. (Bible companion ser. for lesson and sermon preparation) 64-3866 1.00 pap.,
1. Bible. O. T.—Study—Outlines, syllabi, etc. I. Title.

ACKERMAN, James 221'.07'12
Stokes.
Teaching the Old Testament in English classes, by James S. Ackerman, and Alan Wilkin Jenks and Edward B. Jenkinson, with Jan Blough. Bloomington, Indiana University Press [1973] xvii, 494 p. 21 cm. (Indiana University English curriculum study series) Based on On teaching the Bible as literature, by J. S. Ackerman, with J. S. Hawley. Bibliography: p. 443-464. [BS1197.A23 1973] 72-93907 ISBN 0-253-35785-3 4.95 (pbk.)
1. Bible. O.T.—History of Biblical events. 2. Bible. O.T.—Study. I. Title. II. Series.

*FRASER, T. Layton 221.076
A survey of the Old Testament [a study guide 6th ed. rev.] Grand Rapids, Mich., Eerdmans [1965, c.1962] 261p. maps. 24cm. Bibl. 3.75
I. Title.

BARBOUR, Hugh. 221.077
Reading and understanding the Old Testament. New York, Association Press [1965] 320 p. maps. 23 cm. (An Association Press programed instruction book) Includes bibliographies. [BS1194.B3] 65-11090
1. Bible. O.T. — Study. I. Title.

JANZEN, Waldemar. 221'.08 s
Mourning cry and woe oracle / Waldemar Janzen. Berlin ; New York : De Gruyter, 1972. 91 p. ; 24 cm. (Beiheft zur Zeitschrift fur die alttestamentliche Wissenschaft ; 125) "The present monograph represents, by and large, the second part of the author's doctoral dissertation, which was accepted by the Department of Near Eastern Languages and Literatures of Harvard University in the spring of 1969." Includes bibliographical references. [BS410.Z5 vol. 125] [BS1199.D3] 231'.8 75-500109 ISBN 3-11-003848-X
1. Judgment of God—Biblical teaching. 2. Hoi (The Hebrew word) I. Title. II. Series: Zeitschrift fur die alttestamentliche Wissenschaft. Beihefte ; 125.

ROGERSON, John William. 221'.08 s
Myth in Old Testament interpretation / J. W. Rogerson. Berlin ; New York : De Gruyter, 1974. vi, 206 p. ; 24 cm. (Beiheft zur Zeitschrift fur die alttestamentliche Wissenschaft ; 134) Includes indexes. Bibliography: p. [190]-201. [BS410.Z5 vol. 134] [BS1183] 221.6'8 73-78234 ISBN 3-11-004220-7 : 33.80
1. Myth in the Old Testament. I. Title. II. Series: Zeitschrift fur die alttestamentliche Wissenschaft. Beihefte ; 134.

WHYBRAY, R. N. 221'.08 s
The intellectual tradition in the Old Testament / R. N. Whybray. Berlin ; New York : De Gruyter, 1974. xii, 158 p. ; 24 cm. (Beiheft zur Zeitschrift fur die alttestamentliche Wissenschaft ; 135) Includes bibliographical references and index. [BS410.Z5 vol. 135] [BS1455] 223 73-78236 ISBN 3-11-004424-2 : 30.20
1. Wisdom literature—Criticism, Textual. 2. Wisdom—Biblical teaching. I. Title. II. Series: Zeitschrift fur die alttestamentliche Wissenschaft. Beihefte ; 135.

GORDON, Cyrus Herzl, 221.095
1908-
Introduction to Old Testament times. Ventnor, N. J., Ventnor Publishers [c1953] 312p. 21cm. [BS635.G74] 53-5798
1. Bible. O. T.—History of contemporary events, etc. I. Title. II. Title: Old Testament times.

LEWY, Immanuel. 221.1
The birth of the Bible, a new approach. With an introd. by Mordecai M. Kaplan. [New York,] Selling agent: Bloch Pub. Co. [1950] 254 p. 24 cm. [BS1171.L48] 50-3436
1. Bible. O. T—Criticism, interpretation, etc. I. Title.

MOWINCKEL, Sigmund Olaf 221.1
Plytt, 1884-
The Old Testament as Word of God. Translated by Reidar B. Bjornard. New York, Abingdon Press [1959] 144 p. 21 cm. [BT89.M653] 59-10365
1. Bible. O. T.—Evidences, authority, etc. I. Title.

PATTERSON, Charles Henry, 221.1
1897-
The philosophy of the Old Testament. New York, Ronald Press Co. [1953] 557p. 22cm. [BS645.P3] 53-5704
1. Bible—Philosophy. I. Title.

WILSON, Robert Dick, 1856- 221.1
1930.
A scientific investigation of the Old Testament. With revisions by Edward J. Young. Chicago, Moody Press [1959] 194 p. 22 cm. Includes bibliography. [BS1171.W57 1959] 59-11466
1. Bible. O. T. — Evidences, authority, etc. I. Title.

YAMAUCHI, Edwin M. 221.1
Composition and corroboration in classical and Biblical studies [by] Edwin Yamauchi. Philadelphia, Presbyterian and Reformed Pub. Co., 1966. 38 p. 23 cm. (International library of philosophy and theology: Biblical and theological studies) "An expanded revision of a paper read at the Twentieth Annual Convention of the American Scientific Affiliation, August 24, 1965, at the King's College, Briarcliffe, New York." Bibliographical footnotes. [BS1180.Y3] 66-18123
1. Bible. O.T.—Evidences, authority, etc. 2. Bible. O.T.—Criticism, interpretation, etc. I. Title. II. Series.

EPSTEIN, Morris, 1922- 221.105
A book of Torah readings. Paintings by Ezekiel Schloss. [New York 2.] 65 Suffolk St., Ktav Pub. House, c. 1959, 1960. 111 p. illus. (pt. col.) 60-11069 1.50, bds.
1. Bible. O. T. Pentateuch—Paraphrases. I. Title. II. Title: Torah readings.

SUELZER, Alexa 221.106
The Pentateuch; a study in salvation history [New York] Herder & Herder [c.1964] 224p. 22cm. Bibl. 64-19739 4.75
1. Bible. O. T. Pentateuch—Criticism, interpretation, etc. I. Title.

ROUTLEY, Erik. 221.1106
Beginning the Old Testament; studies in Genesis and Exodus for the general reader. Philadelphia, Muhlenberg Press [1962] 159p. 19cm. [BS1235.3.R6 1962] 62-6618
1. Bible. O. T. Genesis—Criticism, interpretation, etc. 2. Bible. O. T. Exodus—Criticism, interpretation, etc. I. Title.

KRAFT, Charles Franklin, 221.1107
1911-
Genesis: beginnings of the Biblical drama [by] Charles F. Kraft. [New York] Woman's Division of Christian Service, Board of Missions, the Methodist Church [1964] v, 226 p. illus. 12 cm. Bibliography: p. 223-226. [BS1235.3.K7] 64-15844
1. Bible, O. T. Genesis — Commentaries. I. Title.

KRAFT, Charles Franklin, 221.1107
1911-
Genesis beginnings of the Biblical drama [New York], 475 Riverside Dr., Woman's Div. of Christian Serv., Bd. of Missions, the Methodist Church. [1964] v. 226p. illus. 19cm. Bibl. 64-15844 1.00 pap.,
1. Bibl. O. T. Genesis—Commentaries. I. Title.

BLENKINSOPP, Joseph, 221.1'2
1927-
Prophecy and canon : a contribution to the study of Jewish origins / Joseph Blenkinsopp. Notre Dame, Ind. : University of Notre Dame Press, c1977. xi, 206 p. ; 21 cm. ([Studies of Judaism and christianity in antiquity] ; No. 3) Includes bibliographical references and indexes. [BS1135.B57] 76-22411 ISBN 0-268-01522-8 : 16.95
1. Bible. O.T.—Canon. 2. Bible. O.T. Prophets—Relation to the Pentateuch. 3. Bible. O.T. Pentateuch—Relation to the Prophets. I. Title. II. Series.

CANON and authority : 221.1'2
essays in Old Testament religion and theology / edited by George W Coats and Burke O. Long ; with contributions by Peter R. Ackroyd ... [et al.]. Philadelphia : Fortress Press, c1977. xvi, 190 p. ; 24 cm. Includes bibliographical references and indexes. [BS480.C34] 76-62614 ISBN 0-8006-0501-2 : 13.50
1. Zimmerli, Walther, 1907- —Addresses, essays, lectures. 2. Bible. O.T.—Evidences, authority, etc.—Addresses, essays, lectures. 3. Bible. O.T.—Canon—Addresses, essays, lectures. 4. Bible. O.T.—Hermeneutics—Addresses, essays, lectures. I. Coats, George W. II. Long, Burke O.

RIDDERBOS, Herman N. 221.12
The authority of the New Testament Scriptures. Tr. by H. De Jongste. Philadelphia, Presbyterian & Reformed, 1963. 93p. 23cm. (Intl. lib. of philosophy and theology. Biblical and theological studies ser.) Bibl. 61-11748 apply
1. Bible. N. T.—Canon. 2. Bible. N. T.—Evidences, authority, etc. I. Title.

SANDERS, James A., 1927- 221.1'2
Torah and canon, by James A. Sanders. Philadelphia, Fortress Press [1972] xx, 124 p. 19 cm. [BS1135.S25] 72-171504 ISBN 0-8006-0105-X 2.95
1. Bible. O.T.—Canon. 2. Tradition (Judaism) I. Title.

AIGRAIN, Rene, 1886-1957. 221.15
Prophecy fulfilled: the Old Testament realized in the New, by Rene Aigrain and Omer Englebert. Translated by Lancelot C. Sheppard. With a pref. by John M. Oesterreicher. New York, D. McKay Co. [1958] 274p. illus. 21cm. [BS2387.A35] 58-12251
1. Bible. N. T.—Relation to O. T. 2. Bible. O. T.—Prohecies. I. Englebert, Omer, 1893- joint author. II. Title.

CLEMENTS, Ronald Ernest, 221.1'5
1929-
Prophecy and tradition [by] R. E. Clements. Atlanta, John Knox Press [1975, c1974] 104 p. 22 cm. (Growing points in theology) Bibliography: p. 93-99. [BS1198.C57 1975] 74-3713 ISBN 0-8042-0110-2 4.95 (pbk.)
1. Prophets. I. Title.

CROWTHER, Duane S. 221.15
Prophets & prophecies of the Old Testament, by Duane S. Crowther. Salt Lake City, Deseret Book Co., 1966. xii, 644 p. col. illus., col. maps. 24 cm. Bibliography: p. 18-19. [BS1505.2.C7] 66-25508
1. Bible. O.T. Prophets—Introductions. I. Title.

MILTON, John Peterson 221.15
Prophecy interpreted; essays in Old Testament in terpretation. Minneapolis. Augsburg Pub. House [c.1960] x, 139p. (bibl.) 22cm. 60-6437 2.75
1. Bible—Prophecies. 2. Jews—Restoration. I. Title.

MILTON, John Peterson, 221.15
1897-
Prophecy interpreted; essays in Old Testament interpretation. Minneapolis, Augsburg Pub. House [1960] 139p. 22cm. Includes bibliography. [BS647.2.M5] 60-6437
1. Bible—Prophecies. 2. Jews—Restoration. I. Title.

SMART, James D. 221.15
Servants of the Word; the prophets of Israel. Philadelphia, Westminster Press [1961, c.1960] 95p. (Westminster guides to the Bible) 60-11066 1.50
1. Prophets. I. Title.

WALVOORD, John F. 221.15
Israel in prophecy. Grand Rapids, Mich., Zondervan [c.1962] 138p. 21cm. Bibl. 62-4367 2.50
1. Bible—Prophecies—Jews. 2. Israel. I. Title.

BROWN,Francis, 1849-1916. 221.2
A Hebrew and English lexicon of the Old Testament, with an appendix containing the Biblical Aramaic, based on the lexicon of William Gesenius as tr., by Edward Robinson. Ed., with constant reference to the Thesaurus of Gesenius as completed by E. Rodiger and with authorized use of the latest German editions of Gesenius' Handworterbuch uber das Alte Testament, by Francis Brown with the co-operation of S. R. Driver and Charles A. Briggs. Boston, Houghton, Mifflin, 1891- v. 27 cm. [PJ4833.B66] 48-33574
1. Hebrew language—Dictionaries—English. 2. English language—Dictionaries—Hebrew. I. Driver, Samuel Rolles, 1846-1914. II. Briggs, Charles Augustus, 1841-1913. III. Robinson, Edward, 1794-1863, tr. IV. Gesenius, Friedrich Heinrich Wilhelm, 1786-1842. Hebraisch-deutsches Handworterbuch. V. Title.

BROWN, Francis, 1849-1916. 221.2
A Hebrew and English lexicon of the Old Testament, with an appendix containing the Biblical Aramaic. Based on the lexicon of William Gesenius as translated by Edward Robinson. Edited with constant reference to the Thesaurus of Gesenius as completed by E. Rodiger, and with authorized use of the latest German editions of Gesenius's Handworterbuch uber das Alte Testament, by Francis Brown with the co-operation of S. R. Driver and Charles A. Briggs. [Reprinted with corrections] Oxford, Clarendon Press [1962] xix, 1127 p. 25 cm. [PJ4833.B68] 66-33161
1. Hebrew language — Dictionaries — English. 2. English language — Dictionaries — Hebrew. I. Robinson, Edward, 1794-1863. II. Gesenius, Friedrich Heinrich Wilheim, 1786-1842. Hebraisch-deutsches Handworterbuch. III. Title.

BROWN, Francis, 1849-1916. 221.2
A Hebrew and English lexicon of the Old Testament, with an appendix containing the Biblical Aramaic, based on the lexicon of William Gesenius as translated by Edward Robinson. Edited, with constant reference to the Thesaurus of Gesenius as completed by E. Rodiger, and with authorized use of the latest German editions of Gesenius's Handworterbuch uber das Alte Testament, by Francis Brown, with the co-operation of S. R. Driver and Charles A. Briggs. Oxford,

Clarendon Press [1952] xix, 1126 p. 25 cm. [PJ4833.G] 53-8441
1. Hebrew language — Dictionaries — English. I. Driver, Samuel Rolles, 1846-1914. II. Briggs, Charles Augustus, 1841-1913. III. Robinson, Edward. 1794-1803, tr. IV. Gesenius, Friedrich Heinrich Wilheim, 1786-1842. Hebraisch-deutsches Handworterbuch. V. Title.

EINSPAHR, Bruce. 221.2
Index to the Brown, Driver and Briggs Hebrew and English lexicon of the Old Testament / compiled by Bruce Einspahr. Chicago : Moody Press, c1976. p. cm. [PJ4833.B683E35] 76-25479 ISBN 0-8024-4082-7 : 24.95
1. Brown, Francis, 1849-1916. A Hebrew and English lexicon of the Old Testament—Indexes. I. Brown, Francis, 1849-1916. A Hebrew and English lexicon of the Old Testament. II. Title.

GESENIUS, Friedrich Heinrich Wilhelm, 1786-1842. 221.2
A Hebrew and English lexicon of the Old Testament, with an appendix containing the Biblical Aramaic, based on the lexicon of William Gesenius as translated by Edward Robinson. Edited, with constant reference to the Thesaurus of Gesenius as completed by E. Rodiger, and with authorized use of the latest German editions of Gesenius's Handworterbuch uber das Alte Testament, by Francis Brown, with the co-operation of S. R. Driver and Charles A. Briggs. iOxford, Clarendon Press [1952] xix, 1126p. 25cm. [PJ4833.G] A53
1. Hebrew language— Dictionaries—English. I. Robinson, Edward, 1794-1863, tr. II. Brown, Francis, 1849-1916. III. Title.

KOHLER, Ludwig Hugo, 1880- 221.2
Lexicon in Veteris Testamenti libros. Leiden, E. J. Brill; Grand Rapids, Eerdmans, 1951-53. Leiden, E. J. Brill; Grand Rapids, Eerdmans, 1958. 2v. 27cm. xi, 227p. 28cm. 'Abkiirzungen und Zeichen'(bibliographical): v. 1, p. [i]-ix (2d group);v. 2, p. [iiii]-lxvi. 'Abkiirzungen und Zeichen' (bibliographical): p. [xix]-xxxiv. [PJ4833.K62] 59-17615
1. Hebrew language—Dictionaries—English. 2. Hebrew language—Dictionaries —German. I. Baumgartner, Walter, 1887- II. Title. III. Title: —Supplementum,
Contents omitted.

ROTH, Leon, 1896- 221.2
God and man in the Old Testament. London, Allen & Unwin; New York, Macmillan [1955] 167p. 19cm. (Ethical and religious classics of East and West, no. 12) [BS432.R64] 55-14390
1. Bible—Indexes, Topical. I. Title.

SCHARFSTEIN, Ben-Ami, 1919- 221.2
English-Hebrew dictionary. Compiled by Ben-Ami Scharfstein and Raphael Sappan. Edited by Zevi Scharfstein. Tel-Aviv, Published by Dvir Pub. Co. for Shilo Pub. House, New York [1961] xx, 825p. 25cm. Added t. p. in Hebrew. [PJ4833.S33] 62-6162
1. English language—Dictionaries—Hebrew. I. Sappan, Raphael, joint author. II. Title.

BIBLE. O.T. English. 1962. Siewert. 221.3
The amplified Old Testament. [1st ed.] Grand Rapids, Zondervan Pub. House, 1962-64 [v. 1, 1964] 2v, 17 cm. Edited and translated by Frances E. Siewert. Contents.CONTENTS.--pt. 1. Genesis-Esther.--pt. 2. Job-Malachi. [BS895.S54] 62-1064
I. Siewert, Frances E., ed. and tr. II. Title.

BIBLE. O.T. English. 1962. Siewert. 221.3
The amplified Old Testament. [1st ed.] Grand Rapids, Zondervan Pub. House. 1962- v. 17cm. Edited and translated by Frances E. Siewert. Contents.pt. 2. Job-Malachi. [BS895.S54] 62-1064
I. Siewert, Frances E., ed. and tr. II. Title.

BOTTERWECK, G. Johannes. 221.3
Theological dictionary of the Old Testament. Edited by G. Johannes Botterweck and Helmer Ringgren. Translator: John T. Willis. Grand Rapids, Eerdmans [1974- v. 25 cm. Translation of Theologisches Worterbuch zum Alten Testament. Includes bibliographical references. [BS440.B5713] 73-76170 ISBN 0-8028-2338-6 18.50 (v. 1)
1. Bible. O.T.—Dictionaries—Hebrew. 2. Hebrew language—Dictionaries—English. I. Ringgren, Helmer, 1917- joint author. II. Title.

NOVAK, Alfons, 1904- 221.3
Hebrew honey; a thesaurus of words found in the Bible, by Al Novak. With an introd. by K. Owen Whitel [1st ed.] New York, Vantage Press [1965] 197 p. 21 cm. [BS525.N6] 64-25876
1. Bible. O.T. — Dictionaries. 2. Hebrew language — Words — Hist. I. Title.

NOVAK, Alfons, 1904- 221.3
Hebrew honey; a thesaurus of words found in the Bible. Introd. by K. Owen White. New York, Vantage [c.1965] 197p. 21cm. [BS525.N6] 64-25876 4.00 bds.,
1. Bible. O.T.—Dictionaries. 2. Hebrew language—Words—Hist. I. Title.

AP-THOMAS, Dafydd Rhys 221.4
A primer of Old Testament text criticism, by D. R. Ap-Thomas. 2d ed. Philadelphia, Fortress [1966] viii, 56p. 19cm. (Facet bks. Biblical ser., 14) Bibl. [BS1136.A6 1966] 66-21731 .85 pap.,
1. Bible. O. T. — Criticism, Textual. I. Title. II. Series.

AP-THOMAS, Dafydd Rhys. 221.4
A primer of Old Testament text criticism, by D. R. Ap-Thomas. 2d ed. Philadelphia, Fortress Press [1966] viii, 56 p. 19 cm. (Facet books. Biblical series, 14) Bibliography: p. 51-54. [BS1136.A6 1966] 66-21731
1. Bible. O.T.—Criticism, Textual. I. Title. II. Series.

BIBLE, O. T. English 221.4
The amplified Old Testament; pt. 1. Grand Rapids, Mich., Zondervan [c.]1964. 1398p. 17cm. Ed., tr., by Frances E. Siewert. Contents.pt.1. Genesis-Esther. 62-1964 4.95
I. Siewert, Frances E., ed. and tr. II. Title.

BROWNLEE, William Hugh. 221.4
The meaning of the Qumran scrolls for the Bible, with special attention to the book of Isaiah. New York, Oxford University Press, 1964. xxi, 309 p. 22 cm. (The James W. Richard lectures in Christian religion, 1958) Bibliographical footnotes. [BM487.B68] 64-10061
1. Dead Sea Scrolls. 2. Bible. O. T. Isaiah—Criticism, Textual. I. Title. II. Series.

BRUCE, Frederick Fyvie, D. D., 1910- 221.4
Second thoughts on the Dead Sea scrolls. [2d ed.] Grand Rapids, Mich., Eerdmans [c.1961] 160p. col. front. Bibl. 62-360 3.00
1. Dead Sea scrolls. I. Title.

COSS, Thurman L. 221.4
Secrets from the caves; a layman's guide to the Dead Sea scrolls. New York, Abingdon Press [1963] 171 p. 23 cm. [BM487.C6] 63-15707
1. Dead Sea scrolls. I. Title.

DANIELOU, Jean 221.4
The Dead Sea scrolls and primitive Christianity. Tr. from French by Salvator Attanasio [New York] New Amer. Lib. [1962, c.1958] 128p. illus. (Mentor omega bk., MP405) Bibl. .60 pap.,
1. Dead Sea scrolls. I. Title.

DANIELOU, Jean. 221.4
The Dead Sea scrolls and primitive Christianity. Translated from the French by Salvator Attanasio. Baltimore, Helicon Press [1958] 128 p. illus. 23 cm. Translation of Les manuscrits de la mer Morte et les origines du christianisme. Includes bibliography. [BM487.D253] 58-14443
1. Dead Sea scrolls.

DEAD Sea scrolls. 221.4
Les grottes de Murabba'at [2v] par P. Benoit, J.T. milik, R. de Vaux. Avec des contributions de G. M. Crowfoot, A. Grohmann. [New York] Oxford 1961[ ] 2v. 303; 107p. illus. 33cm. (Discoveries in the Judaean Desert, 2) At head of title: Jordan Dept. of Antiquities. Ecole biblique et archeologique francaise. Palestine Archaeological Museum. Contents.1. Texte.--2. Planches. Bibl. 61-1884 26.90
I. Benoit, Pierre, 1906- II. Title. III. Series.

DEAD Sea scrolls. 221.4
Les 'petites grottes' de Qumran: exploration de la falaise, les grottes 2Q, 3Q, 5Q, 6Q, 7Q a 10Q, le rouleau de cuivre. Par M. Baillet, J. T. Milik, et R. de Vaux. Avec une contribution de H. W. Baker. Oxford, Clarendon Press[dist. New York, Oxford, c.]1962. 2v. (various p.) illus., map, facsims. 33cm. (Discoveries in the Judaean Desert of Jordan, 3) At head of title: Jordan Dept. of Antiquities. Amer. Schools of Oriental Res. Ecole biblique et archeologique francaise. Palestine Archaeological Museum. Contents.1. Textes.--2. Planches. Bibl. 63-800 26.90 set,
I. Baillet, II. Title. III. Series.

DEAD Sea Scrolls. English. 221.4
The Dead Sea scriptures, in English translation with introd. and notes by Theodor H. Gaster. Rev. and enl. ed. Garden City, N.Y., Anchor Books [1964] x, 420 p. 19 cm. Bibliography: p. [389]-391. 64-11039
I. Gaster, Theodor Herzl, 1906- ed. and tr. II. Title.

DEAD Sea scrolls. English. 221.4
The Dead Sea scriptures, in English translation with introd. and notes by Theodor H. Gaster. Rev. and enl. ed. Garden City, N. Y., Anchor Books [1964] x, 420 p. 19 cm. Bibliography: p. [389]-391. [BM487.A3G3 1964] 64-11039
I. Gaster, Theodor Herzl, 1906- ed. and tr. II. Title.

DEAD Sea scrolls. English. 221.4
The Dead Sea scriptures, in English translation / with introd. and notes by Theodor H. Gaster. 3d ed., rev. and enl. Garden City, N.Y. : Anchor Press, 1976. xvi, 578 p. ; 18 cm. Includes bibliographical references and index. [BM487.A3G3 1976] 76-2840 ISBN 0-385-08859-0 pbk. : 3.50
I. Gaster, Theodor Herzl, 1906- II. Title.

DEAD Sea Scrolls. English. 221'.4
The Dead Sea scrolls. Translated, with an introd. and commentaries, by Geza Vermes and illustrated by Shraga Weil. New York, Heritage Press [1967] 241 p. illus. (part col.) 30 cm. "First published ... 1962. Text revised ... for this edition." 67-6319
I. Vermes, Geza, 1924- ed. II. Weil, Shraga, 1918- illus. III. Title.

DEAD Sea scrolls. English. 221'.4
The Dead Sea scrolls. Translated, with an introd. and commentaries, by Geza Vermes and illustrated by Shraga Weil. New York, Heritage Press [1967] 241 p. illus. (part col.) 30 cm. "First published ... 1962. Text revised ... for this edition." [BM487.A3V4 1967] 67-6319
I. Vermes, Geza, 1924- ed. II. Weil, Shraga, 1918- illus.

DEAD Sea Scrolls. English 221.4
The Dead Sea scrolls in English [by] G. Vermes. Baltimore, Penguin Books [1962] 254 p. 18 cm. (Pelican books) Bibliography: p. [252] 63-2160
I. Vermes, Geza, 1924- ed. and tr. II. Title.

DEAD Sea scrolls. English 221.4
The Dead Sea scrolls in English [by] G. Vermes [Gloucester, Mass., Peter Smith, 1963, c.1962] 254p. 18cm. (Pelican bks., A551 rebound) Bibl. 3.25
I. Vermes, Geza, 1924- ed. and tr. II. Title.

DEAD Sea scrolls. English. 221.4
The Dead Sea scrolls in English [by] G. Vermes. Baltimore, Penguin Books [1962] 254 p. 18 cm. (Pelican books) Bibliography: p. [252] [BM487.A3V4] 63-2160
I. Vermes, Geza, 1924- ed. and tr. II. Title.

DUPONT-SOMMER, Andre 221.4
The Essene writings from Qumran. Tr. [from French] by G. Vermes. Cleveland, World [1962, c.1961] xv, 428p. maps. (Meridian bks., MG44) Bibl. 62-10171 1.95 pap.,
1. Dead Sea scrolls. 2. Essenes. I. Dead Sea scrolls. English. II. Title.

DUPONT-SOMMER, Andre 221.4
The Essene writings from Qumran. Tr. [from French] by G. Vermes. [Gloucester, Mass., Peter Smith, 1963. c.1961] xv, 428p. maps. 21cm. (Meridian bks., MG44 rebound) Bibl. 4.00
1. Dead Sea scrolls. 2. Essenes. I. Dead Sea scrolls. English. II. Title.

EWING, Upton Clary. 221.4
The prophet of the Dead Sea Scrolls. New York, Philosophical Library [1963] 148 p. 22 cm. [BM487.E9] 62-21558
1. Teacher of Righteousness. 2. Dead Sea scrolls. I. Title.

EWING, Upton Clary 221.4
The prophet of the Dead Sea Scrolls. New York, Philosophical [c.1963] 148p. 22cm. Bibl. 62-21558 3.75
1. Teacher of Righteousness. 2. Dead Sea scrolls. I. Title.

GILKES, A. N. 221.4
The impact of the Dead Sea scrolls. London, Macmillan[dist.] New York, St. Martin's [1963, c.1962] 167p. illus. 21cm. Bibl. 63-3456 3.50
1. Dead Sea scrolls. I. Title.

GOODWIN, Donald Watson. 221.4
Text-restoration methods in contemporary U.S.A. Biblical scholarship ... Naples, 1969. x, 178 p. 24 cm. (Istituto orientale di Napoli. Pubblicazioni del Seminario di semitistica. Ricerche, 5) A revision of the author's thesis, Brown University, 1965. Bibliography: p. 161-171. [BS1136.G66 1969] 71-543130
1. Bible. O.T.—Criticism, Textual—History. I. Title. II. Series: Naples. Istituto orientale. Seminario di semitistica. Pubblicazioni: Ricerche 5

HARRISON, Roland Kenneth. 221.4
The Dead Sea scrolls; an introduction. [New York, Harper, 1961] 160p. illus. 21cm. (Harper torchbooks. The Cloister library, TB84) [BM487.H3 1961a] 61-19281
1. Dead Sea scrolls. I. Title.

*HONOUR, Alan 221.4
Cave of riches; the story of the Dead Sea Scrolls. New York, McGraw [1967, c.1956] 157p. illus. 21cm. (Young pioneer bk., 78011) .60 pap.,
1. Dead Sea Scrolls—Juvenille literature. I. Title.

LA SOR, William Sanford. 221.4
The Dead Sea scrolls and the Christian faith. [Rev. ed.] Chicago, Moody Press [c1962] 251 p. 17 cm. First published in 1956 under title: Amazing Dead Sea scrolls and the Christian faith. [BM487.L36 1962] 63-1085
1. Dead Sea scrolls. I. Title.

LA SOR, William Sanford. 221.4
The Dead Sea scrolls and the Christian faith. [Rev. ed.] Chicago, Moody [1963, c.1956, 1962] 251p. 17cm. First pub. in 1956 under title: Amazing Dead Sea scrolls and the Christian faith. Bibl. 63-1085 .89 pap.,
1. Dead Sea scrolls. I. Title.

LA SOR, William Sanford 221.4
The Dead Sea scrolls and the New Testament. Grand Rapids, Mich., Eerdmans [1972] 281 p. 21 cm. Bibliography: p. 265-269. [BM487.L37] 67-28372 ISBN 0-8028-1114-0 3.95
1. Dead Sea scrolls—Relation to the New Testament. I. Title.

MANSOOR, Menahem 221.4
The Dead Sea scrolls; a college textbook and a study guide. Grand Rapids. Mich., Eerdmans [1965, c.]1964. x, 210p. 12cm. Bibl. [BM487.M27] 64-8580 4.00
1. Dead Sea scrolls—Handbooks, manuals, etc. I. Title.

MANUAL of discipline 221.4
The Rule of Qumran and its meaning: introduction, translation, and commentary. R. C. Leaney. Philadelphia, Westminster [c.1966] 310p. 23cm. (New Testament lib.) Bibl. [BM488.M3A3] 66-16966 7.50
I. Leaney, Alfred Robert Clare, ed. and tr. II. Title.

MEDICO, Henri E del, 1896- 221.4
The riddle of the Scrolls. Translated by H. Garner. [1st American ed.] New York, R.M. McBride Co. [1959, c1958] 432p. illus. 23cm. Translation of L enigme des manuscrits de la mer Morte. Includes translations of non-Biblical texts from the Dead Sea scrolls and the Damascus document. Includes bibliography. [BM487.M373 1959] 59-8873
1. Dead Sea scrolls. I. Dead Sea scrolls. English. II. Zadokite documents. III. Title.

MILIK, Jozef Tadeusz, 1922- 221.4
Ten years of discovery in the wilderness of Judaea. Translated by J. Strugnell. [1st English ed.] Naperville, Ill., A. R. Allenson [1959] 160p. illus., maps (part fold.) facsims. 22cm. (Studies in Biblical theology, no. 26) Bibliography: p. 147-150. [BM487.M493] 59-1301
1. Dead sea scrolls. I. Title. II. Series.

MOWRY, Lucetta. 221.4
The Dead Sea scrolls and the early church. [Chicago] University of Chicago Press [1962] 259p. 23cm. [BM487.M6] 62-12637
1. Dead Sea scrolls. 2. Qumran community. 3. Church history— Primitive and early church. 4. Redemption—Comparative studies. I. Title.

MURPHY-O'CONNOR, Jerome, 1935- comp. 221.4
Paul and Qumran; studies in New Testament exegesis [by] Pierre Benoit [and others] Chicago, Priory Press [1968] x, 254 p. 23 cm. Contents.Contents.—Qumran and the New Testament, by P. Benoit.—A feature of Qumran angelology and the angels of 1 Cor. 11:10, by J. A. Fitzmyer.—2 Cor. 6: 14-7: 1 in the light of the Qumran texts and the Testaments of the Twelve Patriarchs, by J. Gnilka.—The courts of the Church of Corinth and the courts of Qumran, by M. Delcor.—The Teacher of Righteousness of Qumran and the question of justification by faith in the theology of the Apostle Paul, by W. Grundmann.—The Epistle to the Ephesians in the light of the Qumran texts, by K. G. Kuhn.—Mystery in the theology of Saint Paul and its parallels at Qumran, by J. Coppens.—Contributions made by Qumran to the understanding of the Epistle to the Ephesians, by F. Mussner.—Truth: Paul and Qumran, by J. Murphy-O'Connor. Bibliographical footnotes. [BM487.M82 1968] 68-57011 5.95
1. Bible. N.T. Epistle of Paul—Criticism, interpretation, etc. 2. Dead Sea scrolls—Addresses, essays, lectures. I. Title.

NOBLE, Iris. ?21.4
Treasure of the caves; the story of the Dead Sea scrolls. New York, Macmillan [1971] 214 p. illus., facsims., maps, ports. 21 cm. [BM487.N6] 69-11303

1. Dead Sea scrolls. I. Title.

PALMER, Geoffrey. 221.4 (j)
Quest for the Dead Sea scrolls. With illus. by Peter Forster. [1st American ed.] New York, John Day Co. [1965, c1964] 88, [8] p. illus. (part col.) 23 cm. Bibliography: p. [91] [BM487.P3 1965] 65-16712
1. Dead Sea scrolls—Juvenile literature. I. Title.

*PEDLEY, Katharine Greenleaf 221.4
The library at Qumran; a librarian looks at the Dead Sea Scrolls. Berkeley 1, Calif., P.O. Box 875, Peacock Pr., 1964. 23p. 22cm. (Peacock biblio ser., no.1) Reprinted from Revue de Qumran, v.2, pt.1. 1.25 pap.,
1. Dead Sea scrolls. I. Title.

PFEIFFER, Charles F. 221.4
The Dead Sea scrolls and the Bible, by Charles F. Pfeiffer. [Enl. ed.] Grand Rapids, Mich., Baker Book House [1969] 152 p. illus., facsims. 22 cm. (Baker studies in biblical archaeology, 7) 1957 ed. published under title: The Dead Sea scrolls. [BM487.P45 1969] 72-76780
1. Dead Sea scrolls. I. Title.

POTTER, Charles Francis, 1885-1962. 221.4
The lost years of Jesus. New Hyde Park, N. Y., University Books [1963] 160 p. 22 cm. [BM487.P7 1963] 63-12601
1. Essenes. 2. Dead Sea scrolls. 3. Christianity and other religions—Judaism. I. Title.

RAPPAPORT, Uriel. 1935- 221.4
The story of the Dead Sea scrolls. Illustrated by Milka Cizik. Irvington-on-Hudson, N. Y. Harvey House [1967] 128 p. illus (part col). facsims., maps. plans. ports. 26 cm. (A story of science series book) Bibliography: p. 124. [BM487.R3] 67-25297
1. Dead Sea scrolls—juvenile literature. I. Title.

RAPPAPORT, Uriel, 1935- 221.4
The story of the Dead Sea scrolls. Illustrated by Milka Cizik. Irvington-on-Hudson, N.Y., Harvey House [1967] 128 p. illus. (part col.), facsims., maps, plans, ports. 26 cm. (A Story of science series book) Bibliography: p. 124. Traces the discovery of the Dead Sea scrolls, describes the painstaking process of preserving and deciphering them, and explains what they have contributed to scholars' knowledge of the period in which they were written. [BM487.R3] AC 68
1. Dead Sea scrolls. I. Cizik, Milka, illus. II. Title.

ROBINSON, O. Preston, 1903- 221.4
The challenge of the scrolls; how old is Christ's gospel? Salt Lake City, Desert Book Co., 1963. 91 p. illus. 23 cm. [BM487.R58] 63-3708
1. Dead Sea scrolls. 2. Christianity—Origin. I. Title. II. Title: How old is Christ's gospel?

ROBINSON, O. Preston, 1903- 221.4
How old is Christ's Gospel?: The challenge of the scrolls. Salt Lake City, Deseret [c.]1963. 91p. illus. 23cm. Bibl. 63-3708 1.95
1. Dead Sea scrolls. 2. Christianity—Origin. I. Title.

ROTH, Cecil, 1899- 221.4
The historical background of the Dead Sea scrolls. New York, Philosophical Library, 1959 [c1958] 87p. 23cm. Includes bibliography. [BM175.Q6R6 1959] 59-16249
1. Qumran community. 2. Zealots (Jewish party) 3. Dead Sea scrolls. I. Title.

TREVER, John C., 1915- 221.4
The Dead Sea scrolls : a personal account / by John C. Trever. Rev. ed. Grand Rapids : Eerdmans, 1977. p. cm. Published in 1965 and 1966 under title: The untold story of Qumran. Includes bibliographical references and index. [BM487.T7 1977] 77-10808 ISBN 0-8028-1695-9 pbk. : 3.95
1. Trever, John C., 1915- 2. Dead Sea scrolls. 3. Qumran. I. Title.

VAUX, Roland de, 1903- 221.4
L'archeologie et les manuscrits de la mer Morte. [New York] Pub. forthe British Acad. by Oxford [c.]1961[ ] xv, 107p. illus., fold. map, 25cm. (Schweich lectures of the British Acad., 1959) Bibl. 62-245 6.90
1. Qumran. 2. Dead Sea scrolls. I. Title. II. Series: The Schweich lectures, 1959

VERMES, Geza, 1924- ed. and tr. 221.4
Dead Sea scrolls. English. Harmondsworth, Penguin, 1968. 3-258 p. 19 cm. 12/6 (B68-68583) Bibliography: p. 253. [BM487.A3V4 1968] 68-121221
I. Title. II. Title: The Dead Sea Scrolls in English

WAARD, Jan de 221.4
A comparative study of the Old Testament text in the Dead Sea scrolls and in the New Testament, by J. De Waard. Leiden, E. J. Brill, 1965. 101p. 25cm. (Studies on the texts of the desert of Judah, v. 4) Bibl. [BM487.W23] 66-6582 7.00
1. Dead Sea scrolls. 2. Bible. O. T. — Quotations, Early. I. Title. II. Series.
Available from Eerdmans, Grand Rapids, Mich.

WILSON, Edmund, 1895- 221.4
The Dead Sea scrolls, 1947-1969. New York, Oxford University Press, 1969. 320 p. 20 cm. 1955-1959 editions published under title: The scrolls from the Dead Sea. Includes bibliographical references. [BM487.W5 1969] 75-83505 6.50
1. Dead Sea scrolls.

WILSON, Edmund, 1895- 221.4
The scrolls from the Dead Sea. New York, Meridian Books [1959, c1955] 121 p. 19 cm. (Meridian books, M69) [BM487.W5 1959] 59-7185
1. Dead Sea scrolls. I. Title.

BOWKER, John Westerdale. 221.4'2
The Targums and Rabbinic literature; an introduction to Jewish interpretations of scripture. London, Cambridge U.P., 1969. xxi, 379 p. 24 cm. Bibliography: p. 326-348. [BS709.4.B6] 71-80817 ISBN 0-521-07415-0 75/-
1. Bible. O.T. Aramaic—Versions. 2. Bible. O.T.—Criticism, interpretation, etc., Jewish. 3. Bible. O.T. Genesis. Aramaic. Targum Pseudo-Jonathan—Translations into English. I. Title.

ALLEGRO, John Marco, 1923- 221.44
The Dead Sea scrolls. [Harmondsworth, Middlesex] Penguin Books [1956] 207p. plates, ports., maps, facsims. 19cm. (Pelican books, A376) Bibliography: p. 185-197. [BM487.A39] A57
1. Dead Sea scrolls. I. Title.

ALLEGRO, John Marco, 1923- 221.44
The Dead Sea scrolls and the origins of Christianity. New York, Criterion Books [1957] 250 p. 42 plates (incl. ports., facsims.) maps. 22 cm. Bibliography: p. 227-239. [BM487.A4] 57-6249
1. Dead Sea scrolls.

ALLEGRO, John Marco, 1923- 221.44
The people of the Dead Sea scrolls in text and pictures by John Marco Allegro. [1st ed.] Garden City, N. Y., Doubleday, 1958. 192p. illus. 27cm. [BM175.Q6A4] 58-13267
1. Qumran community. 2. Dead Sea scrolls. I. Title.

ALLEGRO, John Marco, 1923- 221.44
The people of the Dead Sea scrolls in text and pictures by John Marco Allegro. [1st ed.] Garden City, N. Y., Doubleday, 1958. 192 p. illus. 27 cm. [BM175.Q6A4] 58-13267
1. Dead Sea scrolls. 2. Qumran community. I. Title.

BAPMASA, 221.4'4
1897. 61 p. 23 cm. No more published? [BM45.S65] 51-52016
1. Judaism — Collected works.

BARR, James. 221.4'4
Comparative philology and the text of the Old Testament. Oxford, Clarendon P., 1968. ix, 354 p. 23 cm. Bibliography: p. [310]-319. [PJ4544.B37] 78-356665 65/-
1. Bible. O.T.—Criticism, textual, etc. 2. Hebrew language—Grammar, Comparative. I. Title

BRUCE, Frederick Fyvie, 1910- 221.44
Second thoughts on the Dead Sea scrolls. American ed. Grand Rapids Eerdmans, 1956. 143p. illus. 23cm. [BM487.B7 1956] 57-13523
1. Dead Sea scrolls. I. Title.

BRUCE, Frederick Fyvie, 1910- 221.44
Second thoughts on the Dead Sea scrolls. [American ed.] Grand Rapids, Eerdmans, 1956. 143p. illus. 23cm. [BM487.B7 1956] 57-13523
1. Dead Sea scrolls. I. Title.

BURROWS, Millar, 1889- 221.44
More light on the Dead Sea scrolls; new scrolls and new interpretations, with translations of important recent discoveries. New York, Viking Press, 1958. xiii, 434 p. col. map. 24 cm. Bibliography: p. 411-424. [BM487.B8] 58-8133
1. Dead Sea scrolls. I. Dead Sea scrolls. English. II. Title.

DAVIES, Arthur Powell. 221.44
The meaning of the Dead Sea scrolls. [New York] New American Library [1956] 137p. illus. 19cm. (A Signet key book, Ks 339) [BM487.D3 1956a] 56-9787
1. Dead Sea scrolls. I. Title.

DEAD Sea scrolls. 221.4'4
Qumran cave 4. Oxford, Clarendon P., 1968- v. 31 plates. 32 cm. (Discoveries in the Judaean desert of Jordan, 5) At head of title: Palestine Archaeological Museum. Ecole biblique et archeologique francaise. Contents.Contents.—1. 4Q158-4Q186, by John M. Allegro with the collaboration of Arnold A. Anderson. [BM487.A1 1968] 71-356658 84/- (v. 1)
I. Allegro, John Marco, 1923- II. Jerusalem. Palestine Archaeological Museum. III. Jerusalem. Ecole biblique et archeologique francaise. IV. Title. V. Series.

DEAD Sea scrolls. English. 221.44
The Dead Sea scriptures, in English translation with introd. and notes by Theodor H. Gaster. [1st ed.] Garden City, N. Y., Doubleday, 1956. xii, 350 p. 20 cm. "The Zadokite document": p. [61]-85. Bibliography: p. [323]-326. [BM487.A3 1956] 56-11602
I. Gaster, Theodor Herzl, 1906- ed. and tr. II. Zadokite documents.

DRIVER, Godfrey Rolles, 1892- 221.44
The Hebrew scrolls, from the neighbourhood of Jericho and the Dead Sea. London, Oxford University Press, 1951. 50 p. plates. 22 cm. (Friends of Dr. Williams's Library, 4th lecture, 1950) Bibliographical footnotes. [BM176.D7] 52-92147
1. Manuscripts, Hebrew. 2. Jews—Hist.—586 B. C. to 70 A. D. I. Title. II. Series: Friends of Dr. Williams's Library, London. Lecture, 1950

DRIVER, Godfrey Rolles, 1892- 221.44
The Judaean scrolls; the problem and a solution [by] G. R. Driver. New York, Schocken Books [1966, c1965] x, 624 p. illus., map. 23 cm. Bibliography: p. 593-594. [BM487.D72 1966] 66-13557
1. Dead Sea scrolls. I. Title.

DUPONT-SOMMER, Andre. 221.44
The Dead Sea scrolls, a preliminary survey translated from the French by E. Margaret Rowley Oxford, Blackwell [1952] 100p. illus., map. facsims. 20cm. Translation of Apercus preliminaires sur les manuscrits de la mer Morte. Bibliographical footnotes. [BM487.D813] 52-2760
1. Dead Sea scrolls. 2. Jews— Hist.—586 B. C.-70 A. D. 3. Manuscripts, Heberew. 4. Bible. Manuscripts, Hebrew. O. T. Isaiah. I. Title.

EISENBERG, Azriel Louis, 1903- 221.44
The great discovery. Illustrated by Shane Miller. New York, Abelard-Schuman [1956] 112 p. illus. 22 cm. [BM487.E35] 56-10695
1. Dead Sea scrolls. I. Title.

FRITSCH, Charles Theodore, 1912- 221.44
The Qumran community: its history and scrolls. New York, Macmillan, 1956. viii, 147 p. illus. 22 cm. Bibliography: p. 131-141. [BM487.F7] 56-7302
1. Dead Sea scrolls. I. Title.

GRAYSTONE, Geoffrey, 1922- 221.44
The Dead Sea scrolls and the originality of Christ. New York, Sheed & Ward [1956] 117 p. 20 cm. "Appeared originally as articles in the Irish theological quarterly under the title, 'The Dead Sea scrolls and the New Testament.'" [BM487.G7] 56-7732
1. Dead Sea scrolls. 2. Christianity—Origin. I. Title.

GREENBERG, Simon, 1901- 221.4'4
Foundations of a faith. New York, Burning Bush Press [c1967] x. 340 p. 22 cm. Contents.--The pattern of a faith.--God, man, Torah, and Israel.--A revealed law.--Judaism and the democratic ideal.-- Some of Judaism's eternally relevant contributions to civilization.-- The multiplication of the mitzvot.--Symbols and symbolism.--One people.-- The concept of k'lai Yisrael.--The role of higher Jewish learning: an evaluation of the Jewish Theological Seminary of America.--Building spiritual bridges.--Auto-emancipation and Zionism.--Towards a Jewish version of American civilization. Bibliographical references included in "Notes" (p. 313-334) [BM45.G73] 296 67-31666
1. Judaism—Addresses, essays, lectures. I. Title.

HELINE, Theodore. 221.44
The Dead Sea scrolls. Los Angeles, New Age Press [1957] 75p. 23cm. [BM487.H4] 57-34938
1. Dead Sea scrolls. I. Title.

HONOUR, Alan. 221.44
Cave of riches; the story of the Dead Sea scrolls. Illustrated by P. A. Hutchison. New York, Whittlesey House [1956] 159p. illus. 21cm. [BM487.H6] 56-10318
1. Dead Sea scrolls. I. Title.

HONOUR, Alan. 221.44
Cave of riches; the story of the Dead Sea scrolls. Illustrated by P. A. Hutchison. New York, Whittlesey House [1956] 159 p. illus. 21 cm. [BM487.H6] 56-10318
1. Dead Sea scrolls. I. Title.

HOWIE, Carl Gordon, 1920- 221.44
The Dead Sea scrolls and the living church. Richmond, John Knox Press [1958] 128p. 21cm. Includes bibliography. [BM487.H67] 58-6861
1. Dead Sea scrolls. 2. Qumran community. I. Title.

INTERNATIONAL Organization for Masoretic Studies. 221'.4'4
1972 and 1973 proceedings / IOMS; edited by Harry M. Orlinsky for the International Organization for Masoretic Studies (IOMS) and the society of Biblical Literature. Missoula, Mont. : Society of Biblical Literature : distributed by Scholars' Press, University of Montana, 1974. vi, 171 p. ; 22 cm. (Masoretic studies ; no. 1) Includes bibliographical references. [BS718.I57 1974] 74-16568 ISBN 0-88414-042-3
1. Masorah—Congresses. I. Orlinsky, Harry Meyer, 1908- ed. II. Society of Biblical Literature. III. Title. IV. Series.

JACOB BEN HAYYIM IBN. ADONIJAH, ca.1470-ca.1538. 221.4'4
Introduction to the Rabbinic Bible [by] Jacob ben Chajim ibn Adonijah. Hebrew & English with explanatory notes, by Christian D. Ginsburg, & the Massoreth ha-massoreth of Elias Levita, being an exposition of the Massoretic notes on the Hebrew Bible, or the ancient critical apparatus of the Old Testament in Hebrew with English tr., & critical & explanatory notes, by Christian D. Ginsburg. Prolegomenon by Norman H. Snaith. New York, Ktav [c1968] xxxvi, 91, viii, 307p. 23cm. (Lib., of Biblical studies) Reprint of 1867 ed. except for Prolegomenon. [BS718.J313] HE 68 14.95 2v.,
1. Masorah. 2. Bible. O. T.—Criticism, Textual. I. Ginsburg, Christian David, 1831-1914. II. Elias Levita, 1468-1549. III. Snaith. Norman Henry, 1898- IV. Masoret ha masoret. V. Title. VI. Title: Masoret ha-masoret. VII. Title: The Rabbinic Bible. VIII. Series: Library of Biblical studies

JEWISH Publication Society of America. 221.44
The Holy Scriptures according to the Masoretic text. Philadelphia, Jewish Publication Society of America, 1955. 2 v. (8, 2264 p.) 22 cm. Hebrew and English. [BS715 1955] 55-53514
1. Bible. O. T. Hebrew. 1955.

KAHLE, Paul Ernst, 221.44
The Cairo Geniza. 2d ed. New York, Praeger [1960] 370p. (Bibl. footnotes) illus. 23cm. 60-14602 8.50
1. Cairo Genizah. 2. Bible. O. T.—Criticism, Textual. 3. Targum. 4. Bible. O. T. Greek—Versions—Septuagint. 5. Tatianus, 2d cent. Diatessaron. 6. Bible. N. T. Gospels—Criticism, Textual. I. Title.

LA SOR, William Sanford. 221.44
Amazing Dead Sea scrolls and the Christian faith. Chicago, Moody Press [1956] 251p. 20cm. [BM487.L36] 57-1074
1. Dead Sea scrolls. I. Title.

LA SOR, William Sanford. 221.44
Amazing Dead Sea scrolls and the Christian faith. [2d ed.] Chicago, Moody Press [1959] 251p. 20cm. Bibliographical footnotes. [BM487.L36 1959] 60-296
1. Dead Sea scrolls. I. Title.

LEIMAN, Sid Z., comp. 221.4'4
The Canon and Masorah of the Hebrew Bible : an introductory reader / edited by Sid Z. Leiman. New York : Ktav Pub. House, [1974] x, 877 p. ; 24 cm. (The Library of Biblical studies) Includes bibliographical references. [BS718.L35] 76-149605 ISBN 0-87068-164-8 : 29.50
1. Masorah—Addresses, essays, lectures. 2. Bible. O.T.—Canon—Addresses, essays, lectures. I. Title. II. Series.

MILGROM, Jacob, 1923- 221.4'4
Studies in Levitical terminology. Berkeley, University of California Press, 1970- v. 27 cm. (University of California publications. Near Eastern studies, v. 14) Contents.Contents.—1. The encroacher and the Levite. The term 'Aboda. Bibliography (p. 91-94) [PJ4801.M5] 76-626141 ISBN 0-520-09308-9 (v. 1) 5.50 (v. 1)

1. P document (Biblical criticism) 2. Tabernacle—Desecration. 3. Levites. 4. 'Avodah (The word) I. Title. II. Series: California. University. University of California publications. Near Eastern studies, v. 14

MURPHY, Roland Edmund, 1917- 221.44
The Dead Sea scrolls and the Bible. Westminster, Md., Newman Press, 1956. 119p. illus. 21cm. [BM487.M8] 56-11425
1. Dead Sea scrolls. I. Title.

MURPHY, Roland Edmund, 1917- 221.44
The Dead Sea scrolls and the Bible. Westminster, Md., Newman Press, 1956. 119 p. illus. 21 cm. [BM487.M8] 56-11425
1. Dead Sea scrolls. I. Title.

MURPHY, Roland Edward, 1917- 221.44
The Dead Sea scrolls and the Bible. Westminster, Md., Newman Press, 1956. 119p. illus. 21cm. [BM487.M8] 56-11425
1. Dead Sea scrolls. I. Title.

PFEIFFER, Charles F 221.44
The Dead Sea scrolls. Grand Rapids, Baker Book House 1957. 107p. 20cm. [BM487.P45] 57-10683
1. Dead Sea scrolls. I. Title.

QUMRAN and the history of the Biblical text / edited by Frank Moore Cross and Shemaryahu Talmon. Cambridge, Mass. : Harvard University Press, 1975. 415 p. : ill. ; 24 cm. Includes bibliographical references. [BM487.Q58] 75-12529 ISBN 0-674-74360-1. ISBN 0-674-74362-8 pbk. 221.4'4
1. Dead Sea scrolls—Addresses, essays, lectures. 2. Bible. O.T.—Criticism and interpretation—Addresses, essays, lectures. I. Cross, Frank Moore. II. Talmon, Shmarjahu.

ROBINSON, O Preston, 1903- 221.44
The Dead Sea scrolls and original Christianity. Salt Lake City, Deseret Book Co., 1958. 123p. illus. 23cm. Includes bibliography. [BM487.R6] 58-1868
1. Dead Sea scrolls. 2. Mormons and Mormonism. I. Title.

SAMUEL, Athanasius Yeshue, Abp. 1907- 221.44
Treasure of Qumran; my story of the Dead Sea scrolls. Philadelphia, Westminster [1966] 208p. illus., facsims. ports. 22cm. Autobiographical. [BM487.S 24] 66-18828 2.65 pap.,
1. Dead Sea scrolls. I. Title.

SCHECHTER, Solomon, 1847-1915. 221.4'4
The wisdom of Solomon Schechter, by Bernard Mandelbaum. New York, Burning Bush Press, 1963. 136 p. 28 cm. "A United Synagogue jubilee publications (1913-1963)" [BM45.S35] 63-23895
1. Judaism—Addresses, essays, lectures. I. Mandelbaum, Bernard, 1922- ed. II. Title.

SCHONFIELD, Hugh Joseph, 1901- 221.44
Secrets of the Dead Sea scrolls, studies towards their solution. Gloucester, Mass., Peter Smith. 1962, c.1957] 164p. 21cm. (Perpetua bk. rebound) Bibl. 3.50
1. Dead Sea scrolls. I. Title.

SCHONFIELD, Hugh Joseph, 1901- 221.44
Secrets of the Dead Sea scrolls, studies towards their solution. New York, T. Yoseloff [1957] 164p. 24cm. [BM487.S32 1957] 57-13387
1. Dead Sea scrolls. I. Title.

STENDAHL, Krister, ed. 221.44
The scrolls and the New Testament. [1st ed.] New York, Harper [1957] 308p. 22cm. [BM487.S8] 56-13028
1. Dead Sea scrolls. 2. Bible. N. T.—Criticism, interpretation, etc. I. Title.

STENDAHL, Krister, ed. 221.44
The scrolls and the New Testament. [1st ed.] New York, Harper [1957] 308 p. 22 cm. [BM487.S8] 56-13028
1. Dead Sea scrolls. 2. Bible. N. T. — Criticism, interpretation, etc. I. Title.

TREVER, John C 1915- 221.44
The untold story of Qumran [by] John C. Trever. Westwood, N.J., F. H. Revell Co., [1965] 214 p. illus (part col.) facsima. (part col.) maps (on lining papers) port. (part col.) 26 cm. Bibliographical references included in "Notes" (p. 183-205) [BM487.T7] 65-10559
1. Dead Sea scrolls. I. Title.

TREVER, John C., 1915- 221.44
The untold story of Qumran. Westwood, N.J., Revell [c.1965] 214p. illus. (pt. col.) facsims. (pt. col.) maps (on lining papers) ports. (pt. col.) 26cm. Bibl. [BM487.T7] 65-10559 bds., 8.95; until Jan. 1,7.95
1. Dead Sea scrolls. I. Title.

UNGER, Merrill Frederick, 1909- 221.44
The Dead Sea scrolls, and other amazing archaeological discoveries. Grand Rapids, Zondervan Pub. House [1957] 121 p. 20 cm. [BM487.U5] 58-1026
1. Dead Sea scrolls. I. Title.

VAUX, Roland de, 1903-1971. 221'.44
Archaeology and the Dead Sea scrolls. London, published for the British Academy by the Oxford University Press, 1973. xv, 142 p. illus., fold maps. 26 cm. (The Schweich lectures of the British Academy, 1959) Revised ed. in an English translation of L'archeologie et les manuscrits de la mer Morte. Includes bibliographical references. [DS110.Q8V313 1973] 73-174845 ISBN 0-19-725931-6
1. Qumran. 2. Dead Sea scrolls. I. British Academy, London (Founded 1901). II. Title. III. Series: The Schweich lectures, 1959.
Distributed by Oxford University Press, New York, 12.00.

VERMES, Geza 1924- 221.44
Discovery in the Judean desert. New York, Desclee Co., 1956. 237p. plates, map, facsims. 24cm. 'The texts': p. [121]--202. Bibliography: p.[223]--237. [BM487.V43] 56-12905
1. Dead Sea scrolls. I. Dead Sea scrolls. English. II. Title.

VERMES, Geza, 1924- 221.44
Discovery in the Judean desert. New York, Desclee Co., 1956. 237 p. plates, map, facsims. 24 cm. "The texts": p. [121]-202. Bibliography: p. [223]-237. [BM487.V43] 56-12905
1. Dead Sea Scrolls. I. Dead Sea scrolls. English. II. Title.

WORDS and meanings: essays presented to David Winton Thomas on his retirement from the Regius Professorship of Hebrew in the University of Cambridge, 1968; edited by Peter R. Ackroyd and Barnabas Lindars. London, Cambridge U.P., 1968. xiii, 240 p. plate, port. 23 cm. "Bibliography of the writings of David Winton Thomas compiled by Anthony Phillips": p. 217-228. [BS1192.W63] 68-29649 ISBN 0-521-07270-0 45/- 221.4'4
1. Thomas, David Winton, 1901- — Bibliography. 2. Bible, O.T.—Criticism, interpretation, etc.—Addresses, essays, lectures. I. Thomas, David Winton, 1901- II. Ackroyd, Peter R., ed. III. Lindars, Barnabas, ed.

YADIN, Yigael, 1917- 221.44
The message of the scrolls. New York, Simon and Schuster, 1957. 191p. illus. 23cm. [BM487.Y22] 57-14102
1. Dead Sea scrolls. I. Title.

YADIN, Yigael, 1917- 221.44
The message of the scrolls. New York, Simon and Schuster, 1957. 191 p. illus. 23 cm. [BM487.Y22] 57-14102
1. Dead Sea Scrolls. I. Title.

YADIN, Yigael [Name orig.: Yigal Sukenik] 1917- 221.44
The message of the scrolls. New York, Grosset [1962, c.1957] 191p. illus. 21cm. (Universal lib., UL135) 1.65 pap.,
1. Dead Sea Scrolls. I. Title.

ZEITLIN, Solomon, 1892- 221.44
The Dead Sea scrolls and modern scholarship. Philadelphia, Dropsie College for Hebrew and Cognate Learning, 1956. xvi, 154p. facsims. 25cm. (The Jewish quarterly review. Monograph series, no. 3) Bibliographical footnotes. [BM487.Z4] 56-35990
1. Dead Sea scrolls. I. Title. II. Series.

BIBLE. O. T. English. 1954. Thomson. 221.48
The Septuagint Bible, the oldest versionof the Old Testament, in the translation of Charles Thomson, as edited, rev. and enl. by C. A. Muses. Indian Hills, Colo. [Falcon's Wing Press] 1954. xxvi, 1426p. 22cm. [BS742.T42 1954] 54-11780
1. Bible. O. T. Greek—Versions—Septuagint. 2. Bible. Greek—Translations into English. I. Thomson, Charles, 1729-1824, tr. II. Title.

BIBLE. O. T. English. 1962. Children's version. 221.48
The Children's version of the Holy Old Testament, in the translation of Charles Thomson, as edited, rev. and enl. by C. A. Muses. 2d ed. [Indian Hills, Colo.] Falcon's Wing Press [c1960] xxvi, 1428p. 22cm. [BS742.T42 1960] 59-14771
1. Bible. O. T. Greek—Versions—SeptungingOpt. 2. Bible. Greek—Translations into English. I. Thomson, Charles, 1729-1824, tr. II. Title.

BIBLE. O.T. Greek. Septuagint. 1971. 221.4'8
The Septuagint version of the Old Testament. With an English translation, and with various readings and critical notes [by Sir L. C. L. Brenton] Grand Rapids, Mich., Zondervan Pub. House [1971] vi, 1130 p. 25 cm. Greek and English in parallel columns. [BS742.B74 1971] 70-106440
1. Bible. Greek—Translations into English. I. Brenton, Lancelot Charles Lee, Sir, bart., 1807-1862, tr. II. Bible. O.T. English. Brenton. 1971. III. Title.

BIBLE. O.T. Greek. Septuagint. 1972. 221'.48
The Septuagint version of the Old Testament and Apocrypha. With an English translation and with various readings and critical notes [by Sir L. C. L. Brenton] Grand Rapids, Zondervan Pub. House [1972] vi, 1130, iii, 248 p. 25 cm. Greek and English in parallel columns. [BS742.B74 1972] 73-180309
1. Bible. Greek—Translations into English. I. Brenton, Lancelot Charles Lee, Sir, bart., 1807-1862, tr. II. Bible. O. T. English. Brenton. 1972. III. Bible. O.T. Apocrypha. Greek. Septuagint. 1972. IV. Bible. O.T. Apocrypha. English. Brenton. 1972. V. Title.

JELLICOE, Sidney. 221.4'8
The Septuagint and modern study. Oxford, Clarendon P., 1968. xix, 423 p. 23 cm. Bibliography: p. [370]-400. [BS744.J44] 68-131103 ISBN 0-19-826617-0 65/-
1. Bible. O.T. Greek—Versions—Septuagint. I. Title.

JELLICOE, Sidney, comp. 221.4'8
Studies in the Septuagint : origins, recensions, and interpretations : selected essays, with a prolegomenon / by Sidney Jellicoe. New York : Ktav Pub. House, [1974] lxii, 609 p. ; 24 cm. (Library of Biblical studies) English, French, or German. Includes bibliographical references. [BS744.J45] 73-1344 ISBN 0-87068-219-9 : 25.00
1. Bible. O.T. Greek—Versions—Septuagint. I. Title. II. Series.

KATZ, Peter. 221.4'8
The text of the Septuagint; its corruptions and their emendation, by the late Peter Walters (formerly Katz). Edited by D. W. Gooding. [London] Cambridge University Press, 1973. xx, 418 p. 24 cm. Originally presented as the author's thesis, Cambridge, 1945. Bibliography: p. 347-356. [BS744.K33 1973] 74-161292 ISBN 0-521-07977-2 37.50
1. Bible. O.T. Greek—Versions—Septuagint. 2. Bible. O.T.—Criticism, Textual. I. Title.
Distributed by Cambridge University Press N.Y.

KLEIN, Ralph W. 221.4'8
Textual criticism of the Old Testament : the Septuagint after Qumran / by Ralph W. Klein. Philadelphia : Fortress Press, [1974] xii, 84 p. ; 22 cm. (Guides to Biblical scholarship : Old Testament series) Bibliography: p. 84. [BS1136.K55] 74-80420 ISBN 0-8006-1087-3 : 2.75
1. Bible. O.T.—Criticism, Textual. 2. Bible. O.T. Greek—Versions—Septuagint. I. Title.

MORRISH, George. 221.4'8
A concordance of the Septuagint : giving various readings from Codices Vaticanus, Alexandrinus, Sinaiticus, and Ephraemi, with an appendix of words from Origin's Hexapla, etc., not found in the above manuscripts / compiled by George Morrish. Grand Rapids : Zondervan, 1976. p. cm. [BS744.M67 1976] 76-13490 ISBN 0-85150-174-5 : 12.95
1. Bible. O.T. Greek—Versions—Septuagint—Concordances. I. Origines. Hexapla. II. Title.

SANDERS, Henry Arthur, 1868-1956. 221.4'8
The Old Testament manuscripts in the Freer collection. New York, Macmillan, 1917. [New York, Johnson Reprint Corp., 1972] vii, 357 p. illus. 23 cm. English and Greek. Original ed. issued as v. 8 of the University of Michigan studies. Humanistic series. [BS739.F7S22 1972] 77-39134
1. Bible. Manuscripts, Greek. O.T. Selected books. 2. Manuscripts, Greek—Facsimiles. I. Freer Gallery of Art, Washington, D.C. Mss. (Greek) II. Bible. O.T. Psalms. Greek. 1972. III. Title. IV. Series: Michigan. University. University of Michigan studies. Humanistic series, v. 8.

SWETE, Henry Barclay, 1835-1917. 221.48
An introduction to the Old Testament in Greek. Rev. by Richard Rusden Ottley. With an appendix containing the letter of Aristeas edited by H. St. J. Thackeray. New York, KTAV Pub. House, 1968. xiii, 626 p. 23 cm. Reprint of the 1902 ed. Bibliographical references included in "Additional notes": (p. [498]-530) Bibliographical footnotes. [BS738.S8 1968] 68-31420 12.50
1. Bible. O.T. Greek—History. I. Thackeray, Henry St. John, 1869?-1930. II. Ottley, Richard Rusden, 1864- III. Aristeas' epistle. 1968. IV. Title.

BIBLE. O.T. English. 1952. New American. 221.5'2
The Holy Bible. Translated from the original languages with critical use of all the ancient sources by members of the Catholic Biblical Association of America. Paterson, N.J., St. Anthony Guild Press, 1952-[69. v. 2, 1969] 4 v. 20 cm. Vols. 1, 3-4 sponsored by the Episcopal Committee and v. 2 by the Bishops' Committee of the Confraternity of Christian Doctrine. No more published. Contents.Contents.—v. 1. Genesis to Ruth.—v. 2. Samuel to Maccabees.—v. 3. The sapiental books: Job to Sirach.—v. 4. The prophetic books: Isaia to Malachia. [BS892.3.A1 1952.P3] 52-13526
I. Catholic Bible Association of America. II. Confraternity of Christian Doctrine. Episcopal Committee. III. Confraternity of Christian Doctrine. Bishops' Committee.

BIBLE. O. T. English. 1952. Revised standard. 221.52
The Holy Bible: The Old Testament. Revised standard version, translated from the original tongues; being the version set forth A. D. 1611, revised A. D. 1885 and A. D. 1901; compared with the most ancient authorities and revised A. D. 1952. New York, T. Nelson [c1952] 2v. (xiv, 1957p.) 19cm. [BS891.A1 1952.N4] 53-1318
I. Title.

BIBLE. O. T. English. 1953.NewWorld. 221.52
New World translation of the Hebrew Scriptures, rendered from the original languages by the New World Bible Translation Committee. [1st ed.] Brooklyn, Watchtower Bible Tract Society, 1953-60. 5 v. illus., maps (part col.) 19 cm. [BS895.N4] 53-35201
I. New World Bible Translation Committee. II. Watch Tower Bible and Tract Society. III. Title.

BIBLE. O. T. English. 1953. New World. 221.52
New World translation of the Hebrew Scriptures, rendered from the original languages by the New World Bible Translation Committee, A. D. 1953. [1st ed. Brooklyn, Watchtower Bible and Tract Society] 1953- v. illus., maps (part col.) 19cm. [BS895.N4] 53-35201
I. New World Bible Translation Committee. II. Watch Tower Bible and Tract Society. III. Title.

BIBLE. O. T. English. 1957. Jewish Publication Society. 221.52
The Holy Scriptures; a Jewish family Bible according to the Mosoretic text. Complete with inspirational and information features, including a most comprehensive, encyclopedia dictionary of the Bible and religious terms, a complete section of holidays and their meanings, an inspiring section for strength to meet every human problem, co-ordinated Biblical maps of ancient and modern cities, plus magnificent full color reproductions of paintings of people in the Bible and their stories. Editors: Morris A. Gutstein and David Graubart. Bible text: Jewish Publication Society of America Chicago, Menorah Press [1957] xvi, 942p. illus. (part col.) col. maps. 27cm. [BS895.J4 1957] 57-3220
1. Bible. O. T.—Dictionaries. I. Jewish Publication Society of America. II. Title.

BIBLE. O. T. English. 1962. Children's version. 221.52
The Children's version of the Hly Bible. [1st ed.] New York, McGraw-Hill[1962] 1175, 207p. col. illus. 23cm. Cover title: The Children's Old Testament, with stories. 'The Children's Bible story book: Old Testament. Stories by Peter Palmer. Illustrated by Manning de V. Lee' has special t. p. and separatepaging. [BS897.P3 1962] 62-17788
I. Palmer, Peter. The Children's Bible story book: Old Testament. II. Title. III. Title: The Children's Old Testament, with stories. IV. Title: The Children's Bible story book: Old Testament.

BIBLE. O.T. English. 1962. Children's version 221.52
The Children's version of the Holy Bible. New york, McGraw [c.1962] 1175, 207p. col. illus. 23cm. Cover title: The Children's Old Testament, with stories. 'The Children's Bible story book: Old Testament. Stories by Peter Palmer. Illus. by Manning de V. Lee' has special t.p. and separate paging. 62-17788 7.95
I. Palmer, Peter. The Children's Bible story book: Old Testament. II. Title. III. Title: The Children's Old Testament, with stories. IV.

Title: The Children's Bible story book: Old Testament.

BIBLE. O.T. English. 1963. 221.52
Authorized.
The Holy Bible, Old Testament. Translated out of the original tongues: and with the former translations diligently compared and rev., by His Majesty's special command. Salt Lake City, Deseret Book Co., 1963. iv, 1240 p. illus. (part col.) col. maps. 27 cm. [BS885 1963.S3] 63-25014
I. Title.

BIBLE. O.T. English. 1965. 221.52
Confraternity version.
The Old Testament, complete. With annotations by Joseph A. Grispino. New York, Guild Press [1965] xii, 1802 p. illus., maps. 19 cm. (An Angelus book) "The text is the new translation sponsored by the Episcopal Committee of the Confraternity of Christian Doctrine for the books of Genesis to Ruth, Job to Sirach, and the Prophetical books. The books of Kings to Esther, and 1, 2, Machabees are from the Douay version." [BS880] 65-1930
I. Grispino, Joseph A. II. Confraternity of Christian Doctrine. III. Title.

BIBLE. O. T. English. 221.52
1965. Confraternity version.
The Old Testament. complete. Annotations by Joseph A. Grispino. New York, Guild Pr. [c.1965] xii, 1802p. illus., maps. 19cm. (Angelus bk., 31176) Text is the new tr. sponsored by the Episcopal Comm. of the Confraternity of Christian Doctrine for the books of Genesis to Ruth. Job to Sirach, and the Prophetical books. The books of Kings to Esther, and 1. 2. Machabees are from the Douav version. [BS880] 65-1930 1.50 pap.,
I. Grispino. Joseph A. II. Confraternity of Christian Doctrine. III. Title.

BIBLE. O.T. English. 221.5'2
Birnbaum. 1976.
The concise Jewish Bible / edited and translated by Philip Birnbaum. New York : Sanhedrin Press, c1976. 234 p. ; 24 cm. [BS895.B57] 76-49108 ISBN 0-88482-450-0 : 7.95. ISBN 0-88482-451-9 pbk. : 3.95
I. Birnbaum, Philip. II. Title.

BIBLE. O.T. English. New 221.5'2
English. 1970.
The New English Bible: the Old Testament. London: Oxford U.P./Cambridge U.P., 1970. xxiv, 1366 p. 24 cm. Translated under the supervision of the Joint Committee on the New Translation of the Bible. [BS892.A1 1970.L62] 75-486868 50/-
I. Joint Committee on the New Translation of the Bible. II. Title.

BIBLE. O. T. English. 221.52
Selections. 1950.
Prose and poetry from the Old Testament, edited by James F. Fullington. New York, Appleton-Century-Crofts [1950] xi, 114 p. 18 cm. (Crofts classics) Bibliography: p. 113-114. [BS1091.F8] 50-9988
I. Fullington, James Fitz-James. ed. II. Title.

BIBLE. O. T. English. 221.52
Selections. 1950. Authorized.
Narratives from the Old Testament, edited by James F. Fullington. New York, Appleton-Century-Crofts [1950] ix, 115 p. 18 cm. (Crofts classics) Bibliography: p. 115. [BS1091.F82] 50-9987
I. Fullington, James Fitz-James. ed. II. Title.

BIBLE. O. T. English. 221.52
Selections. 1950. Douai.
In our image; character studies from the Old Testament, selected from the Douay version by Houston Harte. 32 color paintings by Guy Rowe. Pref. by Bishop Fitzsimon of Amarillo, foreword by Kent Cooper. [Roman Catholic ed.] New York, Oxford University Press, 1950. xvi, 205 p. 32 col. plates. 32 cm. [BS1091.H36] 50-12986
1. Bible. O. T.—Pictorial illustrations. I. Harte, Houston, 1893- ed. II. Rowe, Guy, 1894- illus. III. Title.

BIBLE. O. T. English. 221.52
Selections. 1953. Revised standard.
A study of the Old Testament, by Herbert Morrison Gale. East Northfield, Mass., Northfield Schools, 1953. 286p. 26cm. [BS1091.G28] 53-37782
1. Bible. O. T.—Study—Text-books. I. Gale, Herbert Morrison, 1907— II. Title.

BIBLE. O. T. English. 221.52
Selections. 1956. Authorized.
The wisdom of the Torah; edited by Dogobert D. Runes. New York, Philosophical Library [1956] 300p. 22cm. [BS1091.R8] 56-13824
I. Runes, Dagobert David, 1902- ed. II. Title.

BIBLE. O. T. English. 221.52
Selections. 1957.
Bible readings for the synagogue, selected and edited by Robert I. Kahn. Houston, Temple Emanu El, 1957. 96p. 22cm. [BS1091.K3] 58-36611
I. Kahn, Robert I., ed. II. Title.

BIBLE. O.T. English. 221.52
Selections. 1963.Confraternityversion.
The Old Testament. Authorized Catholic ed. Abridged from the Holy Bible sponsored by the Episcopal Committee of the Confraternity of Christian Doctrine. Foreword by Louis A. Gales. The selections were made and arranged by Louis A. Gales and Charles Hartman. New York, Guild Press [1963] xxiv, 455 p. maps. 17 cm. (An Angelus book) [BS880] 63-24747
I. Gales, Louis A., ed. II. Hartman, Charles, ed. III. Confraternity of Christian Doctrine. IV. Title.

BIBLE. O. T. English. 221.52
Selections. 1963. Confraternity version.
The Old Testament. AuthorizedCatholic ed. Abridged from the Holy Bible sponsored by the Episcopal Comm. of the Confraternity of Christian Doctrine. Foreword by Louis A. Gales. The selections were made and arranged by Louis A. Gales, Charles Hartman. New York, Guild [dist. Golden, c.1963] xxiv, 455p. maps. 17cm. (Angelus bk.) 63-24747 .65 pap.,
I. Gales, Louis A., ed. II. Hartman, Charles, ed. III. Confraternity of Christian Doctrine IV. Title.

BIBLE. O.T. English. 221.5'2
Selections. 1976.
The visual Bible : ninety-two drawings / Mortimer Borne. New York : Abaris Books, 1977,c1976 190 p. : ill. ; 29 cm. [BS1091.B67] 77-371322 ISBN 0-913870-15-3 : 12.50
1. Bible—Pictures, illustrations, etc. I. Borne, Mortimer. II. Title.

EDINGTON, Andrew. 221.5'2
The Word made fresh / compiled by Andrew Edington ; with foreword by James A. Wharton. Atlanta : J. Knox Press, c1975-1976. 3 v. ; 23 cm. Contents.Contents.—v. 1. Genesis-Kings.—v. 2. Chronicles-Malachi.—v. 3. The New Testament. [BS195.E3] 75-13457 ISBN 0-8042-0075-0(v.1) pbk. : 3.95 per vol.
1. Bible—Paraphrases, English. I. Title.

EDWARDS, Anne. 221.5'2
The Bible for young readers: the Old Testament. Rewritten for young readers by Anne Edwards. Illustrated by Charles Front and David Christian. New York, Golden Press [1968, c1967] 369 p. col. illus. 19 cm. Originally published under title: A child's Bible. A prose retelling of the Old Testament including highlights of the most important books. [BS551.2.E33 1968] 68-20534 3.95
1. Bible stories, English—O.T. I. Front, Charles, illus. II. Christian, David, illus. III. Title.

*FULLINGTON, James F., ed. 221.52
Prose and poetry from the Old Testament. New York, Appleton [1964, c.1950] 112p. 19cm. (New century classics) Bibl. .95 bds.,
I. Title.

MILTON, John Peterson, 221.52
1897-
God's word to men; an evaluation of the Revised standard version of the Old Testament. Minneapolis, Augsburg Pub. House [1953] 31p. 23cm. [BS891.M5] 54-17879
1. Bible. O. T. English—Versions—Revised standard. I. Title.

NAPIER, Bunyan Davie. 221.5'2
Time of burning [by] B. Davie Napier. Philadelphia, Pilgrim Press [1970] 94 p. 21 cm. [BS1151.5.N3] 74-117723 2.95
1. Bible. O.T.—Paraphrases, English. 2. Bible. O.T.—Meditations. I. Title.

PALMER, Peter 221.52
The children's Bible story book: Old Testament. Illus. by Manning DeV. Lee. New York, McGraw c.1962 207p. col. illus. 23cm. 62-17789 3.95
I. Title.

ROTHWELL, Allen Edward. 221.52
The Old Bible in rhyme. [1st ed.] New York, Pageant Press [1953] 182p. 24cm. [BS559.R67] 53-8805
1. Bible. O. T.—History of Biblical events—Poetry. I. Title.

BIBLE. O.T. English. 221.5'203
Authorized. 1968.
The Oxford illustrated Old Testament; with drawings by contemporary artists. London, New York [etc.] Oxford U.P., 1968- v. illus. 24 cm. Contents.—1. The Pentateuch.—2. The historical books.—3. The poetical books. [BS185 1968.L6] 74-398632 63/- per. vol.
I. Title.

BIBLE. O. T. English 221.5203
Selections. 1966. Authorized
God and His people. Ed. by Harold Bassage, from the King James version of the Old Testament. Illus. by Clark B. Fitz-Gerald. New York, Seabury [c.1966] ix, 212p. illus. 24cm. [BS1091.B35] 66-16656 4.95
I. Bassage, Harold Edwin, 1906- ed. II. Title.

DELL'ISOLA, Frank. 221.52'04
The Old Testament for everyman; edited and rearranged in a continuous narrative. [1st ed.] New York, Meredith Press [1968] xiv, 427 p. 25 cm. The text used is that of the Confraternity of Christian Doctrine and the Revised standard versions of the Bible. [BS1091.D4] 68-11333
I. Title.

ALLEN, Eula. 221.6
Before the beginning. Virginia Beach, Va., A.R.E. Press, 1963. 66 l. illus. 28 cm. Typescript. "Based on a twenty years' study of the Bible and the [Edgar Cayce] readings": pref. [BS1239.A404]
1. Bible. O.T. Genesis I-III—Criticism, interpretation, etc. 2. Creation—Biblical teaching. I. Title.

ANDERSON, Bernhard W., ed. 221.6
Israel's prophetic heritage; essays in honor of James Muilenburg. Ed. by Bernhard W. Anderson, Walter Harrelson. New York, Harper [c.1962] xiv, 242p. port. 22cm. 62-11122 5.00
1. Muilenburg, James. 2. Bible. O. T.—Addresses, essays, lectures. 3. Bible. O. T. Prophets—Criticism, interpretation, etc. I. Harrelson, Walter J., joint ed. II. Title.

ANDERSON, Bernhard W ed. 221.6
Israel's prophetic heritage: essays in honor of James Muilenburg. Edited by Bernhard W. Anderson and Walter Harrelson. 1st ed. New York, Harper [1962] xiv, 242p. port. 22cm. [BS1192.A4] 62-11122
1. Mulleaburg, James. 2. Bible. O. T.—Addresses, essays, lectures. 3. Bible. O. T. Prophets—Criticism. interpretation, etc. I. Harreison, Walter., joint ed. II. Title.
Contents omitted.

BAAB, Otto J. 221.6
The theology of the Old Testament. Nashville, Abingdon [1961, c.1949] 287p. (Apex bk., E1) Bibl. 1.50 pap.,
1. Bible. O T.—Theology. I. Title.

BAMBERGER, Bernard Jacob, 221.6
1904-
The Bible: a modern Jewish approach. 2d ed. New York, Schocken Books [1963] 118 p. 21 cm. (Schocken paperbacks. SB62) Bibliography: p. 116-118. [BS1140.2.B3 1963] 63-18388
1. Bible. O. T.—Introductions.

BEAUCAMP, Evode. 221.6
The Bible and the universe; Israel and the theology of history. [Translation by David Balhatchet] Westminster, Md., Newman Press [1963] xviii, 200 p. 22 cm. Translation of La Bible et le seus religieux de l'univers, based on the author's thesis, Lyons, 1953. Bibliography: p. 187-188. [BR115.II5B413] 62-21498
1. History — Philosophy. 2. Bible. O.T. — Criticism, interpretation, etc. I. Title.

BEAUCAMP, Evode 221.6
The Bible and the universe; Israel and the theology of history. [Tr. from French by David Balhatchet] Westminster, Md., Newman [c.1963] xviii, 200p. 22cm. Bibl. 62-21498 4.75
1. History—Philosophy. 2. Bible. O. T.—Criticism, interpretation, etc. I. Title.

BEWER, Julius August, 1877- 221.6
1953.
The literature of the Old Testament. 3d ed., completely rev. by Emil G. Kraeling. New York, Columbia University Press, 1962. xv, 496 p. 24 cm. (Records of civilization: sources and studies, no. 5) Includes index. Bibliography: p. [464]-480. [BS1140.B45 1962] 62-17061
1. Bible. O.T.—Introductions. I. Title. II. Series.

BICKERMAN, Elias Joseph, 221.6
1897-
Studies in Jewish and Christian history / by Elias Bickerman. Leiden : E. J. Brill, 1976- v. ; 25 cm. (Arbeiten zur Geschichte des antiken Judentums und des Urchristentums ; bd. 9) English, French, or German. Includes bibliographical references and indexes. [BS1192.B45] 76-364097 ISBN 9-00-404395-0 (v. 1)
1. Bible. O.T.—Criticism, interpretation, etc.—Addresses, essays, lectures. 2. Bible. O.T. Greek—Versions—Septuagint—Addresses, essays, lectures. I. Title. II. Series.

BORNKAMM, Heinrich, 1901- 221.6
Luther and the Old Testament. Translated by Eric W. and Ruth C. Gritsch. Edited by Victor I. Gruhn. Philadelphia, Fortress Press [1969] xii, 307 p. 23 cm. Includes bibliographical references. [BR333.B61213] 69-11272 9.75
1. Luther, Martin, 1483-1546. 2. Bible. O.T.—Criticism, interpretation, etc.—History. I. Title.

BRUCE, Frederick Fyvie, 221.6
1910-
Biblical exegesis in the Qumran texts. Grand Rapids, Eerdmans [1959] 82p. 23cm. (Exegetica) [BS1160.B7] 59-3475
1. Bible, O. T.—Criticism, interpretation, etc.—Hist. 2. Dead Sea scrolls. I. Title.

CAMPBELL, D. B. J. 221.6
The Old Testament for modern readers [by] D. B. J. Campbell. Atlanta, John Knox Press [1974, c1972] viii, 135 p. 23 cm. [BS1194.C35 1974] 73-16913 ISBN 0-8042-0197-8 5.95
1. Bible. O.T.—Study—Text-books. 2. Cultus, Jewish. I. Title.

CARMICHAEL, Patrick Henry, 221.6
1889- ed.
Understanding the books of the Old Testament; a guide to Bible study for laymen. Edited by Patrick H. Carmichael, prepared by W. A. Benfield, Jr. [and others] Richmond, John Knox Press [1950] 173 p. illus. 25 cm. [BS1140.C25] 50-58274
1. Bible. O. T.—Introductions. I. Title.
Contents Omitted.

CARMICHAEL, Patrick Henry, 221.6
1889- ed.
Understanding the books of the Old Testament; a guide to Bible study for laymen. Prepared by W. A. Benfield, Jr. [others. Rev. ed.] Richmond, Va., John Knox [1961, c.1950, 1961] 188p. illus. (Aletheia paperbacks) 61-9223 1.95 pap.,
1. Bible. O. T.—Introduction. I. Title.

CASPER, Bernard Moses, 221.6
1916-
An introduction to Jewish Bible commentary. New York, T. Yoseloff [1961, c.1960] 128p. (Popular Jewish library) Bibl. 61-2740 2.95 bds.,
1. Bible. O. T.—Criticism, interpretation, etc.—Hist. I. Title. II. Title: Jewish Bible commentary.

CHARPENTIER, Etienne. 221.6
The Old Testament, always relevant. Translated by Sheila Richards. [Edited by Lisa McGaw] De Pere, Wis., St. Norbert Abbey Press, 1969. 233 p. 19 cm. Translation of Jeunesse du vieux testament. [BS1140.2.C4513] 74-87816 3.95
1. Bible. O.T.—Introductions. I. Title.

CHILDS, Brevard S. 221.6
Memory and tradition in Israel. Naperville, Ill., Allenson [1963] 96p. 22cm. (Studies in Biblical theology, v. 37) Bibl. 63-2478 2.00 pap.,
1. Memory—Biblical teaching. 2. Tradition (Judaism) 3. Zkr (Hebrew root) I. Title.

CROSS, Frank Moore. 221.6
Canaanite myth and Hebrew epic; essays in the history of the religion of Israel. Cambridge, Mass., Harvard University Press, 1973. xviii, 376 p. 25 cm. Includes bibliographical references. [BS1171.2.C76] 72-76564 ISBN 0-674-09175-2 14.00
1. Bible. O.T.—Criticism, interpretation, etc. 2. Canaanites—Religion—Addresses, essays, lectures. 3. Judaism—History—Ancient period—Addresses, essays, lectures. I. Title.

DANIELOU, Jean 221.6
From shadows to reality; studies in the Biblical typology of the Fathers. [Tr. [from French] by Wulstan Hibberd] Westminster, Md., Newman Press [c.1960] 296p. Bibl. 60-14811 5.50
1. Typology (Theology) 2. Bible. O. T. Hexateuch—Hermeneutics. 3. Bible—Criticism, interpretation, etc.—Hist. I. Title.

DAVIDSON, Robert. 221.6
The Old Testament. Philadelphia, Lippincott [1964] 236 p. 21 cm. (Knowing Christianity) Bibliography: p. 233. [BS1192.5.D35] 64-23472
I. Title.

DENTAN, Robert Claude, 221.6
1907-
Preface to Old Testament theology. Rev. ed. New York, Seabury Press, 1963. 146 p. 22 cm. Bibliography: p. [127]-144. [BS1192.5.D4 1963] 63-18696
1. Bible. O.T. — Theology. I. Title.

DENTAN, Robert Claude, 1907- 221.6
Preface to Old Testament theology. Rev. ed. New York, Seabury [c.]1963. 146p. 22cm. Bibl. 63-18696 3.00 bds.,
1. Bible. O. T.—Theology. I. Title.

DODD, Charles Harold, 1884- 221.6
According to the Scriptures; the sub-structure of New Testament theology. New York, Scribner, 1953. 145p. 20cm. [BS2397.D6 1953] 53-11929
1. Bible. N. T.—Theology. 2. Bible. N. T.—Relation to O. T. I. Title.

DRIVER, Samuel Rolles, 1846-1914 221.6
An introduction to the literature of the Old Testament. [Gloucester, Mass., Peter Smith, 1962] xxv, xi, 577p. 21cm. (Meridian lib., ML3 rebound) Bibl. 4.25
1. Bible. O.T.—Introductions. 2. Hebrew literature—Hist. & crit. I. Title.

DRIVER, Samuel Rolles, 1846-1914. 221.6
An introduction to the literature of the Old Testament. New York, Meridian Books, 1956. xxv, 577 p. 21 cm. (The Meridian library, ML3) Includes bibliographical references. [BS1140.D8 1956] 56-10898
1. Bible. O. T.—Introductions. 2. Hebrew literature—History and criticism.

EDWARDS, David Lawrence. 221.6
A key to the Old Testament / David L. Edwards. London : Collins, 1976. 282 p., [8] leaves of plates : ill. (some col.) ; 22 cm. Includes index. Bibliography: p. [273]-274. [BS1171.2.E38] 76-381838 ISBN 0-00-215402-1 : £4.95
1. Bible. O.T.—Criticism, interpretation, etc. I. Title.

EICHRODT, Walther, 1890- 221.6
Theology of the Old Testament: v.2. Tr. by J.A. Baker. Philadelphia, Westminster [1967] v. 23cm. (Old Testament lib.) Bibl. [BS1192.5.E353] 61-11867 7.50
1. Bible—O.T.—Theology. I. Title. II. Series.

EICHRODT, Walther, 1890- 221.6
Theology of the Old Testament. Tr. [from German] by J. A. Baker. Philadelphia, Westminster Pr. [c.1961] 542p. (Old Testament lib.) Bibl. 61-11867 7.50
1. Bible. O. T.—Theology. I. Title. II. Series.

ELLIS, Peter F. 221.6
The men and the message of the Old Testament. Collegeville, Minn., LiturgicalPr. [c.1963] 559p. illus. 24cm. Bibl. 63-3042 8.00
1. Bible. O.T.—Introductions. I. Title.

ELLIS, Peter F 221.6
The men and the message of the Old Testament. Collegeville. Minn., Liturgical Press [1963] 559 p. illus. 24 cm. Includes bibliographies. [BS1140.2.E4] 221 63-3042
1. Bible. O.T. — Introductions. I. Title.

ELLISON, Henry Leopold. 221.6
The message of the Old Testament [by] H. L. Ellison. Grand Rapids, Eerdmans [1969] 94 p. 20 cm. [BS1140.2.E43 1969] 70-12175 1.45
1. Bible. O.T.—Introductions. I. Title.

ESSAYS in honor of George Ernest Wright / edited by Edward F. Campbell and Robert G. Boling. Missoula, MT : Scholars Press, [1976] p. cm. Essays from the Bulletin of the American Schools of Oriental Research, no. 220-221, Dec. 1975, Feb., 1976. [BS1192.E78] 76-10747 ISBN 0-89130-106-2 221.6
1. Wright, George Ernest, 1909-1974. 2. Bible. O.T.—Criticism, interpretation, etc.—Addresses, essays, lectures. 3. Bible—Antiquities—Addresses, essays, lectures. I. Wright, George Ernest, 1909-1974. II. Campbell, Edward Fay. III. Boling, Robert G. IV. American Schools of Oriental Research. Bulletin.

FRANCISCO, Clyde T. 221.6
Introducing the Old Testament; based upon John R. Sampey's Syllabus. Nashville, Broadman Press [1950] xii, 271 p. 21 cm. Bibliography: p. 235-242. [BS1140.F67] 50-58226
1. Bible. O. T.—Introductions. I. Sampey, John Richard, 1863-1946. II. Title. III. Title: Syllabus for Old Testament study.

FRANCISCO, Clyde T. 221.6
Introducing the Old Testament / Clyde T. Francisco. Rev. ed. Nashville : Broadman Press, c1977. 301 p. ; 22 cm. Based on Syllabus for Old Testament study by J. R. Sampey. Bibliography: p. 289-299. [BS1140.2.F67 1977] 76-24060 ISBN 0-8054-1213-1 : 8.95
1. Bible. O.T.—Introductions. I. Sampey, John Richard, 1863-1946. Syllabus for Old Testament study. II. Title.

FRANCISCO, Clyde T. 221.6
Introducing the Old Testament / Clyde T. Francisco. Rev. ed. Nashville : Broadman Press, c1977. 301 p. ; 22 cm. Based on Syllabus for Old Testament study by J. R. Sampey. Bibliography: p. 289-299. [BS1140.2.F67 1977] 76-24060 ISBN 0-8054-1213-1 : 8.95
1. Bible. O.T.—Introductions. I. Sampey, John Richard, 1863-1946. Syllabus for Old Testament study. II. Title.

FREEDMAN, David Noel, 1922- 221.6
God has spoken; an introduction to the Old Testament for young people, by David Noel Freedman and James D. Smart. Philadelphia, Westminster Press [1949] 268p. illus. 22cm. [BS1140.F7] 49-11773
1. Bible, O. T.—Introductions. I. Smart, James D., joint author. II. Title.

FROMM, Erich, 1900- 221.6
You shall be as gods; a radical interpretation of the Old Testament and its tradition. [1st ed.] New York, Holt, Rinehart and Winston [1966] 240 p. 22 cm. [BS1171.2.F7 1966] 66-22066
1. Bible. O.T.—Criticism, interpretation, etc. I. Title.

GASTER, Theodor Herze, 1906- 221.6
Myth, legend, and custom in the Old Testament; a comparative study with chapters from Sir James G. Frazer's Folklore in the Old Testament. [1st ed.] New York, Harper & Row [1969] lv, 899 p. 24 cm. Bibliographical references included in "Notes." [BS625.G3] 69-17018 20.00
1. Bible. Old Testament—Criticism, interpretation, etc. 2. Folk-lore—Jews. 3. Mythology. I. Frazer, James George, Sir, 1854-1941. Folk-lore in the Old Testament. II. Title.

GASTER, Theodor Herze, 1906- 221.6
Myth, legend, and custom in the Old Testament; a comparative study with chapters from Sir James G. Frazer's Folklore in the Old Testament [by] Theodore H. Gaster New York Harper & Row 1975 c1969 2v. (908 p.); 21 cm. Includes bibliographical references. [BS625.G3] 4.95 (ea.)
1. Frazer, Sir James George, 1854-1941. Folk-lore in the Old Testament. 2. Folk-lore—Jews. 3. Bible. Old Testament—Criticism, Interpretation, etc. 4. Mythology. I. Title.
L.C. card no. for original edition: 69-17018. Vol. 1, ISBN 0-06-138640-5, Vol. 2, ISBN 0-06-138641-3

GELIN, Albert. 221'.6
Les Idees maitresses de l'Ancien Testament... [Paris,] Editions du Cerf, 1966. 127 p. 18 cm. (Fol vivante, 30) 3.60 F. Illustrated cover. Bibliography: p. [113]-125. [BS1192.5.G4] 67-100006
1. Bible. O.T.—Theology. I. Title.

GELIN, Albert. 221.6
The key concepts of the Old Testament. Translated by George Lamb. New York, Sheed and Ward, 1955. 94p. 20cm. 'A translation of Les idees maitresses de l'Ancien Testament.' [BS1192.5.G415] 55-9453
1. Bible. O.T.—Theology. I. Title.

GELIN, Albert 221.6
The key concepts of the Old Testament. Tr. [from French] by George Lamb. New York, Paulist Pr. [1963, c.1955] 94p. 18cm. (Deus bk.) .75 pap.,
1. Bible. O.T.—Theology. I. Title.

GOD and history in the Old Testament / Dennis Baly, with the help and advice of the following contributors, T. P. Bronco, Jr. ... [et al.]. 1st ed. New York : Harper & Row, c1976. xiii, 234 p. ; 24 cm. Includes indexes. Bibliography: p. 209-215. [BS1192.6B34 1976] 76-9984 ISBN 0-06-060369-0 pbk. : 6.95 221.6
1. Bible. O.T.—Criticism, interpretation, etc.—Addresses, essays, lectures. 2. God—Biblical teaching—Addresses, essays, lectures. I. Bronco, T. P., joint author.

†GORDIS, Robert, 1908- 221.6
The word and the book : studies in Biblical language and literature / by Robert Gordis. New York : Ktav Pub. House, 1976. xvi, 388, 48 p. ; 24 cm. Reprinted from various journals and Festschriften, 1930-1974. English and Hebrew. Includes bibliographical references and indexes. [BS1192.G67] 75-46617 ISBN 0-87068-456-6 ; 25.00
1. Bible. O.T.—Language, style—Addresses, essays, lectures. 2. Bible. O.T.—Criticism, interpretation, etc.—Addresses, essays, lectures. 3. Bible. O.T. Ecclesiastes—Criticism, interpretation, etc.—Addresses, essays, lectures. I. Title.

GUTHRIE, Harvey H. 221.6
God and history in the Old Testament. Greenwich, Conn., Seabury Press, [c.]1960. viii, 179p. Bibl. notes: p.166-168. 22cm. 60-5886 4.25
1. Bible. O. T.—Criticism, interpretation, etc. 2. God. 3. History—Philosophy. I. Title.

HAHN, Herbert Ferdinand, 1905- 221.6
The Old Testament in modern research [by] Herbert F. Hahn. With a survey of recent literature, by Horace D. Hummel. [2d, expanded ed.] Philadelphia, Fortress Press [1966] xii, 332 p. 22 cm. Includes bibliographical references. [BS1160.H3 1966] 66-18995
1. Bible. O.T.—Criticism, interpretation, etc.—History. I. Hummel, Horace D. II. Title.

HAMLIN, Griffith A 221.6
The Old Testament, its intent and content, including the Apocrypha. Boston, Christopher Pub. House [1958] 113p. 21cm. [BS1140.H32] 58-8663
1. Bible. O. T.— Introductions. 2. Bible. O. T. Apocrypha—Introductions. I. Title.

HANKE, Howard A. 221.6
From Eden to eternity; a survey of Christology and ecclesiology in the Old Testament and their redemptive relationship to man, from Adam to the end of time. Grand Rapids, Eerdmans [c.1960] 196p. (bibl.) 23cm. 59-14585 3.50
1. Bible. N. T.—Relation to O. T. I. Title.

HART, Henry St. John 1912- 221.6
A foreword to the Old Testament; an essay of elementary introduction. New York, Oxford University Press, 1951. xv, 184p. maps. 22cm. 'Books suggested for further reading': p. 180. [BS1140.H] A53
1. Bible. O. T.—Introductions. I. Title.

HEBERT, Arthur Gabriel, 1886- 221.6
The Old Testament from within. New York, Oxford [c.1962, 1965] 153p. 20cm. (100) [BS1140.2.H42] 1.85 pap.,
1. Bible. O. T. — Criticism, interpretation, etc. I. Title.

HEINISCH, Paul, 1878-1956. 221.6
Theology of the Old Testament. William G. Heidt, translator. [Rev. and supplemented. Collegeville, Minn.] Liturgical Press [1957? c1955] 476p. 24cm. Includes bibliography. [BS1192.5.H42 1957] 60-37395
1. Bible. O. T.— Theology. I. Title.

HERBERT, Arthur Gabriel, 1886- 221.6
The Old Testament from within. London, New York, Oxford University Press, 1962. 153p. 20cm. 'A completely revised edition of The Bible from within, which was published ... in 1950. Much of the text ... remains, but it is really a new book.' [BS1140.2.H42] 62-52005
1. Bible. O. T.—Circiticism, interpretation, etc. I. Title.

JACOB, Edmond. 221.6
Theology of the Old Testament. Translated by Arthur W. Heathcote and Philip J. Allcock. New York, Harper [1958] 368p. 22cm. Includes bibliographies. [BS1192.5.J313 1958a] 58-7094
1. Bible. O. T.—Theology. I. Title.

JENKS, Alan W. 221.6
The Elohist and north Israelite traditions / by Alan W. Jenks. Missoula, Mont. : Published by Scholars Press for the Society of Biblical Literature, c1976. p. cm. (Monograph series - Society of Biblical Literature ; no. 22) A revision of the author's thesis, Harvard, 1965. Includes bibliographical references and indexes. [BS1181.2.J46 1976] 76-40189 ISBN 0-89130-088-0
1. E document (Biblical criticism) 2. Prophets. I. Title. II. Series: Society of Biblical Literature. Monograph series ; no. 22.

JENKS, Alan W. 221.6
The Elohist and north Israelite traditions / by Alan W. Jenks. Missoula, Mont. : Published by Scholars Press for the Society of Biblical Literature, c1976. p. cm. (Monograph series - Society of Biblical Literature ; no. 22) A revision of the author's thesis, Harvard, 1965. Includes bibliographical references and indexes. [BS1181.2.J46 1976] 76-40189 ISBN 0-89130-088-0
1. E document (Biblical criticism) 2. Prophets. I. Title. II. Series: Society of Biblical Literature. Monograph series ; no. 22.

JENSEN, Joseph, 1924- 221.6
God's word to Israel. Boston, Allyn and Bacon [1968] xix, 314 p. illus. 22 cm. Includes bibliographies. [BS1140.2.J4] 68-14348
1. Bible. O.T.—Introductions. I. Title.

JOHANSSON, Catherine B. 221.6
Concepts of freedom in the Old Testament, by Catherine Johansson. [1st ed.] New York, Vantage Press [1965] 92 p. 21 cm. [BS1192.J6] 65-26207
1. Bible. O. T. — Addresses, essays, lectures. I. Title.

JONES, Bob, 1911- 221.6
Ancient truths for modern days; sermons on Old Testament subjects that particularly apply to our times. Murfreesboro, Tenn., Box 1099 Sword of the Lord Pubs., 1964, c.1963 187p. port. 21cm. 64-334 2.50 bds.,
1. Bible. O. T.—Sermons. 2. Sermons, American. I. Title.

KEIL, Karl Friedrich, 1807-1888. 221.6
Manual of historico-critical introduction to the canonical scriptures of the Old Testament. Translated from the 2d ed., with supplementary notes from Bleek and others, by George C. M. Douglas. Grand Rapids, W. B. Eerdman, 1952. 2v. 23cm. [BS1140.K] A 53
1. Bible. O. T.—Introductions. 2. Hebrew literature—Hist. & crit. I. Bleek, Friedrich, 1793-1859. Einleitung in das Alte Testament. II. Title. III. Title: Introduction to the canonical scriptures of the Old Testament.

KUHL, Curt. 221.6
The Old Testament, its origins and composition. Translated by C. T. M. Herriott. Richmons, John Knox Press, 1961. viii, 354p. 23cm. Translation of Die Enistehung des Alten Testaments. Bibliography: p. [319]-347. [BS1185.K813 1961] 61-7885
1. Bible. O. T.—Criticism, Textual. 2. Bible. O. T.—Criticism, Interpretation, etc. I. Title.

LARUE, Gerald A. 221.6
Old Testament life and literature [by] Gerald A. Larue. Boston, Allyn and Bacon [1968] xiii, 513 p. illus., maps. 26 cm. Bibliography: p. 461-503. [BS1140.2.L34] 68-18948
1. Bible. O.T.—Introductions. 2. Bible. O.T.—History of Biblical events. I. Title.

A Light unto my path; 221.6
Old Testament studies in honor of Jacob M. Myers. Edited by Howard N. Bream, Ralph D. Heim [and] Carey A. Moore. Philadelphia, Temple University Press [1974] xxv, 529 p. 24 cm. (Gettysburg theological studies, 4) Includes bibliographical references. [BS1192.L53] 73-85042 ISBN 0-87722-026-3 15.00
1. Myers, Jacob Martin, 1904- 2. Myers, Jacob Martin, 1904- —Bibliography. 3. Bible. O.T.—Addresses, essays, lectures. I. Myers, Jacob Martin, 1904- II. Bream, H. N., ed. III. Heim, Ralph Daniel, 1895- ed. IV. Moore, Carey A., 1930- ed. V. Title. VI. Series.

LOVELACE, Marc. 221'.6
Compass points for Old Testament study. Nashville, Abingdon Press [1972] 176 p. illus. 24 cm. Includes bibliographies. [BS1140.2.L68] 72-172816 ISBN 0-687-09275-2 4.95
1. Bible. O.T.—Introductions. I. Title.

MCKANE, William 221.6
Prophets and wise men. Naperville, Ill., A.R. Allenson [c.1965] 136p. 22cm. (Studies in Biblical theol., no.44) Bibl. [BS1198.M18] 65-3390 2.85 pap.,
1. Wisdom. 2. Bible. O. T.—Prophecies. I. Title. II. Series.

MCKANE, William 221.6
Tracts for the times; Ruth, Esther, Lamentations, Ecclesiastes. Song of songs. London, Lutterworth; Nashville, Abingdon [1965]93p. 20cm. (Bible guides, no.12) [BS1309.M22] 65-1372 1.00 pap.,
1. Bible. O. T. Five scrolls—Introductions. I. Title.

MACKENZIE, Roderick A. F. 221.6
Faith and history in the Old Testament; [lects.] New York, Macmillan [1965, c.1963] 124p. 18cm. (MP186) 1.45 pap.,
1. Bible. O. T.—Theology. 2. Bible. O.T.—History of Biblical events. I. Title.

MACKENZIE, Roderick Andrew Francis, 1911- 221.6
Faith and history in the Old Testament; [lectures by] R. A. F. MacKenzie. Minneapolis, University of Minnesota Press [1963] viii, 119 p. 23 cm. [BS1192.5.M3] 63-10585

1. Bible. O. T.—Theology. 2. Bible. O. T.—History of Biblical events. I. Title.

MANASSEH ben Joseph ben Israel, 1604-1657. 221'.6
The conciliator of R. Manasseh ben Israel; a reconcilement of the apparent contradictions in Holy Scripture, to which are added explanatory notes, and biographical notices of the quoted authorities, by E. H. Lindo. New York, Hermon Press [1972 i.e. 1973] 2 v. in 1. 24 cm. Reprint of the 1842 ed. Contents.Contents.—v. 1. The Pentateuch.—v. 2. The prophets and hagiography. [BS1177.M32 1972] 72-83942 ISBN 0-87203-036-9 14.95
1. Bible. O.T.—Criticism, interpretation, etc. I. Title.

MANN, Newton M 1836-1926. 221.6
A rational view of the Bible; five lectures on the date and origin of the various books of the Old Testament. Rochester, N. Y., C. Mann, printer, 1879. 206p. 19cm. [BS1171.M36] 54-52991
1. Bible. O. T.—Criticism, interpretation, etc. I. Title.

MEADOWS, Thomas Burton, 1881- 221.6
Guidance to the study of the Old Testament, an objective approach. New York, Vantage Press [c1954] 291p. 23cm. [BS1194.M348] 54-8378
1. Bible. O. T.—Study—Text-books. I. Title.

MILLER, Adam William, 1896- 221.6
Brief introduction to the Old Testament. Anderson, Ind., Warner Press [1964] 224 p. 19 cm. Includes bibliographies. [BS1140.2.M5] 64-11424
1. Bible. O.T.—Introductions. I. Title.

MILLER, Charles Henry, 1933- 221'.6
"As it is written"; the use of Old Testament references in the documents of Vatican Council II [by] Charles H. Miller. St. Louis, Marianist Communications Center, 1973. viii, 246 p. 25 cm. Bibliography: p. [233]-246. [BX830 1962.M55] 73-161531
1. Vatican Council. 2d, 1962-1965. 2. Bible. O.T.—Criticism, interpretation, etc. I. Vatican Council. 2d, 1962-1965.

MISKOTTE, Kornelis Heiko, 1894- 221.6
When the gods are silent [by] Kornelis H. Miskotte. Translated, with an introd., by John W. Doberstein. New York, Harper and Row [1967] xviii, 494 p. 22 cm. Translation of Als de goden zwijgen. Bibliographical footnotes. [BS476.M573] 66-10229
1. Bible. O. T.—Hermeneutics. 2. Bible. O. T.—Criticism, interpretation, etc. I. Title.

MISKOTTE, Kornelis Heiko, 1894- 221.6
When the gods are silent [by] Kornelis H. Miskotte. Translated, with an introd., by John W. Doberstein. New York, Harper and Row [1967] xviii, 494 p. 22 cm. Translation of Als de goden zwijgen. Bibliographical footnotes. [BS476.M573 1967] 66-10229
1. Bible. O.T.—Hermeneutics. 2. Bible. O.T.—Criticism, interpretation, etc. I. Title.

MORIARTY, Frederick L 221.6
Foreword to the Old Testament books. Weston, Mass, Weston College Press, 1954. 118p. illus. 20cm. [BS1140.M65] 54-14997
1. Bible. O. T.—Introductions. I. Title.

MORIARTY, Frederick L. 221.6
Introducing the Old Testament. Milwaukee, Bruce Pub. Co. [c.1960] xi, 253p. (3p. bibl.) illus. 23cm. (Impact books) 60-7391 4.25
1. Bible. O.T.—Introductions. I. Title.

NAPIER, Bunyan Davie. 221.6
Song of the vineyard; a theological introduction to the Old Testament. New York, Harper [1962] 387p. illus. 22cm. Includes bibliography. [BS1140.2.N3] 62-7435
1. Bible. O. T.—Introductions. 2. Bible. O. T.—Theology. I. Title.

NIELSEN, Eduard. 221.6
Oral tradition, a modern problem in Old Testament introduction; with a foreword by H. H. Fowley. Chicago, A. P. Allenson [1954] 108p. 22cm. (Studies in Biblical theology, no. 11) Translation of 'articles, published in Dansk teologisk tidsskrift, xiii (1950) and xv (1952) [BS1185.N5] 54-10022
1. Oral tradition. 2. Bible. O. T.—Criticism, interpretation, etc. I. Title. II. Series.

NOTH, Martin, 1902-1968. 221'.6
The laws in the Pentateuch, and other studies. Translated by D. R. Ap-Thomas. Introd. by Norman W. Porteous. Philadelphia, Fortress Press [1967] xiv, 289 p. 21 cm. Translation of: Gesammelte Studien zum Alten Testament. Bibliography: p. xiii-xiv. [BS1192.N5713 1967] 67-11111
1. Bible. O.T.—Addresses, essays, lectures. I. Title.

OESTERLEY, William Oscar Emil, 1866- 221.6
An introduction to the books of the Old Testament, by W. O. E. Oesterley and Theodore H. Robinson. New York, Meridian Books [1960] 454 p. 19 cm. (Living age books, LA23) Includes bibliography. [BS1140.O4 1960] 58-11932
1. Bible. O. T.—Introductions. I. Robinson, Theodore Henry, 1881- joint author.

OESTERREICHER, John M 1904- 221.6
The Israel of God: on the Old Testament roots of the church's faith. Englewood Cliffs, N.J., Prentice-Hall [1963] ix, 118 p. 24 cm. (Foundations of Catholic theology series) Bibliography: p. 111. [BS1192.5.O4] 63-21438
1. Bible. O.T. — Theology. I. Title.

OESTERREICHER, John M., 1904- 221.6
The Israel of God; on the Old Testament roots of the church's faith. Englewood Cliffs, N.J., Prentice [c.1963] ix, 118p. 24cm. (Founds. of Catholic theology ser.) Bibl. 63-21438 3.95; 1.50 pap.,
1. Bible. O.T.—Theology. I. Title.

OTWELL, John H. 221'.6
I will be your God; a layman's guide to Old Testament study [by] John H. Otwell. Nashville, Abingdon Press [1967] 224 p. 23 cm. Includes bibliographical references. [BS1197.O78] 67-14990
1. Bible. O. T. — History of Biblical events. 2. Bible. O. T. — Introductions. I. Title.

OTWELL, John H. 221'.6
I will be your God; a layman's guide to Old Testament study [by] John H. Otwell. Nashville, Abington Press [1967] 224 p. 23 cm. Includes bibliographical references. [BS1197.O78] 67-14990
1. Bible. O.T.—History of Biblical events. 2. Bible. O.T.—Introductions. I. Title.

PARRIS, George Keith, 1908- 221.6
Read the Bible with me; a layman's companion and guide to the Old Testament. New York, American Pr. [1961c.1960] 533p. 60-15814 7.50
1. Bible. O. T.—Criticism, interpretation. etc. I. Title.

PAUL Marie de la Croix, Father 221.6
Spirituality of the Old Testament; v.3. Tr. [from French] by Elizabeth McCabe; St. Louis, Herder [c.1963] 347p. 21cm. (Cross and crown ser. of spirituality, no. 24) 61-12115 4.95
1. Spiritual life—Biblical teaching. 2. Bible. O. T.—Criticism, interpretation, etc. I. Title.

PAUL MARIE DE LA CROIX, Father 221.6
Spirituality of the Old Testament. Tr. [from French] by Elizabeth McCabe. St. Louis, Herder [c.1961] xvi, 247p. (Cross and crown ser. of spirituality, no. 18) 61-12115 4.25 bds.,
1. Spiritual life—Biblical teaching. 2. Bible. O. T.—Criticism, interpretation, etc. I. Title.

PAYNE, John Barton, 1922- 221.6
The theology of the Older Testament. Grand Rapids, Zondervan Pub. House [1962] 554 p. 23 cm. Includes bibliography. [B1192.5.P3] 62-13172
1. Bible. O. T.—Theology. I. Title.

PFEIFFER, Robert Henry, 1892- 221.6
The books of the Old Testament. New York, Harper [1957] 335p. 22cm. 'An abridgment of the author's Introduction to the Old Testament.' [BS1140.P475] 56-13173
1. Bible. O. T.—Introductions. I. Title.

PILCHIK, Ely Emanuel. 221.6
From the beginning; a new look at the Bible. New York, Bloch Pub. Co., 1956. 275p. 21cm. [BS1140.P53] 56-13251
1. Bible. O. T.—Introductions. I. Title.

PREUS, James Samuel. 221.6
From shadow to promise; Old Testament interpretation from Augustine to the young Luther. Cambridge, Mass., Belknap Press of Harvard University Press, 1969. vii, 301 p. 22 cm. A revision of the author's thesis, Harvard Divinity School. Bibliography: p. [285]-293. [BR333.5.B5P7 1969] 69-12732 7.50
1. Luther, Martin, 1483-1546. 2. Bible. O.T.—Criticism, interpretation, etc. 3. Theology—Middle Ages, 600-1500. I. Title.

PURKISER, W T ed. 221.6
Exploring the Old Testament [by] W. T. Purkiser, editor [and others] Kansas City, Mo., Beacon Hill Press [1955] 448p. 23cm. Bibliography: p.436-442. [BS1140.P8] 55-13823
1. Bible. O. T.—Introductions. I. Title.

RAD, Gerhard von, 1901- 221.6
Old Testament theology. Translated by D. M. G. Stalker. New York, Harper, 1962-[65] 2 v. 24 cm. Vol. 2 published by Harper & Row. Contents.v. 1. The theology of Israel's historical traditions.--v. 2. The theology of Israel's prophetic traditions. Bibliographical footnotes. [BS1192.5.R3132] 62-7306
1. Bible. O. T.—Theology. I. Title.

RAD, Gerhard von, 1901- 221.6
Old Testament theology. Translated by D. M. G. Stalker. New York, Harper, 1962-[65] 2 v. 24 cm. Vol. 2 published by Harper & Row. Contents.Contents.—v. 1. The theology of Israel's historical traditions.—v. 2. The theology of Israel's prophetic traditions. Bibliographical footnotes. [BS1192.5.R3132] 62-7306
1. Bible. O.T.—Theology. I. Title.

RAD, Gerhard von, 1901- 221.6
The problem of the Hexateuch, and other essays. Tr. [from German] by E. W. Trueman Dicken. New York, McGraw [c.1966] xiii, 340p. port. 23cm. Bibl. [BS1188.R313] 66-11432 9.50
1. Bible. O. T. — Addresses, essays, lectures. I. Title.

RAD, Gerhard von, 1901- 221.6
The problem of the Hexateuch, and other essays. Translated by E. W. Trueman Dicken. New York, McGraw-Hill [1966] xiii, 340 p. port. 23 cm. Translation of Gesammelte Studien zum Alten Testament. Bibliographical footnotes. [BS1188.R313] 66-11432
1. Bible. O. T.—Addresses, essays, lectures. I. Title.

RENDTORFF, Rolf, 1925- 221.6
God's history; a way through the Old Testament. Translated by Gordon C. Winsor. Philadelphia, Westminster Press [1969] 77 p. 21 cm. Translation of Gottes Geschichte. [BS1140.2.R413] 69-18648 ISBN 6-642-48527- 1.85
1. Bible. O.T.—Introductions. I. Title.

ROBERTSON, David A. 221.6
Linguistic evidence in dating early Hebrew poetry, by David A. Robertson. [Missoula, Mont.] Published by Society of Biblical Literature for the Seminar on Form Criticism, 1972. ix, 159 p. 22 cm. (Society of Biblical Literature. Dissertation series, no. 3) Originally presented as the author's thesis, Yale, 1966. Bibliography: p. 157-159. [BS1405.2.R6 1972] 72-87886 ISBN 0-88414-012-1
1. Bible. O.T.—Language, style. 2. Hebrew poetry—History and criticism. I. Society of Biblical Literature. Form Criticism Seminar. II. Title. III. Series.

ROBERTSON, David A. 221.6
The Old Testament and the literary critic / by David Robertson. Philadelphia : Fortress Press, c1977. viii, 87 p. ; 22 cm. (Guides to Biblical scholarship : Old Testament series) Bibliography: p. 86-87. [BS535.R62] 76-62620 ISBN 0-8006-0463-6 pbk. : 3.25
1. Bible. O.T.—Criticism, interpretation, etc. 2. Bible as literature. I. Title.

ROBINSON, H. Wheeler, 1872-1945. 221.6
Inspiration and revelation in the Old Testament. [New York, Oxford, 1962] 298p. 20cm. (Oxford paperbacks, no. 52) Bibl. 1.50 pap.,
1. Bible, O.T.—Theology. 2. Bible. O.T.—Inspiration. 3. Revelation—Biblical teaching. I. Title.

ROSENBERG, Stuart E. 221.6
The Bible is for you; our Biblical heritage reconsidered. New York, Longmans [c.]1961. 179p. Bibl. 61-14220 3.75
1. Bible. O. T.—Criticism, interpretation, etc. I. Title.

ROWLEY, Harold Henry, 1890- 221.6
Men of God: studies in Old Testament history and prophecy. London, New York, Nelson [1963] xii, 306 p. 22 cm. "Essays ... originally delivered as lectures in the John Rylands Library in Manchester." Bibliographical footnotes. [BS1171.2.R64] 63-25727
1. Bible. O. T. — Criticism, interpretation, etc. I. Title.

ROWLEY, Harold Henry, 1890- 221.6
Men of God; studies in Old Testament history and prophecy. New York, Nelson [c.1963] xii, 306p. 22cm. Essays orig. delivered as lects. in the John Rylands Lib. in Manchester. Bibl. 63-25727 8.50
1. Bible. O.T.—Criticism, interpretation, etc. I. Title.

ROWLEY, Harold Henry, 1890- 221.6
The re-discovery of the Old Testament. Freeport, N.Y., Books for Libraries Press [1969, c1946] 314 p. 23 cm. (Essay index reprint series) Bibliographical footnotes. [BS1171.R7 1969] 75-76912 ISBN 8-369-11547-
1. Bible. O.T.—Criticism, interpretation, etc. I. Title.

SANDMEL, Samuel. 221.6
The Hebrew Scriptures; an introduction to their literature and religious ideas. [lst ed.] New York, Knopf, 1963. 552 p. illus. 24 cm. [BS1140.2.S2] 62-19580
1. Bible. O. T.—Introductions. I. Title.

SCHWARTZMAN, Sylvan David. 221.6
The living Bible; a topical approach to the Jewish scriptures by Sylvan D. Schwartzman and Jack D. Spiro. Illustrated by Bruno Frost. New York, Union of American Hebrew Congregations [1962] 299 p. illus. 25 cm. Includes bibliographies. [BS1140.2.S3] 62-14823
1. Bible—O. T.—Introductions. I. Spiro, Jack D., joint author. II. Title.

SCHWARTZMAN, Sylvan David 221.6
The living Bible; a topical approach to the Jewish scriptures by Sylvan D. Schwartzman, Jack D. Spiro. Illus. by Bruno Frost. New York, Union of Amer. Hebrew Congregations [c.1962] 299p. 25cm. Bibl. 62-14823 3.95
1. Bible—O.T.—Introductions. I. Spiro, Jack D., joint author. II. Title.

SCHWARZBACH, Bertram Eugene. 221.6
Voltaire's Old Testament criticism. [New York, 1968] vii, 240, 2 l. 28 cm. Thesis—Columbia University. Photocopy of typescript. Bibliography: leaves 232-240. [B2178.R4S35] 68-4929
1. Voltaire, Francois Marie Arouet de, 1694-1778—Religion and ethics. 2. Bible. O.T.—Criticism, interpretation, etc.—History—18th century. I. Title.

SCOTT, Jack B., 1928- 221.6
God's plan unfolded : a student's introduction to God's written word, the Old Testament / by Jack B. Scott. [Clinton, Miss.] : Scott, c1976. vii, 277 p. ; 24 cm. [BS1140.2.S34] 76-379436
1. Bible. O.T.—Introductions. I. Title.

SCOTT, Robert Balgarnie Young, 1899- 221.6
The way of wisdom in the Old Testament [by] R. B. Y. Scott. New York, Macmillan [1971] xv, 238 p. 22 cm. Includes bibliographical references. [BS1455.S37] 71-150075 7.95
1. Wisdom literature—Criticism, interpretation, etc. I. Title.

SEALE, Morris S. 221.6
The desert Bible: nomadic tribal culture and Old Testament interpretation [by] Morris S. Seale. New York, St. Martin's [1974] ix, 223 p. 23 cm. Includes bibliographical references. [BS1171.2.S4 1974b] 73-87282 8.95
1. Bible. O.T.—Comparative studies. 2. Bedouins. I. Title.

SELLIN, Ernst, 1867-1945. 221.6
Introduction to the Old Testament. Initiated by Ernst Sellin. Completely rev. and rewritten by Georg Fohrer. Nashville, Abingdon Press [1968] 540 p. 24 cm. Translation of Einleitung in des Alte Testament. Includes bibliographical references. [BS1140.S413] 68-20968
1. Bible. O.T.—Introductions. I. Fohrer, Georg, ed. II. Title.

SHEEHAN, John F. X. 221.6
Let the people cry amen! / By John F. X. Sheehan. New York : Paulist Press, c1977. vi, 200 p. ; 21 cm. (An Exploration book) Includes index. Bibliography: p. 179-180. [BS1171.2.S48] 76-45676 ISBN 0-8091-0217-X : 7.95 ISBN 0-8091-2003-8 pbk. : 5.95
1. Bible. O.T.—Criticism, interpretation, etc. I. Title.

SMART, James D. 221.6
The Old Testament in dialogue with modern man. Philadelphia, Westminster Press [1964] 138 p. 21 cm. "Delivered [in Spanish translation] as the Carnahan lectures at Union Theological Seminary, Buenos Aires in Argentina in July, 1963." [BS1171.2.S6] 64-14086
1. Bible. O. T.—Criticism, interpretation, etc. 2. Communications (Theology) I. Title.

SNAITH, Norman Henry, 1898- 221.6
The distinctive ideas of the Old Testament. New York, Schocken [1964] 193p. 21cm. (SB90) Bibl. 64-24013 1.75 pap.,
1. Bible. O. T.—Theology. I. Title.

SOCIETY for Old Testament Study. 221.6
The Old Testament and modern study; a

generation of discovery and research. Essays by members of the Society for Old Testament Study, edited by H.H. Rowley. [London] Oxford University Press [1961] xxxi, 405 p. 20 cm. (Oxford paperbacks, no. 18) Includes bibliographies. [BS1188.S] A63
1. Bible. O.T. — Criticism, interpretation, etc. 2. Bible. O.T. — Addresses, essays, lectures. I. Rowley, Harold Henry, 1890- ed. II. Title.

SOCIETY for Old Testament Study 221.6
The Old Testament and modern study; a generation of discovery and research. Essays by members of the society, ed. by H. H. Rowley. [New York] Oxford Univ. Press [1961] 405p. Bibl. 2.25 pap.,
1. Bible. O.T.—Criticism, interpretation, etc. 2. Bible. O.T.—Addresses, essays, lectures. I. Rowley, Harold Henry, 1890- ed. II. Title.

SOGGIN, J. Alberto. 221.6
Introduction to the Old Testament : from its origins to the closing of the Alexandrian canon / J. Alberto Soggin ; [translated from the Italian by John Bowden]. London : S.C.M. Press, 1976. xxxii, 510 p. ; 23 cm. (Old Testament library) Translation of the 2d rev. and updated ed. of Introduzione all'Antico Testamento. Includes index. Bibliography: p. [xxix]-xxxii. [BS475.2.S613 1976b] 77-363324 ISBN 0-334-00721-6 : £9.50
1. Bible. O.T.—Introductions. I. Title. II. Series.

SPIRO, Jack D., Rabbi 221.6
Teacher's guide for The living Bible. New York, Union of Amer. Hebrew Cong. [c.1963] 101p. 28cm. 2.00 pap.,
I. Title.

STEPHENSON, Maude A. 221.6
A commentary on the five scrolls, Song of Songs, Ruth, Lamentations, Ecclesiastes, Esther. New York, Vantage [c.1962] 130p. 21cm. 2.75
I. Title.

STEVENSON, Dwight Eshelman, 1906- 221.6
Preaching on the books of the Old Testament. [1st ed.] New York, Harper [1961] 267 p. 22 cm. Includes bibliography., [BS1187.S8] 61-7350
1. Bible. O. T. Homiletical use. I. Title.

STEVENSON, Dwight Eshelman, 1906- 221.6
Preaching on the books of the Old Testament. New York, Harper [c.1961] 267p. Bibl. 61-7350 3.95 bds.,
1. Bible. O. T.—Homiletical use. I. Title.

TAYLOR, John Bernard. 221.6
A Christian's guide to the Old Testament, by John B. Taylor. Chicago, Moody Press [1966] 95 p. 19 cm. (Christian forum books) [BS1140.2.T3] 66-9311
1. Bible. O.T.—Introductions. 2. Bible. O.T.—Reading. I. Title.

TOOMBS, Lawrence E 221.6
The Old Testament in Christian preaching. Philadelphia, Westminster Press [1961] 192 p. illus. 21 cm. [BS1187.T6] 61-11635
1. Bible. O. T. — Homiletical use. I. Title.

TOOMBS, Lawrence E. 221.6
The Old Testament in Christian preaching. Philadelphia, Westminster Pr. [c.1961] 192p. illus. 61-11635 3.95
1. Bible. O. T.—Homiletical use. I. Title.

TRANSLATING & understanding 221.6 the Old Testament; essays in honor of Herbert Gordon May. Edited by Harry Thomas Frank and William L. Reed. Nashville [Tenn.] Abingdon Press [1970] 351 p. illus. 25 cm. Includes bibliographical references. [BS1192.T7] 75-115354 11.00
1. May, Herbert Gordon, 1904- — Bibliography. 2. Bible. O.T.—Addresses, essays, lectures. I. Frank, Harry Thomas, ed. II. Reed, William LaForest, 1912- ed. III. May, Herbert Gordon, 1904-

TRAVELS in the world of the 221.6 Old Testament : studies presented to professor M. A. Beek on the occasion of his 65th birthday / edited by M. S. H. G. Heerma van Voss, Ph. H. J. Houwink ten Cate and N. A. van Uchelen. Assen : Van Gorcum, 1974. xviii, 281 p. : port. ; 25 cm. (Studia Semitica Neerlandica ; nr. 16) Dutch or English. "Publications by Professor Dr. M. A. Beek in the period 1935-1973": p. [xiii]-xviii. [BS1192.T74] 74-190238 33.65
1. Beek, Martinus Adrianus, 1909- 2. Bible. O.T.—Addresses, essays, lectures. I. Beek, Martinus Adrianus, 1909- II. Heerma van Voss, Mattieu Sybrand Huibert Gerard, ed. III. Houwink ten Cate, Philo Hendrik Jan, ed. IV. Uchelen, N. A. van, ed. V. Series.
Distributed by International Scholarly Book Services, Beaverton, Or.

UNDERSTANDING the Bible: 221.6 the Old Testament, edited by John P. Bradley and John Quinlan. Gastonia, N.C., Good Will Publishers [1970] xvi, 389 p. illus. (part col.), facsims., maps, ports. 25 cm. (The Catholic layman's library, v. 1) [BS1171.2.U5] 73-92775
1. Bible. O.T.—Criticism, interpretation, etc. I. Bradley, John P., ed. II. Quinlan, John, 1920- ed. III. Title. IV. Series.

UNGER, Merrill Frederick, 1909- 221.6
Introductory guide to the Old Testament. Grand Rapids, Zondervan Pub. House [1951] 420 p. 21 cm. [BS1140.U5] 51-14531
1. Bible O.T. — introductions. I. Title.

UNGER, Merrill Frederick, 1909- 221.6
Introductory guide to the Old Testament. Grand Rapids, Zondervan Pub. House [1951] 420 p. 21 cm. [BS1140.U5] 51-14531
1. Bible. O. T.—Introductions.

WATTS, James Washington, 1896- 221.6
Old Testament teaching [by] J. Wash Watts. Nashville, Broadman [c.1967] First pub. in 1947 under title: A survey of Old Testament teaching. Bibl. [BS1140.W3 1967] 67-12824 5.95
1. Bibl. O.T.—Introductions. 2. Bibl. O.T.—Theology. I.)0cx, 358p. 23cm. II. Title.

WATTS, James Washington, 1896- 221.6
Old Testament teaching [by] J. Wash Watts. Nashville, Broadman Press [c1967] x, 358 p. 23 cm. First published in 1947 under title: A survey of Old Testament teaching. Includes bibliographical references. [BS1140.W3 1967] 67-12824
1. Bible. O.T. — Introductions. 2. Bible. O.T. — Theology. I. Title.

WATTS, John D. W. 221.6
Basic patterns in Old Testament religion [by] John D. W. Watts. [1st ed.] New York, Vantage Press [1971] 162 p. 22 cm. Includes bibliographical references. [BS1192.5.W37] 72-27986 4.50
1. Bible. O.T.—Theology. 2. Judaism—History—To 70 A.D. I. Title.

WEISER, Artur, 1893- 221.6
The Old Testament: its formation and development. [Translated by Dorothea M. Barton] New York, Association Press [1961] 492 p. 22 cm. Translation of Einleitung in das Alte Testament. Includes bibliography. [BS1140.W443] 61-14178
1. Bible. O.T. — Introductions. I. Title.

WEISER, Artur, 1893- 221.6
The Old Testament: its formation and development. [Tr. from German by Dorothea M. Barton] New York, Association [c.1961] 492p. Bibl. 61-14178 5.95
1. Bible. O. T.—Introductions. I. Title.

WESTERMANN, Claus. 221.6
The Old Testament and Jesus Christ. Translated by Omar Kaste. Minneapolis, Augsburg Pub. House [1970?] 80 p. 20 cm. [BS2387.W413] 71-101108 2.25
1. Jesus Christ—Person and offices. 2. Bible. N.T.—Relation to O.T. I. Title.

WIGHT, Fred Hartley, 1899- 221.6
Devotional studies of Old Testament types. Chicago, Moody Press [1956] 255p. illus. 22cm. [BT225.W53] 56-2841
1. Typology (Theology) I. Title.

WIGHT, Fred Hartley, 1899- 221.6
Devotional studies of Old Testament types. Chicago, Moody Press [1956] 255 p. illus. 22 cm. [BT225.W53] 56-2841
1. Typology (Theology) I. Title.

WRIGHT, George Ernest, 1909- ed. 221.6
The Bible and the ancient Near East; essays in honor of William Foxwell Albright. [1st ed.] Garden City, N.Y., Doubleday, 1961. 409 p. illus., port. 25 cm. "Bibliography of W. F. Albright": p. [363]-389. Includes bibliographical references. [BS1188.W7] 61-8699
1. Albright, William Foxwell, 1891- 2. Bible. O.T.—Criticism, interpretation, etc. 3. Near East—History—Addresses, essays, lectures. 4. Religions—History—Addresses, essays, lectures. I. Title.

YOUNG, Edward Joseph. 221.6
An introduction to the old Testament. Grand Rapids, Eerdmans [1958] 456 p. 23 cm. "Outgrowth of a series of forty articles ... which appeared during 1947-1948 in the Southern Presbyterian journal." [BS1140.Y6 1958] 60-20384
1. Bible. O.T. — Introductions. I. Title.

YOUNG, Edward Joseph. 221.6
The study of Old Testament theology today. [Westwood, N.J.] F. H. Revell Co. [1959] 112 p. 20 cm. Includes bibliography. [BS1192.5.Y6 1959] 59-10094
1. Bible. O.T. — Theology. I. Title. II. Title: Old Testament theology today.

ZIMMERLI, Walther, 1907- 221.6
The law and the prophets; a study of the meaning of the Old Testament. Translated by R. E. Clements. New York, Harper & Row [1967, c1965] vi, 101 p. 21 cm. (The James Sprunt lectures, 1963) Harper torchbooks. The Cloister library, TB144 Bibliographical footnotes. [BS1171.2.Z513 1967] 67-1358
1. Bible. O.T.—Criticism, interpretation, etc. I. Title. II. Series.

ZIMMERLI, Walther, 1907- 221.6
The Old Testament and the world / Walther Zimmerli ; translated [from the German] by John J. Scullion. London : S.P.C.K., 1976. vii, 172 p. ; 23 cm. Translation of Die Weltlichkeit des Alten Testaments. Includes bibliographical references and indexes. [BS1199.W74Z5513 1976b] 77-350969 ISBN 0-281-02890-7 : £4.95
1. Bible. O.T.—Theology—Addresses, essays, lectures. 2. World in the Bible—Addresses, essays, lectures. I. Title.

ROWLEY, Harold Henry, 1890- 221.6'08
From Moses to Qumran; studies in the Old Testament, by Harold H. Rowley. Freeport, N.Y., Books for Libraries Press [1971, c1963] xiv, 293 p. 23 cm. (Essay index reprint series) Includes bibliographical references. [BS1192.R64 1971] 74-128307 ISBN 0-8369-2130-5
1. Bible. O.T.—Addresses, essays, lectures. I. Title.

CLEMENTS, Ronald Ernest, 1929- 221.6'09
A century of Old Testament study / by Ronald E. Clements. Guildford [Eng.] : Lutterworth, 1976. viii, 152 p. ; 22 cm. Includes bibliographical references and index. [BS1160.C55 1976] 76-379214 ISBN 0-7188-2235-8 : £2.60
1. Bible. O.T.—Criticism, interpretation, etc.—History—19th century. 2. Bible. O.T.—Criticism, interpretation, etc.—History—20th century. I. Title.

KRAELING, Emil Gottlieb Heinrich, 1892- 221.6'09'03
The Old Testament since the Reformation [by] Emil G. Kraeling. New York, Schocken Books [1969, c1955] 320 p. 21 cm. Bibliographical references included in "Notes" (p. 285-310) [BS1160.K7 1969] 70-83671 7.50
1. Bible. O.T.—Criticism, interpretation, etc.—History—Modern period, 1500- I. Title.

TALMAGE, Frank. 221.6'092'4 B
David Kimhi, the man and the commentaries / Frank Ephraim Talmage. Cambridge, Mass. : Harvard University Press, 1975. viii, 236 p. : map ; 24 cm. (Harvard Judaic monographs ; 1) Includes indexes. Bibliography: p. 189-193. [BS1161.K55T34] 75-1747 ISBN 0-674-19340-7 : 10.00
1. Kimhi, David, 1160?-1235? 2. Bible. O.T.—Criticism, interpretation, etc., Jewish. I. Title. II. Series.

BRIGHT, John. 221'.6'3
The authority of the old testament. Grand Rapids, Baker Book House [1975 c1967] 272 p. 22 cm. (Twin brooks series) Bibliography: p. 253-261 [BS476.B62] 67-14989 ISBN 0-8010-0637-6 4.95 (pbk.)
1. Bible. O.T.—Hermeneutics. 2. Bible. O.T.—Homiletical use. I. Title. II. Series.

BRIGHT, John, 1908- 221'.6'3
The authority of the Old Testament. Nashville, Abingdon Press [1967] 272 p. 24 cm. (Lectures on the James A. Gray Fund of the Divinity School of Duke University, Durham, North Carolina) The James A. Gray lectures at Duke University) Bibliography: p. 253-261. [BS476.B62] 67-14989
1. Bible. O. T. — Hermeneutics. 2. Bible. O. T. — Homiletical use. I. Title. II. Series.

HOW does the Christian 221.6'3 *confront the Old Testament?* Ed. by Pierre Benoit, Roland E. Murphy, Bastiaan van Iersel. New York, Paulist. [1968] 194p. 24cm. (Concilium theol. in the age of renewal: Scripture, v. 30) Includes articles tr. from several languages by various persons. [BS476.H65] 67-31633 4.50
1. Bible. O. T.—Hermeneutics. 2. Bible. O. T.—Use. I. Benoit, Pierre, Aug 3, 1906- ed. II. Murphy, Roland Edmund, 1917- ed. III. Iersel, Bastiaan Martinus Franciscus van. ed. IV. Series: Concilium: theology in the age of renewal, v. 30

LYS, Daniel. 221.6'3
The meaning of the Old Testament; an essay on hermeneutics. Nashville, Abingdon Press [1967] 192 p. 21 cm. Translation of A la recherche d'une methode pour l'exegese de l'Ancien Testament. Bibliography: p. 183-185. [BS476.L913] 67-11016
1. Bible. O.T.—Hermeneutics. I. Title.

PATTE, Daniel. 221.6'3
Early Jewish hermeneutic in Palestine / by Daniel Patte. Missoula, Mont. : Scholars Press, 1975. xiii, 344 p. ; 22 cm. (Dissertation series - Society of Biblical Literature ; 22) Bibliography: p. 327-344. [BS1186.P3] 75-22225 ISBN 0-89130-015-5 pbk. : 4.25
1. Bible. O.T.—Criticism, interpretation, etc., Jewish—History. 2. Bible. O.T.—Hermeneutics. 3. Dead Sea scrolls. 4. Apocalyptic literature. I. Title. II. Series: Society of Biblical Literature. Dissertation series ; 22.

ALTMANN, Alexander, 1906- 221.64
Biblical motifs; origins and transformations. Cambridge, Harvard University Press, 1966. 251 p. illus. 24 cm. (Philip W. Lown Institute of Advanced Judaic Studies, Brandeis University. Studies and texts, v. 3) Bibliographical footnotes. [BS1192.A4] 65-11587
1. Bible. O. T. — Addresses, essays, lectures. 2. Symbolism in the Bible — Addresses, essays, lectures. I. Title. II. Series: Brandeis University, Waltham, Mass. Philip W. Lown Institute of Advanced Judaic Studies. Studies and texts, v. 3

ALTMANN, Alexander, 1906- ed. 221.64
Biblical motifs; origins and transformations. Cambridge, Mass., Harvard [c.]1966. 251p. illus. 24cm. (Philip W. Lown Inst. of Advanced Judaic Studies, Brandeis Univ. Studies and texts, v.3) Bibl. Title. (Series: Brandeis University, Waltham, Mass. Philip W. Lown Instuute of Advanced Judaic Studies. Studies and texts, v.3) [BS1192.A4] 65-11587 7.50
1. Bible. O.T. — Addresses, essays, lectures. 2. Symbolism in the Bible — Addresses, essays, lectures. I. Title. II. Series.

JOINES, Karen Randolph, 1938- 221.6'4
Serpent symbolism in the Old Testament: a linguistic, archaeological, and literary study. Haddonfield, N.J., Haddonfield House [1974] vii, 127 p. 21 cm. Includes bibliographical references. [BS1199.S37J64] 74-11359 ISBN 0-88366-005-9 25.00
1. Serpents in the Bible. 2. Serpents (in religion, folk-lore, etc.) I. Title.

MATHER, Samuel, 1626-1671. 221'.6'4
The figures or types of the Old Testament. With a new introd. by Mason I. Lowance, Jr. New York, Johnson Reprint Corp., 1969. xxv, vii, 540 p. 23 cm. (Series in American studies) Reprint of the 2d ed., 1705. Includes bibliographical references. [BS478.M3 1969] 78-81541
1. Typology (Theology) I. Title. II. Series.

STEVENS, Charles Hadley, 1892- 221.6'4
The wilderness journey; Christian principles illustrated by Israel's desert wanderings [by] Charles H. Stevens. Chicago, Moody Press [1971] 272 p. col. map (on lining papers) 22 cm. Bibliography: p. 271-272. [BS478.S75] 71-143474 4.95
1. Typology (Theology) I. Title.

WOUDSTRA, Marten H 221.64
The Ark of the Covenant from conquest to kingship, by Marten H. Woudstra. [Philadelphia, Presbyterian and Reformed Pub. Co., 1965] 152 p. 23 cm. (International library of philosophy and theology. Biblical and theological studies) Bibliography: p. 147-152. [BM657.A8W6] 65-19019
1. Ark of the Covenant. I. Title. II. Series: International Library of philosophy and theology: Biblical and theological studies series

WOUDSTRA, Marten H. 221.64
The Ark of the Covenant from conquest to kingship [Presbyterian and Reformed Pub Co.; dist. Grand Rapids, Mich., Baker Bk., c.1965] 152p. 23cm. (Intl. lib. of philosophy and theology. Biblical and theological studies) Bibl. Title. (Series: International library of philosophy and theology: Biblical and theological studies series) [BM657.A8W6] 65-19019 3.50 pap.,
1. Ark of the Covenant. I. Title. II. Series.

ACHTEMEIER, Elizabeth Rice, 1926- 221.6'6
The Old Testament and the proclamation of the Gospel, by Elizabeth Achtemeier. Philadelphia, Westminster Press [1973] 224 p. 22 cm. Includes bibliographical references.

[BS1171.2.A25] 73-7863 ISBN 0-664-20974-2 6.95
1. Bible. O.T.—Criticism, interpretation, etc. 2. Bible. N.T.—Relation to O.T. 3. Bible. O.T.—Homiletical use. I. Title.

ALLIS, Oswald Thompson, 1880- 221.6'6
The Old Testament; its claims and its critics, by Oswald T. Allis. [Nutley, N.J.] Presbyterian and Reformed Pub. Co., 1972. xii, 509 p. 23 cm. Includes bibliographical references. [BS1171.2.A43] 72-184265 ISBN 0-8010-0037-8 9.95
1. Bible O.T.—Criticism, interpretation, etc. I. Title.

BECKER, Joachim, 1931- 221.6'6
The formation of the Old Testament. Translated by Walter Wifall. Chicago, Franciscan Herald Press [1972] 77 p. 18 cm. (Herald Biblical booklets) Translation of Wie entstand das Alte Testament? [BS1174.2.B413] 72-77455 ISBN 0-8199-0214-4 0.95
1. Bible. O.T.—Criticism, interpretation, etc. I. Title.

BEN-GURION, David, 1886- 221.6'6
Ben-Gurion looks at the Bible. Translated by Jonathan Kolatch. Middle Village, N.Y., Jonathan David Publishers [1972] 317 p. 24 cm. "Collections of addresses in essay form ... first published in Hebrew in 1969." Translation of 'Iyunim ba-Tanakh. [BS1192.B4313] 70-167600 ISBN 0-8246-0127-0 7.95
1. Bible. O.T.—Addresses, essays, lectures. I. Title.

CLEMENTS, Ronald Ernest, 1929- 221.6'6
One hundred years of Old Testament interpretation / Ronald E. Clements. Philadelphia : Westminster Press, c1976. viii, 152 p. ; 22 cm. Includes bibliographical references and index. [BS1160.C56 1976] 76-23236 ISBN 0-664-24747-4 : 4.95
1. Bible. O.T.—Criticism, interpretation, etc.—History—19th century. 2. Bible. O.T.—Criticism, interpretation, etc.—History—20th century. I. Title.

CRENSHAW, James L. 221.6'6
Prophetic conflict; its effect upon Israelite religion [by] James L. Crenshaw. Berlin, New York, De Gruyter, 1971. xiv, 134 p. 24 cm. (Beiheft zur Zeitschrift für die alttestamentliche Wissenschaft, 124) Bibliography: p. [124]-127. [BS1505.2.C68 1971] 76-877459 ISBN 3-11-003363-1
1. Bible. O.T Prophets—Criticism, interpretation, etc. I. Title. II. Series: Zeitschrift für die alttestamentliche Wissenschaft. Beihefte 124.

DAVIS, O. B. 221.6'6
Introduction to Biblical literature / O. B. Davis. Rochelle Park, N.J. : Hayden Book Co., c1976. 245 p. ; 23 cm. (Hayden series in literature) Includes bibliographical references. [BS1194.D34] 76-16176 ISBN 0-8104-5834-9 : 4.98
1. Bible. O.T.—Study—Text-books. I. Title.

DOSS, Helen (Grigsby) 221.6'6
Jonah. Illustrated by Norman Kohn. New York, Abingdon Press [1964] [BS580.J55D6] 64-14791
I. Title.

DOSS, Helen (Grigsby) 221.6'6
Jonah. Illustrated by Norman Kohn. New York, Abingdon Press [1964] 111 p. illus., map (on lining papers) 25 cm. [BS580.J55D6] 64-14791
1. Jonah, the prophet — Juvenile literature. I. Title.

HANFORD, Thomas W ed. 221.6'6
Favorite poems. Complete ed. Chicago, M. A. Donohue [n.d.] 320p. 19cm. [PR1175.H29] 53-25277
1. English poetry (Collections) I. Title.

HASEL, Gerhard F. 221.6'6
Old Testament theology : basic issues in the current debate / by Gerhard F. Hasel. Rev. ed. Grand Rapids : Eerdmans, 1975, c1972. 163 p. ; 21 cm. Includes indexes. Bibliography: p. 145-155. [BS1192.5.H37 1975] 75-16148 pbk. : 2.95
1. Bible. O.T.—Theology. I. Title.

HASEL, Gerhard F. 221.6'6
Old Testament theology: basic issues in the current debate, by Gerhard F. Hasel. Grand Rapids, Mich., Eerdmans, [1972] 103 p. 21 cm. Bibliography: p. 97-98. [BS1192.5.H37] 72-77181 ISBN 0-8028-1478-6 1.95
1. Bible. O.T.—Theology. I. Title.

HOPKINSON, Alfred Stephan. 221.66
Modern man reads the Old Testament [by] A. Stephan Hopkinson. New York, Association Press [1966] 189 p. 21 cm. [BS1171.2.H6] 65-21963
1. Bible. O.T. — Criticism, interpretation, etc. I. Title.

HOPKINSON, Alfred Stephan 221.66
Modern man reads the Old Testament. New York, Association [c.1966] 189p. 21cm. [BS1171.2.H6 1966a] 65-21963 3.95 bds.,
1. Bible. O. T. — Criticism, interpretation, etc. I. Title.

JACOBS, Louis, comp. 221.6'6
Jewish biblical exegesis. Front. by Eleanor Schick. New York, Behrman House [1973] xii, 196 p. front. 24 cm. (The Chain of tradition series, v. 4) [BS1186.J3] 73-1487 ISBN 0-87441-225-0 3.95
1. Bible. O.T.—Criticism, interpretation, etc., Jewish. 2. Bible. O.T.—Commentaries. I. Title.

JOSEPH and his brethren. 221.6'6 New York, American Tract Society [n. d.] 80p. illus. 16cm. [BS580.J6.J62] 60-57166
1. Joseph, the patriarch—Juvenile literature. I. American Tract Society.

KAISER, Otto, 1924- 221.6'6
Introduction to the Old Testament : a presentation of its results and problems / Otto Kaiser ; translated by John Sturdy. 1st U.S. ed. Minneapolis : Augsburg Pub. House, 1975. xvii, 420 p. ; 23 cm. Translation of Einleitung in das Alte Testament. "Translated from the revised second edition 1970, and incorporating further revisions by the author to 1973." Includes index. Bibliography: p. [414]-415. [BS1140.2.K313 1975] 73-82220 ISBN 0-8066-1400-5
1. Bible. O.T.—Introductions. I. Title.

KAISER, Walter C., comp. 221.6'6
Classical evangelical essays in Old Testament interpretation. Edited by Walter C. Kaiser, Jr. Grand Rapids, Baker Book House [1972] 265 p. 22 cm. Includes bibliographies. [BS1188.K26] 72-191693 ISBN 0-8010-5314-5 3.95
1. Bible. O.T.—Criticism, interpretation, etc.—Addresses, essays, lectures. I. Title.

*KAISER, Walter C. 221.6'6
The Old Testament in contemporary preaching [by] Walter C. Kaiser, Jr. Grand Rapids, Mich.. Baker Book House, [1973] 135 p. 22 cm. (Elmore Harris series, no. 3) [BS1171] ISBN 0-8010-5331-5. 1.95 (pbk.)
1. Bible. O.T.—Criticism, interpretation, etc. I. Title.

KAISER, Walter C. 221.6'6
The Old Testament in contemporary preaching [by] Walter C. Kaiser, Jr. Grand Rapids, Baker Book House [1973] 135 p. 22 cm. (Ontario Bible College. The Elmore Harris series, no. 3) Includes bibliographical references. [BS1171.2.K27] 74-156973 ISBN 0-8010-5331-5 1.95 (pbk.).
1. Bible. O.T.—Homiletical use. 2. Bible. O.T.—Criticism, interpretation, etc. I. Title. II. Series: The Elmore Harris series, no. 3.

KATZ, Paul M., 1933- 221.66
The Bible: myth or reality? A new look at an old book. NewYork, Exposition [c.1966] 153p. 22cm. (Exposition testament bk.) Bibl. [BS1171.2.K3] 66-5639 4.50
1. Bible. O.T. — Criticism, interpretation, etc. I. Title.

KATZ, Paul M 1933- 221.66
The Bible: myth or reality? A new look at an old book [by] Paul M. Katz. [1st ed.] New York, Exposition Press [1966] 153 p. 22 cm. (An Exposition testament book) Bibliography: p. [151]-153. [BS1171.2.K3] 66-5639
1. Bible. O. T. — Criticism, interpretation, etc. I. Title.

LITTLE, Darwin. 221.6'6
What is truth? : An essay on the origin of man and Biblical theology / [Darwin Little]. Charlotte, N.C. : Covenant Press, c1973. 116, 10 p. : maps ; 23 cm. [BS1171.2.L57] 73-88202
1. Bible. O.T.—Criticism, interpretation, etc. 2. Bible. O.T.—History of Biblical events. I. Title.

MCCUNLEY, Foster R. 221.6'6
Proclaiming the promise : Christian preaching from the Old Testament / by Foster R. McCurley, Jr. Philadelphia : Fortress Press, [1974] xi, 160 p. ; 22 cm. Includes bibliographical references. [BS1191.5.M32] 74-76921 ISBN 0-8006-1083-0 : 4.95
1. Bible. O.T.—Homiletical use. I. Title.

MAURO, Philip, 1859-1952. 221.6'6
The wonders of Bible chronolgoy Rev ed. Swengel, Pa., Bible Truth Depot, 1961. 99p. 20cm. First published in 1922 under title: The chronology of the Bible. [BS637.M45 1961] 62-1276
1. Bible—Chronology. I. Title.

PHILLIPS, Arthur Angell, comp. 221.6'6
In fealty to Apollo; an anthology selected by Ian Maxwell [and] A. A. Phillips. [6th ed. Melbourne] Melbourne University Press [1966] xvii, 116 p. 21 cm. Authors' names in reverse order in previous ed. [PR1175.P573 1966] 67-90004 unpriced
1. English poetry. I. Maxwell, Ian Ramsay, joint comp. II. Title.

RAST, Walter E., 1930- 221.6'6
Tradition history and the Old Testament, by Walter E. Rast. Philadelphia, Fortress Press [1971, c1972] xiii, 82 p. 22 cm. (Guides to Biblical scholarship. Old Testament series) Bibliography: p. 80-82. [BS1171.2.R34] 70-171509 ISBN 0-8006-1460-7 2.50
1. Bible. O.T.—Criticism, interpretation, etc. I. Title.

REPRESENTATIVE poetry; 221.6'6 prepared by members of the Dept. of English at the University of Toronto. 3d ed. [Toronto] University of Toronto Press [1962-63] 3 v. 24 cm. "Prefatory note" signed: F. E. L. P. [i.e. F. E. L. Priestley] general editor; F. D. H. [i.e. F. David Hoeniger] assoc. gen. editor. Bibliographical references included in "Notes" at end of each vol. [PR1175.R423] 78-208120
1. English poetry. I. Toronto. University. Dept. of English.

SANDMEL, Samuel. 221.6'6
The enjoyment of Scripture; the Law, the Prophets, and the Writings. New York, Oxford University Press, 1972. x, 300 p. 21 cm. Bibliography: p. 285-286. [BS535.S246] 72-86303 ISBN 0-19-501590-8 8.95
1. Bible. O.T.—Criticism, interpretation, etc. 2. Bible as literature. I. Title.

SHEEHAN, John F. X. 221.6'6
The threshing floor; an interpretation of the Old Testament [by] John F. X. Sheehan. Foreword by J. Coert Rylaarsdam. New York, Paulist Press [1972] xi, 208 p. 23 cm. [BS1171.2.S5] 72-81574 ISBN 0-8091-0167-X 3.95 (pbk)
1. Bible. O. T.—Criticism, interpretation, etc. I. Title.

†SOGGIN, J. Alberto. 221'.6'6
Introduction to the Old Testament, from its origins to the closing of the Alexandrian canon / J. Alberto Soggin ; [translated by John Bowden from the Italian]. Philadelphia : Westminster Press, c1976. xxxii, 510 p. ; 23 cm. Translation of the 2d rev. and updated ed. of Introduzione all'Antico Testamento. Includes bibliographies and index. [BS475.2.S613] 76-20650 ISBN 0-664-21339-1 : 16.50
1. Bible. O.T.—Introductions. I. Title.

SPRIGGS, D. G., 1946- 221.6'6
Two Old Testament theologies : a comparative evaluation of the contributions of Eichrodt and von Rad to our understanding of the nature of Old Testament theology / D. G. Spriggs. Naperville, Ill. : A. R. Allenson, [1974 or 1975] xii, 127 p. ; 22 cm. (Studies in Biblical theology : 2d ser. ; 30) Includes index. Bibliography: p. [ix]-x. [BS1192.5.S67] 74-23022 ISBN 0-8401-3080-5 pbk. : 8.95
1. Eichrodt, Walther, 1890- 2. Rad, Gerhard von, 1901-1971. 3. Bible. O.T.—Theology—History. I. Title. II. Series.

STRANGE, Marcian. 221.6'6
Couples of the Bible. Notre Dame, Ind., Fides Publishers [1963] 192 p. illus. 21 cm. "First appeared as a series in Marriage magazine, St. Meinrad, Indiana." [BS571.S86] 63-20805
1. Bible — Biog. 2. Marriage — Biblical teaching. I. Title.

VAN DOREN, Mark, 1894-1972 221.6'6
In the beginning, love; dialogues on the Bible [by] Mark Van Doren and Maurice Samuel. Edited and annotated by Edith Samuel. New York, John Day Co. [1973] xix, 268 p. 22 cm. Fifteen conversations as presented between 1953 and 1972 on the radio program The words we live by. Includes bibliographical references. [BS1171.2.V35 1973] 72-12076 ISBN 0-381-98236-X 8.95
1. Bible. O.T.—Criticism, interpretation, etc. I. Samuel, Maurice, 1895-1972. II. Samuel, Edith, ed. III. Title.

VERMES, Geza, 1924- 221.6'6
Scripture and tradition in Judaism. Haggadic studies. 2nd, revised ed. Leiden, Brill, 1973. x, 243 p. 25 cm. (Studia post-biblica v. 4) Includes bibliographical references. [BS1186.V47 1973] 74-157393 ISBN 9-00-403626-1
1. Abraham, the patriarch. 2. Balaam, the prophet. 3. Bible. O.T.—Criticism, interpretation, etc., Jewish. 4. Tradition (Judaism) 5. Aggada—Addresses, essays, lectures. I. Title. II. Series.
Distributed by Humanities Press; 19.25.

WALSH, Chad, 1914- 221.6'6
The story of Job. Garden City, N.Y. [Doubleday, 1963] 64 p. illus. (part col.) 21 cm. (Know your Bible program) [BS580.J5W3 1963] 64-1653
1. Job, the patriarch — Juvenile literature. 2. Bible stories, English — O.T. Job. I. Title.

WARREN, Mary. 221.6'6
The boy with a sling: 1 Samuel 16: 1-18:5 for children. Illustrated by Sally Mathews [St. Louis] Concordia Pub. House [1965] 1 v. (unpaged) col. illus. 21 cm. (Arch books) [BS580.D3W3] 65-15143
1. David. King of Israel — Juvenile literature. I. Title.

WEINGREEN, Jacob. 221.6'6
From Bible to Mishna : the continuity of tradition / by J. Weingreen. New York : Holmes & Meier, c1976. p. cm. Includes index. Bibliography: p. [BS1186.W44] 75-37728 ISBN 0-8419-0249-6
1. Bible. O.T.—Criticism, interpretation, etc., Jewish. 2. Mishnah—Criticism, interpretation, etc. 3. Tradition (Judaism) I. Title.

WOLFF, Hans Walter. 221.6'6
The Old Testament: a guide to its writings. Translated by Keith R. Crim. Philadelphia, Fortress Press [1973] iv, 156 p. 20 cm. Translation of Bibel: Das Alte Testament. [BS1140.2.W6313] 73-79010 ISBN 0-8006-0169-6 3.25 (pbk.)
1. Bible. O.T.—Introductions. I. Title.

ZIMMERLI, Walther, 1907- 221.6'6
The Old Testament and the world / Walther Zimmerli ; translated by John J. Scullion. Atlanta : John Knox Press, 1976. 172 p. ; 23 cm. Translation of Die Weltlichkeit des alten Testaments. Includes bibliographical references and indexes. [BS1199.W74Z5513 1976] 75-32946 ISBN 0-8042-0139-0 : 8.50
1. Bible. O.T.—Theology—Addresses, essays, lectures. 2. World in the Bible—Addresses, essays, lectures. I. Title.

MONRO, Margaret Theodora, 1896- 221.660-51327
The Old Testament and our times: a short reading course with subjects for discussion. [New York] Longmans [1960] 105p. "Began as a series of articles contributed during 1959 to the Mercat cross, published in Edinburgh by the Jesuit Fathers." Bibl.: p. 5-6 in "Hints on using this book." 3.50 bds.,
1. Bible. O.T.—Study. I. Title.

WOODS, Clyde M. 221.6'6'08 s
Genesis-Exodus, by Clyde M. Woods. Shreveport, La., Lambert Book House, 1972. 229 p. 23 cm. (His The living way commentary on the Old Testament, v. 1) "The scripture text in this publication is from the Revised Standard Version of the Bible." [BS1151.2.W66 vol. 1] [BS1235.3] 222'.11'077 72-171045
1. Bible. O.T. Genesis—Commentaries. 2. Bible. O.T. Exodus—Commentaries. I. Bible. O.T. Genesis. English. Revised Standard. 1972. II. Bible. O.T. Exodus. English. Revised Standard. 1972. III. Title.

WOODS, Clyde M. 221.6'6'08
The living way commentary on the Old Testament, by Clyde M. Woods. Shreveport, La., Lambert Book House, 1972- v. 23 cm. "The scripture text in this publication is from the Revised Standard Version of the Bible." Contents.Contents.—v. 1. Genesis-Exodus. [BS1151.2.W66] 72-87128
1. Bible. O.T.—Commentaries. I. Bible. O.T. English. Revised Standard. 1972. II. Title.

CULLEY, Robert C. 221.6'7
Studies in the structure of Hebrew narrative / by Robert C. Culley. Philadelphia : Fortress Press, c1976. vi, 122 p. ; 22 cm. (Semeia supplements) Bibliography: p. 119-122. [BS1205.2.C84] 75-37159 ISBN 0-8006-1504-2 pbk. : 3.95
1. Bible. O.T. Historical books—Criticism, Form. 2. Narration in the Bible. I. Title. II. Series.

FRITSCH, Charles 221.6'7
Theodore, 1912-
The Qumran community: its history and scrolls, by Charles T. Fritsch. With a new introd. by the author. New York, Biblo and Tannen, [1973 c1956] viii, 147 p. illus. 22 cm. Bibliography: p. 131-141. [BM487.F7 1972] 72-7327 ISBN 0-8196-0279-5 7.50
1. Dead Sea scrolls. 2. Qumran community.

HAYES, John Haralson, 221.6'7
1934-
Old Testament form criticism. Edited by John H. Hayes. San Antonio, Trinity University Press [1974] xix, 289 p. 24 cm. (Trinity University monograph series in religion, v. 2) Includes bibliographies. [BS1182.H38] 72-97351 ISBN 0-911536-44-2 8.00
1. Bible. O.T.—Criticism, Form. I. Title. II. Series: Trinity University, San Antonio. Monograph series in religion, v. 2.

STUENKEL, Walter W., 221.6'7
1912-
The books of the Old Testament / Walter W. Stuenkel. St. Louis : Concordia Pub. House, c1977. 135 p. : maps ; 19 cm. "Companion volume to The books of the New Testament, edited by Herbert T. Mayer and published ... in 1969." Bibliography: p. [134]-135. [BS1140.2.S88] 76-56246 ISBN 0-570-03749-2 pbk. : 2.95
1. Bible. O.T.—Introductions. I. Title.

TUCKER, Gene M. 221.6'7
Form criticism of the Old Testament, by Gene M. Tucker. Philadelphia, Fortress Press [1971] xii, 84 p. 22 cm. (Guides to Biblical scholarship. Old Testament series) Bibliography: p. 84. [BS1182.T8] 72-154487 ISBN 0-8006-0177-7 2.50
1. Bible. O.T.—Criticism, Form. I. Title.

ROGERSON, John William. 221.6'8
The supernatural in the Old Testament / by John Rogerson. Guildford : Lutterworth Press, 1976. [7], 66 p. : ill. ; 22 cm. (Interpreting the Bible) Includes bibliographical references. [BS1199.S94R63] 76-383981 ISBN 0-7188-2233-1 : £1.90
1. Bible. O.T.—Criticism, interpretation, etc. 2. Supernatural in the Bible. I. Title.

BERKELEY, James Percival, 221.7
1879-
Knowing the Old Testament. Philadelphia, Judson Press [c1954] 171p. illus. 20cm. [BS1171.B46] 54-8201
1. Bible. O. T.—Criticism, interpretation, etc. I. Title.

BIBLE. O. T. English. 1955. 221.7
Authorized.
Notes on the Old Testament, explanatory and practical, by Albert Barnes. Enl. type ed., edited by Robert Frew. Grand Rapids, Baker Book House, 1955-- v. illus., facsim. 23cm. Cover title: Barnes on the Old Testament. [BS1151.B3] 55-11630
1. Bible. O. T.—Commentaries. I. Barnes, Albert, 1798-1870, ed. II. Title.

BRILLET, Gaston 221.7
Meditations on the Old Testament. The narratives. Translated [from the French] by Kathryn Sullivan. New York, Desclee Co., 1959 239p. 22cm. 59-15258 3.50
1. Bible. O. T.—Meditations. I. Title.

BRILLET, Gaston, 1878- 221.7
Meditations on the Old Testament. Tr. [from French]by Kathryn Sullivan. New York, Desclee [c.]1961. 249p. Contents.[4] Wisdom. 59-15258 3.75
1. Bible. O. T.—Meditations. I. Title.

BRILLET, Gaston, 1878- 221.7
Meditations on the Old Testament. [v.3] Tr. [from French] by Jane Wynne Saul. New York, Desclee Co., 1961[c.1958, 1960] 274p. Contents.3. Prophecy. 59-15258 3.75
1. Bible. O. T.—Meditations. I. Title.

FISON, J E 221.7
Understanding the Old Testament; the way of holiness. London, Oxford University Press, 1952. 208p. illus. 20cm. [BS1197.F48] 54-21461
1. Bible. O. T.—History of Biblical events. I. Title.

HARRELSON, Walter J 221.7
Interpreting the Old Testament [by] Walter Harrelson. New York, Holt, Rinehart and Winston [1965] xi, 529 p. 4 col. maps (on lining papers) 24 cm. Bibliography: p. 501-514. [BS1140.2.H3] 64-12820
1. Bible. O.T. — Criticism, interpretation, etc. I. Title.

HARRELSON, Walter J. 221.7
Interpreting the Old Testament. New York, Holt [c.1964] xi, 529p. 4 col. maps (on lining papers) 24cm. Bibl. 64-12820 7.50
1. Bible. O. T.—Criticism, interpretation, etc. I. Title.

HEATON, Eric William. 221.7
The Hebrew kingdoms, by E. W. Heaton. London, Oxford U.P., 1968. xx, 437 p. illus., facsims. 20 cm. (The New Clarendon Bible. Old Testament, v. 3) Maps on lining papers. Bibliography: p. [396]-402. [BS1151.2.N46 vol. 3] 68-133944
1. Jews—History—953-586 B.C. 2. Bible. O.T.—Commentaries. 3. Bible. O.T.—History of Biblical events. I. Title. II. Series.

HEIDT, William George, 221.7
1913- ed.
Old Testament reading guide. [Editorial committee: W. G. Heidt and others] Collegeville, Minn., Liturgical Press [1965-] v. fold. map. 20 cm. [BS1193.O4] 65-2824
1. Bible. O.T. — Study. I. Title.

IRWIN, William Andrew, 221.7
1884-
The Old Testament: keystone of human culture. New York, H. Schuman [1952] 293 p. 22 cm. [BS1192.5.I 7] 52-13853
1. Bible. O. T.—Theology. I. Title.

KOHLER, Ludwig Hugo, 1880- 221.7
Old Testament theology; translated by A. S. Todd. Philadelphia. Westminster Press [c1957] 257p. 24cm. [BS1174.K613] 58-7205
1. Bible. O. T.—Theology. I. Title.

KRAELING, Emil Gottlieb 221.7
Heinrich., 1892-
The Old Testament since the Reformation. New York, Harper [c1955] 320p. 22cm. [BS1160.K7 1955a] 55-11478
1. Bible. O. T.—Criticism, interpretation, etc.—Hist. I. Title.

LAMSA, George Mamishisho, 221.7
1893-
Old Testament light; a scriptural commentary based on the Aramic of the ancient Peshitta text [by] George M. Lamsa. Englewood Cliffs, N.J., Prentice-Hall [1964] xv. 976 p. map (on lining paper) 22 cm. [BS1151.2.L3] 64-12095
1. Bible. O.T. — Commentaries. I. Title.

LAMSA, George Mamishisho, 221.7
1893-
Old Testament light; a scriptural commentary based on the Aramaic of the ancient Peshitta text [by] George M. Lamsa. Englewood Cliffs, N.J., Prentice [c.1964] xv, 976p. map (on linin paper) 22cm. 64-12095 8.95
1. Bible. O. T.—Commentaries. I. Title.

MCKENZIE, John L. 221.7
The two-edged sword; an interpretation of the Old Testament. Milwaukee, Bruce Pub. Co. [1956] 317 p. 23 cm. [BS1171.M347] 56-11153
1. Bible. O.T.—Criticism, interpretation, etc. I. Title.

MCKENZIE, John L. 221.7
The two-edged sword; an intrepretation of the Old Testament. Garden City, N.Y. Doubleday [1966, 1956] 350p. 18cm. (Image bk., D215) 1.25 pap.,
1. Bible. O.T. — Criticism, interpretation, etc. I. Title.

NAPIER, Bunyan Davie. 221.7
From faith to faith; essays on Old Testament literature. [1st ed.] New York, Harper [1955] 223p. 22cm. [BS1171.N35] 55-8525
1. Bible. O. T.—Criticism, interpretation, etc. I. Title.

NEWELL, William Reed, 1868- 221.7
Old Testament studies; lessons given at union Bible classes in the United State and Canada. New ed., rev., enl. Chicago, Moody Press 1950- v. 20 cm. Contents.v. 1 Genesis to Job. [BS1151.N4] 50-2313
1. Bible. O. T. — Commentaries. I. Title.

OLD Testament reading 221.7
guide [Edit. comm.: W. G. Heidt, others] Collegeville, Minn. 56321, Liturgical Pr. St. John's Abbey [1965] iv. (various p.) fold. map. 20cm. [BS1193.O4] 65-2824 price unreported
1. Bible. O. T.—Study. I. Heidt, William George, 1913- ed.

ROWLEY, H. H. 221.7
The growth of the Old Testament. Ed. by E. O. James. New York, Harper [c.1963] 192p. (Harper Torchbk.; Cloister Lib., TB-107) Orig. pub. in London in 1950. Bibl. 1.25 pap.,
I. Title.

SARNA, Nahum M. 1923- 221.7
Understanding Genesis, by Nahum M. Sarna. [1st ed.] New York, Jewish Theol. Seminary of Amer. [1966] xxx, 267p. illus., maps. 22cm. (Heritage of Biblical Israel, v. 1) Bibl. [BS1235.3.S33] 66-23626 6.95
1. Bible. O.T. Genesis — Commentaries. I. Title. II. Series.

WEATHERHEAD, Leslie Dixon, 221.7
1893-
The busy man's Old Testament [by] Leslie D. Weatherhead. Nashville, Tenn., Abingdon Press [1971] 176 p. 20 cm. Includes bibliographical references. [BS1193.W23 1971] 70-158673 ISBN 0-687-04376-X 3.50
1. Bible. O.T.—Reading. I. Title.

SLOTKIN, James Sydney, 221.767
1913-1958
From field to factory; new industrial employees. Glencoe, Ill., Free Press [1960] 156 p. 24 cm. [HF5549.S832] 59-15921
1. Personnel management. 2. Industrial relations. 3. Social adjustment. I. Title.

BIBLE. O.T. English. 221.77
Selections. 1966.
The rabbis' Bible, by Solomon Simon and Morrison David Bial, with the editorial assistance of Hannah Grad Goodman. Woodcuts by Irwin Rosenhouse. New York, Behrman House [1966- v. illus. 24 cm. "An abridged version . . . arranged as a continuous text across the tops of the pages, with a continuing keyed commentary at the bottoms." Contents.CONTENTS.--v. 1. Torah. [BS1151.2.S5] 66-20409
1. Bible. O. T.—Commentaries. I. Simon, Solomon, 1805- II. Bial, Morrison David, 1917- III. Title.

BIBLE. O.T. English. 221.7'7
Selections. 1966.
The rabbis' Bible, by Solomon Simon and Morrison David Bial, with the editorial assistance of Hannah Grad Goodman. Woodcuts by Irwin Rosenhouse. New York, Behrman House [1966- v. illus. 24 cm. Vol. 3 by S. Simon and A. Rothberg. "An abridged version ... arranged as a continuous text across the tops of the pages, with a continuing keyed commentary at the bottoms." Contents.Contents.—v. 1. Torah.—v. 2. Early prophets: Joshua, Judges, Samuel, Kings, Chronicles.—v. 3. The later prophets: Isaiah, Jeremiah, Hosea, Joel, Amos, Obadiah, Jonah, Micah, Nahum, Habakkuk, Zephaniah, Haggai, Zechariah, Malachi. [BS1151.2.S5] 66-20409 ISBN 0-87441-026-6
1. Bible. O.T.—Commentaries. I. Simon, Solomon, 1895- II. Bial, Morrison David, 1917- III. Rothberg, Abraham, ed. IV. Title.

ESSAYS in Old Testament 221.8'17
ethics (J. Philip Hyatt, in memoriam) Edited by James L. Crenshaw and John T. Willis. New York, Ktav Pub. House [1974] xxxvi, 287 p. 24 cm. Chronological list of James Philip Hyatt's works: p. xi-xxxi. Includes bibliographical references. [BS1199.E8E84] 73-15850 ISBN 0-87068-233-4 12.50
1. Hyatt, James Philip, 1909-1972. 2. Hyatt, James Philip, 1909-1972—Bibliography. 3. Bible. O.T.—Ethics. I. Hyatt, James Philip, 1909-1972. II. Crenshaw, James L., ed. III. Willis, John T., 1933- ed.
Contents omitted.

ROLLINS, Marion 221.8'172'4
Josephine (Benedict), 1898-
The God of the Old Testament in relation to war, by Marion J. Benedict. New York, Bureau of Publications, Teachers College, Columbia University, 1927. [New York, AMS Press, 1973] viii, 185 p. 22 cm. Reprint of the 1927 ed., issued in series: Teachers College, Columbia University. Contributions to education, no. 263. Originally presented as the author's thesis, Columbia. Bibliography: p. 185. [BS1199.W2R6 1972] 72-176551 ISBN 0-404-55263-3 10.00
1. Bible. O.T.—Criticism, interpretation, etc. 2. God. 3. War. 4. War and religion—Biblical teaching. I. Title. II. Series: Columbia University. Teachers College. Contributions to education, no. 263.

ROBINSON, Henry Wheeler, 221.8179
1872-1945.
The cross in the Old Testament. Philadelphia, Westminster Press [1955?] 192p. 22cm. 'Originally printed under the titles The cross of Job (1916), The cross of the servant (1926), and The cross of Jeremiah (1925). [BS1199.S8R6] 56-5103
1. Suffering. 2. Job, the patriarch. 3. Servant of Jehovah. 4. Jeremiah, the prophet. I. Title.

KNIGHT, George Angus 221.8231
Fulton, 1909-
A Christian theology of the Old Testament. Richmond, John Knox Press [1959] 383p. 23cm. Includes bibliography. [BS1192.5.K54 1959] 59-83184
1. Bible. O. T.—Theology. I. Title.

MCKAY, John William, 221.8'299'21
1941-
Religion in Judah under the Assyrians, 732-609 BC [by] J. W. McKay. Naperville, Ill., A. R. Allenson [1973] xii, 142 p. illus. 22 cm. (Studies in Biblical theology, 2d ser. 26) Includes bibliographical references. [BM165.M22] 72-97460 ISBN 0-8401-4076-2 9.95
1. Judea—Religion. 2. Judaism—Relations—Assyro-Babylonian. 3. Assyro-Babylonian religion—Relations—Judaism. I. Title. II. Series.
Pbk. 7.45, ISBN 0-8401-3076-7.

SINGER, Richard E 221.8301
If the prophets were alive today; Ruth and Jerry find some answers. New York, Bookman Associates [1957] 191p. illus. 23cm. [BS670.S5] 57-2151
1. Sociology, Biblical—Study and teaching. I. Title.

SINGER, Richard E 221.8301
If the prophets were alive today; Ruth and Jerry find some answers. New York, Bookman Associates [1957] 191 p. illus. 23 cm. [BS670.S5] 57-2151
1. Sociology, Biblical — Study and teaching. I. Title.

DUNSTON, Alfred 221.8'30145'196
G., 1915-
The Black man in the Old Testament and its world / by Alfred G. Dunston, Jr. Philadelphia : Dorrance, [1974] 161 p. ; 22 cm. Bibliography: p. 159-161. [BS1199.N4D86] 74-78665 ISBN 0-8059-2016-1 : 6.95
1. Negro race in the Bible. I. Title.

WELD, Theodore 221.8'30145'22
Dwight, 1803-1895.
The Bible against slavery; or, An inquiry into the genius of the Mosaic system, and the teachings of the Old Testament on the subject of human rights. Pittsburgh, United Presbyterian Board of Publication, 1864. Detroit, Negro History Press, 1970. vii, 154 p. 22 cm. [HT915.W4 1970] 74-92447
1. Slavery. 2. Slavery in the United States—Controversial literature—1864. I. Title.

MCALLISTER, Grace Edna. 221.8396
God portrays women. Chicago, Moody Press [1954] 190p. 22cm. [BS575.M25] 54-3703
1. Women in the Bible. 2. Bible. O.T.—Biog. I. Title.

DOWNIE, Hugh Kerr, 221.839833
1883-
Harvest festivals: Old Testament feasts, types of New Testament truths. [ust ed.] New York, Loizeaux Bros. [1951] 187 p. illus. 20 cm. [BS2387.D64] 51-12674
1. Bible. N. T.—Relation to O. T. 2. Typology (Theology) 3. Fasts and feasts—Judaism. I. Title.

EBSTEIN, Wilhelm, 1836- 221.861
1912
Die Medizin im Alten Testament. Munchen, W. Fritsch [New York, Stechert-Hafner] 1965. viii, 184p. 21cm. Photomechanischer Neudruck der Ausgabe Stuttgart. Ferd. Enke Verlag, 1901. Bibl. [R135.5.E2] 65-26954 5.75 pap.,
1. Bible — Medicine, hygiene, etc. I. Title.

GLENN, Jacob B 1905- 221.861
The Bible and modern medicine; an interpretation of the basic principles of the Bible in the light of present day medical thought. New York, Bloch Pub. Co. [1963] 222 p. 23 cm. [R135.5.G55] 63-6032
1. Pible — Medicine, hygiene, etc. 2. Jewish way of life. 3. Jews — Rites and ceremonies. I. Title.

GLENN, Jacob B., M. D. 221.861
1905-
The Bible and modern medicine; an interpretation of the basic principles of the Bible in the light of present day medical thought. New York, Bloch [c.1963] 222p. 23cm. Bibl. 63-6032 5.00
1. Bible—Medicine, hygiene, etc. 2. Jewish way of life. 3. Jews—Rites and ceremonies. I. Title.

MACHT, David Israel, 221.86161
1882-
The heart and blood in the Bible. Baltimore, 1951. 79 p. 23 cm. [R135.5.M3] 51-5531
1. Bible—Medicine, hygiene, etc. I. Title.

LIGNEE, Hubert 221.87261
The temple of Yahweh. Baltimore, Helicon [1966] 128p. 18cm. (Living word ser., 2) Tr. of Le temple du Seigneur & Vers le sanctuaire du Ciel. [BS680.T4L513] 66-9664 1.25 pap.,
1. Temple of God. I. Lignee, Hubert. Vers le sanctuaire du Ciel. II. Title.
Available from Taplinger, New York.

GOOD, Edwin Marshall 221.88
Irony in the Old Testament. Philadelphia, Westminster [c.1965] 256p. 21cm. Bibl. [BS1199.I7G6] 65-10152 6.50
1. Bible. O. T.—Criticism, interpretation, etc. 2. Irony. I. Title.

GOOD, Edwin Marshall. 221.88
Irony in the Old Testatment, by Edwin M. Good. Philadelphia, Westminster Press [1965] 256 p. 21 cm. Bibliographical footnotes. [BS1199.I7G6] 65-10152
1. Bible. O. T. — Criticism, interpretation, etc. 2. Irony. I. Title.

TRAWICK, Buckner B 221.88
The Bible as literature; Old Testament history and biography. New York, Barnes & Noble [1963] 182 p. illus. 22 cm. (College outline series, no. 56) [BS535.T7] 63-14574
1. Bible. O.T. — Language, style. I. Title.

TRAWICK, Buckner B. 221.88
The Bible as literature; Old Testament history and biography. New York, Barnes & Noble [c.1963] 182p. illus. 22cm. (Coll. outline ser., no.56) Bibl. 63-14574 3.50; 1.25 pap.,
1. Bible. O. T.—Language, style. I. Title.

LA SOR, William 221.8'95694
Sanford.
Israel : a Biblical view/ by William Sanford La Sor. Grand Rapids, Mich. : Eerdmans, c1976. 108 p. ; 18 cm. [BS1199.S4L3] 75-46520 pbk. : 2.45
1. Bible—History of Biblical events—Addresses, essays, lectures. 2. Bible. O.T. Prophets—Criticism, interpretation, etc.—Addresses, essays, lectures. 3. Servant of Jehovah—Addresses, essays, lectures. 4. Church—Biblical teaching—Addresses, essays, lectures. I. Title.

ALBRIGHT, William Foxwell, 221.9
1891-
Archaeology, historical analogy & early Biblical tradition [by] William F. Albright. Baton Rouge, Louisana State University Press [c1966] ix, 69 p. 21 cm. (Rockwell lecture series) Bibliographical footnotes. [BS621.A4] 66-21755
1. Bible. O. T.—Antiq.—Addresses, essays, lectures. 2. Bible. O. T.—Addresses, essays, lectures I. Title. II. Series: Rockwell lectures

ALBRIGHT, William Foxwell, 221.9
1891-
Archaeology, historical analogy & eary Biblical tradition [by] William F. Albright. Baton Rouge, La. State Univ. Pr. [c.1966] ix, 69p. 21cm. (Rockwell lect. ser.) Bibl. [BS621.A4] 66-21755 2.75
1. Bible. O.T.—Antiq.—Addresses, essays, lectures. 2. Bible. O.T.—Addresses, essays, lectures. I. Title. II. Series: Rockwell lectures

ALLEN, Irene. 221.9
A short introduction to the Old Testament; a graded course for middle forms. 2d ed. [London] Oxford University Press, 1963. 191 p. illus., maps, geneal. tables. 19 cm. [BS1194.A55] 64-967
1. Bible. O. T. — Introductions. I. Title.

ALLEN, Irene 221.9
A short introduction to the Old Testament; a graded course for middle forms. 2d ed. [New York] Oxford [c.]1963. 191p. illus., maps, geneal. tables. 19cm. 64-967 1.20 bds.,
1. Bible. O. T.—Introductions. I. Title.

BOWIE, Walter Russell, 221.9
1882-
The living story of the Old Testament. Illustrated by Douglas Rosa. Englewood Cliffs, N. J., Prentice-Hall [1964] x, 214 p. illus. (part col.) 24 cm. [BS1197.B67] 64-13228
1. Bible. O. T. — History of Biblical events. I. Title.

BOWIE, Walter Russell, 221.9
1882-
The living story of the Old Testament. Illus. by Douglas Rosa. Englewood Cliffs, N.J., Prentice [c.1964] x, 214p. illus. (pt. col.) 24cm. 64-13228 4.95 bds.,
1. Bible. O. T.—History of Biblical events. I. Title.

BRICHTO, Sidney. 221.9
A child's first Bible. Arranged by Sidney Brichto. Illustrated by Chet Kalm. New York, Behrman House [c1961] 63 p. col. illus. 18 cm. [BM107.B7] 61-9305
1. Bible stories — O. T. I. Title.

EAKIN, Frank E., 1936- 221.9
The religion and culture of Israel; an introduction to Old Testament thought [by] Frank E. Eakin, Jr. Boston, Allyn and Bacon [1971] xxiv, 335 p. illus., maps. 24 cm. Includes bibliographies. [BS1197.E23] 70-151088
1. Bible. O.T.—History of Biblical events. 2. Judaism—History—Ancient period. I. Title.

FLANDERS, Henry Jackson. 221.9
People of the covenant; an introduction to the Old Testament [by] Henry Jackson Flanders, Jr., Robert Wilson Crapps [and] David Anthony Smith. New York, Ronald Press Co. [1963] 479 p. illus. 22 cm. [BS635.2.F5] 63-9253
1. Bible. O.T. — History of Biblical events. I. Title.

FLANDERS, Henry Jackson, 221.9
Jr.
People of the covenant; an introduction to the Old Testament [by] Henry Jackson Flanders, Jr., Robert Wilson Crapps. David Anthony Smith. New York, Ronald [c.1963] 479p. illus. 22cm. Bibl. 63-9253 6.00
1. Bible. O.T.—History of Biblical events. I. Title.

GILBERT, Miriam. j 221.9
The mighty voice: Isaiah, prophet and poet. Illustrated by Simon Jeruchim. [Philadelphia] Jewish Publication Society of America [1963] 138 p. illus. 22 cm. (Covenant books, 15) [BS580.I 7G5] 63-16055
1. Isaiah, the prophet — Juvenile literature. I. Title.

GILBERT, Miriam 221.9
The mighty voice: Isaiah, prophet and poet. Illus. by Simon Jeruchim. [Philadelphia] Jewish Pubn. Soc. of Amer. [c.1963] 138p. illus. 22cm. (Covenant bks., 15) 63-16055 2.95
1. Isaiah, the prophet—Juvenile literature. I. Title.

HAUGHTON, Rosemary 221.9
A home for God's family, written, illustrated by Rosemary Haughton. New York, Kenedy [1965] 125 p. illus. 23cm. [BS551.2H38] 65-15200 2.95
1. Bible stories, English—O. T. I. Title.

JONES, Clifford Merton. 221.9
Old Testament illustrations; photographs, maps and diagrams, compiled and introduced by Clifford M. Jones. Cambridge [Eng.] University Press, 1971. 189 p. illus., maps, plans. 26 cm. (The Cambridge Bible commentary: New English Bible) Bibliography: p. 177. [BS1180.J65] 76-142131 ISBN 0-521-08007-X £3.00
1. Bible. O.T.—History of contemporary events. 2. Judaism—History—To 70 A.D. I. Title. II. Series.

KELLNER, Esther. 221.9
The background of the Old Testament. [1st ed.] Garden City, N. Y., Doubleday, 1963. 367 p. illus. 22 cm. Includes bibliography. [BS1197.K44] 63-18027
1. Bible. O.T.—History of Biblical events. I. Title.

KELLNER, Esther. 221.9
Solomon the Wise. Garden City, N. Y. [N. Doubleday, 1961] 64p. illus. 21cm. (Know your Bible program) [BS580.S6K4] 61-3964
1. Solomon, King of Israel—Juvenile literature. I. Title.

KLAPERMAN, Libby M. j 221.9
Bible stories from the Old Testament. Illustrated by Geoffrey Biggs. New York, Grosset & Dunlap, c1963. 60 p. illus. 29 cm. [BS551.2.K53] 63-2135
1. Bible stories, English — O.T. I. Title.

KLAPERMAN, Libby M. 221.9
Bible stories from the Old Testament. Illus. by Geoffrey Biggs. New York, Grosset, c.1963. 60p. illus. (pt. col.) 29cm. 63-2135 1.00 bds.,
1. Bible stories, English—O.T. I. Title.

LACE, O. Jessie. 221.9
Understanding the Old Testament; edited by O. Jessie Lace. Cambridge [Eng.] University Press, 1972. x, 190 p. illus. 21 cm. (The Cambridge Bible commentary: New English Bible) [BS1197.L24] 75-178282 ISBN 0-521-08415-6
1. Bible. O.T.—History of contemporary events. 2. Judaism—History. I. Title. II. Series.

LAPPIN, Peter. 221.9
Mightly Samson. Garden City, N. Y. [1961] 63p. illus. 21cm. (The Catholic know-your-Bible program) [BS580.L15L3] 61-65885
1. Samson, Judge of Israel—Juvenile literature. I. Title.

LINK, Mark J. 221.9
These stones will shout : a new voice for the Old Testament / by Mark Link. 1st ed. Niles, Ill. : Argus Communications, [1975] 228 p. : ill. ; 23 cm. Includes bibliographical references and index. Discusses the evidence revealed by modern archaeological discoveries that supports the accuracy of the Old Testament in historical particulars. [BS1197.L53] 75-15829 ISBN 0-913592-53-6 : 5.95
1. Bible. O.T.—History of Biblical events. 2. Bible. O.T.—Criticism, interpretation, etc. I. Title.

MELLOR, Enid B. 221.9
The making of the Old Testament; edited by Enid B. Mellor. Cambridge [Eng.] University Press, 1972. x, 214 p. 21 cm. (The Cambridge Bible Commentary: New English Bible) Bibliography: p. 201. [BS1130.M43] 71-163063 ISBN 0-521-08184-X
1. Bible. O.T.—History. I. Title. II. Series.

*MOUNT, R. H., Jr. 221.9
God's tabernacle in Israel's wilderness journey; for boys & girls [Mansfield, Ohio]1298 Marlin Dr., Author, c.1963. 205p. illus. 24cm. 1.65
I. Title.

NOTH, Martin, 1902- 221.9
The Old Testament world. Translated by Victor I. Gruhn. Philadelphia, Fortress Press [1966] xxii, 404 p. illus., plans, maps. 24 cm. [BS1197.N6513] 65-10061
1. Palestine — Historical geography. 2. Bible. O.T. — Antiq. 3. Bible. O.T. — Criticism, Textual. I. Title.

NOTH, Martin, 1902- 221.9
The Old Testament world. Tr. [from German] by Victor I. Gruhn. Philadelphia, Fortress [c.1962-1966] xxii, 404p. illus., plans, maps. 24cm. [BS1197.N6513] 65-10061 8.00
1. Palestine — Historical geography. 2. Bibl. O. T. — Antiq. 3. Bible. O. T. — Criticism. Textual. I. Title.

PALMER, Peter. 221.9
The children's Bible story book; Old Testament. Illustrated by Manning DeV. Lee. [1st ed.] New York, McGraw-Hill [1962] 207p. illus. 23cm. Issued also with Bible. O. T. English. 1962. Children's version. The Children's version of the Holy Bible. [BS551.2.P37 1962] 62-17789
1. Bible stories ., English— O. T. I. Title.

PFEIFFER, Charles F. 221.9
The divided kingdom, by Charles F. Pfeiffer. Grand Rapids, Baker Book House [1967] 117 p. illus., map. 23 cm. (Old Testament history series) Bibliography: p. 107-111. [DS121.6.P43] 66-18306
1. Jews—History—953-586 B.C. I. Title.

RATTEY, Beatrice Katherine. 221.9
A short history of the Hebrews from the Patriarchs to Herod the Great / B. K. Rattey. 3d ed / rev. by P. M. Binyon. London : Oxford University Press, 1976. 144 p. : ill. ; 22 cm. First-2d ed. published under title: A short history of the Hebrews from Moses to Herod the Great. Includes index. Bibliography: p. [135] [Bs1197.R36 1976] 76-365337 pbk. : 2.50
1. Bible. O.T.—History of Biblical events. I. Binyon, P. M. II. Title.
Distributed by Oxford University Press N.Y. N.Y.

ROBINSON, Theodore Henry, 221.9
1881-
The decline and fall of the Hebrew Kingdoms; Israel in the eighth and seventh centuries B.C., by T. H. Robinson. [1st AMS ed.] Oxford, Clarendon Press, 1926. [New York, AMS Press, 1971] xix, 246, [17] p. illus. 23 cm. (The Clarendon Bible, v. 3) "Chronological table," by E. W. Hippisley: p. [247]-[263] [BS1505.R48 1971] 74-137284 ISBN 0-404-05376-9
1. Jews—History—953-586 B.C. 2. Bible. O.T 2 Kings—Commentaries. 3. Bible. O.T Prophets—Commentaries. I. Title. II. Series.

SALSTRAND, George A. E., 221.9
1908-
The time was right [by] George A. E. Salstrand. Nashville, Broadman Press [1973] 123 p. map. 21 cm. Bibliography: p. 121-123. [DS121.65.S24] 72-97604 ISBN 0-8054-8119-2 1.50 (pbk.)
1. Jews—History—586 B.C.-70 A.D. 2. Christianity—Origin. I. Title.

SCHEDL, Claus. 221.9
History of the Old Testament. Staten Island, N.Y., Alba House [1972-73; v. 1, 1973] 5 v. illus. 22 cm. Translation of Geschichte des Alten Testaments. Contents.Contents.—v. 1. The ancient Orient and ancient Biblical history.—v. 2. God's people of the covenant.—v. 3. The golden age of David.—v. 4. The age of the prophets.—v. 5. The fullness of time. Includes bibliographical references. [BS1197.S3213] 70-38990 45.00
1. Bible. O.T.—History of Biblical events. I. Title.

SOCIETY for Old Testament 221.9
Study.
Documents from Old Testament times. Translated with introductions and notes by members of the old Society for Old Testement [sic] Study and edited by D. Winton Thomas. New York, Harper [1961, c1958] 302 p. illus. 21 cm. (Harper torchbooks. The Cloister library. TB85) [BS1180.S66 1961] 61-19233
1. Bible. O.T. — Evidences, authority, etc. 2. Bible. O.T — Antiq. I. Thomas, David Winton, 1901- ed. II. Title.

SOCIETY for Old Testament 221.9
Study
Documents from Old Testament times. Tr. with introds., notes by members of the Old Society for Old Testament Study and ed. by D. Winton Thomas. New York, Harper [1961, c.1958] 302p. illus. (Harper torchbks. Cloister lib., TB85) Bibl. 61-19233 1.75 pap.,
1. Bible. O.T.—Evidences, authority, etc. 2. Bible. O.T.—Antiq. I. Thomas, David Winton, 1901- ed. II. Title.

STUDIES on the ancient 221.9
Palestinian world; presented to Professor F. V. Winnett on the occasion of his retirement 1 July 1971. Edited by J. W. Wevers and D. B. Redford. [Toronto, Buffalo] University of Toronto Press [1972] 171 p. illus. 24 cm. (Toronto Semitic texts and studies) Contents.Contents.—An incense burner from Tell es-Sa'idiyeh, Jordan Valley, by J. B. Pritchard.—The archaeological history of Elealeh in Moab, by W. L. Reed.—Three Byzantine tombstones from Dhiban. Jordan, by A. D. Tushingham.—The placing of the accent signs in Biblical texts with Palestinian pointing, by E. J. Revell.—The textual affinities of the Arabic Genesis of Bib. Nat. Arab 9, by J. W. Wevers.—Energic verbal forms in Hebrew, by R. J. Williams.—Israel's eschatology from Amos to Daniel, by W. S. McCullough.—Oral tradition and historicity, by R. C. Culley.—Abraham and David? by N. E. Wagner.—Studies in relations between Palestine and Egypt during the first millennium B.C.: I. The taxation system of Solomon, by D. B. Redford.—Cylinder C of Sin-sarra-iskun, a new text from Baghdad, by A. K. Grayson.—Bibliography of Professor Winnett's publications, by A. Bembenek (p. [169]-171) [BS1192.S75] 79-151397 ISBN 0-8020-5254-1 10.00
1. Bible. O.T.—Addresses, essays, lectures. 2. Palestine—Antiquities—Addresses, essays, lectures. 3. Winnett, Frederick Victor—Bibliography. I. Winnett, Frederick Victor. II. Wevers, John William, ed. III. Redford, Donald B., ed.

THEIELE, Edwin Richard, 221.9
1895-.
The mysterious numbers of the Hebrew kings; a reconstruction of the chronology of the kingdoms of Israel and Judah, by Edwin R. Thiele. [Rev. ed.] Grand Rapids, W. B. Eerdmans Pub. Co. [1965] xxvi, 232 p. map. 24 cm. Bibliography: p. 219-226. [BS637.T53 1965] 66-786
1. Bible. O.T. — Chronology. 2. Chronology, Jewish. 3. Jews — Hist. — To 586 a.c. I. Title.

THIELE, Edwin Richard, 221.9
1895-
The mysterious numbers of the Hebrew kings; a reconstruction of the chronology of the kingdoms of Israel and Judah. [Rev. ed.] Grand Rapids, Mich., Eerdmans [c.1951, 1965] xxvi, 232p. map. 24cm. Bibl. [BS637.T53] 66-786 6.00
1. Bible. O. T. — Chronology. 2. Chronology, Jewish. 3. Jews — Hist. — To 586 B. C. I. Title.

VAUX, Roland de, 1903- 221.9
The Bible and the ancient Near East [by] Roland de Vaux. Translated by Damian McHugh. Garden City, N.Y., Doubleday, 1971. 284 p. 22 cm. Selection of 15 articles translated from the author's Bible et Orient. Includes bibliographical references. [BS1192.V34132] 70-97659 6.95
1. Bible. O.T.—Addresses, essays, lectures. I. Title.

WALLIS, Louis, 1876- 221.9
The Bible is human; a study in secular history. New York, Columbia University Press, 1942. [New York, AMS Press, 1972] xvi, 330 p. 23 cm. Bibliography: p. [296]-303. [BS1197.W354 1972] 74-149677 ISBN 0-404-06814-6 8.50
1. Bible. O.T.—History of Biblical events. 2. Bible. O.T.—Historiography. I. Title.

WHITLEY, Charles Francis 221.9
The exilic age. London, Longmans Green [dist. Mystic, Conn., Verry, 1965, c.1957] 160p. 22cm. Bibl. [BM165.W5] 65-3099 3.50
1. Judaism—Hist.—Ancient period. I. Title.

WILLS, Garry, 1934- j221.9
Solomon the Wise. Garden City, N. Y. [N. Doubleday, 1961] 64 p. illus. 21 cm. (The Catholic know-your-Bible program) [BS580.S6W5] 61-3966
1. Solomon, King of Israel — Juvenile literature. I. Title.

ALEXANDER, David S. 221.9'0222
The Old Testament in living pictures; a photo guide to the Old Testament, by David S. Alexander. [1st ed.] Glendale, Calif., G/L Regal Books [1973] 156 p. illus. 25 cm. [DS108.5.A67] 73-85490 ISBN 0-8307-0225-3 5.95
1. Bible. O.T.—Geography. 2. Palestine—Description and travel—Views. I. Title.

MILLER, James Maxwell, 221.9'07'2 1937-
The Old Testament and the historian / J. Maxwell Miller. London : S.P.C.K., 1976. viii, 87 p. ; 22 cm. Includes bibliographical references. [BS1197.M48 1976b] 77-359986 ISBN 0-281-02943-1 : £2.25
1. Bible. O.T.—Historiography. I. Title.

MILLER, James Maxwell, 221.9'07'2 1937-
The Old Testament and the historian / by J. Maxwell Miller. Philadelphia : Fortress Press, c1976. viii, 87 p. ; 22 cm. (Guides to Biblical scholarship : Old Testament series) Includes bibliographical references. [BS1197.M48] 75-10881 ISBN 0-8006-0461-X pbk. : 2.95
1. Bible. O.T.—Historiography. I. Title.

ALT, Albrecht, 1883-1956 221.9/08
Essays on Old Testament history and religion [by] Albrecht Alt. Tr. by R A. Wilson. Garden City, N.Y., Doubleday [1968,c.1966] viii, 352p. 19cm. (Anchor bk., A544) The essays here tr. were pub. in a collection of Alt's essays . . . Kleine Schriften zur Geschichte des Volkes Israel. Bibl. [BS1188A433 1967] 1.45 pap.,
1. Bible—O.T.—Addresses, essays, lectures. 2. Jews—Hist.—To 70 A.D.—Addresses, essays, lectures. I. Title.

ALT, Albrecht, 1883- 221.9'08 1956.
Essays on Old Testament history and religion. Translated by R. A. Wilson. [1st ed. in the U.S.A.] Garden City, N.Y., Doubleday, 1967 [c1966] viii, 352 p. 22 cm. "The essays here translated were published in a collection of Alt's essays ... Kleine Schriften zur Geschichte des Volkes Israel." Bibliographical footnotes. [BS1188.A433 1967] 67-10372
1. Jews—History—To 70 A.D.—Addresses, essays, lectures. 2. Bible. O.T.—Addresses, essays, lectures. I. Title.

MAZAR, Benjamin, 1906- 221.9084 ed.
Views of the Biblical world. [Editorial board: chairman, Benjamin Mazar; editors, Michael Avi-Yonah and Abraham Malamat] 1st international ed. Chicago, Jordan Publications, 1959- v. illus. 30 cm. Contents.The Law [BS621.P414] 59-7767
1. Bible. O.T. — Antiq. 2. Near East — Antiq. 3. Bible. O.T. — Pictures, illustrations, etc. I. Title.

PEOPLES of Old Testament 221.9'1 *times,* edited by D. J. Wiseman for the Society for Old Testament Study. Oxford, Clarendon Press, 1973. xxi, 402 p. illus. 22 cm. Includes bibliographies. [DS57.P44] 73-179589 ISBN 0-19-826316-3 17.75
1. Near East—Civilization. 2. Near East—History—To 622. I. Wiseman, Donald John, ed. II. Society for Old Testament Study.
Distributed by Oxford University Press, New York; Library edition 14.02

ACKLAND, Donald F 221.92
People haven't changed. Grand Rapids, Zondervan Pub. House [1957] 151p. 21cm. [BS571.A3] 58-19108
1. Bible. O.T.—Biog. I. Title.

BARGELLINI, Piero, 1897- 221.92
David; translated by Elisabeth Abbott. New York, P.J. Kenedy [1954] 165p. 22cm. [BS580.D3B22] 54-6528
1. David, King of Israel. I. Title.

BARKER, William Pierson 221.92
Kings in shirtsleeves; men who ruled Israel. [Westwood, N.J.] Revell [c.1961] 119p. 61-13620 2.50 bds.,
1. Bible. O. T.—Biog. 2. Jews—Kings and rulers. I. Title.

BLANK, Sheldon H. 221.92
Jeremiah: man and prophet. [1st ed.] Cincinnati, Hebrew Union College Press, 1961. 260 p. 22 cm. [BS580.J4B48] 61-14333
1. Jeremiah, the prophet.

BLUMENTHAL, Warren B 221.92
Branch of almond; the life and times of Jeremiah. New York, Bookman Associates [1961] 271p. 23cm. [BS580.J4B5] 61-9847
1. Jeremiah, the prophet. I. Title.

BOLLIGER, Max. 221.92
Daniel. Illus. by Edith Schindler. Translated by Marion Koenig. New York, Delacorte Press [1970] 109 p. illus. 22 cm. "A Seymour Lawrence book." Translation of Daniel und ein Volk in Gefangenschaft. Retells the Old Testament story of Daniel's rise from slavery to a position of power in the court of Nebuchadnezzar through his ability to interpret dreams. [BS580.D2B63 1970] 74-87169 3.95
1. Daniel, the prophet—Juvenile literature. I. Schindler, Edith, illus. II. Title.

BOLLIGER, Max. 221.92
David. Drawings by Edith Schindler. Translated by Marion Koenig. [1st American ed.] New York, Delacorte Press [1967] 96 p. illus. 22 cm. Follows David's relationship with King Saul showing how he won the King's favor with the harp and incurred his wrath by gaining popularity in battle. "A Seymour Lawrence Book." Translation of David: Ein Hirtenjunge wird Konig. [BS580.D3B583] AC 67
1. David, King of Israel. I. Schindler, Edith, illus. II. Title.

BORUCH, Behn. 221.92
The coat of many colors; the story of Joseph. Illustrated by Bernard Springsteel. New York, Hebrew Pub. Co., c1959. unpaged. illus. 23cm. [BS580.J6B6] 59-4210
1. Joseph. the patriarch—Juvenile literature. I. Title.

BORUCH, Behn. 221.92
In the beginning; the story of Abraham. Illustrated by Bernard Springsteel. New York, Hebrew Pub. Co., c1958. unpaged. illus. 23cm. [BS580.A3B6] 59-20244
1. Abraham, the patriarch. I. Title.

BORUCH, Behn. 221.92
The patriarchs; the story of Abraham, Isaac and Jacob. Illustrated by Bernard Spingsteel. New York, Hebrew Pub. Co., c1960. unpaged. illus. 23cm. [BS573.B6] 60-2150
1. Patriarchs (Bible)—Juvenile literature. I. Title.

BUBER, Martin, 1878-1965. 221.92
Moses; the revelation and the covenant. New York, Harper [1958] 226 p. 21 cm. (Harper torchbooks, TB27) "First published in 1946 under the title: Moses." Includes bibliography. [BS580.M6B8 1958] 58-5216
1. Moses.

*BURGESS, E. T. 221.92
Other women of the Bible. Little Rock, Ark., Baptist Pubns., 1964. 64p. 23cm. (Topical Bible studies, no. 31) .50 pap.,
I. Title.

CHAPPELL, Clovis Gillham, 221.92 1882-
Living with royalty. New York, Abingdon Press [1962] 124p. 20cm. [BS571.C4] 62-11520
1. Bible. O. T.—Biog. 2. Methodist Church—Sermons. 3. Sermons, American. I. Title.

CORVIN, R O. 221.92
David and his mighty men. Grand Rapids, Eerdmans, 1950. 175 p. 21 cm. [BS580.D3C65] 50-9186
1. David, King of Israel. 2. Bible. O. T.—Biog. I. Title.

DAY, Bertram, 1871- 221.92
Joseph, the dreamer. Boston, Christopher Pub. House [1957] 108p. 21cm. [BS580.J6D3] 57-11960
1. Joseph, the patriarch. I. Title.

DE HAAN, Martin Ralph, 221.92 1891-
Adventures in faith: studies in the life of Abraham. Grand Rapids, Zondervan Pub. House [1953] 192p. 20cm. [BS580.A3D43] 53-28731
1. Abraham, the patriarch. I. Title.

D'HUMY, Fernand Emile, 221.92 1873-
What manner of man was Moses? New York, Library Publishers [1955] 301p. illus. 21cm. [BS580.M6D44] 55-12379
I. Title.

DOANE, Pelagie, 1906- 221.92
Bible children; stories from the old Testament. Philadelphia, Lippincott [1954] 64 p. illus. 26 cm. [BS576.D6] 54-8487
1. Children in the Bible. I. Title.

DONOGHUE, Richard Kingston 221.92
Abraham, friend of God; a religious biography. New York, Exposition Press [c.1960] 128p. illus. 21cm. (An Exposition-testament book) 60-50549 3.00
1. Abraham, the patriarch. I. Title.

FAIRBAIRN, Patrick, 1805- 221.92 1874
Jonah: his life. character and mission. Foreword by Joseph C. Holbrook. Jr. Grand Rapids, Mich., Kregel 1964. 237p. 19cm. 64-16635 3.50
1. Jonah. the prophet. I. Title.

FICHTNER, Joseph. 221.92
Forerunners of Christ; studies of Old Testament characters. Milwaukee, Bruce Pub. Co. [1965] x, 136 p. maps. 21 cm. [BS571.F4] 65-15303
1. Bible. O.T. — Biog. I. Title.

FICHTNER, Joseph 221.92
Forerunners of Christ; studies of Old Testament characters. Milwaukee, Bruce [c.1965] x, 136p. maps. 21cm. [BS571.F4] 65-15303 3.50
1. Bible. O. T.—Biog. I. Title.

FRASER, Gordon Holmes. 221.92
Elijah, the pilgrim prophet; a study of the life and ministry of Elijah the Tishbite. Chicago, Moody Press [1956] 126p. 20cm. [BS580.E4F7] 56-4538
1. Elijah, the prophet. I. Title.

FREEHOF, Lillian B (Simon) 221.92 1906-
Stories of King David; illustrated by Seymour R. Kaplan. Philadelphia, Jewish Publication Society of America [1952] 161p. illus. 28cm. [BS580.D3F7] 52-14766
1. David, King of Israel. I. Title.

FREEHOF, Lillian B (Simon) 221.92 1906-
Stories of King Solomon; illustrated by Seymour R. Kaplan. Philadelphia, Jewish Publication Society of America [c1955] 175p. illus. 28cm. [BS580.S6F7] 55-8423
1. Solomon, King of Israel. I. Title.

FREUD, Sigmund, 1856-1939. 221.92
Moses and monotheism. Translated from the German by Katherine Jones. New York, Vintage Books, 1955 [c1939] viii, 178, iv p. 19cm. (A Vintage book, K-14) Translation of Der Mann Moses und die monotheistische Religion. Bibliographical footnotes. [BS580] 55-152
1. Moses. 2. Monotheism. 3. Judaism—Relations—Egyptian. 4. Psychology, Religious. I. Title.

GEIS, Bernard. 221.92
David and Goliath; adapted for young children from the First Book of Samuel. Pictures by Cliff Young. Philadelphia, J. C. Winston Co [1955] unpaged. illus. 21cm. (Magic talking books, T-12) 'The song of David' (phonodisc. 78 rpm.) on cover. Full orchestra and sound effects; Jimmy Carroll, Musical director. [BS580.D3G4] 56-16952
1. David, King of Israel. I. The song of David. Phonodisc. II. Title.

*GEORGE, J.-M. 221.92
Abraham; story by J.-M. George, Harold Winstone. Pictures by Jacques Le Scanff. New York, Macmillan, c.1966. 1v. (unpaged) col. illus. 20cm. (Dove bks., 13:04562) .59 pap.,
I. Title.

*GEORGE, J.-M. 221.92
Jacob; story by J.-M. George, Harold Winstone. Pictures by Jacques Le Scanff. New York, Macmillan, c.1966. 1v. (unpaged) col. illus. 20cm. (Dove bks., 14:04565) .59 pap.,
I. Title.

GIBSON, Bertha Askew 221.92
The big three, then the big job. New York, Vantage Press [c.1960] 191p. 21cm. 3.50
I. Title.

GRAHAM, James Robert, 221.92 1898-
The prophet-statesman, a drama of Daniel. Butler, Ind., Higley Press [c1955] 240p. 20cm. [BS580.D2G7] 56-28832
1. Daniel, the prophet. I. Title.

GREENE, Carla, 1906- 221.92
Moses; the great lawgiver. Illustrated by Anne Lewis. Irvington-on-Hudson, N.Y., Harvey House [1968] 45 p. illus. 27 cm. A brief biography of the Biblical prophet who led his people out of Egypt to the Promised Land and gave them the Ten Commandments. [BS580.M6G72] AC 68
1. Moses. I. Lewis, Anne, illus. II. Title.

HANNAY, James Owen, 1865- 221.92 1950.
Jeremiah the prophet, by George A. Birmingham (J. O. Hannay) New York, Harper [1956] 256p. 21cm. First published in 1939 under title: God's iron. [BS580] 56-13943
1. Jeremiah, the prophet. I. Title.

HANNAY, James Owen, 1865- 221.92 1950.
Jeremiah the prophet, by George A. Birmingham (J. O. Hannay) New York, Harper [1956] 256p. 21cm. First published in 1939 under title: God's iron. [BS580] 56-13943
1. Jeremiah, the prophet. I. Title.

HASKIN, Dorothy (Clark) 221.92
The royal brickyard. Grand Rapids, Baker Book House, [c.]1959. 69p. 21cm. (Valor series, 4) 59-15529 .50 bds.,
1. Moses—Fiction. I. Title.

HASKIN, Dorothy (Clark) 221.92 1905-
The royal brickyard. Grand Rapids, Baker Book House, 1959. 69p. 21cm. (Valor series, 4) [BS580.M6H36] 59-15529
1. Moses—Fiction. I. Title.

HAUGHTON, Rosemary. 221.92
The young Moses. Illustrated by the author. New York, Roy Publishers [1966] 136 p. illus. 21 cm. The boyhood of Moses of the Bullrushes, who grew up to lead the Jews out of Egypt back to their intended country. [BS580.M6H368] AC 67
1. Moses. 2. Egypt—Social life and customs—To 640 A.D. I. Title.

HAYNES, Carlyle Boynton, 221.92 1882-
God sent a man. Washington, D.C., 6856 Eastern Ave., N.W. Review and Herald Pub. Assn., [1962] 192p. 22cm. 62-9140 3.00
1. Joseph, the patriarch. I. Title.

HAZEN, Barbara Shook 221.92
David and Goliath. Pictures by Robert J. Lee New York, Golden Press, 1974, c1968 1 v. (unpaged) col. illus. 21 cm. [BS580.D3H3] 0.49
1. David, King of Israel—Juvenile literature. I. Title.

HAZEN, Barbara Shook. 221.92 (j)
David and Goliath. Pictures by Robert J. Lee. New York, Golden Press [1968] 1 v. (unpaged) col. illus. 33 cm. (A Big golden book) [BS580.D3H3] 68-6913 1.00
1. David, King of Israel—Juvenile literature. I. Lee, Robert J., 1921- illus. II. Title.

HILL, Dorothy Black, 1893- 221.92
Abraham: his heritage and ours. Introd. by Sophia L. Fahs. Boston, Beacon Press [1957] 208 p. illus. 24 cm. [BS580.A3H5] 57-8852
1. Abraham, the patriarch.

HILL, Dorothy (Black) 221.92 1893-
Abraham: his heritage and ours. Introd. by Sophia L. Fahs. Boston, Beacon Press [1957] 208p. illus. 24cm. [BS580.A3H5] 57-8852
1. Abraham, the patriarch. I. Title.

HILL, John Leonard, 1878- 221.92
From Joshua to David. Nashville, Convention Press [1959, c1934] 113p. 19cm. [BS571.H48 1959] 59-9309
1. Bible. O. T.—Biog. 2. Bible. O. T.—Study—Text-books. I. Title.

HOBBS, Herschel H 221.92
Moses' mighty men. Nashville, Broadman Press [1958] 108p. 21cm. [BS571.H6] 58-5409
1. Bible. O. T.— Biog. 2. Moses. I. Title.

HORTON, Fred L. 221.9'2 B
The Melchizedek tradition : a critical examination of the sources to the fifth century A.D. and in the Epistle to the Hebrews / Fred L. Horton, Jr. Cambridge [Eng.] ; New York : Cambridge University Press, 1976. xi, 191 p. ; 23 cm. (Society for New Testament Studies. Monograph series ; 30) Includes indexes. Bibliography: p. 173-182. [BS580.M4H67] 75-32479 ISBN 0-521-21014-3 : 32.00
1. Melchizedek, King of Salem. 2. Bible. N.T. Hebrews—Criticism, interpretation, etc. I. Title. II. Series: Studiorum Novi Testamenti Societas. Monograph series ; 30.

HUNT, Clark W 221.92
Mighty men of God, with a good word for Cain. New York, Abingdon Press [1959] 144p. 20cm. [BS571.H79] 59-10361
1. Bible. O. T.—Biog. I. Title.

HYATT, James Philip, 1909- 221.92
Jeremiah, prophet of courage and hope. New York, Abingdon Press [1958] 128 p. 20 cm. Includes bibliography. [BS580.J4H9] 58-6593
1. Jeremiah, the prophet.

JAMES FLEMING, 1877-1959 221.92
Personalities of the Old Testament, [Reissue] Foreword by Julius A. Bewer. New York, Scribners [1965, c.1939] xvi p., 632p. maps. 24cm. (Hale lecs.: 4 40451) Bibl. [BS571.J3] 39-24508 3.95 pap.,
1. Bible. O. T.—Biog. I. Title.

JENKINS, Sara Lucile, 221.92
1905-
Amos, prophet of justice. New York, Association Press [1956] 127p. 20cm. (Heroes of God series) [BS580.A6J4] 56-9182
1. Amos, the prophet. I. Title.

JENKINS, Sara Lucile, 221.92
1905-
Amos, prophet of justice. New York, Association Press [1956] 127p. 20cm. (Heroes of God series) [BS580.A6J4] 56-9182
1. Ames, the prophet. I. Title.

JONES, Juanita Nuttall, 221.92
1912-
Deborah, the woman who saved Israel [by] Juanita Nuttall Jones and James Banford McKendry New York, Association Press [1956] 127p. 20cm. (Heroes of God series) [BS580.D4J6] 56-9186
1. Deborah, judge of Israel. I. McKendry, James Banford, joint author. II. Title.

JONES, Mary Alice, 1898- 221.92
Friends of Jesus. Illustrated by Janet Robson Kennedy. Chicago, Rand McNally, 1964, c1954. 1 v. (unpaged) col. illus. 27 cm. [BS2433.J6 1964] 61-15253
1. Jesus Christ—Friends and associates—Juvenile literature. I. Title.

KENNEDY, Gerald 221.92
Witnesses of the spirit. Nashville, Upper Room [c.1961] 64p. .35 pap.,
I. Title.

KING, Marian. 221.92
Coat of many colors, the story of Joseph; illustrated by Steele Savage. [1st ed.] Philadelphia, Lippincott [1950] ix, 165 p. illus. 21 cm. [BS580.J6K5] 50-14665
1. Joseph, the patriarch. I. Title.

KLAPERMAN, Libby M 221.92
Adam and the first Sabbath. Pictures by Lillian Port. New York, Behram House [1953] unpaged. illus. 21cm. [BS580.A4K5] 53-11818
1. Adam (Biblical character) I. Title.

KUMMEL, Sara B 221.92
Esther becomes a queen. Hal Just, illustrator. [New York] Union of American Hebrew Congregations, c1955. unpaged. illus. 16x24cm. [BS580.E8K8] 55-33687
1. Esther, Queen of Persia. I. Title.

LA SOR, William Sanford. 221.92
Great personalities of the Old Testament: their lives and times. [Westwood, N. J.] Revell [1959] 192p. 21cm. Includes bibliography. [BS571.L32] 59-5500
1. Bible. O. T.—Biog. I. Title.

LEE, Robert Greene, 1836- 221.92
Bible fires; messages on Bible characters. Grand Rapids, Zondervan Pub. House [1956] 184p. 20cm. [BS571.L43] 56-40840
1. Bible—Biog. 2. Baptists—Sermons. 3. Sermons, American. I. Title.

LEE, Robert Greene, 1886- 221.92
Bible fires; messages on Bible characters. Grand Rapids, Zondervan Pub. House [1956] 181p. 20cm. [BS571.L43] 56-40840
1. Bible—Biog. 2. Baptists— Sermons. 3. Sermons, American. I. Title.

LEVINGER, Elma (Ehrlich) 221.92
1887-
Elijah, prophet of the one God. New York, Association Press [1956] 123p. 20cm. (Heroes of God series) [BS580.E4L47] 56-9185
1. Elijah, the prophet. I. Title.

LONG, Laura. 221.92
The chosen boy; a story of Moses, who led his people from slavery to the Promised Land. Drawings by Clotilde Embree Funk. [1st ed.] Indianapolis, Bobbs-Merrill [1952] 192 p. illus. 20 cm. [BS580.M6L58] 52-10704
1. Moses. I. Title.

LONG, Laura. 221.92
Queen Esther, star in Judea's crown; a dramatic retelling of the book of Esther. New York, Association Press [1954] 156p. illus. 20cm. (Heroes of God series) [BS580.E8L58] 54-8383
1. Esther, Queen of Persia. I. Title.

MCALLISTER, Grace Edna. 221.92
God portrays more women. Chicago, Moody Press [1956] 188p. 22cm. [BS575.M24] 56-1610
1. Women in the Bible. 2. Bible. O.T.—Biog. I. Title.

MACARTNEY, Clarence Edward 221.92
Noble, 1879-
Sermons on Old Testament heroes. Nashville, Abingdon [1962, c.1935] 247p. 18cm. (Apex bks., J5) .95 pap.,
1. Bible. O.T.—Biog. 2. Bible—Biog.—O.T. 3. Presbyterian church—Sermons. 4. Sermons, American. I. Title.

MCCLINTOCK, Marshall 221.92
David and the giant, by Mike McClintock. Pictures by Fritz Siebel New York, Harper [c.1960] unpaged. illus. (col.) 23cm. (An I can read book) 60-11196 1.95; 2.19 Harpercrest ed.,
I. Title.

MCCLINTOCK, Marshall, 221.92
1906-
David and the giant, by Mike McClintock. Pictures by Fritz Siebel. New York, Harper [1960] unpaged. illus. 23cm. (An I can read book) [BS580.D3M25] 60-11196
1. David, King of Israel—Juvenile literature. I. Title.

MACDUFF, John Ross, 1818- 221.92
1895.
Elijah, the prophet of fire. Grand Rapids, Baker Book House, 1956. 351p. illus. 21cm. [BS580.E4M2 1956] 56-7579
1. Elijah, the prophet. I. Title.

MCLAREN, Alexander, 1826- 221.92
1910.
The life of David as reflected in his Psalms. 7th ed. Grand Rapids, Baker Book House, 1955. 261p. 20cm. [Baker co-operative reprint library] 'Reprinted from the 1888 printing by Hodder & Stonghton, London.' [BS580] 55-8793
1. David, King of Israel. 2. Bible. O. T. Psalms—Criticism, interpretation. etc. I. Title.

*MACVEAGH, Rogers 221.92
Joshua, by Rogers MacVeagh, Thomas B. Costain. Introd. by Norman Vincent Peale. New York, Popular Lib. [1964, c.1943, 1948] 190p. map. 18cm. (M2067) .60 pap.,
1. Joshua. I. Costain, Thomas Bertram, 1885- II. Title.

MAGARY, Alvin Edwin. 221.92
Saints without halos. New York, Abingdon-Cokesbury Press [1951]C176 p. 20 cm. [BS2430.M24] 51-9136
1. Bible. N. T.—Biog. I. Title.

MALVERN, Gladys. 221.92
Behold your queen! Decorations by Corinne Malvern. [1st ed.] New York, Longmans, Green, 1951. 218 p. 22 cm. [BS580.E8M3] 51-11613
1. Esther, Queen of Persia. I. Title.

MEYER, Frederick 221.92
Brotherton, 1847-1929.
David: shepherd, psalmist, king Grand Rapids, Zondervan Pub. House [1953] 160p. 21cm. [BS580.D3M4 1953] 53-13074
1. David, King of Isrsel. I. Title.

MEYER, Frederick 221.92
Brotherton, 1847-1929.
Moses. the servant of God. Grand Rapids, Zondervan Pub. House [1954] 189p. 20cm. [BS580.M6M4 1954] 53-13076
1. Moses. I. Title.

MILLIKIN, Virginia Greene. 221.92
Jeremiah, prophet of disaster; a novel-biography of the Prophet Jeremiah. New York, Association Press [1954] 155p. illus. 20cm. (Heroes of God series) [BS580.J4M5] 54-8247
1. Jeremiah, the Prophet. I. Title.

MUTH, Don. 221.92
Elijah, the man who went to heaven. Illus. by author. Mountain View, Calif., Pacific Press Pub. Association, c1954. 1 v. (unpaged) illus. 29 cm. [BS580.E4M8] 55-16782
1. Elijah, the prophet.

NEHER, Andre. 221.92
Moses and the vocation of the Jewish people. Translated by Irene Marinoff. New York, Harper Torchbooks, c1959. 191p. illus. 18cm. (Men of wisdom, MW7) Includes bibliography. [BS580.M6N43] 59-6652
1. Moses. 2. Judaism—Hist.—Ancient period. I. Title.

PARMITER, Geoffrey de 221.92
Clinton.
King David. [1st American ed.] New York, Nelson [1961, c1960] 195p. illus. 23cm. Bibliographical footnotes. [BS580.D3P3 1961] 61-2156
1. David, King of Israel. I. Title.

PARMITER, Geoffrey Vincent 221.92
de Clinton
King David. New York, T. Nelson [1961, c.1960] 195p. front. Bibl. 3.95
1. David, King of Israel. I. Title.

PETERSHAM, Maud (Fuller) 221.92
1890-
Joseph and his brothers, from the story told in the book of Genesis [by] Maud and Miska Petersham. New York, Macmillan, 1958. [32] p. illus. 24 cm. Retells the Bible story of Joseph, victim of jealous older brothers, who, by his ability to interpret dreams, made a place for himself in the land of Egypt. [BS580.J6P44 1958] AC 68
1. Joseph, the patriarch. 2. Bible stories—Old Testament. I. Petersham, Miska, 1888- joint author. II. Title.

PETERSHAM, Maud (Fuller) 221.92
1890-
Moses, from the story told in the Old Testament [by] Maud and Miska Petersham. New York, Macmillan, 1958 [c1938] [32] p. illus. 24 cm. Retells the Bible story of Moses, who was hidden from the Egyptians as a baby, and who led his people across the Red Sea and into the wilderness in search of the Promised Land. [BS580.M6P45 1958] AC 68
1. Moses. 2. Bible stories—Old Testament. I. Petersham, Miska, 1888- joint author. II. Title.

PETERSHAM, Maud (Fuller) 221.92
1890-
Ruth; from the story told in the book of Ruth [by] Maud and Miska Petersham. New York, Macmillan, 1958 [c1938] [32] p. illus. 24 cm. Presents the Old Testament tale of Ruth who, when her husband died, returned with her mother-in-law to Bethlehem to work in the fields of Boaz. [BS580.R8P45 1958] AC 68
1. Ruth (Biblical character) 2. Bible stories—Old Testament. I. Petersham, Miska, 1888- joint author. II. Title.

PETERSHAM, Maud Fuller, 221.92
1890-1971.
David, from the story told in the First book of Samuel and the First book of Kings [by] Maud and Miska Petersham. New York, Macmillan, 1958. unpaged. illus. 24 cm. [BS580.D3P47 1958] 58-8035
1. David, King of Israel. I. Petersham, Miska, 1888-1960, joint author.

PETERSHAM, Maud Fuller, 221.92
1890-1971.
Joseph and his brothers, from the story told in the book of Genesis [by] Maud and Miska Petersham. New York, Macmillan, 1958. unpaged, illus. 24 cm. [BS580.J6P44 1958] 58-8034
1. Joseph, the patriarch. I. Petersham, Miska, 1888-1960, joint author. II. Title.

PINK, Arthur Walkington, 221.92
1886-1952.
The life of David. Grand Rapids, Zondervan Pub. House [1958] 2v. 22cm. [BS580.D3P54] 58-25453
1. David, King of Israel. I. Title.

PINK, Arthur Walkington, 221.92
1886-1952.
The life of Elijah. Swengel, Pa., Bible Truth Depot [1956] 314p. 22cm. [BS580.E4P45] 56-10688
1. Elijah, the prophet. I. Title.

RAD, Gerhard von 221.92
Moses. New York, Association Press [1960] 80p. 19cm. (World Christian books, no. 32. Second series), 1.00 pap.,
1. Moses. I. Title.

RAD, Gerhard von, 1901- 221.92
Moses. New York, Association Press [1960?] 80p. 19cm. (World Christian books, no. 32. Second series) [BS580.M6R23] 60-8945
1. Moses. I. Title.

REDPATH, Alan. 221.92
The making of a man of God; studies in the life of David. [Westwood, N.J.] Revell [1962] 256 p. 21 cm. [BS580.D3R4] 62-10731
1. David, King of Israel. 2. Devotional literature. I. Title.

ROBERSON, Lee. 221.92
Kings on parade; [striking lessons from Adoni-bezek, David, Asa, Joash, Hezekiah, Manasseh, Zedekiah, and other Bible kings. Wheaton, Ill., Sword of the Lord Publishers [1956] 106p. 21cm. [BS579.K5R6] 57-21802
1. Bible. O. T.—Biog. 2. Jews —Hist.—To 586 B. C. I. Title.

SAMUEL, Maurice, 1895- 221.92
1972.
Certain people of the Book. [1st ed.] New York, Knopf, 1955. 363 p. 22 cm. [BS572.S3] 55-8887
1. Bible. O. T.—Biography. I. Title.

SCHMID, Evan, 1920- 221.92
David; the story of the King of Israel. Illus. by Brother Bernard Howard. Notre Dame, Ind., Dujarie Press [1953] 95p. illus. 24cm. [BS580.D3S35] 53-2903
1. David, King of Israel. I. Title.

SLAUGHTER, Frank G. 221.92
David: warrior and king. New York, Pocket Bks. [1963, c.1962] 389p. 17cm. (Permabk. ed. M5066) .50 pap.,
1. David, King of Israel. I. Title.

SLAUGHTER, Frank Gill, 221.92
1908-
David, warrior and king, a Biblical biography. [1st ed.] Cleveland, World Pub. Co. [1962] 411 p. 22 cm. [BS580.D3S48] 62-9050
1. David, King of Israel. I. Title.

SOUTHON, Arthur Eustace, 221.92
1887-
On eagles' wings. New York, McGraw-Hill [1954, c1939] 296 p. 21 cm. The story of Moses. [BS580.M6S55 1954] 53-12057
1. Moses. I. Title.

SPURGEON, Charles Haddon, 221.92
1834-1892.
Sermons on women of the Old Testament; sel. and ed. by Chas. T. Cook. Grand Rapids, Zondervan Pub. House [c.1960] 256p. (Library of Spurgeon's sermons, v. 11) 61-706 2.95
1. Women in the Bible. 2. Bible. O. T.—Biog. I. Title.

STAACK, Hagen. 221.92
Living personalities of the Old Testament. [1st ed.] New York, Harper & Row [1964] xii, 147 p. 22 cm. Bibliography: p. 147. [BS571.S78] 64-14375
1. Bible. O. T.—Biography. I. Title.

*STIBBS, Alan M. 221.92
God's friend, studies in the life of Abraham. Chicago, Inter-Varsity [1964] 88p. 19cm. .75 pap.,
I. Title.

STRONG, Kendrick. 221.92
Old Testament portraits. Philadelphia, Christian Education Press [1958] 179 p. illus. 23 cm. [BS571.S87] 58-8808
1. Bible. O.T. — Biog. I. Title.

TEULINGS, C. P. 221.92
A gallery of portraits of the Old Testament. New York, Vantage [c.1963] 270p. 22cm. 64-215 3.95 bds.,
1. Bible. O. T.—Biog. I. Title.

TRIBBLE, Harold Wayland, 221.92
1899-
From Adam to Moses. Nashville, Convention Press [1959] 140 p. illus. 19 cm. [BS571.T7] 59-9308
1. Bible. O.T. — Biog. 2. Bible. O.T. — Study — Text-books. I. Title.

TRIMMER, Vincent David 221.92
Elisha prophet extraordinary. Chicago, Moody [c.1963] 80p. 18cm. (Compact bk., 43) .29 pap.,
I. Title.

TURNBULL, Ralph G. 221.92
Personalities of the Old Testament, by Ralph G. Turnbull. Grand Rapids, Baker Book House, 1964. 151 p. 21 cm. [BS571.T85] 64-15681
1. Bible. O. T.—Biography. I. Title.

WEISFELD, Israel Harold, 221.92
1906-
This man Moses, by Israel H. Weisfeld. New York, Bloch Pub. Co. [1966] xxii, 234 p. illus. 25 cm. Bibliography: p. [229]-230. [BS580.M6W43] 66-24260
1. Moses. I. Title.

WEISFELD, Israel Harold, 221.92
1906-
This man Moses. by Israel H. Weisfeld. New York, Bloch [1966] xxii, 234p. illus. 25cm. Bibl. [BS580.M6W43] 66-24260 7.50
1. Moses. I. Title.

WEISS, George Christian, 221.92
1910-
Joseph and his brothers. Sponsored by the Benedictine monks of Belmont Abbey. Garden City, N.Y., [N. Doubleday, 1960] 64 p. illus. 21 cm. (The Catholic know-your-Bible program) [BS580.J6W38 1960] 60-3101
1. Joseph, the patriarch — Juvenile literature. I. Title.

WEYNE, Arthur. 221.92
Joshua, the redeemer; illustrated by Dan Samuels. New York, Behrman House [1952] 116p. illus. 21cm. [BS580.J7W47] 53-50
1. Joshua, son of Nun. I. Title.

WHEMPNER, Verna Huber. 221.92
Little boys of the Bible. Illus. by Delight Whempner Danly. Minneapolis, Denison [1960] 54 p. illus. 29 cm. Includes bibliography. [BS577.W46] 58-13815
1. Children in the Bible. I. Title.

WHEMPNER, Verna Huber 221.92
Little boys of the Bible. Illus. by Delight

Whempner Danly. Minneapolis, Denison [c.1960] 54p. (bibl.) illus. (part col.) 29cm. 58-13815 3.00
1. Children in the Bible. I. Title.

WILLIAMSON, Adolph Ancrum, 1883- 221.92
Moses, who first saw our pyramid of life; a grand philosophy of evolution. New York, Philosophical Library [1950] viii, 231 p. 23 cm. Bibliography: p.229-231. [BS580.M6W5] 50-1115
1. Moses. I. Title.

YATES, Kyle Monroe, 1895- 221.92
From Solomon to Malachi. Nashville, Convention Press [1959, c1934] 126 p. illus. 20 cm. [BS1505.5.Y3 1959] 59-9310
1. Bible. O.T. — Biog. 2. Bible. O.T. — Study — Text-books. I. Title.

AGUILAR, Grace, 1816-1847. 221.9'22 B
The women of Israel; or, Characters and sketches from the Holy Scriptures and Jewish history illustrative of the past history, present duties, and future destiny of the Hebrew females, as based on the Word of God. Plainview, N.Y., Books for Libraries Press [1974] p. cm. (Essay index reprint series) Reprint of the 1879 ed. published by G. Routledge, London, and E. P. Dutton, New York. [BS575.A3 1974] 74-4358 ISBN 0-518-10174-6
1. Bible. O.T.—Biography. 2. Women in the Bible. 3. Women, Jewish. I. Title. II. Title: Characters and sketches from the Holy Scriptures and Jewish history.

BARING-GOULD, Sabine, 1834-1924. 221.9'22 B
Legends of the patriarchs and prophets and other Old Testament characters from various sources. [Folcroft, Pa.] Folcroft Library Editions, 1974. p. cm. Reprint of the 1872 ed. published by Holt & Williams, New York. [BS571.B337 1974] 74-9741 ISBN 0-8414-3205-8 (lib. bdg.)
1. Bible. O.T.—Biography. I. Title.

BARINGGOULD SABINE, 1834-1924. 221.9'22 B
Legends of the patriarchs and prophets and other Old Testament characters from various sources. [Folcroft, Pa.] Folcroft Library Editions, 1974. p. cm. Reprint of the 1872 ed. published by Holt & Williams, New York. [BS571.B337 1974] 74-9741 30.00 (lib. bdg.).
1. Bible. O.T.—Biography. I. Title.

BARRETT, Ethel. 221.9'22 B
I'm no hero. Glendale, Calif., G/L Regal Books [1974] 150 p. illus. 20 cm. (A Regal venture book) [BS571.B37] 73-85395 ISBN 0-8307-0254-7 0.95 (pbk.).
1. Bible. O.T.—Biography. 2. Christian life—1960- I. Title.

BEAUCAMP, Evode. 221.92'2
Prophetic intervention in the history of man. Staten Island, N.Y., Alba House [1971, c1970] xvii, 230 p. 22 cm. Translation of Le prophetisme et l'election d'Israel. [BS1198.B3613] 76-129176 ISBN 0-8189-0191-8 4.95
1. Prophets. I. Title.

BLANK, Sheldon H. 221.92'2
Understanding the prophets, by Sheldon H. Blank. New York, Union of American Hebrew Congregations [1969] 138 p. 20 cm. (Issues of faith) [BS1198.B52] 74-92159 2.50
1. Prophets. I. Title. II. Series.

BOICE, James Montgomery, 1938- 221.9'22 B
How God can use nobodies; small enough to be great: Abraham, Moses, and David. Wheaton, Ill., Victor Books [1974] 156 p. 18 cm. (An Input book) [BS571.B553] 73-91026 ISBN 0-88207-027-4 1.25 (pbk.)
1. Abraham, the patriarch. 2. Moses. 3. David, King of Israel. I. Title.

BROWNE, Earl Zollicoffer. 221.9'22
Let's return to the Mosaic authorship of the Pentateuch. [1st ed.] New York, Greenwich Book Publishers [1962] 131p. 21cm. [BS1225.2.B7] 62-15299
1. Bible. O. T. Pentateuch—Evidences, authority, etc. I. Title.

COMAY, Jean. 221.9'2'2 B
Who's who in the Old Testament, together with the Apocrypha. London, Weidenfeld and Nicolson, 1971. 448 p. illus. (some col.), facsims., maps. 26 cm. [BS570.C64 1971b] 72-195604 ISBN 0-297-00409-3
1. Bible. O.T.—Biography—Dictionaries. I. Title.
Available from Holt, Rinehart and Winston, 14.95, 0-03-086263-9.

COMAY, Joan. 221.92'2 B
Who's who in the Old Testament, together with the Apocrypha. Advisory editors for this volume: Michael Graetz [and] Leonard Cowie. [1st ed.] New York, Holt, Rinehart and Winston [1971] 448 p. illus. 26 cm. [BS570.C64] 79-153655 ISBN 0-03-086263-9 14.95
1. Bible. O.T.—Biography—Dictionaries. I. Title.

CORVIN, R. O. 221.92'2 B
David and his mighty men, by R. O. Corvin. Freeport, N.Y., Books for Libraries Press [1970, c1950] 175 p. 23 cm. (Biography index reprint series) [BS580.D3C65 1970] 74-136646
1. David, King of Israel. 2. Bible. O.T.—Biography. I. Title.

*CULBERTSON, Paul T. 221.922
Contemporary insights from Bible characters [by] Paul T. Culbertson. Grand Rapids, Mich., Baker Book House [1973] 144 p. 20 cm. [BS571.5] ISBN 0-8010-2350-5 2.45 (pbk.)
1. Bible—Biography—Sermons. I. Title.

DAUGHTERS of St. Paul. 221.92'2
Women of the Bible; the Old Testament. Illus. by Gregori. [Boston] St. Paul Editions [1970] 123 p. col. illus., col. maps. 25 cm. Biblical quotations and brief narration recount the deeds of women of the Old Testament. [BS575.D34] 71-145574 5.00
1. Bible. O.T.—Biography—Juvenile literature. 2. Women in the Bible—Juvenile literature. I. Gregori, illus. II. Title.

DIGGES, Mary Laurentia, 1910- 221.922
Adam's haunted sons. With a foreword by Barnabas Ahern. New York, Macmillan [1966] xvi, 302 p. 22 cm. Bibliographical references included in "Notes" (p. 289-292) [BS571.D5] 66-21162
1. Bible. O.T. — Biog. I. Title.

DIGGES, Mary Laurentia Sister 1910- 221.922
Adam's haunted sons. Foreword by Barnabas Ahern. New York, Macmillan [c.1966] xvi, 302p. 22cm. Bibl. [BS571.D5] 66-21162 5.95
1. Bible. O.T. — Biog. I. Title.

ESSES, Michael. 221.9'22
The phenomenon of obedience. Plainfield, N.J., Logos International [1974] x, 189 p. 21 cm. [BS571.E84] 73-92248 ISBN 0-88270-085-5 2.50
1. Bible. O.T.—Biography. I. Title.

FRAINE, Jean de. 221.92'2
Women of the Old Testament, by J. de Fraine. Translated by Forrest L. Ingram. De Pere, Wis., St. Norbert Abbey Press, 1968. 92 p. 20 cm. Translation of Bijbelse Vrouwengestalten. [BS575.F713] 68-58524 ISBN 0-8316-1029-8
1. Bible. O.T.—Biography. 2. Women in the Bible. I. Title.

HUBBARD, David Allan. 221.9'22 B
Strange heroes / David Allan Hubbard. Philadelphia : A. J. Holman Co., c1977. 208 p. ; 18 cm. (Trumpet books) [BS571.H74] 77-1889 ISBN 0-87981-077-7 pbk. : 1.95
1. Bible. O.T.—Biography. I. Title.

KELSO, James Leon, 1892 221.922
Archaeology and our Old Testament contemporaries. Grand Rapids, Mich., Zondervan [c.1966] 191p. illus., map. 23cm. Bibl. [BS572.K4] 66-13691 4.95
1. Bible. O.T. — Biog. I. Title.

KITTEL, Rudolf, 1853-1929. 221.92'2
Great men and movements in Israel. Authorized translation by Charlotte A. Knoch and C. D. Wright. Prolegomenon by Theodor H. Gaster. New York, Ktav Pub. House, 1968. lii, 465 p. 24 cm. (The Library of Biblical studies) Reprint of the 1929 ed. with new prolegomenon by Theodor H. Gaster. Translation of Gestalten und Gedanken in Israel. Includes bibliographies. [BS571.K5 1968] 66-29121
1. Jews—History—To A.D. 70. 2. Bible. O.T.—Biography. I. Title. II. Series.

KRAELING, Emil Gottlieb Heinrich, 1892- 221'.922
The prophets, by Emil G. Kraeling. [Chicago] Rand McNally [1969] 304 p. 22 cm. Bibliographical references included in "Notes and references" (p. 293-297) [BS1198.K7] 75-90839 6.95
1. Prophets.

NADEN, Roy C. 221.9'22 B
Without a doubt / by Roy C. Naden. Mountain View, Calif. : Pacific Press Pub. Association, c1975. 78 p. : ill. ; 19 cm. [BS571.N3 1975] 75-32709
1. Bible. O.T.—Biography. 2. Meditations. I. Title.

PAPE, William H 221.922
I talked with Noah; imaginary conversations with Bible characters, by William H. Pape. Grand Rapids, Baker Book House, 1966. 128 p. 20 cm. [BS572.P3] 66-18317
1. Bible. O.T. — Biog. I. Title.

PAPE, William H. 221.922
I talked with Noah; imaginary conversations with Bible characters. Grand Rapids, Mich., Baker Bk. [c.]1966. 128p. 20cm. [BS572.P3] 66-18317 2.95
1. Bible. O. T. — Biog. I. Title.

PATTERSON, Ward. 221.9'22 B
Yesterday today: answers from the ancients. Cincinnati, New Life Books [1974] 96 p. illus. 18 cm. [BS571.P28] 74-79113 ISBN 0-87239-003-9 1.50 (pbk.).
1. Bible. O.T.—Biography. I. Title.
Available from Standard Pub. Co.

PEARLMAN, Moshe, 1911- 221.9'22 B
In the footsteps of the prophets / Moshe Pearlman. New York : Crowell, 1975. 230 p. : ill. (some col.) ; 29 cm. Includes index. [BS1505.2.P4 1975] 75-11965 ISBN 0-690-00962-3 : 19.95
1. Prophets. I. Title.

PRITCHARD, James Bennett, 1909- 221.9'22
Solomon and Sheba, edited by James B. Pritchard. New York, Praeger [1974] p. cm. [BS580.S6P74] 72-79551 ISBN 0-275-46540-3 15.00
1. Solomon, King of Israel—Legends—History and criticism. 2. Sheba, Queen of—Legends—History and criticism. I. Title.

PRITCHARD, James Bennett, 1909- 221.9'22
Solomon & Sheba / James B. Pritchard, ed. ; [contributors] Gus W. van Beek ... [et al.]. London : Phaidon, 1974. 160 p., [48] p. of plates : ill., facsims., maps, plans ; 26 cm. Distributed in the U.S.A. by Praeger, New York. Includes index. Bibliography: p. 152-158. [BS580.S6P74 1974b] 74-196853 ISBN 0-7148-1613-2 : 17.50
1. Solomon, King of Israel—Legends—History and criticism. 2. Sheba, Queen of—Legends—History and criticism. I. Van Beek, Gus Willard, 1922- II. Title.

ROLSTON, Holmes, 1900- 221.92'2
Personalities around David. Richmond, John Knox PressA [1968] 144 p. 21 cm. (Aletheia paperbacks) [BS580.D3R6] 67-19895
1. David, King of Israel—Friends and associates. I. Title.

SANFORD, John A. 221.9'22 B
The man who wrestled with God; a study of individuation (personal growth toward wholeness) based on four Bible stories [by] John A. Sanford. King of Prussia, Pa., Religious Pub. Co. [1974] 126 p. 22 cm. Errata slip inserted. Includes bibliographical references. [BS571.S26] 74-79994 5.95
1. Jacob, the patriarch. 2. Joseph, the patriarch. 3. Moses. 4. Adam (Biblical character) 5. Eve (Biblical character) I. Title.
Publisher's address: 198 Allendale Road, King of Prussia, Pa. 19406.

WIESEL, Elie, 1928- 221.9'22 B
Messengers of God: Biblical portraits and legends / [by] Elie Wiesel ; translated from the French by Marion Wiesel. New York : Pocket Books, 1977,c1976. 251p. ; 18 cm. (A Kangaroo Book) ob, the patriarch. [BM516.W513 1976] ISBN 0-3711-81097-9 pbk. : 1.95
1. Moss-Legends. 2. Midrash-Legends. 3. Bible. O.T. Genesis-Legends. 4. Aggada. 5. Tales, Hasidic. I. Title. II. Series.
L.C. card no. for 1976 Random House ed.:75-43425

WIESEL, Elie, 1928- 221.9'22 B
Messengers of God : Biblical portraits and legends / Elie Wiesel ; translated from the French by Marion Wiesel. 1st American ed. New York : Random House, c1976. xiv, 237 p. ; 22 cm. Translation of Celebration biblique. Bibliography: p. 237. [BM516.W513 1976] 75-43425 ISBN 0-394-49740-6 : 8.95
1. Moses—Legends. 2. Job, the patriarch. 3. Midrash—Legends. 4. Bible. O.T. Genesis—Legends. 5. Aggada. 6. Tales, Hasidic. I. Title.

WILSON, Clifford A. 221.92'2 B
A greater than Elijah is here, by Clifford Wilson. [Melbourne, Australian Institute of Archaeology in association with Word of Truth Productions, 1969] 36 p. 21 cm. (A word of truth production) Processed. [BS580.E4W54] 75-487928 unpriced
1. Elijah, the prophet. 2. Elisha, the prophet. 3. Jesus Christ—Person and offices. I. Australian Institute of Archaeology. II. Title.

ZELIGS, Dorothy Freda. 221.9'22 B
Psychoanalysis and the Bible; a study in depth of seven leaders [by] Dorothy F. Zeligs. New York, Bloch Pub. Co. [1974] xxiv, 348 p. 24 cm. Includes bibliographical references. [BS571.Z44] 73-85071 ISBN 0-8197-0360-5 10.00
1. Bible. O.T.—Biography. 2. Bible. O.T.—Psychology. I. Title.

ARMSTRONG, William Howard, 1914- 221.9'24 B
Hadassah: Esther the orphan queen [by] William H. Armstrong. Illustrated by Barbara Ninde Byfield. [1st ed.] Garden City, N.Y., Doubleday [1972] 75 p. illus. 22 cm. Retells the Bible story of Esther who, as Queen of Persia and a Jew, was able to save her people from extermination. [BS580.E8A75] 72-76114 ISBN 0-385-08832-9 3.95
1. Esther, Queen of Persia—Juvenile literature. 2. Bible stories, English—O.T. Esther. I. Byfield, Barbara Ninde, illus. II. Title.

BLASI, Anthony. 221.92'4
Jeremy; a story of Jeremiah, the prophet. Notre Dame, Dujarie [c1967] 79p. illus., port. 22cm. [BS580.J4B49] 67-28933 2.75 bds.,
1. Jeremiah, the prophet. I. Title.

BOLLIGER, Max. 221.92'4
Joseph. Illus. by Edith Schindler. Translated by Marion Koenig. New York, Delacorte Press [1969] 109 p. illus. 22 cm. "A Seymour Lawrence book." A retelling of the Old Testament story of Joseph, whose jealous brothers sold him into slavery for twenty pieces of silver. [BS580.J6B563] 68-20107 3.95
1. Joseph, the patriarch—Juvenile literature. 2. Bible stories—Old Testament. I. Schindler, Edith, illus. II. Title.

BOSCH, Juan, Pres. Dominican Republic, 1909- 221.924
David, the biography of a king. Translated by John Marks. [1st American ed.] New York, Hawthorn Books [1966] 224 p. 21 cm. [BS580.D3B633 1966] 66-23401
1. David, King of Israel. I. Title.

BOSCH, Juan, Pres. Dominican Republic 1909- 221.924
David, the biography of a king by John Marks [1st amer. ed] New York, Hawthorn [1966] 224p. 21cm. [BS580.D3B633 1966] 66-23401 4.95
1. David, King of Israel. I. Title.

CONWAY, Moncure Daniel, 1832-1907. 221.9'24 B
Solomon and Solomonic literature. New York, Haskell House, 1973. viii, 248 p. 23 cm. [BS580.S6C6 1973] 72-2032 ISBN 0-8383-1478-3 10.95
1. Solomon, King of Israel. 2. Hebrew literature—History and criticism. I. Title.

DE REGNIERS, Beatrice Schenk. 221.924
David and Goliath. Illustrated by Richard M. Powers. New York, Viking Press, 1965. 1 v. (unpaged) col. illus. 29 cm. [BS580.D3D54] 65-18151
1. David, King of Israel—Juvenile literature. I. Powers, Richard M., illus. II. Title.

GAUBERT, Henri, 1895- 221.9'24 B
Solomon the magnificent. Translated by Lancelot Sheppard and A. Manson. New York, Hastings House [1970] xix, 191 p. illus. 20 cm. (The Bible in history, v. 5) "A Giniger book." Bibliography: p. 187-188. [BS580.S6G313 1970] 69-15815 ISBN 0-8038-6685-2 5.95
1. Solomon, King of Israel. I. Title. II. Series.

GIBBS, Paul T. 221.92'4 B
David and his mighty men [by] Paul T. Gibbs. Washington, Review and Herald Pub. Association [1970] 205 p. 22 cm. [BS580.D3G5] 79-102115
1. David, King of Israel. 2. Bible. O.T.—Biography. I. Title.

GONZALEZ, Angel, of Madrid? 221.92'4
Abraham, father of believers. Translated by Robert J. Olsen. [New York] Herder and Herder [1967] 157 p. 21 cm. Translation of Abraham, padre de los creyentes. Bibliographical footnotes. [BS580.A3G63] 67-25879
1. Abraham, the patriarch. I. Title.

GONZALEZ, Nunez Angel, 1925- 221.92'4
Abraham, father of believers. Translated by Robert J. Olsen. [New York] Herder and Herder [1967] 157 p. 21 cm. Translation of Abraham, padre de los creyentes. Bibliographical footnotes. [BS580.A3G63] 67-25879
1. Abraham, the patriarch. I. Title.

HALL, Joseph, Bp. of Norwich, 1574-1656. 221.9'24 B
Samson; selections from a contemplation on an

historical passage in the Old Testament. With drawings by Fritz Kredel. [Lexington, Ky., Stamperia del Santuccio, 1972] a-c, xix p. illus. 29 cm. Selections from Book 10 in the part dealing with the Old Testament of the work first published 1612-26 under title: Contemplations upon the principall passages of the Holy Storie. [BS580.S15H34] 73-151450
1. Samson, Judge of Israel.

HARDINGE, Leslie. 221.92'4
Elisha, man of God. Washington, Review and Herald Pub. Association [1968] 128 p. 22 cm. [BS580.E5H3] 68-25113
1. Elisha, the prophet. I. Title.

HERCUS, John. 221.92'4
David. [Rev. ed.] Chicago, Inter-varsity Press [1968] ix, 136 p. 20 cm. At head of title: Another "casebook." [BS580.D3H44 1968] 68-28327 4.50
1. David, King of Israel. I. Title.

JOHNSON, Kate Nunez. 221.924
And he prayed. Philadelphia, Dorrance [1966] 44 p. 21 cm. [BS580.E4J6] 66-23409
1. Elijah, the prophet. I. Title.

JORDAN, Cynthia. 221.9'24 B
Little David. [Illus. by Ruby I. Walker. Pasadena, Tex., Charlotte Pub. Co., c1972] [24] p. col. illus. and phonodisc (2 s. 7 in. 45 rpm.) in pocket. 21 cm. Cover title. Musical accompaniment on phonodisc by Charlotte Ophelia; Mike Kiser, narrator. Recounts the feats David was able to perform with God's help. [BS580.D3J58] 73-165489
1. David, King of Israel—Juvenile literature. I. Walker, Ruby I., illus. II. Ophelia, Charlotte. III. Kiser, Mike. IV. Title.

KLAGSBRUN, Francine. 221.92'4
The story of Moses. New York, Watts [1968] xvii., 171p. map. 22cm. Immortals of phil. & religion) [BS580.M6K55] 68-27403 3.95; 2.96 lib. ed.,
1. Moses. I. Title.

LOREDANO, Giovanni 221.92'4
Francesco, 1606-1661
The life of Adam (1640). A facsim. reproduction of the English tr. of 1659 with an introd. by Roy C. Flanagan with John Arthos. Gainesville, Fla., Scholars' Facsimiles, 1967. xxi, 86p. illus. 20cm. Tr. of L'Adamo. [BS580.A4L613 1659a] 67-26617 6.00
I. Roy C. ed. II. Orthos, John, 1908- ed. III. Title.

MCGEE, John Vernon, 221.92'4
1904-
In a barley field, by J. Vernon McGee. Glendale, Calif., G/L Regal Books [1968] 192 p. 18 cm. On cover: Ruth's romance of redemption. 1943 and 1954 editions published under title: Ruth: the romance of redemption. Bibliography: p. 192. [BS580.R8M3 1968] 68-22387
1. Ruth (Biblical character) 2. Redemption—Biblical teaching. I. Title.

MILLER, Amos W., 1927- 221.9'24 B
Abraham: friend of God; an ethical biography of the founder of the Jewish people, by Amos W. Miller. Middle Village, N.Y., J. David [1973] 213 p. 22 cm. [BS580.A3M5] 73-6406 ISBN 0-8246-0156-4 7.95
1. Abraham, the patriarch. I. Title.

PARROT, Andre, 1901- 221.92'4
Abraham and his times. Translated by James H. Farley. Philadelphia, Fortress Press [1968] xiv, 178 p. illus. 22 cm. A translation of Abraham et son temps. Bibliography: p. 160-164. [BS580.A3P3313] 68-18146 4.75
1. Abraham, the patriarch. I. Title.

PINK, Arthur 221.9'24 B
Walkington, 1886-1952.
Gleanings from Elisha; his life and miracles. Chicago, Moody Press [1972] 254 p. 24 cm. Includes bibliographical references. [BS580.E5P55 1972] 79-181591 ISBN 0-8024-2962-9 5.95
1. Elisha, the prophet—Miracles. I. Title.

WALSH, Bill. 221'.92'4
David and Goliath / by Bill Walsh ; with an afterword for parents and teachers by Charlie Shedd. Kansas City [Kan.] : Sheed Andrews and McNeel, c1977. p. cm. (A Cartoon Bible story) A cartoon version of the clash between a giant warrior and a young shepherd armed with a slingshot. [BS580.D3W27] 77-21773 ISBN 0-8362-0729-7 pbk. : 1.95
1. David, King of Israel—Juvenile literature. 2. Bible. O.T.—Biography—Juvenile literature. I. Title.

WILSON, Clifford A. 221.92'4
A greater than David is here, by Clifford Wilson. [Melbourne, Australian Institute of Archaeology in association with Word of Truth Productions, 1968?] 32 p. 23 cm. (A Word of Truth production) [BS580.D3W53] 73-426936 unpriced
1. David, King of Israel. I. Australian Institute of Archaeology. II. Title.

WILSON, Clifford A. 221.92'4
A greater than Solomon is here, by Clifford Wilson. [Melbourne, Australian Institute of Archaeology in association with Word of Truth Productions, 1968] 40 p. 21 cm. (A Word of truth production) [BS580.S6W53] 78-467107 unpriced
1. Solomon, King of Israel. 2. Jesus Christ—Person and offices. I. Australian Institute of Archaeology. II. Title.

WOLFF, Hans Walter. 221.9'24 B
Amos, the prophet; the man and his background. Translated by Foster R. McCurley. Edited, with an introd., by John Reumann. Philadelphia, Fortress Press [1973] xii, 100 p. 18 cm. Translation of Amos' geistige Heimat. Bibliography: p. 90-96. [BS580.A6W6513] 72-87062 ISBN 0-8006-0012-6 2.95
1. Amos, the prophet.

*WOOD, Leon J. 221.924
A commentary on Daniel, by Leon Wood. Grand Rapids, Mich., Zondervan Publishing House [1973] 336 p. illus., table, 23 cm. Bibliography: p. 332-336. [BS1556.3] 72-83884 6.95
1. Bible. O. T. Book of Daniel—Commentaries. I. Title.

WOOD, Leon James. 221.92'4
Elijah, prophet of God, by Leon J. Wood. Des Plaines, Ill., Regular Baptist Pr. [1968] 160p. 22cm. [BS580.E4W6] 67-25970 2.95
1. Elijah, the prophet. I. Title.

ALBRIGHT, William Foxwell, 221.93
1891-
The Biblical period from Abraham to Ezra. New York, Harper [c.1949-1963] 120p. 20cm. (Harper torchbks., Cloister lib.; TB102) Bibl. 1.35 pap.,
1. Bible. O. T.—History of contemporary events, etc. I. Title.

ALBRIGHT, William Foxwell, 221.93
1891-
The Biblical period. Pittsburgh, 1955. 65 p. 24 cm. "Reprinted...from The Jews; their history, culture and religion, edited by Louis Finkelstein. New York, Harper and Brothers, 1949." [BS1180.A42] 57-555
1. Bible. O. T.—History of contemporary events, etc. I. Title.

ALBRIGHT, William 221.9'3
Foxwell, 1891-1971.
Archaeology and the religion of Israel. [5th ed.] Baltimore, Johns Hopkins Press [1968] xviii, 247 p. 24 cm. (The Ayer lectures of the Colgate-Rochester Divinity School, 1941) Includes bibliographical references. [BS1180.A4 1968] 68-58526
1. Bible. O.T.—Evidences, authority, etc. 2. Bible. O.T.—Antiquities. 3. Judaism—History—To 70 A.D. 4. Levant—Religion. I. Title. II. Series: The Ayer lectures, 1941.

BARNETT, Richard David, 221.93
1909-
Illustrations of Old Testament history, by R. D. Barnett. London, British Mus. [1966] 91p. illus. 25cm. Bibl. [BS621.B3] 66-72019 2.10
1. Bible. O.T. — Antiq. I. British Museum. II. Title.
Available from British Info. in New York.

FULLER, Charles Edward, 221.93
1887-
The tabernacle in the wilderness; edited by Grace L. and Daniel P. Fuller. [Westwood, N. J.] F. H. Revell Co. [c1955] 96p. illus. 20cm. [BM654.F8] 55-6632
1. Tabernacle. 2. Typology (Theology) I. Title.

GRAY, John, Rev. 221.93
Archaeology and the Old Testament world. New York, Nelson [c.1962] xi, 256p. illus., maps (pt. fold.) 25cm. Bibl. 62-6804 6.50
1. Bible—O. T.—Antiq. 2. Near East—Antiq. I. Title.

GRAY, John, 1913- 221.93
Archaeology and the Old Testament world. London, New York, T. Nelson [1962] xi, 256 p. illus., maps (part fold.) facsims. 25 cm. Bibliography: p. 231-232. Bibliographical footnotes. [BS621.G67 1962] 62-6804
1. Bible. O.T.—Antiq. 2. Near East—Antiq. I. Title.

HEATON, Eric William. 221.93
Everyday life in Old Testament times. Illustrated from drawings by Marjorie Quennell. New York, Scribner [1956] 240p. illus. 24cm. [BS620.H4 1956] 56-10348
1. Bible. O. T.—Antiq. I. Title.

HEATON, EricWilliam. 221.93
Everyday life in Old Testament times. Illustrated from drawings by Marjorie Quennell. New York, Scribner [1956] 240p. illus. 24cm. [BS620.H4 1956] 56-10348
1. Bible. O. T.—Antiq. I. Title.

HICKS, B R 221.93
Precious gem in the tabernacle. [Jeffersonville? Ind., 1961] 295p. illus. 23cm. [BT225.H5] 61-28193
1. Typology (Theology) 2. Tabernacle. I. Title.

MAGNALIA Dei, the mighty 221.9'3
acts of God : essays on the Bible and archaeology in memory of G. Ernest Wright / edited by Frank Moore Cross, Werner E. Lemke, and Patrick D. Miller, Jr. 1st ed. Garden City, N.Y. : Doubleday, c1976. p. cm. Includes indexes. "The bibliography of G. Ernest Wright": p. [BS1192.M34] 75-35617 ISBN 0-385-05257-X : 24.95
1. Wright, George Ernest, 1909- 2. Wright, George Ernest, 1909- —Bibliography. 3. Bible. O.T.—Addresses, essays, lectures. 4. Bible. O.T.—Antiquities—Addresses, essays, lectures. I. Wright, George Ernest, 1909- II. Cross, Frank Moore. III. Lemke, Werner E. IV. Miller, Patrick D.

NOERDLINGER, Henry S 221.93
Moses and Egypt; the documentation to the motion picture The Ten commandments. With an introd. by Cecil B. deMille. Los Angeles, University of Southern California Press, 1956. 202p. illus. 23cm. [BV4655.N63] 56-12886
1. Commandments, Ten. 2. Moses. 3. Egypt—Civilization. 4. The Ten commandments (Motion picture) I. Title.

PAUL, Shalom M. 221.9'3
Biblical archaeology / edited by Shalom M. Paul and William G. Dever. New York : Quadrangle/New York Times Book Co., [1975] c1974. xiii, 290 p. : ill. ; 25 cm. (The New York times library of Jewish knowledge) Includes index. Bibliography: p. 280. [BS621.P38 1975] 73-77034 ISBN 0-8129-0351-X : 12.50
1. Bible—Antiquities. I. Dever, William G., joint author. II. Title.

PRICE, Ira Maurice, 1856- 221.93
1939.
The monuments and the Old Testament; light from the Near East on the Scriptures, by Ira Maurice Price, Ovid R. Sellers [and] E. Leslie Carlson. Philadelphia, Judson Press [1958] 450p. illus. 24cm. Includes bibliography. [BS1180.P8 1958] 58-7091
1. Bible. O. T.—Antiq. 2. Bible. O. T.—Evidences, authorities, etc. I. Title.

PRITCHARD, James Bennett, 221.93
1909- ed.
The ancient Near East; an anthology of texts and pictures. Translators and annotators: W. F. Albright [and others. Princeton] Princeton University Press, 1958. 380 p. illus. 23 cm. Combined selections from, and condensation of, the editor's Ancient Near Eastern texts relating to the Old Testament, 2d ed., 1955, and The ancient Near East in pictures relating to the Old Testament, 1954. [BS1180.P82 1958] 58-10052
1. Bible. O.T.—History of contemporary events, etc. 2. Bible. O.T.—Anntiquities. 3. Oriental literature—Translations into English. 4. English literature—Translations from Oriental literature. I. Title.

PRITCHARD, James Bennett, 221.93
1909- ed.
Ancient Near Eastern texts relating to the Old Testament. Princeton, Princeton University Press, 1950. xxi, 526 p. 32 cm. [BS1180.P83] 50 12738
1. Bible. O.T.—History of contemporary events, etc. 2. Oriental literature—Translations into English. I. Title.

PRITCHARD, James Bennett, 221.93
1909- ed.
Ancient Near Eastern texts relating to the Old Testament. Translators and annotators: W. F. Albright [and others] 2d ed., corr. and enl. Princeton, Princeton University Press, 1955. xxi, 544p. 29cm. Bibliographical footnotes. [BS1180.P83 1955] 55-9033
1. Bible. O. T.—History of contemporary events, etc. 2. Oriental literature—Translations into English. I. Title.

PRITCHARD, James Bennett, 221.93
1909-
Archaeology and the Old Testament. [Princeton] Princeton University Press, 1958. 263 p. illus. 23 cm. [BS1180.P84] 58-10053
1. Bible. O.T.—History of contemporary events, etc. 2. Bible. O.T.—Antiquities. I. Title.

ROWLEY, Harold Henry, 221.93
1890-
From Joseph to Joshua; Biblical traditions in the light of archaeology. London, Published for the British Academy by Oxford University Press, 1950. xii, 200 p. 25 cm. (The Schweich lectures of the British Academy, 1948) Bibliography: p. [165]-188. [BS1197.R6] 51-9123
1. Bible. O.T. — History of Biblical events. 2. Jews — Hist. — To B.C. 586. I. Title. II. Series: Schweich lectures, 1948

SMITH, Arthur E 221.93
The Temple and its teaching; the Temple of Solomon compared and contrasted with the Tabernacle in the wilderness. Chicago, Moody Press [1956] 155p. illus. 22cm. [BM655.S58] 56-4227
1. Jerusalem. Temple. 2. Tabernacle. 3. Typology (Theology) I. Title.

SMITH, Arthur E 221.93
The Temple and its teaching; the Temple of Solomon compared and contrasted with the Tabernacle in the wilderness. Chicago, Moody Press [1956] 156 p. illus. 22 cm. [BM655.S58] 56-4227
1. Jerusalem. Temple. 2. Tabernacle. 3. Typology (Theology) I. Title.

THOMAS, David Winton, 221.93
1901-
Archaeology and Old Testament study: jubilee volume of the Society for Old Testament Study, 1917-1967, ed. by D. Winton Thomas. Oxford, Clarendon Pr., 1967. xxxvii, 493p. 20 plates, maps, plans. 23cm. Bibl. [BS620.T54] 67-103741 12.00
1. Bible. O.T.—Antiq.—Addresses, essays, lectures. I. Society for Old Testament Study. II. Title.
Available from Oxford Univ. Pr., New York.

THOMPSON, John Arthur, 221.93
1913-
Archaeology and the Old Testament. Grand Rapids, Eerdmans [1957] 121p. illus. 19cm. (A Pathway book) [BS620.T57] 57-11584
1. Bible. O. T.—Antiq. 2. Bible. O. T.—History of contemporary events, etc. I. Title.

THOMPSON, John Arthur, 221.93
1913-
Archaeology and the Old Testament. Grand Rapids, Eerdmans [1957] 121 p. illus. 19 cm. (A Pathway book) [BS620.T57] 57-11584
1. Bible. O.T. — Antiq. 2. Bible. O.T. — History of contemporary events, etc. I. Title.

THOMPSON, John Arthur, 221.93
1913-
Archaeology and the pre-Christian centuries. Grand Rapids, Eerdmans [1958] 139 p. illus. 19 cm. (Pathway books) Continues the author's Archaeology and the Old Testament. Includes bibliography. [BS620.T572] 58-13061
1. Bible. O.T. — Antiq. 2. Bible. O.T. — History of contemporary events, etc. I. Title.

UNGER, Merrill Frederick, 221.93
1909-
Archeology and the Old Testament. Grand Rapids, Zondervan Pub. House [1954] 339p. illus. maps. 23cm. Includes bibliographies. Bibliographical footnotes. [BS1180.U6] 55-136
1. Bible. O. T.—Antiq. 2. Bible. O. T.—History of contemporary events, etc. 3. Bible. O. T.—Evidences, authority, etc. I. Title.

POWELL, Newman Minnich, 221.94
1893-
Time was; a new chronology. Oklahoma City, Modern Publishers, 1955. 173p. illus. 24cm. [BS637.P6] 55-24609
1. Bible. O.T.—Chronology. I. Title.

THIELE, Edwin Richard, 221.94
1895-
The mysterious numbers of the Hebrew kings; a reconstruction of the chronology of the kingdoms of Israel and Judah. [Chicago] University of Chicago Press [1951] xxi, 298 p. tables. 24 cm. Bibliographical footnotes. [BS637.T53] 51-11393
1. Bible. O. T. — Chronology. 2. Chronology, Hebrew. 3. Jews — Hist. — To 586 B. C. I. Title.

ACKROYD, Peter R. 221.95
Exile and restoration; a study of Hebrew thought of the sixth century B.C. by Peter R. Ackroyd. Philadelphia, Westminster Press [1968] xv, 286 p. 23 cm. (The Old Testament library) Bibliography: p. [257]-258. Bibliographical footnotes. [BS1197.A25 1968] 68-27689 8.50
1. Bible. O.T.—History of Biblical events. I. Title. II. Series.

ACKROYD, Peter R. 221.95
Israel under Babylon and Persia, by Peter R. Ackroyd. [London] Oxford University Press, 1970. xvi, 374 p. illus., maps. 19 cm. (The New Clarendon Bible: Old Testament, v. 4) Bibliography: p. 350-354. [BS1151.2.N46 vol. 4] 79-511473 6.00
1. Bible. O.T.—Criticism, interpretation, etc. 2.

Judaism—History—Post-exilic period, 586 B.C.-210 A.D. I. Title. II. Series.

ALTMAN, Addie (Richman) 221.95
The Jewish child's Bible stories. Illustrated by Resa Babin. Rev. and enl. ed. New York, Bloch Pub. Co. [c.1960] 138p. illus. 26cm. 60-6933 2.50 bds.,
1. Bible stories, English—O.T. I. Title.

ALTMAN, Addie (Richman) 221.95
The Jewish child's Bible stories. Illustrated by Resa Babin. Rev. and enl. ed. New York, Bloch Pub. Co. [1960] 138p. illus. 26cm. [BM107.A5 1960] 60-6933
1. Bible stories, English—O. T. I. Title.

ANDERSON, Bernhard W 221.95
Understanding the Old Testament. Englewood Cliffs, N.J., Prentice-Hall, 1957. 551p. illus. 24cm. [BS1197.A63] 57-8704
1. Bible. O. T.—History of Biblical evants. 2. Jews—Hist.—To 70 A. D. I. Title.

ANDERSON, Bernhard W 221.95
Understanding the Old Testament [by] Bernhard W. Anderson. 2d ed. Englewood Cliffs, N.J., Prentice-Hall [1966] xxi, 586 p. illus., maps (part col.) plates. 24 cm. Bibliography: p. 561-578. [BS1197.A63 1966] 66-11713
1. Bible. O.T. — History of Biblical events. 2. Jews — Hist. — To 70 A.D. I. Title.

ANDERSON, Bernhard W. 221.95
Understanding the Old Testament. 2d ed. Englewood Cliffs,N.J., Prentice [c.1957, 1966] xxi, 586p. illus., maps (pt. col.) col. plates. 24cm. Bibl. [BS1197.A63] 66-11713 10.60
1. Bible. O. T. — History of Biblical events. 2. Jews. — Hist. — To 70 A.D. I. Title.

ANDERSON, George Wishart 221.95
The history and religion of Israel by G. W. Anderson. [London] Oxford, 1966. xi, 210p. illus. 2 maps, tables, 20cm. (New Clarendon Bible: Old Testament, v.1) [BS1151.2N46 vol.1] 66-75519 3.75
1. Judaism — Hist. — Ancient period. 2. Bible. O. T. — Hist of Biblical events. I. Title. II. Series.
Available from the publisher's New York office

*ANDERSON, James A. 221.95
Just think. New York, Vantage [1966, c.1965] 93p. 21cm. 2.50 bds.,
I. Title.

ARMSTRONG, April (Oursler) 221.95
The book of God; adventures from the Old Testament. Adapted from The greatest book ever written, by Fulton Oursler. Illustrated by Jules Gotlieb. Garden City, N. Y., Garden City Books [1957] 447p. illus. 25cm. [BS551.2.A72] 57-9849
1. Bible stories, English—O. T. I. Title.

ASCH, Shalom, 1880-1957. 221.95 (j)
In the beginning; stories from the Bible. Translated by Caroline Cunningham. Drawings by Eleanor Klemm. New York, Schocken Books [1966, c1935] 120 p. illus. 21 cm. [BS551.A75 1966] 66-24907
1. Bible stories, English—Old Testament. I. Cunningham, Caroline, tr. II. Title.

BAXTER, Edna M., 1895- 221.95
The beginnings of our religion [by] Edna M. Baxter. Valley Forge [Pa.] Judson [1968] 253p. illus., map. 24cm. Bibl. [BS1197.B3] 67-25890 5.95
1. Bible. O. T.—History of Biblical events. 2. Jews—Hist.—To 70 A.D. I. Title.

BEARMAN, Jane 221.95
Jonathan. Author and illus., Jane Bearman. New York, JonathanDavid [1966] [44] p. illus. (pt. col.) 24cm. (Bible heroes lib. bk.) [BS580.J57B4] 65-21754 1.95
1. Jonathan, son of Saul — Juvenile literature. I. Title.

BEEBE, Catherine, 1898- 221.95
David, the shepherd king. Illus. by Dorothy Koch. Valatie, N.Y., Holy Cross Pr. [1966] 80p. illus. 22cm. [BS580.D3B4] 66-7290 2.75
1. David, King of Israel — Juvenille literature. I. Title.

BEEK, Martinus Adrianus, 1909- 221.95
A journey through the Old Testament. Translated by Arnold J. Pomerans. New York, Harper [1960, c1959] 254 p. illus. 22 cm. Translation of Wegen en voetsporen van het Oude Testament. [BS1197.B383 1960] 60-5401
1. Bible. O.T.—History of Biblical events. 2. Bible. O.T.—Criticism, interpretation, etc. I. Title.

BEEM, Merrill A 221.95
Teacher's guide for The story of the Hebrew people, to use with the pupil's book. New York, Published for the Cooperative Publication Association by Abingdon Press [1959] 188p. illus. 20cm. (The Cooperative series texts for weekday religious education classes and released-time religious education in-struction) [BS1194.B35] 58-13629
1. Bible. O. T.—History of Biblical events. 2. Jews—Hist.—To 70 A. D.—Outlines, sylabi, etc. I. Title. II. Title: The story of the Hebrew people.

BERGER, Mannie. 221.95
Moses and his neighbors, by M. Berger. New York, Philosophical Library [1965] x, 86 p. illus. 22 cm. [BS1187.B4] 64-20424
1. Bible, O.T. — Addresses, essays, lectures. I. Title.

BERGER, Mannie 221.95
Moses and his neighbors. New York, Philosophical [c.1965] x, 86p. illus. 22cm. [BS1187.B4] 64-20424 3.50
1. Bible. O.T.—Addresses, essays, lectures. I. Title.

BIBLE. O. T. English. 221.95
Selections. 1960. Authorized.
The Old Testament. Arr. and illustrated by Marguerite de Angeli. With a pref. by Samuel Terrien. New York, Doubleday [c.1960] 1v. (unpaged) illus. (part col.) endpaper map. 32cm. 60-11621 6.95
1. Bible—Pictures, illustrations, etc. I. De Angeli, Marguerite (Lofft) II. Title.

BLENKINSOPP, Joseph, 1927- 221.9'5
Gibeon and Israel; the role of Gibeon and the Gibeonites in the political and religious history of early Israel. Cambridge [Eng.] University Press, 1972. xi, 151 p. 23 cm. (Society for Old Testament Study. Monograph series, 2) Includes bibliographical references. [BS1199.G58B55] 74-171672 ISBN 0-521-08368-0
1. Bible. O.T. Historical books—History of Biblical events. 2. Gibeonites. 3. Al Jib, Jordan—Antiquities. I. Title. II. Series.

BLOHM, Emily, 1898- 221.95
Children's favorite Bible stories. [1st ed.] New York, Vantage Press [1955] 52p. 21cm. [BS551.2.B55] 55-8396
1. Bible stories, English—O. T. I. Title.

BOOTH, Osborne. 221.95
The chosen people; a narrative history of the Israelites. [St. Louis] Bethany Press [1959] 264p. illus. 23cm. Includes bibliography. [BS1197.B65] 59-13168
1. Bible. O. T.—History of Biblical events. I. Title.

BRO, Margueritte Harmon, 1894- 221.9'5
The book you always meant to read: the Old Testament. [1st ed.] Garden City, N.Y., Doubleday, 1974. xi, 418 p. 22 cm. [BS1197.B76] 72-92193 ISBN 0-385-05667-2 7.95
1. Bible. O.T.—History of Biblical events. I. Title.

BROWN, Wendell, 1905- 221.95
The long view, a study in some of the Hebrew prophets [by] Wendell Brown, George C. Seward [and] Philip Weltner. A class-room test ed. Atlanta, Priv. print. at Foote and Davies [1954] 228p. 24cm. [BS635.B76] 55-18759
1. Bible. O. T.—History of Biblical events. 2. Prophets. I. Title.

BUCK, Harry Merwyn. 221.95
People of the Lord; the history, scriptures, and faith of ancient Israel [by] Harry M. Buck. New York, Macmillian [1965, c1966] xvii, 653 p. illus., maps. 25 cm. "Biblographical essay": p. 619-634. [BS1140.2.B8] 65-16563
1. Bible. O. T. — History of Biblical events. 2. Bible. O. T. — Commentaries. I. Title.

BUCK, Harry Merwyn 221.95
People of the Lord; the history, scriptures, and faith of ancient Israel. New York, Macmillan [c.1966] xvii, 653p. lilus., maps. 25cm. Bibl. [BS1140.2.B8] 65-16563 7.50
1. Bible. O. T. — History of Biblical events. 2. Bible. O. T. — Commentaries. I. Title.

CALLAHAN, Gertrude E, 1911- 221.95
Through the Old Testament and the Apocrypha. New York, Beechhurst Press [1952] 328 p. 22 cm. [BS635.C3] 52-1881
1. Bible. O. T.—History of Biblical events. 2. Bible. O. T. Apocrypha—History of Biblical events. 3. Jews—Hist.—To 70 A. D. I. Title.

CAMPBELL, Gay, 1912- 221.95
Bible stories for Jewish children: from creation to Joshua, by Ruth Samuels [pseud.] Illustrated by Laszlo Matulay. [New York] Ktav Pub. House [1954] 72p. illus. 26cm. [BS551.2.C3] 55-17414
1. Bible stories, English—O. T. I. Title.

CAMPBELL, Gay, 1912- 221.95
The Jewish beginning, by Ruth Samuels [pseud.] New York, Ktav Pub. House [1952- v. illus. 23 cm. [BS551.C36] 52-66038
1. Bible stories, English—O. T. Pentateuch. I. Title.

CAMPBELL, Gaye, 1912- 221.95
Bible stories for Jewish children; from creation to Joshua, by Ruth Samuels [pseud.] Illustrated by Laszlo Matulay. [New York] Ktav Pub. House [1954] 72 p. illus. 26 cm. [BS551.2.C3] 55-17414
1. Bible stories, English—O. T. I. Title.

CAMPBELL, Gaye, 1912- 221.95
The Jewish beginning, by Ruth Samuels [pseud.] New York, Ktav Pub. House [1952- v. illus. 23 cm. [BS551.2.C32] 52-66038
1. Bible stories, English—O. T. Pentateuch. I. Title.

CHEVERTON, Cecil Frank, 1889- 221.95
The Old Testament for new students. Saint Louis, Bethany Press [1951] 224 p. illus. 21 cm. [BS1197.C4] 51-7245
1. Bible. O. T.—History of Biblical events. I. Title.

CHEVERTON, Cecil Frank, 1889-1953. 221.95
The Old Testament for new students. Rev. by Ambrose Edens and George P. Fowler. Saint Louis, Bethany Press [c1956] 224p. illus. 21cm. [BS1197.C4 1956] 56-12890
1. Bible. O. T.—History of Biblical events. I. Title.

COCAGNAC, A M 221.95
Bible for young Christians; the Old Testament, by A. M. Cocagnac and Rosemary Haughton. Illus. by Jacques Lescanff. New York, Macmillan, 1967. 125 p. col. illus. 27 cm. [BS551.2.C6] 67-13292
1. Bible stories, English — O. T. I. Haughton, Rosemary, joint author. II. Lescanff, Jacques, illus. III. Bible. O. T. English. Paraphrases. 1967. IV. Title.

COCAGNAC, A. M. 221.95
Bible for young Christians; the Old Testament, by A. M. Cocagnac, Rosemary Haughton. Illus. by Jacques Lescanff. New York. Macmillan, 1967. 125p. col. illus. 27cm. [BS551.2.C6] 67-13292 4.95 bds.,
1. Bible stories, English—O. T. I. Haughton, Rosemary, joint author. II. Lescanff, Jacques, illus. III. Bible. O. T. English. Paraphrases. 1967. IV. Title.

CONN, Charles W. 221.9'5
Highlights of Hebrew history / Charles W. Conn. Cleveland, Tenn. : Pathway Press, c1975. 112 p. : maps ; 20 cm. (Church training course ; 203) [BS1197.C54] 75-20971 ISBN 0-87148-402-1 pbk. : 2.50
1. Bible. O.T.—History of Biblical events. 2. Bible. O.T.—Study—Text-books. I. Title.

DANIEL-ROPS, Henry, 1901- 221.95
The Book of Books; the story of the Old Testament. Translated by Donal O Kelly. Illustrated by Fritz Kredel. New York, Kenedy [1956] 166p. illus. 25cm. Translation of Histoire sainte de mes filleuis. [BS1197.D33] 56-6428
1. Bible. O. T.—History of Biblical events. I. Title.

DANIEL-ROPS, Henry, 1901- 221.95
Israel and the ancient world (orig.: Sacred history); a history of the Israelites from the time of Abraham to the birth of Christ. Tr. [from French] by K. Madge. Garden City, N.Y., Doubleday [1964] 4)3p. maps, diagrs. 19cm. (Image bk., D6169) 64-1082 1.35 pap.,
1. Bible—History of Biblical events. I. Title.

DE LA MARE, Walter John, 1873-1956 221.95
Stories from the Bible. Illus. by Edward Ardizzone. New York, Knopf, [c.]1961. 420p. 61-6048 4.95
1. Bible stories, English—O. T. I. Title.

DREANY, E. Joseph 221.95
A Maxton book about Bible stories from the Old Testament. New York, Maxton Pub. Corp. [c.1960] unpaged. illus. (part col.) 27cm. (Maxton books for young people, 56) 60-53108 .69; 1.38 bds., lib. ed.,
1. Bible stories, English—O.T. I. Title.

EARLE, Arthur. 221.9'5
The Bible dates itself / by Arthur Earle. 1st ed. Southampton, Pa. : Earle, [1974] 228 p. : ill. ; 24 cm. Includes indexes. Bibliography: p. 216-218. [BS637.2.E18] 73-88548 ISBN 0-9600788-1-9
1. Bible. O.T.—Chronology. I. Title.

ELSPETH, Sister, 1868- 221.95
Old Testament roots of our faith, student resource book, grade 9; materials for Christian education prepared at the direction of General Convention. Greenwich, Conn., Seabury Press [1957] 178p. illus. 22cm. (The Seabury series, R-9) [BS551.2.E4] 57-8345
1. Bible. O.T.—History of Biblical events. I. Title.

FAMOUS forerunners of 221.95
Christ. Charlotte. N. C., Catholic Bible House [1964] xii, 283p. illus. (pt. col.) col. maps. 24cm. Contributions by various authors and artists [BS550.2.F3] 64-56992 sold as set with 'Our BlessedLord,' 24.95
1. Bible stories, English—O. T.

FARGO, Gail B 221.95
Bible stories and you. New York, Philosophical Library [1954] 90p. 22cm. [BS534.F32] 54-8723
I. Title.

FELT, Marie Fox, 1900- 221.95
Sacred stories for children, from the Old Testament. [Salt Lake City, Deseret Book Co., 1954] 151p. illus. 32cm. [BS551.F4] 54-41453
1. Bible stories, English—O. T. I. Title.

FESSENDEN, Katharine 221.95
The Old Testament story: Adam to Jonah. New York, H. Z. Walck, [c.]1960. 155p. illus., diagrs., map 26cm. 60-14039 4.75
1. Bible stories, English—O. T. 2. Bible. O. T.—Pictures, illustrations, etc. I. Title.

FISHMAN, Isidore, 1908- 221.95
Remember the days of old; an introduction to Biblical history. With a foreword by Azriel Eisenberg. Hartford, Conn., Hartmore House [1969] x, 189 p. illus., maps. 25 cm. Includes bibliographical references. [BS1194.F53 1969] 79-100058 4.95
1. Bible. O.T.—Study—Text-books. I. Title.

FRASER, Edith, 1903- 221'.95
A boy hears stories from the Old Testament. Illus. by Jim Padgett. Nashville, Abingdon Press [1967] 96 p. illus. 25 cm. These retold stories from the first books of the Bible include such colorful and well known figures as Moses, David and Goliath, and Joseph. [BS551.2.F72] AC 67
1. Bible stories—O.T. I. Padgett, Jim, illus. II. Title.

GINZBERG, Louis, 1873- 221.95
Legends of the Jews. New York, S. & S. [1961, c.1909-1956] 646p. (Essandess paperback) 2.45 pap.,
1. Legends, Jewish I. Title.

HAZEN, Barbara Shook. 221.95
David and Goliath. Pictures by Robert J. Lee. New York, Golden Press [1968] [26] p. col. illus. 33 cm. (A Big golden book) A retelling of the Bible story about a young boy whose faith in God helped him overcome the Philistine giant. [BS580.D3H3] AC 68
1. David, King of Israel. 2. Bible stories—Old Testament. I. Lee, Robert J., 1921- illus. II. Title.

HECHT, Emanuel, 1821-1862. 221.95
Biblical history for Israelitish schools, with a brief outline of the geography of Palestine. Rev. and corr. by S. Adler. Translated from the German by M. Mayer. 7th ed. New York, M. Thalmessinger, 1958. 144p. 18cm. [BS1197.H36 1874] 58-50326
1. Bible. O. T.—History of Biblical events. I. Title.

HEINISCH, Paul, 1878- 221.95
History of the Old Testament. Translator, William Heidt; artist, Frank Kacmarcik. Collegeville, Minn., Liturgical Press [1952] xviii, 492p. illus., map (on lining papers) 24cm. 'Supplementary reading and notes': p. 436-483. [BS635.H43] 53-862
1. Bible. O. T.—History of Biblical events. 2. Jews—Hist.—To 70A. D. I. Title.

HEINISCH, Paul, 1878-1956. 221.95
History of the Old Testament. William G. Heidt, translator. [Rev. and supplemented. Collegeville, Minn.] Liturgical Press [1957, c1952] 457p. illus. 24cm. Includes bibliography. [BS635.H43 1957] 60-39300
1. Bible. O. T.—History of Biblical events. 2. Jews—Hist.—To 70 A. D. I. Title.

HERRMANN, Siegfried, 1926- 221.9'5
A history of Israel in Old Testament times / Siegfried Herrmann ; translated by John Bowden from the German. 1st American ed. Philadelphia : Fortress Press, 1975. xiii, 364 p. : maps ; 23 cm. Translation of Geschichte Israels in alttestamentlicher Zeit. Includes index. Bibliography: p. [329]-331. [BS1197.H3913 1975] 74-24918 ISBN 0-8006-0405-9 : 15.50

1. Bible. O.T.—History of Biblical events. I. Title.

HESTER, Hubert Inman, 1895- 221.95
The heart of Hebrew history; a study of the Old Testament. [Rev. ed.] Liberty, Mo., Quality Press [c1962] 330p. illus. 24cm. [BS1197.H4 1962] 62-6582
1. Bible. O. T.—History of Biblical events. I. Title.

HINCHMAN, Catharine Sellew 221.95
Adventures with Abraham's children. Illus. by Steele Savage. Boston, Little [c.1964] xii, 179 p. illus. 21 cm. Bibl. 64-16551 3.95
1. Bible stories, English—O. T. I. Title.

HINCHMAN, Catharine Sellew. 221.95
Adventures with Abraham's children, by Catharine F. Sellew, with illus. by Steele Savage. [1st ed.] Boston, Little Brown [1964] xii, 179 p. illus. 21 cm. Bibliography: p. 175. [BS551.2.H53] 64-16551
1. Bible stores, English — O.T. I. Title.

HOLLENDER, Betty Rosett. 221.95
Bible stories for little children. Illustrated by William Steinel. New York, Union of American Hebrew Congregations [1955-60] 3 v. illus. 22cm. (Commission on Jewish Education of the Union of American Hebrew Congregations and Central Conference of American Rabbis. Union graded series) [BS551.2.H6] 56-17893
1. Bible stories, English—O. T. I. Title.

HONNESS, Elizabeth Hoffman, 1904- 221.95
We are His people. Illustrated by Paul V. Lantz and Richard Whitson. Philadelphia, Westminster Press [1960, c.1959] 49p. illus. (part col.) 16x32cm. 59-5610 1.25 bds.,
1. Bible stories, English. I. Title.

HOROWITZ, Caroline, 1909- 221.95
A child's first book of Bible stories, by Ann Day Steeple [pseud.] Illustrated by Hubert Whatley. New York, Hart Pub. Co. [1950] 95 p. col. illus. 22 cm. (Happy hour books) [BS551.H68] 50-11466
1. Bible stories, English.—O. T. I. Title.

HOWIE, Carl Gordon, 1920- 221.95
The Old Testament story [by] Carl G. Howie. [1st ed.] New York, Harper & Row [1965] 183 p. maps. 22 cm. [BS1197.H6] 65-15392
1. Bible. O.T.—History of Biblical events. I. Title.

HOWIE, Carl Gordon, 1920- 221.95
The Old Testament story. New York, Harper [c.1965] 183p. maps. 22cm. [BS1197.H6] 65-15392 4.50
1. Bible. O. T.—History of Biblical events I. Title.

ISRAELITE and Judaean 221.9'5
history / edited by John H. Hayes and J. Maxwell Miller. Philadelphia : Westminster Press, c1977. p. cm. Includes indexes. [BS1197.I85] 76-41913 ISBN 0-664-21291-3 : 25.00
1. Jews—History—To 70 A.D. 2. Bible. O.T.—History of Biblical events. 3. Bible. O.T.—Criticism, interpretation, etc.—History. I. Hayes, John H., 1934- II. Miller, James Maxwell, 1937-

ISRAELITE and Judaean 221.9'5
history / edited by John H. Hayes and J. Maxwell Miller. Philadelphia : Westminster Press, c1977. p. cm. Includes indexes. [BS1197.I85] 76-41913 ISBN 0-664-21291-3 : 25.00
1. Jews—History—To 70 A.D. 2. Bible. O.T.—History of Biblical events. 3. Bible. O.T.—Criticism, interpretation, etc.—History. I. Hayes, John H., 1934- II. Miller, James Maxwell, 1937-

JONES, Mary Alice, 1898- 221.95
Bible stories: Old Testament. Illustrated by Elizabeth Webbe. Chicago, Rand McNally, c1954. unpaged. illus. 21cm. (A Rand McNally book-elf book, 491) [BS551.J72 1954] 54-28238
1. Bible stories, English—O. T. I. Title.

JONES, Mary Alice, 1898- j221.95
Bible stories: Old Testament. Illustrated by Elizabeth Webbe. Chicago, Rand McNally, c1954. 1 v. (unpaged) illus. 33 cm. (A Rand McNally giant book) [BS551.2.J63 1954b] 63-11262
1. Bible stories, English—O.T. I. Title.

JONES, Mary Alice, 1898- 221.95
The story of Joseph, Illus. by Manning de V. Lee. Chicago, Rand McNally [1966] c.1965. 1 v. (unpaged) col. illus. 33cm. (Rand McNally giant bk.) [BS580.J6J55] 66-14816 1.00 bds.,
1. Joseph, the patriarch — Juvenile literature. I. Lee, Manning de Villeneuve, 1894- illus. II. Title.

JUERGENS, Mary. 221.95
The wonder book of Bible stories. Illus. by Bruno Frost. New York, Wonder Books [1951] unpaged. illus. 21 cm. (Wonder books, 577) [BS551.J8] 51-14561
1. Bible stories, English—O. T. I. Title.

KAMM, Josephine 221.95
Kings, prophets, and history; a new look at the Old Testament. Illus. by Gwyneth Cole. New York, McGraw [1966, c.1965] 191p. illus., maps. 23cm. First pub. in England in 1965 by Gollancz under title: A new look at the Old Testament. [BS1197.K26] 66-16413 3.50; 3.06 lib. ed.,
1. Bible. O. T. — History of Biblical events. I. Title.

KEENEY, Virginia Drysdale, 1890- 221.95
Centuries ago; from Genesis to the time of Christ. Philadelphia, Press of Allen, Lane & Scott, 1951. 126 p. illus. 24 cm. [BS1197.K4] 51-38720
1. Bible. O. T.—History of Biblical events. I. Title.

KELSO, James Leon, 1892- 221.95
Archaology and the ancient testament; the Christian's God of the Old Testament vs. Canaanite religion. Written especially for laymen [by] James L. Kelso. Grand Rapids, Zondervan Pub. House [1968] 214 p. illus. 23 cm. Bibliographical footnotes. [BS1197.K46] 68-25144
1. Bible. O.T.—History of Biblical events. I. Title.

KITCHEN, Kenneth Anderson. 221.95
Ancient Orient and Old Testament [by] K. A. Kitchen. [1st English ed.] Chicago, Inter-Varsity Press [1966] 191 p. 23 cm. Bibliographical footnotes. [BS1180.K55 1966a] 66-30697
1. Bible. O.T.—History of contemporary events, etc. 2. Bible. O.T.—Antiq. I. Title.

KLAPERMAN, Libby M 221.95
Stories of the Bible; written and adapted by Libby M. Klaperman. Illustrated in full color by N. Dufourt; selected and arr. by Jorn Sann and Ralph Schonberg. New York, Sann's Pub. Co. [1954- v. illus. 32cm. [BS551.2.K55] 54-11797
1. Bible stories, English—O. T. I. Title.

KNIGHT, Douglas A. 221.9'5
Rediscovering the traditions of Israel : the development of the traditio-historical research of the Old Testament, with special consideration of Scandinavian contributions / by Douglas A. Knight. Rev. ed. [Missoula, Mont.] : Society of Biblical Literature : distributed by Scholars Press, 1975. xv, 439 p. ; 22 cm. (Dissertation series ; no. 9) Originally presented as the author's thesis, Gottingen, 1972. Includes indexes. Bibliography: p. 401-428. [BS1160.K57 1975] 75-6868 ISBN 0-88414-055-5 : 4.20
1. Bible. O.T.—Criticism, interpretation, etc.—History—Modern period, 1500- I. Title. II. Series: Society of Biblical Literature. Dissertation series ; no. 9.

KNIGHT, Douglas A. 221.9'5
Rediscovering the traditions of Israel; the development of the traditio-historical research of the Old Testament, with special consideration of Scandinavian contributions, by Douglas A. Knight. [Missoula, Mont.] Published by Society of Biblical Literature for the Form Criticism Seminar, 1973. xiii, 439 p. 22 cm. (Society of Biblical Literature. Dissertation series, no. 9) Cover title: The traditions of Israel. Originally presented as the author's thesis, Gottingen, 1972. Bibliography: p. 401-428. [BS1160.K57 1973] 73-83724 ISBN 0-88414-020-2
1. Bible. O.T.—Criticism, interpretation, etc.—History—Modern period, 1500- I. Society of Biblical Literature. Form Criticism Seminar. II. Title. III. Title: The traditions of Israel. IV. Series.

KOMROFF, Manuel, 1890- j221.95
Heroes of the Bible. Illustrated by Robert J. Lee. New York, Golden Press [1966] 138 p. illus. (part col.) 29 cm. [BS551.2.K6] 66-5843
1. Bible stories, English — O. T. I. Lee, Robert J., 1921- illus. II. Title.

KOMROFF, Manuel, 1890- 221.95
Heroes of the Bible. Illus. by Robert J. Lee. New York, Golden Pr. [c.1966] 138p. illus. (pt. col.)29cm. [BS551.2.K6] 66-5843 4.95 bds.,
1. Bible stories, English — O. T. I. Lee, Robert J., 1921- illus. II. Title.

KRAUS, Hans Joachim. 221.95
The people of God in the Old Testament. New York, Association Press [1958] 92p. 20cm. (World Christian books) [BV600.K77] 58-11537
1. Church—Biblical teaching. 2. Bible. O.T.—Theology. 3. Jews—Election, Doctrine of. I. Title.

KUNTZ, John Kenneth. 221.9'5
The people of ancient Israel; an introduction to Old Testament literature, history, and thought [by] J. Kenneth Kuntz. New York, Harper & Row [1974] xv, 559 p. illus. 24 cm. Bibliography: p. 510-541. [BS1140.2.K86] 74-8042 ISBN 0-06-043822-3
1. Bible. O.T.—Introductions. 2. Bible. O.T.—History of Biblical events. I. Title.

KUSKIN, Karla. 221.95
The animals and the ark. New York, Harper [1958] [32] p. illus. 18 x 25 cm. A retelling in verse of the Biblical story of Noah and the ark in which he and the animals lived during the flood. [PZ8.3.K96An] AC 68
1. Noah's ark—Poetry. I. Title.

LASAR, Theodore. 221.9'5
The lost tribes of Israel discovered / by Theodore Lasar. New York : Earth Co., 1976. vii, 68 p. ; 23 cm. Includes bibliographical references and index. [DS131.L27] 76-16340
1. Lost tribes of Israel. I. Title.

LESSING, Erich. 221.95 (j)
The story of Noah. [Told in photographs by Erich Lessing. Text from the King James Bible. Pictures and text edited by Barbara Brakeley Miller. New York, Time-Life Books, 1968?] 1 v. (unpaged) illus. (part col.) 26 cm. [BS580.N6L4] 68-23127
1. Noah. 2. Bible. O.T. Genesis—Pictures, illustrations, etc. I. Miller, Barbara Brakeley, ed. II. Title.

LEWITTES, Mordecai Henry, 1911- 221.95
Heroes of Jewish history; with exercises, projects, and games. New York, Hebrew Pub. Co. [1952- v. illus. 22cm. [DS118.L53] 52-43744
1. Jews—History, Juvenile. I. Title.

LONGSTRETH, Edward, 1894- 221.95
Decisive battles of the Bible. Drawings by W. T. Mars. [1st ed.] Philadelphia, Lippincott [1962] 190 p. illus. 21 cm. [BS1197.L72] 62-15200
1. Bible. O. T.—Military history. I. Title.

MCCARTHY, Dennis J. 221.95
Kings and prophets [by] Dennis J. McCarthy. Milwaukee, Bruce Pub. Co. [1968] xix, 203 p. 23 cm. (Contemporary college theology series. Biblical theology) Bibliography: p. 195. [BS1197.M18] 68-24581
1. Jews—History. 2. Bible. O.T.—History of Biblical events. 3. Bible. O.T.—Introductions. I. Title.

MACLEAR, George Frederick, 1833-1902. 221.95
A class-book of Old Testament history. Grand Rapids, Eerdmans, 1953. 508p. illus. 23cm. [BS1197.M25 1953] 52-10584
1. Bible. O. T.—History of Biblical events. I. Title.

MACLEAR, George Frederick, 1833-1902. 221.95
A primer of Old Testament history; a useful condensation of Biblical narratives for busy students of literature. With a detailed index by Kenneth Walter Cameron. Hartford, Transcendental Books [1969] [34], 125-130 l. map. 29 cm. A reproduction (124 p. on [32] l.) of the 1930 ed. (London, Macmillan), issued under title: A primer of Old Testament history for national and elementary schools. With a pref. and index by K. W. Cameron. First published in 1866 under title: A shilling book of Old Testament history for national and elementary schools. [BS1197.M26 1969] 77-10227
1. Bible. O.T.—History of Biblical events. I. Cameron, Kenneth Walter, 1908- II. Title.

MCRAE, Glenn, 1887- 221.95
The story the Old Testament tells. Leadership training text, course 122 A. St. Louis, Bethany Press, c1959. 96p. 20cm. Includes bibliography. [BS1194.M342] 59-6494
1. Bible. O. T.—Study—Text-books. 2. Bible. O. T.—History of Biblical events. I. Title.

MAUS, Cynthia Pearl, 1880- comp. 221.95
The Old Testament and the fine arts; an anthology of pictures, poetry, music, and stories covering the Old Testament. New York, Harper [1954] 826 p. illus., maps. 25 cm. Includes hymns in close score. [BS1197.M35] 54-8970
1. Bible. O.T.—History of Biblical events. 2. Bible. O.T.—Pictures, illustrations, etc. 3. Bible. O.T.—History of Biblical events—Poetry. I. Title.

MENDENHALL, George E. 221.9'5
The tenth generation; essays in early Biblical history [by] George E. Mendenhall. [Baltimore, Johns Hopkins University Press, 1972] p. Bibliography: p. [BS1192.5.M45] 72-3636 ISBN 0-8018-1267-4
1. Bible. O. T.—Theology—Addresses, essays, lectures. I. Title.

MENDENHALL, George E. 221.9'5
The tenth generation; the origins of the Biblical tradition [by] George E. Mendenhall. Baltimore, Johns Hopkins University Press [1973] xviii, 248 p. illus. 24 cm. Bibliography: p. 227-230. [BS1192.5.M45] 79-189068 ISBN 0-8018-1267-4 12.50
1. Bible. O.T.—Theology—Addresses, essays, lectures. I. Title.

MERRILL, Eugene H. 221.95
An historical survey of the Old Testament [by] Eugene H. Merrill. [Nutley, N.J., Craig Press, c1966] viii, 343 p. 23 cm. Bibliography: p. [332]-339. [BS1197.M44] 66-28302
1. Bible. O.T.—History of Biblical events. I. Title.

MONTET, Pierre, 1885-1966. 221.95
Egypt and the Bible. Translated by Leslie R. Keylock. Philadelphia, Fortress Press [1968] xv, 154 p. illus. 22 cm. Bibliography: p. 143-146. [BS1197.M5813] 68-18145 4.75
1. Bible. O.T.—History of contemporary events, etc. I. Title.

MORE stories from the Old 221.95
Testament ... Piet Worm drew the pictures. [New York, Sheed & Ward, 1957] unpaged. illus. 23cm. [BS551.2.M6] 58-3313
1. Bible stories, English—O.T. I. Worm, Piet, illus.

*MOUNT, R. H., Jr. 221.95
The law prophesied. 2d ed. [Mansfield, Ohio]. 1298 Marlin Dr., Author, c.1963. 205p. illus. 24cm. 4.95
I. Title.

ODELL, Mary Elise 221.95
Preparing the way. Illus. by Grace Golden. New York, Hawthorn [1963] 96p. illus. (pt. col.) maps. 26cm. (New lib. of Catholic knowledge, v.1) Bibl. 63-11044 3.95
1. Bible. O.T.—History of Biblical events. I. Title. II. Series.

ORLINSKY, Harry Meyer, 1908- 221.9'5
Understanding the Bible through history and archaeology [by] Harry M. Orlinsky. New York, Ktav Pub. House [1972] ix, 292 p. illus. 29 cm. Based on the author's Ancient Israel, first published in 1954. Includes selections from the Bible in English and Hebrew. Bibliography: p. 277-282. [BS1197.O74] 78-75014 ISBN 0-87068-096-X 7.95
1. Bible. O.T.—History of Biblical events. I. Bible. O.T. English. Selections. 1972. II. Bible. O.T. Hebrew. Selections. 1972. III. Title.

OURSLER, Fulton, 1893- 221.95
The greatest book ever written; the Old Testament story. [1st ed.] Garden City, N.Y., Doubleday [1951] xiii, 489 p. maps. 22 cm. [BS1197.O8] 51-13841
1. Bible. B. T. — History of Biblical events. I. Title.

OURSLER, Fulton, 1893-1952. 221.95
The greatest book ever written; the Old Testament story. Maps by Rafael Palacios. New York, Permabooks [1959, c1951] 522p. illus. 18cm. (Permabooks, M-5014) [BS1197] 59-65225
1. Bible. O. T.—History of Biblical events. I. Title.

PFEIFFER, Charles F. 221.9'5
Old Testament history, by Charles F. Pfeiffer. Grand Rapids, Mich., Baker Book House [1973] 640 p. illus. 24 cm. Bibliography: p. [611]-624. [BS1197.P44] 73-177601 ISBN 0-8010-6945-9 12.95
1. Bible. O.T.—History of Biblical events. 2. Bible. O.T.—History of contemporary events, etc. I. Title.

PFEIFFER, Charles F 221.95
An outline of Old Testament history. Chicago, Moody Press [1960] 160p. illus. 22cm. (Christian handbooks) Includes bibliography. [BS1197.P45] 59-15907
1. Bible. O. T.— History of Biblical events. I. Title.

PHILO Judaeus. Spurious and doubtful works. 221.95
The Biblical antiquities of Philo, now first translated from the old Latin version by M. R. James. Prolegomenon by Louis H. Feldman. New York, Ktav Pub. House, 1971. clxix, 280 p. 23 cm. (Translations of early documents. Ser. I. Palestinian Jewish texts (prerabbinic)) Translation of Antiquitates Biblicae. Reprint of

the 1917 ed., with a new introd. [BS1197.P5 1971] 69-13579 ISBN 0-87068-069-2
1. Bible. O.T.—History of Biblical events. I. James, Montague Rhodes, 1862-1926, tr. II. Feldman, Louis H. III. Title. IV. Series. V. The Library of Biblical studies

*PICHASKE, Donald R., ed. 221.95
The Old Testament for us, by Gustav K. Wiencke, Charles M. Cooper. Philadelphia, Lutheran Church Pr. [c.1965] 216p. col. illus. 24cm. (LCA Sunday Church Sch. ser.) bds., 1.85; project guide, pap., .70
I. Title.

*PICHASKE, Donald R., ed. 221.95
The Old Testament for us, terms 1 & 2; Youth's real life problems, term 3; teacher's guide [for] gr. 8, by Terence Mullins, Edward Uthe, Virginia Westervelt. Philadelphia, Lutheran Church Pr. [c.1965] 320p. 24cm. (LCA Sunday Church Sch. ser.) 2.50
I. Title.

PRITCHARD, James Bennett, 221.95
1909-
The ancient Near East; supplementary texts and pictures relating to the Old Testament, edited by James B. Pritchard. Princeton, N.J., Princeton University Press, 1969. viii, 274 p. illus., plans. 29 cm. Contains supplementary materials for the author's The ancient Near East in pictures and Ancient Near Eastern texts. Bibliographical footnotes. [BS1180.P826] 78-76500 15.00
1. Bible. O.T.—Antiquities. 2. Bible. O.T.—History of contemporary events. 3. Near East—Antiquities. 4. Oriental literature—Translations into English. 5. English literature—Translations from Oriental literature. I. Title.

RAND, Howard B 1889- 221.95
Primogenesis: the story the Bible tells. Haverhill, Mass., Destiny Publishers [1953] 662p. illus. 23cm. [BS1197.R35] 53-31323
1. Bible. O. T.—History of Biblical events. I. Title.

REED, Gwendolyn E. 221.95
Adam and Eve, by Gwendolyn Reed. Illustrated by Helen Siegl. New York, Lothrop, Lee & Shepard Co. [1968] [28] p. illus. 26 cm. Woodcut illustrations. A retelling of the Biblical story. [BS580.A4R4] AC 68
1. Adam (Biblical character) 2. Eve (Biblical character) I. Siegl, Helen, illus. II. Title.

ROSE, Anne K. 221.95
Samson and Delilah [by] Anne K. Rose. Illustrated by Richard Powers. New York, Lothrop, Lee & Shephard [1968] [32] p. col. illus. 26 cm. The Philistines hate Samson for having defeated them in battle and they send Delilah to find the secret of his strength. [BS580.S15R62] AC 68
1. Samson, Judge of Israel. I. Powers, Richard M., illus. II. Title.

RUSSELL, David Syme. 221.95
The Jews from Alexander to Herod, by D.S. Russell. London, Oxford U.P., 1967. xvi, 329 p. illus., maps, tables. 19 1/2 cm. (The New Clarendon Bible: Old Testament, v. 5) 25/- (B 67-23348) Bibliography: p. [303]-305. [BS1151.2.N46 vol. 5] 68-31935
1. Jews—Hist.—586 B.C.-70 A.D. 2. Judaism—Hist.—Post-exilic period. I. Title. II. Series.

RUSSELL, David Syme. 221.95
The Jews from Alexander to Herod, by D. S. Russell. London, Oxford U.P., 1967. xvi, 329 p. illus., maps, tables. 20 cm. (The New Clarendon Bible: Old Testament, v. 5) Bibliography: p. [303]-305. [BS1151.2.N46 vol. 5] 68-31935 25/-
1. Jews—History—586 B.C.-70 A.D. 2. Judaism—History—Post exilic period. I. Title. II. Series.

SCHATZ, Elihu A. 221.9'5
Proof of the accuracy of the Bible [by] Elihu A. Schatz. Middle Village, N.Y., Jonathan David Publishers [1973] p. Bibliography: p. [BS1171.2.S29] 73-10726 ISBN 0-8246-0161-0 15.00
1. Bible. O.T.—Chronology. 2. Bible. O.T.—Evidences, authority, etc. 3. Messiah—Biblical teaching. 4. Jewish law. I. Title.

SCHULTZ, Samuel J 221.95
The Old Testament speaks. [1st ed.] New York, Harper [1960] 436p. illus. 25cm. Includes bibliography. [BS1197.S33] 60-7952
1. Bible. O. T. History of Biblical events. I. Title.

SCHULTZ, Samuel J. 221.95
The Old Testament speaks [by] Samuel J. Schultz. 2d ed. New York, Harper & Row [1970] xii, 436 p. maps. 25 cm. Bibliographical footnotes. [BS1197.S33 1970] 79-10659 6.00
1. Bible. O.T.—History of Biblical events. I. Title.

SEVENTH-DAY Adventists. 221.95
General Conference. Dept. of Education.
Messengers of the promise; Bible stories for grades 5 and 6. Illustrated by Helen Torrey. [Teacher's ed.] Mountain View, Calif., Pacific Press Pub. Assn. [1952] 392, 336p. illus. 21cm. 'Series 111degree, odd year. The main work, also issued. separately, is preceded by 'Teacher's guide and key for Messengers of the promise,' with special t.p. [BS551.2.S4336 1952a] 56-18078
1. Bible stories, English—O.T. I. Title.

SHANNON, David T. 221.9'5
The Old Testament experience of faith / David T. Shannon. Valley Forge, PA. : Judson Press, c1977. 175 p. : maps ; 22 cm. Includes bibliographical references. [BS1197.S48] 76-48512 ISBN 0-8170-0719-9 : 3.50
1. Bible. O.T.—History of Biblical events. 2. Christian life—Biblical teaching. I. Title.

SKOUSEN, Willard Cleon, 221.95
1913-
The fourth thousand years, by W. Cleon Skousen. Salt Lake City, Bookcraft [1966] xvii, 846 p. illus., 2 maps (1 col.) 24 cm. Bibliographical footnotes. [BS1197.S54] 66-29887
1. Bible. O.T.—History of Biblical events. I. Title.

SKOUSEN, Willard Cleon, 221.95
1913-
The Third thousand years, by W. Cleon Skousen. [1st ed.] Salt Lake City, Bookcraft [c1964] xvii, 704 p. illus., maps, ports. 24 cm. Bibliographical footnotes. [BS1197.S55] 65-2511
1. Bible. O. T. — History of Biblical events. I. Title.

SLOAN, William Wilson. 221.95
A survey of the Old Testament. New York, Abingdon Press [1957] 334p. 24cm. Includes bibliographies. [BS1197.S56] 57-5079
1. Bible.O.T.—History of Biblical events. I. Title.

SLOAN, William Wilson. 221.95
A survey of the Old Testament. New York, Abingdon Press [1957] 334 p. 24 cm. Includes bibliographies. [BS1197.S56] 57-5079
1. Bible. O. T. — History of Biblical events. I. Title.

SLOAN, William Wilson 221.95
A survey of the Old Testament. Nashville, Abingdon [1965, c.1957] 334p. 23cm. (Apex bk. S-3) Bibl. [BS1197.S56] 1.50 pap.,
1. Bible. O. T.—History of Biblical events. I. Title.

SLUSSER, Dorothy Mallett. 221.95
Bible stories retold for adults. Philadelphia, Westminster Press [c1960] 128 p. 21 cm. Includes bibliography. [BS550.2.S55] 60-5017
1. Bible. O.T. — History of Biblical events. I. Title.

SLUSSER, Dorothy Mallett 221.95
Bible stories retold for adults. Philadelphia, Westminster Press [c.1960] 128p. 21cm. (bibl.) 60-5017 3.00
1. Bible. O. T.—History of Biblical events. I. Title.

SMITH, Morton, 1915- 221.95
Palestinian parties and politics that shaped the Old Testament. New York, Columbia University Press, 1971. viii, 348 p. 21 cm. (Lectures on the history of religions, new ser., no. 9) Revision of the author's thesis, Harvard, 1957. Bibliography: p. [285]-303. [BS1171.2.S64 1971] 70-161299 ISBN 0-231-02986-1
1. Bible. O.T.—Criticism, interpretation, etc. 2. Judaism—History—Post-exilic period, 586 B.C.-210 A.D. I. Title. II. Series.

SMITH, Ralph Lee, 1918- 221.95
Israel's period of progress [by] Ralph L. Smith. Nashville, Convention Press [1970] xii, 180 p. illus., maps. 21 cm. (Bible survey series, 4) Bibliography: p. 173. [BS1197.S627] 78-88061
1. Jews—History—To 953 B.C. 2. Bible. O.T.—History of Biblical events. 3. Bible. O.T. Psalms—Introductions. I. Title. II. Series.

SMITHER, Ethel Lisle. 221.95
Early Old Testament stories. Illustrated by Kurt Wiese. New York, Abingdon Press [1954] 79 p. illus. 21 cm. [BS551.S63] 54-11967
1. Bible stories, English—O. T. I. Title.

SMITHER, Ethel Lisle. 221.95
Later Old Testament stories. Illustrated by Kurt Wiese. New York, Abingdon Press [c1956] 80p. illus. 21cm. [BS551.2.S55] 56-13773
1. Bible stories, English—O. T. I. Title.

SMITHER, Ethel Lisle. 221.95
Later Old Testament stories. Illustrated by Kurt Wiese. New York, Abingdon Press [c1956] 80 p. illus. 21 cm. [BS551.2.S55] 56-13773
1. Bible stories, English — O.T. I. Title.

SOUTHALL, Ivan. 221.95
The curse of Cain; Bible stories, retold by Ivan Southall [from] Genesis 1:1 to 9:19. Illustrated by Joan Kiddell-Monroe. [New York] St. Martin's Press [1968] 117 p. illus. 22 cm. A retelling of the events in Genesis including the creation of Adam and Eve, the temptation in the Garden of Eden, Cain's murder of Abel, and the building of the ark by Noah. [BS551.2.S66 1968b] AC 68
1. Bible stories—Old Testament. Genesis. I. Kiddell-Monroe, Joan, illus. II. Title.

SOUTHALL, Ivan. 221.95
The sword of Esau; Bible stories retold by Ivan Southall. Illustrated by Joan Kiddell-Monroe. [New York, St. Martin's Press [1968] 116 p. illus. 22 cm. Three detailed retellings of Old Testament stories: The Sword of Esau, about the stealing of a birthright; Gideon, Gideon, What Have You Done? about the Hebrews' victory over the Midianites; and Even Job was not Swallowed by a Fish, about the prophet Jonah. [BS550.2.S62 1968] AC 68
1. Bible stories—Old Testament. I. Kiddell-Monroe, Joan, illus. II. Title.

SPRAGUE, Dorothy. 221.95
Bible stories for children; illustrated by Jon Nielsen. New York, Avon Publications, c1953. unpaged. Illus. 21cm. (Jolly books, 220) [BS551.S725] 53-39555
1. Bible stories, English—O.T. I. Title.

STEVENS, William Wilson. 221.9'5
A guide for Old Testament study [by] William W. Stevens. Nashville, Broadman Press [1974] 282, 31 p. illus. 21 cm. [BS1197.S73] 73-91606 ISBN 0-8054-1210-7 4.95 (pbk.)
1. Bible. O.T.—History of Biblical events. 2. Bible. O.T.—Study—Text-books. I. Title.

STILES, Mervin. 221.9'5
Synchronizing Hebrew originals from available records, 749-740 [B.C.] [Appos? Calif., 1973] [54] l. illus. 46 x 64 cm. At head of title: [Shofar (romanized form)] "A synchronization of selected references and historical incidents which have been recorded in the Holy Scriptures of the Hebrew people." Photocopy of typescript. [BS1197.S74] 73-178322
1. Bible. O.T.—History of contemporary events, etc. 2. Bible. O.T.—Chronology. I. Title.

TAYLOR, Melba B 221.95
Kings and prophets; the Old Testament story retold. [1st ed.] New York, Exposition Press [1952] 123 p. 23 cm. [BX550.T3] 52-7661
1. Bible. O. T. — History of Biblical events. I. Title.

TIME-LIFE Books. 221.9'5
The Israelites / by the editors of Time-Life Books. New York : Time-Life Books, [1975] 159 p. : ill. ; 27 cm. (The Emergence of man) Includes index. Bibliography: p. 155. [BS1197.T53 1975] 75-4101 7.95
1. Jews—History—To 586 B.C. 2. Bible. O.T.—History of Biblical events. 3. Palestine—Antiquities. I. Title.

*TURNBULL, Ralph G. 221.95
The kingdoms of Israel and Judah. Grand Rapids, Mich., Baker Bk. [c.]1966. 90p. 22cm. (Bible companion ser. for lesson and sermon prep.) 1.00 pap.,
I. Title.

WAHL, Jan. 221.9/5
Runaway Jonah, and other tales. Pictures by Uri Shulevitz. New York, Macmillan [1967,c1968] 42p. col. illus. 23cm. [BS551.2.W23] 68-12084 3.95 lib. ed.,
1. Bible stories, English—O. T. I. Title. II. Title: Ages 4-8.

WAHL, Jan. 221.95
Runaway Jonah, and other tales. Pictures by Uri Shulevitz. New York, Macmillan [1967, c1968] 42 p. col. illus. 23 cm. A retelling of the famous Bible adventures of Noah, Daniel, Jonah, David, and Joseph. [BS551.2.W23] AC 68
1. Bible stories—Old Testament. I. Shulevitz, Uri, 1935- illus. II. Title.

WALKER, Elmer Jerry, 1918- 221.95
Stories from the Bible. [Westwood, N. J.] F. H. Revell Co. [c1955- v. 20cm. [BS551.W243] 55-5391
1. Bible stories, English—O. T. I. Title.

WATSON, Jane (Werner) 221.95
1915-
First Bible stories retold by Jane Werner. Pictures by Eloise Wilkin. New York, Simon and Schuster [1954] unpaged. illus. 21cm. (A Little golden book, 198) [BS551.2.W3] 54-14540
1. Bible stories, English—O. T. I. Title.

WATSON, Jane (Werner) 221.95
1915-
Heroes of the Bible. Pictures by Rachel Taft Dixon and Marjorie Hartwell. New York, Simon and Schuster [1955] unpaged. illus. 21cm. (Little golden library, 236) [BS551.W44] 55-3229
1. Bible. O. T.—Biog. I. Title.

WEHRLI, Allen G 221.95
From patriarch to prophet. Philadelphia, Christian Education Press [1960] 207 p. 21 cm. [BS1197.W38] 60-15023
1. Bible. O. T. — History of Biblical events. I. Title.

WEHRLI, Allen G. 221.95
From patriarch to prophet. Philadelphia, Christian Education Press [c.1960] xi, 207p. 21cm. 60-15023 3.00
1. Bible. O. T.—History of Biblical events. I. Title.

WESTERMANN, Claus. 221.95
A thousand years and a day; our time in the Old Testament. Translated by Stanley Rudman. Philadelphia, Muhlenberg Press [1962] 280 p. illus. 21 cm. [BS1197.W413] 62-8544
1. Bible. O.T. — History of Biblical events. I. Title.

WESTERMANN, Claus 221.95
A thousand years and a day; our time in the Old Testament. Tr. [from German] by Stanley Rudman. Philadelphia, Muhlenberg [c.1962] 280p. illus. 62-8544 4.00
1. Bible. O.T.—History of Biblical events. I. Title.

WIESNER, William. 221.95
The Tower of Babel. [Written and illustrated by William Wiesner] New York, Viking Press [1968] [32] p. col. illus. 29 cm. "Based on the book of Genesis and on commentaries ... in the book Hebrew myths by Robert Graves and Raphael Patai." When the proud and insolent people of Babel built a tower to reach into heaven, God confused the languages of mankind and divided one people into many nations. [BS1238.B2W5 1968] AC 68
1. Babel, Tower of. 2. Bible stories—Old Testament. I. Title.

WITT, Lydia Workman, 1902- 221.95
The eclogue; the Bible stories in versification as narrative readings and dramatic monologues;a complete chronology of the Old Testament. [Belmont, Calif., Doxology House, [1953- v. illus. 23cm. [PS3545.I93E3] 54-21581
1. Bible. O. T.—History of Biblical events—Poetry. I. Title.

WOOD, Leon James. 221.95
A survey of Israel's history [by] Leon Wood. Grand Rapids, Zondervan Pub. House [1970] 444 p. maps (part col.) 23 cm. Bibliography: p. 413-416. [BS1197.W66] 70-120041 7.50
1. Bible. O.T.—History of Biblical events. I. Title.

WORM, Piet. 221.95
More stories from the Old Testament ... Piet Worm drew the pictures. [New York, Sheed & Ward, 1957] unpaged. illus. 23 cm. [BS551.2.W65] 58-3313
1. Bible stories, English — O. T. I. Title.

ZACHARIAS, Alfred, 1901- 221.95
The Babylonian dragon, and other tales. With original woodcuts by the author. Translated by Gisela Heinecken. Philadelphia, Muhlenberg Press [1961] 106 p. illus. 20 cm. Translation of Bileams Eselin. [BS550.2.Z313] 61-6749
1. Bible stores, English — O.T. 2. Animals, Legends and stories of. I. Title.

ZACHARIAS, Alfred, 1901- 221.95
The Babylonian dragon, and other tales. Original woodcuts by the author. Tr. by Gisela Heinecken. Philadelphia, Munhlenberg Pr. [c.1961] 106p. 61-6749 2.50 bds.,
1. Bible stories, English—O. T. 2. Animals, Legends and stories of. I. Title.

ADCOCK, Roger. 221.95'05
God's early heroes. Rev. by Elsiebeth McDaniel. Illustrated by Gordon King. Wheaton, Ill., Scripture Press Publications, 1971. 77 p. col. illus. 32 cm. London ed. published in 1969 under title: Great stories from the Bible. Nineteen Bible stories involving prominent characters of the Old Testament. [BS551.2.A33 1971] 70-151700 ISBN 0-361-01110-5
1. Bible. O.T. Biography—Juvenile literature. 2. Bible stories, English—O.T. I. McDaniel, Elsiebeth. II. King, Gordon, fl. 1971- illus. III. Title.

BARRETT, Ethel. 221.95'05
Which way to Nineveh? Glendale, Calif., G/L

Regal Books [1969] 135 p. illus. 20 cm. Retells and interprets various tales from the Old Testament. [BS551.2.B33] 79-96703 0.69
1. Bible stories, English. I. Title.

BIBLE, O.T. English. 221.9505
Selections. 1966. Authorized.
The Old Testament. Arranged and illustrated by Marguerite de Angeli. With a pref. by Samuel Terrien. Garden City, N. Y., Doubleday [1966] viii, 264 p. illus. (part col.) 32 cm. [BS897.D4] 66-28667
1. Bible. O. T.—Pictures, illustrations, etc. I. De Angeli, Marguerite (Lofft) 1889- II. Title.

BIBLE. O.T. English. 221.9505
Selections. 1966. Authorized.
The Old Testament. Arranged and illustrated by Marguerite de Angeli. With a pref. by Samuel Terrien. Garden City, N.Y., Doubleday [1966] viii, 264 p. illus. (part col.) 32 cm. [BS897.D4 1966] 66-28667
1. Bible O.T.—Pictures, illustrations, etc. I. De Angeli, Marguerite (Lofft) 1889- II. Title.

BOLLIGER, Max. 221.9'505
Noah and the rainbow; an ancient story retold by Max Bolliger. Translated by Clyde Robert Bulla. With pictures by Helga Aichinger. New York, Crowell [1972] [25] p. col. illus. 31 cm. Translation of Der Regenbogen. Retells the Old Testament story of Noah who built an ark to hold his family and the animals during the great flood. [BS658.B6513] 72-76361 ISBN 0-690-58448-2 4.50
1. Noah's ark—Juvenile literature. I. Aichinger, Helga, illus. II. Title.

DANIEL, David. 221.95'05
The complete book of Bible stories for Jewish children. Illustrated by Ben Einhorn. [New York] Ktav Pub. House [1971] 2 v. in 1. col. illus., col. maps. 25 cm. Contents.Contents.—pt. 1. From Creation to Joshua.—pt. 2. From Joshua to Judah Maccabee. [BM107.D3] 75-155841 ISBN 0-87068-381-0
1. Bible stories, English—O.T. I. Title.

DANIEL, David. 221.95'05
The Jewish beginning. Illustrated by Ben Einhorn. [New York] Ktav Pub. House [1971] 2 v. col. illus. 25 cm. Contents.Contents.—pt. 1. From creation to Joshua.—pt. 2. From Joshua to Judah Maccabee. Retells the stories of the Old Testament in two volumes. [BM107.D32] 79-30587 ISBN 0-87068-381-0 (pt. 1)
1. Bible stories, English—O.T. I. Einhorn, Ben, illus. II. Title.

KOSSOFF, David, 1919- 221.95'05
Bible stories, retold by David Kossoff. Illustrated by Gino D'Achille. Foreword by William Barclay. Chicago, Follett [1969, c1968] 285 p. illus. (part col.) 26 cm. This illustrated retelling of ninety-six Old Testament stories includes "Jacob in Exile," "The Walls of Jericho," and "The Wisdom of Solomon." [BS551.2.K67 1969] 69-18396 6.95
1. Bible stories, English—O.T. I. D'Achille, Gino, illus. II. Title.

LARSEN, Beverly. 221.9505
Damsel from afar; the story of Ruth. Illustrated by Melva Mickelson. Minneapolis, Augsburg Pub. House [1965] 96 p. illus. 21 cm. [BS580.R8L3] 65-22834
1. Ruth (Bibical character) — Fiction. I. Title.

LARSEN, Beverly 221.9505
Damsel from afar; the story of Ruth. Illus. by Melva Mickelson. Minneapolis, Augsburg [c.1965] 96p. illus. 21cm. [BS580.R8L3] 65-22834 2.95
1. Ruth (Biblical character)—Fiction. I. Title.

PETERSON, Gail. 221.9'505
The Bible storybook / by Gail Mahan Peterson ; illustrated by Fred Klemushin. Kansas City, Mo. : Hallmark Cards, [1974] 44 p. : col. ill. ; 27 cm. (Hallmark children's editions) Retells twelve stories from the Old Testament including those about Noah, Abraham, Jonah, and Esther, Queen of Persia. [BS551.2.P47] 73-90489 ISBN 0-87529-382-4 : 5.95
1. Bible stories, English—O.T. I. Klemushin, Fred, illus. II. Title.

PHIFER, Kenneth G. 221.9'505
Tales of human frailty and the gentleness of God [by] Kenneth G. Phifer. Atlanta, John Knox Press [1974] 127 p. 21 cm. Includes bibliographical references. [BS550.2.P48] 73-16914 ISBN 0-8042-2197-9 3.95 (pbk.)
1. Bible stories, English—O.T. I. Title.

RADIUS, Marianne 221.95'05
Catherine (Vos)
The tent of God; a journey through the Old Testament, by Marianne Radius. Illustrated by Chris Stoffel Overvoorde. Grand Rapids, W. B. Eerdmans Pub. Co. [1968] 368 p. illus. 24 cm. [BS550.2.R33] 68-30984 5.95
1. Bible stories, English—O.T. I. Title.

REDDISH, Robert O. 221.9'505
The burning, burning bush; our story from the rise with Abraham to collapse under Solomon, by Robert O. Reddish, Jr. Illustrated by Toni Reddish. [Evergreen, Colo., Rorge Pub. Co., 1974] 691 p. illus. 22 cm. Bibliography: p. 689-690. [BS1197.R38] 73-85938 11.95
1. Jews—History—To 952 B.C. 2. Bible. O.T.—History of Biblical events. I. Title.

RIEGERT, Norbert. 221.9505
Servers of the Lord. Illustrated by Lee Lindner. Milwaukee, Bruce Pub. Co. [1966] 60 p. illus. 21 cm. [BS551.2.R5] 66-29553
1. Bible stories, English. I. Title.

SOUTHALL, Ivan. 221.95'05
The sword of Esau; Bible stories retold by Ivan Southall. Illustrated by Joan Kiddell-Monroe. [New York] St. Martin's Press [1968] 116 p. illus. 22 cm. Contents.Contents.—The sword of Esau.—Gideon, Gideon, what have you done?—Even Job was not swallowed by a fish. [BS550.2.S62 1968] 68-10847
1. Bible stories, English—O.T. I. Title.

STEVENS, William 221.9'505
Wilson.
A guide for New Testament study / William W. Stevens. Nashville, Tenn. : Broadman Press, c1977. 439 p. : ill. ; 21 cm. Includes index. [BS2407.S73] 76-62920 ISBN 0-8054-1360-X : 7.50
1. Bible. N.T.—History of Biblical events. I. Title.

TRESSELT, Alvin R. 221.95'05
Stories from the Bible, retold by Alvin Tresselt. With lithographs by Lynd Ward. New York, Coward, McCann & Geoghegan [1971] 60 p. illus. (part col.) 32 cm. Retells twelve Old Testament stories including "Joseph and His Brothers," "Ruth and Naomi," and "Shadrach, Meshach, and Abednego." [BS551.2.T73 1971] 72-132597 5.39
1. Bible stories, English—O.T. I. Ward, Lynd Kendall, 1905- illus. II. Title.

VAN EYSSEN, Shirley. 221.9'505
In the beginning; a new interpretation of the Old Testament. With drawings by Nicole Claveloux [and others. New York] H. Quist, c1970. 64 p. col. illus. 34 cm. (A Here-and-there book from Harlin Quist) An illustrated retelling of Old Testament stories including "Cain and Abel," "David and Goliath," and "Jonah and the Whale." [BS551.2.V28] 79-140415 ISBN 0-8252-0051-2 5.95
1. Bible stories, English—O.T. I. Claveloux, Nicole, illus. II. Title.

RADIUS, Marianne 221.95'25
Catherine (Vos)
The tent of God; a journey through the Old Testament, by Marianne Radius. Illustrated by Chris Stoffel Overvoorde. Grand Rapids, W. B. Eerdmans Pub. Co. [1968] 368 p. illus. 24 cm. [BS550.2.R33] 68-30984 5.95
1. Bible stories, English—O. T. I. Title.

KOSSOFF, David, 1919- 221.95'5
Bible stories, retold by David Kossoff. Foreword by William Barclay. [New York] Warner Paperback Lib. [1973, c.1968] 235 p. 18 cm. A retelling of 96 Old Testament stories, including "Jacob in exile," "The Walls of Jericho," and "The wisdom of Solomon." [BS551.2.K67 1969] 1.25 (pbk.)
1. Bible stories, English—O.T. I. Title.
L.C. card no. for the original illustrated, hardbound edition: 68-18396.

222 Historical Books Of Old Testament

BENTON, Patricia. 222
The gift of Christmas, a collection of legends, customs and poems as told as told by Patricia Benton. New York, F. Fell [1962] 48 p. 21 cm. [PS3503.E585G5] 62-18125
I. Title.

BENTON, Patricia. 222
Love is. New York, F. Fell [1963] 45 p. 21 cm. Poems. [PS3503.E585L6] 63-1743
I. Title.

BERGEY, Alyce. 222
The first rainbow. Illus. by Ruth Brophy. Minneapolis, T. S. Denison [1965] 1 v. (unpaged) col. illus. 29 cm. [BS580.N6B4] 64-7705
1. Noah — Juvenile literature. I. Brophy, Ruth, illus. II. Title.

BERGEY, Alyce 222
The first rainbow, Illus. by Ruth Brophy. Minneapolis, Denison [c.1965] 1v. (unpaged) col. illus. 29cm. [BS580.N6B4] 64-7705 2.75
1. Noah—Juvenile literature. I. Brophy, Ruth, illus. II. Title.

BERGEY, Alyce. 222 (j)
The great promise; Genesis 12:1-21:3 for children. Illustrated by Betty Wind. St. Louis, Concordia Pub. House [1968] 1 v. (unpaged) col. illus. 21 cm. (Arch books) In verse. [BS580.A3B42] 68-4309
1. Abraham, the patriarch—Juvenile poetry. I. Wind, Betty, illus. II. Title.

BERGEY, Alyce. 222
The great promise; Genesis 12:1-21:3 for children. Illustrated by Betty Wind. St. Louis, Concordia Pub. House [1968] [32] p. col. illus. 21 cm. (Arch books) A retelling in verse of God's promise to Abraham that he would have a son who would live in the land of Canaan. [BS580.A3B42] AC 68
1. Abraham, the patriarch—Poetry. 2. Bible stories—Old Testament. I. Wind, Betty, illus. II. Title.

BERRIGAN, Daniel. 222
Encounters: poems [by] Daniel Berrigan; etchings [by] Robert E. Marx. New York, Associated Artists, 1965. [7] 1., 9 plates (in portfolio) 40 cm. Title vignette, engr. The poems have been taken from Encounters (Cleveland, New York. World Pub. Co.) published in 1960. "An edition of sixty copies, numbered one through sixty; in addition, five copies marked I through V ... in color and ten copies marked A through J have been printed for the poet and artist ... Copy number 3 [signed] Robert E. Marx." [PS3503.E734E5 1965] 66-57876
I. Marx, Robert Ernst, 1925- illus. II. Title.

BIBLE. O.T. Five scrolls. 222
Hebrew. 1969.
[Hamesh megilot ve-sefer Yonah (romanized form)] The Five megilloth and Jonah; a new translation. Introductions by H. L. Ginsberg, with drawings by Ismar David. [1st ed.] Philadelphia, Jewish Publication Society of America, 1969. xi, 121 p. illus. 24 cm. [BS1309.A2G5 1969] 69-19043 5.00
I. Ginsberg, Harold Louis. II. Jewish Publication Society of America. III. Bible. O.T. Five scrolls. English. Jewish Publication Society. 1969. IV. Bible. O.T. Jonah. Hebrew. 1969. V. Bible. O.T. Jonah. English. Jewish Publication Society. 1969.

BIBLE. O. T. Historical 222
books. English. Selections. 1957. Pfeiffer.
The Hebrew Iliad; the history of the rise of Israel under Saul and Davis. Written during the reign of Solomon probably by the priest. Ahimaaz. Translated from the original Hebrew by Robert H. Pfeiffer, with general and chapter introductions by William G. Pollard Jews History to 953 D.C. New York, Harper [1957] 154p. map. 21cm. [BS1203.P45] 57-9889
1. Jews—Hist.—To 953 D. C. I. Pfeiffer, Robert Henry, 1892- II. Title.

BLUMENTHAL, Walter Hart, 222
1883-
The pepper shaker. [Iowa City? 1964] 18 p. 24 cm. "100 copies." Poems. [PS3503.L93P4] 64-5419
I. Title.

BRAMBLETT, Agnes Cochran. 222
With lifted heart. Boston, Branden Press [1965] 64 p. 21 cm. Poems. [PS3503.R2555255] 65-26246
I. Title.

BREWER, Wilmon, 1895- 222
Still more adventures; [poems] Illus. in color from paintings by Polly Thayer Starr and Mrs. William Armistead Falconer. Francestown, N. H., M. Jones [1966] 436 p. col. illus., col. ports. 21 cm. [PS3503.R513S7] 66-31781
I. Title.

BRIN, Herb. 222
Wild flowers; from a garden of Jewish verse. Illustrated by Eric Ray. New York, J. David [1965] 63 p. illus. 22 cm. [PS3503.R552W5] 65-17365
I. Title.

BRINGS, Erik. 222
Golden arrows. Philadelphia, Dorrance [1962] 32 p. 20 cm. (Contemporary poets of Dorrance, 562) [PS3503.R557G6] 62-21888
I. Title.

BROBECK, Florence Richards, 222
1895-
Against the dark. New York, Ram Press [1962] 41 p. 20 cm. Poems. [PS3503.R6352A3] 62-22282
I. Title.

BROUGHER, William Edward, 222
1889-
Baggy pants and other stories. [1st ed.] New York, Vantage Press [1965] 163 p. 21 cm. [PS3503.R758B3] 66-531
I. Title.

BROUGHTON, James Richard, 222
1913-
Tidings, [poems at the land's edge] San Francisco, Pearce & Bennett [c1965] 57 p. 25 cm. "500 copies" [PS3503.R759T5] 65-28768
I. Title.

BUCK, Pearl (Sydenstricker) 222
1892-
Laba zeme; romans. No anglu valodas tulkojusi Anna Kalnina. [New York] Gramatu draugs, 1953. 264p. 22cm. [PS3503.U198G644] 53-39682
I. Title.

BURFORD, William. 222
A world; [poems. Austin] University of Texas [1962] 46 p. 22 cm. (Tower series, no. 3) [PS3503.U5976W6] 62-19995
I. Title.

BURGESS, Gelett, 1866-1951. 222
The miniature Purple Cow. Pasadena [Calif., S. and K. Dawson [1966]. 21 p. illus 39 x 54 cm. [PS3503.U6P8] 67-91
1. Bibliography — Microscopic and miniature editions — Specimens. I. Title.

BURGESS, Thornton Waldo, 222
1874-
The million little sunbeams, by Thornton W. Burgess. With an illus. by Harrison Cady. Toledo, Six Oaks Press, 1963. 8 p. illus., port 70 mm. "Published by Paul W. Kleser, Toledo, Ohio, as a tribute to . . . Thornton W. Burgess, on the eve of his 90th birthday." [PS3503.U6075M5] 64-5121
1. Bibliography — Microscopic and miniature editors — Specimens. I. Title.

CROSS, Frank Moore. 222
Studies in ancient Yahwistic poetry / by Frank Moore Cross, Jr., David Noel Freedman. [Missoula, Mont.] : Society of Biblical Literature : distributed by Scholars Press, 1975. p. cm. (SBL dissertation series) Bibliography: p. [BS1405.2.C76] 75-28159 ISBN 0-89130-014-7 : 4.20
1. Bible. O.T. Exodus XV—Criticism, Textual. 2. Bible. O.T. Genesis XLIX—Criticism, Textual. 3. Bible. O.T. Deuteronomy XXXIII—Criticism, Textual. 4. Bible. O.T. 2 Samuel XXII—Criticism, Textual. 5. Bible. O.T. Psalms XVIII—Criticism, Textual. 6. Hebrew poetry, Biblical—History and criticism. I. Freedman, David Noel, 1922- joint author. II. Title. III. Series: Society of Biblical Literature. Dissertation series.

DE WELT, Don. 222
Sacred history and geography; a workbook and teaching manual on the seventeen historical books of the Old Testament. Grand Rapids, Baker Book House, 1955. 496p. illus. 25cm. [BS1205.D4] 55-9471
1. Bible. O. T. Historical books—Study—Textbooks. I. Title.

EDWARDS, Josephine 222
Cunnington.
These commandments are mine. Illustrated by Jim Padgett. Nashville, Southern Publishing Association [c1963] 112 p. illus. 19 cm. [BV4656.E3] 63-17061
1. Commandments, Ten — Juvenile literature. I. Title.

HART, Lawrence, ed. 222
Accent on Barlow; a comemmorative [sic] anthology. San Rafael, Calif. [c1962] 72 p. 22 cm. [PS3503.A5732A6] 63-1951
1. American poetry — 20th cent. I. Barlow, Robert Hayward. 1918-1951. II. Title.

HAUGHTON, Rosemary 222
The family God chose, written, illus. by Rosemary Haughton. New York, Kenedy [1964] 128p. illus. 23cm. 64-21855 2.95
1. Bible stories, English—O.T. Pentateuch. 2. Abraham, the patriarch—Juvenile literature. I. Title.

HOGAN, Bernice. j 222
Deborah. Drawings by Joan Berg. New York Abingdon Press [1964] 159 p. illus. 23 cm. [BS580.D4H6] 64-10149
1. Deborah, judge of Israel — Juvenile literature. I. Title.

HOGAN, Bernice 222
Deborah. Drawings by Joan Berg. Nashville. Abingdon [c.1964] 159p. illus. 23cm. 64-10149 2.75
1. Deborah, judge of Israel—Juvenile literature. I. Title.

HOTH, Iva. 222
The captivity; 1 Kings 21:9-Malachi. Script by Iva Hoth. Illus. by Andre Le Blanc. Bible editor: C. Elvan Olmstead. Elgin, IL, D. C. Cook Pub. Co. [1973] 174 p. illus. 18 cm. (Her The picture Bible for all ages, v. 4) Retells in comic book format the Old Testament stories from the time of Elijah to the beginning of King Herod's reign.

[BS551.2.H682] 73-78171 ISBN 0-912692-16-2 0.95 (pbk.)
1. Bible stories, English—O.T. I. Le Blanc, Andre, 1921- illus. II. Title.

JONES, Mary Alice, 1898- 222 (j)
The Bible story of the creation. Illustrated by D. K. Stone. [Chicago] Rand McNally [1967] 44 p. illus. (part col.) 24 cm. [BS651.J63 1967] 67-21608
1. Creation—Juvenile literature. I. Title.

JONES, Mary Alice, 1898- 222
The Bible story of the creation. Illustrated by D. K. Stone. [Chicago] Rand McNally [1967] 44 p. illus. (part col.) 24 cm. Presents the first chapter of Genesis, the story of the creation of the world, with a commentary on its meaning for faith. [BS651.J63 1967] AC 68
1. Creation. I. Stone, D. K., illus. II. Title.

KOCH, Dietrich-Alex. 222
Die Bedeutung der Wundererzahlungen fur die Christologie des Markusevangeliums / Dietrich-Alex Koch. Berlin ; New York : De Gruyter, 1975. xi, 217 p. ; 24 cm. (Beiheft zur Zeitschrift fur die neutestamentliche Wissenschaft und die Kunde der alteren Kirche ; 42) A revision of the author's thesis, Gottingen, 1973. Includes indexes. Bibliography: p. [194]-207. [BS410.Z7 Heft 42] [BT366] 226'.2'066 74-80631 ISBN 3-11-004783-7 : DM90.00
1. Jesus Christ—Miracles. 2. Jesus Christ—History of doctrines—Early church, ca. 30-600. 3. Bible. N.T. Mark—Criticism, interpretation, etc. I. Title. II. Series: Zeitschrift fur die neutestamentliche Wissenschaft und die Kunde der alteren Kirche : Beihefte ; 42.

PFEIFFER, Charles F. 222
The united kingdom, by Charles F. Pfeiffer. Grand Rapids, Baker Book House [1970] 92 p. illus., maps. 23 cm. ([His Old Testament history series]) Bibliography: p. 85-87. [BS1325.2.P45] 68-19214 3.95
1. Jews—History—1200-935 B.C. 2. Bible. O.T. Samuel—History of Biblical events. I. Title.

*PONTIER, Arthur E. 222
The Savior is coming; a study manual of Old Testament revelation from David through the return from exile. Grand Rapids, Mich., Baker Bk. [c.]1965. 84p. 22cm. (Scripture-centered Catechism ser.) .90 pap.,
I. Title.

RICHARDS, Larry. 222
Years of darkness, days of glory : lessons from Israel's history : studies in Joshua through the time of Solomon / Larry Richards. Leader's ed. Elgin, Ill. : D. C. Cook Pub. Co., c1977. 274 p. : ill. ; 22 cm. (His Bible alive series) [BS1286.5.R53] 76-6582 ISBN 0-912692-96-0 : 3.95 ISBN 0-912692-97-9 pbk. : 2.95
1. Jews—History—1200-953 B.C.—Study and teaching. 2. Bible. O.T. Former prophets—Study—Text-books. I. Title. II. Series.

SAPORTA, Raphael, 1913- 222
A basket in the reeds. Illus. by H. Hechtkopf. Minneapolis, Lerner [1965, c.1964] 1v. (unpaged) col. illus. 31cm. [BS580.M6S32] 64-25640 3.79
1. Moses—Juvenile literature. I. Hechtkopf, H., illus. II. Title.

TAYLOR, Kenneth Nathaniel. 222
Living history of Israel; a paraphrase of Joshua, Judges, I and II Samuel, I and II Kings, I and II Chronicles, Ezra, and Nehemiah [by Kenneth N. Taylor] Wheaton, Ill., Tyndale House Publishers [1970] 693 p. 18 cm. [BS1203.T38] 79-123032 ISBN 0-8423-2460-7 4.95
1. Bible. O.T. Historical books—Paraphrases, English. I. Title.

WIESNER, William. 222 (j)
The Tower of Babel. [Written and illustrated by William Wiesner] New York, Viking Press [1968] [32] p. col. illus. 29 cm. "Based on the book of Genesis and on commentaries ... in the book Hebrew myths by Robert Graves and Raphael Patai." [BS1238.B2W5 1968] 68-16069
1. Babel, Tower of.

WILSON, Clifford A. 222
A greater than Joshua is here, by Clifford Wilson. [Melbourne, Australian Institute of Archeology in association with Word of Truth Productions, 1968] 38 p. 23 cm. [BS621.W46] 77-477011 unpriced
1. Bible—Antiquities. I. Australian Institute of Archeology. II. Title.

WYNANTS, Miche. j 222
Noah's ark. 1st American ed. New York, Harcourt, Brace & World [1965] 1 v. (unpaged) illus. (part col.) 28 cm. [BS580.N6W9 1965a] 65-8155
1. Noah — Juvenile literature. I. Title.

WYNANTS, Miche 222
Noah's ark. 1st Amer. ed. New York, Harcourt, c.1965. 1v. (unpaged)illus. (pt. col.) 28cm. [BS580.N6W9] 65-8155 3.25 bds.,
1. Noah—Juvenile literature. I. Title.

GETTYS, Joseph Miller, 222.06
1907-
Surveying the historical books. Richmond, John Knox Press [1963] 163 p. 21 cm. (Surveying the Bible series) [BS1205.5.G4] 63-8701
1. Bible. O. T. Historical books — Introductions. I. Title.

GETTYS, Joseph Miller, 222.06
1907-
Surveying the historical books. Richmond, Va., Knox [c.1963] 163p. 21cm. (Surveying the Bible ser.) 63-8701 2.00 pap.,
1. Bibl. O. T. Historical books—Introductions. I. Title.

GETTYS, Joseph Miller, 222.06
1907-
Teaching the historical books. Richmond, John Knox Press [1963] 63 p. 21 cm. (Surveying the Bible series) [BS1365.5.G4] 63-8700
1. Bible. O. T. Historical books — Study. I. Title.

GETTYS. JOSEPH MILLER, 222.06
1907-
Teaching the historical books. Richmond, Va., Knox [c.1963] 63p. 21cm. (Surveying the Bible ser.) 63-8700 1.25 pap.,
1. Bible. O. T. Historical books—Study. I. Title.

HISTORIANS of Israel; 222.06
v. 1-2. Nashville, Abingdon [1962. 2v.] 88; 87p. Contents.v. 1, 1 and 2 Samuel; 1 and 2 Kings, by Gordon Robinson. v. 2, 1 and 2 Chronicles; Ezra, Nehemiah, by Hugh Anderson. (Bible guides, no. 5 & 6) 62-16048 1.00 pap., ea.,
1. Bible. O. T. Historical books—Criticism, interpretation, etc. I. Robinson, Gordon. II. Anderson, Hugh.

TOOMBS, Lawrence E 222.06
Nation making: Exodus, Numbers, Joshua, Judges. London, Lutterworth Press; New York, Abingdon Press [1962] 86 p. 20 cm. (Bible guides, no. 4) [BS1210.Z72T6] 62-851
1. Bible. O. T. Heptateuch — Criticsm, interpretation, etc. I. Title.

TOOMBS, Lawrence E. 222.06
Nation making: Exodus, Numbers, Joshua, Judges. Nashville, Abingdon [1962] 86p. (Bible guides, no. 4) 62-851 1.00 pap.,
1. Bible. O. T. Heptateuch—Criticism, interpretation, etc. I. Title.

WEIPPERT, Manfred. 222.06
The settlement of the Israelite tribes in Palestine; a critical survey of recent scholarly debate. Naperville, Ill., A. R. Allenson [1971] xx, 171 p. maps. 22 cm. (Studies in Biblical theology, 2d ser., 21) Translation of Die Landnahme der israelitischen Stamme in der neueren wissenschaftlichen Diskussion. Includes bibliographical references. [DS121.55.W413] 74-131587
1. Jews—History—To 1200 B.C. I. Title. II. Series.

MADDUX, Roy Clark. 222'.06'6
Bible history in outline: Genesis-Esther. Grand Rapids, Baker Book House [1972] 133 p. 20 cm. [BS1193.M33] 72-182094 ISBN 0-8010-5895-3 2.50
1. Bible. O.T.—Study—Outlines, syllabi, etc. I. Title.

DAILY Bible commentary 222'.07
: Genesis-Job / [Arthur E. Cundall co-ordinating editor]. Philadelphia : A. J. Holman, [1977], c1973. p. cm. Reprint of the ed. published by Scripture Union, London. [BS1151.2.D32 1977] 76-46493 ISBN 0-87981-068-8 : 8.95
1. Bible. O.T.—Commentaries. I. Cundall, Arthur Ernest.

DAILY Bible commentary 222'.07
: Genesis-Job / [Arthur E. Cundall co-ordinating editor]. Philadelphia : A. J. Holman, [1977], c1973. p. cm. Reprint of the ed. published by Scripture Union, London. [BS1151.2.D32 1977] 76-46493 ISBN 0-87981-068-8 : 8.95
1. Bible. O.T.—Commentaries. I. Cundall, Arthur Ernest.

SZIKSZAI, Stephen. 222.09
The story of Israel, from Joshua to Alexander the Great. Philadelphia, Westminster Press [1960] 96 p. 20 cm. Westminster guides to the Bible] [BS1197.S9] 60-5225
1. Bible. O. T. Historical books — History of Biblical events. I. Title.

SZIKSZAI, Stephen 222.09
The story of Israel, from Joshua to Alexander the Great. Philadelphia, Westminster Press [c.1960] 96p. 20cm. (Westminster guides to the Bible) 60-5225 1.50
1. Bible. O. T. Historical books—History of Biblical events. I. Title.

MAYES, Andrew D. H. 222'.09'5
Israel in the period of the judges [by] A. D. H. Mayes. Naperville, Ill., A. R. Allenson [1974] x, 156 p. 22 cm. (Studies in Biblical theology; 2d series, 29) Bibliography: p. [140]-147. [BS1305.2.M39] 73-85127 ISBN 0-8401-3079-1
1. Jews—History—1200-953 B.C. 2. Bible. O.T. Judges—Criticism, interpretation, etc. I. Title. II. Series.

BARRETT, Ethel. 222'.09'505
If I had a wish ... / by Ethel Barrett. Glendale, Calif. : G/L Regal Books, c1974. 140 p. : ill. ; 20 cm. (A Regal venture book) Includes bibliographical references. [BJ1500.W55B37] 74-83139 ISBN 0-8307-0314-4 pbk. : 1.25
1. Bible. O.T.—Biography. 2. Wishes. I. Title.

SAMUELS, Ruth. 222'.09'505
Bible stories for Jewish children, from Joshua to Queen Esther. Illustrated by Laszlo Matulay. [New York] Ktav Pub. House [1973] 72 p. illus. (part col.) 27 cm. On spine: Joshua to Queen Esther. Retellings of thirty-seven Old Testament stories including that portion from Joshua to Queen Esther. [BS551.2.S324] 73-180210 4.00
1. Bible stories, English—O.T. I. Matulay, Laszlo, illus. II. Title. III. Title: Joshua to Queen Esther.

BLENKINSOPP, Joseph, 1927- 222'.1
Pentateuch. Chicago, ACTA Foundation [1971] viii, 248 p. 22 cm. (Scripture discussion commentary, 1) Contents.Contents.—Genesis 1-50, by J. Blenkinsopp.—Exodus, by J. Challenor.—Deuteronomy, by J. Blenkinsopp. Includes bibliographical references. [BS1235.3.B58] 71-173033 ISBN 0-87946-000-8
1. Bible. O.T. Genesis—Commentaries. 2. Bible. O.T. Exodus—Commentaries. 3. Bible. O.T. Deuteronomy—Commentaries. I. Challenor, John. II. Title. III. Series.

CHILL, Abraham. 222'.1
The mitzvot : the commandments and their rationale / by Abraham Chill. New York : Bloch Pub. Co., 1975 c1974 xxxiv, 508 p. ; 24 cm. Includes bibliographical references and index. [BM520.7.C48 1974] 74-14055 ISBN 0-8197-0376-1 : 15.95
1. Bible. O.T. Pentateuch—Commentaries. 2. Commandments (Judaism) I. Title.

CRISWELL, W A. 222.1
The gospel according to Moses. Nashville, Broadman Press ['1950] 175 p. 20 cm. [BS1225.C75] 51-1400
1. Bible. O. T. Pentateuch—Sermons. 2. Baptists—Sermons. 3. Sermons, American. I. Title.

CRISWELL, Wallie A 222.1
The gospel according to Moses. Nashville, Broadman Press [1950] 175 p. 20 cm. [BS1225.C75] 51-1400
1. Bible. O. T. Pentateuch—Sermons. 2. Baptists— Sermons. 3. Sermons, American. I. Title.

KASHER, Menachem Mendel, 222.1
1895-
Encyclopedia of Biblical interpretation, a millennial anthology; v.6. Tr. under the editorship of Harry Freedman. New York, N.Y., 10024, Amer. Biblical Ency. Soc. 210 W. 91 St. [c.1965] xiv, 267p. 29cm. Text of Pentateuch with commentary and Talmudic-Midrashic interpretations. Abridged tr. of the author's Humash Torah shelemah. Contents.v.6. Genesis. Bible. [BS1225.K363] 53-2813 10.95
1. Bible. O. T. Pentateuch—Commentaries. I. Bible. O. T. Pentateuch. English. 1953. Jewish Publication Society. II. Title.

LEWY, Immanuel. 222.1
The growth of the Pentateuch, a literary, sociological, and biographical approach. Introd. by Robert H. Pfeiffer. New York, Bookman Associates [1955] 288p. 22cm. [BS1225.L47] 55-4051
1. Bible. O. T. Pentateuch—Criticism, interpretation, etc. I. Title.

NEWELL, William Reed, 1868- 222.1
Studies in the Pentateuch; an analysis of Genesis, Exodus, Leviticus, Numbers & Deuteronomy. Chicago, Moody Bible Institute, Correspondence School [1950] 332 p. 21 cm. "A Moody correspondence course." [BS1227.N4] 50-13199
1. Bible O. T. Pentateuch — Study — Text-books. I. Moody Bible Institute of Chicago. II. Title.

PENNELL, George E. 222.1
Jehovah, not the serpent, thy God; a study of the J. document, by George E. Pennell. Denver, Big Mountain [1966] 55p. 23cm. [BS1215.2.P4] 67-617 2.50 bds.,
1. Bible. O. T. Hexateuch—Criticism, interpretation, etc. I. Title.

POLL, Solomon. 222'.1
Ancient thoughts in modern perspective: a contemporary view of the Bible. New York, Philosophical Library [1968] xii, 124 p. 23 cm. [BS1225.4.P64] 68-22349 4.00
1. Bible. O.T. Pentateuch—Meditations. I. Title.

POOL, David de Sola, 1885- 222.1
The Kaddish. 3d printing. Jerusalem, Printed by Sivan Press under the auspices of the Union of Sephardic Congregations. New York, 1964. xiii, 119 p. 23 cm. Reprint of work first published in 1909. Bibliography: p. viii-xi. [BM670.K3P6] 66-989
1. Kaddish (Jewish prayer) I. Title.

TAYLOR, Kenneth Nathaniel. 222'.1
Living books of Moses; a paraphrase of Genesis-Exodus-Leviticus-Numbers-Deuteronomy. Wheaton, Ill., Tyndale House [1969] 531 p. 18 cm. Technical consultant for this v.: H. Hoffner. [BS1226.T3] 70-93076 4.95
1. Bible. O.T. Pentateuch—Paraphrases, English. I. Title.

THOMAS, William Henry 222.1
Griffith, 1861-1924.
Through the Pentateuch chapter by chapter, by W. H. Griffith Thomas, edited by his daughter. Grand Rapids, Eerdmans [1957] 191p. 23cm. [BS1239.T5] 57-7389
1. Bible. O. T. Pentateuch—Study—Outlines, syllabi, etc. I. Title.

THOMAS, William Henry 222.1
Griffith, 1861-1924.
Through the Pentateuch chapter by chapter, by W. H. Griffith Thomas, edited by his daughter. Grand Rapids, Eerdmans [1957] 191 p. 23 cm. [BS1239.T5] 57-7380
1. Bible. O.T. Pentateuch — Study — Outlines, syllabi, etc. I. Title.

TORAH Yesharah; 222.1
a traditional interpretative translation of the Five Books of Moses, and an introd. to each Haftorah. Based on Talmudic and Midrashic sources, as well as from medieval and mod. commentators [v.1] Tr., ed. by Rabbi Chas. Kahane. New York, 30 Canal, Solomon Rabinowitz Bk. Concern [c.1963] unpaged. 21 cm. (Torah Yesharah pubn.) Hebrew and English. 4.50
1. Bible. O. T. Pentateuch. English. 1963. Kahane. I. Kahane, Charles P., ed. and tr. II. Title: Torah yesharah.

TORAH Yesharah; 222.1
a traditional interpretative translation of the Five Books of Moses, and an introd. to each Haftorah. Based on Talmudic and Midrashic sources, as well as from medieval and mod. commentators [v.2] Tr., ed. by Rabbi Chas. Kahane. New York, 30 Canal St. Solomon Rabinowitz Bk. Concern, [c.1964] various p. 21cm. (Torah Yesharah pubn.) Hebrew and Eng. 4.50
1. Bible. O.T. Pentateuch. English. 1963. Kahane. I. Kahane, Charles Ph., ed. and tr.

TORAH 222.1tTorah Yesharah;
Yesharah. New York, 30 Canal Solomon Rabinowitz bk. Concern, [c.1963] unpaged 21cm. (Torah Yesharah pubn.) Hebrew and English. a t 4.50
I. Bible. O.T. Pentateuch. English. 1963. Kahane. II. Kahane, Charles P., ed. and tr.

TUNYOGI, Andrew C., 1907- 222'.1
The rebellions of Israel [by] Andrew C. Tunyogi. Richmond, John Knox Press [1969] 158 p. 21 cm. Bibliographical references included in "Notes" (p. [147]-158) [BM612.5.T85] 69-19471 4.95
1. Bible. O.T. Pentateuch—Criticism, interpretation, etc. 2. Covenants (Jewish theology) I. Title.

**WISDOM of the Torah,* 222.1
ed. New York, Citadel [1967, c.1966] 300p. 21cm. (C236) y Dagobret D. Runes. 2.25 pap.,

COLODNER, Solomon, 222'.1'007
1908-
Concepts and values. New York, Shengold Publishers [1969, c1968] 140 p. 22 cm. [BS1227.C59] 68-58503 3.95
1. Bible. O. T. Pentateuch—Study—Outlines, Syllabi, etc. I. Title.

BROWNE, Earl Zollicoffer, 222.101
M. D.
Let's return to the Mosaic authorship of the Pentateuch. New York, Greenwich [c.1962] 131p. 21cm. 62-15299 3.50

1. Bible. O. T. Pentateuch—Evidences, authority, etc. I. Title.

BIBLE. O.T. 222'.1'042
Pentateuch. English. Etheridge. 1968.
The Targums of Onkelos and Jonathan ben Uzziel on the Pentateuch, with the fragments of the Jerusalem Targum from the Chaldee, by J. W. Etheridge. New York, Ktav Pub. House, 1968. 2 v. in 1. 24 cm. First published in London (Longman), 1862-65. Contents.Contents.—[1] Genesis and Exodus.—[2] Leviticus, Numbers, and Deuteronomy. [BS1223.A2E8] 68-58086
1. Bible O.T. Pentateuch. Aramaic. Targum Onkelos—Translations into English. 2. Bible. O.T. Pentateuch. Aramaic. Targum Pseudo-Jonathan—Translations into English. 3. Bible. O.T. Pentateuch. Aramaic. Targum Yerushalmi—Translations into English. I. Etheridge, John Wesley, 1804-1866, tr. II. Title.

BUTIN, Romain 222.1'04'4
Francois, 1871-1937.
The ten nequdoth of the Torah; or, The meaning and purpose of the extraordinary points of the Pentateuch, (Massoretic text) A contribution to the history of textual criticism among the ancient Jews, by Romain Butin. Prolegomenon by Shemaryahu Talmon. New York, Ktav Pub. House, 1969. xxviii, 136 p. 23 cm. (The Library of Biblical studies) A reissue of the author's thesis (Catholic University, 1904) published in 1906; with a new Prolegomenon. Vita. Bibliography: p. 131-136. [BS718.B77 1969] 67-11895
1. Masorah. 2. Hebrew language—Accents and accentuation. I. Talmon, Shmarjahu. II. Title. III. Series.

POLLAK, Michael. 222'.1'044
The discovery of a missing Chinese Torah scroll. Dallas, Bridwell Library [1973] 36 l. 28 cm. Includes bibliographical references. [BM657.T6P64] 74-177309
1. Torah scrolls. 2. Jews in Kaifeng, China. I. Bridwell Library. II. Title.

SIEGEL, Jonathan Paul. 222'.1'044
The Severus scroll and 1QIs [superscript a] / by Jonathan Paul Siegel. Missoula, Mont. : Published by Scholars Press for the Society of Biblical Literature, c1975. p. cm. (Masoretic studies ; no. 2) Bibliography: p. [BS1222.5.S48S53] 75-28372 ISBN 0-89130-028-7 : 2.80
1. Bible. O.T. Pentateuch. Hebrew. Severus scroll. 2. Bible. O.T. Isaiah. Hebrew. Dead Sea scroll A. 3. Bible. O.T. Pentateuch—Criticism, Textual. 4. Sribes, Jewish. I. Title. II. Series.

BIBLE. O.T. 222'.1'046
Pentateuch. Aramaic. Targum Yerushalmi. Selections. 1977.
Variant versions of Targumic traditions within Codex Neofiti 1 / by Shirley Lund and Julia A. Foster. Missoula, Mont. : Published by Scholars Press for the Society of Biblical Literature, c1977. xii, 174 p. ; 24 cm. (Aramaic studies ; 2) English or Aramaic. Includes bibliographical references and index. [BS1224.A76 1977] 77-5389 ISBN 0-89130-137-2 : 4.50
1. Bible. O.T. Pentateuch. Aramaic. Targum Yerushalmi. I. Lund, Shirley. II. Foster, Julia A. III. Codex Neofiti 1. IV. Bible. O.T. Pentateuch. English. Lund. Selections. 1977. V. Title. VI. Series: Aramaic studies series ; 2.

RHYMER, Joseph, 1927- 222'.1'05
The beginnings of a people. Chart and maps designed and executed by Paul Colsell to the author's specifications. Dayton, Ohio, Pflaum Press, 1967. xi, 168 p. illus., maps. 22 cm. (His A way through the Old Testament [v. 1] The Pentateuch) [BS1225.2.R46 1967b] 67-29764
1. Bible. O.T. Pentateuch—History of Biblical events. I. Title.

RHYMER, Joseph, 1927- 222'.1'05
The covenant and the kingdom. Dayton, Ohio, Pflaum Press, 1968. 149 p., illus., map. 22 cm. (His A Way through the Old Testament, v. 2: Joshua, Judges, Samuel and Kings) [BS1286.5.R5 1968b] 68-22895 4.75
1. Bible. O.T. Former prophets—History of Biblical events. I. Title.

BIBLE. O.T. 222'.1'052
Pentateuch. English. 1963. Jewish Publication Society.
The Torah, [Torah (romanized form)] the five books of Moses. [1st ed., 2d impression] Philadelphia, Jewish Publication Society of America [1963, c1962] 393 p. 22 cm. "A new translation of the Holy Scriptures according to the Masoretic text. First section." [BS1223 1963] 62-12948
I. Jewish Publication Society of America.

BIBLE. O.T. 222'.1'05201
Pentateuch. English. 1967. Tyndale.
William Tyndale's five books of Moses called the Pentateuch, being a verbatim reprint of the edition of MCCCCCXXX. Compared with Tyndale's Genesis of 1534, and the Pentateuch in the Vulgate, Luther, and Matthew's Bible, with various collations and prolegomena, by J. I. Mombert, and newly introduced by F. F. Bruce. Carbondale, Ill., Southern Illinois University Press [1967] cliv, 635 p. facsims. 24 cm. New ed. of the work first compiled by J. I. Mombert in 1884. [BS140 1967] 67-23739
1. Bible. O.T. Pentateuch. English—Versions—Tyndale. I. Tyndale, William, d. 1536, tr. II. Mombert, Jacob Isidor, 1829-1913, ed. III. Bruce, Frederick Fyvie, 1910- ed. IV. Title. V. Title: Five books of Moses.

ASIMOV, Isaac, 1920- 222.106
Words from the Exodus. Decorations by William Barss. Boston, Houghton Mifflin, 1963. 203 p. illus. 22 cm. [BS1225.5.A8] 63-7136
1. Bible. O. T. Pentateuch—Language, style. 2. English language—Words—History. I. Title.

CRISWELL, Wallie A. 222.106
The gospel according to Moses. Grand Rapids, Zondervan Pub. House [1960.c.1950] 175p. 61-708 2.50
1. Bible, O. T. Pentateuch—Sermons. 2. Baptists—Sermons. 3. Sermons, American. I. Title.

EFRON, Benjamin. 222.106
The message of the Torah. [New York] Ktav Pub. House [1963] 152 p. 25cm. Includes selected verses in Hebrew with English translation. [BS1225.2.E35] 63-24006
1. Bible. O. T. Pentateuch—Criticism, interpretation, etc. I. Title.

EFRON, Benjamin 222.106
The message of the Torah. [New York] Ktav [c.1963] 151p. 25cm. Includes selected verses in Hebrew with English tr. 63-24006 3.00
1. Bible. O.T. Pentateuch—Criticism, Interpretation. I. Title.

GETTYS, Joseph Miller, 222.106
1907-
Surveying the Pentateuch. Richmond, Va., Knox [c.1962] 147p. illus. 21cm. (Surveying the Bible ser.) Bibl. 62-11716 1.75 pap.,
1. Bible. O. T. Pentateuch—Study—Outlines, syllabi, etc. I. Title.

GETTYS, Joseph Miller, 222.106
1907-
Teaching the Pentateuch. Richmond, Va., Knox [c.1962] 59p. 21cm. (Surveying the Bible ser.) 62-11715 1.25 pap.,
1. Bible. O. T. Pentateuch—Study. I. Title.

GINSBURG, Christian 222'.1'06
David, 1831-1914, ed. and tr.
The Massorah / compiled from manuscripts, alphabetically and lexically arranged by Christian D. Ginsburg. New York : Ktav Pub. House, [1975] p. cm. (The Library of Biblical studies) Added t.p. (v. 1-3): ha-Masorah. Reprint, with a prolegomenon, analytical table of contents, and list of identified sources and parallels by Aron Dotan, of the 1880-1905 ed. published in London by the author. [BS718.G52 1975] 79-92329 300.00(set)
1. Masorah. I. Title. II. Series.

KAHAN, Samuel 222.106
Heaven on your head; interpretations, legends and parables, comments on the Torah and the holidays, as narrated by S. Z. Kahana. Ed., adapted by Morris Silverman. Illus. by Meir Ben-Uri. Hartmore House [dist. New York, Taplinger, 1964] 287p. illus. 23cm. [BS1225.5.K35] 64-57066 5.95
1. Aggada. 2. Bible. O.T. Pentateuch—Addresses. essays, lectures. 3. Fasts and feasts—Judaism. I. Silverman, Morris, 1894- ed. II. Title.

KELLEY, Page H. 222'.1'06
A nation in the making [by] Page H. Kelley. Nashville, Convention Press [1969] 174 p. map. 21 cm. (Bible survey series, v. 3) "Church study course [of the Sunday School Board of the Southern Baptist Convention] This book is number 3203 in category 2, section for adults and young people." Includes bibliographical references. [BS1227.K4] 77-77619
1. Bible. O.T. Pentateuch—Study—Text-books. I. Title. II. Series.

*KRAJENKE, Robert W. 222'.1'06
Man crowned King: the divine drama unfolds: Edgar Cayce's story of the Old Testament from Joshua to Solomon [by] Robert W. Krajenke. New York, Bantam Books [1974] 209 p. 18 cm. [BF131.1] 1.25 (pbk.)
1. Bible and spiritualism. I. Cayce, Edgar, 1877-1945. II. Title.

*KRAJENKE, Robert W. 222'.106
Man the Messiah: God's plan fulfilled; Edgar Cayce's story of the Old Testament [by] Robert W. Krajenke. New York, Bantam Books [1974] xix, 284 p. 18 cm. [BF1311] 1.25 (pbk.)
1. Cayce, Edgar, 1877-1945. 2. Bible & spiritualism. I. Cayce, Edgar, 1877-1945. II. Title.

KRAJENKE, Robert W. 222'.1'06
A million years to the Promised Land; Edgar Cayce's story of the Old Testament, Genesis through Deuteronomy. [By] Robert W. Krajenke. Toronto, New York, Bantam Books [1973] xxv, 262 p. 18 cm. Bibliography: p. [255] [BF1311.B5K7] 73-10183 1.25 (pbk.)
1. Cayce, Edgar, 1877-1945. 2. Bible and spiritualism. I. Cayce, Edgar, 1877-1945. II. Title.

POLZIN, Robert. 222'.1'06
Late Biblical Hebrew : toward an historical typology of Biblical Hebrew prose / by Robert Polzin. Missoula, Mont. : Published by Scholars Press for the Harvard Semitic Museum, c1976. xii, 170 p. ; 21 cm. (Harvard Semitic monographs ; 12) Bibliography: p. 161-165. [BS1345.5.P64] 76-3559 ISBN 0-89130-101-1 : 6.00
1. Bible. O.T. Chronicles—Language, style. 2. Bible. O.T. Pentateuch—Language, style. 3. P document (Biblical criticism) 4. Hebrew language—Style. I. Title. II. Series.

PURVIS, James D. 222'.1'06
The Samaritan Pentateuch and the origin of the Samaritan sect [by] James D. Purvis. Cambridge, Mass., Harvard University Press, 1968. xiv, 147 p. 22 cm. (Harvard Semitic monographs, v. 2) Based on the author's thesis, Harvard, 1962. Bibliography: p. [130]-142. [BS1225.2.P8] 68-17631 6.00
1. Bible. O.T. Pentateuch—Criticism, interpretation, etc. 2. Samaritans. I. Title. II. Series.

RABINOWITZ, Louis 222'.1'06
Isaac, 1906-
Torah and flora / L. I. Rabinowitz. New York : Sanhedrin Press, c1977. p. cm. Includes index. [BS1225.4.R3] 76-58906 ISBN 0-88482-917-0 : 9.95
1. Bible. O.T. Pentateuch—Sermons. 2. Bible—Natural history. 3. Sermons, Jewish—Israel. 4. Sermons, English—Israel—Jewish authors. I. Title.

SEGAL, Moses Hirsch, 222'.1'06
1877-1968.
The Pentateuch; its composition and its authorship and other Biblical studies. Jerusalem, Magnes Press, Hebrew University, 1967. xiii, 255 p. 25 cm. IL 15.00 "The greater part ... mostly in a different form, appeared originally in ... Scripta Hierosolymitana ... Jewish quarterly review ... Vetus Testamentum ... [and] Journal of Biblical literature." Bibliographical footnotes. [BS1225.2.S38] HE68
1. Bible. O. T. Pentateuch—Criticism, interpretation, etc. 2. Bible. O.T. Criticism, interpretation, etc. I. Title.

SESBOUE, D. 222.106
The message of Moses, by D. Sesboue. Baltimore, Helicon [1966] 80 p. 18 cm. (Living world ser., 1) Tr., of Les traditions bibliques. [BS1225.2.S413] 65-24131 pap., 1.25
1. Bible. O. T. Pentateuch—Theology. I. Title. Availabe from Taplinger in New York.

SILVER, Abba Hillel, 222.106
1893-.
Moses and the original Torah. New York, Macmillan, 1961. 188 p. 22 cm. [BX1225.2.S5] 61-15163
1. Bible O. T. Pentateuch — Criticism, interpretations, etc. 2. Judaism Hist. Ancient period. I. Title.

SILVER, Abba Hillel, 222.106
1893-
Moses and the original Torah. New York, Macmillan [c.] 1961. 188p. 61-15163 3.50
1. Bible. O. T. Pentateuch—Criticism, interpretation, etc. 2. Judaism—Hist.—Ancient period. I. Title.

SILVERMAN, Hillel E., 222'.1'06
1924-
From week to week; reflections on the Sabbath Torah readings, by Hillel E. Silverman. Bridgeport, Conn., Hartmore House [1974] p. cm. [BS1225.4.S54] 74-16211 ISBN 0-87677-156-8
1. Bible. O.T. Pentateuch—Meditations. I. Title.

WANEFSKY, Joseph. 222'.1'06
From the shadow of insight. New York, Philosophical Library [1974] 149 p. 22 cm. [BS1225.4.W28] 73-82166 ISBN 0-8022-2128-9 6.00
1. Bible. O.T. Pentateuch—Sermons. 2. Sermons, American—Jewish authors. 3. Sermons, Jewish—United States. I. Title.

*WARREN, Mary 222.106
The great escape: Exodus 3:1-15: 1 for children. Illus. by Jim Roberts. St. Louis, Concordia, c.1966 1v. (unpaged) col. illus. 21cm. (Arch bks., set 3, no. 59-1125) .35 pap.,
1. Exodus, The — Juvenile literature. 2. Bible stories, O. T. — Juvenile literature. I. Title.

ZERIN, Edward. 222.106
The birth of the Torah. [1st ed.] New York, Appleton-Century-Crofts [1962] 274 p. 21 cm. [BS1225.2.Z4] 62-19143
1. Bible. O. T. Pentateuch—Criticism, interpretation, etc. I. Title.

BRUEGGEMANN, Walter. 222'.1'066
The vitality of Old Testament traditions / by Walter Brueggemann and Hans Walter Wolff. Atlanta : John Knox Press, [1975] 155 p. ; 21 cm. Includes bibliographical references. [BS1225.2.B74 1975] 74-7830 ISBN 0-8042-0111-0 pbk. : 4.95
1. Bible. O.T. Pentateuch—Criticism, interpretation, etc.—Addresses, essays, lectures. I. Wolff, Hans Walter, joint author. II. Title.

CRAGHAN, John F. 222'.1'066
This is the word of the Lord; a promise fulfilled [by] John F. Craghan. Liguori, Mo., Liguori Publications [1972] 128 p. maps. 18 cm. [BS1225.2.C7] 72-78410 1.50
1. Bible. O.T. Pentateuch—Criticism, interpretation, etc. 2. Bible. O. T. Joshua—Criticism, interpretation, etc. I. Title.

FEINSTEIN, Moses, 222'.1'066
1892-
Bastion of faith; a collection of expositions on the Bible and Jewish holidays as heard from Moshe Feinstein. Compiled and edited by Abraham Fishelis. New York [Balshon Printing and Offset Co.] 1973. 256 p. 24 cm. "This work is a translation of some of the excerpts in my two published volumes in Hebrew, entitled Kol rom." [BS1225.3.F38] 74-151226
1. Bible. O. T. Pentateuch—Commentaries. I. Fishelis, Avraham Shelomoh, ed. II. Feinstein, Moses, 1892- Kol ram. III. Title.

NICHOLSON, Ernest 222'.1'066
Wilson.
Exodus and Sinai in history and tradition [by] E. W. Nicholson. Richmond, Va., John Knox Press [1973] xv, 94 p. 22 cm. (Growing points in theology) Bibliography: p. [85]-90. [BS680.E9N52 1973] 73-6595 ISBN 0-8042-0200-1 4.95
1. Bible. O.T. Pentateuch—Criticism, interpretation, etc. 2. Exodus, The. 3. Covenants (Theology)—Biblical teaching. I. Title.

NOTH, Martin, 1902- 222'.1'066
1968.
A history of Pentateuchal traditions. Translated with an introd. by Bernhard W. Anderson. Englewood Cliffs, N.J., Prentice-Hall [1972] xxxv, 296 p. port. 24 cm. Translation of the 1st ed. of Uberlieferungsgeschichte des Pentateuch. Includes bibliographical references. [BS1225.2.N613] 73-132171 ISBN 0-13-391235-3 11.95
1. Bible. O.T. Pentateuch—Criticism, interpretation, etc. I. Title.

RAD, Gerhard von, 222'.1'066
1901-1971.
Wisdom in Israel. Nashville, Abingdon Press [1972] x, 330 p. 23 cm. Translation of Weisheit in Israel. Includes bibliographical references. [BS1455.R2313 1972b] 73-152746 ISBN 0-687-45756-4 12.95
1. Wisdom literature—Criticism, interpretation, etc. I. Title.

*WORKMAN, Edgar John 222.1066
The book of the law; a study of the inspiring word of God. New York, Exposition [c.1966] 164p. 22cm. 3.00
I. Title.

HABEL, Norman C. 222'.1'067
Literary criticism of the Old Testament, by Norman C. Habel. Philadelphia, Fortress Press [1971] x, 86 p. 22 cm. (Guides to Biblical scholarship. Old Testament series) [BS1225.2.H3] 78-157548 ISBN 0-8006-0176-9 2.50
1. Bible. O.T. Pentateuch—Criticism, interpretation, etc. I. Title.

ALLIS, Oswald Thompson, 222.107
1880-
God spake by Moses; an exposition of the Pentateuch. Nutley, N. J., Presbyterian and Reformed Pub. Co., 1958. 159p. 22cm. [BS1225.3.A4 1958] 58-59922
1. Bible O.T. Pentateuch—Commentaries. I. Title.

CHIEL, Arthur A. 222'.1'07
Pathways through the Torah / by Arthur A.

Chiel. [New York] : Ktav Pub. House, [1975- v. : ill. ; 23 cm. [BS1225.3.C45] 75-308407 ISBN 0-87068-620-8 pbk. : 1.95
1. Bible. O.T. Pentateuch—Commentaries. I. Title.

ERDMAN, Charles Rosenbury, 1866-1960 222'.1'07
The Pentateuch; a concise commentary on Genesis, Exodus, Leviticus, Numbers, and Deuteronomy [by] Charles R. Erdman. Old Tappan, N.J., Revell [c.1953] 1v. (various pagings) 21cm. First pub. separately as: The book of Genesis, an exposition. [1950]; The book of Exodus, an exposition. [1949]; The book of Leviticus, an exposition. [1951]; The book of Numbers, an exposition. [1952]; The book of Deuteronomy, an exposition. [1953] [BS1225.3.E7] 68-7562 8.95 bds.,
1. Bible. O.T. Pentateuch—Commentaries. I. Title.

FRYDMAN, Alexander Zusha, 1897-1943, comp. 222'.1'07
Wellsprings of Torah; an anthology of Biblical commentaries, by Alexander Zusia Friedman. Compiled and edited by Nison L. Alpert. Translated from the original Yiddish by Gertrude Hirschler. New York, Judaica Press, 1969. 2 v. (xxiii, 549 p.) 24 cm. Translation of Der Torah-kval (romanized form) Bibliography: p. 521-549. [BM724.F713] 73-10530 12.95
1. Bible. O.T. Pentateuch—Meditations. 2. Jewish devotional literature. I. Title.

HAILPERIN, Herman, 1899- 222.107
Rashi and the Christian scholars. [Pittsburgh] University of Pittsburgh Press [1963] xvii, 379 p. 24 cm. Bibliographical references included in "Notes" (p. 267-358) [BS1161.S58H3] 62-7929
1. Solomon ben Isaac, called RaSHI, 1040-1105. 2. Nicolas de Lyre, d. 1349. 3. Bible — Criticism, interpretation, etc. — Hist. I. Title.

HAILPERIN, Herman, 1899- 222.107
Rashi and the Christian scholars. [Pittsburgh, Pa. Univ. of Pittsburgh Pr. [c.1963] xvii, 379p. 24cm. Bibl. 62-7929 12.50
1. Solomon ben Isaac, called RaSHI, 1040-1105. 2. Nicolas de Lyre. d. 1349. 3. Bible—Criticism, interpretation, etc.—Hist. I. Title.

"IN search of our 222'.1'07
Sephardic roots." Compiled and arr. by David N. Barocas. New York, Foundation for the Advancement of Sephardic Studies and Culture [1970] 103 l. illus. 28 cm. (Foundation for the Advancement of Sephardic Studies and Culture. Tract 5-7) Cover title. Contents.Contents.—Tract 5. An introduction to the Me-'am lo'ez, by M. J. Benardete, with Hulli's thirty principles on the ethics of the soul, translated from the Ladino and edited by P. O. de Benardete.—Tract 6. Hebrew aspects of the Me-'am lo'ez, by N. G. Tarragano, translated from the Ladino by P. O. de Benardete.—Tract 7. The history and culture of the Sephardic Jews—a synthetic analysis, by M. J. Benardete and translated from the Spanish by P. O. de Benardete. [BS1158.L3M434] 74-157553
1. Me-'am lo'ez. 2. Sephardim. I. Barocas, David N., ed. II. Title. III. Series.

MACKINTOSH, Charles Henry, 1820-1896. 222'.1'07
Genesis to Deuteronomy: notes on the Pentateuch. [1st ed. in one v.] Neptune, N.J., Loizeaux Bros. [1973] 928 p. (p. 913-928 blank for reader's notes) 25 cm. "Originally published in six volumes under the titles: Notes on Genesis, 1880; Notes on Exodus, 1881; Notes on Leviticus, 1881; Notes on Numbers, 1882; Notes on Deuteronomy I, 1881; Notes on Deuteronomy II, 1882." [BS1225.M32] 72-75082 ISBN 0-87213-617-5 10.95
1. Bible. O.T. Pentateuch—Commentaries. 2. Bible. O.T. Pentateuch—Commentaries. I. Title.

MOSES ben Nahman, ca.1195-ca.1270. 222'.1'07
Commentary on the Torah [by] Ramban (Nachmanides). Translated and annotated with index by Charles B. Chavel. New York, Shilo Pub. House [1971- v. 26 cm. Translation of Perush ha-Torah. Contents.Contents.—[1] Genesis.—[2] Exodus.—[3] Leviticus.—[4] Numbers. [BS1225.M66553] 71-184043 ISBN 0-88328-007-8 (v. 2)
1. Bible. O.T. Pentateuch—Commentaries. I. Chavel, Charles Ber, 1906- II. Title.

NATIONAL Jewish Music Council. 222'.1'07
Bridging Israel and America through music and honoring four American Jewish composers. [Program guides prepared for the Jewish Music Festival theme, 1963-64. New York, 1963-64] 2 v. ports. 28 cm. Contents.-- v.1. Music of Israel today. -- v.2. The music of Gershon Ephros, Solomon Rowosky, Heinrich Schalit, Jacob Weinburg; edited by Lewis Appleton. [ML3776.N31B7] 65-5865
1. Music, Jewish — Bibl. 2. Composers, Jewish. I. Title. II. Title: Honoring four American Jewish composers.

RICHARDS, Larry. 222'.1'07
Freedom Road : understanding redemption : studies in Exodus, Leviticus, Numbers, and Deuteronomy / Larry Richards. Elgin, Ill. : D. C. Cook Pub. Co., c1976. 286 p. : ill. ; 22 cm. (His Bible alive series) [BS1225.2.R5] 75-45771 ISBN 0-912692-90-1 pbk. : 3.95
1. Bible. O.T. Pentateuch—Criticism, interpretation, etc. I. Title.

WEINBERG, Norbert. 222'.1'07
The essential Torah. New York, Bloch Pub. Co. [1974] xiii, 332 p. 24 cm. [BM670.H3W44] 73-77282 ISBN 0-8197-0282-X 8.95
1. Jews. Liturgy and ritual. Haftorath—Commentaries. 2. Bible. O.T. Pentateuch—Commentaries. I. Title.

PLAUT, W. Gunther, 1912- 222'.1'077
(Torah) [Torah (romanized form)] The Torah, a modern commentary, by W. Gunther Plaut. New York, Union of American Hebrew Congregations [1974- v. 26 cm. Includes original Hebrew text and the Jewish Publication Society's English translation of the Pentateuch and of the Haftaroth, both the traditional ones and two alternatives chosen by the author from a wider range of Biblical sources. Contents.Contents.—1. Genesis. Bibliography: v. 1, p. [504]-[509] [BS1225.3.P55] 75-307497
1. Bible. O.T. Pentateuch—Commentaries. I. Jewish Publication Society of America. II. Jews. Liturgy and ritual. Haftaroth (Reform, Plaut). English & Hebrew. 1974. III. Jews. Liturgy and ritual. Reform rite, Plaut. 1974. IV. Bible. O.T. Pentateuch. Hebrew. 1974. V. Bible. O.T. Pentateuch. English. Jewish Publication Society. 1974.

SOLOMON ben Isaac, called RaSHI, 1040-1105. 222'.1'077
Rashi, commentaries on the Pentateuch. Selected and translated by Chaim Pearl. [1st ed.] New York, Norton [1970] 256 p. 22 cm. (The B'nai B'rith Jewish heritage classics) Translation from Perush 'al ha-Torah (romanized form) Bibliography: p. 247. [BS1225.S5742] 78-108325 6.00
1. Bible. O.T. Pentateuch—Commentaries. I. Pearl, Chaim, 1919- comp. II. Title.

SOLOMON ben Isaac, called RaSHI, 1040-1105. 222'.1'077
Rashi: commentaries on the Pentateuch. Selected and translated by Chaim Pearl. New York, Viking Press [1973, c1970] 256 p. 22 cm. (The B'nai B'rith Jewish heritage classics) (UNESCO collection of representative works. Israel series) Translation from Perush 'al ha-Torah. Bibliography: p. 247. [BS1225.S5742 1973] 72-12619 ISBN 0-670-58967-5 6.95
1. Bible. O.T. Pentateuch—Commentaries. I. Pearl, Chaim, 1919- comp. II. Title. III. Series.

FILBY, Frederick Arthur 222.1085
Creation revealed; a study of Genesis, chapter one, in the light of modern science. Foreword by R. L. F. Boyd. [Westwood, N.J.] Revell [1966, c.1963] 160p. front., chart. 23cm. [BS651.F48] 66-2837 3.50 bds.,
1. Bible and science. 2. Bible. O. T. Genesis I. Criticism, interpretation, etc. II. Title.

LIVINGSTON, George Herbert, 1916- 222'.1'09
The Pentateuch in its cultural environment [by] G. Herbert Livingston. Grand Rapids, Baker Book House [1974] xiv, 296 p. illus. 24 cm. Includes bibliographies. [BS1225.2.L58] 73-92978 ISBN 0-8010-5540-7 8.95
1. Bible. O.T. Pentateuch—History of contemporary events, etc. 2. Bible. O.T.—Criticism, interpretation, etc. I. Title.

AUERBACH, Elias, 1882- 222'.1'0924
Moses. Translated and edited by Robert A. Barclay and Israel O. Lehman, with annotations by Israel O. Lehman. Detroit, Wayne State University Press, 1975. 253 p. ; 24 cm. Includes bibliographical references. [BS580.M6A813] 72-6589 ISBN 0-8143-1491-0
1. Moses. 2. Bible. O.T. Pentateuch—Criticism, interpretation, etc.

BEEGLE, Dewey M. 222'.1'0924 B
Moses, the servant of Yahweh [by] Dewey M. Beegle. Grand Rapids, Mich., Eerdmans [1972] 368 p. illus. (on lining paper) 23 cm. Includes bibliographical references. [BS580.M6B44] 73-162029 ISBN 0-8028-3406-X 7.95
1. Moses. I. Title.

DAICHES, David, 1912- 222'.1'0924 B
Moses, the man and his vision / David Daiches. New York : Praeger, 1975. 264 p. : ill. ; 26 cm. Includes index. Bibliography: p. 257-258. [BS580.M6D3] 74-11918 ISBN 0-275-33740-5 : 19.95
1. Moses. I. Title.

GILPIN, Richard O. 222'.1'0924 B
Moses—born to be a slave, but God ... / Richard O. Gilpin. 1st ed. Hicksville, N.Y. : Exposition Press, c1977. 119 p. ; 22 cm. [BS580.M6G48] 77-366950 ISBN 0-682-48843-7 : 5.50
1. Bible. O.T.—Biography. 2. Moses. I. Title.

GILPIN, Richard O. 222'.1'0924 B
Moses—born to be a slave, but God ... / Richard O. Gilpin. 1st ed. Hicksville, N.Y. : Exposition Press, c1977. 119 p. ; 22 cm. [BS580.M6G48] 77-366950 ISBN 0-682-48843-7 : 5.50
1. Bible. O.T.—Biography. 2. Moses. I. Title.

KLAGSBRUN, Francine. 222'.1'0924 B
The story of Moses. London, New York, Franklin Watts Ltd. [1971] xvii, 171 p. map. 23 cm. (Immortals of philosophy and religion) Bibliography: p. v-vii. [BS580.M6K55 1971] 72-180143 ISBN 0-85166-290-0 £1.25
1. Moses. I. Title.

KLAGSBRUN, Francine. 222'.1'0924 B
The story of Moses. New York, F. Watts [1968] vxii, 171 p. map. 22 cm. (Immortals of philosophy and religion) Presents the life and teachings of the prophet and lawgiver who, after a revelation from God, devoted his life to leading his people out of slavery to the promised land. [BS580.M6K55] 68-27403 3.95
1. Moses—Juvenile literature. I. Title.

MUNOWITZ, Ken. 222'.1'0924 B
Moses, Moses / pictures by Ken Munowitz ; text by Charles L. Mee, Jr.. 1st ed. New York : Harper & Row, c1977. [32] p. : ill. ; 26 cm. Retells the early events in the life of Moses. [BS580.M6M8 1977] 76-41516 ISBN 0-06-024178-0 : 4.95. lib.bdg. : 4.79
1. Bible. O.T.—Biography—Juvenile literature. 2. Moses—Juvenile literature. I. Mee, Charles L. II. Title.

ROSHWALD, Mordecai, 1921- 222'.1'0924
Moses: leader, prophet, man; the story of Moses and his image through the ages [by] Mordecai and Miriam Roshwald. New York, T. Yoseloff [1969] 233 p. illus. 22 cm. Bibliography: p. 215-228. [BS580.M6R62] 69-15773 6.00
1. Moses. I. Roshwald, Miriam, joint author. II. Title.

YOUNG, William Edgar, 1928- 222'.1'0924 B
Moses : God's helper / William E. Young ; illustrated by J. William Myers. Nashville : Broadman Press, c1976. 48 p. : col. ill. ; 24 cm. (Biblearn series) Discusses the life of Moses who led the Hebrews out of Egypt and received the Ten Commandments from God. [BS580.M6Y68] 76-382766 ISBN 0-8054-4225-1 : 3.95
1. Moses—Juvenile literature. 2. Bible. O.T.—Biography—Juvenile literature. I. Myers, James William. II. Title.

LEISHMAN, Thomas Linton, 1900- 222'.1'095
The continuity of the Bible. Boston, Christian Science Pub. Society [1968- v. maps. 24 cm. Articles originally published in the Christian science journal, 1963- Contents.—[1] The patriarchs.—[2] Joshua to Elisha.—[3] Prophetic writings.—[4] The Gospels. [BS1225.2.L4] 68-31635 3.50 (v. 3)
1. Jews—History—To 1200 B.C. 2. Bible. O.T. Pentateuch—History of Biblical events. 3. Prophets. I. Title.

LIBBEY, Scott 222.1095
Rebels and God. Illus. by Shirley Hirsch. [Philadelphia] United Church [1964] 89p. illus. (pt. col.) 22cm. Pt. of the United Church curriculum, prepared, pub by the Div. of Christian Educ. and the Div. of Pubn. of the United Church Bd. for Homeland Ministries. 64-14494 1.50
1. Paul, Saint, apostle—Juvenile literature. 2. Moses—Juvenile literature. I. United Church for Homeland Ministries. Division of Christian Education. II. United Church of Christ. III. United Church Board Division of Publication. IV. Title.

PLASTARAS, James. 222'.1'095
Creation and covenant. Milwaukee, Bruce Pub. Co. [1968] xvii, 202 p. 23 cm. (Contemporary college theology series. Biblical theology) Bibliographical footnotes. [BS1225.2.P55] 68-23526
1. Jews—History. 2. Bible. O.T. Pentateuch—History of Biblical events. 3. Bible. O.T. Pentateuch—Introductions. I. Title.

TRAVIS, Marion M. 222'.1095
The divine drama [by] Marion M. Travis. South Brunswick [N.J.] A. S. Barnes [1967] 494 p. 22 cm. Bibliographical footnotes. [BS1225.5.T7] 67-10592
1. Jews—History—To 1200 B.C. 2. Bible. O.T. Pentateuch—History of Biblical events. I. Title.

HARLOW, Jules. 222'.1'09505
Lessons from our living past. Edited by Jules Harlow. Associate editors: Kelly Cherry, Seymour Rossel, Carol Sanders. Illustrated by Erika Weihs. New York, Behrman House [1972] 128 p. col. illus. 26 cm. A retelling of Old Testament stories and Jewish legends designed to teach the principles of Judaism. [BM107.H37] 72-2055 ISBN 0-87441-085-1
1. Legends, Jewish. 2. Bible stories, English—O.T. 3. Religious education, Jewish—Textbooks for children. I. Weihs, Erika, illus. II. Title.

HOTH, Iva. 222'.1'09505
The promised land; Exodus 20:1-1 Samuel 16:19. Script by Iva Hoth. Illus. by Andre Le Blanc. Bible editor: C. Elvan Olmstead. Elgin, IL, D. C. Cook Pub. Co. [1973] 158 p. illus. 18 cm. (Her The picture Bible for all ages, v. 2) Retells in comic book format the Bible stories, from the Jews' exodus from Egypt to David's anointment as the next King of Israel. [BS551.2.H686] 73-78168 ISBN 0-912692-14-6 0.95
1. Bible stories, English—O.T. I. Le Blanc, Andre, 1921- illus. II. Title.

NEWMAN, Shirley. 222'.1'09505
A child's introduction to Torah. Edited by Louis Newman. Joseph J. Schwab, consultant. Illustrated by Jessica Zemsky. New York, Published by Behrman House for the Melton Research Center of the Jewish Theological Seminary of America [1972] 128 p. col. illus. 26 cm. A retelling of the first five books of the Bible which serve as the religious structure of Judaism. [BS550.2.N48] 72-2056 ISBN 0-87441-067-3
1. Bible stories, English—O.T. Pentateuch. I. Zemsky, Jessica, illus. II. Jewish Theological Seminary of America. Melton Research Center. III. Title.

ALLEN, Don Cameron, 1904- 222.11
The legend of Noah; Renaissance rationalism in art, science, and letters. Urbana, Univ. of Ill. Pr., 1963, [c.1949] 221p. illus. 21cm. (Illini. bk. IB-12) Bibl. 1.45 pap.,
1. Noah. I. Title. II. Series: Illinois. University. Illinois studies in language and literature, v. 33, no. 3-4

ANDERSON, Joseph Lyman. 222.11
The four rivers of Eden; a biological evidence of the truth of the Bible story. Richfield, Utah ,[1954] 176p. 23cm. [BS1237.A6] 54-27098
1. Eden. I. Title.

BALSIGER, Dave. 222'.11
In search of Noah's ark / by Dave Balsiger & Charles E. Sellier, Jr. Los Angeles : Sun Classic Books, c1976. 218 p., [16] leaves of plates : ill. ; 18 cm. Bibliography: p. 216-217. [BS658.B34] 76-151887 ISBN 0-917214-01-3 : 1.95
1. Noah's ark. 2. Deluge. I. Sellier, Charles E., joint author. II. In search of Noah's ark. [Motion picture]

*BERGEY, Alyce 222.11
The boy who saved his family: Genesis: 37-50 for children. Illus. by Betty Wind. St. Louis, Concordia, c.1966. 1v. (unpaged) col. illus. 21cm. (Arch bks., set 3, no. 59-1126) .35 pap.,
1. Bible stories. O.T. — Juvenile literature. I. Title.

BIBLE. O.T. Genesis I-II, 4. English. Jerusalem Bible. 1970. 222'.11
The creation. Illustrated by Jo Spier. [1st ed.] Garden City, N.Y., Doubleday [1970] [25] p. col. illus. 21 x 27 cm. Genesis I, 7, 20, and 27, and parts of other verses omitted. Illustrations accompany passages from the book of Genesis on the creation. [BS1233.S65] 71-94076 3.95
I. Spier, Jo, 1900- illus. II. Title.

BIBLE. O.T. Genesis, I-XI. English. New English. 1973. 222'.11
Genesis 1-11, commentary by Robert Davidson. Cambridge [Eng.] University Press, 1973. 117 p. 21 cm. (The Cambridge Bible commentary: New English Bible) Bibliography: p. 113. [BS1235.3.D3 1973] 72-93675 ISBN 0-521-08618-3
1. Bible. O.T. Genesis, I-XI—Commentaries. I. Davidson, Robert. II. Title. III. Series.
Distributed by Cambridge University Press, New York, 5.95, pbk. 2.95 ISBN 0-521-09760-6

BONHOEFFER, Dietrich, 1906-1945. 222.11
Creation and fall; a theological interpretation of Genesis 1-3. [Translation by John C. Fletcher] New York, Macmillan [1959] 96p. 22c8. [BS1235.B653] 59-4787
1. Bible. O. T. Genesis I-III—Commentaries. 2. Creation. 3. Fall of man. I. Title.

BOONE, Leslie A 222.11
The gift from God's fingers. Illus. by Barry Martin. [1st ed. New York] Pageant Press [c1955] 110p. illus. 21cm. [BS651.B73] 55-12511
1. Creation. I. Title.

BOSLEY, Harold Augustus, 1907- 222.11
Sermons on Genesis. [1st ed.] New York, Harper [1958] 206p. 22cm. Includes bibliography. [BS1235.B667] 58-10371
1. Bible. O. T. Genesis—Sermons. 2. Methodist Church—Sermons. 3. Sermons, American. I. Title.

BOSLEY, Harold Augustus, 1907- 222.11
Sermons on Genesis. Nashville, Abingdon [1964, c.1958] 206p. 21cm. (Apex bk. R-1) Bibl. 1.75 pap.,
1. Bible. O.T. Genesis—Sermons. 2. Methodist Church—Sermons. 3. Sermons, American. I. Title.

COHEN, H. Hirsch. 222'.11
The drunkenness of Noah / by H. Hirsch Cohen. University : University of Alabama Press, [1974] xiii, 177 p. : map (on lining paper) ; 25 cm. (Judaic studies ; 4) Includes indexes. Bibliography: p. 160-164. [BS580.N6C63] 74-194696 ISBN 0-8173-6702-0 : 7.95
1. Noah. 2. Cain. 3. Bible. O.T. Genesis—Criticism, interpretation, etc. I. Title. II. Series.

DANIELOU, Jean 222.11
In the beginning, Genesis I-III. Foreword by Gerard S. Sloyan [Tr. from French by Julien L. Randolf] Helicon [dist. New York, Taplinger, c.1965] 106p. 21cm. (Challenge bk.) [BS1235.2.D313] 64-16130 1.25 pap.,
1. Bible. O. T. Genesis I-III — Criticism, interpretation, etc. I. Title.

DANIELOU, Jean. 222.11
In the beginning ... Genesis I-III With a foreword by Gerard S. Sloyan. (Translated from the French by Julien L. Randolf Baltimore, Helicon [1965] 106 p. 21 cm. (A Challenge book) Bibliography: p. 103-106. [BS1235.2.D313] 64-16130
1. Bible. O. T. Genesis I-III — Criticism, interpretation, etc. I. Title.

EAKIN, Frank, 1885- 222.11
Bible study for grownups; a helping-book based on Genesis and Mathew for individual and group use. New York, Macmillan, 1956. 347p. 22cm. [BS1239.E3] 56-7680
1. Bible. O. T. Genesis—Study—Text-books. 2. Bible. N. T. Mathew—Study—Text-books. I. Title.

ERDMAN, Charles Rosenbury, 1866- 222.11
The book of Genesis, an exposition. New York, Revell [1950] 124 p. 20 cm. [BS1235.E7] 50-8366
1. Bible. O. T. Genesis—Commentaries. I. Title.

FILBY, Frederick Arthur. 222'.11
The flood reconsidered; a review of the evidences of geology, archaeology, ancient literature, and the Bible [by] Fredk. A. Filby. Foreword by Stephen S. Short. Grand Rapids, Zondervan Pub. House [1971, c1970] ix, 148 p. 21 cm. (Contemporary evangelical perspectives) Bibliography: p. 138-141. [BS658.F54 1971] 75-171194
1. Deluge. I. Title.

FORRESTER-BROWN, James S. 222'.11
The two creation stories in Genesis; a study of their symbolism [by] James S. Forrester-Brown. Berkeley, Shambala, 1974. xiii, 284 p. 22 cm. Reprint of the 1920 ed. published by J. M. Watkins, London. Bibliography: p. 282-284. [BS651.F7 1974] 74-75095 ISBN 0-87773-053-9 3.95
1. Bible. O.T. Genesis I-III—Criticsim, interpretation, etc. 2. Creation. I. Title.

GRAHAM, Lorenz B. 222'.11
God wash the world and start again, by Lorenz Graham. Pictures by Clare Romano Ross. New York, Crowell [1971, c1946] [40] p. illus. (part col.) 21 cm. The crisis of the flood and how Noah survived it as told by Liberians who have recently learned English. [BS658.G7 1971] 75-109900 ISBN 0-690-33295-5 3.75
1. Deluge—Juvenile literature. 2. Noah's ark—Juvenile literature. I. Ross, Clare Romano, illus. II. Title.

HANNON, Ruth. 222'.11
Noah's ark. Retold by Ruth Hannon. Pictures by Carolyn Bracken. New York, Golden Press [1973] 33 p. illus. 28 cm. Retells the Old Testament story of Noah, who built an ark which held his family and a pair of every living creature on earth during the forty days of the flood. [BS658.H28] 73-77490 3.95
1. Noah's ark—Juvenile literature. I. Bracken, Carolyn, illus. II. Title.

HANSON, Richard S. 222'.11
The serpent was wiser; a new look at Genesis 1-11 [by] Richard S. Hanson. Minneapolis, Augsburg Pub. House [1972] 128 p. 20 cm. Includes bibliographical references. [BS1235.2.H35] 70-176485 ISBN 0-8066-1214-2 2.95
1. Bible. O.T. Genesis I-XI—Criticism, interpretation, etc. I. Title.

HAPPEL, Robert A 222.11
Altars from Genesis; daily devotions for the family. Philadelphia, Christian Education Press [1961] 115p. 22cm. [BS1235.4.H35] 61-12208
1. Bible. O. T. Genesis— Meditations. I. Title.

HOPKINS, Garland Evans, 1913- ed. 222.11
The mighty beginnings; sermons based on the book of Genesis. St. Louis, Bethany Press [1956] 192p. 21cm. [BS1235.H66] 56-7956
1. Bible. O. T. Genesis—Sermons. 2. Sermons, American. I. Title.

JERUSALMI, Isaac, 1928- 222'.11
[Ma'aseh de-Yosef tsadika (romanized form)] The story of Joseph (Genesis 37; 39-47); a philological commentary. 2d rev. ed. Cincinnati, Hebrew Union College—Jewish Institute of Religion, 1968. xiii, 233 l. 28 cm. (His Auxiliary materials for the study of Semitic languages, no. 1) [BS1239.J4 1968] 70-3521
1. Bible. O.T. Genesis xxxvii, xxxix-xlvii—Study—Outlines, syllabi, etc. I. Title: The story of Joseph.

*LATOURETTE, Jane 222.11
The story of the Noah's Ark: Genesis 6: 5-9: 17 for children. Illus. by Sally Mathews. St. Louis, Concordia, c.1965. 1v. (unpaged) col. illus. 21cm. (Arch bks., set 2, no. 59-1110) .35 pap.,
1. Noah Ark (Story)—Juvenile literature. I. Title.

*LEE, J. W. 222.11
Preaching from Genesis; the perfecting of the believer's faith, by J. W. Lee. Grand Rapids, Baker Book House [1975] 137 p. 22 cm. [BS1235.4] ISBN 0-8010-5542-3 4.95.
1. Bible—Homilectical use—Old Testament—Genesis. 2. Bible—Sermons—Old Testament—Genesis. I. Title.

LEUPOLD, Herbert Carl, 1892- 222.11
Exposition of Genesis. Grand Rapids, Baker Book House, 1956 [c1912] 2v. (1220p.) 22cm. Bibliography: v. 1, p. 30-33. [BS1235.L45 1956] 55-11417
1. Bible. O. T. Genesis—Commentaries. I. Title.

LOGAN, William M 222.11
In the beginning God. Richmond, John Knox Press [1957] 90p. 21cm. Includes bibliography. [BS1235.L58] 57-11746
1. Bible. O. T. Genesis I-XI—Commentaries. I. Title.

LOWENTHAL, Eric I., 1901- 222'.11
The Joseph narrative in Genesis; an interpretation by Eric I. Lowenthal. New York, Ktav Pub. House, 1973. ix, 212 p. 24 cm. "Book interprets ... Genesis 37-50, omitting chapters 38 and 49: 1-27." Bibliography: p. 203-208. [BS1235.3.L69] 72-12044 ISBN 0-87068-216-4 9.50
1. Joseph, the patriarch. 2. Bible. O.T. Genesis XXXVII-L—Commentaries. I. Title.

LUTHER, Martin, 1483-1546. 222.11
Commentary on Genesis. A new translation by J. Theodore Mueller. Grand Rapids, Zondervan Pub. House [1958] 2v. 22cm. Translation of In primum librum Mose enarrationes. [BS1235.L79] 58-3431
1. Bible. O. T. Genesis—Commentaries. I. Title.

MAKRAKES, Apostolos, 1831-1905. 222.11
The Bible and the world; or, God's great Book studied in the light of His small one. Triluminal science, surveying the universe and explaining everything, etc. Proof of the authenticity of the Septuagint. Translated by D. Cummings. Chicago, Orthodox Christian Educational Society, 1950. xii, 483. 32 p. port. 24 cm. [BS652.M3] 51-23624
1. Creation. 2. Bible. O. T. Greek—Versions—Septuagint. I. Title. II. Title: Triluminal science. III. Title: Proof of the authenticity of the Septuagint.

MIYOSHI, Sekiya, 1924- 222'.11
The oldest story in the world. Story and pictures by Sekiya Miyoshi. Adapted by Barbara L. Jensh. Valley Forge [Pa.] Judson Press [1969] [24] p. col. illus. 25 cm. Paraphrases, with illustrations in bright colors, God's creation of the Earth. [BS652.M55] 69-18145 ISBN 0-8170-0436-X 2.95
1. Creation—Juvenile literature. I. Jensh, Barbara L. II. Title.

MONRO, Margaret Theodora, 1896- 222.11
Thinking about Genesis. London, New York, Longmans, Green [1953] 221p. 20cm. [BS1235.M518] 54-2719
1. Bible. O. T. Genesis—Criticism, interpretation, etc. I. Title.

MONRO, Margaret Theodora, 1896- 222.11
Thinking about Genesis. Chicago, Regnery [1966] xxiii, 223p. 18cm (Logos 511-710) [BS1235.M518] 1.45 pap.,
1. Bible. O.T. Genesis — Criticism, interpretation, etc. I. Title.

MUNK, Eli. 222'.11
(Shiv'at yeme Bereshit) = The seven days of the beginning / by Eli Munk. Jerusalem ; New York : Feldheim, 1974. 169 p. ; 23 cm. Text in English; notes in Hebrew and English. Includes bibliographical references and index. [BS1235.3.M86] 75-315624 6.95
1. Bible. O.T. Genesis I-II, 3—Commentaries. 2. Creation—Biblical teaching. I. Title. II. Title: The seven days of the beginning.

*NUTT, Ben. 222.'1'1
Train up a child / Ben Nutt. Chicago : Adams Press, 1976. 126p. ; 16 cm. Contents.Contents: Part I Genesis paraphrased for children. [BS551] pbk. : 2.75
1. Bible O.T. Genesis-Juvenile Literature. I. Title.
Order from : A. & B Products, Berrien Springs, M.I. 49104

PARROT, Andre, 1901- 222.11
The flood and Noah's ark. [Translated by Edwin Hudson] New York, Philosophical Library [1955] 76p. illus., map. 20cm. (Studies in Biblical archaeology, no. 1) Bibliography: p. 73-74. Bibliographical footnotes. [BS658.P345] 55-13875
1. Deluge. 2. Noah's ark. I. Title. II. Series.

PARROT, Andre, 1901- 222.11
The Tower of Babel. [Translated by Edwin Hudson] New York, Philosophical Library [1955] 75p. illus., map. 20cm. (Studies in Biblical archaeology, no. 2) Bibliography: p.71-72. Bibliographical footnotes. [BS1238.B2P315] 55-13876
1. Babel, Tower of. I. Title. II. Series.

PATTEN, Donald Wesley, 1929- 222.11
The Biblical flood and the ice epoch; a study in scientific history, by Donald W. Patten. [1st ed.] Seattle, Pacific Meridian Pub. Co., 1966. xvi, 336 p. illus., maps. 24 cm. Bibliography: p. [326]-330. [BS658.P347] 66-18566
1. Deluge. 2. Bible and geology. I. Title.

REHWINKEL, Alfred Martin, 1887- 222.11
The Flood in the light of the Bible, geology and archaeology. Saint Louis, Concordia Pub. House, 1951. xx, 372 p. illus., map. 24 cm. Bibliography: p. 357-360. [BS658.R4] 51-11785
1. Deluge. 2. Bible and geology. I. Title.

REHWINKEL, Alfred Martin, 1887- 222.11
The Flood in the light of the Bible, geology, and archaeology. [6th slightly rev. print.] Saint Louis, Concordia Pub. House, 1951 [i. e. 1957] 372p. illus. 21cm. Includes bibliography. [BS658.R4 1957] 57-4751
1. Deluge. 2. Bible and geology. I. Title.

REIK, Theodor, 1888- 222.11
The creation of woman. New York, G. Braziller, 1960. 159p. illus. 22cm. Includes bibliography. [BS580.E85R4] 60-5613
1. Eve (Biblical character) 2. Psychoanalysis. 3. Initiations (in religion, folk-lore, etc.) I. Title.

*REIK, Theodor, 1888- 222.11
The creation of woman. New York, McGraw [1973, c.1960] 159 p. front. 21 cm. (McGraw-Hill paperbacks) Includes bibliography. [BS580] ISBN 0-07-051813-0 pap., 1.95
1. Eve (Biblical character) 2. Psychoanalysis. 3. Initiations (in religion, folk-lore, etc.) I. Title.
L.C. card no. for Knopf edition: 60-5613.

REIK, Theodor, 1888-1970. 222.11
The creation of woman. New York, G. Braziller, 1960. 159 p. illus. 22 cm. Includes bibliography. [BS580.E85R4] 60-5613
1. Eve (Biblical character) 2. Psychoanalysis. 3. Initiations (in religion, folk-lore, etc.) I. Title.

REIK, Theodor, 1888-1970. 222.11
The temptation. New York, G. Braziller, 1961. 256 p. 22 cm. Includes bibliography. [BS580.I67R4] 61-12955
1. Isaac, the patriarch. 2. Initiations (in religion, folk-lore, etc.) 3. Psychoanalysis. 4. Typology (Theology) I. Title.

SINGER, Isaac Bashevis, 1904- 222'.11
The wicked city. Pictures by Leonard Everett Fisher. Translated by the author and Elizabeth Shub. New York, Farrar, Straus and Giroux [1972] [39] p. col. illus. 27 cm. Retells the Old Testament tale of the destruction of Sodom. [BS580.A3S4813 1972] 72-175144 ISBN 0-374-38426-6 4.50
1. Abraham, the patriarch—Juvenile literature. 2. Lot (Biblical character)—Juvenile literature. 3. Bible stories—O.T. I. Fisher, Leonard Everett, illus. II. Title.

SMITH, Cushing. 222.11
Behold! Genesis; what the two Bible accounts are all about. [1st ed.] New York, Pagent Press [1958, c1957] 125 p. 21 cm. [BS1235.S57] 58-384
1. Bible. O. T. Genesis — Miscellanea. I. Title.

SWANSTON, Hamish F. G., 1933- 222'.11
God makes the world. Pictures by Emile Probst. Text by Hamish Swanston. Nashville, Abingdon [1970] [28] p. col. illus. 19 x 20 cm. (His The Bible for children, v. 1) Retells, from the Old Testament, the events of the Creation and the Flood. [BS551.2.S95] 77-152774
1. Bible stories, English—O.T.—Genesis. I. Probst, Emile D., illus. II. Title.

SZEKELY, Edmond Bordeaux. 222'.11
The Essene book of creation; our spiritual heritage for the space age. [San Diego, Calif.] First Christians' (Essene) Church, 1968. 71 p. illus., port. 31 cm. Contents.Contents.—Genesis; an Essene interpretation.—Moses; a modern revaluation. [BS580.M6S9] 74-14717
1. Moses. 2. Bible. O.T. Genesis I-III—Criticism, interpretation, etc. I. Title.

VAWTER, Bruce. 222.11
A path through Genesis. New York, Sheed & Ward [1956] 308p. illus. 22cm. [BS1235.V3] 56-9530
1. Bible. O. T. Genesis—Commentaries. I. Title.

VAWTER, Bruce. 222.11
A path through Genesis. New York, Sheed & Ward [1956] 308 p. illus. 22 cm. [BS1235.V3] 56-9530
1. Bible. O.T. Genesis — Commentaries. I. Title.

WARSAW, Philip, 1890- 222.11
Genesis, mother of sciences, an exposition. by Pincas Dov [pseud. Chicago? 1953] 402p. 24cm. [BS652.W3] 53-29340
1. Bible. O. T. Genesis— Miscellanes. I. Title.

WEIL, Lisl. 222'.11
The very first story ever told / Lisl Weil. 1st ed. New York : Atheneum, 1976. [47] p. : col. ill. ; 24 cm. Retells the stories of the creation of the world and the fall of Adam and Eve. [BS551.2W.37 1976] 75-21666 ISBN 0-689-30516-8 : 6.50
1. Bible stories, English—O.T. Gensis. 2. Creation—Juvenile literature. 3. Fall of man—Juvenile literature. I. Title.

WHITCOMB, John Clement, 1924- 222.11
The Genesis Flood; the Biblical record and its scientific implications, by John C. Whitcomb, Jr., and Henry M. Morris. Foreword by John C. McCampbell. Philadelphia, Presbyterian and Reformed Pub. Co., 1961. xxv, 518 p. illus., diagrs. 24 cm. Bibliographical footnotes. [BS658.W5] 60-13463
1. Deluge. I. Morris, Henry Madison, 1918- joint author.

WHITCOMB, John Clement, 1924- 222'.11
The world that perished [by] John C. Whitcomb, Jr. Grand Rapids, Baker Book House [1973] 155 p. illus. 21 cm. Bibliography: p. 145-148. [BS658.W52] 73-84109 ISBN 0-8010-9537-9 1.95
1. Deluge. I. Title.

WORM, Piet. 222.11
Stories from the Old Testament [from Adam to Joseph] ... Piet Worm drew the pictures.

[New York, Sheed and Ward, 1956] unpaged. illus. 23 cm. [(BS551.2.W66)] 57-2122
1. Bible stories, English — O. T. Genesis. I. Title.

YOUNG, Davis A. 222'.11
Creation and the flood : an alternative to flood geology and theistic evolution / Davis A. Young. Grand Rapids : Baker Book House, c1977. 217 p. : ill. ; 24 cm. Includes bibliographical references. [BS657.Y68] 77-151681 ISBN 0-8010-9912-9 : 6.95
1. Bible and geology. 2. Deluge. 3. Catastrophes (Geology) 4. Bible and evolution. I. Title.

BASH, Ewald. 222'.11'00207
Legends from the future. Illustrated and designed by Anne Gayler. New York, Friendship Press [1972] 95 p. illus. 22 cm. [BS1235.4.B376] 71-178892 ISBN 0-377-02101-6 1.75
1. Bible. O.T. Genesis—Meditations. 2. Bible. O.T. Exodus—Meditations. I. Title.

RICHARDS, Larry. 222'.11'007
Let day begin : man in God's universe : studies in Genesis and Job / Larry Richards. Leader's ed. Elgin, Ill. : D. C. Cook Pub. Co., c1976. 284 p. : maps ; 22 cm. (His Bible alive series) Bibliography: p. 256. [BS1239.R5] 75-36697 ISBN 0-912692-86-3 pbk. : 3.95
1. Bible. O.T. Genesis—Study—Outlines, syllabi, etc. 2. Bible. O.T. Job—Study—Outlines, syllabi, etc. I. Title. II. Series.

JOHNSTON, Joseph, 1891- 222.11015
Christ in Genesis; a clergyman's study of the first book of Moses as a scripture of prophecy. [1st ed.] New York, Exposition Press [1959] 75p. 21cm. [BS1238.P7J6] 59-3814
1. Bible. O. T. Genesis—Prophecies. 2. Messiah—Prophecies. I. Title.

BIBLE. O.T. Genesis. 222'.11'044
Hebrew. Baer-Delitzsch. 1970.
The interlinear literal translation of the Hebrew Old Testament, with the King James version and the Revised version conveniently placed in the margins for ready reference, and with explanatory textural footnotes, supplemented by tables of the Hebrew verb, and the Hebrew alphabet, by George Ricker Berry. Genesis and Exodus. Grand Rapids, Mich., Kregel Publications [1970] xii, 404 p. 24 cm. (Kregel reprint library) Cover title: Interlinear Hebrew-English Old Testament: Genesis-Exodus. "The Hebrew text used is, for Genesis, that of Baer and Delitzsch ... For Exodus, the text of Baer and Delitzsch having not yet been published, that of Theile has been used." No more published. Reprint of the 1897 ed. [BS1232.B4 1970] 77-136092 ISBN 0-8254-2214-0 8.95
1. Bible—Interlinear translations. I. Baer, Seligmann, 1825-1897. II. Delitzsch, Franz Julius, 1813-1890. III. Theile, Carl Gottfried Wilhelm, 1799-1854. IV. Berry, George Ricker, 1865-1945. V. Bible. O.T. Exodus. Hebrew. Theile. 1970. VI. Title. VII. Title: Interlinear Hebrew-English Old Testament: Genesis-Exodus.

NAPIER, Bunyan 222'.11'0505
Davie.
Come sweet death; a quintet from Genesis [by] B. D. Napier. Philadelphia, United Church Press [1967] 96 p. 21 cm. [BX1235.4.N3] 67-17793
1. Bible. O. T. Genesis. English. Paraphrases. 1967. 2. Bible. O. T. Genesis—Meditations. I. Title.

BIBLE. O.T. Genesis. 222.11052
English. 1963.Watts.
A distinctive translation of Genesis, by J. Wash Watts. Grand Rapids, Eerdmans [1963] 154 p. 20 cm. [BS1233.W3] 61-17397
I. Watts, James Washington, 1806- tr. II. Title.

BIBLE. O.T. Genesis. 222.11052
English. 1963. Watts.
A distinctive translation of Genesis, by J. Wash Watts, Grand Rapids, Mich., Eerdmans [c.1963] 154p. 20cm. 61-17397 1.95 pap.,
I. Watts, James Washington, 1896- tr. II. Title.

BIBLE, O. T. Genesis. 222.11052
English. 1966. Jewish Publication Society.
Genesis; the N. J. V. translation. Introd. by Harry M. Orlinsky. New York, Harper [c.1962, 1966] 96p. 21cm. (Torchbks. TB736G. Temple lib.) Rev. version of the First book of the Torah, pub. in 1962 by the Jewish Pubn. Soc. of Amer. [BS1233.J42] 66-16605 1.25 pap.,
I. Jewish Publication Society of America II. Title.

BIBLE. O.T. Genesis. 222'.11'052
English. Jerusalem. 1969.
Genesis: the first book of Moses; wood engravings by Hermann Fechenbach. London, Oxford, A. R. Mowbray, 1969. 221 p. illus. 26 cm. [N8027.F4] 70-398859 84/-
1. Bible. O.T. Genesis—Pictures, illustrations, etc. I. Fechenbach, Hermann, 1897- II. Title.

BIBLE. O.T. Genesis I- 222'.11'052
II, 4a. English. 1975.
The story of creation : Genesis 1:1-2:4a / illustrated by Holly and Ivar Zapp. Plainfield, N.J. : Logos International, c1975. [21] p. : col. ill. ; 23 cm. "Text ... translated from the Hebrew text (as edited by Rudolf Kittel)" Illustrations accompany passages from the book of Genesis on the creation. [BS1233.Z36] 75-2799 ISBN 0-88270-119-3 : 2.25
1. Creation. I. Zapp, Holly. II. Zapp, Ivar. III. Title.

CLEAVELAND, Elizabeth 222'.11'052
Whittlesey.
A study of Tindale's Genesis, compared with the Genesis of Coverdale and of the Authorized version. [Hamden, Conn.] Archon Books, 1972. xliii, 258 p. 22 cm. Originally presented as the author's thesis, Yale, 1910. Reprint of the 1911 ed., which was issued as no. 43 of Yale studies in English. [PR2384.T9Z6 1972] 72-341 ISBN 0-208-01126-9
1. Tyndale, William, d. 1536. 2. Coverdale, Miles, Bp. of Exeter, 1488-1568. 3. Bible. O.T. Genesis. English—Versions. I. Title. II. Series: Yale studies in English, 43.

HOTH, Iva. 222'.11'052
Creation; Genesis 1:1—Exodus 19:20. Script by Iva Hoth. Illus. by Andre LeBlanc. Bible editor, C. Elvan Olmstead Elgin, Il., D.C. Cook Pub. Co. [1973] 157 p. illus. 18 cm. (Her The picture Bible for all ages, v. 1) Retells in picture format the events in the Old Testament books of Genesis and Exodus. [BS560.H64] 73-78167 ISBN 0-912692-13-8 0.95 (pbk.)
1. Bible. O.T. Genesis—Picture Bibles. 2. Bible. O.T. Exodus—Picture Bibles. I. Le Blanc, Andre, 1921- illus. II. Title.

BIBLE, O. T. Genesis. 222.1105208
English. 1965
The Genesis octapla; eight English versions of the book of Genesis in the Tyndale-King James tradition. Ed. by Luther A. Weigle. New York, Nelson [1965] xiv, 301p. 8 facsims. 28cm. [BS 1233.9.a2W4] 65-10700 12.50
1. Bible. O. T. Genesis. English — Version — Collections. I. Weigle, Luther Allan, 1880- ed. II. Title.

ANDERSON, Bernhard W. 222.1106
The beginning of history: Genesis. London, Lutterworth Press; Nashville, Abingdon [1963] 96p. 20cm. (Bible guides, no. 2) 63-759 1.00 pap.,
1. Bible. O. T. Genesis—Criticism, interpretation, etc. I. Title.

ASIMOV, Isaac, 1920- 222.1106
Words in Genesis. Decorations by William Barss. Boston, Houghton [c.]1962. 233p. illus, maps, 62-8117 3.00
1. Bible. O. T. Genesis—Language, style. 2. English language—Words—Hist. I. Title.

ASIMOV, Isaac, 1920- 222.1106
Words in Genesis. Decorations by William Barss. Boston, Houghton Mifflin, 1962. 233p. illus. 22cm. [BS1235.5.A8] 62-8117
1. Bible. O. T. Genesis—Language, style. 2. English language—Words—Hist. I. Title.

BOGUSZ, J. G. 222'.11'06
My invisible friend explains the Bible, by J. G. Bogusz. Boston, Branden Press [1971] 38 p. illus., map. 23 cm. [BS1191.B6] 75-130523 ISBN 0-8283-1300-8 4.00
1. Bible. O.T.—Miscellanea. I. Title.

COATS, George W. 222'.11'06
From Canaan to Egypt : structural and theological context for the Joseph story / George W. Coats. Washington : Catholic Bibical Association of America, 1976. ix, 101 p. ; 23 cm. (The Catholic Bibical quarterly. Monograph series ; 4) Includes indexes. Bibliography: p. 93-96. [BS1235.2.C6] 75-11382 ISBN 0-915170-03-5 pbk. : 2.50
1. Joseph, the patriarch. 2. Bible. O.T. Genesis XXXVII-XLVII—Criticism, interpretation, etc. I. Title. II. Series.

ELLIOTT, Ralph H. 222.1106
The message of Genesis. Nashville, Broadman Press [c.1961] 209p. Bibl. 61-7547 4.50
1. Bible. O. T. Genesis—Theology. I. Title.

FINEGAN, Jack, 1908- 222.1106
In the beginning; a journey through Genesis. [1st ed.] New York, Harper [1962] 159 p. 22 cm. Includes bibliography. [BS1235.2.F5] 62-7286
1. Bible. O.T. Genesis—Criticism, interpretation, etc. 2. Bible and science. I. Title.

*GALUSHA, Walter T. 222.1106
Fossils and the word of God. New York, Exposition [c.1964] 115p. 21cm. 3.00
I. Title.

GERBER, Israel Joshua, 222.1106
1918-
Immortal rebels; freedom for the individual in the Bible. New York, Jonathan David [c.1963] xi,267p. 24cm. Bibl. 63-21528 5.95
1. Bible. O. T. Genesis—Psychology. I. Title.

GERBER, Israel Joshua, 222.1106
1918-
Immortal rebels; freedom for the individual in the Bible. New York, Jonathan David [c1963] xi, 267 p. 24 cm. Bibliography: p. 253-257. [BS1235.5.G4] 63-21528
1. Bible. O.T. Genesis—Psychology. I. Title.

GINSBURGH, Irwin. 222'.11'06
First, man ; then, Adam! : A scientific interpretation of the Book of Genesis / Irwin Ginsburgh. New York : Simon and Schuster, c1975. 122 p. ; 22 cm. Includes bibliographical references. [BS1235.5.G5 1975b] 76-53811 ISBN 0-671-22747-5 : 5.95
1. Bible. O.T. Genesis—Miscellanea. 2. Bible and science. I. Title.

GINSBURGH, Irwin. 222'.11'06
First, man—then, Adam! : A scientific interpretation of the Book of Genesis / Irwin Ginsburgh. 1st ed. Morton Grove, Ill. : Dearborn Press, c1975. 122 p. : ill. ; 21 cm. Includes bibliographical references. [BS1235.5.G5] 75-26236 4.95
1. Bible. O.T. Genesis—Miscellanea. 2. Bible and science. I. Title.

GUNKEL, Hermann, 1862- 222.1106
1932.
The legends of Genesis, the Biblical saga and history. [Translated by W. H. Carruth] Introd. by William F. Albright. New York, Schocken Books [1964] xii, 164 p. 21 cm. Translation of the author's Die Sagen der Genesis, the introduction to his translation and commentary on Genesis. [BS1235.G8 1964] 64-22609
1. Bible. O.T. Genesis—Criticism, interpretation, etc. I. Carruth, William Herbert, 1859-1924, tr. II. Title.

GUTZKE, Manford 222'.11'06
George.
Plain talk on Genesis / Manford George Gutzke. Grand Rapids : Zondervan Pub. House, c1975. 143 p. ; 21 cm. [BS1235.2.G87] 74-25330 pbk. : 2.95
1. Bible. O.T. Genesis—Criticism, interpretation, etc. I. Title.

HAURET, Charles. 222.1106
Beginnings: Genesis and modern science. Translated by John F. McDonnell. [2d rev. ed.] Dubuque, Iowa, Priory Press [1964] 240 p. illus. map. 22 cm. Translation of Origines de l'univers et de l'homme d'apres la Bible. Bibliographical footnotes. [BS651.H36] 64-17323
1. Creation — Biblical teaching. 2. Man (Theology) — Biblical teaching. 3. Bible. O.T. Genesis I-III — Criticism, interpretation, etc. I. Title.

HAURET, Charles 222.1106
Beginnings: Genesis and modern science. Tr. [from French] by John F. McDonnell [2d rev. ed.] Dubuque, Iowa, Priory Pr. [1964] 240p. illus., map. 22cm. Bibl. 64-17323 price unreported
1. Creation—Biblical teaching. 2. Man (Theology)—Biblical teaching. 3. Bible. O. T. Genesis I-III—Criticism, interpretation, etc. I. Title.

HESSLER, Bertram. 222.1106
The Bible in in the light of modern science. Translated by Sylvester Saller. Chicago, Franciscan Herald Press [1960] 87p. 19cm. Includes bibliography. [BS651.H453] 60-9293
1. Bible and science. I. Title.

HESSLER, Bertram 222.1106
The Bible in the light of modern science. Translated [from the German] bySylvester Saller. Chicago, Franciscan Herald Press [c.1960] xiii, 87p. Includes bibliography. 19cm. 60-9293 1.75 bds.,
1. Bible and science. I. Title.

JENS, Arlene Johnson. 222'.11'06
I am the Lord thy sex : (an interpretation of Genesis and Exodus) / Arlene Johnson Jens. 1st ed. Hicksville, N.Y. : Exposition Press, c1975. 87 p. ; 22 cm. [BS1235.2.J4] 75-332481 ISBN 0-682-48377-X : 5.00
1. Bible. O.T. Genesis—Criticism, interpretation, etc. 2. Bible. O.T. Exodus—Criticism, interpretation, etc. I. Title.

LAPPLE, Alfred, 1915- 222'.11'06
Key problems of Genesis [Translated by Robert Kress] Glen Rock, N.J., Paulist Press [1967] 127 p. illus. 18 cm. Translation of v. 1 of Biblische Verkundigung in der Zeitenwende. Bibliography: p. 126-127. [BS1235.2.L313] 67-7270
1. Bible. O.T. Genesis I-XII—Criticism, interpretation, etc. I. Title.

LAPPLE, Alfred Karl, 222'.11'06
1915-
Key problems of Genesis [by] Alfred Lapple. [Translated by Robert Kress] Glen Rock, N.J., Paulist Press [1967] 127 p. illus. 18 cm. (Deus books) Translation of Biblische Verkiindigung in der Zeitenwende. Bibliography: p. 126-127. [BS1235.2.L313] 67-7270
1. Bible. O.T. Genesis I-XII — Criticism, interpretation, etc. I. Title.

MURRAY, Ralph L. 222.1106
From the beginning. Nashville, Broadman [1964] xi, 136p. 21cm. Bibl. 64-21161 2.75
1. Bible. O. T. Genesis I-XII—Criticism, interpretation, etc. I. Title.

NILES, Daniel 222.1106
Thambyrajah.
Studies in Genesis. Philadelphia, Westminster Press [1958] 109p. 20cm. First published in Calcutta under title: In the beginning. [BS1235.2.N5 1958] 58-8682
1. Bible. O. T. Genesis—Criticism, interpretation, etc. I. Title.

RENCKENS, Henricus 222.1106
Israel's concept of the beginning: the theology of Genesis 1-3. [New York] Herder & Herder [c.1964] 320p. 22cm. Ser. of articles which orig. appeared in four successive vols. of Verbum (1950-1953) 64-13690 5.95
1. Bible. O. T. Genesis I-III—Criticism, interpretation, etc. I. Title.

SHEED, Francis Joseph, 222'.11'06
1897-
Genesis regained, by F. J. Sheed. New York, Sheed and Ward [1969] ix, 182 p. 22 cm. "Some further reading": p. 175-178. [BS1235.2.S48] 74-89478 4.95
1. Bible. O.T. Genesis I-III—Criticism, interpretation, etc. I. Title.

THIELICKE, Helmut, 1908- 222.1106
How the world began; man in the first chapters of the Bible. Translated with an introd. by John W. Doberstein. Philadelphia, Muhlenberg Press [1961] 308 p. 22 cm. [BS1235.4.T513] 61-6756
1. Bible. O.T. Genesis — Sermons. 2. Lutheran Church — Sermons. 3. Sermons, English — Translations from German. 4. Sermons, German — Translations into English. I. Title.

THIELICKE, Helmut, 1908- 222.1106
How the world began; man in the first chapters of the Bible. Translated with an introd. by John W. Doberstein Philadelphia, Muhlenberg Press [1961] 308 p. 22 cm. [BS1235.4.T513] 61-6756
1. Bible. O. T. Genesis—Sermons. 2. Lutheran Church—Sermons. 3. Sermons, English—Translations from German. 4. Sermons, German—Translations into English. I. Title.

VAN DER ZIEL, Aldert, 222.1106
1910-
Genesis and scientific inquiry. Minneapolis, Denison [c.1965] 209p. 23cm. Bibl. [BS651.V3] 65-19103 4.50
1. Bible. O. T. Genesis—Criticism, interpretation, etc. 2. Bible and science. I. Title.

*WILSON, Clifford A. 222.11'06
In the beginning God; answers to questions on Genesis. By Clifford A. Wilson. Rev. ed. Grand Rapids, Baker Book House, [1975] 142 p. 20 cm. Bibliography: p. 141-142. [BS1235.5] ISBN 0-8010-9571-9 2.50 (pbk.)
1. Bible—Criticism, Interpretation, etc.—O.T. pentateuch I. Title.

YOUNG, Edward Joseph 222.1106
Studies in Genesis one [Nutley, N.J.,] Presbyterian and Reformed Pub. Co., Box 185 [1965] 105p. 23cm. (Intl. lib. of philosophy and theology: Biblical and theological studies) Bibl. Title. (Series: International library of philosophy and theology: Biblical and theological studies series) [BS1235.2.Y6] 64-17028 1.50 pap.,
1. Bible. O.T. Genesis I. Criticism, interpretation, etc. II. Title. III. Series.

DE HAAN, Martin Ralph, 222.11064
1891-
Portraits of Christ in Genesis, by M. R. De Haan. Grand Rapids, Zondervan Pub. House [1966] 192 p. 21 cm. [BT225.D4] 66-21026
1. Typology (Theology) I. Title.

DEHAAN, Martin Ralph, 222.11064
1891-
Portraits of Christ in Genesis, by M. R. De

Haan. Grand Rapids, Mich., Zondervan [1966] 192p. 21cm. [BT225.D4] 66-21026 2.50
1. Typology (Theology) I. Title.

CLEMENTS, Ronald Ernest, 1929- 222'11'066
Abraham and David; Genesis xv and its meaning for Israelite tradition [by] R. E. Clements. Naperville, Ill., A. R. Allenson [1967] 96 p. 22 cm. (Studies in biblical theology, 2d ser., 5) Bibliography: p. 89-93. [BS1235.2.C55] 67-8569
1. Bible. O.T. Genesis xv—Criticism, interpretation, etc. 2. Covenants (Theology)—Biblical teaching. I. Title. II. Series.

CLEMENTS, Ronald Ernest, 1929- 222'.11'066
Abraham and David; Genesis XV and its meaning for Israelite tradition [by] R. E. Clements. Naperville, Ill., A. R. Allenson [1967] 96 p. 22 cm. (Studies in biblical theology, 2d ser., 5) Bibliography: p. 89-93. [BS1235.2.C55] 67-8569
1. Bible. O.T. Genesis XV—Criticism, interpretation, etc. 2. Covenants (Theology)—Biblical teaching. I. Title. II. Series.

DAVIES, John Dudley. 222'.11'066
Beginning now; a Christian exploration of the first three chapters of Genesis [by] John D. Davies. Philadelphia, Fortress Press [1971] 285 p. 23 cm. Includes bibliographical references. [BS1235.2.D36] 70-157535 ISBN 0-8006-0037-1 5.95
1. Bible. O.T. Genesis, I-III—Criticism, interpretation, etc. I. Title.

GAVERLUK, Emil. 222'.11'066
Did Genesis man conquer space? Illustrated by Jack Hamm. Nashville, T. Nelson [1974] 192 p. illus. 21 cm. Includes bibliographical references. [BS1235.5.G34] 74-1262 ISBN 0-8407-5553-8 2.95 (pbk.)
1. Bible. O.T. Genesis—Miscellanea. 2. Plurality of worlds. 3. Civilization, Ancient. I. Title.

JACOBSON, Edith, 1915- 222'.11'066
The light of understanding; a guide to the book of Genesis. [Miami Beach, Fla.] Hadassah, Miami Beach Chapter, Shengold Publishers, Inc. [1972] 48 p. 22 cm. Bibliography: p. 48. [BS1235.2.J23] 72-78513
1. Bible. O.T. Genesis—Criticism, interpretation, etc. I. Title.

KRAVITZ, Nathan 222'.11'066
Genesis: a new interpretation of the first three chapters. New York, Philosophical Library [1967] 83 p. illus. 22 cm. [BS1235.3.K76] 66-23435
1. Bible. O. T. Genesis, I-III — Commentaries. I. Title.

KRAVITZ, Nathan. 222'.11'066
Genesis: a new interpretation of the first three chapters. New York, Philosophical Library [1967] 83 p. illus. 22 cm. [BS1235.3.K76] 66-23435
1. Bible. O.T. Genesis, I-III—Commentaries. I. Title.

*SAXE, Grace, ed. 222'.11'066
Studies in Genesis, arranged by Grace Saxe, rev. by Irving L. Jensen. Chicago, Moody [1967] 96p. 22cm. Cover title 95 pap.,
I. Title.

SCHAEFFER, Francis August. 222'.11'066
Genesis in space and time; the flow of biblical history [by] Francis A. Schaeffer. Downers Grove, Ill., Inter-Varsity Press [1972] 167 p. 21 cm. Includes bibliographical references. [BS1235.2.S32] 72-78405 ISBN 0-87784-636-7 2.25
1. Bible. O.T. Genesis I-XI—Criticism, interpretation, etc. I. Title.

SCHAEFFER, Francis August. 222'.11'066
Genesis in space & time; the flow of Biblical history [by] Francis A. Schaeffer. Glendale, Calif., Regal Books [1972] 174 p. illus. 20 cm. (A Bible commentary for layman) (G/L curriculum edition) Includes bibliographical references. [BS1235.2.S32 1972b] 72-90407 ISBN 0-87784-636-7 2.25
1. Bible. O.T. Genesis I-XI—Criticism, interpretation, etc. I. Title.

SUARES, Carlo. 222'.11'066
The cipher of Genesis; the original code of the Qabala as applied to the Scriptures. [1st ed.] Berkeley, Shambala Publications [1970] 231 p. 23 cm. (The Clear light series) Translation of La Bible restituee. [BS1235.5.S813 1970] 70-11833 5.95
1. Bible. O.T. Genesis—Miscellanea. 2. Gematria. I. Title.

SUARES, Carlo, 1892- 222'.11'066
The cipher of Genesis; the original code of the Qabala as applied to the Scriptures. New York, Bantam [1973, c.1967] xv, 240 p. 18 cm. (Bantam Book, X7720) Translation of La Bible restituee. [BS1235.5.S813 1970] pap., 1.75
1. Gematria. I. Bible. O.T. Genesis—Miscellanea. II. Title.

PLASTARAS, James 222.11067
The God of Exodus; the theology of the Exodus narratives. Milwaukee, Bruce Pub. [1966] ix, 342p. 22cm. (Impact bks.) [BS1245.2.P5] 66-28858 6.75
1. Exodus, The. 2. Bible. O.T. Exodus — Theology. I. Title.

BIBLE. O.T. Genesis. English. 1964. Speiser. 222.1107
Genesis. Introd., translation, and notes by E. A. Speiser. [1st ed.] Garden City, N.Y., Doubleday, 1964. lxxvi, 378 p. 24 cm. (The Anchor Bible, 1) Bibliographical references included in "Principal abbreviations" (p. [xi]-xii) [BS192.2.A1 1964.G3, vol. 1] 64-21724
1. Bible. O.T. Genesis—Commentaries. I. Speiser, Ephraim Avigdor, 1902- ed. and tr. II. Title. III. Series.

DAVIS, John James, 1936- 222'.11'07
Paradise to prison : studies in Genesis / John J. Davis. Grand Rapids, Mich. : Baker Book House, c1975. 363 p. : ill. ; 24 cm. Includes indexes. Bibliography: p. 305-339. [BS1235.3.D34] 74-30753 ISBN 0-8010-2838-8 : 7.95
1. Bible. O.T. Genesis—Commentaries.

ESSES, Michael. 222'.11'07
Jesus in Genesis / Michael Esses. Plainfield, N.J. : Logos International, c1974. xi, 263 p. ; 21 cm. [BS1235.3.E83] 75-309089 ISBN 0-88270-093-6 : 5.95. ISBN 0-88270-100-2 pbk. : 2.95
1. Bible. O.T. Genesis—Commentaries. I. Title.

*HOBBS, Herschel H. 222.'11'07
The origin of all things : studies in Genesis / Herschel H. Hobbs. Waco, Tex. : Word Books [1976]c1975. 159p. ; 23 cm. Bibliography: p. 159. [BS1235.3] 75-36191 ISBN 0-87680-459-8 : 5.95
1. Bible, O.T. Genesis-Commentaries. I. Title.

KIDNER, Derek. 222'.11'07
Genesis; an introduction and commentary. [1st ed.] Chicago, Inter-varsity [1967] 224p. 19cm. (Tyndale Old Testament commentaries [2]) Bibl. [BS1235.3.K47] 67-23333 3.95 bds.,
1. Bible. O. T. Genesis—Commentaries. I. Title.

MORGENSTERN, Julian, 1881- 222.1107
The book of Genesis: a Jewish interpretation. [2d ed.] New York, Schocken Books [1965] 309 p. 21 cm. (Schocken paperbacks) "SB96." First published in 1919 under title: A Jewish interpretation of the book of Genesis. Bibliography: p. [35] [BS1235.M6 1965] 65-14826
1. Bible O. T. Genesis — Commentaries. I. Title.

MORGENSTERN, Julian, 1881- 222.1107
The book of Genesis: a Jewish interpretation [2d ed.] New York, Schocken [c.1965] 309p. 21cm. (SB96) First pub. in 1919 under title: A Jewish interpretation of the book of Genesis. Bibl. [BS1235.M6] 65-14826 5.00; 1.95 pap.,
1. Bible. O. T. Genesis—Commentaries. I. Title.

PAYNE, D. F. 222'.11'07
Genesis, Exodus [by] D. F. Payne. [1st U.S. ed.] Grand Rapids, Mich., W. B. Eerdmans Pub. Co. [1971, c1970] 95 p. 19 cm. (Scripture Union Bible study books) [BS1235.5.P36 1971] 79-150645 1.25
1. Bible. O.T. Genesis—Study—Textbooks. 2. Bible. O.T. Exodus—Study—Textbooks. I. Title.

PFEIFFER, Charles F. 222.1107
The book of Genesis, a study manual. Grand Rapids, Baker Book House [1958] 108 p. 20 cm. (Shield Bible study series) [BS1235.P47] 58-8162
1. Bible. O.T. Genesis—Commentaries.

PLAUT, W. Gunther, 1912- 222'.11'07
[Bereshit (romanized form)] Genesis. Commentary, by W. Gunther Plaut. New York, Union of American Hebrew Congregations [1974, c1973] p. cm. (His Pardes Torah) Includes Biblical text in Hebrew and English. [BS1235.3.P55 1974] 73-16180 5.00
1. Bible. O.T. Genesis—Commentaries. I. Bible. O.T. Genesis. Hebrew. 1974. II. Bible. O.T. Genesis. English. 1974.

RAD, Gerhard von, 1901- 222.1107
Genesis: a commentary. Translated by John H. Marks. Philadelphia, Westminster Press [1961] 434p. 23cm. (The Old Testament library) Translation of Das erste Buch Mose, Genesiz., Bibliography: p. 8. [BS1235.3.R313] 61-5072
1. Bible. O. T. Genesis—Commentaries. I. Title. II. Series.

STIGERS, Harold G., 1917- 222'.11'07
A commentary on Genesis / Harold G. Stigers. Grand Rapids : Zondervan Pub. House, c1976. 352 p. : ill. ; 25 cm. Includes the author's translation of the text of Genesis. Includes index. Bibliography: p. 339-347. [BS1235.3.S76] 75-6187
1. Bible. O.T. Genesis—Commentaries. I. Bible. O.T. Genesis. English. Stigers. 1975. II. Title.

WOOD, Leon James. 222'.11'07
Genesis : a study guide / Leon J. Wood. Grand Rapids, Mich. : Zondervan Pub. House, c1975. 152 p. ; 21 cm. (Study guide series) Bibliography: p. 151-152. [BS1235.3.W58] 74-25352 pbk. : 1.95
1. Bible. O.T. Genesis—Commentaries. I. Title.

WOODSON, Leslie H., 1929- 222'.11'07
The beginning; a study of Genesis [by] Les Woodson. Wheaton, Ill., Victor Books [1974] 154 p. 21 cm. Includes bibliographical references. [BS1235.3.W6] 74-79161 ISBN 0-88207-713-9 1.95 (pbk.).
1. Bible. O.T. Genesis—Commentaries. I. Title.

BARNHOUSE, Donald Grey, 1895-1960. 222'.11'077
Genesis; a devotional exposition. Grand Rapids, Zondervan Pub. House [1973] 208, 253 p. 23 cm. [BS1235.4.B37 1973] 74-151224 8.95
1. Bible. O. T. Genesis—Devotional literature. I. Title.

BARNHOUSE, Donald Grey, 1895-1960. 222'.11'077
Genesis; a devotional commentary. Grand Rapids, Mich., Zondervan Pub. House [1970] 208 p. 23 cm. [BS1235.4.B37] 78-106434 4.95
1. Bible. O.T. Genesis—Devotional literature. I. Title.

BIBLE. O.T. Genesis XLIX. English. Aberbach-Grossfeld. 1976. 222'.11'077
Targum Onqelos on Genesis 49 : translation and analytical commentary / by Moses Aberbach and Bernard Grossfeld. Missoula, Mont. : Published by Scholars Press for the Society of Biblical Literature, c1976. xiv, 84 p. ; 23 cm. (Aramaic studies ; no. 1) Includes indexes. Bibliography: p. 70-73. [BS1233.A25] 76-27271 ISBN 0-89130-078-3
1. Bible. O.T. Genesis XLIX. Aramaic. Targum Onkelos—Criticism, interpretation, etc. 2. Bible. O.T. Genesis XLIX. Aramaic. Targum Onkelos—Translations into English. I. Aberbach, Moses. II. Grossfeld, Bernard. III. Title. IV. Series.

JACOB, Benno, 1862-1945. 222'.11'077
The first book of the Bible: Genesis, interpreted by B. Jacob. His commentary abridged, edited, and translated by Ernest I. Jacob and Walter Jacob. New York, Ktav Pub. House [1974] x, 358 p. 24 cm. Abridged translation of Das erste Buch der Tora: Genesis. "Bibliography of Benno Jacob": p. 350-358. [BS1235.J27213 1974] 74-1007 ISBN 0-87068-246-6 12.50
1. Bible. O.T. Genesis.—Commentaries. I. Jacob, Ernest I., ed. II. Jacob, Walter, 1930- ed. III. Bible. O.T. Genesis. English. 1974. IV. Title.

JACOB, Benno, 1862-1945. 222'.11'077
The first book of the Torah, Genesis, translated [and] with a commentary [in German] by B. Jacob. New York, Ktav Pub. House [1974] 1055 p. 24 cm. Cover title: Das erste Buch der Tora, Genesis. Reprint of the 1934 ed. published by Shocken Verlag, Berlin. Bibliography: p. 1050-1055. [BS1235.J27 1974] 74-2854 ISBN 0-87068-247-4
1. Bible. O.T. Genesis—Commentaries. I. Bible. O.T. Genesis. German. Jacob. 1974. II. Title. III. Title: Das erste Buch der Tora.

LEIBOWITZ, Nehama. 222'.11'077
Studies in Shemot : the Book of Exodus / Nehama Leibowitz ; [translated and adapted from the Hebrew by Aryeh Newman]. Jerusalem : World Zionist Organization, Dept. for Torah Education and Culture in the Diaspora, c1976. 2 v. (xvi, 783 p.) ; 22 cm. Translation of 'Iyunim hadashim be-sefer Shemot, 3d rev. ed. "Biographical notes on Jewish Bible commentators, compiled by Aryeh Newman.": v. 2, p. [711]-737. [BS1245.3.L4413] 76-375548
1. Bible. O.T. Exodus—Commentaries. I. Title.

SWEDENBORG, Emanuel, 1688-1772 222'.11'077
Heavenly secrets (Arcana caelestia), which are contained in the Holy Scripture or word of the Lord disclosed. From the Latin of Emanuel Swedenborg. New York, Swedenborg Found., 1967. v. 18cm. ontents.kv.1. Genesis, chapters 1-7, nos. 1-823. [BX8712.A8 1967] 67-9674 1.00 pap.,
1. New Jerusalem Church—Doctrinal and controversial works. 2. Bible. O.T. Genesis—Commentaries. 3. Bible. O.T. Exodus—Commentaries. I. Title.
Publisher's address: 139 E. 23rd St., New York, N.Y.

VAWTER, Bruce. 222'.11'077
On Genesis : a new reading / by Bruce Vawter. 1st ed. Garden City, N.Y. : Doubleday, 1977. 501 p. : maps (on lining paper) ; 24 cm. Includes index. [BS1235.3.V38] 76-26354 ISBN 0-385-06104-8 : 10.00
1. Bible. O.T. Genesis—Commentaries. I. Title.

GENESIS & 222'.11'0830131
ecology, an exchange [by] Donald E. Gowan [and] Millard Schumaker. Kingston, Ont., Queen's Theological College, 1973. 31 p. 22 cm. (Queen's Theological College. Occasional papers, 1) Cover title. Does "subdue" mean "plunder" first appeared under the title Genesis and ecology: does "subdue" mean "plunder"? in the Oct. 7, 1970 issue of the Christian century. Contents.Contents.—Gowan, D. E. Does "subdue" mean "plunder"?—Schumaker, M. Nature's servant-king.—Gowan, D. E. A rejoinder. [GF80.G46] 74-169103
1. Bible. O.T. Genesis I, 28—Criticism, interpretation, etc.—Addresses, essays, lectures. 2. Human ecology—Moral and religious aspects—Addresses, essays, lectures. I. Gowan, Donald E. Does "subdue" mean "plunder"? 1973. II. Schumaker, Millard. Nature's servant-king. 1973. III. Gowan, Donald E. A rejoinder, 1973. IV. Series: Kingston, Ont. Queen's Theological College. Occasional papers, 1.

CALLAWAY, Elvy E., 1889- 222'.11'09
In the beginning [by] E. E. Callaway. [Dayton, Ohio, ITB Associates, c1971] 141 p. map (on lining papers), port. 23 cm. [BS1237.C26] 71-185694 1.80
1. Eden. 2. Deluge. I. Title.

PONDER, Catherine. 222'.11'0922 B
The millionaires of Genesis, their prosperity secrets for you! / Catherine Ponder. Marina del Rey, Ca. : DeVorss, c1976. 178 p. ; 21 cm. (Her The Millionaires of the Bible) [BJ1611.2.P626] 76-19843 ISBN 0-87516-215-0 pbk. : 3.95
1. Bible. O.T.—Biography. 2. Success. 3. Patriarchs (Bible)—Biography. I. Title.

BULLA, Clyde Robert. 222'.11'0924
Joseph, the dreamer. Illustrated by Gordon Laite. New York, Crowell [1971] [64] p. illus. (part col.) 27 cm. A retelling of the Bible story in which Joseph is reunited with his family many years after being sold into slavery in Egypt. [BS580.J6B8 1971] 75-94791 ISBN 0-690-46554-8 4.95
1. Joseph, the patriarch—Juvenile literature. I. Laite, Gordon, illus. II. Title.

COLE, C. Donald. 222'.11'0924 B
Abraham : God's man of faith / by C. Donald Cole. Chicago : Moody Press, c1977. 223 p. ; 22 cm. [BS580.A3C57] 77-1268 ISBN 0-8024-0033-7 pbk. : 3.95
1. Abraham, the patriarch. 2. Bible. O.T.—Biography. 3. Patriarchs (Bible)—Biography. I. Title.

GAUBERT, Henri, 1895- 222'.11'0924
Abraham, loved by God. Translated by Lancelot Sheppard. New York, Hastings House [1968] xii, 195 p. illus., maps. 20 cm. (The Bible in history, v. 1) "A Giniger book." Translation of Abraham, l'ami de Dieu. Bibliography: p. 185-186. [BS580.A3G33 1968] 68-55435 5.95
1. Abraham, the patriarch. I. Title. II. Series.

RIVES, Elsie. 222'.11'0924 B
Abraham, man of faith / Elsie Rives ; illustrated by William N. McPheeters. Nashville : Broadman Press, c1976. 48 p. : col. ill. ; 24 cm. (Biblearn series) Discusses Abraham's efforts to obey God and establish a new nation in Canaan. [BS580.A3R58] 76-382767 3.95
1. Abraham, the patriarch—Juvenile literature. 2. Patriarchs (Bible)—Biography—Juvenile literature. I. McPheeters, William N. II. Title.

SUMMERS, Jester. 222'.11'0924 B
Joseph the forgiver / Jester Summers ; illustrated by Michael Sloan. Nashville : Broadman Press, c1976. 48 p. : col. ill. ; 24 cm. (Biblearn series) Discusses the events of Joseph's life that enabled him to provide for his family during a famine and forgive his brothers for their cruelties. [BS580.J6S95] 76-383002 ISBN 0-8054-4224-3 : 3.95
1. Joseph, the patriarch—Juvenile literature. 2. Bible. O.T.—Biography—Juvenile literature. I. Sloan, Michael. II. Title.

VAN SETERS, John. 222'.11'0924 B
Abraham in history and tradition / John Van Seters. New Haven : Yale University Press, 1975. xiii, 335 p. ; 25 cm. Includes bibliographical references and index. [BS580.A3V36] 74-20087 ISBN 0-300-01792-8 : 15.00
1. Abraham, the patriarch. 2. Bible. O.T. Genesis XII-XXV—Criticism, interpretation, etc. I. Title.

NAVARRA, Fernand, 1915- 222'.11'093
Noah's ark: I touched it. Edited with Dave Balsiger. Plainfield, N.J., Logos International [1974] xv, 137 p. illus. 21 cm. [DS51.A66N35] 73-91761 ISBN 0-88270-064-2 2.95 (pbk.).
1. Noah's ark. 2. Ararat, Mt. I. Title.

*VOS, Howard F. 222.11093
Genesis and archaeology. Chicago, Moody [c.1963] 127p. 17cm. (Colorportage lib., 499) Bibl. .39 pap.,
I. Title.

BLENKINSOPP, Joseph, 1927- 222.11095
From Adam to Abraham; introduction to sacred history. Glen Rock, N. J., Paulist [1966, c.1965] 127p. 19cm. (Insight ser.) Bibl. [BS1235.2.B5] 66-1730 .95 pap.,
1. Bible. O. T. Genesis I-XI — History of Biblical events. I. Title.

HOLT, John Marshall. 222.11095
The patriarchs of Israel. Nashville, Vanderbilt University Press, 1964. vii, 239 p. 23 cm. Bibliography: p. 219-224. [BS1235.2.H6] 64-13543
1. Bible. O. T. Genesis—Criticism, interpretation, etc. 2. Patriarchs (Bible) I. Title.

HUNT, Ignatius, 1920- 222'.11'095
The world of the patriarchs. Englewood Cliffs, N. J., Prentice [1967] xiii, 178p. maps (on lining papers) 22cm. (Prentice backgrounds to the Bible ser.) Bibl. [BS1180.H8] 67-17371 5.95
1. Bible. O. T. Genesis — History of contemporary events, etc. 2. Patriarchs (Bible) I. Title. II. Series.

PFEIFFER, Charles F. 222.11095
The patriarchal age. Grand Rapids, Mich., Baker Bk. House, 1961. 128p. Bibl. 61-12008 2.95
1. Bible. O. T. Genesis—History of contemporary events, etc. 2. Patriarchs (Bible) I. Title.

SLUSSER, Dorothy Mallet 222.11095
At the foot of the mountain; stories from the book of Exodus. Philadelphia, Westminster Press [c.1961] 156p. Bibl. 61-5397 3.00
1. Bible. O. T. Exodus—History of Biblical events. I. Title.

SLUSSER, Dorothy Mallett. 222.11095
At the foot of the mountain; stories from the book of Exodus. Philadelphia, Westminster Press [1961] 156 p. 21 cm. Includes bibliography. [BS1245.5.S55] 61-5397
1. Bible. O. T. Exodus — History of Biblical events. I. Title.

ADAM'S apple and other stories, 222'.11'09505 as told by teenagers to Marne Breckensiek. Liguori, Mo., Liguorian Books [1970] 86 p. illus. 19 cm. Five Biblical tales retold in modern language by teenagers. [BS551.2.A3] 70-151148 1.00
1. Bible stories, English. I. Breckensiek, Marne.

CHRISTIAN, Mary Blount. 222'.11'09505
When time began : the Creation for beginning readers : Genesis 1:1-2:3 for children / by Mary Blount Christian ; illustrated by Aline Cunningham. St. Louis : Concordia Pub. House, c1976. [48] p. : col. ill. ; 23 cm. (I can read a Bible story) Easy-to-read account of the creation. [BS651.C47] 76-14359 ISBN 0-570-07308-1 : 3.95 ISBN 0-570-07302-2 pbk. : 1.95
1. Creation—Juvenile literature. I. Cunningham, Aline. II. Title.

GOLANN, Cecil Paige, 1921- 222'.11'09505
Mission on a mountain : the story of Abraham and Isaac / Cecil P. Golann ; illustrated by H. Hechtkopf. Minneapolis : Lerner Publications Co., 1975, c1974. [32] p. : col. ill. ; 31 cm. Retells the Old Testament story of Abraham and his son Isaac. [BS580.A3G56 1975] 73-7498 ISBN 0-8225-0363-8 : 4.95
1. Abraham, the patriarch—Juvenile literature. 2. Isaac, the patriarch—Juvenile literature. I. Hechtkopf, H. II. Title.

HANCOCK, Sibyl. 222'.11'09505
An ark and a rainbow : Noah and the ark for beginning readers : Genesis 6-9 for children / by Sibyl Hancock ; illustrated by Aline Cunningham. St. Louis : Concordia Pub. House, c1976. [39] p. : col. ill. ; 23 cm. (I can read a Bible story) Easy-to-read retelling of the story of Noah and the ark he built to withstand a flood which covered the earth. [BS658.H25] 76-14924 ISBN 0-570-07309-X : 3.95
1. Noah's ark—Juvenile literature. 2. Deluge—Juvenile literature. I. Cunningham, Aline. II. Title.

HANCOCK, Sibyl. 222'.11'09505
Climbing up to nowhere : the Tower of Babel for beginning readers : Genesis 10-11:1-9 for children / by Sibyl Hancock ; illustrated by Aline Cunningham. St. Louis : Concordia Pub. House, c1977. [48] p. : col. ill. ; 22 cm. (I can read a Bible story) Retells the story of the Tower of Babel for beginning readers. [BS1238.B2H36] 77-7210 ISBN 0-570-07322-7 : 3.95. ISBN 0-570-07316-2 pbk. : 1.95
1. Babel, Tower of—Juvenile literature. I. Cunningham, Aline. II. Title.

HUTTON, Warwick. 222'.11'09505
Noah and the great flood / Warwick Hutton. New York : Atheneum, 1977. p. cm. "A Margaret K. McElderry book." An interpretation of the familiar Bible story using a simple text based on the King James version. [BS658.H87] 77-3217 ISBN 0-689-50098-X : 7.95
1. Noah—Juvenile literature. 2. Bible. O.T.—Biography—Juvenile literature. 3. Deluge—Juvenile literature. I. Title.

LEMKE, Stefan. 222'.11'09505
The creation / [art by Stefan Lemke and Marie-Luise Lemke-Prickern. Philadelphia : Fortress Press, 1976. [20] p. : col. ill. ; 19 cm. "A Sunshine book." Retells the story of the seven days during which God created the universe. [BS651.L36] 76-11268 ISBN 0-8006-1575-1 pbk. : 1.75
1. Creation—Juvenile literature. I. Lemke-Pricken, Marie-Luise, joint author. II. Title.

LEMKE, Stefan. 222'.11'09505
Noah's ark / [art by Stefan Lemke and Marie-Luise Lemke-Pricken]. Philadelphia : Fortress Press, 1976. [20] p. : col. ill. ; 19 cm. "A Sunshine book." Retells the story of Noah and the huge ark that God asked him to build. [BS658.L45] 76-11269 ISBN 0-8006-1576-X pbk. : 1.75
1. Noah's ark—Juvenile literature. I. Lemke-Pricken, Marie-Luise, joint author. II. Title.

PANA Creation, inc. 222'.11'09505
Beginning : the beginning of Earth, man, and nations / written by Pana Creation. La Mesa, Calif. : Pana Creation, c1976. v, 172 p. : ill. ; 19 cm. "The vice-president of Pana is Melvin D. Hasman ... who wrote the book as it was revealed to him." "Discussion guide for Beginning": p. [135]-163. Includes index. [BS651.P25 1976] 76-9929 ISBN 0-915300-02-8 : 4.95
1. Bible. O.T. Genesis I-XI—Miscellanea. 2. Creation. I. Hasman, Melvin D. II. Title.

WALSH, Bill. 222'.11'09505
Noah and the ark : a cartoon Bible story / by Bill Walsh ; with an afterword for parents and teachers by Charlie Sheed. Kansas City, [Kan.] : Sheed Andrews and McMeel, c1976. p. cm. (Cartoon Bible stories series) A cartoon version of how Noah builds the ark in preparation for the great flood. [BS658.W25] 76-57955 ISBN 0-8362-0697-5 pbk. : 1.95
1. Noah's ark—Caricatures and cartoons—Juvenile literature. I. Title.

*BUTLER, Hugh McKay 222.116.
The Christian and Hebrew atomic bomb; an exposure of the works of the devil Satan. New York, Exposition [c.1964] 91p. 22cm. 3.50
I. Title.

*ANDEEN, G. Kenneth 222.117
Genesis, the book of beginnings. Ed. by Jerome Nilssen. Illus. by Robert McGovern. Philadelphia, Lutheran Church Pr. [c.1966] 112 p. illus. 21 cm. (Sunday Church school ser., term 3) .90; 1.00 pap., teacher's guide
I. Title.

TRAHERNE, Thomas, d.1674 222.117
Meditations on the six days of the creation (1717). Introd. by George Robert Guffey. Los Angeles. William Andrews Clark Memorial Lib., Univ. of Calif., 1966. xvi, 91p. 22cm. (Augustan Reprint Soc. Pubn. no. 119) Pt. 1 of A collection of meditations and devotions reprinted from the British Mus. copy. Bibl. [BS1225.T7 1717a] 66-6698 .90 pap.,
1. Bible. O.T. Genesis I. Title. II. Series.

BAIRD, Jesse Hays, 1889- 222.12
From out of the west; messages from western pulpits. Stockton, Calif., The Lantern Press, 1962. Caldwell, Id., The Caxton printers, ltd., 1931. 156 p. illus. 21 cm. 2 p. l., 134 p. 20 cm. Includes brief biographies of Presbyterian ministers and illustrations of Presbyterian churches. [BX9178.B3294G6] NUC63 31-13256
1. Commandments, Ten—Sermons. 2. Sermons, American. 3. Presbyterian Church Sermons. I. Baird, Jesse Hays, 1889- II. Title. III. Title: God's law of life, thirteen sermons,

BEN-DAVID, Eliezer. 222'.12
Out of the iron furnace : the Jewish redemption from ancient Egypt and the delivery from spiritual bondage / by Eliezer Ben-David ; translated and adapted by Yaakov Feitman. New York : Shengold Publishers, c1975. 144 p. ; 23 cm. An expanded translation of Mateh haElohim. Includes bibliographical references and index. [BS1245.5.B4513] 74-84829 ISBN 0-88400-040-0 : 5.95
1. Plagues of Egypt—Miscellanea. I. Feitman, Yaakov. II. Title.

COATS, George W. 222'.12
Rebellion in the wilderness; the murmuring motif in the wilderness, traditions of the Old Testament [by] George W. Coats. Nashville, Abingdon Press [1968] 288 p. 22 cm. Bibliography: p. 265-275. [BS1245.2.C59] 68-17444
1. Jews—History—To 1200 B.C. 2. Bible. O.T. Exodus—Criticism, interpretation, etc. 3. Bible. O.T. Numbers—Criticism, interpretation, etc. I. Title.

CORNWALL, E. Judson. 222'.12
Let us draw near / Judson Cornwall. Plainfield, N.J. : Logos International, c1977. 168 p. : ill. ; 21 cm. [BM654.C67] 77-24832 ISBN 0-88270-226-2 : 2.95
1. Bible. O.T. Exodus XXV-XXX—Miscellanea. 2. Tabernacle—Miscellanea. I. Title.

GOLDIN, Judah, 1914- 222'.12
The Song at the sea; being a commentary on a commentary in two parts. New Haven, Yale University Press, 1971. xxii, 290 p. 23 cm. "Part II. Shirta: a new translation, with commentary": p. [63]-249. Includes bibliographical references. [BM517.M43G63] 73-140530 ISBN 0-300-01409-0 10.00
1. Mekilta. Massekta de-Shirah—Commentaries. 2. Bible. O.T. Exodus XV, 1-21—Commentaries. I. Mekilta. Massekta de-Shirah. English. 1971. II. Title.

LEE, J Fitzgerald. 222.12
The great migration; the origin of the Jewish people and materials towards the solution of a world problem. 2d ed., rev. and enl. by G. FitzGerald-Lee. London, New York, Skeffington, 1951. 212 p. illus. 19 cm. [BS1245.L37 1951] 51-5458
1. Jews—Origin. 2. Indians of Central America—Antiq. 3. Indians of Mexico—Antiq. 4. Egypt—Antiq. 5. Indians—Origin. 6. Man—Migrations. 7. Bible. O. T. Pentateuch—Evidences, authority, etc. I. Title.

*SAXE, Grace 222.12
Studies in Exodus, arranged by Grace Saxe, rev. by Irving L. Jensen. Chicago. Moody [1967] 111p. diagrs. 22cm. (Bible self-study ser., 30-8411) Cover title. .95 pap.,
1. Bible. O.T. Exodus—Commentaries. I. Jensen, Irving L, ed. II. Title.

RHODES, Daniel D 222.12007
A covenant community; a study of the book of Exodus. Richmond, John Knox Press [1964] 71 p. 23 cm. (The Every member Bible study series) Bibliography: p. 9-11. [BS1245.R5] 64-12503
1. Bible. O.T. Exodus — Study. I. Title.

RHODES, Daniel D. 222.12007
A covenant community; a study of the book of Exodus. Richmond, Va., Knox [c.1964] 71p. 23cm. (Every member Bible study ser.) Bibl. 64-12503 .60 pap.,
1. Bible. O. T. Exodus—Study. I. Title.

OWENS, John Joseph, 1918- 222'.12'044
Exodus / John Joseph Owens. 1st ed. New York : Harper & Row, c1977. p. cm. (His Analytical key to the Old Testament) [BS1245.5.O9 1977] 77-14404 ISBN 0-06-066405-3 pbk. : 4.95
1. Bible. O.T. Exodus—Translating. 2. Hebrew language—Glossaries, vocabularies, etc. 3. Hebrew language—Translating into English. I. Bible. O.T. Exodus. Hebrew. Asher. 1977. II. Title. III. Series.

FINEGAN, Jack, 1908- 222.1206
Let my people go; a journey through Exodus. [1st ed.] New York, Harper & Row [c1963] 148 p. illus. 22 cm. [BS1245.2.F5] 63-7603
1. Bible. O.T. Exodus — Criticism, interpretation, etc. I. Title.

FINEGAN, Jack, 1908- 222.1206
Let my people go; a journey through Exodus. New York, Harper [c.1963] 148p. illus. 22cm. Bibl. 63-7603 3.75
1. Bible. O.T. Exodus—Criticism, interpretation, etc. I. Title.

GUTZKE, Manford George. 222'.12'06
Plain talk on Exodus / Manford George Gutzke. Grand Rapids : Zondervan Pub. House, [1974] 244 p. : ill. ; 21 cm. [BS1245.2.G87] 74-4954 pbk. : 2.95
1. Bible. O.T. Exodus—Criticism, interpretation, etc. 2. Salvation. I. Title.

HABEL, Norman C. 222.1206
Wait a minute, Moses! [Reissue] St. Louis, Concordia [c.1965] 97p. illus. 20cm. (Current perspectives of life for Christian youth, 2) [BV1549.2.H2] 65-23701 1.00 pap.,
1. Religious education—Text-books for young people. 2. Exodus, The—Study and teaching. I. Title.

HEBERT, Arthur Gabriel, 1886- 222.1206
When Israel came out of Egypt. Richmond, Va., John Knox [c.1961. 128p. illus. Bibl. 61-14511 1.75 bds.,
1. Jews—Hist.—To entrance into Canaan. 2. Typology (Theology) I. Title.

HERBERT, Arthur Gabriel, 1886- 222.1206
When Israel came out of Egypt. Richmond, John Knox Pess [1961] 128p. illus. 19cm. Includes bibliography. [BS1245.2.H4 1961] 61-14511
1. Jews—Hist.—To entrance into Canaan. 2. Typology (Theology) I. Title.

KNIGHT, George Angus Fulton, 1909- 222'.12'06
Theology as narration : a commentary on the Book of Exodus / George A. F. Knight. Grand Rapids : Eerdmans, 1977. xiv, 269 p. ; 22 cm. [BS1245.3.K58 1977] 76-20463 ISBN 0-8028-3489-2 : 4.95
1. Bible. O.T. Exodus—Commentaries. I. Title.

LENSSEN, F A 222'.12'06
The Bible on the exodus, by F. A. Lenssen. Translated by F. Vander Heijden. De Pere, Wis., St. Norbert Abbey Press, 1966. 115 p. 17 cm. Translation of De Rijbel over de uittocht. Bibliography: p. [111]-115. [BS680.E9L43] 66-22821
1. Exodus, The — Biblical teaching. I. Title.

O'CONNELL, Kevin G. 222'.12'066
The Theodotionic revision of the Book of Exodus; a contribution to the study of the early history of the transmission of the Old Testament in Greek [by] Kevin G. O'Connell. Cambridge, Harvard University Press, 1972. 329 p. 25 cm. (Harvard Semitic monographs, v. 3) Thesis—Harvard University. Bibliography: p. 327-329. [BS1245.2.O28] 70-160026 ISBN 0-674-87785-3
1. Bible. O.T. Exodus—Criticism, Textual. 2. Bible. O.T. Exodus. Greek—Versions—Theodotion. I. Title. II. Series.

BIBLE. O. T. EXODUS. ENGLISH. 1962. REVISED STANDARD. 222.1207
Exodus; a commentary [by] Martin Noth. Philadelphia, Westminster Press [1962] 283p. 23cm. (The Old Testament library) Translation of the commentary by J. S. Bowden from Das sweite Buch Mose, Exodus. [BS1245.3.N613 1962] 62-7940
1. Bible. O. T. Exodus—Commentaries. I. Noth, Martin, 1902- ed. II. Title. III. Series.

COLE, Robert Alan. 222'.12'07
Exodus; an introduction and commentary, by R. Alan Cole. [1st ed.] Downers Grove, Ill., Inter-Varsity Press [1973] 239 p. 20 cm. (Tyndale Old Testament commentaries) [BS1245.3.C6] 72-97952 ISBN 0-87784-865-3 5.95
1. Bible. O.T. Exodus—Commentaries. I. Title.

GREENBERG, Moshe. 222'.12'07
Understanding Exodus. New York, Published by Behrman House for the Melton Research Center of the Jewish Theological Seminary of America [1969- pt. 28 cm. (Heritage of

Biblical Israel series, v. 2) Bibliography: pt. 1, p. 205-214. [BS1245.3.G7] 76-13628
1. Bible. O.T. Exodus—Commentaries. I. Title. II. Series.

HUEY, F. B., 1925- 222'.12'07
Exodus : a study guide commentary / F. B. Huey, Jr. Grand Rapids : Zondervan Publishing House, c1977. 142 p. ; 21 cm. (Study guide series) Bibliography: p. 141-142. [BS1245.3.H83] 77-9995 ISBN 0-310-36053-6 pbk. : 2.50
1. Bible. O.T. Exodus—Commentaries. I. Bible. O.T. Exodus. English. 1977. II. Title.

JACOB BEN ISAAC, of 222.1207
Janow, 1550-1628.
Tzeenah u-reenah; a Jewish commentary on the Book of Exodus, by Norman C. Gore. [1st ed.] New York, Vantage Press [1965] 258 p. 21 cm. A translation based on the Metz edition of 1768. Bibliography: p. 258. [BS1245.J283] 65-2490
1. Bible. O.T. Exodus—Commentaries. I. Gore, Norman C., ed. and tr. II. Title.

JACOB BEN ISAAC, of 222.1207
Janow, 1550-1628
Tzeenah u-reenah; a Jewish commentary of the Book of Exodus [Tr. from Yiddish] by Norman C. Gore. New York, Vantage [c.1965] 258p. 21cm. Tr. based on the Metz ed. of 1768. Bibl. [BS1245.J283] 65-2490 5.00
1. Bible. O. T. Exodus—Commentaries. I. Gore, Norman C., ed. and tr. II. Title.

PINK, Arthur Walkington, 222.1207
1886-1952
Gleanings in Exodus. Chicago, Moody [1962] 384p. 24cm. 62-1359 4.50
1. Bible. O.T. Exodus—Commentaries. I. Title.

RAMM, Bernard L., 222'.12'07
1916-
His way out. by Bernard L. Ramm. Glendale, Calif., G/L Regal Books [1974] 213 p. 18 cm. (A Bible commentary for laymen) Bibliography: p. 211-213. [BS1245.2.R35] 73-87284 ISBN 0-8307-0277-6 1.45 (pbk.)
1. Bible. O.T. Exodus—Criticism, interpretation, etc. I. Title.

BIBLE. O.T. Exodus. 222'.12'077
English. New English. 1972.
Exodus, commentary by Ronald E. Clements. Cambridge [Eng.] Cambridge University Press, 1972. viii, 248 p. map. 21 cm. (Cambridge Bible commentary: New English Bible) Includes bibliographical references. [BS1243.C55 1972] 77-179983 ISBN 0-521-08218-8
1. Bible. O.T. Exodus—Commentaries. I. Clements, Ronald Ernest, 1929- II. Title. III. Series.

CHILDS, Brevard S. 222'.12'077
The book of Exodus; a critical, theological commentary [by] Brevard S. Childs. Philadelphia, Westminster Press [1974] xxv, 659 p. 23 cm. (The Old Testament library) Bibliography: p. [xxi]-xxv. [BS1245.3.C45] 73-23120 ISBN 0-664-20985-8
1. Bible. O.T. Exodus—Commentaries. I. Bible. O.T. Exodus. English. Childs. 1974. II. Title. III. Series.

NOTH, Martin, 1902- 222.12077
Exodus; a commentary. Philadelphia, Westminster Press [1962] 283 p. 23 cm. (The Old Testament library) "Translated by J. S. Bowden from ... Das zweite Buch Mose, Exodus." [BS1245.3.N613] 62-7940
1. Bible. O.T. Exodus — Commentaries. 2. Bible. O.T. Exodus. English. 1962. Revised standard. I. Title. II. Series.

NOTH, Martin, 1902- 222.12077
1968.
Exodus; a commentary. Philadelphia, Westminster Press [1962] 283 p. 23 cm. (The Old Testament library) "Translated by J. S. Bowden from ... Das zweite Buch Mose, Exodus." [BS1245.3.N613 1962] 62-7940
1. Bible. O.T. Exodus—Commentaries. I. Bible. O.T. Exodus. English. 1962. Revised standard. II. Title. III. Series.

PEARLMAN, Moshe, 1911- 222'.12'09
Moses; where it all began. Photography by David Harris. [1st American ed.] New York, Abelard-Schuman [1974, c1973] 224 p. illus. 28 cm. "An adaptation of the title The first days of Israel by Moshe Pearlman." [BS580.M6P39 1973] 73-21320 ISBN 0-200-00138-8 8.95
1. Moses. 2. Jews—History—To 953 B.C. 3. Levant—Description and travel—Views. I. Pearlman, Moshe, 1911- The first days of Israel in the footsteps of Moses. II. Title.

PFEIFFER, Charles F 222.12095
Egypt and the Exodus. Grand Rapids, Baker Book House, 1964. 96 p. illus., map. 28 cm. ([Old Testament history series]) Bibliography: p. 89-91. [BS1245.5P4] 64-16940
1. Bible. O. T. Exodus—History of Biblical events. I. Title.

PFEIFFER, Charles F. 222.12095
Egypt and the Exodus. Grand Rapids, Mich., Baker Bk. [c.]1964. 96p. illus., map. 23cm. (Old Testament hist. ser.), v.4) Bibl. 64-16940 2.95
1. Bibl. O. T. Exodus—History of Biblical events. I. Title.

GRAHAM, Lorenz B. 222'.12'09505
A road down in the sea [by] Lorenz Graham. Pictures by Gregorio Prestopino. New York, T. Y. Crowell [1970] [48] p. (chiefly col. illus.) 21 cm. The story of the Exodus told in the speech patterns and images of African people newly acquainted with the English language. [BS680.E9G7] 74-113854 ISBN 0-690-70500-X
1. Exodus, The—Juvenile literature. I. Prestopino, Gregorio, illus. II. Title.

ERDMAN, Charles Rosenbury, 222.13
1866-
The book of Leviticus, an exposition. New York, Revell [1951] 144 p. 20 cm. [BS1255.E7] 51-2629
1. Bible. O. T. Leviticus—Commentaries. I. Title.

JUKES, Andrew John, 1815- 222'.13
1901.
The law of the offerings. Grand Rapids, Mich. Kregel Publications [1966] 219 p. 20 cm. "Reprinted complete and unabridged from the 17th edition." First published in 1847 under title: The law of the offerings in Levitieus 1.-vii. considered as the appointed figure of the various aspects of the offering of the body of Jesus Christ. [BS1255.J8] 66-19198
1. Bible. O. T. Leviticus 1-vii — Theology. 2. Sacrifice — Biblical teaching. 3. Typology (Theology) I. Title.

PFEIFFER, Charles F. 222.13
The book of Leviticus, a study manual. Grand Rapids, Baker Book House, 1957. 60 p. 20 cm. (Shield Bible study series) [BS1255.P4] 57-14665
1. Bible. O.T. Leviticus—Study—Outlines, syllabi, etc.

*SAXE, Grace. 222.13
Studies in Leviticus, arranged by Grace Saxe, rev. by Irving L. Jensen. Chicago, Moody [1967] 80p. 22cm. (Bible self-study ser., 30-8413) Cover title. .95 pap.,
1. Bible. O.T. Leviticus—Commentaries. I. Jensen, Irving L. ed. II. Title.

BARCLAY, Robert Anderson 222.1306
The law givers: Leviticus and Deuteronomy. London, Lutterworth Press; Nashville, Abingdon [1964] 85p. 20cm. (Bible guides, no. 3) 64-2418 1.00 pap.,
1. Bible. O. T. Leviticus—Criticism, interpretation, etc. 2. Bible. O. T. Deuteronomy—Criticism, interpretation, etc. I. Title.

BIBLE. O.T. Leviticus. 222.1307
English. 1965.Revisedstandard
Leviticus; a commentary[by] Martin Noth [Tr. from German] Philadelphia, Westminster [c.1962, 1965] 208p. 23cm. (Old Testament lib.) [BS1255.3.N6] 65-11498 5.00
1. Bible. O.T. Leviticus—Commentaries. I. Noth, Martin, 1902- ed. II. Title. III. Series.

BIBLE. O.T. 222'.13'077
Leviticus. English. New English. 1976.
Leviticus / commentary by J. R. Porter. Cambridge ; New York : Cambridge University Press, 1976. x, 231 p. ; 21 cm. (The Cambridge Bible Commentary, New English Bible) Includes index. Bibliography: p. 225-226. [BS1253.P67] 75-20831 ISBN 0-521-08638-8 : 16.50 ISBN 0-521-09773-8 pbk. :
1. Bible. O.T. Leviticus—Commentaries. I. Porter, Joshua Roy. II. Title. III. Series.

DE WELT, Don. 222'.13'077
Leviticus / by Don De Welt ; paraphrase by Kenneth N. Taylor. Joplin, Mo. : College Press, c1975. viii, 498 p. : ill. ; 23 cm. (Bible study textbook series) Includes text of American revised version of Leviticus. Includes index. Bibliography: p. 481-482. [BS1255.3.D4] 75-328945
1. Bible. O.T. Leviticus—Commentaries. I. Taylor, Kenneth Nathaniel. II. Bible. O.T. Leviticus. English. American revised. 1975. III. Title.

NOTH, Martin, 1902- 222.13077
Leviticus; a commentary. Philadelphia, Westminster Press [1965] 208 p. 23 cm. (The Old Testament library) "Translated by J. S. Anderson from ... Das dritte Buch Mose, Leviticus." [BS1255.3.N613] 65-11498
1. Bible. O.T. Leviticus — Commentaries. I. Bible. O.T. Leviticus. English. 1965. Revised standard. II. Title. III. Series.

NOTH, Martin, 1902- 222'.13'077
1968.
Leviticus : a commentary / Martin Noth. Rev. ed. Philadelphia : Westminster Press, c1977. p. cm. (The Old Testament library) Rev. translation of Das dritte Buch Mose, Leviticus. [BS1255.3.N613 1977] 77-7654 ISBN 0-664-20774-X : 10.00
1. Bible. O.T. Leviticus—Commentaries. I. Bible. O.T. Leviticus. English. Revised standard. 1977. II. Title. III. Series.

ERDMAN, Charles Rosenbury, 222.14
1866-
The book of Numbers, an exposition. Westwood, N. J., Revell [1952] 142 p. 20 cm. [BS1265.E7] 52-3463
1. Bible. O. T. Numbers—Commentaries. I. Title.

*JENSEN, Irving L. 222.14
Numbers; journey to God's rest-land. Chicago, Moody [c.1964] 128p. 17cm. (Colportage lib. 505) .39 pap.,
I. Title.

REEVES, James. 222'.14
The angel and the donkey. Illustrated by Edward Ardizzone. New York, McGraw-Hill [1970, c1969] [32] p. illus. (part col.) 20 x 25 cm. A donkey hears a voice that his wise master does not and by doing so saves the man's life. [BS580.B3R4 1970] 75-102453 4.50
1. Balaam, the prophet—Juvenile literature. I. Ardizzone, Edward, 1900- illus. II. Title.

*SAXE, Grace. 222.14
Studies in Numbers and Deuteronomy, arranged by Grace Saxe, rev. by Irving L. Jensen. Chicago, Moody [1967] 111p. 22cm. (Bible self-study ser.) .95 pap.,
1. Bible. O. T. Numbers—Study, outlines, syllabi, etc. 2. Bible. O. T. Deuteronomy—Study, outlines, syllabi, etc. I. Jensen, Irving L. ed. II. Title.

HESLOP, William Greene, 222.1407
1886-
Nuggets from Numbers; studies of selected portions from the book of Numbers. Butler, Ind., Higley Press [c1958954 122p. 20cm. [BS1265.3.H45] 59-43542
1. Bible. O. T. Numbers—Commentaries. I. Title.

BIBLE. O.T. Numbers. 222'.14'077
English. New English. 1976.
Numbers / commentary by John Sturdy. Cambridge, [Eng.] ; New York : Cambridge University Press, 1976. x, 252 p. : maps ; 20 cm. (The Cambridge Bible commentary, New English Bible) Includes index. Bibliography: p. 246. [BS1263.S78] 75-39373 ISBN 0-521-08632-9 : 17.95 ISBN 0-521-09776-2 pbk. :
1. Bible. O.T. Numbers—Commentaries. I. Sturdy, John. II. Title. III. Series.

NOTH, Martin, 1902- 222'.14'077
1968.
Numbers: a commentary. [Translated by James D. Martin from the German.] Philadelphia, Westminster Press [1968] x, 258 p. 24 cm. (The Old Testament library) Translation of Das vierte Buch Mose, Numeri. [BS1265.3.N613 1968] 69-12129 6.50
1. Bible. O.T. Numbers—Commentaries. I. Bible. O.T. Numbers. English. Revised standard. 1968. II. Title. III. Series.

*BLENKINSOPP, Joseph. 222.15
Deuteronomy. Milwaukee, Bruce [1968] 54p. 18cm. (Scripture discussion outlines) .75 pap.,
1. Bible. O. T. Deuteronomy—Commentaries. I. Title.

ERDMAN, Charles Rosenbury, 222.15
1866-
The book of Deuteronomy, an exposition. Westwood, N. J., Revell [1953] 95 p. 20 cm. [BS1275.E7] 53-1989
1. Bible. O. T. Deuteronomy— Commentaries. I. Title.

MANLEY, George Thomas, 222.15
The book of the law; studies in the date of Deuteronomy. [1st American ed.] Grand Rapids, Eerdmans [1957] 192p. map. 23cm. Bibliographical footnotes. [BS1275.M29] 57-14191
1. Bible. O. T. Deuteronomy—Criticism, Interpretation, etc. I. Title.

MITTMANN, Siegfried. 222'.15
Deuteronomium 1:1-6:3 literarkritisch und traditionsgeschichtlich untersucht / Siegfried Mittmann. Berlin ; New York : de Gruyter, 1975. x, 188 p. ; 24 cm. (Beiheft zur Zeitschrift fur die alttestamentliche Wissenschaft ; 139) A revision of the author's Habilitationsschrift, Tubingen, 1972. Bibliography: p. [185]-188. [BS410.Z5 vol. 139] [BS1275.2] 75-522134 ISBN 3-11-005728-X : DM88.00
1. Bible. O.T. Deuteronomy I-VI, 3—Criticism, interpretation, etc. I. Title. II. Series: Zeitschrift fur die alttestamentliche Wissenschaft : Beihefte ; 139.

RAD, Gerhard von, 1901- 222.15
Studies in Deuteronomy; translated by David Stalker. Chicago, H. Regnery Co., 1953. 96p. 22cm. (Studies in Biblical theology, no.9) [BS1275.R32 1953a] 54-1928
1. Bible. O. T. Deuteronomy—Criticism, interpretation, etc. I. Title.

THOMPSON, John Arthur, 222'.15
1913-
Deuteronomy : an introduction and commentary / by J. A. Thompson. London : Inter-Varsity Press, c1974. 320 p. ; 20 cm. (The Tyndale Old Testament commentaries) Includes bibliographical references. [BS1275.3.T46 1974] 74-14303 ISBN 0-87784-882-3 : 7.95
1. Bible. O.T. Deuteronomy—Commentaries.
Distributed by Inter-Vansity Dawners Grove, Il. 60575.

OBERST, Bruce. 222'.15'007
Deuteronomy. Thought questions, by Don DeWelt. Summary by Adam Clarke. Joplin, Mo., College Press [1968] viii, 452 p. illus., maps. 22 cm. (Bible study textbook series) Bibliography: p. 449-452. [BS1275.5.O2] 70-1070 5.95
1. Bible. O.T. Deuteronomy—Study—Outlines, syllabi, etc.

NICHOLSON, Ernest 222'.15'01
Wilson.
Deuteronomy and tradition. by E. W. Nicholson. Oxford, Blackwell, 1967. xii, 145 p. 23 cm. (B 67-11833) Bibliography: p. 126-132. [BS1275.2.N5] 67-91693
1. Bible. O. T. Deuteronomy — Introductions. I. Title.

NICHOLSON, Ernest 222'.15'01
Wilson.
Deuteronomy and tradition, by E. W. Nicholson. [American ed.] Philadelphia, Fortress Press [1967] 145 p. 23 cm. Bibliography: p. 126-132. [BS1275.2.N5 1967b] 67-22200
1. Bible. O.T. Deuteronomy—Introductions. I. Title.

ALLEGRO, John Marco, 222.15044
1923-
The Shapira affair. [1st ed.] Garden City, N.Y., Doubleday, 1965. 139 p. illus., facsims., map. ports. 22 cm. [BS1272.5.S5A55] 65-10640
1. Shapira, Moses Wilheim, 1830?-1884. 2. Bible. Manuscripts, Hebrew. O.T. Deuteronomy. I. Title.

ALLEGRO, John Marco, 222.15044
1923-
The Shapira affair. [1st ed.] Garden City, N.Y., Doubleday, 1965. 139 p. illus., facsims., map, ports. 22 cm. [BS1272.5.S5A55] 65-10640
1. Shapira, Moses Wilheim, 1830?-1884. 2. Bible. Manuscripts, Hebrew. O. T. Deuteronomy. I. Title.

BLIGH, John. 222'.15'06
Christian Deuteronomy : (Luke 9-18) / by John Bligh. Staten Island, N.Y. : Alba House, 1975, c1970. 154 p. ; 13 cm. (Scripture for meditation ; 5) Includes index. [BS1275.4.B55 1975] 74-31349 ISBN 0-8189-0310-4 pbk. : 1.95
1. Bible. O.T. Deuteronomy—Meditations. 2. Bible. N.T. Luke—Criticism, interpretation, etc. I. Title. II. Series.

CLEMENTS, Ronald 222'.15'06
Ernest, 1929-
God's chosen people; a theological interpretation of the book of Deuteronomy [by] R. E. Clements. Valley Forge, Judson Press [1969, c1968] 126 p. 19 cm. Bibliographical footnotes. [BS1275.2.C5 1969] 74-82154 2.50
1. Bible. O.T. Deuteronomy—Theology. I. Title.

CARMICHAEL, Calum M. 222'.15'066
The laws of deuteronomy [by] Calum M. Carmichael. Ithaca, Cornell University Press [1974] 277 p. 22 cm. Includes bibliographical references. [BS1275.2.C34 1974] 73-19206 ISBN 0-8014-0824-5 11.50
1. Bible. O.T. Deuteronomy—Criticism, interpretation, etc. 2. Law (Theology)—Biblical teaching. I. Title.

BIBLE. O. T. 222.1507
Deuteronomy. English. 1966, Revised standard.
Deuteronomy; a commentary [by] Gerhard von Rad. [Tr. by Dorothea Barton] Philadelphia, Westminster [1966] 211p. 23cm. (Old Testament lib.) Tr. of Das funfte Buch Mose: Deuteronomium, which was first pub. in 1964 as v. 8 of Das Alte Testament deutsch,

ed. by V. Herntrich, A. Weiser. Bibl. [BS1275.3.R31966] 66-23088 5.00
1. Bible. O. T. Deuteronomy — Commentaries. I. Rad, Gerhard von, 1901- ed. II. Herntrich, Volkmar, 1908- ed. Das Alte Testament deutsch. (Series.) III. Title.

BIBLE. O.T. 222'.15'07
Deuteronomy. English. Craigie. 1976.
The Book of Deuteronomy / by Peter C. Craigie. Grand Rapids : Eerdmans, c1976. 424 p. ; 22 cm. (The New international commentary on the Old Testament) Includes the text of Deuteronomy. Includes indexes. Bibliography: p. 69-72. [BS1273.C7] 75-45372 ISBN 0-8028-2355-6 : 10.95
1. Bible. O.T. Deuteronomy—Commentaries. I. Craigie, Peter C. II. Title. III. Series.

KLINE, Meredith G. 222.1507
Treaty of the great King; the covenant structure of Deuteronomy: studies and commentary. Grand Rapids, Mich., Eerdmans [c.1963] 149p. 22cm. Bibl. 63-11497 3.50
1. Bible. O. T. Deuteronomy—Commentaries. I. Title.

RAD, Gerhard von, 1901- 222.1507
Deuteronomy; a commentary. [Translated by Dorothea Barton] Philadelphia, Westminster Press [1966] 211 p. 23 cm. (The Old Testament library) Translation of Das funfte Buch Mose: Deuteronomium, which was first published in 1964 as v. 8 of Das Alte Testament deutsch, edited by V. Herntrich and A. Weiser. Bibliographical footnotes. [BS1275.3.R3 1966] 66-23088
1. Bible. O.T. Deuteronomy—Commentaries. I. Bible. O.T. Deuteronomy. English. 1966. Revised standard. II. Title. III. Series.

SCHNEIDER, Bernard N. 222'.15'07
Deuteronomy, a favored book of Jesus, by Bernard N. Schneider. Grand Rapids, Mich., Baker Book House [1970] 163 p. illus., map. 20 cm. Bibliography: p. 163. [BS1275.3.S33] 78-116857 2.95
1. Bible. O.T. Deuteronomy—Commentaries. I. Title.

SCHULTZ, Samuel J. 222'.15'07
Deuteronomy: the gospel of love, by Samuel J. Schultz. Chicago, Moody Press [1971] 127 p. 20 cm. (Everyman's Bible commentary) [BS1275.3.S35] 72-155693 0.95
1. Bible. O.T. Deuteronomy—Commentaries. I. Title. II. Series.

BIBLE. O.T. 222'.15'077
Deuteronomy. English. New English. 1973.
Deuteronomy. Commentary by Anthony Phillips. [Cambridge, Eng.] Cambridge University Press, 1973. xii, 237 p. 20 cm. (The Cambridge Bible commentary: New English Bible) Bibliography: p. 234. [BS1275.3.P47] 73-77172 ISBN 0-521-08636-1
1. Bible. O.T. Deuteronomy—Commentaries. I. Phillips, Anthony. II. Title. III. Series.
Distributed by Cambridge University Press, New York, 11.95.

BROKKE, Harold J. 222.16
The law is holy. Minneapolis, Bethany Fellowship [1963] 175p. 20cm. 63-4471 2.50
1. Commandments, Ten. I. Title.

*CHAPPELL, Clovis G. 222.16
Ten rules for living / Clovis G. Chappell. Grand Rapids : Baker Book House, 1976 c1966. 178 p. ; 20 cm. (Clovis G. Chappell library) [BS1281] ISBN 0-8010-2385-8 pbk. : 2.95
1. Commandments, Ten. I. Title.

CHAPPELL, Clovis G., 1882- 222.16
Ten rules for living. Nashville, Abingdon [1961, c.1938] 178p. (Apex bks., F2) .95 pap.,
1. Commandments. Ten—Sermons. 2. Methodist church—Sermons. 3. Sermons, American. I. Title.

COFFMAN, James Burton. 222.16
The Ten commandments. yesterday and today. [Weste)0wood, N. J.] Revell [1961] 128p. 21cm. Includes bibliography. [BV4655.C58] 61-13617
1. Commandments, Ten. I. Title.

COFFMAN, James Burton 222.16
The Ten commandments, yesterday and today. [Westwood, N. J.] Revell [c.1961] 128p. Bibl. 61-13617 2.50 bds.,
1. Commandments, Ten. I. Title.

CONNERY, John R, 1913- 222.16
Teacher's manual in Ferrell, William F. Loyalty, the Commandments in modern life. Chicago, Loyola University Press, 1949-51. [BV4655.F4 1949] 50-31748
I. Title.

DAVIDMAN, Joy. 222.16
Smoke on the mountain; an interpretation of the Ten commandments. Philadelphia, Westminster Press [1954] 141p. 21cm. [BV4655.D32] 54-6099
1. Commandments, Ten. I. Title.

DAVIES, Arthur Powell. 222.16
The Ten commandments. [New Uork] New American Library [1956] 143p. illus. 18cm. (A Signet key book, Ks343) Includes bibliography. [BV4655.D327] 56-56
1. Commandments, Ten. I. Title.

ELLER, Vernard. 222'.16
The Mad morality; or, the Ten Commandments revisited. Nashville, Abingdon Press [1970] 80 p. illus. 28 cm. [BV4655.E63] 79-112885 ISBN 0-687-22899-9 2.79
1. Commandments, Ten I. Mad. II. Title. III. Title: The Ten Commandments revisited.

FEE, Zephyrus Roy, 1890- 222.16
The great commandments of God. Dallas, Wilkinson Pub. Co. [1954] 281p. illus. 20cm. Includes bibliography. [BV4655.F38] 55-16798
1. Commandments, ten. I. Title.

FORD, William Herschel, 222.16
1900-
Simple sermons on the Ten commandments. Introd. by Robert G. Lee. Grand Rapids, Zondervan Pub. House [1956] 138p. 20cm. [BV4655.F64] 56-25036
1. Commandments, Ten—Sermons. 2. Baptists—Sermons. 3. Sermons, American. I. Title.

FOX, Emmet. 222.16
The Ten commandments the master key to life. 1st ed. New York, Harper [1953] 158 p. 20 cm. [BV4655.F69] 53-8369
1. Commandments, Ten. 2. New Thought.

FROST, Gerhard E. 222.16
The law perfect; ten studies on the Commandments. Minneapolis, Augsburg Pub. House [1952] 96 p. 20 cm. (Ten-week teacher-training course books) [BV4655.F7] 52-10195
1. Commandments, Ten. I. Title.

GOLDMAN, Solomon, 1893- 222.16
1953.
The Ten commandments. Edited and with an introd. by Maurice Samuel. [Chicago] University of Chicago Press [1956] 224 p. illus. 23 cm. Includes bibliography. [BM520.75.G6] 56-10081
1. Bible. O.T. Exodus XIX-XX—Commentaries. 2. Commandments, Ten. I. Title.

GULLIXSON, Thaddeus Frank, 222.16
1882-
God's hall of mirrors; messages based on the Ten commandments, by T. F. Gullixson. Minneapolis, Augsburg [1966] vii, 120p. 20cm. [BV4655.G8] 66-6039 2.50 pap.,
1. Commandments, Ten. I. Title.

HENSEL, Harry W 222.16
The First commandment. San Gabriel, Calif., Willing Pub. Co. [1959] 160p. 20cm. Includes bibliography. [BV4657.H44] 59-43144
1. Commandments, Ten—Other gods. I. Title.

HERKLOTS, Hugh Gerard 222.16
Gibson, 1903-
The Ten commandments and modern man. Fair Lawn, N. J., Essential Books, 1958. 190p. 20cm. [BV4655.H4] 58-778
1. Commandments, Ten. I. Title.

HONEYCUTT, Roy Lee. 222.16
These ten words [by] Roy L. Honeycutt. Nashville, Broadman Press [1966] 128 p. 20 cm. Bibliography: p. 126-128. [BV4655.H53] 66-15530
1. Commendments, Ten. I. Title.

HONEYCUTT, Roy Lee, Jr. 222.16
These ten words. Nashville, Broadman [c.1966] 128p.20cm. Bibl. [BV4655.H53] 66-15530 1.50
1. Commandments, Ten. I. Title.

JONES, Mary Alice, 1898- 222.16
ed.
The Ten commandments. Cover illus. by Mary Murray; inside illus. by Dorothy Grider. Chicago, Rand McNally, '1952. unpaged. illus. 17 cm. [BV4656.J6 1952] 52-3467
1. Commandments. Ten—Juvenile literature. I. Title.

JONES, Mary Alice, 1898- 222.16
ed.
The Ten commandments for children; illustrated by Robert Bonfils. Chicago, Rand McNally, c1956. unpaged. illus. 22cm. (A Rand McNally elf book, 543) [BV4656.J62] 56-7404
1. Commandments, Ten—Juvenile literature. I. Title.

JONES, Mary Alice, 1898- 222.16
ed.
The Ten commandments for children. Illustrated by Robert Bonfils. Chicago, Rand McNally, 1958, c1956. unpaged. illus. 33cm. (A Rand McNally giant book) [BV4656.J62 1958] 58-9648
1. Commandments, Ten—Juvenile literature. I. Title.

KUIPER, Henry J, 1885- ed. 222.16
Sermons on the Ten commandments, Lord's days: XXXIVXLIV, by ministers of the Reformed and Christian Reformed churches. Grand Rapids, Zondervan [1951] 175 p. 20 cm. (Sermons on the Heidelberg catechism, no. 4) [BX9426.A1K8 vol. 4] 51-11411
1. Commandments, Ten—Sermons. 2. Reformed Church—Sermons. 3. Sermons, American. I. Title.

MAURER, Benjamin A 1894- 222.16
The Ten commandements will not budge. Saint Louis, Concordia Pub. House, 1951. 104 p. 20 cm. [BV4655.M423] 51-14014
1. Commandments, Ten. I. Title.

*MORGAN, G. Campbell. 222.16
The ten commandments, [by] G. Campbell Morgan. Grand Rapids, Baker Book House [1974] 126 p. 20 cm. [BV4655] ISBN 0-8010-5954-2 1.95 (pbk.)
1. Commandments, Ten. I. Title.

MORRISON, Joseph 222.16
Pure water from old wells. New York, Vantage [c.1963] 69p. 21cm. 2.50 bds.,
I. Title.

NELSON, Carl Ellis, 1916- 222.16
Love and the law ; the place of the Ten commandments in the Christian faith today. Richmond, Va., John Knox Press [1963] 93 p. 21 cm. [BV4655.N35] 63-17979
1. Commandments, Ten. 2. Christian Life — Presbyterian authors. I. Title.

NELSON, Carl Ellis, 1916- 222.16
Love and the law; the place of the Ten commandments in the Christian faith today. Richmond, Va. Knox [c. 1963] 93p. 21cm. 63-17979 1.50 pap.,
1. Commandments, Ten. 2. Christian life—Presbyterian authors. I. Title.

PALMER, Robert E. 222'.16
Directions for living, by Robert E. Palmer. New York, Carlton Press [1967] 100 p. 22 cm. (A Hearthstone book) [BV4655.P33] 74-263269 2.50
1. Presbyterian Church—Sermons. 2. Commandments, Ten—Sermons. 3. Sermons, American. I. Title.

POTEAT, Edwin McNeill, 222.16
1892-
Mandate to humanity; an inquiry into the history and meaning of the Ten commandments and their relation to contemporary culture. Nashville, Abingdon-Cokesbury Press [1953] 238p. 24cm. [BV4655.P64] 53-5399
1. Commandments, Ten. I. Title.

REICHERT, Gilbert P. 222.16
The ten commandments speak to you. New York, Vantage [c.1962] 86p. 21cm. 2.50
I. Title.

SEALE, Ervin. 222.16
Ten words that will change your life. New York, Morrow, 1954. 188p. 21cm. [BV4655.S4] 54-6796
1. Commandments, Ten. I. Title.

SIMCOX, Carroll Eugene, 222.16
1912-
Living the Ten commandments; a guide to Christian obedience. New York, Morehouse-Gorham Co., 1953. 120p. 21cm. [BV4655.S54] 53-1319
1. Commandments, Ten. I. Title.

SLEMP, John Calvin, 1902- 222.16
Twelve laws of life, a study of the Ten Commandments and related teachings of Jesus. [1st ed.] Philadelphia, Judson Press [1950] 112 p. 20 cm. Bibliographical footnotes. [BV4655.S6] 50-7418
1. Commandments, Ten. 2. Jesus Christ—Teachings. I. Title.

THE Ten commandments 222.16
today a discussion of the Decalog. Salt Lake City, Deseret Book Co., 1955. 149p. 24cm. [BV4655.T4] 55-56948
1. Commandments, Ten.

BERG, Harold Edwin. 222.1606
The Ten commandments and you. Philadelphia, Fortress Press [1964] 119 p. 18 cm. [BV4655.B39] 64-23066
1. Commandments, Ten. I. Title.

BERG, Harold Edwin 222.1606
The Ten commandments and you. Philadelphia, Fortress [c.1964] 119p. 18cm. 64-23066 1.75
1. Commandments, Ten. I. Title.

CUSHING, Richard James, 222.1606
Cardinal
Spiritual guideposts. [Boston, Daughters of St. Paul, 1960] 184p. 22cm. (St. Paul editions) 60-50091 3.00; 2.00 pap.,
1. Commandments, Ten. I. Title.

KAHN, Robert I. 222.1606
The Ten commandments for today [by] Robert I. Kahn. [1st ed.] Garden City, N. Y., Doubleday, 1964. x, 133 p. 22 cm. [BV4655.K25] 64-19315
1. Commandments, Ten. I. Title.

KAHN, Robert I. 222.1606
The Ten commandments for today [by] Robert I. Kahn. New York, Family Library [1974, c1964] 159 p. 18 cm. [BV4655.K25] ISBN 0-515-03405-3 1.25 (pbk.)
1. Commandments, Ten. I. Title.
L.C. card no. for original edition: 64-19315.

KLEIN, Isaac 222.1606
The Ten Commandments in a changing world. Jerusalem, Citadel Pr. [dist. New York 2. 96 E. Bdway, Phillip Feldheim, 1964, c.]1963. 141p. 21cm. 3.50
1. Commandments, Ten—Sermons. 2. Sermons, American—Jewish authors. I. Title.

LOWERY, Daniel L 222.1606
Life and live; the commandments for teenagers. Glen Rock, N.J., Paulist Press (1964) 224 p. 18 cm. (Deus books) [HQ35.L6] 64-14154
1. Sex. 2. Adolescence. I. Title.

LOWERY, Daniel L. 222.1606
Life and love; the commandments for teenagers. Glen Rock, N.J., Paulist Pr. [c.1964] 224p. 18cm. (Deus bks.) 64-14154 .95 pap.,
1. Sex. 2. Adolescence. I. Title.

PETERSEN, Emma Marr. 222.1606
Stories from the Ten commandments for young Latter-Day Saints. Salt Lake City, Bookcraft [1960] 187p. illus. 24cm. [BV4656.P46] 60-44459
1. Commandments, Ten—Juvenile literature. I. Title.

TIPPETT, Harry Moyle. 222.1606
1891-
The voice from Sinai. Illus. by Jim Padgett. Nashville, Southern Pub. Assn. [1964] 141p. illus. 19cm. 63-21242 price unreported
1. Commandments, Ten. I. Title.

TRUEBLOOD, David Elton, 222.1606
1900-
Foundations for reconstruction. Rev. ed. New York, Harper [1961] 109 p. 20 cm. [BV4655.T7] 61-18269
1. Commandments, Ten. I. Title.

WEATHERLY, Owen Milton. 222.1606
The Ten commandments in modern perspective. Richmond, John Knox Press [1961] 160 p. 21 cm. [BV4655.W4] 61-17440
1. Commandments, Ten. I. Title.

NIELSEN, Eduard. 222'.16'066
The Ten commandments in new perspective; a traditio-historical approach. [Translated by David J. Bourke from the German] Naperville, Ill., A. R. Allenson [1968] x, 162 p. 22 cm. (Studies in Biblical theology, 2d ser., 7) Translation of De Ti bud. Bibliography: p. [146]-150. [BS1285.2.N5213] 68-3944
1. Commandments, Ten. I. Title. II. Series.

STAMM, Johann Jakob, 222'.16'066
1910-
The Ten Commandments in recent research [by] J. J. Stamm with M. E. Andrew. Naperville, Ill., A. R. Allenson [1967] 119 p. 22 cm. (Studies in Biblical theology, 2d ser. no. 2) "Translated with additions by M. E. Andrew from the German, Der Dekalog im Lichte der neueren Forschung, second edition, revised and enlarged ... 1962." Bibliography: p. 11-12. [BS1285.2.S713 1967a] 67-5850
1. Commandments, Ten. I. Andrew, Maurice Edward, 1932- tr. II. Title. III. Series.

SUELTZ, Arthur Fay. 222'.16'066
New directions from the Ten Commandments / Arthur Fay Sueltz. 1st ed. New York : Harper & Row, c1976. ix, 101 p. ; 21 cm. Includes bibliographical references. [BV4655.S77 1976] 75-36744 ISBN 0-06-067760-0 : 2.95
1. Commandments, Ten. I. Title.

FINLAY, Terence J. 222.1607
The Ten Commandments. New York, Scribners [c.1961] 123p. 61-13606 2.50
1. Commandments, Ten. I. Title.

GOLDMAN, Solomon, 1893- 222.1607
1953
The Ten commandments. Ed., introd. by

Maurice Samuel [Chicago] Univ. of Chic. Pr. [1963, c.1956] 224p. illus. 21cm. (Phoenix bk., P141) 1.75 pap.,
1. Commandments, Ten. 2. Bible. O. T. Exodus XIX-XX—Commentaries. I. Title.

RUSHDOONY, Rousas John. 222'.16'07
The institutes of Biblical law. A Chalcedon study, with three appendices by Gary North. [Nutley, N.J.] Craig Press, 1973. vii, 890 p. 24 cm. Includes bibliographical references. [BV4655.R8] 72-79485
1. Commandments, Ten. 2. Law (Theology)—Biblical teaching. 3. Jewish law. I. Title.

†DAUGHTERS of St. Paul. 222'.16'077
A brief summary of the Ten commandments / compiled by the Daughters of St. Paul. Boston : St. Paul Editions, c1976. 84 p. ; 18 cm. (Magister paperback series) [BV4655.D318 1975] 75-38796 pbk. : 0.95
1. Commandments, Ten. I. Title.

DISCOVER life : 222'.16'077
a study of the Ten Commandments / J. Laurence Martin, editor. Scottdale, Pa. : Herald Press, c1975. 80 p. : ill. ; 20 cm. [BV4655.D53] 75-18373 ISBN 0-8361-1779-4 : 1.95
1. Commandments, Ten. I. Martin, J. Laurence.

KRAL, Martin A. 222'.16'077
Thou shalt not / by Martin A. Kral. Roslyn Heights, N.Y. : Libra Publishers, c1976. 95 p. ; 22 cm. [BV4655.K7] 76-16322 6.95
1. Commandments, Ten. I. Title.

BEDIER, Mary Juliana, Sister, 1896- 222.19
Listen to God; the Ten commandments explained. Illustrated by Adele Werber. St. Paul, Catechetical Guild Educational Society [1954] unpaged. illus. 17cm. (A First book for little Catholics) [BV4656.B4] 54-27246
1. Commandments, Ten—Juvenile literature. I. Title.

DAVIS, John James, 1936- 222'.2
Conquest and crisis; studies in Joshua, Judges, and Ruth, by John J. Davis. Grand Rapids, Baker Book House [1969] 176 p. illus., geneal. table. 20 cm. Bibliography: p. 171-174. [BS1295.2.D38] 70-88244 2.95 (pbk)
1. Jews—History—1200-953 B.C. 2. Bible. O.T. Joshua—Criticism, interpretation, etc. 3. Bible. O.T. Judges—Criticism, interpretation, etc. 4. Bible. O.T. Ruth—Criticism, interpretation, etc. I. Title.

*HILL, Dave 222.2
The walls came tumbling down; Joshua 1-6 for children. Illus. by Jim Roberts, Art Kirchhoff. St. Louis, Concordia, 1967. 1v. (unpaged) col. illus. 21cm. (Arch bks.) .35 pap.,
1. Bible — O.T. — Joshua — Juvenile literature. I. Title.

IRONSIDE, Henry Allan, 1876- 222.2
Addresses on the book of Joshua. [1st ed.] New York, Loizeaux Bros. [1950] 142 p. 20 cm. Bible. O. T. Joshua--Sermons. [BS1295.I 7] 50-7377
I. Title.

REDPATH, Alan. 222.2
Victorious Christian living; studies in the book of Joshua. [Westwood, N. J.] Revell [1955] 254p. 21cm. [BS1295.R4] 55-8765
1. Bible. O. T. Joshua—Sermons. 2. Holiness. I. Title.

*SAXE, Grace. 222.2
Studies in Joshua., arranged by Grace Saxe, rev. by Irving L. Jensen. Chicago, Moody [1968] 80p. 22cm. (Bible self-study ser.) .95 pap.,
1. Bible. O.T. Joshua—Study, outlines, syllabi, etc. I. Jensen, Irving L. ed. II. Title.

SCHAEFFER, Francis August. 222'.2'06
Joshua and the flow of Biblical history / Francis A. Schaeffer. Downers Grove, Ill. : InterVarsity Press, [1975] 215 p. ; 21 cm. [BS1295.2.S3] 74-31847 ISBN 0-87784-958-7 : 6.95 ISBN 0-87784-773-8 pbk. : 3.95
1. Joshua, son of Nun. 2. Bible. O.T. Joshua—Criticism, interpretation, etc. I. Title.

*ARMERDING, Carl 222'.2066
Conquest and victory; studies in Joshua. Chicago, Moody [1967] 160p. 18cm. (MP96) .59 pap.,
I. Title.

JOHNSON, Alan F. 222'.2'07
Thirty days to spiritual power : insights from Joshua and Judges / Alan F. Johnson. Wheaton, Ill. : Tyndale House Publishers, 1975. [139] p. ; 21 cm. [BS1295.4.J63] 75-13634 ISBN 0-8423-7090-0 : 2.95

1. Bible. O.T. Joshua—Meditations. 2. Bible. O.T. Judges—Meditations. I. Title.

PINK, Arthur Walkington, 1886-1952. 222.207
Gleanings in Joshua. Chicago, Moody Press [1964] 430 p. 24 cm. [BS1295.3P5] 64-20991
1. Bible, O.T. Joshua—Commentaries. I. Title.

PINK, Arthur Walkington, 1886-1952 222.207
Gleanings in Joshua. Chicago, Moody [c.1964] 430p. 24cm. 64-20991 4.95
1. Bible. O. T. Joshua-Commentaries. I. Title.

BIBLE. O.T. Joshua. English. New English. 1974. 222'.2'077
The book of Joshua. Commentary by J. Maxwell Miller and Gene M. Tucker. [London, New York] Cambridge University Press [1974] x, 205 p. maps. 21 cm. (The Cambridge Bible commentary: New English Bible) Bibliography: p. 185. [BS1293 1974] 74-180248 ISBN 0-521-08616-7 11.95
1. Bible. O.T. Joshua—Commentaries. I. Miller, James Maxwell, 1937- II. Tucker, Gene M. III. Title. IV. Series.

SOGGIN, J. Alberto. 222'.2'077
Joshua: a commentary [by] J. Alberto Soggin. Philadelphia, Westminster Press [1972] xvii, 245 p. 23 cm. (The Old Testament library) Translation of Le livre de Josue. Includes bibliographical references. [BS1295.3.S613] 72-76954 ISBN 0-664-20938-6 8.00
1. Bible. O.T. Joshua—Commentaries. I. Bible. O.T. Joshua. English. 1972. II. Title. III. Series.

SCOTT, William Anderson, 1813-1885. 222'.2'0924
Wedge of gold : [the folly and fall of Achan] : a careful look at the sin of covetousness / W. A. Scott. Swengel, Pa. : Reiner Publications, [1974?] 162 p. ; 19 cm. Discourses delivered in the Calvary Church, San Francisco. Reprint of the 1855 ed. [BX9178.S4W4 1974] 74-187954 2.95
1. Presbyterian Church—Sermons. 2. Sermons, American. 3. Achan (Biblical character) I. Title.

MCKENZIE, John L. 222.2095
The world of the Judges [by] John L. McKenzie. Englewood Cliffs, N.J., Prentice-Hall [1966] x, 182 p. maps (on lining papers) 22 cm. (Prentice-Hall backgrounds to the Bible series) Includes bibliographies. [BS1295.2.M3] 66-13728
1. Jews—History—1200-953 B.C. 2. Bible. O.T. Joshau—History of Biblical events. 3. Bible. O.T. Judges—History of Biblical events. I. Title. II. Series.

SANDFORD, Frank W 1862-1948. 222'.2'095
The art of war for the Christian soldier. [A revision] Amherst, N. H., Kingdom Press [c1966] xvii, 165 p. 21 cm. [BS1295.S25] 66-29707
1. Bible. O. T. Joshua—History of Biblical events. I. Title.

WOOD, Leon James. 222'.2'095
Distressing days of the judges / Leon Wood. Grand Rapids, Mich. : Zondervan Pub. House, c1975. 434 p. : ill. ; 23 cm. Includes indexes. Bibliography: p. 404-407. [BS1305.2.W66] 74-25348 9.95
1. Jews—History—From entrance into Canaan to 953 B.C. 2. Bible. O.T. Judges—History of Biblical events. 3. Bible. O.T. Joshua—History of Biblical events. I. Title.

*JENSEN, Irving L. 222.29505
Joshua: rest-land won. Chicago, Moody [1966] 128p. 18cm. (Colportage lib.,530) Bibl. .39 pap.,
I. Title.

BIBLE. O.T. Judges. English. 1970. 222'.3
The book of Judges, with introduction and notes, and Notes on the Hebrew text of the books of Kings, with an introduction and appendix, by C. F. Burney. Prolegomenon by William F. Albright. New York, KTAV Pub. House, 1970. 2 v. in 1. illus., maps, plates. 24 cm. (The Library of Biblical studies) "The book of Judges, with introduction and notes," is a reprint of the 1918 ed. Burney's "Notes on the Hebrew text of the books of Kings" is a reprint of the 1903 ed. Albright's "Prolegomenon" is new. Includes bibliographies. [BS1305.3.B5 1970] 79-9771
1. Bible. O.T. Judges—Commentaries. 2. Bible. O.T. Kings—Commentaries. I. Burney, Charles Fox, 1868-1925. II. Burney, Charles Fox, 1868-1925. Notes on the Hebrew text of the Books of Kings. III. Title. IV. Series.

GIESELER, Carl Albert. 222.3
Ruth the gleaner. St. Louis, Concordia Pub. House [1956] 06p. 20cm. [BS1315.G5] 55-7713

1. Bible. O. T. Ruth—Commentaries. I. Title.

MCGEE, John Vernon, 1904- 222.3
Ruth: the romance of redemption. 2d ed. Wheaton, Ill., Van Kampen Press, 1954. 158p. 20cm. [BS580.R8] 54-2978
1. Ruth (Biblical character) 2. Redemption—Biblical teaching. I. Title.

MCINTIRE, Carl, 1906- 222.3
Better than seven sons. Collingswood, N. J., Christian Beacon Press, 1954. 90p. 21cm. [BS1315.M25] 54-41982
1. Bible. O. T. Ruth—Sermons. 2. Presbyterian Church—Sermons. 3. Sermons, American. I. Title.

*SAXE, Grace. 222.3
Studies in Judges and Ruth, arranged by Grace Saxe, rev. by Irving L. Jensen. Chicago, Moody [1968] 95p. 22cm. (Bible self-study ser., 30-8419) Cover title. .95 pap.,
1. Bible. O.T. Judges—Commentaries. 2. Bible. O.T. Ruth—Commentaries. I. Jensen, Irving L. ed. II. Title.

BIBLE. O.T. Judges. English. 1968. 222'.3'052
The book of Judges. Illustrated by Jacob Shacham. [1st ed.] Philadelphia, Chilton Book Co. [1968] 70 p. col. illus. 27 cm. [BS1303.A3 1968] 68-21073 4.95
1. Bible. O.T. Judges—Pictures, illustrations, etc. I. Shacham, Jacob, illus. II. Title.

SWANSTON, Hamish F. G., 1933- 222'.3'066
Histories. Chicago, ACTA Foundation [1971- v. 22 cm. (Scripture discussion commentary, 3) Contents.Contents.—1. Judges, 1 and 2 Samuel, 1 and 2 Kings, by H. Swanston. Ruth, by L. Bright. Includes bibliographical references. [BS1286.5.S95] 72-178779 ISBN 0-87946-002-4
1. Bible. O.T. Former prophets—Commentaries. 2. Bible. O.T. Ruth—Commentaries. I. Bright, Laurence. II. Title. III. Series.

CUNDALL, Arthur Ernest. 222'.3'07
Judges [and] Ruth. [1st ed.] Chicago, Inter-varsity Press [1968] 318 p. illus., maps. 20 cm. (The Tyndale Old Testament commentaries) Contents.—Judges; an introduction and commentary, by A. E. Cundall.—Ruth; an introduction and commentary, by L. Morris. Includes bibliographies. [BS1305.3.C8 1968b] 68-31426 3.95
1. Bible. O.T. Judges—Commentaries. 2. Bible. O.T. Ruth—Commentaries. I. Morris, Leon. Ruth. 1968. II. Title.

BIBLE. O.T. Judges. English. New English. 1975. 222'.32'077
The book of Judges : commentary / by James D. Martin. Cambridge, Eng. ; New York : Cambridge University Press, 1975. x, 234 p. : map ; 20 cm. (The Cambridge Bible commentary, New English Bible) Includes index. Bibliography: p. 227. [BS1305.3.M37 1975] 74-31797 ISBN 0-521-08639-6 : 15.95
1. Bible. O.T. Judges—Commentaries. I. Martin, James D., 1935- II. Title. III. Series.

HUNTER, John Edward, 1909- 222'.32'0922 B
Judges and a permissive society / John E. Hunter. Grand Rapids : Zondervan Pub. House, c1975. 127 p. ; 18 cm. [BS1305.2.H86] 74-25340 1.50
1. Bible. O.T. Judges—Criticism, interpretation, etc. 2. Bible. O.T. Judges—Biography. I. Title.

HALS, Ronald M., 1864-1926. 222'.35
The theology of the book of Ruth, by Ronald M. Hals. Philadelphia, Fortress Press [1969] xii, 81 p. 20 cm. (Facet books. Biblical series, 23) Includes bibliographical references. [BS1315.2.H3] 69-12996 0.85
1. Bible. O.T. Ruth—Theology. I. Title.

MAURO, Philip, 1859- 222.3506
Ruth: the satisfied stranger. Swengel, Pa., Bible Truth Depot [1963, c.1920] 220p. 19cm. 1.95 pap.,
1. Ruth. I. Title.

ROSENBERG, Israel. 222'.35'066
The world of words; the truth about the Scroll of Ruth, the message of logosophy. New York, Philosophical Library [1973] xiii, 211 p. 22 cm. Includes bibliographical references. [BS1315.2.R67] 72-85035 ISBN 0-8022-2101-7 7.50
1. Bible. O. T. Ruth—Criticism, interpretation, etc. I. Title.

ANDERSON, C. Reuben. 222'.35'07
The books of Ruth and Esther; a study manual, by C. Reuben Anderson. Grand Rapids, Mich., Baker Book House [1970] 93 p. 20 cm. (Shield Bible study series)

Bibliography: p. 93. [BS1315.3.A63] 77-115901 1.95
1. Bible. O.T. Ruth—Commentaries. 2. Bible. O.T. Esther—Commentaries. I. Title.

COLLINS, Stanley, 1916- 222'.35'07
Courage and submission : a study of Ruth & Esther / Stanley Collins. Glendale, Calif. : G/L Regal Books, c1975. 94 p. ; 18 cm. (A Bible commentary for laymen) [BS1315.3.C64] 74-32323 ISBN 0-8307-0310-1
1. Bible. O.T. Ruth—Commentaries. 2. Bible. O.T. Esther—Commentaries. I. Title.

ASIMOV, Isaac, 1920- 222'.35'077
The story of Ruth. [1st ed.] Garden City, N.Y., Doubleday [1972] xii, 102 p. maps. 22 cm. Retells the Old Testament tale of the faithful daughter-in-law showing how the events of the story reveal the history of that period. [BS1315.3.A83] 72-83137 ISBN 0-385-08594-X 3.95
1. Bible. O.T. Ruth—Commentaries—Juvenile literature. I. Title.

GARDINER, George E. 222'.35'0924 B
The romance of Ruth / by George E. Gardiner. Grand Rapids : Kregel Publications, [1977] p. cm. [BS580.R8G37] 77-79187 ISBN 0-8254-2718-5 pbk. : 1.50
1. Bible. O.T.—Biography. 2. Ruth (Biblical character) I. Title.

GARDINER, George E. 222'.35'0924 B
The romance of Ruth / by George E. Gardiner. Grand Rapids : Kregel Publications, [1977] p. cm. [BS580.R8G37] 77-79187 ISBN 0-8254-2718-5 pbk. : 1.50
1. Bible. O.T.—Biography. 2. Ruth (Biblical character) I. Title.

BIBLE. O.T. Historical books. English. Revised. Selections. 1973. 222'.4
Saul and David; with 41 lithographs by Oskar Kokoschka. New York, Putnam [1973] 214 p. illus. 31 cm. German ed. published in 1970. Selections from 1-2 Samuel and 1 Kings. [BS1323.K64 1973] 73-83127 ISBN 0-399-11174-3 17.50
1. Bible—Pictures, illustrations, etc. I. Kokoschka, Oskar, 1886- illus. II. Title.

*BLACKWOOD, Andrew Watterston. 222.4
Preaching from Samuel [by] Andrew W. Blackwood. Grand Rapids, Baker Book House [1975 c1946] 256 p. 20 cm. Includes bibliographical references and index. [BS1321] ISBN 0-8010-0641-4 2.95 (pbk.)
1. Bible—O.T. Samuel—Homiletical use. I. Title.

*SAXE, Grace. 222.4
Studies in I and II Samuel, arranged by Grace Saxe, rev. by Irving L. Jensen. Chicago, Moody [1968] 112p. illus. 22cm. (Bible self-study ser.) .95 pap.,
1. Bible. O. T. Samuel—Commentaries. I. Jensen, Irving L. ed. II. Title.

WHYBRAY, Roger Norman. 222'.4
The succession narrative; a study of II Samuel 9-20, [and] I Kings 1 and 2 [by] R. N. Whybray. Naperville, Ill., A. R. Allenson [1968] ix, 118 p. 22 cm. (Studies in Biblical theology, 2d ser., 9) Bibliographical footnotes. [BS1325.2.W45] 68-4419
1. Bible. O.T. 2 Samuel IX-XX—Criticism, interpretation, etc. 2. Bible. O.T. 1 Kings I-II—Criticism, interpretation, etc. I. Title. II. Series.

KRAFT, Robert A., comp. 222'.4'048
1972 proceedings, edited by Robert A. Kraft for the International Organization for Septuagint and Cognate Studies and the Society of Biblical Literature Pseudepigraphia Seminar. [Missoula, Mont., Society of Biblical Literature] 1972. iv, 245 p. 22 cm. (Septuagint and cognate studies, no. 2) Contains proceedings of the International Organization for Septuagint and Cognate Studies symposium held Sept. 4, 1972 in Los Angeles, and of the Society of Biblical Literature Pseudepigrapha Seminar, held Sept. 5, 1972 in Los Angeles. Includes bibliographical references. [BS1325.2.K7] 74-165169
1. Bible. O.T. Samuel—Criticism, Textual—Congresses. 2. Bible. O.T. Kings—Criticism, Textual—Congresses. 3. Bible. O.T. Apocryphal books. Psalms of Solomon—Congresses. 4. Bible. O.T. Apocryphal books. Testament of Abraham—Congresses. I. International Organization for Septuagint and Cognate Studies. II. Society of Biblical Literature. III. Pseudepigrapha Seminar, Los Angeles, 1972. IV. Title. V. Series.

DAVIS, John James, 1936- 222'.4'06
The birth of a kingdom; studies in I-II Samuel

and I Kings 1-11, by John J. Davis. Grand Rapids, Baker Book House [1970] 209 p. illus., maps. 20 cm. (Old Testament series) Bibliography: p. 191-195. [BS1325.2.D37] 79-129927 2.95
1. Bible. O.T. Samuel—Criticism, interpretation, etc. 2. Bible. O.T. 1 Kings I-XI—Criticism, interpretation, etc. I. Title.

HERTZBERG, Hans Wilhelm, 1895- 222.407
I and II Samuel, a commentary Tr. from German by J.S. Bowden Philadelphia, Westminister [1965, c.1964] 416p. 23cm. (Old Testament lib.) Bible. [BS1325.3H413] 65-10074 7.50
1. Bible. O. T. Samuel—Commentaries. 2. Bible. O. T. Samuel. English. 1964. (Series) I. Title.

GEHRKE, Ralph David, 1919- 222'.4'077
Concordia commentary: 1 and 2 Samuel St. Louis, Concordia Pub. House [1968] 397 p. maps. 20 cm. Bibliography: p. 393-394. [BS1325.3.G4] 68-19904 4.00
1. Bible. O.T. Samuel—Commentaries. I. Bible. O.T. Samuel. II. Title.

LANDAY, Jerry M. 222'.4'09
The House of David [by] Jerry M. Landay. [1st ed.] New York, Saturday Review Press; [distributed by] E. P. Dutton [1973, i.e.1974] 272 p. illus. 26 cm. Bibliography: p. 268. [BS580.D3L34] 73-87729 ISBN 0-8415-0290-0 14.95
1. David, King of Israel. I. Title.

BLENKINSOPP, Joseph, 1927- 222.4095
The promise to David; the anointed king in God's plan. With study-club questions. Glen Rock, N. J., Paulist Press [1964] 78 p. 18 cm. (Insight series) "Suggested reading: p. 77-78. [BS580.D3B55] 64-24523
1. David, King of Israel. I. Title.

BLENKINSOPP, Joseph, 1927- 222.4095
The promise to David; the anointed king in God's plan. With study-club questions. Glen Rock, N.J., Paulist [c.1964] 78p. 18cm. (Insight ser.) Bibl. 64-24523 .50 pap.,
1. David, King of Israel. I. Title.

*COOPER, Duff [Alfred Duff Cooper] 1st Viscount Norwich of Aldwick, 1890-1954 222.4095
David. London, Hart-Davis [dist. Chester Springs, Pa., Dufour, 1965] 224p. map. 21cm. Bibl. 3.25 bds.,
I. David, King of Israel. II. Title.

HOTH, Iva. 222'.4'09505
Kings and prophets; 1 Samuel 16:23-1 Kings 21:8. Script by Iva Hoth. Illus. by Andre Le Blanc. Bible editor: C. Elvan Olmstead. Elgin, IL, D. C. Cook Pub. Co. [1973] 158 p. illus. 18 cm. (Her The picture Bible for all ages, v. 3) Retells in comic book format the Old Testament stories from David's fight with Goliath to the time of the Prophet Elijah. [BS551.2.H684] 73-78170 ISBN 0-912692-15-4 0.95 (pbk.)
1. Bible stories, English—O.T. Historical books. I. Le Blanc, Andre, 1921- illus. II. Title.

WARREN, Mary 222.43
The boy with a sling: 1 Samuel 16:1-18:5 for children. Illus. by Sally Mathews [St. Louis] Concordia [c.1965] 1v. (unpaged) col. illus. 21cm. (Arch bks., set 2 no. 59-1116) [BS580.D3W3] 65-15143 .35 pap.,
1. David King of Israel—Juvenile literature. I. Title.

MILLER, Patrick D. 222'.43'06
The hand of the Lord : a reassessment of the "Ark narrative" of 1 Samuel / Patrick D. Miller Jr., J. J. M. Roberts. Baltimore : Johns Hopkins University Press, c1977. viii, 119 p. ; 26 cm. (The Johns Hopkins Near Eastern studies) Includes indexes. Bibliography: p. 106-111. [BS1325.2.M54] 76-48737 ISBN 0-8018-1920-2 : 11.00
1. Bible. O.T. 1 Samuel II, 12-VII, 1—Theology. 2. Ark of the Covenant. I. Roberts, Jimmy Jack McBee, joint author. II. Title. III. Series: Johns Hopkins University. Near Eastern studies.

BIRCH, Bruce C. 222'.43'07
The rise of the Israelite monarchy : the growth and development of I Samuel 7-15 / by Bruce C. Birch. Missoula, Mont. : Published by Scholars Press for the Society of Biblical Literature, c1976. xi, 170 p. ; 21 cm. (Dissertation series ; no. 27) Bibliography: p. 159-170. [BS1325.2.B57] 76-20680 ISBN 0-89130-112-7 : 4.20
1. Bible. O.T. 1 Samuel VII-XV—Criticism, interpretation, etc. 2. Kings and rulers—Biblical teaching. I. Title. II. Series: Society of Biblical Literature. Dissertation series ; no. 27.

BIBLE. O.T. 1 Samuel. English. New English. 1971. 222'.43'077
The first book of Samuel; commentary by Peter R. Ackroyd. Cambridge, University Press, 1971. xii, 237 p. illus., maps, plan. 21 cm. (The Cambridge Bible commentary: New English Bible) Bibliography: p. 232. [BS1325.3.A3] 77-128636 ISBN 0-521-07965-9 £2.20 ($6.95 U.S.)
1. Bible. O.T. 1 Samuel—Commentaries. I. Ackroyd, Peter R. II. Title.

MCCALL, Yvonne Holloway. 222'.43'0905
The angry king : 1 Samuel 18-2 Samuel 5 for children / written by Yvonne Holloway McCall ; illustrated by Jim Roberts. St. Louis : Concordia Pub. House, c1976. p. cm. (Arch books ; ser. 14) Retells in rhyme how David came to replace Saul as king of Israel with emphasis on the meaning of love, trust in God, and handling competition in a Christian way. [BS580.S3M3] 76-27365 ISBN 0-570-06110-5 pbk. : 0.59
1. Saul, King of Israel—Juvenile literature. 2. David, King of Israel—Juvenile literature. 3. Bible. O.T.—Biography—Juvenile literature. I. Roberts, Jim. II. Title.

NEFF, LaVonne. 222'.43'0905
God's gift baby : 1 Samuel 1-2 for children / written by LaVonne Neff ; illustrated by Don Kueker. St. Louis : Concordia Pub. House, 1977c1976 p. cm. (Arch books ; ser. 14) Retells the story of Hannah's years-long desire for a child and how after she finally gave birth to a son, Samuel, she returned him to God. [BS580.H3N44] 76-27752 ISBN 0-570-06113-X pbk. : 0.59
1. Hannah (Biblical character)—Juvenile literature. 2. Samuel, judge of Israel—Juvenile literature. 3. Bible. O.T.—Biography—Juvenile literature. I. Kueker, Don. II. Title.

BARRETT, Ethel. 222'.43'09505
Rules, who needs them? Glendale, Calif., G/L Regal Books [1974] 150 p. illus. 20 cm. (A Regal venture book) Includes bibliographical references. [BS550.2.B37] 73-90623 ISBN 0-8307-0282-2 0.95 (pbk.)
1. Bible stories, English—O.T. Judges. 2. Bible stories, English—O.T. 1 Samuel. 3. Christian life—1960- I. Title.

*SOLTAU, T. Stanley 222.439505
The God-pointed life; lessons from the life of David. Chicago, Moody [1966] 127p. 18cm. (Colportage lib., 521) .39 pap.,
I. Title.

BIBLE. O.T 1 Kings. Jewish Publication Society 222.5
Book of Kings 1; a commentary of Leo L. Honor. New York, Union of American Hebrew Congregations, 1955. xiii, 367p. 24cm. (The Jewish commentary for Bible readers) Bibliography: p. 361-367. [BS1335.H6] 55-2553
1. Bible. O. T. 1 Kings—Commentaries. I. Honor, Leo Lazarus, 1894- II. Title. III. Series: Commission on Jewish Education of the Union of American Hebrew Congregations and the Central Conference of American Rabbis. The Jewish commentary for Bible readers

HASTINGS, James, 1852-1922 ed. 222.5
The Speaker's Bible. Edited by James Hastings, assisted by B. A. Clark. Grand Rapids, Baker Book House, 1961- v. 25 cm. Contents.[1] Hebrews. -- [2] -- [3] Luke. v. 1-2 -- [4] Deuteronomy. Joshua. Judges. Ruth. -- [5] I and II Peter. Jude. -- [6] Job. Psalms I. Includes bibliographies. [BS491.5.S73] 61-16755
1. Bible — Sermons. I. Title.

MONTGOMERY, James Alan, 1866-1949. 222.5
A critical and exegetical commentary on the Books of Kings. Edited by Henry Snyder Gehman. New York, Scribner, 1951. xlvi, 575p. 21cm. (The International critical commentary) Includes bibliographies. [BS491.I6 vol.10] 52-8522
1. Bible. C T. Kings—Commentaries. I. Title. II. Series.

PROKOP, Phyllis Stillwell 222.5
Conversations with prophets; courage for Christians from two men of God. St. Louis, Concordia [1966] 76p. 15cm. Includes selections from the Bible, largely from First and Second Kings. [BS580.E4P7] 66-25098 1.50
1. Elijah, the prophet. 2. Elisha, the prophet. 3. Bible. O. T. Kings. English. 1966. Authorized. I. Title.

SANGSTER, James S. 222.5
The Chariot of Israel: a tale of Elijah. New York Exposition [c.1963] 183p. 21cm. (Exposition-banner bk.) 3.00
I. Title.

SHENKEL, James Donald. 222'.5
Chronology and recensional development in the Greek text of Kings. Cambridge, Mass., Harvard University Press, 1968. 151 p. 22 cm. (Harvard Semitic monographs, v. 1) A revision of the author's thesis—Harvard, 1964. Bibliography: p. [138]-148. [BS1325.2.S5 1968] 68-21983 6.50
1. Bible. O.T. Kings. Greek—Criticism, textual. 2. Bible. O.T. Kings—Versions. I. Title. II. Series.

WALLACE, Ronald S 222.5
Elijah and Elisha; expositions from the book of Kings. Grand Rapids, W.B. Eerdmans Pub. Co., 1957. 164p. 23cm. [BS530.E4W3 1957] 57-14194
1. Elijah, the prophet, 2. Elisha, the prophet. I. Title.

WALLACE, Ronald S 222.5
Elijah and Elisha; expositions from the book of Kings. Grand Rapids, W. B. Eerdmans Pub. Co., 1957. 164 p. 23 cm. [BS580.E4W3 1957] 57-14194
1. Elijah, the prophet. 2. Elisha, the prophet. I. Title.

WHITCOMB, John Clement, 1924- 222'.5'06
Solomon to the Exile; studies in Kings and Chronicles, by John C. Whitcomb, Jr. Winona Lake, Ind., BMH Books [1971] 182 p. illus., 2 maps, plan. 20 cm. (Old Testament studies) Bibliography: p. 159-161. [BS1335.2.W48] 72-152379 3.95
1. Bible. O.T. Kings—Criticism, interpretation, etc. 2. Bible. O.T. Chronicles—Criticism, interpretation, etc. I. Title.

GRAY, John, 1913- 222.507
I & II Kings; a commentary. Philadelphia, Westminster Press [c1963] 744 p. maps. 23 cm. (The Old Testament library) Bibliography: p. [710]-730. [BS1335.3.G7] 64-10086
1. Bible. O.T. Kings—Commentaries. I. Bible. O.T. Kings. English. 1963. II. Title. III. Series.

GRAY, John, 1913- 222.507
I& II Kings: a commentary. Philadelphia, Westminster Press [c.1963] 744p. maps. 23cm. (Old Testament lib.) Bibl. 64-10086 8.50 [corrected entry]
1. Bible. O. T. Kings—Commentaries. I. Bible. O. T. Kings. English. 1963. II. Title. III. Series.

WIFALL, Walter. 222'.5'07
The court history of Israel : a Commentary on First and Second Kings / Walter Wifall. 1st ed. St. Louis, Mo. : Clayton Pub. House, [1975] 192 p. : ill. ; 22 cm. Includes bibliographical references. [BS1335.3.W53] 75-9271 ISBN 0-915644-02-9 pbk. : 6.50
1. Bible. O.T. 1-2 Kings—Commentaries. I. Title.

GRAY, John, 1913- 222'.5'077
I & II Kings; a commentary. 2d, fully rev. ed. Philadelphia, Westminster Press [1970] xviii, 802 p. maps. 23 cm. (The Old Testament library) Bibliography: p. [777]-802. [BS1335.3.G7 1970b] 73-134271 15.00
1. Bible. O.T. Kings—Commentaries. I. Bible. O.T. Kings. English. 1970. II. Title. III. Series.

THIELE, Edwin Richard, 1895- 222'.5'09
A chronology of the Hebrew kings / by Edwin R. Thiele. Grand Raphids : Zondervan Pub. House, c1977. 93 p. ; 21 cm. (Contemporary evangelical perspectives) Includes bibliographical references and index. [BS637.T48] 77-3276 ISBN 0-310-36001-3 pbk. : 2.95
1. Jews—History—953-586 B.C.—Chronology. 2. Bible. O.T. Kings—Chronology. 3. Bible. O.T. 2 Chronicles—Chronology. I. Title.

KELLNER, Esther. 222.5095
The breakup of Solomon's kingdom. Sponsored by the Benedictine monks of Belmont Abbey. Garden City, N. Y. [1961] 64p. illus. 21cm. (The Catholic know-your-Bible program) [BS551.2.K4 1961] 61-19173
1. Bible stories, English—O. T. Kings. I. Title.

BARRETT, Ethel. 222'.5'09505
The strangest thing happened. Glendale, Calif., G/L Regal Books [1970, c1969] 137 p. illus. 20 cm. (A Regal venture book) [BS551.2.B32] 76-84599 0.69
1. Bible stories, English—O.T. Kings. I. Title.

*SAXE, Grace. 222.53
Studies in I Kings with Chronicles, arranged by Grace Saxe, rev. by Irving L. Jensen. Chicago, Moody [1968] 112p. illus. 22cm. (Bible self-study ser.) .95 pap.,
1. Bible. O. T. Kings I. Commentaries. II. Bible. O. T. Chronicles—Commentaries. III. Jensen, Irving L. ed. IV. Title.

GOODING, David Willoughby. 222'.53'044
Relics of ancient exegesis : a study of the miscellanies in 3 Reigns 2 / D. W. Gooding. Cambridge ; New York : Cambridge University Press, 1976. viii, 132 p. ; 23 cm. (Monograph series - Society for Old Testament Study ; 4) Includes the Greek texts of 1 Kings II, 35 and 46. Includes bibliographical references and indexes. [BS1335.2.G66] 74-19523 ISBN 0-521-20700-2 : 15.00
1. Bible. O.T. 1 Kings II, 35—Criticism, Textual. 2. Bible. O.T. 1 Kings II, 46—Criticism, Textual. I. Bible. O.T. 1 Kings II, 35. Greek. 1976. II. Bible. O.T. 1 Kings II, 46. Greek. 1976. III. Title. IV. Series: Society for Old Testament Study. Monograph series ; 4.

BIBLE. O.T. 1 Kings. English. New English. 1972. 222'.53'077
The first book of Kings. Commentary by J. Robinson. Cambridge [Eng.] University Pr., 1972. xi, 258 p. maps. 21 cm. (Cambridge Bible commentary: New English Bible) Bibliography: p. 253. [BS1333.R6] 72-80592 ISBN 0-521-08619-1 9.95;
1. Bible. O.T. 1 Kings—Commentaries. I. Robinson, Joseph, 1927- II. Title. III. Series. Available from the publisher's New York office. Pbk. 3.95, ISBN 0-521-09734-7.

NAPIER, Bunyan Davie. 222'.53'077
Word of God, word of earth / Davie Napier. Philadelphia : United Church Press, c1976. 105 p. ; 22 cm. "A Pilgrim Press book." Includes the author's edited translation of selected passages from the Old Testament book of 1st Kings. Includes bibliographical references. [BS580.E4N36] 75-45312 ISBN 0-8298-0304-1 : 4.95 ISBN 0-8298-0307-6 pbk. : 3.25
1. Elijah, the prophet—Addresses, essays, lectures. 2. Bible. O.T. 1 Kings XVII-XIX, XXI—Criticism, interpretation, etc.—Addresses, essays, lectures. 3. Pastoral theology—Addresses, essays, lectures. I. Bible. O.T. 1 Kings XVII-XIX, XXI. English. Napier. 1976. II. Title.

*METCALF, Harold E. 222.530924
Elijah; God's mighty witness. Nashville, Southern Pub. [c.1965] 96p. 18cm. 1.00 pap.,
I. Title.

KOLBREK, Loyal. 222'.53'09505
The day God made it rain : I Kings 17-18 for children / written by Loyal Kolbrek ; illustrated by Herb Halpern Productions. St. Louis : Concordia Publishing House, c1976. p. cm. (Arch books, series 14) Relates in rhyme the story of Elijah and how his faith in God was vindicated. [BS580.E4K63] 76-26574 ISBN 0-570-06108-3 : 0.59
1. Elijah, the prophet—Juvenile literature. 2. Bible. O.T.—Biography—Juvenile literature. I. Herb Halpern Productions. II. Title.

*SAXE, Grace. 222.54
Studies in II Kings with Chronicles, arranged by Grace Saxe, rev. by Irving L. Jensen. Chicago, Moody [1968] 112p. illus. 22cm. (Bible self-study ser.) .95 pap.,
1. Bible. O. T. Kings II—Commentaries. 2. Bible. O. T. Chronicles—Commentaries. I. Jensen, Irving L. ed. II. Title.

BIBLE. O.T. 2 Kings. English. New English. 1976. 222'.54'077
The second book of Kings / commentary by J. Robinson. Cambridge ; New York : Cambridge University Press, 1976. xii, 256 p. : maps ; 21 cm. (The Cambridge Bible commentary, New English Bible) Includes index. Bibliography: p. 250. [BS1333.R6 1976] 76-6863 ISBN 0-521-08646-9 : 17.50. ISBN 0-521-09774-6 pbk. : 6.95
1. Bible. O.T. 2 Kings—Commentaries. I. Robinson, Joseph, 1927- II. Title. III. Series.

ELLUL, Jacques. 222'.54'0922
The politics of God and the politics of man. Translated and edited by Geoffrey W. Bromiley. Grand Rapids, Mich., Eerdmans [1972] 199 p. 21 cm. Translation of Politique de Dieu, politiques de l'homme. [BS1335.4.E413] 76-188247 ISBN 0-8028-1442-5 3.45
1. Bible. O.T. 2 Kings—Biography. I. Title.

GREENE, Carol. 222'.54'09505
Seven baths for Naaman : the healing of Naaman for beginning readers : 2 Kings 5:1-15 for children / by Carol Greene ; illustrated by Aline Cunningham. St. Louis : Concordia Pub. House, c1977. [46] p. : col. ill. ; 23 cm. (I can read a Bible story.) Retells the Bible story in which Naaman, a wealthy Syrian travels to Israel in hopes that Elisha will cure him of his illness. [BS580.N2G73] 77-6801 ISBN 0-570-07321-9 : 3.95. ISBN 0-570-07315-4 pbk. : 1.95
1. Naaman, the Syrian—Juvenile literature. 2. Bible. O.T.—Biography—Juvenile literature. I. Cunningham, Aline. II. Title.

GREENE, Carol. 222'.54'09505
Seven baths for Naaman : the healing of Naaman for beginning readers : 2 Kings 5:1-15 for children / by Carol Greene ; illustrated by Aline Cunningham. St. Louis : Concordia Pub. House, c1977. [46] p. : col. ill. ; 23 cm. (I can read a Bible story.) Retells the Bible story in which Naaman, a wealthy Syrian travels to Israel in hopes that Elisha will cure him of his illness. [BS580.N2G73] 77-6801 ISBN 0-570-07321-9 : 3.95. ISBN 0-570-07315-4 pbk. : 1.95
1. Naaman, the Syrian—Juvenile literature. 2. Bible. O.T.—Biography—Juvenile literature. I. Cunningham, Aline. II. Title.

BIBLE. O. T. Historical books. Hebrew. 1954. 222.6
The Chronicler's history of Israel; Chronicles-Ezra-Nehemiah restored to its original form, by Charles C. Torrey. New Haven, Yale University Press, 1954 xxxiv, 207p. 23cm. Based on Seligman Baer's edition of the Hebrew text and the Authorized English version. [BS1202.T6] 54-9523
I. Bible. O. T. Historical books. English. 1954. Authorized. II. Teorey, Charles Cutler, 1863- III. Title.

BIBLE. O.T. Historical books. Hebrew. 1973. 222'.6
The Chronicler's history of Israel; Chronicles-Ezra-Nehemiah restored to its original form, by Charles C. Torrey. Port washington, N.Y., Kennikat Press [1973, c1954] xxxiv, 207 p. 22 cm. Based on Seligman Baer's edition of the Hebrew text and the Authorized English version. [BS1202.T6 1973] 72-85281 ISBN 0-8046-1709-0 10.00
I. Torrey, Charles Cutler, 1863-1956. II. Bible. O.T. Historical books. English. Authorized. 1973.

WILLIAMSON, Hugh Godfrey Maturin, 1947- 222'.6'06
Israel in the Books of Chronicles / H. G. M. Williamson. Cambridge [Eng.] ; New York : Cambridge University Press, 1977. xi, 170 p. ; 22 cm. Based on the author's thesis, University of Cambridge, 1975. Includes indexes. Bibliography: p. 141-154. [BS1345.2.W48] 76-56118 ISBN 0-521-21305-3 : 15.95
1. Bible. O.T. Chronicles—Criticism, interpretation, etc. 2. Twelve tribes of Israel. I. Title.

WILLIAMSON, Hugh Godfrey Maturin, 1947- 222'.6'06
Israel in the Books of Chronicles / H. G. M. Williamson. Cambridge [Eng.] ; New York : Cambridge University Press, 1977. xi, 170 p. ; 22 cm. Based on the author's thesis, University of Cambridge, 1975. Includes indexes. Bibliography: p. 141-154. [BS1345.2.W48] 76-56118 ISBN 0-521-21305-3 : 15.95
1. Bible. O.T. Chronicles—Criticism, interpretation, etc. 2. Twelve tribes of Israel. I. Title.

BIBLE. O.T. Chronicles. English. New English. 1976. 222'.6'077
The first and second books of the Chronicles : commentary / by R. J. Coggins. Cambridge, Eng. ; New York : Cambridge University Press, 1976. x, 314 p. ; 20 cm. (The Cambridge Bible commentary on the New English Bible) Includes index. Bibliography: p. 310. [BS1345.3.C63] 75-17117 ISBN 0-521-08647-7 : 18.95 ISBN 0-521-09758-4 pbk. :
1. Bible. O.T. Chronicles—Commentaries. I. Coggins, R. J., 1929- II. Title. III. Series: The Cambridge Bible commentary, New English Bible.

BIBLE. O.T. 1 Chronicles. English. 1965. Myers. 222.63052
I Chronicles. Introd., translation, and notes by Jacob M. Myers. [1st ed.] Garden City, N.Y., Doubleday, 1965. xciv, 239 p. 25 cm. (The Anchor Bible, v. 12) Bibliography: p. [xci]-xciv. [BS192.2.A1 1964.G3 vol. 12] 65-17226
1. Bible. O.T. 1 Chronicles—Commentaries. I. Myers, Jacob Martin, 1904- ed. and tr. II. Title. III. Series.

BIBLE. O.T. I and II Chronicles. English. 1965. Myers. 222.63052
I Chronicles [and] II Chronicles; 2v. Introd., tr., and notes by Jacob M. Myers. Garden City, N.Y., Doubleday [c.]1965. 2v. (xciv, 239; xxxvi, 268p.) 25cm. (Anchor Bible, v.12-13) Bibl [BS192.2.A1 1964.G3 vol.12-13] 65-17226 6.00 ea.,
1. Bible. O.T. Chronicles—Commentaries. 2. Bible. O.T. Chronicles—Commentaries. I. Myers, Jacob Martin, 1904- ed. and tr. (Series) II. Title.

BIBLE. O.T. Ezra. English. 1965. Myers. 222.7
Ezra. Nehemiah. Introd., translation and notes by Jacob M. Myers. [1st ed.] Garden City, N.Y., Doubleday, 1965. lxxxiii, 268 p. plan. 25 cm. (The Anchor Bible, 14) Bibliography: p. [lxxviii]-lxxxiii. [BS192.2.A1 1964.G3, vol. 14] 65-23788
1. Bible. O.T. Ezra—Commentaries. 2. Bible. O.T. Nehemiah—Commentaries. I. Myers, Jacob Martin, 1904- ed. and tr. II. Bible. O.T. Nehemiah. English. 1965. Myers. III. Title. IV. Series.

BIBLE. O. T. Ezra. English. 1965. Myers 222.7
Ezra. Nehemiah. Introd., Tr. notes by Jacob M. Myers. Garden City, N.Y., Doubleday, [c.] 1965. lxxxiii, 268p. plan. 25cm. (Anchor Bible, 14) Bibl. [BS192.2.A1 1964.G3] 65-23788 6.00
1. Bible. O.T. Ezra—Commentaries. 2. Bible. O. T. Nehemiah—Commentaries. I. Myers, Jacob Martin, 1904- ed. and tr. II. Bible. O. T. Nehemiah. English. 1965. Myers. (Series) III. Title.

GREENFIELD, Moses, comp. 222'.7
150 year calendar, with corresponding English and Hebrew dates including holidays, Sidras and Haftoras. Contains also a Hebrew festival calendar for 2000 years. [Brooklyn? N.Y., 1963] 1 v. (unpaged) 26 cm. [CE35.G7] 63-59822
1. Caldendar, Jewish. I. Title.

IRONSIDE, Henry Allan, 1876-1951. 222.7
Notes on the books of Ezra, Nehemiah, and Esther. New York, Loizeaux Bros. [1951] 101, 126, 123p. 20cm. [BS1205.I7] 54-32893
1. Bible. O. T. Historical books—Commentaries. I. Title.

SEVENTH-DAY Adventists. General Conference. Historical Research Committee. 222.7
The chronology of Ezra 7; a report prepared for the committee by Siegfried H. Horn and Lynn H. Wood. Washington, Review and Herald Pub. Association [1953] 160p. illus. 21cm. Bibliography: p. 146-156. [BS1355.S4] 53-33640
1. Bible. O.T. Ezra VII—Chronology. 2. Seventh-Day Adventists—Doctrinal and controversial works. I. Horn, Siegfried H., 1908- II. Wood, Lynn Harper, 1887- III. Title.

SEVENTH-DAY Adventists. General Conference. Historical Research Committee. 222'.7
The chronology of Ezra 7; [a report of the committee prepared by] Siegfried H. Horn and Lynn H. Wood. 2d ed., rev. Washington, Review and Herald Pub. Association [1970] 192 p. illus., facsims. 21 cm. "The report is based on the work of all the members, and the final product represents the united conclusions of the committee."—First ed. (1953) of the report. [BS1355.2.S48 1970] 70-23756
1. Bible. O.T. Ezra VII—Chronology. 2. Calendar, Jewish. I. Wood, Lynn Harber, 1887- joint author. II. Title.

TORREY, Charles Cutler, 1863-1956. 222'.7'06
Ezra studies. Prolegomenon by William F. Stinespring. New York, Ktav Pub. House, 1970. xxxiv, 346 p. 23 cm. (The Library of Biblical studies) Reprint of the 1910 ed., with Stinespring's prolegomenon added. [BS1355.2.T66 1970] 69-11427
1. Bible. O.T. Ezra—Criticism, Textual. 2. Bible. O.T. Ezra—Criticism, interpretation, etc. I. Title. II. Series.

BIBLE. O.T. Proverbs, English. 1963.Authorized. 222.707
The book of Proverbs, from the authorized King James version, with an introd. by Robert Gordis and decorations by Valenti Angelo. New York, Printed for the members of the Limited Editions Club, 1963. 1 v. (unpaged, on double leaves) illus. 25 cm. [BS1463.G6] 64-1770
I. Gordis, Robert, 1908- II. Angelo, Valenti, 1897- illus. III. Title.

JONES, Edgar 222.707
Proverbs and Ecclesiastes: introduction and commentary. New York, Macmillan [1962, c.1961] 349p. 19cm. (Torch Bible commentaries) 62-16096 4.25
1. Bible. O.T. Proverbs—Commentaries. 2. Bible. O.T. Ecclesiastes—Commentaries. I. Title.

JONES, Edgar, 1912- 222.707
Proverbs and Ecclesiastes; introduction and commentary. New York, Macmillan [1961] 349 p. 19 cm. (Torch Bible commentaries) [BS1465.3.J6] 62-16096
1. Bible. O. T. Proverbs—Commentaries. 2. Bible. O. T. Ecclesiastes—Commentaries. I. Title. II. Series.

BIBLE. O.T. Ezra. English. New English. 1976. 222'.7'077
The books of Ezra and Nehemiah / commentary by R. J. Coggins. Cambridge [Eng.] ; New York : Cambridge University Press, 1976. p. cm. (The Cambridge Bible commentary, New English Bible) Includes index. Bibliography: p. [BS1353.C63] 75-26278 ISBN 0-521-08648-5 : 15.75. ISBN 0-521-09759-2 pbk. : 6.75
1. Bible. O.T. Ezra—Commentaries. 2. Bible. O.T. Nehemiah—Commentaries. I. Coggins, R. J., 1929- II. Bible. O.T. Nehemiah. English. New English. 1976. III. Title. IV. Series.

ANDERSON, Stanley Edwin. 222.8
Nehemiah, the executive. Wheaton, Ill., Van Kampen Press [1954] 168p. 20cm. [BS1365.A5] 54-11937
1. Bible. O. T. Nehemiah—Homiletical use. 2. Nehemiah. I. Title.

MCINTIRE, Carl, 1906- 222.8
The wall of Jerusalem also is broken down. Collngswood, N. J., Christian Beacon Press, 1954. 120p. 21cm. [BS1365.M3] 55-16570
1. Bible. O. T. Nehemiah—Sermons. 2. Presbyterian Chruch—Sermons. 3. Sermons, American. I. Title.

REDPATH, Alan. 222.8
Victorious Christian service; studies in the book of Nehemiah. [Westwood, N. J.] Revell [1958] 190p. 21cm. [BS1365.R4] 58-11020
1. Bible. O. T. Nehemiah—Commentaries. I. Title.

BARBER, Cyril J. 222'.8'06
Nehemiah and the dynamics of effective leadership / by Cyril J. Barber. Neptune, N.J. : Loizeaux Bros., [1976] p. cm. Bibliography: p. [BS1365.2.B37] 76-22567 pbk. : 2.75
1. Nehemiah. 2. Bible. O.T. Nehemiah—Criticism, interpretation, etc. 3. Leadership—Biblical teaching. I. Title.

MCGEE, J Vernon. 222.9
Exposition on the book of Esther. Wheaton, Ill., Van Kampen Press [1951] 76 p. 20 cm. [BS135.M2] 51-2783
1. Bible. O. T. Esther—Sermons. I. Title.

MCGEE, John Vernon, 1904- 222.9
Exposition on the book of Esther. Wheaton, Ill., Van Kampen Press [1951] 76p. 20cm. [BS1375.M2] 51-2783
1. Bible. O. T. Esther—Sermons. I. Title.

NECHES, Solomon Michael, 1891- 222.9
The case of Mordecai vs. Haman. [1st ed.] Los Angeles, De Vorss [1951] 55 p. 21 cm. Bibliographical references included in "Notes" (p. 32-51) [BS580.M57N4] 51-1267
1. Mordecai, cousin of Esther, Queen of Persia. 2. Haman, chief minister of Abasuerus, King of Persia. I. Title.

CARSON, Alexander 222.906
God's providence unfolded in the Book of Esther. Swengel, Pa., Bible Truth, 1962. 132p. 20cm. 1.50 pap.,
I. Title.

DICKINSON, George T. 222'.9'06
Hidden patterns and the grand design [by] George T. Dickinson. Washington, Review & Herald [1967] 126p. 20cm. [BS1375.4.D5] 67-19721 3.50
1. Bible. O. T. Esther—Devotional literature. I. Title.

DICKINSON, George T 222'.9'06
Hidden patterns and the grand design [by] George T. Dickinson. Washington, Review and Herald Pub. Assn [1967] 126 p. 20 cm. [BS1375.4D5] 67-19721
1. Bible, O. T. Esther — Devotional literature. I. Title.

ARMERDING, Carl. 222'.9'066
Esther for such a time as this. Westchester, Ill., Good News Publishers [1974] 96 p. 18 cm. (A One evening book) [BS1375.2.A75] 73-92177 0.95 (pbk)
1. Bible. O.T. Esther—Criticism, interpretation, etc. I. Title.

THOMAS, W. Ian. 222'.9'066
If I perish, I perish; the Christian life as seen in Esther, by W. Ian Thomas. Grand Rapids, Zondervan Pub. House [1967] 126 p. 21 cm. [BS1375.4.T47] 65-19512
1. Bible. O.T. Esther—Devotional literature. I. Title.

BIBLE. O.T. Esther. English. Moore. 1971. 222'.9'077
Esther. Introd., translation, and notes by Carey A. Moore. [1st ed.] Garden City, N.Y., Doubleday, 1971. lxxii, 117 p. illus., facsim., 2 maps. 24 cm. (The Anchor Bible, 7B) Bibliography: p. [lxv]-lxxii. [BS192.2.A1 1964.G3 vol. 7B] 75-140615 6.00
1. Bible. O.T. Esther—Commentaries. I. Moore, Carey A., 1930- ed. II. Title. III. Series.

BRIN, Ruth Firestone. 222'.9'09505
The story of Esther / Ruth F. Brin ; illustrated by H. Hechtkopf. Minneapolis : Lerner Publications Co., 1976. [32] p. : col. ill. ; 31 cm. Retells the story of Esther, a young Jewish girl who became queen of Persia and used her influence to stop the murder of the Jews of her country. [BS580.E8B74 1976] 92 75-743 ISBN 0-8225-0364-6 lib.bdg. : 4.95
1. Esther, Queen of Persia—Juvenile literature. 2. Bible stories, English—O.T. Esther. I. Hechtkopf, H. II. Title.

*WARBLER, J.-M. 222.92
The prophet and the soldier; story by J.-M. Warbler, Harold Winstone. Pictures by Alain Le Foll. New York, Macmillan, c.1965, 1966. 1v. (unpaged) col. illus. 20cm. (Dove bks., 16:04569) .59 pap.,
I. Title.

223 Poetic Books Of Old Testament

ASPECTS of wisdom in Judaism and early Christianity / Robert L. Wilken, editor. Notre Dame, Ind. : University of Notre Dame Press, [1975] xxii, 218 p. ; 21 cm. ([Studies in Judaism and Christianity in antiquity] ; no. 1) Papers presented at a seminar sponsored by the Dept. of theology, University of Notre Dame in 1973. Includes indexes. Bibliography: p. 201-210. [BS1455.A8] 74-27888 ISBN 0-268-00577-X : 13.95 223
1. Philo Judaeus. 2. Bible. N.T.—Relation to Old Testament—Addresses, essays, lectures. 3. Midrash—History and criticism. 4. Wisdom literature—Criticism, interpretation, etc.—Addresses, essays, lectures. 5. Christianity—Early church, ca. 30-600—Addresses, essays, lectures. I. Wilken, Robert Louis, 1936- II. Notre Dame, Ind. University. Dept. of Theology. III. Title. IV. Series.

BEAUCAMP, Evode. 223
Man's destiny in the books of wisdom. [Translated by John Clarke] Staten Island, N.Y., Alba House [1970] xii, 217 p. 22 cm. Translation of La sagesse et la destin des elus, first published in 1957 as v. 2 of the author's Sous la main de Dieu. [BS1455.B3613] 73-110596 ISBN 0-8189-0159-4 4.95
1. Wisdom literature—Criticism, interpretation, etc. I. Title.

BIBLE. O. T. Ecclesiastes. English. 1952. Authorized in Bible. O. T. Psalms. English. 1952. Authorized. 223
The book of Psalms and the First psalm of David, the book of Proverbs [and] the book of Ecclesiastes. Garden City, N. Y., Doubleday [1952] [BS1403.D6] 52-5118
I. Title.

BIBLE. O.T. Ecclesiastes. English. 1965.Authorized. j223
Ecclesiastes; or, The preacher. In the King James translation of the Bible. With drawings by Ben Shahn, engraved in wood by Stefan Martin. Calligraphy by David Soshensky. New York, Spiral Press, 1965. 1 v. (unpaged) illus. 34 cm. 285 numbered copies. No. for copyright. [BS1473] 67-578
1. Shahn, Ben, 1896- illus. I. Title. II. Title: The preacher.

BIBLE. O.T. Ecclesiastes III, 1-8. English. 1966. j223
A time for all things; Ecclesiastes: chapter 3, verses 1-8. Pictures by Tony Palazzo. New York, H. Z. Walck, 1966. 1 v. (unpaged) col. illus. 20 cm. [BS1473] 66-18537
1. Bible. O. T. Ecclesiastes III, 1-8—Pictures, illustrations, etc. I. Palazzo, Tony, Illus. II. Title.

BIBLE. O.T. Ecclesiastes III, 1-8. English. 1966 j223
A time for all things; Ecclesiastes: chapter 3, verses 1-8. Pictures by Tony Palazzo. New York, Walck, c.1966 1 v. (unpaged) col. illus. 20 cm. [B 473 1966] 66-18537 3.75
1. Bible. O.T. Ecclesiastes III, 1-8—Pictures, illustrations, etc. I. Palazzo, Tony, illus. II. Title.

BIBLE. O.T. English. Selections. 1966.Douai. j223
Psalms for children; selections from the Douay Version of the Old Testament, selected by Edith Lowe. Illustrated by Nan Pollard. Chicago, Follett Pub. co. [1966] 44 p. col. illus. 29 x 14 cm. [BS1423.L6] 66-15916
I. Lowe, Edith May (Kovar) 1905- ed. II. Title.

BIBLE. O. T. Proverbs. English. 1952. Authorized in Bible. O. T. Psalms. English. 1952. Authorized. 223
The book of Psalms and the First psalm of David, the book of Proverbs [and] the book of Ecclesiastes. Garden City, N. Y., Doubleday [1952] [BS1403.D6] 52-5118

I. Title.

BIBLE. O. T. Psalms. English. 223
1952. Authorized.
The book of Psalms and the First psalm of David, the book of Proverbs [and] the book of Ecclesiastes; King James version with wood engravings by Clare Leighton. Garden City, N. Y., Doubleday [1952] xii. 304 p. illus. 22 cm. [BS1403.D6] 52-5118
I. Bible. O. T. 1 Chronicles xvi, 8-36. English. 1952. Authorized. II. Bible. O. T. Proverbs. English. 1952. Authorized. III. Bible. O. T. Ecclesiastes. English 1952. Authorized. IV. Leighton, Clare Veronica Hope, 1900- illus. V. Title.

BIBLE. O.T. Psalms. English. j223
Selections. 1966.Authorized.
The child's book of Psalms; selections from the King James Version of the Old Testament, selected by Edith Lowe. Illustrated by Nan Pollard. Chicago, Follett Pub. Co. [1966] 44 p. col. illus. 29 x 14 cm. [BS1423.L58] 66-15917
I. Lowe, Edith May (Kovar) 1905- ed. II. Title.

BIBLE. O.T. Psalms. English. 223
Selections. 1966. Authorized
The child's book of Psalms; selections from the King James Version of the Old Testament, selected by Edith Lowe. Illus. by Nan Pollard. Chicago, Follett [c.1966] 44p. col. illus. 29x14cm. [BS1423.L58] 66-15917 1.00 bds.,
I. Lowe, Edith May (Kovar) 1905- ed. II. Title.

BIBLE. O.T. Psalms. English. 223
Selections. 1966. Douai.
Psalms for children; selections from the Douay Version of the Old Testament, selected by Edith Lowe iIllus. by Nan Pollard. Chicago, Follett [c.1966] llus. 29x14cm. 44p. col. x14cm. [BS1423.L6] 66-15916 1.00 bds.,
I. Lowe, Edith May (Kovar) 1905- ed. II. Title.

BIBLE. O.T. 1 Chronicles XVI 223
8-36. English. 1953. Authorized in Bible O.T. Psalms. English 1952
The book of Psalms and the First psalm of David, the book of Proverbs [and] the book of Ecclesiastes. Garden City. N. Y., Doubleday [1952] [BS1403.D6] 52-5118
I. Title.

COOK, Albert Spaulding. 223
The root of the thing; a study of Job and the Songs [by] Albert Cook. Bloomington, Indiana University Press, 1968. xii, 162 p. 22 cm. [BS1415.2.C65] 68-27340 6.95
1. Bible. O.T. Job—Criticism, interpretation, etc. 2. Bible. O.T. Song of Solomon—Criticism, interpretation, etc. I. Title.

JOHNSON, L. D., 1916- 223
Israel's wisdom : learn and live / L. D. Johnson. Nashville : Broadman Press, [1975] 128 p. ; 20 cm. [BS1455.J63] 74-26312 ISBN 0-8054-8125-7 : 1.95
1. Wisdom literature—Criticism, interpretation, etc. I. Title.

JONES, Mary Alice, 1898- j223
The Twenty-third Psalm. Interpreted by Mary Alice Jones. Illustrated by Manning de V. Lee. Chicago, Rand McNally, 1965, c1964. 1 v. (unpaged) col. illus. 32 cm. [[BS1450 23dJ63]] 65-14639
1. Bible. O. T. Psalms xxiii—Juvenile literature. I. Lee, Manning de Villeneuve 1894- illus. II. Title.

JONES, Mary Alice, 1898- 223
The Twenty-third Psalm. Interpreted by Mary Alice Jones. Illus. by Manning de V. Lee. Chicago, Rand McNally, 1966, c.1964. 1 v. (unpaged) col. illus. 32 cm. [BS145023d.J63] 65-14639 pap., 1.00
1. Bible. O. T. Psalms XXII—Juvenile literature. I. Lee, Manning de Villeneuve, 1894- illus. II. Title.

LITTLE (Arthur D.) inc. 223
An examination of the applicability of microelectronic circuits to the telemetry and command subsystems of several applications spacecraft. Prepared under contract no. NASw-732 for National Aeronautics and Space Administration. [Washington, National Aeronautics and Space Administration]; for sale by the Clearinghouse for Federal Scientific and Technical Information, Springfield, Va [1965] vii, [144] p. illus. 27 cm. [NASA contractor report CR-223] Includes bibliographies. [TL521.3.C6A3 no.] 65-61596
1. Aerospace telemetry. 2. Space vehicles — Command control systems. 3. Astrionics. 4. Microelectronics. I. U.S. National Aeronautics and Space Administration. II. Title. III. Series: U.S. National Aeronautics and Space Administration. NASA contractor report (CR-223

PATERSON, John, 1887- 223
The book that is alive; studies in Old Testament life and thought as set forth by the Hebrew sages. New York, Scribner, 1954. 196p. 21cm. [BS1455.P3] 54-5921
1. Bible. O. T. Wisdom literature—Criticism, interpretation, etc. 2. Bible—Influence. I. Title.

PETERSHAM, Maud (Fuller) 223
1890-
The Shepherd Psalm; Psalm XXIII from the book of Psalms. New York, Macmillan, 1962. 24 p. illus. 24 cm. Tells of King David and the song he sang, the twenty-third Psalm; illustrates and gives the words to the Psalm; and tells what life was like for a shepherd in Old Testament times. [BS1450 23d.P4] AC 68
1. Bible. O.T. Psalms XXIII. I. Title.

RANKIN, Oliver Shaw. 223
Israel's Wisdom literature; its bearing on theology and the history of religion [by] O. S. Rankin. New York, Schocken Books [1969] xvi, 270 p. 21 cm. Reprint of the 1936 ed. Bibliographical footnotes. [BS1455.R27 1969] 69-19620 2.45
1. Bible. O.T. Wisdom literature—Theology. 2. Reward (Theology)—Biblical teaching. 3. Immortality (Judaism) I. Title.

SPRINGETT, J C 223
Telemetry and command techniques for planetary spacecraft [by] J. C. Springett. Pasadena, Jet Propulsion Laboratory, California Institute of Technology, 1965. vi, 32 p. illus. 28 cm. (JPL technical report no. 32-495) Bibliography: p. 31-32. [TL3025.S65] 68-3480
1. Astronautics—Communication systems. 2. Aerospace telemetry. I. Title. II. Series: California Institute of Technology, Pasadena. Jet Propulsion Laboratory. JPL technical report no. 32-495

MADDUX, Roy Clark 223.02
Outline studies of Job, Proverbs, Ecclesiastes, and the Song of Songs. Grand Rapids, Mich., Baker Bk, [c.] 1966. 61p. 20cm. [BS1456.M3] 66-18307 1.95 bds.,
1. Bible. O. T. Wisdom literature — Study — Outlines, syllabi, etc. 2. Bible. O. T. Wisdom literature — Study—Outlines, syllabi, etc. 3. Bible. O. T. Job—Study — outlines, syllabi, etc. I. Title.

BIBLE. O.T. 223'.05'2
Hagiographa. English. Selections. 1973.
The Old Testament books of poetry from 26 translations. Curtis Vaughan, general editor. Grand Rapids, Zondervan Bible Publishers [1973] 710 p. 22 cm. (The Old Testament books from 26 translations) [BS1403.V38] 73-175992 9.95
I. Vaughan, Curtis, ed. II. Title. III. Series: Bible. O.T. English. 1973. The Old Testament books from 26 translations.

GOODWIN, John 223.06
Divine wisdom; an introduction to the Wisdom books of the Bible. New York, Association [1963] 80p. 19cm. (World Christian bks., no. 47) 64-128 1.25 pap.,
1. Bible. O.T. Wisdom literature—Introductions. I. Title.

PERDUE, Leo G. 223'.06
Wisdom and cult : a critical analysis of the views of cult in the wisdom literature of Israel and the ancient Near East / by Leo G. Perdue. Missoula, Mont. : Published by Scholars Press for the Society of Biblical Literature, c1977. xiii, 390 p. ; 22 cm. (Dissertation series ; no. 30) Originally presented as the author's thesis, Vanderbilt University, 1976. Bibliography: p. 365-390. [BS1455.P4 1977] 76-47453 ISBN 0-89130-094-5 : 4.50
1. Wisdom literature—Criticism, interpretation, etc. 2. Cultus, Jewish. 3. Egyptian literature—Relation to the Old Testament. 4. Assyro-Babylonian literature—Relation to the Old Testament. I. Title. II. Series: Society of Biblical Literature. Dissertation series ; no. 30.

ROBINSON, Theodore Henry, 223'.06
1881-
The poetry of the Old Testament / by Theodore H. Robinson. New York : AMS Press, c1977. 231 p. ; 18 cm. Reprint of the 1947 ed. published by Duckworth, London, in series: Studies in theology. Includes index. Bibliography: p. 217-227. [BS1405.2.R63 1977] 75-41233 ISBN 0-404-14593-0 : 15.00
1. Hebrew poetry, Biblical—History and criticism. I. Title. II. Series: Studies in theology (London).

SKEHAN, Patrick William. 223'.06
Studies in Israelite poetry and wisdom, by Patrick W. Skehan. Washington, Catholic Biblical Association of America, 1971. xii, 265 p. 26 cm. (The Catholic Biblical quarterly. Monograph series, 1) Includes bibliographical references. [BS1455.S63] 77-153511
1. Bible. O.T. Psalms—Criticism, interpretation, etc. 2. Bible. O.T. Job—Criticism, interpretation, etc. 3. Wisdom literature—Criticism, interpretation, etc. I. Title. II. Series.

WITHER, George, 1588- 223'.06
1667.
Britain's remembrancer. (cI' I[reverse c] cxxviii). New York, B. Franklin [1967] 580 p. 25 cm. (Burt Franklin research & source works series, no. 150) Reprint of the 1880 ed., which was issued as no. 28-29 of The Spenser Society. [PR2392.B6 1967] 72-184254
1. Plague—England—London, 1625—Poetry. I. Title. II. Series: Spenser Society, Manchester. Publication no. 28-29.

DILLON, Emile Joseph, 223'.06'6
1855-1933.
The sceptics of the Old Testament: Job, Koheleth, Agur; with English text translated for the first time from the primitive Hebrew as restored on the basis of recent philological discoveries. New York, Haskell House Publishers, 1973. xvi, 280 p. 23 cm. Reprint of the 1895 ed. published by Ibister, London. Includes translations of the restored texts of The poem of Job, The speaker, and The sayings of Agur. Includes bibliographical references. [BS1415.D54 1973] 73-16064 ISBN 0-8383-1723-5
1. Bible. O.T. Job—Criticism, interpretation, etc. 2. Bible. O.T. Ecclesiastes—Criticism, interpretation, etc. 3. Bible. O.T. Proverbs—Criticism, interpretation, etc. I. Title.

STUDIES in ancient 223'.06'6
Israelite wisdom / selected with a prolegomenon by James L. Crenshaw. New York : Ktav Pub. House, 1976. xviii, 494 p. ; 24 cm. (The Library of Biblical studies) Bibliography: p. 46-60. [BS1455.S83] 75-31986 ISBN 0-87068-255-5 : 29.50
1. Wisdom literature—Criticism, interpretation, etc.—Addresses, essays, lectures. 2. Wisdom—Biblical teaching—Addresses, essays, lectures. I. Crenshaw, James L. II. Series.

DAILY Bible commentary 223'.07
: Psalms-Malachi / Arthur E. Cundall co-ordinating editor. Philadelphia : A. J. Holman, [1977], c1973. p. cm. Reprint of the ed. published by Scripture Union, London. [BS1151.2.D33 1977] 76-46492 ISBN 0-87981-069-6 : 8.95 (vol. 1)
1. Bible. O.T.—Commentaries. I. Cundall, Arthur Ernest.

DAILY Bible commentary 223'.07
: Psalms-Malachi / Arthur E. Cundall co-ordinating editor. Philadelphia : A. J. Holman, [1977], c1973. p. cm. Reprint of the ed. published by Scripture Union, London. [BS1151.2.D33 1977] 76-46492 ISBN 0-87981-069-6 : 8.95 (vol. 1)
1. Bible. O.T.—Commentaries. I. Cundall, Arthur Ernest.

BENNETT, William, 1818- 223.1
1900.
The trials and triumph of Job. Georgetown, Conn., Glenburgh Co. [1954] 115p. illus. 22cm. In verse. [PS1094.B64T7 1954] 54-25236
I. Bible. O. T. Job. English. Paraphrases. 1964. II. Title.

BIBLE, O. T. Job. English. 223.1
1856.
The book of Job, from the original Hebrew on the basis of the common and earlier English versions. New York, American Bible Union, 1856. 63p. 24cm. [BS1413 1856] 57-52365
I. American Bible Union. II. Title.

BIBLE. O. T. Job. English. 223.1
1926. Authorized.
The book of Job, according to the Authorized version 1926. MDCXI, following the arrangement of the Temple Bible. [San Francisco, Grabhorn Press, 1926] xxix p. col. front. 45 cm. Caption title. 210 copies. No. 66. [BS1413 1926] 57-51871
I. Title.

BIBLE. O. T. Job. English. 223.1
1951. Peterson.
The God that Job had; a reading of the book of Job, by Russell A. Peterson. Minneapolis, Colwell Press [1951] 51 p. 22 cm. [BS1413.P4] 51-39050
I. Peterson, Russell Arthur, 1922- tr. II. Title.

BIBLE. O. T. Job. English. 223.1
1958. Jewish Publication Society.
Book of Job; a commentary, by Solomon B. Freehof. New York, Union of American Hebrew Congregations, 1958. 261p. 24cm. (The Jewish commentary for Bible readers) Union adult series. Includes bibliography. [BS1415.F66] 58-38364
1. Bible. O. T. Job—Commentaries. I. Freehof, Solomon Bennett, 1892- II. Title.

BIBLE. O. T. Job. English. 223.1
1965. Pope
Job. Introd., translation, notes by Marvin H. Pope. Garden City, N.Y., Doubleday [c.]1965. lxxxii, 293p. 25cm. (Anchor Bible, v.15) Bibl. [BS192.2.A1.G3 vol.15] 65-12361 6.00
1. Bible. O. T. Job—Commentaries. I. Pope, Marvin H., ed. II. Title.

BIBLE. O.T. Job. English. 223.1
1965. Pope.
Job. Introd., translation, and notes by Marvin H. Pope. [1st ed.] Garden City, N.Y., Doubleday, 1965. lxxxii, 293 p. 25 cm. (The Anchor Bible, v. 15) Includes bibliographical references. [BS192.2.A1 1964.G3 vol. 15] 65-12361
1. Bible. O.T. Job—Commentaries. I. Pope, Marvin, H., ed. II. Title. III. Series.

BIBLE. O.T. Job. English. 223'.1
Authorized. 1976.
The book of Job / illustrated by William Blake ; with a new introd. by Michael Marqusee. New York : Paddington, c1976. 52 p., [22] leaves of plates : ill. ; 28 cm. (Masterpieces of the illustrated book) [BS1413.B55] 75-22959 ISBN 0-8467-0112-X : 4.95
1. Bible—Pictures, illustrations, etc. I. Blake, William, 1757-1827.

BLAIR, J. Allen 223.1
Living patiently; a devotional study of the Book of Job, by J. Allen Blair. [1st ed.] Neptune. N. J. Loizeaux, 1966. 379p. 20cm. [BS1415.3.B57] 66-25720 4.00 bds.,
1. Bible. O. T. Job—Commentaries. I. Title.

BREAKSTONE, Raymond, ed. 223.1
Job: a case study. New York, Bookman Associates [c1964] 320 p. 22 cm. Contents.CONTENTS. -- The Book of job. -- J. B., by A. MacLeish. -- A masque of reason, by R. Frost. -- A guide to Job's encounter, by J. K. Singer. Bibliography: p. 319-320. [BS1415.5.B7] 64-8607
1. Bible. O. T. Job — Criticism, Interpretation, etc. 2. Suffering. I. MacLeish, Archibald, 1892- J. B. II. Frost, Robert, 1874-1963. The masque of reason. III. Singer, June K. The guide to Job's encounter. IV. Title.

CALVIN, Jean, 1509-1564. 223.1
Sermons from Job; selected and translated by Leroy Nixon. With an introductory essay by Harold Dekker. Grand Rapids, W. B. Eerdmans Pub. Co., 1952. xxxvii, 300 p. 23 cm. [BS1415.C252] 52-13313
1. Bible. O.T. Job—Sermons. I. Title.

CHAPPELL, Clovis Gillham, 223.1
1882-
Sermons from Job. Nashville, Abingdon Press [1957] 158p. 20cm. [BS1415.C48] 57-8353
1. Bible. O. T. Job—Sermons. 2. Methodist Church—Sermons. 3. Sermons, American. I. Title.

GARD, Donald H 1923- 223.1
The exegetical method of the Greek translator of the Book of Job. Philadelphia, Society of Biblical Literature, 1952. vi, 107p. 23cm. (Journal of Biblical literature. Monograph series, v.8) Condensation of thesis--Princeton Theological Seminary. Bibliography: p. 96-106. [BS1414.G72G25] 53-836
1. Bible. O. T. Job. Greek—Versions—Septuagint. 2. Bible. O.T. Job—Theology. 3. God—Biblical teaching. I. Title. II. Series.

GERBER, Israel Joshua. 223.1
The psychology of the suffering mind. [1st ed.] New York, Jonathan David Co. ['1951] 202 p. 24 cm. [BS1415.G44] 52-798
1. Bible. O. T. Job—Psychology. I. Title.

HANSON, Anthony Tyrrell 223.1
The book of Job. Introd., commentary by Anthony and Miriam Hanson. New York, Collier [1962] 127p. 18cm. (Torch Bible commentaries; AS235Y) .95 pap.,
1. Bible. O.T. Job—Commentaries. I. Hanson, Miriam, joint author. II. Title.

KENT, Herbert Harold. 223'.1
Job, our contemporary [by] H. Harold Kent. Grand Rapids, Eerdmans [1967] 65 p. 20 cm. [BS1415.2.K4] 67-30116
1. Bible. O.T. Job—Criticism, interpretation, etc. I. Title.

LAMB, John Alexander 223.1
The Psalms in Christian worship. London, Faith Pr. [dist. Westminster, Md., Canterbury Pr., c.1962] 178p. 23cm. Bibl. 63-597 3.95
1. Bible. O. T., Psalms—Liturgical use. I. Title.

TERRIEN, Samuel. 223.1
Job: poet of existence. [1st ed.] Indianapolis, BobbsMerrill [1957] 249p. 21cm. Includes bibliography. [BS1415.T4] 57-9352
1. Bible. O. T. Job—Commentaries. I. Title.

WARD, William B 223.1
Out of the whirlwind; answers to the problem

of suffering from the book of Job. Richmond, John Knox Press [1958] 123 p. 21 cm. Includes bibliography. [BS1415.W3] 58-7771
1. Bible, O.T. Job — Commentaries. I. Title.

WENDT, A Earnest, 1888- 223.1
A new look at Job. Boston, Christopher Pub. House [1954-56] 2v. 21cm. Vol. 2 published by Greenwich Book Publishers, New York, has special title: job: beneath the surface. [BS1415.W45] 55-18761
1. Bible. O. T. Job— Criticism, interpretation, etc. I. Title.

WENDT, A. Earnest, 1888- 223.1
A new look at Job. Boston, Christopher Pub. House [1954-56] 2 v. 21 cm. Vol. 2 published by Greenwich Book Publishers, New York, has special title: Job: beneath the surface. [BS1415.W45] 53-18761
1. Bible. O.T. Job — Criticism, interpretation, etc. I. Title.

DONN, Thomas 223'.1'052
Mackenzie.
The divine challenge; being a metrical paraphrase of the Book of Job in four-line stanzas of anapaestic tetrameters in rhyme, by Thomas M. Donn. Inverness [Scot.] Printed by R. Carruthers, 1963. xxii, 120 p. 23 cm. Bibliography: p. xiii. [BS1416.D6] 77-232712
1. Bible. O.T. Job—Paraphrases, English. I. Title.

ETHERIDGE, Eugene W. 223'.1'052
The man from Uz; a paraphrase drama of the Book of Job in blank verse, by Eugene W. Etheridge. Francestown, N.H. Golden Quill Press [1972] 94 p. 21 cm. [BS1416.E83] 72-79811 ISBN 0-8233-0178-8 4.00
1. Bible. O.T. Job—Paraphrases, English. I. Title.

CARSTENSEN, Roger N. 223.106
Job: defense of honor. New York, Abingdon Press [1963] 158 p. 23 cm. [BS1415.2.C3] 63-7764
1. Bible. O. T. Job—Criticism, interpretation, etc. I. Title.

CRAWFORD, Harriet A 223.106
A libretto for Job. Boston, Christopher Pub. House [1963] 199 p. 21 cm. [BS1416.C7] 63-20778
I. Bible. O.T. Job. English. 1963 II. Title.

CRAWFORD, Harriet A. 223.106
A libretto for Job. Boston, Christopher [c.1963] 199p. 21cm. 63-20778 3.95
1. Bible. O.T. Job. English. 1963. I. Title.

FINLAY, M. H. 223.106
The arrows of the Almighty: a devotional study of the character of Job. Chicago, Moody [c.1963] 80p. 18cm. (Compact bks., 37) .29 pap.,
I. Title.

GARLAND, D. David. 223'.1'06
Job: a study guide, by D. David Garland. Grand Rapids, Zondervan Pub. House [1971] 107 p. 21 cm. (Study guide series) Includes bibliographical references. [BS1415.5.G3] 70-156242
1. Bible. O.T. Job—Study—Text-books. I. Title.

GLATZER, Nahum Norbert, 223'.1'06
1903- comp.
The dimensions of Job; a study and selected readings, presented by Nahum N. Glatzer. New York, Schocken Books [1969] x, 310 p. 21 cm. Bibliography: p. 299-303. [BS1415.2.G57] 69-11936 7.95
1. Bible. O.T. Job—Criticism, interpretation, etc. I. Title.

GLATZER, Nahum Norbert, 223'.1'06
1903-
The dimensions of Job; a study and selected readings, presented by Nahum N. Glatzer. New York, Schocken Books [1973? c.1969] 310 p. 21 cm. (Schocken paperbacks on Jewish life & religion) Bibliography: p. 299-303. [BS1415.2.G57] ISBN 0-8052-0378-8 pap., 3.95
1. Bible. O.T. Job—Criticism, interpretation, etc. I. Title.
L.C. card for original ed.: 69-11936

GORDIS, Robert, 1908- 223.106
The book of God and man; a study of Job. Chicago, University of Chicago Press [1965] xii, 389 p. 24 cm. Bibliography: p. 367-376. [BS1415.2.G6] 65-25126
1. Bible. O.T. Job—Criticism, interpretation, etc. I. Title.

HONE, Ralph E., ed. 223.106
The voice out of the whirlwind: the book of Job. San Francisco, Chandler Pub. Co. [1960] 333 p. illus. 21 cm. (Materials for analysis) "The Authorized version of the book of Job": p. [2]-56. Includes bibliography. [BS1415.2.H6] 60-12567
1. Job, the patriarch. 2. Bible. O.T. Job—Criticism, interpretation, etc. I. Bible. O.T. Job. English. 1930. Authorized. 1960. II. Title.

JUNG, Carl Gustav, 223'.1'06
1875-1961.
Answer to Job. Translated by R. F. C. Hull. [1st Princeton/Bollingen paperback ed. Princeton, N.J.] Princeton University Press [1972, c1969] xv, 121 p. 21 cm. (Princeton/Bollingen paperbacks, 283) Translation of Antwort auf Hiob. Extracted from v. 11 of the author's Collected works, issued as no. 20 in the Bollingen series. Bibliography: p. 109. [BL51.J853 1972] 72-6097 ISBN 0-691-01785-9 2.95
1. Bible. O.T. Job—Criticism, interpretation, etc. 2. Religion—Philosophy. I. Title.

PATERSON, John, 1887- 223.106
The Wisdom of Israel; Job and Proverbs. Nashville, Abingdon Press [1961] 95 p. (Bible guides, no. 11) 61-2739 1.00, pap.
1. Bible. O. T. Job—Criticism, interpretation, etc. 2. Bible. O. T. Proverbs—Criticism, interpretation, etc. I. Title.

PATERSON, John, 1887- 223.106
The wisdom of Israel: Job and Proverbs. London, Lutterworth Press New York, Abingdon Press [1961] 93p. 20cm. (Bible guides, no. no. 11) [BS1415.2.P35 1961] 61-2739
1. Bible. O. T. Job—Criticism, interpretation, etc. 2. Bible. O. T. Proverbs—Criticism, interoretation, etc. I. Title.

PATRICK, Dale. 223'.1'06
Arguing with God : the angry prayers of Job / by Dale Patrick. St. Louis : Bethany Press, c1977. 121 p. : ill. ; 23 cm. Includes a paraphrastic translation of the book of Job. Includes index. Bibliography: 120-121. [BS1415.2.P37] 77-818 ISBN 0-8272-0013-7 pbk. : 5.95
1. Bible. O.T. Job—Criticism, interpretation, etc. 2. Bible. O.T. Job—Paraphrases, English. I. Title.

PATRICK, Dale. 223'.1'06
Arguing with God : the angry prayers of Job / by Dale Patrick. St. Louis : Bethany Press, c1977. 121 p. : ill. ; 23 cm. Includes a paraphrastic translation of the book of Job. Includes index. Bibliography: 120-121. [BS1415.2.P37] 77-818 ISBN 0-8272-0013-7 pbk. : 5.95
1. Bible. O.T. Job—Criticism, interpretation, etc. 2. Bible. O.T. Job—Paraphrases, English. I. Title.

SCHAPER, Robert N. 223'.1'06
Why me God? By Robert N. Schaper. Glendale, Calif., G/L Regal Books [1974] 146 p. 18 cm. (A Bible commentary for laymen) Bibliography: p. 145. [BS1415.2.S28] 73-82763 ISBN 0-8307-0263-6 1.25 (pbk.)
1. Bible. O.T. Job—Criticism, interpretation, etc. I. Title.

SINGER, Richard E. 223.106
Job's encounter. New York, Bkman [1964, c.1963] 276p. illus. 22cm. Bibl. 63-17402 4.50
1. Bible. O. T. Job—Criticism, interpretation, etc. I. Title.

SNAITH, Norman Henry, 223'.1'06
1898-
The Book of Job; its origin and purpose [by] Norman H. Snaith. Naperville, Ill., A. R. Allenson [1968] x, 116 p. 22 cm. (Studies in Biblical theology, 2d ser., 11) Bibliographical footnotes. [BS1415.2.S6] 75-2997
1. Bible. O.T. Job—Criticism, interpretation, etc. I. Title. II. Series.

GIBBS, Paul T. 223'.1'066
Job and the mysteries of wisdom, by Paul T. Gibbs. Nashville, Southern Pub. Association [1967] 175 p. 22 cm. Bibliography: p. 173-175. [BS1415.3.G5] 67-6132
1. Bible. O.T. Job—Commentaries. I. Title.

HONE, Ralph E., ed. 223'.1'066
The voice out of the whirlwind: the book of Job. Selected and edited by Ralph E. Hone. Rev. ed. San Francisco, Chandler Pub. Co. [1972] viii, 298 p. 21 cm. "The New English Bible version of the book of Job": p. 2-53. Bibliography: p. 295-298. [BS1415.2.H6 1972] 70-140217 ISBN 0-8102-0415-0 4.50
1. Job, the patriarch—Collections. 2. Bible. O.T. Job—Criticism, interpretation, etc.—Collections. I. Bible. O.T. Job. English. New English. 1972. II. Title.

HOWARD, David M. 223'.1'066
How come, God? Reflections from Job about God and puzzled man. [1st ed.] Philadelphia, A. J. Holman Co. [1972] 117 p. 21 cm. [BS1415.2.H67] 72-3477 ISBN 0-87981-010-6 3.95
1. Bible, O.T. Job—Criticism, interpretation, etc. 2. Providence and government of God—Biblical teaching. I. Title.

KAHN, Jack H. 223'.1'066
Job's illness : loss, grief, and integration : a psychological interpretation / by Jack Kahn with Hester Solomon. 1st ed. Oxford ; New York : Pergamon Press, [1975] p. cm. "The book of Job reproduced from The new English Bible": p. Bibliography: p. [BS580.J5K33 1975] 75-4834 ISBN 0-08-018087-6
1. Job, the patriarch. 2. Depression, Mental. I. Solomon, Hester, joint author. II. Bible. O.T. Job. English. New English. 1975. III. Title.

KAHN, Jack H. 223'.1'066
Job's illness : loss, grief, and integration : a psychological interpretation / by Jack Kahn, with Hester Solomon. 1st ed. Oxford ; New York : Pergamon Press, 1975. lxiv, 166 p., [5] leaves of plates : ill. ; 22 cm. (Pergamon international library of science, technology, engineering, and social studies) "The book of Job reproduced from The new English Bible": p. xiv-lxiv. Includes index. Bibliography: p. 159-162. [BS580.J5K33 1975] 75-4834 ISBN 0-08-018087-6 : 14.00
1. Job, the patriarch. 2. Depression, Mental. I. Solomon, Hester, joint author. II. Bible. O.T. Job. English. New English. 1975. III. Title.

KAUNG, Stephen. 223'.1'066
The splendor of his ways : seeing the Lord's end in Job / Stephen Kaung. New York : Christian Fellowship Publishers, [1974] 171 p. ; 21 cm. [BS1415.2.K37] 74-189520
1. Bible. O.T. Job—Criticism, interpretation, etc. I. Title.

LEVENSON, Jon Douglas. 223'.1'066
The Book of Job in its time and in the twentieth century. Cambridge, Mass., Harvard University Press, 1972. 80 p. 19 cm. (The LeBaron Russell Briggs prize honors essays in English, 1971) Bibliography: p. 73-75. [BS1415.2.L47] 73-188971 ISBN 0-674-07860-8
1. Bible. O.T. Job—Criticism, interpretation, etc. I. Title. II. Series.

MORGAN, George 223'.1'066
Campbell, 1863-1945.
The answers of Jesus to Job, by G. Campbell Morgan. Grand Rapids, Mich., Baker Book House [1973] 136 p. 19 cm. (G. Campbell Morgan library) First published in 1935. [BS1415.2] ISBN 0-8010-5917-8 1.95 (pbk.)
1. Bible. O.T. Job—Criticism, interpretation, etc. I. Title.

SANDERS, Paul S., 223'.1'066
comp.
Twentieth century interpretations of the Book of Job; a collection of critical essays, edited by Paul S. Sanders. Englewood Cliffs, N.J., Prentice-Hall [1968] vii, 118 p. 21 cm. (Twentieth century interpretations) (A Spectrum book.) Includes bibliographical references. [BS1415.2.S2] 68-17831
1. Bible. O.T. Job—Criticism, interpretations, etc. I. Title.

ANDERSEN, Francis I., 223'.1'07
1925-
Job : an introduction and commentary / by Francis I. Andersen. London ; Downers Grove, Ill. : Inter-Varsity Press, c1976. 294 p. ; 20 cm. (The Tyndale Old Testament commentaries) Includes bibliographical references. [BS1415.3.A5 1976] 76-12298 ISBN 0-87784-869-6 : 7.95
1. Bible. O.T. Job—Commentaries. I. Title.

BAKER, Wesley C 223.107
More than a man can take; a study of Job, by Wesley C. Baker. Philadelphia, Westminster Press [1966] 154 p. 21 cm. [BS1415.3.B3] 66-13082
1. Bible. O. T. Job—Commentaries. I. Title.

BAKER, Wesley C. 223.107
More than a man can take; a study of Job. Philadelphia, Westminster [c.1966] 154p. 21cm. [BS1415.3.B3] 66-13082 2.25 pap.,
1. Bibl. O.T.Job—Commentaries. I. Title.

BIBLE. O. T. Psalms. 223'.1'07
English. 1760. Authorized.
The New-England Psalter improved, by the addition of a variety of lessons in spelling, accented and divided according to rule. Likewise, rules for reading ... Some account of the books of the Old-Testament: of the books of the Prophets: of the Apocryphal books, and of the books of the New-Testament. The whole being a proper introduction, not only to learning, but to the training up children in the reading of the Holy Scriptures in particular. Philadelphia, Printed and sold by W. Dunlap, 1760. 116p. 16cm. [BS1422 1760] 55-53741
I. Title.

BIBLE. O. T. Psalms. 223'.1'07
English. 1952. Authorized.
The book of Psalms, from the Authorized King James version of the Holy Bible. New York, Priv. print., press of A. Colish, 1952. xii, 195p. 15cm. 'Four hundred and fifty copies. ... number 94.' [BS1422 1952] 53-26242
I. Title.

BLACKWOOD, Andrew 223.107
Watterson
Devotional introduction to Job. Grand Rapids, Baker Book House, [c.]1959. 166p. 23cm. 59-15525 2.95
1. Bible. O.T. Job—Commentaries. I. Title.

BLACKWOOD, Andrew 223.107
Watterson, 1915-
Devotional introduction to Job. [1st ed.] Grand Rapids, Baker Book House, 1959. 166p. 23cm. [BS1415.3.B55] 59-15525
1. Bible. O. T. Job—Commentaries. I. Title.

ELLISON, Henry Leopold. 223.107
From tragedy to triumph, the message of the book of Job. Grand Rapids, Eerdmans [1958] 127 p. 23 cm. Name originally: Henry Leopold Zeckhausen. [BS1415.3.E4] 58-9553
1. Bible. O.T. Job — Commentaries. I. Title.

FROST, Gerhard E. 223'.1'07
The color of the night : reflections on the Book of Job / Gerhard E. Frost. Minneapolis : Augsburg Pub., House, c1977. 144 p. ; 20 cm. [BS1415.4.F75] 77-72458 ISBN 0-8066-1583-4 pbk. : 3.50
1. Bible. O.T. Job—Meditations. I. Title.

FROST, Gerhard E. 223'.1'07
The color of the night : reflections on the Book of Job / Gerhard E. Frost. Minneapolis : Augsburg Pub., House, c1977. 144 p. ; 20 cm. [BS1415.4.F75] 77-72458 ISBN 0-8066-1583-4 pbk. : 3.50
1. Bible. O.T. Job—Meditations. I. Title.

HULME, William Edward, 223'.1'07
1920-
Dialogue in despair; pastoral commentary on the Book of Job [by] William E. Hulme. Nashville, Abingdon Press [1968] 157 p. 21 cm. [BS1415.3.H84] 68-11476
1. Bible. O.T. Job—Commentaries. 2. Pastoral counseling. I. Title.

JOHNSON, L. D., 1916- 223'.1'07
Out of the whirlwind; the major message of Job [by] L. D. Johnson. Nashville, Broadman Press [1971] 94 p. 19 cm. Includes bibliographical references. [BS1415.2.J58] 78-145983 ISBN 0-8054-1208-5
1. Job, the patriarch. 2. Bible. O.T. Job—Criticism, interpretation, etc. I. Title.

MACBEATH, Andrew 223.1'07
The book of Job; a study manual. Grand Rapids, Baker Bk., 1966. 106p. 20cm. (Shield Bible study outlines) Bibl. [BS1415.2.M3] 66-29241 1.50 pap.,
1. Bible. O.T. Job—Study—Outlines, syllabi, etc. I. Title.

MURPHY, Joseph 223.107
Living without strain; inner meaning of the book of Job. San Gabriel, Calif., P.O. Box 51 Willing Pub. Co. [c.1959] 157p. 20cm. 60-877 3.50
1. Bible. O. T. Job—Commentaries. 2. New Thought. I. Title.

MURPHY, Joseph, 1898- 223.107
Living without strain; inner meaning of the book of Job. San Gabriel. Calif., Willing Pub. Co. [c1959] 157p. 20cm. [BS1415.3.M8] 60-877
1. Bible. O. T. Job— Commentaries. 2. New Thought. I. Title.

MURPHY, Roland Edmund, 223'.1'07
1917-
The Psalms, Job / Roland E. Murphy. Philadelphia : Fortress Press, c1977. 96 p. ; 22 cm. (Proclamation commentaries) Includes index. Bibliography: p. 92-93. [BS1430.3.M87] 77-78637 ISBN 0-8006-0588-8 pbk. : 2.95
1. Bible. O.T. Psalms—Commentaries. 2. Bible. O.T. Job—Commentaries. I. Title.

SALMON BEN YERUHIM, fl. 223'.1'07
10th cent.
The Arabic commentary on the book of Psalms, chapters 42-72. Edited from the unique ms. in the State Public Library in Leningrad by Lawrence Marwick. Philadelphia, Dropsie College for Hebrew and Cognate Learning, 1956. 121p. 24cm. In Judeo-Arabic. [BS1429.S27] 58-41504
1. Bible. O. T. Psalms—Commentaries. 2. Karaites. I. Marwick, Lawrence, 1909- ed. II. Title.

BIBLE. O.T. Job. 223'.1'077
English. New English. 1975.
The Book of Job / commentary by Norman C. Habel. London ; New York : Cambridge University Press, 1975. x, 240 p. ; 21 cm. (Cambridge Bible commentary : New English Bible) Includes index. Bibliography: p. 235. [BS1413.H28] 74-82588 ISBN 0-521-20653-7 : 14.95 ISBN 0-521-09943-9 pbk. : 5.95

1. Bible. O.T. Job—Commentaries. I. Habel, Norman C. II. Title. III. Series.

ELLISON, Henry 223'.1'077
Leopold.
A study of Job; from tragedy to triumph [by] H. L. Ellison. Grand Rapids, Zondervan Pub. House [1972, c1958] 127 p. 21 cm. Originally published in Great Britain under title: From tragedy to triumph. [BS1415.3.E4 1972] 73-146577
1. Bible. O.T. Job—Commentaries. I. Title.

SCAMMON, John H. 223'.1'077
If I could find God; anguish and faith in the Book of Job [by] John H. Scammon. Valley Forge [Pa.] Judson Press [1974] 110 p. illus. 22 cm. Bibliography: p. 109-110. [BS1415.5.S3] 74-2894 ISBN 0-8170-0625-7 2.95 (pbk.)
1. Bible. O.T. Job—Study—Text-books. I. Title.

SCHREIBER, Vernon R. 223'.1'077
My servant Job : a devotional guide to the Book of Job : including the complete text of Job for modern man, Today's English version / Vernon R. Schreiber. Minneapolis, Minn. : Augsburg Pub. House, [1974] iv, 139 p. : ill. ; 18 cm. [BS1415.4.S38] 74-14169 ISBN 0-8066-1454-4 pbk. : 0.95
1. Bible. O.T. Job—Devotional literature. I. Bible. O.T. Job. English. Today's English. 1974. II. Title.

BIBLE. O. T. Job. 223.108882
English. 1959.
The book of Job as a Greek tragedy; with an essay by Horace M. Kallen. Introd. by George Foote Moore. core. New York, Hill and Wang [1959] 163p. 19cm. (A Dramabook, D19) [BS1417.K3 1959] 59-12602
I. Kallen, Horace Meyer, 1882- ed. II. Title.

ROSENBERG, David W., 223'.1'09505
1943-
Job speaks : interpreted from the original Hebrew book of Job / David Rosenberg. 1st ed. New York : Harper & Row, c1977. viii, 101 p. ; 21 cm. "A Poet's Bible. [BS1416.R67 1977] 76-62922 ISBN 0-06-067008-8 : 7.95
1. Bible. O.T. Job—Paraphrases, English. I. Title.

ROSENBERG, David W., 223'.1'09505
1943-
Job speaks : interpreted from the original Hebrew book of Job / David Rosenberg. 1st ed. New York : Harper & Row, c1977. viii, 101 p. ; 21 cm. "A Poet's Bible. [BS1416.R67 1977] 76-62922 ISBN 0-06-067008-8 : 7.95
1. Bible. O.T. Job—Paraphrases, English. I. Title.

EWING, Ward B., 223'.1'924 B
1942-
Job, a vision of God / Ward B. Ewing. New York : Seabury Press, c1976. p. cm. "A Crossroad book." Bibliography: p. [BS580.J5E87] 75-45387 ISBN 0-8164-0285-X : 8.95
1. Job, the patriarch. 2. Bible. O.T. Job—Criticism, interpretation, etc. I. Title.

ALLSTROM, Elizabeth C., ed. 223.2
Songs along the way. Woodcuts by Mel Silverman. New York, Abingdon Press [1961] 64 p. illus. 25 cm. [BS1423.A4] 61-5123
I. Bible. O. T. Psalms. English. Revised standard version. Selections. 1961. II. Title.

AUGUSTINUS, Aurelius, 223.2
Saint Bp. of Hippo.
Nine sermons of Saint Augustine on the Psalms. Translated and introduced by Edmund Hill. New York, Kenedy [1959] xi, 176p. 23cm. '[The translator] followed the text of the Maurist edition, as it is printed in Migne's Patrologia Latina.' [BS1429.A78 1959] 59-5636
1. Bible. O.T. Psalms—Sermons. 2. Sermons, Latin—Translations into English. 3. Sermons, English—Translations from Latin. I. Hill, Edmund, ed. and tr. II. Title.

BARNETT, Joe R. 223'.2
Happiness ... day and night [from the psalms, by] Joe R. Barnett [and] John D. Gipson. [1st ed. Fort Worth, Tex., Pathway Pub. House, 1968] 114 p. 21 cm. [BS1433.B3] 68-8926
1. Bible. O.T. Psalms—Meditations. I. Gipson, John D., joint author. II. Title.

BERNADD DE CLAIRVAUX, 223.2
Saint 1091?-1153.
Lent with Saint Bernard. A devotionalcommentary on Psalm ninety-one. Translated and edited by a religious of C. S. M. V. London, Mowbray; New York, Morehouse-Gorham [1953] 79p. 19cm. [BS1450 91st.B4] 53-8032
1. Bible. O. T. Psalms XCI—Commentaries. I. Title.

*BIBLE. O. T. Psalms. 223'.2
English.
Familiar Bible verses. [Valley Forge, Pa.] [Judson Press] [1973] [32] p. col. illus. 18 cm. [BS1423]
1. Bible. O. T. Psalms—Juvenile literature. I. Bentley, Carolyn. II. Title.

BIBLE. O. T. Psalms. 223.2
English. 1955. Fides.
The Psalms; Fides translation, introd. and notes by Mary Perkins Ryan. Chicago, Fides Publishers Association [1955] xxxvii, 306p. 21cm. [BS1424.R9] 55-12647
I. Ryan, Mary Perkins, 1915- ed. II. Title.

BIBLE. O. T. Psalms. 223.2
English. 1960. Authorized.
The book of Psalms, from the Authorized King James version. With a pref. by Mark Van Doren, and decorations by Valenti Angelo. New York, Limited Editions Club, 1960. unpaged. illus. 17cm. [BS1422 1960] 61-3016
I. Title.

BIBLE. O. T. Psalms. 223.2
English. 1961. Authorized.
The book of Psalms, from the Authorized King James version. Pref. by Mark Van Doren. Decorations by Valenti Angelo. New York, Heritage Club [dist. Dial Pr., 1961, c.1960] 1.v. (unpaged) illus. 17cm. 61-19103 5.00
I. Title.

BIBLE. O. T. Psalms. 223.2
English. 1961. Byington.
The book of Psalms, Tr. by Steven T. Byington. Boston, Bruce Humphries [1961, c.1957] 144p. 16cm. (Bible in living English) 54-11537 .50 pap.,
I. Byington, Steven Tracy, 1868-1957. II. Title. III. Series.

BIBLE. O. T. Psalms. 223.2
English. 1963
The Psalms, a new translation. Tr. from Hebrew. Arr. for singing to the psalmody of Joseph Gelineau. Philadelphia, Westminster [1965, c.1963] 255p. 19cm. [BS1440.G68] 64-8765 1.45 pap.,
I. Gelineau, Joseph. II. Title.

BIBLE. O.T. Psalms. 223.2
English. 1964.Hadas.
The book of Psalms for the modern reader. A new translation by Gershon Hadas. New York, J. David [1964] xxii, 266 p. 20 cm. [BS1424.H3] 64-19750
I. Hadas, Gershon, tr. II. Title.

BIBLE. O. T. Psalms. 223.2
English. 1964. Hadas
The book of Psalms for the modern reader. New tr. by Gershon Hadas. New York, J. David [c.1964] xxii, 266p. 20cm. [BS1424.H3] 64-19750 3.95; 1.95 pap.,
I. Hadas, Gershon, tr. II. Title.

BIBLE. O.T. Psalms. 223'.2
English. Authorized. Selections. 1968.
The Psalms; a selection, by Elvajean Hall. Illustrated by Charles Mozley. New York, F. Watts [1968] xv, 78 p. illus. 22 cm. Presents thirty-six well-known psalms arranged in verse form. [BS1423.H3] 68-24125 2.95
I. Hall, Elvajean, comp. II. Mozley, Charles, illus. III. Title.

*BIBLE, O. T. Psalms. 223.2
English. King James
The Book of Psalms, translated out of the original Hebrew: and with the former translations diligently comprared and revised, King James version. Large type ed. New York, Watts [1967] 116p. 29cm. (Keith Jennison bk.) 6.95
1. Bible. O. T. Psalms. I. Title.

BIBLE. O. T. Psalms. 223.2
English. Paraphrases. 1960. Collins.
Here I am, Lord; sixteen Psalms for young readers, by G. Vauthier. Illus. by Josette and Suzanne Boland. Tr. from French by Joseph B. Collins. Westminster, Md., Newman Press, 1960[1961, c.1960] 42p. col. illus. 28cm. 3.00 bds.,
I. Bible. O. T. Psalms. English. Selections. 1960. II. Vauthier, G. III. Collins, Joseph Burns, 1897- tr. IV. Title.

BIBLE. O. T. Psalms. 223.2
English. Selections. 1952. Authorized.
Psalms for daily needs, edited by Raymond Calkins. New York, Austin-Phelps, 1952. xx, 169 p. 21 cm. [BS1423.C3] 52-8806
I. Calkins, Raymond, 1869- ed. II. Title.

BIBLE. O. T. Psalms. 223.2
English. Selections. 1955.
The Psalms; a selection arranged for personal devotion, by Guy Emerson. Foreword by Cuthbert A. Simpson. New York, Harper [1955] xix, 171p. 19cm. [BS1423.E6] 55-9689
I. Emerson, Guy, comp. II. Title.

BIBLE. O. T. Psalms. 223.2
English. Selections. 1956. Authorized.
The child's book of Psalms, selected by Edith Lowe, illustrated by Nan Pollard. Garden City, N. Y., Garden City Books [1956] unpaged. illus. 29 x 14cm. [BS1423.L58] 56-58710
I. Lowe, Edith May (Kovar) 1905- ed. II. Title.

BIBLE. O. T. Psalms. 223.2
English. Selections. 1956. Douai.
The child's book of Psalms, selected by Edith Lowe, illustrated by Nan Pollard. Garden City, N. Y., Garden City Books [1956] unpaged. illus. 29 x 14cm. [BS1423.L6] 56-58397
I. Lowe, Edith May (Kovar) 1905- ed. II. Title.

BIBLE. O. T. Psalms. 223.2
English. Selections. 1960.
Favorite Psalms. [Westwood, N. J.] Revell [c.1960] 64p. 17cm. (A Revell inspirational classic) 60-13100 1.00 bds.,
I. Title.

BIBLE. O.T. Psalms. 223'.2
English. Selections. 1967.Authorized.
Songs of joy from the Book of Psalms. Selected, edited, and with an introd. by Louis Untermeyer. Illustrated by Joan Berg Victor. Cleveland, World Pub. Co. [1967] 1 v. (unpaged) illus. 21 cm. [BS1423.U5] 67-13820
I. Untermeyer, Louis, 1885- II. Title.

BIBLE. O.T. Psalms. 223'.2
English. Selections. 1969.
Fifty psalms; an attempt at a new translation [by] Huub Oosterhuis [and others. New York] Herder and Herder [1969] 156 p. 21 cm. The Psalms in Vijftig Psalmen, proeve van een nieuwe vertaling, published in the Netherlands in 1967, were translated into English for this ed. by F. J. van Beeck who also wrote the commentaries. [BS1423.O6] 71-80273 3.95
1. Bible. O.T. Psalms—Commentaries. I. Oosterhuis, Huub. II. Beeck, Frans Jozef van. III. Title.

BIBLE. O.T. Psalms. 223'.2
English. Selections. 1973.
Fifty psalms; a new translation [by] Huub Oosterhuis [and others] New York, Seabury Press [1973] 156 p. 21 cm. "A Crossroad book." Translation of the Dutch version, Vijftig psalmen, by F. J. van Beeck and others, with introd. and commentaries added. [BS1423.O6 1973] 73-21731 ISBN 0-8164-2581-7 3.50 (pbk.)
1. Bible. O.T. Psalms—Commentaries. I. Oosterhuis, Huub, tr. II. Beeck, Frans Jozef van, tr. III. Title.

BIBLE. O.T. Psalms. 223'.2
English. Taylor. Selections. 1973.
Layman's guide to 70 Psalms [by] Charles L. Taylor. Nashville, Abingdon Press [1973] 128 p. 20 cm. [BS1423.T38] 72-14228 ISBN 0-687-21221-9 3.75
1. Bible. O.T. Psalms—Devotional literature. I. Taylor, Charles Lincoln, 1901- II. Title.

*BIBLE. O. T. Psalms. 223'.2
German. 1658
Die Psalmen des koniglichen Propheten Davids mit einer einleitung von W. G. Marigold. New York, London, Johnson Reprint Corp., 1972. lxxi, 413 p. 18 cm. (Classics in Germanic Literatures and Philosophy.) "This facsimile reprint of the 1658 edition is from a copy at the Graf von Schonbornsche Schlossbibliothek, Pommersfelden, Germany" [BS1430] 72-2291 35.00
1. Bible. O.T. Psalms—German. I. Schonborn, Johann Philipp von. II. Title.

BIBLE. O. T. Psalms. 223.2
Hebrew. 1961
Sefer tehilim; v. 2. title transliterated. New York, Feldheim. [c.1966] 500p. 24cm. title listed in Hebrew Rendered into English by Ggertrude Hirschler. [BS1430.G79] 66-399 8.75
1. Bible. O. T. Psalms—Commentaries. I. Grunwald, Juda, 1849-1920. 'Olelot Yehudah. II. Title.

BIBLE. O. T. Psalms XXIII. 223.2
English. 1965. Authorized.
The Lord is my shepherd; the Twenty-third psalm. Pictures by Tony Palazzo. New York, Walck, c. 1965. 1v. (unpaged) col. illus. 20cm. [BS145023rd.P3] 65-19731 3.75
I. Palazzo, Tony, illus. II. Title.

BIBLE. O.T. Psalms XXIII. 223'.2
English. Authorized. 1970.
The Twentythird psalm, King James version. Illustrated by Marie Angel. New York, Crowell [1970] 19 p. col. illus. 21 cm. [BS1450 23d.A6] 75-106566 ISBN 0-690-84141-8 3.50
I. Angel, Marie, illus. II. Title.

BIBLE. O.T. Psalms. 223'.2
English. Authorized. Selections. 1967.
Songs of joy from the Book of Psalms. Selected, edited, and with an introd. by Louis Untermeyer. Illustrated by Joan Berg Victor. Cleveland, World Pub. Co. [1967] 1 v. (unpaged) illus. 21 cm. [BS1423.U5] 67-13820
I. Untermeyer, Louis, 1885- II. Title.

BLAIR, J Allen. 223.2
Living reliantly; a devotional study of the 23rd Psalm. [1st ed.] New York, Loizeaux Bros., 1958. 125p. 20cm. [BS145023d.B6] 58-14945
1. Bible. O. T. Psalms XXIII. I. Title.

BRANDT, Leslie F. 223'.2
God is here; let's celebrate! In 39 meditations based on Psalms, by Leslie F. Brandt. St. Louis, Concordia Pub. House [1969] 58 p. 21 cm. [BS1430.4.B67] 73-89877 1.75
1. Bible. O.T. Psalms—Meditations. I. Title.

BRANDT, Leslie F. 223'.2
The Lord rules—let's serve Him; meditations on the Psalms [by] Leslie F. Brandt. St. Louis, Concordia Pub. House [1972] 77 p. 21 cm. [BS1430.4.B673] 72-80783 ISBN 0-570-03137-0
1. Bible. O.T. Psalms—Meditations. I. Title.

CARPENTER, Alton E. 223'.2
Twenty-three keys to inner peace from the Twenty-third Psalm / A. E. Carpenter. 1st ed. Hicksville, N.Y. : Exposition Press, [1974] 192 p. ; 22 cm. [BS1450 23d.C34] 74-193335 ISBN 0-682-48058-4 : 7.50
1. Bible. O.T. Psalms XXIII—Meditations. I. Title.

CHAPMAN, Harry. comp. 223.2
Life, wisdom, truth, and happiness in the book of Psalms; a collection of verses in the Psalms ... Appended to each section are quotations from the Jewish sages. [1st ed.] Los Angeles, 1952. 58 p. 17 cm. [BS1434.C5] 52-27707
1. Bible. O. T. Psalms—Indexes, Topical. I. Title.

CLARKE, Maurice, 1882- 223.2
How to read and enjoy the Psalms. Chicago, Wilcox & Follett, '1950. iii, 156 p. 24 cm. Bibliography: p. 1-2. [BS1430.C615] 50-1811
1. Bible. O. T. Psalms—Study. I. Title.

COATES, Thomas, 1910- 223.2
The Psalms for today. Saint Louis, Concordia Pub. House [1957] 118p. 23cm. [BS1433.C6] 57-8853
1. Bible. O. T. Psalms—Meditations. I. Title.

DOERFFLER, Alfred 1884- 223.2
The mind at ease. Saint Louis, Concordia Pub. House [1955] 131p. 20cm. [BS1433.D6] 55-12377
1. Bible. O. T. Psalms—Meditations. I. Title.

ELLIOTT, Norman K. 223'.2
The Lord your shepherd; the Twenty-third psalm for modern man [by] Norman K. Elliott. [1st ed.] Garden City, N.Y., Doubleday, 1969. 152, [1] p. 22 cm. Bibliographical references included in "Notes" (p. [153]) [BS1430.4.E4] 69-20078 4.50
1. Bible. O.T. Psalms XXIII—Devotional literature. I. Title.

EMLEY, Alban Maurice, 1890- 223.2
The magic prayer. Drawings by D. Karsell. Los Angeles, House-Warven [1950] 220 p. illus. 28 cm. (Gusto classics) [BS1450 119th.E5] 51-15091
1. Bible. O. T. Psalms. cxix—Miscellanea. I. Title.

GARRONE, Gabriel Marie 223.2
Abp. 1901-
How to pray the Psalms [by] Gabriel Garonne. Translated by the Benedictine Monks of Mount Saviour Monastery, Elmire, N.Y. Notre Dame, Ind., Fides Publishers [1965] 118 p. 19 cm. (Fides dome books, D-45) Translation of Psaumes et priere. [BS1430.2.G2813] 65-13805
1. Bible. O.T. Psalms — Meditations. 2. Bible. O.T. Psalms — Liturgical use. I. Title.

GUARDINI, Romano, 1885- 223'.2
The wisdom of the Psalms. Translated by Stella Lange. Chicago, H. Regnery Co. [1968] vii, 168 p. 21 cm. Translation of Weisheit der Psalmen. [BS1430.4.G813] 68-26059
1. Bible. O.T. Psalms—Meditations. I. Title.

HAY, David M., 1935- 223'.2
Glory at the right hand: Psalm 110 in early Christianity [by] David M. Hay. Nashville, Abingdon Press [1973] 176 p. 24 cm. (Society of Biblical Literature. Monograph series, 18) A revision of the author's thesis, Yale, 1965. Includes bibliographical references. [BS1430.2.H33 1973] 73-297 ISBN 0-687-20633-2 5.00
1. Bible. O.T. Psalms CX—Criticism, interpretation, etc.—History—Early church. I. Title. II. Series.

HESLOP, William Greene, 1886- 223.2
Sermon seeds from the Psalms. Butler, Ind., Higley Press [c1956] 144p. 20cm. [BS1430.H43] 57-31084
1. Bible. . T. Psalms—Homiletical use. I. Title.

HUBBARD, David Allan. 223'.2
Psalms for all seasons. Grand Rapids, Eerdmans [1971] 96 p. 18 cm. (An Eerdmans evangelical paperback) "[First presented] as a series of talks on the international radio broadcast The joyful sound." [BS1430.3.H8] 76-150639 1.25
1. Bible. O.T. Psalms—Commentaries. I. The Joyful sound. II. Title.

HUNTER, John Edward, 1909- 223'.2
Finding the living Christ in the Psalms [by] John E. Hunter. Grand Rapids, Zondervan Pub. House [1972] 145 p. 18 cm. (Zondervan books) [BS1430.4.H85] 70-189587 1.25
1. Bible. O.T. Psalms—Meditations. I. Title. II. Title: Christ in the Psalms.

JAMES, Fleming, 1877-1959. 223.2
Thirty psalmists; personalities of the Psalter. Edited and with a foreword by R. Lansing Hicks. New York, Seabury Press [1965] xvii, 251 p. 21 cm. (A Seabury paperback, SP19) "A study in personalities of the Psalter as seen against the background of Gunkel's type-study of the Psalms." Bibliography: p. 249-250. [BS1430.G82J35 1965] 65-14646
1. Bible. O.T. Psalms—Commentaries. I. Gunkel, Hermann, 1862-1932. II. Title. III. Title: Einleitung in die Psalmen.

JAMES, Fleming, 1877-1959 223.2
Thirty psalmists; personalities of the Psalter. Ed., foreword by R. Lansing Hicks. New York, Seabury [c.1938, 1965] xvii, 251p. 12cm. (SP19) A study in personalities of the Psalter as seen against the background of Gunkel's type-study of the Psalms. Bibl. [BS1430.G82J35] 65-14646 1.95 pap.,
1. Bible. O. T. Psalms—Commentaries. I. Gunkel, Hermann, 1862-1932. Einleitung in die Psalmen. II. Title.

KEESECKER, William F. 223'.2
The wisdom of the Psalms; selections and expositions based on commentary by John Calvin [by] William F. Keesecker. New York, World Pub. Co. [1970] 60 p. 21 cm. (World inspirational books) [BS1430.4.K4 1970] 79-131564
1. Bible. O.T. Psalms—Devotional literature. I. Calvin, Jean, 1509-1564. Commentarius in librum Psalmorum. II. Title.

*KETCHAM, Robert T. 223'.2
I shall not want; an exposition of Psalm Twenty-three, by R. T. Ketcham. Chicago, Moody [1972, c.1953] 128 p. 18 cm. (Moody pocket bks.) [BS1430.4] ISBN 0-8024-0130-9 pap., 0.75
1. Bible. O.T. Psalms—Devotional literature. 2. Bible. O.T. Psalms—Commentaries. I. Title.

KIMHI, David, 1160?-1235? 223'.2
The commentary of Rabbi David Kimhi on Psalms CXX-CL. Edited and translated by Joshua Baker and Ernest W. Nicholson. Cambridge [Eng.] University Press, 1973. xxxii, 190 p. 23 cm. (University of Cambridge oriental publications, no. 22) Includes Hebrew text and English translation of Perush Radak 'al Tehilim. [BS1429.K54 1973] 72-78889 ISBN 0-521-08670-1
1. Bible. O.T. Psalms CXX-CL—Commentaries. I. Baker, Joshua, ed. II. Nicholson, Ernest Wilson, ed. III. Title. IV. Series. Cambridge. University. Oriental publications, no. 22.
Distributed by Cambridge University Press, New York; 13.50

KNIGHT, William Allen, 1863- 223'.2
The song of our Syrian guest. Philadelphia, United Church Press [1972] 46 p. 16 cm. "A Pilgrim Press book ..." [BS1450 23d.K6 1972] 72-4580 ISBN 0-8298-0239-8
1. Bible. O.T. Psalms XXIII—Criticism, interpretation, etc. I. Title.

KOHN, Harold E 223.2
Through the valley; nature's clues to victorious living. Illustrated with 40 line drawings by the author. Grand Rapids, W. B. Eerdmans Pub. Co. [1957] 172p. illus. 23cm. [BS1450 23d.K755] 57-7390
1. Bible. O. T. Psalms xxiii—Meditations. I. Title.

KOHN, Harold E 223.2
Through the valley; nature's clues to victorious living. Illustrated with 40 line drawings by the author. Grand Rapids, W. B. Eerdmans Pub. Co. [1957] 172p. illus. 23cm. [BS1450 23d.K755] 57-7390
1. Bible. O.T. Psalms XXIII—Meditations. I. Title.

KUHLMANN, Edward, 1882- 223.2
A story a day forty-two stories on the Twenty-third psalm. Illus. by Harvey Fuller iColumbus, Ohio, Wartburg Press [1952] 55p. illus. 27cm. [BV4571.K8] 53-17033
1. Children—Religious life. 2. Bible. O. T. Psalms XXIII— Miscellanea. I. Title.

LESLIE, Elmer Archibald, 1888- 223.2
The Psalms. Tr. and interpreted in the light of Hebrew life and worship. Nashville, Abingdon [1968,c.1949] 448p. 24cm. (Apex bks., AC-275) Bibl. [BS1430.L42] 49-8204 2.75 pap.,
1. Bible. O. T. Psalms—Commentaries. I. Bible. O. T. Psalms. English. 1949. Leslie. II. Title.

LOGSDON, S Franklin. 223.2
Thou art my portion; the life of victory in Psalm 119. Introd. by William Culbertson. Grand Rapids, Zondervan Pub. House [c1956] 121p. 20cm. [BS1450 119th.L6] 57-23344
1. Bible. O. T. Psalms cxix—Commentaries. I. Title.

*LOWE, Edith, comp. 223.2
Psalms for children; selections fromthe Douay version of the Old Testament. Illus. by Nan Pollard. Chicago, Follett [c.1966] 44p. illus. (pt. col.) 29x14cm. (7300) 1.00 bds.,
1. Bible. O.T. Psalms—Juvenile literature. I. Title.

*LOWE, Edith, comp. 223.2
The child's book of psalms; selections from the King James Version of the Old Testament. Illus. by Nan Pollard. Chicago, Follett [c.1966] 44p. illus. (pt. col.) 29x14cm. (1142) 1.00 bds.,
1. Bible. O.T. Psalms—Juvenile literature. I. Title.

MACCAULEY, Rose Agnes. 223'.2
Vision 20/20; twenty psalms for the twentieth century. Notre Dame, Ind., Fides Publishers [1971] 62 p. illus. 22 cm. [BS1440.A1M28] 76-172640 ISBN 0-8190-0078-7 2.95
1. Bible. O.T. Psalms—Paraphrases, English. I. Title.

MERTON, Thomas, 1915- 223.2
Bread in the wilderness. [New York, 1953] 146p. illus. 26cm. 'A New Directions book.' [BS1435.M4] 53-13509
1. Bible. O. T. Psalms—Liturgical use. 2. Contemplation. I. Title.

MEYER, Frederick Brotherton, 1847-1929. 223.2
The Shepherd Psalm. Grand Rapids, Zondervan Pub. House [1953] 128p. 19cm. [BS1450 23d.M4 1953] 55-848
1. Bible. O. T. Psalms xxiii—Commentaries. I. Title.

MORGAN, Dewi 223.2
But God comes first, a meditation on the Te Deum. Foreword by the Bishop of London. Longmans. [dist. New York, McKay, c.1962] 96p. 61-66825 1.50; .90 pap.,
1. Te Deum laudamus. 2. Meditations. I. Title.

NOTHER, Ingo. 223'.2
Luthers Ubersetzungen des zweiten Psalms : ihre Beziehungen zur Ubers.- u. Auslegungstradition, zur Theologie Luthers u. zur Zeitgeschichte / Ingo Nother. 1. Aufl. Hamburg : Buske, 1976. ix, 321 p. : ill. ; 21 cm. (Hamburger philologische Studien ; 41) Includes texts in Latin. Originally presented as the author's thesis, Hamburg, 1975. Bibliography: p. 308-321. [BS1450 2d.N63 1976] 76-460785 ISBN 3-87118-229-X
1. Bible. O.T. Psalms II. German—Versions—Luther. I. Title.

OWEN, George Frederick, 1897- 223.2
The Shepherd Psalm of Palestine. Photos. by G. Eric Matson. Grand Rapids, Eerdmans [1958] 84p. illus. 24cm. Includes bibliography. [BS1450 23d.O85] 58-59784
1. Bible. O. T. Psalms xxiii—Commentaries. I. Title.

PHILLIPS, Ordis E., 1886- 223'.2
Exploring the Messianic Psalms, by O. E. Phillips. Philadelphia, Hebrew Christian Fellowship [1967] 318 p. illus. (on lining papers) 22 cm. [BS1445.M4P5] 67-9431
1. Messianic Psalms. I. Bible. O.T. Psalms. English. Selections. 1967. II. Title.

REDDING, David A. 223'.2
Songs in the night; psalms of David [by] David A. Redding. [2d ed.] Jacksonville, Fla., Paramount Press [1970] xvii, 174 p. 22 cm. 1963 ed. published under title: Psalms of David. Bibliography: p. 167. [BS1430.3.R4 1970] 78-129573
1. Bible. O.T. Psalms.—Commentaries. I. Bible. O.T. Psalms. English. Revised standard. Selections. 1970. II. Title.

RIMAUD, Didier. 223'.2
God's words—our prayer. Translated by Edmond Bonin. St. Meinrad, Ind., Abbey Press, 1973. v, 105 p. 18 cm. (A Priority edition) Translation of Des mots de Dieu pour la priere. [BS1430.4.R5513] 73-85335 1.95
1. Bible. O.T. Psalms—Meditations. 2. Bible. O.T. Psalms—Prayers. I. Title.

ROTHUIZEN, Gerard Theodore, 1926- 223'.2
Landscape; a bundle of thoughts about the Psalms (the first fifty) [by] G. Th. Rothuizen. Translated by John Frederick Jansen. Richmond, John Knox Press [1971] 238 p. illus. 21 cm. Translation of Landschap. [BS1430.4.R6713] 70-133241 ISBN 0-8042-2405-6 6.95
1. Bible. O.T. Psalms I-L—Meditations. I. Title.

*SAXE, Grace. 223.2
Studies in Psalms, arranged by Grace Saxe, rev. by Irving L. Jensen. Chicago, Moody [1968] 128p. 22cm. (Bible self-study ser.) .95 pap.,
1. Bible. O. T. Psalms—Commentaries. I. Jensen, Irving L. ed. II. Title.

SCAMMON, John H. 223'.2
Living with the Psalms [by] John H. Scammon. Valley Forge [Pa.] Judson [1967] 157p. illus. 23cm. Includes music. Bibl. [BS1430.4.S3] 67-14358 3.95
1. Bible. O. T. Psalms—Devotional literature. I. Title.

SCAMMON, John H 223'.2
Living with the Psalms [by] John H. Scammon. Valley Forge [Pa.] Judson Press [1967] 157 p. illus. 23 cm. Includes music. Bibliographical references included in "Notes." [BS1430.4.S3] 67-14358
1. Bible. O. T. Psalms—Devotional literature. I. Title.

SHIRKEY, Albert P 223.2
The Lord is my shepherd. Nashville, The Upper room [1963] 64 p. illus. 20 cm. [BS145023d.S5] 63-16713
1. Bible. O. T. Psalms xxiii—Meditations. I. Title.

SHIRKEY, Albert P. 223.2
The Lord is my shepherd. Nashville, Upper Room [c.1963] 64p. illus. 20cm. 63-16713 1.00
1. Bible. O.T. Psalms xxiii—Meditations. I. Title.

SORG, Rembert, 1908- 223'.2
Ecumenic Psalm 87; original form and two rereadings, with an appendix on Psalm 110,3. [1st ed.] Fifield, Wis., King of Martyrs Priory, 1969. xvi, 83 p. 23 cm. Bibliographical footnotes. [BS1450.87th.S6] 72-93737
1. Bible. O.T. Psalms LXXXVII—Criticism, interpretation, etc. I. Title.

TAYLOR, Charles Lincoln, 1902- 223.2
Let the Psalms speak. Greenwich, Conn., Seabury Press, 1961. 149 p. 20 cm. Includes bibliography. [BS1430.2.T35] 61-11313
1. Bible. O. T. Psalms — Criticism, interpretation, etc. I. Title.

TERRIEN, Samuel. 223.2
The Psalms and their meaning for today. [1st ed.] Indianapolis, Bobbs-Merrill [1952] 278 p. 21 cm. Includes bibliography. [BX1430.T4] 52-5808
1. Bible. O. T. Psalms — Criticism, interpretation, etc. I. Title.

TERRIEN, Samuel. 223.2
The Psalms and their meaning for today. [1st ed.] Indianapolis, Bobbs-Merrill [1952] 278 p. 21 cm. Includes bibliography. [BS1430.T4] 52-5808
1. Bible. O. T. Psalms.—Criticism, interpretation, etc. I. Title.

TERRIEN, Samuel L 1911- 223.2
The Psalms and their meaning for today. [1st ed.] Indianapolis, Bobbs-Merrill [1952] 278 p. 21 cm. Includes bibliography. [BS1430.T4] 52-5808
1. Bible. O. T. Psalms—Criticism, interpretation, etc. I. Title.

WILKINSON, Violet. 223'.2
Israel's praise! a study of the Psalms. London, Oxford U.P., 1967. 96 p. diagrs. 18 1/2 cm. (Approaching the Bible, 1) Bibliography: p. 92-93. [BS1430.5.W5] 68-70106 9/6
1. Bible. O.T. Psalms—Study—Outlines, syllabi,etc. I. Title.

WISLOFF, Fredrick, 1904- 223.2
Streams of gladness;a year's daily meditations based on the book of Psalms. Translated by B. H. J. Habel. Minneapolis, Augsburg Pub. House [1958] 207 p. 18 cm. [BS1433.W513] 57-14796
1. Bible. O.T. Psalms — Meditations. 2. Devotional calendars — Lutheran Church. I. Title.

WORDSWORTH, Ephraim Edward, 1887- 223.2
Freedom from want; meditations on the Twenty-third psalm. Kansas City, Mo., Beacon Hill Press [1960] 128 p. 20 cm. [BS145023d.W64] 60-9358
1. Bible. O. T. Psalms xxiii — Meditations. I. Title.

MADDUX, Roy Clark 223.200202
The Psalms in outline. Grand Rapids, Mich., Baker Bk. [c.]1965. 73p. 21cm. ([Minister's handbk. ser.]) [BS1451.M3] 65-18266 1.95
1. Bible. O. T. Psalms—Study—Outlines, syllabi, etc. I. Title.

THE Psalms around us. 223'.2'00222
Philadelphia, Countryside Press; [distributed to the book trade by] Doubleday, Garden City, N.Y. [1970] 95 p. illus. (part col.) 29 cm. "Quotations from the Psalms are taken from the Revised standard version of the Bible." [BS1423.C68] 72-114340
I. Bible. O.T. Psalms. English. Revised standard. Selections. 1970.

ANDERSON, Bernhard W. 223'.2'007
Out of the depths; the Psalms speak for us today, by Bernhard W. Anderson. Philadelphia, Westminster Press [1974] x, 198 p. 20 cm. Bibliography: p. 194-198. [BS1430.5.A53 1974] 73-11402 ISBN 0-664-24981-7 3.50 (pbk)
1. Bible. O.T. Psalms—Study—Text-books. I. Title.

BARTH, Christoph F. 223.201
Introduction to the Psalms [by] Christoph F. Barth. Tr. by R. A. Wilson. New York, Scribners [1966] 87p. 22cm. Bibl. [BS1430.2.B313] 66-28135 2.95p bds.,
1. Bible. O.T.Psalms — Introductions. I. Title.

MULLEN, William B., 1918- 223'.2'02
Concordance of the Prayer Book Psalter [by] William B. Mullen. Gresham, Or., St. Paul's Press [1969] v, 263 p. 28 cm. [BX5946.M8] 74-11234
1. Bible. O.T. Psalms—Concordances, English. I. Title.

BIBLE. Manuscript, Hebrew. O. T. Psalms. Dead Sea Psalms scroll. 223'.2'044
The Psalms scroll of Qumran Cave 11 (11QPsa) [edited] by J. A. Sanders. Oxford, Clarendon Press, 1965. viii, 99 p., 17 plates (incl. facsims.) 32 cm. Discoveries in the Judaean Desert of Jordon, 4) At head of title: American Schools of Oriental Reserach [and] Palestine Archaeological Museum. Bibliographical footnotes. [BS1420.5.D4A5] 65-8825
1. Dead Sea scrolls. I. Sanders, Jim Alvin, ed. II. American Schools of Oriental Research. III. Jerusalem. Palestine Archaeological Museum. IV. Title. V. Series.

BIBLE. Manuscripts, Hebrew. O. T. Psalms. Dead Sea Psalms scroll. 223'.2'044
The Dead Sea Psalms scroll [edited] by J. A. Sanders. Ithaca, N.Y., Cornell University Press [1967] xi, 174 p. illus., facsims. (part fold.) map. 28 cm. English and Hebrew on opposite pages. "Pre-Masoretic Salter bibliography": p. 151-153. Bibliographical footnotes. [BS1420.5.D4A48] 66-15765
1. Dead Sea scrolls. I. Sanders, Jim Alvin, ed. II. Title.

BIBLE. Manuscripts, Hebrew. O.T. Psalms. Dead Sea Psalms scroll. 223'.2'044
The Dead Sea Psalms scroll [edited] by J. A. Sanders. Ithaca, N.Y., Cornell University Press [1967] xi, 174 p. illus., facsims. (part fold.) map. 28 cm. English and Hebrew on opposite pages. "Pre-Masoretic Psalter bibliography": p. 151-153. Bibliographical footnotes. [BS1420.5.D4A48] 66-15765
1. Dead Sea scrolls. I. Sanders, James A., ed. II. Title.

DEAD Sea scrolls 223.2044
The Psalms scroll of Qumran Cave 11 (11QPsa) ed. by J. A. Sanders Oxford, Clarendon [New York, Oxford, c.]1965. vii, 99p., 17 plates (incl. facsims.) 32cm. (Discoveries in the Judaean Desert of Jordan, 4) At head of title: Amer. Schools of Oriental Res. [and] Palestine Archaeological Mus. Bibl. [BS1420.5.DA5] 65-8825 10.10
I. Sanders, Jim Alvin, ed. II. American Schools of Oriental Research. III. Jerusalem. Palestine Archaeological Museum. IV. Bible. MSS., Hebrew. O.T. Psalms. V. Title. VI. Series.

CATHOLIC Church. Liturgy and ritual. Psalter (Vespasian Psalter) 223.205
The Vespasian psalter. Edited by Sherman M. Kuhn. Ann Arbor, University of Michigan Press [1965] xii, 327 p. 29 cm. Latin, with Anglo-Saxon interlinear translation. "Text ... transcribed from MLAA rotograph no. 332. British Museum MS. Cotton Vespasian A. 1." [BX2033.A3V4 1965] 63-9901
I. Kuhn, Sherman McAllister, 1907- ed. II. Title.

CATHOLIC Church. Liturgy and ritual. Psalter (Vespasian psalter) 223.205
The Vespasian psalter. Ed. by Sherman M. Kuhn. Ann Arbor, Univ. of Mich. Pr. [c.1965] xii, 327p. 29cm. Latin, with Anglo-Saxon interlinear translation. Text transcribed from MLAA rotograph no.332. British Museum MS. Cotton Vespasian A. 1. [BX2033.A3V4] 63-9901 12.50
I. Kuhn, Sherman McAllister, 1907- ed. II. Title.

BIBLE. O. T. Psalms. English. 1963. 223.2052
The Psalms, a new translation. Tr. from Hebrew, arr. for singing to the psalmody of Joseph Gelineau. Glen Rock, N. J., Paulist [1965, c.1963] 256p. 18cm. (Deus bks.) This tr. made from the Hebrew, is the work of a team of scholars in co-operation with the Grail [BS1440] 65-7816 1.25 pap.,
I. Gelineau, Joseph. II. Title.

BIBLE. O.T. Psalms. English. 1963. 223.2052
The Psalms, a new translation. Translated from the Hebrew and arr. for singing to the psalmody of Joseph Gelineau. Glen Rock, N. J., Paulist Press [1965, c1963] 256 p. 18 cm. (Deus books) (This translation ... made from the Hebrew, is the work of a team of scholars in co-operation with the Grail." [BS1440] 65-7816 CD
I. Gelineau, Joseph. II. Title.

BIBLE. O.T. Psalms. English. Jerusalem Bible. 1968. 223'.2'052
The Psalms of the Jerusalem Bible. [General editor: Alexander Jones] Garden City, N.Y., Doubleday [1968, c1966] 281 p. 25 cm. [BS1422 1968] 68-27102 5.95
I. Jones, Alexander, 1906- ed. II. Title.

BIBLE. O.T. Psalms. English. Jerusalem Bible. 1977. 223'.2'052
Illustrated Psalms of the Jerusalem Bible / Alexander Jones, general editor ; Fannie Drossos, illustrator. 1st ed. Garden City, N.Y. : Doubleday, 1977. 379 p. : ill. ; 26 cm. [BS1422 1977] 76-23769 ISBN 0-385-12286-1 : 6.95
I. Jones, Alexander, 1906- II. Drossos, Fannie. III. Title.

BIBLE. O.T. Psalms. English. Selections. 1976. 223'.2'052
Selected Psalms for today / compiled and illustrated by Royal V. Carley. Norwalk, Conn. : C. R. Gibson, c1976. [27] p. : ill. ; 19 cm. [BS1423.C37] 73-38042 ISBN 0-8378-2013-8 : 2.50
I. Carley, Royal V. II. Title.

BIBLE. O.T. Psalms. English. Selections. 1977. 223'.2'052
I find my joy in the Lord! : A treasury of favorite biblical prayers for all the seasons of the heart / edited by Roger J. Radley from the Grail translation of the Psalms. New York : Paulist Press, c1977. vi, 137 p. ; 18 cm. (Emmaus books) [BS1423.R32] 76-24446 ISBN 0-8091-1990-0 pbk. : 1.45
I. Radley, Roger J. II. Title.

BIBLE. O.T. Psalms. English. Today's English. 1970. 223'.2'052
The Psalms for modern man. Today's English version. New York, American Bible Society [1970] 211 p. illus. 19 cm. [BS1422 1970] 75-22760
I. Title.

BIBLE. O.T. Psalms. English. Today's English. Selections. 1974. 223'.2'052
The psalms for worship today [compiled by] Dwight W. Vogel. St. Louis, Concordia Pub. House [1974] 176 p. 23 cm. [BS1436.V6] 74-13761 ISBN 0-570-03239-3
I. Vogel, Dwight W., comp. II. Title.

BIBLE. O.T. Psalms. Hebrew. 1973. 223'.2'052
Tehilim (romanized form). The Psalms; a new English translation. With drawings by Ismar David. New York, prepared by the Jewish Publication Society of America, Union of American Hebrew Congregations, 1973. x, 178 p. illus. 34 cm. "Issued on the occasion of the one-hundredth anniversary of the Union of American Hebrew Congregations." [BS1422 1973b] 74-155411 50.00
I. David, Ismar, illus. II. Jewish Publication Society of America. III. Union of American Hebrew Congregations. IV. Bible. O.T. Psalms. English. Jewish Publication Society. 1973.

BRANDT, Leslie F. 223'.2'052
Psalms/now, by Leslie F. Brandt, with art by Corita Kent. St. Louis, Concordia Pub. House [1973] 222 p. illus. 22 cm. [BS1440.B73] 73-78103 ISBN 0-570-03230-X 4.50
1. Bible. O.T. Psalms—Paraphrases, English. I. Title.

VAN Zeller, Hubert, 1905- 223.2052
The Psalms in other words; a presentation for beginners. Springfield, Ill., Templegate [1964] 94 p. 20 cm. (His [In other words series]) [BX1433.V33] 65-2834
1. Bible. O.T. Psalms — Devotional literature. I. Title.

BIBLE. O.T. Psalms. English. 1967.Authorized. 223'.2'05203
The book of Psalms. King James version; translated out of the original Hebrew, and with the former translations diligently compared and revised. Large type ed., complete and unabridged. New York, F. Watts,[1967] 116 p. 29 cm. "A Keith Jennison book." [BS1422] 68-31907 CD
I. Title.

BIBLE. O.T. Psalms. English. 1967. Authorized. 223'.2'05203
The book of Psalms. Authorized or King James version from the Holy Bible. [Magnatype ed.] Pittsburgh, Stanwix House [1967] 417 p. 29 cm. [BS1422 1967] 66-26066
I. Title.

BIBLE. O.T. Psalms. English. Hanson. 1968. 223'.2'05204
The Psalms in modern speech for public and private use, by Richard S. Hanson. Philadelphia, Fortress Press [1968] 3 v. 18 cm. Includes bibliographical references. [BS1424.H35] 68-29463 5.50
I. Hanson, Richard S., tr. II. Title.

BIBLE. O.T. Psalms. English. Paraphrases. 1967.Taylor. 223'.2'05204
Living ppsalms and Proverbs with the major prophets, paraphrased by Kenneth N. Taylor. [Wheaton, Ill, Tyndale House, 1967] 745 p. 18 cm. [BX1424.T3] 67-6593
I. Bible. O.T. Proverbs. English. Paraphrases. 1967. Taylor. II. Bible. O.T. Prophets. English. Paraphrases. 1967. Taylor. III. Taylor, Kenneth Nathaniel. IV. Title.

BIBLE. O. T. Psalms. English. Paraphrases. 1967. Taylor. 223'.2'05204
Living Psalms and Proverbs with the major prophets, paraphrased by Kenneth N. Taylor. [Wheaton, Ill., Tyndale House, 1967] 745p. 18cm. [BS1424.T3] 67-6593 2.95 pap.,
I. Bible. O. T. Proverbs. English. Paraphrases. 1967. Taylor. II. Bible. O. T. Prophets. English. Paraphrases. 1967. Taylor. III. Taylor, Kenneth Nathaniel. IV. Title.

BIBLE. O.T. Psalms. English. Selections. 1965.Revisedstandardversion. 223.205204
Psalms and proverbs for boys and girls. Selected by Marjorie Ingzel. New York, T. Nelson [1965] 63 p. 16 cm. [BS1423.I 5] 65-22401
I. Bible O. T. Proverbs. English. Selections. 1965. Revised standard version. a. Ingle, Marjorie, comp. II. Title.

BIBLE O. T. Psalms, English 1965.Revisedstandardversionbible.ot.p erbs.englishselections. 1965. revised standard version. ingzel, marjorie, 223.205204
Psalms and proverbs for boys and girls. selected by Marjorie Ingzel. New York, Nelson [1965] 63 p. 16 cm. [bs1423.15] '65 1.25
I. Title.

TAYLOR, Kenneth Nathaniel. 223'.2'05204
Living Psalms and Proverbs with the major prophets, paraphrased by Kenneth N. Taylor. [Wheaton, Ill.] [Tyndale House] [1967] 745 p. 18 cm. [BS1440.T38] 67-6593
1. Bible. O.T. Psalms—Paraphrases, English. 2. Bible. O.T. Proverbs—Paraphrases, English. 3. Bible. O.T. Prophets—Paraphrases, English. I. Title.

BIBLE. O.T. Psalms. English. 1950. New American. 223'.2'05205
The Holy Bible: The book of Psalms and The canticles of the Roman Breviary. Translated from the original languages with critical use of all the ancient sources by members of the Catholic Biblical Association of America. Paterson, N.J., St. Anthony Guild Press, 1950. vi, 302 p. 20 cm. "Sponsored by the Episcopal Committee of the Confraternity of Christian Doctrine." [BS1422 1950] 78-19217
I. Catholic Biblical Association of America. II. Confraternity of Christian Doctrine. Episcopal Committee. III. Title: The book of Psalms. IV. Title: The canticles of the Roman Breviary.

GLASS, Henry Alexander. 223'.2'05209
The story of the Psalters; a history of the metrical versions of Great Britain and America from 1549 to 1885. London, K. Paul, Trench, 1888. [New York, AMS Press, 1972] vii, 208 p. 19 cm. [BS1440.A1G58 1972] 72-1635 ISBN 0-404-08308-0
1. Bible. O.T. Psalms—Paraphrases, English—History and criticism. 2. Psalters. I. Title.

BIBLE. O.T. Psalms. English. Paraphrases. 1963. 223.206
The Psalms of Sir Philip Sidney and the Countess of Pembroke. Edited with an introd. by J. C. A. Rathmell. [1st American ed.] Garden City, N. Y., Doubleday, 1963. xxxviii, 362 p. 18 cm. (Anchor books) First published in 1823 under title: The Psalmes of David translated into divers and sundry kindes of verse ... Bibliography: p. 359-362. [BS1440.S5] 63-8764
I. Sidney, Sir Philip, 1554-1586, tr. II. Pembroke, Mary (Sidney) Herbert, countess of, 1561-1621, tr. III. Rathmell, John C. A. 1935- ed. IV. Title.

BIBLE. O. T. Psalms. English. Paraphrases. 1963. 223.206
The Psalms of Sir Philip Sidney and the Countess of Pembroke. Ed., introd. by J. C. A. Rathmell. Garden City, N. Y., Doubleday [c.] 1963. xxxviii, 362p. 18cm. (Anchor bks. A311) First pub. in 1823 under title: The Psalmes of David translated into divers and sundry kindes of verse. Bibl. 63-8764 1.45 pap.,
I. Sidney, Philip, Sir 1554-1586, tr. II. Pembroke, Mary (Sidney) Herbert, countess of, III. Rathmell, John C. A., 1935- ed. IV. Title.

BIBLE. O.T. Psalms. English. Paraphrases. 1963. 223.206
The Psalms of Sir Sidney and the Countess of Pembroke. Edited with an introd. by J. C. A. Rathmell. [New York] New York University Press, 1963. xxxviii, 362 p. ports. 24 cm. (The Stuart editions) First published in 1823 under title: The Psalmes of David translated into divers and sundry kindes of verse ... Bibliography: p. 359-362. [BS1440.S5] 63-24856
I. Sidney Sir Hillip, 1554-1586, tr. II. Pembroke, Mary (Sidney) Herbert, countess of, 1561-1621, tr. III. Rathmell, John C. A., 1935- ed. IV. Title.

BUTTENWIESER, Moses, 1862-1939. 223'.2'06
The Psalms; chronologically treated with a new trans- lation. Prolegomenon by Nahum M. Sarna. New York, Ktav Pub. House, 1969. xliv, 911 p. 23 cm. (The Library of Biblical studies) Reprint of the 1938 ed. Includes bibliographical references. [BS1430.B87 1969] 69-10409
1. Bible. O.T. Psalms—Commentaries. I. Bible. O.T. Psalms. English. Buttenwieser. 1969. II. Title. III. Series.

CHASE, Mary Ellen, 1887- 223.206
The Psalms for the common reader. [1st ed.] New York, W. W. Norton [1962] 208 p. 22 cm. "Types of Psalms ... arranged according to the form given in the Authorized or King James version": p. 121-159. Includes bibliography. [BS1430.2.C54] 62-8579
1. Bible. O.T. Psalms—Criticism, interpretation, etc. I. Bible. O.T. Psalms. English. Selections. 1962. Authorized. II. Title.

DALTON, Len. 223'.2'06
Psalms in reflection, as seen by Elder Len Dalton. [Waco, Tex., Printed by Texian Press, 1973] viii, 124 p. 24 cm. [BS1430.2.D32] 73-76486 4.00
1. Bible. O.T. Psalms—Criticism, interpretation, etc. I. Title.

DOERFFLER, Alfred, 1884- 223'.2'06
The mind at ease / Alfred Doerffler. St. Louis, Mo. : Concordia Pub. House, [1976] c1957. p. cm. Large print ed. [BS1430.4.D63 1976] 75-43869 ISBN 0-570-03040-4 : 3.95
1. Bible. O.T. Psalms—Meditations. 2. Sight-saving books. I. Title.

DOERFFLER, Alfred, 1884- 223'.2'06
The mind at ease / Alfred Doerffler. St. Louis, Mo. : Concordia Pub. House, [1976] c1957. p. cm. Large print ed. [BS1430.4.D63 1976] 75-43869 ISBN 0-570-03040-4 pbk. : 3.95
1. Bible. O.T. Psalms—Meditations. 2. Sight-saving books. I. Title.

DRIJVERS, Pius 223.206
The Psalms, their structure and meaning [New York] Herder& Herder [c.1965] xii, [2], 269p. 21cm. Bibl. [BS1430.2.D713] 65-19629 5.50
1. Bible. O. T. Psalms—Criticism, interpretation, etc. I. Title.

DRIJVERS, Pius. 223.206
The Psalms, their structure and meaning. [New York] Herder and Herder [1965] xii, [2], 269 p. 21 cm. Translation of Over de Psalmen. Bibliography: 13th prelim. page. [BS1430.2.D713 1965] 65-19629
1. Bible. O.T. Psalms—Criticism, interpretation, etc. I. Title.

EATON, J. H. 223'.2'06
Kingship and the psalms / J. H. Eaton. London : S.C.M. Press, 1976. xii, 227 p. ; 22 cm. (Studies in biblical theology : 2d series ; 32) Includes indexes. Bibliography: p. [213]-219. [BS1430.2.E23] 76-381836 ISBN 0-334-00850-6 : £5.00
1. Bible. O.T. Psalms—Criticism, interpretation, etc. 2. Kings and rulers—Biblical teaching. I. Title. II. Series.

GASNIER, Henri Michel 223.206
The Psalms, school of spirituality. Tr. [from French] by Aldhelm Dean. St. Louis, Herder [c.1962] 160p. 19cm. 62-5608 3.75
1. Bible. O.T. Psalms—Criticism, interpretation, etc. I. Title.

GRIFFITH, Arthur Leonard, 1920- 223'.2'06
God in man's experience; the activity of God in the Psalms, by Leonard Griffith. Waco, Tex., Word Books [1968] 192 p. 23 cm. [BS1430.3.G7 1968] 68-3400
1. Bible. O.T. Psalms—Commentaries. I. Title.

*GROENHOFF, Edwin L. 223.206
It's your choice, by Edwin L. Groenhoff. Minneapolis, His International Service [1975] 64 p. ill. 21 cm. [BS1430.2] ISBN 0-911802-38-X 1.95 (pbk.)
1. Bible. O.T. Psalms—Criticism, interpretation, etc. I. Title.

GUNN, George Sinclair. 223.206
Singers of Israel; the book of Psalms. London, Lutterworth Press; New York, Abingdon Press [1963] 95 p. 20 cm. (Bible guides, no. 10) [BS1433.G8] 63-761
1. Bible. O. T. Psalms — Criticism, interpretation, etc. I. Title.

GUNN, George Sinclair 223.206
Singers of Israel; the book of Psalms. London, Lutterworth Press; Nashville, Abingdon [1963] 95p. 20cm. (Bible guides, no. 10) 63-761 1.00
1. Bible. O. T. Psalms—Criticism, interpretation, etc. I. Title.

GUTHRIE, Harvey H 223.206
Israel's sacred songs; a study of dominant themes [by] Harvey H. Guthrie, Jr. New York, Seabury Press [1966] x, 241 p. 22 cm. Includes bibliographies. [BS1430.2G8] 66-10833
1. Bible. O.T. Psalms — Criticism, interpretation, etc. I. Title.

GUTHRIE, Harvey H., Jr. 223.206
Israel's sacred songs; a study of dominant themes. New York, Eabury [c.1966] x, 241p. 22cm. Bibl. [BS1430.2.g8] 66-10833 5.95
1. Bible. O.T. Psalms—Criticism, interpretation,etc. I. Title.

HAURET, Charles 223.206
The songs of the people of God. Tr. by John F. McDonnell. Chicago, Priory Pr. [1966, c.1965] 178p. 19cm. Bibl. [BS1430.2.h313] 65-19360 2.95
1. Bible. O.T. Psalms—Criticism, interpretation, etc. I. Title.

HAYES, John Haralson, 1934- 223'.2'06
Understanding the Psalms / John H. Hayes. Valley Forge, Pa. : Judson Press, [1976] p. cm. [BS1430.2.H35] 75-22034 ISBN 0-8170-0683-4 : 4.50
1. Bible. O.T. Psalms—Introductions. I. Title.

HIERONYMUS, Saint. 223.206
The homilies of Saint Jerome. Translated by Marie Liguori Ewald. Washington, Catholic University of America Press [1964-66] 2 v. 22 cm. (The Fathers of the church, a new translation, v. 48, 57) Contents.Contents.—v. 1. 1-59 on the Psalms.—v. 2. Homilies 60-96. Bibliography: v. 1, p. xxxi. [BR60.F3H5] 64-13360
1. Bible. O.T. Psalms—Sermons. 2. Sermons, Latin—Translations into English. 3. Sermons, English—Translations from Latin. I. Ewald, Marie Liguori, 1905- tr. II. Title. III. Series: The Fathers of the church, a new translation, v. 48, [etc.]

KNIGHT, William Allen, 1863- 223.206
The song of our Syrian guest [by] William Allen Knight, and a shepherd's song [by]

Henry Van Dyke. [Westwood, N. J.] Revell [1964] 62 p. 17 cm. (A Revell inspirational classic) Bible. O. T. Psalms XXIII--Criticism, interpretation, etc. [BS145023d.K6 1964] 64-21463
I. Van Dyke, Henry, 1952-1933. II. Title. III. Title: A shepherd's song.

KNIGHT, William Allen, 1863- 223.206
The song of our Syrian guest [by] William Allen Knight, and A shepherd's song [by] Henry Van Dyke [Westwood, N. J.] Revell [c.1964] 62p. 17cm. (Revell inspirational classic) 64-21463 1.00 bds.,
1. Bible. O. T. Psalms xxiii—Criticism, interpretation, etc. I. Van Dyke, Henry, 1852-1933. II. Title. III. Title: A shepherd's song.

MCKILLOP, Sybil L. 223.206
Twenty psalms for schools, from the Prayer Book, the Scottish Psalter and a fresh tr., selected and arranged for singing at morning worship. Foreword by M. E. Popham [dist. Westminster, Md., Canterbury, c.1962] 63p. 22cm. 1.00 pap.,
I. Title.

MISCHKE, Bernard C 223.206
Meditations on the Psalms. New York, Sheed and Ward [1963] 298 p. 22 cm. [BS1430.2.M5] 63-8549
1. Bible. O.T. Psalms — Meditations. I. Title.

MISCHKE, Bernard C. 223.206
Meditations on the Psalms. New York, Sheed [c.1963] 298p. 22cm. 63-8549 4.95 bds.,
1. Bible. O.T. Psalms—Meditations. I. Title.

MOWINCKEL, Sigmund Olaf Plytt, 1884- 223.206
The Psalms in Israel's worship. New York, Abingdon Press [c1962] 2 v. 26 cm. Translation and revision by D. R. Ap-Thomas of Offersang og sangoffer. Bibliography: v. 2, p. [271]-289. [BS1430.2.M613] 63-3665
1. Bible. O.T. Psalms — Criticism, interpretations, etc. 2. Bible. O.T. Psalms — Liturgical use. I. Title.

NICHOLS, J. W. H. 223'.2'06
Musings in the psalms / by J. W. H. Nichols. New York : Loizeaux Bros., [1954?] 91 p. ; 19 cm. [BS1430.2.N5] 75-319387
1. Bible. O.T. Psalms—Criticism, interpretation, etc. I. Title.

RINGGREN, Helmer [Karl Vilhelm Helmer Ringgren] 1917- 223.206
The faith of the psalmists. Philadelphia, Fortress Pr. [1963] 138p. 22cm. Bibl. 63-7906 3.50
1. Bible. O.T. Psalms—Criticism, interpretation, etc. I. Title.

SABOURIN, Leopold. 223'.2'06
The Psalms: their origin and meaning. Staten Island, N.Y., Alba House [1969] 2 v. 22 cm. Bibliography: v. 2, p. [337]-367. [BS1430.2.S23] 71-77647 17.50
1. Bible. O.T. Psalms—Criticism, interpretation, etc. I. Title.

STRADLING, Leslie E. 223'.2'06
Praying the psalms / Leslie E. Stradling ; foreword by George E. Sweazey. 1st American ed. Philadelphia : Fortress Press, 1977. vii, 119 p. ; 19 cm. Bibliography: p. 119. [BS1430.2.S83 1977] 76-46340 ISBN 0-8006-1247-7 pbk. : 3.50
1. Bible. O.T. Psalms—Criticism, interpretation, etc. I. Title.

TESSIER, Albert Denis 223.206
'I shall not want . . .' Los Angeles, 4029 Wilshire Blvd. Harbor House, [c.1963] 76p. illus. 17cm. gift ed., 2.95
I. Title.

WILLIS, John T., 1933- 223'.2'06
Insights from the Psalms, by John T. Willis. Abilene, Tex., Biblical Research Press [1974- v. 22 cm. (The Way of life series, no. 131) On spine: The Psalms. [BS1430.5.W53] 73-93946 1.50
1. Bible. O.T. Psalms—Study—Text-books. I. Title.

WORDEN, Thomas 223.206
The Psalms are Christian prayer. New York, Sheed [1962, c.1961] 219p. 22cm. Bibl. 62-4812 3.95
1. Bible. O.T. Psalms—Criticism, interpretation, etc. 2. Prayer (Judaism) I. Title.

CULLEY, Robert C. 223/.2/061
Oral formulaic language in the Biblical psalms [by] Robert C. Culley. [Toronto] Univ. of Toronto Pr. [c1967] viii. 137p. 24cm. (Near & Middle East ser. 4) Bibl. [BS1430.2.C8] 67-1094443 6.50
1. Bible. O. T. Psalms—Criticism, Form. I. Title. II. Series.

GUNKEL, Hermann, 1862-1932. 223'.2'061
The Psalms; a form-critical introduction. With an introd. by James Muilenburg. Translated by Thomas M. Horner. Philadelphia, Fortress Press [1967] xi, 52 p. 20 cm. (Facet books. Biblical series 19) "Translated from volume I of the second edition of Die Religion in Geschichte und Gegenwart." Bibliography: p. 42-50. [BS1430.2.G7813] 67-22983
1. Bible. O.T. Psalms—Criticism, Form. I. Title. II. Series.

ANDERS-RICHARDS, Donald. 223'.2'066
The drama of the Psalms. Valley Forge [Pa.] Judson Press [1970, c1968] 118, [1] p. 20 cm. Bibliography: p. [119] [BS1430.2.A5 1970] 79-100965 1.95
1. Bible. O.T. Psalms—Criticism, interpretation, etc. I. Title.

BONHOEFFER, Dietrich, 1906-1945. 223'.2'066
Psalms: the prayer book of the Bible. With a sketch on the life of Dietrich Bonhoeffer by Eberhard Bethge. Translated by James H. Burtness. Minneapolis, Augsburg Pub. House [1970] 86 p. 17 cm. Translation of Das Gebetbuch der Bibel. [BS1430.2.B613 1970] 73-101111 2.75
1. Bible. O.T. Psalms—Introductions. I. Bethge, Eberhard, 1909- II. Title.

JOHNSON, Aubrey Rodway. 223'.2'066
Sacral Kingship in ancient Israel, by Aubrey R. Johnson. 2nd ed. Cardiff, Wales Univ. Pr., 1967. xiv, 167p. 23cm. Discussion of 'the hymns which celebrate the Kingship of Yahweh, and the so-called royal psalms.'--Preface. Bibl. [BS1445.M4J6 1967] 67-100203 6.00
1. Bibl. O. T. Pslams—Commentaries. 2. Jews—Kings and rulers. 3. Messianic psalms. I. Title.
Distributed by Verry, Mystic, Conn.

ROUTLEY, Erik. 223'.2'066
Exploring the Psalms / by Erik Routley. Philadelphia : Westminster Press, [1975] 172 p. ; 20 cm. "The thirteen chapters of this study were originally written for Crossroads ... " Includes index. [BS1430.2.R68] 74-20674 ISBN 0-664-24999-X pbk. : 3.25
1. Bible. O.T. Psalms—Criticism, interpretation, etc. I. Title.

SABOURIN, Leopold. 223'.2'066
The Psalms: their origin and meaning. New, enl., updated ed. Staten Island, N.Y., Alba House [1974] xx, 450 p. port. 21 cm. Bibliography: p. [411]-441. [BS1430.2.S23 1974] 73-16459 ISBN 0-8189-0121-7 5.95 (pbk.)
1. Bible. O.T. Psalms—Criticism, interpretation, etc. I. Title.

WESTERMANN, Claus. 223.2066
The praise of God in the Psalms. Translated by Keith R. Crim. Richmond, John Knox Press [1965] 172 p. 21 cm. Bibliography: p. 169-172. [BS1430.2.W413] 65-10553
1. Bible. O.T. Psalms — Criticism, interpretation, etc. I. Title.

WESTERMANN, Claus 223.2066
The praise of God in the Psalms. Tr. [from German] by Keith R. Crim. Richmond, Va., Knox [c.1965] 172p. 21cm. Bibl. [BS1430.2.W413] 65-10553 4.25 bds.,
1. Bible. O. T. Psalms—Criticisms, interpretations, etc. I. Title.

WITHER, George, 1588-1667. 223'.2'067
A preparation to the Psalter. New York, B. Franklin [1967] 160 p. illus. 35 cm. (Burt Franklin research & source works series #150) Reprint of the 1884 ed. which was issued as no. 37 of Publications of the Spencer Society. [PR2392.P6 1967] 72-184503
1. Bible. O.T. Psalms—Criticism, interpretation, etc. 2. Bible—Criticism, interpretation, etc.—O.T. Psalms. I. Title. II. Series: Spenser Society, Manchester. Publications, no. 37.

ALDEN, Robert. 223'.2'07
Psalms : songs of devotion / by Robert Alden. Chicago : Moody Press, c1974- v. ; 19 cm. (Everyman's Bible commentary) Contents.Contents.—v. 1. Psalms 1-50. [BS1430.3.A4] 74-15348 ISBN 0-8024-2018-4 pbk. : 1.95
1. Bible. O.T. Psalms—Commentaries. I. Title. II. Series.

ARMERDING, Carl. 223'.2'07
Psalms in a minor key. Chicago, Moody Press [1973] 159 p. 22 cm. [BS1430.4.A8] 73-7330 ISBN 0-8024-6936-1 3.95
1. Bible. O.T. Psalms—Meditations. I. Title.

BIBLE. O.T. Psalms. English. 1966. Dahood. 223.207
Psalms. Introd., translation, and notes, by Mitchell Dahood. [1st ed.] Garden City, N.Y., Doubleday, 1966-70. 3 v. 24 cm. (The Anchor Bible, 16-17A) Contents.Contents.—1. 1-50.—2. 51-100.—3. 101-150. Includes bibliographies. [BS192.2.A1 1964.G3 vol. 16-17A] 66-11766
1. Bible. O.T. Psalms—Commentaries. I. Dahood, Mitchell J., ed. and tr. II. Title. III. Series.

BIBLE. O.T. Psalms. English. 1966. Dahood 223.2'07
Psalms II. Introd., trs., notes, by Mitchell Dahood. Garden City, N.Y., Doubleday, 1968. v. 29cm. (Anchor Bible. 1-) [BS192.2.A1 1965 G3 vol. 17] 66-11764 6.00
1. Bible. O.T. Psalms—Commentaries. I. Dahood, Mitchell J. ed. and tr. II. Title.
Contents Omitted.

BLAIKLOCK, E. M. 223'.2'07 s
Psalms for living / E. M. Blaiklock. Philadelphia : A. J. Holman, c1977. 136 p. ; 21 cm. (His Commentary on the Psalms ; v. 1) [BS1430.3.B53 vol. 1] 223'.2'07 77-1122 ISBN 0-87981-080-7 : 4.5
1. Bible. O.T. Psalms I-LXXII—Commentaries. I. Title.

BLAIKLOCK, E. M. 223'.2'07 s
Psalms in Worship Psalms 73-150 / E. M. Blaiklock. Philadelphia : A. J. Holman, 1977. 144 p. ; 21 cm. (His Commentary on the Psalms ; v. 2) [BS1430.3.B53 vol. 2] 223'.2'07 77-2875 ISBN 0-87981-081-5 : 4.95
1. Bible. O.T. Psalms LXXIII-CL—Commentaries. I. Title.

A Commentary on the 223'.2'07
Psalms from primitive and mediaeval writers : and from the various office-books and hymns of the Roman, Mozarabic, Ambrosian, Gallican, Greek, Coptic, Armenian, and Syriac rites / by J. M. Neale and R. F. Littledale. New York : AMS Press, [1976] p. cm. With Psalms in the Coverdale version. Reprint of the editions published by J. Masters & Co., London. Contents.Contents.—v. 1. Psalm I to Psalm XXXVIII. 4th ed. 1884.—v. 2. Psalm XXXIX to Psalm LXXX. 3d ed. 1879.—v. 3. Psalm LXXXI to Psalm CXVIII. 3d ed. 1887.—v. 4. Psalm CXIX to Psalm CL with indexes of Scripture references and of subjects. 2d ed. 1883. [BS1429.C65] 78-130990 ISBN 0-404-04680-0 145.00
1. Bible. O.T. Psalms—Commentaries. I. Neale, John Mason, 1818-1866. II. Littledale, Richard Frederick, 1833-1890. III. Coverdale, Miles, Bp. of Exeter, 1488-1568. IV. Bible. O.T. Psalms. English. Coverdale. 1976.

CRIM, Keith R. 223.207
The royal Psalms. Richmond, John Knox Press [1962] 127 p. 21 cm. "Unless...[Revised standard version is] indicated the Scripture quotations are in the author's translation." [BS1445.M4C7] 62-10237
1. Bible. O.T. Psalms—Commentaries. 2. Messianic Psalms. 3. Jews—Kings and rulers. I. Title.

KIDNER, Derek. 223'.2'07
Psalms 73-150 : a commentary on Books III-V of the Psalms / by Derek Kidner. London : Inter-Varsity Press, [1975] p. 259-492 ; 19 cm. (The Tyndale Old Testament commentaries) Includes bibliographical references. [BS1430.3.K53 1975] 76-3948 ISBN 0-87784-959-5 : 7.95 (U.S.)
1. Bible. O.T. Psalms LXXIII-CL—Commentaries.

KIDNER, Derek. 223'.2'07
Psalms 73-150 : a commentary on Books III-V of the Psalms / by Derek Kidner London : Inter-Varsity Press, [1975] p. 259-492 ; 19 cm. (The Tyndale Old Testament commentaries) Includes bibliographical references. [BS1430.3.K53 1975] 76-3948 ISBN 0-87784-959-5 : 7.95
1. Bible. O.T. Psalms LXXIII-CL—Commentaries.
Distributed by Inter-Varsity, Illinois.

MEYER, Frederick Brotherton, 1847-1929. 223'.2'07
Gems from the Psalms / F. B. Meyer. Westchester, Ill. : Good News Publishers, c1976. 254 p. ; 21 cm. [BS1430.3.M49 1976] 76-17670 ISBN 0-89107-146-6 : 2.95
1. Bible. O.T. Psalms—Commentaries. I. Title.

REDDING, David A 223.207
Psalms of David. [Westwood, N.J., F.H. Revell Co. [1963] xvii, 174 p. 21 cm. Bibliography: p. 167. [BS1430.2.R4] 63-7593
1. Bible. O.T. Psalms — Commentaries. I. Title.

REDDING, David A. 223.207
Psalms of David. [Westwood, N.J.] Revell [c.1963] xvii, 174p. 21cm. Bibl. 63-7593 3.00 bds.,
1. Bible. O.T. Psalms—Commentaries. I. Title.

WEISER, Artur, 1893- 223.207
The Psalms, a commentary. [Translated by Herbert Hartwell from the German, Die Psalmen, Das Alte Testament, deutsch 14/15] Philadelphia, Westminster Press 1962] 841 p. 23 cm. (The Old Testament library) Bibliography: p. 14-15. [BS1430.W353] 62-16760
1. Bible. O.T. Psalms — Commentaries. I. Title. II. Series.

WEISER, Artur, 1893- 223.207
The Psalms, a commentary. [Tr. by Herbert Hartwell from German] Philadelphia, Westminster [c.1962] 841p. 23cm. (Old Testament lib.) Bibl. 62-16760 9.50
1. Bible. O.T. Psalms—Commentaries. I. Title. II. Series.

BIBLE. O.T. Psalms. English. Authorized. 1973. 223'.2'077
Psalms and Proverbs in two versions with commentary. Produced for Moody monthly. New York, Iversen-Norman Associates, 1973. 378 p. 25 cm. Contains texts of Psalms and Proverbs in both the King James and the Living Bible versions with commentary from C. F. Pfeiffer's The Wycliff Bible commentary. Includes bibliographies. [BS1422 1973] 72-97786
1. Bible. O.T. Psalms—Commentaries. 2. Bible. O.T. Proverbs—Commentaries. I. Pfeiffer, Charles F. The Wycliff Bible commentary. Psalms-Proverbs. 1973. II. Moody monthly. III. Bible. O.T. Psalms. English. Living Bible. 1973. IV. Bible. O.T. Proverbs. English. Authorized. 1973. V. Bible. O.T. Proverbs. English. Living Bible. 1973. VI. Title.

BIBLE. O.T. Psalms. English. Perowne, 1976. 223'.2'077
The book of Psalms / a new translation with introductions and notes, explanatory and critical by J. J. Stewart Perowne. Grand Rapids, Mich. : Zondervan Pub. House, 1976. 2 v. in 1 ; 23 cm. Reprint of the 1878-79 ed. published by D. Bell, London. Includes indexes. [BS1430.P4 1976] 76-381689 19.95
1. Bible. O.T. Pslams—Commentaries. I. Perowne, John James Stewart, 1823-1904.

VAN DOREN, Mark, 1894-1972. 223'.2'077
The book of praise; dialogues on the Psalms [by] Mark Van Doren and Maurice Samuel. Edited and annotated by Edith Samuel. New York, John Day Co. [1975] xix, 265 p. 22 cm. Includes bibliographical references. [BS1430.2.V36 1975] 74-9362 ISBN 0-381-98271-8
1. Bible. O.T. Psalms—Criticism, interpretation, etc. I. Samuel, Maurice, 1895-1972. II. Samuel, Edith, ed. III. Title.

INCH, Morris A., 1925- 223'.2'08815
Psychology in the Psalms; a portrait of man in God's world [by] Morris A. Inch. [1st ed.] Waco, Tex., Word Books [1969] 202 p. 23 cm. Bibliography: p. 196-202. [BS1430.2.I5] 69-20221 4.95
1. Bible. O.T. Psalms.—Criticism, interpretation, etc. 2. Man (Theology)—Biblical teaching. I. Title.

ROSENBERG, David W., 1943- 223'.2'09505
Blues of the sky : interpreted from the original Hebrew Book of Psalms / David Rosenberg. 1st ed. New York : Harper & Row, c1976. 53 p. ; 21 cm. "A Poet's Bible." [BS1440.A1R67 1976] 76-9991 ISBN 0-06-067009-6 : 6.95
1. Bible. O.T. Psalms—Paraphrases, English. I. Title.

ROUTLEY, Erik. 223.2406
Ascent to the cross. New York, Abingdon Press [1962] 94p. 20cm. [BS1445.S6R6] 62-52163
1. Bible. O. T. Psalms cxx-cxxxiv—Meditations. I. Title.

BIBLE. O.T. Psalms. English. 1911. 223'.2'52
The Hexaplar Psalter. Edited by William Aldis Wright. Hildesheim, New York, G. Olms, 1969. vi, 389 p. 22 cm. (Anglistica & Americana, 55) Reprint of the ed. published in Cambridge by University Press in 1911. Coverdale (1535) Great Bible (1539) Geneva (1560) Bishops (1568) Authorised (1611) Revised (1885) in parallel columns. [BS1421.W7 1969] 72-483998
I. Wright, William Aldis, 1831-1914, ed. II. Title. III. Series.

BIBLE. O.T. Psalms. I-XXXIV, XL-XLI. English. 1963.Kendon. 223.252
Thirty-six Psalms, an English version, by Frank Kendon. Cambridge [Eng.] University

Press, 1963. vii, 63 p. 28 cm. [BS1424.K4] 63-24935
I. Kendon, Frank, 1893- tr. II. Title.

BIBLE. O.T. Psalms I-XXXIV, XL-XLI. English. 1963. Kendon 223.252
Thirty-six Psalms, an English version, by Frank Kendon. Cambridge [Eng.] University Pr. [dist. New York, Cambridge, c.] 1963. viii, 63p. 28cm. 63-24935 5.00
I. Kendon, Frank, 1893- tr. II. Title.

BIBLE. O.T. Psalms XXIII. English 1965.Authorized. 223.25203
The Twenty third psalm. Illustrated by Tasha Tudor. Worcester, A. J. St. Onge [1965] 1 v. (unpaged) col. illus. 93 mm. [BS145023d.T8] 66-89
1. Bible. O. T. Psalms—Pictures, illustrations, etc. 2. Bibliography—Microscopic and miniature editions—Specimens. I. Tudor, Tasha, illus. II. Title.

BIBLE. O.T. Psalms XXIII. English. 1965 Authorized. 223.252'03
The Lord is my shepherd; the Twenty-third psalm. Pictures by Tony Palazzo. New York, Walck [1973 c.1965] 1 v. (unpaged) col. illus. 20 cm. [BS1450.23rd.P3] 66-89 ISBN 0-8098-1804-3 pap., 1.50
I. Palazzo, Tony, illus. II. Title.

BIBLE. O.T. Psalms xxiii. English. 1965. Authorized. 223.25203
The Twenty-third psalm. Illus. by Tasha Tudor. Worcester, Mass., A. J. St. Onge [c.1965] 1v. (unpaged) col. illus. 10x7cm. [BS1450 23d.T8] 66-89 5.00 bds.,
1. Bible. O.T. Psalms — Pictures, illustrations, etc. 2. Bibliography—Microscopic and miniature editions—Specimens. I. Tudor, Tasha illus. II. Title.

MORGAN, Dewi 223.266
Arising from the Psalms. [1st Amer. ed] New York, Morehouse [1966, c.1965] xii. 145p. 21cm. [BS1430.4.M6 1966] 66-5523 3.75
1. Bible, O.T. Psalms—Devotional literature. I. Title.

*JOWETT, J. H. 223.'2'77
Spring in the desert : studies in the Psalms / J. H. Jowett. Grand Rapids : Baker Book House, 1976c1924. viii, 300p. ; 20 cm. (His Libbrary) [BS 1430] ISBN 0-8010-5065-0 pbk. : 3.95.
1. Bible. O. T. Psalms-Criticism, interpretation, etc. I. Title.

*POPEJOY, Bill. 223.'2'77
Goodness, you're following me! : a devotional commentary on Psalm 23. Springfield, Mo. : Gospel Pub House [1976]c1975. 120p. ; 18 cm. (Radiant books) [BS1450] ISBN 0-88243-519-1 pbk. : 1.45
1. Bible. O.T. Psalms xxiii-Commentaries. I. Title.

SWANK, Calvin Peter, 1880- 223.306
Sermons from the Psalms. Grand Rapids, Baker Book House, 1962. 122 p. 20 cm. (Evangelical pulpit library) [BS1445.P4S9] 62-12670
1. Penitential Psalms. 2. Sermons, American. 3. Lutheran Church—Sermons. 4. Evangelistic sermons. I. Title.

SWANK, Calvin Peter, 1880- 223.306
Sermons from the Psalms. Grand Rapids, Mich., Baker [c.]1962. 122p. 20cm. (Evangelical pulpit lib.) 62-12670 2.50
1. Penitential Psalms. 2. Sermons, American. 3. Lutheran Church—Sermons. 4. Evangelistic sermons. I. Title.

BIBLE. O. T. Psalms. English. Selections. 1960. Ward. 223.4
Seasons of the soul, by Archibald F. Ward, Jr. Richmond. John Knox Press [c.1960] 135p. illus. 24cm. Selections from the Psalms, rendered into English from French and German versions. 60-15656 3.00
I. Ward, Archibald Floyd, 1912- tr. II. Title.

GUDNASON, Kay, comp. 223.4
Psalms of the heavens, earth, and sea. Text from the book of Psalms, arr. by Kay Gudnason, with selected photos. Natick, Mass., W. A. Wilde Co. [1964] 1 v. (unpaged) illus. 19 x 26 cm. [BS1433.G83] 64-19917
1. Bible. O.T. Psalms — Pictures, illustrations, etc. I. Title.

GUDNASON, Kay, comp. 223.4
Psalms of the heavens, earth, and sea. Text from the book of Psalms, arr. by Kay Gudnason, with selected photos. Natick, Mass., W. A. Wilde [c.1964] 1v. (unpaged) illus. 19x26cm. 64-19917 4.50
1. Bible. O. T. Psalms—Pictures, illustrations, etc. I. Title.

MCCALL, Thomas S. 223'.4
The coming Russian invasion of Israel / Thomas S. McCall and Zola Levitt. Chicago : Moody Press, [1974] 96 p. : ill. ; 21 cm. Includes bibliographical references. [BS649.P3M3] 74-192548 ISBN 0-8024-1606-3 pbk. : 3.95
1. Bible—Prophecies—Israel. 2. Bible—Prophecies—Russia. I. Levitt, Zola, joint author. II. Title.

RODD. CYRIL S. 223.406
Psalms 73-150 London. Epworth Pr.[dist. Naperville. Ill., Allenson. c.1964] 136p. 19cm. (Epworth preacher's commentaries. v 11) 64-2024 3.00
1. Bible. O. T. Psalms 1-LXXII—Commentaries. I. Title.

BIBLE. O. T. Psalms. English. Paraphrases. 1954. Kleist-Lynam. 223.5
The Psalms in rhythmic prose. Translation based on the authorized Latin version rendered from the original texts by members of the Pontifical Biblical Institute. Translated by James A. Kleist and Thomas J. Lynam. Milwaukee, Bruce [1954] xii, 236p. 23cm. [BS1440.K53] 54-9335
I. Kleist, James Aloysius, 1873- tr. II. Lynam, Thomas J., tr. III. Title.

BIBLE. O. T. Psalms. English. Paraphrases. 1955. 223.5
Songs from one hundred Psalms [by] Ethel Riner Sublette. [1st ed.] New York, Exposition Press [1955] 160p. 21cm. [BS1440.S9] 55-9416
I. Sublette, Ethel Riner. II. Title.

CECILIA, Sister, 1892- 223.5
The Psalms in modern life. Chicago, H. Regnery Co., 1960. 259p. 21cm. [S1430.2.C4] 60-14058
1. Bible. O. T. Psalms—Meditations. I. Title.

CECILIA, Sister 223.5
The Psalms in modern life. Chicago, H. Regnery Co., [c.1960] xi, 259p. 21cm. (bibl. footnotes) 60-14058 4.50 bds.,
1. Bible. O. T. Psalms—Meditations. I. Title.

HARASZTI, Zoltan, 1892- 223.5
The enigma of the Bay Psalm book. [Chicago] University of Chicago Press [1956] xiii, 143 p. port., facsims. 20 cm. Companion volume to The Bay Psalm book, a facsimile reprint of the first edition of 1640, published in 1956. Bibliographical references included in "Notes" (p. 119-139) [BS1440.B415H3] 56-5128
1. Bible. O.T. Psalms. English—Paraphases—Bay Psalm book. 2. Bay Psalm book. I. Title.

HARASZTI, Zoltan, 1892- 223.5
The gnigma of the Bay Psalm book. [Chicago] University of Chicago Press [1956] xiii, 143p. port., facsims. 20cm. Companion volume to The Bay Psalm book, a facsimile reprint of the first edition of 1640, published in 1956. Bibliographical references included in 'Notes' (p. 119-139) [BS1440.B415H3] 56-5128
1. Bible. O. T. Psalms. English—Paraphrases—Bay Psalm book. 2. Bay Psalm book. I. Title.

MERTON, Thomas 223.5
Bread in the wilderness [New York] New Directions [1960. c.1953] 146p. (Bibl. notes: p.141-146) 24cm. 53-13509 3.50; 1.65 pap.,
1. Bible. O. T. Psalms—Liturgical use. 2. Contemplation. I. Title.

PETERSHAM, Maud Sylvia (Fuller) 1890- 223.5
The Shepherd Psalm; Psalm xxiii from the book of Psalms. New York, Macmillan [c.] 1962. 24p. illus. 24cm. 62-17339 2.50 bds.,
1. Bible. O.T. Psalms. xxiii. English. 1962. Authorized. I. Title.

RYAN, Mary Perkins, 1915- 223.5
Key to the Psalms. Chicago, Fides Publishers Association [1957] 187p. 21cm. (Fides family readers) [BS1435.R9] 57-13166
1. Bible. O. T. Psalms— Liturgical use. 2. Bible. O. T. Psalms—Theology. I. Bible. O. T. Psalms. English. Selections. 1957. Fides. II. Title.

ALLEN, Charles Livingstone, 1913- 223.6
The Twenty-third psalm; an interpretation. [Illus. by Ismar David. Westwood, N. J.] Revell [1961] 62p. illus. 20cm. [BS1450 23d.A55] 61-9843
1. Bible. O. T. Psalms XXIII—Criticism, interpretation, etc. I. Title.

ALLEN, Charles Livingstone, 1913- 223.6
The Twenty-third psalm; an interpretation. [Illus. by Ismar David. Westwood, N. J.] Revell [c.1961] 62p. illus. (part col.) 61-9843 1.50 bds.,
1. Bible. O. T. Psalms XXIII—Criticism, interpretation, etc. I. Title.

AUGUSTINUS, Aurelius, Saint. Bp. of Hippo. 223.6
St. Augustine on the Psalms. Translated and annotated by Scholastica Hebgin and Felicitas Corrigan. Westminster, Md., Newman Press, 1960- v. 23cm. (Ancient Christian writers: the works of the Fathers in translation, no. 29 Contents.v. 1. Psalms 1-29. Bibliography: v. 1. p. 15-16. [BR60.A35 no.29] 60-10722
1. Bible. O. T. Psalms—Commentaries. I. Hebgin, Scholastica, ed. and tr. II. Corrigan, Felicitas, ed. and tr. III. Title. IV. Series.

AUGUSTINUS, Aurelius, Saint, Bp. of Hippo. 223.6
St. Augustine on the Psalms. v. 1. Psalms 1-29. Translated [from the Latin] and annotated by Scholastica Hebgin and Felicitas Corrigan. Westminster, Md., Newman Press [c.] 1960 vi, 354p. (Bibl.: p.15-16, bibl. notes: p.315-341) 23cm. (Ancient Christian writers; the works of the Fathers in translation, no. 29) 60-10722 4.50 bds.,
1. Bible. O. T. Psalms—Commentaries. I. Hebgin, Scholastica, ed. and tr. II. Corrigan, Felicitas, ed. and tr. III. Title. IV. Series.

BOSLEY, Harold Augustus, 1907- 223.6
Sermons on the Psalms. New York, Harper [c1956] 208p. 22cm. [BS1430.B68] 55-6781
1. Bible. O. T. Psalms—Sermons. 2. Methodist Church—Sermons. 3. Sermons, American. I. Title.

DANIEL, Robert T 1904- 223.6
How to study the Psalms; based on an exposition of twelve favorite psalms. Westwood, N. J., Revell [1953] 271p. 21cm. [BS1430.D34] 53-2393
1. Bible. O. T. Psalms—Commentaries. I. Bible. O. T. Psalms. English. 1953. Revised standard. II. Title.

IRONSIDE, Henry Allan, 1876-1951. 223.6
Studies on book one of the Psalms. [1st ed.] New York, Loizeaux Bros. [1952] 250 p. 20 cm. [BS1430.I 7] 52-8574
1. Bible. O. T. Psalms I-XIL—Commentaries. I. Title.

KALT, Edmund, 1879-1943. 223.6
Herder's commentary on the Psalms. Tr. by Bernard Fritz. Westminster, Md., Newman Pr. [c.]1961. xxii, 559p. 61-9903 6.75
1. Bible. O. T. Psalms—Commentaries. I. Bible. O. T. Psalms. English. 1961. Kalt. II. Title.

KISSANE, Edward J., 1886- 223.6
The book of Psalms. Tr. from a critically rev. Hebrew text, with a commentary [dist. Mystic. Conn., Verry, 1965] 656p. 22cm. Bibl [BS1430.K55] 10.00
1. Bible. O. T. Psalms—Commentaries. I. Bible. O. T. Psalms English. 1953. Kissane. II. Title.

LEUPOLD, Herbert Carl, 1892- 223.6
Exposition of the Psalms. Columbus, Ohio, Wartburg Press [1959] 1010 p. 23 cm. Includes bibliography. [BS1430.2.L47] 59-9289
1. Bible. O. T. Paslms—Commentaries. I. Title.

LEWIS, Clive Staples, 1898- 223.6
Reflections on the Psalms. [1st American ed.] New York, Harcourt, Brace [c1958] 151p. 21cm. [BS1433.L4] 58-10910
1. Bible. O.T. Psalms—Criticism, Interpretation, etc. I. Title.

MAKRAKES, Apostolos, 1831-1905. 223.6
Commentary on the Psalms of David; translated out of the original Greek by D. Cummings. Chicago, Orthodox Christian Educational Society, 1950. xxxi, 960 p. port. 24 cm. "Commentary on the nine Odes of the church, by Apostolos Makrakis, translated out of the original Greek by D. Cummings" (p.[871]-960) has special t. p. [BS1430.M33] 51-615
1. Bible. O. T. Psalms—Commentaries. 2. Canticles. I. Title. II. Title: Commentary on the nine Odes of the church.

MILTON, John Peterson, 1897- 223.6
The Psalms. Rock Island, Ill., Augustana Book Concern [1954] 252p. 22cm. [BS1430.M5] 54-38492
1. Bible. O. T. Psalms—Theology. 2. Bible. O. T. Psalms—Sermons. 3. Lutheran Church—Sermons. 4. Sermons, American. I. Title.

O'SULLIVAN, Kevin. 223.6
My daily psalter; a short explanation and application of the psalms as they occur each day in the Breviary,[by] Kevin O'Sullivan. Chicago, Franciscan Herald Press [c1963] xi, 258 p. 23 cm. [BS1430.2.O8] 63-21387
1. Bible. O. T. Psalms — Commentaries. I. Catholic Church. Liturgy and ritual. Psalter. II. Title.

PATERSON, John, 1887- 223.6
The praises of Israel; studies, literary and religious, in the Psalms. New York, Scribner, 1950. x, 256 p. 21 cm. Bibliography: p. 247-249. [BS1430.P28] 50-4212
1. Bible. O.T. Psalms — Criticism, interpretation, etc. I. Title.

SCOTT, Robert Balgarnie Young, 1899- 223.6
The Psalms as Christian praise. New York, Association Press [1958] 94p. 20cm. (World Christian books) [BS1430.S38] 58-11538
1. Bible. O. T. Psalms— Criticism, interpretation, etc. I. Title.

SPURGEON, Charles Haddon 223.6
Sermons on the Psalms. Selected and edited by Chas. T. Cook. Grand Rapids, Mich., Zondervan Pub. House [1960] 255p. 23cm. (Library of Spurgeon's sermons, v. 9) 60-3453 2.95
1. Bible. O. T. Psalms—Sermons. 2. Baptists—Sermons. 3. Sermons. English. I. Title.

TONER, Helen L 223.6
Discovering the unshakeable through psalmists' eyes. St. Louis, Bethany Press [1956] 64p. 18cm. [BS1433.T6] 55-12155
1. Bible. O. T. Psalms—Meditations. I. Title.

TONER, Helen L 223.6
Discovering the unshakeable through psalmists' eyes. St. Louis, Bethany Press [1956] 64 p. 18 cm. [BS1433.T6] 55-12155
1. Bible. O. T. Psalms — Meditations. I. Title.

WEVERS, John William. 223.6
The way of the righteous; Psalms and the books of Wisdom. Philadelphia, Westminster Press [1961] 96 p. 20 cm. (Westminster guides to the Bible) [BS1430.2.W45] 61-13971
1. Bible. O. T. Psalms—Criticism, interpretation, etc. 2. Bible. O. T. Wisdom literature—Criticism, interpretation, etc. I. Title.

YATES, Kyle Monroe, 1895- 223.6
Studies in Psams. Nashville, Broadman Press [1953] 146p. 20cm. [BS1451.Y3] 53-13325
1. Bible. O. T. Psalms—Study—Text-books. I. Title.

BARNETT, Joe R. 223'.7
Paths to peace [by] Joe R. Barnett [and] John D. Gipson. [1st ed. Fort Worth, Tex., Pathway Pub. House, 1969] 114 p. 21 cm. [BS1465.4B37] 76-80845
1. Bible. O.T. Proverbs—Meditations. I. Gipson, John D., joint author. II. Title.

BIBLE. O. T. Proverbs. English. 1950. 223.7
Proverbs, with commentary by Julius H. Greenstone. Philadelphia, Jewish Publication Society of America, 1950. xiii, 354 p. 22 cm. (The Holy Scriptures, with commentary) Bibliography: p. xxxi-xiii. [BS1463.G67] 51-196
I. Greenstone, Julius Hillel, 1873- II. Jewish Publication Society of America. III. Title.

BIBLE. O.T. Proverbs. English. 1963. Authorized 223.7
The book of Proverbs, from the authorized King James version, with an introd. by Robert Gordis and decorations by Valenti Angelo. New York, Heritage [dist. Dial, 1965, c.1963] 1v. (unpaged, on double leaves) illus. 25cm. [BS1463.G6] 6.50
I. Gordis, Robert, 1908- II. Angelo, Valenti, 1897- illus. III. Title.

BIBLE. O.T. Proverbs. English. 1965. Scott. 223.7
Proverbs. Ecclesiastes. Introd., translation, and notes by R. B. Y. Scott. [1st ed.] Garden City, N.Y., Doubleday, 1965. liii, 255 p. 25 cm. (The Anchor Bible, 18) Includes bibliographies. [BS192.2.A1 1964.G3, vol. 18] 65-13988
1. Bible. O.T. Proverbs—Commentaries. 2. Bible. O.T. Ecclesiastes—Commentaries. I. Scott, Robert Balgarnie Young, 1899- ed. and tr. II. Bible. O.T. Ecclesiastes. English. 1965. Scott. III. Title. IV. Title: Ecclesiastes. V. Series.

BIBLE. O. T. Proverbs. English. 1965. Scott. 223.7
Proverbs. Ecclesiastes. Introd., tr., note by R. B. Y. Scott. Garden City, N. Y., Doubleday, [c.]1965. liii, 255p. 25cm. (Anchor Bible, 18) Bibl. [BS192.2.A1 1964. G3, vol.18] 65-13988 6.00
1. Bible. O. T. Proverbs—Commentaries. 2. Bible. O. T. Ecclesiastes—Commentaries. I. Scott, Robert Balgarnie Young, 1899- ed. and tr. II. Bible. O. T. Ecclesiastes. English. 1965. Scott. III. Title. IV. Title: Ecclesiastes. (Series)

BIBLE. O.T. Proverbs. English. New American Standard. Selections. 1973. 223'.7
Insight; uncommon sense for common people.

Selected proverbs from the New American Standard Bible arr. topically. Compiled by Bryce D. Bartruff. Minneapolis, Minn., Bethany Fellowship [1973] 108 p. illus. 18 cm. (Dimension books) [BS1463.B37] 73-10830 ISBN 0-87123-248-0 1.25 (pbk.)
I. Bartruff, Bryce D. II. Title.

BIBLE. O.T. Proverbs. 223'.7
English. Selections. 1968.
The little book of Proverbs. Selected by Carol Wilkins Giniger. Illustrated by Barbara Werner. New York, Golden Press [1968] 64 p. illus. 17 cm. (The Golden library of faith & inspiration) "A Giniger book." [BS1463.G5] 68-17171
I. Giniger, Carol Wilkins, comp. II. Title.

IRONSIDE, Henry Allan, 223.7
1876-1951.
Notes on the book of Proverbs. [1st ed.] New York, Loizeaux Bros. [1952] 485p. 19cm. [BS1465.I7] 54-32889
1. Bible. O. T. Proverbs—Commentaries. I. Title.

WILSON, Herman O. 223'.7
Studies in Proverbs [by] Herman O. Wilson. Austin, Tex., Sweet Pub. Co. [1969] 104 p. 22 cm. (The Living Word series, 210) [BS1467.W5] 71-92631
1. Bible. O.T. Proverbs—Study—Text-books. I. Title.

*GEE, Donald. 223.7'007
A word to the wise. Springfield, Mo., Gospel Publishing House, [1975] 78 p. 19 cm. (Radiant books) Original title: "Proverbs for Pentecost" [BS1467] ISBN 0-88243-632-5 0.95 (pbk.)
1. Bible—Commentaries—O.T. Poetical Books. I. Title.

BIBLE. O.T. Proverbs. 223'.7'052
English. Today's English. 1974.
Ancient wisdom for modern man : Proverbs and Ecclesiastes in Today's English version. New York : Simon and Schuster, [1974] c1972. 69 p. : ill. ; 22 cm. [BS1463 1974] 75-300640 ISBN 0-671-21893-X pbk. : 3.95
I. Bible. O.T. Ecclesiastes. English. Today's English. 1974. II. Title.

BIBLE, O.T. 223'.7'05204
Proverbs. English. 1966. Sperka.
Proberbs to live by, arranged by topics, and the Book of proverbs in a modern translation with resumes preceeding [sic] each chapter. Translated, edited, and compiled by Joshua S. Sperka. New York, Block Pub. Co. [1967, c1966] 246 p. 24 cm. [BS1463.S6] 66-30571
I. Sperka, Joshua Sidney, 1904- ed. and tr. II. Title.

AMMERMAN, Leila 223'.7'06
Tremaine.
The golden ladder of stewardship. Natick, Mass., W. A. Wilde Co. [1962] 66p. 20cm. [BV772.A48] 62-13688
1. Stewardship, Christian. I. Title.

BRAZELL, George. 223'.7'06
This is stewardship. Springfield, Mo., Gospel Pub. House [1962] 127 p. 20 cm. Includes bibliographies. [BV772.B7] 62-20510
1. Stewardship, Christian. I. Title.

DRAPER, James T. 223'.7'06
Proverbs : the secret of beautiful living / James T. Draper, Jr. Wheaton, Ill. : Tyndale House Publishers, c1977. 159 p. ; 22 cm. Bibliography: p. 159. [BS1465.4.D73] 76-58132 ISBN 0-8423-4925-1 : 5.95
1. Bible. O.T. Proverbs—Sermons. 2. Baptists—Sermons. 3. Sermons, American. I. Title.

DRAPER, James T. 223'.7'06
Proverbs : the secret of beautiful living / James T. Draper, Jr. Wheaton, Ill. : Tyndale House Publishers, c1977. 159 p. ; 22 cm. Bibliography: p. 159. [BS1465.4.D73] 76-58132 ISBN 0-8423-4925-1 : 5.95
1. Bible. O.T. Proverbs—Sermons. 2. Baptists—Sermons. 3. Sermons, American. I. Title.

FRASER, Neil McCormick. 223'.7'06
The glory of His rising: a closer look at the Resurrection. [1st ed.] Neptune, N.J., Loizeaux Brothers [1963] 127 p. 20 cm. [BT481.F7] 63-13778
1. Jesus Christ — Resurrection. I. Title.

FRASER, Neil McCormick. 223'.7'06
The glory of His rising: a closer look at the Resurrection. [1st ed.] Neptune, N.J., Loizeaux Brothers [1963] 127 p. 20 cm. [BT481.F7] 63-13778
1. Jesus Christ — Resurrection. I. Title.

GOPPELT, Leonhard, 223'.7'06
1911-
The Easter message today: three essays by Leonhard Goppelt, Helmut Thielicke, and Hans-Rudolf Muller-Schwefe. Translated by Salvator Atanasio and Darrell Likens Guder. With an introd. by Markus Barth. London, New York, Nelson [1964] 156 p. 21 cm. Bibliographical footnotes. [BT481.G613] 64-17738
1. Jesus Christ — Resurrection. 2. Easter. I. Title.

GREAT sermons on the 223'.7'06
Resurrection, by Alexander Maclaren [and others] Grand Rapids, Baker Book House, 1963. 127 p. 20 cm. ([Minister's handbook series]) First published in 1896 under title: The Resurrection. [BT481.G7] 63-21469
1. Jesus Christ—Resurrection—Sermons. 2. Maclaren, Alexander.

GREENE, Oliver B 223'.7'06
The Epistle of Paul the apostle to the Colossians, by Oliver B. Greene. Greenville, S.C., Gospel Hour, inc. [1964, c1963] 235 p. 20 cm. [BS2715.3.G7] 63-21467
1. Bible. N.T. Colossians — Commentaries. I. Bible. N.T. Colossians. English. 1964. II. Title.

HATCH, Clarence W 1903- 223'.7'06
1960.
Stewardship enriches life. Rev. by Mildred Hatch. Anderson, Ind., Warner Press [1962] 96p. 21cm. [BV772.H34 1962] 62-13335
1. Stewardship, Christian. I. Title.

HOLT, Ivan Lee, Bp., 223'.7'06
1886-
Yesterday speaks to today. New York, Abingdon Press [1956] 96p. 20cm. [BS1505.H63] 56-10147
1. Prophets. I. Title.

HOLT, Ivan Lee, Bp., 223'.7'06
1886-
Yesterday speaks to today. New York, Abingdon Press [1956] 96p. 20cm. [BS1505.H63] 56-10147
1. Prophets. I. Title.

HOUGH, John E T 223'.7'06
The service of our lives [by] John E. T. Hough and Ronald W. Thomson. London, SCM Press [1962] 120 p. 19 cm. (The Living church books) Bibliography: p. [115]-117. [BV772.H59] 64-36023
1. Stewardship, Christian. I. Thomson, Ronald William, joint author. II. Title.

HYATT, James Philip, 223'.7'06
1909-
The prophetic criticism of Israelite worship [by] J. Philip Hyatt. Cincinnati, Hebrew Union College Press [1963] 24 p. 23 cm. (The Goldenson lecture of 1963) Bibliographical references included in "Notes" (p. 23-24) [BS1505.2.G6] 68-6987
1. Prophets. 2. Worship (Judaism) I. Title. II. Series: The Goldenson lecture, 1963

HYATT, James Philip, 223'.7'06
1909-
The prophetic criticism of Israelite worship [by] J. Philip Hyatt. Cincinnati, Hebrew Union College Press [1963] 24 p. 23 cm. (The Goldenson lecture of 1963) Bibliographical references included in "Notes" (p. 23-24) [BS1505.2.G6 1963] 68-6987
1. Prophets. 2. Worship (Judaism) I. Title. II. Series: The Goldenson lecture, 1963

JONES, Bob, 1911- 223'.7'06
Ancient truths for modern days; sermons on Old Testament subjects that particularly apply to our times. Murfreesboro, Tenn., Sword of the Lord Publishers [1963] 187 p. port. 21 cm. [BS1151.5.J6] 64-334
1. Bible. O. T. Sermons. 2. Sermons, American. I. Title.

LARSEN, Paul E. 223'.7'06
Wise up & live! Wisdom from Proverbs [by] Paul E. Larsen. Glendale, Calif., G/L Regal Books [1974] 239 p. 18 cm. "A Bible commentary for laymen." Includes bibliographical references. [BS1465.4.L37] 73-86222 ISBN 0-8307-0219-9 1.25 (pbk.).
1. Bible. O.T. Proverbs—Sermons. 2. Sermons, American. I. Title.

LAYTON, Mac, 1931- 223'.7'06
This grace also. 1st ed. Includes bibliographical references. [BV772.L38] 65-5011
1. Stewardship, Christian. I. Title.

LAYTON, Mac, 1931- 223'.7'06
This grace also. 1st ed. Dallas, Christian Pub. Co. [c1964] xi, 279 p. 23 cm. Includes bibliographical references. [BV772.L38] 65-5011
1. Stewardship, Christian. I. Title.

NEW Clarendon Bible: 223'.7'06
Old Testament. v. 1- [London, Oxford University Press, 1966- v. illus. 20 cm. [BS1151.2.N46] 66-7969
1. Bible. O. T. — Commentaries.

20 stewardship 223'.7'06
sermons, by pastors of the Evangelical Lutheran Church Minneapolis, Augusburg Pub. House [1954] 227p. 21cm. [BV772.T9] 54-13222
1. Stewardship, Christian—Sermons. 2. Lutheran Church—Sermons. 3. Sermons, American. I. Evangelical Lutheran Church.

WHITE, Kenneth Owen. 223'.7'06
1902.
Messages on stewardship, by K. Owen White, Herschel H. Hobbs, J. Ralph Grant, and others. Grant Rapids, Baker Book House, 1963. 141 p. 20 cm. [BV772.M48] 63-23043
1. Stewardship, Christian — Sermons. I. Title.

JENSEN, Kenneth L., 223'.7'066
1932-
Wisdom, the principal thing; studies in proverbs, by Kenneth L. Jensen. [1st ed.] Seattle, Pacific Meridian Pub. Co. [1971] xv, 167 p. illus. 23 cm. Bibliography: p. 164. [BS1465.2.J46] 77-171461 2.95
1. Bible. O.T. Proverbs—Criticism, interpretation, etc. I. Title.

WHYBRAY, Roger Norman. 223.7066
Wisdom in Proverbs; the concept of wisdom in Proverbs 1-9 [by] R. N. Whybray. Naperville, Ill., A. R. Allenson [1965] 120 p. 22 cm. (Studies in Biblical theology no. 45) Bibliography: p. 108-110. Bibliographical footnotes. [BS1465.2.W5] 65-5299
1. Bible. O.T. Proverbs I-IX — Criticism, interpretation, etc. 2. Wisdom. I. Title. II. Series.

WHYBRAY, Roger Norman 223.7066
Wisdom in Proverbs; the concept of wisdow in Proverbs 1-9. Naperville, Ill., A. R. Allenson [c.1965] 120p. 22cm. Studies in Biblical theology no. 45) Bibl. [BS1465.2.W5] 65-5299 2.85 pap.,
1. Bible. O. T. Proverbs I-IX—Criticism, interpretation, etc. 2. Wisdom. I. Title.

BIBLE. O. T. Proverbs. 223.707
English. 1961. Jewish Publication Society.
Book of Proverbs; a commentary, by W. Gunther Plaut. New York, Union of American Hebrew Congregations [c.] 1961. xi, 339 p. (Jewish commentary for Bible readers; Union adult ser.) Bibl. 61-9760 4.75
1. Bible. O. T. Proverbs—Commentaries. I. Plaut, W. Gunther, 1912- II. Title. III. Series: Commission on Jewish Education of the Union of American Hebrew Congregations and the Central Conference of American Rabbis. The Jewish commentary for Bible readers. Series: Commission on Jewish Education of the Union of American Hebrew Congregations and the Central Conference of American Rabbis. Union adult series

BIBLE. O.T. Proverbs. 223.707
English. 1961. Jewish Publication Society
Book of Proverbs; a commentary, by W. Gunther Plaut. New York, Union of American Hebrew Congregations, 1961. xi, 339p. 24cm. (The Jewish commentary for Bible readers) Union adult series. Bibliography: p. 321-324. [BS1465.3.P5] 61-9760
1. Bible. O. T. Proverbs—Commentaries. I. Pusey, Edward Bouverie II. Title. III. Series: Commission on Jewish Education of the Union of American Hebrew Congregations and the Central Conference of American Rabbis. The Jewish commentary for Bible readers. Series: Commission on Jewish Education of the Union of American Hebrew Congregations and the Central Conference of American Rabbis. Union adult series

COATES, Thomas 223.707
The Proverbs for today. Saint Louis, Concordia Pub. House [c.1960] xi,116p. 22cm. 60-13113 2.00 half cloth,
1. Bible. O. T. Proverbs—Meditations. I. Title.

COATES, Thomas, 1910- 223.707
The Proverbs for today. Saint Louis, Concordia Pub. House [1960] 116p. 22cm. [BS1465.4.C6] 60-13113
1. Bible. O. T. Proverbs—Meditations. I. Title.

BIBLE. O.T. Proverbs. 223'.7'077
English. New English. 1972.
The book of Proverbs; commentary by R. N. Whybray. Cambridge [Eng.] University Press, 1972. x, 196 p. 21 cm. (The Cambridge Bible commentary: New English Bible) Bibliography: p. 190-191. [BS1463.W48 1972] 70-171687 ISBN 0-521-08364-8
1. Bible. O.T. Proverbs—Commentaries. I. Whybray, Roger Norman. II. Title. III. Series.

HIRSCH, Samson 223'.7'077
Raphael, 1808-1888.
From the wisdom of Mishle / Samson Raphael Hirsch ; [rendered into English by Karin Paritzky-Joshua]. Jerusalem ; New York : Feldheim Publishers, 1976. 260 p. ; 24 cm. First published in Der Neue Jeschurun, 1883-1885, under title: Salomonische Spruchweisheit. Includes index. [BS1465.H57 1976] 77-372209
1. Bible. O.T. Proverbs—Commentaries. I. Bible. O.T. Proverbs. English. Selections. 1976. II. Title.

KIDNER, Derek. 223'.7'077
The Proverbs : an introduction and commentary / by Derek Kidner. Downers Grove, Ill. : InterVarsity Press, 1975, c1964. 192 p. ; 20 cm. (Tyndale Old Testament commentaries) [BS1465.3.K52 1975] 75-326397 ISBN 0-87784-861-0 : 5.95
1. Bible. O.T. Proverbs—Commentaries. I. Title.

MCKANE, William. 223'.7'077
Proverbs, a new approach. Philadelphia, Westminster Press [1970] xxii, 670 p. 23 cm. (The Old Testament library) Bibliography: p. xi-xxii. [BS1465.3.M25 1970b] 75-108185 12.50
1. Bible. O.T. Proverbs—Commentaries. I. Title. II. Series.

GINSBERG, Harold Louis. 223.8
Studies in Koheleth. New York, Jewish Theological Seminary of America, 1950. vii, 46 p. 21 cm. (Texts and studies of the Jewish Theological Seminary of America, v. 17) Bibliographical footnotes. [BS1475.G55] 50-12943
1. Bible. O. T. Ecclesiastes—Criticism, interpretation, etc. I. Title. II. Series: Jewish Theological Seminary of America. Texts and studies, v. 17

GORDIS, Robert, 1908- 223.8
Koheleth, the man and his world. New York, Jewish Theological Seminary of America, 1951. xi, 396 p. 24 cm. (Texts and studies of the Jewish Theological Seminary of America, v. 19) "The book of Koheleth, Hebrew text and a new translation": p. [135]-191. Bibliography: p. 387-396. [BS1475.G63] 51-7222
1. Bible. O. T. Ecclesiastes—Commentaries. I. Bible. O. T. Ecclesiastes. English. 1951. Gordis. II. Bible. O. T. Ecclesiastes. Hebrew. 1951. III. Title. IV. Series: Jewish Theological Seminary of America. Texts and studies, v. 19

GORDIS, Robert, 1908- 223.8
Koheleth, the man and his world. [2d augm. ed.] New York, Published for the Jewish Theological Seminary of America by Bloch Pub. Co., 1955. xi, 404p. 24cm. (Texts and studies of the Jewish Theological Seminary of America, v. 19) 'The book of Koheleth, Hebrew text and a new translation;: p. [135]-191. Bibliography: p. 387-396. [BS1475.G63 1955] 55-5448
1. Bible. O. T. Ecclesiastes—Commentaries. I. Bible. O. T. Ecclesiastes. English. 1951. Gordis. II. Bible. O. T. Ecclesiastes. Hebrew. 1951. III. Title. IV. Series: Jewish Theological Seminary of America, Texts and studies, v. 19

LEE, G Avery. 223.8
Preaching from Ecclesiastes. Nashville, Broadman Press [1958] 142p. 21cm. [BX6333.L395P7] 58-5410
1. Baptists—Sermons. 2. Sermons, American. 3. Bible. O. T. Ecclesinstes— Homlletical use. I. Title.

LEUPOLD, Herbert Carl, 223.8
1892-
Exposition of Ecclesiastes. Columbus, Ohio, Wartburg Press [1952] 304p. 23cm. [BS1475.L46] 53-17034
1. Bible. O. T. Ecclesiastes—Commentaries. I. Title.

BIBLE. O.T. 223'.8'044
Ecclesiastes. Hebrew. 1968.
Koheleth (romanized form) The book of Ecclesiastes [by Koheleth the preacher, the son of David, king in Jerusalem] In the revised King James version. With an introd. by Kenneth Rexroth and illus. by Edgar Miller. New York, Limited Editions Club, 1968. 53 p. col. illus. 31 cm. Half title: Ecclesiastes; or, The preacher. Hebrew and English. [BS1472.M5] 74-21890
I. Miller, Edgar, 1900- illus. II. Limited Editions Club, inc., New York. III. Bible. O.T. Ecclesiastes. English. Authorized. 1968. IV. Title: The book of Ecclesiastes.

BIBLE. O.T. 223.8052
Ecclesiastes. English 1958. Authorized
Ecclesiastes. With a wood engraving and eight trial drawings by Hans Foy. [Designed and directed by Lester Douglas. Washington? 1958] [55]p. illus., plates. 31cm. [BS1473 1958] 59-28502
I. Foy, Hans, illus. II. Douglas, Lester Charles, 1893- III. Title.

BIBLE. O.T. 223'.8'05203
Ecclesiastes. English. Authorized. 1971.
Ecclesiastes; or, The preacher. Handwritten and illuminated by Ben Shahn. New York, Grossman [1971] [33] p. 9 plates (part col.) 32

cm. Cover title: Ben Shahn's Ecclesiastes. [BS1473 1971] 77-121371 25.00
1. Bible—Pictures, illustrations, etc. I. Shahn, Ben, 1898-1969, illus.

DEHAAN, Richard W. 223'.8'06
The art of staying off dead-end streets [by] Richard W. DeHaan and Herbert Vande Lugt. Wheaton, Ill., Victor Books [1974] 156 p. 18 cm. [BS1475.2.D43] 74-79163 ISBN 0-88207-710-4 1.75 (pbk.)
1. Bible. O.T. Ecclesiastes—Criticism, interpretation, etc. I. Vander Lugt, Herbert, joint author. II. Title.

HUBBARD, David Allan. 223'.8'06
Beyond futility / by David Allan Hubbard. Grand Rapids : Eerdmans, c1976. p. cm. "First used as Bible studies on the Joyful sound, an international radio broadcast sponsored by the Fuller Evangelistic Association." [BS1475.2.H82] 76-21696 ISBN 0-8028-1650-9 pbk. : 2.65
1. Bible. O.T. Ecclesiastes—Criticism, interpretation, etc. I. The Joyful sound. II. Title.

*MALLOTT, Floyd, 1897- 223.806
1871.
Is life worth living? The inquiry of the book of Ecclesiastes discussed [by] Floyd E. Mallott. Elgin, Ill., The Brethren Pr. [1972] 124 p. 21 cm. [BS1475.5] ISBN 0-87178-000-3 4.25
1. Bible. O.T. Ecclesiastes—Study. I. Title.

STEESE, Peter B ed. 223.806
Ecclesiastes, edited by Peter B. Steese. Boston, Allyn and Bacon, 1966. vi, 202 p. 22 cm. (Allyn and Bacon casebook series) Includes Biblical text of Ecclesiastes, King James Version, together with related writings and critical essays. Bibliography: p. 201-202. [BS1475.5.S7] 66-14157
1. Bible. O.T. Ecclesiastes—Study. I. Bible. O.T. Ecclesiastes. English. II. Title.

STEESE, Peter B., ed 223.806
Ecclesiastes. Boston, Allyn [c.] 1966. vi, 202p. 22cm. (Allyn casebk. ser.) Includes Biblical text of Ecclesiastes, King James Version, together with related writings and critical essays. Bibl. [BS1475.5.S7] 66-14157 2.95 pap.,
1. Bible. O. T. Ecclesiastes—Study. I. Bible. O. T. II. Title.

BIBLE. O.T. 223'.8'066
Ecclesiastes. English. Jastrow. 1972.
A gentle cynic; being a translation of the Book of Koheleth, commonly known as Ecclesiastes, its origin, growth, and interpretation, by Morris Jastrow, Jr. New York, Oriole Editions, 1972. 254 p. 23 cm. Reprint of the 1919 ed. Includes bibliographical references. [BS1475.J3 1972] 72-84809 ISBN 0-88211-030-6 8.00
1. Bible. O.T. Ecclesiastes—Commentaries. I. Jastrow, Morris, 1861-1921, ed. II. Title.

GORDIS, Robert, 1908- 223'.8'066
Koheleth, the man and his world; a study of Ecclesiastes. 3d augm. ed. New York, Schocken [1968] x, 321p. 21cm. (Schocken paperbacks) The book of Koheleth; Hebrew text & a new tr.: p. [145]-201. Bibl. [BS1475.3G6 1968] 67-26988 2.45 pap.,
1. Bible. O. T. Ecclesiastes—Commentaries. I. Bible. O. T. Ecclesiastes. English. Gordis. 1968. II. Bible. O. T. Ecclesiastes. Hebrew. 1968. III. Title.

SHORT, Robert L. 223'.8'066
A time to be born—a time to die [by] Robert L. Short. [1st ed.] New York, Harper & Row [1973] viii, 117 p. illus. 29 cm. Includes bibliographical references. [BS1475.2.S56 1973] 72-78058 ISBN 0-06-067676-0 5.95
1. Bible. O.T. Ecclesiastes—Criticism, interpretation, etc. I. Title.
Pbk. 2.95.

SPERKA, Joshua Sidney, 223'.8'066
1904- comp.
Ecclesiastes: stories to live by. A modern translation with a story illustrating each verse translated, edited, and compiled by Joshua S. Sperka. New York, Bloch Pub. Co. [1972] 232 p. 23 cm. Bibliography: p. 215-222. [BS1475.4.S64] 73-150613 5.95
1. Bible. O.T. Ecclesiastes—Homiletical use. 2. Rabbinical literature—Translations into English. 3. Tales, Jewish. I. Bible. O.T. Ecclesiastes. English. Sperka. 1972. II. Title.

ZIMMERMANN, Frank. 223'.8'066
The inner world of Qohelet. With translation and commentary. New York, Ktav Pub. House, 1973. xiv, 196 p. 24 cm. Translation of Ecclesiastes: p. 164-176. "Notes and bibliography": p. 177-188. [BS1475.3.Z55] 72-5823 ISBN 0-87068-181-8 10.00
1. Bible. O.T. Ecclesiastes—Psychology. 2. Bible. O.T. Ecclesiastes—Commentaries. I. Bible. O.T. Ecclesiastes. English. Zimmermann. 1973. II. Title.

EICHHORN, David Max. 223.807
Musings of the old professor; the meaning of Koheles; a new translation of and commentary on the Book of Ecclesiastes. New York, J. David [1963] 267 p. 23 cm. Bibliography: p. 255-267. [BS1475.3.E4] 63-15803
1. Bible. O.T. Ecclesiastes — Commentaries. I. Bible. O.T. Ecclesiastes. English. 1963. II. Title.

EICHHORN, David Max 223.807
Musings of the old professor; the meaning of Koheles; a new translation of and commentary on the Book of Ecclesiastes. New York, Jonathan David [c.1963] 267p. 23cm. Bibl. 63-15803 5.95
1. Bible. O.T.—Ecclesiastes—Commentaries. I. Bible. O.T. Ecclesiastes. English. 1963. II. Title.

KIDNER, Derek. 223'.8'077
A time to mourn, and a time to dance : Ecclesiastes & the way of the world / Derek Kidner. Downers Grove, Ill. : InterVarsity Press, 1976. 110 p. ; 21 cm. (The Bible speaks today) Includes bibliographical references. [BS1475.3.K52] 76-21460 ISBN 0-87784-647-2 pbk. : 2.50
1. Bible. O.T. Ecclesiastes—Commentaries. I. Title.

BERNARD DE CLAIRVAUX, 223.9
Saint, 1091?-1153.
Saint Bernard on the Song of songs; Sermones in Cantica canticorum. Translated and edited by a religious of C. S. M. V., with an introd. and notes. London, A. R. Mowbray; New York, Morehouse-Gorham [1952] 272 p. facsim. 20 cm. [BS1485.B45] 52-12714
1. Bible. O. T. Song of Solemon—Sermons. 2. Sermons, Latin—Translations into English. 3. Sermons, English—Translations from Latin. I. Title.

BIBLE. O.T. Song of Solomon 223.9
The song of songs. Translated from the original Hebrew with an introduction and explanations by Hugh J. Schonfield. [New York] New American Library [c.1959] 128p. 19cm. (Mentor religious classic MD277) .50 pap.,
I. Title.

BIBLE. O. T. Song of 223.9
Solomon. English. Paraphases. 1952. Wragg.
The Song of songs, with drawings by Arthur Wragg. London, New York, Selwyn &Blount [1952] 64p. illus. 26 cm. 'A fragmentary wedding idyll.' [BS1486.W7 1952] 53-27625
I. Wragg, Arthur. II. Title.

BIBLE. O.T. Song of 223'.9
Solomon. English. Revised standard. Selections. 1970.
Song of love; selections from the Song of songs. Edited by Maureen P. Collins. With photos. by Fortune Monte and Sylvia Plachy. New York, Association Press [1970] 1 v. (unpaged) illus. 24 cm. [BS1483.C64 1970] 77-129424 4.95
I. Collins, Maureen P., ed. II. Title.

GORDIS, Robert, 1908- 223.9
The Song of songs: a study, modern translation, and commentary. New York, Jewish Theological Seminary of America, 1954. xii, 108p. 24cm. (Texts and studies of the Jewish Theological Seminary of America, v. 20) Bibliography: p. 99-106. [BS1485.G63] 54-765
1. Bible. O. T. Song of Solomon—Commentaries. I. Bible. O. T. Song of Solomon. English. 1954. Gordis. II. Title. III. Series: Jewish Theological Seminary of America. Texts and studies, v. 20

IRONSIDE, Henry Allan, 223.9
1876-1951.
Addresses on the Song of Solomon. [1st ed.] New York, Loizeaux Bros. [1950] 137p. 19cm. [BS1485.I7] 54-32894
1. Bible. O. T. Song of Solomon—Commentaries. I. Title.

MCPHEE, Louise Mapes, 1889- 223.9
The romance of the ages; meditations on the Song of songs. Oak Park, Ill., Designed Products [1950] 111 p. 19 cm. [BS1485.M3] 50-36695
1. Bible. O. T. Song of Solomon—Meditations. I. Title.

ORIGENES. 223.9
The Song of songs: Commentary and Homilies. Translated and annotated by R. P. Lawson. Westminster, Md., Newman Press, 1957. 385p. 23cm. (Ancient Christian writers; the works of the Fathers in translation, no. 26) Bibliographical references included in 'Notes' (p. [307]-371) [BR60.A35 no.26] 57-11826
1. Bible. O. T. Song of Solomon—Commentaries. I. Origenes. The Song of songs: Homilies. II. Lawson, R. P., ed. and tr. III. Title. IV. Series.

ORIGENES. 223.9
The Song of songs: Commentary and Homilies. Translated and annotated by R. P. Lawson. Westminster, Md., Newman Press, 1957. 385p. 23cm. (Ancient Christian writers; the works of the Fathers in translation, no.26) Bibliographical references included in 'Notes' (p.[307]-371) [BR60.A35 no.26] 57-11826
1. Bible, O. T. Song of Solomon—Commentaries. I. Origenes. The Song of songs: Homilies. II. Lawson, R. P., ed. and tr. III. Title. IV. Series.

SIEGEL, Abraham M 223.9
The sublime songs of love; a new commentary on the Song of songs, and related essays. [1st ed.] New York, Exposition Press [1955] 93p. 21cm. [BS1485.S55] 54-12481
1. Bible. O. T. Song of Solomon—Commentaries. 2. Judaism—Addresses, essays, lectures. I. Title.

SLOAN, Maxine. 223.9
What will ye see in the Shulamite? [1st ed.] New York, Pageant Press [1956] 96p. 21cm. Includes the author's dramatic arrangement of the Song of Solomon. [BS1490.S57] 56-12505
1. Bible. O.T. Song of Solomon—Criticism. interpretation, etc. I. Bible. O. T. Song of Solomon. English. 1956. II. Title.

SLOAN, Maxine. 223.9
What will ye see in the Shulamite? [1st ed.] New York, Pageant Press [1956] 96 p. 21 cm. Includes the author's dramatic arrangement of the Song of Solomon. [BS1490.S57] 56-12505
1. Bible. O. T. Song of Solomon — Criticism, interpretation, etc. I. Bible. O. T. Song of Solomon. English. 1956 II. Title.

WILLIRAM, Abbot of 223'.9'047
Ebersberg, d.1085.
The "Expositio in Cantica canticorum" of Williram, abbot of Ebersberg, 1048-1085. A critical ed.[by] Erminnie Hollis Bartelmez. Philadelphia, American Philosophical Society, 1967 xxvii, 573 p. illus., facsims. 31 cm. (Memoirs of the American Philosophical Society, v. 69) An interpretation of the Vulgate text of the Song of Solomon, paraphrased in Latin hexameters and translated into German prose. Bibliography: p. 572-573. [BS1489.G4W5] 67-19648
I. Bible. O. T. Song of Solomon. Latin. Paraphrases 1967. Williram. II. Bible O.T.Song of Solomon. German (Old High German) Paraphrases. 1967, William. III. iii. Bartelmez, Erminnie Holles ed. IV. Title. V. Series: American Philosophical Society, Philadelphia. Memoirs. v. 69

WILLIRAM, Abbot of 223'.9'047
Ebersberg, d.1085.
The "Expositio in Cantica canticorum" of Williram, abbot of Ebersberg, 1048-1085. A critical ed. [by] Erminnie Hollis Bartelmez. Philadelphia, American Philosophical Society, 1967. xxviii, 573 p. illus., facsims. 31 cm. (Memoirs of the American Philosophical Society, v. 69) An interpretation of the Vulgate text of the Song of Solomon, paraphrased in Latin hexameters and translated into German prose. Bibliography: p. 572-573. [BS1489.G4W5 1967] 67-19648
I. Bartelmez, Erminnie Hollis, ed. II. Bible. O.T. Song of Solomon. Latin. Paraphrases. 1967. Williram. III. Bible. O.T. Song of Solomon. German (Old High German) Paraphrases. 1967. Williram. IV. Title. V. Series: American Philosophical Society, Philadelphia. Memoirs, v. 69.

BIBLE. O.T. Song of 223'.9'052
Solomon. English. Falk. 1977.
The Song of songs : love poems from the Bible / translated from the original Hebrew by Marcia Falk. New York : Harcourt Brace Jovanovich, c1977. p. cm. Based on the translator's thesis, Stanford. [BS1487.F34 1977] 77-73049 ISBN 0-15-183770-8 : 4.95
I. Falk, Marcia. II. Title.

BIBLE. O.T. Song of 223'.9'052
Solomon. English. Selections. 1975.
Arise my love : Song of Solomon / drawings by Dhimitri Zonia. St. Louis, Mo. : Concordia Pub. House, c1975. [56] p. : ill. ; 23 x 31 cm. [BS1483 1975] 75-4077 ISBN 0-570-03253-9 : 12.50 ISBN 0-570-03712-3 pbk. : 4.95
1. Bible—Pictures, illustrations, etc. I. Zonia, Dhimitri. II. Title.

DILLOW, Joseph C. 223'.9'06
Solomon on sex / Joseph C. Dillow. New York : T. Nelson, c1977. 196 p. ; 24 cm. Includes bibliographical references. [BS1485.3.D55] 77-1049 ISBN 0-8407-5117-6 : 6.95
1. Bible. O.T. Song of Solomon—Commentaries. 2. Sex (Theology)—Biblical teaching. I. Title.

GLICKMAN, S. Craig. 223'.9'06
A song for lovers : including a new paraphrase and a new translation of the Song of Solomon / S. Craig Glickman ; [foreword by Howard G. Hendricks]. Downers Grove, Ill. : InterVarsity Press, c1976. 188 p. ; 21 cm. Includes bibliographical references. [BS1485.2.G55] 75-21454 ISBN 0-87784-768-1 : 3.95
1. Bible. O.T. Song of Solomon—Criticism, interpretation, etc. 2. Bible. O.T. Song of Solomon—Paraphrases, English. I. Bible. O.T. Song of Solomon. English. Glickman. 1976. II. Title.

GORDIS, Robert, 1908- 223'.9'066
The Song of songs and Lamentations; a study, modern translation and commentary. Rev. and augm. ed. New York, Ktav Pub. House [1974] xv, 203 p. 24 cm. A revision, with new material, of the author's The Song of songs (1954) and of A commentary on the text of Lamentations (1958). Includes bibliographies. [BS1485.3.G64 1974] 74-4194 ISBN 0-87068-256-3 12.50
1. Bible. O.T. Song of Solomon—Commentaries. 2. Bible. O.T. Lamentations—Commentaries. I. Bible. O.T. Song of Solomon. English. Gordis. 1974. II. Bible. O.T. Lamentations. English. Gordis. 1974. III. Title.

SUARES, Carlo. 223'.9'066
The Song of Songs; the canonical Song of Solomon deciphered according to the original code of the Qabala. Berkeley [Calif.] Shambala, 1972. 161 p. 22 cm. Translation of Le Cantique des cantiques. [BS1485.3.S913 1972] 79-146506 ISBN 0-87773-027-X 6.95
1. Bible. O.T. Song of Solomon—Commentaries. 2. Cabala. I. Bible. O.T. Song of Solomon. Hebrew. 1972. II. Bible. O.T. Song of Solomon. English. Revised standard. 1972. III. Title.

WEBBER, Charles 223.907
The Song of Solomon, by Charles and David Webber. Grand Rapids, Mich., Zondervan [1963, c.1962] 64p. 21cm. 63-2162 1.00 pap.,
1. Bible. O.T. Song of Solomon—Commentaries. I. Webber, David, joint author. II. Title.

BIBLE. O.T. Song of 223.9077
Solomon. English. 1965.
Song of songs [by] Watchman Nee. Translated by Elizabeth K. Mei and Daniel Smith. Fort Washington, Pa. Christian Literature Crusade [1965] 155 p. 23 cm. "This commentary is a composition of notes recorded by a brother ... the manuscript has never been proofread for correction by Mr. Nee." [BS1485.3.N4] 66-4200
1. Bible. O. T. Song of Solomon—Commentaries. I. Nee, Watchman. II. Title.

BIBLE. O.T. Song of 223.9077
Solomon. English. 1966.
Lo! The bridegroom. The song of heavenly love; fifty meditations on the Song of Solomon, by Peter C. Krey. [Houston, Tex., St. Thomas Press, 1966] xii. 141 p. 20 cm. [BS1485.4.K7] 66-20393
1. Bible. O. T. Song of Solomon—Meditations. I. Krey, Peter C. II. Title.

BIBLE. O.T. Song of 223'.9'077
Solomon. English. Ginsburg. 1970.
The Song of Songs and Coheleth (commonly called the Book of Ecclesiastes) Translated from the original Hebrew, with a commentary, historical and critical, by Christian D. Ginsburg. Prolegomenon by Sheldon H. Blank. 2 v. in 1. New York, Ktav Pub. House, 1970. xlvi, 191, viii, 528 p. 23 cm. (The Library of Biblical studies) Reprints of the 1857 and 1861 editions respectively, with a new prolegomenon by S. H. Blank. Includes bibliographical references. [BS1483.G5 1970] 68-19725
1. Bible. O.T. Song of Solomon—Commentaries. 2. Bible. O.T. Ecclesiastes—Commentaries. I. Ginsburg, Christian David, 1831-1914. II. Bible. O.T. Ecclesiastes. English. Ginsburg. 1970. III. Title. IV. Series.

BIBLE. O.T. Song of 223'.9'077
Solomon. English. Graves. 1973.
The Song of songs. Text and commentary by Robert Graves. Illustrated by Hans Erni. [1st American ed.] New York, C. N. Potter; distributed by Crown Publishers [1973] 16, [34] p. illus. 28 cm. [BS1483.G72 1973] 73-82331 ISBN 0-517-50801-X 5.95
1. Bible—Pictures, illustrations, etc. I. Graves, Robert, 1895- II. Erni, Hans, 1909- illus.

COTTON, John, 1584- 223'.9'077
1652.
A brief exposition, with practical observations, upon the whole Book of Canticles / John Cotton. New York : Arno Press, 1972. 238 p. ; 24 cm. (Research library of colonial Americana) Reprint of the 1655 ed. published by R. Smith, London. [BS1485.C7 1972] 71-141106 ISBN 0-405-03320-6 : 16.00
1. Bible. O.T. Song of Solomon—Commentaries. I. Title. II. Series.

DRYBURGH, Bob. 223'.9'077
Lessons for lovers in the Song of Solomon / Bob Dryburgh. New Canaan, Conn. : Keats Pub., 1975. 222 p. ; 18 cm. (A Pivot family reader) (A Pivot book) [BS1485.3.D79] 75-7807 pbk. : 1.75
1. Bible. O.T. Song of Solomon—Commentaries. I. Bible. O.T. Song of Solomon. II. Title.

LABOTZ, Paul, 1900- 223.9077
The romance of the ages; an exposition of the Song of Solomon. Foreword by M. R. De Haan. Grand Rapids, Kregel Publications [1965] 291 p. 21 cm. [BS1485.3L3] 65-23678
1. Bible. O.T. Song of Solomon — Commentaries. I. Title.

LABOTZ, Paul, 1900- 223.9077
The romance of the ages; an exposition of the Song of Solomon. Foreword by M. R. De Haan. Grand Rapids, Mich., kregel [c.1965] 291p. 21cm. [BS1485.3.L3] 65-23678 3.50
1. Bible. O.T.Song of Solomon—Commentaries. I. Title.

MASON, Clarence E. 223'.9'077
Love song / Clarence E. Mason, Jr. Chicago : Moody Press, c1976. 96 p. ; 22 cm. [BS1485.3.M35] 76-56121 pbk. : 1.95
1. Bible. O.T. Song of Solomon—Commentaries. I. Title.

224 Prophetic Books Of Old Testament

BIBLE. O.T. Daniel III. j224
English. 1965.Authorized.
Shadrach, Meshach, and Abednego. From the Book of Daniel. Illustrated by Paul Galdone. New York, Whittlesey House [c1965] 32 p. illus. (part col.) 26 cm. [BS1533.G3] 64-20528
I. Galdone, Paul, illus. II. Title.

BIBLE. O. T. Minor prophets. 224
English. 1953.
The Minor prophets; a commentary, explanatory and practical, by E. B. Pusey. Grand Rapids, Baker Book House 1953-57. 2v. 23cm. Contents.v. 1. Hoses, Joel, Ames. Obadiah, and Jonah.--v. 2. Micah, Nahum, Habakkuk, Zephaniah, Haggai, Zechariah, and Milachi. [BS1560.P82] 55-11418
1. Bible. O. T. Minor prophets—Commentaries. I. Pusey, Edward Bouverie, 1800-1882. II. Title.

BIBLE. O.T. Minor prophets, 224
English. 1958.Deere.
The twelve speak; a translation...with exegetical and interpretative footnotes and an introductory section on prophecy, by Derward William Deere. [1st ed.] New York, American Press, 1958-[61] 2. v. 22 cm. Bibliographical footnotes. [BS1560.A3D4] 58-6615
I. Deere, Derward William, ed. and tr. II. Title.

BIBLE. O. T. Minor prophets. 224
English. 1958. Deere.
The twelve speak; a translation ... with exegetical and interpretative footnotes and an introductory section on prophecy, by Derward William Deere. [1st ed.] New York, American Press, 1958- v. 22cm. Bibliographical footnotes. [BS1560.A3D4] 58-6615
I. Deere, Derward William, ed. and tr. II. Title.

BIBLE. O.T. Minor prophets. 224
English. Paraphrases. 1965.Taylor.
Living prophecies; the Minor prophets paraphrased with Daniel and the Revelation. [Wheaton, Ill., Tyndale House, 1965] 232 p. 18 cm. Prepared by Kenneth N. Taylor with the assistance of Harry Hoffner, Berkeley Mickelsen, and Warren Harbeck. Cf. Dust jacket. Paraphrases. 1965. Taylor. [BS1560.A3T3] 65-4360
I. XX Bible, N. T. Revelation. English. Paraphrases. 1965. Taylor. II. Title.

BIBLE. O. T. Minor prophets. 224
English. Paraphrases. 1965. Taylor.
Living prophecies; the Minor prophets paraphrased with Daniel and the Revelation [Wheaton, Ill., Tyndale House, c.1965] 232p. 18cm. Prepared by Kenneth N. Taylor with the assistance of Harry Hoffner, Berkeley Mickelsen, Warren Harbeck [BS1560.A3T3] 65-4360 2.95
I. Taylor, Kenneth Nathaniel. II. Bible. O. T. Daniel. English. Paraphrases. 1965. Taylor. III. Bible. N. T. Revelation. English. Paraphrases. 1965. Taylor. IV. Title.

BIBLE. O. T. Prophets. 224
English. 1956. Authorized.
The Prophets; in the King James version, with introd. and critical notes by Julius A. Bewer. New York, Harper [1956] viii, 663p. 25cm. (Harper's annotated Bible series) [BS491.B42] 57-4414
1. Bible. O. T. Prophets—Commentaries. I. Bewer, Julius August, 1877-1953, ed. II. Title.

BIBLE. O. T. Minor 224
prophets. English. Paraphrases. 1965. Taylor.
Living prophecies; the Minor prophets paraphrased with Daniel and the Revelation. [Wheaton, Ill.] [Tyndale House] [1965] 232 p. 18 cm. Prepared by Kenneth N. Taylor with the assistance of Harry Hoffner, Berkeley Michelsen, and Warren Harbeck. Cf. Dust jacket. [BS1560.A3T3] 65-4360
1. Bible. O. T. Daniel. English. Paraphrases. 1965. Taylor. 2. Bible. N. T. Revelation. English. Paraphrases. 1965. Taylor. I. Taylor, Kenneth Nathaniel. II. Title.

BIBLE. O. T. Daniel iII. 224
English. 1965 Authorized.
Shadrach, Meshach, and Abednego. From the Book of Daniel. Illus. by Paul Galdone. New York, Whittlesey-McGraw, c.1965. 32p. illus. (pt. col.) 26cm. [BS1553.G3] 64-20528 2.75
I. Galdone, Paul, illus. II. Title.

BLACKWOOD, Andrew Watterson, 224
1882-
Preaching from prophetic books. New York, Abingdon-Cokesbury Press [1951] 224 p. 21 cm. [BS1505.B57] 51-13076
1. Bible. O. T. Prophets—Homiletical use. I. Title.

BOYD, Frank Mathews, 1883- 224
The books of the Minor prophets. Springfield, Mo., Gospel Pub. House [1954, c1953] 249p. 20cm. [BS1560.B6] 54-38488
1. Bible. O.T. Minor prophets—Introductions. I. Title.

BUBER, Martin 224
The prophetic faith, [trans. from the Hebrew by Carlyle Witton-Davies] New York, Harper, [1960, c.1949] 247p. 21cm. (Harper Torchbooks, The Cloister library TB 73) (Bibl. footnotes) 1.45 pap.,
1. Bible. O.T. Prophets—Theology. I. Title.

BUBER, Martin, 1878- 224
The prophetic faith [tr. from Hebrew by Carlyle Witton-Davies. Gloucester, Mass., Peter Smith, 1961, c.1941] 247p. (Harper Torchbook: Cloister lib. TB73 rebound in cloth) Bibl. 3.50
1. Bible. O.T. Prophets—Theology. I. Witton Davies, Carlyle, tr. II. Title.

CHAINE, Joseph, 1888-1948. 224
God's heralds; a guide to the prophets of Israel. Translated by Brendan McGrath. New York, J. F. Wagner [c1955] 236p. illus. 21cm. Translation of Introduction a la lecture des prophetes. [BS1505.C443] 56-1032
1. Bible. O. T. Prophets—Criticism, interpretation, etc. 2. Prophets. I. Title.

CHURCH, Brooke (Peters) 1885- 224
The private lives of the prophets and the times in which they lived. New York, Rinehart [1953] 246 p. 21 cm. [BS1505.C56] 52-14190
1. Prophets. I. Title.

CLEMENTS, Ronald Ernest, 224
1929-
The conscience of the nation: a study of early Israelite prophecy, by R. E. Clements. London, Oxford U. P., 1967. 119 p. maps, diagrs. 18 1/2 cm. (Approaching the Bible) (B 67-12744) Bibliography: p. 111-113. [BS1198.C55] 68-106116
1. Prophets. 2. Bible. O. T. Prophets—Study—Outlines, syllabi, etc. I. Title.

COATES, Thomas, 1910- 224
The prophets for today. St. Louis, Concordia [1966, c.1965] xii, 115 p., 22 cm [BS1505.4.C6] 65-21219 2.00 bds.,
1. Bible. O. T. Prophets—Meditions. I. Title.

CORBETT, Jack Elliott, 1920- 224
The Prophets on Main Street / J. Elliott Corbett. Rev. and exp. Atlanta : John Knox Press, c1977. p. cm. Bibliography: p. [BS1505.7.C67 1977] 77-79597 ISBN 0-8042-0841-7 pbk. : 5.95
1. Bible. O.T. Prophets—Paraphrases, English. 2. Prophets. I. Title.

DI CESARE, Mario A. 224
Poetry and prophecy : reflections on the word / Mario A. Di Cesare. Amherst, Mass : Published for the Friends of the Amherst College Library, c1977. 42 p. ; 22 cm. (The Robert Frost lecture : 1976) [BS1198.D53] 77-150847
1. Prophets—Addresses, essays, lectures. 2. Poetry—Addresses, essays, lectures. I. Amherst College. Library. Friends. II. Title. III. Series.

GIRDWOOD, James. 224
Look up! A fresh consideration of the judgment of God that falls upon His people when they disobey Him and the hope-inspiring promises He extends to those who turn back to Him. Cincinnati, Standard Pub. [1972] 96 p. 18 cm. (Fountain books) [BS1505.5.G57] 70-180747
1. Bible. O.T. Jeremiah—Study—Text-books. 2. Bible. O.T. Ezekiel—Study—Text-books. 3. Bible. O.T. Haggai—Study—Text-books. 4. Bible. O.T. Zechariah—Study—Text-books. I. Title.

GOLDBERG, David, 1886- 224
Meet the prophets. In collaboration with Samuel Halevi Baron and Leonard R. Sussman. Illustrated by F. Dzubas. New York, Bookman Associates [1956] 211p. illus. 23cm. [BS1505.G57] 56-2168
1. Prophets. I. Title.

HAMILTON, Edith, 1867- 224
Spokesmen for God; the great teachers of the Old Testament. New York, Norton [1962, c.1936, 1949] 259p. 20cm. (Norton lib. N169) 1.25 pap.,
1. Bible. O. T. Prophets—Criticism, interpretations, etc. 2. Prophets. I. Title.

HOENIG, Sidney Benjamin. 224
A guide to the Prophets, by Sidney B. Hoenig and Samuel H. Rosenberg. New York, Yeshiva University, Dept. of Adult Education, Community Service Division, 1957. 224p. 21cm. Includes bibliography. [BS1505.H6 1957] 57-7991
1. Bible. O. T. Prophets—Introductions. 2. Bible. O. T. Historical books— Introductions. I. Rosenberg, Samuel H., joint author. II. Title.

HOENIG, Sidney Benjamin. 224
A guide to the Prophets, by Sidney B. Hoenig ... and Samuel H. Bosenberg ... New York, Bloch publishing co., 1942. xiv p., 1 l., 191p. 21cm. 'References' at end of most of the chapters. Bibliography: p. 185-191. [BS1505.H6] 62-23107
1. Bible. O. T. Prophets—Introductions. 2. Bible. O. T. Historical books—Introductions. I. Rosenberg, Samuel H., joint author. II. Title.

INTERPRETING the prophetic 224
tradition. Introd. by Harry M. Orlinsky. Cinn. [i.e. Cincinnati] Hebrew Union College Press, 1969. xii, 343 p. 23 cm. (The Goldenson lectures, 1955-1966) Contents.Contents.—"Of a truth the Lord hath sent me": an inquiry into the source of the prophet's authority, by S. H. Blank.—The prophets: our concurrence and our dissent, by A. Cronbach.—The prophet in modern Hebrew literature, by J. B. Agus.—Prophets and philosophers: the scandal of prophecy, by L. H. Silberman.—The voice of prophecy in this satellite age, by E. F. Magnin.—The stone which the modern builders rejected, by L. A. Olan.—Samuel and the beginnings of the prophetic movement, by W. F. Albright.—Prophetic religion in an age of revolution, by L. I. Feuer.—The prophetic criticism of Israelite worship, by J. P. Hyatt.—The so-called "suffering servant" in Isaiah 53, by H. M. Orlinsky.—Jerusalem and the prophets, by R. De Vaux.—The changing image of the prophet in Jewish thought, by B. J. Bamberger. Includes bibliographical references. [BS1505.2.I5] 68-58444
1. Bible. O.T. Prophets—Addresses, essays, lectures. 2. Prophets. I. Orlinsky, Harry Meyer, 1908- ed. II. Title. III. Series. IV. Library of Biblical studies.

IRONSIDE, Henry Allan, 1876- 224
1951.
Notes on the Minor Prophets. [1st ed.] New York, Loiseaux Bros. [1950] 464p. 20cm. [BS1560.I7] 54-32918
1. Bible. O. T. Minor Prophets—Commentaries. I. Title.

*JOHNSON, Kate Nunez 224
And he prayed. Philadelphia, Dorrance [1966] 44p. 21cm. 3.00
I. Title.

KEVIN, Robert Oliver. 224
The Religious demand upon society, a study of the prophetic tradition ... Lectures ... delivered at the Washington Cathedral Library ... 1950- Authorized recording and production by Henderson Services. Washington [1950- v. in 28 cm. (Christianity and modern man, course 7) Cover title. [BS1505.R4] 51-31766
1. Bible. O. T. Prophets — Theology. 2. Reformation. I. Title. II. Series.
Contents omitted.

KUHL, Curt 224
The prophets of Israel. Translated [from the German] by Rudolf J. Ehrlich and J. P. Smith. Richmond, John Knox Press, 1960[ ] vii, 199p. Bibl.: p.192-196. 23cm. 60-11624 3.50 bds.,
1. Prophets. I. Title.

LAETSCH, Theodore Ferdinand 224
Karl, 1877-
Bible commentary: the minor prophets. Saint Louis, Concordia Pub. House [1956] xiv, 566p. 25cm. [BS1560.L25] 55-7444
1. Bible. O.T. Minor prophets—Commentaries. I. Title.

LAETSCH, Theodore Ferdinand 224
Karl, 1877-
Bible commentary: the minor prophets. Saint Louis, Concordia Pub. House [1956] xiv, 566 p. 25 cm. [BS1560.L25] 55-7444
1. Bible. O. T. Minor prophets — Commentaries.

LEAVELL, Roland Quinche, 224
1891-1963.
Prophetic preaching, then and now. Grand Rapids Mich., Baker Bk. [c.]1963. 96p. 20cm. 63-19098 2.25
1. Preaching. 2. Bible. O. T. Prophets—Homiletical use. I. Title.

LEAVELL, Roland Quinche, 224
1891-1963.
Prophetic preaching, then and now. Grand Rapios, Baker Book House, 1963. 96 p. 20 cm. [BV4211.2.L4] 63-19098
1. Preaching. 2. Bible. O.T. Prophets — Homiletical use. I. Title.

MATTUCK, Israel Isidor 224
The thought of the prophets. New York, Collier [1962] 158p. 18cm. (AS349V) .95 pap.,
1. Bible. O.T. Prophets—Theology. I. Title.

PROPHETS. 224
Chicago, ACTA Foundation [1971- v. 22 cm. (Scripture discussion commentary, 2) Contents.Contents.—1. Amos and Hosea, by A. Macpherson. Isaiah 1-39, by J. Rhymer. Jeremiah, by J. Challenor. Isaiah 40-66, by J. Challenor. Includes bibliographical references. [BS1585.3.P76] 72-178778 ISBN 0-87946-001-6
1. Bible. O.T. Amos—Commentaries. 2. Bible. O.T. Hosea—Commentaries. 3. Bible. O.T. Isaiah—Commentaries. 4. Bible. O.T. Jeremiah—Commentaries. I. Macpherson, Ann. II. Title. III. Series.

RAD, Gerhard von, 1901-1971. 224
The message of the prophets. [1st U.S. ed.] New York, Harper & Row [1972, c1965] 289 p. 22 cm. Translation of Die Botschaft der Propheten, a revised version of material from the author's Theologie des Alten Testaments. Includes bibliographical references. [BS1505.2.R313 1972] 72-183633 3.95
1. Bible. O.T. Prophets—Theology. 2. Prophets. I. Title.

RUST, Eric Charles. 224
Covenant and hope; a study in the theology of the prophets [by] Eric C. Rust. Waco, Tex., Word Books [1972] 192 p. 23 cm. [BS1198.R87] 72-84170 5.95
1. Prophets. I. Title.

SCHULTZ, Samuel J. 224
The prophets speak; law of love, the essence of Israel's religion, by Samuel J. Schultz. [1st ed.] New York, Harper & Row [1968] 159 p. 21 cm. [BS1198.S35] 69-10478 5.00
1. Bible O.T. Prophets—Theology. 2. Prophets. I. Title.

SCOTT, Robert Balgarnie 224
Young, 1899-
The relevance of the prophets [by] R. B. Y. Scott. Rev. ed. New York, Macmillan [1968] viii, 248 p. 20 cm. Includes bibliographical references. [BS1505.S36 1968] 68-17519
1. Bible. O.T. Prophets—Criticism, interpretation, etc. 2. Prophets. I. Title.

SILVERMAN, Althea Osber. 224
Behold my messengers! The lives and teachings of the prophets. Illus. by Reuben Leaf. New York, Bloch Pub. Co., 1955. 239p. illus. 21cm. [BS1505.S416] 55-11056
1. Prophets. I. Title.

SKELTON, Eugene. 224
Meet the prophets! Nashville, Tenn., Broadman Press [1972] 160 p. illus. 22 cm. [BS1198.S5] 72-79176 ISBN 0-8054-1510-6
1. Prophets. I. Title.

SPERRY, Sidney Branton, 1895- 224
The voice of Israel's prophets; a Latter-Day Saint interpretation of the Major and Minor Prophets of the Old Testament. [Salt Lake City] Deseret Book Co., 1952 [i. e. 1953] 457p. 24cm. [BS1505.S66] 53-27622
1. Bible. O. T. Prophets—Commentaries. I. Title.

STAACK, Hagen. 224
Prophetic voices of the Bible. Cleveland, World Pub. Co. [1968] 121 p. illus. 21 cm. [BS1198.S65 1968] 68-26840 3.50
1. Prophets. I. Title.

UNTERMAN, Isaac, 1889- 224
The Hebrew prophets. New York, Bloch Pub. Co., 1970. xxiii, 298 p. illus., port. 24 cm. Bibliography: p. 283-288. [BS1505.3.U5] 79-14962 7.50

1. Bible. O.T. Prophets—Commentaries. I. Title.

VAN ZELLER, Hubert, 1905- 224
The outspoken ones; twelve prophets of Israel and Juda. New York, Sheed & Ward [1955] 195p. illus. 21cm. [BS1560.V37] 55-9449
1. Bible. O. T. Minor prophets—Introductions. I. Title.

VCOLE, Clifford Adair, 1915- 224
The Prophets speak. Independence, Mo., Herald House, 1954. 199p. 21cm. [BS1505.C574] 54-11777
1. Bible. O. T. Prophets—Introductions. I. Title.

WANEFSKY, David. 224
The Prophets speak to us anew. New York, Philosophical Library [1952] 232p. 22cm. [BS1505.W3] 52-14283
1. Bible. O. T. Prophets—Commentaries. I. Title.

WEBB, Daniel, 1719?-1798. 224
Literary amusements, in verse and prose. New York, Garland Pub., 1970. 76 p. 22 cm. Facsim. of a Yale University Library copy with imprint: London, Printed for J. Dodsley, 1787. Bound with Langhorne, John. Letters on the eloquence of the pulpit. New York, 1970. Contents.Contents.—Imitation of the fourth satire of Boileau.—Further thoughts on manners and language.—Essay on party-writing.—Hymn to health.—To Mira, on her wedding day.—Miss A. to Miss D.—On a red-breast.—Strictures on Florus. [BV4210.L34 1765a] 77-112260
I. Title.

WHALLEY, Peter, 1722-1791. 224
An essay on the manner of writing history. New York, Garland Pub., 1970. 28 p. 22 cm. Facsim. of a Yale University Library copy with imprint: London, Printed for M. Cooper, 1746. Bound with Langhorne, John. Letters on the eloquence of the pulpit. New York, 1970. [BV4210.L34 1765a] 78-112263
1. Historiography—Early works to 1800. I. Title.

WHITLEY, Charles Francis. 224
The exilic age / by Charles Francis Whitley. Westport, Conn. : Greenwood Press, 1975, c1957. 160 p. ; 22 cm. Reprint of the 1958 ed. published by the Westminster Press, Philadelphia. Includes bibliographical references and index. [BS1525.2.W48 1975] 74-29795 ISBN 0-8371-8002-3 lib.bdg. : 10.25
1. Jews—History—Babylonian captivity, 598-515 B.C. 2. Bible. O.T. Jeremiah—Criticism, interpretation, etc. 3. Bible. O.T. Ezekiel—Criticism, interpretation, etc. 4. Bible. O.T. Isaiah XL-LXVI—Criticism, interpretation, etc. I. Title.

WILLIAMS, Walter George, 1900- 224
The prophets: pioneers to Christianity. New York, Abingdon Press [1956] 23p. 23cm. [BS1505.W57] 56-6358
1. Prophets I. Title.

WILLIAMS, Walter George, 1900- 224
The prophets; pioneers to Christianity. New York, Abingdon Press [1956] 223 p. 23 cm. [BS1505.W57] 56-6358
1. Prophets. I. Title.

WILLIAMS, Walter George, 1903- 224
The prophets, pioneers to Christianity. New York, Abingdon Press [1956] 223 p. 23 cm. [BS1505.W57] 56-6358
1. Prophets. I. Title.

WILLIS, John T., 1933- 224
My servants, the prophets, by John T. Willis. Abilene, Tex., Biblical Research Press [1971- v. 22 cm. (The Way of life series, no. 116) [BS1198.W53] 76-180789
1. Prophets—Study and teaching. I. Title.

WOLFE, Rolland Emerson, 1902- 224
Men of prophetic fire; with illus. by Phillips E. Osgood. Boston, Beacon Press [1951] 316 p. illus. 22 cm. [BS1505.W67] 51-14955
1. Prophets I. Title.

YOUNG, Edward Joseph. 224
My servants, the prophets. Grand Rapids, W. B. Eerdmans Pub. Co., 1952. 231 p. 23 cm. [BS1505.Y6] 52-14505
1. Prophets. 2. Bible. O. T. Prophets — Criticism, interpretation, etc. I. Title.

MADDUX, Roy Clark. 224'.002'02
The Prophets in outline. Grand Rapids, Baker Book House [1967] 110 p. 20 cm. (Minister's handbook series) [BS1505.5.M3] 67-18184
1. Bible. O.T. Prophets—Study—Outlines, syllabi, etc. I. Title.

MURPHY, Dennis J. 224'.007
His servants, the prophets, by Dennis J. Murphy. [Melbourne] Central Catholic Library for the Catholic Biblical Association in Victoria, 1965. 137 p. 23 cm. [BS1506.M8] 74-422057 unpriced
1. Bible. O.T. Prophets—Study—Text-books. I. Title.

BEECHER, Willis Judson, 1838-1912 224.06
The prophets and the promise. Grand Rapids, Mich., Baker Bk., 1963. xiv, 427p. 23cm. 63-19837 3.95
1. Prophets. 2. Messiah. I. Title.

BRIGHT, John, 1908- 224'.06
Covenant and promise : the prophetic understanding of the future in pre-exilic Israel / John Bright. Philadelphia : Westminster Press, c1976. p. cm. Includes bibliographical references and indexes. [BS1505.2.B74] 76-13546 ISBN 0-664-20752-9 : 10.95
1. Jews—History—953-586 B.C. 2. Bible. O.T. Prophets—Theology. 3. Prophets. I. Title.

CHAPPELL, Clovis Gillham, 1882- 224.06
And the prophets . . . [by] Clovis G. Chappell. Nashville, Abingdon [1962, c.1946] 208p. 18cm. (Apex bk. J1) .95 pap.,
1. Prophets. I. Title.

CHASE, Mary Ellen, 1887-1962. 224.06
The Prophets for the common reader. [1st ed.] New York, Norton [1963] 183 p. 22 cm. "Selected books on prophecy and the prophets": p. 181-183. [BS1505.2.C5] 63-15878
1. Bible. O. T. Prophets—Criticism, interpretation, etc. I. Title.

CLEMENTS, Ronald Ernest, 1929- 224.06
Prophecy and covenant [by] R. E. Clements. Naperville, Ill. A. R. Allenson [1965] 135 p. 22 cm. (Studies in Biblical theology, no. 43) Bibliographical footnotes. [BS1505.2.C55] 65-3306
1. Bible. O. T. Prophets — Criticism, interpretation, etc. 2. Covenants (Theology) I. Title. II. Series.

CLEMENTS, Ronald Ernest, 1929- 224.06
Prophecy and covenant. Naperville, Ill., A. R. Allenson [c.1965] 135p. 22cm. (Studies in Biblical theology, no. 43) Bibl. [BS1505.2.C55] 65-3306 2.85 pap.,
1. Bible, O. T. Prophets—Criticism, interpretation, etc. 2. Covenants (Theology) I. Title. II. Series.

COHON, Beryl D. 224.06
God's angry men; a student's introduction to the Hebrew prophets. New York, Bloch [c.1961] 109p. front. 2.75
I. Title.

COHON, Beryl David 224.06
The prophets: their personalities and teachings. New York, Bloch Pub. Co. [c.1960] xiii, 232p. 23cm. Bibl.:p225-228. 60-14901 3.75
1. Bible. O.T. Prophets—Criticism, interpretation, etc. I. Title.

COHON, Beryl David, 1898- 224.06
The prophets. their personalities and teachings. New York, Bloch Pub. Co. [1960] 232p. 22cm. Includes bibliography. [BS1505.C573 1960] 60-14901
1. Bible. O. T. Prophets— Criticism, interpretation, etc. I. Title.

CORBETT, Jack Elliott, 1920- 224.06
The prophets on Main Street. Richmond, Va., Knox [c.1965] 155, [5]p. 21cm. Bibl. [BS1505.5.C6] 65-10428 2.00 pap.,
1. Bible. O.T. Prophets—Addresses, essays, lectures. I. Title.

DHEILLY, Joseph, 1902- 224.06
The prophets; tr. from French by Rachel Attwater. New York, Hawthorn Books [c.1960] 158p. (Twentieth century encyclopedia of Catholicism, v. 66. Section 6: The word of God) Bibl. 60-53577 3.50 bds.,
1. Bible. O. T. Prophets—Theology. 2. Prophets. I. Title.

FREEMAN, Hobart E. 224'.06
An introduction to the Old Testament Prophets, by Hobart E. Freeman. Chicago, Moody Press [1969, c 1968] 384 p. 24 cm. Bibliography: 356-361. [BS1505.2.F73] 68-26412 6.95
1. Bible. O.T. Prophets—Criticism, interpretation, etc. I. Title.

HEATN, Eric William. 224.06
The Old Testament Prophets. 53Harmondsworth, Middlesex] Penguin Books [1958] 186p. 18cm. *A Pellcan book, A414) 'Completely revised and largely rewritten edition of [the author's] His servants the Prophets, published ... in 1949.' [BS1198.H4 1958] 59-4547
1. Prophets. 2. Bible. O. T. Prophets—Theology. I. Title.

HEATON, Eric William. 224'.06
The Old Testament prophets / E. W. Heaton. Atlanta : John Knox Press, c1977. p. cm. Includes indexes. Bibliography: p. [BS1198.H4 1977] 77-79589 ISBN 0-8042-0140-4 pbk. : 3.95
1. Bible. O.T. Prophets—Theology. 2. Prophets. I. Title.

HESCHEL, Abraham Joshua, 1907- 224.06
The prohpets. [1st ed.] New York, Harper & Row [1962] 518 p. 25 cm. [BS1505.2.H4] 62-7290
1. Bible. O. T. Prophets — Criticism, interpretation, etc. 2. Prophets. I. Title.

HESCHEL, Abraham Joshua, 1907- 224.06
The Prophets. [1st ed.] New York, Harper & Row [1962] 518 p. 25 cm. [BS1505.2.H4] 62-7290
1. Bible. O.T. Prophets—Criticism, interpretation, etc. 2. Prophets. I. Title.

HESCHEL, Abraham Joshua, 1907- 224'.06
The Prophets, by Abraham J. Heschel. New York, Harper & Row [1969, c1962] xv, 235 p. 21 cm. (Harper torchbooks, TB 1421) "This edition comprises the first 220 pages of the Prophets, originally published in 1962." Bibliographical footnotes. [BS1505.2] 78-2376 1.75
1. Bible. O.T. Prophets—Criticism, interpretation, etc. 2. Prophets.

JURGENSEN, Barbara. 224'.06
The prophets speak again : a brief introduction to Old Testament prophecy / Barbara Jurgensen. Minneapolis : Augsburg Pub. House, c1977. 128 p. ; 20 cm. [BS1505.2.J87] 76-27084 ISBN 0-8066-1566-4 : 2.95
1. Bible. O.T. Prophets—Criticism, interpretation, etc. 2. Prophets. I. Title.

JURGENSEN, Barbara. 224'.06
The prophets speak again : a brief introduction to Old Testament prophecy / Barbara Jurgensen. Minneapolis : Augsburg Pub. House, c1977. 128 p. ; 20 cm. [BS1505.2.J87] 76-27084 ISBN 0-8066-1566-4 : 2.95
1. Bible. O.T. Prophets—Criticism, interpretation, etc. 2. Prophets. I. Title.

LINDBLOM, Johannes, 1882- 224.06
Prophecy in ancient Israel. Philadelphia, Muhlenberg [1963, c.1962] 472p. 23cm. Bibl. 63-907 10.00
1. Bible. O. T. Prophets—Criticism, interpretation, etc. 2. Prophets. I. Title.

MALY, Eugene H. 224'.06
Prophets of salvation [by] Eugene H. Maly. [New York] Herder & Herder [1967] 191p. 21cm. Orig. appeared in Hi-time magazine. [BS1198.M27] 67-14146 4.50
1. Prophets. 2. Bible. O.T. Prophets—Criticism, interpretation, etc. I. Title.

MILLEY, C Ross. 224.06
The prophets of Israel. New York, Philosophical Library [1959] 143p. 22cm. Includes bibliography. [BS1505.5.M5] 59-16478
1. Prophets. 2. Bible. O. T. Prophets—Theology. I. Title.

MURRAY, Ralph L 224.06
Plumb lines and fruit baskets; sixteen timely, provocative sermons on the prophets [by] Ralph L. Murray. Nashville, Broadman Press [1966] viii, 134 p. 21 cm. Includes bibliographical references. [BS1505.4.M8] 66-15145
1. Bible. O.T. Prophets — Sermons. 2. Sermons, American. 3. Baptists — Sermons. I. Title.

MURRAY, Ralph L. 224.06
Plumb lines and fruit baskets; sixteen timely, provocative sermons on the prophets. Nashville, Broadman [c.1966] viii, 134p. 21cm. Bibl. [BS1505.4.M8] 66-15145 2.95 bds.,
1. Bible. O.T. Prophets — Sermons. 2. Sermons, American. 3. Baptists — Sermons. I. Title.

NAPIER, Bunyan Davie 224.06
Prophets in perspective. Nashville, Abingdon [c.1962, 1963] 128p. 20cm. Bibl. 63-15711 2.75 bds.,
1. Bible. O.T. Prophets—Criticism, interpretation, etc. 2. Prophets. I. Title.

NEHER, Andre. 224'.06
The prophetic existence. Translated from the French by William Wolf. South Brunswick [N.J.] A. S. Barnes [1969] 355 p. 22 cm. Translation of L'essence du prophetisme. Includes bibliographical references. [BS1198.N413] 68-27259 10.00
1. Bible. O.T. Prophets—Theology. 2. Mysticism—Judaism. I. Title.

PETERSEN, David L. 224'.06
Late Israelite prophecy : studies in deutero-prophetic literature and in Chronicles / by David L. Petersen. Missoula, Mont. : Published by Scholars Press for the Society of Biblical Literature, c1976. p. cm. (Monograph series - Society of Biblical Literature ; no. 23) Based on the author's thesis, Yale, 1972. Includes bibliographical references. [BS1505.2.P47 1976] 76-26014 ISBN 0-89130-076-7 : 2.80
1. Bible. O.T. Prophets—Criticism, interpretation, etc. 2. Bible. O.T. Chronicles—Criticism, interpretation, etc. I. Title. II. Series: Society of Biblical Literature. Monograph series ; no. 23.

RAUD, Elsa. 224.06
Introduction to prophecy. Findlay, Ohio, Dunham Pub. Co. [c1960] 236p. 22cm. [BS647.2.R3] 62-3769
1. Bible—Prophecies. I. Title.

REID, John Calvin, 1901- 224'.06
We spoke for God. Grand Rapids, Eerdmans [1967] 122 p. 23 cm. [BS1505.2.R4] 67-28376
1. Bible. O. T. Prophets—Introductions. 2. Prophets. I. Title.

REID, John Calvin, 1901- 224'.06
We spoke for God. Grand Rapids, Eerdmans [1967] 122 p. 23 cm. [BS1505.2.R4] 67-28376
1. Bible. O.T. Prophets—Introductions. 2. Prophets. I. Title.

SEILHAMER, Frank H. 224'.06
Prophets and prophecy : seven key messengers / Frank H. Seilhamer. Philadelphia : Fortress Press, c1977. x, 85 p. ; 22 cm. Bibliography: p. 84-85. [BS1198.S42] 76-62603 ISBN 0-8006-1254-X pbk. : 2.95
1. Bible. O.T. Prophets—Criticism, interpretation, etc. 2. Prophets. I. Title.

STUHLMUELLER, Carroll. 224.06
The Prophets and the word of God With a foreword by Bernard Cooke. Notre Dame, Ind., Fides [1964] 324 p. 21 cm. [BS1505.2.S8] 64-16501
1. Bible. O. T. Prophets — Criticism, interpretation, etc. I. Title.

STUHLMUELLER, Carroll 224.06
The Prophets and the word of God. Foreword by Bernard Cooke. Notre Dame, Ind., Fides [c.1964] 324p. 21cm. 64-16501 4.95
1. Bible. O. T. Prophets—Criticism, interpretation, etc. I. Title.

VAWTER, Bruce. 224.06
The conscience of Israel; pre-exilic prophets and prophecy. New York, Sheed & Ward [1961] 308 p. illus. 22 cm. [BS1505.2.V35] 61-11788
1. Bible. O.T. Prophets — Criticism, interpretation, etc. I. Title.

VAWTER, Bruce 224.06
The conscience of Israel; pre-exilic prophets and prophecy. New York, Sheed & Ward [c.1961] 308p. illus. 61-11788 5.00
1. Bible. O. T. Prophets — Criticism, interpretation, etc. I. Title.

WIFALL, Walter. 224'.06
Israel's prophets : envoys of the King / by Walter Wifall. Chicago : Franciscan Herald Press, [1975] p. cm. (Herald Biblical booklets) Bibliography: p. [BS1198.W5] 74-31167 ISBN 0-8199-0521-6 pbk. : 0.95
1. Prophets. I. Title.

WINWARD, Stephen F. 224'.06
A guide to the prophets, by Stephen F. Winward. Richmond, Va., John Knox Press [1969, c1968] 255 p. 23 cm. Bibliographical footnotes. [BS1505.2.W55 1969] 68-55819 5.00
1. Bible. O.T. Prophets—Introductions. I. Title.

YODER, Sanford Calvin Bp., 1879- 224.06
He gave some prophets; the Old Testament prophets and their message. Scottsdale, Pa., Herald Press [1964] 252 p. 20 cm. [BS1505.2.Y6] 64-18733
1. Bible. O. T. Prophets — Introduction. I. Title.

YODER, Sanford Calvin, Bp., 1879- 224.06
He gave some prophets; the Old Testament prophets and their message. Scottdale, Pa., Herald Pr. [c.1964] 252p. 20cm. [BS1505.2.Y6] 64-18733 4.50
1. Bible. O. T. Prophets—Introductions. I. Title.

CHRISTENSEN, Duane L. 224'.06'6
Transformations of the war oracle in Old Testament prophecy : studies in the oracles against the nations / by Duane L. Christensen. Missoula, Mont. : Published by Scholars Press for Harvard theological review, 1976c1975 xii, 305 p. : maps ; 22 cm. (Harvard dissertations in religion ; no. 3) Originally presented as the author's thesis, Harvard, 1971. Bibliography: p. 285-305. [BS1199.N3C4 1975] 75-34264 ISBN 0-89130-064-3 pbk. : 6.00
1. Bible. O.T. Prophets—Criticism, interpretation, etc. 2. Bible. O.T. Prophets—History of contemporary events, etc. 3. Nationalism—Biblical teaching. 4. War—Biblical teaching. I. Title. II. Series.

ELLISON, Henry Leopold. 224'.06'6
The Old Testament prophets: a study guide; studies in the Hebrew prophets, by H. L. Ellison. [3d ed.] Grand Rapids, Mich., Zondervan Pub. House [1971, c1966] 160 p. 21 cm. "Previously published under the title: Men spake from God." Bibliography: p. 155. [BS1505.E57 1971] 79-156239 Pap. $1.95
1. Bible. O.T. Prophets—Introductions. I. Title.

JOHNSON, Aubrey Rodway 224.066
The cultic prophet in ancient Israel [2d ed.] Cardiff, Univ. of Wales Pr. Mystic, Conn., Verry, 1965] viii, 91p. 22cm. First pub. in 1960. Bibl. [BS1198.J6] 65-8444 3.50
1. Prophets. I. Title.

WESTERMANN, Claus. 224'.06'6
Basic forms of prophetic speech. Translated by Hugh Clayton White. Philadelphia, Westminster Press [1967] 222 p. 21 cm. Bibliographical references included in "Notes" (p. 211-222) [BS1505.2.W413] 67-10512
1. Bible. O.T. Prophets—Criticism, Form. I. Title.

EATON, J. H. 224.07
Obadiah, Nahum, Habakkuk and Zephaniah. Introd., commentary by J. H. Eaton. [Dist. New York, Macmillan, 1962, c.1961] 159p. 19cm. (Torch Bible commentaries) Bibl. 62-5843 3.00
1. Bible. O.T. Minor prophets—Commentaries. I. Title.

HIRSCH, Mendel, 1833- 224'.07
1898.
The Haphtoroth; translated & explained by Mendel Hirsch, rendered into English by Isaac Levy. London [I. Levy; sole American selling agent: Bloch Pub. Co., New York] 1966. 703 p. 25 cm. (B67-8946) With Haftaroth in Hewbrew. [BS1287.H513] HE67
1. Bible. O.T. Haftaroth — Commentaires. I. Bible. O.T. Haftaroth. English. 1966. II. BBle. O. T. Haftaroth. Hebrew. 1966. III. Levy, Isaac, tr. IV. Title.

BIBLE. O.T. Prophets. 224.077
English. 1966.Revisedstandard.
Commentary on the prophets [by] Emil G. Kraeling. Based on the Revised standard version. Camden, N.J., T. Nelson [1966] 2 v. 22 cm. Contents.CONTENTS.-- v. 1. Issiah, Jeremiah, Ezekiel.--v. 2. Daniel-Malachi. Includes bibliographies. [BS1503.K7] 66-14425
I. Kraeling, Emil Gottlieb Heinrich, 1802- II. Title.

GOTTWALD, Norman Karol, 224.08327
1926-
All the kingdoms of the earth; Israelite prophecy and international relations in the ancient Near East [by] Norman K. Gottwald. [1st ed.] New York, Harper & Row [1964] 448 p. illus., maps. 22 cm. Bibliography: p. 395-418. [BS1199.P6G6] 64-19499
1. Bible. O.T. — Political science. 2. Bible. O.T. — Prophecies. 3. Near East — Hist. I. Title.

GOTTWALD, Norman Karol, 224.08327
1926-
All the kingdoms of the earth: Israelite prophecy and international relations in the ancient Near East. New York, Harper [c.1964] xiii, 448p. illus., maps. 22cm. Bibl. 64-19499 7.00
1. Bible. O. T.—Political science. 2. Bible. O.T.—Prophecies. 3. Near East—Hist. I. Title.

NEWMAN, Shirley. 224'.092'2 B
A child's introduction to the early Prophets / by Shirley Newman ; edited by Louis Newman ; illustrated by Lucille Wallace. New York : Behrman House, c1975. 128 p. : col. ill. ; 26 cm. Twenty-eight Bible stories featuring Joshua, Gideon, Samuel, and David. [BS551.2.N45] 75-14052 ISBN 0-87441-244-7
1. Bible stories, English—O.T. Former prophets. I. Wallace, Lucille. II. Title.

VAN DOLSON, Bobbie 224'.09'22
Jane.
Prophets are people, believe it or not / Bobbie Jane Van Dolson. Washington : Review and Herald Pub. Association, [1974] 92 p. : ill. ; 21 cm. [BS1560.V36] 74-78394 ISBN pbk. : 2.50
1. Prophets. I. Title.

GOODMAN, Hannah Grad. 224.095
The story of Prophecy. Edited by Eugene B. Borowitz. Iilustrated by Eli Levin and Robert Cenedella; maps by Stephen Kraft. New York,Behram House [1963] 248 p. illus., maps. 24 cm. [BS1198G6] 65-24925
1. Prophets. I. Title.

GOODMAN, Hannah Grad. 224.095
The story of prophecy. Ed. by Eugene B. Borowitz. Illus. by Eli Levin, Robert Cenedella; maps by Stephen Kraft. New York, Behrman [c.1965] 248p. illus., maps. 24cm. [BS1198.G6] 65-24925 3.95
1. Prophets. I. Title.

ALEXANDER, Joseph Addison, 224.1
1809-1860.
Commentary on the prophecies of Isaiah. Introd. by Merrill F. Unger. Editor's pref. by John Eadie. Grand Rapids, Zondervan Pub. House [1953] 2 v. in 1. 23 cm. (Zondervan classic commentary series) Originally pubished in 1846-47 in 2 v., with titles: The earlier prophecies of Isaiah, and The later prophecies of Isaiah. Revised and edited in 1865 by John Eadie, with title: The prophecies of Isaiah. [BS1515.A42] 55-15157
1. Bible. O. T. Isaiah—Commentaries.

ALLIS, Oswald Thompson, 224.1
1880-
The unity of Isaiah; a study in prophecy. [Special ed., with foreword by Clarence Edward Macartney] Philadelphia, Presbyterian and Reformed Pub. Co., 1950 [i. e. 1951] 134 p. 21 cm. Bibliographical footnotes. [BS1515.A44 1951] 51-1982
1. Bible. O. T. Isaiah—Criticism, interpretation, etc. 2. Bible. O. T. Isaiah—Prophecies. I. Title.

ASTON, Frederick Alfred. 224'.1
The challenge of the ages; new light on Isaiah 53. 21st ed., rev. Scarsdale, N.Y., Research Press, 1970 [c1963] 24 p. 24 cm. Includes bibliographical references. [BS1520.A87 1970] 74-99176
1. Bible. O.T. Isaiah LIII—Criticism, interpretation, etc. 2. Servant of Jehovah. I. Bible. O.T. Isaiah LIII. English. 1970. II. Title.

BENNETT, Fredna W. 224'.1
Christian living from Isaiah, by Fredna W. Bennett. Grand Rapids, Baker Book House [1968] 114 p. 19 cm. [BS1515.4.B45] 68-7171 1.50
1. Bible. O.T. Isaiah—Devotional literature. I. Title.

BIBLE. O.T. Isaiah. 224'.1
English. Jewish Publication Society. 1973.
The book of Isaiah. A new translation with drawings by Chaim Gross. Introd. by H. L. Ginsberg. [1st ed.] Philadelphia, Jewish Publication Society of America, 1973 [c1972] 192 p. illus. 30 cm. Bibliography: p. [24] [BS1513.G76 1973] 78-188581 ISBN 0-8276-0005-4 12.50
1. Bible—Pictures, illustrations, etc. I. Jewish Publication Society of America.

BIBLE. O.T. Isaiah. 224'.1
English. McKenzie. 1968.
Second Isaiah. Introd., translation, and notes by John L. McKenzie. [1st ed.] Garden City, N.Y., Doubleday, 1968. lxxiv, 221 p. 25 cm. (The Anchor Bible, v. 20) Bibliographical footnotes. [BS192.2.A1 1964.G3 vol. 20] 68-10565
1. Bible. O.T. Isaiah XL-LXVI—Commentaries. I. McKenzie, John L. II. Title. III. Series.

BIBLE. O.T. Isaiah XL- 224'.1
LXVI. English. New English. 1975.
The book of the Prophet Isaiah, chapters 40-66 / commentary by A. S. Herbert. Cambridge ; New York : Cambridge University Press, 1975. x, 204 p. : maps ; 21 cm. (The Cambridge Bible commentary, New English Bible) Includes index. Bibliography: p. 201. [BS1520.H47 1975] 74-16997 ISBN 0-521-20721-5 : 14.95 ISBN 0-521-09933-1 pbk. : 5.95
1. Bible. O.T. Isaiah XL-LXVI—Commentaries. I. Herbert, Arthur Sumner. II. Title. III. Series.

BLANK, Sheldon H 224.1
Prophetic faith in Isaiah. [1st ed.] New York, Harper 1958 241p. 22cm. [BS1515.B58] 57-9887
1. Bible. O. T. Isaiah—Criticism, interpretation, etc. I. Title.

BLANK, Sheldon H. 224.1
Prophetic faith in Isaiah. Detroit, Wayne State Univ. Pr., 1967[c.1958] 241p. 21cm. (WB24) [BS1515.B58] 2.50 pap.,
1. Bible. O.T. Isaiah—Criticism, interpretation, etc. I. Title.

BOYD, Frank Mathews, 1883- 224.1
Book of the prophet Isaiah. Springfield, Mo., Gospel Pub. House [1950] 248 p. 20 cm. Bibliography: p. 248. [BS1515.B63] 51-24094
1. Bible. O. T. Isaiah—Commentaries. I. Title.

CALVIN, Jean, 1509-1564. 224.1
The Gospel according to Isaiah, seven sermons on Isaiah 53 concerning the Passion and death of Christ; translated by Leroy Nixon. Grand Rapids, W. B. Eerdmans Pub. Co., 1953. 133p. 23cm. Translation of Sermons sur la prophetie d'Esale, chap. 53, published in 1887 in the author's Opera quae supersunt omnia, v. 35. [BS1515.C324] 53-8039
1. Bible. O. T. Isaiah LIII— Sermons. 2. Sermons, French—Translations into English. 3. Sermons, English— Translations from French. I. Title.

COLTMAN, William George, 224.1
1887-
Musings in Isaiah. Oak Park, Ill., Designed Products [1950] 239 p. 20 cm. [BS1515.C63] 50-57761
1. Bible. O. T. Isalah XL-LXVI—Sermons. 2. Baptists—Sermons. . 3. Sermons, American. I. Title.

ERDMAN, Charles Rosenbury, 224.1
1866-
The book of Isaiah, an exposition. [Westwood, N. J.] Revell [1954] 160 p. 20 cm. [BS1515.E7] 54-9687
1. Bible. O. T. Isaiah— Commentaries. I. Title.

IRONSIDE, Henry Allan, 224.1
1876-1951.
Expository notes on the prophet Isaiah. [1st ed.] New York, Loizeaux Bros. [1952] 369p. 20cm. [BS1515.I74] 53-18202
1. Bible. O. T. Isaiah— Commentaries. I. Title.

KAISER, Otto, 1924- 224'.1
Isaiah 1-12: a commentary. Philadelphia, Westminster Press [1972] xx, 170 p. 23 cm. (The Old Testament library) Translation of Der Prophet Jesaja/Kap. 1-12. Includes bibliographical references. [BS1515.3.K3313 1972] 77-189464 ISBN 0-664-20939-4 6.50
1. Bible. O.T. Isaiah I-XII—Commentaries. I. Bible. O.T. Isaiah. English. 1972. II. Title. III. Series.

KAISER, Otto, 1924- 224'.1
Isaiah 13-39; a comentary. [Translated by R. A. Wilson from the German] Philadelphia, Westminster Press [1974] xix, 412 p. 23 cm. (The Old Testament library) Translation of v. 2 of Der Prophet Jesaja. Includes bibliographical references. [BS1515.3.K3313 1974] 73-21949 ISBN 0-664-20984-X 12.50
1. Bible. O.T. Isaiah XIII-XXXIX—Comentaries. I. Bible. O.T. Isaiah XIII-XXXIX. English. 1974. II. Title. III. Series.

KELLEY, Page H. 224'.1
Judgment and redemption in Isaiah; [studies in Isaiah 1-12 and 40-55, by] Page H. Kelley. Nashville, Broadman Press [1968] 95 p. 19 cm. "Suggestions for further study": p. 15-16. [BS1515.2.K4] 68-9028
1. Bible. O.T. Isaiah—Theology. 2. Judgment Day—Biblical teaching. 3. Redemption—Biblical teaching. I. Title.

MARTIN, Alfred, 1916- 224.1
Isaiah. 'the salvation of Jehovah'; a survey of the book of Isaiah the prophet. Chicago, Moody Press [c1956] 127p. 17cm. (Colportage library, 311) [BS1515.M28] 57-49205
1. Bible. O. T. Isaiah—Study—Outlines, syllabi, etc. I. Title.

MILTON, John Peterson, 224.1
1897-
Preaching from Isaiah. Minneapolis, Augsburg Pub. House [1953] 187p. 22cm. [BS1515.M45] 53-13370
1. Bible. O. T. Isalah—Homiletical use. I. Title.

MUCKLE, J. Yeoman 224.1
Isaiah 1-39, London, Epworth Press[dist. Naperville, Ill., Alec R. Allenson, 1959] xi, 135p. 19cm. (Epworth preacher's commentaries) 60-1972 2.75 bds.,
1. Bible. O. T. Isaiah I-XXXIX—Commentaries. I. Title.

NEUBAUER, Adolf, 1832- 224'.1
1907, comp.
The "suffering servant" of Isaiah, according to the Jewish interpreters. Translated by Samuel R. Driver and Adolf Neubauer, with an introd. by Edward B. Pusey. New York, Hermon Press [1969] lxxvi, 574 p. 22 cm. Reprint of the 1877 ed. which was published under title: The fifty-third chapter of Isaiah according to the Jewish interpreters. II. Translations. Includes bibliographical references. [BS1520.N49] 68-9533 13.95
1. Bible. O.T. Isaiah LII, 13-LIII—Commentaries—Collections. 2. Servant of Jehovah. 3. Bible. O.T.—Criticism, interpretation, etc., Jewish. I. Driver, Samuel Rolles, 1846-1914, tr. II. Title.

NORTH, Christopher Richard, 224.1
1888-
The suffering servant in Deutero-Isaiah; an historical and critical study. 2d ed. London, Oxford University Press, 1956. xi, 264p. 23cm. Bibliography: p. [240]-253. [BS1515.N6 1956] 56-59025
1. Servant of Jehovah. 2. Bible. O. T. Isaiah XL-LXVI—Criticism, interpretation, etc. I. Title.

NORTH, Christopher Richard, 224.1
1888-
The suffering servant in Deutero-Isainh; an historical and critical study. 2d ed. London, Oxford University Press, 1956. xi, 264p. 23cm. Bibliography: p. [240]-253. [BS1515.N6 1956] 56-59025
1. Servant of Jehovah. 2. Bible. D.T. Isaiah XI-LXVI—Criticism. interpretation, etc. I. Title.

ODENDAAL, Dirk H. 224'.1
The eschatological expectation of Isaiah 40-66 with special reference to Israel and the nations, by Dirk H. Odendaal. [Nutley, N.J., Presbyterian and Reformed Pub. Co., c1970] x, 202 p. 23 cm. (International library of philosophy and theology: Biblical and theological studies) Bibliography: p. 196-197. [BS1199.E75O3] 72-186102
1. Bible. O.T. Isaiah XL-LXVI—Criticism, interpretation, etc. 2. Eschatology—Biblical teaching. I. Title. II. Series: International library of philosophy and theology: Biblical and theological studies series.

REDPATH, Alan. 224'.1
Faith for the times; studies in the prophecy of Isaiah, chapters 40 to 66. Old Tappan, N.J., Revell [1972- v. 21 cm. Contents.Contents.—pt. 1. The promise of deliverance. [BS1520.R4] 72-4621 ISBN 0-8007-0550-5 3.95
1. Bible. O.T. Isaiah XL-LXVI—Sermons. 2. Sermons, American. I. Title.

REDPATH, Alan. 224'.1
Faith for the times/deliverance / by Alan Redpath. Old Tappan, N.J. : Revell, 1977. p. cm. Originally published 1972-76 in 3 v. with collective title Faith for the times: studies in the prophecy of Isaiah, chapters 40 to 66. [BS1520.R4 1977] 77-22980 ISBN 0-8007-0855-5 : 3.95
1. Bible. O.T. Isaiah XL-LXVI—Sermons. 2. Sermons, British. I. Title.

REDPATH, Alan. 224'.1 s
The fruit of deliverance : studies in the prophecy of Isaiah, chapters 55 to 66 / Alan Redpath. Old Tappan, N.J. : Revell, c1976. 93 p. ; 21 cm. (His Faith for the times ; pt. 3) [BS1520.R4 pt. 3] [BS1520.5] 224'.1 75-42352 ISBN 0-8007-0779-6 : 3.95
1. Bible. O.T. Isaiah LV-LXVI—Sermons. 2. Sermons, American. I. Title.

REDPATH, Alan. 224'.1 s
The Plan of deliverance; studies in the prophecy of Isaiah, chapters 49 to 54. Old Tappan, N.J., Revell [1974] 127 p. 21 cm. (His Faith for the times, pt. 2) [BS1520.R4 pt. 2] [BS1520] 224'.1 74-4033 ISBN 0-8007-0657-9 3.95
1. Bible. O.T. Isaiah XLIX-LIV—Sermons. 2. Sermons, American. I. Title. II. Series.

REDPATH, Alan. 224'.1 s
The promise of deliverance; studies in the prophecy of Isaiah, chapters 40 to 66. Old Tappan, N.J., Revell [1972] 160 p. 21 cm. (His Faith for the times, pt. 1) [BS1520.R4 pt. 1] [BS1520] 224'.1 74-160894 ISBN 0-8007-0550-5 3.95
1. Bible. O.T. Isaiah XL-LXVI—Sermons. 2. Sermons, American. I. Title. II. Series.

RENCKENS, Henricus. 224'.1
The prophet of the nearness of God: Isaiah, by H. Ren[c]kens. [Edited by Lisa McGaw] Translated by James M. Boumans. De Pere, Wis., St. Norbert Abbey Press, 1969. 276 p. 20 cm. Translation of De profeet van de nabijheid Gods. [BS1515.3.R413] 77-87814 4.95
1. Bible. O.T. Isaiah I-XII—Commentaries. I. McGaw, Lisa, ed. II. Title.

ROBINSON, George 224.1
Livingstone, 1864-
The book of Isaian in fifteen studies. Rev. ed. Grand Rapids, Baker Book House, 1954. 175p. 20cm. [BS1515] 54-11078
1. Bible. O. T. Isalah—Study—Text-books. I. Title.

SCHILLING, Sylvester Paul, 1904- 224.1
Isaiah speaks. [New York] Woman's Division of Christian Service, Board of Missions of the Methodist Church [1958] 154p. 19cm. Includes bibliography. [BS1515.S36] 57-10955
1. Bible. O. T. Isalah—Criticism, interpretation, etc. I. Title.

*TASSELL, Paul 224.1
Outline studies of Isaiah. Grand Rapids, Mich., Baker Bk. [1967] 79p. 22cm. ((1.00 sermon lib.) 1.00 pap.,
I.)OsProphets—Isaiah—Commentaries. II. Title.

THEXTON, S. Clive 224.1
Isaiah 40-66. London, Epworth Press [dist. Naperville, Ill., Alec R. Allenson, 1959] xii, 160p. 19cm. (Epworth preacher's commentaries) 60-1993 2.75 bds.,
1. Bible. O. T. Isaiah XL-LXVI—Commentaries. I. Title.

TODD, Virgil H. 224'.1
Prophet without portfolio; a study and interpretation of the prophecy of Second Isaiah, by Virgil H. Todd. North Quincy, Mass., Christopher Pub. House [1972] 161 p. 21 cm. Includes bibliographical references. [BS1520.T6] 77-178202 4.95
1. Bible. O. T. Isaiah XL-LV—Theology. 2. Eschotology—Biblical teaching. I. Title.

TSCHIRHART, Mary J. 224'.1
Hasten to take away the spoils: make haste to take away the prey (Isaiah 8:3) by Mary J. Tschirhart. New York, Philosophical Library [1972] 88 p. illus. 23 cm. Excerpts from the book of Isaiah with brief interpretations by the author, together with the author's interpretation of her recent book "The kingdom and the golden calves." [BS1515.2.T78] 72-75323 ISBN 0-8022-2087-8 6.00
1. Bible. O.T. Isaiah—Criticism, interpretation, etc. 2. Bible—Prophecies. I. Title.

VAN ZELLER, Hubert, Father, 1905- 224.1
Isaias, man of ideas. Westminster, Md., Newman Press, 1951. 123 p. 19 cm. [BS580.I7V3] 51-13745
1. Issiah, the prophet. I. Title.

WESTERMANN, Claus. 224'.1
Isaiah 40-66; a commentary. [Translated by David M. G. Stalker from the German] Philadelphia, Westminster Press [1969] xv, 429 p. 23 cm. (The Old Testament library) Translation of Das Buch Jesaia, 40-66. Bibliography: p. [xiii]-xv. [BS1520.W413 1969b] 69-18647 8.50
1. Bible. O.T. Isaiah XL-LXVI—Commentaries. I. Title. II. Series.

WHYBRAY, Roger Norman. 224'.1
The heavenly counsellor in Isaiah xl 13-14; a study of the sources of the theology of Deutero-Isaiah [by] R. N. Whybray. Cambridge [Eng.] University Press, 1971. viii, 90 p. 23 cm. (Society for Old Testament Study. Monograph series, 1) Includes bibliographical references. [BS1520.W47 1971] 77-132286 ISBN 0-521-08044-4
1. Bible. O.T. Isaiah XL, 13-14—Criticism, interpretation, etc. I. Title. II. Series.

YOUNG, Edward Joseph. 224.1
Isaiah fifty-three, a devotional and expository study. Grand Rapids, W. B. Eerdmans Pub. Co., 1952. 91 p. 23 cm. [BS1515.Y6] 52-7095
1. Bible. O. T. Isaiah. LIII — Commentaries. 2. Servant of Jehovah. I. Title.

YOUNG, Edward Joseph. 224.1
Studies in Isaiah. Grand Rapids, Eerdmans, 1954. 206p. 23cm. [BS1515] 54-4436
1. Bible. O. T. Isaiah— Criticism, interpretation, etc. 2. Bible. O. T. Isaiah—Prophecies. I. Title.

YOUNG, Edward Joseph. 224.1
Who wrote Isaiah? Grand Rapids, Eerdmans [1958] 88 p. 19 cm. (Pathway books; a series of contemporary evangelical studies) Includes bibliography. [BS1515.Y63] 57-14945
1. Bible. O.T. — Criticism, interpretation, etc. I. Title.

MARGULIES, Rachel 224.1014
The indivisible Isaiah: evidence for the single authorship of the prophetic book. Jerusalem, Sura Inst. for Res.; New York, Yeshiva Univ. [c.]1964. x, 245p. 24cm. Completely renewed rev, ed., based on the Bible tr. of the Jewish Bible Soc. Bibl. 64-18572 4.75
1. Bible. O. T. Isaiah—Criticism, interpretation, etc. I. Title.

ROSENBLOOM, Joseph R. 224'.1'044
The Dead Sea Isaiah scroll: a literary analysis. A comparison with the Masoretic text and the Biblia Hebraica, by Joseph R. Rosenbloom. Grand Rapids, Mich., Eerdmans [1970] xiii, 88 p. 23 cm. Bibliography: p. 85-88. [BS1515.2.R67] 68-28855 4.50
1. Bible. O.T. Isaiah. Hebrew. Dead Sea scroll A—Criticism, Textual. I. Title.

BIBLE. O.T. Isaiah. 224'.1'052
English. Jewish Publication Society. 1973.
The book of Isaiah; a new translation. Introd. by H. L. Ginsberg. [1st ed.] Philadelphia, Jewish Publication Society of America, 1973 [c1972] 116 p. 27 cm. [BS1513.J48 1973] 73-163827 ISBN 0-8276-0005-4 4.00
I. Jewish Publication Society of America.

BIBLE. O.T. Isaiah. 224'.1'052
English. New international. 1975.
The Book of Isaiah from the New international version. Grand Rapids, Mich. : Zondervan Bible Publishers, c1975. 162 p. ; 22 cm. Preface signed: Committee on Bible Translation. [BS1513.N48 1975] 75-24237
I. Committee on Bible Translation. II. Title.

KNIGHT, George Angus Fulton, 1909- 224.106
Isaiah. Nashville, Abingdon [1961] 96p. (Prophets of Israel, 1, Bible guides, no. 7) 61-2733 1.00 pap.,
1. Bible. O. T. Isaiah—Criticism, interpretation, etc. I. Title.

MACRAE, Alan A. 224'.1'06
The gospel of Isaiah / by Alan A. MacRae. Chicago : Moody Press, c1977. 192 p. ; 22 cm. Includes indexes. [BS1520.M3] 77-3045 ISBN 0-8024-3189-5 : 2.95
1. Bible. O.T. Isaiah XL-LVI, 8—Commentaries. I. Bible. O.T. Isaiah XL-LVI, 8. II. Title.

MELUGIN, Roy F. 224'.1'06
The formation of Isaiah 40-55 / Roy F. Melugin. Berlin ; New York : W. de Gruyter, 1976. (Beihefte zur Zeitschrift fur die alttestamentliche Wissenschaft ; 141) Bibliography: p. [BS401.Z5 vol. 141] [BS1520] 76-13519 ISBN 3-11-005820-0
1. Bible. O.T. Isaiah XL-LV—Criticism, interpretation, etc. I. Title. II. Series: Zeitschrift fur die alttestamentliche Wissenschaft. Beihefte ; 141.

MORGENSTERN, Julian, 1881- 224.106
The message of Deutero-Isaiah in its sequential unfolding. Hebrew Union College Pr. [dist. New York, University Pubs., c.]1961. 169p. Bibl. 61-30604 5.00
1. Bible. O. T. Isaiah—Criticism, interpretation, etc. I. Title.

SPYKERBOER, Hendrik Carel. 224'.1'06
The structure and composition of Deutero-Isaiah with special reference to the polemics against idolatry / door Hendrik Carel Spykerboer. Meppel : Krips Repro, 1976. vi, 242 p. ; 24 cm. Thesis - Groningen. "Stellingen": [2] p. inserted. Summary in Dutch. Bibliography: p. 237-240. [BS1520.S75] 77-364795
1. Bible. O.T. Isaiah XL-LV—Criticism, interpretation, etc. 2. Idols and images—Worship—Biblical teaching. I. Title: The structure and composition of Deutero-Isaiah ...

STUHLMUELLER, Carroll. 224'.1'06
Isaiah / by Carroll Stuhlmueller. Chicago : Franciscan Herald Press, [1976] p. cm. (Read and pray) [BS1515.3.S88] 76-879 ISBN 0-8199-0628-X pbk. : 0.95
1. Bible. O.T. Isaiah—Commentaries. 2. Bible. O.T. Isaiah—Meditations. 3. Prayers. I. Bible. O.T. Isaiah. English. Selections. 1976. II. Title. III. Series.

WATERMAN, Leroy 224.106
Forerunners of Jesus. New York, Philosophical Library [c.1959] 156p. 23cm. (10p. bibl. notes) 60-16009 3.00
1. Bible. O. T. Isaiah—Theology. 2. Jesus Christ—Person and offices. 3. John the Baptist. I. Title.

WATERMAN, Leroy, 1875- 224.106
Forerunners of Jesus. New York, Philosophical Library [c1959] 156 p. 23 cm. Includes bibliography. [BS1515.5.W3] 60-16009
1. Bible. O. T. Isaiah — Theology. 2. Jesus Christ — Person and offices. 3. John the Baptist. I. Title.

WHEDBEE, J. William. 224'.1'06
Isaiah & wisdom [by] J. William Whedbee. Nashville, Abingdon Press [1971] 172 p. 23 cm. Bibliography: p. 155-164. [BS1515.2.W47] 75-134250 ISBN 0-687-19706-6 5.95
1. Bible O.T. Isaiah—Criticism, interpretation, etc. 2. Wisdom. I. Title.

GREEN, James Leo. 224'.1'066
God reigns; expository studies in the prophecy of Isaiah. Nashville, Broadman Press [1968] viii, 178 p. 21 cm. Bibliography: p. 175-178. [BS1515.2.G7] 68-9026 4.50
1. Bible. O.T. Isaiah—Criticism, interpretation, etc. I. Title.

GUFFIN, Gilbert Lee. 224'.1'066
The gospel in Isaiah, by Gilbert L. Guffin. Nashville, Convention Press [1968] x, 148 p. 19 cm. Bibliography: p. 135-136. [BS1515.5.G8] 68-25507
1. Bible. O.T. Isaiah—Criticism, interpretation, etc. I. Title.

JENSEN, Joseph, 1924- 224'.1'066
The use of tora by Isaiah; his debate with the wisdom tradition. Washington, Catholic Biblical Association of America, 1973. ix, 156 p. 26 cm. (The Catholic biblical quarterly. Monograph series, 3) Bibliography: p. 136-146. [BS1515.2.J46] 73-83134 3.00
1. Bible. O.T. Isaiah—Criticism, interpretation, etc. 2. Torah (The word) I. Title. II. Series.

WARD, James Merrill, 1928- 224'.1'066
Amos & Isaiah: prophets of the word of God [by] James M. Ward. Nashville, Abingdon Press [1969] 287 p. 23 cm. Bibliography: p. 281-283. Bibliographical footnotes. [BS1585.2.W28] 69-18456
1. Bible. O.T. Amos—Criticism, interpretation, etc. 2. Bible. O.T. Isaiah—Criticism, interpretation, etc. I. Title.

BIBLE. O.T. Isaiah XL-LV. 224.107
English. 1964.North.
The second Isaiah; introduction, translation, and commentary to chapters XL-LV, by Christopher R. Nort. Oxford, Clarendon Press, 1964. xi, 290 p. 23 cm. Bibliography: p. [30]-31. [BS1520.A3N6] 65-300
1. Bible. O. T. Isaiah XL-LV—Commentaries. I. North Christopher Richard, 1888- II. Title.

FREEHOF, Solomon Bennett, 1892- 224'.1'07
Book of Isaiah; a commentary, by Solomon B. Freehof. New York, Union of American Hebrew Congregations, 1972. 333 p. 25 cm. (The Jewish commentary for Bible readers) Bibliography: p. 333. [BS1515.3.F74] 72-2156
1. Bible. O.T. Isaiah—Commentaries. I. Bible. O.T. Isaiah. English. 1972. II. Series: Commission on Jewish Education of the Union of American Hebrew Congregations and the Central Conference of American Rabbis. The Jewish commentary for Bible readers

GARLAND, D. David. 224'.1'07
Isaiah; a study guide, by D. David Garland. Grand Rapids, Zondervan Pub. House [1968] 115 p. 21 cm. (A Zondervan paperback) [BS1515.5.G3] 68-58077 0.95
1. Bible. O.T. Isaiah—Study—Outlines, syllabi, etc. I. Title.

GUTZKE, Manford George. 224'.1'07
Plain talk on Isaiah / Manford George Gutzke. Grand Rapids : Zondervan Pub. House, c1977. 256 p. ; 21 cm. [BS1515.2.G87] 76-53766 ISBN 0-310-25551-1 pbk. : 2.95
1. Bible. O.T. Isaiah—Commentaries. I. Title.

LESLIE, Elmer Archibald, 1888- 224.107
Isaiah; chronologically arranged, translated, and interpreted. New York, Abingdon Press [1963] 288 p. 24 cm. Bibliography: p. 279-282. [BS1515.3.L4] 63-7765
1. Bible. O.T. Isaiah — Commentaries. I. Bible. O.T. Isaiah. English. 1963. Leslie. II. Title.

LESLIE, Elmer Archibald, 1888- 224.107
Isaiah; chronologically arranged, tr., interpreted. Nashville, Abingdon [c.1963] 288p. 24cm. Bibl. 63-7765 5.00
1. Bible. O. T. Isaiah—Commentaries. I. Bible, O. T. Isaiah. English. 1963. Leslie. II. Title.

MAUCHLINE, John 224.107
Isaiah 1-39: introduction and commetary. New York, Macmillan [c.1962] 237p. 20cm. (Torch Bible commentaries) 62-51997 3.50
1. Bible. O.T. Isaiah I—Commentaries. I. Title.

MAUCHLINE, John. 224.107
Isaiah 1-39: introduction and commentary. New York, Macmillan [1962] 237p. 20cm. (Torch Bible commentaries) [BS1515.3.M3] 62-51997
1. Bible. O. T. Isaiah I-xxxix— Commentaries. I. Title.

SCHILLING, Sylvester Paul, 1904- 224.107
Isaiah speaks. New York, Crowell [1959] 148p. 21cm. Includes bibliography. [BS1515.2.S36 1959] 59-12506
1. Bible. O. T. Isaiah—Criticism, interpretation, etc. I. Title.

SMART, James D 224.107
History and theology in Second Isaiah, a commentary on Isaiah 35, 40-66, by James D. Smart. Philadelphia, Westminster Press [1965] 304 p. 24 cm. Bibliographical references included in footnotes. [BS1520.Z72S5] 65-17000
1. Bible. O. T. Isaiah XL-LXVI — Commentaries. I. Title.

SMART, James D. 224.107
History and theology in Second Isaiah; a commentary on Isaiah 35, 40-66. Philadelphia, Westminster [c.1965] 304p. 24cm. Bibl. [BS1520.Z72S5] 65-17000 6.50
1. Bible. O. T. Isaiah XL-LXVI—Commentaries. I. Title.

VINE, William Edwy, 1873-1949. 224'.1'07
Isaiah; prophecies, promises, warnings. Grand Rapids, Mich., Zondervan Pub. House [1971] 222 p. 21 cm. Reprint of the 1946 ed. [BS1515.2.V5 1971] 70-146560
1. Bible. O.T. Isaiah—Criticism, interpretation, etc. 2. Bible. O.T. Isaiah—Prophecies. I. Title.

BIBLE. O.T. Isaiah. 224.1077
English. 1965.Young.
The book of Isaiah: the English text, with introd., exposition, and notes by Edward J. Young. Grand Rapids, Eerdmans [1965- v. 23 cm. (The New international commentary on the Old Testament) Contents.CONTENTS.--v. 1. Chapters 1 to 18. Bibliography: v. 1, p. 501-512. [BS1515.3.Y6] 63-17786
1. Bible. O. T. Isaiah—Commentaries. I. Young, Edward Joseph, ed. and tr. II. Title. III. Series.

BIBLE. O.T. Isaiah. 224.1077
English. 1965. Young
The book of Isaiah: the English text; v.1. Introd., exposition, and notes by Edward J. Young. Grand Rapids, Mich., Eerdmans [c.1965] xii, 534p. 23cm. (New intl. commentary on the Old Testament) Bibl. Contents.v.1. Chapters 1 to 18 [BS1515.3.Y6] 63-17786 7.95
1. Bible. O.T. Isaiah—Commentaries. I. Young, Edward Joseph, ed. and tr. II. Title. III. Series.

BIBLE. O.T. Isaiah I-XXXIX. 224'.1'077
English. New English. 1973.
The book of the prophet Isaiah, chapters 1-39. Commentary by A. S. Herbert. Cambridge [Eng.] University Press, 1973. x, 218 p. maps. 21 cm. (The Cambridge Bible commentary: New English Bible) Bibliography: p. 216. [BS1515.3.H47] 73-79495 ISBN 0-521-08624-8
1. Bible. O.T. Isaiah I-XXXIX—Commentaries. I. Herbert, Arthur Sumner. II. Title. III. Series.
Distributed by Cambridge University Press, N.Y., 9.95

BUTLER, Paul T. 224'.1'077
Isaiah / by Paul T. Butler. Joplin, Mo. : College Press, c1975- v. : ill. ; 23 cm. (Bible study textbook series) Bibliography: v. 1, p. 371-372. [BS1515.3.B87] 75-328170
1. Bible. O.T. Isaiah—Commentaries. 2. Bible—Prophecies. I. Title.

KNIGHT, George Angus Fulton, 1909- 224.1077
Deutero-Isaiah: a theological commentary on Isaiah 40-55 [by] George A. F. Knight. New York, Abingdon Press [1965] 283 p.24 cm. Bibliography: p. 275-279. [BS152-.Z72K5] 65-20363
1. Bible. O. T. Isaiah XL-LV—Commentaries. I. Bible. O. T. Isaiah XL-LV, English. 1965. Knight. II. Title.

KNIGHT, George Angus Fulton, 1909- 224.1077
Deutero-Isaiah: a theological commentary on Isaiah 40-55. Nashville. Abingdon [c.1965] 283p. 24cm. Bibl. [BS1520.Z72K5] 65-20363 5.50
1. Bible. O. T. Isaiah XL-LV—Commentaries. I. Bible. O. T. Isaiah XL-LV. English. 1965. Knight. II. Title.

LEUPOLD, Herbert Carl, 1892- 224'.1'077
Exposition of Isaiah, by H. C. Leupold. Grand Rapids, Baker Book House [1968- v. 23 cm. [BS1515.3.L43] 68-29786 7.95
1. Bible. O.T. Isaiah—Commentaries. I. Title.

MILLAR, William R. 224'.1'077
Isaiah 24-27 and the origin of apocalyptic / by William R. Millar. Missoula, Mont. : Published by Scholars Press for the Harvard Semitic Museum, c1976. p. cm. (Harvard Semitic monographs ; 11) Bibliography: p. [BS1515.2.M52] 76-3561 ISBN 0-89130-102-X : 5.60
1. Bible. O.T. Isaiah XXIV-XXVII—Criticism, interpretation, etc. 2. Apocalyptic literature. I. Title. II. Series.

MILLAR, William R. 224'.1'077
Isaiah 24-27 and the origin of apocalyptic / by William R. Millar. Missoula, Mont. : Published

by Scholars Press for the Harvard Semitic Museum, c1976. xii, 125 p. ; 23 cm. (Harvard Semitic monographs ; 11) Bibliography: p. 121-125. [BS1515.2.M52] 76-3561 ISBN 0-89130-102-X : 5.60
1. Bible. O.T. Isaiah XXIV-XXVII—Criticism, interpretation, etc. 2. Apocalyptic literature. I. Title. II. Series.

BIBLE. O. T. Jeremiah. 224.2
English. 1952.Revised.
The book of the prophet Jeremiah together with the Lamentations, in the Revised version. With introduction and notes by A. W. Streane. Cambridge, University Press, 1952. liii, 381 p. fold. col. map. 17 cm. (Cambridge Bible for schools and colleges) Includes bibliographical references. [BS1525] 63-6938 CD
1. Bible. O. T. Jeremiah—Commentaries 2. Bible. O. T. Lamentations—Commentaries. I. Bible. O. T. Lamentations. English. 1952. Revised. II. Streane, Annesley William, 1844-1915. III. Title. IV. Series.

BIBLE. O. T. Jeremiah. 224.2
English. 1964. Bright.
Jeremiah. Introd., tr., notes by John Bright. Garden City, N.Y., Doubleday [c.]1965. cxliv, 372p. 24cm. (Anchor Bible, 21) Bibl. [BS192.2.A1 1964.G3 v.21] 65-13603 7.00
1. Bible. O. T. Jeremiah—Commentaries. I. Bright, John, 1908- ed. and tr. II. Title. III. Series.

BIBLE. O.T. Jeremiah. 224.2
English. 1964. Bright.
Jeremiah. Introd., translation, and notes by John Bright. [1st ed.] Garden City, N.Y., Doubleday, 1965. cxliv, 372 p. 24 cm. (The Anchor Bible, 21) Bibliography: p. [cxliii]-cxliv. [BS192.2.A1 1964.G3, vol. 21] 65-13603
1. Bible. O.T. Jeremiah—Commentaries. I. Bright, John, 1908- ed. and tr. II. Title. III. Series.

BIBLE. O.T. Jeremiah I- 224'.2
XXV. English. New English. 1973.
The book of the Prophet Jeremiah, chapters 1-25. Commentary by Ernest W. Nicholson. Cambridge [Eng.] University Press, 1973. xii, 221 p. 20 cm. (The Cambridge Bible commentary: New English Bible) Bibliography: p. 218. [BS1523.N52 1973] 73-80477 ISBN 0-521-08625-6 9.95
1. Bible. O.T. Jeremiah I-XXV—Commentaries. I. Nicholson, Ernest Wilson. II. Title. III. Series.
Distributed by Cambridge University Press, New York, 3.95 (pbk.), ISBN 0521-09769-X.

CASE, Harold Claude, 1902- 224.2
The prophet Jeremiah. [Cincinnati] Woman's Division of Christian Service, Board of Missions of the Methodist Church [1953] 225p. 19cm. 'The book of Jeremiah. King James version, with headings, paragraphing, poetical arrangement, and punctuation, by Julius A. Bewer: p. [75]-225. Includes bibliography. [BS580.J4C37] 53-29140
1. Jeremiah, the prophet. I. Bible. C. T. Jeremiah. English. 1953. Authorized. II. Bewer, Julius August, 1877- III. Title.

ERDMAN, Charles Rosenbury, 224.2
1866-
The book of Jeremiah and Lamentations, an exposition. [Westwood, N. J.] F. H. Revell Co. [1955] 126p. 20cm. [BS1525.E7] 55-6630
1. Bible. O. T. Jeremiah—Commentaries. 2. Bible. O. T. Lementations—Commentaries. I. Title.

HABEL, Norman C. 224'.2
Concordia commentary: Jeremiah, Lamentations [by] Norman C. Habel. St. Louis, Concordia Pub. House [1968] 416 p. 21 cm. [BS1525.3.H3] 68-19474 4.00
1. Bible. O.T. Jeremiah—Commentaries. 2. Bible. O.T. Lamentations—Commentaries. I. Title.

HOLLADAY, William Lee. 224'.2
The architecture of Jeremiah 1-20 / William L. Holladay. Lewisburg : Bucknell University Press, [1975] p. cm. Includes index. Bibliography: p. [BS1525.2.H63] 74-204 ISBN 0-8387-1523-0 : 10.00
1. Bible. O.T. Jeremiah I-XX—Criticism, interpretation, etc. I. Title.

IRONSIDE, Henry Allan, 224.2
1876-1951.
Notes on the prophecy and Lamentations of Jeremiah, 'the weeping prophet.' [1st ed.] New York, Loizeaux Bros. [1952] 358p. 20cm. [BS1525.I7] 54-32890
1. Bible. O. T. Jeremiah—Commentaries. 2. Bible. O. T. Lamentations— Commentaries. I. Title.

LAETSCH. THEODORE FERDINAND
224.2
KARL, 1877-
Bible commentary: Jeremiah. Saint Louis, Concordia Pub. House [1953, c1952] 412p. 25cm. [BS1525.L2] 53-23899
1. Bible. O. T. Jeremiah—Commentaries. 2. Bible. O. T. Lamentations—Commentaries. I. Title.

LESLIE, Elmer Archibald, 224.2
1888-
Jeremiah; chronologically arranged, translated, and interpreted. Nahsville, Abingdon Press [1954] 349p. 24cm. Bibliography: p. 341-343. [BS1525.L383] 54-7030
1. Bible. O. T. Jeremiah—Commentaries. I. Bible. O. T. Jeremiah. English. 1954. Leslie. II. Title.

LESLIE, Elmer Archibald, 224.2
1888-
Jeremiah; chronologically arranged, tr., interpreted. Nashville, Abingdon [1961, c.1954] 349p. (Apex bks., G3) Bibl. 2.25 pap.,
1. Bible. O.T. Jeremiah—Commentaries. I. Bible. O.T. Jeremiah. English. 1954. Leslie. II. Title.

PARALIPOMENA Jeremiae. 224'.2
English and Greek.
Paraleipomena Jeremiou. Edited and translated by Robert A. Kraft and Ann-Elizabeth Purintun. [Missoula, Mont.] Society of Biblical Literature, 1972. 49 p. 24 cm. (Society of Biblical Literature. Texts and translations, 1. Pseudepigrapha series, 1) Bibliography: p. 7-10. [BS1830.P22 1972] 72-88436
I. Kraft, Robert A., ed. II. Purintun, Ann-Elizabeth, ed. III. Series: Society of Biblical Literature. Texts and translations, 1. IV. Series: Pseudepigrapha series, 1.

SKINNER, John, 1851-1925 224.2
Prophecy and religion; studies in the life of Jeremiah [New York] Cambridge, 1961[ ] 360p. 1.45 pap.,
1. Jeremiah, the prophet. 2. Bible. O.T.—Criticism, interpretation, etc. I. Title.

SIRE, James W. 224'.2'007
Jeremiah, meet the 20th century : 12 studies in Jeremiah / James W. Sire. Downers Grove, Ill. : InterVarsity Press, [1975] 116 p. ; 21 cm. [BS1525.5.S57] 74-31846 ISBN 0-87784-641-3 pbk. : 2.50
1. Bible. O.T. Jeremiah—Study—Outlines, syllabi, etc. I. Title.

WHITE, Kenneth Owen, 224.2007
1902-
The book of Jeremiah; a study manual. Grand Rapids, Baker Book House, 1961. 101 p. 20 cm. (Shield Bible study series) Includes bibliography. [BS1525.5.W5] 61-17552
1. Bible. O.T. Jeremiah—Study—Text-books. I. Title.

LUNDBOM, Jack R. 224'.2'044
Jeremiah : a study in ancient Hebrew rhetoric / by Jack R. Lundbom. [Missoula, Mont.] : Society of Biblical Literature : distributed by Scholars Press, 1975. xiv, 195 p. ; 22 cm. (Dissertation series ; no. 18) Thesis—Graduate Theological Union, Berkeley, 1973. Includes indexes. Bibliography: p. 163-183. [BS1525.2.L85] 75-15732 ISBN 0-89130-011-2 : 4.20
1. Bible. O.T. Jeremiah—Language, Style. 2. Bible. O.T. Jeremiah—Criticism, interpretation, etc. I. Series: Society of Biblical Literature. Dissertation series ; no. 18.

BULLOCK, Robert H 224.206
Hammer on the rock; the message of the prophet Jeremiah. Richmond, John Knox Press [1962] 64p. 23cm. (Every member Bible study) [BS1525.5.B8] 62-12767
1. Bible. O.T. Jeremiah—Study. I. Title.

HARRELSON, Walter J 224.206
Jeremiah, prohphet to the nations. Philadelphia, Judson Press [1959] 80p. 19cm. Includes bibliography. [BS1525.5.H35] 59-14168
1. Bible. O. T. Jeremiah—Study— Text-books. I. Title.

JANZEN, John Gerald, 224'.2'06
1932-
Studies in the text of Jeremiah [by] J. Gerald Janzen. Cambridge, Harvard University Press, 1973. 242 p. 25 cm. (Harvard Semitic monographs, v. 6) Originally presented as the author's thesis, Harvard, 1963. Includes bibliographical references. [BS1525.2.J36 1973] 73-81265 ISBN 0-674-85260-5 5.95 (pbk.)
1. Bible. O.T. Jeremiah—Criticism, Textual. I. Title. II. Series.

NICHOLSON, Ernest 224'.2'06
Wilson.
Preaching to the exiles; a study of the prose tradition in the book of Jeremiah [by] E. W. Nicholson. New York, Schocken Books [1971, c1970] 154 p. 23 cm. Bibliography: p. 140-144. [BS1525.2.N5 1971] 74-146021 ISBN 0-8052-3389-X
1. Bible. O.T. Jeremiah—Criticism, interpretation, etc. I. Title.

RAITT, Thomas M. 224'.2'06
A theology of exile : judgment/deliverance in Jeremiah and Ezekiel / Thomas M. Raitt. Philadelphia : Fortress Press, c1977. x, 271 p. ; 24 cm. Includes index. Bibliography: p. 232-234. [BS1525.5.R34] 76-62610 ISBN 0-8006-0497-0 : 15.95
1. Bible. O.T. Jeremiah—Theology. 2. Bible. O.T. Ezekiel—Theology. I. Title.

STEDMAN, Ray C. 224'.2'06
Death of a nation / Ray C. Stedman. Waco, Tex. : Word Books, c1976. 242 p. ; 22 cm. (Discovery books) [BS1525.2.S74] 75-36190 ISBN 0-87680-458-X : 5.95
1. Bible. O.T. Jeremiah—Criticism, interpretation, etc. I. Title.

TOV, 'Imanu'el. 224'.2'06
The Septuagint translation of Jeremiah and Baruch : a discussion of an early revision of the LXX of Jeremiah 29-52 and Baruch 1:1-3:8 / by Emanuel Tov. Missoula, Mont. : Published by Scholars Press for Harvard Semitic Museum, c1976. 199 p. ; 22 cm. (Harvard Semitic monographs ; no. 8) A revision of the author's thesis, Hebrew University, 1973. Includes indexes. Bibliography: p. 179-185. [BS1524.G7S45 1976] 75-43872 ISBN 0-89130-070-8 : 4.00
1. Bible. O.T. Jeremiah. Greek. Septuagint—Criticism, Textual. 2. Bible. O.T. Apocrypha. Baruch. Greek. Septuagint—Criticism, Textual. I. Title. II. Series.

WOOD, Fred M 224.206
Fire in my bones. Nashville, Broadman Press, [1959] 172 p. 21 cm. Includes bibliography. [BS1525.W6] 59-5864
1. Jeremiah, the prophet. 2. Bible. O. T. Jeremiah — Criticism, interpretation, etc. I. Title.

PLOTKIN, Albert. 224'.2'066
The religion of Jeremiah. [New York] Bloch Pub. Co. [1974] 153 p. 23 cm. Bibliography: p. 147-153. [BS580.J4P56] 73-93045 3.95
1. Jeremiah, the prophet. 2. Bible. O.T. Jeremiah—Criticism, interpretation, etc. I. Title.

BLACKWOOD, Andrew 224'.2'07
Watterson, 1915-
Commentary on Jeremiah : the word, the words, and the world / Andrew W. Blackwood, Jr. Waco, Tex. : Word Books, c1977. 326 p. ; 24 cm. Bibliography: p. 324-326. [BS1525.3.B55] 76-48509 ISBN 0-87680-416-4 : 8.95
1. Bible. O.T. Jeremiah—Commentaries. I. Title.

HARRISON, Roland 224'.2'07
Kenneth.
Jeremiah and Lamentations; an introduction and commentary, by R. K. Harrison. [1st ed.] Downers Grove, Ill., Inter-Varsity Press [1973] 240 p. 19 cm. (The Tyndale Old Testament commentaries) Includes bibliographies. [BS1525.3.H37] 72-97951 ISBN 0-85111-626-4 5.95
1. Bible. O.T. Jeremiah—Commentaries. 2. Bible. O.T. Lamentations—Commentaries. I. Title.

HOLLADAY, William Lee. 224'.2'07
Jeremiah: spokesman out of time [by] William L. Holladay. Philadelphia, United Church Press [1974] 158 p. 22 cm. "A Pilgrim Press Book." Bibliography: p. 151-152. [BS1525.2.H64] 74-7052 ISBN 0-8298-0283-5 2.95 (pbk.).
1. Jeremiah, the prophet. 2. Bible. O. T. Jeremiah—Criticism, interpretation, etc. I. Title.

JENSEN, Irving L. 224.207
Jeremiah; profet of judgment. Chicago, Moody [c.1966] 127 p. 18 cm. (col portage lib. 515) pap., .39
I. Title.

BIBLE. O.T. Jeremiah 224'.2'077
XXVI-LII. English. New English. 1975.
The book of the prophet Jeremiah, chapters 26-52 / commentary by Ernest W. Nicholson. London ; New York : Cambridge University Press, 1975. xi, 247 p. ; 21 cm. (Cambridge Bible commentary, New English Bible) Bibliography: p. 237. [BS1523.N54 1975] 74-80337 ISBN 0-521-20497-6. ISBN 0-521-09867-X pbk.
1. Bible. O.T. Jeremiah XXVI-LII—Commentaries. I. Nicholson, Ernest Wilson. II. Title. III. Series.

BIBLE. O.T. Jeremiah 224'.2'077
XXVI-LII. English. New English. 1975.
The book of the prophet Jeremiah, chapters 26-52 / commentary by Ernest W. Nicholson London ; New York : Cambridge University Press, 1975. xi, 247 p. ; 21 cm. (Cambridge Bible commentary, New English Bible) Bibliography: p. 237. [BS1523.N54 1975] 74-80337 ISBN 0-521-20497-6 : 14.95 ISBN 0-521-09867-X pbk. : 5.95
1. Bible. O.T. Jeremiah XXVI-LII—Commentaries. I. Nicholson, Ernest Wilson. II. Title. III. Series.

COX, Hugh S. 224'.2'077
Jeremiah: a helping hand for Bible students. [Action, Me., 1967] ll. 60602. 278p. 23cm. Foreword signed: Hugh S. Cox [BS1525.3.C6] 67-12484 5.00 pap.,
1. Bible. O. T. Jeremiah— Commentaries. I. Title.

HOWARD, David M. 224'.2'0924 B
Words of fire, rivers of tears : the man Jeremiah / David M. Howard. Wheaton, Ill. : Tyndale House Publishers, 1976. 139 p. ; 21 cm. [BS580.J4H66] 75-37233 ISBN 0-8423-8480-4 : 2.95
1. Jeremiah, the prophet. I. Title.

LEVINE, Etan. 224'.3'04
The Aramaic version of Lamentations / Etan Levine. New York : Hermon Press, 1976. 203 p. ; 25 cm. Aramaic text of Lamentations and English translation : p. 25-74. Includes index. Bibliography: p. 203. [BS1535.3.L48] 76-276212 14.95
1. Bible. O.T. Lamentations—Commentaries. I. Bible. O.T. Lamentations. Aramaic. 1976. II. Bible. O.T. Lamentations. English. Levine. 1976. III. Title.

WRIGHT, John Stafford. 224'.3'07
Lamentations, Ezekiel, Daniel [by] J. Stafford Wright. [1st U.S. ed.] Grand Rapids, Mich., Eerdmans [1970, c1969] 93 p. 19 cm. (Scripture Union Bible study books) Cover title: Lamentations—Daniel. [BS1535.3.W75 1970] 70-112951 1.25
1. Bible. O.T. Lamentations—Commentaries. 2. Bible. O.T. Ezekiel—Commentaries. 3. Bible. O.T. Daniel—Commentaries. I. Title.

BOYD, Frank Mathews, 1883- 224.4
Book of the Prophet Ezekiel. Springfield, Mo., Gospel Pub. House [1951] 232 p. illus., map. 20 cm. [BS1545.B68] 51-4501
1. Bible. O. T. Ezekiel—Commentaries. I. Title.

ERDMAN, Charles Rosenbury, 224.4
1866-
The book of Ezekiel, an exposition. [Westwood, N. J., Revell [1956] 156 p. 20 cm. [BS1545.E7] 56-7442
1. Bible. O. T. Ezekiel—Commentaries. I. Title.

LEVENSON, Jon Douglas. 224'.4'06
Theology of the program of restoration of Ezekiel 40-48 / by Jon Douglas Levenson. Cambridge, Mass. : Published by Scholars Press for the Harvard Semitic Museum, 1976. p. cm. (Harvard Semitic monograph ; 10) Thesis—Harvard University, 1975. Bibliography: p. [BS1545.5.L48 1976] 76-3769 ISBN 0-89130-105-4 : 5.60
1. Bible. O.T. Ezekiel XL-XLVIII—Theology. I. Title. II. Series.

TORREY, Charles Cutler, 224'.4'06
1863-1956.
Pseudo-Ezekiel and the original prophecy. New York, Ktav Pub. House, 1970. xxxix, 11-261 p. 24 cm. (The Library of Biblical studies) Reprint of the 1930 ed. issued as Yale oriental series, researches, v. 18, with critical articles by S. Spiegel and C. C. Torrey (p. [121]-261) and a prolegomenon by M. Greenberg. Bibliography: p. xxxix. [BS1545.2.T6 1970] 72-78785
1. Bible. O.T. Ezekiel—Criticism, interpretation, etc. I. Spiegel, Shalom, 1899- II. Title. III. Series.

CARLEY, Keith W. 224'.4'066
Ezekiel among the prophets : a study of Ezekiel's place in prophetic tradition / Keith W. Carley. Naperville, Ill. : A. R. Allenson, [1974 or 1975] x, 112 p. ; 22 cm. (Studies in Biblical theology : 2d ser. ; 31) Includes bibliographical references and indexes. [BS1545.2.C37] 74-23023 ISBN 0-8401-3081-3 pbk. : 8.25
1. Bible. O.T. Ezekiel—Criticism, interpretation, etc. I. Title. II. Series.

ALEXANDER, Ralph. 224'.4'07
Ezekiel / by Ralph Alexander. Chicago : Moody Press, c1976. 160 p. : ill. ; 19 cm. Bibliography: p. 160. [BS1545.3.A43] 75-45234 ISBN 0-8024-2026-5 pbk. : 1.95
1. Bible. O.T. Ezekiel—Commentaries. I. Title.

BLACKWOOD, Andrew 224.407
Watterson, 1915-
Ezekiel; Prophecy of hope, by Andrew W. Blackwood, Jr. Grand Rapids, Baker Book House, 1965. 274 p. 23 cm. Bibliography: p. 8. [BS1545.3.B55] 65-18261

1. Bible. O. T. Ezekiel—Commentaries. I. Title.

BLACKWOOD, Andrew 224'.4'07
Watterson 1915-
The other son of man: Ezekiel/Jesus, by Andrew W. Blackwood, Jr. Grand Rapids, Baker Bk. [c.1966] 165p. 23cm. [BS1545.2.B55] 66-27967 3.95
1. Bible. O. T. Ezekiel—Criticism, interpretation, etc. 2. Son of Man. I. Title.

BLACKWOOD, Andrew 224'.4'07
Watterson, 1915-
The other son of man: Ezekiel/Jesus, by Andrew W. Blackwood, Jr. Grand Rapids, Baker Book House [c1966] 165 p. 23 cm. [BS1545.2.B55] 66-27967
1. Bible. O. T. Ezekiel—Criticism, interpretation, etc. 2. Son of Man I. Title.

BLACKWOOD, Andrew 224.407
Watterson, Jr., 1915-
Ezekiel; prophecy of hope. Grand Rapids, Mich., Baker Bk. [c.]1965. 274p. 23cm. Bibl. [BS1545.3.B55] 65-18261 4.50
1. Bible. O.T. Ezekiel—Commentaries. I. Title.

FAIRBAIRN, Patrick 224.407
An exposition of Ezekiel. Grand Rapids, Mich., zondervan Pub. House [1960] 504p. 23cm. (Classic commentary library) Previous editions published under title: Ezekiel and the book of his prophecy. 60-2521 5.95
1. Bible. O. T. Ezekiel—Commentaries. I. Title.

FEINBERG, Charles Lee. 224'.4'07
The prophecy of Ezekiel; the glory of the Lord. Chicago, Moody Press [1969] 286 p. 24 cm. Bibliography: p. 280-283. [BS1545.3.F4] 79-11270 4.95
1. Bible. O.T. Ezekiel—Commentaries. I. Title.

TAYLOR, John Bernard. 224'.4'07
Ezekiel; an introduction and commentary, by John B. Taylor. [1st ed.] Downers Grove, Ill., Inter-Varsity Press [1969] 285 p. illus. 19 cm. (The Tyndale Old Testament commentaries) Bibliographical footnotes. [BS1545.3.T34 1969b] 75-98041 3.95
1. Bible. O.T. Ezekiel—Commentaries.

BIBLE. O.T. Ezekiel. 224'.4'077
English. New English. 1974.
The book of the prophet Ezekiel / commentary by Keith W. Carley. London ; New York : Cambridge University Press, 1974. x, 331 p. : ill. ; 21 cm. (The Cambridge Bible commentary : New English Bible) Includes index. Bibliography: p. 323. [BS1543.C37] 73-94352 ISBN 0-521-08653-1 15.50 ISBN 0-521-09755-X pbk. : 5.95
1. Bible. O.T. Ezekiel—Commentaries. I. Carley, Keith W. II. Title. III. Series.

EICHRODT, Walther, 224'.4'077
1890-
Ezekiel; a commentary. [Translated by Cosslett Quin from the German] Philadelphia, Westminster Press [1970] xiv, 594 p. 23 cm. (The Old Testament library) Translation of Der Prophet Hesekiel, originally published as v. 22 of Das Alte Testament deutsch. Bibliography: p. [xiii]-xiv. [BS1545.3.E3713 1970b] 71-117646 12.50
1. Bible. O.T. Ezekiel—Commentaries. I. Bible. O.T. Ezekiel. English. 1970. II. Title. III. Series.

GAEBELEIN, Arno 224'.4'077
Clemens, 1861-1945.
The prophet Ezekiel; an analytical exposition. [2d ed., rev.] Neptune, N.J., Loizeaux Bros. [1972, c1918] 346 p. 22 cm. [BS1545.G3 1972] 72-88419 ISBN 0-87213-217-X 4.25
1. Bible. O.T. Ezekiel—Commentaries. I. Title.

GAEBELEIN, Arno 224'.4'077
Clemens, 1861-1945.
The prophet Ezekiel; an analytical exposition. [2d ed., rev.] Neptune, N.J., Loizeaux Bros. [1972, c1918] 346 p. 22 cm. [BS1545.G3 1972] 72-88419 ISBN 0-87213-217-X 4.25
1. Bible. O.T. Ezekiel—Commentaries. I. Title.

BIBLE. O.T. Daniel. 224.5
English. 1948. Westminster version.
The book of Daniel, by C. Lattey. Dublin, Browne & Nolan [dist. Mystic, Conn., Lawrence Verry, 1964] lii, 143p. 22cm. Bibl. 50-36293 3.00
1. Bible. O.T. Daniel—Commentaries. I. Lattey, Cuthbert, 1877- ed. II. Title.

CRISWELL, Wallie A. 224'.5
Expository sermons on the book of Daniel, by W. A. Criswell. Grand Rapids, Mich., Zondervan Pub. Co. [1968-72] 4 v. 22 cm. Contents.Contents.—v. 1. Introductory materials and discussion.—v. 2. Daniel I-III.—v. 3. Daniel IV-VI.—v. 4. Daniel VII-XII. [BS1555.4.C7] 68-27468
1. Bible. O.T. Daniel—Sermons. 2. Sermons, American. 3. Baptists—Sermons. I. Title.

CROWTHER, Duane S 224.5
Prophecy, key to the future. [1st ed.] Salt Lake City, Bookcraft [1962] 355 p. illus. 24 cm. [BT891.C7] 62-53407
1. Bible — Prophecies. 2. Millennium I. Title.

CULVER, Robert D 224.5
Daniel and the latter days. [Westwood, N. J.] F. H. Revell Co. [1954] 221p. 21cm. [BT885.C89] 54-5434
1. Millennium. 2. Bible. O. T. Daniel—Prophecies. I. Title.

GAEBELEIN, Arno Clemens, 224.5
1861-
The Prophet Daniel; a key to the visions and prophecies of the book of Daniel. Grand Rapids, Kregel Publications, 1955. 212p. 20cm. [BS1556] 55-9465
1. Bible. O. T. Daniel—Prophecies. I. Title.

IRONSIDE, Henry Allan, 224.5
1876-1951.
Lectures on Daniel the Prophet. [2d ed.] New York, Loizeaux Bros. [1953] 253p. illus. 20cm. [BS1556.I68 1953] 54-32509
1. Bible. O. T. Daniel—Prophecies. I. Title.

KEMPIN, Albert J, 1900- 224.5
Daniel for today. Anderson, Ind., Gospel Trumpet Co. [1952] 159 p. 20 cm. [BS1555.K37] 52-29313
1. Bible. O. T. Daniel—Criticism, interpretation, etc. I. Title.

*MAXWELL, Arthur S. 224.5
God and the future. Mountain View, Calif., Pacific Pr. Pub. [1967] 80p. illus. 18cm. T.p. and text in Russian. .50 pap.,
1. Bible. O.T. Daniel—Criticism, interpretation, etc. 2. Seventh-Day Adventists—Doctrinal and controversial works. I. Title.

NEWELL, Philip Rutherford, 224.5
1902-
Daniel: the man greatly beloved, and his prophecies. Chicago, Moody Press, 1951. 191 p. 20 cm. [BS1556.N35] 51-4099
1. Bible. O. T. Daniel — Prophecies. I. Title.

PRICE, George McCready, 224.5
1870-
The greatest of the prophets; a new commentary on the book of Daniel. Mountain View, Calif., Pacific Press Pub. Association [1955] 342p. 23cm. [BS1555.P68] 55-7093
1. Bible. O. T. Daniel—Commentaries. 2. Bible. O. T. Daniel—Prophecies. I. Title.

ROWLEY, Harold Henry, 1890- 224.5
Darius the Mede and the four world empires in the book of Daniel; a historical study of contemporary theories. Cardiff, Univ. of Wales Pr. Bd. [dist. Mystic, Conn., Verry, 1965] xxxiii, 195p. 23cm. Bibl. [BS1555.R6] 4.50
1. Darius, the Mede. 2. Bible. O. T. Daniel—Criticism, interpretation, etc. 3. Bible—Criticism, interpretation, etc.—O. T. Daniel. I. Title.

*SCHENCK, Joann 224.5
Three men who walked in fire; Daniel 3 for children. Illus. by Sally Mathews. St. Louis, Concordia, 1967. 1v. (unpaged) col. illus. 21cm. (Arch bks.) .35 pap.,
1. Bible—O.T.— Daniel—Juvenile literature. I. Title.

TALBOT, Louis Thompson, 224.5
1889-
The prophecies of Daniel in the light of past, present, and future events. [3d ed.] Wheaton, Ill., Van Kampen Press [1954, c1940] 234p. illus. 20cm. [BS1556] 54-13527
1. Bible. O. T. Daniel—Prophecies. I. Title.

TULGA, Chester Earl, 1896- 224.5
Premillennialists and their critics. Somerset, Ky., Eastern Baptist Institute [1961] 62 p. 19 cm. [BT891.T8] 62-3612
1. Millennium. I. Title.

VAN Zeller, Hubert, Father, 224.5
1905-
Daniel: man of desires. Westminster, Md., Newman Press, 1951. 231 p. 19 cm. [BS1555.V3] 51-14577
1. Bible. O.T. Daniel — Commentaries. I. Title.

WORDEN, Hazel Irene, 1899- 224.5
Our falling image, fulfilling Daniel's prophecy. Art work by Francis Sutherland. [Los Angeles 1950] 81 p. illus. 19 cm. [BS1556.W65] 50-31158
1. Bible. O. T. Daniel — Prophecies. I. Title.

ANDERSON, Roy Allan. 224'.5'015
Unfolding Daniel's prophecies / Roy Allan Anderson. Mountain View, Calif. : Pacific Press Pub. Association, c1975. 192 p. ; 22 cm. (Dimension ; 120) Includes index. Bibliography: p. 182-185. [BS1556.A65] 75-16526 pbk. : 2.95
1. Daniel, the prophet. 2. Bible. O.T. Daniel—Prophecies. I. Title.

BLOOMFIELD, Arthur 224.5015
Edward, 1895-
The end of the days; a study of Daniel's visions. Minneapolis, Bethany Fellowship [1961] 279p. illus. 22cm. [BS1556.B55] 61-42470
1. Bible. O. T. Daniel—Prophecies. I. Title.

LANG, George Henry, 224'.5'015
1874-1958.
The histories and prophecies of Daniel. Grand Rapids, Kregel Publications [1973, c1940] 224 p. 23 cm. Reprint of the 4th ed. published in 1950 by Paternoster Press, London. [BS1555.2.L36 1973] 73-81797 ISBN 0-8254-3104-2 4.95
1. Bible. O.T. Daniel—Criticism, interpretation, etc. I. Title.

LOWE, Marmion L. 224'.5'015
Christ in the Book of Daniel, by Marmion L. Lowe. Bible School Park, N.Y. [1968] xv, 193 p. 20 cm. [BS1556.L6] 68-3309
1. Bible. O.T. Daniel—Prophecies. 2. Messiah—Prophecies. I. Title.

BIBLE. O.T. Daniel. 224'.5'0524
English. Concordant version. 1968.
Concordant literal Old Testament: the book of Daniel. Saugus, Calif., Concordant Pub. Concern [1968] 64 p. 19 cm. [BS895.C6] 68-3510
I. Title.

ANDERSON, Robert, Sir 224.506
1841-1918.
The coming Prince; the marvellous prophecy of Daniel's seventy weeks concerning the Antichrist. 15th ed. Grand Rapids, Kregel Publication, 1963. liv, 311 p. 22 cm. Bibliographical footnotes. [BS1556.A64 1963] 63-1164
1. Bible. O. T. Daniel — Prophecies. 2. Antichrist. I. Title.

BOUTFLOWER, Charles, 224.506
1846-
In and around the book of Daniel. Pref. by Theophilus G. Pinches. Grand Rapids, Mich., Zondervan [1963] 312p. illus. map. 23cm. Bibl. 63-2120 4.95
1. Bible. O. T. Daniel—Criticism, Interpretation, etc. 2. Babylonia—Hist. I. Title.

BOUTFLOWER, Charles, 224'.5'06
1846-1936.
In and around the book of Daniel / by Charles Boutflower. Grand Rapids : Kregel Publications, 1977. xxiii, 314 p., [12] leaves of plates : ill. ; 23 cm. (Kregel reprint library) Reprint of the 1923 ed. published by Society for Promoting Christian Knowledge, London; Macmillan, New York. Includes indexes. Bibliography: p. 297-301. [BS1555.B6 1977] 77-7648 ISBN 0-8254-2229-9 : 9.95
1. Bible. O.T. Daniel—Criticism, interpretation, etc. 2. Babylonia—History. I. Title.

COLLINS, John Joseph, 224'.5'06
1946-
The apocalyptic vision of the book of Daniel / by Bob Devine ; [pictures by Carlyn Bowser]. Missoula, Mont. : Published by Scholars Press for Harvard Semitic Museum, c1977. xx, 239 p. ; 23 cm. (Harvard semitic monographs ; no. 16) Bibliography: p. 225-239. [BS1555.2.C64] 77-23124 ISBN 0-89130-133-X : 6.00
1. Bible. O.T. Daniel—Criticism, interpretation, etc. I. Bowser, Carolyn Ewing. II. Harvard University. Semitic Museum. III. Title. IV. Series.

CULVER, Robert Duncan. 224'.5'06
Daniel and the latter days / by Robert Duncan Culver. Rev. ed. Chicago : Moody Press, c1977. p. cm. Includes index. Bibliography: p. [BT891.C84 1977] 77-10027 ISBN 0-8024-1755-8 pbk. : 3.95
1. Bible. O.T. Daniel—Prophecies. 2. Millennium. I. Title.

CULVER, Robert Duncan. 224'.5'06
Daniel and the latter days / by Robert Duncan Culver. Rev. ed. Chicago : Moody Press, c1977. p. cm. Includes index. Bibliography: p. [BT891.C84 1977] 77-10027 ISBN 0-8024-1755-8 pbk. : 3.95
1. Bible. O.T. Daniel—Prophecies. 2. Millennium. I. Title.

KELLY, William, 1821- 224'.5'06
1906.
Notes on the Book of Daniel, a most valuable and lucid exposition of the prophecies of this book, with practical applications of its moral lessons. [8th ed.] New York, Loizeaux Bros. [1952] 270p. 19cm. [BS1555.K36 1952] 55-41735
1. Bible. O. T. Daniel —Commentaries. I. Title.

KEPLER, Thomas Samuel, 224.506
1897-
Dream of the future: Daniel and Revelation. London, Lutterworth Press Nashville, Abingdon [1963] 94p. 20cm. (Bible guides, no. 22) 63-483 1.00 pap.,
1. Bible. O. T. Daniel—Introductions. 2. Bible. N. T. Revelation—Introductions. I. Title.

NEWELL, Philip 224.506
Rutherford, 1902-
Daniel, the man greatly beloved and his prophecies. Chicago, Moody [c.]1962. 199p. 22cm. 62-52000 3.00
1. Bible. O. T. Daniel—Prophecies. I. Title.

WHITCOMB, John Clement, 224.506
1924-
Darius the Mede; a study in historical identification. Grand Rapids, Eerdmans [1959] 84 p. illus. 23 cm. "An Evangelical Theological Society publication." Includes bibliography. [BS1555.W5] 59-8746
1. Darius, the Mede. 2. Bible. O.T. Daniel — Criticism, interpretation, etc. I. Title.

BLAIR, J. Allen. 224'.5'066
Living courageously; a devotional study of the book of Daniel, by J. Allen Blair. [Chicago] Moody Press [1971] 251 p. 20 cm. [BS1555.4.B53] 70-140898 ISBN 0-87213-030-4 3.95
1. Bible. O.T. Daniel—Devotional literature. I. Title.

SILVA, Antone R. 224'.5'066
Emanuel.
A critical analysis of the historicity of the Book of Daniel, by Antone R. Emanuel Silva. [Boston, Thompson's Academy, 1968] 32, [4] p. 24 cm. Bibliography: p. [35]-[36] [BS1555.2.S5] 68-3918
1. Bible. O.T. Daniel—Criticism, interpretation, etc. I. Title.

WILSON, Robert Dick, 224'.5'066
1856-1930.
Studies in the book of Daniel. Grand Rapids, Mich., Baker Book House [1972, c1917-38] 2 v. in 1. 23 cm. (Limited editions library) Vol. 2 originally edited by O. T. Allis. Bibliography: v. 1, p. 391-396. [BS1555.W69 1972] 72-195915 ISBN 0-8010-9530-1 9.95
1. Bible. O.T. Daniel—Criticism, interpretation, etc. I. Allis, Oswald Thompson, 1880- ed. II. Title.

BIBLE. O. T. Daniel. 224.507
English. 1959. Authorized.
The book of Daniel. [By H. Deane] Rapids, Zondervan Pub. House [1960] 108p. geneal. table. 18cm. (The Layman's handy commentary series) 'The contents of this commentary appear ... in Ellicott's commentary on the whole Bible.'--Jacket. Bibliographical footnotes. [BS1555.E5 1960] 60-2759
1. Bible. O. T. Daniel—Commentaries. I. Deane, Henry, 1838—1894. II. Ellicott, Charles John, Bp. of Gloucester, 1819-1905, ed. III. Title.

BIBLE. O. T. Daniel. 224.507
English. 1959. Authorized.
The book of Daniel. [By H. deane] Edited by Charles John Ellicott. [New ed.] Grand Rapids, Mich., Zondervan Pub. House [1959, i.e., 1960] 108 p. geneal. table. 18 cm. (The Layman's handy commentary series) "The contents of this commentary appear...in Ellicott's commentary on the whole Bible."—Jacket. Bibliographical footnotes. 60-2759 1.95
1. Bible. O. T. Daniel—Commentaries. I. Deane, Henry, 1838-1894. II. Ellicott, Charles John, Bp. of Gloucester, 1819-1905, ed. III. Title.

HIERONYMUS, Saint. 224.507
Jerome's commentary on Daniel. Translated by Gleason L. Archer, Jr. Grand Rapids, Baker Book House, 1958. 189p. 20cm. [BS1555.H453] 58-59818
1. Bible. O. T. Daniel—Commentaries. I. Archer, Gleason Leonard, 1916- tr. II. Title.

*JOHNSON, Philip C. 224.507
The book of Daniel; a study manual. Grand Rapids, Mich., Baker Bk. [c.]1964. 96p. 19cm. (Shield Biblestudy ser.) 1.50 pap.,
I. Title.

KING, Geoffrey R. 224'.5'07
Daniel; a detailed explanation of the book, by Geoffrey R. King. [Corr. and rev.] Grand Rapids, Eerdmans [1966] 248 p. 20 cm. "First given [as] weekly [lectures] at the author's Bible School in connection with the East London Tabernacle." [BS1555.2.K54 1966] 67-4081
1. Bible. O.T. Daniel—Criticism, interpretation, etc. I. Title.

PHILIP, James. 224'.5'07
By the rivers of Babylon: studies in the Book of Daniel. Aberdeen (60 Union Row,

Aberdeen, AB1 1SA), Didasko Press, [1971- v. 21 cm. Contents.—pt. 1. Chapters 1-6. [BS1555.2.P47] 72-186716 ISBN 0-903120-02-X (v. 1) £0.20 (v. 1)
1. Bible. O.T. Daniel. I-VI—Criticism, interpretation, etc. I. Title.

PORTEOUS, Norman W. 224.507
Daniel: a commentary. Philadelphia, Westminster [c.1962, 1965] 173p. 23cm. (Old Testament lib.) Bibl. [BS1555.3.P613] 65-21071 4.00
1. Bible. O.T. Daniel—Commentaries. I. Bible. O.T. Daniel. English. 1965. II. Title. III. Series.

TATFORD, Frederick A., 1901- 224.507
The climax of the ages; studies in the prophecy of Daniel. Appendix by F. F. Bruce. Grand Rapids, Mich., Zondervan [1964, c.1953] 256 p. 19 cm. 64-2547 1.50, pap.
1. Bible. O. T. Daniel—Prophecies. I. Title.

WOOD, Leon James. 224'.5'07
Daniel : a study guide / by Leon J. Wood. Grand Rapids : Zondervan Pub. House, c1975. 160 p. : ill. ; 20 cm. Bibliography: p. 159-160. [BS1555.3.W67] 74-11864 pbk. : 1.95
1. Bible. O.T. Daniel—Commentaries. 2. Bible. O.T. Daniel—Study—Text-books. I. Title.

BIBLE. O. T. Daniel. English. New English. 1976. 224'.5'077
The Book of Daniel / commentary by Raymond Hammer. Cambridge ; New York : Cambridge University Press, [1976] p. cm. (The Cambridge Bible commentary, New English Bible) Includes index. Bibliography: p. [BS1553.H35] 76-4241 ISBN 0-521-08654-X. pbk. : 3.95
1. Bible. O.T. Daniel—Commentaries. I. Hammer, Raymond. II. Title. III. Series.

KNOCH, Adolf E. 224'.5'077
Concordant studies in the book of Daniel [by] A. E. Knoch. Saugus, Calif., Concordant Pub. Concern [1968] 464 p. (p. [460]-464, advertisements) 19 cm. [BS1555.3.K59] 72-261
1. Bible. O.T. Daniel—Commentaries. I. Title.

STRAUSS, Lehman. 224'.5'077
The prophecies of Daniel. [1st ed.] Neptune, N.J., Loizeaux Bros. [1969] 384 p. 20 cm. On spine: Daniel. Bibliography: p. 371-372. [BS1555.3.S8] 70-85293 4.95
1. Bible. O.T. Daniel—Commentaries. I. Title.

WALVOORD, John F. 224'.5'077
Daniel, the key to prophetic revelation. A commentary by John F. Walvoord. Chicago, Moody Press [1971] 317 p. 24 cm. Bibliography: p. 298-304. [BS1555.3.W33] 75-123161 6.95
1. Bible. O.T. Daniel—Commentaries. I. Title.

ZIMMERMANN, Felix H. 224'.5'077
Daniel in Babylon [by] Felix H. Zimmermann. [1974 revision] Broadview, Ill., Gibbs Pub. Co. [1974] xiii, 195 p. 22 cm. [BS1555.2.Z55] 73-86013 4.95
1. Bible. O.T. Daniel—Commentaries. I. Bible. O.T. Daniel. English. 1974. II. Title.

KRENTEL. MILDRED. 224.5095
I see 4; a story based on the third chapter of Daniel. Illustrated by William Lent. New York, Loizeaux Bros., c1959. unpaged illus. 26cm. in verse. [BS580.D2K7] 59-4876
1. Daniel. the prophet—Juvenile literature. I. Title.

CHRISTIAN, Mary Blount. 224'.5'09505
Daniel, who dared : Daniel in the lions' den for beginning readers : Daniel 1:1-8, 6 for children / by Mary Blount Christian ; illustrated by Aline Cunningham. St. Louis : Concordia Pub. House, c1977. [48] p. : col. ill. ; 23 cm. (I can read a Bible story) Tells the story of Daniel in the lions' den. [BS580.D2C47] 77-6412 ISBN 0-570-07325-1 : 3.95. ISBN 0-570-07319-7 pbk. : 1.95
1. Daniel, the prophet—Juvenile literature. 2. Bible. O.T.—Biography—Juvenile literature. I. Cunningham, Aline. II. Title.

BIBLE. O.T. Prophets. English. 1963. Phillips. 224.52
Four prophets: Amos, Hosea, First Isaiah, Micah; a modern translation from the Hebrew, by J. B. Phillips. New York, Macmillan, 1963. xxvii, 161 p. maps. 22 cm. [BS1503.P5] 63-16748
I. Phillips, John Bertram, 1906- tr. II. Title.

RAND, Howard B 1889- 224.6
Study in Hosea. Haverhill, Mass., Destiny Publishers [1955] 154p. 21cm. [BS580.H6R3] 55-12181
1. House, the prophet. 2. Angio-Israelism. I. Title.

WHITE, Kenneth Owen, 1902- 224.6
Studies in Hosea; God's incomparable love. Nashville, Convention Press [1957] 142 p. 19 cm. [BS1565.W48] 57-12144
1. Bible. O.T. Hosea — Study — Text-books. I. Title.

*BENNETT, T. Miles 224'.6'07
Hosea: prophet of God's love; a study guide and exposition of the Book of Hosea, [by] T. Miles Bennett. Grand Rapids, Baker Book House, [1975] 116 p. 18 cm. [BS1565.3] ISBN 0-8010-0645-7 1.25 (pbk.)
1. Bible. O.T. Hosea—Commentaries. I. Title.

GARLAND, D. David. 224'.6'07
Hosea : a study guide commentary / D. David Garland. Grand Rapids : Zondervan Pub. House, c1975. 81 p. ; 21 cm. (The "Study guide" series) Includes bibliographical references. [BS1565.3.G37] 75-6180 pbk. : 1.95
1. Bible. O.T. Hosea—Commentaries. I. Title.

HONEYCUTT, Roy Lee. 224'.6'07
Hosea and his message / Roy L. Honeycutt. Nashville : Broadman Press, [1975] 96 p. ; 19 cm. [BS1565.3.H66] 74-33075 ISBN 0-8054-1212-3 pbk. : 1.50
1. Bible. O.T. Hosea—Commentaries. I. Title.

HUBBARD, David Allan. 224'.6'07
With bands of love; lessons from the Book of Hosea. Grand Rapids, W. B. Eerdmans Pub. Co. [1968] 114 p. maps. 20 cm. [BS1565.3.H8] 67-19320
1. Bible. O. T. Hosea—Commentaries. I. Title.

KNIGHT, George Angus Fulton 224.607
Hosea introduction and commentary. London, SCM Press[dist New York, Macmillan, 1960] 127p. (Bibl.) 20cm. (Torch Bible commentaries) 60-3070 2.25 bds.,
1. Bible. O. T. Hosea—Commentaries. I. Title.

LOGSDON, S Franklin. 224.607
Hosea: people who forgot God; an exposition of Hosea. Chicago, Moody Press [c1959] 127p. 18cm. (Colportage library, 386) [BS1565.L6] 60-765
1. Bible. O. T. Hosea— Commentaries. I. Title.

VALLOWE, Ed. F. 224.607
Preaching from Hosea. Grand Rapids, Mich., Baker Bk. [c.]1963. 98p. 20cm. (Minister's handbk. ser.) 63-20015 1.95 bds.,
1. Bible. O.T. Hosea—Commentaries. I. Title.

MAYS, James Luther. 224'.6'07'7
Hosea, a commentary. Philadelphia, Westminster Press [1969] x, 190 p. 23 cm. (The Old Testament library) Bibliographical footnotes. [BS1565.3.M36 1969b] 75-79618 6.00
1. Bible. O.T. Hosea—Commentaries. I. Bible. O.T. Hosea. English. Revised Standard. 1969. II. Title. III. Series.

WOLFF, Hans Walter. 224'.6'077
Hosea : a commentary on the book of the Prophet Hosea / by Hans Walter Wolff ; translated by Gary Stansell ; edited by Paul D. Hanson. Philadelphia : Fortress Press, [1974] xxxii, 259 p. : facsim. ; 25 cm. (Hermeneia) Translation of Dodekapropheton 1: Hosea (2. Aufl.) Includes bibliographies and indexes. [BS1565.3.W64213] 70-179634 ISBN 0-8006-6004-8 : 19.95
1. Bible. O.T. Hosea—Commentaries. I. Bible. O.T. Hosea. English. Wolff. 1974. II. Title. III. Series.

WARD, James Merrill, 1928- 224.67
Hosea; a theological commentary, by James M. Ward [1st ed.] New York, Harper & Row [1966] xxi, 264 p. 22 cm. Bibliography: p. 249. [BS1565.2.W3] 66-13917
1. Bible. O. T. Hosea — Theology. I. Title.

WARD, James Merrill, 1928- 224.67
Hosea; a theological commentary. New York, Harper [c.1966] xxi, 264p. 22cm. Bibl. [BS1565.2.W3] 66-13917 5.00
1. Bible. O. T. Hosea—Theology. I. Title.

PRICE, Walter K. 224'.7'066
The Prophet Joel and the day of the Lord / by Walter K. Price. Chicago : Moody Press, c1976. p. cm. Includes bibliographical references. [BS1575.2.P74] 76-23253 ISBN 0-8024-6904-3 : 3.95
1. Bible. O.T. Joel—Criticism, interpretation, etc. 2. Day of Jehovah. I. Title.

DI GANGI, Mariano. 224'.7'07
The book of Joel; a study manual. Grand Rapids, Mich., Baker Book House [1970] 78 p. 20 cm. (Shield Bible study series) Bibliography: p. 77-78. [BS1575.3.D53] 73-115900 1.95
1. Bible. O.T. Joel—Commentaries. I. Title.

GARLAND, D. David. 224.8007
Amos; a study guide with questions for discussion, by D. David Garland. Grand Rapids, Zondervan Pub. House [1966] 96 p. 21 cm. [BS1585.5.G3] 66-18948
1. Bible. O.T. Amos—Study. I. Title.

YATES, Kyle M 1924- 224.8007
Studies in Amos [by] Kyle M. Yates, Jr. Nashville, Convention Press [1966] vii, 136 p. 19 cm. "Church study course [of the Sunday School Board of the Southern Convention] This book is number 31 in category 2, section for adults and young people." Includes bibliographies. [BS1585.5.Y3] 66-22775
1. Bible. O. T. Amos — Study. I. Southern Baptist Convention. Sunday School Board. II. Title.

WEITZNER, Emil. 224*.8*02
The book of Amos; prologue, paraphrase, epilogue. New York, 1963. 1 v. (unpaged) illus. 21 cm. [BS1586.W44] 72-222364
1. Bible. O.T. Amos—Paraphrases, English. I. Title.

CRENSHAW, James L. 224'.8'06
Hymnic affirmation of divine justice : the doxologies of Amos and related texts in the Old Testament / by James L. Crenshaw. Missoula, Mont. : Published by Scholars Press for the Society of Biblical Literature, c1975. xii, 178 p. ; 22 cm. (Dissertation series ; no. 24) Originally presented as the author's thesis, Vanderbilt University, 1964. Bibliography: p. 159-178. [BS1585.2.C73 1975] 75-22349 ISBN 0-89130-016-3 pbk. : 4.20 4.20
1. Bible. O.T. Amos—Criticism, interpretation, etc. 2. Praise of God—Biblical teaching. 3. Doxology. I. Title. II. Series: Society of Biblical Literature. Dissertation series ; no. 24.

ROUTTENBERG, Hyman J. 224'.8'06
Amos of Tekoa; a study in interpretation [by] Hyman J. Routtenberg. With a foreword by Louis Finkelstein. [1st ed.] New York, Vantage Press [1971] 194 p. 22 cm. Bibliography: p. 190-194. [BS1585.3.R65] 72-21643 4.95
1. Bible. O.T. Amos—Commentaries. 2. Bible. O.T. Amos—Criticism, interpretation, etc., Jewish. I. Title.

WATTS, John D W 224.806
Studying the book of Amos [by] John D. W. Watts. Nashville, Broadman Press [1966] 93 p. 21 cm. Includes bibliographical references. [BS1585.2.W3] 66-19904
1. Bible. O.T. Amos — Criticism, interpretation, etc. I. Title.

WATTS, John D. W. 224.806
Studying the book of Amos. Nashville, Broadman [c.1966] 93p. 21cm. Bibl. [BS1585.2.W3] 66-19904 1.50 pap.,
1. Bible. O.T. Amos—Criticism, interpretation, etc. I. Title.

WATTS, John D W 224.806
Vision and prophecy in Amos. Grand Rapids, Eerdmans [1958] viii, 89 p. 23 cm. (Riischilkon, Switzerland. Baptist Theological Seminary. Faculty lectures, 1955) Includes bibliography. [BS1585.W3] 58-13511
1. Bible. O. T. Amos — Criticism, interpretation, etc. I. Title. II. Series.

HAMMERSHAIMB, Erling, 1904- 224'.8'07
The book of Amos: a commentary. Translated by John Sturdy. New York, Schocken Books [1970] 148 p. 23 cm. Translation of Amos. Bibliography: p. [145]-148. [BS1585.3.H313] 70-124678 ISBN 8-05-233741- 8.50
1. Bible. O.T. Amos—Commentaries. I. Title.

HONEYCUTT, Roy Lee 224.807
Amos and his message, an expository commentary Nashville, Broadman [c.1963] viii, 182p. 22cm. Bibl. 63-19071 3.75
1. Bible. O.T. Amos—Commentaries. I. Title.

HONEYCUTT, Roy Lee. 224.807
Amos and his message, an expository commentary. Nashville, Broadman Press [1963] viii, 182 p. 22 cm. Bibliography: p. 178-182. [BS1585.3.H6] 63-19071
1. Bible O.T. Amos — Commentaries. I. Title.

KELLEY, Page H. 224.807
The Book of Amos; a study manual, by Page H. Kelley. Grand Rapids, Baker Bk. [1966] 98p. 20 cm. (Shield Bible study outlines) Bibl. [BS1585.3.K4] 66-18310 1.50 pap.,
1. Bible. O. T. Amos — commentaries. I. Title.

KELLEY, Page H. 224.807
The Book of Amos; a study manual, by Page H. Kelley. Grand Rapids, Baker Book House [1966] 98 p. 20 cm. (Shield Bible study outlines) Bibliography: p. 11. [BS1585.3.K4] 66-18310
1. Bible. O.T. Amos—Commentaries. I. Title.

MOTYER, J. A. 224'.8'07
The day of the lion : the message of Amos / J. A. Motyer. Downers Grove, Ill. : InterVarsity Press, 1974. 208 p. ; 21 cm. (The Voice of the Old Testament) Includes bibliographical references. [BS1585.3.M67] 74-14300 ISBN 0-87784-766-5 : 3.95
1. Bible. O.T. Amos—Commentaries. I. Title. II. Series.

THOROGOOD, Bernard. 224'.8'07
A guide to the Book of Amos : with theme discussions on judgement, social justice, priest and prophet / Bernard Thorogood. Valley Forge : Judson Press, 1977, c1971. x, 118 p. : ill. ; 22 cm. Reprint of the ed. published by S.P.C.K., London. Includes index. Bibliography: p. x. [BS1585.5.T48 1977] 76-48551 ISBN 0-8170-0725-3 pbk. : 3.95
1. Bible. O.T. Amos—Study. I. Title.

HOWARD, James Keir, 1934- 224'.8'077
Amos among the prophets [by] J. K. Howard. Grand Rapids, Baker Book House [1968, c1967] viii, 119 p. 20 cm. ([The New minister's handbook series) First published in 1967 under title: Among the prophets. Includes bibliographical references. [BS1585.3.H9 1968] 79-2529 2.95
1. Bible. O. T. Amos—Commentaries. I. Title.

MAYS, James Luther. 224'.8'077
Amos; a commentary. Philadelphia, Westminster Press [1969] viii, 168 p. 23 cm. (The Old Testament library) Includes bibliographical references. [BS1585.3.M34 1969b] 79-76885 5.50
1. Bible. O.T. Amos—Commentaries. I. Title. II. Series.

ALLEN, Leslie C. 224'.9
The books of Joel, Obadiah, Jonah, and Micah / by Leslie C. Allen. Grand Rapids, Mich. : Eerdmans, [1975] p. cm. (The New international commentary on the Old Testament) Bibliography: [BS1560.A65] 75-22484 ISBN 0-8028-2373-4 : 12.50
1. Bible. O.T. Minor prophets—Commentaries. I. Bible. O.T. Minor prophets. English. Selections. 1975. II. Title. III. Series.

BIBLE. O.T. Minor prophets. English. New English. 1971. 224.9
The books of Amos, Hosea and Micah; commentary by Henry McKeating. Cambridge, University Press, 1971. x, 198 p. 21 cm. (The Cambridge Bible commentary: New English Bible) Cover title: Amos, Hosea, Micah. Bibliography: p. 194. [BS1560.A3M26 1971] 72-170286 ISBN 0-521-08133-5 £2.20 ($6.95 U.S.)
1. Bible. O.T. Amos—Commentaries. 2. Bible. O.T. Hosea—Commentaries. 3. Bible. O.T. Micah—Commentaries. I. McKeating, Henry. II. Title. III. Title: Amos, Hosea, Micah. IV. Series.

BIBLE. O. T. Minor prophets. English. Paraphrases. 1967.Taylor. 224'.9
Men who dared; a modern retelling of the lives and messages of the Minor prophets, by Barbara Jurgenson. Paraphrase by Kenneth N. Taylor. Wheaton, Ill., Tyndale House [1967] 133 p. illus. 22 cm. [BS1560.A3T32] 67-28428
I. Taylor, Kenneth Nathaniel-. II. Jurgenson, Barbara. III. Title.

BIBLE. O.T. Minor prophets. English. Paraphrases. 1967. Taylor. 224'.9
Men who dared; a modern retelling of the lives and messages of the Minor prophets, by Barbara Jurgenson. Paraphrase by Kenneth N. Taylor. Wheaton, Ill., Tyndale House [1967] 133 p. illus. 22 cm. [BS1560.A3T32] 67-28428
I. Taylor, Kenneth Nathaniel. II. Jurgenson, Barbara. III. Title.

EDIGER, Peter J. 224'.9
The Prophets' report on religion in North America [by] Peter J. Ediger. Newton, Kan., Faith and Life Press [1971] 56 p. illus. 18 x 19 cm. [BS1606.E3] 78-150650 ISBN 0-87303-686-7
1. Bible. O.T. Prophets—Paraphrases, English. I. Title.

GAEBELEIN, Frank Ely, 1899- 224'.9
Four minor prophets: Obadiah, Jonah, Habakkuk, and Haggai; their message for today, by Frank E. Gaebelein. Chicago, Moody Press [1970] 253 p. 22 cm. Bibliography: p. 249-253. [BS1595.3.G3] 76-104828 4.95
1. Bible. O.T. Obadiah—Commentaries. 2. Bible. O.T. Jonah—Commentaries. 3. Bible. O.T. Habakkuk—Commentaries. 4. Bible. O.T. Haggai—Commentaries. I. Title.

JENSEN, Irving Lester. 224.'9
Haggai, Zechariah, Malachi : a self-study guide / Irving L. Jensen. [Chicago] : Moody Press, c1976. 96 p. : diagrs. ; 22 cm. (Bible self-study guides) Cover title. Bibliography: p. 90-91. [BS1655.5.J46] 75-36502 ISBN 0-8024-1037-5 pbk. : 1.95

1. Bible. O.T. Haggai—Study—Outlines, syllabi, etc. 2. Bible. O.T. Zechariah—Study—Outlines, syllabi, etc. 3. Bible. O.T. Malachi—Study—Outlines, syllabi, etc. I. Title.

LEWIS, Jack Pearl, 1919- 224.90007
The minor prophets. Grand Rapids, Mich., Baker Bk. [c.1966] 103p. 20cm. Bibl. [BS1560.L4] 66-18308 1.95
1. Bible. O. T. Minor prophets—Study. I. Title.

BUTLER, Paul T. 224'.9'007
The Minor prophets; the prophets of the decline: Obadiah, Joel, Jonah, Amos [and] Hosea, by Paul T. Butler. Joplin, Mo., College Press [1968] xiv, 606 p. illus., maps. 23 cm. (Bible study textbook series) Bibliography: p. 605-606. [BS1560.B8] 79-1493 6.95
1. Bible. O.T. Minor prophets—Study—Outlines, syllabi, etc.

LEWIS, Jack Pearl, 1919- 224.9007
The minor prophets, by Jack P. Lewis. Grand Rapids, Baker Book House [1966] 106. p. 20 cm. Includes bibliographies. [BS1560.L4] 66-18308
1. Bible. O. T. Minor prophets — Study. I. Title.

FEIGON, Gershon J., 1916- 224'.9'042
Yemenite Targum manuscript to the twelve Minor prophets, by Gershon J. Feigon. An ancient handwritten Hebrew Bible discovered in Yemen: containing an Aramaic Targum translation; and, the Arabic translation of R. Saadye Gaon. San Diego, Calif., Bureau of Jewish Education [1971] 54 p. facsims. 22 cm. [BS1560.A4A75] 79-157662
1. Bible. O.T. Minor prophets. Aramaic. Targum Jonathan—Criticism, Textual. 2. Bible. O.T. Hebrew. Jewish Theol. Sem. Libr. MSS. (Enelow Memorial Collection, no. 27) I. Title.

HUNTER, John Edward, 1909- 224'.9'06
Major truths from the minor prophets / John E. Hunter. Grand Rapids : Zondervan Pub. House, c1977. 128 p. ; 18 cm. [BS1560.H8] 76-26968 pbk :
1. Bible. O.T. Minor prophets—Criticism, interpretation, etc. I. Title.

HUNTER, John Edward, 1909- 224'.9'06
Major truths from the minor prophets / John E. Hunter. Grand Rapids : Zondervan Pub. House, c1977. 128 p. ; 18 cm. [BS1560.H8] 76-26968 pbk :
1. Bible. O.T. Minor prophets—Criticism, interpretation, etc. I. Title.

WOOD, Fred M. 22'4.9'06
Yesterday's voices for today's world [by] Fred M. Wood. Nashville, Broadman [1967] 128p. 20cm. Bibl. [BS1560.W6] 67-17431 150 bds.,
1. Bible. O. T. Minor Prophets—Introductions. I. Title.

HAILEY, Homer, 1904- 224'.9'066
A commentary on the Minor Prophets. Grand Rapids, Baker Book House [1972] 428 p. 23 cm. Bibliography: p. 427-428. [BS1560.H3] 72-80331 ISBN 0-8010-4049-3 6.95
1. Bible. O.T. Minor prophets—Commentaries. I. Title.

BIBLE. C. T. MINOR PROPHETS. ENGLISH. 1960. 224.907
The Minor prophets; the men and their messages [by] G. Campbell Morgan. [Westwood, N. J.] Revell [1960] 157p. 22cm. [BS1560.M58] 60-5500
1. Bible. O. T. Minor prophets—Commentaries. I. Morgan. George Campbell. 1863-1945. II. Title.

BIBLE. O. T. Minor prophets. English. 1960. 224.907
The minor prophets; the men and their messages [by] G. Campbell Morgan. [Westwood, N.J.] Revell [c.1960] 157p. 22cm. 60-5500 2.75
1. Bible. O. T. Minor prophets—Commentaries. I. Morgan, George Campbell, 1863-1945. II. Title.

TAYLOR, John Bernard. 224'.9'07
The Minor Prophets [by] John B. Taylor. [1st U.S. ed.] Grand Rapids, Eerdmans [1970] 94 p. 19 cm. (Scripture Union Bible study books) [BS1560.T37 1970] 70-127629 1.25
1. Bible. O.T. Minor prophets—Commentaries. I. Title.

BIBLE. O.T. Daniel. English. Authorized. 1975. 224'.9'077
Daniel and Minor prophets, with Wycliffe Bible commentary : produced for Moody monthly. Parallel ed. New York : Iversen-Norman Associates, 1975. xxiii, 275 p. ; 25 cm. Includes bibliographies. [BS1553.P44] 75-18808
1. Bible. O.T. Daniel—Commentaries. 2. Bible. O.T. Minor prophets—Commentaries. I. Pfeiffer, Charles F. The Wyclif Bible commentary: Daniel and Minor prophets. 1975. II. Bible. O.T. Minor prophets. English. Authorized. 1975. III. Moody monthly. IV. Title.

BIBLE. O.T. Minor prophets. English. New English. 1975. 224'.9'077
The books of Joel, Obadiah, Jonah, Nahum, Habakkuk, and Zephaniah / commentary by John D. W. Watts. Cambridge, [Eng.] ; New York : Cambridge University Press, 1975. x, 190 p. ; 22 cm. (The Cambridge Bible commentary, New English Bible) Includes index. Bibliography: p. 186. [BS1560.W355] 74-80355 ISBN 0-521-20505-0 : 12.50 ISBN 0-521-09870-X pbk. : 5.95
1. Bible. O.T. Minor prophets—Commentaries. I. Watts, John D. W. II. Title. III. Series.

THE Minor prophets: 224'.9'077
Hosea to Malachi; a helping hand for Bible students. [Acton, Me., 1967] 390 p. 23 cm. [BS1560.M48] 67-21817
1. Bible. O.T. Minor prophets—Commentaries. I. Title: Bible, O.T. Minor prophets. English. 1967.

MINOR prophets (The) 224'.9'077
Hosea to Malachi& a helping hand for Bible students. [Acton, Me., 1967] 390p. 23cm. [BS1560.M48] 67-21817 3.50 pap.,
1. Bible. O. T. Minor prophets — Commentaries. I. Bible. O. T. Minor prophets. English. 1967.
Available from E. T. Lenfest, P. O. Box 35, Acton, Maine 04001

WATTS, John D. W. 224'.91
Obadiah: a critical exegetical commentary, by John D. W. Watts. Grand Rapids, Eerdmans [1969] 78 p. 23 cm. Includes text in English and Hebrew. Includes bibliographical references. [BS1595.3.W37] 67-13983 3.50
1. Bible. O.T. Obadiah—Commentaries. I. Bible. O.T. Obadiah. English. Watts. 1969. II. Bible. O.T. Obadiah. Hebrew. 1969. III. Title.

HILLIS, Don W. 224'.91'066
The book of Obadiah, by Don W. Hillis. Grand Rapids, Mich., Baker Book House [1969, c1968] 75 p. 21 cm. (Shield Bible study series) Bibliography: p. 74-75. [BS1595.3.H54 1969] 68-19687 1.95
1. Bible. O.T. Obadiah—Commentaries. I. Title.

*BREM, M. M. 224.92
The man caught by a fish; the Book of Jonah for children. Illus. by Jim Roberts. St. Louis, Concordia, 1967. 1v. (unpaged) col. illus. 21cm. (Arch bks.) .35 pap.,
1. Bible— O.T.—Jonah—Juvenile literature. I. Title.

DE HAAN, Martin Ralph, 1891- 224.92
Jonah, fact or fiction? Grand Rapids, Zondervan Pub. House [1957] 168p. 20cm. [BS580.J55D4] 57-41651
1. Jonah, the prophet. I. Title.

FISCHER, James A. 224.92
Jonas and the whale. Paterson, New Jersey, St. Anthony's Guild [c.1959] iii, 43p. 18cm. (Catholic Bible Association pamphlet) .25 pap.,
I. Title.

FORCE, Maynard Alfred, 1904- 224.92
Jonah speaks; devotional meditations from the Book of Jonah. Minneapolis, Lutheran Bible Institute [1950] 174 p. 21 cm. [BS1605.F6] 50-4058
1. Bible. O. T. Jonah—Meditations. I. Title.

*HILLIS, Don W. 224.92
The Book of Jonah: a discussion guide to the Book of Jonah. Grand Rapids, Baker Book House [1973] 104 p. 18 cm. (Contemporary discussion series) Originally published in 1967 under title: The Book of Jonah, a study manual. Bibliography: p. 8. [BS1605.2] 1.25 (pbk.)
1. Bible. O. T. Jonah—Commentaries. I. Title.

KENNEDY, James Hardee. 224.92
Studies in the book of Jonah. Nashville, Broadman Press [1956] 103 p. 21 cm. [BS1605.K4] 56-8677
1. Bible. O. T. Jonah—Commentaries.

MACBETH, George. 224'.92
Jonah and the Lord, by George MacBeth. Pictures by Margaret Gordon. New York, Holt, 1970. [31] p. col. illus. 22 x 27 cm. A retelling of the Bible story in which a man has to be swallowed by a whale before he learns to respect the command of the Lord. [BS580.J55M26 1970] 72-80320 ISBN 0-03-081612-2 3.95
1. Jonah, the prophet—Juvenile literature. I. Gordon, Margaret, 1939- illus. II. Title.

PICKARD, William M., 1921- 224'.92'007
Rather die than live—Jonah [by] William M. Pickard. [New York, Education and Cultivation Division, Board of Global Ministries, United Methodist Church, 1974] xi, 140 p. port. 19 cm. Bibliography: p. 137-138. [BS1605.5.P52] 74-4352 1.45 (pbk.)
1. Bible. O.T. Jonah—Study—Text-books. I. Title.

BIBLE. O.T. Jonah. English. Authorized. 1974. 224'.92'05203
The book of Jonah / transcribed from the Holy Bible, translated out of the original tongues at the royal behest of that most high & mighty prince, James, King of Great Britain, etc. ; and also illuminated, by the humble hand of Judith Anne Duncan. Minneapolis : Scholar-Gipsy Press, 1974. [29] p. : col. ill. ; 27 cm. [BS1603 1974] 74-21628
I. Duncan, Judith A., ill. II. Title.

BROOKES, James Hall, 1830-1897. 224'.92'06
Did Jesus rise? A book written to remove doubts. New York, Loizeaux Bros. [1945] 126p. 20cm. [Treasury of truth, no. 78] [BT480.B78] 55-15389
1. Jesus Christ— Resurrection. I. Title.

FRETHEIM, Terence E. 224'.92'06
The message of Jonah : a theological commentary / Terence E. Fretheim. Minneapolis : Augsburg Pub. House, c1977. 142 p. ; 20 cm. Bibliography: p. 141-142. [BS1605.2.F73] 77-72461 ISBN 0-8066-1591-5 pbk. : 4.95
1. Bible. O.T. Jonah—Theology—Addresses, essays, lectures. I. Title.

FRETHEIM, Terence E. 224'.92'06
The message of Jonah : a theological commentary / Terence E. Fretheim. Minneapolis : Augsburg Pub. House, c1977. 142 p. ; 20 cm. Bibliography: p. 141-142. [BS1605.2.F73] 77-72461 ISBN 0-8066-1591-5 pbk. : 4.95
1. Bible. O.T. Jonah—Theology—Addresses, essays, lectures. I. Title.

HILLIS, Don W 224'.92'06
The book of Jonah: Jonah speaks again; a study manual, by Don W. Hillis. Grand Rapids, Baker Book House [1967] 71 p. 20 cm. (Shield Bible study outlines) Text of Jonah from the Living prophecies, by K. N. Taylor and others, 1965. Bibliography: p. [8] [BS1605.3.H5] 67-18180
1. Bible. O. T. Jonah—Commentaries. I. Bible. O. T. Jonah. English. 1967. Taylor. II. Title.

HILLIS, Don W. 224'.92'06
The book of Jonah: Jonah speaks again; a study manual, by Don W. Hillis. Grand Rapids, Baker Book House [1967] 71 p. 20 cm. (Shield Bible study outlines) Text of Jonah from the Living prophecies, by K. N. Taylor and others, 1965. Bibliography: p. [8] [BS1605.3.H5] 67-18180
1. Bible. O.T. Jonah—Commentaries. I. Bible. O.T. Jonah. English. 1967. Taylor. II. Title.

MAGONET, Jonathan, 1942- 224'.92'06
Form and meaning : studies in literary techniques in the book of Jonah / Jonathan Magonet. Bern : Herbert Lang, 1976. 169 p. ; 21 cm. (Beitrage zur biblischen Exegese und Theologie ; Bd. 2) Thesis—Heidelberg. Bibliography: p. 155-169. [BS1605.2.M33] 77-460992 ISBN 3-261-01762-7 : 30.00F
1. Bible. O.T. Jonah—Criticism, interpretation, etc. I. Title. II. Series.

WILSON, Clifford A. 224'.92'06
A greater than Jonah is here; a survey of the archaeological and historical background to the times of Jonah, and a devotional commentary as to the One "to Whom all prophets bear witness." (Acts 10:43), by Clifford Wilson. [Melbourne, Australian Institute of Archaeology in association with Word of Truth Productions, 1969?] 53, [3] p. 23 cm. (A Word of Truth production) [BS1605.2.W5] 74-466247 unpriced
1. Jesus Christ—Resurrection. 2. Bible. O.T. Jonah—Criticism, interpretation, etc. I. Australian Institute of Archaeology. II. Title.

*BULL, Geoffrey T. 224'.92'066
The city and the sign; an interpretation of the Book of Jonah. Grand Rapids, Mich., Baker Book House [1972, c.1970] 157 p. 21 cm. Bibliography: p. [157] [BS1605.2] ISBN 0-8010-0589-2 3.95
1. Bible. O.T. Jonah—Criticism, interpretation, etc. I. Title.

SIMPSON, William, 1823-1899. 224'.92'066
The Jonah legend; a suggestion of interpretation. London, G. Richards, 1899. Detroit, Grand River Books, 1971. 182 p. illus. 22 cm. Includes bibliographical references. [BS1605.2.S55 1971] 72-176496
1. Bible. O.T. Jonah—Criticism, interpretation, etc. I. Title.

*BANKS, William L. 224.9207
Jonah, the reluctant prophet. Chicago, Moody [1966] 123p. 17cm. (Colportage lib. 519) p.39 pap.,
I. Title.

BANKS, William L. 224.9207
Jonah, verse by verse. New York, Vantage [c.1963] 103p. 21cm. 2.50
I. Title.

BLAIR, J. Allen. 224.9207
Living obediently; a devotional study of the book of Jonah. [1st ed.] Neptune, N. J., Loizeaux Bros., 1963. 190 p. 20 cm. [BS1605.3.B55] 63-18265
1. Bible. O. T. Jonah — Commentaries. I. Title.

BLAIR, J. Allen 224.9207
Living obediently; a devotional study of the book of Jonah. Neptune, N. J., Loizeaux [c.] 1963. 190p. 20cm. 63-18265 2.75 bds.,
1. Bible. O. T. Jonah—Commentaries. I. Title.

HASEL, Gerhard F. 224'.92'07
Jonah, messenger of the eleventh hour / by Gerhard F. Hasel. Mountain View, Calif. : Pacific Press Pub. Association, c1976. 112 p. ; 22 cm. (Dimension ; 119) Includes bibliographical references and index. [BS1605.3.H36] 76-12907 pbk. : 3.95
1. Bible. O.T. Jonah—Commentaries. I. Title.

MARKUS, J. Ondrej. 224'.92'07
Prophet Jonah / by J. Ondrej Markus ; [translated from the Slovak by A. P. Slabey]. 1st English ed. Medford, Wis. : V. Uhri, 1975. 82 p. ; 15 cm. Includes bibliographical references. [BS580.J55M2813] 75-16663
1. Jonah, the prophet. 2. Bible. O.T. Jonah—Commentaries. I. Title.

ELLUL, Jacques. 224'.92'077
The judgment of Jonah. Translated by Geoffrey W. Bromiley. Grand Rapids, Mich., Eerdmans [1971] 103 p. 22 cm. Translation of Le livre de Jonas. [BS580.J55E4413] 70-142901 1.95
1. Jonah, the prophet. I. Title.

LEMKE, Stefan. 224'.92'0924 B
Jonah / [art by Stefan Lemke and Marie-Luise Lemke-Pricken]. Philadelphia : Fortress Press, 1976. [20] p. : col. ill. ; 19 cm. "A Sunshine book." Retells the story of Jonah who was sent by God to warn the people of Nineveh about their evil ways. [BS580.J55L45] 76-11275 ISBN 0-8006-1577-8 pbk. : 1.75
1. Jonah, the prophet—Juvenile literature. 2. Bible. O.T.—Biography—Juvenile literature. I. Lemke-Pricken, Marie-Luise, joint author. II. Title.

BULLA, Clyde Robert. 224'.92'09505
Jonah and the great fish. Illustrated by Helga Aichinger. New York, Crowell [1970] [39] p. col. illus. 27 cm. More than once stubborn Jonah had to be taught not to question the will of the Lord. [BS580.J55B8] 69-13636 4.50
1. Jonah, the prophet—Juvenile literature. I. Aichinger, Helga, illus. II. Title.

CHRISTIAN, Mary Blount. 224'.92'09505
Jonah, go to Nineveh! : Jonah and the whale for beginning readers : the Book of Jonah for children / by Mary Blount Christian ; illustrated by Aline Cunningham. St. Louis : Concordia Pub. House, c1976. [48] p. : col. ill. ; 23 cm. (I can read a Bible story) An easy-to-read retelling of the trials of Jonah, who has trouble understanding the essence of God's love. [BS580.J55C48] 76-15286 ISBN 0-570-07307-3 : 3.95
1. Jonah, the prophet—Juvenile literature. I. Cunningham, Aline. II. Title.

HAIZ, Danah. 224'.92'09505
Jonah's journey. Illustrated by H. Hechtkopf. Minneapolis, Lerner Publications Co. [1973] [32] p. col. illus. 31 cm. Relates the events of Jonah's journey to warn the people of Nineveh that God was going to destroy their wicked city. [BS580.J55H33 1973] 72-268 ISBN 0-8225-0362-X 4.50 (lib. bdg.)
1. Jonah, the prophet—Juvenile literature. I. Hechtkopf, H., illus. II. Title.

WALSH, Bill. 224'.92'09505
Jonah and the whale / by Bill Walsh ; with an afterword for parents and teachers by Charlie Shedd. Kansas City : Sheed Andrews and McMeel, c1976. p. cm. (A Cartoon Bible story for children) With some reluctance, Jonah agrees to warn the citizens of Nineveh of God's displeasure. [BS580.J55W34] 76-41009 ISBN 0-8362-0689-4 pbk. : 1.95
1. Jonah, the prophet—Juvenile literature. 2.

Bible. O.T.—Biography—Juvenile literature. I. Title.

COPASS, Benjamin Andrew, 1865-1950. 224.93
A study of the Prophet Micah; power by the spirit, by B. A. Copass and E. L. Carlson. Grand Rapids, Baker Book House, 1950. 169 p. 20 cm. Bibliography: p. [165]-166. [BS1615.C6] 50-37008
1. Bible. O. T. Micah—Commentaries. I. Carlson, Ernest Leslie, 1893- joint author. II. Title.

BENNETT, T. Miles. 224'.93'07
The book of Micah; a study manual, by T. Miles Bennett. Grand Rapids, Baker Book House [1968] 75 p. 20 cm. (Shield Bible study outlines) Bibliography: p. 75. [BS1615.3.B4] 68-16890
1. Bible. O.T. Micah—Commentaries. I. Title.

MAYS, James Luther. 224'.93'07
Micah : a commentary / [by] James Luther Mays. London : S.C.M. Press, 1976. xii, 169 p. ; 23 cm. (The Old Testament library) Bibliography: p. 34-35. [BS1615.3.M39 1976b] 76-380854 ISBN 0-334-01026-8 : £5.75
1. Bible. O.T. Micah—Commentaries. I. Title. II. Series.

MAYS, James Luther. 224'.93'07
Micah : a commentary / James Luther Mays. Philadelphia : Westminster Press, c1976. xii, 169 p. ; 23 cm. (The Old Testament library) Bibliography: p. 34-35. [BS1615.3.M39 1976] 76-2599 ISBN 0-664-20817-7 : 10.95
1. Bible. O.T. Micah—Commentaries. I. Bible. O.T. Micah. English. 1976. II. Title. III. Series.

MAIER, Walter Arthur, 1893-1950. 224.94
The book of Nahum, a commentary. Saint Louis, Concordia Pub. House [1959] 386p. 24cm. Includes bibliography. [BS1625.M2] 57-14474
1. Bible. O. T. Nahum—Commentaries. I. Bible. O. T. Nahum. English. 1959. Maier. II. Title.

FREEMAN, Hobart E. 224'.94'07
Nahum, Zephaniah, Habakkuk; minor prophets of the seventh century B.C., by Hobart E. Freeman. Chicago, Moody Press [1973] 126 p. 20 cm. (Everyman's Bible commentary) Bibliography: p. 125-126. [BS1560.F7] 72-95031 ISBN 0-8024-2034-6 1.50 (pbk.)
1. Bible. O.T. Nahum—Commentaries. 2. Bible. O.T. Zephaniah—Commentaries. 3. Bible. O.T. Habakkuk—Commentaries. I. Title. II. Series.

MCKAY, Charles Lloyd, 1908- 224.95
The hand of God in human experience. Nashville [1955] 67p. 20cm. [BS1635.M2] 55-58702
1. Bible. O. T. Habakkuk—Commentaries. I. Title.

BROWNTEE, William Hugh. 224.950
The Habakkuk in the ancient commentary from Qumran Philadelphia, Society of Biblical Literature and Exegesis, 1959. viii, 130p. 23cm. (Journal of Biblical literature. Monograph series, v.11) Includes bibliographical references. [BS1635.H3B72] 59-2782
1. Habakkuk commentary. 2. Bible. O. T. Habakkuk— Criticism, Textual. I. Title. II. Series.

HABAKKUK commentary. English & Hebrew. 224'.95'06
The Midrash Pesher of Habakkuk / text, translation, exposition with an introduction by William H. Brownlee. Missoula, Mont. : Published by Scholars Press for the Society of Biblical Literature, c1977. p. cm. (Monograph series - Society of Biblical Literature ; no. 24) Includes index. Bibliography: p. [BS1635.H28 1977] 76-30560 ISBN 0-89130-096-1
1. Bible. O.T. Habakkuk—Commentaries. 2. Habakkuk commentary—Criticism, interpretation, etc. I. Browlee, William Hugh. II. Title. III. Series: Society of Biblical Literature. Monograph series ; no. 24.

SORG, Rembert, 1908- 224'.95'06
Habaqquq III and Selah Fifield, Wis., King of Martyrs Priory, 1968 [c1969] vii, 81 p. illus. 24 cm. Bibliographical footnotes. [BS1635.2.S64] 76-93738
1. Bible. O.T. Habakkuk III—Criticism, Textual. I. Title.

GOWAN, Donald E. 224'.95'066
The triumph of faith in Habakkuk / Donald E. Gowan. Atlanta : John Knox Press, c1976. p. cm. Bibliography: p. [BS1635.2.G68] 75-32843 ISBN 0-8042-0195-1 : 5.95
1. Bible. O.T. Habakkuk—Criticism, interpretation, etc. I. Title.

KAPELRUD, Arvid Schou, 1912- 224'.96'06
The message of the prophet Zephaniah : morphology and ideas / by Arvid S. Kapelrud. Oslo; [Boston]: Universitetsforlaget, [1975] 116 p. ; 22 cm. Includes index. Bibliography: p. 110-[112] [BS1645.2.K36] 75-323147 ISBN 8-200-01373-1 : 9.00
1. Bible. O.T. Zephaniah—Criticism, interpretation, etc. I. Bible. O.T. Zephaniah. English. 1975. II. Title.

WOLFF, Richard, 1927- 224'.97'066
The book of Haggai, a study manual. Grand Rapids, Baker Book House [1967] 85 p. 20 cm. (Shield Bible study outlines) Bibliography: p. 83-85. [BS1655.5.W6] 67-18202
1. Bible. O.T. Haggai—Study—Outlines, syllabi, etc. I. Title.

BALDWIN, Joyce G. 224'.97'07
Haggai, Zechariah, Malachi; an introduction and commentary, by Joyce G. Baldwin. [1st ed.] Downers Grove, Ill., Inter-varsity Press [1972] 253 p. 19 cm. (The Tyndale Old Testament commentaries) Includes bibliographical references. [BS1655.3.B34] 72-75980 5.95
1. Bible. O.T. Haggai—Commentaries. 2. Bible. O.T. Zechariah—Commentaries. 3. Bible. O.T. Malachi—Commentaries. I. Title.

WOLF, Herbert, 1938- 224'.97'07
Haggai and Malachi / by Herbert Wolf. Chicago : Moody Press, c1976. 128 p. ; 19 cm. (Everyman's Bible commentary) Bibliography: p. 128. [BS1655.3.W58] 76-356962 ISBN 0-8024-2037-0 pbk. : 1.95
1. Bible. O.T. Haggai—Commentaries. 2. Bible. O.T. Malachi—Commentaries. I. Title. II. Series.

FEINBERG, Charles Lee. 224.98
God remembers; a study of the Book of Zechariah. Wheaton, Ill., Van Kampen Press [1951, '1950] xii, 283 p. 20 cm. Bibliography: p. 281-283. [BS1665.F4] 51-1181
1. Bible. O. T. Zechariah—Commentaries. I. Title.

LEUPOLD, Herbert Carl, 1892- 224.98
Exposition of Zechariah. Columbus, Ohio, WartburgPress [1956] 280p. 23cm. [BS1665.L45] 57-17483
1. Bible. O. T. Zechariah—Commentaries. I. Title.

BARON, David. 224'.98'07
The visions & prophecies of Zechariah. Grand Rapids, Kregel Publications [1972] x, 555 p. 23 cm. (Kregel reprint library) Reprint of the 1918 ed., which first appeared as articles in the Scattered nation, 1907-1918. Includes the text of the Book of Zechariah. Includes bibliographical references. [BS1665.5.B37 1972] 70-180834 ISBN 0-8254-2216-7 6.95
1. Bible. O.T. Zechariah—Prophecies. I. Bible. O.T. Zechariah. English. American standard. 1972. II. Title.

RULER, Arnold Albert van, 1908- 224.9807
Zechariah speaks today: studies in Zechariah, chapters 1-8 [Abridged tr. from Dutch] New York, Association [1963] 79p. 19 cm. (World Christian bks. no. 43, 2d ser.) 63-3229 1.00 pap.,
1. Bible. O. T. Zechariah—Commentaries. I. Title.

UNGER, Merrill Frederick, 1909- 224.9807
Zechariah. Grand Rapids, Zondervan Pub. House [1963] 275 p. 25 cm. (His Bible commentary) Bibliography: p. 273-275. [BS1665.3.U5] 63-4321
1. Bible. O.T. Zechariah — Commentaries. I. Title.

*MORGAN, George Campbell, 1863-1945. 224.99
Malachi's message for today [by] G. Campbell Morgan. Grand Rapids, Mich., Baker Book House [1972] 131 p. 20 cm. (The Morgan library) [BS1655] 0-8010 pap., 1.95
1. Bible. O.T. Malachi—Criticism, interpretation, etc. I. Title.

BAILEY, Robert W. 224'.99'06
God's questions and answers : contemporary studies in Malachi / Robert W. Bailey. New York : Seabury Press, 1977. p. cm. "A Crossroad book." Includes bibliographical references. [BS1675.4.B34] 76-56513 ISBN 0-8164-1231-6 pbk. : 3.95
1. Bible. O.T. Malachi—Meditations. I. Title.

DELAUGHTER, Thomas J. 224'.99'06
Malachi, messenger of divine love / Thomas J. Delaughter. New Orleans : Insight Press, c1976. 158 p. ; 22 cm. Bibliography: p. 149-158. [BS1675.3.D44] 75-40410 ISBN 0-914520-07-5 pbk. : 4.00
1. Bible. O.T. Malachi—Commentaries. I. Title.

225 New Testament

BARCLAY, William, Lecturer in the University of Glasgow. 225
Many witnesses, one Lord. Grand Rapids, Mich., Baker Book House [1973, c.1963] 128 p. 20 cm. [BS2361.2.B3] ISBN 0-8010-0595-7 pap., 1.50
1. Bible. N.T.—Criticism, interpretation, etc. I. Title.
L.C. card no. for original ed.: 63-10831.

BIBLE. N. T. English. 1954. Kleist-Lilly. 225
The New Testament, rendered from the original Greek with explanatory notes. Pt.1: The four Gospels, translated by James A. Kleist. Pt. 2: Acts of the Apostles, Epistles, and Apocalypse, translated by Joseph L. Lilly. Milwaukee, Bruce Pub. Co. [1954] xii, 690p. maps. 23cm. [BS2095.K5] 54-7889
I. Kleist, James Aloyslus. 1873- tr. II. Lilly, Joseph L. tr. III. Title.

BIBLE. N. T. English. 1956. Kleist-Lilly. 225
The New Testament, rendered from the original Greek with explanatory notes. Pt. 1: The four Gospels, translated by James A. Kleist. Pt. 2: Acts of the Apostles, Epistles, and Apocalypse, translated by Joseph L. Lilly. Milwaukee, Bruce Pub. Co. [c1956] xii, 690p. maps. 23cm. [BS2095.K 1956] 56-58008
I. Kleist, James Aloysius, 1873- tr. II. Lilly, Joseph L., tr. III. Title.

BIBLE. N. T. English. 1962. Authorized. 225
The personal worker's New Testament. With notes and marked plan of salvation arr. and compiled [sic] by Clifton W. Brannon using the edition of 1611 A.D. commonly known as the Authorized King James version Longview, Tex., Clift Brannon Evangelistc Association, 1962. vii, 585p. 12cm. [BS2085 1962.L6] 62-4749
I. Brannon, Clifton Woodrow, comp. II. Title.

BIBLE. N.T. English. 1963. Beck. 225
The New Testament, in the language of today, by William F. Beck. Saint Louis, Concordia Pub. House [1963] xi, 459 p. 24 cm. [BS2095.B4] 63-8909
I. Beck. William F., tr. II. Title.

BIBLE. N. T. English. 1963. Beck. 225
The New Testament, in the language of today, by William F. Beck. St. Louis, Concordia [c.1963] xi, 459p. 24cm. 63-8909 4.75
I. Beck, William F., tr. II. Title.

BIBLE. N. T. English. Selections. 1953. Authorized. 225
The golden Bible for children: the New Testament, edited and arr. by Elsa Jane Werner; illustrated by Alice and Martin Provensen. New York, Simon and Schuster [1953] 96p. illus. 34cm. (A Giant golden book. 705) [BS2097.W4] 53-4393
I. Werner, Jane. 1915- ed. II. Title.

BRUCE, Frederick Fyvie, 1910- 225
The message of the New Testament [by] F. F. Bruce. Grand Rapids, Eerdmans [1973, c1972] 120 p. 20 cm. Bibliography: p. 117. [BS2330.2.B78 1973] 73-161149 1.95
1. Bible. N.T.—Introductions. I. Title.

CONZELMANN, Hans. 225
An outline of the theology of the New Testament. [1st U.S. ed.] New York, Harper & Row [1969] xviii, 373 p. 22 cm. Translation of Grundriss der Theologie des Neuen Testaments. Includes bibliographical references. [BS2397.C6513 1969] 69-17019 8.50
1. Bible. N.T.—Theology. I. Title.

CULLMANN, Oscar. 225
The New Testament: an introduction for the general reader. Philadelphia, Westminster Press [1968] 138 p. 19 cm. Translation of Le Nouveau Testament. Bibliography: p. [137]-138. [BS2330.2.C813] 68-12796
1. Bible. N.T.—Introductions. I. Title.

DALPADADO, J. Kingsley, 1922- 225
Reading the Acts, Epistles, and Revelation : (a guide to readers and teachers) / by J. Kingsley Dalpadado. Boston : St. Paul Editions, c1977. p. cm. Includes index. Bibliography: p. [BS2617.8.D34] 77-24484 6.95 pbk. : 5.95
1. Bible. N.T. Acts, Epistles, and Revelation—Criticism, interpretation, etc. I. Title.

DALPADADO, J. Kingsley, 1922- 225
Reading the Acts, Epistles, and Revelation : (a guide to readers and teachers) / by J. Kingsley Dalpadado. Boston : St. Paul Editions, c1977. p. cm. Includes index. Bibliography: p. [BS2617.8.D34] 77-24484 6.95 pbk. : 5.95
1. Bible. N.T. Acts, Epistles, and Revelation—Criticism, interpretation, etc. I. Title.

FITZWATER, Perry Braxton, 1871- 225
Preaching and teaching the New Testament. Chicago, Moody Press [1957] 622p. 24cm. [BS2341.F5] 57-44046
1. Bible. N.T.—Sermons—Outlines. I. Title.

GRANT, Frederick Clifton, 1891- 225
An introduction to New Testament thought. New York, Abingdon-Cokesbury Press [1950] 339 p. 24 cm. [BS2361.G65] 50-8047
1. Bible. N.T.—Theology.

HARRINGTON, Wilfrid J 225
Record of the fulfillment: the New Testament [by] Wilfrid J. Harrington. Chicago, Priory Press [1966, c1965] xii, 533 p. map. 24 cm. "The Bible text ... is from the Revised standard version." Bibliography: p. 491-498. [BS2330.2.H32] 66-24107
1. Bible. N.T. — Introductions. I. Title.

HARRINGTON, Wilfrid J. 225
Record of the fulfillment: the New Testament [by]Wilfrid J. Harrington. Chicago, Priory Pr. [1966, c.1965] xii, 533p. map. 24cm. The Bible Text is from the Rev. standard version. Bibl. [BS2330.2.H32] 66-24107 7.50
1. Bible. N. T.—Introductions. I. Title.

HARRISON, Everett Falconer, 1902- 225
Introduction to the New Testament, by Everett F. Harrison. [Rev. ed.] Grand Rapids, Eerdmans [1971] xiv, 508 p. maps (on lining papers). 24 cm. Includes bibliographies. [BS2330.2.H33 1971] 76-29311 7.95
1. Bible. N.T.—Introductions. I. Title.

HESTER, Hubert Inman, 1895- 225
The heart of the New Testament. Liberty, Mo., W. Jewell Press [1950] xiv, 350, [1] p. 5 maps. 24 cm. Bibliography: p. [351] [BS2330.H4] 50-35186
1. Bible. N. T.—Introductions. 2. Jesus Christ—Biog. 3. Bible. N. T.—History of Biblical events. I. Title.

HOPPER, Myron Taggart, 1903- 225
New Testament life and literature; a course for students of high school age in weekday church schools. Teacher's ed. St. Louis, Published for the Cooperative Pub. Association by the Bethany Press [1950] 159 p. 20 cm. [BS2535.H6] 50-32162
1. Bible. N. T.—Study—Text-books. I. Title.

HUDSON, Roland V, 1913- 225
The New Testament outlined. Wilmore, Ky., Wilmore Press, '1951. 80 p. port. 19 cm. [BS2525.H8] 51-27495
1. Bible. N. T.—Study—Outlines, syllabl, etc. I. Title.

HUDSON, Roland Vernon, 1913- 225
The New Testament outlined. Wilmore, Ky., Wilmore Press, c1951. 80). port. 19cm. [BS2525.H8] 51-27495
1. Bible. N. T.—Study—Outlines, syllabi, etc. I. Title.

*KRUPP, Nate 225
A world to win: secrets of New Testament evangelism. Minneapolis, Bethany [1966] 94p. 21cm. pap., price unreported
I. Title.

LEITCH, Addison H. 225
A reader's introduction to the New Testament [by] Addison H. Leitch. [1st ed.] Garden City, Doubleday, 1971. viii, 160 p. 22 cm. Includes bibliographical references. [BS2330.2.L4] 77-131088 5.95
1. Bible. N.T.—Introductions. I. Title.

MCNEILE, Alan Hugh, 1871-1933. 225
An introduction to the study of the New Testament. 2d ed. rev. by C. S. C. Williams. Oxford, Clarendon Press, 1953. viii, 486p. 23cm. Includes bibliographies. [BS2330.M33 1953] 53-3555
1. Bible. N. T.—Introductions. I. Title.

MANSON, William, 1882-1958 225
Jesus and the Christian. Grand Rapids, Eerdmans [1967] 236p. 23cm. [BS2395.M3 1967] 67-13986 5.95
1. Bible. N.T.—Addresses, essays, lectures. I. Title.

MARXSEN, Willi, 1919- 225
Introduction to the New Testament; an approach to its problems, by W. Marxsen. Translated by G. Buswell. Philadelphia, Fortress Press [1968] xiv, 284 p. 23 cm. Translation of Einleitung in das Neue Testament. Includes bibliographical references. [BS2330.2.M313 1968] 68-15419

1. Bible. N.T.—Introductions. I. Title.

*MEARS, Henrietta C. 225
A look at the New Testament; an abridged survey of Matthew-Revelation. Glendale, Calif. [Gospel Pubns., 1966] 275p. illus. 18cm. (Regal bks., GL952) ap.,
I. Title.

METZGER, Bruce Manning. 225
The New Testament: its background, growth, and content. New York, Abingdon Press [1965] 288 p. illus., maps. 24 cm. Bibliography: p. 277-279. [BS2535.2.M4] 65-21981
1. Bible. N. T.—Study. I. Title.

MORGAN, Carl Hamilton, 1901- 225
The layman's introduction to the New Testament [by] Carl H. Morgan. Valley Forge [Pa.] Judson Press [1968] 126 p. illus., maps. 22 cm. Includes bibliographies. [BS2330.2.M58] 68-22756 2.50
1. Bible. N.T.—Introductions. I. Title.

MORGAN, Robert, 1940- 225
The nature of New Testament theology. The contribution of William Wrede and Adolf Schlatter, edited, translated, and with an introd. by Robert Morgan. Naperville, Ill., A. R. Allenson [1973] 196 p. 22 cm. (Studies in Biblical theology, 2d ser., 25) Contents.Contents.—Morgan, R. Introduction: The nature of New Testament theology.—Wrede, W. The task and methods of "New Testament theology."—Schlatter, A. The theology of the New Testament and dogmatics.—Bibliographical note (p. [167]-168) [BS2397.M63 1973] 72-97459 ISBN 0-8401-3075-9 7.95 (pbk.)
1. Bible. N.T.—Theology. I. Wrede, William, 1859-1906. Uber aufgabe und Methode der sogenannten neutestamentlichen Theologie. English. 1973. II. Schlatter, Adolf von, 1852-1938. Die Theologie des Neuen Testaments und die Dogmatik. English. 1973. III. Title. IV. Series.

NEW dimensions in New 225
Testament study / edited by Richard N. Longenecker and Merrill C. Tenney. Grand Rapids : Zondervan Pub. House, c1974. xiii, 377 p. ; 25 cm. "The twenty-four articles ... were originally presented at the sessions of the twenty-fifth annual meeting of the Evangelical Theological Society, December 27-29, 1973, at Wheaton College, Wheaton, Illinois." Includes bibliographical references and indexes. [BS2395.N49] 74-11857 8.95
1. Bible. N.T.—Addresses, essays, lectures. I. Longenecker, Richard N. II. Tenney, Merrill Chaplin, 1904- III. Evangelical Theological Society.

QUESNELL, Quentin. 225
This good news; an introduction to the Catholic theology of the New Testament. Milwaukee, Bruce Pub. Co. [1964] xiv, 224 p. 22 cm. (Impact books) [BS2397.Q4] 64-15782
1. Bible. N. T.—Theology. I. Title.

QUESNELL, Quentin 225
This good news; an introduction to the Catholic theology of the New Testament. Milwaukee, Bruce [c.1964] xiv, 224p. 22cm. (Impact bks.) 64-15782 4.50
1. Bible. N.T.—Theology. I. Title.

RICHARDSON, Alan, 1905- 225
An introduction to the theology of the New Testament. New York, Harper [1959, c1958] 423 p. 22 cm. Includes bibliography. [BS2397.R48 1959] 59-5153
1. Bible. N.T.—Theology. I. Title: The theology of the New Testament.

RIFE, John Merle, 1895- 225
The nature and origin of the New Testament / by J. Merle Rife. New York : Philosophical Library, [1975] 158 p. ; 22 cm. Includes bibliographical references and index. [BS2330.2.R56] 74-80276 ISBN 0-8022-2148-3 : 8.75
1. Bible. N.T.—Introductions. I. Title.

SAVOY, Gene. 225
The decoded New Testament, authorized version : an authoritative translation of the sacred teachings of light as contained in the encoded writings of the Gospels, Acts, and Epistles / by Gene Savoy. Reno, New. : International Community of Christ, Pub. Dept., 1977, c1974. xix, 120 p. ; 29 cm. (The Sacred teachings of light ; codex 2, v. 1) "An unabridged printing of the King James version of the New Testament is ... presented in the margins for readers reference." Includes index. [BS2390.S27 1977] 77-368891
1. Bible. N.T.—Miscellanea. 2. Gnosticism. 3. Essenes. I. International Community of Christ. II. Bible. N.T. English. Authorized. 1977. III. Title. IV. Series.

SELBY, Donald Joseph. 225
Introduction to the New Testament: "the Word became flesh" [by] Donald J. Selby. [New York, Macmillan, 1971] xxiii, 530 p. illus., facsims., maps, ports. 24 cm. "This book and its companion Introduction to the Old Testament: 'Hear O Israel,' by James King West are available in a one-volume edition entitled Introduction to the Bible, by Donald J. Selby and James King West." Includes bibliographies. [BS2330.2.S44] 71-152822
1. Bible. N.T.—Introductions. I. Title.

SOLI Deo gloria; 225
New Testament studies in honor of William Childs Robinson. Edited by J. McDowell Richards. Richmond, John Knox Press [1968] 160 p. 21 cm. Contents.Contents.—Foreword, by J. McDowell Richards.—The relevance of redemptive history, by O. Cullmann.—"Jesus is Lord," by F. F. Bruce.—Paul's understanding of righteousness, by B. Reicke.—Paul and the law, by G. E. Ladd.—Word and power, by W. C. Robinson, Jr.—Lampades in Matthew 25: 1-13, by J. Jeremiah.—World in modern theology and in New Testament theology, by J. M. Robinson.—John Calvin's polemic against idolatry, by J. H. Leith.—Theological persuasion, by T. F. Torrance.—William Childs Robinson.—Notes and acknowledgements (p. [141]-155).—Tabula gratulatoria. [BS2395.S6] 68-20620
1. Bible. N.T.—Addresses, essays, lectures. I. Richards, James McDowell, 1902- ed. II. Robinson, William Childs, 1897-

TASKER, Randolph Vincent 225
Greewood, 1895-
The Old Testament in the New Testament. [2d ed. Grand Rapids, Mich., Eerdmans, 1963, c.1946, 1954] 159p. 19cm. 1.45 pap.,
1. Bible. N. T.—Relation to O. T. I. Title.

TENNEY, Merrill Chapin, 1904- 225
The New Testament, an historical and analytic survey. Grand Rapids, W. B. Eerdmans Pub. Co., 1953. 474p. illus. 23cm. Includes bibliography. [BS2330.T4] 53-9742
1. Bible. N. T.—Introductions. 2. Bible. N. T.—History of contemporary events, etc. I. Title.

TITUS, Eric Lane, 1909- 225
Essentials of New Testament study. New York, Ronald Press Co. [1958] 261 p. 22 cm. Includes bibliography. [BS2530.T58] 58-7374
1. Bible. N.T.—Study—Text books. 2. Bible. N.T. — History of Biblical events. 3. Bible. N.T. — Introductions. I. Title.

TURNER, John Clyde, 1878- 225
The New Testament doctrine of the church. Nashville, Broadman Press [c1951] 118 p. 20 cm. [BS2545.C5T8] 51-14865
1. Church — Biblical teaching. 2. Bible. N.T. — Theology. I. Title.

THE Use of the Old Testament 225
in the New and other essays; studies in honor of William Franklin Stinespring. Edited by James M. Efird. Durham, N.C., Duke University Press, 1972. xv, 332 p. illus. 25 cm. Contents.Contents.—Smith, D. M., Jr. The use of the Old Testament in the New.—Tucker, G. M. The Rahab saga (Joshua 2): some form-critical and traditio-historical observations.—Eakin, F. E., Jr. Spiritual obduracy and parable purpose.—Williams, D. L. The Israelite cult and Christian worship.—Cresson, B. C. The condemnation of Edom in post-exilic Judaism.—Polley, M. E. H. Wheeler Robinson and the problem of organizing an Old Testament theology.—Pope, M. H. A divine banquet at Ugarit.—Strugnell, J. "Of cabbages and kings"—or queans: notes on Ben Sira 36:18-21.—Brownlee, W. H. Anthropology and soteriology in the Dead Sea scrolls and in the New Testament.—Wintermute, O. A study of gnostic exegesis of the Old Testament.—Charlesworth, J. H. Ba'uta [romanized form] in earliest Christianity.—Anderson, H. The Old Testament in Mark's Gospel.—Efird, J. M. Note on Mark 5:43.—Davies, W. D. The moral teaching of the early church.—Bibliography (p. xiv-xv) [BS2387.U8] 70-185463 ISBN 0-8223-0288-8
1. Stinespring, William Franklin, 1901- — Bibliography. 2. Bible. N.T.—Relation to O.T.—Addresses, essays, lectures. I. Stinespring, William Franklin, 1901- II. Efird, James M., ed.

WERNER, Emily J 225
Answer to the Word- Studies in four New Testament books, for young people and adults. Philadelphia, Muhlenberg Press [1953] 96p. illus. 18cm. (Faith and action series) [BS2535.W42] 54-1750
1. Bible N. T.—Study—Text-books. I. Title.

REES, Howard. 225.007
Handbook on Bible study. Nashville, Broadman Press [1959] 62p. 16cm. (Alpha Omega series) Includes bibliography. [BS2530.R4] 59-9689
1. Bible. N. T.—Study. I. Title.

VIOLI, Unicio Jack. 225.02
Review notes and study guide to the New Testament. New York, Monarch Pr. [1966, c.1964] 171p. 21cm. (Monarch review notes and study guides, 625) Bibl. [BS2525] 65-7191 2.50
1. Bible. N.T.—Study—Outlines, syllabi, etc. I. Title.

RHEIN, Francis Bayard. 225'.02'02
Barron's simplified approach to the New Testament. Woodbury, N.Y., Barron's Educational Series [1968] 155 p. 22 cm. Bibliography: p. 153-155. [BS2330.2.R52] 68-28825 0.95
1. Bible. N.T.—Introductions. I. Title. II. Title: Simplified approach to the New Testament.

TRAWICK, Buckner B. 225'.02'02
The New Testament as literature (Gospels and Acts) [by] Buckner B. Trawick. [2d ed.] N[ew] Y[ork] Barnes & Noble [1968] vii, 176 p. map. 21 cm. (Barnes & Noble college outline series, no. 57) "The King James ... version ... has been chosen as the basis for this book." Includes bibliographical references. [BS2525.T7 1968] 78-312 1.50 (1.65 Can)
1. Bible. N.T.—Study—Outlines, syllabi, etc. I. Title.

WESTERMANN, Claus. 225'.02'02
Handbook to the New Testament. Translated and edited by Robert H. Boyd. Minneapolis, Augsburg Pub. House [1969] xi, 180 p. col. maps (on lining papers) 22 cm. "A translation of the introduction and New Testament sections of [the author's] Abriss der Bibelkunde." Bibliographical footnotes. [BS2525.W413] 69-14190 4.95
1. Bible. N.T.—Study—Outlines, syllabi, etc. I. Title.

DODD, Charles Harold, 225.04
1884-
New Testament studies. New York, Scribner [1954] 182p. 23cm. [BS2393.D58] 54-6301
1. Bible. N. T.—Addresses, essays, lectures. I. Title.

JOHNSON, Sherman Elbridge, 225.04
1908- ed.
The joy of study; papers on New Testament and related subjects presented to honor Frederick Clifton Grant. New York, Macmillan, 1951. xii, 163 p. 21 cm. Bibliographical footnotes. [BS2280.J6] 51-14486
1. Bible. N. T.—Addresses, essays. lectures. 2. Grant, Frederick Clifton, 1891- I. Title.
Contents Omitted.

STONEHOUSE, Ned Bernard, 225.04
1902-
Paul before the Areopagus, and other New Testament studies. Grand Rapids, Eerdmans, 1957. 197p. 23cm. [BS2393.S8] PP13683
1. Paul, Saint, apostle. 2. Bible. N. T.—Addresses, essays, lectures. I. Title.

STONEHOUSE, Ned Bernard, 225.04
1902-
Paul before the Areopagus, and other New Testament studies. Grand Rapids, Eerdmans, 1957. 197 p. 23 cm. [BS2393.S8] HP13683
1. Paul, Saint, apostle. 2. Bible. N.T. — Addresses, essays, lectures. I. Title.

BIBLE. N.T. English. 225'.05'2
Layman's parallel. 1970.
The layman's parallel New Testament: King James version, the Amplified New Testament, the Living New Testament. Revised Standard version. Grand Rapids, Mich., Zondervan Pub. House [1970] xv, 943 p. 25 cm. [BS2025 1970.Z65] 78-132518 7.95
1. Bible. N.T. English—Versions. I. Title.

AMS Press, 1967] xvi, 64 p. 23 cm. (The English scholar's library of old and modern works [v. 1] no. 3) Bibliography: p. [ix]-x. [PR1121.A72 no. 3] [PR2337.R6] 655.1'421 72-194939
1. Songs, English—Texts. 2. English poetry—Early modern, 1500-1700. I. Title. II. Series.

DUNNETT, Walter M 225.06
New Testament survey. [1st ed.] Wheaton, Ill., Evangelical Teacher Training Association [1963] 94 p. maps. 23 cm. [(Evangelical Teacher Training Association] Textbook of the certificate course, unit 3) Includes bibliographical references. [BS2330.2.D8] 63-7410
1. Bible. N.T. — Introductions. I. Title.

FRANZMANN, Martin H. 225.06
The word of the Lord grows; a first historical introduction to the New Testament. St. Louis, Concordia [c.]1961. 324p. Bibl. 61-13453 4.00
1. Bible. N. T.—Introductions. I. Title.

LIEFELD, Theodore S. 225.06
Search: New Testament survey. Minneapolis, Augsburg, c.1962. 55p. 22cm. pap., .75; instructor's guide, pap., .75
I. Title.

NEW Testament survey. 225.06
[1st ed.] Wheaton, Ill., Evangelical Teacher Training Association [1963] 94 p. maps. 23 cm. [(Evangelical Teacher Training Association] Textbook of the certificate course, unit 3) Includes bibliographical references. [BS2330.2.D8] 63-7410
1. Bible. N.T. — Introductions.

ROBINSON, John Arthur 225.06
Thomas, Bp., 1919-
Twelve New Testament studies. Naperville, Ill., A. R. Allenson [1962] 180 p. 22 cm. (Studies in Biblical theology, no. 34) [BS2395.R6] 62-6184
1. Bible. N.T.—Criticism, interpretation, etc. I. Title.

ALVES, Colin. 225.07
The kingdom; a New Testament course. Cambridge [Eng.] University Press, 1959. 203p. illus. 20cm. [BS2535.2.A4] 60-16013
1. Bible. N. T.—Study—Text-books. 2. Religious education—Text-books for adolescents. I. Title.

ALVES, Colin 225.07
The kingdom; a New Testament course. [New York] Cambridge University Press, 1959 [i. e., 1960] xix, 203p. illus. 20cm. 60-16043 1.75 bds.,
1. Bible. N. T.—Study—Text-books. 2. Religious education—Text-books for adolescents. I. Title.

BAXTER, Edna M., 1895- 225.07
Teaching the New Testament. Philadelphia, Christian Education Press [1960] 309 p. illus. 21 cm. Includes bibliography. [BS2530.B3] 60-6662
1. Bible. N. T.—Study. I. Title.

BIBLE. N. T. English. 225.07
1959. American revised.
Teachers' New Testament, with notes and helps. American standard version. Grand Rapids, Baker Book House, 1959. xvi, 656p. 17cm. Published in 1912 under title: Nelson's explanatory Testament. [BS2090.A1 1959.G7] 59-8335
1. Bible. N. T.—Commentaries. I. Title.

BIBLE. N. T. English. 225.07
1960. Confraternity version.
New Testament reading guide. Collegeville, Minn., Liturgical Press [c1960-62] 14 v. maps. 20 cm. Text and commentaries. [BS2341.2.N4] 63-3511
1. Bible. N. T. — Commentaries. I. Title.

BROWN, Raymond Bryan. 225.07
A study of the New Testament [by] Raymond B. Brown [and] Velma Darbo. Teacher's book for use with 14 year olds, may be adapted for other intermediates. Nashville, Broadman Press [1965] 192 p. 21 cm. (The Weekday Bible study series) [BS2535.2.B7] 65-16573
1. Bible. N.T. — Study — Text-books. I. Darbo, Velma, joint author. II. Title.

BROWN, Raymond Bryan 225.07
A study of the New Testament [by] Raymond B. Brown, Velma Darbo. Teacher's bk. for use with 14 year olds, may be adapted for other intermediates. Nashville. Broadman [c.1965] 192p. 21cm. (Weekday Bible study ser.) [BS2535.2.B7] 65-16573 pap., 2.75; student's bk., pap., 1.00
1. Bible. N. T.—Study—Textbooks. I. Darbo, Velma, joint author. II. Title.

GUNDRY, Robert Horton. 225'.07
A survey of the New Testament [by] Robert H. Gundry. [Grand Rapids] Zondervan Pub. House [1970] xvi, 400 p. illus., maps. 25 cm.

Includes bibliographical references. [BS2535.2.G85] 78-106442 6.95
1. Bible. N.T.—Study—Text-books. I. Title.

HAM, Wayne. 225.07
Enriching your New Testament studies; a study guide to treasure in earthen vessels. [Independence, Mo., Herald Pub. House, 1966] 198 p. illus. 21 cm. [BS2525.H3] 66-22598
1. Bible, N.T.—Study—Outlines, syllabi, etc. I. Title.

HAM, Wayne 225.07
Enriching your New Testament studies; a study guide to treasure in earthen vessels. [Independence, Mo., Herald Pub. [c.1966] 198p. illus. 21cm. [BS2525.H3] 66-22598 2.75;1.75 pap.,
1. Bible. N. T.—Study—Outlines, syllabi, etc. I. Title.

HARTSHORN, Chris Benson. 225'.07
The development of the early Christian church; a study based on the Acts of the Apostles and the Epistles, by Chris B. Hartshorn. [Independence, Mo.] Reorganized Church of Jesus Christ of Latter Day Saints, 1967. 341 p. 21 cm. Includes bibliographical references. [BS2617.5.H3] 67-11907
1. Bible. N.T. Acts and Epistles—Study—Outlines, syllabi, etc. 2. Church history—Primitive and early church, ca. 30-600. I. Title.

KIMBALL, Warren Young 225.07
Search the Scriptures. [Dedham, Mass., 302 Mt. Vernon St. Author, 1959, c.1958] 106p. 22cm. 60-84 2.75
1. Bible. N. T.—Study. I. Title.

LACE, O. Jessie 225.07
Teaching the New Testament. Foreword by Frederick C. Grant. Greenwich, Conn., Seabury Press [c.]1961. 96p. Bibl. 61-5795 1.95 pap.,
1. Bible. N. T.—Study. I. Title.

THE New Testament student 225'.07
at work / John H. Skilton, editor. [Nutley, N.J.] : Presbyterian and Reformed Pub. Co., 1975. xiv, 258 p. ; 21 cm. (The New Testament student ; v. 2) Includes bibliographical references. [BS2395.N54] 75-24949
1. Bible. N.T.—Addresses, essays, lectures. I. Skilton, John H.

PERRIN, Norman. 225'.07
The New Testament, an introduction; proclamation and parenesis, myth and history. New York, Harcourt Brace Jovanovich [1974] xii, 385 p. illus. 24 cm. Bibliography: p. 353-359. [BS2330.2.P46] 73-18623 ISBN 0-15-565725-9 4.95 (pbk.)
1. Bible. N.T.—Introductions. I. Title.

PIET, John H. 225'.07
The key to the Good news [by] John H. Piet. Grand Rapids, Mich., Eerdmans [1974] 62 p. 18 cm. [BS2525.P5] 73-18239 ISBN 0-8028-1541-3
1. Bible. N.T.—Study—Outlines, syllabi, etc. I. Title.

STUDYING the New 225'.07
Testament today / edited by John H. Skilton. [Nutley, N.J.] : Presbyterian and Reformed Pub. Co., 1974. viii, 198 p. ; 21 cm. (The New Testament student ; v. 1) Includes bibliographical references. [BS2395.S84] 74-21691
1. Bible. N.T.—Addresses, essays, lectures. I. Skilton, John H.

WARE, Russell. 225'.07
The new Israel; a guide for studying the New Testament. Denton, Tex. [1969] iv, 136 p. illus. 23 cm. Includes bibliographies. [BS2535.2.W36] 74-8746
1. Bible. N.T.—Study. I. Title.

*HORNER, Jerry 225'.076
An outline of New Testament survey. Berkeley, Calif., McCutchan [1967] 85p. maps. 28cm. 2.55 pap.,
I. Title.

PONTIER, Arthur E. 225.076
The Savior and the church: A catechism manual of New Testament Revelation. Grand Rapids, Mich., Baker Bk. [c.]1962. 81p. 22cm. .75 pap.,
I. Title.

*BECK, Madeline H. 225'.077
Mastering New Testament facts; programmed reading, art and activities to get it all down pat [by] Madeline H. Beck [&] Lamar Williamson, Jr. Sketches by Stan Williams [&] Martha Williamson. Richmond, Va., John Knox Press [1973-] 4 v. illus. 28 cm. "Designed for Good news for modern man—easily used with other versions of the Bible. Contents.Contents: Book 1: Introduction. Matthew. Mark. Luke.—book 2: John. Acts.—Book 3: Romans to Hebrews.—Book 4: James to Revelation. ISBN 0-8042-0326-1 2.45 ea (pbk.)
1. Bible. N.T.—Programmed instruction. I. Williamson, Lamar, joint author. II. Title.
Book 2 (ISBN 0-8042-0327-X); Book 3 (ISBN 0-8042-0328-8); Book 4 (ISBN 0-8042-0329-6)

BATEY, Richard A., 1933- 225'.08
comp.
New Testament issues. Edited by Richard Batey. [1st U.S. ed.] New York, Harper & Row [1970] 241 p. 21 cm. (Harper forum books, RD 11) Contents.Contents.—Interpreting the New Testament: The challenge of New Testament theology today, by N. Perrin. On the problem of demythologizing, by R. Bultmann. Prolegomena to a commentary on Mark, by S. Sandmel.—Jesus of Nazareth: Concerning Jesus of Nazareth, by F. W. Beare. The interpreter and the parables: the centrality of the kingdom, by A. M. Hunter. The Lord's Prayer in modern research, by J. Jeremias. Did Jesus really rise from the dead? By W. Pannenberg.—The world of Paul: Dissensions within the early Church, by O. Cullmann. Current problems in Pauline research, by H. Conzelmann. St. Paul and the law, by C. E. B. Cranfield. Dying and rising with Christ, by E. Schweizer.—The world of John: The destination and purpose of St. John's Gospel, by J. A. T. Robinson. The kerygma of the Gospel according to John, by R. E. Brown. The search for the theology of the Fourth Evangelist, by J. L. Price. Includes bibliographical references. [BS2395.B35 1970] 75-109079 3.95
1. Bible. N.T.—Addresses, essays, lectures. I. Title.

CLARK, Kenneth Willis, 225'.08
1898-
Studies in the history and text of the New Testament in honor of Kenneth Willis Clark [edited] by Boyd L. Daniels and M. Jack Suggs. Salt Lake City, University of Utah Press, 1967. 187 p. port. 25 cm. (Studies and documents, 29) [BS2395.S8] 68-981
1. Bible. N. T.—Addresses, essays, lectures. I. Daniels, Boyd L., ed. II. Suggs, M. Jack ed. III. Title. IV. Series.
Contents omitted

DODD, Charles Harold, 225'.08
1884-
More New Testament studies [by] C. H. Dodd. Grand Rapids, Eerdmans [1968] vii, 157 p. 23 cm. Bibliographical footnotes. [BS2393.D57 1968] 73-1237 4.50
1. Bible. N.T.—Addresses, essays, lectures. I. Title.

RYAN, Rosalie. 1915- ed. 225.08
Contemporary Testament studies. Collegeville. Minn., Liturgical [1965] xiii,489p. 24cm. Bibl. [BS2395.R9] 65-29881 price unreported
1. Bibl N.T.—Addresses, essays, lectures. I. Title.

SCHLIER, Heinrich, 1900- 225'.08
The relevance of the New Testament. [New York] Herder and Herder [1968, c1967] x, 258 p. 22 cm. Translation of Besinnung auf das Neue Testament. Bibliographical footnotes. [BS2395.S2513] 67-21849
1. Bible. N. T.—Addresses, essays, lectures. I. Title.

STUDIES in the history 225'.08
and text of the New Testament in honor of Kenneth Willis Clark [edited] by Boyd L. Daniels and M. Jack Suggs. Salt Lake City, University of Utah Press, 1967. 187 p. port. 25 cm (Studies and documents, 29) Contents.Contents.—Bibliography (p. ix-xi).—External evidence and New Testament criticism, by E. C. Colwell.—Ho de dikaios ek pisteos zesetai, by D. M. Smith, Jr.—The Claremont profile-method for grouping New Testament minuscule manuscripts, by E. J. Epp.—Matthew as Eirenopoios, by M. P. Brown, Jr.—Codex 1867, by J. Geerlings.—Tatian's influence on the developing New Testament, by K. L. Carroll.—An analysis of the textual variations between Pap75 and Codex Vaticanus in the text of John, by C. L. Porter.—The problem of Christian origins: a programmatic essay, by W. L. Farmer.—A magical amulet for curing fevers, by B. M. Metzger.—Aspects of Paul's theology and their bearing on literary problems of Second Corinthians, by T. L. Price.—Matthew's Beatitudes and the Septuagint, by J. M. Rife.—La provenance Athonite, by J. Duplacy.—The purpose of John 21, by S. Agourides.—The Colossian heresy and Qumran theology, by E. W. Saunders.—Some problems in Jude 5, by A. Wikgren.—Style and text in the Greek New Testament, by G. D. Kilpatrick.—Uber die Bedeutung eines Punktes, by K. Aland. [BS2395.S8] 68-981
1. Bible. N.T.—Addresses, essays, lectures. I. Clark, Kenneth Willis, 1898- II. Daniels, Boyd L., ed. III. Suggs, M. Jack, ed. IV. Title. V. Series.

EHRHARDT, Arnold 225.081
The framework of the New Testament stories. Cambridge, Mass., Harvard [c.]1964. ix, 336p. 23cm. Bibl. [BS2395.E4] 65-79 7.00
1. Bible. N. T.—Addresses, essays, lectures. I. Title.

EHRHARDT, Arnold, 1903- 225.081
The framework of the New Testament stories. Cambridge, Mass., Harvard University Press, 1964. ix, 336 p. 23 cm. Bibliography: p. 313-324. [BS2395.E4] 65-79
1. Bible. N.T. — Addresses, essays, lectures. I. Title.

STUDIORUM Novi Testamenti 225.082
Societas
Bulletin. no. 1-3 [New York] Cambridge, 1963. 1v. 22cm. Reissue, orig. pub. 1950-52. 64-62 4.50 pap.,
1. Bible—Societies, etc. I. Title.

BRUCE, Frederick Fyvie, 225.1
1910-
Are the New Testament documents reliable? [4th ed.] Grand Rapids, Eerdmans, 1954. 122p. 23cm. [BS2332.B7 1954] 54-4811
1. Bible. N. T.—Evidences, authority, etc. I. Title.

BRUCE, Frederick Fyvie, 225.1
1910-
Are the New Testament documents reliable? [3d ed.] Chicago, Inter-varsity Christian Fellowship [1950] 118 p. 19 cm. [BS2332.B7 1950] 51-33891
1. Bible. N. T.—Evidences, authority, etc. I. Title.

BRUCE, Frederick Fyvie, 225.1
1910-
The New Testament documents: are they reliable? [5th rev. ed.] Grand Rapids, Eerdmans [1960] 120p. 18cm. (Eerdmans pocket editions) Includes bibliography. [BS2332.B7 1960] 60-2355
1. Bibel. N. T.—Evidences, authority, etc. I. Title.

HAMLIN, Griffith A 225.1
The New Testament, its intent and content. Goldsboro, N. C., Carolina Print. Co. [1959] 69p. 20cm. [BS2330.2.H3] 59-11378
1. Bible. N. T.—Introductions. I. Title.

ROBINSON, John Arthur 225.1
Thomas, Bp., 1919-
Can we trust the New Testament? / John A. T. Robinson. Grand Rapids : Eerdmans, 1977. 142 p. ; 18 cm. [BS2332.R6 1977] 76-49640 ISBN 0-8028-1682-7 pbk. : 1.95
1. Bible N.T.—Evidences, authority, etc. I. Title.

GRANT, Robert McQueen, 225.12
1917-
The formation of the New Testament [by] Robert M. Grant. [1st ed.] New York, Harper & Row [1965] 194 p. 21 cm. Bibliography: p. [188]-190. [BS2320.G78] 65-20451
1. Bible. N. T.—Canon. I. Title.

ROBINSON, John Arthur 225.1'4
Thomas, Bp., 1919-
Redating the New Testament / by John A. T. Robinson. Philadelphia : Westminster Press, c1976. p. cm. Includes bibliographical references and indexes. [BS2315.5.R67] 76-17554 ISBN 0-664-21336-7 : 15.00
1. Bible—Authorship—Date of authorship. I. Title.

BIBLE. N.T. Matthew. 225.1'5'08 s
English. Authorized. 1972.
The beginning of sorrows: the complete King James version of Matthew; with special emphasis on tomorrow's events in prophecy, by Salem Kirban. [Huntingdon Valley, Pa., S. Kirban, 1972] 142 p. illus. (part col.) 21 cm. (Prophecy New Testament series, no. 1) Cover title. [BS2545.P7P75 no. 1] [BS2573] 226'.2 72-197091 ISBN 0-912582-02-2 3.95
1. Bible. N.T. Matthew—Criticism, interpretation, etc. I. Kirban, Salem. II. Title.

PROPHECY New Testament 225.1'5'08
series, by Salem Kirban. Huntingdon Valley, Pa., S. Kirban [1972- v. illus. (part col.) 21 cm. Contents.Contents.—no. 1. The beginning of sorrows: the complete King James version of Matthew. [BS2545.P7P75] 72-79800
1. Bible—Prophecies. I. Kirban, Salem.

ELDER, E., comp. 225.2
Concordance to the New English Bible, New Testament. Grand Rapids, Mich., Zondervan [1965] 401p. 24cm. Concordance of words not in, or not in the same verses as the King James version. Supplement to existing concordances of other versions, First pub. in 1964 under title: New English Bible, New Testament: concordance. [BS2305.E4] 65-4322 4.95
1. Bible. N. T.—Concordances, English—New English. I. Title.

ELDER, E. 225.2
New English Bible, New Testament: concordance. Comp. by E. Elder. Grand Rapids, Mich., Zondervan [1965, c.1964] 401p. 22cm. A concordance of words not in, or not in the same verses as the Authorized version. Supplement to existing concordances of other versions. [BS2305.E4] 65-1490 4.95
1. Bible. N.T.—Concordances, English—New English. I. Title.

GALL, James, 1784?-1874. 225.2
Bible student's English-Greek concordance and Greek-English dictionary. Grand Rapids, Baker Book House, 1953. vii, 334, 32p. 25cm. [BS2305.G3] 54-14369
1. Bible. N. T.— Concordances, English. I. Title. II. Title: English-Greek concordance.

MODERN concordance to the 225.2
New Testament / edited and revised following all current English translations of the New Testament by Michael Darton. 1st ed. Garden City, N.Y. : Doubleday, c1976. xviii, 786 p. ; 29 cm. English or Greek. "Based on the French Concordance de la Bible, Nouveau Testament produced under the aegis of the Association de la Concordance francaise de la Bible." Includes indexes. [BS2305.M6 1976b] 77-365063 ISBN 0-385-07901-X : 27.50
1. Bible—Concordances, English. I. Darton, Michael. II. Bible, N.T.

SEUBERT, Aloysius H 225.2
The index to the New Testament and The topical analysis to the New Testament. [San Diego, Calif., 1953] vii, 122, v. 142p. 21cm. 'A Universal publication.' [BS2310.S45] 53-32188
1. Bible. N.T.—Indexes, Topical. I. Title.

SEUBERT, Aloysius H 225.2
The index to the New Testament, and The topical analysis to the New Testament. [Student ed. San Diego, Universal Publications 1954] 122, 142p. 21cm. [BS2310.S45 1954] 55-24547
1. Bible. N.T.—Indexes, Topical. I. Title. II. Title: The topical analysis to the New Testament.

SEUBERT, Aloysius H. 225.2
The index to the New Testament, and The topical analysis to the New Testament. [Library ed. Lemon Grove, Calif., Universal Publications, c1955] vii, 122, 142 p. 21 cm. Bibliography: p. vii. [BS2310.S45 1955] 58-26854
1. Bible. N.T. — Indexes, Topical. I. Title. II. Title: The topical analysis to the New Testament.

SMITH, Jacob Brubaker, 225.2
1870-1951.
Greek-English concordance to the New Testament: a tabular and statistical Greek-English concordance based on the King James version, with an English-to-Greek index. Introd. by Bruce M. Metzger. Scottdale, Pa., Herald Press, 1955. 430 p. 29 cm. [BS2302.S54] 55-12260
1. Bible. N.T.—Concordances, Greek. 2. Greek language, Biblical—Dictionaries—English. I. Title.

STEGENGA, J. 225.2
La concordancia analitica greco-espanola del Nuevo Testamento greco-espanol / compilada en griego-ingles por J. Stegenga ; [traducci on y compilaci on] en griega-espanol por A. E. Tuggy. Maracaibo, Venezuela : Editorial Libertador, c1975. xiii, 845, vi, 207 p. ; 27 cm. Translation of The Greek-English analytical concordance of the Greek-English New Testament. "Apendices de lecturas variantes": p. [i]-207 (last groups) [BS2302.S718] 75-21139
1. Bible. N.T.—Concordances, Greek. 2. Greek language, Biblical—Dictionaries—Spanish. I. Tuggy, A. E. II. Title.

STEGENGA, J., comp. 225.2
The Greek-English analytical concordance, supplementary of various readings from early and late Greek texts; v.2. Prep. for those using the Greek texts of Westcott & Hort, Eberhard Nestle (21st ed.), Augustinus Merk (5th ed.) Jackson, Miss. 39209, Hellenes-English Biblical Found., Box 10412 [c.1965] 115p. 28cm. [BS2302.S7 Suppl.] 63-1737 2.60 pap.,
1. Bible. N.T.—Concordances. 2. Greek language—Biblical—Dictionaries—English. I. Title.

STEGENGA, J 225.2
The Greek-English analytical concordance of the Greek-English New Testament. [Jackson, Miss., Hellenes-English Biblical Foundation 1963] [Jackson, Miss., Hellenes-English Biblical Foundation 1964-65] xv, 832 p. 28

cm. 2 v. 28 cm. Contents.Contents.--v. 1. Sustitutions and additions.--v. 2. Omissions and transpositions. [BS2302.S7] 63-1737
1. Bible. N.T.—Concordances, Greek. 2. Greek language Biblical—Dictionaries—English. I. Title. II. Title: The Greek-English analytical concordance, supplementary of various readings from early and late Greek texts. Prepared for those using the Greek texts of Westcott & Hort; Eberhard Nestle

STEGENGA, J. 225.2
The Greek-English analytical concordance [of the Greek-English New Testament. Supplement.] v.1. [Jackson 9, Miss., P.O. Bx. 10412, Hellenes-English Biblical Found., c.1964] 86p. 28cm. 63-1737 1.95 pap.,
1. Bible. N.T.—Concordances. I. Greek language—Biblical—Dictionaries—English. II. Title.
Contents omitted.

TOLLENAERE, F. de. 225.2
Word-indices and word-lists to the Gothic Bible and minor fragments / by Felicien de Tollenaere, Randall L. Jones, in cooperation with Frans van Coetsem, Philip H. Smith and Hon Tom Wong. Leiden : Brill, 1976. xvi, 581, [2] p. ; 30 cm. Bibliography: p. [583] [BS428.G67T64] 76-373996 ISBN 9-00-404360-8 : fl 245.00
1. Bible—Concordances, Gothic. 2. Gothic language—Word frequency. 3. Gothic language—Glossaries, vocabularies, etc. I. Jones, Randall L., joint author. II. Title.

VOLLSTANDIGE Konkordanz 225.2
zum griechischen Neuen Testament : unter Zugrundelegung aller modernen kritischen Textausgaben und des Textus receptus / in Verbindung mit H. Riesenfeld, H.-U. Rosenbaum, Chr. Hannick, neu zusammengestellt unter der Leitung von K. Aland. Berlin ; New York : De Gruyter, 1975- v. ; 31 cm. (Arbeiten zur neutestamentlichen Textforschung ; Bd. 4) Issued in parts. [BS2302.V64] 75-521776 ISBN 3-11-002258-3 (v. 1/1)
1. Bible. N.T.—Concordances, Greek. I. Aland, Kurt.

WIGRAM, George V. 225.2
The Englishman's Greek concordance of the New Testament; being an attempt at a verbal connexion between the Greek and the English texts: including a concordance to the proper names; with indexes, Greek-English and English-Greek; and a concordance of various readings [by George V. Wigram] 9th ed., in which is added a vocabulary of New Testament Greek. Grand Rapids, Mich., Zondervan Pub. House [1970] xxxv, 1020, 14, iv, 71 p. 25 cm. Ninth ed. first published in 1903. [BS2341.W65 1970] 71-106435
1. Bible. N.T.—Concordances, English. I. Title.

KILLINGER, John. 225'.2'06
A sense of His presence / by John Killinger ; drawings by Andy Bacon. 1st ed. Garden City, N.Y. : Doubleday, 1977. xii, 129 p. : ill. ; 22 cm. (The Devotional commentary : Matthew) [BS2575.4.K54] 77-1038 ISBN 0-385-12715-4 : 5.95
1. Bible. N.T. Matthew—Devotional literature. I. Title. II. Series.

GUY, Harold A 225.3
Who's who in the gospels [by] H. A. Guy. London, Melbourne [etc.] Macmillan; New York, St. Martin's P., 1966. v, 152 p. 19 1/2 cm. 12/6 (8/6 school ed.) [BS2312.G8] 66-15481
1. Bible. N.T. — Dictionaries. I. Title.

GUY, Harold A. 225.3
Who's who in the gospels [by] H. A. Guy. London, Melbourne New [etc.] Macmillan, New York, St. Martin's 1966. v, 152p. 19 cm. [BS2312.G8 1966] 66-15481 2.99
1. Bible. N. T.—Dictionaries. I. Title.

THE New international 225.3
dictionary of New Testament theology / Colin Brown, general editor. Grand Rapids, Mich. : Zondervan Pub. House, c1975- v. ; 25 cm. Dictionary of New Testament theology. "Translated, with additions and revisions, from the German Theologisches Begriffslexikon zum Neuen Testament, edited by Lothar Coenen, Erich Beyreuther and Hans Bietenhard." "Companion volume: The new international dictionary of the Christian Church." Includes bibliographical references and indexes. [BS2397.N48] 75-38895 ISBN 0-85364-177-3 : 24.95
1. Bible. N.T.—Theology—Dictionaries. 2. Bible. N.T.—Dictionaries. I. Brown, Colin. II. Title: Dictionary of New Testament theology.

PARTRIDGE, Eric, 1894- 225.3
A New Testament word book; a glossary. Freeport, N.Y., Books for Libraries Press [1970] xi, 215 p. 23 cm. Reprint of the 1940 ed. [BS440.P34 1970] 70-117907
1. Bible—Dictionaries. I. Title.

COLWELL, Ernest Cadman, 225.4
1901-
Studies in methodology in textual criticism of the New Testament, by Ernest C. Colwell. Grand Rapids, Eerdmans, 1969. 175 p. 25 cm. (New Testament tools and studies, v. 9) Includes bibliographical references. [BS2325.C6 1969b] 70-14515
1. Bible. N.T.—Criticism, Textual—Addresses, essays, lectures. I. Title. II. Series.

EARLE, Ralph. 225.4
Word meanings in the New Testament. Grand Rapids, Baker Book House [1974- v. 20 cm. Contents.Contents.— —v. 3. Romans. [BS2665.2.E24] 74-174439 4.95 (per vol.)
1. Bible. N.T. Romans—Language, style. I. Title.

GREENLEE, Jacob Harold, 225.4
1918-
Introduction to New Testament, textual criticism. Grand Rapids, Mich., Eerdmans [c.1964] 160p. illus., facsims. 22cm. Bibl. 63-20679 3.50
1. Bible. N.T.—Criticism, Textual. I. Title.

GREENLEE, Jacob Harold, 225.4
1918-
Introduction to New Testament textual criticism, by J. Harold Greenlee. Grand Rapids, Eerdmans [1964] 160 p. illus., facsims. 22 cm. Bibliography: p. 151-154. [BS2325.G67] 63-20679
1. Bible. N.T. — Criticism, Textual. I. Title.

METZGER, Bruce Manning. 225.4
The text of the New Testament; its transmission, corruption, and restoration. New York, Oxford University Press, 1964. ix, 268 p. 16 plates. 22 cm. Bibliography: p. [257]-259. [BS2325.M4] 64-2530
1. Bible. N.T. — Criticism, Textual. 2. Bible. N.T. — Hist. I. Title.

METZGER, Bruce Manning 225.4
The text of the New Testament; its transmission, corruption, and restoration. New York, Oxford [c.]1964. ix, 268p. 16 plates. 22cm. Bibl. 64-2530 7.00
1. Bible. N.T.—Criticism, Textual. 2. Bible. N.T.—Hist. I. Title.

METZGER, Bruce Manning. 225.4
The text of the New Testament; its transmission, corruption, and restoration by Bruce M. Metzger. 2d ed. New York, Oxford University Press, 1968. ix, 281 p. illus. 22 cm. Includes bibliographical references. [BS2325.M4 1968] 68-7852 7.00
1. Bible. N.T.—Criticism, Texual. 2. Bible. N.T.—History. I. Title.

METZGER, Bruce Manning. 225.4
The text of the New Testament: its transmission, corruption, and restoration, by Bruce M. Metzger. 2nd ed. Oxford, Clarendon P., 1968. xi, 284 p. 16 plates, illus., facsims., 23 cm. Bibliography: p. [257]-260. [BS2325.M4 1968b] 79-385648 45/-
1. Bible. N.T.—Criticism, Textual. 2. Bible. N.T.—History. I. Title.

PICKERING, Wilbur N. 225.4
The identity of the New Testament text / Wilbur N. Pickering. Nashville : T. Nelson, c1977 191 p. : ill. ; 21 cm. Includes index. Bibliography: p. 181-186. [BS2325.P52] 77-1559 ISBN 0-8407-5113-3 : 7.95
1. Bible. N.T.—Criticism, Textual. I. Title.

WILDER, Amos Niven, 1895- 225.4
The language of the Gospel; early Christian rhetoric. New York, Harper & Row [1964] 143 p. 22 cm. Bibliographical footnotes. [BS2370.W5] 64-15479
1. Bible, N.T. — Language, style. I. Title.

WILDER, Amos Niven, 1895- 225.4
The language of the Gospel; early Christian rhetoric. New York, Harper [c.1964] 143p. 22cm. Bibl. 64-15479 3.50
1. Bible. N. T.—Language, style. I. Title.

FULLER, Reginald Horace. 225.406
Luke's witness to Jesus Christ. New York, Association Press [c1958] 80 p. 19 cm. (World Christian books, no. 26, 2d ser.) [BS2596.F8] 59-14240
1. Bible. N. T. Luke — Study — Text-books. I. Title.

BIBLE. N. T. Gospels. 225.47
Greek. Selections. 1956.
Codex Climaci rescriptus Graecus; a study of portions of the Greek New Testament comprising the underwriting of part of a palimpsest in the library of Westminister College, Cambridge (Ms. Gregory 1561, L) By Ian A. Moir. Cambridge [Eng.] University Press, 1956. xi, 116p. diagrs., facsims., tables. 22cm. (Texts and studies: contributions to Biblical and pastristic literature, new ser. 2) Bibliography: p. 21.sBible. N. T. Gospels--Criticism, Textual. [BR45.T43 n.s., vol. 2] 62-38842
I. Moir, Ian A. II. Bible. Manuscripts, Greek, N. T. Codex Climaci rescriptus Graecus. III. Title. IV. Series.

HARDING LECTURES. 225.47
Nashville, Christian Family Books. v. ports. 21 cm. annual. "Harding College lectureship." Editor: W. J. Hacker. [BR45.H3] 64-1305
1. Christianity — 20th cent. — Addresses, essays, lectures. 2. Christian life — Addresses, essays, lectures. I. Hacker, W. Joe, ed. II. Harding College, Searcy, Ark. III. Title.

JANIC, Vojislav, 1890- ed. 225.47
and tr.
Lives of the Serbian saints, by Voyeslav Yanich and C. Patrick Hankey. London, Society for Promoting Christian Knowledge. New York, Macmillan, 1921. xx, 108 p. plate, ports. 19 cm. (Translations of Christian literature, ser. 7) Translated from a martyrology issued, in the middle of the last century, for the use of the church throughout Serbia. [BR45.T67L5] 21-21903
1. Saints, Serbian. I. Hankey, Cyril Patrick, joint ed. II. Title. III. Series.

LANCASTER, Pa. Theological 225.47
Seminary of the United Church of Christ.
Occasional papers, no. 1- Lancaster, Pa., 1962- [BR45.L25] 62-21931
I. Title.

LANCASTER, Pa. Theological 225.47
Seminary of the United Church of Christ.
Occasional papers, no. 1- Lancaster, Pa., 1962- v. in 22 cm. [BR45.L25] 62-21931
1. Theology — Collections. I. Title.

LIVESEY, Derek, Leonard, 225.47
1923-
Lives of the Serbian saints, by Voyeslav Yanich and C. Patrick Hankey. London, Society for Promoting Christian Knowledge. New York, Macmillan, 1921. xx, 108 p. plate, ports. 19 cm. (Translations of Christian literature, ser. 7) Translated from a martyrology issued, in the middle of the last century, for the use of the church throughout Serbia. [BR45.T67L5] 21-21903
1. Saints, Serbian. I. Title. II. Series.

MUNCEY, Raymond Waterville 225.47
Luke, ed.
The New Testament text of Saint Ambrose. Cambridge [Eng.] University Press, 1959. lxxviii, 118p. 23cm. (Texts and studies; contributions to biblical and patristic literature, new ser., 4) 'The New Testament text of St. Ambrose is predominantly Old Latin.--p. xxiv. [BR45.T43 n. s., 4] 59-16076
1. Ambrosius, Saint, Bp. of Milan. 2. Bible. N. T.—Quotations, Early. 3. Bible. N. T. Latin—Criticism, Textual. I. Title. II. Series.

BIBLE. N.T. Acts. English. 225.48
1964.
The Acts of the apostles; an exposition, by Richard Belward Rackham. Grand Rapids, Baker Book House, 1964. cxv, 524 p. 23 cm. (Westminster commentaries) Limited editions library. Reprint of the 14th ed., published in 1951. [BS2625.R3] 64-23176
1. Bible. N.T. Acts—Commentaries. I. Rackham, Richard Belward, 1863-1912. II. Title. III. Series.

BIBLE. N. T. Greek. 1958. 225.48
The Greek Testament; with a critically revised text, a digest of various readings, marginal references to verbal and idiomatic usage, prolegomena, and a critical and exegetical commentary, by Henry Alford. With revision by Everett F. Harrison. Chicago, Moody Press [1958] 4v. in 2. tables. 24cm. Contents.[1] The four Gospels. Acts-Corinthiana--[2] Galatiana--Philemon, Hebrewa--Revelation. Includes bibliographies. [BS1965 1958] 58-3073
1. Bible. N. T.— Commentaries. I. Alford, Henry, 1810-1871. ed. II. Title.

BIBLE. N.T. Greek. 1966. 225'.4'8
The Greek New Testament; edited by Kurt Aland [and others] New York, American Bible Society; London, British & Foreign Bible Society, 1966. iv, 920 p. tables. 19 1/2 cm. 21/- Bibliography: p. xiix-iv. [BS1965] 67-80007
I. Aland, Kurt, ed. II. Title.

BIBLE. N.T. Greek. 1969. 225.4'8
The Kingdom interlinear translation of the Greek Scriptures. Produced by New World Bible Translation Committee. [1st ed. Brooklyn, Watchtower Bible and Tract Society of New York] 1969. 1165 p. illus., facsims., maps, plans. 19 cm. "A literal word-for-word translation into English under the Greek text as set out in 'The New Testament in the original Greek—the text revised by Brooke Foss Westcott, D.D., and Fenton John Anthony Hort, D.D.' ... together with the New World translation of the Christian Greek Scriptures, revised edition, a modern-language translation of the Westcott and Hort Greek text." [BS1965 1969] 77-11484 2.00
I. Westcott, Brooke Foss, Bp. of Durham, 1825-1901. II. Hort, Fenton John Anthony, 1828-1892. III. New World Bible Translation Committee. IV. Bible. N.T. English. New World. 1969. V. Title.

BIBLE. N.T. Greek. 1975. 225.4'8
The Greek-English New Testament : King James version, New International version, Greek text, Literal interlinear. Washington : Christianity Today, [1975] xxxix, 777 p. ; 24 cm. The King James and New International versions, and the Nestle Greek text with a literal English translation by A. Marshall, on opposite pages. [BS1965 1975] 75-4148
1. Bible—Interlinear translations. I. Bible. N.T. English. 1975. II. Title.

BIBLE. N.T. Greek. 1976. 225.4'8
The New International Version interlinear Greek-English New Testament : the Nestle Greek text with a literal English translation by Alfred Marshall, and a foreword by J. B. Phillips, also a marginal text of the New international version. Grand Rapids : Zondervan, c1976. xx, 1027 p. ; 23 cm. [BS1965 1976] 76-13493 13.95
1. Bible—Interlinear translations. I. Marshall, Alfred. II. Bible. N.T. English. Marshall. 1976. III. Bible. N.T. New international version. 1976. IV. Title. V. Title: Interliner Greek-English New Testament.

BRUGGEN, J. van, 1936- 225'.4'8
The ancient text of the New Testament / by Jakob van Bruggen. Winnipeg : Premier, 1976. 40 p. ; 23 cm. Translation of De tekst van het Nieuwe Testament. Includes bibliographical references. [BS2325.B7813] 77-365178 ISBN 0-88756-005-9
1. Bible. N.T.—Criticism, Textual—Addresses, essays, lectures. I. Title.

GREENLEE, Jacob Harold, 225.4'8
1918-
Nine uncial palimpsests of the Greek New Testament, by J. Harold Greenlee. Salt Lake City, University of Utah Press, 1968. 131 p. illus., facsims. 25 cm. (Studies and documents, 39) Includes bibliographical references. [BS1939.G73] 72-13138
1. Bible. Manuscripts, Greek. N.T. I. Title. II. Series.

HAN, Nathan E. 225.4'8
A parsing guide to the Greek New Testament. Compiled by Nathan E. Han. With an introd. by Merrill C. Tenney. Scottdale, Pa., Herald Press [1971] xv, 479 p. 23 cm. [PA847.H3] 77-158175 ISBN 0-8361-1653-4 12.95
1. Greek language, Biblical—Verb. I. Title.

HARRISVILLE, Roy A. 225.48
The concept of newness in the New Testament. Minneapolis, Augsburg Pub. House [1960] viii, 126p. Bibl. 20cm. (An Augsburg Publishing House theological monograph) 60-8895 1.95 pap.,
1. Kainos (The word). 2. Neos (The word). 3. Bible. N.T.—Theology. I. Title. II. Title: Newness in the New Testament.

HATCH, William Henry 225.48
Paine, 1875-
Facsimiles and descriptions of minuscule manuscripts of the New Testament. Cambridge, Harvard University Press, 1951. [xii], 289 p. 100 facsims. 31 cm. "Companion to the author's ... The principal uncial manuscripts of the New Testament." Bibliographical footnotes. Bibliography: p. [xi]-[xii] [BS1938.H28] 52-220
1. Bible. Manuscripts, Greek. N.T. 2. Bible. Manuscripts, Greek—Facsimiles—N.T. 3. Manuscripts, Greek—Facsimiles. 4. Writing, Minuscule. I. Title. II. Title: Minuscule manuscripts of the New Testament.

HOBBS, Herschel H 225.48
Preaching values from the papyri. Grand Rapids, Baker Book House, 1964. 123 p. 20 cm. [BS525.H6] 64-14305
1. Greek language. Biblical — Words — Hist. 2. Greek language, Helenistic (300 B.C.-600 A.D.) — Words — Hist. I. Title.

HOBBS, Herschel H. 225.48
Preaching values from the papyri. Grand Rapids, Mich., Baker Bk. [c.]1964. 123p. 20cm. 64-14305 2.95
1. Greek language, Biblical—Words—Hist. 2. Greek language, Hellenistic (300 B.C.-600 A.D.)—Words—Hist. I. Title.

METZGER, Bruce Manning. 225.48
Chapters in the history of New Testament textual criticism. Grand Rapids, W. B. Eerdmans, 1963. x, 164 p. 25 cm. (New Testament tools and studies, v. 4) Includes bibliographical references. [BS471.M4] 63-25909

1. Bible — Criticism, Textual — Hist. I. Title. II. Series.

METZGER, Bruce Manning 225.48
Chapters in the history of New Testament textual criticism. Grand Rapids, Mich., Eerdmans [c.]1963. x, 164p. 25cm. (New Testament tools and studies, v.4) Bibl. 63-25909 4.00
1. Bible—Criticism, Textual—Hist. I. Title. II. Series.

METZGER, Bruce Manning. 225.48
A textual commentary on the Greek New Testament; a companion volume to the United Bible Societies' Greek New Testament (3d ed.), by Bruce M. Metzger. London, New York, United Bible Societies [1971] xxxi, 775 p. 19 cm. Includes bibliographical references. [BS2325.M43] 73-160110 ISBN 3-438-06010-8
1. Bible. N.T.—Criticism, Textual. I. United Bible Societies. II. Bible. N.T. Greek. 1968. III. Title.

MORRIS, Leon. 225.48
The apostolic preaching of the cross. [1st ed.] Grand Rapids, Eerdmans [1955] 296p. 23cm. Bibliographical footnotes. [BS2385.M63] 56-13629
1. Bible. N. T.—Language, style. 2. Greek language, Biblical—Semantics. 3. Theology—Terminology. I. Title.

RICE, John R., 1895- 225.48
Filled with the spirit; a verse-by-verse commentary on Acts of the Apostles. Murfreesboro, Tenn., Sword of the Lord Publishers [c1963] 555 p. 21 cm. [BS2625.3.R5] 64-1990
1. Bible. N.T. Acts — Commentaries. I. Title.

RIENECKER, Fritz. 225.4'8
A linguistic key to the Greek New Testament / Fritz Rienecker ; translated, with additions and revisions, from the German Sprachlicher Schluessel zum griechischen Neuen Testament, edited by Cleon L. Rogers, Jr. Grand Rapids, Mich. : Zondervan, c1976- v. ; 23 cm. Contents.Contents.—v. 1. Matthew through Acts. [BS1938.R513] 75-45486 6.95
1. Bible. N.T.—Criticism, Textual. 2. Bible. N.T. Greek—Versions. I. Rogers, Cleon L. II. Title.

SANDERS, Henry Arthur, 225.4'8
1868-1956.
The New Testament manuscripts in the Freer collection. New York, Macmillan, 1918. [New York, Johnson Reprint Corp., 1972] x, 323 p. illus. 23 cm. Original ed. issued as v. 9 of University of Michigan studies. Humanistic series. Contents.Contents.—Pt. I. The Washington manuscript of the Gospels.—Pt. II. The Washington fragments of the Epistles of Paul. [BS1939.F7S2 1972] 73-39271
1. Bible. Manuscripts, Greek. N.T. 2. Manuscripts, Greek—Facsimiles. I. Freer Gallery of Art, Washington, D.C. Mss. (Greek) II. Bible. N.T. Epistles of Paul. Greek. 1972. III. Title. IV. Series: Michigan. University. University of Michigan studies. Humanistic series, v. 9.

WILCOX, Max. 225.48
The Semitisms of Acts. Oxford, Clarendon Press, 1965. xiii, 206 p. illus. 23 cm. "Originally presented as a thesis ... University of Edinburgh, in 1955, under the title: The Semitisms of Acts I-XV." Bibliography: p. [186]-189. [BS2625.2.W5] 65-2131
1. Bible. N.T. Acts — Criticism, Textual. I. Title.

YODER, James D 225.48
Concordance to the distinctive Greek text of Codex Bezae. Grand Rapids, Eerdmans, 1961. vi, 73 p. 28 cm. (New Testament tools and studies, v. 2) [BS1964.B4Y6] 61-66468
1. Bible. Manuscripts. Greek. N.T. Codex Bezae. 2. Bible N.T. — Concordances, Greek. I. Title. II. Series.

YODER, James D. 225.48
Concordance to the distinctive Greek text of Codex Bezae. Grand Rapids, Mich., Eerdmans [c.]1961. vi, 73p. 28cm. (New Testament tools and studies, v.2) 61-66468 5.00
1. Bible, Manuscripts, Greek. N. T. Codex Bezae. 2. Bible. N. T.—Concordances, Greek I. Title. II. Series.

BIBLE. N. T. English. 1961. 225.5
Norlie.
Simplified New Testament in plain English for today's reader. A new tr. from the Greek by Olaf M. Norlie. With The Psalms for today, a new tr. in current English, by R. K. Harrison. Grand Rapids, Mich., Zondervan [c.1961] 603, xiv, 160p. 61-16512 4.95
I. Norlie, Olaf Morgan, 1876- tr. II. Bible. O. T. Psalms. English. 1961. III. Title. IV. Title: The Psalms for today.

BIBLE. N. T. English. 1962. 225.5
The New Testament octapla; eight English versions of the New Testament in the Tyndale-King James tradition. Ed. by Luther A. Weigle. New York, Nelson [1962] xvi, 1489p. 8 facsims. 29cm. 62-10331 20.00
1. Bible. N. T. English—Versions. I. Weigle, Luther Allen, 1880- II. Title.

COLWELL, Ernest Cadman, 225.5
1901-
What is the best New Testament? [Chicago] University of Chicago Press [1952] 126 p. illus. 20 cm. [BS2385.C64] 52-8690
1. Bible. N. T.—Criticism, Textual. 2. Bible. N. T. English—Versions. I. Title.

DENNETT, Herbert. 225.5
A guide to modern versions of the New Testament; how to understand and use them. Chicago, Moody Press [1966, c1965] xiii, 142 p. 22 cm. First published in 1965 under title: Graphic guide to modern versions of the New Testament. Bibliography: p. 137. [BS455.D45 1966] 67-1987
1. Bible. N.T. English—Versions. I. Title. II. Title: Modern versions of the New Testament.

GROSSOUW, Willem Karel 225.5
Maria, 1906-
Revelation and redemption; a sketch of the theology of St. John. Translated and edited from the Dutch by Martin W. Schoenberg. Westminster, Md., Newman Press, 1955. 133p. 22cm. Translation of Het Christendom van Johannes. [BS2615.G945] 55-8010
1. Bible. N. T. John—Commentaries. I. Title.

TAYLOR, Vincent, 1887- 225.5
The text of the New Testament; a short introduction. [New York] St. Martin's Press, 1961. 113 p. 22 cm. Includes bibliography. [BS2325.T35 1961] 61-3731
1. Bible. N. T. — Criticism, Textual. I. Title.

TAYLOR, Vincent, 1887- 225.5
The text of the New Testament; a short introduction. New York, St. Martin's Press [c.] 1961. 113p. Bibl. 61-3731 3.50
1. Bible, N.T.—Criticism, Textual. I. Title.

BIBLE. N. T. English. 225.5/04
1965. Revised Standard.
The New Testament of our Lord and Savior Jesus Christ. Rev. standard version, Catholic ed. Prepd. by the Catholic Biblical Assn. of Gt. Brit. Pref. by Albert Cardinal Meyer. Large type ed. New York, Watts [1697,c.1965] 999p. 28cm. (Keith Jennison bk.) Tr. from the Greek, being the version set forth A.D. 1611, rev. A.D.1881 and A.D. 1901 compared with the most ancient authorities and rev. A.D. 1946 [BS2091.A1 1965 T6] 12.50
I. Catholic Biblical Association of Gt. Brit. II. Title.

BIBLE. N.T. Polyglot. 225.51
1964.
New Testament students' workbook: Greek, Latin, English. Collegeville, Minn., Liturgical Press [1964, c1963] 671 p. 32 cm. The Greek and Latin text is from the 21st ed. of Novum Testamentum Graece et Latine edited by D. Eberhard Nestle, revised by D. Erwin Nestle and d. Kurt Aland, published in Stuttgart, 1962. The English text is the Confraternity version of the 1958 printing, Paterson, N.J., of the New Testament of Our Lord and Saviour, Jesus Christ, a revision of the Challoner-Rheims version. [BS1901] 64-56533
I. Title.

BIBLE. English. 225.52
Selections. 1953.
Biblical book; quotations from the New Testament and quotations from Bible themes, selected and compiled by A. Pfeiffer. New York, William-Frederick Press, 1953. 127p. illus. 19cm. [BS391.P47] 52-8638
I. Pfeiffer, Adolph, ed. II. Title.

BIBLE. N. T. English. 225.52
1903. Twentieth century.
The twentieth century New Testament; a translation into modern English. Chicago, Moody Pr. [1961] 449p. 3.50; 1.29 pap.,
I. Title.

BIBLE. N. T. English. 225.52
1946. Revised standard.
The new covenant, commonly called the New Testament of Our Lord and Savior Jesus Christ. Rev. standard version, tr. from Greek, being the version set forth A. D. 1611, rev. A. D. 1881 and A. D. 1901, compared with the most ancient authorities, rev. A. D. 1946. New York, Harper [1962, c.1946] 638p. 11cm. Cover title: New Testament. Psalms. 4.00, bxd.
I. Title.

BIBLE. N. T. English. 225.52
1950. Confraternity version.
The New Testament of Our Lord and Savior Jesus Christ, translated from the Latin Vulgate; a revision of the Challoner-Rheims version, edited by Catholic scholars under the patronage of the Episcopal Committee of the Confraternity of Christian Doctrine . . . Special student ed. New York, Catholic Book Pub. Co. [1950] 379p. col. illus., col. maps. 26cm. [BS2080 1950.N42] 51-441
I. Confraternity of Christian Doctrine. II. Title.

BIBLE. N. T. English. 225.52
1950. Confraternity version.
The New Testament of Our Lord and Savior Jesus Christ, translated from the Latin Vulgate; a revision of the Challoner-Rheims version, edited by Catholic scholars under the patronage of the Episcopal Committee of the Confraternity of Christian Doctrine . . . With the words of Christ printed in red. New York, Catholic Book Pub. Co. [1950] 383p. col. illus., col. maps. 21cm. [BS2080 1950.N4] 50-575
I. Confraternity of Christian Doctrine. II. Title.

BIBLE. N. T. English. 225.52
1950. Moffatt.
The New Testament and the Psalms; a new translation by James Moffatt. New York, Harper [c1950] 561p. 11cm. [BS2095] 51-12525
I. Bible. O. T. Psalms. English. 1950. Moffatt. II. Moffatt, James, 1870-1944, tr. III. Title.

BIBLE. N. T. English. 225.52
1950. New World.
New World translation of the Christian Greek Scriptures, rendered from the original language by the New World Bible Translation Committee. [Brooklyn, Watchtower Bible and Tract Society] 1950. 792 p. illus., maps (part col.) facsims. 19 cm. [BS2095.N44] 50-14033
I. New World Bible Translation Committee. II. Watch Tower Bible and Tract Society. III. Title.

BIBLE. N. T. English. 225.52
1950. Rheims.
The New Testament of Our Lord and Savior Jesus Christ, translated from the Latin Vulgate; a revision of the Challoner-Rheims version, edited by Catholic scholars under the patronage of the Episcopal Committee of the Confraternity of Christian Doctrine ... With the words of Christ printed in red. New York, Catholic Book Pub. Co. [1950] 383 p. col. illus., col. maps. 21 cm. [BS2080 1950.N4] 50-575
I. Challoner, Richard, Bp., 1691-1781. ed. II. Confraternity of Christian Doctrine. III. Title.

BIBLE. N. T. English. 225.52
1950. Sacred Name version.
The New Testament of our Messiah and Saviour Yahshua. Sacred Name version, critically compared with ancient authorities and divers manuscripts. Irvington, N. J., Scripture Research Association, 1950. 566 p. 17 cm. Cover title: Sacred Name New Testament. [BS2095.S23 1950] 50-55680
I. Title. II. Title: Sacred Name New Testament.

BIBLE. N. T. English. 225.52
1950. Williams.
The New Testament; a translation in the language of the people, by Charles B. Williams. Chicago, Moody Press, 1950. 575 p. 21 cm. [BS2095.W] A 51
I. Williams, Charles Bray, 1869- tr. II. Title.

BIBLE. N. T. English. 225.52
1951. Authorized.
The New Testament of Our Lord and Saviour Jesus Christ. The authorized King James version. Self pronouncing ed. with a guide to the parables and an index to the words and wisdom of Jesus as applied to everyday problems of life. Chicago, Spencer Press [1951] x, 308 p. 12 cm. [BS2085 1951.C5] 51-5410
I. Title.

BIBLE. N. T. English. 225.52
1951. Brotherhood Authentic Bible Society.
The New Testament of Our Lord and Savior Jesus Christ. The authentic version. Plattsburg, Mo., Brotherhood Authentic Bible Society, '1951. 475 p. 18 cm. [BS2095.B7] 51-30185
I. Title.

BIBLE. N. T. English. 225.52
1952. Confraternity version.
The New Testament of Our Lord and Savior Jesus Christ. The words of Our Lord printed in red; new Confraternity text . . . Holy Land ed. New York, C. Wildermann Co. [1952] x, 310p. illus. (part col.) col. maps. 23cm. 'Study outline of the New Testament':p. 256-310. [BS2080 1952.N4] 53-476
I. Title.

BIBLE. N. T. English. 225.52
1953. Confraternity version.
The New Testament of Our Lord and Savior Jesus Christ, translated from the Latin Vulgate; a revision of the Challoner-Rheims version edited by Catholic scholars under the patronage of the Episcopal Committee of the Confraternity of Christian Doctrine. St. Paul, Catechetical Guild Educational Society [1953] 480p. 17cm. [BS2080 1953.S3] 53-30049
I. Confraternity of Christian Doctrine. II. Title.

BIBLE. N. T. English. 225.52
1953. Wesley.
John Wesley's New Testament, compared with the Authorized version; with an introd. by Fred Pierce Corson. Anniversary ed. Philadelphia, Winston [1953] xiv, 391p. port., facsims. 19cm. [BS2095.W424] 53-7376
I. Wesley. John 1703-1791. tr. II. Title.

BIBLE. N. T. English. 225.52
1953. Weymouth.
The New Testament in modern speech [by] Richard Francis Weymouth. [6th ed.] New York, Harper [1953] 456p. map (on lining papers) 19cm. [BS2095.W45 1953] 53-6529
I. Weymouth, Richard Francis, 1822-1902, tr. II. Title.

BIBLE. N.T. English. 1954. 225.52
Montgomery.
The New Testament in modern English. Translated by Helen Barrett Montgomery. Philadelphia, Judson Press [1954, c1924] 724 p. 17 cm. At head of title: Centenary translation. First published in 1924 under title: Centenary translation of the New Testament, published to signalize the completion of the first hundred years of work of the American Baptist Publication Society. [BS2095] 63-6810
I. Montgomery, Helen (Barrett) 1861-1934, tr. II. Title.

BIBLE. N. T. English. 225.52
1954. Moore.
The New Testament, a new, independent, individual translation from the Greek by George Albert Moore. [Collector's ed.] Chevy Chase, Md., Country Dollar Press [1954, c1953] 353 p. port. 30 cm. (The Moore series of source books, translations, and commentaries) 'Limited to 250 copies . . . no. 3.' aMoore, George Albert, [BS2095.M78] 54-1019
I. Title.

BIBLE. N. T. English. 225.52
1956. Authorized.
The New Testament and book of Psalms, translated out of the original tongues and with the former translations diligently compared and revised. Authorized King James version. Red letter ed., with all the words recorded therein as having been spoken by Our Lord printed in red. Cleveland, World Pub. Co. [1956] 636p. plates (part col.) 19cm. [BS2085 1956.C5] 56-592506
I. Bible. O. T. Psalms. English. 1956. Authorized. II. Title.

BIBLE. N. T. English. 225.52
1956. Confraternity version.
The New Testament of Our Lord and Savior Jesus Christ. Translated from the Latin Vulgate; a revision of the Challoner-Rheims version edited by Catholic scholars under the patronage of the Episcopal Committee of the Confraternity of Christian Doctrine. [Official Catholic ed. complete and unabridged] Garden City, Image Books [1956, c1941] x 549p. 18cm. (A Doubleday image book D39) [BS2080] 56-4825
I. Confraternity of Christian Doctrine. II. Title.

BIBLE N.T. English. 1958. 225.52
Phillips.
The New Testament in modern English. Translated by J. B. Phillips. New York, Macmillan [1967? c1958] xii, 574 p. maps. 28 cm. "Macmillan large print edition." [BS2095] 67-7185
I. Phillips, John Bertram, 1906- tr. II. Title.

BIBLE. N. T. English. 225.52
1958. Phillips.
The New Testament in modern English. Translated by J. B. Phillips. New York, Macmillan, 1958. 575p. maps. 22cm. [BS2095.P5] 58-10922
I. Phillips, John Bertram, 1906- tr. II. Title.

BIBLE. N.T. English. 1958. 225.52
Phillips.
The New Testament in modern English. Tr. by J. B. Phillips. New York, Macmillan 1962[c.1952-1958] 575p. maps. 21cm. (mp 105) 1.45 pap.,
I. Phillips, John Bertram, 1906- tr. II. Title.

BIBLE. N.T. English. 1958. 225.52
Phillips.
The New Testament in modern English. Translated by J. B. Phillips. New York, Macmillan [1967? c1958] xii, 574 p. maps. 28 cm. "Macmillan large print edition." [BS2095] 67-7185

I. Phillips, John Bertram, 1906- tr. II. Title.

BIBLE. N. T. English. 225.52
1958. Schonfield.
The authentic New Testament, edited and translated from the Greek for the general reader by Hugh J. Schonfield. Maps and illus. by J. F. Horrabin. [New York] New American Library [1958] xiviii, 478p. illus., Maps, plan, 18cm. (A Mentor religious classic, MD215) 'Index of references' :p. [476]-478. [BS2095.S37 1958] 58-577
I. Schonfield, Hugh Joseph, 1901- ed. and tr. II. Title.

BIBLE. N. T. English. 225.52
1958. Siewert.
Amplified New Testament. Grand Rapids, Zondervan Pub. House [1958] 989, [21]p. 18cm. Translated by Frances E. Siewert, pages 997- 1010 blak for "Notes." Bibliography: p. [991]-[994] [BS2095.S45] 58-2457
I. Siewert, Frances E., ed. and tr. II. Title.

BIBLE, N. T. English. 225.52
1958. Siewert
Amplified New Testament. Grand Rapids, Mich., Zondervan [1964, c.1958] 989, [21]p. 18cm. Tr. by Frances E. Siewert. On cover: Student ed. complete. Bibl. price unreported
I. Siewert, Frances E., ed. and tr. II. Title.

BIBLE. N. T. English. 225.52
1958. Tomanek.
The New Testament of Our Lord and Savior Jesus Anointed, by James L. Tomanek. Pocatello, Idaho, Printed by Arrowhead Press [1958] 462p. 23cm. [BS2095.T6] 59-17605
I. Tomanek, James L., tr. II. Title.

BIBLE. N. T. English. 225.52
1959. Authorized.
Christian worker's New Testament. Authorized King James version. Indexed and marked by the best methods of Bible marking on all subjects connected with the theme of salvation. Edited by J. Gilchrist Lawson. Philadelphia, Winston [c1959] xvi, 336p. 13cm. [BS2085. 1959.P5] 60-1375
I. Lawson, James Gilchrist, 1874-1946, ed. II. Title.

BIBLE. N. T. English. 1959 225.52
Authorized.
The New Testament, with special arrangement by Holland Evans, Jr. Paducah, Ky., H. Evans, Jr., c1959. 470p. 28cm. [BS2085 1959.P3] 60-22433
I. Evans, Holland. II. Title. III. Title: 'A correlation of parallel quotations located in both the Old and New Testaments of the Bible as related to the New Testament.'

BIBLE. N.T. English. 1959. 225.52
Rotherham.
The emphasized New Testament; a translation designed to set forth the exact meaning, the proper terminology, and the graphic style of the sacred original, by Joseph Bryant Rotherham. Grand Rapids, Kregel Publications, 1959. 272p. 25cm. 59-7561 3.95
I. Rotherham, Joseph Bryant, 1828-1910, tr. II. Title.

BIBLE. N. T. English. 225.52
1960. Confraternity version.
The New Testament of Our Lord and Savior Jesus Christ, translated from the Latin Vulgate; a revision of the Challoner-Rheims version edited by Catholic scholars under the patronage of the Episcopal Committee of the Confraternity of Christian Doctrine. [Official Catholic ed.] New York, Guild Press; distributed by Golden Press [1960, c1953] 480p. 17cm. (A Catechetical Guild book) [BS2080 1960.N4] 60-2422
I. Confraternity of Christian Doctrine. II. Title.

BIBLE, N.T. English. 1961. 225.52
Authorized.
Dake's annotated reference Bible--the New Testament (with the addition of Daniel, Psalms, and Proverbs) By Finis J. Dake. Grand Rapids, Zondervan Pub. House [c.] 1961. 488p. 28cm. 61-577 7.95
I. Dake, Finis Jennings. II. Title. III. Title: Annotated reference Bible.

BIBLE. N. T. English. 225.52
1961. Authorized.
New Testament translated out of the original tongues and with the former translations diligently compared and revised. Special arrangement. Paducah, Ky., Midwestern Pub. Co. [1961] Bible. N. T.--Reference editions. [BS2096.5.A1 1961] 61-45610
I. Title.

BIBLE. N. T. English. 225.52
1961. Authorized.
New Testament translated out of the original tongues (with the addition of Daniel, Psalms, and Proverbs) By Finis J. Dake. Grand Rapids, Zondervan Pub. House, 1961. 488p. 28cm. [BS2085 1961.D3] 61-577
I. Dake, Finis, Jennings II. Title. III. Title: Annoted references Bible

BIBLE. N. T. English. 225.52
1961. Noli.
The New Testament of Our Lord and Savior Jesus Christ. Translated into English from the approved Greek text of the Church of Constantinople and the Church of Greece, by Fan S. Noli. Boston, Albanian Orthodox Church in America, 1961. 508p. 24cm. [BS2095.N57] 61-2819
I. Noli, Fan Stylian Abp., 1882- tr., II. Title.

BIBLE. N. T. English. 225.52
1961. Noli.
The New Testament of Our Lord and Savior Jesus Christ. Tr. into English from the approved Greek text of the Church of Constantinople and the Church of Greece, by Fan S. Noli. Boston, Albanian Orthodox Church in America, [c.]1961. 508p. 61-28194 8.00
I. Noli, Fan Stylian, Abp., 1882- tr. II. Title.

BIBLE. N. T. English. 225.52
1961. Norlie.
Simplified New Testament in plain English for today's reader. A new translation from the Greek by Olaf M. Norlie. With The Psalms for today, a new translation in current English, by R. K. Harrison. Grand Rapids, Zondervan Pub. House [1961] 603, xiv, 160p. 18cm. [BS2095.N58] 61-16512
I. Norlie, Olaf Morgan, 1876- tr. II. Bible. O. T. Psalms. Ebglish. 1961. III. Title. IV. Title: The Psalms for today.

BIBLE. N. T. English. 225.52
1961. Wuest.
The New Testament; an expanded translation, by Kenneth S. Wuest. Grand Rapids, Eerdmans [c.1961] xvii, 624p. First published in 3 vols., 1956-59, under title: Expanded translation of the Greek New Testament. 61-17398 5.95
I. Wuest, Kenneth Samuel, 1893- tr. II. Title.

BIBLE. N. T. English. 225.52
1961. Wuest.
The New Testament; an expanded translation, by Kenneth S. Wuest. Grand Rapids, Eerdmans [1961] xvii, 624p. 23cm. First published in 3 vols., 1956-59, under title: Expanded translation of the Greek New Testament. [BS2095.W72] 61-17398
I. Wuest, Kenneth Samuel, 1893- tr. II. Title.

BIBLE. N.T. English. 1962. 225.52
The Holy Bible: The New Testament of Our Lord and Savior Jesus Christ. Tr. out of the original Greek and with the former trs. diligently compared and rev. . . Authorized King James version. New York, Paperback Lib. [1962] 327p. 18cm. (55-151) .95 pap.,
1. Bible. N.T.—English. I. Title.

BIBLE. N.T. English. 1962. 225.52
Revised standard.
The New Covenant commonly called the New Testament, of our Lord and Savior Jesus Christ. Translated from the Greek, being the version set forth A.D. 1611; rev. A.D. 1881 and A.D. 1901. Compared with the most ancient authorities and rev. A.D. 1946. With reading aids by Frederick C. Grant. New York, Published by T. Nelson for Bantam Books [1962] xxix, 576 p. maps. 18 cm. (Bantam classic) Bibliography: p. 541-548. [BS2091.A11962.N4] 62-20937
I. Title.

BIBLE. N. T. English. 225.52
1962. Authorized
The personal worker's New Testament, with notes and marked plan of salvation, arranged, comp. by Clifton W. Brannon, using the ed. of 1611 A.D., commonly known as the Authorized King James Version . . . Philadelphia, Natl. Bible Pr. for Clift Brannon Evangelistic Assoc., inc. [c.1962] 585p. 12cm. 1.00
I. Brannon, Clift W., comp. II. Title.

BIBLE. N.T. English. 1963. 225.52
New American standard.
New American standard Bible; New Testament. 3d ed. La Habra, Calif., Foundation Press, publisher for the Lockman Foundation [c1963] 441 p. 24 cm. [BS2095.N35] 64-3823
I. Lockman Foundation, La Habra, Calif. II. Title.

BIBLE. N.T. English. 1963. 225.52
New American standard.
New American standard Bible. New Testament. [2d ed] Chicago, Moody Press [c1963] 441 p. 24 cm. A revision of the American revised edition of 1901 prepared by the Editorial Board of the Lockman Foundation. [BS2095.N35] 64-2439
I. Lockman Foundation, La Habra, Calif. II. Title.

BIBLE. N.T. English. 1963. 225.52
New American standard.
New American Standard Bible: New Testament. [2d ed.] Nashville, Broadman Press [1963] 441 p. 24 cm. A revision of the American revised edition of 1901 prepared by the Editorial Board of the Lockman Foundation. [BS2095.N35] 64-1154
I. Lockman Foundation, La Habra, Calif. II. Title.

BIBLE. N.T. English. 1963. 225.52
New American Standard.
New American standard Bible: New Testament. [Pilot ed.] La Habra, Calif., Produced and published by the Lockman Foundation 1963 441 p. 23 cm. A revision of the American revised edition of 1901 prepared by the Editorial Board of the Lockman Foundation. [BS2095.N35] 64-244
I. Lockman Foundation, La Habra, Calif. II. Title.

BIBLE. N.T. English. 1963. 225.52
Williams.
The New Testament; a new translation in plain English, by Charles Kingsley Williams. Grand Rapids, Eerdmans [1963] 8, 545, 9-27 p. 21 cm. "Translation ... made from the Greek text lying behind the English revised version of 1881, published as Novum Testamentum Graece (Souter, Oxford Press, 1910)" [BS2095.W517] 63-20687
I. Williams, Charles Kingsley, tr. II. Title.

BIBLE. N.T. English. 1963. 225.52
The New Testament in four versions: King James, Revised standard, Phillips modern English, New English Bible. [Washington, Christianity today, 1963] xxx, 831 p. 25 cm. [BS20251963.C5] 63-23127
I. Title.

BIBLE. N. T. English. 225.52
1963. New American standard.
New American standard Bible: New Testament. [Pilot ed.] La Habra, Calif., Box 277 Produced, pub. by the Lockman Found., [1964, c.1960-1963] 441p. 23cm. Rev. of the Amer. rev. ed. of 1901 prep. by the Edit. Board of the Lockman Found. 64-244 4.95
I. Lockman Foundation, La Habra, Calif. II. Title.

BIBLE. N. T. English. 225.52
1963. New American Standard.
New American Standard Bible; New Testament. [2d ed.] Nashville, Broadman & Chicago, Moody [1964, c.1960-1963] 441p. 24cm. Rev. of the Amer. rev. ed. of 1901 prepared by the Edit. Bd. of the Lockman Found. 4.95
I. Lockman Foundation, La Habra, Calif. II. Title.

BIBLE. N.T. English. 1964. 225.52
Confraternity version.
Illustrated New Testament. Collegvile, Minn., Liturgical Press [c1964] 255 p. illus., facsims., maps. 29 cm. "The English text of this edition of the New Testament is that of the Confraternity of Christian Doctrine." [BS2080 1964.C6] 65-2683
1. Bible. N.T.—Pictures, illustrations, etc. I. Confraternity of Christian Doctrine. II. Title.

BIBLE. N.T. English. 225.52
1964.Beck.
The New Testament, in the language of today, by William F. Beck. Concordia paperbacks ed. Saint Louis, Concordia Pub. House [1964, c1963] xi, 459 p. 21 cm. [BS2095.B4] 64-8139
I. Beck, William F., tr. II. Title.

BIBLE. N.T. English. 1964. 225.52
Revised standard.
The Protestant and Roman Catholic New Testament. Revised standard version. Confraternity version. [New York, Iversen-Ford Associates, 1964] xix, 435 p. 25 cm. In parallel columns. Revised standard version has special t.p.: The New Covenant, commonly called the New Testament of Our Lord and Savior Jesus Christ ... translated from the Greek ... compared with the most ancient authorities and revised A.D 1946. New York, Harper & Row. Confraternity version has special t.p.: The New Testatment of Our Lord and Savior Jesus Christ, translated from the Latin Vulgate; a revision of the Challoner-Rheims version, edited by Catholic scholars under the patronage of the Episcopal Committee of the Confraternity of Christian Doctrine. [New York, Catholic Book Pub. Co.] [BS2091.A3 1964.N4] 64-8226
I. Bible. N.T. English. 1964. Confraternity version. II. Confraternity of Christian Doctrine. III. Title. IV. Title: The New Covenant.

BIBLE. N.T. English. 1964. 225.52
Beck.
The New Testament, in the language of today. by William F. Beck. St. Louis, Concordia [1964, c.1963] xi, 459p. 21cm. 64-8139 1.45 pap.,
I. Beck, William F., tr. II. Title.

BIBLE. N.T. English. 1965. 225.52
Phillips.
The New Testament in modern English. Student ed. [translated by] J. B. Phillips. [1st American ed.] New York, Macmillan Co. [1965, c1960] xvii, 558 p. maps. 20 cm. [BS2095.P5] 65-1408
I. Phillips, John Bertram, 1906- tr. II. Title.

BIBLE. N. T. English. 225.52
1965. Phillips.
The New Testament in modern English. Student ed. [tr. by] J. B. Phillips [1st Amer. ed.] New York, Macmillan [1965, c.1952-1960] xvii, 558p. maps. 20cm. Pub. in Great Britain under the title The New Testament in modern English for schools [BS2095.P5] 65-1408 3.00; 2.45 bds., pap.,
I. Phillips, John Bertram, 1906- tr. II. Title.

BIBLE, N.T. English. 1966. 225.52
The four translation New Testament: King James; New standard Bible; williams in the language of the people; Beck, in the language of today. [Chicago, Moody c. 1966] xxviii, 739 p 25 cm [bs2025 1966.m6] 66-15920 9.95
1. Bible N. T. English version. I. Title.

BIBLE. N.T. English. 1966. 225.52
The four translation New Testament: King James; New American standard Bible; Williams, in the language of the people; Beck, in the language of today. [Chicago, Moody Press, 1966] xxviii, 739 p. 25 cm. [BS2025 1966.M6] 66-15920
1. Bible. N.T. English—Versions. I. Title.

BIBLE. N.T. English. 1966. 225.52
Williams.
The New Testament in the language of the people, by Charles B. Williams. Chicago, Moody Press [c1966] 572 p. 20 cm. "Our translation is based on the Westcott and Hort Greek text ... When there are conflicting variations in the Greek manuscripts we have generally followed the Vatican manuscript." [BS2095] 67-2440
I. Williams, Charles Bray, 1869-1952, tr. II. Title.

BIBLE, N.T.English. 1966. 225.52
The York, St. Martin's 1966. [Chicago, Moody c.1966] v,152p. 19 cm. xxviii, 739p. 25cm. [BS2025 1966.M6] 66-15920 2.99 9.95
1. Bible. N. T.— four translation New Testament: 2. Bible. N.T.English—Versions. I. Title.

BIBLE. N. T. ENGLISH. 225.52
1966. WILLIAMS
The New Testament in the language of the people, by Charles B. Williams. Chicago, Moody [c.1966] 572p. 20cm. Our tr. conflicting variations in the Greek ms. we have generally followed the Vatican ms.' [BS2095] 67-2440 3.95
I. Williams, Charles Bray, 1869-1952, tr. II. Title.

BIBLE. N.T. English. 1967. 225.52
The New Testament from 26 translations. General editor: Curtis Vaughan. Grand Rapids, Zondervan Pub. House [1967] 1237 p. 22 cm. [BS2025.1967.V3] 67-22689
I. Vaughan, Curtis, ed. II. Title.

BIBLE. N.T. ENGLISH., 1967 225.52
The New Testament from 26 translations. General ed.: Curtis Vaughan. Grand Rapids, Zondervan [1967] 1237p. 22cm. [BS2025 1967.V3] 67-22689 12.50
I. Vaughan, Curtis. ed II. Title.

BIBLE. N. T. English. 225.5'2
1967.
The New Testament in four versions: King James, Revised Standard, Phillips modern English, New English Bible. London, New York [etc.] Collins [1967] xxx, 831 p. 24 1/2 cm. 60/- (B 67-26299) Parallel texts. [BS2025 1967.C6] 68-77288
I. Title.

BIBLE. N.T. English. 225.5'2
1967.
The New Testament in four versions: King James, Revised standard, Phillips Modern English, New English Bible. London, New York, Collins' Clear-type Press [1967] xxx, 831 p. 25 cm. [BS2025 1967.C5] 67-8644
I. Title.

BIBLE. N.T. English. 225.5'2
1967.
The New Testament in four versions: King James, Revised standard, Phillips modern English, New English Bible. London, New

York, Collins' Clear-type Press [1967] xxx, 831 p. 25 cm. [BS2025.1967.C5] 67-8644
I. Title.

BIBLE. N. T. English. 225.52
1967.
The New Testament from 26 translations. General editor: Curtis Vaughan Grand Rapids, Zondervan Pub. House [1967] 1237 p. 22 cm. [BS2025 1967.V3] 67-22689
I. Vaughan, Curtis, ed. II. Title.

BIBLE. N.T. English. 225.5'2
1967. Jerusalem Bible.
The New Testament of the Jerusalem Bible / general editor, Alexander Jones. Large-type reader's ed. Garden City, N.Y. : Doubleday, [1975] c1967. 1112 p. ; 24 cm. [BS2095.J4 1975] 75-329095 ISBN 0-385-04868-8 : 12.95
1. Sight-saving books. I. Jones, Alexander, 1906- II. Title.

BIBLE. N.T. English. 225.5'2
1974.
Eight translation New Testament : King James version, the Living Bible, Phillips modern English, Revised standard version, Today's English version, New international version, Jerusalem Bible, New English Bible. Wheaton, Ill. : Christian Reader, 1974. li, 1897 p. ; 24 cm. [BS2025 1974.C48] 74-21060
1. Bible. N.T. English—Versions. I. Title.

BIBLE. N.T. English. 225.5'2
1975.
The parallel four translation New Testament : King James version, New American standard, New international version, Amplified. New York : Produced for Back to the Bible Broadcast [by] Iversen-Norman Associates, 1975. xxviii, 897 p. ; 25 cm. [BS2025 1975.I9] 75-2894
1. Bible. N.T. English—Versions. I. Title.

BIBLE. N.T. English. 225.5'2
Catholic Biblical Association of America. Selections. 1972.
New Testament prayer book; the prayers contained in the Gospels, the Acts of the Apostles, the Epistles, and the Book of Revelation, compiled by Marion A. Habig. Chicago, Franciscan Herald Press [1972] p. [BS192.3.A1 1972.C48] 72-6221 ISBN 0-8199-0438-4
1. Bible. N.T.—Prayers. I. Habig, Marion Alphonse, 1901- comp. II. Title.

BIBLE. N.T. English. 225.5'2
Concordant version. 1976.
Concordant literal New Testament : with keyword concordance. 6th ed. Canyon Country, CA : Concordant Pub. Concern, 1976. 624, 368 p. ; 20 cm. Includes index. [BS2095.C58 1976] 76-378085
I. Title.

BIBLE. N.T. English. 225.5'2
International. 1973.
The Holy Bible; new international version. The New Testament. Grand Rapids, Mich., Zondervan Bible Publishers [1973] x, 573 p. 23 cm. [BS2095.I57 1973] 73-174297
I. Title.

BIBLE. N.T. English. 225.5'2
Klingensmith. 1972.
Today's English New Testament [Translated by] Don Klingensmith. [1st ed.] New York, Vantage Press [1972] 446 p. 21 cm. [BS2095.K544] 72-197790 7.50
I. Klingensmith, Don J., tr. II. Title.

BIBLE. N.T. English. 225.5'2
Klingensmith. 1974.
The New Testament. [Translated by Don Klingensmith] Fargo, N.D., Printed by Kaye's Inc. [1974] ii, 477 p. 16 cm. Cover title: The New Testament in everyday English. [BS2095.K544 1974] 74-174361
I. Klingensmith, Don J., tr. II. Title: The New Testament in everyday English.

BIBLE. N.T. English. 225.5'2
Klingensmith. Selections. 1969.
The New Testament. Don J. Klingensmith, chief editor. Fargo, N.D., Kaye's, inc., Printers [1969- v. 18 cm. "A young people's translation." Contents.Contents.—v. 1. According to Matthew, Mark, Luke—Acts. [BS2095.K543] 75-13704
I. Klingensmith, Don J., ed. II. Title.

BIBLE. N.T. English. New 225.5'2
Berkeley version. 1970.
The modern language New Testament. The new Berkeley version. [Rev. ed.] Grand Rapids, Zondervan Pub. House [1970] 291 p. 21 cm. A revision of G. Verkuyl's translation of the New Testament originally published in 1945 under title: Berkeley version of the New Testament from the original Greek. [BS2095.N36 1970] 70-106432 3.95
I. Verkuyl, Gerrit, 1872- II. Title.

BIBLE. N.T. English. New 225.5'2
English. 1970.
The New English Bible: the New Testament. 2nd ed. London: Oxford U.P./Cambridge U.P., 1970. xv, 447 p. 24 cm. Translated under the supervision of the Joint Committee on the New Translation of the Bible. [BS2092.A1 1970.L62] 74-485797 ISBN 0-19-180013-9 25/-
I. Joint Committee on the New Translation of the Bible. II. Title.

BIBLE. N.T. English. New 225.5'2
international. 1976.
The Holy Bible : New international version, the New Testament. Grand Rapids, Mich. : Zondervan Bible Publishers, [1976], c1974. x, 597 p., [3] leaves of plates : 5 maps ; 19 cm. Pref. signed: The Committee on Bible Translation. On cover: New Testament, with study helps. Includes index. [BS2095.N37 1976] 76-151540 2.95
I. Committee on Bible Translation.

BIBLE. N. T. English. 225.5'2
Norlie. 1972.
One way; the Jesus People New Testament; a new translation in modern English [by Olaf M. Norlie] Pasadena, Calif., Compass Press [1972] 603 p. illus. 19 cm. "A Jesus People book." [BS2095.N58 1972] 72-78871
I. Norlie, Olaf Morgan, 1876-1962, tr. II. Title. III. Title: Jesus People New Testament.

BIBLE. N.T. English. 225.5'2
Phillips. Selections. 1970.
The New Testament in shorter form. In modern translation [by] J. B. Phillips. Selected and introduced by Samuel Terrien. [New York] Macmillan [1970] vii, 211 p. col. maps. 22 cm. Bibliography: p. 211. [BS2095.P5 1970] 73-95182 7.95
I. Terrien, Samuel L., 1911- ed. II. Phillips, John Bertram, 1906- III. Title.

BIBLE. N.T. English. 225.5'2
Restoration of original name version. 1968.
The New Testament of Our Master and Saviour Yahvahshua the Messiah (commonly called Jesus Christ): Restoration of original name New Testament. [Junction City, Or., Missionary Dispensary Bible Research, 1968] xxi, 323 p. 23 cm. Cover title: Restoration of original name New Testament. "Designed to restore to the Scriptures the sacred name of the Most High and His Son from the sacred original on the basis of the Rotherham version revised by Missionary Dispensary Bible Research." [BS2095.R4] 79-2021
I. Missionary Dispensary Bible Research. II. Title. III. Title: Restoration of original name New Testament.

BIBLE. N.T. English. 225.5'2
Revised standard. 1955.
The new covenant commonly called the New Testament of our Lord and Savior Jesus Christ. Illustrated ed. London ; New York : T. Nelson, 1955. 293 p., [8] leaves of plates : ill. ; 22 cm. "Translated from the Greek, being the version set forth A.D. 1611, rev. A.D. 1881 and A.D. 1901, compared with the most ancient authorities and rev. A.D. 1946." [BS2091.A1 1955.L6] 75-314196
I. Title.

BIBLE. N. T. English. 225.52
Selections. 1955.
Golden nuggets from the New Testament, by Ezra L. Marler. [1st ed.] Salt Lake City, Bookcraft Publishers [1955] 197p. 24cm. [BS2261.M35] 56-27353
I. Marler, Ezra L. ed. II. Title.

BIBLE. N.T. English. 225.5'2
Today's English. 1970.
Good news for modern man; the New Testament in Today's English version. New church member edition. Nashville, Broadman Press [1970] iv, 600 p. illus. 18 cm. Scripture, text, and illus. by American Bible Society. "With a presentation page and special helps for new church members." First published in 1966 under title: Today's English version of the New Testament. [BS2095.T56 1970] 77-16586
I. American Bible Society. II. Title.

BIBLE. N.T. English. 225.5'2
Today's English. 1971.
Good news for modern man; the New Testament in Today's English version. 3d ed. New York, American Bible Society [1971] vi, 658 p. illus., maps, plan. 18 cm. First published in 1966 under title: Today's English version of the New Testament. "The text from which this translation was made is the Greek New Testament prepared by an international committee of New Testament scholars, sponsored by several members of the United Bible Societies, and published in 1966." [BS2095.T56 1971] 76-27096
I. Title.

BIBLE. N.T. English. 225.5'2
Today's English. 1971.
Today's English version of the New Testament and Psalms. A translation made by the American Bible Society. New York, Macmillan [1971] vi, 874 p. illus. 21 cm. [BS2095.T56 1971b] 72-175147 3.95
I. American Bible Society. II. Bible. O.T. Psalms. English. Today's English. 1971. The Psalms for modern man. 1971. III. Title.

BIBLE. N.T. English. 225.5'2
Today's English. 1972.
The blue denim Bible: the New Testament in Today's English version, Good news for modern man, third edition. New York, World Arts Foundation; distributed by A. J. Holman, Philadelphia [1972, c1971] vi, 658 p. illus., maps. 18 cm. [BS2095.T56 1972] 73-150440 1.95
I. Title.

BIBLE. N.T. English. 225.5'2
Today's English. 1974.
Good news for modern man; Today's English version New Testament in color. [New York] American Bible Society [1974] vi, 428 p. illus. 27 cm. "The text from which this translation was made is the Greek New Testament prepared by an international committee of New Testament scholars, sponsored by the United Bible Societies, and published first in 1966." [BS2095.T56 1974] 74-175993
I. Title.

BIBLE. N.T. English. 225.5'2
Today's English. Selections. 1972.
My sweet Lord; selections from Good news for modern man, the new English version of the New Testament. Illustrated by Norman Laliberte. Edited by Lois Huffmon. [Kansas City, Mo., Hallmark Cards, 1972] [47] p. illus. (part col.) 16 cm. (Hallmark editions) [BS2261.H83] 73-168972 ISBN 0-87529-239-9 2.00
I. Laliberte, Norman, illus. II. Huffmon, Lois, comp. III. Title.

BIBLE. N.T. Greek. 225.5'2
Scholz. 1975.
The English hexapla : exhibiting the six important English translations of the New Testament scriptures ... the original Greek text after Scholz, with the various readings of the textus receptus and the principal Constantinopolitan and Alexandrine manuscripts, and a complete collation of Scholz's text with Griesbach's edition of M.DCCC.V, preceded by an historical account of the English translations. New York : AMS Press, 1975. ca. 1300 p. ; 29 cm. Includes the Wycliffe, Tyndale, Cranmer, Genevan, Anglo-Rhemish, and Authorized English versions. Reprint of the 1841 ed. published by S. Bagster, London. [BS2025 1975.S36 1975] 74-39440 ISBN 0-404-00798-8 : 195.00
1. Bible. N.T. English—Versions. I. Scholz, Johann Martin Augustin, 1794-1852. II. Bible. N.T. English. Hexapla. 1975. III. Title.

BIBLE. N. T. English. 225.52
1950. New World.
New World translation of the Christian Greek Scriptures, rendered from the original language by the New World Bible Translation Committee. [Brooklyn] [Watchtower Bible and Tract Society] 1950. 792 p. illus., maps (part col.) facsims. 19 cm. [BS2095.N44] 50-14033
I. New World Bible Translation Committee. II. Watch Tower Bible and Tract Society. III. Title.

BIBLE. N. T. English. 225.52
1955.
The New Testament of Our Lord and Saviour Jesus Christ. With over 500 illus. and with 14 maps. New York, American Bible Society, 1955 [c1946-55] 1 v. (various pagings) illus., maps, facsims. 29 cm. On spine: The good news; the New Testament, King James and Revised Standard version. [BS2085 1955.N4] 55-14657
1. Bible. N.T.—Pictures, illustrations, etc. I. Title: The good news.

BIBLE. N. T. English. 225.52
1963.
The New Testament in four versions: King James, Revised standard, Phillips modern English, New English Bible. [Washington] [Christianity today] [1963] xxx, 831 p. 25 cm. [BS2025 1963.C5] 63-23127
I. Title.

BIBLE. N. T. English. 225.52
Authorized. 1954.
The New Testament in cadenced form. Designed by Morton C. Bradley, Jr. Cambridge [Mass.] Bradley Press; distributed by Rinehart, New York [1954] viii, 675 p. 24 cm. At head of title: The King James version. [BS185 1954.C3] 54-13105
I. Bradley, Morton Clark, 1912- II. Title.

BIBLE. N.T. English. 225.52
Phillips. 1962.
The New Testament in modern English. Translated by J. B. Phillips. New York, Macmillan, 1962. 575 p. maps. 22 cm. [BS2095.P5] 58-10922
I. Phillips, John Bertram, 1906- tr. II. Title.

BIBLE. N. T. English. 225.52
Phillips. 1965
The New Testament in modern English. Student ed. [translated by] J. B. Phillips. [1st American ed.] New York, Macmillan [1965, c1960] xvii, 558 p. maps. 20 cm. [BS2095.P5 1965] 65-1408
I. Phillips, John Bertram, 1906- tr. II. Title.

225.52
Amplified New Testament. Grand Rapids, Zondervan Pub. House [1958] 989, [21] p. 18 cm. Translation by Frances E. Siewert. Pages [997]-[1010] blank for "Notes." Bibliography: p. [991]-[994] [BS2095.S45] 58-2457
I. Siewert, Frances E., ed. and tr. II. Title.

BIBLE. N.T. English. 225.52
Williams. 1963.
The New Testament; a new translation in plain English, by Charles Kingsley Williams. Grand Rapids, Eerdmans [1963] 8, 545, 9-27 p. 21 cm. "Translation...made from the Greek text lying behind the English revised version of 1881, published as Novum Testamentum Graece (Souter, Oxford Press, 1910)" [BS2095.W517 1963] 63-20687
I. Williams, Charles Kingsley, tr. II. Title.

INTERNATIONAL Council of 225.52
Religious Education. American Standard Bible Committee.
An introduction to the Revised standard version of the Old Testament, by members of the revision committee. Luther A. Weigle, chairman. New York, Nelson [1952] 92 p. 21 cm. [BS891.I 5] 52-4178
1. Bible. O. T. English—Versious—Revised standard. I. Weigle, Luther Allan, 1880- II. Title.

STRAND, Kenneth Albert, 225.52
1927-
Reformation Bible pictures; woodcuts from early Lutheran and Emserian New Testaments. Compilation and commentary by Kenneth A. Strand. [Rev. and enl.] Ann Arbor, Mich., Ann Arbor Publishers [1963] 104 p. 58 illus. (incl. facsims.) 23 cm. Woodcuts by Cranach and Lemberger. Published in 1962 under title: Woodcuts from the earliest Lutheran and Emserian New Testaments. [NE1205.S8A54 1963] 63-14417
1. Bible. N. T. — Pictures, illustrations, etc. 2. Bible. N. T. German, 1522. Luther. 3. Bible. N. T. Low German. 1527. Emser. I. Cranach, Lucas, 1472-1553. II. Lemberger, Georg, 1495?-1540? III. Title.

TAYLOR, Kenneth 225.5'2
Nathaniel.
The Jesus book. [Paraphrase: Ken Taylor. Additional text: Dean Merrill] Wheaton, Ill., Tyndale House Publishers [1971] 440 p. illus. 18 cm. 1967 ed. published under title: The living New Testament. [BS2095.T37 1971] 72-183266 ISBN 0-8423-1860-7
1. Bible. N.T.—Paraphrases, English. I. Title.

THOMAS, Cecil K 1911- 225.52
Alexander Campbell and his new version. St. Louis, Bethany Press [1958] 224 p. 23 cm. [Bethany history series] Includes bibliography. [BS2095.C33T5] 58-13226
1. "Based upon a dissertation presented to the faculty of Princeton Theological Seminary in fulfillment of the requirements for the degree of doctor of theology." 2. Campbell, Alexander, 1788-1866. 3. Bible. N.T. English — Versions — Campbell. I. Title.

WEIGLE, Luther Allan, 225.5'2
1880-
The English New Testament from Tyndale to the Revised standard version [by] Luther A. Weigle. New York, Greenwood Press [1969, c1949] 158 p. 23 cm. "Based on a series of Cole lectures at Vanderbilt University." Contents.Contents.—The English Bible to 1611.—The church and the English vernacular.—Tyndale and the King James version.—The King James version in three centuries.—The Revised standard version of the New Testament.—The use of the New Testament in worship. Includes bibliographical references. [BS2317.W4 1969] 71-97323
1. Bible. N.T. English—History. I. Title.

BIBLE. N.T. English 225.5'201
(Middle English). Selections. 1974.
A fourteenth century English Biblical version, edited by Anna C. Paues. Cambridge [Eng.] University Press, 1904. [New York, AMS Press, 1974] lxxxvi, 263 p. 23 cm. Includes bibliographical references. [BS2038.P3 1974] 76-178573 ISBN 0-404-56528-X 14.50
I. Paues, Anna Carolina, 1867- ed. II. Title.

ORMULUM. 225.5'201
The Ormulum, with the notes and glossary of Dr. R. M. White; edited by Rev. Robert Holt. Oxford, Clarendon Press, 1878. [New York, AMS Press, 1974] 2 v. facsims. 19 cm. Reprint of the 1878 ed. Includes bibliographical references. [PR2101.W5 1974] 72-178548 ISBN 0-404-56654-5
I. White, Robert Meadows, 1798-1865, ed. II. Holt, Robert, 1827-1906, ed. III. Bible. N.T. English (Middle English) Paraphrases. 1974.

BIBLE. N.T. English. 225.52'03
1961? Authorized.
New Testament of Our Lord and Saviour Jesus Christ. Translated out of the original Greek and with the former translations diligently compared and revised. Set forth in 1611 and commonly known as the King James version. New York, American Bible Society [1961?] 844 p. 25 cm. [BS2085 1961.N4] 72-5722
I. Title.

BIBLE. N.T. English. 225.5'2'03
1967. Craddock.
The Christ Emphasis New Testament of Our Lord and Saviour Jesus Christ. Translated out of the original tongues and with the former translations diligently compared and rev., King James version, 1611. By Edward J. Craddock. Nashville, Bible Emphasis Publishers [1967] 532 p. 21 cm. [BS2085 1967.N3] 67-16877
I. Bible. N.T. English. 1967. Authorized II. Title.

BIBLE. N. T. English. 225.52'03
1967. Authorized.
The New Testament of Our Lord and Saviour Jesus Christ. King James version; translated out of the original Greek, and with the former translations diligently compared and revised. Appointed to be read in churches. New York, F. Watts [1967] 457 p. 29 cm. "A Keith Jennison book." [BS2085] 68-31905
I. Title.

BIBLE. N.T. English. 225.52'03
1967. Authorized.
The New Testament of Our Lord and Saviour Jesus Christ. King James version; translated out of the original Greek, and with the former translations diligently compared and revised. Appointed to be read in churches. Large type ed., complete and unabridged. New York, F. Watts [1967] 457 p. 29 cm. "A Keith Jennison book." [BS2085] 68-31905
I. Title.

BIBLE. N. T. English. 225.5'2'03
1967. Craddock.
The Christ Emphasis New Testament of Our Lord and Saviour Jesus Christ. Tr. out of the original tongues and with the former translations diligently compared and rev., King James version, 1611. By Edward J. Craddock. Nashville, Bible Emphasis Pubs. [1967] 532p. 21cm. [BS2085 1967. N3] 67-16877 7.95; flexible bdg., p9.95
I. Bible. N. T. English. 1967. Authorized. II. Title.
Publisher's address: R. E. Lee Apts., 2108 Hayes St., Nashville, Tenn. 37203.

BIBLE. N.T. English. 225.52'03
Authorized. 1971.
The guide-to-God New Testament. Little Rock, Ark., Baptist Publications Committee, 1971. 67x, 500, 501x-575x p. 12 cm. The study-guide sections (designated "x") are prepared by C. W. Brannon. [BS2085 1971.L58] 73-180721
I. Brannon, Clifton Woodrow. II. Title.

BIBLE. N.T. English. 225.5'203
Authorized. 1971.
The New Testament of Our Lord and Saviour Jesus Christ. Translated out of the original Greek and with the former translations diligently compared and revised, set forth in 1611 and commonly known as the King James version. Valparaiso, Fla., Glad Tidings, inc. [1971] 435 p. 21 cm. [BS2085 1971.V3] 75-27306

BIBLE. N.T. English. 225.52'04
1953. Knox.
The New Testament of Our Lord and Saviour Jesus Christ; a new translation. New York, Sheed & Ward, 1953 [c1944] 573 p. 22 cm. On spine: The New Testament in English. Translated by R. A. Knox. [BS2095.K62] 72-8235
I. Knox, Ronald Arbuthnott, 1888-1957, tr.

BIBLE, N. T. English. 225.5204
1965. Revised standard.
The New Testament of Our Lord and Savior Jesus Christ. Revised standard version, Catholic ed. Prepared by the Catholic Biblical Assn. of Great Britain. Pref. by Albert Cardinal Meyer. New York, Nelson [1965] xvi, 250p. 22cm. Tr. from the Greek, being the version set forth 1611 A. D., revised 1881 A. D. and 1901 A. D. compared with the most ancient authorities and revised 1946 A. D. [BS2091.A1 1965.T6] 65-5050 3.50
I. Catholic Biblical Association of Great Britain. II. Title.

BIBLE. N.T. English. 225.5'2'04
1966. Concordant version.
Concordant literal New Testament. Memorial ed. Saugus, Calif., Cocordant Pub. Concern [1966] 639 p. facsims. 20 cm. Compiled by A. E. Knoch [BS2095.C58] 67-8636
I. Knoch, Adolf E., comp. II. Title.

BIBLE, N. T. English., 225.5204
1966
Today's English version of the New Testament. Tr. by the American Bible Soc. New York, Macmillan [1968,c.1966] iv, 611p. illus. maps 20cm. Also pub. as Good news for modern man. [BS2095.T56] 66-28212 1.95 pap.,
I. American Bible Society. II. Title.

BIBLE. N.T. English. 225.5204
1966. Today's English.
Today's English version of the New Testament. A translation made by the American Bible Society. New York, Macmillan [1966] viii, 568 p. 19 cm. "Also published as Good news for modern man." The text from which this translation was made is the Greek New Testament prepared by an international committee of New Testament scholars, sponsored by several members of the United Bible Societies, and published in 1966." [BS2095.T56] 66-28212
I. American Bible Society. II. Title.

BIBLE. N.T. English. 225.5204
1966. Today's English.
Today's English version of the New Testament. A translation made by the American Bible Society. New York, Macmillan [1966] viii, 568 p. 19 cm. "Also published as Good news for modern man." The text from which this translation was made is the Greek New Testament prepared by an international committee of New Testament scholars, sponsored by several members of the United Bible Societies, and published in 1966." [BS2095.T56] 66-28212
I. American Bible Society.

BIBLE. N.T. English. 225.5'2'04
1967. Jerusalem Bible.
The New Testament of the Jerusalem Bible. General editor: Alexander Jones. [1st ed.] Garden City, N.Y., Doubleday [1967, c1966] xi, 462 p. maps (part col.) 24 cm. "The principal collaborators in translation and literary revision were: Joseph Leo Alston [and others]" [BS2095.J4 1967] 67-24835
I. Jones, Alexander, 1906- ed. II. Title.

BIBLE. N.T. English. 225.52'04
1967. Revised standard.
The New Testament of Our Lord and Savior Jesus Christ. Revised standard version, Catholic ed. Prepared by the Catholic Biblical Association of Great Britain. With a pref. by Albert Cardinal Meyer. New York, F. Watts [1967, c1965] 999 p. 29 cm. "A Keith Jennison book." "Large type edition, complete and unabridged." "Translated from the Greek, being the version set forth A.D. 1611, revised A.D. 1881 and A.D. 1901, compared with the most ancient authorities and revised A.D. 1946." [BS2091.A1] 68-31906
I. Catholic Biblical Association of Great Britain. II. Title.

BIBLE. N.T. English. 225.5'204
1967. Today's English.
Good news for modern man; the New Testament in Today's English version, with easy-to-use, marked references to guide you to a new life of peace and happiness through Jesus Christ. Nashville, Broadman Press [1967] iv, 597 p. illus. 18 cm. First published in 1966 under title: Today's English Version of the New Testament. [BS2095.T56 1967] 67-8142
I. Title.

BIBLE. N.T. English. 225.52'04
Barclay. 1968.
The New Testament: a new translation by William Barclay. London, New York, Collins, 1968- v. 24 cm. Contents.Contents.—v. 1. The Gospels and the Acts of the Apostles. Bibliographical footnotes. [BS2095.B33] 68-54594 25/- ($4.95) (v. 1)
I. Barclay, William, lecturer in the University of Glasgow, tr.

BIBLE. N.T. English. 225.52'04
Ledvard. 1969.
The children's New Testament. Translated by Gleason H. Ledyard. Waco, Word Books [1969] viii, 628 p. col. illus., maps. 24 cm. [BS2097.L4] 69-20228 6.95
I. Ledyard, Gleason H., tr. II. Title.

BIBLE. N.T. English. 225.5'2'04
New American Standard. 1971.
New American Standard Bible: New Testament, Psalms. Text ed. La Habra, Calif., Foundation Press Publications, publisher for the Lockman Foundation [1971] ix, 431, 146 p. 20 cm. [BS2095.N35 1971] 72-178787 2.45
I. Lockman Foundation, La Habra, Calif. II. Bible. O.T. Psalms. English. New American Standard. 1971. III. Title.

BIBLE. N.T. English. 225.5'204
New American Standard. 1975.
New American standard New Testament. Soul winner's ed. Philadelphia : Holman Co., c1975. xiv, 401 p. ; 18 cm. [BS2095.N35 1975] 76-350112
I. Title.

BIBLE. N.T. English. 225.5'204
Revised standard. 1971.
Concordia Bible with notes: the New Covenant, commonly called the New Testament of Our Lord and Savior Jesus Christ. Revised standard version ... [Introductions, notes, and references prepared by Martin H. Franzmann] 2d ed. Saint Louis, Published by W. Collins Sons for Concordia Pub. House, 1971. x, 541 p. col. maps. 27 cm. [BS2091.A1 1971.S3] 71-152384 ISBN 0-570-00500-0
I. Franzmann, Martin H., ed. II. Title.

BIBLE. N.T. English. 225.5'2'04
Selections. 1967. Klingensmith.
The New Testament. Don J. Klingensmith [translator and] chief editor. Fargo, N.D., Kaye's, inc., printers, [1967- v. 22 cm. Contents.Contents.—v. 1. According to Matthew, Mark, Luke—Acts. [BS2095.K54] 68-2095
I. Klingensmith, Don J., ed. II. Title.

BIBLE. N.T. English. 225'.52'04
Today's English. 1969.
Today's English version of the New Testament. A translation made by the American Bible Society. [Illustrated ed. New York] Macmillan [1969, c1966] iv, 605 p. illus., maps. 22 cm. "Also published as Good news for modern man." "The text from which this translation was made is the Greek New Testament prepared by an international committee of New Testament scholars, sponsored by several members of the United Bible Societies, and published in 1966." [BS2095.T56 1969] 70-7539 4.95
I. American Bible Society. II. Title.

BIBLE. N.T. English. 225.5'204
Today's English. 1972.
The blue denim Bible: the New Testament in Today's English version, Good news for modern man, third edition. New York, World Arts Foundation; distributed by A. J. Holman, Philadelphia [1972, c1971] vi, 658 p. illus., maps. 18 cm. [BS2095.T56 1972] 73-150440 1.95
I. Title.

THE Greek elements; 225.5'2'04
designed to complement the Concordant literal New Testament, the Concordant Greek text and keyword concordance; and consisting of Tables of the grammatical forms and their English standards with a reverse index, A complete analysis of the vocabulary with English equivalents, and a Short Greek course. Saugus, Calif., Concordant Pub. Concern [1971] 176 p. 21 cm. On spine: Concordant library: the Greek elements. [PA817.G67] 72-28888
1. Greek language, Biblical—Grammar. 2. Greek language—Glossaries, vocabularies, etc. I. Title: Concordant library: the Greek elements.

GREENLEE, Jacob 225.5'2'04
Harold, 1918-
A concise exegetical grammar of New Testament Greek. [3d ed., rev.] Grand Rapids, Eerdmans [1963] 79 p. 23 cm. Includes bibliography. [PA817.G7 1963] 63-2182
1. Greek language, Biblical — Grammar. I. Title.

HALE, Clarence 225.5'2'04
Benjamin, 1905-
Let's read Greek; a graded reader [by] Clarence B. Hale. Chicago, Moody Press [1968] iv, 173 p. 24 cm. [PA817.H28] 68-18887
1. Greek language, Biblical—Readers. I. Title.

TAYLOR, Kenneth 225.52'04
Nathaniel.
The living New Testament; paraphrased. Wheaton, Ill., Tyndale House [1967] 650 p. 21 cm. "The basic translation was done by Kenneth N. Taylor."—Jacket. An illustrated ed. published in 1971 under title: The Jesus book. [BS2095.T37 1967] 67-28431
1. Bible. N.T.—Paraphrases, English. I. Title.

BIBLE. N.T. English. 225'.52'05
1967. Confraternity Version.
The New Testament of Our Lord and Savior Jesus Christ. with introductions and annotations by Joseph A. Grispino. A revision of the Challoner-Rheims version, edited by Catholic scholars under the patronage of the Episcopal Committee of the Confraternity of Christian Doctrine. New York, Guild Press [1967] xi, 860 p. maps. 18 cm. (An angelus book) "31177." "The Biblical text is translated from the Latin Vulgate." [BS2080 1967.N4] 66-24853
I. Grispino, Joseph A. II. Confraternity of Christian Doctrine. III. Title.

BIBLE. N.T. English. 225'.52'05
1967. Confraternity Version.
The New Testament of Our Lord and Savior Jesus Christ, with introductions and annotations by Joseph A. Grispino. A revision of the Challoner-Rheims version, edited by Catholic scholars under the patronage of the Episcopal Committee of the Confraternity of Christian Doctrine. New York, Guild Press [1967] xi, 860 p. maps. 18 cm. (An angelus book) "31177." "The Biblical text is translated from the Latin Vulgate." [BS2080.1967.N4] 66-24853
I. Grispino, Joseph A. II. Confraternity of Christian Doctrine. Episcopal Committee.

BIBLE. N.T. English. 225.5'205
New American. 1970.
The new American Bible: the New Testament. Newly translated from the original Greek with critical use of the ancient sources by members of the Catholic Biblical Association of America. Paterson, N.J., St. Anthony Guild Press [1970] viii, 835 p. 4 maps. 20 cm. "Sponsored by the Bishops' Committee of the Confraternity of Christian Doctrine." [BS2092.3.A1 1970.P37] 78-141767 ISBN 0-87236-311-2 5.95
I. Catholic Biblical Association of America. II. Confraternity of Christian Doctrine. Bishops' Committee. III. Title.

BIBLE, N.T. German. 1963. 225.53
Neue-Welt-Ubersetzung der Christlichen Griechischen Schriften, Ubersetz nach der englischen Wiedergabe von 1961, doch unter getreuer Berucksichtigung des griechischen Urtextes [Brooklyn, N. Y., 124 Columbia Heights, Watchtower Bible & Tract Soc. of New York, c.1963] 352p. 19cm. 63-23289 .50
1. Watch Tower Bible and Tract Society of New York. I. Title.

STRAND, Kenneth Albert, 225.53
1927-
Reformation Bibles in the crossfire; the story of Jerome Emser, his anti-Lutheran critique and his Catholic Bible version. Ann arbor, Mich., Ann Arbor Publishers [1961] 116 p. illus. 24 cm. Includes bibliography. [BR350.E5S8] 61-3965
1. Emser, Hieronymus, 1477 or 8-1527. 2. Luther, Martin, 1483-1527. 3. Bible. N.T. — Versions, Catholic vs. Protestant. I. Title.

STRAND, Kenneth Albert, 225.53
1927-
Reformation Bibles in the crossfire; the story of Jerome Emser, his anti-Lutheran critique and his Catholic Bible version. Ann Arbor, Mich., 711 N. Univ. Ave. Ann Arbor Pubs., [c.1961] 116p. illus. Bibl. 61-3965 2.50
1. Emser, Hieronymus, 1477 or 8-1527. 2. Luther, Martin, 1483-1527. 3. Bible. N. T.— Versions, Catholic vs. Protestant. I. Title.

BIBLE. N.T. Dutch. 225.53931
1963. New World
Nieuwe-Wereldvertaling van de Christelijke Griekse Geschriften. Vertaald uit de Engelse vertaling van 1961, maar met getrouwe raadpleging van de oude Griekse tekst. [New York, Watchtower Bible & Tract Soc., c.]1963. 352p. 19cm. 63-24961 .50 bds.,
I. Watch Tower Bible and Tract Society. II. Title.

STRAND, Kenneth Albert, 225.5394
1927-
A Reformation paradox; the condemned New Testament of the Rostock Brethren of the Common Life. With plates providing facsim. reproduction of the first 20 chapters of the Gospel of Matthew from this rare work. With a foreword by Albert Hyma. Ann Arbor, Mich., Ann Arbor Publishers [1960] 101 p. facsims. 28 cm. Bibliographical references included in "Notes" (p. 51-58) [BS2169 1530b] 60-3132
1. Emser, Hieronymus, 1477 or 8-1527. 2. Bible. N.T. Low German. 1530. 3. Brothers of the Common Life. 4. Luther, Martin, 1483-1546. I. Bible. N.T. Matthew. Low German (1530) 1960. II. Title.

BIBLE, N.T. French. 1963. 225.54
New World
Les Ecritures grecques chretiennes; traduction du Monde Nouveau. Traduites d'apres la

version anglaise de 1961 mais avec consultation fidele de l'ancien texte grec. [New York, Watchtower Bible & Tract Soc. of New York, c.]1963. 320p. 19cm. 63-24960 .50 bds., *I. Title.*

BIBLE. N.T. Italian. 1963. 225.55
New World
Traduzione del Nuovo Mondo delle Scritture greche cristiane. Tradotta dalla versione inglese del 1961 ma con la fedele consultazione dell'antico testo greco. [New York, Watchtower Bible Tract Soc. of New York, c.]1963. 320p. 19cm. 63-24959 .50 bds., *I. Title.*

BIBLE. N.T. Spanish. 1963. 225.56
New World
Traduccion del Nuevo Mundo de las Escrituras griegas cristianas. Traducidas de la version en ingles de 1961, pero consultando fielmente el antiguo texto griego. [New York, Watchtower Bibl & Tract Soc. of New York, c.]1963. 320p. 19cm. 63-24957 .50 bds., *I. Title.*

BIBLE. N.T. PORTUGUESE. 225.569
1963. NEW WORLD
Traducao do Novo Mundo das Escrituras gregas cristas. Traducao da versao inglesa de 1961 mediante consulta constante ao antigo texto grego, Edicao brasileira. [New York, Watchtower Bible & Tract Soc. of New York, c.]1963. 320p. 19cm. 63-24958 .50 bds., *I. Title.*

PARVIS, Merrill Mead, 225.58
1906- ed.
New Testament manuscript studies; the materials and the making of a critical apparatus, edited by Merrill M. Parvis [and] Allen P. Wikgren. [Chicago] University of Chicago Press [1950] xi, 220 p. 32 plates. 25 cm. Bibliographical references included in "Notes" (p. 175-220) [BS1938.P3] 50-6832
1. Bible. Manuscripts, Greek. N.T. 2. Bible. N.T. — Criticism, Textual. I. Wikgren, Allen Paul, 1906- joint ed. II. Title.
Contents omitted.

ALDRIDGE, John William. 225'.6
The hermeneutic of Erasmus. Richmond, John Knox Press [1966] 134 p. 21 cm. (Basel studies of theology no. 2) Bibliography: p. 129-134. [BR350.E7A7] 66-20331
1. Erasmus, Desiderius, d. 1536. 2. Bible—Criticism, interpretation, etc.—History—16th century. I. Title. II. Series.

BARCLAY, William lecturer 225.6
in the University of Glasgow
Many witnesses, one Lord. Philadelphia, Westminster Press [1963] 128 p. 20 cm. [BS2361.2.B3] 63-10831
1. Bible. N.T. — Criticism, interpretation, etc. I. Title.

BARCLAY, William 225.6
Many witnesses, one Lord. Philadelphia, Westminster [c.1963] 128p. 20cm. Bibl. 63-10831 2.50
1. Bible. N.T.—Criticism, interpretation, etc. I. Title.

BARKER, Glenn W., 1920- 225.6
The New Testament speaks [by] Glenn W. Barker, William L. Lane [and] J. Ramsey Michaels. [1st ed.] New York, Harper & Row [1969] 448 p. maps. 25 cm. Includes bibliographies. [BS2330.2.B33] 69-10477 6.50
1. Bible. N.T.—Introductions. 2. Bible. N.T.—Theology. I. Lane, William L., 1931- joint author. II. Michaels, J. Ramsey, joint author. III. Title.

BARNETT, Albert Edward, 225.6
1895-
The New Testament, its making and meaning. Rev. ed. New York, Abingdon Press [1958] 304p. illus. 22cm. Includes bibliography. [BS2330.B34 1958] 58-9921
1. Bible. N. T.—Introductions. I. Title.

BARTSCH, Hans Werner, ed. 225.6
Kerygma and myth; a theological debate, by Rudolf Bultmann [and others] Rev. ed. of this translation by Reginald H. Fuller. New York, Harper & Row [1961] xii, 228 p. 21 cm. (Harper Torchbooks. The Cloister library. TB80) The English edition was first published 1953. Bibliography: p. 224-228. [BS2364.B313 1961] 54-2914
1. Bible. N.T.—Criticism, interpretation, etc. I. Bultmann, Rudolf Karl, 1884- II. Title.

BAUM, Gregory, 1923- 225.6
The Jews and gospel, a re-examination of the New Testament. Westminster, Md., Newman Press [1961] 288p. 21cm. [BM535.B3 1961] 61-8969
1. Christianity and other religions—Judaism. 2. Bible. N. T.— Criticism, interpretation, etc: I. Title.

BAUM, Gregory, 1923- 225.6
The Jews and the gospel, a re-examination of the New Testament. Westminster, Md., Newman Press [1961] 288 p. 21 cm. [BM535.B3] 61-8969
1. Christianity and other religions — Judaism. 2. Bible. N.T. — Criticism, interpretation, etc. I. Title.

BAUMAN, Edward W. 225.6
An introduction to the New Testament. Philadelphia, Westminster Press [1961] 189 p. 22 cm. [BS2330.2.B35] 61-10616
1. Bible. N.T.—Introductions.

BEARDSLEE, William A. 225'.6
Literary criticism of the New Testament, by William A. Beardslee. Philadelphia, Fortress Press [1970] x, 86 p. 22 cm. (New Testament series) (Guides to biblical scholarship.) Includes bibliographical references. [BS2361.2.B4] 77-94817 2.50
1. Bible. N.T.—Criticism, interpretation, etc. I. Title.

BENDER, Harold Stauffer, 225.6
1897-
These are my people; the nature of the church and its discipleship according to the New Testament. Scottdale, Pa., Herald Press [1962] 126p. 20cm. (The Conrad Grebel lectures, 1960) Includes bibliography. [BS2545.C5B4] 62-12947
1. Church—Biblical teaching. 2. Bible. N. T.—Theology. I. Title.

BIBLE. N. T. English. 225.6
Selections. 1963. Authorized.
The Bible speaks about faith, daily readings from the authorised or King James version and the New English Bibl. Chosen, arr. by Cecil Northcott. New York, Association [1963] unpaged. 20cm. 63-17419 1.50 bds.,
1. Devotional calendars. I. Northcott, William Cecil, 1902- II. Bible. N. T. English. Selections. 1963. New English. III. Title.

BIBLE. N.T. English. 225'.6
Selections. 1967. Authorized.
Literature from the New Testament. Edited by James F. Fullington. New York, Appleton-Century-Crofts [1967] xxi, 138 p. 18 cm. (Crofts classics) Bibliography: p. 137-138. [BS2261.F8] 67-11442
I. Fullington, James Fitz-James, ed. II. Title.

BLACKWALL, Anthony, 1674- 225'.6
1730.
The sacred classics defended and illustrated. New York, Garland Pub., 1970. 2 v. port. 20 cm. "Facsimile ... made from a copy in the Harvard University Library." Original t.p. for v. 1 reads: The sacred classics defended and illustrated: or, An essay humbly offer'd towards proving the purity, propriety, and true eloquence of the writers of the New Testament ... by A. Blackwall, M.A. The second edition, corrected. London: Printed for C. Rivington ... MDCCXXVII. Original t.p. for v. 2. reads: The sacred classics defended and illustrated ... With a preface, wherein is shewn the necessity and usefulness of a new version of the sacred books. By the late Reverend and learned A. Blackwall ... London: Printed for Charles Rivington ... MDCCXXXI. Includes bibliographical references. [BS2360.B62] 73-112077
1. Bible. N.T.—Criticism, interpretation, etc. I. Title.

BONSIRVEN, Joseph 225.6
Theology of the New Testament. [Tr. from French by S.F.L. Tye] Westminster, Md., Newman [1963] xxiv, 413p. 23cm. Bibl. 63-23790 9.75
1. Bible. N.T.—Theology. I. Title.

BRANDEIS, Donald, 1928- 225.6
The Gospel in the Old Testament. Grand Rapids, Baker Book House, 1960. 188p. 23cm. [BS2387.B68] 60-15711
1. Bible. N.T.—Relation to O.T. I. Title.

BRATT, John H. 225.6
New Testament guide. Rev. and enl. Grand Rapids, Mich., Eerdmans [c.1946, 1961] 144p. Bibl. 61-10852 3.00
1. Bible. N. T.—Introductions. I. Title.

BULTMANN, Rudolf Karl, 225.6
1884-
Jesus Christ and mythology. New York, Scribner [1958] 96 p. 21 cm. [BS2378.B8] 58-8247
1. Demythologization. I. Title.

CARMICHAEL, Patrick Henry, 225.6
1889- ed.
Understanding the books of the New Testament; a guide to Bible study for laymen. Prepared by Felix B. Gear [and others] Richmond, John Knox Press [1952] 205 p. 25 cm. [BS2330.C27] 52-1865
1. Bible. N. T.—Introductions. I. Title.

CARMICHAEL, Patrick Henry, 225.6
1889- ed.
Understanding the books of the New Testament; a guide to Bible study for laymen. Prepared by Felix B. Gear [others. Rev. ed.] Richmond, Va., John Knox Pr. [1961, c.1952, 1961] 224p. illus. (Aletheia paperbacks) Bibl. 61-9583 1.95 pap.,
1. Bible. N. T.—Introductions. I. Title.

CHARPENTIER, Etienne. 225.6
The New Testament, always news. Translated by Philip G. Roets. [Edited by Lisa McGaw] De Pere, Wis., St. Norbert Abbey Press, 1969. 311 p. 19 cm. Translation of Ce testament toujours nouveau. [BS2330.2.C4813] 78-87817 4.95
1. Bible. N.T.—Criticism, interpretation, etc. I. Title.

CHATZEANTONIOU, Georgios A 225.6
New Testament introduction, by George A. Hadjiantoniou. Chicago, Moody Press [1957] 352p. 22cm. Includes bibliography. [BS2330.C372] 57-22419
1. Bible. N. T. —Introductions. I. Title.

COGGAN, Frederick Donald, 225.6
Bp. of Bradford
Five makers of the New Testament. London, Hodder & Stoughton [dist. New York, Morehouse, 1963, c.1962] 95p. 18cm. 63-1830 .75 pap.,
1. Bible. N.T.—Introductions. I. Title.

CONNICK, C. Milo. 225.6
The New Testament : an introduction to its history, literature, and thought / C. Milo Connick. 2d ed. Encino, Calif. : Dickenson Pub. Co., [1977] p. cm. Includes index. Bibliography: p. [BS2330.2.C65 1977] 77-23599 ISBN 0-8221-0205-6 : 12.95
1. Bible. N.T.—Introductions. I. Title.

CONNICK, C. Milo. 225.6
The New Testament; an introduction to its history, literature, and thought [by] C. Milo Connick. Encino, Calif., Dickenson Pub. Co. [1972] xiv, 444 p. illus. 25 cm. Bibliography: p. 426-438. [BS2330.2.C65] 76-180754 ISBN 0-8221-0007-X
1. Bible. N.T.—Introductions. I. Title.

CRAIG, Clarence Tucker, 225.6
1895-
The study of the New Testament. Nashville, Abingdon [1963, c.1939] 131p. 21cm. (Apex bks., N2) Bibl. 1.00 pap.,
1. Bibl. N. T.—Study—Text-books. 2. Bible—Study—Text-books—N. T. I. Title.

CROWNFIELD, Frederic C. 225.6
A historical approach to the New Testament. New York, Harper [c.1960] 420p. illus. Includes bibl. 60-15344 5.50
1. Bible. N. T.—Criticism, interpretation, etc. I. Title.

DANA, Harvey Eugene, 1888- 225.6
1945.
Interpreting the New Testament [by] H. E. Dana and R. E. Glaze, Jr. Based on Searching the Scriptures. Nashville, Broadman Press [c.1936, 1961] 165p. Bibl. 61-56284 3.25 bds.,
1. Bible. N. T.—Hermeneutics. I. Glaze, R. E., joint author. II. Title.

DAUGHTERS of St. Paul. 225.6
Introduction to the books of the New Testament / by Daughters of St. Paul. Boston : St. Paul Editions, 1977. p. cm. [BS2330.2.D34 1977] 77-10872 pbk. : 1.00
1. Bible. N.T.—Introductions. I. Title.

DAUGHTERS of St. Paul. 225.6
Introduction to the books of the New Testament / by Daughters of St. Paul. Boston : St. Paul Editions, 1977. p. cm. [BS2330.2.D34 1977] 77-10872 pbk. : 1.00
1. Bible. N.T.—Introductions. I. Title.

DAVIES, William David, 225.6
1911-
Invitation to the New Testament, a guide to its main witnesses, by W. D. Davies. [1st ed.] Garden City, N.Y., Doubleday, 1966. xii, 540 p. 25 cm. Bibliography: p. [523]-530. [BS2330.2.D35] 65-17223
1. Bible. N.T.—Introductions. I. Title.

DOTY, William G., 1939- 225.6
Contemporary New Testament interpretation [by] William G. Doty. Englewood Cliffs, N.J., Prentice-Hall [1972] vii, 176 p. 24 cm. Bibliography of works by Rudolf Bultmann cited in the text: p. 163-165. [BS2350.D67] 71-38839 ISBN 0-13-170142-8 7.95
1. Bible. N.T.—Criticism, interpretation, etc.—History—20th century. I. Title.

FEINE, Paul, 1859-1933. 225.6
Introduction to the New Testament, founded by Paul Feine and Johannes Behm. Completely re-edited by Werner Georg Kummel. 14th rev. ed. Translated by A. J. Mattill, Jr. Nashville, Abingdon Press [1966] 444 p. 24 cm. Includes bibliographical references. [BS2330.F413] 66-11944
1. Bible. N.T.—Introductions. I. Behm, Johannes, 1883- joint author. II. Kummel, Werner Georg, 1905- ed. III. Title.

FEINE, Paul, 1859-1933 225.6
Introduction to the New Testament, founded by Paul Feine, Johannes Behm. Completely re-ed. by Werner Georg Kummel. 14th rev. ed. Tr. [from German] by A. J. Mattill, Jr. Nashville, Abingdon [c.1965, 1966] 444p. 24cm. Bibl. [BS2330.F413] 66-11944 7.50
1. Bible. N. T. — Introductions. I. Behm, Johannes, 1883- joint author. II. Kummel, Werner Georg, 1905- ed. III. Title.

FILSON, Floyd Vivian, 1896- 225.6
Opening the New Testament. Philadelphia, Westminster Press [1952] 224 p. illus. 22 cm. [BS2330.F5] 52-7116
1. Bible. N. T.—Introductions. I. Title.

FULLER, Reginald Horace 225.6
The New Testament in current study. New York, Scribners [1966. c.1962] 147p. 21cm. (Scribner studies in biblical interpretation. 4-3125) 2.95 pap.,
1. Bible. N.T.— Criticism, interpretation, etc.—Hist. I. Title.

GASQUE, W. Ward 225.6
Sir William M. Ramsay, archaeologist and New Testament scholar; a survey of his contribution to the study of the New Testament, by W. Ward Gasque. Foreword by F. F. Bruce. Grand Rapids, Baker Bk. [1966] 95p. 22cm. (Baker studies in Biblical archaeology) Issued also as thesis (Master of Theol.) Fuller Theol. Seminary. Bibl. [BS2351.R3G3 1966] 66-18312 1.50 pap.,
1. Ramsay, Sir William Mitchell, 1851-1939. I. Title.

GOGARTEN, Friedrich, 1887- 225.6
Demythologizing and history. [1st English ed.] New York, Scribner [1955] 92 p. 23 cm. "Translation by Neville Horton Smith...based on the first German edition published in Stuttgart in 1953 under the title Entmythologisierung und Kirche." [BS2364.G65] 55-14922
1. Bultmann, Rudolf Karl, 1884- 2. Bible. N.T.—Criticism, interpretation, etc. 3. History—Philosophy. I. Title.

GRANT, Robert McQueen, 225.6
1917-
A historical introduction to the New Testament. [1st ed.] New York, Harper & Row [1963] 447 p. 22 cm. [BS2330.2.G7] 63-12162
1. Bible. N.T.—Introductions. I. Title.

GRANT, Robert McQueen, 225.6
1917-
A historical introduction to the New Testament. New York, Harper [c.1963] 447p. 22cm. 63-12162 5.00
1. Bible. N. T.—Introductions. I. Title.

GROMACKI, Robert Glenn. 225'.6
New Testament survey / Robert G. Gromacki. Grand Rapids : Baker Book House, [1974] xi, 433 p. : ill. ; 24 cm. Includes index. Bibliography: p. 414-425. [BS2330.2.G76] 74-83793 ISBN 0-8010-3677-1 : 9.95
1. Bible. N.T.—Introductions. I. Title.

GROOM, M S 1872- 225.6
Vital teachings of the New Testament, a handbook of Christian faith. [1st ed.] New York, Exposition Press [1962] 208p. 22cm. (An Exposition-Testament book) [BS2361.G58] 62-15680
1. Bible. N. T.—Theology. I. Title.

GROSSOUW, Willem Karel 225.6
Maria, 1906-
Spirituality of the New Testament. Translated by Martin W. Schoenberg. St. Louis, Herder [1961] 203p. 21cm. (Cross and crown series of spirituality, no. 19) Translation of Bijbelse vroomheid; beschouwingen over de spiritualiteit vanhet Nieuwe Testament. [BS2361.2.G753] 61-12285
1. Bible. N. T.—Criticism, interpretation, etc. I. Title.

HAMANN, Henry Paul. 225.6
A popular guide to New Testament criticism / Henry P. Hamann. St. Louis : Concordia Pub. House, c1977. 78 p. ; 23 cm. Bibliography: p. 78. [BS2393.H34] 77-9627 ISBN 0-570-03760-3 : 2.95
1. Bible. N.T.—Criticism, interpretation, etc. I. Title.

HAZELTON, Roger, 1909- 225.6
New Testament heritage. Philadelphia, United Church [c.1955, 1962] 111p. 19cm. (Pilgrim bk.) 62-19783 1.45 pap.,
1. Bible. N. T.—Introductions. I. Title.

HEAD, Eldred Douglas, 1892- 225.6
New Testament life and literature as reflected in the papyri. Nashville, Broadman Press [1952] 148 p. 20 cm. Includes bibliography. [BS2375.H4] 52-9166
1. Bible. N. T.—Criticism, interpretation, etc. 2. Bible. N. T.—History of contemporary events, etc. 3. Manuscripts, Greek (Papyri) I. Title.

HEARD, Richard Grenville. 225.6
An introduction to the New Testament. New York, Harper [1950?] 268 p. 22 cm. Includes bibliography. [BS2330.H35 1950a] 51-12786
1. Bible. N. T.—Introductions. I. Title.

HERKLOTS, Hugh Gerard Gibson, 1903- 225.6
A fresh approach to the New Testament. New York, Abingdon-Cokesbury Press ['1950] 176 p. 20 cm. [BS2330.H39] 51-5323
1. Bible. N. T.—Introductions. I. Title.

HERMANN, Ingo, 1932- 225.6
Encounter with the New Testament, an initiation. Translated from the German by Raymond Meyerpeter. New York, P. J. Kenedy [1965] 140 p. 22 cm. Translation of Begegnung mit der Bibel. Bibliographical references included in "Notes" (p. 129-140) [BS2330.2.H453] 64-21847
1. Bible. N.T. — Introductions. I. Title.

HERMANN, Ingo, 1932- 225.6
Encounter with the New Testament, an initiation. Tr. from German by Raymond Meyerpeter. New York, Kenedy [c.1965] 140p. 22cm. Bibl. [BS2330.2.H453] 64-21847 3.95
1. Bible. N.T.—Introductions. I. Title.

HUNTER, Archibald Macbride. 225.6
Gleanings from the New Testament / A. M. Hunter. Philadelphia : Westminster Press, c1975. vi, 182 p. ; 22 cm. Includes bibliographical references. [BS2395.H79 1975] 75-33652 ISBN 0-664-24794-6 : 5.45
1. Bible. N.T.—Addresses, essays, lectures. I. Title.

HUNTER, Archibald Macbride. 225.6
Introducing New Testament theology. Philadelphia, Westminster Press [1958] 160 p. 20 cm. [BS2397.H8] 58-5130
1. Bible. N.T.—Theology. I. Title.

HUNTER, Archibald Macbride. 225.6
Introducing the New Testament. 2d ed., rev. and enl. Philadelphia, Westminster Press [1957] 208p. 20cm. Includes bibliography. [BS2330.H8 1957] 58-5256
1. Bible. N. T.—Introductions. I. Title.

HUNTER, Archibald Macbride. 225.6
The New Testament for today / A. M. Hunter. Atlanta : John Knox Press, 1975, c1974. p. cm. [BS2361.2.H86 1975] 74-31491 ISBN 0-8042-0351-2 pbk. : 2.45
1. Bible. N.T.—Criticism, interpretation, etc. I. Title.

HUNTER, Archibald Macbride 225.6
Teaching and preaching the New Testament. Philadelphia, Westminster [c.1963] 191p. 23cm. Bibl. 63-12596 3.75
1. Forsyth, Peter Taylor, 1848-1921. 2. Sermons, English—Scotland. 3. Bible. N. T.—Addresses, essays, lectures. I. Title.

HUNTER, Archibald Macbridge. 225.6
Teaching and preaching the New Testament. Philadelphia. Westminister Press [1963] 191 p. 23 cm. Bibliographical references included in footnotes. [BS2395.H8] 63-12596
1. Sermons, English — Scotland. 2. Bible.N. T. — Addresses, essays, lectures. 3. Forsyth, Peter Taylor, 1848-1921. I. Title.

KASEMANN, Ernst. 225.6
Essays on New Testament themes [Translated by W. J. Montague] Naperville, Ill. A. R. Allenson [1964] 200 p. 22 cm. (Studies in Biblical theology, no. 41) "Translated ... from selections from ... [the author's] ... Exegetische Versuche and Besinnungen, erster Band (2nd edition, Vandenhoeck and Ruprecht, 1960)" Bibliographical footnotes. [BS2395.K313] 65-106
1. Bible. N.T. — Addresses, essays, lectures. I. Title. II. Series.

KASEMANN, Ernst 225.6
Essays on New Testament themes [Tr. from German by W. J. Montague] Naperville, Ill., Allenson [c.1964] 200p. 22cm. (Studies in Biblical theology, no. 41; 2d ed. Vandenhoeck und Ruprecht, 1960) Bibl. [BS2395.K313] 65-106 3.95 pap.,
1. Bible. N. T.—Addresses, essays, lectures. I. Title. II. Series.

KASEMANN, Ernst. 225.6
New Testament questions of today. Philadelphia, Fortress Press [1969] xi, 305 p. 24 cm. "Translated ... from selections from ... Exegetische Versuche und Besinnungen, zweiter Band." Bibliographical footnotes. [BS2395.K3132] 70-81531 6.75
1. Bible. N.T.—Addresses, essays, lectures. I Title.

KECK, Leander E. 225.6
The New Testament experience of faith / by Leander E. Keck. St. Louis : Bethany Press, c1976. 160 p. ; 22 cm. [BS2361.2.K42] 76-46491 ISBN 0-8272-2507-5 pbk. : 2.95
1. Bible. N.T.—Criticism, interpretation, etc. 2. Christianity—Origin. I. Title.

KEE, Howard Clark. 225.6
Understanding the New Testament [by] Howard Clark Kee, Franklin W. Young [and] Karlfried Froehlich. 2d ed. Englewood Cliffs, N.J., Prentice-Hall [1965] xxii, 490 p. illus., maps (3 col. on lining papers) 24 cm. Bibliography: p. 455-463. [BS2407.K37 1965] 65-12336
1. Bible. N.T.—History of Biblical events. 2. Bible. N.T.—Introductions. I. Young, Franklin W., joint author. II. Froehlich, Karlfried, joint author. III. Title.

KLASSEN, William, ed. 225.6
Current issues in New Testament interpretation; essays in honor of Otto A. Piper. Ed. by William Klassen, Graydon F. Snyder. New York, Harper [c.1962] xiv, 302p. 22cm. front. port. 62-11132 5.00
1. Piper, Otto A., 1891- 2. Bible. N.T.—Addresses, essays, lectures. I. Snyder, Graydon F., joint ed. II. Title.

KNUDSEN, Ralph Edward, 1897- 225.6
Knowing the New Testament. Phaldelphia, Judson Press [1954] 192p. 20cm. [BS2330.K63] 54-8200
1. Bible. N. T.—Introductions. I. Title.

KUMMEL, Werner Georg, 1905- 225.6
Introduction to the New Testament / by Werner Georg Kummel ; translated by Howard Clark Kee. Rev. ed. Nashville, Tenn. : Abingdon Press, [1975] 629 p. ; 23 cm. Revised and updated translation of Einleitung in das Neue Testament by P. Feine and J. Behm. Includes bibliographies and indexes. [BS2330.F413 1975] 74-26804 ISBN 0-687-19575-6. : 15.95.
1. Bible. N.T.—Introductions. I. Feine, Paul, 1859-1933. Einleitung in das Neue Testament. II. Title.

KUSKE, Martin. 225.6
The Old Testament as the Book of Christ : an appraisal of Bonhoeffer's interpretation / by Martin Kuske ; translated by S. T. Kimbrough, Jr. Philadelphia : Westminster Press, c1976. p. cm. Translation of Das Alte Testament als Buch von Christus. "List of D. Bonhoeffer sources": p. [BS1160.K8713] 76-25495 ISBN 0-664-20772-3 : 12.95
1. Bonhoeffer, Dietrich, 1906-1945. 2. Bible. O.T.—Criticism, interpretation, etc.—History—20th century. 3. Bible. N.T.—Relation to the Old Testament. I. Title.

LACE, O Jessie. 225.6
Understanding the New Testament, edited by O. Jessie Lace. Cambridge [Eng.] University Press, 1965. ix, 167 p. maps 21 cm. (The Cambridge Bible commentary: New English Bible) [BS 2530.L32] 65-19153
1. Bible. N.T. — Study. I. Title. II. Series.

LACE, O. Jessie, ed. 225.6
Understanding the New Testament [New York] Cambridge [c.]1965. ix, 167p. maps. 21cm. (Cambridge Bible commentary: New Eng. Bible) [BS2530.L32] 65-19153 3.50; 1.65 pap.,
1. Bibl. N.T. — Study. I. Title. II. Series.

LADD, George Eldon, 1911- 225'.6
The New Testament and criticism. Grand Rapids, W. B. Eerdmans Pub. Co. [1967] 222 p. 22 cm. Bibliographical footnotes. [BS2361.2.L3] 66-18728
1. Bible. N.T.—Criticism, interpretation, etc. I. Title.

LADD, George Eldon, 1911- 225.6
The pattern of New Testament truth. Grand Rapids, Mich., Eerdmans [1968] 119 p. 22 cm. Originally delivered as the Nils W. Lund memorial lectures, Nov. 15-16, 1966, North Park Seminary, Chicago. Bibliographical footnotes. [BS2397.L3] 68-16256
1. Bible. N.T.—Theology. I. Title.

LAMSA, George Mamishisho, 1893- 225.6
More light on the Gospel; over 400 New Testament passages explained [by] George M. Lamsa. [1st ed.] Garden City, N.Y., Doubleday, 1968. xxx, 377 p. 22 cm. [BS2361.2.L35] 68-27125 6.95
1. Bible. N.T.—Criticism, interpretation, etc. I. Title.

LOHMEYER, Ernst Johannes, 1890-1946 225.6
Lord of the Temple; a study of the relation between cult and Gospel. Tr. by Stewart Todd. Richmond, Va., Knox, 1962. 116p. 23cm. 62-18409 3.00 bds.,
1. Bible. N.T.—Theology. 2. Cults, Jewish. I. Title.

MACQUARRIE, John 225.6
The scope of demythologizing; Bultmann and his critics. New York, Harper [1961, c.1960] 255p. (The Library of philosophy and theology) Bibl. 61-7344 4.50
1. Bultmann, Rudolf Karl, 1884- 2. Demythologization. I. Title.

MACQUARRIE, John 225.6
The scope of demythologizing; Baultmann and his critics [Magnolia, Mass., P. Smith, 1966, c.1960] 225p. 21cm. (Torchbk., Cloister lib., TB134J rebound) Bibl. [BS2873.M26 1961] 3.75
1. Bultmann, Rudolf Karl, 1884- 2. Demythologization. I. Title.

MALEVEZ, Leopold 225.6
The Christian message and myth; the theology of Rudolf Bultmann. [Translated from the French by Olive Wyon] Westminster, Md., Newman Press [1958 i.e. 1959] 215p. (Bibl. footnotes) 22cm. 59-14800 4.50
1. Bultmann, Rudolf Karl. 2. Demythologization. I. Title.

MANSON, Thomas Walter, 1893-1958. 225.6
Studies in the Gospels and Epistles. Edited by Matthew Black. Philadelphia, Westminster Press [1962] 293p. 23cm. [BS2555.2.M3] 62-14176
1. Bible. N. T. Gospels—Criticism, interpretation, etc. 2. Bible. N. T. Epistles of Paul—Criticism, interpretation, etc. I. Title.

MARXSEN, Willi, 1919- 225.6
The New Testament as the church's book. Translated by James E. Mignard. Philadelphia, Fortress Press [1971, c1972] vi, 154 p. 18 cm. Translation of Das Neue Testament als Buch der Kirche. [BS2364.2.M3713] 70-164554 ISBN 0-8006-0102-5 3.95
1. Bible. N.T.—Criticism, interpretation, etc. I. Title.

MENDENHALL, George Newton, 1879- 225.6
The basic teachings of the New Testament. New York, Vantage [c.1962] 173p. 21cm. 62-4591 3.50
1. Bible. N. T.—Theology. I. Title.

MENDENHALL, George Newton, 1879- 225.6
The basic teachings of the New Testament. [1st ed.] New York, Vantage Press [1962] 173p. 21cm. [BS2397.M4] 62-4591
1. Bible. N. T.—Theology. I. Title.

MINEAR, Paul Sevier, 1906- 225.6
Images of the church in the New Testament. Philadelphia, Westminster Press [c.1960] 294p. 24cm. 60-11331 6.00
1. Church—Biblical teaching. 2. Bible. N. T.—Theology. I. Title.

MONRO, Margaret T. 225.6
Enjoying the New Testament, Foreword by the Rev, Cuthbert Lattey, Garden City, N. Y., Doubleday [1962, c.1961] 197p. illus. 18cm. (Image bk., D147) Bibl. 62-51428 .75 pap.,
1. Bible. N.T.—Study. I. Title.

MOULE, Charles Francis Digby. 225'.6
The phenomenon of the New Testament; an inquiry into the implications of certain features of the New Testament [by] C. F. D. Moule. Naperville, Ill., A. R. Allenson [1967] viii, 120 p. 22 cm. (Studies in Biblioical theology, 2d ser., 1) Bibliographical footnotes. [BS2361.2.M6 1967a] 67-4984
1. Bible. N.T.—Criticism, interpretation, etc. I. Title. II. Series. III. The David S. Schaff lectures, 1966.

MOUNCE, Robert H 225.6
The essential nature of New Testament preaching 1st ed. Grand Rapids, Eerdmans [1960] 168p. 22cm. Includes bibliography. [BS2397.M65] 60-10093
1. Bible. N. T.— Theology. I. Title.

MOUNCE, Robert H. 225.6
The essential nature of New Testament preaching. Grand Rapids, Mich., Eerdmans [c.1960] 168p. (bibl. and bibl. footnotes) 22cm. 60-10093 3.50
1. Bible. N.T.—Theology. I. Title.

NEILL, Stephen Charles, Bp. 225.6
Jesus through many eyes : introduction to the theology of the New Testament / Stephen Neill. Philadelphia : Fortress Press, c1976. ix, 214 p. ; 23 cm. Includes indexes. Bibliography: p. 196-205. [BS2397.N44] 75-36455 ISBN 0-8006-1220-5 : 5.50
1. Jesus Christ—Person and offices. 2. Bible. N.T.—Theology. I. Title.

†THE New Testament and structuralism : 225.6
a collection of essays / by Corina Galland ... [et al.] ; edited and translated by Alfred M. Johnson, Jr. Pittsburgh : Pickwick Press, 1976. ix, 338 p. : ill. ; 22 cm. (Pittsburgh theological monograph series ; 11) "Originally published in 1971 as number 22 (June) issue of Langages, entitled Semiotique narrative : recits Bibliques." Includes index. Bibliography: p. 325-332. [BS2325.N48] 76-25447 ISBN 0-915138-13-1 pbk. : 7.95
1. Bible. N.T.—Criticism Textual—Addresses essays lectures. 2. Structuralism (Literary analysis)—Addresses essays lectures. I. Galland, Corina. II. Johnson, Alfred M., 1942- III. Series.

NEW Testament studies : 225.6
essays in honor of Ray Summers in his sixty-fifth year / edited by Huber L. Drumwright and Curtis Vaughan. Waco, Tex. : Markham Press Fund, c1975. xii, 195 p., [1] leaf of plates : port. ; 24 cm. Bibliography: p. 177-195. [BS2395.N56] 75-29815
1. Summers, Ray. 2. Summers, Ray—Bibliography. 3. Bible. N.T.—Criticism, interpretation, etc.—Addresses, essays, lectures. I. Summers, Ray. II. Drumwright, Huber L. III. Vaughan, Curtis.

OGDEN, Schubert Miles, 1928- 225.6
Christ without myth; a study based on the theology of Rudolf Bultmann. New York, Harper [c.1961] 189p. Bibl. 61-12831 3.75 bds.,
1. Bultmann, Rudolf Karl, 1884- 2. Demythologization. I. Title.

OWEN, Huw Parri 225.6
Revelation and existence; a study in the theology of Rudolf Bultmann. Cardiff, Univ. of Wales Pr. [dist. Mystic, Conn., Verry, 1964] 160 p. 22 cm. 58-37072 3.50
1. Bultmann, Rudolf Karl, 1884- 2. Demythologization. 3. Existentialism. I. Title.

PARKER, Pierson. 225.6
Inherit the promise; six keys to New Testament thought. Greenwich, Conn., Seabury Press, 1957. 243p. 22cm. [BS2397.P3] 57-10127
1. Bible. N. T.—Theology. I. Title.

PATTE, Daniel. 225.6
What is structural exegesis? / By Daniel Patte. Philadelphia : Fortress Press, c1976. vi, 90 p. : diagrs. ; 22 cm. (Guides to Biblical scholarship : New Testament series) Includes index. Bibliography: p. 86-88. [BS2361.2.P36] 75-36454 ISBN 0-8006-0462-8 pbk. : 2.95
1. Bible. N.T.—Criticism, interpretation, etc. 2. Bible. N.T.—Hermeneutics. I. Title.

PHILLIPS, John Bertram, 1906- 225.6
Ring of truth; a translator's testimony [by] J. B. Phillips. New York, Macmillan [1967] 125 p. 21 cm. [BS501.P5A3] 67-12799
1. Bible. N.T. English—Versions—Phillips. 2. Bible—Translating. I. Title.

PRICE, James Ligon, 1915- 225.6
Interpreting the New Testament. New York, Holt, Rinehart and Winston [1961] 572p. illus. 25cm. Includes bibliography. [BS2330.2.P7] 61-8590
1. Bible, N. T.—Introductions. I. Title.

PRICE, James Ligon, 1915- 225.6
Interpreting the New Testament [by] James L. Price. 2d ed. New York, Holt, Rinehart and Winston [1971] xv, 624 p. illus., maps. 25 cm. Bibliography: p. 601-615. [BS2330.2.P7 1971] 72-138401 ISBN 0-03-085261-7
1. Bible. N.T.—Introductions. I. Title.

RHEIN, Francis Bayard. 225.6
An analytical approach to the New Testament. Woodbury, N.Y., Barron's Educational Series, inc. [1966] xiv, 387 p. maps. 20 cm. Bibliography: p. 379-381. [BS2330.2.R5] 65-23532
1. Bible. N.T.—Introductions. I. Title.

RHEIN, Francis Bayard 225.6
Understanding the new testament rev. ed. Woodbury, New York, Barron's Educational Series [1974, c1966] xiii, 387 p. maps 20 cm. Bibliography: p. 379-381. [BS2330.2.R5] ISBN 0-8120-0027-7 3.25 (pbk.)
1. Bible. New Testament—Introductions. I. Title.
L.C. card number for original edition: 65-23532.

RIDDERBOS, Herman N 225.6
When the time had fully come; studies in New Testament theology. Grand Rapids, Eerdmans [1957] 104p. 19cm. (Pathway books) [BS2397.R5] 57-9772
1. Bible. N. T.— Theology. I. Title.

RIDDERBOS, Herman N 225.6
When the time had fully come; studies in New Testament theology. Grand Rapids, Eerdmans [1957] 104p. 19cm. (Pathway books) [BS2397.R5] 57-9772
1. Bible. N. T.— Theology. I. Title.

ROBERT, Andre, 1883-1955, 225.6
ed.
Introduction to the New Testament [ed. by] A. Robert, A. Feuillet. Tr. from French by Patrick W. Skehan [others] New York, Desclee, 1965. xviii, 912p. illus. facsims. 3 maps (in pocket (2 col.)) 23cm. Bibl. [BS2330.2.R613] 65-15631 15.75
1. Bibl. N. T. — Introductions. I. Feuillet, Andre, joint ed. II. Title.

ROBINSON, Gordon. 225.6
New Testament detection. New York, Oxford University Press, 1964. 269 p. 22 cm. [BS2370.R6] 64-25238
1. Bible. N.T. — Criticism, interpretation, etc. I. Title.

ROBINSON, Gordon 225.6
New Testament detection. New York, Oxford [c.] 1964. 269p. 22cm. 64-25238 4.50 pap.,
1. Bible. N. T.—Criticism, interpretation, etc. I. Title.

ROSTAGNO, Sergio, 1934- 225.6
Essays on the New Testament : a "materialist" approach / by Sergio Rostagno ; transl. by Dave Macey. Geneva : World Student Christian Federation, [1976] 76 p. ; 21 cm. Includes bibliographical references. [BS2395.R67] 77-367478
1. Bible. N.T.—Criticism, interpretation, etc.—Addresses, essays, lectures. I. Title.

ROWLINGSON, Donald T 225.6
Introduction to New Testament study. New York, Macmillan, 1956. 246p. 22cm. [BS2330.R63] 56-7682
1. Bible. N. T.—Introductions. I. Title.

RUEF, John Samuel. 225.6
Understanding the Gospels. New York, Seabury Press, 1963. 61 p. 21 cm. [BS2555.5.R8] 63-19450
1. Bible. NT. Gospels — Criticism, interpretation, etc. 2. Jesus Christ — Person and offices. I. Title.

RUEF, John Samuel 225.6
Understanding the Gospels. New York, Seabury [c.]1963. 61p. 21cm. 63-19450 1.25 pap.,
1. Bible. N.T. Gospels—Criticism, interpretation, etc. 2. Jesus Christ—Person and offices. I. Title.

RUSSELL, William D 1938- 225.6
Treasure in earthen vessels; an introduction to the New Testament, by William D. Russell. [Independence, Mo.] Dept. of Religious Education, Reorganized Church of Jesus Christ of Latter Day Saints [1966] 286 p. illus., facsims., maps, ports. 21 cm. Bibliography: p. 274-280. [BS2535.2.R8] 65-28007
1. Bible. N.T.—Study. I. Reorganized Church of Jesus Christ of Latter-Day Saints. Dept. of Religious Education. II. Title.

RUSSELL, William D., 1938- 225.6
Treasure in earthen vessels; an introduction to the New Testament. [Independence, Mo] Dept. of Religious Educ., Reorganized Church of Jesus Christ of Latter Day Saints [dist. Herald Pub. House, c.1966] 286p. illus., facsims., maps, ports. 21cm. Bibl. [BS2535.2.R8] 65-28007 3.00
1. Bible. N.T. — Study. I. Reorganized Church of Jesus Christ of Latter-Day Saints. Dept. of Religious Education. II. Title.

SCAER, David P., 1936- 225.6
The Apostolic Scriptures [by] David P. Scaer. St. Louis, Concordia Pub. House [1971] 68 p. 23 cm. (Contemporary theology series) [BS480.S325] 70-162533 ISBN 0-570-06716-2
1. Bible—Inspiration. 2. Apostles. I. Title.

*SCHACHER, James A. 225.6
Conversational Bible studies; New Testament, [by] James A. Schacher. Grand Rapids, Baker Book House, [1975] 154 p. 18 cm. (Contemporary discussion series) [BS2544] ISBN 0-8010-8054-1 1.65 (pbk.)
1. Bible—Study—Outlines, syllabi, etc. 2. Bible. NT—Criticism, interpretation, etc. I. Title.

SCHLIER, Heinrich, 1900- 225.6
Principalities and powers in the New Testament. [New York] Herder & Herder [c.1961] 88p. (Quaestiones disputatae, 3) 61-9373 1.95 pap.,
1. Spirits. 2. Bible. N.T.—Theology. I. Title.

SCHLIER, Heinrich, 1900- 225.6
The relevance of the New Testament; tr., [from German] by W. J. O'Hara. London, Burns & Oates; New York, Herder & Herder 1968. x, 258p. 22cm. Tr. of: Besinnung auf das Neue Testament. Bibl. [BS2395.S27] 68-98292 6.50
1. Bible. N. T.—Criticism, interpretation, etc.—Addresses, essays, lectures. I. Title.

SCHLIER, Heinrich, 1900- 225.6
The relevance of the New Testament: translated [from the German] by W. J. O'Hara. London. Burns & Oates; New York, Herder and Herder 1968. x, 258 p. 22 cm. 45/- (SBN 223 17901 9) (B 68-05658) Translation of: Besinnung auf das Neue Testament. Bibliographical footnotes. [BS2395.S27] 68-98292
1. Bible. N. T.—Criticism, interpretation, etc.—Addresses, essays, lectures. I. Title.

SCHNACKENBURG, Rudolf, 225.6
1914-
Christian existence in the New Testament. [Translated by F. Wieck. Notre Dame, Ind.] University of Notre Dame Press, 1968- v. 20 cm. Translation of Christliche Existenz nach dem Neuen Testament. Bibliographical footnotes. [BS2397.S3513] 68-27576 6.95
1. Bible. N.T.—Theology—Addresses, essays, lectures. I. Title.

SCHNACKENBURG, Rudolf, 225.6
1914-
New Testament theology today. Translated by David Askew. [New York] Herder and Herder [1963] 133 p. 23 cm. Includes bibliography. [BS2397.S413] 63-9559
1. Bible. N.T.—Theology. I. Title.

SCHNACKENBURG, Rudolf, 225.6
1914-
New Testament theology today. Tr. by David Askew. New York, Herder & Herder [c.1963] 133p. 23cm. Bibl. 63-9559 2.95
1. Bible. N.T.—Theology. I. Title.

SHEIL, Leonard. 225.6
Pray like this. Pray with St. Paul. [Boston] St. Paul Editions [1963] 330 p. 19 cm. [BS2341.2.S5] 62-20703
1. Bible. N. T.—Meditations. I. Title. II. Title: Pray with St. paul.

SHEIL, Leonard 225.6
Pray like this. Pray with St. Paul. [Boston] St. Paul Eds. [dist. Daughters of St. Paul, c.1963] 330p. 19cm. 62-20703 4.00
1. Bible. N. T.—Meditations. I. Title. II. Title: Pray with St. Paul.

SPARKS, Hedley Frederick 225.6
Davis.
The formation of the New Testament. New York, Philosophical Library [1953] 172p. 22cm. Includes bibliography. [BS2330.S64] 53-7915
1. Bible. N. T.—Introductions. I. Title.

SPIVEY, Robert A., 1931- 225.6
Anatomy of the New Testament; a guide to its structure and meaning [by] Robert A. Spivey [and] D. Moody Smith, Jr. [New York] Macmillan [1969] xvii, 510 p. illus., maps. 24 cm. Includes bibliographical references. [BS2330.2.S65] 69-14271
1. Bible. N.T.—Introductions. I. Smith, Dwight Moody, joint author. II. Title.

STAUFFER, Ethelbert, 1902- 225.6
New Testament theology; translated from the German by John Marsh. [1st American ed.] New York, Macmillan [1956, c1955] 373 p. 24 cm. [HD9705.U64S77] [BS2397.S8 1956] 59-44724 56-11575
1. Bible. N. T. — Theology I. Title.

STAUFFER, Ethelbert, 1902- 225.6
New Testament theology translated from the German by John Marsh. 1st American ed. New York, Macmillan [1956, c1955] 373p. 24cm. Includes bibliographies. [BS2397.S815 1956] 56-11575
1. Bible. N. T.—Theology I. Title.

STEVENSON, Dwight Eshelman, 225.6
1906-
Preaching on the books of the New Testament. [1st ed.] New York, Harper [1956] 268p. 22cm. [BS2330.S687] 56-6117
1. Bible. N. T.—Introductions. 2. Bible. N. T.—Homiletical use. I. Title.

STEVENSON, Dwight Eshelman, 225.6
1906-
Preaching on the books of the New Testament. [1st ed.] New York, Harper 1956] 268 p. 22 cm. [BS2330.S687] 56-6117
1. Bible. N. T. — Introductions. 2. Bible. N. T.==Homiletical use. I. Title.

*STOTT, John R. W. 225.6
Basic introduction to the New Testament. Grand Rapids, Mich., Eerdmans, 1964. 179p. 18cm. 1.45 pap.,
I. Title.

STOTT, John R W 225.6
Men with a message. With a foreword by the Bishop of London. London, New York, Longmans, Green [1954] 179p. 17cm. [BS2330.S69] 54-964
1. Bible. N. T.—Introductions. I. Title.

STUDIES in New Testament 225.6
language and text : essays in honour of George D. Kilpatrick on the occasion of his sixty-fifth birthday / edited by J. K. Elliott. Leiden : Brill, 1976. x, 400 p. : port. ; 25 cm. (Supplements to Novum Testamentum ; v. 44) English, French, or German. Bibliography of works by G. Kilpatrick: p. [4]-13. [BS2395.S78] 76-362782 ISBN 9-00-404386-1 : fl 150.00
1. Kilpatrick, George Dunbar. 2. Kilpatrick, George Dunbar—Bibliography. 3. Bible. N.T.—Criticism, interpretation, etc.—Addresses, essays, lectures. I. Kilpatrick, George Dunbar. II. Elliott, James Keith. III. Series: Novum Testamentum : Supplements ; v. 44.

TENNEY, Merrill Chapin, 225.6
1904-
New Testament survey. [Rev. ed.] Grand Rapids, Eerdmans [1961] 464 p. illus. 24 cm. "A revision of The New Testament, an historical and analytic survey...1953." [BS2330.T4 1961] 61-10862
1. Bible. N.T. — Introduction. 2. Bible. N.T. — History of contemporary events, etc. I. Title.

TENNEY, Merrill Chapin, 225.6
1904-
New Testament survey. [Rev. ed.] Grand Rapids, Eerdmans [1961] 464 p. illus. 24 cm. "A revision of The New Testament, and historical and analytic survey ... 1953." [BS2330.T4 1961] 61-10862
1. Bible. N. T.—Introductions. 2. Bible. N. T.—History of contemporary events, etc. I. Title.

THROCKMORTON, Burton 225.6
Hamilton, 1921-
The New Testament and mythology. Philadelphia, Westminster Press [1959] 255 p. 21 cm. Includes bibliography. [BS2378.T5] 59-9545
1. Demythologization. I. Title.

TWILLEY,L D 225.6
The origin and transmission of the New Testament; a short introduction, Grand Rapids, Eerdmans [c1957] 69 p. illus. 19 cm. (A Pathway book) [BS2330.T85] 58-9550
1. Bible. N.T. — Introductions. 2. Bible. N.T. — Criticism, Textual. I. Title.

UNDERSTANDING the Bible: 225.6
the New Testament, edited by John P. Bradley and John Quinlan. Gastonia, N.C., Good Will Publishers [1970] xi, 375 p. illus. (part col.), facsims., maps, plan, ports. 25 cm. (The Catholic layman's library, v. 2) [BS2361.2.U53] 77-92776
1. Bible. N.T.—Criticism, interpretation, etc. I. Bradley, John P., ed. II. Quinlan, John, 1920- ed. III. Title. IV. Series.

VOS, Howard Frederic, 1925- 225.6
Simple survey of the New Testament for the layman. Grand Rapids, Zondervan Pub. House [1957] 92 p. 20 cm. Includes bibliography. [BS2330.V6] 57-38377
1. Bible. I. Title.

VOS, Howard Frederic, 1925- 225.6
Simple survey of the New Testament for the layman. Grand Rapids, Zondervan Pub. House [1957] 92p. 20cm. Includes bibliography. [BS2330.V6] 57-38377
1. Bible. N. T.—Introductions. I. Title.

WARD, Ronald Arthur. 225.6
Hidden meaning in the New Testament; new light from the old Greek [by] Ronald A. Ward. Foreword by Paul S. Rees. Introd. by Marcus Ward. Old Tappan, N.J., F. H. Revell Co. [1969] 190 p. 21 cm. Bibliography: p. 181. [BS2370.W3] 78-2183 4.95
1. Bible. N.T.—Criticism, interpretation, etc. 2. Greek language, Biblical—Grammar. I. Title.

WIKENHAUSER, Alfred, 1883- 225.6
New Testament introduction. Translated by Joseph Cunningham. [New York] Herder and Herder [1958] 579 p. 23 cm. An English translation based on the 2d rev and enl. German ed. published in 1956 under title: Einleitung in das Neue Testament. Includes bibliography. [BS2330.W463 1958a] 58-5870
1. Bible. N.T.—Introductions. I. Title.

WILDER, Amos Niven, 1895- 225.6
New Testament faith for today. [1st ed.] New York, Harper [1955] 186p. 22cm. [BR121.W528] 55-8530
1. Christianity—Essence, genius, nature. 2. Bible. N. T.— Theology. I. Title.

BROWN, Buford B. 225.607
From Jerusalem to Rome. New York, Vantage [c.1963] 103p. 21cm. 2.95
I. Title.

ROBINSON, James 225.6'08
McConkey, 1924-
Trajectories through early Christianity [by] James M. Robinson [and] Helmut Koester. Philadelphia, Fortress Press [1971] xii, 297 p. 23 cm. Includes bibliographical references. [BS2395.R59] 79-141254 ISBN 0-8006-0058-4 9.95
1. Bible. N.T.—Addresses, essays, lectures. 2. Christian literature, Early—Addresses, essays, lectures. I. Koester, Helmut, 1926- II. Title.

JEREMIAS, Joachim, 1900- 225.6081
The central message of the New Testament. New York, Scribner [1965] 95 p. 22 cm. Bibliographical footnotes. [BS2395.J4] 65-16695
1. Bible. N.T.—Addresses, essays, lectures. I. Title.

KUMMEL, Werner Georg, 225.6'09
1905-
The New Testament: the history of the investigation of its problems. Translated by S. McLean Gilmour and Howard C. Kee. Nashville, Abingdon Press [1972] 510 p. 24 cm. Translation of Das Neue Testament: Geschichte der Erforschung seiner Probleme. Bibliography: p. 462-465. [BS2350.K813] 74-185554 ISBN 0-687-27926-7 10.95
1. Bible. N.T.—Criticism, interpretation, etc.—History. I. Title.

NEILL, Stephen Charles, 225.609
Bp.
The interpretation of the New Testament, 1861-1961, by Stephen Neill. New York, Oxford [c.]1964. vi, 360p. 23cm. (Firth lects., 1962) Bibl. 64-3980 7.00
1. Bible. N. T.—Criticism, interpretation, etc.—Hist. I. Title. II. Series: The Firth lectures in the University of Nottingham, 1962

NEILL, Stephen Charles, 225'.6'09
Bp.
The interpretation of the New Testament, 1861-1961, by Stephen Neill. [1st ed. reprinted with corrections] London, Oxford U.P., 1966. xii, 360 p. 20 cm. (The Firth lectures, 1962) 10/6 (B 66-21456) Oxford paperbacks. Bibliographical footnotes. [BS2350.N4 1966] 67-82380
1. Bible. N.T. — Criticism, interpretation, etc. — Hist. I. Title. II. Series: The Firth lectures in the University of Nottingham, 1962

DILLISTONE, 225.6'092'4 B
Frederick William, 1903-
C. H. Dodd, interpreter of the New Testament / by F. W. Dillistone. Grand Rapids : Eerdmans, c1977. 255 p. ; 25 cm. Includes index. Bibliography: p. 249-251. [BS2351.D6D54 1977] 76-54324 ISBN 0-8028-3496-5 : 11.95
1. Dodd, Charles Harold, 1884-1973. 2. New Testament scholars—England—Biography. I. Title.

PETERS, Clarence H 225.6095
The early years of the Christian church. Garden City, N.Y. [N. Doubleday, 1963] 64 p. illus. 21 cm. (Know your Bible program) [BS551.2.P45] 63-3840
1. Bible stores, English—N.T. Acts. I. Title.

*COLE, Alan 225.61
A Christian's guide to the New Testament. Chicago, Moody [1966, c.1965] 96p. 18cm. .95 pap.,
I. Title.

FINEGAN, Jack, 1908- 225.6'1
Encountering New Testament manuscripts; a working introduction to textual criticism. Grand Rapids, Mich., Eerdmans [1974] 203 p. illus. 26 cm. Includes bibliographical references. [BS2325.F56 1974] 74-1297 ISBN 0-8028-3445-0 10.00
1. Bible. N.T.—Criticism, Textual. 2. Bible. N.T. Manuscripts. I. Title.

WILDER, Amos Niven, 1895- 225.6'1
Early Christian rhetoric; the language of the Gospel [by] Amos N. Wilder. Cambridge, Mass., Harvard University Press, 1971 [c1964] xxx, 135 p. 22 cm. A reissue of the 1964 ed., with a new introd. by the author. Original ed. also published under title: The language of the Gospel. "The present volume, with the exception of the concluding chapter, represents the text of the Haskell lectures for 1961-1962, ... Oberlin College". Includes bibliographical

references. [BS2370.W5 1971] 78-134949 ISBN 0-674-22002-1 5.50
1. Bible. N.T.—Language, style. I. Title.

ACHTEMEIER, Paul J. 225.6'3
An introduction to the new hermeneutic, by Paul J. Achtemeier. Philadelphia, Westminster Press [1969] 190 p. 21 cm. Bibliographical references included in "Notes" (p. [166]-183) [BS2331.A23] 74-79666 6.50
1. Fuchs, Ernst, 1903- 2. Bible. N.T.—Hermeneutics. 3. Religion and language. I. Title.

FISHER, Fred L. 225.63
How to interpret the New Testament, by Fred L. Fisher. Philadelphia, Westminster Press [1966] 172 p. 21 cm. [BS2331.F5] 66-12912
1. Bible. N. T.—Hermeneutics. I. Title.

TURNER, Nigel. 225.63
Grammatical insights into the New Testament. Edinburgh, Clark [1966] viii, 198 p. tables. 22 1/2 cm. 27/6 (B 66-8250) [BS2361.2.T8] 66-71386
1. Bible. N.T. — Criticism, interpretation, etc. I. Title.

VIA, Dan Otto, 1928- 225.6'3
Kerygma and comedy in the New Testament : a structuralist approach to hermeneutic / by Dan O. Via, Jr. Philadelphia : Fortress Press, [1975] xii, 179 p. ; 24 cm. Includes bibliographical references and index. [BS2361.2.V5] 74-80425 ISBN 0-8006-0281-1 : 8.95
1. Bible. N.T.—Criticism, interpretation, etc. 2. Bible. N.T. Epistles of Paul—Criticism, interpretation, etc. 3. Bible. N.T. Mark—Criticism, interpretation, etc. I. Title.

BORNKAMM, Gunther. 225.6'6
The New Testament; a guide to its writings. Translated by Reginald H. Fuller and Ilse Fuller. Philadelphia, Fortress Press [1973] viii, 166 p. 19 cm. Translation of Bibel, das Neue Testament. Bibliography: p. 151-156. [BS2330.2.B6713] 73-79009 ISBN 0-8006-0168-8 3.25 (pbk.)
1. Bible. N.T.—Introductions. I. Title.

BRIGGS, Robert Cook, 1915- 225.6'6
Interpreting the New Testament today; an introduction to methods and issues in the study of the New Testament [by] R. C. Briggs. [Rev. ed.] Nashville, Abingdon Press [1973] 288 p. 22 cm. Published in 1969 under title: Interpreting the Gospels. Includes bibliographical references. [BS2555.2.B7 1973] 73-8024 ISBN 0-687-19327-3 4.75 (pbk.)
1. Bible. N.T.—Criticism, interpretation, etc. I. Title.

COGGAN, Frederick Donald, 1909- 225.6'6
The prayers of the New Testament, by Donald Coggan. Washington, Corpus Books [1968, c1967] 190 p. 21 cm. [BV228.C65 1968] 68-29838 4.50
1. Bible. N.T.—Prayers. I. Title.

DAUBE, David. 225.6'6
The New Testament and rabbinic Judaism. New York, Arno Press, 1973 [c1956] xviii, 460 p. 23 cm. (The Jewish people: history, religion, literature) Reprint of the ed. published by University of London, Athlone Press, London, which was issued as no. 2 of Jordan lectures in comparative religion. Includes bibliographical references. [BM535.D34 1973] 73-2191 ISBN 0-405-05257-X 25.00
1. Bible. N.T.—Criticism, interpretation, etc. 2. Rabbinical literature—Relation to the New Testament. I. Title. II. Series. III. Series: Jordan lectures in comparative religion, 2.

FITZMYER, Joseph A. 225.6'6
Essays on the Semitic background of the New Testament / Joseph A. Fitzmyer. Missoula, Mont. : Society of Biblical Literature : distributed by Scholars' Press, [1974] xix, 524 p. ; 22 cm. (Sources for Biblical study; 5) Includes bibliographical references and indexes. [BS2395.F57 1974] 74-83874 ISBN 0-88414-040-7
1. Bible. N.T.—Criticism, interpretation, etc.—Addresses, essays, lectures. 2. Dead Sea scrolls—Addresses, essays, lectures. I. Title. II. Series.

HUNTER, Archibald Macbride. 225'.6'6
Introducing the New Testament, by Archibald M. Hunter. 3d rev. ed. Philadelphia, Westminster Press [1972] viii, 216 p. 21 cm. Bibliography: p. [209]-212. [BS2330.H8 1972] 72-7110 ISBN 0-664-24965-5 3.50
1. Bible. N.T.—Introductions. I. Title.

JONSSON, Jakob 225.66
Humour and irony in the New Testament: an exegetic study. [Copenhagen] Munksgaard [New York, Humanities, 1966] 236p. 24cm. Bibl. [BS2545.W5J6] 63-6117 10.50 pap.,
1. Bible. N.T. — Criticism, interpretation, etc. 2. Wit and humor, Ancient. I. Title.

KEE, Howard Clark. 225.6'6
Understanding the New Testament [by] Howard Clark Kee, Franklin W. Young [and] Karlfried Froehlich. 3d ed. Englewood Cliffs, N.J., Prentice-Hall [1973] xv, 446 p. illus. 24 cm. Bibliography: p. 411-419. [BS2407.K37 1973] 72-13877 ISBN 0-13-936104-9 9.95
1. Bible. N.T.—History of Biblical events. 2. Bible. N.T.—Introductions. I. Young, Franklin W., joint author. II. Froehlich, Karlfried, joint author. III. Title.

KUMMEL, Werner Georg, 1905- 225.6'6
The theology of the New Testament according to its major witnesses: Jesus-Paul-John [Translated by John E. Steely] Nashville, Abingdon Press [1973] 350 p. 24 cm. Translation of Die Theologie des Neuen Testaments nach seinen Hauptzeugen Jesus, Paulus, Johannes. Bibliography: p. 19-21. [BS2397.K8313] 73-6961 ISBN 0-687-41552-7 14.95
1. Bible. N.T.—Theology. I. Title.

LADD, George Eldon, 1911- 225.6'6
A theology of the New Testament. Grand Rapids, Mich., Eerdmans [1974] 661 p. 25 cm. Includes bibliographical references. [BS2397.L33] 74-766 ISBN 0-8028-3443-4 2.50
1. Bible. N.T.—Theology. I. Title.

MARTIN, Ralph P. 225.6'6
New Testament foundations: a guide for Christian students, by Ralph P. Martin. Grand Rapids, Eerdmans [1975- v. 25 cm. Contents.Contents.—v. 1. The four Gospels. Bibliography: v. 1, p. 314-316. [BS2330.2.M28] 74-19163 ISBN 0-8028-3444-2 8.95
1. Bible. N.T.—Introductions. I. Title.

PRITCHARD, John Paul, 1902- 225.6'6
A literary approach to the New Testament. [1st ed.] Norman, University of Oklahoma Press [1972] xi, 355 p. maps. 22 cm. Bibliography: p. 334-345. [BS2361.2.P75] 72-1793 ISBN 0-8061-1011-2
1. Bible. N.T.—Criticism, interpretation, etc. 2. Bible. N.T.—Language, style. I. Title.

SANDMEL, Samuel. 225.6'6
A Jewish understanding of the New Textament. Augmented ed. New York, Ktav Pub. House [1974] p. cm. Reprint of the 1956 ed. published by Hebrew Union College Press, Cincinnati, with a new introd. and an updated bibliography. Bibliography: p. [BS2361.2.S26 1974] 74-8041 ISBN 0-87068-262-8 10.00; 3.95 (pbk.)
1. Bible. N.T.—Criticism, interpretation, inc. 2. Judaism—Relations—Christianity. 3. Christianity and other religions—Judaism. I. Title.

SPIVEY, Robert A., 1931- 225.6'6
Anatomy of the New Testament; a guide to its structure and meaning [by] Robert A. Spivey [and] D. Moody Smith, Jr. 2d ed. New York, Macmillan [1974] xvii, 539 p. illus. 24 cm. Bibliography: p. 507-513. [BS2330.2.S65 1974] 73-7679 ISBN 0-02-415280-3 9.95
1. Bible. N.T.—Introductions. I. Smith, Dwight Moody, joint author. II. Title.

STENDAHL, Krister, ed. 225.6'6
The scrolls and the New Testament / edited by Krister Stendahl. Westport, Conn. : Greenwood Press, 1975, c1957. ix, 308 p. ; 22 cm. Reprint of the ed. published by Harper, New York. Includes bibliographical references and indexes. [BM487.S8 1975] 73-15167 ISBN 0-8371-7171-7 lib.bdg. 15.25
1. Dead Sea scrolls—Relation to the New Testament. I. Title.

TRIMINGHAM, John Spencer. 225.6'6
Two worlds are ours; a study of time and eternity in relation to the Christian Gospel freed from the tyranny of the Old Testament reference, by J. Spencer Trimingham. Beirut, Librairie de Liban, 1971. xiii, 174 p. 22 cm. Includes bibliographical references. [BS2387.T75] 72-176343
1. Bible. N.T.—Relation to O.T. 2. Christianity, Essence, genius, nature. 3. Christianity and other religions. I. Title.
Dist. by Verry for 5.00.

*WINTER, Bob R. 225.66
New Testament survey; pt. 2. Austin, Tex., R. B. Sweet Co. 120p. 22cm. (Living word ser.) .75 pap.,
1. Bible. N. T.—Commentaries. I. Title.
Publisher's address: Box 4055, Austin, Tex. 78751

YOHN, David Waite. 225.6'6
The Christian reader's guide to the New Testament. Grand Rapids, Mich., Eerdmans [1973] 200 p. 22 cm. [BS2341.3.Y64] 73-76532 ISBN 0-8028-1505-7 3.45
1. Bible. N.T.—Sermons. 2. Sermons, American. I. Title.

KERTELGE, Karl. 225.6'6'08 s
The Epistle to the Romans. [Translated by Francis McDonagh. New York] Herder and Herder [1972] 144 p. 22 cm. (New Testament for spiritual reading, 12) Translation of Der Brief an die Romer. Includes the text of the Epistle. [BS2341.2.N38 vol. 12] [BS2665.3] 227'.1'077 73-151028 6.00
1. Bible. N.T. Romans—Commentaries. I. Bible. N.T. Romans. English. 1972. II. Title. III. Series.

BEASLEY, Walter J. 225.6'7
These extra-ordinary documents, by W. J. Beasley and J. A. Thompson. Melbourne, Australian Institute of Archaeology, 1969. 32 p. illus., diagrs. 19 cm. [BS2332.B4] 73-157476
1. Bible. N.T.—Evidences, authority, etc. I. Thomspon, John Arthur, 1913- joint author. II. Title.

MAYER, Herbert T. 225.6'7
The books of the New Testament [by] Herbert T. Mayer. Saint Louis, Concordia Pub. House [1969] 133 p. 20 cm. [BS2330.2.M33] 69-12766 2.00
1. Bible. N.T.—Introductions. I. Title.

NEWMAN, Barclay Moon, 1931- 225.67
The meaning of the New Testament [by] Barclay M. Newman. Nashville, Broadman Press [1966] xii, 331 p. illus., maps. 23 cm. Includes bibliographical references. [BS2361.2.N4] 66-19906
1. Bible. N.T.—Criticism, interpretation, etc. I. Title.

MACQUARRIE, John. 225.6'8
The scope of demythologizing; Bultmann and his critics. Gloucester, Mass., P. Smith, 1969 [c1960] 256 p. 21 cm. Includes bibliographical references. [BS2378.M26 1969] 79-11333
1. Bultmann, Rudolf Karl, 1884- 2. Demythologization. I. Title.

BENGEL, Johann Albrecht, 1687-1752. 225.7
New Testament word studies, by John Albert Bengel. A new translation by Charlton T. Lewis and Marvin R. Vincent. Grand Rapids, Kregel [1971] 2 v. 24 cm. (Kregel reprint library) Translation of Gnomon Novi Testamenti. Reprint of the 1864 ed. Contents.Contents.—v. 1. Matthew-Acts.—v. 2. Romans-Revelation. Bibliography: v. 1, p. 9-10; v. 2, p. 7-8. [BS2335.B413 1971] 70-155250 ISBN 0-8254-2215-9 29.95
1. Bible. N.T.—Commentaries. I. Lewis, Charlton Thomas, 1834-1904, tr. II. Vincent, Marvin Richardson, 1834-1922, tr. III. Title.

BERGER, Henry William, 1871-1948. 225.7
Toward the New Testament of the future; an attempt to separate theological interpolations from the teachings of Jesus. With a tentative diatessaron compiled from the author's notes. [1st ed.] New York, Exposition Press [1953] 295p. 21cm. [BS2332.B45] 53-6706
1. Bible. N. T.—Evidences, authority, etc. I. Title.

BIBLE. N. T. English. 1952. Authorised. 225.7
The New Testament of Our Lord Jesus Christ, King James version; with notes intended to point out the essential truths it contains, by Fernand Faivre. Notes translated from the 5th French ed. by Alice Fontannaz. 3d ed. Butler, Ind., Higley Press [1952] 480p. 19cm. [BS2085 1952.B8] 53-16584
1. Bible. N. T.—Commentaries. I. Faivre, Fernand. II. Title.

BIBLE. N. T. English. 1962. Authorized. 225.7
Barnes' notes on the New Testament, by Albert Barnes. Ed., headings, improved readings, biographical sketch by Ingram Cobbin. Complete, unabridged. Grand Rapids, Mich., Kregel [1962] xi, 1763p. illus. maps. 26cm. A62 14.95;; until Dec. 31, 12.95
1. Bible. N. T.—Commentaries. I. Barnes, Albert, 1789-1870, ed II. Title.

BIBLE. N.T. English. 1964. American revised. 225.7
Compact commentary on the New Testament. Grand Rapids, Baker Book House, 1964. xvi, 656 p. 17 cm. Published in 1912 under title: Nelson's explanatory Testament. [BS2090.A1 1964.G7] 64-6010
1. Bible. N.T.—Commentaries. I. Title.

BIBLE. N.T. English. 1964. American revised. 225.7
Compact commentary on the New Testament. Grand Rapids, Mich., Baker Bk., 1964. xvi, 656p. 17cm. 64-6010 3.95
1. Bible. N. T.—Commentaries. I. Title.

CAMBRON, Mark Gray, 1911- 225.7
The New Testament; a book-by-book survey. Introd. by Lee Roberson. Grand Rapids, Zondervan Pub. House [c1958] 472p. 23cm. Includes bibliography. [BS2525.C3] 59-29215
1. Bible. N. T.—Study—Outlines, syllabi, etc. I. Title.

CULLMANN, Oscar. 225.7
The early church; studies in early Christian history and theology. Edited by A. J. B. Higgins. Philadelphia, Westminster Press [1956] 217p. 24cm. Translations by A. J. B. Higgins and S. Godman. [BS2395.C8 1956] 56-5476
1. Bible. N. T.—Addresses. essays. lectures. 2. Church history— Primitive and early church—Addresses. essays. lectures. I. Title.

CULLMANN, Oscar. 225.7
The early church; studies in early Christian history and theology. Edited by A. J. B. Higgins. Abridged ed. Philadelphia, Westminster Press [1966, c1956] 162 p. 23 cm. Bibliographical footnotes. [BS2395.C82] 66-20093
1. Bible. N.T.—Addresses, essays, lectures. 2. Church history—Primitive and early church, 30-600—Addresses, essays, lectures. I. Title.

EARLE, Ralph, ed. 225.7
Exploring the New Testament. Ralph Earle, editor, Harvey J. S. Blaney [and] Carl Hanson. Kansas City, Mo., Beacon Hill Press [c1955] 467p. maps. 23cm. Bibliography: p. 452-458. [BS2525.E35] 56-1551
1. Bible. N. T.—Study—Outlines, syllabi, etc. I. Title.

FILSON, Floyd Vivian, 1896- 225.7
Jesus Christ, the risen Lord. New York, Abingdon Press [1956] 288 p. 24 cm. [BS2397.F48] 56-8740
1. Bible. N. T.—Theology. 2. Jesus Christ—Resurrection.

GRAVES, Robert, 1895- 225.7
The Nazarene Gospel restored, by Robert Graves and Joshua Podro. [1st American ed.] Garden City, N. Y., Doubleday, 1954 [c1953] xxiv, 982 p. 24 cm. Includes bibliographical references. [BS2555.G686 1954] 54-7314
1. Bible. N.T. Gospels—Criticism, interpretation, etc. 2. Christianity—Origin. I. Podro, Joshua, joint author. II. Title.

HARRISON, Everett Falconer, 1902- 225'.7
The New Testament and Wycliffe Bible commentary. [Parallel ed.] New York, Iversen Associates, 1971. xxi, 1104 p. 24 cm. The author's commentary first published in 1962 in C. F. Pfeiffer's The Wycliffe Bible commentary. Includes bibliographies. [BS2341.2.H36] 72-183345
1. Bible. N.T.—Commentaries. I. Pfeiffer, Charles F. The Wycliffe commentary. II. Bible. N.T. English. Authorized. 1971. III. Title. IV. Title: The Wycliffe Bible commentary.

HARVEY, Anthony Ernest. 225.7
The new English Bible, companion to the New Testament, by A. E. Harvey. [2d ed. Oxford, Eng.] Oxford University Press, 1970. vii, 850 p. maps. 24 cm. [BS2341.2.H37 1970] 73-141049 9.95
1. Bible. N.T.—Commentaries. I. Title.

HENDRIKSEN, William, 1900- 225.7
New Testament commentary [v.6] Grand Rapids, Mich., Baker Bk. [1965, c.1964] 243p. illus., map. 24cm. Accompanying Biblical text is author's tr. Bibl. Contents.[v.6] Exposition of Colossians and Philemon. [BS2341.H4] 54-924 6.95
1. Bible. N.T.—Commentaries. I. Bible. N.T. English. Hendriksen. II. Title.

HUFFMAN, Jasper Abraham, 1880- 225.7
Golden treasures from the Greek New Testament for English readers. Winona Lake, Ind., Standard Press [1951] 160 p. 20 cm. [BS2361.H75] 51-5042
1. Bible. N. T.—Criticism, interpretation, etc. I. Title.

HUNTER, Archibald Macbride. 225.7
Probing the New Testament, by A. M. Hunter. [American ed.] Richmond, John Knox Press [1972, c1971] 156 p. 19 cm. First published in 1971 under title: Exploring the New Testament. [BS2393.H85 1972] 71-37421 ISBN 0-8042-0388-1 2.45
1. Bible. N.T.—Criticism, interpretation, etc.—Addresses, essays, lectures. I. Title.

KNOCH, Adolf E. 225.7
Concordant commentary on the New Testament [by] A. E. Knoch. Saugus, Calif., Concordant Pub. Concern [1968] 407 p. 21 cm. First published in 1926 as a part of the Concordant version of the Sacred Scriptures, compiled by A. E. Knoch. "The version used in this commentary is the Concordant literal New Testament." [BS2341.2.K6] 68-3573
1. Bible. N.T.—Commentaries. I. Title.

KNOX, Ronald Arbuthnott, 225.7
1888-
A commentary on the Gospels. New York, Sheed & Ward, 1952-56. 3v. 22cm. 'Meant to be read in conjunction with the Knox New Testament.' Vols. 2-3 have title: A New Testament commentary for English readers. Vol. 1 published in London in 1953 under title: A New Testament commentary for English readers. [BS2341.K6] 52-10614
1. Bible. N. T.—Commentaries. I. Title. II. Title: A New Testament commentary for English readers.

KRAELING, Emil Gottlieb 225.7
Heinrich, 1892-
The clarified New Testament; v. 1. New York, McGraw [1962] 337p. 24cm. Contents.v. 1. The four Gospels. Bibl. 62-17887 8.95
1. Bible. N. T.—Commentaries. I. Title.

LEBRETON, Jules, 1873-1956. 225.7
The spiritual teaching of the New Testament. Translated by James E. Whalen. Westminster, Md., Newman Press, 1960. 382p. 22cm. Translation of Lumen Christl: la doctrine spiritucIle de Nouveau Testament. Includes bibliography. [BS2397.L383] 60-10725
1. Bible. N. T.—Theology. 2. Spiritual life—Catholic authors. I. Title.

LEBRETON, Jules [Marie 225.7
Leon] 1873-1956.
The spiritual teaching of the New Testament. Translated [from the French] by James E. Whalen. Westminster, Md., Newman Press, [c.]1960. 382p. (bibl. footnotes) 22cm. 60-10725 5.50
1. Bible. N. T.—Theology. 2. Spiritual life—Catholic authors. I. Title.

LOISY, Alfred Firman, 1857- 225.7
1940.
The origins of the New Testament. Tr. [from French] by L. P. Jacks. New York. Collier [1962] 384p. 18cm. (BS119V) 1.50 pap.,
1. Bible. N. T.—Criticism, interpretation, etc. I. Title.

MAKRAKES, Apostolos, 1831- 225.7
1905.
Interpretation of the entire New Testament. [Translated from the original Greek by Albert George Alexander] Chicago, Orthodox Christian Educational [sic] Society, 1949-50 [i. e. 1951] 2 v. (x. 2042 p.) port. 24 cm. Omits that part of the work covering the book of Revelation, which was published in 1948 under title: Interpretation of the Revelation of St. John the Divine. [BS2333.M315] 51-30532
1. Bible. N. T.—Commentaries. I. Title.

MEADOWS, Thomas Burton, 225.7
1881-
Guidance to the study of the New Testament an objective approach. [1st ed.] New York, Vantage Press [c1955] 513p. 21cm. [BS2535.M4] 55-9523
1. Bible. N.T.—Study—Text-books. I. Title.

MIEGGE, Giovanni 225.7
Gospel and myth in the thought of Rudolf Bultmann. Translated [from the Italian] by Stephen Neill. Richmond, John Knox Press [1960] 152p. (4p. bibl.) 23cm. 60-6937 4.00
1. Bultmann, Rudolf Karl, 1884- 2. Demythologization. I. Title.

MINEAR, Paul Sevier, 1906- 225.7
The kingdom and the power; an exposition of the New Testament gospel. Philadelphia, Westminster Press [1950] 269 p. 24 cm. Bibliographical references included in "Notes" (p. [247]-280) [BS2361.M55] 50-9919
1. Bible. N. T. — Theology. I. Title.

ONE volume New Testament 225.7
commentary, by John Wesley, Adam Clarke, Matthew Henry, and others. Grand Rapids, Baker Book House, 1957. 1v. (unpaged) 23cm. 'Previously printed under the title The Methodist commentary on the New Testament in the year 1893, by Charles H. Kelley, London.' [BS2341.M45 1957] 57-10157
1. Bible. N. T.—Commentaries. I. Wesley, John, 1703-1791.

PARKER, Thomas Henry Louis. 225.7
Calvin's New Testament commentaries [by] T. H. L. Parker. Grand Rapids, Eerdmans [1971] xiii, 208 p. 23 cm. Bibliography: p. [153]-195. [BS2350.P37] 79-27977 7.95
1. Calvin, Jean, 1509-1564. 2. Bible. N.T.—Criticism, interpretation, etc.—History—16th century. I. Title.

*PATTERSON, Charles H. 225.7
The New Testament; notes, including introduction, historical background of the New Testament, outline of the life of Jesus, summaries and commentaries. Lincoln, Neb., Cliff's Notes [c.1965] 101p. 21cm. Bibl. 1.00 pap.,
1. Bible. N.T.—Interpretations, etc. I. Title.

RYRIE, Charles Caldwell, 225.7
1925-
Biblical theology of the New Testament. Chicago, Moody Press [1959] 384p. 24cm. Includes bibliography. [BS2397.R9] 59-11468
1. Bible. N. T.— Theology. I. Title.

SANDERS, Joseph Newbould. 225.7
The foundations of the Christian faith; a study of the teaching of the New Testament in the light of historical criticism. New York, Philosophical Library [1952] 199p. 22cm. [BS2397] 52-8401
1. Bible. N. T.— Theology. I. Title.

SANDMEL, Samuel. 225.7
A Jewish understanding of the New Testament. Cincinnati, Hebrew Union College Press, 1956. 321 p. 25 cm. [BS2361.S24] 56-8371
1. Bible. N.T.—Criticism, interpretation, etc. 2. Judaism—Relations—Christianity. 3. Christianity and other religions—Judaism. I. Title.

WOLFENBUTTEL Herzog-August- 225.7
Bibliothek. Mass. (Aug. 11.2)
The Wolfenbuttel Lithuanian Postile manuscript of the year 1573; v.1. Ed. by Gordon B. Ford, Jr. Louisville, Ky., 40202, Pyramid Pr., 820 Ky. Home Life Bldg., c.1965. 1v. (unpaged 1.) 41cm. Facsim. ed. from a microfilm of the MS. Original t.p. reads: Ischgvldimas evangeliv per wisvs mettvs. [BS2547.W62] 66-4719 36.00
1. Bible. N.T. Epistles and Gospels, Liturgical — Commentaries. 2. Sermons, Lithuanian. I. Ford, Gordon B., ed. II. Title. III. Title: Ischgvldimas evangeliv per wisvs mettvs.

AIRHART, Arnold E. 225.7'7 s
Acts / by Arnold E. Airhart. Kansas City, Mo. : Beacon Hill Press of Kansas City, c1977. 304 p. ; 20 cm. (Beacon bible expositions ; v. 5) Bibliography: p. 303-304. [BS491.2.B42 vol. 5] [BS2625.3] 226'.6'077 77-151058 ISBN 0-8341-0316-8 : 5.95
1. Bible. N.T. Acts—Commentaries. I. Title. II. Series.

BIBLE. N.T. English. 225.7'7
Authorized. 1975.
The parallel New Testament and Unger's Bible handbook : produced for Moody monthly. New York : Iversen-Norman Associates, 1975. xxiii, 711 p. : ill. ; 24 cm. Includes the texts of the King James and New American Standard versions of the N.T., and the corresponding commentary from Unger's Bible handbook on opposite pages. [BS2085 1975.N48] 75-2893
1. Bible. N.T.—Handbooks, manuals, etc. I. Unger, Merrill Frederick, 1909- Unger's Bible handbook. New Testament. 1975. II. Moody monthly. III. Bible. N.T. English. New American Standard. 1975. IV. Title.

ERASMUS, Desiderius, 225.7'7
d.1536.
The first tome or volume of the Paraphrase of Erasmus upon the Newe Testament / Desiderius Erasmus ; with an introd. by John N. Wall, Jr. Delmar, N.Y. : Scholars' Facsimiles & Reprints, 1975. p. cm. Translation of the Gospels and Acts from Erasmus' Paraphrases in Novum Testamentum. Reprint of the 1548 ed. published by E. Whitechurche, London. "STC 2854." [BS2335.E7132 1975] 75-23361 ISBN 0-8201-1159-7
1. Bible. N.T.—Commentaries. I. Title.

ERASMUS, Desiderius, 225.7'7
d.1536.
The first tome or volume of the Paraphrase of Erasmus upon the Newe Testamente / [Desiderius Erasmus]. A facsim. reproduction / with an introd. by John N. Wall, Jr. Delmar, N.Y. : Scholars' Facsimiles & Reprints, 1975. 25, ca. 1350 p. ; 21 cm. Translation of the Gospels and Acts from Erasmus' Paraphrases in Novum Testamentum. Reprint of the 1548 ed. published by E. Whitechurche, London. "STC 2854." Includes bibliographical references. [BS2335.E7132 1975] 75-23361 ISBN 0-8201-1159-7 lib.bdg. : 75.00
1. Bible. N.T.—Commentaries. I. Title.

GREATHOUSE, William M. 225.7'7 s
Romans / by William M. Greathouse. Kansas City, Mo. : Beacon Hill Press of Kansas City, c1975. 224 p. ; 20 cm. (Beacon Bible expositions ; v. 6) Bibliography: p. 222-224. [BS491.2.B42 vol. 6] [BS2665.3] 227'.1'077 75-328403
1. Bible. N.T. Romans—Commentaries. I. Title. II. Series.

KIRBAN, Salem. 225.7'7
Kirban's prophecy New Testament, including Revelation visualized, King James version. Huntingdon Valley, Pa., Kirban, inc., c1973. 873, 480 p. illus. 21 cm. [BS2341.2.K54] 71-145767 ISBN 0-912582-00-6 19.95
1. Bible. N.T.—Commentaries. 2. Bible. N.T.—Prophecies. I. Cohen, Gary G. Revelation visualized. 1973. II. Bible. N.T. English. Authorized. 1973. III. Title. IV. Title: Prophecy New Testament. V. Title: Revelation visualized.

MCCONKIE, Bruce R. 225.77
Doctrinal New Testament commentary. Salt Lake City, Bookcraft [1965?- v. map. 24 cm. Contents.-- v. 1. The Gospels, by B. R. McConkie. [BS2341.2.D6] 65-29174
1. Bible. N.T. — Commentaries. I. Title.

MCCUMBER, W. E. 225.7'7 s
Matthew / by William E. McCumber. Kansas City, Mo. : Beacon Hill Press of Kansas City, c1975. 224 p. ; 20 cm. (Beacon Bible expositions ; v. 1) Bibliography: p. 224. [BS491.2.B42 vol. 1] [BS2575.3] 226'.2'077 76-354198 ISBN 0-8341-0312-5
1. Bible. N.T Matthew—Commentaries. I. Title. II. Series.

NEW Testament for 225.7'7
spiritual reading, edited by John L. McKenzie. New York, Herder and Herder [1969- v. 21 cm. [BS2341.2.N382] 70-77601
1. Bible. N.T.—Commentaries. I. McKenzie, John L., ed.

PURKISER, W. T. 225.7'7 s
Hebrews, James, Peter, by W. T. Purkiser. Kansas City, Mo., Beacon Hill Press [1974] 232 p. 20 cm. (Beacon Bible exposition, v. 11) Bibliography: p. 230-232. [BS491.2.B42 vol. 11] [BS2775.3] 227'.87'077 74-78052 4.95
1. Bible. N.T Hebrews—Commentaries. 2. Bible. N.T. James—Commentaries. 3. Bible. N.T. Peter—Commentaries. I. Bible. N.T. Catholic epistles. English. Selections. 1974. II. Bible. N.T. Hebrews. English. 1974. III. Title. IV. Series.

WELCH, Reuben. 225.7'7 s
Luke / by Reuben Welch. Kansas City, Mo. : Beacon Hill Press of Kansas City, c1974. 223 p. ; 20 cm. (Beacon Bible expositions ; v. 3) Bibliography: p. 222-223. [BS491.2.B42 vol. 3] [BS2595.3] 226'.4'077 75-328404
1. Bible. N.T. Luke—Commentaries. I. Title. II. Series.

MCCASLAND, Selby 225.81334
Vernon, 1896-
By the finger of God; demon possession and exorcism in early Christianity in the light of modern views of mental illness. With and introd. by David Cole Wilson. New York, Macmillan, 1951. xi, 146 p. 21 cm. Bibliographical footnotes. [BS2545.D5M2] 51-9691
1. Demoniac possession. 2. Exorcism. 3. Bible. N. T.—Psychology. I. Title.

HOULDEN, James Leslie. 225.8'17
Ethics and the New Testament [by] J. L. Houlden. Harmondsworth, Penguin, 1973. ix, 134 p. 18 cm. (Pelican books) Includes bibliographical references. [BS2545.E8H6] 73-168470 ISBN 0-14-021573-5 £0.35
1. Bible. N.T.—Ethics. I. Title.

KNOX, John, 1900- 225.817
The ethic of Jesus in the teaching of the church; its authority and its relevance. Nashville, Abingdon Press [c.1961] 124p. Bibl. 61-5195 2.00 bds.,
1. Jesus Christ—Ethics. 2. Christian ethics. I. Title.

KNOX, John, 1900- 225.817
The ethic of Jesus in the teaching of the church: its authority and its relevance. New York, Abingdon Press [1961] 124p. 20cm. Includes bibliography. [BS2417.E8K56] 61-5195
1. Jesus Christ—Ethics. 2. Christian ethics.s8 I. Title.

LILLIE, William 225.817
Studies in New Testament ethics. Philadelphia, Westminster [1963, c.1961] 189p. 22cm. Bibl. 63-7504 3.95
1. Bible. N.T.—Ethics. I. Title. II. Title: New Testament ethics.

SANDERS, Jack T. 225.8'17
Ethics in the New Testament : change and development / Jack T. Sanders. Philadelphia : Fortress Press, c1975. xiii, 144 p. ; 24 cm. Includes indexes. Bibliography: p. 133-136. [BS2545.E8S22] 74-26342 ISBN 0-8006-0404-0 : 6.95
1. Bible. N.T.—Ethics. I. Title.

MACGREGOR, George 225.81724
Hogarth Carnaby, 1892-
The New Testament basis of pacifism and The relevance of an impossible ideal. Nyack, N. Y., Fellowship Publications, 1956. 160p. 22cm. Includes bibliography. [BS2545.P4M32] 60-7634
1. Peace—Biblical arguments. 2. Pacifism. 3. War and religion. I. Niebuhr, Reinhold, 1892- II. Macgregor, George Hogarth Carnaby, 1892- The relevance of an impossible ideal. III. Title. IV. Title: The relevance of an impossible ideal.

SEITZ, Oscar J F 225.82
One body and one spirit; a study of the church in the New Testament. Greenwich. Conn., Seabury Press, 1960. 188p. 22cm. Includes bibliography. [BS2545.C5S46] 60-11084
1. Church— Biblical teaching. I. Title.

SEITZ, Oscar J. F. 225.82
One body and one spirit; a study of the church in the New Testament. Greenwich, Conn., Seabury Press [c.]1960. 188p. Bibl.: p.176-177. 22cm. 60-11084 4.25
1. Church—Biblical teaching. I. Title.

HAMERTON-KELLY, R. G. 225.8'232
Pre-existence, wisdom, and the Son of Man; a study of the idea of pre-existence in the New Testament, by R. G. Hamerton-Kelly. Cambridge [Eng.] University Press, 1973. xii, 310 p. 23 cm. (Society for New Testament Studies. Monograph series, 21) Bibliography: p. 281-294. [BS2545.P684H35] 72-78890 ISBN 0-521-08629-9 23.50
1. Son of Man. 2. Pre-existence—Biblical teaching. I. Title. II. Series: Studiorum Novi Testamenti Societas. Monograph series, 21.
Distributed by Cambridge University Press N.Y.

IRONSIDE, Henry Allan, 225.82323
1876-1951.
The mysteries of God. New York, Loizeaux Bros. 1946. 124p. 20cm. [BS2545.M8I7] 54-32728
1. Mysticism. I. Title.

MORRIS, Leon. 225.82323
The Cross in the New Testament. Grand Rapids, W. B. Eerdmans Pub. Co. [1965] 454 p. 24 cm. Bibliographical footnotes. [BT262.M6] 64-22026
1. Atonement — Biblical teaching. I. Title.

MORRIS, Leon 225.82323
The Cross in the New Testament. Grand Rapids, Mich., Eerdmans [c.1965] 454p. 24cm. Bibl. [BT262.M6] 64-22026 6.95
1. Atonement—Biblical teaching. I. Title.

CANTINAT, Jean. 225.823291
Mary in the Bible. Translated by Paul Barrett. Westminster, Md., Newman Press, 1965. 245 p. 23 cm. Includes bibliographical references. [BT605.2.C313] 65-24591
1. Mary, Virgin. I. Title.

CANTINAT, Jean 225.823291
Mary in the Bible. Tr. by Paul Barrett. Westminster, Md, Newman [c.]1965. 245p. 23cm. Bibl. [BT605.2.C313] 65-24591 5.50
1. Mary, Virgin. I. Title.

SCHELKLE, Karl Hermann. 225.825
Discipleship and priesthood. [Rev. ed. translated by Joseph Disselhorst. New York] Herder and Herder [1965] 142 p. 21 cm. Translation of Jungerschaft und Apostelamt. Bibliographical footnotes. [BX1912.S2883] 65-13483
1. Priesthood—Biblical teaching. I. Title.

SCHELKLE, Karl Hermann 225.825
Discipleship and priesthood [Rev. ed. tr. from German by Joseph Disselhorst New York] Herder & Herder [c.1965] 142p. 21cm. Bibl. [BX1912.S2883] 65-13483 3.50
1. Priesthood—Biblical teaching. I. Title.

BRUCE, Gustav Marius, 225.826
1879-
The Apostolic Church: founding, nature, polity, worship, impact. Minneapolis, T. S. Denison [c.1963] 198p. 23cm. Bibl. 63-21757 3.50
1. Church—Biblical teaching. 2. Church polity—Early church. I. Title.

BRUCE, Gustav Marius, 225.826
1879-
The Apostolic Church: founding, nature, polity, worship, impact. Minneapolis, T. S. Denison [1963] 198 p. 23 cm. Bibliography: p. 197. [BV597.B7] 63-21757
1. Church — Biblical teaching. 2. Church polity — Early church. I. Title.

CLARKE, Arthur G. 1887- 225.826
New Testament church principles. [3d ed.]

New York, Loizeaux [c.1962] 102p. 19cm. 62-53125 2.50
1. Church—Biblical teaching. I. Title.

CLARKE, ArthurG 1887- 225.826
New Testament church principles. [3d ed.] New York, Loizeaux Bros. [1962] 102p. 19cm. [BV597.C5 1962] 62-53125
1. Church—Biblical teaching. I. Title.

MUIRHEAD, Ian A 225.826
Education in the New Testament, by Ian A. Muirhead. New York, Association Press [1965] 94 p. 22 cm. (Monographs in Christian education, no. 2) "The basis of this study was a working-paper contributed to the Church of Scotland Special Committee on Religious Education." Bibliographical references included in "Notes" (p. 89-94) [BV1465.M8] 65-11082
1. Religious education — Biblical teaching. I. Title.

MUIRHEAD, Ian A. 225.826
Education in the New Testament. New York, Association [c.1965] 94p. 22cm. (Monographs in Christian educ., no. 2) The basis of this study was a working-paper contributed to the Church of Scotland Special Comm. on Religious Educ. Bibl. [BV1465.M8] 65-11082 2.50 pap.,
1. Religious education—Biblical teaching. I. Title.

AKERMAN, John Yonge, 225.82617
1806-1873
Numismatic illustrations of the narrative portions of the New Testament. Chicago, Argonaut [c.]1966. vii, 62p. illus. 22cm. (Argonaut libr. of antiquities) Bibl. [CJ255.A5 1966] 66-19185 3.00
1. Bible — Numismatics. I. Title.

CULLMANN, Oscar. 225.82617
The state in the New Testament. New York, Scribner [1956] 123p. 21cm. [BS2545.C55C8] 56-7123
1. Church and state—Biblical teaching. I. Title.

MCKELVEY, R. J. 225.8'262
The new Temple: the Church in the New Testament by R. J. McKelvey. London, Oxford U.P., 1969. xix, 238 p. 23 cm. (Oxford theological monographs) Bibliography: p. [207] -216. [BV597.M3] 73-393136 42/-
1. Church—Biblical teaching. 2. Temple of God. I. Title. II. Series.

SCHNACKENBURG, Rudolf, 225.8262
1914-
The church in the New Testament. [Translated by W. J. O'Hara. New York] Herder and Herder [1965] 221, [1] p. 23 cm. "Notes and bibliography": p. 197-[222] [BS2545.C5S383] 65-13368
1. Church—Biblical teaching. I. Title.

SCHNACKENBURG, Rudolf, 225.8262
1914-
The church in the New Testament. [Translated by W. J. O'Hara] New York, Seabury Press [1974, c1965] [222 p.] 21 cm. (A Crossroad book) Originally published under title: "Die Kirche im Neuen Testament." Includes bibliographical references. [BS2545.C5S383] 65-18368 ISBN 0-8164-2585-X. 4.95 (pbk.)
1. Church—Biblical teaching. I. Title.

COGGAN, Donald, Abp. 225.8'264'1
of Canterbury, 1909-
The prayers of the New Testament. New York, Harper & Row, [1975 c1967] xiv, 15-190 p. 22 cm. Includes index of authors. [BV228.C65] 74-25683 ISBN 0-06-061511-7 6.95
1. Bible. N.T.—Prayers. I. Title.

LUMIERE et vie. 225.82651
Baptism in the New Testament; a symposium [by] A. George [and others] Translated by David Askew. Baltimore, Helicon [1964] 238 p. 21 cm. Originally published as a special study in two issues of Lumiere et vie. France, 1956." Bibliographical footnotes. [BV806.L913 1964] 64-20014
1. Baptism — Biblical teaching. I. George, Augustin. II. Title.

LUMIERE et vie 225.82651
Baptism in the New Testament; a symposium [by] A. George [others] Tr.[from French] by David Askew. Helicon[dist. New York, Taplinger, c.1964] 238p. 21cm. Orig. pub. as a special study in two issues of Lumiere et vie, France, 1956. Bibl. 64-20014 4.50
1. Baptism—Biblical teaching. I. George, Augustin. II. Title.

HAHN, Ferdinand, 1926- 225.8266
Mission in the New Testament. [Translated by Frank Clarke from the German] Naperville, Ill., A. R. Allenson [1965] 184 p. 22 cm. (Studies in Biblical theology, no. 47) Translation of Das Verstandnis der Mission im Neuen Testament. Bibliographical footnotes. [BV2073.H313] 65-6444
1. Missions — Biblical teaching. I. Title. II. Series.

HAHN, Ferdinand, 1926- 225.8266
Mission in the New Testament. [Tr. from German by Frank Clarke] Naperville, Ill., A. R. Allenson [c.1965] 184p. 22cm. (Studies in Biblical theology, no.47) Bibl. [BV2073.H313] 65-6444 4.50 pap.,
1. Missions—Biblical teaching. I. Title. II. Series.

HENDERSON, Ian, 1910- 225.829
Myth in the New Testament. Chicago, H. Regnery Co., 1952. 57p. 22cm. (Studies in Biblical theology, no. 7) [BS2397.H4] 53-1724
1. Bible. N. T.—Theology. 2. Mythology. 3. Existentialism. I. Title.

BAUM, Gregory, 1923- 225.8296
Is the New Testament anti-Semitic? A re-examination of the New Testament. Rev. ed. Glen Rock, N.J., Paulist [c.1965] 350p. 18cm. (Deus bks.) First pub. in 1961 under title: The Jews and the gospel. Bibl. [BM535.B3] 65-21761 1.25 pap.,
1. Christianity and other religions—Judaism. 2. Bible. N.T.—Criticism, interpretation, etc. I. Title.

FAXON, Alicia 225.8'30141'2
Craig.
Women and Jesus. Philadelphia, United Church Press [1973] 126 p. 22 cm. "A Pilgrim Press book." Bibliography: p. 119-126. [BT590.W6F38] 72-11868 ISBN 0-8298-0244-4 4.95
1. Jesus Christ—Attitude towards women. 2. Women in the Bible. I. Title.

KNIGHT, George 225.8'30141
William.
The New Testament teaching on the role relationship of men and women / George W. Knight III. Grand Rapids, Mich. : Baker Book House, c1977. 76 p. ; 22 cm. Includes bibliographical references and indexes. [BS2545.M39K59] 76-56492 ISBN 0-8010-5383-8 pbk. : 3.95
1. Bible. N.T.—Criticism, interpretation, etc.—Addresses, essays, lectures. 2. Men (Christian theology)—Biblical teaching—Addresses, essays, lecturs. 3. Woman (Christian theology)—Biblical teaching—Addresses, essays, lectures. I. Title.

AMSON, Peter 225.855146
Frederick, 1889-
Christ and the sailor; a study of the maritime incidents in the New Testament. Foreword by Thomas D. Roberts. Fresno, Calif., Acad. Lib. [1963] 198p. 20cm. Bibl. 1.50 pap.,
1. Sea in the Bible. 2. Fishing in the Bible. 3. Galilee, Sea of. 4. Apostles. 5. Bible—Concordances, English. I. Title.

ANSON, Peter 225.855146
Frederick, 1889-
Christ and the sailor; a study of the maritime incidents in the New Testament. With a foreword by Thomas D. Roberts. Fresno, Calif., Academy Library Guild [1956?] 198p. 20cm. [BS2545] 56-13886
1. Sea in the Bible. 2. Fishing in the Bible. 3. Galilee, Sea of. 4. Apostles. 5. Bible—Concordances. English. I. Title.

AKERMAN, John Yonge, 225.87374
1806-1873.
Numismatic illustrations of the narrative portions of the New Testament. Chicago, Argonaut, 1966. vii, 62 p. illus. 22 cm. (Argonaut library of antiquities) Bibliographical footnotes. [CJ255.A5 1966] 66-19185
1. Bible—Numismatics. I. Title.

DAUGHTERS of St. Paul. 225.9
The great hero, St. Paul the apostle. Written and illustrated by the Daughters of St. Paul. [Boston] St. Paul Editions [1963] 170 p. illus. 22 cm. [BS2506.5.D38] 63-15968
1. Paul, Saint, apostle — Juvenile literature. I. Title.

DAUGHTERS OF ST. PAUL. 225.9
The great hero, St. Paul the apostle. Written, illus. by the Daughters of St. Paul. [Boston] St. Paul Eds. [dist. Author, c.1963] 170p. col. illus. 22cm. 63-15968 2.50
1. Paul, Saint, apostle—Juvenile literature. I. Title.

DEISSMANN, Gustav Adolf, 225.9
1866-1937
Light from the ancient East; the New Testament illustrated by recently discovered texts of the Graeco-Roman world. Tr. [from German] by Lionel R. M. Strachan. New, completely rev. ed. with eighty-five illus. from the latest German ed. Grand Rapids, Mich., Baker Bk. [1966] xxxii, 535p. plates, facsims. 23cm. (Limited eds lib.) [BS2375.D45] 7.95
1. Bible. N. T. — History of contemporary events, etc. 2. Bible. N. T. — Language, style. I. Strachan, Lionel Richard Mortimer, 1876- tr. II. Title.

DERRETT, John Duncan 225.9
Martin, 1922-
Jesus's audience: the social and psychological environment in which He worked; prolegomena to a restatement of the teaching of Jesus. Lectures at Newquay, 1971 [by] J. Duncan M. Derrett. With a foreword by the Bishop of Truro. New York, Seabury Press [1974, c1973] 240 p. 22 cm. "A Crossroad book." Includes bibliographical references. [DS112.D4 1974] 73-17893 ISBN 0-8164-1148-4 5.95
1. Jews—Social life and customs. 2. Jesus Christ—Teachings. I. Title.

EWING, Joseph Franklin, 225.9
1905-
The ancient way: life and landmarks of the Holy Land [by] J. Franklin Ewing. New York, Scribner [1964] 224 p. illus., map, plan. 22 cm. [BS621.E9] 64-23524
1. Bible—History of contemporary events, etc. 2. Near East—Social life and customs. I. Title.

FOSDICK, Harry Emerson, 225.9
1878-
The life of Saint Paul. Illus. by Leonard Everett Fisher. New York, Random [c.1962] 175p. col. illus. 22cm. (World landmark bks., W-53) 62-7881 1.95
1. Paul, Saint, apostle—Juvenile literature. I. Title.

GRANT, Frederick Clifton, 225.9
1891-
The economic background of the Gospels, by Frederick C. Grant. New York, Russell & Russell [1973] 156 p. 19 cm. Reprint of the 1926 ed. published by the Oxford University Press, London. [BS2555.G68 1973] 72-84987 ISBN 0-8462-1712-0 12.00
1. Bible. N.T. Gospels—Economics. I. Title.

*INSLEE, Joseph W. 225.9
God's way in the New Testament. Illus. by James Heugh, Davis Meltzer. Philadelphia, Luthera iPhiladelphia, Lutheran Church Pr. [c.1965] 156p. illus. (pt. col.) 22cm. (LCA weekday church sch. ser. WCS-6) 1.75; teachers guide, gr.6, 2.75; workbk., pap., price unreported.
I. Title.

REYNOLDS, Ruth (Sutton) 225.9
The wonder of the New Testament; the story of where and how it grew. [1st ed.] New York, Exposition Press [1961] 138p. 22cm. (An Exposition-testament book) Includes bibliography. [BS2410.R4] 61-4211
1. Bible. N.T.—History of Biblical events. 2. Bible N.T.—Biog. I. Title.

SMITH, Betty 225.9
Stories of Jesus [bks. 5, 6, 7, 8] Illus. by Cicely Steed. Philadelphia, Westminster [c.1963] various p. illus. (pt. col.) 21cm. Contents.b. 5. People Jesus loved.--bk. 6. Jesus and the children.--bk. 7. Jesus, the healer.--bk. 8. Jesus, the King of Kings. 75 bds., ea.,
I. Title.

STUMP, Gladys Sims. j225.9
Six dreams and a golden collar. Illustrated by Dick Cole. Mountain View, Calif., Pacific Press Pub. Association [1962] 181 p. illus. 22 cm. [BS580.J6S8] 62-14314
1. Joseph, the patriarch—Juvenile literature. I. Title.

STUMP, Gladys Sims. 225.9
Six dreams and a golden collar. Illus. by Dick Cole. Mountain View, Calif., Pac. Pr. Pub. [c.1962] 181p. illus. (pt. col.) 22cm. 62-14314 3.00
1. Joseph, the patriarch—Juvenile literature. I. Title.

TENNEY, Merrill Chapin, 225.9
1904-.
New Testament times, by Merrill C. Tenney. Grand Rapids, W. B. Eerdmans Pub. Co. [1965] xv, 396 p. illus., maps (part fold.) 24 cm. Bibliography: p. 373-380. [BS2410.T4] 65-18099
1. Bible. N.T. — History of contemporary events, etc. 2. Bible. N.T — History of Biblical events. I. Title.

TENNEY, Merrill Chapin, 225.9
1904-
New Testament times, by Merrill C. Tenney. Grand Rapids, W. B. Eerdmans Pub. Co. [1965] xv, 396 p. illus., maps (part fold.) 24 cm. Bibliography: p. 373-380. [BS2410.T4] 65-18099
1. Bible. N. T.—History of contemporary events, etc. 2. Bible. N. T.—History of Biblical events. I. Title.

UNNIK, Willem Cornelis van 225.9
The New Testament, its history and message. Tr. by H. H. Hoskins. New York, Harper [1965, c.1962, 1964] 192p. illus., maps. 20cm. Bibl. [BS2407.U513] 65-10202 3.95
1. Bible. N. T.—History of Biblical events. I. Title.

WILK, Gerd. 225.9
Journeys with Jesus and Paul. Translated by Victor I. Gruhn. Philadelphia, Fortress Press [1970] 127 p. col. illus., col. maps. 22 cm. Translation of Strassen der Bibel. Traces the events recorded in the New Testament with emphasis on the life of Jesus, the journeys of Paul, and the way of life in ancient Palestine. [BS633.W513] 74-116462 4.95
1. Jesus Christ—Biography—Juvenile literature. 2. Paul, Saint, apostle—Juvenile literature. 3. Bible—Geography—Juvenile literature. I. Title.

WILLETT, Franciscus. j225.9
The fisherman saint, a story of Saint Peter, by Brother Franciscus. Illustrations by Rita McCann. Notre Dame, Ind., Dujarie Press [1947] 89 p. illus. 24 cm. [BS2515.W48] 47-23431
1. Peter, Saint, apostle — Juvenile literature. I. Title.

WILLETT, Franciscus. j225.9
The tentmaker from Tarsus, a story of St. Paul, by Brother Franciscus. Illus. by Rosemary Donatino. Notre Dame, Ind., Dujarie Press [1950] 95 p. illus. 24 cm. [BS2505.W486] 50-2575
1. Paul, Saint, apostle — Juvenile literature. I. Title.

ALEXANDER, David, 1937- 225.9'1
The New Testament in living pictures; a photo guide to the New Testament, by David S. Alexander. [2d ed.] Glendale, Calif., G/L Regal Books [1973, c1972] 155 p. col. illus. 25 cm. [BS630.A58 1973] 73-79755 ISBN 0-8307-0172-9 5.95
1. Bible. N.T.—Geography. 2. Palestine—Description and travel—Views. 3. Near East—Description and travel—Views. I. Bible. N.T. English. Selections. 1973. II. Title.

BLAIKLOCK, E. M. 225.91
Cities of the New Testament. [Westwood, N.J.] Revell [1966, c.]1965. 128p. illus. (pt. col.) 23cm. [DS44.9.B55] 66-2278 3.95
1. Cities and towns — Levant. 2. Bible — Geography. I. Title.

BOUQUET, Alan Coates, 225.91
1884-
Everyday life in New Testament times; illustrated from drawings by Marjorie Quennell. New York, Scribner, 1954 [c1953] 235 p. illus. 24 cm. [DS112.B64 1954] 54-7082
1. Bible. N.T.—History of contemporary events, etc. 2. Palestine—Social life and customs. I. Title.

HAKIM, George, Abp., 1908- 225.91
Reading the good news in Galilee [Tr. from French by James A. Corbett] Helicon [dist. New York, Taplinger, c.1965] 126p. illus. 21cm. [BT296.H313] 64-20232 3.50 bds.,
1. Jesus Christ—Biog. I. Title.

LUDWIG, Charles, 1918- 225.9'1
Cities in New Testament times / Charles Ludwig. Denver : Accent Books, c1976. 128 p. : ill. ; 20 cm. Bibliography: p. 127-128. [BS630.L75] 75-41480 ISBN 0-916406-16-4 pbk. : 2.25
1. Bible. N.T.—Geography. 2. Cities and towns, Ancient—Near East. I. Title.

SHEETS, Herchel H. 225.91
Places Christ hallowed; on seeing the Holy Land. Nashville, Upper Room [1965] 64p. illus. 20cm. [BT303.9.S5] 65-19532 price unreported
1. Jesus Christ—Journeys. 2. Bible. N. T. Gospels—Geography. I. Title.

AGNEW, Edith J 1897- 225.92
People of the way. Illustrated by Johannes Troyer. Philadelphia. Westminster Press [c1959] 47p. illus. 16x23cm. [BS2628.A3] 60-5618
1. Apostles—Juvenile literature. 2. Bible stories, English—N. T. Acts. I. Title.

AGNEW, Edith J., 1897- 225.92
People of the way. Illustrated by Johannes Troyer. Philadelphia, Westminster Press [c.1959] 47p. illus. (part col.) 16x23cm. 60-5618 1.25 bds.,
1. Apostles—Juvenile literature. 2. Bible stories, English—N. T. Acts. I. Title.

BARCLAY, William lecturer 225.92
in the University of Glasgow.
The master's men. New York, Abingdon Press [c1959] 127p. 20cm. Includes bibliography. [BS2440.B33 1959a] 60-5471

1. Apostles. I. Title.

BARCLAY, William, lecturer in the University of Glasgow. 225.92
The Master's men. New York, Abingdon Press [c.1959] 127p. Includes bibliography 20cm. 60-5471 2.00 bds.,
1. Apostles. I. Title.

BARKER, William Pierson. 225.92
Saints in aprons and overalls: friends of Paul [Westwood, N. J.] Revell [1959] 128p. 21cm. [BS2430.B37] 59-11520
1. Paul, Saint, apostole. 2. Bible. N. T.—Biog. I. Title.

BARKER, William Pierson 225.92
Saints in aprons and overalls: friends of Paul. [Westwood, N.J.] Revell [c.1959] 128p. 21cm. 59-11520 2.00 bds.,
1. Bible. N. T.—Biog. 2. Paul, Saint, apostle. I. Title.

BARKER, William Pierson. 225.92
Twelve who were chosen; the disciples of Jesus. [Westwood, N. J.] F. H. Revell Co. [1958, c1957] 127p. 21cm. [BS2440.B34] 58-5342
1. Apostles. I. Title.

BAUMGAERTNER, John H 225.92
Meet the twelve. Minneapolis, Augsburg Pub. House [1960] 122p. illus. 21cm. [BS2440.B36] 60-6440
1. Apostles. I. Title.

BAUMGAERTNER, John H. 225.92
Meet the twelve [Rev. ed.] Minneapolis, Augsburg [1966, c.1960] xiii, 130p. illus. 20cm. [BS2440.B36] 60-6440 1.95 pap.,
1. Apostles. I. Title.

BERGEAUD, Jean 225.92
Saint John the Baptist. Tr. by Jane Wynne Saul. New York, Macmillan [1963, c.1962] 126p. 18cm. (Your name--your saint ser.) 63-7475 2.50
1. John the Baptist. I. Title.

BIBLE. N.T. Acts and Epistles. English. Harmonies. 1964. Authorized. 225.92
A harmony of the life of St. Paul according to the Acts of the Apostles and the Pauline Epistles, by Frank J. Goodwin. Grand Rapids, Baker Book House, 1964. 240 p. maps. 23 cm. First ed. published in 1895. [BS2505.A3] 65-7472
1. Paul, Saint, apostle. I. Goodwin, Frank Judson, 1862-1953. II. Title.

BIBLE. N. T. Acts and Epistles. English Harmonies. 1964. Authorized 225.92
A harmony of the life of St. Paul according to the Acts of the Apostles and the Pauline Epistles, by Frank J. Goodwin. Grand Rapids, Mich., Baker Bk. [1965] 240p. maps. 23cm. [BS2505.A3] 65-7472 3.95
1. Paul, Saint, apostle. I. Goodwin, Frank Judson, 1861-1953. II. Title.

BLACKWELDER, Boyce W. 225.92
Toward understanding Paul. Anderson, Ind., Warner Press [dist. Gospel Trumpet Press, c.1961] 127p. Bibl. 61-9720 2.95
1. Paul, Saint, apostle. I. Title.

BORGWARDT, Robert G 225.92
Men who knew Jesus. Minneapolis, T. S. Denison [1958] 115p. 22cm. [BS2430.B6] 58-9507
1. Bible. N. T. —Biog. I. Title.

BROWN, Slater, 1896- 225.92
John the Baptist, prophet of Christ. New York, Association Press [1955] 125p. illus. 20cm. (Heroes of God series) [BS2456.B75] 55-7409
1. John the Baptist. I. Title.

BROWN, Slater, 1896- 225.92
Luke, missionary doctor. New York, Association Press [1956] 121p. 20cm. (Heroes of God series) [BS2465.B7] 225.92 56-9184
1. Luke, Saint. I. Title.

BRUCE, Janet 225.92
The life of Saint Paul. Pictures by Emile Probst. London, Burns & Oates; New York, Herder & Herder [c.1965] [27]p. col. illus. 19cm. (Men of God 4) [BS2506.5.B7] 65-21948 1.50 bds.
1. Paul, Saint, apostle—Juvenile literature. I. Probst, Emile, illus. II. Title. III. Series.

BRUCKBERGER, Raymond Leopold, 1907- 225.92
Mary Magdalene. Translated by H. L. Binsse. New York, Pantheon [1953] 192p. illus. 22cm. [BS2485.B753] 53-6127
1. Mary Magdalene, Saint. I. Title.

BRUCKBERGER, Raymond Leopold, 1907- 225.92
Mary Magdalene; translated by H. L. Binsse. Annotated ed. New York, Pantheon [1953] 263p. illus. 22cm. [BS2485.B753 1953a] 53-7153
1. Mary Magdalene, Saint. I. Title.

BRUNOT, Amedee. 225.92
Saint Paul and his message. Translated from the French by Ronald Matthews. [1st ed.] New York, Hawthorne Books [1959] 140p. 21cm. (The Twentieth century encyclopedia of Catholicism, v. 70. Section 6: The word of God) Includes bibliography. [BS2505.B773] 59-8204
1. Paul, Saint, apostle. I. Title.

BUNCH, Taylor Grant. 225.92
Valiant in fight. Mountain View, Calif., Pacific Press Pub. Association [1956] 264p. 21cm. [BS2430.B77] 56-10342
1. Bible. N. T.—Biog. I. Title.

CAPALDI, Isaias G 225.92
Andrew of Galilee, apostle of Christ. London , New York, Longmans, Green [1955] 276p. illus. 19cm. [BS2451.C36 1955] 55-2321
1. Andrew, Saint, apostle. I. Title.

CHAPPELL, Clovis Gillham, 1882- 225.92
Sermons on Simon Peter. New York, Abingdon Press [1959] 128p. 20cm. [BS2515.C5] 59-10357
1. Peter, Saint, apostle—Sermons. 2. Methodist Church—Sermons. 3. Sermons, American. I. Title.

CHRYSOSTOMUS, Joannes, Saint, Patriarch of Constantinople, d. 407. 225.92
In praise of Saint Paul. Tr. [from Greek] by Thomas Halton. [Boston] St. Paul Eds. [dist. Daughters of St. Paul, c.1963] 123p. 20cm. 63-14467 2.00; 1.00 pap.,
1. Paul, Saint, Apostle—Sermons. 2. Sermons, Greek—Translations into English. 3. Sermons, English—Translations from Greek. I. Halton, Thomas, tr. II. Title.

COAKLEY, Mary Lewis, 1907- 225.92
Famous women of the New Testament. Sponsored by the Benedicitine monks of Belmont Abbey. Garden City, N. Y. [N. Doubleday, 1960] 64p. illus. 21cm. (The Catholic know-Your-Bible program) [BS2445.C6] 60-3653
1. Women in the Bible—Juvenile literature. 2. Bible. N. T.—Biog.—Juvenile literature. I. Title.

CORNELL, George W. 225.92
They knew Jesus. New York, Morrow, 1957. 288 p. illus. 21 cm. Includes bibliography. [BS2430.C55] 57-10930
1. Bible. N. T.—Biography. I. Title.

CULLMANN, Oscar 225.92
Peter; disciple, apostle, martyr: a historical and theological study. Tr from German by Floyd V. Filson. 2d rev.,)expanded ed. Philadelphia, Westminster [c.1962] 252p. 22cm. (Lib of hist. and doctrine) Bibl. 62-10169 5.00
1. Peter, Saint, apostle. I. Title.

DALY, Emily Joseph, comp. 225.92
Paul, trumpet of the spirit; an anthology. With a foreword by Edward J. Maginn. Paterson, N.J., St. Anthony Guild Press [1963] 249 p. illus. 20 cm. [BS2506.D3] 63-15296
1. Paul, Saint, Apostle — Collections. I. Title.

DALY, Emily Joseph, comp. 225.92
Paul, trumpet of the spirit; an anthology. Foreword by Edward J. Maginn. Paterson, N.J., St. Anthony [c.1963] 249p. illus. 20cm. 63-15296 3.50
1. Paul, Saint, apostle—Collections. I. Title.

DAUGHTERS of St. Paul. 225.92 (j)
The fisher prince; the story of St. Peter, Apostle, written and illustrated by the Daughters of St. Paul. [Boston] St. Paul Editions [1966] 69 p. illus. 22 cm. (Their Encounter books) [BS2515.D29] 66-29163
1. Peter, Saint, apostle—Juvenile literature. I. Title.

DEISSMANN, Gustav Adolf, 1866-1937. 225.92
Paul; a study in social and religious history. Translated by William E. Wilson. [1st Harper torchbook ed.] New York, Harper [1957] 323 p. illus. 21 cm. (Harper torchbooks, TB15) [BS2505.D42 1957] 922.1 57-7533
1. Paul, Saint, apostle.

DRUMWRIGHT, Huber L. 225.9'2 B
Saints alive! The humble heroes of the New Testament [by] Huber L. Drumwright. Nashville, Tenn., Broadman Press [1972] 128 p. 21 cm. [BS2430.D78] 72-79169 ISBN 0-8054-8116-8 1.95
1. Bible. N.T.—Biography. I. Title.

EMMERICH, Anna Katharina, 1774-1824 225.92
And she was called Magdalen; the life of Saint Mary Magdalen, as revealed in the visions of the most outstanding stigmatist-mystic of the last century, Sister Anna Catharina Emmerick. Ed. by Robert Emmet Curtiss. New York, Vantage [c.1962] 47p. illus. 21cm. 62-5295 2.00
1. Mary Magdalene, Saint. I. Title.

ENSLIN, Morton Scott, 1897- 225.92
The ethics of Paul. Nashville, Abingdon [1962, c.1957] 335p. 21cm. (Apex Bks. K 1) 2.25 pap.,
1. Paul, Saint, apostle. I. Title.

FOOTE, Gaston, 1902- 225.92
The transformation of the twelve. New York, Abingdon Press [1958] 128 p. 20 cm. [BS2440.F6] 58-10457
1. Apostles. I. Title.

GARTH, Helen Meredith, 1916- 225.92
Saint Mary Magdalene in mediaeval literature. Baltimore, Johns Hopkins Press, 1950. 114 p. 24 cm. (The Johns Hopkins University studles in historical and political science, ser. 67, no. 3) Pages also numbered 348-452. Bibliographical footnotes. [H31.J6 ser. 67, no. 3] 51-9492
1. Mary Magdslene, Saint, in literature. I. Title. II. Series.

GIORDANI, Igino, 1894- 225.92
St. Paul, apostle and martyr. Tr. from Italian by Clelia Maranzana, Mary Paula Williamson. Foreword by Richard Cardinal Cushing. [Boston] St. Paul Eds. [dist. Daughters of St.Paul, c.1961] 277p. illus. 61-11836 6.50; 5.00 pap.,
1. Paul, Saint, apostle. I. Title.

GOODSPEED, Edgar Johnson, 1871- 225.92
The twelve, the story of Christ's apostles. New York, Collier [1962, c.1957] 190p. 18cm. (AS314) .95 pap.,
1. Apostles. 2. Bible. N.T.—Criticism, interpretation, etc. 3. Christian literature, Early—Hist. & crit. I. Title.

GOODSPEED, Edgar Johnson, 1871- 225.92
The twelve, the story of Christ's apostles. [1st ed.] Philadelphia, J. C. Winston Co. [1957] 182p. 22cm. [BS2440.G6] 57-5197
1. Apostles. 2. Bible. N. T.— Criticism, interpretation, etc. 3. Christian literature, Early—Hist. & crit. I. Title.

GOODSPEED, Edgar Johnson, 1871-1962. 225.92
Matthew, apostle and evangelist. [1st ed.] Philadelphia, Winston [1959] 166 p. 22 cm. [BS2495.G6] 59-6599
1. Matthew, Saint, apostle. 2. Bible. N.T. Matthew—Criticism, interpretation, etc.

GOODSPEED, Edgar Johnson, 1871-1962. 225.92
Paul; [a biography drawn from the evidence in the apostle's writings] Nashville, Abingdon Press [1962, c1947] 246 p. 21 cm. (Apex books, D2) Includes bibliography. [BS2505] A62
1. Paul, Saint, apostle. I. Title.

GOODSPEED, Edgar Johnson, 1871-1962. 225.92
The twelve, the story of Christ's apostles. [1st ed.] Philadelphia, J. C. Winston Co. [1957] 182 p. 22 cm. [BS2440.G6] 57 5197
1. Bible. N.T.—Criticism, interpretation, etc. 2. Christian literature, Early—History and criticism. I. Title.

GREENE, Genard, Brother, 1921- 225.92
A cry in the wilderness; a story of St. John the Baptist. Illus. by Brother Bernard Howard. Notre Dame, Ind., Dujarie Press [1952] 86 p. illus. 24 cm. [BS2456.G7] 52-39266
1. John the Baptist. I. Title.

GUARDUCCI, Margherita. 225.92
The tomb of St. Peter; the new discoveries in the sacred grottoes of the Vatican. With an introd. by H. V. Morton. Translated from the Italian by Joseph McLellan. [1st ed.] New York, Hawthorn Books [1960] 198 p. illus. 24 cm. [BS2515.G813] 60-5898
1. Peter, Saint, apostle—Tomb. 2. Vatican City. San Pietro in Vaticano (Basilica) I. Title.

HALL, Asa Zadel 225.92
A cloud of witnesses; pen portraits and character sketches of people around Paulthe great apostle: his friends and enemies. Grand Rapids, Mich., Zondervan [c.1961] 88p. illus. 61-66713 1.95
1. Paul, Saint, apostle. 2. Bible. N. T.—Biog. I. Title.

HARGROVE, Hubbard Hoyt, 1895- 225.92
Personalities around the Cross. Grand Rapids, Baker Book House, 1963. 138 p. 20 cm. [BT431.H27] 63-21468
1. Jesus Christ — Passion. 2. Bible. N.T. — Biog. I. Title.

HARGROVE, Hubbard Hoyt, 1895- 225.92
Personalties around the Cross. Grand Rapids, Mich., Baker Bk. [c.]1963. 138p. 20cm. 63-21468 2.50
1. Jesus Christ—Passion. 2. Bible. N.T.—Biog. I. Title.

HENDERSON, Zelpha. 225.92
Jesus was their friend. Anderson, Ind., Warner Press [1958] 64p. illus. 23cm. [BS2433.H4] 58-12693
1. Bible. N. T.—Biog. I. Title.

HOMAN, Helen Mary (Walker) 1893- 225.92
By post to the apostles. New York, All Saints [1962, c.1931-1952] 146p. (AS225) .50 pap.,
1. Apostles. I. Title.

HOMAN, Helen (Walker), 1893- 225.92
By post to the apostles. New York, McKay [1952] 260 p. 21 cm. [BS2440.H6 1952] 52-7934
1. Apostles. I. Title.

HOSPODAR, Blaise, 1893- 225.92
Salome: virgin or prostitute? [1st ed.] New York, Pageant Press [1953] 79p. 24cm. [BS2520.S6H6] 53-7032
1. Salome. I. Title.

HUFFMAN, Jasper Abraham, 1880- 225.92
Judas; the biography of a soul. Marion, Ind., Wesley Press [1958] 166p. 20cm. [BS2460.J8H8] 58-48847
1. Judas Iscariot. I. Title.

HUNT, Clark W 225.92
Living in the light of the Cross. New York, Abingdon Press [1964] 142 p. 20 cm. Bible. N. T. -- Biog. -- Sermons. [BS2431.H8] 64-12958
1. Methodist Church — Sermons. 2. Sermons, American. I. Title.

HUNT, Clark W. 225.92
Living in the light of the Cross. Nashville, Abingdon [c.1964] 142p. 20cm. 64-12958 2.75 bds.,
1. Bible. N. T.—Biog.—Sermons. 2. Methodist Church—Sermons. 3. Sermons, American. I. Title.

JONES, Mary Alice, 1898- 225.92
Friends of Jesus; illustrated by Janet Robson Kennedy. Chicago, Rand McNally, c1954. unpaged. illus. 17cm. (Rand-McNally book-elf juniors, 687) [BS2433.J6] 54-11678
1. Jesus Christ—Friends and associates. I. Title.

KENDRICK, Thomas Downing Sir 225.92
St. James in Spain [dist. New York, Hillary House, 1961, c.1960] 223p. illus., maps. Bibl. 5.00
1. James, Saint, apostle—Cultus. 2. Catholic Church in Spain. 3. Santiago de Compostela. I. Title.

KIK, Jacob Marcellus, 1903- 225.92
Voices from heaven and hell. Philadelphia, Presbyterian and Reformed Pub. Co., 1955 [i. e. 1956] 192p. 21cm. [BS2430.K5] 55-12209
1. Bible. N. T.—Biog. I. Title.

KNOX, John, 1900- 225.92
Chapters in a life of Paul. Nashville, Abingdon [1964, c.1950] 168p. 23cm. (Apex bks., P2) 1.25 pap.,
1. Paul, Saint, apostle. I. Title.

KRAELING, Carl Hermann, 1897- 225.92
John the Baptist. New York, Scribner, 1951. xii, 218 p. 21 cm. Bibliographical references included in "Notes" (p. [189]-210) [BS2456.K67] 51-13626
1. John the Baptist. I. Title.

LAPIDE, Cornelius A, 1567-1637. 225.92
The personality of St. Paul. Translated by the Daughters of St. Paul. [Boston] St. Paul Editions [1959] 153p. illus. 22cm. [BS2505.L27] 59-33736
1. Paul, Saint, apostle. I. Title.

LA SOR, William Sanford. 225.92
Great personalities of the New Testament: their lives and times. [Westwood, N. J.] Revell [1961] 192p. 21cm. Includes bibliography. [BS2430.L23] 61-9239
1. Bible. N. T.—Biog. I. Title.

LASOR, Williams Sanford 225.92
Great personalities of the New Testament: their lives and times. Westwood, N. J., Revell [c.1961] 192p. Bibl. 61-9239 3.00
1. Bible. N. T.—Biog. I. Title.

LEAVELL, Roland Quinche, 225.92
1891-
The Apostle Paul, Christ's supreme trophy. Grand Rapids, Mich., Baker Bk. [1964, c.] 1963. 128p. illus. 23cm. 63-14400 1.50 pap.,
1. Paul, Saint, Apostle. I. Title.

LEAVELL, Roland Quinche, 225.92
1891-1963
The Apostle Paul, Christ's supreme trophy. Grand Rapids, Mich., Baker Bk. [c.]1963. 128p. illus. 23cm. 63-14400 2.95
1. Paul, Saint, Apostle. I. Title.

LEVY, Rosalie Marie, 1889- 225.92
The man in chain; Saint Paul, vessel of election. [n.p.] St. Paul Editions [c1957] 248p. illus. 22cm. [BS2505.L38] 59-23935
1. Paul, Saint, aposite. 2. Devotional calendars—Catholic Church. I. Title.

LILLIE, Amy Morris. 225.92
Run the good race. Illus. by Steele Savage. New York, Abingdon Press [1965] 72 p. illus. 22 cm. [BX2520.T5L5] 65-14091
1. Timothy (Biblical character) — Juvenile literature. I. Title.

LILLIE, Amy Morris 225.92
Run the good race. Illus. by Steele Savage. Nashville, Abingdon [c.1962, 1965] 72p. illus. 22cm. [BS2520T5L5] 65-14091 2.50
1. Timothy (Biblical character)—Juvenile literature. I. Title.

•LONGENECKER, Richard N. 225.92
Paul: apostle of liberty. New York, Harper [c.1964] 1v. 24cm. 4.50
I. Title.

MACARTNEY, Clarence Edward 225.92
Noble, 1879-
Peter and his Lord; sermons on the life of Peter. Nashville, Abingdon Press [1961, c.1937] 247 p. .95, pap.
1. Peter, Saint, apostle. 2. Presbyterian church—Sermons. 3. Sermons, American. I. Title.

MCCORRY, Vincent P 1909- 225.92
More blessed than kings; essays on certain minor characters in the four Gospels. Westminster, Md., Newman Press, 1954. 242p. 21cm. [BS2430.M2] 54-12082
1. Bible. N. T. Gospels—Biog. I. Title.

MARSHALL, Effie Lawrence, 225.92
1873-
Mary of Bethany. Manchester, Me., Falmouth Pub. House [1954] 197p. 21cm. [BS2490.M2M3] 54-7446
1. Mary of Bethany. I. Title.

MARTIN, Ira Jay, 1911- 225.92
The faith of Paul, a study for inquiring Christians. NewYork, Pageant [1965, c.1964] 350p. 21cm. [BS2506.M37] 64-66331 6.00
1. Paul, Saint, apostle. I. Title.

MARY SIMEON, Mother, 225.92
Simon called Peter. Decorations by John F. Kelly. Westminster, Md., Newman Press, 1959[i.e., 1960] 111p. illus. 19cm. 60-1823 2.25 bds.,
1. Peter, Saint, apostle. I. Title.

MARY SIMEON, Mother 1894- 225.92
Personalities in the Gospel story. Milwaukee, Bruce [c.1963] 140p. 23cm. 63-20156 3.50
1. Bible. N.T. Gospels—Biog. I. Title.

MATHEWS, Basil Joseph, 225.92
1879-1951.
Paul the dauntless. [Westwood, N. J.,] Revell [1959] 375p. 21cm. Includes bibliography. [BS2505.M35 1959] 59-4741
1. Paul, Saint, apostle. I. Title.

MILLER, Donald G. 225.92
Conqueror in chains, a story of the apostle Paul; illustrated by Albert De Mee Jousset. Philadelphia, Westminster Press [1951] 271 p. illus. 22 cm. [BS2505.M52] 922.1 51-12690
1. Paul, Saint, apostle. I. Title.

MOE, Olaf Edvard, 1876- 225.92
The apostle Paul. Translated by L. A. Vigness. Minneapolis, Augsburg Pub. House [1950-54] 2 v. maps. 22 cm. Contents.Contents.—1. His life and his work.—2. His message and doctrine. Includes bibliographies. [BS2505.M5494] 922.1 50-7291
1. Paul, Saint, apostle.

MORLEY, John P. 225.92
Beyond the bar; the story of the Apostle Barnabas. New York, Vantage [c.1961] 303p. 3.95
I. Title.

MOSLEY, Jean (Bell) 1913- 225.92
Famous women of the New Testament. Garden City, N. Y. [N. Doubleday, 1960] 64p. illus. 21cm. (Know your Bible program) [BS2445.M6] 60-3654
1. Women in the Bible—Juvenile literature. 2. Bible. N. T.—Biog.—Juvenile literature. I. Title.

MUNCK, Johannes, 1904- 225.92
Paul and the salvation of mankind. [Translated by Frank Clarke from the German Paulus und die Heilsgeschichte. 1st English ed.] Richmond, John Knox Press [1959] 351 p. 24 cm. Includes bibliography. [BS2505.M933 1959] 60-5412
1. Paul, Saint, apostle.

NEELEY, Deta Petersen. 225.92
A child's story of the New Testament, by Deta Petersen Neeley and Nathan Glen Neeley. Salt Lake City. Printed by Deseret News Press, 1956-57. 2v. illus. 20cm. Contents.v. 1. Jesus of Nazareth.--v. 2. Paul of Trasus. [BX8630.A28N4] 57-19522
1. Bible stories, English—N. T. I. Neeley, Nathan Glen, joint author. II. Title.

NICOLE, Albert. 225.92
Judas, the betrayer. Translated from the French. Grand Rapids, Baker Book House, 1957. 81p. 20cm. [BS2160.J8N513] 57-14759
1. Judas Iscariot. I. Title.

NOCK, Arthur Darby, 1902- 225.92
St. Paul. New York, Harper & Row [1963] 255 p. 21 cm. (Harper torchbooks. The Cloister library) "TB 104." Bibliography: p. 249-251. [[BS2506]]
1. Paul, Saint, apostle.

PARKS, William J 225.92
Paul, his Master's champion. [1st ed.] New York, Vantage Press [1961] 330p. 21cm. [BS2506.P36] 61-66797
1. Paul, Saint, apostle. I. Title.

PARKS, William J. 225.92
Paul, his Master's champion. New York, Vantage [c.1961] 300p. 4.50 bds.,
I. Title.

PETERSON, Finis Paul. 225.92
Peter's tomb recently discovered in Jerusalem. McKeesport, Pa. [1960] 87p. illus. 20cm. [BS2515.P48] 61-23402
1. Peter, Saint, apostle—Tomb. 2. Catholic Church— Doctrinal and controversial works—Protestant authors. I. Title.

PITTENGER, William Norman, 225.92
1905-
The life of Saint Paul [by] W. Norman Pittenger. New York, F. Watts [1968] ix, 141 p. map. 22 cm. (Immortals of philosophy and religion) Bibliography: p. 137-138. A biography of the man known as "the first Christian missionary and theologian," including discussions of the world he lived in, other religions of the time, our sources of information about him, his teachings, and his influence on religious history. [BS2506.P5] AC 68
1. Paul, Saint, apostle. I. Title.

RENGERS, Christopher. 225.92
They played in Calvary's drama. Milwaukee, Bruce Pub. Co. [1962] 106p. 20cm. [BT431.R4] 62-10345
1. Jesus Christ—Passion. 2. Bible. N. T.—Biog. I. Title.

RETIF, Andre. 225.92
John the Baptist, missionary of Christ. Westminster, Md., Newman Press, 1953. 122p. 22cm. Translated by Francis Murry. [BS2456.R413] 53-10383
1. John the Baptist. I. Title.

ROLSTON, Holmes, 1900- 225.92
Faces about the Christ. Richmond, John Knox Press [c1959] 215p. 20cm. [BS2430.R62] 58-9909
1. Bible. N. T. Gospels—Biog. I. Title.

ROLSTON, Holmes, 1900- 225.92
Faces about the Christ. Richmond, Knox [1967, c.1959] 215p. 21cm. (Aletheia ed.) [BS2430.R62] 58-9909 1.95 pap.,
1. Bible. N.T. Gospels—Biog. I. Title.

ROLSTON, Holmes, 1900- 225.92
Personalities around Paul; men and women who helped or hindered the Apostle Paul. Richmond, John Knox Press [1954] 206 p. 21 cm. [BS2430.R63] 54-8504
1. Bible. N. T.—Biography. 2. Paul, Saint, apostle. I. Title.

SANDMEL, Samuel. 225.92
The genius of Paul, a study in history. New York, Farrar, Straus & Cudahy [1958] 239 p. 22 cm. Includes bibliography. [BS2505.S38] 58-12485
1. Paul, Saint, apostle. I. Title.

SAPONARO, Michele, 1885- 225.92
The fishers of men. [1st ed.] New York, Hawthorn Books [1962] 282 p. 24 cm. Translation of I discepoli. [BS2618.S253] 62-9232
1. Aposties. 2. Bible. N.T.—History of Biblical events. I. Title.

SATTERFIELD, Lawrence. 225.92
Paul, soldier of the cross. Philadelphia, Dorrance [1963] 340 p. 21 cm. [BS2506.S2] 63-16011
1. Paul, Saint, Apostle. I. Title.

SATTERFIELD, Lawrence 225.92
Paul, soldier of the cross. Philadelphia, Dorrance [c.1963] 340p. 21cm. 63-16011 3.95
1. Paul, Saint, Apostle. I. Title.

SCOBIE, Charles Hugh Hope. 225.92
John the Baptist [by] Charles H. H. Scobie. Philadelphia, Fortress Press [1964] 224 p. map. 23 cm. Bibliographical footnotes. [BS2456.S36] 64-55082
1. John the Baptist. I. Title.

SCOBIE, Charles Hugh Hope 225.92
John the Baptist. Philadelphia, Fortress [c.1964] 224p. map. 23cm. Bibl. 64-55082 3.25
1. John the Baptist. I. Title.

SEGERHAMMAR, Carl William. 225.92
They talked with God; sermon studies on New Testament characters. Rock Island, Ill., Augustana Book Concern [1954] 190p. 21cm. [BS2430.S4] 54-9965
1. Bible. N. T.—Biog. I. Title.

SELBY, Donald Joseph. 225.92
Toward the understanding of St. Paul. Englewood Cliffs, N. J., Prentice-Hall, 1962. 355 p. 22 cm. [BS2506.S4] 62-8561
1. Paul, Saint, apostle. I. Title.

SIMON, Marcel. 225.92
St. Stephen and the Hellenists in the primitive church. London, New York, Longmans, Green [1958] 130 p. 21 cm. (The Haskell lectures, 1956] Includes bibliography. [BS2520.S8S5] 59-16126
1. Stephen, Saint, martyr I. Title.

SMITH, Asbury. 225.92
The twelve Christ chose. [1st ed.] New York, Harper [1958] 178 p. illus. 22 cm. Includes bibliography. [BS2440.S53] 58-7103
1. Apostles. I. Title.

SMITH, Asbury. 225.92
The twelve Christ chose. [1st ed.] New York, Harper [1958] 178 p. illus. 22 cm. Includes bibliography. [BS2440.S53] 58-7103
1. Apostles. I. Title.

STALKER, James 225.92
Life of St. Paul; handbook for Bible classes. Grand Rapids, Mich., Zondervan [1960] 160p. Bibliographical references included in 'Hints to teachers and questions for pupils (p. 145-160)20cm. 1.25 bds.,
1. Paul, Saint, apostle. I. Title.

STEINMANN, Jean. 225.92
Saint John the Baptist and the desert tradition. Translated from the French by Michael Boyes. New York, Harper [1958] 191 p. illus. 18 cm. (Men of wisdom, 5) Includes bibliography. [BS2456.S773] 58-11727
1. John the Baptist. 2. Dead Sea scrolls. I. Title.

STEWART, James Stuart, 225.92
1896-
A man in Christ: the vital elements of St. Paul's religion. New York, Harper [1963?] xv, 331 p. 21 cm. Bibliographical footnotes. [BS2651.S85] 63-6330
1. Paul, Saint, apostle. 2. Bible. N. T. Epistles of Paul — Theology. I. Title.

STEWART, James Stuart, 225.92
1896-
A man in Christ; the vital elements of St. Paul's religion. New York, Harper [c.1963] xv, 331p. 21cm. Bibl. 63-6330 3.00
1. Paul, Saint, apostle. 2. Bible. N.T. Epistles of Paul—Theology. I. Title.

TAYLOR, William Mackergo, 225.92
1829-1895.
Paul, the missionary. Grand Rapids, Baker Book House, 1962. 570 p. 21 cm. (Bible biographies) [BX2505.T37 1962] 62-21707
1. Paul, Saint, apostle. I. Title.

TAYLOR, William Mackergo, 225.92
1829-1895
Paul, the missionary. Grand Rapids, Mich., Baker Bk-House, 1962. 570p. 21cm. (Bible biographies) 62-21707 3.95
1. Paul, Saint, apostle. I. Title.

THOMPSON, Blanche 225.92
Jennings, 1887-.
Peter and Paul; the rock and the sword. Illustrated by Harry Barton. New York, Vision Books [1964] 177 p. illus. 22 cm. "62." [BS2515.T48] 64-11634
1. Peter, Saint, apostle — Juvenile literature. 2. Paul, Saint, apostle — Juvenile literature. I. Title.

THOMPSON, Blanche 225.92
Jennings, 1887-
Peter and Paul; the rock and the sword. Illus. by Harry Barton. New York, Farrar [c.1964] 177p. illus. 22cm. (Vision bk., 62) 64-11634 2.25
1. Peter, Saint, apostle—Juvenile literature. 2. Paul, Saint, apostle—Juvenile literature. I. Title.

TURNBULL, Ralph G. 225.92
Personalities of the New Testament. Grand Rapids, Mich., Baker Bk. House [c.]1961. 114p. 61-10000 1.95 bds.,
1. Bible N. T.—Biog. I. Title.

TURNBULL, Ralph G 225.92
Personalities of the New Testaments. Grand Rapids, Baker Book House, 1961. 114 p. 20 cm. [BS2430.T85] 61-10000
1. Bible. N. T. — Biog. I. Title.

VAN ETTEN, Isabel Upton. 225.92
Who was Saul of Tarsus. Los Angeles, Cole-Holmquist Press, 1957. 92p. 24cm. [BS2505.V3 922.1] [BS2505.V3] 57-28029 57-28029
1. Paul, Saint, apostle. I. Title.

WAGNER, Harold E 225.92
"Were you there?" Personalities whose sins helped crucify our Lord or whose virtues helped sustain Him in His Passion. New York, Morehouse-Gorham Co., 1951. 110 p. 19 cm. [BT430.W14] 51-1882
1. Jesus Christ-Passion — Meditations. 2. Bible. N.T. Gospels — Biog. I. Title.

WAHLSTROM, Eric Herbert. 225.92
Let's look at Paul; studies in the life and teachings of St. Paul. Rock Island, Ill., Augustana Press [1960] 90 p. 20 cm. Includes bibliography. [BS2507.W3] 60-16831
1. Paul, Saint, apostle — Study. I. Title.

WAHLSTROM, Eric Herbert 225.92
Let's look at Paul; studies in the life and teachings of St. Paul. Rock Island, Ill.. Augustana Press [c.1960] ix, 90p. Includes bibl. 20cm. 60-16831 1.50 pap.,
1. Paul, Saint, apostle—Study. I. Title.

•WALSTON, Marie 225.92
Paul from Tarsus to Rome. New York, Vantage [c.1964] 101p. 21cm 2.75
I. Title.

WHITE, Reginald E O 225.92
Apostle extraordinary, a modern portrait of St. Paul. Grand Rapids, W. B. Eerdmans Pub. Co. [1962] 200 p. 22 cm. [BS2506.W5] 62-18955
1. Paul, Saint, apostle. I. Title.

WHITE, Reginald E. O 225.92
Apostle extraordinary, a modern portrait of St. Paul. Grand Rapids, Mich., Eerdmans [c.1962] 209p. 22cm. 62-18955 3.50 bds.,
1. Paul, Saint, apostle. I. Title.

•WILKINSON, Henrietta T. 225.92
Living as disciples [Gr. 1] Illus, by W. K. Plummer. Richmond, Va., CLC Pr. [dist. Knox, 1966, c.1965] 128p. col. illus. 20cm. 1.95 pap.,
I. Title.

WILLIAMS, Albert 225.92
Nathaniel, 1914-
John Mark, first Gospel writer. New York, Association Press [1956] 127p. 20cm. (Heroes of God series) [BS2475.W5] 56-9183
1. Mark, Saint. I. Title.

WILLIAMS, Albert 225.92
Nathaniel, 1914-
John Mark, first Gospel writer. New York, Association Press [1956] 127 p. 20 cm. (Heroes of God series) [BS2475.W5] 56-9183
1. Mark, Saint. I. Title.

WOOD, Katharine Marie, 225.92
1910-
The four evangelists: St. Matthew, St. Mark, St. Luke, St. John; story and pictures by Katharine Wood. New York. Kenedy [1959] unpaged. illus. 29 cm. [BS2441.W6] 59-7934
1. Evangelists (Bible) I. Title.

WOOD, Katharine Marie, 225.92
1910-
The holy apostles: Peter and Paul. Story and pictures by Katharine Wood. New York, P. J. Kenedy [1960] unpaged. illus. 29 cm. [BS2515.W64] 60-13883
1. Peter, Saint, apostle — Juvenile literature. 2. Paul, Saint, apostle — Juvenile literature. I. Title.

WOOD, Katharine Marie, 1910- 225.92
The holy apostles: Peter and Paul. Story and pictures by Katharine Wood. New York, P. J. Kenedy [c.1960] unpaged. 29cm. 60-13883 2.50
1. Peter, Saint, apostle—Juvenile literature. 2. Paul, Saint, apostle—Juvenile literature. I. Title.

WOOD, Katharine Marie, 1910- 225.92
The twelve apostles. New York, Kenedy [1956] unpaged. illus. 29cm. [BS2440.W6] 56-5752
1. Apostles—Juvenile literature. I. Title.

WOOD, Katharine Marie, 1910- 225.92
The twelve apostles. New York, Kenedy [1956] unpaged. illus. 29 cm. [BS2440.W6] 56-3752
1. Apostles — Juvenile literature. I. Title.

YALE, Alfred H. 225.92
Life and letters of Paul; a study course for adults. [Independence? Mo.] Dept. of Religious Education, Reorganized Church of Jesus Christ of Latter Day Saints [1959] 304 p. illus. 21 cm. Includes bibliography. [BS2505.Y3] 59-8360
1. Paul, Saint, apostle. 2. Bible. N.T. Epistles of Paul — Study — Text-books. I. Title.

ZUZIC, Marko 225.92
A short history of St. John in Ephesus, the first and greatest metropolis of Asia, the cradle of the Hellenic civilization, a nursery and garden of Christianity, the second province of God after Jerusalem, with a precious unique common Christian-Moslem shrine. Lima, Ohio, Priv. print., Amer. Soc. of Ephesus[dist. Fresno, Calif., Amer. Lib. Guild, 1962, c.] 1960. xi, 96p. illus., group port. 19cm. 62-51999 2.50
1. John, Saint, apostle—Tomb. 2. Ephesus. I. Title.

I. Title.

BATTLE, Gerald N. 225.9'22 B
Armed with love; stories of the disciples [by] Gerald N. Battle. Chapter decorations by Charles Cox. Nashville, Abingdon Press [1973] 222 p. illus. 25 cm. Bibliography: p. 221-222. Biographical profiles of the twelve disciples describing the influence of Christ's teachings on each of them. [BS2440.B35] 73-626 ISBN 0-687-01741-6 4.95
1. Apostles—Juvenile literature. I. Title.

BIETZ, Arthur Leo. 225.922
When God met men, by Arthur L. Bietz. Mountain View, Calif., Pacific Press Pub. Association [1966] 106 p. 22 cm. [BS2430.B47] 66-29071
1. Bible. N.T.—Biography. I. Title.

BROWNRIGG, Ronald. 225.9'22 B
The twelve apostles. [1st American ed.] New York, Macmillan [1974] 248 p. illus. 26 cm. [BS2440.B68 1974] 73-21569 12.95
1. Apostles. I. Title.

BROWNRIGG, Ronald. 225.92'2 B
Who's who in the New Testament. Advisory editors for this volume: Canon E. Every [and] Wolfgang E. Pax. [1st ed.] New York, Holt, Rinehart and Winston [1971] 448 p. illus. 26 cm. [BS2430.B67] 75-153654 ISBN 0-03-086262-0 14.95
1. Bible. N.T.—Biography—Dictionaries. I. Title.

CHAPPELL, Clovis Gillham, 1882- 225.92'2
Men that count, by Clovis G. Chappell. Grand Rapids, Baker Book House [1967] 164 p. 20 cm. (Ministers paperback library) Reprint of the 1929 ed. Sermons. Contents.Contents.—Needless poverty: James.—Worry and its cure: Paul.—All things new: Paul.—A great believer: Paul.—At the cross: Paul.—A successful service: Peter.—Kept: Peter.—A pilgrim's progress: the man born blind.—The glory of the ordinary: Andrew.—A fighter: Zacchaeus.—A woman's revenge: John the Baptist.—A beautiful vocation: Onesiphorus.—Making life count: author of Hebrews.—A wholehearted saint: Caleb.—Mr. Sorrowful: Jabez.—The spoiled dream: Jeremiah. [BS571.5.C46 1967] 67-18173
1. Bible—Biography. 2. Sermons, American. I. Title.

DAVIDSON, Donald. 225.922
God chose them; thirty informative character studies of New Testament men and women. Grand Rapids, Zondervan Pub. House [1965] 142 p. 23 cm. [BS2430.D28 1965] 65-6000
1. Bible. N.T. — Biog. I. Title.

DAVIDSON, Donald 225.922
God chose them; thirty informative character studies of New Testament men and women. Grand Rapids, Mich., Zondervan [c.1965] 142p. 23cm. [BS2430.D28] 65-6000 2.95 bds.,
1. Bible. N. T.—Biog. I. Title.

GADLA Hawaryat. English & Ethiopic. 225.9'22 B
The contendings of the apostles (Mashafa gadla hawaryat) : being the Ethiopic version of the histories of the lives, martyrdoms and deaths of the twelve apostles and evangelists : Ethiopic texts, edited from manuscripts in the British Museum / Sir Ernest A. Wallis Budge. Amsterdam : APA : Philo Press, 1976. 2 v. ; 23 cm. Reprint of the 1899-1901 ed. published by H. Frowde, London. Contents.Contents.—v. 1. Ethiopic text.—v. 2. English translation. Includes bibliographical references and indexes. [BS2440.G313 1976] 77-359993 ISBN 9-06-022482-5 : fl 228.80
1. Apostles—Legends. I. Budge, Ernest Alfred Thompson Wallis, Sir, 1857-1934. II. Title.

GRIFFITH, Arthur Leonard, 1920- 225.9'22 B
Gospel characters : the personalities around Jesus / by Leonard Griffith. Grand Rapids, Mich. : Eerdmans, c1976. p. cm. [BS2430.G74 1976] 76-12412 ISBN 0-8028-1646-0 pbk. : 3.95
1. Jesus Christ—Friends and associates. 2. Bible. N.T. Gospels—Biography. I. Title.

GUTHRIE, Donald, 1916- 225.9'22 B
The apostles / Donald Guthrie. Grand Rapids : Zondervan Pub. House, c1975. 422 p. : ill. ; 25 cm. Includes indexes. Bibliography: p. 413-416. [BS2618.G87] 74-11856 8.95
1. Bible. N.T.—History of Biblical events. 2. Apostles. I. Title.

HILL, David C. 225.922
These met the Master; 40 portraits of persons who encountered the Christ [by] David C. Hill. Minneapolis. Augsburg [c.1967] 95p. 20cm. [BS2430.H5] 67-11716 1.95 pap.,
1. Bible. N.T.—Biog. I. Title.

HILL, David C 225.922
These met the Master; 40 portraits of persons who encountered the Christ [by] David C. Hill. Minneapolis, Augsburg Pub. House [1967] 95 p. 20 cm. [BS2430.H5] 67-11716
1. Bible. N.T. — Biog. I. Title.

HOMAN, Helen (Walker) 1893- 225.9'22
By post to the Apostles. Freeport, N.Y., Books for Libraries Press [1971, c1933] xi, 260 p. 23 cm. (Biography index reprint series) [BS2440.H6 1971] 74-148219 ISBN 0-8369-8066-2
1. Apostles. I. Title.

HUBBARD, David Allan. 225.9'22 B
They met Jesus. [1st ed.] Philadelphia, A. J. Holman Co. [1974] 120 p. 21 cm. Originally presented as a series of radio talks on the international broadcast the Joyful sound. [BS2430.H8] 74-2312 ISBN 0-87981-030-0 2.95 (pbk.)
1. Bible. N.T.—Biography. I. The Joyful sound. II. Title.

*HUNTER, John 225.92'2
Impact. Glendale, Calif., Regal Bks. [1966] 221p. 18cm. (GL 95-12) .95 pap.,
I. Title.

JONES, George Curtis, 1911- 225.9'2'2 B
We knew His power / G. Curtis Jones. Nashville : Abingdon, c1976. 128 p. ; 20 cm. [BS2430.J66] 75-44181 ISBN 0-687-44315-6 : 5.95
1. Jesus Christ—Biography. 2. Bible. N.T. Gospels—Biography. I. Title.

KORTREY, Walter A., 1923- 225.9'22 B
People around Jesus [by] Walter A. Kortrey. Philadelphia, United Church Press [1974] 128 p. illus. 22 cm. "A Pilgrim Press book." Bibliography: p. 113. [BS2430.K65] 74-16400 ISBN 0-8298-0288-6
1. Jesus Christ—Friends and associates. I. Title.

KRAELING, Emil Gottlieb Heinrich, 1892- 225.92'2
The disciples, by Emil G. Kraeling. [Chicago] Rand McNally [1966] 301 p. 22 cm. "Apocrypha bibliography": p. 247-250. "Notes and references": p. 251-289. [BS2440.K7] 66-26635
1. Apostles. I. Title.

KRAELING, Emil Gottlieb Heinrich, 1892- 225.92'2
The disciples, by Emil G. Kraeling. [Chicago] Rand McNally [1966] 301 p. 22 cm. "Apocrypha bibliography": p. 247-250. "Notes and references": p. 251-289. [BS2440.K7] 66-26635
1. Apostles. I. Title.

LA SOR, William Sanford. 225.9'22
Men who knew Christ. Glendale, Calif., G/L Regal Books [1971] 167 p. illus. 18 cm. Bibliography: p. 162-167. [BS2430.L24] 70-135026 ISBN 0-8307-0086-2 0.95
1. Bible. N.T.—Biography. I. Title.

LEAVELL, Landrum P. 225.9'22 B
Twelve who followed Jesus / Landrum P. Leavell. Nashville : Broadman Press, [1975] 125 p. ; 21 cm. [BS2440.L38] 74-18655 ISBN 0-8054-1352-9 : 3.95
1. Apostles. I. Title.

LOCKYER, Herbert. 225.9'22 B
All the apostles of the Bible; studies in the characters of the apostles, the men Jesus chose, and the message they proclaimed. Grand Rapids, Mich., Zondervan Pub. House [1972] 278 p. illus. 24 cm. Bibliography: p. 271. [BS2440.L6] 70-180837 5.95
1. Apostles. I. Title.

PAPE, William H. 225.92'2
I talked with Paul; imaginary conversations with Bible characters, by William H. Pape. Grand Rapids, Baker Book House [1967] 112 p. 19 cm. [BS2430.P28] 67-18192
1. Bible. N.T.—Biography. I. Title.

PARMELEE, Alice 225.92'2
They beheld his glory; stories of the men and women who knew Jesus. [1st ed.] New York, Harper [1967] xii, 275p. 22cm. [BS2430.P3] 67-11504 4.95
1. Bible. N.T. Gospels—Biog. I. Title.

PARMELEE, Alice. 225.92'2
They beheld his glory; stories of the men and women who knew Jesus. [1st ed.] New York, Harper & Row [1967] xii, 275 p. 22 cm. [BS2430.P3] 67-11504
1. Bible. N. T. Gospels—Biog. I. Title.

PERRY, Earl. 225.92'2
These first called Him Master. Nashville, Broadman Press [1968] 128 p. 20 cm. Bibliography: p. 128. [BS2440.P4] 68-12131
1. Bible. N.T.—Biograpy. 2. Apostles. I. Title.

POLING, David, 1928- 225.9'2'2 B
They walked with Christ; illuminating portraits of the men and women who knew Jesus Christ during His ministry on earth. With illus. by John Lane. Forewords by Norman Vincent Peale and Bishop Fulton J. Sheen. New York, Enterprise Publications [1972] v, 62 p. illus. 28 cm. [BS2430.P64] 74-188521
1. Bible. N.T. Gospels—Biography. I. Title.

*ROBERTSON, A. T. 225.9'22
Some minor characters in the New Testament / by A. T. Robertson. Grand Rapids : Baker Book House, 1976c1928 182p. ; 20 cm. (His LibraryII) [BS2430] ISBN 0-8010-7637-4 pbk. : 2.95.
1. Bible-Biography. I. Title.

ROLSTON, Holmes, 1900- 225.922
Faces about the Christ. Richmond, John Knox Press [1966] 215 p. 21 cm. (Aletheia paperbacks) [BS2430.R62] 67-644
1. Bible. N.T. Gospels—Biog. I. Title.

ROUNER, Arthur Acy. 225.922
Master of men, by Arthur A. Rouner, Jr. Minneapolis, T. S. Denison [1966] 106 p. 22 cm. [BX2431.R68] 65-29144
1. Bible. N. T. — Blog. — Sermons. 2. Sermons, American. I. Title.

SMITH, Woodrow W. 225.9'22 B
The twelve who walked in Galilee: character studies of the members of Jesus' cabinet [by] Woodrow W. Smith. Old Tappan, N.J., Revell [1974] 128 p. 21 cm. Bibliography: p. 126-128. [BS2440.S55] 73-16410 ISBN 0-8007-0636-6 3.95
1. Apostles. I. Title.

*VIGEVENO, H. S. 225.92'2
13 men who changed the world. Glendale, Calif., Regal Bks. [1966] 159p. illus. 18cm. (G195-5) .95 pap.,
I. Title.

ARMSTRONG, April (Oursler) 225.9'24
The conversion of St. Paul. Sponsored by the Benedictine monks of Belmont Abbey. Garden City, N.Y. [N. Doubleday, 1963] 64 p. illus. (part col.) fold. map. 21 cm. (The Catholic know-your-Bible program) Full name: Grace April (Oursler) Armstrong. [BS2506.5.A7] 63-25273
1. Paul, Saint, apostle — Conversion — Juvenile literature. I. Title.

BARCLAY, William, lecturer in the University of Glasgow. 225.9'24 B
Ambassador for Christ; the life and teaching of Paul. Valley Forge, [Pa.] Judson Press [1974, c1973] 183 p. 22 cm. "Originally published in 1951 by the Church of Scotland Youth Committee." [BS2506.B34 1974] 73-9762 ISBN 0-8170-0631-1 1.95 (pbk)
1. Paul, Saint, apostle. I. Title.

BLACKWELL, Muriel Fontenot. 225.9'24 B
Peter, the prince of apostles / Muriel F. Blackwell ; illustrated by Paul Karch. Nashville : Broadman Press, c1976. 48 p. : col. ill. ; 24 cm. (Biblearn series) Discusses the conversion and ministry of Peter, the apostle chosen to lead Jesus' followers after the crucifixion. [BS2515.B52] 76-382762 ISBN 0-8054-4227-8 : 3.95
1. Peter, Saint, apostle—Juvenile literature. 2. Bible. N.T.—Biography—Juvenile literature. 3. Apostles—Biography—Juvenile literature. I. Karch, Paul. II. Title.

BLENKINSOPP, Joseph, 1927- 225.92'4
Jesus is Lord; Paul's life in Christ. New York, Paulist Press [1967] 126 p. 19 cm. (Deus books) Bibliography: p. 119-121. [BS2506.B57] 67-23602
1. Paul, Saint, Apostle. I. Title.

BORNKAMM, Gunther. 225.9'24 B
Paul, Paulus. Translated by D. M. G. Stalker. [1st U.S. ed.] New York, Harper & Row [1971] xxviii, 259 p. 22 cm. [BS2506.B6213] 75-22728 7.50
1. Paul, Saint, apostle. 2. Bible. N.T. Epistles of Paul—Theology.

BRADFORD, Ernle Dusgate Selby. 225.9'24 B
Paul the traveller / Ernle Bradford. 1st American ed. New York : Macmillan, 1976, c1974. vii, 246 p., [6] leaves of plates : ill. ; 22 cm. Includes index. [BS2506.B7 1976] 75-28451 ISBN 0-02-514390-5 : 9.95
1. Paul, Saint, Apostle. I. Title.

BUCK, Charles Henry, 1915- 225.92'4
Saint Paul; a study of the development of his thought, by Charles Buck and Greer Taylor. New York, Scribner [1969] x, 278 p. 24 cm. Bibliographical footnotes. [BS2506.B78 1969] 69-17054 7.95
1. Paul, Saint, apostle. I. Taylor, Greer, 1917- joint author. II. Title.

BUCKMASTER, Henrietta, pseud. 225.924
Paul, a man who changed the world. New York, McGraw [c.1965] ix, [1] 213p. maps. 21cm. Bibl. [BS2506.B8] 65-24889 4.95
1. Paul, Saint, apostle. I. Title.

BUCKMASTER, Henrietta, pseud. 225.924 (B)
Paul, a man who changed the world. New York, McGraw-Hill [1965] ix, [1], 213 p. maps. 21 cm. Bibliography: p. [x] [BS2506.B8] 65-24889
1. Paul, Saint, apostle. I. Title.

CLIFFORD, T. A., 1893- 225.9'24 B
Peter and the keys, by T. A. Clifford. Philadelphia, Dorrance [1972] 58 p. 22 cm. Includes bibliographical references. [BS2515.C54] 72-171930 ISBN 0-8059-1615-6 3.50
1. Peter, Saint, apostle. 2. Papacy. I. Title.

DRANE, John William. 225.9'24 B
Paul : [an illustrated documentary on the life and writings of a key figure in the beginnings of Christianity] / John W. Drane. Berkhamsted : Lion Publishing, 1976. 127 p. : ill., facsims., maps ; 24 cm. Includes index. Bibliography: p. 123-125. [BS2506.D7] 77-373988 ISBN 0-85648-043-6 : £1.75
1. Paul, Saint, Apostle. 2. Bible. N.T. Epistles of Paul—Criticism, interpretation, etc. 3. Christian saints—Turkey—Tarsus—Biography. 4. Tarsus, Turkey—Biography.

ENSLIN, Morton Scott, 1897- 225.9'24 B
Reapproaching Paul. Philadelphia, Westminster Press [1972] 159 p. 21 cm. Includes bibliographical references. [BS2506.E57] 72-4941 ISBN 0-664-20951-3 5.95
1. Paul, Saint, apostle. I. Title.

GIBBS, Paul T. 225.9'24 B
Paul the Conqueror [by] Paul T. Gibbs. Washington, Review and Herald Pub. Association [1972] 124 p. 22 cm. (Discovery paperbacks) [BS2506.G5] 75-178160
1. Paul, Saint, apostle. I. Title.

GRANT, Michael, 1914- 225.9'24 B
Saint Paul / Michael Grant. London : Weidenfeld and Nicolson, c1976. 250 p. : maps ; 24 cm. Includes index. Bibliography: p. 242-244. [BS2506.G68] 76-364100 ISBN 0-297-77082-9 : £5.95
1. Paul, Saint, Apostle.

GRANT, Michael, 1914- 225.9'24 B
Saint Paul / Michael Grant. New York :

Scribner, c1976. 250 p. : maps ; 25 cm. Includes index. Bibliography: p. 242-244. [BS2506.G68 1976b] 76-6024 ISBN 0-684-14682-7 : 14.95
1. Paul, Saint, Apostle. 2. Bible. N.T.—Biography. I. Title.

GUNTHER, John J. 225.9'2'4 B
Paul: messenger and exile; a study in the chronology of his life and letters [by] John J. Gunther. Valley Forge, Judson Press [1972] 190 p. map. 23 cm. Includes bibliographical references. [BS2506.G85] 70-181022 ISBN 0-8170-0504-8 6.95
1. Paul, Saint, apostle. I. Title.

HAUGHTON, Rosemary. 225.924 B
Paul and the world's most famous letters. [Nashville, Abingdon Press, 1970] 110 p. illus., maps. 27 cm. 1969 ed., London, published under title: Why the Epistles were written. Bibliography: p. 107. [BS2506.H3 1970] 72-105063 3.75
1. Paul, Saint, apostle. 2. Bible. N.T. Epistles of Paul—Criticism, interpretation, etc. I. Title.

HAUGHTON, Rosemary 225.924
The young Saint Mark. Illus. by the author. New York, Roy [1965, c.1964] 136p. illus. 21cm. (Young biographies) [BS2475.H3] 65-18879 3.25 bds.,
1. Mark, Saint—Juvenile literature. I. Title.

HIEBERT, David Edmond, 225.9'24 B
1910-
Personalities around Paul [by] D. Edmond Hiebert. Chicago, Moody Press [1973] 270 p. 24 cm. Bibliography: p. 252-266. [BS2430.H48] 72-95028 ISBN 0-8024-6473-4 5.95
1. Paul, Saint, apostle—Friends and associates. I. Title.

KALLAS, James G 225.924 (B)
The story of Paul, by James G. Kallas. Minneapolis, Augsburg Pub. House [1966] 151 p. 22 cm. Includes bibliographies. [BS2506.K3] 66-19206
1. Paul, Saint, apostle. I. Title.

KALLAS, James G. 225.924
The story of Paul. Minneapolis, Augsburg [c.1966] 151p. 22cm. Bibl. [BS2506.K3] 66-19206 1.50, pap.,
1. Paul, Saint, apostle. I. Title.

KELSO, James Leon, 225.92'4 B
1892-
An archaeologist follows the Apostle Paul [by] James L. Kelso. Waco, Tex., Word Books [1970] 142 p. illus., map. 23 cm. Includes bibliographical references. [BS2506.K44] 78-128446 3.95
1. Paul, Saint, apostle. 2. Bible. N.T. Epistles of Paul—Antiquities. I. Title.

KRAELING, Emil 225.924 (B)
Gottlieb Heinrich, 1892-
I have kept the faith; the life of the apostle Paul, by Emil G. Kraeling. Chicago, Rand McNally [1965] 320 p. maps (on lining papers) 22 cm. "Notes and references": p. 276-307. [BS2506.K7] 65-15357
1. Paul, Saint, apostle. I. Title.

KRAELING, Emil Gottlieb 225.924
Heinrich, 1892-
I have kept the faith; the life of the apostle Paul, by Emil G. Kraeling. Chicago, Rand McNally [c.1965] 320p. maps (on lining papers) 22cm. Bibl. [BS2506.K7] 65-15357 3.95
1. Paul, Saint, apostle. I. Title.

LECROY, Ruth Brooks. 225.9'24
Sunrise in Syria; a fact and fiction story about Saul of Tarsus who became Paul the Apostle. Little Rock, Ark., Pioneer Books [1972] ix, 250 p. 24 cm. [BS2506.L43] 74-189490 5.95
1. Paul, Saint, apostle. I. Title.

LOHFINK, Gerhard, 225.9'24 B
1934-
The conversion of St. Paul : narrative and history in Acts / by Gerhard Lohfink; translated and edited by Bruce J. Malina Chicago : Franciscan Herald Press, [1975] p. cm. (Herald scriptural library) Translation of Paulus vor Damaskus, 3d. ed. (1967) Bibliography: p. [BS2506.L5713] 75-12796 ISBN 0-8199-0572-0 : 5.95
1. Paul, Saint, apostle. 2. Bible. N.T. Acts—Criticism, interpretation, etc. I. Title.

LONGENECKER, Richard 225.92'4 B
N.
The ministry and message of Paul [by] Richard Longenecker. Grand Rapids, Mich., Zondervan Pub. House [1971] 130 p. 21 cm. (Contemporary evangelical perspectives) Bibliography: p. 113-122. [BS2506.L598] 77-159661
1. Paul, Saint, apostle. I. Title.

MUGGERIDGE, Malcolm, 225.9'24 B
1903-
Paul, envoy extraordinary [by] Malcolm Muggeridge & Alec Vidler. [1st U.S. ed.] New York, Harper & Row [1972] 159 p. illus. 23 cm. [BS2506.M84 1972] 73-184408 5.95
1. Paul, Saint, apostle. I. Vidler, Alexander Roper, 1899- II. Title.

O'CONNOR, Daniel 225.92'4
William, 1925-
Peter in Rome: the literary, liturgical, and archeological evidence. New York, Columbia University Press, 1969. xiv, 242 p. illus., plans. 29 cm. Bibliography: p. 214-226. [BS2515.O28] 68-17552 20.00
1. Peter, Saint, apostle. I. Title.

PEROWNE, Stewart, 225.9'24 B
1901-
The journeys of St. Paul. London, New York, Hamlyn, 1973. 144 p. illus. (some col.), col. maps (on lining papers), ports. 29 cm. Bibliography: p. 142. [BS2506.P45 1973] 73-162279 £2.25
1. Paul, Saint, apostle—Journeys. I. Title.

PETER in the New 225.9'24 B
Testament; a collaborative assessment by Protestant and Roman Catholic scholars. Edited by Raymond E. Brown, Karl P. Donfried, and John Reumann, from discussions by Paul J. Achtemeier [and others] Minneapolis, Augsburg Pub. House, 1973. ix, 181 p. 21 cm. Bibliography: p. 169-177. [BS2615.P47] 73-83787 ISBN 0-8066-1401-3 1.95 (pbk.)
1. Peter, Saint, apostle. 2. Bible. N.T.—Criticism, interpretation, etc. I. Brown, Raymond Edward, ed. II. Donfried, Karl P., ed. III. Reumann, John Henry Paul, ed.

PITTENGER, William 225.92'4
Norman, 1905-
The life of Saint Paul [by] W. Norman Pittenger. New York, F. Watts [1968] ix, 141 p. map. 22 cm. (Immortals of philosophy and religion) Bibliography: p. 137-138. [BS2506.P5] 68-22145 3.95
1. Paul, Saint, apostle.

PITTENGER, William 225.9'24 B
Norman, 1905-
The life of Saint Peter, by W. Norman Pittenger. New York, Watts [1971] x, 116 p. 22 cm. (Immortals of philosophy and religion) Includes bibliographical references. The life of the disciple who founded the Christian Church. [BS2515.P58] 92 70-134659 ISBN 0-531-00963-7
1. Peter, Saint, apostle. I. Title.

POLLOCK, John Charles. 225.9'24
The apostle: a life of Paul, by John Pollock. [1st ed.] Garden City, N.Y., Doubleday, 1969. xiv, 244 p. maps (on lining papers) 22 cm. Bibliographical references included in "Notes" (p. [239]-244) [BS2506.P58] 69-15194 4.95
1. Paul, Saint, apostle. I. Title.

PRIESTER, Gertrude 225.92'4 B
Ann.
Who are you, Lord? [By] Gertrude Priester. Illustrated by Shannon Stirnweis. Richmond, CLC Press [1969] 126 p. col. illus. 21 cm. (The Covenant life curriculum) A biography of the Apostle Paul based largely on the Book of Acts telling how he traveled throughout the Biblical world preaching about Jesus Christ. [BS2506.5.P73] 92 70-13550
1. Paul, Saint, apostle—Juvenile literature. I. Stirnweis, Shannon, illus. II. Title.

ROBERTSON, Archibald 225.9'24
Thomas, 1863-1934.
Epochs in the life of Paul : a study of development in Paul's career / A. T. Robertson. Nashville : Broadman Press, 1974. xi, 337 p. ; 20 cm. (A. T. Robertson library) Reprint of the 1909 ed. published by Scribner, New York. Includes indexes. Bibliography: p. 321-327. [BS2505.R57 1974] 74-192551 ISBN 0-8054-1348-0 : pbk. 3.45
1. Paul, Saint, apostle. I. Title.

RUBENSTEIN, Richard L. 225.9'24 B
My brother Paul [by] Richard L. Rubenstein. [1st ed.] New York, Harper & Row [1972] x, 209 p. 22 cm. Includes bibliographical references. [BS2506.R8 1972] 72-124704 ISBN 0-06-067014-2 5.95
1. Paul, Saint, apostle. I. Title.

SANDMEL, Samuel. 225.924
The genius of Paul; a study in history. With a new introd. by the author. New York, Schocken Books [1970, c1958] xvi, 239 p. 21 cm. Includes bibliographical references. [BS2506.S15 1970] 76-111287
1. Paul, Saint, apostle. I. Title.

SANNESS, Palmer. 225.924
The incomparable Paul. Boston, Branden Press [1969] 39 p. 22 cm. [BS2506.S17] 78-83704 1.00
1. Paul, Saint, apostle. I. Title.

SMITH, Roy Lemon, 1887- 225.9'24
From Saul to Paul; the making of an apostle. Nashville, Tidings [1962] 104 p. 19 cm. [BS2506.S5] 62-20562
1. Paul, Saint, apostle. I. Title.

SMITH, Roy Lemon, 1887- 225.9'24
The tentmakers, a story. New York, Abingdon Press [1963] 112 p. illus. 19 cm. [BS2506.5.S4] 63-7332
1. Paul, Saint, apostle — Fiction. I. Title.

STENDAHL, Krister. 225.9'2'4
Paul among Jews and Gentiles, and other essays / Krister Stendahl. Philadelphia : Fortress Press, c1976. ix, 133 p. ; 22 cm. Includes bibliographical references. [BS2506.S76] 75-36450 ISBN 0-8006-1224-8 : 3.75
1. Paul, Saint, Apostle—Addresses, essays, lectures. 2. Bible. N.T. Epistles of Paul—Theology—Addresses, essays, lectures. 3. Christian saints—Turkey—Tarsus—Addresses, essays, lectures. 4. Tarsus, Turkey—Biography—Addresses, essays, lectures. I. Title.

TRENT, Robbie, 1894- 225.9'24 B
Paul, God's adventurer / Robbie Trent ; [ill. by Ron Adair]. Waco, Tex. : Word Books, c1975. 224 p. : ill. ; 23 cm. Includes bibliographical references. [BS2506.T73] 75-10089 ISBN 0-87680-381-8 : 6.95
1. Paul, Saint, apostle. I. Title.

TUCKER, Iva Jewel. 225.9'24 B
Paul, the missionary / Iva Jewel Tucker ; illustrated by Ron Hester. Nashville : Broadman Press, c1976. 46 p. : col. ill. ; 24 cm. (Biblearn series) Discusses the conversion and ministry of Paul the missionary. [BS2506.5.T82] 76-382994 ISBN 0-8054-4228-6 : 3.95
1. Paul, Saint, Apostle—Juvenile literature. 2. Evangelists (Bible)—Biography—Juvenile literature. 3. Bible. N.T.—Biography—Juvenile literature. I. Hester, Ronald. II. Title.

BLAIKLOCK, E. M. 225.93
The archaeology of the New Testament, by E. M. Blaiklock. Grand Rapids, Zondervan Pub. House [1970] 192 p. illus., facsims., maps (part col.), ports. 23 cm. [BS2375.B49] 70-95046 4.95
1. Bible. N.T.—Antiquities. I. Title.

BLAIKLOCK, E M 225.93
Out of the earth; the witness of archaeology to the New Testament. Grand Rapids, Mich., W. B. Eerdmans Pub. Co., 1957. 80p. illus. 19cm. [BS2375.B5] 57-4346
1. Bible. N. T.—Antiq. I. Title.

BLAIKLOCK, E. M. 225.93
Out of the earth; the witness of archaeology to the New Testament. 2d ed. Grand Rapids, Eerdmans, 1961[ ] 92p. 61-4761 2.00
1. Bible. N. T.—Antiq. I. Title.

BLAIKLOCK, E M 225.93
Out of the earth; the witness of archaeology to the New Testament. Grand Rapids, Mich., W. B. Eerdmans Pub. Co., 1957. 80p. illus. 19cm. [BS2375.B5] 57-4346
1. Bible. N. T.—Antiq. I. Title.

FINEGAN, Jack, 1908- 225.93
The archeology of the New Testament; the life of Jesus and the beginning of the early church. Princeton, N.J., Princeton University Press, 1969. xxiv, 273 p. illus., maps. 29 cm. Bibliographical footnotes. [BS2375.F5] 69-18057 ISBN 6-910353-42- 20.00
1. Bible. N.T.—Antiquities. I. Title.

HARRISON, Roland Kenneth 225.93
Archaeology of the New Testament. New York, Association [c.1964] xii, 138p. illus., maps. 23cm. Bibl. 64-19484 3.95
1. Bible. N.T.—Antiq. I. Title.

HARRISON, Roland Kenneth. 225.93
Archaeology of the New Testament [by] R. K. Harrison. New York, Association Press [1964] xii, 138 p. illus., maps. 23 cm. Bibliographical references included in "notes to chapters" (p. [95]-134) Bibliography: p. [135]-136. [BS2375.H3] 64-19484
1. Bible. N. T. — Antiq. I. Title.

KIRSCHBAUM, Engelbert, 225.93
1902-
The tombs of St. Peter & St. Paul. Translated from the German by John Murray. New York, St. Martin's Press [1959] 247 p. illus. 24 cm. Translation of Die Graeber der Apostelfuersten. Includes bibliography. [BS2515.K513 1959] 59-11406
1. Peter, Saint, apostle—Tomb. 2. Paul, Saint, apostle. 3. Vatican (City) San Pietro in Vaticano (Basilica) I. Title.

RAMSAY, William Mitchell, 225.93
Sir 1851-1939.
The bearing of recent discovery on the trustworthiness of the New Testament. Grand Rapids, Mich., Baker Book House, 1953. xiv, 427p. illus., map. 22cm. (The JamesSprunt lectures eor 1911) Bibliographical footnotes. [BS2375.R] A54
1. Bible. N. T.—Evidences, authority, etc. I. Title. II. Series: The James Sprunt lectures, 1911

THOMPSON, John Arthur, 225.93
1913-
Archaeology and the New Testament. Grand Rapids, Eerdmans [1960] 154 p. illus. 19 cm. (A Pathway book) Includes bibliography. [BS621.T5] 59-14588
1. Bible. N.T. — Antiq. 2. Bible — History of contemporary events, etc. I. Title.

THOMPSON, John Arthur, 225.93
1913-
Archaeology and the New Testament. Grand Rapids, Eerdmans [1960] 151 p. illus. 19 cm. (A Pathway book) Includes bibliography. [BS621.T5] 59-14588
1. Bible. N. T.—Antiquities. 2. Bible—History of contemporary events, etc. I. Title.

UNGER, Merrill Frederick, 225.93
1909-
Archaeology and the New Testament. Grand Rapids, Zondervan Pub. House [1962] 350 p. illus., maps. 23 cm. A companion volume to Archaeology and the Old Testament. [BS2375.U5] 62-7371
1. Bible. N.T. — Antiq. 2. Bible. N.T. — History of contemporary events. 3. Bible. N.T. — Evidences, authority, etc. I. Title.

UNGER, Merrill Frederick, 225.93
1909-
Archaeology and the New Testament. Grand Rapids, Zondervan Pub. House [1962] 350 p. illus., maps. 23 cm. A companion volume to Archaeology and the Old Testament. [BS2375.U5] 62-7371
1. Bible. N. T.—Antiquities. 2. Bible. N. T.—History of contemporary events. 3. Bible. N. T.—Evidences, authority, etc. I. Title.

BARRETT, Ethel. 225.95
The people who couldn't be stopped. Glendale, Calif., G/L Regal Books [1970] 138 p. illus. 20 cm. (A Regal venture book) [BS2400.B36] 79-108817 0.69
1. Bible. N.T.—History of Biblical events. I. Title.

BEARDSLEY, Samuel B. 225.95 (j)
The first night of Christmas. Story by Samuel B. Beardsley. Illus. by Margaret Jervis. Norwalk, Conn., C. R. Gibson Co. [1968] 1 v. (unpaged) illus. (part col.) 19 cm. Poem. [PZ8.3.B383Fi] 67-29315
I. Jervis, Margaret, illus. II. Title.

BEEBE, Catherine, 1898- 225.95
The apostles of the Lord. Story by Catherine Beebe; pictures by Robb Beebe. Milwaukee, Bruce Pub. Co. [1958] 126p. illus. 21cm. [BS2401.B44] 58-11343
1. Bible stories, English—N. T. I. Title.

BIBLE. N. T. Gospels. 225.95
English. Selections. 1956. Authorized.
The life of Christ Jesus in Bible language, from the King James Version of the Bible; arr. by Genevieve P. Olson. [San Diego, Calif.] Printed [by] Arts and Crafts Press, c1956. 52p. 19cm. [BT302.I52-121.9] 56-36567
1. Jesus Christ—Biog.—Juvenile literature. I. Olson, Genevieve P. II. Title.

BLIGH, John. 225.95
Historical information for New Testament students. Baltimore, Helicon [1967, c1965] viii, 120 p. illus., maps. 20 cm. Bibliography: p. 118. [BS2410.B6 1967b] 68-476
1. Bible. N.T.—History of contemporary events, etc. I. Title.

BOWIE, Walter Russell, 225.95
1882-1969.
The living story of the New Testament. Illustrated by Douglas Rosa. Englewood Cliffs, N. J., Prentice-Hall [1959] 183 p. illus. 24 cm. [BS2407.B6] 59-13092
1. Bible. N.T.—History of Biblical events. I. Title.

BRUCE, Frederick Fyvie, 225'.95
1910-
New Testament history [by] F. F. Bruce. [1st U.S. ed.] Garden City, N.Y., Doubleday, 1971 [c1969] xiv, 462 p. 22 cm. Bibliography: p. [431]-438. [BS2407.B69 1971] 78-144253 8.95
1. Bible. N.T.—History of Biblical events. 2. Bible. N.T.—History of contemporary events. I. Title.

THE church seasons; 225.95
Christ and the Christian year. [1st ed.] New York, Morehouse-Barlow, 1962. 144p. illus.

21cm. (Episcopal Church fellowship series, course 5-A, reader) [BS2401.C45] 62-8019
1. Church year. 2. Bible stories, English—N. T. I. Series.

CHURCH seasons (The); 225.95
Christ and the Christian year. Course 5-A Reader [and] Teacher's guide. New York, Morehouse [c.1962. 2v.] 144; 160p. col. illus. 21cm. (Episcopal Church fellowship ser.) 62-8019 pap., reader, 1.80; teacher's guide, 2.10
1. Church year. 2. Bible stories, English—N.T. I. Series.

COCAGNAC, A. M. 225.95 (j)
Bible for young Christians; the New Testament, by A. M. Cocagnac and Rosemary Haughton. Illus. by Jacques Lescanff. New York, Macmillan [1967] 125 p. col. illus. 27 cm. Translation of La Bible pour les jeunes. [BS2401.C57] 67-20890
1. Bible stories, English—N.T. I. Haughton, Rosemary, joint author. II. Lescanff, Jacques, illus. III. Bible. N.T. English. Paraphrases. 1967. IV. Title.

CRAIG, Clarence Tucker, 1895- 225.95
The beginning of Christianity [by] Clarence Tucker Craig. Nashville, Abingdon Press [c.1943] 366p. Bibl.: p.343-346. 44-170 1.75 pap.,
1. Bible. N. T.—History of Biblical events. I. Title.

CRAPPS, Robert W., 1925- 225.95
Introduction to the New Testament [by] Robert W. Crapps, Edgar V. McKnight [and] David A. Smith. New York, Ronald Press Co. [1969] xii, 566 p. illus., facsims., maps, plan. 24 cm. Bibliography: p. 532-543. [BS2330.2.C7] 72-75637
1. Bible. N.T.—Introductions. I. McKnight, Edgar V., joint author. II. Smith, David Anthony, 1928- joint author. III. Title.

DAVIS, Sadie Holcombe. 225.95
When Jesus was here. Pictures by Dorothy Handsaker Scott. Nashville, Broadman Press, c1957. unpaged. illus. 25cm. (Little treasure series, 11) [BS2401.D35] 57-13968
1. Bible stories, English—N. T. Gospels. I. Title.

FILSON, Floyd Vivian, 1896- 225.95
A New Testament history; the story of the emerging church [by] Floyd V. Filson. Philadelphia, Westminster Press [1964] xi, 435 p. 16 col. maps. 25 cm. (Westminster aids to the study of the Scriptures) Bibliographical footnotes. [BS2407.F5] 64-15360
1. Bible. N.T.—History of Biblical events. I. Title. II. Series.

FREMANTLE, Anne (Jackson), 1909- ed. 225.95
The greatest Bible stories; a Catholic anthology from world literaturs. New York, Stephen Daye Press [1951] 382 p. 21 cm. [BS2430.F7] 51-3886
1. Bible. N. T.—History of Biblical events—Fiction. 2. Bible. N. T.—Biog. 3. Catholic literature. I. Title.
Contents Omitted.

GLOVER, Gloria (Diener) 1902- 225.95
The story of Jesus. Illustrated by Priscilla Pointer. Chicago, Rand McNally, 1965, c1949. 1 v. (unpaged) col. illus. 26 cm. (A Rand McNally book) [BT302.G5] 65-13184
1. Jesus Christ — Biog. — Juvenile literature. I. Title.

HOLLINSON, Harry 225.95
Background to the New Testament. Illustrated by Leslie Butler. [London] Perry Colour Books [1960[ ] stamped: distributed by SportShelf, New Rochelle, N.Y. 22p. Includes bibliography. illus. (part col.) 19cm. (A Do-you-know book) 60-1842 1.50 bds.,
1. Bible. N.T.—History of contemporary events, etc. I. Title.

JOHNSON, Ethel A. 225.95
My book about Jesus. [Washington] Review and Herald Pub. Assocation, c1962. 61 p. illus. 24 cm. [BT302.J583] 62-14167
1. Jesus Christ — Biog. — Juvenile literature. I. Title.

JOHNSTON, George, June9,1913- 225.95
The secrets of the kingdom. Illus. by Charles E. Hewins. Philadelphia, Westminster Press [1954] 222 p. illus. 22 cm. [BS2407.J6] 54-7083
1. Bible. N.T.—History of Biblical events. I. Title.

JOHNSTON, George, June9,1913- 225.95
The secrets of the kingdom. Illus. by Charles E. Hewins. Philadelphia, Westminster Press [1954] 222p. illus. 22cm. [BS2407.J6] 54-7083
1. Bible. N. T.—History of Biblical events. I. Title.

JONES, Mary Alice, 1898- 225.95
Jesus who helped people, Illustrated by Manning de V. Lee. Chicago, Rand McNally, 1965, c1964. 1 v. (unpaged) col. illus. 27 cm. [BT302.J5885 1965] 65-13186
1. Jesus Christ—Biog.—Juvenile literature. I. Title.

KEE, Howard Clark, comp. 225.9'5
The origins of Christianity; sources and documents. Englewood Cliffs, N.J., Prentice-Hall [1973] xi, 270 p. illus. 23 cm. Bibliography: p. 266-267. [BR129.K44] 73-4830 ISBN 0-13-642553-4 3.95
1. Bible. N.T.—History of contemporary events—Sources. 2. Hebrew literature (Selections: Extracts, etc.) 3. Apocryphal books. I. Title.

KEITH, Alphas William, 1873- 225.95
Back to God and His church. [Oaktown? Ind., 1956] 350p. 23cm. [BS2407.K4] 56-38600
1. Bible. N. T.—History of Biblical events. 2. Bible—Examinations, questions, etc. I. Title.

KOTKER, Norman. 225.95
The Holy Land in the time of Jesus, by the editors of Horizon magazine. Author: Norman Kotker. Consultant: Frederick C. Grant. 1st ed. New York, American Heritage Pub. Co.; book trade and institutional distribution by Harper & Row [1967] 151 p. illus. (part col.) col. maps. 27 cm. (A Horizon caravel book) Bibliography: p. 151. [BS2407.K6] 67-12487
1. Bible. N.T.—History of Biblical events. 2. Bible. N.T.—History of contemporary events, etc. I. Horizon (New York, 1958-) II. Title.

LIETZMANN, Hans, 1875-1942. 225.9'5
The beginnings of the Christian Church. Translated by Bertram Lee Woolf. New York, Scribner [1952] 303p. 23cm. Translation of Die Anfange, published as v. 1 of the author's Geschichte der alten Kirche. [BR129.L53 1952] 53-3008
1. Church history—Primitive and early church. 2. Bible. N.T.—History of contemporary events, etc. 3. Christian literature, Early—Hist. & crit. I. Title.

LOHSE, Eduard, 1924- 225.9'5
The New Testament environment / Eduard Lohse ; translated by John E. Steely. Nashville : Abingdon, c1976. 296 p. : ill. ; 22 cm. Translation of Umwelt des Neuen Testaments. Includes indexes. Bibliography: p. 281-285. [BS2410.L6413] 75-43618 ISBN 0-687-27945-3 : 12.95 pbk. : 6.95
1. Bible. N.T.—History of contemporary events, etc. I. Title.

MACKAIL, John William, 1859-1945. 225.95
The Holy Bible for young readers; the New Testament, being the story of God's chosen people after the coming of Our Lord Jesus Christ upon earth, together with stories of saints and martyrs. Illustrated by Fritz Kredel. Mount Vernon, N. Y., Peter Pauper Press [1951] 157 p. col. illus. 27 cm. First published in 1901 under title: Biblia innocentium: part second. [BS2410.M32 1951] 52-3164
1. Bible. N. T.—History of Biblical events. I. Title.

MACLEAR, George Frederick, 1833-1902. 225.95
A class-book of New Testament history. Grand Rapids, Eerdmans, 1953. 550p. illus. 23cm. [BS2407] 52-10585
1. Bible. N. T.—History of Biblical events. I. Title.

MCMINN, Janie Lancaster. 225.95
The great surprise! Children's stories of the Resurrection and the Holy Spirit. Illustrated by Sybil Brunner Loffland. [1st ed.] New York, Loizeaux Bros. [1960] 145p. illus. 22cm. [BS2401.M25] 60-16104
1. Bible stories, I. Title.

MALHERBE, Abraham J., ed. 225.95
The World of the New Testament. Editor: Abraham J. Malherbe. Austin, Tex., R. B. Sweet [c1967] v. 186 p. 21 cm. (The Living word commentary, 1) Includes bibliographies. [BS2410.W67] 68-5578
1. Bible. N. T.—History of contemporary events, etc. I. Title.

MEYER, Edith Patterson. 225.95
Stories from the Bible: New Testament, retold by Edith Patterson Meyer. Illustrated by Lis Linge. New York, Grosset & Dunlap [1957] 92p. illus. 31cm. [BS2401.M4] 57-12413
1. Bible stories, English—N. T. I. Title.

MORRILL, Madge (Haines) 225.95
Stories Jesus told, and how Bobby and Ruth loved them. Mountain View, Calif., Pacific Press Pub. Association [1950] 128 p. illus. 21 cm. Full name: Madge Arty (Haines) Morrill. [BS2401.M6] 50-2983
1. Bible stories, English — N.T. Gospels I. Title.

OURSLER, Fulton, 1893-1952. 225.95
A child's life of Jesus. Picutres by Elinore Blaisdell. Garden City, N.Y., Doubleday [1959?] c1951. 1 v. (unpaged) illus. (part col.) 22 cm. [BT302.O83] 66-1015
1. Jesus Christ — Biog. — Juvenile literature. I. Blaisdell, Elinore, 1904- illus. II. Title.

OURSLER, Fulton, 1893-1952. 225.95
The greatest faith ever known; the story of the men who first spread the religion of Jesus and of the momentous times in which they lived, by Fulton Oursler and April Oursler Armstrong. [1st ed.] Garden City, N.Y., Doubleday, 1953. 383 p. illus. 22 cm. [BS2618.O8] 53-9979
1. Bible. N.T.—History of Biblical events. 2. Apostles. I. Armstrong, April (Oursler) joint author. II. Title.

POOL, Elizabeth (Routh) 1909- 225.95
The unexpected Messiah. New York, I. Washburn [1961] 294p. 22cm. [BS2407.P65] 61-14131
1. Bible. N. T.—History of Biblical events. I. Title.

POOL, Elizabeth (Routh) 225.95
[Alice Elizabeth (Routh) Pool] 1909-
The unexpected Messiah. New York, Washburn [c.1961] 294p. 61-14131 5.00
1. Bible. N.T.—History of Biblical events. I. Title.

PROCTER, Rosalie. 225.95
Told to Patrick; Bible bed-time stories. Photos. by Ronald Procter. New York, Roy Publishers [1957] 93p. illus. 23cm. [BS2401] 57-9899
1. Bible stories. English—N. T. I. Procter, Patrick. II. Title.

RAMSAY, William Mitchell Sir 225.95
Pictures of the apostolic church; studies in the book of Acts. Grand Rapids, Baker Book House, 1959. xv, 367p. 20cm. 60-1113 3.50
1. Bible. N.T.—History of Biblical events. 2. Church history—Primitive and early church. I. Title.

†SARNO, Ronald A. 225.9'5
The cruel Caesars : their impact on the early church / by Ronald A. Sarno. [Canfield, Ohio] : Alba Books, c1976. 165 p. : maps ; 18 cm. Includes bibliographical references and indexes. [BS2410.S24] 76-21587 ISBN 0-8189-1140-9 pbk. : 1.85
1. Bible. N.T.—History of contemporary events, etc. 2. Church and state—History. 3. Roman emperors. I. Title.

SCHULTZ, Samuel J. 225.9'5
The gospel of Moses [by] Samuel J. Schultz. [1st ed.] New York, Harper & Row [1974] x, 165 p. 21 cm. Bibliography: p. 66-67. [BS635.2.S32 1974] 74-4619 ISBN 0-06-067132-7 5.95
1. Moses. 2. Bible—History of Biblical events. I. Title.
Pbk. 2.95, ISBN 0-06-067133-5.

SHERWIN-WHITE, Adrian Nicholas. 225.95
Roman society and Roman law in the New Testament. Oxford, Clarendon Press, 1963. 204 p. 20 cm. (The Sarum lectures, 1960-1961) [BS2390.S45] 63-2896
1. Bible. N. T.—History of contemporary events, etc. 2. Roman law—Antiq. I. Title.

SHERWIN-WHITE, Adrian Nicholas 225.95
Roman society and Roman law in the New Testament. Oxford Clarendon[dist. New York, Oxford, c.1963. 204p. 20cm. (Sarum lects., 1960-1961) Bibl. 63-2896 4.00
1. Bible. N. T.—History of contemporary events, etc. 2. Roman law—Antiq. I. Title.

SLOAN, William Wilson. 225.95
A survey of the New Testament. Paterson, N.J., Littlefield, Adams, 1962. 302 p. 21 cm. (New students outline series, no. 146) Includes bibliography. [BS2407.S47 1962] 62-3053
1. Bible.N. T. — History of Biblical events. I. Title.

SLOAN, William Wilson. 225.95
A survey of the New Testament. New York, Philosophical Library [1961] 302 p. 22 cm. Includes bibliography. [BS2407.S47] 61-10614
1. Bible. N. T.—History of Biblical events. I. Title.

SLOAN, William Wilson 225.95
A survey of the New Testament. Paterson, N. J., Littlefield [c.] 1962. 302p. 21cm. (New students outline ser., no. 146) Bibl. 62-3053 1.95 pap.,
1. Bible. N. T.—History of Biblical events. I. Title.

WEISS, Johannes, 1863-1914. 225.95
Earliest Christianity; a history of the period A.D. 30-150. English translation edited with a new introd. and bibliography by Frederick C. Grant. New York, Harper [1959] 2 v. 21 cm. (Harper torchbooks, TB53-54) Includes bibliography. [BS2410.W2822] 59-6651
1. Bible. N.T.—History of Biblical events. 2. Bible. N.T.—Theology. 3. Church history—Primitive and early church, ca. 30-600. 4. Theology, Doctrinal—History—Early church, ca. 30-600. I. Title.

WIEMER, Rudolf Otto, 1905- 225.95
The prodigal son. Illus. and design by Reinhard Hermann. Translation by Paul T. Martinsen. Minneapolis, Augsburg Pub. House [1967] [24] p. col. illus. 27 cm. Translation of Der verlorene Sohn. The Bible story of the philandering son whose father celebrated with joy his return home. Modern illustrations. [BT378.P8W483] AC 67
1. Prodigal son (Parable) 2. Bible stories—N.T. I. Title.

WORM, Piet. 225.95
Stories from the New Testament in which Piet Worm tells the stories of St. John the Baptist and the Annunciation of the birth of Jesus in Bethlehem, of His teaching and miracles, His twelve apostles and His death and resurrection. Piet Worm drew the pictures too. [New York, Sheed and Ward, 1958] unpaged. illus. 23 cm. [BS2401.W65] 59-16388
1. Bible stories, English — N. T. Gospels I. Title.

JONES, Clifford Merton. 225.9500222
New Testament illustrations: photographs, maps, and diagrams compiled and introduced by Clifford M. Jones. Cambridge, Cambridge U.P., 1966. 189 p. illus., maps, facsims., tables, diagrs. 26 cm. (The Cambridge Bible commentary: New English Bible) Bibliography: p. 177-178. [BS2410.J6] 66-10046 25/-
1. Bible. N.T.—History of contemporary events, etc. 2. Church history—Primitive and early church, ca. 30-600. I. Title. II. Series.

REICKE, Bo Ivar, 1914- 225.95'009'014
The New Testament era; the world of the Bible from 500 B.C. to A.D. 100, by Bo Reicke. Translated by David E. Green. Philadelphia, Fortress Press [1968] x, 336 p. maps. 23 cm. Translation of Neutestamentliche Zeitgeschichte. Includes bibliographical references. [BS2410.R383] 68-15864 5.75
1. Bible. N.T.—History of contemporary events, etc. I. Title.

DAUGHTERS of St. Paul. 225.95'05
The Bible for young people. Illustrated by De Luca. [Boston] St. Paul Editions [1969, c1968] 136 p. col. illus. 25 cm. Stories from the New Testament recount the birth, youth, miracles, teachings, death, Resurrection, and Ascension of Christ. Includes a separate section on the Acts of the Apostles. [BS2401.D33] 67-29694
1. Bible stories, English—N.T. I. De Luca, Sister, illus. II. Title.

GOSSETT, Bob. 225.9'505
The stranger at Emmaus, and other New Testament stories. [Independence, Mo., Herald Pub. House, 1972] 92 p. 21 cm. Fictionalized retellings of ten New Testament stories. [BS2401.G64] 72-83275 ISBN 0-8309-0076-4 3.00
1. Bible stories, English—N.T. I. Title.

HEEG, Aloysius Joseph, 1895- 225.9'5'05
Jesus and I [by] Aloysius J. Heeg. Chicago, Loyola University Press [1972] 138 p. illus. 16 cm. Includes question-and-answer text of the First communion catechism prepared from the Baltimore catechism. [BS2401.H4 1972] 72-178996 ISBN 0-8294-0214-4
1. Bible stories, English—N.T. 2. First communion—Instruction and study. I. Baltimore catechism. II. Title.

*IVERS, Richard H. 225.9505
His name was Joseph. New York, Vantage [c.1966] 109p. 21cm. 2.95 bds.,
I. Title.

MULLAN, Carol. 225.9'505
New Testament Bible stories / as told by Carol Mullan ; illustrated by Dan Waring. Racine, Wis. : Golden Press, [1975] [20] p. : col. ill. ; 32 cm. Retells simply some events from the life of Jesus and several of His

parables. [BS2401.M77] 75-312224 ISBN 0-307-10502-4 : 1.25
1. Bible stories, English—N.T. I. Waring, Dan. II. Title.

PATCH, Robert C. 225.9'505
Illustrated stories about the New Testament / Robert C. Patch, narrative ; Stuart Heimdal, artist and art director ; Paul R. Cheesman, correlator and writer, director of research and photography. 1st ed. Provo, Utah : Promised Land Publications, 1973- , c1972- v. : col. ill. ; 32 cm. The volumes chronicle the life of Jesus and the work of the apostles and include photographic essays of the Holy Land. [BS2401.P35] 75-312226
1. Bible stories, English—N.T. I. Heimdal, Stuart, ill. II. Cheesman, Paul R. III. Title.

226 Gospels & Acts

ALLSTROM, Elizabeth C j226
Truly, I say to you, by Elizabeth Allstrom. Woodcuts by Mel Silverman. New York, Abingdon Press [1966] 62 p. illus. (part col.) 25 cm. [BT380.2.A65] 66-10565
1. Sermon on the Mount — Juvenile literature. I. Silverman, Mel, illus. II. Title.

ALLSTROM, Elizabeth C. 226
Truly, I say to you. Woodcuts by Mel Silverman. Nashville, Abingdon [c.1966] 62p. illus. (pt. col.) 25cm. [BT380.2.A65] 66-10565 3.00
1. Sermon on the Mount — Juvenile literature. I. Silverman, Mel, illus. II. Title.

BARCLAY, William, lecturer in the University of Glasgow. 226
Introduction to the first three Gospels / by William Barclay. A rev. ed. of The first three Gospels. Philadelphia : Westminster Press, c1975. p. cm. Includes indexes. Bibliography: p. [BS2555.2.B27 1975] 75-37545 ISBN 0-664-24798-9 : 5.95
1. Bible. N.T. Gospels—Introductions. I. Title.

BARRETT, Charles Kingsley. 226
Luke the historian in recent study, by C. K. Barrett. With a new, select bibliography. [New ed.] Philadelphia, Fortress Press [1970, c1961] 80 p. 20 cm. (Facet books. Biblical series, 24) Bibliography: p. [77]-80. [BS2465.B27 1970] 75-81527 1.00
1. Luke, Saint. I. Title.

BARTELS, Robert A 226
Kerygma or Gospel tradition--which came first? Minneapolis, Augsburg Pub. House [1961] 126p. 22cm. (An Augsburg theological monograph) Includes bibliography. [BS2555.2B3] 61-14963
1. Bible, N. T. Gospels—Criticism, Form. 2. Preaching—Hist.—Early church. I. Title.

BECK,Dwight Marion. 226
Through the Gospels to Jesus. [1st ed.] New York, Harper [1954] 468p. 22cm. [BS2555.B49] 54-5847
1. Bible. N. T. Gospels—Criticism, interpretation, etc. 2. Jesus Christ—Biog. 3. Bible. N. T.—History of contemporary events, etc. I. Title.

BEERS, Victor Gilbert, 1928- 226
Patterns for prayer from the Gospels [by] V. Gilbert Beers. Old Tappan, N.J., Revell [1972] 95 p. 18 cm. [BV228.B4] 72-3909 ISBN 0-8007-0545-9 2.95
1. Bible. N.T. Gospels—Prayers. I. Title.

*BERGEY, Alyce 226
The fisherman's surprise; Luke 5:1-11 and John 21 for children. Illus. by Bill Behm. St. Louis, Concordia, 1967. 1v. (unpaged) col. illus. 21cm. (Arch bks.) .35 pap.,
1. Bible—N.T.—Luke—Juvenile literature. 2. Bible-N.T.—John—Juvenile literature. I. Title.

BIBLE. N. T. English. 1956. Wuest. 226
Expanded translation of the Greek New Testament [by] Kenneth S. Wuest. Grand Rapids, W. B. Eerdmans Pub. Co., 1956- v. 23cm. Contents.v. 1. The Gospels. [BS2095.W7] 56-12804
I. Wuest, Kenneth Samuel, 1893- tr. II. Title.

BIBLE. N. T. English. 1956. Wuest. 226
Expanded translation of the Greek New Testament [by] Kenneth S. Wuest. Grand Rapids, Eerdmans, 1956-[59] 3 v. 23cm. Contents.v. 1. The Gospels.--v. 2. Acts through Ephesians. --v. 3. Phillippians through the Revelation. [BS2095W7] 56-12804
I. Wuest, Kenneth Samuel, 1893- tr. II. Title.

BIBLE. N.T. English. Haugerud. Selections. 1977. 226
The word for us : the Gospels of John and Mark, Epistles to the Romans and the Galatians / restated in inclusive language by Joann Haugerud. 1st ed. Seattle : Coalition on Women and Religion, c1977. iv, 119 p. ; 22 cm. [BS2261.H38] 77-83418
I. Haugerud, Joann. II. Title.

BIBLE. N. T. Epistles and Gospels, Liturgical. Lithuanian (1579) 1966. Vilentas 226
Baltramiejus Vilentas' Lithuanian translation of the Gospels and Epistles, 1579; Ed. by Gordon B. Ford, Jr. Louisville, Ky., Pyramid Pr., 1966 v. 28cm. Includes facsim. of the 1579 Konigsberg ed., propd. from the Vilnius State Univ. copy Lr 1387) with t.p. reading: Euangelias bei Epistolas, nedeliu ir schwentuju dienosu skaitomosias, BazniczosuChrikszonischkosu, pilnai ir wiernai perguldita ant lietuwischka szodzia, per Baltramieju Willenta . . .Ischspaustas Karalauczui per J. Osterbergera, 1579. Text in Gothic type, with a transcription in roman type. The life and works of Baltramiejus Vilentas (20 1.) included in v. 1. [BS2547.A4L5 1966] 66-1610 36.00
I. Vilentas, Baltramiejus, 1525 (ca.)-1587, tr. II. Ford, Gordon B., ed. III. Bible. N.T. Epistles and Gospels, Liturgical. Lithuanian. 1966. IV. Title. V. Title: Euangelias bei Epistoals.

BIBLE. N. T. Gospels and Acts. English. 1959. Authorized. 226
The Gospels of Saint Matthew, Saint Mark, Saint Luke & Saint John, together with the Acts of the apostles, according to the Authorized King James version, with reproductions of religious paintings in the Samuel H. Kress collection. New York, Arranged & printed by R. Ellis for the Samuel H. Kress Foundation, 1959. 253p. col. illus. 33cm. [BS2548.A3 1959] 60-828
1. Bible. N. T.—Pictures, illustrations etc. I. Samuel H. Kress Foundation. II. Title.

BIBLE. N. T. Gospels. English. 1953. Rieu. 226
The four Gospels, a new translation from the Greek by E. V. Rieu. Baltimore, Penguin Books [1953] xxxiii, 250p. 19cm. (The Penguin classics, L 32) [BS2553.R42 1953] 53-8747
I. Rieu, Emile Victor, 1887- tr. II. Title.

BIBLE. N. T. Gospels. English. 1954. Authorized. 226
Miracles, parables, and teachings of Jesus; arr. to show the teachings of Jesus in red letters. Redwood City, Calif., West Trade Bindery and Pub. Co. [1954] xxii, 223p. 17cm. 'The Book of Revelation':p. 197-223. [BS2553.A3 1954] 54-26093
I. Bible. N. T. Revelation. English. 1954. Authorized. II. Title.

BIBLE. N. T. Gospels. English. 1957. Heenan. 226
The word of salvation. Translated into English by John J. Heenan. Milwaukee, Bruce Pub. Co. [1957- I. The Gospel according to Saint Mark, by J. Huby. I.aDurand, Alfred, 1857?-1928. II.aHuby, Joseph, 1878-1948. v. 23cm. Translated from a series of French commentaries entitled Verbum salutis. Contents.[1] Translation and explanation of I. The Gospel according to Saint Matthew, by A. Durand, and [BS2555.H372] 57-7757
1. Bible. N. T. Gospels—Commentaries. I. Heenan, John J., tr. II. Title.

BIBLE. N. T. Gospels. English. 1957. Heenan. 226
The word of salvation. Translated into English by John J. Heenan. Milwaukee, Bruce Pub. Co. [1957] 2v. 28cm. Translatated from a series of French commentaries entitled Verbum salutis. Contents.[1] Translation and explanation of 1. The Gospel according to Saint Matthew, by A. Durand, and II. The Gospel according to Saint Mark, by J. Huby.--[2] Translation and explanation of III. The Gospel according to Saint Luke, by A. Valensin and J. Huby, and IV. The Gospel according to Saint John, by A. Durand. [BS2555.H372] 57-7757
1. Bible. N. T. Gospels—Commentaries. I. Heenan, John J., tr. II. Durand, Alfred, 1857?-1928. III. Huby, Joseph, 1878-1948. IV. Valensin, Albert, 1873-1944. V. Title.

BIBLE. N.T. Gospels. English. 1958. Phillips 226
The Gospels, translated into modern English, by J. B. Phillips. New York, Macmillan, 1958 [c1957] ix, 252p. map (on lining paper) 22cm. Bibliography: p. viii. [BS2553.P5 1958] 57-14426
I. Phillips, John Bertram, 1906- tr. II. Title.

BIBLE. N.T. Gospels. English. Authorized. Selections. 1968. 226
The life and morals of Jesus of Nazareth, extracted textually from the Gospels of Matthew, Mark, Luke, and John, by Thomas Jefferson. New York, Eakins Press [1968] 152 p. 14 cm. "Jefferson's original volume with his notes, is in the collection of the United States National Museum, Washington, D.C." [BT299.2.J4] 68-27400 3.95
1. Jesus Christ—Biography—Sources, Biblical. 2. Jesus Christ—Teachings. I. Jefferson, Thomas, Pres. U.S., 1743-1826, comp. II. Title.

BIBLE. N.T. Gospels. English. Selections. 1902 226
The Jefferson Bible; being the life & morals of Jesus Christ of Nazareth, extracted textually from the Gospels of Matthew, Mark, Luke & John. By Thomas Jefferson. Greenwich, Conn., Fawcett [1961, c.1946] 128p. illus. (Premier bk. d145) .50 pap.,
I. Jefferson, Thomas, pres. U. S., 1743-1826, ed. II. Bible. English Selections. N.T. Gospels. 1902. III. Title.

BIBLE. N. T. Gospels. English. Selections. 1951. 226
The life and morals of Jesus of Nazareth, extracted textually from the Gospels of Matthew, Mark, Luke and John. by Thomas Jefferson; edited, with an introd., by Henry Wilder Foote. Boston, Beacon Press, 1951. 151 p. facsims. 19 cm. With facsim. of original t. p.: The life and morals of Jesus of Nazareth extracted textually from the Gospels in Greek, Latin, French & English. [BS2549.J4E5 1951] 51-10842
I. Jefferson, Thomas, Pres. U. S., 1743-1826, comp. II. Foote, Henry Wilder, 1875- ed. III. Title.

BIBLE. N.T. Gospels. English. Selections. 1966. Revised standard. j226
Parables for boys and girls. Selected by Marjorie Ingzel. [Camden, N.J.] T. Nelson [1966] 64 p. 16 cm. [BT373.E5] 66-14895
1. Jesus Christ—Parables—Texts. 2. Jesus Christ—Parables—Juvenile literature. I. Ingzel, Marjorie, comp. II. Title.

BIBLE. N.T. Gospels. English. Selections. 1966. Revised standard version. 226 (j)
Parables for boys and girls. Selected by Marjorie Ingzel. [Camden, N.J.] T. Nelson [1966] 64 p. 16 cm. [BT373.E5 1966] 66-14895
1. Jesus Christ—Parables—Texts. 2. Jesus Christ—Parables—Juvenile literature. I. Ingzel, Marjorie, comp. II. Title.

BIBLE. N.T. Gospels. English. Selections. 1967. Revised standard. 226
The story of Jesus; a little New Testament. Bible text selected from the Revised standard version. With illus. by Maud and Miska Petersham. New York, Macmillan [1967] vii, 103 p. col. illus. 20 cm. Illustrations accompany excerpts from Biblical text tracing the life of Jesus. Combined ed. of Jesus' story, first published in 1942, and The story of Jesus, first published in 1944. [BT302.P443] 67-25223
1. Jesus Christ—Biography—Juvenile literature. 2. Bible stories, English—N.T. Gospels. I. Petersham, Maud (Fuller) 1890- illus. II. Petersham, Miska, 1888-1960, illus. III. Title.

BIBLE. N.T. Gospels. Greek. Nestle-Aland. 1969. 226
Synopticon: the verbal agreement between the Greek texts of Matthew, Mark and Luke contextually exhibited [edited by] William R. Farmer. London, Cambridge U.P., 1969. [11], 229 p. 25 cm. [BS2551.A2 1969] 78-77287 10/-/-
1. Bible. N.T. Gospels—Harmonies. I. Farmer, William Reuben, ed. II. Title.

BIBLE. N. T. Gospels. English. 1953. Phillips. 226
The Gospels, translated into modern English by J. B. Phillips. New York, Macmillan, 1953 [c1952] x, 243 p. map (on lining paper) 22 cm. Bibliography: p. ix-x. [BS2553.P5 1953] 53-964
I. Phillips, J. B., tr.

BLACK, Matthew. 226
An Aramaic approach to the Gospels and Acts. 2d ed. Oxford, Clarendon Press, 1954. vii, 304p. 23cm. Bibliographical footnotes. [BS2555.B] A 55
1. Bible. N. T. Gospels and Acts—Criticism, interpretation, etc. I. Title.

BORGONGINI-DUCA, Francesco, Cardinal. 226
The Word of God; short meditations of the Sunday Gospels. A translation by Francis Cardinal Spellman. New York, J. J. Crawley [1957] 243p. illus. 22cm. [BX2185.B7 1957] 58-17804
1. Bible. N. T. Epistles and Gospels, Liturgical— Meditations. I. Speliman, Francis Joseph, Cardinal, 1889- tr. II. Title.

BRIGGS, Robert Cook, 1915- 226
Interpreting the Gospels; an introduction to methods and issues in the study of the Synoptic Gospels [by] R. C. Briggs. Nashville, Abingdon Press [1969] 188 p. 23 cm. Rev. ed. published in 1973 under title: Interpreting the New Testament today. Includes bibliographical references. [BS2555.2.B7] 69-19738 ISBN 0-687-19326-5 4.50
1. Bible. N.T. Gospels—Criticism, interpretation, etc. I. Title.

BULTMANN, Rudolf 226
The History of the synoptic tradition / Rudolf Bultmann ; translated by John Marsh ; revised edition. New York : Harper & Row, 1976 c1963. 462 p. ; 21 cm. Includes index. Bibliography: p. 381-455 [BS2555.B723] ISBN 0-06-06-1172-3 pbk. : 4.95
1. Bible. N.T. Gospels—Criticism, Form. I. Title. II. Title: Title: The synoptic tradition.
L.C. card no. for original edition: 62-7282.

BULTMANN, Rudolf Karl, 1884- 226
The history of the synoptic tradition. Tr. by John Marsh. New York, Harper [c.1963] viii, 456p. 24cm. Bibl. 62-7282 8.50
1. Bible. N. T. Gospels—Criticism, Form. I. Title. II. Title: The synoptic tradition.

BULTMANN, Rudolf Karl, 1884- 226
The history of the synoptic tradition [by] Rudolf Bultmann. Translated by John Marsh. Rev. ed. New York, Harper & Row [1968, c1963] viii, 462 p. 24 cm. Translation of Die Geschichte der synoptischen Tradition. "Second edition 1968 with corrections and with additions from the 1962 supplement." Includes bibliographical references. [BS2555.B7233 1968] 68-27093 9.50
1. Bible. N.T. Gospels—Criticism, Form. I. Title.

BULTMANN, Rudolf Karl, 1884- 226
The history of the synoptic trandition. Translated by John Marsh. New York, Harper & Row [1963] vii, 456 p. 24 cm. Bibliographical footnotes. [BS2555.B7233] 62-7282
1. Bible. N.T. Gospels — Criticism, Form. I. Title. II. Title: The synoptic tradition.

BUNDY, Walter Ernest, 1889- 226
Jesus and the first three Gospels; an introduction to the synoptic tradition. Cambridge, Harvard University Press, 1955. xxiii, 598p. 25cm. Bibliographical footnotes. [BS2555.B725] 53-10868
1. Bible. N. T. Gospels—Criticism, interpretation, etc. I. Title.

CADBURY, Henry Joel, 1883- 226
Behind the Gospels [by] Henry J. Cadbury. [Wallingford, Pa., Pendle Hill Publications, 1968] 31 p. 20 cm. (Pendle Hill pamphlet 160) Bibliographical footnotes. [BS2555.2.C27] 68-8591 0.55
1. Bible. N. T. Gospels—Criticism, Form. I. Title.

CALLIES, Fritz A. 226
God's children pray; the Lord's prayer in children's words. Milwaukee, Northwestern Pub. House, 1963. 31p. illus. 28cm. 63-14673 .98
1. Lord's prayer—Juvenile literature. I. Title.

CAMPBELL, D. B. J. 226
The Synoptic Gospels; a commentary for teachers and students [by] D. B. J. Campbell. Foreword by Adam Fox. New York, Seabury Press [1969, c1966] 166 p. 21 cm. (A Seabury paperback, SP64) [BS2555.3.C3 1969] 74-6898 2.25
1. Bible. N.T. Gospels—Commentaries. I. Title.

DIBELIUS, Martin, 1883-1947 226
From tradition to Gospel [Tr. from the German rev. 2d ed. in collaboration with the author by Bertram Lee Woolf] New York, Scribners [1965] 311p. 21cm. (Scribner lib., SL124) Bibl. [BS2555.D52] 1.65 pap.,
1. Bible. N. T. Gospels—Criticism, interpretation, etc. 2. Bible—Criticism, interpretation, etc.—N. T. Gospels. I. Woolf, Bertram Lee, 1884- tr. II. Title.

EDWARDS, Richard Alan. 226
A concordance to Q / Richard A. Edwards. Missoula, Mont. : Society of Biblical Literature : distributed by Scholars Press, [1975] p. cm. (Sources for Biblical study ; 7) [BS2555.5.E38] 75-6768 ISBN 0-88414-052-0 (Society of Biblical Literature) : 7.00
1. Q document (Biblical criticism)—Concordances. I. Title. II. Series.

ELLINGSEN, Harald F J. 226
Homiletic thesaurus on the Gospels. Grand Rapids, Baker Book House, 1949-50. 3 v. 24 cm. Contents.[1] Matthew.--[2] Mark-Luke.--[3] John. [BS2555.E5] 50-2106
1. Bible. N. T. Gospels—Sermons—Outlines. I. Title.

ELMER, Irene 226
The boy who ran away; Luke 15: 1-2 for

children. Illustrated by Sally Mathews. St. Louis, Concordia Pub. House [1964] [32] p. col. illus. 21 cm. (Arch books) Quality religious books for children. [BT378.P8E48] 63-23143
1. Prodigal son (Parable) — Juvenile literature. I. Title.

ELMER, Irene 226
The boy who ran away: Luke 15:1-2 for children. Illus. by Sally Mathews. St. Louis, Concordia [c.1964] [32]p. col. illus. 21cm. (Arch bks.) 63-23143 .35 pap.,
1. Prodigal son (Parable)—Juvenile literature. I. Title.

FANNON, Patrick, 1929- 226
The four Gospels; a short introduction to their making and message. Notre Dame, Ind., Fides Publishers [1966, c1964] 113 p. 18 cm. (A Fides dome book, D-49) [BS2555.2.F27 1966] 66-20179
1. Bible. N.T. Gospels—Introductions. I. Title.

FARMER, James Leonard. 226
John and Jesus in their day and ours; social studies in the Gospels. New York, Psychomedical Library, 1956. 304p. 22cm. (Religion and society) [BS2456.F3] 56-28904
1. John the Baptist. 2. Jesus Christ—Biog. 3. Sociology, Biblical. I. Title.

FERRE, Nels Fredrick Solomon, 1908- 226
A theology for Christian prayer. Nashville, Tenn., Tidings [1963] 71 p. illus. 19 cm. [BV210.2.F4] 63-21518
1. Prayer. I. Title.

FERRE, Nels Fredrick Solomon, 1908- 226
A theology for Christian prayer. Nashville, Tenn., Tidings [1963] 71 p. illus. 19 cm. [BV210.2.F4] 63-21518
1. Prayer. I. Title.

*FIELDHOUSE, Marvin L. 226
Another gospel [by] Marvin L. Fieldhouse. 2nd ed. Jericho, N.Y., Exposition Press [1974] 141 p. 22 cm. [BS2555.3] ISBN 0-682-47912-8 5.50
1. Bible. N.T. Gospels—Criticism. I. Title.

FORELL, Betty 226
Little Benjamin and the first Christmas: Luke 2:1-18 for children. Illus. by Betty Wind. St. Louis, Concordia [c.1964. 32]p. col. illus. 21cm. (Arch bks.) 63-23146 .35 pap.,
1. Jesus Christ—Nativity—Juvenile literature. I. Title.

FORESTIER, Peter, 1882- 226
The kingdom is yours; Gospel commentary. Translated by Angeline Bouchard. Chicago, Fides Publishers [1954-cv. 21cm. Translation of Meditations sur l Evengile. [BS2555.F613] 54-745
1. Bibl. N. T. Gospels—Commentaries. I. Title.

GILMOUR, Samuel MacLean, 1905- 226
The gospel Jesus preached. Philadelphia, Westminster Press [1957] 238p. 21cm. Includes bibliography. [BS2415.G57] 57-5075
1. Jesus Christ—Teachings. 2. Bible. N. T. Gospels—Criticism, interpretation, etc. I. Title.

GLUNZ, Hans. 226
Die lateinische vorlage der Westsachsischen evangelienversion, von dr. Hans Glunz. Leipzig, B. Tauchnitz, 1928 New York Johnson Reprint, 1967. 104p. 24cm. (Added t.-p.: Beitrage zur englischen philologie . . . 9. hft.) The author's inaugural dissertation, Munich. Verzeichnis der zu vorliegender arbeit benutzten literatur: p. [10]-12. [BS132.G5] 29-21353 4.00 pap.,
1. Bible. N.T. Gospels—Versions, Anglo-Saxon. 2. Bible. N.T. Gospels—Versions, Latin. 3. Bible. N.T.—Criticism, Textual. I. Title.

GRANT, Frederick Clifton, 1891- ed. & tr. 226
Form criticism; two essays on New Testament research. [Tr. from German. Gloucester, Mass., Peter Smith, 1963, c.1934, 1962] 161p. 21cm. (Harper torch-bk., Acad. lib. rebound) 3.25
1. Bible. N.T. Gospels—Criticism, interpretation, etc. 2. Church history—Primitive and early church. I. Bultmann, Rudolph Karl, 1884- II. Kundzins, Karlis, 1883- III. Title.
Contents omitted.

GRANT, Frederick Clifton, 1891- 226
The Gospels: their origin and their growth. [1st ed.] New York, Harper [1957] 216p. 22cm. Includes bibliography. [BS2555.G684] 57-7352
1. Bible. N.T. Gospels—Criticism, interpretation, etc. I. Title.

GRAY, George, 1872- 226
One mediator, a fourfold revelation; the one mediator in Matthew, Mark, Luke, and John. [1st ed.] New York, Loizeaux Bros. [1951] 192 p. illus. 20 cm. [BS2555.G688] 52-20828
1. Bible. N. T. Gospels—Introductions. I. Title.

*HEIM, Ralph D. 226
Four pictures of Christ, by Ralph D. Heim, Frank W. Klos. Philadelphia, Lutheran Church Pr. [c.1965] 143p. illus. 21cm. (LCA sch. of religion ser.) 1.50; 1.25, pap., teachers guide, pap.,
I. Title.

*HILL, Dave. 226
The most wonderful King: Luke 19:28--24:43 and John 12:12--20:31 for children. Written by Dave Hill, illus. by Betty Wind. St. Louis, Concordia, 1968. 1v. (unpaged) illus. (pt. col.) 21cm. (Arch bks., set no. 5, 59-1154) .35 pap.,
1. Bible. N.T. Luke—Juvenile literature. I. Title.

IRONSIDE, Henry Allan, 1876-1951. 226
The mission of the Holy Spirit; and, Praying in the Holy Spirit. [Combined ed.] New York, Loizeaux Bros. [1950] 61, 64p. 20cm. [BV210.I7] 55-41750
1. Prayer. 2. Holy Spirit. I. Title. II. Title: Praying in the Holy Spirit.

KEE, Howard Clark. 226
Jesus in history; an approach to the study of the Gospels. New York, Harcourt, Brace & World [1970] viii, 280 p. 21 cm. Includes bibliographical references. [BS2555.2.K43] 73-97266
1. Jesus Christ—Biography—Sources. 2. Bible. N.T. Gospels—Criticism, interpretation, etc. I. Title.

KEENE, James Calvin. 226
Meditations on the Gospels. New York, Abingdon Press [1959] 96 p. 21 cm. [BS2555.4.K4] 59-10363
1. Bible. N. T. Gospels—Meditations. I. Title.

KELLY, William, 1821-1906. 226
Lectures on the Gospel of Matthew. New ed., rev. New York, Loizeaux Bros. [1950] 519p. 19cm. [BS2575.K4 1950] 55-41749
1. Bible. N. T. Matthew—Commentaries. I. Title.

KEVIN, Neil. 226
Out of Nazareth. New York, D.McKay [1953] 189p. 21cm. [BS550.K4] 53-7545
1. Bible stories, English—N. T. Gospels. I. Title.

KLEVER, Anita. 226
Stories Jesus told. Illustrated by Jo Polseno. [Chicago] Rand McNally [1967] 45 p. illus. (part col.) 24 cm. Stories retold from the many parables accredited to Jesus. [BT376.K6] AC 67
1. Jesus Christ—Parables. 2. Bible stories. I. Polseno, Jo, illus. II. Title.

KNOX, Wilfred Lawrence, 1886- 226
The sources of the Synoptic Gospels. Edited by H. Chadwick. Cambridge [Eng.] University Press, 1953- v. 23cm. [BS2555.K58] 53-8788
1. Bible. N. T. Gospels— Criticism, interpretation, etc. I. Title.

KRAMER, Janice 226
Eight bags of gold: Matthew 25: 14-30 for children. Illus. by Sally Mathews. St.Louis, Concordia, c.1964 [32]p. col. illus. 21cm. (Arch bks.) 64-16985 .35 pap.,
1. The talents (Parable) Juvenile literature. I. Title.

KRAMER, Janice 226
The good Samaritan: Luke 10:25-37 for children. Illus. by Sally Mathews. St. Louis, Concordia, c.1964. [32]p. col. illus. 21cm. (Arch bks.) 63-23369 .35 pap.,
1. Good Samaritan (Parable)—Juvenile literature. I. Title.

KRAMER, Janice 226
The rich fool: Luke 12: 16-21 for children. Illus. by Sally Mathews. St. Louis, Concordia, c.1964 [32]p. col. illus. 21cm. (Arch bks., Quality religious bks. for children, 59-1109) 64-16984 .35 pap.,
1. Rich fool (Parable)—Juvenile literature. I. Title.

*KRAMER, Janice. 226
The unforgiving servant: Matthew 18:23-35 for children. Written by Janice Kramer, illus. by Sally Matthews. St. Louis, Concordia, 1968. 1v. (unpaged) illus. (pt. col.) 21cm. (Arch bks., set no. 5, 59-1154) .35 pap.,
1. Bible. N.T. Matthew—Juvenile literature. I. Title.

*LANE, Thomas Clifford 226
The parables. New York, Vantage [c.1964] 127p. 21cm. 2.50
I. Title.

LOCKWOOD, Myna 226
Jesus tells a story; the parables. Illus. by Mae Gerhard. New York, Guild [dist. Golden, c.1962] 46p. col. illus. 29cm. (Bk. for young Catholics) 62-3915 2.95
1. Jesus Christ—Parables—Juvenile Literature. I. Title.

LOVE, Julian Price, 1894- 226
The gospel and the Gospels. Nashville, Abingdon-Cokesbury Press [1953] 191p. 21cm. [BS2555.L65] 53-6352
1. Bible. N. T. Gospels—Criticism, interpretation, etc. 2. Bible. N. T. Gospels—Theology. I. Title.

MAIER, Walter A., 1925- 226
Form criticism reexamined [by] Walter A. Maier. St. Louis, Concordia Pub. House [1973] 46 p. 23 cm. (Contemporary theology series) Includes bibliographical references. [BS2555.2.M28 1973] 73-80314 ISBN 0-570-06722-7
1. Bible. N.T. Gospels—Criticism, Form. I. Title.

*MAXWELL, Arturo S. 226
Las bellas historias de la biblia, v.7-10. Mexico, D.F., Ediciones Interamericanas [Mountain View, Calif., Pacific Pr. Pub., c.1956, 1965] 4v. (various p.) col. illus. 26cm. Spanish text. 8.75 ea.,
I. Title.

MILLER, Fred, 1908- 226
Meditations from Matthew. New York, Carlton Press, 1961. 97p. 21cm. (A Reflection book) [BS2575.4.M5] 61-66698
1. Bible. N. T. Matthew—Meditations. I. Title.

MONTEFIORE, Claude Joseph Goldsmid, 1858-1938. 226
Rabbinic literature and Gospel teachings. New York, Ktav Pub. House, 1970. xlii, 442 p. 24 cm. (The Library of Biblical studies) Reprint of the 1930 ed. with Prolegomenon by Eugene Mihaly. Bibliography: p. xxxiii-xxxiv. [BS2555.M632 1970] 68-19731 ISBN 0-87068-088-9
1. Bible. N.T. Gospels—Criticism, interpretation, etc. 2. Rabbinical literature—Relation to the New Testament. I. Title. II. Series.

MOON, Alleen. 226
A study of the Gospels, teacher's guide for use with senior high school pupils in weekday church school classes. Nashville, Published for the Cooperative Publication Association by Abingdon-Cokesbury Press [1952] 123p. 20cm. (The Cooperative series texts for weekday religious education) [BS2556.M6] 53-6353
1. Bible. N. T. Gospels—Study—Text-books. I. Title.

MUELLER, Virginia. 226
The king's invitation; Matthew 22:1-14 for children. Illustrated by Jim Roberts. St. Louis, Concordia Pub. House [1968] [32] p. col. illus. 21 cm. (Arch books) A retelling in verse of Jesus' parable about the king who gave a wedding feast for his son. [BS2575.5.M8] AC 68
1. Bible. N.T. Matthew XXII, 1-14—Poetry. 2. Bible stories—New Testament. I. Roberts, Jim, illus. II. Title.

MUELLER, Virginia. 226
The secret journey; Matthew 2:13-23 for children. Illustrated by Betty Wind. St. Louis, Concordia Pub. House [1968] [32] p. col. illus. 21 cm. (Arch books) Tells in verse of Joseph and Mary's flight into Egypt with their newborn child and their return to Nazareth when Jesus was a small boy. [BS2575.5.M82] AC 68
1. Bible. N.T. Matthew II, 13-23—Poetry. 2. Bible stories—New Testament. I. Wind, Betty, illus. II. Title.

OLSEN, Kermit Robert, 1914- 226
The magnitude of prayer. [Westwood, N.J. [Revell [1962] 94p. 20cm. Sequel to First steps in prayer. [BV210.2.O4] 62-10737
1. Prayer. I. Title.

*OLTMANN, George 226
Hjalmar's Christmas story. New York, Vantage [1967] 92p. front. 21cm. 2.75 bds.,
I. Title.

PALMER, Humphrey. 226
The logic of Gospel criticism: an account of the methods and arguments used by textual, documentary, source, and form critics of the New Testament. London, Melbourne [etc.] Macmillan; New York, St. Martin's, 1968 x, 260p. illus. 23cm. Bibl. [BS2555.2.P27] 68-15304 10.00 lib. ed.,
1. Bible, N. T. Gospels—Criticism, interpretation, etc. 2. Bible, N. T.—Criticism, interpretation, etc. I. Title.

PARKER, Pierson. 226
The Gospel before Mark. Chicago, University of Chicago Press [1953] 266 p. 24 cm. [BS2555.P27] 53-11443
1. Bible. N.T. Gospels—Criticism, interpretation, etc. I. Title.

PATTON, Carl Safford, 1866-1939 226
Sources of the synoptic Gospels, by Carl S. Patton . . . New York, London, Macmillan 1915; New York, Johnson Reprint, 1967. xiii, 263p. 23cm. (Half-title: Univ. of Mich. studies. Humanistic ser., vol. v.) The author's doctoral dissertation, Univ. of Mich., but not pub. as a thesis, [BS2555.P35] 15-19244 20.00 pap.,
1. Title.

PERRIN, Norman. 226
What is redaction criticism? Philadelphia, Fortress Press [1969] ix, 86 p. 22 cm. (Guides to Biblical scholarship) Bibliography: p. 82-86. [BS2555.2.P47] 72-81529 2.25
1. Bible. N.T. Gospels—Criticism, interpretation, etc. I. Title. II. Title: Redaction criticism.

PITTSBURGH Festival on the Gospels, 1970. 226
Jesus and man's hope. [Pittsburgh] Pittsburgh Theological Seminary [1970-71] 2 v. 24 cm. A Perspective book. Includes bibliographical references. [BS2555.2.P58 1970] 74-22638 7.00 (v. 1)
1. Bible. N.T. Gospels—Addresses, essays, lectures. I. Pittsburgh. Theological Seminary. II. Title.

PRENTICE, William Kelly, 1871- 226
The gospel of the kingdom of God, a study. Boston, Christopher Pub. House [1953] 200p. 21cm. [BT303.P7] 53-9089
1. Bible. N. T. Gospels—Criticism, interpretation, etc. 2. Jesus Christ—Teachings. 3. Christianity—Origin. I. Title.

PRICE, Eugenia. 226
Learning to live from the Gospels. [1st ed.] Philadelphia, Lippincott, [1968] 222 p. 21 cm. The author's favorite Gospel verses with her reflections on them. [BS2555.4.P7] 68-29733 3.95
1. Bible. N.T. Gospels—Meditations. 2. Christian life. I. Title.

PROHASZKA, Ottokar, Bp., 1858-1927. 226
Meditations on the Gospels; authorized translation from the Hugarian by M. de Pal. Foreword by C. C. Martindale. [2d ed.] Westminster, Md., Newman Press, 1951. 3 v. in 1. port 19 cm. [BS2555.P72 1951] 51-11044
1. Bible. N.T. Gospels—Meditations. I. Title.

QUADFLIEG, Josef, 1924- 226
The book of the twelve apostles. Illustrated by Johannes Gruger. [Translated from the German by Isabel and Florence McHugh. New York] Pantheon Books [1961] 168p. illus. 21cm. [BS2440.Q313] 60-11475
1. Apostles—Juvenile literature. I. Title.

SANDERS, E. P. 226
The tendencies of the synoptic tradition [by] E. P. Sanders. London, Cambridge U.P., 1969. xiv, 328 p. 23 cm. (Society for New Testament Studies. Monograph series, 9) Revision of thesis, Union Theological Seminary. Bibliography: p. 307-318. [BS2555.2.S24] 77-77292 90/- ($14.50)
1. Bible. N.T. Gospels—Criticism, Textual. I. Title. II. Series: Studiorum Novi Testamenti Societas. Monograph series, 9

**SAYINGS of Jesus (The).* 226
Decorated by Valenti Angelo. Mt. Vernon, N.Y., Peter Pauper [1968?] 61p. 19cm. 1.25 bds.,
1. Bible—N.T.—Gospels—Selections.

SCHECK, Joann. 226 (j)
2 men in the temple; Luke 18:9-14 for children. Illustrated by Jim Roberts. St. Louis, Concordia Pub. House [1968] 1 v. (unpaged) col. illus. 21 cm. (Arch books) In verse. [BS2595.5.S3] 68-4305
1. Bible. N.T. Luke XVIII, 9-14—Juvenile poetry. I. Roberts, Jim, illus. II. Title.

SCHECK, Joann. 226
2 men in the temple; Luke 18:9-14 for children. Illustrated by Jim Roberts. St. Louis, Concordia Pub. House [1968] [32] p. col. illus. 21 cm. (Arch books) A retelling, in verse, of a parable which contrasts two men, a dishonest one who recognizes his faults, repents, and is forgiven, and one who proudly parades his false piety. [BS2595.5.S3] AC 68
1. Bible. N.T. Luke XVIII, 9-14—Poetry. 2. Bible stories—New Testament. I. Roberts, Jim, illus. II. Title.

SMITH, Morton. 226
Tannaitic parallels to the Gospels. Philadelphia, Society of Biblical Literature, 1951. xii, 215 p. 23 cm. (Journal of Biblical literature. Monograph series, v. 6) "Revised form of a dissertation written in Hebrew, for ... the degree of doctor of philosophy from the Hebrew University in Jerusalem." Bibliography: p. 190-206. [BS2555.S55] 51-5571
1. Bible. N. T. Gospels—Language, style 2. Literature, Comparative—Greek and Hebrew. 3. Literature, Comparative—Hebrew and Greek. 4. Tannaim. I. Title. II. Series.

SMITH, Morton, 1915- 226
Tannaitic parallels to the Gospels. Philadelphia, Society of Biblical Literature, 1951. xii, 215 p. 23 cm. (Journal of Biblical literature. Monograph series. v. 6) "Revised form of a dissertation written in Hebrew, for ... the degree of doctor of philosophy from the Hebrew University in Jerusalem." Bibliography: p. 199-206. [BS2555.S55] 51-5571
1. Bible. N.T. Gospels — Language, style. 2. Literature. Comparative — Greek and Hebrew. 3. Literature, Comparative — Hebrew and Greek. 4. Tannaim. I. Title. II. Series.

SMITH, William Benjamin, 226
1850-1934.
The birth of the Gospel; a study of the origin and purport of the primitive allegory of the Jesus. Edited by Addison Gulick. New York, Philosophical Library [1957] xxi, 232p. 24cm. [BS2555.S56] 57-1331
1. Bible. N. T. Gospels—Criticism, interpretation, etc. 2. Christianity—Origin. I. Title.

SMITH, William Benjamin, 226
1850-1934.
The birth of the Gospel; a study of the origin and purport of the primitive allegory of the Jesus. Edited by Addison Gulick. New York, Philosophical Library [1957] xxi, 232 p. 24 cm. [BS2555.S56] 57-1331
1. Bible. N.T. Gospels — Criticism, interpretation, etc. 2. Christianity — Origin. I. Title.

STEERE, Douglas Van, 1901- 226
Dimensions of prayer. [New York] Woman's Division of Christian Service Board of Missions, Methodist Church [1962] 126 p. 19 cm. Includes bibliography. [BV210.2.S7] 62-11822
1. Prayer. I. Title.

TENNEY, Merrill Chapin, 1904- 226
The genius of the Gospels. Grand Rapids, Eerdmans, 1951. 124 p. 23 cm. (The Mid-year lectures ... Western Conservative Baptist Theological Seminary of Portland, Oregon, 1951) [BS2555.T34] 51-8079
1. Bible. N. T. Gospels — Criticism, interpretation, etc. I. Title.

TOAL, M F ed. and tr. 226
Patristic homilies on the Gospels. Chicago, Regnery, 1955- v. 23cm. Contents.v.1. From the first Sunday of Advent to Quinquagesima. Includes bibliographical references. [BS2555.A2T6] 56-86
1. Bible. N. T. Gospels—Commentaries. 2. Church year sermons. 3. Christian literature, Early (Selections: I. Title.

TOAL, M F ed. and tr. 226
The Sunday sermons of the great Fathers. Translated and edited by M. F. Toal. Chicago, Regnery [1958- v. 23 cm. "First published 1955 ... under the title Patristic homilies on the Gospels." [BS2555.T575] 58-59974
1. Bible. N. T. Gospels — Commentaries. 2. Church year sermons. 3. Christian literature, Early (Selections: Extracts, etc.) I. Title.

TOAL, M. F., ed. and tr. 226
The Sunday sermons of the great Fathers; a manual of preaching, spiritual reading and meditation; v.4. Tr., ed. by M. F. Toal. Chicago, Regnery [c.1963] 491p. 22cm. Contents.v. 4. From the eleventh Sunday after Pentecost to the twenty-fourth and last Sunday after Pentecost. First pub. 1955 under the title Patristic homilies on the Gospels. 58-59974 4.50; 7.50 deluxe ed.,
1. Bible. N.T. Gospels—Commentaries. 2. Church year sermons. 3. Christian literature, Early (Selections: Extracts, etc.) I. Title.

TRAWICK, Buckner B. 226
The new Testament as literature (Gospels and Acts). N[ew] Y[ork] Barnes & Noble [c.1964] vii, 132p. maps. 22cm. (Coll. outline ser., no. 57) The King James version has ben chosen as the basis for this book. Bibl. [BS2525.T7] 65-459 2.95; 1.25 pap.,
1. Bible. N. T.—Study—Outlines, syllabi, etc. I. Title.

TRAWICK, Buckner B 226
The New Testament as literature (Gospels and Acts) [by] Buckner B. Trawick,. N[ew] Y[ork] Barnes & Noble [1964] vii, 132 p. maps. 22 cm. "The King James...version...has been chosen as the basis for this book." Bibliography: p. 120-123. [BS2525.T7] 65-459
1. Bible. N.T. — Study — Outline, syllab. etc. I. Title.

TRENT, Robbie, 1894- 226
The boy's lunch. Pictures by Howard Simon. Nashville, Abingdon [1964] 32p. illus. 21cm. 64-10154 1.35
1. Bible stories, English—N. T. John vi. 2. Feeding of the five thousand (Miracle)—Juvenile literature. I. Title.

WARD, Maisie, 1889- 226
They saw His glory; an introduction to the Gospels and Acts. New York, Sheed and Ward [1956] 278p. 22cm. [BS2548.W3] 56-6127
1. Bible. N. T. Gospels and Acts—Introductions. I. Title.

WARD, Maisie, 1889- 226
They saw His glory; an introduction to the Gospels and Acts. New York, Sheed and Ward [1956] 278 p. 22 cm. [BS2548.W3] 56-6127
1. Bible. N.T. Gospels and Acts — Introductions. I. Title.

WARREN, Mary. 226
The great surprise Luke 19: 2-10 for children Illustrated by Betty Wind. St. Louis, Concordia Pub. House, 1964. [32] p. col. illus. 21 cm. (Arch books) Quality religious books for children. [BS2520.Z3W3] 63-23147
1. Zacchaeus (Biblical character) — Juvenile literature. I. Title.

WARREN, Mary 226
The great surprise: Luke 19: 2-10 for children. Illus. by Betty Wind. St. Louis, Concordia, c.1964 [32]p. col. illus. 21cm. (Arch bks.) 63-23147 .35 pap.,
1. Zacchaeus (Biblical character)—Juvenile literature. I. Title.

WIEMER, Rudolf Otto, 1905- 226
The prodigal son. Illus. and design by Reinhard Herrmann. Tr. by Paul T. Martinsen. Minneapolis, Augsburg [c.1967] 1v. (unpaged) col. illus. 27cm. Tr. of Der verlorene Sohn. [BT378.P8 W483] 67-8420 1.75 bds.,
1. Prodigal son (Parable)—Juvenile literature. I. Title.

WILKIN, Eloise (Burns) illus. 226
The Lord's prayer. Illus. by Eloise Wilkin with commentary by Esther Wilkin. New York, Golden Pr., c.1961. unpaged. col. illus. 29cm. (Guild Pr. bk., Catholic child's bk.) 61-66232 1.95 bds.,
1. Lord's prayer—Juvenile literature. I. Wilkin, Esther (Burns) II. Title.

WILKIN, Eloise (Burns) j226
Illus.
The Lord's prayer, Illustrated by Eloise Wilkin with commentary by Esther Wilkin. New York, Golden Press, c1961. unpaged. illus. 29 cm. (A Guild Press book) A Catholic child's book [BV232.W5] 61-66232
1. Lord's prayer — Juvenile literature. I. Wilkin, Esther (Burns) II. Title.

WILSON, Clifford A. 226
New light on the Gospels [by] Clifford A. Wilson. Foreward by F. F. Bruce. Grand Rapids, Baker Book House [1975 c1970] 128 p. 18 cm. Bibliography: p. 117-120. [BS2555.5.W54] ISBN 0-8010-9567-0 1.25 (pbk.)
1. Bible. N.T. Gospels—Antiquities. I. Title.
L.C. no. of original edition: 78-864904.

WORLLEDGE, Arthur John, 1848- 226
Prayer, by A. J. Worlledge. 2d ed. London, New York, Longmans, Green, 1902. xvi. 378 p. 20 cm. (The Oxford library of practical theology) Bibliographical footnotes. [BV210.W65 1902] 65-79424
1. Prayer. I. Title.

ZODIATES, Spyros. 226
The pursuit of happiness; an exposition of the Beatitudes of Christ in Matthew 5:1-11 and Luke 6:20-26, based upon the original Greek text. Grand Rapids, Eerdmans [1966] x, 671 p. 20 cm. Includes bibliographies. [BT382.Z6] 66-7351
1. Beatitudes. I. Title.

ALCOTT, Amos Bronson, 226'.007
1799-1888.
Conversations with children on the Gospels. Conducted and edited by A. Bronson Alcott. New York, Arno Press, 1972 [c1836] 2 v. in 1. illus. 22 cm. (The Romantic tradition in American literature) Reprint of the 1836-1837 ed. Added t.p. reads: Record of conversations on the Gospels .... [BS2555.A62] 72-4948 ISBN 0-405-04621-9 27.00 2 vol.
1. Bible. N.T. Gospels—Catechisms, question-books. I. Title. II. Series.

*FAGERLIN, Elsie 226.007
Bible notebook. Illus. by Alex Stein. Gustav K. Wiencke, ed. Philadelphia, Lutheran Church Pr. [c.1964] various p. col. illus., maps. 23cm. (The Gospel story of Jesus, 2) .35 pap.,
I. Title.

HAMILTON, William 226.007
[Hughes]
The modern reader's guide to the Gospels. New York, Association Press [1960, c.1959] 190p. 20cm. 60-6562 3.50 bds.,
1. Bible. N. T. Gospels—Study—Outlines, syllabi, etc. I. Title.

INTERNATIONAL Congress 226.0082
on 'The Four Gospels in 1957,' Oxford, 1957.
The Gospels reconsidered; a selection of papers. New York, Humanities Pr. [1961] 222p. Bibl. 61-4645 5.50
1. Bible. N. T. Gospels—Congresses. I. Title.

STONEHOUSE, Ned Bernard, 226.01
1902-1962.
Origins of the Synoptic Gospels; some basic questions. Grand Rapids, Eerdmans [1963] xiii, 201 p. 23 cm. (The Payton lectures, 1962) Bibliographical footnotes. [BS2555.S74] 63-11495
1. Bible. N. T. Gospels — Criticism, interpretation, etc. I. Title. II. Series.

FARMER, William Reuben. 226.04
The Synoptic problem, a critical analysis [by] William R. Farmer. New York, Macmillan [1964] xi, 306 p. 24 cm. Bibliographical footnotes. [BS2555.2.F3] 64-17374
1. Bible. N.T. Gospels — Criticism, interpretation, etc. I. Title.

FARMER. WILLIAM REUBEN 226.04
The Synoptic problem, a critical analysis. New York, Macmillan [c.1964] xi, 308p. 24cm. Bibl. 64-17374 10.00
1. Bible. N. T. Gospels—Criticism, interpretation, etc. I. Title.

MARTINEZ DALMAU, Eduardo, 226.04
Bp., 1892-
A study on the Synoptic Gospels; a new solution to an old problem: the dependence of the Greek Gospels of St. Matthew and St. Luke upon the Gospel of St. Mark. New York, Speller [c.1964] xiii, 122 p. 23 cm. 63-22674 3.00
1. Bible. N. T. Gospels—Criticism, interpretation, etc. I. Title.

BLASS, Friedrich 226'.04'8
Wilhelm, 1843-1907.
Philology of the Gospels. Chicago, Argonaut, 1969. viii, 249 p. 23 cm. Title on spine: Gospels. Reprint of the 1898 ed. Bibliographical footnotes. [BS2555.B55 1969] 71-5186
1. Bible. N.T. Gospels—Criticism, Textual. I. Title. II. Title: Gospels.

ELDRIDGE, Lawrence 226'.04'8
Allen, 1937-
The Gospel text of Epiphanius of Salamis. Salt Lake City, University of Utah Press, 1969. 191 p. 25 cm. (Studies and documents, 41) Based on the author's thesis, Princeton Theological Seminary, 1967. Bibliography: p. [183]-191. [BS2555.2.E43 1969] 77-278217
1. Epiphanius, Saint, Bp. of Constantia in Cyprus. 2. Bible N.T. Gospels—Criticism, Textual—History. I. Title. II. Series.

BIBLE. N. T. Gospels. 226.051
Polyglot. Selection. (1904) 1964.
The Jefferson Bible. With annotated commentaries on religion of Thomas Jefferson. Introd. by Henry Wilder Foote. Foreword by Donald S. Harrington. Ed by O. I. A. Roche. New York, Potter [dist. Crown, c.1964] 384p. maps (on lining papers) 24cm. Facsimile of The life and morals of Jesus of Nazareth extracted textually from the Gospels in Greek, Latin, French & English: p.149-321. 63-19900 7.50
I. Bible. N. T. Gospels. Polyglot. Selections. 1964. II. Bible. N. T. Gospels. English. Selections. 1964. Authorized. III. Jefferson, Thomas, Pres. U. S., 1743-1826. IV. Title. V. Title: The life and morals of Jesus of Nazareth.

BIBLE. N.T. Gospels. 226.051
Polyglot. Selections. (1904)1964.
The Jefferson Bible. With the annotated commentaries on religion of Thomas Jefferson. Introd. by Henry Wilder Foote. Forward by Donald S. Harrington. Edited by O. I. A. Roche. [1st ed.] New York, C. N. Potter [1964] 384 p. maps (on lining papers) 24 cm. A facsimile of "The life and morals of Jesus of Nazareth extracted textually from the Gospels in Greek, Latin, French & English": p. 149-321. [BS2549.J3] 63-19900
I. Bible. N.T. Gospels. Polyglot. Selections. 1964. II. Bible. N.T. Gospels. English. Selections. 1964. Authorized. III. Jefferson, Thomas, Pres. U.S., 1743-1826. IV. Title. V. Title: The life and morals of Jesus of Nazareth.

BIBLE. N.T. Gospels. 226'.052
English. Alba House. 1970.
The Alba House New Testament; the accounts of Matthew, Mark, Luke, and John. Prepared by Kevin Condon. Staten Island, N.Y., Alba House [1970] 384 p. illus., ports. 18 cm. "A version of the New Testament in modern English." "The present edition is substantially the same ... as that published ... under the title the Mercier New Testament." [BS2553.C58] 79-140281 2.95
I. Condon, Kevin. II. Title.

BIBLE. N. T. Gospels. 226.052
English. Phillips
The Gospels, tr. into modern English by J. B. Phillips. New York, Macmillan 1961 [c.1952, 1957] 252p (Macmillan paperback, Mp 49) Bibl. 1.25 pap.,
I. Phillips, John Bartram, 1906- tr. II. Title.

CUMMING, William 226'.05'2
Kenneth.
"Follow me" / compiled and edited by William Kenneth Cumming. 1st ed. Cocoa, Fla. : Mustardseed Press, c1977. 120 p. ; 19 cm. Includes bibliographical references. [BT306.C85] 76-47721 ISBN 0-917920-01-5 : 6.95 ISBN 0-917920-00-7 pbk. : 1.95
1. Jesus Christ—Words. 2. Bible. N.T. Gospels—Paraphrases, English. I. Title.

CUMMING, William 226'.05'2
Kenneth.
"Follow me" / compiled and edited by William Kenneth Cumming. 1st ed. Cocoa, Fla. : Mustardseed Press, c1977. 120 p. ; 19 cm. Includes bibliographical references. [BT306.C85] 76-47721 ISBN 0-917920-01-5 : 6.95 ISBN 0-917920-00-7 pbk. : 1.95
1. Jesus Christ—Words. 2. Bible. N.T. Gospels—Paraphrases, English. I. Title.

BIBLE. N.T. Gospels. 226'.05'203
English. Authorized. 1971.
The Holy Gospels. King James version, 1611. [Prepared and compiled for publication by Paul Holoviak. South Canaan, Pa.] St. Tikhon's Seminary Press [1971] 458 p. col. illus. 33 cm. Pages 457-458 are blank. [BS2565.A3H64] 72-182597
I. Holoviak, Paul, ed. II. Title.

BIBLE. N.T. Gospels. 226'.05'206
English. New English. Selections. 1973.
Love in the words and life of Jesus, by the editors of Country beautiful. Illustrated with the art of Ivan Mestrovic. Waukesha, Wis., Country Beautiful Corp. [1973] 143 p. illus. 22 cm. [BS2415.A2M45] 73-79617 ISBN 0-87294-046-2 8.95
1. Jesus Christ—Teachings. 2. Jesus Christ—Art. I. Mestrovic, Ivan, 1883-1962, illus. II. Country beautiful. III. Title.

BIBLE. N.T. Gospels. 226'.053
Pennsylvania German dialect. Wood. 1968.
The four gospels, translated into the Pennsylvania German dialect by Ralph Charles Wood. Daniel Schumacher's Baptismal register, translated with an introd. by Frederick S. Weiser. Allentown, Pa., Pennsylvania German Society, 1968. 407 p. col. facsims. 24 cm. (Publications of the Pennsylvania German Society, v. 1) "Es Evangelium vum Matthaeus" (p. [11]-59) is a revision of the translation published previously in Stuttgart in 1955. "Daniel Schumacher's Baptismal register": p. [185]-407. Includes bibliographical references. [GR110.P4A372 vol. 1] 68-25357
I. Wood, Ralph Charles, 1904- tr. II. Weiser, Frederick Sheely, 1935- ed. III. Schumacher, Daniel, d. 1787. Baptismal register. 1968. IV. Series: Pennsylvania-German Society. Publications, v. 1

ABRAHAMS, Israel, 1858- 226'.06
1925.
Studies in Pharisaism and the Gospels. First and second series. [Prolegomenon by Morton S. Enslin. New York, Ktav Pub. House, 1967] 2 v. in 1. 24 cm. (Library of Biblical studies) Half title; each vol. has also special t. p. Includes bibliographical references. [BS2555.A32] 67-11899
1. Pharisees. 2. Bible, N. T. Gospels—Criticism, interpretation, etc. I. Title. II. Title: Pharisaism and the Gospels. III. Series.

ABRAHAMS, Israel, 1858- 226'.06
1925.
Studies in Pharisaism and the Gospels. First and second series. [Prolegomenon by Morton S. Enslin. New York, Ktav Pub. House, 1967] 2 v. in 1. 24 cm. (Library of Biblical studies) Half title; each vol. has also special t.p.

Includes bibliographical references. [BS2555.A32] 67-11899
1. Bible. N.T. Gospels—Criticism, interpretation, etc. 2. Pharisees. I. Title. II. Title: Pharisaism and the Gospels. III. Series.

ARENS, Eduardo. 226'.06
The [Greek characters for Elthon (romanized form)]-sayings in the synoptic tradition : a historico-critical investigation / Eduardo Arens. Freiburg/Schweiz : Universitatsverlag, 1976. 370 p. ; 25 cm. (Orbis biblicus et orientalis ; 10) Originally presented as the author's thesis, Fribourg, 1975/76. Bibliography: p. [351]-370. [BS2555.2.A73 1976] 76-483762 ISBN 3-7278-0148-4 : 48.00F
1. Jesus Christ—Words. 2. Bible. N.T. Gospels—Criticism, interpretation, etc. 3. Elthon (The Greek word) I. [(The elthon-sayings in the synoptic tradition] II. Title. III. Series.

BAIRD, Joseph Arthur. 226'.06
Audience criticism and the historical Jesus, by J. Arthur Baird. Philadelphia, Westminster Press [1969] 208 p. 21 cm. Bibliographical references included in "Notes" (p. [197]-208) [BS2555.2.B267] 69-10426 6.50
1. Jesus Christ—Historicity. 2. Bible. N.T. Gospels—Criticism, interpretation, etc. 3. Electronic data processing—Theology. I. Title.

BALY, Denis 226.06
Discipleship. Greenwich, Conn., Seabury [c.1962] 64p. 21cm. (Bible study unit) .85 pap.,
I. Title.

BARCLAY, William lecturer 226.06
in the University of Glasgow
The first three Gospels. Philadelphia, Westminster [1966] 317p. 22cm. Based on a ser. of articles entitled The making and meaning of the Gospels, which appeared in The British weekly. Bibl. [BS2555.2.B27 1966a] 67-11493 2.65 pap.,
1. Bible. N. T. Gospels—Introductions. I. The British weekly. II. Title.

BASSET, Bernard. 226.06
200 Gospel questions and inquiries. New York, Sheed and Ward [1959] 240p. 21cm. [BS2556.B3] 59-10659
1. Bible. N. T. Gospels—Study—Text-books. I. Title.

BEAVERBROOK, William 226.06
Maxwell Aitken, baron, 1879-
The Divine propagandist. [1st ed.] New York, Duell, Sloan and Pearce [1962] 83p. 21cm. [BS2415.B42] 62-12165
1. Jesus Christ—Teachings. I. Title.

BIBLE. N.T. Gospels. 226.06
English. Harmonies. 1964. Revised.
A synopsis of the Gospels; the Synoptic Gospels with the Johannine parallels[by] H. F. D. Sparks. Philadelphia, Fortress Press [1964] xxv, 248 p. 29 cm. [BT299.2.S6] 64-15950
1. Jesus Christ—Biog.—Sources. Biblical. I. Sparks, Hedley Frederick Davis. II. Title.

BIBLE. N. T. Gospels. 226.06
English. Harmonies. 1964. Revised.
A synopsis of the Gospels; the Synoptic Gospels with the Johannine parallels [by] H. F. D. Sparks. Philadelphia Fortress [c.1964] xxv, 248p. 29cm. 64-15950 6.50
1. Jesus Christ—Biog.—Sources. Biblical. I. Sparks, Hedley Frederick Davis. II. Title.

BLACK, Matthew. 226/.06
An Aramaic approach to the Gospels and Acts; with an appendix on The Son of Man, by Geza Vermes. 3rd ed. Oxford, Clarendon Pr., 1967. [10] 359p. 23cm. Bibl. [BS2555.2.B55 1967] 67-113310 9.60
1. Bible. N. T. Gospels and Acts—Criticism, interpretation, etc. I. Title.

BOUSSUET, Jacques Benigne, 226.06
Bp. of Meaux, 1627-1704
Selections from Meditations on the Gospel [2v.] Tr. by Lucille Corinne Franchere. Special introd. by L. Colin, Th. Rey-Mermet. Chicago, Regnery, 1962. 2v. (various p.) 21cm. 62-15230 10.00 set.,
1. Bible. N. T. Gospels—Meditations. I. Title. II. Title: Meditations on the Gospel.

BROWN, Raymond Edward. 226.06
New Testament essays. Garden City, N.Y., Doubleday [1968,c.1965] 351p. 18cm. (Image bk. D251) Bibl. [BS2395 B7] 65-26969 1.35 pap.,
1. Bible, N. T.—Addresses, essays, lectures. 2. Bible. N. T.—Criticism, interpretation, etc.—Hist. I. Title.

BROWN, Raymond Edward. 226.06
New Testament essays, by Raymond E. Brown. Milwaukee, Bruce Pub. Co. [1965] xvi, 280 p. 22 cm. (Impact books) Bibliographical footnotes. [BS2395.B7] 65-26969
1. Bible. N.T. — Addresses, essays, lectures. 2. Bible. N.T. — Criticism, interpretation, etc. — Hist. I. Title.

CARDENAL, Ernesto. 226'.06
The Gospel in Solentiname / Ernesto Cardenal ; translated by Donald D. Walsh. Maryknoll, N.Y. : Orbis Books, c1976. x, 265 p. ; 20 cm. Translation of El Evangelio en Solentiname. Dialogues on the Gospels between the author and community members of Solentiname. [BS2555.2.C27713] 76-2681 ISBN 0-88344-168-3 : 6.95
1. Bible. N.T. Gospels—Criticism, interpretation, etc. I. Title.

CARTLIDGE, David R., 226'.06
comp.
Sourcebook of texts for the comparative study of the Gospels: literature of the Hellenistic and Roman period illuminating the milieu and character of the Gospels. [Translated and edited by] David R. Cartlidge [and] David L. Dungan. 2d ed., rev. and augm. [Missoula, Mont.] Society of Biblical Literature; [distributed by University of Tennessee Book & Supply Store, Knoxville] 1972 [c1971] 285 p. map. 28 cm. (Sources for Biblical study, 1) "Text editions used for the translations": p. 284-285. [BS2555.5.C37 1972] 72-88435
1. Bible. N.T. Gospels—Extra-canonical parallels. I. Dungan, David L., joint comp. II. Title. III. Series.

CERFAUX, Lucien, 1883- 226.06
The four Gospels, an historical introduction; the oral tradition; Matthew, Mark, Luke, and John; the apocryphal gospels. Translated [from the French] by Patrick Hepburne-Scott, with an introd. by Leonard Johnston. Westminster, Md., Newman Press [1960] 145p. Bibl. footnotes 60-14818 3.00
1. Bible. N. T. Gospels—Introduction. 2. Bible. N. T. Aprocryphal books. Gospels—Criticism, interpretation, etc. I. Title.

CHABANEL Mother 226.06
Gospel initiations for each Sunday of the year. Foreword by Philip F. Pocock. Introd. by Gregory Baum. Glen Rock, N.J., Paulist Pr. [1964, c.1963] 231p. illus. 23cm. Bibl. 63-23212 2.95 pap.,
1. Bible. N.T. Epistles and Gospels, Liturgical—Commentaries. 2. Church year—Meditations. I. Title.

DALPADADO, J. Kingsley, 226'.06
1922-
Reading the Gospels—a guide to readers and teachers / J. Kingsley Dalpadado. [Boston] : St. Paul Editions, c1976. 310 p. : ill. ; 22 cm. (Contemporary New Testament series) Includes index. Bibliography: p. 299-302. [BS2555.2.D23] 75-42378 5.00 pbk. : 4.00
1. Bible. N.T. Gospels—Criticism, interpretation, etc. I. Title.

DUNGAN, David L., comp. 226'.06
Sourcebook of texts for the comparative study of the Gospels : literature of the Hellenistic and Roman period illuminating the milieu and character of the Gospels / [translated and edited] by David L. Dungan and David R. Cartlidge. 4th ed., corr. Missoula, Mont. : Published by Scholars Press for the Society of Biblical Literature, c1975. p. cm. (Sources for Biblical study ; no. 1) Bibliography: p. [BS2555.5.D86 1975] 75-43845 ISBN 0-89130-068-6 : 5.00
1. Bible. N.T. Gospels—Extra-canonical parallels. I. Cartlidge, David R. II. Title. III. Series.

DUNGAN, David L., comp. 226'.06
Sourcebook of texts for the comparative study of the Gospels : literature of the Hellenistic and Roman period illuminating the milieu and character of the Gospels / [translated and edited] by David L. Dungan and David R. Cartlidge. 4th ed., corr. Missoula, Mont. : Published by Scholars Press for the Society of Biblical Literature, 1976c1974 x, 378 p. ; 23 cm. (Sources for Biblical study ; no. 1) Bibliography: p. 355-374. [BS2555.5.D86 1974] 75-43845 ISBN 0-89130-068-6 : 7.00
1. Bible. N.T. Gospels—Extra-canonical parallels. I. Cartlidge, David R. II. Title. III. Series.

DUNGAN, David L., comp. 226'.06
Sourcebook of texts for the comparative study of the Gospels; literature of the Hellenistic and Roman period illuminating the milieu and character of the Gospels. [Translated and edited by] David L. Dungan [and] David R. Cartlidge. 3d ed., completely rev. and augm. [Cambridge, Mass.] Society of Biblical Literature, 1973 [c1971] ix, 378 p. 29 cm. (Sources for Biblical study, 1) Second ed., 1972, is entered under Cartlidge. "Mystery religions of the Greco-Roman world, a preliminary bibliography of secondary literature in English, compiled by Eldon J. Epp": p. 355-374; "Text editions used for the translations": p. 375-378. [BS2555.5.D86 1973] 73-92210 ISBN 0-88414-035-0 7.00
1. Bible. N.T. Gospels—Extra-canonical parallels. I. Cartlidge, David R., joint author. II. Title. III. Series.

EDWARDS, Richard Alan. 226'.06
A theology of Q : eschatology, prophecy, and wisdom / Richard A. Edwards. Philadelphia : Fortress Press, c1976. xiii, 173 p. ; 24 cm. Includes indexes. Bibliography: p. 159-164. [BS2555.2.E34] 75-13042 ISBN 0-8006-0432-6 : 11.95
1. Q document (Biblical criticism) I. Title.

EVELY, Louis, 1910- 226'.06
The Gospels without myth. Translated by J. F. Bernard. Garden City, N.Y., Doubleday, 1971. 167 p. 22 cm. Translation of L'Evangile sans mythes. Includes bibliographical references. [BS2363.E913] 79-131067 4.95
1. Bible. N.T. Gospels—Criticism, interpretation, etc. I. Title.

GILMOUR, George Peel 226.06
The memoirs called Gospels. Chicago, Judson Press [1960, c.1959] x, 299p. Bibl. notes: p.277-293 60-15407 3.50
1. Bible. N. T. Gospels—Criticism, interpretation, etc. I. Title.

GLOEGE, Gerhard, 1901- 226.06
The day of His coming; the Man in the Gospels. [Translated by Stanley Rudman from Aller Tage Tag] Philadelphia, Fortress Press [1963] 302 p. 23 cm. Bibliography: p. [297]-298. [BS2555.2.G563] 63-13876
1. Bible. N.T. Gospels-Criticism, interpretation, etc. I. Title.

GLOEGE, Gerhard, 1901- 226.06
The day of His coming; the Man in the Gospels. [Tr. by Stanley Rudman from Aller Tage Tag] Philadelphia, Fortress [c.1963] 302p. 23cm. Bibl. 63-13876 4.25
1. Bible. N. T. Gospels—Criticism, interpretation, etc. I. Title.

GRANT, Frederick Clifton, 226.06
1891- ed. and tr.
Form criticism; two essays on New Testament research: The study of the Synoptic gospels, by Rudolf Bultmann, and Primitive Christianity in the light of Gospel research, by Karl Kundsin; tr. by Frederick C. Grant. New York, Harper & Row [1962, c.1934] 161p.21cm. (Harper torchbks. Cloister Lib. TB 96) 1.25 pap.,
1. Bible, N.T. Gospels—Criticism, interpretation. etc. 2. Church history—Primitive and early church. I. Bultmann, Rudolf Karl, 1884- II. Kundzins, Karlis, 1883- III. Title.

GUY, Harold A 226.06
The Synoptic Gospels. London, Macmillan; New York, St. Martin's Press, 1960 [i. e. 1961] 183p. illus. 19cm. Includes bibliography. [BS2555.2.G8] 61-870
1. Bible. N. T. Gospels—Criticism, interpretation, etc. I. Title.

HANSON, Anthony Tyrrell, 226.06
ed.
Vindications: essays on the historical basis of Christianity, edited by Anthony Hanson. London, S.C.M. Pr. 1966. 192p. 21cm. (Living Church bks) [BS2350.H3] 66-72378 5.00 bds.,
1. Bible. N.T. — Criticism, interpretation, etc. — Hist. 2. Theology — 20th cent. 3. Apologetics — 20th cent. I. Title.
Available from Morehouse in New York.

HARRINGTON, Wilfrid J 226.06
Explaining the Gospels. New York, Paulist Press [1963] 190 p. 18 cm. (Deus books) Includes bibliography. [BS2555.2.H3] 63-4450
1. Bible. N.T. Gospels — Introductions. I. Title.

HARRINGTON, Wilfrid J. 226.06
Explaining the Gospels. New York, Paulist Pr. [c.1963] 190p. 18cm. (Deus bks.) Bibl. 63-4450 .95 pap.,
1. Bible. N. T. Gospels—Introductions. I. Title.

JUKES, Andrew John, 1815- 226'.06
1901.
Four views of Christ. Edited by James Shiffer Kiefer. Grand Rapids, Kregel Publications [1966] 128 p. 20 cm. Newly edited from the work originally published in 1853 under title: The characteristic differences of the four Gospels. [BS2555.J8 1966] 66-19197
1. Bible. N.T. Gospels—Criticism, interpretation, etc. 2. Jesus Christ I. Kiefer, James Shiffer, ed. II. Title.

KEE, Howard Clark. 226.06
Jesus and God's new people; the four Gospels. Philadelphia, Westminster Press [1959] 92p. 20cm. (Westminster guides to the Bible) [BS2555.2.K4] 59-9522
1. Bible. N. T. Gospels —Criticism, interpretation, etc. I. Title.

KEE, Howard Clark. 226'.06
Jesus in history : an approach to the study of the Gospels / Howard Clark Kee. 2d ed. New York : Harcourt Brace Jovanovich, c1977. vii, 312 p. ; 21 cm. Includes bibliographical references and indexes. [BS2555.2.K43 1977] 77-75349 ISBN 0-15-547382-4 pbk. : 7.95
1. Jesus Christ—Biography—Sources. 2. Bible. N.T. Gospels—Criticism, interpretation, etc. I. Title.

KEE, Howard Clark. 226'.06
Jesus in history : an approach to the study of the Gospels / Howard Clark Kee. 2d ed. New York : Harcourt Brace Jovanovich, c1977. vii, 312 p. ; 21 cm. Includes bibliographical references and indexes. [BS2555.2.K43 1977] 77-75349 ISBN 0-15-547382-4 pbk. : 7.95
1. Jesus Christ—Biography—Sources. 2. Bible. N.T. Gospels—Criticism, interpretation, etc. I. Title.

LUCA, Giuseppe de, 1898- 226'.06
1962.
Altar, gift, and Gospel; 53 meditations on certain Gospel passages. Springfield, Ill., Templegate [1967] 175 p. 22 cm. Translation of Commento al vangelo quotidiano dal mercoledi delle ceneri al sabato in albis. [BS2555.4.L813] 67-21048
1. Bible. N.T. Gospels—Meditations. I. Title.

MITTON, C. Leslie 226.06
The good news; Matthew, Mark, and Luke. Nashville, Abingdon Press [1961] 96p. (Bible guides, no. 13) 61-2738 1.00 pap.,
1. Bible. N.T. Gospels—Criticism, interpretation, etc. I. Title.

NICOLL, Maurice, 1884- 226.06
1953.
The mark. New York, T. Nelson [1956] 219 p. illus. 23 cm. Full name: Henry Maurice Dunlop Nicoll. [BS2415] A62
1. Jesus Christ — Teachings. 2. Bible. N. T. Gospels — Theology. I. Title.

PAUPERT, Jean Marie, 1927- 226.06
What is the Gospel? Translated from the French by A. Manson. [1st ed.] New York, Hawthorn Books [1962] 150p. 22cm. (Twentieth century encyclopedia of Catholicism, v. 69. Section 6: The Word of God) Translation of Quelle est donc cette bonne nouvelle' Includes bibliography. [BS25552.P313] 62-21418
1. Jesus Christ—Teachings. 2. Bible. N. T. Gospels—Criticism, Interpretation, etc. I. Title.

PAUPERT, Jean Marie, 1927- 226.06
What is the Gospel? Tr. from French by A. Manson. New York, Hawthorn [c.1962] 150p. 22cm. (Twentieth century encyclopedia of Catholicism, v. 69. Section 6: The Word of God) Bibl. 62-21418 3.50
1. Bible. N.T. Gospels—Criticism, Interpretation, etc. 2. Jesus Christ—Teachings. I. Title.

REID, John Calvin, 1901- 226.06
We wrote the Gospels. Grand Rapids, Mich., Eerdmans [1960] 61p. illus. 22cm. [BS2555.5.R4] 60-15301
1. Bible. N. T. Gospels—Introductions. 2. Evangelists (Bible) I. Title.

ROLLINS, Wayne G. 226.06
The Gospels; portraits of Christ. Philadelphia, Westminster [1964, c.1963] 128p. 21cm. Bibl. 64-10044 3.00
1. Bible. N.T. Gospels—Criticism, interpretation, etc. I. Title.

ROPES, James Hardy, 1866- 226.06
1933.
The Synoptic gospels. 2d impression, with new pref. London, Oxford University Press [c1960] 117p. 19cm. [BS2555.R64 1960] 61-663
1. Bible. N. T. Gospels— Criticism, interpretation, etc. I. Title.

SHEETS, Herchel H. 226'.06
Enemy versions of the Gospel; the Gospel according to Jesus' enemies, by Herchel H. Sheets. [Nashville] Upper Room [1973] 72 p. 20 cm. [BT306.3.S53] 73-80050 1.00
1. Jesus Christ—Biography—Sermons. 2. Methodist Church—Sermons. 3. Sermons, American. I. Title.

SUGGS, M. Jack. 226.06
The Gospel story. St. Louis, Bethany Press [1960] 95 p. illus. 21 cm. [BS2555.2.S8] 60-14652
1. Bible. N. T. Gospels—Criticism, Interpretation, etc. I. Title.

SUGGS, M. Jack 226.06
The Gospel story. St. Louis, Bethany Press [c.1960] 95p. illus. 21cm. 60-14652 2.50

1. *Bible. N. T. Gospels—Criticism, interpretation, etc. I. Title.*

TALBERT, Charles H. 226'.06
What is a Gospel? : The genre of the canonical Gospels / Charles H. Talbert. Philadelphia : Fortress Press, c1977. p. cm. Includes indexes. [BS2555.2.T34] 77-78645 ISBN 0-8006-0512-8 : 9.95
1. *Bible. N.T. Gospels—Criticism, interpretation, etc. 2. Biography (as a literary form) 3. Bible as literature. I. Title.*

TASKER, Randolph Vincent 226.06
Greenwood, 1895-
The nature and purpose of the Gospels. [Rev. ed.] Richmond, John Knox Press [1962] 111 p. 19 cm. Includes bibliography. [BX2555.T28 1962] 62-16634
1. *Bible. N. T. Gospels — Criticism, interpretation, etc. I. Title.*

TASKER, Randolph Vincent 226.06
Greenwood, 1895-
The nature and purpose of the Gospels. [Rev. ed.] Richmond, Va., Knox [1962] 111p. 19cm. Bibl. 62-16634 1.50 pap.,
1. *Bible. N. T. Gospels—Criticisms, interpretation. etc I. Title.*

VITA laudanda : 226'.06
essays in memory of Ulrich S. Leupold / edited by Erich R. W. Schultz. Waterloo, Ont. : Wilfrid Laurier University Press, c1976. x, 192 p. : port. ; 23 cm. Contents.Contents.—Granskou, D. The unity and variety of the Gospel.—Reumann, J. Redaktionsgeschichte and Roman Ordo: some principles and problems in pericope reform.—Riegert, E. R. The death-resurrection motif.—Himmelman, D. Jesus' eschatological concern for poor folk: an exegetical study of Luke 6:20-21, 24-25.—Vajta, V. The new mass in Protestant perspective.—Anders, C. R. The search for a new song: developments in contemporary hymnody in the American Lutheran churches.—Brown, E. S. Revision of the collects: an experiment.—Kemp, W. The "polyphony of life": references to music in Bonhoeffer's Letters and papers from prison.—Buszin, W. Heinrich Schuetz (sagittarius). "A bibliography of books, articles, and book reviews by Ulrich S. Leopold [sic]": p. 173-192. [BS2555.2.V57] 76-364988 ISBN 0-88920-021-1
1. *Leupold, Ulrich, 1909-1970. 2. Leupold, Ulrich, 1909-1970—Bibliography. 3. Bible. N.T. Gospels—Criticism, interpretation, etc.—Addresses, essays, lectures. 4. Liturgics—Addresses, essays, lectures. 5. Church music—Addresses, essays, lectures. I. Leupold, Ulrich, 1909-1970. II. Schultz, Erich R. W.*

VOERMAN, Arthur H. 226.06
The story of the good news, an explanatory paraphrase of the four Gospels. New York, Exposition [c.1962] 279p. 21cm. 4.50
I. Title.

WINK, Walter. 226'.06
John the Baptist in the gospel tradition. London, Cambridge U.P., 1968. xii, 132 p. 23 cm. (Society for New Testament Studies. Monograph series, 7) Bibliography: p. 117-123. [BS2456.W5] 68-21401 ISBN 0-521-07143-7 30/-
1. *John the Baptist. 2. Bible. N.T. Gospels—Criticism, interpretation, etc. I. Title. II. Series: Studiorum Novi Testamenti Societas. Monograph series, 7*

MCKNIGHT, Edgar V. 226'.06'1
What is form criticism? By Edgar V. McKnight. Philadelphia, Fortress Press [1969] x, 86 p. 22 cm. (Guides to Biblical scholarship) Bibliography: p. 80-86. [BS2555.2.M26] 71-81526 2.25
1. *Bible. N.T. Gospels—Criticism, Form. I. Title.*

BENOIT, Pierre, 226'.06'6
Aug.3,1906-
Jesus and the gospel. Translated by Benet Weatherhead. [New York] Herder and Herder [1973-74] 2 v. 23 cm. "A translation of selected articles from ... Exegese et theologie." Vol. 2 published by Seabury Press, New York, as A Crossroad book. Includes bibliographical references. [BS2555.2.B4613] 72-94303 ISBN 0-07-073770-3 (v. 1) 9.75 (v. 1) varies
1. *Peter, Saint, apostle. 2. Bible. N.T. Gospels—Addresses, essays, lectures. 3. Bible. N.T. Epistles of Paul—Theology. I. Title.*

CIUBA, Edward J., 1935- 226'.06'6
Who do you say that I am? An adult inquiry into the first three Gospels [by] Edward J. Ciuba. New York, Alba House [1974] xvi, 155 p. 21 cm. Bibliography: p. [145]-152. [BS2555.2.C54] 74-10808 ISBN 0-8189-0295-7
1. *Bible. N.T. Gospels—Criticism, interpretation, etc. I. Title.*

DIBELIUS, Martin, 1883- 226'.06'6
1947.
From tradition to gospel / by Martin Dibelius ; translated from the revised second edition of Die Formgeschichte des Evangeliums in collaboration with the author by Bertram Lee Woolf. Cambridge [Eng.] : James Clarke, 1971. xv, 311 p. ; 22 cm. (Library of theological translations) Includes bibliographical references and indexes. [BS2555.D52 1971] 75-324588 ISBN 0-227-67752-8 : £4.00
1. *Bible. N.T. Gospels—Criticism, Form. I. Title.*

*ELLIS, Maie Lenora, 226.06'.6
1890, comp.
The old testament prophecies as fulfilled in the gospels, compiled by Maie L. Ellis. Illus. by Lucile Ellings. [First ed.] New York, Vantage [1972] xii, 112 p., illus., 21 cm. [BS2555.2] ISBN 0-533-00354-7 3.95
1. *Bible N.T. Gospels—Criticism, interpretation, etc. 2. Bible—prophecies. I. Title.*

HULL, John M. 226'.06'6
Hellenistic magic and the synoptic tradition [by] John M. Hull. Naperville, Ill., A. R. Allenson [1974] xii, 192 p. 22 cm. (Studies in Biblical theology, 2d ser., 28) Bibliography: p. [171]-179. [BS2555.2.H85] 73-77369 ISBN 0-8401-3078-3
1. *Bible. N.T. Gospels—Criticism, interpretation, etc. 2. Magic, Greek. I. Title.*

KENNEDY, Gerald 226'.06'6
Hamilton, Bp., 1907-
The preacher and the New English Bible, by Gerald Kennedy. New York, Oxford University Press, 1972. viii, 183 p. 22 cm. [BS2555.4.K44] 76-185612 ISBN 0-19-501561-4 5.95
1. *Bible. N.T. Gospels—Meditations. I. Title.*

KISTEMAKER, Simon. 226'.06'6
The Gospels in current study. Grand Rapids, Baker Book House [1972] 171 p. 22 cm. Bibliography: p. 161-165. [BS2555.2.K55] 72-78255 ISBN 0-8010-5316-1 2.95
1. *Bible. N.T. Gospels—Criticism, interpretation, etc. I. Title.*

MONAGHAN, Forbes J. 226'.06'6
Reflections on the synoptic gospels, and their special design [by] Forbes J. Monaghan. Staten Island, N.Y., Alba House [1970] xvii, 204 p. 22 cm. Includes bibliographical references. [BS2555.5.M65] 70-110595 4.95
1. *Synoptic problem. I. Title.*

ROHDE, Joachim. 226'.06'6
Rediscovering the teaching of the evangelists. Philadelphia, Westminster Press [1968] viii, 278 p. 23 cm. (The New Testament library) Translation of Die redaktionsgeschichtliche Methode, a revision of the author's thesis, Berlin, 1962 with title Formgeschichte und Redaktionsgeschichte in der neutestamentlichen Forschung der Gegenwart. Bibliography: p. [259]-270. [BS2555.2.R5813 1968b] 69-14423 ISBN 0-664-20856-8 7.50
1. *Bible. N.T. Gospels—Criticism, interpretation, etc.—History—20th century. 2. Bible. N.T. Gospels—Criticism, Form. I. Title.*

SMITH, Charles William 226'.06'6
Frederick, 1905-
The paradox of Jesus in the Gospels, by Charles W. F. Smith. Philadelphia, Westminster Press [1969] 236 p. 22 cm. Includes bibliographical references. [BT202.S58] 69-14201 6.50
1. *Jesus Christ—Person and offices. 2. Bible. N.T. Gospels—Criticism, interpretation, etc. I. Title.*

TANNEHILL, Robert C. 226'.06'6
The sword of His mouth / by Robert C. Tannehill. Philadelphia : Fortress Press, c1975. vi, 224 p. ; 22 cm. (Semeia supplements ; no. 1) Includes index. Bibliography: p. 205-215. [BS2555.2.T36] 75-18948 ISBN 0-8006-1501-8 pbk. : 4.95
1. *Jesus Christ—Words. 2. Bible. N.T. Gospels—Criticism, interpretation, etc. I. Title. II. Series.*

WAND, John William 226'.06'6
Charles, Bp. of London, 1885-
Christianity: a historical religion? By William Wand. Valley Forge, Pa., Judson Press [1972] 176 p. 21 cm. Includes bibliographical references. [BR115.H5W35 1972] 77-180505 ISBN 0-8170-0554-4 4.95
1. *Jesus Christ—Historicity. 2. History (Theology) 3. Christianity—Essence, genius, nature. I. Title.*

BEA, Augustin, Cardinal, 226.067
1881-
The study of the synoptic Gospels; new approaches and outlooks. English version edited by Joseph A. Fitzmyer. New York, Harper & Row [1965] 95 p. 21 cm. Translation of La storicita del Vangeli. Bibliographical footnotes. [BS2555.2.B413] 65-20447
1. *Bible. N. T. Gospels—Historiography. 2. Bible. N. T. Gospels—Hermeneutics. 3. Catholic Church. Commissio Pontificia de Re Biblica. Instructio de historica Evangeliorum veritate. I. Title.*

BEA, Augustin, Cardinal, 226.067
1881-
The study of the synoptic Gospels; new approaches and outlooks. [Tr. from Italian] Eng. version ed. by Joseph A. Fitzmyer. New York, Harper [c.1964. 1965] 95p. 21cm. Bibl. [BS2555.2,B413] 65-20447 3.50 bds.,
1. *Bible. N.T. Gospels—Historiography. 2. Bible. N.T. Gospels—Hermeneutics. 3. Catholic Church. Commissio Pontifico de Re Biblica: Instructio de historica Evangeliorum veritate. I. Title.*

BEARE, Francis Wright, 226.07
1902-
The earliest records of Jesus. Companion to the Synopsis of the first three Gospels, by Albert Huck. Nashville, Abingdon [1962] 254p. 26cm. Bibl. 62-52293 6.50
1. *Bible. N. T. Gospels—Commentaries. I. Title.*

BIBLE. N.T. Gospels 226.07
English Harmonies. 1961. American standard
A layman's harmony of the Gospels [by] John Franklin Carter. Based on the American standard version of the Bible. Nashville, Broadman Press [1961] ix, 364p. illus., maps. 24cm. [BS2560.C38] 61-7546
1. *Bible. N. T. Gospels— Commentaries. I. Carter, John Franklin. II. Title.*

BIBLE. N. T. Gospels. 226.07
English. Harmonies. 1961. American standard.
A layman's harmony of the Gospels [by] John Franklin Carter. Based on the American standard version of the Bible. Nashville, Tenn., Broadman Press [c.1961] ix, 364p. illus., maps. 61-7546 4.50
1. *Bible. N. T. Gospels—Commentaries. I. Carter, John Franklin. II. Title.*

DAILY Bible commentary 226'.07
: St. Matthew to Acts / [Arthur E. Cundall co-ordinating editor]. Philadelphia : A. J. Holman, [1977], c1973. p. cm. Reprint of the ed. published by Scripture Union, London. [BS2341.2.D34 1977] 76-46441 ISBN 0-87981-070-X : 8.95
1. *Bible. N.T.—Commentaries. I. Cundall, Arthur Ernest.*

DAILY Bible commentary 226'.07
: St. Matthew to Acts / [Arthur E. Cundall co-ordinating editor]. Philadelphia : A. J. Holman, [1977], c1973. p. cm. Reprint of the ed. published by Scripture Union, London. [BS2341.2.D34 1977] 76-46441 ISBN 0-87981-070-X : 8.95
1. *Bible. N.T.—Commentaries. I. Cundall, Arthur Ernest.*

HARVEY, Anthony Ernest. 226'.07
The new English Bible, companion to the New Testament: the Gospels, by A. E. Harvey. [Oxford, Eng.] Oxford University Press, 1972 [c1970] 399 p. 23 cm. Cover title: The new English Bible, companion to the Gospels. "First published 1970 as part of Companion to the New Testament." [BS2555.3.H37 1972] 72-169309 ISBN 0-19-826168-3 3.95 (U.S.)
1. *Bible. N.T. Gospels—Commentaries. I. Title.*

HEROD, Frederic George. 226'.07
The Gospels : a first commentary / F. G. Herod. Atlanta : John Knox Press, 1977, c1976. p. cm. Includes indexes. Bibliography: p. [BS2555.2.H43 1977] 77-79590 ISBN 0-8042-0255-9 pbk. : 2.95
1. *Bible. N.T. Gospels—Criticism, interpretation, etc. I. Title.*

HIEBERT, David Edmond, 226'.07
1910-
The Gospels and Acts / by D. Edmond Hiebert. Chicago : Moody Press, c1975. 298 p. ; 24 cm. (His An introduction to the New Testament ; v. 1) Includes index. Bibliography: p. 282-296. [BS2555.2.H48] 75-332628 ISBN 0-8024-4137-8 : 7.95
1. *Bible. N.T. Gospels—Introductions. 2. Bible. N.T. Acts—Introductions. I. Title.*

LYNCH, William E. 226'.07
Jesus in the Synoptic Gospels, by William E. Lynch. Milwaukee, Bruce Pub. Co. [1967] xvi, 132 p. 22 cm. (Impact books) Bibliography: p. 115-119. [BS2555.3.L8] 67-26340
1. *Bible. N.T. Gospels—Commentaries. I. Title.*

MURPHY, Richard Thomas 226.07
Aquinas, 1908-
The Sunday Gospels. Milwaukee, Bruce Pub. Co. [1960] 266p. illus. 24cm. [BS2565.Z73M8] 60-15481
1. *Bible. N. T. Epistles and Gospels, Liturgical— Commentaries. I. Title.*

HODSON, Geoffrey. 226'.077
The Christ life from Nativity to Ascension / Geoffrey Hodson. Wheaton, Ill. : Theosophical Pub. House, c1975. 460 p. : ill. ; 21 cm. (A Quest book) Includes index. Bibliography: p. [459]-460. [BT304.97.H6] 75-4169 ISBN 0-8356-0467-5 : 5.50
1. *Jesus Christ—Theosophical interpretations. 2. Bible. N.T. Gospels—Criticism, interpretation, etc. I. Title.*

MONTEFIORE, Claude 226.07'7
Joseph Goldsmid, 1858-1938, ed.
The Synoptic Gospels, edited with an introd. and a commentary by C. G. Montefiore. 2d ed. rev. and partly rewritten. New York, Ktav Pub. House, 1968. 2 v. 23 cm. (Library of Biblical studies) Reprint of the 1927 edition with a new prolegomenon by Lou H. Silberman. Contents.Contents.—v. 1. Introduction. The Gospel according to Mark.—2. The Gospel according to Matthew. The Gospel according to Luke. 'Am ha-'Arec, by I. Abrahams. Includes bibliographical references. [BS2555.M63 1968] 67-18256
1. *Bible. N.T. Gospels—Commentaries. I. Abrahams, Israel, 1858-1925. II. Title. III. Series.*

LESLIE, Robert 226.0813134
Campbell, 1917-
Jesus and logotherapy; the ministry of Jesus as interpreted through the psychotherapy of Viktor Frankl. Abingdon [c.1965] 143p. 21cm. Bibl. [BT590.P9L4] 65-11077 3.00 bds.,
1. *Frankl, Viktor Emil. 2. Jesus Christ—Psychology I. Title.*

WAHLBERG, Rachel 226'.08'301412
Conrad.
Jesus according to a woman / by Rachel Conrad Wahlberg. New York : Paulist Press, [1975] 106 p. ; 18 cm. (Paulist Press/Deus book) Bibliography: p. 104-106. [BT590.W6W33] 74-27461 ISBN 0-8091-1861-0 pbk. : 1.45
1. *Jesus Christ—Attitude towards women. I. Title.*

PARROT, Andre, 1901- 226'.09
Land of Christ; archaeology, history, geography. Translated by James H. Farley. Philadelphia, Fortress Press [1968] ix, 166 p. illus., maps, plans. 22 cm. Translation of Terre du Christ, archeologie, histoire, geographie. Bibliography: p. 147-[150] [DS107.4.P2813] 68-15863 5.95
1. *Bible. N.T. Gospels—Geography. 2. Palestine—Description and travel. I. Title.*

ELTON, Godfrey Elton, 226.0905
baron, 1892-
Simon Peter [by] Lord Elton. [1st ed. in the U.S.A.] Garden City, N.Y., Doubleday, 1966 [c1965] xvii, 236 p. 22 cm. Bibliographical footnotes. [BS2515.E45 1966] 66-10918
1. *Peter, Saint, apostle. I. Title.*

ELTON, Godfrey Elton, 226.0905
baron, 1892-
Simon Peter [1st ed. in the U.S.A.] Garden City, N.Y., Doubleday, 1966 [c.1965] xvii, 236p. 22cm. Bibl. [BS2515.E45] 66-10918 4.50
1. *Peter, Saint, apostle. I. Title.*

BARKER, William Pierson 226.092
Personalities around Jesus [Westwood, N.J.] Revell [c.1963] 156p. 20cm. 63-17108 2.95 bds.,
1. *Bible. N.T.—Biog. I. Title.*

KELSO, James Leon, 1892- 226'.093
An archaeologist looks at the Gospels [by] James L. Kelso. [1st ed.] Waco, Tex., Word Books [1969] 143 p. illus. 23 cm. Bibliographical footnotes. [BS2375.K4] 69-20232 3.95
1. *Bible. N.T.—Antiquities. I. Title.*

BEDENBAUGH, J. Benjamin 226.095
The gospel story of Jesus, by J. Benjamin Bedenbaugh, Gustav K. Wiencke. Illus. by Gustav Rehberger. Philadelphia, Lutheran Church Pr. [c.1964] 224p. illus. (pt. col.) 24cm. 1.75
I. Title.

BIBLE. N. T. Gospels. 226.095
English. Selections. 1960. Confraternity version.
The Holy Gospel children, by Richard Cardinal Cushing. Illustrated by the Daughters of St. Paul. [Boston] St. Paul Editions [1960] 172p. illus. 21cm. [BS2401.C85] 60-50090
1. *Bible stories. English—N. T. Gospels. I. Cushing, Richard James, Cardinal, 1895- II. Title.*

BIBLE. N. T. Gospels. 226.095
English. Selections. 1960. Confraternity version.
The Holy Gospel for children, by Richard Cardinal Cushing. Illustrated by the Daughters of St. Paul. [Boston, Daughters of St. Paul, c.1960] 172p. col. illus. 21cm. (St. Paul editions) 60-50090 3.00
1. Bible stories, English—N. T. Gospels. I. Cushing, Richard James, Cardinal. II. Title.

JESUS in his time 226'.095
[by] Joseph Vogt [and others] Edited by Hans Jurgen Schultz. Translated by Brian Watchorn. Foreword by William Neil. [1st American ed.] Philadelphia, Fortress Press, 1971. xi, 148 p. 22 cm. Translation of Die Zeit Jesu. [BS2555.5.Z413 1971] 70-99613 3.75
1. Jesus Christ—Biography—Addresses, essays, lectures. 2. Bible. N.T. Gospels—History of contemporary events—Addresses, essays, lectures. I. Vogt, Joseph, 1895- II. Schultz, Hans Jurgen, ed.

ROBO, Etienne 226.095
In the margins of the Gospel. Westminster, Md., Newman [1964] 191p. 19cm. 64-970 3.95
1. Bible. N.T. Gospels—History of Biblical events. I. Title.

GIBBS, Paul T. 226'.095'05
Crossroads of the cross [by] Paul T. Gibbs. Washington, Review and Herald Pub. Association [1969] 126 p. 22 cm. [BS2430.G5] 73-84992
1. Jesus Christ—Friends and associates. 2. Jesus Christ—Passion. I. Title.

VAN Zeller, Hubert, 226.09505
1905-
The Gospel in other words; a presentation for beginners. Springfield, Ill., Templegate [1965] 127 p. 20 cm. [[BT301.2]] 65-29934
1. Jesus Christ — Biog. I. Bible, N.T. Gospels. English. Paraphrases. 1965. Van Zeller. II. Title.

VAN ZELLER, Hubert, 226.09505
1905-
The Gospel in other words; a presentation for beginners. Springfield, Ill., Templegate [c.1965] 127p. 20cm. 127p. 20cm. [BT301.2] 65-29934 2.95 bds.,
1. Jesus Christ — Biog. I. Bible. N. T. Gospels. English. Paraphrases. 1965. Van Zeller II. Title.

BIBLE. N.T. Gospels. 226'.1
English. Authorized. 1973.
The witnesses [by] Arthur Markve. With an apologetic critique of the Bible by Ernest o'Neill. [3d ed.] Minneapolis, Bethany Fellowship [1973, c1957] xxii, 409 p. 22 cm. First ed. published in 1957 under title: A new harmony of the Gospels. [BT299.2.M3 1973] 73-172148 ISBN 0-87123-393-2 3.95
1. Jesus Christ—Biography—Sources, Biblical. I. Markve, Arthur. II. Title.

BIBLE. N.T. Gospels. 226'.1
English. Coulter. 1974.
A harmony of the Gospels in modern English; the life of Jesus Christ, by Frederick R. Coulter. [Los Angeles,] York Pub. Co. [1974] viii, 264 p. illus. 27 cm. [BT299.2.C68] 73-93940 12.50
1. Jesus Christ—Biography—Sources, Biblical. I. Coulter, Frederick R. II. Title.

BIBLE. N. T. Gospels 226.1
English. Harmonies.(1874) 1965
The testimony of the Evangelists, examined by the rules of evidence administered in courts of justice, by Simon Greenleaf. Appendix containing a hist. of the most ancient manuscript copies of the New Testament, a comparison of their text with that of the King James' Bible, by Constantine Tischendorff, also review of the trial of Jesus. Grand Rapids, Mich. Baker Bk., 1965. xxiii, 613p. 23cm. (Lim. eds. lib.) Reprinted from the 1874 ed. printed in New York by James Cockcroft & Co. [BS2560.G72] 65-18267 7.95
1. Bible. N. T. Gospels—Evidences, authority, etc. 2. Jesus Christ.—Trial. 3. Bible. N. T. Gospels. English. Harmonies. 1874. Authorized. I. Greenleaf, Simon, 1783-1853, ed. II. Tischendorf, Constantin von, 1815-1874. III. Bible. N.T. Gospels. English. Harmonies.1874. Authorized. IV. Title.

BIBLE. N.T. Gospels. 226.1
English. Harmonies. (1874)1965.Authorized.
The testimony of the Evangelists examined by the rules of evidence administered in courts of justice, by Simon Greenleaf. With an appendix containing a history of the most ancient manuscript copies of the New Testament, and a comparison of their text with that of the King James' Bible, by Constantine Tischendorff; also a review of the trial of Jesus. Grand Rapids, Baker Book House, 1965. xxiii, 613 p. 23 cm. (Limited editions library) "Reprinted from the 1874 edition printed in New York by James Cockcroft & Company." [BS2560.G74] 65-18267
1. Bible. N.T. Gospels—Evidences, authority, etc. 2. Jesus Christ—Trial. I. Greenleaf, Simon, 1783-1853, ed. II. Tischendorf, Constantin von, 1815-1874. III. Bible. N.T. Gospels. English, Harmonies. 1874. Authorized. IV. Title.

BIBLE. N. T. Gospels. 226.1
English. Harmonies. 1950. Revised standard.
Gospel records of the message and mission of Jesus Christ; a harmony of the Gospels in the text of the Revised standard version, arr. for comparative study [by] Albert Cassel Wieand. [Rev. ed.] Elgin, Ill., Brethren Pub. House [1950] 268 p. illus. maps. 29 cm. [BS2560.W52 1950] 51-17276
I. Wieand, Albert Cassel., 1871- II. Title.

BIBLE. N. T. Gospels. 226.1
English. Harmonies. 1951. Peterson.
The Synoptic New Testament; a new translation and harmony of the four Gospels from the original Greek, by Russell A. Peterson. Boston, Meador [1951] 159 p. 21 cm. [BT299.P4] 51-14722
1. Jesus Christ—Biog.—Sources, Biblical. I. Peterson, Russell Arthur, 1922- II. Title.

BIBLE. N. T. Gospels. 226.1
English. Harmonies. 1953.
The life of Christ as compiled from the four Gospels [by] Powell B. Trotter. [1st ed.] New York, Pageant Press [1953] 155p. 24cm. [BT299.T75] 53-8106
1. Jesus Christ—Sources, Biblical. I. Trotter, Powell B., comp. II. Title.

BIBLE. N. T. Gospels. 226.1
English. Harmonies. 1957. Revised standard.
Gospel parallels; a synopsis of the first three Gospels, with alternative readings from the manuscripts and noncanoncil parallels. Textused is the Revised standard version, 1952; the arrangement follows the Huck-Lietzmann synopsis, 9th ed., 1936. Edited by Burton H. Throckmorton, Jr. [2d ed., rev.] New York, Nelson [1957] xxv, 191p. 27cm. Prepared by a subcommittee of the American Standard Bible Committee. [BS2560.I5 1957] 57-3558
I. Throckmorton, Burton Hamilton, 1921- ed. II. International Council of Religious Education. American Standard Bible Committee. III. Title.

BIBLE. N.T. Gospels. 226.1
English. Harmonies. 1963.Knox.
A harmony of the Gospels in the Knox translation. Edited by Leonard Johnston and Aidan Pickering. New York, Sheed and War [1963, c1944] xii, 252 p. 22 cm. [BS2560.J63] 63-17147
I. Knox, Ronald Arbuthnott, 1888-1957, tr. II. Johnston, Leonard, ed. III. Pickering, Aidan, ed. IV. Title.

BIBLE. N.T. Gospels. 226.1
English. Harmonies. 1963. Knox
A harmony of the Gospels in the Knox translation. Ed. by Leonard Johnston, Aidan Pickering. New York, Sheed & Ward [1963, c.1944] xii, 252p. 22cm. 63-17147 6.00
I. Knox, Ronald Arbuthnott, 1888-1957, tr. II. Johnston, Leonard ed. III. Pickering, Aidan, ed. IV. Title.

BIBLE. N. T. Gospels. 226'.1
English. Harmonies, 1967. Revised standard.
Gospel parallels; a synopsis of the first three Gospels with alternative readings from the manuscripts and noncanonical parallels. Text used is the Revised standard version, 1952, the arrangement follows the Huck-Lietzmann synopsis, 9th ed., 1936. Ed. by Burton H. Throckmorton, Jr. [3d ed., rev.] Toronto, Camden, N. J., Nelson [1967] xxv, 191p. 27cm. Prepd. by a subcomm. of the Amer. Standard Bible Comm. [BS2560.I5 1967] 67-9322 5.50
I. Throckmorton, Burton Hamilton, 1921- ed. II. International Council of Religious Education. American Standard Bible Committee. III. Title.

BIBLE. N.T. Gospels. 226'.1
English. Harmonies. 1967. Revised standard.
Gospel parallels; a synopsis of the first three Gospels with alternative readings from the manuscripts and noncanonical parallels. Text used is the Revised standard version. 1952; the arrangement follows the Huck-Lietzmann synopsis, 9th ed., 1936. Edited by Burton H. Throckmorton, Jr. [3d ed., rev.] Toronto, Camden, N.J., T. Nelson [1967] xxv, 191 p. 27 cm. Prepared by a subcommittee of the American Standard Bible Committee. [BS2560.I5] 67-9322
I. Throckmorton, Burton Hamilton, 1921- ed. II. International Council of Religious Education. American Standard Bible Committee. III. Title.

BIBLE. N.T. Gospels. 226'.1
English. Revised. Harmonies. 1975.
The Johannine synopsis of the Gospels / H. F. D. Sparks. 1st U.S. ed. New York : Harper & Row, [1975] c1974. xiii, 96 p. ; 29 cm. Includes indexes. [BT299.2.S6 1975] 75-24182 ISBN 0-06-067474-1 : 15.00
1. Jesus Christ—Biography—Sources, Biblical. I. Sparks, Hedley Frederick Davis. II. Title.

BIBLE. N.T. Gospels. 226'.1
English. Today's English. Selections. 1970.
The man who turned history upside down; the life and teachings of Jesus from Good news for modern man. Illustrated by Ken Rice. New York, Morehouse-Barlow Co. [1970] 111 p. col. illus. 19 cm. [BT299.2.R5] 78-125105
1. Jesus Christ—Biography—Sources, Biblical. 2. Jesus Christ—Teachings. I. Title.

BIBLE. N.T. Gospels. 226'.1
Greek. 1976.
Synopsis of the four gospels : Greek-Engl. ed. of the synopsis quattuor evangeliorum ; completely rev. on the basis of the Greek text of Nestle-Aland 26th ed. and Greek New Testament 3rd ed. ; the Engl. text is the 2. ed of the rev. standard version United Bible Societies / ed. by Kurt Aland. Stuttgart : Wurttembergische Bibelanstalt, 1976. xxx, 338, 361 p. ; 28 cm. On t.p.: United Bible Societies. Opposite pages numbered in duplicate up to p. 338. [BS2560.A2A35 1976] 76-380511 ISBN 3-438-05405-1 (United Bible Societies) : DM44.00
1. Bible. N.T. Gospels—Harmonies. I. Aland, Kurt, ed. II. Bible. N.T. Gospels. English. Revised Standard. 1976. III. Title.

BIBLE. N. T. Gospels. 226.1
Harmonies. English. Authorized. 1954
Our Lord of the Gospels; a harmony of the Gospels, being a life of Jesus Christ while He dwelt upon the earth in mortality and in the days immediately following His resurrection, as recorded in the Sacred Autographs as they have come down to us, and in the Book of Mormon, chronologically arranged. King James version, variorum text. By J. Reuben Clark, Jr. Salt Lake City, Desert Book Co., 1954. xii, 549, [2] p. maps (part col.) geneal. table, plan. 24 cm. Bibliography: p. [551] [BX8630.A27G6] 55-689
1. Bible—Harmonies. I. Clark, Joshua Reuben, 1871- II. Book of Mormon. III. Title.

*DAVIES, Benjamin, ed. 226.1
Baker's pocket harmony of the gospels. Grand Rapids, Baker Book House [1975] viii, 184 p. 18 cm. [BS2560] ISBN 0-8010-2843-4 1.45 (pbk.)
1. Bible—Harmonies. 2. Bible—N.T. Gospels. I. Title.

NEVIUS, Richard C 226'.1'04
The divines [i. e. divine] names in the Gospels, by Richard C. Nevins. Salt Lake City, University of Utah Press, 1967. v, 135 p. 25 cm. (Studies and documents, 30) Includes bibliographies. [BS2555.2.N48] 68-2325
1. Bible. N. T. Gospels—Criticism, Textual. I. Title. II. Series.

NEVIUS, Richard C. 226'.1'04
The divines [i.e. divine] names in the Gospels, by Richard C. Nevius. Salt Lake City, University of Utah Press, 1967. v, 135 p. 25 cm. (Studies and documents 30) Includes bibliographies. [BS2555.2.N48] 68-2325
1. Bible. N.T. Gospels—Criticism, Textual. I. Title. II. Series.

COLWELL, Ernest Cadman, 226'.1'06
1901-
New or old? The Christian struggle with change and tradition, by Ernest C. Colwell. Philadelphia, Westminster Press [1970] 128 p. 21 cm. (The Sprunt lectures, 1969) Includes bibliographical references. [BS2555.2.C57] 70-111039 2.65
1. Bible. N.T. Gospels—Criticism, interpretation, etc.—Addresses, essays, lectures. 2. Gnosticism—Addresses, essays, lectures. I. Title. II. Series.

ALLEN, Charles 226'.2
Livingstone, 1913-
The Beatitudes, an interpretation [by] Charles L. Allen. Westwood, N.J., Revell [1967] 61 p. col. illus. 20 cm. "From [the author's] 'God's psychiatry.' " [BT382.A4] 67-11071
1. Beatitudes.

ANDREWS, Charles Freer, 226.2
1871-1940
The Sermon on the Mount. Foreword by Rabindranath Tagore, introd. note by Agatha Harrison. New York, Collier [1962] 157p. 18cm. (AS341V) .95 pap.,
1. Sermon on the Mount. I. Ravindranatha Thakura, Sir, 1861-1941. II. Title.

AUGUSTINUS, Aurelius, 226.2
Saint, Bp. of Hippo.
Commentary on the Lord's Sermon on the Mount, with seventeen related sermons; translated by Denis J. Kavanagh. New York, Fathers of the Church, inc., 1951. vi, 382 p. 22 cm. (Writings of Saint Augustine, v. 3) The Fathers of the Church, a new translation, v. 11. Translation of De Sermone Domini in Monte, and other sermons. [BR60.F3A8 vol. 3] 52-1735
1. Sermon on the Mount. 2. Sermons, Latin—Translations into English. 3. Sermons, English—Translations from Latin. I. Title.

AUGUSTINUS, Aurelius, 226.2
Saint, Bp. of Hippo.
Commentary on the Lord's Sermon on the Mount, with seventeen related sermons. Translated by Denis J. Kavanaugh. Washington, Catholic University of America Press [1963, c195a] vi. 382 p. 22 cm. (Writings of Saint Augustine., v. 3) The fathers of the church, a new translation, v. 11. Translation of De Sermone Domini in Monte, and other sermons. [BR60.F3A8] 63-18826
1. Sermon on the mount. 2. Sermons, Latin — Translations in English. 3. Sermons, English — Translations from Latin. I. Kavanagh, Denis Joseph, 1886- II. Title. III. Series: The Fathers of the church, a new translation, v. 11

AUGUSTINUS, Aurelius, 226.2
Saint, Bp. of Hippo.
Commentary on the Lord's Sermon on the Mount, with seventeenth related sermons. Tr. by Denis J. Kavanagh. Washington, D.C., Catholic Univ. of America Pr. [1963, c.1951] vi, 382p. 22cm. (Writings of Saint Augustine, v.3; The Fathers of the church, a new translation, v.11) 63-18826 5.00
1. Sermon on the Mount. 2. Sermons, Latin—Translations into English. 3. Sermons, English—Translations from Latin. I. Kavanagh, Denis Joseph, 1886- tr. II. Title. III. Series.

BAKER, Eric W 226.2
The neglected factor; the ethical element in the Gospel. New York, Abingdon Press [1963] ix, 100 p. 21 cm. [BT382.B36] 63-24997
1. Beatitudes. 2. Religion and ethics. I. Title. II. Title: (The Cato lecture, 1963)

BAKER, Eric W. 226.2
The neglected factor; the ethical element in the Gospel. Nashville, Abingdon [c.1963] ix, 100p. 21cm. (Cato lect., 1963) 63-24997 2.25
1. Beatitudes. 2. Religion and ethics. I. Title.

BAKER, Gordon Pratt. 226.2
In the school of Christ; the meaning of the Beatitudes for today. Nashville, Tidings [1962] 96 p. 19 cm. Includes bibliography. [BT382.B35] 62-20173
1. Beatitudes. I. Title.

BATDORF, Irvin W 226.2
Interpreting the Beatitudes, by Irvin W. Batdorf. Philadelphia, Westminster Press [1966] 160 p. 21 cm. Includes bibliographies. [BT382.B37] 66-11518
1. Beatitudes. I. Title.

BATDORF, Irvin W. 226.2
Interpreting the Beatitudes. Philadelphia, Westminster [c.1966] 160p. 21cm. Bibl. [BT382.B37] 66-11518 2.25 pap.,
1. Beatitudes. I. Title.

BIBLE. N. T. Matthew. 226.2
English. 1957. Douai
The Gospel according to Saint Matthew. With an introd. and commentary by C. C. Martindale. Westminster, Md. Newman Press 1957 Newm :n P-ess [1 57] 224p. illus. 19cm. (Stonyhurst Scripture manuals) [BS2575 M37] 58 484
1. Bible. N. T. Matthew—Commentaries. I. Martindale, Cyril Charlie, 1879- II. Title.

BIBLE. N.T. Matthew. 226.2
English. 1958. Authorized.
The book of Matthew. With special arrangement by Holland Evans, Jr. Carbondale, Ill., Dunaway-Sinclair, 1958. 171p. 27cm. 'A correlation of parallel quotations located in both the Old and New Testaments of the Bible as related to Matthew.' [BS2573 1958] 58-26554
1. Bible. O. T.—Quotations in the N. T. I. Evans, Holland. II. Title.

BIBLE. N.T. Matthew. 226.2
English. 1962. Noli.
The port of Nazareth; a revised version of the Gospel of St. Matthew, with a rhythmical translation of the sayings and parables of Our Lord and Savior Jesus Christ, by Metropolitan Fan S. Noli. Boston, 1962. 111 p. 19 cm. [BS2573] 63-349
I. Noli, Fan Stylian, Abp., 1882- tr. II. Title.

BIBLE. N.T. Matthew. 226'.2
English. Einspruch. 1971?
The good news according to Matthew. Translated by Henry Einspruch. [5th ed.] Baltimore, Lewis and Harriet Lederer

Foundation [1971? c1964] vi, 83 p. illus. 21 cm. [BS2573 1971] 72-168657
I. Einspruch, Henry, 1892- tr. II. Title.

BIBLE N. T. Matthew V-VII. 226.2
English. 1957. Bowman-Tapp
The Gospel from the Mount; a new translation and interpretation of Matthew, chs, 5 to 7, by John Wick Bowman and Roland W. Tapp. Philadelphia, Westminster Press [1957] 189p. 21cm. [BT380.B67] 57-9708
1. Sermon on the Mount. I. bowman, John Wick, 1894- ed. and tr. II. Tapp, oland W., ed. and t-. III. Title.

BIBLE N. T. Matthew V-VII. 226.2
English. Paraphrases. 1954. Scher
The Master-speech: the Sermon in the Mount; a nonsectarian interpretation of Matthew 5-7, with questions and answers for study, by Andrew R. Scher. [1st ed.] New York, Exposition Press [1954] 60p. 21cm. [BT380.S33] 54-5753
1. Sermon on the Mount. I. Scher, Andrew R. II. Title.

BIBLE. N.T. Matthew 23-VIII 226.2
1. English. 1955. Authorized.
The Sermon on the Mount. Introd. by Norman Vincent Peale. Wood engravings by John De Pol. [1st ed.] Cleveland, World Pub. Co. [1955] 50p. illus. 21cm. [BT380.A3 1955] 55-8255
1. Sermon on the Mount. I. Title.

BONHOEFFER, Dietrich, 1906- 226.2
1945
The cost of discipleship. [Tr. from German] Rev., unabridged [6th] ed. containing material not previously tr. New York, Macmillan [1963, c.1959] 352p. 18cm. (MP131) Bibl. 1.45 pap.,
1. Sermon on the Mount. I. Title.

BONHOEFFER, Dietrich, 1906- 226.2
1945.
The cost of discipleship. [Translated from the German by R. H. Fuller, with some revision by Irmgard Booth] Rev. [i.e. 2d] & unabridged ed. containing material not previously translated. New York, Macmillan [1959] 285 p. 23 cm. Translation of Nachfolge. [BT380.B66 1959] 60-677
1. Sermon on the Mount. I. Title.

*BOOTY, John. 226.2
Yearning to be free; verses and homilies for meditation on the Christian life. Cambridge, Mass., Greeno, Hadden, [1974] 72 p. 21 cm. [BV4500] ISBN 0-913550-03-5. 2.25 (pbk.)
1. Christian life. I. Title.

BUNCH, Taylor Grant. 226.2
The road to happiness. Washington, Review and Herald Pub. Association [c1960] 128p. 21cm. [BT382.B79] 60-15508
1. Beatitudes—Sermons. 2. Seventh-Day Adventists—Sermons. I. Title.

BUTLER, Basil Christopher. 226.2
The originality of St. Matthew; a critique of the twodocument hypothesis. Cambridge [Eng.] University Press, 1951. vii. 178 p. 23 cm. [BS2575.B8] 51-13171
1. Bible. N. Y. Matthew—Criticism, interpretation, etc. I. Title.

BUTTRICK, George Arthur, 226'.2
1892-
The Beatitudes; a contemporary meditation [by] George A. Buttrick. Design and illus. by Diana Blank. Nashville, Abingdon Press [1968] 63 p. illus. 19 cm. [BT382.B83] 68-25366 2.50
1. Beatitudes—Meditations. I. Title.

COHON, Beryl David, 1898- 226.2
Jacob's well; some Jewish sources and parallels to the Sermon on the Mount. New York, Bookman Associates [1956] 112p. 23cm. [BT380.C57] 56-4459
1. Sermon on the Mount. I. Title.

COHON, Beryl David, 1898- 226.2
Jacob's well; some Jewish sources and parallels to the Sermon on the Mount. New York, Bookman Associates [1956] 112p. 23cm. [BT380.C57] 56-4459
1. Sermon on the Mount. I. Title.

CONNICK, C. Milo 226.2
Build on the rock; you and the Sermon on the Mount. [Westwood, N.J.] Revell [c.1960] 191p. Includes bibliography. 22cm. 60-5503 2.95
1. Sermon on the Mount. I. Title.

CROCK, Clement Henry, 1890- 226.2
The eight Beatitudes. New York, J. F. Wagner [1953] 149 p. 21 cm. [BT382.C7] 53-2128
1. Beatitudes. I. Title.

CROWE, Charles M 226.2
Sermons from the Mount. Nashville, Abingdon Press [1954] 159p. 21cm. [BT380.C7] 54-5941
1. Sermon on the Mount—Sermons. 2. Methodist Church—Sermons. 3. Sermons, American. I. Title.

DAVIES, William David, 226.2
1911-
The Sermon on the Mount, by W. D. Davies. Cambridge [Eng.] University Press, 1966. 163 p. 19 cm. [BT380.2.D35] 66-17057
1. Sermon on the Mount. I. Title.

DAVIES, William David, 226.2
1911-
The setting of the Sermon on the Mount. [New York] Cambridge [c.]1964. xiii, 546p. 24cm. Bibl. 64-630 12.50
1. Sermon on the Mount. I. Title.

DELIMAT, Casimir A. 226.2
Ascent; spiritual progress according to the Beatitudes. New York, St. Paul Publications [1961, c.1960] 188p. 60-14931 3.25
1. Beatitudes. I. Title.

EDDLEMAN, H Leo. 226.2
Teachings of Jesus in Matthew 5-7. Nashville, Convention Press [1955] 146p. 20cm. [BT380.E3] 56-21488
1. Sermon on the Mount. I. Title.

FITCH, William 226.2
The Beatitudes of Jesus. Illus. by Armand Merizon. Grand Rapids, Mich., Eerdmans [1962, c.1961] 132p. 61-18336 3.00 bds.,
1. Beatitudes. I. Title.

FITZGERALD, Ernest A. 226'.2
There's no other way [by] Ernest A. Fitzgerald. Nashville, Abingdon Press [1970]. 144 p. 20 cm. [BT380.2.F55] 75-124753 3.50
1. Sermon on the Mount—Sermons. 2. Methodist Church—Sermons. 3. Sermons, American. I. Title.

FRIEDLANDER, Gerald, 1871- 226'.2
1923.
The Jewish sources of the Sermon on the Mount. New York, Ktav Pub. House, 1969. lviii, 301 p. 24 cm. (The Library of Biblical studies) Reprint of the 1911 ed., with a new "Prolegomenon, by Solomon Zeitlin." Includes bibliographical references. [BT380.F67 1969] 67-11897
1. Sermon on the Mount. I. Title. II. Series.

GRAHAM, William Franklin, 226.2
1918-
The secret of happiness; Jesus' teaching on happiness as expressed in the Beatitudes. [1st ed.] Garden City, N.Y., Doubleday, 1955. 117 p. illus. 22 cm. [BT382.G7] 55-11331
1. Beatitudes. 2. Happiness. I. Title.

GYLDENVAND, Lily M., 1917- 226'.2
Invitation to joy, by Lily M. Gyldenvand. Minneapolis, Augsburg Pub. House [1969] 111 p. 17 cm. [BT382.G9] 73-84803 2.95
1. Beatitudes—Meditations. I. Title.

HUBBARD, Benjamin Jerome. 226'.2
The Matthean redaction of a primitive apostolic commissioning : an exegesis of Matthew 28:16-20 / by Benjamin Jerome Hubbard. [Missoula? Mont.] : Society of Biblical Literature, 1974. xiii, 187 p. ; 21 cm. (Dissertation series - Society of Biblical Literature ; no. 19) Thesis—University of Iowa, 1973. Bibliography: p. 181-187. [BS2575.2.H82] 74-16566 ISBN 0-88414-047-4
1. Bible. N.T. Matthew XXVIII, 16-20—Criticism, interpretation, etc. I. Title. II. Series: Society of Biblical Literature. Dissertation series ; no. 19.

HUNTER, Archibald Macbride. 226.2
A pattern for life; an exposition of the Sermon on the Mount. Philadelphia, Westminster Press [1953] 124p. 20cm. 'First published in Great Britain in 1953 ... under the title: Design for life.' [BT380.H85 1953a] 53-11817
1. Sermon on the Mount. I. Title.

HUNTER, Archibald Macbride. 226.2
A pattern for life; an exposition of the Sermon on the Mount: its making,its exegesis, and its meaning, by Archibald M. Hunter. Rev. ed. Philadelphia, Westminister Press [1965] 127 p. 19 cm. First published in London in 1953 under title: Design for life. [BT380.2.H85] 66-11517
1. Sermon on the Mount. I. Title.

HUTCHISON, Harry. 226.2
The Beatitudes and modern life. New York, Morehouse-Barlow [1960] 127p. 20cm. Includes bibliography. [BT382.H85] 60-6204
1. Beatitudes—Study and teaching. I. Title.

JORDAN, Clarence. 226'.2
Sermon on the Mount. [Rev. ed.] Valley Forge [Pa.], Judson Press [1970, c1952] 126 p. 20 cm. (A Koinonia publication) [BT380.2.J67 1970] 78-17614 1.95
1. Sermon on the Mount. I. Title.

KEPLER, Thomas Samuel, 226.2
1897-
Jesus' design for living. Nashville, Abingdon Press [c1955] 127p. 20cm. [BT380.K4] 55-5045
1. Sermon onthe Mount—Meditations. I. Title.

KINGSBURY, Jack Dean. 226'.2
The parables of Jesus in Matthew 13; a study in redaction-criticism. [1st ed.] Richmond, John Knox Press [1969] xii, 180 p. 23 cm. "Revised version of a doctoral dissertation ... submitted to the ... University of Basel ... 1966." Bibliography: p. [167]-170. [BS2575.2.K5 1969] 69-17512 5.95
1. Jesus Christ—Parables. 2. Bible. N.T. Matthew XIII—Criticism, interpretation, etc. I. Title.

LAMSA, George Mamishisho, 226.2
1893-
The kingdom on earth, by George M. Lamsa. Lee's Summit, Mo., Unity Books [distributed by Hawthorn Books, New York] 1966. 192 p. 20 cm. [BT380.2.L3] 66-25237
1. Sermon on the Mount. I. Title.

LAWSON, William, 1904- 226.2
Good Christian men rejoice; the meaning and attainment of happiness. New York, Sheed and Ward, 1955. 202p. 20cm. [BT382.L35] 55-9456
1. Beatitudes. 2. Happiness. I. Title.

LLOYD-JONES, David Martyn 226.2
Studies in the Sermon on the Mount. [v.1] Grand Rapids, Eerdmans [1959] 320p. v. 23cm. 60-34 4.50
1. Sermon on the Mount—Sermons. I. Title.

LLOYD-JONES, David Martyn. 226.2
Studies in the Sermon on the Mount. [1st ed.] Grand Rapids, Eerdmans [1959-60] 2v. 23cm. [BT380.L56] 60-34
1. Sermon on the Mount—Sermons. I. Title.

LLOYD-JONES, David Martyn 226.2
Studies in the Sermon on the Mount. v.2. Grand Rapids, Mich., Eerdmans [1961] 337p. 60-34 4.50
1. Sermon on the Mount—Sermons. I. Title.

MCARTHUR, Harvey K. 226.2
Understanding the Sermon on the Mount. New York, Harper [c.1960] 192p. 22cm. Bibl.: p.181-186 60-11783 3.50 half cloth,
1. Sermon on the Mount. I. Title.

MCMILLAN, Robert M. 226'.2
Happiness is God's gift [by] Robert M. McMillan. Nashville, Broadman Press [1970] 95 p. illus. 18 cm. [BT382.M282] 71-95408 2.95
1. Beatitudes. I. Title.

MARTIN, Hugh, 1890- 226.2
The Beatitudes. New York, Harper [1953] 92p. 20cm. [BT382.M285 1953] 52-11077
1. Beatitudes. I. Title.

MATURIN, Basil William, 226.2
1847-1915.
Laws of the spiritual life. Baltimore, Carroll Press, 1951. v, 281 p. 18 cm. [BT382.M37 1951] 51-7430
1. Beatitudes 2. Spiritual life—Catholic authors. I. Title.

MERCHANT, Jane. 226.2
Blessed are you. New York, Abingdon Press [1961] 112p. 16cm. [BT382.M39] 61-12767
1. Beatitudes—Meditations. I. Title.

MEYER, Frederick 226.2
Brotherion, 1847-1929.
Blessed are ye: talks on the Beatitudes. GrandRapids, Baker Book House, 1955. 142p. 21cm. [BT382] 55-8794
1. Beatitudes—Sermons. 2. Baptists—Sermons. 3. Bermons, English. I. Title.

MEYER, Frederick 226.2
Brotherton, 1847-1929.
The directory of the devout life; meditations on the Sermon on the Mount. Grand Rapids, Baker Book House, 1954. 191p. 21cm. [Co-operative reprint library] [BV4501] 54-11074
1. Christian life. 2. Sermon on the Mount—Meditations. I. Title.

MEYER, Frederick 226.2
Brotherton, 1847-1929.
The Sermon on the Mount; the directory of the devout life. Grand Rapids, Baker Book House, 1959. 191p. 21cm. [BT380.M46 1959] 60-2245
1. Sermon on the Mount —Meditations. 2. Christian life. I. Title.

MILLER, John W., 1926- 226'.2
The Christian way; a guide to the Christian life based on the Sermon on the Mount, by John W. Miller. Scottdale, Pa., Herald Press [1969] 136 p. 18 cm. Bibliography: p. 136. [BT380.2.M5] 78-76622
1. Sermon on the Mount. I. Title.

MORGAN, Edward J 1906- 226.2
No thought for tomorrow. Grand Rapids, Eerdmans [1961] 123p. 23cm. [BT380.2.M65] 60-53087
1. Sermon on the Mount. I. Title.

MORRIS, Leon. 226.2
The story of the cross; a devotional study of St. Matthew, chapters 26-28. Grand Rapids, Eerdmans, 1957. 128p. 21cm. [BS2575] 57-13714
1. Bible. N. T. Matthew XXVI-XXVIII—Commentaries. 2. Jesus Christ—Passion—Devotional literature. I. Title.

MYRES, William V 226.2
Design for happiness. Nashville, Broadman Press [1961] 124p. 21cm. Includes bibliography. [BT380.2.M9] 61-12416
1. Sermon on the Mount. I. Title.

PENNINGTON, Chester A. 226'.2
A more excellent way [by] Chester A. Pennington. Design and illus. by David Dawson. Nashville, Abingdon Press [1969] 47 p. illus. 19 cm. [BS2675.4.P45] 71-86163 2.25
1. Bible. N.T. 1 Corinthians XIII—Meditations. 2. Love (Theology)—Meditations. I. Title.

PINK, Arthur Walkington, 226.2
1886-1952.
An exposition of the Sermon on the Mount. Grand Rapids, Baker Book House, 1959 [c1953] 422p. 23cm. [BT380.P5 1959] 59-8344
1. Sermon on the Mount. I. Title.

PINK, Arthur Walkington, 226.2
1886-1952
An exposition of the Sermon on the Mount. [1st ed.] Swengel, Pa., Bible Truth Depot, 1950. 442 p. 22 cm. [BT380.P5] 51-3606
1. Sermon on the Mount. I. Title.

PRICE, Walter K. 226'.2
Jesus' prophetic sermon: the Olivet key to Israel, the church, and the nations, by Walter K. Price. Chicago, Moody Press [1972] 160 p. 22 cm. [BS2575.2.P74] 70-175493 ISBN 0-8024-4330-3 4.95
1. Jesus Christ—Prophecies. 2. Bible. N.T. Matthew XXIV-XXV—Criticism, interpretation, etc. I. Title.

PROCHNOW, Herbert Victor, 226.2
1897-
Meditations on the Beatitudes. Boston, W. A. Wilde Co. [1952] 66 p. 17 cm. [BT382.P7] 52-12608
1. Beatitudes. I. Title.

RICE, John R., 1895- 226.2
The King of the Jews; a verse-by-verse commentary on the Gospel according to Matthew. Wheaton, Ill., Sword of the Lord Publishers [1955] c504p. 21cm. [BS2575.R52] 55-42711
1. Bible. N. T. Matthew—Commentaries. I. Title.

RIDDERBOS, Herman N 226.2
Matthew's witness to Jesus Christ; the King and the kingdom. New York, Association Press [1958] 94p. 20cm. (World Christian books) [BS2575.R47] 58-11536
1. Bible. N. T. Matthew—Commentaries. I. Title.

RONGLONE, Louis A 226.2
Conferences on the beatitudes. Philadelphia, P. Relily Co. [1959] 175p. 21cm. [BT382.R65] 59-4794
1. Beatitudes—Sermons. 2. Monastic and religious life of women. I. Title.

RUF, Peter, 1890- 226.2
What He said: a concordance of the words of Christ as they appear in the four Gospels. New York, Carlton Press, 1962. 116p. 21cm. (A Reflection book) [BT306.R73] 62-52077
1. Jesus Christ—Words. 2. Bible. N. T. Gospels—Concordances, English. I. Title.

SCHUMM, Robert William. 226'.2
Gifts of grace; 13 Beatitudes. Foreword by Arlo L. Schilling. Danville, Ill., Interstate Printers & Publishers [1969] 78 p. 23 cm. Bibliographical references included in "Notes" (p. 73-78) [BT382.S38] 73-79734
1. Beatitudes—Meditations. I. Title.

SHINN, Roger Lincoln. 226.2
Sermon on the Mount. Philadelphia. United Church Press [1962] 112 p. 19 cm. (A Pilgrim book) [RT380.2.S5] 62-19785
1. Sermon on the Mount. I. Title.

SHINN, Roger Lincoln 226.2
Sermon on the Mount. Philadelphia, United Church [c.1959, 1962] 112p. 19cm. (Pilgrim bk.) 62-19785 1.45 pap.,
1. Sermon on the Mount. I. Title.

SMITH, Charles Zachariah. 226.2
The divine constitution. [1st ed.] Los Angeles, De Vorss [1952] 152p. 23cm. [BT382.S62] 52-67066
1. Beatitudes. I. Title.

SOARES Prabhu, George M. 226.2
The formula quotations in the infancy narrative of Matthew : an enquiry into the tradition history of Mt 1-2 / George M. Soares Prabhu. Rome : Biblical Institute Press, 1976. xv, 346 p., [2] leaves of plates ; 24 cm. (Analecta biblica ; 63) Includes indexes. Bibliography: p. [301]-318. [BS2575.2.S65] 76-379131
1. Bible. N.T. Matthew I-II—Criticism, interpretation, etc. I. Title. II. Series.

SOCKMAN, Ralph Washington, 226.2
1889-
The higher happiness. New York, Abingdon-Cokesbury Press [1950] 174 p. 21 cm. [BT382.S64] 49-50398
1. Beatitudes. I. Title.

SUGGS, M. Jack. 226'.2
Wisdom, christology, and law in Matthew's Gospel [by] M. Jack Suggs. Cambridge, Harvard University Press, 1970. 132 p. 22 cm. [BS2545.W45S9] 75-95930 6.00
1. Jesus Christ—Person and offices. 2. Bible. N.T. Matthew—Criticism, interpretation, etc. 3. Wisdom—Biblical teaching. 4. Law (Theology)—Biblical teaching. I. Title.

THIELICKE, Helmut, 1908- 226.2
Life can begin again; sermons on the Sermon on the Mount. Translated by John W. Doberstein. Philadelphia, Fortress Press [1963] 215 p. 22 cm. [BT380.2.T513] 63-12535
1. Sermon on the Mount — Sermons. 2. Lutheran Church — Sermons. 3. Sermons, English — Translations from German. 4. Sermons, German — Translations into English. I. Title.

THIELICKE, Helmut, 1908- 226.2
Life can begin again; sermons on the Sermon on the Mount. Tr. [from German] by John W. Doberstein. Philadelphia, Fortress [c.1963] 215p. 22cm. 63-12535 3.75
1. Sermon on the Mount—Sermons. 2. Lutheran Church—Sermons. 3. Sermons. English—Translations from German. 4. Sermons, German—Translations into English. I. Title.

THOMAS, David, 1813-1894. 226.2
The Gospel of St. Matthew; an expository and homiletic commentary. Edited by William Webster. Grand Rapids, Baker Book House, 1956. xvi, 506p. 23cm. [Baker reprint library, 5] 'A reprint of the 1873 printing by Dickinson and Higham, London, under the title The genius of the Gospel.' [BS2575.T5 1956] 56-7587
1. Bible. N. T. Matthew—Commentaries. I. Title.

THOMAS, David, 1813-1894. 226.2
The Gospel of St. Matthews; an expository and homiletic commentary. Edited by William Webster. Grand Rapids, Baker Book House, 1956. xvi, 560 p. 23 cm. [Baker reprint library, 5] "A reprint of the 1873 printing by Dickinson and Higham, London, under the title The genius of the Gospel." [BS2575.T5 1956] 56-7587
1. Bible. N.T. Matthews — Commentaries. I. Title.

THOMPSON, Ernest Trice, 226.2
1894-
The Sermon on the Mount and its meaning for today [Rev. ed.] Richmond, John Knox Press [1961] 128 p. 21 cm. (Aletheia paperbacks) Includes bibliography. [BT380.T46 1961] 61-3735
1. Sermon on the Mount. I. Title.

THOMPSON, Ernest Trice, 226.2
1894-
The Sermon on the Mount and its meaning for today. [Rev. ed.] Richmond, John Knox Press [1953, c1946] 154 p. 21 cm. [BT380.T46 1953] 53-11761
1. Sermon on the Mount.

THOMPSON, Ernest Trice, 226.2
1894-
The Sermon on the Mount and its meaning for today. [Rev. ed.] Richmond, va., John Knox [1961, c.1946, 1961] 128p. (Aletheia paperbacks) Bibl. 61-3735 1.45 pap.,
1. Sermon on the Mount. I. Title.

VAN RYN, August, 1800- 226.2
Meditations in Matthew. [1st ed.] New York, Loizeaux Bros. [1958] 319 p. 20 cm. [BS2575.V2] 58-45397
1. Bible. N.T. Matthew — Meditations. I. Title.

VIGEVENO, H. S. 226'.2
Climbing up the mountain, children, by H. S. Vigeveno. Glendale, Calif., G/L Regal Books [1968] 184 p. 18 cm. [BT380.2.V5] 68-18058
1. Sermon on the Mount. I. Title.

WALKER, Harold Blake. 226.2
Ladder of light; the meaning of the Beatitudes. New York, Revell [1951] 192 p. 21 cm. [BT382.W27] 51-9442
1. Beatitudes — Sermons. 2. Presbyterian Church — Sermons. 3. Sermons, American. I. Title.

WEST, Edward N. 226.2
God's image in us; a meditation on Christ's teachings in His Sermon on the Mount. [1st ed.] Cleveland, World Pub. Co. [1960] 181 p. 21 cm. [BT380.2.W45] 60-5809
1. Sermon on the Mount. I. Title.

WEST, Edward N. 226.2
God's image in us; a meditation on Christ's teachings in His Sermon on the Mount. Cleveland, World Pub. Co. [c.1960] 181p. 21cm. 60-5809 3.50
1. Sermon on the Mount. I. Title.

*WHITE, Elena G. de 226.2
El discurso maestro de Jesucristo. Mexico, Ediciones Interamericanas [dist. Mountain View, Calif., Pacific Pr. Pub. Assn., c.1964] 128p. illus. 20cm. 1.25 pap.,
I. Title.

WHITE, Ellen Gould (Harmon) 226.2
1827-1915.
Thoughts from the Mount of Blessing. Mountain View, Calif., Pacific Press Pub. Association [c1956] 172p. 18cm. [BT380.W45 1956] 56-7169
1. Sermon on the Mount. I. Title.

WHITE, Ellen Gould (Harmon) 226.2
1827-1915.
Thoughts from the Mount of Blessing. Mountain View, Calif., Pacific Press Pub. Association [c1956] 172 p. 18 cm. [BT380.W45 1956] 56-7169
1. Sermon on the Mount. I. Title.

WIRT, Sherwood Eliot. 226.2
The cross on the mountain. Foreword by Eugenia Price. New York, Crowell [1959] 129 p. 21 cm. [BT382.W56] 59-7761
1. Beatitudes. I. Title.

FOWLER, Harold. 226'.2'007
The Gospel of Matthew. Joplin, Mo., College Press [1968- v. map. 23 cm. (Bible study textbook series) [BS2576.F6] 78-1064 6.95
1. Bible. N.T. Matthew—Study—Outlines, syllabi, etc. I. Title.

BIBLE. N.T. Matthew. 226'.2'048
Greek. 1964.
Family II in Matthew, by Russell Champlin. Salt Lake City, University of Utah Press, 1964. vii, 170 p. facsims. 25 cm. (Studies and documents, 24) "This study ... is an essential portion of a thesis submitted to the Language Department, University of Utah, in partial fulfillment of the requirements for a doctor of philosophy degree." Introductory and explanatory matter in English; text in Greek. Includes bibliographical references. [BS2571 1964] 73-168366
I. Champlin, Russell. II. Title. III. Series.

BIBLE. N.T. Matthew. 226'.2'048
Greek. 1966.
Family E and its allies in Matthew, by Russell Champlin. With collation of codex 903 by Jacob Geerlings. Salt Lake City, University of Utah Press, 1966. viii, 200 p. 25 cm. (Studies and documents, 28) Introductory matter in English; text in Greek. Includes bibliographical references. [BS2571 1966] 72-17240
I. Champlin, Russell, ed. II. Geerlings, Jacob, ed. III. Title. IV. Series.

JORDAN, Clarence. 226'.2'052
The cotton patch version of Matthew and John; including the Gospel of Matthew (except for the "begat" verses) and the first eight chapters of the Gospel of John. New York, Association Press [1970] 128 p. 22 cm. (A Koinonia publication) Paraphrased from the Nestle-Aland Greek text, 23d ed., 1957. [BS2577.J65] 70-129422 2.50
1. Bible. N.T. Matthew—Paraphrases, English. 2. Bible. N.T. John I-VIII—Paraphrases, English. I. Title.

BIBLE. N.T. Matthew. 226'.2'0529
Anglo-Saxon. 1904.
Euangelium secundum Mattheum. The Gospel of Saint Matthew in West-Saxon; edited from the manuscripts, by James Wilson Bright. Boston, Heath, 1904. [New York, AMS Press, [1973 c.1972] 147 p. 19 cm. Original ed. issued in series: The Belles-lettres series. Section 1. English literature. [BS2573 1904a] 78-144446 ISBN 0-404-53604-2 7.50
I. Bright, James Wilson, 1852-1926, ed. II. Bible. N.T. Matthew. Anglo-Saxon. Bright. 1972. III. Title.

BLAIR, Edward Payson 226.206
Jesus in the Gospel of Matthew. Nashville, Abingdon Press [c.1960] 176p. 21cm. 60-12067 3.00
1. Bible. N. T. Matthew—Theology. 2. Jesus Christ—Person and offices. I. Title.

BLAIR, Edward Payson, 226.206
1910-
Jesus in the Gospel of Matthew. New York, Abingdon Press [1960] 176p. 21cm. [BS2575.5.B55] 60-12067
1. Bible. N. T. Matthew—Theology. 2. Jesus Christ—Person and office. I. Title.

BORNKAMM, Gunther. 226.206
Tradition and interpretation in Matthew [by] Gunther Bornkamm, Gerhard Barth [and] Heinz Joachim Held. [Translated by Percy Scott from the German] Philadelphia, Westminster Press [1963] 307 p. 23 cm. (The New Testament library) Bibliographical footnotes. [BS2575.2.B613] 63-10495
1. Bible. N.T. Matthew—Theology. I. Title.

CERFAUX, Lucien, 1883- 226.206
Apostle and apostolate, according to the Gospel of St. Matthew. Translated by Donald D. Duggan. New York, Desclee Co., 1960. 183p. 22cm. Translation of Discours de mission. [BV2073.C433] 60-6515
1. Missions—Biblical teaching. 2. Bible. N. T. Matthew IX, 35-x, 15—Meditations. I. Title.

COPE, O. Lamar, 1938- 226'.2'06
Matthew, a scribe trained for the kingdom of heaven / by O. Lamar Cope. Washington : Catholic Biblical Association of America, 1976. p. cm. (The Catholic Biblical quarterly monograph series ; 5) Originally presented as the author's thesis, Union Theological Seminary, 1971. Includes index. Bibliography: p. [BS2575.2.C66 1976] 75-36778 ISBN 0-915170-04-3 : 3.00
1. Bible. N.T. Matthew—Criticism, interpretation, etc. I. Title. II. Series: The Catholic Biblical quarterly. Monograph series ; 5.

CRISWELL, Wallie A. 226.206
Expository notes on the Gospel of Matthew. Grand Rapids, Mich., Zondervan [c.1961] 168p. 61-66712 2.95
1. Bible. N. T. Matthew—Commentaries. I. Title.

DAILY, Starr, pseud. 226.206
The magnificent love; a gospel of divine love based on the Sermon on the Mount. Westwood, N.J., Revell [1964] 144 p. 20 cm. 64-16604
1. Sermon on the Mount. 2. Love (Theology) I. Title.

DAILY, Starr, pseud. 226.206
The magnificent love; a gospel of divine love based on the Sermon on the Mount. Westwood, N. J., Revell [c.1964] 144p. 20cm. 64-16604 2.95 bds.,
1. Sermon on the Mount. 2. Love (Theology) I. Title.

FORD, William Herschel, 226.206
1900-
Simple sermons from the Gospel of Matthew. Grand Rapids, Zondervan Pub. House, [1963] 242 p. 21 cm. [BS2575.4.F6] 63-15742
1. Bible. N. T. Matthew—Sermons. 2. Sermons, American. 3. Baptists—Sermons. I. Title.

FORD, William Herschel, 226.206
1900-
Simple sermons from the Gospel of Matthew. Grand Rapids, Mich., Zondervan [c.1963] 242p. 21cm. 63-15742 3.95 bds.,
1. Bible. N.T. Matthew—Sermons. 2. Sermons, American. 3. Baptists—Sermons. I. Title.

GAEBELIEN, Arno Clemens, 226.206
1861-1945.
The Gospel of Matthew; an exposition. New York, Loizeaux Bros., [1961, c1910] 624 p. 21 cm. [BS2575.G3 1961] 61-17223
1. Bible. N.T. Matthew — Devotional literature. I. Title.

GRAHAM, William Franklin, 226.206
1918-
The secret of happiness; Jesus' teaching on happiness as expressed in the Beatitudes. New York, Pocket Bks. [1963, c.1955] 145p. 17cm. (M4274) .35 pap.,
1. Beatitudes. 2. Happiness. I. Title.

GRIFFITH, Arthur Leonard, 226.206
1920-
Pathways to happiness; a devotional study of the Beatitudes. New York, Abingdon Press [1964] 127 p. 20 cm. [BT382.G75] 64-10601
1. Beatitudes. I. Title.

GRIFFITH, Arthur Leonard, 226.206
1920-
Pathways to happiness; a devotional study of the Beatitudes. Nashville, Abingdon [c.1964] 127p. 20cm. 64-10601 2.50 bds.,
1. Beatitudes. I. Title.

HARGROVE, Hubbard Hoyt, 226.206
1895-
At the master's feet; expository sermons on the Sermon on the Mount. Grand Rapids, Mich., Baker Bk. 1963 [c.1944] 211p. 21cm. (Evangelical pulpit lib.) 63-12028 2.95
1. Sermon on the Mount—Sermons. 2. Baptists—Sermons. 3. Sermons, English. I. Title.

HASTINGS, Robert J. 226'.2'06
Take heaven now! [By] Robert J. Hastings. Nashville, Broadman Press [1968] 126 p. 21 cm. Bibliographical references included in "Notes" (p. 124-126) [BT382.H28] 68-12130
1. Beatitudes. I. Title.

HORACE, J. Gentry, Rev. 226.206
None good but God; a general introduction to scientific Christianity in the form of a spiritual key to Matthew 19:16-22. New York, Exposition [c.1962] 105p. 21cm. 3.00
I. Title.

KINGSBURY, Jack Dean. 226'.2'06
Matthew : structure, christology, kingdom / by Jack Dean Kingsbury. London : S.P.C.K., 1976. xiv, 178 p. ; 24 cm. Includes bibliographical references and indexes. [BS2575.2.K49 1976] 77-355759 ISBN 0-281-02916-4 : £6.50
1. Jesus Christ—History of doctrines—Early church, ca. 30-600. 2. Bible. N.T. Matthew—Criticism, interpretation, etc. I. Title.

MEIER, John P. 226'.2'06
Law and history in Matthew's Gospel : a redactional study of Mt.5:17-48 / John P. Meier. Rome : Biblical institute press, 1976. xi, 206 p. ; 24 cm. (Analecta Biblica ; 71) Originally presented as the author's thesis, Biblical Institute, 1975 (S.S.L.) Includes indexes. Bibliography: p. [172]-192. [BS2575.2.M44 1976] 76-380938
1. Bible. N.T. Matthew V, 17-48—Criticism, interpretation, etc. I. Title. II. Series.

MILLER, Fred 226.206
Meditations from Matthew. New York, Carlton [dist. Comet, c.]1961. 97p. (Reflection bk.) 3.00
I. Title.

O'CONNOR, Daniel, 1933- 226'.2'06
The images of Jesus : exploring the metaphors in Matthew's Gospel / by Daniel O'Connor and Jacques Jimenez ; [ill. by Tomie de Paola]. Minneapolis : Winston Press, c1977. 187 p. : ill. ; 24 cm. [BS2575.2.O27] 77-72549 ISBN 0-03-021326-6 pbk. : 5.95
1. Bible. N.T. Matthew—Criticism, interpretation, etc. 2. Metaphor. I. Jimenez, Jacques, joint author. II. Title.

PENDLETON, Winston K 226.206
Pursuit of happiness, a study of the Beatitudes. St. Louis, Bethany Press [1963] 79 p. 21 cm. [BT382.P43] 63-8824
1. Beatitudes. I. Title.

PENDLETON, Winston K. 226.206
Pursuit of happiness, a study of the Beatitudes. St. Louis, Bethany [c.1963] 79p. 21cm. 63-8824 1.95
1. Beatitudes. I. Title.

PLOTZKE, Urban Werner, 226.206
1907-
God's own Magna charta. [Tr. from German by J. Holland Smith] Westminster, Md., Newman [1964, c.1963] 198p. 19cm. 64-1943 4.25
1. Sermon on the Mount—Sermons. 2. Beatitudes—Sermons. I. Title.

POOVEY, William Arthur, 226'.2'06
1913-
The power of the kingdom; meditations on Matthew [by] W. A. Poovey. Minneapolis, Augsburg Pub. House [1974] 128 p. 20 cm. [BS2575.4.P66] 74-77682 ISBN 0-8066-1433-1 2.95 (pbk.)
1. Bible. N.T. Matthew—Meditations. I. Title.

PRABHAVANANDA, Swami, 226.206
1893-
The Sermon on the Mount according to Vedanta. Hollywood, Calif., Vedanta Press [1964] 110 p. 19 cm. [BT304.94.P68] 64-8660
1. Sermon on the Mount. 2. Jesus Christ—Hindu interpretations. I. Title.

PRABHAVANANDA, Swami, 226.206
1893-
The Sermon on the Mount according to Vedanta. Hollywood, Calif., Vedanta [c.1964] 110p. 19cm. [BT304.94.P68] 64-8660 2.50 bds.,

1. Sermon on the Mount. 2. Jesus Christ—Hindu interpretations. I. Title.

RIST, John M. 226'.2'06
On the independence of Matthew and Mark / John M. Rist. Cambridge [Eng.] ; New York : Cambridge University Press, 1977. p. cm. (Monograph series - Society for New Testament Studies ; 32) Includes bibliographical references and index. [BS2575.2.R58] 76-40840 ISBN 0-521-21476-9 : 11.50
1. Bible. N.T. Matthew—Relation to Mark. 2. Bible. N.T. Mark—Relation to Matthew. I. Title. II. Series: Studorium Novi Testamenti Societas. Monograph series ; 32.

STEDMAN, Ray C. 226'.2'06
Behind history / Ray C. Stedman. Waco, Tex. : Word Books, c1976. 166 p. ; 22 cm. (Discovery books) [BT375.2S68] 75-36181 ISBN 0-87680-450-4 : 5.95
1. Jesus Christ—Parables. 2. Bible. N.T. Matthew XIII—Criticism, interpretation, etc. I. Title.

STONEHOUSE, Ned Bernard, 1902- 226.206
The witness of Matthew and Mark to Christ. [2d ed.] Grand Rapids, Eerdmans [1958] 269 p. 20 cm. [BS2585.S8 1958] 59-16048
1. Bible. N.T. Mark — Criticism, interpretation, etc. 2. Bible. N.T. Matthew — Criticism, interpretation, etc. I. Title.

THURNEYSEN, Eduard, 1888- 226.206
The Sermon on the Mount. Translated by William Childs Robinson, Sr. with James M. Jobinson. Richmond, John Knox Press [1964] 82 p. 19 cm. (Chime paperbacks) Bibliographical references included in "Notes" (p. 79-82) [BT380.2.T523] 64-12625
1. Sermon on the Mount. 2. Bible. N. T. Matthew v-vii-Criticism, interpretation, etc. I. Title.

THURNEYSEN, Eduard, 1888- 226.206
The Sermon on the Mount. Tr. [from German] by William Childs Robinson, Sr., with James M. Robinson. Richmond, Va., Knox [c.1964]. 82p. 19cm. (Chime paperbacks) Bibl. 64-12625 1.00 pap.,
1. Sermon on the Mount. 2. Bible. N. T. Matthew v-vii—Criticism, interpretation, etc. I. Title.

WAETJEN, Herman C. 226'.2'06
The origin and destiny of humanness : an interpretation of the Gospel according to Matthew / Herman C. Waetjen. Corte Madera, Calif. : Omega Books, c1976. 266 p. ; 22 cm. Includes bibliographical references and indexes. [BS2575.2.W28] 77-350351 ISBN 0-89353-016-6 pbk. : 5.00
1. Bible. N.T. Matthew—Criticism, interpretation, etc. I. Title.

HARMS, Ray 226.2061
The Matthean weekday lessons in the Greek Gospel lectionary. [Chicago] Dept. of New Testament & Early Christian Lit., Univ. of Chicago [1966] vii, 55p. 24cm. (Studies in the lectionary text of the Greek New Testament, v.2, no. 6) Revision of authors' Thesis, Princeton Theological Seminary. Bibl. [BS2575.2.H3] 66-27028 1.25
1. Bible. N. T. Matthew — Criticism. Textual. 2. Lectionaries — Hist. & crit. I. Title. II. Series.

BARCLAY, William, lecturer in the University of Glasgow. 226'.2'066
The Beatitudes and the Lord's prayer for everyman. [1st U.S. ed.] New York, Harper & Row [1968, c1964] 256 p. 22 cm. Combined ed. of the author's The plain man looks at the Beatitudes, and The plain man looks at the Lord's prayer. [BT382.B369 1968] 68-17595
1. Beatitudes. 2. Lord's prayer. I. Title.

BONHAM, Tal D., 1934- 226'.2'066
The demands of discipleship; the relevance of the Sermon on the Mount, by Tal D. Bonham. [1st ed.] Pine Bluff, Ark., Discipleship Book Co. [1967] 178 p. 23 cm. Bibliography: p. [155]-172. [BT380.2.B6] 67-28446
1. Sermon on the Mount. I. Title.

BONHAM, Tal D., 1934- 226'.2'066
The demands of discipleship; the relevance of the Sermon on the Mount, by Tal D. Bonham. [1st ed.] Pine Bluff, Ark., Discipleship Bk. Co. [1967] 178p. 23cm. Bibl. [BT380.2.B6] 67 28446 3.95
1. Sermon on the Mount. I. Title.
The author is Southern Baptist. Publisher's address: 2604 W. 40th St., Pine Bluff, Ark. 71601.

BROWN, Raymond Edward. 226'.2'066
The birth of Messiah : a commentary on the infancy narratives in Matthew and Luke / by Raymond E. Brown. Garden City, N.Y. : Doubleday, c1977. p. cm. Includes bibliographies and indexes. [BS2575.2.B76] 76-56271 ISBN 0-385-05907-8 : 12.50
1. Jesus Christ—Nativity. 2. Bible. N.T. Matthew I-II—Criticism, interpretation, etc. 3. Bible. N.T. Luke I-II—Criticism, interpretation, etc. I. Title.

CHRYSOSTOMUS, Joannes, Saint, Patriarch of Constantinople, d.407. 226'.2'066
The preaching of Chrysostom; Homilies on the Sermon on the mount. Edited with an introd. by Jaroslav Pelikan. Philadelphia, Fortress Press [1967] ix, 230 p. 18 cm. (The Preacher's paperback library) Part of a larger work, Homilies on the Gospel of Saint Matthew, Homiliae in Matthaeum. Bibliographical footnotes. [BR65.C45H63] 67-13057
1. Sermon on the Mount—Sermons. 2. Bible. N. T. Matthew v-vii—Sermons. 3. Sermons, Greek—Translations into English. 4. Sermons, English—Translations from Greek. I. Pelikan, Jaroslav Jan 1923- ed. II. Title.

CHRYSOSTOMUS, Joannes, Saint, Patriarch of Constantinople, d.407. 226'.2'066
The preaching of Chrysostom; Homilies on the Sermon on the mount. Edited with an introd. by Jaroslav Pelikan. Philadelphia, Fortress Press [1967] ix, 230 p. 18 cm. (The Preacher's paperback library) Part of a larger work, Homilies on the Gospel of Saint Matthew, Homiliae in Matthaeum. Bibliographical footnotes. [BR65.C45H63 1967] 67-13057
1. Sermon on the Mount—Sermons. 2. Sermons, Greek—Translations into English. 3. Sermons, English—Translations from Greek. I. Pelikan, Jaroslav Jan, 1923- ed. II. Title.

FREYNE, Sean. 226'.2'066
Mark and Matthew. Chicago, ACTA Foundation [1971] viii, 245 p. 22 cm. (Scripture discussion commentary, 7) Contents.Contents.—Mark, by S. Freyne.—Matthew, by H. Wansbrough. Includes bibliographical references. [BS2585.3.F74] 72-178780
1. Bible. N.T. Mark—Commentaries. 2. Bible. N.T. Matthew—Commentaries. I. Wansbrough, Henry, 1934- II. Title. III. Series.

KINGSBURY, Jack Dean. 226'.2'066
Matthew / Jack Dean Kingsbury. Philadelphia : Fortress Press, c1977. xii, 116 p. ; 22 cm. (Proclamation commentaries) Includes index. Bibliography: p. 110-112. [BS2575.2.K47] 76-46732 ISBN 0-8006-0586-1 pbk. : 3.50
1. Bible. N.T. Matthew—Criticism, interpretation, etc. 2. Bible. N.T. Matthew—Homiletical use.

METZLER, Burton. 226'.2'066
Light from a hillside; the message of the Sermon on the Mount. Elgin, Ill., Brethren Press [1968] 140 p. 21 cm. [BT380.2.M4] 68-1648
1. Sermon on the Mount. I. Title.

REDHEAD, John A. 226'.2'066
Finding meaning in the Beatitudes [by] John A. Redhead. Nashville, Abingdon Press [1968] 109 p. 20 cm. [BT382.R38] 68-11467
1. Beatitudes. I. Title.

BIBLE. N. T. Matthew. English. 1958. Barclay. 226.207
The Gospel of Matthew. Translated with an introd. and interpretation by William Barclay. [2d ed.] Philadelphia, Westminster Press [1958] 2v. 18cm. (The Daily study Bible series) [BS2575.B35 1958] 59-8233
1. Bible. N. T. Matthew—Commentaries. I. Barclay, William. lecturer in the University of Glasgow, ed. and tr. II. Title. III. Series.

BIBLE. N.T. Matthew. English. 1963. New English. 226.207
The Gospel according to Matthew. Commentary by A. W. Argyle. Cambridge, University Press, 1963. ix, 227 p. maps. 20 cm. (The Cambridge Bible commentary: New English Bible) [BS2575.3.A7] 63-23728
1. Bible. N.T. Matthew—Commentaries. I. Argyle, Aubrey William, 1910- II. Title. III. Series.

BIBLE. N. T. Matthew. English. 1963. New English. 226.207
The Gospel according to Matthew. Commentary by A. W. Argyle. [New York] Cambridge [c.]1963. ix, 227p. maps. 20cm. (Cambridge Bible commentary: New English Bible) 63-23728 1.65 pap.,
1. Bible. N. T. Matthew—Commentaries. I. Argyle, Aubrey William, 1910- II. Title. III. Series.

BIBLE. N. T. Matthew. English. 1963. New English. 226.207
The Gospel according to Matthew. Commentary by A. W. Argyle. [New York] Cambridge [c.]1963. ix, 227p. maps. 20cm. (Cambridge Bible commentary: New English Bible) 63-23728 2.75 1.95 text ed. bds.,
1. Bible. N. T. Matthew—Commentaries. I. Argyle, Aubrey William, 1910- II. Title. III. Series.

BIBLE. N.T. Matthew. English. 1965. Revised standard. 226.207
The Gospel according to St. Matthew; a text and commentary for students [by] Alexander Jones. New York, Sheed & Ward [1965] 334 p. 21 cm. Bibliography: p. 323. [BS2575.3.J6 1965a] 65-12212
1. Bible. N.T. Matthew—Commentaries. I. Jones, Alexander, 1906- II. Title.

BIBLE. N. T. Matthew. English. 1965. Revised standard. 226.207
The Gospel according to St. Matthew; a text and commentary for students by Alexander Jones. New York, Sheed [c.1965] 334p. 21cm. Bibl. [BS2575.3.J6] 65-12212 5.00 bds.,
1. Bible. N. T. Matthew—Commentaries. I. Jones, Alexander, 1906- II. Title.

BIBLE. N.T. Matthew. English. Albright-Mann. 1971. 226'.2'07
Matthew; introduction, translation, and notes by W. F. Albright and C. S. Mann. [1st ed.] Garden City, N.Y., Doubleday, 1971. cxcviii, 366 p. 25 cm. (The Anchor Bible, v. 26) Bibliography: p. cxci-cxcviii. [BS192.2.A1 1964.G3 vol. 26] [BS2575.3] 77-150875 8.00
1. Bible. N.T. Matthew—Commentaries. I. Albright, William Foxwell, 1891-1971, ed. II. Mann, Christopher Stephen, ed. III. Title. IV. Series.

COX, G. E. P. 226.207
The Gospel according to Saint Matthew, a commentary. New York, Collier [1962] 191p. (Torch Bible commentary, AS236Y) Bibl. .95 pap.,
I. Title.

DAVIS, William Hersey, 1887- 226.207
Davis' notes on Matthew. Nashville, Broadman [c.1962] 109p. 21cm. 62-15325 1.50 pap.,
1. Bible. N.T. Matthew—Commentaries. I. Title.

ERDMAN, Charles Rosenbury, 1866-1960 226.207
The gospel of Matthew, an exposition. Pref. by Earl F. Zeigler. Philadelphia. Westminster [1966] 253p. 19cm. (His Commentaries on New Testament bks.) [BS2575.E7 1966] 66-9720 1.25 pap.,
1. Bible. N. T. Mathew —Commentaries. 2. Bible. N. T. Mathew. English. 1966. American standard. I. Title.

FENTON, John C., 1921- 226.207
The Gospel of St. Matthew. Baltimore, Penguin [1964, c.1963] 487p. map. 18cm. (Pelican Gospel commentaries, A488) Bibl. 64-1437 1.95 pap.,
1. Bible. N. T. Matthew—Commentaries. I. Bible. N.T. Matthew. English. 1964. Revised standard. II. Title.

FILSON, Floyd Vivian, 1896- 226.207
A commentary on the Gospel according to St. Matthew. New York, Harper [1961, c.1960] vi, 314p. (Harper's New Testament commentaries) Bibl.: p. 45-47. 61-5260 5.00
1. Bible. N. T. Matthew—Commentaries. I. Bible. N. T. Matthew. English. 1961. II. Title.

FRANZMANN, Martin H. 226.207
Follow Me; discipleship according to Saint Matthew. St. Louis, Concordia Pub. House, [c.]1961. 240p. Bibl. 60-53149 3.50
1. Bible. N. T. Matthew—Commentaries. I. Title.

GREEN, H. Benedict. 226'.2'07
The Gospel according to Matthew in the revised standard version : introduction and commentary / by H. Benedict Green. Oxford : University Press, 1975. 264 p. ; 18 cm. (The New Clarendon Bible : New Testament) Includes bibliographical references and index. [BS2575.3.G73] 76-357234 ISBN 0-19-836918-2 : 15.50
1. Bible. N.T. Matthew—Commentaries. I. Title. II. Series.

HAMILTON, William, 1924- 226.207
The modern reader's guide to Matthew and Luke. New York, Association Press [1959] 125p. 16cm. (An Association Press reflection book) [BS2576.H35] 59-8073
1. Bible, N.T. Matthew—Study—Outlines, syllabi, etc. 2. Bible, N.T. Luke—Study—Outlines, syllabi, etc. I. Title.

HOBBS, Herschel H 226.207
An exposition of the Gospel of Matthew, by Herschel H. Hobbs. Grand Rapids, Baker Book House, 1965. 422 p. 23 cm. [BS2575.3.H6] 65-18263
1. Bible. N.T. Matthew — Commentaries. I. Title.

HOBBS, Herschel H 226.207
An exposition of the Gospel of Matthew. Grand Rapids, Mich., Baker Bk. [c.]1965. 422p. 23cm. [BS2575.3.H6] 65-18263 6.95
1. Bible. N. T. Matthew—Commentaries. I. Title.

HOBBS, Herschel H. 226.207
The Gospel of Matthew. Grand Rapids, Mich., Baker Bk. 135p. (Proclaiming the New Testament) Bibl. 61-10006 2.50 bds.,
1. Bible. N. T. Matthew—Homiletical use. I. Title.

ISRAEL, Menachem. 226'.2'07
The record of Christ's life and doctrine; related by Saint Matthew. Interpretation and comments by Menachem Israel. [1st ed.] New York, Exposition Press [1968] viii, 190 p. 21 cm. [BS2575.3.I8] 68-5120
1. Bible. N.T. Matthew—Commentaries. I. Title.

LEAVELL, Roland Quinche, 1891-1963. 226.207
Studies in Matthew: the King and the kingdom. Nashville, Convention Press [c1962] 146 p. 20 cm. "Church study course [of the Sunday School Board of the Southern Baptist Convention] This book is number 0226 in category 2, section for adults and young people." [BS2575.3.L4] 62-10285
1. Bible. N.T. Matthew — Commentaries. I. Southern Baptist Convention. Sunday School Board. II. Title.

RICHARDS, Lawrence O. 226'.2'07
The Servant King : the life of Jesus on Earth : studies in Matthew / Larry Richards. Leader's ed. Elgin, Ill. : D. C. Cook Pub. Co., c1976. 278 p. ; 22 cm. (His Bible alive series) Includes bibliographical references. [BS2576.R53] 76-6581 ISBN 0-912692-98-7 pbk. : 3.95
1. Bible. N.T. Matthew—Study—Text-books. I. Title. II. Series.

SIMCOX, Carroll Eugene, 1912- 226.207
The first Gospel, its meaning and message. Greenwich, Conn., Seabury Press [1963] 311 p. 22 cm. With the author's translation of the Gospel according to St. Matthew at beginning of each chapter. [BS2575.3.S5] 63-8463
1. Bible. N. T. Matthew—Commentaries. I. Bible. N. T. Matthew. English. 1963. Simcox. II. Title.

SIMCOX, Carroll Eugene, 1912- 226.207
The first Gospel, its meaning and message. Greenwich, Conn., Seabury [c.1963] 311p. 22cm. 63-8463 5.75
1. Bible. N. T. Matthew—Commentaries. I. Bible. N. T. Matthew. English 1963 Simcox II. Title.

SMITH, Chuck, 1927- 226'.2'07
The Gospel of Matthew for growing Christians. Edited by Hugh and Norma Steven. Old Tappan, N.J., Revell [1973] 158 p. 21 cm. Retells the Gospel of Matthew in everyday language, elaborating on its important points and relating its message to Christian life today. [BS2575.3.S6] 73-9979 ISBN 0-8007-0617-X 2.45 (pbk.)
1. Bible. N.T. Matthew—Commentaries. I. Bible. N.T. Matthew. English. II. Title.

SPURGEON, Charles Haddon, 1834-1892 226.207
Popular exposition of Matthew. Introductory note by Mrs. C. H. Spurgeon. Includes textual index of sermons. etc., by Spurgeon on various passages in Matthew. Grand Rapids, Mich., Zondervan [1962] 263p. 23cm. A62 2.95
1. Bible. N. T. Matthew—Commentaries. I. Title.

TASKER, Randolph Vincent Greenwood, 1895- 226.207
The Gospel according to St. Matthew, an introduction and commentary. [1st ed.] Grand Rapids, Eerdmans [1961] 285 p. 20 cm. (The Tyndale New Testament commentaries) [BS2575.3.53] 61-18907
1. Bible. N.T. Matthew — Commentaries. I. Title.

THOMAS, William Henry Griffith, 1861-1924. 226.207
Outline studies in the Gospel of Matthew by W. H. Griffith Thomas, edited by his daughter. Grand Rapids, Eerdmans [1961] 476 p. 23 cm. [BS2576.T5] 61-10861
1. Bible. N.T. Matthew — Study — Outlines, Syllabi, etc. I. Title.

THOMAS, William Henry Griffith, 1861-1924. 226.207
Outline studies in the Gospel of Matthew, by W. H. Griffith Thomas, ed. by his daughter. Grand Rapids, Mich., Eerdmans [c.1961] 476p. 61-10861 5.50

1. Bible. N. T. Matthew—Study—Outlines, Syllabi, etc. I. Title.

TOLBERT, Malcolm. 226'.2'07
Good news from Matthew / Malcolm O. Tolbert. Nashville : Broadman Press, c1975. 248 p. ; 19 cm. [BS2575.3.T6] 75-2537 ISBN 0-8054-1353-7 pbk. : 3.50
1. Bible. N.T. Matthew—Commentaries. I. Title.

TRASKER, Randolph Vincent Greenwood, 1895- 226.207
The Gospel according to St. Matthew, an introduction and commentary [1st ed.] Grand Rapids, Eerdmans [1961] 285 p. 20 cm. (The Tyndale New Testament commentaries) [BS2575.3.T3] 61-18907
1. Bible. N. T. Matthew—Commentaries.

WARD, Arthur Marcus, 1906- 226.207
The Gospel according to St. Matthew. London, Epworth Press [1961; distributed in U.S.A. by Allenson, Naperville, Ill. stamped] 162 p. 19 cm. (Epworth preacher's commentaries) [BS2575.3.W3] 61-1635
1. Bible. N.T. Matthew — Commentaries. I. Title.

WILLETT, Franciscus. 226.207
St. Matthew and his Gospel. Valatie, N.Y., Holy Cross Press, 1964. xii, 169 p. 24 cm. (Holy Cross Bible series) Bibliography: p. ix-x. [BS2575.3.W5] 64-8536
1. Bible. N.T. Matthew — Commentaries. I. Title.

WILLETT, Franciscus 226.207
St. Matthew and his Gospel. Valatie, N.Y., Holy Cross Pr. [c.]1964. xii, 169p. 24cm. (Holy Cross Bible ser.) Bibl. [BS2575.3.W5] 64-8536 3.95
1. Bible. N. T. Matthew—Commentaries. I. Title.

BIBLE. N.T. Matthew. English. Barclay. 1975. 226'.2'077
The Gospel of Matthew / translated with an introd. and interpretation by William Barclay. Rev. ed. Philadelphia : Westminster Press, [1975- v. ; 20 cm. (The Daily study Bible series) Bibliography: v. 1, p. [401] [BS25731975b] 74-28251 ISBN 0-664-21300-6(v.1) : 6.25 ISBN 0-664-24100-X pbk. : 3.45
1. Bible. N.T. Matthew—Commentaries. I. Barclay, William, lecturer in the University of Glasgow, ed. II. Title. III. Series.

*BIBLE N. T. MATTHEW ENGLISH. REVISED STANDARD, 1975. 226'.2'077
The Gospel according to Matthew in the revised standard version. Introd. and commentary by H. Benedict Green. [London, New York.] Oxford University Press, 1975 xiv, 264 p. map. 19 cm. (New Clarendon Bible) Includes bibliographical references and index. [BS2573] ISBN 0-19-836918-2 15.50.
1. Bible. N.T. Matthew—Commentaries. I. Green, H. Benedict. II. Title.

BOLES, Henry Leo, 1874- 226'.2'077
A commentary on the Gospel according to Matthew / by H. Leo Boles. Nashville, Tenn. : Gospel Advocate Co., [1976?] c1952. 574 p. ; 23 cm. A companion volume to A commentary on the New Testament Epistles by David Lipscomb. Includes index. Bibliography: p. [567]-569. [BS2575.B59 1976] 76-370462 5.95
1. Bible. N.T. Matthew—Commentaries. I. Title.

GREENE, Oliver B. 226'.2'077
The Gospel according to Matthew, by Oliver B Greene. Greenville, S.C., Gospel Hour [1971- v. 21 cm. [BS2575.3.G74] 72-187237 6.00 per vol.
1. Bible. N.T. Matthew—Commentaries. I. Title.

GUTZKE, Manford George. 226.2077
Plain talk on Matthew. Grand Rapids, Zondervan Pub. House [1966] 245 p. 23 cm. [BS2575.4.G78] 66-13689
1. Bible. N.T. Matthew — Devotional literature. I. Title.

GUTZKE, Manford George 226.2077
Plain talk on Matthew. Grand Rapids, Mich., Zondervan [c.1966] 245p. 23cm. [BS2575.4.G78] 66-13689 3.95 bds.,
1. Bible. N.T. Matthew — Devotional literature. I. Title.

KINGSBURY, Jack Dean. 226'.2'077
Matthew : structure, Christology, kingdom / by Jack Dean Kingsbury. Philadelphia : Fortress Press, c1975. xiv, 178 p. ; 24 cm. Includes bibliographical references and indexes. [BS2575.2.K49] 75-13043 ISBN 0-8006-0434-2 : 10.95
1. Jesus Christ—History of doctrines—Early church, ca. 30-600. 2. Bible. N.T. Matthew—Criticism, interpretation, etc. I. Title.

KUNKEL, Fritz, 1889-1956. 226'.2'077
Creation continues. Edited by Elizabeth Kunkel and Ruth Spafford Morris. [Rev. ed.] Waco, Tex., Word Books [1973] 284 p. port. 22 cm. Bibliography: p. 279-281. [BS2575.K8 1973] 73-76257 5.95
1. Bible. N.T. Matthew—Commentaries. 2. Bible. N.T. Matthew—Psychology. I. Kunkel, Elizabeth, ed. II. Morris, Ruth Spafford, ed. III. Title.

SCHWEIZER, Eduard, 1913- 226'.2'077
The good news according to Matthew / Eduard Schweizer ; translated by David E. Green. Atlanta : John Knox Press, [1975] 572 p. ; 21 cm. Translation of Das Evangelium nach Matthaus. "New Testament Scripture quotations are from Good news for modern man, the New Testament in Today's English." Includes bibliographical references and indexes. [BS2575.3.S3313] 74-3717 ISBN 0-8042-0251-6 : 12.95
1. Bible. N.T. Matthew—Commentaries. I. Bible. N.T. Matthew. English. Today's English. 1975. II. Title.

SENIOR, Donald. 226'.2'077
Invitation to Matthew : a commentary on the Gospel of Matthew with complete text from the Jerusalem Bible / Donald Senior. 1st ed. Garden City, N.Y. : Image Books, 1977. p. cm. Bibliography: p. [BS2575.3.S46] 77-73337 ISBN 0-385-12211-X pbk. : 2.95
1. Bible. N.T. Matthew—Commentaries. I. Bible. N.T. Matthew. English. Jerusalem Bible. 1977. II. Title.

TRILLING, Wolfgang. 226'.2'077
The Gospel according to St. Matthew: [Translated by Kevin Smyth. New York] Herder and Herder [1969- v. 21 cm. (New Testament for spiritual reading, 1-) Translation of Das Evangelium nach Matthaus. [BS2341.2.N382 vol. 1, etc.] 70-10741 6.00 (v. 1)
1. Bible. N.T. Matthew—Commentaries. I. Bible. N.T. Matthew. English. 1969. II. Title. III. Series.

MCNEELY, Jeannette. 226'.2'09505
Led by a star : the Wise men for beginning readers : Matthew 2:1-12 for children / by Jeannette McNeely ; illustrated by Aline Cunningham. St. Louis : Concordia Pub. House, c1977. [46] p. : col. ill. ; 23 cm. (I can read a Bible story) The three Wise Men follow a bright new star believing it will lead them to the new King of the Jews. [BT315.M33] 77-6308 ISBN 0-570-07326-X : 3.95. ISBN 0-570-07320-0 pbk. : 1.95
1. Jesus Christ—Nativity—Juvenile literature. I. Cunningham, Aline. II. Title.

ARNOLD, Eberhard, 1883-1935. 226'.2'206
Salt and light; talks and writings on the Sermon on the Mount. [Ed. & tr. from German by the Society of Brothers] Rifton, N. Y., Plough 1967. xxxi, 309p. 20cm. [BT380.A7] 67-18009
1. Sermon on the Mount. I. Bruderhof Communities. II. Title.

AMBROZIC, Aloysius M., 1930- 226'.3
The hidden kingdom; a redaction-critical study of the references to the kingdom of God in Mark's Gospel, by Aloysius M. Ambrozic. Washington, Catholic Biblical Association of America, 1972. xi, 280 p. 25 cm. (The Catholic Biblical quarterly. Monograph series, 2) Bibliography: p. 248-265. [BS2417.K5A43] 72-89100 9.00
1. Bible. N.T. Mark—Criticism, interpretation, etc. 2. Kingdom of God—Biblical teaching. I. Title. II. Series.

BARNETT, Albert Edward, 1895- 226.3
Disciples to such a Lord: the Gospel according to St. Mark. [New York] Woman's Division of Christian Service, Board of Missions, the Methodist Church [1957] 162p. 19cm. Includes bibliography. [BS2585.B37] 57-7701
1. Bible. N. T. Mark—Commentaries. I. Title.

BEASLEY-MURRAY, George Raymond, 1916- 226.3
A commentary on Mark thirteen, by G. R. Beasley-Murray. London, New York Macmillan, 1957. 124p. 23cm. [BS2585.B39] 57-3717
1. Bible. N. T. Mark XIII— Commentaries. I. Title.

BIBLE. N. T. Mark. English. 1952. Vernon. 226.3
The Gospel of St. Mark; a new translation in simple English from the Nestle Greek text, by Edward Vernon. [1st American ed.] New York, Prentice-Hall [1952] v, 115 p. 18 cm. [BS2583 1952] 52-8110
I. Vernon, Edward Thomson, 1890- tr. II. Title.

BIBLE. N. T. Mark. English. 1956. Douai. 226.3
The gospel according to Saint Mark. With an introd. and commentary by C. C. Martindale. Westminster, Md., Newman Press, 1956. xxxii, 177p. maps. 19cm. (Stonyhurst Scripture manuals) [BS2585.M35] 56-14231
1. Bible. N. T. Murk—Commentaries. I. Martindale, Cyril Charlie, 1879- II. Title.

BIBLE. N. T. Mark. English. 1957. 226.3
The Gospel of Mark; translated with an introd. and interpretation by William Barclay. [2d ed.] Philadelphia Westminster Press [1957] xxi, 390p. 18cm. (The Daily study Bible series) [BS2585.B36 1957] 57-6029
1. Bible. N. T. Mark—Commentaries. I. Barclay, William lecturer in the University of Glasgow, ed. and tr. II. Title. III. Series.

BIBLE. N.T. Mark. English. 1957. 226.3
The Gospel of Mark; translated with an introd. and interpretation by William Barclay. [2d ed.] Philadelphia, Westminster Press [1957] xxi, 390 p. 18 cm. (The Daily study Bible series) [BS2585.B36 1957] 57-6029
1. Bible. N.T. Mark—Commentaries. I. Barclay, William, lecturer in the University of Glasgow, ed. and tr. II. Title. III. Series.

BIBLE. N. T. Mark. English. Selections. 1957. Revised standard. 226.3
The Son of God; readings from the Gospel according to St. Mark. With background information by Edric A. Weld and William Sydnor. Illustrated by Leonard Weisgard. Greenwich, Conn., Seabury Press [1957] vi, 122p. illus. 21cm. (The Seabury series, R-6) [BS2586.W4] 57-8343
1. Bible. N. T. Mark—Study—Text-books. I. Weld, Edric A. II. Sydnor, William. III. Title.

CARRINGTON, Philip, Bp., 1892- 226.3
The primitive Christian calendar; a study in the making of the Marcan Gospel. Cambridge [Eng.] University Press, 1952- v. facsims. 23cm. Contents.v. 1. Introduction & text. [BS2585.C32] 52-9796
1. Bible. N. T. Mark—Criticism, interpretaion etc. 2. Church year. I. Title.

FARMER, William Reuben. 226'.3
The last twelve verses of Mark, by William R. Farmer. [London, New York] Cambridge University Press [1974] xii, 123 p. facsim. 23 cm. (Society for New Testament Studies. Monograph series, 25) Bibliography: p. 110-112. [BS2585.2.F35] 73-89003 ISBN 0-521-20414-3
1. Bible. N.T. Mark XVI, 9-20—Criticism, interpretation, etc. I. Title. II. Series: Studiorum Novi Testamenti Societas. Monograph series, 25.

FARMER, William Reuben. 226'.3
The last twelve verses of Mark, by William R. Farmer. [London, New York] Cambridge University Press [1974] xii, 123 p. facsim. 23 cm. (Society for New Testament Studies. Monograph series, 25) Bibliography: p. 110-112. [BS2585.2.F35] 73-89003 ISBN 0-521-20414-3 9.50
1. Bible. N.T. Mark XVI, 9-20—Criticism, interpretation, etc. I. Title. II. Series: Studiorum Novi Testamenti Societas. Monograph series, 25.

FARRER, Austin Marsden. 226.3
A study in St. Mark. New York, Oxford University Press, 1952. 398 p. 23 cm. [BS2585.F3] 52-12001
1. Bible. N. T. Mark—Criticism, interpretation, etc. I. Title.

GRANT, Frederick Clifton, 1891- 226.3
The earliest gospel; studies of the evangelic tradition at its point of crystallization in writing, by Frederick C. Grant. Nashville, Abingdon [1962, c.1943] 270p. (Apex bks., H3) Bibl. 1.25 pap.,
1. Bible. N. T. Mark—Criticism, interpretation, etc. I. Title.

GUTZKE, Manford George. 226'.3
Go Gospel; daily devotions and Bible studies in the Gospel of Mark. Glendale, Calif., G/L Regal Books [1968] 183 p. map. 18 cm. Bibliography: p. 182-183. [BS2585.4.G8] 68-8389
1. Bible. N.T. Mark—Devotional literature. I. Title.

GUY, Harold A 226.3
The origin of the Gospel of Mark. New York, Harper [1955] 176p. 19cm. [BS2585.G8 1955] 56-307
1. Bible. N. T. Mark—Criticism, interpretation, etc. I. Title.

HUNTER, Archibald Macbride 226.3
The Gospel according to Saint Mark, a commentary. New York, Collier [1962] 160p. (Torch Bible commentary, AS237Y) Bibl. .95 pap.,
1. Bible—N.T. Mark—Commentaries. I. Title.

LIGHTFOOT, Robert Henry, 1883- 226.3
The Gospel message of St. Mark. Oxford, Clarendon Press, 1950. 116 p. 23 cm. [BS2585.L48] 51-9265
1. Bible. N. T. Mark—Criticism interpretation, etc. 2. Bible. N. T. Mark—Theology. I. Title.

LOHSE, Eduard, 1924- 226.3
Mark's witness to Jesus Christ. [Translated from the German by Stephen Neill] New York, Association Press [1955] 93p. 20cm. (World Christian books) [BS2585.L57] 55-7567
1. Bible. N. T. Mark—Criticism, interpretation, etc. I. Title.

LOHSE, Eduard, 1924- 226.3
Mark's witness to Jesus Christ. [Translated from the German by Stephen Neill] New York, Association Press [1955] 93 p. 20 cm. (World Christian books [3]) [BS2585.L57] 55-7567
1. Bible. N. T. Mark — Criticism, interpretation, etc. I. Title.

NEVIUS, Richard C. 226'.3
The divine names in Mark, by Richard C. Nevius. Salt Lake City, University of Utah Press, 1964. v, 84 p. 25 cm. (Studies and documents, 25) Bibliography: p. 50-52. [BS2545.N3N48] 72-196578
1. Bible. N.T. Mark—Criticism, interpretation, etc. 2. God—Name—Biblical teaching. I. Title. II. Series.

PETERSON, Hugh R 1903- 226.3
A study of the Gospel of Mark. Nashville, Convention Press [1958] 150p. 19cm. [BS2586.P4] 58-10534
1. Bible. N. T. Mark—Study—Text-books. I. Title.

ROBERTSON, Archibald Thomas, 1863-1934. 226.3
Studies in Mark's Gospel. Rev. and edited by Heber F. Peacock. Nashville, Broadman Press [1958] 134p. 21cm. [BS2585.R65 1958] 58-8925
1. Bible. N. T. Mark —Criticism, interpretation, etc. 2. Bible—Criticism, interpretation, etc.— N. T. Mark. I. Title.

ROBINSON, James McConkey, 1924- 226.3
The problem of history in Mark. Naperville, Ill., A. R. Allenson [1957] 95p. 22cm. (Studies in Biblical theology, no. 21) Bibliographical footnotes. [BS2585.R68] 57-857
1. Bible. N. T. Mark—Criticism. interpretation, etc. I. Title. II. Series.

THOMPSON, Ernest Trice, 1894- 226.3
The Gospel according to Mark and its meaning for today. Richmond, John Knox Press [1954] 255p. 21cm. [BS2585.T55] 53-11760
1. Bible. N. T. Mark—Commentaries. I. Title.

VAN RYN, August, 1890- 226.3
Mediations in Mark, [1st ed.] New York, Loizeaux Bros. [1957] 247 p. 20 cm. [BS2585.V3] 57-14195
1. Bible, N.T. Mark — Meditations. I. Title.

VAN LINDEN, Philip 226'.3'007
Knowing Christ through Mark's gospel : an adult study guide to the Gospel of Mark / Philip Van Linden. Chicago : Franciscan Herald Press, [1976] p. cm. (Herald Biblical booklet series) Bibliography: p. [BS2585.5.V36] 76-21787 ISBN 0-8199-0727-8 pbk. : 0.95
1. Bible. N.T. Mark—Study—Text-books. I. Title.

BIBLE. N.T. Mark. English. Price. 1976. 226'.3'052
The good news according to Mark / translated by Reynolds Price. [s.l. : s.n.], 1976 (s.l. : West Coast Print Center) 50 p. ; 21 cm. "Three hundred copies." [BS2583.P74] 77-359043
I. Price, Reynolds, 1933- II. Title.

BIBLE. N.T. Mark. Anglo-Saxon. 1905. 226'.3'0529
Euangelium secundum Marcum. The Gospel of Saint Mark in West-Saxon; edited from the manuscripts, by James Wilson Bright. Boston, Heath, 1905. [New York, AMS Press, 1973] 84 p. 19 cm. Original ed. issued in series: The Belles-lettres series. Section 1. English literature. [BS2583 1905a] 74-144445 ISBN 0-404-53603-4 65.00
I. Bright, James Wilson, 1852-1926, ed. II.

Bible. N.T. Mark. Anglo-Saxon. Bright. 1972. III. Title.

ACHTEMEIER, Paul J. 226'.3'06
Mark / Paul J. Achtemeier ; Gerhard Krodel, editor. Philadelphia : Fortress Press, c1975. vi, 122 p. ; 22 cm. (Proclamation commentaries) Includes index. Bibliography: p. 118-119. [BS2585.2.A25] 74-26333 ISBN 0-8006-0581-0 pbk. : 2.95
1. Bible. N.T. Mark—Criticism, interpretation, etc. I. Title.

BEST, Ernest. 226.306
The Temptation and the Passion: the Markan soteriology. Cambridge [Eng.] University Press, 1965. xiii, 221 p. 23 cm. (Society for New Testament Studies. Monograph series, 2) Bibliography: p. 192-200. [BS2585.2.B47] 65-15312
1. Bible. N. T. Mark — Criticism, interpretation, etc. 2. Bible. N.T. Mark — Theology. 3. Jesus Christ — Passion. 4. Jesus Christ — Temptation. 5. Salvation — Biblical teachng. I. Title. II. Series: Studlorum Novi Testamenti Societas. Monograph series, 2

BEST, Ernest 226.306
The Temptation and the Passion: the Markan soteriology. [New York] Cambridge [c.]1965. xiii, 221p. 23cm. (Soc. for New Testament Studies. Monograph ser., 2) Bibl. Title. (Series: Studiorum Novi Testamenti Societas. Monograph series, 2) [BS2585.2.B47] 65-15312 6.50
1. Bible. N. T. Mark—Criticism, interpretation, etc. 2. Bible. N. T. Mark—Theology. 3. Jesus Christ—Passion. 4. Jesus Christ—Temptation. 5. Salvation—Biblical teaching. I. Title. II. Series.

BURKILL, T. Alec. 226.306
Mysterious revelation; an examination of the philosophy of St. Mark's Gospel. Ithaca, N.Y., Cornell University Press [1963] xii, 337 p. 24 cm. Bibliography:p. 325-332. [BS2585.2.B8] 63-11306
1. Bible. N.T. Mark — Criticism, interpretation, etc. I. Title.

BURKILL, T. Alec 226.306
Mysterious revelation; an examination of the philosophy of St. Mark's Gospel. Ithaca, N.Y., Cornell Univ. Pr. [c.1963] xii, 337p. 24cm. Bibl. 63-11306 6.50
1. Bible. N.T. Mark—Criticism, interpretation, etc. I. Title.

CENTER for 226'.3'06
Hermeneutical Studies in Hellenistic and Modern Culture.
The aretalogy used by Mark : protocol of the sixth colloquy, 12 April 1973 / The Center for Hermeneutical Studies in Hellenistic and Modern Culture ; Morton Smith. Berkeley, CA : The Center, [1975] p. cm. (Protocol series of the collogules of the Center for Hermeneutical Studies in Hellenistic and Modern Culture ; no. 6) Bibliography: p. [BS2585.2.C38 1975] 75-34344
1. Bible. N.T. Mark—Criticism, interpretation, etc.—Congresses. I. Smith, Morton, 1915- II. Title. III. Series: Center for Hermeneutical Studies in Hellenistic and Modern Culture. Protocol series of the colloquies ; no. 6.

CHURCH, Ivor F. 226'.3'06
A study of the Marcan Gospel / by Ivor F. Church. 1st ed. New York : Vantage Press, c1976. 200 p. ; 22 cm. Includes bibliographical references. [BS2585.2.C47] 76-380759 ISBN 0-533-02038-7 : 7.50
1. Bible. N.T. Mark—Criticism, interpretation, etc. I. Title.

FULLER, Reginald 226'.3'06
Horace.
Longer Mark : forgery, interpolation, or old tradition? / Reginald Horace Fuller ; W. Wuellner, editor. Berkeley, Calif. : Center for Hermeneutical Studies, 1975. p. cm. (Protocol of the eighteenth colloquy) Bibliography: p. [BS2585.2.F84] 76-12558 ISBN 0-89242-017-0 : 2.00
1. Bible. N.T. Mark—Criticism, interpretation, etc.—Congresses. 2. Secret Gospel according to Mark—Congresses. I. Title. II. Series: Center for Hermeneutical Studies. Protocol series of the colloquies ; 18.

KEE, Howard Clark. 226'.3'06
Community of the new age : studies in Mark's Gospel / by Howard Clark Kee. Philadelphia : Westminster Press, c1977. xi, 225 p. ; 24 cm. Includes bibliographical references and indexes. [BS2585.2.K43] 76-49484 ISBN 0-664-20770-7 : 13.95
1. Bible. N.T. Mark—Criticism, interpretation, etc. I. Title.

KEE, Howard Clark. 226'.3'06
Community of the new age : studies in Mark's Gospel / by Howard Clark Kee. Philadelphia : Westminster Press, c1977. xi, 225 p. ; 24 cm. Includes bibliographical references and indexes. [BS2585.2.K43] 76-49484 ISBN 0-664-20770-7 : 13.95
1. Bible. N.T. Mark—Criticism, interpretation, etc. I. Title.

LIGHTFOOT, Robert Henry, 226.306
1883-
The Gospel message of St. Mark. [New York] Oxford [1962] 118p. 20cm. (41) 1.50 pap.,
1. Bible. N. T. Mark—Criticism, interpretation, etc. 2. Bible. N. T. Mark—Theology. I. Title.

MAUSER, Ulrich W., 1926- 226.306
Christ in the wilderness; the wilderness theme in the second Gospel and its basis in the Biblical tradition. Naperville, Ill., Allenson [1963] 159p. 22cm. (Studies in Biblical theology, no. 39) Bibl. 63-5689 2.75 pap.,
1. Bible. N. T. Mark—Criticism, interpretation, etc. 2. Wilderness (Theology) I. Title.

MILLER, Dale, 1923- 226'.3'06
The adult Son. [Des Moines, Iowa, Printed by Wallace-Homestead Co., 1974] 163 p. 23 cm. [BS2585.2.M54] 74-77418 ISBN 0-9600726-1-6
1. Bible. N.T. Mark—Criticism, interpretation, etc. I. Title.

THE Passion in Mark : 226'.3'06
studies on Mark 14-16 / edited by Werner H. Kelber ; with contributions by John R. Donahue ... [et al.]. Philadelphia : Fortress Press, c1976. xvii, 203 p. ; 24 cm. Includes indexes. Bibliography: p. 181-189. [BS2585.2.P3] 75-36453 ISBN 0-8006-0439-3 : 10.95
1. Bible. N.T. Mark XIV-XVI—Criticism, interpretation, etc.—Addresses, essays, lectures. I. Kelber, Werner H. II. Donahue, John R.

TROCME, Etienne. 226'.3'06
The formation of the Gospel according to Mark / by Etienne Trocme ; translated by Pamela Gaughan. Philadelphia : Westminster Press, [1975] viii, 293 p. ; 22 cm. Translation of La formation de l'Evangile selon Marc. Includes indexes. Bibliography: p. 262-278. [BS2585.2.T7513] 75-15510 ISBN 0-664-20803-7 : 12.95
1. Bible. N.T. Mark—Criticism, interpretation, etc. I. Title.

COUNTERFEIT or 226'.3'061
genuine? : Mark 16? John 8? / Edited by David Otis Fuller. 1st ed. Grand Rapids : Grand Rapids International Publications, 1975. 217 p. ; 21 cm. Includes bibliographical references. [BS2585.2.C65] 74-82807 ISBN 0-8254-2615-4 pbk. : 3.50
1. Bible. N.T. Mark XVI, 9-20—Criticism, interpretation, etc. 2. Bible. N.T. John VII, 53-VIII, 11—Criticism, interpretation, etc. 3. Bible—Evidences, authority, etc. I. Fuller, David Otis, 1903-

BIBLE. N.T. Mark. 226'.3'066
English. 1974.
The Gospel according to Mark; the English text with introduction, exposition, and notes, by William L. Lane. Grand Rapids, Eerdmans [1974] xvi, 652 p. 23 cm. (The New international commentary on the New Testament, v. 2) Includes bibliographical references. [BS2585.3.L36] 73-76529 ISBN 0-8028-2340-8 10.00
1. Bible. N.T. Mark—Commentaries. I. Lane, William L., 1931- II. Title. III. Series.

BURKILL, T. Alec. 226'.3'066
New light on the earliest Gospel: seven Markan studies, by T. A. Burkill. Ithaca [N.Y.] Cornell University Press [1972] xi, 275 p. 22 cm. Bibliography: p. 265-270. [BS2585.2.B83] 74-37777 ISBN 0-8014-0706-0 11.50
1. Bible. N.T. Mark—Criticism, interpretation, etc.—Addresses, essays, lectures. I. Title.

DONAHUE, John R. 226'.3'066
Are you the Christ? The trial narrative in the Gospel of Mark, by John R. Donahue. [Missoula, Mont.] Published by Society of Biblical Literature for the Seminar on Mark, 1973. xi, 269 p. 22 cm. (Society of Biblical Literature. Dissertation series, no. 10) Originally presented as the author's thesis, University of Chicago, 1972. Bibliography: p. 245-260. [BS2585.2.D66 1973] 73-81373 ISBN 0-88414-021-0
1. Jesus Christ—Trial. 2. Bible. N.T. Mark XIV, 53-65—Criticism, interpretation, etc. I. Society of Biblical Literature. Seminar on Mark. II. Title. III. Series.

HARRISVILLE, Roy A 226'.3'066
The miracle of Mark; a study in the Gospel [by] Roy a. Harrisville. Minneapolis, Augsburg Pub. House [1967] 128 p. 20 cm. (A Tower book) Bibliographical references included in "Notes" (p. 118-121) [BS2585.2.H3] 67-11725
1. Bible. N. T. Mark — Criticism interpretation etc. I. Title.

HARRISVILLE, Roy A. 226'.3'066
The miracle of Mark; a study in the Gospel [by] Roy A. Harrisville. Minneapolis, Augsburg Pub. House [1967] 128 p. 20 cm. (A Tower book) Bibliographical references included in "Notes" (p. 118-121) [BS2585.2.H3] 67-11725
1. Bible. N.T. Mark—Criticism, interpretation, etc. I. Title.

RIGAUX, Beda 226'.3'066
The testimony of Carroll. Chicago, Franciscan Herald [c.1966] xvi, 138p. 21cm. Bibl. [BS2585.2.R513] 66-2877 3.95
1. Bible. N. T. Mark--Criticism, interpretation, etc. I. Title.

RIGAUX, Beda. 226'.3'066
The testimony of St. Mark. Pref. by Lucien Cerfaux. Translated from the French by Malachy Carroll. Chicago, Franciscan Herald Press [c1966] xvi, 138 p. 21 cm. "Bibliographical note": p. 135-138. [BS2585.2.R513] 66-28770
1. Bible. N.T. Mark — Criticism, interpretation, etc. I. Title.

SCHENKE, Ludger, 1940- 226'.3'066
Glory and the Way of the Cross: the Gospel of Mark. Translated by Robin Scroggs. Chicago, Franciscan Herald Press [1972] 71 p. 18 cm. (Herald Biblical booklets) Translation of Herrlichkeit und Kreuz. [BS2585.2.S26413] 72-77454 ISBN 0-8199-0213-6 0.95
1. Jesus Christ—History of doctrines—Early church, ca. 30-600. 2. Bible. N.T. Mark—Criticism, interpretation, etc. I. Title.

WEEDEN, Theodore J. 226'.3'066
Mark-traditions in conflict [by] Theodore J. Weeden. Philadelphia, Fortress Press [1971] x, 182 p. 23 cm. Based on the author's thesis, Claremont Graduate School and University Center, 1964. Bibliography: p. 169-176. [BS2585.2.W4] 70-157543 ISBN 0-8006-0041-X 6.95
1. Bible. N.T. Mark—Criticism, interpretation, etc. I. Title.

MARXSEN, Willi, 1919- 226'.3'067
Mark the Evangelist; studies on the redaction history of the Gospel. Translated by James Boyce [and others] Nashville, Abingdon Press [1969] 222 p. 23 cm. Translation of Der Evangelist Markus. Bibliographical footnotes. [BS2585.2.M2713] 69-12022 5.50
1. Bible. N.T. Mark—Criticism, interpretation, etc. I. Title.

ANDERSON, Hugh, 1920- 226'.3'07
The Gospel of Mark / Hugh Anderson. London : Oliphants, 1976. xviii, 366 p. ; 23 cm. (New century Bible) Includes indexes. Bibliography: p. xii-xviii. [BS2585.3.A52] 76-377165 ISBN 0-551-00579-3 : £6.95
1. Bible. N.T. Mark—Commentaries. I. Title. II. Series.

BEACH, Curtis. 226.307
The Gospel of Mark, its making and meaning. [1st ed.] New York, Harper [1959] 124p. 20cm. Includes bibliography. [BS2585.2.B4] 59-7144
1. Bible. N. T. Mark—Criticism, interpretation, etc. I. Title.

BIBLE. N.T. Mark. 226.307
English. 1963. Revised standard.
The gospel according to St. Mark; a text and commentary for students [by] Alexander Jones. New York, Sheed & Ward [1963] 255 p. illus. 21 cm. Bibliography: p. 251. [BS2585.3.J65] 63-23021
1. Bible. N.T. Mark—Commentaries. I. Jones, Alexander, 1906- II. Title.

BIBLE. N.T. Mark, 226.307
English, 1963. Revised standard.
The gospel according to St. Mark; a text and commentary for students [by] Alexander Jones. New York, Sheed [1964, c.1963] 255p. illus. 21cm. Bibl. 63-23021 4.50 bds.,
1. Bible. N. T. Mark—Commentaries. I. Jones, Alexander, 1906— II. Title.

CARRINGTON, Philip, 226.307
Abp., 1892-
According to Mark; a running commentary on the oldest Gospel. [New York] Cambridge University Press, 1960[ ] 384p. Bibl. footnotes. 60-51429 9.50
1. Bible. N. T. Mark—Commentaries. I. Title.

COLE, Robert Alan. 226.307
The Gospel according to St. Mark, an introduction and commentary. [1st American ed.] Grand Rapids, Eerdmans [1961] 263 p. 21 cm. (The Tyndale New Testament commentaries [2]) [BS2585.3.C6 1961] 61-18908
1. Bible. N. T. Mark—Commentaries.

CRANFIELD, C.E.B. 226.307
The Gospel according to Saint Mark; an introduction and commentary. 2d [ed.] with supplementary notes. [New York] Cambridge, 1963 [c.1959] xv, 493p. 18cm. (Cambridge Greek Testament commentary) Bibl. 63-25954 2.95 pap.,
1. Bible. N.T. Mark—Commentaries. I. Title. II. Series.

CRANFIELD, C. E. B. 226.307
The Gospel according to Saint Mark, an introducton and commentary. [New York] Cambridge [Eng.] University Press, 1959 [i.e. 1960] xv, 479p. Includes bibliography. 19cm. (Cambridge Greek testament commentary) 60-16015 7.50
1. Bible. N. T. Mark—Commentaries. I. Title. II. Series.

EARLE, Ralph. 226.307
The Gospel according to Mark. Grand Rapids, Mich., Zondervan Pub. House [1957] 192 p. map. 25 cm. (The Evangelical commentary on the Bible [2]) Bibliography: p. 11-17. [BS491.E8 vol. 2] 64-56824
1. Bible, N.T. Mark. English. 1957. American standard. I. Title. II. Series.

EARLE, Ralph 226.307
The Gospel of Mark. Grand Rapids, Mich., Baker Bk. House, [c.] 1961. 119 p. (Proclaiming the New Testament) Bibl. 61-11088 2.50
1. Bible. N. T. Mark—Homiletical use. I. Title.

EARLE, Ralph. 226'.3'07
Mark: the gospel of action. Chicago, Moody Press [1970] 127 p. 19 cm. (Everyman's Bible commentary) Bibliography: p. 127. [BS2585.3.E24] 71-104824 0.95
1. Bible. N.T. Mark—Commentaries. I. Title. II. Series.

GUY, Harold A. 226'.3'07
The Gospel of Mark [by] H. A. Guy. London Melbourne Macmillan; New York, St. Martin's 1968. viii, 191p. map. 19cm. [BS2585.3G88 1968] 68-20757 2.95
1. Bible. N.T. Mark—Commentaries. I. Title.

HAMILTON, William, 1924- 226.307
The modern reader's guide to Mark. New York, Association Press [1959] 125p. 16cm. (An Association Press reflection book) [BS2586.H3] 59-8075
1. Bible, N. T. Mark—Study—Outlines, syllabi, etc. I. Title.

HIEBERT, David Edmond, 226'.3'07
1910-
Mark, a portrait of the servant; a commentary by D. Edmond Hiebert. Chicago, Moody Press [1974] 437 p. 24 cm. Bibliography: p. 432-437. [BS2585.3.H5] 73-15084 ISBN 0-8024-5182-9 7.95
1. Bible. N.T. Mark—Commentaries. I. Title.

HOBBS, Herschel H. 226'.3'07
An exposition of the Gospel of Mark, by Herschel H. Hobbs. Grand Rapids, Baker Book House [1970] 261 p. 23 cm. Bibliography: p. 9. [BS2585.3.H6] 70-106483 6.95
1. Bible. N.T. Mark—Commentaries. I. Title.

HOBBS, Herschel H. 226'.3'07
The Gospel of Mark; a study manual, by Herschel H. Hobbs. Grand Rapids, Baker Book House [1971] 79 p. 20 cm. (Shield Bible study series) [BS2585.3.H62] 75-156743 ISBN 0-8010-4017-5 1.95
1. Bible. N.T. Mark—Commentaries. I. Title.

JOHNSON, Sherman 226.307
Elbridge, 1908-
A commentary on the Gospel according to St. Mark. New York, Harper [1961, c.1960] viii, 279p. (Harper's New Testament commentaries) Bibl. 61-7342 5.00
1. Bible. N. T. Mark—Commentaries. I. Bible. N. T. Mark. English. 1960. Johnson. II. Title.

MURRAY, Ralph L. 226'.3'07
Can I believe in miracles? [By] Ralph L. Murray. Nashville, Broadman Press [1967] 140 p. 20 cm. [BT366.M8] 67-22031
1. Jesus Christ—Miracles. 2. Bible. N.T. Mark—Commentaries. I. Title.

NINEHAM, D. E. 226.307
The Gospel of St. Mark. Baltimore, Penguin [1964, c.1963] 477p. map. 18cm. (Pelican Gospel commentaries, A489) Bibl. 64-1423 1.95 pap.,
1. Bible. N.T. Mark—Commentaries. I. Bible. N.T. Mark. English. 1964. Revised standard. II. Title.

NINEHAM, Dennis Eric, 226'.3'07
1921-
The Gospel of St. Mark [by] D. E. Nineham. New York, Seabury Press [1968, c1963] 477 p. map. 22 cm. (The Pelican Gospel

commentaries) Includes bibliographical references. [BS2585.3.N5] 68-14135
1. Bible. N.T. Mark—Commentaries. I. Title.

NINEHAM, Dennis Eric, 1921- 226.307
The Gospel of St. Mark. Baltimore, Penguin Books [1964, c1963] 477 p. map. 18 cm. (The Pelican Gospel commentaries) "A489." Pelican books. Includes bibliographical references. [BS2585.3.N5] 64-1423
1. Bible, N.T. Mark — Commentaries. I. Bible, N.T. Mark. English. 1964. Revised standard. II. Title.

SLUSSER, Dorothy Mallett. 226'.3'07
The Jesus of Mark's Gospel, by Dorothy M. Slusser and Gerald H. Slusser. Philadelphia, Westminster Press [1967] 157 p. 19 cm. Bibliographical references included in "Notes" (p. [155]-157) [BS2585.3.S58] 68-10227
1. Bible. N. T. Mark—Commentaries. I. Slusser, Gerald H., joint author. II. Title.

SLUSSER, Dorothy Mallett. 226'.3'07
The Jesus of Mark's Gospel, by Dorothy M. Slusser and Gerald H. Slusser. Philadelphia, Westminster Press [1967] 157 p. 19 cm. Bibliographical references included in "Notes" (p. [155]-157) [BS2585.3.S58] 68-10227
1. Bible. N.T. Mark—Commentaries. I. Slusser, Gerald H., joint author. II. Title.

THOMPSON, Ernest Trice, 1894- 226.307
The Gospel according to Mark and its meaning for today. [Rev. ed.] New York, Longman, Green, 1957. 255 p. 21 cm. (Aletheia paperbacks) Includes bibliography. [BS2585.3.T55 1962] 62-5299
1. Bible. N.T. Mark — Commentaries. I. Title.

THOMPSON, Ernest Trice, 1894- 226.307
The Gospel according to Mark and its meaning for today. [Rev. ed.] Richmond, Va., Knox [1962] 255p. 21cm. (Aletheia paperbacks) 62-5299 1.95 pap.,
1. Bible. N.T. Mark—Commentaries. I. Title.

TRUEBLOOD, David Elton 226.307
Confronting Christ. New York, Harper [c.1960] xi, 180p. 20cm. 60-7955 3.00 half cloth,
1. Bible. N. T. Mark—Commentaries. I. Title.

TRUEBLOOD, David Elton, 1900- 226.307
Confronting Christ. [1st ed.] New York, Harper [1960] 180 p. 20 cm. [BS2585.3.T75] 60-7955
1. Bible. N.T. Mark — Commentaries. I. Title.

BEASLEY-MURRAY, George Raymond, 1916- 226'.3'077
Jesus and the future; an examination of the criticism of the eschatological discourse, Mark 13, with special reference to the little apocalypse theory. London, Macmillan; New York, St. Martin's Press, 1954. 287p. 23cm. [BS2585.B4] 226 54-2013
1. Bible. N. T. Mark xiii-Criticism, interpretation. etc. 2. Jesus Christ —Teachings. 3. Eschatology—Biblical teaching. I. Title.

BIBLE. N.T. Mark. English. 1965. New English. 226.3077
The Gospel according to Mark. Commentary by C. F. D. Moule. Cambridge [Eng.] University Press, 1965. x, 133 p. map. 21 cm. (The Cambridge Bible commentary: New English Bible) [BS2585.3.M6] 65-19152
1. Bible. N.T. Mark—Commentaries. I. Moule, Charles Francis Digby. II. Title. III. Series.

BIBLE. N.T. Mark. English. 1965. New English. 226.3077
The Gospel according to Mark. Commentary by C. F. D. Moule. Cambridge [Eng.] University Press, 1965. x, 133 p. map. 21 cm. (The Cambridge Bible commentary: New English Bible) [BS2585.3.M6] 65-19152
1. Bible. N.T. Mark—Commentaries. I. Moule, Charles Francis Digby. II. Title. III. Series.

BIBLE. N.T. Mark. English. 1976. 226'.3'077
The Gospel of Mark / introd. and notes by W. Graham Scroggie. Grand Rapids : Zondervan Pub. House, 1976. 285 p. ; 17 cm. (Study hour commentaries) Reprint of the ed. published by Marshall, Morgan & Scott, London, under title: The Gospel of St. Mark; issued in the study hour series. [BS2583 1976] 75-42112
1. Bible. N.T. Mark—Commentaries. I. Scroggie, William Graham, 1877-1958. II. Title. III. Series: The Study hour series.

BIBLE. N.T. Mark. English. Barclay. 1975. 226'.3'077
The Gospel of Mark / translated with an introd. and interpretation by William Barclay. Philadelphia : Westminster Press, [1975] x, 371, [2] p. ; 20 cm. (The Daily study Bible series. — Rev. ed.) Bibliography: p. [373] [BS2583 1975] 74-28250 ISBN 0-664-21302-2 : 6.25 ISBN 0-664-24102-6 pbk. 3.45
1. Bible. N.T. Mark—Commentaries. I. Barclay, William, lecturer in the University of Glasgow, ed. II. Title. III. Series.

BIBLE. N.T. Mark. Greek. 1977. 226'.3'077
The Gospel according to St. Mark : the Greek text / with introd., notes, and indices by Henry Barclay Swete. Grand Rapids, Mi : Kregel Publications, [1977] p. cm. (Kregel reprint library series) Reprint of the 1905 ed. published by Macmillan, London. Includes bibliographical references and indexes. [BS2581 1977] 77-79193 ISBN 0-8254-3715-6 : 12.95
1. Bible. N.T. Mark—Commentaries. I. Swete, Henry Barclay, 1835-1917. II. Title.

GREENE, Oliver B. 226'.3'077
The second epistle of Paul the Apostle to the Corinthians / by Oliver B. Greene. Greenville, S.C. : Gospel Hour, inc., 1976. 667 p. ; 20 cm. [BS2675.3.G73] 76-376787 10.00
1. Bible. N.T. 2 Corinthians—Commentaries. I. Bible. N.T. 2 Corinthians. English. Authorized. 1976. II. Title.

*GUTZKE, Manford George 226'.3'077
The go Gospel a discussion guide to the Book of Mark [by] Manford G. Gutzke. Grand Rapids, Baker Book House [1975 c1968] 183 p. 18 cm. (Contemporary Discussion Series) [BS2585] 63-8389 ISBN 0-8010-3694-1 1.65 (pbk.)
1. Bible. N.T. Mark—Criticism, interpretation, etc. I. Title.

GUTZKE, Manford George. 226'.3'077
Plain talk on Mark / Manford George Gutzke. Grand Rapids : Zondervan Pub. House, c1975. 192 p. ; 21 cm. [BS2585.3.G87] 75-6181 pbk. : 2.95
1. Bible. N.T. Mark—Commentaries. I. Title.

JOHNSON, Barton W., 1833-1894. 226'.3'077
The Gospel of Mark; a new commentary, workbook, teaching manual [by] B. W. Johnson and Don DeWelt. Joplin, Mo., College Press [1965] 516 p. maps. 23 cm. (Bible study textbook series) "Acknowledgements" (bibliographical): p. 5-6. [BS2586.J6] 76-1069 6.95
1. Bible. N.T. Mark—Study—Outlines, syllabi, etc. I. DeWelt, Don. II. Title.

*LINK, Mark 226'.3'077
The mustard seed: a prayer guide to Mark's gospel. Niles, Ill., Argus Communications [1974] 203 p. illus. 19 cm. [BS2585.3] ISBN 0-913592-49-8 1.95 (pbk.)
1. Bible. N.T. Mark. 2. Prayers. I. Title.

MCMILLAN, Earle. 226'.3'077
The Gospel according to Mark. Austin, Tex., Sweet Pub. Co. [1973] 192 p. 22 cm. (The Living word commentary, 3) Includes the text in the Revised standard version. Bibliography: p. 18. [BS2585.3.M29] 72-86991 ISBN 0-8344-0066-9
1. Bible. N.T. Mark—Commentaries. I. Bible. N.T. Mark. English. Revised standard. 1973. II. Title. III. Series.

MCMILLAN, Earle. 226'.3'077
The Gospel according to Mark. Austin, Tex., Sweet Pub. Co. [1973] 192 p. 22 cm. (The Living word commentary, 3) Includes the text in the Revised standard version. Bibliography: p. 18. [BS2585.3.M29] 72-86991 ISBN 0-8344-0066-9 3.95
1. Bible. N.T. Mark—Commentaries. I. Bible. N.T. Mark. English. Revised standard. 1973. II. Title. III. Series.

NINEHAM, Dennis Eric, 1921- 226'.3'077
The Gospel of St. Mark [by] D. E. Nineham. New York, Seabury Press [1968, c1963] 477 p. map. 22 cm. (The Pelican Gospel commentaries) Includes bibliographical references. [BS2585.3.N5 1968] 68-14135
1. Bible. N.T. Mark—Commentaries. I. Title.

PIKE, Kenneth Lee, 1912- 226'.3'077
Mark my words, by Kenneth L. Pike. Grand Rapids, Eerdmans [1971] 123 p. 18 cm. (An Eerdmans evangelical paperback) The author's comments, in verse, accompany the complete King James text of Mark. [BS2585.2.P54] 74-150641 1.75
1. Bible. N.T. Mark—History of Biblical events—Poetry. I. Bible. N.T. Mark. English. Authorized. 1971. II. Title.

SCHMID, Josef, 1893- 226'.3'077
The Gospel according to Mark. A version and commentary by Josef Schmid. Edited by Alfred Wikenhauser and Otto Kuss. Translated from the German [and] edited in English by Kevin Condon. Staten Island, N.Y., Alba House [1968?] 310 p. 22 cm. (The Regensburg New Testament) [BS2585.3.S2813] 71-4339 5.95
1. Bible. N.T. Mark—Commentaries. I. Wikenhauser, Alfred, 1883-1960, ed. II. Kuss, Otto, 1905- ed. III. Condon, Kevin, ed. IV. Bible. N.T. Mark. English. Schmid. 1968? V. Title. VI. Series.

SCHWEIZER, Eduard, 1913- 226'.3'077
The good news according to Mark. Translated by Donald H. Madvig. Richmond, John Knox Press [1970] 395 p. 21 cm. Translation of Das Evangelium nach Markus. "The English language edition is based on the text of Today's English version (Good news for modern man)" [BS2585.3.S3613] 77-93828 9.95
1. Bible. N.T. Mark—Commentaries. I. Bible. N.T. Mark. English. Today's English. 1970. II. Title.

SMITH, Chuck, 1927- 226'.3'077
The Gospel of Mark for growing Christians. Edited by Hugh Steven. Old Tappan, N.J., Revell [1974] 127 p. 21 cm. [BS2585.3.S6] 74-8927 ISBN 0-8007-0675-7 1.95 (pbk.)
1. Bible. N.T. Mark—Commentaries. I. Bible. N.T. Mark. English. II. Title.

STANDARD Bible commentary: Mark, by Enos Dowling [and others] Edited by Kenton K. Smith. Cincinnati, Standard Pub. [1968] xxvii, 155 p. illus., maps, plan. 24 cm. Bibliography: p. xxvii. [BS2585.3.S7] 68-5387 5.95 226'.3'077
1. Bible. N.T. Mark—Commentaries. I. Dowling, Enos Everett, 1905- II. Smith, Kenton K., ed.

STEDMAN, Ray C. 226'.3'077
The ruler who serves / Ray C. Stedman. Waco, Tex. : Word Books, c1976. 231 p. ; 21 cm. (Discovery books) Companion volume to the author's The servant who rules. [BS2585.3.S74] 76-20972 ISBN 0-87680-487-3 : 5.95
1. Bible. N.T. Mark VIII, 34-XVI—Commentaries. I. Title.

STEDMAN,Ray C. 226'.3'077
The servant who rules / Ray C. Stedman. Waco, Tex. : Word Books, c1976. 223 p. ; 21 cm. (Discovery books) Continued by The ruler who serves. [BS2585.3.S75] 76-20967 ISBN 0-87680-480-6 : 5.95
1. Bible. N.T. Mark I-VIII, 26—Commentaries. I. Title.

WHISTON, Lionel A. 226'.3'077
New beginnings : relational studies in Mark / Lionel Whiston. Waco, Tex. : Word Books, c1976. 125 p. ; 21 cm. [BS2585.3.W44] 75-19905 ISBN 0-87680-995-6 pbk. : 2.95
1. Bible. N.T. Mark I-IV, 34—Commentaries. 2. Christian life—Congregational authors. I. Title.

WHISTON, Lionel A. 226'.3'077
Power of a new life : relational studies in Mark / Lionel Whiston. Waco, Tex. : Word Books, c1976. 117 p. ; 21 cm. [BS2585.3.W442] 75-19906 pbk. : 2.95
1. Bible. N.T. Mark IV, 35-IX—Commentaries. 2. Christian life—Congregational authors. I. Title.

WHISTON, Lionel A. 226'.3'077
Through suffering to victory : relational studies in Mark / Lionel Whiston. Waco, Tex. : Word Books, c1976. 157 p. ; 21 cm. [BS2585.3.W443] 75-19907 pbk. : 3.50
1. Bible. N.T. Mark X-XVI, 8—Commentaries. 2. Christian life—Congregational authors. I. Title.

CRAIGHILL, Marian G. 226'.3'0922 B
The Craighills of China [by] Marian G. Craighill. Ambler, Pa., Trinity Press [1972] xii, 285 p. illus. 21 cm. [BV3427.C68C7] 72-92010 ISBN 0-912046-08-2 3.95
1. Craighill, Lloyd Rutherford, 1886-1971. I. Title.

BIBLE, N.T. Mark, Greek, 1966. 226.37
The Gospel according to St. Mark; the Greek text with introduction, notes, and indexes by Vincent Taylor 2nd ed. London, Macmillan; New York, St. Martin's [c.]1966. xxi, 700p. 23cm. Bibl. [BS2585.I34 1966] 66-15271 10.00
1. Bible. N.T. Mark—Commentaries. I. Taylor, Vincent, 1887- ed. II. Title.

BIBLE. N.T. Mark. Greek. 1966. 226.37
The Gospel according to St. Mark: the Greek text with introduction, notes, and indexes by Vincent Taylor. 2d ed. London, Melbourne, [etc.] Macmillan; New York, St. Martin's P., 1966. xxi, 700 p. 22 1/2 cm. 50/- (B 66-10233) Bibliography: p. xiii-xxi. [BS2585.T34] 66-15271
1. Bible. N.T. Mark—Commentaries. I. Taylor, Vincent, 1887- ed. II. Title.

ARNDT, William, 1880- 226.4
Bible commentary: the Gospel according to St. Luke. Saint Louis, Concordia Pub. House [1956] ix, 523p. 25cm. Bibliography: p.34-36. [BS2595.A6] 55-12191
1. Bible. N. T. Luke—Commentaries. I. Bible. N. T. Luke. English. 1956. Arndt. II. Title.

BAILEY, Kenneth E. 226'.4
The cross and the prodigal; the 15th chapter of Luke, seen through the eyes of Middle Eastern peasants [by] Kenneth E. Bailey. St. Louis, Concordia Pub. House [1973] 133 p. 23 cm. "All Biblical quotations are from the Revised standard version." Contents.Contents.—Commentary on the 15th chapter of the Gospel, according to Luke.—"Two sons have I not;" a one-act play in four scenes.—Music for Shaluk's song (p. 133) [BS2595.3.B27 1973] 72-90957 ISBN 0-570-03139-7 2.95
1. Bible. N.T. Luke XV—Commentaries. 2. Bible plays. I. Bailey, Kenneth E. Two sons have I not. 1973. II. Bible. N.T. Luke XV. English. Revised standard. 1973. III. Title.

BIBLE. N. T. Luke. English. 1952. Confraternity version. 226.4
The Gospel according to St. Luke; from the revision of the Challoner-Rheims version, edited by Catholic scholars under the patronage of the Episcopal Committee of the Confraternity of Christian Doctrine. [3d ed.] Paterson, N. J., St. Anthony Guild Press [1952,c1941] 148-239p. 16cm. [BS2593 1952] 53-19356
I. Confraternity of Christian Doctrine. II. Title.

BIBLE, N T. Luke. English. 1956. Barclay. lecturer at the University of Glasgow, ed. and tr. 226.4
The Gospel of Luke. Translated with an introd. and interpretation by William Barclay. [2d ed.] Philadelphia, Westminster Press [1956] 314p. 18cm. (The Daily study Bible) [BS2595.B35 1956] 57-9567
1. Bible. N.T. Luke—Commentaries. I. Title.

BIBLE. N. T. Luke. English. 1957. Douai. 226.4
The Gospel according to Saint Luke. With an introd. and commentary by C. C. Martindale. Westminster, Md., Newman Press [1957] 203p. illus. 19cm. (Stonyhurst-Scripture manuals) [BS2595.M375] 58-483
1. Bible. N. T. Luke—Commentaries. I. Martindale, Cyril Charlie, 1879 — II. Title.

BIBLE. N.T. Luke. English. Paraphrases. 1955. Taylor. 226.4
St. Luke's life of Jesus, retold in modern language by G. Aiken Taylor. New York, Macmillan, 1955. 161p. 22cm. [BS2597.T39] 55-14500
I. Taylor, George Aiken, 1920- II. Title.

*BREM M. M. 226.4
Mary's story; Luke 1: 5-2: 18 for children. Illus. by Sally Mathews. St. Louis, Concordia, 1967. 1v. (unpaged) col. illus. 21cm. (Arch bks.) .35 pap.,
1. Bible— N.T.—Luke—Juvenile literature. I. Title.

*BROOKS, Keith L. 226.4
Ephesians, the epistle of Christian maturity [Chicago] Moody [c.1964] 64p. 22cm (Teach yourself the Bible ser.) .80 pap.,
I. Title.

BUNYAN, John, 1628-1688. 226'.4
The groans of a damned soul. Swengel, Pa., Reiner Publications, 1967. 108 p. 19 cm. An exposition of Luke XVI, 19-31. An abridgement of Sighs from hell; or, The groans of a damned soul, first published in 1658 under title: A few sighs from hell; or, The groans of a damned soul. [BR75.B852] 68-6571
1. Dives and Lazarus (Parable) 2. Future punishment—Early works to 1800. I. Title.

BUNYAN, John, 1628-1688. 226'.4
The groans of a damned soul. Swengel, Pa., Reiner Publications, 1967. 108 p. 19 cm. An exposition of Luke XVI, 19-31. An abridgement of Sighs from hell; or, The groans of a damned soul, first published in 1658 under title: A few sighs from hell; or, The groans of a damned soul. [BR75.B852] 68-6571
1. Dives and Lazarus (Parable) 2. Future punishment—Early works to 1800. I. Title.

HOBART, William Kirk. 226.4
The medical language of St. Luke. Grand Rapids, Baker Book House, 1954. xxxvi, 305p.

23cm. [Co-operative reprint library] [BS2595.H6] 54-11071
1. Luke, Saint. 2. Bible, N. T. Luke and Acts—Criticism, interpretation, etc. I. Title.

JORDAN, Clarence. 226'.4
The cotton patch version of Luke and Acts: Jesus' doings and The happenings. New York, Association Press [1969] 159 p. 23 cm. (A Koinonia publication) A colloquial modern translation, based on the Nestle-Aland Greek text, 23d ed. 1957. [BS2589.A3J65] 69-18840 4.50
1. Bible. N.T. Luke and Acts—Paraphrases, English. I. Title.

MATSON, Archie. 226.4
A month with the Master, for twentieth-century Christians; a manual for spiritual growth based on the Gospel of Luke and suggested by the Spiritual exercises of Ignatius Loyola. [1st ed.] New York, Harper [1958] 252p. 22cm. [BS2595.M38] 57-12935
1. Bible. N. T. Luke—Meditations. I. Title.

NORTH, Brownlow, 1810-1875. 226.4
The rich man and Lazarus; a practical exposition of Luke xvi, 19-31. [London] Banner of Truth Trust, [stamped: distributed by Bible Truth Depot, Swengel, Pa.] 1960 127p. 19cm. [BT378.D5N6] 61-1207
1. Dives and Lazarus (Parable) I. Title.

REICKE, Bo Ivar, 1914- 226.4
The Gospel of Luke, by Bo Reicke. Translated by Ross Mackenzie. Richmond, John Knox Press [1964] 89 p. 19 cm. (Chime paperbacks) Bibliography: p. 89. [BS2595.2.R413] 64-12263
1. Bible. N.T. Luke — Introductions. 2. Bible. N.T. Luke — Theology. I. Title.

REICKE, Bo Ivar, 1914- 226.4
The Gospel of Luke. Tr. [from Swedish] by Ross Mackenzie. Richmond, Va., Knox [c.1964] 89p. 19cm. (Chime paperbacks) Bibl. 64-12263 1.00 pap.,
1. Bible. N. T. Luke—Introductions. 2. Bible. N. T. Luke—Theology. I. Title.

ROBINSON, William Childs, 1922- 226.4
The way of the Lord; a study of history and eschatology in the Gospel of Luke. [Dallas? 1962] ll. 117 p. 23 cm. Diss.--Basel. Vita. Bibliographical footnotes. [BS2595.2.R6] 63-35506
1. Bible. N. T.—Like—Criticism, interpretation, etc. 2. Eschatology—Biblical teaching. I. Title.

*STEINER, Rudolf 226.4
The Gospel of St. Luke; a course of lectures given at Basel, Sept. 1909. Tr. from German by Andrew Lissovsky. Blauvelt, N. Y., Author [c.1965] 198p. 28cm. T.p. in Russian with Eng. tr.: text in Russian. 5.00, pap.,
1. Bible. N. T. Luke—Addresses, essays, lectures. I. Title.

STOCK, Eugene, 1836-1928. 226.4
Talks on St. Luke's Gospel. Grand Rapids, Baker Book House, 1955. 296p. 21cm. [BS2595.S76 1955] 55-10433
1. Bible. N.T. Luke—Commentaries. I. Title.

TAYLOR, Vincent, 1887-1968. 226'.4
The passion narrative of St. Luke; a critical and historical investigation. Edited by Owen E. Evans. Cambridge [Eng.] University Press [1971] 1972. xii, 141 p. 22 cm. (Society for New Testament Studies monograph series, 19) Includes bibliographical references. [BT431.T34 1972] 79-163057 ISBN 0-521-08295-1
1. Jesus Christ—Passion. 2. Bible. N.T. Luke—Criticism, interpretation, etc. I. Title. II. Series: Studiorum Novi Testamenti Societas. Monograph series, 19.

THOMAS, William Henry Griffith, 1861-1924. 226.4
Outline studies in the Gospel of Luke, by W. H. Griffith Thomas, edited by his daughter. Grand Rapids, Eerdmans, 1950. 406 p. 21 cm. [BS2596.T5] 50-7471
1. Bible. N. T. Luke — Study — Outlines, syllabi, etc. I. Title.

TITTLE, Ernest Fremont, 1885-1949. 226.4
The Gospel according to Luke; exposition & application. With a foreword by Halford E. Luccock. New York, Harper [1951] 274 p. 22 cm. [BS2595.T5] 51-13352
1. Bible. N. T. Luke — Commentaries. I. Title.

VAN RYN, August, 1890- 226.4
Meditations in Luke. lstied 1st ed. New York, Loizeaux Bros. [1953] 278p. 20cm. [BS2595.V33] 53-11028
1. Bible. N. T. Luke—Meditations. I. Title.

VARNER, Paul Nolan. 226.4
Case histories from the files of Dr. Luke. Columbus, Ohio, Wartburg Press [1957] 154p. 20cm. [BS2595.V36] 57-685
1. Bible. N. T. Luke—Criticism, interpretation, etc. I. Title.

WALSH, Bill. 226'.4
The good Samaritan / by Bill Walsh ; with an afterword for parents and teachers by Charlie Shedd. Mission, Kan. : Sheed Andrews and McMeel, c1977. p. cm. (A Cartoon Bible story) A retelling of the parable of the Good Samaritan in cartoon format. [BT378.G6W34] 77-21218 ISBN 0-8362-0731-9 pbk. : 1.95
1. Good Samaritan (Parable)—Juvenile literature. I. Title.

WILKINSON, Violet. 226'.4
The centre of history: a study of Luke's Gospel. London, Oxford U. P., 1967. 93 p. tables. 18 1/2 cm. (Approaching the Bible, 4) Bibliography: p. 83. [BS2595.5.] [5] 68-70107 9/6
1. Bible. N. T. Luke—Study—Outlines, syliabi, etc. I. Title.

KUNZ, Marilyn. 226'.4'007
The Gospel of Luke; 13 discussions for group Bible study, by Marilyn Kunz and Catherine Schell. Wheaton, Ill., Tyndale House Publishers [1973] 63 p. map. 19 cm. (Neighborhood Bible studies) [BS2595.5.K86] 72-97661 ISBN 0-8423-3880-2
1. Bible. N.T. Luke—Study—Text-books. I. Schell, Catherine, joint author. II. Title.

MINEAR, Paul Sevier, 1906- 226'.4'015
To heal and to reveal : the prophetic vocation according to Luke / Paul S. Minear. New York : Seabury Press, c1976. ix, 179 p. ; 21 cm. "A Crossroad book." Includes index. [BS2545.P72M56] 75-42213 ISBN 0-8164-0295-7 : 8.95
1. Bible. N.T. Luke—Criticism, interpretation, etc.—Addresses, essays, lectures. 2. Prophecy (Christianity)—Biblical teaching—Addresses, essays, lectures. 3. Gifts, Spiritual—Biblical teaching—Addresses, essays, lectures. I. Title.

BIBLE. N.T. Luke. Greek. 1968. 226'.4'048
Family E and its allies in Luke, by Jacob Geerlings. Appendix A: Collation of Sinai 148 (Greg. 1185) by Kenneth W. Ogden. Salt Lake City, University of Utah Press, 1968. iii, 164 p. 3 facsims. 25 cm. (Studies and documents, 35) Introductory matter in English; text in Greek. [BS2591 1968] 74-18889
I. Geerlings, Jacob, ed. II. Ogden, Kenneth W., ed. III. Title. IV. Series.

MORTON, Andrew Queen 226.4048
The structure of Luke and Acts [by] A. Q. Morton, G. H. C. Macgregor. New York, Harper [1965, c.1964] 155p. 22cm. [BS2589.Z72M6] 65-15401 3.50
1. Bible N.T. Luke and Acts—Criticism, textual. I. Macgregor, George Hogarth Carnaby, 1892-1963. II. Bible. N.T. Luke and Acts. English. 1964. Revised standard. III. Title.

BIBLE. N. T. Luke. English. 1960. Authorized. 226.4052
Gospel of St. Luke; Authorized King James version. Glendale, Calif., [P.O. Box 405] International Pub. Co., c.1960. 165p. illus. (part col.) 21cm. (A Little prince Bible book) 60-4696 2.79
I. Title.

BIBLE. N.T. Luke. English. Revised standard. 1972. 226'.4'05204
The Gospel according to Luke in the Revised Standard Version. With introd. and commentary by G. H. P. Thompson. Oxford, Clarendon Press, 1972. [16], 291 p. illus. 20 cm. (The New Clarendon Bible: New Testament.) Bibliography: 11th-12th prelim. page. [BS2593 1972] 72-193490 ISBN 0-19-836910-7 £3.00 ($10.25 U.S.)
1. Bible. N.T. Luke—Commentaries. I. Thompson, George Harry Packwood. II. Title. III. Series.

BIBLE. N.T. Luke. Anglo-Saxon. Corpus Christi College Library. MSS. (140) 226'.4'0529
Euangelium secundum Lucam. The Gospel of Saint Luke in West-Saxon; edited from the manuscripts, by James Wilson Bright. Boston, Heath, 1906. [New York, AMS Press, 1972] viii, 143 p. 19 cm. Original ed. issued in series: The Belles-lettres series. Section 1. English literature. [BS2594.A5B74 1972] 75-144448 ISBN 0-404-53602-6
I. Bright, James Wilson, 1852-1926, ed. II. Cambridge. University. Corpus Christi College. Library. MSS. (140) III. Title.

BIBLE. N.T. Luke. Anglo-Saxon. Corpus Christi College Library. MSS. (140) 226'.4'0529
Euangelium secundum Lucam. The Gospel of Saint Luke in West-Saxon. Edited from the mss. by James Wilson Bright. [Folcroft, Pa.] Folcroft Library Editions, 1973. p. Reprint of the 1906 ed. published by Heath, Boston, in series: The Belles-lettres series, section 1, English literature. [BS2594.A5B74 1973] 73-15860 10.00
I. Bright, James Wilson, 1852-1926, ed. II. Cambridge. University. Corpus Christi College. Library. MSS. (140) III. Title.

BARCLAY, William, lecturer in the University of Glasgow. 226'.4'06
Jesus Christ for today. Nashville, Tidings [1973] 86 p. 19 cm. Page 86 blank for "Notes." Bibliography: p. 5. [BS2595.2.B37] 73-86376 1.00 (pbk.)
1. Bible. N.T. Luke—Criticism, interpretation, etc. 2. Evangelistic works. I. Title.

CONZELMANN, Hans 226.406
The theology of St. Luke. Tr. by Geoffrey Buswell. New York, Harper [1961, c.1960] 255p. Bibl. 61-7354 5.00
1. Bible. N. T. Luke—Theology. I. Title.

DANKER, Frederick W. 226'.4'06
Luke / Frederick W. Danker. Philadelphia : Fortress Press, c1976. vii, 120 p. ; 22 cm. (Proclamation commentaries) Includes index. Bibliography: p. 115-116. [BS2595.2.D36] 75-36446 ISBN 0-8006-0583-7 pbk. : 2.95
1. Bible. N.T. Luke—Criticism, interpretation, etc.

DRURY, John. 226'.4'06
Tradition and design in Luke's Gospel : a study in Early Christian historiography / [by] John Drury. London : Darton, Longman and Todd, 1976. xiii, 208 p. ; 22 cm. Includes index. Bibliography: p. 193-196. [BS2595.2.D78 1976] 76-384063 ISBN 0-232-51316-3 : £3.95
1. Bible. N.T. Luke—Criticism, interpretation, etc. I. Title.

EGELKRAUT, Helmuth L. 226'.4'06
Jesus' mission to Jerusalem : a redaction critical study of the travel narrative in the Gospel of Luke, Lk 9:51-19:48 / Helmuth L. Egelkraut. Frankfurt/M. : Peter Lang, 1976. iv, x, 257 p. ; 22 cm. (Europaische Hochschulschriften : Reihe 23, Theologie ; Bd. 80) Originally presented as the author's thesis, Princeton Theological Seminary. Bibliography: p. 238-257. [BS2595.2.E33 1976] 77-367476 ISBN 3-261-02133-0 : 44.00F
1. Bible. N.T. Luke IX, 51-XIX—Criticism, interpretation, etc. I. Title. II. Series.

FLENDER, Helmut 226'.4'06
St. Luke, theologian of redemptive history. Tr. by Reginald H., & Ilse Fuller. [Amer. ed.] Philadelphia, Fortress [1967] x, 179p. 23cm. Tr. of the author's thesis, pub. under title: Heil und Geschichte in der Theologie des Lukas. Bibl. [BS2595.2.F513 1967] 67-18245 4.95 bds.,
1. Bible. N. T. Luke— Theology. I. Title.

HARVEY, Anthony Ernest. 226'.4'06
Jesus on trial : a study in the fourth gospel / A. E. Harvey. London : SPCK, 1976. viii, 140 p. ; 20 cm. Includes indexes. Bibliography: p. viii. [BT440.H37] 76-374954 ISBN 0-281-02918-0 : 2.95
1. Jesus Christ—Trial. 2. Bible. N.T. John—Criticism, interpretation, etc. I. Title.

HASTINGS, Adrian. 226.406
Prophet and witness in Jerusalem; a study of the teachings of Saint Luke. Baltimore, Helicon Press [1958] 200p. 21cm. Includes bibliography. [BS2589.H35] 58-13822
1. Bible. N.T. Luke and Acts—Theology. I. Title.

KECK, Leander E., ed. 226.406
Studies in Luke-Acts; essays presented in honor of Paul Schubert, edited by Leander E. Keck [and] J. Louis Martyn. Nashville, Abingdon Press [1966] 316 p. port. 24 cm. Contents.Contents.—Paul Schubert at Yale, by R. L. Calhoun.—Luke-Acts, a storm center in contemporary scholarship, by W. C. van Unnik.—On the Paulinism of Acts, by P. Vielhauer.—The perspective of Acts, by E. R. Goodenough.—Interpreting Luke-Acts in a period of existentialist theology, by U. Wilckens.—Four features of Lucan style, by H. J. Cadbury.—In search of the original text of Acts, by A. F. J. Klikn.—Luke's use of the birth stories, by P. S. Minear.—On preaching the Word of God, by W. C. Robinson, Jr.—The story of Abraham in Luke-Acts, by N. A. Dahl.—The Christology of Acts, by C. F. D. Moule.—The concept of the Davidic Son of God in Acts and its Old Testament background, by E. Schweizer.—The missionary stance of Paul in I Corinthians 9 and in Acts, by G. Bornkamm.—Concerning the speeches in Acts, by E. Schweizer.—The address of Paul on the Aeropagus, by H. Conzelmann.—Jewish Christianity in Acts in light of the Qumran scrolls, by J. A. Fitzmyer.—The Book of Acts as source material for the history of early Christianity, by E. Haenchen.—Acts and the Pauline letter corpus, by J. Knox.—Ephesians and Acts, by E. Kasemann.—Luke's place in the development of early Christianity, by H. Conzelmann. Includes bibliographies. [BS2589.Z72K4] 66-14998
1. Schubert, Paul, 1900- 2. Bible. N.T. Luke and Acts—Addresses, essays, lectures. I. Schubert, Paul, 1900- II. Martyn, James Louis, 1925- joint ed. III. Title.

PAOLI, Arturo. 226'.4'06
Meditations on Saint Luke / Arturo Paoli ; translated by Bernard F. McWilliams. Maryknoll, N.Y. : Orbis Books, c1977. p. cm. Rev. translation of La radice dell'uomo, originally published in 1972. [BS2595.4.P3313 1977] 76-58539 ISBN 0-88344-384-8 : 8.95 ISBN 0-88344-385-6 pbk. : 4.95
1. Bible. N.T. Luke—Meditations. I. Title.

TALBERT, Charles H 226.406
Luke and the gnostics; an examination of Lucan purpose [by] Charles H. Talbert. Nashville, Abingdon Press [1966] 127 p. 23 cm. "In part based upon research done for a doctoral dissertation (Vanderbilt, 1963)." Bibliographical footnotes. [BS2589.Z72T3] 66-10855
1. Bible. N. T. Luke and Acts—Criticism, interpretation, etc. I. Title.

TALBERT, Charles H. 226.406
Luke and the gnostics; an examination of Lucan purpose. Nashville, Abingdon [c.1966] 127p. 23cm. Bibl. [BS2589.Z72T3] 66-10855 2.75
1. Bibl). N. T. Luke and Acts—Criticism, interpretation, etc. I. Title.

WILLIAMS, Walter Rollin. 226'.4'06
The rich heritage of Quakerism, by Walter R. Williams. Grand Rapids, Eerdmans [c1962] 279 p. illus., 3 fold., maps, port. 23 cm. Addendum slip mounted on p. 232. Bibliography: p. 263-264. Bibliographical references included in "Notes" (p. 257-262) [BX7731.2.W5] 61-18338
1. Friends. Society of — Addresses, essays, lectures. I. Title.

,wingo, Earle L 226'.4'06
A lawyer reviews the illegal trial of Jesus. [Hattiesburg? Miss. 1954] 116p. 19cm. [BT440.W72] A55
1. Jesus Christ—Trial. I. Title.

EARLE, Ralph. 226'.4'066
The Gospel of Luke. Grand Rapids, Baker Book House [1968] 109 p. 20 cm. (Proclaiming the New Testament) Bibliography: p. 108-109. [BS2595.4.E37] 68-14968
1. Bible. N.T. Luke—Homiletical use. I. Title.

JERVELL, Jacob. 226'.4'066
Luke and the people of God; a new look at Luke-Acts. Foreword by Nils Dahl. Minneapolis, Augsburg Pub. House [1972] 207 p. 23 cm. Includes bibliographical references. [BS2589.J47] 72-78565 ISBN 0-8066-1232-0 8.50
1. Luke, Saint. 2. Bible. N.T. Luke and Acts—Criticism, interpretation, etc. I. Title.

MACPHERSON, Duncan. 226'.4'066
Luke. Chicago, ACTA Foundation [1971] viii, 184 p. 22 cm. (Scripture discussion commentary, 8) Contents.Contents.—Luke, by D. Macpherson.—Acts, by N. Lash.—1 Peter, by B. Robinson. Includes bibliographical references. [BS2589.M23] 72-178782
1. Bible. N.T. Luke—Commentaries. 2. Bible. N.T. Acts—Commentaries. 3. Bible. N.T. 1 Peter—Commentaries. I. Lash, Nicholas. II. Robinson, Bernard. III. Title. IV. Series.

TURLINGTON, Henry E. 226'.4'066
Luke's witness to Jesus [by] Henry E. Turlington. Nashville, Broadman Press [1967] 93 p. 20 cm. Bibliographical footnotes. [BS2595.2.T8] 67-22035
1. Bible. N.T. Luke—Introductions. I. Title.

WILSON, Stephen G. 226'.4'066
The Gentiles and the Gentile mission in Luke-Acts, by Stephen G. Wilson. Cambridge [Eng.] University Press, 1973. xi, 294 p. 23 cm. (Society for New Testament Studies. Monograph series 23) Based on the author's thesis, Durham University, 1969. Bibliography: p. 268-276. [BS2545.G4W54] 72-90489 ISBN 0-521-20134-9
1. Bible. N.T. Luke and Acts—Criticism, interpretation, etc. 2. Gentiles in the New Testament. I. Title. II. Series: Studiorum Novi Testamenti Societas. Monograph series, 23. Distributed by Cambridge University Press, N.Y; 17.50

ANDREWS, Charles Richard 226.407
King of the ends of the earth. Valley Forge [Pa.] Judson [c.1962] 125p. 20cm. 62-11742 1.25 pap.,

1. Bible. N.T. Luke I-VI—Criticism, interpretation, etc. 2. Christian life. I. Title.

BARTH, Karl, 1886- 226.407
The great promise, Luke I. [Translated by Hans Freund] New York, Philosophical Library [1963] 70 p. 22 cm. Translation of Die Verheissung. [BS2595.3.B313] 61-15239
1. Bible. N.T. Luke I — Commentaries. I. Title.

BARTH, Karl, 1886- 226.407
The great promise, Luke I. [Tr. from German by Hans Freund] New York, Philosophical [c.1963] 70p. 22cm. 61-15239 2.75
1. Bible. N.T. Luke I—Cometaries. I. Title.

BIBLE. N.T. Luke. 226.407
English. 1965. New Enlgish.
The Gospel according to Luke. Commentary by E. J. Tinsley. Cambridge [Eng.] University Press, 1965. ix, 216 p. map, plan. 21 cm. (The Cambridge Bible commentary: New English Bible) "A note on further study": p. 213-214. [BS2595.3.T5] 65-3522
1. Bible. N.T. Luke-Commentaries. I. Tinsley, Ernest John. II. Title. III. Series.

BIBLE. N. T. Luke. 226.407
English. 1965. New English
The Gospel according to Luke. Commentary by E. J. Tinsley [New York] Cambridge [c.] 1965. ix, 216p. map, plan. 21cm. (Cambridge Bible commentary: New English Bible) Bibl. [BS2595.3.T5] 65-3522 3.50; 1.65
1. Bible. N. T. Luke—Commentaries. I. Tinsley, Ernest John. II. Title. III. Series.

BOWIE, Walter Russell, 226.407
1882-
The compassionate Christ; reflections from the Gospel of Luke. Nashville. Abingdon [c.1965] 320p. 24cm. Bibl. [BS2595.3.B6] 65-13144 5.50
1. Bible. N. T. Luke—Commentaries. I. Title.

BOWIE, Walter Russell, 226.407
1882-1969.
The compassionate Christ; reflections from the Gospel of Luke. New York, Abingdon Press [1965] 320 p. 24 cm. Bibliographical footnotes. [BS2595.3.B6] 65-13144
1. Bible. N.T. Luke—Commentaries. I. Title.

BROWNING, Wilfrid Robert 226.407
Francis.
The Gospel according to Saint Luke, a commentary. New York, Collier [1962, c.1960] 159p. (Torch Bible commentaries, AS238Y) Bibl. .95 pap.,
1. Bible. N. T. Luke—Commentaries. I. Title.

BROWNING, Wilfrid Robert 226.407
Francis.
The Gospel according to Saint Luke: introduction and commentary. New York, Macmillan [1960] 176p. (Bibl.) 20cm. (Torch Bible commentaries) 60-3804 3.00 bds.,
1. Bible. N. T. Luke—Commentaries. I. Title.

CAIRD, George Bradford 226.407
The Gospel of St. Luke. Baltimore, Penguin [1964, c.1963] 271p. map. 18cm. (Pelican Gospel commentaries, A490) 64-1438 1.65 pap.,
1. Bible. N. T. Luke—Commentaries. I. Bible. N. T. Luke. English. 1964. Revised standard. II. Title.

CANNON, William 226'.4'07
Ragsdale, 1916-
A disciple's profile of Jesus : from the Gospel of Luke / William R. Cannon. Nashville : Upper Room, [1975] ix, 118 p. ; 22 cm. [BS2595.4.C36] 75-2956 pbk. : 1.50
1. Bible. N.T. Luke—Meditations. I. Title.

DANKER, Frederick W. 226' 4'07
Jesus and the new age, according to St. Luke; a commentary on the third Gospel [by] Frederick W. Danker. St. Louis, Mo., Clayton Pub. House [1972] xxiii, 255 p. 23 cm. [BS2595.3.D35] 72-83650
1. Bible. N.T. Luke—Commentaries. I. Title.

FORD, Douglas William 226'.4'07
Cleverley.
A reading of Saint Luke's gospel, by D. W. Cleverley Ford. Philadelphia, Lippincott [1967] 255 p. 20 cm. [BS2595.3.F6] 67-24006
1. Bible. N.T. Luke—Commentaries. I. Title.

GIDEON, Virtus E. 226'.4'07
Luke, a study guide, by Virtus E. Gideon. [1st ed.] Grand Rapids, Zondervan Pub. House [1967] 128 p. 21 cm. Includes bibliographies. [BS2595.5.G5] 67-22691
1. Bible. N.T. Luke—Study—Outlines, syllabi, etc. I. Title.

GUTZKE, Manford George. 226.407
Plain talk on Luke. Grand Rapids, Zondervan Pub. House [1966] 180 p. 23 cm. [BS2595.3.G8] 66-18949
1. Bible. N.T. Luke—Commentaries. I. Title.

HOBBS, Herschel H. 226'.4'07
An exposition of the Gospel of Luke, by Herschel H. Hobbs. Grand Rapids, Baker Bk. [1966] 355p. 23cm. Bibl. [BS2595.3.H6] 66-28804 6.95
1. Bible. N. T. Luke —Commentaries. I. Title.

HOBBS, Herschel H 226'.4'07
An exposition of the Gospel of Luke, by Herschel H. Hobbs. Grand Rapids, Baker Book House [1966] 355 p. 23 cm. Bibliographical references included in "Introduction" (p. 8-9) [BS2595.3.H6] 66-28804
1. Bible. N.T. Luke — Commentaries. I. Title.

LEANEY, Alfred Robert 226.407
Clare.
A commentary on the gospel according to St. Luke. New York, Harper [1958] xii, 300p. 22cm. (Harper's New Testament commentaries) Includes bibliography. [BS2595.L35 1958a] 58-10376
1. Bible. N. T. Luke—Commentaries. I. Bible. N. T. Luke. English. 1958. II. Title.

MOORMAN, John Richard 226.407
Humpidge. Bp. of Ripon.
The path to glory; studies in the Gospel according to Saint Luke. [London] S. P. C. K.; [Greenwich, Conn.] Seabury Press, 1960. 300p. 23cm. [BS2595.3.M65] 60-51608
1. Bible. N. T. Luke—Commentaries. I. Bible. N. T. Luke. English. 1960. Revised. II. Title.

MOORMAN, John Richard 226.407
Humpidge, Bp of Ripon.
The path to glory; studies in the Gospel according to Saint Luke. [London] S.P.C.K.; [Greenwich, Conn.] Seabury Press, 1960[ ] 300p. 23cm. 60-51608 4.75
1. Bible. N.T. Luke—Commentaries. I. Bible. N.T. Luke. English. 1960. Revised. II. Title.

MORRIS, Leon. 226'.4'07
The Gospel according to St. Luke : an introduction and commentary / by Leon Morris. 1st American ed. Grand Rapids : Eerdmans, 1974. 350 p. ; 20 cm. (The Tyndale New Testament commentaries) Includes bibliographical references. [BS2595.3.M67 1974] 75-300668 ISBN 0-8028-2253-3 : 6.95. ISBN 0-8028-1402-6 pbk. : 3.45
1. Bible. N.T. Luke—Commentaries. I. Title.

RICHARDS, Larry. 226'.4'07
You can be transformed! a study of Luke: God's gospel of new life. [Wheaton, Ill.] Victor Books [1973] 159 p. 18 cm. (An Input book) [BS2595.4.R52] 73-78691 ISBN 0-88207-236-6 1.25
1. Bible. N.T. Luke—Meditations. I. Title.

STAGG, Frank, 1911- 226'.4'07
Studies in Luke's Gospel. Nashville, Convention Press [1967] xii, 148 p. maps. 19 cm. "Church study course [of the Sunday School Board of the Southern Baptist Convention] This book is number 32 in category 2, section for adults and young people." Bibliography: p. 141. [BS2596.S84] 67-14440
1. Bible. N.T. Luke—Study—Outlines, syliabi, etc. I. Title.

WEEDMAN, Gary. 226'.4'07
Jesus; an interesting, to-the-point digest of: what Jesus did for you, what Jesus says to you. Cincinnati, Standard Pub. [1971] 96 p. 18 cm. (Fountain books) [BS2595.5.W38] 74-164740
1. Bible. N.T. Luke—Study—Text-books. I. Title.

WEISIGER, Cary N. 226'.4'07
The gospel of Luke; a study manual, by Cary N. Weisiger, III. Grand Rapids, Baker Book House [1966] 128 p. 20 cm. (Shield Bible study outlines.) [BS2595.5.W4] 66-29242
1. Bible. N.T. Luke—Study—Outlines, syllabi, etc. I. Title.

APPLEBURY, T. R. 226'.4'077
Studies in Luke, by T. A. Applebury. Joplin, Mo., College Press [1965] 397 p. 23 cm. (Bible study textbook series) [BS2596.A58] 79-1067
1. Bible. N.T. Luke—Study—Outlines, syllabi, etc. I. Title.

ASH, Anthony Lee. 226'.4'077
The Gospel according to Luke. Austin, Tex., Sweet Pub. Co. [1972-73] 2 v. 22 cm. (The Living word commentary, 4) Contents.Contents.—pt. 1. 1:1-9:50.—pt. 2. 9:51-24:53. [BS2595.3.A8] 72-77838 ISBN 0-8344-0067-7 (v. 1) 3.50 (v. 1)
1. Bible. N.T. Luke—Commentaries. I. Title. II. Series.

BIBLE. N.T. Luke. 226'.4'077
English. Barclay. 1975.
The Gospel of Luke / translated with an introd. and interpretation by William Barclay. Philadelphia : Westminster Press, [1975] x, 300 p. ; 20 cm. (The Daily study Bible series. — Rev. ed.) [BS2593 1975] 74-30042 6.25 ISBN 0-664-24103-4 pbk. : 3.45
1. Bible. N.T. Luke—Commentaries. I. Barclay, William, lecturer in the University of Glasgow, ed. II. Title. III. Series.

*BROWNSON, William C. 226.4'077
Distinctive lessons from Luke. [by] William C. Brownson, Jr. Grand Rapids, Baker Book House [1974] 128 p. 18 cm. (Contemporary Discussion Series) [BS2595] ISBN 0-8010-0626-0 1.25 (pbk.)
1. Bible. N.T. Luke—Criticism, interpretation. I. Title.

CAIRD, George 226'.4'077
Bradford.
The Gospel of St. Luke [by] G. B. Caird. New York, Seabury Press [1968, c1963] 271 p. map. 22 cm. (The Pelican Gospel commentaries) [BS2595.3.C3 1968] 68-14136
1. Bible. N.T. Luke—Commentaries. I. Title.

DRURY, John. 226'.4'077
Luke. New York, Macmillan [1973] 220 p. 18 cm. (The J. B. Phillips' commentaries, 3) Cover title: The Gospel of Luke. [BS2595.3.D78] 74-154441 1.50 (pbk.)
1. Bible. N.T. Luke—Commentaries. I. Bible. N.T. Luke. English. Phillips. 1973. II. Title. III. Title: The Gospel of Luke.

HARRINGTON, Wilfrid J. 226'.4'077
The Gospel according to St. Luke; a commentary, by Wilfrid J. Harrington. Westminster, Md., Newman Press [1967] vi, 297 p. 22 cm. Bibliography: p. 295-297. [BS2595.3.H35] 67-28700
1. Bible. N.T. Luke—Commentaries. I. Bible. N.T. Luke. English. 1967. Revised standard. II. Title.

KARRIS, Robert J. 226'.4'077
Invitation to Luke : a commentary on the Gospel of Luke with complete text from the Jerusalem Bible / Robert J. Karris. 1st ed. Garden City, N.Y. : Image Books, 1977. 279 p. ; 18 cm. Bibliography: p. [278]-279. [BS2595.3.K38] 77-73331 ISBN 0-385-12210-1 pbk. : 1.95
1. Bible. N.T. Luke—Commentaries. I. Bible. N.T. Luke. English. Jerusalem Bible. 1977. II. Title.

KARRIS, Robert J. 226'.4'077
Invitation to Luke : a commentary on the Gospel of Luke with complete text from the Jerusalem Bible / Robert J. Karris. 1st ed. Garden City, N.Y. : Image Books, 1977. 279 p. ; 18 cm. Bibliography: p. [278]-279. [BS2595.3.K38] 77-73331 ISBN 0-385-12210-1 pbk. : 1.95
1. Bible. N.T. Luke—Commentaries. I. Bible. N.T. Luke. English. Jerusalem Bible. 1977. II. Title.

POWELL, Ivor. 226.4077
Luke's thrilling Gospel. Grand Rapids, Zondervan Pub. House [1966, c1965] 507 p. 23 cm. [BS2595.3.P6] 66-2319
1. Bible. N. T. Luke—Commentaries 2. Bible. N. T. Luke—Homiletical use. I. Title.

POWELL, Ivor 226.4077
Luke's thrilling Gospel. Grand Rapids, Mich., Zondervan [1966, c.1965] 507p. 23cm. [BS2595.3.P6] 66-2319 9.95
1. Bible, N. T. Luke—Commentaries. 2. Bible. N. T. Luke—Homiletical use. I. Title.

STOGER, Alois. 226'.4'077
The Gospel according to St. Luke. [Translated by Benen Fahy. New York] Herder and Herder [1969] 2 v. 21 cm. (New Testament for spiritual reading, 5-6) Translation of Das Evangelium nach Lukas. [BS2341.2.N382 vol. 5-6] 74-10742 6.00 per vol.
1. Bible. N.T. Luke—Commentaries. I. Bible. N.T. Luke. English. 1969. II. Title. III. Series.

HERMANS, L 226.40823292
The Bible on the childhood of Jesus, by L. Hermans. Translated by H. J. J. Vaughan. De Pere, Wis., St. Norbert Abbey Press, 1965. 112 p. 17 cm. Bibliographical references included in "Notes" (p. [101]-112) [BT315.2.H413] 65-22862
1. Jesus Christ — Biog. — Early life. I. Title.

HERMANS, L. 226.4082392
The Bible on the childhood of Jesus. Tr. by H. J. J. Vaughan. De Pere, Wis., St. Norbert Abbey Pr. [c.]1965. 112p. 17cm. Bibl. [BT315.2.H413] 65-22862 .95 pap.,
1. Jesus Christ—Biog.—Earlylife. I. Title.

NIXON, Joan Lowery. 226'.4'09505
The son who came home again : the prodigal son for beginning readers : Luke 15:11-32 for children / by Joan Lowery Nixon ; illustrated by Aline Cunningham. St. Louis : Concordia Pub. House, c1977. [48] p. : col. ill. ; 23 cm. (I can read a Bible story) Retells the parable of the son, who, after squandering his inheritance, returns home to a forgiving father. [BT378.P8N57] 77-6651 3.95
1. Prodigal son (Parable)—Juvenile literature. I. Cunningham, Aline. II. Title.

NIXON, Joan Lowery. 226'.4'09505
Who is my neighbor? : The Good Samaritan for beginning readers : Luke 10:29-37 for children / retold by Joan Lowery Nixon ; illustrated by Aline Cunningham. St. Louis : Concordia Pub. House, [1976] p. cm. (I can read a Bible story) [BT378.G6N59] 76-13232 ISBN 0-570-07310-3 : 3.95
1. Good Samaritan (Parable)—Juvenile literature. I. Cunningham, Aline. II. Title.

ULMER, Louise. 226'.4'09505
The man who learned to give : Luke 5:27-32 for children / written by Louise Ulmer ; illustrated by John D. Firestone & Associates. St. Louis : Concordia Pub. House, 1977,c1976. p. cm. (Arch books ; ser. 14) Retells in verse the story of Matthew's conversion from tax collector to a disciple of Jesus. [BS2495.U45] 76-27272 ISBN 0-570-06109-1 pbk. : 0.59
1. Matthew, Saint, apostle—Juvenile literature. 2. Bible. N.T.—Biography—Juvenile literature. I. John D. Firestone & Associates. II. Title.

VAN WOERKOM, Dorothy 226'.4'09505
Let us go to Bethlehem! : The first Christmas for beginning readers : Luke 2:1-20 for children / by Dorothy Van Woerkom ; illustrated by Aline Cunningham. St. Louis : Concordia Pub. House, c1976. [48] p. : col. ill. ; 23 cm. (I can read a Bible story) Easy-to-read retelling of the birth of Jesus Christ. [BT315.2.V34] 76-14918 3.95
1. Jesus Christ—Nativity—Juvenile literature. I. Cunningham, Aline. II. Title.

MARQUARDT, Mervin A. 226'4'09595
Jesus' second family : Luke 10:38-42 for children / written by Mervin A. Marquardt ; illustrated by Alice Hausner. St. Louis : Concordia Publishing House, c1976. p. cm. (Arch books, series 14) Retells in verse the story of a visit Jesus made to his close friends Mary, Martha, and Lazarus who lived in Bethany. [BS2433.M37] 76-26578 ISBN 0-570-06111-3 : 0.59
1. Jesus Christ—Friends and associates—Juvenile literature. 2. Bible. N.T.—Biography—Juvenile literature. I. Hausner, Alice, illus. II. Title.

ERDMAN, Charles 226'.4'77
Rosenbury, 1866-1960.
The Gospel of Luke; an exposition, by Charles R. Erdman. Pref. by Earl F. Zeigler. Philadelphia, Westminster Press [1966] 257 p. 19 cm. (His Commentaries on the New Testament books) [BS2595.E7 1966] 67-1989
1. Bible. N.T. Luke—Commentaries. I. Title.

APPLETON, George. 226.5
John's witness to Jesus. New York, Association Press [1955] 96p. 10cm. (World Christian books) [BS2615.A58] 55-9118
1. Bible. N. T. John—Theology. I. Title.

BERKELEY, James Percival, 226.5
1879-
Reading the Gospel of John, [1st ed.] Chicago, Judson Press [1958] 290p. 21cm. Includes bibliography. [BS2615.B47] 58-9989
1. Bible. N.T. John—Commentaries. I. Title.

BERKELEY, James Percival, 226.5
1879-
Reading the Gospel of John. [Valley Forge, Pa.] Judson [1966, c.1958] 290p. 20cm. Bibl. [BS2615.B47] 58-9989 2.00 pap.,
1. Bible. N.T.John— Commentaries. I. Title.

BIBLE. N.T. John Coptic 226.5
(Fayumic) 1962.
The Gospel of John in Fayumic Coptic (P. Mich. Inv. 3521) Edited by Elinor M. Husselman. Ann Arbor, 1962. 96 p. 6 facsims. 23 cm. (University of Michigan. Kelsey Museum of Archaeology. Studies, 2) [BS2614.C6H8] 63-63384
I. Husselman, Elinor (Mullett) 1900- ed. II. Michigan. University. Kelsey Museum of Archaeology. Mss. (P. Mich. Inv. 3521) III. Title. IV. Series. V. Series: Michigan. University. Kelsey Museum of Archaeology. Studies, w

BIBLE. N. T. John. English. 226.5
1952. Confraternity version.
The Gospel according to St. John; from the revision of the Challoner-Rheims version, edited by Catholic scholars under the patronage of the Episcopal Committee of the Confraternity of Christian Doctrine. [3d ed.] Paterson, N. J., St. Anthony Guild Press [1952, c1941] 240-310p. 16cm. [BS2613 1952] 53-19355
I. Confraternity of Christian Doctrine. II. Title.

BIBLE. N. T. John. English. 226.5
1956. Barclay.
The Gospel of John. Translated, with an introd. and interpretation by William Barclay. [2d ed.] Philadelphia, Westminster Press [1956] 2v. 18cm. (The Daily study Bible) [BS2615.B34 1956] 58-5035
1. Bible. N. T. John—Commentaries. I. Barclay, William, lecturer in the University of Glasgow, ed and tr. II. Title.

BIBLE. N. T. John. English. 226.5
1956. Revised.
St. John's Gospel, a commentary by R. H. Lightfoot. Edited by C. F. Evans. With the text of the Revised version. Oxford, Clarendon Press, 1956. 368p. 23cm. [BS2615.L45] 56-4968
1. Bible. N. T. John—Commentaries. I. Lightfoot, Robert Henry, 1883-1953. II. Title.

BIBLE. N. T. John. English. 226.5
1957. Douai.
The Gospel according to Saint John. With an introd. and commentary by C. C. Martindale. Westminster, Md., Newman Press [1957] 175p. illus. 19cm. (Stonyhurst Scripture manuals) [BS2615.M374] 57-8611
1. Bible. N. T. John—Commentaries. I. Martindale, Cyril Charlie, 1879- II. Title.

BIBLE. N. T. John. English. 226.5
1958. Authorized.
The light that lighteth every man, by Paul W. Harrison. Grand Rapids, Eerdmans [1958] 329p. 23cm. [BS2615.H372] 58-14822
1. Bible N. T. John—Commentaries. I. Harrison, Paul Wilberforce, 1883- II. Title.

BIBLE. N. T. John. English. 226.5
1960. Confraternity version.
The Gospel of St. Johnand the Johannine Epistles; introduction and commentary by Liturgical Press [1960] 128p. 20cm. (New Testament reading guide, 13) [BS2615.H372] 58-14822
1. Bible. N. T. John—Commentaries. 2. Bible. N. T. Epistles of John—Commentaries. I. Brown, Raymond Edward. II. Title.

BISAGNO, John R. 226'.5
The Word made flesh / John Bisagno. Waco, Tex. : Word Books, [1975] 128 p. ; 23 cm. [BS2615.4.B57] 74-27482 4.95
1. Bible. N.T. John I, 1-18—Meditations. I. Title.

BOISMARD, M E 226.5
St. John's prologue; [commentary] by M. E. Boismard. Translated by Carisbrooke Dominicans. Westminster, Md., Newman Press [1957] 152p. 19cm. Includes bibliography. [BS2615.B6] 57-2467
1. Bible. N. T. John. I, 1-18— Commentaries. 2. Bible. N. T. John—Theology. I. Title.

BUCK, Harry Merwyn. 226.5
The Johannine lessons in the Greek Gospel lectionary. Chicago, University of Chicago Press [1958] viii, 83p. 25cm. (Studies in the lectionary text of the Greek New Testament, v. 2. no. 4) Bibliography: p.78-83. [BS1938.5.S8 vol. 2,no.4] 58-5537
1. Bible. N. T. John—Criticism, Textual. 2. Lectionaries—Hist. & crit. 3. Bible. N. T. Epistles and Gospels, Liturgical—Criticism, Textual. I. Title. II. Series.

CHILTON, Charles George 226.5
Eric, 1885-
Satisfaction from the Scriptures. Boston, Wilde [1950] 208 p. 22 cm. [BS2615.C45] 50-10655
1. Bible, N. T. John—Sermons. 2. Bible. N. T. Acts—Sermons. I. Title.

CLYMER, Reuben Swinburne, 226.5
1878-
The interpretation of St. John: an exposition of the divine drama; the Nazarene's life, and what it teaches to man. The glory or tragedy of man's soul in teh exercise of its inherent capability to become divine. Nonpolitical and without creed other than the absoluteness of the Christos within man. The recognition of the achievement of all men irrespetive of race, color, or creed. Quakertown, Pa., Philosophical Pub. Co. [1953] 266p. 24cm. [BS2615.C62] 53-12812
1. bBible. N. T. John—Commentaries. I. Title.

COATES, Thomas, 1910- 226'.5
Gospel of John for today; meditations on the Fourth Gospel. Saint Louis, Concordia Pub. House [1968] 144 p. 20 cm. [BS2615.4.C6] 68-31560 1.95
1. Bible. N.T. John—Meditations. I. Title. II. Title: Meditations on the Fourth Gospel.

COLWELL, Ernest Cadman, 226.5
1901-
The Gospel of the Spirit a study in the Fourth Gospel, by Ernest Cadman Colwell and Eric Lane Titus. [1st ed.] New York, Harper [1953] 190p. 22cm. [BS2615.C64] 53-8367
1. Bible. N. T. John—Criticism, interpretation, etc. I. Titus, Eric Lane, 1909- joint author. II. Title.

COTTON, John, 1584-1652. 226'.5
Christ, the fountaine of life / John Cotton. New York : Arno Press, 1972. 256 p. ; 23 cm. (Research library of colonial Americana) Reprint of the 1651 ed. printed by R. Ibbitson, London. [BS2805.C595 1972] 75-141107 ISBN 0-405-03321-4
1. Bible. N.T. 1 John V, 12-17—Sermons. 2. Congregational churches—Sermons. 3. Sermons, American. I. Title. II. Series.

DODD, Charles Harold, 1884- 226.5
The interpretation of the Fourth Gospel. Cambridge [Eng.] University Press, 1953. xi, 477p. 24cm. [BS2615.D57] 53-7686
1. Bible. N. T. John—Criticism, interpretation, etc. I. Title.

FEE, Gordon D. 226'.5
Papyrus Bodmer II (P66): its textual relationships and scribal characteristics, by Gordon D. Fee. Salt Lake City, University of Utah Press, 1968. vii, 146 p. 25 cm. (Studies and documents, 34) "The substance of this study formed part of a larger dissertation on text-critical methodology accepted by the Graduate School of Religion at the University of Southern California in the summer of 1966." Includes bibliographical references. [BS2615.2.F375] 78-13193
1. Bible. N.T. John—Criticism, Textual. 2. Papyrus Bodmer II (P66) I. Title. II. Series.

FRIELING, Rudolf. 226'.5
Agape, by Rudolph Frieling. [Edited by Lisa McGaw] Translated by Jeffrey Kay. De Pere, Wisc., St. Norbert Abbey Press, 1969. 72 p. 19 cm. [BS2615.2.F7313] 70-87812 1.95
1. Bible. N.T. John—Criticism, interpretation, etc. 2. Love—Biblical teaching. I. McGaw, Lisa, ed. II. Title.

GIBSON, Charles Knight. 226.5
Christ before Calvary: ten portraits. [1st ed.] New York, Vantage Press [c1956] 85p. 21cm. [BS2614.G47] 56-12312
1. Bible, N. T. John XVII—Meditations. I. Title.

HARRISON, Everett Falconer, 226.5
1902-
The Son of God among the sons of men; studies in the Gospel according to John. Boston, W. A. Wilde Co. [1949] 251p. 20cm. [BS2615H34] 49-48444
1. Bible. N. T. John—Criticism, interpretation, etc. 2. Bible. N. T.—Biog. I. Title.

•HILL, Dave 226(5
The boy who gave his lunch away; John 6:1-15 for children. Illus. by Betty Wind. St. Louis, Concordia, 1967. 1.v (unpaged) col. illus. 21cm. (Arch bks.) .35 pap.,
1. Bible—N. T.—John—Juvenile literature. I. Title.

MCLAREN, Alexander, 1826- 226.5
1910.
With Christ in the upper room; sermons on fourteenth, fifteenth, and sixteenth chapters of the Gospel of John. Grand Rapids, Baker Book House, 1956. 379p. 21cm. Published in 8190 under title: Holy of holies. [BS2615.M28 1956] 56-11839
1. Bibl. N. T. John xiv-xvi—Sermons. 2. Baptists—Sermons. 3. Sermons, English. I. Title.

MURPHY, Joseph, 1898- 226.5
Peace within yourself. San Gabriel, Calif, Willing Pub. Co. [1956] 300p. 20cm. [BS2615.M83] 57-18409
1. Bible. N. T. John—Miscellanea. I. Title.

NUNN, Henry Preston 226.5
Vaughan.
The authorship of the Fourth Gospel. [Windsor, Berks.] Alden & Blackwell (Eton) 1952. 152p. 19cm. [BS2615.N8] 52-11949
1. Bible. N. T. John—Evidences, authority, etc. 2. Bible. N. T. John—Criticism, interpretation, etc. I. Title.

ODEBERG, Hugo, 1898- 226'.5
The Fourth Gospel; interpreted in its relation to contemporaneous religious currents in Palestine and the Hellenistic-Oriental world. Chicago, Argonaut, 1968. 336 p. 23 cm. On spine: Gospel. Reprint of 1929 ed.; covers John I, 5 [superscript 1]-XII. No more published? Includes some passages from Rabbinic literature in Aramaic and Hebrew. Bibliography: p. [7]-31. [BS2615.2.O3 1968] 76-3012
1. Bible. N.T. John—Criticism, interpretation, etc. I. Title.

RAINSFORD, Marcus, 1820?- 226.5
1897.
Our Lord prays for His own; thoughts on John 17. With a biographical introd. by S. Maxwell Coder. Chicago, Moody Press, 1950. 476 p. 23 cm. (The Wycliffe series of Christian classics) First published in 1873 under title: Lectures on St. John 17. "Gospel dialogues between Mr. D. L. Moody and the Rev. Marcus Rainsford": p. 455-476. Bibliography: p. 29. [BS2615.R27 1950] 50-14886
1. Bible. N. T. John XVII — Commentaries. I. Title. II. Series.

RIPLEY, Francis J. 226.5
The last Gospel; doctrinal and spiritual conferences on the opening verses of St John's Gospel. New York, Sheed [1962, c.1961] 225p. 62-11095 3.50 bds.,
1. Bibl. N. T. John I, 1-14—Meditations. I. Title.

ROSSCUP, James E. 226'.5
Abiding in Christ: studies in John 15 [by] James E. Rosscup. Grand Rapids, Mich., Zondervan Pub. House [1973] 254 p. 22 cm. Includes bibliographical references. [BV4501.2.R67 1973] 72-85570 5.95
1. Bible. N.T. John 15—Criticism, interpretation, etc. 2. Christian life—1960- I. Title.

SALSTRAND, George A E 1908- 226.5
How to preach from the Gospel of John. Grand Rapids, Baker Book House, 1953. 114p. 21cm. [BS2615.S28] 53-35203
1. Bible. N. T. John—Sermons—Outlines. I. Title.

STEDMAN, Ray C. 226'.5
Secrets of the spirit / Ray C. Stedman. Old Tappan, N.J. : F. H. Revell, [1975] 160 p. ; 21 cm. [BS2615.2.S73] 74-20925 ISBN 0-8007-0721-4 : 4.95
1. Bible. N.T. John XIII-XVII—Criticism, interpretation, etc. I. Title.

STEVENSON, Dwight Eshelman, 226.5
1906-
The fourth witness. St. Louis, Bethany Press, c1954. 96p. 20cm. (A Bethany Bible course) [BS2616.S8] 55-14556
1. Bible. N. T. John—Study—Text-books. I. Title.

TITUS, Eric Lane, 1909- 226.5
The message of the Fourth Gospel. New York, Abingdon Press [1957] 253p. 23cm. [BS2615.T56] 57-5282
1. Bible. N.T. John—Commentaries. I. Title.

TITUS, Eric Lane, 1909- 226.5
The message of the Fourth Gospel. New York, Abingdon Press [1957] 253 p. 23 cm. [BS2615.T56] 57-5282
1. Bible. N.T. John — Commentaries. I. Title.

WEST, Edward N 226.5
Meditations on the Gospel of St. John. [1st ed.] New York, Harper [c1955] 189p. 20cm. [BS2615.W48] 54-12331
1. Bible. N. T. John—Meditations. I. Title.

GETTYS, Joseph Miller 226.5007
How to study John. Richmond, Va., John Knox Press [c.1960] 153p. (Bibls.) 23cm. 60-14141 1.75 pap.,
1. Bible. N.T. John—Study. I. Title.

GETTYS, Joseph Miller, 226.5007
1907-
How to teach John. Richmond, Va., John Knox Press [c.1960] 80p. 23cm. 60-50590 1.50 pap.,
1. Bible. N. T. John—Study. I. Title.

HUNT, Gladys M. 226'.5'007
Eyewitness: John's view of Jesus [by] Gladys Hunt. Wheaton, Ill., H. Shaw Publishers [1971] 87 p. map. 22 cm. [BS2616.H78] 70-158130 ISBN 0-87788-245-2
1. Bible. N.T. John—Study. I. Title.

KYSAR, Robert. 226'.5'007
The fourth evangelist and his Gospel : an examination of contemporary scholarship / Robert Kysar. Minneapolis : Augsburg Pub. House, c1975. 296 p. ; 22 cm. Includes bibliographical references and indexes. [BS2615.2.K9] 75-22711 ISBN 0-8066-1504-4 : 4.95
1. Bible. N.T. John—Criticism, interpretation, etc.—History—20th century. I. Title.

NIXON, Robin E. 226.5'007
St. John [by] R. E. Nixon. [1st U.S. ed.] Grand Rapids, Eerdmans [1968] 85 p. 19 cm. (Bible study books) [BS2616.N5 1968] 68-56122 1.25
1. Bible. N.T. John—Study—Outlines, syllabi, etc. I. Title.

†CULLMANN, Oscar. 226'.5'01
The Johannine circle / Oscar Cullmann ; translated by John Bowden. Philadelphia : Westminster Press, c1976. xi, 124 p. ; 24 cm. Translation of Der johanneische Kreis. Includes indexes. Bibliography: p. [100]-101. [BS2615.2.C8413 1976] 75-42249 ISBN 0-664-20744-8 : 6.95
1. Bible. N.T. John—Criticism, interpretation, etc. 2. Johannine school. I. Title.

CULLMANN, Oscar. 226'.5'01
The Johannine circle : its place in Judaism, among the disciples of Jesus and in early Christianity : a study in the origin of the Gospel of John / [by] Oscar Cullmann ; [translated from the German by John Bowden] . London : S.C.M. Press, 1976. xii, 124 p. ; 23 cm. (New Testament library) Translation of Der johanniesche Kreis. Includes index. Bibliography: p. 100-101. [BS2615.2.C8413 1976b] 76-372897 ISBN 0-334-00797-6 : £3.50
1. Bible. N.T. John—Criticism, interpretation, etc. 2. Johannine school. I. Title.

FORTNA, Robert Tomson. 226'.5'01
The gospel of signs: a reconstruction of the narrative source underlying the Fourth Gospel. London, Cambridge U.P., 1970. xiii, 274 p. 23 cm. (Society for New Testament Studies. Monograph series, 11) A revision of the author's thesis, Union Theological Seminary. Bibliography: p. 246-256. [BS2615.2.F65 1970] 74-93708 95/- ($11.50)
1. Bible. N.T. John—Criticism, interpretation, etc. I. Title. II. Series: Studiorum Novi Testamenti Societas. Monograph series, 11

SMITH, Dwight Moody. 226.504
The composition and order of the fourth Gospel; Bultmann's literary theory. New Haven, Yale University Press, 1965. xx, 272 p. 26 cm. (Yale publications in religion, 10) Based on the author's thesis. Yale University. "The hypothetical original text of the fourth Gospel (as arranged by Bultmann]": p. 179-212. Bibliography: p. 251-255. [BS2615.2.S6] 64-20936
1. Bultmann, Rudolf Karl, 1884- Das Evangelium des Johannes. 2. Bible. N. T. John — Criticism, textual. I. Title. II. Series.

BIBLE. N.T. John. 226'.5'047
Latin. Stonyhurst. 1969.
The Stonyhurst Gospel of Saint John. Edited by T. Julian Brown, with a technical description of the binding by Roger Powell and Peter Waters. Oxford [University Press] for the Roxburghe Club, 1969. 62 p. [91] p. facsims., plates. 25 cm. Introd. in English. Text of the gospel reproduced in facsimile from the copy in possession of Stonyhurst College. [PR1105.R7 1969] 70-505470
1. Bookbinding—England. I. Brown, Thomas Julian, ed. II. Title.

SALMON, Victor. 226'.5'048
The fourth Gospel : a history of the textual tradition of the original Greek Gospel / by Victor Salmon ; translated by Matthew J. O'Connell. Collegeville, Minn. : Liturgical Press, c1976. 112 p. : 64 ill. ; 23 cm. Translation of Histoire de la tradition textuelle de l'original grec du quatrieme Evangile. Includes bibliographies. [BS2611.3.S2313] 77-364581 ISBN 0-8146-0926-0
1. Bible. N.T. John—Manuscripts, Greek. 2. Bible. N.T. Greek—Versions. I. Title.

BIBLE. N.T. John. 226.5052
English. 1965. Crawford.
The good news of Jesus Christ, by His follower John. Translation by William Raymond Crawford. Forword by Jim Vaus. Tarrytown, N.Y., Tarrytown Publishers [1965, c1964] 100 p. 15 cm. [BS2613] 65-22662
I. Crawford, William Raymond, tr. II. Title.

BIBLE. N. T. John. 226'.5'05203
English. 1967. Authorized.
The Gospel according to Saint John, in the words of the King James version of the year 1611. Ed. in conformity with the true ecumenical spirit of His Holiness, Pope John XXIII, by Dagobert D. Runes. New York, Philosophical Lib. [1967] vi, 97p. 22cm. [BS2613 1967] 67-20465 2.75
I. Runes, Dagobert David, 1902- ed. II. Title.

BIBLE. N.T. John. 226'.5'05203
English. 1967. Authorized.
The Gospel according to Saint John, in the words of the King James version of the year 1611. Edited in conformity with the true ecumenical spirit of His Holiness, Pope John xxiii, by Dagobert D. Runes. New York, Philosophical Library [1967] vi, 97 p. 22 cm. [BS2613] 67-20465
I. Runes, Dagobert Daivd, 1902- ed. II. Title.

BIBLE. N.T. John. 226'.5'0529
Anglo-Saxon. 1904.
Euangelium secundum Iohannem. The Gospel of Saint John in West Saxon; edited from the manuscripts, with introd. and notes by James Wilson Bright. With a glossary by Lancelot Minor Harris. [Folcroft, Pa.] Folcroft Library Editions, 1973. p. Reprint of the 1904 ed. published by D. C. Heath, Boston and issued in The Belles-lettres series. Section 1. English

literature. Bibliography: p. [BS2613 1904c] 73-9893 11.50 (lib. ed.)
1. Anglo-Saxon language—Glossaries, vocabularies, etc. I. Bright, James Wilson, 1852-1926, ed. II. Harris, Lancelot Minor, 1868-1941. III. Title.

BIBLE. N.T. John. 226'.5'0529
Anglo-Saxon. 1904.
Euangelium secundum Iohannem. The Gospel of Saint John in West-Saxon; edited from the manuscripts, with introduction and notes, by James Wilson Bright. With a glossary by Lancelot Minor Harris. Boston, Heath, 1904. [New York, AMS Press, 1973 c1972] xxxix, 260 p. 19 cm. Original ed. issued in series: The Belles-lettres series. Section 1. English literature. Bibliography: p. [183]-188. [BS2613 1904a] 71-144447 ISBN 0-404-53605-0 12.00
1. Anglo-Saxon language—Glossaries, vocabularies, etc. I. Bright, James Wilson, 1852-1926, ed. II. Harris, Lancelot Minor, 1868-1941. III. Bible. N.T. John. Anglo-Saxon. Bright. 1972. IV. Title.

BIBLE. N.T. John. 226'.5'0529
Anglo-Saxon. 1973.
Euangelium secundum Iohannem. The Gospel of Saint John in West-Saxon, edited from the manuscripts, with introd. and notes by James Wilson Bright. With a glossary by Lancelot Minor Harris. [Folcroft, Pa.] Folcroft Library Editions, 1973. 260 p. 23 cm. Reprint of the 1904 ed. published by D.C. Heath, Boston, and issued in The Belles-lettres series. Section 1. English literature. Bibliography: p. [183]-188. [BS2613 1973] 73-9893 ISBN 0-8414-3179-5 (lib. bdg.)
1. Anglo-Saxon language—Glossaries, vocabularies, etc. I. Bright, James Wilson, 1852-1926, ed. II. Harris, Lancelot Minor, 1868-1941. III. Title.

*KENT, Homer A. 226'.5'0529
Light in the darkness; studies in the gospel of John, [by] Homer A. Kent, Jr. Grand Rapids, Baker Book House [1974] 239 p. illus. 20 cm. (New Testament studies.) Bibliography: p. 231-239. [BS2616] ISBN 0-8010-5342-0
1. Bible. N.T. John—Commentaries. I. Title.
Pbk. 2.95, ISBN 0-8010-5343-9

APPOLD, Mark L. 226'.5'06
The oneness motif in the fourth gospel : motif analysis and exegetical probe into the theology of John / by Mark L. Appold. 1. Aufl. Tubingen : Mohr, 1976. ix, 313 p. ; 24 cm. (Wissenschaftliche Untersuchungen zum Neuen Testament : Reihe 2 ; 1) A revision of the author's inaugural dissertation, Faculty of Evangelical Theology, University of Tubingen, 1973. Bibliography: p. [295]-313. [BS2615.2.A66 1976] 76-382939 ISBN 3-16-138371-0 : DM48.00
1. Jesus Christ—History of doctrines—Early church, ca. 30-600. 2. Bible. N.T. John—Criticism, interpretation, etc. I. Title. II. Series.

AUGUSTINUS, Aurelius, 226.506
Saint Bp. of Hippo.
John shines through Augustine; selections from the sermons of Augustine on the Gospel according to Saint John. Tr. [from Latin] by A. P. Carleton. New York, Association Press [1961] 79p. (World Christian books, no. 34., 2d ser.) 61-8212 1.00 pap.,
1. Bible. N. T. John—Sermons. 2. Sermons, Latin—Translations into English. 3. Sermons, English—Translation from Latin. I. Carleton, Arthur Patrick, ed. and tr. II. Title.

BIBLE, N. T. John. 226.506
English. 1961. Vann.
The Eagle's word; a presentation of the Gospel according to St. John, introductory essay by Gerald Vann. New York, Harcourt [c.1961] 247p. (Helen and Kurt Wolff bk.) 61-15809 4.50
1. Bible. N. T. John—Criticism, Interpretation, etc. I. Vann, Gerald, 1906- II. Title.

BOWMAN, John, 1916- 226'.5'06
The fourth Gospel and the Jews : a study in R. Akiba, Esther, and the Gospel of John / by John Bowman. Pittsburgh : Pickwick Press, 1975. xii, 409 p. : 22 cm. (Pittsburgh theological monograph series ; 8) Includes index. Bibliography: p. 375-379. [BS2615.2.B65] 75-40461 ISBN 0-915138-10-7
1. Akiba ben Joseph, ca. 50-ca. 132. 2. Bible. N.T. John—Criticism, interpretation, etc. 3. Bible. O.T. Esther—Criticism, interpretation, etc. I. Title. II. Series.

BROWN, Jeff D. 226.506
Sermon outlines on the Gospel of John 1-7. Grand Rapids, Mich., Baker Book House [c.] 1960. 85p. 22cm. 1.00 pap.,
I. Title.

BROWN, Jeff D. 226.506
Sermon outlines on the Gospel of John 8-21. Grand Rapids, Mich., Baker Book House [c.] 1960. 89p. 22cm. 1.00 pap.,
I. Title.

BRUNS, J. Edgar, 1923- 226'.5'06
The art and thought of John [by] J. Edgar Bruns. [New York] Herder and Herder [1969] 152 p. 22 cm. Includes bibliographies. [BS2615.2.B78] 70-87752 4.95
1. Bible. N.T. John—Criticism, interpretation, etc. I. Title.

BRUNS, J. Edgar, 1923- 226'.5'06
The Christian Buddhism of St. John; new insights into the Fourth Gospel, by J. Edgar Bruns. Foreword by Gregory Baum. New York, Paulist Press [1971] xiv, 80 p. 21 cm. Based on a series of lectures given in the Institute of Christian Thought at St. Michael's of Toronto, Spring, 1969-70. Includes bibliographical references. [BS2615.2.B783] 76-151660 2.50
1. Bible. N.T. John—Criticism, interpretation, etc. 2. Buddha and Buddhism—Relations—Christianity. 3. Christianity and other religions—Buddhism. I. Title.

DANA, Harvey Eugene, 226.506
1888-
The heavenly guest an expository analysis of the Gospel of John. Nashville, Tenn., Broadman Press [1960, c.1943] 152p. (Broadman starbooks) Bibl. 1.00 pap.,
1. Bible. N. T. John—Commentaries. 2. Bible—Commentaries—N. T. John. I. Title.

DODD, Charles Harold, 226.506
1884-
Historical tradition in the Fourth Gospel. [New York] Cambridge [c.]1963. xii, 453p. 25cm. 63-23896 10.00
1. Bible. N. T. John—Criticism, interpretation, etc. I. Title.

ELLIS, Edward Earle. 226.506
The world of St. John; the Gospel and the Epistles, by E. Earle Ellis. London, Lutterworth Press; New York, Abingdon Press [1965] 96 p. 20 cm. (Bible guides, no. 14) [BS2601.E55] 65-1134
1. Bible. N.T. Johannine literature. I. Title.

ELLIS, edward Earle 226.506
The world of St. John; the Gospel and the Epistles, by E. Earle Ellis. London, Lutterworth Pr.; Nashville, Abingdon [1965] 96p. 20cm. (Bible guides, no. 14) [BS2601.E55] 65-1134 1.00 pap.,
1. Bible. N. T. Johannine literature. I. Title.

FEUILLET, André. 226.506
Johannine studies. Staten Island, N.Y., Alba House [1965] 202 p. 22 cm. Translated by Thomas E. Crane from French articles formerly published in periodicals, memorial volumes, and melanges. Bibliographical footnotes. [BS2601.F45] 64-20112
1. Bible. N.T. Johannine literature—Criticism, interpretation, etc. I. Title.

FEUILLET, Andre 226.506
Johannine studies [Tr. from French by Thomas E. Crane] Staten Island, N.Y., Alba [c.1965] 292p. 22cm. Bibl. [BS2601.F45] 64-20112 5.95
1. Bible. N. T. Johannine literature—Criticism, interpretation, etc. I. Title.

GLASSON, Thomas Francis. 226.506
Moses in the fourth Gospel. Naperville, Ill., A. R. Allenson [1963] 115 p. 22 cm. (Studies in Biblical theology, no. 40) Includes bibliography. [BS2615.2.G6] 63-5666
1. Moses. 2. Bible. N.T. John — Theology 3. Wilderness (Theology) 4. Typology (Theology) I. Title.

GLASSON, Thomas Francis. 226.506
Moses in the fourth Gospel. Naperville. Ill., Allenson [c.1963] 115p. 22cm. (Studies in Biblical theology, no. 40) Bibl. 63-5666 2.00 pap.,
1. Bible. N.T. John—Theology. 2. Moses. 3. Wilderness (Theology) 4. Typology (Theology) I. Title.

GUILDING, Aileen. 226.506
The Fourth Gospel and Jewish worship; a study of the relation of St. John's Gospel to the ancient Jewish lectionary system. Oxford, Clarendon Press, 1960. 247p. 25cm. Bibliographical footnotes. [BS2615.2.G8] 60-2897
1. Bible. N. T. John— Criticism, interpretation, etc. 2. Bible, O. T.—Liturgical use. I. Title.

GUTZKE, Manford George. 226'.5'06
Plain talk on John. Grand Rapids, Zondervan Pub. House [1968] 213 p. 23 cm. [BS2615.3.G8] 69-11646 3.95
1. Bible. N.T. John—Commentaries. I. Title.

GUY, Harold A 226.506
The Gospel and letters of John. London, Macmillan; New York, St. Martin's Press, 1963. vii, 136 p. map. 20 cm. Bibliography: p. 134. [BS2601.Z72G8] 64-214
1. Bible. N.T. Johannine literature — Introductions. I. Title.

GUY, Harold A. 226.506
The Gospel and letters of John. London, Macmillan; New York, St. Martin's [1964, c.] 1963. vii, 136p. map. 20cm. Bibl. 64-214 1.75
1. Bible. N. T. Johannine literature—Introductions. I. Title.

HARNER, Philip B. 226'.5'06
The "I am" of the fourth Gospel: a study in Johannine usage and thought, by Philip B. Harner. Philadelphia, Fortress Press [1970] vi, 66 p. 20 cm. (Facet books. Biblical series -26) Includes bibliographical references. [BS2615.2.H36] 72-123506 1.00
1. Bible. N.T. John—Criticism, interpretation, etc. 2. I am (Biblical phrase) I. Title.

HARVEY, Anthony Ernest. 226'.5'06
Jesus on trial : a study in the Fourth Gospel / A. E. Harvey. Atlanta : John Knox Press, 1977, c1976. p. cm. Reprint of the ed. published by SPCK, London. Includes indexes. Bibliography: p. [BT440.H37 1977] 77-79588 ISBN 0-8042-0335-0 : 6.95
1. Jesus Christ—Trial. 2. Bible. N.T. John—Criticism, interpretation, etc. I. Title.

HUNTER, Archibald 226'.5'06
Macbride.
According to John; the new look at the fourth Gospel, by Archibald M. Hunter. Philadelphia, Westminster Press [1968] 128 p. 21 cm. Bibliography: p. [119]-122. [BS2615.2.H8] 69-14199 1.65
1. Bible. N.T. John—Criticism, interpretation, etc. I. Title.

KOGLIN, Anna E 226.506
That you may believe; a study in the Gospel of John, by Anna E. Koglin. Anderson, Ind., Warner Press [1964] 96 p. 21 cm. [BS2615.5.K6] 64-22158
1. Bible. N. T. John—Study. I. Title.

KOGLIN. ANNA E. 226.506
That you may believe; a study in the Gospel of John. Anderson. Ind., Warner [c.1964] 96p. 21cm. 64-22158 1.25 pap.,
1. Bible. N. T. John—Study I. Title.

KYSAR, Robert. 226'.5'06
John, the maverick Gospel / Robert Kysar. Atlanta : John Knox Press, c1976. 118 p. ; 23 cm. Bibliography: p. [119] [BS2615.2.K93] 76-12393 ISBN 0-8042-0302-4 pbk. : 4.95
1. Bible. N.T. John—Criticism, interpretation, etc. I. Title.

MOLONEY, Francis J. 226'.5'06
The Johannine Son of Man / Francis J. Moloney. Roma : LAS, 1976. xv, 265 p. ; 24 cm. (Biblioteca di scienze religiose ; 14) Originally presented as the author's thesis, Oxford, 1975. Includes indexes. Bibliography: p. [221]-240. [BT232.M64 1976] 77-368906
1. Bible. N.T. John—Criticism, interpretation, etc. 2. Son of Man. I. Title.

MORRIS, Leon. 226'.5'06
Studies in the fourth Gospel. Grand Rapids, W. B. Eerdmans Pub. Co. [1969] 374 p. 23 cm. Bibliographical footnotes. [BS2615.2.M6] 68-12790 8.95
1. Bible. N.T. John—Criticism, interpretation, etc. I. Title.

MORRIS, Leon. 226'.5'06
Studies in the Fourth Gospel. Devon, Paternoster P., 1969. 374 p. 23 cm. Includes bibliographical references. [BS2615.2.M6 1969b] 72-458008 35/-
1. Bible. N.T. John—Criticism, interpretation, etc. I. Title.

ONE way for modern man 226.506
[the Gospel of John in modern English, tr. by J. B. Phillips] New York, Amer. Bible Soc. [1963, c.1952, 1957] 76p. illus. 20cm. .15 pap.,

PAUL Marie de la Croix, 226'.5'06
Father.
The Biblical spirituality of St. John. [Translated by John Clarke] Staten Island, N.Y., Alba House [1966] 425 p. 24 cm. Translation of L'Evangile de Jean et son temoignage spirituel. Bibliographical footnotes. [BS2615.2.P313] 66-13033
1. Bible. N.T. John—Theology. 2. Spiritual life—Biblical teaching. I. Title.

PERKINS, Pheme. 226'.5'06
Gospel of St. John / by Pheme Perkins Chicago : Franciscan Herald Press, [1975] p. cm. (Read and pray series) [BS2615.4.P4] 75-2360 pbk. : 0.95 0.95
1. Bible. N.T. John—Devotional literature. I. Title. II. Series: Read and pray.

SELF, Jerry M. 226'.5'06
Men & women in John's Gospel / Jerry M. Self. Nashville : Broadman Press, [1974] 126 p. ; 19 cm. [BS2615.4.S44] 74-79487 ISBN 0-8054-8123-0 pbk. : 1.95
1. Bible. N.T. John—Meditations. 2. Bible. N.T. John—Biography. I. Title.

SMITH, Dwight Moody. 226'.5'06
John / D. Moody Smith. Philadelphia : Fortress Press, c1976. xiii, 114 p. ; 22 cm. (Proclamation commentaries) Includes index. Bibliography: p. 109-110. [BS2615.2.S62] 75-13046 ISBN 0-8006-0582-9 pbk. : 2.95
1. Bible. N.T. John—Criticism, interpretation, etc.

STEINER, Rudolf 226.506
The Gospel of St. John, in relation to the three other Gospels, particularly to the Gospel of St. Luke: a course of 14 lectures given at Kassel, 15th June to 7th July 1909. [in Russian] Tr. from German. West Nyack, N.Y., Author [c.]1962. 289p. 28cm. 5.00 pap.,
I. Title.

STEVENS, William Wilson. 226.506
That ye may believe; a distinctive study of the Gospel of John. [1st ed.] New York, American Press [1959] 176 p. 21 cm. Includes bibliography. [BS2615.5.S8] 59-9557
1. Bible. N. T. John — Theology. I. Title.

TEMPLE, William, Abp., 226.506
1881-1944
Readings in St. John's gospel, first and second series. [New York, St. Martin's, 1962] 391p. 18cm. (St. Martin's lib.) 1.75
1. Bible. N. T. John—Readings. I. Title.

WARD, Ronald Arthur 226.506
The Gospel of John. Grand Rapids, Mich., Baker Bk. House, 1961. 142p. (Proclaiming the New Testament) Bibl. 61-15592 2.50
1. Bible. N. T. John—Homiletical use. I. Title.

WILES, Maurice F 226.506
The spirtual Gospel; the interpretation of the Fourth Gospel in the early church. Cambridge [Eng.] University Press, 1960. x, 181 p. 22 cm. Bibliography: p. 162-166. [BS2615.2.S5] 60-1484
1. Bible. N. T. John — Criticism, interpretations, etc. — Hist. I. Title.

CULPEPPER, R. Alan. 226'.5'061
The Johannine school : an evaluation of the Johannine-school hypothesis based on an investigation of the nature of ancient schools / by R. Alan Culpepper. Missoula, Mont. : Published by Scholars Press for the Society of Biblical Literature, c1975. p. cm. (Society of Biblical Literature. Dissertation series ; no. 26) Originally presented as the author's thesis, Duke, 1974. Includes index. Bibliography: p. [BS2615.2.C86 1975] 75-34235 ISBN 0-89130-063-5 4.20
1. Bible. N.T. John—Authorship. 2. Johannine school. 3. Philosophy, Ancient. I. Title. II. Series.

CULPEPPER, R. Alan. 226'.5'061
The Johannine school : an evaluation of the Johannine-school hypothesis based on an investigation of the nature of ancient schools / by R. Alan Culpepper. Missoula, Mont. : Published by Scholars Press for the Society of Biblical Literature, c1975. p. cm. (Society of Biblical Literature. Dissertation series ; no. 26) Originally presented as the author's thesis, Duke, 1974. Includes index. Bibliography: p. [BS2615.2.C86 1975] 75-34235 ISBN 0-89130-063-5 4.20
1. Bible. N.T. John—Authorship. 2. Johannine school. 3. Philosophy, Ancient. I. Title. II. Series.

TEEPLE, Howard Merle, 226'.5'061
1911-
The literary origin of the Gospel of John, by Howard M. Teeple. Evanston, Religion and Ethics Institute, 1974. x, 297 p. 22 cm. Bibliography: p. [274]-293. [BS2615.2.T43] 73-87487 6.00 (pbk.)
1. Bible. N.T. John—Criticism, interpretation, etc. I. Title.
Publishers Address: P.O. Box 664, Evanston, Illinois, 60204.

BARRETT, Charles 226'.5'066
Kingsley.
The gospel of John and Judaism / C. K. Barrett ; translated from the German by D. M. Smith. 1st American ed. Philadelphia : Fortress Press, 1975. ix, 101 p. ; 20 cm. (Franz Delitzsch lectures ; 1967) Translation of Das Johannesevangelium und das Judentum. Includes bibliographical references and indexes. [BS2615.2.B3513 1975] 75-15435 ISBN 0-8006-0431-8 : 5.95
1. Bible. N.T. John—Criticism, interpretation, etc. 2. Jews in the New Testament. I. Title. II. Series.

BOICE, James 226'.5'066
Montgomery, 1928-
Witness and revelation in the Gospel of John. Grand Rapids, Zondervan Pub. House [1970]

192 p. 21 cm. (Contemporary evangelical perspectives) Includes bibliographical references. [BS2615.2.B57] 78-106426
1. Bible. N.T. John—Criticism, interpretation, etc. 2. Witness bearing (Christianity)—Biblical teaching. 3. Revelation—Biblical teaching. I. Title.

CRANNY, Titus F., 1921 226.5066
John 17; As we are one; an exposition and interpretation of the seventeenth chapter of St. John's Gospel of Our Lord, containing His prayer for the unity all His followers, by Titus Cranny. Garrison, N.Y., Unity Apostolate, 1965, c.1966. 176p. 22cm. [BS261.5.2C7] 66-26469 3.25
1. Bibl . N.T. John xvii—Criticism, interpretation, etc. 2. Christian union. I. Title.

CREHAN, Joseph. 226'.5'066
The theology of St. John. New York, Sheed and Ward [1966, c1965] 160 p. 20 cm. Bibliography: p. 9-10. [BS2601.C7 1966] 66-12266
1. Bible. N.T. Johannine literature—Theology. I. Title.

CROSSAN, John Dominic. 226'.5'066
The Gospel of eternal life; reflections on the theology of St. John [by] Dominic Crossan. Milwaukee, Bruce Pub. Co. [1967] xvi, 180 p. 22 cm. (Impact books) Bibliography: p. 171-173. [BS2601.C76] 67-21897
1. Bible. N.T. Johannine literature—Theology. I. Title.

DODD, Charles Harold, 226'.5'066
1884-
The interpretation of the fourth Gospel, by C. H. Dodd. Cambridge, Cambridge U.P., 1968. xii, 478 p. 23 cm. Bibliographical footnotes. [BS2615.D57 1968] 68-105178 ISBN 0-521-09517-4 17/6
1. Bible. N.T. John—Criticism, interpretation, etc. I. Title.

HAILEY, Homer, 1904- 226'.5'066
That you may believe; studies in the Gospel of John. Grand Rapids, Mich., Baker Book House [1973] 196 p. 23 cm. Bibliography: p. 195-196. [BS2615.2.H33] 73-81248 ISBN 0-8010-4078-7 3.95
1. Bible. N.T. John—Criticism, interpretation, etc. I. Title.

HERZOG, Frederick. 226'.5'066
Liberation theology; liberation in the light of the fourth Gospel. New York, Seabury Press, [1972] xv, 272 p. 22 cm. Bibliography: p. 267-269. [BS2615.2.H47] 72-81026 ISBN 0-8164-0241-8 6.95
1. Bible. N.T. John—Theology. 2. Freedom (Theology) I. Title.

JAUNCEY, James H. 226'.5'066
The compelling indwelling, by James H. Jauncey. Foreword by Grady B. Wilson. Chicago, Moody Press [1972] 127 p. 22 cm. [BS2615.2.J38] 72-77941 ISBN 0-8024-1605-5
1. Bible. N.T. John XV—Criticism, interpretation, etc. I. Title.

MARTYN, James Louis, 226'.5'066
1925-
History and theology in the Fourth Gospel [by] J. Louis Martyn. [1st ed.] New York, Harper & Row [1968] xxi, 168 p. 21 cm. Bibliographical footnotes. [BS2615.2.M34] 68-17588
1. Bible. N.T. John—Criticism, interpretation, etc. 2. Bible. N.T. John—Theology. I. Title.

PAGELS, Elaine H., 226'.5'066
1943-
The Johannine Gospel in gnostic exegesis: Heracleon's commentary on John [by] Elaine H. Pagels. Nashville, Abingdon Press [1973] 128 p. 24 cm. (Society of Biblical Literature. Monograph series, no. 17) Based on the author's thesis, Harvard, 1970. Includes bibliographical references. [BS2615.2.P24] 72-10120 ISBN 0-687-20632-4 3.50
1. Heracleon, the Gnostic. 2. Bible. N.T. John—Criticism, interpretation, etc.—History—Early church. 3. Gnosticism. I. Title. II. Series.

SAUNDERS, Ernest W. 226'.5'066
John celebrates the Gospel; [a study of the fourth Gospel, by] Ernest W. Saunders. Nashville, Abingdon Press [1970, c1968] x, 187 p. 19 cm. "Originally published as Coming to life." Bibliography: p. 184-186. [BS2615.3.S2 1970] 77-109677 ISBN 0-687-20306-6
1. Bible. N.T. John—Commentaries. I. Title.

SCHNEIDERFRANKEN, 226'.5'066
Joseph Anton, 1876-1943.
The wisdom of St. John / B Yin Ra (Joseph Anton Schneiderfranken) Berkeley, Calif. : Kober Press, c1975. xii, 92 p. ; 21 cm. Translation of Die Weisheit des Johannes. [BS2615.S35413 1975] 74-15272 ISBN 0-915034-01-8 : 5.00
1. Bible. N.T. John—Miscellanea. I. Title.

SCHNEIDERFRANKEN, 226'.5'066
Joseph Anton, 1876-1943.
The wisdom of St. John / Bo Yin Ra (Joseph Anton Schneiderfranken) ; translated from the German by B. A. Reichenbach. Berkeley, Calif. : Kober Press, c1975. xii, 92 p. ; 21 cm. Translation of Die Weisheit des Johannes. [BS2615.S35413 1975] 74-15272 ISBN 0-915034-01-8 : 5.00
1. Bible. N.T. John—Miscellanea. I. Title.

SMITH, F. Sherwood. 226'.5'066
A philosopher looks at Jesus; light for Christian living from John's Gospel, by F. Sherwood Smith and Orrin Root. Cincinnati, Standard Pub. [1973] 96 p. illus. 18 cm. (Fountain books) [BS2615.2.S63] 73-80992
1. Bible. N.T. John—Criticism, interpretation, etc. I. Root, Orrin, joint author. II. Title.

VANDERLIP, George. 226'.5'066
Christianity according to John / by D. George Vanderlip. Philadelphia : Westminister Press, [1975] 224 p. ; 22 cm. Bibliography: p. 203-215. [BS2615.2.V36] 74-34585 ISBN 0-664-20737-5 : 8.50
1. Bible. N.T. John—Theology. I. Title.

MUSSNER, Franz 226'.5'067
The historical Jesus in the Gospel of St. John. [Tr. by W. J. O'Hara. New York] Herder & Herder [1967] 115p. 22cm. (Quaestiones disputatae) Tr. of Die Johanneische Schweise und die Frage nach dem historischen Jesus. Bibl. [BS2601.M7913] 66-2881 2.50 pap.,
1. Bible. N. T. Johannine literature—Historiography. 2. Jesus Christ—Biog.—Sources.s8 I. Title.

BIBLE. N. T. John. 226.507
English. 1956. Revised.
St. John's Gospel, a commentary by R. H. Lightfoot. Edited by C. F. Evans. With the text of the Revised version. New York, Oxford University Press [1960] xii, 368p. Bibl.: p.[357]-365. 23cm. (Oxford Paperback No. 5) 2.25 pap.,
1. Bible. N. T. John—Commentaries. I. Lightfoot, Robert Henry, 1883-1953. II. Title.

BIBLE. N. T. John. 226.507
English. 1965. New English.
The Gospel according to John. Commentary by A. M. Hunter [New York] Cambridge [c.] 1965. ix, 204p. map. plan. 21cm. (Cambridge Bible commentary: New English Bible) [BS2615.3.H8] 65-3521 3.50; 1.65 pap.,
1. Bible. N. T. John—Commentaries. I. Hunter, Archibald Macbride. II. Title. III. Series.

BOUYER, Louis, 1913- 226.507
The Fourth Gospel. Tr. [from French] by Patrick Byrne. Westminster. Md., Newman. 1964[c.1955, 1964] 233p. 22cm. 63-12249 4.50
1. Bible. N. T. John—Commentaries. I. Title.

BROWN, Jeff D. 226.507
Sermon outlines on the Gospel of John [2.] 1-7; 8-21. Grand Rapids, Michigan, Baker Book House [c.1960] 85p.; 89p. 22cm. 1.00 pap., ea., *I. Title.*

BULTMANN, Rudolf Karl, 226'.5'07
1884-
The Gospel of John; a commentary, by Rudolf Bultmann. Translated by G. R. Beasley-Murray, general editor, R. W. N. Hoare, and J. K. Riches. Philadelphia, Westminster Press [1971] xii, 744 p. 24 cm. "Translated from the 1964 printing of Das Evangelium des Johannes (with the Supplement of 1966)" Bibliography: p. 725-731. [BS2615.3.B7813 1971b] 70-125197 ISBN 0-664-20893-2 15.00
1. Bible N.T. John—Commentaries. I. Title.

BUSSCHE, Henri van 226'.5'07
den., 1920-
The Gospel of the Word [by] H. van den Bussche. Chicago, Priory Pr. [1967] 211p. 21cm. Orig. text apeared first in Dutch in the weekly. De Bazuin. This tr. is made from the authorized French version. . .L'Evangile du Verbe . . . Chapters 1-5 tr. by Sister M. Marta. Chapters 6-15 tr. by John C. Guinness. [BS2615.3.B813] 67-14013 4.95
1. Bible. N. T. John—Commentaries. I. Title.

CARLSON, G. Raymond. 226'.5'07
The life worth living / G. Raymond Carlson ; adapted from Gospel of John by Stanley M. Horton. Springfield, Mo. : Gospel Pub. House, c1975. 127 p. ; 18 cm. (Radiant books) [BS2615.C354] 75-22607 ISBN 0-88243-876-X pbk. : 1.25
1. Bible. N.T. John—Criticism, interpretation, etc. 2. Christian life—Biblical teaching. I. Horton, Stanley M. Gospel of John. II. Title.

CHRYSOSTOMUS, Joannes, 226.507
Saint, Patriarch of Constantinople, d.407.
Commentary on Saint John the apostle and evangelist; homilies [1-88] Translated by Sister Thomas Aquinas Goggin. New York, Fathers of the Church, inc., 1957-60 [c1957-59] 2 v. 22 cm. (The Fathers of the church, a new translation, v. 33 and 41) Translation of Homiliae in Ioannem. Bibliography: v. 1, p. xx. [BR60.F3C4] 57-1545
1. Bible. N.T. John—Sermons. 2. Sermons, Greek—Translations into English. 3. Sermons, English—Translations from Greek. I. Goggin, Thomas Aquinas, Sister, 1911- tr. II. Title. III. Series.

CHRYSOSTOMUS, Joannes, 226.507
Saint, Patriarch of Constantinople, d. 407.
Commentary on Saint John the apostle and evangelist; homilies [1-88] Translated by Sister Thomas Aquinas Goggin. New York, Fathers of the Church, inc., 1957-60 [c1957-59] 2v. 22cm. (The Fathers of the church, a new translation, v. 33 and 41) Translation of Homillae in Ioannem. Bibliography: v. 1, p. xx. [BR60.F3C4] 57-1545
1. Bible. N. T. John—Sermons. 2. Sermons, Greek—Translations into English. 3. Sermons, English—Translations from Greek. I. Goggin, Thomas Aquinas, Sister 1911- tr. II. Title. III. Series.

DIETRICH, Suzanne de. 226'.5'07
And he is lifted up; meditations on the Gospel of John, by Suzanne de Dietrich. Translated by Dennis Pardee. Philadelphia, Westminster Press [1969] 171 p. 21 cm. Translation of L'heure de l'elevation. "Explanatory and bibliographical notes": p. 163-164. [BS2615.4.D513] 69-18649 2.65
1. Bible. N.T. John—Devotional literature. I. Title.

GAEBELEIN, Arno Clemens, 226.507
1861-1945.
The Gospel of John; a complete analytical exposition. [2d ed., rev.] Neptune, N.J., Loizeaux Bros. [1965] 414 p. 21 cm. [BS2615.G25 1965] 65-26586
1. Bible. N. T. John — Commentaries. I. Title.

GAEBELEIN, Arno Clemens, 226.507
1861-1945
The Gospel of John; a complete analytical exposition [2d ed., rev.] Neptune, N. J., Loizeaux [c.1965] 414p. 21cm. [BS2615.G25] 65-26586 4.50
1. Bible. N.T. John—Commentaries. I. Title.

HAMILTON, William, 1924- 226.507
The modern reader's guide to John. New York, Association Press [1959] 124p. 16cm. (An Association Press reflection book) [BS2616.H35] 59-8074
1. Bible, N. T. John—Study—Outline, syllabi, etc. I. Title.

HOBBS, Herschel H. 226'.5'07
An exposition of the Gospel of John, by Herschel H. Hobbs. Grand Rapids, Baker Book House [1968] 297 p. 23 cm. Includes bibliographical references. [BS2615.3.H6] 68-23454 6.95
1. Bible. N.T. John—Commentaries. I. Title.

HOBBS, Herschel H 226.507
The Gospel of John; a study guide, by Herschel H. Hobbs Grand Rapids, Zondervan Pub. House [1965] 96 p. 21 cm. [BS2615.5.H6] 66-418
1. Bible. N.T. John — Study. I. Title.

*HOBBS, Herschel H. 226.507
The Gospel of John; a study guide. Grand Rapids, Mich., Zondervan [c.1965] 96p. 22cm. 1.95 bds.,
I. Title.

*HOBBS, Herschel H. 226.507
The Gospel of St. John; a study guide. Grand Rapids, Mich., Zondervan [c.1965] 96p. 21cm. 1.00 pap.,
I. Title.

HUTCHESON, George, 226.507
minister at Edinburgh.
An exposition of the Gospel according to John. Grand Rapids, Kregel Publications, 1959. 439p. 23cm. First published in London in 1657 under title: An exposition of the Gospel of jesus Christ according to John. [BS2615.H8 1959] 60-1056
1. Bible. N. T. John—Commentaries. I. Title.

LAURIN, Roy Leonard, 226'.5'07
1898-1966.
John, life eternal; a devotional commentary. Chicago, Moody Press [1972] 287 p. 22 cm. [BS2615.3.L37 1972] 74-175497 ISBN 0-8024-4350-8 4.95
1. Bible. N.T. John—Commentaries. I. Title.

LUTHI, Walter 226.507
St. John's Gospel an exposition. Translated [from the German] by Kurt Schoenenberger. Richmond, John Knox Press, 1960[ ] vii, 348p. 23cm. 60-9273 5.00 bds.,
1. Bible. N. T. John—Commentaries. I. Title.

LUTHI, Walter, 1901- 226.507
St. John's Gospel, an exposition. Translated by Kurt Schoenenberger. Richmond, John Knox Press, 1960. 348p. 23cm. Translation of Johannes, das vierte Evangelium. [BS2615.L763 1960] 60-9273
1. Bible. N. T. John—Commentaries. I. Title.

MCLAREN, Alexander, 1826- 226.507
1910.
The Gospel of St. John. Grand Rapids, Zondervan Pub. House, 1960. 231p. 18cm. (His Bible class expositions) 'These chapters were written as a commentary on the International Sunday school lessons for the American Sunday school times, from which they are reprinted.' [BS2615.M26] 60-51235
1. Bible.. N. T. John—Commentaries. I. Title.

MARSH, John, 1904- 226'.5'07
The Gospel of St. John. Harmondsworth, Penguin, 1968. 704 p. map 18 cm. (The Pelican Gospel commentaries) Bibliography: p. [83] [BS2615.3.M37] 68-141039 10/6
1. Bible. N.T. John—Commentaries. I. Title.

PINK, Arthur 226'.5'07
Walkington, 1886-1952.
Exposition of the Gospel of John / Arthur W. Pink. Grand Rapids : Zondervan Pub. House, 1975. 411, 409, 340 p. ; 23 cm. [BS2616.P5 1975] 76-360819
1. Bible. N.T. John—Study—Text-books. I. Title.

POWELL, Ivor. 226.507
John's wonderful Gospel. Grand Rapids, Zondervan Pub. House [1962] 443p. 23cm. [BS2615.3.P6] 62-51604
1. Bible. N. T. John—Commentaries. I. Title.

RICHARDSON, Alan 226.507
The Gospel according to Saint John: introduction and commentary. London, SCM Press. [New York, Macmillan, 1960] 220p. Bibl.: p.33-34. 19cm. (Torch Bible commentaries) 59-358 3.00
1. Bible. N.T. John—Commentaries. I. Title.

RICHARDSON, Alan, 1905- 226.507
The Gospel according to Saint John, a commentary. New York, Collier [1962, c.1959] 224p. (Torch Bible comentary, AS239Y) Bibl. .95 pap.,
1. Bible. N.T. John—Commentaries. I. Title.

SANDERS, John Oswald. 226'.5'07
105 days with John / J. Oswald Sanders. Chicago : Moody Press, c1976. 222 p. ; 22 cm. [BS2615.3.S185] 76-12540 ISBN 0-8024-6066-6 : 5.95
1. Bible. N.T. John—Commentaries. I. Title.

SAUNDERS, Ernest W. 226'.5'07
Coming to life; a study of the Gospel of John [by] Ernest W. Saunders. [New York, Joint Commn. on Educ. and Cultivation, Board of Missions, United Methodist Church, 1968] x, 190p. 19cm. Bibl [BS2615.3.S2] 68-23404 1.25; .50 guidebk.,
1. Bible. N. T. John—Commentaries. I. Title.
Publisher's address: 475 Riverside Drive, New York, N.Y. 10027.

STEWART, Irma. 226.507
Annotations from John. New York, Priv. print., I. H. Still, publisher's agent [1960] 63 p. 20 cm. Includes bibliography. [BS2615.3.S8] 60-13134
1. Bible. N. T. John XIII, 31-XVII — Commentaries. 2. Christian Science. I. Title.

TASKER, Randolph Vincent 226.507
Greenwood, 1895-
The Gospel according to St. John, an introduction and commentary. [1st ed.] Grand Rapids, Eerdmans [1960] 237 p. 21 cm. (The Tyndale New Testament commentaries) Includes bibliography. [BX2615.3.T3] 60-10268
1. Bible. N. T. John — Commentaries. I. Title.

TASKER, Randolph Vincent 226.507
Greenwood, 1895-
The Gospel according to St. John, an introduction and commentary [1st ed.] Grand Rapids, Eerdmans [1960] 237 p. 21 cm. (The Tyndale New Testament commentaries) Includes bibliography. [BS2615.3.T3] 60-10268
1. Bible. N.T. John—Commentaries.

TURNER, George Allen 226.507
The Gospel according to John [by] George Allen Turner, Julius R. Mantey. Grand Rapids, Mich., Eerdmans [1964] xi, 420p. maps. 25cm. (Evangelical commentary on the Bible, v.4) Bibl. 64-16592 8.95
I. Mantey, Julius R., joint author. II. Bible. N. T. John. English. 1964 American standard III. Title. IV. Series.

YATES, Kyle Monroe, 1895- 226.507
Preaching from John's Gospel. Nashville, Broadman [1964] x, 181p. 21cm. 64-19977 3.25

1. Bible. N. T. John—Homiletical use. I. Title.

ZODIATES, Spyros. 226.507
Was Christ God? An exposition of John I: 1-18 from the original Greek text, by Spiros Zodhiates. Grand Rapids, W. B. Eerdman [c1966] ix, 350 p. 21 cm. Originally broadcast on New Testament Light radio program and published in twelve booklets. [BS2615.3.Z6] 66-31308
1. Bible. N.T. John I. 1-18 — Commentaries. I. New Testament light (Radio program) II. Title.

BARCLAY, William, 226'.5'077
lecturer in the University of Glasgow.
Introduction to John and the Acts of the apostles / by William Barclay. Philadelphia : Westminster Press, c1976. p. cm. Published in Great Britain as vol. 2 of The Gospels and Acts, entitled: The fourth Gospel and Acts of the apostles. Includes indexes. Bibliography: p. [BS2615.2.B33] 75-38902 ISBN 0-664-24771-7 : 5.95
1. Bible. N.T. John—Introductions. 2. Bible. N.T. Acts—Introductions. I. Title.

BEHLER, G. M. 226.5077
The last discourse of Jesus. Foreword by F. M. Braun. [Tr. from French by Robert T. Francoeur] Helicon [dist., New York, Taplinger, 1966] 286p. 21cm. Bibl. [BT420.B3613] 65-24121 5.95 bds.,
1. Bible. N.T. John XIII-XVII—Commentaries. I. Bible. N.T. John XIII-XVII. English, 1965. II. Title.

BEHLER, Gebhard Maria. 226.5077
The last discourse of Jesus [by] G. M. Behler. With a foreword by F. M. Braun. [Translated from the French by Robert T. Francoeur] Baltimore, Helicon [1965] 286 p. 21 cm. Translation of Les paroles d'adieux du Seigneur. A verse by verse commentary on chapters 13-17 of the Gospel according to St. John. Bibliography: p. 15-16. [BT420.B3613] 65-24121
1. Bible. N.T. John XIII-XVII—Commentaries. 2. Bible. N.T. John XIII-XVII. English. 1965. I. Title.

BIBLE. N.T. John. 226.5077
English. 1966. Brown.
The Gospel according to John. Introd., translation, and notes by Raymond E. Brown. [1st ed.] Garden City, N.Y., Doubleday, 1966- - v. 25 cm. (The Anchor Bible, no. 29 Contents.CONTENTS.--[1] Chapters 1-12. Includes bibliographies. [BS192.2.A1 1964.G3] 66-12209
1. Bible. N.T. John—Commentaries. I. Brown, Raymond Edward, ed. and tr. II. Title. III. Series.

BIBLE. N.T. John. 226'.5'077
English. 1966. Brown
The Gospel according to John. Introd., translation, and notes by Raymond E. Brown. [1st ed.] Garden City, N.Y., Doubleday, 1966-70. 2 v. (cxlvi, 1208 p.) 25 cm. (The Anchor Bible, no. 29-29A) Contents.Contents.—[1] Chapters 1-12.—[2] Chapters 13-21. Includes bibliographies. [BS192.2.A1 1964.G3, no. 29-29A] 66-12209
1. Bible. N.T. John—Commentaries. I. Brown, Raymond Edward, ed. II. Title. III. Series.

BIBLE. N.T. John. 226'.5'077
English. Authorized. 1976.
The Gospel of John / introd. and notes by W. Graham Scroggie. Grand Rapids : Zondervan Pub. House, 1976. 131 p. ; 17 cm. (Study hour commentaries) Reprint of the ed. published by Marshall, Morgan & Scott, London, under title: St. John; issued in the Study hour series. [BS2613 1976] 75-42049 9.95
1. Bible. N.T. John—Commentaries. I. Scroggie, William Graham, 1877-1958. II. Title. III. Series: The Study hour series.

BIBLE. N.T. John. 226'.5'077
English. Barclay. 1975.
The Gospel of John / translated with an introd. and interpretation by William Barclay. Philadelphia : Westminster Press, [1975] p. cm. (The Daily study Bible series. — Rev. ed.) [BS2613 1975] 74-30031 ISBN 0-664-21304-9(v.1) : 6.25 ISBN 0-664-24104-2 (v. 1) pbk. : 3.45
1. Bible. N.T. John—Commentaries. I. Barclay, William, lecturer in the University of Glasgow, ed. II. Title. III. Series.

BOICE, James 226'.5'077
Montgomery, 1938-
The Gospel of John : an expositional commentary / James Montgomery Boice. Grand Rapids : Zondervan Pub. House, [1975- v. ; 23 cm. Contents.Contents.—v. 1. John 1:1-4:54. Includes bibliographical references and indexes. [BS2615.3.B55] 74-25327 9.95 (v. 1)
1. Bible. N.T. John—Commentaries. I. Title.

BONAR, Horatius, 1808- 226'.5'077
1889.
Studies in the Gospel of John. Grand Rapids, Zondervan Pub. House [1972] 110 p. 21 cm. (A Zondervan book) "Originally published as part of a larger series: Light and truth; or, Bible thoughts and themes ... in 1869, and has now been carefully revised and up-dated for a new generation of Bible students." [BS2615.B627 1972] 70-171202 1.95
1. Bible. N.T. John—Criticism, interpretation, etc. I. Title.

BULTMANN, Rudolf Karl, 226'.5'077
1884-
The Johannine epistles; a commentary on the Johannine epistles, by Rudolf Bultmann. Translated by R. Philip O'Hara with Lane C. McGaughy and Robert Funk. Edited by Robert W. Funk. Philadelphia, Fortress Press [1973] xiv, 143 p. illus. 25 cm. (Hermeneia) Translation of Die drei Johannesbriefe. Bibliography: p. 118-132. [BS2805.3.B8413] 75-171510 ISBN 0-8006-6003-X
1. Bible. N.T. Epistles of John—Commentaries. I. Bible. N.T. Epistles of John. 1973. II. Title. III. Series.

ERDMAN, Charles 226'.5'077
Rosenbury, 1866-1960.
The Gospel of John; an exposition. Pref. by Earl F. Zeigler. Philadelphia, Westminster Press [1966] 189 p. 19 cm. (His Commentaries on the New Testament books) [BS2615.E7 1966] 67-2150
1. Bible. N. T John — Commentaries. I. Title.

FENTON, John C., 1921- 226'.5'077
The Gospel according to John in the Revised standard version; with introduction and commentary by J. C. Fenton. Oxford, Clarendon P., 1970. [10] 221 p. illus., maps, facsims. 19 cm. (New Clarendon Bible: New Testament) Bibliography: p. [10] (1st group) [BS2615.3.F4 1970] 70-538626 ISBN 0-19-836908-5 30/-
1. Bible. N.T. John—Commentaries. I. Bible. N.T. John. English. Revised standard. 1970. II. Title. III. Series.

HOSIER, Helen Kooiman. 226'.5'077
The caring Jesus : a woman's view of the Gospel of John / Helen Kooiman Hosier. New York : Hawthorn Books, c1975. xv, 207 p. ; 21 cm. Includes bibliographical references. [BT198.H67 1975] 74-33587 ISBN 0-8015-1084-8 : 3.95
1. Jesus Christ—History of doctrines—Early church, ca. 30-600. 2. Bible. N.T. John—Criticism, interpretation, etc. I. Title.

LIPSCOMB, David, 1831- 226'.5'077
1918.
A commentary on the Gospel according to John / by David Lipscomb ; edited, with additional notes by C. E. W. Dorris. Nashville : Gospel Advocate Co., 1971, c1939. 338 p. ; 23 cm. Includes index. [BS2615.L49 1971] 76-366532 5.95
1. Bible. N.T. John—Commentaries. I. Dorris, Charles Elias Webb, 1871- II. Title.

MARSH, John, 1904- 226'.5'077
The Gospel of St John. Baltimore, Penguin Books [1968] 700 p. map. 19 cm. (The Pelican Gospel commentaries) (Pelican books.) "A491." "The Bible text in this publication is from the revised standard version." Includes bibliographical references. [BS2615.3.M37 1968b] 77-328 2.65
1. Bible. N.T. John—Commentaries. I. Bible. N.T. John. English. Revised standard. 1968. II. Title.

MORRIS, Leon, 1914- 226'.5'077
The Gospel according to John; the English text with introduction and notes. Grand Rapids, Eerdmans [1971] xi, 936 p. 23 cm. (The New international commentary on the New Testament) Includes bibliographical references. [BS2615.3.M67] 70-120845 12.50
1. Bible. N.T. John—Commentaries. I. Bible. N.T. John. English. American revised. 1971. II. Title.

SANDERS, Joseph 226'.5'077
Newbould.
A commentary on the Gospel according to St. John [by] J. N. Sanders. Edited and completed by B. A. Mastin. [1st United States ed.] New York, Harper & Row [1968] x, 480 p. 22 cm. (Harper's New Testament commentaries) Bibliographical footnotes. [BS2615.3.S19 1968b] 69-10469 10.00
1. Bible. N.T. John—Commentaries. I. Mastin, B. A., ed. II. Title.

RINGENBERG, Loyal R. 226'.5'095
Who is Jesus? : a study of John's Gospel revealing the most amazing person of history / Loyal R. Ringenberg. Broadview, Ill. : Gibbs Pub. Co., 1974. 128 p. ; 23 cm. Edition of 1971 published under title: The Christ of Christianity. Bibliography: p. 127-128. [BS2616.R56 1974] 73-86017 4.95

1. Bible. N.T. John—Study—Textbooks. I. Title.

NIXON, Joan Lowery. 226'.5'09505
Five loaves and two fishes : feeding of five thousand for beginning readers : John 6:1-15 for children / by Joan Lowery Nixon ; illustrated by Aline Cunningham. St. Louis : Concordia Pub. House, c1976. [48] p. : col. ill. ; 23 cm. (I can read a bible story) An easy-to-read account of the Bible story in which Jesus fed the crowds of people on the shores of the Sea of Galilee with five loaves of bread and two fishes. [BT367.F4N59] 76-15288 ISBN 0-570-07311-1 : 3.95 ISBN 0-570-07305-7 pbk. :
1. Feeding of the five thousand (Miracle)—Juvenile literature. I. Cunningham, Aline. II. Title.

*ADAMS, Jay E. 226.'6
Audience adaptations in the sermons and speeches of Paul / Jay E. Adams Grand Rapids : Baker Book House, c1976. [vii], 107 p. ; 22 cm. (Studies in preaching ; 2). Bibliography: pp. [72] - 77, [103] - 107. [BS2655.A6] ISBN 0-8010-0104-8 pbk. : 2.95
1. Paul, Saint, Apostle—Sermons. 2. Bible—Homiletical use. I. Title.

ALEXANDER, Joseph Addison, 226.6
1809-1860.
Commentary on the Acts of the Apostles. Grand Rapids, Zondervan Pub. House [1956] 2v. in 1 (xxiii, 960p.) 23cm. (Classic commentary library) 'Reprinted complete and unabridged from the third edition published by Scribner, Armstrong & Company in 1875.' [BS2625.A58] 58-1066
1. Bible. N. T. Acts—Commentaries. I. Title.

BIBLE. N. T. Acts. English. 226.6
1957.
The Acts of the Apostles: text and commentary. Translated by Laurence E. Byrne. Milwaukee, Bruce Pub. Co. [1958] xii, 420p. maps. 25cm. At head of title: Giuseppe Ricciotti. 'The scripture text used is mainly the Confraternity version with an occasional direct translation of Ricciottl's translation from the Greek.'--Dust Jacket. [BS2625.R48] 57-12920
1. Bible. N. T. Acts—Commentaries. I. Ricciotti, Giuseppe, 1890- ed. and tr. II. Byrne, Laurence E., tr. III. Title.

BIBLE. N. T. Acts. English. 226.6
1957. Barclay.
The Acts of the Apostles; translated with an introd. and interpretation by William Barclay. [2d ed.] Philadelphia, Westminster Press [1957] xix, 213p. 18cm. (The Daily study Bible series) [BS2625.B27 1957] 57-6030
1. Bible. N. T. Acts—Commentaries. I. Barclay, William, lecturer in the University of Glasgow., ed. and tr. II. Title. III. Series.

BIBLE. N. T. Acts. English. 226.6
1958. Douai.
The Acts of the Apostles. With an introd. and commentary by C. C. Martindale. Westminster, Md., Newman Press [1958] 199p. illus. 19cm. (Stonyhurst Scripture manuals) [BS2625.M36] 58-3966
1. Bible. N. T. Acts—Commentaries. I. Martindale, Cyril Charile, 1879- II. Title.

BIBLE. N. T. Acts. 226.6
English. Phillips. 1955
The young church in action; a translation of the Acts of the Apostles by J. B. Phillips. New York, Macmillan, 1955. xvi, 103 p. maps. 22 cm. [BS2623.P45] 55-13575
I. Phillips, John Bertram, 1906- tr. II. Title.

BIBLE N. T. PROPHETS. 226.6
GREEK. 1920
The Acts of the Apostles; v.4, ed. by F. J. Foakes Jackson, D.D., Kirsopp Lake. Grand Rapids, Mich., Baker Bk. [1966] 420p. map. 23cm. (Beginnings of Christianity, pt. 1) Contents.v. 4 English tr. & commentary, by Kirsopp Lake, H. J. Cadbury. [BS2625.F6] 7.95
1. Bible. N.T. Acts—Commentaries. I. Foakes-Jackson, Frederick John, ed. II. Lake, Kirsopp, joint ed. III. Title.

BLAIR, Edward Payson, 1910- 226.6
A study of the book of Acts. New York, Abingdon-Cokesbury Press [1951] 128 p. 19 cm. "Adapted from [the author's] The Acts and Apocalyptic literature." "Text of the book of Acts [Revised standard veraion]"; p. 72-128. [BS2626.B52] 51-4456
1. Bible. N. T. Acts—Study—Text-books. I. Bible. N. T. Acts. English. 1951. Revised standard. II. Title.

BRUCE, Frederick Fyvie, 226.6
1910-
The Acts of the Apostles; the Greek text with introd. and commentary. [1st American ed.] Chicago, Inter-varsity Christian Fellowship [1952] viii, 491p. 22cm. 'The Greek text on which the commentary is based is Westcott and Hort's.' Bibliography: p. 49-55. [BS2625.B7 1952] 54-25
1. Bible. N. T.—Commentaries. I. Bible. N. T. Acts. Greek. 1952. II. Title.

BRUCE, Frederick Fyvie, 226.6
1910-
Commentary on the book of the Acts; the English text, with introduction, exposition, and notes. Grand Rapids, Eerdmans, 1954. 555p. 22cm. (The New international commentary on the New Testament) [BS2625.B72] 54-12695
1. Bible. N. T. Acts—Commentaries. I. Bible. N. T. Acts. English. 1954. American standard. II. Title.

CADBURY, Henry Joel, 1883- 226.6
The book of Acts in history. New York, Harper [1955] 170p. 22cm. [BS2625.C27 1955a] 55-9829
1. Bible. N. T. Acts—History of contemporary events, etc. 2. Bible. N. T. Acts—Criticism, interpretation, etc. I. Title.

CHAPPELL, Clovis Gillham, 226.6
1882-
When the church was young. New York, Abingdon-Cokesbury Press [1950] 184 p. 20 cm. [BS2625.C48] 49-50301
1. Bible. N. T. Acts—Sermons. 2. Methodist Church—Sermons. 3. Sermons, American. I. Title.

CHARLIER, Jean Pierre. 226'.6
The gospel of the church's infancy, by J. P. Charlier. Translated by John L. Sullivan. De Pere, Wis., St. Norbert Abbey Press, 1969. viii, 133 p. 19 cm. Translation of L'Evangile de l'enfance de l'Eglise. Bibliography: p. [130]-133. [BS2625.3.C513] 73-87813 2.95
1. Bible. N.T. Acts I-II—Commentaries. I. Title.

DIBELIUS, Martin, 1883- 226.6
1947.
Studies in the Acts of the Apostles. Edited by Heinrich Greeven. [Translated by Mary Ling from the German] New York, Scribner's [1956] 228p. 24cm. [BS2625] 56-13941
1. Bible. N. T. Acts—Criticism, interpretation, etc. I. Title.

EASTON, Burton Scott, 1877- 226.6
Early Christianity: The purpose of Acts, and other papers. Edited by Frederick C. Grant. Greenwich, Conn., Seabury Press, 1954. 158p. illus. 21cm. [BS2625.E27] 54-9212
1. Bible. N. T. Acts—Criticism, interpretation, etc. 2. Christianlty— Early church. I. Title. II. Title: The purpose of Acts.

FORD, William Herschel, 226.6
1900-
Simple sermons from the book of Acts; introd. by Robert G. Lee. (Grand Rapids, Zondervan [1950] 2 v. 20 cm. [BS2625.F67] 50-4483
1. Bible. N. T. Acts—Sermons. 2. Baptists—Sermons. 3. Sermons, American. I. Title.

HUNT, Marigold. 226.6
The first Catholics; the Acts of the Apostles for children. New York, Sheed and Ward, 1953. 146p. illus. 21cm. [BS2628.H85] 53-12268
1. Bible stories, English—N. T. Acts. I. Title.

IRONSIDE, Henry Allan, 226.6
1876-1951.
Lectures on the Book of Acts. New York, Loizeaux Bros. [1951] 651p. 19cm. [BS2625.I7] 55-21221
1. Bible. N. T. Acts—Commentaries. I. Title.

*LASH, Nicholas. 226.6
Acts of the Apostles. Milwaukee, Bruce [1968] 53p. 18cm. [Scripture discussion outlines) .75 pap.,
1. Bible. N.T. Acts—Commentaries. I. Title.

*MARTIN, Robert J. 226.6
All about witnessing; a study of the Book of Acts; by Robert J. Martin. Grand Rapids, Baker Book House [1975] 89 p. 18 cm. [BS2626] ISBN 0-8010-5970-4 1.65 (pbk.)
1. Bible—Commentaries—New Testament—Acts. 2. Bible—Criticism, interpretation, etc.—New Testament, Acts. I. Title.

MORGAN, George Campbell, 226'.6
1863-1945.
The birth of the church. Edited by Jill Morgan. Old Tappan, N.J., F. H. Revell Co. [1968] 189 p. 21 cm. [BS2625.3.M6 1968] 68-28437 4.95
1. Bible. N.T. Acts II—Commentaries. I. Title.

MOULE, Charles Francis 226.6
Digby.
Christ's messengers; studies in the Acts of the apostles. New York, Association Press [1957] 94p. 20cm. (World Christian books) [BS2625.M64] 57-11611
1. Bible. N. T. Acts—Criticism, interpretation, etc. I. Title.

MOULE, Charles Francis Digby. 226.6
Christ's messengers; studies in the Acts of the apostles. New York, Association Press [1957] 94p. 20cm. (World Christian books) [BS2625.M64] 57-11611
1. Bible. N. T. Acts—Criticism, interpretation, etc. I. Title.

PROTESTANT Episcopal Church in the U. S. A. National Council. Dept. of Christian Education. 226.6
Traveling the way. Illustrated by Alexander McDonnell. Greenwich, Conn., Seabury Press [1956] 210p. illus. 22cm. (The Seabury series, R-5) [BS2619.P7] 56-7850
1. Bible. N. T. Acts—Study—Text-books. 2. Church history— Primitive and early church—Fiction. I. McGowen, Drusilla. Cleon makes his choice. II. Title.
Contents omitted.

STAGG, Frank, 1911- 226.6
The book of Acts; the early struggle for an unhindered gospel. Nashville, Broadman Press [1955] 281p. 22cm. [BS2625.S67] 55-14948
1. Bible. N. T. Acts—Commentaries. I. Title.

STAM, Cornelius Richard, 1908- 226.6
Acts, dispensationally considered. Chicago, Berean Bible Society [1954- v. 20cm. [BS2625.S68] 55-15391
1. Bible. N. T. Acts—Commentaries. 2. Covenants (Theology) I. Title.

STEDMAN, Ray C. 226'.6
Birth of the body : [Acts 1-12] / Ray C. Stedman ; [foreword by Hal Lindsey]. Santa Ana, Calif. : Vision House, c1974. 200 p. ; 21 cm. [BS2625.4.S73] 74-82549 ISBN 0-88449-019-X. ISBN 0-88449-013-0 pbk. : 2.95
1. Bible. N.T. Acts I-XII—Sermons. 2. Sermons, American. I. Title.

THOMAS, David, 1813-1894. 226.6
Acts of the Apostles; a homiletic commentary. Grand Rapids, Baker Book House, 1955. 493p. 23cm. [Co-operative reprint library, 18] 'A reprint of the 1870 printing by Richard D. Dickinson, London.' [BS2625.T43] 55-8795
1. Bible. N. T. Acts— Commentaries. I. Title.

THOMAS, William Henry Griffith, 1861-1924. 226.6
Outline studies in the Acts of the Apostles, by W. H. Griffith Thomas, edited by his daughter. Grand Rapids, Eerdmans, 1956. 555p. 23cm. [BS2625.T53] 54-6237
1. Bible. N. T. Acts—Sermons—Outlines. I. Title.

THOMAS, William Henry Griffith, 1861-1924. 226.6
Outline studies in the Acts of the Apostles, by W. H. Griffith Thomas, edited by his daughter. Grand Rapids, Eerdmans, 1956. 555 p. 23 cm. [BS2625.T53] 54-6237
1. Bible. N.T. Acts — Sermons — Outlines. I. Title.

WAND, John William Charles, Bp. of London, 1885- 226.6
A history of the early church to A.D. 500 by J. W. C. Wand. [4th ed. London] Methuen [1963] ix, 300 p. 20 cm. Bibliography: p. 264-268. [BR165.W35 1963] 65-84476
1. Church history — Primitive and early church. I. Title.

WILLIAMS, Charles Stephen Conway. 226.6
A commentary on the Acts of the Apostles. New York, Harper [1958, c1957] 301 p. 22 cm. (Harper's New Testament commentaries) Includes bibliography. [BS2625.W53 1958] 58-5197
1. Bible. N. T. Acts — Commentaries. I. Bible. N. T. Acts. English. 1957. Williams. II. Title.

ZEHNLE, Richard F. 226'.6
Peter's Pentecost discourse; tradition and Lukan reinterpretation in Peter's speeches of Acts 2 and 3 [by] Richard F. Zehnle. Nashville, Published for the Society of Biblical Literature by Abingdon Press [1971] 144 p. 24 cm. (Society of Biblical Literature. Monograph series, 15) Includes bibliographical references. [BS2625.2.Z4] 72-148063 ISBN 0-687-20629-4 3.25
1. Bible. N.T. Acts II-III—Criticism, interpretation, etc. I. Title. II. Series.

DEMARAY, Donald E. 226.6007
The book of Acts, a study manual. Grand Rapids, Baker Book House [c.]1959. 66p. 20cm. (The Shield Bible study series) 60-1142 1.25 pap.,
1. Bible. N. T. Acts—Study—Text-books. I. Title.

JENSEN, Irving Lester. 226'.6'007
Acts: an inductive study; a manual of Bible-study-in-depth, by Irving L. Jensen. Chicago, Moody Press [1968] 253 p. illus., maps. 22 cm. "Companion [to the author's] Independent Bible study." Bibliography: p. 248-253. [BS2616.J45] 67-14390 4.95
1. Bible. N.T. Acts—Study—Outlines, syllabi, etc. I. Title.

KECK, Leander E. 226.6007
Mandate to witness; studies in the book of Acts. Valley Forge, Pa., Judson [c.1964] 173p. 21cm. Bibl. 64-15796 3.75
1. Bible. N. T. Acts—Study. I. Title. II. Title: Studies in the book of Acts.

POTTOFF, Harvey H 226.6007
Acts, then and now, by Harvey H. Potthoff. New York, Joint Commission on Education and Cultivation, Board of Missions of the Methodist Church, 1965] xvi, 128 p. illus. maps. 19 cm. Includes bibliographical references. [BS2625.5.P65] 65-15721
1. Bible. N. T. Acts—Study. I. Title.

JACOBS, J. Vernon 226.60076
Workbook on the Book of Acts. Cincinnati, Standard Pub. Co., c.1960. 64p. maps 27cm. .75 pap.,
I. Title.

DUPONT, Jacques, 1915- 226.604
The sources of the Acts. [English translation by Kethleen Pond. New York] Herder and Herder [1964] 180 p. 23 cm. Translation of Les source du livre des Actes. Bibliographical footnotes. [BS2625.2.D813] 63-18149
1. Bible. N.T. Acts — Criticism, interpretation, etc. I. Title.

DUPONT, Jacques, 1915- 226.604
The sources of the Acts. Tr. [from French] by Kathleen Pond. New York, Herder & Herder [c.1964] 180p. 23cm. Bibl. 63-18149 4.75 bds.,
1. Bible. N. T. Acts—Criticism, interpretation. etc. I. Title.

WILCOX, Max 226.604
The Semitisms of Acts. Oxford, Clarendon Pr. [dist. New York, Oxford, c.1965] xiii, 206p. illus. 23cm. Bibl. [BS2625.2.W5] 65-2131 8.00 bds.,
1. Bible. N. T. Acts—Criticism, Textual. I. Title.

BIBLE. N. T. Acts. English. 1955. Phillips. 226.6052
The young church in action; a translation of the Acts of the Apostles by J. B. Phillips. New York, Macmillan, 1961[c.1955] xvi, 103p. maps. .95 pap.,
I. Phillips, John Bertram, 1906- II. Title.

BARNETT, Albert Edward, 1895- 226.606
The modern reader's guide to Acts. New York, Association Press [1962] 125p. 16cm. (An Association Press reflection book) Includes bibliography. [BS2626.B3] 62-9380
1. Bible. N. T. Acts—Study—Outlines, syllabi, etc. I. Title.

BARNETT, Albert Edward, 1895- 226.606
The modern reader's guide to Acts. New York, Association [c.1962] 125p. 16cm. (Association Pr. reflection bk.) Bibl. 62-9380 .50 pap.,
1. Bible. N.T. Acts—Study—Outlines, syllabi, etc. I. Title.

BROOKS, Keith L. 226.606
Acts--adventures of the early church. Chicago, Moody [c.1963] 96p. 22cm. (Teach yourself the Bible ser.) 1.00 pap.,
I. Title.

BROWN, Stanley C 226.606
Evangelism in the early church; a study in the book of the Acts of the apostles. Grand Rapids, Mich. [1963] 73 p. 22 cm. [BS2625.2.B7] 63-3826
1. Bible, N.T. Acts — Criticism, interpretation, etc. 2. Evangelistic work. I. Title.

BROWN, Stanley C. 226.606
Evangelism in the early church: a study in the book of the Acts of the apostles. Grand Rapids, Mich. Eerdmans [c.1963] 73p. 22cm. Bibl. 63-3826 2.00
1. Bible. N. T. Acts—Criticism, interpretation, etc. 2. Evangelistic work. I. Title.

CHRISTENSEN, Chuck. 226'.6'06
Acts, God working with us / Chuck & Winnie Christensen. Wheaton, Ill. : H. Shaw, c1974. 95 p. ; 21 cm. (A Fisherman Bible studyguide) [BS2625.5.C47] 74-83512 ISBN 0-87788-319-X
1. Bible. N.T. Acts—Study—Outlines, syllabi, etc. I. Christensen, Winnie, joint author. II. Title.

DE HAAN, Martin Ralph, 1891- 226.606
Pentecost and after, by M. R. De Haan. Grand Rapids, Zondervan Pub. House [1964] 184 p. 20 cm. [BS2625.2.D4] 64-15553
1. Bible N.T. Acts — Criticism, interpretation, etc. I. Title.

DEHAAN, Martin Ralph, 1891- 226.606
Pentecost and after. Grand Rapids, Mich., Zondervan [c.1964] 184p. 20cm. 64-15553 2.50 bds.,
1. Bible. N.T. Acts—Criticism, interpretation, etc. I. Title.

DESJARDINS, Lucile 226.606
The story of the early church; a study of the Book of Acts. Leader's guide, for use with ninth and tenth grade classes in teaching religion through the week. Nashville, Published for the Cooperative Publication Association by Abingdon Press [c.1959] 109p. 20cm. (The Cooperative series) Includes bibliography. illus. 60-186 1.00 pap.,
1. Bible. N.T. Acts—Study—Text-books. I. Title. II. Title: Early church.

JAMISON, Albert Leland, 1911- 226.606
Light for the Gentiles; Paul and the growing church. Philadelphia, Westminster Press [1961] 91p. 20cm. (Westminster guides to the Bible) [BS2625.2.J3] 62-7483
1. Bible. N. T. Acts—Criticism, interpretation, etc. 2. Paul, Saint, apostle. 3. Bible. N. T. Epistles of Paul—Criticism, interpretation, etc. I. Title.

JAMISON, Leland 226.606
Light for the Gentiles; Paul and the growing church. Philadelphia, Westminster Pr. [c.1961] 91p. (Westminster guides to the Bible) 62-7483 1.50
1. Paul, Saint, apostle. 2. Bible. N. T. Acts—Criticism, interpretation, etc. 3. Bible. N. T. Epistles of Paul—Criticism, interpretation, etc. I. Title.

KILGALLEN, John J. 226'.6'06
The Stephen speech : a literary and redactional study of Acts 7, 2-53 / [di] John Kilgallen. Rome : Biblical Institute Press, 1976. xiii, 187 p. ; 24 cm. (Analecta biblica ; 67) "Developed from a doctoral dissertation entitled A literary and redactional study of Acts 7, 2-53 (Pontifical Biblical Institute, Roma, 1974)" Includes indexes. Bibliography: p. [165]-170. [BS2625.2.K5] 77-364631
1. Stephen, Saint, Martyr. 2. Bible. N.T. Acts VII, 2-53—Criticism, interpretation, etc. I. Title. II. Series.

LADD, George Eldon, 1911- 226.606
The young church; Acts of the Apostles. London, Lutterworth Press; New York, Abingdon Press [1964] 96 p. 20 cm. (Bible guides, no. 15) [BS2625.2.L3] 64-1537
1. Bible. N.T. Acts — Criticism, interpretation, etc. I. Title.

LADD, George Eldon, 1911- 226.606
The young church; Acts of the Apostles. London, Lutterworth Pr.; Nashville, Abingdon [1964] 96p. 20cm. (Bible guides, no. 15) 64-1537 1.00 pap.,
1. Bible. N. T. Acts—Criticism, interpretation, etc. I. Title.

MOULE, Charles Francis Digby 226.606
A chosen vessel: studies in the Acts of the Apostles. pt. 2. New York, Association [1962] 79p. 19cm. (World Christian bks., no. 37, second ser.) 1.00 pap.,
1. Bible. N. T. Acts—Criticism, interpretation, etc. I. Title.

MOULE, Charles Francis Digby. 226.606
Studies in the Acts of the apostles. New York, Association Press [1957- v. 20 cm. (World Christian books, [19], 37 Contents.[pt. 1] Christ's messengers. -- pt. 2 A chosen vessel. [BS2625.M64] 57-11611
1. Bible. N.T. Acts — Criticism, interpretation, etc. I. Title. II. Title: Christ's messengers. III. Title: A chosen vessel.

PARKER, Robert P. 226.606
The church on the move: studies in the book of Acts. Nashville, Tenn., Tidings. 1908 Grand Ave. [1964] 71p. 19cm. Bibl. [BS2625.5.P3] 64-8055 .60
1. Bible. N.T. Acts—Study. I. Title.

SUGDEN, Howard F. 226'.6'06
Storming the gates of hell : action in acts / Howard F. Sugden. Denver : Accent Books, c1977. 128 p. ; 18 cm. [BS2625.2.S93] 75-50296 ISBN 0-916406-63-6 pbk. : 1.45
1. Bible. N.T. Acts—Criticism, interpretation, etc. I. Title.

VAN RYN, August, 1890- 226.606
Acts of the Apostles; the unfinished work of Christ. [1st ed.] New York, Loizeaux Bros. [1961] 253 p. 20 cm. [BS2625.4.V3] 61-14601
1. Bible. N.T. Acts — Meditations. I. Title.

VAN RYN, August, 1890- 226.606
Acts of the Apostles; the unfinished work of Christ. New York, Loizeaux [c.1961] 253p. 61-14601 3.50
1. Bible. N. T. Acts—Meditations. I. Title.

WHITESELL, Faris Daniel, 1895- 226.606
Sermon outlines from the book of Acts. [Westwood, N.J.] Revell [1961] 64 p. 21 cm. (Revell's sermon outline series) [BS2625.4.W5] 61-9245
1. Bible. N.T. Acts — Sermons — Outlines. I. Title.

WHITESELL, Faris Daniel, 1895- 226.606
Sermon outlines from the book of Acts. [Westwood, N. J.] Revell [c.1961] 64p. (Revell's sermon outline series) 61-9245 1.00 pap.,
1. Bible. N. T. Acts—Sermons—Outlines. I. Title.

GASQUE, W. Ward. 226'.6'0609
A history of the criticism of the Acts of the Apostles / by W. Ward Gasque. Grand Rapids : Eerdmans, [1975] p. cm. [BS2625.2.G37] 75-9654 ISBN 0-8028-3461-2 : 12.50
1. Bible. N.T. Acts—Criticism, interpretation, etc.—History. I. Title.

†BIBLE. N.T. Acts. English. 1976. 226'.6'066
The Acts of the Apostles / introd. and notes by W. Graham Scroggie. Grand Rapids, Mich. : Zondervan Pub. House, 1976. 186 p. ; 17 cm. (Study hour commentaries) Reprint of the 1931 ed. published by Marshall, Morgan & Scott, London, in series: The Study hour series. [BS2623.S38 1976] 75-38802 ISBN 0-310-22310-5 : 9.95
1. Bible. N.T. Acts—Commentaries. I. Scroggie, William Graham, 1877-1958. II. Title. III. Series: The Study hour series.

BIBLE. N.T. Acts. Greek. 1966. 226.6066
The Acts of the Apostles, edited by F. J. Foakes Jackson and Kirsopp Lake. Grand Rapids, Baker Book House [1966-] v. facsims., geneal, table, map. 23 cm. Contents.CONTENTS.-- v. 5. Additional notes to the commentary, edited by K. Lake and H. B. Cadbury. Bibliographical footnoes. [BS2625] 66-9683
1. Bible. N.T. Acts—Commentaries. I. Foakes-Jacson, Frederick John, 1855- ed. II. Lake, Kirsopp, 1872- ed. III. Cadbury, Henry Joel, 1883- ed. IV. Title. V. Title: (The Beginnings of Christianity, pt. 1) Limited editions library

BIBLE. N.T. Acts. Greek. 1966. 226.6066
The Acts of the Apostles, edited by F. J. Foakes Jackson and Kirsopp Lake. Grand Rapids, Baker Book House [1966- v. facsims., geneal. table, map. 23 cm. (The Beginnings of Christianity, pt. 1) Limited editions library. Contents.Contents.—v. 5. Additional notes to the commentary, edited by K. Lake and H. J. Cadbury. Bibliographical footnotes. [BS2625] 66-9683
1. Bible. N.T. Acts—Commentaries. I. Foakes-Jackson, Frederick John, 1855- ed. II. Lake, Kirsopp, 1872- ed. III. Cadbury, Henry Joel, 1883- ed. IV. Title.

EPP, Eldon Jay 226.6066
The theological tendency of Codex Bezae Cantabrigtensis in Acts. Cambridge, London, Cambridge Univ. Pr., 1966. xvi, 210p. 23cm. (Soc. for New Testament Studies. Monograph ser. 3) Bibl. [BS2625.2.E6] 66-17055 8.50
1. Bible. Manuscripts, Greek. N. T. Codex Bezae. 2. Bibl. N.T. Acts—Criticism, Textual. I. Title. II. Series: Studiorum Novi Testamenti Societas. Monograph series, 3
Available from the publisher's New York office.

LA SOR, William Sanford. 226'.6'066
Church alive. Glendale, Calif., G/L Regal Books [1972] 429 p. 18 cm. (Layman's Bible commentary: Acts) Bibliography: p. 406-411. [BS2625.3.L37 1972] 78-185799 ISBN 0-8307-0145-1 1.95
1. Bible. N.T. Acts—Commentaries. I. Title.

LA SOR, William Sanford. 226'.6'066
Church alive. Glendale, Calif., G/L Regal Books [1972] 429 p. 18 cm. (Layman's Bible commentary: Acts) Bibliography: p. 406-411. [BS2625.3.L37 1972] 78-185799 ISBN 0-8307-0145-1 1.95
1. Bible. N.T. Acts—Commentaries. I. Title.

MANN, Christopher Stephen. 226'.6'066
The message delivered [by] C. S. Mann. New York, Morehouse-Barlow Co. [1973] 121 p. illus. 19 cm. Includes bibliographical

references. [BS2625.2.M36] 73-84097 ISBN 0-8192-1143-5 1.95 (pbk.)
1. Bible. N.T. Acts—Criticism, interpretation, etc. I. Title.

BARKER, William Pierson. 226'.6'07
They stood boldly; men and women in the Book of Acts [by] William P. Barker. Westwood, N.J., F. H. Revell Co. [1967] 188 p. 21 cm. [BS2625.4.B3] 67-11063
1. Bible. N.T. Acts—Sermons. I. Title.

BIBLE. N.T. Acts. 226.607
English. 1966. Confraternity version.
Our Christian beginnings; the Acts of the Apostles; the couple's text, with a commentary, for high schools [by] Franciscus Willett. Illustrated by Dorothy Koch. Valatie, N.Y., Holy Cross Press [1966] viii, 139 p. illus. maps. 24 cm. (Holy Cross Bible series [2]) Bibliography: p. viii. [BS2625.3.W5] 66-8136
1. Bible. N.T. Acts—Commentaries. I. Willett, Franciscus, ed. II. Title.

BIBLE, N.T. Acts. 226.607
English. 1966. Confraternity version.
Our Christian beginnings; the Acts of the Apostles; the complete text, with a commentary, for high schools [by] Franciscus Willett. Illus. by Dorothy Koch. Valatie, N.Y., Holy Cross Pr. [1966] viii, 139p. illus., maps. 24cm. (Holy Cross Bible ser. 2) Bibl. [BS2625.3.W5] 66-8136 3.50
1. Bible. N.T. Acts—Commentaries. I. Willett, Franciscus, ed. II. Title.

BIBLE. N.T. Acts. 226'.6'07
English. 1967. Revised standard.
The Acts in the Revised standard version. With introd. and commentary by R. P. C. Hanson. Oxford, Clarendon Press, 1967. [11], 262 p. illus., map (on lining paper), plan. 19 cm. (The New Clarendon Bible: New Testament) Bibliography: 11th prelim. page. [BS2625.3.H34] 67-3224
1. Bible. N.T. Acts—Commentaries. I. Hanson, Richard Patrick Crosland. II. Title. III. Series.

BIBLE. N.T. Acts. 226'.6'07
English. 1967. Munck.
The Acts of the Apostles. Introd., translation, and notes by Johannes Munck. Rev. by William F. Albright and C. S. Mann. [1st ed.] Garden City, N.Y., Doubleday, 1967. xc, 317 p. 24 cm. (The Anchor Bible, 31) Bibliography: p. [ixxxviii]-xc. [BS2625.3.B5] 66-20918
1. Bible. N.T. Acts—Commentaries. I. Munck, Johannes, 1904-1965. II. Title. III. Series.

BIBLE. N.T. Acts. 226'.6'07
English. 1967. Munck.
The Acts of the Apostles. Introd., translation, and notes by Johannes Munck. Rev. by William F. Albright and C. S. Mann. [1st ed.] Garden City, N.Y., Doubleday, 1967. xc, 317 p. 24 cm. (The Anchor Bible 31) Bibliography: p. [lxxxviii]-xc. [BS192.2.A1 1967.G3 vol. 31] 66-20918
1. Bible. N.T. Acts—Commentaries. I. Munck, Johannes, 1904-1965. II. Title. III. Series.

BIBLE. N.T. Acts. 226'.6'07
English. 1967. Revised standard.
The Acts in the Revised standard version. With introd. and commentary by R. P. C. Hanson. Oxford, Clarendon Press, 1967. [11], 262 p. illus., map (on lining paper), plan. 19 cm. (The New Clarendon Bible: New Testament) Bibliography: 11th prelim. page. [BS2625.3.H34] 67-3224
1. Bible. N.T. Acts—Commentaries. I. Hanson, Richard Patrick Crosland. II. Title. III. Series.

BLAIKLOCK, E M 226.607
The Acts of the Apostles; an historical commentary. [1st ed.] Grand Rapids, Eerdmans [1959] 197p. 21cm. (The Tyndale New Testament commentaries) Includes bibliography. [BS2625.3.B55] 59-8752
1. Bible. N. T. Acts—Commentaries. I. Title.

CARTER, Charles Webb, 1905- 226'.6'07
The Acts of the Apostles, by Charles W. Carter and Ralph Earle. Grand Rapids, Zondervan Pub. House [1973] 435 p. illus. 23 cm. (Zondervan commentary series) Published in 1959 as a vol. in the Evangelical commentary on the Bible series, and now republished with new introductory matter and updated bibliography. Bibliography: p. 427-434. [BS2625.3.C33 1973] 73-160588 7.95
1. Bible. N.T. Acts—Commentaries. I. Earle, Ralph. II. Bible. N.T. Acts. English. American standard. 1973. III. Title.

DICKSON, Kwesi A. 226'.6'07
The story of the early Church as found in the Acts of the Apostles / by Kwesi A. Dickson. London : Darton, Longman and Todd, 1976. 160 p. : maps ; 19 cm. Bibliography: p. [160] [BS2625.2.D52] 76-378117 ISBN 0-232-51333-3 : £1.20
1. Bible. N.T. Acts—Criticism, interpretation, etc. I. Title.

GAEBELEIN, Arno Clemens, 1861-1945. 226.607
The Acts of the Apostles, an exposition. New York, Loizeaux Bros. [1961, c1912] 429 p. 21 cm. [BS2625.G3 1961] 61-17224
1. Bible: N. T. Acts — Commentaries. I. Title.

GRECH, Prospero. 226'.6'07
Acts of the Apostles explained; a doctrinal commentary. [Translated by Gregory Carnevale] Staten Island, N.Y., Alba House [1966] 151 p. map (on lining papers) 22 cm. Translation of Atti degli Apostoli. Bibliographical references included in "Preface" (p. 7-8) [BS2625.3.G713] 66-27531
1. Bible. N.T.—Commentaries. I. Title.

GUTZKE, Manford George. 226.607
Plain talk on Acts. Grand Rapids, Zondervan Pub. House [1966] 221 p. 23 cm. [BS2625.3.G8] 66-13688
1. Bible. N.T. Acts — Commentaries. I. Title.

GUTZKE, Manford George 226.607
Plain talk on Acts. Grand Rapids, Mich., Zondervan [c.1966] 221p. 23cm. [BS2625.3.G8] 66-13688 3.95 bds.,
1. Bible. N.T. Acts—Commentaries I. Title.

JACOBSEN, Henry, 1908- 226'.6'07
The Acts then and now. [Wheaton, Ill.] Victor Books [1973] 224 p. 18 cm. (An Input book) [BS2625.2.J27] 72-96738 ISBN 0-88207-239-0 1.45
1. Bible. N.T. Acts—Criticism, interpretation, etc. I. Title.

JACOBSEN, Henry, 1908- 226'.6'07
The Acts then and now. [Wheaton, Ill.] Victor Books [1973] 224 p. 18 cm. (An Input book) [BS2625.2.J27] 72-96738 ISBN 0-88207-239-0 1.45 (pbk.)
1. Bible. N.T. Acts—Criticism, interpretation, etc. I. Title.

JONES, J. Estill. 226'.6'07
Acts: working together in Christ's mission [by] J. Estill Jones. [Nashville] Convention Press [1974] 144 p. illus. 20 cm. On cover: January Bible study. "Text for course 3215 of the New church study course." Includes bibliographical references. [BS2625.3.J66] 74-180416
1. Bible. N.T. Acts—Commentaries. I. Title.

KENT, Homer Austin, 1926- 226'.6'07
Jerusalem to Rome; studies in the Book of Acts, by Homer A. Kent, Jr. Grand Rapids, Baker Book House [1972] 202 p. illus. 20 cm. (New Testment studies) Bibliography: p. 198-202. [BS2625.5.K44] 77-187723 ISBN 0-8010-5313-7 2.95 (pbk.)
1. Bible. N.T. Acts—Study—Text-books. I. Title.

MCBRIDE ALFRED 226'.6'07
The Gospel of the Holy Spirit : [a commentary on the Acts of the Apostles] / Alfred McBride. New York : Arena Lettres, c1975. ix, 144 p. ; 18 cm. [BS2625.3.M27 1975b] 74-24276 1.50
1. Bible. N.T. Acts—Commentaries. I. Title.

MCBRIDE, Alfred. 226'.6'07
The Gospel of the Holy Spirit : a commentary on the Acts of the Apostles / Alfred McBride. New York : Hawthorn Books, c1975. vi, 145 p. ; 21 cm. [BS2625.3.M27 1975] 75-217 ISBN 0-8015-3098-9 : 2.95
1. Bible. N.T. Acts—Commentaries. I. Title.

MACKENZIE, Ross, 1927- 226'.6'07
The word in action; the Acts of the Apostles for our time. Richmond, John Knox Press [1973] 128 p. map. 21 cm. (Covenant life curriculum) (Bible studies for modern man) Includes bibliographical references. [BS2625.2.M33] 72-6968 ISBN 0-8042-9088-1 pap. 1.95
1. Bible. N.T. Acts—Criticism, interpretation, etc. I. Title. II. Series.

*ROBERTS, J. W. 226.6'07
Act of the Apostles pt. 2. Austin, Texas, R.B. Sweet Co. [1967] 94p. 22cm. (Living word ser.) .75 pap.,
1. Bible.N.T.Acts—Commentaries. I. Title.
Publisher's address: Box 4055, Austin, Tex. 78751.

TURNBULL, Ralph G 226.607
The Acts of the apostles. Grand Rapids, Baker Book House, 1961. 161 p. 20 cm. (Proclaiming the New Testament) Includes bibliography. [BS2625.4.T85] 61-1001
1. Bible, N.T. Acts — Homiletical use. I. Title.

TURNBULL, Ralph G. 226.607
The Acts of the apostles. Grand Rapids, Mich., Baker Book House [c.]1961. 161p. (Proclaiming the New Testament) Bibl. 61-10001 2.75
1. Bible. N. T. Acts—Homiletical use. I. Title.

VAUGHAN, Curtis. 226'.6'07
Acts, a study guide / Curtis Vaughan. Grand Rapids : Zondervan Pub. House, [1974] 159 p. ; 21 cm. Bibliography: p. 157-159. [BS2625.5.V38] 74-4953 pbk. : 1.75
1. Bible. N.T. Acts—Study—Text-books. I. Title.

BIBLE. N.T. Acts. 226.6077
English. 1965. Authorized.
The Acts of the Apostles [with commentary] by Thomas Walker. Introd. and biographical sketch by Wilbur M. Smith. Chicago, Moody Press [1965] xxix, 586 p. 20 cm. First published in 1910 by the Society for Promoting Christian Knowledge Depository in Madras as part of the Indian church commentaries series. [BS2625.W3] 65-14609
1. Bible. N.T. Acts—Commentaries. I. Walker, Thomas, ed. II. Title.

BIBLE. N.T.Acts. 226.6077
English. 1965. Authorized
The Acts of the Apostles [commentary] by Thomas Walker. Introd., biographical sketch by Wilbur M. Smith. Chicago, Moody [1965] xxix, 586p. 20cm. First pub. in 1910 by the Soc. for Promoting Christian Knowledge Depository in Madras as part of the Indian church commentaries ser. [BS2625.W3] 65-14609 4.95
1. Bible. N.T. Acts—Commentaries. I. Walker, Thomas, ed. II. Title.

BIBLE. N.T. Acts. 226'.6'077
English. 1976. Barclay.
The Acts of the Apostles / translated with an introduction and interpretation by William Barclay. Rev. ed. Philadelphia : Westminster Press, c1976. x, 193, [2] p. ; 19 cm. (The Daily study Bible series) Bibliography: p. [1]. [BS2623.B37 1976] 76-22671 ISBN 0-664-21306-5 deluxe ed. : 6.25 ISBN 0-664-24106-9 pbk. : 3.45
1. Bible. N.T. Acts—Commentaries. I. Title. II. Series.

HAENCHEN, Ernst, 1894- 226'.6'077
The Acts of the Apostles; a commentary. [Translated by Bernard Noble and Gerald Shinn, under the supervision of Hugh Anderson, and with the translation rev. and brought up to date by R. McL. Wilson] Philadelphia, Westminster Press [1971] xxiii, 737 p. col. map. 24 cm. Translation of 14th ed. of Die Apostelgeschichte. Includes bibliographies. [BS2625.3.H313] 78-161218 ISBN 0-664-20919-X 17.50
1. Bible. N.T. Acts—Commentaries. I. Bible. N.T. Acts. English. II. Title.

HARRISON, Everett Falconer, 1902- 226'.6'.077
Acts : the expanding church / by Everett F. Harrison. Chicago : Moody Press, [1976] c1975. p. cm. Includes index. Bibliography: p. [BS2625.3.H37] 75-28445 ISBN 0-8024-0035-3 : 7.95
1. Bible. N.T. Acts—Commentaries. I. Bible. N.T. Acts. II. Title.

KEACH, Richard L. 226'.6'077
God's spirit in the church [by] Richard L. Keach. Valley Forge [Pa.] Judson Press [1974] 59 p. 22 cm. Based on material first published in Adult class, v. 68, no. 3. Includes bibliographical references. [BS2625.2.K4] 73-19512 ISBN 0-8170-0632-X 1.75 (pbk.)
1. Bible. N.T. Acts—Criticism, interpretation, etc. I. Title.

PRICE, Eugenia. 226'.6'077
Learning to live from the acts. [1st ed.] Philadelphia, Lippincott [1970] 160 p. 21 cm. [BS2625.3.P7] 72-118977 3.95
1. Bible. N.T. Acts—Commentaries. I. Title.

SMITH, Robert H., 1932- 226'.6'077
Concordia commentary: Acts [by] Robert H. Smith. Saint Louis, Concordia Pub. House [1970] 395 p. maps. 20 cm. Bibliography: p. 388-390. [BS2625.3.S6] 70-98297
1. Bible. N.T. Acts—Commentaries. I. Bible. N.T. Acts. English. Revised standard. 1970. II. Title.

WEST, Maude De Joseph. 226'.6'077
Saints in sandals / Maude De Joseph West. Grand Rapids : Baker Book House, c1975. 250 p. ; 23 cm. [BS2625.3.W47] 76-353727 ISBN 0-8010-9570-0 : 6.95
1. Bible. N.T. Acts—Commentaries. I. Title.

REES, Paul Stromberg 226.60922
Men of action in the book of Acts [by] Paul S. Rees. Westwood, N.J., Revell [1966] ix, 102p. 21cm. [BS2625.4.R4] 66-21903 2.95
1. Bible. N. T. Acts—Biog. I. Title.

REES, Paul Stromberg. 226.60922
Men of action in the book of Acts [by] Paul S. Rees. Westwood, N.J., Revell [1966] ix, 102 p. 21 cm. [BS2625.4.R4] 66-21903
1. Bible. N.T. Acts—Biography. I. Title.

AUTREY, C E 226.6095
Evangelism in the Acts. Grand Rapids, Zondervan Pub. House, [c1964] 87 p. 22 cm. Bibliographical references included in "Notes" (p. 86-87) [BS2625.5.A8] 63-17752
1. Bible N. T. Acts — History of Biblical events. 2. Evangelistic work. I. Title.

AUTREY, C. E. 226.6095
Evangelism in the Acts. Grand Rapids, Mich., Zondervan [c.1964] 87p. 22cm. Bibl. 63-17752 2.50
1. Bible N. T. Acts—History of Biblical events. 2. Evangelistic work. I. Title.

FILSON, Floyd Vivian, 1896- 226.6095
Three crucial decades; studies in the book of Acts. Richmond, John Knox Press [1963] 118 p. 22 cm. "Present[s] in slightly revised form the Smyth lectures delivered at Columbia Theological Seminary, Decatur, Georgia, on November 5-9, 1962." Bibliographical footnotes. [BS2625.5.F5] 63-15197
1. Bible. N. T. Acts — History of Biblical events. I. Title.

FILSON, Floyd Vivian, 1896- 226.6095
Three crucial decades; studies in the book of Acts. Richmond, Va., Knox [c.1963] 118p. 22cm. Present[s] in slightly rev. form the Smyth lects. delivered at Columbia Theological Seminary, Decatur, Georgia, on November 5-9, 1962. Bibl. 63-15197 3.00
1. Bible. N.T. Acts—History of Biblical events. I. Title.

SCHMITHALS, Walter. 226.6095
Paul and James. [Translated by Dorothea M. Barton] Naperville, Ill., A. R. Allenson [1965] 125 p. 22 cm. (Studies in Biblical theology, no. 46) Bibliography: p. 119-122. [BS2635.2.S313] 65-5431
1. Bible. N. T. Epistles—Criticism, interpretation, etc. 2. Jewish Christians—Early church. 3. Bible. N. T. Acts and Epistles—History of Biblical events. I. Title. II. Series.

SCHMITHALS, Walter 226.6095
Paul and James [Tr. by Dorothea M. Barton] Naperville, Ill., A. R. Allenson [c.]1965. 125p. 22cm. (Studies in Biblical theology, no.46) Bibl. [BS2635.2.S313] 65-5431 4.95 pap.,
1. Bible. N. T. Epistles—Criticism, interpretation, etc. 2. Jewish Christians—Early church. 3. Bible. N. T. Acts and Epistles—History of Biblical events I. Title. II. Series.

GOSPELS in study and preaching (The): Trinity Sunday to the ninth Sunday after Trinity. Exegetical studies, by Arthur Voobus. Homiletical studies, by Henry Grady Davis. Philadelphia, Fortress [c.1966] xi, 300p. 24cm. Bibl. [BS2547.G6] 66-14245 5.50 226.66
1. Bible. N. T. Epistles and gospels, Liturgical—Commentaries. I. Voobus, Arthur. II. Davis, Henry Grady.

VOOBUS, Arthur. 226.66
The Gospels in study and preaching; Trinity Sunday to the ninth Sunday after Trinity. Exegetical studies, by Arthur Voobus. Homiletical studies, by Henry Grady Davis. Philadelphia, Fortress Press [1966] xi, 300 p. 24 cm. Bibliographical footnotes. [BS2547.G6] 66-14245
1. Bible. N.T. Epistles and gospels, Liturgical — Commentaries. I. Davis, Henry Grady. II. Title.

BIBLE. N.T. Acts. English. 226.67
1966. New English.
Acts of the Apostles: commentary, by J. W. Packer. Cambridge, Cambridge U.P., 1966. x, 233 p. maps, plans, tables, diagrs. 20 1/2 cm. (B 66-12797) (Cambridge Bible commentary: New English Bible) 18/6 Bibliography: p. 227-228. [BS2625.3.P3] 66-13639
1. Bible. N.T. Acts—Commentaries. I. Packer, John William. II. Title. III. Series.

BIBLE. N.T. Acts. English. 226.67
1966. New English.
Acts of the Apostles: commentary, by J. W. Packer. Cambridge, Cambridge U.P., 1966. x, 233 p. maps, plans, tables, diagrs. 21 cm. (Cambridge Bible commentary: New English Bible) Bibliography: p. 227-228. [BS2625.3.P3] 66-13639 18/6
1. Bible. N.T. Acts—Commentaries. I. Packer, John William. II. Title. III. Series.

ALLEN, Charles Livingstone, 1913- 226.7
The touch of the Master's hand; Christ's miracles for today. [Westwood, N.J.] Revell [1956] 158p. 22cm. [BT365.A4] 56-13218
1. Jesus Christ—Miracles—Sermons. 2.

Baptists—Sermons. 3. Sermons, American. I. Title.

CHAPPELL, Clovis Gillham, 1882- 226.7
Sermons from the miracles. Nashville, Abingdon [1965, c.1937] 224p. 18cm. (Apex bk., T2) [BT365.C45] 1.25 pap.,
1. Jesus Christ—Miracles—Sermons. 2. Methodist church—Sermons. 3. Sermons. American. I. Title.

FOREMAN, Dennis Walden, 1900- 226.7
The miracles of Jesus. Boston, Christopher Pub. House [1954] 314p. 21cm. [BT365.F6] 54-12570
1. Jesus Christ—Miracles. I. Title.

FULLER, Reginald Horace. 226.7
Interpreting the miracles. Philadelphia, Westminster Press [1963] 127 p. 20 cm. [BS2545.M5F8] 63-14638
1. Jesus Christ—Miracles. 2. Miracles. I. Title.

GAIRNS, David Smith, 1862-1946. 226.7
The faith that rebels; a re-examination of the miracles of Jesus. [6th ed.] New York, Harper [1954] 260p. 20cm. [BT365.C3 1954] 55-14048
1. Jesus Christ— Miracles. I. Title.

LAIDLAW, John, 1832-1906- 226.7
The miracles of Our Lord; expository and homiletic. Grand Rapids, Baker Book House 1956. o88p. 20cm. [Baker reprint library, 6] 'A reprint of the 1900 printing by Hodder and Stoughton, London.' [BT365.L27 1956] 56-7578
1. Jesus Christ—Miracles. I. Title.

NICOLL, Maurice, 1884- 226.7
The new man; an interpretation of some parables and miracles of Christ. [1st American ed.] New York, Hermitage House, 1951 [c1950] 235 p. 21 cm. Full name: Henry Maurice Dunlop Nicoll. [BT375.N48] 51-11662
1. Jesus Christ — Parables. 2. Jesus Christ — Miracles. I. Title.

REDDING, David A 226.7
The miracles of Christ. Westwood, N.J., F.H. Revell Co. [1964] xiv, 186 p. 21 cm. Bibliography: p. [177] [BT366.R4] 64-16603
1. Jesus Christ — Miracles. I. Title.

REDDING, David A. 226.7
The miracles of Christ. Westwood. N.J., Revell [c.1964] xiv. 186p. 21cm. Bibl. 64-16603 3.50
1. Jesus Christ—Miracles. I. Title.

STEWART, John J 226.7
The miracles of Christmas, by John J. Stewart. Salt Lake City, Deseret Book Co., 1965. 63 p. illus. 16 cm. [BT336S7] 65-28865
1. Jesus Christ — Miracles. I. Title.

TRENCH, Richard Chenevix, Abp. of Dublin, 1807-1886. 226.7
Notes on the miracles of Our Lord. Westwood, N. J., F. H. Revell Co. [1953] 517p. 22cm. [BT365.T7 1953] 53-4069
1. Jesus Christ— Miracles. I. Title.

WALLACE, Ronald S 226.7
The Gospel miracles; studies in Matthew, Mark, and Luke. Grand Rapids, Eerdmans [1960] 161 p. 23 cm. [BT366.W3 1960] 60-15613
1. Jesus Christ — Miracles. I. Title.

WALLACE, Ronald S. 226.7
The Gospel miracles; studies in Matthew, Mark, and Luke. Grand Rapids, Eerdmans [c.1960] 161p. 60-15613 3.50
1. Jesus Christ—Miracles. I. Title.

WALLACE, Ronald S 226.7
Many things in parables [and] The Gospel miracles. Grand Rapids, Eerdmans [1963] 218, 161 p. 22 cm. Includes bibliography. [BT375.2.W3 1963] 63-4584
1. Jesus Christ — Parables. 2. Jesus Christ — Miracles. I. Title: The Gospel miracles. II. Title.

WALLACE, Ronald S. 226.7
Many things in parables [and] The Gospel miracles. Grand Rapids, Mich., Eerdmans [c.1963] 218, 161p. 22cm. Bibl. 63-4584 1.95 pap.,
1. Jesus Christ—Parables. 2. Jesus Christ—Miracles. I. Title. II. Title: The Gospel miracles.

WEISER, Alfons, 1934- 226'.7
The miracles of Jesus, then and now. Translated by David L. Tiede. Chicago, Franciscan Herald Press [1972] 44 p. 18 cm. (Herald Biblical booklets) Translation of Jesu Wunder, damals und heute. [BT366.W4413] 72-77452 ISBN 0-8199-0211-X 0.95
1. Jesus Christ—Miracles. I. Title.

REDDING, David A. 226'.7'06
The miracles and the parables; two best sellers complete in one volume: The miracles of Christ, The parables He told [by] David A. Redding. Old Tappan, N.J., F. H. Revell Co. [1971] x, 186, iv, 177 p. 21 cm. Includes bibliographies. [BT366.R4 1971] 77-145676 ISBN 0-8007-0424-X 5.95
1. Jesus Christ—Miracles. 2. Jesus Christ—Parables. I. Redding, David A., The parables He told. 1971. II. Title.

BARTLETT, David Lyon, 1941- 226'.7'066
Fact and faith / David L. Bartlett. Valley Forge, Pa. : Judson Press, [1975] 144 p. ; 22 cm. Includes index. Bibliography: p. 141-142. [BS2545.M5B37] 74-22517 ISBN 0-8170-0654-0 pbk. : 3.95
1. Jesus Christ—Resurrection. 2. Miracles. I. Title.

TAYLOR, William Mackergo, 1829-1895. 226'.7'07
Miracles of our Saviour / by William M. Taylor. Grand Rapids : Kregel Publications, 1975. vi, 449 p. ; 22 cm. Reprint of the 1906 ed. published by Doran, New York. Includes bibliographical references. [BT365.T23 1975] 74-79944 ISBN 0-8254-3806-3 : 5.95
1. Jesus Christ—Miracles. I. Title.

ALLEN, Charles Livingstone, 1913- 226.8
When the heart is hungry; Christ's parables for today. [Westwood, N. J.] Revell [1955] 159p. 22cm. [BT375.A65] 55-6625
I. Title.

ARMSTRONG. APRIL (OURSLER) 226.8
The tales Christ told. [1st ed.] Garden City, N. Y., Doubleday, 1959. 256p. 22cm. [BT375.2.A7] 59-6346
1. Jesus Christ—Parables. I. Title.

ARMSTRONG, April (Oursler) 226.8
[Full name: Grace April (Oursler) Armstrong].
The tales Christ told. Garden City, N.Y., Doubleday [1968, c.1959] 198p. 18cm. (Echo bk., E56) 59-6346 .95 pap.,
1. Jesus Christ—Parables. I. Title.

BAILEY, Kenneth E. 226'.8
Poet and peasant : a literary-cultural approach to the parables in Luke / by Kenneth Ewing Bailey. Grand Rapids : Eerdmans, c1976. 238 p. ; 25 cm. Includes indexes. Bibliography: p. 217-229. [BT375.2.B23] 75-41405 ISBN 0-8028-3476-0 pbk. : 3.95
1. Jesus Christ—Parables. 2. Bible. N.T. Luke—Criticism, interpretation, etc. I. Title.

BASH, Ewald. 226'.8
Visit to five brothers, and other double exposures. [St. Louis] Concordia Pub. House [1968] 104 p. illus. 21 cm. (The Perspective series, 5) [BS680.P3B3] 68-20134
1. Bible—Parables. I. Title.

BASH, Ewald. 226'.8
Visit to five brothers, and other double exposures. [St. Louis] Concordia Pub. House [1968] 104 p. illus. 21 cm. (The Perspective series, 5) [BS680.P3B3] 68-20134
1. Bible—Parables. I. Title.

BRUNNER, Heinrich Emil, 1889- 226.8
Sowing and reaping; the parables of Jesus. Translated by Thomas Wieser. Richmond, John Knox Press [1964] 91 p. 21 cm. [BT375.B753] 64-12989
1. Jesus Christ — Parables — Sermons. 2. Reformed Church — Sermons. 3. Sermons, German. I. Title.

BRUNNER, Heinrich Emil, 1889- 226.8
Sowing and reaping; the parable of Jesus. Tr. [from German] by Thomas Wieser Richmond, Va., Knox [c.1964] 91p. 21cm. 64-12987 1.50 pap.,
1. Jesus Christ—Parables—Sermons. 2. Reformed Church—Sermons. 3. Sermons. German. I. Title.

BUNYAN, John, 1628-1688. 226'.8
The barren fig-tree; or, The doom and downfall of the fruitless professor, shewing that the day of grace may be past with him long before his life is ended, the signs also by which such miserable mortals may be known. Swengel, Pa., Reiner Publications, 1968. 76 p. 19 cm. [BT378.B2B8 1968] 68-5558
1. Barren fig tree (Parable) I. Title. II. Title: The doom and downfall of the fruitless professor.

CHAPPELL, Clovis Gillham, 1882- 226.8
In parables. Nashville, Abingdon-Cokesbury [1953] 153p. 20cm. [BT375.C48] 53-8132
1. Jesus Christ—Parables. I. Title.

COX, Norman Wade, 1888- 226.8
God and ourselves. Nashville, Broadman Press [c.1960] x, 139p. 21cm. 60-5191 2.75 bds.,
1. Prodigal son (Parable)—Sermons. 2. Baptists—Sermons. 3. Sermons, American. I. Title.

CROWE, Charles M 226.8
Sermons on the parables of Jesus. Nashville, Abingdon-Cokesbury Press [c1953] 186p. 21cm. [BT375.C75] 52-11314
1. Jesus Christ—Parables—Sermons. 2. Methodist Church—Sermons. 3. Sermons, American. I. Title.

DANNEMILLER, Lawrence. 226.8
Stories told by Our Lord; [23 parables] Pref. by Lawrence Dannemiller. Illustrated by Osborn Woods. [1st ed.] Baltimore, Helicon Press, 1960. unpaged. illus. 24 x 31 cm. [BT376.S75] 60-15629
1. Jesus Christ — Parables — Jevenile literature. I. Title.

DIGNAM, F Philip. 226.8
The boy who changed his name, and other stories. New York, Morehouse-Gorham [1956] 60p. illus 24cm. [BT376.D5] 56-13454
1. Jesus Christ—Parables—Juvenile literature. I. Title.

DUNCAN, Cleo. 226'.8
Woofy is forgiven, and The prodigal son. Illustrated by Beryl Bailey Jones. Boston, United Church Press, 1964. 1 v. (unpaged) col. illus. 21 cm. "Part of the United Church curriculum, prepared and published by the Church Board for Homeland Ministries." [BT378.P8D75] 64-19469
1. Prodigal son (Parable) — Juvenile literature. I. i. United Church Board for Homeland Ministries. Division of Christian Education. II. ii. United Church Board for Homeland Ministries. Division of Publication. The prodigal son. III. Title.

DUNCAN, Cleo. 226'.8
Woofy is forgiven, and The prodigal son. Illustrated by Beryl Bailey Jones. Boston, United Church Press, 1964. 1 v. (unpaged) col. illus. 21 cm. "Part of the United Church curriculum, prepared and published by the Division of Christian Education and the Division of Publication of the United Church Board for Homeland Ministries." [BT378.P8D75] 64-19469
1. Prodigal son (Parable) — Juvenile literature. I. i. United Church Board for Homeland Ministries. Division of Christian Education. II. ii. United Church Board for Homeland Ministries. Division of Publication. The prodigal son. III. Title.

ELLIOTT, William Marion, 1903- 226.8
Two sons. Richmond, John Knox Press [1955] 62p. 21cm. [BT378.P8E47] 55-6742
1. Prodigal son (Parable) I. Title.

GLEN, John Stanley, 1907- 226.8
The parables of conflict in Luke. Philadelphia, Westminster [c.1962] 160p. 21cm. Bibl. 62-9811 3.50
1. Jesus Christ—Parables. I. Title.

GRAHAM, Lorenz B. 226'.8
Hongry catch the foolish boy, by Lorenz Graham. Pictures by James Brown, Jr. New York, Crowell [1973] [40] p. illus. (part col.) 21 x 22 cm. Story first appeared in the author's How God fix Jonah, published in 1946. Retells the parable of the prodigal son in the speech patterns and images of African people newly acquainted with the English language. [BT378.P8G68 1973] 77-184981 ISBN 0-690-40111-6 3.95
1. Prodigal son (Parable)—Juvenile literature. I. Brown, James, illus. II. Title.

HAMILTON, James Wallace, 1900- 226.8
Horns and halos in human nature. [Westwood, N. J.] Revell [1954] 173p. 22cm. [BR121.H213] 54-9685
1. Christianity—Essence, genius, nature. I. Title.

JEREMIAS, Joachim, 1900- 226.8
The parables of Jesus. Translated by S. H. Hooke. New York, Scribner [1955] 178p. 24cm. [BT375] 55-2375
1. Jesus Christ-Parables. I. Title.

*JORDAN, Clarence 226.'8
Cotton patch parables of liberation / Clarence Jordan, Bill Lane Doulos. Scottdale, Pa. : Herald Press, c1976. 160 p. ; 18 cm. (A Koinonia publication.) Includes bibliographical notes. [BT373] ISBN 0-8361-1334-9 pbk. : 1.95
1. Jesus Christ—Parables. I. Doulos, Bill Lane joint author. II. Title.

LANG, George Henry, 1874- 226.8
The parabolic teaching of Scripture. Grand Rapids, Eerdmans, 1955. 400p. 23cm. London ed. (Paternoster Press) has title: Pictures and parables. [BS680.P3L3 1955a] 55-13855
1. Bible—Parables. I. Title.

LATOURETTE, Jane, 226'.8
Jon and the little lost lamb: Luke 15: 1-7 for children. Illustrated by Betty Wind. St. Louis, Concordia Pub. House [1965] St. Louis, Concordia Pub. House [1965] 1 v. (unpaged) col. illus. 21 cm. [32] p. col. illus. 21 cm. (Arch books) (Arch books) [BT378.L6L3] [PZ7.L3699St] 917.41'45 65-15144 63-23144
1. I. Mathews, Sally, Illus. 2. Lost sheep (Parable) — Juvenile literature. 3. Noah's ark — Juvenile literature. I. Latourette, Jane. II. Title. III. Title: The story of Noah's ark,

LATOURETTE, Jane 226.8
Jon and the little lost lamb: Luke 15: 1-7 for children. Illus. by Betty Wind. St. Louis, Concordia c.1965. 1v. (unpaged) col. illus. 21cm. (Arch bks., set 2, no. 59-11106) [BT378.L6L3] 65-15144 .35 pap.,
1. Lost sheep (Parable)—Juvenile literature. I. Title.

*LATOURETTE, Jane R. 226.8
The house on the rock; Matthew 7: 24-27 for children, Illus. by Sally Mathews. St. Louis, Concordia, [c.1966] 1v. (unpaged) col. illus. 21cm. (Arch bks., set 3, no. 59-1128) .35 pap.,
1. Parables,Biblical—Juvenile literature. 2. Bible stories, English—N.T.—Juvenile literature. I. Title.

MATURIN, Basil William, 1847-1915. 226.8
Practical studies on the parables of Our Lord. Baltimore, Carroll Press, 1951. 295 p. 18 cm. [BT377.M35 1951] 51-7012
1. Jesus Christ—Parables—Study. I. Title.

MOON, Robert D. 226.8
Love's conquest. Mountain View, Calif., Pacific Press Pub. Association [c.1960] xvii, 116p. 21cm. 60-8300 3.00
1. Prodigal son (Parable) I. Title.

MOSCHNER, Franz Maria 226.8
The kingdom of heaven in parables. Translated [from the German] by David Heimann. St. Louis, Herder [c.1960] x, 326p. 21cm. (Cross and crown series of spirituality, no. 17) 60-14100 4.75
1. Jesus Christ—Parables. 2. Kingdom of God. I. Title.

MOSCHNER, Franz Maria, 1896- 226.8
The kingdom of heaven in parables. Translated by David Heimann. St. Louis, Herder [1960] 326p. 21cm. (Cross and crown series of spirituality, no. 17) [BT375.2.M653] 60-14100
1. Jesus Christ—Parables. 2. Kingdom of God. I. Title.

MUSSNER, Franz 226.8
The use of parables in catechetics. Tr. [from German] by Maria von Eroes. Notre Dame, Ind., Univ. of Notre Dame Pr., 1965. 107p. 18cm. (Contemp. catechetics ser.) Bibl. [BV4225.2.M813] 65-14736 1.25
1. Homiletical illustrations. 2. Jesus Christ—Parables. I. Title.

POTEAT, Edwin McNeil, 1892- 226.8
Parables of crisis. New York, Harper [1950] 255 p. 22 cm. [BT375.P6] 50-7490
1. Jesus Christ—Parables. I. Title.

REID, John Calvin, 1901- 226.8
Parables from nature; earthly stories with a heavenly meaning. The parables of Jesus retold and interpreted for young minds; illustrated by Reynold H. Weidenaar. Grand Rapids, Eerdmans, 1954. 89p. illus. 21cm. [BT376.R4] 54-10729
1. Jesus Christ—Parables— Juvenile literature. I. Title.

SCHMANDT, Henrietta Elizabeth. 226.8
Parables of the Master. [1st ed.] New York, Vantage Press [1956] 80p. illus. 21cm. [BT375.S33] 56-11214
1. Jesus Christ—Parables. I. Title.

SCHROEDER, Frederick W 226.8
Far from home. Philadelphia, Christian Education Press [1961] 123p. 20cm. [BT378.P8S314] 61-10557
1. Prodigal son (Parable)—Meditations. I. Title.

SEALE, Ervin. 226.8
Learn to live; the meaning of the parables. New York, Morrow, 1955. 256 p. 21 cm. [BT375.S36] 55-7113
1. Jesus Christ—Parables. I. Title.

STORIES told by Our Lord; 226.8
[23 parables] Pref. by Lawrence Dannemiller. Illustrated by Osborn Woods. Baltimore,

Helicon Press [c.]1960. unpaged. illus. 24x31cm. 60-15629 5.00
1. Jesus Christ—Parables—Juvenile literature. I. Dannemiller, Lawrence.

STRATON, Hillyer Hawthorne, 1905- 226.8
A guide to the parables of Jesus. Grand Rapids, Eerdmans [1959] 198 p. 23 cm. Includes bibliography. [BT375.2.S7] 59-8750
I. Jesus Christ — Parables. II. Title.

TRENCH, Richard Chenevix, Abp. of Dublin, 1807-1886. 226.8
Notes on the parables of Our Lord. Westwood, N. J., F. H. Revell Co. [1953] 518p. 22cm. [BT375.T7 1953] 53-4140
1. Jesus Christ— Parables. I. Title. II. Title: Parables of Our Lord.

WALLACE, Ronald S 226.8
Many things in parables, expository studies. New York, Harper [1956, c1955] 218 p. 22 cm. [BT375.W3 1956] 55-11485
1. Jesus Christ — Parables. I. Title.

WALLEY, Barbara Ann. 226'.8
Mustard seed faith; an exposition of the Biblical mustard seed. Menomonie, Wis., Mustard Seed Press [1968] 3 p. illus. 15 cm. "One hundred and sixty copies were printed ... number 5." [BT378.M8W3] 68-7795
1. Mustard seed (Parable) 2. Faith—Biblical teaching. I. Title.

WALSH, Bill. 226'.8
The prodigal son / Bill Walsh ; edited with an introduction by Charlie Shedd. Kansas City, Kan. : Sheed Andrews and McMeel, c1977. p. cm. (A Cartoon Bible story) A cartoon version of the parable of the prodigal son who, after squandering his inheritance, returns home to his forgiving father. [BT378.P8W24] 77-1146 ISBN 0-8362-0693-2 pbk. : 1.95
1. Prodigal son (Parable)—Caricatures and cartoons—Juvenile literature. I. Title.

*WELLS, Edmund E. 226.8
The gospel according to Mother Goose, [by] Edmund E. Wells. Anderson, Indiana, Warner Press [1973, c1969] 59 p. 18 cm. (A Portal book) [BT375.2] 0.75 (pbk.)
1. Parables. I. Title.

WHITE, Ellen Gould (Harmon) 1827-1915 226.8
Highways to heaven. Washington, Review and Herald Pub. Association.[1952] 384 p. illus. 22 cm. Previous editions published under title: Christ's object lessons. [BT375.W5] 52-3468
1. Jesus Christ—Parables. 2. Jesus Christ—Pictures, illustrations, etc. I. Title.

WHITE, John Wesley. 226'.8
The runaway / John Wesley White. [Dallas : Crescendo Publications], c1976. 198 p. ; 18 cm. [BT378.P8W46] 77-371317 ISBN 0-89038-028-7 pbk. : 1.95
1. Prodigal son (Parable) I. Title.

WHITING, Thomas A 226.8
Sermons on the prodigal son. New York, Abingdon Press [1959] 111 p. 20 cm. [BT378.P8W47] 60-5237
1. Prodigal son (Parable) — Sermons. 2. Methodist Church — Sermons. 3. Sermons, American. I. Title.

WHITING, Thomas A. 226.8
Sermons on the prodigal son. Abingdon Press [c.1959] 111p. Bibl. footnotes: p2.00 bds., 60-5237
1. Prodigal son (Parable)—Sermons. 2. Methodist Church—Sermons. 3. Sermons, American. I. Title.

HARGREAVES, John Henry Monsarrat, 1911- 226'.8'007
A guide to the parables / John Hargreaves ; with a foreword by C. H. Dodd. Valley Forge, PA : Judson Press, 1975, c1968. [11], 132 p. : ill. ; 22 cm. Includes index. Bibliogrpahy: 11th prelim. page. [BT377.H3 1975] 74-20518 ISBN 0-8170-0653-2 pbk. : 3.95
1. Jesus Christ—Parables—Study and teaching. I. Title.

BIBLE. N.T. Gospels. English. Selections. 1975. Authorized. 226'.8'05203
The parables of Our Lord and Saviour Jesus Christ / with pictures by John Everett Millais ; engraved by the brothers Dalziel ; with a new introd. by Mary Lutyens. New York : Dover Publications, 1975. xxxvi, 76 p. : ill. ; 24 cm. Reprint of the 1864 ed. published by Routledge, Warne, and Routledge, London. Bibliography: p. xxxv. [BT373.E5 1975] 74-20328 ISBN 0-486-20494-4 pbk. : 2.50
1. Jesus Christ—Parables—Texts. 2. Jesus Christ—Parables—Pictures, illustrations, etc. I. Mallais, John Everett, Sir, bart., 1829-1896.

BARCLAY, William, lecturer in the University of Glasgow. 226'.8'06
And Jesus said; a handbook on the parables of Jesus. Philadelphia, Westminster Press [1970] 222, [2] p. 19 cm. Bibliography: [223-224] [BT375.2.B27] 77-120410 2.75
1. Jesus Christ—Parables.

BROOKS, Melvin R 226.806
Parables of the Kingdom [by] Melvin R. Brooks. Salt Lake City, Deseret Book Co., 1965. xiii, 172 p. col. illus. 24 cm. Bibliography: p. [159]-162. [BS680.P3B7] 65-29166
1. Bible — Parables. I. Title.

CARGILL, Robert L. 226'.8'06
All the parables of Jesus; an inspirational interpretation of the parables and how they relate to life today [by] Robert L. Cargill. Nashville, Broadman Press [1970] 127 p. 20 cm. [BT375.2.C35] 73-117302 2.95
1. Jesus Christ—Parables. I. Title.

DEEVER, Philip O. 226'.8'06
The kingdom is ... / Philip O. Deever. Nashville : Tidings, c1976. ix, 80 p. ; 19 cm. [BT375.2.D37] 74-18588
1. Jesus Christ—Parables. I. Title.

DODD, Charles Harold, 1884- 226.806
The parables of the kingdom. [Rev. ed.] New York, Scribner [1961] 176 p. 21 cm. [BT375.D55 1961] 61-3521
1. Jesus Christ—Parables. 2. Kingdom of God—Biblical teaching. I. Title.

DODD, Charles Harold, 1884- 226.806
The parables of the kingdom [Rev. ed.] New York, Scribners [1965, c.1961]; 176p. 21cm. (Scribner lib., SL125) [BT375.D55] 61-3521 1.45 pap.,
1. Jesus Christ—Parables. 2. Kingdom of God—Biblical teaching. I. Title.

FLOOD, Edmund. 226'.8'06
Parables of Jesus. New York, Paulist Press [1971] 64 p. 17 cm. [BT375.2.F55 1971] 79-147905 0.75
1. Jesus Christ—Parables. I. Title.

GOOD, Charles M. 226.806
The parables-of-Jesus. Boston, Christopher Pub. House [c.1961] 142p. Bibl. 61-15193 3.00
1. Jesus Christ—Parables. I. Title.

GOOD, Charles Martin. 226.806
The parables of Jesus. Boston, Christopher Pub. House [1961] 142 p. 21 cm. Includes bibliography. [BT375.2.G6] 61-15193
1. Jesus Christ—Parables. I. Title.

GUTZWILLER, Richard 226.806
The parables of the Lord [Tr. from German by Arlene Swidler. New York] Herder & Herder [c.1964] 144p. 21cm. Bibl. 64-19729 3.75
1. Jesus Christ—Parables. I. Title.

GUTZWILLER, Richard. 226.806
The parables of the Lord [Translated by Arlene Swidler. New York] Herder and Herder [1964] 144 p. 21 cm. Bibliographical footnotes. [BT375.2.G813] 64-19729
1. Jesus Christ — Parables. I. Title.

HABERSHON, Ada Ruth, 1861- 226.806
The study of the parables. Pref. by Robert Anderson. Grand Rapids, Mich., Kregel, 1963. 366p. 23cm. 62-19175 3.95
1. Bible—Parables. I. Title.

HARRINGTON, Wilfrid J 226.806
A key to the parables, by Wilfrid J. Harrington. Glen Rock, N.J., Paulist Press [1964] 160 p. 19 cm. (Deus books) Bibliography: p. 160. [BT375.2.H3] 64-24516
1. Jesus Christ — Parables. I. Title.

HARRINGTON, Wilfrid J. 226.806
A key to the parables. Glen Rock, N.J., Paulist [c.1964] 160p. 19cm. (Deus bks.) Bibl. 64-24516 95 pap.,
1. Jesus Christ—Parables. I. Title.

HUNTER, Archibald Macbride. 226.806
Interpreting the parables. Philadelphia, Westminster Press [1961, c1960] 126 p. 20 cm. Includes bibliography. [BT375.2.H8] 61-5122
1. Jesus Christ—Parables. I. Title.

JAVELET, Robert. 226.806
The Gospel paradox. [Translation by Donald Antoine. New York] Herder and Herder [1966] 224 p. 21 cm. Translation of Les paraboles contra la loi. [BT375.2.J313] 66-16943
1. Jesus Christ—Parables. I. Title.

JEREMIAS, Joachim, 1900- 226.806
The parables of Jesus. [Tr. by S. H. Hooke] Rev. ed. New York, Scribners [1966, c.1963] 248p. 23cm. (Scribner Studies in Biblical Interpretation, 4-4055) Bibl. [BT375.J413 1963] 63-22114 2.95 pap.,
1. Jesus Christ—Parables. I. Title.

JONES, Geraint Vaughan 226.806
The art and truth of the parables: a study in their literary form and modern interpretation. London, S.P.C.K. [dist. New York, Seabury, c.]1964. xii, 250p. 23cm. Bibl. 64-5589 7.00
1. Jesus Christ—Parable. 2. Bible. N.T. Gospels—Criticism, interpretation, etc.—Hist. 3. Prodigal son (Parable) I. Title.

KAHLEFELD, Heinrich. 226.806
Parables and instruction in the Gospels. Translated by Arlene Swidler. [New York] Herder and Herder [1966- v. 21 cm. Bibliographical references included in "Notes" (v. 1., p. 156-167) [BT375.2.K313] 66-13073
1. Jesus Christ — Parables. I. Title.

KAHLEFELD, Heinrich 226.806
Parables and instructions in the Gospels. Tr. [from German] by Arlene Swidler. [New York] Herder & Herder [c.1966] 174p. 21cm. Bibl. [BT375.2.K313] 66-13073 3.95
1. Jesus Christ—Parables. I. Title.

KENNEDY, Gerald [Hamilton] 226.806
The parables: sermons on the stories Jesus told. New York, Harper [c.1960] ix, 213p. 22cm. (bibl. footnotes) 60-7959 3.50 half cloth,
1. Jesus Christ—Parables. I. Title.

KENNEDY, Gerald Hamilton, Bp., 1907- 226.806
The parables: sermons on the stories Jesus told. New York, Harper [1967,c.1960] vii, 213p. 21cm. (Chapelbks, CB35) [BT375.2.K4] 60-7959 1.60 pap.,
1. Jesus Christ—Parables. I. Title.

KEYES, Nelson Beecher, 1894- 226.806
The parables. Garden City, N. Y. [N. Doubleday, 1963] 63 p. illus. (part mounted col.) 21 cm. (Know your Bible program) [BT375.2.K44 1963] 63-5830
1. Jesus Christ — Parables. I. Title.

LIGHTFOOT, Neil R 226.806
Lessons from the parables, by Neil R. Lightfoot. Grand Rapids, Baker Book House, 1965. 184 p. 22 cm. Bibliography: p. 185. [BT375.2.L5] 65-18264
1. Jesus Christ — Parables, I. Title.

LIGHTFOOT, Neil R. 226.806
Lessons from the parables. Grand Rapids, Mich., Baker Bk. [c.]1965. 184p. 22cm. Bibl. [BT375.2.L5] 65-18264 3.50
1. Jesus Christ—Parables. I. Title.

LINNEMANN, Eta. 226'.8'06
Jesus of the parables; introduction and exposition. [Translated by John Sturdy. 1st U.S. ed.] New York, Harper & Row [1967, c1966] xv, 218 p. 22 cm. Translation of Gleichnisse Jesu, Einfuhrung und Auslegung. Bibliography: p. [199]-208. [BT375.2.L5313 1967] 67-11499
1. Jesus Christ—Parables. I. Title.

LOCKYER, Herbert. 226.806
All the parables of the Bible; a study and analysis of the more than 250 parables in Scripture, including those in the Old Testament, as well as those of Our Lord, and others, in the New Testament. Grand Rapids, Zondervan Pub. House [1963] 381 p. 24 cm. Bibliography: p. 373-374. [BS680.P3L6] 63-15746
1. Bible—Parables. I. Title. II. Title: Parables of the Bible.

O'SULLIVAN, Kevin. 226.806
Living parables. Milwaukee, Bruce Pub. Co. [1963] 120 p. 23 cm. [BT375.2.O7] 63-11879
1. Jesus Christ — Parables. I. Title.

O'SULLIVAN, Kevin 226.806
Living parables. Milwaukee, Bruce [c.1963] 120p. 23cm. 63-11879 3.75
1. Jesus Christ—Parables. I. Title.

PARABLES for our world; 226.806
sermons preached at St. Aldate's, Oxford, by the Bishop of London [others] London. A. R. Mowbray [dist. Westminster, Md., Court Pl., Canterbury Pr.,] c.1962] 68p. 18cm. (Star bks.) 63-630 .95 pap.,
1. Bible—Parables. 2. Church of England—Sermons. 3. Sermons, English. I. Stopford, Robert Wright, Bp. of London, 1901-

*PAULSON, John F. 226.806
Parables of the kingdom, by John F. Paulson. Donald R. Pichaske. John Gretzer, illus. Philadelphia, Lutheran Church Pr. [c.1964] 112p. 21cm. 1.25; pap., teacher's ed., pap., 1.50
I. Title.

REDDING, David A 226.806
The parables He told. [Westwood, N. J.] Revell [1962] 177p. 21cm. Includes bibliography. [BT375.2.R4] 62-10729
1. Jesus Christ—Parables. I. Title.

SCHARLEMANN, Martin Henry, 1910- 226.806
Proclaiming the parables. Saint Louis, Concordia Pub. House [1963] 94 p. 21 cm. (The Witnessing church series) [BT375.2.S3] 63-12300
1. Jesus Christ—Parables. I. Title.

SCHARLEMANN, Martin Henry, 1910- 226.806
Proclaiming the parables. Saint Louis, Concordia [1963] 94p. 21cm. (Witnessing church ser.) 63-123007 1.75 pap.,
1. Jesus Christ—Parables. I. Title.

†*SEMIOLOGY and parables* 226'.8'06
: exploration of the possibilities offered by structuralism for exegesis : papers of the conference sponsored by the Vanderbilt Interdisciplinary Project, "Semiology and Exegesis," and supported by a grant from the National Endowment for the Humanities, held at Vanderbilt University, Nashville, Tennessee, May 15-17, 1975 / edited by Daniel Patte. Pittsburgh : Pickwick Press, 1976. xx, 384 p. : diagrs. ; 22 cm. (Pittsburgh theological monograph series ; 9) Includes bibliographical references. [BT375.2.S45] 76-20686 ISBN 0-915138-11-5 pbk. : 7.50
1. Jesus Christ—Parables—Congresses. 2. Parables—Congresses. 3. Semiotics—Congresses. I. Patte, Daniel. II. Vanderbilt University, Nashville. III. Series.

SMITH, Charles William Frederick, 1905- 226'.8'06
The Jesus of the parables / Charles W. F. Smith. Rev. ed. Philadelphia : United Church Press, [1975] 255 p. ; 21 cm. "A Pilgrim Press book." "In this edition the revised version texts [of the Bible] have been replaced by those of the revised standard version." Includes bibliographical references and indexes. [BT375.S735 1975] 74-26816 ISBN 0-8298-0267-3 : 8.95
1. Jesus Christ—Parables. I. Bible. N.T. Gospels. English. Selections. Revised standard. 1975. II. Title.

THIELICKE, Helmut, 1908- 226.806
The waiting Father; sermons on the parables of Jesus. Translated with an introd. by John W. Doberstein. [1st ed.] New York, Harper [1959] 192 p. 22 cm. Translation of Das Bilderbuch Gottes; Reden uber die Gleichnisse Jesu. [BT375.2.T5] 59-7164
1. Jesus Christ — Parables — Sermons. 2. Lutheran Church — Sermons. 3. Sermons, German — Translations into English. 4. Sermons, English — Translations from German. I. Title.

*TRENCH, Eichard Chenevix 226.806
Notes on the Parables of our Lord; popular ed. Grand Rapids, Mich., Baker Bk. [1965, c.1948] 211p. 20cm. 1.95 pap.,
I. Title.

WEHRLI, Eugene S 226.806
Exploring the parables. Boston, United Church Press [1963] 126 p. illus. 21 cm. (An Adult resource book) [BT375.2.W4] 63-13560
1. Jesus Christ — Parables. I. Title.

WEHRLI, Eugene S. 226.806
Exploring the parables. Philadelphia, United Church [c.1963] 126p. illus. 21cm. (Adult resource bk.) 63-13560 1.50 pap.,
1. Jesus Christ—Parables. I. Title.

WEHRLI, Eugene S 226.806
The parables of Jesus; a coursebook for leaders of adults. Boston, United Church Press [1963] 123 p. illus. 21 cm. [BT377.W4] 63-17255
1. Jesus Christ — Parables — Study and teaching. I. Title.

WEHRLI. EUGENE S. 226.806
The parables of Jesus: a coursebook for leaders of adults. Philadelphia. United Church [c.1963] 123p. illus. 21cm. 63-17255 1.50 pap.,
1. Jesus Christ—Parables—Study and teaching. I. Title.

VIA, Dan Otto, 1928- 226'.8'063
The parables; their literary and existential dimension. Philadelphia, Fortress Press [1967] xii, 217 p. 22 cm. Bibliographical footnotes. [BT375.2.V5] 67-11910
1. Jesus Christ—Parables. I. Title.

*BUTTRICK, George A. 226.8'066
The parables of Jesus. Grand Rapids, Baker Book House [1973, c.1928] xxx, 274 p. 20 cm. (Minister's paperback library) Bibliographical footnotes. [BT375.2] ISBN 0-8010-0597-3 pap., 2.95
1. Jesus Christ—Parables. I. Title.

CARLSTON, Charles E. 226'.8'066
The parables of the triple tradition / Charles E. Carlston. Philadelphia : Fortress Press, c1975. xviii, 249 p. ; 24 cm. Includes indexes. Bibliography: p. 213-231. [BT375.2.C354] 74-26347 ISBN 0-8006-0402-4 : 11.95
1. Jesus Christ—Parables. 2. Bible. N.T. Gospels—Criticism, interpretation, etc. I. Title.

CERFAUX, Lucien, 1883- 226'.8'066
The treasure of the parables. Translated by M. Bent. De Pere, Wis., St. Norbert Abbey Press, 1968. 143 p. 20 cm. Translation of Le tresor des paraboles. [BT375.2.C413] 68-58123 ISBN 0-8316-1026-3 2.95
1. Jesus Christ—Parables. I. Title.

COATES, Thomas, 1910- 226'.8'066
The parables for today. St. Louis, Concordia Pub. House [1971] 73 p. 23 cm. [BT375.2.C6 1971] 71-163071 ISBN 0-570-03011-0
1. Jesus Christ—Parables—Meditations. I. Title.

CROSSAN, John Dominic. 226'.8'066
In parables: the challenge of the historical Jesus. [1st ed.] New York, Harper & Row [1973] xvi, 141 p. 21 cm. Bibliography: p. 132-135. [BT375.2.C76] 73-7067 ISBN 0-06-061606-7 5.95
1. Jesus Christ—Parables. I. Title.

DEEVER, Philip O. 226'.8'066
Lending the parables our ears : toward a meaningful experience with the Gospel parables / Philip O. Deever. Nashville : Tidings, c1975. x, 148 p. ; 19 cm. Includes bibliographical references and index. [BT375.2.D38] 74-19960
1. Jesus Christ—Parables. I. Title.

GRANSKOU, David M. 226'.8'066
Preaching on the parables [by] David M. Granskou. Philadelphia, Fortress Press [1972] xii, 129 p. (p. 129 advertisement) 18 cm. (The Preacher's paperback library) Includes bibliographical references. [BT375.2.G7] 74-165512 ISBN 0-8006-4011-X 3.50
1. Jesus Christ—Parables. I. Title.

HARRINGTON, Wilfrid J. 226'.8'066
Parables told by Jesus; a contemporary approach to the parables, by Wilfrid J. Harrington. New York, Alba House [1975, c1974] vi, 135 p. 21 cm. Bibliography: p. 135. [BT375.2.H33 1975] 74-12395 ISBN 0-8189-0296-5 1.95 (pbk.).
1. Jesus Christ—Parables. I. Title.

HUNTER, Archibald Macbride. 226'.8'066
The parables then and now [by] A. M. Hunter. Philadelphia, Westminster Press [1971] 128 p. 21 cm. Bibliography: p. [122] [BT375.2.H82] 72-170113 ISBN 0-664-24940-X 2.25
1. Jesus Christ—Parables. I. Title.

JEREMIAS, Joachim, 1900- 226'.8'066
Rediscovering the parables. New York, Scribners [c.1966] 191p. 21cm. Tr. of Die Gleichnisse Jesu. [BT375.J423 1966a] 67-13197 4.95
1. Jesus Christ—Parables. I. Title.

JEREMIAS, Joachim, 1900- 226'.8'066
Rediscovering the parables. New York, Scribner [c1966] 191 p. 21 cm. Translation of Die Gleichnisse, Jesu. [BT375.J413 1966a] 67-13197
1. Jesus Christ — Parables. I. Title.

KEACH, Benjamin, 1640-1704. 226'.8'066
Exposition of the parables in the Bible / by Benjamin Keach ; foreword by Herbert Lockyer. Grand Rapids : Kregel Publications, [1974] xiv, 904 p. ; 25 cm. (Kregel reprint library) Reprint of the 1856 ed. published by W. H. Collingridge, London, under title: Exposition of the parables and express similitudes of our Lord and Saviour Jesus Christ. Includes index. [BT374.K4 1974] 73-85297 ISBN 0-8254-3016-X : 12.95
1. Jesus Christ—Parables. I. Title.

WAY, Robert E., 1912- 226'.8'066
The garden of the beloved [by] Robert E. Way. Illus. by Laszlo Kubinyi. [1st ed.] Garden City, N.Y., Doubleday, 1974. 71 p. illus. 24 cm. [BL624.W38] 74-8 ISBN 0-385-02117-8 5.95
1. Parables. I. Title.

TAYLOR, William Mackergo, 1829-1895. 226'.8'07
The parables of our Saviour / by William M. Taylor. Grand Rapids : Kregel Publications, 1975. vi, 445 p. ; 22 cm. Reprint of the 1906 ed. published by A. C. Armstrong, New York. Includes bibliographical references. [BT375.T3 1975] 74-79943 ISBN 0-8254-3805-5 : 5.95
1. Jesus Christ—Parables. I. Title.

DRAPER, James T. 226'.87'07
Hebrews : the life that pleases God / James T. Draper, Jr. Wheaton, Ill. : Tyndale House Publishers, 1976. 393 p. ; 22 cm. Bibliography: p. 393. [BS2775.3.D72] 76-8675 ISBN 0-8423-1409-1 : 7.95
1. Bible. N.T. Hebrews—Commentaries. I. Title.

BECKER, Karl, 1907- ed. 226.9
Our Father; a handbook for meditation, compiled and edited by Karl Becker and Marie Peter. Translated from the German by Ruth Mary Bethell. Chicago, H. Regnery Co., 1956. 334p. 22cm. Translation of Das hellige Vaterunser. [BV230.B432] 56-7621
1. Lord's prayer. I. Peter, Maria, joint ed. II. Title.

BIETZ, Arthur L. 226.9
The Lord's Prayer. Washington, D.C., Review & Herald [c.1963] 32p. 14cm. .15 pap.,
1. Lord's Prayer. I. Title.

BOEGNER, Marc, 1881- 226.9
The prayer of the church universal; translated by Howard Schomer. Nashville, Abingdon Press [1954] 128p. 18cm. [BV230.B632] 53-11342
1. Lord's prayer—Meditations. I. Title.

DAY, Gardiner Mumford, 1900- 226.9
The Lord's prayer; an interpretation. With a foreword byDavid R. Hunter. Illustrated by Allan R. Crite. Greenwich, Conn., Seabury Press, 1954. 98p. illus. 20cm. [BV230.D3] 54-9211
1. Lord's prayer. I. Title.

EVELY, Louis, 1910- 226.9
We dare to say our father. Translated by James Langdale. Garden City, N. Y., Image Books 1975 [c1965] 118 p., 18 cm. Translation of: Notre Pere-Aux sources de notre fraternite. [BV230.E853] ISBN 0-385-06274-5 1.45 (pbk.)
1. Lord's prayer. I. Title.
L.C. card no. for original ed.: 64-21005.

GUARDINI, Romano, 1885- 226.9
The Lord's prayer. Translated from the German by Isabel McHugh. [New York] Pantheon Books [1958] 124p. 21cm. [BV230.G773] 58-6095
1. Lord's prayer. I. Title.

JEFFRIES, J Campbell, 1910- 226.9
The law in the prayer; the Ten commandments in the Lord's prayer. With a foreword by Clyde T. Francisco. New York, Exposition Press [1952] 97 p. 23 cm. [BV230.J4] 52-5702
1. Lord's prayer. I. Title.

JORDAN, Gerald Ray, 1896- 226.9
Life-giving words; thoughts on the prayer Jesus gave us, by G. Ray Jordan. Anderson, Inds.,Warner Press [1964] xi, 112 p. (p. 110-112 blank) 19 cm. Bibliographical footnotes. [BV230.J6] 64-22157
1. Lord's prayer. I. Title.

JORDAN, Gerald Ray, 1896- 226.9
Life-giving words; thoughts on the prayer Jesus gave us. Anderson, Ind., Warner [c.1964] xi, 112p. 19cm. Bibl. 64-22157 1.50 pap.,
1. Lord's prayer. I. Title.

KERR, Clarence Ware, 1893- 226.9
Pattern for powerful praying. Los Angeles, Cowan Publications [1958] 155p. 22cm. [BV230.K4] 58-42574
1. Lord's prayer. I. Title.

KLAVER, Richard. 226.9
When you pray; an analysis of the Our Father. Westminster, Md., Newman Press, 1955. 209p. 22cm. [BV230.K57] 55-11167
1. Lord's prayer. I. Title.

KUIPER, Henry J 1885- ed. 226.9
Sermons on the Lord's prayer, by ministers in the Reformed and Christian Reformed Churches. Grand Rapids, Zondervan Pub. House [1956] 138p. 21cm. [BV230.K8] 56-13594
1. Lord's prayer—Sermons. 2. Reformed Church— Sermons. 3. Sermons, American. I. Title.

LAYMON, Charles M. 226'.9
The Lord's prayer in its Biblical setting [by] Charles M. Laymon. Nashville, Abingdon Press [1968] 160 p. 20 cm. Bibliographical footnotes. [BV230.L384] 68-25362 3.50
1. Lord's prayer. I. Title.

LORD'S prayer (The). 226.9
Designs by J. Jane Gates. Freeport, Me., Bond Wheelwright [1965] unpaged rag bk. col. illus. 28cm. Protestant and Catholic versions. unbound, ea., 2.95

MCCORD, Hugo, 1911- 226.9
The disciples' prayer. Murfreesboro, Tenn., De Hoff Publications, 1954. 89p. 20cm. [BV230.M2516] 55-27327
1. Lord's prayer. I. Title.

MCGEE, John Vernon, 1904- 226.9
The prayer the Lord did not pray. Wheaton, Ill., Van Kampen Press [1953] 95p. 20cm. [BV230.M2518] 53-10678
1. Lord's prayer. I. Title.

MCNABB, Vincent Joseph, 1868-1943. 226.9
The craft of prayer. Westminster, Md., Newman Press [1951] 105 p. 18 cm. [BV210.M283 1951] 52-9738
1. Lord's prayer. 2. Prayer. I. Title.

PROCHNOW, Herbert Victor, 1897- 226.9
Meditations on the Lord's prayer. Natick, Mass., W. A. Wilde Co. [1959] 60p. 17cm. [BV230.P7] 59-14834
1. Lord's prayer—Meditations. I. Title.

REDPATH, Alan. 226.9
Victorious praying; studies in the family prayer. [Westwood, N.J.] F. H. Revell [1957] 151 p. 20 cm. [BV230.R33] 57-5404
1. Lord's prayer. I. Title.

RICH, Joseph Walter, 1881- 226.9
The Lord's prayer. Illus. by Stanley Dunlap, Jr. Washington, Review and Herald [1956] 127p. illus. 18cm. [BV230.R47] 56-58614
1. Lord's prayer. I. Title.

SCOTT, Ernest Findlay, 1868- 226.9
The Lord's prayer; its character, purpose, and interpretation. New York, Scribner, 1951. vii, 126 p. 21 cm. [BV230.S367] 51-440
1. Lord's prayer. I. Title.

STRONG, Kendrick. 226.9
A layman's guide to Our Lord's prayer. Nashville, The Upper room [1958] 80 p. 19 cm. [BV230.S784] 58-14095
1. Lord's Prayer. I. Title.

THOMAS, Joan Gale. 226.9
Our Father; the Lord's prayer, arranged in picture and rhyme for people who are still very young. Roman Catholic ed. New York, Lothrop, Lee & Shepard [1952] unpaged. illus. 21 cm. [BV232.T52] 52-12615
1. Lord's praryer — Juvenile literature. I. Title.

THOMAS AQUINAS, Saint, 1225?-1274. 226.9
The three greatest prayers; commentaries on the Our Father, the Hail Mary, and the Apostles' Creed. Translated by Laurence Shapcote. With an introd. by Thomas Gilby. Westminster, Md., Newman Press, 1956. vii, 89p. 20cm. [BX890.T62E6 1956] 56-13844
1. Lord's prayer—Early works to 1800. 2. Ave Maria—Early works to 1800. 3. Apostles' Creed—Early works to 1800. I. Title.

THOMAS AQUINAS, Saint, 1225?-1274. 226.9
The three greatest prayers; commentaries on the Our Father, the Hail Mary, and the Apostles' Creed. Translated by Laurence Shapcote. With an introd. by Thomas Gilby. Westminster, Md., Newman Press, 1956. vii, 89 p. 20 cm. [BX890.T62E6 1956] 56-13844
1. Lord's prayer — Early works to 1800. 2. Ave Maria — Early works to 1800. 3. Apostles' Creek — Early works to 1800. I. Title.

VANDEUR, Eugene, 1875- 226.9
Living the Lord's prayer. Translated by M. Angeline Bouchard. St. Louis, Herder [1961] 192 p. 21 cm. Translation of L'abandon a Dieu voie de la paix. [BV230.V283] 61-12116
1. Lord's prayer — Meditations. I. Title.

VANDEUR, Eugene, Dom, 1875- 226.9
Living the Lord's prayer. Tr. [from French] by M. Angeline Bouchard. St. Louis, B. Herder [c.1961] 192p. 61-12116 3.75
1. Lord's prayer.—Meditations. I. Title.

VEUTHEY, Leon. 226.9
The Our Father; translated by James Meyer. Chicago, Franciscan Herald Press [1955] 92p. 20cm. (Franciscan spirituality, no.2) Translation of Le Notre Pere des ames Interieures. [BV230.V455] 55-5745
1. Lords's prayer. I. Title.

VICEDOM, Georg F. 226'.9
A prayer for the world; the Lord's Prayer, a prayer for mission [by] Georg F. Vicedom. Tr. by Edward and Marie Schroeder. St. Louis, Concordia [1967] v, 168p. 21cm. Tr. of Gebet fur die Welt. Bibl. [BV230.V5] 67-18122 2.95 pap.,
1. Lord's prayer. I. Title.

VICEDOM, Georg F. 226'.9
A prayer for the world; the Lord's Prayer, a prayer for mission [by] Georg F. Vicedom. Translated by Edward and Marie Schroeder. St. Louis, Concordia Pub. House [1967] v. 168 p. 21 cm. Translation of Gebet fur die Weit. Bibliography: p. 167-168. [BV230.V5] 67-18122
1. Lord's prayer. I. Title.

LORD'S prayer. English. 226'.9'00222
The Lord's prayer. Pictures by George Kraus. [New York] Windmill Books [1970] [30] p. col. illus. 11 x 14 cm. The text of the Lord's Prayer accompanied by fifteen illustrations of Amish life. [BV232.K7] 78-107273 2.95
1. Lord's prayer—Juvenile literature. I. Kraus, George, 1909- illus.

A monk of the Eastern Church. 226'.9'009
The Prayer of Jesus; its genesis, development, and practice in the Byzantine-Slavic religious tradition [by] a monk of the Eastern Church. Translated from the 4th French ed. By a monk of the Western Church. New York, Desclee Co.[1967] 124 p. 20 cm. Bibliographical footnotes. [BV230.P6813] 67-17677
1. Lord's prayer. I. A monk of the Western Church, tr. II. Title.

PRAYER of Jesus (The); 226'.9'009
its genesis, development, and practice in the Byzantine-Slavic religious tradition [by] a monk of the Eastern Church. Tr. from the 4th French ed. By a monk of the Western Church. New York, Desclee [1967] 124p. 20 cm. Bibl. [BV230.P6813] 67-17677 2.95
1. Lord's prayer. I. A monk of the Eastern Church. II. A monk of the Western Church, tr.

SERMON on the Mount. English. 226.9'05203
The Sermon on the Mount, being the fifth, sixth & seventh chapters of the Gospel according to St. Matthew in the King James version of the Holy Bible. Chicago, Monastery Hill Bindery, 1968. [21] p. 1 col. illus. 27 cm. Limited ed. issued with season's greetings by Hertzberg-New Method, inc., to commemorate their 100 years of service, 1868-1968, especially that of the Monastery Hill Bindery which was founded in 1868. [BT380.A3 1968] 76-289196

ALLEN, Charles Livingstone, 1913- 226.906
The Lord's prayer, an interpretation. [Westwood, N.J.] Revell [1963] 64 p. illus. 20 cm. "From [the author's] 'God's psychiatry.'" [BV230.A55] 63-10396
1. Lord's prayer. I. Title.

ALLEN, Charles Livingstone, 1913- 226.906
The Lord's prayer, an interpretation. [Illus. by Ismar David. Westwood, N.J.] Revell [c.1963] 64p. col. illus. 20cm. From the author's God's psychiatry. 63-10396 2.00 bds.,
1. Lord's prayer. I. Title.

ARNOLD, Eberhard, 1883-1935. 226'.9'06
Salt and light : talks and writings on the Sermon on the Mount / by Eberhard Arnold ; [edited and translated from the German by the Hutterian Society of Brothers]. 2d ed. Rifton, N.Y. : Plough Pub. House, 1977. xxvii, 309 p. ; 18 cm. [BT380.A7 1977] 77-1204 ISBN 0-87486-170-5 pbk. : 3.00
1. Sermon on the Mount. I. Title.

BARCLAY, William, lecturer in the University of Glasgow. 226'.9'06
The Beatitudes and the Lord's prayer for everyman / William Barclay. New York : Harper & Row, 1975, c1964. 256 p. ; 20 cm. Combined ed. of the author's The plain man looks at the Beatitudes, and The plain man looks at the Lord's prayer. [BT382.B369 1975] 75-9309 ISBN 0-06-060393-3 pbk. : 2.95
1. Beatitudes. 2. Lord's prayer. I. Title.

*BLAIKLOCK, E. M. 226.906
Our Lord's teaching on prayer. Grand Rapids, Mich., Zondervan [c.1964] 60p. 19cm. (49) 1.25 pap.,
I. Title.

BUSSCHE, Henri van den, 1920- 226.906
Understanding the Lord's prayer. Tr. by Charles Schaldenbrand. New York, Sheed [c.1963] 144p. 21cm. 63-8536 3.00 bds.,
1. Lord's prayer. I. Title.

CLARKSON, Edith Margaret, 1915- 226.906
Our Father; the Lord's prayer for children. Grand Rapids, Mich., Eerdmans [c.1961] 117p. illus. 61-10864 2.50 bds.,
1. Lord's prayer—Juvenile literature. I. Title.

ELLIOTT, Norman K 226.906
How to be the Lord's prayer. [Westwood, N.J.] Revell [1964] 127 p. 21 cm. [BV230.E4] 64-16605
I. Title.

ELLIOTT, Norman K. 226.906
How to be the Lord's prayer [Westwood, N. J.] Revell [c.1964] 127p. 21cm. 64-16605 2.50
1. Lord's prayer. I. Title.

FISHER, Fred L. 226'.9'06
The Sermon on the mount / Fred L. Fisher. Nashville : Broadman Press, c1976. 154 p. ; 22 cm. Includes bibliographical references. [BT380.2.F545] 75-8373 ISBN 0-8054-1355-3 bds. : 5.95
1. Sermon on the mount.

GIVE us this day; 226'.9'06
a boy learns the meaning of the Lord's Prayer. Narrated and illustrated by Jussi Aarnio [and others. English language ed. Camden, N.J.] T. Nelson [1970] [73] p. illus. (part col.) 36 cm. Through his adventures with the stray cat he adopts, a young boy discovers the meaning of the Lord's Prayer. [BV232.G59] 74-127070 4.95
1. Lord's prayer—Juvenile literature. I. Aarnio, Jussi.

KISSINGER, Warren S., 226'.9'06
1922-
The Sermon on the Mount : a history of interpretation and bibliography / by Warren S. Kissinger. Metuchen, N.J. : Scarecrow Press, 1975. xiii, 296 p. ; 22 cm. (ATLA bibliography series ; no. 3) Includes indexes. Part II was developed and greatly expanded from the bibliography and books of the late W. Harold Row. [BT380.2.K5 1975] 75-29031 ISBN 0-8108-0843-9 : 12.50
1. Sermon on the Mount. 2. Sermon on the mount—Bibliography. 3. Beatitudes—Bibliography. I. Title. II. Series: American Theological Library Association. ATLA bibliography series ; no. 3.

LOWE, John, 1899-1960 226.906
The Lord's prayer. Oxford, Clarendon Pr. [dist. New York, Oxford, c.]1962. 68p. 19cm. 63-1294 1.60
1. Lord's prayer. I. Title.

LUTHI, Walter, 1901- 226.906
The Lord's prayer, an exposition. Tr. by Kurt Schoenenberger. Richmond, Va., John Knox Pr. [c.1961] 103p. 62-7170 2.50 bds.,
1. Lord's prayer. I. Title.

MARITAIN, Raissa. 226.906
Notes on the Lord's prayer. Foreword by Thomas Merton. New York, P. J. Kenedy [1964] 122 p. 21 cm. Bibliographical footnotes. [BV230.M293] 64-13204
1. Lord's prayer. I. Title.

MATTHEWS, Walter Robert 226.906
The Lord's prayer; an exposition for today. New York, Morehouse-Barlow Co. [1960, c.1958] 59p. 19cm. 'A series of short essays on the Lord's prayer which appeared in the Daily telegraph in the autumn of 1958.' 60-50287 .85 pap.,
1. Lord's prayer. I. Title.

SCHURMANN, Heinz. 226.906
Praying with Christ; the "Our Father" for today. [Translated by William Michael Ducey and Alphonse Simon. New York] Herder and Herder [1964] vi, 140, [1] p. 21 cm. Translation of Das Gebet des Herrn. Bibliographical references included in "Notes" (p. 109-[141]) [BV230.S36] 63-21841
1. Lord's prayer. I. Title.

SCHURMANN, Heinz 226.906
Praying with Christ; the 'Our Father' for today. [Tr. from German by William Michael Ducey, Alphonse Simon. New York] Herder & Herder [c.1964] vi, 140, [1]p. 21cm. Bibl. 63-21841 3.50
1. Lord's prayer. I. Title.

SCOTT, Ernest Findlay, 226.906
1868-1954
The Lord's prayer; its character, purpose, and interpretation. New York, Scribners [1962, c.1951] vii, 126p. (Scribner lib. SL-59) 1.25 pap.,
1. Lord's prayer. I. Title.

SUTPHIN, Wyn Blair. 226.906
Thine the glory. [Sermons] Foreword by Norman Victor Hope. [1st ed.] New York, Dutton, 1962. 121 p. 20 cm. [BV230.S85] 62-9127
1. Lord's prayer—Sermons. 2. Presbyterian Church—Sermons. 3. Sermons, American. I. Title.

SUTPHIN, Wyn Blair 226.906
Thine the glory. [Sermons] Foreword by Norman Victor Hope. New York, Dutton [c.] 1962. 121p. 62-9127 3.00
1. Lord's prayer—Sermons. 2. Presbyterian Church—Sermons. 3. Sermons, American. I. Title.

*THIELICKE, Helmut. 226.906
Our heavenly Father; sermons on the Lord's prayer. Translated [from the German] with an introduction by John W. Doberstein. Grand Rapids, Mich., Baker Book House [1974, c1960] 157 p, 20 cm. (Minister's paperback library) [BV233] 60-11788 ISBN 0-8010-8814-3 2.95 (pbk.)
1. Lord's prayer—Sermons. 2. Lutheran Church—Sermons. 3. Sermons, English—Translations from German. 4. Sermons, German—Translations into English. I. Title.

THIELICKE, Helmut, 1908- 226.906
Our Heavenly Father; sermons on the Lord's prayer. Translated with an introd. by John W. Doberstein. [1st American ed.] New York, Harper [1960] 157 p. 22 cm. Translation of Das Gebet, das die Welt umspaunt. [BV230.T453] 60-11788
1. Lord's prayer — Sermons. 2. Lutheran Church — Sermons. 3. Sermons, English — Translations from German. 4. Sermons, German — Translations into English. I. Title.

AUGUSTINUS, Aurelius, 226'.9'066
Saint, Bp. of Hippo.
The preaching of Augustine; "Our Lord's Sermon on the mount". Edited and with an introd. by Jaroslav Pelikan. Translated by Francine Cardman. Philadelphia, Fortress Press [1973] xxi, 186 p. 18 cm. (The Preacher's paperback library, 13) Translation of De Sermone Domini in monte. Includes bibliographical references. [BT380.A8513] 72-87061 ISBN 0-8006-4012-8 3.75 (pbk.)
1. Sermon on the Mount. I. Cardman, Francine, tr. II. Title.

BOICE, James 226'.9'07
Montgomery, 1938-
The Sermon on the Mount; an exposition. Grand Rapids, Zondervan Pub. House [1972] 328 p. 23 cm. Includes bibliographical references. [BT380.2.B56] 72-83882 5.95
1. Sermon on the Mount.

LEWIS, Donald Earle 226.907
Prayer power; living the Lord's prayer. [Westwood, N.J.] Revell [c.1960] 64p. 20cm. (2p. bibl. notes) 60-8455 1.50 bds.,
1. Lord's prayer. I. Title.

O'DONNELL, Clement Maria. 226.907
St. Cyprian on the Lord's prayer. Washington, CatholicUniversity of America Press, 1960. xv, 52p. 23cm. (Catholic University of America. Studies in sacred theology, 2d ser., no. 124A) Abstract of thesis Catholic University of America. Bibliography: p. x-xv. [Hbv230.O3] 61-2605
1. Lord's prayer—Early works to 1800. 2. Cyprianus, Saint. Bp. of Carthage. De Dominica oratione. I. Title. II. Series: Catholic University of America. School of Sacred Theology. Studies in sacred theology, 2d ser., no. 124A

PENTECOST, J. Dwight. 226'.9'07
Design for living : the Sermon on the mount / by J. Dwight Pentecost. Chicago : Moody Press, [1975] 208 p. ; 22 cm. [BT382.P44] 75-12818 ISBN 0-8024-2128-8 : 5.95
1. Sermon on the mount. I. Title.

SIKORSKY, Igor Ivan, 226.907
1889-
The message of the Lord's prayer. [New York] I. Obolensky [1963] 87 p. 22 cm. [BV230.S43 1963] 63-20482
1. Lord's prayer. I. Title.

SOCKMAN, Ralph 226.907
Washington, 1889-
The Lord's prayer; an interpretation. Design and illus. by Jean Penland. New York, Abingdon Press [c1962] unpaged. illus. 19 cm. [BV233.S62 1962] 62-14669
1. Lord's prayer. I. Title.

SOCKMAN, Ralph 226.907
Washington, 1889-
The Lord's prayer; an interpretation. Design, illus. by Jean Penland. Nashville, Abingdon [1963, c.1947, 1962] unpaged. col. illus. 19cm. 62-14669 1.50
1. Lord's prayer. I. Title.

WHISTON, Charles Francis, 226.907
1900-
When ye pray, say Our Father; a devotional study of the Lord's prayer. Boston, Pilgrim Press [1960] 117 p. 19 cm. [BV230.W45] 60-13349
1. Lord's prayer. I. Title.

WHISTON, Charles Francis, 226.907
1900-
When ye pray, say Our Father; a devotional study of the Lord's prayer. Boston, Pilgrim Press [c.1960] 117p. 60-13349 1.35 pap.,
I. Title.

READ, David Haxton 226'.9'077
Carswell.
Holy common sense; the Lord's prayer for today [by] David H. C. Read. Nashville, Abingdon Press [1968] 96 p. 20 cm. [BV230.R32] 68-11466
1. Lord's prayer. I. Title.

SANDERS, John Oswald, 226'.9'077
1902-
Real discipleship; a devotional exposition of the Sermon on the Mount [by] J. Oswald Sanders. Grand Rapids, Zondervan Pub. House [1973, c1972] 160 p. 18 cm. London ed. published under title: The world's greatest sermon. Includes bibliographies. [BT380.2.S26 1972] 73-2653 1.25 (pbk.)
1. Sermon on the Mount. I. Title.

BIBLE. N.T. James. 226.91
English. 1954. Johnstone
Lectures, exegetical and practical, on the Epistle of James; with a new translation of the Epistle and notes on the Greek text, by Robert Johnstone. Grand Rapids, Baker Book House, 1954. 433p. 21cm. [Co-operative reprint library] Cover title: The Epistle of James. [BS2785.J6 1954] 54-2944
1. Bible. N. T. James—Commentaries. I. Johnstone, Robert professor in United Presbyterian College of Edinburgh. II. Title.

BARBIERI, Louis A. 226'.92'07
First and Second Peter / by Louis A. Barbieri. Chicago : Moody Press, c1977. 126 p. ; 19 cm. (Everyman's Bible commentary) Bibliography: p. 126. [BS2795.3.B29 1977] 76-53760 ISBN 0-8024-2061-3 pbk. : 1.95
1. Bible. N.T. Peter—Commentaries. I. Title. II. Series.

BARRETT, George West. 226'.93
Christ's keys to happiness, by George W. Barrett. New York, World Pub. Co. [1970] 60 p. 21 cm. (World inspirational books) [BT382.B3694 1970] 74-131560
1. Beatitudes—Meditations. I. Title.

*LAWLOR, George L. 226.93
The beatitudes are for today; an exposition of Mathew 5:1-16, by George L. Lawlor. Grand Rapids, Baker Book House, [1974]. 131 p. 22 cm. [BT382] ISBN 0-8010-5541-5. 2.95 (pbk.)
1. Beatitudes. I. Title.

MURPHY, Charles. 226'.93
Blessed are you; beatitudes for modern man. [New York] Herder and Herder [1971] 110 p. 21 cm. Includes bibliographical references. [BT382.M87] 74-146301 4.50
1. Beatitudes. I. Title.

MARY Francis, Mother, 226'.93'06
1921-
Blessed are you / by Mother Mary Francis. St. Bonaventure, N.Y. : Franciscan Institute of St. Bonaventure University, c1976. vii, 84 p. ; 23 cm. Includes bibliographical references. [BT382.M288] 76-6815
1. Beatitudes. I. Title.

VAN DOLSON LEO R. 226'.93'06
God's footprint on my floor / by Leo R. Van Dolson. Nashville : Southern Pub. Association, c1977. 124 p. ; 20 cm. (Horizon) [BT382.V28] 76-56996 ISBN 0-8127-0132-1 pbk. : 4.95
1. Beatitudes. 2. Christian life—Seventh-Day Adventist authors. I. Title.

WIERSBE, Warren W. 226'.93'06
Live like a king : making the Beatitudes work in daily life / by Warren W. Wiersbe. Chicago : Moody Press, c1976. 159 p. ; 22 cm. [BT382.W53] 76-17576 ISBN 0-8024-4908-5 : 4.95
1. Beatitudes. I. Title.

ALLEN, R. Earl. 226'.93'066
Divine dividends; an inspirational reading of the Sermon on the mount [by] R. Earl Allen. Nashville, T. Nelson [1974] 160 p. 21 cm. [BT382.A42] 74-4474
1. Beatitudes—Sermons. 2. Baptists—Sermons. 3. Sermons, American. I. Title.

AUGSBURGER, Myron S. 226'.93'066
The expanded life [by] Myron S. Augsburger. Nashville, Abingdon Press [1972] 127 p. 20 cm. [BT382.A9] 72-689 ISBN 0-687-12419-0 3.25
1. Beatitudes. 2. Christian life—Mennonite authors. I. Title.

LOVETTE, Roger, 1935- 226'.93'066
For the dispossessed. Philadelphia, United Church Press [1973] 127 p. 22 cm. "A Pilgrim Press book." Includes bibliographical references. [BT382.L68] 73-12511 ISBN 0-8298-0258-4 4.95
1. Beatitudes—Sermons. I. Title.

WATSON, Thomas, 226'.93'066
d.1686.
The Beatitudes: an exposition of Matthew 5: 1-12. New ed., revised in layout. London, Banner of Truth Trust, 1971. 307 p. 23 cm. Originally published, London, 1660. [BS2575.2.W35 1971] 74-26846 ISBN 0-85151-035-3 £1.20
1. Beatitudes. 2. Bible. N.T. Matthew V, 1-12—Criticism, interpretation, etc. I. Title.

CANDLISH, Robert Smith, 226.94
1806-1873.
The First epistle of John. Grand Rapids, Mich., Zondervan Pub. House [1952] 577p. 23cm. First ed. published in 1866 under title: The First epistle of John expounded in a series of lectures. [BS2805.C3 1952] 53-3954
1. Bible. N. T. I John—Commentaries. I. Title.

FROHLICH, Samuel Heinrich, 226.94
1803-1857.
Meditations on the Epistles of John; meditations delivered in Zurich in the years 1840-1842. New York, Carlton Press [1963] v. 21 cm. (A Reflection book) Extracts of sermons on the three Epistles of John taken from [the author's] diary and translated from the German. [BS2805.4.F7 1963] 63-6420
1. Bible. N. T. Epistles of John — Sermons. I. Title.

FROHLICH, Samuel Heinrich, 226.94
1803-1857.
Meditations on the Epistles of John: meditations delivered in Zurich in the years 1840-1842. New York, Carlton [c.1963] 272p. 21cm. (Reflection bk.) Extracts of sermons on the three Epistles of John taken from [the author's [diary and tr. from German 63-6420 3.00
1. Bible. N. T. Epistles of John—Sermons. I. Title.

COBURN, John B. 226'.96
Deliver us from evil : the prayer of our Lord / John B. Coburn ; photos. by Ray Ellis. New York : Seabury Press, c1976. 93 p. : ill. ; 23 cm. "A Crossroad book." [BV230.C65] 76-20198 ISBN 0-8164-2124-2 pbk. : 4.95
1. Lord's prayer. I. Title.

DAVIDSON, John A., 1919- 226'.96
The Lord's prayer, by John A. Davidson. New York, World Pub. Co. [1970] 60 p. 21 cm. (World inspirational books) Includes bibliographical references. [BV230.D27 1970] 78-131561
1. Lord's prayer.

CROSBY, Michael, 226'.96'066
1940-
Thy will be done : praying the Our Father as subversive activity / Michael H. Crosby. Maryknoll, N.Y. : Orbis Books, c1977. p. cm. Includes bibliographical references. [BV230.C76] 77-5118 ISBN 0-88344-496-8 : 8.95
1. Lord's prayer. I. Title.

HARNER, Philip B. 226'.96'066
Understanding the Lord's prayer / Philip B. Harner. Philadelphia : Fortress Press, c1975. x, 149 p. ; 22 cm. Includes bibliographical references and indexes. [BV230.H39] 75-13035 ISBN 0-8006-1213-2 : 4.25
1. Lord's prayer. I. Title. II. Title: The Lord's prayer.

LOMASNEY, Eileen. 226'.96'07
My book of the Lord's prayer / by Eileen Lomasney ; art by Alice Hausner. St. Louis : Concordia Pub. House, c1976. [31] p. : col. ill. ; 26 cm. Includes text of the Lord's prayer. Text and rhyming commentary of the Lord's Prayer. [BV232.L58] 76-2707 ISBN 0-570-03456-6 : 4.95
1. Lord's prayer—Juvenile literature. I. Hausner, Alice. II. Lord's prayer. English. 1976. III. Title.

KELLER, Weldon 226'.96'077
Phillip, 1920-
A layman looks at the Lord's prayer / by W. Phillip Keller. Chicago : Moody Press, c1976. 155 p. ; 22 cm. [BV230.K36] 75-31635 ISBN 0-8024-4643-4 : 4.95
1. Lord's prayer. I. Title.

SHEED, Francis 226'.96'077
Joseph, 1897-
The Lord's prayer : the prayer of Jesus / F. J. Sheed ; photos. by Catherine Hughes. New York : Seabury Press, c1975. 92 p. : ill. ; 23 cm. "A Crossroad book." [BV230.S4] 75-13521 ISBN 0-8164-2597-3 : 4.95
1. Lord's prayer. I. Title.

227 Epistles

AMIOT, Francois 227
The key concepts of St. Paul. [Tr. by John Dingle. New York] Herder & Herder [c.1944, 1962] 297p. 21cm. Bibl. 61-17458 4.95

1. Salvation. 2. Bible. N. T. Epistles of Paul—Theology I. Title.

ANDERSON, Bernhard W ed. 227
The Old Testament and Christian faith; a theological discussion. [1st ed.] New York, Harper & Row [c1963] xii, 271 p. 22 cm. Bibliography: p. 265-266. [BS2387.A6] 63-15952
1. Bible. N.T. — Relation to O.T. 2. Bible. O. T. — Use. I. Title.

BEARE, Francis Wright, 1902- 227
St. Paul and his letters. London, A. & C. Black [1962] 152 p. 24 cm. [BS2650.3.B4] 63-414
1. Bible. N. T. Epistles of Paul — Commentaries. I. Title.

BIBLE. N. T. Epistles. 227
English. 1956. Laubach.
The inspired letters, in clearest English. Prepared by Frank C. Laubach. New York, T. Nelson [1956] 221p. 19cm. [BS2633.L36] 56-7958
I. Laubach, Frank Charles, 1884- ed. II. Title.

BIBLE. N. T. Epistles. 227
English. 1957. Phillips.
Letters to young churches; a translation of the New Testament Epistles, by J. B. Phillips. With an introd. by C. S. Lewis. New York, Macmillan, 1957. xiv, 225p. map (on lining paper) 22cm. [BS2633.P5 1957] 57-12598
I. Phillips, John Bertram, 1906- tr. II. Title.

BIBLE, N. T. Epistles. 227
English. 1957. Phillips.
Letters to young churches; a translation of the New Testament Epistles, by J. B. Phillips. With an introd. by C. S. Lewis. New York, Macmillan 1960[c.1947, 1957] 225p. (Macmillan paperbacks 28) 1.25 pap.,
I. Phillips, John Bertram, 1960- tr. II. Title.

BIBLE. N.T. Epistles. 227
English. 1957. Phillips.
Letters to young churches; a translation of the New Testament Epistles, by J. B. Phillips. With an introd. by C. S. Lewis. New York, Macmillan, 1957. xiv, 225 p. map (on lining paper) 22 cm. [BS2633.P5 1957] 57-12598
I. Phillips, John Bertram, 1906- tr. II. Title.

BIBLE. N.T. Epistles of Paul. 227
English. Barclay. 1975.
The letters to the Philippians, Colossians, and Thessalonians / translated with an introd. and interpretation by William Barclay. Rev. ed. Philadelphia : Westminster Press, c1975. xv, 219 p. ; 20 cm. (The Daily study Bible series. — Rev. ed.) [BS2643.B37 1975] 75-26525 ISBN 0-664-24110-7 pbk. : 3.45
1. Bible. N.T. Philippians—Commentaries. 2. Bible. N.T. Colossians—Commentaries. 3. Bible. N.T. Thessalonians—Commentaries. I. Barclay, William, lecturer in the University of Glasgow. II. Title. III. Series.

BIBLE. N.T. Epistles of Paul. 227
English. Selections. 1973.
The wisdom of Paul. [Compiled by Rudolph F. Norden] St. Louis, Concordia Pub. House [1973] 64 p. 18 cm. [BS2643.N67 1973] 73-78852 ISBN 0-570-03165-6 0.75 (pbk.)
I. Norden, Rudolph F., comp. II. Title.

BRANDT, R. L. 227
Praying with Paul, by R. L. Brandt. Grand Rapids, Baker Book House [1966] 106 p. 20 cm. [BV210.2.B7] 66-18316
1. Prayer. I. Title.

BRANDT, R. L. 227
Praying with Paul, by R. L. Brandt. Grand Rapids, Baker Bk. [1966] 106p. 20cm. [BV210.2.B7] 66-18316 2.50
1. Prayer. I. Title.

BROX, Norbert, 1935- 227
Understanding the message of Paul. Translated by Joseph Blenkinsopp. Notre Dame [Ind.] University of Notre Dame Press [1968] 138 p. 18 cm. (Contemporary catechics series) Translation of Paulus und seine Verkundigung. Includes bibliographical references. [BS2651.B6813] 68-14141
1. Bible. N.T. Epistles of Paul—Theology. I. Title.

BULLOUGH, Sebastian. 227
Saint Paul and apostolic writings; with a foreword by the Cardinal Archbishop of Westminster. Westminster, Md., Newman Press, 1950. xviii, 338 p. 19 cm. (Scripture textbooks for Catholic schools, v, 6) Bibliography: p. xii-xv. [BS2636.B8] 50-8385
1. Bible. N. T. Epistles and Revelation—Study—Text-books. I. Title. II. Series.

CAIRD, George Bradford. 227
Paul's letters from prison : Ephesians, Philippians, Colossians, Philemon, in the Revised standard version / introd. and commentary by G. B. Caird. Oxford : Oxford University Press, 1976. 223 p. ; 19 cm. (The New Clarendon Bible) "The actual text of the letters is not included." Includes index. Bibliography: p. [7]-8. [BS2650.3.C28] 76-368451 ISBN 0-19-836919-0 : 10.50
1. Bible. N.T. Ephesians—Commentaries. 2. Bible. N.T. Philippians—Commentaries. 3. Bible. N.T. Colossians—Commentaries. 4. Bible. N.T. Philemon—Commentaries. I. Title. II. Series.
Distributed by Oxford, New York.

DE WITT, Norman Wentworth, 227
1876-
St. Paul and Epicurus. Minneapolis, University of Minnesota Press [1954] 201p. 24cm. Sequel to Epicurus and his philosophy. [BS2651.D4] 54-12314
1. Paul, Saint, apostle. 2. Epicurus. 3. Bible. N. T. Epistles of Paul—Theology. I. Title.

DODD, Charles Harold, 1884- 227
The Old Testament in the New. Philadelphia, Fortress Press [1963] x, 33 p. 19 cm. (Facet books. Biblical series, 3) Bibliography: p. 31-32 [BS2387.D58 1963] 63-17880
1. Bible. O.T. — Quotations in the N.T. I. Title. II. Series.

*DOTY, Brant Lee 227
The apostle Paul: study course for youth and adults. Cincinnati, Ohio, Standard c.1964 112p. 22cm. (Training for service ser.) 1.25 pap.,
I. Title.

ELLIS, Edward Earle. 227
Paul's use of the Old Testament. Edinburgh, Oliver and Boyd [1957] xii, 204p. 23cm. Bibliographical footnotes. [BS2387.E5] 57-3758
1. Bible. N. T. Epistles of Paul-Relation to O. T. 2. Bible. O. T.-Use. I. Title.

ELLIS, Edward Earle. 227
Paul's use of the Old Testament. Grand Rapids, W. B. Eerdmans Pub. Co., 1957. xii, 204p. 23cm. Bibliographical footnotes. [BS2387.E5 1957a] 57-14160
1. Bible. N. T. Epistles of Paul-Relation to O. T. 2. Bible. O. T.-Use. I. Title.

ENSLEY, Francis Gerald, Bp. 227
Paul's letters to local churches. [New York, 1956] 175p. illus. 29 cm. [BS2650.E65] 56-7572
1. Paul, Saint, apostle. 2. Bible. N. T. Epistles of Paul—Criticism, interpretation, etc. 3. Bible, N. T. Epistles of Paul—Theology. I. Title.

FIELDS, Wilbur. 227
Philippians-Colossians-Philemon; a new commentary, workbook, teaching manual. Joplin, Mo., College Press [1969] x, 279 p. illus., map. 23 cm. (Bible study textbook series) [BS2705.5.F5] 78-8763 4.95
1. Bible. N.T. Philippians—Study—Outlines, syllabi, etc. 2. Bible. N.T. Colossians—Study—Outlines, syllabi, etc. 3. Bible. N.T. Philemon—Study—Outlines, syllabi, etc. I. Title.

FUCHS, Emanuel, 1902- 227
Speak, Lord. Tripoli, Iowa, Crane Creek Press [1951] 200 p. 21 cm. [BS2635.F8] 51-33896
1. Bible. N.T. Epistles—Introductions. I. Title.

FURNISH, Victor Paul. 227
Theology and ethics in Paul. Nashville, Abingdon Press [1968] 304 p. 23 cm. Bibliography: p. 280-294. [BS2655.E8F8] 68-17445
1. Bible. N.T. Epistles of Paul—Ethics. I. Title.

GIBLIN, Charles Homer. 227
In hope of God's glory; Pauline theological perspectives. [New York] Herder and Herder [1970] xv, 424 p. maps. 22 cm. Bibliography: p. 407-416. [BS2651.G5] 78-127875 13.50
1. Bible. N.T. Epistles of Paul—Theology. I. Title.

GROSSOUW, Willem Karel Maria, 227
1906-
In Christ a sketch of the theology of Saint Paul translated and edited from the 2d rev Dutch ed by Martin W Schoenberg Westminster, Md., Newman Press, 1952. 138p. 21cm. [BS2651.G753] 52-10389
1. Bible. N. T. Epistles of Paul— Theology. I. Title.

*HOGG, Charles F. 227'.
The Epistle to the Galatians, with notes exegetical and expository, by C. F. Hogg, W. E. Vine. Grand Rapids, Kregel [1967] viii, 352p. 23cm. First pub. 1921. [BS2685.H6 1967] 81'07 67-9445 4.50
1. Bible. N.T. Galations— Commentaries. I. Vine,William Edwy. 1873-1949, joint author. II. Title.

HOULDEN, James Leslie. 227
Paul's letters from prison: Philippians, Colossians, Philemon and Ephesians [by] J. L. Houlden. Harmondsworth, Penguin, 1970. 357 p. 18 cm. (Pelican New Testament commentaries) (Pelican books) Includes the Revised standard text of the Epistles. [BS2650.3.H65] 79-22824 ISBN 0-14-021198-5 10/- ($2.65 U.S.)
1. Bible. N.T. Epistles of Paul—Commentaries. I. Bible. N.T. Epistles of Paul. English. Revised standard. 1970. II. Title.

HUNTER, Archibald Macbride. 227
The gospel according to St. Paul, by Archibald M. Hunter. Rev. ed. Philadelphia, Westminster Press [1967, c1966] 126 p. 19 cm. Previous editions published under title: Interpreting Paul's gospel. Includes bibliographical footnotes. [BS2651.H78 1967] 67-10511
1. Bible. N.T. Epistles of Paul—Theology. I. Title.

HUNTER, Archibald Macbride. 227
Interpreting Paul's gospel. Philadelphia, Westminster Press [1955?] 144 p. 21 cm. (The James Sprunt lectures, 1954) [BS2651.H78] 55-5023
1. Bible. N.T. Epistles of Paul—Theology. I. Title.

HUNTER, John Edward, 1909- 227
Faith and courage for today; writings of faith and encouragement; daily devotions and Bible studies, by John Hunter. Glendale, Calif., G/L Regal Books [1968] 131 p. 18 cm. Bibliography: p. 131. [BS2629.H8] 68-28901
1. Bible. N.T. Epistles and Revelation—Study—Outlines, syllabi, etc. 2. Devotional exercises. I. Title.

JORDAN, Clarence. 227
The cotton patch version of Paul's Epistles. New York, Association Press [1968] 158 p. 22 cm. (A Koinonia publication) A colloquial modern translation with a Southern accent, based on the Nestle-Aland Greek text, 23d ed., 1957. [BS2643.J67] 68-11487
1. Bible. N.T. Epistles of Paul—Paraphrases, English. I. Title.

KEITH, Noel Leonard. 227
Paul's message for today; echoes from William C. Morro & Granville T. Walker, by Noel Keith. Fort Worth, Texas Christian University Press [1970] xv, 103 p. 21 cm. (Texas Christian University. Monographs in religion, no. 1) Bibliography: p. 95-96. [BS2651.K43] 71-127431
1. Bible. N.T. Epistles of Paul—Theology. I. Morro, William Charles, 1871-1943. II. Walker, Granville T. III. Title. IV. Series: Texas Christian University, Fort Worth. Monographs in religion, no. 1

KELLER, Edmund B. 227
Some paradoxes of Paul / by Edmund B. Keller. New York : Philosophical Library, [1974] xi, 263 p. ; 22 cm. Originally presented as the author's thesis, Boston University. Bibliography: p. 207-229. [BS2652.K44 1974] 74-75085 ISBN 0-8022-2144-0 : 8.50
1. Paul, Saint, apostle. 2. Bible. N.T. Epistles of Paul—Theology. 3. Paradox. I. Title.

KEPLER, Thomas Samuel, 1897- 227
comp.
Contemporary thinking about Paul, an anthology. New York, Abingdon-Cokesbury Press [1950] 442 p. 24 cm. Bibliography: p. 419-422. [BS2505.K37] 50-5469
1. Paul, Saint, apostle. 2. Bible. N. T. Epistles of Paul—Criticism, interpretation, etc. I. Title.

KINSEY, Robert S 227
With Paul in Greece. Nashville, Parthenon Press [1957] 208p. illus. 21cm. Includes bibliography. [BS2505.K48] 57-59249
1. Paul, Saint, apostle. 2. Bible. N. T. Epistles of Paul—Criticism, 3. Greece, Modern—Descr. & trav.—1951- I. Title.

KNOX, Ronald Arbuthnott, 227
1888-
St. Paul's gospel. New York, Sheed & Ward, 1950. 72 p. 20 cm. [BS2651.K63 1950a] 51-1983
1. Bible. N. T. Epistles of Paul—Theology. 2. Paul, Saint, apostle. I. Title.

LAWLER, Brendan, 1909- 227
The Epistles in focus. New York, P. J. Kenedy [1954] 165p. illus. 23cm. [BS2618.L3] 54-6167
1. Bible. N. T. Acts and Epistles—Introductions. I. Title.

LOANE, Marcus L. 227
Three letters from prison; studies in Ephesians, Colossians and Philemon [by] Marcus L. Loane. Waco, Tex., Word Books [1972] 157 p. 23 cm. Bibliography: p. 156-157. [BS2695.2.L6] 79-160300 4.95
1. Bible. N.T. Ephesians—Criticism, interpretation, etc. 2. Bible. N.T. Colossians—Criticism, interpretation, etc. 3. Bible. N.T. Philemon—Criticism, interpretation, etc. I. Title.

LUCCOCK, Halford Edward, 227
1885-
More preaching values in the Epistles of Paul v.2. New York, Harper [c.1961] 255p. Contents.vol. 2. Second Corinthians, Galatians, Philippians, Colossians. 61-12828 3.95 bds.,
1. Bible. N.T. Epistles of Paul—Homiletical use. I. Title.

LUCCOCK, Halford Edward, 227
1885-
Preaching values in the Epistles of Paul. [1st ed.] New York, Harper [1959-61] 2v. 22cm. Vol. 2 has title: More preaching values in the Epistles of Paul. Contents.v. 1. Romans and First Corinthians--v. 2. Second Corinthians, Galatians, Philippians, Colossians. [BS2650.4.L8] 61-12828
1. Bible. N. T. Epistles of Paul—Homlletical use. I. Title. II. Title: More preaching values in the Epistles of Paul.

MCCUMBER, W. E. 227
Holiness in the prayers of St. Paul. Kansas City, Mo., Beacon Hill Press [1955] 121p. 20cm. [BS2655.H6M3] 55-14591
1. Holiness—Biblical teaching. 2. Bible. N. T. Epistles of Paul—Theology. I. Title.

MANSON, Thomas Walter, 1893- 227
1958
On Paul and John. some selected theological themes. Ed. by Matthew Black. Naperville. Ill., Allenson [c.1963] 168p. 22cm. (Studies in Biblical theology. no. 38) Bibl. 63-5688 2.85 pap.,
1. Bible. N. T. Epistles of Paul—Theology. 2. Bible. N. T. Johannine literature—Theology. 3. Jesus Christ—History of doctrines—Early church. I. Title.

MICHELS, Florence. 227
Paul and the law of love. Milwaukee, Bruce Pub. Co. [1967] xiv, 151 p. 23 cm. Bibliography: p. 143-148. [BS2655.E8M5] 67-30099
1. Bible. N. T. Epistles of Paul—Ethics. 2. Christian ethics—Catholic authors. I. Title.

MICHELS, Florence. 227
Paul and the law of love. Milwaukee, Bruce Pub. Co. [1967] xiv, 151 p. 23 cm. Bibliography: p. 143-148. [BS2655.E8M5] 67-30099
1. Bible. N.T. Epistles of Paul—Ethics. 2. Christian ethics—Catholic authors. I. Title.

*PAUL, Saint 227
Saint Paul [selections from his writings. Introd. by] Jacques Maritain. New York, McGraw [1965, c.1941] 161p. 19cm. 1.95 pap.,
I. Title.

RICHARDS, Lawrence O. 227
The great adventure : the first days of the church : studies in Acts, James, Galatians, and Romans / Larry Richards. Leader's ed. Elgin, Ill. : D. C. Cook Pub. Co., c1977. 252 p. ; 22 cm. (His Bible alive series) [BS2626.R5] 76-11474 pbk. : 3.95
1. Bible. N.T. Acts—Study—Text-books. 2. Bible. N.T. James—Study—Text-books. 3. Bible. N.T. Galatians—Study—Text-books. 4. Bible. N.T. Romans—Study—Text-books. I. Title. II. Series.

RIDDERBOS, Herman N 227
Paul and Jesus; origin and general character of Paul's preaching of Christ. Translated by David H. Freeman. Philadelphia, Presbyterian and Reformed Pub. Co., 1958 [c1957] 155p. 21cm. Includes bibliography. [BS2653.R5] 57-8807
1. Bible. N. T. Epistles of Paul—Theology. 2. Demythologization. 3. Christianity— Origin. I. Title.

RIGAUX, Beda. 227
The letters of St. Paul; modern studies. Editor and translator Stephen Yonick. Chicago, Franciscan Herald Press [1968] xviii, 272 p. 21 cm. ([Herald scriptural library]) Translation of Saint Paul et ses lettres. Bibliographical references included in "Notes" (p. 182-261) [BS2650.2.R513] 68-54395 6.95
1. Paul, Saint, apostle. 2. Bible. N.T. Epistles of Paul—Criticism, interpretation, etc. I. Title.

ROBINSON, John A T 227
The body; a study in Pauline theology. Chicago, H. Regnery Co., 1952. 95p. 22cm. (Studies in Biblical theology, no.5) Bibliographical footnotes. [BS2651.R615] 52-9987
1. Bible. N. T. Epistles of Paul—Theology. I. Title. II. Series.

ROBINSON, John Arthur Thomas, 227
Bp., 1919-
The body; a study in Pauline theology. Chicago, Regnery, 1952. 95p. 22cm. (Studies in Biblical theology, no. 5) Bibliographical footnotes. [BS2651.R615] 52-9987
1. Bible. N. T. Epistles of Paul— Theology. I. Title. II. Series.

ROLSTON, Holmes, 1900- 227
Consider Paul, apostle of Jesus Christ; revelation and inspiration in the letters of Paul. Richmond, John Knox Press [1951] 217 p. 21 cm. "References and acknowledgments": p. [195]-209. [BS2651.R63] 51-2823
1. Bible. N.T. Epistles of Paul — Theology. 2. Paul, Saint, apostle. I. Title.

ROLSTON, Holmes, 1900- 227
Stewardship in the New Testament church; a study in the teachings of Saint Paul concerning Christian stewardship. [Rev. ed.] Richmond, John Knox Press [1959] 160p. 21cm. Includes bibliography. [BS2655.S65R6 1959] 59-6078
1. Bible. N. T. Epistles of Paul—Theology. 2. Stewardship, Christian—Biblical teaching. I. Title.

SCHWEITZER, Albert, 1875- 227
Paul and his interpreters; a critical history. [Translated from the German by W. Montgomery] New York, Macmillan, 1951. xii, 252 p. 22 cm. Includes bibliographies. [BS2651.S3 1951] 51-10193
1. Paul, Saint, apostle. 2. Bible. N.T. Epistles of Paul — Criticism, interpretation, etc. — Hist. I. Title.

SCHWEITZER, Albert, 1875- 227
1965.
The mysticism of Paul the apostle. Translated into English by William Montgomery. With a prefatory note by F. C. Burkitt. New York, Macmillan, 1955 [c1931] xv, 411 p. 22 cm. [BS2655.M9S43 1955] 56-967
1. Paul, Saint, apostle. 2. Bible. N. T. Epistles of Paul—Theology. 3. Mysticism. I. Title.

SCOTT, Charles Archibald 227
Anderson, 1859-1941
Christianity according to St. Paul. by Charles A. Anderson Scott. Cambridge [Eng. The Univ. Pr. 1966. xiii, 283p. 19cm. (CAM405) Bibl. [BS2651.S35] 28-5574 5.00 1.95 pap.,
1. Paul, Saint. apostle. 2. Bible. N. T. Epistles of Paul—Theology. 3. Christianity. 4. Salvation—Biblical teaching. I. Title.
Available from Cambridge Univ. Pr., New York.

SERMONIC studies; 227
the standard epistles. Saint Louis, Concordia Pub. House [1957- v.illus. 23cm. Contents.v.1. From the first Sunday in Advent to Trinity Sunday. [BS2635.S4] 56-12707
1. Bible. N.T. Epistles and Gospels, Liturgical—Commentaries. 2. Sermons—Outlines.

SERMONIC studies; the 227
standard epistles. Saint Louis, Concordia Pub. House [1956- v. illus. 23 cm. Contents.v. 1. From the first Sunday in Advent to Trinity Sunday. [BS2635.S4] 56-12707
1. Bible. N.T. Epistles and Gospels, Liturgical — Commentaries. 2. Sermons — Outlines.

SHEPARD, John Watson, 1879- 227
The life and letters of St. Paul; an exegetical study. 1st ed. Grand Rapids, Eerdmans, 1950. 605 p. 24 cm. Bibliography: p. [601]-605. Bibliographical footnotes. [BS2650.s55] 50-11380
1. Paul, Saint, apostle. 2. Bible. N. T. Epistles of Paul—Commentaries. I. Title.

THOMPSON, George Harry 227
Packwood.
The letters of Paul to the Ephesians. to the Colossians and to Philemon: commentary by G. H. P. Thompson. London, Cambridge Univ. Pr., 1967. x, 198p. 3 maps. 21cm. (Cambridge Bible commentary: New English Bible) [BS2695.3.T46] 67-1710 1.65 pap.,
1. Bible. N. T. Ephesians—Commentaries. 2. Bible. N. T. Colossians—Commentaries. 3. Bible. N. T. Philemon—Commentaries. I. Bible. N. T. Epistles of Paul. English, 1967. II. Title.
Available from the publisher's New York office.

*TRUETT, George Washington, 227
1867-1944.
Sermons from Paul, by George W. Truett. Edited by Powhatan W. James. Grand Rapids, Mich., Baker Book House [1973, c.1947] 213 p. 20 cm. (George W. Truett library) At head of title: Vol. 11 in the Truett memorial series [BS2765.3] ISBN 0-8010-8796-1 2.95 (pbk.)
1. Paul, Saint, apostle—Sermons. I. James, Powhatan W., ed. II. Title. III. Series: Truett memorial series, v. 11

WAHLSTROM, Eric Herbert. 227
The new life in Christ. Philadelphia, Muhlenberg Press [1950] xx, 295 p. 22 cm. Bibliographical footnotes. [BS2651.W3] 50-3501
1. Bible. N.T. Epistles of Paul — Theology. I. Title.

WAND, John William Charles, 227
Bp. of London, 1885-
What St. Paul really said [by] J. W. C. Wand. New York, Schocken Books [1969, c1968] 173 p. 21 cm. (What they really said series) "Suggestions for further reading": p. 165-166. [BS2651.W33 1969b] 69-11188 4.00
1. Paul, Saint, apostle. 2. Bible. N.T. Epistles of Paul—Theology. I. Title.

WAND, John William Charles, 227
Bp of London, 1885-
What St. Paul said; or, The teaching of St. Paul. London, New York, Oxford University Press, 1952. 108 p. 21 cm. [BS2650.W36] 52-8918
1. Bible, N. T. Epistles of Paul — Introductions. I. Title.

WEED, Michael R. 227
The letters of Paul to the Ephesians, the Colossians, and Philemon [by] Michael R. Weed. Austin [Tex.] R. B. Sweet Co. [1971] 190 p. 21 cm. (The Living word commentary, 11) Includes bibliographies. [BS2765.3.W4] 79-134688 ISBN 0-8344-0055-3
1. Bible. N.T. Philemon—Commentaries. 2. Bible. N.T. Colossians—Commentaries. 3. Bible. N.T. Ephesians—Commentaries. I. Bible. N.T. Ephesians. English. Revised standard. 1971. II. Bible. N.T. Colossians. English. Revised standard. 1971. III. Bible. N.T. Philemon. English. Revised standard. 1971. IV. Title. V. Series.

WILES, Gordon P. 227
Paul's intercessory prayers; the significance of the intercessory prayer passages in the letters of St Paul [by] Gordon P. Wiles. Cambridge [Eng.] University Press [1974] xii, 351 p. 23 cm. (Society for New Testament Studies. Monograph series, 24) Based on the author's dissertation presented to the Yale University faculty in 1965, entitled The function of intercessory prayer in Paul's apostolic ministry with special reference to the First Epistle to the Thessalonians. Bibliography: 303-317. [BS2650.5.W54] 73-79310 ISBN 0-521-20274-4
1. Bible. N.T. Epistles of Paul—Prayers. I. Title. II. Series: Studiorum Novi Testament Societas. Monograph series, 24.
Distributed by Cambridge University Press, N.Y., 19.50.

WILLIAMS, Charles Bray, 1869- 227
1952.
A commentary on the Pauline Epistles. Chicago, Moody Press [1953] 507p. 24cm. [BS2650.W55] 54-43
1. Bible. N. T. Epistles of Paul—Commentaries. I. Title.

ZUNTZ, Gunther, 1902- 227
The text of the Epistles; a disquisition upon the Corpus Paulinum. London, Published for the British Academy by Oxford University Press, 1953. xvii, 295p. diagr., tables. 25cm. (The Schweich lectures of the British Academy, 1946) [BS2650.Z85] 54-1106
1. Bible. N. T. Epistles of Paul—Criticism, Textual. I. Title. II. Series: The Schwelch lectures, 1946

*NELSON, P. C. 227.'0020'2
The letters of Paul / P. C. Nelson. Springfield, Mo. : Gospel Pub House [1976]c1945. 143p. ; 22 cm. Includes bibliographical references. [BS2657] ISBN 0-88243-546-9 pbk. : 2.00
1. Bible N.T. Epistles of Paul-study. I. Title.

GETTYS, Joseph Miller, 227.007
1907-
How to study Philippians, Colossians, and Philemon. Richmond, John Knox Press [1964] 87 p. 23 cm. (How to study the Bible series) Includes bibliographies. [BS2650.5.G4] 64-11256
1. Bible. N. T. Epistles of Paul — Study — Outlines, syllabi, etc. I. Title.

GETTYS, Joseph Miller, 227.007
1907-
How to study Philippians, Colossians, and Philemon. Richmond,Va., Knox [c.1964] 87p. 23cm. (How to study the Bible ser.) Bibl. 64-11256 1.50 pap.,
1. Bible. N. T. Epistles of Paul—Study—Outlines, syllabi, etc. I. Title.

MOORE, Hight C, 1871- 227.007
1957.
From Pentecost to Patmos. Nashville, Convention Press [1959, c1934]*145p. illus. 19cm. [BS2619.M65 1959] 59-9311
1. Paul, Saint, apostle. 2. Bible. N. T. Acts and Epistles—Study—Text-books. I. Title.

SCHWEITZER, Albert, 1875- 227.007
Paul and his interpreters, a critical history [Tr. from German by W. Montgomery] New York, Schocken [1964] xiii, 255p. 21cm. (SB79) Bibl. 64-16461 1.95 pap.,
1. Paul, Saint, apostle. 2. Bible. N.T. Epistles of Paul—Criticism, interpretation, etc.—Hist. I. Title.

MORTON, Andrew Queen. 227.014
Paul, the man and the myth: a study in the authorship of Greek prose, by A. Q. Morton and James McLeman. London, Hodder & Stoughton [1966] 217 p. 54 tables, diagr. 23 1/2 cm. (B 66-15008) [BS2650.2.M6] 66-74525
1. Bible. N. T. Epistles of Paul — Authorship. 2. Greek language — Word frequency. 3. Greek language — Sentences. 4. Paul, Saint, apostel. I. McLeman, James, joint author. II. Title.

MORTON, Andrew Queen. 227'.01'4
Paul, the man and the myth; a study in the authorship of Greek prose, by A. Q. Morton and James McLeman. New York, Harper & Row [1966] 217 p. 22 cm. [BS2650.2.M6 1966] 67-10053
1. Paul, Saint, apostle. 2. Bible. N.T. Epistles of Paul—Authorship. 3. Greek language—Word frequency. 4. Greek language—Sentences. I. McLeman, James, joint author. II. Title.

MORTON, Andrew Queen 227.04
Christianity in the computer age, by A. Q. Morton, James McLeman. New York, Harper [1965, c.1964] 95p. 20cm. First pub. under title: Christianity and the computer. [BR121.2.M6] 64-15483 2.50
1. Christianity—20th cent. 2. Bible—Criticism, Textual. I. McLeman, James, joint author. II. Title.

DAVIES, Margaret, 1941- 227'.04'8
The text of the Pauline Epistles in manuscript 2344 and its relationship to the text of other known manuscripts in particular to 330, 436, and 462. Salt Lake City, University of Utah Press, 1968. v, 176 p. 25 cm. (Studies and documents, 38) "Substantially the same as the doctoral thesis submitted ... [to] Birmingham University." Bibliography: p. 173-176. [BS2641.7 Codex 2344.D38 1968] 70-633772
1. Bible. N.T. Epistles of Paul. Greek. Codex 2344 (Gregory-Dobs.) I. Title. II. Series.

BIBLE. N.T. Epistles. 227'.052
English. Phillips. 1968.
Letters to young churches; a translation of the New Testament Epistles, by J. B. Phillips. With an introd. by C. S. Lewis. 21st anniversary ed. New York, Macmillan [1968] xx, 248 p. 18 cm. [BS2633.P5 1968] 68-22129 1.45
I. Phillips, John Bertram, 1906- tr. II. Title.

BIBLE. N.T. Epistles of 227'.052
Paul. English. Blackwelder. 1971.
Letters from Paul. An exegetical translation by Boyce W. Blackwelder. Anderson, Ind., Warner Press [1971] 160 p. 22 cm. "Translation ... from the Greek text edited by Professor Eberhard Nestle." Includes bibliographical references. [BS2643.B54 1971] 78-158423 ISBN 0-87162-123-1
I. Blackwelder, Boyce W., tr. II. Title.

BIBLE. N.T. Epistles of 227.052
Paul. English. Paraphrases. 1965. Bruce.
The letters of Paul; an expanded paraphrase, by F. F. Bruce. Printed in parallel with the Revised version, with fuller references by Drs. Scrivener, Moulton & Greenup. [American ed.] Grand Rapids, Eerdmans [1965] 323 p. 23 cm. [BS2643.B7] 65-18089
I. Bible. N.T. Epistles of Paul. English. 1965. Revised. II. Bruce, Frederick Fyvie, 1910- III. Title.

BIBLE. N. T. Epistles of 227.052
Paul English. Paraphrases. 1965. Bruce.
The letters of Paul; an expanded paraphrase, by F. F. Bruce. Printed in parallel with the Revised version, with fuller references by Drs. Scrivener, Moulton & Greenup [Amer. ed.] Grand Rapids, Mich., Eerdmans [c.1965] 323p. 23cm. [BS2643.B7] 65-18089 4.95
I. Bible. N. T. Epistles of Paul. English. 1965. Revised. II. Bruce, Frederick Fyvie, 1910- III. Title.

BIBLE. N. T. Epistles 227.052
of Paul. English. Paraphrases. 1965.
Bruce.
The letters of Paul; an expanded paraphrase, by F. F. Bruce. Printed in parallel with the Revised version, with fuller references by Drs. Scrivener, Moulton & Greeup. [American ed.] Grand Rapids, Eerdmans [1965] 323 p. 23 cm. [BS2643.B7 1965] 65-18089
I. Bruce, Frederick Fyvie, 1910- II. Bible. N.T. Epistles of Paul. English. Revised. 1965. III. Title.

BRANDT, Leslie F. 227'.05'2
Epistles/now / Leslie F. Brandt. St. Louis : Concordia Pub. House, c1976. p. cm. [BS2637.B69 1976] 75-38711 ISBN 0-570-03258-X : 5.95
1. Bible. N.T. Epistles—Paraphrases, English. I. Title.

BRANDT, Leslie F. 227'.05'2
Living through loving : reflections on letters of the New Testament / Leslie F. Brandt. St. Louis : Concordia Pub. House, c1974. 80 p. ; 21 cm. [BS2637.B7] 73-88949 ISBN 0-570-03173-7 pbk. : 1.75
1. Bible. N.T. Epistles—Paraphrases, English. I. Title.

JOHNSON, Ben Campbell. 227'.05'2
The heart of Paul / Ben Campbell Johnson. Waco, Tex. : Word Books, c1976. 174 p. ; 23 cm. (His A relational paraphrase of the New Testament ; v. 1) [BS2637.J64] 76-19531 ISBN 0-87680-475-X : 5.95
1. Bible. N.T. Epistles of Paul—Paraphrases, English. I. Title. II. Series.

LETTERS to street 227'.05'2
Christians, by two brothers from Berkeley. Drawings by Lee Hardy. Grand Rapids, Zondervan Pub. House [1971] 224 p. illus. 22 cm. [BS2637.L48] 78-171192 3.95
1. Bible. N.T. Epistles—Paraphrases, English. I. Two brothers from Berkeley.

BIBLE. N.T. Epistles. 227'.052'04
English. Paraphrases. 1967.
Revised Epistles of the New Testament; a twentieth century version; revisiion of 1964-1966, by Robert L. Fogel. [1st ed.] New York, Vantage Press [1967, c1966] 172 p. 21 cm. [BS2637.B5] 65-28652
1. Fogel, Robert L., ed. I. Title.

BIBLE. N.T. Epistles. 227'.052'04
English. Paraphrases. 1967.
Revised Epistles of the New Testament; a twentieth-century version; revision of 1964-1966, by Robert L. Fogel. [1st ed.] New York, Vantage Press [1967, c1966] 172 p. 21 cm. [BS2637.B5] 65-28652
I. Fogel, Robert L., ed. II. Title.

BIBLE. N.T. Epistles 227'.05'205
of Paul. English. New American Bible. Selections. 1976.
Drawing near Him with confidence / compiled by the Daughters of St. Paul. Boston : St. Paul Editions, c1976. p. cm. [BS2643.D38 1976] 75-44217
I. Daughters of St. Paul. II. Title.

AMIOT, Francois. 227.06
How to read St. Paul. Translated by Michael D. Meilach. Chicago. Franciscan Herald Press [1964] 120 p. 24 cm. Translation of Lire Saint Paul. Bibliography: p. 117-120. [BS2650.5.A513] 64-24282
1. Bible. N.T. Epistles of Paul — Study. I. Title.

AMIOT, Francois 227.06
How to read St. Paul. Tr. [from French] by Michael D. Meilach. Chicago, Franciscan Herald [c.1964] 120p. 21cm. Bibl. [BS2650.5.A513] 64-24282 2.95
1. Bible. N. T. Epistles of Paul—Study. I. Title.

AUSTGEN, Robert J. 227.06
Natural motivation in the Pauline Epistles [by] Robert J. Austgen. Notre Dame, Ind., University of Notre Dame Press, 1966. viii, 156 p. 23 cm. Thesis—University of Fribourg. Bibliography: p. 137-146. [BS2652.A88] 66-31813
1. Bible. N.T. Epistles of Paul—Theology. 2. Bible. N.T. Epistles of Paul—Psychology. 3. Motivation (Psychology) I. Title.

BAIRD, William, 1924- 227.06
Paul's message and mission. New York, Abingdon Press [1960] 176p. 21cm. Includes bibliography. [BS2506.B3] 60-12066
1. Paul, Saint, apostle. 2. Bible. N. T. Epistles of Paul—Theology. I. Title.

BAIRD, William [Robb] 227.06
Paul's message and mission. Nashville, Abingdon Press [c.1960] 176p. 21cm. (Bibl. footnotes) 60-12066 3.00
1. Paul, Saint, apostle. 2. Bible. N. T. Epistles of Paul—Theology. I. Title.

BARCLAY, William, 227.06
lecturer in the University of Glasgow.
The mind of St Paul. New York, Harper [c1958] 256p. 22cm. [BS2651.B35 1958] 59-10327
1. Bible. N. T. Epistles of Paul—Theology. 2. Paul, Saint, apostle. I. Title.

BARNLUND, A W 227.06
Paul interpreted; or, A new approach to the Pauline mind; a study in spiritual relationships (an argument) Boston, Bruce Humphries [1959] 265p. 22cm. [BS2650.5.B3] 58-11334
1. Bible. N. T. Epistles of Paul—Theology. I. Title.

BEARDSLEE, William A. 227.06
Human achievement and divine vocation in the message of Paul. Naperville, Ill., A. R. Allenson [1961] 142p. (Studies in Biblical theology, 31) 61-4760 2.25 pap.,
1. Bible. N. T. Epistles of Paul—Theology. 2. Vocation—Biblical teaching. I. Title.

BEKER, Johan Christian, 227.06
1924-
The church faces the world; late New Testament writings. Philadelphia, Westminster Press [1961, c.1960] 96p. (Westminster guides to the Bible) 60-13176 1.50
1. Bible. N. T. Epistles and Revelation—Introductions. I. Title.

BIBLE. N.T. Epistles. 227.06
English. Paraphrases. 1962.
Living letters; the paraphrased Epistles. [Wheaton, Ill., Tyndale House, 1962] 338 p. 18 cm. [BS2637.T9] 63-142
I. Title. II. Title.

BIBLE. N. T. Epistles. 227.06
English. Paraphrases. 1962
Living letters; the paraphrased Epistles. [Wheaton, Ill.] [Tryndal House] [1962] 338 p. 18 cm. [BS2637.T9] 63-142
I. Title.

BRUCE, Frederick Fyvie, 227.06
1910-
Paul and his converts: 1 and 2 Thessalonians. 1 and 2 Corinthians. Nashville, Abingdon [1962] 87p. (Bibl. guides, no. 17) 62-856 1.00 pap.,
1. Bible. N. T. Thessalonians—Criticism, interpretation, etc. 2. Bibl. N. T. Corinthians—Criticism, interpretaion, etc. I. Title.

*BURNSIDE, L. Brooks 227.06
The Apostle Paul speaks to this age. New York, Exposition [c.1965] 173p. 22cm. 4.00
I. Title.

CENTER for Hermeneutical 227'.06
Studies in Hellenistic and Modern Culture.
The Pauline basis of the concept of Scriptural form in Irenaeus : protocol of the eighth colloquy, 4 November 1973 / The Center for Hemeneutical Studies in Hellenistic and Modern Culture ; John S. Coolidge. Berkeley, CA : The Center, c1975. 59 p. ; 21 cm. (Protocol series of the colloquies of the Center for Hermeneutical Studies in Hellenistic and Modern Culture ; nr. 8 ISSN 0098-0900s) Includes bibliographical references..[BS500.C43 1975]X75-34343ISBN 0-89242-007-3VI
1. Irenaeus, Saint, Bp. of Lyons—Congresses. 2. Bible—Criticism, interpretation, etc.—History—Early church, ca. 30-600—Congresses. 3. Bible. N.T. Epistles of Paul—Criticism, interpretation, etc.—Congresses. I. Coolidge, John S. II. Title. III. Series: Center for Hermeneutical Studies in Hellenistic and Modern Culture. Protocol series of the colloquies ; nr. 8.

CERFAUX, Lucien, 1883- 227'.06
The Christian in the theology of St. Paul. [New York] Herder & Herder [1967] 568 p. 23 cm. Translation of Le chretien dans la theologie paulinienne. Bibliographical footnotes. [BS2651.C3913 1967b] 67-29672
1. Bible. N. T. Epistles of Paul—Theology. I. Title.

CERFAUX, Lucien, 1883- 227.06
The church in the theology of St. Paul. English translation by Geoffrey Webb and Adrian Walker. [New York] Herder and Herder [1959] 419p. 23cm. Includes bibliography. [BS2655.C5C43 1959a] 59-5741
1. Church—Biblical teaching. 2. Bible. N. T. Epistles of Paul—Theology. I. Title.

CERFAUX, Lucien, 1883- 227'.06
The spiritual journey of Saint Paul. Translated by John C. Guinness. New York, Sheed and Ward [1968] xviii, 236 p. 22 cm. Translation of L'itineraire spirituel de saint Paul. [BS2651.C4213] 68-13847
1. Bible. N.T. Epistles of Paul—Theology. I. Title.

DUNGAN, David L. 227'.06
The sayings of Jesus in the churches of Paul; the use of the Synoptic tradition in the regulation of early church life, by David L. Dungan. Philadelphia, Fortress Press [1971] xxxiii, 180 p. 22 cm. Bibliography: p. [156]-170. [BT306.D85] 70-155785 ISBN 0-8006-0056-8 6.95
1. Jesus Christ—Words. 2. Bible. N.T. Epistles of Paul—Criticism, interpretation, etc. I. Title.

ELLIS. EDWARD EARLE 227.06
Paul and his recent interpreters. Grand Rapids, Mich., Eerdmans [c.1961] 63p. Bibl. 61-10853 1.75 pap.,
1. Paul, Saint, apostle. 2. Eschatology—Biblical teaching. 3. Bible. N. T. Pastoral epistles—Criticism, interpretaion, etc. I. Title.

FITZMYER, Joseph A. 227'.06
Pauline theology, a brief sketch [by] Joseph A. Fitzmyer. Englewood Cliffs, N.J., Prentice-Hall [1967] viii, 88 p. 22 cm. Includes bibliographies. [BS2651.F5] 67-19295
1. Bible. N.T. Epistles of Paul—Theology. I. Title.

FULTON, Mary Beth. 227.06
This love on which I speak; worship with St. Paul. Valley Forge [Pa.] Judson [c.1962] 129p. 21cm. 62-12902 2.50
1. Paul, Saint, apostle—Meditations. 2. Worship programs. I. Title.

GALE, Herbert Morrison, 227.06
1907-
The use of analogy in the letters of Paul, by Herbert M. Gale. Philadelphia, Westminster Press [1964] 282 p. 21 cm. Bibliography: p. 271-275. [BS2655.A5G3] 64-15581
1. Bible. N. T. Epistles of Paul — Criticism, interpretation, etc. 2. Analogy. I. Title.

GALE, Herbert Morrison, 227.06
1907-
The use of analogy in the letters of Paul. Philadelphia, Westminster [c.1964] 282p. 21cm. Bibl. 64-15581 6.00
1. Bible. N. T. Epistles of Paul—Criticism, interpretation, etc. 2. Analogy. I. Title.

GUTHRIE, Donald, 1916- 227.06
Epistles from prison; Philippians, Ephesians, Colossians, Philemon. London, Lutterworth Pr.; Nashville, Abingdon [1964] 95p. 20cm. (Bible guides, no. 19) 64-1538 1.00 pap.,
1. Bible. N.T. Epistles of Paul—Criticism, interpretation, etc. I. Title.

GUTHRIE, Donald, 1916- 227.06
Epistles from prison; Philippians, Ephesians, Colossians, Philemon. London, Lutterworth Press; New York, Abington Press [1964] 95 p. 20 cm. (Bible guides, no. 19) [BS2650.2G84] 64-1538
1. Bible. N. T. Epistles of Paul — Criticism, interpretation, etc. I. Title.

GUTHRIE, Donald, 1916- 227.06
New Testament introduction; the Pauline Epistles. Chicago, Inter-varsity Press, 1519 North Astor [c.1961] 319p. Bibl. 61-3563 4.95
1. Bible. N. T. Epistles of Paul—Introductions. I. Title.

HIEBERT, David Edmond, 227'.06
1910-
The Pauline Epistles / by D. Edmond Hiebert. Rev. ed. Chicago : Moody Press, c1977. 381 p. ; 24 cm. (His An introduction to the New Testament ; v. 2) Published in 1954 under title: An introduction to the Pauline Epistles. Includes index. Bibliography: p. 364-377. [BS2650.2.H53 1977] 77-150161 ISBN 0-8024-4138-6 : 7.95
1. Bible. N.T. Epistles of Paul—Introductions. I. Title.

HILLSDALE, Paul, ed. 227.06
Prayers from Saint Paul. New York, Sheed and War [1964] xv, 238 p. 22 cm. [BV235.H5] 64-16122
1. Bible. N.T. Epistles of Paul — Prayers. 2. Prayer — Biblical teaching. I. Title.

HILSDALE, Paul, ed. 227.06
Prayers from Saint Paul. New York, Sheed [c.1964] xv, 238p. 22cm. 64-16122 4.50 bds.,
1. Bible. N. T. Epistles of Paul—Prayers. 2. Prayer—Biblical teaching. I. Title.

HUNTER, Archibald 227.06
Macbride.
Paul and his predecessors. [New rev. ed.] Philadelphia, Westminster Press [1961] 154 p. 22 cm. Includes bibliography. [BS2651.H8 1961] 61-13073
1. Bible. N.T. Epistles of Paul—Theology. 2. Paul, Saint, apostle. I. Title.

KASEMANN, Ernst. 227'.06
Perspectives on Paul. [Translated by Margaret Kohl. 1st American ed.] Philadelphia, Fortress Press [1971] 173 p. 23 cm. Translation of Paulinische Perspektiven. [BS2651.K3213 1971] 79-157540 ISBN 0-8006-0030-4 6.95
1. Bible. N.T. Epistles of Paul—Addresses, essays, lectures. I. Title.

LONGENECKER, Richard N. 227.06
Paul, apostle of liberty, by Richard N. Longenecker. [1st ed.] New York, Harper & Row [1964] x. 310 p. 22 cm. Bibliographical footnotes. [BS2506.L6] 64-19500
1. Paul, Saint, apostle. I. Title.

MATHEWS, Horace Frederick, 227.06
1914-
According to St. Paul; a study course on the New Testament letters. New York, Collier [1962] 124p. 18cm. (AS206Y) Bibl. 62-3494 .95 pap.,
1. Bible. N. T. Epistles of Paul—Study—Outlines. syllabi, etc. I. Title.

MONTAGUE, George T 227.06
The living thought of Saint Paul an introduction to Pauline theology through intensive study of key texts, by George T. Montague. Milwaukee, Bruce Pub. Co. [1966] xxi, 242 p. maps. 23 cm. (Contemporary college theology series: Biblical theology) Bibliography: p. 219-221. [BS2650.5.M6] 66-17718
1. Bible. N.T. Epistles of Paul — Study. I. Title.

MONTAGUE, George T. 227.06
The living thought of Saint Paul; an introduction to Paulinetheology through intensive study of key texts. Milwaukee, Bruce [c.1966] xxi, 242p. maps. 23cm. (Contemp. coll. theol. ser.: Biblical theol.) Bibl. [BS2650.5.M6] 66-17718 4.50; 2.25 pap.,
1. Bible. N.T. Epistles of Paul—Study. I. Title.

MONTAGUE, George T 227.06
Maturing in Christ; Saint Paul's program for Christian growth, by George T. Montague. Milwaukee, Bruce Pub. Co. [1964] x, 244 p. 22 cm. (Impact books) [BS2651.M6] 64-20635
1. Bible. N.T. Epistles of Paul — Theology. 2. Spiritual life — Biblical teaching. I. Title.

MONTAGUE, George T. 227.06
Maturing in Christ; Saint Paul's program for Christian growth. Milwaukee [c.1964] x, 244p. 22cm. (Impact bks.) 64-20635 3.95
1. Bible. N.T. Epistles of Paul—Theology. 2. Spiritual life—Biblical teaching. I. Title.

NICKLE, Keith Fullerton. 227.06
1933-
The collection: a study in Paul's strategy [by] Keith F. Nickle. Naperville. Ill., A.R.Allenson [1966] 176p. 22cm. (Studies in Biblical theol. no. 48) Thesis--Basel. Vita: p. [2] of cover Bibl. [BS2655.C53N5 1966a] 66-7322 3.75 pap.,
1. Church finance—Early church. 2. Bible. N. T. Epistles of Paul—Criticism, interpretation. etc. I. Title. II. Series.

NIELSON, John B 227.06
In Christ; the significance of the phrase 'In Christ' in the writings of St. Paul. Kansas City, Mo., Beacon Hill Press [1960] 133p. 20cm. Includes bibliography. [BS2651.N5] 60-13196
1. Bible. N. T. Epistles of Paul—Theology. I. Title.

PEARCE, J. Winston 227.06
Paul and his letters. Nashville, Broadman Press [c.1961] 168p. 61-7549 2.75 bds.,
1. Bible. N. T. Epistles of Paul—Sermons. 2. Baptists—Sermons. I. Title.

PEARCE J WINSTON. 227.06
Paul and his letters. Nashville, Broadman Press [1961] 168p. 21cm. [BS2650.4.P4] 61-7549
1. Bible. N. T. Epistles of Paul—Sermons. 2. Baptists—Sermons. I. Title.

PINK, Arthur Walkington, 227.06
1886-1952.
Gleanings from Paul: studies in the prayers of the Apostle, by Arthur W. Pink Chicago, Moody Press [1967] 351 p. 24 cm. [BV235.P5] 67-14379
1. Bible., N. T. Epistles of Paul—Prayers. I. Title.

*ROBERTSON, A. T. 227.' 06
Paul the interpreter of Christ / By A. T. Robertson. Grand Rapids : Baker Book House, 1976c1921. 155p. ; 20 cm. (His Library II) [BS2651] ISBN 0-8010-7638-2 pbk. : 2.95.
1. Paul, Saint, apostle. 2. Bible. N. T. Epistles of Paul-Theology. I. Title.

ROBINSON, John Arthur 227'.06
Thomas, Bp., 1919-
The body : a study in Pauline theology / by John A. T. Robinson. Philadelphia : Westminster Press, [1977] c1952. p. cm. Includes bibliographical references and indexes. [BS2651.R615 1977] 77-7221 ISBN 0-664-24149-2 pbk. : 3.95
1. Bible. N.T. Epistles of Paul—Theology. I. Title.

ROLSTON, Holmes, 1900- 227.06
The "we knows" of the apostle Paul. Richmond, John Knox Press [1966] 101 p. 21 cm. Includes bibliographical references. [BS2650.4.46] 66-12114
1. Bible. N.T. Epistles of Paul—Sermons. 2. Presbyterian Church—Sermons. 3. Sermons, American. I. Title.

ROLSTON, Holmes, 1900- 227.06
The 'we knows' of the apostle Paul. Richmond, Va., Knox [c.1966] 101p. 21cm. Bibl. [BS2650.4.R6] 66-12114 1.65 pap.,
1. Bible. N.T. Epistles of Paul—Sermons. 2. Presbyterian Church—Sermons. 3. Sermons, American. I. Title.

SCHOEPS, Hans Joachim 227.06
Paul; the theology of the apostle in the light of Jewish religious history. Tr. by Harold Knight. Philadelphia, Westminster [1961] 303p. Bibl. 61-10284 6.50
1. Bible. N.T. Epistles of Paul—Theology. 2. Christianity and other religions—Judaism. I. Title.

SCROGGS, Robin. 227'.06
The last Adam; a study in Pauline anthropology. Philadelphia, Fortress Press [1966] xxiv, 139 p. 23 cm. "Errata" slip inserted. Bibliography: p. [123]-128. [BS2651.S37] 66-23416
1. Jesus Christ—History of doctrines—Early church, ca. 30-600. 2. Bible. N.T. Epistles of Paul—Theology. 3. Adam (Biblical character) I. Title.

WHITELEY, Denys Edward 227.06
Hugh.
The theology of St. Paul [by] D. E. H. Whiteley. [1st ed.] Philadelphia, Fortress Press, 1964. xvi, 205 p. 23 cm. Bibliography: p. [277]-282. [BS2651.W47] 64-15398
1. Bible. N.T. Epistles of Paul — Theology. I. Title.

WHITELEY, Denys Edward 227.06
Hugh
The theology of St. Paul. Philadelphia, Fortress [c.] 1964. xvi, 295p. 23cm. Bibl. 64-15398 5.25
1. Bible. N. T. Epistles of Paul—Theology. I. Title.

WIKENHAUSER. ALFRED 227.06
Pauline mysticism; Christ in the mystical teaching of St. Paul.. [New York] Herder and Herder [c.1960] 255p. 23cm. Translation by Joseph Cunningham . . . based on the second German edition of 'Die Christusmystik des Apostels Paulus,' published by Herder, Freiburg, 1956.' Bibl.: p.243-246. 60-8328 4.50
1. Bible. N.T. Epistles of Paul—Theology. 2. Mysticism—Biblical teaching. I. Title.

WIKENHAUSER, Alfred, 1883- 227.06
Pauline mysticism; Christ in the mystical teaching of St. Paul. [New York] Herder and Herder [1960] 255 p. 23 cm. Includes bibliography. [BS2655.M9W53 1960a] 60-8328
1. Bible. N.T. Epistles of Paul — Theology. 2. Mysticism — Biblical teaching. I. Title. II. Title: "Translation by Joseph Cunningham ... based on the second German edition of 'Die Christusmystik des Apostels Paulus,' published by Herder, Freiburg, 1956."

WILSON, Clifford A. 227'.06
New light on New Testament letters [by] Clifford A. Wilson. Grand Rapids, Baker Book House [1975 c1971] 125 p. 18 cm. Bibliography: p. 115-116. [BS2629.W54] ISBN 0-8010-9563-8 1.25 (pbk.)
1. Bible. N.T. Epistles and Revelation—Criticism, interpretation, etc. I. Title.
L.C. no. of original edition: 73-157305.

BIBLE. N.T. Epistles of 227'.06'5
Paul. English. Revised standard. 1975.
Pauline parallels / designed and edited by Fred O. Francis and J. Paul Sampley. Philadelphia : Fortress Press, c1975. ix, 388 p. ; 24 x 36 cm. (Sources for Biblical study ; 9) Includes indexes. [BS2643.F7 1975] 74-26346 ISBN 0-8006-1206-X pbk. : 10.95
1. Bible. N.T. Epistles of Paul—Harmonies. I. Francis, Fred O. II. Sampley, J. Paul. III. Title. IV. Series.

BOUTTIER, Michel, 1921- 227.066
Christianity according to Paul. [Translated by Frank Clarke from the French] Naperville, Ill., A. R. Allenson [1966] 127 p. 22 cm. (Studies in Biblical theology 49) Bibliography: p. 120-121. [BS2651] 67-47
1. Bible. N.T. Epistles of Paul—Theology. I. Title. II. Series.

DOTY, William G., 1939- 227'.06'6
Letters in primitive Christianity, by William G. Doty. Philadelphia, Fortress Press [1973] xi, 84 p. 22 cm. (Guides to Biblical scholarship. New Testament series) Includes bibliographical references. [BS2635.2.D68] 72-87058 ISBN 0-8006-0460-1 2.50
1. Bible. N.T. Epistles—Criticism, interpretation, etc. 2. Christian literature, Early—History and criticism. 3. Letters—History and criticism. I. Title.

FISHER, Fred L. 227'.06'6
Paul and his teachings [by] Fred L. Fisher. Nashville, Broadman Press [1974] 160 p. 22 cm. Includes bibliographical references. [BS2506.F55] 73-83829 ISBN 0-8054-1339-1 5.25
1. Paul, Saint, apostle. 2. Bible. N.T. Epistles of Paul—Theology. I. Title.

HANSON, Anthony 227'.06'6
Tyrrell.
Studies in Paul's technique and theology.

[American ed.] Grand Rapids, Eerdmans [1974] xiv, 329 p. 22 cm. Bibliography: p. [305]-313. [BS2650.2.H36 1974] 74-7491 ISBN 0-8028-3452-3 8.95
1. Bible. N.T. Epistles of Paul—Criticism, interpretation, etc. 2. Bible—Criticism, interpretation, etc.—History—Early church, ca. 30-600. I. Title.

MEEKS, Wayne A., comp. 227'.06'6
The writings of St. Paul. Edited by Wayne A. Meeks. [1st ed.] New York, Norton [1972] xvii, 454 p. 22 cm. (A Norton critical edition) Bibliography: p. 445-446. [BS2505.A3M43] 77-95542 ISBN 0-393-04338-X 4.95
1. Paul, Saint, apostle—Collections. 2. Bible. N.T. Epistles of Paul—Theology—Collections. I. Title.

RIDDERBOS, Herman N. 227'.06'6
Paul : an outline of his theology / Herman Ridderbos ; translated by John Richard de Witt. Grand Rapids, Mich. : W. B. Eerdmans Pub. Co., [1975] 587 p. ; 24 cm. Translation of Paulus. Includes bibliographical references and indexes. [BS2651.R513] 73-2292 ISBN 0-8028-3438-8 : 12.95
1. Bible. N.T. Epistles of Paul—Theology. I. Title.

ROETZEL, Calvin J. 227'.06'6
The letters of Paul : conversations in context / by Calvin J. Roetzel. Atlanta : John Knox Press, [1975] viii, 114 p. ; 23 cm. Includes bibliographical references and index. [BS2650.2.R63] 74-21901 ISBN 0-8042-0208-7 pbk. : 4.95
1. Paul, Saint, apostle. 2. Bible. N.T. Epistles of Paul—Criticism, interpretation, etc. I. Title.

AUGRAIN, Charles. 227'.07
Paul, master of the spiritual life. [Translated by Sr. M. Paul Purcell] Staten Island, N.Y., Alba House [1967-68] 3 v. map. 19 cm. Vol. 2 has imprint: Cork [Ire.] Mercier Press. Translation of Paul, maitre de vie spirituelle. [BS2650.3.A8513] 67-24923 3.95
1. Bible. N.T. Epistles of Paul—Commentaries. I. Title.

BARRETT, Charles Kingsley. 227.07
From first Adam to last; a study in Pauline theology. New York, Scribner [1962] 124p. 22cm. (Hewett lectures, 1961) [BS2651.B38] 62-19850
1. Bible, N. T. Epistles of Paul—Theology. I. Title.

BEARE, Francis Wright, 227.07
1902-
St. Paul and his letters. New York, Abingdon Press [1962] 142 p. 21 cm. [BS2650.3.B4] 62-17500
1. Bible. N.T. Epistles of Paul—Commentaries. I. Title.

BIBLE. N. T. Epistles of 227.07
Paul. English. 1958. Conybeare.
The Epistles of Paul; a translation, and notes, by W. J. Conybeare. Grand Rapids, Baker Book House, 1958. 231p. 21cm. [BS2650.C57] 58-12740
1. Bible. N. T. Epistles of Paul—Commentaries. I. Conybeare, William John., 1815-1857, tr. II. Title.

BIBLE. N. T. Epistles of 227.07
Paul. English. 1959. Barclay.
The letters to thePhilippians, Colossians, and Thessalonians. Translated, with introductions and interpretations, by William Barclay. [2d ed.] Philadelphia, Westminster Press [1959] 253p. 18cm. (The Daily study Bible) [BS2650.3.B35 1959] 59-10146
1. Bible. N. T. Epistles of Paul—Commentaries. I. Barclay, William, lecturer in the University of Glasgow., ed. and tr. II. Title.

BIBLE. N.T. Acts and 227.07
Epistles. English. Knox. 1959.
It is Paul who writes, based on the translation of the Epistles of Saint Paul & of the Acts of the Apostles by Ronald Knox, arranged in a continuous narrative with explanations by Ronald Cox. New York, Sheed and Ward [1959, c1944] x, 487 p. maps. 22 cm. [BS2617.5.A3K6] 59-10654
1. Paul, Saint, apostle. 2. Bible. N. T. Acts and Epistles—Commentaries. 3. Bible—Harmonies. I. Knox, Ronald Arbuthnott, 1888-1957, tr. II. Cox, Ronald. III. Title.

CANTINAT, Jean. 227'.07
The Epistles of St. Paul explained. Staten Island, N.Y., Alba House [1967] 204 p. map (on lining papers) 22 cm. Bibliography: p. [201]-204. [BS2650.3.C313] 66-17220
1. Bible. N.T. Epistles of Paul—Commentaries. I. Title.

DAILY Bible commentary 227'.07
: Romans to Revelation / Arthur E. Cundall co-ordinating editor. Philadelphia : A. J. Holman, [1977], c1973. p. cm. Reprint of the ed. published by Scripture Union, London. [BS2341.2.D33 1977] 76-46442 ISBN 0-87981-071-8 : 8.95
1. Bible. N.T.—Commentaries. I. Gundall, Arthur Ernest.

DAILY Bible commentary 227'.07
: Romans to Revelation / Arthur E. Cundall co-ordinating editor. Philadelphia : A. J. Holman, [1977], c1973. p. cm. Reprint of the ed. published by Scripture Union, London. [BS2341.2.D33 1977] 76-46442 ISBN 0-87981-071-8 : 8.95
1. Bible. N.T.—Commentaries. I. Gundall, Arthur Ernest.

HOVEN, Victor Emanuel, 227.07
1871-
The New Testament Epistles: analysis and notes. Grand Rapids, Baker Book House, 1959. 161p. 21cm. [BS2635.H6] 59-8341
1. Bible. N. T. Epistles—Study—Outlines, syllabi, etc. I. Title.

MCCORRY, Vincent P., 1909- 227.07
Everyman's St. Paul. New York, Farrar, Straus and Cudahy [c.1961] 215p. 61-5898 3.95 half cloth,
1. Paul, Saint, apostle. 2. Bible. N.T. Epistles and Gospels, Liturgical—Commentaries. I. Title.

MACKAY, Brain S. 227.07
Freedom of the Christian: Galatians and Romans. London, Lutterworth; Nashville, Abingdon [1965] 96p. 20cm. (Bible guides, no. 16 [BS2665.2.M22] 65-1370 1.00 pap.,
1. Bible. N. T. Romans—Introductions. 2. Bible. N. T. Galatians—Introductions. I. Title.

MURPHY, Richard Thomas 227.07
Aquinas, 1908-
The Sunday Epistles. Milwaukee, Bruce Pub. Co. [1961] 274p. illus. 24cm. [BS2638.Z73M8] 61-16516
1. Bible. N. T. Epistles and gospels, Liturgical— Commentaries. I. Title.

SERMONIC studies; 227.07
the standard epistles; v. 2 Saint Louis, Concordia [c.1963] 616p. 23cm. Contents.v. 2. The Trinity Season. 56-12707 7.50
1. Bible. N. T. Epistles and Gospels, Liturgical—Commentaries. 2. Sermons—Outlines.

SMITH, Earl C 1894- 227.07
Paul's Gospel; an analysis and exposition of Paul's Epistles to the Romans, to the Galatians, to the Ephesians, to the Philippians, to the Colossians. [1st ed.] New York, Greenwich Book Publishers [1960] 103 p. 22 cm. [BS2650.5.S6] 60-13394
1. Bible. N.T. Epistles of Paul — Study — Outlines, syllabi, etc. 2. Bible. N.T. Epistles of Paul — Commentaries. I. Title.

SMITH, Earl C. 1894- 227.07
Paul's Gospel; an analysis and exposition of Paul's Epistles to the Romans, to the Galatians, to the Ephesians, to the Philippians, to the Colossians. New York, Greenwich Book Publishers [c.1960] 103p. 60-13394 2.50
1. Bible. N. T. Epistles of Paul—Study—Outlines, syllabi, etc. 2. Bible. N. T. Epistles of Paul—Commentaries. I. Title.

WIRT, Sherwood Eliot. 227.07
Open your Bible to the New Testament letters. [Westwood, N. J., Revell [1962] 128 p. 21 cm. [BS2635.3.W5] 62-17103
1. Bible. N. T. Epistles — Commentaries. I. Title.

WIRT, Sherwood Eliot 227.07
Open your Bible to the New Testament letters. [Westwood. N. J.] Revell [c.1962] 128p. 21 cm. 62-17103 2.50 bds.,
1. Bible. N. T. Epistles—Commentaries. I. Title.

PAGELS, Elaine H., 227'.07'7
1943-
The gnostic Paul : gnostic exegesis of the Pauline letters / Elaine Hiesey Pagels. Philadelphia : Fortress Press, c1975. xii, 180 p. ; 24 cm. Includes indexes. Bibliography: p. 167-170. [BS2650.2.P33] 74-26350 ISBN 0-8006-0403-2 : 10.95
1. Bible. N.T. Epistles of Paul—Criticism, interpretation, etc. 2. Gnosticism. I. Title.

SCHWEITZER, Albert, 227'.08'24822
1875-1965.
The mysticism of Paul the apostle. With a prefatory note by F. C. Burkitt. [Translated from the German by William Montgomery] New York, Seabury Press [1968, c1931] xv, 411 p. 21 cm. (A Seabury paperback, SP51) Translation of Die Mystik des Apostels Paulus. Bibliographical footnotes. [BS2655.M9S43 1968] 68-28707 2.95
1. Paul, Saint, apostle. 2. Bible. N.T. Epistles of Paul—Theology. 3. Mysticism—Biblical teaching. I. Title.

MURPHY-O'CONNOR, 227.08251
Jerome, 1935-
Paul on preaching. New York, Sheed and Ward [1964] xx, 314 p. 20 cm. Bibliography: p. [303]-305. [BS2655.P8M8] 64-19908
1. Preaching — Biblical teaching. 2. Bible. N.T. Epistles of Paul — Criticism, interpretation, etc. I. Title.

MURPHY-O'CONNOR, 227.08251
Jerome, 1935-
Paul on preaching. New York, Sheed [1964] xx, 314p. 20cm. Bibl. 64-19908 4.50
1. Preaching—Biblical teaching. 2. Bible. N. T. Epistles of Paul—Criticism, interpretation, etc. I. Title.

SCHNACKENBURG, Rudolf, 227.082651
1914-
Baptism in the thought of St. Paul; a study in Pauline theology. Tr. [from German] by G. R. Beasley-Murray [New York] Herder & Herder [c.1964] xii, 228p. 23cm. Bibl. 64-25228 5.95
1. Baptism—Biblical teaching. 2. Bible. N.T. Epistles of Paul—Theology. I. Title.

MUELLER, Herman. 227'.08'37
A critical analysis of the Jewish educational philosophy in relationship to the Epistles of St. Paul. (St. Augustin b. Siegburg) Steyler, 1967. 80 p. 24 cm. (Veroffentlichungen des Missionspriesterseminars St. Augustin, Siegburg, Nr. 17) Bibliography: p. 72-76. [BS2655.E3M8] 72-362928 14.00
1. Jews—Education. 2. Bible. N.T. Epistles of Paul—Theology. I. Title. II. Series: Sankt Augustin, Ger. Missionspriesterseminar. Veroffentlichungen, Nr. 17

ROSENBERG, Meyer 227'.08'37
Joshua.
The historical development of Hebrew education from ancient times to 135 C. E. Long Branch, N. J., 1927. 135p. port. 21cm. Bibliography:p. 133-135. [LA47.R83] 27-18409
1. Jews—Education—Hist. I. Title.

ALLEN, Clifton J 1901- 227.1
The gospel according to Paul; a study of the Letter to the Romans. Nashville, Convention Press [c1956] 148p. 20cm. [BS2665.A5] 57-13893
1. Bible. N. T. Romans—Study—Text-books. I. Title.

ALLEN, Clifton J., 1901- 227.1
The Gospel according to Paul; a study of the Letter to the Romans. Nashville, Broadman Pr. [1973, c.1956] iv, 136 p. 19 cm. [BS2665.A5] ISBN 0-8054-1342-1 1.95 (pbk.)
1. Bible. N.T. Romans—Study—Text-books. I. Title.
L.C. card no. for hardbound ed.: 57-13893.

BARNHOUSE, Donald Grey 227.1
Exposition of Bible doctrines, taking the Epistle to the Romans as a point of departure; v.8. Grand Rapids, Mich., Eerdmans [c.1963] 176p. 22cm. Contents.v.8. Romans 9:1-11:36 58-13516 3.50
1. Bible. N.T. Romans—Sermons. I. Title.

BARNHOUSE, Donald Grey, 227.1
1895-
Exposition of Bible doctrines, taking the Epistle of the Romans as point of departure; v.7. Grand Rapids, Mich., Eerdmans [c.1963] 243p. 22cm. Contents.v.7. God's heirs, Romans 8:1-39. 58-13516 4.50
1. Bible. N.T. Romans—Sermons. I. Title.

BARNHOUSE, Donald Grey, 227.1
1895-
Exposition of Bible doctrines, taking the Epistle to the Romans as a point of departure. Grand Rapids, Mich., Eerdmans [c.1964] 202p. 22cm. First pub., 1952 under title: Expository messages on the whole Bible, taking the Epistle to the Romans as a point of departure. Contents.v. 10. Romans 14:13-16:27. 58-13516 4.50
1. Bible. N. T. Romans—Sermons. I. Title.

BARNHOUSE, Donald Grey, 227.1
1895-
Expository messages on the whole Bible, taking the Epistle to the Romans as a point of departure. Wheaton, Ill., Van Kampen Press [1952- v. 22 cm. Contents.v. 1. Man's ruin, Romans 1 : 1-82.-- v. 2. God's wrath, Romans 2:1-3:20. [BS2665.B32] 52-22280
1. Bible. N. T. Romans—Sermons. I. Title.

BARNHOUSE, Donald Grey, 227.1
1895-
Man's ruin; expository messages on the whole Bible taking the Epistle to the Romans as a point of departure. Wheaton, Ill., Van Kampen Press [1952] Urbana, 1952. v. 301 p. 22 cm. 267-350 p. illus., map. 26 cm. (His Romans, v. 1) (Illinois. Natural History Survey. Bulletin. v. 25, article 5) Bibliography: p. 348-350. [BS2665.B32] 52-22280
1. Bible. N. T. Romans—Sermons. 2. Fishes—Mississippi River. I. Starrett, William Charles. joint author. II. Title. III. Title: Commercial and sport fishes of the Mississippi River between Paul G. Barnickol [and] William C. Starrett. IV. Series.

BARRETT, Charles Kingsley. 227.1
A commentary on the Epistle to the Romans. New York, Harper [1958, c1957] 294p. 22cm. (Harper's New Testament commentaries) [BS2665.B325 1957a] 57-12722
1. Bible, N. T. Romans—Commentaries. I. Bible, N. T. Romans. English. 1957. Barrett. II. Title.

BARTH, Karl, 1886- 227.1
Christ and Adam; man and humanity in Romans 5. Translated by T. A. Smail. [1st ed.] New York, Harper [1957] 96p. 20cm. [BS2665.B3272] 57-9875
1. Bible. N. T. Romans v—Theology. 2. Man (Theology)—Biblical teaching. I. Title.

BARTLETT, Charles Norman, 227.1
1891-
Right in Romans; studies in the Epistle of Paul to the Romans. Chicago, Moody Press [1953] 128p. 18cm. (Colportage library, 246) [BS2665.B36] 54-1162
1. Bible. N. T. Romans—Commentaries. I. Title.

BIBLE. N. T. Romans. 227.1
English. 1957. Barclay.
The Letter to the Romans. Translated with an introd. and interpretation by William Barclay. [2d ed.] Philadelphia, Westminster Press [1957] xxxi, 243p. 18cm. (The Daily study Bible) [BS2665.B25 1957] 58-5148
1. Bible. N. T.Romans—Commentaries. I. Barclay, William, lecturer in the University of Glasgow, ed. and tr. II. Title. III. Series: The Daily studt Bible series

BULTMANN, Rudolf Karl, 227'.1
1884-
The old and new man in the letters of Paul, by Rudolf Bultmann. Translated by Keith R. Crim. Richmond, John Knox Press [1967] 79 p. 19 cm. Translation of Der alte und der neue Mensch in der Theologie des Paulus. Includes bibliographical references. [BS2651.B8713] 67-24123
1. Bible. N.T. Epistles of Paul—Theology. 2. Bible. N.T. Romans VII—Commentaries. 3. Bible. N.T. Romans V—Commentaries. I. Title.

ELLISON, Henry Leopold. 227.1
The mystery of Israel; an exposition of Romans 9-11, by H. L. Ellison. Grand Rapids, Eerdmans [1966] 96 p. 21 cm. Bibliographical footnotes. [BS2665.3.E4] 66-27404
1. Bible. N.T. Romans IX-XI — Commentaries. I. Title.

ELLISON, Henry Leopold 227.1
The mystery of Israel; an exposition of Romans 9-11, by H. L. Ellison. Grand Rapids, Eerdmans [1966] 96p. 21cm. Bibl. [BS2665.3E11] 66-27404 1.25 pap.,
1. Bible. N. T. Romans IX-XI—Commentaries. I. Title.

GREENE, Oliver B 227.1
The Epistle of Paul, the apostle to the Romans. Greenville, S.C., Gospel Hour, inc. [1962] 334 p. 20 cm. "Series of radio sermons as delivered day by day over ... Gospel hour broadcast[s]" [BS2665.4.G7] 62-58314
1. Bible. N.T. Romans — Sermons. 2. Sermons, American. I. Bible. N.T. Epistles of Paul. English. 1962. II. Title.

HESLOP, William Greene, 227.1
1886-
Pen pictures from Paul; great passages in Romans. Butler, Ind., Higley Press [1958] 142p. 20cm. [BS2650.H4] 58-31874
1. Bible. N. T. Epistles of Paul—Commentaries. I. Title.

IRONSIDE, Henry Allan, 227.1
1876-1951.
Lectures on the Epistle to the Romans. [1st ed.] New York, Loizeaux Bros. [1951] 176p. 20cm. [BS2665.I75] 55-53754
1. Bible. N. T. Romans—Commentaries. I. Title.

*LLOYD-JONES, D. M. 227.1
Romans An exposition of chapters 7. 1-8. 4. The Low: its functions and limits [by] D. M. Lloyd-Jones. Grand Rapids, Zondervan, [1974 c1973] [xii, 358 p.] 23 cm. [S2665.4] 7.95
1. Bible. N. T. Romans—Commentaries. I. Title.

LLOYD-JONES, David Martyn. 227'.1
Romans; an exposition of chapters 3.20-4.25, atonement and justification [by] D. M. Lloyd-Jones. [Grand Rapids, Mich.] Zondervan Pub. House [1971, c1970] xiii, 250 p. 23 cm. "Sermons ... apart from the first ... delivered during the Friday nights of the period, February to October, 1957 [at Westminster

Chapel, London]" [BS2665.4.L57 1971] 72-25015 5.95
1. Bible. N.T. Romans III, 20-IV, 25—Sermons. 2. Sermons, English. I. Title.

LLOYD-JONES, David Martyn. 227'.1
Romans; an exposition of chapter 6, the new man [by] D. M. Lloyd-Jones. Grand Rapids, Mich., Zondervan Pub. House [1973, c1972] xii, 313 p. 23 cm. Sermons delivered on Friday nights in Westminister Chapel, Oct. 1958-Apr. 1959. [BS2665.4.L58 1973] 74-161756 6.95
1. Bible. N.T. Romans VI—Sermons. 2. Sermons, English. I. Title.

LUTHER, Martin, 1483-1546. 227.1
Commentary on the Epistle to the Romans; a new translation by J. Theodore Mueller. Grand Rapids, Zondervan Pub. House [1954] 207p. 23cm. A digest in English of Luther's manuscript published in the Weimar ed. of his works, v. 56, under title: Divi Pauli apostoll ad Romance Epistola. [BS2665.L7512] 55-572
1. Bible. N. T. Romans—Commentaries. I. Title.

MERCHANT, Jane. 227.1
The mercies of God; meditations on Romans 12. New York, Abingdon Press [1963] 110 p. 18 cm. [BS2665.4.M4] 63-15709
1. Bible. N.T. Romans XII — Meditations. I. Title.

MERCHANT, Jane 227.1
The mercies of God; meditations on Romans 12. Nashville. Abingdon [c.1948-1963] 110p. 18cm. 63-15709 1.75
1. Bible. N. T. Romans XII—Meditations. I. Title.

MORRISON, Clinton 227.1
The powers that be: earthly rulers and demonic powers in Romans 13, 1-7. Naperville, Ill., A. A. Allenson [1960] 144 p. 22 cm. (Studies in Biblical theology, no. 29) Bibl. footnotes. 60-4219 2.25 pap.,
1. Bible, N. T. Romans xiii, 1-7—Theology. 2. Church and state—Biblical teaching. 3. Emperor worship. I. Title. II. Series.

MOULE, Handley Carr Glyn, 227.1
Bp. of Durham, 1841-1920.
The Epistle to the Romans [by] Handley C. G. Moule. [New ed.] Grand Rapids, Zondervan Pub. House [19] x, 437 p. 22 cm. Previous editions published under title: The Epistle of St. Paul to the Romans. [BS2665.3.M6] 67-121248
1. Bible. N.T. Romans — Commentaries. I. Title.

MUNCK, Johannes, 1904-1965 227.1
Christ & Israel; an interpretation of Romans 9-11. Foreword by Krister Stendahl. [Tr. from Danish by Ingeborg Nixon] Philadelphia, Fortress [1967] xviii, 156p. 22cm. Bibl. [BS 2665.3.M7513] 67-17401 4.25
1. Bibl.N.T. Romans IX-XI—Commentaries. I. Title.

QUIMBY, Chester Warren, 227.1
1891-
The great redemption; a living commentary on Paul's Epistle to the Romans. New York, Macmillan, 1950. ix ,213 p. 21 cm. Bibliography: p. 211-213. [BS2665.Q5] 50-5451
1. Bible. N. T. Romans — Commentaries. I. Title.

RICHARDSON, John R 227.1
The Epistle to the Romans, by John R. Richardson and Knox Chamblin. Grand Rapids, Baker Book House, 1963. 166 p. 20 cm. (Proclaiming the New Testament) [BS2665.5.R5] 63-12948
1. Bible. N.T. Romans — Homiletical use. I. Chamblin, Knox, joint author. II. Title.

RICHARDSON, John R. 227.1
The Epistle to the Romans, by John R. Richardson, Knox Chamblin. Grand Rapids, Mich., Baker Bk. House [c.]1963. 166p. 20cm. (Proclaiming the New Testament) Bibl. 63-12948 2.95
1. Bible. N. T. Romans—Homiletical use. I. Chamblin, Knox. joint author. II. Title.

STOTT, John R. W. 227.1
Men made new: an exposition of Romans 5-8, by John R. W. Stott. [1st ed.] Chicago, Inter-Varsity Press [1966] 108 p. 18 cm. Based on "the Bible Readings on Romans 5-8 [given by the author] at the Keswick Convention in July 1965." [BS2665.3.S8 1966a] 66-24396
1. Bible. N.T. Romans V-VIII—Commentaries. I. Title.

TALBOT, Louis Thompson, 227.1
1889-
Addresses on Romans. [2d ed.] Wheaton, Ill., Van Kampen Press [1954? c1936] 237p. illus. 20cm. [BS2665] 53-13427
1. Bible. N. T. Romans—Sermons. 2. Sermons, American. I. Title.

TAYLOR, Kenneth Nathaniel. 227'.1
A living letter for the children's hour, by Kenneth N. Taylor. Illustrated by Robert G. Doares. [Rev. ed.] Chicago, Moody Press [1968] 167 p. illus. 24 cm. 1959 ed. published under title: Romans for the children's hour, with I and II Timothy. Presents the teachings of Paul's epistles by paraphrasing them and telling short stories based on their themes. Includes study questions and a prayer pertinent to each story. [BS2665.4.T3 1968] 68-26407 3.95
1. Bible. N.T. Romans—Meditations. 2. Bible. N.T. Timothy—Meditations. I. Doares, Robert G., illus. II. Bible. N.T. Romans. English. Paraphrases. 1968. Taylor. III. Bible. N.T. Timothy. English. Paraphrases. 1968. Taylor. IV. Title.

WOOD, Arthur Skevington. 227.1
Life by the spirit (formerly published as Paul's Pentecost) by A. Skevington Wood. Grand Rapids Zondervan Pub. House [c1963] 144 p. 21 cm. [BS2665.5.W6 1963] 64-57999
1. Bible. N. T. Romans VIII — Devotional literature. I. Title.

WUEST, Kenneth Samuel, 227.1
1893-
Romans in the Greek New Testament for the English reader. [1st ed.] Grand Rapids, Eerdmans, 1955. 399p. 21cm. (His Word studies in the Greek New Testament, 16) [BS2665.W8] 55-13728
I. Title.

BLAIKLOCK, E. M. 227'.1'007
Romans [by] E. M. Blaiklock. Grand Rapids, Mich., W. B. Eerdmans Pub. Co. [1971] 92 p. 19 cm. (Scripture Union Bible study books) [BS2665.5.B63] 76-151983 1.25
1. Bible. N.T. Romans—Study—Outlines, syllabi, etc. I. Title.

GAMBLE, Harry, 1941- 227'.1'04
The textual history of the letter to the Romans : a study in textual and literary criticism / by Harry Gamble, Jr. Grand Rapids : Eerdmans, 1977. 151 p. ; 25 cm. A revision of the author's thesis, Yale, 1970. Bibliography: p. 147-151. [BS2665.2.G35 1976] 76-44484 ISBN 0-8028-1670-3 : 15.00
1. Bible. N.T. Romans—Criticism, Textual. I. Title.

GAMBLE, Harry, 1941- 227'.1'04
The textual history of the letter to the Romans : a study in textual and literary criticism / by Harry Gamble, Jr. Grand Rapids : Eerdmans, 1977. 151 p. ; 25 cm. A revision of the author's thesis, Yale, 1970. Bibliography: p. 147-151. [BS2665.2.G35 1976] 76-44484 ISBN 0-8028-1670-3 : 15.00
1. Bible. N.T. Romans—Criticism, Textual. I. Title.

BARNEY, Kenneth D. 227.1'06
Freedom, a guarantee for everybody : adapted from Romans by G. Raymond Carlson / Kenneth D. Barney. Springfield, Mo. : Gospel Pub. House, c1975. 125 p. ; 18 cm. (Radiant books) [BS2665.2.B37] 75-34644 ISBN 0-88243-891-3 pbk. : 1.25
1. Bible. N.T. Romans—Criticism, interpretation, etc. I. Carlson, G. Raymond. Romans. II. Title.

BARNHOUSE, Donald Grey, 227.106
1895-
Exposition of Bible doctrines, taking the Epistle to the Romans as a point of departure. v. 9. Grand Rapids, Mich., Eerdmans [c.1964] v. 22cm. First pub., 1952- under title: Expository messages on the whole Bible, taking the Epistle to the Romans as a point of departure. Contents.v.9. God's discipline: Romans 12:1-14:12, by Donald Grey Barnhouse. 58-13516 4.50
1. Bible. N.T. Romans—Sermons. I. Title.

BARNHOUSE, Donald Grey, 227.106
1895-
God's freedom; exposition of Bible doctrines, taking the Epistle to the Romans as a point of departure. Grand Rapids, Mich., Eerdmans [c.1961] 260p. Contents.v.6. Romans 6:1-7:25. 58-13516 4.50
1. Bible. N.T. Romans—Sermons. I. Title.

BARTH, Karl, 1886- 227.106
Christ and Adam; man and humanity in Romans 5. Tr. by T. A. Smail. New York, Collier [1962, c.1956, 1957] 123p. 18cm. (AS205V) .95 pap.,
1. Bible. N. T. Romans v—Theology. 2. Man (Theology)—Biblical teaching. I. Title.

BIBLE. N.T. Romans. 227.106
English. 1962. Blackwelder.
Toward understanding Romans; an introduction and exegetical translation, by Boyce W. Blackwelder. Anderson, Ind., Warner [dist. Gospel Trumpet, c.1962] 101p. 22cm. Bibl. 62-15373 3.50
I. Blackwelder, Boyce W. II. Title.

BRYAN, Christopher, 227'.1'06
1935-
Way of freedom : an introduction to the Epistle to the Romans with study guide / by Christopher Bryan. New York : Seabury Press, [1975] 124 p. ; 21 cm. "A Crossroad book." Bibliography: p. 123-124. [BS2665.2.B79] 74-28392 ISBN 0-8164-2111-0 pbk. : 2.95
1. Bible. N.T. Romans—Criticism, interpretation, etc. I. Title.

*ERICKSEN, Fred M. 227.106
Search. Minneapolis, Augsburg, c.1963. 56p. 22cm. .75 pap.,
I. Title.
Contents omitted.

KNOX, John, 1900- 227.106
Life in Christ Jesus; reflections on Romans, 5-8. Greenwich, Conn., Seabury Press, 1961. 128p. 22cm. [BS2665.4.K55] 61-11616
1. Bible. N. T. Romans v-viii—Meditations. I. Title.

KNOX, John, 1900- 227.106
Life in Christ Jesus; reflections on Romans, 5-8. New York, Seabury [1966, c.1961] 128p. 21cm. (SP26) [BS2665.4.K55] 61-11616 1.25 pap.,
1. Bible. N.T. Romans V-VIII—Meditations. I. Title.

†LLOYD-JONES, David 227'.1'06
Martyn.
Romans : an exposition of chapter 8:17-39 : the final perseverance of the saints / D. M. Lloyd-Jones. Grand Rapids : Zondervan Pub. House, 1976. xii, 457 p. ; 23 cm. Sermons delivered on Friday nights in Westminster Chapel, May 1961-May 1962. Includes text of Romans VIII, 17-39. [BS2665.4.L59] 76-2574 ISBN 0-310-33573-6 pbk. : 1.95
1. Bible. N.T. Romans VIII, 17-39—Sermons. 2. Sermons, English. I. Bible. N.T. Romans VIII, 17-39. English. 1976. II. Title.

PRICE, Walter K 227.106
Revival in Romans; an exposition of the Epistle to the Romans, chapters 1 through 8, with emphasis on its evangelistic thrust. Grand Rapids, Zondervan Pub. House [1962] 160p. 21cm. Includes bibliography. [BS2665.4.P7] 62-948
1. Bible. N. T. Romans— Sermons. 2. Evangelistic sermons. I. Title.

STEINKE, Peter L. 227'.1'06
With eyes wide open : biblical studies in Romans for young people / Peter L. Steinke. St. Louis : Concordia Pub. House, c1974. 78 p. ; 21 cm. Originally presented as a television program under same title. Unacc. melody, With eyes wide open, by J. Ylvisaker (p. 18-19) Brief stories and commentary explore the meaning of the New Testament book of Romans. [BS2665.2.S84] 74-3735 ISBN 0-570-03180-X pbk. : 1.50
1. Bible. N.T. Romans—Criticism, interpretation, etc.—Juvenile literature. I. Title.

VAUGHAN, Curtis. 227'.1'06
Romans : a study guide / by Curtis Vaughan. Grand Rapids : Zondervan Pub. House, c1976. p. cm. (Study guide series) Bibliography: p. [BS2665.5.V38] 76-26485 pbk. : 1.95
1. Bible. N.T. Romans—Study—Text-books. I. Title.

DALTON, Len. 227'.1'066
Searchlights from the Roman letter. [Waco, Tex., printed by Davis Bros. Pub. Co., 1967] x, 214 p. 16 cm. [BS2665.3.D34] 67-25161
1. Bible. N. T. Romans—Commentaries. I. Title.

DALTON, Len. 227'.1'066
Searchlights from the Roman letter. [Waco, Tex., printed by Davis Bros. Pub. Co., 1967] x, 214 p. 16 cm. [BS2665.3.D34] 67-25161
1. Bible, N.T. Romans—Commentaries. I. Title.

LOANE, Marcus L. 227'.1'066
The hope of glory; an exposition of the eighth chapter in the Epistle to the Romans, by Marcus L. Loane. Waco, Tex., Word Books [1969, c1968] 160 p. 23 cm. Bibliographical footnotes. [BS2665.3.L6 1969] 77-5734 3.95
1. Bible. N.T. Romans VIII—Commentaries. I. Title.

MINEAR, Paul Sevier, 227'.1'066
1906-
The obedience of faith; the purposes of Paul in the Epistle to the Romans [by] Paul S. Minear. Naperville, Ill., A. R. Allenson [1971] x, 115 p. 22 cm. (Studies in biblical theology, 2d ser., 19) [BS2665.2.M55 1971b] 76-131590 ISBN 0-8401-3069-4
1. Bible. N.T. Romans—Criticism, interpretation, etc. I. Title. II. Series.

SMART, James D. 227'.1'066
Doorway to a new age; a study of Paul's Letter to the Romans, by James D. Smart. [Cincinnati, Service Center, Board of Missions, United Methodist Church, 1972] xi, 196 p. 19 cm. Bibliography: p. 176-178. [BS2665.2.S6] 76-188673 1.25
1. Bible. N.T. Romans—Criticism interpretation, etc. I. Title.

STARKEY, Lycurgus 227'.1'066
Monroe.
Romans: a revolutionary manifesto [by] Lycurgus M. Starkey, Jr. Nashville, Abingdon Press [1973] 128 p. 19 cm. Includes bibliographical references. [BS2665.2.S8] 73-5870 ISBN 0-687-36604-6 2.75
1. Bible. N.T. Romans—Criticism, interpretation, etc. I. Title.

ARCHER, Gleason Leonard, 227.107
1916-
The Epistle to the Romans; a study manual. Grand Rapids, Baker Book House, 1959. 103 p. 20 cm. (Shield Bible study series) Includes bibliography. [BS2665.A7] 58-8382
1. Bible. N.T. Romans—Commentaries. I. Title.

BARNHOUSE, Donald Grey 227.107
Exposition of Bible doctrines, taking the Epistle to the Romans as a point of departure; v.3, God's remedy, Romans 3:21-4:25 Grand Rapids, Eerdmans [1959, c.1954] 387p. 22cm. First published, 1952- under title: Expository messages on the whole Bible, taking the Epistle to the Romans as a point of departure. 58-13516 3.50
1. Bible. N. T. Romans—Sermons. I. Title.

BARTH, Karl, 1886- 227.107
A shorter commentary on Romans. Richmond, John Knox Press [1959] 188p. 23cm. A translation by D. H. van Daalen of Kurze Erklarung des Romerbriefs. [BS2665.B32773 1959] 59-7419
1. Bible. N. T. Romans—Commentaries. I. Title.

*BERKEMEYER, William C. 227.1'07
Paul's Gospel; an adult study book on the Epistle to Romans, by William C. Berkemeyer. William A. Dudde, ed. Illus. by Johanna Sperl. Philadelphia, Lutheran Church Pr. [1968] 110p. illus. 21cm. (LCA Sunday church sch. ser.) .90 pap.,; 1.00 tchrs. guide.
1. Bible. N.T. Romans—Study, outlines, syllabi, etc. I. Dudde, William A. ed. II. Title.

BIBLE. N.T. Romans. 227'.1'07
Greek. 1967.
A critical and doctrinal commentary on the Epistle of St. Paul to the Romans. by William G. T. Shedd. Grand Rapids, Zondervan Pub. House [1967] viii, 439 p. 21 cm. "Reprinted from the 1879 edition." [BS2665.S5] 67-17235
1. Bible. N.T. Romans—Commentaries. I. Shedd, William Greenough Thayer, 1820-1894, ed. II. Title.

BIBLE. N. T. Romans. 227.107
English. 1961. Rhys.
The Epistle to the Romans, by Howard Rhys. New York, Macmillan [c.]1961. 250p. Bibl. 61-13522 3.50
1. Bible. N. T. Romans—Commentaries. I. Rhys, Howard, 1917- ed. II. Title.

BIBLE. N.T. Romans. 227'.1'07
English. 1967. New English.
The letter of Paul to the Romans; commentary by Ernest Best. Cambridge, Cambridge U.P., 1967. viii, 181 p. map. 20 1/2 cm. (B 67-3270) (The Cambridge Bible commentary: New English Bible) 17/6 (9/6 pbk.) Bibliography: p. 180. [BS2665.3.B4] 66-24289
1. Bible. N.T. Romans—Commentaries. I. Best, Ernest. II. Title. III. Series.

BIBLE. N.T. Romans. 227'.1'07
English. 1967. New English.
The letter of Paul to the Romans; commentary by Ernest Best. Cambridge, Cambridge U.P., 1967. viii, 184 p. map. 20 1/2 cm. (The Cambridge Bible commentary: New English Bible) Bibliography: p. 180. [BS2665.3.B4] 66-24289
1. Bible. N.T. Romans—Commentaries. I. Best, Ernest. II. Title. III. Series.

BIBLE. N.T. Romans. 227'.1'07
English. 1977.
Studies in Romans / by H. C. G. Moule. Grand Rapids : Kregel Publications, 1977. 270 p. ; 19 cm. (Kregel popular commentary series) Reprint of the 1892 ed. published at the University Press, Cambridge, Eng., under title The Epistle of Paul the Apostle to the Romans, and issued in series: The Cambridge Bible for schools and colleges. Includes bibliographical references and index. [BS2663.M68 1977] 77-79180 ISBN 0-8254-3215-4 pbk. : 3.50
1. Bible. N.T. Romans—Commentaries. I.

Moule, Handley Carr Glyn, Bp. of Durham, 1841-1920. II. Title.

BRAUCH, Manfred T. 227'.1'07
Set free to be / Manfred T. Brauch. Valley Forge, Pa. : Judson Press, [1975] 96 p. ; 22 cm. Includes bibliographical references. [BS2665.2.B73] 75-4721 ISBN 0-8170-0663-X : 2.95
1. Bible. N.T. Romans—Criticism, interpretation, etc. I. Title.

*BROKKE, Harold J. 227.107
Saved by his life. Minneapolis, 6820 Auto Club Rd. Bethany Fellowship, [c.1964] 211p. 19cm. 1.50 pap.,
I. Title.

BRUCE, Frederick Fyvie, 1910- 227.107
The Epistle of Paul to the Romans; an introduction and commentary. [1st ed.] Grand Rapids, Eerdmans [1963] 288 p. 21 cm. (The Tyndale New Testament commentaries [v. 6]) [BS2665.3.B69] 63-25766
1. Bible. N. T. Romans — Commentaries. I. Title.

BRUCE, Frederick Fyvie, 1910- 227.107
The Epistle of Paul to the Romans: an introduction and commentary. Grand Rapids, Mich., Eerdmans [c.1963] 288p. 21cm. (Tyndale New Testament commentaries v.6) Bibl. 63-25766 3.00
1. Bible. N. T. Romans—Commentaries. I. Title.

BRUNNER, Heinrich Emil, 1889- 227.107
The Letter to the Romans; a commentary. Philadelphia, Westminster Press [1959] 168 p. 23 cm. "This English translation is based upon one made by H. A. Kennedy from the 1956 German edition." [BS2665.3.B713] 59-9193
1. Bible. N. T. Romans. English. 1959. Revised standard. 2. Bible. N. T. Romans—Commentaries.

DAVIS, Thomas A. 227'.1'07
Romans for the everyday man [by] Thomas A. Davis. Washington, Review and Herald Pub. Association [1972, c1971] 186 p. illus. 22 cm. (Discovery paperbacks) Includes bibliographical references. [BS2665.3.D36 1972] 70-180601
1. Bible. N.T. Romans—Commentaries. I. Title.

DEHAAN, Richard W. 227'.1'07
The world on trial; studies in Romans [by] Richard W. De Haan. Grand Rapids, Zondervan Pub. House [1970] 192 p. 22 cm. [BS2665.2.D43] 76-121360 4.00
1. Bible. N.T. Romans—Criticism, interpretation, etc. I. Title.

GODET, Frederic, 1812-1900. 227'.1'07
Commentary on the Epistle to the Romans / F. Godet ; translated from the French by A. Cusin ; the translation rev. and edited with an introd. and appendix, Talbot W. Chambers. Grand Rapids : Kregel Publications, [1977] p. cm. Originally published in 1883 under title: Commentary on St. Paul's Epistle to the Romans. Reprint of the 1956 ed. published by Zondervan Pub. House, Grand Rapids, in series: Classic commentary library. [BS2665.G55 1977] 77-79189 ISBN 0-8254-2715-0 : 12.95
1. Bible. N.T. Romans—Commentaries. I. Title.

GRIFFITH, Arthur Leonard, 1920- 227.107
The Roman letter today. Nashville, Abingdon [1961, c.1959] 77p. 61-65437 1.00 pap.,
1. Bible. N. T. Romans—Criticism, interpretation, etc. I. Title.

HALVERSON, Richard C. 227.1'07
God's way out of futility; a concise discussion of Romans; its application to life here and now, with questions for discussion. Grand Rapids, Mich., Zondervan [1973, c.1964] 239 p. 18 cm. "Formerly published as Prologue to prison, and The gospel for the whole of life." [BS2665.2] 1.25 (pbk.)
1. Bible. N.T. Romans—Criticism, interpretation, etc. I. Title.

HAMILTON, Floyd Eugene, 1890- 227.107
The Epistle to the Romans; an exegetical and devotional commentary. Grand Rapids, Baker Book House, 1958. 235p. 23cm. [BS2665.H15] 58-12329
1. Bible. N. T. Romans— Commentaries. I. Title.

HOBBS, Herschel H. 227'.1'07
Romans : a verse by verse study / Herschel H. Hobbs. Waco, Tex. : Word Books, c1977. 168, [1] p. ; 23 cm. Bibliography: p. [169] [BS2665.3.H59] 76-48547 ISBN 0-87680-513-6 : 5.95
1. Bible. N.T. Romans—Commentaries. I. Title.

JOHNSON, Alan F. 227'.1'07
The freedom letter : a contemporary analysis of Paul's Roman letter that changed the course of Christianity / by Alan F. Johnson. Chicago : Moody Press, [1974] 220 p. : ill. ; 22 cm. Bibliography: p. 219-220. [BS2665.3.J63] 74-184822 ISBN 0-8024-2874-6 : 4.95
1. Bible. N.T. Romans—Commentaries. I. Title.

JOHNSON, Alan F. 227'.1'07
Romans : the freedom letter / by Alan F. Johnson. Chicago : Moody Press, 1976, c1974. p. cm. (Everyman's Bible commentary) Edition of 1974 published under title: The freedom letter. Includes bibliographies. [BS2665.3.J63 1976] 76-45368 ISBN 0-8024-2063-X (v. 1) : 1.95 per vol.
1. Bible. N.T. Romans—Commentaries. I. Title. II. Series.

LIDDON, Henry Parry, 1829-1890. 227.107
Explanatory analysis of St. Paul's Epistle to the Romans. Grand Rapids, Mich. Zondervan Pub. House [1961] 309p. 61-1476 4.95
1. Bible. N. T. Romans—Commentaries. I. Title.

LUTHER, Martin, 1483-1546 227.107
Lectures on Romans, v.15. Newly tr., ed. by Wilhelm Pauck. Philadelphia, Westminster Press [c.1961] lxvi, 444p. (Library of Christian classics, v.15) 'Translation is based on the critical edition of Luther's Romerbriefvorlesung by Johannes Ficker, published as vol. 56 of the so-called Weimar edition.' Bibl. 61-13626 6.50
1. Bible. N. T. Romans—Commentaries. I. Pauck, Wilhelm, 1901- ed. and tr. II. Title. III. Series.

LUTHI, Walter, 1901- 227.107
The Letter to the Romans, an exposition. Tr. [from German] by Kurt Schoenenberger. Richmond, Va., John Knox [c.]1961. 61-10283 4.00 bds.,
1. Bible. N. T. Romans—Commentaries. I. Title.

LUTHI, Walter, 1901- 227.107
The Letter to the Romans, an exposition. Translated by Kurt Schoenenberger. Richmond, John Knox Press, 1961. 221p. 23cm. Translation of Der Romerbrief, ausgelegt fur die Gemeinde. [BS2665.3.L813] 61-10283
1. Bible. N. T. Romans—Commentaries. I. Title.

MCCLAIN, Alva J. 227'.1'07
Romans: the gospel of God's grace; the lectures of Alva J. McClain. Compiled and edited by Herman A. Hoyt. Chicago, Moody Press [1973] 253 p. 22 cm. [BS2665.3.M24] 72-95027 ISBN 0-8024-7373-3 4.95
1. Bible. N.T. Romans—Commentaries. I. Title.

MALONE, A Hodge. 227.107
God's eternal power; the Epistle to the Romans in an intensive study. Epworth, Ga. [1959] 232p. 21cm. [BS2665.3.M3] 59-52130
1. Bible. N. T. Romans—Commentaries. I. Title.

MURRAY, John, 1898- 227.107
The Epistle to the Romans; the English text with introduction, exposition, and notes. Grand Rapids, Mich., Eerdmans [1960] (New international commentary on the New Testament) Includes bibliography. 59-14593 5.00
1. Bible. N.T. Romans—Commentaries. I. Title.

MURRAY, John, 1898- 227.107
The Epistle to the Romans; the English text with introduction, exposition, and notes, v.2; chapters IX-XVI. Grand Rapids, Mich., Eerdmans [1966, c.1965] xvi, 286p. 23cm. (New intl. commentary on the New Testament) Bibl. [BS2665.3.M8] 59-14593 5.00
1. Bible. N.T. Romans—Commentaries. I. Title.

PALMER, Earl F. 227'.1'07
Salvation by surprise : studies in the Book of Romans / Earl F. Palmer. Waco, Tex. : Word Books, c1975. 198 p. : ill. ; 23 cm. Includes bibliographical references. [BS2665.3.P34] 75-10090 5.95
1. Bible. N.T. Romans—Commentaries. I. Bible. N.T. Romans. English. Revised standard. 1975. II. Title.

SCHELKLE, Karl Hermann. 227.107
The Epistle to the Romans; theological meditations. [New York] Herder and Herder [1964] 269 p. 21 cm. Translation of Meditationen uber den Romerbrief. "The Epistle to the Romans reprinted from the New Testament, translated by James A. Kleist s. j. and Joseph I. Lilly c. m., 1956." [BS2665.3.S213] 64-19735
1. Bible. N. T. Romans—Commentaries. I. Bible. N. T. Romans. English. 1964. Kleist-Lilly. II. Title.

SCHELKLE, Karl Hermann 227.107
The Epistle to the Romans; theological meditations [Tr. from German. New York] Herder & Herder [c.1964] 269p. 21cm. The Epistle to the Romans reprinted from the New Testament, tr. by James A. Kleist, S. J., Joseph I. Lilly, C. M., 1956. 64-19735 4.95
1. Bible. N. t. Romans—Commentaries. I. Bible. N. T. Romans. English. 1964. Kleist-Lilly. II. Title.

STEELE, David N. 227.107
Romans, an interpretive outline; a study manual of Romans, including a series of interpretive notes and charts on the major doctrines of the epistle, by David N. Steele, Curtis C. Thomas. Pref. by Gordon H. Clark, Philadelphia, Presbyterian & Reformed [c.] 1963. xiv, 200p. diagrs. 26cm. Bibl. 63-21694 5.00
1. Bible. N. T. Romans—Study—Outlines, syllabi, etc. I. Thomas, Curtis C., joint author. II. Title.

STEELE, David N 227.107
Romans, an interpretive outline; a study manual of Romans, including a series of interpretive notes and charts on the major doctrines of the epistle, by Daivd N. Steele [and] Curtis C. Thomas. Pref. by Gordon H. Clark. Philadelphia, Presbyterian and Reformed Pub. Co., 1963. xiv, 200 p. diagrs. 26 cm. Includes bibliographies. [BS2665.5.S8] 63-21694
1. Bible. N.T. Romans—Study—Outlines, syllabi, etc. I. Thomas, Curtis C., joint author. II. Title.

STIFLER, James Madison, 1839-1902. 227.107
The Epistle to the Romans; a commentary, logical and historical. Chicago, Moody Press [1960] 256 p. 22 cm. [BS2665.S7 1960] 61-195
1. Bible. N. T. Romans — Commentaries. I. Title.

TAYLOR, Kenneth Nathaniel. 227.107
Romans for the children's hour, with I and II Timothy; a family devotions book. illustrated by JoAnn Brubaker. Chicago, Moody Press [1959] 190 p. illus. 24 cm. [BX2665.4.T3] 59-65319
1. Bible. N. T. Romans — Meditations. 2. Bible. N. T. Timothy — Meditations. I. Bible. N. T. Romans English. Paraphrases. 1959. Taylor. II. Bible. N. T. Timothy. English. Paraphrases. 1959. Taylor. III. Title.

THROCKMORTON, Burton Hamilton, 1921- 227.107
Romans for the layman. Philadelphia, Westminster Press [1961] 109 p. illus. 19 cm. [BS2665.3.T5] 61-5398
1. Bible. N. T. Romans—Commentaries. I. Title.

THROCKMORTON, Burton Hamilton, Jr., 1921 227.107
Romans for the layman. Philadelphia, Westminster Press [c.1961] 109p. illus. 61-5398 1.25 pap.,
1. Bible. N. T. Romans Commentaries. I. Title.

VANDERLIP, George 227'.107
Paul and Romans. Valley Forge [Pa.] Judson [1967] 112p. 20cm. Bibl. [BS2665.3.V3] 67-14360 2.00 pap.,
1. Bible. N.T. Romans—Commentaries. I. Title.

VANDERLIP, George. 227'.107
Paul and Romans. Valley Forge [Pa.] Judson Press [1967] 112 p. 20 cm. Bibliography: p. 112. [BS2665.3.V3] 67-14360
1. Bible. N T. Romans — Commentaries. I. Title.

BARRETT, Charles Kingsley. 227'.1'077
Reading through Romans / C. K. Barrett. 1st American ed. Philadelphia : Fortress Press, 1977. 85 p. ; 20 cm. [BS2665.3.B34 1977] 76-55828 ISBN 0-8006-1250-7 pbk. : 2.95
1. Bible. N.T. Romans—Commentaries. I. Title.

BARTH, Karl, 1886- 227'.1'077
The epistle to the Romans; tr. from the 6th ed. by Edwyn C. Hoskyns. London, New York Oxford Univ. Pr., 1968. xxi, 547p. 21cm. (Galaxy bk., GB261) Tr. of Der Romerbrief. [BS2665.B34 1968] 68-120958 2.95 pap.,
1. Bible. N. T. Romans—Commentaries. I. Title.

BATEY, Richard A., 1933- 227'.1'077
The letter of Paul to the Romans [by] Richard A. Batey. Austin, Tex., R. B. Sweet Co. [1969] 189 p. 21 cm. (The Living word commentary, 7) Bibliography: p. 15. [BS2665.3.B35] 68-58865
1. Bible. N.T. Romans—Commentaries. I. Bible. N.T. Romans. English Revised standard. 1969. II. Title. III. Series.

BIBLE. N.T. Romans. English. Barclay. 1975. 227'.1'077
The Letter to the Romans / translated with an introd. and interpretation by William Barclay. Rev. ed. Philadelphia : Westminster Press, c1975. p. cm. (Daily study Bible series.—Rev. ed.) [BS2663.B37 1975] 75-26523 ISBN 0-664-24107-7 pbk. : 3.45
1. Bible. N.T. Romans—Commentaries. I. Barclay, William, lecturer in the University of Glasgow. II. Title. III. Series.

DE WELT, Don. 227'.1'077
Romans realized; a new commentary, workbook, teaching manual. Paraphrase by James MacKnight. Summary by Moses E. Lard. Joplin, Mo., College Press [1964, c1959] 270 p. 23 cm. (Bible study textbook) Bibliography: p. 269-270. [BS2665.3.D4 1964] 72-1068
1. Bible. N.T. Romans—Commentaries. I. Title.

ERDMAN, Charles Rosenbury, 1866-1960. 227'.1'077
The Epistle of Paul to the Romans; an exposition. Pref. by Earl F. Zeigler. Philadelphia, Westminster Press [1966] 173 p. 19 cm. (His Commentaries on the New Testament books) On spine: The Epistle to the Romans. First published in 1925 under title: The Epistle to the Romans. [BS2665.E7 1966] 67-2104
1. Bible. N.T. Romans—Commentaries. I. Title. II. Title: The Epistle to the Romans.

FORELL, George Wolfgang. 227'.1'077
The Christian lifestyle : reflections on Romans 12-15 / by George Wolfgang · Forell. Philadelphia : Fortress Press, c1975. vii, 88 p. ; 22 cm. Includes bibliographical references. [BS2665.4.F67] 75-13033 ISBN 0-8006-1200-0 : 2.95
1. Bible. N.T. Romans XII-XV—Meditations. 2. Christian life—Biblical teaching. I. Title.

FRANZMANN, Martin H. 227'.1'077
Concordia commentary: Romans, by Martin H. Franzmann. St. Louis, Concordia Pub. House [1968] 289 p. 20 cm. Bibliography: p. 283-288. [BS2665.3.F7] 68-19990 4.00
1. Bible. N.T. Romans—Commentaries. I. Title.

GREENE, Oliver B. 227'.1'077
The Epistle of Paul the apostle to the Romans / by Oliver B. Greene. Enl. ed. Greenville, S.C. : Gospel Hour, inc., 1974. vii, 512 p. ; 21 cm. [BS2665.3.G73 1974] 74-187903 8.00
1. Bible. N.T. Romans—Commentaries. I. Bible. N.T. Romans. English. 1974.

LEENHARDT, Franz J., 1902- 227.1077
The Epistle to the Romans; a commentary. [Tr. from French by Harold Knight] Cleveland, World [1965, c.1957, c.1961] 389p. 22cm. [BS2665.3.L413] 65-18003 6.00
1. Bible. N.T. Romans—Commentaries I. Title.

MILLS, Sanford C. 227'.1'077
A Hebrew Christian looks at Romans [by] Sanford C. Mills. Grand Rapids, Mich., Dunham Pub. Co. [1968] 507 p. 23 cm. Bibliography: p. 493-[494] [BS2665.3.M5] 68-22830 7.95
1. Bible. N.T. Romans—Commentaries. I. Title.

O'NEILL, J. C. 227'.1'077
Paul's letter to the Romans / J. C. O'Neill. Harmondsworth; Baltimore Penguin 1975 315 p. ; 18 cm. (The Pelican New Testament commentaries) (A Pelican book) Includes the Revised standard text of the Epistle of Paul. Bibliography: p. 285-315. [BS2665.3.O5] 75-328864 ISBN 0-14-021810-6 pbk. : 3.25
1. Bible. N.T. Romans—Commentaries. I. Bible. N.T. Epistles of Paul. English. Revised standard. 1975. II. Title.

PLUMER, William Swan, 1802-1880. 227'.1'077
Commentary on Romans. Grand Rapids, Mich., Kregel [1971] 646 p. 23 cm. (Kregel reprint library) Reprint of the 1870 ed., which was issued under title: Commentary on Paul's Epistle to the Romans. [BS2665.P6 1971] 73-155251 ISBN 0-8254-3501-3 8.95

1. Bible. N.T. Romans—Commentaries. I. Title.

SWANEY, Richard A. 227'.1'09505
Out of darkness, light! / Richard A. Swaney. Mountain View, Calif. : Pacific Press Pub. Association, c1975. 62 p. ; 19 cm. Translation and paraphrase of the N.T. book of Romans. [BS2667.S87] 75-18106
1. Bible. N.T. Romans—Paraphrases, English. I. Title.

BARTCHY, S. Scott. 227'.2
[Mallon chresai (romanized form)] first-century slavery and the interpretation of 1 Corinthians 7:21, by S. Scott Bartchy. [Missoula, Mont.] Published by Society of Biblical Literature for the Seminar on Paul, 1973. ix, 199 p. 22 cm. (SBL dissertation series, 11) Originally presented as the author's thesis, Harvard. Bibliography: p. 185-199. [BS2675.2.B33 1973] 73-83723 ISBN 0-88414-022-9
1. Bible. N.T. 1 Corinthians VII, 21—Criticism, interpretation, etc. 2. Slavery in the Bible. 3. Slavery—History. I. Title. II. Title: First-century slavery and the interpretation of 1 Corinthians 7:21. III. Series: Society of Biblical Literature. Dissertation series, 11.

BIBLE. N.T. 1 Corinthians 227'.2
XIII. English. New English. 1975.
The greatest is love : St. Paul's wonderful words about faith, hope, and love / illustrated by Lois Jackson. Kansas City, Mo. : [Hallmark, 1975] [32] p. : ill. (some col.) ; 11 cm. (Hallmark editions) [BS2673 1975] 74-15378 ISBN 0-87529-421-9 : 2.00
1. Love (Theology)—Biblical teaching. I. Title.

BIBLE. N. T. Corinthians. 227.2
English. 1956. Barclay.
The Letters to the Corinthians. Translated with an introd. and interpretation by William Barclay. [2d ed.] Philadelphia, Westminster Press [1956] 297p. 18cm. (The Daily study Bible) [BS2675.B28 1956] 57-9566
1. Bible. N. T. Corinthians—Commentaries. I. Barclay, William, lecture in the University of Glasgow, ed. and tr. II. Title.

*BRIGHT, Laurence. 227.2
1 Corinthians Milwaukee, Bruce [1968] 54p. 18cm. (Scripture discussion outlines) .75 pap.,
1. Bible. N. T. Corinthians 1—Commentaries. I. Title.

BUNCH, Taylor Grant. 227.2
Love; a comprehensive exposition of 1 Corinthians 13. Washington, Review and Herald [1952] 128 p. 21 cm. [BS2675.B8] 52-30626
1. Bible. N. T. 2. Corinthians XIII—Commentaries. 3. Love (Theology)—Biblical teaching. I. Title.

CAMPBELL, Robert C. 227'.2
The Gospel of Paul [by] Robert B. [sic] Campbell. Valley Forge [Pa.] Judson Press [1973] 62 p. 22 cm. "Based upon material first published in Adult class, volume 68, number 1." [BS2675.2.C35] 73-7582 ISBN 0-8170-0587-0 1.50 (pbk.)
1. Bible. N.T. 1 Corinthians—Theology. 2. Bible. N.T. Romans—Theology. I. Title.

DE HAAN, Martin Ralph, 227.2
1891-
Studies in I Corinthians; messages on practical Christian living. Grand Rapids, Zondervan Pub. House [1956] 192p. 20cm. [BS2675.D43] 56-42852
1. Bible. N. T. I. Corinthians—Commentaries. II. Title.

EVANS, Colleen Townsend. 227'.2
Love is an everyday thing. Old Tappan, N.J., Revell [1974] 128 p. 21 cm. [BS2675.2.E9] 74-19046 ISBN 0-8007-0687-0
1. Bible. N.T. 1 Corinthians XIII—Criticism, interpretation, etc. 2. Love (Theology)—Biblical teaching. I. Title.

GETTYS, Joseph Miller, 227.2
1907-
How to study I Corinthians. Richmond, John Knox Press [1951] 128 p. 23 cm. [BS2675.G4] 51-2782
1. Bible. N. T. I. Corinthians—Study. II. Title.

GROSHEIDE, Frederik Willem, 227.2
1881-
Commentary on the First epistle to the Corinthians. Grand Rapids, W. B. Eerdmans Pub. Co., 1953. 415p. 23cm. (The New international commentary on the New Testament) [BS2675.G85] 53-8670
1. Bible. N.T. 1 Corinthians—Commentaries. 2. Corinthians. English. 1953. American revised. I. Bible. N.T. II. Title.

GUDER, Eileen L. 227'.2
To live in love [by] Eileen Guder. Foreword by Helmut Thielicke. Introd. by Richard C. Halverson. Grand Rapids, Zondervan [1967] 192p. 23cm. [BS2675.4.G8] 67-17240 3.95
1. Bible. N. T. 1. Corinthians XIII — Devotional literature. I. Title.

IRONSIDE, Henry Allan, 227.2
1876-1951.
Addresses on the First Epistle to the Corinthians. New York, Loizeaux Bros. [1952] 564p. 20cm. [BS2675.I68] 55-18729
1. Bible. N. T. 1 Corinthians— Commentaries. I. Title.

JACKSON, Lois. 227.2
The greatest is love; St. Paul's wonderful words about faith, hope, and love. Illustrated by Lois Jackson. [Kansas City, Mo., Hallmark, 1971] [47] p. illus. (part col.) 16 cm. (Hallmark editions) "From the new English Bible, New Testament, second edition." [BS2673.J33 1971] 75-131520 ISBN 0-87529-163-5 2.25
1. Bible—Pictures, illustrations, etc. I. Bible. N.T. 1 Corinthians. XIII. English. 1971. II. Title.

MORRIS, Leon. 227.2
The First epistle of Paul to the Corinthians; an introduction and commentary. [1st ed.] Grand Rapids, Eerdmans [1958] Corinthians--Commentaries. 249p. 21cm. (The Tyndale New Testament commentaries) Includes bibliography. [BS2675.M67] 58-10233
1. Bible. N. T. I. Title.

RULER, Arnold Albert van, 227.2
1908-
The greatest of these is love. [Translated by Lewis B. Smedes] Grand Rapids, Eerdmans [1958] 111p. 21cm. [BV4639.R773] 58-9541
1. Bible. N. T. 1 Corinthians XIII—Commentaries. 2. Love (Theology) I. Title.

WOYCHUK, N A 227.2
For all eternity; being a devotional exposition of I Cor. 3:8-15. Foreword by L. S. Chafer; foreword to 2d ed. by T. R. Dunham. New York, Books, inc. [1955] 173p. 20cm. First published under title: Building gold, silver, and precious stones. [BV4832.W64 1955] 56-19294
1. Bible, N. T. 2. Corinthians III, 8-15 — Commentaries. 3. Devotional literature I. Title.

ZODIATES, Spyros. 227'.2
Conquering the fear of death; an exposition of I Corinthians 15, based upon the original Greek text, by Spiros Zodhiates. Grand Rapids, Mich., Eerdmans [1970] x, 869 p. 20 cm. [BS2675.2.Z6] 74-17613 9.95
1. Bible. N.T. 1 Corinthians XV—Criticism, interpretation, etc. I. Title.

ZODIATES, Spyros. 227'.2
To love is to live; an exposition of I Corinthians 13, based upon the original Greek text, by Spiros Zodhiates. Grand Rapids, Eerdmans [1967] ix, 350 p. 20 cm. [BS2675.3.Z6] 67-9657
1. Bible. N. T. 1Corinthians XIII—Commentaries. I. Title.

ZODIATES, Spyros. 227'.2
To love is to live; an exposition of I Corinthians 13, based upon the original Greek text, by Spiros Zodhiates. Grand Rapids, Eerdmans [1967] ix, 350 p. 20 cm. [BS2675.3.Z6] 67-9657
1. Bible. N.T. 1 Corinthians XIII—Commentaries. I. Title.

BERQUIST, Millard J 227.2007
Studies in First Corinthians. Nashville, Convention Press [c1960] 148p. 19cm. [BS2675.5.B4] 60-13304
1. Bible. N. T. I. Corinthians-Study-Textbooks II. Title.

HOBBS, Herschel H. 227.2007
The Epistles to the Corinthians, a study manual. Grand Rapids, Baker Book House, 1960. 127 p. 20 cm. (Shield Bible study series) [BS2675.5.H6] 60-15785
1. Bible. N.T. Corinthians—Study—Textbooks. I. Title.

BAIRD, William, 1924- 227.206
The Corinthian church, a Biblical approach to urban culture. New York, Abingdon [c.1964] 224p. 24cm. Bibl. 64-20519 4.75
1. Bible. N.T. I Corinthians—Criticism, interpretation, etc. 2. City churches. I. Title.

BAIRD, William, 1924- 227.206
The Corinthian church, a Biblical approach to urban culture. New York, Abingdon Press [1964] 224 p. 24 cm. Bibliograhical footnotes. [BS2675.2.B3] 64-20519
1. Bible. N. T. Corinthians—Criticism, interpretation, etc. 2. City churches. I. Title.

BARTH, Karl, 1886-1968. 227'.2'06
The resurrection of the dead / by Karl Barth ; translated by H. J. Stenning. New York : Arno Press, 1977, c1933. 213 p. ; 23 cm. (The Literature of death and dying) Translation of Die auferstehung der toten. Reprint of the ed. published by Revell, New York. [BS2675.B32 1977] 76-19559 ISBN 0-405-09555-4 : 15.00
1. Jesus Christ—Resurrection. 2. Bible. N.T. 1 Corinthians XV—Commentaries. 3. Resurrection. I. Title. II. Series.

DAHL, Murdoch E., 1914- 227.206
The resurrection of the body; a study of I Corinthians 15. Naperville, Ill., Allenson [c.1962] 148p. 22cm. (Studies in Biblical theology, v.36) Bibl. 62-51198 2.75 pap.,
1. Bible. N. T. I Corinthians xv—Criticism, interpretation, etc. 2. Resurrection—Biblical teaching. I. Title.

HURD, John Coolidge. 227.206
The origin of I Corinthians New York, Seabury Press, 1965. xvi, 355 p. map. 23 cm. Bibliography: p. [306]-334. [BS2675.2.H8 1965] 65-3386
1. Bible. N. T. Corinthians — Criticism, interpretation, etc. I. Title.

HURD, John Coolidge 227.206
The Origin of I Corinthians New York, Seabury [c.]1965. xvi, 355p. map. 23cm. Bibl. [BS2675.2.H8] 65-3386 7.95
1. Bible. N. T. Corinthians—Criticism, interpretation, etc. I. Title.

KINNEY, Laurence F 227.206
Not like ordinary men, a study of First corinthians. Richmond, John Knox Press [1961] 76p. 23cm. Includes bibliography. [BS2675.5.K5] 61-11069
1. Bible. N. T. 2. Corinthians —Study. I. Title.

LEE, Robert Greene, 1886- 227.206
Beds of pearls, by Robert G. Lee. Grand Rapids, Mich. Zondervan [1960, c.1936] 120p. 20cm. 1.95 bds.,
1. Bible. N.T. I. Corinthians, xv 3-4—Criticism, interpretation, etc. I. Title.

SNOWDEN, Rita Frances. 227.206
The kindled flame. Philadelphia, Muhlenberg Press [1959] 127 p. 18 cm. [BS2675.4.S6] 60-962
1. Bible. N.T. 1 Corinthians XIII — Meditations. I. Title.

SNOWDEN, Rita Frances 227.206
The kindled flame. Philadelphia, Muhlenberg Press [1960] 127p. 18cm. 60-962 1.50 bds.,
1. Bible. N. T. I. Corinthians XIII—Meditations. I. Title.

SPITTLER, Russell P. 227'.2'06
The Corinthian correspondence / Russell P. Spittler. Springfield, Mo. : Gospel Pub. House, c1976. 125 p. : map ; 18 cm. (Radiant books) [BS2675.2.S67] 75-43157 ISBN 0-88243-892-1 pbk. : 1.25
1. Bible. N.T. Corinthians—Criticism, interpretation, etc. I. Title.

DEAN, Robert James, 227'.2'066
1932-
First Corinthians for today [by] Robert J. Dean. Nashville, Broadman Press [1972] 160 p. 21 cm. Includes bibliographical references. [BS2675.2.D4] 72-79165 ISBN 0-8054-1337-5
1. Bible. N.T. 1 Corinthians—Criticism, interpretation, etc. I. Title.

PAUL. 227'.2'066
Chicago, ACTA Foundation [1971- v. 22 cm. (Scripture discussion commentary, 11) Contents.Contents.— —2. 1 Corinthians, by L. Bright. 2 Corinthians, by H. Wansbrough. Philippians, by J. Murray-O'Connor. Colossians, by J. Murray-O'Connor. Philemon, by L. Bright. Includes bibliographical references. [BS2675.3.P36] 72-178777 ISBN 0-87946-010-5
1. Bible. N.T. Corinthians—Commentaries. 2. Bible. N.T. Philippians—Commentaries. 3. Bible. N.T. Colossians—Commentaries. 4. Bible. N.T. Philemon—Commentaries. I. Title. II. Series.

PEARSON, Birger 227'.2'066
Albert.
The pneumatikos-psychikos terminology in 1 Corinthians; a study in the theology of the Corinthian opponents of Paul and its relation to gnosticism. [Missoula, Mont.] Published by Society of Biblical Literature for the Nag Hammadi Seminar, 1973. xii, 147 p. 22 cm. (Society of Biblical Literature. Dissertation series, 12) Thesis—Harvard University, 1968. Bibliography: p. 137-147. [BS2675.2.P4] 73-92209 ISBN 0-88414-034-2
1. Bible. N.T. 1 Corinthians—Criticism, interpretation, etc. 2. Gnosticism. I. Title. II. Series.

WAGNER, C. Peter. 227'.2'066
A turned-on church in an uptight world; a study guide on First Corinthians with questions for discussion groups [by] C. Peter Wagner. Grand Rapids, Zondervan Pub. House [1971] 124 p. 21 cm. (A Zondervan horizon book) [BS2675.2.W3] 77-156241
1. Bible. N.T. 1 Corinthians—Criticism, interpretation, etc. 2. Christianity—20th century. I. Title.

BIBLE. N. T. Corinthians. 227.207
English. 1965. New English
The First and second letters of Paul to the Corinthians. Commentary by Margaret E. Thrall [New York] Cambridge [c.]1965. viii, 197p. map. 21cm. (Cambridge Bible commentary: New English Bible) [BS2675.3.T5] 65-14357 3.50; 1.65 pap.,
1. Bible. N. T. Corinthians—Commentaries. I. Thrall, Margaret Eleanor. II. Title. III. Series.

BLAIR, J. Allen. 227'.2'07
Living wisely; a devotional study of the First Epistle to the Corinthians, by J. Allen Blair. [1st ed.] Neptune, N.J., Loizeaux Bros., 1969. 381 p. 20 cm. [BS2675.4.B53] 68-58844 4.50
1. Bible. N.T. 1 Corinthians—Devotional literature. I. Title.

BOYER, James L. 227'.2'07
For a world like ours; studies in I Corinthians, by James L. Boyer. Grand Rapids, Baker Book House [1971] 153 p. illus. 20 cm. (New Testament studies) Bibliography: p. 152-153. [BS2675.5.B68] 70-174807 ISBN 0-8010-0553-1 2.95 (pbk.)
1. Bible. N.T. 1 Corinthians—Study—Textbooks. I. Title.

FISHER, Fred L. 227'.2'07
Commentary on 1 & 2 Corinthians / Fred Fisher. Waco, Tex. : Word Books, [1975] 453 p. ; 25 cm. Bibliography: p. 447-453. [BS2675.3.F57] 74-27486 9.95
1. Bible. N.T. Corinthians—Commentaries. I. Title.

FISHER, Fred L. 227'.2'07
Commentary on 1 & 2 Corinthians / Fred Fisher. Waco, Tex. : Word Books, [1975] 453 p. ; 25 cm. Bibliography: p. 447-453. [BS2675.3.F57] 74-27486 9.95
1. Bible. N.T. Corinthians—Commentaries. I. Title.

GLEN, John Stanley, 1907- 227.207
Pastoral problems in First Corinthians. Philadelphia, Westminster Press [1964] 224 p. 21 cm. "References and notes": p. 220-224. [BS2675.3.G55] 64-16521
1. Bible. N.T. 1 Corinthians — Commentaries. 2. Pastoral Theology — Biblical teaching. I. Title.

GLEN. JOHN STANLEY, 1907- 227.207
Pastoral problems in First Corinthians. Philadelphia, Westminster [c.1964] 224p. 21cm. Bibl. 64-10521 5.00
1. Bible. N. T. I. Corinthians—Commentaries. 2. Pastoral theology—Biblical teaching I. Title.

GODET, Frederic, 227'.2'07
1812-1900.
Commentary on I Corinthians / by Frederic Godet. Grand Rapids : Kregel Publications, 1977. p. cm. (Kregel reprint library) Translation of Commentaire sur la premiere epitre aux Corinthiens. Reprint of the 1898? ed. published by T. & T. Clark, Edinburgh, under title: Commentary on St. Paul's First Epistle to the Corinthians, which was issued as v. 27 and 30, new ser., of Clark's foreign theological library. [BS2675.G6913] 77-79190 ISBN 0-8254-2716-9 : 14.95
1. Bible. N.T. 1 Corinthians—Commentaries. I. Title.

*LUCK, G. Coleman 227'.2'07
First Corinthians. Chicago, Moody [1967,c.1958] 128p. 19cm. (Everyman's Bible commentary) .95 pap.,
1. Bible. N.T. Corinthians—Commentaries. I. Title.

REDPATH, Alan. 227.207
The royal route to heaven; studies in First Corinthians. [Westwood, N. J.] Revell [1960] 248p. 21cm. [BS2675.3.R4] 60-13094
1. Bible. N. T. 2. Corinthians—Commentaries. I. Title.

SIMON, William Glyn 227.207
Hughes
The First epistle to the Corinthians; introduction and commentary. London, SCM Press [New York, Macmillan, 1959, i.e.1960] 157p. Includes bibliography p.11-12. 19cm. (Torch Bible commentaries) 60-4218 2.50 bds.,
1. Bible. N. T. I. Corinthians—Commentaries. I. Title.

VAN GORDER, Paul R. 227'.2'07
The church stands corrected / Paul R. Van Gorder. Wheaton, Ill. : Victor Books, c1976. 156 p. ; 18 cm. (An Input book) [BS2675.3.V36] 76-10505 ISBN 0-88207-733-3 pbk. : 1.75
1. Bible. N.T. 1 Corinthians—Commentaries. I. Title.

BARRETT, Charles Kingsley. 227'.2'077
A commentary on the First Epistle to the Corinthians [by] C. K. Barrett. [1st ed.] New York, Harper & Row [1968] xi, 410 p. 22 cm. (Harper's New Testament commentaries) Bibliographical footnotes. [BS2675.3.B3] 68-17594
1. Bible. N. T. 1 Corinthians—Commentaries. I. Title.

BARRETT, Charles Kingsley. 227'.2'077
A commentary on the First Epistle to the Corinthians [by] C. K. Barrett. [1st ed.] New York, Harper & Row [1968] xi, 410 p. 22 cm. (Harper's New Testament commentaries) Bibliographical footnotes. [BS2675.3.B3] 68-17594
1. Bible. N.T. 1 Corinthians—Commentaries.

BIBLE. N.T. Corinthians. English. Barclay. 1975. 227'.2'077
The Letters to the Corinthians / translated with an introd. and interpretation by William Barclay. Rev. ed. Philadelphia : Westminster Press, c1975. xv, 268, [2] p. ; 20 cm. (The Daily study Bible series.—Rev. ed.) Bibliography: p. [270] [BS2673.B37 1975] 75-26563 ISBN 0-664-24108-5 pbk. : 3.45
1. Bible. N.T. Corinthians—Commentaries. I. Barclay, William, lecturer in the University of Glasgow. II. Title. III. Series.

BITTLINGER, Arnold, 1928- 227'.2'077
Gifts and graces; a commentary on I Corinthians 12-14. Translation from German by Herbert Klassen and supervised by Michael Harper. [1st U.S. ed.] Grand Rapids, [1968, c1967] 122 p. 21 cm. Translation of Gnadengaben. [BS2675.3.B513 1968] 68-28848 1.95
1. Bible. N.T. 1 Corinthians XII-XIV—Commentaries. I. Title.

CONZELMANN, Hans. 227'.2'077
1 Corinthians : a commentary on the First Epistle to the Corinthians / by Hans Conzelmann; translated by James W. Leitch; bibliography and references by James W. Dunkly; edited by George W. MacRae. Philadelphia : Fortress Press, [1975] xxii, 323 p. ; 25 cm. (Hermeneia) Translation of Der erste Brief an die Korinther. Includes the text of 1 Corinthians in a translation produced for this edition. Includes indexes. Bibliography: p. 304-308. [BS2675.3.C6613] 73-88360 ISBN 0-8006-6005-6 : 19.95
1. Bible. N.T. 1 Corinthians—Commentaries. I. Bible. N.T. 1 Corinthians. English. Leitch-MacRae. 1975. II. Title. III. Series.

GODET, Frederic, 1812-1900. 227'.2'077
The First Epistle to the Corinthians. Translated from the French by A. Cusin. Foreword to 1971 ed. by Donald W. Burdick. Grand Rapids, Zondervan Pub. House [1971] 2 v. in 1. 23 cm. Translation of Commentaire sur la premiere epitre aux Corinthiens. Reprint of the 1886 ed. [BS2675.3.G613 1971] 70-23547 11.95
1. Bible. N.T. 1 Corinthians—Commentaries. I. Title.

ROBERTSON, Edwin Hanton. 227'.2'077
Corinthians 1 and 2, by E. H. Robertson New York, Macmillan [1973] 154 p. 19 cm. (The J. B. Phillips' commentaries, 7) Cover title: The epistles to the Corinthians. [BS2675.3.R6] 74-153422 1.50 (pbk.).
1. Bible. N.T. Corinthians—Commentaries. I. Title. II. Title: The epistles to the Corinthians.

RUEF, John Samuel. 227'.2'077
Paul's first letter to Corinth [by] J. S. Ruef. [Harmondsworth, Eng., Baltimore] Penguin Books [1971] xxix, 197 p. 19 cm. (Pelican New Testament commentaries) Includes bibliographical references. [BS2675.3.R8 1971] 77-31980 ISBN 0-14-021329-5 £0.40
1. Bible. N.T. 1 Corinthians—Commentaries. I. Bible. N.T. 1 Corinthians. English. New English. 1971. II. Title.

ERDMAN, Charles Rosenbury, 1866-1960. 227'.2'77
The First epistle of Paul to the Corinthians; an exposition. Pref. by Earl F. Zeigler. Philadelphia, Westminster Press [1966] 176 p. 19 cm. (His Commentaries on the New Testament books) On spine: The First epistle to the Corinthians. [BS2675.E7 1966] 67-1998
1. Bible. N.T. 1 Corinthians—Commentaries. I. Title.

*REDPATH, Alan 227.3
Blessings out of buffetings: studies in Corinthians II. Westwood, N.J., Revell [c.1965] 240p. 21cm. 3.95 bds.,
1. Bible. N. T. Corinthians II—Commentaries. I. Title.

TASKER, Randolph Vincent Greenwood, 1895- 227.3
The Second epistle of Paul to the Corinthians, an introduction and commentary. [1st ed.] Grand Rapids, Eerdmans [1958] 192 p. 21 cm. (The Tyndale New Testament commentaries) Includes bibliography. [BX2675.T3] 58-10234
1. Bible. N. T. 2 Corinthians — Commentaries. I. Title.

*JAMES, Edgar C. 227.3007
II Corinthians: keys to triumphant living. Chicago, Moody [c.1964] 64p. 22cm. .80 pap.,
I. Title.

*WOYCHUK, N. A. 227.306
God's glory displayed: devotional exposition of II Corinthians 4:1-18. Chicago, Moody [1964, c.1962] 159p. 18cm. (89) .59 pap.,
I. Title.

CENTER for Hermeneutical Studies in Hellenistic and Modern Culture. 227'.3'066
Paul's Apology, II Corinthians 10-13, and the Socratic tradition / Hans Dieter Betz ; W. Wuellner, editor. Berkeley, CA : The Center, c1975. 30 p. ; 22 cm. (Protocol series of the colloquies of the Center ; no. 2 ISSN 0098-0900s) Includes bibliographical references..[BS2675.2.C44 1975] 75-35038 ISBN 0-89242-001-4
1. Bible. N.T. 2 Corinthians X-XIII—Criticism, interpretation, etc.—Congresses. I. Betz, Hans Dieter. II. Wuellner, Wilhelm H., 1927- III. Title. IV. Series: Center for Hermeneutical Studies in Hellenistic and Modern Culture. Protocol series of the colloquies ; no. 2.

HUGHES, Philip Edgcumbe 227.307
Paul's Second epistle to the Corinthians; the English text with introd., exposition, notes. Grand Rapids, Mich., Eerdmans [c.1962] 508p. 23cm. (New intl. commentary on the New Testament) Bibl. 61-17390 6.00
1. Bible. N. T. 2. Corinthians—Commentaries. I. Bible. N. T. 2. Corinthians. English. 1962. American revised. II. Title.

*KELCY, Raymond C. 227.3'07
Second Corinthians. 79p. 22cm. (Living word ser.) .75 pap.,
1. Bible—N.T.—Corinthians. 2. Commentaries. I. ustin, Texas, R. B. Sweet Co. [1967] II. Title.
Publisher's address: Box 4055, Austin, Tex.78751.

ERDMAN, Charles Rosenbury, 1866-1960. 227'.3'077
The Second epistle of Paul to the Corinthians; an exposition. Pref. by Earl F. Zeigler. Philadelphia, Westminster Press [1966] 136 p. 19 cm. (His Commentaries on the New Testament books) On spine: The Second epistle to the Corinthians. [BS2675.E73 1966] 67-2101
1. Bible. N. T. 2. Corinithians — Commentaries. I. Title.

ERDMAN, Charles Rosenbury, 1866-1960. 227'.3'077
The Second epistle of Paul to the Corinthians; an exposition. Pref. by Earl F. Zeigler. Philadelphia, Westminster Press [1966] 136 p. 19 cm. (His Commentaries on the New Testament books) On spine: The Second epistle to the Corinthians. [BS2675.E73 1966] 67-2101
1. Bible. N.T. 2 Corinthians—Commentaries. I. Title.

SCHELKLE, Karl Hermann. 227'.3'077
The Second Epistle to the Corinthians [by] Karl Schelkle. [Translated by Kevin Smyth. New York] Herder and Herder [1969] xx, 220 p. 22 cm. (New Testament for spiritual reading, 14) Translation of: Der sweite Brief an die Korinther. [BS2675.3.S3313] 76-17197 6.00
1. Bible. N.T. 2 Corinthians—Commentaries. I. Title. II. Series.

THOMPSON, James, 1942- 227'.3'077
The second letter of Paul to the Corinthians. Austin, Tex., R. B. Sweet Co. [1970] 192 p. 21 cm. (The Living word commentary, 9) Bibliography: p. 18. [BS2675.3.T48] 75-113159 ISBN 0-8344-0054-5
1. Bible. N.T. 2 Corinthians—Commentaries. I. Bible. N.T. 2 Corinthians. English. Revised standard. 1970. II. Title. III. Series.

RIDDERBOS, Herman N 227.4
The Epistle of Paul to the churches of Galatia. Grand Rapids, W. B. Eerdmans Pub. Co., 1953. 238p. 22cm. (The New International commentary on the New Testament) Translated by H. Zylstra from the Dutch ms. [BS2685.R5] 53-8671
1. Bible. N. T. Galatians—Commentaries. I. Bible. N. T. Galatians. English. 1953. American revised. II. Title.

STRAUSS, Lehman. 227.4
Devotional studies in Galatians and Ephesians. [1st ed.] New York, Loizeaux Bros. [1957] 256p. 20cm. Includes bibliography. [BS2685.S75] 57-4789
1. Bible. N. T. Galatians—Commentaries. 2. Bible. N. T. Ephesians—Commentaries. I. Title.

STRAUSS, Lehman. 227.4
Devotional studies in Galatians and Ephesians. [1st ed.] New York, Loizeaux Bros. [1957] 256 p. 20 cm. Includes bibliography. [BS2685.S75] 57-4789
1. Bible. N.T. Galatians — Commentaries. 2. Bible. N.T. Ephesians — Commentaries. I. Title.

TENNEY, Merrill Chapin, 1904- 227.4
Galatians; the charter of Christian liberty. Grand Rapids, Eerdmans, 1950. 200 p. map. 23 cm. Bibliography: p. [195]-200. [BS2685.T4] 50-8671
1. Bible. N. T. Galatians — Criticism, interpretation, etc. I. Title.

BLIGH, John. 227'.4'048
Galatians in Greek; a structural analysis of St. Paul's Epistle to the Galatians, with notes on the Greek. [Detroit] University of Detroit Press, 1966. 239 p. 23 cm. Bibliography: p. 72-73. [BS2685.2.B55] 67-9287
1. Bible. N.T. Galatians—Criticism, interpretation, etc. 2. Bible. N.T. Galatians—Language, style. I. Bible. N.T. Galatians. Greek. 1966. II. Title.

BIBLE. N.T. Galatians. English. Paraphrases. 1958. Neill. 227.4052
Paul to the Galatians [by] Stephen Neill. Ne York, Association Press [c1958] 74 p. 19 cm. (World Christian books, ser. 2, no 25) [BS2687.N4] 59-14241
I. Neill, Stephen Charles, Bp. II. Title.

BARCLAY, William, lecturer in the University of Glasgow. 227.406
Flesh and spirit, an examination of Galatians 5: 19-23. Nashville, Abingdon Press [1962] 127p. 19cm. [BS2685.2.B3] 62-52340
1. Bible. N. T. Galatians v, 19-23—Criticism, interpretation, etc. I. Title.

BLACKWOOD, Andrew Watterson, Jr., 1915- 227.406
The Epistles to the Galatians and Ephesians. Grand Rapids, Mich., Baker Bk. [c.]1962. 210p. 21cm. (Proclaiming the New Testament) Bibl. 62-11027 3.50
1. Bible. N. T. Galatians—Homiletical use. 2. Bible. N. T. Ephesians—Homiletical use. I. Title.

HUBBARD, David Allan. 227'.4'06
Galatians : gospel of freedom / David Allan Hubbard. Waco, Tex. : Word Books, 1977. 118 p. ; 21 cm. [BS2685.2.H8] 77-75451 ISBN 0-8499-2800-1 pbk. : 3.50
1. Bible. N.T. Galatians—Criticism, interpretation, etc. I. Title.

SANDERSON, John W. 227'.4'06
The fruit of the spirit : a study guide / by John W. Sanderson. Grand Rapids : Zondervan Pub. House, 1976. 189 p. ; 18 cm. Includes index. Bibliography: p. 180-182. [BS2685.2.S26 1976] 76-370964 pbk. : 1.75
1. Bible. N.T. Galatians v, 22-23—Criticism, interpretation, etc. 2. Christian life—Biblical teaching. I. Title.

MCDONALD, Hugh Dermot. 227'.4'066
Freedom in faith; a commentary on Paul's Epistle to the Galatians, by H. D. McDonald. Old Tappan, N.J., F. H. Revell Co. [1974, c1973] 157 p. 20 cm. [BS2685.3.M32 1974] 73-23076 ISBN 0-8007-0656-0 3.95
1. Bible. N.T. Galatians—Commentaries. I. Title.

SKAGGS, Fred R. 227'.4'066
The sound of falling chains; studies in Galatians, by Fred B. Skaggs [and] Robert J. Paciocco. Richmond, Skipworth Press [1972] iii, 140 p. maps. 21 cm. [BS2685.2.S57] 72-90687
1. Bible. N.T. Galatians—Criticism, interpretation, etc. I. Paciocco, Robert J., joint author. II. Bible. N.T. Galatians. III. Title.

BIBLE. N. T. Galatians. English. 1959. Barclay. 227.407
The letters to the Galatians and Ephesians. Translated, with introductions and interpretations, by William Barclay. Philadelphia, Westminster Press [1959] xviii, 219p. 18cm. (The Daily study Bible) [BS2685.3.B3 1959] 59-10145
1. Bible. N. T. Galatians—Commentaries. 2. Bible. N. T. Ephesians—Commentaries. I. Bible. N. T. Ephesians. English. 1959. Barclay. II. Barclay, William, lecture in the University of Glasgow, ed. and tr. III. Title. IV. Series: The Daily study Bible series

BIBLE. N.T. Galatians. English. 1967. New English. 227'.4'07
The letter of Paul to the Galatians; commentary by William Neil. Cambridge, Cambridge U.P., 1967. viii, 96 p. map. 20 1/2 cm. (The Cambridge Bible commentary: New English Bible) 17/6 (9/6 pbk.) [BS2685.3.N4] 66-29271
1. Bible. N.T. Galatians—Commentaries. I. Neil, William, 1909- II. Title. III. Series.

BIBLE. N.T. Galatians. English. 1967. New English 227'.4'07
The letter of Paul to the Galations; commentary by William Neil. Cambridge, Cambridge Univ. Pr., 1967. viii, 96p. map. 21cm. (Cambridge Bible commentary:New English Bible) [BS2685.3.N4] 66-29271 1.65 pap.,
1. Bible. N.T. Galatians—Commentaries. I. Neil. William, 1909- II. Title.
Available from publisher's New York office.

BRING, Ragnar, 1895- 227.407
Commentary on Galatians. Translated by Eric Wahlstrom. Philadelphia, Muhlenberg Press [1961] 296p. 23cm. Translation of Pauli Brev till Galaterna. [BS2685.3.B713] 61-6750
1. Bible. N. T. Galatians—Commentaries. I. Title.

BRING RAGNAR, [Anders Ebbe Ragner Bring] 1895- 227.407
Commentary on Galatians. Trans. [from Swedish] by Eric Wahlstrom. Philadelphia, Muhlenberg Press [c.1961] 296p. 61-6750 4.50
1. Bible. N.T. Galations—Commentaries. I. Title.

DE WOLF, Lotan Harold, 1905- 227'.4'07
Galatians; a letter for today, by L. Harold DeWolf. Grand Rapids, Eerdmans [1971] 86 p. 21 cm. [BS2685.2.D48] 78-162030 1.95
1. Bible. N.T. Galatians—Criticism, interpretations, etc. I. Title.

HAMILTON, Floyd Eugene, 1890- 227.407
The Epistle to the Galatians; a study manual. Grand Rapids, Baker Book House, 1959. 66p. 20cm. (Shield Bible study series) Includes bibliography. [BS2685.H26] 59-9127
1. Bible. N. T. Galatians—Commentaries. I. Title.

KOEHLER, John Philipp, 1859-1951. 227.407
The Epistle of Paul to the Galatians, a commentary by Joh. Ph. Koehler. Translated from the German by E. E. Sauer. Milwaukee, Northwestern Pub. House [c1957] 167p. 21cm. [BS2685.K613] 57-11477
1. Bible. N. T. Galatians— Commentaries. I. Bible. N. T. Galatians. English. 1957. II. Title.

RAMSAY, Sir William Mitchell, 1851-1939. 227.407
A historical commentary on St. Paul's epistle to the Galatians. Grand Rapids, Baker Book House, 1965. xi, 478 p. maps (on lining papers) 23 cm. "First ... published in the Expositor, June, 1898 -- September, 1899." "Reprinted from the 1900 edition." Bibliographical footnotes. [BS2685] 65-23751
1. Bible. N. T. Galatians — Commentaries. I. Title.

RAMSAY, Sir William Mitchell, 1851-1939 227.407
A historical commentary on St. Paul's epistle to the Galatians. Grand Rapids, Mich., Baker Bk., 1965. xi, 478p. maps (on lining papers) 23cm. First pub. in the Expositor, June, 1898 September, 1899. Reprinted from the 1900 ed. Bibl. [BS2685] 65-23751 6.95
1. Bible. N.T. Galatians—Commentaries. I. Title.

VOS, Howard Frederic, 1925- 227'.4'07
Galatians; a call to Christian liberty, by Howard F. Vos. Chicago, Moody Press [1971] 124 p. 20 cm. (Everyman's Bible commentary) Bibliography: p. 123-124. [BS2685.3.V68] 77-123159 0.95
1. Bible. N.T. Galatians—Commentaries. I. Title. II. Series.

WOOD, Fred M. 227'.4'07
The glory of Galatians [by] Fred M. Wood. Nashville, Broadman Press [1972] 147, [2] p. 20 cm. Bibliography: p. [149] [BS2685.3.W66] 70-178069 ISBN 0-8054-1335-9 2.95
1. Bible. N.T. Galatians—Commentaries. I. Title.

BIBLE. N.T. Galatians. English. Barclay. 1976. 227'.4'077
The letters to the Galatians and Ephesians / translated with an introd. and interpretation by William Barclay. Rev. ed. Philadelphia : Westminster Press, c1976. p. cm. (The Daily study Bible series — Rev. ed.) [BS2683.B37

1976] 76-22672 ISBN 0-664-21309-X deluxe ed. : 6.25 ISBN 0-664-24109-3 pbk. :
1. Bible. N.T. Galatians—Commentaries. 2. Bible. N.T. Ephesians—Commentaries. I. Barclay, William, lecturer in the University of Glasgow. II. Bible. N.T. Ephesians. English. Barclay. 1976. III. Title. IV. Series.

COLE, Robert Alan. 227.4077
The Epistle of Paul to the Galatians; an introduction and commentary, by R. A. Cole. [1st ed.] Grand Rapids, Eerdmans [1965] 188 p. 20 cm. (The Tyndale New Testament commentaries [v. 9]) Bibliographical references included in "Chief abbreviations" (p. 9-10) [BS2685.3.C6] 65-9502
1. Bible. N. T. Galatians — Commentaries. I. Title.

COLE, Robert Alan 227.4077
The Epistle of Paul to the Galatians; an introduction and commentary. Grand Rapids, Mich., Eerdmans [1965] 188p. 20cm. (Tyndale Testament commentaries, v.9) Bibl. [BS2685.3.C6] 65-9502 3.50
1. Bible. N. T. Galatians—Commentaries. I. Title.

ERDMAN, Charles Rosenbury, 1866-1960. 227.4077
The Epistle of Paul to the Galatians; an exposition. Pref. by Earl F. Zeigler. Philadelphia, Westminster Press [1966] 139 p. 19 cm. (His Commentaries on the New Testament books) On spine: The Epistle to the Galatians. [BS2685.E7 1966] 67-2106
1. Bible. N. T. Galatians — Commentaries. I. Title.

JOHNSON, Robert Lee, 1919- 227'.4'077
The letter of Paul to the Galatians [by] Robert L. Johnson. Austin, Tex., R. B. Sweet [1969] 182 p. 21 cm. (The Living Word commentary, 10) Bibliography: p. 30-32. [BS2685.3.J6] 76-95018
1. Bible. N.T. Galatians—Commentaries. I. Title. II. Series.

PINNOCK, Clark H., 1937- 227'.4'077
Truth on fire; the message of Galatians [by] Clark H. Pinnock. Grand Rapids, Mich., Baker Book House [1972] 94 p. 22 cm. [BS2685.3.P56] 72-85672 ISBN 0-8010-6927-0 1.95 (pbk.)
1. Bible. N.T. Galatians—Commentaries. I. Title.

QUESNELL, Quentin. 227'.4'077
The gospel of Christian freedom. [New York] Herder and Herder [1969] ix, 134 p. 21 cm. [BS2685.3.Q4] 70-75698 4.50
1. Bible. N.T. Galatians—Commentaries. I. Title.

SCHNEIDER, Gerhard, 1926- 227'.4'077
The epistle to the Galatians. [Translated by Kevin Smyth. New York] Herder and Herder [1969] xx, 142 p. 22 cm. (New Testament for spiritual reading, 15) Translation of Der Brief an die Galater. [BS2341.2.N382 vol. 15] 75-13609 5.00
1. Bible. N.T. Galatians—Commentaries. I. Title. II. Series.

WAGGONER, Ellet Joseph. 227'.4'077
The glad tidings; studies in Galatians, by E. J. Waggoner. Edited by Robert J. Wieland. [Rev. ed.] Mountain View, Calif., Pacific Press Pub. Association [1973?] 144 p. 22 cm. [BS2685.W3 1973] 72-81729
1. Bible. N.T. Galatians—Commentaries. I. Title.

WIERSBE, Warren W. 227'.4'077
Be free : an expository study of Galatians / Warren W. Wiersbe. Wheaton, Ill. : Victor Books, c1975. 160 p. ; 18 cm. (An Input book) [BS2685.3.W52] 74-33824 ISBN 0-88207-716-3 pbk. : 1.75
1. Bible. N.T. Galatians—Commentaries. 2. Christian life—Biblical teaching. I. Title.

WILLIAMS, Don. 227'.4'077
Celebrate your freedom : an inductive Bible study on Galatians / Don Williams. Waco, Tex. : Word Books, c1975. 148 p. ; 23 cm. [BS2685.3.W53] 75-19900 pbk. : 4.95
1. Bible. N.T. Galatians—Commentaries. I. Bible. N.T. Galatians. English. 1975. II. Title.

*KENT, Homer A. 227.'4'77
The freedom of God's sons : studies in Galtians / by Homer A. Kent, Jr. Grand Rapids : Baker Book House, 1976. 191p. : ill. ; 20 cm. (New Testament studies) Bibliography:p.187-191. [BS2685.3] ISBN 0-8010-5376-5 pbk. : 2.95.
1. Bible-Commentaries-N.T. Galatians 2. Bible-Criticism, interpretation, etc.- N.T. Epistles. I. Title.

ERDMAN, Charles Rosenbury, 1866-1960. 227'.5
The Epistle of Paul to the Ephesians; an exposition. Pref. by Earl F. Zeigler. Philadelphia, Westminster Press [1966] 143 p. 19 cm. (His Commentaries on the New Testament books) On spine: The Epistle to the Ephesians. [BS2695.E7 1966] 67-1971
1. Bible. N.T. Ephesians—Commentaries. I. Title.

GETTYS, Joseph Miller, 1907- 227.5
How to study Ephesians. Richmond, John Knox Press [1954] 64p. 23cm. [BS2695.G4] 54-7427
1. Bible. N.T. Ephesians—Study. I. Title.

GOODSPEED, Edgar Johnson, 1871-1962. 227.5
The key to Ephesians. [Chicago] University of Chicago Press [1956] xvi, 75 p. 25 cm. Suggests that the author of Ephesians was Onesimus. [BS2695.G58] 56-6550
1. Onesimus, Saint, d. 109. 2. Bible. N. T. Ephesians—Criticism, interpretation, etc. I. Bible. N. T. Ephesians. English. American Revised. 1956 II. Title.

*HOBBS, Herschel H. 227.5
New men in Christ [by] Herschel H. Hobbs Waco, Texas, Word Books [1974] 130 p. 23 cm. (studies in Ephesians) [BS2695.4] 73-85522 4.95
1. Bible. N. T. Ephesians—Commentaries. I. Title.

IRONSIDE, Henry Allan, 1876-1951. 227.5
In the heavenlies; practical expository addresses on the Epistle to the Ephesians. [1st ed.] New York, Loizeaux Bros. [1953] 341p. 20cm. [BS2695.I7] 54-32508
1. Bible. N. T. Ephesians—Commentaries. I. Title.

LLOYD-JONES, David Martyn. 227'.5
God's way of reconciliation (studies in Ephesians, chapter 2) [by] D. Martyn Lloyd-Jones. Grand Rapids, Baker Book House [1972] vii, 380 p. 22 cm. [BS2695.4.L54] 73-160675 ISBN 0-8010-5519-9 7.95
1. Bible. N. T. Ephesians II—Sermons. 2. Sermons, English. I. Title.

LLOYD-JONES, David Martyn. 227'.5
Life in the spirit in marriage, home & work; an exposition of Ephesians 5:18 to 6:9 [by] D. M. Lloyd-Jones. Grand Rapids, Baker Book House, [1975 c1973] 371 p. 22 cm. Series of sermons preached in Westminster Chapel, London during 1959 and 1960. [BS2695.4.L56] ISBN 0-8010-5550-4 8.95
1. Bible. N.T. Ephesians V, 18-V1,9—Sermons. 2. Sermons, English. 3. Church of England—Sermons. I. Title.
L.C. card no. for original ed.: 74-189728.

MACKAY, John Alexander, 1889- 227.5
God's order; the Ephesian letter and this present time. New York, Macmillan, 1953. 214p. 21cm. [BS2695.M32] 53-6695
1. Bible. N. T. Ephesians—Theology. I. Title.

MEYER, Frederick Brotherton, 1847-1929. 227.5
Ephesians: a devotional commentary. Grand Rapids, Zondervan Pub. House [1953] 126p. 20cm. (The F. B. Meyer library] Published in 1893 under title: Key-words of the inner life. [BS2695.M4 1953] 55-2861
1. Bible. N. T. Ephesians—Commentaries. I. Title.

MITTON, C Leslie. 227.5
The Epistle to the Ephesians; its authorship, origin, and purpose. Oxford, Clarendon Press, 1951. x, 346 p. 23 cm. "This book ... apart from the omission of two ... essays ... is in the same form as a thesis which was accepted by ... the University of London for the degree of doctor of philosophy." Bibliography: p. [ix]-x. [BS2695.M52] 52-7259
1. Bible. N. T. Ephesians — Criticism, interpretation, etc. I. Title.

PARKER, Joseph, 1830-1902. 227.5
The Epistle to the Ephesians. Grand Rapids, Baker Book House, 1956. 272p. 22cm. [BS2695.P27 1956] 56-7582
1. Bible. N. T. Ephesians—Commentaries. I. Title.

QUIMBY, Chester Warren, 1891- 227.5
The unity of mankind; a discussion of the central theme of the Epistle to the Ephesians in the light of present-day experience. Anderson, Ind., Warner Press [1958] 160p. 21cm. [BS2695.Q5] 58-8214
1. Bible. N. T. Ephesians—Theology. 2. Christian union. I. Title.

SIMPSON, Edmund Kidley. 227.5
Commentary on the Epistles to the Ephesians and the Colossians. The English text with introd., exposition and notes by E. K. Simpson and F. F. Bruce. Grand Rapids, Eerdmans [1957] 328 p. 23 cm. (The New international commentary on the New Testament) [BS2695.S5] 57-13040
1. Bible.N.T. Ephesians — Commentaries. 2. Bible. N.T. Colossians — Commentaries. I. Bruce, Frederick Fyvie, 1910- II. Bible. N.T. Ephesians. English. 1957. III. Bible. N.T. Colossians. English. 1957. IV. Title.

STOCKHARDT, George, 1842-1913. 227.5
Commentary on St. Paul's Letter to the Ephesians; done into English by Martin S. Sommer. Saint Louis, Concordia Pub. House, 1952. 271 p. 24 cm. [BS2695.S8] 52-43232
1. Bible. N. T. Ephesians — Commentaries. I. Title.

WEBB, Barbara Owen. 227'.5
Devotions for families : building blocks of Christian life / Barbara Owen Webb ; cover and ill. by Bill Hamilton Associates. Valley Forge, Pa. : Judson Press, c1976. 48 p. : ill. ; 28 cm. [BS2695.4.W4] 75-22162 ISBN 0-8170-0680-X pbk. : 1.95
1. Bible N.T. Ephesians—Meditations. 2. Family—Prayer-books and devotions—English. I. Title.

WRIGHT, Walter, Coleman, 1877- 227.5
Ephesians; an encyclical letter from the heart of Christ through the heart of Paul to the heart of the church of all time. Chicago, Moody Press [c1954] 128p. 18cm. (Colportage library, 258) [BS2695.W7] 55-32282
1. Bible. N. T. Ephesians—Commentaries. I. Title.

WUEST, Kenneth Samuel, 1893- 227.5
Ephesians and Colossians in the Greek New Testament for the English reader. Grand Rapids, W. B. Eerdmans Pub. Co., 1953. 254p. 21cm. [BS2695.W8] 53-7835
1. Bible. N. T. Ephesians—Commentaries. 2. Bible. N. T. Colossians —Commentaries. I. Title.

FIELDS, Wilbur. 227'.5'007
The glorious church, a study of Ephesians. [2d ed.] Joplin, Mo., College Press [1966, c1960] 213 p. illus., map. 23 cm. (Bible study textbook series) [BS2695.5.F5 1966] 71-1065 3.95
1. Bible. N.T. Ephesians—Study—Outlines, syllabi, etc. I. Title.

BARNEY, Kenneth D. 227'.5'06
A faith to live by / Kenneth D. Barney. Springfield, Mo. : Gospel Pub. House, 1977c1976 125 p. ; 18 cm. (Radiant books) [BS2695.2.B35] 76-27929 ISBN 0-88243-899-9 pbk. : 1.25
1. Bible. N.T. Ephesians—Criticism, interpretation, etc. 2. Christian life—1960- I. Title.

BARTH, Markus. 227.506
The broken wall; a study of the Epistle to the Ephesians. [1st ed.] Chicago, Judson Press [1959] 272p. 21cm. [BS2695.B33] 59-6574
1. Bible. N. T. Ephesians—Criticism, Interpretation, etc. I. Title.

CRISWELL, Wallie A. 227'.5'06
Ephesians, an exposition / by W. A. Criswell. Grand Rapids, Mich. : Zondervan Pub. House, [1974] 308 p. ; 22 cm. [BS2695.4.C74] 74-11852 pbk. : 6.95
1. Bible. N.T. Ephesians—Sermons. 2. Baptists—Sermons. 3. Sermons, American. I. Title.

HOWARD, Fred D. 227.506
Preaching and teaching from Ephesians. Grand Rapids, Baker Book House, 1963. 106 p. 21 cm. ([Minister's handbook series]) Bibliographical footnotes. [BS2695.3.H6] 63-20012
1. Bible. N.T. Ephesians—Commentaries. I. Title.

HOWARD, Fred D. 227.506
Preaching and teaching from Ephesians. Grand Rapids, Mich., Baker Bk. [c.]1963. 106p. 21cm. (Minister's handbk. ser.) Bibl. 63-20012 1.95 bds.,
1. Bible. N. T. Ephesians—Commentaries. I. Title.

MOODY, Dale. 227.506
Christ and the church an exposition of Ephesians with special application to some present issued. Grand Rapids, Eerdmans [1963] 153 p. 22 cm. Bibliographical footnotes. [BS2695.4.M6] 63-22533
1. Bible. N.T. Ephesians — Sermons. 2. Baptists — Sermons. 3. Sermons, American. I. Title.

MOODY, Dale 227.506
Christ and the church, an exposition of Ephesians with special application to some present issues. Grand Rapids, Mich., Eerdmans [c.1963] 153p. 22cm. Bibl. 63-22533 2.95; 1.45 pap.,
1. Bible. N. T. Ephesians—Sermons. 2. Baptists—Sermons. 3. Sermons, American. I. Title.

PUTNAM, Roy C., 1928- 227'.5'06
Getting it all together / Roy C. Putnam. Nashville : Abingdon, c1977. 112 p. ; 20 cm. [BS2695.2.P87] 76-28456 ISBN 0-687-14114-1 pbk. : 3.95
1. Bible. N.T. Ephesians—Criticism, interpretation, etc. I. Title.

SAMPLEY, J. Paul. 227'.5'06
"And the two shall become one flesh"; a study of traditions in Ephesians 5:21-33 [by] J. Paul Sampley. Cambridge [Eng.] University Press, 1971. viii, 177 p. 23 cm. (Society for New Testament Studies. Monograph series, 16) Bibliography: p. 164-168. [BS2695.2.S25 1971] 77-152644 ISBN 0-521-08131-9
1. Bible. N.T. Ephesians V, 21-33—Criticism, interpretation, etc. I. Title. II. Series: Studiorum Novi Testamenti Societas. Monograph series, 16.

ALLAN, John A. 227.507
The Epistle to the Ephesians: introduction and commentary. London, SCM Press [New York, Macmillan, 1960] 142p. 19cm. (Torch Bible commentaries) 59-357 2.25
1. Bible. N. T. Ephesians—Commentaries. I. Title.

BRUCE, Frederick Fyvie, 1910- 227.507
The Epistle to the Ephesians: a verse-by-verse exposition. [Westwood, N.J.] Revell [1962, c.1961] 139p. 21 cm. Bibl. 62-3295 3.00 bds.,
1. Bible. N. T. Ephesians—Commentaries. I. Bible. N. T. Ephesians. English. 1961. Revised II. Title.

FOULKES, Francis. 227.507
The Epistle of Paul to the Ephesians, an introduction and commentary. [1st ed.] Grand Rapids, Eerdmans [1963] 181 p. 21 cm. (The Tyndale New Testament commentaries) [BS2695.F66] 63-25958
1. Bible. N. T. Ephesians — Commentaries. I. Title.

FOULKES, Francis 227.507
The Epistle of Paul to the Ephesians, an introduction and commentary. Grand Rapids, Mich., Eerdmans [c.1963] 181p. 21cm. (Tyndale New Testament commentaries) 63-25958 3.00
1. Bible. N. T. Ephesians—Commentaries. I. Title.

GERSTNER, John H. 227.507
The Epistle to the Ephesians, a study manual. Grand Rapids, Baker Book House, 1958. 84 p. 21 cm. (Shield Bible study series) Includes bibliography. [BS2695.G38] 58-8385
1. Bible. N.T. Ephesians—Commentaries.

GUTZKE, Manford George. 227'.5'07
Plain talk on Ephesians. Grand Rapids, Mich., Zondervan Pub. House [1973] 191 p. 21 cm. [BS2695.3.G87] 72-85571 pap. 1.95
1. Bible. N.T. Ephesians—Commentaries. I. Title.

KENT, Homer Austin, 1926- 227'.5'07
Ephesians; the glory of the church, by Homer A. Kent, Jr. Chicago, Moody Press [1971] 128 p. 20 cm. (Everyman's Bible commentary) [BS2695.3.K4] 77-155689 0.95
1. Bible. N.T. Ephesians—Commentaries. I. Title. II. Series.

MITTON, C. Leslie. 227'.5'07
Ephesians / [by] C. Leslie Mitton. London : Oliphants, 1976. xiv, 235 p. ; 23 cm. (New century Bible) Includes index. Bibliography: p. xiii-xiv. [BS2695.3.M57] 76-379732 ISBN 0-551-00594-7 : £5.95
1. Bible. N.T. Ephesians—Commentaries. I. Title. II. Series.

MOULE, Handley Carr Glyn, Bp. of Durham, 1841-1920. 227'.5'07
Ephesian studies : lessons in faith and work. Handley C. G. Moule. 2d ed. Grand Rapids : Zondervan Pub. House, [1962?] ix, 340 p. ; 22 cm. Reprint of the 2d ed., originally published in 1908 by Hodder & Stoughton, London. [BS2695.H63 1962] 75-321752
1. Bible. N.T. Ephesians—Commentaries. I. Title.

POOVEY, William Arthur, 1913- 227'.5'07
Stand still & move ahead; meditations on Ephesians [by] W. A. Poovey. Minneapolis, Augsburg Pub. House [1973] 128 p. 20 cm.

[BS2695.4.P66] 72-90258 ISBN 0-8066-1305-X 2.75
1. Bible. N.T. Ephesians—Meditations. I. Title.

STEDMAN, Ray C. 227'.5'07
Riches in Christ / Ray C. Stedman. Waco, Tex. : Word Books, c1976. 215 p. ; 21 cm. (Discovery books) [BS2695.4.S73] 76-2860 ISBN 0-87680-462-8 : 5.95
1. Bible. N.T. Ephesians I-III—Sermons. 2. Sermons, American. I. Title.

SUMMERS, Ray. 227.507
Ephesians: pattern for Christian living. Nashville, Broadman Press [c.1960] xii, 156p. 21cm. (bibl.: p.153-156) 60-5195 3.00
1. Bible. N. T. Ephesians—Commentaries. I. Title.

SUMMERS, Ray. 227.507
Ephesians: pattern for Christian living. Nashville, Broadman Press [1960] 156 p. 24 cm. Includes bibliography. [BS2695.3.S9] 60-5195
1. Bible. N.T. Ephesians—Commentaries. I. Title.

TANNER, Paul A 227.507
The church, the body of Christ; the Epistle to the Ephesians speaks to us. Anderson, Ind., Warner Press [1959] 111 p. 19 cm. [BS2695.T34] 59-6604
1. Bible. N. T. Ephesians — Commentaries. I. Title.

VAUGHAN, Curtis. 227'.5'07
Ephesians : a study guide commentary / Curtis Vaughan. Grand Rapids : Zondervan Pub. House, c1977. 137 p. ; 21 cm. Bibliography: p. 135-137. [BS2695.3.V33] 76-44821 pbk. : 1.95
1. Bible. N.T. Ephesians—Commentaries. I. Title.

BIBLE. N.T. Ephesians. 227'.5'077
English. Authorized. 1977.
Studies in Ephesians / by H. C. G. Moule. Grand Rapids : Kregel Publications, 1977. 175 p. ; 19 cm. (Kregel popular commentary series) Reprint of the 1893 ed. published at the University Press, Cambridge, under title: The Epistle to the Ephesians, and in series: The Cambridge Bible for schools and colleges. Includes index. [BS2693.M68 1977] 77-79179 ISBN 0-8254-3218-9 pbk. : 2.95
1. Bible. N.T. Ephesians—Commentaries. I. Moule, Handley Carr Glyn, Bp. of Durham, 1841-1920. II. Title. III. Series: The Cambridge Bible for schools and colleges.

MACDONALD, William, 227'.5'077
1917-
Ephesians, the mystery of the church; a commentary. Wheaton, Ill., H. Shaw Publishers [1968] 144 p. 22 cm. Bibliography: p. 144. [BS2695.3.M3] 68-2809
1. Bible. N.T. Ephesians—Commentaries. I. Title.

WIERSBE, Warren W. 227'.5'077
Be rich : are you losing the things that money can't buy? : An expository study of the Epistle to the Ephesians / Warren W. Wiersbe. Wheaton, Ill. : Victor Books, c1976. 175 p. ; 18 cm. [BS2695.3.W53] 76-6833 ISBN 0-88207-730-9 pbk. : 1.75
1. Bible. N.T. Ephesians—Commentaries. I. Title.

ZERWICK, Maximilian. 227'.5'077
The epistle to the Ephesians [Translated by Kevin Smyth. New York] Herder and Herder [1969] xxii, 181 p. 22 cm. (New Testament for spiritual reading, 16) Translation of Der Brief an die Epheser. [BS2341.2.N382 vol. 16] 70-13610 6.00
1. Bible. N.T. Ephesians—Commentaries. I. Title. II. Series.

BIBLE. N.T. Philippians. 227'.6
English. 1977.
Studies in Philippians / by H. C. G. Moule. Grand Rapids, MI : Kregel Publications, 1977. p. cm. (Kregel popular commentary series) Originally published under title: The Epistle to the Philippians. Reprint of the 1893 ed. published by the University Press, Cambridge, in series: The Cambridge Bible for schools and colleges. [BS2703.M68] 77-79184 ISBN 0-8254-3216-2 pbk. : 2.45
1. Bible. N.T. Philippians—Commentaries. I. Moule, Handley Carr Glyn, Bp. of Durham, 1841-1920. II. Bible. N.T. Philippians. English. 1893. The Epistle to the Philippians. III. Title.

BIBLE N. T. Phillipians. 227.6
English. 1955. Johnstone
Lectures, exegetical and practical, on the Epistle of Paul to the Philippians; with a revised translation of the Epistle and notes on the Greek text, by Robert Johnstone. Grand Rapids, Baker Book House, 1955. 490p. 21cm. [Co-operative reprint library. 17] 'Reprinted from the 1875 printing by William Oliphant and Co., Edinburgh.' [BS2705.J57 1955] 55-8792
1. Bible. N. T. Philippians—Commentaries. I. Johnstone, Robert, professor in United Presbyterian College of Edinburgh. II. Title.

BIBLE. N. T. Philippians. 227.6
Greek. 1913.
Saint Paul's Epistle to the Philippians; a revised text with introductions, notes, and dissertations, by J. B. Lightfoot. Grand Rapid, Mich. Zondervan Pub. House [1965] xvi, 350 p. 23 cm. (Half-title: The Epistles of St. Paul. III. The first Roman captivity. I.) "First edition printed 1868." Dissertations: The Christian ministry; St. Paul and Seneca: p. [179]-328. [BS2705.L7 1913] 19-5674
1. Bible. N. T. Philippians—Commentaries. I. Lightfoot, Joseph Barber, bp. of Durham, 1828-1889, ed.

BLAIR, J Allen. 227.6
Living victoriously; a devotional study of Philippians. Grand Rapids, W. B. Eerdmans Pub. Co., 1956. 129 p. 23cm. [BS2705.B55] 56-58066
1. Bible. N. T. Philippians—Commentaries. I. Title.

GETTYS, Joseph Miller, 227.6
1907-
How to teach Philippians, Colossians, and Philemon. Richmond, Va. Knox [1964] 45p. 23cm. (How to study the Bible ser) 64-11257 1.00 pap.,
1. Bible. N. T. Epistles of Paul—Study—Outlines, syllabi, etc. I. Title.

GRAY, Henry David, 1908- 227.6
The upward call; a daily devotional study of Philippians for youth. New York, Abingdon-Cokesbury Press [1952] 95 p. 18 cm. [BS2705.G7] 52-8842
1. Bible. N. T. Philippians—Meditations. 2. Devotional exercises. I. Title.

GREENWAY, Alfred L. 227.6
The Epistle to the Philippians; a study manual. Grand Rapids, Baker Book House, 1957. 75 p. 20 cm. (Shield Bible study series) [BS2705.G73] 58-7711
1. Bible. N.T. Philippians—Commentaries.

HERKLOTS, Hugh Gerard 227.6
Gibson, 1903-
The Epistle of St. Paul to the Philippians; a devotional commentary. London, Lutterworth Press [lable: Chicago, A. R. Allennson, 1946] 136p. 19cm. [BS2705.H43] 53-32464
1. Bible. N. T. Phillippians—Commentaries. I. Title.

HERRING, Ralph A 227.6
Studies in Philippians. Nashville, Broadman Press [1952] 106p. 19cm. [BS2705.H45] 52-14760
1. Bible. N. T. Philippians—Study—Text-books. I. Title.

HERRING, Ralph A 227.6
To live is Christ; studies in Philippians. Nashville, Broadman Press [1953] 106p. 19cm. First published in 1952 under title: Studies in Philippians. [BS2705.H45 1953] 53-32186
1. Bible. N. T. Philippians—Study—Text-books. I. Title.

IRONSIDE, Henry Allan, 227.6
1876-1951.
Notes on Philippians. New ed., rev. New York, Loizeaux Bros. [1954] 126p. 19cm. [BS2705.I7] 54-33305
1. Bible. N. T. Philippians—Commentaries. I. Title.

MALTE, Eric C. 227'.6
New joy for daily living, by Eric C. Malte. Saint Louis, Concordia Pub. House [1969] 86 p. 20 cm. [BS2705.4.M3] 76-96216 1.95
1. Bible. N.T. Philippians—Devotional literature. I. Bible. N.T. Philippians. English. 1969. II. Title.

MARTIN, Ralph P 227'.6
Carmen Christi; Philippians ii. 5-11 in recent interpretation and in the setting of early Christian worship, by R. P. Martin. London, Cambridge U. P., 1967. xii, 364 p. 22 1/2 cm. (Society for New Testament Studies. Monograph series, 4) (B 67-15547) Bibliography: p. 320-339. [BS2705.2.M3] 67-12321
1. Bible. N. T. Philippians II, 5-11—Criticism, interpretation, etc. I. Title. II. Series: Studiorum Novi Testamenti Societas. Monograph series, 4

MARTIN, Ralph P. 227'.6
Carmen Christi; Philippians ii. 5-11 in recent interpretation and in the setting of early Christian worship. by R. P. Martin. London, Cambridge U. P., 1967. xii, 364 p. 22 1/2 cm. (Society for New Testament Studies. Monograph series, 4) Bibliography: p. 320-339. [BS2705.2.M3] 67-12321
1. Bible. N.T. Philippians II, 5-11—Criticism, interpretation, etc. I. Title. II. Series: Studiorum Novi Testamenti Societas. Monograph series, 4.

MULLER, Jacobus Johannes, 227.6
1906-
The Epistles of Paul to the Phillippians and to Philemon. Grand Rapids, Eerdmans, 1955. 200p. 23cm. (The New international commentary on the New Testament) [BS2705.M8] 55-2520
1. Bible. N. T. Philippians— Commentaries. 2. Bible. N. T. Philemon—Commentaries. I. Title.

PAINE, Stephen William, 227.6
1908-
Toward the mark; studies in Philippians Westwood, N. J., Revell [1953] 191p. 21cm. [BS2705.P2] 53-9087
1. Bible. N. T. Philippians—Commentaries. I. Title.

SIMCOX, Carroll Eugene, 227.6
1912-
They met at Philippi; a devotional commentary on philippians. New York, Oxford University Press, 1958 174 p. 21 cm. [BS2705.S5] 58-7989
1. Bible. N. T. Philippians — Commentaries I. Bible, N. T. Philippians, English, 1958. Simcox. II. Title.

WUEST, Kenneth Samuel, 227.6
1893-
Philippians in the Greek New Testament for the English reader. by Kenneth S. Wuest. Grand Rapids, Mich., Wm. B. Eerdmans publishing company, 1942. 119 [1] p. 20cm. The fifth in a series of word studies by the author. [BS2705.W8] 42-19628
1. Bible.N. T. Philippians—Commentaries. I. Bible. N. T. Philippians. English 1942 Wuest. II. Title.

BLIGH, John. 227'.6'06
Philippians / by John Bligh. Staten Island, N.Y. : Alba House, 1975, c1969. 129 p. ; 18 cm. (Scripture for meditation ; 2) Includes bibliographical references. [BS2705.4.B57 1975] 74-31317 ISBN 0-8189-0307-4 pbk. : 1.95
1. Bible. N.T. Philippians—Meditations. I. Title. II. Series.

DUNCAN, George B. 227.606
The life of continual rejoicing; studies in the Epistle to the Philippians. Chicago, Moody [c*65] 127p. 18cm. (Colportage lib., 510) [BS2705.5D8] 65-3625 .39 pap.,
1. Bible. N. T. Philippians—Addresses, essays, lectures. I. Title.

GETZ, Gene A. 227'.6'06
A profile of Christian maturity : a study of Philippians / by Gene A. Getz. Grand Rapids : Zondervan, c1976. 185 p. : map ; 18 cm. Includes bibliographical references. [BS2705.5.G47] 76-12096 pbk. : 1.95
1. Bible. N.T. Philippians—Study—Text-books. I. Title.

GRAY, Henry David, 1908- 227.606
The upward call; a daily devotional study of Philippians for youth. Nashville, Abingdon [1963, c.1952] 95p. 17cm. (Apex bk. M3) .69 pap.,
1. Bible. N.T. Philippians—Meditations. 2. Devotional exercises. I. Title.

VOS, Howard Frederic, 227'.6'06
1925-
Philippians : a study guide / Howard Vos. Grand Rapids : Zondervan Pub. House, c1975. 95 p. ; 21 cm. (Study guide series) Bibliography: p. 93-95. [BS2705.5.V67] 74-25349 pbk. : 1.95
1. Bible. N.T. Philippians—Study—Text-books. I. Title.

GRIFFITH, Arthur 227'.6'066
Leonard, 1920-
This is living; Paul's letter to the Philippians [by] Leonard Griffith. Nashville, Abingdon Press [1967, c1966] 158 p. 23 cm. [BS2705.3.G7] 67-4182
1. Bible. N.T. Philippians—Commentaries. I. Title.

AVERY, Margaret, 1890- 227.607
St. Paul's letter to the Philippians. London, Oxford U. P., 1967. 93 p. tables 19 cm. (Approaching the Bible, 3) 9/6 (B 67-12301) Bibliography: p. 89-90. [BS2705.5.A812271b0.6] 68-71638
1. Bible. N T. Philippians—Study—Outlines, syllabi, etc. I. Title.

BARTH, Karl, 1886- 227.607
The epistle to the Philippians. [Translated by James W. Leitch] Richmond, John Knox Press [1962] 128p. 22cm. Translation of Erklarung des Philipperbriefs. Bibliography: p. 128. [BS2705.B253 1962] 62-8213
1. Bible. N. T. Philippians—Commentaries. I. Title.

BEARE, Francis Wright, 227.607
1902-
A commentary on the Epistle to the Philippians. New York, Harper [1959] 182p. 22cm. (Harper's New Testament commentaries) Includes bibliography. [BS2705.3.B4 1959a] 59-7145
1. Bible. N. T. Philippians—Commentaries. I. Title.

BLAIKLOCK, E. M. 227.607
From prison in Rome; letters to the Philippians and Philemon. Grand Rapids, Mich., Zondervan [c.]1964 viii, 71p. map. 19cm. 64-55385 1.95 bds.,
1. Bible. N. T. Philippians—Commentaries. 2. Bible. N. T. Philemon—Commentaries. I. Title.

BLAIR, J. Allen. 227.607
Living victoriously; a devotional study of Philippians, by J. Allen Blair. New York, Loizeaux Bros. [1962] c1956] 129 p. 20 cm. [BS2705.4.B55 1962] 65-8826
1. Bible. N. T. Phillippians — Meditations. I. Title.

BOICE, James 227'.6'07
Montgomery, 1938-
Philippians; an expositional commentary. Grand Rapids, Zondervan Pub. House [1971] 314 p. 23 cm. [BS2705.3.B63] 79-146573 5.95
1. Bible. N.T. Philippians—Commentaries. I. Title.

DIETRICH, Suzanne de. 227.607
Toward fullness of life; studies in the letter of Paul to the Philippians. Philadelphia, Westminster [1966] 94p. 19cm. [BS2705.3.D5] 66-17604 1.25 pap.,
1. Bible. N.T. Philippians—Commentaries. I. Title.

MARTIN, Ralph P. 227.607
The Epistle of Paul to the Philippians, an introduction and commentary. Grand Rapids, Mich., Eerdmans 1960[c.1959] 186p. Includes bibliography. 21cm. (The Tyndale New Testament commentaries) 59-15971 3.00
1. Bible, N. T. Philippians — Commentaries. I. Title.

MOTYER, J. A. 227.607
Philippian studies; the richness of Christ [by] J. A. Motyer. [1st ed.] Chicago, Inter-Varsity Press [1966] 188 p. 23 cm. [BS2705.3.M58] 66-24395
1. Bible. N.T. Philippians—Commentaries. I. Title.

PENTECOST, J. Dwight. 227'.6'07
The joy of living; a study of Philippians [by] J. Dwight Pentecost. Grand Rapids, Zondervan Pub. House [1973] 245 p. 21 cm. [BS2705.3.P46] 73-2664 2.95 (pbk.)
1. Bible. N.T. Philippians—Commentaries. I. Title.

REES, Paul Stromberg. 227.607
The adequate man: Paul in Philippians. [Westwood, N. J.] Revell [1959] 127p. 20cm. Includes bibliography. [BS2705.R4 1959] 59-8720
1. Bible. N. T. Philippians—Commentaries. I. Title.

ROBERTSON, Archilbald 227.607
Thomas, 1863-1934.
Paul's joy in Christ studies in Philippians. Rev. and edited by W. C. Strickland. Nashville, Broadman Press [1959] 149p. 21cm. Includes bibliography. [BS2705.R6 1959] 59-5860
1. Bible. N. T. Philippians—Commentaries. I. Title.

STRAUSS, Lehman. 227.607
Devotional studies in Philippians. [1st ed.] New York, Loizeaux Bros. [1959] 253 p. 20 cm. Includes bibliography. [BS2705.3.S8] 59-49514
1. Bible. N.T. Philippians — Commentaries. I. Title.

TENNEY, Merrill Chapin, 227.607
1904-
Philippians: the gospel at work. Grand Rapids, Mich., W. B. Eerdmans Pub. Co., 1956. 102 p. 23 cm. [BS2705.3.T4] 56-10408
1. Bibl. N.T. Philippians — Commentaries. I. Title.

WALVOORD, John F. 227'.6'07
Philippians; triumph in Christ [by] John F. Walvoord. Chicago, Moody Press [1971] 127 p. 19 cm. (Everyman's Bible commentary) Bibliography: p. 125-127. [BS2705.3.W29] 78-143473 0.95
1. Bible. N.T. Philippians—Commentaries. I. Title. II. Series.

WALVOORD, John F 227.607
To live is Christ; an exposition of the Epistle

of Paul to the Philippians. Findlay, Ohio, Dunham Pub. Co. [1961] 93 p. 20 cm. [BS2705.3.W3] 62-3613
1. Bible. N.T. Philippians — Commentaries. I. Title.

WIERSBE, Warren W. 227'.6'07
Be joyful; a practical study of Philippians [by] Warren W. Wiersbe. Wheaton, Ill., Victor Books [1974] 130 p. 18 cm. (An Input book) [BS2705.3.W5] 74-76328 ISBN 0-88207-705-8 1.75 (pbk.)
1. Bible. N.T. Philippians—Commentaries. I. Title.

BERKELEY, James 227'.6'077
Percival, 1879-
Paul and Philippians [by] James P. Berkeley. Valley Forge [Pa.] Judson Press [1969] 62 p. 20 cm. [BS2705.3.B47] 69-16384 1.50
1. Bible. N.T. Philippians—Commentaries. I. Title.

BITTLINGER, Arnold, 227'.6'077
1928-
Letter of joy : an exploration of the letter Philippi / by Arnold Bittlinger ; translated from the German language by Susan Wiesmann. Minneapolis : Bethany Fellowship, [1975] 124 p. ; 21 cm. Translation of Ratschlage fur eine Gemeinde. [BS2705.3.B5613] 75-2265 ISBN 0-87123-338-X pbk. : 2.45
1. Bible. N.T. Philippians—Commentaries. I. Title.

ERDMAN, Charles 227'.6'077
Rosenbury, 1866-1960.
The Epistle of Paul to the Philippians; an exposition. Pref. by Earl F. Zeigler. Philadelphia, Westminster Press [1966] 155 p. 19 cm. (His Commentaries on the New Testament books) On spine: The Epistle to the Philippians. [BS2705.E7 1966] 67-2105
1. Bible. N.T. Philippians—Commentaries. I. Title.

HARRELL, Pat Edwin. 227'.6'077
The letter of Paul to the Philippians. Austin, Tex., R. B. Sweet [1969] 150 p. 21 cm. (The Living word commentary, 12) Bibliography: p. 41-42. [BS2705.3.H37] 71-79956
1. Bible. N.T. Philippians—Commentaries. I. Title. II. Series.

OGILVIE, Lloyd John. 227'.6'077
Let God love you. Waco, Tex., Word Books [1974] 160 p. 23 cm. Includes bibliographical references. [BS2705.4.O37] 73-91546 4.95
1. Bible. N.T. Philippians—Meditations. I. Title.

WILES, Maurice F. 227'6'6
The divine apostle: the interpretation of St. Paul's Epistles in the Early Church, by Maurice F. Wiles. London, Cambridge Univ. Pr., 1967. vi, 162p. 23cm. Bibl. [BS2650.2.W5] 67-13809 6.50
1. Bible. N. T. Epistles of Paul—Criticism, interpretation, etc.—Hist.—Early church. I. Title.
Available from publisher's New York office.

IRONSIDE, Henry Allan, 227.7
1876-1951.
Lectures on the Epistle to the Colossians. New York, Loizeaux Bros. [194-?] 186p. 19cm. [BS2715.I7] 54-32727
1. Bible. N. T. Colossians—Commentaries. I. Title.

PICKELL, Charles N 1927- 227.7
The Epistle to the Colossians; a study manual, by Charles N. Pickell. Grand Rapids, Baker Book House, 1965. 70 p. 20 cm. (The Shield Bible study series) Bibliography: p. 69-70. [BS2715.5.P5] 65-16287
1. Bible. N.T. Colossians—Study—Outlines, syllabi, etc. I. Title.

PICKELL, Charles N. 1927- 227.7
The Epistle to the Colossians; a study manual. Grand Rapids, Mich., Baker Bk. [c]1965. 70p. 20cm. (Shield Bible study ser.) Bibl. [BS2715.5.P5] 65-16287 1.50 pap.,
1. Bible. N. T. Colossians—Study—Outlines, syllabi, etc. I. Title.

SCHMIDT, Otto Henry, 1886- 227.7
Saint Paul shows us how; the pastor and missionary worker looks at his task in the light of St. Paul's Epistle to the Colossians. St. Louis, Concordia Pub. House [1950] viii, 118 p. 20 cm. Bibliography: p. 119. [BS2715.S3] 50-54734
1. Bible. N.T. Collossians — Commentaries. I. Title.

BIBLE. N.T. Colossians. 227.7052
English. Paraphrases. 1964.Neill.
Paul to the Colossians, by Stephen Neill. New York, Association Press [1964] 76 p. 19 cm. (World Christian books, no. 50. 3d ser.) [BS2717.N4] 65-729
I. Neill, Stephen Charles, Bp. II. Title.

BIBLE. N.T. Colossians. 227.7052
English. Paraphrases. 1964. Neill.
Paul to the Colossians by Stephen Neill. New York, Association [1964] 76p. 19cm. (World Christian bks., no. 50. 3d ser.) [BS2717.N4] 65-729 1.25 pap.,
I. Neill, Stephen Charles, Bp. II. Title.

BARCLAY, William 227.706
lecturer in the University of Glasgow
The all-sufficient Christ; studies in Paul's Letter to the Colossians. Philadelphia, Westminster Press [1963] 142 p. 19 cm. [BS2715.2.B3] 63-18385
1. Bible. N.T. Colossians — Criticism, interpretation, etc. I. Bible. N.T. Colossians. 1963. Revised standard. II. Title.

BARCLAY, William 227.706
The all-sufficient Christ; studies in Paul's Letter to the Colossians. Philadelphia, Westminster [c.1963] 142p. 19cm. 63-18385 1.45 pap.,
1. Bible. N. T. Colossians—Criticism, interpretation, etc. I. Bible. N. T. Colossians. 1963. Revised standard. II. Title.

BLIGH, John. 227'.7'06
Colossians / by John Bligh. Staten Island, N.Y. : Alba House, 1975, c1969. 125 p. ; 18 cm. (Scripture for meditation ; 4) Includes index. [BS2715.4.B55 1975] 74-31318 ISBN 0-8189-0309-0 pbk. : 1.95
1. Bible. N.T. Colossians—Meditations. I. Title. II. Series.

FRANZMANN, Martin H 227.706
New courage for daily living; devotions for adults. Saint Louis, Concordia Pub. House [1963] 95 p. 20 cm. (The Family worship series) [BX2715.4.F7] 63-19962
1. Bible. N. T. Colossians — Meditations. I. Title.

FRANZMANN, Martin H. 227.706
New courage for daily living: devotions for adults. St. Louis, Concordia [c.1963] 95p. 20cm. (Family worship ser.) 63-19962 1.00 pap.,
1. Bible. N. T. Colossians—Meditations. I. Title.

HOBBS, Herschel H. 227.706
Christ in you; an exposition of the Epistle to the Colosians. Grand Rapids, Mich., Baker Bk. House, 1961. 128p. (Evangelical pulpit lib.) 61-17546 2.50
1. Bible. N. T. Colossians—Sermons. 2. Evangelistic sermons. 3. Baptists—Sermons. 4. Sermons, American. I. Title.

TRENTHAM, Charles 227.7'06
Arthur, 1919-
The Shepherd of the Stars [by] Charles A. Trentham. Nashville, Broadman Pr. [1973, c.1962] x, 172 p. 19 cm. "An exploration of Colossians and its relevance for modern man." Includes bibliography. [BS2715.4.T7] 62-9200 ISBN 0-8054-1343-X
1. Bible. N.T. Colossians—Meditations. I. Title.

BENSON, David V. 227'.7'066
A new look at Colossians [by] David V. Benson. Carol Stream, Ill., Creation House [1973] 75 p. 18 cm. (New leaf library) [BS2715.2.B46] 73-82859 ISBN 0-88419-050-1 1.25 (pbk.)
1. Bible. N.T. Colossians—Criticism, interpretation, etc. I. Title.

FRANCIS, Fred O., 227'.7'066
comp.
Conflict at Colossae; a problem in the interpretation of early Christianity, illustrated by selected modern studies. Edited and translated, with an introd. and epilogue by Fred O. Francis and Wayne A. Meeks. [Missoula, Mont.] Society of Biblical Literature, 1973. viii, 222 p. 28 cm. (Sources for Biblical study, 4) Contents.Contents.—Lightfoot, J. B. The Colossian heresy.—Dibelius, M. The Isis initiation in Apuleius and related initiatory rites.—Bornkamm, G. The heresy of Colossians.—Lyonnet, S. Paul's adversaries in Colossae.—Francis, F. O. Humility and angelic worship in Col 2:18. The background of Embateuein (Col 2:18) in legal papyri and oracle inscriptions. Bibliography (p. 219-222) [BS2715.2.F72] 73-89169 ISBN 0-88414-032-6
1. Bible. N.T. Colossians—Criticism, interpretation, etc. I. Meeks, Wayne A., joint comp. II. Title. III. Series.

WHITE, Reginald E. O. 227'.7'066
In Him the fullness; homiletic studies in Paul's Epistle to the Colossians [by] R. E. O. White. Old Tappan, N.J., Revell [1973] 156 p. 21 cm. [BS2715.4.W5] 73-8801 ISBN 0-8007-0620-X 2.95 (pbk.)
1. Bible. N.T. Colossians—Sermons. 2. Baptists—Sermons. 3. Sermons, English. I. Title.

BIBLE. N.T. Colossians. 227'.7'07
English. 1977.
Studies in Colossians and Philemon / by H. C. G. Moule. Grand Rapids : Kregel Publications, [1977] p. cm. (Kregel popular commentary series) Reprint of the 1893 ed. published by The University Press, Cambridge, under title: The epistles to the Colossians and to Philemon, in series: The Cambridge Bible for schools and colleges. Includes bibliographical references and index. [BS2713.M68 1977] 77-79185 ISBN 0-8254-3217-0 pbk. : 2.95
1. Bible. N.T. Colossians—Commentaries. I. Moule, Handley Carr Glyn, Bp. of Durham, 1841-1920. II. Bible. N.T. Philemon. English. 1977. III. Title.

CARSON, Herbert M. 227.707
The Epistles of Paul to the Colossians and Philemon: an introduction and commentary. Grand Rapids, Mich., Eerdmans [1960] 112p. 112p. (Tyndale New Testament commentaries) 60-11127 2.00
1. Bible. N. T. Colossians—Commentaries. 2. Bible. N. T. Philemon—Commentaries. I. Title.

CRAGG, Herbert W. 227.707
The sole sufficiency of Jesus Christ; studies in the Epistle to the Colossians. [Dist. New York, Revell, 1962, c.1961] 110p. 62-1875 2.50 bds.,
1. Bible. N. T. Colossians—Commentaries. I. Title.

ERDMAN, Charles 227.707
Rosenbury, 1866-1960.
The Epistles of Paul to the Colossians and to Philemon: an exposition. Pref. by Earl F. Zeigler. Philadelphia, Westminster Press [1966] 152 p. 19 cm. (His Commentaries on the New Testament books) On spine: The Epistles to the Colossians and to Philemon. [BS2715.E7 1966] 67-131
1. Bible. N.T. Colossians—Commentaries. 2. Bible. N.T. Philemon—Commentaries. I. Title.

LOHSE, Eduard, 1924- 227.7'07
Colossians and Philemon; a commentary on the Epistles to the Colossians and to Philemon. Translated by William R. Poehlmann and Robert J. Karris. Edited by Helmut Koester. Philadelphia, Fortress Press [1971] xviii, 233 p. 25 cm. (Hermeneia) Translation of Die Briefe an die Kolosser und an Philemon. Bibliography: p. 210-219. [BS2715.3.L6413] 76-157550
1. Bible. N.T. Colossians—Commentaries. 2. Bible. N.T. Philemon—Commentaries. I. Bible. N.T. Colossians. English. Poehlmann & Karris. 1971. II. Bible. N.T. Philemon. English. Poehlmann & Karris. 1971. III. Title. IV. Series.

MOULE, Charles Francis 227.707
Digby.
The Epistles of Paul the apostle to the Colossians and to Philemon; an introduction and commentary. Cambridge [Eng.] University Press, 1958. 169 p. 19 cm. (Cambridge Greek Testament commentary) Includes bibliography. [BS2715.M6 1958] 59-16057
1. Bible. N. T. Colossians—Commentaries. 2. Bible. N. T. Philemon—Commentaries.

ROBERTSON, Archibald 227.707
Thomas, 1863-1934.
Paul and the intellectuals; the Epistle to the Colossians. Rev. and edited by W. C. Strickland. Nashville, Broadman Press [1959] 145 p. 21 cm. Includes bibliography. [BS2715.3.R6 1959] 59-5859
1. Bible. N. T. Colossians—Commentaries. I. Title.

MARTIN, Ralph P. 227'.7'077
Colossians: the church's Lord and the Christian's liberty; an expository commentary with a present-day application, by Ralph P. Martin. Grand Rapids, Zondervan Pub. House [1973, c1972] p. Bibliography: p. [BS2715.3.M37 1973] 72-13058 ISBN 0-85364-125-0
1. Bible. N.T. Colossians—Commentaries. I. Bible. N.T. Colossians. English. Revised standard. 1973.

*NICHOLSON, William 227.'7'077
R., Bp., d. 1901
Popular studies in Colossians; oneness with Christ, by W. R. Nicholson. Ed. by James D. Gray. Fincastle, Va., Scripture Truth Bk. Co. [1967, c.1903] 284p. port. 22cm. 3.95
1. Bible. N.T. Colossians—Study. I. Gray, James D., ed. II. Title.
Distributed by Kregel Pubns., 525 Eastern Ave. S. E., Grand Rapids, Mich. 49503.

TAYLOR, Preston. 227'.7'077
Philippians : joy in Jesus / by Preston Taylor. Chicago : Moody Press, c1976. p. cm. Bibliography: p. [BS2705.4.T39] 76-25128 ISBN 0-8024-6507-2 : 1.50
1. Bible. N.T. Philippians—Meditations. I. Title.

BIBLE. N.T. Pastoral 227.8
epistles. English. 1966. New English.
The pastoral letters: commentary on the first and second letters to Timothy and the letter to Titus, by Anthony Tyrrell Hanson. Cambridge, Cambridge U.P., 1966. viii, 126 p. map. 20 1/2 cm. (Cambridge Bible commentary: New Nelgish Bible) 15/- Bibliography: p. 123-124. [BSt2735.3.H3] 66-11281
1. Bible. N.T. Pastoral epistles—Commentaries. I. Hanson, Anthony Tyrrell. II. Title. III. Series.

BIBLE. N.T. Pastoral 227.8
epistles. English. 1966. New English
The pastoral letters; commentary on the first and second letters to Timothy and the letter to Titus, by Anthony Tyrell Hanson. Cambridge, Cambridge Univ. Pr., 1966. viii, 125p. map. 21cm. (Cambridge Bible commentary; New English Bible) Bibl. [BS2735.3.H3] 66-11281 3.00; 1.65 pap.,
1. Bible. N.T. Pastoral epistles—Commentaries. I. Hanson, Anthony Tyrrell. II. Title. III. Series.
For the general reader. Available from the publisher's New York office.

BIBLE. N. T. Pastoral 227.8
epistles. English. 1966. New English.
The pastoral letters; commentary on the first and second letters to Timothy and the letter to Titus, by Anthony Tyrrell Hanson. Cambridge, Cambridge U. P., 1966. viii, 126 p. map. 21 cm. (Cambridge Bible commentary: New English Bible) Bibliography: p. 123-124. [BS2735.3.H3] 66-11281 15/-
1. Bible. N. T. Pastoral epistles—Commentaries. I. Hanson, Anthony Tyrrell. II. Title. III. Series.

*CUNNINGHAM, Charles B. 227.8
Simple studies in Timothy, Titus, and Philemon. Grand Rapids, Mich., Baker Bk. [c.] 1964. 108p. 22cm. (Dollar sermon lib.) 1.00 pap.,
I. Title.

DIBELIUS, Martin, 1883- 227'.8
1947.
The Pastoral epistles; a commentary on the Pastoral epistles, by Martin Dibelius and Hans Conzelmann. Translated by Philip Buttolph and Adela Yarbro. Edited by Helmut Koester. Philadelphia, Fortress Press [1972] xx, 175 p. illus. 25 cm. (Hermeneia) Translation of Die Pastoralbriefe, 4th rev. ed. by H. Conzelmann. Bibliography: p. 161-163. [BS2735.D513 1972] 71-157549 ISBN 0-8006-6002-1
1. Bible. N.T. Pastoral epistles—Commentaries. I. Conzelmann, Hans. II. Bible. N.T. Pastoral epistles. English. Koester. 1972. III. Title. IV. Series.

IRONSIDE, Henry Allan, 227.8
1876-1951.
Addresses, lectures, expositions on Timothy, Titus, and Philemon. New York, Loizeaux Bros. [1951] 288p. 19cm. First ed. published in 1947 under title: Addresses on the First and Second Epistles of Timothy; also, lectures on the Epistle to Titus. [BS2735.I7 1951] 54-32891
1. Bible. N. T. Pastoral Epistles—Commentaries. 2. Bible. N. T. Philemon—Commentaries. I. Title.

LIGHTFOOT, Joseph Barber, 227.8
Bp. of Durham, 1828-1889.
Notes on the Epistles of St. Paul (I and II Thessalonians, I Corinthians 1-7, Romans 1-7, Ephesians 1: 1-14) Based on the Greek text from previously unpublished commentaries. Grand Rapids, Zondervan Pub. House, 1957. 336p. 23cm. (Classic commentary library) [BS2650.L53] 58-3456
1. Bible. N. T. Epistles of Paul—Commentaries. I. Title.

MOELLERING, Howard Armin. 227'.8
Concordia commentary: 1 Timothy, 2 Timothy, Titus [by] H. Armin Moellering. Philemon [by] Victor A. Bartling. Saint Louis, Concordia Pub. House [1970] 288 p. 20 cm. Includes bibliographies. [BS2735.3.M6] 71-121107
1. Bible. N.T. Pastoral epistles—Commentaries. I. Bartling, Victor A. Philemon. 1970. II. Title: Concordia commentary: 1 Timothy, 2 Timothy, Titus, Philemon.

VINE, William Edwy, 1873- 227.8
1949
The Epistles to Timothy and Titus; faith and conduct. Grand Rapids, Mich., Zondervan [c.1965] 176p. 20cm. [BS2735.3.V5] 66-132 2.95 bds.,
1. Bible. N.T. Pastoral epistles—Commentaries. I. Title.

ELLIOTT, Willis Edwin, 227.8007
1918-
The pastoral letters; a guide for adult group study of 1 and 2 Timothy, and Titus, by Willis E. Elliott and Willard W. Wetzel. Boston,

United Church Press [1964] 156 p. illus. 21 cm. [BS2735.5.E5] 64-14498
1. Bible. N.T. Pastoral epistles — Study. I. Wetzel, Willard W., joint author. II. Title.

JOHNSON, Philip C. 227.8007
The epistles to Titus and Philemon; a study manual, by Philip C. Johnson. Grand Rapids, Baker Book House [1966] 100 p. 20 cm. (Shield Bible study outlines) [BS2755.5.J6] 66-18302
1. Bible. N.T. Titus—Study. 2. Bible. N.T. Philemon—Study. I. Title.

AMIOT, Francois. 227'.8'06
The key concepts of St. Paul. [Translated by John Dingle. New York] Herder and Herder [1962] 297 p. 21 cm. Translation of Les idees maitresses de saint Paul. [BS2651.A643] 61-17458
1. Bible. N.T. Epistles of Paul—Theology. 2. Salvation. I. Title.

WHITE, John Lee. 227'.8'06
The form and function of the body of the Greek letter: a study of the letter-body in the non-literary papyri and in Paul the Apostle [Missoula, Mont.] Society of Biblical Literature for the Seminar on Paul, 1972. ix, 166 p. 22 cm. ([Society of Biblical Literature] Dissertation series, no. 2) On cover: The body of the Greek letter. Originally presented as the author's thesis, Vanderbilt University, 1970. Bibliography: p. 165-166. [BS2650.2.W43 1972] 72-87360
1. Bible. N.T. Epistles of Paul—Criticism, interpretation, etc. 2. Greek letters—History and criticism. I. Title. II. Title: The body of the Greek letter. III. Series.

WHITE, John Lee. 227'.8'06
The form and function of the body of the Greek letter : a study of the letter-body in the non-literary papyri and in Paul the Apostle / by John Lee White. 2d ed., corr. Missoula, Mont. : Published by Scholars Press for the Society of Biblical Literature, 1976c1972 xiv, 131 p. ; 22 cm. (Dissertation series - Society of Biblical Literature ; no. 2) Originally presented as the author's thesis, Vanderbilt University, 1970. Bibliography: p. 129-131. [BS2650.2.W43 1972b] 75-33088 ISBN 0-89130-048-1 pbk. : 4.50
1. Bible. N.T. Epistles of Paul—Criticism, interpretation, etc. 2. Greek letters—History and criticism. I. Title. II. Series: Society of Biblical Literature. Dissertation series ; no. 2.

BIBLE. N. T. Pastoral 227.807
epistles. English. 1960. Barclay.
The letters to Timothy, Titus, and Philemon. Translated, with introductions and interpretations, by William Barclay. [2d ed.] Philadelphia, Westminster Press [1960] xv, 324 p. 18 cm. (The Daily study Bible) [BS2735.3.B3 1960] 61-5396
1. Bible. N. T. Pastoral epistles—Commentaries. 2. Bible. N. T. Philemon—Commentaries. I. Bible. N. T. Philemon. English. 1960. Barclay. II. Barclay, William, lecturer in the University of Glasgow, ed. and tr. III. Title. IV. Series: The Daily Study Bible series

CARLETON, Arthur Patrick 227.807
Pastoral epistles; a commentary. New York, Association [1964] 77p. 19cm. (World Christian bks., no. 51. 3d ser.) [BS2735.3.C3] 65-709 1.25 pap.,
1. Bible. N.T. Pastoral epistles—Commentaries. I. Title.

HORNE, Charles M. 227.807
The Epistles to the Thessalonians, a study manual. Grand Rapids, Mich., Baker Bk. House, 1961. 78p. (Shield Bible study ser.) Bibl. 61-11307 1.50 pap.,
1. Bible. N. T. Thessalonians—Study—Textbooks. I. Title.

KELLY, John Norman 227.807
Davidson
A commentary on the pastoral epistles; I Timothy, II Timothy, Titus. New York, Harper [1964, c.1963] 264p. 22cm. (Harper's New Testament commentaries) Bibl. 64-10751 5.00
1. Bible. N.T. Pastoral epistles—Commentaries. I. Title.

LEANEY, Alfred Robert 227.807
Clare
The epistles to Timothy, Titus, and Philemon; introduction and commentary. London, SCM Press [dist. New York, Macmillan, 1960] 144p. (Bibl.: p.38-39) 20cm. (Torch Bible commentaries) 60-3071 2.50 bds.,
1. Bible. N.T. Pastoral epistles—Commentaries. I. Title.

BIBLE. N.T. Pastoral 227'.8'077
epistles. English. Barclay. 1975.
The letters to Timothy, Titus, and Philemon / translated with an introd. and interpretation by William Barclay. Rev. ed. Philadelphia : Westminster Press, c1975. xvii, 283, [1] p. ; 19 cm. (The Daily study Bible series. — Rev. ed.) Bibliography: p. [284] [BS2733.B28 1975] 75-26553 ISBN 0-664-24111-5 pbk. : 3.45
1. Bible. N.T. Pastoral epistles—Commentaries. 2. Bible. N.T. Philemon—Commentaries. I. Barclay, William, lecturer in the University of Glasgow. II. Bible. N.T. Philemon. English. Barclay. 1975. III. Title. IV. Series.

GRAY, W. Arthur. 227'.81
Sanctified common sense, by W. Arthur Gray. Boston, Christopher Pub. House [1968] 112 p. 21 cm. Bibliographical footnotes. [BS2725.3.G7] 68-31021 ISBN 0-8158-0007-X 3.00
1. Bible. N.T. 1 Thessalonians V, 13-22—Commentaries. I. Title.

MORRIS, Leon. 227.81
The Epistles of Paul to the Thessalonians; an introduction and commentary. [1st ed.] Grand Rapids, Eerdmans, 1957. 152p. 21cm. (The Tyndale New Testament commentaries) [BS2725] 57-13634
1. Bible. N. T. Thessalonians—Commentaries. I. Title.

MORRIS, Leon. 227.81
The Epistles of Paul to the Thessalonians; an introduction and commentary. [1st ed.] Grand Rapids, Eerdmans, 1957. 152p. 21cm. (The Tyndale New Testament commentaries) [BS2725] 57-13634
1. Bible N. T. Thessalonians—Commentaries. I. Title.

NEIL, William, 1909- 227.81
The Epistle of Paul to the Thessalonians. New York, Harper [1950] xivii, 204 p. 21 cm. (The Moffatt New Testament commentary) [BS2341.M6 vol. 12] 50-7263
1. Bible. N.T. Thessalonians — Commentaries. I. Title. II. Series.

NEIL, William, 1909- 227.81
St. Paul's Epistles to the Thessalonians; introduction and commentary. Naperville, Ill., Allenson [1957] 151p. 19cm. (Torch Bible commentaries) Includes bibliography. [BS2725.N4] 58-14534
1. Bible. N. T. Thessalonians— Commentaries. I. Title.

OCKENGA, Harold John, 227.81
1905-
The church in God; expository values in Thessalonians. [Westwood, N. J.] [Revell [c1956] 350p. 21cm. [BS2725.O25] 56-5240
1. Bible. N. T. Thessalonians— Sermons. I. Title.

OCKENGA, Harold John, 227.81
1905-
The Epistles to the Thessalonians. Grand Rapids, Baker Book House, 1962. 142 p. 20 cm. (Proclaiming the New Testament [10]) [BS2725.4.03] 62-20643
1. Bible. N.T. Thessalonians — Homiletical use. I. Title.

BARNHOUSE, Donald 227'.81'07
Grey, 1895-1960.
Thessalonians—an expositional commentary / Donald Grey Barnhouse. Grand Rapids : Zondervan Pub. House, c1977. 111 p. ; 21 cm. [BS2725.B37 1977] 77-1507 5.95
1. Presbyterian Church—Sermons. 2. Bible. N.T. Thessalonians—Sermons. 3. Sermons, American. I. Title.

BIBLE. N.T. 227'.81'07
Thessalonians. English. Revised standard. 1969.
Thessalonians in the Revised standard version; with introduction & commentary by D. E. H. Whiteley. London, Oxford U.P., 1969. x, 115 p. illus., facsims., maps. 20 cm. (New Clarendon Bible, New Testament) Bibliography: p. 31. [BS2725.3.W5] 73-437875 ISBN 0-19-836906-9 20/-
1. Bible. N.T. Thessalonians—Commentaries. I. Whiteley, Denys Edward Hugh. II. Title. III. Series.

BRISTOL, Lyle O 227.8107
1913or14-1963.
Paul and Thessalonians [by] Lyle O. Bristol. Valley Forge, Judson Press [1965] 95 p. 20 cm. Bibliography: p. 95. [BS2725.3.B68] 64-24075
1. Bible. N. T. Thessalonians — Commentaries. I. Title.

BRISTOL, Lyle O., 227.8107
1913or14-1963
Paul and Thessalonians. Valley Fovge, Pa., Judson [c.1965] 95p. 20cm. Bibl. [BS2725.3B68] 64-24075 1.50 pap.,
1. Bible. N. T. Thessalonians—Commentaries. I. Title.

ERDMAN, Charles 227.8107
Rosenbury, 1866-1960.
The Epistles of Paul to the Thessalonians; an exposition. Pref. by Earl F. Zeigler. Philadelphia, Westminster Press [1966] 105 p. 19 cm. (His Commentaries on the New Testament books) On spine: The Epistles to the Thessalonians. [BS2725.E7 1966] 67-140
1. Bible. N.T. Thessalonians—Commentaries. I. Title. II. Title: The Epistles to the Thessalonians.

*HOGG, Charles F. 227'.81'07
The epistles to the Thessalonians;
I. Title.

HORTON, Stanley M. 227'.81'07
It's getting late : a practical commentary on the Epistles to the Thessalonians / Stanley M. Horton. Springfield, Mo. : Gospel Pub. House, [1975] iii, 124 p. ; 18 cm. (Radiant books) Bibliography: p. 124. [BS2725.3.H67] 74-33869 1.25
1. Bible. N.T. Thessalonians—Commentaries. I. Title.

LINEBERRY, John 227.8107
Vital word studies in I Thessalonians: a sound scriptural presentation based upon the original Greek text. Grand Rapids, Mich. Zondervan Pub. House [c.1960] 131p. 23cm. Bibl.: p. 131i132 60-4100 2.00 bds.,
1. Bible. N. T. I Thessalonians—Commentaries. I. Bible. N. T. I. Thessalonians. English. 1960. Lineberry. II. Bible. N. T. I. Thessalonians. 1960. Authorized. III. Title.

LINEBERRY, John, 1926- 227.8107
Vital word studies in I Thessalonians: a sound scriptural presentation based upon the original Greek text. Grand Rapids, Zondervan Pub. House [1960] 131p. 23cm. Includes bibliography. [BS2725.3.L5] 60-4100
1. Bible. N. T. I Thessalonians—Commentaries. I. Bible. N. T. I Thessalonians. English. 1960. Lineberry. II. Bible. N. T. 1 Thessalonians. English. 1960. Authorized. III. Title.

LINEBERRY, John, 1926- 227.8107
Vital word studies in II Thessalonians: a sound Scriptural presentation based upon the original Greek text. Introd. by G. Arthur Woolsey. Grand Rapids, Mich., Zondervan [1962, c.1961] 93p. 23cm. Bibl. 62-3454 2.50
1. Bible. N.T. 1 Thessalonians—Commentaries. I. Bible. N.T. 2 Thessalonians. English. 1961. Lineberry. II. Bible. N.T. 2 Thessalonians English. 1961. Authorized. III. Title.

MORRIS, Leon. 227.8107
The first and second Epistles to the Thessalonians; the English text with introd., exposition, and notes. Grand Rapids, Eerdmans [1959] 274 p. 23 cm. (The New international commentary on the New Testament) Bibliographical footnotes. [BS2725.M65] 58-9549
1. Bible. N. T. Thessalonians—Commentaries.

BIBLE. N.T. 227.81077
Thessalonians. English. 1965. Blackwelder.
Toward understanding Thessalonians; an introduction, oxegetical translation, and commentary, by Boyce W. Blackwelder. Anderson, Ind., Warner Press [1965] 160 p. 21 cm. The translation is based on Eberhard Nestle's edition of the Greek text (London, British and Foreign Bible Society, 1934) bibliography: p. 155-156. [BS2725.3.B53] 65-14973
1. Bible. N.T. Thessalonians—Commentaries. I. Blackwelder, Boyce W. II. Title.

BIBLE. N.T. 227'.81'077
Thessalonians. English. Revised standard. 1969.
1 and 2 Thessalonians / edited by A. L. Moore. London ; Camden, N.J. : Nelson, 1969. ix, 127 p. ; 23 cm. (The Century Bible ; new ser.) Includes indexes. Bibliography: p.[viii]-ix. [BS2723.M66 1969] 75-322844 ISBN 0-551-00580-7
1. Bible. N.T. Thessalonians—Commentaries. I. Moore, Arthur Lewis. II. Title. III. Series.

HIEBERT, David 227'.81'077
Edmond, 1910-
The Thessalonian epistles, a call to readiness; a commentary by D. Edmond Hiebert. Chicago, Moody Press [1971] 383 p. 24 cm. Includes the text of the epistles interwoven with the commentary. Bibliography: p. 376-383. [BS2725.3.H5] 76-143478 6.95
1. Bible. N.T. Thessalonians—Commentaries. I. Bible. N.T. Thessalonians. English. American revised. 1971. II. Title.

KELCY, Raymond C., 227'.81'077
1916-
The letters of Paul to the Thessalonians [by] Raymond C. Kelcy. Austin, Tex., R. B. Sweet Co. [1968] 182 p. 21 cm. (The Living word commentary, 13) "Based on the text of the Revised standard version of the Bible." Bibliography: p. 19-20. [BS2725.3.K4] 68-55947
1. Bible. N.T. Thessalonians—Commentaries. I. Title.

BIBLE. N. T. 227.81077065-14973
Thessalonians. English. 1965. Blackwelder.
Toward understanding Thessalonians; an introduction, exegetical translation, and commentary, by Boyce W. Blackwelder. Anderson, Ind., Warner [c.1965] 160p. 21cm. Tr. is based on Eberhard Nestle's ed. of the Greek text (London, British and Foreign Bible Soc., 1934) Bibl. [BS2725.3.B53] 3.95
1. Bible. N. T. Thessalonians—Commentaries. I. Blackwelder, Boyce W. II. Title.

BIBLE. N.T. Pastoral 227.83
epistles. English. 1963.
The Pastoral epistles in the new English Bible. Introd., commentary by C. K. Barrett. Oxford, Clarendon Pr. [New York, Oxford] 1963. 151p. illus., map (on lining paper) facsim. 20cm. (New Clarendon Bible. New Testament) Bibl. 63-5605 2.50
1. Bible. N.T. Pastoral epistles—Commentaries. I. Barrett, Charles Kingsley. II. Title.

BIBLE. N.T. Pastoral 227.83
epistles. English. 1963.
The Pastoral epistles in the new English Bible. With Introd. and commentary by C. K. Barrett. Oxford, Clarendon Press, 1963. 151 p. illus., map (on lining paper) facsim. 20 cm. (The New Clarendon Bible (New Testament)) Bibliography: p. [35] [BS2733.B3] 63-5605
1. Bible. N.T. Pastoral epistles—Commentaries. I. Barrett, Charles Kingsley. II. Title.

BIBLE. N. T. Pastoral 227.83
epistles. Greek. 1954.
The Pastoral epistles; the Greek text, with introd. and commentary by E. K. Simpson. [1st ed.] Grand Rapids, Eerdmans [1954] vii, 173p. 22cm. Bibliography: p. 169-170. [BS2735.S5] 55-252
1. Bible. N. T. Pastoral epistles—Commentaries. I. Simpson, Eerdnd Kidley. II. Title.

GUTHRIE, Donald, 1916- 227.83
The Pastoral epistles, an introduction and commentary. [1st ed.] Grand Rapids, Eerdmans [1957] 228 p. 20 cm. (Tyndale New Testament commentaries) [BS2735.G8] 57-14483
1. Bible. N. T. Pastoral epistles—Commentaries.

HIEBERT, David Edmond, 227.83
1910-
First Timothy. Chicago, Moody Press [1957] 127p. 17cm. (Colportage library, 327) [BS2745.H5] 57-3561
1. Bible. N.T. I. Timothy—Commentaries. II. Title.

WUEST, Kenneth Samuel, 227.83
1893-
The Pastoral Epistles in the Greek New Testament for the English reader. Grand Rapids, W. B. Eerdmans Pub. Co. 1952. 207 p. 21 cm. The twelfth in a series of word studies by the author. [BS2735.W8] 52-12762
1. Bible. N. T. Pastoral Epistles — Commentaries. I. Title.

BLAIKLOCK, E. M. 227'.83'007
The Pastoral epistles; a study guide to the epistles of I and II Timothy and Titus [by] E. M. Blaiklock. Grand Rapids, Mich., Zondervan Pub. House [1972] 127 p. 21 cm. [BS2735.5.B56] 74-180838
1. Bible. N.T. Timothy—Study—Outlines, syllabi, etc. 2. Bible. N.T. Titus—Study—Outlines, syllabi, etc. I. Title.

ELLIOTT, James Keith. 227'.83'048
The Greek text of the epistles to Timothy and Titus, by J. K. Elliott. Salt Lake City, University of Utah Press, 1968. v, 257 p. 25 cm. (Studies and documents, 36) Introductory matter and commentary in English; variant textual readings in Greek. "Substantially in content the thesis submitted ... [to] Oxford University." Bibliography: p. 250-257. [BS2745.2.E4] 76-17643
1. Bible. N.T. Timothy—Criticism, Textual. 2. Bible. N.T. Titus—Criticism, Textual. I. Title. II. Series.

BARACKMAN, Paul F 227.8306
The Epistles to Timothy and Titus. Grand Rapids, Baker Book House, 1962. 155p. 21cm. (Proclaiming the New Testament) Includes bibliography. [BS2735.4.B3] 62-11026
1. Bible. N. T. Pastoral epistles —Homiletical use. I. Title.

ENSLIN, Morton Scott, 227.8306
1897-
Letters to the churches: 1 and 2 Timothy,

Titus. London, Lutterworth Press; New York, Abingdon Press [1964] 94 p. 20 cm. (Bible guides, no. 18) [BS2735.2E5] 63-760
1. Bible, N.T. Pastoral epistles — Criticism, interpretation, etc. I. Title.

ENSLIN, Morton Scott, 1897- 227.8306
Letters to the churches: 1 and 2 Timothy, Titus. London, Lutterworth Pr., Nashville, Abingdon [1963] 94p. 20cm. (Bible guides, no. 18) 63-760 1.00 pap.,
1. Bible. N.T. Pastoral epistles—Criticism, interpretation, etc. I. Title.

ERDMAN, Charles Rosenbury, 1866-1960. 227.8307
The Pastoral epistles of Paul; an exposition. Pref. by Earl F. Zeigler. Philadelphia, Westminster Press [1966] 170 p. 19 cm. (His Commentaries on the New Testament books) Cover title: The Pastoral Epistles of Paul (I and II Timothy, Titus) [BS2735.E7 1966] 67-141
1. Bible. N.T. Pastoral epistles—Commentaries. I. Title.

JONES, Russell Bradley, 1894- 227.8307
The Epistles to Timothy, a study manual. Grand Rapids, Baker Book House, 1959. 81p. 20cm. (Shield Bible study series) [BS2745.J6] 59-11729
1. Bible. N. T. Timothy—Commentaries. I. Title.

TRENTHAM, Charles Arthur, 1919- 227.8307
Studies in Timothy. Nashville, Convention Press [c1959] 144 p. 19 cm. Includes bibliography. [BS2745.5.T7] 59-9965
1. Bible. N.T. Timothy — Study — Text-books. I. Title.

WARD, Ronald Arthur. 227'.83'07
Commentary on 1 & 2 Timothy & Titus by Ronald A. Ward. Waco, Tex. : Word Books, [1974] 284 p. ; 25 cm. Bibliography: p. 281-284. [BS2735.3.W37] 74-82661 7.95
1. Bible. N.T. Pastoral epistles—Commentaries. I. Title.

WARD, Ronald Arthur. 227'.83'07
Commentary on 1 & 2 Timothy & Titus by Ronald A. Ward. Waco, Tex. : Word Books, [1974] 284 p. ; 25 cm. Bibliography: p. 281-284. [BS2735.3.W37] 74-82661 7.95
1. Bible. N.T. Pastoral epistles—Commentaries. I. Title.

GREENE, Oliver B 227'.83'077
The Epistles of Paul, the Apostle to Timothy and Titus, by Oliver B. Greene. Greenville, S.C., Gospel Hour [c1964] 496 p. 20 cm. [BS2735.3.G7] 64-20145
1. Bible. N.T. Pastoral epistles — Commentaries. I. Bible. N.T. Pastoral epistles. English. 1964. II. Title.

HOULDEN, James Leslie. 227'.83'077
The pastoral Epistles : I and II Timothy, Titus / [by] J. L. Houlden. Harmondsworth : Penguin, 1976. 168 p. ; 19 cm. (The Pelican New Testament commentaries) (A Pelican book) Includes indexes. Includes an introductory essay by the editor and the Revised Standard Version text of the Epistles. Bibliography: p. 13-14. [BS2735.3.H68] 76-383585 ISBN 0-14-021814-9 pbk. : 1.95
1. Bible. N.T. Pastoral epistles—Commentaries. I. Bible. N.T. Pastoral epistles. English. Revised standard. 1976. II. Title.
Distributed by Penguin, Baltimore, Md.

SPAIN, Carl. 227'.83'077
The letters of Paul to Timothy and Titus. Austin, Tex., R. B. Sweet Co. [1970] 192 p. 21 cm. (The Living word commentary, 14) Bibliography: p. 17-18. [BS2735.3.S65] 75-133509
1. Bible. N.T. Pastoral epistles—Commentaries. I. Title. II. Series.

WOYCHUK, N. A. 227'.84'066
An exposition of Second Timothy, inspirational and practical, by N. A. Woychuk. Old Tappan, N.J., Revell [1974, c1973] 172 p. 21 cm. Includes the Authorized version of Second Timothy. [BS2745.3.W69 1974] 73-14535 ISBN 0-8007-0637-4 4.50
1. Bible. N.T. 2 Timothy—Commentaries. I. Bible. N.T. 2 Timothy. English. Authorized. 1974. II. Title.

BIBLE. N.T. 2 Timothy. English. 1977. 227'.84'07
Studies in Second Timothy / by H. C. G. Moule. Grand Rapids : Kregel Publications, [1977] p. cm. (Kregel popular commentary series) Reprint of the ed. published by Religious Tract Society, London, under title: The second epistle to Timothy, in series: A devotional commentary. [BS2473.M68 1977] 77-79182 ISBN 0-8254-3219-7 pbk. : 2.95
1. Bible. N.T. 2 Timothy—Commentaries. I. Moule, Handley Carr Glyn, Bp. of Durham, 1841-1920. II. Title. III. Series: A Devotional commentary.

STOTT, John R. W. 227'.84'077
Guard the Gospel; the message of 2 Timothy [by] John R. W. Stott. Downers Grove, Ill., Inter Varsity Press [1973] 127 p. 22 cm. (The Bible speaks today) Includes bibliographical references. [BS2745.3.S76] 73-75890 ISBN 0-87784-481-X 1.95
1. Bible. N.T. 2 Timothy—Commentaries. I. Title.

PATTERSON, Paige. 227'.85'077
Living in hope of eternal life; an exposition of the Book of Titus. Foreword by Wayne E. Ward. Grand Rapids, Zondervan Pub. House [1968] 56 p. 23 cm. Bibliography: p. 55-56. [BS2755.3.P36] 68-24197
1. Bible. N.T. Titus—Commentaries. I. Bible. N.T. Titus. II. Title.

KNOX, John, 1900- 227.8606
Philemon among the letters of Paul; a new view of its place and importance. Rev. ed. New York, Abingdon Press [1959] 110p. 20cm. Includes bibliography. [BS2765.K6 1959] 59-7248
1. Bible. N. T. Philemon—Criticism, Interpretation, etc. I. Title.

SCROGGIE, William Graham, 1877-1958. 227'.86'07
Studies in Philemon / W. Graham Scroggie. Grand Rapids : Kregel Publications, 1977. p. cm. Reprint of the 1927 ed. publshed by Hulbert Pub. Co., London, under title: A note to a friend. [BS2765.3.S39 1977] 77-79186 ISBN 0-8254-3718-0 : 3.95
1. Bible. N.T. Philemon—Commentaries. I. Title.

ARCHER, Gleason Leonard, 1916- 227.87
The Epistle to the Hebrews; a study manual. Grand Rapids, Baker Book House, 1957. 108 p. 21 cm. (Shield Bible study series) [BS2775.A7] 57-8565
1. Bible. N.T. Hebrews—Study—Outlines, syllabi, etc. I. Title.

BIBLE. N. T. Hebrews. English. 1957. Barclay. 227.87
The Letter to the Hebrews. Translated with an introd. and interpretation by William Barclay. [2d ed.] Philadelphia, Westminster Press [1957] xxiii, 231p. 18cm. (The Daily study Bible) [BS2775.B3 1957] 58-5149
1. Bible, N. T. Hebrews— Commentaries. I. Barclay, William, lecturer in the University of Glassow, ed. and tr. II. Title. III. Series: The Daily study Bible series

GLAZE, R E 227.87
No easy salvation; [a careful examination of the question of apostasy in Hebrews, by] R. E. Glaze, Jr. Nashville, Broadman Press [c1966] 71 p. 22 cm. (A Broadman theological monograph) [BS2775.2.G55] 66-10708
1. Bible. N.T. Hebrews — Criticism, interpretation, etc. 2. Apostasy — Biblical teaching. I. Title.

GLAZE, R. E., Jr. 227.87
No easy salvation; [a careful examination of the question of apostasy in Hebrews] Nashville, Broadman [c.1966] 71p. 22cm. (Broadman theol. monograph) [BS2775.2.G55] 66-10708 1.25 pap.,
1. Bible. N.T. Hebrews—Criticism, interpretation, etc. 2. Apostasy—Biblical teaching. I. Title.

GREENE, Wilda. 227'.87
The disturbing Christ. Nashville, Broadman Press [1967,c1968] 127 p. 20 cm. bibliography: p. 127. [BS2775.4.G7] 68-12560
1. Bible. N. T. Hebrews—Devotional literature. I. Title.

GREENE, Wilda. 227'.87
The disturbing Christ. Nashville, Broadman Press [1967, c1968] 127 p. 20 cm. Bibliography: p. 127. [BS2775.4.G7] 68-12560
1. Bible. N.T. Hebrews—Devotional literature. I. Title.

HOBBS, Herschel H 227.87
Studies in Hebrews. Nashville, Sunday School Board, Southern Baptist Convention [c1954] 139p. 20cm. [BS2775.H58] 55-18767
1. Bible. N. T. Hebrews—Study—Text-books. I. Title.

LEMONS, Frank W., 1901- 227'.87
Profiles of faith [by] Frank W. Lemons. [1st ed.] Cleveland, Tenn., Pathway Press [1971] 103 p. 16 cm. [BS1199.F3L45] 70-167942
1. Church of God—Sermons. 2. Bible. N.T. Hebrews XI—Sermons. 3. Faith—Biblical teaching. 4. Sermons, American. I. Title.

*MORGAN, G. Campbell. 227.87
God's last word to man; studies in Hebrews, [by] G. Campbell Morgan. Grand Rapids, Baker Book House [1974] 160 p. 20 cm. (G. Campbell Morgan library) [BS2775] ISBN 0-8010-5955-0 2.45 (pbk.)
1. Bible. New Testement. Hebrews—Commentaries. I. Title.

SCHNEIDER, Johannes, 1895- 227.87
The letter to the Hebrews. Translated by William A. Mueller. Grand Rapids, Eerdmans [1957] 139p. 23cm. [BS2775.S332] 57-13845
1. Bible. N. T. Hebrews—Commentaries. I. Title.

SEISS, Joseph Augustus, 1823-1904. 227.87
Lectures on Hebrews. Grand Rapids, Baker Book House, 1954. 408p. 23cm. [Co-operative reprint library] [BS2775.S38] 54-11079
1. Bible. N. T. Hebrews— Commentaries. I. Title.

VOS, Geerhardus, 1862-1949. 227.87
The teaching of the Epistle to the Hebrews. Edited and re-written by Johannes G. Vos. Grand Rapids. W. B. Eerdmans Pub. Co., 1956. 124p. 23cm. [BS2775.V6] 56-13889
1. Bible. N. T. Hebrews—Theology. I. Vos, Johannes Geerhardus, ed. II. Title.

VOS GEERHARDUS, 1862-1940. 227.87
The teaching of the Epistle to the Hebrews. Edited and re-written by Johannes G. Vos. Grand Rapids. W. B. Eerdmans Pub. Co., 1956. 124 p. 23 cm. [BS2775.V6] 56-13889
1. Bible. N. T. Hebrews — Theology. I. Title.

WRIGHT, Walter Coleman, 1877- 227.87
Hebrews; a guide for Bible students in busy days. Chicago, Moody Press [1952] 191 p. 20 cm. [BS2775.W7] 52-64448
1. Bible. N.T. Hebrews — Commentaries. I. Title.

SCHAAL, John H. 227'.87'007
Better living through Christ; studies in the Book of Hebrews, by John H. Schaal. Grand Rapids, Reformed Bible Institute [1968] vii, 128 p. 22 cm. (Bible study course) [BS2775.5.S3] 68-57683
1. Bible. N.T. Hebrews—Study—Outlines, syllabi, etc. I. Title. II. Series.

HARBIN, Albert Leroy, 1903- 227'.87'0071
Harbin's notes on the Epistle to the Hebrews. Vallejo, Calif., Mrs. A. L. Harbin [1970] 157 p. group port. 19 cm. [BS2775.5.H34] 70-14925
1. Bible. N.T. Hebrews—Study—Outlines, syllabi, etc. I. Title.

HOPPIN, Ruth. 227'.87'014
Priscilla, author of the Epistle to the Hebrews, and other essays. [1st ed.] New York, Exposition Press [1969] 158 p. 21 cm. Contents.Contents.—Priscilla, author of the Epistle to the Hebrews.—The sovereignty of God and the spiritual status of women.—Four devotions.—More than a day's journey. Includes bibliographies. [BS2775.2.H6] 72-8428 6.00
1. Priscilla, Saint, wife of Saint Aquila. 2. Bible. N.T. Hebrews—Criticism, interpretation, etc. 3. Woman (Theology)—Biblical teaching. 4. Devotional exercises. I. Title.

BRISTOL, Lyle O., 1913or14-1963. 227'.87'017
Hebrews: a commentary [by] Lyle O. Bristol with the editorial cooperation of Melvyn R. Hillmer. Valley Forge [Pa.] Judson Press [1967] 192 p. 21 cm. Thesis—Emmanuel College, Toronto. Bibliography: p. 191-192. [BS2775.3.B66] 67-25891
1. Bible. N.T. Hebrews.—Commentaries. I. Bible. N.T. Hebrews. English. 1967. Revised standard. II. Title.

RODDY, Clarence Stonelynn. 227.8703
The Epistle to the Hebrews. Grand Rapids, Baker Book House, 1962. 141 p. 20 cm. [BS2775.4R6.]
1. Bible. N.T. Hebrews—Homilectical use. I. Title.

JORDAN, Clarence. 227'.87'052
The cotton patch version of Hebrews and the general Epistles [by] Clarence Jordan. New York, Association Press [1973] 93 p. 23 cm. Paraphrased from the Nestle-Aland Greek text, 23d ed., 1957. [BS2773.J67] 73-14856 ISBN 0-8096-1878-8 4.95
1. Bible. N.T. Hebrews—Paraphrases, English. 2. Bible. N.T. Epistles—Paraphrases, English. I. Title.
Pbk. 2.95; ISBN 0-8096-1879-6

BARCLAY, William lecturer in the University of Glasgow 227.8706
Epistle to the Hebrews. London, Lutterworth Press New York, Abingdon Press [1965] 96 p. 20 cm. (Bible guides, no. 20) [BS2775.2.B3] 65-1135
1. Bible. N.T. Hebrews — Introductions. I. Title.

BARCLAY, William 227.8706
Epistle to the Hebrews. London, Lutterworth Pr.; Nashville, Abingdon [1965] 96p. 20cm. (Bible guides, no. 20) [BS2775.2B3] 65-1135 1.00 pap.,
1. Bible. N. T. Hebrews—Introductions. I. Title.

BROOKS, Keith L. 227.8706
Hebrews--the beauty of Christ unveiled. Chicago Moody [c.1963] 64p. 22cm. (Teach yourself the Bible ser.) .80 pap.,
I. Title.

FILSON, Floyd Vivian, 1896- 227'.87'066
"Yesterday"; a study of Hebrews in the light of chapter 13 [by] Floyd V. Filson. Naperville, Ill., A. R. Allenson [1967] 88 p. 22 cm. (Studies in Biblical theology, 2d ser. 4) Bibliographical footnotes. [BS2775.3.F5 1967b] 67-7015
1. Bible. N.T. Hebrews XIII—Commentaries. I. Title. II. Series.

BRUCE, Frederick Fyvie, 1910- 227.8707
The Epistle to the Hebrews; the English text with introduction, exposition, and notes, by F. F. Bruce. Grand Rapids, W. B. Eerdmans Pub. Co. [1964] ixiv, 447 p. 23 cm. (The New international commentary on the New Testament) Bibliography: p. iix-ixii. [BS2775.3.B7] 64-16596
1. Bible. N. T. Hebrews — Commentaries. I. Bible. N. T. Hebrews. English. 1964. American revised. II. Title.

BRUCE, Frederick Fyvie, 1910- 227.8707
The Epistle to the Hebrews; the English text with introduction, exposition, and notes. Grand Rapids, Mich., Eerdmans [c.1964] lxiv, 447p. 23cm. (New intl. commentary on the New Testament) Bibl. [BS2775.3.B7] 64-16596 6.00
1. Bible. N. T. Hebrews—coommentaries. 2. Bible. N. T. Hebrews—Commentaries. I. Bible. N. T. p6.00 II. Bible. N. T. Hebrews. English. 1964. American revised. III. Title.

CARGILL, Robert L. 227/.87/07
Understanding the book of Hebrews [by] Robert L. Cargill. Nashville, Broadman [1967] 133p. 20cm. On cover: An inspirational commentary. [BS2775.3.C3] 67-30489 1.95 pap.,
1. Bible. N. T. Hebrews—Commentaries. I. Title.

GUTZKE, Manford George. 227'.8707
Plain talk on Hebrews / Manford George Gutzke. Grand Rapids, Mich. : Zondervan Pub. House, c1976. 122 p. ; 21 cm. [BS2775.3.G87] 75-21129 pbk. : 2.95
1. Bible. N.T. Hebrews—Commentaries. I. Title.

GUTZKE, Manford George. 227'.87'07
Plain talk on Romans / Manford George Gutzke. Grand Rapids, Mich. : Zondervan Pub. House, c1976. p. cm. [BS2665.3.G87] 76-22516 pbk. : 3.95
1. Bible. N.T. Romans—Commentaries. I. Title.

HEWITT, Thomas, 1909- 227.8707
The Epistle to the Hebrews, an introduction and commentary. Grand Rapids, Mich., Eerdmans [c.1960] 217p. (Tyndale New Testament commentaries) 61-8379 3.00
1. Bible. N.T. Hebrews—Commentaries. I. Title.

HEWITT, Thomas, 1909- 227.8707
The Epistle to the Hebrews, an introduction and commentary. [1st ed.] 217p. 21cm. (The Tynadale New Testament commentaries) [BS2775.3.H45 1960] 61-8379
1. Bible. N. T. Hebrews—Commentaries. I. Title. II. Title: Grand Rapids,

HOBBS, Herschel H. 227'.87'07
How to follow Jesus; the challenge of Hebrews for Christian life and witness today [by] Herschel H. Hobbs. Nashville, Broadman Press [1971] 144 p. 22 cm. Bibliography: p. [143]-144. [BS2775.3.H6] 74-178062 ISBN 0-8054-1334-0 4.50
1. Bible. N.T. Hebrews—Commentaries. I. Title.

LIGHTFOOT, Neil R. 227'.87'07
Jesus Christ today : a commentary on the book of Hebrews / Neil R. Lightfoot. Grand

Rapids, Mich. : Baker Book House, c1976. 274 p. ; 24 cm. Includes indexes. [BS2775.3.L53] 76-45239 ISBN 0-8010-5563-6 : 8.95
1. Bible. N.T. Hebrews—Commentaries. I. Title.

MONTEFIORE, Hugh 227.8707
A commentary on the Epistle to the Hebrews. New York, Harper [1965, c.1964] ix, 272p. 22cm. (Harper's New Testament commentaries) On spine: The Epistle to the Hebrews. Tr. of the Biblical text by the author. Bibl. [BS2775.3.M6] 65-10372 5.00
1. Bible. N. T. Hebrews—Commentaries. I. Bible. N. T. Hebrews. English. 1964. Montefiore. II. Title. III. Title: The Epistle to the Hebrews.

MOULE, Handley Carr 227'.87'07
Glyn, Bp. of Durham, 1841-1920.
Studies in Hebrews / by H. C. G. Moule. Grand Rapids : Kregel Publications, [1977] p. cm. Reprint of the 1909 ed. published by Hodder and Stoughton, New York, under title: Messages from the Epistle to the Hebrews. [BS2775.M65 1977] 77-79181 ISBN 0-8254-3223-5 pbk. : 2.45
1. Bible. N.T. Hebrews—Commentaries. I. Title.

PHILLIPS, John, 1927- 227'.87'07
Exploring Hebrews / John Phillips. Chicago : Moody Press, c1977. 222 p. ; 24 cm. Includes bibliographical references. [BS2775.3.P47] 76-39908 ISBN 0-8024-2406-6 : 6.95
1. Bible. N.T. Hebrews—Commentaries. I. Title.

PINK, Arthur Walkington, 227.8707
1886-1952
An exposition of Hebrews [2v.] Grand Rapids, Mich., Baker Bk. [1964, c.1954] 2v. (1307p.) 23cm. 54-11076 11.95 set,
1. Bible. N. T. Hebrews—Commentaries. I. Title.

THOMAS, William Henry 227.8707
Griffith, 1861-1924.
Hebrews; a devotional commentary. Grand Rapids, Eerdmans [1961?] 186 p. 21 cm. Includes bibliogrpahy. [BS2775.3.T5] 61-66231
1. Bible. N.T. Hebrews — Commentaries. I. Title.

THOMAS, William Henry 227.8707
Griffith, 1861-1924
Hebrews; a devotional commentary. Grand Rapids, Mich., Eeromans [1961] 186p. Bibl. 61-66231 3.00
1. Bible. N.T. Hebrews—Commentaries. I. Title.

TURNER, George Allen. 227'.87'07
The new & living way : a fresh exposition of the Epistle to the Hebrews / George Allen Turner. Minneapolis : Bethany Fellowship, [1974] c1975. 238 p. ; 21 cm. Bibliography: p. 235-238. [BS2775.3.T87] 74-23104 pbk. : 2.45
1. Bible. N.T. Hebrews—Commentaries. I. Title.

WILEY, Henry Orton, 1877- 227.8707
The Epistle to the Hebrews. Kansas City, Mo., Beacon Hill Press [1959] 438 p. 23 cm. [BS2775.3W5] 59-5493
1. Bible. N. T. Hebrews — Commentaries. I. Title.

BIBLE. N.T. Hebrews. 227'87'077
English. Barclay. 1976.
The Letter to the Hebrews / translated with an introd. and interpretation by William Barclay. Rev. ed. Philadelphia : Westminster Press, c1976. p. cm. (The Daily study Bible series — Rev. ed.) [BS2775.3] ISBN 0-664-24112-3 pbk. : 3.45
1. Bible. N.T. Hebrews—Commentaries. I. Barclay, William, lecturer in the University of Glasgow. II. Title. III. Series.

DAVIES, John Howard. 227'.87'077
A letter to Hebrews; commentary by J. H. Davies. London, Cambridge U.P., 1967 vii, 146 p. 20 1/2 cm. (Cambridge Bible commentary: New English Bible) Bibliographical note: p. 142. [BS2775.3.D3] 67-18311
1. Bible. N.T. Hebrews—Commentaries. I. Bible. N.T. Hebrews. English. 1967. II. Title.

ERDMAN, Charles 227'.87'077
Rosenbury, 1866-1960.
The Epistle to the Hebrews; an exposition. Pref. by Earl F. Zeigler. Philadelphia, Westminster Press [1966] 145 p. 19 cm. (His Commentaries on the New Testament books) [BS2775.E7 1966] 67-2103
1. Bible. N.T. Hebrews—Commentaries. I. Title.

KENT, Homer Austin, 227'.87'077
1926-
The Epistle to the Hebrews: a commentary [by] Homer A. Kent, Jr. Grand Rapids, Baker Book House [1972] 303 p. illus. 23 cm. Includes the text of the Epistle to the Hebrews. Bibliography: p. 297-303. [BS2775.3.K46] 72-84121 ISBN 0-8010-5322-6 5.95
1. Bible N.T. Hebrews—Commentaries. I. Bible. N.T. Hebrews. English. 1972. II. Title.

*MORGAN, George 227'.87'077
Campbell, 1863-1945.
The triumphs of faith [by] G. Campbell Morgan. Grand Rapids, Mich., Baker Book House [1973] 192 p. 19 cm. (G. Campbell Morgan library) First published in 1934. [BS2775.3] ISBN 0-8010-5918-6 2.95 (pbk.)
1. Bible. N.T. Hebrews—Commentaries. I. Title.

OWEN, John, 1616- 227'.87'077
1683.
Hebrews, the epistle of warning. Pref. by Herbert Lockyer. [Reprint ed.] Grand Rapids, Kregel Publications [1968] 283 p. 22 cm. "An abridgment by M. J. Tryon of John Owen's Exposition of the Epistle to the Hebrews." [BS2775.O8 1968] 68-57719 3.95
1. Bible. N.T. Hebrews—Commentaries. I. Tryon, M. J. II. Title.

STEDMAN, Ray C. 227'.87'077
What more can God say? A fresh look at Hebrews [by] Ray C. Stedman. Glendale, Calif., G/L Regal Books [1974] 247 p. 18 cm. [BS2775.3.S75] 74-176002 ISBN 0-8307-0296-2 1.45 (pbk.)
1. Bible. N.T. Hebrews—Commentaries. I. Title.

THOMPSON, James, 227'.87'077
1942-
The letter to the Hebrews. Austin, Tex., R. B. Sweet [1971] 184 p. 21 cm. (Living word commentary, 15) Bibliography: p. 18-19. [BS2775.3.T53] 70-163750 ISBN 0-8344-0071-5
1. Bible. N.T. Hebrews—Commentaries. I. Bible. N.T. Hebrews. English. Revised standard. 1971. II. Title. III. Series.

AINSLIE, Edgar. 227.876
Christ, the anchor; a study of themes in the Epistle to the Hebrews. Orange, Calif., Published and distributed by the Ralph E. Welch Foundation [1966] 177 p 22 cm. [BS2775.2.A35] 66-23200
1. Bible. N.T. Hebrews—Criticism, interpretations, etc. 2. Jesus Christ—History of doctrines—Early church. I. Title.

BIBLE. N. T. Jude. Greek, 227.9
1965
The Epistle of St. Jude and the Second epistle of St. Peter. Greek text with introd., notes, comments, by Joseph B. Mayor. Grand Rapids, Mich., Baker Bk., 1965. ccii, 239p. 23cm. (Limited eds. lib.) Orig. ed. printed in 1907 in London. Cover title: The Epistles of Jude and II Peter Bibl. [BS2815.M3] 65-16378 6.95
1. Bible. N. T. Jude—Commentaries. 2. Bible. N. T. 3. Peter—Commentaries. 4. Bible. N.T. Jude—Commentaries. 5. Bible. N.T. II. Peter—Commentaries I. Bible. N. T. 2 Peter. Greek. 1965. II. Mayor, Joseph Bickersteth, 1828-1916, ed. III. Title. IV. Title: The Epistles of Jude and II Peter.

BIBLE. N.T. Jude. Greek. 227.9
1965.
The Epistle of St. Jude and the Second epistle of St. Peter. Greek text with introd., notes, and comments, by Joseph B. Mayor. Grand Rapids, Baker Book House, 1965. ccii, 239 p. 23 cm. (Limited editions library) "Reprinted ... from the original edition printed in 1907 in London." Cover title: The Epistles of Jude and II Peter. Bibliographical footnotes. [BS2815.M3 1965] 65-16378
1. Bible. N.T. Jude—Commentaries. 2. Bible. N.T. Peter—Commentaries I. Bible. N.t. 2 Peter. Greek. 1965. II. Mayor, Joseph Bickersteth, 1828-1916, ed. III. Title. IV. Title: The Epistles of Jude and II Peter.

EDWARDS, Clifford Walter 227.9
Christian being and doing; a study-commentary on James andI Peter. [Joint Commn. on Education and Cultivation, Bd. of Missions, the Methodist Church, [dist. Cincinnati, Ohio 45237, Service Ctr., 7820 Reading Rd., 1966] xiv, 177p. 19cm. Bibl. [BS2785.3.E3] 66-13568 1.00 pap.,
1. Bible. N. T. James—Commentaries. 2. Bible. N.T. I. Peter—Commentaries. II. Title.

KUBO, Sakae, 1926- 227.9
Pa and the Codex vaticanus. Salt Lake City, University of Utah Press, 1965. 196 p. 25 cm. (Studies and documents, 27) Based on the author's thesis, University of Chicago. Includes bibliographical references. [BS2811.7] 66-5522
1. Bible. Manuscripts, Greek. N. T. Jude. (Papyrus 72) 2. Bible.Manuscripts, Greek. N. T. Peter (Papyrus 72) 3. Bible. Manuscripts, Greek, N. T. Jude. Codex vaticanus. 4. Bible. Manuscripts, Greek. N. T. Peter. Codex vaticanus. I. Title. II. Series.

*REEDER, W. Donald 227.9
The letters of John and Jude. Chicago, Moody [c.1965] 64p. 22cm. (Teach yourself the Bible ser., 81-4680.MP80) cover title. .80 pap.,
I. Title.

*ROBERTSON, A. T. 227.9
Epochs in the life of Paul [by] A. T. Robertson. Grand Rapids, Baker Book House, [1974]. xi, 337 p. 20 cm. [BS2505.A3] ISBN 0-8010-7625-0. 3.45 (pbk.)
1. Bible—Biography. I. Title.

*ROBERTSON, A. T. 227.9
Epochs in the life of Simon Peter [by] A. T. Robertson. Grand Rapids, Baker Book House, [1974]. xvi, 342 p. 20 cm. [BS2520.S7] ISBN 0-8010-7626-9. 3.45 (pbk.)
1. Bible—Biography. I. Title.

*ROBERTSON, A. T. 227.9
Epochs in the life of the Apostle John [by] A. T. Robertson. Grand Rapids, Baker Book House, [1974] 253 p. 20 cm. [BS2455] ISBN 0-8010-7627-7. 2.95 (pbk.)
1. Bible—Biography. I. Title.

VINE, William Edwy, 1873- 227.9
1949
The Epistles of John: light. love. life. Grand Rapids. Mich., Zondervan [1965] 128p. 20cm. [BS2805.3.V5] 65-5806 2.95 bds.,
1. Bible. N. T. Epistles of John—Commentaries. I. Title.

WUEST, Kenneth Samuel, 227.9
1893-
In these last days: II Peter, I, II, III John, and Jude in the Greek New Testament for the English reader. Gran Rapids, W. B. Eerdmans Pub. Co., 1954. 283p. 21cm. The fourteenth in a series of word studies by the author. [BS2777.W8] 53-9735
1. Bible. N. T. Catholic epistles—Commentaries. I. Title.

BEASLEY-MURRAY, G. R. 227.906
The general Epistles: James, 1 Peter, Jude, 2 Peter. London, Lutterworth Pr., Nashville, Abingdon [c.1965] 96p. 20cm. (Bible guides, no. 21) [BS2777.B4] 65-1176 1.00 pap.,
1. Bible. N.T. Catholic epistles—Introductions. I. Title.

BEASLEY-MURRAY, George 227.906
Raymond, 1916-
The general Epistles: James, 1 Peter, Jude, 2 Peter, by G. R. Beasley-Murray. London, Lutterworth Press; New York, Abingdon Press [1965] 96 p. 20 cm. (Bible guides, no. 21) [BS2777.B4] 65-1176
1. Bible. N.T. Catholic Epistics — Introductions. I. Title.

HEBREWS, James, 1 and 2 227'.9'06
Peter, Jude, Revelation / Reginald H. Fuller ... [et al.]. Philadelphia : Fortress Press, c1977. vi, 122 p. ; 22 cm. (Proclamation commentaries) Bibliography: p. 121-122. [BS2775.2.H4] 76-7864 ISBN 0-8006-0584-5 pbk. : 3.50
1. Bible. N.T. Hebrews—Criticism, interpretation, etc. 2. Bible. N.T. Catholic epistles—Criticism, interpretation, etc. 3. Bible. N.T. Revelation—Criticism, interpretation, etc. I. Fuller, Reginald Horace.

HIEBERT, David Edmond, 227.906
1910-
An introduction to the non-Pauline epistles. Chicago, Moody Press [1962] 252p. 22cm. Includes bibliography. [BS2635.2.H5] 62-4767
1. Bible. N. T. Epistles—Introductions. I. Title. II. Title: The non-Pauline epistles.

HIEBERT, David Edmond, 227'.9'06
1910-
The non-Pauline epistles and Revelation / by D. Edmond Hiebert. Rev. and enl. ed. Chicago : Moody Press, 1977. 294 p. ; 24 cm. (His An introduction to the New Testament ; v. 3) Published in 1962 under title: An introduction to the non-Pauline epistles. Includes index. Bibliography: p. 282-291. [BS2635.2.H5 1977] 77-2236 ISBN 0-8024-4139-4 : 7.95
1. Bible. N.T. Epistles—Introductions. 2. Bible. N.T. Revelation—Introductions. I. Title.

JONES, Russell Bradley, 227.906
1894-
The Epistles of James, John, and Jude. Grand Rapids, Mich., Baker Bk. House, 1961. 164. (Proclaiming the New Testament) Bibl. 61-15847 2.50
1. Bible. N. T. Catholic epistles—Homiletical use. I. Title.

BIBLE. N.T. Catholic 227.907
epistles. English. 1964. Reicke.
The Epistles of James, Peter, and Jude. Introd., translation, and notes by Bo Reicke. [1st ed.] Garden City, N.Y., Doubleday, 1964. xxxviii, 221 p. 24 cm. (The Anchor Bible, 37) Bibliography: p. [220]-221. [BS192.2 1964.G3, vol. 37] 63-8221
1. Bible. N.T. Catholic epistles—Commentaries. I. Reicke, Bo Ivar, 1914- ed. and tr. II. Title. III. Series.

BIBLE. N.T. Catholic 227.907
epistles. English. 1964.Reicke.
The Epistles of James, Peter, and Jude. Introd., translation, and notes by Bo Reicke. [1st ed.] Garden City, N.Y., Doubleday, 1964. xxxviii, 221 p. 24 cm. (The Anchor Bible, 37) Bibliography: p. [220]-221. [BS192.2 1964.G3, vol. 37] 63-8221
1. Bible. N.T. Catholic epistles—Commentaries. I. Reicke, Bo Ivar, 1914- ed. and tr. II. Title. III. Series.

BIBLE. N.T. Epistles of 227.907
John. English. 1965. New English.
The letters of John and James. Commentary on the three letters of John and the letter of James by R. R. Williams, bishop of leicester. Cambridge [Eng.] University Press, 1965. vii, 143 p. 21 cm. (The Cambridge Bible commentary: New English Bible) [BS2805.3W5] 65-3523
1. Bible. N.T. Epistles of John—Commentaries. 2. Bible. N.T. James—Commentaries. I. Williams, Ronald, Ralph, Bp. of Leicester, 1906- II. Bible. N.T. James. English. 1965. New English. III. Title. IV. Series.

BIBLE, N. T. Epistles of 227.907
John. English. 1965. New English
The letters of John and James. Commentary on the three letters of John and the letter of James by R. R. Williams, bishop of Leicester [New York] Cambridge [c.1965] vii, 143p. 21cm. (Cambridge Bible commentary: New Eng. Bible) [BS2805.3.W5] 65-3523 3.00; 1.65 pap.,
1. Bible. N. T. Epistles of John—Commentaries. 2. Bible. N. T. James—Commentaries. I. Williams, Ronald, Ralph, Bp. of Leicester, 1906- II. Bible. N. T. James. English. 1965. New English. III. Title. IV. Series.

CRANFIELD, C. E. B. 227.907
I & II Peter and Jude; introd. and commentary. [New York, Macmillan] [c.1960] 192p. (Torch Bible commentaries) Bibl. 61-784 3.00 bds.,
1. Bible. N. T. Peter—Commentaries. 2. Bible. N. T. Jude—Commentaries. I. Title.

STOTT, John R W 227.907
The Epistles of John, an introduction and commentary, by J. R. W., Scott [1st ed.] Grand Rapids, W. B. Eerdmans Pub. Co. [1964] 230 p. 21 cm. (The Tyndale New Testament commentaries [v. 19]) Includes bibliographical references. [BS2805.3.S74] 64-8801
1. Bible. N. T. Epistles of John — Commentaries. I. Title.

STOTT, John R. W. 227.907
The Epistles of John, an introduction and commentary. Grand Rapids, Mich., Eerdmans [c.1964] 230p. 21cm. (Tyndale New Testament commentaries, v.19) Bibl. [BS2805.3.S74] 64-8801 3.00
1. Bible. N.T. Epistles of John—Commentaries. I. Title.

*WARD, Ronald A. 227.907
The epistles of John and Jude; a study manual. Grand Rapids, Mich., Baker Bk. [c.]1965. 102p. 20om. (Shield Bible study ser.) 1.50 pap.,
I. Title.

ERDMAN, Charles 227'.9'077
Rosenbury, 1866-1960.
The General epistles; an exposition. Pref. by Earl F. Zeigler. Philadelphia, Westminster Press [1966] 228 p. 19 cm. (His Commentaries on the New Testament books) Cover title: The General epistles (James; I and II Peter; I, II, and III John; Jude) [BS2777.E7 1966] 67-2102
1. Bible. N. T. Catholic epistles — Commentaries. I. Title.

BIRD, John L. 227'.91
Faith that works; a study guide on the Book of James, by John L. Bird. Grand Rapids, Zondervan Pub. House [1968, c1965] 94 p. 21 cm. "Addresses ... delivered ... at Duke Street Baptist Church, Richmond, Surrey." [BS2785.4.B5] 68-22174
1. Bible. N.T. James—Sermons. 2. Sermons, American. 3. Baptists—Sermons. I. Title.

BLACKMAN, Edwin Cyril. 227.91
The Epistle of James: introduction and commentary. Naperville, Ill., Allenson [1957] 159p. 19cm. (Torch Bible commentaries) [BS2785.B5] 58-14532
1. Bible. N. T. James—Commentaries. I. Title.

CHITWOOD, Billy J. 227'.91
A faith that works; an inspirational study of James [by] B. J. Chitwood. Nashville, Broadman Press [1969] 128 p. 21 cm. (A Broadman inner circle book) [BS2785.4.C46] 77-78833
1. Bible. N.T. James—Meditations. I. Title.

EVANS, Louis Hadley, 1897- 227.91
Make your faith work; a letter from James. [Westwood, N. J.] Revell [1957] 159p. 21cm. [BS2785.E9] 57-5406
1. Bible. N.T. James—Commentaries. I. Title.

GAEBELEIN, Frank Ely, 1899- 227.91
The practical Epistle of James; studies in applied Christianity. Great NEck, N. Y., Doniger Raughley [c1955] 127p. 22cm. [BS2785.G3] 55-7558
1. Bible. N. T. James—Commentaries. I. Title.

GUTZKE, Manford George. 227'.91
Plain talk on James. Grand Rapids, Zondervan Pub. House [1969] 189 p. 22 cm. (The Plain talk series) [BS2785.4.G8] 73-81059
1. Bible. N.T. James—Commentaries. I. Title.

NIEBOER, Joe. 227.91
Practical exposition of James. Erie, Pa., Our Daily Walk Publishers [1950] 436 p. 20 cm. [BS2785.N5] 50-29279
1. Bible. N. T. James — Commentaries. I. Title.

ROSS, Alexander, 1888- 227.91
The Epistles of James and John. Grand Rapids, Eerdmans, 1954. 249p. 23cm. (The New international commentary on the New Testament) [BS2785.R68] 54-14953
1. Bible. N. T. James—Commentaries. 2. Bible. N. T. Epistles of John— Commentaries. I. Title.

STRAUSS, Lehman. 227.91
James, your brother; studies in the Epistle of James. [1st ed.] New York, Loizeaux Bros. [1956] 243p. 20cm. [BS2785.S85] 56-45703
1. Bible. N. T. James— Commentaries. I. Title.

STRAUSS, Leo. 227.91
Natural right and history. Chicago, University of Chicago Press [1957] 327 p. 22 cm. (Charles R. Walgreen Foundation lectures) [BS2785.S85] 56-45703
1. Natural law. I. Title.

STRINGFELLOW, William. 227'.91
Count it all joy; reflections on faith, doubt, and temptation seen through the Letter of James. Grand Rapids, Eerdmans [1967] 101 p. 23 cm. [BS2785.4.S76] 64-16588
1. Bible. N.T. James I—Meditations. I. Title.

SWEETING, George, 1924- 227.91
How to solve conflicts Chicago, Moody Press [1975 c1973] 153 p. 21 cm. [BS2785.2] ISBN 0-8024-3654-4 2.50 (pbk.)
I. Title.
L.C. card number for original edition: 75-129039.

TASKER, Randolph Vincent Greenwood, 1895- 227.91
The general Epistle of James, an introduction and commentary. [1st ed.] Grand Rapids, Eerdmans, 1957. 144p. 21cm. (The Tyndale New Testament commentaries) [BS2785.T3] 57-698
1. Bible. N. T. James— Commentaries. I. Title.

TASKER, Randolph Vincent Greenwood, 1895- 227.91
The general Epistle of James, an introduction and commentary. (1st ed.] Grand Rapids, Eerdmans, 1957. 144 p. 21 cm. (The Tyndale New Testament commentaries) [BX2785.T3] 57-698
1. Bible. N. T. James — Commentaries. I. Title.

CRISWELL, Wallie A. 227'.91'06
Expository sermons on the Epistle of James / W. A. Criswell. Grand Rapids : Zondervan Pub. House, c1975. 128 p. ; 21 cm. [BS2785.4.C74] 75-21120
1. Bible. N.T. James—Sermons. 2. Baptists—Sermons. 3. Sermons, American. I. Title.

HULME, William Edward, 1920- 227'.91'06
The fire of little Jim : power for growth from the letter of James / William E. Hulme. Nashville : Abingdon, c1976. 158 p. ; 19 cm. [BS2785.2.H84] 76-13535 ISBN 0-687-13090-5 pbk. : 3.95
1. Bible. N.T. James—Criticism, interpretation, etc. I. Title.

KENYON, Don J 227.9106
The double mind; an expository and devotional study from the Epistle of James. Grand Rapids, Zondervan Pub. House [1959] 83p. 20cm. [BS2785.5.K4] 59-2859
1. Bible. N. T. James—Addresses, essays, lectures. I. Title.

SHIFFLETT, Alvin. 227'.91'06
Blue jeans theology of James / by Alvin Shifflett. Cincinnati, Ohio : New Life Books, [1975] 94 p. ; 18 cm. [BS2785.2.S54] 74-28724 ISBN 0-87239-010-1 : 1.50
1. Bible. N.T. James—Theology. I. Title.

VALENTINE, Foy. 227'.91'06
Where the action is; studies in James. Waco, Tex., Word Books [1969] 192 p. 23 cm. Includes bibliographical references. [BS2785.2.V3] 76-96291 4.95
1. Bible. N.T. James—Criticism, interpretation, etc. I. Title.

DOWNEY, Murray W. 227'.91'066
James, a practical faith, by Murray W. Downey. Chicago, Moody Press [1972] 143 p. 22 cm. Bibliography: 142-143. [BS2785.2.D68] 72-77959 ISBN 0-8024-4228-5 Pap. $2.25
1. Bible. N.T. James—Criticism, interpretation, etc. 2. Bible. N.T. James—Sermons. I. Title.

KELLY, Earl. 227'.91'066
James; a practical primer for Christian living. Nutley, N.J., Craig Press, 1969. 282 p. 22 cm. Bibliography: p. 278-282. [BS2785.4.K44] 77-105931
1. Bible. N.T. James—Sermons. 2. Baptists—Sermons. 3. Sermons, American. I. Title.

KRUTZA, William J. 227'.91'066
Living that counts: a study guide to the Book of James [by] William J. Krutza and Philip P. Di Cicco. Grand Rapids, Mich., Baker Book House [1972] 120 p. 18 cm. (Contemporary discussion series) [BS2785.5.K7] 72-85714 ISBN 0-8010-5318-8 1.25
1. Bible. N.T. James—Study—Text-books. I. Di Cicco, Philip P., joint author. II. Title.

*LUCK, G. Coleman. 227'.91'066
James: Faith in action. Chicago, Moody [1967,c.1954] 124p. 19cm. (Everyman's Bible commentary) .95 pap.,
1. Bible. N.T. James—Criticism, interpretation, etc. I. Title.

STEVENSON, Herbert F. 227.91066
James speaks for today [by] Herbert F. Stevenson. Foreword by Paul S. Rees. [Westwood, N.J.] Revell [1966] 127 p. 23 cm. [BS2785.4.S7 1966a] 66-9711
1. Bible. N.T. James—Sermons. I. Title.

†ADAMSON, James B. 227'.91'07
The Epistle of James / by James B. Adamson. Grand Rapids : Erdmans, c1976. 227 p. ; 23 cm. (The New international commentary on the New Testament ;) Includes indexes. Bibliography: p. 40-45. [BS2785.3.A3] 76-9840 ISBN 0-8028-2377-7 : 8.95
1. Bible. N.T. James—Commentaries. I. Bible. N.T. James. 1976. II. Title.

BIBLE, N. T. James. 227.9107
English. 1961. Barclay.
The letters of James and Peter. Tr. with introd. and interpretations, by William Barclay. Philadelphia, Westminster Press [1961] xviii, 415p. (Daily study Bible) 61-7023 2.50
1. Bible. N. T. James—Commentaries. 2. Bible. N. T. Peter—Commentaries. I. Barclay, William, lecturer in the University of Glasgow, ed. and tr. II. Bible. N. T. Peter. English. 1961. Barclay. III. Title. IV. Series: The Daily study Bible series

COLSON, Howard P., 1910- 227'.91'07
The practical message of James [by] Howard P. Colson. Nashville, Broadman Press [1969] 90 p. 20 cm. Includes bibliographical references. [BS2785.3.C6] 70-78834
1. Bible. N.T.James—Commentaries. I. Title.

HARROP, Clayton K. 227'.91'07
The letter of James [by] Clayton K. Harrop. Nashville, Convention Press [1969] 156 p. 20 cm. "Church study course [of the Sunday School Board of the Southern Baptist Convention] This book is number 3204 in subject area 2, courses for adults and young people." Bibliography: p. 151-152. [BS2785.3.H37] 73-77618
1. Bible. N.T. James—Commentaries. I. Title.

JACOBSEN, Henry, 1908- 227'.91'07
The good life; Epistle of James. Wheaton, Ill., Scripture Press Publications [1968] 96 p. 22 cm. [BS2785.5.J3] 68-11556
1. Bible. N.T. James—Study—Outlines, syllabi, etc. I. Title.

ROBERTSON, Archibald Thomas, 1863-1934. 227.9107
Studies in the Epistle of James. Rev. and edited by Herber F. Peacock. Nashville, Broadman Press [1959] 200p. 21cm. 'First published as Practical and social aspects of Christianity.' Includes bibliography. [BS2785.R6 1959] 59-5861
1. Bible. N.T. James—Commentaries. I. Title.

ROPER, David H. 227'.91'07
The law that sets you free! : Book of James / David H. Roper. Waco, Tex. : Word Books, c1977. 123 p. ; 21 cm. (Discovery books) [BS2785.3.R66] 77-75455 ISBN 0-8499-0003-4 : 5.95
1. Bible. N.T. James—Commentaries. I. Title.

ROPER, David H. 227'.91'07
The law that sets you free! : Book of James / David H. Roper. Waco, Tex. : Word Books, c1977. 123 p. ; 21 cm. (Discovery books) [BS2785.3.R66] 77-75455 ISBN 0-8499-0003-4 : 5.95
1. Bible. N.T. James—Commentaries. I. Title.

VAUGHAN, Curtis. 227'.91'07
James; a study guide. [1st ed.] Grand Rapids, Zondervan Pub. House [1969] 128 p. 21 cm. Bibliography: p. 126-128. [BS2785.3.V38] 79-95032
1. Bible. N.T. James—Commentaries. I. Title.

ZODHIATES, Spiros 227.9107
The epistle of James and the life of faith [v.1], The work of faith, an exposition of James 1:1-2:13. Grand Rapids, Mich., Eerdmans [1960, c.1959] 223p. 23cm. (bibl. p.195-202) 59-14584 3.50
1. Bible. N.T. James—Commentaries. I. Title.

BIBLE. N.T. James. 227'.91'077
English. Barclay. 1976.
The letters of James and Peter / translated with an introd. ed. and interpretation by William Barclay. Rev. ed. Philadelphia : Westminster Press, c1976. xi, 351, [1] p. ; 19 cm. (The Daily study Bible series. — Rev. ed.) Bibliography: p. [352] [BS2783.B37 1976] 75-37601 6.25
1. Bible. N.T. James—Commentaries. 2. Bible. N.T. Peter—Commentaries. I. Barclay, William, lecturer in the University of Glasgow. II. Bible. N.T. Peter. English. Barclay. 1976. III. Title. IV. Series.

BLANCHARD, John, 1932- 227'.91'077
Bible studies in the epistle of James / [by] John Blanchard. London ; Waco, Tex. : Word Books, 1971- v. ; 19 cm. Contents.Contents.—v. 1. Not hearers only. [BS2785.3.B58] 74-193615 ISBN 0-85009-032-6 (v. 1) : £0.50 (v. 1)
1. Bible. N.T. James—Commentaries. I. Title.

DIBELIUS, Martin, 1883-1947. 227'.91'077
James : a commentary on the Epistle of James / by Martin Dibelius ; rev. by Heinrich Greeven ; translated by Michael A. Williams ; edited by Helmut Koester. Philadelphia : Fortress Press, c1976. xxii, 285 p. ; 25 cm. (Hermeneia) Translated from Der Brief des Jakobus, 11th rev. ed. prepared by H. Greeven. Bibliography: p. 262-271. [BS2785.D513] 74-80428 ISBN 0-8006-6006-4 : 16.95
1. Bible. N.T. James—Commentaries. I. Greeven, Heinrich, 1906- II. Bible. N.T. James. English. 1976. III. Title. IV. Series.

GWINN, Ralph A. 227'.91'077
The Epistle of James; a study manual, by Ralph A. Gwinn. Grand Rapids, Baker Book House [1967] 68 p. 20 cm. (Shield Bible study outlines) Includes bibliographical references. [BS2785.3.G8] 67-18176
1. Bible. N.T. James—Commentaries. I. Title.

MITTON, C Leslie. 227.91077
The Epistle of James; [a commentary, by] C. Leslie Mitton. Grand Rapids, Eerdmans [1966] 255 p. 23 cm. Bibliography: p. 247-249. [BS2785.3.M5 1966a] 66-31291
1 Bible N.T. James — Commentaries. I. Title.

SIMMONS, Billy. 227'.91'077
A functioning faith; expositions on the Epistle of James. Waco, Tex., Word Books [1967] 144 p. 22 cm. Bibliographical footnotes. [BS2785.4.S5] 67-26936
1. Bible N.T. James—Sermons. 2. Sermons, American. 3. Baptists—Sermons. I. Title.

WOLFF, Richard, 1927- 227'.91'077
General epistles of James & Jude. Wheaton, Ill., Tyndale House, 1969. 113 p. 21 cm. (His Contemporary commentaries) [BS2785.3.W6] 74-103947
1. Bible. N.T. James—Commentaries. 2. Bible. N.T. Jude—Commentaries. I. Title.

MAYCOCK, Edward A 227.92
A letter of wise counsel; studies in the First epistle of Peter. New York, Association Press [1957] 93p. 20cm. (World Christian books) [BS2795.M3 1957] 57-6881
1. Bible. N. T. 2. Peter—Commentaries. I. Title.

*MULLER, John H. 227'.92
Exciting Christianity. New York, Vantage [1973] 87 p. 21 cm. Bibliography: p. 86-87. [BS2785] ISBN 0-533-00715-1 3.50
1. Bible. N.T. 1 Peter—Commentaries. I. Title.

NIEBOER, Joe. 227.92
Practical exposition of I Peter, verse by verse. [2d ed.] Erie, Pa., Our Daily Walk Publishers [1952, c1951] 328 p. 21 cm. [BS2795.N5] 52-27055
1. Bible N. T. Peter — Commentaries. I. Title.

WOYCHUK, N A 227.92
The faith of experience; devotional exposition of I Peter 1;3-8. Grand Rapids, W. B. Eerdmans Pub. Co., 1953. 92p. 23cm. [BS2795.W65] 53-8144
1. Bible. N. T. 2. Peter I, 3-8 Commentaries I. Title.

CRISWELL, Wallie A. 227'.92'06
Expository sermons on the Epistles of Peter / W. A. Criswell. Grand Rapids : Zondervan Pub. House, c1976. p. cm. [BS2795.4.C74] 76-26486 5.95
1. Baptists—Sermons. 2. Bible. N.T. Peter—Sermons. 3. Sermons, American. I. Title.

WEISIGER, Cary N. 227.9206
The Epistles of Peter. Grand Rapids, Mich., Baker Bk. House, 1961. 141p. (Proclaiming the New Testament) Bibl. 61-16816 2.50
1. Bible. N. T. Peter—Homiletical use. I. Title.

BIBLE. N.T. Peter. 227'.92'.07
English. 1967. New English.
The letters of Peter and Jude; a commentary on the first letter of Peter, a letter of Jude and the second letter of Peter [by] A. R. C. Leaney. Cambridge, Cambridge U.P., 1967. vii, 144 p. map. 20 1/2 cm. (B 67-3272) (The Cambridge Bible commentary: New English Bible) 17/6 (9/6 pbk.) Bibliography: p. 143. [BS2695.3.L4] 66-29214
1. Bible. N.T. Peter—Commentaries. 2. Bible. N.T. Jude—Commentaries. I. Leaney, Alfred Robert Clare. II. Bible. N.T. Jude. English. 1967. New English. III. Title. IV. Series.

BIBLE. N.T. Peter. 227.9207
English. English. 1967. New English
The letters of Peter and Jude; a commentary on the first letter of Peter, a letter of Jude and the second letter of Peter [by] A. R. C. Leaney. Cambridge, Cambridge Univ. Pr., 1967. vii, 144p. map. 21cm. (Cambridge Bible commentary: New English Bible) Bibl. [BS2695.3.L4] 66-29214 3.50 1.65 pap.,
1. Bible, N.T. Peter —Commentaries. 2. Bible.—Commentaries. I. Leaney, Al-fred Robert Clare. II. Bible. N.T. Jude.English. 1967. New English. III. Title. IV. Series.
Available from publisher's New York office.

BLAIR, J Allen. 227.9207
Living peacefully; a devotional study of the First Epistle of Peter. [1st ed.] New York, Loizeaux Bros., 1959. 255p. 20cm. [BS2795.4.B5] 59-3887
1. Bible. N. T. 2. Peter—Meditations. I. Title.

COCHRANE, Elvis E. 227.9207
The Epistles of Peter; a study manual, by Elvis E. Cochrane. Grand Rapids, Baker Book House, 1965. 96 p. 20 cm. (The Shield Bible study series) [BS2595.3.C6] 65-16288
1. Bible. N.T. Peter—Commentaries.

DEHAAN, Richard W. 227'.92'07
Good news for bad times : a study of 1 Peter / Richard W. De Haan and Herbert Vander Lugt. Wheaton, Ill. : Victor Books, c1975. 156 p. ; 18 cm. (An Input book) [BS2795.3.D4] 75-6146 ISBN 0-88207-719-8 pbk. : 1.75
1. Bible. N.T. 1 Peter—Commentaries. I. Vander Lugt, Herbert, joint author. II. Title.

FICKETT, Harold L. 227'.92'07
Peter's principles [by] Harold L. Fickett, Jr. Glendale, Calif., G/L Regal Books [1974] 223 p. 18 cm. (A Bible commentary for laymen) [BS2795.3.F5] 73-90620 ISBN 0-8307-0276-8 1.45 (pbk.)
1. Bible. N.T. Peter—Commentaries. I. Title.

HORTON, Stanley M. 227'.92'07
Ready always; a devotional commentary on the Epistles of Peter [by] Stanley M. Horton. Springfield, Mo., Gospel Pub. House [1974] 126, [1] p. 18 cm. (Radiant books) Bibliography: p. [127] [BS2795.3.H67] 74-76802 1.25
1. Bible. N.T. Peter—Commentaries. I. Title.

KELLY, John Norman Davidson. 227'.92'07
A commentary on the epistles of Peter and of Jude [by] J. N. D. Kelly. [1st U.S. ed.] New York, Harper & Row [1969] x, 387 p. 22 cm. (Harper's New Testament commentaries) [BS2795.3.K4 1969b] 75-85061 8.00
1. Bible. N.T. Peter—Commentaries. 2. Bible. N.T. Jude—Commentaries. I. Title.

REES, Paul Stromberg 227.9207
Triumphant in trouble; studies in I Peter. [Westwood, N.J.] Revell [1963, c.1962] 144p. 21cm. 63-7596 3.00
1. Bible. N. T. 1 Peter—Commentaries. I. Title.

ROLSTON, Holmes, 1900- 227'.92'07
The Apostle Peter speaks to us today / Holmes Rolston. Atlanta : John Knox Press, c1977. 99 p.; 21 cm. [BS2795.4.R64] 76-44974 ISBN 0-8042-0201-X pbk. : 2.95
1. Presbyterian Church—Sermons. 2. Bible. N.T. 1 Peter—Sermons. 3. Sermons, American. I. Title.

STIBBS, Alan Marshall. 227.9207
The First epistle general of Peter; a commentary by Alan M. Stibbs, and an introd. by Andrew F. Walls, [1st ed.] Grand Rapids, Eerdmans [1959] 192 p. 20 cm. (The Tyndale New Testament commentaries) Includes bibliography. [BX2795.3.S7] 59-8753
1. Bible. N. T. 1 Peter — Commentaries. I. Title.

BROWNSON, William 227.92077
Clarence 1928-
Tried by fire; the message of 1 Peter [by] William C. Brownson. Revised edition. Grand Rapids, Baker Book House [1975] 109 p. 17 cm. (Contemporary Discussion Series) [BS2795.3] ISBN 0-8010-0592-2 1.65 (pbk.)
1. Bible—Commentaries—N. T. Catholic epistles. I. Title.
L.C. card no. for original edition: 74-136819.

CLARK, Gordon Haddon. 227'.92'077
Peter speaks today; a devotional commentary on First Peter, by Gordon H. Clark. Phildelphia, Presbyterian and Reformed Pub. Co. [1967] x, 159 p. 23 cm. [BS2795.3.C55] 67-28971
1. Bible. N.T. 1 Peter—Commentaries. I. Title.

CLARK, Gordon Haddon. 227'.92'077
Peter speaks today; a devotional commentary on First Peter, by Gordon H. Clark. Philadelphia, Presbyterian and Reformed Pub. Co. [1967] x, 159 p. 23 cm. [BS2795.3.C55] 67-28971
1. Bible. N.T. 1 Peter—Commentaries. I. Title.

LEIGHTON, Robert, 227'.92'077
Abp. of Glasgow, 1611-1684.
Commentary on First Peter. Grand Rapids, Kregel Publications [1972] 511 p. 23 cm. (The Kregel reprint library) Previous editions published under title: A practical commentary on the First Epistle of St. Peter. Reprint of the 1853 ed. [BS2795.L42 1972] 74-165058 ISBN 0-8254-3103-4 8.95
1. Bible. N.T. 1 Peter—Commentaries. I. Title.

GREEN, Edward Michael 227'.93
Bankes.
The second epistle general of Peter, and the general epistle of Jude; an introduction and commentary, by Michael Green. [1st ed.] Grand Rapids, Eerdmans [1968] 192 p. 20 cm. (The Tyndale New Testament commentaries [v. 18]) Bibliographical footnotes. [BS2795.3.G7 1968] 68-4086
1. Bible. N.T. 2 Peter—Commentaries. 2. Bible. N.T. Jude—Commentaries. I. Title.

NIEBOER, Joe. 227.93
Practical exposition of II Peter, verse by verse. Erie, Pa., Our Daily Walk Publishers [1952] 276 p. 21 cm. [BS2795.N52] 52-38631
1. Bible. N. T. Peter — Commentaries. I. Title.

BLAIR, J. Allen 227.9307
Living faithfully, a devotional study of the Second epistle of Peter. New York, Loizeaux Bros. [c.]1961. 256p. 61-14600 3.00
1. Bible. N. T. 2 Peter—Meditations. I. Title.

CONNER, Walter Thomas, 227.94
1877-1952.
The epistles of John [2d and rev. ed.] Nashville, Broadman Press [1957] 151p. 21cm. [BS2805.C57 1957] 57-8658
1. Bible. N. T. Epistles of John—Commentaries. I. Title.

FINDLAY, George 227.94
Gillanders, 1849-1919.
Fellowship in the life eternal; an exposition of the Epistles of St. John. Grand Rapids, Eerdmans, 1955. 431p. 23cm. [BS2805.F5] 57-4111
1. Bible. N. T. Epistles of John—Commentaries. I. Title.

FULCO, William J. 227'.94
Maranatha; reflections on the mystical theology of John the Evangelist, by William J. Fulco. New York, Paulist Press [1973] v, 90 p. 19 cm. (Paulist Press/Deus books) [BS2601.F8] 73-82225 ISBN 0-8091-1778-9 1.25 (pbk.)
1. Bible. N.T. Johannine literature—Theology. I. Title.

IRONSIDE, Henry Allan, 227.94
1876-1951.
Addresses on the Epistles of John, and an Exposition of the Epistle of Jude. [2d ed.] New York, Loizeaux Bros. [1954] 235, 61p. 19cm. [BS2805.I7 1954] 54-3577
1. Bible. N. T. Epistles of John—Sermons. 2. Bible, N. T. Jude— Sermons. I. Title.

*FRIEDERICHSEN, Mrs. 227.9406
Paul
God's truth made simple. Written, illus. by Mrs. Paul Friederichsen. Chicago, Moody [c.1966] 256p. illus. 17cm. (MP89) .89 pap.,
I. Title.

GUTZKE, Manfred 227'.94'06
George.
Plain talk on the Epistles of John / by Manford George Gutzke. Grand Rapids : Zondervan Corp., c1977. p. cm. [BS2805.3.G87] 77-21942 ISBN 0-310-25631-3 pbk. : 3.95
1. Bible. N.T. Epistles of John—Commentaries. I. Title.

TORREY, Reuben Archer, 227.9406
1856-1928.
Outline studies on I. John... Grand Rapids, Zondervan Pub. House [1963] 84 p. 21 cm. [BS2805.T6] 63-3367
1. Bible, N.T. 1 John — Criticism, interpretation, etc. I. Title.

TORREY, Reuben Archer, 227.9406
1856-1928
Outline studies on I John. Grand Rapids, Mich., Zondervan [c.1963] 84p. 21cm. 63-3367 1.95 bds.,
1. Bible, N. T aJohn—Criticism, interpretation, etc. I. Title.

LEAVELL, Landrum P. 227'.94'066
John's letters—light for living [by] Landrum P. Leavell. Nashville, Broadman Press [1970] 96 p. 19 cm. [BS2805.2.L4] 71-113210
1. Bible. N.T. Epistles of John—Criticism, interpretation, etc. I. Title.

ALEXANDER, Neil 227.9407
The Epistles of John: introduction and commentary. New York, Macmillan [c.1962] 173p. 20cm. (Torch Bible commentaries) 62-51907 3.00
1. Bible. N. T. Epistles of John—Commentaries. I. Title.

ALEXANDER, Neil. 227.9407
The Epistles of John: introduction and commentary. New York, Macmillan [1962] 178p. 20cm. (Torch Bible commentaries) [BS2805.3.A4] 62-51907
1. Bible. N. T. Epistles of John—Commentaries. I. Title.

BIBLE. N. T. EPISTLES OF 227.9407
JOHN. ENGLISH. 1960. BARCLAY.
The letters of John and Jude. Tr.with introductions and interpretations by William Barclay. [2d ed.] Philadelphia, Westminster Press [1960] xiii, 245p. (Daily study Bible) 61-10838 2.50
1. Bible. N. T. Epistles of John—Commentaries. 2. Bible. N. T. Jude—Commentaries. I. Barclay, William, lecturer in the University of Glasgow, ed. and tr. II. Bible. N. T. Jude. English. 1960 Barclay. III. Title. IV. Series: The Daily study Bible series

BLAIKLOCK, E. M. 227.9407
Faith is the victory; studies in the First epistle of John. Grand Rapids, Eerdmans [1959, i.e.1960] 64p. 20cm. 60-16103 2.00
1. Bible. N. T. 1 John—Commentaries. I. Title.

BURDICK, Donald W. 227'.94'07
The Epistles of John / by Donald W. Burdick. Chicago : Moody Press, [1970] 127 p. ; 20 cm. (Everyman's Bible commentary) Bibliography: p. 126-127. [BS2805.3.B87] 78-104823 ISBN 0-8024-2062-1
1. Bible. N.T. Epistles of John—Commentaries. I. Title. II. Series.

DAMMERS, A. H. 227.9407
God is light, God is love; a running commentary on the First Letter of John. New York, Association [1963] 80p. 19cm. (World Christian bks., no. 48, ser. 2) 64-129 1.25 pap.,
1. Bible. N. T. 1 John—Commentaries. I. Title.

DIETRICH, Suzanne de. 227.9407
This we know; a study of the letters of John. Richmond, John Knox Press [1963] 60 p. 23 cm. [BS2805.3D5] 63-8708
1. Bible. N.T. Epistles of John — Commentaries. I. Title.

DIETRICH, Suzanne de 227.9407
This we know a study of the letters of John. Richmond, Va., Knox [c.1963] 60p. 23cm. Bibl. 63-8708 .60 pap.,
1. Bible. N.T. Epistles of John—Commentaries. I. Title.

HENDRICKS, William L., 227'.94'07
1929-
The letters of John, by William L. Hendricks. Nashville, Convention Press [1970] 156 p. illus. 20 cm. (Tapestries of truth) "Text for course 3206 of subject area Biblical revelation of the New church study course." Bibliography: p. [151] [BS2805.3.H45] 73-110746
1. Bible. N.T. Epistles of John—Commentaries. I. Title.

STRAUSS, Lehman. 227.9407
The Epistles of John. [1st ed.] New York, Loiseaux Bros. [1962] 188 p. 20 cm. [BS2805.3.S75] 62-17542
1. Bible. N.T. Epistles of John — Commentaries. I. Title.

STRAUSS, Lehman. 227.9407
The Epistles of John. New York, Loizeaux [c.1962] 188p. 20cm. 62-17542 3.00
1. Bible. N. T. Epistles of John—Commentaries. I. Title.

TOLBERT, Malcolm. 227'.94'07
Walking with the Lord; the relevance of First John to the contemporary Christian life. Nashville, Tenn., Broadman Press [1970] 124 p. 21 cm. (A Broadman book) [BS2805.2.T64] 76-117299
1. Bible. N.T. 1 John—Criticism, interpretation, etc. 2. Christian life—Baptist authors. I. Title.

VAUGHAN, Curtis. 227'.94'07
1, 2, 3 John; a study guide. [1st ed. Grand Rapids, Zondervan Pub. House [1970] 139 p. 21 cm. Bibliography: p. 137-139. [BS2805.3.V38] 74-120037
1. Bible. N.T. Epistles of John—Commentaries. I. Title.

†VINES, Jerry. 227'.94'07
Family followship / by Jerry Vines. Dallas : Crescendo Publications, c1976. 384 p. ; 18 cm. [BS2805.4.V56] 76-11290 ISBN 0-89038-029-5 pbk. : 2.95
1. Bible. N.T. 1 John—Sermons. 2. Baptists—Sermons. 3. Sermons, American. I. Title.

WHITE, Reginald E. O. 227.9407
Open letter to Evangelicals; a devotional and homiletic commentary on the First Epistle of John. Grand Rapids, Mich., Erdman's [1965, c.1964] 276p. 21cm. [BS2805.5.W45] 64-22024 4.95
1. Bible, N. T. I. John—Commentaries. I. Title.

BIBLE. N.T. Epistles 227'.94'077
of John. English. Barclay. c1976.
The letters of John and Jude / translated with an introd. and interpretation by William Barclay. Rev. ed. Philadelphia : Westminster Press, c1976. ix, 207 p. ; 20 cm. (The Daily study Bible series. — Rev. ed.) Includes bibliographical references. [BS2803.B37 1976] 75-37760 ISBN 0-664-21314-6 : 6.25 ISBN 0-664-241:4-X pbk. : 3.45
1. Bible. N.T. Epistles of John—Commentaries. 2. Bible. N.T. Jude—Commentaries. I. Barclay, William, lecturer in the University of Glasgow. II. Bible. N.T. Jude. English. Barclay. c1976. III. Title. IV. Series.

BRUCE, Frederick 227'.94'077
Fyvie, 1910-
The Epistles of John. Introd., exposition, and notes, by F. F. Bruce. Old Tappan, N.J., F. H. Revell [1971, c1970] 160 p. 21 cm. "The Bible text ... is the Revised version of 1881." "The substance of this commentary appeared in twenty-four instalments in the Witness during 1967 and 1968." Bibliography: p. 20-21. [BS2805.3.B77 1971] 75-149373 ISBN 0-8007-0447-9 4.95
1. Bible. N.T. Epistles of John—Commentaries. I. Bible. N.T. Epistles of John. English. Revised. 1971. II. Title.

HOULDEN, James 227'.94'077
Leslie.
A commentary on the Johannine Epistles / J. L. Houlden. 1st U.S. ed. New York : Harper & Row, [1974] c1973. xi, 164 p. ; 22 cm. (Harper's New Testament commentaries) Includes translation of the Epistles of John. Includes indexes. Bibliography: p. 43-44. [BS2805.3.H68 1974] 74-4634 ISBN 0-06-064020-0 : 6.95
1. Bible. N.T. Epistles of John—Commentaries. I. Bible. N.T. Epistles of John. English. Houlden. 1974. II. Title.

MOODY, Dale. 227'.94'077
The letters of John. Waco, Tex., Word Books [1970] 136 p. 23 cm. Bibliography: p. 136. [BS2805.3.M6 1970] 77-141433 3.95
1. Bible. N.T. Epistles of John—Commentaries. I. Title.

RINGENBERG, Loyal R. 227'.94'077
Who is a Christian? : forty-eight theses derived from a deductive study of the First letter of John / Loyal R. Ringenberg. Broadview, Ill. : Gibbs Pub. Co., [1974] 143 p. ; 22 cm. Bibliography: p. 141-143. [BS2805.3.R54] 73-86016 4.95
1. Bible. N.T. 1 John—Commentaries. 2. Christian life—Biblical teaching. I. Title.

ROBERTS, J. W., 1918- 227'.94'077
The letters of John [by] J. W. Roberts. Austin, Tex., R. B. Sweet Co. [1968] 182 p. 21 cm. (The Living word commentary, 18) "Based on the text of the Revised standard version of the Bible." Bibliography: p. 15-17. [BS2805.3.R6] 78-162
1. Bible. N.T. Epistles of John—Commentaries. I. Title.

VINE, William Edwy, 227'.94'077
1873-1949.
The Epistles of John: light, love, life. [U.S.A. paperback ed.] Grand Rapids, Mich., Zondervan Pub. House [1970] 128 p. 21 cm. [BS2805.3.V5] 73-136355
1. Bible. N.T. Epistles of John—Commentaries. I. Title.

WALKER, Doak, 1927- 227.9633
Dork Walker, three-time all-American, by Dorothy Kendall Bracken as told by Doak Walker. Austin, Tex., Steck Co., [1950] ix, 258 p. illus., ports. 24 cm. [GV939.W3A3] 50-9513
I. Bracken, Dorothy Kendall. II. Title.

AUSTIN, William R. 227'.97
Clouds without water [by] Bill R. Austin. Nashville, Broadman Press [1968] 128 p. 20 cm. On cover: A study of Jude as it deals with unregenerate church members. [BS2815.3.A9] 68-15850
1. Bible. N.T. Jude—Commentaries. I. Title.

*CODER, S. Maxwell. 227.97
Jude, the Acts of the Apostles. Chicago, Moody [1968] 127p. 19cm. (Everyman's Bible commentary) .95 pap.,
1. Bible—N.T.—Acts of the Apostles—Jude—Criticism, interpretation, etc. I. Title.

EVANS, Robert Llewelyn. 227.97
The Epistle of Jude; a message for the last days. 3d ed. [enl.] Alhambra, Calif, [1950] 52 p. 20 cm. [BS2815.E9 1950] 50-33739
1. Bible. N. T. Jude—Commentaries. I. Title.

WOLFF, Richard 227.9707
A commentary on the Epistle of Jude. Grand Rapids, Mich., Zondervan Pub. House [c.1960] 150 p. 21 cm. Bibl.: p. 147-150. 60-4760 147-150 21cm. 2.50 bds.,
1. Bible. N. T. Jude—Commentaries. I. Title.

WOLFF, Richard, 1927- 227.9707
A commentary on the Epistle of Jude. Grand Rapids, Zondervan Pub. House [1960] 150 p. 21 cm. Includes bibliography. [BS2815.3.W6] 60-4766
1. Bible. N.T. Jude — Commentaries. I. Title.

LAWLOR, George L. 227'.97'077
Translation and exposition of the Epistle of Jude, by George Lawrence Lawlor. [Nutley, N.J.] Presbyterian and Reformed Pub. Co., 1972. vi, 151 p. 23 cm. (An International library of philosophy and theology: Biblical and theological studies) Bibliography: p. 149-151. [BS2815.3.L38] 74-187331 3.95
1. Bible. N.T. Jude—Commentaries. I. Bible. N.T. Jude. English. Lawlor. 1972. II. Title. III. Series: International library of philosophy and theology: Biblical and theological studies series.

228 Revelation (Apocalypse)

AINSLIE, Edgar. 228
The dawn of the scarlet age; studies in the book of Revelation. Philadelphia, Sunday School Times Co. [1954] 150p. 21cm. Originally published as a series of articles in the Sunday school times, Mar. 13-Sept. 4, 1954. [BS2825.A46] 54-13331
1. Bible. N. T. Revelation—Commentaries. I. Title.

ALLEN, Elliott Douglass, 228
1874-
Armageddon; studies in the Revelation of St. John [by] E. D. Allen. Philadelphia, Presbyterian and Reformed Pub. Co. [c1964] 116 p. 23 em. [BS2825.2.A6] 64-24572
1. Bible. N.T. Revelation — Prophecies. I. Title.

ANDERSON, Roy Allan. 228
Unfolding the Revelation; evangelistic studies for public presentation. Mountain View, Calif., Pacific Press Pub. Association [1953] 216p. illus. 20cm. [BS2825.A485] 53-12519

1. Bible. N. T. Revelation—Commentaries. I. Title.

ANDREWS, John Nevins, 1829-1883. 228
The three messages of Revelation XIV, 6-12, particularly the third angel's message, and two-horned beast. 5th ed., rev. Battle Creek, Mich., Review and Herald Pub. Co., 1892. [Nashville, Southern Pub. Association, 1970] viii, 141 p. 21 cm. (Heritage library) [BS2825.2.A67 1970] 70-19893
1. Bible. N.T. Revelation XIV, 6-12—Criticism, interpretation, etc. I. Title.

ARMERDING, Carl. 228
The four and twenty elders. New York, Loizeaux Bros. [19--] 11p. 19cm. (Treasury of truth, no. 227) [BS2825.A66] 56-26036
1. Bible. N. T. Revelation—Criticism, interpretation, etc. I. Title.

BARCLAY, William, lecturer in the University of Glasgow. 228
Letters to the seven churches. New York, Abingdon Press [1958, c1957] 111p. 20cm. [BS2825.B32 1958] 58-5146
1. Bible. N. T. Revelation II-III—Commentaries. I. Title.

BARCLAY, William, lecturer in the University of Glasgow. 228
Letters to the seven churches. London, SCM Press [1957] 127p. 20cm. Bibliography: p. 8-9. [BS2825.B32] 57-3759
1. Bible. N. T. Revelation II-III—Commentaries. I. Title.

BELEW, Pascal P 228
Seven golden candlesticks. Butler,Ind., Higley Press [c1956] 99p. illus. 20cm. [BS2825.B432] 57-20740
1. Bible. N. T. Revelation II-III—Sermons. 2. Church of the Nazarene—Sermons. 3. Sermons, american. I. Title.

BENSON, Hamar. 228
The coming Lord Jesus Christ, devotional meditations on the book of Revelation. [1st ed.] New York, American Press [1961] 77p. 22cm. [BS2825.4.B4] 61-8749
1. Bible. N. T. Revelation—Meditations. I. Title.

BIBLE. N. T. Revelation. English. 1957. Phillips. 228
The book of Revelation; a new translation of the Apocalypse by J. B. Phillips. New York, Macmillan, 1957. 50p. 22cm. Includes bibliography. [BS2823.P5] 57-8104
I. Phillips, John Berham, 1906- tr. II. Title.

BIBLE. N. T. Revelation. English. 1957. Phillips. 228
The book of Revelation; a new translation of the Apocalypse by J. B. Phillips. New York, Macmillan, 1961[c.1957] . 50p. (Macmillan paperback) Bibl. .95 pap.,
I. Phillips, John Bertram, 1906- tr. II. Title.

BIBLE, N. T. Revelation. English. 1958. Authorized. 228
The analysis of Revelation, by Alva W. Sherman. [1st ed.] New York, Greenwich Book Publishers [1958] 172p. 22cm. [BS2825.S383] 58-8143
1. Bible. N. T. Revelation—Commentaries. I. Sherman, Alva W. II. Title.

BIBLE. N. T. Revelation. English. 1958. Torrey. 228
The Apocalypse of John. New Haven, Yale University Press, 1958. xvi, 210p. 21cm. Bibliography: p. 203-207. [BS2825.T64] 58-6547
1. Bible. N. T. Revelation—Commentaries. I. Torrey, Charles Cutler, 1863-1956, ed. and tr. II. Title.

BIBLE. N. T. Revelation. English. Paraphrases. 1950. Rogers. 228
The Book of Revelation in plain language, by W. H. Rogers. Phoenix, Ariz., W. H. Rogers [1950] 117 p. 21 cm. [BS2823.R6] 50-3970
1. Bible. N. T. Revelation—Commentaries. I. Rogers, William Hubert, 1883- II. Title.

BIBLE. N. T. Revelation. English. Paraphrases. 1952. Scher. 228
The book of life opened; the hidden meaning of the Revelation of St. John the Divine: a nonsectarian interpretation with questions and answers for study, by Andrew R. Scher. [1st ed.] New York, Exposition Press [1952] 212 p. 21 cm. [BS2825.B386] 52-10986
1. Bible. N. T. Revelation—Miscellanca. I. Scher, Andrew R. II. Title.

BIBLE. N. T. Revelation. English. Paraphrases. 1955. Bowman. 228
The drama of the book of Revelation: an account of the book, with a new translation in the language of today, by John Wick Bowman. Philadelphia, Westminster Press [1955] 159p. 21cm. [BS2825.B65] 55-8595
1. Bible. N. T. Revelation—Commentaries. I. Bowman, John Wick, 1894- II. Title.

BIBLE. N. T. Revelation. English. Phillips. 1957 228
The book of Revelation; a new translation of the Apocalypse by J. B. Phillips. New York, Macmillan, 1957. 50 p. 22 cm. Includes bibliography. [BS2823.P5] 57-8104
I. Phillips, John Bertram, 1906- tr.

BURNS, Thomas Joseph, 1878- 228
The urge of man; dedicated to mankind. Manchester, Iowa, Philipp Drug Store [1951] 125 p. 25 cm. [BS2827.B77] 51-38570
1. Bible. N. T. Revelation—Prophecies. I. Title.

CHAPPELL, Clovis Gillham, 1882- 228
Sermons from Revelation [by] Clovis G. Chappell. New York, Nashville, Abingdon [1967,c.1943] 215p. 18cm. (Apex bks., AA-1-125) [BS2825.C44] 43-2914 1.25 pap.,
1. Bible N. T. Revelation—Sermons. 2. Methodist church—Sermons. 3. Sermons, American. I. Title.

COMBLIN, Joseph, 1923- 228
Le Christ dans l'Apocalypse, par J. Comblin Paris, Tournai, Rome, New York, Desclee, 1965. xii, 268 p. 22 cm. (Bibliotheque de theologie. Serie 8: Theologie biblique, 6) 30 F. Bibliography: p. [vii] -- xii. [BS2825.2C6] 67-73215
1. Bible. N.T. Revelation — Theology. I. Title. II. Series.

CORKE, Helen, 1882- 228
Lawrence & Apocalypse. New York, Haskell House, 1966. 130 p. 22 cm. Reprint of work first published in 1933. [PR6023.A93A76 1966] 68-1141
1. Lawrence, David Herbert, 1885-1930. Apocalypse. I. Title.

COX, Clyde C 228
Prophetical events and the great tribulation; a study of prophecy in Revelation. [1st ed.] New York, Exposition Press [1957] 126p. illus. 21cm. [BS2825.C62] 57-9217
1. Bible. N. T. Revelation—Prophecies. I. Title.

CRISWELL, Wallie A. 228
Expository sermons on Revelation; v.5. Grand Rapids, Mich., Zondervan [1966] 183p. 21cm. Contents.v.5. Revelation chapters eighteen through twenty-two [BS2825.4C7] 63-1760 2.95 bds.,
1. Bible N.T.—Revelation—Sermons. 2. Baptists—Sermons. 3. Sermons, American. I. Title.

FEUILLET, Andre. 228
The Apocalypse, [Translated from the French by Thomas E. Crane] Staten Island, N.Y., Alba House [1965] 143 p. 22 cm. Includes bibliographical references. [BS2825.2F413] 65-15728
1. Bible. N.T. Revelation—Criticism, interpretation, etc.—Hist. I. Title.

FEUILLET, Andre 228
The Apocalypse [Tr. from French by Thomas E. Crane] Staten Island, N.Y., Alba [c.1965] 143p. 22cm. Bibl. [BS2825.2.F413] 65-15728 3.95
1. Bible. N. T. Revelation—Criticism, interpretation, etc.—Hist. I. Title.

GETTYS, Joseph Miller, 1907- 228
How to teach the Revelation. Richmond, John Knox Press [1955] 56p. illus. 23cm. [BS2825.G43] 55-7100
1. Bible. N. T. Revelation—Study. I. Title.

GETTYS, Joseph Miller, 1907- 228
How to teach the Revelation. [Rev. ed.] Richmond, John Knox Press [1964, c1963] 56 p. diagr. 23 cm. (How to study the Bible series) Bibliography: p. 56. [BS2825.G43 1964] 63-20158
1. Bible. N. T. Revelation — Study. I. Title.

HARNLY, Joseph W 1870- 228
Har-Magedon, before and after; a study of prophecy and its fulfilment in history. [1st ed.] New York, Exposition Press [1955] 90p. illus. 21cm. [BS2825.H253] 55-11384
1. Bible. N. T. Revelation—Prophecies. I. Title.

HAVNER, Vance, 1901- 228
Repent or else! Westwood, N.J. Revell, 1958. 121p. 17cm. [BS2825.H33] 58-11023
1. Bible. N. T. Revelation II-III—Sermons. 2. Baptists—Sermons. 3. Sermons, American. I. Title.

HOYT, Edyth Viola (Sage) Armstrong, 1888- 228
Studies in the Apocalypse of John of Patmos, a noninterpretive and literary approach to the last book of the English Bible, based on the well known lecture series by Edyth Armstrong Hoyt, together with a free modern paraphrase and glossary prepared by a group of research students. Columbus, Ohio, 1950. ix, 240 p. (p. 240 advertisement) illus. 29 cm. Bibliography: p. 232. [BS2825.H775 1950] 51-1266
1. Bible. N. T. Revelation—Criticism, interpretation, etc. I. Bible. N. T. Revelation. English. Paraphrases. 1949. II. Title.

IRONSIDE, Henry Allan, 1876-1951. 228
Lectures on the book of Revelation, delivered in the Gospel Auditorium, Oakland, Calif. From shorthand notes, revised by the author. [1st ed.] New York, Loizeaux Bros. [1953] 366p. illus. 20cm. [BS2825.I68] 54-32888
1. Bible. N. T. Revelation—Commentaries. I. Title.

KEPLER, Thomas Samuel, 1897- 228
The book of Revelation; a commentary for laymen. New York, Oxford University Press, 1957. 232p. illus. 21cm. Includes bibliography. [BS2825.K42] 57-10384
1. Bible. N. T. Revelation—Commentaries. I. Bible. N. T. Revelation. English. 1957. Revised standard. II. Title.

KIK, Jacob Marcellus, 1903- 228
Revelation twenty, an exposition. Philadelphia, Presbyterian and Reformed Pub. Co. [1955] 92p. 23cm. [BS2825.K45] 55-7632
1. Bible. N. T. Revelation XX—Commentaries. I. Title.

KNIGHT, Paul S. 228
The upper room of God's house. Boston, Christopher Pub. House [1951] 213 p. 21 cm. [BS2825.K67] 51-9519
1. Bible. N. T. Revelation—Criticism, interpretation, etc. I. Title.

LAWRENCE, David Herbert, 1885-1930 228
Apocalypse. Introd. by Richard Aldington. New York, Viking [1966, c.1931] xxxii, 200p. 20cm. (Compass bk. C191) [BS2825.L35] 32-5886 1.45 pap.,
1. Bible, N. T. Revelation—Criticism, interpretation, etc. 2. Bible—Criticism, interpretation, etc.—N. T. Revelation. I. Aldington, Richard, 1892- II. Title.

LEONARD, Bernard F 228
The book of destiny; an open statement of the authentic and inspired prophecies of the Old and New Testament. Belleville, Ill., Buechler Pub. Co., 1955 [i. e. 1956] 271p. 23cm. [BS2825.L457] 56-27360
1. Bible. N. T. Revelation—Commentaries. I. Title.

LILJE, Hanns, 1899- 228
The last book of the Bible; the meaning of the Revelation of St. John. Tr. by Olive Wyon. Philadelphia, Fortress [1967,c.1957] 286p. 19cm. Tr. from Das letzle Buch der Bibel . . . 4th ed. 1955. [BS2825.L495] 57-9591 2.25 pap.,
1. Bible. N. T. Revelation— Commentaries. I. Title.

LILJE, Hanns, 1899- 228
The last book of the Bible; the meaning of the Revelation of St. John. Translated by Olive Wyon. Philadelphia, Muhlenberg Press [1957] 286p. 22cm. 'Translated from Das letxte Buch der Bibel ... fourth edition. 1955.' [BS2825.L495] 57-9591
1. Bible. N. T. Revelation—Commentaries. I. Title.

LITTLE, Carroll Herman, 1872- 228
Explanation of the book of Revelation. St. Louis, Concordia Pub. House [c1950] vi, 232 p. 21 cm. [BS2825.L53] 51-3484
1. Bible. N. T. Revelation—Commentaries. 2. Bible. N. T. Revelation. English. 1950. I. Title.

MCCALL, Druie Anselm, 1896- 228
The language of heaven, and other gospel messages from the book of Revelation. Wheaton, Ill., Sword of the Lord Publishers [1953, c1952] 142p. 21cm. [BS2825.M23] 53-19921
1. Bible. N. T. Revelation—Sermons. 2. Baptists—Sermons. 3. Sermons, American. I. Title.

MCDOWELL, Edward Allison, 1898- 228
The meaning and message of the book of Revelation. Nashville. Broadman Press [1951] 224 p. 21 cm. [BS2825.M315] 51-11141
1. Bible. N. T. Revelation—Commentaries. I. Title.

MCKNIGHT, William John, 1865- 228
What is bound to happen; the disclosure made to the apostle John and transmitted to the church in the book of Revelation. An interpretation. Boston, Meador Pub. Co. [1951] 319 p. 21 cm. [BS2825.M344] 51-5037
1. Bible. N. T. Revelation—Commentaries. I. Title.

MACNAIR, A Stanley 228
To the churches, with love; Biblical studies of the letters to the seven churches. Chicago, Judson Press [1960] 109p. 19cm. [BS2825.3.M3] 60-8793
1. Bible. N. T. Revelation I-III—Commentaries. I. Title.

MARTIN, Hugh, 1890- 228
The seven lettors. Philadelphia, Westminster Press [1957] 122p. illus. 20cm. [BS2825.M348] 58-5023
1. Bible. N. T. Revelation—Commentaries. I. Title.

*MAXWELL, Arthur S. 228
Christ and tomorrow. Mountain View, Calif., Pacific Pr. Pub. [1968] 80p. illus. 18 cm. T.p. and text in Russian. .50 pap.,
1. Bible. N.T. Revelations—Criticism, interpretation, etc. 2. Seventh-Day Adventists—Doctrinal and controversial works. I. Title.

MURPHY, Joseph, 1898- 228
Pray your way through it. San Gabriel, Calif., Willing Pub. Co. [1958] 173p. 20cm. [BS2825.M79] 59-29210
1. New Thought. 2. Bible. N. T. Revelation—Miscellanea. I. Title.

NILES, Daniel Thambyrajah. 228
As seeing the invisible; a study of the book of Revelation. [1st ed.] New York, Harper [1961] 192p. 21cm. Includes bibliography. [BS2825.4.N5] 61-7347
1. Bible. N. T. Revelation-Meditations. I. Bible. N. T. Revelation. English. 1961. Niles. II. Title.

PINN, James R C 228
Revelation today; a homiletical exposition of the book of Revelation. [1st ed.] New York, Vantage Press [1958, c1957] 337p. 22cm. Includes bibliography. [BS2825.P53] 57-8554
1. Bible, N. T. Revelation—Commentaries. I. Title.

PLOGER, Otto. 228
Theocracy and eschatology. Translated by S. Rudman. Richmond, John Knox Press [1968] viii, 123 p. 23 cm. Translation of the 2d ed. of Theokratie und Eschatologie. Bibliographical footnotes. [BS646.P5513 1968b] 68-12142
1. Apocalyptic literature. 2. Eschatology—Biblical teaching. 3. Theocracy. I. Title.

RICHARDSON, Donald William, 1879- 228
The Revelation of Jesus Christ: an interpretation. [4th ed.] Richmond, John Knox Press [1957] 195p. 21cm. Includes bibliography. [BS2825.R45 1957] 57-8522
1. Bible. N. T. Revelation—Commentaries. I. Title.

RISSI, Mathias. 228
The future of the world; an exegetical study of Revelation 19.11-22.15. Naperville, Ill., A. R. Allenson [1972?] 120 p. 22 cm. (Studies in biblical theology, 2d ser., 23) "An expanded and revised version of the original German edition, Die Zukunft der Welt." Includes bibliographical references. [BS2825.2.R47] 72-186007 ISBN 0-8401-3073-2
1. Bible. N.T. Revelation XIX, 11-XXII, 15—Criticism, interpretation, etc. I. Title. II. Series.

ROBERSON, Charles Heber, 1879- 228
Studies in the Revelation. 1st ed. Tyler, Tex., P. D. Wilmeth [1957] 200p. 21cm. [BS2825.R59] 57-58254
1. Bible. N. T. Revelation—Commentaries. I. Title.

ROWLEY, Harold Henry, 1890- 228
The relevance of apocalyptic; a study of Jewish and Christian apocalypses from Daniel to the Revelation. Rev. ed. New York, Harper [1955?] 205p. 20cm. [BS646] 55-143041
1. Apocalyptic literature. I. Title.

RUST, Ella Arjenette, 1884- 228
An exposition of the Revelation of Jesus Christ. [2d corr. ed.] New York, Exposition Press [1957] 448p. 21cm. [BS2825.R845 1957] 56-12383
1. Bible. N. T. Revelation—Commentaries. I. Title.

SEISS, Joseph Augustus, 1823-1904. 228
Letters to the seven churches. Grand Rapids, Baker Book House, 1956. 343p. 20cm. (Barker reprint library 4) First published in 1889 under title: The letters of Jesus. [BS2825.S375 1956] 56-7585
1. Bible. N. T. Revelation II-III— Sermons. 2. Lenten sermons. 3. Lutheran Church—Sermons. 4. Sermons, American. I. Title.

SHANK, F O 228
The great day. Elgin, Ill., Printed for the author by Brethren Pub. House [1954] 106p. 20cm. [BS2825.S379] 55-16551
1. Bible N. T. Revelation—Prophecies. I. Title.

STOTT, John R. W 228
What Christ thinks of the church; expository addresses on the first three chapters of the book of Revelation. [1st ed.] Grand Rapids, Eerdmans [1958] 128 p. illus. 21 cm. (Preaching for today) [BS2825.S76] 58-9548
1. Bible. N.T. Revelation I-III — Sermons. 2. Church of England — Sermons. 3. Sermons, English. I. Title.

SUMMERS, Ray. 228
Worthy is the Lamb; an interpretation of revelation. Nashville, Broadman Press [1951] 224 p. 22 cm. [BS2825.S775] 51-10833
1. Bible. N. T. Revelation — Commentaries. I. Title.

TENNEY, Merrill Chapin, 1904- 228
The book of Revelation. Grand Rapids, Baker Book House, 1963. 116 p. 20 cm. (Proclaiming the New Testament) [BS2825.5.T4] 63-12949
1. Bible, N.T. Revelation — Homiletical use. I. Title.

TENNEY, Merrill Chapin, 1904- 228
The book of Revelation. Grand Rapids, Mich., Baker Bk. [c.]1963. 116p. 20cm. (Proclaiming the New Testament) 63-12949 2.75
1. Bible. N.T. Revelation—Homiletical use. I. Title.

TENNEY, Merrill Chapin, 1904- 228
Interpreting Revelation. Grand Rapids, Eerdmans [1957] 220p. 23cm. Includes bibliography. [BS2825.T4] 57-7391
1. Bible. N. T. Revelation—Commentaries. I. Title.

TENNEY, Merrill Chapin, 1904- 228
Interpreting Revelation. Grand Rapids, Eerdmans [1957] 220 p. 23 cm. Includes bibliography. [BS2825.T4] 57-7391
1. Bible, N.T. Revelation — Commentaries. I. Title.

*[VALENCE, Louis O.] 228
Four riders of the Apocalypse; the revelation, by L.O.V. [pseud.] New York, Vantage [c.1965] 106p. 21cm. 2.50
I. Title.

VAN GORDER, John Jay, 1881- 228
ABC's of the Revelation. Hendersonville, N. C., Maranatha Book Stall [1952] 186p. 20cm. [BS2825.V25] 53-16591
1. Bible. N. T. Revelation—Commentaries. I. Title.

WALKER, Barney, 1895- 228
Seven spiritual ships; the stewardships given to the seven churches of Christ as told in St. John's revelation (Revelation 1-3) [1st ed.] New York, Exposition Press [1959] 59 p. 21 cm. [BS2825.W13] 59-16049
1. Bible. N. T. Reveation I-III — Sermons. 2. Stewardship, Christian. I. Title.

WERNECKE, Herbert Henry, 1895- 228
The book of Revelation speaks to us. With a foreword by Elmer G. Homrighausen. Philadelphia, Westminster Press [1954] 176p. 21cm. Includes bibliography. [BS2825.W33] 54-9402
1. Bible. N. T. Revelation—Commentaries. I. Title.

GETTYS, Joseph Miller, 1907- 228.007
How to study the Revelation [Rev.] Richmond, Knox [1963] 117p. 23cm. (How to study the Bibl ser.) Bibl. 63-20157 2.00 pap.,
1. Bible. N. T. Revelation—Study—Text-books. I. Title.

GETTYS, Joseph Miller, 1907- 228.007
How to teach the Revelation [Rev. ed.] Richmond, Knox [1964, c.1963] 56p. diagr. 23cm. (How to study the Bible ser.) Bibl. 63-20158 1.00 pap.,
1. Bible. N. T. Revelation—Study. I. Title.

HUNT, Gladys M. 228'.007'6
The lamb who is the lion [by] Gladys Hunt. Wheaton, Ill., H. Shaw Publishers [1973] 73 p. map. 21 cm. (A Fisherman Bible studyguide) [BS2825.3.H86] 73-78032 ISBN 0-87788-486-2 1.25 (pbk.)
1. Bible. N.T. Revelation—Commentaries. 2. Bible—Study. I. Title.

BLOOMFIELD, Arthur Edward, 1895- 228.015
All things new; a study of Revelation. Minneapolis, Bethany Fellowship [c1959] 272p. illus. 24cm. [BS2825.5.B55] 60-20383
1. Bible. N. T. Revelation—Prophecies. I. Title.

BIBLE. N. T. Revelation. English. 1962. Lattimore. 228.052
The Revelation of John. Tr. by Richmond Lattimore. New York, Harcourt [c.1962] v, 51p. 22cm. 62-19029 3.25
I. Lattimore, Richmond Alexander, 1906- tr. II. Title.

BIBLE. N.T. Revelation. English. Durham. 1973. 228'.05'204
The Book of Revelation; a private translation from the original Greek into simple English language, with the meanings of the symbols given in the chapter headings, by Thomas Ernest Durham. Minneapolis, Denison [1973] 87 p. 22 cm. [BS2823.D87] 73-77731
I. Durham, Thomas Ernest, tr. II. Title.

BALDINGER, Albert H., D. D. 228.06
Preaching from Revelation; timely messages for troubled hearts. Grand Rapids, Mich., Zondervan Pub. House [c.1960] 128p. 21cm. 60-1440 2.00 bds.,
1. Bible. N. T. Revelation—Sermons. I. Title.

BALDINGER, Albert H 228.06
Preaching from Revelation; timely messages for troubled hearts. Grand Rapids, Zondervan Pub. House [1960] 128p. 21cm. A revision of the author's Sermons on Revelation. [BS2825.B3 1960] 60-1440
1. Bible. N. T. Revelation—Sermons. I. Title.

BIBLE. N.T. Revelation. Latin. Cloisters Apocalypse. 228'.06
The Cloisters Apocalypse. New York, Metropolitan Museum of Art [1971] 2 v. illus. 32 cm. Facsim. of a slightly imperfect MS. in the Metropolitan Museum of Art. Lacunae completed from the closely related MS. Lat. 14410 in the Bibliotheque nationale, Paris. The English text of the Confraternity Bible is used in v. 2 in lieu of translation of the Latin text of the MS. Contents.Contents.—v. 1. An early fourteenth-century manuscript in facsimile.—v. 2. Commentaries on an early fourteenth-century manuscript, by E. Deuchler, J. M. Hoffeld and H. Nickel. Bibliography: v. 2, p. 28. [BS2822.5.C58D48] 77-162342 ISBN 0-87099-110-8
1. Bible—Pictures, illustrations, etc. I. Deuchler, Florens, 1931- II. Hoffeld, Jeffrey M. III. Nickel, Helmut. IV. New York (City). Metropolitan Museum of Art. The Cloisters. V. Bible. N.T. Revelation. Latin. 1971. VI. Bible. N.T. Revelation. English. Confraternity. 1971. VII. Title.

BOYCOTT, John L. 228.06
Of things to come. New York, Vantage [c.1962] 83p. 21cm. 2.75
I. Title.

CHATZEANTONIOU, Georgios A. 228.06
The postman of Patmos; striking messages of the seven letters to the seven churches of Revelation, by G. A. Hadjiantoniou. Grand Rapids, Mich., Zondervan Pub. House [c.1961] 149p. 61-4321 2.50
1. Bible. N.T. Revelation I-III—Meditations. I. Title.

CHRISTENSEN, Anton M. 228.06
The United States in Bible prophecy; Bible prophecy today and our citizenship in heaven. New York, Exposition [c.1962] 115p. 21cm. 3.00
I. Title.

COLLINS, Adela Yarbro. 228'.06
The combat myth in the Book of Revelation / by Adela Yarbro Collins. Missoula, Mont. : Published by Scholars Press for Harvard theological review, c1976. xvi, 292 p. : 22 cm. (Harvard dissertations in religion ; no. 9) Originally presented as the author's thesis, Harvard, 1975. Bibliography: p. 271-292. [BS2825.2.C58 1976] 76-26969 ISBN 0-89130-077-5 : 4.20
1. Bible. N.T. Revelation—Criticism, interpretation, etc. 2. Bible. N.T. Revelation XII—Criticism, interpretation, etc. 3. Combat in the Bible. I. Title. II. Series.

CRISWELL, W. A. 228.06
Expository sermons on Revelation. Grand Rapids, Mich., Zondervan [c.1962] 184p. 21cm. 2.95
I. Title.

CRISWELL, W. A. 228.06
Expository sermons on Revelation volume two (Revelation chapters two and three) Grand Rapids, Mich., Zondervan [c.1963] 184p. 21cm. 2.95
I. Title.

CRISWELL, Wallie A. 228.06
Expository sermons on Revelation; v.3. Grand Rapids, Mich., Zondervan [c.1964] 184p. 21cm. [BS2825.4.C7] 63-1760 2.95 bds.,
1. Bible. N. T. Revelation—Sermons. 2. Baptists—Sermons. 3. Sermons, American. I. Title.

CRISWELL, Wallie A. 228.06
Expository sermons on Revelation; v4. Grand Rapids, Mich., Zondervan [c.1965] 189p. 21cm. Contents.v.4. Revelation, chapters eleven through seventeen [BS2825.4.C7] 63-1760 2.95 bds.,
1. Bible. N.T. Revelation—Sermons. 2. Baptists—Sermons. 3. Sermons, American. I. Title.

ELLUL, Jacques. 228'.06
Apocalypse : the Book of revelation / Jacques Ellul ; translated by George W. Schreiner. New York : Seabury Press, 1977. 283 p. ; 22 cm. Translation of L'Apocalypse, architecture en mouvement. "A Crossroad book." Includes bibliographical references. [BS2825.2.E4413] 76-54322 ISBN 0-8164-0330-9 : 10.95
1. Bible. N.T. Revelation—Criticism, interpretation, etc. I. Title.

FARRER, Austin Marsden 228.06
A rebirth of images; the making of St. John's Apocalypse Gloucester, Mass., P. Smith, 1964 348p. illus. 21cm. (Beacon paperback, BP152 rebound) 4.25
1. Bible. N. T. Revelation—Criticism, interpretation, etc. I. Title.

FARRER, Austin Marsden. 228'.06
A rebirth of images; the making of St. John's Apocalypse, by Austin Farrer. Gloucester, Mass., P. Smith, 1970. 348 p. illus. 21 cm. "First published in 1949." [BS2825.2.F3 1970] 74-21038 5.00
1. Bible. N.T. Revelation—Criticism, interpretation, etc. I. Title.

FARRER, Austin Marsden. 228.06
A rebirth of images; the making of St. John's Apocalypse. Boston, Beacon Press [1963] 348 p. illus. 21 cm. (A Beacon paperback) [BS2825.2.F3] 63-2992
1. Bible. N. T. Revelation—Criticism, interpretation, etc. I. Title.

FIORENZA, Elisabeth Schussler, 1938- 228'.06
The apocalypse / by Elisabeth Schuessler Fiorenza. Chicago : Franciscan Herald Press, 1976. p. cm. (Herald Biblical booklets) [BS2825.2.F5 1976] 76-16802 ISBN 0-8199-0726-X : 0.95
1. Bible. N.T. Revelation—Criticism, interpretation, etc. I. Title.

GRANT, James Ralph, 1908- 228.06
Letters to the seven churches, and other sermons. Grand Rapids, Mich., Baker Bk. [c.] 1962. 113p. 20cm. 62-19235 1.95
1. Bible. N.T. Revelation—Sermons. 2. Baptists—Sermons. 3. Sermons, American. I. Title.

GUILD, Daniel R 228.06
Rich revelations of Jesus which meet a man's practical need in the twentieth century, by Daniel R. Guild. Nashville, Southern Pub. Association [1965] 287 p. 22 cm. [BS2825.5.G8] 64-18173
1. Bible, N. T. Revelation — Prophecies. I. Title.

GUILD, Daniel R. 228.06
Rich revelations of Jesus which meet a man's practical need in the twentieth century. Nashville, Southern Pub. [c.1965] 287p. 22cm. [BS2825.5.G8] 64-18173 4.95)4s*SBible. N. T. Revlaation--Prophecies.
1. Bible. N. T. Revlaation—Prophecies. I. Title.

LAWRENCE, David Herbert, 1885-1930. 228'.06
Apocalypse / D. H. Lawrence ; with an introduction by Richard Aldington. Harmondsworth : Penguin, 1974. xxvii, 126 p. ; 19 cm. "First published 1931." [BS2825.L35 1974] 75-322797 ISBN 0-14-003856-6 : £0.35
1. Bible. N.T. Revelation—Criticism, interpretation, etc. I. Aldington, Richard, 1892-1962. II. Title.

LAYMON, Charles M. 228.06
The book of Revelation, its message and meaning. Nashville, Abingdon Press [c.1960] 176p. 23cm. Bibl.: p165-166 illus. 60-10911 3.oo
1. Bible. N. T. Revelation—Criticism, interpretation, etc. I. Title.

LAYMON, Charles M 228.06
The book of Revelation, its message and meaning. New York, Abingdon Press [1960] 176p. illus. 23cm. Includes bibliography. [BS2825.2.L3] 60-10911
1. Bible. N. T. Revelation —Criticism, interpretation, etc. I. Title.

MCCAN, Robert L 228.06
A vision of victory. Nashville, Broadman Press [1959] 139p. 21cm. Includes bibliography. [BS2825.4.M25] 59-9685
1. Bible. N. T. Revelation—Sermons. 2. Baptists—Sermons. 3. Sermons, American. I. Title.

*MARTIN, Oliver S. 228.06
A study in the Revelation. New York, Exposition [c.1964] 209p. 22cm. (EP 42101) 4.00
I. Title.

MOUNCE, Robert H. 228'.06
The Book of Revelation / by Robert H. Mounce. Grand Rapids : Eerdmans, c1977. p. cm. (The New international commentary on the New Testament ; 17) Includes indexes. Bibliography: p. [BS2825.3.M69] 77-7664 ISBN 0-8028-2348-3 : 10.95
1. Bible. N.T. Revelation—Commentaries. I. Bible. N.T. Revelation. English. American revised. 1977. II. Title.

NEWMAN, Barclay Moon, 1931- 228'.06
Rediscovering the Book of Revelation [by] Barclay M. Newman, Jr. Valley Forge [Pa.] Judson Press [1968] 127 p. 21 cm. Bibliography: p. 123-127. [BS2825.3.N4] 68-20434 3.95
1. Bible. N.T. Revelation—Commentaries. I. Title.

PAULSON, J. Sig. 228'.06
Revelation, the book of unity / by J. Sig Paulson, Ric Dickerson. Unity Village, Mo. : Unity Books, c1976. 199 p. ; 20 cm. Based on a series of dialogues between J. S. Paulson and R. Dickerson. [BS2825.2.P38] 75-46149 3.95
1. Bible. N.T. Revelation—Criticism, interpretation, etc. I. Dickerson, Ric, joint author. II. Title.

RAMSAY, Sir William Mitchell, 1851-1939. 228.06
The letters to the seven churches of Asia and their place in the plan of the apocalypse. Grand Rapids, Mich., Baker Book House, 1963. 446 p. illus. 23 cm. [BS2825.R33] 63-12950
1. Bible. N.T. Revelation — Criticism, interpretation, etc. I. Title.

RAMSAY, William Mitchell, Sir 1851-1939. 228.06
The letters to the seven churches of Asia and their place in the plan of the apocalypse. Grand Rapids, Mich., Baker Bk., 1963. 446p. illus. 23cm. 63-12950 4.95
1. Bible. N. T. Revelation—Criticism, interpretation, etc. I. Title.

RICHARDS, Edward H. 228'.06
The Revelation letters : expository sermons on the Seven Churches / by E. H. Richards. Nashville, Tenn. : Eric Publishers, c1975. x, 188 p. ; 23 cm. Bibliography: p. 187-188. [BS2825.4.R5] 75-330251 5.95
1. The seven churches—Sermons. 2. Baptists—Sermons. 3. Sermons, American. I. Title.

RISSI, Mathias. 228.06
Time and history; a study on the Revelation. Translated by Gordon C. Winsor. Richmond, John Knox Press [1966] x, 147 p. 21 cm. Translation of Was ist und was geschehen soli danach. Bibliographical footnotes. [BS2825.2.R493] 66-11904
1. Bible. N.T. Revelation — Criticism, interpretation, etc. 2. Time (Theology) I. Title.

RISSI, Mathias 228.06
Time and history; a study on the Revelation. Tr. [from German] by Gordon C. Winsor. Richmond, *va., Knox [c.1966] x, 147p. 21cm. Bibl. [BS2825.2.R493] 66-11904 4.50
1. Bible. N. T. Revelation—Criticism, interpretation, etc. 2. Time (Theology) I. Title.

SMITH, Chuck, 1927- 228'.06
What the world is coming to / Chuck Smith. Costa Mesa, Calif. : Maranatha Evangelical Association of Calvary Chapel, c1977. 227 p. ; 21 cm. Includes bibliographical references. [BS2825.3.S57] 77-3186 ISBN 0-89337-007-X : 3.95
1. Bible. N.T. Revelation—Commentaries. I. Title.

SWEDENBORG, Emanuel, 1688-1772. 228.06
The Apocalypse explained; the Apocalypse explained according to the spirtual sense in which the arcana there predicted by heretofore concealed are revealed. A posthumous work of Emanuel Swedenborg. Standard ed. New York, Swedenborg Foundation, 1960- v. 22 cm. Revised by John Whitehead. [BX8712.A4 1960] 63-3838
1. Bible. N.T. Revelation — Commentaries. I. Bible. N.T. Revelation. English. 1960. II. Title.

TORRANCE, Thomas Forsyth 228.06
The Apocalypse today. Grand Rapids, Eerdmans [c.1959] 155p. 22cm. 59-8755 3.00
1. Bible. N. T. Revelation—Sermons. 2. Church of Scotland—Sermons. 3. Sermons, English—Scotland. I. Title.

TORRANCE, Thomas Forsyth, 228.06
1913-
The Apocalypse today. [1st ed.] Grand Rapids, Eerdmans [1959] 155 p. 22 cm. [BS2825.4.T65] 59-8755
1. Bible. N.T. Revelation — Sermons. 2. Church of Scotland — Sermons. 3. Sermons, English — Scotland. I. Title.

*UNJHEM, Arne 228.06
The Book of Revelation by Arne Unjhem. Frank W. Klos, ed. Iajos Szalay, artist [Philadelphia] Lutheran Church Pr. [1967] 141p. illus. 21cm. (LCA Sch. of religion ser.) 1.25 pap.,
1. Bible—N.T.—Revelation—Criticism, interpretation, etc. 2. Bible— Criticism, interpretation, etc. I. Klos, Frank W., ed. II. Title.

WATCH Tower Bible and 228'.06
Tract Society of Pennsylvania.
"Then is finished the mystery of God." [1st ed. Brooklyn, Watchtower Bible and Tract Society of New York, 1969] 380 p. illus. (part col.) 19 cm. [BS2825.2.W3] 74-11104
1. Bible. N.T. Revelation—Prophecies. 2. Jehovah's Witnesses—Doctrinal and controversial works. I. Title.

STRAND, Kenneth Albert, 228'.06'3
1927-
Interpreting the Book of Revelation : hermeneutical guidelines, with brief introduction to literary analysis / by Kenneth A. Strand. Rev. and enl. ed. of The open gates of heaven. Worthington, Ohio : Ann Arbor Publishers, 1976. 88 p. : diagrs. ; 24 cm. Includes bibliographical references and indexes. [BS2825.2.S77 1976] 76-378092 ISBN 0-89039-167-X pbk. : 2.75
1. Bible. N.T. Revelation—Criticism, interpretation, etc. I. Title.

BEASLEY-MURRAY, George 228'.06'6
Raymond, 1916-
Highlights of the Book of Revelation [by] George R. Beasley-Murray. Nashville, Tenn., Broadman Press [1972] vi, 86 p. 20 cm. Includes bibliographical references. [BS2825.2.B43] 70-189501 ISBN 0-8054-1336-7 2.95
1. Bible. N.T. Revelation—Criticism, interpretation, etc. I. Title.

COOPER, David Lipscomb, 228'.06'6
1886-
An exposition of the Book of Revelation, by David L. Cooper. Los Angeles, Biblical Research Society [1972] xvii, 274 p. illus. 20 cm. [BS2825.2.C64] 74-115875
1. Bible. N.T. Revelation—Criticism, interpretation, etc. I. Title.

JENKINS, Ferrell. 228'.06'6
The Old Testament in the Book of Revelation. Foreword by Homer Hailey. Marion, Ind., Cogdill Foundation Publications [1972] 151 p. illus. 23 cm. Originally presented as the author's thesis (M.A.), Harding Graduate School of Religion. Bibliography: p. 133-141. [BS2825.2.J4 1972] 71-176201
1. Bible. N.T. Revelation—Relation to O.T. I. Title.

*LINDEMAN, Lucile 228'.06'6
Wells.
God's incomparable plan. New York, Carlton Press [1973] 138 p. 22 cm. (A Hearthstone Book) [BS2825] 3.00
1. Bible. N.T. Revelation—Criticism, interpretation, etc. I. Title.

PRICE, George McCready, 228'.06'6
1870-
The time of the end. Nashville, Southern Pub. Association [1967] 171 p. 22 cm. [BS2825.2.P74] 67-31686
1. Bible. N. T. Revelation, XIII-XVII—Criticism, interpretation, etc. 2. Seventh-Day Adventists—Doctrinal and controversial works. I. Title.

PRICE, George McCready, 228'.06'6
1870-
The time of the end. Nashville, Southern Pub. Association [1967] 171 p. 22 cm. [BS2825.2.P74] 67-31686
1. Seventh-Day Adventists—Doctrinal and controversial works. 2. Bible. N.T. Revelation, XIII-XVII—Criticism, interpretation, etc. I. Title.

ANDERSON, Roy Allan 228.07
Unfolding the Revelation; evangelistic studies for public presentation. Mountain View, Calif., Pacific Pr. Pub. Assn. [c.1953, 1961] 223p. illus. 61-10884 3.00
1. Bible. N. T. Revelation—Commentaries. I. Title.

ANDERSON, Roy Allan. 228.07
Unfolding the Revelation; evangelistic studies for public presentation. Mountain View, Calif., Pacific Press Pub. Association [1961] 223p. illus. 20cm. [BS2825.A485 1961] 61-10884
1. Bible. N. T. Revelation—Commentaries. I. Title.

BECKWITH, Isbon Thaddeus, 228'.07
1843-1936.
The Apocalypse of John; studies in introduction with a critical and exegetical commentary. Grand Rapids, Baker Book House [1967, c1919] xv, 794 p. 23 cm. Includes bibliographical references. [BS2825.B4 1967] 67-18171
1. Bible. N.T. Revelation—Commentaries. I. Title.

BIBLE. N. T. Revelation. 228.07
English. 1961. Barclay.
The Revelation of John. [2 v.] Tr. with an introd. and interpretation by William Barclay. 2d ed. Philadelphia, Westminster Press [1961] 231;297p. (Daily study Bible) 61-8293 2.50 ea.,
1. Bible. N. T. Revelation—Commentaries. I. Barclay, William, lecturer in the University of Glasgow, ed. and tr. II. Title. III. Series: The Daily study Bible series

BIBLE. N.T. Revelation. 228.07
English. 1965. New English.
The Revelation of John. Commentary by T. F. Glasson. Cambridge [Eng.] University Press, 1965. xi, 127 p. map. 21 cm. (The Cambridge Bible commentary: New English Bible) "Books for further reading": p. 125. [BS2825.3.G55] 65-3524
1. Bible. N.T. Revelation—Commentaries. I. Glasson, Thomas Francis. II. Title. III. Series.

BIBLE, N. T. Revelation. 228.07
English. 1965. New English
The revelation of John Commentary by T. F. Glasson [New York] Cambridge [c.]1965. xi, 127p. map. 21cm. (Cambridge Bible commentary: New English Bible) Bibl. [BS2825.3.G55] 65-3524 3.00; 1.65 pap.,
1. Bible. N. T. Revelation—Commentaries. I. Glasson, Thomas Francis. II. Title. III. Series.

BIBLE. N.T. Revelation. 228.07
English. 1966.
A commentary on the Revelation of St. John the Divine. [by] G. B. Caird. [1st ed.] New York, Harper [1966] x, 316p. 22cm. (Harper's New Testament commentaries) Bibl. [BS2825.3.C3 1966a] 66-20774 6.50
1. Bible. N.T. Revelation—Commentaries. I. Caird, George Bradford. II. Title.

BIBLE. N.T. Revelation. 228.07
English. 1966.
A commentary on the Revelation of St. John the Divine [by] G. B. Caird. [1st ed.] New York, Harper & Row [1966) x, 316 p. 22 cm. (Harper's New Testament commentaries) Bibliography: p. ix-x. [BS2825.3.C3] 66-20774
1. Bible. N.T. Revelation—Commentaries. I. Caird, George Bradford. II. Title.

BOWMAN, John Wick, 1894- 228'.07
The first Christian drama; the Book of Revelation. Philadelphia, Westminster Press [1968] 159 p. 21 cm. [BS2825.3.B6 1968] 68-19049
1. Bible. N.T. Revelation—Commentaries. I. Title.

COCKRELL, U C 228.07
Omega in symbols: from Jesus Christ to John the Divine. [1st ed.] New York, Vantage Press [1961] 138p. 21cm. [BS2825.5.C6] 61-66714
1. Bible. N. T. Revelation— Prophecies. I. Title.

COHEN, Gary G. 228'.07
Understanding Revelation; an investigation of the key interpretational and chronological questions which surround the Book of Revelation, by Gary G. Cohen. Collingswood, N.J., Christian Beacon Press [1968] 186 p. 18 cm. A revision of the author's thesis, Grace Seminary, Winona Lake, Ind. Bibliography: p. 180-186. [BS2825.2.C56 1968] 68-4413
1. Bible. N.T. Revelation—Prophecies. I. Title.

CONSTAS, Constantine J. 228.07
The Revelation of Jesus Christ. Tr. from his orig. Greek by the author. New York, Carlton [c.1963] 638p. 21cm. (Reflection bk.) 63-5555 6.50
1. Bible. N. T. Revelation—Commentaries. I. Bible. N. T. Revelation. English. 1963. Constas. II. Title.

COWARD, Parnell C. 228'.07
Revelation systematically studied : a study with the layman in mind / by Parnell C. Coward. Cleveland, Tenn. : Pathway Press, [1974] 300 p. ; 22 cm. Bibliography: p. 300. [BS2825.3.C65] 73-88325 ISBN 0-87148-730-6 : 5.95
1. Bible. N.T. Revelation—Commentaries. I. Title.

DE SANTO, Charles. 228'.07
The book of Revelation, a study manual. Grand Rapids, Baker Book House [1967] 112 p. 20 cm. (Shield Bible study outlines) [BX2825.5.D4] 67-18174
1. Bible. N.T. Revelation — Study — Outlines, syllabi, etc. I. Title.

DE SANTO, Charles. 228'.07
The book of Revelation, a study manual. Grand Rapids, Baker Book House [1967] 112 p. 20 cm. (Shield Bible study outlines) [BS2825.5.D4] 67-18174
1. Bible. N.T. Revelation—Study—Outlines, syllabi, etc. I. Title.

FARRER, Austin Marsden. 228.07
The Revelation of St. John the Divine; commentary on the English text, by Austin Farrer. Oxford, Clarendon Press, 1964. viii, 233 p. 23 cm. [BS2825.3.F3] 64-4740
1. Bible. N.T. Revelation — Commentaries. I. Bible. N.T. Revelation. English. 1964. II. Title.

FARRER, Austin Marsden 228.07
The revelation of St. John the Divine; commentary on the English text. [New York] Oxford [c.]1964. viii, 233p. 23cm. 64-4740 4.80
1. Bible. N. T. Revelation—Commentaries. I. Bible. N. T. Revelation. English. 1964. II. Title.

FRANZMANN, Martin H. 228'.07
The Revelation to John : a commentary / by Martin H. Franzmann. St. Louis : Concordia Pub. House, c1976. 148 p. ; 21 cm. Includes bibliographical references. [BS2825.3.F68] 76-3749 ISBN 0-570-03728-X : 6.95
1. Bible. N.T. Revelation—Commentaries. I. Title.

GAEBELEIN, Arno Clemens, 228.07
1861-1945.
The Revelation; an analysis and exposition of the last book of the Bible. New York, Loizeaux Bros. [1961] 225 p. 21 cm. Bible. N.T. Revelation -- Prophecies. [BS2825.G3 1961] 61-17225
I. Title.

GRAHAM, Catherine. 228'.07
Revelation simplified, verse by verse. Corpus Christi, Tex., W. S. Graham, c1972. 211 p. 21 cm. [BS2825.3.G66] 74-178197
1. Bible. N.T. Revelation—Commentaries. I. Title.

HAYWARD, Otis Madison. 228.07
The story of the Revelation. Cambridge, Md., Revelation Press; distributed by Tidewater Publishers, 1959. 363p. 23cm. [BS2825.3.H35] 59-12837
1. Bible. N. T. Revelation—Commentaries. I. Title.

HOBBS, Herschel H. 228'.07
The cosmic drama; an exposition of the Book of Revelation [by] Herschel H. Hobbs. Waco, Tex., Word Books [1971] 212 p. 23 cm. Bibliography: p. 210-212. [BS2825.3.H6] 75-160298 5.95
1. Bible. N.T. Revelation—Commentaries. I. Title.

JACOBSEN, Henry, 1908- 228'.07
The war we can't lose; a devotional guide to the Revelation. [Wheaton, Ill.] Victor Books [1972] 96 p. 18 cm. (An Input book) [BS2825.3.J33] 72-77013 ISBN 0-88207-047-9 0.95
1. Bible. N.T. Revelation—Commentaries. I. Title.

JACOBSEN, Henry, 1908- 228'.07
The war we can't lose; a devotional guide to the Revelation. [Wheaton, Ill.] Victor Books [1972] 96 p. 18 cm. (An Input book) [BS2825.3.J33] 72-77013 ISBN 0-88207-047-9 0.95
1. Bible. N.T. Revelation—Commentaries. I. Title.

KINCHELOE, Raymond 228'.07
McFarland.
A personal adventure in prophecy; understanding Revelation. Wheaton, Ill., Tyndale House Publishers [1974] x, 214 p. 22 cm. Bibliography: p. 205-214. [BS2825.3.K55] 74-80149 ISBN 0-8423-4815-8 4.95
1. Bible. N.T. Revelation—Commentaries. I. Title.

KUYPER, Abraham, 1837-1920 228.07
The Revelation of St. John. Tr. from Dutch by John Hendrick de Vries. Grand Rapids, Eerdmans [1964, c.1963] 360p. 22cm. The Revelation of St. John, presented here in English garb, forms the greater part of the fourth and last volume of Dr. Kuyper's work: 'The consummation of the world.' 64-3804 2.25 pap.,
1. Bible. N. T. Revelation—Commentaries. I. De Vries, John Hendrik, 1859- tr. II. Title.

LADD, George Eldon, 1911- 228'.07
A commentary on the Revelation of John. Grand Rapids, Eerdmans [1972] 308 p. 23 cm. Bibliography: p. 297-299. [BS2825.3.L28] 70-150640 6.95
1. Bible. N.T. Revelation—Commentaries. I. Title.

LAWRENCE, John Benjamin, 228.07
1873-
A new heaven and a new earth; a contemporary interpretation of the book of Revelation. New York, American Press [c.1960] 165p. 22cm. 60-12191 2.75
1. Bible. N. T. Revelation—Commentaries. I. Title.

LAWRENCE, John Benjamin, 228.07
1873-
A new heaven and new earth: a contemporary interpretation of the book of Revelation. [1st ed.] New York, American Press [1960] 165p. 22cm. [BS2825.3.L35] 60-12191
1. Bible. N. T. Revelation—Commentaries. I. Title.

MAURO, Philip, 1859-1952. 228'.07
Of things which soon must come to pass; a commentary on the Book of Revelation. Swengel, Pa., Reiner Publications, 1971. xxviii, 623 p. 21 cm. Reprint of the 1933 ed. of the work first published in 1925 under title: The Patmos visions. [BS2825.3.M38 1971] 79-24076 6.95
1. Bible. N.T. Revelation—Commentaries. I. Title.

MINEAR, Paul Sevier, 228'.07
1906-
I saw a new earth; an introduction to the visions of the Apocalypse [by] Paul S. Minear. Foreword by Myles M. Bourke. Washington, Corpus Books [1968] xxvi, 385 p. illus. 21 cm. Translation of the book of Revelation with annotations: p. [299]-365. Bibliography: p. 367-384. [BS2825.3.M5] 68-18711 10.00
1. Bible. N.T. Revelation—Commentaries. I. Bible. N.T. Revelation. English. Minear. 1968. II. Title.

MORRIS, Leon. 228'.07
The Revelation of St. John; an introduction and commentary. [1st ed.] Grand Rapids, Eerdmans [1969] 263 p. 21 cm. (The Tyndale New Testament commentaries [v. 20]) Bibliographical footnotes. [BS2825.3.M67] 70-9509 4.50
1. Bible. N.T. Revelation—Commentaries. I. Title.

NJEIM, George A. 228'.07
Insights into the book of Revelation; as illuminated by the Book of Mormon, by George A. Njeim. [Lawrence? Kan., 1970] 247 p. 21 cm. Includes bibliographical references. [BS2825.3.N54] 75-114838
1. Bible. N.T. Revelation—Commentaries. I. Title.

ONSTAD, Esther. 228'.07
Courage for today, hope for tomorrow : a study of the Revelation / Esther Onstad. Minneapolis, Minn. : Augsburg Pub. House, [1975] c1974. 144 p. : ill. ; 22 cm. Bibliography: p. 94. [BS2825.3.O57 1975] 75-2829 ISBN 0-8066-1474-9 pbk. : 2.95
1. Bible. N.T. Revelation—Commentaries. 2. Bible. N.T. Revelation—Study. I. Title.

OTTMAN, Ford Cyrinde, 228'.07
1859-
The unfolding of the ages in the Revelation of John. Grand Rapids, Kregel Pubns. [1967] xxx, 510p. 22cm. Reprint of the 1905 ed. [BS2825.O75 1967] 67-25850 5.95
1. Bible. N. T. Revelation—Commentaries. I. Title.

PHILLIPS, John, 1927- 228'.07
Exploring Revelation / John Phillips. Chicago : Moody Press, [1974] 282 p. : 24 cm. Includes bibliographical references. [BS2825.3.P47] 74-15330 ISBN 0-8024-2407-4 : 5.95
1. Bible. N.T. Revelation—Commentaries. I. Title.

POELLOT, Luther. 228.07
Revelation, the last book in the Bible. St. Louis, Concordia Pub. House, 1962. 314p. 24cm. Includes bibliography. [BS2825.3.P6 1962] 61-18228
1. Bible. N. T. Revelation—Commentaries. I. Title.

RAYMER, Ethel G. 228.07
Seed of the City. New York, Vantage Press. [c.1959] 184p. 22cm. 3.00 bds.,
I. Title.

RICHARDS, Hubert J. 1921- 228'.07
What the Spirit says to the churches; a key to the Apocalypse of John, by Hubert J. Richards. New York, Kenedy [1967] c141p. illus. 23cm. [BS2825.3.R5] 67-14149 4.50 bds.,
1. Bible. N. T. Revelation—Commentaries. I. Bible. N. T. Revelation. English. 1967. II. Title.

RICHARDSON, Donald William, 1879- 228.07
The Revelation of Jesus Christ: an interpretation [Rev. ed.] Richmond, Va., Knox [c.1939, 1964] 140p. 21cm. (Aletheia ed.) Bibl. 1.45 pap.,
1. Bible. N.T. Revelation—Commentaries. I. Title.

RIST, Martin, 1896- 228.07
The modern reader's guide to the book of Revelation. New York, Association Press [1961] 128p. 15cm. (An Association Press reflection book, 546) Includes bibliography. [BS2825.2.R5] 61-7115
1. Bible. N. T. Revelation—Criticism, interpretation, etc. I. Title.

RUSHDOONY, Rousas John. 228'.07
Thy kingdom come; studies in Daniel and Revelation. [Philadelphia] Presbyterian and Reformed Pub. Co., 1971 [c1970] iv, 256 p. 21 cm. Includes bibliographical references. [BS1555.2.R88] 70-139853 4.95
1. Bible. O.T. Daniel—Criticism, interpretation, etc. 2. Bible. N.T. Revelation—Criticism, interpretation, etc. I. Title.

RYRIE, Charles Caldwell. 228'.07
Revelation. Chicago, Moody [1968] 127p. 19cm. (Everyman's Bible commentary, 3966) .95 pap.,
1. Bible. N. T. Revelation—Study, outlines, syllabi, etc. I. Title.

*SHERMAN, Alva W. 228.07
The analysis of revelation. New York, Vantage [c.1964] 211p. 21cm. 4.50
I. Title.

SMITH, Jacob Brubaker, 1870-1951. 228.07
A revelation of Jesus Christ; a commentary on the book of Revelation. Edited by J. Otis Yoder. Introd. by Merrill C. Tenney. Scottdale, Pa., Herald Press [1961] 369 p. illus. 24 cm. [BS2825.5.S56] 61-7091
1. Bible. N.T. Revelation — Commentaries. I. Title.

SMITH, Jacob Brubaker, 1870-1951. 228.07
A revelation of Jesus Christ; a commentary on the book of Revelation. Ed. by J. Otis Yoder. Introd. by Merrill C. Tenney. Scottdale, Pa., Herald Press [c.1961] 369p. illus. 61-7091 5.75
1. Bible. N. T. Revelation—Commentaries. I. Title.

STRAUSS, Lehman 228.07
The book of the Revelation, outlined studies. Neptune, N. J., Loizeaux [c.1964] 381p. 20cm. Bibl. [BS2825.3.S7] 64-8641 4.50
1. Bible. N.T. Revelation—Commentaries. I. Title.

STRAUSS, Lehman. 228.07
The book of the Revelation, outlined studies. [1st ed.] Neptune, N.J., Loizeaux Bros. [1964] 381 p. 20 cm. Bibliography: p. 365-366. [BS2825.3.S7] 64-8641
1. Bible. N. T. Revelation — Commentaries. I. Title.

SWEDENBORG, Emanuel, 1688-1772 228.07
The Apocalypse explained according to the spiritual sense in which the arcana there predicted but heretofore concealed are revealed; v. 2. Standard ed. A posthumous work of Emanuel Swedenborg. New York, Swedenborg Found., 1963. 586, iii p. 22cm. Contents.v.2, Chapters 5;6. 2.50
1. Bible. N. T. Revelation—Commentaries. I. Bible. N. T. Revelation. English. 1949. II. Title.

TATE, Jesse. 228.07
Patmos wonderland; the book of Revelation in explanatory language with commentary (Wonderland workship) [1st ed.] Roanoke, Va., Morning Star [1965] 120 p. 22 cm. [BS2825.3.T3] 65-23925
1. Bible N. T. Revelation—Criticism, interpretation, etc. I. Title.

TICONIUS, 4th cent. 228.07
The Turin fragments of Tyconius' commentary on Revelation, Edited by Francesco Lo Bue, and prepared for the press by G. G. Willis. Cambridge [Eng.] University Press, 1963. xv, 196 p. 4 facsims. 23 cm. (Texts and studies: contributions to Biblical and patristic literature, new ser., 7) In Latin. Bibliography: p. 39-42. [BR45.T43] 63-5497
1. Bible. N.T. Revelation — Commentaries. I. Lo Bue, Francesco, 1914-1955, ed. II. Willis, Geoffrey Grimshaw. III. Title. IV. Series.

TICONIUS, 4th cent. 228.07
The Turin fragments of Tyconius' commentary on Revelation. Ed. by Francesco Lo Bue. Prepared for pr. by G. G. Willis. [New York] Cambridge [c.]1963. xv, 198p. 4 facsims. 23cm. (Texts & studies; contributions to Biblical and patristic lit., new ser., 7) In Latin. Bibl. 63-5497 11.00
1. Bible. N. T. Revelation—Commentaries. I. Lo Bue, Francesco, 1914-1955, ed. II. Willis, Geoffrey Grimshaw, III. Title. IV. Series.

VAN GORDER, John Jay, 1881- 228'.07
ABC's of the Revelation, by John J. Vangorder. Grand Rapids, Mich., Zondervan Pub. House [1969] 186 p. 21 cm. [BS2825.3.V35 1969] 75-81054
1. Bible. N.T. Revelation—Commentaries. I. Title.

WALVOORD, John F. 228.07
The Revelation of Jesus Christ; a commentary, by John F. Walvoord. Chicago, Moody [1966] 347p. 24cm. Bibl. [BS2825.3.W33] 66-16227 5.95
1. Bible. .. N.T. RVelation—Commenatries. I. Bible. N.T. Revelation. English. 1966. Authorized. II. Title.

WILCOCK, Michael. 228'.07
I saw heaven opened : the message of Revelation / Michael Wilcock. Downers Grove, Ill. : InterVarsity Press, c1975. 223 p. ; 22 cm. (The Bible speaks today) [BS2825.3.W53] 74-31845 ISBN 0-87784-774-6 pbk. : 3.95
1. Bible. N.T. Revelation—Commentaries. I. Title.

*BARNEY, Kenneth D. 228'.0766
We interrupt this crisis/ Kenneth D. Barney. Springfield, Mo.: Gospel Pub. House [1976] c1970. 63 p.; 18 cm. (Radiant Books) Original title "Christ speaks to the church." [BS2825.2] ISBN 0-88243-704-6 pbk.: 1.25
1. Bible. N.T. Revelation—Criticism, interpretation, etc. I. Title.

BARNHOUSE, Donald Grey, 1895-1960. 228'.07'7
Revelation; an expository commentary, "God's last word." Grand Rapids, Zondervan Pub. House [1971] 432 p. 23 cm. "The earlier chapters first appeared serially in Revelation magazine under the title of 'God's last word' in the years between 1934 and 1942." [BS2825.3.B2 1971] 77-120051
1. Bible. N. T. Revelation—Commentaries. I. Title. II. Title: God's last word.

BIBLE. N.T. Revelation. English. Barclay. 1976. 228'.077
The Revelation of John / translated with an introd. and interpretation by William Barclay. Rev. ed. Philadelphia : Westminster Press, c1976. v. ; 19 cm. (The Daily study Bible series. — Rev. ed.) Contents.Contents.—V. 1. Chapters 1 to 5. Bibliography: v. 1, p. [184] [BS2823.B37 1976] 75-37600 ISBN 0-664-21315-4(v.1). : 6.25 pbk. : 3.45
1. Bible. N.T. Revelation—Commentaries. I. Barclay, William, lecturer in the University of Glasgow. II. Title. III. Series.

BIBLE. N.T. Revelation. Greek. 1977. 228'.07'7
The Apocalypse of St. John : the Greek text, with introduction, notes, and indices / by Henry Barclay Swete. Grand Rapids : Kregel Publications, [1977] p. cm. (Kregel reprint library) Reprint of the 2d ed., 1907, published by Macmillan, London, New York. Includes bibliographical references and indexes. [BS2821.S96 1977] 77-79192 ISBN 0-8254-3716-4 : 12.95
1. Bible. N.T. Revelation—Commentaries. I. Swete, Henry Barclay, 1835-1917. II. Title.

CAIRD, George Bradford. 228'.07'7
A commentary on the Revelation of St. John the Divine [by] G. B. Caird. [1st ed.] New York, Harper & Row [1966] x, 316 p. 22 cm. (Harper's New Testament commentaries) Bibliography: p. ix-x. [BS2825.3.C3 1966b] 66-20774
1. Bible. N. T. Revelation—Commentaries. I. Title.

COHEN, Gary G. 228'.07'7
Revelation visualized; never before so crystal clear and current an explanation of the last book of the Bible! Verse by verse King James version. Each verse includes a commentary by Gary G. Cohen and background by Salem Kirban. Huntingdon Valley, Pa., S. Kirban [1971] 480 p. illus. (part col.), facsims., maps (part col.), ports. (part col.) 19 cm. [BS2825.3.C57] 78-146684
1. Bible N.T. Revelation—Commentaries. I. Kirban, Salem, joint author. II. Bible. N.T. Revelation. English. Authorized. 1971. III. Title.

ELLER, Vernard. 228'.07'7
The most revealing book of the Bible: making sense out of Revelation. Grand Rapids, Eerdmans [1974] 214 p. illus. 23 cm. [BS2825.3.E57] 74-2495 ISBN 0-8028-1572-3 3.95 (pbk.).
1. Bible. N.T. Revelation—Commentaries. I. Title.

HARRINGTON, Wilfrid J. 228'.07'7
Understanding the Apocalypse [by] Wilfrid J. Harrington. Washington, Corpus Books [1969] ix, 278 p. 22 cm. Bibliography: p. 277-278. [BS2825.3.H34] 75-83513 5.95
1. Bible. N.T. Revelation—Commentaries. I. Title.

HOEKSEMA, Herman. 228'.07'7
Behold, He cometh; an exposition of the book of Revelation. Edited and partially rev. by Homer C. Hoeksema. Grand Rapids, Mich. Reformed Free Pub. Association; distributed by Kregel Publications [1969] viii, 726 p. 23 cm. [BS2825.H65] 70-82449 9.95
1. Bible. N.T. Revelation—Commentaries. I. Title.

LAHAYE, Tim F. 228'.07'7
Revelation / illustrated and made plain by Tim LaHaye. Rev. ed. Grand Rapids, Mich. : Zondervan Pub. House, [1975] 323, [3] p. : ill. ; 22 cm. Bibliography: p. [326] [BS2825.3.L33 1975] 74-9323 pbk. : 4.95
1. Bible. N.T. Revelation—Commentaries. I. Title.

NORELLI-BACHELET, Patrizia. 228'.07'7
The hidden manna, being the Revelation called Apocalypse of John the Divine with complete text and commentaries / by Patrizia Norelli-Bachelet. 1st ed. Panorama City, Calif. : Aeon Books, 1976. 385 p. ; 20 cm. [BS2825.3.N67] 77-150764
1. Bible. N.T. Revelation—Commentaries. I. Bible. N.T. Revelation. English. Authorized. 1976. II. Title.

ROBBINS, Ray F., 1915- 228'.07'7
The revelation of Jesus Christ / Ray Frank Robbins. Nashville : Broadman Press, c1975. 260 p. ; 20 cm. Bibliography: p. 251-260. [BS2825.3.R59] 75-1739 ISBN 0-8054-1354-5 pbk. : 3.95
1. Bible. N.T. Revelation—Commentaries. I. Title.

ROBERTS, J. W., 1918- 228'.07'7
The Revelation to John (the Apocalypse) / J. W. Roberts. Austin, Tex. : Sweet Pub. Co., c1974. 203 p. ; 22 cm. (The Living word commentary ; 19) Includes the text in the Revised standard version. Bibliography: p. 24-26. [BS2825.3.R6] 73-20857 ISBN 0-8344-0074-X : 4.25
1. Bible. N.T. Revelation—Commentaries. I. Bible. N.T. Revelation. English. Revised standard. 1974. II. Title. III. Series.

SCOTT, Walter, 1838-1933. 228'.07'7
Exposition of the Revelation of Jesus Christ. [4th ed.] Westwood, N.J., F. H. Revell Co. [1968] 456 p. 22 cm. Bibliography: p. [3]-[4] [BS2825.3.S3 1968] 71-2369 7.95
1. Bible. N.T. Revelation—Commentaries. I. Title.

SWEDENBORG, Emanuel, 1688-1772. 228'.07'7
The Apocalypse revealed. Translated from the Latin of Emanuel Swedenborg. Translation rev. and edited by Alice Spiers Sechrist. New York, Swedenborg Foundation [1969] ix, 1157 p. 18 cm. [BX8712.A6 1969] 78-5623 2.50
1. Bible. N.T. Revelation—Commentaries. I. Sechrist, Alice Spiers, ed. II. Bible. N.T. Revelation. English. Swedenborg. 1969. III. Title.

SWEDENBORG, Emanuel, 1688-1772. 228'.07'7
The Apocalypse revealed : wherein are disclosed the arcana there foretold which have hitherto remained concealed / translated from the Latin of Emanuel Swedenborg ; a translation by John Whitehead. Standard ed. New York : Swedenborg Foundation, 1968. 2 v. ; 21 cm. Translation of Apocalypsis revelata. Includes indexes. [BX8712.A6 1968] 74-186368
1. Bible. N.T. Revelation—Commentaries. I. Title.

TATE, Jesse. 228'.07'7
Patmos. Boyce, Va., Christianity Tomorrow [1972] xx, 318 p. 21 cm. (A Tomorrow book) A finished version of an incomplete, preliminary work published in 1965 under title: Patmos wonderland. [BS2825.3.T29] 72-89600 4.95
1. Bible. N.T. Revelation—Commentaries. 2. Bible. N.T. Revelation—Paraphrases, English. I. Title.

UMPHREY, Clyde Ellis. 228'.07'7
Challenge and witness in revelation / by Clyde Ellis Umphrey. 1st ed. Portland, Or. : Metropolitan Press, [1974] xviii, 121 p. ; 22 cm. [BS2825.3.U47] 74-80516 1.95
1. Bible. N.T. Revelation—Commentaries. I. Title.

WALLACE, Foy Esco, 1896- 228.077
The Book of Revelation, consisting of a commentary on the Apocalypse of the New Testament, by Foy E. Wallace, Jr. Nashville, F. E. Wallace Publications, 1966. ix, 477 p. ports. 24 cm. [BS2825.3.W3] 66-4975
1. Bible. N.T. Revelation — Commentaries. I. Title.

ERDMAN, Charles Rosenbury, 1866-1960. 228'.77
The Revelation of John; an exposition. Pref. by Earl F. Zeigler. Philadelphia, Westminster Press [1966] 181 p. 19 cm. (His Commentaries on the New Testament books) [BS2825.E63 1966] 67-1999
1. Bible. N.T. Revelation—Commentaries. I. Title.

*ANDERSON, Evelyn. 228.8'5
Good morning, Lord; devotions for the mature years [by] Evelyn Amderson. Grand Rapids, Mich., Baker Book House [1973] 95 p. 20 cm. (Good morning, Lord series) [BX2372] 1.95
1. Aged—Religious life. 2. Aged—Prayer-Books and devotions. I. Title.

229 Apocrypha & Pseudepigrapha

ANDREWS, Herbert Tom, 1864-1928. 229
An introduction to the Apocryphal books of the Old and New Testament, by H. T. Andrews. Rev. and edited by Charles F. Pfeiffer. Grand Rapids, Baker Book House, 1964. 141 p. 21 cm. First published in London in 1908 under title: The Apocryphal books of the Old and New Testament. Bibliography: p. 135-137. [BS1700.A63] 64-15679
1. Bible. O. T. Apocrypha and Apocryphal books — Introductions. I. Pfeiffer, Charles F., ed. II. Title.

ANDREWS, Herbert Tom, 1864-1928 229
An introduction to the Apocryphal books of the Old and New Testament. Rev., ed. by Charles F. Pfeiffer. Grand Rapids, Mich., Baker Bk. [c.]1964. 141p. 21cm. First pub. in London in 1908 under title: The Apocryphal books of the Old and New Testament. Bibl. 64-15679 2.95
1. Bible. O. T. Apocrypha and Apocryphal books—Introductions. I. Pfeiffer, Charles F., ed. II. Title.

BIBLE. Apocryphal books. English. 1963. 229
The lost books of the Bible and The forgotten books of Eden. Cleveland, World [1963] 293, xii, 269p. plates. 21cm. (Forum bks.; F256) Each pt. has special t. p. The forgotten books of Eden, edited by Rutherford H. Platt, Jr. 63-19519 2.25 pap.,
I. Bible. N. T. Apocryphal books. English. 1963. The lost books of the Bible. II. Bible. O. T. Apocryphal books. English. 1963. The forgotten books of Eden. III. Platt, Rutherford Hayes, 1894- ed. IV. Title. V. Title: The forgotten books of Eden.

BIBLE. N.T. Apocryphal books. English. 1963. 229
The lost books of the Bible and The forgotten books of Eden. Cleveland, World Pub. Co. [1963] 293, xii, 269 p. plates. 21 cm. (Forum books) "F256." Each part has special t.p. The forgotten books of Eden, edited by Rutherford H. Platt, Jr. [BS1692] 63-19519
I. Bible. O.T. Apocryphal books. English. 1963. The forgotten books of Eden. II. Platt, Rutherford Hayes, 1894- ed. III. Title. IV. Title: The forgotten books of Eden.

BIBLE. N.T. Apocryphal books. English. 1963. 229
New Testament Apocrypha, edited by Wilhelm Schneemelcher. English translation [by A. J. B. Higgins and others] edited by R. McL. Wilson. Philadelphia, Westminster Press [1963-66, c1963-65] 2 v. 24 cm. Original German ed., edited by Edgar Hennecke. Contents.CONTENTS.--v. 1. Gospels and related writings.--v. 2. Writings relating to the Apostles, apocalypses, and related subjects. Includes bibliograhpical footnotes. [BS2832.S3] 63-7492
I. Hennecke, Edgar, 1865-1951, ed. II. Schneemelcher, Wilhelm, 1914- ed. III. Wilson, Robert McLachian, ed. IV. Title.

BIBLE. N. T. APOCRYPHAL BOOKS. ENGLISH. 1963. 229
New Testament Apocrypha; v.1. ed. by Wilhelm Schneemelcher. Eng. tr. [by A. J. B. Higgins, others] ed. by R. McL. Wilson. Philadelphia, Westminster [c.1963] 531p. 24cm. Orig. German ed., by Edgar Hennecke. Contents.v.1. Gospels and related writings. Bibl. 63-7492 7.50
I. Hennecke, Edgar, 1865-1951, ed. II. Scheemelcher, Wilhelm, 1914- ed. III. Wilson, Robert McLachlan, ed. IV. Title.

BIBLE. O.T. Apocrypha. English. 1936. Authorized. 229
The Apocrypha; or, Non-canonical books of the Bible. The King James version. Edited by Manuel Komroff. New York, Arno Press, 1972. 350 p. 24 cm. (The Atheist viewpoint) Reprint of the 1936 ed. [BS1692 1936b] 70-161319 ISBN 0-405-03622-1
I. Komroff, Manuel, 1890- ed. II. Bible. O.T. Apocrypha. English. Authorized. 1972. III. Title. IV. Series.

BIBLE. O. T. Apocrypha. English. 1957. Revised standard. 229
The Apocrypha, Revised standard version of the Old Testament. Translated from the Greek and Latin tongues, being the version set forth A. D. 1611, rev. A. D. 1894, compared with the most ancient authorities and rev. A. D. 1957. New York, Nelson, 1957. 250p. 22cm. [BS1692 1957] 57-10132
I. Title.

BIBLE. O. T. Apocrypha. English. 1957 Revised standard. 229
The Apocrypha Revised standard version of the Old Testament. Translated from the Greek and Latin tongues, being the version set forth A. D. 1611, rev. A. D. 1894, compared with the most ancient authorities and rev. A. D. 1957. New York, Nelson, 1957. 250p. 22cm. [BS1692 1957] 57-10132
I. Title.

BIBLE. O.T. Apocrypha. English. 1959. Goodspeed. 229
The Apocrypha; an Amer. tr. by Edgar J. Goodspeed. Introd. by Moses Hadas. New York, Modern Lib. [dist. Random, 1962, c.1938, 1961] xxvi, 493p. 19cm. (326) 62-4258 1.95
I. Goodspeed, Edgar Johnson, 1871-1962, tr. II. Title.

BIBLE. O.T. Apocrypha. English. 1962. Authorized. 229
The Apocrypha; a facsimile of the famous Nonesuch ed. of 1924. New Hyde Park, N.Y., University Bks. [1963, c.1962] xv, 237. 29cm. Orig. t.p. reads: The Apocrypha reprinted according to the authorized version 1611. London, Nonesuch Press; New York, Dial Press, 1924. Lithographed facsimile reproduction, with introd. by Morton Enslin. 62-12335 15.00, bxd.
I. Title.

BIBLE. O. T. Apocrypha. English. 1965. Revised standard 229
The Apocrypha of the Old Testament. Rev. stanard version. Tr. from Greek and Latin tongues, being the version set forth A. D. 1611, rev. A. D. 1894, compared with the most ancient authorities and rev. A. D. 1957. With introds. comments, cross references, tables of chronology, index. Ed. by Bruce M. Metzger. New York. Oxford. 1965 [c.1957, 1965] xxii, 298p. maps (on lining papers)23cm. At head of title: The Oxford annotated Apocrypha. [BS1692] 65-12463 3.50
I. Metzger, Bruce Manning, ed. II. Title. III. Title: The Oxford annotated Apocrypha.

BIBLE. O. T. Apocrypha. English. Selections. 1957. 229
The hidden books; selections from the Apocrypha for the general reader. Based upon the King James version, with omissions, rearrangement, and modernization in the interest of increased understanding and enjoyment, by Adele Bildersee. New York, Abelard-Schuman [1957, c1956] 183p. illus. 22cm. [BS1695.B5] 56-12169
I. Bildersee, Adele, 1888- II. Title.

BIBLE. O. T. Apocrypha. English. Selections. 1957. 229
The hidden books; selections from the Apocrypha for the general reader. Based upon the King James version, with omissions, rearrangement, and modernization in the interest of increased understanding and enjoyment, by Adele Bildersee. New York, Abelard-Schuman [1957, c1956] 183 p. illus. 22 cm. [BS1695.B5] 56-12169
I. Bildersee, Adele, 1883- II. Title.

DENTAN, Robert Claude, 1907- 229
The Apocrypha, bridge of the Testaments; a reader's guide to the Apocryphal books of the Old Testament. Greenwich, Conn., Seabury Press, 1954. 122p. 20cm. [BS1700.D4] 54-2142
1. Bible. O. T. Apocrypha—Introductions. I. Title.

DENTAN, Robert Claude, 1907- 229
The Apocrypha, bridge of the Testaments; a reader's guide to the apocryphal books of the Old Testament [Rev. ed.] New York, Seabury [c.1954, 1964] v, 122p. 21cm. (Seabury paperback, SP13) Bibl. 64-23900 1.25 pap.,
1. Bible. O.T. Apocrypha—Introductions. I. Title.

DENTAN, Robert Clause, 1907- 229
The Apocrypha, bridge of the Testaments; a reader's guide to the apocryphal books of the Old Testament, by Robert C. Dentan. [Rev. ed.] New York, Seabury Press [1964] v. 122 p. 21 cm. (A Seabury paperback, SP13) Bibliography: p. 112-116. [BS1700.D4 1964] 64-23900
1. Bible. O.T. Apocrypha — Introductions. I. Title.

DIMIER, Catherine. 229
The Old Testament Apocrypha. Translated from the French by S. J. Tester. [1st American ed.] New York, Hawthorn Books [1964] 154, [1] p. 21 cm. (The Twentieth century encyclopedia of Catholicism, v. 71. Section 6: The word of God) Translation of Ce que l'Ancien Testament ne dit pas. Bibliography: p. [155] [BS1700.D513] 64-14157
1. Bible. O.T. Apocryphal books — Criticism, interpretation, etc. I. Title. II. Series. III. Series: The Twentieth century encyclopedia of Catholicism, v. 71

DIMIER, Catherine 229
The Old Testament Apocrypha. Tr. from French by S. J. Tester. New York, Hawthorn [c.1964] 154,[1]p. 21cm. (20th cent. ency. of Catholicism. v.71. Sect. 6: The word of God) Bibl. 64-14157 3.50 bds.,
1. Bible. O. T. Apocryphal books—Criticism. interpretation. etc. I. Title. II. Series: The Twentieth century encyclopedia of Catholicism, v.71

METZGER, Bruce Manning. 229
An introduction to the Apocrypha. New York, Oxford University Press, 1957. 274 p. 22 cm. [BS1700.M4] 57-11636
1. Bible. O.T. Apocrypha—Introductions.

MEYER, Edith Patterson 229
The three guardsmen, and other stories from the Apocrypha. Illus. by Howard Simon. Nashville, Abingdon Press [c.1960] 128p. illus., endpaper map 22cm. 60-6817 2.50
1. Bible stories, English—O. T. Apocrypha. I. Title.

MEYER, Edith Patterson. 229
The three guardsmen, and other stories from the Apocrypha. Illus. by Howard Simon. New York, Abingdon Press [1960] 128p. illus. 22cm. [BS1700.M45] 60-6817
1. Bible stories, English—O. T. Apocrypha. I. Title.

ROST, Leonhard, 1896- 229
Judaism outside the Hebrew canon : an introduction to the documents / by Leonhard Rost ; translated by David E. Green. Nashville : Abingdon, [1976] p. cm. Translation of Einleitung in die alttestamentlichen Apokryphen und Pseudepigraphen einschliesslich der grossen Qumran-Handschriften. Bibliography: p. [BS1700.R6213] 76-15006 ISBN 0-687-20654-5 : 16.95 pbk. : 5.95
1. Dead Sea scrolls. 2. Apocryphal books (Old Testament)—Criticism, interpretation, etc. I. Title.

SMALLWOOD, E. Mary. 229
The Jews under Roman rule : from Pompey to Diocletian / by E. Mary Smallwood. Leiden : Brill, 1976. xiv, 595 p. : ill. ; 25 cm. (Studies in Judaism in late antiquity ; v. 20) Includes bibliographical references and index. [DS122.S62] 76-371075 ISBN 9-00-404491-4 : fl 276.00
1. Jews—History—168 B.C.—135 A.D. 2. Rome—History—Empire, 30 B.C.-284 A.D. I. Title. II. Series.

TORREY, Charles Cutler, 1863-1956 229
The apocryphal literature; a brief introduction. Hamden, Conn., Archon [dist. Shoe String] 1963[c.1945] 151p. 24cm. Bibl. 63-13089 5.50
1. Bible. O. T. Apocrypha and apocryphal books—Introductions. I. Title.

WALSH, Mary Ellen, 1892- 229
The Apocrypha, by Mary E. Walsh. Nashville, Southern Pub. Association [1968] 111 p. 22 cm. Bibliography: p. 105-106. [BS1700.W33] 68-19193
1. Bible. O.T. Apocrypha—Introductions. 2. Bible. O.T. Apocrypha—Canon. I. Title.

BIBLE. O.T. Apocrypha. English. New English. 1970. 229'.052
The New English Bible: the Apocrypha. London: Oxford U.P./Cambridge U.P., 1970. xiv, 362 p. 24 cm. Translated under the supervision of the Joint Committee on the New Translation of the Bible. [BS1692 1970] 72-486074 25/-
I. Joint Committee on the New Translation of the Bible. II. Title.

†CHARLESWORTH, James H. 229'.06
The pseudepigrapha and modern research / by James H. Charlesworth, assisted by P. Dykers. Missoula, Mont. : Scholars Press for the Society of Biblical Literature, c1976. xiv, 245 p. ; 22 cm. (Septuagint and cognate studies ; no. 7) Includes bibliographies and index. [BS1700.C45] 76-25921 ISBN 0-89130-075-9 : 2.80
1. Apocryphal books (Old Testament)—Criticism, interpretation, etc. I. Dykers, P., joint author. II. Title. III. Series.

THE Legacy of Zion : 229'.06
intertestamental texts related to the New Testament / Henry R. Moeller, editor. Grand Rapids : Baker Book House, 1977. 212 p. ; 24 cm. Bibliography: p. 209-212. [BM176.L36] 76-47313 ISBN 0-8010-6002-8 : 8.95
1. Judaism—History—Post-exilic period, 586 B.C.-210 A.D.—Sources. I. Moeller, Henry R.

TURNER, Henry Ernest William, 1907- 229.06
Thomas and the Evangelists [by] H. E. W. Turner and Hugh Montefiore. Naperville, Ill., A. R. Allenson [1962] 128 p. 22 cm. (Studies in Biblical theology, no. 35) Includes bibliography. [BS2860.T52T8] 62-51200
1. Bible. N.T. Apocryphal books. Coptic Gospel of Thomas — Criticism, interpretation, etc. 2. Bible, N. T. Gospels — Criticism, interpretation, etc. 3. Montefiore, Hugh. I. Title.

TURNER, Henry Ernest William, 1907- 229.06
Thomas and the Evangelists [by] H. E. W. Turner, Hugh Montefiore. Naperville, Ill., 635 E. Ogden Ave. Allenson, [c.1962] 128p. 22cm. (Studies in Biblical theology, no. 35) Bibl. 62-512009 2.00 pap.,
1. Bible. N.T. Apocryphal books. Coptic Gospel of Thomas—Criticism, interpretation, etc. 2. Bible. N.T. Gospels—Criticism, interpretation, etc. I. Montefiore, Hugh. II. Title.

ELLISON, Henry Leopold. 229'.09'5
From Babylon to Bethlehem : the Jewish people from the exile to the Messiah / by H. L. Ellison. Exeter : Paternoster Press, 1976. viii, 136 p. : geneal. tables ; 22 cm. Includes indexes. Bibliography: p. 126. [DS121.65.E38] 76-365007 ISBN 0-85364-190-0 : 1.80
1. Jews—History—586 B.C.-70 A.D. 2. Judaism—History—Post-exilic period, 586 B.C.-210 A.D.

THOMPSON, Alden Lloyd. 229'.1
Responsibility for evil in the theodicy of IV Ezra : a study illustrating the significance of form and structure for the meaning of the book / by Alden Lloyd Thompson. Missoula, Mont. : Published by Scholars Press for the Society of Biblical Literature, c1977. p. cm. (Dissertation series - Society of Biblical Literature ; no. 29) Originally presented as the author's thesis, University of Edinburgh, 1974. Bibliography: p. [BS1715.2.T48 1977] 76-40915 ISBN 0-89130-091-0 : 4.20
1. Bible. O.T. Apocrypha. 2 Esdras—Criticism, interpretation, etc. I. Title. II. Series: Society of Biblical Literature. Dissertation series ; no. 29.

GRAY, Simon James Holliday. B22.9'14
Otherwise engaged and other plays / Simon Gray. [New York] : Penguin Books, [1976] c1975. p. cm. [PR6057.R33A19 1976] 76-18816 ISBN 0-14-048136-2 pbk. : 2.50
I. Title.
Contents omitted

BIBLE. O. T. Apocrypha. Tobit. English. 1958. Zimmermann. 229.2
The book of Tobit. An English translation with introd. and commentary by Frank Zimmermann. New York Published for the Dropsie College for Hebrew and Cognate Learning by Harper [1958] xii, 190p. 21cm. (Jewish Apocryphal literature) Greek and English. Bibliography: p. 179-180. [BS1725.Z5] 58-11288
1. Bible. O. T. Apocrypha. Tobit—Commentrries. I. Bible. O. T. Apocrypha. Tobit. Greek. 1958. II. Zimmermann, Frank, ed. and tr. III. Title. IV. Series.

BIBLE. O.T. Apocrypha. English. New English. Selections. 1972. 229'.22'05206
The shorter books of the Apocrypha: Tobit, Judith, Rest of Esther, Baruch, Letter of Jeremiah, additions to Daniel and Prayer of Manasseh. Commentary by J. C. Dancy, with contributions by W. J. Fuerst and R. J. Hammer. Cambridge [Eng.] University Press, 1972. ix, 252 p. 21 cm. (The Cambridge Bible commentary: New English Bible) [BS1695.D3 1972] 72-76358 9.95
I. Dancy, John Christopher. II. Fuerst, Wesley J., 1930- III. Hammer, Raymond. IV. Title. V. Series.
Distributed by Cambridge University Press N.Y. pap 3.95

CENTER for Hermeneutical Studies in Hellenistic and Modern Culture. 229'.24'063
Narrative structures in the book of Judith : protocol of the eleventh colloquy, 27 January [i.e. 17 March] 1974 / the Center for Hermeneutical Studies in Hellenistic and Modern Culture ; Luis Alonso-Schokel ; W. Wuellner, editor. Berkeley, CA : The Center, c1975. 72 p. ; 21 cm. (Protocol series of the colloquies of the Center for Hermeneutical Studies in Hellenistic and Modern Culture ; nr. 11) Includes bibliographical references. [BS1735.2.C46 1975] 75-24155
1. Bible. O.T. Apocrypha. Judith—Criticism, interpretation, etc.—Congresses. I. Alonso-Schokel, Luis, 1920- II. Wuellner, Wilhelm H., 1927- III. Title. IV. Series: Center for Hermeneutical Studies in Hellenistic and Modern Culture. Protocol series of the colloquies ; nr. 11.

BIBLE. O. T. Apocrypha. Windom of Solomon. English. 1957. 229.3
The book of Wisdom. An English translation with introd. and commentary by Joseph Reider. New York, Published for Dropsie College for Hebrew and Cognate Learning by Harper [1957] 233p. 21cm. (Jewish apocryphal literature) Greek and English. Bibliography: p. 43-46. [BS1755.R4] 57-2212
1. Bible. O. T. Apocrypha, Wisdom of Solomon—Commentaries. I. Bible. O. T. Apocrypha. Wisdom of Solomon. Greek. 1957. II. Reider, Joseph, 1884- ed. and tr. III. Title. IV. Series.

BIBLE. O. T. Apocrypha. Wisdom of Solomon. English, 1957. 229.3
The book of Wisdom. An English translation with introd. and commentary by Joseph Reider. New York, Published for Dropsie College for Hebrew and Cognate Learning by Harper [1957] 233p. 21cm. (Jewish apocryphal literature) Greek and English. Bibliography: p.43-46. [BS1755.R4] 57-2212
1. Bible. O. T. Apocrypha. Wisdom of Solomon—Commentaries. I. Bible. O. T. Apocrypha. Wisdom of Solomon. Greek, 1957. II. Reider, Joseph, 1884- ed. and tr. III. Title. IV. Series.

MURPHY, Roland Edmund, 1917- 229.306
Seven books of wisdom. Milwaukee, Bruce Pub. Co. [1960] 163 p. 23 cm. (Impact books) [B1455.Z72M8] 60-14446
1. Bible. O. T. Wisdom literature—Introductions. I. Title.

MURPHY, Roland Edward, 1917- 229.306
Seven books of wisdom. Milwaukee, Bruce Pub. Co. [c.1960] x, 163p. 23cm. (Impact books) 60-14446 3.75
1. Bible. O. T. Wisdom literature—Introductions. I. Title.

CLARKE, Ernest George. 229'.3'077
The Wisdom of Solomon; commentary by Ernest G. Clarke. Cambridge [Eng.] University Press, 1973. xii, 136 p. 21 cm. (The Cambridge Bible commentary: New English Bible) Includes bibliographical references. [BS1755.3.C55] 74-155266 ISBN 0-521-08635-3 6.95
1. Bible. O.T. Apocrypha. Wisdom of Solomon—Commentaries. I. Bible. O.T. Apocrypha. Wisdom of Solomon. II. Title. III. Series.
Distributed by Cambridge University Press, N.Y.

BIBLE. O.T. Apocrypha. Ecclesiasticus. English. Revised Standard. Selections. 1973. 229'.4
Wisdom from the Apocrypha; selections from Ecclesiasticus. [Compiled by N. Alfred Balmer. Edited by Rudolph F. Norden] St. Louis, Concordia Pub. House [1973] 63 p. 18 cm. [BS1763.B34 1973] 73-78851 ISBN 0-570-03164-8 0.75 (pbk.)
I. Balmer, N. Alfred, comp. II. Title.

BIBLE. O. T. Ecclesiastes. English. 1952. Power. 229.4
Ecclesiastes; or, The preacher. A new translation, with introd., notes, glossary and index, by A. D. Power. London, New York, Longmans, Green [1952] viii, 156p. 19cm. [BS1473 1952] 53-2060

1. Bible. O. T. Ecclesiastes—Commentaries. I. Power, Arnold Danvers, ed. II. Title.

WINTER, Michael M. 229'.4'02
A concordance to the Peshitta version of Ben Sira / by Michael M. Winter. Leiden : Brill, 1976. ix, 656 p. ; 25 cm. (Monographs of the Peshitta Institute, Leiden ; v. 2) English or Syriac. Includes bibliographical references. [BS1764.S96W55] 76-370423 fl 96.00
1. Bible. O.T. Apocrypha. Ecclesiasticus. Syriac. Peshitta—Concordances. I. Title. II. Series: Leyden. Rijksuniversiteit. Peshitta Institute. Monographs ; v. 2.

DI LELLA, Alexander A. 229.406
The Hebrew text of Sirach; a text-critical and historical study, by Alexander A. DiLella. The Hague, Mouton, 1966. 183p. 22cm. (Studies in classical lit., 1) Rev. of thesis, Catholic Univ., first pub. in 1963 under title A text-critical and historical study of the Hebrew text of Sirach. Bibl. [BS1765.2.D5 1966] 65-28167 10.25 pap.,
1. Bible. O.T. Apocrypha. Ecclesiasticus — Criticism, Textual. 2. Cairo Genizah. I. Title.
American distributor: Humanities, New York.

SNAITH, John G. 229'.4'077
Ecclesiasticus, or the wisdom of Jesus son of Sirach, commentary by John G. Snaith. [London, New York] Cambridge University Press, [1974] x, 271 p. 21 cm. (The Cambridge Bible commentary: New English Bible) Bibliography: p. 263. [BS1765.3.S6] 73-82459 ISBN 0-521-08657-4 4.95
1. Bible. O.T. Apocrypha. Ecclesiasticus—Commentaries. I. Bible. O.T. Apocrypha. Ecclesiasticus. New English Bible. 1974. II. Title. III. Series.
Pbk. 2.95; ISBN 0-521-09775-4.

BIBLE. O.T. Apocrypha. 229'.5
Baruch. Polyglot. 1975.
The book of Baruch : also called I Baruch : (Greek and Hebrew) / edited, reconstructed, and translated by Emanuel Tov. Missoula, Mont. : Scholars Press, c1975. p. cm. (Society of Biblical Literature texts and translations series ; 8) (Pseudepigrapha series ; 6) English, Greek, and Hebrew. Based on I. Tov's thesis, Hebrew University, Jerusalem, 1973. Bibliography: p. [BS1771.T68] 75-30775 ISBN 0-89130-043-0 : 2.80
1. Bible. O.T. Apocrypha. Baruch—Concordances, Greek. 2. Bible. O.T. Apocrypha. Baruch—Concordances, Hebrew. I. Tov, 'Imanu'el. II. Title. III. Series. IV. Series: Society of Biblical Literature. Texts and translations ; 8.

BIBLE. O. T. Apocrypha. 1 229.7
Maccabees. English. 1950.
The first book of Maccabees, an English translation by Sidney Tedesche. Introd. and commentary by Solomon Zeitlin. New York, Published for the Dropsie College for Hebrew and Cognate Learning by Harper [1950] xvi, 221 p. 21 cm. (Jewish apocryphal literature) Text in Greek and English. Bibliography: p. 269-271. [BS1823.T4 1950] 50-8265
1. Bible. O. T. Apocrypha. 2. Maccabees—Commentaries. I. Bible. O. T. Apocrypha. II. Maccabees, Greek, 1950. III. Tedesche,Sidney Saul, 1890- tr. IV. Zeitlin, Solomon, 1892- V. Title. VI. Series.

BIBLE. O. T. Apocrypha. 1 229.7
Maccabees. English. 1950.Tedesche.
The first book of Maccabees, an English translation by Sidney Tedesche. Introd. and commentary by Solomon Zeitlin. New York, Published for the Dropsie College for Hebrew and Cognate Learning by Harper [1950] xvi, 291 p. 21 cm. (Jewish apocryphal literature) Text in Greek and English. Bibliography: p. 269-271. [BS1823.T4] 50-8265
1. Bible. O. T. Apocrypha. 2. Maccabees—Commentarics. I. Bible. O.T. Apocrypha. Maccabees. Greek, 1950. II. Tedesche, Sidney Saul. 1890- tr. III. Zeitlin, Solomon, 1892- IV. Title.

BIBLE. O. T. Apocrypha. 2 229.7
Maccabees. English. 1954- Tedesche.
The second book of Maccabees, edited by Solomon Zeitlin with introd. and commentary. English translation by Sidney Tedesche. New York, Published for the Dropsie College for Hebrew and Cognate Learning by Harper [1954] xiii, 271p. 21cm. (Jewish apocryphal literature) Text in Greek and English. Includes bibliographical references. [BS1823.T42 1954] 54-13230
1. Bible. O. T. Apocrypha. 2. Maccabees. Greek, 1954. I. Tedesche, Sidney Saul, 1890- tr. II. Zeltlin, Solomon, 1892- ed. III. Title. IV. Series.

BIBLE. O. T. Apocryphal 229.7
books. 3-4 Maccabees. English. 1953. Hadas.
The third and fourth books of Maccabees; edited and translated by Moses Hadas. New York, Published for the Dropsie College for Hebrew and Cognate Learning by Harper [1953] xii, 248p. 21cm. (Jewish apocryphal literature) Greek and English. Includes bibliographical references. [BS1823.H2 1953] 53-5114
I. Bible. O. T. Apocryphal books. 3-4 Maccabees. Greek. 1953, Hadas. II. Hadas, Moses, 1900- ed. and tr. III. Title. IV. Series.

BIBLE. O. T. Apocrypha. 229.707
1. Maccabees. English. 1962. Tedesche.
The book of Maccabees. Tr. by Sidney Tedesche. Illus. by Jacob Shacham. Prayer Bk. Pr.[dist. New York, Taplinger, 1962] 78p. col. illus. 27cm. 62-52362 7.50 bds.,
I. Tedesche, Sidney Saul, 1890- tr. II. Title.

BIBLE. O.T. Apocrypha. 229'.73'07
1-2 Maccabees. English. New English. 1973.
The First and Second Books of the Maccabees. Commentary by John R. Bartlett. Cambridge [Eng.] University Press, 1973. xiv, 357 p. 21 cm. (The Cambridge Bible commentary: New English Bible) Bibliography: p. 348. [BS1825.3.B37] 72-87436 ISBN 0-521-08658-2
1. Bible. O.T. Apocrypha. 1-2 Maccabees—Commentaries. I. Bartlett, John Raymond. II. Title. III. Series.
Distributed by Cambridge University Press N.Y. 14.95.

BIBLE. N.T. Apocryphal 229.8
books. Coptic Gospel of Philip. English. 1962.
The Gospel of Philip. Translated from the Coptic text, with an introd. and commentary, by R. McL. Wilson. New York, Harper & Row [c1962] vii, 198 p. 22 cm. Bibliolgraphy: p. 195-196. [BS2860.P66A3] 63-7612
I. Wilson, Robert McLachian, ed. and tr. II. Title.

BIBLE. N. T. Apocryphal 229.8
books. Coptic Gospel of Philip. English. 1962.
The Gospel of Philip. Tr. from the Coptic, introd., commentary by R. McL. Wilson. New York, Harper [1963, c.1962] vii, 198p. 22cm. Bibl. 63-7612 3.75 bds.,
I. Wilson, Robert McLachlan ed. and tr. II. Title.

BIBLE. N. T. APOCRYPHAL 229.8
BOOKS. COPTIC GOSPEL OF THOMAS. COPTIC (SAHIDIC) 1959.
The Gospel according to Thomas. Coptic text established and translated by A. Guillamont [and others] Leiden, E. J. Brill; New York, Harper [1959] vii, 62p. 25cm. Bibliography: p. vii. [BS2860.T5A3 1959] 59-4875
I. Guillaumont, Antoine., ed. and tr. II. Bible. N. T. Apocryphal books. Coptic Gospel of Thomas. English. 1959. III. Title.

BRUNS, J. Edgar, 1923- 229'.8
The forbidden Gospel / J. Edgar Bruns. 1st ed. New York : Harper & Row, c1976. 64 p. ; 20 cm. [BT520.B83 1976] 75-9315 ISBN 0-06-061149-9 : 5.95
1. Jesus Christ—Biography—Apocryphal and legendary literature. 2. Gnosticism. I. Title.

DOWLING, Levi H., 1844- 229'.8
1911.
The aquarian gospel of Jesus the Christ; the philosophic and practical basis of the religion of the aquarian age of the world and of the church universal, transcribed from the Book of God's remembrances, known as the Akashic records, by Levi. With introd. by Eva S. Dowling. 1st paperback ed. Tucson, Ariz., Omen Press, 1972. 260 p. 21 cm. Reprint of the 1907 ed. [BT520.D75 1972] 72-180074
1. Jesus Christ—Biography—Apocryphal and legendary literature. I. Title.

GARTNER, Bertil 229.8
The theology of the Gospel according to Thomas. Tr. [from Swedish] by Eric J. Sharpe. New York, Harper [c.1961] 286p. Bibl. 61-5261 5.00
1. Bible. N. T. Apocryphal books. Coptic Gospel of Thomas—Theology. 2. Gnosticism. I. Title.

MURDOCH, Iris. 229'.8
The sovereignty of good over other concepts. London, Cambridge U.P., 1967. [2], 37 p. 18 1/2 cm. (Leslie Stephen lectures, 1967) [BJ1401.M8] 68-131619 5/-
1. Good and evil. I. Title. II. Series.

SMITH, Morton, 1915- 229'.8
Clement of Alexandria and a secret Gospel of Mark. Cambridge, Mass., Harvard University Press, 1973. x, 452 p. illus. 25 cm. English, Greek, or Latin. Bibliography: p. 423-444. [BS2860.S42S53] 72-148938 ISBN 0-674-13490-7
1. Clemens, Titus Flavius, Alexandrinus. 2. Secret Gospel according to Mark. I. Title.

SMITH, Morton, 1915- 229'.8
The Secret Gospel; the discovery and interpretation of the Secret Gospel according to Mark. [1st ed.] New York, Harper & Row [1973] ix, 148 p. illus. 22 cm. [BS2860.S42S55 1973] 72-11363 ISBN 0-06-067411-3 5.95
1. Secret Gospel according to Mark. I. Title.

SUMMERS, Ray. 229'.8
The secret sayings of the living Jesus; studies in the Coptic Gospel according to Thomas. Waco, Tex., Word Books [1968] 159 p. 23 cm. Bibliography: p. 157-159. [BS2860.T52S8] 68-19486
1. Bible. N. T. Apocryphal books. Coptic Gospel of Thomas—Criticism, Interpretation, etc. I. Title.

SZEKELY, Edmond Bordeaux. 229'.8
The Essene Gospel of peace. Translation based on the first century Aramaic and ancient Slavonic texts. [13th ed. San Diego, Calif.] Academy of Creative Living, 1971. 64 p. (p. 60-64 advertisements) illus. 31 cm. Published in 1937 under title: The Gospel of peace of Jesus Christ by the disciple John. [BT295.S95 1971] 72-27604
1. Jesus Christ—Miscellanea. I. Title.

FINEGAN, Jack, 1908- 229'.8'06
Hidden records of the life of Jesus; an introduction to the New Testament Apocrypha and to some of the areas through which they were transmitted, namely, Jewish, Egyptian, and Gnostic Christianity, together with the earlier Gospel-type records in the Apocrypha, in Greek and Latin texts [with] translations and explanations. Philadelphia, Pilgrim Press [1969] xxxi, 320 p. facsims. 23 cm. Includes bibliographical references. [BS2840.F53] 69-19286 12.00
1. Apocryphal books (New Testament)—Criticism, interpretation, etc. I. Title.

GOODSPEED, Edgar Johnson, 229.9
1871-
Famous "biblical" hoaxes. (Orig. title: Modern apocrypha) Grand Rapids. Mich., Baker Bk. [1968, c.1956] 124p. 20cm. (Twin Brooks ser.) [BS2840.G59] 1.95 pap.,
1. Bible. N.T. Apocryphal books—Criticism, interpretation, etc. 2. Jesus Christ—Biog.—Apocryphal and legendary literature. I. Title.

GOODSPEED, Edgar Johnson, 229.9
1871-
Modern apocrypha. Boston, Beacon Press [1956] 124p. illus. 22cm. [BS2840.G59] 56-10075
1. Bible. N. T. Apocryphal books—Criticism, interpretation, etc. 2. Jesus Christ—Biog.—Apocryphal and legendary literature. I. Title.

HERVIEUX, Jacques, 1927- 229.9
The New Testament Apocrypha. Translated from the French by Wulstan Hibberd. [1st ed.] New York, Hawthorn Books [1960] 188 p. 21 cm. (Twentieth century encyclopedia of Catholicism, v. 72. Section 6 : The Word of God) Translation of Ce que l'Evangile ne dit pas. Includes bibliography. [BS2840.H453] 60-53117
1. Bible. N.T. Apocryphal books—Criticism, interpretation, etc. I. Title.

HYMN of Jesus. English. 229'.9
The hymn of Jesus; echoes from the gnosis. Translated with comments by G. R. S. Mead. Wheaton, Ill., Theosophical Pub. House [1973] 75, [1] p. 15 cm. (A Quest miniature) Bibliography: p. [76] [BS2880.J62M4 1973] 73-159392 ISBN 0-8356-0432-2 1.00
I. Mead, George Robert Stow, 1863-1933.

ROWLEY, Harold Henry, 1890- 229.9
The relevance of apocalyptic; a study of Jewish and Christian apocalypses from Daniel to the Revelation [New rev., 3d, ed.] New York, Association [1964, c.1963] 240p. 23cm. Bibl. 64-12221 5.95
1. Apocalyptic literature. I. Title.

GOODSPEED, Edgar 229'.9'06
Johnson, 1871-1962.
Strange new gospels. Freeport, N.Y., Books for Libraries Press [1971] xi, 111 p. 23 cm. (Essay index reprint series) [BS2840.G6 1971] 70-156652 ISBN 0-8369-2364-2
1. Jesus Christ—Biography—Apocryphal and legendary literature. 2. Apocryphal books (New Testament)—Criticism, interpretation, etc. I. Title.

FEINBERG, Charles Lee. 229'.9'066
The minor prophets / Charles Lee Feinberg. Combined ed. Chicago : Moody Press, 1976. 360 p. ; 24 cm. Formerly published in the series: The Major messages of the minor prophets, c1948-c1952. Includes indexes. [BS1560.F4] 75-44088 ISBN 0-8024-5306-6 : 7.95
1. Bible. O.T. Minor prophets—Commentaries. I. Title.
Contents omitted

ARISTEAS' epistle. 229'.91
Aristeas to Philocrates (letter of Aristeas) Edited and translated by Moses Hadas. New York, Ktav Pub. House, 1973 [i.e. 1974, c1951] vii, 233 p. 22 cm. Reprint of the ed. published for the Dropsie College for Hebrew and Cognate Learning by Harper, New York, in series: Jewish apocryphal literature. Greek and English. Includes bibliographical references. [BS744.A7 1974] 73-16051 ISBN 0-87068-229-6 12.50
1. Bible. O.T. Greek—Versions—Septuagint. I. Hadas, Moses, 1900-1966, ed. II. Title. III. Series: Jewish apocryphal literature.

BIBLE. O. T. Apocrypha. 229.91
English. 1913.
The apocrypha and pseudepigrapha of the Old Testament in English, with introductions and critical and explanatory notes to the several books; 2v. Ed., in conjuction with many scholars, by R. H. Charles. [New York, Oxford, 1963] 2v. (683;871p.) 28cm. Contents.v.1. Apocrypha.--v.2. Pseudepigrapha. A14 v.1, 12.80; v.2, p19.20.
I. Bible. O. T. Apocryphal books. English. 1913. II. Charles, Robert Henry, 1855- ed. III. Title.

[ELEAZAR ben Asher ha- 229'.911
Levi] 14thcent.
The chronicles of Jerahmeel; or, The Hebrew Bible historiale. Being a collection of apocryphal and pseudo-epigraphical books dealing with the history of the world from the creation to the death of Judas Maccabeus. Translated for the first time from an unique manuscript in the Bodleian Library by M. Gaster. Together with an introd., critical notes, a full index, and five facsims. Prolegomenon by Haim Schwarzbaum. New York, Ktav Pub. House, 1971 [i.e. 1972] 124, cxii, 341 p. facsims. 23 cm. A translation of the first part of the manuscript, entitled Sefer ha-zikhronot. cf. Catalogue of the Hebrew manuscripts in the Bodleian Library. Reprint, with prolegomenon, of the 1899 ed., which was issued as New series, v. 4 (i.e. 11) of the Oriental translation fund. Bibliography: p. 112-124. [BM530.E53132 1972] 77-147926 ISBN 0-87068-162-1
1. Legends, Jewish. I. Jerahmeel ben Solomon, 12th cent. II. Gaster, Moses, 1856-1939, ed. III. Oxford. University. Bodleian Library. Mss. (Hebrew d. 11) IV. Title. V. Title: The Hebrew Bible historiale. VI. Series: Oriental Translation Fund, London. Publications, new ser., v. 11.

[ELEAZAR ben Asher ha- 229'.911
Levi] 14thcent.
The Hebrew fragments of Pseudo-Philo's Liber antiquitatum Biblicarum preserved in the Chronicles of Jerahmeel. Edited and translated by Daniel J. Harrington. [Missoula, Mont.] Society of Biblical Literature, 1974. vi, 74 p. 24 cm. (Society of Biblical Literature. Texts and translations, 3. Pseudepigrapha series, 3) English and Hebrew. The original manuscript of the Chronicles is preserved in the Bodleian Library, Oxford (Ms. Heb. d. 11) Includes bibliographical references. [BM530.E53132 1974] 73-89170 ISBN 0-88414-036-9
1. Legends, Jewish. I. Philo Judaeus. Spurious and doubtful works. Antiquitates Biblicae. II. Jerahmeel ben Solomon, 12th cent. III. Oxford. University. Bodleian Library. Mss. (Hebrew d. 11) IV. Title. V. Series: Society of Biblical Literature. Texts and translations, 3. VI. Series: Pseudepigrapha series, 3.

VANDERKAM, James C. 229'.911
Textual and historical studies in the Book of Jubilees / by James C. VanderKam. Missoula, Mont. : Published by Scholars Press for Harvard Semitic Museum, c1977. xv, 307 p. ; 22 cm. (Harvard Semitic monographs ; no. 14) Originally presented as the author's thesis, Harvard, 1976. Bibliography: p. 289-307. [BS1830.J8V36 1977] 76-45388 ISBN 0-89130-118-6 : 6.00
1. Bible. O.T. Apocryphal books. Book of Jubilees—Criticism, Textual. I. Title. II. Series.

BIBLE. O.T. Apocryphal 229'.912
Books. Odes of Solomon. Syriac. 1973.
The Odes of Solomon, edited, with translation and notes, by James Hamilton Charlesworth. Oxford, Clarendon Press, 1973. xv, 167 p. 23 cm. Bibliography: p. [149]-157. [BS1830.O3S9 1973] 74-158467 ISBN 0-19-826162-4
I. Charlesworth, James H., ed. II. Bible. O.T. Apocryphal Books. Odes of Solomon. English. 1973.
Distributed by Oxford University Press, New York; 19.25.

BIBLE. O.T. Apocryphal 229'.913
books. 1 Enoch. English. Laurence. 1972.
The Book of Enoch the prophet [translated] by Richard Laurence. Minneapolis, Wizards Bookshelf, 1972. xlviii, 180 p. 22 cm. (Secret doctrine reference series) Reprint of the 1883 ed. published by Kegan Paul, Trench & Co., London. [BS1830.E6A3 1972] 72-95273 ISBN 0-913510-01-7 6.00
I. Laurence, Richard, Abp. of Cashel, 1760-1838, tr. II. Title.

BIBLE. O.T. Apocryphal books. 3 Enoch. Hebrew. 1973. 229'.913
3 Enoch; or, The Hebrew Book of Enoch. Edited and translated for the first time with introd., commentary & critical notes, by Hugo Odeberg. Prolegomenon by Jonas C. Greenfield New York, Ktav Pub. House, 1973. xlvii, 192, 179, 74, 34 p. 24 cm. (The Library of Biblical studies) Reprint of the 1928 ed. published by the University Press, Cambridge; with new prolegomenon. "Translation with notes" (179 p. (3d group)) and "Hebrew text with critical notes" (74 p. (4th group)) from H. Odeberg's thesis—University of London, 1924. "The ms. which is made the basis of the present edition is the ... Bodleian MS. Opp. 556, foll. 314 seqq. ... entitled 'Book of Enoch by R. Ishmael ben Elisha, high priest.'" Bibliography: p. [3]-18 (2d group) [BS1830.E82A3 1973] 69-10670 ISBN 0-87068-093-5 22.50
1. Bible. O.T. Apocryphal books. 3 Enoch—Commentaries. I. Odeberg, Hugo, 1898- ed. II. Bible. O.T. Apocryphal books. 3 Enoch. English. Odeberg. 1973. III. Title. IV. Title: The Hebrew Book of Enoch. V. Series.

BLOCH, Joshua, 1890- 229.913
On the apocalyptic in Judaism. Philadelphia, Dropsie College for Hebrew and Cognate Learning, 1952. vi, 154 p. 25 cm. (The Jewish quarteriy review. Monograph series, no. 2) Bibliographical footnotes. [BS646.B45] 52-4967
1. Apocalyptic literature. 2. Eschatology, Jewish. I. Title. II. Series.

KOCH, Klaus. 229'.913
The rediscovery of Apocalyptic; a polemical work on a neglected area of Biblical studies and its damaging effects on theology and philosophy. Naperville, Ill., A. R. Allenson [1972?] 157 p. 22 cm. (Studies in Biblical theology, 2d ser., 22) Translation of Ratlos vor der Apokalyptik. Includes bibliographical references. [BS646.K613] 72-186002 ISBN 0-8401-3072-4
1. Apocalyptic literature. I. Title. II. Series.

POTTER, Charles Francis, 1885-1962 229.913
Did Jesus write this book? Greenwich, Conn., Fawcett [1967,c.1965] 159p. 18cm. (Crest bk., t1047) .75 pap.,
1. Bible. O. T. Apocryphal books. 2. Enoch-Criticism, interpretation,etc. I. Title.

POTTER, Charles Francis, 1885-1962. 229.913
Did Jesus write this book? New York, University Books [1966, c1965] 159 p. 24 cm. [BS1830.E81P6] 65-27644
1. Bible. O. T. Apocryphal books. 2. Enoch—Criticism, interpretation, etc. I. Title.

RUSSELL, David Syme 229.91306
The method & message of Jewish Apocalyptic, 200 BC-AD 100. Philadelphia, Westminster [c.1964] 464p. 23cm. (Old Testament lib.) Bibl. 64-18683 7.50
1. Apocalyptic literature. I. Title.

RUSSELL, David Syme. 229.91306
The method & message of Jewish Apocalyptic, two hundred BC-Ad one hundred by D.S. Russell. Philadelphia, Westminster Press [1964] 464 p. 23 cm. (The Old Testament library) Bibliography: p. 406-480. [BS1705.R8] 64-18683
1. Apocalyptic literature. I. Title.

BIBLE. O.T. Apocryphal books. Testament of Abraham. English. 1972. Stone. 229'.914
The Testament of Abraham, the Greek recensions. Translated by Michael E. Stone. [New York] Society of Biblical Literature, 1972. viii, 89 p. 24 cm. (Texts and translations, 2) (Pseudepigrapha series, 2) Includes texts in Greek. [BS1830.T31A3 1972] 72-88770
I. Stone, Michael E., 1938- tr. II. Bible. O.T. Apocryphal books. Testament of Abraham. Greek. 1972. III. Title. IV. Series. V. Series: Society of Biblical Literature. Texts and translations, 2.

BIBLE. O.T. Apocryphal books. Testaments of the twelve patriarchs. Joseph. Armenian. 1975. 229'.914
The Armenian version of the Testament of Joseph : introduction, critical edition, and translation / by Michael E. Stone. Missoula, Mont. : Published by Scholars Press for the Society of Biblical Literature, c1975. p. cm. (Texts and translations ; 6) (Pseudepigrapha series ; 5) Bibliography: p. [BS1830.T4A75 1975] 75-29210 ISBN 0-89130-035-X : 2.80
I. Stone, Michael E., 1938- II. Bible. O.T. Apocryphal books. Testaments of the twelve patriarchs. Joseph. English. Stone. 1975. III. Bible. O.T. Apocryphal books. Testaments of the twelve patriarchs. Armenian. 1975. IV. Title. V. Series. VI. Series: Society of Biblical Literature. Texts and translations ; 6.

SLINGERLAND, Howard D. 229'.914
The Testaments of the twelve patriarchs : a critical history of research / by Howard D. Slingerland. Missoula, Mont. : Published by Scholars Press for the Society of Biblical Literature, c1975. p. cm. (Monograph series - Society of Biblical Literature ; no. 21) A revision of the author's thesis, Union Theological Seminary, 1973. Includes index. Bibliography: p. [BS1830.T5S57 1975] 75-34233 ISBN 0-89130-062-7
1. Bible. O.T. Apocryphal books. Testaments of the twelve patriarchs—Criticism, interpretation, etc.—History. I. Title. II. Series: Society of Biblical Literature. Monograph series ; no. 21.

STUDIES on the Testament of Abraham / edited by George W. E. Nickelsburg, Jr. Missoula, Mont. : Published by Scholars Press for the Society of Biblical Literature, c1976. x, 340 p. : 21 cm. (Septuagint and cognate studies ; no. 6) Revised papers of the Society of Biblical Literature Pseudepigrapha Seminar held at the International Congress of Learned Societies in the Field of Religion, held in 1972, and published as part II of the 1972 proceedings, compiled by R. A. Kraft. Includes bibliographical references. [BS1830.T32S88 1976] 76-44205 ISBN 0-89130-117-8 : 4.50 229'.914
1. Bible. O. T. Apocryphal books. Testament of Abraham—Criticism, interpretation, etc.—Addresses, essays, lectures. I. Nickelsburg, George W. E., 1934- II. Kraft, Robert A., comp. 1972 proceedings. III. Pseudepigrapha Seminar, Los Angeles, 1972. IV. International Congress of Learned Societies in the Field of Religion, Los Angeles, 1972. V. Title. VI. Series.

STUDIES on the Testament of Joseph : seminar papers / edited by George W. E. Nickelsburg, Jr., for the Society of Biblical Literature, Pseudepigrapha Group. Missoula, Mont. : Society of Biblical Literature : distributed by Scholars Press, 1975. p. cm. (Septuagint and cognate studies ; no. 5) "Working papers prepared for the sessions of the Society of Biblical Literature Pseudepigrapha Group, to be held October 30-November 2, 1975, at the Palmer House, Chicago." Includes bibliographical references. [BS1830.T5S78] 75-26923 ISBN 0-89130-027-9 : 2.80 229'.914
1. Bible. O.T. Apocryphal books. Testaments of the twelve patriarchs. Joseph—Addresses, essays, lectures. I. Nickelsburg, George W. E., 1934- II. Society of Biblical Literature. Pseudepigrapha Group. III. Title. IV. Series.

SEFER ha-Yashar. English. 229'.915
The Book of Yashar. Translated from the Hebrew and published by Mordecai Manuel Noah. With an introductory essay: Mordecai M. Noah and the Book of Yashar. New York, Hermon Press [1973 c1840] xxiii, 267 p. 24 cm. Reprint of the ed. published by M. M. Noah and A. S. Gould under title: The Book of Jashar. [BS1830.J2A3 1972] 72-83943 ISBN 0-87203-034-2 9.75
1. Jews—History—To entrance into Canaan. I. Noah, Mordecai Manuel, 1785-1851, ed. II. Title.

SEFER HA-YASHAR. 229.915
The Book of Jasher; faithfully translated from the original. Dedicated to the world and all religions. [1st ed.] Philadelphia, BibleCorp. of America, c1954. xxiii, 267p. illus. 20cm. 'In order to hold fast to the purest translation, Hebrew words have been left intact as they are in the original Scriptures.' Copyright date on mounted label. A reprint of the 1840 ed., edited by M. M. Noah. [BS1830.J2A3 1954] 54-42583
I. Bible. O. T. Pentateuch. English. Paraphrases. 1954. II. Noah, Mordecal Manuel, 1785-1851, ed. III. Title.

DEAD Sea scrolls. English & Aramaic. 229'.918
Aramaic texts from Qumran / with translations and annotations by B. Jongeling, C. J. Labuschagne and A. S. van der Woude. Leiden : Brill, 1976- v. ; 19 cm. (Semitic study series ; new series no. 4) Contents.Contents.—v. 1. The Job Targum from Cave II. The Genesis Apocryphon from Cave I. The Prayer of Nabonidus from Cave 4. Includes bibliographies. [BM487.A3J66 1976] 76-364963 ISBN 9-00-404452-3 : fl 28.00 (v. 1)
I. Jongeling, Bastiaan. II. Labuschagne, C. J. III. Woude, A. S. van der. IV. Title. V. Series.

MORRIS, Leon, 1914- 229'.94
Apocalyptic. Grand Rapids, Mich., Eerdmans [1972] 87 p. 21 cm. Includes bibliographical references. [BS646.M67] 72-75572 ISBN 0-8028-1455-7
1. Apocalyptic literature. I. Title.

EVANGELIUM VERITATIS. 229.95
The Gospel of truth, a Valentinian meditation on the gospel. Translation from the Coptic and commentary by Kendrick Grobel. Nashville, Abingdon Press [c.1960] 206p. Bibliography: p.203-206 20cm. 60-5231 4.00
1. Valentinians. I. Grobel, Kendrick, ed. and tr. II. Title.

GRANT, Robert McQueen, 1917- 229.951
The secret sayings of Jesus; the Gnostic Gospel of Thomas, by Robert M. Grant, David Noel Freeman. With an English tr. of the Gospel of Thomas, by William R. Schoedel. Garden City, N.Y., Doubleday [c.1960] 198p. (Dolphin bk. C 163) Bibl. .95 pap.,
1. Bible. N. T. Apocryphal books. Gospels—Criticism, interpretation, etc. 2. Gnosticism. I. Schoedel, William R., tr. II. Bible. N. T. Apocryphal books. Coptic Gospel of Thomas. English. 1960. Schoedel. III. Title.

GRANT, Robert McQueen, 1917- 229.951
The secret sayings of Jesus, by Robert M. Grant in collaboration with David Noel Freedman. With an English translation of the Gospel of Thomas by William R. Schoedel. [1st ed.] Garden City, N. Y., Doubleday, 1960. 206 p. 22 cm. Includes bibliography. [BS2851.G7] 60-6876
1. Bible. N. T. Apocryphal books. Gospels—Criticism, interpretation, etc. 2. Gnosticism. I. Schoedel, William R., tr. II. Bible. N. T. Apocryphal books. Coptic Gospel of Thomas. English. 1960. Schoedel. III. Title.

230 CHRISTIAN DOCTRINAL THEOLOGY

ADAMS, James Luther, 1901- 230
On being human religiously : selected essays in religion and society / James Luther Adams ; edited and introduced by Max L. Stackhouse. Boston : Beacon Press, c1976. xxx, 257 p. ; 21 cm. Includes bibliographical references and index. [BR50.A28] 75-36037 ISBN 0-8070-1122-3 : 9.95
1. Theology—Addresses, essays, lectures. 2. Social ethics—Addresses, essays, lectures. 3. Liberty—Addresses, essays, lectures. I. Stackhouse, Max L. II. Title.

ALEXANDER, David K ed. 230
What can you believe? Edited by David K. Alexander and C. W. Junker. Nashville, Broadman Press [1966] 119 p. 20 cm. [BT77.A33] 66-19907
1. Theology, Doctrinal—Popular works. I. Junker, Charles William, joint ed. II. Title.

ALEXANDER, David K. ed. 230
What can you believe? Ed. by David K. Alexander. C. W. Junker. Nashville, Broadman Pr. [c.1966] 119p. 20cm. [BT77.A33] 66-19907 1.75 pap.,
1. Theology, Doctrinal—Popular wo-ks. I. Junker, Charles William, joint ed. II. Title.

ALTIZER, Thomas J. J. 230
Radical theology and the death of God [by] Thomas J. J. Altizer and William Hamilton. [New ed. with new preface and bibliography]. Harmondsworth, Penguin, 1968. 208 p. 18 cm. (Pelican books, A957) Bibliography: p. 189-208. [BT83.5.A46 1968] 70-393537 5/-
1. Death of God theology. I. Hamilton, William, 1924- joint author. II. Title. III. Title: The death of God.

AMES, William, 1576-1633 230
The marrow of theology. Tr. from the 3d Latin ed., 1629, by John D. Eusden. Boston, Pilgrim Pr. [1968] xiii, 353p. port. 23cm. [Milestone lib.] Tr. of Medulla theologica. Bibl. [BT70.A5513] 67-26186 7.95
1. Theology, Doctrinal. I. Eusden, John Dykstra. ed. II. Title.

ANDERSEN, Wilhelm, 1911- 230
Law and gospel: a study in Biblical theology. New York, Association Press [c1961] 80p. 19cm. (World Christian books, 2d ser., no. 40) [BT85.A5] 62-10270
1. Law and gospel. I. Title.

ANDERSON, Bernhard W. 230
Creation versus chaos: the reinterpretation of mythical symbolism in the Bible [by] Bernhard W. Anderson. New York, Association [1967] 192p. 21cm. Bibl. [BT695.A4] 67-14578 4.95
1. Bible. O.T.—Theology. 2. Creation. 3. Chaos (Theology) I. Title.

ANDERSON, James Norman Dalrymple. 230
A lawyer among the theologians, by Norman Anderson. [1st American ed.] Grand Rapids, W. B. Eerdmans Pub. Co. [1974, c1973] 240 p. 20 cm. Includes bibliographical references. [BR85.A623 1974] 73-21894 ISBN 0-8028-1565-0 3.95 (pbk.)
1. Jesus Christ—Resurrection. 2. Theology—Addresses, essays, lectures. I. Title.

ANDERSON, Margaret J. 230
Bible doctrines for teenagers, by Margaret J. Anderson. Grand Rapids, Zondervan Pub. House [1968] 93 p. 20 cm. [BT77.A48] 67-22694
1. Theology, Doctrinal—Popular works. I. Title.

ANDERSON, Robert T 1928- 230
An introduction to Christianity [by] Robert T. Anderson [and] Peter B. Fischer. New York, Harper & Row [1966] x 234 p. 23 cm. Includes bibliographies. [BT75.2.A5] 66-11260
1. Theology. Doctrinal. I. Fischer, Peter B., joint author. II. Title.

ANDERSON, Robert T., 1928- 230
An introduction to Christianity [by] Robert T. Anderson, Peter B. Fischer. New York, Harper [c.1966] x, 234p. 23cm. Bibl. [BT75.2.A5] 66-11260 4.95
1. Theology, Doctrinal. I. Fischer, Peter B., joint author. II. Title.

ANDERSON, Wilhelm, 1911- 230
Law and gospel; a study in Biblical theology. New York, Association 1962, c.1961 80p. 19cm. (World Christian bks., 2d ser., no. 40) 62-10270 1.00 pap.,
1. Law and gospel. I. Title.

ANSELM, Saint, Abp. of Canterbury, 1033-1109. 230
Trinity, incarnation, and redemption; theological treatises. Edited with introd. by Jasper Hopkins and Herbert Richardson. New York, Harper & Row [1970] xxii, 199 p. 21 cm. (Harper Torchbooks, TB 1513) [BR765.A82E575 1970] 71-111082 2.75
1. Catholic Church—Collected works. 2. Theology—Collected works—Middle Ages, 600-1500. I. Title.

ARGOW, Waldemar. 230
The case for liberal religion. [Yellow Springs, Ohio] Antioch Press [1954] 155p. 22cm. [BR1615.A68] 54-6800
1. Liberalism (Religion) I. Title.

ASHBROOK, James B., 1925- 230
Christianity for pious skeptics / James B. Ashbrook, Paul W. Walaskay. Nashville : Abingdon, c1977. 160 p. : ill. ; 21 cm. Includes bibliographical references. [BS2506.A83] 77-911 ISBN 0-687-07646-3 pbk. : 4.95
1. Paul, Saint, Apostle. 2. Bible. N.T.—Biography. 3. Christian saints—Turkey—Tarsus—Biography. 4. Tarsus, Turkey—Biography. 5. Faith and reason. 6. Christian life—1960- I. Walaskay, Paul W., 1939- II. Title.

ASKING them question; 230
a selection from the three series. Edited by Ronald Selby Wright. London, New York, Oxford University Press, 1953. 254p. 19cm. [BR96.A815] 54-22119
1. Questions and answers—Theology. I. Wright, Ronald Selby, 1908- ed.

ASKING them questions. 230
3d ser. Edited by Ronald Selby Wright. London, New York, Oxford University Press, 1950. xviii, 194 p. 19 cm. [BR96.A83] 50-8143
1. Questions and answers—Theology. I. Wright, Ronald Selby, 1908- ed.

ASKING them questions; 230
new series, edited by Ronald Selby Wright. London, New York, Oxford University Press, 1972- v. 19 cm. Bibliography: v. 1, p. [159]-160. [BR96.A833] 72-190704 ISBN 0-19-213423-X £1.00
1. Theology—Miscellanea. I. Wright, Ronald Selby, 1908- ed.

AULEN, Gustaf Emanuel Hildebrand, Bp., 1879- 230
The faith of the Christian church. Translated from the 5th Swedish ed. by Eric H. Wahlstrom. Philadelphia, Muhlenberg Press [c1960] 403p. 22cm. Translation of Den allmllnneliga kristna tron. Includes bibliography. [BT75.A763 1960] 61-5302
1. Theology, Doctrinal. I. Title.

AULEN, Gustaf Emanuel Hilderbrand, Bp., 1879- 230
The faith of the Christian church. Tr. from the 5th Swedish ed. by Eric H. Wahlstrom. Philadelphia, Muhlenberg Press [c.1960] 403p. Bibl. 61-5302 6.95
1. Theology, Doctrinal. I. Title.

AVERILL, Lloyd James, 1923- 230
American theology in the liberal tradition [by] Lloyd J. Averill. Philadelphia, Westminster'

[1967] 173p. 21cm. Bibl. [BR1615.A9] 67-13164 4.50
1. Liberalism (Religion)—U. S. 2. Theology, Doctrinal—Hist.—19th cent. 3. Theology, Doctrinal—Hist.—20th cent. I. Title.

BABBAGE, Stuart Barton. 230
The vacuum of unbelief, and other essays. Grand Rapids, Zondervan Pub. House [1969] 152 p. 21 cm. Bibliographical footnotes. [BR85.B28] 69-11660 3.95
1. Christianity—Addresses, essays, lectures. I. Title.

BAILEY, Charles James Nice. 230
Ground work for comparative metatheology; a roadmap for ecumenical analytics. Ann Arbor, University Microfilms, 1965. xi, 435 p. (on double leaves) illus. 22 cm. Supplement. [Ann Arbor, University Microfilms, 1965] S-40 p. (on double leaves) 22 cm. Bibliographical references includes in "Notes" (p. S-81--S-88) BT78.B25 Suppl. Bibliographical references included in "Notes" (p. [861]-432]) [BT78.B25] 65-2555
1. Theology—Methodology. I. Title. II. Title: Methatheology.

BAILEY, John Amedee. 230
The ministry of the Church in the world. London, New York [etc.] Oxford U.P., 1967. [9], 125 p. 20 cm. [BR121.2.B28] 67-89274
1. Christianity—20th century. 2. Theology, Doctrinal—Popular works. I. Title.

BAKER, Charles F 230
Bible truth what we believe and why we believe it. Milwaukee, Milwaukee Bible College [1956] 123p. 20cm. [BT77.B26] 57-28034
1. Theology, Doctrinal—Popular works. I. Title.

BAKER, Charles F. 230
A dispensational theology, by Charles F. Baker. Pref. by Peter Veltman. Grand Rapids, Mich., Grace Bible College Publications [1971] xiii, 688 p. 25 cm. Bibliography: p. 659-666. [BT75.2.B3] 71-150312 ISBN 0-912340-01-0 9.95
1. Theology, Doctrinal. 2. Dispensationalism. I. Title.

BAKER, Thomas Eugene, 1929- 230
Christ and the even balance; a manual on fundamentalism, by Thomas E. Baker. Millersburg, Pa., Bible Truth Mission [1968] ix, 168 p. 24 cm. [BT82.2.B3] 68-56294 3.50
1. Fundamentalism. I. Title.

BALTAZAR, Eulalio R. 230
God within process [by] Eulalio R. Baltazar. Paramus, N.J., Newman Press [1970] 186 p. 24 cm. Includes bibliographical references. [BT83.6.B3 1970] 73-118701 5.95
1. Process theology. I. Title.

BALTHASAR, Hans Urs von, 230
1905-
The God question and modern man. Foreword by John Macquarrie. [Translation from the original German by Hilda Graef] New York, Seabury Press [1967] xvi, 155 p. 21 cm. (A Seabury paperback) [BR121.B2417 1967] 67-11275
1. Christianity—20th century. I. Title.

BALTHASAR, Hans Urs von, 230
1905-
Science, religion, and Christianity. [Translation from the original German by Hilda Graef] Westminster, Md., Newman Press [c1958] 155p. 22cm. Translation of Die Gottesfrage des heutigen Menschen. [BR121.B2417] 59-1092
1. Christianity—20th cent. I. Title.

BANCROFT, Emery Herbert. 230
Christian theology, systematic and Biblical / by Emery H. Bancroft. 2d rev. ed. / edited by Ronald B. Mayers. Grand Rapids : Zondervan Pub. House, c1976. 410 p. ; 23 cm. Includes bibliographical references and index. [BT77.B3 1976] 76-150619
1. Theology, Doctrinal. I. Mayers, Ronald B. II. Title.

BARNEY, Kenneth D. 230
You'd better believe it! / Kenneth D. Barney ; adapted from The fundamentals of the faith by Donald Johns. Springfield, Mo. : Gospel Pub. House, c1975. 126 p. ; 18 cm. (Radiant books) [BT77.B334] 75-22608 ISBN 0-88243-887-5 pbk. : 1.25
1. Theology, Doctrinal—Popular works. 2. Christian life—1960- I. Johns, Donald. The fundamentals of the faith. II. Title.

BARREAU, Jean Claude. 230
The faith of a pagan. Translated by Jules G. Viau. New York, Paulist Press [1968] v, 89 p. 19 cm. Translation of La foi d'un paien. [BT77.B3423] 68-20850
1. Theology, Doctrinal—Popular works. I. Title.

BARRY, Mack C. 230
Every wind of doctrine. Boston, Christopher Pub. House [1952] 155 p. 21 cm. [BT78.B27] 52-25939
1. Theology, Doctrinal. I. Title.

BARTH, Karl, 1886- 230
Church dogmatics. [Authorised translation by G. T. Thomson. New York, Scribner, 1955- v. in 23cm. Half title: each pt. has also special t.p. Contents.v. 1. The doctrine of the word of God. 2 pts. [BT75.B283] 57-1428
1. TeOlogy, Doctrinal. I. Title.

BARTH, Karl, 1886- 230
Church dogmatics; a selection. Introd. by Helmut Gollwitzer. Tr. [from German] ed. by G. W. Bromiley. New York, Harper & Row [1962, c.1961] 262p. 21cm. (Harper torchbks. TB95: Cloister lib.) 1.50 pap.,
1. Theology, Doctrinal. I. Title.

BARTH, Karl, 1886- 230
Church dogmatics; a selection. Introd. by Helmut Gollwitzer. Tr. [from German] ed. by G. W. Bromiley [Gloucester, Mass., Peter Smith, 1963, c.1961] 262p. 21cm. (Harper torchbk., Cloister lib., TB95 rebound) 3.50
1. Theology, Doctrinal. I. Title.

BARTH, Karl, 1886-1968. 230
Final testimonies / by Karl Barth ; edited by Eberhard Busch ; translated by Geoffrey W. Bromiley. Grand Rapids : Eerdmans, c1977. 67 p. ; 22 cm. Translation of Letzte Zeugnisse. [BR85.B41913 1977] 77-8088 ISBN 0-8028-3497-3 : 3.95
1. Theology—Addresses, essays, lectures. I. Title.
Contents omitted

BARTH, Karl, 1886-1968. 230
Protestant thought: from Rousseau to Ritschl, being a translation of eleven chapters of Die protestantische Theologie im 19. Jahrhundert. [Translated by Brian Cozens] Freeport, N.Y., Books for Libraries Press [1971, c1959] 435 p. 23 cm. (Essay index reprint series) Bibliography: p. [423]-425. [BT30.G3B313 1971] 73-142606 ISBN 0-8369-2102-X
1. Theology, Doctrinal—History—Germany. 2. Theology, Doctrinal—History—18th century. 3. Theology, Doctrinal—History—19th century. 4. Theology, Protestant—Germany. I. Title.

BAVINCK, Johan Herman, 1895- 230
The riddle of life. [Translated by J. J. Lamberts] Grand Rapids, Eerdmans [1958] 128p. 21cm. [BR121.B293] 58-7567
1. Christianity—20th cent. I. Title.

BAYLE, Pierre, 1647-1706. 230
The great contest of faith and reason; selections from the writings of Pierre Bayle. Translated and edited, with an introd. by Karl C. Sandberg. New York, Ungar [1963] xv. 108 p. 21 cm. (Milestones of thought in the history of ideas) Bibliography: p. xv. [BT50.B313] 63-12901
1. Faith and reason. I. Sandberg, Karl C., ed. and tr. II. Title. III. Series.

BAYLE, Pierre, 1647-1706 230
The great contest of faith and reason; selections from the writings of Pierre Bayle. Tr. [from French] ed., introd. by Karl C. Sandberg. New York, Ungar [c.1963] xv, 108p. 21cm. (Milestones of thought in the hist. of ideas) Bibl. 63-12901 3.75
1. Faith and reason. I. Sandberg, Karl C., ed. and tr. II. Title. III. Series.

BEARDSLEE, William A 230
A house for hope; a study in process and Biblical thought, by William A. Beardslee. Philadelphia, Westminster Press [1972] 192 p. 21 cm. Includes bibliographical references. [BT83.6.B4] 75-181724 ISBN 0-664-20931-9 5.95
1. Process theology. 2. Hope. I. Title.

BERGER, Peter L. 230
A rumor of angels; modern society and the rediscovery of the supernatural [by] Peter L. Berger. [1st ed.] Garden City, N.Y., Doubleday, 1969. xi, 129 p. 22 cm. Bibliographical references included in "Notes" (p. [125]-129) [BL100.B43] 69-10979 4.50
1. Supernatural. 2. Religion and sociology. I. Title.

BERKOUWER, Gerrit Cornelis, 230
1903-
A half century of theology : movements and motives / by G. C. Berkhouwer ; translated and edited by Lewis B. Smedes. Grand Rapids : Eerdmans, c1977. 268 p. ; 22 cm. Translation of Een halve eeuw theologie. Includes index. [BT28.B44713] 76-56798 pbk. : 4.95
1. Theology, Doctrinal—History—20th century. I. Title.

BERNARD, Thomas Dehany, 1815- 230
1904
The progress of doctrine in the New Testament; eight lectures delivered before the Univ. of Oxford on the Bampton Found. Introd. by Wilbur M. Smith. Grand Rapids, Mich., Zondervan [1962] 244p. 21cm. 1.95 pap.,
1. Bible. N.T.—Theology I. Title.

BERRY, William G. 230
To be honest [by] William G. Berry. Philadelphia, Westminister Press [1965] 150 p. 19 cm. (Adventures in faith) Bibliographical references includes in "Notes" (p. [153]-159) [BT77.B46] 65-19778
1. Theology, Doctrinal — Popular works. I. Title.

BERRY, William G. 230
To be honest. Philadelphia, Westminster [c.1965] 2159p. 19cm. (Adventures in faith) Bibl. [BT77.B46] 65-19778 1.45 pap.,
1. Theology, Doctrinal—Popular works. I. Title.

BLANSHARD, Paul, 1892- 230
Some of my best friends are Christians. La Salle, Ill., Open Court [1974] 190 p. 21 cm. Bibliography: p. 187-190. [BL2775.2.B53] 74-744 ISBN 0-87548-149-3 5.95
1. Christianity—Controversial literature. I. Title.

BOA, Kenneth. 230
God, I don't understand / Kenneth Boa. Wheaton, Ill. : Victor Books, c1975. 154 p. : ill. ; 21 cm. (An Input book) Includes bibliographical references. [BT77.B63] 75-173 ISBN 0-88207-722-8 pbk. : 2.25
1. Theology, Doctrinal—Popular works. I. Title.

BOHME, Jakob, 1575-1624. 230
The works of Jacob Behmen, the Teutonic theosopher : to which is prefixed the life of the author ; with figures illustrating his principles, left by the Reverend William Law, M.A. New York : Gordon Press, 1976. p. cm. Reprint of the 1764-1781 ed. printed for M. Richardson, London and other publishers. Contents.Contents.—v. 1. The aurora. The three principles.—[2] The threefold life of man. The answers to forty questions concerning the soul. The treatise of the Incarnation. The clavis.—v. 3. The mysterium magnum; or, An explanation of the first Book of Moses, called Genesis. Four tables of divine revelation.—v. 4. Signatura rerum. Of the election of grace; or, Of God's will towards man, commonly called predestination. The way to Christ. A discourse between a soul hungry and thirsty after the fountain of life, the sweet love of Jesus Christ; and a soul enlightened. Of the four complexions. Of Christ's testaments, baptism, and the supper. [BV5072.B58 1976] 76-21647 ISBN 0-87968-465-8 lib.bdg. : 600.00(4 vols.)
1. Mysticism—Collected works. 2. Theology—Collected works—16th century.

BONHOEFFER, Dietrich, 1906- 230
1945.
Act and being. Translated by Bernard Noble. Introd. by Ernst Wolf. [1st American ed.] New York, Harper [1962, c1961] 192 p. 22 cm. [BT83.B613 1962a] 62-7951
1. Dialectical theology. 2. Act (Philosophy) I. Title.

BOROS, Ladislaus, 1927- 230
You can always begin again / Ladislaus Boros ; translated by David Smith. New York : Paulist Press, c1977. 94 p. ; 19 cm. (A Deus book) Translation of Gedanken uber das Christliche. [BR85.D74513 1977] 76-49324 ISBN 0-8091-2006-2 pbk. : 1.75
1. Theology—Addresses, essays, lectures. I. Title.

BOSLEY, Harold Augustus, 230
1907-
A firm faith for today. [1st ed.] New York, Harper [1950] 283 p. 22 cm. Bibliography: p. 273-278. [BT75.B59] 50-6190
1. Theology, Doctrinal. I. Title.

BOWMAN, John Wick, 1894- 230
Prophetic realism and the gospel; a preface to Biblical theology. Philadelphia, Westminister Press [1955] 288p. illus. 24cm. (The James Sprunt lectures, 1951) [BS543.B6] 55-6002
1. Bible—Theology. I. Title.

BRAATEN, Carl E., 1929- 230
The futurist option, by Carl E. Braaten and Robert W. Jenson. New York, Newman Press [1970] vi, 183 p. 21 cm. Includes bibliographical references. [BT15.B66] 73-127792 2.95
1. Theology, Doctrinal—Addresses, essays, lectures. I. Jenson, Robert W. II. Title.

BRADLEY, Rolland, 1896- 230
Our basic faith. [Austin, Tex.] Von Boeckmann-Jones Co., 1964. x 122 p. 19 cm. Bibliographical footnotes. [BT78.B72] 64-8144
1. Theology, Doctrinal. 2. Religions. I. Title.

BRADSHAW, Marion John, 1886- 230
Baleful legacy, a faith without foundations; an examination of neo-orthodoxy. Oklahoma City, Modern Publishers, 1955. 113p. 24cm. Includes bibliography. [BT78.B7] 56-17870
1. Neo-orthodoxy. I. Title.

BRAVO, Francisco, 1934- 230
Christ in the thought of Teilhard de Chardin. Translated by Cathryn B. Larme. Notre Dame, Ind., University of Notre Dame Press [1967] xviii, 163 p. 22 cm. Translation of Cristo en el pensamiento del padre Teilhard de Chardin. Includes bibliographical references. [B2430.T374B6813] 67-22140
1. Teihard de Chardin, Pierre. I. Title.

BROGLIE, Guy de, 1889- 230
Revelation and reason. Translated from the French by Mark Pontifex. [1st ed.] New York, Hawthorn Books [1965] 188, [1] p. 21 cm. (The Twentieth century encyclopedia of Catholicism, v. 9. Section 1: Knowledge and faith) Translation of Les signes de credibilite de la revelation chretienne. Bibliography: p. [189] [BT50.B6813] 65-22785
1. Faith and reason. 2. Church — Credibility. I. Title. II. Series: The Twentieth century encyclopedia of Catholicism, v. 9

BROGLIE, Guy de, 1889- 230
Revelation and reason. Tr. from French by Mark Pontifex. New York, Hawthorn [c.1965] 188, [1]p. 21cm. (Twentieth cent. ency. of Catholicism, v.9. Section 1: Knowledge and faith) Bibl. Title. (Series: The Twentieth century encyclopedia of Catholicism, v.9) [BT50.B6813] 65-22785 3.50 bds.,
1. Faith and reason. 2. Church—Credibility. I. Title. II. Series.

BROWN, Robert McAfee, 1920- 230
The Presbyterians. Glen Rock, J.J., Paulist Press [1966] 29 p. illus. 19 cm. (Ecumenical series) Bibliography: p. 29. [BX9177.B73] 66-6284
1. Presbyterian Church. 2. Presbyterian Church — Relations — Catholic Church. 3. Catholic Church — Relations — Presbyterian Church. I. Title.

BROWN, William Adams, 1865- 230
1943.
Christian theology in outline / by William Adams Brown. New York : AMS Press, 1976. xiv, 468 p. ; 19 cm. Reprint of the 1906 ed. published by Scribner, New York. Includes index. "A classified bibliography": p. [427]-454. [BT75.B83 1976] 75-41044 ISBN 0-404-14648-1 : 26.00
1. Theology, Doctrinal. I. Title.

BRUMM, Ursula. 230
American thought and religious typology. [Translated from the German by John Hooglund] New Brunswick, N.J., Rutgers University Press [1970]. x, 265 p. 22 cm. Translation of Die religiose Typologie im amerikanischen Denken. Bibliography: p. [253]-262. [BS478.B7713] 76-97737 9.00
1. Typology (Theology)—History of doctrines. 2. Symbolism. 3. U.S.—Intellectual life. I. Title.

BRUNNER, Heinrich Emil, 1889- 230
Our faith, by Emil Brunner. Tr. by John W. Rilling. New York, Scribners [1963] 153p. 21cm. (SL87) 1.25 pap.,
1. Theology, Doctrinal—Popular works. I. Rilling, John William, 1906- tr. II. Title.

BRUNNER, Heinrich Emil, 1889- 230
The scandal of Christianity. Philadelphia, Westminster Press [1951] 116 p. 20 cm. (The Andrew C. Zenos memorial lectures. 1946) [BT75.B847] 51-12829
1. Theology. Doctrinal. 2. Apologetics—20th cent. I. Title.

BRUNNER, Heinrich Emil, 1889- 230
The Word of God and modern man [by] Emil Brunner. Translated by David Cairns. Richmond, John Knox Press [1964] 87 p. 21 cm. Contents.CONTENTS. -- The Word of God and modern man. -- Faith in the Creator and the scientific world-picture. -- Jesus Christ and historical life. -- The body of Christ and the problem of fellowship. [BR85.B8923] 64-16280
1. Man (Theology) 2. Religion and science — 1926-1945. 3. Incarnation. 4. Church. I. Title.

BRUNNER, Heinrich Emil, 1889- 230
The word of God and modern man. Tr. [from German] by David Cairns. Richmond. Va., Knox [c.1964] 87p. 21cm. 64-16280 1.50 pap.,
1. Man (Theology) 2. Religion and science—1926-1945. 3. Incarnation. 4. Church. I. Title.
Contents omitted.

BRUNNER, Heinrich Emil, 1889-1966. 230
Dogmatics. Translated by Olive Wyon. Philadelphia, Westminster Press [1950- v. 24 cm. Contents.Contents.—v. 1. The Christian doctrine of God. —v. 3. The Christian doctrine of the church, faith, and the consummation. [BT75.B842] 50-6821
1. Theology, Doctrinal. I. Title.

BUBE, Richard H 1927- 230
To every man an answer; a systematic study of the scriptural basis of Christian doctrine. Chicago, Moody Press [1955] 510p. 24cm. [BT75.B848] 55-4050
1. Theology, Doctrinal. I. Title.

BULTMANN, Rudolf Karl, 1884- 230
Theology of the New Testament; translated by Kendrick Grobel. New York, Scribner, 1951-55. 2v. 22cm. Includes bibliographies. [BS2397.B813] 51-14678
1. Bible. N. T.—Theology. I. Title.

BURI, Fritz, 1907- 230
Theology of existence, Tr. by Harold H. Oliver, Gerhard Onder. Greenwood, S. C., Attic Pr., 1965. xiv, 112p. 23cm. Bibl. [BT75.2.B7813] 65-29261 4.00
1. Theology, Doctrinal. 2. Existentialism. I. Title.

BURKE, Thomas Patrick, 1934- ed. 230
The Word in history; the St. Xavier symposium, edited by T. Patrick Burke. New York, Sheed and Ward [1966] ix, 180 p. 22 cm. "[Symposium] held at Saint Xavier College, Chicago, March 31st to April 3rd, 1966, under the auspices of the John XXIII Institute." Includes bibliographical references. [BT80.B8] 66-27571
1. Theology, Doctrinal—Addresses, essays, lectures. I. St. Xavier College, Chicago. II. John XXIII Institute, Chicago. III. Title.

BUSWELL, James Oliver, 1895- 230
A systematic theology of the Christian religion. Grand Rapids, Zondervan Pub. House [1962-63] 2 v. 23 cm. [BT75.2.B8] 62-16807
1. Theology, Doctrinal. I. Title.

BUSWELL, James Oliver, 1895- 230
A Systematic theology of the Christian religion. Grand Rapids, Zondervan Pub. House [1962-63] 2 v. 23 cm. [BT75.2.B8] 62-16807
1. Theology, Doctrinal. I. Title.

BUTTRICK, George Arthur, 1892- 230
So we believe, so we pray. New York, Abingdon-Cokesbury [1951] 256 p. 23 cm. "References": p. 233-248. [BT75.B96] 51-9467
1. Theology, Doctrinal. 2. Lord's prayer. I. Title.

BUTTRICK, George Arthur, 1892- 230
So we believe, so we pray. Nashville, Abingdon [1962, c.1951] 256p. (Apex bks., H2) Bibl. 1.25 pap.,
1. Theology, Doctrinal. 2. Lord's prayer. I. Title.

CAIRD, George B. 230
The truth of the gospel. London, New York, Oxford University Press, 1950. vii, 168 p. 20 cm. (A Primer of Christianity, pt. 3) [BT77.C19] 50-12101
1. Theology, Doctrinal—Popular works. 2. Apologetics—20th cent. I. Title. II. Series.

CAIRD, George Bradford. 230
The truth of the gospel. London, New York, Oxford University Press, 1950. vii, 168p. 20cm. (A Primer of Christianity, pt. 3) [BT77.C19] 50-12101
1. Theology, Doctrinal— Popular works. 2. Apologetics—20th cent. I. Title. II. Series.

CALLAHAN, Daniel J., ed. 230
Christianity divided, Protestant and Roman Catholic theological issues; edited by Daniel J. Callahan, Heiko A. Oberman [and] Daniel J. O'Hanlon. New York, Sheed and Ward [1961] xiv, 335 p. 22 cm. Includes bibliographies. [BX4818.3.C3] 61-11789
1. Protestant churches—Relations—Catholic Church. 2. Catholic Church—Relations—Protestant churches. 3. Creeds—Comparative studies. I. Title.

CALLAHAN, Daniel J. 230
The role of theology in the university [by] Daniel Callahan, William Scott [and] F. X. Shea. Milwaukee, Bruce Pub. Co. [1967] xii, 163 p. 23 cm. (Contemporary college theology series) Bibliographical footnotes. [BT65.C3] 67-28215
1. Theology—Study and teaching—Catholic Church. 2. Theology, Doctrinal—Introductions. I. Scott, William A., 1920- II. Shea, Francis X., 1926-

CAMBRON, Mark G 1911- 230
Bible doctrines; beliefs that matter. Introd. by Herbert Lockyer. Grand Rapids, Zondervan Pub. House [1954] 288p. 23cm. [BT75.C18] 55-248
1. Theology, Doctrinal. I. Title.

CAMBRON, Mark Gray, 1911- 230
Bible doctrines beliefs that matter. Introd. by Herbert Lockyer. Grand Rapids, Zondervan Pub. House [1954] 288p. 23cm. [BT75.C18] 55-248
1. Theology, Doctrinal. I. Title.

CAMPBELL, Dennis M., 1945- 230
Authority and the renewal of American theology / Dennis M. Campbell. Philadelphia : United Church Press, c1976. viii, 144 p. ; 22 cm. "A Pilgrim Press book." Originally presented as the author's thesis, Duke, 1973. Includes bibliographical references. [BT88.C247 1976] 75-40340 ISBN 0-8298-0303-3 : 6.00
1. Authority (Religion)—History of doctrines. 2. Theology, Doctrinal—History—United States. I. Title.

CAMPBELL, Donald James, Bp. 230
If I believe. Philadelphia, Westminster Press [1959] 157p. 20cm. [BT77.C22] 59-8071
1. Theology, Doctrinal—Popular works. I. Title.

CAPON, Robert Farrar. 230
Hunting the divine fox; images and mystery in Christian faith. New York, Seabury Press [1974] 167 p. 22 cm. "A Crossroad book." [BT77.C227] 73-17891 ISBN 0-8164-0252-3 5.95
1. Theology, Doctrinal—Popular works. I. Title.

CARNELL, Edward John, 1919- 230
The case for orthodox theology. Philadelphia, Westminster Press [1959] 162 p. 22 cm. Includes bibliography. [BR121.2.C3] 59-5515
1. Christianity—Essence, genius, nature. I. Title.

CARNELL, Edward John, 1919- 230
A philosophy of the Christian religion. Grand Rapids, W. B. Eerdmans Pub. Co., 1952. 523 p. 23 cm. Bibliographical footnotes. [BT40.C3] 52-804
1. Christianity—Philosophy. I. Title.

CARNELL, Edward John, 1919-1967. 230
The case for biblical Christianity. Edited by Ronald H. Nash. Grand Rapids, Mich., W. B. Eerdmans Pub. Co. [1969] 186 p. 22 cm. Contents.Contents.—Christian fellowship and the unity of the church.—The nature of the unity we seek.—Conservatives and liberals do not need each other.—Orthodoxy: cultic vs. classical.—On faith and reason.—Becoming acquainted with the person of God.—On Reinhold Niebuhr and Billy Graham.—Reinhold Niebuhr's view of Scripture.—Niebuhr's criteria of verification.—Reflections on aspects of a Christian ethic.—The virgin birth of Christ.—Jesus Christ and man's condition.—Reflections on contemporary theology.—The government of the church.—The case for orthodox theology.—The fear of death and the hope of the resurrection.—Bibliography of books and articles by Edward John Carnell (p. 183-186) Bibliographical footnotes. [BT15.C3] 68-20584 3.50
1. Theology—Collected works—20th century. I. Title.

CASALIS, Georges 230
Portrait of Karl Barth. Tr., introd., by Robert McAfee Brown. Garden City, N. Y., Doubleday [c.] 1963. 135p. 22cm. Bibl. 63-7483 3.50
1. Barth, Karl, 1886- I. Title.

CASALIS, Georges 230
Portrait of Karl Barth. Tr. [from French] introd. by Robert McAfee Brown. Garden City, N.Y., Doubleday [1964, c.1963] 114p. 18cm. (Anchor bk. A422) Bibl. .95 pap.,
1. Barth, Karl, 1886- I. Title.

CASSELS, Louis 230
Christian primer. Garden City, N. Y. Doubleday [1967,c.1964] 108p. 21cm. (Waymark bk., W3) Bibl. 1.45 pap.,
1. Theology, Doctrinal—Popular works. 2. Christian life. I. Title.

CASSELS, Louis. 230
Christian primer. [1st ed.] Garden City, N. Y., Doubleday, 1964. 108 p. 22 cm. Bibliography: p. [105]-108. [BT77.C24] 64-13848
1. Theology, Doctrinal—Popular works. 2. Christian life. I. Title.

CASSERLEY, Julian Victor Langmead, 1909- 230
The death of man; a critique of Christian atheism, by J. V. Langmead Casserley. New York, Morehouse-Barlow Co. [1967] 159 p. 21 cm. [BT83.5.C3] 67-12969
1. Death of God theology. 2. Christianity—20th century. I. Title.

CAUTHEN, Kenneth. 230
The impact of American religious liberalism. [1st ed.] New York, Harper Row [1962] xiii, 290p. 22cm. Bibliographical references included in 'Notes' (p. 257-283) [BR1615.C35] 62-14573
1. Liberalism (Religion) 2. U. S.—Church history—20th cent. I. Title.

CAUTHEN, Wilfred Kenneth. 230
The impact of American religious liberalism, by Kenneth Cauthen. [1st ed.] New York, Harper & Row [1962] xiii, 290 p. 22 cm. Bibliographical references included in "Notes" (p. 257-283) [BR1615.C35] 62-14573
1. Liberalism (Religion) 2. U.S. — Church history — 20th cent. I. Title.

CHADWICK, Owen. 230
From Bossuet to Newman; the idea of doctrinal development. Cambridge [Eng.] University Press, 1957. 253p. 22cm. (The Birkbeck lectures, 1955-56) [BX1747.C4] 58-865
1. Dogma, Development of. I. Title.

CHAFER, Lewis Sperry, 1871-1952. 230
Major Bible themes; 52 vital doctrines of the Scripture simplified and explained. Rev. by John F. Walvoord. Grand Rapids, Mich., Zondervan Pub. House [1974] 374 p. 23 cm. [BT77.C452] 73-17641 5.95
1. Theology, Doctrinal—Popular works. I. Walvoord, John F. II. Title.

CHANCE, Roger James Ferguson, Sir, 1893- 230
Apple and Eve / [by] Roger Chance. London : Villiers Publications, 1976. 91 p. ; 23 cm. [BT720.C38] 77-359988 ISBN 0-900777-08-7 : £3.00
1. Jesus Christ—Person and offices—Miscellanea. 2. Sin, Original—Miscellanea. I. Title.

*CHARLES, Rodger 230
The church and the world, by Rodger Charles S. J. General editor: Edward Yarnold. Notre Dame, Ind., Fides Publishers [1973] 89, [4] p. 18 cm. (Theology today series no. 43) [BT28] ISBN 0-85342-333-4 0.95 (pbk.)
1. Theology. Doctrinal—History—19th-20th centuries. I. Yarnold, Edward. ed. II. Title.

CHARLOT, John. 230
New Testament disunity; its significance for Christianity today. [1st ed.] New York, E. P. Dutton, 1970. 260 p. 22 cm. Bibliography: p. [255]-260. [BS2397.C47 1970] 79-92617 7.95
1. Bible. N.T.—Theology. I. Title.

CHENU, Marie Dominique, 1895- 230
Nature, man, and society in the twelfth century; essays on new theological perspectives in the Latin West, by M. D. Chenu, with a pref. by Etienne Gilson. Selected, edited, and translated by Jerome Taylor and Lester K. Little. Chicago, University of Chicago Press [1968] xxi, 361 p. 25 cm. Translation of nine essays selected from La theologie au douzieme siecle. Bibliographical footnotes. [BT26.C513] 68-15574
1. Theology, Doctrinal—History—Middle Ages, 600-1500. 2. Philosophy, Medieval—History. 3. Scholasticism—History. I. Title.

CHESNUT, D Lee. 230
The atom speaks, and echoes the word of God. Art work by Leech Illustrators. Grand Rapids, Eerdmans, 1951. 232 p. illus. 23 cm. Bibliography: p. 231-232. [BR115.A85C5] 51-2189
1. Atomic bomb—Moral and religious aspects. I. Title.

CHESTERTON, Gilbert Keith, 1874-1936. 230
The everlasting man. Garden City, N.Y., Image Books [1974, c1925] 280 p. 18 cm. [BL48.C5 1974b] 74-2114 ISBN 0-385-07198-1 1.95 (pbk.)
1. Catholic Church—Apologetic works. 2. Religion. 3. Christianity and other religions. I. Title.

CHIFFLOT, Th. G. 230
Approaches to a theology of history. Tr. from French by Mary Perkins Ryan. New York, Desclee [1966, c.1965] 110p. 22cm. Bibl. [BR115.H5C513] 66-13369 3.50
1. History (Theology) I. Title.

CHILDS, Brevard S. 230
Biblical theology in crisis, by Brevard S. Childs. Philadelphia, Westminster Press [1970] 255 p. 22 cm. Includes bibliographical references. [BS543.C45] 74-96698 8.00
1. Bible—Theology. I. Title.

CHRISTIAN, C. W. 230
Shaping your faith; a guide to a personal theology [by] C. W. Christian. Waco, Tex., Word Books [1973] 254 p. 23 cm. Bibliography: p. 242-245. [BT77.C458] 72-84156 5.95
1. Theology, Doctrinal—Popular works. I. Title.

THE Christian faith; 230
essays in explanation and defence. Edited by W. R. Matthews. Freeport, N.Y., Books for Libraries Press [1971] 339 p. 23 cm. (Essay index reprint series) Reprint of the 1936 ed. Includes bibliographical references. [BT77.C46 1971] 73-152162 ISBN 0-8369-2348-0
1. Theology, Doctrinal—Popular works—Addresses, essays, lectures. I. Matthews, Walter Robert, 1881- ed.

CHRISTIAN history and interpretation; studies presented to John Knox. 230
Ed. by W. R. Farmer, C. F. D. Moule, R. R. Niebuhr. Cambridge [Eng.] Univ. Pr., 1967. xxxv, 428p. port. 24cm. [BR50.C52] 67-15306 9.50
1. Knox, John, 1900- 2. Theology—Addreses, essays, lectures. I. Knox, John, 1900- II. Farmer, William Reuben. ed. III. Moule, Charles Francis Digby, ed. IV. Niebuhr, Richard R. ed.
Available from Cambridge Univ. Pr., New York.

CHRISTIAN theology : 230
a case method approach / editors, Robert A. Evans, Thomas D. Parker ; consulting editors, Keith R. Bridston, John B. Cobb, Jr., Gordon D. Kaufman. 1st ed. New York : Harper & Row, c1976. p. cm. (A Harper forum book) Includes bibliographies. [BT78.C455 1976] 76-9963 ISBN 0-06-062251-2 : 10.00. ISBN 0-06-062252-0 pbk. : 4.95
1. Theology, Doctrinal—Case studies. I. Evans, Robert A., 1937- II. Parker, Thomas D.

CLARK, Chester A 230
Man and his Maker. [1st ed.] New York, Vantage Press [1956] 96p. 21cm. [BF639.C53] 56-7512
1. New Thought. I. Title.

*CLARK, Frank H. 230
Where is heaven? New York, Vantage [c.1965] 114p. 21cm. 2.75 bds.,
I. Title.

CLARK, Gordon Haddon 230
Karl Barth's theological method. Philadelphia. Presbyterian & Reformed, 1963. 229p. 24cm. Bibl. 63-12648 apply
1. Barth, Karl, 1886- 2. Theology—Methodology. I. Title.

CLARKE, Oliver Fielding. 230
For Christ's sake; a reply to the Bishop of Woolwich's book Honest to God, and a positive continuation of the discussion. [2d ed.] New York, Morehouse-Barlow Co. [1963] 103 p. 18 cm. Bibliographical footnotes. [BT55.R63C5 1963] 63-25421
1. Robinson, John Arthur Thomas, Bp. 1919- Honest to God. 2. Christianity — Essence, genius, nature. I. Title.

CLARKE, Oliver Fielding 230
For Christ's sake; a reply to the Bishop of Woolwich's book Honest to God, and a positive continuation of the discussion [2d ed.] New York, Morehouse [c.1963] 103p. 18cm. Bibl. 63-25421 1.50 pap.,
1. Robinson, John Arthur Thomas, Bp., 1919- Honest to God. 2. Christianity—Essence; genius, nature. I. Title.

COBB, John B. 230
God and the world, by John B. Cobb, Jr. Philadelphia, Westminster Press [1969] 138, [1] p. 21 cm. Bibliography: p. [139] [BT75.2.C6] 69-11374 ISBN 6-642-48608-2.95
1. Theology, Doctrinal—Addresses, essays, lectures. I. Title.

COBB, John B 230
Living options in Protestant theology: a survey of methods. Philadelphia, Westminster Press [1962] 336p. 24cm. [BX4811.C6] 62-10568
1. Protestanitism. 2. Theology, Doctrinal. I. Title. II. Title: Protestant theology.

COBB, John B. 230
Process theology : an introductory exposition / John B. Cobb, Jr., and David Ray Griffin. Philadelphia : Westminster Press, c1976. p. cm. Includes index. Bibliography: p. [BT83.6.C6] 76-10352 ISBN 0-664-24743-1 pbk. : 6.95
1. Process theology. I. Griffin, David, 1939- joint author. II. Title.

COFFIN, Henry Sloane, 1877-1954. 230
Some Christian convictions; a practical restatement in terms of present-day thinking.

Freeport, N.Y., Books for Libraries Press [1972] ix, 222 p. 23 cm. (Essay index reprint series) Reprint of the 1915 ed. [BT77.C59 1972] 79-167328 ISBN 0-8369-2763-X
1. Theology, Doctrinal—Popular works—Addresses, essays, lectures. I. Title.

COLE, Stewart Grant, 1892- 230
The history of fundamentalism. Hamden, Conn., Archon [dist. Shoe String] 1963 [c.1931] 360p. 22cm. 63-13761 9.00
1. Fundamentalism. 2. Protestants in the U.S. I. Title.

COLE, Stewart Grant, 1892- 230
The history of fundamentalism, by Stewart G. Cole. Westport, Conn., Greenwood Press [1971, c1931] xiv, 360 p. 23 cm. Bibliography: p. 341-350. [BT82.2.C6 1971] 70-138107 ISBN 0-8371-5683-1
1. Fundamentalism. I. Title.

COLLINS, Anthony, 1676-1729. 230
A discourse of the grounds and reasons of the Christian religion / Anthony Collins. New York : Garland Pub., 1976. xlii [i.e. lxii], 284 p. ; 19 cm. (British philosophers and theologians of the 17th and 18th centuries) Reprint of the 1724 ed. Includes bibliographical references. [BL2773.C63 1976] 75-11212 ISBN 0-8240-1766-8 lib.bdg. : 25.00
1. Whiston, William, 1667-1752. An essay towards restoring the true text of the Old Testament. 2. Bible. O.T.—Quotations in the New Testament. 3. Bible. O.T.—Prophecies. 4. Christianity—Controversial literature. 5. Messiah—Prophecies. 6. Liberty. I. Title. II. Series.

A Companion to John : 230
readings in Johannine theology (John's Gospel and Epistles) / edited by Michael J. Taylor. New York : Alba House, c1977. xv, 281 p. ; 21 cm. Includes bibliographical references. [BS2601.C56] 77-7042 ISBN 0-8189-0348-1 : 5.95
1. Bible. N.T. Johannine literature—Theology—Addresses, essays, lectures. I. Taylor, Michael J.

CONGAR, Yves Marie Joseph, 1904- 230
The meaning of tradition, by Yves Congar. Translated from the French by A. N. Woodrow. [1st ed.] New York, Hawthorn Books [1964] 155 p. 22 cm. (The Twentieth century encyclopedia of Catholicism, v. 3. Section 1: Knowledge and faith) Translation of Tradition et la vie de l'eglise. [BT90.C593] 64-14159
1. Tradition (Theology) I. Title. II. Series: The Twentieth century encyclopedia of Catholicism, v. 3

THE Context of contemporary 230
theology; essays in honor of Paul Lehmann. Edited by Alexander J. McKelway and E. David Willis. Atlanta, John Knox Press [1974] 270 p. 21 cm. [BT10.C64] 73-16916 ISBN 0-8042-0513-2 10.00
1. Lehmann, Paul Louis, 1906- —Addresses, essays, lectures. 2. Theology—20th century—Addresses, essays, lectures. I. Lehmann, Paul Louis, 1906- II. McKelway, Alexander J., ed. III. Willis, Edward David, ed.
Contents omitted

COOKE, Bernard J. 230
The God of space and time [by] Bernard J. Cooke. New York, Holt, Rinehart and Winston [1969] ix, 208 p. 22 cm. [BS543.C6] 73-87856 4.95
1. Bible—Theology. I. Title.

COOPER, John Charles. 230
The roots of the radical theology. Philadelphia, Westminster Press [1967] 172 p. 21 cm. Bibliographical references included in "Notes" (p. [160]-172) [BT28.C6] 67-12013
1. Theology, Doctrinal—History—19th century. 2. Theology, Doctrinal—History—20th century. 3. Death of God theology. I. Title.

CORNELL, George W. 230
The Way and its ways. New York, Association [c.1963] 251p. 21cm. Bibl. 63-17417 4.50
1. Christianity—Essence, genius, nature. 2. Theology, Doctrinal—Popular works. I. Title.

COSTAS, Peter J 230
The voice of the living God; a study of the Biblical basis of various Christian beliefs today. [1st ed.] New York, Exposition Press [1956] 182p. 21cm. [BT78.C7] 56-11584
1. Theology, Doctrinal. I. Title.

COURTENAY, Walter Rowe, 1902- 230
"I believe, but ...!" A reaffirmation of faith. Richmond, John Knox Press [1950] 182 p. 21 cm. "References and acknowledgments": p. 173-182. [BT77.C79] 50-7761
1. Theology, Doctrinal—Popular works. I. Title.

COUSINS, Ewert H., comp. 230
Process theology: basic writings. Edited by Ewert H. Cousins. New York, Newman Press [1971] vii, 376 p. 23 cm. Contents.Contents.—Preface, by E. H. Cousins.—Introduction: process models in culture, philosophy, and theology, by E. H. Cousins.—Process thought: a contemporary trend in theology, by W. N. Pittenger.—Faith and the formative imagery of our time, by B. E. Meland.—The development of process philosophy, by C. Hartshorne.—Whitehead's method of empirical analysis, by B. M. Loomer.—God and the world, by A. N. Whitehead.—Philosophical and religious uses of "God," by C. Hartshorne.—The reality of God, by S. M. Ogden.—A Whiteheadian reflection on God's relation to the world, by W. E. Stokes.—The world and God, by J. B. Cobb.—God and man, by D. D. Williams.—The new creation, by B. E. Meland.—Bernard E. Meland, process thought, and the significance of Christ, by W. N. Pittenger.—The human predicament, by H. N. Wieman.—Teilhard de Chardin and the orientation of evolution: a critical essay, by T. Dobzhansky.—My universe, by P. Teilhard de Chardin.—The cosmic Christ, by H. de Lubac.—Cosmology and Christology, by N. M. Wildiers.—The problem of evil in Teilhard's thought, by G. Crespy.—Teilhard de Chardin and Christian spirituality, by C. F. Mooney.—Teilhard's process metaphysics, by I. G. Barbour.—Bibliography on process theology (p. 351-369) Includes bibliographies. [BT83.6.C68] 78-171961 4.95
1. Teilhard de Chardin, Pierre—Addresses, essays, lectures. 2. Process theology—Addresses, essays, lectures. I. Title.

COUTTS, John James. 230
This we believe : a study of the background and meaning of Salvation Army doctrines / by John J. Coutts. London : Salvation Army International Headquarters, 1976. 133 p. ; 19 cm. (Challenge books) Includes bibliographical references. [BX9721.2.C68] 76-373787 ISBN 0-85412-282-6 : £0.60
1. Salvation Army—Doctrinal and controversial works. I. Title.

COX, David, 1920- 230
What Christians believe. London, Darton, Longman & Todd [dist. Westminster, Md., Canterbury, c.1963] ix, 187p. 19cm. A 63 2.75 bds.,
1. Theology, Doctrinal—Popular works. I. Title.

COX, Harvey Gallagher. 230
The feast of fools; a theological essay on festivity and fantasy, by Harvey Cox. Cambridge, Harvard University Press, 1969. xii, 204 p. 24 cm. Bibliographical references included in "Notes" (p. [179]-197) [BT28.C65] 75-95914 5.95
1. Festivals. 2. Fantasy. 3. Theology—20th century. I. Title.

CRANOR, Phoebe. 230
Why did God let grandpa die? / Phoebe Cranor. Minneapolis : Bethany Fellowship, c1976. 128 p. ; 18 cm. (Dimension books) [BR96.C72] 76-17737 ISBN 0-87123-603-6 pbk. : 1.95
1. Theology. 2. Children—Religious life. I. Title.

CREATION, Christ, and culture 230
: studies in honour of T. F. Torrance / edited by Richard W. A. McKinney. Edinburgh : Clark, 1976. ix, 321 p., plate : port. ; 23 cm. Contents.Contents.—Clements, R. E. Covenant and Canon in the Old Testament.—Black, M. The New Creation in I Enoch.—Barbour, R. S. Creation, wisdom, and Christ.—Heron, A. Logos, image, son. Ritschl, D. Some comments on the backbround and influence of Augustine's Lex Aeterna doctrine.—Jenson, R. W. The body of God's presence.—MacKinnon, D. M. The relation of the doctrines of the Incarnation and the Trinity.—Galloway, A. D. Creation and covenant.—Moltmann, J. Creation and redemption.—O'Donoghue, N. D. Creation and participation.—Jaki, S. L. Theological aspects of creative science.—Langford, T. A. Authority, community, and church.—Houston, J. Precepts and counsels.—McDonagh, E. Morality and prayer.—McIntyre, J. Theology and method.—Jungel, E. The truth of life.—McKinney, R. W. A. Historical relativism, the appeal to experience and theological reconstruction.—Sykes, S. W. Life after death.—Thomas, J. H. The problem of defining a theology of culture with reference to the theology of Paul Tillich.—Newbigin, L. All in one place or all of one sort? Bibliography: p. 307-321. [BR50.C66] 76-379213 ISBN 0-567-01019-8 : £5.60
1. Torrance, Thomas Forsyth, 1913- 2. Torrance, Thomas Forsyth, 1913- —Bibliography. 3. Theology—Addresses, essays, lectures. I. Torrance, Thomas Forsyth, 1913- II. McKinney, Richard W. A.

CRISTIANI, Leon [Augustin Louis Leon Pierre Cristiani] 1879- 230
Catholics and Protestants, separated brothers, [an exchange of letters by] Leon Cristiani and Jean Rilliet. Translated from the French by Joseph I. Holland and Gilbert V. Tutungi. Westminster, Md., Newman Press [c.]1960. 161p. 60-14815 3.95
1. Catholic Church—Doctrinal and controversial works—Debates, etc. I. Rilliet, Jean Horace, joint author. II. Title.

CULLMANN, Oscar. 230
Christ and time; the primitive Christian conception of time and history. Translated from the German by Floyd V. Filson. Rev. ed. Philadelphia, Westminster Press [1964] xvi, 253 p. 21 cm. [BT78.C83 1964] 64-2336
1. Theology, Doctronal. 2. Church history — Philosophy. 3. Salvation. I. Title.

CULLMANN, Oscar. 230
Christ and time; the primitive Christian conception of time and history. Translated from the German by Floyd V. Filson. Philadelphia, Westminster Press [1950] 253 p. 21 cm. Bibliographical footnotes. [BT78.C83] 50-6855
1. Theology, Doctrinal. 2. Church history—Philosophy. 3. Salvation. I. Title.

CUMMING, James T., 1938- 230
Hey, God, what about ...? / James T. Cumming, Hans Moll ; art by Kathy Counts. St. Louis : Concordia Pub. House, c1977. 104 p. : ill. ; 22 cm. Includes index. [BR96.C85] 77-9932 ISBN 0-570-037581-1 pbk. : 2.95
1. Theology—Miscellanea. I. Moll, Hans, 1938- joint author. II. Title.

CUMMING, James T., 1938- 230
Hey, God, what about ...? / James T. Cumming, Hans Moll ; art by Kathy Counts. St. Louis : Concordia Pub. House, c1977. 104 p. : ill. ; 22 cm. Includes index. [BR96.C85] 77-9932 ISBN 0-570-037581-1 pbk. : 2.95
1. Theology—Miscellanea. I. Moll, Hans, 1938- joint author. II. Title.

CUSTANCE, Arthur C. 230
The doorway papers / Arthur C. Custance. Grand Rapids : Zondervan Pub. House, [1975- v. ; 23 cm. Contents.Contents.—v. 1. Noah's three sons. [BS543.A1C87] 75-311880
1. Bible—Theology—Collected works. I. Title.

CUSTANCE, Arthur C. 230 s
Evolution or creation? / Arthur C. Custance ; drawings by the author. Grand Rapids : Zondervan Pub. House, 1976. 329 p. : ill. ; 23 cm. (His The doorway papers ; v. 4) Includes bibliographical references. [BS543.A1C87 vol. 4] [BL226] 213 75-23370 8.95
1. Creation. 2. Evolution. 3. Monotheism. 4. Polytheism. 5. Man. I. Title.

CUSTANCE, Arthur C. 230 s
Hidden things of God's revelation / Arthur C. Custance. Grand Rapids : Zondervan Pub. House, c1977. p. cm. (His The doorway papers ; v. 7) Bibliography: p. [BS543.A1C87 vol. 7] [BS540] 231'.74 77-22036 ISBN 0-310-23020-9 : 8.95
1. Bible—Criticism, interpretation, etc.—Addresses, essays, lectures. 2. Revelation—Biblical teaching—Addresses, essays, lectures. I. Title.

CUSTANCE, Arthur C. 230 s
Hidden things of God's revelation / Arthur C. Custance. Grand Rapids : Zondervan Pub. House, c1977. p. cm. (His The doorway papers ; v. 7) Bibliography: p. [BS543.A1C87 vol. 7] [BS540] 231'.74 77-22036 ISBN 0-310-23020-9 : 8.95
1. Bible—Criticism, interpretation, etc.—Addresses, essays, lectures. 2. Revelation—Biblical teaching—Addresses, essays, lectures. I. Title.

CUSTANCE, Arthur C. 230 s
Man in Adam and in Christ / Arthur C. Custance. Grand Rapids : Zondervan Pub. House, [1975] 350 p. ; 23 cm. (His The doorway papers ; v. 3) Includes bibliographical references. [BS543.A1C87 vol. 3] [BT703] 233 76-1817 8.95
1. Man (Theology)—Addresses, essays, lectures. I. Title.

CUSTANCE, Arthur C. 230 s
Noah's three sons : human history in three dimensions / Arthur C. Custance. Grand Rapids : Zondervan Pub. House, [1975] 368 p. : ill. ; 23 cm. (His The doorway papers ; v. 1) Includes bibliographical references. [BS543.A1C87 vol. 1] [BS661] 233 74-4957 8.95
1. Japheth (Biblical character) 2. Ham (Biblical character) 3. Shem (Biblical character) 4. Man (Theology)—Biblical teaching. I. Title.

CUSTANCE, Arthur C. 230 s
Time and eternity and other biblical studies / Arthur C. Custance. Grand Rapids : Zondervan Pub. House, c1977. 240 p. ; 23 cm. (His the doorway papers ; v. 6) Includes bibliographical references. [BS543.A1C87 vol. 6] [BS540] 220.6 76-46443 ISBN 0-310-23000-4 : 8.95
1. Bible—Criticism, interpretation, etc.—Addresses, essays, lectures. I. Title.

CUSTANCE, Arthur C. 230 s
Time and eternity and other biblical studies / Arthur C. Custance. Grand Rapids : Zondervan Pub. House, c1977. 240 p. ; 23 cm. (His the doorway papers ; v. 6) Includes bibliographical references. [BS543.A1C87 vol. 6] [BS540] 220.6 76-46443 ISBN 0-310-23000-4 : 8.95
1. Bible—Criticism, interpretation, etc.—Addresses, essays, lectures. I. Title.

CUSTANCE, Arthur C. 230 s
The Virgin birth and the Incarnation / by Arthur C. Custance ; ill. by the author. Grand Rapids : Zondervan Pub. House, c1976. p. cm. (His The doorway papers ; v. 5) "Each of these papers was previously published separately." Bibliography: p. [BS543.A1C87 vol. 5] [BR85] 230 76-14968 8.95
1. Theology—Addresses, essays, lectures. I. Title.
Contents omitted. Contents omitted.

DAVIS, George Washington. 230
Existentialism and theology; an investigation of the contribution of Rudolf Bultmann to theological thought. New York, Philosophical Library [1957] 88p. 23cm. [BT40.B83D3] 57-2668
1. Bultmann, Rudolf Karl, 1884- 2. Existentialism. I. Title.

DAWE, Donald G. 230
No orthodoxy but the truth; a survey of Protestant theology, by Donald G. Dawe. Philadelphia, Westminster Press [1969] 185 p. 21 cm. Bibliographical references included in "Notes" (p. 173-180) [BX4805.2.D34] 69-10424 ISBN 0-664-20844-4 5.95
1. Theology, Protestant. 2. Theology, Doctrinal—History—Modern period, 1500- I. Title.

*DEAL, William S. 230
The christian's daily manna. [by] William S. Deal. Grand Rapids, Mich., Baker book, [1973] [122] p., 18 cm. [BS482] ISBN 0-8010-2832-9 0.95 (pbk.)
1. Christian life—Biblical teaching. 2. Bible—Commentary. I. Title.

DEJEAN, Edgar K. 230
Tom, Dick, and Jane in theology land / with Edgar DeJean. Corte Madera, Calif. : Omega Books, c1976. 109 p. ; 22 cm. Includes bibliographical references. [BT77.D395] 76-24109 ISBN 0-89353-010-7 pbk. : 4.00
1. Theology, Doctrinal—Popular works. I. Title.

DENIS, Henri, priest. 230
Where is theology going? Translated by Theodore DuBois. Westminster, Md., Newman Press [1968] v, 106 p. 21 cm. Translation of Pour une prospective theologique. [BT78.D413] 68-20851
1. Theology, Doctrinal. I. Title.

*DENNEY, James. 230
Studies in theology : lectures delivered in Chicago Theological Seminary. Grand Rapids : Baker Book House, 1976 xxvii, 272p. : port. ; 20 cm. (Notable books on theology) Includes bibliographical references. [BT75] ISBN 0-8010-2850-7 pbk. : 3.95.
1. Theology, Doctrinal-Addresses, essays, lectures. I. Title.

THE Development of 230
fundamental theology. Edited by Johannes B. Metz. New York, Paulist Press [1969] viii, 180 p. 24 cm. (Concilium: theology in the age of renewal. Fundamental theology, v. 46) Bibliographical footnotes. [BX1747.D48] 74-92116 4.50
1. Theology, Catholic. 2. Apologetics—History. I. Metz, Johannes Baptist, 1928- ed. II. Series: Concilium: theology in the age of renewal, v. 46

DE WOLF, Lotan Harold, 1905- 230
The case for theology in liberal perspective. Philadelphia, Westminster Press [1959] 206 p. 21 cm. Includes bibliography. [BT75.2.D4] 59-6062
1. Theology, Doctrinal. 2. Liberalism (Religion) I. Title.

DE WOLF, Lotan Harold, 1905- 230
A theology of the living church. [1st ed.] New York, Harper [1953] 383p. 25cm. [BT77.D4] 53-5989
1. Theology, Doctrinal—Popular works. I. Title.

DE WOLF, Lotan Harold, 1905- 230
Trends and frontiers of religious thought.

Nashville, National Methodist Student Movement [1955] 139p. 20cm. [BT28.D48] 55-14429
1. Religious thought—20th cent. 2. Theology, Doctrinal—Hist.—20th cent. I. Title.

DIBRANDI, Herman A. 230
Introduction to Christian doctrine / Herman A. diBrandi. New York : Morehouse-Barlow Co., c1976. iv, 90 p. ; 19 cm. Bibliography: p. 89-90. [BT77.D45] 75-43430 ISBN 0-8192-1194-X pbk. : 3.50
1. Theology, Doctrinal—Popular works. I. Title.

DIETRICH, Suzanne de. 230
God's word in today's world. Valley Forge, Judson Press [1967] 110 p. 20 cm. (Lake view books) [BT77.D47] 67-25894
1. Theology, Doctrinal — Popular works. 2. Bible — Theology. I. Title.

DIETRICH, Suzanne de 230
God's word in today's world. Valley Forge. Judson [1967] 110p. 20cm. (Lake view bks.) Bible-- Theology. [BT77.D47] 67-25894 2.50 pap.,
1. Theology. Doctrinal—Popular works. I. Title.

DIEZ-ALEGRIA, Jose Maria, 1911- 230 B
I believe in hope. Translated by Gary MacEoin. [1st ed.] Garden City, N.Y., Doubleday, 1974. 187 p. 22 cm. Translation of Yo creo en la esperanza. [BX4705.D537A313] 73-82244 ISBN 0-385-08448-X 5.95
1. Diez-Alegria, Jose Maria, 1911- 2. Catholic Church—Doctrinal and controversial works—Catholic authors. 3. Christianity—Controversial literature. I. Title.

DILLISTONE, Frederick William, 1903- ed. 230
Scripture and tradition; essays by F. W. Dillistone [and others] Greenwich Conn., Seabury Press, 1955. 150p. 19cm. [BT89.D5 1955a] 55-14612
1. Bible—Evidences, authority, etc. 2. Tradition (Theology) I. Title.

DIMENSIONS in religious education / contributors, Avery Dulles ... [et al.] ; edited by John R. McCall. Havertown, Pa. : CIM Books, c1973. iv, 183 p. ; 26 cm. Includes bibliographical references. [BR50.D52] 75-322209 230
1. Theology—Addresses, essays, lectures. 2. Christian education—Addresses, essays, lectures. I. Dulles, Avery Robert, 1918- II. McCall, John R., 1920-

THE Divine principle. 230
[Washington] Holy Spirit Association for the Unification of World Christianity [1973] 643 p. port. 24 cm. Translation of Wolli haeje. [BT75.2.W6313] 73-78869
1. Theology, Doctrinal. 2. History (Theology) I. Segye Kidokkyo T'ongil Sillyong Hyophoe.

DODD, Charles Harold, 1884- 230
Gospel and law; the relation of faith and ethics in early Christianity. New York, Columbia University Press, 1951. 83 p. 21 cm. (Bampton lectures in America, no. 3) [BT85.D6] 51-11458
1. Law and Gospel. I. Title. II. Series.

DOGMA and pluralism. 230
Edited by Edward Schillebeeckx. [New York] Herder and Herder [1970] 155 p. 23 cm. (Concilium: theology in the age of renewal, v. 51, Dogma) Includes bibliographical footnotes. [BX885.D6] 74-98258 2.95
1. Catholic Church—Addresses, essays, lectures. 2. Creeds—Addresses, essays, lectures. I. Schillebeeckx, Edward Cornelis Florentius Alfons, 1914- ed. II. Series: Concilium (New York) v. 51

DONNE, John, 1573-1631. 230
Essays in divinity, edited by Evelyn M. Simpson. Oxford, Clarendon Press, 1952. xxix, 137 p. facsim. 23 cm. [BT70.D65] 52-9892
1. Theology, Doctrinal. I. Title.

DUTHIE, Charles S. 230
Outline of Christian belief, by Charles S. Duthie. Nashville, Abingdon Press [1968] 116 p. 21 cm. A series of articles which appeared in The British Weekly from Oct. 1966 to June 1967. Bibliography: p. [115]-116. [BT77.D8] 68-7990 2.75
1. Theology, Doctrinal—Popular works. I. The British weekly. II. Title.

DWIGHT E. Stevenson : 230
a tribute by some of his former students / editor, William R. Barr. Lexington, Ky. : Lexington Theological Seminary, 1975. 67 p. ; 25 cm. On spine: Stevenson tribute volume. Contents.Contents.—White, R. C. Dwight E. Stevenson, teacher of preachers.—Reid, M. K. On identifying the word of God today.—Spainhower, J. I. It occurs to me.—Blanton, Betty L. God's continuing incarnation through us.—Wilson, G. H. Always a pilgrim?—Barr, W. R. The presentation of Christ.—Pierson, R. M. A selected listing of some of the literary productions of Dwight E. and Deloris Stevenson. Includes bibliographical references. [BR50.D85] 75-330964
1. Stevenson, Dwight Eshelman, 1906- 2. Stevenson, Dwight Eshelman, 1906- — Bibliography. 3. Theology. I. Stevenson, Dwight Eshelman, 1906- II. Barr, William R. III. Title: Stevenson tribute volume.

EASTON, William Burnet, 1905- 230
Basic Christian beliefs. Philadelphia, Westminster Press [1957] 196p. 21cm. [BT77.E14] 57-8930
1. Theology, Doctrinal—Popular works. I. Title.

EASTWOOD, Charles Cyril, 1916- 230
The priesthood of all believers; an examination of the doctrine from the Reformation to the present day. Minneapolis, Augsburg Pub. House [1962, 1960] 268 p. 22 cm. Includes bibliography. [BT767.5.E3 1962] 62-3573
1. Priesthood. Universal. I. Title.

EASTWOOD, Cyril 230
The priesthood of all believers; an examination of the doctrine from the Reformation to the present day. Minneapolis, Augsburg [1962, c.1960] 268p. 22cm. Bibl. 62-3573 4.50
1. Priesthood. Universal. I. Title.

EBELING, Gerhard, 1912- 230
The problem of historicity in the church and its proclamation. Tr. by Grover Foley. Philadelphia, Fortress [1967] vi, 120p. illus. 20cm. Tr. of Die Geschichtlichken der Kirche und ihre Verkundigung als theologisches Problem. Bibl. [BR115.H5F23] 67-11850 3.00
1. Church—Credibility. 2. History (Theology) 3. Tradition (Theology) I. Title.

EBELING, Gerhard, 1912- 230
Theology and proclamation; dialogue with Bultmann. Tr. byJohn Riches. Philadelphia, Fortress [1966] 186p. 21cm. Bibl. [BX4827.B78E213] 66-7851 3.95 bds.,
1. Bultmann, Rudolf Karl, 1884- 2. Theology—Methodology. I. Title.

EBELING, Gerhard, 1912- 230
The word of God and tradition; historical studies interpreting the divisions of Christianity. Translated by S. H. Hooke. Philadelphia, Fortress Press [1968] 272 p. 21 cm. Translation of Wort Gottes und Tradition. Bibliographical references included in "Notes" (p. 237-261) [BT15.E2413] 68-29130 3.95
1. Theology, Doctrinal—Addresses, essays, lectures. 2. Tradition (Theology)—Addresses, essays, lectures. I. Title.

EBERSOLE, Mark C. 230
Christian faith and man's religion. New York, Crowell [1961] 206 p. 21 cm. Includes bibliography. [BT77.E18] 61-14526
1. Theology, Doctrinal—Popular works. 2. Religious thought—Modern period. 3. Religion. I. Title.

ECCLES, David McAdam Eccles, 1st viscount, 1904- 230
Half-way to faith, by David Eccles. Philadelphia, Westminster [1966] 128p. 19cm. (Adventures in faith) [BR124.E351966] 66-20092 1.45 pap.,
1. Christianity—20th cent. I. Title.

EDINGTON, Andrew. 230
The big search. [1st ed.] New York, Pageant Press [1955] 51p. 21cm. [BT77.E24] 55-10115
1. Theology, Doctrinal—Popular works. I. Title.

EDWARDS, David Lawrence, ed. 230
The "Honest to God" debate; some reactions to the book "Honest to God." With a new chapter by its author, John A. T. Robinson. Philadelphia, Westminster Press [1963] 287 p. 18 cm. Bibliographical footnotes. [BT55.R63E4 1963a] 63-22614
1. Robinson, John Arthur Thomas, Bp., 1919- Honest to God. I. Title.

EDWARDS, Francis Henry, 1897- 230
The joy in creation and judgment / F. Henry Edwards. Independence, Mo. : Herald Pub. House, c1975. 255 p. ; 21 cm. Includes bibliographical references and index. [BT75.2.E38] 75-12821 ISBN 0-8309-0147-7 : 10.00
1. Theology, Doctrinal. I. Title.

ELERT, Werner, 1885-1955 230
Law and gospel, by Werner Elert. Tr. by Edward H. Schroeder. Philadelphia, Fortress [1967] 52p. 19cm. (Facet books. Social ethics ser., 16) Tr. of an essay in the v. Zwischen Gnade und Ungnade . . . 1948. A reply to Karl Barth's . . . essay, Gospel and law. [BT79.E413] 66-25263 .85 pap.,
1. Law and gospel. 2. Barth, Karl, 1886- Evangelium und Gesetz. I. Title.

ELFENBEIN, Hiram. 230
Organized religion; the great game of make-believe. New York, Philosophical Library [1968] 239 p. 22 cm. Bibliographical footnotes. [BL2775.2.E43] 67-27264
1. Religion—Controversial literature. I. Title.

ERB, Margaret. 230
Basic Christianity. [Chicago, Inter-Varsity Press, 1967? c1952] 88 p. 18 cm. (An Inter-Varsity guide for Bible discussions) [BT60.E7] 67-28874
1. Christianity—Essence, genius, nature. 2. Bible—Study—Outline, syllabi, etc. I. Title.

ESSAYS in honor of Joseph P. 230
Brennan / by members of the faculty, Saint Bernard's Seminary ; edited by Robert F. McNamara. Rochester, N.Y. : The Seminary, 1976, c1977. 158 p. ; 22 cm. "The sheaf, Bicentennial issue, (part one)." Contents.Contents.—Turvasi, F. Charles Briggs, a pioneer of theological ecumenism.—Healy, J., Carm, O. Empathy with the cross.—Falcone, S. A. The kind of bread we pray for in the Lord's prayer.—Kelly, J. G. The interpretation of Amos 4:13 in the early Christian community.—Jankowiak, J. M. The American seminary.—Graf, W. Some reflections on reconciliation.—Pennington, J. G. Fulton John Sheen, a chronology and bibliography.—Brennan, J. P. Some hidden harmonies of the Fifth Book of Psalms. Includes bibliographical references. [BR50.E84] 76-51644
1. Brennan, Joseph P.—Addresses, essays, lectures. 2. Sheen, Fulton John, Bp., 1895- Bibliography. 3. Theology—Addresses, essays, lectures. I. Brennan, Joseph P. II. McNamara, Robert Francis, 1910- III. St. Bernard's Seminary, Rochester, N.Y. IV. The Sheaf.

EVANS, Donald D. 230
The logic of self-involvement; a philosophical study of everyday language with special reference to the Christian use of language about God as Creator [by] Donald D. Evans. [New York] Herder and Herder [1969, c1963] 293 p. 22 cm. Bibliography: p. [269]-275. [BT695.E8 1969] 69-17776 8.50
1. Creation. 2. Semantics (Philosophy) 3. Analysis (Philosophy) 4. Theology—Terminology. I. Title.

EVANS, William, 1870-1950. 230
The great doctrines of the Bible / by William Evans. Enl. ed. / with eighty additional entries by S. Maxwell Coder. Chicago : Moody Press, [1974] 325 p. ; 24 cm. Includes index. [BT77.E82 1974] 74-185534 ISBN 0-8024-3301-4 : 5.95
1. Bible—Theology. 2. Theology, Doctrinal—Popular works. I. Coder, Samuel Maxwell, 1902- II. Title.

FANT, David Jones, 1897- ed. 230
Foundations of the faith; twelve studies in the basic Christian revelation. Westwood, N. J., Revell ['1951] 189 p. 21 cm. [BT75.F25] 51-14857
1. Theology, Doctrinal. I. Title.

FARLEY, Edward, 1929- 230
Ecclesial man : a social phenomenology of faith and reality / by Edward Farley. Philadelphia : Fortress Press, [1975] xvii, 282 p. ; 21 cm. Includes bibliographical references and index. [BR100.F34] 73-88359 ISBN 0-8006-0272-2 : 10.50
1. Husserl, Edmund, 1859-1938. 2. Christianity—Philosophy. 3. Phenomenology. I. Title.

FARRER, Austin Marsden. 230
Interpretation and belief / Austin Farrer ; edited by Charles C. Conti ; foreword by E. L. Mascall. London : SPCK, 1976. xiv, 210 p. ; 23 cm. Includes bibliographical references. [BR85.F37] 76-379459 ISBN 0-281-02889-3 : £5.95
1. Theology—Addresses, essays, lectures. I. Title.

FEINER, Johannes. 230
The common catechism : a book of Christian faith / [edited by Johannes Feiner and Lukas Vischer ; with the cooperation of Josef Blank ... et al.] New York : Seabury Press, 1975. xxv, 690 p. ; 22 cm. "A Crossroad book." Translation of Neues Glaubensbuch: der gemeinsame christliche Glaube. Includes index. [BT75.2.F4213] 75-1070 ISBN 0-8164-0283-3 : 10.95
1. Theology, Doctrinal. I. Vischer, Lukas, joint author. II. Title.

THE ferment in the Church 230
[by] Roger Lloyd. New York, Morehouse-Barlow Co. [1964] 124 p. 19 cm. Bibliography: p. [123]-124. [BT55.L57] 64-7225
1. Christianity — Essence, genius, nature.

FERRE, Nels Frederick Solomon, 1908- 230
Reason in religion. [Edinburgh, New York] Nelson [1963] 336 p. 23 cm. (Nelson's library of theology) [BT50.F42] 63-5247
1. Faith and reason. I. Title.

FERRE, Nels Fredrick Solomon, 1908- 230
The living God of nowhere and nothing, by Nels F.S. Ferre. Philadelphia, Westminster Press [1967, c1966] vii 237 p. 23 cm. [BR121.2.F43] 67-18727
1. Christianity—20th cent. I. Title.

FERRE, Nels Fredrick Solomon, 1908- 230
The living God of nowhere and nothing, by Nels F. S. Ferre. Philadelphia, Westminster Press [1967, c1966] vii, 237 p. 23 cm. [BR121.2.F43 1967] 67-18727
1. Christianity—20th century. I. Title.

FERRE, Nels Fredrick Solomon, 1908- 230
Searchlights on contemporary theology. New York, Harper [c.1961] 241p. Bibl. 61-7355 4.50 bds.,
1. Theology, Doctrinal. I. Title.

FERRIS, Theodore Parker, 1908- 230
When I became a man. New York, Oxford University Press, 1937. 228p. 20cm. [BR121.F5473] 57-6479
1. Christianity—Essence, genius, nature. I. Title.

FEUERBACH, Ludwig Andreas, 1804-1872. 230
The essence of Christianity. Translated from the German by George Eliot. Introductory essay by Karl Barth. Foreword by H. Richard Niebuhr. New York, Harper [1957] xiiv, 339p. 21cm. (The Library of religion and culture) Harper torchbooks, TB 11. [B2971.W4E5 1957] 57-13606
1. Religion—Philosophy. 2. Christianity—Controversial literature. I. Title.

FIELD, Benjamin, d. 1869. 230
The student's handbook of Christian theology. New ed., edited, with extensive additions by John C. Symons. Also considerable new material never heretofore published, added to the chapter, The final perseverance of the saints, by Peter Wiseman. Freeport, Pa., Fountain Press [1955] 332p. 21cm. [BT75.F45 1955] 55-27321
1. Theology, Doctrinal. I. Title.

FINEGAN, Jack 230
First steps in theology. New York, Association Press [c.1960] 128p. 16cm. (An Association Press reflection book) 'A reflection book drawn from the author's Beginning in theology.' 60-12719 .50 pap.,
1. Theology, Doctrinal—Popular works. I. Title.

FINEGAN, Jack, 1908- 230
Beginnings in theology. New York, Association Press [c1956] 244p. 20cm. [BT77.F5] 56-5029
1. Theology, Doctrinal—Popular works. I. Title.

FINEGAN, Jack, 1908- 230
Step by step in theology; adapted from Jack Finegan's First steps in theology. Prepared by Hal and Jean Vermes. New York, Association [c.1962] 120p. 26cm. (Association programed instruction bk.) 62-11032 3.00 pap.,
1. Theology, Doctrinal—Popular works. I. Vermes, Hal G. II. Vermes, Jean Campbell (Pattison) III. Title.

FINEGAN, Jack, 1908- 230
The three R's of Christianity. Richmond, John Knox Press [1964] 125 p. 20 cm. Bibliographical references included in "Notes" (p. [119]-125) [BT127.2.F5] 64-10078
1. Revelation. 2. Redemption. I. Title.

FINEGAN, Jack, 1908- 230
The three R's of Christianity. Richmond, Va., Knox [c.1964] 125p. 20cm. Bibl. 64-10078 1.75 pap.,
1. Revelation. 2. Redemption. I. Title.

FINNEY, Charles Grandison, 1792-1875. 230
Finney's systematic theology / Charles Finney ; edited by J. H. Fairchild. Abridged. Minneapolis : Bethany Fellowship, 1976. xx, 435 p. ; 22 cm. First published in 1846 under title: Finney's Lectures on systematic theology. [BT80.F5 1976] 76-3500 ISBN 0-87123-153-0 pbk. : 4.95
1. Theology, Doctrinal—Addresses, essays, lectures. 2. Christian ethics—Addresses, essays, lectures. I. Title.

FINNEY, Charles Grandison, 1792-1875. 230
The heart of truth : Finney's lectures on theology / by Charles G. Finney. New bicentennial ed. Minneapolis : Bethany Fellowship, 1976. 248 p. ; 21 cm. Originally published in 1840 under title: Skeletons of a course of theological lectures. [BR85.F427 1976] 75-46128 ISBN 0-87123-226-X pbk. : 3.50
1. Theology—Addresses, essays, lectures. 2. Christian ethics—Addresses, essays, lectures. I. Title.

FISKE, Charles, Bp., 1868-1942. 230
The confessions of a puzzled parson, and other pleas for reality. Freeport, N.Y., Books for Libraries Press [1968] vii, 273 p. 22 cm. (Essay index reprint series) Reprint of the 1928 ed. [BR85.F46 1968] 68-54345
1. Christianity—Addresses, essays, lectures. I. Title.

FITZER, Joseph, 1939- 230
Moehler and Baur in controversy, 1832-38: romantic-idealist assessment of the Reformation and Counter-Reformation. Tallahassee, Fla., American Academy of Religion, 1974. 116 p. 23 cm. (AAR studies in religion, no. 7) Includes bibliographical references. [BT28.F48] 74-77619 ISBN 0-88420-111-2 3.00 (pbk.)
1. Mohler, Johann Adam, 1796-1838. 2. Baur, Ferdinand Christian, 1792-1860. 3. Theology, Doctrinal—History—19th century. I. Title. II. Series: American Academy of Religion. AAR studies in religion, no. 7.

FLETCHER, M. J. 230
The altar; a study of the tenets of Christianity as taught by Jesus Christ. New York, Exposition [c.1963] 96p. 21cm. 3.00
I. Title.

FORDE, Gerhard O. 230
The Law-Gospel debate; an interpretation of its historical development, by Gerhard O. Forde. Minneapolis, Minn., Augsburg Pub. House [1968, c1969] xv, 248 p. 22 cm. Bibliography: p. 235-240. [BT79.F6] 68-25804 5.95
1. Law and gospel—History of doctrines. I. Title.

FORELL, George Wolfgang. 230
The Protestant faith / by George Wolfgang Forell. With revisions. Philadelphia : Fortress Press, 1975, c1960. xii, 308 p. ; 22 cm. Originally published by Prentice-Hall, Englewood Cliffs, N.J. Includes bibliographical references and index. [BX4811.F65 1975] 74-26341 ISBN 0-8006-1095-4 : 5.95
1. Protestant churches—Doctrinal and controversial works. 2. Theology, Doctrinal. 3. Creeds. I. Title.

FORSTER, Roger T. 230
That's a good question; reasonable answers about living faith [by] Roger T. Forster and V. Paul Marston. Wheaton, Ill., Tyndale House [1974, c1971] 160 p. 18 cm. "First published in Great Britain under the title: Yes, but." Includes bibliographical references. [BR96.F8 1974] 72-96217 ISBN 0-8423-7030-7 1.45
1. Theology—Miscellanea. I. Marston, V. Paul, joint author. II. Title.

FORSTER, Roger T. 230
That's a good question; reasonable answers about living faith [by] Roger T. Forster and V. Paul Marston. Wheaton, Ill., Tyndale House [1974, c1971] 160 p. 18 cm. "First published in Great Britain under the title: Yes, but." Includes bibliographical references. [BR96.F8 1974] 72-96217 ISBN 0-8423-7030-7 1.95 (pbk.)
1. Theology—Miscellanea. I. Marston, V. Paul, joint author. II. Title.

FORSYTH, Peter Taylor, 1848-1921. 230
The principle of authority in relation to certainty, sanctity, and society; an essay in the philosophy of experimental religion. [2d ed.] London, Independent Press [1952; label: Chicago, A. R. Allenson] 430p. 21cm. [BT88.F6 1952] 53-32191
1. Authority (Religion) I. Title.

FOUNDATIONS; 230
a statement of Christian belief in terms of modern thought, by seven Oxford men; B. H. Streeter [and others] Freeport, N.Y., Books for Libraries Press [1971] xi, 538 p. 23 cm. (Essay index reprint series) Reprint of the 1912 ed. Includes bibliographical references. [BT78.F65 1971] 77-152171 ISBN 0-8369-2189-5
1. Modernism. 2. Theology, Doctrinal—Addresses, essays, lectures. I. Streeter, Burnett Hillman, 1874-1937.

FREEDOM : 230
heritage, accomplishments, and prospects in Christ / director of lectureship and editor of the book, William Woodson ; lectureship committee, Brad Brumley ... [et al.]. Henderson, Tenn. : Freed Hardeman College, c1976. 409 p. : ports. ; 23 cm. (Freed-Hardeman College lectures ; 1976) Includes bibliographical references. [BT810.2.F7] 76-356022
1. Freedom (Theology)—Addresses, essays, lectures. 2. Theology—Addresses, essays, lectures. I. Woodson, William. II. Series: Freed-Hardeman College. Lectures ; 1976.

FREEDOM : 230
heritage, accomplishments, and prospects in Christ / director of lectureship and editor of the book, William Woodson ; lectureship committee, Brad Brumley ... [et al.]. Henderson, Tenn. : Freed Hardeman College, c1976. 409 p. : ports. ; 23 cm. (Freed-Hardeman College lectures ; 1976) Includes bibliographical references. [BT810.2.F7] 76-356022
1. Freedom (Theology)—Addresses, essays, lectures. 2. Theology—Addresses, essays, lectures. I. Woodson, William. II. Series: Freed-Hardeman College. Lectures ; 1976.

FREEDOM : 230
heritage, accomplishments, and prospects in Christ / director of lectureship and editor of the book, William Woodson ; lectureship committee, Brad Brumley ... [et al.]. Henderson, Tenn. : Freed Hardeman College, c1976. 409 p. : ports. ; 23 cm. (Freed-Hardeman College lectures ; 1976) Includes bibliographical references. [BT810.2.F7] 76-356022
1. Freedom (Theology)—Addresses, essays, lectures. 2. Theology—Addresses, essays, lectures. I. Woodson, William. II. Series: Freed-Hardeman College. Lectures ; 1976.

FUCHS, William A 1885-1954. 230
Mystery of God and man. [1st ed.] New York, Vantage Press [1956] 344p. illus. 21cm. [BS652.F8] 56-7523
I. Title.

FURNESS, John Malcolm. 230
Vital doctrines of the faith, by Malcolm Furness. [1st U.S. ed.] Grand Rapids, Eerdmans [1974, c1973] 128 p. 18 cm. Includes bibliographical references. [BT77.F84 1974] 73-22310 ISBN 0-8028-1573-1 2.45 (pbk.)
1. Theology, Doctrinal—Popular works. I. Title.

FURNISS, Norman F 230
The fundamentalist controversy, 1918-1931. New Haven, Yale University Press, 1954. viii, 199p. 25cm. (Yale historical publications. Miscellany, 59) 'The outgrowth of ... [the author's] dissertation presented ... for the pH. D. degree at Yale University.' Bibliographical footnotes. 'Bibliographical note': p. [183]-191. [BT78.F82] 54-5082
1. Modernist fundamentalist controversy. I. Title. II. Series.

FURNISS, Norman F. 230
The fundamentalist controversy, 1918-1931. Hamden, Conn., Archon Bks. [dist. Shoe String] 1963[c.1954] viii, 199p. 23cm. Bibl. 63-16554 6.00
1. Modernist-fundamentalist controversy. I. Title.

THE Future of empirical theology, 230
by Fred Berthold [and others] Edited by Bernard E. Meland. Chicago, University of Chicago Press [1969] x, 387 p. 24 cm. (Essays in divinity, v. 7) "Several ... of the essays ... were presented at the Alumni Conference of the Theological Field of Divinity School, November 7-9, 1966." Bibliographical footnotes. [BT83.53.F8] 78-83980
1. Empirical theology—Addresses, essays, lectures. I. Berthold, Fred, 1922- II. Meland, Bernard Eugene, 1899- ed. III. Title. IV. Series.

GEISELMANN, Josef Rupert, 1890- 230
The meaning of tradition. [Translated by W. J. O'Hara. New York] Herder and Herder [1966] 123 p. 22 cm. (Quaestiones disputatae, 15) Translation of the first 3 chapters of Die Hellge Schrift und die Tradition. Bibliographical references included in "Notes" (p. 113-123) [BT90.G413 1966] 66-10597
1. Tradition (Theology) I. Title.

GEISELMANN, Josef Rupert, 1890- 230
The meaning of tradition. [Tr. from German by W. . O'Hara. New York] Herder & Herder [c.1966] 123p. 22cm. (Quaestiones disputatae, 15) Bibl. [BT90.G413] 66-10597 2.50 pap.,
1. Tradition (Theology) I. Title.

GELDENHUYS, Johannes Norval, 1918- 230
Supreme authority; the authority of the Lord, His apostles and the New Testament. Foreword by Ned B. Stonehouse. Grand Rapids, Eerdmans, 1953. 128p. 23cm. Bibliography: p.123-125. [BT88.G4] 53-9738
1. Authority (Religion) 2. Jesus Christ—Person and offices. 3. Apostles. 4. Bible. N. T.—Evidences, authority, etc. I. Title.

*GERSTNER, John H. 230
Theology for everyman. Chicago. Moody [c.1965] 127p. 18cm. (Colportage lib. 512) .39 pap.,
I. Title.

GIBSON, Raymond E. 230
God, man, and time; human destiny in American theology [by] Raymond E. Gibson. Philadelphia, United Church Press [1966] 187 p. 21 cm. Bibliographical references included in "Notes" (p. 179-187) [BT821.2.G5] 66-17662
1. Theology, Doctrinal — Hist. — U.S. 2. Man (Theology) — History of doctrines. 3. Eschatology — History of doctrines. I. Title.

GIBSON, Raymond E. 230
God, man, and time; human destiny in American theology. Philadelphia, United Church Pr. [c.1966] 187p. 21cm. Bibl. [BT821.2.G5] 66-17662 3.95
1. Theology, Doctrinal—Hist.—U. S. 2. Man (Theology)—History of doctrines. 3. Eschatology—History of doctrines. I. Title.

GOD and the good : 230
essays in honor of Henry Stob / edited by Clifton Orlebeke and Lewis Smedes. Grand Rapids : Eerdmans, [1975] 227 p. : port. ; 23 cm. Bibliography of Henry Stob compiled by Peter DeKlerk": p. 221-227. [BR50.G538] 74-31479 ISBN 0-8028-3454-X : 6.95
1. Stob, Henry, 1908- —Bibliography. 2. Theology—Addresses, essays, lectures. I. Stob, Henry, 1908- II. Orlebeke, Clifton, ed. III. Smedes, Lewis B., ed.
Contents omitted.

GODWIN, William, 1756-1836. 230
Essays / by William Godwin. Folcroft, Pa. : Folcroft Library Editions, 1977. viii, 293 p. ; 23 cm. Reprint of the 1873 ed. published by H. S. King, London. Contents.Contents.—Preliminary essay.—Preface to essay I.—On a state of future retribution.—On the present life of man considered as a state of probation for a future world.—On contrition.—On the death of Jesus considered as an atonement for sin.—On providence.—Note to essay V (fragment).—On the question, what shall we do to be saved? (fragment).—On faith and works.—On the character of Jesus.—On the history and effects of the Christian religion. [BR85.G577 1977] 77-23245 ISBN 0-8414-4502-8 : 35.00
1. Theology—Addresses, essays, lectures. I. Title.

GOGARTEN, Friedrich, 1887- 230
Despair and hope for our time. Translated by Thomas Wieser. Philadelphia, Pilgrim Press [1970] v, 170 p. 22 cm. Translation of Verhangnis und Hoffnung der Neuzeit. Includes bibliographical references. [BR115.W6G613] 72-115305 7.95
1. Church and the world. 2. Secularism. I. Title.

THE Gospel as history / 230
edited by Vilmos Vajta. Philadelphia : Fortress Press, [1975] viii, 247 p. ; 22 cm. (The Gospel encounters history series) Includes bibliographical references. [BR50.G584] 74-263348 ISBN 0-8006-0410-5 : 10.95
1. Theology—Addresses, essays, lectures. I. Vajta, Vilmos. II. Series.

GRAHAM, William Franklin, 1918- 230
Peace with God. [1st ed.] Garden City, N.Y., Doubleday, 1953. 222 p. 22 cm. [BT77.G78] 53-5967
1. Theology, Doctrinal—Popular works. I. Title.

GRANT, Frederick Clifton, 1891- 230
Basic Christian beliefs. New York, Macmillan, 1961 [c.1960] 126p. Bibl. 61-14707 2.95
1. Theology, Doctrinal—Popular works. I. Title.

GREEN, Joseph Franklin 230
Faith to grow on. Nashville, Broadman Press [c.1960] 123p. 21cm. 60-9532 2.50 bds.,
1. Theology, Doctrinal—Popular works. I. Title.

GREEN, Joseph Franklin, 1924- 230
Faith to grow on. Nashville, Broadman Press [1960] 123p. 21cm. [BT77.G84] 60-9532
1. Theology, Doctrinal—Popular works. I. Title.

GREEN, Joseph Franklin, 1924- 230
The heart of the Gospel [by] Joseph F. Green. Nashville, Broadman Press [1968] 128 p. 21 cm. [BT77.G842] 68-20675
1. Theology, Doctrinal—Popular works. I. Title.

GROFF, Warren F. 230
The shaping of modern Christian thought, by Warren F. Groff and Donald E. Miller. Cleveland, World Pub. Co. [1968] xii, 489 p. 24 cm. Bibliographical footnotes. [BR450.G7] 68-23018
1. Religious thought—Modern period, 1500- I. Miller, Donald Eugene, joint author. II. Title.

GUPTILL, Nathanael M 230
Christianity does make sense; a theology for laymen. [2d ed.] New York, American Press [c1956] 128p. 22cm. [BR121.G885 1956] 56-12423
1. Christianity—20th cent. I. Title.

GUTZKE, Manford George 230
Plain talk about Christian words. Johnson City, Tenn., Royal Pubns. Box 47 [1964] 222p. 21cm. [BV3797.G8] 65-932 3.95
1. Evangelistic sermons. 2. Sermons, American. 3. Theology—Terminology. I. Title.

HALL, Douglas John, 1928- 230
Lighten our darkness : toward an indigenous theology of the cross / by Douglas John Hall. Philadelphia : Westminster Press, c1976. 253 p. ; 24 cm. Includes bibliographical references and index. [BR121.2.H317] 75-38963 ISBN 0-664-20808-8 : 10.95
1. Christianity—20th century. 2. Theology—20th century. 3. North America—Civilization. I. Title.

HAMILTON, Kenneth. 230
The system and the gospel; a critique of Paul Tillich. [1st American ed.] New York, Macmillan [1963] 247 p. 23 cm. (The Library of philosophy and theology) [BX4827.T53H3] 63-17633
1. Tillich, Paul, 1886- I. Title.

HAMILTON, Kenneth 230
The system and the gospel; a critique of Paul Tillich. New York, Macmillan [c.1963] 247p. 23cm. (Lib. of phil. and theology) 63-17633 4.95
1. Tillich, Paul, 1886- I. Title.

HAMILTON, Kenneth. 230
To turn from idols. Grand Rapids, Mich., Eerdmans [1973] 232 p. 21 cm. Includes bibliographical references. [BL485.H35] 73-76533 ISBN 0-8028-1528-6 3.95
1. Idols and images—Worship. 2. Christianity—20th century. I. Title.

HAMILTON, William, 1924- 230
The new essence of Christianity. [Rev. ed.] New York, Association Press [1966] 159 p. 20 cm. Includes bibliographical references. [BR481.H25 1966] 66-18857
1. Theology—20th century. 2. Christianity—20th century. I. Title.

HAMILTON, William, 1924- 230
On taking God out of the dictionary. New York, McGraw-Hill [1974] 255 p. 23 cm. [BR481.H26] 73-19691 ISBN 0-07-025802-3 8.95
1. Theology—20th century. 2. Christianity—20th century. I. Title.

HANSON, Richard Patrick Crosland, ed. 230
Difficulties for Christian belief, ed. by R. P. C. Hanson. London, Melbourne [etc.] Macmillan; New York, St. Martin's, 1967.[6], 154p. 19cm. Bibl. [BT80.H26 1967] 67-10580 4.95 bds.,
1. Theology, Doctrinal —Addresses, essays, lectures. I. Title.

HANSON, Richard Patrick Crosland, ed. 230
Difficulties for Christian belief, edited by R. P. C. Hanson. London, Melbourne [etc.] Macmillan; New York, St. Martin's Press, 1967. [6], 154 p. 19 cm. (B 67-548) Bibliography: p. [150]-151. [BT80.H26 1967] 67-10580
1. Theology, Doctrinal — Addresses, essays, lectures. I. Title.

HANSON, Richard Patrick Crosland 230
Tradition in the early church. Philadelphia, Westminster [1963, c.1962] 288p. 23cm. (Lib. of hist. and doctrine) Bibl. 63-7925 5.75
1. Tradition (Theology)—Early church. I. Title.

HARD questions / 230
edited by Frank Colquhoun. [1st American ed.]. Downers Grove, Ill. : InterVarsity Press, 1977, c1976. 131 p. ; 21 cm. Includes bibliographical references. [BR96.H32 1977] 77-150604 ISBN 0-87784-720-7 : 2.95
1. Theology—Addresses, essays, lectures. I. Colquhoun, Frank.

HARKNESS, Georgia Elma, 1891- 230
Beliefs that count. New York, Abingdon Press [1961] 125 p. 20 cm. [BT77.H268] 61-65438
1. Theology, Doctrinal—Popular works. I. Title.

HARKNESS, Georgia Elma, 1891- 230
Foundations of Christian knowledge. New York, Abingdon Press [1955] 160p. 21cm. Includes bibliography. [BT88.H3] 55-9139
1. Authority (Religion) 2. Knowledge, Theory of (Religion) I. Title.

HARKNESS, Georgia Elma, 1891- 230
Our Christian hope [by] Georgia Harkness. New York, Abingdon Press [1964] 176 p. 21 cm. Bibliographical footnotes. [BT77.H269] 64-19346
1. Theology, Doctrinal—Popular works. I. Title.

HARKNESS, Georgia Elma, 1891- 230
What Christians believe [by] Georgia Harkness. New York, Abingdon Press [1965] 72 p. 19 cm. [BT77.H273] 65-15232
1. Theology, Doctrinal — Popular works. I. Title.

HARKNESS, Georgia Elma, 1891- 230
What Christians believe. Nashville, Abingdon [c.1965] 72p. 19cm. [BT77.H273] 65-15232 .75 pap.,
1. Theology, Doctrinal—Popula works. I. Title.

HARLE, Wilfried, 1941- 230
Sein und Gnade : die Ontologie in Karl Barths kirchlicher Dogmatik / von Wilfried Harle. Berlin ; New York : De Gruyter, 1975. x, 428 p. ; 22 cm. (Theologische Bibliothek Topelmann ; Bd. 27) Habilitationsschrift—Kiel, 1973. Includes bibliographies and indexes. [BT75.B286H33 1975] 75-522676 ISBN 3-11-005706-9 : DM92.00
1. Barth, Karl, 1886-1968. Die kirchliche Dogmatik. 2. Ontology—History. I. Title.

HARNACK, Adolf von, 1851- 230
1930.
What is Christianity? Translated by Thomas Bailey Saunders. Introd. by Rudolf Bultmann. [1st Harper torchbook ed.] New York, Harper [1957] 301 p. 21 cm. (The Library of religion and culture) (Harper torchbooks, TB17) Translation of Das Wesen des Christentums. [BR121.H3 1957] 57-7534
1. Christianity—Essence, genius, nature. I. Title.

HARNER, Nevin Cowger, 1901- 230
I believe, a Christian faith for youth. Philadelphia, Christian Education Press [1950] 127 p. 21 cm. [BT77.H282] 50-6216
1. Theology, Doctrinal—Popular works. I. Title.

HAROUTUNIAN, Joseph, 1904- 230
God with us; a theology of transpersonal life. Philadelphia, Westminister Press, [1965] 318 p. 21 cm. Bibliographical references included in "notes" (p. [305]-314) [BT78.H29] 65-19279
1. Theology, Doctrinal. I. Title.

HAROUTUNIAN, Joseph, 1904- 230
God with us; a theology of transpersonal life. Philadelphia, Westminster [c.1965] 318p. 21cm. Bibl. [BT78.H29] 65-19279 6.00
1. Theology, Doctrinal. I. Title.

HARRIS, Horton. 230
The Tubingen School / by Horton Harris. Oxford : Clarendon Press, 1975. viii, 288 p., [5] leaves of plates : ill. ; 22 cm. Includes index. Bibliography: p. [263]-283. [BS2350.H33] 75-328998 ISBN 0-19-826642-1 : £9.50
1. Bible. N.T.—Criticism, interpretation, etc.—History—19th century. 2. Tubingen School (Protestant theology) I. Title.

HARRIS, Horton. 230
The Tubingen School / by Horton Harris. Oxford : Clarendon Press, 1975. viii, 288 p., [5] leaves of plates : ill. ; 22 cm. Includes index. Bibliography: p. [263]-283. [BS2350.H33] 75-328998 ISBN 0-19-826642-1 : 30.00
1. Bible. N.T.—Criticism, interpretation, etc.—History—19th century. 2. Tubingen School (Protestant theology) I. Title.
Distributed by Oxford University Press, N.Y.

HARRIS, Thomas Lake, 1823- 230
1906.
Arcana of Christianity : an unfolding of the celestial sense of the Divine Word through T. L. Harris. New York : AMS Press, 1976- v. : ill. ; 23 cm. Reprint ed.: v. 1 first published in 2 v. in 1858 by New Church Pub. Association, New York, as v. 1, pt. 1, and an appendix; v. 2 in 1867 by the Brotherhood of the New Life, New York, as v. 1, pt. 3. No more published. Includes index. Contents.Contents.—v. 1. Genesis, 1st chapter. Appendix to the Arcana of Christianity: the Song of Satan.—v. 2. The Apocalypse. [BX9998.H25 1976] 72-2955 ISBN 0-404-10720-6
1. Bible. O.T. Genesis I—Criticism, interpretation, etc. 2. Bible. N.T. Revelation—Criticism, interpretation, etc. I. Title. II. Title: Song of Satan.

HARTT, Julian Norris 230
A Christian critique of American culture; an essay in practical theology [by] Julian N. Hartt. [1st ed.] New York, Harper [1967] xix, 425p. 22cm. [BR115.C8H38] 67-14932 8.50
1. Christianity and culture. 2. Church and the world. I. Title.

HARTT, Julian Norris. 230
The restless quest / Julian N. Hartt. Philadelphia : United Church Press, [1975] 189 p. 21 cm. "A Pilgrim Press book." Includes bibliographical references. [BR85.H29] 74-26836 ISBN 0-8298-0289-4 : 6.95
1. Theology—Addresses, essays, lectures. I. Title.

HAYWARD, John F. 230
Existentialism and religious liberalism. Boston, Beacon [c.1962] 131p. 21cm. 62-13634 3.95 bds.,
1. Liberalism (Religion) 2. Existentialism. I. Title.

HAZELTON, Roger, 1909- 230
Christ and ourselves; a clue to Christian life today. [1st ed.] New York, Harper & Row [1965] xii, 145 p. 22 cm. [BT202.H3] 65-15391
1. Jesus Christ. 2. Christian life. I. Title.

HAZELTON, Roger, 1909- 230
Christ and ourselves; a clue to Christian life today. New York, Harper [c.1965] xii, 145p. 22cm. [BT202.H3] 65-15391 3.00
1. Jesus Christ. 2. Christian life. I. Title.

HEBERT, Arthur Gabriel, 1886- 230
Fundamentalism and the church. Philadelphia, Westminster Press [BT78.H43] 57-9602
I. Title.

HECK, James Arthur, 1892- 230
A theology for laymen. Harrisburg, Pa., Evangelical Press [1956] 185p. 18cm. 'First appeared as a series of fifty-three weekly columns in the Telescope-messenger ... during the year 1955, under the title, Fireside talks on our Christian beliefs.' [BT77.H39] 56-58925
1. Theology, Doctrinal—Popular works. I. Title.

HENRY, Carl Ferdinand Howard, 230
1913-
God, revelation, and authority / Carl F. H. Henry. Waco, Tex. : Word Books, c1976- v. ; 24 cm. Contents.Contents.—v. 1- God who speaks and shows. Includes bibliographies and indexes. [BR1640.A25H45] 76-19536 ISBN 0-87680-477-6 (v. 1) : 12.95 per vol.
1. Evangelicalism—Collected works. I. Title.

HENRY, Carl Ferdinand 230 s
Howard, 1913-
God who speaks and shows : / Carl F. H. Henry. Waco, Tex. : Word Books, c1976- v. in ; 24 cm. (His God, revelation, and authority ; v. 1-) Contents.Contents.—[1] Preliminary considerations.—[2] Fifteen theses. v. Includes bibliographies and indexes. [BR1640.A25H45 vol. 1-2, etc.] [BR118] 230 77-353143 12.95
1. Theology. 2. Christianity—Philosophy. 3. Revelation. I. Title.

HENRY, Carl Ferdinand Howard, 230
1913-
Personal idealism and Strong's theology. Wheaton, Ill., Van Kampen Press [1951] 233 p. 24 cm. Bibliography: p. 230-233. [BT75.S874H4] 51-8679
1. Strong, Augustus Hopkins, 1836-1921. 2. Personalism. I. Title.

HERBERG, Will. 230
Faith enacted as history : essays in Biblical theology / by Will Herberg ; edited with an introduction by Bernard W. Anderson. Philadelphia : Westminster Press, c1976. 281 p. : port. ; 22 cm. Includes bibliographical references. [BS543.H45] [Contents omitted.] 76-26899 ISBN 0-664-21335-9 : 12.00
1. Bible—Theology—Addresses, essays, lectures. I. Title.
Contents omitted

HERBERT, Arthur Gabriel, 230
1886-
Fundamentalism and the church. Philadelphia, Westminster Press [1957] 156p. 24cm. [BT78.H43] 57-9602
1. Fundamentalism. I. Title.

HERRMANN, Wilhelm, 1846-1922. 230
The communion of the Christian with God; described on the basis of Luther's statements. Edited and with an introd. by Robert T. Voelkel. Philadelphia, Fortress Press [1971] lxviii, 370 p. 20 cm. (Lines of Jesus series) Translation of Der Verkehr des Christen mit Gott. Bibliography: p. [lxiii]-lxiv. [BT771.H43 1971] 78-154491 ISBN 0-8006-1270-1 (pbk) 6.95
1. Faith. 2. Experience (Religion) I. Voelkel, Robert T., ed. II. Title.

HEUSS, John, 1908- 230
Have a lively faith. New York, Morehouse-Barlow [c1963] 191 p. 21 cm. [BT77.H46] 63-21702
1. Theology, Doctrinal — Popular works. I. Title.

HEUSS, John, 1908- 230
Have a lively faith. New York, Morehouse [c.1963] 191p. 21cm. 63-21702 4.95
1. Theology. Doctrinal—Popular works. I. Title.

HOBBS, Herschel H. 230
Fundamentals of our faith. Nashville, Broadman Press [1960] x, 161p. Includes bibliography. 20cm. 60-5200 1.95 pap.,
1. Theology, Doctrinal—Popular works. I. Title.

HOBBS, Herschel H. 230
A layman's handbook of Christian doctrine / Herschel H. Hobbs. Nashville : Broadman Press, [1974] 142 p. ; 20 cm. [BR96.H55] 74-78615 ISBN 0-8054-1927-6 pbk. : 2.50
1. Theology—Dictionaries. I. Title.

HODGE, Archibald Alexander, 230
1823-1886.
Outlines of theology. Grand Rapids, Mich., Zondervan Pub. House [1972] 678 p. 23 cm. Reprint of the rewritten and enl. ed. of 1879. [BT75.H6 1972] 73-150624 9.95
1. Presbyterian Church—Doctrinal and controversial works. 2. Theology, Doctrinal. I. Title.

HODGSON, Leonard, 1889- 230
Christian faith and practice; seven lectures. New York, Scribner, 1951. 116 p. 23 cm. [BT7.H55] 51-12463
1. Theology, Doctrinal—Popular works. I. Title.

HOEKSEMA, Herman. 230
Reformed dogmatics. Grand Rapids, Reformed Free Pub. Association [1966] xvii, 917 p. 23 cm. Bibliography: p. 915-917. [BT75.2.H6] 66-24047
1. Theology, Doctrinal. I. Title.

HOLBACH, Paul Henri Thiry, 230
baron d', 1723-1789.
Christianity unveiled : being an examination of the principles and effects of the Christian religion / by Baron d'Holbach (Paul Henri Thiry Holbach) ; translated from the French of Boulanger by W. M. Johnson. New York : Gordon Press, 1974. vi, 98 p. ; 24 cm. Translation of Le christianisme devoile. Reprint of the 1819 ed. published by R. Carlile, London. Includes bibliographical references. [BL2773.H67 1974] 73-8280 ISBN 0-87968-068-7
1. Christianity—Controversial literature. I. Title.

HOLMES, Arthur Frank, 1924- 230
Faith seeks understanding; a Christian approach to knowledge, by Arthur F. Holmes. Grand Rapids, Eerdmans [1971] 175 p. 22 cm. Bibliography: p. 163-170. [BT50.H63] 72-150638 2.95
1. Faith and reason. 2. Knowledge, Theory of (Religion) I. Title.

HOLMES, Kenneth A, 1917- 230
Foes of the Spirit; a critique of religious formalism. New York, Exposition Press [1952] 87 p. 23 cm. [BT78.H56] 52-6090
1. Modernism. I. Title.

HOLMES, Urban Tigner, 1930- 230
To speak of God; theology for beginners [by] Urban T. Holmes, III. New York, Seabury Press [1974] xix, 153 p. 22 cm. "A Crossroad book." [BR118.H64] 74-8917 ISBN 0-8164-1169-7 6.95
1. Theology—Methodology. I. Title.

HOMANS, Peter. 230
Theology after Freud; an interpretive inquiry. Indianapolis, Bobbs-Merrill [1970] xvii, 254 p. 21 cm. Bibliography: p. 233-245. [BF175.H64] 76-84162 4.25
1. Freud, Sigmund, 1856-1939. 2. Psychoanalysis and religion. I. Title.

HORDERN, William. 230
The case for a new reformation theology. Philadelphia, Westminster Press [1959] 176p. 22cm. Includes bibliography. [BT78.H58] 59-5410
1. Neo-orthodoxy. I. Title. II. Title: New reformation theology.

HORTON, Walter Marshall, 230
1895-
Christian theology, an ecumenical approach. [1st ed.] New York, Harper [1955] 304p. 22cm. Includes bibliography. [BT75.H68] 54-12329
1. Theology, Doctrinal. 2. Ecumenical movement. I. Title.

HORTON, Walter Marshall, 230
1895-
Christian theology, an ecumenical approach. Rev. and enl. ed. New York, Harper [1958] 320p. illus. 22cm. Includes bibliography. [BT75.H68 1958] 57-14903
1. Theology, Doctrinal. 2. Ecumenical movement. I. Title.

HOULDEN, James Leslie. 230
Patterns of faith : a study in the relationship between the New Testament and Christian doctrine / J. L. Houlden. Philadelphia : Fortress Press, c1977. 87 p. ; 20 cm. Includes bibliographical references and index. [BT78.H67] 76-55829 ISBN 0-8006-0493-8 pbk. : 3.25
1. Bible. N.T.—Criticism, interpretation, etc. 2. Theology, Doctrinal. I. Title.

HUFFMAN, Jasper Abraham, 230
1880-
The meanings of things believed by Christians. Winona.Lake, Ind., Standard Press [1953] 184p. 20cm. [BT75.H9] 53-29144
1. Theology, Doctrinal. I. Title.

HUMPHREYS, Fisher. 230
Thinking about God : an introduction to Christian theology / Fisher Humphreys. New Orleans : Insight Press, [1974] 224 p. 22 cm. Includes bibliographical references. [BT77.H83] 74-81556 ISBN 0-914520-00-8 : 5.00
1. Theology, Doctrinal—Popular works. I. Title.

HUNT, F. Olen. 230
Heaven is my home, by F. Olen Hunt, Sr. [1st ed.] Atlanta, Spiritual Life Publishers [1967] xi, 106 p. 22 cm. [BT77.H84] 67-18480
1. Theology, Doctrinal—Popular works. I. Title.

HUNT, George Laird, comp. 230
Twelve makers of modern Protestant thought. Edited with introd. by George L. Hunt. New York, Association Press [1971] 140 p. 18 cm. 1958 ed. published under title: Ten makers of modern Protestant thought. Contents.Contents.—Albert Schweitzer, by H. A. Rodgers.—Walter Rauschenbusch, by R. T. Handy.—Soren Kierkegaard, by F. J. Denbeaux.—Karl Barth, by T. F. Torrance.—Reinhold Niebuhr, by C. Welch.—Paul Tillich, by R. C. Johnson.—Rudolph Bultmann, by C. Michalson.—Martin Buber, by W. E. Wiest.—Dietrich Bonhoeffer, by T. A. Gill.—Martin Heidegger, by J. Macquarrie.—Jurgen Moltmann, by D. L. Migliore.—Alfred North Whitehead, by J. B. Cobb, Jr. Includes bibliographical references. [BX4825.H8 1971] 70-152897 ISBN 0-8096-1824-9 2.25
1. Theologians. I. Title.

HUNTER, Archibald Macbride. 230
Jesus : Lord and Saviour / [by] A. M. Hunter. London : S.C.M. Press, 1976. vii, 182 p. ; 22 cm. Includes bibliographical references. [BR85.H743] 77-355602 ISBN 0-334-00804-2 : 2.50
1. Theology—Addresses, essays, lectures.

HUNTER, Archibald Macbride. 230
Taking the Christian view [by] A. M. Hunter. Atlanta, John Knox Press [1974] viii, 84 p. 21 cm. [BT77.H85 1974] 73-16919 ISBN 0-8042-0721-6
1. Theology, Doctrinal—Popular works. 2. Christian life—1960- I. Title.

HUNTER, William M. 230
God and you; a faith to live. [Westwood, N. J.] Revell [1957] 159 p. 21 cm. [BR121.H84] 57-5407
1. Christianity—Essence, genius, nature. I. Title.

HUNTER, William Musbach, 230
1914-.
God and you; a faith to live. [Westwood, N. J.] Revell [1957] 159 p. 21 cm. [BR121.2.H84] 57-5407
1. Christanity — Essence, genius, nature. I. Title.

HUTCHISON, Harry. 230
A faith to live by. Natick, Mass., W. A. Wilde Co. [1959] 92p. 21cm. [BR121.2.H86] 59-14833
1. Christianity—Essence, genius, nature. I. Title.

IMSCHOOT, Paul van 230
Theology of the Old Textament; v.1 Pref. by Lucien Cerfaux. Tr. [from French] by Kathryn

Sullivan, Fidelis Buck. New York, Desclee [1966, c.1954] 300p. 23cm. Contents.v.1. God. Bibl. [BS1192.5.1513] 65-20538 6.75
1. Bible. O. T.—Theology. I. Title.

IRESON, Gordon Worley. 230
Strange victory; the gospel of the resurrection [by] Gordon W. Ireson. New York, Seabury Press [1970] 128 p. 21 cm. (A Seabury paperback SP 69) Includes bibliographical references. [BT77.I67] 70-120367
1. Theology, Doctrinal—Popular works. I. Title.

IRONSIDE, Henry Allan, 1876- 230
1951.
The only two religions and other Gospel papers. New York, Loizeaux Bros. [194-?] 95p. 20cm. [BR123.I68] 54-32892
1. Christianity—Addresses, essays, lectures. I. Title.

IRONSIDE, Henry Allan, 1876- 230
1951.
Sailing with Paul; simple papers for young Christians. [1st ed.] New York, Loizeaux Bros. [1953] 78p. 19cm. [BT77.I74] 54-43122
1. Theology, Doctrinal—Popular works. I. Title.

*ISSETT, Lu Nell. 230
Color me legitimate [first ed.] Van Nuys, Calif., Bible Voice Books, [1975] 88 p. 18 cm. Includes bibliographical references. [BT771.2] 1.50 (pbk.)
1. Theology, Doctrinal—Popular works. I. Title.
Pub. address: P.O. Box 7491 91409.

JAEGER, Werner Wilhelm, 1888- 230
Two rediscovered works of ancient Christian literature: Gregory of Nyssa and Macarius. Leiden, E. J. Brill, 1954. vi, 301p. 25cm. English and Greek. Bibl. [Br65.G76J28] A54 12.50
1. Gregorius, Saint, Bp. of Nyssa, fl. 379-394. 2. Macarius, Saint, the Elder, of Egypt, 4rh cent. I. Gregorius, Saint, Bp. of Nyssa, fl, 379-394. De instituto christiano. II. Macarius, Saint, the Elder, of Egypt, 4th cent. Epistola magna. III. Title.
Contents omitted. Available from Heinman in New York.

JANSEN, G. M. A. 230
An existential approach to theology [by] G. M. A. Jansen. Milwaukee, Bruce Pub. Co. [1966] xii, 128 p. 23 cm. (Impact books) Bibliography: p. 125-126. [BT77.J3] 66-26657
1. Theology, Doctrinal—Popular works. I. Title.

JAY, John Edwin, 1868- 230
Tell me--my quest. Detroit, c1953. 217p. 23cm. [BR125.J28] 54-20750
1. Christianity—20th cent. I. Title.

JENSON, Robert W 230
Alpha and Omega; a study in the theology of Karl Barth. New York, Nelson [1963] 175 p. 22 cm. Bibliography: p. 173-175. [BX4827.B3J4] 63-11567
1. Barth, Karl, 1886- I. Title.

JENSON, Robert W. 230
Alpha and Omega; a study in the theology of Karl Barth. New York, Nelson [c.1963] 175p. 22cm. Bibl. 63-11567 4.00 bds.,
1. Barth, Karl, 1886- I. Title.

JENSON, Robert W. 230
Story and promise; a brief theology of the gospel about Jesus, by Robert W. Jenson. Philadelphia, Fortress Press [1973] ix, 198 p. 20 cm. Includes bibliographies. [BT77.J38] 72-87060 ISBN 0-8006-0143-2 3.95
1. Theology, Doctrinal—Popular works. I. Title.

JESSOP, Thomas Edmund, 1896- 230
An introduction to Christian doctrine. New York, T. Nelson [1961, c.1960] 133p. Bibl. 61-2472 3.00
1. Theology, Doctrinal—Introductions. I. Title.

JOHNSON, Early Ashby, 1917- 230
The crucial task of theology. Richmond, John Knox Press [1958] 222p. 21cm. Includes bibliography. [BT40.J6] 58-7773
1. Theology. 2. Knowledge, Theory of (Religion) I. Title.

JOHNSON, Robert Clyde. 230
Authority in Protestant theology. Philadelphia, Westminster Press [1959] 224p. 22cm. Includes bibliography. [BT88.J6] 59-9824
1. Authority (Religion) I. Title.

JONES, Edgar, 1912- 230
The living word; an introd. to Old Testament theology. Oxford [Eng.] Religious Education Press [1970] xi, 136 p. 21 cm. (Understanding the Bible, 3) Includes bibliographical references. [BS1192.5.J64] 76-115401
1. Bible. O.T.—Theology. I. Title. II. Series.

JONES, William Paul, 1930- 230
The recovery of life's meaning; understanding creation and the incarnation. New York, Association Press [1963] 254 p. 20 cm. (Haddam House books) [BR121.2.J6] 63-10383
1. Christianity—20th cent. I. Title.

JONES, William Paul, 1930- 230
The recovery of life's meaning; understanding creation and the incarnation. New York, Association [c.1963] 254p. 20cm. (Haddam House bks.) 63-10383 4.50 bds.,
1. Christianity—20th cent. I. Title.

JOYCE, J Daniel. 230
The living Christ in our changing world. St. Louis, Bethany Press [1962] 95p. 20cm. [BT80.J68] 62-17917
1. Theology, Doctrinal. 2. Christian life. 3. Sermons, American. I. Title.

KAGAWA, Toyohiko 230
Kagawa, Japanese prophet, his witness in life and word. [Edited by] Jessie M.Trout. New York, Association Press [1960] 80p. [2p. bibl. notes] 19cm. (World Christian books, no. 30. Second series) 60-6574 1.00 pap.,
1. Theology—Collected works. I. Trout, Jessie M., ed. II. Title.

KAISER, Edwin G 1893- 230
Sacred doctrine: an introduction to theology. Westminster, Md., Newman Press, 1958. 344p. 24cm. [BT65.K2] 57-11816
1. Theology, Doctrinal—Introductions. 2. Catholic Church— Doctrinal and controversial works. I. Title.

KALLAS, James G. 230
A layman's introduction to Christian thought, by James Kallas. Philadelphia, Westminster Press [1969] 140 p. 21 cm. [BT77.K23] 69-16919 2.45
1. Theology, Doctrinal—Popular works. I. Title.

KASEMANN, Ernst. 230
Jesus means freedom. [Translated by Frank Clarke. 1st American ed.] Philadelphia, Fortress Press [1970, c1969] 158 p. 22 cm. Translation of Der Ruf der Freiheit. [BS2545.F7K313 1970] 75-94357 2.75
1. Jesus Christ—Person and offices. 2. Freedom (Theology)—Biblical teaching. I. Title.

KASEY, Thomas David 230
Yoke in freedom. New York, Vantage Press [c.1960] 163p. 21cm. 3.00
I. Title.

KAUFMAN, Edmund George. 230
Basic Christian convictions, by Edmund G. Kaufman. North Newton, Kan., Bethel College [1972] xxiv, 338 p. 24 cm. Includes bibliographies. [BT75.2.K36] 72-86406 6.50
1. Theology, Doctrinal. I. Title.

KAUFMAN, Edmund George. 230
Basic Christian convictions, by Edmund G. Kaufman. North Newton, Kan., Bethel College [1972] xxiv, 338 p. 24 cm. Includes bibliographies. [BT75.2.K36] 72-86406 6.50
1. Theology, Doctrinal. I. Title.

KAUFMAN, Gordon D. 230
An essay on theological method / by Gordon D. Kaufman. Missoula, Mont. : Published by Scholars Press for the American Academy of Religion, c1975. xiii, 72 p. ; 24 cm. (AAR studies in religion ; no. 11) Includes bibliographical references. [BR118.K38] 75-31656 ISBN 0-89130-046-5 : 4.20
1. Theology—Methodology. I. Title. II. Series: American Academy of Religion. AAR studies in religion ; no. 11.

KAUFMAN, Gordon D. 230
An essay on theological method / by Gordon D. Kaufman. Missoula, Mont. : Published by Scholars Press for the American Academy of Religion, c1975. p. cm. (AAR studies in religion ; no. 11) Includes bibliographical references. [BR118.K38] 75-31656 ISBN 0-89130-046-5 : 4.20
1. Theology—Methodology. I. Title. II. Series: American Academy of Religion. AAR studies in religion ; no. 11.

KAUFMAN, Gordon D. 230
Systematic theology; a historicist perspective, by Gordon D. Kaufman. New York, Scribner [1969, c1968] xxii, 543 p. 24 cm. Bibliographical footnotes. [BT75.2.K38 1969] 68-27789 8.95
1. Theology, Doctrinal. I. Title.

KAVANAUGH, James J. 230
The birth of God, by James Kavanaugh. New York, Trident Press [1969] 191 p. 22 cm. [BR124.K35] 69-16054 4.95
1. Christianity—20th century. I. Title.

KEE, Alistair, 1937- comp. 230
A reader in political theology. Philadelphia, Westminster Press [1975, c1974] xiii, 171 p. 22 cm. [BT28.K4 1975] 74-19047 ISBN 0-664-24816-0
1. Theology—20th century—Collected works. I. Title.

KELSEY, David H. 230
The fabric of Paul Tillich's theology, by David H. Kelsey. New Haven, Yale University Press, 1967. x, 202 p. 21 cm. (Yale publications in religion, 13) Bibliographical footnotes. [BX4827.T53K43] 67-12994
1. Tillich, Paul, 1886-1965. I. Title. II. Series.

KENNEDY, Dennis James, 1930- 230
Truths that transform / D. James Kennedy. Old Tappan, N.J. : F. H. Revell Co., [1974] 160 p. ; 26 cm. Includes index. [BT77.K277] 74-20923 ISBN 0-8007-0655-2 : 4.95
1. Theology, Doctrinal—Popular works. I. Title.

KENNEDY, Gerald Hamilton, 230
Bp., 1907-
I believe. New York, Aningdon Press [1958] 94p. 29cm. [Know your faith series] [BR121.K342] 58-5400
1. Christianity—Essence, genius, nature. I. Title.

*KEROACK, Louis J. 230
Hell is what you make it. New York, Vantage [1967] 69p. 21cm. 2.50 bds.,
I. Title.

KESWICK Convention, 1976. 230
Keswick seventysix / [Keswick Convention] ; edited by J. Hywel-Davies ; [black and white photographs by K. W. Coates]. London : Coverdale House, 1976. 255 p., [8] p. of plates : ill., ports. ; 18 cm. [BV4487.K5K42 1976] 77-355397 ISBN 0-902088-86-6 : £1.50
1. Keswick movement—Congresses. I. Hywel-Davies, J. II. Title.

*KIDD, Elizabeth 230
We believe. Art by Johanna Sperl. Ed.: Walter A. Kortrey. Philadelphia, Lutheran Church Pr. [c.1965] 63p. illus. 20cm. (LCA church camp ser.) pap., .85; teacher's guide, pap., 1.00
I. Title.

KIM, Young Oon. 230
Unification theology & Christian thought / Young Oon Kim. 1st ed. New York : Golden Gate Pub. Co., 1975. xi, 302 p. ; 21 cm. Includes bibliographies and index. [BT75.2.K53] 74-32590
1. Segye Kidokkyo T'ongil Sillyong Hyophoe—Doctrinal and controversial works. 2. Theology, Doctrinal. 3. Theology, Doctrinal—History. I. Title.

*KING, Norman 230
White paper on the Bible. Minneapolis, Denison [c.1964] 81p. 22cm. 1.00 pap.,
I. Title.

KING, Rachel Hadley, 1904- 230
Theology you can understand. New York, Morehouse-Gorham Co. [1956] 223p. illus. 21cm. [BT77.K4] 56-9732
1. Teeology, Doctrinal—Popular works. I. Title.

KIRK, Kenneth Escott, Bp. of 230
Oxford, 1886-1954
The vision of God: the Christian doctrine of the summumbonum [Magnolia, Mass., P. Smith, 1966] xxiv, 582p. 21cm. (Torchbk., Cloister lib., TB137Q rebound) First pub. in 1931. Bibl. [BT848.K5 1966] 5.00
1. Beatific vision — History of doctrines. 2. Christian ethics — Hist. 3. Asceticism — Hist. I. Title.

KIRK, Kenneth Escott, Bp. of 230
Oxford, 1886-1954
The vision of God: the Christian doctrine of the summumbonum. New York, Harper [1966] xxiv, 582p. 21cm. (Torchbks., TB137Q. Cloister Lib.) First. pub. in 1931. 2d ed. pub. in 1932. Bibl [BT848.K5] 66-4591 2.95 pap.,
1. Beatific vision — History of doctrines. 2. Christian ethics — Hist. 3. Asceticism — Hist. I. Title.

KLIEVER, Lonnie D. 230
Radical Christianity; the new theologies in perspective, with readings from the radicals, by Lonnie D. Kliever and John H. Hayes. [1st ed. Anderson, S.C., Droke House, 1968] 282 p. 23 cm. Bibliography: p. 277-282. [BT83.5.K55] 68-13827 3.50
1. Death of God theology. 2. Theology, Doctrinal—History—20th century. I. Hayes, John Haralson, 1934- joint author. II. Title.

KNIGHT, George Angus Fulton, 230
1909- ed.
Jews and Christians: preparation for dialogue. Philadelphia, Westminster [c.1965] 191p. 21cm. Bibl. [BM535.K57] 65-11614 2.45 pap.,
1. Christianity and other religions—Judaism. 2. Judaism—Relations—Christianity. I. Title.

KNUDSON, Albert Cornelius, 230
1873-
Basic issues in Christian thought. New York, Abingdon-Cokesbury Press [1950] 220 p. 21 cm. Bibliographical footnotes. [BT40.K6] 50-8538
1. Christianity—Philosophy. I. Title.

KOEHLER, Alfred W. 230
Light from above; Christian doctrine explained and applied. Saint Louis, Mo., Concordia Pub. House [c.1960] 165p. 23cm. 60-50142 1.50 pap.,
1. Theology, Doctrinal—Popular works. I. Title.

KRAEMER, Hendrik, 1888- 230
Why Christianity of all religions? Tr. [from Dutch] by Hubert Hoskins. Philadelphia, Westminster [c.1962] 125p. 21cm. 62-14048 2.75
1. Christianity—Essence, genius, nature. 2. Christianity and other religions. I. Title.

KRIEG, Carl E. 230
What to believe? : The questions of Christian faith / Carl E. Krieg. Philadelphia : Fortress Press, [1974] viii, 113 p. ; 19 cm. [BT77.K65] 74-80415 ISBN 0-8006-1085-7 pbk. : 3.25
1. Theology, Doctrinal—Popular works. 2. Apologetics—20th century. I. Title.

KRONER, Richard, 1884- 230
Between faith and thought: reflections and suggestions. New York, Oxford University Press, 1966. ix, 203 p. 21 cm. [BT80.K7] 66-22264
1. Theology, Doctrinal — Addresses, essays, lectures. I. Title.

KRONER, Richard, 1884- 230
Between faith and thought: reflections and suggestions. New York, Oxford, 1966. ix, 203p. 21cm. [BT80.K7] 66-22264 4.95
1. Theoiogy, Doctrinal — Addresses, essays, lectures. I. Title.

KRONER, Richard, 1884- 230
Between faith and thought : reflections and suggestions / Richard Kroner. Westport, Conn. : Greenwood Press, 1975, c1966. ix, 203 p. ; 21 cm. Reprint of the ed. published by Oxford University Press, New York. Includes index. [BT80.K7 1975] 75-3995 ISBN 0-8371-7430-9 lib.bdg. : 12.00
1. Theology, Doctrinal—Addresses, essays, lectures. I. Title.

KUITERT, Harminus Martinus. 230
The necessity of faith : or, Without faith you're as good as dead / by Harry M. Kuitert ; translated by John K. Tunistra. Grand Rapids, Mich. : W. B. Eerdmans Pub. Co., c1976. 159 p. ; 18 cm. Translation of Zonder geloof vaart niemand wel. Bibliography: p. 154-159. [BR85.K8413] 76-17837 ISBN 0 ISBN 0-8028-1616-9 pbk. : 3.95
1. Theology—Addresses, essays, lectures. I. Title.

LAIDLAW, Robert A. 230
The reason why, by Robert A. Laidlaw. Grand Rapids, Zondervan Pub. House [1970] 64 p. 14 cm. [BT1105.L33] 79-19374
1. Apologetics—20th century. I. Title.

*LAIDLAW, Roberto A. 230
Fe que razona; curso Biblico [Chicago] Moody [c.1966] 63p. 22cm. (Ser. estudios por cuenta propia) .65 pap.,
I. Title.

LAURIN, Robert B., 1927- 230
Contemporary Old Testament theologians, by Robert B. Laurin. Valley Forge [Pa.] Judson Press [1970] 223 p. 23 cm. Contents.Contents.—W. Eichrodt: Theology of the Old Testament, by N. K. Gottwald.—Gerhard von Rad: Old Testament theology, by G. H. Davies.—Otto Procksch: Theology of the Old Testament, by J. N. Schofield.—Theodorus C. Vriezen: An outline of Old Testament theology, by R. E. Clements.—Edmond Jacob: Theology of the Old Testament, by R. B. Laurin.—George A. F. Knight: A Christian theology of the Old Testament, by J. I. Durham.—Paul van Imschoot: Theology of the Old Testament, by D. A Hubbard. Includes bibliographies. [BS1192.5.L38] 70-116725 ISBN 0-8170-0488-2 8.95
1. Bible. O.T.—Theology—History. I. Title.

LAWSON, John. 230
Comprehensive handbook of Christian doctrine. Englewood Cliffs, N.J., Prentice-Hall [1967] xiii, 287 p. 24 cm. Includes bibliographies. [BT75.2.L38] 67-10011
1. Theology, Doctrinal. I. Title.

LAWTON, Stewart. 230
Pastoral implications of Biblical theology;

truths that compelled. [New York] Seabury Press [1968] 189 p. 23 cm. (The Library of practical theology) London ed. (Hodder & Stoughton) has title: Truths that compelled; contemporary implications of Biblical theology. [BS543.L3 1968b] 68-25319 3.95
1. Bible—Theology. 2. Bible—Criticism, interpretation, etc.—History. I. Title.

LEE, Ernest George, 1896- 230
Christianity and the new situation Boston, Beacon Press [1954] 157p. 22cm. [BR127.L38] 54-7698
1. Christianity—20th cent. 2. Secularism. I. Title.

LE GUILLOU, M J 230
Christ and church; a theology of the mystery, by M. J. Le Guillou. Pref. by M. D. Chenu. Foreword by J. Bosc. Translated by Charles E. Schaldenbrand. New York, Desclee Co., 1966, c1963] 375 p. 22 cm. Bibliographical footnotes. [BT75.2.L413] 66-17859
1. Theology, Doctrinal. 2. Mystery. I. Title.

LE GUILLOU, M. J. 230
Christ and church; a theology of the mystery, by M. J. Le Guillou. Pref. by M. D. Chenu. Foreword by J. Bosc. Translated by Charles E. Schaldenbrand. New York, Desclee Co., 1966 [c1963] 375 p. 22 cm. Bibliographical footnotes. [BT75.2.L413] 66-17859
1. Theology, Doctrinal. 2. Mystery. I. Title.

LEIBRECHT, Walter, ed. 230
Religion and culture; essays in honor of Paul Tillich. Edited by Walter Leibrecht. Freeport, N.Y., Books for Libraries Press [1972, c1959] xi, 399 p. port. 24 cm. (Essay index reprint series) Bibliography: p. 367-396. [BR50.L38 1972] 78-167376 ISBN 0-8369-2558-0
1. Theology—Addresses, essays, lectures. 2. Civilization, Modern—Addresses, essays, lectures. I. Tillich, Paul, 1886-1965. II. Title.

LEITCH, Addison H. 230
Interpreting basic theology, Great Neck, N.Y., Channel Pr. [c.1961] 208p. 61-17159 3.50 bds.,
1. Theology, Doctrinal—Popular works. I. Title.

LEWIS, Gordon Russell, 1926- 230
Decide for yourself; a theological workbook [by] Gordon R. Lewis. Downers Grove, Ill., Inter-Varsity Press [1970] 174 p. 21 cm. Includes bibliographical references. [BT77.L43] 71-116046
1. Theology, Doctrinal—Popular works. I. Title.

LEWIS, Gordon Russell, 1926- 230
Judge for yourself; a workbook on contemporary challenges to Christian faith [by] Gordon R. Lewis. Downers Grove, Ill., InterVarsity Press [1974] 127 p. 21 cm. Includes bibliographical references. [BT1102.L45] 73-81575 ISBN 0-87784-637-5 2.25 (pbk.)
1. Apologetics—20th century. I. Title.

LEWIS, J. P. 1868- 230
The divine order and the immortalization of man; a treatise on God's practical demonstration of life and immortality. [1st ed.] New York, Exposition Press [1959] 178p. 21cm. [BR125] 59-65209
1. Christianity—20th cent. I. Title.

LIGHTNER, Robert Paul 230
Neo-evangelism [2d ed.] Des Plaines, Ill., Regular Baptist Pr. [1965] 190p. 20cm. Bibl. [BR479.L5] 65-3741 2.95
1. Theology—20th cent. 2. Evangelism. I. Title.

LIGHTNER, Robert Paul. 230
Neo-liberalism. Chicago, Regular Baptist Press [1959] 100p. 20cm. Includes bibliography. [BR1617.L5] 59-50051
1. Liberalism (Religion) I. Title.

LINDSELL, Harold, 1913- 230
A handbook of Christian truth, by Harold Lindsell and Charles J. Woodbridge. Westwood, N. J., F. H. Revell Co. [1952] 351p. 21cm. [BT75.L55] 53-9083
1. Theology, Doctrinal. I. Woodbridge, Charles Jahleel, 1902- joint author. II. Title.

LITTLE, Ganse. 230
Beliefs that matter. Philadelphia, Westminster Press [1957] 142p. 21cm. [BT77.L55] 57-9603
1. Theology, Doctrinal—Popular works. I. Title.

LITTLE, Paul E. 230
Know what you believe [by] Paul E. Little. Wheaton, Ill., Scripture Press Publications [1970] 192 p. 18 cm. Includes bibliographical references. [BT77.L555] 76-105667
1. Theology, Doctrinal—Popular works. I. Title.

LITTLE, William Herbert, 1876- 230
God's plan for man; Christian doctrines in verse. [1st ed.] New York, Pageant Press [1959] 152p. 21cm. [BS85.L5] 59-13333
1. Theology, Doctrinal—Poetry. I. Title.

LLOYD-JONES, David Martyn. 230
Authority. Chicago, Inter-varsity Press [1958] 94p. 18cm. [BT88.L6] 58-59555
1. Authority (Religion) I. Title.

LLOYD, Roger Bradshaigh, 1901- 230
The ferment in the Church [by] Roger Lloyd. New York, Morehouse-Barlow Co. [1964] 124 p. 19 cm. Bibliography: p. [123]-124. [BT55.L57] 64-7225
1. Christianity — Essence, genius, nature. I. Title.

LLOYD, Roger Bradshaigh, 1901- 230
The ferment in the Church. New York, Morehouse [c.1964] 124p. 19cm. Bibl. 64-7225 1.75 pap.,
1. Christianity—Essence, genius, nature. I. Title.

LOCKE, John, 1632-1704 230
The reasonableness of Christianity, as delivered in the Scriptures complete and unabridged. Annotated with some reference to other works of the author. Ed., introd. by George W. Ewing Chicago, Regnery [1965] xxvii, 228p. 17cm. (Gateway ed., 6087) Bibl. [BR120.L6] 65-2632 1.65 pap.,
1. Christianity—17th cent. 2. Apologetics—17th cent. I. Ewing, George W., ed. II. Title.

LOCKE, John, 1632-1704. 230
The reasonableness of Christianity, with A discourse of miracles, and part of A third letter concerning toleration. Edited, abridged, and introduced by I. T. Ramsey. Stanford, Calif., Stanford University Press [1958] 102p. 22cm. (A Library of modern religious thought) [BR120.L62] 58-8595
1. Christianity—17th cent. 2. Philosophy and religion. I. Ramsey, Ian T. II. Title. III. Series.

LOEW, Cornelius Richard. 230
Modern rivals to Christian faith. Philadelphia, Westminster Press [1956] 96p. 20cm. (The Layman's theological library) [BR121.L59] 56-6173
1. Christianity—Essence, genius, nature. 2. U. S.—Religion. I. Title.

LOISY, Alfred Firmin, 1857-1940. 230
The Gospel and the church / by Alfred Loisy ; with an introd. by Bernard B. Scott. Philadelphia : Fortress Press, c1976. lxxiii, 277 p. ; 20 cm. (Lives of Jesus series) Translation of L'Evangile et l'Eglise. Bibliography: p. lxxi-lxxiii. [BR121.H35L63 1976] 75-13050 ISBN 0-8006-1274-4 : 8.95
1. Harnack, Adolf von, 1851-1930. Das Wesen des Christentums. 2. Christianity—Essence, genius, nature. I. Title.

LORNELL, Ruby. 230
We live by faith. [a layman's guide to Christian belief] Philadelphia, Muhlenberg Press [c1955] 143p. 20cm. [BR121.L625] 54-11474
1. Christianity—Essence, genius, nature. I. Title.

LOTZ, David W., 1937- 230
Ritschl & Luther; a fresh perspective on Albrecht Ritschl's theology in the light of his Luther study [by] David W. Lotz. Nashville, Abingdon Press [1974] 215 p. 24 cm. Bibliography: p. 203-211. [BR333.2.L67] 73-14962 ISBN 0-687-36449-3 10.50
1. Luther, Martin, 1483-1546—Theology. 2. Ritschl, Albrecht Benjamin, 1822-1889. I. Title.

LOUTH, Andrew. 230
Theology and spirituality : a paper read by Andrew Louth to the Origen Society in St. John's College on 30 October 1974 ; also, Contemporary doctrinal criticism and Catholic theology : an article first published in Faith and Unity, Autumn 1975. Oxford : S.L.G. Press, 1976. [2], 24 p. ; 21 cm. (Fairacres publications ; 55 ISSN 0307-1405s) [BT80.L68]i76-368449 ISBN 0-7283-0057-5 : £0.35
1. Theology—Addresses, essays, lectures. 2. Spirituality—Addresses, essays, lectures. I. Title.

LOWRIE, Walter, 1868- 230
What is Christianity? [New York] Pantheon [1953] 192p. 21cm. [bR123.L695] 53-6128
1. Christianity—Addresdes, essays, lectures. I. Title.

LOWTHER, Edgar A 1881- 230
The road ahead; the Christian way to world peace. [1st ed.] New York, Exposition Press [1956] 107p. 21cm. [BR121.L69] 56-8717
1. Christianity—Essence, genius, nature. I. Title.

LUCAS, John Randolph. 230
Freedom and grace : essays / by J. R. Lucas. Grand Rapids : Eerdmans, 1976. xiv, 138 p. ; 23 cm. [BR50.L77 1976] 75-43843 ISBN 0-8028-3482-5 : 7.95
1. Theology—Addresses, essays, lectures. I. Title.

LUCAS, John Randolph. 230
Freedom and grace / essays by J. R. Lucas. London : SPCK, 1976. xiv, 138 p. ; 22 cm. Includes bibliographical references. [BR85.L878] 76-376729 ISBN 0-281-02932-6 : £3.95
1. Theology—Addresses, essays, lectures. I. Title.

*LUNDY, C. A. 230
The life entity. New York, Exposition [1966] 56p. 21cm. 3.00
I. Title.

LUTZ, Milton Charles. 230
Human footprints on the divine highroad. Boston, Christopher Pub. House [1956] 123p. 21cm. [BR121.L8] 56-41456
1. Christianity—20th cent. I. Title.

MCCALLUM, James Ramsay. 230
Abelard's Christian theology / by J. Ramsey McCallum. Merrick, N.Y. : Richwood Pub. Co., 1976. vii, 117 p. ; 23 cm. Reprint of the 1948 ed. published by Blackwell, Oxford. Includes a translation of a substantial portion of Abelard's Theologiae christianae. Includes index. Bibliography: p. 115-116. [BT70.M23 1976] 76-1128 ISBN 0-915172-07-0 lib.bdg. : 12.50
1. Abailard, Pierre, 1079-1142. Theologiae christiane. 2. Theology, Doctrinal. I. Abailard, Pierre, 1079-1142. Theologiae chritianae. English. Selections. 1976. II. Title.

MACDONALD, George, 1824-1905. 230
Life essential : the hope of the Gospel / George MacDonald ; edited by Rolland Hein. Wheaton, Ill. : H. Shaw Publishers, c1974. 102 p. ; 22 cm. (The Wheaton literary series) Abridgment of The hope of the Gospel. [BR85.M162 1974] 74-16732 ISBN 0-87788-499-4 : 1.95
1. Theology—Addresses, essays, lectures. I. Hein, Rolland. II. Title.

MCDONALD, Hugh Dermot. 230
Living doctrines of the New Testament [by] H. D. McDonald. Grand Rapids, Zondervan Pub. House, 1972 [c1971] 319 p. 21 cm. (Contemporary evangelical perspectives) Bibliography: p. 307-319. [BS2397.M3 1972] 77-180836
1. Bible. N.T.—Theology. I. Title.

MACDONALD, Murdo Ewen 230
The need to believe. New York, Scribner [1960 c.1959] viii, 128p. (2p. bibl.) 22cm. 60-7345 2.95
1. Apologetics—20th cent. I. Title.

MCGIFFERT, Arthur Cushman, 1861-1933 230
Protestant thought before Kant [Gloucester, Mass., Peter Smith, 1962, c.1961] 265p. 21cm. (Harper torchbks. Cloister lib., TB93 rebound) Bibl. 3.50
1. Religious thought—Modern period. 2. Theology, Doctrinal—Hist.—Modern period. 3. Rationalism—Hist. I. Title.

MACHEN, John Gresham 230
Christianity and liberalism. Grand Rapids, Mich., Eerdmans [c.1923] 189p. 20cm. 1.75 pap.,
1. Liberalism (Religion) I. Title.

MACHEN, John Gresham, 1881-1937 230
The origin of Paul's religion. Grand Rapids, Mich., Eerdmans [1966, c.1925] 239p. 20cm. (James Sprunt lects., 9th ser.) Bibl. [BS2651.M3] 66-2845 1.95 pap.,
1. Paul, Saint, apostle. 2. Bible. N. T. Epistles of Paul — Theology. I. Title.

MACKAY, John Alexander, 1889- 230
Christian reality & appearance [by] John A. Mackay. Richmond, John Knox Press [1969] 108 p. 21 cm. [BR121.2.M28] 69-19474 3.75
1. Christianity—20th century. I. Title.

MCKELWAY, Alexander J. 230
The Systematic theology of Paul Tillich, a review and analysis. Richmond, Knox [c.1964] 280p. 21cm. Bibl. 64-13969 5.50
1. Tillich, Paul, 1886- Systematic theology. 2. Theology, Doctrinal. I. Title.

MACKEY, James Patrick 230
The grace of God, the response of man a study in basic theology [by] J. P. Mackey. Albany, Magi Bks. [c.1966] 192p. 21cm. First ed., 1966, has title: Life and grace. [BT77.M155 1966] 67-21468 3.95
1. Theology, Doctrinal— Popular works. I. Title.

MACKEY, James Patrick. 230
Tradition and change in the church [by] J. P. Mackey. Dayton, Ohio, Pflaum Press, 1968. xxiv, 192 p. 21 cm. Includes bibliographical references. [BT90.M33] 68-21238
1. Tradition (Theology) 2. Church renewal—Catholic Church. I. Title.

*MCNEILLY, Elizabeth H. 230
The three greatest mysteries. New York, Carlton [c.1964] 70p. 21cm. 2.50
I. Title.

MACPHAIL, James Russell. 230
The Way, the Truth, and the Life; an outline of Christian doctrine. New York, Oxford University Press, 1954. 208p. 20cm. [BT77.M165] 54-6910
1. Theology, Doctrinal—Popular works. I. Title.

MACQUARRIE, John. 230
An existentialist theology: a comparison of Heidegger and Bultmann. Harmondsworth, Penguin, 1973. x, 239 p. 18 cm. (Pelican books) Previous ed. London, SCM Press, 1955. Includes bibliographical references. [BT84.M32 1973] 74-163184 ISBN 0-14-021535-2 £0.45
1. Heidegger, Martin, 1889- 2. Bultmann, Rudolf Karl, 1884- 3. Christianity and existentialism. I. Title.

MCQUARRIE, John. 230
The faith of the people of God; a lay theology. New York, Scribner [1973? c.1972] 191 p. 21 cm. (Lyceum Editions, SL367) Bibliography: p. 181-187. [BT77.M166] 72-1224 ISBN 0-68413060-2 2.45 (pbk.)
1. Theology, Doctrinal—Popular works. I. Title.

MACQUARRIE, John. 230
Principles of Christian theology. New York, Scribner [1966] xiv, 477 p. 24 cm. Bibliographical footnotes. [BT75.2.M3] 66-18545
1. Theology, Doctrinal. I. Title.

MACQUARRIE, John. 230
Principles of Christian theology / John Macquarrie. 2d ed. New York : Scribner, c1977. xiii, 544 p. ; 24 cm. Includes bibliographical references and index. [BT75.2.M3 1977] 76-23182 ISBN 0-684-14776-9 : 15.00. ISBN 0-684-14777-7 pbk. : 6.95
1. Theology, Doctrinal. I. Title.

MACQUARRIE, John. 230
Studies in Christian existentialism; lectures and essays. Philadelphia, Westminster Press [1966, c1965] 278 p. 21 cm. [BT80.M 1966a] 66-21808
1. Theology, Doctrinal—Addresses, essays, lectures. I. Title.

MCQUILKIN, Robert Crawford, 1886-1952. 230
God's law and God's grace. Grand Rapids, Eerdmans [1958] 90p. 23cm. [BT85.M3] 58-14596
1. Law and gospel. 2. Grace (Theology) I. Title.

MAN'S need and God's gift : 230
readings in Christian theology / Millard J. Erickson, editor. Grand Rapids, Mich. : Baker Book House, 1977,c1976 382 p. ; 22 cm. Includes bibliographical references. [BT80.M36] 77-150993 ISBN 0-8010-3324-1 : 7.95
1. Theology, Doctrinal—Addresses, essays, lectures. I. Erickson, Millard.

MARLE, Rene. 230
Identifying Christianity / by Rene Marle ; translated by Jeanne Marie Lyons. St. Meinrad, Ind. : Abbey Press, 1975. xi, 175 p. ; 21 cm. (A Priority edition) Translation of La Singularite chretienne. Includes bibliographical references. [BT28.M27713] 75-209 ISBN 0-87029-043-6 : 4.75
1. Theology—20th century. I. Title.

MARNACK, Adolf von 1851-1930. 230
History of dogma. Tr. from the 3d German ed., by Neil Buchanan. New York, Dover [1961] 4 v. various p. (T904, T905, T906, T907) 2.50 pap., ea.,
1. Theology, Doctrinal—Hist. I. Title.

MARNEY, Carlyle, 1916- 230
The coming faith. Nashville, Abingdon Press [1970] 176 p. 21 cm. [BR121.2.M34] 72-112886 4.00
1. Christianity—20th century. I. Title.

MARROU, Henri Irenee. 230
Time and timeliness, by H. I. Marrou. Translated by Violet Nevile. New York, Sheed and Ward [1969] vi, 178 p. 21 cm. Translation of Theologie de l'histoire. Bibliographical footnotes. [BR115.H5M2483] 78-82601 5.00
1. History (Theology) I. Title.

MARROW, Stanley B. 230
The Christ in Jesus, by Stanley B. Marrow. New York, Paulist Press [1968] vii, 100 p. 18 cm. (Deus books) [BS2525.M3] 68-16666
1. Bible. N.T.—Study—Outlines, syllabi, etc. I. Title.

MARSTON, George W 230
The voice of authority. [Nutley, N.J.,] Presbyterian and Reformed Pub. Co., 1960. 110p. 21cm. Includes bibliography. [BT88.M35] 60-8196
1. Authority (Religion) I. Title.

MARTIN, Walter Ralston, 1928- 230
Essential Christianity; a handbook of basic Christian doctrines. Grand Rapids, Zondervan Pub. House [1962] 114p. 21cm. [BT77.M28] 62-51869
1. Theology, Doctrinal— Popular works. I. Title.

MASCALL, Eric Lionel, 1905- 230
The secularization of Christianity; an analysis and a critique [by] E. L. Mascall. New York, Holt [1966, c.1965] xiii, 286p. 23cm. Bibl. [BT28.M28 1966] 66-15656 6.00
1. Robinson, John Arthur Thomas, Bp., 1919- Honest to God. 2. Van Buren, Paul Matthew, 1924- The secular meaning of the Gospel. 3. Christianity — 20th cent. 4. Death of God theology. I. Title.

MASCALL, Eric Lionel, 1905- 230
Words and images; a study in theological discourse. New York, Ronald Press Co. [1957] 132p. 21cm. Includes bibliography. [BT40.M38 1957] 57-4542
1. Christianity—Philosophy. 2. Knowledge, Theory of (Religion) I. Title.

MATHEWS, Shailer, 1863-1941. 230
The faith of modernism. New York, AMS Press [1969] vii, 182 p. 23 cm. Reprint of the 1924 ed. [BT82.M3 1969] 71-108117
1. Modernism. I. Title.

MAURICE, Frederick Denison, 1805-1872. 230
What is revelation? : A series of sermons on the Epiphany, to which are added letters to a student of theology on the Bampton lectures of Mr. Mansel / by Frederick Denison Maurice. New York : AMS Press, [1975] p. cm. Reprint of the 1859 ed. published by Macmillan, Cambridge. [BL51.M33M3 1975] 76-173061 ISBN 0-404-04276-7 : 37.50
1. Mansel, Henry Longueville, 1820-1871. The limits of religious thought. 2. Religion—Philosophy. 3. Rationalism. 4. Revelation. I. Title.

MELLERT, Robert B. 230
What is process theology? / By Robert B. Mellert. New York : Paulist Press, [1975] 141 p. ; 18 cm. (Deus books) Includes bibliographical references. [BT83.6.M44] 74-28933 ISBN 0-8091-1867-X pbk. : 1.95
1. Whitehead, Alfred North, 1861-1947. 2. Process theology. I. Title.

MELLONE, Sydney Herbert, 1869- 230
Leaders of early Christian thought. Boston, Beacon Press [1955] 243p. 23cm. [BT23] 55-14644
1. Theology, Doctrinal—Hist.—Early church. I. Title.

MICHALSON, Carl. 230
The witness of radical faith / by Carl Michalson. Nashville : Tidings, [1974] 108 p. ; 19 cm. [BR85.M479] 74-80895 pbk. : 1.75
1. Theology—Addresses, essays, lectures. I. Title.

MICHALSON, Carl. 230
Worldly theology; the hermeneutical focus of an historical faith. New York, Scribner [1967] xii, 243 p. 24 cm. Bibliographical references included in "Notes" (p. 227-238) [BT15.M48] 67-21348
1. Theology, Doctrinal—Addresses, essays, lectures. I. Title.

*MICHELMORE, Peter. 230
Back to Jesus. Greenwich, Conn., Fawcett Publications [1973] 192 p., 18 cm. [BT771] 0.95 (pbk.)
1. Faith. 2. Experience (Religion). I. Title.

MICKLEM, Nathaniel, 1888- 230
Faith and reason. London, G. Duckworth[dist. Naperville, Ill., Alec R. Allenson, 1963] 196p. 19cm. Bibl. 64-2073 3.50
1. Faith and reason. 2. Theology, Doctrinal—Popular works. I. Title.

MICKS, Marianne H. 230
Introduction to theology. New York, Seabury [1967,c.1964] xiv, 204p. 21cm. (SP40) [BT77.M524] 64-19622 2.25 pap.,
1. Theology. I. Title.

MIEGGE, Giovanni. 230
Christian affirmations in a secular age. Translated by Stephen Neill. New York, Oxford University Press, 1958. 170p. 23cm. Translation of Per una fede. [BR121.M583 1958] 58-59950
1. Christianity—Essence, genius, nature. 2. Theology, Doctrinal. I. Title.

MILFORD, Theodore Richard. 230
Foolishness to the Greeks. Greenwich, Conn., Seabury Press [1953] 112p. 23cm. [BT15.M5] 54-2078
1. Theology, Doctrinal—Addresses, essays, lectures. I. Title.

MILLER, Allen O 230
Invitation to theology; resources for Christian nurture and discipline. Philadelphia, Christian Education Press [1958] 278p. 21cm. Includes bibliography. [BT77.M53] 58-11704
1. Theology, Doctrinal—Popular works. 2. Religious education. I. Title.

MILTON, John Peterson, 1897- 230
Our Hebrew-Christian heritage, by John P. Milton. [1st ed.] Madison, Wisc., Straus Print. & Pub. Co. [1973] 156 p. 21 cm. Bibliography: p. 155-156. [BT60.M52] 73-85714
1. Christianity—Essence, genius, nature. I. Title.

MIRANDA, Jose Porfirio. 230
Being and the Messiah : the message of St. John / Jose Porfirio Miranda ; translated by John Eagleson. Maryknoll, N.Y. : Orbis Books, c1977. ix, 245 p. ; 22 cm. Translation of El ser y el Mesias. Includes indexes. Bibliography: p. 227-233. [BS2601.M5413] 77-5388 ISBN 0-88344-027-X : 8.95 ISBN 0-88344-028-8 pbk. : 4.95
1. Bible. N.T. Johannine literature—Criticism, interpretation, etc. 2. Existentialism. 3. Communism. I. Title.

MITCHELL, W A A 230
Getting back to God; or, The truth about religion, by Alexander Angell [pseud] Boston, Christopher Pub. House [1951] 200 p. 21 cm. [BR126.M54] 51-8946
1. Christianity — Miscellanea. I. Title.

MOLTMANN, Jurgen. 230
The experiment hope / Jurgen Moltmann ; edited, translated, with a foreword by M. Douglas Meeks. Philadelphia : Fortress Press, [1975] xvii, 190 p. ; 24 cm. Translation of Das Experiment Hoffnung. Includes bibliographical references. [BV4638.M5513] 74-26339 ISBN 0-8006-0407-5 : 8.95
1. Hope—Addresses, essays, lectures. 2. Theology—Addresses, essays, lectures. I. Title.

MOLTMANN, Jurgen. 230
Religion, revolution, and the future. Translated by M. Douglas Meeks. New York, Scribner [1969] xvii, 220 p. 24 cm. Bibliographical footnotes. [BT15.M62] 69-17053 5.95
1. Theology—Addresses, essays, lectures. I. Title.

MONSMA, Peter Halman, 1902- 230
The message of Christianity. New York, Bookman Associates [1954] 124p. 23cm. [BR121.M7175] 54-11994
1. Christianity—Essence, genius, nature. I. Title.

MOON, Sun Myung. 230
Christianity in crisis: new hope. [Washington] HSA-UWC, 1974. ix, 123 p. illus. 19 cm. Translation of 3 speeches from the author's 1973 tour delivered Oct. 20, 21, and 28, 1973. Contents.Contents.—God's hope for man.—God's hope for America.—The future of Christianity. [BR85.M617] 74-76156
1. Theology—Addresses, essays, lectures. I. Title.

MOON, Sun Myung. 230
The new future of Christianity / Sun Myung Moon. Washington : Unification Church International, 1974. vii, 144 p., [1] fold. leaf of plates : ill. ; 20 cm. Translation of 2 speeches delivered at the Waldorf Astoria, and Madison Square Garden, New York on Sept. 17 and 18, 1974 respectively. Contents.Contents.—God's new way of life.—The new future of Christianity. [BX9750.S4M66] 74-24931
1. Segye Kidokkyo T'ongil Sillyong Hyophoe—Sermons. 2. Sermons, Korean—Translations into English. 3. Sermons, English—Translations from Korean. I. Title.

MOONEY, Christopher F., 1925- comp. 230
The presence and absence of God. Edited by Christopher F. Mooney. New York, Fordham University Press [1969] xi, 178 p. 23 cm. (The Cardinal Bea lectures) "The lectures ... were delivered between 1966 and 1968 under the sponsorship of Fordham University's Cardinal Bea Institute." Includes bibliographies. [BT771.2.M596] 68-8748 6.00
1. Faith—Addresses, essays, lectures. 2. Belief and doubt—Addresses, essays, lectures. 3. God—Addresses, essays, lectures. I. Cardinal Bea Institute. II. Title. III. Series.

MORGAN, Claude M 230
Seeking the truth. [1st ed.] New York, Pageant Press [1955] 104 p. 21cm. [BR121.M76] 55-12325
1. Christianity—20th cent. I. Title.

MORGAN, Richard 230
Bible must be retaught. Nashville, Printed by the Parthenon Pr. [1967] 70p. 23cm. [BS543.M58] 67-18976 2.00 pap.,
1. Bible—Theology. I. Title.

MOSLEY, Nicholas, 1923- 230
Experience and religion; a lay essay in theology. Philadelphia, United Church Pr. [1967,c.1965] 156p. 20cm. [BT77.M87 1967] 67-22945 1.95 pap.,
1. Theology, Doctrinal — Popular works. 2. Experience (Religion) I. Title.

MOUBARAC, Youakim. 230
Bible, liturgy, and dogma, by Yves Moubarac and P. Lucien. Notre Dame, Ind., Fides Publishers [1966, c1965] 160 p. 21 cm. (Saint Severin series for adult Christians, v. 2) Fides paperback textbooks, PBT-18. Translation of Dogme, Bible, et liturgie. [BS543.M613] 66-3235
1. Bible — Theology. 2. Church year. I. Lucien P., joint author. II. Title.

MOW, Anna B. 230
Find your own faith / Anna B. Mow. Grand Rapids : Zondervan Pub. House, c1977. 192 p. ; 18 cm. [BS571.M68] 77-23821 ISBN 0-310-29652-8 pbk. : 1.95
1. Bible—Study. I. Title.

MURPHY, John L 1924- 230
The notion of tradition in John Driedo. Dissertatio ad lauream in Facultate Theologica Pontificiae Universitatis Gregorianae. Milwaukee, 1959. 321p. 23cm. At head of title: Pontificia Universitas Gregoriana. Includes bibliography. [BT90.M8] 59-9908
1. Dridoens, Jean, 1480?-1535. 2. Tradition (Theology) I. Title.

MURPHY, John L 1924- 230
With the eyes of faith [by] John L. Murphy. Milwaukee, Bruce Pub. Co. [c1966] xxiii, 333 p. 22 cm. (Impact books) Bibliographical references included in "Notes" (p. 277-315) [BT50.M85] 65-27903
1. Faith and reason. I. Title.

MURPHY, John L., 1924- 230
With the eyes of faith. Milwaukee, Bruce [c.1966]cxxiii, 333p. 22cm. (Impact bks.) Bibl. [BT50.M85] 65-27903 6.75
1. Faith and reason. I. Title.

MURPHY, William B 230
God and His creation, by William B. Murphy [and others] Dubuque [Iowa] Priory Press, 1958. 516p. 24cm. (College texts in theology) At head of title: Theology, a basic synthesis for the college. Includes bibliography. [BT101.M945] 58-9913
1. God. 2. Creation. I. Title.

MURRAY, Irving Russell. 230
A religion of their own; aims and techniques of the liberal church and church school. Boston, Beacon Press [1952] 54p. 21cm. (Beacon reference series) [BR1615.M8] 53-6500
1. Liberalism (Religion) I. Title.

MUYBARAC, Youakim 230
Bible, liturgy, and dogma, by Yves Moubarac, P. Lucien, v.2 [Tr.from French] Notre Dame, Ind., Fides Pub. [1966, c.1965] 160p. 21cm. (Saint Severin ser., for adult Christians, v.2; PBT-18) [BS543.M613] 66-3235 1.75 pap.,
1. Bible — Theology. 2. Church year. I. Lucien P., joint author. II. Title.

NACHANT, Theresa Elsa. 230
The overcomer. Boston, Christopher Pub. House [1951] 276 p. 21 cm. [BR126.N2] 51-1881
1. Christianity — 20th cent. I. Title.

NATIONAL Holiness Association. 230
Projecting our heritage; papers and messages delivered at the centennial convention of the National Holiness Association, Cleveland, Ohio, April 16-19, 1968. Compiled by Myron F. Boyd and Merne A. Harris. Kansas City, Mo., Beacon Hill Press of Kansas City [1969] 157 p. 20 cm. [BT10.N35] 75-79957
1. Theology—Addresses, essays, lectures. 2. Sanctification—Addresses, essays, lectures. I. Boyd, Myron F., comp. II. Harris, Merne A., comp. III. Title.

NAVONE, John J. 230
A theology of failure / by John Navone. New York : Paulist Press, [1974] 129 p. ; 21 cm. Includes bibliographical references. [BT730.5.N38] 74-82720 ISBN 0-8091-1839-4 pbk. : 3.50 3.50
1. Failure (Christian theology) I. Title.

*NEF, E. 230
God and man. New York, Vantage [1967] 195p. 21cm. 3.95 bds.,
I. Title.

NESBITT, Ralph Beryl. 230
A Protestant believes. New York, 1962. 126p. 23cm. [BX4811.N4] 62-21475
1. Protestant churches— Doctrinal and controversial works. I. Title.

NEW heaven? New earth? : 230
an encounter with Pentecostalism / [by] Simon Tugwell ... [et al.] ; preface by Walter Hollenweger. London : Darton, Longman and Todd, 1976. 206 p. ; 22 cm. Includes bibliographical references. [BR1644.N48] 77-353539 ISBN 0-232-51350-3 : £2.25
1. Pentecostalism—Addresses, essays, lectures. I. Tugwell, Simon.

*NEWMAN, Paul S., comp. 230
In God we trust; America's heritage of faith. compiled by Paul S. Newman. Designed by Herman Zuckerman. Norwalk, Conn., Published by the C. R. Gibson Company, [1974] 89 p. col. illus. 21 cm. Bibliography: p. 89 [BT77] 73-88091 ISBN 0-8378-1754-4 3.95
1. Theology 2. United States—Social life and customs. I. Title.

NICHOL, Charles Ready, 1876- 230
The possibility of apostasy. Clifton, Tex., Nichol Pub. Co., 1951. 104 p. illus. 23 cm. [BT783.N5] 52-25577
1. Apostasy. I. Title.

NICHOLS, James Hastings, 1915- ed. 230
The Mercersburg theology. New York, Oxford University Press, 1966. viii, 384 p. 24 cm. (A Library of Protestant thought) Consists chiefly of works and articles by John W. Nevin and Phillip Schaff. Bibliography: p. 372-375. [BX9571.N5] 66-24435
1. Mercersburg theology. I. Nevin, John Williamson, 1803-1886. II. Schaff, Phillip, 1819-1893. III. Title. IV. Series.

NICHOLS, James Hastings, 1915- ed. 230
The Mercersburg theology. New York, Oxford University Press, 1966. viii, 384 p. 24 cm. (A Library of Protestant thought) Consists chiefly of works and articles by John W. Nevin and Philip Schaff. Bibliography: p. 372-375. [BX9571.N5] 66-24435
1. Mercersburg theology. I. Nevin, John Williamson, 1803-1886. II. Schaff, Philip, 1819-1893. III. Title. IV. Series.

NO famine in the land : 230
studies in honor of John L. McKenzie / edited by James W. Flanagan, Anita Weisbrod Robinson. Missoula, Mont. : Published by Scholars Press for the Institute for Antiquity and Christianity—Claremont, c1975. xii, 349 p. : ill. ; 24 cm. Contents.Contents.—Munson, T. N. Biographical sketch of John L. McKenzie.—Robinson, A. W. Letters from life.—Freedman, D. N. The Aaronic benediction (numbers 6:24-26).—Bellefontaine, E. The curses of Deuteronomy 27.—Mendenhall, G. E. Samuel's "broken rib".—Blenkinsopp, J. The quest of the historical Saul.—Flanagan, J. W. Judah in all Israel.—Murphy, R. E. Wisdom and Yahwism.—Vawter, B. Prophecy and the redactional question.—Wicker, K. O. First century marriage ethics.—Fitzmyer, J. A. Reconciliation in Pauline theology.—Brown, R. E. Luke's method in the Annunciation narratives of chapter one.—Crossan, J. D. Jesus and pacifism.—Funk, R. W. The significance of discourse structure for the study of the New Testament.—Sloyan, G. S. Postbiblical development of the Petrine Ministry.—Cooke, B. The "war-myth" in 2nd century Christian teaching.—Burkhart, J. E. Authority, candor, and ecumenism.—Baum, G. An ecclesiological principle.—Cahill, P. J. Myth and meaning.—Robinson, J. M. The internal word in history. "A bibliography of the books, articles, and reviews of John L. McKenzie, by Donald H. Wimmer": p. 301-322. [BR50.N55] 75-33108 ISBN 0-89130-051-1 : 7.00
1. McKenzie, John L. 2. McKenzie, John L.—Bibliography. 3. Theology—Addresses, essays, lectures. I. McKenzie, John L. II. Flanagan, James W. III. Robinson, Anita Weisbrod. IV. Institute for Antiquity and Christianity.

NOGAR, Raymond J. 230
The Lord of the absurd [by] Raymond J. Nogar. [New York] Herder & Herder [1966] 157p. 21cm. [BT80.N6] 66-22608 3.95
1. Theology — Addresses, essays, lectures. I. Title.

NORDEN, Rudolph F. 230
The Gospel: love it & live it [by] Rudolph F. Norden. St. Louis, Concordia Pub. House [1973] 79 p. 19 cm. [BT77.N67 1973] 72-94850 ISBN 0-570-03146-X
1. Theology, Doctrinal—Popular works. I. Title.

NORQUIST, N Leroy. 230
The Bible and our Christian beliefs. Rock Island, Ill., Augustana Press [c1962] ix, 206 p. 20 cm. [BS543.N6] 63-11991
1. Bible — Theology. 2. Theology, Doctrinal — Popular works. I. Title.

NOTRE Dame Colloquium, 230
University of Notre Dame, 1967.
The spirit and power of Christian secularity Albert Schlitzer, editor. Contributors: Bernard Cooke [and others] Notre Dame [Ind.] University of Notre Dame Press [1969] xi, 216 p. 24 cm. Bibliographical footnotes. [BT83.7.N6 1967] 75-75154 10.00
1. Secularization (Theology)—Addresses, essays, lectures. 2. Secularism—Addresses, essays, lectures. I. Schlitzer, Albert L., 1902- ed. II. Cooke, Bernard J. III. Title.

NOVAK, Michael. 230
A time to build; [essays] New York, Macmillan [1967] xii, 493 p. 21 cm. Includes bibliographical references. [BT15.N6] 67-23484
1. Theology, Doctrinal—Addresses, essays, lectures. I. Title.

OGDEN, Schubert Miles, 1928- 230
The reality of God, and other essays, by Schubert M. Ogden. [1st ed.] New York, Harper [1966] xii, 237p. 22cm. Bibl. [BT80.04] 66-20783 6.00
1. Theology, Doctrinal — Addresses, essays, lectures. I. Title.

OGLETREE, Thomas W 230
Christian faith and history, a critical comparison of Ernst Troeltsch and Karl Barth [by] Thomas W. Ogletree. New York, Abingdon Press [1965] 236 p. 23 cm. Bibliographical footnotes. [BX4827.T703] 65-20364
1. Troeltsch, Ernst, 1865-1923. 2. Barth, Karl, 1886- 3. History — Philosophy. I. Title.

OGLETREE, Thomas W. 230
Christian faith and history; a critical comparison of Ernst Troeltsch and Karl Barth. Nashville, Abingdon [c.1965] 236p. 23cm. Bibl. [BX4827.T703] 65-20364 4.00
1. Troeltsch, Ernst, 1865-1923. 2. Barth, Karl, 1886- 3. History—Philosophy. I. Title.

OMAN, John Wood, 1860-1939. 230
Grace and personality. [New York] Association [1961, c.1917] 255p. (Giant reflection bks., 701) 61-14175 1.50 pap.,
1. Theology, Doctrinal. I. Title.

OMMEN, Thomas B. 230
The hermeneutic of dogma / by Thomas B. Ommen. Missoula, Mont. : Published by Scholars Press for the American Academy of Religion, 1976c1975 xii, 250 p. ; 22 cm. (Dissertation series - American Academy of Religion ; no. 11) Originally presented as the author's thesis, Marquette University, 1973. Bibliography: p. 243-250. [BT22.O49 1975] 75-29493 ISBN 0-89130-039-2 pbk. : 4.50
1. Theology—Methodology. 2. Hermeneutics. 3. Dogma. I. Title. II. Series: American Academy of Religion. Dissertation series — American Academy of Religion ; no. 11.

ORIGENES. 230
On first principles; being Koetschau's text of the De principiis, translated into English, together with an introd. and notes by G. W. Butterworth. Introd. to the Torchbook ed. by Henri De Lubac. [1st ed.] New York, Harper & Row [1966] lxiv, 342 p. 21 cm. (Harper torchbooks. The Cathedral library, TB 311N) Bibliography: p. [lix]-lxi. Bibliographical footnotes. [BR65.O568E5 1966] 66-3604
I. Koetschau, Paul, 1857- II. Butterworth, George William, 1879- tr. III. Title.

ORIGENES. 230
On first principles; being Koetschav's text of the De Principiis, translated into English, together with an introduction and notes by G. W. Butterworth. Introd. to the Torchbook edition by Henri de Lubac. Gloucester, Mass., Peter Smith, 1973 [c1966] lxiv, 342 p. 21 cm. Reprint of the Cathedral Library edition, Harper Torchbooks, TB 311 N. Bibliography: p. [lix]-lxi. Bibliographical footnotes. [BR65.O568E5] ISBN 0-8446-2685-6 5.75
1. Koetschav, Paul, 1857- I. Butterworth, George William, 1879- tr. II. Title.
L.C. card no. for the Torchbook edition: 66-3604.

ORR, James Edwin, 1912- 230
Faith that makes sense. Valley Forge [Pa.] Judson [1962, c.1960] 109p. 19cm. 62-14809 1.45 pap.,
1. Theology, Doctrinal—Popular works. I. Title.

ORTIZ, Juan Carlos, 1934- 230
Disciple / by Juan Carlos Ortiz. Carol Stream, Ill. : Creation House, [1975] 158 p. ; 23 cm. [BV4501.2.O725] 74-29650 ISBN 0-88419-101-X : 5.95
1. Christian life—1960- I. Title.

OSGOOD, Phillips Endecott, 230
1882-
Religion without magic. Boston, Beacon Press [1954] 204p. 22cm. [BR1615.O77] 54-8427
1. Liberalism (Religion) I. Title.

OUR common history as 230
Christians : essays in honor of Albert C. Outler / edited by John Deschner, Leroy T. Howe, and Klaus Penzel. New York : Oxford University Press, 1975. xxi, 298 p. ; 22 cm. [BR50.O7] 74-83988 ISBN 0-19-501865-6 : 9.50
1. Outler, Albert Cook, 1908- 2. Outler, Albert Cook, 1908- —Bibliography. 3. Theology—Addresses, essays, lectures. I. Deschner, John. II. Howe, Leroy T., 1936- III. Penzel, Klaus.
Contents omitted

OXNAM, Garfield Bromley, 230
Bp., 1891-
A testament of faith. [1st ed.] Boston, Little, Brown [1958] 176 p. 20 cm. [BR124.O9] 58-6027
1. Christianity—Essence, genius, nature. I. Title.

PACKER, James Innell. 230
"Fundamentalism" and the word of God; some evangelical principles. Grand Rapids, Eerdmans Pub. Co. [1958] 191 p. 18 cm. Includes bibliography. [BT78.P15] 58-13512
1. Fundamentalism. I. Title.

PAGE, Kirby, 1890-1957. 230
Kirby Page and the social gospel : an anthology / edited, with an introd., by Charles Chatfield and Charles DeBenedetti. New York : Garland Pub., 1976. p. cm. (The Garland library of war and peace) Bibliography: p. [BR85.P23 1976] 70-147695 ISBN 0-8240-0451-5 lib.bdg. : 25.00
1. Page, Kirby, 1890-1957. 2. Page, Kirby, 1890-1957—Bibliography. 3. Theology—Addresses, essays, lectures. 4. Church and social problems—Addresses, essays, lectures. I. Title. II. Series.

PALMER, Bennett William. 230
World democracy [by] Bin Dir Woor [pseud. 1st ed.] New York, Greenwich Book Publishers [1961] 92p. 21cm. [BX9998.P3] 61-11625
I. Title.

PALMER, E H 230
This thing called religion. [1st ed.] New York, Exposition Press [1952] 132 p. 23 cm. Includes bibliography. [BL48.P26] 52-9241
1. Religion. I. Title.

PANA Creation, inc. 230
Panorama : how God sees life on Earth : a true story / written by Pana Creation. Woodland Hills, Calif. : Pana Creation, [1975] v, 138 p. ; 20 cm. "The vice-president of Pana is Melvin D. Hasman ... who wrote the book as it was revealed to him." "Discussion guide for Panorama": p. [41]-127. [BT175.P25 1975] 74-33972 ISBN 0-915300-01-X pbk. : 4.95
1. God. 2. Devil. 3. Theology—Miscellanea. I. Hasman, Melvin D. II. Title.

PANNENBERG, Wolfhart, 1928- 230
Spirit, faith, and church, by Wolfhart Pannenberg, Avery Dulles [and] Carl E. Braaten. Philadelphia, Westminster Press [1970] 123 p. 21 cm. (The Walter and Mary Tuohy Chair lectures, 1969) Includes bibliographical references. [BV603.P3] 78-93000 4.50
1. Church—Addresses, essays, lectures. 2. Theology, Doctrinal—Addresses, essays, lectures. I. Braaten, Carl E., 1929- II. Dulles, Avery Robert, 1918- III. Title. IV. Series.

PASCHALL, Henry Franklin. 230
The Gospel for an exploding world [by] H. Franklin Paschall. Nashville, Broadman Press [1967] 128 p. 21 cm. Bibliographical footnotes. [BX6331.2.P3] 68-13360
1. Baptists—Doctrinal and controversial works. I. Title.

PASCHALL, Henry Franklin. 230
The Gospel for an exploding world [by] H. Franklin Paschall. Nashville, Broadman Press [1967] 128 p. 21 cm. Bibliographical footnotes. [BX6331.2.P3] 68-13360
1. Baptists—Doctrinal and controversial works. I. Title.

PATTERSON, Lloyd George, 230
1929-
God and history in early Christian thought [by] L. G. Patterson. New York, Seabury Press [1967] viii, 181 p. 22 cm. ([Studies in patristic thought, v. 2]) Companion vol. to God and world in early Christian theology, by R. A. Norris. Bibliography: p. [167]-181. [BR115.H5P3] 67-10847
1. History (Theology)—History of doctrines. I. Title.

PEARSON, Roy Messer, 1914- 230
The believer's unbelief; a layman's guide through Christian doubts. New York, Nelson [c.1963] 175p. 22cm. Bibl. 63-10926 3.95
1. Theology, Doctrinal—Popular works. I. Title.

PEARSON, Roy Messer, 1914- 230
The beliver's unbelief; a layman's guide through Christian doubts. New York, T. Nelson [1963] 175 p. 22 cm. [BT77.P37] 63-10926
1. Theology, Doctrinal—Popular works. I. Title.

*PECK, Mabel B. 230
You are that. New York, Vantage [c.1965] 148p. 21cm. 3.50 bds.,
I. Title.

PELIKAN, Jaroslav, 1923- 230
Fools for Christ; essays on the true, the good, and the beautiful. Philadelphia, Muhlenberg Press [1955] 172p. 20cm. [BT45.P4] 55-7766
1. Religion. 2. Worth. 3. Holiness. 4. Truth. 5. Good and evil. 6. Aesthetics. I. Title.
Contents omitted.

PELIKAN, Jaroslav Jan, 1923- 230
Fools for Christ; essays on the true, the good, and the beautiful. Philadelphia, Muhlenberg Press [1955] 172 p. 20 cm. [BT45.P4] 55-7766
1. Religion. 2. Worth. 3. Holiness. 4. Truth 5. Good and evil. 6. Aesthetics. I. Title.
Contents Omitted

PELIKAN, Jaroslav Jan, 1923- 230
Historical theology: continuity and change in Christian doctrine [by] Jaroslav Pelikan. New York, Corpus [1971] xxiii, 228 p. 24 cm. (Theological resources) Bibliography: p. 219-223. [BT21.2.P43 1971b] 77-93572 ISBN 0-664-20909-2 9.95
1. Theology, Doctrinal—History. I. Title.

PENTECOST, J Dwight. 230
Things which become sound doctrine [by] J. Dwight Pentecost. Westwood, N. J., F. H. Revell Co. [1965] 159 p. 21 cm. [BV4501.2.P4] 65-10558
1. Christian life. 2. Theology, Doctrinal—Popular works. I. Title.

PENTECOST, J. Dwight 230
Things which become sound doctrine. Westwood, N.J., Revell [c.1965] 159p. 21cm. [BV4501.2.P4] 65-10558 3.50 bds.,
1. Christian life. 2. Theology, Doctrinal—Popular works. I. Title.

THE people of the way; 230
from a saint to the saints. Swengel, Pa., Bible Truth Depot, 1961. 278p. 20cm. [BX9998.P45] 61-11026

PIEPER, Franz August Otto, 230
1852-1931.
Christian dogmatics. Saint Louis, Concordia Pub. House, 1950- v. 24 cm. Bibliographical footnotes. [BT75.P53] 50-8650
1. Theology, Doctrinal. 2. Lutheran Church — Doctrinal and controversial works. I. Title.

PIEPER, Franz August Otto, 230
1852-1931.
Christian dogmatics. Saint Louis, Concordia Pub. House, 1950-57. 4v. 24cm. Vol. 4: Index. Bibliographical footnotes. [BT75.P53] 50-8650
1. Theology. Doctrinal. 2. Lutheran Church—Doctrinal and controversial works. I. Title.

PIKE, James Albert, Bp., 230
1913-
What is this treasure? New York, Harper [c.1966] 90p. 22cm. [BT77.P47] 66-11484 3.00 bds.,
1. Theology, Doctrinal — Popular works. I. Title.

PIKE, James Albert, Bp., 230
1913-1969.
What is this treasure? [By] James A. Pike. [1st ed.] New York, Harper & Row [1966] 90 p. 22 cm. [BT77.P47] 66-11484
1. Theology, Doctrinal—Popular works. I. Title.

PIKE, Kenneth Lee, 1912- 230
With heart and mind; a personal synthesis of scholarship and devotion. Grand Rapids, Mich., Eerdmans [c.1962] 140p. illus. 21cm. 62-21374 1.75 pap.,
1. Modernist-fundamentalist controversy. 2. Evangelicanism. I. Title.

PITCAIRN, Theodore. 230
My Lord and my God; essays on modern religion, the Bible, and Emanuel Swedenborg. [1st ed.] New York, Exposition Press [1967] ix, 298 p. illus. (part col.), col. ports. 21 cm. [BX8721.2.P5] 67-9668
1. Theology, Doctrinal—Popular works. 2. New Jerusalem Church—Doctrinal and controversial works. I. Title.

PITCAIRN, Theodore. 230
My Lord and my God; essays on modern religion, the Bible, and Emanuel Swedenborg. [1st ed.] New York, Exposition Press [1967] ix, 298 p. illus. (part col.), col. ports. 21 cm. [BX8721.2.P5] 67-9668
1. New Jerusalem Church—Doctrinal and controversial works. 2. Theology, Doctrinal—Popular works. I. Title.

PITTENGER, William Norman, 230
1905-
Christ in the haunted wood; the Christian foundation for the good life. Greenwich, Conn., Seabury Press, 1953. 180p. 22cm. [BR121.P556] 53-12960
1. Christianity— Essence, genius, nature. 2. Christian life. I. Title.

PITTENGER, William Norman, 230
1905-
Christian affirmations. New York, Morehouse-Gorham Co., 1954. 159p. 21cm. [BT15.P55] 55-15152
1. Theology, Doctrinal—Addresses, essays, lectures. 2. Worship. I. Title.

PITTENGER, William Norman, 230
1905-
Christian faith and the question of history [by] Norman Pittenger. Philadelphia, Fortress Press [1973] 151 p. 19 cm. [BK115.H5P57] 73-79353 ISBN 0-8006-1057-1 3.75
1. History (Theology) I. Title.

PITTENGER, William Norman, 230
1905-
God's way with men; a study of the relationship between God and man in providence, "miracle," and prayer, by Norman Pittenger. Valley Forge [Pa.] Judson Press [1969] 184 p. 22 cm. [BT135.P54 1969] 71-86853 4.95
1. Providence and government of God. 2. Miracles. 3. Prayer. I. Title.

PITTENGER, William Norman, 230
1905-
The historic faith and a changing world. New York, Oxford University Press, 1950. viii, 181 p. 21 cm. [BR481.P5] 50-8289
1. Christianity — 20th cent. I. Title.

PITTENGER, William Norman, 230
1905-
Theology and reality; essays in restatement. Greenwich, Conn., Seabury Press, 1955. 235p. 22cm. [BT15.P554] 55-6356
1. Theology. Doctrinal—Addresses, essays, lectures. I. Title.

PITTENGER, William Norman, 230
1905-
Unbounded love : God and man in process, with study guide / by Norman Pittenger. New York : Seabury Press, c1976. x, 115 p. ; 21 cm. (The First Stephen Fielding Bayne memorial lectures) "A Crossroad book." [BT77.P56] 76-2083 ISBN 0-8164-2119-6 pbk. : 3.95
1. Theology, Doctrinal—Popular works—Addresses, essays, lectures. 2. Process theology—Addresses, essays, lectures. I. Title. II. Series: Stephen Fielding Bayne memorial lectures ; 1st.

POWELL, Ivor 230
This I believe; the essential truths of Christianity. Grand Rapids, Mich., Zondervan Pub. House [1961] 222p. 61-1490 2.50
1. Theology, Doctrinal—Popular works. I. Title.

*POWELL, John Joseph, 1925- 230
A reason to live! A reason to die! [by] John Powell, S. J. Niles, Ill., Argus Communications [1972] 207 p. illus. (some col.) 23 cm. [BT77] 2.95
1. Theology, Doctrinal—Popular works. I. Title.

POWER, John, 1927- 230
Look toward the East; some aspects of Old Testament theology. Dublin, Gill and

Macmillan [1969] 167 p. 21 cm. [BS1192.5.P64] 77-15877 ISBN 0-7171-0238-6 36/-
1. Bible. O.T.—Theology. I. Title.

POWYS, Llewelyn, 1884-1939. 230
The pathetic fallacy : a study of Christianity / by Llewelyn Powys. Folcroft, Pa. : Folcroft Library Editions, 1977. viii, 115 p. ; 24 cm. Reprint of the 1930 ed. published by Watts, London, which was issued as no. 22 of the Thinker's library. [BL2775.2.P66 1977] 77-828 ISBN 0-8414-6797-8 lib. bdg. : 12.50
1. Christianity—Controversial literature. I. Title. II. Series: The Thinker's library ; no. 22.

PRENTER, Regin, 1907- 230
The church's faith; a primer of Christian beliefs. Translated by Theodor I. Jensen. Philadelphia, Fortress Press [1968] xxxii, 224 p. 18 cm. (A Fortress paperback original) Translation of Kirkens tro: en kristenlaere for laegfolk. [BT77.K4313] 68-17708 2.75
1. Theology, Doctrinal—Popular works. I. Title.

PRENTER, Regin, 1907- 230
Creation and redemption. Tr. by Theodor I. Jensen. Philadelphia, Fortress [1967] xi, 596p. 23cm. Bibl. [BT75.2.P713] 66-17342 9.00
1. Theology, Doctrinal. I. Title.

PRENTER, Regin, 1907- 230
Creation and redemption. Translated by Theodor I. Jensen. Philadelphia, Fortress Press [1967] xi, 596 p. 23 cm. Bibliographical footnotes. [BT75.2.P713] 66-17342
1. Theology. Doctrinal. I. Title.

*PRIME, Derek 230
Tell me about the Holy Spirit, about the church. Chicago, Moody [1967,c.1965] 64p. illus. 19cm. (Moody arrows: devotional, no. 19) .50 pap.,
1. Christianity—Study and teaching—Juvenile literature. I. Title.

PROPHET, Mark. 230
My soul doth magnify the Lord! Revelations of Mary the mother of Jesus to the messengers Mark and Elizabeth Prophet. Sons and Daughters of Dominion ed. Colorado Springs [Colo.] Summit Lighthouse [1974- v. col. illus. 23 cm. (Their The golden word of Mary series, book 1-) [BF1311.M42P76] 73-83759
1. Mary, Virgin—Miscellanea. 2. Spirit writings. I. Prophet, Elizabeth, joint author. II. Title.

QUESNELL, Quentin. 230
AAR Seminar in Dialectic / Quentin Quesnell, William P. Loewe. [s.l. : s.n.], 1976. vi, 54 p. ; 22 cm. Cover title. Includes Two theologians of the cross, by W. P. Loewe. Includes bibliographical references and indexes. [BT78.Q47] 77-356495
1. Barth, Karl, 1886-1968—Congresses. 2. Moltmann, Jurgen—Congresses. 3. Dialectical theology—Congresses. I. American Academy of Religion. II. Loewe, William P. Two theologians of the cross. 1976. III. Title.

RAHNER, Hugo, 1900- 230
A theology of proclamation. Tr. by Richard Dimmler [others] Adapted by Joseph Halpin. [New York] Herder & Herder [1968] 216p. 22cm. Tr. of Eine Theologie der Verkundigung. Bibl. [BT78.R2813] 67-29677 5.95
1. Theology, Doctrinal. 2. Communication (Theology) 3. Preaching. I. Halpin, Joseph. II. Title.

RAHNER, Karl, 1904- 230
Kerygma and dogma [by] Karl Rahner and Karl Lehmann. [New York] Herder and Herder [1969] 105 p. 22 cm. (Mysterium salutis) (Series: Feiner, Johannes. Mysterium salutis. English) Translation of Kerygma und Dogma, originally published in 1965 as p. 622-703 of Die Grundlagen heilsgeschichtlicher Dogmatik, edited by H. U. von Balthasar. Bibliographical footnotes. [BT19.R33] 68-55090 4.50
1. Dogma. 2. Kerygma. I. Lehmann, Karl, 1936- joint author. II. Title. III. Series.

RAHNER, Karl, 1904- 230
On heresy [Tr. from German by W. J. O'Hara, New York] Herder & Herder [c.1964] 66p. 22cm. (Quaestiones disputatae, 11) 64-12719 1.75 pap.,
1. Heresy. I. Title.

RAHNER, Karl, 1904- 230
Opportunities for faith; elements of a modern spirituality. Translated by Edward Quinn. New York, Seabury Press [1975, c1974] x, 229 p. 22 cm. Translation of Chancen des Glaubens. "A Crossroad book." Bibliography: p. [227]-229. [BR85.R22913 1975] 74-13973 ISBN 0-8164-1180-8 8.95
1. Theology—Addresses, essays, lectures. I. Title.

RALL, Harris Franklin, 1870- 230
The God of our faith. New York, Abingdon Press [1955] 158p. 21cm. [BT75.R16] 55-10271
1. Theology, Doctrinal. 2. God. I. Title.

RAMM, Bernard, 1916- 230
The pattern of authority. Grand Rapids, Eerdmans, 1957. 117p. 19cm. (A Pathway book) Includes bibliography. [BT88.R24] 57-7388
1. Authority (Religion) I. Title.

RAMSDELL, Edward Thomas. 230
The Christian perspective. New York, Abingdon-Cokesbury Press [1950] 218 p. 22 cm. Bibliographical footnotes. [BT75.R213] 50-6922
1. Theology, Doctrinal. I. Title.

RAMSEY, Arthur Michael 230
Introducing the Christian faith. [New York, Morehouse, 1963, c.1961] 95p. 19cm. (SCM paperback) .75 pap.,
I. Title.

RASHDALL, Hastings, 1858-1924. 230
Ideas and ideals. Selected by H. D. A. Major and F. L. Cross. Freeport, N.Y., Books for Libraries Press [1968] 238 p. 22 cm. (Essay index reprint series) Reprint of 1928 ed. Contents.Contents.—The validity of religious experience.—The rights of the state.—The rights of the church.—The rights of the individual.—The idea of progress.—Modernism.—The life of Newman.—George Tyrrell.—The atonement.—The scholastic theology.—The alleged immanence of God.—The metaphysic of Mr. Bradley. [BR85.R25 1968] 68-16970
1. Theology—Addresses, essays, lectures. I. Major, Henry Dewsbury Alves, 1872- ed. II. Cross, Frank Leslie, 1900- ed. III. Title.

READ, David Haxton Carswell. 230
The Christian faith. New York, Scribner [c1956] 175p. 18cm. [BT77.R36 1956] 56-7129
1. Theology, Doctrinal—Popular works. I. Title.

REARDON, Bernard M. G., comp. 230
Liberal Protestantism, edited and introduced by Bernard M. G. Reardon. Stanford, Calif., Stanford University Press [1968] 244 p. 23 cm. (A Library of modern religious thought) Bibliographical footnotes. [BR1615.R4 1968] 68-17139
1. Liberalism (Religion) 2. Theology—Collections. I. Title. II. Series.

REDWOOD, Hugh, 1883- 230
Residue of days; a confession of faith. New York, Macmillan, 1959 [c1958] 127p. 20cm. [BR1725.R38A3] 59-8172
I. Title.

RELIGIOUS experience and process theology : the pastoral implications of a major modern movement / edited by Harry James Cargas and Bernard Lee. New York : Paulist Press, c1976. xvi, 438 p. ; 23 cm. Includes bibliographies. [BT83.6.R4] 75-46065 ISBN 0-8091-1934-X : 9.95 230
1. Process theology—Addresses, essays, lectures. I. Cargas, Harry J. II. Lee, Bernard.

REST, Karl. 230
Put your faith to work. Philadelphia, Muhlenberg Press [1956] 186p. 20cm. [BT77.R43] 56-9338
1. Theology, Doctrinal—Popular works. 2. Church membership. I. Title.

REST, Karl H A 230
Put your faith to work [by] Karl H. A. Rest. Philadelphia, Muhlenberg Press [1956] xii, 186 p. 20 cm. Bibliographical footnotes. [BT77.R43] 56-9338
1. Theology, Doctrinal — Popular works. 2. Church membership. I. Title.

RICHARD, Robert L 230
Secularization theology [by] Robert L. Richard. [New York] Herder and Herder [1967] x, 190 p. 21 cm. [BT83.7.R5] 67-25882
1. Secularization (Theology) 2. Theology, Doctrinal—Hist.—20th cent. I. Title.

RICHARD, Robert L 230
Secularization theology [by] Robert L. Richard. London, Burns & Oates; [New York] Herder and Herder, 1967 [i. e. 1968,] 192 p. 21 cm. 30/- (SBN 223 29847 5) [BT83.7.R5 1968] 68-90879
1. Secularization (Theology) 2. Theology, Doctrinal—Hist.—20th cent. I. Title.

RICHARD, Robert L. 230
Secularization theology [by] Robert L. Richard. [New York] Herder and Herder [1967] x, 190 p. 21 cm. [BT83.7.R5] 67-25882
1. Secularization (Theology) 2. Theology, Doctrinal—History—20th century. I. Title.

RICHARDSON, Herbert Warren. 230
Toward an American theology [by] Herbert W. Richardson. [1st ed.] New York, Harper & Row [1967] xii, 170 p. 22 cm. Bibliographical footnotes. [BT15.R5] 67-14942
1. Theology, Doctrinal—Addresses, essays, lectures. I. Title.

ROARK, Dallas M., 1931- 230
The Christian faith : an introduction to Christian thought / Dallas M. Roark. Grand Rapids, Mich. : Baker Book House, 1977,c1969. 352p. ; 20 cm. Includes indexes. Bibliographical footnotes. [BT65.R6] ISBN 0-8010-7652-8 pbk. : 4.95
1. Theology, Doctrinal-Introductions. I. Title.
L.C. card no. for 19699 Broadman Press ed.: 69-14369.

ROARK, Dallas M., 1931- 230
The Christian faith [by] Dallas M. Roark. Nashville, Broadman Press [1969] 328 p. 22 cm. Bibliographical footnotes. [BT65.R6] 69-14369 7.50
1. Theology, Doctrinal—Introductions. I. Title.

ROBERTS, Arthur Wayne, 1934- 230
Assumption and faith : you have to begin somewhere / A. Wayne Roberts. Broadview, Ill. : Gibbs Pub. Co., [1974] ix, 97 p. ; 21 cm. Includes bibliographical references. [BT1102.R575] 74-22298 1.95
1. Apologetics—20th century. I. Title.

ROBERTS, James Deotis. 230
A Black political theology, by J. Deotis Roberts. Philadelphia, Westminster Press [1974] 238 p. 19 cm. Includes bibliographical references. [BT75.2.R6] 74-4384 ISBN 0-664-24988-4 3.95 (pbk.).
1. Theology, Doctrinal. 2. Negroes—Religion. I. Title.

ROBINSON, Godfrey Clive. 230
Here is the answer [by] Godfrey C. Robinson [and] Stephen F. Winward. Valley Forge, Judson Press [1970, c1949] 110 p. 20 cm. [BT77.R627] 70-123472 2.50
1. Theology, Doctrinal—Popular works. I. Winward, Stephen F., joint author. II. Title.

ROBINSON, James McConkey, 1924- 230
The beginnings of dialectic theology. Edited by James M. Robinson. Richmond, John Knox Press [1968- v. 24 cm. Vol. 1 contains a translation of p. 37-49, 77-218, and 322-347 of Teil 1 and p. 11-218 of Teil 2, of Anfange der dialektischen Theologie, Munchen, 1962-63, comp. by J. Moltmann. Vol. 1, pt. 1 translated by Keith R. Crim; pt. 2 translated by Louis De Grazia and Keith R. Crim. Includes bibliographical references. [BT83.R63] 67-12941 12.50 (v. 1)
1. Dialectical theology—Collections. 2. Theology—Collections—20th century. I. Moltmann, Jurgen, ed. Anfange der dialektischen Theologie. English. 1968. II. Title.

ROBINSON, John Arthur Thomas, Bp., 1919- 230
But that I can't believe! [By] John A. T. Robinson [New York] New American Library [1967] 170 p. 21 cm. (Perspectives in humanism) Bibliographical footnotes. [BT77.R63 1967] 67-24793
1. Theology, Doctrinal—Popular works. I. Title. II. Series.

ROBINSON, John Arthur Thomas, Bp., 1919- 230
But that I can't believe! [By] John A. T. Robinson. [New York] New American Library [1967] 170 p. 21 cm. (Perspectives in humanism) Bibliographical footnotes. [BT77.R63 1967] 67-24793
1. Theology, Doctrinal—Popular works. I. Title. II. Series.

ROBINSON, John Arthur Thomas, Bp., 1919- 230
Honest to God. Philadelphia, Westminster Press [1963] 143 p. 19 cm. [BT55.R6] 63-13819
1. Christianity — Essence, genius, nature. 2. Apologetics — 20th cent. I. Title.

ROBINSON, John Arthur Thomas, Bp., 1919- 230
Honest to God. Philadelphia, Westminster Press [1963] 143 p. 19 cm. [BT55.R6] 63-13819
1. Christianity—Essence, genius, nature. 2. Apologetics—20th century. I. Title.

ROELLIG, Harold F. 230
The God who cares; a Christian interpretation of time, life, and man. A narrative, by Harold F. Roellig. New York, Branch Press [1971] 176 p. 22 cm. Includes bibliographical references. [BS635.2.R6] 70-160224 4.50
1. Bible—History of Biblical events. 2. Christianity—20th century. 3. Evolution. I. Title.

ROSS, Murray G 230
Religious beliefs of youth; a study and analysis of the structure and function of the religious beliefs of young adults, based on a questionnaire sample of 1,935 youth and intensive interviews with 100 young people. Foreword by Gordon W. Allport. New York, Association Press, 1950. xviii, 251 p. 24 cm. ([Young Men's Christian Associations] National Council. Studies) Bibliography: p. 246-248. [BR516.R66] 50-7756
1. U.S. — Religion. 2. Youth — Religious life. I. Title.

RUETHER, Rosemary Radford. 230
Liberation theology: human hope confronts Christian history and American power. New York, Paulist Press [1972] vi, 194 p. 21 cm. Includes bibliographical references. [BT810.2.R8] 72-92263 ISBN 0-8091-1744-4 3.95
1. Freedom (Theology)—Addresses, essays, lectures. 2. Sociology, Christian—Addresses, essays, lectures. 3. Theology—Addresses, essays, lectures. I. Title.
Contents Omitted.

RUPERT, Hoover. 230
What's good about God? Nashville, Abingdon Press [1970] 173 p. 21 cm. Includes bibliographical references. [BT77.R86] 70-124749 ISBN 6-87448-700- 4.50
1. Theology, Doctrinal—Popular works. I. Title.

RUSSELL, Frederick H. 230
The just war in the middle ages / Frederick H. Russell. Cambridge ; New York : Cambridge University Press, 1975. xi, 332 p. ; 23 cm. (Cambridge studies in life and thought ; 3d ser., v. 8) Includes index. Bibliography: p. 311-320. [BT736.2.R85] 74-25655 ISBN 0-521-20690-1 : 32.50
1. Just war doctrine—History of doctrines. I. Title. II. Series.

RUST, Eric Charles. 230
Nature—garden or desert? An essay in environmental theology, by Eric C. Rust. Waco, Tex., Word Books [1971] 150 p. 23 cm. Includes bibliographical references. [BT695.5.R88] 76-157751 4.95
1. Nature (Theology) I. Title.

RYRIE, Charles Caldwell, 1925- 230
Neo-orthodoxy [Rev. ed.] Chicago, Moody [1966, c.1956] 64p. 18cm. (Christian forum bk.) [BT78.R9] 58-44331 .95 pap.,
1. Neo-orthodoxy. I. Title.

RYRIE, Charles Caldwell, 1925- 230
Neo-orthodoxy: what it is and what it does. Chicago, Moody Press [1956] 62p. 22cm. [BT78.R9] 58-44331
1. Neo-orthodoxy. I. Title.

RYRIE, Charles Caldwell, 1925- 230
A survey of Bible doctrine. Chicago, Moody Press [1972] 191 p. 22 cm. (Christian handbooks) Bibliography: p. 187. [BS543.R9] 72-77958 ISBN 0-8024-8435-2 2.25
1. Bible—Theology. I. Title.

SANDEEN, Ernest Robert, 1931- 230
The origins of fundamentalism: toward a historical interpretation, by Ernest R. Sandeen. Philadelphia, Fortress Press [1968] viii, 31 p. 20 cm. (Facet books. Historical series, 10) "Originally published as Toward a historical interpretation of the origins of fundamentalism, in Church history, XXXVI, 1967." Includes bibliographical references. [BT82.2.S2] 68-31337
1. Fundamentalism. I. Title.

SATPRAKASHANANDA, Swami. 230
Hinduism and Christianity : Jesus Christ and his teachings in the light of Vedanta / by Swami Satprakashananda. St. Louis : Vedanta Society of St. Louis, 1975. 196 p. ; 20 cm. Includes bibliographical references and index. [BR128.H5S26] 75-32598 ISBN 0-916356-53-1 : 7.50
1. Jesus Christ—Hindu interpretations. 2. Christianity and other religions—Hinduism. 3. Hinduism—Relations—Christianity. I. Title.

SAUNDERSON, Henry Hallam, 1871- 230
The way called heresy. Boston, Starr King Press [1956] 376p. 22cm. [BR1615.S28] 56-2696
1. Liberalism (Religion) 2. Heresies and heretics. I. Title.

SCHILLING, Sylvester Paul, 1904- 230
Contemporary continental theologians [by] S. Paul Schilling. Nashville, Abingdon Press [1966] 288 p. 24 cm. [BT28.S37] 66-10854
1. Theology—20th cent. I. Title.

SCHILLING, Sylvester Paul, 1904- 230
Contemporary continental theologians. Nashville, Abingdon [c.1966] 288p. 24cm. [BT28.S37] 66-10854 5.00
1. Theology — 20th cent. I. Title.

SCHLEIERMACHER, Friedrich Ernst Daniel, 1768-1834. 230
The Christian faith / by Friedrich Schleiermacher ; edited by H. R. Mackintosh and J. S. Stewart. Philadelphia : Fortress Press, 1976. xii, 760 p. ; 23 cm. Translation of the 2d ed. of Der christliche Glaube. Includes bibliographical references and indexes. [BT75.S58513 1976] 76-53313 ISBN 0-8006-0487-3
1. Theology, Doctrinal. I. Title.

SCHMAUS, Michael, 1897- 230
The essence of Christianity. Foreword by Kevin McNamara. [Translation by J. Holland Smith] Chicago, Scepter [1961] 288 p. 22 cm. Translation of Vom Wesen des Christentums. [BR121.S353] 64-1330
1. Christianity—Essence, genius, nature. I. Title.

SCHNACKENBURG, Rudolf, 1914- 230
Present and future; modern aspects of New Testament theology. Notre Dame, University of Notre Dame Press, 1966. viii, 212 p. 22 cm. (The Cardinal O'Hara series, v. 3) First delivered as a series of lectures at the University of Notre Dame in the fall of 1965. Bibliographical footnotes. [BS2397.S42] 66-24923
1. Bible. N.T.—Theology—Addresses, essays, lectures. I. Title. II. Series.

SCHNACKENBURG, Rudolf, 1914- 230
The truth will make you free. [Translated by Rodelinde Albrecht. New York, Herder and Herder [1966] 126 p. 21 cm. Translation of Von der Wahrheit die Freimacht. Bibliographical footnotes. [BT50.S3913] 66-22611
1. Truth (Theology) I. Title.

SCHNEIDER, Reinhold, 1903-1958. 230
Messages from the depths : selections from the writings of Reinhold Schneider / edited by Curt Winterhalter ; translated by Robert J. Cunningham. Chicago : Franciscan Herald Press, [1977] p. cm. Translation of Worte aus der Tiefe. Bibliography: p. [BR85.S27613] 77-12809 ISBN 0-8199-0683-2 pbk. : 4.95
1. Theology—Addresses, essays, lectures. I. Title.

SCHROEDER, W. Widick. 230
Where do I stand? Living theological options for contemporary Christians, by W. Widick Schroeder and Keith A. Davis. Chicago, Exploration Press [1973] ix, 158 p. 28 cm. [BT77.S384] 72-97252 3.00
1. Theology, Doctrinal—Popular works. I. Davis, Keith A., joint author. II. Title.

SCHROEDER, W. Widick. 230
Where do I stand? : living thelogical options for contemporary Christians / W. Widick Schroeder and Keith A. Davis. Rev. ed. Chicago : Exploration Press, [1975] ix, 157 p. ; 23 cm. (Studies in ministry and parish life) Includes bibliographical references. [BT77.S384 1975] 75-5284 ISBN 0-913552-02-X : 7.50 pbk. : 4.00
1. Theology, Doctrinal—Popular works. I. Davis, Keith A., joint author. II. Title. III. Series.

SCRIVEN, Charles. 230
The demons have had it : a theological ABC / by Charles Scriven. Nashville : Southern Pub. Association, c1976. 125 p. ; 21 cm. Includes bibliographical references. [BT77.S386] 76-2926 ISBN 0-8127-0111-9
1. Theology, Doctrinal—Popular works. I. Title.

SCROGGS, Robin. 230
Paul for a new day / Robin Scroggs. Philadelphia : Fortress Press, c1977. xi, 84 p. ; 22 cm. Includes bibliographical references and index. [BS2651.S373] 76-9719 ISBN 0-8006-1242-6 pbk. : 2.95
1. Bible. N.T. Epistles of Paul—Theology—Addresses, essays, lectures. I. Title.

SEGUNDO, Juan Luis. 230
Liberation of theology / Juan Luis Segundo ; translated by John Drury. Maryknoll, N.Y. : Orbis Books, c1976. p. cm. Translation of Liberation de la teologia. Includes bibliographical references. [BT83.S4413] 76-7049 ISBN 0-88344-285-X. ISBN 0-88344-286-8 pbk.
1. Liberation theology. 2. Sociology, Christian. 3. Theology—20th century. I. Title.

SENARCLENS, Jacques de, 1914- 230
Heirs of the Reformation. Tr. [from French] ed. by G. W. Bromiley. Foreword by T. F. Torrance. Philadelphia, Westminster [1964, c.1959] 343p. 23cm. (Lib. of hist. and doctrine) Bibl. 63-20956 6.50
1. Theology, Doctrinal—Hist.—20th cent. I. Title.

SETZER, J. Schoneberg. 230
What's left to believe? [By] J. Schoneberg Setzer. Nashville, Abingdon Press [1968] 236 p. 25 cm. [BT77.S45] 68-11473
1. Theology, Doctrinal—Popular works. I. Title.

*SHARP, Gladys M. 230
The undivided God. New York, Carlton [1967] 70p. 21cm. (Hearthstone bk.) 2.00
I. Title.

SHEED, Francis Joseph, 1897- 230
God and the human condition; v. 1 [by] F. J. Sheed. New York, Sheed [1966] 301p. 22cm. Contents.v. 1. God and the human mind. [BT75.2.S5] 66-22027 5.00
1. Theology, Doctrinal. I. Title.

SHELDON, Wilmon Henry, 1875- 230
Rational religion: the philosophy of Christian love. New York, Philosophical Library [1962] 138 p. 22 cm. [BT50.S5] 62-15035
1. Faith and reason. I. Title.

SHELDON, Wilmon Henry, 1875- 230
Rational religion: the philosophy of Christian love. New York, Philosophical [c.1962] 138p. 22cm. 62-15035 4.75
1. Faith and reason. I. Title.

SHELLEY, Bruce Leon, 1927- 230
By what authority? The standards of truth in the early church, by Bruce Shelley. Grand Rapids, Mich., W. B. Eerdmans Pub. Co. [1965] 166 p. 21 cm. Bibliography: p. 159-162. Bibliographical footnotes. [BT88.S48] 65-18097
1. Authority (Religion) I. Title.

SHELLEY, Bruce Leon, 1927- 230
By what authority? The standards of truth in the early church. Grand Rapids, Mich., Eerdmans [c.1965] 166p. 21cm. Bibl. [BT88.S48] 65-18097 1.95 pap.,
1. Authority (Religion) I. Title.

SHOWERS, Renald E. 230
What on earth is God doing? Satan's conflict with God, by Renald E. Showers. [1st ed.] Neptune, N.J., Loizeaux Bros. [1973] 128 p. 21 cm. Bibliography: p. 127-128. [BS680.H47S54] 73-81551 ISBN 0-87213-784-8 1.59 (pbk.)
1. Bible—History of Biblical events. 2. History (Theology)—Biblical teaching. 3. Devil. I. Title.

SHROYER, Montgomery J., 1888- 230
The authority of the Bible in Christian belief. Nashville, Tidings [1961] 72 p. 19 cm. [BT77.S53] 61-9130
1. Theology, Doctrinal — Popular works. I. Title.

SHROYER, Montgomery J., 1888- 230
The authority of the Bible in Christian belief. Nashville, 1908 Girard Ave. Tidings, [c.1961] 72p. illus. 61-9130 .50 pap.,
1. Theology, Doctrinal—Popular works. I. Title.

SHUTE, John Raymond. 230
The quest. [Essays] Monroe, N.C., Nocalore Press, 1951. 78 p. 21 cm. [BR1616.S5] 51-31459
1. Liberalism (Religion) I. Title.

SIEMENS, David F., Jr. 230
Exploring Christianity, a guided tour. Chicago, Moody [1963, c.1962] 156p. 18cm. (Moody pocket bks., 78) Bibl. 62-21957 .59 pap.,
1. Questions and answers—Theology. I. Title.

SLUSSER, Gerald H. 230
The local church in transition: theology, education, and ministry. Philadelphia, Westminster [c.1964] 204p. 21cm. Bibl. 64-16351 4.75
1. Pastoral theology. I. Title.

SLUSSER, Gerald H 230
The local church in transition: theology, education, and ministry, by Gerald H. Slusser. Philadelphia, Westminster Press [1964] 204 p. 21 cm. Bibliographical references included in "Notes" (p. [199]-204) [BV4011.S57] 64-16351
1. Pastoral theology. I. Title.

SMART, James D. 230
The ABC's of Christian faith, by James D. Smart. Philadelphia, Westminster Press [1968] 140 p. 19 cm. [BT77.S58] 68-13958
1. Theology, Doctrinal—Popular works. I. Title.

SMITH, Charles Henry, 1875-1948. 230
Mennonite country boy; the early years of C. Henry Smith. Newton, Kan., Faith and Life Press [1962] 261 p. illus. 24 cm. (Mennonite historical series) Includes bibliography [BR139.S6A3] 62-2760
I. Title.

SMITH, Harold D 230
A criticism of Christian dogma; a plea for a revitalized morality based on rational principles, by Harold D. Smith. [1st ed.] New York, Exposition Press [1964] 119 p. 21 cm. Bibliography: [117]-119. [BT75.2.S6] 65-2514
1. Theology, Doctrinal. I. Title.

*SMITH, Harold D. 230
A criticism of Christian dogma; a plea for revitalized morality based on rational principles. New York, Exposition [c.1964] 119p. 21cm. Bibl. 3.50
I. Title.

SMITH, Ronald Gregor. 230
Secular Christianity. [1st ed.] New York, Harper & Row [1966] 222 p. 22 cm. Bibliography: p. 213-215. [BT55.S55 1966a] 66-20785
1. Faith. 2. History (Theology) 3. Secularism. I. Title.

SPANN, John Richard, 1891- ed. 230
Fruits of faith. New York, Abingdon-Cokesbury Press [1950] 240 p. 23 cm. Lectures of 18 scholars at the 30th Annual Conference on Ministerial Training. Evanston, Ill., rev. and adapted to book form. [BT765.S63] 50-9179
1. Sanctification — Addresses, essays, lectures. I. Title.

SPARKES, Vernone M., 1938- 230
The theological enterprise, by Vernone M. Sparkes. [Independence, Mo., Herald Pub. House, 1969] 272 p. 21 cm. Includes bibliographical references. [BT75.2.S65] 73-89842 5.95
1. Theology, Doctrinal. I. Title.

SPIRIT and light : 230
essays in historical theology / edited by Madeleine L'Engle and William B. Green. New York : Seabury Press, c1976. p. cm. "Crossroad books." [BR50.S67] 76-17834 ISBN 0-8164-0310-4 : 8.95
1. West, Edward N. 2. Theology—Addresses, essays, lectures. I. L'Engle, Madeleine. II. Green, William B., 1927-

THE Spirituality of Western Christendom / introd. by Jean Leclerq : edited by E. Rozanne Elder. Kalamazoo : Published for the Medieval Institute & the Institute of Cisterian Studies, Western Michigan University, [by] Cisterian Publications, 1976. xxxv, 217 p. ; 23 cm. (Cistercian studies series ; no. 30) "A special volume of the series: Studies in medieval culture." Includes bibliographical references. [BV4490.S73] 76-22615 ISBN 0-87907-987-8 pbk. : 7.95 230
1. Spirituality. I. Elder, Ellen Rozanne. II. Studies in medieval culture. III. Series.

SPURRIER, William A. 230
Guide to the Christian faith, an introduction to Christian doctrine. New York, Scribner [c.1952] xii, 242p. 21cm. (Scribner library SL19) 1.25 pap.,
1. Theology, Doctrinal—Popular works. I. Title.

SPURRIER, William Atwell. 230
Guide to the Christian faith, an introduction to Christian doctrine. New York, Scribner, 1952. 242 p. 21 cm. [BT77.S72] 52-554
1. Theology, Doctrinal — Popular works. I. Title.

STAGG, Frank, 1911- 230
New Testament theology. Nashville, Groadman Press [1961] 361 p. 22cm. [BS2341.S68] 62-15328
1. Bible. N.T. — Theology. I. Title.

STAGG, Frank, 1911- 230
New Testament theology. Nashville, Broadman [c.1962] 361p. 22cm. Bibl. 62-15328 5.95
1. Bible. N. T.—Theology I. Title.

STANLEY, Clifford L. 230
Conflicting reports about God; nine lectures, by Clifford L. Stanley, given June 14-23, 1966. Washington, Lectern Press; sales outlet: Seminary Book Service, Alexandria, Va., [1967] vi, 70 p. 29 cm. [BT83.5.S8] 67-4173
1. Death of God theology. 2. Theology, Doctrinal—History—20th century. I. Title.

STARRATT, Alfred B. 230
The real God [by] Alfred B. Starratt. Philadelphia, Westminister Press [1965] 124 p. 19 cm. (Adventure in faith) [BT60.S7] 65-16999
1. Christianity—Essence, genius, nature. I. Title.

STARRATT, Alfred B. 230
The real God. Philadelphia, Westminister [c.1965] 124p. 19cm. (Adventures in faith) [BT60.S7] 65-16999 1.45 pap.,
1. Christianitiy—Essence, genius, nature. I. Title.

STEEVES, Paul D. 230
Getting to know your faith / Paul Steeves. Downers Grove, Ill. : InterVarsity Press, c1977. 126 p. : forms ; 21 cm. Includes bibliographical references. [BT77.S733] 76-55555 ISBN 0-87784-629-4 pbk. : 2.95
1. Theology, Doctrinal—Popular works. I. Title.

STERLING, Chandler W., Bp., 1911- 230
The eighth square, by Chandler Sterling. Artwork and cover design by Don Crouse. Ambler, Pa., Trinity Press [1970] xii, 106 p. illus. 22 cm. [BT77.S737] 75-111643
1. Theology, Doctrinal—Popular works. I. Title.

STEVENS, William Wilson 230
Doctrines of the Christian religion. Grand Rapids, Eerdmans [1967] 435p. 24cm. Bibl. [BT75.S.S7] 67-13977 6.95
1. Theology, Doctrinal. I. Title.

STEVENS, William Wilson. 230
Doctrines of the Christian religion. Grand Rapids, Eerdmans [1967] 435 p. 24 cm. Bibliography: p. 411-413. [BT75.2.S7] 67-13977
1. Theology, Doctrinal. I. Title.

STEVICK, Daniel B. 230
Beyond fundamentalism. Richmond, John Knox Press [1964] 239 p. 21 cm. Bibliography: p. 237-239. [BT78.S815] 64-10645
1. Fundamentalism. I. Title.

THE Story of the Fort Worth Norris-Wallace debate; a documentary record of the facts concerning the Norris-Wallace debate, held in Fort Worth, Texas, November, 1934. Nashville, Tenn., F. E. Wallace, Jr. Publications [1969?] c1968. 346 p. facsims., ports. 24 cm. Compiled by F. E. Wallace. [BX6495.N59S7] 72-268696 230
1. Norris, John Franklyn, 1877-1952. 2. Wallace, Foy Esco, 1896- 3. Disputations, Religious. I. Wallace, Foy Esco, 1896- comp.

STOTT, John R. 230
Basic Christianity. [1st ed., reprinted] Grand Rapids, Eerdmans [1958] 144 p. 18 cm. (Eerdmans pocket editions) [BT77.S74 1958] 58-13513
1. Theology, Doctrinal — Popular works. I. Title.

STOTT, John R W 230
Fundamentalism and evangelism. [1st American ed.] Grand Rapids, Eerdmans [1959] 80 p. 20 cm. [BT82.2.S7 1959] 59-6952
1. Fundamentalism. 2. Evangelistic work. I. Title.

STRENG, William D. 230
Faith for today : a brief outline of Christian thought / William D. Streng. Minneapolis : Augsburg Pub. House, c1975. 64 p. ; 20 cm. [BT77.S743] 75-2843 ISBN 0-8066-1488-9 pbk. : 1.25
1. Theology, Doctrinal—Popular works. I. Title.

STROOP, John Ridley, 1897- 230
God's plan and me. Nashville [1950- v. 20 cm. Contents.book 1. Jesus' mission and method. [BT77.S77] 51-18847
1. Theology, Doctrinal. I. Title.

STUDIES honoring Ignatius Charles Brady, Friar Minor / edited by Romano Stephen Almagno and Conrad L. Harkins. St. Bonaventure, N.Y. : Franciscan Institute, 1976. 494 p. : port. ; 25 cm. (Franciscan Institute publications : Theology series ; no. 6) English, French, German, Italian, or Spanish. Includes bibliographical references. [BR50.S819] 76-1318 230
1. Brady, Ignatius C. 2. Brady, Ignatius C.—Bibliography. 3. Theology—Addresses, essays, lectures. I. Brady, Ignatius C. II. Almagno, Romano Stephen. III. Harkins, Conrad L. IV. Series: St. Bonaventure University, St. Bonaventure, N.Y. Franciscan Institute. Theology series ; no. 6.

*SURDU, Elena. 230
My talk with the Lord. New York, Exposition 132p. 21cm. 4.50
I. Title.

SWANN, Doris Cutter. 230
Bible teachings. Nashville, Broadman Press [1970] 46 p. 21 cm. [BT77.S785] 79-117309
1. Theology, Doctrinal—Popular works. I. Title.

SWEAZEY, George Edgar, 1905- 230
The Christian answer to life's urgent questions. St. Louis, Bethany Press [1962] 192 p. 23 cm. [BT77.S79] 62-8757
1. Theology, Doctrinal — Popular works. I. Title.

SWEAZEY, George Edgar, 1905- 230
The Christian answer to life's urgent questions. St. Louis, Bethany [c.1962] 192p. 23cm. 62-8757 3.50
1. Theology, Doctrinal—Popular works. I. Title.

SWIDLER, Leonard J 230
Scripture and ecumenism; Protestant, Catholic, Orthodox, and Jewish. Edited and introd. by Leonard J. Swidler. Pittsburgh, Duquesne University Press, 1965. vii, 197 p. 23 cm. (Duquesne studies. Theological series, 8) Nine papers delivered at the annual ecumenical seminar held at Duquesne University, spring, 1964. Bibliographical footnotes. [BT90.S9] 64-8867
1. Tradition (Theology) 2. Bible — Evidences, authority, etc. 3. Christian union. I. Duquesne University, Pittsburgh. II. Title. III. Series.

SWIDLER, Leonard J. ed. 230
Scripture and ecumenism: Protestant, Catholic, Orthodox, and Jewish. Pittsburgh, Duquesne [c.]1965. vii, 197p. 23cm. (Duquesne studies. Theological ser., 3) Nine papers delivered at the annual ecumenical seminar held at Duquesne Univ., spring, 1964. Bibl. [BT90.S9] 64-8867 4.95
1. Tradition (Theology) 2. Bible—Evidences, authority, etc. 3. Christian union. I. Duquesne University, Pittsburgh. II. Title. III. Series.

SYKES, Stephen. 230
An introduction to Christian theology today. Atlanta, John Knox Press [1974, c1971] 153 p. 21 cm. First published under title: Christian theology today. Bibliography: p. 149-153. [BT28.S93 1974] 73-16911 ISBN 0-8042-0474-8 3.50
1. Theology—20th century. I. Title.

TAVARD, Georges Henri 230
Holy Writ or Holy Church; the crisis of the Protestant Reformation. New York, Harper [1960] x, 250 p. 22 cm. (bibl. footnotes) 60-5299 5.00
1. Authority (Religion). 2. Catholic Church—Relations—Protestant churches. 3. Protestant churches—Relations—Catholic Church. I. Title.

TAVARD, Georges Henri, 1922- 230
Holy Writ or Holy Church; the crisis of the Protestant Reformation. New York, Harper [1960, c1959] 250 p. 22 cm. Includes bibliography. [BT88.T35 1960] 60-5299
1. Authority (Religion) 2. Catholic Church — Relations — Protestant churches. 3. Protestant churches — Relations — Catholic Church I. Title.

TAVARD, Georges Henri, 1922- 230
Meditation on the word; perspectives for a renewed theology, by George H. Tavard. Glen Rock, N.J., Paulist Press Paperback [1968] v, 169 p. 21 cm. [BT77.T34] 68-24813 3.50
1. Theology, Doctrinal—Popular works. I. Title.

TAYLOR, Kenneth Nathaniel. 230
Devotions for the children's hour; illustrated by JoAnne Brubaker. Chicago, Moody Press [1954] 189p. illus. 24cm. [BV4870.T3] 54-1887
1. Children—Prayer-books and devotions — English. I. Title.

TAYLOR, Oral E. 230
Christianity vs. communistic atheism [Bebee, W. Va.] Author, c.1963. 72p. illus. 23cm. 63-22174 1.00 pap.,
1. Bible—Prophecies—Addresses, essays, lectures. I. Title.

TEMPLE, William, Abp. of Canterbury, 1881-1944 230
About Christ: the Archbishop's lectures in 1921 and 1925 on 'The universality of Christ' and 'Christ's revelation of God.' reprinted with a preface by the Archbishop of York, essay by J. Eric Fenn. London, SCM Pr. [dist. New York, Morehouse, 1963, c.1962] 143p. 19cm. (Living church bks.) 63-1831 1.30 pap.,
1. Christianity—Addresses, essays, lectures. 2. Jesus Christ—Teaching. I. Title. II. Title: The universality of Christ. III. Title: Christ's revelation of God.

THEOLOGY of joy / 230
edited by Johann Baptist Metz and Jean-Pierre Jossua. New York : Herder and Herder, 1974. 158 p. ; 23 cm. (Concilium ; new, ser., v. 5, no. 10 (95), Fundamental theology) Series statment also appears as: Concilium: religion in the seventies. Includes bibliographical references. [BJ1481.T49] 73-17903 ISBN 0-8164-2579-5 pbk. : 3.95
1. Joy—Addresses, essays, lectures. I. Metz, Johannes Baptist, 1928- ed. II. Jossua, Jean Pierre, ed. III. Series: Concilium (New York) ; 95.

THE Theology of liberation. 230
Washington : Division for Latin America, USCC, [197-]. 60 p. ; 23 cm. (LADOC 'Keyhole' series ; 2) Cover title. [BT83.57.T47] 75-330890 1.00
1. Liberation theology—Addresses, essays, lectures. I. Title. II. Series.

THIELICKE, Helmut, 1908- 230
Between heaven and earth : conversations with American Christians / by Helmut Thielicke ; translated and edited by John W. Doberstein. Westport, Conn. : Greenwood Press, 1975, c1965. xvii, 192 p. ; 22 cm. Translation of Gesprache uber Himmel und Erde. Reprint of the ed. published by Harper & Row, New York. Includes bibliographical references and index. [BR85.T48413 1975] 73-16609 ISBN 0-8371-7185-7
1. Theology—Addresses, essays, lectures. I. Title.

THIELICKE, Helmut, 1908- 230
Between heaven and earth : conversations with American Christians / by Helmut Thielicke ; translated and edited by John W. Doberstein. Westport, Conn. : Greenwood Press, 1975, c1965. xvii, 192 p. ; 22 cm. Translation of Gesprache uber Himmel und Erde. Reprint of the ed. published by Harper & Row, New York. Includes bibliographical references and index. [BR85.T48413 1975] 73-16609 ISBN 0-8371-7185-7 lib.bdg. : 12.00
1. Theology—Addresses, essays, lectures. I. Title.

THIELICKE, Helmut, 1908- 230
The evangelical faith. Translated and edited by Geoffrey W. Bromiley. Grand Rapids, Eerdmans [1974- v. 25 cm. Translation of Der evangelische Glaube. Contents.Contents.—v. 1. Prolegomena: the relation of theology to modern thought forms. Includes bibliographical references. [BT75.2.T4513] 74-7010 ISBN 0-8028-2342-4 (v. 1)
1. Theology, Doctrinal. I. Title.

THIELICKE, Helmut, 1908- 230 s
Prolegomena: the relation of theology to modern thought forms. Translated and edited by Geoffrey W. Bromiley. Grand Rapids, Eerdmans [1974] 420 p. 25 cm. (His The evangelical faith, v. 1) Includes bibliographical references. [BT75.2.T4513 vol. 1] [BT28] 230'.09'04 74-7011 ISBN 0-8028-2342-4
1. Theology—20th century. I. Title.

THIRD world theologies / 230
edited by Gerald H. Anderson and Thomas F. Stransky. New York : Paulist Press, c1976. viii, 254 p. ; 19 cm. (Mission trends ; no. 3) Bibliography: p. 250-254. [BR50.T47] 76-24451 ISBN 0-8091-1984-6 pbk. : 3.45
1. Theology—Addresses, essays, lectures. I. Anderson, Gerald H. II. Stransky, Thomas F.

THOMAS, John Heywood. 230
Paul Tillich: an appraisal. Philadelphia, Westminster Press [1963] 216 p. 22 cm. Bibliographical references included in footnotes. [BX4827.T53T5] 63-12599
1. Tillich, Paul, 1886-1965.

THOMAS, Owen C. 230
Introduction to theology [by] Owen C. Thomas. Cambridge, Mass., Greeno, Hadden [1973] 218 p. 23 cm. Bibliography: p. 216-218. [BT77.T455] 73-76599 ISBN 0-913550-02-7
1. Theology, Doctrinal—Popular works. I. Title.

THOMPSON, Egbert Herron, 1895- 230
The kingdom of heaven. [1st ed.] New York, Pageant Press, 1955. 58p. 21cm. [BT77.T48] 54-10887
1. Theology, Doctrinal—Popular works. I. Title.

THURIAN, Max. 230
Love and truth meet. Translated by C. Edward Hopkin. Philadelphia, Pilgrim Press [1968] x, 166 p. 22 cm. Translation of Amour et verite se rencontrent. [BT77.T4913] 68-59100 6.50
1. Theology, Doctrinal—Popular works. I. Title.

TILLICH, Paul, 1886-1965. 230
Systematic theology. Chicago, University of Chicago Press [1951-63] 3 v. 24 cm. Contents.Contents.—v. 1. Reason and revelation. Being and God.—v. 2. Existence and the Christ.—v. 3. Life and the spirit. History and the kingdom of God. [BT75.T56] 51-2235
1. Theology, Doctrinal.

TORRANCE, Thomas Forsyth, 1913- 230
Theology in reconstruction Grand Rapids, Mich., Eerdmans [1966, c.1965] 288p. 23cm. Bibl. [BT80.T6] 66-2894 5.00 bds.,
1. Theology, Doctrinal—Addresses, essays, lectures. I. Title.

TRACY, David. 230
Blessed rage for order, the new pluralism in theology / David Tracy. New York : Seabury Press, [1975] p. cm. "A Crossroad book." Includes index. [BT28.T65] 75-8803 ISBN 0-8164-0277-9 : 12.95
1. Theology—20th century. 2. Religion and language. I. Title.

TRADITION and theology in the Old Testament / 230
edited by Douglas A. Knight ; with contributions by Walter Harrelson ... [et al.]. Philadelphia : Fortress Press, c1977. xiv, 336 p. ; 24 cm. Includes bibliographical references and indexes. [BS1199.T68T73] 76-7872 ISBN 0-8006-0484-9 : 16.95
1. Bible. O.T.—Criticism, interpretation, etc.—Addresses, essays, lectures. 2. Tradition (Theology)—Biblical teaching—Addresses, essays, lectures. I. Knight, Douglas A. II. Harrelson, Walter J.

TULGA, Chester Earl, 1896- 230
The case against neo-orthodoxy. Chicago, Conservative Baptist Fellowship [1951] 64 p. 18 cm. (His Little books on big subjects) [BT78.T815] 51-23627
1. Neo-orthodoxy. I. Title.

TZANGAS, George J. 230
Have you talked to Him? / By John Christian [i.e. G. J. Tzangas]. Akron, Ohio : J. Christian, [1974] 66 leaves ; 23 cm. [BF1301.T95] 74-84034
1. Spirit writings. 2. Theology—Miscellanea. I. Title.

UNGERSMA, Aaron J 1905- 230
Handbook for Christian believers [by] A. J. Ungersma. Richmond, John Knox Press [1964] x, 215 p. 21 cm. (Aletheia paperbacks) [BT77.U5 1964] 64-16285
1. Theology, Doctrinal — Popular works. 2. Christianity — 20th cent. I. Title.

UNGERSMA, Aaron J., 1905- 230
Handbook for Christian believers. Richmond, Va., Knox [c.1964] x, 215p. 21cm. (Aletheia paperbacks) 64-16285 1.95 pap.,
1. Theology, Doctrinal—Popular works. 2. Christianity—20th cent. I. Title.

UNGERSMA, Aaron J., 1905- 230
Handbook for Christian believers; faith explained for today's needs. [1st ed.] Indianapolis, Bobbs-Merrill [1953] 215 p. 21 cm. [BT77.U5] 53-5233
1. Theology, Doctrinal—Popular works. 2. Christianity—20th century. I. Title.

VALEN-SONDSTAAN, Olav 230
The word that can never die. Tr. [from Norwegian] by Norman A. Madson, Sr., Ahlert H. Strand. [Licensed Eng. ed.] St. Louis, Concordia [1966, c. 1949] 164p. 24cm. Lects. delivered in Sweden in 1947. [BT80.V313] 66-22419 3.95
1. Theology—Addresses, essays, lectures. I. Title.

VAN BUREN, Paul Matthews, 1924- 230
The secular meaning of the gospel, based on an analysis of its language. New York, Macmillan [1963] 205 p. 22 cm. [BR121.2.V3 1963] 63-15701
1. Christianity—20th century. I. Title.

VAN BUREN, Paul Matthews, 1924- 230
The burden of freedom : Americans and the God of Israel / Paul M. van Buren. New York : Seabury Press, c1976. p. cm. "A Crossroad book." [BT810.2.V36] 76-15181 ISBN 0-8164-0318-X : 6.95
1. Freedom (Theology)—Addresses, essays, lectures. 2. Judaism—United States—Addresses, essays, lectures. I. Title.

VAN DUSEN, Henry Pitney, 1897- 230
The vindication of liberal theology; a tract for the times. Based upon the Eugene William Lyman memorial lecture, Sweet Briar College. New York, Scribner [1963] 192 p. 21 cm. [BR1615.V3] 63-12024
1. Liberalism (Religion) I. Title.

VAN DUSEN, Henry Pitney, 1897- 230
The vindication of liberal theology; a tract for the times. Based upon the Eugene William Lyman memorial lecture, Sweet Briar College. New York, Scribners [c.1963] 192p. 21cm. 63-12024 3.50
1. Liberalism (Religion) I. Title.

VASS, Pearl, 1907- 230
The spiritual message of Hebrews; the lessons of the law and the gospel for Israel of old and for those who seek God in our day. [1st ed.] New York, Greenwich Book Publishers [1958] 150 p. 21 cm. [BR126.V35] 57-13309
I. Title.

VASSADY, Bela. 230
Light against darkness. Philadelphia, Christian Education Press [1961] 176 p. 21 cm. [BT77.V34] 61-13471
1. Theology, Doctrinal — Popular words. 2. Christianity — Essence, genius, nature. I. Title.

VASSADY, Bela 230
Light against darkness. Philadelphia, Christian Education Pr. [c.1961] 176p. Bibl. 61-13471 3.00
1. Theology. Doctrinal—Popular works. 2. Christianity—Essence, genius, nature. I. Title.

VERITY, George Bersford, 1887- 230
Life in Christ; a study of coinherence. Greenwich, Conn., Seabury Press [1954] 224p. 20cm. [BT75.V44 1954] 54-13344
1. Theology. Doctrinal. I. Title. II. Title: Coinherence.

VERITY, Geroge Beresford 1887- 230
Life in Christ; a study of coinherence. London, New York, Longmans, Green [1954] 224p. 20cm. [BT75.V44 1954a] 55-153
1. Theology, Doctrinal. I. Title. II. Title: Coinherence.

VIDLER, Alexander Roper, 1899- 230
Christian belief; a course of open lectures delivered in the University of Cambridge. New York, Scribner [1950] 129 p. 22 cm. Includes btbliographical references. [BT75.V48] 50-13220
1. Theology, Doctrinal. I. Title.

VOS, Geerhardus, 1862-1949. 230
Biblical theology : Old and New Testaments / Geerhardus Vos. Edinburgh ; Carlisle, Pa. : Banner of Truth Trust, 1975. x, 426 p. ; 23 cm. First published in 1948. Includes indexes. [BS543.V67 1975] 75-328208
1. Bible—Theology. I. Title.

WAGNER, James Edgar, 1900- 230
Incarnation to ascension: a pastoral interpretation. Philadelphia, Christian Education Press [1962] 111 p. 20 cm. [B777.W25] 62-18103
1. Theology, Doctrinal — Popular works. I. Title.

WAGNER, James Edgar, 1900- 230
Incarnation to ascension: a pastoral interpretation. Philadelphia, Christian Educ. Pr. [dist. United Church Pr., c.1962] 111p. 20cm. 62-18103 2.50
1. Theology, Doctrinal—Popular works. I. Title.

WALTON, Alfred Grant, 1887- 230
This I can believe; an outline of essentials of the Christian faith. With a foreword by Hugh L. Cooper. Freeport, N.Y., Books for Libraries Press [1971, c1935] xiv, 256 p. 23 cm. (Essay index reprint series) [BT1101.W16 1971] 79-142708 ISBN 0-8369-2207-7
1. Apologetics—20th century. I. Title.

WAMBLE, G. Hugh, 1923- 230
The shape of faith. Nashville, Broadman [c.1962] 88p. 20cm. (Broadman starbk.) 62-9201 1.00 pap.,
1. Protestant churches—U.S. I. Title.

WARD, William B. 230
Beliefs that live. Richmond, John Knox Press [1963] 126 p. 21 cm. [BT77.W33] 63-13832
1. Theology, Doctrinal — Popular works. I. Title.

WARD, William B. 230
Beliefs that live. Richmond, Va., John Knox [c.1963] 126p. 21cm. 63-13832 1.75 pap.,
1. Theology, Doctrinal—Popular works. I. Title.

WARFIELD, Benjamin Breckinridge, 1851-1921. 230
Biblical foundations. Grand Rapids, Eerdmans [1958] 350 p. 23 cm. (Selected theological studies) [BT15.W343 1958] 58-13059
1. Theology, Doctrinal — Addresses, essays, lectures. I. Title.

WATERMAN, Leroy, 1875- 230
The religion of Jesus; Christianity's unclaimed heritage of prophetic religion [1st ed.] New

York, Harper [1952] 251 p. 22 cm. [BR121.W265] 52-8493
1. Christianity — Essence, genius, nature. I. Title.

WATTS, Alan Wilson, 1915- 230
Myth and ritual in Christianity. New York, Vanguard Press [1953] ix. 262p. illus. 23cm. (Myth and man) A Thames and Hudson book. [BR135.W3] 54-6992
1. Mythology. 2. Christian art and symbolism. I. Title. II. Series.

WEATHERHEAD, Leslie Dixon, 1893- 230
The Christian agnostic. Nashville, Abingdon [c1965] 368p. 23cm. Bibl. [BT78.W4] 65-26733 4.75
1. Theology, Doctrinal. I. Title.

WEATHERHEAD, Leslie Dixon, 1893- 230
The Christian agnostic [by] Leslie D. Weatherhead. New York, Abingdon Press [1965] 368 p. 23 cm. Bibliographical footnotes. [BT78.W4] 65-26733
1. Theology, Doctrinal. I. Title.

WEAVER, Horace R 230
The everlasting covenant, content and value of the Old Testament [by] Horace R. Weaver. Nashville, Graded Press [1965] 231 p. 19 cm. [BS1151.2.W4] 65-4751
1. Bible. O.T. — Commentaries. I. Title.

WEBER, Otto, 1902- 230
Karl Barth's Church dogmatics; an introductory report on volumes I: 1 to III: 4. Translated by Arthur C. Cochrane. Philadelphia, Westminster Press [1953] 253p. 24cm. [BT75.B286W42] 53-6528
1. Barth, Karl, 1886- Die Kirchllche Dogmatik. 2. Theology. Doctrinal. I. Title.

WEDEL, Theodore Otto, 1892- 230
The Christianity of Main Street. New York, Macmillan, 1950. x, 112 p. 21 cm. [BR121.W42] 50-11672
1. Christianity — Essence, genius, nature. 2. Christianity — 20th cent. I. Title.

WEIGEL, Gustave, 1906- 230
A survey of Protestant theology in our day. Westminster, Md., Newman Press, 1954. 56p. 22cm. [BX 4820.W37] 54-12085
1. Protestantism. 2. Catholic Church—Doctrinal and controverstal works—Catholic authors. 3. Theology, Doctrinal—Hist. I. Title.

*WESTON, Sidney A. 230
Life problems in a changing world [a discussion unit for high school ages and young adults. Rev. ed.] Boston, Whittemore Assocs. [c.1964] 96p. illus. 17cm. .75 pap.,
I. Title.

WHALE, John Seldon, D. D. 1896- 230
Christian doctrine: eight lectures delivered in the University of Cambridge to undergraduates of all faculties. [reissue, New York4 Cambridge, 1963. 196p. 19cm. Bibl. 1.25 pap.,
1. Theology, Doctrianal. I. Title.

WHAT the Bible says / 230
compiled and edited by Lewis Drummond ; with a foreword by Billy Graham. Nashville : Abingdon Press, 1975, c1974. xx, 201 p. ; 23 cm. Includes index. [BS543.W48 1975] 75-17736 ISBN 0-687-44585-X : 5.95
1. Bible—Theology. I. Drummond, Lewis A.

WHITE, Hugh Vernon, 1889- 230
Truth and the person in Christian theology; a theological essay in terms of the spiritual person. New York, Oxford University Press, 1963. 240 p. 21 cm. [BT75.2.W5] 63-12821
1. Theology, Doctrinal — Introductions. I. Title.

WHITE, Hugh Vernon, 1889- 230
Truth and the person in Christian theology; a theological essay in terms of the spiritual person. New York, Oxford [c.]1963. 240p. 21cm. Bibl. 63-12821 6.00
1. Theology, Doctrinal—Introductions. I. Title.

WICKENDEN, Arthur Consaul, 1893- 230
The concerns of religion. New York, Harper [1959] 185 p. 22 cm. First ed. published in 1939 under title: Youth looks at religion. Includes bibliography. [BR121.W526 1959] 59-7167
1. Christianity — 20th cent. I. Title.

WILDER, Amos Niven, 1895- 230
Otherworldliness and the New Testament. [1st ed.] New York, Harper [1954] 124p. 20cm. [BT15.W5] 54-11661
1. Theology, Doctrinal— Addresses, essays, lectures. I. Title.

WILES, Maurice F. 230
Jerusalem, Athens, and Oxford, by Maurice Wiles, an inaugural lecture delivered before the University of Oxford on 18 May, 1971. Oxford, Clarendon Press, 1971. 21 p. 22 cm. Includes bibliographical references. [BT21.2.W54] 72-188636 ISBN 0-19-951289-2 £0.40
1. Theology, Doctrinal—History. I. Title.

WILES, Maurice F. 230
Working papers in doctrine / [by] Maurice Wiles. London : S.C.M. Press, 1976. ix, 213 p. ; 23 cm. Contents.Contents.—Some reflections on the origins of the doctrine of the Trinity.—Eternal generation.—In defence of Arius.—The doctrine of Christ in the patristic age.—The nature of the early debate about Christ's human soul.—The theological legacy of St. Cyprian.—One baptism for the remission of sins.—The consequences of modern understanding of reality for the relevance and authority of the tradition of the early Church in our time.—The unassumed is the unhealed.—Does Christology rest on a mistake?—Religious authority and divine action.—Jerusalem, Athens, and Oxford.—The criteria of Christian theology. Includes bibliographical references and index. [BT80.W53] 76-376862 ISBN 0-334-01807-2 : £4.95
1. Theology, Doctrinal—Addresses, essays, lectures. I. Title.

WILEY, Henry Orton, 1877- 230
Christian theology, by H. Orton Wiley. Kansas City, Mo., Beacon Hill Press of Kansas City [1969] 3 v. 24 cm. Reprint of the 1940 ed. Bibliography: v. 3, p. 394-436. [BT75.W5 1969] 75-14807
1. Theology, Doctrinal. I. Title.

WILLIAMS, Carl Carnelius, 1903- 230
Things most surely believed. Anderson, Ind., Gospel Trumpet Co. [1955] 144p. 19cm. [BT77.W55] 55-28918
1. Theology, Doctrinal— Popular works. 2. Church of God (Anderson, Ind.)—Doctrinal and controversial works. I. Title.

WILLIAMS, Daniel Day, 1910- 230
God's grace and man's hope. New York, Harper [1965, c.1949] 215p. 21cm. (Chapel bks., CB17J) Bibl. [BR121.W53] 1.60 pap.,
1. Christianity—Essence, genius, nature. I. Title.

WILLIAMS, Daniel Day, 1910- 230
What present-day theologians are thinking. Rev. ed. [New York] Harper [1959] 190 p. 20 cm. Includes bibliography. [BT28.W55 1959] 58-13946
1. Theology, Doctrinal — Hist. — 20th cent. 2. Religious thought — 20th cent. I. Title.

WILLIAMS, Daniel Day, 1910- 230
What present-day theologians are thinking. [1st ed.] [New York] Harper [1952] 158 p. 20 cm. [BT28.W55] 52-8494
1. Theology, Doctrinal—History—20th cent. 2. Religious thought—20th cent. I. Title.

WILLIAMS, John Rodman. 230
10 teachings / J. Rodman Williams. Carol Stream, Ill. : Creation House, [1974] 121 p. ; 18 cm. (New leaf library) [BT77.W57] 73-82858 ISBN 0-88419-051-X : 1.95
1. Theology, Doctrinal—Popular works. I. Title.

WINGREN, Gustaf, 1910- 230
The flight from creation. Minneapolis, Augsburg Pub. House [1971] 91 p. 20 cm. Includes bibliographical references. [BT695.W55] 79-135232 ISBN 0-8066-1114-6
1. Creation. I. Title.

WINGREN, Gustaf, 1910- 230
Theology in conflict; Nygren, Barth, Bultmann. Translated by Eric II. Wahlstrom. Philadelphia, Muhlenberg Press [1958] 170 p. 21 cm. Translation of Teologiens metodfraga. [BT28.W573] 58-5750
1. Nygren, Anders Bp., 1890- 2. Barth, Karl, 1886- 3. Bultmann, Rudolf Karl, 1884- 4. Theology, Doctrinal — Hist. — 20th cent. 5. Law and gospel. I. Title.

WISE, Carroll Alonzo, 1903- 230
The meaning of pastoral care, by Carroll A. Wise. [1st ed.] New York, Harper & Row [1966] xi, 144 p. 21 cm. Bibliographical references included in "Notes" (p. 137-142) [BV4011.W55] 66-15048
1. Pastoral theology. I. Title.

WISE, Carroll Alonzo, 1903- 230
The meaning of pastoral care. New York, Harper [c.1966] xi,144p. 21cm. Bibl. [BV4011.W55] 66-15048 3.50 bds.,
1. Pastoral theology. I. Title.

WOLFSON, Harry Austryn, 1887- 230
The philosophy of the church fathers. Cambridge, Harvard University Press, 1956- v. 23 cm. (His Structure and growth of philosophic systems from Plato to Spinoza, 3) Contents.v. 1. Faith, Trinity, Incarnation. Bibliographical footnotes. [BT25.W6] 56-5176
1. Theology, Doctrinal — Hist. — Early church. 2. Christian literature, Early — Hist. & crit. 3. Christianity — Philosophy. 4. Trinity — History of doctrines. 5. Heresies and heretics — Early church. I. Title.

WOLFSON, Harry Austryn, 1887- 230
The philosophy of the Church fathers; v.1. 2d ed. rev. Cambridge, Mass., Harvard, 1964. v. 23cm. (His Structure and growth of philosophic systems from Plato to Spinoza, 3) Contents.v.1. Faith, Trinity, Incarnation. Bibl. 64-5600 10.00
1. Theology, Doctrinal—Hist.—Early church. 2. Incarnation—History of doctrines. 3. Trinity—History of doctrines. 4. Heresies and heretics—Early church. I. Title.

WOLFSON, Harry Austryn, 1887- 230
The philosophy of the Church fathers. 3d ed., rev. Cambridge, Harvard University Press [1970- v. 23 cm. (His Structure and growth of philosophic systems from Plato to Spinoza, 3) Contents.Contents.—v. 1. Faith, Trinity, Incarnation. Includes bibliographical references. [BT25.W63] 70-119077 ISBN 0-674-66551-1 12.50
1. Theology, Doctrinal—History—Early church, ca. 30-600. 2. Incarnation—History of doctrines. 3. Trinity—History of doctrines. 4. Heresies and heretics—Early church, ca. 30-600. I. Title.

WOOD, Barry, 1940- 230
The magnificent frolic. Philadelphia, Westminster Press [1970] 223 p. 20 cm. Bibliography: p. [215]-223. [BL182.W65] 78-101698 ISBN 0-664-20886-X 4.95
1. Natural theology. I. Title.

WOOD, Frederic C. 230
Living in the now; spirit-centered faith for 20th century man, by Frederic C. Wood, Jr., New York, Association Press [1970] 159 p. 21 cm. Includes bibliographical references. [BR123.W68] 74-93428 4.95
1. Theology—Addresses, essays, lectures. I. Title.

WOODS, Guy N., 1908- 230
Questions and answers, open forum, Freed-Hardeman College lectures / by Guy N. Woods. Henderson, Tenn. : The College, c1976. 381 p. : ill. ; 24 cm. (Freed-Hardeman College lectures) Includes indexes. [BR96.W66] 76-359613
1. Theology—Miscellanea. I. Title. II. Series: Freed-Hardeman College. Lectures.

WOODSON, Leslie H., 1929- 230
What you believe and why; Bible doctrines made understandable to the man-on-the-street, by Leslie Woodson. Grand Rapids, Zondervan Pub. House [1972] 160 p. 21 cm. [BS543.W66] 73-189585
1. Bible—Theology. I. Title.

WUERL, Donald W. 230
Fathers of the church / Donald W. Wuerl. Huntington, Ind. : Our Sunday Visitor, c1975. 144 p. ; 18 cm. [BR1706.W83] 75-329621 ISBN 0-87973-765-4 pbk. : 2.50
1. Fathers of the church. I. Title.

WYCLIFFE, John, d.1384. 230
Wycliffe : select English writings / edited by Herbert E. Winn ; with a pref. by H. B. Workman. New York : AMS Press, [1976] p. cm. Reprint of the 1929 ed. published by Oxford University Press, London. [BR75.W84 1976] 75-41303 ISBN 0-404-14635-X : 14.00
1. Theology—Collected works—Middle Ages, 600-1500. I. Title.

YOUNGS, Robert W 230
What it means to be a Christian. New York, Farrar, Straus & Cudahy [1960] 192 p. 22 cm. [BR121.2.Y6] 60-5652
1. Christianity — 20th cent. I. Title.

YOUNGS, Robert W. 230
What it means to be a Christian. New York, Farrar, Straus & Cudahy [c.1960] xxiv, 192p. 22cm. 60-5652 3.50 half cloth,
1. Christianity—20th cent. I. Title.

ZAHRNT, Heinz, 1915- 230
The question of God; Protestant theology in the twentieth century. Translated from the German by R. A. Wilson. [1st ed.] New York, Harcourt, Brace & World [1969] 398 p. 23 cm. "A Helen and Kurt Wolff book." Translation of Die Sache mit Gott. Bibliographical references included in "Notes" (p. [361]-383) [BT28.Z313 1969] 69-14847
1. Theology, Protestant—History—20th century. 2. Theology, Doctrinal—History—20th century. 3. God—History of doctrines—20th century. I. Title.

PIKE, James Albert, 1913-1969. 230.0081
A time for Christian candor [by] James A. Pike. [1st ed.] New York, Harper & Row [1964] 160 p. 22 cm. Bibliographical references included in footnotes. [BT55.P5] 64-20196
1. Christianity—Essence, genius, nature. 2. Apologetics—20th cent. I. Title.

AUSTIN, William H. 230'.01
Waves, particles, and paradoxes [by] William H. Austin. Houston, Tex., William Marsh Rice University, 1967. 103 p. 23 cm. (Monograph in philosophy) (Rice University studies, v. 53, no. 2) Bibliographical references included in "Notes" (p. 99-103) [HS36.W65 vol. 53 no. 2] 67-9342
1. Theology. 2. Paradox. I. Title. II. Series. III. Series: William Marsh Rice University, Houston, Tex. Monograph in philosophy.

BARRETT, Earl E. 230.01
A Christian perspective of knowing. Kansas City, Mo. 64109, Beacon Hill Pr., 2923 Troost Av., Box 527 [1965] 224p. 23cm. Bibl. [BT40.B3] 65-10656 4.95
1. Knowledge, Theory of (Religion) I. Title.

BLAMIRES, Harry 230.01
The tryanny of time; a defence of dogmatism. New York, Morehouse [c.1965] ix, 131p. 20cm. [BT28.B6] 65-9031 3.00 bds.,
1. Dogma. 2. Theology.—Methodology. I. Title.

BLAMIRES, Harry. 230.01
The tyranny of time; a defense of dogmatism. New York, Morehouse-Barlow Co. [1965] ix, 131 p. 20 cm. [BT28.B6] 65-9031
1. Dogma. 2. Theology — Methodology. I. Title.

BURI, Fritz, 1907- 230'.01
Thinking faith; steps on the way to a philosophical theology. Translated by Harold H. Oliver. Philadelphia, Fortress Press [1968] xii, 100 p. 22 cm. Translation of Denkender Glaube. Bibliographical footnotes. [BT40.B8513] 68-10984
1. Philosophical theology. I. Title.

CAUTHEN, Wilfred Kenneth. 230.01
The triumph of suffering love [by] Kenneth Cauthen. Valley Forge [Pa.] Judson Press [1966] 78 p. 17 cm. Includes bibliographical references. [BR121.2.C35] 66-28294
1. Christianity—Essence, genius, nature. I. Title.

CURTIS, Charles J. 230'.01
The task of philosophical theology [by] C. J. Curtis. New York, Philosophical Lib. [1967] xxvi, 165p. 23cm. Bibl. [BT40.C8] 67-17634 4.50
1. Philosophical theology. 2. Process theology. I. Title.

FARRER, Austin Marsden 230'.01
Faith and speculation; an essay in philosophical theology, by Austin Farrer. New York, N.Y.U. Pr., 1967. vii, 175p. 23cm. (Deems lects., 1964) [BT40.F35] 67-16975 5.00
1. Philosophical theology. I. Title. II. Series: The Deems lectures, 1964

FLEW, Antony Garrard Newton, 1923- ed. 230.01
New essays in philosophical theology. Edited by Antony Flew [and] Alasdair MacIntyre. New York, Macmillan [1964] x, 274 p. 22 cm. (Macmillan paperback edition) "MP184." [BT40.F54 1964] 64-57338
1. Philosophical theology. I. MacIntyre, Alasdair O., joint ed. II. Title.

FLEW, Antony Garrard Newton, 1923- ed. 230.01
New essays in philosophical theology. Ed. by Antony Flew, Alasdair MacIntyre. New York, Macmillan [c.1964] x, 274p. 22cm. (MP184) 64-57338 3.25 pap.,
1. Philosophical theology. I. MacIntyre, Alasadair C., joint ed. II. Title.

HALL, Charles A. M. 230.01
The common quest, theology and the search for truth. Philadelphia, Westminster [1965, c.1961] 332p. 24cm. [BR118.H35] 65-19780 8.50
1. Theology—Methodology. I. Title.

HENRY, Carl Ferdinand Howard, 1913- 230.01
Frontiers in modern theology Chicago, Moody [1966. c1964. 1965] 160p. 18cm. (Christian forum bks.) Bibl. [BT28.H394 1966] 66-6298 1.45 pap.,
1. Theology—20th cent. I. Title.

MITCHELL, Basil, ed. 230.01
Faith and logic; Oxford essays in philosophical theology. Boston, Beacon Press [1957] v.

222p. 23cm. Bibliographical footnotes. [BT40] 57-2513
1. Christianity—Philosophy. I. Title.
Contents omitted.

MITCHELL, Nasil, ed. 230.01
Faith and logic; Oxford essays in philosophical theology. Boston, Beacon Press [1957] v, 222p. 23cm. Bibliographical footnotes. [BT40] 57-2513
1. Christianity—Philosophy. I. Title.
Contents omitted.

PANNENBERG, Wolfhart, 230'.01
1928-
Theology and the philosophy of science / by Wolfhart Pannenberg ; translated by Francis McDonagh. Philadelphia : Westminster Press, c1976. p. cm. Translation of Wissenschaftstheorie und Theologie. Includes index. [BR118.P2713 1976] 76-20763 ISBN 0-664-21337-5 : 17.50
1. Theology. 2. Religion and science—1946- I. Title.

RAMSEY, Ian T 230.01
Christian discourse, some ligical explorations, by Ian T. Ramsey. London, New York. Oxford University Press, 1965. 92 p. 19 cm. (Riddell memorial lectures, 35th ser.) University of Newcastle upon Tyne. Publications. Lectures delivered at the University of Newcastle upon Tyne, November 5-7, 1963. Bibliographical footnotes. [BR96.5.R29] 65-6792
1. Theology — Terminology. I. Title. II. Series.

RAMSEY, Ian T. 230.01
Christian discourse; some logical explorations. New York, Oxford [c.]1965. 92p. 19cm. (Riddell memorial lects., 35th ser,) Lects. delivered at the Univ. of Newcastle upon Tyne, Nov. 5-7, 1963. Bibl. [BR96.5.R29] 65-6792 2.00
1. Theology—Terminology. I. Title. II. Series.

RAMSEY, Ian T 230.01
Models and mystery. London, New York, Oxford University Press, 1964. ix, 74 p. 19 cm. (The Whidden lectures, 1963) Bibliographical footnotes. [BR118.R34] 64-2871
1. Theology — Methodology. I. Title. II. Series.

RAMSEY, Ian T. 230.01
Models and mystery. New York, Oxford [c.] 1964. ix, 74p. 19cm. (Whidden lects. 1963) Bibl. 64-2871 1.55 bds.,
1. Theory—Methodology. I. Title. II. Series.

ROSS, James F., 1931- 230'.01
Philosophical theology, by James F. Ross. Indianapolis, Bobbs-Merrill [1969] x, 326 p. 24 cm. Bibliographical footnotes. [BT40.R6] 68-17707 8.50
1. Philosophical theology.

SCHLEIERMACHER, Friedrich 230.01
Ernst Daniel, 1768-1834.
Brief outline on the study of theology. Translated, with introductions and notes, by Terrence N. Tice. Richmond, John Knox Press [1966] 132 p. 21 cm. "Bibliographical note": p. 127-128. [BR118.S3513] 66-10301
1. Theology—Methodology. I. Title.

SCHLEIERMACHER, Friedrich 230.01
Ernst Daniel, 1768-1834
Brief outline on the study of theology. Tr. [from German] introds., notes, by Terrence N. Tice. Richmond, Va., Knox [c.1966] 132p. 21cm. Bibl. [BR118.S3513] 66-10301 2.25
1. Theology—Methodology. I. Title.

TORRANCE, Thomas Forsyth, 230'.01
1913-
Theological science [by] Thomas F. Torrance. London, New York [etc.] Oxford U.P., 1969. xx, 368 p. 23 cm. "Based on the Hewett lectures for 1959." Bibliographical footnotes. [BT40.T65 1969] 76-413012 84/-
1. Philosophical theology. I. Title.

WICKER, Brian, 1929- 230.01
Toward a contemporary Christianity. [1st American ed. Notre Dame, Ind.] University of Notre Dame Press [1967] xi, 305 p. 21 cm. First published in 1966 under title: Culture and theology. Bibliography: p. 279-291. [BR115.C8W5 1967] 67-11836
1. Christianity and culture. I. Title.

ADAMS, Hampton, 1897- 230.014
Vocabulary of faith. St. Louis, Bethany Press [1956] 124p. 21cm. [BR96.5.A3] 55-12224
1. Theology— Terminology. I. Title.

BIGLER, Vernon. 230.014
Key words in Christian thinking; a guide to theological terms and ideas. New York, Association Press [1966] 125 p. 16 cm. (A Reflection book) [BR96.5.B5] 66-20477
1. Theology—Terminology. I. Title.

FERGUSON, Charles 230'.01'4
Wright, 1901-
A is for Advent [by] Charles W. Ferguson. [1st ed.] Boston, Little, Brown [1968] viii, 149 p. illus. 22 cm. [BR96.5.F4] 68-30879 4.95
1. Theology—Terminology. I. Title.

HORDERN, William. 230.014
Speaking of God; the nature and purpose of theological language. New York, Macmillan [1964] viii, 209 p. 21 cm. Includes bibliographical references. [BV4319.H6] 64-21167
1. Theology — Terminology. 2. Communication (Theology) I. Title.

HORDERN, William 230.014
Speaking of God; the nature and purpose of theological language. New York, Macmillan [c.1964] viii, 209p. 21cm. Bibl. 64-21167 4.95 bds.,
1. Theology—Terminology. 2. Communication (Theology) I. Title.

PING, Charles J. 230.014
Meaningful nonsense, by Charles J. Ping. Philadelphia, Westminster [1966] 143p. 21cm. Bibl. [BL65.L2P5] 66-15545 2.25 pap.,
1. Religion and language. 2. Theology—Terminology. I. Title.

RAMSEY, Ian T. 230.014
Religious language; an empirical placing of theological phrases. New York, Macmillan [1963] 221p. 18cm. (MP129) Bibl. 1.45 pap.,
1. Theology—Terminology. 2. Semantics (Philosophy) 3. Christianity—Philosophy. I. Title.

SARDESON, Charles Thomas. 230.014
Rediscovering the words of faith. New York, Abingdon Press [1956] 124p. 20cm. [BR96.5.S3] 56-7766
1. Theology—Terminology. I. Title.

MOUROUX, Jean 230.01529
The mystery of time, a theological inquiry. Tr. [from French] by John Drury. New York, Desclee [1964, c.1962] 319p. 22cm. Bibl. 64-12768 5.50
1. Time (Theology) I. Title.

HELFAER, Philip M. 230'.01'9
The psychology of religious doubt, by Philip M. Helfaer. Boston, Beacon Press [1972] xiv, 345 p. illus. 21 cm. "Most of this book was originally presented as a doctoral dissertation in the Department of Social Relations at Harvard University." "Twelve ... case studies of Protestant seminarians." Bibliography: p. 333-336. [BF773.H43] 72-75539 ISBN 0-8070-1134-7 9.95
1. Belief and doubt. 2. Psychology, Religious. I. Title.

BRUCKBERGER, Raymond 230.02
Leopold, 1907-
Toward the summit. Translated by Sister M. Camille and Alastair Guinan. New York, Kenedy [1956] 160p. 22cm. [BX1751.B75] 56-10777
1. Catholic Church—Doctrinal and controversial works. I. Title.

MARSHALL, I. Howard 230.02
Christian beliefs: a brief introduction. Chicago, Intervarsity Pr. [c.1963] 96p. 18cm. (Christian bks. for the mod. world) Bibl. 63-23670 1.25 pap.,
1. Theology, Doctrinal—Introductions. I. Title.

WATKIN, Edward Ingram, 230.02
1888-
The Catholic center, an abridgement. New York, Sheed [1962] 95p 19cm. (Canterbury bks.) 62-15641 .75 pap.,
1. Catholic Church—Doctrinal and controversial works—Catholic authors. 2. Religion—Philosophy. 3. Worship. I. Title.

WILLIAMS, George Huntston, 230.02
1914-
The Norman anonymous of 1100 A.D.; toward the identification and evaluation of the so-called Anonymous of York. Cambridge, Harvard University Press, 1951. xiii, 236 p. 24 cm. (Harvard theological studies, 18) "Issued as an extra number of the Harvard theological review." "A reworking of . . . [the author's] doctoral dissertation, 'The bearings of Christology on the relationship between church and state as illustrated by the so-called Anonymous of York,' Union Theological Seminary, New York, 1946." Bibliographical footnotes. [BV629.W61] 51-11559
1. Cambridge. University. Corpus Christi college. Library. Ms. 415. 2. Church and state. I. Title. II. Series.

SPYKMAN, Gordon J. 230'.02'02
Christian fath in focus, by Gordon J. Spykman. Grand Rapids, Baker Bk. [1967] 164p. 20cm. [BT77.3.S6] 67-29071 1.95 pap.,
1. Theology, Doctrinal—Outlines, syllabi, etc. I. Title.

TURNBULL, Ralph G 230.0202
What Christians believe, by Ralph G. Turnbull. Grand Rapids, Mich., Baker Book House, 1965. 86 p. 22 cm. (Bible companion series for lesson and sermon preparation) [BT77.3.T8] 65-29502
1. Theology, Doctrinal — Outlines, syllabi, etc. I. Title.

TURNBULL, Ralph G. 230.0202
What Christians believe. Grand Rapids, Mich., Baker Bk. [c.]1965. 86p. 22cm. (Bible companion ser. for lesson and sermon prep.) [BT77.3.T8] 65-29502 1.00 pap.,
1. Theology, Doctrinal—Outlines, syllabi, etc. I. Title.

AID to Bible 230'.03
understanding, containing historical, geographical, religious, and, social facts concerning Bible persons, peoples, places, plant and animal life, activities, and so forth. [New York, Watchtower Bible and Tract Society of New York, 1971] 1696 p. illus. (part col.), facsims., maps (part col.) 24 cm. [BS440.A43 1971] 72-26875
1. Bible—Dictionaries. I. Watchtower Bible and Tract Society of New York.

CHRISTIAN word book 230'.03
[by] J. Sherrell Hendricks [and others] Nashville, Abingdon Press [1969, c1968] 320 p. 24 cm. [BR95.C53 1969] 69-19739 ISBN 6-87076-498- 3.95
1. Theology—Dictionaries. I. Hendricks, John Sherrell, 1931-

CHRISTIAN word book. 230'.03
[Nashville] Graded Press [1968] 320 p. 23 cm. Prepared by the Editorial Division, Methodist Board of Education for use in the United Methodist Church. Authors: J. Sherrell Hendricks and others. [BR95.C53] 70-302
1. Theology—Dictionaries. I. Hendricks, John Sherrell, 1931- II. United Methodist Church (United States) Board of Education. Editorial Division.

ELLER, Vernard. 230'.03
Cleaning up the Christian vocabulary / Vernard Eller. Elgin, Ill. : Brethren Press, c1976. 121 p. ; 18 cm. [BR96.5.E43] 76-10984 ISBN 0-87178-153-0 pbk. : 2.95
1. Theology—Terminology. I. Title.

GIESEN, Heinrich, ed. 230.03
When you are asked about faith and life. Translated by Elmer Foelber. Philadelphia, Fortress Press [1963] 190 p. 18 cm. [BR96.G513] 63-7903
1. Questions and answers — Theology. I. Title.

GIESEN, Heinrich, ed. 230.03
When you are asked about faith and life. Tr. [from German] by Elmer Foelber. Philadelphia, Fortress [c.1963] 190p. 18cm. 63-7903 3.75
1. Questions and answers—Theology. I. Title.

A Handbook of Christian 230.03
theology; definition essays on concepts and movements of thought in contemporary Protestantism. New York, Meridian Books [1958] 380 p. 18 cm. (Living age books, LA18) Edited by Marvin Halverson and Arthur A. Cohen. [BR95.H3] 57-10852
1. Theology—Dictionaries. I. Halverson, Marvin, 1913- ed. II. Cohen, Arthur Allen, 1928- ed.

HANDBOOK of Christian 230.03
theology (A); definition essays on concepts and movements of thought in contemporary Protestantism. Cleveland, World [1965, c.1958] 380p. 21cm. Ed. by Marvin Halverson, Arthur A. Cohen. [BR95.H3] 5.00
1. Theology—Dictionaries. I. Halverson, Marvin, 1913- ed. II. Cohen, Arthur A., ed.

HARVEY, Van Austin. 230.03
A handbook of theological terms [by] Van A. Harvey. New York, Macmillan [1964] 253 p. 18 cm. "168." [BR95.H32] 64-25193
1. Theology—Dictionaries. I. Title.

RICHARDSON, Alan, 1905- 230'.03
A dictionary of Christian theology. Philadelphia, Westminster Press [1969] xii, 364 p. 26 cm. Includes bibliographical references. [BR95.R47] 69-19153 8.50
1. Theology—Dictionaries. I. Title.

ADAMS, James Luther, 1901- 230.04
Taking time seriously. [Articles] Glencoe, Ill., Free Press [1957] 74p. 24cm. [BR123.A35] 57-4296
1. Theology—Addresses, essays, lectures. I. Title.

BARTH, Karl, 1886- 230.04
The word of God and the word of man. Translated with a new foreword by Douglas Horton. New York, Harper [1957] vii, 327 p. 21 cm. (Harper torchbooks, TB13) Translation of Das Wort Gottes und die Theologie. [BR121.B2455 1957] 57-7531
1. Christianity—Addresses, essays, lectures. 2. Christianity—20th cent. I. Title.

BELLARMINE theolotical 230.04
lectures. vv. 1- St. Meinard, Ind. [St. Meinard Archabbey, 1955- v. 22cm. (A Grall publication) [BX885.B44] k5-9040
1. Catholic Church—Addresses, essays, lectures. 2. Theology—Addresses, essays, lectures. I. Bellarmine College, Louisville, Ky. II. St. Meinard Archabbey, St. Meinard, Ind.

BULTMANN, Rudolf 230.04
Existence and faith; shorter writings. Selected, translated [from the German], and introduced by Schubert M. Ogden. New York, Meridian Books [c.1960] 320p. (bibl. p. [317]-320) 18cm. (Living age books LA29) 4.00; 1.45 pap.,
I. Title.

HENRY, Carl Ferdinand 230.04
Howard, 1913- ed.
Contemporary evangelical thought [by] Andrew W. Blackwood [and others] Great Neck, N. Y., Channel Press [1957] 320p. 24cm. Includes bibliography. [BR118.H46] 57-7630
1. Theology—20th cent. 2. Evangelicalism. I. Title.

KENNEDY, Gerald Hamilton, 230.04
Bp., 1907-
Go inquire of the Lord. [1st ed.] New York, Harper [1952] 125 p. 20 cm. [BR123.K34] 51-11928
1. Christianity—Addresses, essays, lectures. I. Title.

KITCHIN, Samuel S 1877- 230.04
The gate of the kingdom; a new approach to eternal truths. With a foreword by William H. Sill. [1st ed.] New York, Exposition Press [1955] 141p. 21cm. [BR121.K56] 55-5718
1. Christianity—20th cent. I. Title.

LEE, Robert Greene, 1886- 230.04
Great is the Lord. [Westwood, N. J.] F. H. Revell Co. [1955] 160p. 21cm. [BT15.L38] 55-5393
1. Theology. Doctrinal—Addresses, essays, lectures. I. Title.

LEIBRECHT, Walter, ed. 230.04
Religion and culture; essays in honor of Paul Tillich. [1st ed.] New York, Harper [1959] xi, 399p. port. 25cm. Bibliographical references included in 'Notes' (p.355-363) 'A bibliography of Paul Tillich, complied by Peter H. John': p.367-396. [BR50.L38] 58-5193
1. Tillich, Paul, 1886- 2. Theology—Addresses, essays, lectures. 3. Civilization, Modern—Addresses, essays, lectures. I. Title.

MAURICE, Frederick 230.04
Denison, 1805-1872.
Theological essays. Introd. by Edward F. Carpenter. New York, Harper [c1957] 331p. illus. 21cm. [BR85.M33 1957a] 58-5194
1. Theology—Addresses, essays, lectures. I. Title.

MYERS, Edward De Los, ed. 230.04
Christianity and reasons, seven essays. New York, Oxford University Press, 1951. xiii, 172 p. 21 cm. Includes bibliographical references. [BT10.M9] 51-9721
I. Title.
Contents omitted.

RAMSEY, Paul, ed. 230.04
Faith and ethics; the theology of H. Richard Niebuhr [by] Waldo Beach [and others. 1st ed.] New York, Harper [1957] xiv, 306p. port. 22cm. [BX4827.N47R3] 57-9882
1. Niebuhr, Helmut Richard, 1894- 2. Niebuhr, Helmut Richard, 1894- —Bibl. 3. Theology, Doctrinal—Addresses, essays, lectures. I. Title.
Onconnts omitted.

RAMSEY, Paul, ed. [Robert 230.04
Paul Ramsey]
Faith and ethics: the theology of H. Richard Niebuhr [by] Waldo Beach [others.] [Magnolia, Mass., P. Smith, 1967,c.1957] xii, 314p. port. 21cm. [BX4827.N47R3] 4.00
1. Niebuhr, Helmut Richard. 1894- 2. Niebuhr, Helmut Richard, 1894-;Bibl. 3. Theology, Doctrinal — Addresses, essays, lectures. I. Title.
Contents omitted,

THE Root of the vine; 230.04
essays in Biblical theology, by Anton Fridrichsen and other members of Uppsala University. Introd. by A. G. Hebert. New York, Philosophical Library [1953] vii, 160p. 23cm. [BS543.A1R6] 53-12506
1. Bible—Theology—Addresses, essays, lectures. I. Fridrichsen, Anton Johnson, 1888-

SPENCER, Sidney, 1888- 230.04
The deep things of God; essays in liberal religion. London, Allen & Unwin [dist. Mystic, Conn., Verry, 1965] 118p. 19cm. [BR85.S634] 2.00 bds.,
1. Theology—Addresses, essays, lectures. I. Title.

YOUNG, William, 1918- 230.04
Toward a reformed philosophy; the development of a Protestant philosophy in Dutch Calvinistic thought since the time of Abraham Kuyper. Grand Rapids, Piet Hein Publishers, 1952. 155p. 24cm. Includes bibliography. [BT30.N5Y6] 54-35628
1. Religious thought—Netherlands. 2. Theology, Doctrinal—Hist.—Netherlands. 3. Philosophy, Dutch. 4. Calvinism. I. Title. II. Title: Protestant philosophy.

AMERICAN Association of Theological Schools. 230'.07
Horizons of theological education: essays in honor of Charles L. Taylor, edited by John B. Coburn, Walter D. Wagoner [and] Jesse H. Ziegler. Dayton, Ohio [1966] xvii. 133 p. 27 cm. "Published [also] in paper covers as vol. II, number 4 of Theological education." Includes bibliographical references. [BV4020.A63] 67-3969
1. Taylor, Charles Lincoln, 1901- 2. Theology — Study and teaching — Addresses, essays, lectures. I. Coburn, John B., ed. II. Wagoner, Walter D., joint ed. III. Ziegler, Jesse H., joint ed. IV. Taylor, Charles Lincoln, 1901- V. Title.
Contents omitted

CONE, Cecil Wayne. 230'.07
The identity crisis in Black theology / Cecil Wayne Cone. Nashville, Tenn. : AMEC, c1975. 173 p. ; 20 cm. Bibliography: p. 165-173. [BT82.7.C66] 76-350001
1. Black theology—History. 2. Negroes—Religion. I. Title.

COULSON, John, 1919- ed. 230.0711
Theology and the university, an ecumenical investigation [Contributors: Christopher Butler, others] Helicon [dist. New York, Taplinger, c.1964] x, 286p. 23cm. Bibl. 64-15968 4.95
1. Theology—Study and teaching—Catholic Church. 2. Religious education of adults—Catholic. 3. Catholic Church—Education. I. Title.

SOUTHARD, Samuel. 230'.07'2
Religious inquiry : an introduction to the why and how / Samuel Southard. Nashville : Abingdon, c1976. 127 p. ; 19 cm. Includes index. Bibliography: p. 117-121. [BV4.S68] 76-20449 ISBN 0-687-36090-0 pbk. : 3.95
1. Theology, Practical—Research. I. Title.

ANDERSON, Roy Allan 230'.073
Faith that conquers fear. Nashville, Southern Pub. [1967] 171p. 21cm. (His God's eternal plan, v. 1) [BX6154.A567] 67-25226 2.50 pap.,
1. Seventh-Day Adventists— Doctrinal and controversial works. I. Title.

*BRINK, William P. 230.076
Learning doctrine from the Bible. Grand Rapids, Mich., Baker Bk. [c.1965] 82p. illus. 28cm. 1.00 pap.,
I. Title.

CHAPLIN, Dora P 230.076
We want to know; originally intended for young people but frequently borrowed by the other generation especially parents, godparents, clergy, and other leaders. Foreword by Lawrence Rose. New York, Morehouse-Gorham, 1957. 216p. 21cm. Includes bibliography. [BR96.C5] 57-6775
1. Questions and answers— Theology. I. Title.

CLARKE, William R. 230'.076
Pew ask pulpit answers. by W. R. Clarke. Boston, Christopher Pub. House [c.1967] 161p. 21cm. [BR96.C55] 67-13543 3.95
1. Questions and answers—Theology. I. Title.

CLARKE, William R. 230'.076
Pew asks; pulpit answers, by W. R. Clarke. Boston, Christopher Pub. House [c1967] 161 p. 21 cm. [BR96.C55] 67-13543
1. Questions and answers — Theology. I. Title.

FITZGERALD, Lawrence P. 230'.076
Questions that bother me [by] Lawrence P. Fitzgerald. Valley Forge [Pa.] Judson [1967] 94p. 20cm. [BR96.F75] 67-14359 1.95 pap.,
1. Question sQuestion and answers Theology. 2. Questions and answers—Christian life. I. Title.

KNIGHT, Marcus. 230.076
There's an answer somewhere, by Marcus Knight and L. S. Hawkes. With a foreword by the Bishop of Portsmouth. London, New York, Longmans, Green [1953] 134p. 19cm. [BR96.K5] 53-13316
1. Questions and answers—Theology. I. Hawkes, Leonard Stephen, joint author. II. Title.

POLING, Daniel Alfred, 1884- 230.076
Your questions answered with comforting counsel. Great Neck, N.Y., Channel Press [1956] 312p. 21cm. [BR96.P57] 56-12006
1. Questions and answers—Theology. I. Title.

PRIME, Derek. 230'.076
Questions on the Christian faith answered from the Bible. [1st U.S.A. ed.] Grand Rapids, Eerdmans [1968, c1967] 128 p. 21 cm. [BR96.P73 1968] 68-18834
1. Theology—Miscellanea. I. Title.

STONE, Nathan J 230.076
Answering your questions. Chicago, Moody Press [c1956] 509p. 22cm. [BR96.S86] 57-23348
1. Questions and answers—Theology. I. Title.

STONE, Nathan J 230.076
Answering your questions. Chicago, Moody Press [1956] 509 p. 22 cm. [BR96.S86] 57-23348
1. Questions and answers — Theology. I. Title.

UTT, Charles D 230.076
Answers to 343 bible questions Mountain View, Calif., Pacific Press Pub. Association [1957] 383p. 18cm. (Christian home library) [BR96.U8] 57-7780
1. Questions and answers—Theology. I. Title.

WIESE, Walter, fl.1966- 230'.076
Where is God? and other questions children ask. Translated by George Williams. Philadelphia, Fortress Press [1969] 54 p. illus. 19 cm. Translation of Wo ist Gott, Mutter? [BR96.W513] 78-76807 1.95
1. Theology—Miscellanea. 2. Children's questions and answers. I. Title.

WOODBRIDGE, Charles Jahleel, 1902- 230.076
Tell us, please; answers to Life's great questions. [Westwood, N.J.] Revell [1958] 127 p. 21 cm. [BR96.W63] 58-8601
1. Questions and answers — Theology. I. Title.

BEARDSLEE, William A., ed. 230.08
America and the future of theology, ed. by William A. Beardslee. Philadelphia, Westminster [1967] 206p. 21cm. (Adventures in faith) Bibl. [BT15.B4] 67-11861 2.25 pap.,
1. Theology, Doctrinal—Addresses, essays, lectures. 2. U. S.—Religion—Addresses, essays, lectures. I. Title.
Contents omitted.

BEARDSLEE, William A ed. 230.08
America and the future of theology, edited by William A. Beardslee. Philadelphia, Westminster Press [1967] 206 p. 21 cm. (Adventures in faith) includes bibliographical references. [BT15.B4] 67-11861
1. Theology, Doctrinal — Addresses, essays, lectures. 2. U.S. — Religion — Addresses, essays, lectures. I. Title.
Contents omitted

BOWDEN, John Stephen, comp. 230'.08
A reader in contemporary theology, ed. by John Bowden, James Richmond. Philadelphia, Westminster [1967] 190p. 19cm. Bibl. [BT10.B6 1967 a] 67-16281 1.95 pap.,
1. Theology, Doctrinal—Addresses, essays, lectures. I. Richmond, James, 1931- joint comp. II. Title.

BOWDEN, John Stephen, comp. 230'.08
A reader in contemporary theology, edited by John Bowden and James Richmond. Philadelphia, Westminister Press [1967] 190 p. 19 cm. Includes bibliographies. [BT10.B6] 67-16281
1. Theology. Doctrinal — Addresses, essays, lectures. I. Richmond, James, 1931- joint comp. II. Title.

BRUNNER, Heinrich Emil, 1889- 230.08
The scandal of Christianity; the gospel as stumbling block to modern man [by] Emil Brunner. Richmond, John Knox Press [1965] 115 p. 19 cm. "Five lectures . . . delivered as the Robertson lectures . . . Trinity College, Glasgow . . . March, 1948." [BT75.B847] 65-12729
1. Theology, Doctrinal. 2. Apologetics — 20th cent. I. Title.

BRUNNER, Heinrich Emil, 1889- 230.08
The scandal of Christianity; the gospel as stumbling block to modern man [by] Emil Brunner. Richmond, Va., Knox [c.1965] 115p. 19cm. Five lect. delivered as the Robertson lectures, Trinity College, Glasgow, March, 1948. [BT75.B847] 65-12729 1.25 pap.,
1. Theology, Doctrinal. 2. Apologetics—20th cent. I. Title.

BULTMANN, Rudolf Karl, 1884- 230'.08
Faith and understanding, [by] Rudolf Bultmann. Edited with an introd. by Robert W. Funk. Translated by Louise Pettibone Smith. [1st U.S. ed.] New York, Harper & Row [1969- v. 22 cm. Essays. Translation of Glauben und verstehen. Bibliographical footnotes. [BT15.B8213] 69-10471 7.50
1. Bible—Theology. 2. Theology—Addresses, essays, lectures. I. Title.

BUNYAN, John, 1628-1688. 230'.08 s
The doctrine of the law and grace unfolded and I will pray with the Spirit / [by] John Bunyan ; edited by Richard L. Greaves. Oxford : Clarendon Press, 1976. xliv, 303 p., plate : facsims. ; 23 cm. (The miscellaneous works of John Bunyan ; v.2) [BR75.B73 1976 vol. 2] [BT760] 234'.1 77-351855 ISBN 0-19-811871-6 : 31.25
1. Grace (Theology)—Early works to 1800. 2. Law and gospel. I. Greaves, Richard L. II. Bunyan, John, 1628-1688. I will pray with the Spirit and with the understanding also. 1976. III. Title: The doctrine of the law and grace unfolded.
Distributed by Oxford University Press New York N.Y.

BUNYAN, John, 1628-1688. 230'.08
The miscellaneous works of John Bunyan / general editor, Roger Sharrock. Oxford : Clarendon Press, 19 v. : facsims. ; 23 cm. Contents.Contents.— —v.2. The doctrine of the law and grace unfolded and I will pray with the spirit. [BR75.B73 1976] 77-351856 ISBN 0-19-811871-6 (v.2) : 31.25
I. Title.
Dist. by Oxford University Press NY NY

CALLAHAN, Daniel J., comp. 230'.08
God, Jesus, and Spirit. Edited by Daniel Callahan. [New York] Herder and Herder [1969] xix, 352 p. 22 cm. A collection of articles which originally appeared in the Commonweal, 1967-68. Bibliographical footnotes. [BT10.C3] 70-75256 8.50
1. Theology, Doctrinal—Addresses, essays, lectures. I. The Commonweal. II. Title.

CHRISTIANITY and crisis. 230'.08
Witness to a generation; significant writings from Christianity and crisis, 1941-1966, edited by Wayne H. Cowan. With a pref. by Herbert Butterfield. Indianapolis, Bobbs-Merrill [1966] xxi, 272 p. 24 cm. [BT10.C5] 66-29152
1. Theology—Collections. I. Cowan, Wayne H., ed. II. Title.

A Companion to Paul : 230'.08
readings in Pauline theology / Michael J. Taylor, editor. New York : Alba House, [1975] xiv, 245 p. ; 21 cm. Includes bibliographical references. [BS2651.C65] 75-19261 ISBN 0-8189-0304-X pbk. : 4.95
1. Bible. N.T. Epistles of Paul—Collected works. I. Taylor, Michael J.

ECKARDT, Arthur Roy, 1918- comp. 230'.08
The theologian at work; a common search for understanding, edited by A. Roy Eckardt. [1st ed.] New York, Harper & Row [1968] xxx, 253 p. 21 cm. (Harper forum books) [BR118.E25] 68-11745
1. Theology—Methodology. I. Title.

EDWARDS, Jonathan, 1703-1758. 230'.08
The works of President Edwards. [Edited by Edward Williams and Edward Parsons] New York, B. Franklin [1968] 10 v. port. 23 cm. (Burt Franklin research and source work series no. 271) Reprint of the 1817 ed. (8 v.) and of the 2 supplementary vols. published in 1847. [BX7117.E3 1968] 68-56782
1. Congregational churches—Collected works. 2. Theology—Collected works—18th century. I. Williams, Edward, 1750-1813, ed. II. Parsons, Edward, 1762-1833, ed. III. Title.

FAITH, fact, and fantasy 230.08
[by] C.F.D. Moule [others] Pref. by C.F.D. Moule. Philadelphia, Westminster Pr. [1966,c.1964] 125p. 19cm. (Adventures in faith) [BR123.F24] 66-10108 1.45 pap.,
1. Christianity—20th cent.—Addresses, essays, lectures. I. Moule, Charles Francis Digby.

FULLER, Edmund, 1914- 230'.08
Affirmations of God and man; writings for modern dialogue. New York, Association [1967] 160p. 23cm. 160p. 23cm. Bibl. [BR53.F8] 67-14584 4.95 4.95
1. Christian literature 2. Christian literature (Selections: Extracts, etc. I. Title.

GALLOWAY, Allan Douglas, 1920- ed. 230'.08
Basic readings in theology. Edited by A. D. Galloway. Cleveland, Meridian Books [1968, c1964] 316 p. 21 cm. Includes bibliographical references. [BT10.G3 1968] 68-15658
1. Theology—Collections. I. Title.

HARTSOCK, Donald E., comp. 230'.08
Contemporary religious issues, edited by Donald E. Hartsock. Belmont, Calif., Wadsworth Pub. Co. [1968] ix, 422 p. 23 cm. (Wadsworth continuing education series) [BL25.H33] 68-29159
1. Religious thought—20th century. I. Title.

HENRY, Carl Ferdinand Howard, 1913- comp. 230'.08
Fundamentals of the faith [by] Gordon H. Clark [and others] Edited by Carl F. H. Henry. Grand Rapids, Zondervan Pub. House [1969] 291 p. 24 cm. (Contemporary evangelical thought) Each essay also published separately in Christianity today as a pamphlet bind-in, Sept. 1965-Aug. 1968. Contents.Contents.—Revealed religion, by G. H. Clark.—God, his names and nature, by H. B. Kuhn.—The triune God, by S. J. Mikolaski.—The creation of matter, life, and man, by A. H. Leitch.—Jesus Christ, his life and ministry, by J. Schneider.—Jesus Christ, the divine redeemer, by C. D. Linton.—The Holy Spirit, by G. W. Bromiley.—Christ and his church, by M. L. Loane.—The new birth, by B. Graham.—The Reformed doctrine of sanctification, by C. N. Weisiger, 3d.—Heaven or hell? By F. C. Kuehner.—The second advent of Christ, by W. M. Smith.—The glorious destiny of the believer, by M. C. Tenney. Includes bibliographies. [BT10.H4] 72-81056 5.95
1. Theology, Doctrinal—Addresses, essays, lectures. I. Clark, Gordon Haddon. II. Christianity today. III. Title.

HODGSON, Leonard, 1889- 230.08
Christian faith and practice; seven lectures. Grand Rapids, Mich., Eerdmans [1965, c.1950] xii, 113p. 20cm. [BT77.H55] 65-9540 2.50
1. Theology, Doctrinal—Popular works. I. Title.

HUGHES, Philip Edgcumbe, ed. 230.08
Creative minds in contemporary theology; a guidebook to the principal teachings of Karl Barth, G. C. Berkouwer, Emil Brunner, Rudolf Bultmann, Oscar Cullmann, James Denney, C. H. Dodd, Herman Dooyeweerd, P. T. Forsyth, Charles Gore, Reinhold Niebuhr, Pierre Teilhard de Chardin, and Paul Tillich. Grand Rapids, Eerdmans [1966] 488 p. 24 cm. Includes bibliographies. [BT28.H8] 64-22029
1. Theology—20th century. I. Title.

JENKINS, Daniel Thomas, 1914-ed. 230.08
The scope of theology. Cleveland, World [1968,c.1965] 270p. 270p. 21cm. (Meridian bk., M254) Bibl. [BT75.2.J4] 65-25777 2.95 pap.,
1. Theology, Doctrinal. I. Title.

KARLSTADT, Andreas Rudolf, 1480(ca.)-1541. 230'.08
Karlstadt's battle with Luther : documents in a liberal-radical debate / edited by Ronald J. Sider. Philadelphia : Fortress Press, c1977. p. cm. Includes index. Bibliography: p. [BR301.K3] 77-78642 ISBN 0-8006-1312-0 pbk. : 5.95
1. Karlstadt, Andreas Rudolf, 1480 (ca.)-1541. 2. Luther, Martin, 1483-1546. 3. Theology—Collected works—16th century. 4. Reformation—History—Sources. I. Sider, Ronald J. II. Luther, Martin, 1483-1546. Selections. 1977. III. Title.

KARLSTADT, Andreas Rudolf, 1480(ca.)-1541. 230'.08
Karlstadt's battle with Luther : documents in a liberal-radical debate / edited by Ronald J. Sider. Philadelphia : Fortress Press, c1977. p. cm. Includes index. Bibliography: p. [BR301.K3] 77-78642 ISBN 0-8006-1312-0 pbk. : 5.95
1. Karlstadt, Andreas Rudolf, 1480 (ca.)-1541. 2. Luther, Martin, 1483-1546. 3. Theology—Collected works—16th century. 4. Reformation—History—Sources. I. Sider, Ronald J. II. Luther, Martin, 1483-1546. Selections. 1977. III. Title.

KERR, Hugh Thomson, 1909- ed. 230.08
Readings in Christian thought, edited by Hugh T. Kerr. Nashville, Abingdon Press [1966] 382 p. 26 cm. [BR50.K4] 66-14992
1. Theology—Collections. I. Title.

LEWIS, Clive Staples, 1898-1963. 230'.08
A mind awake; an anthology of C. S. Lewis,

edited by Clyde S. Kilby. [1st American ed.] New York, Harcourt, Brace & World [1969, c1968] 252 p. 21 cm. [BT15.L48 1969] 70-78866
1. Theology—Collections—20th century. I. Kilby, Clyde S., ed. II. Title.

MARTY, Martin E. 1928- ed. 230.08
New theology. no. 1- New York, Macmillan. 1964 v. 18 cm. Editors: 1964- M. E. Marty and D. G. Peerman. Consists of reprints from various religious journals. [BR53.N5] 64-3132
1. Theology — Addresses, essays, lectures. 2. Christianity — 20th cent. — Addresses, essays, lectures. I. Peerman, Dean G., ed. II. Title.

MILLER, William Robert. 230'.08
comp.
The new Christianity; an anthology of the rise of modern religious thought, Ed., introds. by William Robert Miller. [New York, Dell, 1968,c.1967] xxi, 393p. 20cm. (Delta bk., 6317) Bibl. [BR115.C8W5 1967] 2.45 pap.,
1. Theology—Collections. I. Title.

MILLER, William Robert, 230'.08
comp.
The new Christianity; an anthology, of the rise of modern religious thought, edited and with introductions by William Robert Miller. New York, Delacorte Press [1967] xxi, 303 p. 21 cm. Includes bibliographies. [BT10.M] 67-14998
1. Theology — Collections. I. Title.

NEW theology. 230.08
no. 5- 1968- New York, Macmillan. v. 18cm. Eds.: 1964-68 M. E. Marty, D. G. Peerman. Consists of reprints from various religious journals. [BR53.N5] 64-3132 1.95 pap.,
1. Theology—Addresses, essays, lectures. 2. Christianity—20th cent.—Addresses, essays, lectures. I. Marty, Martin E., 1928- ed. II. Peerman, Dean G. ed.

NORRIS, Richard Alfred, 230.08
ed.
Lux in lumine; essays to honor W. Norman Pittenger, ed. by R. A. Norris, Jr. New York, Seabury [1966] vi, 186p. 22cm. Bibl. [BR50.N58] 66-16650 4.50
1. Theology—Addresses, essays, lectures. 2. Pittenger, William Norman, 1905—Bibl. I. Pittenger, William Norman, 1905- II. Title.
Contents omitted.

OBERMAN, Heiko Augustinus, 230.08
ed.
Forerunners of the Reformation: the shape of late medieval thought illustrated by key documents. Translations by Paul L. Nyhus. [1st ed.] New York, Holt, Rinehart and Winston [1966] x, 333 p. 22 cm. Bibliography: p. 319-327. [BT10.O23] 66-13496
1. Theology — Collections. I. Title.

OBERMAN, Heiko Augustinus, 230.08
ed.
Forerunners of the Reformation; the shape of late medieval thought, illustrated by key documents. Tr. by Paul L. Nyhus. [1st ed.] New York, Holt [1966] x, 333p. 22cm. Bibl. [BT10.O23] 66-13496 7.95
1. Theology—Collections. I. Title.

PEERMAN, Dean G. ed. 230'.08
Frontline theology, ed. by Dean Peerman. Introd. essay by Martin E. Marty. Richmond. Knox [1967] 172p. 21cm. [BT80.P4] 67-10615 4.50
1. Theology. Doctrinal —Addresses, essays, lectures. I. Title.

RAMSEY, Paul, ed. [Full 230.08
name: Robert Paul Ramsey]
Faith and ethics; the theology of H. Richard Niebuhr [by] Waldo Beach [others] New York, Harper [1965, c.1957] 306p. port. 20cm. (Harper torchbk. TB129L) [BX4827.N47R3] 1.95 pap.,
1. Niebuhr, Helmut Richard, 1894- 2. Niebuhr, Helmut Richard, 1894- —Bibl. 3. Theology, Doctrinal—Addresses, essays, lectures. I. Title.

RAMSEY, Paul [Robert Paul 230.08
Ramsey]
Faith and ethics; the theology of H. Richard Niebuhr [by] Waldo Beach [others] Ed. Paul Ramsey [Gloucester, Mass., P. Smith, 1965, c.1957] xii, 314p. port. 21cm. (Harper torchbk., Cloister lib., TB129L rebound) Bibl. [BX4827.N47R3] 4.00
1. Niebuhr, Helmut Richard, 1894- 2. Niebuhr, Helmut Richard, 1894- —Bibl. 3. Theology, Doctrinal—Addresses, essays, lectures. I. Title.

SCOTT, William A., 1920- 230'.08
comp.
Sources of Protestant theology. Edited by William A. Scott. New York, Bruce Pub. Co. [1971] xviii, 392 p. 23 cm. (Contemporary theology series) [BT10.S3 1971] 70-143783
1. Theology, Protestant—Collections. 2. Theology, Doctrinal—Collections. I. Title.

TROELTSCH, Ernst, 1865- 230'.08
1923.
Writings on theology and religion / Ernst Troeltsch ; translated and edited by Robert Morgan and Michael Pye. Atlanta : John Knox Press, 1977, c1976. p. cm. "The first three essays ... translated ... from Gesammelte Schriften II, Tubingen, 1913 and 1922 ... The fourth was published separately." Bibliography: p. [BR85.T7613] 77-79596 ISBN 0-8042-0554-X : 17.50
1. Troeltsch, Ernst, 1865-1923—Addresses, essays, lectures. 2. Theology—Addresses, essays, lectures. I. Title.
Contents omitted

VAN BUREN, Paul Matthews, 230'.08
1924-
Theological explorations [by] Paul M. van Buren. New York, Macmillan [1968] 181 p. 22 cm. Includes bibliographies. [BT80.V34] 68-16766
1. Theology, Doctrinal—Addresses, essays, lectures. I. Title.

BARTH, Karl 230.081
Evangelical theology, an introduction. Tr. [from German] by Grover Foley. Garden City, Doubleday [1964, c.1963] 184p. 19cm. (Anchor Bk. A408) 1.25 pap.,
1. Theology, Doctrinal—Introductions. I. Title.

BARTH, Karl, 1886-1968. 230.081
Evangelical theology, an introduction. Translated by Grover Foley. [1st ed.] New York, Holt, Rinehart and Winston [1963] xiii, 206 p. 22 cm. Translation of Einfuhrung in die evangelische Theologie. "The first five lectures of this volume were delivered under the auspices of the Divinity School, the University of Chicago, and were 'The Annie Kinkead Warfield lectures of 1962' at the Princeton Theological Seminary." [BT65.B313] 63-7268
1. Theology, Doctrinal—Introductions. I. Title.

FERM, Vergilius Ture 230.081
Anselm, 1896-
Toward an expansive Christian theology, by Vergilius Ferm. New York, Philosophical Library [1964] xv, 186 p. illus. 21 cm. Bibliographical references included in "Notes" (p. 169-177) [BT80.F4] 64-16359
1. Theology—Addresses, essays, lectures. I. Title.

FERM, Vergilius Ture 230.081
Anselm, 1896-
Toward an expansive Christian theology. New York, Philosophical [c.1964] xv, 186p. illus. 21cm. Bibl. 64-16459 5.00 bds.,
1. Theology—Addresses, essays, lectures. I. Title.

HUDDLESTON, Trevor, Bp., 230.081
1913-
The true and living God. Garden City, N.Y., Doubleday, 1965[c.1964] 120p. 22cm. 8 addresses which formed the basis of a mission to Oxford Univ. in the Hilary term, 1963. [BR123.H78] 65-10646 2.95
1. Christianity—20th cent.—Addresses, essays, lectures. I. Title.

LESSING, Gotthold 230.081
Ephraim, 1729-1781.
Theological writings; selections in translation with an introductory essay, by Henry Chadwick. Stanford, Calif. Stanford University Press [1957] 110p. 23cm. (A Library of modern religious thought) Bibliography: p. 107. [BR75.L47 1957] 57-9374
1. Theology—Collected works—18th cent. I. Title.

MONTEFIORE, Hugh 230.081
Awkward questions on Christian love. Philadelphia, Westminster [1965, c.1964] 124p. 19cm. (Adventures in faith) Bibl. [BV4639.M586] 65-15073 1.45 pap.,
1. Theology, Doctrinal—Addresses, essays, lectures. 2. Love (Theology)—Addresses, essays, lectures. I. Title.

BARTH, Karl, 1886- 230.082
God here and now. Translated by Paul M. van Buren. [1st ed.] New York, Harper & Row [1964] xviii, 108 p. 22 cm. (Religious perspectives, v. 9 [i.e. 10]) [BT80.B353] 64-10750
1. Theology, Doctrinal — Addresses, essays, lectures. I. Title. II. Series.

BARTH, Karl, 1886- 230.082
God here and now. Tr. by Paul M. van Buren. New York, Harper [c.1964] xviii, 108p. 22cm. (Religious perspectives, v.9 [i. e. 10]) 64-10750 3.75
1. Theology, Doctrinal—Addresses, essays, lectures. I. Title. II. Series.

BEVAN, R J W ed. 230.082
Steps to Christian understanding. New York, Oxford University Press, 1958. 212p. 19cm. [BT1102.B4 1958] 58-14996
1. Apologetics —20th cent. 2. Theology, Doctrinal — Addresses, essays, lectures. I. Title.

CHRISTIANITY today. 230.082
Basic Christian doctrines by Oswald T. Allis [others] Ed. by Carl F. H. Henry. New York, Holt [c.1962] 302p. 24cm. (Contemporary evangelical thought) First pub. as a ser. in Christianity today. Bibl. 62-18752 6.00
1. Theology, Doctrinal—Addresses, essays, lectures. I. Christianity today. II. Henry, Carl Ferdinand Howard, 1913- ed.

CHRISTIANITY today. 230.082
Basic Christian doctrines [by] Oswald T. Allis [and others] Edited by Carl F. H. Henry. [1st ed.] New York, Holt, Rinehart and Winston [1962] 302p. 24cm. (Contemporary evangelical thought) 'First published as a series in Christianity today.' [BT80.C5] 62-18752
1. Theology, Doctrinal— Addresses, essays, lectures. I. Henry, Carl Ferdinand Howard, 1913- ed. II. Title.

COMMUNITY of the 230.082
Resurrection
Mirfield essays in Christian belief. London, Faith Pr. New York, Morehouse [1963, c.1962] 308p. 23cm. Bibl. 63-2424 5.00
1. Theology, Doctrinal—Addresses, essays, lectures. I. Title.

CUSHMAN, Robert Earl, ed. 230.082
The heritage of Christian thought; essays in honor of Robert Lowry Calhoun. Edited by Robert E. Cushman and Egil Grislis. [1st ed.] New York, Harper & Row [1965] ix, 243 p. port. 25 cm. Contents.-- Preface, by R. E. Cushman. -- A biographical sketch. To recall in gratitude Robert Lowry Calhoun. By V. Corwin. -- The sense of tradition in the ante-Nicene church, by A. C. Outler. -- St. Anselm on the harmony between God's mercy and God's justice, by G. S. Heyer, Jr. -- The a priori in St. Thomas' theory of knowledge, by G. A. Lindbeck. -- The role of consensus in Richard Hooker's method of theological enquiry, by E. Grislis. -- Spinoza on theology and truth, by W. A. Christian. -- Pascal's wager argument, by R. Hazelton. -- The hermeneutics of holiness in Wesley, by C. Michalson. -- Original sin and the enlightenment, by C. A. Holbrook -- The Christology of Paul Tillich, by R. E. Cushman. -- Two models of transcendence: An inquiry into the problem of theological meaning, by G. D. Kaufman. -- Analogy as a principle of theological method historically considered, by N. C. Nielsen, Jr. -- Modern Papal social teaching, by R. P. Ramsey. -- A select bibliography of Robert Lowry Calhoun's writings, by R. P. Morris and J. E. McFarland (p. 239-243) Bibliographical footnotes. [BR50.C8] 65-15390
1. Theology — Addresses, essays, lectures. I. Calhoun, Robert Lowry, 1896- II. Grislis, Egil, joint ed. III. Title.

EBELING, Gerhard, 1912- 230.082
Word and faith. [1st English ed. Translated by James W. Leitch] Philadelphia, Fortress Press [1963] 442 p. 23 cm. Bibliography: p. [16] Bibliographical footnotes. [BT15.E213] 63-13878
1. Theology, Doctrinal—Addresses, essays, lectures. I. Title.

EBELING, Gerhard, 1912- 230.082
Word and faith. Tr. [from German] by James W. Leitch. Philadelphia, Fortress [c.1963] 442p. 23cm. Bibl. 63-13878 6.25
1. Theology, Doctrinal—Addresses, essays, lectures I. Title.

FAITH and order 230.082
findings; the final report of the theological commissions to the Fourth World Conference on Faith and Order, Montreal, 1963. Minneapolis, Augsburg [c.1963] 31, 62, 63, 64p. 22cm. (Faith and order paper, no. 37-40) On jacket: Ed. by Paul S. Minear. Bibl. 63-16608 4.50
1. Theology—Addresses, essays, lectures. 2. Institutionalism (Religion)—Addresses, essays, lectures. 3. Worship—Addresses, essays, lectures. 4. Church—Addresses, essays, lectures. 5. Tradition (Theology)—Addresses, essays, lectures. I. World Conference on Faith and Order, 4th, Montreal, 1963. II. Minear, Paul Sevier, 1906- ed. III. Title.
Contents omitted.

FERM, Robert L., ed. 230.082
Readings in the history of Christian thought. New York, Holt, Rinehart and Winston [1964] xix, 619 p. 24 cm. Bibliography: p. 613-619. [BT10.F4] 64-10211
1. Theology—Collections. I. Title.

GALLOWAY, Allan Douglas, 230.082
1920- ed.
Basic readings in theology. London, Allen & Unwin [dist. New York. Humanities, c.1964] 316p. 23cm. Bibl. [BT10.G3] 64-7244 7.50
1. Theology—Collections. I. Title.

HENRY, Carl Ferdinand 230.082
Howard, 1913- ed.
Christian faith and modern theology: contemporary evangelical thought [by] J. Oliver Buswell, Jr. [and others] Edited by Carl F. H. Henry. [1st ed.] New York, Channel Press [1964] xi, 426 p. 25 cm. Bibliography: p. 421-426. [BR118.H45] 63-23360
1. Theology—20th cent. 2. Evangelicalism. I. Buswell, James Oliver. II. Title. III. Title: Contemporary evangelical thought.

KIMMEL, William 230.082
Breyfogel, ed.
Dimensions of faith; contemporary prophetic Protestant theology. [by] Karl Barth [and others] Edited by William Kimmel and Geoffrey Clive. With a foreword by James Luther Adams. New York, Twayne Publishers [c.1960] 507p. Includes bibliography. 21cm. 60-8551 6.95
1. Theology, Doctrinal—Addresses, essays, lectures. I. Clive, Geoffrey, joint ed. II. Title.

KIMMEL, William 230.082
Breyfogel, 1908- ed.
Dimensions of faith; contemporary prophetic Protestant theology. [By] Karl Barth [and others] Edited by William Kimmel and Geoffrey Clive. With a foreword by James Luther Adams. New York, Twayne Publishers [1960] 507p. 21cm. Includes bibliography. [BT10.K5] 60-8551
1. Theology, Doctrinal—Addresses, essays, lectures. I. Clive, Geoffrey, 1927- joint ed. II. Title.

MCCRACKEN, George 230.082
Englert, 1901- ed.
Early medieval theology. Newly translated and edited by George E. McCracken in collaboration with Allen Cabaniss. Philadelphia, Westminster Press [1957] 430p. 24cm. (The Library of Christian classics, v. 9) Includes bibliographies. [BR50.M18 1957] 57-5015
1. Theology—Middle Ages. I. Title. II. Series.

MCCRACKEN, George 230.082
Englert, 1904- ed.
Early medieval theology. Newly translated and edited by George E. McCracken in collaboration with Allen Cabaniss. Philadelphia, Westminster Press [1957] 430p. 24cm. (The Library of Christian classics, v. 9) Includes bibliographies. [BR50.M18 1957] 57-5015
1. Theology—Middle Ages. I. Title. II. Series.

MARTY, Martin E., 1928- 230.082
ed.
New theology, no. 4. ed. by Martin E. Marty. Dean G. Peerman. New York, Macmillan [1967] v. 19cm. (MP 08742) Bibl. [BR53.M37] 64-3132 1.95 pap.,
1. Theology—Addresses, essays, lectures. 2. christianity—20th Cent. —Addresses, essays, lectures. I. Peerman, Dean G., joint ed. II. Title.

MARTY, Martin E., 1928- 230.082
ed.
New theology no. 1, Ed. by Martin E. Marty, Dean G. Peerman. New York, Macmillan [c.1964] 256p. 18cm. (147) Bibl. 64-3132 1.95 pap.,
1. Theology—Addresses, essays, lectures. 2. Christianity—20th cent.—Addresses, essays, lectures. I. Peerman, Dean, G., joint ed. II. Title.

MARTY, Martin E., 1928- 230.082
ed.
New theology, no. 3. Ed. by Martin E. Marty, Dean G. Peerman. New York, Macmillan [c.1966] 190p. 18cm. (08741) Bibl. [BR53.M37] 64-3132 1.95 pap.,
1. Theology—Addresses, essays, lectures. 2. Christianity—20th cent.—Addresses, essays, lectures. I. Peerman, Dean G., joint ed. II. Title.

MARTY, Martin E., 1928- 230.082
ed.
New theology, no. 2. Ed. by Martin E. Marty, Dean G. Peerman. New York, Macmillan [c.1965] 316p. 18cm. (185) Bibl. [BR53.M37] 64-3132 1.95 pap.,
1. Theology—Addresses, essays, lectures. 2. Christianity—20th cent.—Addresses, essays, lectures. I. Peerman, Dean G., joint ed. II. Title.

RAHNER, Karl, 1904- 230.082
The Word; readings in theology [by] Karl Rahner [and others] Foreword by R. A. F. MacKenzie. Compiled at the Canisianum, Innsbruck. New York, P. J. Kenedy [1964] xii, 301 p. 22 cm. Articles translated from French,

German, or Italian. Includes bibliographical references. [BV4319.W6] 64-21849
1. Communication (Theology) — Addresses, essays, lectures. I. Title.

RODDY, Clarence Stonelynn, ed. 230.082
Things most surely believed. [Westwood, N.J.] Revell [1963] 191 p. 21 cm. 63-10395
1. Theology, Doctrinal—Addresses, essays, lectures. I. Title.

RODDY, Clarence Stonelynn, ed. 230.082
Things most surely believed. [Westwood, N. J.] Revell [c.1963] 191p. 21cm. 63-10395 3.95 bds.,
1. Theology, Doctrinal—Addresses, essays, lectures. I. Title.

TENNEY, Merrill Chapin, ed. 230.082
The word for this century [by] Carl F. H. Henry [and others] New York, Oxford University Press, [c.]1960. 184p. 20cm. (7p. Bibl. notes) 60-5275 4.00 bds.,
1. Theology, Doctrinal—Addresses, essays, lectures. 2. Evangelicalism. I. Henry, Carl Ferdinand Howard. II. Title.

TENNEY, Merrill Chapin, 1904- ed. 230.082
The word for this century [by] Carl F. H. Henry [and others] New York, Oxford University Press, 1960. 184 p. 20 cm. Includes bibliography. [BT15.T4] 60-5275
1. Theology, Doctrinal — Addresses, essays, lectures. 2. Evangelicalism. I. Henry, Carl Ferdinand Howard, 1913- II. Title.

VORGRIMLER, Herbert, ed. 230.082
Dogmatic vs. Biblical theology. Helicon [dist. New York, Taplinger, 1965, c.1964] 274p. 21cm. [BS543.V613] 64-24242 5.50
1. Bible—Theology. 2. Bible—Hermeneutics. I. Title.

WICKS, Robert S., ed. 230.082
The edge of wisdom; a source book of religious and secular writers. New York, Scribners [1965, c.1964] xv, 278p. 24cm. [BT10.W55] 64-24235 3.50 pap.,
1. Theology—Collections I. Title.

WORD (The); 230.082
readings in theology [by] Karl Rahner [others] Foreword by R. A. F. MacKenzie, Comp. at the Canisianum, Innsbruck. New York, Kenedy [c.1964] xii, 301p. 22cm. Articles tr. from French, German, or Italian. 64-21849 4.95
1. Communication (Theology)—Addresses, essays, lectures. I. Rahner, Karl, 1904-

*BERKHOF, Louis. 230.09
The history of Christian doctrines. Grand Rapids, Baker Book House [1975 c1937] 285 p. 21 cm. (Twin Brooks Series) Includes indexes. Bibliography: p. 273-275. [BT21.2] ISBN 0-8010-0636-8 4.95 (pbk.)
1. Dogma, development of. 2. Theology, doctrinal—History. I. Title.

BULL, Robert J 230'.09
Tradition in the making [by] Robert J. Bull. Philadelphia, Geneva Press [1967, c1968] 128 p. 21 cm. (Decade books) [BT21.2.B8] 68-10624
1. Theology, Doctrinal—Hist. I. Title.

BULL, Robert J. 230'.09
Tradition in the making [by] Robert J. Bull. Philadelphia, Geneva Press [1967, c1968] 128 p. 21 cm. (Decade books) [BT21.2.B8] 68-10624
1. Theology, Doctrinal—History. I. Title.

CHRISTIANITY and history 230.09
... Lectures ... delivered at the Washington Cathedral Library ... 1948- Authorized recording and production by Henderson Services. Washington [1950- v. ir 28 cm. (Christianity and modern man, course 3) Cover title. Contents.pt. 1. The Christian movement in history: A. The historical Jesus and the Christian revelation, by A. T. Mollegen and S. Brown-Serman. B. The development of Christian thought, by C. L. Stanley. 2 v. [BT21.C5] 51-33006
1. Theology, Doctrinal—Hist. 2. Religious thought—Hist. 3. Jesus Christ—Messiahship. 4. Christianity—Origin. I. Mollegen, Albert T. II. Series.

CONGAR, Yves Marie Joseph, 1904- 230'.09
A history of theology [by] Yves M. J. Congar. Translated and edited by Hunter Guthrie. [1st ed. in the U.S.A.] Garden City, N.Y., Doubleday, 1968. 312 p. 22 cm. "Based on the article Theologie ... which first appeared in volume 15 of Dictionnaire de theologie catholique." Includes bibliographical references. [BT21.2.C6] 68-19008 5.95
1. Theology, Doctrinal—History. I. Title.

CONGAR, Yves Marie Joseph, 1904- 230.09
Tradition and traditions; an historical and a theological essay, by Yves M. J. Congar. New York, Macmillan [1967, c1966] xx, 536 p. 22 cm. Bibliography: p. 521-523. [BT90.C613] 67-11630
1. Tradition (Theology) 2. Theology, Doctrinal—Hist. I. Title.

CONGAR, Yves Marie Joseph, 1904- 230.09
Tradition and traditions; an historical and a theological essay, by Yves M.-J. Congar. New York, Macmillan [1967, c1966] xx, 536 p. 22 cm. Bibliography: p. 521-523. [BT90.C613 1967] 67-11630
1. Tradition (Theology) 2. Theology, Doctrinal—History. I. Title.

CONTEMPORARY Theology Institute, 2d, Loyola College, Montreal, 1965. 230'.09
The convergence of traditions, Orthodox, Catholic, Protestant. Edited by Elmer O'Brien. [New York] Herder and Herder [1967] 141 p. 22 cm. (Contemporary theology, v. 2) Sponsored by Dept. of Theology, Loyola College. Bibliographical footnotes. [BT22.C65] 67-25880
1. Theology. Doctrinal—Hist. 2. Theology, Eastern Church. 3. Theology, Catholic. 4. Theology, Protestant. I. O'Brien, Elmer, ed. II. Loyola College, Montreal. Dept. of Theology. III. Title.

CONTEMPORARY Theology Institute, 2d, Loyola College, Montreal, 1965. 230'.09
The convergence of traditions, Orthodox, Catholic, Protestant. Edited by Elmer O'Brien. [New York] Herder and Herder [1967] 141 p. 22 cm. (Contemporary theology, v. 2) Sponsored by Dept. of Theology, Loyola College. Bibliographical footnotes. [BT22.C65 1965] 67-25880
1. Theology, Doctrinal—History. 2. Theology, Eastern Church. 3. Theology, Catholic. 4. Theology, Protestant. I. O'Brien, Elmer, ed. II. Loyola College, Montreal. Dept. of Theology. III. Title.

DE WOLF, Lotan Harold 230.09
Present trends in Christian thought. New York, Association Press [c.1960] 128p. 16cm. (an Association Press reflection book) (bibl. notes) 60-6569 .50 pap.,
1. Theology, Doctrinal—Hist.—20th cent. 2. Religious thought—20th cent. I. Title.

DILLENBERGER, John. 230'.09
Contours of faith; changing forms of Christian thought. Nashville, Abingdon Press [1969] 176 p. 21 cm. Bibliography: p. 166-168. [BT80.D47] 69-18451 ISBN 0-687-09588-3 4.00
1. Theology—20th century. 2. Theology, Doctrinal—History—Modern period, 1500- I. Title.

FINLAYSON, R. A. 230.09
The story of theology, by R. A. Finlayson. Chicago, Inter-Varsity Pr. [1964, c.1963] 55p. 22cm. Bibl. 64-4510 1.25 pap.,
1. Theology, Doctrinal—Hist.—Addresses, essays, lectures. I. Title.

FISHER, George Park, 1827-1909. 230'.09
History of Christian doctrine / by George Park Fisher. New York : AMS Press, [1976] p. cm. Reprint of the 1901 ed. published by Scribner, New York, in series: International theological library. [BT21.F5 1976] 75-41095 ISBN 0-404-14663-5 : 32.50
1. Theology, Doctrinal—History. I. Title.

GONZALEZ, Justo L. 230'.09
A history of Christian thought [by] Justo L. Gonzalez. Nashville, Abingdon Press [1970-75] 3 v. 24 cm. Contents.Contents.—v. 1. From the beginnings to the Council of Chalcedon.—v. 2. From Augustine to the eve of the Reformation.—v. 3. From the Protestant Reformation to the twentieth century. Includes bibliographical references. [BT21.2.G6] 74-109679 ISBN 0-687-17174-1 (v. 1) 9.00 (v. 1) varies
1. Theology, Doctrinal—History. I. Title.

HAGGLUND, Bengt, 1920- 230'.09
History of theology. Translated by Gene J. Lund. St. Louis, Concordia Pub. House [1968] 425 p. 24 cm. Translation of Teologins historia. [BT21.2.H313] 68-13365
1. Theology, Doctrinal—History. I. Title.

HARNACK, Adolf von, 1851-1930 230.09
History of dogma. Tr. from 3d German ed. by Neil Buchanan [Gloucester, Mass., Peter Smith, 1961] 7 v. in 4. various p. (Dover bks. rebound) Bibl. 18.00 set
1. Theology, Doctrinal—Hist. I. Title.

HARNACK, Adolf von, 1851-1930. 230.09
Outlines of the history of dogma. Translated by Edwin Knox Mitchell. With an introd. by Philip Rieff. [Boston] Starr King Press [c1957] 567p. 22cm. [BT21.H27 1957a] 58-26851
1. Theology, Doctrinal—Hist. I. Title.

HARNACK, Adolf von, 1851-1930. 230.09
Outlines of the history of dogma. Translated by Edwin Knox Mitchell. With an introd. by Philip Rieff. Boston, Beacon Press [1957] xii, [25], 567p. 21cm. (Beacon paperback no. 49) [BT21.H27 1957] 57-3270
1. Theology, Doctrinal—Hist. I. Title.

HORDERN, William. 230.09
A layman's guide to protestant theology. New York, Macmillan, 1955. 222 p. 22 cm. [BT21.H67] 55-14264
1. Theology, Doctrinal—History. I. Title.

HORDERN, William. 230'.09
A layman's guide to Protestant theology. Rev. ed. New York, Macmillan [1968] xx, 265 p. 22 cm. Bibliography: p. 259-262. [BT21.2.H67 1968] 68-11862
1. Theology, Doctrinal—History. 2. Theology, Protestant. I. Title.

HORDERN, William Edward 230.09
A layman's guide to protestant theology. New York, Macmillan [1962, c.1955] 222p. 18cm. (110) 1.45 pap.,
1. Theology, Doctrinal—Hist. I. Title.

LADNER, Gerhart Burian 230.09
The idea of reform, its impact on Christian thought and action in the age of the Fathers. Cambridge, Mass., Harvard University Press, [c.] 1959. xiii, 553 p. 23 cm. (bibl. notes: p. 477-492) 56-6159 10.00
1. Theology, Doctrinal—Hist.—Early church. I. Title.

LADNER, Gerhart Burian, 1905- 230.09
The idea of reform; its impact on Christian thought and action in the age of the Fathers [Magnolia, Mass., Peter Smith, 1968,c. 1959] 553p. 23cm. Bibl. [BT25.L3 1959] 5.75
1. Theology, Doctrinal—Hist.—Early church. I. Title.

LADNER, Gerhart Burian, 1905- 230.09
The idea of reform, its impact on Christian thought and action in the age of the Fathers. Cambridge, Harvard University Press, 1959. 553p. 23cm. Includes bibliography. [BT25.L3 1959] 59-6159
1. Theology, Doctrinal—Hist.—Early church. I. Title.

LADNER, Gerhart Burian, 1905- 230.09
The idea of reform, its impact on Christian thought and action in the age of the Fathers. [Rev. ed.] New York, Harper [1967,c.1959] 561p. 21cm. (Torchbook, TB149) Bibl. [BT25.I.3] 3.75 pap.,
1. Theology, Doctrinal—Hist.—Early church. 2. Title. I. Title.

LOHSE, Bernhard, 1928- 230'.09
A short history of Christian doctrine. Translated by F. Ernest Stoeffler. Philadelphia, Fortress Press [1966] xiv, 304 p. 23 cm. Translation of Epochen der Dogmengeschichte. Bibliography: p. 267-273. [BT21.2.L613] 66-21732
1. Theology, Doctrinal—History. I. Title.

MORGAN, Richard 230.09
Will the church pay the price? Nashville, Printed by the Parthenon Pr. [1966] 64p. 23cm. [BR125.M7525] 66-30408 2.00 pap.,
1. Christianity—20th cent. I. Title.
Available from Methodist Pub. House, Nashville.

NEVE, Juergen Ludwig, 1865-1943. 230.09
A history of Christian thought, by Otto W. Heick. Philadelphia, Fortess Press [1965- v. 24 cm. In the earlier edition Neve's name appeared first on the title page. Includes bibliographies. [BT21.N482] 65-23839
1. Theology, Doctrinal — Hist. I. Heick, Otto William. II. Title.

NEVE, Juergen Ludwig 1865-1943 Heick, Otto William 230.09
a history of christian thought; v. 2 by Otto W. Heick. Philadelphia, Fortress [c.1966] x 517 p. 24 cm -continues the work beg. by Juergen Ludwig Neve and Otto W. H first published in 1943. bibl. [BT21.N482] 66-23839 7.75
1. theology, doctrinal—hist. I. Title.

[NEVE, Juergen Ludwig] 1865-1943 230.09
A history of Christian thought [v.1. Rev. ed.] by Otto W. Heick. Philadelphia, Fortress [c.1965] 508p. 24cm. In the earlier ed. Neve's name appeared first on the title page. Bibl. [BT21.N482] 65-23839 8.75
1. Theology, Doctrinal—Hist. I. Heick, Otto William. II. Title.

ORR, James, 1844-1913. 230.09
The progress of dogma, being the Elliot lectures, delivered at the Western Theological Seminary, Allegheny, Penna., U.S.A., 1897. Grand Rapids, Eerdmans, 1952. 365p. 22cm. [BT21] 52-9919
1. Theology, Doctrinal—Hist. I. Title.

PELIKAN, Jaroslav Jan, 1923- 230.09
The Christian intellectual New York, Harper [1966,c.1965] 151p. 22cm. (Religious perspectives, v.14) Bibl. [BR115.C8P35] 66-10235 3.75
1. Christianity and culture. 2. Faith and reason. 3. Religion and science—1946- I. Title. II. Series.

PELIKAN, Jaroslav Jan, 1923- 230.09
The Christian intellectual, by Jaroslav Pelikan. [1st ed.] New York, Harper & Row [1965] 151 p. 22 cm. (Religious perspectives, v. 14) Bibliographical references included in "Notes" (p. 131-148) [BR115.C8P35] 66-10235
1. Christianity and culture. 2. Faith and reason. 3. Religion and science—1946- I. Title. II. Series.

PELIKAN, Jaroslav Jan, 1923- 230'.09
Development of Christian doctrine; some historical prolegomena, by Jaroslav Pelikan. New Haven, Yale University Press, 1969. xiii, 149 p. 23 cm. Bibliographical footnotes. [BT19.P4] 69-14864 6.00
1. Dogma, Development of. I. Title.

PICKMAN, Edward Motley, 1886- 230.09
The sequence of belief; a consideration of religious thought from Homer to Ockham. New York, St. Martin's Press [1962] ix, 741p. 22cm. Bibliography: p.727-730. [BT21.2.P5] 61-6699
1. Theology, Doctrinal—Hist. 2. Religious thought—Hist. I. Title.

RELTON, Herbert Maurice, 1882- 230.09
Studies in Christian doctrine. London, Macmillan; New York, St. Martin's Press, 1960. 269p. 23cm. Includes bibliography. [BT15.R4 1960] 60-50585
1. Theology, Doctrinal—Addresses, essays, lectures. 2. Theology, Doctrinal—Hist. I. Title.

SEEBERG, Reinhold, 1859-1935. 230.09
Text-book of the history of doctrines. Translated by Charles E. Hay. Grand Rapids, Baker Book House, 1956. 2 v. in 1. 23cm. Contents.v. 1. History of doctrines in the ancient church.--v. 2. History of doctrines in the middle and early modern ages. Bibliographical footnotes. [BT21.S4 1956] 56-75849
1. Theology, Doctrinal— Hist. I. Title.

TILLICH, Paul, 1886- 230.09
A history of Christian thought. Recorded and edited by Peter H. John. 2d ed. [Providence? R. I.] 1956. 309p. 28cm. 'Lectures ... stenographically recorded and transcribed during the spring semester. 1953, at Union Theological Seminary in New York.' [BT21.T5 1956] 57-32588
1. Theology, Doctrinal —Hist. I. Title.

TILLICH, Paul, 1886- 230.09
A history of Christian thought. Recorded and edited by Peter H. John. 2d ed. [Providence? R.I.] 1956. 309 p. 28 cm. "Lectures ... stenographically recorded and transcribed during the spring semester, 1953, at Union Theological Seminary in New York." [BT21.T5 1956] 57-32588
1. Theology, Doctrinal—Hist. I. Title.

TILLICH, Paul, 1886-1965. 230'.09
A history of Christian thought. [2d ed., rev. and] edited by Carl E. Braaten. New York, Harper & Row [1968] xvii, 300 p. 22 cm. Lectures delivered in 1953 at Union Theological Seminary, New York, recorded and originally edited by P. H. John. [BT21.2.T5 1968] 68-17592
1. Theology, Doctrinal—History. I. Title.

TILLICH, Paul, 1886-1965. 230'.09
A history of Christian thought, from its Judaic and Hellenistic origins to existentialism. Edited by Carl E. Braaten. [New York] Simon and Schuster [1972] xlii, 550 p. 21 cm. (A Touchstone book) Previously published in two separate volumes entitled A history of Christian thought and Perspectives on 19th and 20th century Protestant theology. Includes

bibliographical references. [BT21.2.T53] 72-171021 ISBN 0-671-21426-8 4.95
1. Theology, Doctrinal—History. I. Braaten, Carl E., 1929- ed. II. Tillich, Paul, 1886-1965. Perspectives on 19th and 20th century Protestant theology. 1972. III. Title. IV. Title: Perspectives on 19th and 20th century Protestant theology.

WALGRAVE, Jan Henricus, 1911- 230'.09
Unfolding revelation; the nature of doctrinal development [by] Jan Hendrik Walgrave. Philadelphia, Westminster [1972] xii, 418 p. 24 cm. (Theological resources) Bibliography: p. 403-412. [BT19.W35 1972] 76-102204 ISBN 0-664-20915-7 9.95
1. Dogma, Development of. I. Title.

WILES, Maurice F. 230.09
The Christian fathers, by Maurice Wiles. Philadelphia, Lippincott [1966] 190 p. 21 cm. (Knowing Christianity) Bibliography: p. 186-187. [BR67.W53 1966a] 66-25412
1. Fathers of the church. 2. Theology, Doctrinal—History—Early church, ca. 30-600. I. Title.

WORKMAN, Herbert Brook, 1862- 230'.09
Christian thought to the Reformation. Freeport, N.Y., Books for Libraries Press [1973] p. Reprint of the 1911 ed., issued in series: Studies in theology. Bibliography: p. [BR162.W8 1973] 72-10865 ISBN 0-8369-7127-2
1. Religious thought—Ancient period. 2. Religious thought—Middle Ages. I. Title. II. Series: Studies in theology (London).

AUGUSTINUS, Aurelius, Saint, Bp. of Hippo. 230'.09'015 s
Against Julian. Translated by Matthew A. Schumacher. New York, Fathers of the Church, inc., 1957. xx, 407 p. 22 cm. (Writings of Saint Augustine, v. 16) (The Fathers of the church, a new translation, v. 35.) Bibliography: p. xix-xx. [BR60.F3A8 vol. 16] [BR65.A65] 233'.14 74-168247
1. Sin, Original. 2. Apologetics—Early church, ca. 30-600. I. Title. II. Series.

AUGUSTINUS, Aurelius, Saint, Bp. of Hippo. 230'.09'015 s
Against Julian. Translated by Matthew A. Schumacher. Washington, Catholic University of America Press [1974, c1957] p. cm. (Writings of Saint Augustine, v. 16) Reprint of the ed. published by Fathers of the Church, inc., New York, which was issued as v. 35 of the Fathers of the church, a new translation. Bibliography: p. [BR60.F3A82 vol. 16] [BR65.A65] 233'.14 74-10838 ISBN 0-8132-0035-0
1. Sin, Original. 2. Apologetics—Early church, ca. 30-600. I. Title. II. Series: The Fathers of the church, a new translation, v. 35.

LADNER, Gerhart Burian, 1905- 230'.09'015
The idea of reform; its impact on Christian thought and action in the age of the Fathers [by] Gerhart B. Ladner. [Rev. ed.] New York, Harper & Row [1967] x, 561 p. 21 cm. (Harper torchbooks, TB149) Bibliography: p. 469-489. Bibliographical footnotes. [BT25.L3 1967] 68-732
1. Theology, Doctrinal—Hist.—Early church. I. Title.

LADNER, Gerhart Burian, 1905- 230'.09'015
The idea of reform; its impact on Christian thought and action in the age of the Fathers [by] Gerhart B. Ladner. [Rev. ed.] New York, Harper & Row [1967] x, 561 p. 21 cm. (Harper torchbooks, TB149) Bibliography: p. 469-489. Bibliographical footnotes. [BT25.L3 1967] 68-732
1. Theology, Doctrinal—History—Early church, ca. 30-600. I. Title.

MURRAY, Albert Victor, 1890- 230'.0902
Abelard and St. Bernard: a study in twelfth century 'modernism,' by A. Victor Murray. Manchester, Manchester Univ. Pr.; New York, Barnes & Noble [1967]. viii, 168p. 23cm. Bibl. [BX4705.A2M8 1967] 67-95567 6.75
1. Abailard, Pierre, 1079-1142. 2. Bernard de Clairvaux, Saint, 1091?-1153. 3. Theology, Doctrinal — Hist. — Middle Ages. I. Title.

MURRAY, Albert Victor, 1890- 230'.09'02
Abelard and St. Bernard: a study in twelfth century "modernism." by A. Victor Murray. Manchester, Manchester U.P.; New York, Barnes & Noble [1967] viii, 169 p. 22 1/2 cm. (B 67-14113) Bibliography: p. 164-166. [BX4705.A2M8] 67-95567
1. Aballard, Pierre, 1079-1142. 2. Bernard de Clairvaux, Saint, 1091?-1153. 3. Theology, Doctrinal — Hist. — Middle Ages. I. Title.

OBERMAN, Heiko Augustinus. 230'.09'02
The harvest of medieval theology; Gabriel Biel and late medieval nominalism.[Rev. ed.] Grand Rapids, Eerdmans [1967] xv, 495p. 22cm. (Robert Troup Paine prizetreatise, 1962) Bibl. [BT26.O2] 67-19313 3.95 pap.,
1. Biel, Gabriel, d. 1495. 2. Theology, Doctrinal—Hist.—Middle Ages. 3. Nominalism. I. Title. II. Series.

OBERMAN, Heiko Augustinus. 230.0902
The harvest of medieval theology; Gabriel Biel and late medieval nominalism. Cambridge, Harvard University Press, 1963. xv, 495 p. illus. 24 cm. (The Robert Troup Paine prize-treatise, 1962) Bibliography: p. 431-456. [BT26.O2] 63-9553
1. 1. Biel, Gabriel, d. 2. Theology, Doctrinal — Hist. — Middle Ages. 3. Nominalism. I. Title. II. Series.

OBERMAN, Heiko Augustinus. 230'.09'02
The harvest of medieval theology; Gabriel Biel and late medieval nominalism. [Rev. ed.] Grand Rapids, W. B. Eerdmans Pub. Co. [1967] xv, 495 p. 22 cm. (The Robert Troup Paine prize-treatise, 1962) Bibliography: p. 431-456. [BT26.O2] 67-19313
1. Biel, Gabriel, d. 1495. 2. Theology, Doctrinal—Hist.—Middle Ages. 3. Nominalism. I. Title. II. Series.

OBERMAN, Heiko Augustinus 230.0902
The harvest of medieval theology; Gabriel Biel and late medieval nominalism. Cambridge, Mass., Harvard [c.]1963. xv, 495p. illus. 24cm. (Robert Troup Paine prize-treatise, 1962) Bibl. 63-9553 9.25
1. Biel, Gabriel, d. 1495. 2. Theology, Doctrinal—Hist.—Middle Ages. 3. Nominalism. I. Title. II. Series.

BARTH, Karl, 1886- 230.0903
The humanity of God [Reissue] Richmond, Va., Knox [1963, c.1960] 96p. 21cm. 1.50 pap.,
1. Theology, Doctrinal—Hist.—19th cent. 2. Theology, Doctrinal—Hist.—20th cent. 3. Liberty. I. Title.

BARTH, Karl, 1886-1968. 230.0903
The humanity of God. Richmond, John Knox Press [1960] 96 p. 21 cm. Contents.Contents.—Evangelical theology in the 19th century—The humanity of God.—The gift of freedom. [BT28.B273] 60-5479
1. Theology, Doctrinal—History—19th century. 2. Theology, Doctrinal—History—20th century. 3. Freedom (Theology) I. Title.

HUGHES, Philip Edgcumbe. 230'.09'03
Theology of the English reformers. Grand Rapids, Eerdmans [1966, c1965] 283 p. 23 cm. Bibliographical footnotes. [BT27.H8 1966] 67-1745
1. Theology, Doctrinal—History—16th century. 2. Theology, Anglican. I. Title.

ZIEGLER, Donald Jenks, comp. 230'.09'031
Great debates of the Reformation, edited, with commentaries, by Donald J. Ziegler. New York, Random House [1969] vii, 358 p. map. 21 cm. [BR301.Z5] 69-11973
1. Reformation—Sources. I. Title.

BARTH, Karl, 1886-1968. 230'.09'034
Protestant theology in the nineteenth century; its background & history. Valley Forge [Pa.] Judson Press [1973, c1972] 669 p. 23 cm. "The first complete translation of Die protestantische Theologie im 19. Jahrhundert." Includes bibliographical references. [BT30.G3B313 1973] 72-1956 ISBN 0-8170-0572-2 15.00
1. Theology, Doctrinal—History—Germany. 2. Theology, Doctrinal—History—18th century. 3. Theology, Doctrinal—History—19th century. 4. Theology, Protestant—Germany. I. Title.

REARDON, Bernard M. G. ed. 230.09034
Religious thought in the nineteenth century [by] Bernard M. G. Reardon. Illus. from writers of the period. London, Cambridge 1966. ix, 406p. 24cm. Bibl. [BR477.R4] 66-10542 11.00; 3.95 pap.,
1. Religious thought—19th cent. 2. Theology—Collections. I. Title.
Available from the Publisher's New York office.

ALTIZER, Thomas J. J. 230'.09'04
The descent into hell; a study of the radical reversal of the Christian consciousness [by] Thomas J. J. Altizer. [1st ed.] Philadelphia, Lippincott [1970] 217 p. 22 cm. [BR121.2.A48] 79-105551 5.00
1. Christianity—20th century. I. Title.

BARNETTE, Henlee H. 230'.09'04
The new theology and morality, by Henlee H. Barnette. Philadelphia, Westminster Press [1967] 120 p. 21 cm. Bibliographical references included in "Notes" (p. [109]-120) [BT28.B27] 67-11671
1. Theology, Doctrinal—History—20th century. 2. Christian ethics. I. Title.

BRAATEN, Carl E., 1929- 230.0904
History and hermeneutics, by Carl E. Braaten. Philadelphia, Westminster Press [1966] 205 p. 21 cm. (New directions in theology today, v. 2) Bibliographical references included in "Notes" (p. [183]-196) [BT28.N47 vol. 2] 66-18336
1. Bible—Hermeneutics. 2. Bible—Criticism, interpretation, etc.—History. 3. History (Theology) I. Title. II. Series.

CONN, Harvie M. 230'.09'04
Contemporary world theology; a layman's guidebook, by Harvie M. Conn. [Nutley, N.J.] Presbyterian and Reformed Pub. Co., 1973. x, 155 p. 21 cm. Includes bibliographical references. [BT28.C56] 72-97711 2.95
1. Theology, Doctrinal—History—20th century. I. Title.

CONN, Harvie M. 230'.09'04
Contemporary world theology; a layman's guidebook, by Harvie M. Conn. [Nutley, N.J.] Presbyterian and Reformed Pub. Co., 1973. x, 155 p. 21 cm. Includes bibliographical references. [BT28.C56] 72-97711 2.95 (pbk.)
1. Theology, Doctrinal—History—20th century. I. Title.

CONN, Harvie M. 230'.09'04
Contemporary world theology : a layman's guidebook / by Harvie M. Conn. 2d rev. ed. [Nutley, N.J.] : Presbyterian and Reformed Pub. Co., 1974, c1973. x, 155 p. ; 21 cm. Includes bibliographical references and index. [BT28.C56 1974] 75-317574 2.95
1. Theology, Doctrinal—History—20th century. I. Title.

CONN, Harvie M. 230'.09'04
Contemporary world theology : a layman's guidebook / by Harvie M. Conn. 2d rev. ed. [Nutley, N.J.] : Presbyterian and Reformed Pub. Co., 1974, c1973. x, 155 p. ; 21 cm. Includes bibliographical references and index. [BT28.C56 1974] 75-317574 2.95
1. Theology, Doctrinal—History—20th century. I. Title.

COOPER, John Charles. 230'.09'04
Radical Christianity and its sources. Philadelphia, Westminster Press [1968] 171 p. 21 cm. Bibliographical references included in "Notes" (p. [151]-164) [BT28.C58] 68-21411 5.95
1. Theology, Doctrinal—History—20th century. 2. United States—Religion—1946- 3. Christianity—20th century. 4. Death of God theology. I. Title.

ERICKSON, Millard. 230'.09'04
The new evangelical theology. Westwood, N.J., Revell [1968] 254 p. 21 cm. Bibliography: p. [237]-250. [BR1640.E7] 68-17088
1. Evangelicalism—United States. 2. Theology, Doctrinal—History—20th century. I. Title.

FLETCHER, William C. 230.0904
The moderns: molders of contemporary theology. Grand Rapids, Mich., Zondervan [c.1962] 160p. 23cm. 62-13173 3.00
1. Theologians. 2. Theology, Doctrinal—Hist.—20th cent. I. Title.

FUNK, Robert Walter, 1926- 230.0904
Language, hermeneutic, and word of God; the problem of language in the New Testament and contemporary theology [by] Robert W. Funk. [1st ed.] New York, Harper & Row [1966] xvi, 317 p. 22 cm. Bibliographical footnotes. [BT28.F8] 66-20776
1. Jesus Christ—Parables. 2. Theology, Doctrinal—History—20th century. 3. Communication (Theology) 4. Religion and language. I. Title.

GEFFRE, Claude. 230'.09'04
A new age in theology / by Claude Geffre ; translated by Robert Shillenn, with Francis McDonagh and Theodore L. Westow. New York : Paulist Press, [1974] v, 119 p. ; 20 cm. Translation of Un nouvel age de la theologie. Includes bibliographical references. [BT28.G3613] 74-12634 ISBN 0-8091-1844-0 pbk. : 3.95
1. Theology, Doctrinal—History—20th century. 2. Theology, Catholic—History. I. Title.

GILKEY, Langdon Brown, 1919- 230'.09'04
Naming the whirlwind; the renewal of God-language, by Langdon Gilkey. Indianapolis, Bobbs-Merrill [1969] x, 483 p. 22 cm. Bibliographical footnotes. [BL65.L2G5] 68-11146 2.75
1. Religion and language. 2. Theology—20th century. I. Title.

HAMILTON, Kenneth 230.0904
Revolt against heaven; an enquiry into anti-supernaturalism. Grand Rapids, Mich., Eerdmans [1966,c.1965] 193p. 21cm. Bibl. [BT28.H3] 65-25189 2.45 pap.,
1. Theology —20th cent. I. Title.

HAMILTON, Kenneth. 230'.09'04
What's new in religion? A critical study of new theology, new morality, and secular Christianity. Grand Rapids, Eerdmans [1968] 176 p. 22 cm. Bibliography: p. 175-176. [BT28.H32] 67-28382
1. Theology, Doctrinal—History—20th century. I. Title.

HARVEY, Van Austin. 230.0904
The historian and the believer; the morality of historical knowledge and Christian belief. New York, Macmillan [1966] xv, 301 p. 22 cm. Includes bibliographical references. [BT28.H34] 66-14692
1. Theology — 20th cent. 2. Bible — Ciriticism, interpretation, etc — Hist. 3. History — Philosophy. I. Title.

HARVEY, Van Austin 230.0904
The historian and the believer; the morality of historical knowledge and Christian belief. New York, Macmillan [c.1966] xv,301p. 22cm. Bibl. [BT28.H34] 66-14692 6.95
1. Theology—20th cent. 2. Bible—Criticism, interpretation, etc.—Hist. 3. History—Philosophy. I. Title.

HENRY, Carl Ferdinand Howard, 1913- 230.0904
Fifty years of Protestant theology. Boston, Wilde [1950] 113 p. 20 cm. Bibliographical footnotes. [BT28.H39] 50-10665
1. Theology. Doctrinal—Hist.—20th cent. I. Title.

HERZOG, Frederick 230.0904
Understanding God, the key issue in present-day Protestant thought. New York, Scribners [1966] 191p. 22cm. Bibl. [BT28.H44] 66-25565 4.50
1. Theology, Doctrinal—Hist. — 20th cent. 2. God—History of doctrines. I. Title.

HEUVEL, Albert H. van den. 230.0904
The humiliation of the church, by Albert H. van den Heuvel. Philadelphia, Westminister Press [1966] 192 p. 19 cm. (Adventures in faith) Includes bibliographical references. [BR121.2H43] 66-20095
1. Christianity — 20th cent. 2. Church in the world. I. Title.

HEUVEL, Albert H. van den 230.0904
The humiliation of the church, by Albert H. vanden Philadelphia Westminster [1966] 192 p. (Adventures in faith) bibl. [br121.2.h] 66-20095
1. Christianity—20th cent. 2. Church in the World. Title. I. Title.

ICE, Jackson Lee, comp. 230.0904
The death of God debate, edited by Jackson Lee Ice and John J. Carey. Philadelphia, Westminster Press [1967] 267 p. 19 cm. Includes bibliographical references. [BT83.5.I2] 67-15088
1. Death of God theology. I. Carey, John Jesse, joint comp. II. Title.

IDINOPULOS, Thomas A., comp. 230'.09'04
The erosion of faith; an inquiry into the origins of the contemporary crisis in religious thought, by Thomas A. Idinopulos. Chicago, Quadrangle Books, 1971. xii, 265 p. 22 cm. Contents.Contents.—The theology of feeling, by F. Schleiermacher.—The theology of the individual, by S. Kierkegaard.—The theology of the word, by K. Barth.—The theology of correlation, by P. Tillich.—Theocentric humanism: the Thomistic philosophy of Jacques Maritain.—The theology of Godmanhood, by N. Berdyaev.—The theology of dialogue, by M. Buber.—Theologians in a world come of age.—Bibliography (p. 253-258) [BT28.I34 1971] 74-152094 ISBN 0-8129-0197-5 8.95
1. Theology, Doctrinal—History—19th century. 2. Theology, Doctrinal—History—20th century. I. Title.

LEITCH, Addison H. 230.0904
Winds of doctrine; the theology of Barth, Brunner, Bonhoeffer, Bultmann, Niebuhr, Tillich. Westwood, N.J., Revell [c.1966] 62p. 21cm. [BT28.L4] 66-17050 2.50 bds.,
1. Theology, Doctrinal—20th cent. I. Title.

MASCALL, Eric Lionel, 1905- 230'.09'04
Theology and the future [by] E. L. Mascall. [1st American ed.] New York, Morehouse-Barlow [1968] 183 p. 19 cm. (Charles A. Hart memorial lectures, 1968) Bibliographical footnotes. [BT28.M29 1968] 72-190
1. Theology, Doctrinal—History—20th century. I. Title. II. Series.

MEHTA, Ved Parkash. 230.0904
The new theologian [by] Ved Mehta. [1st ed.] New York, Harper & Row [1966, c1965] 217 p. 22 cm. [BT28.M4] 66-13913
1. Bonhoeffer, Dietrich, 1906-1945. 2. Theology, Doctrinal — Hist. — 20th cent. I. Title.

MEHTA, Ved Parkash. 230.0904
The new theologian [by] Ved Mehta, New York, Harper [1968,c.1965] 217p. 20cm. (Colophon Bks. CN 131) [BT28.M4] 66-13913 2.45 pap.,
1. Bonhoeffer, Dietrich, 1906-1945. 2. Theology, Doctrinal—Hist.—20th cent. I. Title.

NEW directions in theology today. 230.0904
William Hordern, editor. [Philadelphia, Westminster Press, 1966- v. 21 cm. Contents.Contents.—v. 1. Introduction, by W. Hordern.—v. 2. History and hermeneutics, by C. E. Braaten.—v. 3. God and secularity, by J. Macquarrie.—v. 4. The church, by C. W. Williams.—v. 5. Christian life, by P. Hessert.—v. 6. Man: the new humanism, by R. L. Shinn. Includes bibliographical references. [BT28.N47] 66-15544
1. Theology, Doctrinal—History—20th century. I. Hordern, William, ed.

ODEN, Thomas C. 230'.09'04
Contemporary theology and psychotherapy, by Thomas C. Oden. Philadelphia, Westminster Press [1967] 158 p. 23 cm. Bibliographical references included in "Notes" (p. [143]-158) [BV4012.O26] 67-11798
1. Pastoral psychology. 2. Theology, Doctrinal—History—20th century. I. Title.

O'MEARA, Thomas F., 1935- 230'.09'04
Projections; shaping an American theology for the future. Edited by Thomas F. O'Meara and Donald M. Weisser. [1st ed.] Garden City, N.Y., Doubleday, 1970. vi, 233 p. 22 cm. Includes bibliographical references. [BT28.O5] 71-89086 5.95
1. Theology—20th century. 2. Religious thought—U.S. I. Weisser, Donald M., joint author. II. Title.

OSBORN, Robert T. 230'.09'04
Freedom in modern theology, by Robert T. Osborn. Philadelphia, Westminster Press [1967] 273 p. 21 cm. Contents.Contents.—Introduction.—Rudolf Bultmann: Freedom as existence.—Paul Tillich: Freedom to be.—Karl Barth: Freedom in Christ.—Nicolas Berdyaev: Freedom to create.—A theology of freedom. Bibliographical footnotes. [BT28.O7] 67-11862
1. Freedom (Theology)—History of doctrines. 2. Theology, Doctrinal—History—20th century. I. Title.

PITTENGER, William Norman, 1905- 230'.09'04
Reconceptions in Christian thinking, 1817-1967 [by] W. Norman Pittenger New York, Seabury Press [1968] 127 p. 22 cm. (The Paddock lectures, 1967) [BT28.P53] 68-11591
1. Theology, Doctrinal—History—19th century. 2. Theology, Doctrinal—History—20th century. I. Title. II. Series.

POL, Willem Hendrik van de, 1897- 230'.09'04
The end of conventional Christianity, by W. H. van de Pol. Translated by Theodore Zuydwijk. New York, Newman Press [1968] vi, 297 p. 22 cm. Translation of Het einde van het conventionele christendom. Bibliographical footnotes. [BR121.2.P5813] 68-24811
1. Christianity—20th century. 2. Theology, Doctrinal—History—20th century. I. Title.

PORTEOUS, Alvin C. 230.0904
Prophetic voices in contemporary theology; the theological renaissance and the renewal of the church. Nashville, Abingdon [c.1966] 224p. 21cm. Bibl. [BT28.P6] 66-15000 4.00
1. Theology, Doctrinal—20th cent. I. Title.

RAMM, Bernard, 1916- 230.0904
A handbook of contemporary theology. Grand Rapids, Eerdmans [1966] 141 p. 22 cm. Bibliographical references included in "List of abbreviations" (p. 139-141) [BT28.R3] 65-28565
1. Theology, Doctrinal—Hist.—20th cent. I. Title. II. Title: Contemporary theology.

RAMM, Bernard, 1916- 230.0904
A handbook of contemporary theology. Grand Rapids, Mich., Eerdmans [c.1966] 141p. 22cm. Bibl. [BT28.R3] 65-28565 1.95 pap.,
1. Theology, Doctrinal—Hist.—20th cent. I. Title. II. Title: Contemporary theology.

RAMSEY, Arthur Michael, Abp. of Canterbury, 1904- 230'.09'04
God, Christ, and the world; a study in contemporary theology. [1st American ed.] New York, Morehouse-Barlow Co. [1969] 125 p. 19 cm. Bibliography: p. [119]-121. [BT28.R34 1969b] 75-3935
1. Theology, Doctrinal—History—20th century. I. Title.

REINISCH, Leonhard, ed. 230.0904
Theologians of our time: Karl Barth [others] Foreword by Charles H. Henkey [Notre Dame, Ind.] Univ of Notre Dame Pr. [c.1964] x, 235p. 21cm. Orig. pub. in Munich in 1960. Bibl. [BT28.R413] 64-17067 2.25
1. Theologians. 2. Theology, Doctrinal—Hist.—20th cent. I. Title.

REINISCH, Leonhard, ed. 230.0904
Theologians of our time: Karl Barth [and others] Foreword by Charles H. Henkey. [Notre Dame, Ind.] University of Notre Dame Press [1964] x, 235 p. 21 cm. ([Theology today, v. 1]) Bibliography: p. 203-235. [BT28.R413] 64-17067
1. Theologians. 2. Theology, Doctrinal—History—20th century. I. Title.

REYMOND, Robert L. 230'.09'04
Introductory studies in contemporary theology [by] Robert L. Reymond. [Philadelphia] Presbyterian and Reformed Pub. Co. [1968] 242 p. 20 cm. Includes bibliographical references. [BT28.R48] 68-25834
1. Theology, Doctrinal—History—20th century. I. Title.

RICHARDSON, Alan, 1905- 230.0904
Religion in contemporary debate. Philadelphia, Westminster [1966] 124p. 20cm. Lects. given in Queen's College Hall, Dundee, between November 17 and 24, 1965. [BT28.R5 1966] 66-22987 2.75
1. Theology, Doctrinal—Hist—20th cent. I. Title.

ROBINSON, James McConkey, 1924- 230'.09'04
Theology as history, ed. by James M. Robinson, John B. Cobb, Jr. [1st ed.] New York, Harper [1967] x, 276p. 22cm. (New frontiers in theol.; discussions among Continental and 0 Bibl. [BT28.R58] 67-14936 6.00
1. Pannenberg, Wolfhart, 1928- 2. Theology, Doctrinal—Hist.—20th cent. 3. History (Theology)—History of doctrines. I. mer. theologians, v. 3) II. Cobb, John B., joint author. III. Title. IV. Series: New frontiers in theology, v. 3
Contents omitted.

ROBINSON, James McConkey, 1924- 230'.09'04
Theology as history, edited by James M. Robinson [and] John B. Cobb, Jr. [1st ed.] New York, Harper & Row [1967] x, 276 p. 22 cm. (New frontiers in theology: discussions among Continental and American theologians, v. 3) Contents.Revelation as word and as history, by J. M. Robinson. -- Focal essay: The revelation of God in Jesus of Nazareth, by W. Pannenberg. -- The meaning of history, by M. J. Buss -- Revelation and resurrection, by K. Grobel. -- The character of Pannenberg's theology, by W. Hamilton. -- Past, present, and future, by J. B. Cobb. -- Response to the discussion, by W. Pannenberg. Includes bibliographical references. [BT28.R58] 67-14936
1. Pannenberg, Wolfhart, 1928- 2. Theology, Doctrinal — Hist. — 20th cent. 3. History (Theology) — History of doctrines. I. Cobb, John B., joint author. II. Title. III. Series. IV. Series: New frontiers in theology. v. 3

ROSE, Stephen C., ed. 230.0904
Who's killing the church? A Renewal reader, edited by Stephen C. Rose. Selections by Don Benedict [and others. Chicago, Association Press, 1966] 141 p. 21 cm. "With one exception all of the articles ... appeared originally in Renewal magazine." [BR123.R68] 66-9292
1. Christianity—20th century—Addresses, essays, lectures. I. Benedict, Donald L. II. Renewal. III. Title.

RUMSCHEIDT, Martin. 230'.09'04
Revelation and theology: an analysis of the Barth-Harnack correspondence of 1923 [by] H. Martin Rumscheidt. Cambridge [Eng.] University Press, 1972. x, 219 p. 22 cm. (Monograph supplements to the Scottish journal of theology) Bibliography: p. 216-217. [BT28.R85] 78-166947 ISBN 0-521-08365-6 £3.40 ($11.95 U.S.)
1. Barth, Karl, 1886-1968. 2. Harnack, Adolf von, 1851-1930. 3. Theology, Doctrinal—History—20th century. I. Title. II. Series: Scottish journal of theology. Monograph supplements.

RYAN, Michael D., comp. 230'.09'04
The contemporary explosion of theology : ecumenical studies in theology / Langdon Gilkey ... [et al.] ; edited and introduced by Michael D. Ryan. Metuchen, N.J. : Scarecrow Press, 1975. viii, 190 p. ; 22 cm. Includes bibliographical references and index. [BT75.2.R9] 74-34125 ISBN 0-8108-0794-7 : 7.50
1. Theology, Doctrinal. 2. Theology, Doctrinal—History—20th century. I. Gilkey, Langdon Brown, 1919- II. Title.

SHINER, Larry E. 230.0904
The secularization of history; an introduction to the theology of Friedrich Gogarten [by] Larry Shiner. Nashville, Abingdon Press [1966] 236 p. 23 cm. Bibliography: p. 223-228. [BX4827.G6S48] 66-22918
1. Gogarten, Friedrich, 1887- 2. Theology, Doctrinal—History—20th century. I. Title.

SMART, James D. 230'.0904
The divided mind of modern theology, Karl Barth and Rudolf Bultmann, 1908-1933, by James D. Smart. Philadelphia, Westminster Press [1967] 240 p. 24 cm. Bibliographical references included in "Notes" (p. [229]-238) [BT28.S6] 67-10614
1. Barth, Karl, 1886- 2. Bultmann, Rudolf Karl, 1884- 3. Theology, Doctrinal—History—20th century. I. Title.

SPERNA WEILAND, Jan. 230'.09'04
New ways in theology [by] J. Sperna Weiland. Translated by N. D. Smith. Glen Rock, N.J., Newman Press [1968] xv, 222 p. 22 cm. Translation of Orientatie. Includes bibliographies. [BT28.S6513 1968] 68-55398 5.95
1. Theology, Doctrinal—History—20th century. I. Title.

TENSIONS in contemporary theology 230'.09'04
/ edited by Stanley N. Gundry and Alan F. Johnson foreword by Roger Nicole. Chicago : Moody Press, c1976. 366 p. ; 24 cm. Includes bibliographies and index. [BT28.T4] 76-7629 ISBN 0-8024-8585-5 : 8.95
1. Theology, Doctrinal—History—20th century—Addresses, essays, lectures. I. Gundry, Stanley N. II. Johnson, Alan F.

TWENTIETH century theology in the making. 230'.09'04
Edited by Jaroslav Pelikan. Translated by R. A. Wilson. [1st Harper pbk. ed.] New York, Harper & Row [1971] 3 v. 21 cm. Selections from the 2d ed. of Die Religion in Geschichte und Gegenwart. Contents.Contents.—v. 1. Themes of biblical theology.—v. 2. The theological dialogue: issues and resources.—v. 3. Ecumenicity and renewal. Includes bibliographies. [BR45.R4235] 72-178974 ISBN 0-06-139220-0 (v. 1)
1. Theology—20th century—Collections. I. Pelikan, Jaroslav Jan, 1923- ed.

VIDLER, Alexander Roper, 1899- 230.0904
20th century defenders of the faith [by]Alec R. Vidler New York, Seabury Press [1965] 127 p. 20 cm. (Robertson lectures [1964]) Bibliographical footnotes. [BT28.V5] 65-29702
1. Theology, Doctrinal — Hist. — 20th cent. 2. Apologetics — Hist. I. Title. II. Series: Robertson lectures, 1964

VIDLER, Alexander Roper, 1899- 230.0904
20th century defenders of the faith [by] Alex R. Vidler. New York, Seabury [c.1965] 127p. 20cm. (Robertson lects. 1964) Title. (Series: Robertson lectures, 1964) Bibl. [BT28.V5] 65-29702 2.50 bds.,
1. Theology, Doctrinal—Hist.—20th cent. 2. Apologetics—Hist. I. Title. II. Series.

VOGEL, Arthur Anton. 230.0904
The next Christian epoch, by Arthur A. Vogel. [1st ed.] New York, Harper & Row [1966] xii, 111 p. 22 cm. Bibliographical footnotes. [BT28.V6] 66-12647
1. Theology—20th cent. I. Title.

VOGEL, Arthur Anton 230.0904
The next Christian epoch. New York, Harper [c.1966] xii, 111p. 22cm. Bibl. [BT28.V6] 66-12647 3.50 bds.,
1. Theology—20th cent. I. Title.

WILLIAMS, Daniel Day, 1910- 230'.0904
What present-day theologians are thinking. 3d ed., rev. New York, Harper & Row [1967] 227 p. 21 cm. (Harper chapelbooks, CB32) Includes bibliographies. [BT28.W55 1967] 67-1206
1. Theology, Doctrinal—History—20th century. 2. Religious thought—20th century. I. Title.

GATEWOOD, Willard B., comp. 230'.09'042
Controversy in the twenties; fundamentalism, modernism, and evolution. Willard B. Gatewood, Jr., editor. Nashville, Vanderbilt University Press [1969] ix, 459 p. 25 cm. Includes bibliographical references. [BT82.3.G3] 69-11279 10.00
1. Modernist-fundamentalist controversy. I. Title.

BRYAN, Mary Givens. 230'.0922
Passports issued by Governors of Georgia, 1810 to 1820. Index of persons receiving passports, 1785 to 1820, by Wm. H. Dumont, Washington, 1964. 59-112 p. 26 cm. (Special publications of National Genealogical Society, no. 28) "The Passports' issued from 1785 through 1909 were . . . issued in 1959 as a special publication no. 21 [of the National Genealogical Society]" [CS42.N43] 66-6269
1. Registers of births, etc., — Georgia. I. Title. II. Series: National Genealogical Society. Special publications, no. 28

CHARMOT, Francois. 230.0922
Ignatius Loyola and Francis de Sales: two masters, one spirituality [by] F. Charmot. Translated by Sister M. Renelle. St. Louis, B. Herder Book Co. [1966] x, 251 p. 21 cm. (Cross and crown series of spirituality, no. 32) Translation of Deux maitres, une spiritualite: Ignace de Loyola, Francois de Sales. Bibliography: p. 250-251. [BX4700.L7C53] 66-17096
1. Loyola, Ignacio de. Saint, 1491-1556. 2. Francois de Sales, Saint, Bp. of Geneva, 1567-1622. 3. Spiritual life — History of doctrines. I. Title. II. Series.

CHARMOT, Francois 230.0922
Ignatius Loyola and Francis de Sales: two masters, one spirituality. Tr. [from French] by Sister M. Renelle. St. Louis, B. Herder [c. 1966] x, 251p. 21cm. (Cross and crown ser. of spirituality, no. 32) Bibl. [BX4700.L7C53] 66-17096 4.75
1. Loyola, Ignaio de, Saint, 1491-1556. 2. Francois de Sales, Saint, Bp. of Geneva, 1567-1622. 3. Spiritual life—History of doctrines. I. Title. II. Series.

GRANFIELD, Patrick. 230'.0922
Theologians at work. New York, Macmillan [1967] xxvi, 262 p. 21 cm. Interviews. [BT28.G7 1967] 67-27515
1. Theologians. 2. Theology, Doctrinal — Hist. — 20th cent. I. Title.
Contents omitted

GRANFIELD, Patrick 230'.0922
Theologians at work. New York, Macmillan [1967] xxvi, 262p. 21cm. Interviews. [BT28.G7 1967] 67-27515 5.95
1. Theologians. 2. Theology, Doctrinal—Hist.—20th Century. I. Title.
Contents omitted.

GRAY, Joseph M. M., 1877- 230'.0922
Prophets of the soul [by] Joseph M. M. Gray. Freeport, N.Y., Books for Libraries Press [1971] 267 p. 23 cm. (Essay index reprint series) Reprint of the 1936 ed. Contents.Contents.—Those Mathers and the Puritan Commonwealth.—Jonathan Edwards, his God.—George Whitefield and his Master's voice.—Methodist itinerants: creators of climate.—William Ellery Channing: a theological hamlet.—Horace Bushnell: the beloved heretic.—Phillips Brooks: a prophetic goodness.—George A. Gordon: the magnificent rebel.—Washington Gladden and applied Christianity.—What of the light? Includes bibliographies. [BR569.G7 1971] 71-156655 ISBN 0-8369-2277-8
1. Clergy—United States—Biography. I. Title.

HUGHES, Philip Edgcumbe, ed. 230'.0922
Creative minds in contemporary theology; a guidebook to the principal teachings of Karl Barth, G. C. Berkouwer, Dietrich Bonhoeffer, Emil Brunner, Rudolf Bultmann, Oscar Cullmann, James Denney, C. H. Dodd., Herman Dooyeweerd, P. T. Forsyth, Charles Gore, Reinhold Niebuhr, Pierre Teilhard de Chardin, and Paul Tillich. 2d, rev. ed. Grand Rapids, Eerdmans [1969] 522 p. 24 cm. Includes bibliographies. [BT28.H8 1969] 74-3017 6.95
1. Theology—20th century. I. Title.

KERSHNER, Frederick Doyle, 1875-1953. 230'.0922
Pioneers of Christian thought [by] Frederick D. Kershner. Freeport, N.Y., Books for Libraries Press [1968, c1930] 373 p. 23 cm. (Essay index reprint series) Contents.Contents.—Philo.—Paul of Tarsus.—Marcion.—Origen.—Athanasius.—Theodore.—Augustine.—Anselm.—Abelard.—Aquinas.—

Erasmus.—Luther.—Calvin.—Arminius.—Schleiermacher.—Ritschl.—Bibliography (p. 351-355) [BR1700.K45 1968] 68-57327
1. Theologians. 2. Theology, Doctrinal—History. I. Title.

MERTENS, Nora May (Turner) 1896- comp. 230'.0922
Indiana genealogical directory. no.1- Indianapolis, Indiana Historical Society. v. 28 cm. "Compiled by Mrs. F. C. Mertens with the cooperation of members of the Genealogical Section of the Indiana Historical Society." 1962- [CS42.I 5] 63-3743
1. Indiana — General. — Direct. I. Indiana Historical Society. Genealogical Section. II. Title.

PEERMAN, Dean G., ed. 230.0922
A handbook of Christian theologians, edited by Dean G. Peerman and Martin E. Marty. Cleveland, World Pub. Co. [1965] 506 p. 21 cm. "Companion volume to A handbook of Christian theology." Includes bibliographical references. [BT28.P36] 65-18010
1. Theologians. I. Marty, Martin E., 1928- joint ed. II. Title.

RUSSELL, Charles Allyn. 230'.092'2 B
Voices of American fundamentalism : seven biographical studies / by C. Allyn Russell. Philadelphia : Westminster Press, c1976. p. cm. Includes index. Bibliography: p. [BT82.2.R87] 76-5886 ISBN 0-664-20814-2 : 12.50
1. Fundamentalism. 2. Christian biography. I. Title.

SEVERSMITH, Herbert Furman, 1904- 230'.0922
Long Island genealogical source material; a bibliography, by Herbert F. Seversmith and Kenn Stryker-Rodda. Washington. National Genealogical Society, 1962. iv, 121 p. 27 cm. (National Genealogical Society. Special publications, no. 24) [CS42.N43 no. 24] 62-4252
1. Registers of births, etc. — Long Island — Bibl. I. Stryker-Rodda, Kenn, joint author. II. Title. III. Series.

SOPER, David Wesley, 1910- 230'.0922
Major voices in American theology. Port Washington, N.Y., Kennikat Press [1969, c1953-55] 2 v. 22 cm. (Essay and general literature index reprint series) Contents.Contents.—[1] Six contemporary leaders.—v. 2. Men who shape belief. [BR569.S652] 72-86060 ISBN 0-8046-0587-4
1. Theologians—United States. 2. Theology, Doctrinal—History—United States. I. Title. II. Title: Six contemporary leaders. III. Title: Men who shape belief.

STEWART, William C 1907- 230'.0922
Gone to Georgia: Jackson and Gwinnett Counties and their neighbors in the western migration, compiled and with an introd. by William C. Stewart. Washington, National Genealogical Society, 1965. 326 p. 27 cm. (Special publications of the National Genealogical Society, no. 30) [CS42.N43] 65-8587
1. Jackson Co., Ga. — Geneal. 2. Gwinnett Co., Ga. — Geneal. I. Title. II. Series: National Genealogical Society. Special publications, no. 30

ANDERSON, James Francis, 1910- 230'.092'4 B
Paul Tillich; basics in his thought [by] James F. Anderson. Albany, Magi Books [1972] x, 83 p. 20 cm. Includes bibliographical references. [BX4827.T53A75] 70-176127 ISBN 0-87343-040-9 4.95
1. Tillich, Paul, 1886-1965. I. Title.

ARMBRUSTER, Carl J., 1929- 230'.0924
The vision of Paul Tillich [by] Carl J. Armbruster. New York, Sheed [1967] xxii, 328p. 22cm. Bibl. [BX4827.T53A8] 67-13774 6.95
1. Tillich, Paul, 1886-1965. I. Title.

ARMBRUSTER, Carl J., 1929- 230'.0924
The vision of Paul Tillich [by] Carl J. Armbruster. New York, Sheed and Ward [1967] xxii, 328 p. 22 cm. Includes bibliographical references. [BX4837.T53A8] 67-13774
1. Tillich, Paul, 1886-1965. I. Title.

BARTH, J. Robert. 230'.0924
Coleridge and Christian doctrine [by] J. Robert Barth. Cambridge, Mass., Harvard University Press, 1969. xi, 215 p. 25 cm. Bibliography: p. 201-206. [PR4487.R4B3] 75-75426 7.50
1. Coleridge, Samuel Taylor, 1772-1834—Religion and ethics. I. Title.

BINGHAM, June, 1919- 230'.0924 B
Courage to change; an introduction to the life and thought of Reinhold Niebuhr. New York, Scribner [1972] xii, 414 p. illus. 24 cm. "Books by Reinhold Niebuhr": p. 405-406. Includes bibliographical references. [BX4827.N5B5 1972] 72-37467 ISBN 0-684-12789-X 10.00
1. Niebuhr, Reinhold, 1892-1971. I. Title.

BONHOEFFER, Dietrich, 1906-1945. 230'.092'4 B
Letters and papers from prison. Edited by Eberhard Bethge. Rev. ed. New York, Macmillan [1967] 240 p. illus., ports. 22 cm. Translation of Widerstand und Ergebung. [BX4827.B57A43 1967a] 67-19951
I. Title.

BONHOEFFER, Dietrich, 1906-1945. 230'.092'4 B
Letters and papers from prison. Edited by Eberhard Bethge. [1st American] enl. ed. New York, Macmillan [1972, c1971] x, 437 p. maps. 22 cm. Translation of Widerstand und Ergebung. [BX4827.B57A43 1972] 78-184531
I. Title.

BONHOEFFER, Dietrich, 1906-1945. 230'.092'4 B
True patriotism; letters, lectures, and notes, 1939-45, from the Collected works of Dietrich Bonhoeffer, volume III. Edited and introduced by Edwin H. Robertson. Translated by Edwin H. Robertson and John Bowden. [1st U.S. ed.] New York, Harper and Row [1973] 256 p. 21 cm. Includes bibliographical references. [BX4827.B57A2513 1973] 73-6421 ISBN 0-06-060801-3 6.95
1. Bonhoeffer, Dietrich, 1906-1945. 2. Lutheran Church—Collected works. 3. Theology—Collected works—20th century. I. Robertson, Edwin Hanton, ed. II. Title.

BRATT, John H., comp. 230'.092'4
The heritage of John Calvin; Heritage Hall lectures, 1960-70. Edited by John H. Bratt. Grand Rapids, Eerdmans [1973] 222 p. 23 cm. (Heritage Hall publications, no. 2) Includes bibliographical references. [BX9418.B73] 72-92718 ISBN 0-8028-3425-6 5.95
1. Calvin, Jean, 1509-1564. 2. Calvinism. I. Title. II. Series.

BUSCH, Eberhard, 1937- 230'.092'4 B
Karl Barth : his life from letters and autobiographical texts / Eberhard Busch ; translated by John Bowden. Philadelphia : Fortress Press, c1976. xvii, 569 p. : ill. ; 23 cm. Translation of Karl Barths Lebenslauf. Includes bibliographical references and indexes. [BX4827.B3B86313] 76-15881 ISBN 0-8006-0485-7 : 19.95
1. Barth, Karl, 1886-1968. 2. Theologians—Switzerland—Basel—Biography. 3. Basel—Biography.

CHERRY, C. Conrad 230.0924
The theology of Jonathan Edwards: a reappraisal [by] Conrad Cherry [Magnolia, Mass., P. Smith. 1967.c.] 1966. 270p. 19cm. (Anchor bk. rebound) Bibl. [BX7260.E3C5] 3.25
1. Edwards, Jonathan, 1703-1758. I. Title.

CHERRY, C. Conrad. 230.0924
The theology of Jonathan Edwards: a reappraisal [by] Conrad Cherry. Garden City, N.Y., Anchor Books, 1966. 270 p. 18 cm. Bibliographical references included in "Notes" (p. [218]-249) Bibliography: p. [250]-260. [BX7260.E3C5] 66-24336
1. Edwards, Jonathan, 1703-1758. I. Title.

CRESPY, Georges. 230'.0924
From science to theology; an essay on Teilhard de Chardin. Translated by George H. Shriver. Nashville, Abingdon Press [1968] 174 p. 21 cm. Translation of De la science a la theologie. Bibliography: p. 169-170. [B2430.T374C683] 68-25367 4.00
1. Teilhard de Chardin, Pierre. I. Title.

CROMWELL, Richard S. 230'.092'4 B
David Friedrich Strauss and his place in modern thought, by Richard S. Cromwell. Foreword by Wilhelm Pauck. Fair Lawn, N.J., R. E. Burdick [1974] 232 p. 23 cm. "A Carl Hermann Voss book." Bibliography: p. 219-224. [BX4827.S8C76 1974] 73-88620 ISBN 0-913638-05-6 12.50
1. Strauss, David Friedrich, 1808-1874. I. Title.

DAVIDSON, Edward Hutchins. 230.0924
Jonathan Edwards; the narrative of a Puritan mind [by] Edward H. Davidson. Boston, Houghton Mifflin Co. [1966] xii, 161 p. 21 cm. (Riverside studies in literature, L7) Bibliographical references included in "Notes" (p. 149-158) [BX7260.E3D3] 66-3058
1. Edwards, Jonathan, 1708-1758. I. Title.

DAVIDSON, Edward Hutchins 230.0924
Jonathan Edwards; the narrative of a Puritan mind. Boston, Houghton [c.1966] xii,161p. 21cm. (Riverside studies in lit., L7) Bibl. [BX7260.E3D3] 66-3058 1.95 pap.,
1. Edwards, Jonathan, 1703-1758. I. Title.

DAVIDSON, Edward Hutchins. 230'.0924
Jonathan Edwards; the narrative of a Puritan mind [by] Edward H. Davidson. Cambridge, Harvard University Press, 1968 [c1966] xii, 161 p. 22 cm. Bibliographical references included in "Notes" (p. 149-158) [BX7260.E3] 68-7254 6.00
1. Edwards, Jonathan, 1703-1758.

DAVIES, David Richard, 1889-1958. 230'.0924
Reinhold Niebuhr; prophet from America. Freeport, N.Y., Books for Libraries Press [1970, c1945] 94 p. 23 cm. "Books by Reinhold Niebuhr": p. [9] [BX4827.N5D3 1970] 71-117871
1. Niebuhr, Reinhold, 1892-

DIEM, Hermann, 1900- 230.0924
Kierkegaard: an introduction. Tr. by David Green. Richmond, John Knox [1966] 124p. 21cm. Bibl. [BX4827.K5D523] 66-17278 3.50
1. Kierkegaard, Soren Aabye, 1813-1855. I. Title.

ELLER, Vernard. 230'.0924
Kierkegaard and radical discipleship, a new perspective. Princeton, N.J., Princeton University Press, 1968. xii, 445 p. 23 cm. Bibliographical footnotes. [BX4827.K5E4] 67-21021
1. Kierkegaard, Soren Aabye, 1813-1855. 2. Church of the Brethren. I. Title.

ERNST Troeltsch and 230'.092'4
the future of theology / edited by John Powell Clayton. Cambridge ; New York : Cambridge University Press, 1976. xiii, 217 p. ; 23 cm. Essays based on a colloquium sponsored by the Dept. of Religious Studies, University of Lancaster. Includes index. "Bibliography, compiled by Jacob Klapwijk": p. 196-214. [BX4827.T7E76] 75-44576 ISBN 0-521-21074-7 : 18.95
1. Troeltsch, Ernst, 1865-1923—Congresses. I. Clayton, John Powell. II. Lancaster, Eng. University. Dept. of Religious Studies.

ERNST Troeltsch and 230'.092'4
the future of theology / edited by John Powell Clayton. Cambridge : Cambridge University Press, 1976. xiii, 217 p. ; 23 cm. Essays based on a colloquium sponsored by the Dept. of Religious Studies, University of Lancaster. Includes index. Bibliography: p. 196-214. [BX4827.T7E76 1976b] 76-383265 ISBN 0-521-21074-7 : 18.95
1. Troeltsch, Ernst, 1865-1923—Congresses. I. Clayton, John Powell. II. Lancaster, Eng. University. Dept. of Religious Studies.
Distributed by Cambridge University Press N.Y. N.Y.

FACKRE, Gabriel J. 230'.0924
The promise of Reinhold Niebuhr, by Gabriel Fackre. [1st ed.] Philadelphia, Lippincott [1970] 101 p. 21 cm. (The Promise of theology) "A selected bibliography of works by Reinhold Niebuhr": p. 100-101. Includes bibliographical references. [BX4827.N5F3] 79-120329 3.50
1. Niebuhr, Reinhold, 1892- I. Title.

FADNER, Donald Edward. 230'.092'4
The responsible God : a study of the Christian philosophy of H. Richard Niebuhr / by Donald Edward Fadner. Missoula, Mont. : Scholars Press for the American Academy of Religion, c1975. p. cm. (Dessertation series - American Academy of Religion ; no. 13) Originally presented as the author's thesis, University of Chicago, 1974. Bibliography: p. [BX4827.N47F3 1975] 75-29373 ISBN 0-89130-041-4 : 4.20
1. Niebuhr, Helmut Richard, 1894-1962. I. Title. II. Series: American Academy of Religion. Dissertation series — American Academy of Religion ; no. 13.

FADNER, Donald Edward. 230'.092'4
The responsible God : a study of the Christian philosophy of H. Richard Niebuhr / by Donald Edward Fadner. Missoula, Mont. : Published by Scholars Press for the American Academy of Religion, c1975. xvi, 276 p. ; 21 cm. (Dissertation series - American Academy of Religion ; no. 13) Originally presented as the author's thesis, University of Chicago, 1974. Bibliography: p. 273-276. [BX4827.N47F3 1975] 75-29373 ISBN 0-89130-041-4 : 4.20
1. Niebuhr, Helmut Richard, 1894-1962. I. Title. II. Series: American Academy of Religion. Dissertation series — American Academy of Religion ; no. 13.

FANT, Clyde E. 230'.092'4
Bonhoeffer : worldly preaching / Clyde E. Fant. Nashville : T. Nelson, [1975] xi, 180 p. ; 21 cm. Includes 10 lectures delivered by D. Bonhoeffer (p. 123-180). Includes bibliographical references. [BV4207.F36] 74-26806 ISBN 0-8407-5087-0 : 6.95 ISBN 0-8407-5586-4 pbk. :
1. Bonhoeffer, Dietrich, 1906-1945. 2. Preaching—History. I. Bonhoeffer, Dietrich, 1906-1945.

FARICY, Robert L. 1926- 230'.0924
Teilhard de Chardin's theology of the Christian in the world, by Robert L. Faricy. New York, Sheed [1967] xviii, 235p. 22cm. Bibl. [B2430.T374F37] 67-13767 6.00
1. Teilhard de Chardin, Pierre—Theology. I. Title.

FERRE, Nels Fredrick Solomon, 1908- 230'.0924
Paul Tillich: retrospect and future. [Articles by] Nels F. S. Ferre [and others] Introd. by T. A. Kantonen. Nashville, Abingdon Press [1967, c1966] 63 p. 19 cm. "Reprinted from Religion in life, winter 1966." [BX4827.T53P3] 67-31858
1. Tillich, Paul, 1886-1965. I. Title. II. Title: Religion in life.

FLYGT, Sten Gunnar, 1911- 230'.0924
The notorious Dr. Bahrdt. Nashville, Vanderbilt, 1963. ix, 428 p. illus. 24 cm. Bibliography: p. 389-402. [BX4827.B25F5] 63-14648
1. Bahrdt, Karl Friedrich, 1741-1792. 2. Enlightenment. I. Title.

FORSTMANN, Jack. 230'.092'4
A romantic triangle : Schleiermacher and early German romanticism / by Jack Forstman. Missoula, Mont. : Published by Scholars Press for the American Academy of Religion, c1977. xiv, 122 p. ; 24 cm. (AAR studies i2 religion ; no. 13) Includes bibliographical references. [BX4827.S3F68] 76-55709 ISBN 0-89130-124-0 : 4.50
1. Schleiermacher, Friedrich Ernst Daniel, 1768-1834. 2. Schlegel, Friedrich von, 1772-1829. 3. Hardenberg, Friedrich, Freiherr von, 1772-1801. 4. Romanticism—Germany. I. Title. II. Series: American Academy of Religion. AAR studies in religion ; no. 13.

FOWLER, James W., 1940- 230'.092'4 B
To see the kingdom; the theological vision of H. Richard Niebuhr [by] James W. Fowler. Nashville, Abingdon Press [1974] xii, 292 p. illus. 24 cm. Bibliography: p. 277-286. [BX4827.N47F68] 74-688 ISBN 0-687-42300-7 10.95
1. Niebuhr, Helmut Richard, 1894-1962. I. Title.

GALLOWAY, Allan Douglas, 1920- 230.0924
Wolfhart Pannenberg [by] Allan D. Galloway London, George Allen and Unwin [1975 c1973] 143 p. 22 cm. (Contemporary religious thinkers) Includes index. Bibliography: p. 139-140. [BX4827.P3G34] ISBN 0-04-230011-8
1. Pannenberg, Wolfhart, 1928- I. Title.
Distributed by Humanities Press for 9.75. L.C. card no. for original edition: 73-179423.

GELPI, Donald L 1934- 230.0924
Life and light; a guide to the theology of Karl Rahner, by Donald L. Gelpi. New York, Sheed and Ward [1966] xiv, 301 p. 22 cm. Includes bibliographies. [BX4705.R287G4] 66-12274
1. Rahner, Karl, 1904- I. Title.

GELPI, Donald L., 1934- 230.0924
Life and light; a guide to the theology of Karl Rahner, by Donald L. Gelpi. New York, Sheed [c.1966] xiv,301p. 22cm. Bibl. [BX4705.R287G4] 66-12274 6.00
1. Rahner, Karl, 1904- I. Title.

GILL, Jerry H., comp. 230'.0924
Essays on Kierkegaard. Edited by Jerry H. Gill. Minneapolis, Burgess Pub. Co. [1969] iii, 197 p. illus., facsims., ports. 23 cm. Includes bibliographies. [B4377.G5] 72-88030 ISBN 8-08-707248-
1. Kierkegaard, Soren Aabye, 1813-1855. I. Title.

GODDARD, Donald. 230'.092'4 B
The last days of Dietrich Bonhoeffer / Donald Goddard. 1st ed. New York : Harper & Row, c1976. 245 p. ; 24 cm. [BX4827.B57G58 1976] 75-25106 ISBN 0-06-011564-5 : 12.50
1. Bonhoeffer, Dietrich, 1906-1945. I. Title.

GODSEY, John D. 230'.0924 B
The promise of H. Richard Niebuhr, by John D. Godsey. [1st ed.] Philadelphia, Lippincott [1970] 122 p. 22 cm. (The Promise of theology) Bibliography: p. 119-122. [BX4827.N47G6] 75-103600 3.95

1. Niebuhr, Helmut Richard, 1894-1962. I. Title.

GRAGG, Alan. 230'.092'4 B
Charles Hartshorne. Waco, Tex., Word Books [1973] 127 p. 23 cm. (Makers of the modern theological mind) Bibliography: p. 124-127. [B945.H354G72] 70-188063 3.95
1. Hartshorne, Charles, 1897-

GRAGG, Alan. 230'.092'4 B
Charles Hartshorne. Waco, Tex., Word Books [1973] 127 p. 23 cm. (Makers of the modern theological mind) Bibliography: p. 124-127. [B945.H354G72] 70-188063 3.95
1. Hartshorne, Charles, 1897-

GREEN, Clifford J. 230'.092'4
The sociality of Christ and humanity : Dietrich Bonhoeffer's early theology, 1927-1933 / by Clifford J. Green. Missoula, Mont. : Published by Scholars Press for the American Academy of Religion, c1972. xv, 356 p. ; 22 cm. (Dissertation series - American Academy of Religion ; no. 6) Originally presented as the author's thesis, Union Theological Seminary, New York, 1972. Includes bibliographical references. [BX4827.B57G7 1972b] 75-33816 ISBN 0-89130-055-4 : 4.20
1. Bonhoeffer, Dietrich, 1906-1945. I. Title. II. Series: American Academy of Religion. Dissertation series — American Academy of Religion ; no. 6.

GREEN, Clifford J. 230'.092'4
The sociality of Christ and humanity : Dietrich Bonhoeffer's early theology, 1927-1933 / by Clifford J. Green. Missoula, Mont. : Published by Scholars Press for the American Academy of Religion, 1976c1972 xv, 356 p. ; 22 cm. (Dissertation series - American Academy of Religion ; no. 6) Originally presented as the author's thesis, Union Theological Seminary, New York, 1972. Includes bibliographical references. [BX4827.B57G7 1972b] 75-33816 ISBN 0-89130-055-4 pbk. : 4.50
1. Bonhoeffer, Dietrich, 1906-1945. I. Title. II. Series: American Academy of Religion. Dissertation series — American Academy of Religion ; no. 6.

HAMILTON, Kenneth. 230'.0924
The promise of Kierkegaard. [1st ed.] Philadelphia, Lippincott [1969] 116 p. 21 cm. (The Promise of theology) Bibliography: p. 112-116. [B4377.H34] 69-14495 1.50
1. Kierkegaard, Soren Aabye, 1813-1855. 2. Christianity—Philosophy. I. Title.

HAMILTON, Kenneth. 230'.0924
The system and the Gospel; a critique of Paul Tillich. Grand Rapids, Eerdmans [1967, c1963] 249 p. 21 cm. Bibliographical footnotes. [BX4827.T53H3 1967] 67-19318
1. Tillich, Paul, 1886-1965. I. Title.

HAMILTON, Peter Napier. 230'.0924
The living God and the modern world; Christian theology based on the thought of A. N. Whitehead, by Peter Hamilton. Philadelphia, United Church Pr. [1968,c.1967] 256p. 21cm. Bibl. [BT75.2.H35 1968] 67-28283 2.95 pap.,
1. Whitehead, Alfred North, 1861-1947. 2. Theology, Doctrinal. 3. Process theology. I. Title.

HARRIS, Horton. 230'.092'4 B
David Friedrich Strauss and his theology. Cambridge [Eng.] University Press, 1973. xv, 301 p. illus. 22 cm. (Monograph supplements to the Scottish journal of theology) Bibliography: p. 295-298. [BX4827.S8H33] 72-93137 ISBN 0-521-20139-X
1. Strauss, David Friedrich, 1808-1874. I. Title. II. Series: Scottish journal of theology. Monograph supplements.
Distributed by Cambridge University Press, New York, 16.00.

HARTMANN, Franz, d. 1912. 230'.092'4 B
Jacob Boehme : life and doctrines / by Franz Hartmann. 1st ed. Blauvelt, N.Y. : Steinerbooks, c1977. xii, 338 p. ; 22 cm. Published in 1891 under title: The life and doctrines of Jacob Boehme; in 1919 and in 1957 or 8 under title: Personal Christianity. Reprint of the 1891 ed. published by K. Paul, Trench, Trubner, London. Includes bibliographical references and index. [BV5095.B7H3 1977] 76-53631 ISBN 0-8334-1734-7 : 6.50
1. Bohme, Jakob, 1575-1624. I. Bohme, Jakob, 1575-1624.

HEFNER, Philip J 230.0924
Faith and the vitalities of history: a theological study based on the work of Albrecht Ritschl [by] Philip Hefner. [1st ed.] New York, Harper & Row [1966] xi, 192 p. port. 22 cm. (Makers of modern theology) Bibliography: p. 187-190. [BX4827.R5H4] 66-15038
1. Ritschl, Albrecht Benjamin, 1822-1889. 2. Theology — Methodology. 3. History (Theology) 4. Theology — 20th cent. I. Title.

HEFNER, Philip 230.0924
J.Ritschl, Albrecht Benjamin 1822-1899
Faith and the vitalities of history; a theological study based on the work of albrecht ritschl. New York, Harper [c.1966] xi, 192 p. port. 22 cm (Makers mod. theol.) bibl. [bx4827.r5h4-] 66-15038 4.50
1. Theology-Methodology. History (Theology. Theology. Theology—20th cent. I. Title.

HENDERSON, Ian, 1910- 230.0924
Rudolf Bultmann. Richmond, Va., Knox [1966] viii, 47p. 19cm. (Makers of contemp. theol.) [BX4827.B78H4] 66-11071 1.00 pap.,
1. Bultmann, Rudolf Karl, 1884- I. Title.

HODGSON, Peter Crafts, 1934- 230.0924
The formation of historical theology; a study of Ferdinand Christian Baur. New York, Harper [c.1966] xv,299p. port. 22cm. (Makers of modern theol.) Bibl. [BX4827.B33H6] 66-15039 5.50
1. Baur, Ferdinand Christian, 1792-1860. 2. History (Theology) I. Title.

HOPPER, David. 230'.092'4
A dissent on Bonhoeffer / David H. Hopper. Philadelphia : Westminster Press, [1975] p. cm. Includes bibliographical references and index. [BX4827.B57H67] 75-22120 ISBN 0-664-20802-9 : 8.50
1. Bonhoeffer, Dietrich, 1906-1945. I. Title.

HOPPER, David. 230'.0924
Tillich; a theological portrait. [1st ed.] Philadelphia, Lippincott, 1968 [c1967] 189 p. 21 cm. [BX4827.T53H6] 68-10618
1. Tillich, Paul, 1886-1965.

HUMPHREY, James Edward. 230'.092'4
Emil Brunner / by J. Edward Humphrey. Waco, Tex. : Word Books, c1976. 183 p. ; 23 cm. (Makers of the modern theological mind) Bibliography: p. 180-183. [BX4827.B67H85] 75-36186 ISBN 0-87680-453-9 : 6.95
1. Brunner, Heinrich Emil, 1889-1966.

THE Intellectual legacy of Paul Tillich. 230'.0924 Editor, James R. Lyons. Detroit, Wayne State University Press, 1969. 115 p. port. 22 cm. (Slaughter Foundation lectures, 1966) Contents.Contents.—Paul Johannes Tillich, biographical note, by J. R. Lyons.—The philosophical legacy of Paul Tillich, by J. H. Randall, Jr.—Paul Tillich as a contemporary theologian, by R. L. Shinn.—The psychiatric legacy of Paul Tillich, by E. A. Loomis.—Appendix, Tillich-to-Thomas Mann letter (23 May 1943) [BX4827.T53I5] 68-63714 3.95
1. Tillich, Paul, 1886-1965. I. Tillich, Paul, 1886-1965. II. Lyons, James R., ed. III. Title. IV. Series.

JAMES, Ralph E 230'.0924
The concrete God; a new beginning for theology; the thought of Charles Hartshorne, by Ralph E. James. Indianapolis, Bobbs-Merrill [1967] xxviii, 236 p. 22 cm. Bibliography: p. 195-223. [B945.H354J3] 67-25172
1. Hartshorne, Charles, 1897- 2. Process theology. I. Title.

JAMES, Ralph E. 230'.0924
The concrete God; a new beginning for theology; the thought of Charles Hartshorne, by Ralph E. James. Indianapolis, Bobbs-Merrill [1967] xxviii, 236 p. 22 cm. Bibliography: p. 195-223. [B945.H354J3] 67-25172
1. Hartshorne, Charles, 1897- 2. Process theology. I. Title.

JOHN Cobb's theology in process 230'.092'4 / edited by David Ray Griffin and Thomas J. J. Altizer. Philadelphia : Westminster Press, c1977. x, 201 p. ; 24 cm. "Bibliography of John B. Cobb's writings": p. 193-201. [BX4827.C6J63] 77-23135 ISBN 0-664-21292-1 : 15.00
1. Cobb, John B.—Addresses, essays, lectures. 2. Cobb, John B.—Bibliography. I. Griffin, David, 1939- II. Altizer, Thomas J. J.

KALLAS, James 230.0924
The Satanward view; a study in Pauline theology. Philadelphia, Westminster [c. 1966] 152p. 21cm. Bibl. [BS2650.2.K3] 66-10162 4.50
1. Bible. N. T. Epistles of Paul—Theology. I. Title.

KALLAS, James G 230.0924
The Satanward view; a study in Pauline theology. Philadelphia, Westminster Press [1966] 152 p. 21 cm. Bibliographical footnotes. [BS2650.2.K3] 66-10162
1. Bible. N.T. Epistles of Paul — Theology. I. Title.

KARL Barth and the future of theology; 230'.0924 a memorial colloquium held at the Yale Divinity School, January 28, 1969. Edited by David L. Dickerman. New Haven, Yale Divinity School Association [1969] 71 l. 28 cm. Includes bibliographies. [BX4827.B3K35] 75-10954
1. Barth, Karl, 1886-1968. 2. Barth, Karl, 1886-1968—Bibliography. I. Dickerman, David L., ed. II. Yale University. Divinity School. III. Yale Divinity School Association.

KEGLEY, Charles W., 1912- ed. 230.0924
The theology of Rudolf Bultmann, edited by Charles W. Kegley. [1st ed.] New York, Harper & Row [1966] xxv, 320 p. port. 22 cm. Bibliographical footnotes. "Bibliography of the publications of Rudolf Bultmann to 1965": p. 289-310. [BX4827.B78K4] 66-11483
1. Bultmann, Rudolf Karl, 1884- I. Title.

LADD, George Eldon, 1911- 230'.0924
Rudolf Bultmann. Chicago, Inter-Varsity Press [c1964] vii, 52 p. 21 cm. (IVP series in contemporary Christian thought, 7) Bibliography: p. 51-52. [BX4827.B78L3] 64-7860
1. Bultmann, Rudolf Karl, 1884- I. Title.

LANDON, Harold R., ed. 230'.092'4 B
Reinhold Niebuhr: a prophetic voice in our time. Essays in tribute by Paul Tillich, John C. Bennett [and] Hans J. Morgenthau. Harold R. Landon, editor. Plainview, N.Y., Books for Libraries Press [1974, c1962] 126 p. 22 cm. (Essay index reprint series) Papers and discussions from the colloquium in honor of Reinhold Niebuhr on October 20, 1961, at the Cathedral Church of St. John the Divine, New York City. Reprint of the ed. published by the Seabury Press, Greenwich, Conn. Includes bibliographical references. [BX4827.N5L3 1974] 74-841 ISBN 0-518-10150-9 9.50
1. Niebuhr, Reinhold, 1892-1971.

THE Legacy of Reinhold Niebuhr 230'.092'4 / edited by Nathan A. Scott, Jr. Chicago : University of Chicago Press, 1975. xxiv, 124 p. : port. ; 24 cm. "This work also appeared as volume 54, number 4 (Oct. 1974), of the Journal of religion." Bibliography: p. 111-112. [BX4827.N5L4] 74-30714 ISBN 0-226-74297-0 : 6.95
1. Niebuhr, Reinhold, 1892-1971—Addresses, essays, lectures. I. Scott, Nathan A. II. The Journal of religion.

LEWIS, Clive Staples, 1898-1963. 230'.092'4
The joyful Christian : one hundred readings from C. S. Lewis. New York : Macmillan Pub. Co., c1977. p. cm. Bibliography: p. [BX5037.L4 1977] 77-21685 ISBN 0-02-570900-3 : 7.95
1. Church of England—Collected works. 2. Theology—Collected works—20th century. 3. Christian life—Anglican authors—Collected works. I. Title.

LIEM, Ann. 230'.092'4
Jacob Boehme : insights into the challenge of evil / Ann Liem. Wallingford, Pa. : Pendle Hill Publications, 1977. 32 p. ; 19 cm. (Pendle Hill pamphlet ; 214 ISSN 0031-4250s) Includes bibliographical references. [BV5095.B7L53] 77-79823 ISBN 0-87574-214-9 : 0.95
1. Bohme, Jakob, 1575-1624. I. Title.

MAHAN, Wayne W. 230'.092'4
Tillich's system / by Wayne W. Mahan. San Antonio : Trinity University Press, 1974. 148 p. ; 24 cm. Includes bibliographical references and index. [BX4827.T53M25] 73-91170 ISBN 0-911536-52-3 : 7.50
1. Tillich, Paul, 1886-1965. I. Title.

MARLE, Rene. 230'.0924
Bultmann and Christian faith. Translated by Theodore DuBois. Westminster, Md., Newman Press [1967, c1968] vi, 106 p. 21 cm. Translation of Bultmann et la foi Chretienne. Bibliographical footnotes. [BX4827.B78M333] 68-16663
1. Bultmann, Rudolf Karl, 1884- I. Title.

MAY, Rollo. 230'.092'4 B
Paulus; reminiscences of a friendship. [1st ed.] New York, Harper & Row [1973] vii, 113 p. 21 cm. Includes bibliographical references. [BX4827.T53M34] 72-78075 ISBN 0-06-065535-6 5.95
1. Tillich, Paul, 1886-1965. I. Title.

MEEKS, M. Douglas. 230'.092'4
Origins of the theology of hope [by] M. Douglas Meeks. Foreword by Jurgen Moltmann. Philadelphia, Fortress Press [1974] xiv, 178 p. 24 cm. Bibliography: p. 164-174. [BX4827.M6M43] 73-88351 ISBN 0-8006-0265-X 8.50
1. Moltmann, Jurgen. 2. Theology, Doctrinal—History—20th century. 3. Hope—History of doctrines. I. Title.

MINOR, William Sherman, 1900- 230'.092'4
Creativity in Henry Nelson Wieman / by William Sherman Minor ; with a foreword by Bernard E. Meland. Metuchen, N.J. : Scarecrow Press, 1977. xix, 231 p. ; 23 cm. (ATLA monograph series ; no. 11) Includes index. Bibliography: p. 216-224. [BX4827.W45M55 1977] 77-8087 ISBN 0-8108-1041-7 : 10.00
1. Wieman, Henry Nelson, 1884- I. Title. II. Series: American Theological Library Association. ATLA monograph series ; no. 11.

MONTGOMERY, John Warwick. 230'.0924
In defense of Martin Luther; essays. Milwaukee, Northwestern Pub. House [1970] 175 p. illus., facsim. 21 cm. Contents.Contents.—Luther's theology today: The 95 theses then and now. Luther's hermeneutic vs. the new hermeneutic.—Luther and science; Cross, constellation, and crucible.—Luther, libraries, and learning.—Luther on politics and race: Shirer's re-Hitlerizing of Luther. A day in East German Luther country.—Luther and the missionary challenge. Includes bibliographical references. [BR326.M65] 72-123731
1. Luther, Martin, 1483-1546—Addresses, essays, lectures. I. Title.

NETH, John Watson. 230'.0924
Walter Scott speaks; a handbook of doctrine. Milligan College, Tenn., Emmanuel School of Religion, 1967. 156 p. 20 cm. Revision of author's thesis, Butler University. Bibliography:p. 146-147. [BX7343.S3N4 1967] 67-25396
1. Scott, Walter, 1796-1861. I. Title.

NIEBUHR, Reinhold, 1892-1971. 230'.092'4 B
Leaves from the notebook of a tamed cynic / by Reinhold Niebuhr. New York : Da Capo Press, 1976, c1929. p. cm. (Prelude to depression) Reprint of the ed. published by Willett, Clark & Colby, Chicago. [BX4827.N5A34 1976] 76-27833 ISBN 0-306-70852-3 : 15.00
1. Niebuhr, Reinhold, 1892-1971. 2. Clergy—Michigan—Detroit—Biography. 3. Detroit—Biography. I. Title.

OLIVE, Don H. 230'.092'4 B
Wolfhart Pannenberg [by] Don H. Olive. Waco, Tex., Word Books [1973] 120 p. 23 cm. (Makers of the modern theological mind) Bibliography: p. 117-120. [BX4827.P3O44] 78-188068 4.95
1. Pannenberg, Wolfhart, 1928- I. Title.

O'MEARA, Thomas F., 1935- comp. 230'.0924
Rudolf Bultmann in Catholic thought, edited by Thomas F. O'Meara and Donald M. Weisser. [New York] Herder and Herder [1968] 254 p. 22 cm. Contents.Contents.—A prefatory letter from Rudolf Bultmann.—Introduction by the editors.—Demythologizing and theological truth, by H. Fries.—Demythologizing in the school of Alexandria, by J. Danielou.—Form-criticism and the Gospels, by R. Schnackenburg.—Bultmann and the Gospel according to John, by J. Blank.—Bultmann and the Old Testament, by R. Marle.—New insights into faith, by G. Hasenhuttl.—The sacraments in Bultmann's theology, by J. L. McKenzie.—Bultmann on Kerygma and history, by C. Geffre.—Bultmann and Heidegger, by H. Peukert.—Bultmann and tomorrow's theology, by T. F. O'Meara. Bibliographical footnotes. [BX4827.B78O4] 68-55089 5.95
1. Bultmann, Rudolf Karl, 1884- —Addresses, essays, lectures. I. Weisser, Donald M., joint comp. II. Title.

ONIMUS, Jean. 230'.0924
Albert Camus and Christianity. Translated by Emmett Parker. University, University of Alabama Press [1970] xiv, 159 p. 21 cm. Translation of Camus. Selection from Camus' works: p. [107]-148. Bibliography: p. [149]-156. [PQ2605.A3734Z72313] 77-92654 ISBN 0-8173-7601-1
1. Camus, Albert, 1913-1960. I. Title.

OTT, Heinrich. 230'.092'4 B
Reality and faith: the theological legacy of Dietrich Bonhoeffer. [1st American ed.] Philadelphia, Fortress Press [1972] 456 p. 23 cm. Translation of Wirklichkeit und Glaube, 1. Bd. Zum theologischen Erbe Dietrich Bonhoeffers. Includes bibliographical references. [BX4827.B57O86133 1972] 78-165513 ISBN 0-8006-0059-2 11.50
1. Bonhoeffer, Dietrich, 1906-1945. I. Title.

PATTERSON, Bob E. 230'.092'4 B
Reinhold Niebuhr / by Bob E. Patterson. Waco, Tex. : Word Books, c1977. 163 p. ; 23

cm. (Makers of the modern theological mind) Bibliography: p. 161-163. [BX4827.N5P37] 76-46783 ISBN 0-87680-508-X : 6.95
1. Niebuhr, Reinhold, 1892-1971.

PAUCK, Wilhelm, 1901- 230'.0924
Harnack and Troeltsch; two historical theologians. New York, Oxford University Press, 1968. x, 131 p. 21 cm. (Drew University, Madison, N.J. Drew lectureship in biography, 1967) Contents.Contents.—Adolf von Harnack.—Ernst Troeltsch.—Appendix. Adolf von Harnack and Ferdinand Christian von Baur; Troeltsch's contribution to a Festschrift dedicated to Harnack.—Ernst Troeltsch; a funeral address delivered by A. von Harnack. Bibliographical footnotes. [BX4827.H3P3] 68-17617
1. Harnack, Adolf von, 1851-1930. 2. Troeltsch, Ernst, 1865-1923. I. Title. II. Series.

PAUCK, Wilhelm, 1901- 230'.092'4 B
Paul Tillich, his life & thought / Wilhelm & Marion Pauck. 1st ed. New York : Harper & Row, c1976- v. : ill. ; 22 cm. Contents.Contents.—v. 1. Life. Includes bibliographical references and index. [BX4827.T53P28 1976] 74-25709 ISBN 0-06-066474-6 (v. 1) : 15.00
1. Tillich, Paul, 1886-1965. 2. Theologians—United States—Biography. 3. Theologians—Germany—Biography. I. Pauck, Marion, joint author.

PAUL Tillich: 230'.0924
retrospect and future. [Articles by] Nels F. S. Ferre [and others] Introd. by T. A. Kantonen. Nashville, Abingdon Press [1967, c1966] 63 p. 19 cm. "Reprinted from Religion in life, winter 1966." [BX4827.T53P3 1967] 67-31858
1. Tillich, Paul, 1886-1965. I. Ferre, Nels Fredrick Solomon, 1908- II. Religion in life.

PERKINS, Robert L., 1930- 230'.0924
Soren Kierkegaard, by Robert L. Perkins. Richmond, John Knox Press [1969] ix, 46 p. 19 cm. (Makers of contemporary theology) [B4377.P36] 69-14337 1.25
1. Kierkegaard, Soren Aabye, 1813-1855.

PIKE, James Albert, Bp., 1913-1969. 230'.0924
If this be heresy [by] James A. Pike. [1st ed.] New York, Harper & Row [1967] x, 205 p. 22 cm. Bibliographical footnotes. [BT77.P46] 67-21551
1. Theology, Doctrinal—Popular works. I. Title.

REEVES, Marjorie. 230'.0924
The influence of prophecy in the later Middle Ages; a study in Joachimism. Oxford, Clarendon Press, 1969. xiv, 574 p. facsim. 23 cm. Bibliography: p. [541]-546. [BR115.H5R4] 75-452029 unpriced
1. Joachim, Abbot of Fiore, 1135(ca.)-1202. 2. Bible—Prophecies. 3. History (Theology)—History of doctrines. I. Title.

REIST, Benjamin A 230.0924
Toward a theology of involvement; the thought of Ernst Troeltsch, by Benjamin A. Reist. Philadelphia, Westminster Press [1966] 264 p. 21 cm. Bibliography: p. [257]-264. [BX4827.T7R4] 66-11919
1. Troeltsch, Ernst, 1865-1923. I. Title.

REIST, Benjamin A. 230.0924
Toward a theology of involvement; the thought of Ernst Troeltsch. Philadelphia, Westminster [c.1966] 264p. 21cm. Bibl. [BX4827.T7R4] 66-11919 6.00
1. Troeltsch, Ernst, 1865-1923. I. Title.

REX, Walter 230.0924
Essays on Pierre Bayle and religious controversy. The Hague, M. Nijhoff [New York, Humanities, c.1965] xv,271p. port. 24cm. (Intl. archives of the hist. of ideas, 8) Bibl. [BX9419.B3R4] 66-1628 9.50
1. Bayle, Pierre, 1647-1706. 2. Theology—Hist.—17th cent. I. Title. II. Title: Title. (Series: Archives internationales d'histoire des idees, 8)

REYMOND, Robert L. 230'.0924
Brunner's dialectical encounter [by] Robert L. Reymond. Philadelphia, Presbyterian and Reformed Pub. Co., 1967. 29 p. 23 cm. (International library of philosophy and theology: Biblical and theological studies) Bibliographical references included in "Footnotes" (p. 27-29) [BX4827.B67R4] 67-20833
1. Brunner, Heinrich Emil, 1889-1966. I. Title. II. Series.

REYMOND, Robert L. 230'.0924
Bultmann's demythologized kerygma [by] Robert L. Reymond. Philadelphia, Presbyterian and Reformed Pub. Co., 1967. 30 p. 23 cm. (International library of philosophy and theology: Biblical and theological studies) Bibliographical references included in "Notes" (p. 29-30) [BX4827.B78R4] 67-30465
1. Bultmann, Rudolf Karl, 1884- I. Title. II. Series.

ROBERTS, Robert Campbell, 1942- 230'.092'4
Rudolf Bultmann's theology : a critical interpretation / by Robert Campbell Roberts. Grand Rapids, Mich. : Eerdmans, c1976. p. cm. Bibliography: p. [BX4827.B78R6] 75-45382 ISBN 0-8028-1631-2 pbk. : 4.50
1. Bultmann, Rudolf Karl, 1884- I. Title.

ROWE, William L 230'.0924
Religious symbols and God: a philosophical study of Tillich's theology [by] William L. Rowe. Chicago, University of Chicago Press [1968] ix, 245 p. 22 cm. Bibliographical footnotes. [BX4827.T53R6] 68-16715
1. Tillich, Paul, 1886-1965. I. Title.

ROWE, William L. 230'.0924
Religious symbols and God; a philosophical study of Tillich's theology [by] William L. Rowe. Chicago, University of Chicago Press [1968] ix, 245 p. 22 cm. Bibliographical footnotes. [BX4827.T53R6] 68-16715
1. Tillich, Paul, 1886-1965. I. Title.

SANDBERG, Karl C 230.0924
At the crossroads of faith and reason; an essay on Pierre Bayle, by Karl C. Sandberg. Tucson, University of Arizona Press [1966] x, 125 p. 24 cm. Bibliography: p. 115-122. [B1825.Z7S2] 66-18531
1. Bayle, Pierre, 1647-1706. 2. Faith and reason. I. Title.

SANDBERG, Karl C. 230.0924
At the crossroads of faith and reason; an essay on Pierre Bayle. Tucson, Univ. of Ariz. Pr. [c.1966] x, 125p. 24cm. Bibl. [B1825.Z7S2] 66-18531 6.00
1. Bayle, Pierre, 1647-1706. 2. Faith and reason. I. Title.

SCHMITHALS, Walter. 230'.0924
An introduction to the theology of Rudolf Bultmann. Minneapolis, Augsburg Pub. House [1968] xv, 334 p. 23 cm. Translation of Die Theologie Rudolf Bultmanns; eine Einfuhrung. Bibliography: p. 325-328. [BX4827.B78S273 1968b] 68-31995 6.50
1. Bultmann, Rudolf Karl, 1884- I. Title.

SCHRADER, Robert William. 230'.092'4
The nature of theological argument : a study of Paul Tillich / by Robert William Schrader. Missoula, Mont. : Published by Scholars Press for Harvard theological review, c1975. xii, 147 p. ; 22 cm. (Harvard dissertations in religion ; no. 4) Bibliography: p. 147. [BX4827.T53S34] 75-43784 ISBN 0-89130-071-6 : 4.20
1. Tillich, Paul, 1886-1965. I. Title. II. Series.

SIKES, Walter W. 230.0924
On becoming the truth; an introduction to the life and thought of Soren Kierkegaard. St. Louis, Bethany Press, 1968. 190 p. 20 cm. (The Library of contemporary theology) Bibliography: p. 181-184. [BX4827.K5S55] 68-26112 2.95
1. Kierkegaard, Soren Aabye, 1813-1855. I. Title.

SPIEGLER, Gerhand 230'.0924
The eternal covenant; Schleiermacher's experiment in cultural theology. [1st ed.] New York, Harper [1967] xvii, 205p. port. 22cm. (Makers of modern theol.) Bibl. [BX4827.S3S65] 67-21553 5.50
1. Schleiermacher, Friedrich Ernst Daniel, 1768-1834. I. Title.

SPONHEIM, Paul R. 230'.0924
Kierkegaard on Christ and Christian coherence [by] Paul Sponheim. [1st ed.] New York, Harper & Row [1968] xix, 332 p. port. 22 cm. (Makers of modern theology) Includes bibliographical references. [BX4827.K5S6 1968b] 68-17590
1. Kierkegaard, Soren Aabye, 1813-1855. I. Title.

SPONHEIM, Paul R. 230'.092'4
Kierkegaard on Christ and Christian coherence / Paul Sponheim. Westport, Conn. : Greenwood Press, 1975, c1968. xix, 332 p. ; 23 cm. Reprint of the ed. published by Harper & Row, New York. Includes index. Bibliography: p. [321]-327. [BX4827.K5S6 1975] 75-3999 ISBN 0-8371-7455-4 lib.bdg. : 18.25
1. Kierkegaard, Soren Aabye, 1813-1855. I. Title.

STEPHENS, W. Peter. 230'.0924
The holy spirit in the theology of Martin Bucer, by W. P. Stephens. [London] Cambridge University Press, 1970. ix, 291 p. 23 cm. Bibliography: p. 275-283. [BR350.B93S7] 79-96100 90/- ($14.50)
1. Butzer, Martin, 1491-1551. 2. Holy Spirit—History of doctrines. I. Title.

STONE, Ronald H. 230'.0924
Reinhold Niebuhr, prophet to politicians [by] Ronald H. Stone. Nashville, Abingdon Press [1971, c1972] 272 p. 24 cm. Includes bibliographical references. [BX4827.N5S74 1972] 71-172813 ISBN 0-687-36272-5 8.00
1. Niebuhr, Reinhold, 1892-1971. 2. Christianity and politics. I. Title.

*STOUDT, John Joseph, 1911- 230'.0924
Jacob Boehme: His life and thought. Foreword by Paul Tillich. New York, Seabury [1968, c. 1957] 317p. 20cm. (SP 46) Orig. pub. under the title Sunrise to eternity. Bibl. 2.75 pap.,
I. Title.

STRINGFELLOW, William. 230.0924
The Bishop Pike affair; scandals of conscience and heresy, relevance and solemnity in the contemporary church [by] William Stringfellow [and] Anthony Towne. [1st ed.] New York, Harper & Row [1967] xxii, 266 p. 21 cm. Bibliographical references included in "Notes" (p. 251-266) [BX5995.P54S8] 67-21554
1. Pike, James Albert, Bp., 1913- I. Towne, Anthony, joint author. II. Title.

STRINGFELLOW, William. 230'.0924
The Bishop Pike affair; scandals of conscience and heresy, relevance and solemnity in the contemporary church [by] William Stringfellow [and] Anthony Towne. [1st ed.] New York, Harper & Row [1967] xxii, 266 p. 21 cm. Bibliographical references included in "Notes" (p. 251-266) [BX5995.P54S8] 67-21554
1. Pike, James Albert, Bp., 1913- I. Towne, Anthony, joint author. II. Title.

SYKES, Stephen. 230'.0924 B
Friedrich Schleiermacher. Richmond, John Knox Press [1971] viii, 51, [1] p. 19 cm. (Makers of contemporary theology) Bibliography: p. [52] [BX4827.S3S85 1971] 75-158145 ISBN 0-8042-0556-6
1. Schleiermacher, Friedrich Ernst Daniel, 1768-1834.

TAIT, Leslie Gordon, 1926- 230'.0924
The promise of Tillich, by L. Gordon Tait. [1st ed.] Philadelphia, Lippincott [1971] 127 p. 21 cm. (The Promise of theology) Bibliography: p. 123-127. [BX4827.T53T25] 79-146687 3.95
1. Tillich, Paul, 1886-1965. I. Title.

THOMAS, John Heywood. 230.0924
Paul Tillich, by J. Heywood Thomas. [American ed.] Richmond, John Knox Press [1966] 48 p. 19 cm. (Makers of contemporary theology) [BX4827.T53T49 1966] 66-11072
1. Tillich, Paul, 1886-1965. I. Title.

THOMAS, John Heywood 230.0924
Paul Tillich. [Amer. ed.] Richmond, Va., Knox [1966] 48p. 19cm. (Makers of contemp. theol.) 1st pub. in England by the Carey Kingsgate Pr., 1965. [BX4827.T53T49] 66-11072 1.00 pap.,
1. Tillich, Paul, 1886-1965. I. Title.

TILLICH, Hannah. 230'.092'4 B
From time to time. New York, Stein and Day [1973] 252 p. 24 cm. [BX4827.T53T53] 73-79225 ISBN 0-8128-1626-9 7.95
1. Tillich, Paul, 1886-1965. I. Title.

TILLICH, Hannah. 230'.092'4 B
From time to time. New York, Stein and Day [1974 c1973] 252 p. 18 cm. [BX4827.T53T53] ISBN 0-8128-1742-7 1.95 (pbk.)
1. Tillich, Paul, 1886-1965. I. Title.
L.C. card no. for original edition: 73-79225

TILLICH, Paul, 1886-1965. 230.0924
The future of religions. Edited by Jerald C. Brauer. [1st ed.] New York, Harper & Row [1966] 94 p. illus., ports. 22 cm. Contents.Contents.—Tributes to Paul Tillich: Paul Tillich's impact on America, by J. C. Brauer. The sources of Paul Tillich's richness, by W. Pauck. Paul Tillich and the history of religions, by M. Eliade.—Essays by Paul Tillich: The effects of space exploration on man's condition and stature. Frontiers. The decline and the validity of the idea of progress. The significance of the history of religions for the systematic theologian. [BR123.T54] 66-15864
1. Tillich, Paul, 1886-1965. 2. Christianity—20th century—Addresses, essays, lectures. I. Brauer, Jerald C., ed. II. Title.

TILLICH, Paul, 1886-1965. 230'.092'4
The future of religions / Paul Tillich ; edited by Jerald C. Brauer. Westport, Conn. : Greenwood Press, 1976, c1966. 94 p., [8] leaves of plates : ill. ; 23 cm. Reprint of the ed. published by Harper & Row, New York. Contents.Contents.—Tributes to Paul Tillich: Brauer, J. C. Paul Tillich's impact on America. Pauck, W. The sources of Paul Tillich's richness. Eliade, M. Paul Tillich and the history of religions.—Essays by Paul Tillich: The effects of space exploration on man's condition and stature. Frontiers. The decline and the validity of the idea of progress. The significance of the history of religions for the systematic theologian. [BR123.T54 1976] 76-7566 ISBN 0-8371-8861-X lib.bdg. : 10.50
1. Tillich, Paul, 1886-1965—Addresses, essays, lectures. 2. Christianity—20th century—Addresses, essays, lectures. I. Brauer, Jerald C. II. Title.
Contents omitted.

TILLICH, Paul, 1886-1965. 230'.0924
My search for absolutes. With drawings by Saul Steinberg. New York, Simon and Schuster [1967] 143 p. illus. 23 cm. (Credo perspectives) [BX4827.T5A3] 67-16722
1. Absolute, The. I. Title.

TILLICH, Paul, 1886-1965. 230.0924
On the boundary; an autobiographical sketch. New York, Scribner [1966] 104 p. 22 cm. "A revision, newly translated, of Part I of [the author's] The interpretation of history." Bibliography: p. 102-104. [BX4827.T53A33] 66-18546
1. Theology—Addresses, essays, lectures. 2. Protestantism—Addresses, essays, lectures. I. Title.

TILLICH, Paul, 1886-1965. 230'.0924
Systematic theology. [Chicago] University of Chicago Press [1967] c1951-63] 3 v. in 1. 24 cm. [BT75.2.T5] 66-20786
1. Theology, Doctrinal. I. Title.

TILLICH, Paul, 1886-1965. 230'.0924
Systematic theology. [Chicago] University of Chicago Press [1967, c1951-63] 3 v. in 1. 24 cm. [BT75.2.T5 1967] 66-20786
1. Theology, Doctrinal. I. Title.

VOELKEL, Robert T. 230'.0924 B
The shape of the theological task, by Robert T. Voelkel. Philadelphia, Westminster Press [1968] 171 p. 21 cm. Bibliographical references included in "Notes" (p. [165]-171) [BX4827.H44V6] 68-10986
1. Herrmann, Wilhelm, 1846-1922. 2. Theology, Doctrinal—History—20th century. I. Title.

WALSH, Chad, 1914- 230'.092'4 B
C. S. Lewis: apostle to the skeptics. [Norwood, Pa.] Norwood Editions, 1974. p. cm. Reprint of the 1949 ed. published by Macmillan, New York. Bibliography: p. [BX5199.L53W3 1974] 74-10834 ISBN 0-88305-779-4 (lib. bdg.)
1. Lewis, Clive Staples, 1898-1963.

WEISS, Michel P. 230'.0924
Survival through the moral law; an inquiry into Christian precepts and the political order, by Michel P. Weiss. [1st ed.] New York, Exposition Press [1967] 139 p. 21 cm. [BX1765.2.W4] 67-24273
1. Catholic Church—Doctrinal and controversial works—Protestant authors. I. Title.

WERNAER, Robert Maximilian, 1865- 230'.092'4
Romanticism and the romantic school in Germany. New York, Haskell House, 1966. xv. 373 p. 22 cm. First published in 1910. Bibliography: p. 335-350. [PT361.W5] 68-681
1. Romanticism—Germany. I. Title.

BRADY, Frank, comp. 230'.0942
Twentieth century interpretations of Gulliver's travels; a collection of critical essays. Englewood Cliffs, N.J., Prentice-Hall [1968] vii, 118 p. 21 cm. (Twentieth century interpretations) (A Spectrum book.) Includes bibliographical references. [PR3724.G8B7] 68-23699 3.95
1. Swift, Jonathan, 1667-1745. Gulliver's travels. I. Title.

ELLIOTT-BINNS, Leonard Elliott, 1885- 230.0942
English thought, 1860-1900; the theological aspect. London, New York, Longmans, Green [1956] 388p. 23cm. Includes bibliography. [BR759.E496] 56-4136
1. Gt. Brit.-Church history-19th cent. 2. Theology-19th cent. 3. Theology, Doctrinal-Hist.-Gt. Brit. 4. Religious thought-Gt. Brit. I. Title.

LANGFORD, Thomas A. 230'.0942
In search of foundations; English theology, 1900-1920 [by] Thomas A. Langford. Nashville, Abingdon Press [1969] 319 p. 24 cm. Bibliography: p. 299-311. [BT28.L3] 79-84720 6.95

1. Theology, Doctrinal—History—20th century. 2. Theology, Doctrinal—History—Gt. Brit. I. Title.

MCLACHLAN, Herbert, 1876- 230'.0942
The religious opinions of Milton, Locke, and Newton, by H. McLachlan. New York, Russell & Russell [1972] 217 p. 20 cm. (Publications of the University of Manchester, no. 276. Theological series no. 6) Reprint of the 1941 ed. Includes bibliographical references. [PR145.M27 1972] 74-173539
1. Milton, John, 1608-1674—Religion and ethics. 2. Locke, John, 1632-1704. 3. Newton, Isaac, Sir, 1642-1727. 4. Religion in literature. I. Title. II. Series: Victoria University of Manchester. Publications, no. 276. III. Series: Victoria University of Manchester. Publications. Theological series, no. 6.

NEW, John F H 230.0942
Anglican and Puritan; the basis of their opposition, 1558-1640 [by] John F. H. New. Stanford, Calif., Stanford University Press, 1964. 140 p. 23 cm. Bibliographical references included in "Notes" (p. [115]-132) [BR756.N48] 64-12075
1. Theology, Doctrinal — Hist. — Gt. Brit. I. Title.

NEW, John F. H. 230.0942
Anglican and Puritan: the basis of their opposition, 1558-1640 [by] John F. H. New. Stanford, Calif., Stanford Univ. Pr. [c.]1964. 140p. 23cm. Bibl. 64-12075 4.50
1. Theology, Doctrinal—Hist.—Gt. Brit. I. Title.

TULLOCH, John, 1823-1886. 230'.0942
Movements of religious thought in Britain during the nineteenth century. With an introd. by A. C. Cheyne. New York, Humanities Press, 1971. 34, xi, 338 p. 20 cm. (The Victorian library) Reprint of the London, 1885 ed. Includes bibliographical references. [BR759.T8 1971] 72-178660 ISBN 0-7185-5017-X 9.75
1. Religious thought—Great Britain. I. Title.

PALMER, Robert Roswell, 1909- 230.0944
Catholics & unbelievers in eighteenth century France. [2d ed.] New York, Cooper Square Publishers, 1961 [c1939] 236 p. 24 cm. Includes bibliography. [[BR845]] 61-13266
1. Religious thought — France. 2. Religious thought — 18th cent. 3. Apologetics — 18th cent. I. Title.

FERRE, Nels Fredrick Solomon, 1908- 230.09485
Swedish contributions to modern theology, with special reference to Lundensian thought, by Nels F. S. Ferre. With a new chapter, Developments in Swedish theology, 1939-1966 by William A. Johnson. New York, Harper [1967,c.1939] x, 304p. 21cm. (Torchbk., TB147) [BT30.S8F4] 2.45 pap.,
1. Theology, Doctrinal—Hist.—Sweden. I. Title.

FERRE, Nels Fredrick Solomon, 1908- 230'.09485
Swedish contributions to modern theology, with special reference to Lundensian thought [by] Nels F.S. Ferre. With a new chapter, "Developments in Swedish theology, 1939-1966," by William A. Johnson. New York, Harper & Row [1967] x, 304, 6 p. 21 cm. (Harper torchbooks, TB147) Bibliography: p. 296-301. [BT30.S8F4] 67-9656
1. Theology. Doctrinal—Hist.—Sweden. I. Title.

ASIAN voices in 230'.095
Christian theology / edited and with an introd. by Gerald H. Anderson. Maryknoll, N.Y. : Orbis Books, c1976. 321 p. ; 22 cm. Bibliography: p. 264-321. [BT30.A8A78] 75-13795 ISBN 0-88344-017-2 : 15.00. ISBN 0-88344-016-4 pbk. : 7.95
1. Theology, Doctrinal—History—Asia—Addresses, essays, lectures. I. Anderson, Gerald H.

MICHALSON, Carl. 230.0952
Japanese contributions to Christian theology. Philadelphia, Westminster Press [1960] 192p. 21cm. Includes bibliography. [BT30.J3M5] 60-7487
1. Theology, Doctrinal—Hist.—Japan. I. Title.

BOYD, Robin H. S., 1924- 230'.0954
India and the Latin captivity of the Church; the cultural context of the Gospel [by] R. H. S. Boyd. [London] Cambridge University Press [1974] xiv, 151 p. 23 cm. (Monograph supplements to the Scottish journal of theology no. 3) Includes bibliographical references. [BR1155.B66] 73-86049 ISBN 0-521-20371-6
1. Theology, Doctrinal—History—India. I. Title. II. Series: Scottish journal of theology. Monograph supplements, no. 3.
Distributed by Cambridge University Press, New York; 10.50.

KOYAMA, Kosuke, 1929- 230'.0959
Waterbuffalo theology / Kosuke Koyama. Maryknoll, N.Y. : Orbis Books, [1974] ix, 239 p. : ill. ; 22 cm. Includes bibliographical references. [BR85.K68 1974] 74-80980 ISBN 0-88344-702-9 : 4.95
1. Theology—Addresses, essays, lectures. I. Title.

SHORTER, Aylward. 230'.096
African Christian theology : adaptation or incarnation? / Aylward Shorter. Maryknoll, N.Y. : Orbis Books, 1977, c1975. viii, 167 p. ; 22 cm. Includes bibliographical references and index. [BL2400.S42 1977] 77-23325 ISBN 0-88344-002-4 : 7.95 pbk. : 4.95
1. Africa—Religion. 2. Christianity—Africa. 3. Theology, Doctrinal—History—Africa. I. Title.

MOORE, Basil, comp. 230'.0968
The challenge of Black theology in South Africa. Atlanta, John Knox Press [1974, c1973] xii, 156 p. 22 cm. First published in 1973 under title: Black theology. Includes bibliographical references. [BR50.M63 1974] 73-16918 ISBN 0-8042-0794-1 4.95
1. Theology—Addresses, essays, lectures. 2. Blacks—South Africa—Religion—Addresses, essays, lectures. I. Title.

THEOLOGY in the Americas 230'.097
/ edited by Sergio Torres and John Eagleson. Maryknoll, N.Y. : Orbis Books, c1976. xxviii, 438 p. ; 22 cm. Includes papers prepared for a conference held in Detroit, August 1975. Includes bibliographical references. [BT30.A5T46] 76-22545 ISBN 0-88344-479-8 : 12.95. pbk. :
1. Theology, Doctrinal—History—America—Congresses. I. Torres, Sergio. II. Eagleson, John.

AHLSTROM, Sydney E. comp. 230'.0973
Theology in America; the major Protestant voices from puritanism to neo-orthodoxy. Ed. by Sydney E. Ahlstrom. Indianapolis, Bobbs [1967] 630p. 21cm. (American heritage ser., 73) Bibl. [BT30.U55A6] 67-21401 4.75 pap.,
1. Theology, Doctrinal—Hist.—U. S. 2. Theology—Collections—Protestant authors. I. Title.

AHLSTROM, Sydney E. comp. 230'.0973
Theology in America; the major Protestant voices from puritanism to neo-orthodoxy. Edited by Sydney E. Ahlstrom. Indianapolis, Bobbs-Merrill Co. [1967] 630 p. 21 cm. (The American heritage series, 73) Bibliographical footnotes. Bibliography: p. 93-107. [BT30.U55A6] 67-21401
1. Theology. Doctrinal—Hist.—U. S. 2. Theology—Collections—Protestant authors. I. Title.

FOSTER, Frank Hugh, 1851-1935. 230'.0973
The modern movement in American theology; sketches in the history of American protestant thought from the Civil War to the World War. Freeport, N.Y., Books for Libraries Press [1969] 219 p. 23 cm. (Essay index reprint series) Reprint of the 1939 ed. Includes bibliographical references. [BT30.U6F6 1969] 76-86751 ISBN 0-8369-1131-8
1. Protestant theology—United States. 2. New England theology. I. Title.

MILLER, Randolph Crump, 1910- 230'.0973
The American spirit in theology. Philadelphia, United Church Press [1974] 252 p. 22 cm. "A Pilgrim Press book." Bibliography: p. 241-244. [BT30.U6M54] 74-11099 ISBN 0-8298-0285-1 8.50
1. Theology, Doctrinal—History—United States. 2. Empiricism. 3. Process philosophy. I. Title.

NICHOLS, James Hastings, 1915- 230.0973
Romanticism in American theology; Nevin and Schaff at Mercersburg. [Chicago] University of Chicago Press [1961] 322 p. illus. 22 cm. [BT30.U6N5] 61-5609
1. Schaff, Philip, 1819-1893. 2. Nevin, John Williamson, 1803-1886. 3. Mercersburg theology. 4. Theology, Doctrinal—History—United States. I. Title.

SONTAG, Frederick. 230'.0973
The American religious experience; the roots, trends, and future of American theology, by Frederick Sontag and John K. Roth. [1st ed.] New York, Harper & Row [1972] xiii, 401 p. 22 cm. Bibliography: p. [387]-394. [BT30.U6S65 1972] 73-163164 10.95
1. Theology, Doctrinal—History—U.S. 2. Philosophy, American. I. Roth, John K., joint author. II. Title.

SOPER, David Wesley, 1910- 230.0973
Major voices in American Theology. Philadelphia, Westminster Press [1953-55] 2 v. 21 cm. Contents.Contents.—[v. 1] Six contemporary leaders.—v. 2. Men who shape belief. [BR569.S65] 52-13140
1. Theologians, American. 2. Theology, Doctrinal—History—U. S. I. Title. II. Title: Men who shape belief.

KRAFT, Heinrich, 1918- 230.1
Early Christian thinkers; an introduction to Clement of Alexandria and Origen, by H. Kraft. New York, Association Press [1964] 77 p. 19 cm. (World Christian books. 3d ser., no 52) [BT25.K7] 65-546
1. Clements, Titus Flavius, Alexandrinus. 2. Origenes. 3. Alexandrian school, Christian. I. Title.

KRAFT, Heinrich, 1918- 230.1
Early Christian thinkers; an introduction to Clement of Alexandria and Origen. New York, Association [1964] 77p. 19cm. (World Christian bks. 3d ser., no. 52) [BT25.K7] 65-546 1.25 pap.,
1. Clemens, Titus Flavius, Alexandrinus. 2. Alexandrian school, Christian. 3. Origenes. I. Title.

MURPHY, Chuck, 1922- 230'.1
Fundamentals of the faith / Chuck Murphy. Nashville : Abingdon Press, c1976. 94 p. ; 19 cm. [BV4501.2.M85] 75-30505 ISBN 0-687-13699-7 pbk. : 2.95
1. Christian life—Anglican authors. 2. Theology, Doctrinal—Popular works. I. Title.

WERNER, Martin, 1887- 230.1
The formation of Christian dogma; an historical study of its probelem. New York, Harper [1957] 352p. illus. 23cm. 'Rewritten in shortened form by the author from his Die Entstehung des christlichen Dogmas, and translated, with an introduction by S. G. F. Brandon.' [BT23.W413] 57-10528
1. Theology, Doctrinal—Hist.—Early church. I. Title.

WERNER, Martin, 1887- 230.1
The formation of Christian dogma; an historical study of its problem. New York, Harper [1957] 352 p. illus 23 cm. "Rewritten in shortened form by the author from his Die Entstehung des christlichen Dogmas, and translated, with an introduction by S. G. F. Brandon." [BT23.W413] 57-10528
1. Theology, Doctrinal — Hist. — Early church. I. Title.

WERNER, Martin, 1887- 230.1
The formation of Christian dogma; an historical study of its problem. Boston, Beacon [1965, c.1957] 352p. 21cm. (BP191) [BT23.W413] 2.45 pap.,
1. Theology, Doctrinal—Hist.—Early Church. I. Title.

WILES, Maruice F. 230'.1
The making of Christian doctrine: a study in the principles of early doctrinal development, by Maurice Wiles. London, New York, Cambridge University Press, 1975 c1967. viii, 184 p. 18 cm. Bibliographical footnotes. [BT25.W48] ISBN 0-521-09962-5. 5.95 (pbk.)
1. Dogma Development. 2. Theology, Doctrinal—Hist.—Early Church. I. Title.
L.C. card no. for original edition: 67-10018

WILES, Maurice F. 230'.1
The making of Christian doctrine: a study in the principles of early doctrinal development, by Maurice Wiles. London, Cambridge U.P., 1967. viii, 184 p. 19 cm. Bibliographical footnotes. [BT25.W48] 67-10081
1. Dogma, Development of. 2. Theology, Doctrinal—History—Early church ca. 30-600. I. Title.

BARR, Robert R. 230.11
Main currents in early Christian thought, by Robert Barr. Pref. by Jean Danielou. Glen Rock, N.J., Paulist Press [1966] vi, 122 p. illus. 20 cm. (Guide to the Fathers of the church, 1) Bibliographical footnotes. [BT25.B24] 66-22055
1. Theology, Doctrinal—History—Early church, ca. 30-600. I. Title.

CRUTTWELL, Charles Thomas, 1847-1911. 230.1'1
A literary history of early Christianity; including the fathers and the chief heretical writers of the ante-Nicene period, for the use of students and general readers. New York, AMS Press [1971] 2 v. (xxvi, 685 p.) 23 cm. Reprint of the 1893 ed. [BR67.C8 1971] 76-129369 ISBN 0-404-01877-7(Set)
1. Fathers of the church. I. Title.

KELLY, John Norman Davidson. 230.11
Early Christian doctrines. New York, Harper [1959, c1958] 500p. 22cm. Includes bibliography. [BT25.K4] 58-12933
1. Theology, Doctrinal—Hist.—Early church. I. Title.

WILLIS, John Randolph. 230'.1'1
A history of Christian thought : from apostolic times to Saint Augustine / John R. Willis. 1st ed. Hicksville, N.Y. : Exposition Press, c1976. 410 p. ; 24 cm. (An Exposition-university book) Includes index. Bibliography: p. 389-397. [BT25.W53] 76-16237 ISBN 0-682-48583-7 : 16.00
1. Theology, Doctrinal—History—Early church, ca. 30-600. I. Title.

STANLEY, David M. 230.12
The apostolic church in the New Testament. Westminster, Md., Newman [c.]1965. xiv, 472p. 23cm. Essays. Bibl. [BV597.S7] 65-19453 6.95
1. Church—History of doctrines—Early church. I. Title.

STANLEY, David Michael, 1914- 230.12
The apostolic church in the New Testament, by David M. Stanley. Westminster, Md., Newman Press, 1965. xiv, 472 p. 23 cm. Essays. Bibliographical references included in "Notes" (p. 395-462) [BV597.S7] 65-19453
1. Church—History of doctrines—Early church. I. Title.

BARNARD, Leslie William. 230'.13
Justin Martyr: his life and thought, by L. W. Barnard. London, Cambridge U.P., 1967. viii, 193 p. 22 1/2 cm. Bibliography: p. 180-183. [BR65.J86B3] 66-16665
1. Justinus Martyr, Saint.

CYPRIANUS, Saint, Bp. of Carthage. 230'.1'3
De lapsis; and, De ecclesiae catholicae unitate, [by] Cyprian; text and translation by Maurice Bevenot. Oxford, Clarendon Press, 1971. xxiii, 127 p. 21 cm. (Oxford early Christian texts) Parallel Latin text and English translation. Bibliography: p. [xxi]-xxiii. [BR65.C84D4] 72-177386 ISBN 0-19-826804-1 £1.75
1. Church discipline—Early church, ca. 30-600. 2. Church—Unity. I. Bevenot, Maurice, 1897- tr. II. Title. III. Title: De ecclesiae catholicae unitate. IV. Series.

DANIELOU, Jean. 230.13
The theology of Jewish Christianity [by] Jean Danielou. Translated and edited by John A. Baker. London, Darton, Longman & Todd, Chicago, H. Regnery Co. [1964] xvi, 446 p. 25 cm. (The Development of Christian doctrine before the Council of Nicaea, v. 1) Alterations have been made in the content and arrangement of the French edition. Bibliography: p. [411]-422. [BT25.D313 1964] 64-25658
1. Jewish Christians — Early church. 2. Theology, Doctrinal — Hist. — Early church. I. Title. II. Series.

FILSON, Floyd Vivian, 1896- 230'.1'3
The New Testament against its environment: the gospel of Christ the risen Lord. Chicago, Regnery, 1950. 103 p. 22 cm. (Studies in Biblical theology, no. 3) [BS2397.F] A 52
1. Bible. N. T.—Theology. I. Title. II. Series.

MURRAY, Robert, 1908- 230'.1'3
Symbols of church and kingdom : a study in early Syriac tradition / Robert Murray. London ; New York : Cambridge University Press, 1975. xv, 394 p. ; 23 cm. Includes indexes. Bibliography: p. 364-376. [BV598.M87] 74-80363 ISBN 0-521-20553-0 : 25.00
1. Jesus Christ—History of doctrines—Early church, ca. 30-600. 2. Church—History of doctrines—Early church, ac. 30-600. 3. Fathers of the church, Syriac. I. Title.

NOVATIANUS. 230'.1'3
The Trinity, The spectacles, Jewish foods, In praise of purity, Letters, by Novatian. Translated by Russell J. DeSimone. Washington, Catholic University of America Press [1973] p. (The Fathers of the church, a new translation, v. 67) [BR65.N62E5 1973] 73-9872 ISBN 0-8132-0066-0
1. Trinity—Early works to 1800. 2. Christian ethics—Early church. I. DeSimone, Russell J., tr. II. Title. III. Series.

THEOPHILUS, Saint, Bp. of Antioch, 2dcent. 230'.1'3
Ad Autolycum [by] Theophilus of Antioch; text and translation [from the Greek] by Robert M. Grant. Oxford, Clarendon Press, 1970. xxix, 153 p. 21 cm. (Oxford early Christian texts) Parallel Greek text and English translation, English introduction.

[BT1116.T7 1970] 70-570259 ISBN 0-19-826802-5 £2.00
1. Apologetics—Early church, ca. 30-600. I. Grant, Robert McQueen, 1917- II. Title. III. Series.

WARFIELD, Benjamin 230.1'3'0922
Breckinridge, 1851-1921.
Studies in Tertullian and Augustine. Westport, Conn., Greenwood Press [1970] v, 412 p. 23 cm. Reprint of the 1930 ed. Includes bibliographical references. [BR1720.T3W3 1970] 73-109980
1. Tertullianus, Quintus Septimius Florens. 2. Augustinus, Aurelius, Saint, Bp. of Hippo—Addresses, essays, lectures. 3. Trinity—History of doctrines. 4. Knowledge, Theory of (Religion) 5. Pelagianism. I. Title.

ATHANASIUS, Saint, 230.1'4
Patriarch of Alexandria, d.373.
Contra gentes; and, De Incarnatione [by] Athanasius; edited and translated by Robert W. Thomson. Oxford, Clarendon Press, 1971. xxxvi, 288 p. 21 cm. (Oxford early Christian texts) English and Greek. Bibliography: p. ix-x. [BT1116.A82C6 1971] 74-858321 ISBN 0-19-826801-7 £3.25
1. Jesus Christ—Person and offices—Early works to 1800. 2. Apologetics—Early church, ca. 30-600. 3. Paganism. I. Athanasius, Saint, Patriarch of Alexandria, d. 373. De Incarnatione. 1971. II.

AUGUSTINUS, Aurelius, 230'.1'4
Saint, Bp. of Hippo.
An Augustine reader. Edited, with an introd., by John J. O'Meara. [1st ed.] Garden City, N.Y., Image Books [1973] 556 p. 19 cm. (An Image book original, D322) Bibliography: p. [545]-553. [BR65.A52E6 1973] 73-80800 ISBN 0-385-06585-X 2.45
1. Theology—Collected works—Early church, ca. 30-600. I. O'Meara, John Joseph, comp. II. Title.

BETTENSON, Henry 230.1'4
Scowcroft, comp.
The later Christian fathers; a selection from the writings of the fathers from St. Cyril of Jerusalem to St. Leo the Great. Ed. & translated by Henry Bettenson. New York, Oxford Univ. Pr. [1973, c.1970] vii, 294 p. 20 cm. (Oxford pbks., 293) Bibl. footnotes. [BR63.B42] 70-498722 ISBN 0-19-283012-0 pap., 2.95
1. Christian literature, Early—(Selections, extracts etc.) I. Title.

GRABOWSKI, Stanislaus J 230.14
The church; an introduction to the theology of St. Augustine. St. Louis, Herder [1957] 673p. 22cm. [BR65.A9G73] 57-12148
1. Church—History of doctrines—Early church. 2. Augustinus, Aurelius, Saint, Bp. of Hippo—Theology. I. Title.

POLMAN, Andries Derk 230.14
Rietema, 1897-
The Word of God according to St. Augustine. [Translated by A. J. Pomerans] Grand Rapids, Eerdmans [1961] 242 p. 24 cm. [BR65.A9P613] 62-51011
1. Augustinus, Aurelius, Saint, Bp. of Hippo—Theology. 2. Bible—Introductions. I. Title.

AMBROSIUS, Saint, 230.1'4'0924
Bp. of Milan.
Letters. Translated by Mary Melchior Beyenka. [Reprinted with corrections] Washington, Catholic University of America [1967, c1954] xix, 515 p. 22 cm. (The Fathers of the Church, a new translation v. 26) Contents.Contents.—Letters to emperors.—Letters to bishops.—Synodal letters.—Letters to Priests.—Letters to his sister.—Letters to laymen. Bibliography: p. xiv. [BR60.F3A5612] 67-28583
1. Theology—Collected works—Early church, ca. 30-600. I. Title. II. Series.

AMBROSIUS, Saint, 230.1'4'0924
Bp. of Milan.
Letters. Translated by Mary Melchior Beyenka. [Reprinted with corrections] Washington, Catholic University of America [1967, c1954] xix, 515 p. 22 cm. (The Fathers of the Church, a new translation, v. 26) Contents.Letters to emperors.--Letters to bishops.--Synodal letters.--Letters to Priests.--Letters to his sister.--Letters to layment. Bibliography: p. xiv. [BR60.F3A5612] 67-28583
1. Theology—Collected works—Early church. I. Title. II. Series.

AUGUSTINUS, 230.1'4'0924
Aurelius, Saint, Bp. of Hippo.
Writings of Saint Augustine. Washington, Catholic University of America Press, 1966-c1947- v. 22 cm. (The Fathers of the church, a new translation, v 2, 21) Contents.v. 4. Christian instruction. Admonition and grace. The Christian combat. Faith, hope and charity.--v. 5. Confessions. Includes bibliographies. [BR60.F3A82] 66-20314
1. Theology—Collected works—Early church. I. Title. II. Series: The Fathers of the church, a new translation, v. 2 [etc.]

AUGUSTINUS, 230.1'4'0924
Aurelius, Saint, Bp. of Hippo.
Writings of Saint Augustine. Washington, Catholic University of America Press, 1966-c1947- v. 22 cm. (The Fathers of the church, a new translation, v. 2, 12, 21) Contents.Contents.— —v. 4. Christian instruction. Admonition and grace. The Christian combat. Faith, hope and charity.—v. 5. Confessions. —v. 9- Letters. Includes bibliographies. [BR60.F3A82] 66-20314
1. Theology—Collected works—Early church, ca. 30-600. I. Series: The Fathers of the church, a new translation, v. 2 [etc.]

LOOFS, Friedrich, 230'.1'40924 B
1858-1928.
Nestorius and his place in the history of Christian doctrine / by Friedrich Loofs. New York : B. Franklin, [1975] p. cm. Reprint of the 1914 ed. published by the University Press, Cambridge, Eng. [BR65.N384L66 1975] 75-1225 ISBN 0-8337-4903-X
1. Nestorius, Patriarch of Constantinople, fl. 428. I. Title.

MARKUS, Robert 230.1'4'0924
Austin, 1924-
Saeculum: history and society in the theology of St. Augustine [by] R. A. Markus. Cambridge [Eng.], University Press, 1970. ix, 252 p. 22 cm. Bibliography: p. 233-248. [BR65.A9M33 1970] 71-87136 ISBN 0-521-07621-8 75/- ($12.50)
1. Augustinus, Aurelius, Saint, Bp. of Hippo. 2. History (Theology)—History of doctrines. 3. Sociology, Christian—Early church, ca. 30-600. 4. Church—History of doctrines—Early church, ca. 30-600. I. Title.

PORTALIE, Eugene, 230'.1'40924
1852-1909.
A guide to the thought of Saint Augustine / by Eugene Portalie ; with an introd. by Vernon J. Bourke ; translated by Ralph J. Bastian. Westport, Conn. : Greenwood Press, 1975, c1960. xxxvii, 428 p. ; 22 cm. "Translation ... from the article, Saint Augustin, ... in the Dictionnaire de theologie catholique, published by Editions Letouzey et Ane, Paris." Reprint of the ed. published by H. Regnery, Chicago, in series: Library of living Catholic thought. Includes index. Bibliography: p. 407-418. [BR65.A9P63 1975] 75-1182 ISBN 0-8371-7992-0 lib.bdg. : 21.50
1. Augustinus, Aurelius, Saint, Bp. of Hippo—Theology. 2. Augustinus, Aurelius, Saint, Bp. of Hippo—Philosophy. I. Title.

TESELLE, Eugene, 230.14'0924
1931-
Augustine, the theologian. [New York] Herder and Herder [1970] 381 p. 22 cm. "Chronological table of Augustine's works": p. [11]-14. Bibliography: p. [351]-360. [BR65.A9T4 1970] 75-87772 12.50
1. Augustinus, Aurelius, Saint, Bp. of Hippo—Theology.

AGAT'ANGEGHOS. 230.1'62
The teaching of Saint Gregory; an early Armenian catechism. Translation and commentary by Robert W. Thomson. Cambridge, Mass., Harvard University Press, 1970. 206 p. 24 cm. (Harvard Armenian texts and studies, 3) Translation of Vardapetowt'iwn Srboyn Grigori (romanized form) which forms part 2 of the author's Patmowt'iwn (romanized form) Bibliography: p. 184-190. [BT70.A3813 1970] 78-115482 ISBN 0-674-87038-7 8.00
1. Gregorius Illuminator, Saint. 2. Theology, Doctrinal. 3. Theology, Doctrinal—History—Armenia. I. Thomson, Robert W., 1934- ed. II. Title. III. Series.

DUDKO, Dmitrii. 230'.1'9
Our hope / Dmitrii Dudko ; translated by Paul D. Garrett ; foreword by John Meyendorff. Crestwood, N.Y. : St. Vladimir's Seminary Press, 1977, c1975. 292 p. ; 22 cm. Translation of O nashem upovanii. Includes bibliographical references. [BX512.D8213] 77-1051 ISBN 0-913836-35-4 pbk. : 6.95
1. Orthodox Eastern Church, Russian—Doctrinal and controversial works—Miscellanea. 2. Theology—Miscellanea. I. Title.

DUDKO, Dmitrii. 230'.1'9
Our hope / Dmitrii Dudko ; translated by Paul D. Garrett ; foreword by John Meyendorff. Crestwood, N.Y. : St. Vladimir's Seminary Press, 1977, c1975. 292 p. ; 22 cm. Translation of O nashem upovanii. Includes bibliographical references. [BX512.D8213] 77-1051 ISBN 0-913836-35-4 pbk. : 6.95
1. Orthodox Eastern Church, Russian—Doctrinal and controversial works—Miscellanea. 2. Theology—Miscellanea. I. Title.

†LOSSKY, Vladimir, 1903- 230'.1'9
1958.
The mystical theology of the Eastern Church / by Vladimir Lossky ; [translated from the French by members of the Fellowship of St. Alban and St. Sergius]. Crestwood, N.Y. : St. Vladimir's Seminary Press, 1976, c1957. p. cm. Translation of Essai sur la theologie mystique de l'Eglise d'Orient. Reprint of the ed. published by J. Clarke, London. Includes bibliographical references. [BV5082.2.L6713 1976] 76-25448 ISBN 0-913836-31-1 pbk. : 5.95
1. Mysticism—Orthodox Eastern Church. I. Title.

MAKRAKES, Apostolos, 230'.1'9
1831-1905.
Orthodox Christian meditations, by Apostolos Makrakis (1831-1905). Translated out of the original Greek by D. Cummings. [Chicago, Orthodox Christian Educational Society, 1965] 143 p. 21 cm. [BX320.2.M3313 1965] 74-172642
1. Orthodox Eastern Church—Doctrinal and controversial works. 2. Meditations. I. Cummings, Denver, 1889- tr. II. Title.

MEYENDORFF, Jean, 1926- 230'.1'9
Byzantine theology : historical trends and doctrinal themes / John Meyendorff. 1st ed. New York : Fordham University Press, 1974. 243 p. ; 22 cm. Includes index. Bibliography: p. [229]-237. [BX320.2.M47] 72-94167 ISBN 0-8232-0965-2 : 20.00
1. Theology, Eastern Church. I. Title.

MPRATSIOTES, 230.1'9
Panagiotes Ioannou, 1889-
The Greek Orthodox Church, by Panagiotis Bratsiotis. Translated by Joseph Blenkinsopp. Notre Dame [Ind.] University of Notre Dame Press [1968] xi, 120 p. 24 cm. Translation of Von der griechischen Orthodoxie. Includes bibliographies. [BX320.2.M6513] 68-27579
1. Orthodox Eastern Church—Doctrinal and controversial works. I. Title.

PLATON, Metropolitan of 230.1'9
Moscow, 1737-1812.
The Orthodox doctrine of the Apostolic Eastern Church; or, A compendium of Christian theology. Translated from the Greek. To which is prefixed an Historical and expalnatory essay on general catechism; and appended, a Treatise on Melchisedec. New York, AMS Press [1969] vi, 239 p. 22 cm. Historical and explanatory essay on general catechism signed: A. Coray. Reprint of the London ed. published in 1857. Translation of Pravoslavnoe uchenie (romanized form); translated from the Greek translation of A. Koraes by G. Potessaro. [BX320.P5613 1969] 70-81772
1. Orthodox Eastern Church—Doctrinal and controversial works. I. Potessaro, G., tr. II. Koraes, Adamantios, 1748-1833, tr. III. Title. IV. Title: A compendium of Christian theology.

STEPHANOU, Eusebius A 230.19
Belief and practice in the Orthodox Church, by Eusebius A. Stephanou. [New York, Minos Pub. Co.] 1965. 124 p. 18 cm. [BX320.2.S8] 66-6801
1. Orthodox Eastern Church. I. Title.

ABRAMTSOV, David 230'.1'907
Feodor, 1924-
Complete directory of Orthodox Catholic churches in the United States. Philadelphia, Orthodox Cathllic Literature Association, 1953. unpaged. 10cm. [BX732.A6] 53-12476
1. Orthodox Eastern Church—U. S. 2. Churches—U. S.—Direct I. Title. II. Title: Orthodox Catholic churches in the United States.

CONIARIS, Anthony M. 230'.1'907
80 talks for Orthodox young people : for parents, Sunday school teachers, and pastors / by Anthony M. Coniaris. Minneapolis : Light and Life Pub. Co., [1975] 142 p. ; 21 cm. [BX270.C66] 75-11110
1. Christian education—Text-books—Orthodox Eastern. I. Title.

FLOROVSKII, 230'.1'908 s
Georgii Vasil'evich, 1893-
Christianity and culture. Belmont, Mass., Nordland Pub. Co. [1974] 245 p. 23 cm. (Collected works of Georges Florovsky, v. 2) Includes bibliographical references. [BX260.F55 vol. 2] [BR155] 270 73-88870 8.95
1. Church history—Addresses, essays, lectures. 2. Christianity and culture—Addresses, essays, lectures. I. Title.
Contents omitted.

FLOROVSKII, 230'.1'908 s
Georgii Vasil'evich, 1893-
Christianity and culture. Belmont, Mass., Nordland Pub. Co. [1974] 245 p. 23 cm. (Collected works of Georges Florovsky, v. 2) Contents.Contents.—Faith and culture.—The predicament of the Christian historian.—Antinomies of Christian history: empire and desert.—The iconoclastic controversy.—Christianity and civilization.—The social problem in the Eastern Orthodox Church.—Patriarch Jeremiah II and the Lutheran divines.—The Greek version of the Augsburg confession.—The Orthodox churches and the ecumenical movement prior to 1910. Includes bibliographical references. [BX260.F55 vol. 2] [BR155] 270 73-88870
1. Church history—Addresses, essays, lectures. 2. Christianity and culture—Addresses, essays, lectures. I. Title.

FLOROVSKII, Georgii 230'.1'908
Vasil'evich, 1893-
Collected works of Georges Florovsky. Belmont, Mass., Nordland Pub. Co. [1972- v. 23 cm. Contents.Contents.—v. 1. Bible, church, tradition: an Eastern Orthodox view. [BX260.F55] 72-197090
1. Orthodox Eastern Church—Collected works. 2. Theology—Collected works—20th century. I. Title.

FLOROVSKII, Georgii 230'.1'908
Vasil'evich, 1893-
Collected works of Georges Florovsky. Belmont, Mass., Nordland Pub. Co. [1972- v. 23 cm. Contents.Contents.—v. 1. Bible, church, tradition: an Eastern Orthodox view. [BX260.F55] 72-197090
1. Orthodox Eastern Church—Collected works. 2. Theology—Collected works—20th century. I. Title.

FLOROVSKII, Georgii 230'.1'908 s
Vasil'evich, 1893-
Creation and redemption / Georges Florovsky. Belmont, Mass. : Nordland Pub. Co., c1976. 317 p. ; 23 cm. (Collected works of Georges Florovsky ; v. 3) Includes bibliographical references. [BX260.F55 vol. 3] [BT695] 231'.7 76-379190 ISBN 0-913124-10-9 : 18.50
1. Creation. 2. Redemption. I. Title.

MALONEY, George A., 230'.1'909
1924-
A history of Orthodox theology since 1453 / by George A. Maloney. Belmont, Mass. : Nordland Pub. Co., 1977 388 p. ; 23 cm. Includes bibliographical references and index. [BX320.2.M34] 75-27491 ISBN 0-913124-12-5 : 22.50
1. Theology, Eastern church—History. I. Title.

BULGAKOV, Sergei 230'.1'93
Nikolaevich, 1871-1944.
A Bulgakov anthology / Sergius Bulgakov ; edited by James Pain and Nicholas Zernov. Philadelphia : Westminster Press, 1976. p. cm. Bibliography: p. [BX480.B78 1976] 76-23245 ISBN 0-664-21338-3 : 12.50
1. Orthodox Eastern Church, Russian—Collected works. 2. Bulgakov, Sergei Nikilaevich, 1871-1944. 3. Theology—Collected works—20th century. I. Title.

BULGAKOV, Sergei 230'.1'93
Nikolaevich, 1871-1944.
A Bulgakov anthology / Sergius Bulgakov ; edited by James Pain and Nicolas Zernov. London : SPCK, 1976. xxv, 191, [2] p. ; 22 cm. Bibliography: p. [193] [BX480.B78 1976b] 76-379873 ISBN 0-281-02933-4 : £5.50
1. Orthodox Eastern Church, Russian—Collected works. 2. Bulgakov, Sergei Nikolaevich, 1871-1944. 3. Orthodox Eastern Church, Russian—Biography. 4. Theology—Collected works—20th century. I. Title.

EXETASTES. 230'.1'93
Contemporary issues : Orthodox Christian perspectives / by "Exetastes". New York : Greek Orthodox Archdiocese Press, 1976. 103 p. ; 23 cm. Articles republished from the Orthodox observer. [BX325.E86 1976] 76-151121
1. Orthodox Eastern Church—Doctrinal and controversial works—Addresses, essays, lectures. 2. Church and social problems—Orthodox Eastern Church—Addresses, essays, lectures. I. Title.

PLATON, Metropolitan 230'.1'947
of Moscow, 1737-1812.
The present state of the Greek Church in Russia; or, A summary of Christian divinity. Translated from the Slavonian. With a preliminary memoir on the ecclesiastical establishment in Russia; and an appendix, containing an account of the origin and different sects of Russian dissenters. By Robert Pinkerton. New York, Printed and sold by Collins, 1815. [New York, AMS Press, 1973] xi, 276 p. 19 cm. [BX510.P6 1973] 75-131031 ISBN 0-404-05059-X 15.00
1. Orthodox Eastern Church, Russian—

Doctrinal and controversial works. 2. Dissenters, Religious—Russia. I. Pinkerton, Robert. II. Title.

ABAILARD, Pierre, 1079- 1142. 230'.2
Sic et non : a critical edition / Peter Abailard ; [edited by] Blanche B. Boyer and Richard McKeon. Chicago : University of Chicago Press, 1975. p. cm. Includes indexes. [BT70.A2 1975] 74-7567 ISBN 0-226-00058-3
1. Theology, Doctrinal. I. Boyer, Blanche Beatrice. II. McKeon, Richard Peter, 1900- III. Title.

ADAM, Karl, 1876- 230.2
The spirit of Catholicism. Translated by Justin McCann. Rev. ed. Garden City, N. Y., Image Books [1954] 260p. 18cm. (Image books, P502) [BX1751.A4 1954] 54-12995
1. Catholic Church—Doctrinal and controversial works—Crholic authors. I. Title.

ALEXANDER, Anthony F., 1920- 230.2
College dogmatic theology. Chicago, Regnery, 1962. 267p. 21cm. 62-15609 3.00
1. Theology, Doctrinal—Introductions. I. Title.

ANTI-CATHOLICISM in America, 1841-1851 : three sermons. 230'.2 New York : Arno Press, 1977. 370 p. ; 21 cm. (Anti-movements in America) Reprint of Is there any ground to apprehend the extensive and dangerous prevalence of Romanism in the United States? By H. A. Boardman, first published by Hooker & Agnew, Philadelphia, 1841; of An humble but earnest address to the bishops, clergy, and laity of the Protestant Episcopal Church in the United States, on the tolerating among our ministry of the doctrines of the Church of Rome, by J. H. Hopkins, first published by Harper, New York, 1846; and of The declining of popery and its causes, by N. Murray, first published by Harper, New York, 1851. [BX1767.A57] 76-46109 ISBN 0-405-09980-0 : 12.00
1. Catholic Church—Doctrinal and controversial works—Protestant authors—Addresses, essays, lectures. I. Boardman, Henry Augustus, 1808-1880. Is there any ground to apprehend the extensive and dangerous prevalence of Romanism in the United States. 1977. II. Hopkins, John Henry, 1820-1891. An humble but earnest address to the bishops, clergy, and laity of the Protestant Episcopal Church in the United States. 1977. III. Murray, Nicholas, 1802-1861. The decline of popery and its causes. 1977. IV. Series.

BALTIMORE CATECHISM. 230.2
A catechism of Christian doctrine. Rev. ed. of the Baltimore catechism no. 2. [Paterson, N. J., St. Anthony Guild Press, 1961] 137p. 18cm. Includes 'Supplement' (p. 131-137) [BX1961.B26 no. 2 1961] 62-70
1. Catholic Church—Catechisms and creeds—English. I. Title.

BARREAU, Jean Claude 230.2
The good news of Jesus. Tr. [from French] by Roma Rudd Turkel. New York, Paulist [c.1964, 1965] 159p. 18cm. (Deus bks.) [BT77.B3363] 65-21763 .95 pap.,
1. Theology. Doctrinal—Popular works. I. Title.

BARRES, Oliver. 230.2
One shepherd, one flock. New York, Sheed and Ward [c1956] 203p. 21cm. [BX4668.B29] 56-6122
1. Converts, Catholic. I. Title.

BARRES, Oliver. 230.2
One shephered, one flock. New York, Sheed and Ward [c1956] 203p. 21cm. [BX4668.B29] 56-6122
1. Converts, Catholic. I. Title.

BAUM, Gregory, 1923- 230.2
Faith and doctrine; a contemporary view. Paramus, N.J., Newman Press [1969] vi, 136 p. 22 cm. (The David S. Schaff lectures, 1968) Bibliography: p. 135-136. [BX1751.2.B3] 72-76957 4.25
1. Catholic Church—Doctrinal and controversial works. 2. Catholic Church—Apologetic works. I. Title. II. Series.

BAUM, Gregory, 1923- comp. 230.2
The future of belief debate. [New York] Herder & Herder [1967] 232p. 21cm. [BT102.D44B3] 67-28836 2.45 pap.,
1. Dewart, Leslie. The future of belief. I. Title.

BAUM, Gregory, 1923- 230.2
Man becoming; God in secular language. [New York] Herder and Herder [1970] xiv, 285 p. 22 cm. Includes bibliographical references. [BT75.2.B35] 71-110889 6.95
1. Theology, Doctrinal. I. Title.

BAUM, Gregory, 1923- 230'.2
New horizon: theological essays. New York, Paulist Press [1972] viii, 152 p. 18 cm. (Deus books) "The articles [were] for the most part previously published in The Ecumenist." [BX1756.B349N48] 74-188284 1.45
1. Theology, Catholic—Addresses, essays, lectures. I. Title.

BAUSCH, William J. 230'.2
Positioning : belief in the mid-seventies / William J. Bausch. Notre Dame, Ind. : Fides Publishers, [1975] viii, 176 p. ; 23 cm. Includes bibliographical references. [BX1751.2.B33] 75-5679 ISBN 0-8190-0606-8 : 7.95
1. Theology, Catholic. 2. Theology, Doctrinal. I. Title.

BEECHER, Edward, 1803- 1895. 230'.2
The Papal conspiracy exposed / Edward Beecher. New York : Arno Press, 1977, [c1854] 432 p. ; 23 cm. (Anti-movements in America) Reprint of the 1855 ed. published by M. W. Dodd, New York. [BX1770.B38 1977] 76-46066 ISBN 0-405-09940-1 : 24.00
1. Catholic Church—Doctrinal and controversial works—Protestant authors. I. Title. II. Series.

BELLARMINO, Roberto Francesco Romolo, Saint, 1542-1621. 230'.2 s
The art of dying well / [by] St. Robert Bellarmine ; [translated from the Latin by C. E. i.e. Edward Coffin]. Ilkley [etc.] : Scolar Press, 1976. [21], 416 p. ; 20 cm. (English recusant literature, 1558-1640 ; v. 314) (Series: Rogers, David Morrison, comp. English recusant literature, 1558-1640 ; v. 314.) Translation of De arte bene moriendi. Reprint of the 2d ed. of this translation, St. Omer, 1622. "Reproduced (original size) from a copy in the library of Emmanuel College, Cambridge ... STC 1839/5477." [BX1750.A1E5 vol. 314] [BT825] 236'.1 77-355088 ISBN 0-85967-326-X
1. Death—Early works to 1800. 2. Christian life—Catholic authors. I. Title. II. Series.

BENT, Charles N. 230.2
Interpreting the doctrine of God, by Charles N. Bent. Glen Rock, N.J., Paulist Press [1969] vi, 344 p. 21 cm. (Paulist Press exploration books) Bibliography: p. 335-344. [BT19.B4] 68-59158 3.95
1. Dogma, Development of. 2. Theology, Doctrinal—History—20th century. I. Title.

BERKOUWER, Gerrit Cornelis, 1903- 230.2
The conflict with Rome. Translated [by H. De Jongste] under the supervision of David H. Freeman. Philadelphia, Presbyterian and Reformed Pub. Co., 1958 [c1957] 319p. 24cm. Includes bibliography. [BX1765.B523] 57-8809
1. Catholic Church—Doctrinal and controversial works— Protestant authors. I. Title.

BERKOUWER, Gerrit Cornelis, 1903- 230.2
The Second Vatican Council and the new Catholicism, by G. C. Berkouwer. Translated by Lewis B. Smedes. Grand Rapids, Eerdmans [1965] 264 p. 23 cm. Translation of Vatikaans Concille en nieuwe theologie. Bibliographical footnotes. [BX830 1962.B453] 64-8581
1. Vatican Council, 2d. I. Title.

BERNARD de Clairvaux, Saint, 1091?-1153. 230'.2 s
On the Songs of Songs. Translated by Kilian Walsh. Introd. by M. Corneille Halfants. Spencer, Mass., Cistercian Publications, 1971- v. 23 cm. (The works of Bernard of Clairvaux, v. 2,) (Cistercian Fathers series, no. 4,) [BX890.B5 1970 vol. 2, etc.] [BS1485] 223'.9'07 73-168262 ISBN 0-87907-104-4 (v. 1) 7.95 (v. 1)
1. Bible. O.T. Song of Solomon—Sermons. 2. Sermons, Latin—Translations into English. 3. Sermons, English—Translations from Latin. I. Title. II. Series: Bernard de Clairvaux, Saint, 1091?-1153. Works. English. 1970, v. 2 [etc.]

BERNARD de Clairvaux, Saint, 1091?-1153. 230'.2 s
Treatises. Washington, Cistercian Publications, 1973- p. cm. (The works of Bernard of Clairvaux, v.) (Cistercian Fathers series, no.) Contents.Contents.— —2. The steps of humility and pride. On loving God. Includes bibliographies. [BX890.B5 1970 vol. 5, etc.] 230'.2 74-4147 ISBN 0-87907-113-3 8.95
1. Bible. O.T. Song of Solomon—Sermons. 2. God—Worship and love. 3. Humility. 4. Pride and vanity. I. Series: Bernard de Clairvaux, Saint, 1091?-1153. The works of Bernard of Clairvaux, v. [etc.]

BERNARD de Clairvaux, Saint, 1901?-1153. 230'.2 s
Five books on consideration : advice to a Pope / translated by John D. Anderson & Elizabeth T. Kennan. Kalamazoo, Mich. : Cistercian Publications, 1976. 222 p. ; 22 cm. (Cistercian Fathers series ; no. 37) (His The works of Bernard of Clairvaux ; v. 13) Translation of De consideratione. Includes index. Bibliography: p. 211-215. [BX890.B5 1970 vol. 13] [BX953] 262'.13 75-27953 ISBN 0-87907-737-9 pbk. : 4.00
1. Papacy. I. Title. II. Series.

BERRIGAN, Daniel. 230.2
The bow in the clouds; man's covenant with God. New York, Coward-McCann [1961] 220p. 22cm. [BT155.B44] 61-16722
1. Covenants (Theology) 2. Christian life — Catholic authors. I. Title.

BERRIGAN, Daniel 230.2
The bow in the clouds; man's covenat with God. New York, Coward [c.1961] 220p. 61-16722 4.50
1. Covenants (Theology) 2. Christian life—Catholic authors. I. Title.

BERRIGAN, Daniel. 230.2
The bride; essays in the church. New York, Macmillan, 1959. 142p. 22cm. [BX1751.2.B4] 59-6980
1. Church. 2. Catholic Church. I. Title.

BIONDO, Giuseppe. 230'.2 s
A relation of the death of ... Troilo Savelli / [by] Giuseppe Biondo ; [and] Holy philosophy / [by] Guillaume Du Vair ; [translated from the French by J. H.]. Ilkley [etc.] : Scolar Press, 1976. 464 p. (in various pagings) ; 20 cm. (English recusant literature, 1558-1640 ; v. 293) (Series: Rogers, David Morrison, comp. English recusant literature, 1558-1640 ; v. 293.) Biondo's work reprinted from a copy in the library of Downside Abbey of the 1620 ed.; references: Allison and Rogers 112; STC 3134. Du Vair's work reprinted from a copy in the library of Heythrop College of the 1636 ed.; reference: Allison and Rogers 290. [BX1750.A1E5 vol. 293] [BX4705.S367] 248'.246 B 77-356063 ISBN 0-85967-294-8 : £10.00
1. Savelli, Troilo, d. 1592. 2. Christian martyrs—Italy—Rome (City)—Biography. 3. Rome (City)—Biography. 4. Christian life—Catholic authors. I. Du Vair, Guillaume, 1556-1621. De la sainte philosophie. English. 1976. II. Title. III. Series.

BLANSHARD, Paul, 1892- 230.2
My Catholic critics. Boston, Beacon Press [1952] 53 p. 21 cm. (Beacon reference series) [BX1765.B625] 52-11927
1. Catholic Church— Doctrinal and controversial works—Protestant authors. I. Title.

BLENKINSOPP, Joseph, 1927- 230.2
A sketchbook of Biblical theology. [New York] Herder and Herder [1968] viii, 148 p. 22 cm. Bibliographical footnotes. [BS543.B55 1968] 68-29885 3.95
1. Bible—Theology—Addresses, essays, lectures. I. Title.

BOAT, William J., 1896- 230.2
What do you know? The true doctrine of the Catholic Church explained for non-Catholics. New York, Exposition Press [1961, c.1960] 101p. (Exposition-testament book) 61-1492 3.00
1. Catholic Church—Apologetic works. I. Title.

BOOME, Martha. 230.2
Peace through spirituality? By Martha-Maria [pseud.] Translated from the German by Rudolph Weiss. New York, Comet Press Book, 1961. 306p. 21cm. (A Reflection book) [BX1752.B59] 61-18951
1. Catholic Church—Apologetic works. I. Title.

BORLEIS, Harry F 230.2
The Pope speaks. New York, Christ's Mission, 1956. 286p. 22cm. [BX1765.B672] 56-43430
1. Catholic Church —Doctrinal and controversial works—Protestant authors. I. Title.

BOTHWELL, Mary de Angelis. 230'.2
God guides us; teacher's manual for perform-a-text 3 [by] Mary de Angelis Bothwell [and] Mary Margarette Harwood. Theological advisor: John A. Hardon. Consultant: Vincent G. Horrigan. Chicago, Loyola University Press [1974] 32, 435 p. illus. 23 cm. (Christ our life series, 3) [BX930.B64245] 74-167306 ISBN 0-8294-0226-8 4.95; 2.00 (for text without manual)
1. Religious education—Text-books—Catholic. I. Harwood, Mary Margarette, joint author. II. Title.

BOUYER, Louis 230.2
Christian initiation. [Translation from the French by J. R. Foster] New York, Macmillan, 1960[ ] 148p. 20cm. 60-3591 3.50 bds.,
1. Catholic Church—Apologetic works. I. Title.

BOUYER, Louis, 1913- 230.2
Christian humanism. Translated by A. V. Littledale. Westminster, Md., Newman Press, 1959 [c1958] 110p. 20cm. [BZ0px1751.2.B613] 59-1451
1. Catholic Church—Apologetic works. I. Title.

BOUYER, Louis, 1913- 230.2
Christian initiation. Tr. [from French] by J. R. Foster. New York, Collier [1962, c.1960] 128p. 18cm. (AS231Y) .95 pap.,
1. Catholic Church—Apologetic works. I. Title.

BOVIS, Andre de. 230.2
What is the church? Translated from the French by R. F. Trevett. [1st American ed.] New York, Hawthorn Books [1961] 155p. 21cm. (The Twentieth century encyclopedia of Catholicism, v. 48. Section 5: The life of faith) Translation of Leglise et son mystere. Includes bibliography. [BX1746.B633] 61-17756
1. Church. 2. Jesus Christ—Mystical body. I. Title.

BRANTL, George, ed. 230.2
Catholicism. New York, Washington Sq. [1962, c.1961] 277p. 17cm. (W 804) .60 pap.,
1. Catholic Church—Doctrinal and controversial works—Catholic authors. I. Title.

BRANTL, George. 230.2
Catholicism. New York, G. Braziller, 1961. 256 p. 21 cm. (Great religions of modern man) Includes bibliography. [BX1751.2.B7] 61-15501
1. Catholic Church—Doctrinal and controversial works—Catholic authors.

BROWN, Raymond Edward. 230'.2
Biblical reflections on crises facing the church / by Raymond E. Brown. New York : Paulist Press, 1975. x, 118 p. ; 21 cm. Includes bibliographical references. [BX1751.2.B76] 75-19861 ISBN 0-8091-1891-2 pbk. : 2.45
1. Catholic Church—Doctrinal and controversial works—Catholic authors. I. Title.

BRUNGS, Robert A., 1931- 230.2
Building the city; Christian response and responsibility, by Robert A. Brungs. New York, Sheed and Ward [1967] 249 p. 22 cm. Includes bibliographies. [BX2350.2.B75] 67-21900
1. Christian life—Catholic authors. I. Title.

BRUNINI, John Gilland, 1899- 230.2
What Catholics believe--and why (Whereon to stand) With an introd. by Francis Cardinal Spellman. Garden City, N. Y., Garden City Books [1952, '1946] 302 p. 21 cm. [BX1754.B745 1952] 52-3074
1. Catholic Church—Doctrinal and controversial works, Popular. I. Title.

BRUNINI, John Gilland, 1899- 230.2
Whereon to stand: what Catholics believe and why. Introd. by Francis Cardinal Spellman. [New York, Dell, 1961, c.1946, 1961] 351p. (Chapel book, F123) .50 pap.,
1. Catholic church—Doctrinal and controversial works, Popular. I. Title.

BUDDY, Charles Francis, Bp. 230.2
For them also, a resume of Catholic doctrine; fundamentals to live by. San Diego, Calif., Univ. of San Diego Pr. [c.1963] xx, 462p. 20cm. 63-24157 3.00; 1.75 pap.,
1. Catholic Church—Catechisms and creeds—English. 2. Theology, Doctrinal—Popular works. I. Title.

BUDDY, Charles Francis, Bp. 230.2
For them also, a resume of Catholic doctrine; fundamentals to live by. San Diego, University of San Diego Press [1963] xx, 462 p. 20 cm. [BX1754.B772] 63-24157
1. Catholic Church — Catechisms and creeds — English. 2. Theology; Doctrinal — Popular works I. Title.

BURGHARDT, Walter J., ed. 230.2
The idea of Catholicism; an introduction to the thought and worship of the church, edited by Walter J. Burghardt and William F. Lynch. [New York] Meridian Books [1960] 479 p. 22 cm. (Greenwich editions) Includes bibliography. [BX1747.5.B8] 60-6768
1. Catholic Church—Doctrinal and controversial works. I. Lynch, William F., 1908- joint ed. II. Title.

BUTCHER, John M A. 230.2
Outline study theology; for college students: sophomore, junior, and senior years. [New York! 1951] 215, 182, 156 p. 24 cm. [BX1751.B93] 51-39632
1. Catholic Church—Doctrinal and controverslal works. 2. Theology, Doctrinal. I. Title.

BUTLER, Basil Christopher. 230.2
Christians in a new era [by] Christopher Butler. [Maryknoll, N.Y.] Maryknoll Publications [1969] 102 p. 22 cm. [BX1751.2.B85] 77-96724 1.95
1. Catholic Church—Doctrinal and controversial works—Catholic authors. I. Title.

BUTLER, Basil Christopher. 230.2
Why Christ. Baltimore, Helicon Press [1960] viii, 164p. 20cm. 60-8692 3.50 bds.,
1. Catholic Church—Apologetic works. I. Title.

CASSILLY, Francis Bernard, 230.2
1860-1938.
Religion: doctrine and practice. Chicago, Loyola University Press [1958] 535p. illus. 20cm. [BX930.C3 1958] 58-8650
1. Catholic Church—Doctrinal and controversial works—Text-books. I. Title.

CATHOLIC Church. 230.2
The Church teachers; documents of the Church in English translation. The selections in this book were translated and prepared for publication by John F. Clarkson [and others of] St. Mary's College, St. Marys, Kansas. St. Louis, B. Herder Book Co. [c1955] xiv, 400p. 21cm. Documents used in the text are taken principally from the 24th, 28th, and 29th editions of Heinrich Denzinger's Enchiridion symbolorum. [BX1749.A4] 55-10397
1. Catholic Church—Doctrinal and controversial works. I. Clarkson, John F., ed. and tr. II. St. Mary's College, St. Marys, Kan. III. Catholic Church. Canons, decretals, etc. IV. Denzinger, Heinrich Joseph Dominik, 1819-1883. Enchiroidiom symbolorum. V. Title.

CATHOLIC Church. Byzantine 230.2
rite (Ruthenian) Liturgy and ritual. English.
The liturgy of St. John Chrysostom, Ruthenian form; historical background, introd., and commentary by Basil Shereghy. Collegeville, Minn., Liturgical Press [1961] 64p. col. illus. (on cover) 19cm. Cover title: The divine liturgy of St. John Chrysostom. [BX4711.662.S5] 62-1065
I. Shereghy, Basil, ed. II. Title. III. Title: The divine liturgy of St. John Chrysostom.

CATHOLIC Church. National 230'.2
Conference of Catholic Bishops.
Basic teachings for Catholic religious education. Washington, Publications Office, U.S. Catholic Conference, 1973. 36 p. 22 cm. Includes bibliographical references. [BX1755.C34 1973] 73-172147
1. Catholic Church—Doctrinal and controversial works—Catholic authors. 2. Religious education. I. Title.

CATHOLIC Church. Pope, 1939- 230.2
(Pius XII) Humani generis (12 Aug. 1950)
The encyclical "Humani generis"; with a commentary [by] A. C. Cotter. Weston, Mass., Weston College Press, 1951. 100 p. 20 cm. Latin and English. [BX873 1950 Aug. 12.A33] 52-18569
1. Catholic Church—Doctrinal and controversial works—Catholic authors. I. Cotter, Anthony Charles, 1879- II. Title.

CATHOLIC Church. Pope, 1939- 230.2
(Pius XII) Humani generis (12 Aug. 1950)
The encyclical "Humani generis"; with a commentary [by] A. C. Cotter. 2d ed. Weston, Mass., Weston College Press, 1952. ix, 114 p. 20 cm. Latin and English. [BX873 1950 Aug. 12.A34] 52-33493
1. Catholic Church—Doctrinal and controversial works—Catholic authors. I. Cotter, Anthony Charles, 1879- II. Title.

CEGIELKA, Francis A. 230.2
Handbook of ecclesiology and Christology; a concise, authoritative review of the mystery of the church and the incarnation in the light of Vatican II [by] Francis A. Cegielka. Staten Island, N.Y., Alba House [1971] ix, 178 p. 21 cm. Includes bibliographical references. [BX1746.C4] 77-158569 ISBN 0-8189-0201-9 1.95
1. Jesus Christ—Person and offices. 2. Church. I. Title.

CHENU, Marie Dominique, 230.2
1895-
Toward understanding Saint Thomas [by] M.-D. Chenu. Translated with authorized corrections and bibliographical additions by A.-M. Landry and D. Hughes. Chicago, H. Regnery Co. [1964] viii, 386 p. 25 cm. (The Library of living Catholic thought) Translation of Introduction a l'etude de saint Thomas d'Aquin. Bibliographical footnotes. [[B765.T54C513]] 64-14598
1. Thomas Aquinas, Saint, 1225?-1274 I. Title.

CHENU, Marie Dominique, 230.2
1895-
Toward understanding Saint Thomas. Tr. [from French] with authorized corrections, bibl. additions by A.M. Landry, D. Hughes. Chicago, Regnery [c.1964] viii, 386p. 25cm. (Lib. of living Catholic thought) Bibl. 64-14598 6.00
1. Thomas Aquinas, Saint, 1225?-1274. I. Title.

CHESTERTON, Gilbert Keith, 230.2
1874-1936.
The thing. [New York] S[heed] & W[ard, 1957] 255p. 21cm. (A Thomas More book to live) [BX1754.C45 1957] 57-6043
1. Catholic Church—Doctrinal and controversial works—Catholic authors. I. Title.

CHILSON, Richard. 230'.2
The faith of Catholics. New York, Paulist Press [1972] vi, 182 p. 19 cm. (Deus books) [BX1751.2.C45] 72-81229 1.25
1. Theology, Catholic. I. Title.

CHILSON, Richard. 230'.2
An introduction to the faith of Catholics / Richard Chilson. Newly rev. and expanded. New York : Paulist Press, c1975. xi, 303 p. : ill. ; 19 cm. (Deus books) Edition of 1972 published under title: The faith of Catholics. [BX1751.2.C45 1975] 75-329397 ISBN 0-8091-1907-2 pbk. : 2.45
1. Theology, Catholic. I. Title.

THE Christian faith in the 230'.2
doctrinal documents of the Catholic Church / edited by J. Neuner & J. Dupuis. 1st U.S.A. ed., corr. Westminster, Md. : Christian Classics, 1975. xxxi, 687 p. ; 21 cm. The 1st ed. of forerunner of this book, edited by J. Neuner and H. Roos, published in 1938 under title: Der Glaube der Kirche in den Urkunden der Lehrverkundigung. Includes indexes. [BX1747.5.N413 1975] 75-319948 12.50
1. Catholic Church—Doctrinal and controversial works. 2. Catholic Church—Catechisms and creeds—English. I. Neuner, Josef. II. Dupuis, Jacques, 1923-

CHURCH (The;) 230.2
readings in theology [by] Hugo Rahner [others] Foreword by Gustave Weigel. Comp. at the Canisianum, Innsbruck. New York, Kenedy [c.1963] xii, 242p. 22cm. Tr. from German or French. 63-19022 4.95
1. Church—Addresses, essays, lectures. 2. Catholic Church—Addresses, essays, lectures. I. Rahner, Hugo, 1900-

COLACCI, Mario 230.2
The doctrinal conflict between Roman Catholic and Protestant Christianity. Foreword by Alvin N. Rogness. Minneapolis, Denison [c.1962] 269p. 22cm. Bibl. 62-14150 4.50
1. Catholic Church—Doctrinal and controversial works—Protestant authors. I. Title.

COLLEGE Theology Society. 230.2
The paradox of religious secularity. Katharine T. Hargrove, editor. Englewood Cliffs, N.J., Prentice-Hall [1968] x, 203 p. 22 cm. Proceedings of the 13th national convention of the College Theology Society, held in Pittsburgh, Mar. 26-28, 1967. Bibliographical footnotes. [BV1610.C584] 68-24092
1. Universities and colleges—Religion—Societies, etc. 2. Theology—Study and teaching—Societies, etc. 3. Secularism. I. Hargrove, Katharine T., ed. II. Title.

COLLETON, John. 230'.2 s
A just defence of the slandered priestes : 1602 / John Colleton. [A defence of the appendix : 1624 / John Sweet]. Ilkley [Eng.] : Scolar Press, 1976. 303, 72 p. ; 21 cm. (English recusant literature, 1558-1640 ; v. 317) (Series: Rogers, David Morrison, comp. English recusant literature, 1558-1640 ; v. 317.) [BX1750.A1E5 vol. 317] [BX1492] 282'.42 77-356064 ISBN 0-85967-331-6
1. Catholic Church—Clergy. 2. Catholic Church—Doctrinal and controversial works—Catholic authors. 3. Clergy—England. I. Sweet, John. A defence of the appendix. 1976. II. Title. III. Series.

COME to Jesus; 230.2
first steps in religious instruction. Tr., partly adapted by Desmond A. D'Abreo from a German text by Albert Thomas. Ed. by Gunter Biemer, I. M. J. Kern. New York, Herder & Herder [1965, c.1964] 64p. col. illus. 22cm. cover title. 1.25 pap.,

CONGAR, Marie Joseph 230.2
[secular name: Georges Yves Congar]
The mystery of the church; studies by Yves Congar. Translated by A. V. Littledale. Baltimore, Helicon Press, 1960. xii, 186p. Includes bibliography. 23cm. 'Orignally published in French as two separate books: Esquisses du mystere de l'Eglise and La Pentecote: Chartres.' 60-7793 4.75
1. Church. 2. Catholic Church. I. Title.

CONGAR, Yves Marie Joseph, 230.2
1904-
The mystery of the church; studies by Yves Congar. Translated by A. V. Littledale. Baltimore, Helicon Press, 1960. 186 p. 23 cm. "Originally published in French as two separate books: Esquisses du mystere de l'Eglise and La Pentecote: Chartres." Includes bibliography. [BX1746.C6] 60-7793
1. Church. 2. Catholic Church. I. Title.

CONNELL, Francis Jeremiah 230.2
Father Connell answers moral questions. Edited by Eugene J. Weitzel. Washington, Catholic University of America Press, [c.] 1959. xiii, 210p. 23cm. 59-16744 3.95
1. Questions and answers—Theology. 2. Christian ethics—Catholic authors. 3. Catholic Church—Doctrinal and controversial works. I. Title.

CONNOLLY, James M. 230.2
The voices of France; a survey of contemporary theology in France. New York, Macmillan [c.]1961. 231p. Bibl. 61-6686 5.50
1. Theology—20th cent. 2. Catholic Church—Doctrinal and controversial works. 3. Theologians, French. I. Title.

CONWAY, Bertrand Louis, 230.2
1872-1959
The miniature question box. Abridged version of The question box. New York, Paulist Pr. [c.1962] 256p. (Deus bk.) .75 pap.,
1. Catholic Church—Doctrinal and controversial works—Catholic authors. I. Title.

CONWAY, Bertrand Louis, 230.2
1872-1959.
The question box. Pref. by Francis Cardinal Spellman. [New ed., completely rev.] New York, Paulist Press [c.1961] 448p. 61-11249 1.45 pap.,
I. Title.

CONWAY, Bertrand Louis, 230.2
1872-1959
The question box. Pref. by Francis Cardinal Spellman [New rev., enl. ed.] New York, All Saints [c.1961, 1962] 463p. 17cm. (AS703) .75 pap.,
1. Catholic Church—Doctrinal and controversial works—Catholic authors. I. Title.

CONWAY, John Donald, 1905- 230.2
Facts of the faith. New York, All Saints Pr. [1961, c.1959] 371p. (AS-701) .75 pap.,
1. Catholic Church—Doctrinal and controversial works, Popular. I. Title.

COONEY, Cyprian. 230.2
Understanding the new theology. Milwaukee, Bruce Pub. Co. [1968, c1969] xii, 193 p. 22 cm. Includes bibliographies. [BX1751.2.C65] 68-55278 4.95
1. Catholic Church—Doctrinal and controversial works—Catholic authors. 2. Theology, Doctrinal—20th century. I. Title.

COVENTRY, John. 230'.2
Christian truth / John Coventry. New York : Paulist Press, 1975. vi, 104 p. ; 22 cm. Includes bibliographical references. [BT1102.C64 1975b] 75-332944 ISBN 0-8091-1903-X pbk. : 2.45
1. Apologetics—20th century. I. Title.

COWAN, Wayne H., ed. 230.2
Facing Protestant-Roman Catholic tensions; how to think clearly about them as suggested by leading Roman Catholics and Protestants. New York, Association Press [1960] 125 p. 16 cm. (An Association Press reflection book) Includes bibliography. [BX1779.C63] 60-12718
1. Catholic Church—Doctrinal and controversial works—Debates, etc. I. Title.

CRASHAW, William, 1572- 230'.2
1626.
The sermon preached at the cross, Feb. 14, 1607. Introductory note by Peter Davison. New York, Johnson Reprint Corp., [1973 c.1972] 174 p. 22 cm. (Theatrum redivivum) Reprint of the 1608 ed. imprinted by H. L. for E. Weaver, London under title: The sermon preached at the crosse, Feb. xiiij. 1607 (STC 6027) Includes bibliographical references. [BX1763.C65 1972] 70-175654 14.50
1. Catholic Church—Doctrinal and controversial works—Protestant authors. 2. Theater—Moral and religious aspects. I. Title.

CUMMINGS, Daniel Malachy. 230.2
Facts about the Catholic Church [by] Rev. D. M. Cummings. Revised ed. Dublin, Catholic Truth Society of Ireland, 1968. 220 p. 18 cm. [BX1752.C8 1968] 74-354651 5/-
1. Catholic Church—Apologetic works. I. Catholic Truth Society of Ireland. II. Title.

CUSKELLY, Eugene James 230.2
God's gracious design; a new look at Catholic doctrine. Westminster, Md., Newman, 1965. x,311p. 23cm. Bibl. [BX1754.C83] 65-25979 5.95
1. Theology, Doctrinal—Popular works. I. Title.

DANIEL-ROPS, Henry, 1901- 230.2
ed.
The Twentieth century encyclopedia of Catholicism. [Edited by Henri Daniel-Rops. New York, Hawthorn Books, 1958- v. 21 cm. 1 v. (unpaged) 21 cm. Half title; each vol. has also special t. p. Index to the first sixteen volumes. Joseph W. Sprug, index editor. [New York] Hawthorn Books [1959] 58-14327
1. Theology — Collections — Catholic authors. I. Title.

DANIEL-ROPS, Henry, 1901- 230.2
ed.
The Twentieth century encyclopedia of Catholicism. [Edited by Henri Daniel-Rops. New York, Hawthorn Books, 1958- v. 21 cm. v. 21 cm. (BX841.T85 Index Half title: each vol. has also special t. p. -- Index ... Joseph W. Sprug, index editor. [New York] Hawthorn Books [1959- Cover title. Indexes issued semi-annually with annual cumulations. 58-14327
1. Theology — Collections — Catholic authors. I. Title.

DANIELOU, Jean. 230.2
The faith eternal and the man of today. Translated by Paul Joseph Oligny. [Chicago] Franciscan Herald Press [1970] vii, 111 p. 21 cm. Translation of La foi de toujours et l'homme d'aujourd'hui. [BX1751.2.D313] 78-123596
1. Catholic Church—Doctrinal and controversial works—Catholic authors. I. Title.

DAVIS, Charles 230.2
The study of theology. New York, Sheed [1962] 348p. 23cm. 63-4548 5.00
1. Theology, Doctrinal—Popular works. I. Title.

DAVIS, Charles 230.2
Theology for today. New York, Sheed [1963, c. 1962] 310p. 22cm. ibl. 63-8550 5.00
1. Theology, Doctrinal—Introductions. I. Title.

DEFERRARI, Roy Joseph, 230.2
1890-
A complete index of the Summa theologica of St. Thomas Aquinas, by Roy J. Deferrari and Sister M. Inviolata Barry. [Baltimore? 1956] ix, 386p. 28cm. [BX1749.T6D4] 56-4980
1. Thomas Aquinas, Saint, 1225?-1274. Summa theologica. 2. Thomas Aquinas, Saint, 1225?-1274 —Dictionaries, indexes, etc. I. Barry, Inviolata, joint author. II. Title.

DEVINE, George, 1941- 230'.2
American Catholicism: where do we go from here? Englewood Cliffs, N.J., Prentice-Hall [1974, c1975] x, 117 p. 24 cm. Includes bibliographical references. [BX1406.2.D45] 74-11182 ISBN 0-13-023986-0. 6.95
1. Catholic Church in the United States. 2. Catholic Church—Doctrinal and controversial works—Catholic authors. I. Title.
Pbk. 3.50; ISBN 0-13-023978-X.

DEWAN, Wilfrid F. 230.2
Catholic belief and practice in an ecumenical age, with study-club questions, by Wilfrid F. Dewan. Glen Rock, N.J., Paulist Press [1966] 93 p. 19 cm. (Deus books) [BX1751.2.D4] 66-29817
1. Catholic Church—Dectrinal and controversial works—Catholic authors. 2. Christian union—Catholic Church. I. Title.

DEWART, Leslie. 230.2
The future of belief; theism in a world come of age. [New York] Herder and Herder [1966] 223 p. 21 cm. Bibliographical footnotes. [BT102.D42] 66-26482
1. God. 2. Theism. I. Title.

DOORNIK, Nicolaas Gerardus 230.2
Maria van.
The meeting with Christ: a layman's guide to Catholic faith today, by N. G. M. van Doornik. Translated and adapted by Janet Paton. New York, P. J. Kenedy [1964] xii, 237 p. 22 cm. [BX1754.D62] 64-14561
1. Catholic Church — Doctrinal and controversial works, Popular. I. Paton, Janet, tr. II. Title.

DOORNIK, Nicolaas, Gerardus 230.2
Maria van
The meeting with Christ: a layman's guide to Catholic faith today, by N. G. B. van Doornik. Tr. [from Dutch] and adapted by Janet Paton. New York, Kenedy [c.1964] xii, 237p. 22cm. 64-14561 4.95
1. Catholic Church—Doctrinal and controversial works, Popular. I. Paton, Janet, tr. II. Title.

DREXEL, Jeremias, 1581- 230'.2 s
1638.
The angel-guardian's clock, 1630 / Hieremias Drexelius [i.e. J. Drexel] ; [and, An embassage from heaven, 1611 / Ralph Buckland]. Ilkley

[Eng.] : Scolar Press, 1976. 311, 124 p. ; 20 cm. (English recusant literature, 1558-1640 ; v. 298) (Series: Rogers, David Morrison, comp. English recusant literature, 1558-1640 ; v. 298.) Drexel's work is a translation of Horologium auxiliaris tutelaris angeli. Drexel's work reprinted from a copy in the Bodleian Library of the 1630 ed.; references: Allison and Rogers 283; STC 7234. Buckland's work reprinted from a copy in the library of Lambeth Palace of the 1611 ed.; references: Allison and Rogers 180; STC 4007. [BX1750.A1E5 vol. 298] [BT965] 235'.3 76-382908 ISBN 0-85967-299-9
1. Catholic Church—Doctrinal and controversial works—Catholic authors. 2. Christian life—Catholic authors. 3. Angels. I. Buckland, Ralph. An embassage from heaven. 1976. II. Title. III. Series.

DUBITSKY, Cora Marie. 230'.2
Building the faith community / by Cora Marie Dubitsky. New York : Paulist Press, [1974] vi, 177 p. ; 18 cm. (Deus books) [BV1471.2.D8] 74-12632 ISBN 0-8091-1848-3 pbk. : 1.95
1. Religious education. 2. Theology, Catholic. I. Title.

DUGGAN, G. H., 1912- 230.2
Hans Kung and reunion. Westminster, Md., Newman [1965] 96p. 18cm. Bibl. [BX4705.K82D8] 65-933 .95 pap.,
1. Kung, Hans, 1928- I. Title.

DUNS, Joannes, Scotus, 230'.2
1265?-1308?
God and creatures; the quodlibetal questions [by] John Duns Scotus. Translated with an introd., notes, and glossary by Felix Alluntis and Allan B. Wolter. [Princeton, N.J.] Princeton University Press, 1975. xxxiv, 548 p. 25 cm. Translation of Quodlibeta. Includes bibliographical references. [BX1749.D8213] 73-2468 ISBN 0-691-07195-0 25.00
1. Theology, Doctrinal. I. Alluntis, Felix, tr. II. Wolter, Allan Bernard, 1913- tr. III. Title. IV. Title: The quodlibetal questions.

EBNER, James H. 230'.2
God present as mystery : a search for personal meaning in contemporary theology / by James H. Ebner ; [foreword by Andrew M. Greeley]. Winona, Minn. : St. Mary's College Press, c1976. 168 p. ; 21 cm. Includes bibliographical references and index. [BX1751.2.E25] 76-13750 ISBN 0-88489-084-8 pbk. : 4.95
1. Theology, Catholic. 2. Theology, Doctrinal—Popular works. I. Title.

EDMUND Rich, Saint, Abp. of 230.2
Canterbury, d.1240.
Speculum religiosorum; and, speculum ecclesie [by] Edmund of Abingdon; edited by Helen P. Forshaw. London, Oxford University Press for the Academy [1973 i.e.1974] ix, 125 p. 26 cm. (Auctores Britannici Medii Aevi, 3) Includes bibliographical references and indexes. English introd., Latin text. The original Latin text is printed parallel to the vulgate Latin text, which is a translation of an Anglo-Norman version. [BX2349.E35] 74-204756 ISBN 0-19-725935-9 16.00
1. Spiritual life—Catholic authors. I. Forshaw, Helen P., ed. II. Title. III. Title: Speculum ecclesie. IV. Series.
Distributed by Oxford University Press, N.Y.

FAITH and reform; 230.2
a reinterpretation of aggiornamento. Edited by Jonathan Robinson. New York, Fordham University Press, 1969. vi, 172 p. 22 cm. "A selection from a series of papers ... given at Marianopolis College, Montreal, during the winter of 1968." Includes bibliographical references. [BX1751.2.A1F3] 70-75039 6.00
1. Catholic Church—Doctrinal and controversial works—Catholic authors. I. Robinson, Jonathan, ed.

FANNON, Patrick, 1929- 230.2
The changing face of theology. Milwaukee, Bruce Pub. Co. [1968] vii, 105 p. 22 cm. Includes bibliographies. [BX1754.F27] 68-8284
1. Catholic Church—Doctrinal and controversial works, Popular. I. Title.

FARRER, Austin Marsden. 230.2
Saving belief; a discussion of essentials, by Austin Farrer. [1st American ed.] New York, Morehouse-Barlow Co. [1965] 157 p. 21 cm. [BT77.F3] 65-26999
I. Theology, Doctrinal — Popular works. II. Title.

FERNAN, John Joseph, 1908- 230.2
Theology, a course for college students. [Syracuse? N. Y., 1952-55] 4v. maps (on lining papers, v. 3) 24cm. Contents.v. 1. Christ as prophet and king.--v. 2. Christ. our high priest.--v. 3. The mystical Christ.--v. 4. Christ in His Members, by B. J. Murray, J. J. Ferman, and E. J. Messemer. [BX904.F4] 52-4098
1. Theology, Doctrinal. 2. Catholic Church—Doctrinal and controversial works. I. Murray, Bernard J. II. Title.

FLOYD, John. 230'.2 s
The church conquerant over humane wit, [1639?] / John Floyd. [Ilkley, Eng.] : Scolar Press, 1976. 6, 143 p. ; 21 cm. (English recusant literature, 1558-1640 ; v. 320) (Series: Rogers, David Morrison, comp. English recusant literature, 1558-1640 ; v. 320.) Reproduced (original size) from a copy in the Gillow Library. [BX1750.A1E5 vol. 320] [BX1750] 230'.2 77-352545 ISBN 0-85967-335-9
1. Catholic Church—Doctrinal and controversial works—Catholic authors. I. Title. II. Series.

FRANCOIS de Sales, 230'.2 s
Saint, Bp. of Geneva, 1567-1622.
An introduction to a devoute life, 1613 / St. Francis of Sales. Ilkley : Scolar Press, 1976. 135 p. ; 19 cm. (English recusant literature, 1558-1640 ; v. 279) (Series: Rogers, David Morrison, comp. English recusant literature, 1558-1640 ; v. 279.) Reprint of the 1613 ed. [BX1750.A1E5 vol. 279] [BX2179.F8] 242 76-360039 ISBN 0-85967-280-8
1. Meditations. I. Title. II. Series.

FRIES, Heinrich 230.2
Bultmann-Barth and Catholic theology. Tr., introd. [by] Leonard Swidler. Pittsburgh. Duquesne [1967] 182p. 22cm. (Duquesne studies. Theological ser., 8) Bibl. [BX4827.B78F73] 67-9153 4.50
1. Bultmann, Rudolf Karl, 1884- 2. Barth, Karl, 1866- 3. Theology, Catholic. I. Title. II. Series.

FULTON, Justin Dewey, 230'.2
1828-1901.
The fight with Rome / Justin D. Fulton. New York : Arno Press, 1977. viii, 397 p. ; ill. ; 23 cm. (Anti-movements in America) Reprint of the 1889 ed. published by Pratt Bros., Marlboro, Mass. [BX1765.F96 1977] 76-46077 ISBN 0-405-09950-9 : 22.00
1. Catholic Church—Doctrinal and controversial works—Protestant authors. I. Title. II. Series.

FULTON, Justin Dewey, 230'.2
1828-1901.
The fight with Rome / Justin D. Fulton. New York : Arno Press, 1977. viii, 397 p. ; ill. ; 23 cm. (Anti-movements in America) Reprint of the 1889 ed. published by Pratt Bros., Marlboro, Mass. [BX1765.F96 1977] 76-46077 ISBN 0-405-09950-9 : 22.00
1. Catholic Church—Doctrinal and controversial works—Protestant authors. I. Title. II. Series.

GAFFNEY, James. 230'.2
Focus on doctrine / by James Gaffney. New York : Paulist Press, [1975?] 148 p. ; 18 cm. (Paulist Press/Deus book) "The articles ... originally appeared in Service, vol. 1." Bibliography: p. 141-148. [BX1751.2.G26] 74-28635 ISBN 0-8091-1863-7 pbk. : 1.65
1. Theology, Catholic. I. Title.

GARRIGOU-LAGRANGE, 230.2
Reginald, 1877-
Beatitude, a commentary on St. Thomas' Theological summa, Ia IIae, qq. 1-54. Translated by Patrick Cummins. St. Louis, B. Herder Book Co. [1956] 397p. 22cm. Translation of De beatitudine, de actibus humanis et habitibus. [B765.T54G337] 56-9440
1. Thomas Aquinas, Saint, 1225?-1274—Ethics. 2. Thomas Aquinas, Saint, 1225?-1274. Summa theologics. 3. Christian ethics—Catholic authors. I. Title.

GARRIGOU-LAGRANGE, 230.2
Reginald, Father, 1877-
Grace; commentary on the Summa theologica of St. Thomas, Ia IIae, q. 109-14. Translated by the Dominican Nuns, Corpus Christi Monastery, Menlo Park, Calif. St. Louis, B. Herder Book Co., 1952. 535 p. 25 cm. Translation of De gratia. [BX1749T6G34] 52-13198
1. Thomas Aquinas, Saint, 1225?-1274. Summa theologica 2. Grace (Theology) I. Title.

GARRIGOU-LAGRANGE, 230.2
Reginald, Father, 1877-
Reality; a synthesis of Thomistic thought. Translated by Patrick Cummins. St. Louis, Herder, 1950. xiii, 419 p. 25 cm. Translation of La synthese thomiste. Bibliographical footnotes. [BX1749.T6G343] 50-14837
1. Thomas Aqulnas, Saint, 1225?-1274. I. Title.

GARRIGOU-LAGRANGE, 230.2
Reginald, 1877-1964.
The last writings of Reginald Garrigou-Lagrange. Translated by Raymond Smith and Rod Gorton. New York, New City Press [1969] xiii, 224 p. 22 cm. [BX3503.G33 1969] 75-77439 5.95
1. Dominicans—Spiritual life. 2. Spiritual life—Catholic authors. I. Title.

GARVER, Stuart P. 230'.2
Watch your teaching! A comparative study of Roman Catholic and Protestant teaching since Vatican Council II, by Stuart P. Garver. Hackensack, N.J., Christ's Mission [1973] xvi, 167 p. illus. 22 cm. (Christian heritage series) Bibliography: p. 166-167. [BX1751.2.G36] 73-90020 2.95
1. Catholic Church—Doctrinal and controversial works. 2. Protestant churches—Doctrinal and controversial works. I. Title. II. Series.

GARVER, Stuart P. 230'.2
Watch your teaching! A comparative study of Roman Catholic and Protestant teaching since Vatican Council II, by Stuart P. Garver. Hackensack, N.J., Christ's Mission [1973] xvi, 167 p. illus. 22 cm. (Christian heritage series) Bibliography: p. 166-167. [BX1751.2.G36] 73-90020 2.95
1. Catholic Church—Doctrinal and controversial works. 2. Protestant churches—Doctrinal and controversial works. I. Title. II. Series.
Publisher's address: 275 State Street, Hackensack, N.J. 07601

GOD among men; 230.2
translated and edited by Bernard Murchland. Notre Dame, Fides Publishers Association [c.1960] 315p. 20cm. (Themes of theology) 59-14095 4.50
1. Catholic Church—Doctrinal and controversial works, Popular. I. Murchland, Bernard, ed. and tr.

GRAEF, Hilda C. 230.2
Adult Christianity. Chicago, Franciscan Herald [1966] 140p. 21cm. [BX1754.G6845] 65-22872 3.50
1. Theology, Doctrinal—Popular works. I. Title.

GRANT, Dorothy (Fremont), 230.2
1900-
Born again. Milwaukee, Bruce [1950] xi, 254 p. 22 cm. Bibliography: p. 253-254. [BX4668.G65] 50-10440
1. Converts. Catholic. I. Title.

GRATSCH, Edward J 230.2
The basis of Roman Catholicism, by Edward J. Gratsch. [1st ed.] New York, Pageant Press [1967] 275 p. 21 cm. Bibliographical footnotes. [BX1754.G694] 68-3341
1. Catholic Church—Doctrinal and controversial works, Popular. I. Title.

GRATSCH, Edward J. 230.2
The basis of Roman Catholicism, by Edward J. Gratsch. [1st ed.] New York, Pageant Press [1967] 275 p. 21 cm. Bibliographical footnotes. [BX1754.G694] 68-3341
1. Catholic Church—Doctrinal and controversial works, Popular. I. Title.

GRAY, Ronald F., Rev. 230.2
Catholic living in a nutshell: how to bring Christ into your life. Downers Grove,Ill., Carmelite Third Order Pr. [1963] 57p. 19cm. .50 pap.,
I. Title.

GREELEY, Andrew M., 1928- 230'.2
The great mysteries : an essential of catechism / Andrew M. Greeley. New York : Seabury Press, [1976] p. cm. "A Crossroad book." Bibliography: p. [BT77.G837] 76-13208 ISBN 0-8164-0309-0 : 7.95. ISBN 0-8164-2128-5 pbk. : 3.95
1. Theology, Doctrinal—Popular works. 2. Theology, Catholic. I. Title.

GREELEY, Andrew M., 1928- 230'.2
The new agenda [by] Andrew M. Greeley. [1st ed.] Garden City, N.Y., Doubleday, 1973. 312 p. 22 cm. Bibliography: p. [307]-312. [BX1751.2.G73] 72-89309 6.95
1. Catholic Church—Doctrinal and controversial works—Catholic authors. I. Title.

GREELEY, Andrew M., 1928- 230'.2
The new agenda. Garden City, N. Y., Image Books 1975 [c1973] 279 p., 18 cm. Bibliography p.: 275-279. [BX1751.2.G73] ISBN 0-385-02790-7 1.95 (pbk.)
1. Catholic Church—Doctrinal and controversial works—Catholic authors. I. Title.
L.C. card no. for original ed.: 72-89309.

GREGORIUS I, The Great, 230'.2 s
Saint, Pope, 540(ca.)-604.
The second booke of the dialogues [of] St. Gregory / [translated from the Latin by C. F., i.e. Cuthbert Fursdon]. Ilkley [etc.] : Scolar Press, 1976. 319 p. in various pagings ; 20 cm. (English recusant literature, 1558-1640 ; v. 294) (Series: Rogers, David Morrison, comp. English recusant literature, 1558-1640 ; v. 294.) Translation of Book 2 of Dialogi de vita. "STC 12350." Reprint of 1638 ed. Includes A short treatise touching the confraternitie of the scapular of St. Benedicts Order, published in 1639. [BX1750.A1E5 vol. 294] [BX4700.B3] 271'.1'024 B 76-380157 ISBN 0-85967-295-6
1. Benedictus, Saint, Abbot of Monte Cassino. 2. Christian saints—Italy—Biography. 3. Benedictines. I. Fursdon, Cuthbert. II. Batt, Anthony. A short treatise touching the confraternitie of the scapular of St. Benedicts Order. 1976. III. Title. IV. Series.

GUARDINI, Romano, 1885- 230.2
The Faith and modern man; translated from the German by Charlotte E. Forsyth. [New York] Pantheon Books [1952] 166p. 21cm. Translation of Glaubenserkenntnis. [BX1751.G8513] 52-10121
1. Catholic Church—Apologetic works. I. Title.

GUERRY, Emile Maurice, 230.2
Abp., 1891-
In the whole Christ; prayerful meditations on the mystery of the church. Translated from French by M. G. Carroll. New York, Society of St. Paul [1959] 351p. 22cm. [BX2183.G7413 1959] 59-10133
1. Meditations. 2. Jesus—Christ— Mystical body. I. Title.

GUERRY, Emile Maurice, 230.2
Abp., 1891-
In the whole Christ; prayerful meditations on the mystery of the church. Tr. from French by M. G. Carroll. Staten Island, N. Y., Alba [1963] 351p. 22cm. 63-3510 4.00
1. Meditations. 2. Jesus Christ—Mystical body. I. Title.

GUZIE, Tad W. 230.2
For adult Catholics only [by] Tad W. Guzie. Milwaukee, Bruce Pub. Co. [1969] 111 p. 21 cm. [BX1754.G8] 69-17920 1.75 (pbk)
1. Catholic Church—Doctrinal and controversial works, Popular. I. Title.

HALLETT, Garth. 230'.2
Darkness and light : the analysis of doctrinal statements / by Garth L. Hallett. New York : Paulist Press, c1975. vi, 174 p. ; 23 cm. Includes bibliographical references. [BX1753.H23] 75-21734 ISBN 0-8091-1897-1 pbk. : 6.95
1. Wittgenstein, Ludwig, 1889-1951. 2. Religion and language. 3. Theology, Catholic. I. Title.

HARDING, Thomas, 1516- 230'.2 s
1572.
A briefe answere : 1565 / Thomas Harding.Apologia Cardinalis Bellarmini : 1611 / Thomas Preston [i.e. R. Widdrington]. Ilkley [Eng.] : Scolar Press, 1976. [28], 359 p. ; 20 cm. (English recusant literature, 1558-1640 ; v. 309) (Series: Rogers, David Morrison, comp. English recusant literature, 1558-1640 ; v. 309.) Reprint of the 1565 ed. of T. Harding's work, in English, printed by Aegid, Diest, Antverpiae (Antwerp), and the 1611 ed. of T. Preston's work, in Latin, printed by Apud Theophilum Pratum, Cosmopoli. Includes bibliographical references. [BX1750.A1E5 vol. 309] 230'.2 77-351854 ISBN 0-85967-321-9
1. Catholic Church—Doctrinal and controversial works—Catholic authors. 2. Jewel, John, Bp. of Salisbury, 1522-1571. 3. Bellarmino, Roberto Francesco Romolo, Saint, 1542-1621. I. Widdrington, Roger, 1563-1640. Apologia Cardinalis Bellarmini. 1976. II. Title. III. Series.

HARDING, Thomas, 1516- 230'.2 s
1572.
A confutation of a booke intituled An apologie of the Church of England / Thomas Harding. Ilkley [Eng.] : Scolar Press, 1976. 734 p. in various pagings ; 21 cm. (English recusant literature, 1558-1640 ; v. 310) (Series: Rogers, David Morrison, comp. English recusant literature, 1558-1640 ; v. 310.) Reprint of the 1565 ed. published by Ihon Laet, Antwerpe [i.e. Antwerp] "STC 12762." [BX1750.A1E5 vol. 310] [BX5130] 283'.42 76-380275 ISBN 0-85967-322-7
1. Jewel, John, Bp. of Salisbury, 1522-1571. Apologia Ecclesiae Anglicanae. 2. Church of England—Doctrinal and controversial works. I. Jewel, John, Bp. of Salisbury, 1522-1571. Apologia Ecclesiae Anglicanae. II. Title. III. Series.

HARDING, Thomas, 1516- 230'.2 s
1572.
A reiondre to M. Iewels replie, 1566 / Thomas Harding. Ilkley [Eng.] : Scolar Press, 1976. 315 p. ; 22 cm. (English recusant literature ; v. 303) (Series: Rogers, David Morrison, comp. English recusant literature, 1558-1640 ; v. 303.) Reprint of the 1566 ed. published by Ioannis Fouleri, Antverpiae (Antwerp). S.T.C. 12760. [BX1750.A1E5 Vol. 303] [BX2230] 265'.3 76-375713 ISBN 0-85967-310-3

1. Mass—Early works to 1800. I. Jewel, John, Bp. of Salisbury, 1522-1571. II. Title. III. Series.

HARDON, John A. 230'.2
The Catholic catechism / John A. Hardon. 1st ed. Garden City, N.Y. : Doubleday, 1975. 623 p. ; 22 cm. Includes bibliographical references and index. [BX1751.2.H36] 73-81433 ISBN 0-385-08039-5 : 9.95
1. Catholic Church—Doctrinal and controversial works—Catholic authors. 2. Theology, Catholic. I. Title.

HARENBERG, Werner, 1929- 230.2
Der Spiegel on the New Testament; a guide to the struggle between radical and conservative in European university and parish. Translated by James H. Brutness. [New York] Macmillan [1970] x, 246 p. 21 cm. Translation of Jesus und die Kirchen. A series of articles which appeared in Der Spiegel in 1960. Bibliography: p. [240]-246. [BT202.H27513] 75-99022 6.95
1. Jesus Christ—Person and offices—Addresses, essays, lectures. 2. Theology, Doctrinal—Addresses, essays, lectures. I. Title.

HARVEY, Rudolf John, 1910- 230'.2
Uncommon sense / Rudolf Harvey. Huntington, Ind. : Our Sunday Visitor, c1975. 256 p. ; 21 cm. Includes index. [BX1754.H38] ISBN 0-87973-787-5 -87973-787-5 pbk. : 2.50
1. Catholic Church—Doctrinal and controversial works—Catholic authors. 2. Meditations. I. Title.

HASTINGS, Cecily. 230.2
Questions and answers: Catholic evidence. New York, Sheed and Ward [1956] 245p. 21cm. [BX1754.H39] 56-6125
1. Catholic Church—Doctrinal and controversial works, Popular. 2. Questions and answers—Theology. I. Title. II. Title: Catholic evidence.

HAYES, Edward J 230.2
Catholicism and reason, by Edward J. Hayes and Paul J. Hayes. [1st ed.] New York, Vantage Press [1961] 137p. illus. 22cm. Includes bibliography. [BX1752.H3] 60-11702
1. Catholic Church—Apologetic works. I. Hayes, Paul James, 1922- joint author. II. Title.

HAYES, Edward J. 230'.2
Catholicism & reason [by] Edward J. Hayes, Paul J. Hayes & James J. Drummey. Huntington, Ind., Our Sunday Visitor, inc. [1973] 256 p. illus. 21 cm. Bibliography: p. [247]-254. [BX1752.H3 1973] 72-97853 ISBN 0-87973-839-1 4.95
1. Catholic Church—Apologetic works. I. Hayes, Paul James, 1922- joint author. II. Drummey, James J., joint author. III. Title.

HAYES, Edward J 230.2
Three keys to happiness, by Edward and Paul Hayes. Buffalo, Society of Saint Paul [c1952] 308p. 22cm. [BX1754.H42] 57-33559
1. Catholic Church—Doctrinal and controversial works, Popular. I. Hayes, Paul James, 1922- joint author. II. Title.

HAYES, Edward J 230.2
Three keys to happiness, by Edward and Paul Hayes. Index by Ellen Varbel and Florence McElligott. [2d ed.] New York, St. Paul Publications [1961?] 317p. 19cm. [BX1754.H42 1961] 61-13085
1. Catholic Church—Doctrinal and controversial works, Popular. I. Hayes, Paul James, 1922- joint author. II. Title.

HEENAN, John Carmel, Cardinal, 1905- 230.2
The Faith makes sense. New York, Sheed & Ward, 1948. 274 p. 21 cm. [BX1752.H4] 48-9281
1. Catholic Church—Apologetic works. 2. Apologetics—20th cent. I. Title.

HENRY, A. M., ed. 230.2
Theology library, by a group of theologians under the editorship of A. M. Henry; translated by William Storey [and others] Chicago, Fides Publishers Association [1954-58] 6 v. in 7. illus. 20 cm. Translation of Initiation theologique. Contents.v. 1. Introduction to theology. -- Supplementary vol.: Chronology. -- v. 2. God and His creation. -- v. 3. Man and his happiness. -- v. 4. The virtues and states of life. -- v. 5. The historical and mystical Christ. -- v. 6. Christ in His Sacraments. Includes bibliographies. [BX1751.I53] 54-10891
1. Catholic Church — Doctrinal and controversial works. I. Title.

HESBURGH, Theodore Martin, 1917- 230.2
God and the world of man. [2d ed.] Notre Dame, Ind., University of Notre Dame Press [1960] 249p. 24cm. (University religion series. Theology for the layman) [BX1754.H48 1960] 60-8647
1. Catholic Church—Doctrinal and controversial works—Catholic authors. I. Title.

HESBURGH, Theodore Martin, 1917- 230.2
God and the world of man. Notre Dame, University of Notre Dame Press [1950] viii, 318 p. 24 cm. (University religion series. Texts in theologyfor the layman) Bibliography: p. 307-310. [BX1754.H48] 51-3638
1. Catholic Church—Doctrinal and controversial works—Catholic authors. I. Title. II. Series: University religion series

HESKYNS, Thomas. 230'.2 s
The parliament of Chryste, 1566 / Thomas Heskyns. Ilkley [Eng.] : Scolar Press, 1976. Ca. 850 p. ; 27 cm. (English recusant literature, 1558-1640 ; v. 313) (Series: Rogers, David Morrison, comp. English recusant literature, 1558-1640 ; v. 313.) Reprint of the 1566 ed. published by W. Silvius, Antwerp from a copy in the library of Downside Abbey. STC 13250/13842. Includes index. [BX1750.A1E5 vol. 313] [BX2215] 265'.3 77-350532 ISBN 0-85967-325-1
1. Lord's Supper—Catholic Church. I. Title. II. Series.

HIGGINS, Thomas J., 1899- 230.2
Dogma for the layman. Milwaukee, Bruce [c.1961] 218p. 61-17437 3.95
1. Catholic Church—Doctrinal and controversial works, Popular. I. Title.

HILL, Thomas, 1564-1644. 230'.2 s
A plaine path-way to heaven / Thomas Hill. Ilkley [Eng.] : Scolar Press, 1976. 2 v. ; 20 cm. (English recusant literature, 1558-1640 ; v. 324-325) (Series: Rogers, David Morrison, comp. English recusant literature, 1558-1640 ; v. 324-325.) Reprint of the 1634 and 1637 ed. Contents.Contents.—pt. 1. Advent sondaie unto Easter.—pt 2. From Easter untill advent Sonday. [BX1750.A1E5 vol. 324-325] [BX2170.C55] 242'.3 77-355605 ISBN 0-85967-339-1 (v. 1)
1. Church year—Meditations. I. Title. II. Series.

HIRE, Richard P. 230'.2
Our Christian faith : one, holy, catholic, and apostolic / Richard P. Hire. Huntington, IN : Our Sunday Visitor, c1977. 320 p. ; 21 cm. [BX1751.2.H57] 76-56918 ISBN 0-87973-855-3 pbk. : 4.95
1. Theology, Catholic. I. Title.

HISLOP, Alexander, 1807-1865. 230.2
The two Babylons; or, The papal worship proved to be the worship of Nimrod and his wife. With 61 woodcut illus. from Ninevah, Babylon, Egypt, Pompeii, etc. New York, Loizeaux Bros. [1953] 330 p. illus. 22 cm. [BX1765.H45 1953] 54-39027
1. Catholic Church—Doctrinal and controversial works—Protestant authors. 2. Papacy. I. Title.

HOPKINS, Jasper. 230'.2
A companion to the study of St. Anselm. Minneapolis, University of Minnesota Press [1972] ix, 291 p. 24 cm. Cover title: Study of St. Anselm. Appendixes (p. [213]-253): 1. Anselm's Philosophical fragments.—2. Anselm's Methods of arguing. Bibliography: p. 260-275. [BX4700.A58H66 1972] 72-79097 ISBN 0-8166-0657-9 10.50
1. Anselm, Saint, Abp. of Canterbury, 1033-1109. I. Title. II. Title: Study of St. Anselm.

HORVATH, Tibor, 1927(July28)- 230'.2
Faith under scrutiny / Tibor Horvath. Notre Dame, Ind. : Fides Publishers, [1975] p. cm. Includes bibliographical references. [BT1102.H67] 75-11797 ISBN 0-8190-0073-6 : 6.00
1. Catholic Church—Apologetic works. 2. Apologetics—20th century. I. Title.

HOUGHTON, Walter Edwards, 1904- 230.2
The art of Newman's Apologia, by Walter E. Houghton. [Hamden, Conn.] Archon Books, 1970 [c1945] ix, 116 p. port. 21 cm. Includes bibliographical references. [BX4705.N5A38 1970] 78-120369
1. Newman, John Henry, Cardinal, 1801-1890. Apologia pro vita sua. I. Title.

HUGHES, Philip, 1895- 230.2
The Catholic faith in practice. [1st American ed.] Wilkes-Barre, Pa., Dimension Books [1965] vii, 285 p. 21 cm. First ed. published in London in 1938 under title: The faith in practice; Catholic doctrine and life. [BX11751.H84] 65-25560
1. Catholic Church—Doctrinal and controversial works—Catholic authors. 2. Christian life—Catholic authors. I. Title.

HUGHES, Philip, 1895- 230.2
The Catholic faith in practice. [1st Amer. ed.] Wilkes-Barre, Pa., Dimension Bks. [c.1965] viii, 285p. 21cm. First ed. pub. in London in 1938 under title: The faith in practice; Catholic doctrine and life. [BX1751.H84] 65-25560 5.95
1. Catholic Church—Doctrinal and controversial works—Catholic authors. 2. Christian life—Catholic authors. I. Title.

HUNT, Marigold. 230.2
St. Patrick's summer. New York, Sheed and Ward, 1950. viii, 273 p. illus. 22 cm. [BX1754.H86] 50-9857
1. Catholic Church—Doctrinal and controversial works, Popular. I. Title.

JOANNES XXIII, Pope, 1881-1963. 230.2
The teachings of Pope John XXIII. Edited by Michael Chinigo. Translated from the Italian by Arthur A. Coppotelli. [1st American ed. New York] Grosset & Dunlap [1967] 300 p. 20 cm. "A Giniger book." Translation of Gli insegnamenti di Papa Giovanni. [BX891.J5713] 66-25714
1. Catholic Church—Addresses, essays, lectures. I. Chinigo, Michael, ed. II. Title.

JOURNET, Charles. 230.2
What is dogma? Translated from the French by Mark Pontifex. [1st ed.] New York, Hawthorn Books [1964] 109 p. 21 cm. (The Twentieth century encyclopedia of Catholicism, v. 4. Section 1: Knowledge and faith) Translation of Le dogme, chemin de la fol. Bibliography: p. [110]-111. [BT19.J613] 64-14160
1. Dogma. I. Title. II. Series. III. Series: The Twentieth century encyclopedia of Catholicism, v. 4

JOURNET, Charles 230.2
What is dogma? Tr. from French by Mark Pontifex. New York, Hawthorn [c.1964] 109p. 21cm. (Twentieth cent. ency. of Catholicism, v.4. Section 1: Knowledge and faith) Bibl. 64-14160 3.50 bds.,
1. Dogma. I. Title. II. Series: The Twentieth century encyclopedia of Catholicism, v.4

KALE, Roy Addison. 230.2
Only one true church? An historical study of the exclusive claims of the Roman Catholic Church. New York, Vantage Press [1954] 104p. 22cm. [BX1765.K2] 54-9814
1. Catholic Church—Doctrinal and controversial works—Protestant authors. 2. Church. I. Title.

KASCHMITTER, William A. 230'.2
The spirituality of Vatican II : conciliar texts concerning the spiritual life of all Christians / assembled and annotated by William A. Kaschmitter. Huntington, Ind. : Our Sunday Visitor, inc., [1975] 271 p. ; 24 cm. Includes index. [BX1747.5.K37] 74-29344 ISBN 0-87973-868-5 : 7.95
1. Vatican Council. 2d, 1962-1965. 2. Theology, Catholic—Collected works. I. Vatican Council. 2d, 1962-1965. II. Title.

KAVANAUGH, James J. 230'.2
A modern priest looks at his outdated church, by James Kavanaugh. New York, Trident Press, 1967. xiii, 190 p. 22 cm. Bibliographical references included in "Notes" (p. 180-190) [BX1751.2.K34] 67-23591
1. Catholic Church—Doctrinal and controversial works—Catholic authors. I. Title.

KEKEISEN, Robert E 230.2
Ask and learn; questions and answers on the life of the Church. With a foreword by Matthew Smith. Westminster, Md., Newman Press, 1957. 293p. 22cm. [BX1754.K34] 57-11819
1. Catholic Church—Doctrinal and controversial works, Popular. 2. Questions and answers —Theology. I. Title.

KELLEY, Bennet. 230'.2
Catholic faith today : a simple presentation of Catholic thought based on modern Bible studies, Church history, and the Second Vatican Council / by Bennet Kelley. New York : Catholic Book Pub. Co., c1976. 158 p. : ill. ; 21 cm. [BX1961.K43] 77-151263
1. Catholic Church—Catechisms and creeds—English. I. Title.

KILLGALLON, James, 1914- 230.2
Life in Christ; instructions in the Catholic faith [by] James Killgallon and Gerard Weber. Chicago [1959, c1958] 286p. illus. 20cm. Includes bibliography. [BX1754.K518] 59-2559
1. Catholic Church—Doctrinal and controversial works, Popular. I. Weber, Gerard, 1918- joint author. II. Title.

KILLGALLON, James, 1914- 230.2
You are the Church. Westminster, Md., Newman Pr. [c.]1961. 136p. 61-16571 2.95
1. Catholic Church—Doctrinal and controversial works, Popular. I. Title.

KILLGALLON, James J 1914- 230.2
Life in Christ; instructions in the Catholic faith [by] James Killgallon and Gerard Weber. Chicago [1959, c1958] 286 p. illus. 20 cm. Includes bibliography. [BX1754.K518] 59-2559
1. Catholic Church — Doctrinal and controversial works, Popular. I. Weber, Gerard P., 1918- joint author. II. Title.

KILLGALLON, James J., 1914- 230'.2
Life in Christ / James Killgallon, Gerard Weber, and Leonard Ziegmann. 2d ed. Chicago : Life in Christ, 1976. 280 p. ; 19 cm. [BX1754.3.K54 1976] 76-26451 ISBN 0-914070-08-8 pbk. : 1.95
1. Catholic Church—Doctrinal and controversial works, Popular. I. Weber, Gerad P., 1918- joint author. II. Ziegmann, Leonard, joint author. III. Title.

KNOX, Ronald Arbuthnott, 1888- 230.2
In soft garments; a collection of Oxford conferences. [2d ed.] New York, Sheed & Ward [1953] 214p. 22cm. [BX1751] 56-3335
1. Catholic Church—Apologetic works. I. Title.

*KNOX, Ronald Arbuthnott, 1888-1957 230.2
In soft garments. Garden City, N.Y., Doubleday [1964] 200p. 18cm. (Image bk., D166) .75 pap.,
1. Catholic Church—Doctrinal works—Addresses, essays, lectures. I. Title.

KUNG, Hans, 1928- 230.2
That the world may believe. Translated by Cecily Hastings. New York, Sheed and Ward [1963] 149 p. 20 cm. [BX1754.K78] 63-10676
1. Questions and answers — Theology. 2. Catholic Church — Apologetic works. I. Title.

KUNG, Hans, 1928- 230.2
That the world may believe. Tr. by Cecily Hastings. New York, Sheed [c.1963] 149p. 20cm. 63-10676 3.00 bds.,
1. Questions and answers—Theology. 2. Catholic Church—Apologetic works. I. Title.

LAMBERT, Orlando Clayton, 1890- 230.2
Catholicism against itself. Abridged. Winfield, Ala., Fair Haven Publishers, 1963- v. 17 cm. Complete ed. first published in 1954 under title: Roman Catholicism against itself. [BX1765.L2552] 63-17090
1. Catholic Church—Doctrinal and controversial works—Protestant authors. I. Title.

LAMBERT, Orlando Clayton, 1890- 230.2
Roman Catholicism against itself, by O. C. Lambert. Winfield, Ala. [1954-65] 2 v. illus., ports. 24 cm. Cover title: Catholicism against itself. Includes bibliographies. [BX1765.L255] 55-16841
1. Catholic Church — Doctrinal and controversial works — Protestant authors. I. Title. II. Title: Catholicism against itself.

LANG, Martin A. 230'.2
The inheritance: what Catholics believe, by Martin A. Lang. Dayton, Ohio, G. A. Pflaum, 1970. 128 p. illus. 18 cm. (Christian identity series) (Witness book, CI 7) Bibliography: p. 124-125. [BX1751.2.L34] 71-114723 0.95
1. Theology, Catholic. I. Title.

LASH, Nicholas. 230'.2
Newman on development : the search for an explanation in history / Nicholas Lash. Shepherdstown, W. Va. : Patmos Press, 1975. xiii, 264 p. ; 23 cm. Includes indexes. Bibliography: p. [209]-243. [BT21.L3] 75-16649 ISBN 0-915762-01-3 : 17.50
1. Newman, John Henry, Cardinal, 1801-1890. An essay on the development of Christian doctrine. 2. Catholic Church—Doctrinal and controversial works—Catholic authors. 3. Dogma, Development of. I. Title.

LAWRENCE, Emeric Anthony, 1908- 230'.2
Understanding our neighbor's faith / by Emeric A. Lawrence. Collegeville, Minn. : Liturgical Press, c1975. xii, 281 p. ; 20 cm. Includes bibliographical references. [BX1751.2.L38] 76-353618 ISBN 0-8146-0868-X
1. Catholic Church—Doctrinal and controversial works—Catholic authors. 2. Protestantism. I. Title.

LEVY, Rosalie Marie, 1889- 230.2
What do you think of Christ 7th, rev. ed. [Boston] St. Paul Eds. [dist. Daughters of St. Paul, c.1962] xviii, 92p. front. 22cm. 62-18506 1.50; 1.00 pap.,
1. Catholic Church—Doctrinal and controversial works. 2. Jews—Converts to Christianity. I. Title.

LEVY, Rosalie Marie, 1889- 230.2
What think you of Christ? 7th and rev. ed. [Boston] St. Paul Editions [1962] xviii, 92p. front. 22cm. First ed. published in 1919 under title: The heavenly road. [BX1755.L5 1962] 62-18506
1. Catholic Church—Doctrinal and controversial works. 2. Jews—Converts to Christianity. I. Title.

LINDBECK, George A. 230.2
The future of Roman Catholic theology; Vatican II - catalyst for change [by] George A. Lindbeck. Philadelphia, Fortress Press [1970] xvi, 125 p. 22 cm. Includes bibliographical references. [BX830 1962.L513] 75-83678 4.75
1. Vatican Council. 2d, 1962-65. 2. Catholic Church—Relations—Protestant churches. 3. Theology, Catholic. 4. Protestant churches—Relations—Catholic Church. I. Title.

LINK, Mark J 230.2
We are God's people [by] Mark J. Link. Chicago, Loyola University Press [1966] ix. 226 p. illus. 24 cm. [BX930.L4858] 66-5787
1. Religious education — Text-books for youth — Catholic. I. Title.

LINK, Mark J. 230.2
We are God's people. Chicago, Loyola [c.1966] ix, 226p. illus. 24cm. [BX930.L4858] 66-5787 3.00
1. Religious education—Text-books for youth—Catholic I. Title.

LOGAL, Nelson William, 230'.2
1910-
On the rubble of renewal : a pastoral lament / Nelson W. Logal. Chicago : Franciscan Herald Press, c1975. ix, 120 p. ; 22 cm. [BX1751.2.L63] 75-5508 ISBN 0-8199-0563-1 : 6.95
1. Catholic Church—Doctrinal and controversial works—Catholic authors. 2. Catholic Church—History—1965- I. Title.

LONERGAN, Bernard J. F. 230'.2
Collection; papers by Bernard Lonergan. Edited by F. E. Crowe. [New York] Herder and Herder [1967] xxxv. 280 p. 22 cm. Includes bibliographical references. [BX891.L64] 67-13294
1. Catholic Church — Collected works. 2. Theology — Collected works — 20th cent. I. Title.

LONERGAN, Bernard J. F. 230'.2
Philosophy of God, and theology, by Bernard J. F. Lonergan. Philadelphia, Westminster Press [1974, c1973] xi, 74 p. 22 cm. Lectures delivered at the St. Michael's Jesuit School of Philosophy and Letters, Gonzaga University in the fall of 1972. Includes bibliographical references. [BT102.L57 1974] 73-22011 ISBN 0-664-20888-6 4.50
1. God. 2. Theology, Doctrinal. 3. Philosophy and religion. I. Title.

LONERGAN, Bernard J. F. 230'.2
Collection; papers by Bernard Lonergan. Ed. by F. E. Crowe. [New York] Herder & Herder [1967] xxxv, 280p. 22cm. Bibl. [BX891.L64] 67-13294 8.50
1. Catholic Church—Collected works. 2. Theology—Collected works— 20th cent. I. Title.

LUBAC, Henri de, 1896- 230.2
Further paradoxes. Translated from the French by Ernest Beaumont. London, Longmans, Green; Westminster, Md., Newman Press [1958] x, 128p. 19cm. [BX1755.L913] A58
1. Catholic Church—Doctrinal and controversial works—Catholic authors. I. Title.

MCBRIEN, Richard P. 230.2
What do we really believe? [by] Richard P. McBrien. Dayton, Ohio, G. A. Pflaum [1969] 123, [2] p. illus. 17 cm. (Christian experience series, no. 6) (Witness books, W-9.) Bibliography: p. [125] [BX1751.2.M25] 69-20295
1. Catholic Church—Doctrinal and controversial works—Catholic authors. 2. Discussion in Christian education. I. Title.

MCCARTHY, John, 1909- 230.2
Problems in theology. Westminister, Md., Newman Press [1956- v. 22cm. Contents.v.1. The sacraments. [BX1751.M14] 57-8610
1. Questions and answers—Theology. 2. Catholic Church—Doctrinal and controversial works. I. Title.

MCCARTHY, John, 1909- 230.2
Problems in theology. vol. II. Westminster, Md., Newman Press, 1960. 22cm. Contents.v. 2, The commandments. 57-8610 7.50
1. Questions and answers—Theology. 2. Catholic Church—Doctrinal and controversial works. I. Title.

MCCOOL, Gerald A. 230'.2
Catholic theology in the nineteenth century : the quest for a unitary method / Gerald A. McCool. New York : Seabury Press, 1977. p. cm. "A Crossroad book." Includes bibliographical references and index. [BX1747.M25] 76-30493 ISBN 0-8164-0339-2 : 14.95
1. Theology, Catholic—History. 2. Theology, Doctrinal—History—19th century. I. Title.

MCKENZIE, John L. 230.2
The power and the wisdom; an interpretation of the New Testament, by John L. McKenzie. Milwaukee, Bruce Pub. Co. [1965] xvi, 300 p. 23 cm. [BS2361.2.M2] 65-20338
1. Bible. N.T.—Criticism, interpretation, etc. I. Title.

MCKENZIE, Leon. 230.2
Process catechetics; basic directions for catechists. Paramus, N.J., Paulist Press [1970] v, 106 p. 18 cm. (Deus books) Includes bibliographical references. [BR115.H5M23] 75-112659 1.45 (pbk)
1. History (Theology) I. Title.

MCKENZIE, John L. 230'.2
Did I say that? By John L. McKenzie. [Chicago] Thomas More Press [1973] 222 p. 24 cm. "The material in this book appeared in different form in the Critic magazine." [BX1751.2.M255] 73-163352 ISBN 0-88347-026-8 7.95
1. Catholic Church—Doctrinal and controversial works—Catholic authors. I. Title.

MACKEY, James Patrick 230.2
The modern theology of tradition. [New York] Herder & Herder [1963, c.1962] 219p. 23cm. Bibl. 62-19789 4.75
1. Tradition (Theology) I. Title.

MCLOUGHLIN, Emmett 230.2
American culture and Catholic schools. New York, Lyle Stuart [c.1960] 288p. Bibl.: p.273-276 21cm. 60-1141 4.95
1. Catholic Church—Doctrinal and controversial works—Miscellaneous authors. 2. Catholic Church in the U. S.—Education. I. Title.

MCLOUGHLIN, Emmett, 1907- 230.2
American culture and Catholic schools. [1st ed.] New York, L. Stuart [1960] 288 p. 21 cm. Includes bibliography. [BX1770.M17] 60-11141
1. Catholic Church—Doctrinal and controversial works—Miscellaneous authors. 2. Catholic Church in the U.S.—Education. I. Title.

MACLOUGHLIN, James. 230.2
Catholic faith in outline, a summary of instruction; a guide for preacher and teacher. Westminster, Md., Newman Press [1956] 298p. 22cm. [BX1751.M22] 56-11430
1. Catholic Church —Doctrinal and controversial works. I. Title.

MAKRAKES, Apostolos, 1831- 230.2
1905.
The innovations of the Roman Church; based on the reply of the great church of Constantinople to the encyclical issued by Pope Leo XIII in 1894 concerning the union of the churches. [2d ed. Chicago, Orthodox Christian Educational Society, 1966] 82 p. 23 cm. The main text has been taken from the periodical Logos. Includes bibliographical references. [BX1765.M263] 67-9691
1. Catholic Church—Doctrinal and controversial works—Orthodox Eastern authors. I. Title.

MAKRAKES, Apostolos, 1831- 230.2
1905.
The innovations of the Roman Church; based on the reply of the great church of Constantinople to the encyclical issued by Pope Leo XIII in 1894 concerning the union of the churches. [2d ed. Chicago, Orthodox Christian Educational Society, 1966] 82 p. 23 cm. The main text has been taken from the periodical Logos. Includes bibliographical references. [BX1765.M263 1966] 67-9691
1. Catholic Church—Doctrinal and controversial works—Orthodox Eastern authors. I. Title.

MANTON, Joseph E., 1904- 230'.2
Stay with us, Lord / Joseph Manton. Huntington, Ind. : Our Sunday Visitor, inc., c1975. 192 p. ; 21 cm. [BX1751.2.M317] 74-28505 ISBN 0-87973-786-7 : 2.95
1. Catholic Church—Doctrinal and controversial works—Catholic authors. I. Title.

MARIA triumphans / 230'.2 s
[by] N. N. Ilkley [Eng.] : Scolar Press, 1976. [6], 336 p. : 1 ill. ; 20 cm. (English recusant literature, 1558-1640 ; v. 283) (Series: Rogers, David Morrison, comp. English recusant literature, 1558-1640 ; v. 283.) Reprint of the 1635 ed. [BX1750.A1E5 vol. 283] [BT600] 232.91 76-381621 ISBN 0-85967-284-0 : £10.00
1. Mary, Virgin—Early works to 1800. I. N. N. II. N., N. III. Series.

MARITAIN, Jacques, 1882- 230'.2
Ransoming the time. Translated by Harry Lorin Binsse. New York, Gordian Press, 1972 [c1941] xii, 322 p. 22 cm. Published in 1943 under title: Redeeming the time. Includes bibliographical references. [BX890.M28 1972] 70-165665 ISBN 0-87752-153-0
1. Catholic Church—Addresses, essays, lectures. 2. Bergson, Henri Louis, 1859-1941—Addresses, essays, lectures. I. Title.

MARTHA-MARIE 230.2
Peace through spirituality? Tr. from German by Rudolph Weiss. New York, Comet [c.]1961 306p. (Reflection bk.) 4.00
1. Catholic Church—Apologetic works. I. Title.

MARTINDALE, Cyril Charlie, 230.2
1879-
The faith of the Roman Church, New York, Sheed & Ward, 1951 [c1950] x, 134 p. 20 cm. [BX1751.M37 1950a] 51-2142
1. Catholic Church—Doctrinal and controversial works—Catholic authors. I. Title.

MASTERSON, Reginald, ed. 230.2
Theology in the Catholic college. Dubuque, Iowa, Priory Press, Asbury Rd. [c.1961] 343p. Bibl. 61-11123 3.95
1. Theology—Study and teaching—U. S. 2. Theology—Study and teaching—Catholic Church. 3. Universities and colleges—Curricula. I. Title.

MATTHEW, Tobie, Sir, 230'.2 s
1577-1655.
The widdowes mite [by] Sir Tobie Matthew ; [and] A treatise of the holy sacrifice of the masse / [by] Antonio de Molina ; [translated from the Spanish by John Floyd]. Ilkley [etc.] : Scolar Press, 1976. [12], 199 p., [18], 288 p. ; 20 cm. (English recusant literature, 1558-1640 ; v. 284) (Series: Rogers, David Morrison, comp. English recusant literature, 1558-1640 ; v. 284.) Matthew's work reprinted from a copy in the library of Heythrop College of the 1619 ed.; references: Allison and Rogers 539; STC 11490. Molina's work reprinted from a copy in the library of Heythrop College of the 1623 ed.; references: Allison and Rogers 547; STC 18001. [BX1750.A1E5 Vol. 284] [BT600] 232.91 77-354219 ISBN 0-85967-285-9 : £10.00
1. Mary, Virgin—Early works to 1800. 2. Mass. I. Molina, Antonio de, d. 1619? A treatise of the holy sacrifice of the masse. English. 1976. II. Title. III. Series.

MAURIAC, Francois, 1885- 230.2
The stumbling block. New York, Philosophical Library [1952] 83 p. 19 cm. [BX1779.5.M313] 52-8393
1. Catholic Church—Doctrinal and controversial works—Catholic authors. I. Title.

MAYNARD, Theodore, 1890- 230.2
The Catholic way. New York, Appleton-Century-Crofts [1952] 302 p. 21 cm. [BX1754.M37] 52-14347
1. Catholic Church—Doctrinal and controversial works, Popular. I. Title.

MEER, Frederik van der, 230.2
1904-
The faith of the Catholic Church; theology for the layman [by] F. van der Meer. Tr. by John Murray. Wilkes-Barre, Pa., Dimension Bks. [1966] xi, 580p. 22cm. Tr. of Catechismus [BX1754.M4213] 66-17194 9.95
1. Catholic Church—Doctrinal and controversial works, Popular. I. Title.

**MESSAGE of joy (The);* 230.2
An elementary reader for religious instruction [Tr. from German by Desmond A. D'Abreo, illus. by Johannes Gruger. New York. Herder & Herder, 1965, c.1964] 85p. illus. (pt. col.) 21cm. 1.50 pap.,

MILLER, Charles R. 230.2
A dominant Romanism; its religious and political significance. New York, Vantage Press [c.1959] 112p. 21cm. (bibl.) 2.75 bds., *I. Title.*

MILLER, Charles Richard, 230.2
1880-
A dominant Romanism: its religious and political significance. [1st ed.] New York, Vantage Press [c1959] 112p. 22cm. Includes bibliography. [BX1765.2.M5] 60-2609
1. Catholic Church—Doctrinal and controversial works—Protestant authors. I. Title.

MODERN questions, timeless 230'.2
answers / answers by Kenneth Ryan and J. D. Conway. New York : Pillar Books, 1976. 320 p. ; 18 cm. [BX1754.3.M62] 76-15938 ISBN 0-89129-162-8 pbk. : 1.95
1. Catholic Church—Doctrinal and controversial works, Popular. I. Ryan, Kenneth. II. Conway, John Donald, 1905-

MODRAS, Ronald E. 230'.2
Paul Tillich's theology of the church : a Catholic appraisal / by Ronald E. Modras ; with a foreword by Hans Kung. Detroit : Wayne State University Press, 1976. p. cm. Includes index. Bibliography: p. [BV598.M6] 76-6082 ISBN 0-8143-1552-6 : 17.50
1. Tillich, Paul, 1886-1965. 2. Church—History of doctrines—20th century. I. Title.

MOELLER, Charles. 230.2
Modern mentality and evangelization. Translated by E. Mike-Bekassy. Staten Island, N.Y., Alba House [1968, c1967-68] 3 v. 22 cm. Mainly articles from the periodical Lumen vitae. Contents.Contents.—pt. 1. God.—pt. 2. The church.—pt. 3. Jesus & Mary. Bibliographical footnotes. [BX1751.2.M6] 68-15380 2.95 (v. 1) varies
1. Catholic Church—Doctrinal and controversial works—Catholic authors. I. Lumen vitae. II. Title.

MOONEY, Christopher F., 230.2
1925-
Teilhard de Chardin and the mystery of Christ. Garden City, N. Y., Doubleday [1968, c1964] 318 p. (Image books, D252) Bibliography: p. [289]-304. [B2430.T34M606]
1. Teilhard de Chardin, Pierre. I. Title.

MOORE, Sebastian, 1917- 230'.2
God is a new language. Westminster, Md., New man Press [1967] 184 p. 20 cm. [BX1754.M67] 67-18308
1. Catholic Church — Doctrinal and controversial works. Popular. I. Title.

MOORE, Sebastian, 1917- 230.2
God is a new language. Westminster, Md., Newman Press [1967] 184 p. 20 cm. [BX1754.M67] 67-18308
1. Catholic Church—Doctrinal and controversial works, Popular. I. Title.

MORE, Paul Elmer, 1864- 230'.2
1937.
The Catholic faith. Port Washington, N.Y., Kennikat Press [1972, c1931] 312 p. 21 cm. Original ed. issued in his series: The Greek tradition. Includes bibliographical references. [BR85.M63 1972] 70-159094 ISBN 0-8046-1637-X
1. Christianity—Addresses, essays, lectures. I. Title.

MORRISS, Frank. 230'.2
The conservative imperative. Denver, CLA Publishers [1970] ii, 144 p. 18 cm. [BX1753.M66] 71-119529 2.00
1. Catholic Church—Doctrinal and controversial works—Catholic authors. 2. Conservation. I. Title.

MULLER, Martin M 230.2
God, religion and faith; a study of the reasons behind faith, for Catholics and non-Catholics, by Martin M. Muller [1st ed.] New York, Exposition Press [1965] xvi, 141 p. illus. 22 cm. (An Exposition-testament book) [BX1751.2.M8] 65-5022
1. Catholic Church — Apologetic works. 2. Theology, Doctrinal. I. Title.

MULLER, Martin M. 230.2
God, religion and faith; a study of the reasons behind faith, for Catholics and non-Catholics. New York, Exposition [c.1965] xvi. 141p. illus. 22cm. (Exposition-testament bk.) [BX1751.2.M8] 65-5022 4.50
1. Catholic Church—Apologetic works. 2. Theology, Doctrinal. I. Title.

MURRAY, Jane Marie, 1896- 230.2
The Christian life series [by] Jane Marie Murray and Vincent J. Giese. Confraternity ed. Chicago, Fides Publishers Association [1959-61] 4v. illus. 23cm. Books 2 and 4 by J. M. Murray and T. Barrosse; book 3 by J. M. Murray. Books 2-4: 'Abridged and arranged for Confraternity classes by Vincent J. Giese.' Contents.book 1. On the way to God.--book 2. God's people.--book 3. God and man.--book 4. Christ and His church. [BX1754.M76] 59-12211
1. Catholic Church—Doctrinal and controversial works, Popular. I. Giese, Vincent J. II. Barrosse, Thomas. III. Title.

MURRAY, Nicholas, 1802- 230'.2
1861.
Letters to the Right Rev. John Hughes, Roman Catholic bishop of New York / Kirwan, pseudonym of Nicholas Murray. New York : Arno Press, 1977. 329 p. ; 22 cm. (First published in three series in the New York observer, 1847-1848.) (Anti-movements in America) Reprint of the 1855 ed. published by Harper, New York. [BX1765.M82 1977] 76-46091 ISBN 0-405-09964-9 : 21.00
1. Catholic Church—Doctrinal and controversial works—Protestant authors. 2.

Hughes, John, Abp., 1797-1864. I. Title. II. Series.

MURRAY, Rosalind, 1890- 230.2
The further journey. New York, McKay [1952] 185 p. 21 cm. [BX4668.M8] 52-9404
1. Converts, Catholic. I. Title.

NEUNER, Josef 230'.2
The teaching of the Catholic Church as contained in her documents. Orig. prep. by Josef Neuner & Heinrich Roos. Ed. by Karl Rahner. [Tr. by Geoffrey Stevens. Staten Island, N.Y., Alba, 1967] 456p. 22cm. Tr. of Der Glaube der Kirche in den Urkunden der Lehrverkundigung. [BX1747.5.N413] 67-15199 6.95
1. Catholic Church—Doctrinal and controversial works. 2. Catholic Church—Cathechisms and creeds—English. I. Catholic Church. Canons, decretals, etc. II. Roos, Heinrich, 1904- joint author. III. Title.

NEVINS, William, 1797- 230'.2
1835.
Thoughts on popery / William Nevins. New York : Arno Press, 1977. 216 p. ; 21 cm. (Anti-movements in America) Reprint of the 1836 ed. published by American Tract Society, New York. [BX1765.N48 1977] 76-46093 ISBN 0-405-09966-5 : 12.00
1. Catholic Church—Doctrinal and controversial works—Protestant authors. I. Title. II. Series.

NEWMAN, John Henry, 230.2
Cardinal, 1801-1890
Apologia pro vita sua. An authoritative text, basic texts of the Newman-Kingsley controversy, origin and reception of the Apologia [and] essays in criticism. Ed. by David J. DeLaura. [1st ed.] New York, Norton [1968] xviii, 506p. 21cm. (Norton Critical eds.) Bibl. ref. [BX4705.N5A3 1968] 67-16618 5.97; 1.95 pap.,
1. Catholic Church—Doctrinal and controversial works—Catholic authors. I. DeLaura, David J. ed. II. Title.

NEWMAN, John Henry, 230.2
Cardinal, 1801-1890.
Apologia pro vita sua: being a history of his religious opinions; edited, with an introduction and notes, by Martin J. Svaglic. Oxford, Clarendon P., 1967. lx, 604 p. 22 1/2 cm. Bibliographical references. [BX4705.N5A3 1967] 68-75872 5/5/-
1. Catholic Church—Doctrinal and controversial works—Catholic authors. I. Svaglic, Martin J., ed. II. Title.

NEWMAN, John Henry, 230.2
Cardinal, 1801-1890.
Certain difficulties felt by Anglicans in Catholic teaching considered. New ed. Westminster, Md., Christian Classics, 1969. 2 v. 21 cm. (His Works) Title on spine: Difficulties of Anglicans. Contents.Contents.—Twelve lectures addressed in 1850 to the party of the religious movement of 1833.—v. 2. Letter addressed to the Rev. E. B. Pusey, D.D., on occasion of his Eirenicon of 1864. Letter addressed to the Duke of Norfolk, on occasion of Mr. Gladstone's expostulation of 1874. [BX1751.A1N4 1969] 75-3856
1. Catholic Church—Doctrinal and controversial works—Catholic authors. I. Title. II. Title: Difficulties of Anglicans.

NEWMAN, John Henry, 230'.2
Cardinal, 1801-1890.
An essay in aid of a grammar of assent. Westminster, Md., Christian Classics, 1973. viii, 503 p. 21 cm. (His The Works of Cardinal Newman) On spine: Grammar of assent. [BR100.N4 1973] 73-85623 8.75
1. Theism. 2. Faith. I. Title. II. Title: Grammar of assent.

NEWMAN, John Henry, 230.2
Cardinal, 1801-1890.
An essay on the development of Christian doctrine. Westminster, Md., Christian Classics, 1968. xvi, 445 p. 21 cm. Reprint of the 1878 ed. Bibliographical footnotes. [BT21.N5 1968] 68-24083
1. Catholic Church—Doctrinal and controversial works—Catholic authors. 2. Dogma, Development of. I. Title.

NEWMAN, John Henry, 230.2
Cardinal 1801-1890
The heart of Newman, a synthesis arranged by Erich Przywara. Introd. by H. Francis Davis. Springfield, Ill., Templegate [1963] xx, 361p. port. 17cm. Pub. in 1931 under title: A Newman synthesis. 63-25651 3.95
1. Theology, Doctrinal. I. Przywara, Erich, 1889- comp. II. Title.

NEWMAN, John Henry, 230'.2
Cardinal, 1801-1890.
The heart of Newman's Apologia. Arr. by Margaret R. Grennan. With an introd. by Joseph J. Reilly. New York, Russell & Russell [1970] 195 p. 20 cm. Reprint of the 1934 ed. with new pref. by M. R. Grennan. "This edition follows the 1864 text, based on Newman's original pamphlets." [BX4705.N5A3 1970] 71-102523
1. Catholic Church—Doctrinal and controversial works—Catholic authors. I. Grennan, Margaret Rose, 1912- ed. II. Title.

NOLL, John Francis, Bp., 230.2
1875-
Father Smith instructs Jackson, by John Francis Noll and Lester J. Fallon. 60th large ed. Huntington, Ind., Our Sunday Visitor Press, 1952. 227p. 21cm. [BX1754.N6 1952] 53-38039
1. Catholic Church—Doctrinal and controversial works, Popular. I. Fallon, Lester J., joint author. II. Title.

NOLL, John Francis, Abp., 230'.2
1875-1956.
Father Smith instructs Jackson / by John Francis Noll. 2d rev. ed., revised in the light of Vatican Council II and the Credo of the People of God / by Albert J. Nevins. Huntington, Ind. : Our Sunday Visitor, inc., 1975. 299 p. ; 21 cm. Includes index. [BX1754.N6 1975] 75-628 ISBN 0-87973-864-2 pbk. : 3.95
1. Catholic Church—Doctrinal and controversial works, Popular. I. Nevins, Albert J., 1915- II. Title.

O'BRIEN, John Anthony, 230.2
1893-
The Catholic way of life. Englewood Cliffs, N.J., Prentice-Hall [c.1962] 211p. illus. 61-16838 3.95
1. Catholic Church—Doctrinal and controversial works, Popular. 2. Catholic Church—Ceremonies and practices. I. Title.

O'COLLINS, Gerald. 230'.2
The case against dogma / Gerald O'Collins. New York : Paulist Press, [1975] xiv, 110 p. ; 22 cm. Includes index. Bibliography: p. [107] [BT19.O25] 74-15495 ISBN 0-8091-1853-X pbk. : 3.50
1. Dogma. I. Title.

O'CONNELL, David A 230.2
Notes from the Summa on God and His creatures. Providence, Providence College Press [1956] 187p. 28cm. [BX1749.T6O25] 56-13085
1. Thomas Aquinas, Saint, 1225?-1274. Summa theologica. 2. Thomas Aquinas, Saint, 1225?-1274—Theology. 3. God. I. Title.

O'REILLY, Philip 230.2
1000 question and answers on Catholicism. [Rev. ed.] New York, Guild Press; distributed by Golden Press [c.1956, 1960] 384p. 17cm. (An Angelus book) 60-4878 1.25 bds.,
1. Questions and answers—Theology. 2. Catholic Church—Doctrinal and controversial works—Catholic authors. I. Title.

O'REILLY, Philip. 230.2
1000 questions and answers on Catholicism. [1st d.] New York, Holt [1956] 351p. 22cm. [BX1754.O7] 56-7727
1. Catholic Church—Doctrinal and controversial works—Catholic authors. I. Title.

O'REILLY, Philip. 230.2
1000 questions and answers on Catholicism. [Rev. ed.]iNew York, Guild Press; distributed by Golden Press [1960] 384p. 17cm. (An Angelus book) [BX1754.3.O7 1960] 60-4878
1. Questions and answers—Theology. 2. Catholic Church—Doctrinal and controversial works— Catholic authors. I. Title.

O'REILLY, Philip. 230.2
1000 questions and [BX1754.C7] 56-7727
I. Title.

OSORIO, Jeronymo, Bp. 230'.2 s
of Silves, 1506-1580.
A learned and very eloquent treatie / [by] Osorio da Fonseca ; [translated from the Latin by John Fen]. Ilkley [etc.] : Scolar Press, 1976. [13] p., 283 leaves, [2] p. ; 20 cm. (English recusant literature 1558-1640 ; v. 318) (Series: Rogers, David Morrison, comp. English recusant literature, 1558-1640 ; v. 318.) Reprint of the 1568 ed. of this translation, published by Apud J. Fouleram, Lovanii. Reproduced (original size) from a copy in the Library of Lambeth Palace, in which the title page is slightly damaged; in this reprint the title page is reproduced from a copy in the British Library. "STC 18889." [BX1750.A1E5 vol. 318] 230'.2 77-355607 ISBN 0-85967-332-4
1. Catholic Church—Doctrinal and controversial works—Catholic authors. I. Title. II. Series.

PADOVANO, Anthony T. 230.2
The estranged God; modern man's search for belief, by Anthony T. Padovano. New York, Sheed [1966] xviii, 300p. 22cm. Bibl. [BT28.P25] 66-14154 6.00
1. Religious thought—20th cent. 2. Existentialism. 3. Theology—20th cent. I. Title.

PANIZON, Leo A. Hope. 230'.2
The pleasures of being a Catholic : are you thinking of becoming a Catholic? / Leo A. Hope Panizon. [1st ed.] Albuquerque : American Classical College Press, [1975] [35] leaves, [12] leaves of plates : ill. ; 28 cm. "A Science of man book." Includes index. [BX1752.P25] 74-32485 ISBN 0-913314-23-4 : 9.00
1. Catholic Church—Apologetic works. I. Title. II. Title: Are you thinking of becoming a Catholic?

PARIS, Charles W 230.2
The what and why of Catholicism. New York City, J. F. Wagner [1961] 324p. 24cm. [BX1754.P35] 62-473
1. Catholic Church—Doctrinal and controversial works, Popular. I. Title.

PARSONS, Robert, 1546- 230'.2 s
1610.
A treatise of three conversions, 1603-1604 / Robert Persons. Ilkley [Eng.] : Scolar Press, 1976. 3 v. ; 20 cm. (English recusant literature, 1558-1640 ; v. 304-306) (Series: Rogers, David Morrison, comp. English recusant literature, 1558-1640 ; v. 304-306.) Reprint of the 1603-1604 ed. from a copy in the library of Stonyhurst College. [BX1750.A1E5 vol. 304-306] [BX1492] 282'.42 76-374618 ISBN 0-85967-316-2 (v. 1)
1. Catholic Church in England. 2. Catholic Church—Doctrinal and controversial works—Catholic authors. 3. Foxe, John, 1516-1587. Actes and monuments. 4. Persecution. 5. Church history. I. Title. II. Series.

PARSONS, Robert, 1546- 230'.2 s
1610.
The warn-word to Sir Francis Hastinges Westword, 1602 / Robert Persons. Ilkley [Eng.] : Scolar Press, 1976. 131 [i.e. 262], 138, [39] p. ; 21 cm. (English recusant literature, 1558-1640, v. 302) (Series: Rogers, David Morrison, comp. English recusant literature, 1558-1640 ; v. 302.) "Allison and Rogers 642; STC 19418." Reprint of the 1602 ed. [BX1750.A1E5 vol. 302] [BX1750] 230'.2 76-375995 ISBN 0-85967-309-X
1. Catholic Church—Doctrinal and controversial works—Catholic authors. 2. Catholics in England. 3. Protestantism—Controversial literature. I. Title. II. Series.

PASCAL, Blaise, 1623-1662. 230'.2
The heart of Pascal, being his meditations & prayers, notes for his anti-Jesuit campaign, remarks on language and style, etc. Drawn from the Pensees by H. F. Stewart. [Folcroft, Pa.] Folcroft Library Editions, 1973. p. Text in French; preface and notes in English. Reprint of the 1945 ed. published by the University Press, Cambridge. [B1901.P42S77 1973] 73-16024 17.50
I. Stewart, Hugh Fraser, 1863-1948, ed. II. Title.

PASCAL, Blaise, 1623-1662. 230'.2
The heart of Pascal, being his meditations & prayers, notes for his anti-Jesuit campaign, remarks on language and style, etc. Drawn from the Pensees by H. F. Stewart. [Folcroft, Pa.] Folcroft Library Editions, 1973. p. Text in French; preface and notes in English. Reprint of the 1945 ed. published by the University Press, Cambridge. [B1901.P42S77 1973] 73-16024 ISBN 0-8414-7697-7 (lib. bdg.)
I. Stewart, Hugh Fraser, 1863-1948, ed. II. Title.

PATERSON, F. William. 230'.2 s
The Protestants theologie / [by] William Paterson. Ilkley [etc.] : Scolar Press, 1976. [29], 309, [3] p. ; 21 cm. (English recusant literature, 1558-1640 ; v. 316) (Series: Rogers, David Morrison, comp. English recusant literature, 1558-1640 ; v. 316.) Reprint of the 1620 ed. STC 19461; Ailison and Rogers 597. [BX1750.A1E5 vol. 316] [BX1752] 230'.2 77-362661 ISBN 0-85967-330-8
1. Catholic Church—Apologetic works. 2. Protestantism—Controversial literature. I. Title. II. Series.

PAULUS VI Pope, 1897- 230.2
Faith; response to the dialogue of God [by] Pope Paul VI. Compiled by the Daughters of St. Paul. [Boston] St. Paul Editions [1967] 139 p. 22 cm. [BX891.P33] 67-29166
1. Catholic Church—Addresses, essays, lectures. I. Daughters of St. Paul. II. Title.

PAULUS VI, Pope, 1897- 230'.2
The teachings of Pope Paul VI, 1970. Washington, Publications Office, United States Catholic Conference, 1971. x, 518 p. 22 cm. Reprint of the volume for1970 of The teachings of Pope Paul VI, published by Libreria editrice vaticana, Citta del Vaticano. [BX891.P355] 74-152586
1. Catholic Church—Addresses, essays, lectures. I. Title.

PEGUES, Thomas, 1866-1936. 230.2
Catechism of the "Summa theologica" of Saint Thomas Aquinas, for the use of the faithful. Adapted from the French and done into English by Elred Whitacre. Westminster, Md., Newman Press, 1950. xvi, 314 p. 20 cm. [BX1749.T6P383 1950] 51-5980
1. Thomas Aquinas, Saint, 1225-1274. Summa theologica. 2. Catholic Church — Doctrinal and controversial works, Popular. I. Title.

PELIKAN, Jaroslav Jan, 230.2
1923-
The Christian tradition; a history of the development of doctrine [by] Jaroslav Pelikan. Chicago, University of Chicago Press [1971- v. 24 cm. Contents.Contents.—v. 1. The emergence of the Catholic tradition (100-600) Bibliography: v. 1, p. 358-376. [BT21.2.P42] 79-142042 ISBN 0-226-65370-6
1. Theology, Doctrinal—History. I. Title.

PENTECOST, J Dwight. 230.2
Romanism in the light of Scripture. Chicago, Moody Press [1962] 127p. 21cm. [BX1765.2.P42] 62-4722
1. Catholic Church—Doctrinal and controversial works—Protestant authors. I. Title.

PESCH, Otto Hermann. 230'.2
Questions and answers : a shorter Catholic catechism / Otto Pesch. Chicago : Franciscan Herald Press, [1976?] p. cm. Translation of Kleines katholisches Glaubensbuch. [BX1754.P4613] 76-23402 2.95
1. Theology, Catholic. I. Title.

PETRUS THOMAE, ca.1280- 230.2
ca.1340.
Quodlibet. Edited by Sister M. Rachel Hooper and Eligius M. Buytaert. St. Bonaventure, N.Y., Franciscan Institute, 1957. xiv, 242 p. 24 cm. (Franciscan Institute publications. Text series, no. 11) Text based chiefly on MS. 1494, fol. 67-103, of the Nationalbibliothek, Vienna. Includes bibliographical references. [BX1749.P46] 75-261555
1. Catholic Church—Doctrinal and controversial works. 2. Theology, Doctrinal. I. Hooper, Mary Rachel, ed. II. Buytaert, Eloi Marie, 1913- ed. III. Vienna. Nationalbibliothek. MSS. (1494) IV. Title. V. Series: St. Bonaventure University, St. Bonaventure, N.Y. Franciscan Institute. Text series, no. 11

PINELLI, Luca, 1542- 230'.2 s
1607.
Breife meditations / Luca Pinelli ; [translated from the Italian]. Ilkley [etc.] : Scolar Press, 1976. [14], 290, 36 p. ; 20 cm. (English recusant literature, 1558-1640 ; v. 289) (Series: Rogers, David Morrison, comp. English recusant literature, 1558-1640 ; v. 289.) Reprint of the 1600? ed. "STC19937." [BX1750.A1E5 vol. 289] [BX2215] 265'.3 76-379246 ISBN 0-85967-290-5 : £10.00
1. Lord's Supper—Catholic Church. I. Title. II. Series.

PITTSBURGH. St. John 230.2
Chrysostom Greek Catholic Church.
Golden anniversary and solemn re-dedication of newly decorated St. John Chrysostom Greek Catholic Church ... 1960. Pastor: Very Rev. Msgr. John Bilock. [Pittsburgh, 1960] unpaged. illus. 27cm. [BX4711.238.P5] 62-42002
I. Bilock, John. II. Title.

POLE, Reginald, 230'.2 s
Cardinal, 1500-1558.
A treatie of justification, 1569 / Reginald Pole. Ilkley [Eng.] : Scolar Press, 1976. 279 p. in various pagings ; 21 cm. (English recusant literature, 1558-1640 ; v. 281) (Series: Rogers, David Morrison, comp. English recusant literature, 1558-1640 ; v. 281.) Reprints. Includes the first part of The resolution of religion by R. Broughton, 1603; 104 p. [BX1750.A1E5 vol. 281] [BT763] 234'.7 76-361224 ISBN 0-85967-282-4
1. Catholic Church—Apologetic works. 2. Justification. 3. Theology—Early church, ca. 30-600. 4. Religion. I. Broughton, Richard. The resolution of religion, pt. 1. 1603. II. Title. III. Series.

POPE, or president? : 230'.2
Facts for Americans. New York : Arno Press, 1977. 360 p. ; 21 cm. (Anti-movements in America) Reprint of the 1859 ed. published by R. L. Delisser, New York. [BX1765.P6 1977] 76-46094 ISBN 0-405-09967-3 : 20.00
1. Catholic Church—Doctrinal and controversial works. I. Series.

POULLART DES PLACES, Claude Francois, 1679-1709. 230.2
Spiritual writings. Edited by Henry J. Koren. Pittsburgh, Duquesne University, 1959. 297p. illus. 26cm. (Duquesne studies, Spiritan series, 3) English and French. Includes bibliography. [BX890.P597] 60-3235
1. Catholic Church—Collected works. 2. Theology—Collected works—18th cent. 3. Congregation of the Holy Ghost. I. Title.

PREMM, Mathias, 1890- 230.2
Dogmatic theology for the laity. Staten Island, N. Y., Alba [1967] 456p. 23cm. Tr. of Weltuberwindender Glaube. [BX1751.2.P713] 67-21425 9.50
1. Theology, Doctrinal. 2. Catholic Church—Doctrinal and controversial work. I. Title.

PREPOSITINUS Cremonensia, dca.1210, supposed author. 230.2
The Summa contra haereticos; ascribed to Praepositinus of Cremona, by Joseph N. Garvin and James A. Corbbett. [Notre Dame, Ind., University of Notre Dame Press 1958] 302 p. 24 cm. [BX1750.S8 1958] 57-11374
1. Catholic Church—Doctrinal and controversial works. I. Garvin, Joseph N., 1906- . II. Title. III. Title: (Publications in mediaeval studies, The University of Notre Dame, 15) IV. Series: Notre Dame, Ind. University. Publications in mediaeval studies, 15

PRICE, John, 1576- 230'.2 s
Anti-Mortonus / [by] John Price. Ilkley [etc.] : Scolar Press, 1976. [33], 768 p. ; 21 cm. (English recusant literature, 1558-1640 ; v. 288) (Series: Rogers, David Morrison, comp. English recusant literature, 1558-1640 ; v. 288.) Reprint of the 1640 ed. STC 20308. Includes bibliographical references. [BX1750.A1E5 vol. 288] [BX1752] 230'.2 76-381976 ISBN 0-85967-289-1 : £10.00
1. Catholic Church—Apologetic works. 2. Morton, Thomas, 1564-1659. I. Title. II. Series.

PUENTE, Luis de la, 1554-1624. 230'.2 s
Meditations upon the mysteries of our faith ... abbridged, 1624 / Luis de la Puente. Ilkley [Eng.] : Scolar Press, 1976. 679 p. ; 20 cm. (English recusant literature, 1558-1640 ; v. 295) (Series: Rogers, David Morrison, comp. English recusant literature, 1558-1640 ; v. 295.) Abridged translation of Meditaciones de los mysterios de nuestra sancta fe. Reprint of the 1624 ed. "Reproduced (original size) from a copy in the library of Stonyhurst College ... references: Allison and Rogers 699; STC 20487." [BX1750.A1E5 vol. 295] [BX2181] 242 76-382258 ISBN 0-85967-296-4
1. Meditations. I. Title. II. Series.

PUENTE, Luis de la, 1554-1624. 230'.2 s
Meditations upon the mysteries of our holie faith, 1619 / Luis de la Puente. Ilkley [Eng.] : Scolar Press, 1976- v. ; 23 cm. (English recusant literature, 1558-1640 ; v. 296) (Series: Rogers, David Morrison, comp. English recusant literature, 1558-1640 ; v. 296.) Translation of Meditaciones de los mysterios de nuestra sancta fe. Reprint of the 1619 ed. [BX1750.A1E5 vol. 296] [BX2186] 242 76-369250 ISBN 0-85967-297-2 (v. 1) : £13.67 (v. 1)
1. Meditations. I. Title. II. Series.

QUESNELL, Quentin. 230'.2
His Word endures. Canfield, Ohio, Alba Books [1973] 120 p. 18 cm. Selections from the author's syndicated column Know your faith. [BX1751.2.Q47] 72-13196 0.95 (pbk.)
1. Catholic Church—Doctrinal and controversial works—Catholic authors. I. Title.

QUILL, James E. 230'.2
Restitution to the poor: its origin, nature, and extent. Milwaukee, Bruce Pub. Co. [1961] 141 p. 23 cm. [BX1753.Q57] 281'.5 74-240619
1. Restitution. I. Title.

RAEMERS, Sidney Albert, 1892- 230.2
The convert's basic guide. Foreword by William J. Devlin. [1st ed.] New York, Exposition Press [1963] 115 p. 21 cm. (An Exposition-testament book) [BX1754.3.R28] 63-23576
1. Catholic Church—Doctrinal and controversial works, Popular. I. Title.

RAEMERS, Sidney Albert, 1892- 230.2
The convert's basic guide. Foreword by William J. Devlin. NewYork, Exposition [c.1963] 115p. 21cm. (Exposition-testament bk.) 63-23576 2.75
1. Catholic Church—Doctrinal and controversial works, Popular. I. Title.

RAEMERS, Sidney Albert, 1892- 230.2
The convert's manual. Foreword by Thomas K. Gorman. [3d ed.] New York, Exposition Press [1961] 317p. 21cm. (An Exposition-testament book) [BX1754.3.R3 1961] 61-3769
1. Catholic Church—Doctrinal and controversial works, Popular. 2. Questions and answers—Theology. I. Title.

RAEMERS, Sidney Albert, 1892- 230.2
The convert's vade mecum. Foreword by Joseph F. Marbach. New York, Exposition [c.1963] 148p. 22cm. (Exposition-testament bk.) 62-21059 3.00
1. Catholic Church—Doctrinal and controversial works, Popular. I. Title.

RAHNER, Hugo, 1900- 230.2
The Church; readings in theology [by] Hugo Rahner [and others] Foreword by Gustave Weigel. Compiled at the Canisianum, Innsbruck. New York, P.J. Kenedy [1963] xii, 242 p. 22 cm. Translated from German or French. [BV600.A1C5] 63-19022
1. Church — Addresses, essays, lectures. 2. Catholic Church — Addresses, essays, lectures. I. Title.

RAHNER, Karl, 1904- 230'.2
A Rahner reader. Edited by Gerald A. McCool. New York, Seabury Press [1975] xxviii, 381 p. 24 cm. "A Crossroad book." Bibliography: p. 363-372. [BX891.R253 1975] 74-16138 ISBN 0-8164-1173-5
1. Catholic Church—Collected works. 2. Theology—Collected works—20th century. I. McCool, Gerald A., ed. II. Title.

RAHNER, Karl, 1904- 230'.2
Theological investigations. Translated with an introd. by Cornelius Ernst. Baltimore, Helicon Press [1961- v. 22 cm. Vol. 7-8 has imprint: London, Darton, Longman & Todd; New York, Herder and Herder. Vol. 13 published by Seabury Press, New York, as a Crossword book. Vol. 11 has imprint: London, Darton, Longman & Todd; New York, Seabury Press. Translation of Schriften zur Theologie. Translators vary. Contents.Contents.—v. 1. God, Christ, Mary, and grace.—v. 2. Man in the church.—v. 3. The theology of the spiritual life.—v. 4. More recent writings.—v. 5. Later writings.—v. 6. Concerning Vatican Council II.—v. 7. Further theology of the spiritual life, 1.—v. 8. Further theology of the spiritual life, 2.— —v. 11. Confrontations 1. —v. 13. Theology, anthropology, christology. Bibliographical footnotes. [BX1751.2.R313] 61-8189 ISBN 0-232-35616-5 (v. 6)
1. Catholic Church—Doctrinal and controversial works.—Catholic authors. 2. Theology, Catholic. I. Title.

RATZINGER, Joseph. 230.2
Introduction to Christianity. Translated by J. R. Foster. [New York] Herder and Herder [1970, c1969] 280 p. 22 cm. Translation of Einfuhrung in das Christentum. Includes bibliographical references. [BT993.2.R313 1970] 71-105403 6.50
1. Apostles' Creed. 2. Apologetics—20th century. 3. Theology, Doctrinal. I. Title.

RAYMOND, Father, 1903- 230.2
The mysteries in your life [by] M. Raymond. Milwaukee, Bruce Pub. Co. [1965] 200 p. 23 cm. [BX1754.R37] 65-20547
1. Theology, Doctrinal — Popular works. 2. Catholic Church — Doctrinal and controversial works, Popular. 3. Mystery. I. Title.

RAYMOND, Father M., 1903- 230.2
The mysteries in your life. Milwaukee, Bruce [c.1965] vi, 200p. 24cm. [BX1754.R37] 65-20547 4.25
1. Theology, Doctrinal—Popular works. 2. Catholic Church—Doctrinal and controversial works, Popular. 3. Mystery. I. Title.

REGAN, Cronan. 230'.2
Signpost. Chicago, Franciscan Herald Press [1972] xvii, 322 p. 22 cm. Essays originally appeared in the question and answer column "Signpost" in the monthly magazine The Sign. [BX1754.3.R4] 70-169056 ISBN 0-8199-0432-5 7.50
1. Catholic Church—Doctrinal and controversial works, Popular. 2. Theology—Miscellanea. I. The Sign. II. Title.

REGAN, James Wilfred, 1911- 230.2
A primer of theology, by James W. Regan, John A. Henry [and] Thomas C. Donlan. Dubuque, Priory Press, 1954-[v. 1, 1955] v. 24cm. [BX930.R42] 55-12847
1. Catholic Church—Doctrinal and controversial works—Text-books. 2. Religious education—Text-books for adolescents—Catholic. I. Title.

A Reply to M. [i.e. Mr.] Nicholas Smith [i.e. M. Wilson], 1630. 230'.2 s Ilkley : Scolar Press, 1976. [4], 304 p. ; 20 cm. (English recusant literature, 1558-1640 ; v. 290) (Series: Rogers, David Morrison, comp. English recusant literature, 1558-1640 ; v. 290.) Reprint of the 1630 ed. "Reproduced (original size) from a copy in the library of Ampleforth Abbey ... references: Allison and Rogers 710; STC 6929." [BX1750.A1E5 vol. 290] [BX1800] 262'.14 76-383462 ISBN 0-85967-291-3 : £10.00
1. Catholic Church—Government. 2. Catholic Church—Clergy. 3. Kellison, Matthew. Treatise of the Hierarchie. 4. Wilson, Matthew, 1582?-1656. I. Wilson, Matthew, 1582?-1656. II. Series.

RETIF, Andre. 230.2
The Catholic spirit. Translated from the French by Dom Aldhelm Dean. [1st ed.] New York, Hawthorn Books [1959] 126p. 21cm. (The Twentieth century encyclopedia of Catholicism, v. 88. Section 8: The organization of the church) Translation of Catholicite. Includes bibliography. [BX1751.2.R453] 59-6729
1. Catholic Church. I. Title.

REYNOLDS, Arthur G 230.2
What's the difference in Protestant and Roman Catholic beliefs? New York, Abingdon Press [c1954] 63p. 19cm. [BX1765.R42 1954] 55-4169
1. Catholic Church—Doctrinal and controversial works—Protestant authors. I. Title.

RICHEOME, Louis, 1544-1625. 230'.2 s
The pilgrime of Loreto / Louis Richeome ; [translated from the French by E. W. i.e. Edward Worsley]. Ilkley : Scolar Press, 1976. 23, 456 p. : 1 ill. ; 21 cm. (English recusant literature, 1558-1640 ; v. 285) (Series: Rogers, David Morrison, comp. English recusant literature, 1558-1640 ; v. 285.) Translation of Le pelerin de Lorete. Reprint of the 1629 translation, Paris. [BX1750.A1E5 vol. 285] [BT660.L7] 248'29 76-381622 ISBN 0-85967-286-7 : £10.00
1. Loreto, Madonna di. 2. Christian pilgrims and pilgrimages—Loreto, Italy. I. Title. II. Series.

RIGA, Peter. 230.2
Catholic thought in crisis. Milwaukee, Bruce Pub. Co. [1963] xiv, 198 p. 23 cm. (Impact books) Includes bibliographical references. [BX1751.2.R5] 63-14921
1. Christianity — 20th cent. 2. Laity — Catholic Church. 3. Religious liberty. I. Title.

RIGA, Peter 230.2
Catholic thought in crisis. Milwaukee, Bruce [c.1963] xiv, 198p. 23cm. (Impact bks.) Bibl. 63-14921 3.50
1. Christianity—20th cent. 2. Laity—Catholic Church. 3. Religious liberty. I. Title.

RIGA, Peter J 230.2
Catholic thought in crisis. Milwaukee, Bruce Pub. Co. [1963] xiv, 198 p. 23 cm. (Impact books) Includes bibliographical references. [BX1751.2.R5] 63-14921
1. Christianity—20th cent. 2. Laity—Catholic Church. 3. Religious liberty. I. Title.

RIPLEY, Francis J. 230.2
This is the faith. Foreword by Richard Downey. New York, Guild Press: distributed by Golden Press [c.1960] xiv, 416p. 17cm. (Angelus Books) .95 bds.,
1. Catholic Church—Doctrinal and controversial works, Popular. I. Title.

RIPLEY, Francis Joseph, 1912- 230.2
One Christ, one church. London, Burns & Oates; Westminster, Md., Newman Press [c1960] 112p. 18cm. [BX1746.R55 1960] 61-404
1. Church—Unity. 2. Catholic Church—Relations. I. Title.

RIPLEY, Francis Joseph, 1912- 230.2
This is the faith. Foreword by Richard Downey. Westminster, Md., Newman Press, 1962. 414 p. 22 cm. [BX1754.R54] 52-10975
1. Catholic Church — Doctrinal and controversial works, Popular. I. Title.

RIVADENEIRA, Pedro de, 1527-1611. 230'.2 s
The life of B. Father Ignatius of Loyola, 1616 / Pedro de Ribadeneira. Ilkley [Eng.] : Scolar Press, 1976. 358 p. ; 19 cm. (English recusant literature 1558-1640 ; v. 300) (Series: Rogers, David Morrison, comp. English recusant literature, 1558-1640 ; v. 300.) Translation of Vita Ignatii Loiolae. Reprint of the 1616 ed. STC 20967 [BX1750.A1E5 Vol. 300] [BX4700.L7] 271'.53'024 B 76-378334 ISBN 0-85967-301-4
1. Loyola, Ignacio de, Saint, 1491-1556. 2. Christian saints—Biography. I. Title. II. Series.

ROBERTS, Thomas D'Esterre, Abp., 1893- 230.2
Black popes authority: its use and abuse. New York, Sheed and Ward, 1954. 139p. illus. 20cm. [BX1780.R6] 54-11141
1. Catholic Church—Doctrinal and controversial works—Catholic authors. 2. Obedience. 3. Jesuits. I. Title.

ROBERTUS, Prior of Shrewsbury. 230'.2 s
The admirable life of Saint Wenefride / Robert, Prior of Shrewsbury. Ilkley [Eng.] : Scolar Press, 1976. 5, 5, 275 p. : ill. ; 20 cm. (English recusant literature, 1558-1640 ; v. 319) (Series: Rogers, David Morrison, comp. English recusant literature, 1558-1640 ; v. 319.) "STC 21102." Reprint of the 1635 ed. [BX1750.A1E5 vol. 319] [BX4700.W58] 270.2'092'4 B 77-351171 ISBN 0-85967-333-2
1. Winifred, Saint. 2. Christian saints—Wales—Biography. I. Title. II. Series.

RODRIGUEZ, Alonso, 1526-1616. 230'.2 s
A treatise of mentall prayer ; [A treatise of the presence of God] / [by] Alfonso Rodriguez ; [translated from the Spanish by T. B.]. Ilkley : Scolar Press, 1976. [21], 303 p. ; 20 cm. (English recusant literature, 1558-1640 ; v. 291) (Series: Rogers, David Morrison, comp. English recusant literature, 1558-1640 ; v. 291.) Translation of Tratados 5-6 of the author's Ejercicio de perfeccion y virtudes cristianas. Reprint of the 1st ed. of the translation, Douai, 1627. [BX1750.A1E5 vol. 291] [BV209] 248'.3 76-380514 ISBN 0-85967-292-1 : £10.00
1. Prayer—Early works to 1800. 2. Spiritual life—Catholic authors. I. Rodriguez, Alonso, 1526-1616. Ejercicio de perfeccion y virtudes cristianas. Tratado 6. English. 1976. II. Title. III. Series.

*ROMAIN, Sister H. H. S. 230.2
Tell my people; a handbook for catechists. Notre Dame, Ind., Fides [1966,c.1965] xv, 191p. illus. 22cm. 1.95 pap.,
I. Title.

RONDET, Henri, 1898- 230.2
Do dogmas change? Tr. from French by Mark Pontifex. New York, Hawthorn Books [c.1961] 125p. (Twentieth century encyclopedia of Catholicism, v. 5. Section 1: Knowledge and faith) Bibl. 61-12973 3.50 bds.,
1. Dogma, Development of. I. Title.

RYAN, Mary Perkins, 1915- 230.2
Christ and the church; a guide to the church and the sacraments as sources of light and strength for a full, rich life according to God's will. Chicago, Catholic Press [1960] 371p. illus. 18cm. (Library of Catholic devotion) [BX1754.R88] 60-51589
1. Catholic Church—Doctrinal and controversial works, Popular. 2. Sacraments—Catholic Church. I. Title.

SALET, Gaston, 1891- 230.2
The wonders of our faith. Tr. from French by John Leonard. Westminster,Md., Newman [c.1961] 187p. 61-65434 3.50
1. Catholic Church—Doctrinal and controversial works, Popular. I. Title.

SANDERS, Nicholas, 1530?-1581. 230'.2 s
A treatise of the images of Christ / [by] Nicholas Sander. Ilkley : Scolar Press, 1976. [117], 196 [i.e. 392] p. ; 20 cm. (English recusant literature, 1558-1640 ; v. 282) (Series: Rogers, David Morrison, comp. English recusant literature, 1558-1640 ; v. 282.) Reprint of the 1567 ed., Apud Joannem Foulerum, Lovanii [Louvain]. [BX1750.A1E5 vol. 282] [BX2312] 246'.53 76-382257 ISBN 0-85967-283-2 : £10.00
1. Image (Theology)—Catholic Church. I. Title. II. Series.

SCHILLEBEECKX, Edward Cornelis Florentius Alfons, 1914- 230.2
God and man; by E. Schillebeeckx. Translated by Edward Fitzgerald and Peter Tomlinson. New York, Sheed and Ward [1969] xii, 308 p. 22 cm. (His Theological soundings, 3) Bibliographical footnotes. [BT60.S313] 69-16994
1. God—Addresses, essays, lectures. 2. Spiritual life—Catholic authors. 3. Secularization (Theology) I. Title.

SCHILLEBEECKX, Edward Cornelis Florentius Alfons, 1914- 230'.2
Truth and certainty, edited by Edward Schillebeeckx and Bas van Iersel. [New York] Herder and Herder [1973] 138 p. 23 cm. (Concilium, 83) Series statement also appears as: The New concilium: religion in the seventies. Includes bibliographical references. [BV601.6.I5S34] 72-12421 ISBN 0-8164-2539-6 3.95
1. Catholic Church—Infallibility. 2. Catholic Church—Doctrinal and controversial works—

Catholic authors. I. Iersel, Bastiaan Martinius Franciscus van, ed. II. Title. III. Series: Concilium (New York) 83.

SCHMAUS, Michael, 1897- 230.2
Dogma. [Translated by Ann Laeuchli, and others] New York, Sheed and Ward [1968- v. 21 cm. "A project of John XXIII Institute, Saint Xavier College, Chicago." Translation of Der Glaube der Kirche. Contents.Contents.—v. 1. God in revelation.—v. 2. God and creation.—v. 3. God and His Christ.—v. 4. The Church: its origin and structure. Includes bibliographical references. [BT75.2.S3513] 68-26033 ISBN 0-8362-0385-2 (v. 3) 3.95 per vol.
1. Theology, Doctrinal. I. John XXIII Institute, Chicago.

SCHOONENBERG, Peter, 1911- 230.2
God's world in the making. Techny, Ill., Divine Word Punbs. [1967,c.1964] ix, 207p. 21cm. (DWP101) Bibl. 1.85
1. Man (Theology) 2. Evolution. 3. Marriage—Catholic Church. 4. Work (Theology) I. Title.

SCHOONENBERG, Peter, 1911- 230.2
God's world in the making. Pittsburgh, Pa., Duquesne University Press, 1964. ix, 207 p. 23 cm. (Duquesne studies. Theological series, 2) Bibliographical footnotes. [BT701.2.S36] 64-12599
1. Man (Theology) 2. Evolution. 3. Marriage—Catholic Church. 4. Work (Theology) I. Title. II. Series.

SCHOONENBERG, Peter, 1911- 230.2
God's world in the making. Pittsburgh, Pa., Duquesne [c.]1964. ix, 207p. 23cm. (Duquesne studies. Theological ser., 2) Bibl. 64-12599 3.95
1. Man (Theology) 2. Evolution. 3. Marriage—Catholic Church. 4. Work (Theology) I. Title. II. Series.

SCHOONENBERG, Piet J. A. M., 1911- 230.2
Covenant and creation [by] Piet Schoonenberg. [1st American ed. Notre Dame, Ind.] University of Notre Dame Press [1969, c1968] xxiii, 213 p. 21 cm. Translation of Verbond en schepping. Bibliographical footnotes. [BS543.S383 1969] 74-75119 5.95
1. Bible—Theology. I. Title.

SEGUNDO, Juan Luis. 230'.2 s
The community called church, by Juan Luis Segundo in collaboration with the staff of the Peter Faber Center in Montevideo, Uruguay. Translated by John Drury. Maryknoll, N.Y. [Orbis Books, 1973] xi, 172 p. 24 cm. (His A theology for artisans of a new humanity, v. 1) (Series: Segundo, Juan Luis. Teologia abierta para el laico adulto. English. v. 1.) Translation of Esa comunidad llamada iglesia. Includes bibliographical references. [BX1751.2.A1S413 vol. 1] [BX1746] 282 72-85795 ISBN 0-88344-481-X 6.95
1. Church. 2. Christian life—Catholic authors. 3. Church and the world. I. Centro Pedro Fabro de Montevideo. II. Title. III. Series.

SEGUNDO, Juan Luis. 230'.2 s
Evolution and guilt / by Juan Luis Segundo, in collaboration with the staff of the Peter Faber Center in Montevideo, Uruguay ; translated by John Drury. Maryknoll, N.Y. : Orbis Books, [1974] vi, 148 p. ; 24 cm. (His A theology for artisans of a new humanity ; v. 5) (Series: Segundo, Juan Luis. Teologia abierta para el laico adulto. English ; v. 5.) Translation of Evolucion y culpa. Includes bibliographical references. [BX1751.2.A1S413 vol. 5] 233'.2 73-89054 ISBN 0-88344-485-2 : 7.95. ISBN 0-88344-491-7 pbk. : 4.95
I. Centro Pedro Fabro de Montevideo. II. Title. III. Series.

SEGUNDO, Juan Luis. 230'.2 s
Grace and the human condition, by Juan Luis Segundo in collaboration with the staff of the Peter Faber Center in Montevideo, Uruguay. Translated by John Drury. Maryknoll, N.Y. [Orbis Books, 1973] viii, 213 p. 24 cm. (His A theology for artisans of a new humanity, v. 2) (Series: Segundo, Juan Luis. Teologia abierta para el laico adulto. English. v. 2.) Translation of Gracia y condicion humana. Includes bibliographical references. [BX1751.2.A1S413 vol. 2] [BT761.2] 234'.1 72-85794 ISBN 0-88344-482-8 6.95
1. Grace (Theology) 2. Man (Theology) I. Centro Pedro Fabro de Montevideo. II. Title. III. Series.

SEGUNDO, Juan Luis. 230'.2 s
Our idea of God, by Juan Luis Segundo, in collaboration with the staff of the Peter Faber Center in Montevideo, Uruguay. Translated by John Drury. Maryknoll, N.Y., [Orbis Books, 1974] vi, 206 p. 24 cm. (His A theology for artisans of a new humanity, v. 3) (Series: Segundo, Juan Luis. Teologia abierta para el laico adulto. English, v. 3.) Translation of Nuestra idea de Dios. Includes bibliographical references. [BX1751.2.A1S413 vol. 3] [BT102] 231 73-77358 ISBN 0-88344-483-6 6.95
1. God. I. Centro Pedro Fabro de Montevideo. II. Title. III. Series.

SEGUNDO, Juan Luis. 230'.2 s
The sacraments today, by Juan Luis Segundo, in collaboration with the staff of the Peter Faber Center in Montevideo, Uruguay. Translated by John Drury. Maryknoll, N.Y. [Orbis Books, 1974] vi, 154 p. 24 cm. (His A theology for artisans of a new humanity, v. 4) (Series: Segundo, Juan Luis. Teologia abierta para el laico adulto. English, v. 4.) Translation of Los sacramentos hoy. Includes bibliographical references. [BX1751.2.A1S413 vol. 4] [BX2200] 234'.16 73-77359 ISBN 0-88344-484-4 6.95
1. Sacraments—Catholic Church. I. Centro Pedro Fabro de Montevideo. II. Title. III. Series.
Pbk. 3.95, ISBN 0-88344-490-9.

SEGUNDO, Juan Luis. 230'.2
A theology for artisans of a new humanity. [Maryknoll, N.Y.] Orbis Books [1973- v. 24 cm. Translation of Teologia abierta para el laico adulto. Includes bibliographical references. [BX1751.2.A1S413] 73-160586 ISBN 0-88344-480-1 6.95 per vol.
1. Theology, Catholic—Collections. I. Title.

SHANNON, William Henry, 1917- 230.2
The church of Christ. Rochester, N.Y., Christopher Press, 1959. 232 p. illus. 23 cm. Includes bibliography. [BX1752.S5 1959] 59-14685
1. Catholic Church — Apologetic works. 2. Jesus Christ — Mustical body. I. Title.

SHANNON, William Henry, 1917- 230.2
The Church of Christ, [2d ed] Rochester, N.Y., Christopher Press, 1960. xviii, 232 p. illus. 23 cm. Bibliography: p. 194-197. [BX17562.S5 1960] 61-4592
1. Catholic Church — Apologetic works. 2. Jesus Christ — Mystical body. I. Title.

SHEED, Francis Joseph, 1897- 230.2
Thelogy for beginners. New York, Sheed & Ward [1957] 241 p. 21 cm. [BS1754.S553] 57-10174
1. Catholic Church — Doctrinal and controversial works, Popular. I. Title.

SHEED, Francis Joseph, 1897- 230.2
Theology for beginners. New York, Sheed & Ward [1957] 241p. 21cm. [BX1754.S553] 57-10174
1. Catholic Church—Doctrinal and controversial works, Popular. I. Title.

SHERIDAN, John Desmond, 1903- 230'.2
The hungry sheep; Catholic doctrine restated against contemporary attacks [by] John D. Sheridan. New Rochelle, N.Y., Arlington House [1974] 175 p. 23 cm. Includes bibliographical references. [BX1752.S53] 73-17003 ISBN 0-87000-265-1 7.95
1. Catholic Church—Apologetic works. I. Title.

SHERIDAN, John V. 230.2
Questions and answers on the Catholic faith. Foreword by James Francis Cardinal McIntyre. New York, Hawthorn [c.1963] 319p. 21cm. Bibl. 63-11862 4.95
1. Questions and answers—Theology. 2. Catholic Church—Doctrinal and controversial works—Catholic authors. I. Title.

SIMMONS, Ernest. 230.2
Kingdom come; the plain man's guide to the Catholic faith. London, Burns and Oates; Westminster, Md., Newman Press [1961] 197 p. 22 cm. [BX1754.S574 1961] 61-65047
1. Catholic Church — Doctrinal and controversial works — Catholic authors. I. Title.

SMITH, Elwood F. 230.2
A guidebook to the Summa, by Elwood F. Smith and Louis A. Ryan. New York, Benziger, 1950- v. 23 cm. Contents.v. 2. Preface to happiness. includes bibliographies. [BX1749.T6S62] 50-35716
1. Thomas Aquinas, Saint, 1225?-1274. Summa theologica. I. Ryan, Louis A., 1913- joint author. II. Title.

SMITH, Richard, Bp. of Chalcedon, 1566-1655. 230'.2 s
An answer to Thomas Bels late challeng / [by] Richard Smith. Ilkley [etc.] : Scolar Press, 1976. [69], 446, [34] p. ; 20 cm. (English recusant literature, 1558-1640 ; v. 315) (Series: Rogers, David Morrison, comp. English recusant literature, 1558-1640 ; v. 315.) Original t.p. has author statement: by S. R. "Reproduced (original size) from a copy in the library of the Brompton Oratory." Reprint of the 1605 ed. published by L. Kellam, Doway. "STC 22809." Includes index. [BX1750.A1E5 vol. 315] 282 77-355604 ISBN 0-85967-329-4
1. Catholic Church—Doctrinal and controversial works—Catholic authors. 2. Bell, Thomas, fl. 1593-1610. The downefall of poperie. I. Title. II. Series.

SMITH, Robert D 230.2
The mark of holiness. Westminster, Md., Newman Press, 1961. 323 p. 23 cm. Includes bibliography. [BX1751.2.S5] 61-8974
1. Catholic Church — Doctrinal and controversial works — Catholic authors. 2. Church — Holiness. I. Title.

SMITH, Robert D. 230.2
The mark of holiness. Westminster, Md., Newman Press [c.]1961. 323p. Bibl. 61-8974 4.50
1. Catholic Church—Doctrinal and controversial works—Catholic authors. 2. Church—Holiness. I. Title.

SOUTHERN, A. C. 230'.2
Elizabethan recusant prose, 1559-1582 : a historical and critical account of the books of the Catholic refugees printed and published abroad and at secret presses in England together with an annotated bibliography of the same / by A. C. Southern ; with a foreword by H. O. Evennett. Norwood, Pa. : Norwood Editions, 1976. xxxv, 553 p., [10] leaves of plates : ill. ; 24 cm. Reprint of the 1950 ed. published by Sands, London. "Presents in an abridged form a thesis which was originally submitted and approved for the degree of Ph.D. of the University of London." Includes bibliographies and index. [PR428.C3S6 1976] 76-2676 ISBN 0-8414-7642-X lib. bdg. : 45.00
1. English prose literature—Catholic authors—History and criticism. 2. English prose literature—Early modern, 1500-1700—History and criticism. 3. English prose literature—Catholic authors—Bibliography. 4. English prose literature—Early modern, 1500-1700—Bibliography. 5. Bibliography—Early printed books—16th century. I. Title.

STANFORD, Edward V. 230.2
Foundations of Christian belief; an introductory course in apologetics. Westminster, Md., Newman Press, 1960. 241p. illus. Bibl.: p.229-233. 60-10729 1.95 pap.,
1. Catholic Church—Apologetic works. I. Title.

STAPLETON, Thomas, 1535-1598. 230'.2 s
A returne of untruthes upon M. Iewelles replie : 1566 / Thomas Stapleton. Ilkley [Eng.] : Scolar Press, 1976. 134, 196 p. ; 21 cm. (English recusant literature, 1558-1640 ; v. 308) (Series: Rogers, David Morrison, comp. English recusant literature, 1558-1640 ; v. 308.) Reprint of the 1566 ed., printed by J. Latius, Antwerpe. [BX1750.A1E5 vol. 308] 230'.2 76-380406 ISBN 0-85967-320-0
1. Catholic Church—Doctrinal and controversial works—Catholic authors. 2. Jewel, John, Bp. of Salisbury, 1522-1571. I. Title. II. Series.

STEINMANN, Jean. 230.2
A Christian faith for today. Translated by Edmond Bonin. Paramus, N.J., Newman Press [1969] v, 135 p. 21 cm. Translation of Une foi chretienne pour aujourd'hui. Bibliographical footnotes. [BT77.S73513] 70-79038 4.50
1. Theology, Doctrinal—Popular works. I. Title.

STEVENS, Eldred N 1921- 230.2
Stevens-Beevers debate on the New Testament and Roman Catholicism, a public discussion. Nashville [1952] 231p. illus. 21cm. [BX1779.S86] 52-67724
1. Catholic Church—Doctrinal and controversial works—Debates, etc. I. Beevers, Eric, 1907- II. Title.

STEVENS, Eldred N 1921- 230.2
Stevens-Beevers debate on the New Testament and Roman Catholicism, a public discussion. 2d print. Nashville [c1953] 231p. illus. 21cm. [BX1779.S86 1953] 53-20709
1. Catholic Church—Doctrinal and controversial works—Debates, etc. I. Beevers, Eric, 1907- II. Title.

STRAVINSKAS, Peter M. J. 230'.2
The Church after the Council : a primer for adults / Peter M. J. Stravinskas, Robert A. McBain ; photography by Philip Dattilo. New York : Alba House, [1975] xi, 113 p. : ill. ; 21 cm. Includes bibliographies. [BX1751.2.S75] 75-4720 ISBN 0-8189-0316-3 pbk. : 2.95
1. Catholic Church—Doctrinal and controversial works—Catholic authors. I. McBain, Robert A., joint author. II. Title.

STUBER, Stanley Irvin, 1903- 230.2
How Protestants differ from Roman Catholics. New York, Association Press [1961] 126 p. 15 cm. (An Association Press reflection book, 544) "An adaptation of the author's full length Primer on Roman Catholicism for Protestants." [BX1765.2.S8] 61-7112
1. Catholic Church — Doctrinal and controversial works — Protestant authors. I. Title.

STUBER, Stanley Irving, 1903- 230.2
How Protestants differ from Roman Catholics. New York, Association [c.1961] 126p. 15cm. (Association Pr. reflection bk., 544) 'An adaption of the author's full length Primer on Roman Catholicism for Protestants.' 61-7112 .50 pap.,
1. Catholic Church—Doctrinal and controversial works—Protestant authors. I. Title.

STUBER, Stanley Irving, 1903- 230.2
Primer on Roman Catholicism for Protestants; an appraisal of the basic differences between the Roman Catholic Church and Protestantism. New York, Association Press [1953] 276p. 21cm. [BX1765.S84] 53-8727
1. Catholic Church—Doctrinal and controversial works—Protestant authors. I. Title.

STUBER, Stanley Irving, 1903- 230.2
Primer on Roman Catholicism for Protestants: an appraisal of the basic differences between the Roman Catholic Church and Protestantism. New rev. ed. New York, Association Press [1960] 276 p. 21 cm. Includes bibliography. [BX1765S84 1960] 60-6563
1. Catholic Church — Doctrinal and controversial works — Protestant authors. I. Title.

STUBER, Stanley Irving, 1903- 230.2
Primer on Roman Catholicism for Protestants; an appraisal of the basic differences between the Roman Catholic Church and Protestantism. New rev. ed. New York, Association Press [1960] 276 p. 21 cm. Includes bibliography. [BX1765.S84 1960] 60-6563
1. Catholic Church—Doctrinal and controversial works—Protestant authors. I. Title.

SYNAVE, Paul. 230.2
Prophecy and inspiration; a commentary on the Summa theologica II-II, questions 171-178, by Paul Synave and Pierre Benoit. [Translation by Avery R. Dulles and Thomas L. Sheridan] New York, Desclee Co., 1961. 185 p. 22 cm. Translation of Traite de la prophetle. Includes bibliography. [BS480.S953] 60-10164
1. Bible — Inspiration. 2. Prophets. 3. Thomas Aquinas, Saint 1224!-1274. Summa theologica. I. Benoit, Pierre 1906- II. Title.

SYNAVE, Paul 230.2
Prophecy and inspiration; a commentary on the Summa theologica II-II, questions 171-178, by Paul Synave and Pierre Benoit. Tr. [from French] by Avery R. Dulles and Thomas L. Sheridan. New York, Desclee Co., 1961. 185p. Bibl. 60-10164 3.75
1. Thomas Aquinas, Saint, 1225?-1274. Summa theologica. 2. Bible—Inspiration. 3. Prophets. I. Benoit, Pierre, 1906- II. Title.

TANIS, Edward J 230.2
What Rome teaches; a comparison of some of the teachings of the Roman Catholic Church with Holy Scripture. Grand Rapids, Baker Book House, 1954. 56p. 22cm. [BX1765.T23] 54-2720
1. Catholic Church—Doctrinal and controversial works— Protestant authors. I. Title.

TANQUEREY, Adolphe, 1854-1932. 230.2
A manual of dogmatic theology. Translated by John J. Byrnes. New York, Desclee Co., 1959. 2 v. 22 cm. Translation of Brevior synopsis theologiae dogmaticae. Bibliographical footnotes. [BX1751.T313 1959] 59-13235
1. Theology, Doctrinal. 2. Catholic Church — Doctrinal and controversial works. Full name: Adolphe Alfred Tanquerey. I. Title.

THE Teaching of Christ : 230'.2
a Catholic catechism for adults / edited by Ronald Lawler, Donald W. Wuerl, Thomas Comerford Lawler. Huntington, IN : Our Sunday Visitor, c1976. 640 p. ; 22 cm. Includes indexes. Bibliography: p. 582-612. [BX1751.2.T4] 75-34852 ISBN 0-87973-899-5 : 9.95 ISBN 0-87973-858-8 pbk. : 5.95
1. Theology, Catholic. I. Lawler, Ronald David, 1926- II. Wuerl, Donald W. III. Lawler, Thomas Comerford.

TEILHARD de Chardin, Pierre. 230.2
How I believe. Translated by Rene Hague. New York, Harper & Row [1969] 91 p. 19 cm. (Perennial library, 156) Translation of Comment je crois. [B2430.T373C593] 76-7823 0.75
1. Theology—Addresses, essays, lectures. I. Title.

THEODORETUS, Bp. of Cyrrhus. 230'.2 s
The ecclesiasticall history [of] Theodoret / [translated from the Greek]. Ilkley [etc.] : Scolar Press, 1976. [29], 406 p. ; 21 cm. (English recusant literature, 1558-1640 ; v. 287) (Series: Rogers, David Morrison, comp. English recusant literature, 1558-1640 ; v. 287.) Translation of Ekklesiastike historia. Reprint of the 1612 ed. published at St. Omer. STC 23938. [BX1750.A1E5 vol. 287] [BR165] 270.2 76-381977 ISBN 0-85967-288-3 : £10.00
1. Church history—Primitive and early church, ca. 30-600. I. Title. II. Series.

THEOLOGY digest. v. 1- winter 1953- 230.2
[St. Marys, Kan., St. Mary's College] v. in 23 cm. 3 no. a year. Includes two unnumbered preliminary issues dated Dec. 1951 and May 1952. [BX801.T48] 60-17035
1. Theology — Period. 2. Catholic Church — Period. I. St. Mary's College, St. Marys, Kan. II. Title.

THEOLOGY library, 230.2
by a group of theologians under the editorship of A. M. Henry; translated by William Storey. Chicago, Fides Publishers Association [1954- v. 20cm. Translation of Initiation théologique. Contents.v. 1. Introduction to theology. [BX1751.I53] 54-10891
1. Catholic Church—Doctrinal and controversial works. 2. Theology, Doctrinal—Introductions. I. Henry, A. M., ed.

THOMAS Aquinas, Saint, 1225?-1274. 230.2
The Summa theologica. Translated by fathers of the English Dominican Province. Rev. by Daniel J. Sullivan. Chicago, Encyclopaedia Britannica [1955, c1952] 2 v. 25 cm. (Great books of the Western World, v. 19-20) Bibliographical footnotes. [AC1.G72 vol. 19-20] 55-10328
1. Catholic Church—Doctrinal and controversial works. 2. Dominicans. English Province. I. Sullivan, Daniel James, 1909- ed. II. Title.

THOMAS Aquinas, Saint, 1225?-1274. 230.2
Middle High German translation of the Summa theologica; edited with a Latin-German and a German- Latin glossary, by Bayard Quincy Morgan and Friedrich Wilhelm Strothmann. Stanford, Calif., Stanford University Press, 1950. 400 p. facsim. 26 cm. (Stanford University publications. University series. Language and literature. v. 8, no. 1) German and Latin on opposite pages. "[The original ms. of] the Middle High German translation ... is found in Codex H B III 32 of the Landesbibliothek in Stuttgart ... The present edition is based on a photostatic copy made in 1937 ... now ... in the Stanford Library." [PT1658.T39M6] 50-8471
1. Catholic Church — Doctrinal and controversial works. I. Morgan, Bayard Quincy, 1883- ed. II. Title. III. Title: Summa theologica. IV. Series: Stanford University. Stanford University publications. University series. Language and literature, v. 8, no. 1

THOMAS Aquinas, Saint, 1225?-1274. 230.2
Of God and His creatures; an annotated translation (with some abridgement) [of the] Summa contra gentiles of Saint Tho Aquinas, by Joseph Rickaby. Westminster, Md., Carroll Press, 1950. xxi, 423 p. 28 cm. [BX1749.T4] 51-3991
1. Apologetics — Middle Ages. I. Title.

THOMAS, Aquinas, Saint, 1225?-1274 230.2
Summa theologiae. Latin text, English tr., introd., notes, appendices & glossary. London, Eyre & Spottiswoode; New York, McGraw [1966] 23cm. Contents.v.33, 2a2ae. 17-22: Hope, ed., tr., William J. Hill. Bibl. [BX1749.T48] 63-11128 6.75
1. Theology, Doctrinal. I. Title.

THOMAS Aquinas, Saint, 1225?-1274. 230.2
The wisdom of Thomas Aquinas, transcribed from his writings. Mount Vernon, N.Y., Peter Pauper Press [1951] 106 p. 23 cm. "The books ... from which the quotations have been drawn are: Summa theologica and Summa contra gentiles." [BX1749.T324] 51-8366
1. Catholic Church — Doctrinal and controversial works. 2. Apologetics — Middle Ages. I. Title.

THOMAS Aquinas, Saint, 1225?-1274. 230'.2
An Aquinas reader. Edited, with an introd., by Mary T. Clark. [1st ed.] Garden City, N.Y., Image Books, 1972. 597 p. 19 cm. (An Image book original) Bibliography: p. [555]-575. [BX890.T62E6 1972] 72-76709 ISBN 0-385-02505-X 2.45
1. Catholic Church—Collected works. 2. Theology—Collected works—Middle Ages. I. Clark, Mary T., R.S.C.J., ed. II. Title.

THOMAS AQUINAS, Saint, 1225?-1274. 230.2
My way of life, pocket edition of St. Thomas; the Summa simplified for everyone, by Walter Farrell and Martin J. Healy. Brooklyn, Confraternity of the Precious Blood, 1952. vi. 630p. 14cm. [BX1749.T515 1952] 52-67723
1. Catholic Church—Doctrinal and controversial works. I. Farrell, Walter, 1902-1951, tr. II. Healy, Martin J., 1909-tr. III. Title.

THOMAS AQUINAS, Saint, 1225?-1274. 230.2
Nature and grace; selections from the Summa theologica of Thomas Aquinas. Translated and edited by A. M. Fairweather. Philadelphia, Westminster Press [1954] 386p. 24cm. (The Library of Christian classics, v. 11) On spine: Aquinas on nature and grace. Bibliography: p. 369-374. [BX1749.T515 1954] 54-10259
1. Catholic Church—Doctrinal and controversial works. I. Fairweather, Alan M., ed. and tr. II. Title. III. Series: The Library of Christian classics (Philadelphia) v. 11

THOMAS AQUINAS, Saint, 1225?-1274. 230.2
On the truth of the Catholic faith. Summa contra Gentiles. Translated, with an introd. and notes, by Anton C. Pegis. Garden City, N. Y., Hanover House [1955- v. 20cm. Bibliography: book 1, p. 53-56. [BX1749.T413] 55-8490
1. Apologetics—Middle Ages. I. Title.
Contents omitted.

THOMAS AQUINAS, Saint, 1225?-1274. 230.2
On the truth of the Catholic faith. Summa contra Gentiles. Translated, with an introd. and notes, by Anton C. Pegis. Garden City, N. Y., Image Books [1955- v. 19cm. (A Doubleday image book, D26) Bibliography: book 1, p. 53-56. [BX1749.T414] 55-9753
1. Apologetics—Middle Ages. I. Title.
Contents omitted.

THOMAS AQUINAS, Saint, 1225?-1274. 230.2
On the truth of the Catholic faith. Summa contra Gentiles. Translated, with an introd. and notes, by Anton C. Pegis. Garden City, N.Y., Hanover House [1955- v. 20 cm. Contents.book 1. God. -- book 2. Creation. -- book 3. Providence. 2 v. -- book 4. Salvation. Includes bibliographies. [BX1749.T413] 55-8490
1. Apologetics — Middle Ages. I. Title.

THOMAS Aquinas, Saint, 1225?-1274. 230'.2
Pattern for a Christian, according to St. Thomas Aquinas / by A. I. Mennessier; introd. by M. D. Chenu ; translated by Nicholas Halligan. New York : Alba House, [1975] xi, 225 p. ; 21 cm. Translation of L'homme chretien. Includes bibliographical references. [BX890.T62E6 1975] 74-23677 ISBN 0-8189-0299-X pbk. : 4.95
1. Catholic Church—Collected works. 2. Theology—Collected works—Middle Ages, 600-1500. I. Mennessier, Ignatius, 1902-1965. II. Halligan, Francis Nicholas, 1917- tr. III. Title.

THOMAS AQUINAS, Saint, 1225?-1274 230.2
Summa theologiae. Latin text and English tr., introds., notes, appendices, glossaries. London, Eyre & Spottiswoode; New York, McGraw. v. 23cm. Contents.v.8 (1a. 44-49) Creation, variety, and evil, ed., tr. by Thomas Gilby.--v. 19 (1a2ae.22-30; The emotions, ed., tr. by Eric D'Arcy. Bibl. [BX1749.T48 1964] 63-11128 6.75 v.8,; 6.00 v.19,
1. Theology, Doctrinal. I. Title.

THOMAS Aquinas, Saint, 1225?-1274. 230.2
Summa theologiae. General editor: Thomas Gilby. Garden City, N.Y., Image Books [1969- v. 18 cm. The Blackfriars English translation. Contents.Contents.—v. 1. The existence of God (pt. 1, questions 1-13) Bibliographical footnotes. [BX1749.T5 1969] 70-84399 1.45 (v. 1)
1. Theology, Doctrinal. I. Gilby, Thomas, 1902- ed. II. Title.

THOMAS AQUINAS, Saint, 1225?-1274 230.2
Summa theologica [vs. 1, 2, 13] Latin text and English tr., introds., notes, appendices, glossaries. Blackfriars. London, Eyre & Spottiswoode: dist. New York, McGraw [1964] 3v. (various p.) 23cm. Bibl. 63-11128 v.1, 5.50; vs.2 & 13, ea., 6.75
1. Theology, Doctrinal. I. Title.

THOMAS AQUINAS, Saint, 1225?-1274 230.2
Treatise on happiness. Tr. [from Latin] by John A. Oesterle. Englewood Cliffs, N.J., Prentice [c.] 1964. xvi, 208p. 21cm. Bibl. 64-12547 2.75 pap.,
1. Happiness. 2. Ethics. I. Oesterle, John A., tr. II. Title.

THOMAS AQUINAS, Saint, 122?-1274 230.2
Summa theologiae. Latin text and English tr., introds., notes, appendices, glossaries. New York, McGraw; London, Eyre & Spottiswoode [1967] v. 23cm. Contents.v.5 (Ia. 19-26) God's will and providence, ed., tr. by Thomas Gilby.--v.10 (Ia. 65-74) Cosmogony, ed., tr. by William A. Wallace. Bibl. [BX1749.T48 1964] 63-11128 v.5, 6.75; v.10,p7.25
1. Theology, Doctrinal. I. Title.

THOMAS AQUINAS, Saint, 1225?-1274 230.2
Summa theologiae. Latin text. English tr., introd., notes, appendices & glossary. London, Eyre & Spottiswoode; New York, McGraw [1966] 23cm. Contents.v.46, 2a2ae. 179-182: Action and contemplation, ed. tr., Jordan Aumann. Bibl. [BX1749.T48] 63-1128 6.00
1. Theology, Doctrinal. I. Title.

THOMAS AQUINAS, Saint, 1225?-1274. 230.2
Treatise on happiness. Translated by John A. Oesterle. Englewood Cliffs, N.J., Prentice-Hall, 1964. xvi, 208 p. 21 cm. Selections from the Summa theologiae. Bibliographical footnotes. [BX1749.T515 1964] 64-12547
1. Happiness. 2. Ethics. I. Oesterle, John A., tr. II. Title.

THE Thomist. 23022
From an abundant spring; the Walter Farrell memorial volume of the Thomist. Edited by the staff. New York, P. J. Kenedy [1952] xii, 555 p. port. 23 cm. Includes bibliographical references. [BX880;T54] 52-14540
1. Farrell, Walter, 1902-1951. 2. Catholic Church — Addresses, essays, lectures. I. Title.

THE Thomist reader. 230.2
1957- [Baltimore] v. 23cm. Published by the Dominicans, Province of St. Joseph. [BX801.T52] 57-1468
1. Thomas Aquinas, Saint—Societies, periodicals, etc. 2. Theology—Period. 3. Scholasticism—Period. 4. Catholic Church—Period. I. Dominicans, Province of St. Joseph.

TIERNEY, Michael F 1889- 230.2
This mystery which is Christ, essays. [1st ed.] New York, Exposition Press [1958] 197 p. 21 cm. [BX890.T66] 58-14575
1. Catholic Church—Addresses, essays, lectures. I. Title.

TORSELLINO, Orazio, 1545-1599. 230'.2 s
The admirable life of S. Francis Xavier, 1632 / Orazio Torsellino Ilkley [Eng.] : Scolar Press, 1976. 616 p. : ill. ; 21 cm. (English recusant literature, 1558-1640 ; v. 299) (Series: Rogers, David Morrison, comp. English recusant literature, 1558-1640 ; v. 299.) "Reproduced (original size) from a copy in Cambridge University Library ... References: Allison and Rogers 824; STC 24140" Reprint of the 1632 ed. [BX1750.A1E5 vol. 299] [BX4700.F8] 282'.092'4 B 76-377650
1. Francisco Xavier, Saint, 1506-1552. 2. Christian saints—Biography. I. Title. II. Series.

TORSELLINO, Orazio, 1545-1599. 230'.2 s
The history of our B. Lady of Loreto / Orazio Torsellino. Ilkley [Eng.] : Scolar Press, 1976. 540 p. : facsim. ; 20 cm. (English recusant literature, 1558-1640 ; v. 307) (Series: Rogers, David Morrison, comp. English recusant literature, 1558-1640 ; v. 307.) Translated from the Latin. Reprint of the 1608 ed. "STC 24141." Includes index. [BX1750.A1E5 vol. 307] [BT660.L7] 232.91 77-351164 ISBN 0-85967-319-7
1. Loreto, Madonna di. I. Title. II. Series.

TOURVILLE, Henri de, 1842-1903. 230.2
Light and life; notes and letters. [Translated by Vincent Girling] New York, Crowell [1961] 143 p. 16 cm. [BX890.T753] 61-10889
1. Catholic church — Doctrinal and controversial works — Catholic authors. I. Title.

TOURVILLE, Henri de, 1842-1903 230.2
Light and life; notes and letters, by Abbe de Tourville. [Tr. from French by Vincent Girling] New York, Crowell [c.1961] 143p. 16cm. 61-10889 2.50 pap.,
1. Catholic Church—Doctrinal and controversial works—Catholic authors. I. Title.

A Treatise of auricular confession. The fore-runner of Bels downefall 230'.2 s
/ [by] Philip Woodward. Ilkley [etc.] : Scolar Press, 1976. 429 p. in various pagings ; 20 cm. (English recusant literature, 1558-1640 ; v. 322) (Series: Rogers, David Morrison, comp. English recusant literature, 1558-1640 ; v. 322.) "A treatise of auricular confession ... from a copy in the library of the Abbey, Fort Augustus ... references: Allison and Rogers 828; STC 13036 ... Philip Woodward, The fore-runner of Bels downefall ... from a copy in Cambridge University Library ... references: Allison and Rogers 909; STC 19407." Reprint of the 1622 ed. published by J. Heigham, S. Omers, and the 1605 ed. of P. Woodward's work. [BX1750.A1E5 vol. 322] [BX2264] 265'.62 77-362658 ISBN 0-85967-338-3
1. Bell, Thomas, fl. 1593-1610. 2. Catholic Church—Doctrinal and controversial works—Catholic authors. 3. Confession. I. Heigham, John. II. Woodward, Philip. The fore-runner of Bels downefall. 1976. III. Series.

TRESE, Leo John, 1902- 230.2
The faith and Christian living, four-volume religion program. [Discussion questions by James Carroll. Notre Dame, Ind., Fides dome bks., D-21, 22, 23, 24) Reprinting of The faith explained, Many are one, More than many sparrows, and Everyman's road to heaven, by L. J. Trese, and of God so loved the world, by J. J. Castelot. Contents.v.1. The Creed, summary of the faith.--v.2. Salvation, history and the Commandments, by L. J. Trese, J. J. Castelot.--v.3. The sacraments and prayer.--v.4. Guide to Christian living. 63-114u4 1.25 pap., ea.,
1. Theology, Doctrinal—Introductions. I. Title.

TRESE, Leo John, 1902- 230.2
The faith and Christian living, four-volume religion program. [Discussion questions by James Carroll. Notre Dame, Ind., Fides Publishers, 1963] 4 v. 18 cm. (A Fides dome book) A reprinting of The faith explained, Many are one, More than many sparrows, and Everyman's road to heaven, by L. J. Trese and J. J. Castelot -- v.3. The sacraments and prayer. -- v. 4. Guide to Christian living. [BT77.T76] 63-11404
1. Theology, Doctrinal — Introductions. I. Title.

TRESE, Leo John, 1902- 230.2
Many are one. Chicago, Fides Publishers [1952] 147p. 21cm. [BX1754.T7] 52-8414
1. Catholic Church— Doctrinal and controversial works, Popular. I. Title.

TRESE, Leo John, 1902- 230.2
Wisdom shall enter. Chicago, Fides Publishers [1954] 144p. 21cm. [BX1754.T73] 54-7838
1. Catholic Church—Apologetic works. I. Title.

TRUTH and life, an outline of modern theology 230.2
[by] Donal Flanagan [and others. 1st. American ed.] Milwaukee, Bruce Pub. Co. [1969, c1968] xi, 213 p. 20 cm. Bibliographical footnotes. [BT80.T7 1969] 69-12674 4.95
1. Theology, Doctrinal—Addresses, essays, lectures. 2. Christian life—Catholic authors. I. Flanagan, Donal, 1929-

TWENTIETH century 230.2
Catholicism; a periodical supplement to The Twentieth Century Ency. of Catholicism. No. 2 Ed.: Lancelot Sheppard. Managing ed.: Paul Fargis. European ed.: Arthur Coppotelli. New York, Hawthorn [c.1965] 248p. 21cm. Bibl. [BX841.T85] 58-14327 6.00 bds.,
1. Theology—Collections—Catholic authors.

VARILLON, Francois, 1905- 230.2
Announcing Christ through Scripture to the church [Tr. from French] by Stephen Deacon, Jennifer Nicholson] Westminster, Md., Newman, 1964. 503p. 23cm. Bibl. 64-2531 6.95
1. Theology, Doctrinal—Popular works. I. Title.

VAWTER, Bruce. 230.2
New paths through the Bible; some essays in Biblical theology. [1st American ed.] Wilkes-Barre, Pa., Dimension Books [1968] 140 p. 21 cm. Bibliographical footnotes. [BS543.A1V35 1968] 68-31389 4.50
1. Bible—Theology—Addresses, essays, lectures. I. Title.

VERSTEGEN, Richard, 1548(ca.)-1640. 230'.2 s
A restitution of decayed intelligence / Richard Verstegan. Ilkley [Eng.] : Scolar Press, 1976. 338 p. : ill. ; 22 cm. (English recusant

literature, 1558-1640 ; v. 323) (Series: Rogers, David Morrison, comp. English recusant literature, 1558-1640 ; v. 323.) On original t.p.: Nationum origo. "STC 21361." Reprint of the 1605 ed. published by R. Bruney, Antvverp [i.e. Antwerp] Includes index. [BX1750.A1E5 Vol. 323] [DA152] 941.01 77-355702 ISBN 0-85967-340-5
1. Great Britain—History—Anglo-Saxon period, 449-1066. 2. Anglo-Saxon language. I. Title. II. Series.

VILLACASTIN, Tomas de, 1570-1649. 230'.2 s
A manuall of devout meditations, 1618 / Tomas de Villacastin. Ilkley : Scolar Press, 1976. 558 p. ; 20 cm. (English Recusant Literature, 1558-1640 ; v. 326) (Series: Rogers, David Morrison, comp. English recusant literature, 1558-1640 ; v. 326.) Original Spanish title: Manual de consideraciones y ejercicios espirituales. "Allison and Rogers 848; STC 16877." Includes original t.p.: A manuall of devout meditations and exercises, instructing how to pray mentally, drawne for the most part, out of the spiritual exercises of B. F. Ignatius ... Includes index. [BX1750.A1E5 vol. 326] [BX2186] 242 77-371652 ISBN 0-85967-342-1
1. Spiritual exercises. I. Loyola, Ignacio de, Saint, 1491-1556. Exercitia spiritualia. II. Series.

VON HILDEBRAND, Dietrich, 1889- 230'.2
The new Tower of Babel : essays / by Dietrich Von Hildebrand. New ed. Chicago : Franciscan Herald Press, c1977. 243 p. ; 21 cm. Reprint of the 1953 ed. published by P. J. Kenedy, New York. [BX891.V64 1977] 76-998 ISBN 0-8199-0600-X : 5.95
1. Catholic Church—Addresses, essays, lectures. 2. Civilization, Modern—20th century—Addresses, essays, lectures. I. Title.

VONIER, Anscar, Father, 1875-1938. 230.2
Collected works. With a foreword by Pruno Fehrenbacher, o.s.b. [Rev. ed.] Westminster, Md., Newman Press [1952-] v. 22 cm. Contents.CONTENTS. -- v. 1. The Incarnation and redemption. [BX890.V67] A52
1. Catholic Church — Collected works. 2. Theology — Collected works — 20th cent I. Fehrenbacher, Bruno, 1805- ed. II. Title.

WALGRAVE, J. H. 230.2
Newman the theologian; the nature of belief and doctrine as exemplified in his life and works. Translated [from the French] by A. V. Littledale. New York, Sheed & Ward [1960] 378p. Bibl.: p.373-378. 60-16895 8.50
1. Newman, John Henry, Cardinal, 1801-1890. 2. Dogma, Development of. I. Title.

WALGRAVE, Jan Henricus, 1911- 230.2
Newman the theologian; the nature of belief and doctrine as exemplified in his life and works, by J. H. Walgrave. Translated by A. V. Littledale. New York, Sheed & Ward [1960] xi, 378 p. 22 cm. "Translation of Newman, le developpement du dogme." Bibliography: p. 373-378. [BX4705.N5W233 1960] 60-16895
1. Newman, John Henry, Cardinal, 1801-1890. 2. Dogma, Development of. I. Title.

WALKER, John Baptist. 230.2
For all men; Catholic teaching for today based on Vatican II. Chicago, Franciscan Herald Press [1970] xi, 190 p. 21 cm. [BX1754.W27 1970] 79-10186 2.50
1. Catholic Church—Doctrinal and controversial works, Popular. I. Title.

WALSINGHAM, Francis. 230'.2 s
A search made into matters of religion / [by] Francis Walsingham. Ilkley : Scolar Press, 1976. [29], 520 p. ; 21 cm. (English recusant literature, 1558-1640 ; v. 286) (Series: Rogers, David Morrison, comp. English recusant literature, 1588-1640 ; v. 286.) Reprint of the 1609 ed. "Reproduced ... from a copy in the library of Stonyhurst College." STC 25002 Includes index. [BX1750.A1E5 vol. 286] [BX1752] 230'.2 76-380512 ISBN 0-85967-287-5 : £10.00
1. Catholic Church—Apologetic works. 2. Walsingham, Francis. 3. Protestantism—Controversial literature. I. Title. II. Series.

WEDGE, Florence. 230.2
That your joy may be full. Pulaski, Wis., Franciscan Publishers, 1960. 191 p. 22 cm. [BT993.2.W4] 59-13501
1. Apostle's Creed. 2. Catholic Church — Doctrinal and controversial works, Popular. I. Title.

*WEIGEL, Gustave 230.2
Catholic theology in dialogue. New York, Harper [1965, c.1960, 1961] 126p. 21cm. (Harper torchbks.; Cathedral lib., TB301) .95 pap.,
I. Title.

WEIGEL, Gustave, 1906- 230.2
Catholic theology in dialogue. [1st ed.] New York, Harper [1961] 126 p. 20 cm. [BX4818.3.W4] 61-13284
1. Catholic Church — Relations — Protestant churches. 2. Protestant churches — Relations — Catholic Church. 3. Catholic Church — Doctrinal and controversial works — Catholic authors. I. Title.

WEIGEL, Gustave, 1906- 230.2
Catholic theology in dialogue. New York, Harper [c.1960, 1961] 126p. 61-13281 2.75 bds.,
1. Catholic Church—Relations—Protestant churches. 2. Protestant churches—Relations—Catholic Church. 3. Catholic Church—Doctrinal and controversial works—Catholic authors. I. Title.

WELLS, David F. 230'.2
Revolution in Rome [by] David F. Wells. Downers Grove, Ill., InterVarsity Press [1972] 149 p. 22 cm. Bibliography: p. 139-145. [BX1751.2.W43] 72-78404 ISBN 0-87784-910-2 4.95
1. Catholic Church—Doctrinal and controversial works—Protestant authors. I. Title.

WERNER, Maria Assunta 230'.2
CSMC study guide: Concilium library, vs. 11-20. Cincinnati, CSMC Pr. [1967] viii, 88p. 22cm. To be used with readings in the vs. of Concilium: theology in the age of renewal. [BX880.C68W4] 67-5598 1.50 pap.,
1. Concilium: theology in the age of renewal. I. Concilium: theology in the age of renewal. II. Title.

WESTHEIMER, Karl. 230'.2
The historical role of the Catholic Church in times of mental chaos & moral decay. [1st ed. Albuquerque, N.M., American Classical College Press, 1973] 1 v. (various pagings) illus. 28 cm. Cover title. "An American Idea study." [BX1751.2.W46] 73-76434
1. Catholic Church—Doctrinal and controversial works—Catholic authors. 2. Civilization, Modern—20th century. I. Title.
Publisher's Address: P.O. Box 4526 Albuquerque, N.M. 87106

WHITE, Thomas, 1925- 230'.2
Renewal of faith; adult instruction in the Catholic faith [by] Thomas White and Desmond O'Donnell. Notre Dame, Ind., Ave Maria Press [1974] 239 p. 21 cm. "Originally published in serial form by the Catholic Enquiry Centre of Australia." [BX930.W46] 74-76320 ISBN 0-87793-068-6 2.95
1. Christian education—Text-books for adults—Catholic. I. O'Donnell, Desmond, joint author. II. Title.

WIDDRINGTON, Roger, 1563-1640. 230'.2 s
Roger Widdrington last reioynder, 1619 / Thomas Preston. Ilkley : Scolar Press, 1976. 645, [35] p. ; 26 cm. (English recusant literature, 1558-1640 ; v. 280) (Series: Rogers, David Morrison, comp. English recusant literature, 1580-1640 ; v. 280.) Photoreprint ed. Includes original t.p.: Roger Widdringtons last reioynder to Mr. Thomas Fitz-Herberts reply concerning to oath of allegiance, and the Popes power to depose princes. [BX1750.A1E5 vol. 280] [BX1810] 262'.132 76-359810 ISBN 0-85967-281-6
1. Catholic Church—Doctrinal and controversial works—Catholic authors. 2. Popes—Temporal power. 3. Oaths. I. Title. II. Series.

WILHELM, Anthony J. 230'.2
Christ among us; a modern presentation of the Catholic faith, by Anthony J. Wilhelm. Rev. ed. New York, Newman Press [1972, c1973] viii, 440 p. 21 cm. Includes bibliographies. [BX1754.W47 1973] 72-86595 ISBN 0-8091-1746-0 1.95
1. Catholic Church—Doctrinal and controversial works, Popular. I. Title.

WILHELM, Anthony J. 230'.2
Christ among us : a modern presentation of the Catholic faith / by Anthony J. Wilhelm. 2d rev. ed. New York : Paulist Press, 1975. viii, 440 p. ; 21 cm. Includes bibliographies and index. [BX1754.W47 1975] 75-330120 ISBN 0-8091-1746-0 pbk. : 2.95
1. Catholic Church—Doctrinal and controversial works, Popular. I. Title.

WILLIAM, Franz Michel, 1894- 230.2
Our way to God; a book of religious self-education. Translated by Ronald Walls. Milwaukee, Bruce Pub. Co. [1964] xv, 400 p. 23 cm. [BX930.W513] 64-22859
1. Religious education — Text-books for adults — Catholic. I. Title.

WILLIAM, Franz Michel, 1894- 230.2
Our way to God; a book of religious self-education. Tr. [from German] by Ronald Walls. Milwaukee, Bruce [c.1964] xv, 400p. 23cm. 64-22859 5.75
1. Religious education—Text-books for adults—Catholic. I. Title.

WITCUTT, William Purcell. 230.2
Return to reality. New York, Macmillan [1956?] 62p. 23cm. [BX1765] 56-9712
1. Catholic Church—Doctrinal and controversial works—Protestant authors. I. Title.

WITCUTT, William Purcell. 230.2
Return to reality. New York, Macmilla [1956?] 62 p. 23 cm. [BX1765] 56-9712
1. Catholic Church — Doctrinal and controversial works — Protestant authors. I. Title.

WOODS, Ralph Louis, 1904- ed. 230.2
A treasury of Catholic thinking. Introd. by James M. Gillis. New York, Crowell [1953] 378p. 24cm. [BX880.W65] 53-8443
1. Theology—Collections—Catholic authors. I. Title.

WOODS, Ralph Louis, 1904- ed. 230.2
A treasury of Catholic thinking. Introd. by James M. Gillis. New York [Apollo Eds., 1962, c.1953] 378p. (A-36) 1.95 pap.,
1. Theology—Collections—Catholic authors. I. Title.

WRIGHT, Thomas, d.1624? 230'.2 s
Certaine articles or forcible reasons, 1600 / Thomas Wright ; [and] The lives and singular virtues of Saint Elzear ... and of his wife, 1638 / Etienne Binet. Ilkley, Eng. : Scolar Press, 1976. 461 p. ; 19 cm. (English recusant literature, 1558-1640 ; v. 301) (Series: Rogers, David Morrison, comp. English recusant literature, 1558-1640 ; v. 301.) "Reproduced with permission: 1. Thomas Wright, Certaine articles, 1600, from a copy in the library of St. Mary's Seminary, Oscott .... Reference: Allison and Rogers 920; not in STC. 2. Etienne Binet, The lives and singular virtues ..., 1638, from a copy in the Bodleian Library .... Reference: Allison and Rogers 111; not in STC." [BX1750.A1E5 vol. 301] [BX4700.E45] 282'.092'2 B 77-357172
1. Elzear de Sabran, Saint, 1285-1328. 2. Delphine, ca. 1284-ca. 1358. 3. Christian biography—France. 4. Protestantism—Controversial literature. I. Binet, Stephen, 1569-1639. The lives and singular virtues of Saint Elzear ... and of his wife. 1976. II. Title: Certaine articles or forcible reasons, 1600. III. Series.

ZATKO, James J., comp. 230'.2
The valley of silence; Catholic thought in contemporary Poland, edited by James J. Zatko. Notre Dame [Ind.] University of Notre Dame Press [1967] xiv, 391 p. illus. 24 cm. Includes bibliographical references. [BT10.Z3] 67-12125
1. Catholic Church in Poland—Addresses, essays, lectures. 2. Theology—Addresses, essays, lectures. I. Title.

ZUNDEL, Maurice. 230.2
In search of the unknown God. Translated by Margaret Clark. [New York] Herder and Herder [1959] 194 p. 19 cm. [BX1754.3Z833 1959] 58-6990
1. Catholic Church—Doctrinal and controversial works. Popular. 2. Questions and answers—Theology. I. Title.

LONERGAN, Bernard J. F. 230'.2'018
Method in theology, [by] Bernard J. F. Lonergan. London, Darton, Longman and Todd, 1972. xii, 405 p. 23 cm. Includes bibliographical references. [BR118.L65 1972b] 72-195722 ISBN 0-232-51139-X
1. Theology—Methodology. I. Title.
Available from Herder & Herder, 10.00, ISBN 0-07-073198-5.

BOUYER, Louis, 1913- 230.203
Dictionary of theology. Tr. [from French] by Charles Underhill Quinn. [New York, Desclee, 1966, c.1965] xi, 470p. 25cm. [BR95.B6413] 66-13370 9.75
1. Theology—Dictionaries. 2. Catholic Church—Dictionaries. I. Title.

A Catholic dictionary of theology; a work projected with the approval of the Catholic hierarchy of England and Wales. London, New York, Nelson [1962- v. illus. 27cm. Contents.v. 1. Abandonment-casuistry. Includes bibliographies. [BR95.C27] 62-52257 230.203
1. Theology—Dictionaries. 2. Catholic Church—Dictionaries.

CATHOLIC dictionary of theology (A); a work projected with the approval of the Catholic hierarchy of England and Wales. London, New York, Nelson [1967] v. illus. 27cm. Contents.v.2.Cathechism-heaven. Bibl. [BR95.C27] 62-52257 15.00 230.203
1. Theology — Dictionaries. 2. Catholic Church — Dictionaries.

CATHOLIC dictionary of theology (A); a work projected with the approval of the Catholic hierarchy of England and Wales. New York, Nelson [c.1962] 332p. illus. 27cm. Contents.v.1. Abandonment--easuistry. Bibl. 62-52257 9.25 230.203
1. Theology—Dictionaries. 2. Catholic Church—Dictionaries.

RAHNER, Karl, 1904- 230.203
Theological dictionary [by] Karl Rahner [and] Herbert Vorgrimler. Edited by Cornelius Ernst. Translated by Richard Strachan. [New York] Herder and Herder [1965] 493 p. 22 cm. Translation of Kleines theologisches Worterbuch. [BR95.R313] 65-26562
1. Catholic Church—Dictionaries. 2. Theology—Dictionaries. I. Vorgrimler, Herbert, joint author. II. Title.

STOCKHAMMER, Morris, ed. 230.203
Thomas Aquinas dictionary. With an introd. by Theodore E. James. New York, Philosophical Library [1965] xiii, 219 p. 22 cm. "Based on Aquinas' Opera omnia (1882) and on two English translations by Joseph Rickaby ... Aquinas ethicus [and] Of God and His creatures." [BX1749.T324S7] 64-21468
1. Thomas Aquinas, Saint, 1225?-1274—Dictionaries, indexes, etc. I. Title.

THOMAS AGUINAS, Saint 1225?-1274 230.203
Summa Theologiae, vs. 18; 42, 60. Latin text, English tr., introds., notes., appendices, glossaries. Blackfriars, london, eyre & spottiswood; new york, mcgraw 1966. 3 v. (various p) 23 cm Contents.—v. 18 (ia2ae 18-21) Principles of murality, ed. tr. by Thomas Gilby. v. 42 (2a 2ae) 123.140) courage, ed., tr. by Antony Ross. p. 6 Walsh—v.60 (3a. 84-90) the Sacrament of penace, ed. tr by Reginald masterson, T.C. O'Brien. Bibl. [bx1749.t48] 63-11128 19 & 42 ea., 6.75 v. 60 7.00
1. theology, doctrinal. I. Title.

CASTER, Marcel van. 230.207
The structure of catechetics. [2d augum. ed., adapted by the author and translated by Edward J. Dirkswager, Jr., Olga Guedetarian, and Mother Nicolas Smith. New York] Herder and Herder [1965] 253 p. 22 cm. Translation of Dieu nous parie. 1. Structures de la catechese. Includes bibliographies. [BV1471.2.C312] 65-13487
1. Religious education. I. Title.

CASTER, Marcel van 230.207
The structure of catechetics [2d augm. ed., adapted by the author, tr. from French by Edward J. Dirkswager, Jr., Olga Guedetarian, Mother Nicolas Smith. New York] Herder & Herder [c.1965] 253p. 22cm. [BV1471.2.S312] 65-13487 4.95
1. Relgious education. I. Title.

HOFINGER, Johannes, ed. 230.207
Pastoral catechetics edited by Johannes Hofinger and Theodore C. Stone. [New York Herder and Herder [1964] 287 p. 22 cm. Bibliographical footnotes. [BX921.H62] 64-19730
1. Religious education. I. Stone, Theodore C., joint ed. II. Title.

HOFINGER, Johannes, ed. 230.207
Pastoral catechetics, ed. by Johannes Hofinger, Theodore C. Stone [New York] Herder & Herder [c.1964] 287p. 22cm. Bibl. 64-19730 4.95
1. Religious education. I. Stone, Theodore C., joint ed. II. Title.

LANCE, Derek. 230.207
Teaching the history of salvation, an introduction for teachers. With study-club questions. [Rev. American ed.] Glen Rock, N.J., Paulist Press [1964] 127 p. 18 cm. (Insight series) First published in 1964 under title: Till Christ be formed. Bibliography: p. 125-127. [BX926.L3] 64-24522
1. Religious education. I. Title.

LANCE, Derek 230.207
Teaching the history of salvation, an introduction for teachers. With study-club questions [Rev. Amer. ed.] Glen Rock, N.J., Paulist [c.1964] 127p. 18cm. (Insight ser.) First pub. in 1964 under title: Till Christ be formed. Bibl. 64-245221 .95 pap.,
1. Religious education. I. Title.

**BODY of Christ (The);* our meeting with Jesus, teacher's ed. New York, Sadlier, C.1965. 56p. music. 22x21cm. 230.2076

(Our life with God ser., Vatican II ed.) .40 pap.,

*GOD'S gifts to us; 230.2076
gr. 2. New York, Sadlier, c.1965. 96p. col. illus. music. 28cm. (Our life with God ser., Vatican II ed.) 1.08 pap.,

HARING, Bernhard, 230'.2'076
1912-
Bernard Haring replies; answers to 50 moral and religious questions [by] Bernard Haring. Staten Island, N.Y., Alba [1967] 205p. 19cm. Tr. of Padre Bernard Haring risponde. [BX1754.3.H313] 67-15201 3.95
1. Questions and answers—Theology. 2. Catholic Church—Doctrine and controversial works—Catholic authors. I. Title.

HARING, Bernhard, 1912- 230'.2'076
Bernard Haring replies; answers to 50 moral and religious questions [by] Bernard Haring. Staten Island, N.Y., Alba House [1967] 205 p. 19 cm. Translation of Padre Bernard Haring risponde. [BX1754.3.H313] 67-15201
1. Questions and answers — Theology. 2. Catholic Church — Doctrinal and controversal works — Catholic authors. I. Title.

*IN Christ Jesus; 230.2076
gr. 3, teacher's ed. New York, Sadlier, c. 1965. 224p. music 22x21cm. (Our life with God ser., Vatican II ed.) 2.00 pap.,

BALTHASAR, Hans Urs 230'.2'08
von, 1905-
Hans Urs von Balthasar [compiled by Martin Redfern] London, New York, Sheed & Ward, 1972. 126 p. 20 cm. (Theologians today: a series selected and edited by Martin Redfern) (Series: Redfern, Martin Theologians today.) [BX891.B33] 72-2166 ISBN 0-7220-7240-6 3.95
1. Catholic Church—Collected works. 2. Theology—Collected works—20th century. I. Series.
Pbk; 1.95, ISBN 0-7220-0538-3; Contents omitted.

CONGAR, Yves Marie 230'.2'08
Joseph, 1904-
Yves M.-J. Congar, O.P. [compiled by Martin Redfern] London, New York, Sheed & Ward, 1972. 128 p. 20 cm. (Theologians today: a series selected and edited by Martin Redfern) (Series: Redfern, Martin. Theologians today.) [BX891.C62] 72-2167 ISBN 0-7220-7241-4 3.95
1. Catholic Church—Collected works. 2. Theology—Collected works—20th century. I. Series.
Pbk; 1.95, ISBN 0-7220-0533-2; Contents omitted.

DURRWELL, F. X. 230'.2'08
F. X. Durrwell, C.S.S.R. [compiled by Martin Redfern] London, New York, Sheed & Ward, 1972. 125 p. 20 cm. (Theologians today: a series selected and edited by Martin Redfern) Contents.Contents.—The Resurrection of Christ, birth of the Church.—The Sacrament of Scripture.—The Mass in our lives.—Creation and the apostolate. [BX891.D87] 72-2163 ISBN 0-7220-7242-2 £1.25
1. Catholic Church—Collected works. 2. Theology—Collected works—20th century. I. Redfern, Martin. Theologians today.

ETHELRED, Saint, 230'.2'08 s
1109?-1166.
Spiritual friendship / translated by Mary Eugenia Laker. [Kalamazoo, Mich.] : Cistercian Publications, 1974. 144 p. ; 23 cm. (Aelred of Rievaulx ; v. 2) (Cistercial Fathers series ; no. 5) Translation of De spirituali amicitia. Stamped on t.p.: Cistercian Publications, Kalamazoo, Mich. Includes index. Bibliography: p. 137-139. [BX890.E83 1974 vol. 2] [BX2349] 248'.48'2 75-152480 ISBN 0-87907-205-9 : 7.95. pbk.
1. Spiritual life—Middle Ages, 600-1500. 2. Friendship. I. Title.

GLEASON, Robert W ed. 230.208
A theology reader, edited py Robert W. Gleason. New York, Macmillan [1966] xii, 333 p. 21 cm. Includes bibliographical references. [BT80.G5] 66-14691
1. Theology. Doctrinal — Addresses, essays, lectures. I. Title.

GLEASON, Robert W. ed. 230.208
A theology reader. New York, Macmillan [c.1966] xii,333p. 21cm. Bibl. [BT80.G5] 66-14691 6.95
1. Theology, Doctrinal—Addresses, essays, lectures. I. Title.

KUNG, Hans, 1928- 230'.2'08
Hans Kung [compiled by Martin Redfern] London, New York, Sheed & Ward, 1972. 128 p. 20 cm. (Theologians today: a series selected and edited by Martin Redfern) (Series: Redfern, Martin. Theologians today.) Contents.Contents.—Justification and sanctification according to the New Testament.—Liturgical reform and Christian unity.—Freedom in the world.—Truthfulness as a demand of the message of Jesus. [BX891.K83] 72-2159 ISBN 0-7220-7243-0 £1.25
1. Catholic Church—Collected works. 2. Theology—Collected works—20th century. I. Series.

LONERGAN, Bernard J. F. 230'.2'08
A second collection; [papers] by Bernard J. F. Lonergan. Edited by William F. J. Ryan and Bernard J. Tyrrell. Philadelphia, Westminster Press [1975, c1974] 300, [2] p. 23 cm. Bibliography: p. [302] [BX891.L644 1975] 74-14798 ISBN 0-664-20721-9 12.00
1. Catholic Church—Collected works. 2. Theology—Collected works—20th century. I. Title.

LUBAC, Henri de, 1896- 230'.2'08
Henri de Lubac, S.J. [compiled by Martin Redfern] London, New York, Sheed & Ward, 1972. 127 p. 20 cm. (Theologians today: a series selected and edited by Martin Redfern) (Series: Redfern, Martin. Theologians today.) [BX891.L8] 72-2164 ISBN 0-7220-7244-9 3.95
1. Catholic Church—Collected works. 2. Theology—Collected works—20th century. I. Series.
Pbk; 1.95, ISBN 0-7220-0539-3. Contents omitted. Contents omitted.

LUBAC, Henri de, 1896- 230'.2'08
Henri de Lubac, S.J. [compiled by Martin Redfern] London, New York, Sheed & Ward, 1972. 127 p. 20 cm. (Theologians today: a series selected and edited by Martin Redfern) (Series: Redfern, Martin. Theologians today.) Contents.Contents.—Christianity and history.—The sacraments as instruments of unity.—Ludwig Feuerbach, protagonist of atheist humanism.—The family of God. [BX891.L8] 72-2164 ISBN 0-7220-7244-9 £1.25
1. Catholic Church—Collected works. 2. Theology—Collected works—20th century. I. Series.

NEWMAN, John Henry, 230'.2'08
Cardinal, 1801-1890.
Characteristics from the writings of John Henry Newman : being selections personal, historical, philosophical, and religious, from his various works / arranged by William Samuel Lilly, with the author's approval. Folcroft, Pa. : Folcroft Library Editions, 1976. p. cm. Reprint of the 1875 ed. published by Scribner, Wilford & Armstrong, New York. Includes bibliographical references and index. [BX890.N39 1976] 76-45366 ISBN 0-8414-5813-8 lib. bdg. : 40.00
1. Catholic Church—Collected works. 2. Theology—Collected works—19th century. I. Title.

NEWMAN, John Henry, 230'.2'08
Cardinal, 1801-1890.
A Newman treasury : selections from the prose works of John Henry Cardinal Newman / selected and edited by Charles Frederick Harrold. New Rochelle, N.Y. : Arlington House, 1975, c1943. xii, 404 p. ; 24 cm. Reprint of the ed. published by Longmans, Green, London. Bibliography: p. 397-404. [PR5106.H3 1975] 74-31080 ISBN 0-87000-300-3 : 8.95
I. Harrold, Charles Frederick, 1897-1948, ed. II. Title.

RAHNER, Karl, 1904- 230'.2'08
Karl Rahner, S.J. [compiled by Martin Redfern] London, New York, Sheed & Ward, 1972. 128 p. 20 cm. (Theologians today: a series selected and edited by Martin Redfern) (Series: Redfern, Martin. Theologians today.) Contents.Contents.—The propect for Christianity.—The sacrifice of the Mass.—The inspiration of the Bible.—Action in the Church. Includes bibliographical references. [BX891.R32] 72-2165 ISBN 0-7220-7245-7 £1.65
1. Catholic Church—Collected works. 2. Theology—Collected works—20th century. I. Series.

SCHILLEBEECKX, Edward 230'.2'08
Cornelis Florentius Alfons, 1914-
Edward Schillebeeckx, O.P. [compiled by Martin Redfern] London, New York, Sheed and Ward, 1972. 128 p. 20 cm. (Theologians today: a series selected and edited by Martin Redfern) (Series: Redfern, Martin. Theologians today.) Contents.Contents.—The Sacraments: an encounter with God.—Marriage in the Divine Revelation of the Old Testament.—Revelation, scripture, tradition, and teaching authority.—Secular worship and Church liturgy. Includes bibliographical references. [BX891.S354] 72-2162 ISBN 0-7220-7246-5 £1.25
1. Catholic Church—Collected works. 2. Theology—Collected works—20th century. I. Series.

SHEED, Francis Joseph, 230'.2'08
1897-
F. J. Sheed [compiled by Martin Redfern.] London, New York, Sheed and Ward, 1972. 127 p. 20 cm. (Theologians today: a series selected and edited by Martin Redfern) (Series: Redfern, Martin. Theologians today.) Contents.Contents.—Man and his context.—Born of a woman.—Scripture in the Church.—Mass and Eucharist. [BX891.S53] 72-2161 ISBN 0-7220-7247-3 £1.25
1. Catholic Church—Collected works. 2. Theology—Collected works—20th century. I. Series.

SUENENS, Leon Joseph, 230'.2'08
Cardinal, 1904-
Ways of the spirit : the spirituality of Cardinal Suenens / drawn from the writings of Cardinal Suenens and edited with an introduction by Elizabeth Hamilton. London : Darton, Longman and Todd, 1976. 124 p. ; 19 cm. Bibliography: p. 123-[124] [BX891.S85 1976b] 77-368905 ISBN 0-232-51359-7 : £1.20
1. Catholic Church—Collected works. 2. Theology—Collected works—20th century. I. Hamilton, Elizabeth, 1906- II. Title.

SUENENS, Leon Joseph, 230'.2'08
Cardinal, 1904-
Ways of the spirit : the spirituality of Cardinal Suenens / drawn from the writings of Cardinal Suenens and edited with an introd. by Elizabeth Hamilton. New York : Seabury Press, 1976. 123, [1] p. ; 21 cm. "A Crossroad book." Bibliography: p. 123-[124] [BX891.S85] 76-46307 ISBN 0-8164-1218-9 : 5.95
1. Catholic Church—Collected works. 2. Theology—Collected works—20th century. I. Hamilton, Elizabeth, 1906- II. Title.

WARD, Wilfrid Philip, 230.2'08
1856-1916.
Problems and persons, by Wilfrid Ward. Freeport, N.Y., Books for Libraries Press [1968] liv, 377 p. 22 cm. (Essay index reprint series) Reprint of the 1903 ed. Contents.Contents.—Introduction.—Analytical summary.—The time-spirit of the nineteenth century.—The rigidity of Rome.—Unchanging dogma and changeful man.—The foundations of belief.—Candour in biography.—Tennyson.—Thomas Henry Huxley.—Two mottoes of Cardinal Newman.—Newman and Renan.—The life-work of Cardinal Wiseman.—The life of Mrs. Augustus Craven. [AC8.W356 1968] 68-29254
I. Title.

BALTHASAR, Hans Urs von, 230.2081
1905-
Word and redemption. [Translated by A. V. Littledale in cooperation with Alexander Dru. New York] Herder and Herder [1965] 175 p. 22 cm. (His Essays in theology, 2) Translation of Verbum caro. Bibliographical footnotes. [BT80.B333 1965] 65-14591
1. Theology, Doctrinal—Addresses, essays, lectures. I. Title.

BALTHASAR, Hans Urs von, 230.2081
1905-
Word and redemption [Tr. by A. V. Littledale with Alexander Dru. New York] Herder & Herder [c.1965] 175p. 22cm. (His Essays in theology, 2) Bibl. [BT80.B333] 65-14591 3.95
1. Theology, Doctrinal—Addresses, essays, lectures. I. Title.

JARRETT, Bede, 1881- 230.2081
1934.
Bede Jarrett anthology. Edited by Jordan Aumann. Dubuque, Priory Press, 1961. 506 p. 23 cm. [BX890.J35] 64-937
1. Catholic Church—Collected works. 2. Theology—Collected works—20th cent. I. Title.

FEINER, Johannes, ed. 230.2082
Theology today. Edited by Johannes Feiner, Josef Trutsch, and Franz Bockle. Translated by Peter White and Raymond H. Kelly. Milwaukee, Bruce Pub. Co. [1965- v. 22 cm. Translation of Fragen der Theologie heute. Contents.v. 1. Renewal in dogma. Bibliography: v. 1, p. 245-276. [BT10.F353] 64-24337
1. Theology—Addresses, essays, lectures. 2. Catholic Church—Addresses, essays, lectures. I. Trutsch, Josef, joint ed. II. Bockle, Franz, joint ed. III. Title.

FEINER, Johannes, ed. 230.2082
Theology today. v.1. Ed. by Johannes Feiner, Josef Trutsch, Franz Bockle. Tr. [from German] by Peter White, Raymond H. Kelly. Milwaukee, Bruce [c.1965] 282p. Bibl. Contents.v.1. Renewal in dogma. [BT10.F353] 64-24337 5.00
1. Theology—Addresses, essays, lectures. 2. Catholic Church—Addresses, essays, lectures. I. Trutsch, Josef, joint ed. II. Bockle, Franz, joint ed. III. Title.

O'NEILL, Joseph Eugene, 230.2082
1910- ed.
The encounter with God; aspects of modern theology. Foreword by John Courtney Murray. New York, Macmillan [c.1960-1962] 205p. 22cm. Bibl. 62-19426 4.00
1. Theology, Doctrinal—Addresses, essays, lectures. I. Title.

NEWMAN, John Henry, 230'.2'09
Cardinal, 1801-1890.
An essay on the development of Christian doctrine. Edited with an introd. by J. M. Cameron. The ed. of 1845. [Harmondsworth, Baltimore] Penguin Books [1974, c1973] 448 p. 18 cm. (Pelican classics) Reprint of the 1st ed. Includes bibliographical references. [BT21.N5 1974] 74-174355 3.45 (pbk.).
1. Catholic Church—Doctrinal and controversial works—Catholic authors. 2. Dogma, Development of. I. Title.

BIEL, Gabriel, d. 1495 230.20902
Epitome et collectorium ex Occamo circa quatuor Sententiarum libros. Tiibingen, 1501 [i.e. Basel, 1508] Frankfurt/ Maim, Minerva, New York, Johnson Reprint, 1965 iv. (unpaged) 27cm. Facsim. reprod. of the 1508 ed. printed by Jacob de Pfortzen. Based on Ockham's commentary on Sententiarum libri quattuor of Petrus Lombardus, ed. by V. Steinbach, the work first pub. in 1501 in Tiibingen, with title generally quoted as Collectorium super IV libros Sententiarum. Cf. Goff. 3d census. [BX1749.P4B5] 65-7869 43.75
1. Petrus Lombardus, Bp. of Paris, 12th cent. Sententiarum libri quattuor. I. Steinbach, Vendelinus, fl. 1490-1515, ed. II. Ockham, William, d. ca. 1349. Quaestiones et decisiones in quattuor libros Sententiarum. iII. Title. IV. Title: Collectorium super quattuor libros Sententiarum.

O'BRIEN, Elmer ed. 230.209045
Theology in transition; a bibliographical evaluation of the 'decisive decade,' 1954-1964 [New York] Herder & Herder [1965] 282p. 22cm. (Contemp. theol., v.1) Bibl. [BT28.O2] 65-13486 5.95
1. Theology—20th cent. 2. Theology—Bibl. I. Title.

BONEY, William Jerry. 230.2'0922
The new day; Catholic theologians of the renewal. Edited by Wm. Jerry Boney and Lawrence E. Molumby. Richmond, John Knox Press [1968] 142 p. 21 cm. Includes bibliographical references. [BT28.B62] 68-13664
1. Catholic Church—Biography. 2. Theologians. 3. Theology, Doctrinal—History—20th century. I. Molumby, Lawrence E., joint author. II. Title.

JOURNEYS : 230'.2'0922 B
the impact of personal experience on religious thought / edited by Gregory Baum. New York : Paulist Press, c1975. vi, 271 p. ; 23 cm. [BX4651.2.J68] 75-31401 ISBN 0-8091-0204-8 : 10.95 ISBN 0-8091-1909-9 pbk. : 6.95
1. Catholic Church—Biography. 2. Theologians. I. Baum, Gregory, 1923-

STADLER, Johann 230.2'0922
Evangelist, 1804-1868.
Vollstandiges Heiligen-Lexikon / hrsg. von Johann Evangelist Stadler und Franz Joseph Heim. Hildesheim ; New York : G. Olms, 1975- v. ; 20 cm. Reprint of the 1858- ed. published by B. Schmid, Augsburg. Contents.Contents.—Bd. 1. A-D. [BX4655.8.S7 1975] 75-514628 ISBN 3-487-05597-X (v. 1)
1. Christian saints—Dictionaries. I. Heim, Franz Joseph, joint author. II. Title.

THE Tradition of 230'.2'0922
Aquinas and Bonaventure : text and commentary during seven centuries : [catalogue of] an exhibition of manuscripts, incunabula, and scholarly editions selected principally from the collections of the University of Chicago Library and the Newberry Library and held on the occasion of a celebration of the Medieval heritage, the University of Chicago, the Joseph Regenstein Library, November 1974 / sponsored by the University of Chicago, in cooperation with the Jesuit School of Theology in Chicago and the Catholic Theological Union. [Chicago : s.n.], c1974. [23] p. : ill. ; 28 cm. Bibliography: p. [23] [BX4700.T6T7] 75-308795
1. Thomas Aquinas, Saint, 1225?-1274—Exhibitions. 2. Bonaventura, Saint, Cardinal, 1221-1274—Exhibitions. I. Joseph Regenstein Library. II. Jesuit School of Theology in Chicago. III. Catholic Theological Union.

AQUINAS and problems 230'.2'0924
of his time / edited by G. Verbeke and D. Verhelst. Louvain, Belgium : Leuven

University Press, 1976. viii, 229 p. ; 25 cm. (Mediaevalia Lovaniensia ; series 1 : studia 5) English, French, or German. Includes bibliographical references and index. [B765.T54A65] 77-364753 ISBN 9-06-186050-4
1. Thomas Aquinas, Saint, 1225?-1274—Addresses, essays, lectures. I. Verbeke, Gerard. II. Verhelst, D. III. Title. IV. Series.

BARMANN, Lawrence F. 230'.2'0924 B
Baron Friedrich Von Hugel and the modernist crisis in England [by] Lawrence F. Barmann. Cambridge [Eng.] University Press, 1972. xiii, 278 p. 24 cm. Bibliography: p. 253-271. [BX4705.H77B37] 77-153014 ISBN 0-521-08178-5
1. Hugel, Friedrich, Freiherr von, 1852-1925. 2. Modernism—Catholic Church—England.

BETT, Henry, 1876-1953. 230'.2'0924 B
Joachim of Flora / by Henry Bett. Merrick, N.Y. : Richwood Pub. Co., 1976. vii, 184 p. : frontispiece ; 23 cm. Reprint of the 1931 ed. published by Methuen, London, in series: Great medieval churchman. Includes bibliographical references and index. [BX4705.J6B4 1976] 76-20693 ISBN 0-915172-24-0 lib.bdg. : 12.50
1. Joachim, abbot of Fiore, 1132 (ca.)-1202. I. Title. II. Series: Great medieval churchman.

BETT, Henry, 1876-1953. 230'.2'0924 B
Nicholas of Cusa / by Henry Bett. Merrick, N.Y. : Richwood Pub. Co., 1976. x, 210 p. ; 23 cm. Reprint of the 1932 ed. published by Methuen & Co., London, issued in series: Great medieval churchmen. Includes bibliographical references and index. [BX4705.N58B4 1976] 76-1131 ISBN 0-915172-05-4 lib.bdg. : 18.50
1. Nicolaus Cusanus, Cardinal, 1401-1464. I. Title. II. Series: Great medieval churchmen.

BOROS, Ladislaus, 1927- 230'.2'0924 B
Open spirit / Ladislaus Boros ; translated by Erika Young. New York : Paulist Press, [1974] 204 p. ; 21 cm. Translation of Denken in der Begegnung. [BX4705.B663A313 1974] 74-192513 ISBN 0-8091-1856-4 pbk. : 3.95.
1. Boros, Ladislaus, 1927- I. Title.

CARR, Anne. 230'.2'0924
The theological method of Karl Rahner / by Anne Carr. Missoula, Mont. : Published by Scholars Press for the American Academy of Religion, c1977. vii, 281 p. ; 22 cm. (Dissertation series - American Academy of Religion ; no. 19) Originally presented as the author's thesis, University of Chicago, 1971. Bibliography: p. 271-281. [BX4705.R287C37 1977] 76-51639 ISBN 0-89130-129-1 : 4.50
1. Rahner, Karl, 1904- I. Title. II. Series: American Academy of Religion. Dissertation series — American Academy of Religion ; no. 19.

COPLESTON, Frederick Charles. 230'.2'0924
Aquinas / F. C. Copleston. Harmondsworth ; Baltimore : Penguin, 1975. 272 p. : 19 cm. (Pelican books ; A349) Includes index. Bibliography: p. 265-267. [B765.T54C64 1975] 75-327650 ISBN 0-14-020349-4 pbk. : 3.50
1. Thomas Aquinas, Saint, 1225?-1274—Philosophy.

CORBISHLEY, Thomas. 230'.2'0924
The spirituality of Teilhard de Chardin. Paramus, N.J., Paulist Press [1971] 126 p. 18 cm. Includes bibliographical references. [B2430.T374C63 1971b] 72-78440 1.45
1. Teilhard de Chardin, Pierre. 2. Spirituality. I. Title.

COUSINS, Ewert H. 230'.2'0924
Coincidence of opposites : the theology of St. Bonaventure / Ewert H. Cousins. Chicago : Franciscan Herald Press, [1977] p. cm. Includes bibliographical references and index. [BX4700.B68C68] 77-2604 ISBN 0-8199-0580-1 : 7.95
1. Bonaventura, Saint, Cardinal, 1221-1274. I. Title.

DECHANET, Jean Marie. 230'.2'0924 B
William of St. Thierry the man and his work. Translated by Richard Strachan. Spencer, Mass., Cistercian Publications, 1972. x, 172 p. 23 cm. (Cistercian studies series, no. 10) Translation of Guillaume de Saint-Thierry: l'homme et son oeuvre. Bibliography: p. 165-166. [BX4705.G7464D413 1972] 73-152485 ISBN 0-87907-810-3 10.95
1. Guillaume de Saint-Thierry, 1085 (ca)-1148? I. Title. II. Series.

FARICY, Robert L 1926- 230.2'0924
Teilhard de Chardin's theology of the Christian in the world, by Robert L. Faricy. New York, Sheed and Ward [1967] xviii, 235 p. 22 cm. Bibliography: p. 217-226. [[B2430.T374F37]] 67-13767
1. Teilhard de Chardin, Pierre—Theology. I. Title.

HEANEY, John J. 230.2'0924
The modernist crisis: von Hugel, by John J. Heaney. Washington, Corpus Books [1968] 304 p. 21 cm. Bibliographical references included in "Notes" (p. 235-284) "Bibliography of von Hugel's works": p. 285-295. [BX1396.H4] 68-15780 8.50
1. Hugel, Friedrich, Freiherr von, 1852-1925. 2. Modernism—Catholic Church. I. Title.

INTERNATIONAL Lonergan Congress, St. Leo College, 1970. 230'.2'0924 s
Foundations of theology. Edited by Philip McShane. [American ed. Notre Dame, Ind.] University of Notre Dame Press [1972, c1971] xx, 257 p. 23 cm. (Papers from the International Lonergan Congress, 1970, v. 1) Includes bibliographical references. [BX4705.L7133I57 1970, Vol. 1] 230'.2'0924 76-167705 ISBN 0-268-00456-0 10.00
1. Lonergan, Bernard J. F.—Congresses. 2. Theology—Congresses. I. McShane, Philip, ed. II. Title. III. Series.

INTERNATIONAL Lonergan Congress, St. Leo College, 1970. 230'.2'0924 s
Language, truth, and meaning. Edited by Philip McShane. [American ed. Notre Dame, Ind.] University of Notre Dame Press [1972, c1971] 343 p. 23 cm. (Papers from the International Lonergan Congress, 1970, v. 2.) Includes bibliographical references. [BX4705.L7133I57 1970, vol. 2] 121 72-3507 ISBN 0-268-00478-1
1. Lonergan, Bernard J. F.—Congresses. 2. Meaning (Philosophy)—Congresses. 3. Methodology—Congresses. I. McShane, Philip, ed. II. Title. III. Series.

INTERNATIONAL Lonergan Congress, St. Leo College, 1970. 230'.2'0924
Papers from the International Lonergan Congress, 1970. Edited by Philip McShane. [American ed.] Notre Dame, Ind.] University of Notre Dame Press [1972- c1971 v. 23 cm. [BX4705.L7133I57 1970] 74-166474 10.00 (v. 1)
1. Lonergan, Bernard J. F.—Congresses. 2. Theology—Congresses. I. McShane, Philip, ed.

JOHNS, Roger Dick, 1940- 230'.2'0924
Man in the world : the political theology of Johannes Baptist Metz / by Roger Dick Johns. Missoula, Mont. : Published by Scholars Press for the American Academy of Religion, c1976. xiii, 206 p. ; 22 cm. (Dissertation series - American Academy of Religion ; no. 16) Originally presented as the author's thesis, Duke University, 1973. "Works by Johannes Baptist Metz:" p. 193-196. [BX4705.M545J63 1976] 76-26491 ISBN 0-89130-079-1 pbk. : 4.50
1. Metz, Johannes Baptist, 1928- I. Title. II. Series: American Academy of Religion. Dissertation series — American Academy of Religion ; no. 16.

LEPP, Ignace, 1909-1966. 230'.2'0924
The faith of men; meditations inspired by Teilhard de Chardin. Translated by Bernard Murchland. New York, Macmillan [1967] 117 p. 22 cm. Translation of Teilhard et la foi des hommes. [B2430.T374L43] 67-24287
1. Teilhard de Chardin, Pierre—Theology. I. Title.

LUBAC, Henri de, 1896- 230'.2'0924
The religion of Teilhard de Chardin. Translated by Rene Hague. New York, Desclee Co [1967] 380 p. 22 cm. Translation of La pensee religieuse du pere Teilhard de Chardin. [B2430.T374L783 1967a] 67-17675
1. Teilhard de Chardin, Pierre. I. Title.

LUBAC, Henri de, 1896- 230.2'0924
The religion of Teilhard de Chardin. Translated by Rene Hague. Garden City, N.Y., Image Books [1968, c1967] 432 p. 18 cm. Translation of La pensee religieuse du pere Teilhard de Chardin. Bibliographical references included in "Notes" (p. [319]-422) [B2430.T374L783 1968] 68-7165 1.65
1. Teilhard de Chardin, Pierre. I. Title.

LUBAC, Henri de, 1896- 230.20924
Teilhard de Chardin the man and his meaning. Translated by Rene Hague, [1st American ed.] New York Hawthorn Books [1965] x, 203 p. 22 cm. Translation of La priere du Pere Teilhard de Chardin. Bibliographical footnotes. [B2430.T374L813] 65-22914
1. Teilhard de Chardin, Pierre. I. Title.

LUBAC, Henri de, 1896- 230.20924
Teilhard de Chardin: the man and his meaning. Tr. [from French] by Rene Hague. [1st Amer. ed.] New York, Hawthorn [c.1964, 1965] x, 203p. 22cm. Bibl. [B2430.T374L813] 65-22914 4.95
1. Teilhard de Chardin, Pierre. I. Title.

LUBAC, Henri Henri de, 1896- 230'.2'0924
The religion of Teilhard de Chardin. Tr. by Rene Hague. New York, Desclee [1967] 380p. 22cm. Tr. of La pensee religieuse du pere Teilhard de Chardin. [B2430.T374L783 1967a] 67-17675 5.95
1. Teilhard de Chardin, Pierre. I. Title.

LUPTON, Joseph Hirst, 1836-1905. 230'.2'0924 B
A life of John Colet, D.D., dean of St. Paul's, and founder of St. Paul's school. With an appendix of some of his English writings. New York, B. Franklin [1974] xiv, 323 p. port. 23 cm. (Burt Franklin research and source works series. Studies in the history of education 12) Reprint of the 1887 ed. published by G. Bell, London. Includes bibliographical references. [BR754.C6L8 1974] 74-18291 ISBN 0-8337-4243-4 16.50
1. Colet, John, 1467?-1519. I. Title.

MACDONALD, Allan John Macdonald, 1887- 230'.2'0924 B
Berengar and the reform of sacramental doctrine / by A. J. Macdonald. Merrick, N.Y. : Richwood Pub. Co., [1977] xii, 444 p. ; 23 cm. Reprint of the 1930 ed. published by Longmans, Green, London. Includes index. Bibliography: p. [415]-430. [BX4705.B32M3 1977] 77-10031 ISBN 0-915172-25-9 lib.bdg. : 28.50
1. Berengarius, of Tours, 1000 (ca.)-1088. 2. Theologicans—France—Tours—Biography. 3. Tours—Biography. 4. Lord's Supper—History. I. Title.

MCINERNY, Ralph M. 230'.2'0924
St. Thomas Aquinas / by Ralph McInerny. Boston : Twayne Publishers, c1977. 197 p. : port. ; 21 cm. (Twayne's world authors series ; TWAS 408 : Italy) Includes index. Bibliography: p. 183-189. [B765.T54M244] 76-25959 ISBN 0-8057-6248-5 lib.bdg. : 8.95
1. Thomas Aquinas, Saint, 1225?-1274.

MERTON, Thomas, 1915-1968. 230'.2'0924 B
The Asian journal of Thomas Merton. Edited from his original notebooks by Naomi Burton, Patrick Hart & James Laughlin. Consulting editor: Amiya Chakravarty. [New York, New Directions Pub. Corp., 1973] xxviii, 445 p. illus. 24 cm. (A New Directions book) Bibliography: p. 357-361. [BX2350.2.M449 1973] 71-103370 ISBN 0-8112-0464-2 12.50
1. Spiritual life—Catholic authors. 2. Meditation. I. Title.

MURRAY, Michael H 230.20924
The thought of Teihard de Chardin; an introduction [by] Michael H. Murray. New York, Seabury Press [1966] x, 177 p. 22 cm. [B2430.T374M8] 66-13466
1. Teilhard de Chardin, Pierre. I. Title.

MURRAY, Michael H. 230.20924
The thought of Teilhard de Chardin; an introduction. New York, Seabury [c. 1966] x, 177p. 22cm. [B2430.T374M8] 66-13466 4.95
1. Teilhard de Chardin, Pierre. I. Title.

NEWMAN, John Henry, 230.2'0924
Apologia pro vita sua: being a history of his religious opinions; ed. introd. notes, by Martin J. Svaglic. Oxford, Clarendon. Pr., 1967. ardinal, 1801-1890 1x, 604p. 23cm. Bibl. [BX4705.N5A3 1967] 68-75872 bds., price unreported
1. Catholic Church—Doctrinal and controversial works—Catholic authors. I. Svaglic, Martin J. ed. II. Title.
Available from Oxford Univ. Pr., New York.

NEWMAN, John Henry, Cardinal, 1801-1890. 230.2'0924
Apologia pro vita sua: being a history of his religious opinions; edited, with an introduction and notes, by Martin J. Svaglic. Oxford, Clarendon P., 1967. ix, 604 p. 22 1/2 cm. (B67-17788) Bibliographical references. [BX4705.N5A3] 68-75872
1. Catholic Church—Doctrinal and controversial works—Catholic authors. I. Svaglic, Martin J., ed. II. Title.

PERSSON, Per Erik, 1923- 230.20924
Sacra doctrina; reason and revelation in Aquinas. Translated by Ross Mackenzie. Philadelphia, Fortress Press [1970] xii, 317 p. 23 cm. Bibliography: p. 299-312. [BT126.5.P47 1970] 69-12992 9.75
1. Thomas Aquinas, Saint, 1225?-1274—Theology. 2. Revelation—History of doctrines. 3. Reason. I. Title.

RAHNER, Hugo, 1900- 230.2'0924
Ignatius the theologian. Translated by Michael Barry. [New York] Herder and Herder [1968] viii, 238 p. 22 cm. Translation of Ignatius von Loyola als Mensch und Theologe, chapters 11-16. Bibliographical footnotes. [BX4700] 68-22567 6.95
1. Loyola, Ignacio de, Saint, 1491-1556. I. Title.

REEVES, Marjorie. 230'.2'0924
Joachim of Fiore and the prophetic future / [by] Marjorie Reeves. London : S.P.C.K., 1976. ix, 212 p., [4] p. of plates : ill., facsims. ; 22 cm. Includes index. Bibliography: p. [198]-202. [BX4705.J6R43 1976] 77-371375 ISBN 0-281-02887-7 : £3.95
1. Joachim, Abbot of Fiore, 1132 (ca.)-1202. 2. History (Theology) I. Title.

REEVES, Marjorie. 230'.2'0924
Joachim of Fiore and the prophetic future / Marjorie Reeves. New York : Harper & Row, 1977, c1976. 212 p., [2] leaves of plates : ill. ; 21 cm. (Harper torchbooks) Includes index. Bibliography: p. [198]-202. [BX4705.J6R43 1977] 76-55498 ISBN 0-06-131924-4 pbk. : 4.95
1. Joachim, Abbot of Fiore, 1132(ca.)-1202. 2. History (Theology) I. Title.

SELBY, Robin C. 230'.2'0924
The principle of reserve in the writings of John Henry Cardinal Newman / by Robin C. Selby. London ; New York : Oxford University Press, 1975. 108 p. ; 23 cm. (Oxford theological monographs) Includes indexes. Bibliography: p. [106]-108. [B1745.S44] 75-322798 ISBN 0-19-826711-8 : 16.00
1. Newman, John Henry, Cardinal, 1801-1890. 2. Reserve (Christian theology)—History of doctrines. I. Title. II. Series.

SHEPHERD, William C. 230.2'0924
Man's condition; God and the world process [by] William C. Shepherd. [New York] Herder and Herder [1969] 266 p. 22 cm. Bibliographical footnotes. [BT761.2.S5] 68-55091
1. Rohner, Karl, 1904- 2. Natural theology—History of doctrines. 3. Grace (Theology)—History of doctrines. I. Title.

SPEAIGHT, Robert, 1904- 230.2'0924
Teilhard de Chardin: re-mythologization; three papers on the thought of Teilhard de Chardin presented at a symposium at Seabury-Western Theological Seminary, Evanston, Illinois, September, 1968. By Robert Speaight, Robert V. Wilshire [and] J. V. Langmead Casserley. [Chicago, Argus Communications, 1970] 101 p. illus. 23 cm. (Peacock books) Cover title: Chardin: remytholi[sic]gization. Includes bibliographical references. [B2430.T374S75] 73-113275 2.45
1. Teilhard de Chardin, Pierre. I. Wilshire, Robert V. II. Casserley, Julian Victor Langmead, 1909- III. Title. IV. Title: Chardin: remytholi[sic]gization.

TOWERS, Bernard. 230.20924
Teilhard de Chardin. Richmond, Knox [1966] xi, 45p. 19cm. (Makers of contemp. theol.) Bibl. [B2430.T374T6] 66-15515 1.00 pap.,
1. Teilhard de Chardin, Pierre. I. Title.

TRACY, David. 230.2'0924
The achievement of Bernard Lonergan. [New York] Herder and Herder [1970] xv, 302 p. 22 cm. Bibliography: p. 270-287. [BX4705.L7133T7] 79-87773 9.50
1. Lonergan, Bernard J. F. I. Title.

VORGRIMLER, Herbert. 230.20924
Karl Rahner; his life, thought and works. Translated by Edward Quinn. Glen Rock, N.J., Paulist Press [1966, c1965] 96 p. 19 cm. (Deus books) Translation of Karl Rahner; Denkers over God en Wereld. "Notes and bibliography": p. 89-95. "Books by Karl Rahner available in English": p. 96. [BX4705.R287V63 1966a] 66-4765
1. Rahner, Karl, 1904- I. Title. II. Series.

VORGRIMLER, Herbert 230.20924
Karl Rahner; his life, thought and works. Tr. by Edward Quinn. Glen Rock, N.J., Paulist [1966,c.1965] 96p. 19cm. (Deus bks.) Bibl. [BX4705.R287 V63] 66-4765 .75 pap.,
1. Rahner, Karl, 1904- I. Title.

WEST, Delno C., 1936- comp. 230'.2'0924
Joachim of Fiore in Christian thought; essays on the influence of the Calabrian prophet, edited by Delno C. West. New York, B. Franklin [1974, i.e.1975] p. cm. [BX4705.J6W47] 74-18104 ISBN 0-8337-5489-0 28.50
1. Joachim, Abbot of Fiore, 1132 (ca.)-1202—Addresses, essays, lectures. I. Title.

REARDON, Bernard M. G. 230'.2'44
Liberalism and tradition : aspects of Catholic thought in nineteenth-century France /

Bernard Reardon. Cambridge ; New York : Cambridge University Press, 1975. viii, 308 p. ; 24 cm. Includes bibliographical references and index. [DC33.6.R4 1975] 75-7214 ISBN 0-521-20776-2 : 23.50
1. France—Intellectual life. 2. Theology, Catholic—France. 3. Religious thought—19th century—France. I. Title.

CHEVILLE, Roy Arthur, 1897- 230.293'3
When teen-agers talk theology; a guide in exploring together, by Roy A. Cheville [Independence, Mo., Herald Pub. House, 1968] 445 p. 21 cm. At head of title: For youth ... and all who live with youth. [BX8643.Y6C5] 68-57672
1. Mormons and mormonism—Doctrinal and controversial works. 2. Youth—Religious life. I. Title.

RICKS, Eldin, comp. 230.293'3
New Bible ready reference; a compilation of useful Bible passages for Latter-Day Saint missionaries, teachers, and students. A companion volume to the Combination reference. [1st ed. Salt Lake City] Deseret Book Co., 1961. 262p. 15cm. [BX8631.R5] 61-45730
1. Mormons and Mormonism—Doctrinal and controversial works. 2. Bible—Indexes, Topical. I. Title.

CHURCH of England. Archbishops' Commission on Christian Doctrine. 230'.3
Christian believing : the nature of the Christian faith and its expression in Holy Scripture and creeds : a report / by the Doctrine Commission of the Church of England. London : S.P.C.K., 1976. xii, 156 p. ; 22 cm. [BX5131.2.C53 1976] 76-370993 ISBN 0-281-02937-7 : £2.50
1. Bible—Criticism, interpretation, etc.—Addresses, essays, lectures. 2. Theology, Anglican—Addresses, essays, lectures. 3. Creeds—Addresses, essays, lectures. I. Title.

CLARK, Howard Gordon. 230.3
Friends, Romans, countrymen; a friendly answer to questions Roman Catholics ask concerning the relationship of the Anglican churches to the one, holy, catholic, and apostolic church of Jesus Christ. New York, Morehouse- Gorham [1956] 58p. 19cm. [BX5132.C57] 56-11862
1. Protestant Episcopal Church in the U.S. A.—Doctrinal and controversial works. 2. Catholic Church—Doctrinal and controversial works—Protestant authors. I. Title.

CLARKE, Oliver Fielding 230.3
For Christ's sake: a reply to the Bishop of Woolwich's book, Honest to God, and a positive continuation of the discussion. New York, Morehouse [1963] 103p. 19cm. 1.50 pap.,
I. Title.

CLARKE, Samuel, 1675-1729. 230'.3
The works, 1738 / Samuel Clarke. New York : Garland Pub., 1976. p.cm. (British philosophers and theologians of the 17th & 18th centuries ; no. 12) Reprint of the 1738 ed. printed for J. and P. Knapton, London, under title: The works of Samuel Clarke. Contents.Contents.—v. 1. Sermons on several subjects.—v. 2. Sermons on several subjects. Eighteen sermons on several occasions. Sixteen sermons on the being and attributes of God, the obligations of natural religion, and the truth and certainty of the Christian revelation.—v. 3. A paraphrase on the four Evangelists. Three practical essays on baptism, confirmation, and repentance. An exposition of the church catechism. A letter to Mr. Dodwell concerning the immortality of the soul. Reflections on Amyntor.—v. 4. The scripture doctrine of the Trinity. Several tracts relating to the subject of the Trinity. A collection of papers which passed between the late learned M. Leibnitz and Dr. Clarke. A letter to Benjamin Hoadly. [BX5037.C5 1976] 75-11207 ISBN 0-8240-1762-5 : 25.00 per vol.
1. Church of England—Sermons. 2. Church of England—Doctrinal and controversial works—Collected works. 3. Clarke, Samuel, 1675-1729. 4. Bible. N.T. Gospels—Paraphrases, English. 5. Sermons, English. 6. Trinity—Early works to 1800—Collected works. I. Title. II. Series.

COCKSHUT, A. O. J., ed. 230.3
Religious controversies of the nineteenth century: selected documents. Lincoln, Univ. of Neb. Pr. [c.1966] v,246p. 23cm. Bibl. [BR759.C57] 66-18225 5.50
1. Religious thought—England. 2. Religious thought—19th cent. I. Title.
Contents omitted.

COGGAN, Frederick Donald, 1909- 230'.3
Convictions / by Donald Coggan. Grand Rapids : Eerdmans, c1975. 320 p. ; 23 cm. [BX5199.C567A33] 75-42458 ISBN 0-8028-3481-7 : 9.95
1. Coggan, Frederick Donald, 1909- 2. Theology—Addresses, essays, lectures. 3. England—Biography. I. Title.

DUBOIS, Albert Julius, 1906- ed. 230.3
The truth and the life; essays on doctrine by priests of the American Church Union [by] Robert F. Capon [others] Foreword by Henry I. Louttit. New York, Published for the American Church Union by Morehouse-Barlow Co. [c.1961] 207p. 61-7805 4.25 lea. cl.,
1. Protestant Episcopal Church in the U. S. A.—Doctrinal and controversial works. I. Title.

DU BOSE, William Porcher, 1836-1918. 230.3
Unity in the faith. Edited by W. Norman Pittenger. Greenwich, Conn., Seabury Press, 1957. 244p. 22cm. [BX5845.D78] 57-9536
1. Protestant Episcopal Church in the U. S. A.—Addresses, essays, lectures. 2. Theology—Addresses, essays, lectures. I. Title.

FARRER, Austin Marsden. 230'.3
Reflective faith; essays in philosophical theology. Edited by Charles C. Conti. Grand Rapids, Eerdmans [1974, c1972] xv, 234 p. 21 cm. "Chronological list of published writings: 1933-1973": p. [227]-234. [BT40.F36 1974] 73-14737 ISBN 0-8028-1519-7 3.45 (pbk.)
1. Philosophical theology. I. Title.

FERGUSON, Franklin C. 230'.3
A pilgrimage in faith / by Franklin C. Ferguson. New York : Morehouse-Barlow Co., [1975] 170 p. ; 22 cm. Bibliography: p. 165-170. [BX5930.2.F47 1975] 75-5220 ISBN 0-8192-1200-8 pbk. : 3.95
1. Protestant Episcopal Church in the U.S.A.—Doctrinal and controversial works. I. Title.

FRIENDS, Romans, 230.3
countrymen a friendly answer to questions Roman Catholics ask concerning the relationship of the Anglican churches to the one, holy catholic, and apostolic church of Jesus Christ. New York, Morehouse-Gorham [1956] 58p. 19cm. [BX5132.C57] 56-11862
1. Protestant Episcopal Church in the U. S. A.—Doctrinal and constroversial works. 2. Catholic Church—Doctrinal and controversial works—Protestant authors.

GREEN, Bryan S W 230.3
Being and believing. New York, Scribner [1956] 121p. 21cm. [BX5933.G7] 56-10346
1. Church of England—Doctrinal and controversial works. 2. Apostles' Creed. 3. Lord's prayer. 4. Sermon on the Mount. 5. Commandments, Ten. I. Title.

GRISWOLD, Latta, 1876-1931. 230.3
The Episcopal church, its teaching and worship; instructions given at the Chapel of the intercession, New York, for churchmen and confirmation classes, by the Reverena Latta Griswold ... New York, E. S. Gorham, 1916. 111p. 19cm. [BX5933.G] 17-9139
I. Title.

HOOKER, Richard, 1553or4-1600. 230'.3
The Folger Library edition of the works of Richard Hooker / W. Speed Hill, general editor. Cambridge : Belknap Press of Harvard University Press, 1976- c1975- p. cm. Contents.Contents.—v. 1- . Of the laws of ecclesiastical polity. Includes bibliographical references and index. [BX5037.A2 1976] 76-24879 ISBN 0-674-63205-2 (v.1-2) : 60.00(set)
1. Church of England—Collected works. 2. Theology—Collected workks—16th century. I. Hill, William Speed, 1935- II. Title.

HOOKER, Richard, 1553or4-1600. 230'.3 s
Of the laws of ecclesiastical polity / Richard Hooker ; Georges Edelen [et al.] editor[s]. Cambridge : Belknap Press of Harvard University Press, 1976- c1975- p. cm. (The Folger Library edition of the works of Richard Hooker ; v. 1-) Contents.Contents.—v. 1. Preface and books one to four.—v. 2. Book five. Includes bibliographical references and index. [BX5037.A2 1976 vol.1, etc.] [BV649] 262.9'8'3 76-24883 ISBN 0-674-63205-2 (v.1-2) : 60.00(set)
1. Church of England—Doctrinal and controversial works. 2. Ecclesiastical law. 3. Church polity. I. Edelen, Georges. II. Title.

HURD, Richard, Bp. of Worcester, 1720-1808. 230'.3
The works of Richard Hurd, Lord Bishop of Worcester. London, Printed for T. Cadell and W. Davies, Strand, 1811. New York, AMS Press, 1967. 8 v. port. 23 cm. Contents.Contents.—v. 1-2. Critical works.—v. 3-4. Moral and political dialogues.—v. 5-8. Theological works. [PR3517.H78 1967] 72-189751

INGRAM, Tolbert Robert, 1913- 230.3
Lambeth, unity and truth. A reply to the pastoral letter issued by the House of Bishops meetings in General Convention, Miami Beach, Florida, October 1958. Bellaire, Tex., St. Thomas Press [1959] 52p. 24cm. [BX5835 1958] 59-14078
1. Protestant Episcopal Church in the U. S. A.—Pastoral letters and charges. I. Title.

JAY, Eric George 230.3
Friendship with God; the way of the Anglican Communion. New York, Morehouse-Barlow Co. [1959] 96p. 19cm. 59-65373 1.25 pap.,
1. Anglican Communion—Doctrinal and controversial works. 2. Theology. Doctrinal—Popular works. I. Title.

JEWEL, John, Bp. of Salisbury, 1522-1571. 230.3
An apology of the Church of England. Edited by J. E. Botty. Ithaca, N.Y., Published for the Folger Shakespeare Library by Cornell University Press [1963] xivii, 157 p. 23 cm. (Folger documents of Tudor and Stuart civilization) Based on the 1564 translation from the Latin by Lady Ann Bacon. Bibliography: p. 147-151. [BX5130.J362] 63-11494
1. Church of England — Doctrinal and controversial works. I. Folger Shakespeare Library, Washington, D.C. II. Title. III. Series.

JEWEL, John, Bp. of Salisbury, 1522-1571 230.3
An apology of the Church of England. Ed. by J. E. Booty. Ithaca, N.Y., Pub. for Folger Shakespeare Lib. by Cornell [c.1963] xlvii, 157p. 23cm. (Folger documents of Tudor and Stuart civilization) Based on the 1564 tr. from Latin by Lady Ann Bacon. Bibl. 63-11494 4.00
1. Church of England—Doctrinal and controversial works. I. Folger Shakespeare Library, Washington, D.C. II. Title. III. Series.

MOSS, Claude Beaufort, D. D. 1888- 230.3
A summary of the faith. New York, Morehouse-Barlow [c.]1961. 47p. 61-13583 1.25 bds.,
1. Protestant Episcopal Church in the U. S. A.—Doctrinal and controversial works. I. Title.

PIKE, James Albert, 1913- 230.3
The faith of the church, by James A. Pike and W. Norman Pittenger, with the editorial collaboration of Arthur C. Lichtenberger, and with the assistance of the Authors' Committee of the Dept. of Christian Education. New York, The National Council, Protestant Episcopal Church, 1951. 214 p. 22 cm. (The Church's teaching, v. 3) Bibliography: p. 193-207. [BX5930.P5] 51-13489
1. Protestant Episcopal Church in the U.S.A. — Doctrinal and controversial works. I. Pittenger, William Norman, 1905- joint author. II. Title. III. Series.

RAMSEY, Arthur Michael, Abp. of Canterbury, 1904- 230'.3
Canterbury pilgrim / Michael Ramsey. New York : Seabury Press, [1974] x, 188 p. : ill. ; 22 cm. "A Crossroad book." [BX5037.R28] 74-20800 ISBN 0-8164-1192-1 : 7.95
1. Church of England—Collected works. 2. Theology—Collected works—20th century. I. Title.

RAMSEY, Arthur Michael, Abp. of York, 1904- 230.3
An era in Anglican theology, from Gore to Temple; the development of Anglican theology between Lux Mundi and the Second World War, 1889-1939. New York, Scribners [c.1960] ix, 192p. Bibl. footnotes 22cm. (The Hale memorial lectures of Seabury-Western Theological Seminary, 1959) 60-14014 3.50
1. Theology, Doctrinal—Hist.—Gt. Brit. 2. Theology, Doctrinal—Addresses, essays, lectures. I. Title.

RAMSEY, Arthur Michael, Abp. of Canterbury, 1904- 230.3
An era in Anglican theology, from Gore to Temple; the development of Anglican theology between Lux Mundi and the Second World War, 1889-1939. New York, Scribner [1960] 192 p. 22 cm. (The Hale memorial lectures of Seabury-Western Theological Seminary, 1959) Includes bibliography. [BT30.G7R3] 60-14014
1. Theology, Doctrinal — Hist. — Gt. Brit. I. Title.

RAMSEY, Ian T. 230.3
On being sure in religion [London] Univ. of London, Athlone Pr. [dist. New York, Oxford, c.]1963. vii, 92p. 21cm. Rev. and slightly expanded version of the Frederick Denison Maurice lects. for 1961-2, given at King's Coll., London. Bibl. 64-21 2.00 bds.,
I. Theology, Doctrinal—Addresses, essays, lectures. II. Title. III. Title: Being sure in religion.

RIGBY, Fred Frankland 230.3
Anglicanism for parents. Greenwich, Conn., Seabury c.1962 121p. 19cm. A62 1.25 pap.,
1. Church of England—Doctrine and controversial works. I. Title.

SOUTHGATE, Wyndham Mason, 1910- 230.3
John Jewel and the problem of doctrinal authority. Cambridge,.Harvard University Press, 1962. 236 p; illus. 20 cm. (Harvard historical monographs, 49) Includes bibliography. [BX5199.J4S6] 62-9430
1. Jewel, John, Bp. of Salisbury, 1522-1571. 2. Authority (Religion) 3. Church of England — Doctrinal and controversial works. I. Title.

SOUTHGATE, Wyndham Mason, 1910- 230.3
John Jewel and the problem of doctrinal authority. Cambridge, Mass., Harvard [c.]1962. 236p. illus. (Harvard historical monographs, 49) Bibl. 62-9430 6.00
1. Jewel, John, Bp. of Salisbury, 1522-1571. 2. Authority (Religion) 3. Church of England—Doctrinal and controversial works. I. Title.

SUTER, John Wallace. 1890- 230.3
To know and believe; a senior high school resource book. Greenwich, Conn., Seabury Press [1958] 81 p. 21 cm. (The Seabury series, R-10) [BX5930.S8] 58-9266
1. Theology, Doctrinal-Popular works. 2. Protestant Episcopal Church in the U.S.A.—Doctrinal and controversial works. I. Title.

TAYLOR, Jeremy, Bp. of Down and Connor, 1613-1667. 230'.3
Jeremy Taylor: a selection from his works made by Martin Armstrong. Waltham Saint Lawrence, Berkshire, Golden Cockerel Press, 1923. [Folcroft, Pa., Folcroft Library Editions, 1972] p. [BR75.T29 1972] 72-13174 ISBN 0-8414-1165-4 (lib. bdg.)
1. Church of England—Collected works. 2. Theology—Collected works—17th century. I. Armstrong, Martin Donisthorpe, 1882- ed.

THOMPSON, James Nevill. 230.3
I want to live; the Christian answer. New ed., rev. and abridged. [New ed., rev. and abridged] London, A. R. Mowbray [New York, Morehouse-Barlow, 1959] 128p. 19cm. 59-6540 1.50 pap.,
1. Church of England—Doctrinal and controversial works. I. Title.

THORNTON, Martin. 230.3
Christian proficiency. New York, Morehouse-Gorham, 1959. 200 p. 22 cm. [BX5131.2.T5] 59-10485
1. Church of England—Doctrinal and controversial works. I. Title.

WHICHCOTE, Benjamin, 1609-1683. 230'.3
The works / Benjamin Whichcote. New York : Garland Pub., 1976. p. cm. (British philosophers and theologians of the 17th & 18th centuries ; no. 64) Reprint of the 1751 ed. printed by J. Chalmers for A. Thomson, Aberdeen. [BX5037.W53 1976] 75-11265 ISBN 0-8240-1814-1 lib. bdg. : 25.00 per vol.
1. Church of England—Collected works. 2. Theology—Collected works—17th century. I. Title. II. Series.

MCADOO, Henry Robert, Bp. of Ossory 230.3018
The spirit of Anglicanism: a survey of Anglican theological method in the seventeenth century. New York, Scribners [c.1965] ix, 422p. 22cm. (Hale lects. of Seabury-Western Theological Seminary) Bibl. [BT27.M22] 65-16696 5.95
1. Theology, Doctrinal—Hist.—17th cent. 2. Theology—Methodology. I. Title. II. Title: Anglican theological method. III. Series: Seabury-Western Theological Seminary, Evanston, Ill. The Hale lectures

MCADOO, Henry Robert, Bp. of Ossory. 230.3018
The spirit of Anglicanism: a survey of Anglican theological method in the seventeenth century [by]Henry R. McAdoo. New York, Scribner [1965] ix, 422 p. 22 cm. (The Hale lectures of Seabury-Western Theological Seminary) Bibliography: p. 415-417. [BT27.M22 1965a] 65-16696
1. Theology, Doctrinal — Hist. — 17th cent. 2. Theology — Methodology. I. Anglican theological method. (Series: Seabury-Western Theological Seminary, Evanston, Ill. The Hale lectures) II Title.

HARPER, Howard V. 230'.3'03
The Episcopalian's dictionary: church beliefs, terms, customs, and traditions explained in

layman's language [by] Howard Harper. New York, Seabury Press [1975, c1974] viii, 183 p. 21 cm. "A Crossroad book." [BX5007.H37 1975] 74-12105 ISBN 0-8164-1166-2 5.95
1. Protestant Episcopal Church in the U.S.A.—Dictionaries. I. Title.
Pbk. 3.95, ISBN 0-8164-2100-5.

CRAMMER, Thomas, Bp. of Canterbury, 1489-1556 230.308
The work of Thomas Cranmer. Introd. by J. I. Packer. Ed. by G. E. Duffield. Philadelphia, Fortress [1965] xiv, 370p. ports. (1 col.) 23cm. (Courtenav lib. of Reformation classics) Bibl. [BX5037.C76] 65-8827 6.25
1. Church of England—Collected works. 2. Theology—Collected works—16th cent. 3. Lord's Supper—Anglican Communion. I. Duffield, Gervase E., ed. II. Title.

FORSYTH, Peter Taylor, 1848-1921. 230.3'08
The creative theology of P. T. Forsyth; selections from his works. Edited by Samuel J. Mikolaski. Grand Rapids, Mich., Eerdmans [1969] 264 p. 22 cm. Bibliography: p. 262-264. [BX7117.F6 1969] 68-16257 6.95
1. Theology—Collected works—20th century. 2. Congregational churches—Collected works. I. Title.

GUERRY, William Alexander, 1861-1928. 230'.3'08
A 20th century prophet : being the life and thought of William Alexander Guerry, eighth Bishop of South Carolina / edited by Edward B. Guerry. Sewanee, Tenn. : University Press, c1976. 199 p. [1] leaf of plates : ports. ; 24 cm. Includes bibliographical references. [BX5995.G9A25 1976] 76-382338
1. Theology—Addresses, essays, lectures. I. Guerry, Edward B., 1902- II. Title.

HANSON, Richard Patrick Crosland. 230'.3'08
The attractiveness of God; essays in Christian doctrine [by] R. P. C. Hanson. Richmond, Va., John Knox Press [1973] 202 p. 23 cm. Includes bibliographical references. [BT75.2.H37 1973] 73-5345 ISBN 0-8042-0473-X 9.95
1. Theology, Doctrinal. I. Title.

LAUD, William, Abp. of Canterbury, 1573-1645. 230'.3'08
The works of the Most Reverend Father in God, William Laud, D.D. New York : AMS Press, [1975] p. cm. (LACT ; #11) Reprint of the 1847-1860 ed. published by J. H. Parker, Oxford. Contents.Contents.—v. 1. Sermons.—v. 2. Conference with Fisher.—v. 3. Devotions, diary, and history.—v. 4. History of troubles and trial, &c.—v. 5 [pt. 1] History of his chancellorship. pt. 2. Accounts of province, &c.—v. 6. pt. 1. Miscellaneous papers. Letters. pt. 2. Letters. Notes on Bellarmine.—v. 7. Letters. [BX5037.L3 1975] 74-5373 ISBN 0-404-52120-7 : 270.00
1. Church of England—Collected works. 2. Theology—Collected works—17th century. I. Title. II. Series: The Library of Anglo-Catholic theology ; #11.

LAW, William, 1686-1761. 230'.3'08
Freedom from a self-centered life/dying to self : selections from the writings of William Law / edited by Andrew Murray. Minneapolis : Bethany Fellowship, 1977. 144 p. ; 18 cm. (Dimension books) (Classics of devotion) Originally published in 1898 under title: Dying to self. [BV4500.L27 1977] 77-152373 ISBN 0-87123-104-2 pbk. : 1.95
1. Christian life—Anglican authors. I. Murray, Andrew, 1828-1917. II. Title. III. Series.

LAW, William, 1688-1761. 230'.3'08
The power of the spirit : selections from the writings of William Law / edited by Andrew Murray. Minneapolis : Bethany Fellowship, 1977. xv, 218 p. ; 18 cm. (Dimension books) (Classics of devotion) Reprint of the 1896 ed. published by J. Nisbet. [BR75.L346 1977] 76-57110 ISBN 0-87123-463-7 pbk. : 2.25
1. Theology—Collected works—18th century. I. Title. II. Series.

ALLISON, Christopher FitzSimons, 1927- 230.309032
The rise of moralism; the proclamation of the Gospel from Hooker to Baxter [by] C. F. Allison. New York, Seabury Press [1966] xii, 250 p. 23 cm. "Select bibliography": p. [239]-244. [BT27.A4 1966a] 66-22996
1. Theology, Doctrinal—History—17th century. 2. Theology, Anglican. I. Title.

GLICK, Garland Wayne, 1921- 230'.3'0921
The reality of Christianity; a study of Adolf von Harnack a historian and theologian [by] G. Wayne Glick. [1st ed.] New York, Harper & Row [1967] xvii, 359 p. 22 cm. (Makers of modern theology) Based on thesis, University of Chicago. Bibliography: p. 351-354. [BR139.H3G5] 67-14931
1. Harnack, Adolf von, 1851-1930. I. Title.

DE PAULEY, William Cecil, 1893- 230.3'0922
The candle of the Lord; studies in the Cambridge Platonists. Freeport, N.Y., Books for Libraries Press [1970] vii, 248 p. 23 cm. (Essay index reprint series) Reprint of the 1937 ed. Contents.Contents.—Benjamin Whichcote.—Benjamin Whichcote and Jeremy Taylor.—John Smith.—Ralph Cudworth.—Henry More.—Richard Cumberland.—Nathanael Culverwel.—George Rust.—Edward Stillingfleet.—Additional notes: John Calvin.—Lancelot Andrewes: Excerpt on the candle of the Lord.—William Laud: Excerpt on Scripture. Includes bibliographical references. [B1133.C2D46 1970] 75-107693
1. Cambridge Platonists. 2. Philosophy and religion. I. Title.

DILLISTONE, Frederick William, 1903- 230'.3'0924 B
Charles Raven : naturalist, historian, theologian / by F. W. Dillistone. 1st ed. Grand Rapids, Mich. : Eerdmans, [1975] 448 p., [4] leaves of plates : ill. ; 24 cm. Includes index. "Bibliography of Charles Raven": p. 439-440. [BX5199.R26D54 1975] 74-20580 ISBN 0-8028-3455-8 : 12.95
1. Raven, Charles Earle, 1885-1964.

GLICK, Garland Wayne; 1921- 230'.3'0924
The reality of Christianity; a study of Adolf von Harnack as historian and theologian [by] G. Wavne Glick. [1st ed.] New York, Harper [1967] xvii, 359p. 22cm. (Makers of modern theol.) Based on thesis, Univ. of Chicago. Bibl. [BR139.H3G5] 67-1493 7.50
1. Harnack, Adolf von, 1851-1930. I. Title.

LEMAHIEU, D. L., 1945- 230'.3'0924
The mind of William Paley : a philosopher and his age / D. L. LeMahieu. Lincoln : University of Nebraska Press, c1976. xi, 215 p. ; 23 cm. Based on the author's thesis, Harvard University. Includes bibliographical references and index. [BL182.L45] 75-22547 ISBN 0-8032-0865-0 : 12.95
1. Paley, William, 1743-1805. Natural theology. 2. Paley, William, 1743-1805. 3. Natural theology—History of doctrines. I. Title.

OWEN, Huw Parri. 230'.3'0924
W. R. Matthews : philosopher and theologian / H. W. Owen. London : Athlone Press, 1976. ix, 84 p. ; 22 cm. Distributed in the USA by Humanities Press, New Jersey. Includes bibliographical references and index. [BX5199.M29O85] 77-354007 ISBN 0-485-12027-5 pbk. : 3.50
1. Matthews, Walter Robert, 1881-1973.

ACHTEMEIER, Paul. 230.4
The Old Testament roots of our faith [by] Paul and Elizabeth Achtemeier. New York, Abingdon Press [1962] 158 p. 21 cm. [BT180.P7A25] 62-11518
1. God-Promises. I. Achtemeier, Elizabeth Rice, 1926- joint author. II. Title.

ACHTEMEIER, Paul J 230.4
The Old Testament roots of our faith [by] Paul and Elizabeth Achtemeier. New York, Abingdon Press [1962] 158 p. 21 cm. [BT180.P7A25] 62-11518
1. God—Promises. I. Achtemeier, Elizabeth Rice, 1926- joint author. II. Title.

BARTH, Karl, 1886- 230.4
God in action. Introd. by Elmer G. Homrighausen. Tr. by E. G. Homrighausen, Karl J. Ernst. Manhasset, N. Y., Round Table Pr.; dist. Channel, 1963. 143p. 20cm. 63-15798 3.00
1. Dialectical theology. 2. Theology, Doctrinal—Addresses, essays, lectures. I. Title.

BARTH, Karl, 1886-1968. 230.4
Protestant thought: from Rousseau to Ritschl, being the translation of eleven chapters of Die protestantische Theologie im 19. Jahrhundert. [Translated by Brian Cozens] New York, Harper [1959] 435 p. 22 cm. Includes bibliography. [BT30.G3B313 1959] 59-10931
1. Theology, Doctrinal—History—Germany. 2. Theology, Doctrinal—History—18th century. 3. Theology, Doctrinal—History—19th century. I. Title.

BARTH, Karl, 1886-1968. 230.4
Protestant thought: from Rousseau to Ritschl; being the translation of eleven chapters of Die protestantische Theologie im 19. Jahrhundert. [Translated by Brian Cozens. New York] Simon and Schuster [1969, c1959] 435 p. 21 cm. Bibliography: p. [423]-425. Bibliographical footnotes. [BT30.G3B313 1969] 70-4455 2.95
1. Theology, Doctrinal—History—Germany. 2. Theology, Doctrinal—History—18th century. 3. Theology, Doctrinal—History—19th century. I. Title.

BERKOUWER, Gerrit Cornelis, 1903- 230.4
The triumph of grace in the theology of Karl Barth. [Translated from the Dutch by Harry R. Boer. American ed.] Grand Rapids, W. B. Eerdmans Pub. Co., 1956. 414p. 23cm. [BX4827.B3B433] 56-9380
1. Barth, Karl, 1886- 2. Grace (Theology) 3. Dialectical theology. I. Title.

BERKOUWER, Gerrit Cornelis, 1903- 230.4
The triumph of grace in the theology of Karl Barth. [Translated from the Dutch by Harry R. Boer. American ed.] Grand Rapids, W. B. Eeromans Pub. Co., 1956. 414p. 23cm. [BX4827.B3B433] 56-9380
1. Barth. Karl. 1886- 2. Grace (Theology) 3. Dialectical theology. I. Title.

BORNKAMM, Heinrich, 1901- 230.4
The heart of Reformation faith; the fundamental axioms of Evangelical belief. Translated by John W. Doberstein. [1st ed.] New York, Harper & Row [1965] 126 p. 22 cm. Translation of Das bleibende Recht der Reformation. Bibliographical references included in "Notes" (p. 123-124) [BT27.B613] 65-15388
1. Theology—16th century. 2. Protestantism. I. Title.

BULTMANN, Rudolf Karl, 1884- 230.4
Existence and faith; shorter writings of Rudolf Bultmann. Selected, translated, and introduced by Schubert M. Ogden. New York, Meridian Books [1960] 320 p. 19 cm. (Living age books) Includes bibliography. [BT15.B78] 60-6774
1. Theology—Addresses, essays, lectures. I. Title.

FORELL, George Wolfgang 230.4
The Protestant faith. Englewood Cliffs, N.J., Prentice [1967,c.1960] 321p. 22cm. Bibl. [BX4811.F65] 60-10133 2.95 pap.,
1. Protestantism. 2. Theology, Doctrinal. 3. Creeds. I. Title.

HAMMOND, Guyton B., 1930- 230.4
The power of self-transcendence; an introduction to the philosophical theology of Paul Tillich, by Guyton B. Hammond. St. Louis, Bethany Press, 1966. 160 p. 20 cm. (The Library of contemporary theology) Bibliography: p. 148-155. [BX4827.T53H35] 66-19813
1. Tillich, Paul, 1886-1965. I. Title.

HARTWELL, Herbert. 230.4
The theology of Karl Barth: an introduction. Philadelphia, Westminster Press [1964] xiv, 201 p. 19 cm. (Studies in theology series) Bibliography: p. 191-193. [BX4827.B3H3] 65-10167
1. Barth, Karl, 1886- I. Title.

HARTWELL, Herbert 230.4
The theology of Karl Barth: an introduction. Philadelphia, Westminster [c.1964] xiv, 201p. 19cm. (Studies in theology ser.) Bibl. [BX4827.B3H3] 65-10167 1.85 pap.,
1. Barth, Karl, 1886- I. Title.

HENDERLITE, Rachel 230.4
Forgiveness and hope; toward a theology for Protestant Christian education. Richmond, Va., Knox [1966,c.1961] 127p. 21cm. (Aletheia ed.) Bibl. [BT78.H44] 61-13518 1.45 pap.,
1. Theology, Doctrinal—Popular works. 2. Religious education. I. Title.

JONG, Pieter de 230.4
Evangelism and contemporary theology; a study of the implications for evangelism in the thoughts of six modern theologians. Nashville 1908 Grand Ave. Tidings. [c. 1962] 116p. 22cm. Bibl. 62-13349 1.25 pap.,
1. Theology, Doctrinal—Hist.—20th cent. 2. Evangelistic work. I. Title.

KEGLEY, Charles W. ed. 230.4
The theology of Paul Tillich, ed. by Charles W. Kegley, Robert W. Bretall. New York, Macmillan, 1961 [c.1952] xiv, 370p. (Library of living theology, v.1.) Bibl. 1.95 pap.,
1. Tillich, Paul, 1886- I. Bretall, Robert Walter, 1913- joint ed. II. Title.

KEGLEY, Charles W. ed. 230.4
The theology of Paul Tillich, edited by Charles W. Kegley & Robert W. Bretall. New York, Macmillan, 1952. xvi, 370 p. port. 22 cm. (The Library of living theology, v. 1) "Bibliography of the writings of Paul Tillich to March, 1952": p. [351]-362. [BX4827.T53K4] 52-13200
1. Tillich, Paul, 1886- I. Betall, Robert Walter, 1913- joint editor.

LUTHER, Martin, 1483-1546. 230'.4
The wisdom of Martin Luther. The wisdom of John Calvin. The wisdom of John Wesley. [Selected and with commentary by David Poling] New Canaan, Conn., Keats Pub. [1973] 145 p. 18 cm. (Inspiration three, v. 3) (A Pivot family reader) [BR315.L8 1973] 73-169420 1.25 (pbk.)
1. Luther, Martin, 1483-1546. 2. Calvin, Jean, 1509-1564. 3. Wesley, John, 1703-1791. I. Calvin, Jean, 1509-1564. II. Wesley, John, 1703-1791. III. Poling, David, 1928- comp. IV. Title. V. Title: The wisdom of John Calvin. VI. Title: The wisdom of John Wesley.

MARTIN, Bernard, 1928- 230.4
The existentialist theology of Paul Tillich. New York, Bookman [c.1963] 221p. 21cm. Bibl. 62-10275 5.00
1. Tillich, Paul, 1886- I. Title.

MARTIN, Bernard, 1928- 230.4
The existentialist theology of Paul Tillich. New Haven, Conn., Coll. & Univ.Pr. [1964, c.1963] 221p. 21cm. Bibl. 1.95 pap.,
1. Tillich, Paul, 1886- I. Title.

MATCZAK, Sebastian A 230.4
Karl Barth on God; the knowledge of the divine existence. New York, St. Paul Publications [1962] 358p. 21cm. [BT101.B2718M3] 62-15994
1. Barth, Karl, 1886- 2. God—History of doctrines. I. Title.

MAVIS, W Curry. 230.4
Beyond conformity. Winona Lake, Ind., Light and Life Press [1958] 160p. 22cm. [BR1640.M3] 58-49552
1. Evangelicalism. I. Title.

MELANCHTHON, Philipp, 1497-1560 230.4
Melanchthon on Christian doctrine: Loci communes, 1555. Tr., ed. by Clyde L. Manschreck. Introd. by Hans Engelland. New York, Oxford [c.]1965. lvii, 356p. 24cm. (Lib. of Protestant thought) Bibl. [BR336.L62M3] 65-20803 7.00
1. Theology, Doctrinal. 2. Lutheran Church—Doctrinal and controversial works. I. Manschreck, Clyde Leonard, 1917- ed. II. Title. III. Title: Loci communes, 1555. (Series)

MELANCHTHON, Philipp, 1497-1560. 230.4
Melanchthon on Christian doctrine: Loci communes, 1555. Translated and edited by Clyde L. Manschreck. Introd. by Hans Engelland. New York, Oxford University Press, 1965. lvii, 356 p. 24 cm. (A Library of Protestant thought) Bibliography: p. 345-348. [BR336.L62M3] 65-20803
1. Theology, Doctrinal. 2. Lutheran Church—Doctrinal and controversial works. I. Manschreck, Clyde Leonard, 1917- ed. II. Title. III. Title: Loci communes, 1555.

NASH, Ronald H. 230.4
The new evangelicalism. Grand Rapids, Zondervan Pub. House [1963] 188 p. 23 cm. Bibliography: p. 181-183. [BR1640.N3] 63-15740
1. Evangelicalism. I. Title.

NEIBUHR, Richard R 230.4
Schleiermacher on Christ and religion, a new introduction [by] Richard R. Niebuhr. New York, Scribner [1964] xv, 267 p. 24 cm. Bibliograpical footnotes. [BX4827.S3N5] 64-22393
1. Schleiermacher, Friedrich Ernst Daniel, 1768-1834. I. Title.

NIEBUHR, Richard R. 230.4
Schleiermacher on Christ and religion, a new introduction. New York, Scribners [c.1964] xv, 267p. 24cm. Bibl. [BX4827.S3N5] 64-22393 5.95
I. Schleiermacher, Friedrich Ernst Daniel, 1768-1834. II. Title.

O'MEARA, Thomas A ed. 230.4
Paul Tillich in Catholic thought. Thomas A. O'Meara [and] Celestin D. Weisser, editors. Foreword by J. Heywood Thomas, with an afterword by Paul Tillich. Dubuque, Iowa, Priory Press [1964] xxiii, 323 p. 24 cm. Bibliographical footnotes. [BX4827.T53O45] 64-22796
1. Tillich, Paul, 1886- I. Weissner, Celestin D., joint ed. II. Title.

O'MEARA, Thomas A. ed. 230.4
Paul Tillich in Catholic thought. Thomas A. O'Meara Celestin D. Weisser, eds. Foreword by J. Heywood Thomas, afterword by Paul Tillich. Dubuque, Iowa, Priory Pr. [c.1964] xxiii, 323p. 24cm. Bibl. 64-22796 5.95; 2.95 pap.,
1. Tillich, Paul, 1886- I. Weisser, Celestin D., joint ed. II. Title.

O'MEARA, Thomas F., 1935- comp. 230'.4
Paul Tillich in Catholic thought. Editors: Thomas F. O'Meara [and] Donald M. Weisser.

Foreword by J. Heywood Thomas; an afterword by Paul Tillich. Rev. ed. Garden City, N.Y., Image Books [1969] 395 p. 19 cm. Bibliographical footnotes. [BX4827.T53O45 1969] 78-78749 1.45
1. Tillich, Paul, 1886-1965. I. Weisser, Donald M., joint comp. II. Title.

RITSCHL, Albrecht 230'.4
Benjamin, 1822-1889.
Three essays. Translated and with an introd. by Philip Hefner. Philadelphia, Fortress Press [1972] 301 p. 24 cm. Contents.Contents.—Theology and metaphysics.—"Prolegomena" to The history of pietism.—Instruction in the Christian religion. Includes bibliographical references. [B85.R58] 72-75654 ISBN 0-8006-0224-2 10.50
1. Ritschl, Albrecht Benjamin, 1822-1889. 2. Pietism. 3. Christianity—Philosophy. 4. Theological, Doctrinal. I. Title.

TILLICH, Paul, 1886- 230.4
Ultimate concern; Tillich in dialogue. [Ed. by] D. Mackenzie Brown. New York, Harper [1965] xvi, 234p. 22cm. Ed. from tape recordings made during a seminar held at Union of Calif, Santa Barbara, in the spring of 1964. Bibl. [BX4811.T5] 65-15389 3.95
1. Theology. 2. Protestantism. I. Brown, Donald Mackenzie, 1908- ed. II. California. University, Santa Barbara. III. Title. IV. Title: Tillich in dialogue.

TILLICH, Paul, 1886-1965. 230'.4
Perspectives on 19th and 20th century Protestant theology. Edited and with an introd. by Carl E. Braaten. [1st ed.] New York, Harper & Row [1967] xxiv, 252 p. 22 cm. "Lectures ... delivered at the Divinity School of the University of Chicago ... spring ... 1963." Bibliographical footnotes. [BT28.T5] 67-11507
1. Theology, Protestant—History. 2. Theology, Doctrinal—History—19th century. 3. Theology, Doctrinal—History—20th century. I. Braaten, Carl E., 1929- ed. II. Title.

UNHJEM, Arne. 230.4
Dynamics of doubt; a preface to Tillich. Philadelphia, Fortress Press [1966] 128 p. 20 cm. Includes bibliographies. [BX4827.T53U5] 66-23223
1. Tillich, Paul, 1886-1965. I. Title.

VAN Til, Cornelius, 1895- 230.4
Christianity and Barthianism. Philadelphia, Presbyterian and Reformed Pub. Co., 1962. 450 p. 22 cm. [BX4827.B3V3 1962a] 62-15431
1. Barth, Karl, 1886- I. Title.

VAN Til, Cornelius, 1895- 230.4
Christianity and Barthianism. Grand Rapids, Baker Book House [1962] xiii, 450 p. 22 cm. Bibliographical footnotes. [BX4827.B3V3] 62-19849
1. Barth, Karl, 1886- I. Title.

VAN TIL, Cornelius, 1895- 230.4
Christianity and Barthianism. Grand Rapids, Baker Book House [1962] xiii, 450 p. 22 cm. Bibliographical footnotes. [BX4827.B3V3] 62-15431
I. Title.

VAN TIL, Cornelius, 1895- 230.4
Christianity and Barthianism. Grand Rapids, Mich., Baker Bk. [c.1962] xiii, 450p. 22cm. Bibl. 62-15431 6.95
1. Barth, Karl, 1886- I. Title.

WILSON, Theron D. 230.4
Religion for tomorrow. New York, Philosophical [c.1963] x, 138p. 23cm. Bibl. 62-9776 4.75 bds.,
1. Christianity—Addresses, essays, lectures. I. Title.

WINWARD, Stephen F 230.4
A modern ABeCedary for Protestants. New York, Association Press [1964, c1963] 128 p. 24 cm. [BT77.W74 1964] 64-11595
1. Theology, Doctrinal — Popular works. I. Title.

WINWARD, Stephen F. 230.4
A modern ABeCedary for Protestants. New York, Association [1964, c.1963] 128p. 24cm. 64-11595 3.50
1. Theology, Doctrinal—Popular works. I. Title.

ANDREWS, James F., 230.4'0924
1936- comp.
Karl Barth. Edited by James F. Andrews. Contributors: Daniel Jenkins [and others] St. Louis, Herder [1969] ix, 119, 2 p. 18 cm. (The Christian critic series) Bibliography: p. [121] [BX4827.B3A63] 76-79294 1.25
1. Barth, Karl, 1886-1968. I. Jenkins, Daniel Thomas, 1914-

KARL Barth and 230'.4'0924
radical politics / edited and translated by George Hunsinger. Philadelphia : Westminster Press, c1976. 236 p. ; 20 cm. Contents.Contents.—Hunsinger, G. Introduction.—Barth, K. Jesus Christ and the movement for social justice (1911).—Marquardt, F.-W. Socialism in the theology of Karl Barth.—Gollwitzer, H. Kingdom of God and socialism in the theology of Karl Barth.—Diem, H. Karl Barth as socialist: controversy over a new attempt to understand him.—Schellong, D. On reading Karl Barth from the left.—Bettis, J. Political theology and social ethics.—Hunsinger, G. Conclusion: toward a radical Barth. Includes bibliographical references. [BX4827.B3K34] 76-976 ISBN 0-664-24797-0 : 6.00
1. Barth, Karl, 1886-1968—Addresses, essays, lectures. 2. Socialism and religion—History—Addresses, essays, lectures. I. Hunsinger, George.
Contents omitted.

MCCONNACHIE, John, 230'.4'0924 B
1875-
The Barthian theology and the man of to-day. Freeport, N.Y., Books for Libraries Press [1972] 335 p. 22 cm. Reprint of the 1933 ed. Includes bibliographical references. [BX4827.B3M23 1972] 72-2493 ISBN 0-8369-6861-1
1. Barth, Karl, 1886-1968. 2. Dialectical theology. I. Title.

MCCONNACHIE, John, 230'.4'0924 B
1875-
The Barthian theology and the man of to-day. Freeport, N.Y., Books for Libraries Press [1972] 335 p. 22 cm. Reprint of the 1933 ed. Includes bibliographical references. [BX4827.B3M23 1972] 72-2493 ISBN 0-8369-6861-1 12.50
1. Barth, Karl, 1886-1968. 2. Dialectical theology. I. Title.

MUELLER, David 230.4'0924
Livingstone, 1929-
An introduction to the theology of Albrecht Ritschl, by David L. Mueller. Philadelphia, Westminster Press [1969] 214 p. 24 cm. Bibliographical references included in "Notes" (p. 181-214) [BX4827.R5M8] 77-80978 ISBN 6-642-08738- 8.50
1. Ritschl, Albrecht Benjamin, 1822-1889. I. Title.

MUELLER, David 230'.4'0924 B
Livingstone, 1929-
Karl Barth, by David L. Mueller. Waco, Tex., Word Books [1972] 172 p. 23 cm. (Makers of the modern theological mind) Bibliography: p. 169-172. [BX4827.B3M8] 70-188066 4.95
1. Barth, Karl, 1886-1968.

ODEN, Thomas C. 230.4'0924
The promise of Barth; the ethics of freedom, by Thomas C. Oden. [1st ed.] Philadelphia, Lippincott [1969] 109 p. 22 cm. (The Promise of theology) "Selected bibliography of works by Karl Barth": p. 109. Bibliographical references included in "Notes" (p. 103-107) [BX4827.B3O3] 79-86078 3.50
1. Barth, Karl, 1886-1968. I. Title.

PARKER, Thomas Henry 230.4'0924 B
Louis.
Karl Barth, by T. H. L. Parker. Grand Rapids, Eerdmans [1970] 125 p. 22 cm. Includes bibliographical references. [BX4827.B3P28] 70-103449 2.45
1. Barth, Karl, 1886-1968.

ALTHAUS, Paul, 1888-1966. 230.41
The theology of Martin Luther. Translated by Robert C. Schultz. Philadelphia, Fortress Press [1966] xv 464 p. 23 cm. Bibliographical footnotes. [BR333.A513] 66-17345
1. Luther, Martin, 1483-1546—Theology. I. Title.

ANDERSON, Charles S. 230'.4'1
Faith and freedom : the Christian faith according to the Lutheran Confessions / Charles S. Anderson. Minneapolis : Augsburg Pub. House, c1977. 160 p. ; 20 cm. Bibliography: p. 158-160. [BX8068.A1A5] 76-27087 ISBN 0-8066-1558-3 pbk. : 3.95
1. Lutheran Church—Catechisms and creeds. 2. Theology, Lutheran. 3. Justification. I. Title.

ARNDT, Elmer J F. ed. 230.41
The heritage of the Reformation; essays commemorating the centennial of Eden Theological Seminary. New York, R. R. Smith, 1950. 264 p. 23 cm. [BT10.A7] 50-1259
1. Theology, Doctrinal—Addresses, essays, lectures. 2. Evangelical and Reformed Church—Addresses, essays, lectures. 3. Eden Theological Seminary, St. Louis. I. Title.
Contents Omitted.

BERTRAM, Martin H ed. 230.41
Stimmen der Kirche. St. Louis, Concordia Pub. House, 1961. 240p. illus. 23cm. [BX8015.B45] 61-66363
1. Religious education—Text-books for adults—Lutheran. 2. German language—Chrestomathies and readers. I. Title.

BERTRAM, Martin H., ed. 230.41
Stimmen der Kirche. St. Louis, Concordia [c.] 1961. 240p. illus. 61-66363 3.20 pap.,
1. Religious education—Text-books for adults—Lutheran. 2. German language—Chrestomathies and readers. I. Title.

BONHOEFFER, Dietrich, 230.4'1
1906-1945.
The way to freedom; letters, lectures, and notes, 1935-1939, from the Collected works of Dietrich Bonhoeffer, volume II. Edited and introduced by Edwin H. Robertson. Translated by Edwin H. Robertson and John Bowden. [1st U.S. ed.] New York, Harper & Row [1966] 272 p. 22 cm. Bibliographical footnotes. [BX8011.B65 1966] 67-11501
1. Lutheran Church—Collected works. 2. Theology—Collected works—20th century. I. Robertson, Edwin Hanton, ed. II. Title.

CARNELL, Edward John 230.41
The theology of Reinhold Niebuhr. [Rev. ed.] Grand Rapids, Eerdmans [c.1950, 1960] 250p. 22cm. (B2bl. footnotes) 60-16193 2.45 pap.,
1. Niebuhr, Reinhold. 2. Dialectical theology. 3. Neo-orthodoxy. I. Title.

CARNELL, Edward John, 230.41
1919-
The theology of Reinhold Niebuhr. Grand Rapids, Eerdmans, 1951 ['1950] 250 p. 23 cm. Bibliographical footnotes. [BT78.N5C3] 51-9746
1. Niebuhr, Reinhold, 2. Dialectical theology. 3. Neo-orthodoxy. I. Title.

CARNELL, Edward John, 230.41
1919-
The theology of Reinhold Niebuhr. [Rev. ed.] Grand Rapids, Eerdmans [1960] 250p. 22cm. Includes bibliography. [BX4827.N5C3 1960] 60-16193
1. Niebuhr, Reinhold, 1892- 2. Dialectical theology. 3. Neo-orthodoxy. I. Title.

DOCTRINAL declarations; 230.41
a collection of official statements on the doctrinal position of various Lutheran bodies in America. Saint Louis, Mo., Concordia Pub. House, 1957. 116p. 23cm. [BX8065.D6 1957] 57-2051
1. Lutheran Church—Doctrinal and controversial works. 2. Lutheran Church in the U. S.

EMCH, William N 230.41
The question box. Columbus, Ohio, Wartburg Press [1956] 188 p. 20 cm. Compiled from 'The question box, conducted by ... [the author, as] a regular feature of the Lutheran standard. [BR96.E5] 57-16411
1. Questions and answers—Tehology. 2. Lutheran Church—Doctrinal and controversial works. I. Title.

GERRISH, Brian Albert, 230.41
1931-
Grace and reason; a study in the theology of Luther. Oxford, Clarendon Pr. [dist. New York, Oxford, c.] 1962. ix, 188p. 22cm. Bibl. 62-2979 6.75
1. Luther, Martin—Theology. 2. Reason. I. Title.

GRAEBNER, Theodore Conrad, 230.41
1876-
The borderland of right and wrong. [8th ed.] Saint Louis, Concordia Pub. House, 1951. 178 p. 19 cm. [BT32.G7 1951] 51-6989
1. Adiaphora. 2. Lutheran Church—Doctrinal and controversial works. I. Title.

GRITSCH, Eric W. 230'.4'1
Lutheranism : the theological movement and its confessional writings / Eric W. Gritsch and Robert W. Jenson. Philadelphia : Fortress Press, c1976. x, 214 p. ; 24 cm. Includes index. [BX8065.2.G74] 76-7869 ISBN 0-8006-0458-X : 7.50
1. Theology, Lutheran. I. Jenson, Robert W., joint author. II. Title.

HAKER, Milton Albert. 230.41
Preparing for church membership; Biblical and catechitical studies to prepare older young people and adults for membership in the Lutheran Church. [Study book] Arthur H. Getz [and] Gerhard H. Doermann, editors. Philadelphia, Muhlenberg Press [1956] 93 p. illus. 19 cm. "Prepared under the auspices of the boards of parish education of the American Evangelical Lutheran Church [and other Lutheran churches]" [BX8065.H264] 56-58954
1. Lutheran Church — Membership. 2. Lutheran Church — Doctrinal and controversial works. I. Title.

HAKER, Milton Albert. 230.41
Preparing for church membership; a pastor's guide for Biblical and catechetical studies. Arthur H. Getz [and] Gerhard H. Doermann, editors. Philadelphia, Muhlenberg Press [1956] 64p. 20cm. 'Prepared under the auspices of the boards of parish education of the American Evangelical Lutheran Church [and other Lutheran churches]' Bound with the author's Preparing for church membership; Biblical and catechetical studies to prepare older young people and adults for membership in the Lutheran Church. Philadelphia [1956] Includes bibliographies. [BX8065.H264] 56-58955
1. Church membership—Study and teaching. 2. Lutheran Church—Membership. Lutheran Church—Doctrinal and controversial works. I. Title.

HAKER, Milton Albert. 230.41
Preparing for church membership; Biblical and catechetical studies to prepare older young people and adults for membership in the Lutheran Church. [Study book] Arthur H. Getz. [and] Gerhard H. Doermann, editors. Philadelphia, Muhlenberg Press [1956] Philadelphia [1956] 93p. illus. 19cm. 'Prepared under the auspices of the boards of parish education of the American Evangelical Lutheran Church [and other Lutheran churches]' [BX8065.H265] 56-58954
1. Church membership—Study and teaching. 2. Lutheran Church—Membership. 3. Lutheran Church—Doctrinal and controversial works. I. Title. II. Title: —Another issue. Bound with the author's Preparing for church membership;

HEINECKEN, Martin J. J. 230.4'1
Christian teachings; affirmations of faith for laypeople [by] Martin J. Heinecken. Philadelphia, Fortress [1967] ix, 302p. 18cm. (Fortress paperback orig.) Bibl. [BX8065.2.H4] 67-21529 3.50 pap.,
1. Lutheran Church— Doctrinal and controversial works. 2. Theology, Doctrinal—Popular works. I. Title.

HOFFMANN, Oswald C. J. 230'.4'1
God's joyful people—one in the spirit [by] Oswald C. J. Hoffmann. St. Louis, Concordia Pub. House [1973] 103 p. 18 cm. [BV600.2.H574] 72-96742 1.50 (pbk.)
1. Church. I. Title.

HOFMANN, Hans, 1923- 230.41
The theology of Reinhold Niebuhr. Translated by Louise Pettibone Smith. New York, Scribner, 1956. 269p. 22cm. [BX4827.N5H63] 56-5663
1. Niebuhr, Reinhold, 1892- 2. Sin—History of doctrines. I. Title.

HOFMANN, Hans F., 1923- 230.41
The theology of Reinhold Niebuhr Translated by Louise Pettibone Smith. New York Scribner 1956. 269 p. 22 cm. [BX4827.N5H63] 56-5663
1. Niebuhr, Reinhold, 1892- 2. Sin — History of doctrines. I. Title.

HOYER, Robert. 230'.4'1
He calls me by my name : a pre-membership course for adults / Robert Hoyer. St. Louis : Clayton Pub. House, c1977. 103 p. ; 23 cm. [BV1488.H69] 77-74385 ISBN 0-915644-09-6 pbk. : 4.75
1. Christian education—Text-books for adults—Lutheran. I. Title.

HUGGENVIK, Theodore, 1889- 230.41
We believe; an elementary re-affirmation of the fundamentals of the evangelical Christian religion. Minneapolis, Augsburg Pub. House [1950] x, 149 p. 22 cm. "Parts of this handbook ... were published as a series of articles in the Lutheran teacher from October, 1948, to and including October, 1949." [BT77.H79] 50-14975
1. Theology. Doctrinal—Popular works. 2. Lutheran Church—Doctrinal and controversial works. 3. Luther, Martin. Catechismus, Kleiner. I. Title.

KELLER, Paul F. 230.41
Studies in Lutheran doctrine. [Rev. ed. St. Louis, Concordia Pub. House, c.1960] 129p. illus. 28cm. 60-15574 pap., 2.50; comprehensive tests, .10; correction key and profile chart, .10
1. Confirmation—Instruction and study. 2. Lutheran Church—Catechisms and creeds—English. I. Title.

KING, Rachel Hadley, 1904- 230.41
The omission of the Holy Spirit from Reinhold Niebuhr's theology. New York, Philosophical Library [1964] 209 p. 22 cm. Bibliography: p. 207-209. [BX4827.N63K5] 64-13324
1. Niebuhr, Rienhold, 1892- I. Title.

KING, Rachel Hadley, 1904- 230.41
The omission of the Holy Spirit from Reinhold Niebuhr's theology. New York, Philosophical [c.1964] 209p. 22cm. Bibl. 64-13324 5.75
1. Niebuhr, Reinhold, 1892- I. Title.

KNUTSON, Kent S. 230'.4'1
Gospel, church, mission / Kent S. Knutson. Minneapolis : Augsburg Pub. House, c1976. 160 p. ; 21 cm. "Bibliography of Kent S. Knutson material": p. 140-160. [BX8011.K55] 75-40632 ISBN 0-8066-1522-2 : 4.95
1. Lutheran Church—Collected works. 2. Theology—Collected works—20th century. 3. Knutson, Kent S. 4. Knutson, Kent S.—Bibliography. I. Title.

KOEHLER, Edward Wilhelm August, 1875-1951. 230.41
A summary of Christian doctrine; a popular presentation of the teachings of the Bible. 2d rev. ed. prepared for publication by Alfred W. Koehler. Detroit, L. H. Koehler [1952] 328 p. 24 cm. [BX8065.K58 1952] 52-22789
1. Theology, Doctrinal—Popular works. 2. Lutheran Church—Doctrinaland controversial works. I. Title.

KRAUTH, Charles Porterfield, 1823-1883. 230.41
The Conservative Reformation and its theology. Minneapolis, Augsburg Pub. House [1963, c1899] xvii, 840 p. 24 cm. Bibliographical references included in footnotes. [BX8065.K7] 63-16600
1. Reformation. 2. Lutheran Church — Doctrinal and controversial works. I. Title.

KRAUTH, Charles Porterfield, 1823-1883. 230.41
The Conservative Reformation and its theology. Minneapolis, Augsburg Pub. House [1963, c1899] xvii, 840 p. 24 cm. Bibliographical references included in footnotes. [BX8065.K7 1963] 63-16600
1. Reformation. 2. Lutheran Church—Doctrinal and controversial works. I. Title.

LAETSCH, Theodore Ferdinand Karl, 1877- ed. 230.41
The abiding word; an anthology of doctrinal essays for the year 1945-1946, v. 3. St. Louis, Concordia Pub. House, 1960. At head of title: The Centennial series. Bibl. 47-19571 4.75 rev
1. Theology, Doctrinal—Addresses, essays, lectures. 2. Evangelical Lutheran Synod of Missouri, Ohio, and Other States—Doctrinal and controversial works. 3. Lutheran Church—Doctrinal and controversial works. I. Title.

LAVIK, John Rasmus, 1881- 230.41
The way, the truth, and the life; the basic teachings of the Bible concerning God, man, and the way of salvation Minneapolis, Augsburg Pub. House [1957] 258p. 23cm. [BT77.L32] 57-9724
1. Theology, Doctrinal —Popular works. 2. Lutheran Church—Doctrinal and controversial works. I. Title.

LOHE, Wilhelm, 1808-1872. 230.4'1
Three books about the church. Translated, edited, and with an introd. by James L. Schaaf. Philadelphia, Fortress Press [1969] viii, 183 p. 21 cm. (Seminar editions) Translation of Drei Bucher von der Kirche. Bibliographical footnotes. [BX8065.L7 1969] 79-84538 2.95
1. Church. 2. Lutheran Church—Doctrinal and controversial works. I. Title.

LUTHER, Martin, 1483-1546 230.4'1
A compend of Luther's theology. Ed. by Hugh T. Kerr. Philadelphia, Westminster [1966, c.1943] xxi, 253p. 1.95 pap.,
I. Title.

LUTHER, Martin, 1483-1546 230.41
Early theological works. Ed., tr. by James Atkinson. Philadelphia, Westminster [c.1962] 380p. 24cm. (Lib. of Christian classics, v. 16) Bibl. 62-12358 6.50
1. Theology—Collected works. I. Atkinson, James, 1914- ed. and tr. II. Title. III. Series. Content omitted.

LUTHER, Martin, 1483-1546. 230.4'1
Readings in Luther for laymen. With introductions and notes by Charles S. Anderson. Minneapolis, Augsburg Pub. House [1967] ix, 304 p. 22 cm. Bibliographical footnotes. [BR331.E5A6] 67-25367
1. Theology — Collected works — 16th cent. 2. Luthern Church — Collected works. I. Anderson, Charles S., comp. II. Luther, Martin, 1483-1546. III. Title.

LUTHER, Martin, 1483-1546. 230.4'1
Readings in Luther for laymen. With introductions and notes by Charles S. Anderson. Minneapolis, Augsburg Pub. House [1967] ix, 304 p. 22 cm. Bibliographical footnotes. [BR331.E5A6] 67-25367
1. Lutheran Church—Collected works. 2. Theology—Collected works—16th century. I. Anderson, Charles S., comp. II. Title.

LUTHER, Martin, 1483-1546. 230.41
What Luther says, an anthology; compiled by Ewald M. Plass. Saint Louis, Concordia Pub. House [c1959] 3 v. (xxvi, 1667p.) 25cm. Selections from Luther's works translated into English and arranged alphabetically by subject. 'Luther editions and the reformer's principal writings': v. 3. p. 1588-1624. 'A selected bibliography': v. 3, p. 1628-1638. [BR324.P6] 57-8854
1. Luther, Martin— Dictionaries, indexes, etc. I. Plass, Ewald Martin, 1898- II. Title.

LUTHER, Martin, 1483-1546. 230'.4'1
The wisdom of Martin Luther. [Compiled by N. Alfred Balmer] St. Louis [Published by Pyramid Publications for] Concordia Pub. House [1973] 62 p. 18 cm. [BR331.E5B34 1973] 73-78850 ISBN 0-570-03166-4 0.75 (pbk.)
I. Title.

MELANCHTHON, Philipp, 1497-1560. 230.41
Selected writings. Translated by Charles Leander Hill. Edited by Elmer Ellsworth Flack and Lowell J. Satre. Minneapolis, Augsburg Pub. House [1962] 190p. 22cm. Bibliography: p. 189-190. [BR336.A33 1962] 62-9092
1. Theology— Collected works—16th cent. 2. Lutheran Church—Collected works. I. Hill, Charles Leander, tr. II. Flack, Elmer Ellsworth, 1894- ed. III. Satre, Lowell J., ed. IV. Title.

MILLER, Samuel Martin, 1890- 230.41
The Word of Truth; the gospel of your salvation. Rock Island, Ill., Augustana Book Concern [1952] 158 p. 20 cm. [BT77.M57] 52-7237
1. Theology, Doctrinal — Popular works. 2. Lutheran Church — Doctrinal and controversial works. I. Title.

MONTGOMERY, John Warwick. 230'.4'1
Crisis in Lutheran theology; the validity and relevance of historic Lutheranism vs. its contemporary rivals. With a pref. by J. A. O. Preus. Grand Rapids, Baker Book House [1967] 2 v. 22 cm. Bibliography: v. 2, p. 166-168. Bibliographical footnotes. [BX8065.2.M6] 67-6517
1. Theology. Lutheran. 2. Theology. Doctrinal—Hist.—20th cent. I. Title.

MONTGOMERY, John Warwick. 230'.4'1
Crisis in Lutheran theology; the validity and relevance of historic Lutheranism vs. its contemporary rivals. With a pref. by J. A. O. Preus. Grand Rapids, Baker Book House [1967] 2 v. 22 cm. Bibliography: v. 2, p. 166-168. Bibliographical footnotes. [BX8065.2.M6] 67-6517
1. Theology, Lutheran. 2. Theology, Doctrinal—History—20th century. I. Title.

MONTGOMERY, John Warwick. 230'.4'1
Crisis in Lutheran theology; the validity and relevance of historic Lutheranism vs. its contemporary rivals. With a pref. by J. A. O. Preus. [2d ed., rev., with additional material] Minneapolis, Bethany Fellowship [1973] 2 v. 22 cm. Contents.Contents.—v. 1. Essays.—v. 2. An anthology. Bibliography: v. 2, p. 166-168. [BX8065.2.M6 1973] 73-161393 ISBN 0-87123-073-9 1.95 (v.1), (pbk); 2.95 (v.2) (pbk)
1. Theology, Lutheran. 2. Theology, Doctrinal—History—20th century. I. Title.

MONTGOMERY, John Warwick. 230.4'1
History & Christianity. Downers Grove, Ill., InterVarsity Press [1971] 110 p. 18 cm. Contains 4 articles published Dec. 1964 to Mar. 1965 in His magazine. Includes bibliographical references. [BR85.M615 1971] 78-160367 ISBN 0-87784-437-2
1. Theology—Addresses, essays, lectures. I. Title.

PAUCK, Wilhelm, 1901- comp. 230'.4'1
Melanchthon and Bucer. Philadelphia, Westminster Press [1969] xx, 406 p. 24 cm. (The Library of Christian classics, v. 19) Contents.Contents.—Loci communes theologici, by P. Melanchthon.—De regno Christi, by M. Bucer.—Selected bibliography (p. 395-399) [BR336.L62 1969] 69-12309 ISBN 6-642-20193- 7.50
1. Theology—16th century. I. Melanchthon, Philipp, 1497-1560. Loci communes theologici. II. Butzer, Martin, 1491-1551. De regno Christi. III. Title. IV. Series.

PELIKAN, Jaroslav, 1923- 230.41
From Luther to Kierkegaard; a study in the history of theology. Saint Louis, Concordia Pub. House [1950] vii, 171 p. 21 cm. Bibliographical references included in "Notes" (p. 121-166) [BT27.P4] 50-58133
1. Theology, Doctrinal — Hist. 2. Philosophy, Modern. 3. Lutheran Church — Hist. I. Title.

PELIKAN, Jaroslav, 1923- 230.41
From Luther to Kierkegaard; a study in the history of theology. [2d. ed.] St. Louis, Concordia [1963, c.1950] xiii, 171p. 21cm. Bibl. 63-15352 1.75 pap.,
1. Theology, Doctrinal—Hist. 2. Philosophy, Modern—Hist. 3. Lutheran Church—Hist. I. Title.

PELIKAN, Jaroslav Jan, 1923- 230.41
From Luther to Kierkegaard; a study in the history of theology. Saint Louis, Concordia Pub. House [1950] vii. 71 p. 21 cm. Bibliographical references included in "Notes" (p. 121-166) [BT27.P4] 50-58133
1. Theology, Doctrinal—Hist. 2. Philosophy, Modern—Hist. 3. Lutheran Church—Hist. I. Title.

PELIKAN, Jaroslav Jan, 1923- 230.41
From Luther to Kierkegaard; a study in the history of theology, [2d ed.] Saint Louis, Concordia Pub. House [1963, c1950] xiii, 171 p. 21 cm. Bibliographical references included in "Notes" (p.121-166) [BT27.P4] 63-15352
1. Theology, Doctrinal—Hist. 2. Philosophy, Modern—Hist. 3. Lutheran Church—Hist. I. Title.

PINOMAA, Lennart. 230.41
Faith victorious; an introduction to Luther's theology. Translated by Walter J. Kukkonen. Philadelphia, Fortress Press [1963] 216 p. 21 cm. Includes bibliography. [BR333.P4993] 63-7904
1. Luther, Martin—Theology. I. Title.

PINOMAA, Lennart 230.41
Faith victorious; an introduction to Luther's theology. Tr. [from Finnish] by Walter J. Kukkonen. Philadelphia, Fortress [c.1963] 216p. 21cm. Bibl. 63-7904 4.75
1. Luther, Martin—Theology. I. Title.

PREUS, Herman Amberg, 1896- 230'.4'1
A theology to live by : the practical Luther for the practicing Christian / Herman A. Preus. St. Louis : Concordia Pub. House, c1977. 198 p. ; 23 cm. Includes bibliographical references. [BR333.2.P73] 76-42203 ISBN 0-570-03739-5 pbk. : 6.95
1. Luther, Martin, 1483-1546—Theology. I. Title.

PREUS, Robert D., 1924- 230'.4'1
The theology of post-Reformation Lutheranism [by] Robert D. Preus. Saint Louis, Concordia Pub. House [1970-72] 2 v. 24 cm. Contents.Contents.—[1] A study of theological prolegomena.—v. 2. God and His creation. Bibliography: v. 1, p. 421-435; v. 2, p. [259]-264. [BX8065.2.P7 1970] 70-121877 ISBN 0-570-03226-1 (v. 2)
1. Theology, Lutheran—History. I. Title.

REIMANN, Henry William, 1926-1963. 230.41
Let's study theology; [an invitation to the excitement of Christian thought in the 20th century] Saint Louis, Concordia Pub. House [1964] 102 p. 21 cm. Bibliography of Reimann's works: p. 8-9. [BX8065.2.R4] 64-19894
1. Lutheran Church — Catechisms and creeds. 2. Theology, Doctrinal — Popular works. I. Title.

REIMANN, Henry William, 1926-1963 230.41
Let's study theology [an invitation to the excitement of Christian thought in the 20th century] St. Louis, Concordia [c.1964] 102p. 21cm. Bibl 64-19894 1.50 pap.,
1. Lutheran Church—Catechisms and creeds. 2. Theology, Doctrinal—Popular works. I. Title.

RUDNICK, Milton L 230.41
Christianity is for you; a manual of instruction in Christian teaching and worship for those who are considering membership in the Lutheran Church. Saint Louis, Concordia Pub. House [1961] 110p. illus. 22cm. [BX8065.2.R8] 61-2741
1. Lutheran Church—Membership— Study and teaching. 2. Lutheran Church—Doctrinal and controversial works. I. Title.

SAUER, Chuck. 230.41
Heading for the center of the universe. St. Louis, Concordia Pub. House [1965] 95 p. illus. 21 cm. (Perspectives of life for Christian youth, 1) Bibliography: p. 95. [BV4501.2.S27] 65-22697
1. Christian life. I. Title.

SAUER, Chuck 230.41
Heading for the center of the universe. St. Louis, Concordia [c.1965] 95p. illus. 21cm. (Perspectives of life for Christian youth, 1) [BV4501.2.S27] 65-22697 1.00 pap.,
1. Christian life. I. Title.

SCHARLEMANN, Martin Henry 230.41
Toward tomorrow. Saint Louis, Mo., Concordia Pub. House [c.]1960. 160p. 21cm. (bibl.) 60-4034 1.95 pap.,
1. Theology—Addresses, essays, lectures. 2. Lutheran Church—Doctrinal and controversial works. I. Title.

SCHARLEMANN, Martin Henry, 1910- 230.41
Toward tomorrow. Saint Louis, Mo., Concordia Pub. House, 1960. 160p. 21cm. [BX8065.2.S35] 60-4034
1. Theology—Addresses, essays, lectures. 2. Lutheran Church—Doctrinal and controversial works. I. Title.

SCHMID, Heinrich Friedrich Ferdinand, 1811-1885. 230.41
The doctrinal theology of the Evangelical Lutheran Church. 3d ed. rev., tr. from German and Latin by Charles A. Hay, Henry E. Jacobs. Minneapolis, Augsburg Pub. House [1961, c.1875-1889] 692p. 61-4256 4.75
1. Lutheran Church—Doctrinal and controversial works. 2. Theology, Doctrinal. I. Title.

SCOTT, Nathan A. 230.41
Reinhold Niebuhr. Minneapolis, University of Minnesota Press; [distributed to high schools in the U.S. by McGraw-Hill, New York, 1963] 48 p. 21 cm. (University of Minnesota pamphlets of American writers, no. 31) Bibliography: p. 46-48. [BX4827.N5S3] 63-64003
1. Niebuhr, Reinhold, 1892-1971. I. Series: Minnesota. University. Pamphlets on American writers, no. 31

SOHN, Otto E 230.41
What's the answer? Saint Louis, Concordia Pub. House [1960] 210 p. 20 cm. Selections from the author's column with the same title, which has appeared regularly in the Lutheran witness since Jan. 1954. [BR96.S6] 60-44457
1. Questions and answers — Theology. 2. Lutheran Church — Doctrinal and controversial works. I. Title.

SOLOMONSON, Gordon O. 230.41
The faith we teach: parish leader's manual. (with 2 charts in separate envelope) Minneapolis, Augsburg, c.[1962] 63p. 21cm. 1.50 pap.,
I. Title.

TANNER, Jacob, 1865- 230.41
Exploring God's word; a study guide to Bible teachings. Minneapolis, Augsburg Pub. House [1950] viii, 168 p. 22 cm. [B[cpp.T325] 50-10774
1. Theology, Doctrinal — Popular works. 2. Lutheran Church — Doctrinal and controversial works. I. Title.

VAJTA, Vilmos, ed. 230.41
The church and the confessions; the role of the confessions in the life and doctrine of the Lutheran churches, edited by Vilmos Vajta and Hans Weissgerber. Philadelphia, Fortress Press [1963] vi, 218 p. 24 cm. Bibliographical references includes in "Notes" (p. 189-216) [BX8068.A1V3] 63-17267
1. Lutheran Church — Catechisms and creeds. I. Weissgerber, Hans, joint ed. II. Title.

VAJTA, Vilmos, ed. 230.41
The church and the confessions; the role of the confessions in the life and doctrine of the Lutheran churches, edited by Vilmos Vajta, Hans Weissgerber. Philadelphia, Fortress [c.1963] vi, 218p. 24cm. Bibl. 63-17267 5.00
1. Lutheran Church—Catechisms and creeds. I. Weissgerber, Hans, joint ed. II. Title.

WALTHER, Carl Ferdinand Wilhelm, 1811-1887. 230'.4'1
God's no and God's yes; the proper distinction between law and gospel [by] C. F. W. Walther. Condensed by Walter C. Pieper. St. Louis, Concordia Pub. House [1973] 118 p. 22 cm. Condensation of the English translation of Die rechte Unterscheidung von Gesetz und Evangelism. [BT79.W3413 1973] 72-94585 ISBN 0-570-03515-5 1.95 (pbk.)
1. Law and gospel. I. Pieper, Walter C. II. Title.

WALTHER, Carl Ferdinand Wilhelm, 1811-1887. 230.41
The true visible church; an essay for the convention of the general Evangelical Lutheran Synod of Missouri, Ohio, and Other States, for its sessions at St. Louis, Mo., October 31, 1866. Translated by John Theodore Mueller. St. Louis, Concordia Pub. House [1961] 137 p. 24 cm. Translation of Die Evangelisch-Lutherische Kirche, die wahre sichtbare Kirche Gottes auf Erden. [BX8065.W3353] 61-18822
1. Lutheran Church — Doctrinal and controversial works. I. Lutheran Church — Missouri Synod. II. Title.

WARFIELD, Benjamin 230.41
Breckinridge, 1851-1921.
Calvin and Augustine. Edited by Samuel G. Craig; with a foreword by J. Marcellus Kik. Philadelphia, Presbyterian and Reformed Pub. Co., 1956. 507p. 24cm. [BX9418.W32] 56-7349
1. Calvin, Jean, 1509-1564—Theology. 2. Augustinus, Aurelius, Saint, Bp. of Hippo—Theology. I. Title.

WARFIELD, Benjamin 230.41
Breckinridge, 1851-1921.
Calvin and Augustine. Edited by Samuel G. Craig; with a foreword by J. Marcellus Kik. Philadelphia, Presbyterian and Reformed Pub. Co., 1956. 507 p. 24 cm. [BX9418.W32] 56-7349
1. Calvin, Jean, 1509-1564 — Theology. 2. Augustinus, Aurelius. Saint, Bp. of Hippo — Theology. I. Title.

WESSLING, Edward W. 230.41
What's the good word! Explaining and applying basic words used in worship and Christian life. Saint Louis, Concordia Pub. House [1961] 95 p. illus. 19 cm. [BX8065.2.W45] 61-11240
1. Lutheran Church — Doctrinal and controversial works. 2. Theology, Doctrinal — Popular works. I. Title.

WESSLING, Edward W. 230.41
What's the good word? Explaining and applying basic words used in worship and Christian life. Saint Louis, Concordia [c.1961] 95p. illus. 61-11240 1.00 pap.,
1. Lutheran Church—Doctrinal and controversial works. 2. Theology, Doctrinal—Popular works. I. Title.

WINGREN, Gustaf, 1910- 230.41
Gospel and church. Tr. [from Swedish] by Ross Mackenzie. Philadelphia, Fortress [1965, c.1964] viii, 271p. 22cm. Bibl. [BT75.2.W5613] 64-18152 6.25
1. Theology, Doctrinal. 2. Law and gospel. I. Title.

WINGREN, Gustaf, 1910- 230.41
The living word; a theological study of preaching and the church. [Tr. from Swedish by Victor C. Pogue] Philadelphia, Fortress [1965, c.1960] 223p. 18cm. (Preacher's paperback lib., 5) [BV4216.W513] 65-21821 3.00 pap.,
1. Preaching. 2. Lutheran Church—Doctrinal and controversial works. I. Title.

WINGREN, Gustaf, 1910- 230.41
Luther on vocation. Translated by Carl C. Rasmussen. Philadelphia, Muhlenberg Press [1957] 256p. 22cm. [BR333.W512] 57-57561
1. Luther, Martin—Theology. 2. Vocation. I. Title.

WINGREN, Gustaf, 1910- 230.41
Luther on vocation. Translated by Carl C. Rasmussen. Philadelphia, Muhlenberg Press [1957] 256 p. 22 cm. [BR333.W512] 57-5756
1. Luther, Martin — Theology. 2. Vocation. I. Title.

WINGREN, Gustaf [Fredrik] 230.41
1910-
The living word; a theological study of preaching and the church. [Translated by Victor C. Pogue from the Swedish] Philadelphia, Muhlenberg Press [1960] 223p. 23cm. Bibl. footnotes 60-51230 3.75 bds.,
1. Preaching. 2. Lutheran Church—Doctrinal and controversial works. I. Title.

PRENTER, Regin, 1907- 230.41082
The Word and the Spirit; essays on inspiration of the Scriptures. Translated by Harris E. Kaasa. Minneapolis, Augsburg Pub. House [1965] 163 p. 22 cm. [BR85.P653] 65-12135
1. Theology—Addresses, essays, lectures. I. Title.

PRENTER, Regin, 1907- 230.41082
The Word and the Spirit; essays on inspiration of the Scriptures. Tr. by Harris E. Kaasa. Minneapolis, Augsburg [c.1965] 163p. 22cm. [BR85.P653] 65-12135 4.00
1. Theology—Addresses, essays, lectures. I. Title.

JUNGKUNTZ, 230'.4'10922 B
Theodore R., 1932-
The formulators of the Formula of concord : four architects of Lutheran unity / Theodore R. Jungkuntz. St. Louis : Concordia Pub. House, c1977. p. cm. Bibliography: p. [BX8079.J86] 76-40948 ISBN 0-570-03740-9 pbk. : 5.95
1. Andreae, Jakob, 1528-1590. 2. Chemnitz, Martin, 1522-1586. 3. Selnecker, Nikolaus, 1530-1592. 4. Chytraeus, David, 1531-1600. 5. Lutheran Church—Biography. 6. Lutheran Church. Formula of concord. I. Title.

LILJE, Hanns, 1899- 230'.4'10922
The valley of the shadow, translated with an introd. by Olive Wyon. Philadelphia, Muhlenberg Press [1950] 128 p. 20 cm. [BX8080.L] A51
I. Title.

MEDLER, William H. 230'.4'10922
Pages written in a hospital; a personal testimony, [1st ed.] New York, American Press [1963] 145 p. 21 cm. [BX8080.M415A3] 63-13387
1. Tuberculosis — Personal narratives. I. Title.

ACCENTS in Luther's 230.4'1'0924
theology; essays in commemoration of the 450th anniversary of the Reformation. Heino O. Kadai, editor. St. Louis, Concordia Pub. House [1967] 272 p. 22 cm. Planned by the Lutheran Church—Missouri Synod. Contents.Contents.—The abiding validity of the Reformation, by J. H. Tietjen.—Luther and the Word of God, by H. Sasse.—Man: simul justus et peccator, by E. B. Koenker.—The theology of the means of grace, by J. Pelikan.—Christianhood, priesthood, and brotherhood, by G. W. Hoyer. —Luther on ethics: man free and slave, by M. E. Marty.—Luther's theology of the Cross, by H. O. Kadai. Includes bibliographical references. [BR333.2.A3] 67-30309
1. Luther, Martin, 1483-1546—Theology. I. Lutheran Church Missouri Synod. II. Kadai, Heino O., ed.

ASHCRAFT, Morris. 230'.4'10924 B
Rudolf Bultmann. Waco, Tex., Word Books [1972] 123 p. 23 cm. (Makers of the modern theological mind) Bibliography: p. 121-123. [BX4827.B78A83] 74-188059 3.95
1. Bultmann, Rudolf Karl, 1884-

DUMAS, Andre. 230.4'1'0924
Dietrich Bonhoeffer, theologian of reality. Translated by Robert McAfee Brown. New York, Macmillan [1971] xii, 306 p. 22 cm. Translation of Une theologie de la realite: Dietrich Bonhoeffer. Bibliography: p. [296]-301. [BX4827.B57D813] 75-155273
1. Bonhoeffer, Dietrich, 1906-1945. I. Title.

EBELING, Gerhard, 230.4'1'0924
1912-
Luther; an introduction to his thought. Translated by R. A. Wilson. Philadelphia, Fortress Press [1970] 287 p. 22 cm. Includes bibliographical references. [BR333.2.E313 1970] 77-99612 5.95
1. Luther, Martin, 1483-1546—Theology.

FORDE, Gerhard O. 230'.4'10924
Where God meets man; Luther's down-to-earth approach to the Gospel [by] Gerhard O. Forde. Minneapolis, Augsburg Pub. House [1972] 128 p. 20 cm. [BR333.2.F65] 72-78569 ISBN 0-8066-1235-5 2.95
1. Luther, Martin, 1483-1546—Theology. I. Title.

GRISAR, Hartmann, 230'.4'10924 B
1845-1932.
Martin Luther: his life and work. Adapted from the 2d German ed. by Frank J. Eble. New York, AMS Press [1971] x, 609 p. 23 cm. Reprint of the 1930 ed. Bibliography: p. 586-600. [BR325.G75 1971] 71-137235 ISBN 0-404-02935-3
1. Luther, Martin, 1483-1546. 2. Reformation—Germany.

GRUNDTVIG, Nicolai 230'.4'10924 B
Frederik Severin, 1783-1872.
Selected writings / N. F. S. Grundtvig ; edited and with an introd. by Johannes Knudsen ; translated by Johannes Knudsen, Enok Mortensen, Ernest D. Nielsen. Philadelphia : Fortress Press, c1976. vii, 184 p. ; 22 cm. Includes index. Bibliography: p. 182. [BX8011.G78213 1976] 76-7873 ISBN 0-8006-1238-8 : 5.95
1. Lutheran Church—Collected works. 2. Theology—Collected works—19th century.

HOFFMAN, Bengt Runo, 230'.4'10924
1913-
Luther and the mystics : a re-examination of Luther's spiritual experience and his relationship to the mystics / Bengt R. Hoffman. Minneapolis : Augsburg Pub. House, c1976. 285 p. ; 23 cm. Includes indexes. Bibliography: p. 273-278. [BR333.5.M9H63] 75-22724 ISBN 0-8066-1514-1 : 9.95
1. Luther, Martin, 1483-1546—Mysticism. 2. Luther, Martin, 1483-1546—Theology. I. Title.

HOLL, Karl, 1866- 230'.4'10924
1926.
What did Luther understand by religion? / Karl Holl ; edited by James Luther Adams and Walter F. Bense ; translated by Fred W. Meuser and Walter R. Wietzke. Philadelphia : Fortress Press, c1977. iv, 123 p. ; 22 cm. "Translation of the essay 'Was verstand Luther unter Religion?' found in ... Gesammelte Aufsatze zur Kirchengeschichte, volume 1, pp. 1-110." Includes bibliographical references and indexes. [BR333.2.H6413] 76-62611 ISBN 0-8006-1260-4 pbk. : 4.25
1. Luther, Martin, 1483-1546—Theology. 2. Luther, Martin, 1483-1546—Religion. I. Title.

HYMA, Albert, 1893- 230.4'1'0924
Luther's theological development from Erfurt to Augsburg. New York, AMS Press [1971] vi, 90 p. 19 cm. (Landmarks in history) Reprint of the 1928 ed. Bibliography: p. 7-9. [BR333.H93 1971] 76-137247 ISBN 0-404-03479-9
1. Luther, Martin, 1483-1546—Theology. I. Title.

INTERPRETERS of 230.4'1'0924
Luther; essays in honor of Wilhelm Pauck. Edited by Jaroslav Pelikan. Philadelphia, Fortress Press [1968] viii, 374 p. port. 23 cm. Contents.Contents.—Wilhelm Pauck: a tribute, by J. Pelikan.—Martin Luther on Luther, by K. Holl.—Robert Barnes on Luther, by C. S. Anderson.—John Calvin on Luther, by B. A. Gerrish.—The Elizabethans on Luther, by W. A. Clebsch.—Joseph Priestly on Luther, by G. H. Williams.—N. F. S. Grundtvig on Luther, by E. D. Nielsen.—Walther, Schaff, and Krauth on Luther, by E. T. Bachmann.—Soren Kierkegaard on Luther, by E. B. Koenker.—Adolf von Harnack on Luther, by J. Pelikan.—Ernst Troeltsch on Luther, by K. Penzel.—Paul Tillich on Luther, by J. L. Adams.—Wilhelm Pauck: a biographical essay, by M. H. Pauck.—Bibliography of the published writings of Wilhelm Pauck, by M. H. Pauck (p. 362-366) Includes bibliographical references. [BR333.2.I58] 68-23992 8.25
1. Luther, Martin, 1483-1546—Criticism and interpretation—History. 2. Pauck, Wilhelm, 1901- I. Pauck, Wilhelm, 1901- II. Pelikan, Jaroslav Jan, 1923- ed.

JENSEN, De Lamar, 230'.4'10924 B
1925-
Confrontation at Worms: Martin Luther and the Diet of Worms. With a complete English translation of the Edict of Worms. [Provo, Utah, Brigham Young University Press, 1973] 119 p. illus. 29 cm. The Edict is translated from the copy in the J. Reuben Clark, Jr., Library at Brigham Young University, "a French version published in Paris, apparently by the printer Pierre Gromors." Includes bibliographical references. [BR326.6.J45] 73-5906 ISBN 0-8425-1524-0 10.50
1. Luther, Martin, 1483-1546. 2. Worms, Diet of, 1521. I. Holy Roman Empire. Laws, statutes, etc., 1519-1556 (Charles V). Edict of Worms. English. 1973. II. Title.

KADAI, Heino O., ed. 230.4'1'0924
Accents in Luther's theology; essays in commemoration of the 450th anniversary of the Reformation. Heino O. Kadai, editor. St. Louis, Concordia Pub. House [1967] 272 p. 22 cm. Planned by the Lutheran Church--Missouri Synod. Includes bibliographical references. [BR333.2.A3] 67-30309
1. Luther, Martin, 1483-1546—Theology. I. Lutheran Church—Missouri Synod. II. Title. Contents omitted.

KOENIGSBERGER, 230'.4'10924 B
Helmut Georg, comp.
Luther; a profile. Edited by H. G. Koenigsberger. [1st ed.] New York, Hill and Wang [1973] xxi, 234 p. 21 cm. (World profiles) Contents.Contents.—Brief biography of Martin Luther.—Ranke, L. von. The beginning of the Reformation.—Febvre, L. The crisis of 1521-1525.—Ritter, G. The founder of the Evangelical churches.—Engels, F. The Marxist interpretation of Luther.—Erikson, E. H. The search for identity.—Rupp, G. Luther and government.—Hagglund, B. The doctrine of justification.—Ebeling, G. Luther's words.—Pinomaa, L. The doctrine of predestination.—Gerrish, B. A. Luther's belief in reason.—Bornkamm, H. Luther's translation of the New Testament. —Blume, F. Luther the musician.—Bibliography (p. 227-229) [BR326.K575 1973] 76-184946 ISBN 0-8090-6702-1 7.95
1. Luther, Martin, 1483-1546—Addresses, essays, lectures. I. Title.

KOLB, Robert, 230'.4'10924 B
1941-
Andreae and the Formula of concord : six sermons on the way to Lutheran unity / Robert Kolb. St. Louis, Mo. : Concordia Pub. House, c1977. 134 p. ; 23 cm. Confession and brief explanation of certain disputed articles, by J. Andreae: p. 58-60. Six Christian sermons, by J. Andreae: p. 61-66. Includes bibliographical references. [BX8080.A55K64] 76-28542 ISBN 0-570-03741-7 pbk. : 5.95
1. Andreae, Jakob, 1528-1590. 2. Lutheran Church. Formula of concord. 3. Lutheran Church—Clergy—Biography. 4. Clergy—Germany—Biography. I. Andreae, Jakob, 1528-1590. Bekenntnis und kurze Erklarung etlicher zwiespaltiger Artikel. English. 1977. II. Andreae, Jakob, 1528-1590. Sechs christlicher Predig. English. 1977. III. Title.

LOESCHEN, John R., 230'.4'10924
1940-
Wrestling with Luther : an introduction to the study of his thought / John R. Loeschen. St. Louis : Concordia Pub. House, c1976. p. cm. A revision of the author's thesis, Graduate Theological Union, 1968. Includes index. Bibliography: p. [BR33.2.L56 1976] 75-33815 ISBN 0-570-03256-3 : 9.50
1. Luther, Martin, 1483-1546—Theology. I. Title.

LOEWENICH, Walther 230'.4'10924
von, 1903-
Luther's theology of the cross / Walther von Loewenich ; translated by Herbert J. A. Bouman. Minneapolis : Augsburg Pub. House, c1976. 224 p. ; 23 cm. Translation of 5th ed. of Luthers theologia crucis. Bibliography: p. 209-215. [BR333.L6313] 75-2845 ISBN 0-8066-1490-0 : 8.95
1. Luther, Martin, 1483-1546—Theology. I. Title.

LUTHER, Martin., 1483- 23.0410924
1546
Selected writings of Martin Luther. Theodore G. Tappert, ed. Philadelphia, Fortress [1967] 4v. 18cm. Includes music. Contents.v. 1.] 1517-1520.--[v.2.] 1520-1523.--[v.3.] 1523-1526--[v.4.] 1529-1546 Bibl. [BR331.E5T32] 67-25835 2.95 pap., ea.,; 10.00 set, bxd.
1. Theology—Collected works—16th cent. 2. Lutheran Church—Collected works. I. Tappert, Theodore Gerhardt, 1904- ed. II. Title.

MARIUS, Richard. 230'.4'10924 B
Luther. [1st ed.] Philadelphia, Lippincott [1974] 269 p. 24 cm. Bibliography: p. 257-264. [BR325.M29] 74-12134 ISBN 0-397-01048-6 8.95
1. Luther, Martin, 1483-1546.

MARLE, Rene. 230.4'1'0924
Bonhoeffer; the man and his work. Translated by Rosemary Sheed. New York, Newman Press [1968] 141 p. 22 cm. Translation of Dietrich Bonhoeffer. Temoin de Jesus-Christ parmi ses freres. Bibliographical footnotes. [BX4827.B57M33] 68-8395 4.50
1. Bonhoeffer, Dietrich, 1906-1945.

MOISE, Anutza. 230'.4'10924 B
A ransom for Wurmbrand. Edited by Myrtle Powley. Grand Rapids, Mich., Zondervan Pub. House [1972] 126 p. 18 cm. (Zondervan books) [BR1725.W88M6] 72-83869 0.95
1. Wurmbrand, Richard. 2. Wurmbrand, Sabina. I. Title.

MOLTMANN, Jurgen. 230.4'1'0924
Two studies in the theology of Bonhoeffer, by Jurgen Moltman and Jurgen Weissbach. Introd. by Reginald H. Fuller. Translation by Reginald H. Fuller and Ilse Fuller. New York, Scribner [1967] 159 p. 22 cm. The lordship of Christ and human society, by J. Moltmann, is a translation of Herrschaft Christi und soziale Wirklichkeit nach Dietrich Bonhoeffer. Christology and ethics, by J. Weissbach, is a translation of Christologie und Ethik bei Dietrich Bonhoefferi. Bibliographical footnotes. [BX4827.B57M63] 67-24043
1. Bonhoeffer, Dietrich, 1906-1945. I. Moltmann, Jurgen. The lordship of Christ and human society. II. Weissbach, Jurgen. Christology and ethics. III. Title.

PERRIN, Norman. 230.4'1'0924
The promise of Bultmann. [1st ed.] Philadelphia, Lippincott [1969] 116 p. 21 cm. (The Promise of theology) Bibliography: p. 110-116. [BX4827.B78P4] 70-75174 1.75 (pbk)
1. Bultmann, Rudolf Karl, 1884- I. Title.

PHILLIPS, John A. 230'.4'10924
Christ for us in the theology of Dietrich Bonhoeffer [by] John A. Phillips. [1st American ed.] New York, Harper & Row [1967] 303 p. 22 cm. First published in London under title: The form of Christ in the world. Bibliographical references included in "Notes" (p. 257-297) [BX4827.B57P5] 67-14934
1. Bonhoeffer, Dietrich, 2. Jesus Christ—History of doctrines. I. Title.

PSYCHOHISTORY and 230'.4'10924
religion : the case of Young man Luther / edited by Roger A. Johnson ; with contributions by Roland H. Bainton ... [et al.]. Philadelphia : Fortress Press, c1977. vii, 198 p. ; 23 cm. Bibliography: p. 197-198. [BR325.E73P74] 76-7870 ISBN 0-8006-0459-8 : 10.95
1. Erikson, Erik Homburger, 1902- Young man Luther. 2. Luther, Martin, 1483-1546. I. Johnson, Roger A., 1930- II. Bainton, Roland Herbert, 1894-

RASMUSSEN, Larry L. 230.4'1'0924
Dietrich Bonhoeffer: reality and resistance [by] Larry L. Rasmussen. Nashville, Abingdon

Press [1972] 222 p. 23 cm. (Studies in Christian ethics) (An Original Abingdon paperback) Includes bibliographical references. [BX4827.B57R37] 70-173948 ISBN 0-687-10765-2
1. Bonhoeffer, Dietrich, 1906-1945.

REIST, Benjamin A. 230.4'1'0924
The promise of Bonhoeffer, by Benjamin A. Reist. [1st ed.] Philadelphia, Lippincott [1969] 128 p. 21 cm. (The Promise of theology) Bibliographical references included in "Notes" (p. 122-126) Bibliography: p. 127-128. [BX4827.B57R4] 75-86077 3.50
1. Bonhoeffer, Dietrich, 1906-1945. I. Title.

ROARK, Dallas M., 1931- 230'.4'10924 B
Dietrich Bonhoeffer, by Dallas M. Roark. Waco, Tex., Word Books [1972] 141 p. 23 cm. (Makers of the modern theological mind) Bibliography: p. 140-141. [BX4827.B57R6] 72-76439 3.95
1. Bonhoeffer, Dietrich, 1906-1945.

ROBERTSON, Edwin Hanton. 230.410924
Dietrich Bonhoeffer, by E. H. Robertson. Richmond, John Knox Press [1966] ix, 54 p. 19 cm. (Makers of contemporary theology) [BX8080.B645R6 1966a] 66-15514
1. Bonhoeffer, Dietrich, 1906-1945.

SMITH, Ronald Gregor, comp. 230'.4'10924
World come of age. Philadelphia, Fortress Press [1967] 288 p. illus. 22 cm. Contents.Contents.—Introduction, by R. G. Smith.—The challenge of Dietrich Bonhoeffer's life and theology. The first period: foundation; The second period: concentration; The third period: liberation, by E. Bethge.—From a letter to Superintendent Herrenbruck, by K. Barth.—Dietrich Bonhoeffer and Karl Barth's positivism of revelation, by R. Prenter.—'The letters are a particular thorn,' by W. Hamilton.—Bonhoeffer and the young Luther, by R. Prenter.—The problem of the reception and interpretation of Dietrich Bonhoeffer, by H. Muller.—The cross of reality? by H. Schmidt.—The idea of God and modern man, by R. Bultmann. Bibliographical footnotes. [BX4827.B57S6] 67-10438
1. Bonhoeffer, Dietrich, 1906-1945. I. Title.

THIELICKE, Helmut, 1908- 230.4'1'0924
How modern should theology be? Translated by H. George Anderson. Philadelphia, Fortress Press [1969] v, 90 p. 20 cm. Translation of Wie modern darf die Theologie sein? [BX8066.T46W513] 69-14620 2.50
1. Lutheran Church—Sermons. 2. Sermons, German—Translations into English. 3. Sermons, English—Translations from German. I. Title.

TUPPER, Elgin Frank, 1941- 230'.4'10924
The theology of Wolfhart Pannenberg, by E. Frank Tupper. Postscript by Wolfhart Pannenberg. Philadelphia, Westminster Press [1973] 322 p. 25 cm. Based on the author's thesis, Southern Baptist Theological Seminary, 1971. Bibliography: p. 307-316. [BX4827.P3T86] 73-6662 ISBN 0-664-20973-4 10.95
1. Pannenberg, Wolfhart, 1928- I. Title.

WICKS, Jared, 1929- 230.4'1'0924
Man yearning for grace; Luther's early spiritual teaching. Foreword by George A. Lindbeck. Washington, Corpus Books [1968] xvi, 410 p. 21 cm. Bibliography: p. 399-405. [BR333.2.W5] 68-25762 12.50
1. Luther, Martin, 1483-1546—Theology. I. Title.

WINGREN, Gustaf, 1910- 230.4'1'0924
An exodus theology; Einar Billing and the development of modern Swedish theology. Translated by Eric Wahlstrom. Philadelphia, Fortress Press [1969] viii, 181 p. port. 22 cm. Translation of Einar Billing. En studie i svensk teologi fore 1920. Bibliography: p. 173-174. [BX8080.B47W513] 69-14616 4.75
1. Billing, Einar, Bp., 1871-1939. 2. Theology, Doctrinal—History—Sweden. I. Title.

WOELFEL, James W. 230.410924
Bonhoeffer's theology; classical and revolutionary [by] James W. Woelfel. Nashville [Tenn.] Abingdon Press [1970] 350 p. 25 cm. Includes bibliographical references. [BX4827.B57W6 1970] 77-97571 6.95
1. Bonhoeffer, Dietrich, 1906-1945. I. Title.

WOOD, Arthur Skevington. 230.4'1'0924
Captive to the Word; Martin Luther, Doctor of Sacred Scripture, by A. Skevington Wood. Grand Rapids, W. B. Eerdmans Pub. Co. [1969] 192 p. 23 cm. Bibliography: p. 181-186. [BR333.5.B5W6 1969] 75-5704 4.50
1. Luther, Martin, 1483-1546—Theology. 2. Bible—Criticism, interpretation, etc.—History—16th century. I. Title.

YOUNG, Norman James. 230.4'1'0924
History and existential theology; the role of history in the thought of Rudolf Bultmann, by Norman J. Young. Philadelphia, WestminsterPress [1969] 174 p. 21 cm. Bibliographical references included in "Notes" (p. 157-170) [BX4827.B78Y63] 69-16303 5.95
1. Bultmann, Rudolf Karl, 1884- 2. History—Philosophy. I. Title.

WALTHER, Carl Ferdinand Wilhelm, 1811-1887. 230'.4'1322
Walther speaks to the church; selected letters. Edited by Carl S. Meyer. St. Louis, Concordia Pub. House [1973] 104 p. illus. 22 cm. Includes bibliographical references. [BX8080.W3A4 1973] 72-94583 ISBN 0-570-03514-7 1.95 (pbk.)
1. Walther, Carl Ferdinand Wilhelm, 1811-1887. 2. Lutheran Church—Doctrinal and controversial works. I. Title.

TAPPERT, Theodore Gerhardt, 1904- comp. 230'.4'173
Lutheran confessional theology in America, 1840-1880. Edited by Theodore G. Tappert. New York, Oxford University Press, 1972. viii, 364 p. 24 cm. (A Library of Protestant thought) Contents.Contents.—Krauth, C. P. The conservative Reformation and its confessions.—Walther, C. F. W. The kind of confessional subscription required.—Fritschel, S. The doctrinal agreement essential to church unity.—Krauth, C. P. The right relation to denominations in America.—Fritschel, G. Concerning objective and subjective justification.—Walther, C. F. W. God's grace alone the cause of man's election. Election is not in conflict with justification.—Loy, M. Is God's election arbitrary or in view of faith?—Krauth, C. P. Issues in the controversy over predestination.—Walther, C. F. W. Theses on the church and ministry. The proper form of a local congregation.—Krauth, C. P. Fundamental principles of faith and church polity.—Loy, M. The significance of ordination to the ministry.—Walther, C. F. W. The laity in the government of the congregation.—Loy, M. Restoration of the cultus in the Lutheran Church.—Fritschel, S. A proper understanding of freedom in worship.—An order of service for Sundays and festivals.—Selected bibliography (p. 353-358) [BX8065.T33] 72-81463 10.75
1. Theology, Lutheran—United States—Collections. 2. Theology—19th century—Collections. I. Title. II. Series.

BAVINCK, Herman, 1854-1921. 230.42
Our reasonable faith. [Translated from the Dutch ed., Magnalia Dei, by Henry Zylstra] Grand Rapids, Mich., W. B. Eerdmans Pub. Co., 1956. 568p. 23cm. A digest of the author's Gereformeerde dogmatiek. [BX9474.B33] 56-11128
1. Gereformeerde Kerken in Nederland—Doctrinal and controversial works. 2. Theology, Doctrinal. I. Title.

BERKOUWER, Gerrit Cornelis, 1903- 230.42
Modern uncertainty and Christian faith. Grand Rapids, W. B. Eerdmans Pub. Co., 1953. 86p. 23cm. (The Calvin Foundation lectures, 1952) [BX9422.B4] 53-13122
1. Reformed Church—Doctrinal and controversial works. 2. Apologetics—20th cet. I. Title. II. Series.

CALVIN, Jean, 1509-1564. 230.42
By John Calvin, a reflection book introduction to the writings of John Calvin. Selected and edited by Hugh T. Kerr. New York, Association Press [c.1960] 124p. (An Association Press reflection book) Bibl.: p. [123]-124. 16p. 60-12725 .50 pap.,
1. Reformed Church—Collected works. 2. Theology—Collected works—16th cent. I. Title.

CALVIN, Jean, 1509-1564. 230.42
By John Calvin, a reflection book introduction to the writings of John Calvin. Selected and edited by Hugh T. Kerr. New York, Association Press [1960] 124p. 16cm. (An Association Press reflection book) Bibliography: p. [123]-124 [BX9420.A32K4] 60-12725
1. Reformed Church—Colleced works. 2. Theology—Collected works—16th cent. I. Title.

CALVIN, Jean, 1509-1564. 230.42
A Calvin treasury; selections from Industries of the Christian religion. Ed. by William F. Keesecker. New York, Harper [c.1961] v. 152p. 62-7292 3.50
1. Calvin, Jean, 1509-1564. Institutio christianae religionis—Indexes I. Keesecker, William F., ed. II. Title.

CALVIN, Jean, 1509-1564. 230.42
A compend of the Institutes of the Christian religion. Edited by Hugh T. Kerr. Philadelphia, Westminister Press [1964] viii, 228 p. 23 cm. [BX9420.I652] 65-3389
1. Reformed Church—Doctrinal and controversial works. 2. Theology, Doctrinal. I. Kerr, Hugh Thomson, 1900- ed. II. Title.

CALVIN, Jean, 1509-1564. 230.42
Institutes of the Christian religion. A new translation by Henry Beveridge. Grand Rapids, Eerdmans, 1953. 2v. 23cm. [BX9420] 54-3576
1. Reformed Church—Doctrinal and controversial works. 2. Theology, Doctrinal. I. Title.

CALVIN, Jean, 1509-1564. 230.42
Institutes of the Christian religion. Translated by Haenry Beveridge. Grand Rapids, Eerdmans, 1957. 2v. 22cm. [BX9420.I 65 1957] 59-2119
1. Reformed Church— Doctrinal and controversial works. 2. Theology, Doctrinal. I. Title.

CALVIN, Jean, 1509-1564 230.42
Institutes of the Christian religion. Ed. by John T. McNeill. Tr. by Ford Lewis Battles, in collaboration with the ed. and a committee of advisers. Philadelphia, Westminster Press [c.1960] 2 v. (lxxi, 1734 p.) (Library of Christian classics, v.20-21) bibl. 60-5379 12.50, set.
1. Reformed Church—Doctrinal and controversial works. 2. Theology, Doctrinal. I. Title. II. Series.

CALVIN, Jean, 1509-1564. 230'.4'2
Institution of the Christian religion : embracing almost the whole sum of piety & whatever is necessary to know the doctrine of salvation : a work most worthy to be read by all persons zealous for piety, and recently published ; Preface to the most Christian King of France, wherein this book is offered to him as a confession of faith / John Calvin of Noyon, author ; translated and annotated by Ford Lewis Battles. Atlanta : John Knox Press, 1975. p. cm. Translation of Christianae religionis institutio ... published in 1536. Includes indexes. [BX9420.I65 1975] 74-3718 ISBN 0-8042-0489-6 : 9.95
1. Reformed Church—Doctrinal and controversial works. 2. Theology, Doctrinal. I. Battles, Ford Lewis. II. Title.

CALVIN, Jean, 1509-1564. 230.42
On the Christian faith; selections from the Institutes, Commentaries, and Tracts, edited with an introd. by John T. McNeil. New York, Liberal Arts Press [c1957] xxxiii, 219p. 21cm. (The Library of liberal arts, no. 93) Bibliography: p. xxxi-xxxiii. Bibliographical references included in 'Biographical index' (p. 213-219) [BX9420.A32M25] 58-7660
1. Christianity—16th cent. 2. Calvin, Jean, 1509-1564—Theology. I. Title.

FORSTMAN, H. Jackson. 230.42
Word and spirit; Calvin's doctrine of Biblical authority. Stanford, Calif., Stanford University Press, 1962. 178 p. 23 cm. Includes bibliography. [BX9418.F6] 62-8665
1. Calvin, Jean, 1509-1564—Theology. 2. Bible—Evidences, authority, etc. I. Title.

KLOOSTER, Fred H 230.42
The significance of Barth's theology; an appraisal: with special reference to election and reconciliation. Grand Rapids, Baker Book House, 1961. 98p. 21cm. Includes bibliography. [BX4827.B3K5] 61-18636
1. Barth, Karl, I. Title.

MURRAY, John, 1898- 230.42
Calvin on Scripture and divine sovereignty. Grand Rapids, Baker Book House, 1960. 71p. 21cm. 'The three lectures, here reproduced in slightly revised form, were given under the auspices of the Reformed Fellowship, inc., in Grand Rapids, Michigan, on May 21, 22, 26, 1959.' [BX9418.M85] 60-2706
1. Calvin, Jean, 1509-1561—Theology. 2. Bible—Evidences, authority, etc. 3. Providence and government of God—History of doctrines. I. Title. II. Title: Scripture and divine sovereignty.

NIESEL, Wilhelm. 230.42
The theology of Calvin. Translated by Harold Knight. Philadelphia, Westminster Press [1956] 254p. 23cm. [BX9418.N53] 56-8047
1. Valvin, Jean, 1509-1564—Theology. I. Title.

NIXON, Leroy. 230.42
Complete indexes to the Institutes of the Christian religion by John Calvin. Grand Rapids, Eerdmans, 1950 (i.e. 1951) 50 p. 22 cm. Includes any of the 2-vol. American editions. [BX9420.I653] 51-23628
I. Calvin, Jean, 1509-1564. Institutes of the Christian religion. II. Title.

NIXON, Leroy. 230.42
John Calvin's teachings on human reason; a synthesis from Calvin's writings according to established categories, and a study of their implications for the theory of Reformed Protestant Christian education. Foreword by Lee A. Belford. [1st ed.] New York, Exposition Press [1963] xi, 276 p. 22 cm. (An Exposition-testament book) Revision of thesis -- New York University. Bibliography: p. [267] -276. [BX9418.N58] 63-11689
1. Calvinm Jean, 1509-1564. 2. Reason. 3. Religious education. I. Title.

NIXON, Leroy 230.42
John Calvin's teachings on human reason; a synthesis from Calvin's writings according to established categories, and a study of their implications for theory of Reformed Protestant Christian education. Foreword by Lee A. Belford. New York, Exposition [c1963] xi, 276p. 22cm. (Exposition-testament bks.) Bibl. 63-11689 6.00
1. Calvin, Jean, 1509-1564. 2. Reason. 3. Religious education. I. Title.

PALMER, Edwin H. 230'.4'2
The five points of Calvinism; a study manual, by Edwin H. Palmer. Grand Rapids, Baker Book House [1972] 109 p. 22 cm. Bibliography: p. 109. [BX9422.2.P34] 72-85671 ISBN 0-8010-6926-2 1.95
1. Calvinsim. I. Title.

SPIER, J M 1902- 230.42
What is Calvinistic philosophy? Translated from the Dutch by Fred H. Klooster. Grand Rapids, W. B. Erdmans Pub. Co., 1953. 86p. 23cm. [BX9422.S65] 53-8144
1. Calvinism. 2. Religion—Philosophy. 3. Philosophy and religion. I. Title.

STEELE, David N. 230.42
The five points of Calvinism; defined, defended, documented, by David N. Steele, Curtis C. Thomas. Pref. by Roger Nicole. Philadelphia, Presbyterian & Reformed, 1963. 95 p. 23 cm. (Intl. lib. of philosophy and theology: Biblical and theological studies) Bibl. 63-21695 price unreported
1. Calvinism. I. Thomas, Curtis C., joint author. II. Title. III. Series.

STEELE, David N 230.42
The five points of Calvinism; defined, defended, documented, by David N. Steele [and] Curtis C. Thomas. Pref. by Roger Nicole. Philadelphia, Presbyterian and Reformed Pub. Co., 1963. 95 p. 23 cm. (International library of philosphy and theology: Biblical and theological studies) Includes bibliographies. [BX9422.5.S8] 63-21695
1. Calvinism. I. Thomas, Curtis C., joint author. II. Title. III. Series.

VAN Til, Cornelius, 1895- 230.42
The case for Calvinism. Philadelphia, Presbyterian and Reformed Pub. Co. 1964. xviii, 153 p. 22 cm. (International library of philosophy and theology. Philosophical and historical studies series) Bibliographical footnotes. [BX9422.2.V3] 63-21698
1. Calvinism. I. Title.

WALLACE, Ronald S. 230.42
Calvin's doctrine of the Christian life. Grand Rapids, Mich., Eerdmans [1959] xvi, 349p. Includes bibliography 23cm. 59-65442 5.00
1. Christian life. 2. Calvin, Jean, 1509-1564—Theology. I. Title.

WALLACE, Ronald S 230.42
Calvin's doctrine of the Word and sacrament. Grand Rapids, W.B. Eerdmans Pub. Co., 1957. xii, 253p. 23cm. Bibliographical footnotes. [BX9418.W314 1957] 57-14162
1. Calvin, Jean, 1509-1564—Theology. 2. Revelation—History of doctrines. 3. Sacraments—History of doctrines. I. Title.

WALLACE, Ronald S 230.42
Calvin's doctrine of the Word and sacrament. Grand Rapids, W. B. Eerdmans Pub. Co., 1957. xii, 253 p. 23 cm. Bibliographical footnotes. [BX9418.W314] 57-14162
1. Calvin, Jean, 1509-1564 — Theology. 2. Revelation — History of doctrines. 3. Sacraments — History of doctrines. I. Title.

WHITNEY, Harold J 230.42
The teaching of Calvin for today; the substance of the Institutes of the Christian religion, in handy, understandable form. Including a profile of John Calvin. Grand Rapids, Zondervan Pub. House [1959] 205 p. ports. 21 cm. Australian ed. (Brisbane, W. R. Smith & Patterson) has title: Profile of John Calvin and the Institutes. Bibliography: p. 205. [BX9418.W5 1959] 60-4225
1. Calvin, Jean, 1500-1564. 2. Calvin, Jean,

1500-1564. Institute christianae religionis. I. Title.

BEARDSLEE, John W ed. and tr. 230.4208
Reformed dogmatics; J. Wollebius, G. Voetius [and] F. Turretin. Edited and translated by John W. Beardslee, III New York, Oxford University Press, 1965. xi. 471 p. 24 cm. (A Library of Protestan thought) [BX9409.B4] 65-28036
1. Theology — Collections — Reformed authors. 2. Reformed Church — Collections. I. Wolleb, Johannes, 1586-1629. Compendium thelogiae Christianae. II. Voet, Gijsbert, 1589-1676. Selectac Disputations theologicae. III. Turrettini, Francois, 1623-1687. Institutio theologiae elencticae. IV. Title. V. Series.
Contents omitted.

BEARDSLEE, John W. III, ed. and tr. 230.4208
Reformed dogmatics: J. Wollebius. G. Voetius, F. Turretin. New York, Oxford [c.]1965. xi,471p. 24cm. (Lib. of Protestant thought) Bibl. [BX9409.B4] 65-28036 2.50
1. Theology—Collections—Refrmed authors. 2. Reformed Church—Collections. I. Wolleb. Johannes, 1586-1629. Compendium theologiae Christianae. II. Voet, Giisbert, 1589-1676. Selectae disputationes theologicae. III. Turrettini, Francois. 1623-1687. Institutio theologiae elencticae. IV. Title. V. Series.
Contents omitted.

BARTH, Karl, 1886- 230.420924
How I changed my mind. Introd., epilogue by John D. Godsey. Richmond, Knox [1966] 96p. ports. 21cm. Three autobiographical articles which first appeared in issues of the Christian Century. Bibl. [BX4827.B3A3] 66-17277 3.00
I. Title.

DUFFIELD, Gervase E ed. 230.420924
John Calvin. G. E. Duffield, editor. Grand Rapids, Eerdmans [1966] xii, 228 p. facsim., col. port. 23 cm. (Courtenay studies in reformation theology, 1) Contents.Contents. -- The Calvin legend, by B. Hall. -- Calvin against Calvinists, by B. Hall -- The sources of Calvin's Seneca commentary, by F. L. Battles. -- Calvin the letter writer, by J. D. Benoit. -- The history and development of Instituto: how Calvin worked, by J. D. Benoit. -- Calvin and the union of the churches, by J. Cadier. -- The Lord's Supper in the theology and practice of Calvin, by G. S. M. Walker. -- Calvin the theologian, by J. I. Packer. -- Calvin the Biblical expositor, by T. H. L. Parker. -- Calvin and Louis Bude's translation of the Psalms, by R. Peter. -- Calvin's view of ecclesiastical discipline, by R. N. Caswell. Includes bibliographical references. [BX9418.D77] 66-5600
1. Calvin, Jean, 1500-1564 — Addresses, essays, lectures. I. Title. II. Series.

DUFFIELD, Gervase E., ed. 230.420924
John Calvin. Grand Rapids, Mich., Eerdmans [c.1966] xii, 228p. facsim., col. port. 23cm. (Courtenay studies in reformation theol., 1) Bibl. [BX9418.C77 1966a] 66-5600 5.95
1. Calvin, Jean, 1509-1564—Addresses, essays, lectures. I. Title.
Contents omitted.

EXPLORING the 230'.4'20924
heritage of John Calvin / David E. Holwerda, editor. Grand Rapids : Baker Book House, c1976. 317 p. ; 23 cm. "Published to honor John Bratt." "A bibliography of John Bratt [by] Peter De Klerk": p. 304-317. [BX9418.E86] 76-3919 ISBN 0-8010-4146-5 : 7.95
1. Calvin, Jean, 1509-1564—Theology—Addresses, essays, lectures. 2. Bratt, John H. 3. Bratt, John H.—Bibliography. I. Holwerda, David Earl. II. Bratt, John H.
Contents omitted

HALL, Charles A. M. 230.42'0924
With the spirit's sword; the drama of spiritual warfare in the theology of John Calvin, by Charles A. M. Hall. Richmond, Va., John Knox Press [1970, c1968] 227 p. 21 cm. (Basel studies of theology, no. 3) Bibliography: p. 221-227. [BX9418.H26] 68-13492 3.95
1. Calvin, Jean, 1509-1564—Theology. I. Title. II. Series.

PARKER, Thomas Henry Louis. 230'.4'20924 B
John Calvin : a biography / by T. H. L. Parker. Philadelphia : Westminster Press, c1975. xviii, 190 p., [5] leaves of plates : ill. ; 24 cm. Includes indexes. Bibliography: p. 175-180. [BX9418.P344] 75-33302 ISBN 0-664-20810-X : 10.95
1. Calvin, Jean, 1509-1564.

RICHARD, Lucien Joseph. 230'.4'20924
The spirituality of John Calvin / Lucien Joseph Richard. Atlanta : John Knox Press, [1974] 207 p.; 23 cm. Includes index. Bibliography: p. 195-203. [BV4490.R5] 73-16920 pbk. : 5.00 ISBN 0-8042-0711-9
1. Calvin, Jean, 1509-1564. 2. Spiritual life—History of doctrines. I. Title.

ROLSTON, Holmes, 1932- 230.4'2'0924
John Calvin versus the Westminster Confession. Richmond, John Knox Press [1972] 124 p. 21 cm. Includes bibliographical references. [BX9183.R63] 75-37422 ISBN 0-8042-0488-8 2.95
1. Westminster Assembly of Divines. The Confession of faith. 2. Calvin, Jean, 1509-1564—Theology. I. Title.

SNYDER, Dale Norman. 230'.4'20924
Karl Barth's struggle with anthropocentric theology. Gravenhage, Boekhandel Wattez. 1966. 224 p. 22 cm. unpriced (Ne66-40) Bibliography: p. [221]-[(223]) [BX4827.B3S6] 67-95170
1. Barth, Karl, 1886- 2. Proefschrift — Amsterdam. I. Title.

STAUFFER, Richard, 1921- 230'.4'20924 B
The humanness of John Calvin. Translated by George H. Shriver. Nashville, Abingdon Press [1971] 96 p. 20 cm. Translation of L'humanite de Calvin. Includes bibliographical references. [BX9418.S69713] 79-148070 ISBN 0-687-18033-3
1. Calvin, Jean, 1509-1564. I. Title.

WALKER, Williston, 1860-1922. 230'.4'20924 B
John Calvin, the organiser of reformed Protestantism, 1509-1564. New York, Schocken Books [1969] lxxvii, 456 p. 21 cm. Reprint of the 1906 ed., with a bibliographical essay by J. T. McNeill. Bibliographical footnotes. [BX9418.W3 1969] 69-20336
1. Calvin, Jean, 1509-1564.

WALKER, Williston, 1860-1922. 230'.4'20924 B
John Calvin, the organiser of reformed Protestantism, 1509-1564. New York, Putnam, 1906. [New York, AMS Press, 1972] xvi, 456 p. 19 cm. Original ed. issued in series: Heroes of the Reformation. Includes bibliographical references. [BX9418.W3 1972] 78-177878 ISBN 0-404-06807-3 8.50
1. Calvin, Jean, 1509-1564. I. Title.

WILLEMS, Boniface A 1926- 230.420924
Karl Barth; an ecumenical approach to his theology, by B. A. Willems. Translated by Matthew J. van Velzen. Glen Rock, N.J., Paulist Press [1965] 128 p. (p. 119-128 advertisements) 18 cm. (Deus books) [BX4827.B3W53] 65-24044
1. Barth, Karl, 1886- I. Title.

BROWN, Hubert L. 230'.4'3
Black and Mennonite : a search for identity / Hubert L. Brown ; introduction by Katie Funk Wiebe. Scottdale, Pa. : Herald Press, c1976. 124 p. ; 20 cm. (The John F. Funk lectures) Bibliography: p. [121]-124. [BX8143.B76A32] 76-44043 ISBN 0-8361-1801-4 : 3.95
1. Brown, Hubert L. 2. Black theology. 3. Anabaptists. 4. Race problems. I. Title. II. Series: John F. Funk lectures.

†DENCK, Johannes, 1495(ca.)-1527. 230'.4'3
Selected writings of Hans Denck / edited and translated from the text as established by Walter Fellman by Edward J. Furcha, with Ford Lewis Battles. Pittsburgh : Pickwick Press, 1975 [i.e. 1976] 153 p. ; 21 cm. (Pittsburgh original texts and translations series ; 1) Translation of Exegetische Schriften. Includes bibliographical references and index. [BX4929.D4613] 76-7057 ISBN 0-915138-15-8 : 3.75
1. Anabaptists—Collected works. 2. Theology—Collected works—16th century. I. Title.

FRIEDMANN, Robert, 1891-1970. 230'.4'3
The theology of Anabaptism; an interpretation. Scottdale, Pa., Herald Press, 1973. 183 p. 23 cm. (Studies in Anabaptist and Mennonite history, no. 15) Bibliography: p. [163]-174. [BX4931.2.F74] 73-7886 ISBN 0-8361-1194-X 7.95
1. Anabaptists. I. Title. II. Series.

FRIEDMANN, Robert, 1891-1970. 230'.4'3
The theology of Anabaptism; an interpretation. Scottdale, Pa., Herald Press, 1973. 183 p. 23 cm. (Studies in Anabaptist and Mennonite history, no. 15) Bibliography; p. [163]-174. [BX4931.2.F74] 73-7886 ISBN 0-8361-1194-X 7.95
1. Anabaptists. I. Title. II. Series.

KLASSEN, William. 230.4'3
Covenant and community; the life, writings, and hermeneutics of Pilgram Marpeck. Grand Rapids, Eerdmans [1968] 211p. 23cm. Bibl. p.187-202. [BX4946.M3K55] 66-27407 4.95
1. Marbeck, Pilgram, d. 1556. 2. Bible—Criticism, interpretation, etc.—Hist.—16th cent. 3. Anabaptists. I. Title.

PACKULL, Werner O., 1941- 230'.4'3
Mysticism and the early South German-Austrian Anabaptist movement, 1525-1531 / Werner O. Packull. Scottdale, Pa. : Herald Press, 1977. 252 p. ; 23 cm. (Studies in Anabaptist and Mennonite history ; no. 19) Includes index. Bibliography: p. [230]-246. [BX4931.2.P3] 76-46557 ISBN 0-8361-1130-3 : 12.95
1. Anabaptists—History. 2. Mysticism—1450-1800. I. Title. II. Series.

WENGER, John Christian, 1910- 230'.4'3
Our Christ-centered faith; a brief summary of New Testament teaching, by J. C. Wenger. Scottdale, Pa., Herald Press, 1973. 64 p. 18 cm. Bibliography: p. 14-15. [BX4931.2.W42] 72-5942 ISBN 0-8361-1703-4 1.50
1. Anabaptists. 2. Theology, Doctrinal—History—16th century. I. Title.

KUKKONEN, Walter J 230.4773
Faith of our fathers; a guide for the study of the Evangelical Lutheran faith. [1st ed.] New York, American Press [c1957] 203p. 21cm. [BX8065.K78] 57-14554
1. Lutheran Church—Doctrinal and controversial works. 2. Finnish Evangelical Lutheran Church of America—Doctrinal and controversial works. I. Title.

GOLDEN, Samuel A. 230'.4'9 B
Jean LeClerc, by Samuel A. Golden. New York, Twayne Publishers [1972] 183 p. 21 cm. (Twayne's world author series, TWAS 209. Netherlands) Bibliography: p. 169-176. [BX4827.L4G65] 71-169635
1. Le Clerc, Jean, 1657-1736.

GEAR, Felix B. 230.5
Basic beliefs of the reformed faith; a Biblical study of Presbyterian doctrine. Richmond, Va., John Knox Press [c.1960] 80p. (bibls.) 21cm. 60-9774 .60 pap.,
1. Presbyterian Church—Doctrinal and controversial works. I. Title.

OXTOBY, Gurdon C. 230.5
Biblical foundations for belief and action, by Gurdon C. Oxtoby. Philadelphia, Westminster Press [1968] 139 p. 17 cm. [BS543.O9] 68-17149 2.25
1. Bible—Theology. I. Title.

WARD, William B 230.5
Toward responsible discipleship. Richmond, John Knox Press [c1960] 86 p. 20 cm. [BX9175.2.W3] 61-7078
1. Presbyterian Church — Doctrinal and controversial works. I. Title.

DABNEY, Robert Lewis, 1820-1898. 230'.5'1
Lectures in systematic theology. Grand Rapids, Zondervan Pub. House [1972] 903 p. 25 cm. Reprint of the 1878 ed. published under title: Syllabus and notes of the course of systematic and polemic theology taught in Union Theological Seminary, Virginia. [BT75.D2 1972] 73-171200 12.95
1. Presbyterian Church—Doctrinal and controversial works. 2. Theology, Doctrinal. I. Title.

LEITCH, Addison H. 230.51
A layman's guide to Prebyterian beliefs. by Addison H. Leitch. Added feature: an analysis of the Confession of 1967. [1st ed.] Grand Rapids, Zondervan [1967] 158p. 21cm. [BX9175.2.L4] 66-11617 1.95 pap.,
1. Presbyterian Church —Doctrinal and controversial works. I. Title.

LEITCH, Addison H. 230.51
A layman's guide to Presbyterian beliefs, by Addison H. Leitch. Added feature: an analysis of the Confession of 1967. [1st ed.] Grand Rapids, Zondervan Pub. House [1967] 158 p. 21 cm. [BX9175.2.L4] 67-11617
1. Presbyterian Church—Doctrinal and controversial works. I. Title.

PRESBYTERIAN Church in the U. S. A. Board of Christian Education. 230.51
The pastor's guide for the training of church members. Philadelphia [c1957] 205p. illus. 27cm. Includes bibliography. [BX9177.A35] 57-5028
1. Presbyterian Church—Membership. 2. Presbyterian Church— Doctrinal and controversial works. 3. Church membership—Study and teaching. I. Title.

PRESBYTERIAN Church in the U. S. A. Board of Christian Education. 230.51
The way of discipleship; the meaning of membership in the Presbyterian Church. [Philadelphia, c1957] 91p. 19cm. [BX9177.A4] 57-5027
1. Presbyterian Church—Doctrinal and controversial works. I. Title.

SCHAEFFER, Francis August. 230.5'1
The church before the watching world; a practical ecclesiology [by] Francis A. Schaeffer. Downers Grove, Ill., Inter-Varsity Press [1971] 105 p. 18 cm. Includes bibliographical references. [BT1102.S275] 76-166121 ISBN 0-87784-542-5
1. Apologetics—20th century. 2. Liberalism (Religion) I. Title.

WARFIELD, Benjamin Breckinridge, 1851-1921. 230.51
Biblican and theological studies; edited by Samuel G. Craig. Philadelphia, Presbyterian and Reformed Pub. Co., 1952. 580 p. illus. 21 cm. [BT15.W34] 52-6506
1. Theology, Doctrinal — Addresses, essays, lectures. 2. Presbyterian Church — Doctrinal and controversial works. I. Title.

WARFIELD, Benjamin Breckinridge, 1851-1921. 230.5'1
Selected shorter writings of Benjamin B. Warfield, edited by John E. Meeter. Nutley, N.J., Presbyterian and Reformed Pub. Co., 1970-73. 2 v. 23 cm. Includes bibliographical references. [BX8915.W3] 76-110499 7.50 (v. 1) 8.95 (v. 2)
1. Presbyterian Church—Collected works. 2. Theology—Collected works—20th century.

COFFIN, William Sloane. 230'.5'10924 B
Once to every man : an autobiography / William Sloane Coffin. 1st ed. New York : Atheneum, 1977. p. cm. [BX9225.C6243A34 1977] 77-76547 ISBN 0-689-10811-7 : 10.95
1. Coffin, William Sloane. 2. Presbyterian Church—Clergy—Biography. 3. Clergy—United States—Biography. I. Title.

STUDIES in Richard 230'.5'2
Hooker; essays preliminary to an edition of his works. Edited by W. Speed Hill. Cleveland, Press of Case Western Reserve University, 1972. xiv, 363 p. 24 cm. Bibliography: p. 279-320. [BX5199.H813S85] 74-170151 ISBN 0-8295-0220-3 12.50
1. Hooker, Richard, 1553 or 4-1600. I. Hill, William Speed, 1935- ed.

WOTHERSPOON, Henry Johnstone 230.52
A manual of church doctrine according to the Church of Scotland [by] H. J. Wotherspoon and J. M. Kirkpatrick. 2d ed., rev. and enl. by T. F. Torrance and Ronald Selby Wright. New York, Oxford University Press, 1960[ ] viii, 132p. bibl. footnotes 23cm. 60-3016 2.40
1. Church of Scotland—Doctrinal and controversial works. I. Kirkpatrick, James Mackenzie, joint author II. Title.

DAVIES, Ebenezer Thomas. 230'.5'20924 B
The political ideas of Richard Hooker [by] E. T. Davies. With a pref. by R. H. Malden. New York, Octagon Books, 1972. xii, 98 p. 21 cm. Reprint of the 1946 ed. Includes bibliographical references. [JC137.H7D3 1972] 75-159177 ISBN 0-374-92073-7
1. Hooker, Richard, 1553 or 4-1600. I. Title.

BINKLEY, Luther John, 1925- 230.57
The Mercersburg theology; with an introd. by John B. Noss. [Lancaster? Pa., 1953] 156 p. 21 cm. (Franklin and Marshall College studies, no. 7) "A shortened version of [the author's] ... thesis ... Harvard University ... 1950." [BX9571.B55] 53-1551
1. Mercersburg theology. I. Title.

BLOESCH, Donald G., 1928- 230.5'7
The ground of certainty; toward an evangelical theology of revelation, by Donald G. Bloesch. Grand Rapids, Eerdmans [1971] 212 p. 21 cm. Includes bibliographical references. [BR100.B517] 76-142899 3.25
1. Philosophy and religion. I. Title.

EMPIE, Paul E., ed. 230.57
Marburg revisited; a reexamination of Lutheran and Reformed traditions, Editors: Paul C. Empie & James I. McCord. Minneapolis, Augsburg [1966] 193p. 22cm. Papers and summaries prepd. in connection with a ser. of annual meetings held from Feb. 1962 through Feb. 1966. sponsored by the North Amer. Area of the World Alliance of Reformed Churches Holding the Presbvterian Order and the U.S.A. Natl. Comm. of the Lutheran World Fed. Bibl. [BX9171.L8E4] 67-11715 1.75 pap.,
1. elations — Presbyterian Church. 2.

Presbyterian Church — Relations — Lutheran Church. I. McCord. James I., joint ed. II. Alliance of Reformed Churches throughout the World Holding the Presbyterian System. North American Area. III. National Lutheran Council. IV. Title.

LEITH, John H. 230'.5'7
An introduction to the reformed tradition : a way of being the Christian community / John H. Leith. Atlanta : John Knox Press, c1977. 253 p., [8] leaves of plates : ill. ; 22 cm. Includes bibliographical references and indexes. [BX9422.2.L45] 76-12392 ISBN 0-8042-0471-3 : 12.95
1. Theology, Reformed Church. I. Title.

VAN TIL, Cornelius, 1895- 230.57
The defense of the faith. Philadelphia, Presbyterian andReformed Pub. Co., 1955. 436p. 23cm. [BT1101.V3] 55-7140
1. Apologetics. 2. Reformed Church—Doctrinal and controversial works. I. Title.

EDWARDS, Jonathan, 1703-1758. 230'.5'8
Images or shadows of divine things / by Jonathan Edwards ; edited by Perry Miller. Westport, Conn. : Greenwood Press, 1977, c1948. viii, 151 p. ; 23 cm. Reprint of the ed. published by Yale University Press, New Haven. Includes bibliographical references. [BL210.E3 1977] 73-8157 ISBN 0-8371-6952-6 lib. bdg. : 11.75
1. Analogy (Religion) 2. Typology (Theology) I. Miller, Percy, 1905-1963. II. Title.

ELWOOD, Douglas J. 230.58
The philosophical theology of Jonathan Edwards. New York, Columbia University Press, 1960. xii, 220 p. port. 21 cm. "Bibliography of Jonathan Edwards": p. [199]-202. Bibliography: p. [203]-214. [BX7260.E3E5 1960] 60-12503
1. Edwards, Jonathan, 1703-1758. I. Title.

HOOKER, Thomas, 1586-1647. 230'.5'8
Thomas Hooker : writings in England and Holland, 1626-1633 / edited, with introductory essays, by George H. Williams ... [et al.]. Cambridge : Harvard University Press, 1975. viii, 435 p., [1] leaf of plates : ill. ; 24 cm. (Harvard theological studies ; 28) Includes indexes. "A bibliography of the published writings of Thomas Hooker": p. 390-425. [BX7117.H58 1975] 75-30570 ISBN 0-674-88520-1 : 10.00
1. Hooker, Thomas, 1586-1647. 2. Hooker, Thomas, 1586-1647—Bibliography. 3. Theology—Collected works—17th century. 4. Congregational churches—Collected works. I. Williams, George Huntston, 1914- II. Title. III. Series.
Contents omitted

BUSHNELL, Horace, 1802-1876. 230.5808
Horace Bushnell; [twelve selections] edited by H. Shelton Smith. New York, Oxford University Press, 1965. xi, 407 p. 24 cm. (A Library of Protestant thought) Bibliography: p. 392-399. [BX7117.B8S6] 65-28037
1. Congregational churches — Collected works. 2. Theology — Collected works — 19th cent. I. Smith, Hilrie Shelton. 1803- ed. II. Title.

BUSHNELL, Horace, 1802-1876 230.5808
Horace Bushnell [12 selections] ed. by H. Shelton Smith. New York, Oxford [c.]1965. xi, 407p. 24cm. (Lib. of Protestant thought) Bibl. [BX7117.B8S6] 65-28037 7.00
1. Congregational churches—Collected works. 2. Theology—Collected works—19th cent. I. Smith, Hilrie Shelton, 1893- ed. II. Title. III. Series.

EDWARDS, Jonathan, 1703-1758. 230.5'8'08
Selected writings of Jonathan Edwards. Edited, with an introd., by Harold P. Simonson. New York, F. Ungar Pub. Co. [1970] 188 p. 20 cm. (Milestones of thought in the history of ideas) [BX7117.E33S5 1970] 78-115064 ISBN 8-04-461325- 2.45 (pbk)
1. Congregational churches—Collected works. 2. Theology—Collected works—18th century. I. Title. II. Series.

SHINN, Roger Lincoln. 230.5834
We believe; an interpretation of the United Church Statement of faith [by] Roger Lincoln Shinn and Daniel Day Williams. Philadelphia, United Church Press [1966] 132 p. 21 cm. Statement of faith in German, Spanish, and New Testament Greek translations (p. 127-132) [BX9886.S5] 66-23992
1. United Church of Christ—Catechisms and creeds. I. Williams, Daniel Day, 1910- II. United Church of Christ. Statement of faith. 1966. III. Title.

BENES, Peter. 230'.5'9
The masks of orthodoxy : an ecclesiological interpretation of Puritan spirit carvings in Plymouth County, Massachusetts / by Peter Benes. Amherst : University of Massachusetts Press, [1977] p. cm. Includes index. Bibliography: p. [BV153.U6B46] 76-57984 ISBN 0-87023-237-1 : 20.00
1. Christian art and symbolism—Massachusetts—Plymouth Co. 2. Stone carving—Massachusetts—Plymouth Co. 3. Sepulchral monuments—Massachusetts—Plymouth Co. 4. Plymouth Co., Mass.—History. I. Title.

THE Golden treasury of 230'.5'9
Puritan quotations / compiled by I. D. E. Thomas. Chicago : Moody Press, c1975. 321 p. ; 24 cm. Includes index. [PN6084.R3G6] 75-333021 ISBN 0-8024-3080-5 : 7.95
1. Religion—Quotations, maxims, etc. 2. Theology, Puritan. I. Thomas, Isaac David Ellis.

INTRODUCTION to Puritan 230'.5'9
theology : a reader / Edward Hindson, editor ; foreword by James I. Packer. Grand Rapids : Baker Book House, c1976. 282 p. : ill. ; 23 cm. "A Canon Press book." Includes index. Contents.Contents.—Preston, J. Natural theology.—Jewel, J. Scripture.—Charnock, S. God.—Manton, T. Man and sin.—Ussher, J. Christ.—Perkins, W. Salvation: introduction.—Owen, J. The atonement.—Hopkins, S. Regeneration and conversion.—Downame, G. Justification.—Bunyan, J. Sanctification.—Baxter, R. The church.—Edwards, J. Eschatology. Bibliography: p. 267-275. [BX9327.I58] 75-38235 ISBN 0-8010-4143-0 : 8.95
1. Puritans—Addresses, essays, lectures. 2. Theology, Doctrinal—Addresses, essays, lectures. I. Hindson, Edward E.

STANNARD, David E. 230'.5'9
The Puritan way of death : a study in religion, culture, and social change / David E. Stannard. New York : Oxford University Press, 1977. p. cm. Includes bibliographical references and index. [BT825.S76] 76-42647 ISBN 0-19-502226-2 : 11.95
1. Death. 2. Puritans—New England. I. Title.

LOWRIE, Ernest Benson. 230'.5'90924
The shape of the Puritan mind : the thought of Samuel Willard / Ernest Benson Lowrie. New Haven : Yale University Press, 1974. xi, 253 p. ; 21 cm. Includes index. Bibliography: p. 235-248. [BX7260.W5L68 1974] 74-76650 ISBN 0-300-01714-6
1. Willard, Samuel, 1640-1707. I. Title.

BRANDEIS, Donald Asa, 1928- 230.6
A faith for modern man. Grand Rapids, Mich., Baker Bk. House [c.]1961. 129p. 61-18798 2.95 bds.,
1. Theology, Doctrinal—Popular works. I. Title.

*BUNYAN, John, 1628-1688 230.6
Justification by an imputed righteousness. Swengel, Pa., Reiner Pubns., 1967. 89p. 19cm. 1.50 pap.,
I. Title.

*BUNYAN, John, 1628-1688 230.6
The strait gate; or, Great difficulty in going to Heaven. Swengel' Pa., Remer Pubns., 1967 71p. 19cm. With facsim. t.p.: Works of the English divines. Bunyan. 1.00 pap.,
I. Title.

*BUNYAN, John, 1628-1688 230.6
The water of life; or, A discourse showing the richness and glory of the grace and spirit of the gospel. Pref. by C.H. Spurgeon. Swengel, Pa., Reiner Pubns., 1967. vii, 93p. 19cm. 1.50 pap.,
I. Title.

FISHER, Fred L. 230.6
Christianity is personal. Nashville, Broadman Press ['1951] 151 p. 21 cm. [BX6331.F5] 51-14551
1. Baptists—Doctrinal and controversial works. 2. Theology, Doctrinal—Popular works. 3. Christianity—Essence, Genius, nature. I. Title.

FOREMAN, Lawton Durant, 1913- ed. 230.6
Credenda: being a treatise of thirteen Bible doctrines; fundamental of basic beliefs of Missionary Baptists. Writer: Ben M. Bogard [and others] Little Rock, Ark., Seminary Press [1950] 250 p. 23 cm. [BX6349.57.F6] 51-17275
1. American Baptist Association—Doctrinal and controversial works. I. Title.

GAINES, David P. 230.6
Beliefs of Baptists. New York, R. R. Smith, 1952. 295 p. 22 cm. [BX6331.G2] 52-14568
1. Baptists—Doctrinal and controversial works. 2. Theology, Doctrinal—Popular works. I. Title.

GASKIN, Jesse Marvin, 1917- 230.6
The Baptist witness. Shawnee, Printed by Oklahoma Baptist University Press [1950] 94 p. 19 cm. [BX6332.G3] 50-2384
1. Baptists—Doctrinal and controversial works. I. Title.

GRAYUM, H. Frank. 230.6
Bible truths for today. H. Frank Grayum, editor. Nashville, Convention Press [1970] 69 p. 20 cm. "Reprinted from Baptist adults, January, February, March, 1964." "This book is the text for course number 3301 of subject area Christian theology in the New church study course." [BX6225.G67] 71-118304
1. Religious education—Text-books for adults—Baptist. I. Title.

HEFLIN, Jimmie H., ed. 230.6
These folks called Baptist. Grand Rapids, Mich., Baker Bk. House, 1962. 84p. 61-18637 2.00
1. Baptists—Doctrinal and controversial works. I. Title.

HOBBS, Herschel H 230.6
What Baptists believe. Nashville, Broadman Press [1964] 128 p. 20 cm. [BT77.H542] 64-12411
1. Theology, Doctrinal — Popular works. 2. Baptists — Doctrinal and controversial works. I. Title.

HOBBS, Herschel H. 230.6
What Baptists believe. Nashville, Broadman [c.1964] 128p. 20cm. (Broadman inner circle bk.) 64-12411 1.50 bds.,
1. Theology, Doctrinal—Popular works. 2. Baptists—Doctrinal and controversial works. I. Title.

HORNE, Hugh R 230.6
Light on great Bible themes. Grand Rapids, Eerdmans [1964] 103 p. 23 cm. [BX6333.H65L5] 63-20682
1. Sermons, American. 2. Baptists — Sermons. I. Title.

HORNE, Hugh R. 230.6
Light on great Bible themes. Grand Rapids, Mich., Eerdmans [c.1964] 103p. 23cm. 63-20682 2.50
1. Sermons, American. 2. Baptists—Sermons. I. Title.

HUDSON, Winthrop Still, 1911- ed. 230.6
Baptist concepts of the church; a survey of the historical and theological issues which have produced changes in church order. Chicago, Judson Press [1959] 236p. 21cm. [BX6331.H8] 59-12816
1. Church. 2. Baptists—Doctrinal and controversial works. I. Title.

HUDSON, Winthrop Still, 1911- 230.6
Baptist convictions. Valley Forge [Pa.] Judson Press [1963] 85 p. 20 cm. [BX6332.H84] 62-20952
1. Baptists—Doctrinal and controversial works. I. Title.

KATTERJOHN, Arthur D. 230'.6
The tribulation people / by Arthur D. Katterjohn, with Mark Fackler. Carol Stream, Ill. : Creation House, c1975. 137 p. ; 21 cm. Bibliography: p. 135-137. [BT886.K34] 75-24586 ISBN 0-88419-115-X : 3.50
1. Second Advent. 2. Rapture (Christian eschatology) 3. Tribulation (Christian eschatology) I. Fackler, Mark, joint author. II. Title.

KNUDSEN, Ralph Edward, 1897- 230.6
Theology in the New Testament, a basis for Christian faith. Valley Forge [Pa.] Judson Press [1964] 442 p. 23 cm. Includes bibliographies. [BX6331.2.K55] 63-13987
1. Baptists—Doctrinal and controversial works. 2. Bible. N. T.—Theology. I. Title.

KNUDSEN, Ralph Edward, 1897- 230.6
Theology in the New Testament, a basis for Christian faith. Valley Forge, Pa., Judson [c.1964] 442p. 23cm. Bibl. 63-13987 6.95
1. Baptists—Doctrinal and controversial works. 2. Bible. N. T.—Theology. I. Title.

MCBIRNIE, William Steuart, 1920- 230.6
Introduction in the Baptist faith. San Antonio, Naylor Co. [1955] 115p. 23cm. [BX6331.M15] 55-30115
1. Baptists—Doctrinal and controversial works. I. Title.

ROSE, Delbert R. 230'.6
Vital holiness : a theology of Christian experience : interpreting the historic Wesleyan message / Delbert R. Rose. 3d ed. Minneapolis : Bethany Fellowship, c1975. 322 p. ; 22 cm. Originally presented as the author's thesis, State University of Iowa; rev. 1st-2d ed. published under title: A theology of Christian experience. Includes index. Bibliography: p. 311-318. [BX8495.S583R67 1975] 75-328165 ISBN 0-87123-539-0 pbk. : 3.95
1. Smith, Joseph H. 2. National Holiness Association. I. Title.

SHANK, Robert, 1918- 230.6
Life in the Son; a study of the doctrine of perseverance. Introd. by William W. Adams. Springfield, Mo. Westcott Publishers [1960] 380 p. 23 cm. Includes bibliography. [BT768.S5] 59-15488
1. Perseverance (Theology) I. Title.

SHANK, Robert, 1918- 230.6
Life in the Son, a study of the doctrine of perseverance. Introd. by William W. Adams. 2d ed. Springfield, Mo., Westcott Publishers [1961] 380 p. 23 cm. Includes bibliography. [BT768.S5 1961] 61-3734
1. Perseverance (Theology) I. Title.

SHANK, Robert [Lee] 230.6
Life in the Son: a study of the doctrine of perseverance. Introd. by William W. Adams. Springfield, Mo., [P.O. Box 803, Westcott Publishers c.1960] xix 3,80p. (3p. bibl.) 23cm. 50-15488 4.95
1. Perseverance (Theology) I. Title.

SRYGLEY, Fletcher Douglas, 1856-1900. 230.6
The New Testament church; editorials of F. D. Srygley which appeared in the Gospel advocate from 1889 to 1900, comp. and ed. by F. B. Srygley. Nashville, Tenn., McQuiddy printing company, 1910. 319 p. 2 port. (incl. front.) 19 1/2 cm. [BX7076.S72] 10-13187
1. Churches of Christ — Addresses, essays, lectures. I. Srygley, Filo Bunyan, 1859-1940, ed. II. Title.

TURNER, John Clyde, 1878- 230.6
These things we believe. Nashvinne, Convention Press [1956] 134p. 20cm. [BT77.T83] 56-23822
1. Theology, Doctrinal—Popular works. 2. Baptists—Doctrinal and controversial works. I. Title.

TURNER, John Clyde, 1878- 230.6
These things we believe. Nashville, Conventions Press [1956] 134 p. 20 cm. [BT77.T83] 56-23822
1. Theology Doctrinal — Popular works. 2. Baptists — Doctrinal and controversial works. I. Title.

WAHKING, Harold L. 230.6
Being Christlike [by] Harold L. Wahking. Nashville, Tenn., Broadman Press [1970] 96 p. illus. 19 cm. (Being books) Includes bibliographical references. [BT77.W27] 73-113216
1. Theology, Doctrinal—Popular works. 2. Youth—Religious life. I. Title.

WARREN, Thomas B 230.6
Warren- Ballard debate, held in Fort Worth, Texas, July 23-26, 1952, between Thomas B. Warren, Fort Worth, Texas, and L. S. Ballard, Dallas, Texas. Tape recorded; transcribed by Betty Sue Baker. 1st ed. Longview, Wash., Telegram Book Co., 1953. 242p. illus. 20cm. [BX7094.C95W3] 54-19589
1. Churches of Christ—Doctrinal and controversial works. 2. Baptists—Doctrinal and controversial works. I. Ballard, L. S. II. Title.

NEW York State Baptist Convention. 230'.6'09747
God's doing; man's undoing [edited by] Ralph H. Elliott. [Contributors:] Kenneth D. Blazier [and others] Valley Forge, Judson Press [1967] 157 p. 23 cm. Includes papers presented at the annual meeting of the New York State Baptist Convention, October 1966, and a summary of the "study session" following each. Contents.Contents. -- The revelation of God in history, by R. H. Elliott. -- Critique, by A. K. Wise. -- The covenant of God in history, by W. R. Nelson. -- Critique, by K. D. Blazier. -- The society of God in history. by H. E. Williams. -- Critique, by J. M. Dick. -- The ministry of God in history, by G. L. Earnshaw. -- Critique, by J. C. Miller. -- The new morality in contemporary history, by A. L. Whitaker. -- Critique, by N. O. Kelm. -- Notes (p. 149-157) [BX6248.N7A55] 67-17168
1. Baptists — New York (State) — Congresses. 2. Theology, Doctrinal — Congresses. I. Elliott, Ralph H., ed. II. Blazier, Kenneth D. III. Title.

EVANGELISM men : 230'.6'1
proclaiming the doctrines of salvation / compiled by James A. Ponder. Nashville : Broadman Press, c1975. 104 p. : ports. ; 19 cm. Contents.Contents.—Autrey, C. E.

Repentance.—Lee, R. G. The curse.—Hobbs, H. H. God's gracious salvation.—Dossey, C. Y. The new birth.—Meigs, P. A. The sure foundation.—Ford, W. H. The world's need of a supernatural man.—Havner, V. On this rock I stand.—Pennington, J. A. Life's most important question.—James, P. S. The sins of the saints.—Stigler, W. L. Starting life all over again. [BV3797.A1E83] 75-35395 ISBN 0-8054-2226-9 : 2.25
1. Evangelistic sermons. 2. Baptists—Sermons. 3. Sermons, American. I. Ponder, James A. II. Title: Proclaiming the doctrines of salvation.

FORD, William Herschel, 1900- 230.61
Simple sermons on the great Christian doctrines. Nashville, Broadman Press [1951] 137 p. 20 cm. [BX6333.F568S5] 51-11554
1. Baptists—Sermons. 2. Sermons, American. I. Title.

FORD, William Herschel, 1900- 230'.6'1
Simple sermons on the great Christian doctrines / W. Herschel Ford. Grand Rapids : Zondervan Pub. House, [1976], c1951. p. cm. Reprint of the ed. published by Broadman Press, Nashville. [BX6333.F568S5 1976] 75-38795 pbk. : 1.95
1. Baptists—Sermons. 2. Sermons, American. I. Title.

FUNDAMENTAL Baptist Congress of North America, Detroit, 1963. 230'.6'1
The Biblical faith of Baptists: messages. Detroit, Mich. [c1964-66] 2 v. 23 cm. Vol. 2 contains messages presented at the 1966 Congress held in Grand Rapids. Vol. 2 has imprint: Des Plains, Ill., Regular Baptist Press. [BX6207.A22] 67-5756
1. Baptists — Congresses. 2. Baptists — Sermons. 3. Sermons, American. I. Fundamental Baptist Congress of North America, Grand Rapids, 1966. II. Title.

FUNDAMENTAL Baptist Congress of North America, Detroit, 1963. 230'.6'1
The Biblical faith of Baptists; messages. Detroit, Mich. [c1964-66] 2 v. 23 cm. Vol. 2 contains messages presented at the 1966 Congress held in Grand Rapids. Vol. 2 has imprint: Des Plains, Ill., Regular Baptist Press. [BX6207.A22] 67-5756
1. Baptists—Congresses. 2. Baptists—Sermons. 3. Sermons, American. I. Fundamental Baptist Congress of North America, Grand Rapids, 1966. II. Title.

GREEN, Joseph Franklin, 1924- 230.61
God wants you [by] Joe and Janie Green. [Teacher's ed.] Nashville, Convention Press [1966] 84 p. forms. 19 cm. "Church study course [of the Sunday School Board of the Southern Baptist Convention] This book is number 0792 in category 7, section for juniors." "Helps for the teacher": [19] p. bound in. [BX6225.G7] 66-10256
1. Religious education—Text-books for children—Baptist. I. Green, Janie, joint author. II. Southern Baptist Convention. Sunday School Board. III. Title.

JONES, Ora L. 230.61
How the Baptists got their doctrines; a restatement of some almost forgotten church history and doctrines that should be remembered, by Ora L. Jones. Detroit, Harlo Press [1966] 227 p. 23 cm. [BX6331.2.J6] 66-26929
1. Theology, Doctrinal—History. 2. Baptists—Doctrinal and controversial works. I. Title.

MCCALL, Duke K ed. 230.61
What is the church? A symposium of Baptist thouhgt. Nashville, Broadman Press [1958] 189p. 21cm. [BX6331.M17] 58-5411
1. Baptists—Doctrinal and controversial works. 2. Church. I. Title.

MATTHEWS, Victor M. 230.6'1
Personal success; the promise of God [by] Victor M. Matthews. [Grand Rapids, Diadem Productions, c1970] 142 p. 23 cm. [BV4501.2.M385] 72-136754 3.95
1. Christian life—1960- 2. Christianity—Essence, genius, nature. I. Title.

RICE, John R., 1895- 230.6'1
Some serious, popular false doctrines answered from the Scriptures, by John R. Rice. Murfreesboro, Tenn., Sword of the Lord Publishers [1970] 442 p. 21 cm. On spine: False doctrines answered. Includes articles by R. L. Sumner, G. A. Weniger, and J. S. Wimbish. Includes bibliographical references. [BT1102.R5] 73-126630 5.25
1. Apologetics—20th century. I. Title. II. Title: False doctrines answered.

SHANNON, Harper. 230.6'1
Beliefs that are basic. Grand Rapids, Zondervan Pub. House [1969] 96 p. 22 cm. Bibliography: p. 95-96. [BX6333.S45B4] 73-81040 2.95
1. Baptists—Sermons. 2. Sermons, American. I. Title.

TAYLOR, Kenneth Nathaniel. 230.6'1
Devotions for the children's hour, by Kenneth N. Taylor. Illustrated by Robert G. Doares. [Rev. ed.] Chicago, Moody Press [1968] 175 p. illus. 24 cm. Brief anecdotes discuss questions relating to God and the Bible. A prayer, a hymn, and suggested readings from the Bible follow each chapter. [BV4870.T3 1968] 68-26406 3.95
1. Children—Prayer-books and devotions—English—1961- I. Doares, Robert G., illus. II. Title.

JAEHN, Klaus Juergen. 230'.6'10924 B
Rauschenbusch, the formative years / [Klaus Juergen Jaehn]. Valley Forge, PA : Judson Press, c1976. 58 p. ; 22 cm. A revision of the author's thesis (Master of Divinity) which was first published in two parts in Foundations, Oct.-Dec., 1973, v. 16, no. 4 and Jan.-Mar., 1974, v. 17, no. 1. Bibliography: p. 49-52. [BX6495.R3J3 1976] 75-38191 ISBN 0-8170-0707-5 pbk. : 1.50
1. Rauschenbusch, Walter, 1861-1918. I. Title.

FUTURISTIC Conference, Ridgecrest, N.C., 1977. 230'.6'132
Proceedings of major presentations : Futuristic Conference / sponsored by the Sunday School Board of the Southern Baptist Convention, March 21-25, 1977, Ridgecrest, North Carolina. Nashville : The Board, c1977. v, 140 leaves : ill. ; 29 cm. Includes bibliographical references. [CB161.F795 1977] 77-155217
1. Southern Baptist Convention—Congresses. 2. Twentieth century—Forecasts—Congresses. 3. Baptists—Southern States—Congresses. I. Southern Baptist Convention. Sunday School Board.

SHURDEN, Walter B. 230'.6'132
Not a silent people; controversies that have shaped Southern Baptists [by] Walter B. Shurden. Nashville, Broadman Press [1972] 128 p. 21 cm. (A Broadman inner circle book) "Most of the following chapters were first published in the Student in a somewhat revised form during 1970-1971." Includes bibliographical references. [BX6331.2.S53] 79-178066 ISBN 0-8054-8801-4
1. Southern Baptist Convention. 2. Baptists—Doctrinal and controversial works. I. Title.

KNIGHT, Henry. 230.63
One God, one country, one church. [1st ed.] New York, VantagePress [1956] 116p. 21cm. [BX6154.K58] 55-11663
1. Seventh-Day Adventists —Doctrinal and controversial works. I. Title.

REBOK, Denton Edward, 1897- 230.63
Believe His prophets. Washington, Review and Herald Pub. Association [1956] 320p. 18cm. (Christian home library) [BX6154.R338] 56-38678
1. Seventh-Day Adventists—Doctrinal and controversial works. I. Title.

HOLDER, J D 230.64
Principles and practices of the church. Elon College, N. C., Primitive Baptist Pub. House [1961] 222p. 22cm. [BX6387.H6] 61-36014
1. Primitive Baptists—Doctrinal and controversial works. I. Title.

BARCLAY, Robert, 1648-1690 230'.6'6
Barclay's apology in modern English, ed. by Dean Freiday. [Alburtis, Pa., Hemlock Pr.; dist. Friends Bk. Store, Philadelphia, [1967] xli, 465p. 21cm. Tr. of Theologiae vere christianae apologia. Bibl. [BX7730.B3 1967] 67-18796 3.50
1. Friends, Society of—Doctrinal and controversial works. I. Freiday, Dean, ed. II. Title.
Distributor's address: 302 Arch St., Philadelphia, Pa. 19106.

BEAZLEY, George G., 1914- 230'.6'6
The Christian Church (Disciples of Christ): an interpretative examination in the cultural context, edited by George G. Beazley, Jr. [St. Louis, Bethany Press, 1973] 417 p. 23 cm. Includes bibliographical references. [BX7321.2.B42] 73-14748 ISBN 0-8272-0436-1 7.95
1. Disciples of Christ. I. Title.

BLAKELY, Fred Orville, 1910- 230.66
The Apostles' doctrine; a book of sermon-studies in the field of basic Christian teaching. Highland, Ind., 1951- v. 22 cm. [BX7321.B55] 51-4742
1. Disciples of Christ—Doctrinal and controversial works. I. Title.

BLAKELY, Fred Orville, 1910- 230.66
The Apostles' doctrine; a book of sermon-studies in the field of basic Christian teaching. Highland, Ind., 1951-53. 2v. 22cm. [BX7321.B55] 51-4742
1. Disciples of Christ—Doctrinal and controversial works. I. Title.

BLAKELY, Fred Orville, 1910- 230.66
The Apostles' doctrine; a book of sermon-studies in the field of basic Christian teaching. Rev. and enl. Highland, Ind., 1957- v. 22cm. [BX7321.B56] 58-17610
1. Disciples of Christ—Doctrinal and controversial works. I. Title.

CAMPBELL, Alexander, 1788-1866. 230.6'6
The Christian system. New York, Arno Press, 1969. 358 p. 23 cm. (Religion in America) Reprint of the 1866 ed. [BX7321.C2 1969] 73-83412
1. Disciples of Christ—Doctrinal and controversial works. I. Title.

CAMPBELL, Alexander, 1788-1866. 230.66
A compend of Alexander Campbell's theology, with commentary in the form of critical and historical footnotes. Ed. by Royal Humbert. St. Louis, Bethany [c.1961] 295p. 61-15529 4.00
I. Humbert, Royal, ed. II. Title.

CHRISTIAN-EVANGELIST. 230.66
What we believe, edited by James M. Flanagan. St. Louis, Bethany Press [1956] 126p. 20cm. From the 'What we believe ' series of articles published in the Christian-evangelist during 1956.' Includes bibliography. [BX7321.C53] 56-12347
1. Disciples of Christ—Doctrinal and controversial works. I. Flanagan, James M., ed. II. Title.

CHRISTIAN-EVENGELIST. 230.66
What we believe, edited by James M. Flanagan. St. Louis, Beathany Press [1956] 126p. 20cm. From the "What we believe' series of articles published in the Christian-evangelist during 1956.' Includes bibliography. [BX7321.C53] 56-12347
1. Disciples of Christ—Doctrinal and controversial works. I. Flanagan, James M., ed. II. Title.

COGGINS, James Caswell, 1865- 230.66
Christian philosophy and science; a vindication of Bible teaching. Boston, Christopher Pub. House [1950] 315 p. 21 cm. [BX7321.C56] 50-58221
1. Disciples of Christ—Doctrinal and controversial works. I. Title.

DE GROOT, Alfred Thomas 230.66
The restoration principle. St. Louis, Bethany Press [c.1960] 191p. 23cm. bibl. 60-6228 4.00
1. Disciples of Christ. 2. Theology, Doctrinal—Hist. I. Title.

DE GROOT, Alfred Thomas, 1903- 230'.66
Disciple thought: a history [by] A. T. De Groot. Fort Worth, Texas Christian University, 1965. 277 l. 28 cm. Includes bibliographical references. [BX7321.2.D44] 201'.1 77-246172
1. Disciples of Christ—Doctrinal and controversial works. I. Title.

DISCIPLES of Christ. Study Commission on Ministerial Education. 230'.6'6
The imperative is leadership; a report on ministerial development in the Christian Church (Disciples of Christ), by Carroll C. Cotten. With recommendations by the Study Commission on Ministerial Education, Christian Church (Disciples of Christ). St. Louis, Mo., Bethany Press [1973] 125 p. 23 cm. Includes bibliographical references. [BX7311.D57] 73-8893 ISBN 0-8272-1604-1 2.95
1. Disciples of Christ—Clergy. 2. Theology—Study and teaching—Disciples of Christ. I. Cotten, Carroll C., 1936- II. Title.

FLANAGAN, James M., ed. 230.66
The Christian. What we believe, edited by James M. Flanagan. St. Louis, Bethany Press [1956] 126 p. 20 cm. From the "'What we believe' series of articles published in the Christian-evangelist during 1956." Includes bibliography. [BX7321.C53] 56-12347
1. Disciples of Christ — Doctrinal and controversial works. I. Title.

HIGGINS, Albert Sidney, 1881- 230.66
What the Bible says. 2d ed. [Texline? Tex., 1961] 243p. illus. 23cm. [BX7076.H5 1961] 61-35099
1. Churches of Christ—Doctrinal and controversial works. I. Title.

JOHNSON, H. Eugene. 230'.6'6
The Christian church plea / by H. Eugene Johnson. Cincinnati : New Life Books, c1975. 95 p. ; 22 cm. Bibliography: p. [92]-95. [BX7321.2.J63] 75-12012 ISBN 0-87239-053-5 pbk. : 4.95
1. Christian Church (Disciples of Christ)—Doctrinal and controversial works. I. Title.

PORTER, W Curtis, 1897- 230.66
Porter-Myers debate, between W. Curtis Porter, Monette, Arkansas, representing Church of Christ and B. Sunday Myers, Opelika, Alabama, representing Pentecostal Church of God.A written discussion: Is the Church of Christ a denomination? or is it the exclusive New Testament church? Monette, Ark., Porter's Book Shop [c1956] 240p. 23cm. [BX7094.C95P58] 57-25428
1. Churches of Christ—Doctrinal and controversial works. I. Myers, B. Sunday. II. Title.

PORTER, W Curtis, 1897- 230.66
Porter- Myers debate, between W. Curtis Porter, Monette, Arkansas, representing Church of Christ and B. Sunday Myers, Opelika, Alabama, representing Pentecostal Church of God. A written discussion: Is the Church of Christ a denomination? or is it the exclusive New Testament church? Monette, Ark., Porter's Book Shop [c1956] 240p. 23cm. [BX7094.C95P58] 57-25428
1. Churches of Christ— Doctrinal and controversial works. I. Myers, B. Sunday. II. Title.

SCUDDER, John Ralph. 230'.6'6
A history of Disciple theories of religious education. Lexington, Ky., College of the Bible, 1963. 80 p. 23 cm. Based on thesis, Duke University. Bibliographical footnotes. [BX7311.S35] 64-2022
1. Disciples of Christ—Education. I. Title. II. Title: Disciple theories of religious education.

SQUIRE, Russel Nelson, 1908- 230'.6'6
Where is the Bible silent; essays on the Campbell-Stone religious restoration of America, by Russel N. Squire. Los Angeles, Southland Press [1973] xiv, 143 p. 24 cm. Bibliography: p. 59-60. [BX7315.S68] 73-76639
1. Disciples of Christ—History. 2. Churches of Christ—History. 3. Disciples of Christ—Doctrinal and controversial works. 4. Churches of Christ—Doctrinal and controversial works. I. Title.

ANDREASEN, Milian Lauritz, 1876- 230.67
What can a man believe? Mountain View, Calif., Pacific Press Pub. Association [1951] vii, 211 p. 18 cm. [BX6154.A63] 51-5268
1. Seventh-Day Adventists—Doctrinal and controversial works. I. Title.

BIBLE readings for the home; 230.67
a study of 200 vital Scripture topics in question and answer form, contributed by a large number of Bible scholars. Rev., newly illus. Nashville, Southern Pub. Assn., 1963. 568p. illus. (pt. col.) 27cm. Bibl. 63-12806 apply
1. Seventh-Day Adventists—Doctrinal and controversial works.

BIETZ, Arthur Leo 230.67
Exploring God's answers. Mountain View, Calif., Pacific Press Pub. Association [c.1960] 182p. diagr. 23cm. 60-11199 3.95
1. Seventh-Day Adventists—Doctrinal and controversial works. I. Title.

BIRD, Herbert S. 230.67
Theology of Seventh-Day Adventism. Grand Rapids, Mich., Eerdmans [c.1961] 137p. Bibl. 61-10858 3.00
1. Seventh-Day Adventists—Doctrinal and controversial works. I. Title.

BRANSON, William Henry, 1887- 230.67
Drama of the ages. Nashville, Southern Pub. Association [1953] 544p. 18cm. (Christian home library) [B6154.B7 1953] 53-24295
1. Seventh-Day Adventists— Doctrinal and controversial works. I. Title.

BRANSON, William Henry, 1887- 230.67
Drama of the ages. Nashville, Southern Pub. Association, 1950. 584 p. illus. 23 cm. [BX6154.B7] 50-13648
1. Seventh-Day Adventists—Doctrinal and controversial works. I. Title.

CAMPBELL, George A 230.67
How many ways to heaven? Why so many

denominations? Mountain View, Calif., Pacific Press Pub. Association [1953] 86p. illus. 19cm. (Stories that win series) [BX6154.C23] 53-6428
1. Seventh-Day Adventists—Doctrinal and controversial works. 2. Sects. I. Title.

CANRIGHT, Dudley Marvin, 1840-1919. 230.67
Seventh-day Adventism refuted, in a nutshell. Grand Rapids, Mich. Baker Bk., 1962. 83p. 19cm. A reprint of a series of ten tracts. . . published . . . in 1889. 62-6808 .75 pap.,
1. Seventh-Day Adventists—Doctrinal and controversial works. I. Title.

EMMERSON, W. L. 230.67
The Bible speaks; scripture readings systematically arranged for home and class study, answering nearly one thousand questions. Addit. notes gathered, prepd. by Francis A. Soper. Abridged. Mountain View, Calif., Pacific Pr. Pub. [1967,c.1949] 250p. illus. 19cm. [BX6154.E55] .95 pap.,
1. Seventh-Day Adventists—Doctrinal and controversial works. 2. Bible—Examinations, questions, etc. I. Title.

HARDE,. Frederick E J 230.67
Giants of faith. Washington, Review and Herald Pub. Association [1961] 100p. 22cm. [BX6154.H3] 61-119816
1. Seventh-Day Adventists—Doctrinal and controversial works. I. Title.

HOEHN, Edward, 1893- 230.67
God's plan for your life. Mountain View, Calif., Pacific Press Pub. Association [1953] 135p. 20cm. [BX6154.H54] 53-8824
1. Seventh-Day Adventists—Doctrinal and controversial works. I. Title.

JEMISON, T Housel. 230.67
Christian beliefs; fundamental Biblical teachings for Seventh-Day Adventist college classes, by T. H. Jemison. Prepared by the Dept. of Education, General Conference of Seventh-Day Adventists. Mountain View, Calif., Pacific Press Pub. Association [1959] 481p. 23cm. Includes bibliography. [BX6154.J4] 59-14248
1. Theology, Doctrinal. 2. Seventh-Day Adventists—Doctrinal and controversial works. I. Seventh-Day Adventists. General Conference, Dept. of Education. II. Title.

LEE, Leonard C. 230.67
I found the way. Cover and illus. by James Converse. Mountain View, Calif., Pacific Press Pub. Association [c.1961] 122p. 61-10878 .50 pap.,
1. Seventh-Day Adventists—Doctrinal and controversial works. I. Title.

LEWIS, Richard Burton, 1906- 230.67
The Protestant dilemma; how to achieve unity in a completed reformation. Mountain View, Calif., Pacific Press Pub. Association [1961] 106p. 20cm. [BV125.L47] 61-6481
1. Sabbath. 2. Seventh-Day Adventists—Doctrinal and controversial works. I. Title.

LICKEY, Arthur E. 230.67
God speaks to modern man. Washington, D.C., Review & Herald, 1963[c.1952, 1963] 448p. col. illus. 27cm. 63-3624 15.75
1. Seventh-Day Adventists—Doctrinal and controversial works. I. Title.

LICKEY, Arthur E. 230.67
Highways to truth; God speaks to modern man. Washington, Review and Herald Pub. Association [1952] 544 p. illus. 22 cm. [BX6154.L52] 52-33808
1. Seventh-Day Adventists—Doctrinal and controversial works. I. Title.

MARTIN, Walter Ralston 230.67
The truth about Seventh-Day Adventism. Grand Rapids, Mich., Zondervan Pub. House [c.1960] 248p. 23cm. (6p. bibl.) 60-10154 3.50
1. Seventh-Day Adventists—Doctrinal and controversial works. I. Title.

MARTIN, Walter Ralston, 1928- 230.67
The truth about Seventh-Day Adventism Grand Rapids, Zondervan Pub. House [1960] 248p. 23cm. Includes bibliography. [BX6154.M27] 60-10154
1. Seventh-Day Adventists—Doctrinal and controversial works. I. Title.

MAXWELL, Arthur Stanley, 1896- 230.67
Your Bible and you; priceless treasures in the Holy Scriptures. Washington, Review and Hearld Pub. Association [1959] 480p. illus. 26cm. [BX6154.M33] 59-4846
1. Seventh-Day Adventists—Doctrinal and controversial works. I. Title.

NICHOL, Francis David, 1897- 230.67
Answers to objections; an examination of the major objections raised against the teachings of Seventh-Day Adventists. Foreword by W. H. Branson. Rev. and greatly enl. Washington, Review and Herald Pub. Association [1952] 895 p. 24 cm. [BX6154.N5] 52-43231
1. Seventh-Day Adventists — Doctrinal and controversial works. I. Title.

OCHS, William Benjamin. 23067
Living faith. Washington, Review and Herald [1954] 192p. 21cm. [BX6154.O3] 54-27846
1. Seventh-Day Adventists—Doctrinal and controversial works. I. Title.

READ, Walter E 1883- 230.67
The Bible, the spirit of prophecy, and the church. Washington, Review and Herald Pub. Association [1952] 192p. 20cm. [BX6154.R33] 52-68266
1. Seventh-Day Adventists—Doctrinal and controversial works. 2. Bible— Evidences, authority, etc. 3. Prophets. 4. Church. I. Title.

REBOK, Denton Edward, 1897- 230.67
God and I are partners. Washington, Review and Herald Pub. Association [1951] 126 p. illus. 16 cm. (Little giant pocket series) [BX6154.R34] 51-27688
1. Seventh-Day Adventists — Doctrinal and controversial works. I. Title.

RICHARDS, Harold Marshall Sylvester, 1894- 230.67
Look to the stars, by H. M. S. Richards. Washington, Review and Herald Pub. Association [1964] 156 p. 21 cm. [BL254.R5] 64-17663
1. Religion and astronautics. I. Title.

RICHARDS, Harold Marshall Sylvester, 1894- 230.67
Look to the stars, Washington, D. C, Review & Herald [c.1964] 156p. 21cm. [BL254.R5] 64-17663 3.00
1. Religion and astronautics. I. Title.

RICHARDS, Harold Marshall Sylvester, 1894- 230.67
What Jesus said. Nashville, Southern Pub. Association [1957] 576p. illus. 18cm. [BX6154.R45] 57-28028
1. Seventh-Day Adventists—Doctrinal and controversial works. I. Title.

RICHARDS, Harold Marshall Sylvester, 1894- 230.67
Why I am a Seventh-Day Adventist [by] H. M. S. Richards. Washington, Review and Herald Pub. Association [1965] 128 p. illus., ports. 21 cm. [BX6154.R47] 66-3284
1. Seventh-Day Adventists — Doctrinal and controversial works. I. Title.

SEVENTH-DAY Adventists 230.67
answer questions on doctrine; an explanation of certain major aspects of Seventh-Day Adventist belief, prepared by a representative group of Seventh-Day Adventist leaders, Bible teachers, and editors. Washington, Review and Herald Pub. Association [1957] 720 p. 21 cm. Includes bibliography. [BX6154.S4] 57-4838
1. Seventh-Day Adventists — Doctrinal and controversial works. 2. Questions and answers — Theology. I. Title: Questions on doctrine.

SEVENTH-DAY Adventists 230.67
answer questions on doctrine; an explanation of certain major aspects of Seventh-Day Adventist belief, prepared by a representative group of Seventh-Day Adventist leaders, Bible teachers, and editors. Washington, Review and Herald Pub. Association [1957] 720 p. 21 cm. Includes bibliography. [BX6154.S4] 57-4838
1. Seventh-Day Adventists—Doctrinal and controversial works. 2. Questions and answers—Theology. I. Title: Questions on doctrine.

SEVENTH-DAY Adventists. General Conference. 230.67
Our firm foundation; a report of the Seventh-Day Adventist Bible conference held September 1-13, 1952, in the Sligo Seventh-Day Adventist Church, Takoma Park, Maryland. Washington, Review and Herald Pub. Association [1953] 2v. 22cm. Bibliographical footnotes. Bibliography: v. 1, p. 714-716. [BX6154.A45 1952] 53-21443
1. Seventh-Day Adventists—Doctrinal and controversial works. I. Title.

SEVENTH-DAY Adventists. General Conference. Dept. of Education. 230.67
Principles of life from the Word of God; a systematic study of the major doctrines of the Bible. Mountain View, Calif., Pacific Press Pub. Association, for the Dept. of Education, General Conference of Seventh-Day Adventists [1952] 508p. illus. 24cm. [BX6155.S44] 52-14728
1. Seventh-Day Adventists—Doctrinal and controversial works. 2. Theology, Doctrinal—Popular works. I. Title.

TAYLOR, Clifton L 230.67
Outline studies from the Testimonies. 5th ed., rev. Washington, Review and Herald Pub. Association [1955] 480p. 18cm. (Christian home library) [BX6111.W625T3 1955] 56-17895
1. Seventh-Day Adventists—Doctrinal and controversial works. 2. White, Ellen Gould (Harmon) 1827-1915. I. Title.

VANDEMAN, George E. 230.67
Planet rebellion. Nashville, Southern Pub. Association [1960] 448 p. illus. 18 cm. Includes bibliography. [BX6154.V26] 60-2151
1. Seventh-Day Adventists — Doctrinal and controversial works. I. Title.

WALKER, Allen. 230.67
Last-day delusions. Nashville, Southern Pub. Association [1957] 128p. 18cm. [BX6154.W298] 57-40146
1. Seventh-Day Adventists—Doctrinal and controversial works. I. Title.

WALKER, Allen. 230.67
Last-day delusions. Nashville, Southern Pub. Association [1956] 128 p. 18 cm. [BX6154.W298] 57-40146
1. Seventh Day Adventists. — Doctrinal and controversial works. I. Title.

WHITE, Ellen Gould (Harmon) 1827-1915. 230.67
The story of patriarchs and prophets; the conflict of the ages illustrated in the lives of holy men of old. Washington, Review and Herald Pub. Association, 1958. 832 p. illus. 23 cm. [BX6111.W599 1958] 58-1760
1. Seventh-Day Adventists — Doctrinal and controversial works. 2. Patriarchs (Bible) 3. Prophets. I. Title.

ANDERSON, Roy Allan. 230.6'73
A better world. Nashville, Southern Pub. Association [1968] 206 p. 21 cm. (His God's eternal plan, v. 3) [BX6154.A565] 68-18210
1. Seventh-Day Adventists—Doctrinal and controversial works. I. Title.

ANDERSON, Roy Allan. 230.6'73
Love finds a way. Nashville, Southern Pub. Association [1967] 184 p. 21 cm. (His God's eternal plan, v. 2) [BX6154.A5672] 67-23319
1. Seventh-Day Adventists—Doctrinal and controversial works. I. Title.

CLEVELAND, Earl E. 230.6'73
Mine eyes have seen [by] E. E. Cleveland. Washington, Review and Herald Pub. Association [1968] 126 p. 20 cm. [BX6154.C55] 68-18742
1. Seventh-Day Adventists—Doctrinal and controversial works. I. Title.

FORD, Desmond. 230'.6'73
Answers on the way : scriptural answers to your questions / by Desmond Ford. Mountain View, Calif. : Pacific Press Pub. Association, c1977. 155 p. ; 22 cm. (Dimension ; 121) Includes bibliographical references. [BX6154.F57] 76-17704 pbk. : 3.95
1. Seventh-Day Adventists—Doctrinal and controversial works—Adventist authors—Miscellanea. I. Title.

FORD, Desmond. 230'.6'73
Answers on the way : scriptural answers to your questions / by Desmond Ford. Mountain View, Calif. : Pacific Press Pub. Association, c1977. 155 p. ; 22 cm. (Dimension ; 121) Includes bibliographical references. [BX6154.F57] 76-17704 pbk. : 3.95
1. Seventh-Day Adventists—Doctrinal and controversial works—Adventist authors—Miscellanea. I. Title.

HETZELL, M. Carol. 230'.6'73
Gelebter Glaube = Foi vecue = Faith alive / M. Carol Hetzell. Hamburg : Saatkorn-Verlag, c1975. 163 p. : ill. (some col.) ; 30 cm. [BX6154.H4] 75-516307
1. Seventh-Day Adventists—Doctrinal and controversial works. 2. Seventh-Day Adventists—Pictorial works. I. Title. II. Title: Foi vecue. III. Title: Faith alive.

LEROY, Douglas. 230'.6'73
I didn't know that! Cleveland, Tenn., Pathway Press [1973] 144 p. illus. 18 cm. [BX7034.L47] 73-84639 ISBN 0-87148-425-0 1.75 (pbk.)
1. Church of God (Cleveland, Tenn.)—Doctrinal and controversial works. I. Title.

LIBBY, Raymond H. 230'.6'73
What! No God? And other brief Bible messages, by Raymond H. Libby. Mountain View, Calif., Pacific Press Pub. Association [1967] 76 p. front. 19 cm. [BX6154.L47] 66-29535
1. Seventh-Day Adventists—Doctrinal and controversial works. 2. Theology—Miscellanea. I. Title.

LORENZ, Felix A. 230'.6'73
The only hope / by Felix A. Lorenz. Nashville, Tenn. : Southern Pub. Association, c1976. 112 p. ; 21 cm. [BX6154.L66] 75-43059 ISBN 0-8127-0108-9
1. Seventh-Day Adventists—Doctrinal and controversial works. I. Title.

*MAXWELL, Arthur S. 230.673
Bible made plain. Mountain View, Calif., Pacific Pr. Pub. [1968] 128p. illus., 18cm. T.p. and text in Russian. .50 pap.,
1. Seventh-Day Adventists—Doctrinal and controversial works. I. Title.

MAXWELL, Arthur Stanley, 1896- 230.6'73
Good news for you, by Arthur S. Maxwell. Washington, Review and Herald Pub. Association [1966] 256 p. col. illus. 21 cm. [BX6154.M29] 66-25273
1. Seventh-Day Adventists. I. Title.

PIERSON, Robert H. 230'.6'73
We still believe / Robert H. Pierson. Washington : Review and Herald Pub. Association, [1975] 254 p. ; 22 cm. [BX6154.P5] 75-312405 6.95
1. Seventh-Day Adventists—Doctrinal and controversial works. 2. Christian life—Seventh-Day Adventist authors. I. Title.

PROVONSHA, Jack W. 230'.6'73
God is with us [by] Jack W. Provonsha. Washington, Review and Herald Pub. Association [1974] 157 p. 22 cm. [BT1102.P76] 79-174643 3.50
1. Apologetics—20th century. I. Title.

REVIVAL and 230'.6'73
reformation [by] Robert H. Pierson [and others] Washington, Review and Herald Pub. Association [1974] 156 p. 22 cm. Speeches presented at the 1973 Annual Council of the Seventh-day Adventists. [BX6154.R39] 74-77806 4.95
1. Seventh-Day Adventists—Doctrinal and controversial works—Addresses, essays, lectures. I. Pierson, Robert H.

BIBLE. N. T. English. 1955. Authorized. 230.7
Selections from John Wesley's Notes on the New Testament, systematically arr. with explanatory comments [by] John Lawson. Chicago, A. R. Allenson [1955] 219p. 20cm. [BX8330.W36] 55-1584
1. Theology. Doctrinal. 2. Methodist Church—Doctrinal and controversial works. I. Wesley, John, 1703-1791. II. Lawson, John. III. Title.

LUCCOCK, Halford Edward, 1885-1960. 230.7
Halford Luccock treasury. Edited by Robert E. Luccock. New York, Abingdon Press [1963] 446 p. illus. 24 cm. [BX8217.L8] 63-11378
1. Theology — Collected works — 2oth cent. I. Title.

LUCCOCK, Halford Edward, 1885-1960 230.7
Halford Luccock treasury. Ed. by Robert E. Luccock. Nashville, Abingdon [c.1950-1963] 446p. illus. 24cm. 63-11378 6.00
1. Theology—Collected works—20th cent. I. Title.

LYLES, Albert M. 230.7
Methodism mocked; the satiric reaction to Methodism in the eighteenth century. London, Epworth Pr. [dist. Mystic, Conn., Verry, 1964, c.1960] 191p. illus. 23cm. Bibl. 61-4127 2.00
1. Methodist Church—Doctrinal and controversial works. 2. Satire, English—Hist. & crit. I. Title.

POTTHOFF, Harvey H. 230.7
Current theological thinking: an elective unit for adults, with Leader's guide by Howard M. Ham. Nashville, Abingdon [1963, c.1962] 64p. 23cm. .75 pap.,
I. Title.

SLAATTE, Howard Alexander. 230.7
Fire in the brand, an introduction to the creative work and theology of John Wesley. Foreword by Paul V. Galloway. [1st ed.] New York, Exposition Press [1963] 157 p. 22 cm. (An Exposition-university book) "EP41125." [BX8495.W5S545] 63-4965
1. Wesley, John, 1703-1791. I. Title.

SLAATTE, Howard Alexander 230.7
Fire in the brand, an introduction to the creative work and theology of John Wesley. Foreword by Paul V. Galloway. New York, Exposition [c.1963] 157p. 22cm. (Exposition-univ. bk. EP41124) 63-4965 4.00
1. Wesley, John, 1703-1791. I. Title.

STOKES, Mack B 230.7
Major Methodist beliefs. Nashville, Methodist

Pub. House [1956] 96p. 19cm. [BX8332.S685] 56-8745
1. Methodist Church—Doctrinal and controversial works. I. Title.

STOKES, Mack B 230.7
Major Methodist beliefs. Nashville, Methodist Pub. House [1956] 96 p. 19 cm. [BX8332.S685] 56-8745
1. Methodist Church — Doctrinal and controversial works. I. Title.

TOGETHER. 230.7
We believe; twelve articles on Methodist beliefs from the Together series. New York, Abingdon Press [1962] 95 p. 19 cm. [BX8332.T6] 62-51603
1. Methodist Church — Doctrinal and controversial works. I. Title.

TOGETHER 230.7
We believe; twelve articles on Methodist beliefs from the Together series. Nashville, Abingdon [c.1961, 1962] 95p. 19cm. 62-51603 .65 pap.,
1. Methodist Church—Doctrinal and controversial works. I. Title.

WHEDON, Daniel Denison, 230'.7
1808-1885.
Essays, reviews, and discourses, by Daniel D. Whedon. With a biographical sketch by his son, J. S. Whedon, and his nephew, D. A. Whedon. Freeport, N.Y., Books for Libraries Press [1972] 352 p. 23 cm. (Essay index reprint series) Reprint of the 1887 ed. [BX8217.W7 1972] 72-8504 ISBN 0-8369-7339-9
1. Methodist Church—Collected works. 2. Theology—Collected works—19th century. I. Title.

WILLIAMS, Colin W. 230.7
John Wesley's theology today. New York, Abingdon Press [1960] 252 p. 23 cm. Bibliography: p. 243-246. [BX8495.W5W62] 60-5238
1. Wesley, John, 1703-1791. I. Title.

WILLIAMS, Colin Wilbur, 230.7
1921-
John Wesley's theology today. New York, Abingdon Press [1960] 252 p. 23 cm. Bibliography: p. 243-246. [BX8495.W5W62] 60-5238
1. Wesley, John, 1703-1791. I. Title.

BUCKE, Emory Stevens, ed. 230.709
The History of American Methodism. Editorial Board: Emory Stevens Bucke, general editor [and others] New York, Abingdon Press [1964] 3 v. illus., ports., facsims. 24 cm. Issued in a case. Includes bibliographies. [BX8235.H5] 64-10013
1. Methodism — Hist. 2. Methodist Church in the U.S. — Hist. 3. Methodist Church (United States) — Hist. I. Title. II. Title: American Methodism.

CHILES, Robert Eugene 230.709
Theological transition in American Methodism, 1790-1935. Nashville, Abingdon [c.1965] 238p. 22cm. Bibl. [BX8331.2C5] 65-21979 4.00
1. Methodism—Hist. 2. Theology, Doctrinal—Hist.—U.S. I. Title.

CHILES, Robert Eugene. 230.709
Theological transition in American Methodism, 1790-1935 [by] Robert E. Chiles. New York, Abingdon Press [1965] 238 p. 22 cm. Bibliography: p. 215-226. [BX8331.2.C5] 65-21979
1. Methodism—History. 2. Theology, Doctrinal—History—U.S. I. Title.

OUTLER, Albert Cook, 230'.7'1
1908-
Theology in the Wesleyan spirit / Albert C. Outler. Nashville : Tidings, [1975] ix, 101 p. ; 19 cm. Includes bibliographical references. [BX8331.2.O9] 74-24509
1. Methodist Church—Doctrinal and controversial works. 2. Theology, Doctrinal—Popular works. I. Title.

WESLEY, John, 1703-1791. 230.71
A compend of Wesley's theology; edited by Robert W. Burtner and Robert E. Chiles. Nashville, Abingdon Press [1954] 302p. 24cm. Biblipgraphy: p. 291-292. [BX8217.W54B8] 54-5227
1. Theology, Doctrinal. 2. Methodist Church—Doctrinal and controversial works. I. Burtner, Robert Wallace, ed. II. Chiles, Robert Eugene, ed. III. Title.

WYNKOOP, Mildred Bangs. 230'.7'1
A theology of love; the dynamic of Wesleyanism. Kansas City, Mo., Beacon Hill Press of Kansas City [1972] 372 p. 23 cm. Bibliography: p. 369-372. [BX8495.W5W9] 72-197997
1. Wesley, John, 1703-1791. I. Title.

WESLEY, John, 1703- 230'.7'108
1791.
Fire of love : the spirituality of John Wesley / [selected by] Gordon Wakefield. New Canaan, Conn. : Keats Pub., 1977, c1976. 124 p. ; 18 cm. (A Pivot family reader) Includes bibliographies. [BX8217.W54W3 1977] 76-58765 1.95
1. Methodist Church—Collected works. 2. Theology—Collected works—18th century. I. Title.

SELLERS, Ian. 230'.7'10924 B
Adam Clarke, controversialist : Wesleyanism and the historic faith in the age of Bunting / [by] Ian Sellers. [St Columb Major] : [Wesley Historical Society], [1976] [9], 21, a-h p. ; 30 cm. (Lecture - Wesley Historical Society ; 1975) Bibliography: p. [9] (1st group) [BX8495.C57S44] 77-351857 ISBN 0-900798-08-4
1. Clarke, Adam, 1760?-1832—Addresses, essays, lectures. 2. Methodists in England—Biography—Addresses, essays, lectures. I. Title. II. Series: Wesley Historical Society. The Wesley Historical Society lectures ; 1975.

COLAW, Emerson S. 230'.7'6
Beliefs of a United Methodist Christian, by Emerson Colaw. [Nashville, Tidings, 1972] 133 p. 19 cm. [BX8382.2.Z5C64] 72-95656 1.00
1. United Methodist Church (United States) I. Title.

MCCUTCHEON, 230'.7'6320924 B
William John, 1928-
Essays in American theology: the life and thought of Harris Franklin Rall, by W. J. McCutcheon. New York, Philosophical Library [1973] xii, 345 p. 22 cm. Includes bibliographical references. [BX8495.R24M33] 72-190198 ISBN 0-8022-2085-1 12.50
1. Rall, Harris Franklin, 1870-1964. I. Title.

COLLINS, Judge Gould 230.78
Practical theology. New York, Comet Press Books [c. 1960] 75p. 21cm. (A Reflection book) 59-65287 2.75
1. Christian Methodist Episcopal Church—Doctrinal and controversial works. I. Title.

DIRKS, John Edward, 1919- 230.8
The critical theology of Theodore Parker. Westport, Conn., Greenwood Press [1970, c1948] viii, 173 p. port. 23 cm. (Columbia studies in American culture, no. 19) Bibliography: p. [161]-164. [BX9869.P3D5 1970] 70-100156
1. Parker, Theodore, 1810-1860. I. Title. II. Series.

HOLMES, John Haynes, 1879- 230'.8
1964.
The enduring significance of Emerson's divinity school address. [Folcroft, Pa.] Folcroft Library Editions, 1973. 32 p. 24 cm. "Delivered as the Ware lecture on May 25, 1938." "No. 349." Reprint of the 1938 ed. published by the American Unitarian Association, Boston. [BX9842.E553H64 1973] 73-9537 ISBN 0-8414-2073-6 (lib. bdg.)
1. Emerson, Ralph Waldo, 1803-1882. An address delivered before the senior class in Divinity College, Cambridge. I. American Unitarian Association. II. Title.

MENDELSOHN, Jack, 1918- 230.8
Why I am a Unitarian. New York, Nelson [1960] 214 p. 21 cm. [BX9841.M55] 60-7294
1. Unitarian churches—Doctrinal and controversial works. I. Title.

PARKER, Theodore, 1810- 230'.8
1860.
A discourse of matters pertaining to religion. New York, Arno Press, 1972 [c1842] vii, 504 p. 22 cm. (The Romantic tradition in American literature) [BX9841.P3 1972] 72-4968 ISBN 0-405-04639-1 24.00
1. Unitarianism. 2. Religion. 3. Christianity. I. Title. II. Series.

PATTERSON, Robert Leet. 230.8
The philosophy of William Ellery Channing. New York, Bookman Associates [1952] 298 p. port. 24 cm. Includes bibliographical references. [D908.C44P3] 52-12088
1. Channing, William Ellery, 1780-1842. I. Title.

PATTERSON, Robert Leet. 230'.8
The philosophy of William Ellery Channing. New York, Bookman Associates, 1952. [New York, AMS Press, 1973] 298 p. port. 23 cm. Includes bibliographical references. [B908.C44P3 1973] 76-153342 ISBN 0-404-04916-8 12.50
1. Channing, William Ellery, 1780-1842. I. Title.

SCHOLEFIELD, Harry Barron, 230.8
ed.
The Unitarian Universalist pocket guide. Boston, Beacon Press [1965] viii, 69 p. 19 cm. Bibliography: p. 63-68. [BX9841.2.S3 1965] 66-31585
1. Unitarian Universalist Association—Handbooks, manuals, etc. I. Title.

WINN, Arthur Harmon, 1874- 230.8
1949.
Beyond yesterday: to the memory of Rev. Arthur Harmon Winn, A. M., his life and character, with selections from his works. Compiled and edited by Dorothy Q. Deley. [Peterborough? N. H., c1959] 251 p. illus. 23 cm. [BX9815.W52] 60-19255
1. Unitarian churches — Collected works. 2. Theology — Collected works — 20th cent. I. Daley, Dorothy Q., ed. II. Title.

FERM, Robert L. 230'.8'0924 B
Jonathan Edwards the Younger, 1745-1801 : a colonial pastor / by Robert L. Ferm. Grand Rapids, MI : Eerdmans, c1976. 214 p. ; 23 cm. Includes index. Bibliography: p. 195-210. [BX7260.E3F4] 76-12408 ISBN 0-8028-3485-X : 7.95
1. Edwards, Jonathan, 1745-1801. I. Title.

BARTH, Karl, 1886- 230.81
Theology and church; shorter writings, 1920-1928. Translated by Louise Pettibone Smith. With an introd. by T. F. Torrance. [1st American ed.] New York, Harper & Row [1962] 358p. 22cm. Bibliographical footnotes. [BT80.B373] 62-14572
1. Theology, Doctrinal—Addresses, essays, lectures. I. Title.

*DEWEY, Robert D. 230.82
The language of faith. Illus. by Roger Martin. Philadelphia. United Church [1964, c.1963] 96p. illus. 22cm. 1.50 pap.,
I. Title.

ROBINSON, James McConkey, 230.82
1924- ed.
The later Heidegger and theology, edited by James M. Robinson [and] John B. Cobb, Jr. [1st ed.] New York, Harper & Row [1963] xii, 212 p. 22 cm. (New frontiers in theology: discussions among German and American theologians, v. 1) Bibliographical footnotes. [B3279.H49R6] 63-10506
1. Heldegger, Martin, 1889- 2. Theology, Doctrinal — 20th Cent. — Addresses, essays, lectures. I. Cobb, John B., joint ed. II. Title. III. Series.

ROBINSON, James McConkey, 230.82
1924- ed.
The later Heidegger and theology, ed. by James M. Robinson, John B. Cobb, Jr. New York, Harper [c.1963] xii, 212p. 22cm. (New frontiers in theology: discussions among German and Amer. theologians, v. 1) Bibl. 63-10506 4.50
1. Heidegger, Martin, 1889- 2. Theology, Doctrinal—20th cent.—Addresses, essays, lectures. I. Cobb, John B., joint ed. II. Title. III. Series.

JACKSON, Paul Rainey, 230.86'1
1903-
The doctrine and administration of the church, by Paul R. Jackson. Des Plaines, Ill., Regular Baptist Press [1968] 210 p. 22 cm. Rev. and enl. ed. of the author's Doctrine of the local church. Bibliography: p. 209-210. [BX6389.37.J3 1968] 68-28699 3.95
1. Regular Baptists—Doctrinal and controversial works. I. Title.

TAPP, Robert B. 230'.8'7
Religion among the Unitarian Universalists; converts in the stepfathers' house [by] Robert B. Tapp. New York, Seminar Press, 1973. xii, 268 p. 24 cm. (Quantitative studies in social relations) Bibliography: p. 257-259. [BX9841.2.T36 1973] 72-82127 ISBN 0-12-914650-1 10.00
1. Unitarian Universalist Association—Doctrinal and controversial works—Statistics. I. Title.

ROBINSON, Christine 230.893
Hinckley.
Living truths from the Doctrine and covenants. Salt Lake City, Deseret Book Co., 1961. 151p. 20cm. [BX8639.R6L5] 61-2976
1. Mormons and Mormonism— Addresses, essays, lectures. 2. Smith, Joseph, 1806-1844. Doctrine and covenants. I. Title.

ROBINSON, Christine 230.893
Hinckley
Living truths from the Doctrine and covenants. Salt Lake City, Utah, Deseret [c.] 1961. 151p. 61-2976 2.00
1. Smith, Joseph, 1805-1984. Doctrine and covenants. 2. Mormons and Mormonism—Addresses, essays, lectures. I. Title.

BRADFORD, Reed H. 230'.8'933
And they shall teach their children. Salt Lake City, Deseret Book Co., 1964. 218 p. illus. 24 cm. "Formerly published in the Instructor magazine." [BX8643.F3B7] 64-3336
1. Family — Religious life. 2. Christian life — Mormon authors. I. Title.

PETERSEN, Mark E. 230'.8'933
Adam, who is he? / Mark E. Petersen. Salt Lake City : Deseret Book Co., 1976. 96 p. ; 24 cm. Includes index. [BS580.A4P47] 76-7299 ISBN 0-87747-592-X : 4.95
1. Church of Jesus Christ of Latter-Day Saints—Doctrinal and controversial works. 2. Adam (Biblical character) I. Title.

TALMAGE, James Edward, 230'.8'933
1862-1933.
The house of the Lord; a study of holy sanctuaries, ancient and modern. Salt Lake City, Bookcraft Publishers [1962] 333 p. illus. 23 cm. [BX8643.T4T3 1962] 62-6078
1. Mormons and Mormonism. 2. Temples. I. Title.

MACKINTOSH, Charles Henry, 230'.9
1820-1896.
Short papers : reprinted from Things new and old / by C. H. Mackintosh. Sunbury, Pa. : Believers Bookshelf, c1975. 2 v. ; 21 cm. [BR85.M19 1975] 75-29527
1. Theology—Collected works—19th century. I. Things new and old. II. Title.

CHAUNCY, Charles, 1705- 230.9'1
1787.
The mystery hid from ages and generations. New York, Arno Press, 1969. xvi, 406 p. 23 cm. (Religion in America) Reprint of the 1784 ed. The authorship of Charles Chauncy is affirmed by Richard Eddy in his Universalism in America, v. 1, 1884, p. 90-93; Dict. of Amer. biog.; Brit. Mus. Gen. cat. Erroneously attributed to Isaac Chauncy by Halkett & Laing. Includes bibliographical references. [BX9940.C5 1969] 70-83414
1. Universalism. I. Chauncy, Isaac, 1632-1712. II. Title.

HUBERT, Father, O.F.M. 230.91
Cap.
Mystical love for Mary, by Father Hubert. Baltimore, Reparation Society of the Immaculate Heart of Mary [1973] ii, 59 p. 18 cm. [BT640.H8] 73-88069
1. Mary, Virgin—Motherhood (Spiritual) I. Title.

VINS, Georgii Petrovich, 2.3092B
1928-
Testament from prison / Georgi Vins ; translated by Jane Ellis ; edited by Michael Bourdeaux. Elgin, Ill. : D. C. Cook Pub. Co., c1975. 283 p. ; 18 cm. [BX6495.V5A3713]
1. Vins, Georgii Petrovich, 1928- 2. Baptists in Russia—Biography. 3. Persecution—Russia. I. Title.

BLAIR, Peter Hunter. 230'.924
The world of Bede. New York, St. Martin's Press [1971, c1970] x, 340 p. 23 cm. Bibliography: p. 310-327. [PR1578.B6 1971] 73-135524 10.00
1. Beda Venerabilis, 673-735. 2. Great Britain—History—To 1066. I. Title.

SAVON, Herve 230.924
Johann Adam Mohler, the father of modern theology. Tr. by Charles McGrath. Glen Rock, N.J., Paulist [1966] 128p. 19cm. (Deus bks.) Bibl. [BX4705.M59S33] 66-28321 .95 pap.,
1. Mohler, Johann Adam, 1796-1838. I. Title.

ANDERSON, Einar, 1909- 230'.9'3
Inside story of Mormonism. Grand Rapids, Kregel Publications [1973] 162 p. illus. 22 cm. [BX8645.A67] 72-93354 ISBN 0-8254-2111-X 2.95
1. Mormons and Mormonism—Doctrinal and controversial works. I. Title.

BARKER, James Louis, 1880- 230.93
1958.
Apostasy from the divine church. [Salt Lake City?] K. M. Barker [1960] 805p. 24cm. Includes bibliography. [BX8635.2.B3] 60-32793
1. Mormons and Mormonism—Doctrinal and controversial works. 2. Church history. I. Title.

BARNES, Kathleen H. 230'.9'3
Today I saw a prophet / Kathleen H. Barnes & Virginia H. Pearce. Salt Lake City : Deseret Book Co., c1977. 30 p. : col. ill. ; 26 cm. Identifies Biblical prophets from Moses to Peter, explains the role of prophet and lists the men who have served in this capacity for the Church of Jesus Christ of Latter-Day Saints. [BX8643.P7B37] 77-4986 ISBN 0-87747-646-2 : 4.95
1. Prophets (Mormonism)—Juvenile literature. 2. Prophets—Juvenile literature. I. Pearce, Virginia H., joint author. II. Title.

BERRETT, William Edwin. 230.93
Teachings of the Doctrine and covenants. Salt Lake City, Deseret Book Co., 1956. 280p. 24cm. Bibliographical footnotes. [BX8628.B4] 57-640

1. Smith, Joseph, 1805-1844. Doctrine and covenants. I. Title.

BERRETT, William Edwin. 230.93
Teachings of the Doctrine and covenants. Salt Lake City, Deseret Book Co., 1956. 289p. 24cm. Bibliographical footnotes. [BX8628.B4] 57-640
1. Smith, Joseph, 1805-1844. Doctrine and covenants. I. Title.

BUDVARSON, Arthur 230.93
The Book of Mormon, true or false? Grand Rapids, Mich., Zondervan [1961, c.1959] 63p. illus. 61-66230 1.00 pap.,
1. Book of Mormon. 2. Mormons and Mormonism—Doctrinal and controversial works. I. Title.

BURTON, Alma P. 1913- 230.93
Understanding the things of God [by] Alma P. Burton. 1st ed. Salt Lake City, Deseret, 1966. x, 206p. 24cm. [BX8635.2.B8] 66-20704 2.95
1. Mormons and Mormonism—Doctrinal and controversial works. I. Title.

CANNON, George Quayle, 1827-1901. 230.93
Gospel truth; discourses and writings. Selected, arr. and edited by Jerreld L. Newquist. [Salt Lake City] Zion's Book Store, 1957- v. illus. 24cm. [BX8609.C29] 57-35445
1. Mormons and Mormonism—Collected works. I. Title.

CANNON, George Quayle, 1827-1901. 230'.9'3
Gospel truth; discourses and writings of president George Q. Cannon. Selected, arr., and edited by Jerreld L. Newquist. [2d ed.] [Salt Lake City] Deseret Book Co., 1974- c1957- v. 24 cm. [BX8609.C292] 74-165262 ISBN 0-87747-519-9 4.95 (v. 1)
1. Mormons and Mormonism—Collected works. I. Newquist, Jerreld L., ed. II. Title.

CHEVILLE, Roy Arthur, 1897- 230.93
By what authority? A series of lectures delivered to the Melchisedec priesthood of Independence, Missouri, January 8-13, 1956. Reorganized Church of Jesus Christ of Latter Day Saints. [Independence] Herald House [c1956] 96p. 21cm. [BX8674.C48] 56-12878
1. Reorganized Church of Jesus Christ of Latter-Day Saints—Doctrinal and controversial works. 2. Authority (Religion) I. Title.

CHEVILLE, Roy Arthur, 1897- 230.93
The field of theology; an introductory study. [Independence, Mo.] Dept. of Religious Education, Reorganized Church of Jesus Christ of Latter Day Saints [1959] 144p. 21cm. (Restoration theology series) [BX8674.C5] 59-11403
1. Reorganized Church of Jesus Christ of Latter-Day Saints— Doctrinal and controversial works. 2. Theology. I. Title.

DE JONG, Gerrit, 1892- 230.93
Greater dividends from religion; a discussion of the practicality of some religious teachings of a peculiar people. Foreword by Milton Bennion. Salt Lake City, Deseret Book Co. [1950] 137 p. 23 cm. [BX8635.D4] 51-696
1. Mormons and Mormonism—Doctrinal and controversial works. I. Title.

DOXEY, Roy Watkins, 1908- 230.93
The Doctrine and convenants and the future. [Salt Lake City] Desert Book Co., 1954. 96p. 20cm. [BX8628.D68] 54-38486
1. Smith, Joseph, 1805-1844. Doctrine and covenants. 2. Eachatology. I. Title.

DOXEY, Roy Watkins, 1908- 230'.93
The Word of Wisdom today / Roy W. Doxey. Salt Lake City : Deseret Book Co., c1975. x,142 p. ; 24 cm. Includes index. Bibliography: p. 136-138. [BX8629.W6D68] 75-26334 ISBN 0-87747-571-7 : 4.95
1. Word of wisdom. I. Title.

DOXEY, Roy Watkins, 1908- 230'.93
The Word of Wisdom today / Roy W. Doxey. Salt Lake City : Deseret Book Co., c1975. x,142 p. ; 24 cm. Includes index. Bibliography: p. 136-138. [BX8629.W6D68] 75-26334 ISBN 0-87747-571-7 : 4.95
1. Word of wisdom. I. Title.

DYER, Alvin Rulon. 230.9'3
The meaning of truth, by Alvin R. Dyer. [Rev. ed.] Salt Lake City, Deseret Book Co., 1961 [i.e. 1970] 199 p. illus., maps (part col.), ports. 24 cm. 1961-62 ed. published under title: The day of the gentile. Contains three articles: The day of the gentile, The meaning of truth, and The kingdom of evil. Includes bibliographical references. [BX8635.2.D923 1970] 72-130324 4.95
1. Mormons and Mormonism—Doctrinal and controversial works. 2. Demonology. I. Title.

DYER, Alvin Rulon 230.93
Who am I? A sequel volume to This age of confusion. Revealed answers to whence am I? Who am I? and whither am I going? Salt Lake City, Deseret 1966. xxix, 589p. port. 24cm. Bibl. [BX8635.2.D93] 66-21408 5.95
1. Mormons and Mormonism—Doctrinal and controversial works. 2. Man (Theology) I. Title.

FOUNTAIN, J. O., Jr. 230.93
The restitution of all things. New York, Vantage [c.1963] 67p. 21cm. 2.50 bds.,
I. Title.

FRASER, Gordon Holmes. 230'.9'3
Is Mormonism Christian? / By Gordon H. Fraser. Chicago : Moody Press, c1977. p. cm. A consolidation and revision of the author's 1965 ed. of Is Mormonism Christian? and 1964 ed. of What does the Book of Mormon teach? Bibliography: p. [BX8645.F73] 77-6227 ISBN 0-8024-4169-6 pbk. : 1.75
1. Mormons and Mormonism—Controversial literature. I. Fraser, Gordon Holmes. What does the Book of Mormon teach? II. Title.

FRASER, Gordon Holmes. 230'.9'3
Is Mormonism Christian? / By Gordon H. Fraser. Chicago : Moody Press, c1977. p. cm. A consolidation and revision of the author's 1965 ed. of Is Mormonism Christian? and 1964 ed. of What does the Book of Mormon teach? Bibliography: p. [BX8645.F73] 77-6227 ISBN 0-8024-4169-6 pbk. : 1.75
1. Mormons and Mormonism—Controversial literature. I. Fraser, Gordon Holmes. What does the Book of Mormon teach? II. Title.

GREEN, Forace, comp. 230.93
Testimonies of our leaders, compiled and rev. by Forace Green. Salt Lake City, Bookcraft, 1958. 336p. illus. 23cm. [BX8637.G83] 59-24140
1. Momons and Mormonism— Doctrinal and controversial works. I. Title.

HARTSHORN, Chris B. 230.93
Prophetic guidance to the Church of Jesus Christ: selections from the book of Doctrine and Covenants; selected, arranged by Chris B. Hartshorn, Fred L. Young, Paul A. Wellington [Independence, Mo., Herald House c.1962] 56p. 17cm. .50 pap.,
I. Title.

HILTON, Lynn M 230.93
A concordance of the Pearl of great price. [Provo, Utah] Brigham Young University, Extension Publications] c1961. iv, 91p. 28cm. [BX8629.P6H5] 61-59897
1. Smith, Joseph, 1805-1844. Pearl of great price—Concordances. I. Title.

HOLMES, Reed M 230.93
Seek this Christ; the Reorganized Church of Jesus Christ of Latter Day Saints. [Independence, Mo., Herald Pub. House, 1954] 112p. 18cm. [BX8671.H6] 54-11778
1. Reorganized Church of Jesus Christ of Latter-Day Saints—Doctrinal and controversial works. I. Title.

THE Instructor (Salt Lake City) 230.93
Our prophets and principles; writings on our Articles of faith and prophets who made them live. Salt Lake City [1956] 172p. illus. 24cm. [BX8693.I5] 56-2876
1. Mormons and Mormonism—Biog. 2. Smith, Joseph, 1805-1844. The pearl of great price. 3. Apostles. I. Title.

JENSEN, Nephi, 1876- 230.93
The world's greatest need: salvation from the evils of the world through the restored saving power of Jesus Christ. Salt Lake City, Deseret News Press, 1950. xi, 216 p. 20 cm. [BX8635.J4] 51-18539
1. Mormons and Mormonism—Doctrinal and controversial works. I. Title.

JEPSON, Winston F. 230'.93
The plan of salvation, by Winston F. Jepson and Richard T. White. Salt Lake City, Utah, Distributed by Hawkes Publications [1973] 432 p. illus. 22 cm. Includes bibliographical references. [BX8635.2.J46] 73-76888 5.95
1. Church of Jesus Christ of Latter-Day Saints—Doctrinal and controversial works. I. White, Richard T., joint author. II. Title.

JONAS, Larry W. 230.93
Mormon claims examined. Grand Rapids, Mich., Baker Book House, 1961. 85p. 61-4439 1.00 pap.,
1. Mormons and Mormonism—Doctrinal and controversial works. I. Title.

JOURNAL of discourses digest / compiled by Joseph Fielding McConkie. Salt Lake City : Bookcraft, c1975- v. ; 24 cm. Includes index. [BX8639.A1J682] 75-29769 ISBN 0-88494-290-2 (v. 1) : 6.95 (v. 1) 230'.9'3
1. Mormons and Mormonism—Addresses, essays, lectures. I. McConkie, Joseph F.

JOURNAL of discourses digest / compiled by Joseph Fielding McConkie. Salt Lake City : Bookcraft, c1975- v. ; 24 cm. Includes index. [BX8639.A1J682] 75-29769 ISBN 0-88494-290-2 (v. 1) : 6.95 (v. 1) 230'.9'3
1. Mormons and Mormonism—Addresses, essays, lectures. I. McConkie, Joseph F.

LEE, Harold B., 1899- 230'.9'3
Stand ye in holy places; selected sermons and writings of president Harold B. Lee. Salt Lake City, Deseret Book Co., 1974. 398 p. port. 24 cm. [BX8609.L43] 74-77591 ISBN 0-87747-526-1 5.95
1. Mormons and Mormonism—Collected works. I. Title.

LUNDSTROM, Harold, comp. 230.93
Motherhood, a partnership with God. Salt Lake City, Bookcraft [1956] 348p. 24cm. [BX8641.L8] 56-57282
1. Mormons and Mormonism—Doctrinal and controversial works. 2. Mothers— Religious life. I. Title.

LUNDWALL, Nels Benjamin, 1884- comp. 230.93
Masterpieces of Latter-Day Saint leaders; a compilation of discourses and writings of prominent leaders of the Church of Jesus Christ of Latter-Day Saints. Salt Lake City, Deseret Book Co. [1954, c1953] 151p. 24cm. [BX8635.L8] 54-20749
1. Mormons and Mormonism— Doctrinal and controversial works. I. Title.

MCCONKIE, Bruce R 230.93
Mormon doctrine. Salt Lake City, Bookcraft, 1958. 776p. 24cm. [BX8605.5.M3] 58-10837
1. Mormons and Mormonism— Dictionaries. I. Title.

MCCONKIE, Bruce R. 230.9'3
Mormon doctrine, by Bruce R. McConkie. 2d ed. Salt Lake City, Bookcraft, 1966. 856 p. 24 cm. [BX8605.5.M3 1966] 67-2237
1. Mormons and Mormonism—Dictionaries. I. Title.

MCMURRIN, Sterling M. 230.93
The Theological foundations of the Mormon religion. Salt Lake City, Univ. of Utah Pr. [c.1965] 151p. 21cm. Bibl. [BX8635.2.M3] 65-26131 3.00; 2.00 pap.,
1. Mormons and Mormonism—Doctrinal and controversial works. I. Title.

MORGAN, Stephen G., 1940- 230.9'3
Are you Mormons ignoramuses? By Stephen G. Morgan. [Salt Lake City] N. G. Morgan, Sr. [1966] xviii, 256 p. illus., map, port. 24 cm. [BX8635.2.M6] 67-2016
1. Mormons and Mormonism—Doctrinal and controversial works. I. Title.

OAKMAN, Arthur A. 230.93
God's spiritual universe. Independence, Mo., Herald House [c.1961] 188p. Bibl. 61-9684 2.50
1. Reorganized Church of Jesus Christ of Latter-Day Saints—Doctrinal and controversial works. I. Title.

PEARSON, Glenn Laurentz. 230.93
Know your religion. Salt Lake City, Bookcraft [1961] 248p. 24cm. [BX8635.2.P4] 61-30602
1. Mormons and Mormonism—Doctrinal and controversial works. I. Title.

RALSTON, Russell F. 230.93
Fundamental differences between the Reorganized Church and the Church in Utah; a series of lects. delivered to the Melchisedec priesthood of Independence, Mo., Jan. 4-11, 1959, Reorganized Church of Jesus Christ of Latter Day Saints [Rev. ed. Independence, Mo.] Herald House, 1963. 328p. 21cm. Bibl. 63-25860 price unreported
1. Reorganized Church of Jesus Christ of Latter-Day Saints—Doctrinal and controversial works. 2. Mormons and Mormonism—Doctrinal and controversial works. I. Title.

REORGANIZED Church of Jesus Christ of Latter Day Saints. 230.93
Book of doctrine and covenants. Enl. and improved ed. Independence, Mo., Herald Pub. House, 1952. 380, 39 p. 19 cm. "Contains a historical preface for each revelation or section." [BX8628.A4 1952] 52-43442
I. Title. II. Title: Doctrine and covenants.

RICHARDS, Claude. 230.93
The temple letters; a rewarding path to happiness on earth and everlasting treasures in heaven. Salt Lake City, Deseret Book Co., 1956. 198p. illus. 24cm. [BX8638.R5] 56-30631
1. Mormons and Mormonism—Doctrinal and controversial works. I. Title.

RICKS, Eldin. 230.93
The case of the Book of Mormon witnesses. [1st ed.] Salt Lake City, Olympus Pub. Co. [c1961] 77 p. 19 cm. Bibliographical footnotes. [BX8627.R46] 64-26091
1. Book of Mormon — Evidences, authority, etc. I. Title.

SMITH, Joseph, 1805-1844. 230.93
Discourses. Compiled and arr. by Alma P. Burton. 1st ed. Salt Lake City, Deseret Book Co., 1956. 237p. illus. 24cm. [BX8621.S5] 57-17601
1. Mormons and Mormonism—Doctrinal and controversial works. I. Title.

SMITH, Joseph, 1805-1844. 230.93
Discourses. Compiled and arr. by Alma P. Burton. 1st ed. Salt Lake City, Descret Book Co., 1956. 237 p. illus. 24 cm. [BX8621.S5] 57-17601
1. Mormons and Mormonism — Doctrinal and controversial works. I. Title.

SMITH, Joseph, 1805-1844. 230.93
Discourses. Compiled and arr. by Alma P. Burton. 3d ed., Rev and enl. Salt Lake City, Deseret Bolk Co., 1965. viii, 280 p. col. port. 27 cm. [BX8621.S5 1965] 65-29687
1. Mormons and Mormonism — Doctrinal and controversial works. I. Burton, Alma P., 1913- comp. II. Title.

SMITH, Joseph, 1805-1844. 230.9'3
Doctrine and covenants of the Church of the Latter Day Saints: carefully selected from the revelations of God, and compiled by Joseph Smith, Jr. [and others] Kirtland, Ohio, Printed by F. G. Williams, 1835. [Independence, Mo., Herald House, 1971] 257, xxv p. 16 cm. [BX8628.A3 1971] 77-26627 ISBN 0-8309-0041-1
1. Mormons and Mormonism—Doctrinal and controversial works. I. Church of Jesus Christ of Latter-Day Saints. II. Title.

SMITH, Joseph, 1805-1844. 230.93
Lectures on faith, delivered in Kirtland Temple in 1834 and 1835; with the revelation on the Rebellion as an appendix. Independence, Mo., Herald House, 1952 [i.e. 1953] 56p. illus. 20cm. 'These lectures were published as part one of the first edition (1835) of the Book of doctrine and covenants.' [BX8628.A4 1953] 53-32190
1. Mormons and Mormonism—Doctrinal and controversial works. 2. Faith. I. Title.

SMITH, Joseph Fielding, 1876- 230.93
Answers to gospel questions. Salt Lake City, Deseret Book Co. [1957- v. 23cm. [BX8638.S48] 57-29432
1. Mormons and Mormonism—Doctrinal and controversial works. 2. Questions and answers—Theology. I. Title.

SMITH, Joseph Fielding, 1876- 230.93
Answers to gospel questions. Salt Lake City, Deseret Book Co. [1957- v. 23 cm. [BX8638.S48] 57-29432
1. Mormons and Mormonism — Doctrinal and controversial works. 2. Questions and answers — Theology. I. Title.

SMITH, Joseph Fielding, 1876- 230.93
Doctrines of salvation: sermons and writings. Compiled by Bruce R. McConkie. Salt Lake City, Bookcraft [c1954-56] 3v. port. 24cm. Bibliographical footnotes. [BX8609.S63] 56-34495
1. Mormons and Mormonism—Collected works. I. Title.

SMITH, Joseph Fielding, 1876- 230.93
Doctrines of salvation; sermons and writings. Compiled by Bruce R. McConkie. Salt Lake City, Bookcraft [c1954-56] 3 v. port. 24 cm. Bibliographical footnotes. [BX8609.S63] 56-34495
1. Mormons and Mormonism — Collected works. I. Title.

SMITH, Joseph Fielding, 1876- 230.93
Elijah the prophet and his mission. Salt Lake City, Deseret Book Co., 1957. 123p. 20cm. [BX8638.S484] 57-31389
1. Elijah, the prophet. 2. Mormons and Mormonism—Doctrinal and controversial works. I. Title.

SMITH, Joseph Fielding, 1876- 230.93
Elijah the prophet and his mission. Salt Lake City, Deseret Book Co., 1957. 123 p. 20 cm. [BX8638.S484] 57-31389
1. Elijah, the prophet. 2. Mormons and Mormonism — Doctrinal and controversial works. I. Title.

SMITH, Joseph Fielding, 1913- 230.93
Religious truths defined; a comparison of religious faiths with the restored gospel. Salt Lake City, Bookcraft [1959] 411 p. 24 cm. [BX8635.2.S55] 59-48894
1. Mormons and Mormonism — Doctrinal and controversial works. I. Title.

SPERRY, Sidney Branton, 1895- 230.93
Problems of the Book of Mormon. Salt Lake City, Bookcraft [1964] 253 p. 24 cm. Includes bibliographical references. [BX8627.S77] 64-3036
1. Book of Mormon. I. Title.

STARKS, Arthur E 1911- 230.93
A complete concordance to the doctrine and covenants. Independence, Mo., Herald Pub. House, 1951. 212 p. 23 cm. [BX8628.S8] 51-4179
1. Smith, Joseph, 1805-1844. Doctrine and convenants — Concordances. I. Title.

STEWART, Ora (Pate) 1910- 230.93
A letter to my son. [3d ed.] Salt Lake City, Bookcraft [1951] 109p. 17cm. [BX8643.Y6S7 1951] 54-31772
1. Mormons and Mormonism—Doctrinal and controversial works. 2. Young men—Religious life. 3. Sexual ethics. I. Title.

STILSON, Max. 230.93
How to deal with Mormons. Grand Rapids, Zondervan Pub. House [1965] 61 p. 21 cm. Bibliography: p. 61-62. [BX8645.S7] 64-15557
1. Mormons and Mormonism — Doctrinal and controversial works. I. Title.

UNOPULOS, James J., 1919- 230'.93'
Reasoning, fevelation, and you! 'Project Temple' principles of sMormons and Mormonism--Doctrinal and controversial works. [Bx8635.2.U5] 67-21352
I. Title.

WIDTSOE, John Andreas, 1872-1952. 230.93
Evidences and reconciliations. Arr. by G. Homer Durham. Salt Lake City, Bookcraft [1960] 412 p. 24 cm. [BX8635.W582] 60-29867
1. Mormons and Mormonism — Doctrinal and controversial works. I. Title.

YARN, David H. 230.93
The Gospel: God, man, and truth [by] David H. Yarn. Salt Lake City, Deseret, 1965. viii, 211p. 24cm. [BX8635.2.Y3] 65-18575 price unreported
1. Mormons and Mormonism—Doctrinal and controversial works. I. Title.

ANDRUS, Hyrum Leslie, 1924- 230.9'3'0924
Foundations of the millennial kingdom of Christ [by] Hyrum L. Andrus. Salt Lake City, Bookcraft, 1968- v. 24 cm. Contents.—v. 1. God, man, and the universe.—v. 2. Principles of perfection.—v. 3. Doctrines of the kingdom. Bibliographical footnotes. [BX8635.2.A5] 68-56891 5.95 (v. 1)
1. Smith, Joseph, 1805-1844. 2. Mormons and Mormonism—Doctrinal and controversial works. I. Title.

BENSON, Ezra Taft. 230'.9'33
God, family, country : our three great loyalties / Ezra Taft Benson. Salt Lake City : Deseret Book Co., 1974. ix, 422 p., [1] leaf of plates : col. port. ; 24 cm. Includes bibliographical references and index. [BX8635.2.B43] 74-84477 pbk. : 4.95
1. Church of Jesus Christ of Latter-Day Saints—Doctrinal and controversial works. 2. Family. 3. Patriotism. I. Title.

BURTON, Theodore M. 230'.9'33
God's greatest gift / Theodore M. Burton. Salt Lake City : Deseret Book Co., 1976. ix, 291 p. ; 24 cm. Includes index. [BX8635.2.B83] 76-25324 ISBN 0-87747-617-9 : 5.95
1. Church of Jesus Christ of Latter-Day Saints—Doctrinal and controversial works. 2. Future life. I. Title.

DELAPP, G. Leslie. 230'.9'33
In the world ... By G. Leslie DeLapp. [Independence, Mo., Herald Pub. House, 1973] 250 p. 21 cm. Includes bibliographical references. [BX8678.D44A34] 73-75884 ISBN 0-8309-0099-3 6.95
1. DeLapp, G. Leslie. 2. Reorganized Church of Jesus Christ of Latter-Day Saints—Doctrinal and controversial works. I. Title.

JUDD, Peter A., 1943- 230'.9'33
An introduction to the Saints Church : including user's guide / by Peter A. Judd and A. Bruce Lindgren. Independence, Mo. : Christian Education Office, Reorganized Church of Jesus Christ of Latter Day Saints, c1976. 228, 108 p. ; 21 cm. Includes bibliographical references and index. [BX8674.J82] 75-35763 ISBN 0-8309-0154-X
1. Reorganized Church of Jesus Christ of Latter Day Saints—Doctrinal and controversial works. I. Lindgren, A. Bruce, joint author. II. Title.

MARTIN, George Vivian, 1897- 230'.9'33
Revelation is for everyone / by George V. Martin. Salt Lake City : Martin Pub. Co., [1974- v. ; 29 cm. [BX8635.2.M35] 75-301781
1. Church of Jesus Christ of Latter-Day Saints—Doctrinal and controversial works. I. Title.

MAXWELL, Neal A. 230'.9'33
Deposition of a disciple / Neal A. Maxwell. Salt Lake City : Deseret Book Co., 1977 104 p. ; 24 cm. Includes index. [BX8637.M42] 76-50477 3.95
1. Church of Jesus Christ of Latter-Day Saints—Doctrinal and controversial works. 2. Christian life—Mormon authors. I. Title.

PEARL of Great Price Symposium, Brigham Young University, 1975. 230'.9'33
Pearl of Great Price Symposium : a centennial presentation, November 22, 1975 / sponsored by the Department of Ancient Scripture. 1st ed. Provo, Utah : Brigham Young University, 1976. iii leaves, 103 p. ; 28 cm. Includes bibliographical references. [BX8629.P5P4 1975] 76-370968 pbk. : 2.00
1. Smith, Joseph, 1805-1844. The pearl of great price—Congresses. 2. Mormons and Mormonism—Doctrinal and controversial works—Congresses. I. Brigham Young University, Provo, Utah. Dept. of Ancient Scripture.

PETERSEN, Mark E. 230'.9'33
The way of the Master / Mark E. Petersen. Salt Lake City, : Bookcraft, 1974. 186 p. ; 24 cm. Includes index. [BX8635.2.P47] 74-19505 ISBN 0-88494-271-6 : 3.95
1. Church of Jesus Christ of Latter-Day Saints—Doctrinal and controversial works. I. Title.

REORGANIZED Church of Jesus Christ of Latter-Day Saints. Committee on Basic Beliefs. 230.93'3
Exploring the faith; a series of studies in the faith of the Church, prepared by a Committee on Basic Beliefs. [Independence, Mo., Herald Pub. House, 1970] 248 p. 21 cm. Includes bibliographical references. [BX8674.R43] 76-101570
1. Reorganized Chruch of Jesus Christ of Latter-Day Saints—Doctrinal and controversial works. I. Title.

REORGANIZED Church of Jesus Christ of Latter-Day Saints. Dept. of Religious Education. 230.933
Facing today's frontiers; a foundational guide to the theological thinking of older youth, young adults and adults in the Reorganized Church of Jesus Christ of Latter Day Saints. Ed. by the Dept. of Religious Educ. [Independence, Mo.] Herald House [c.]1965 112p. 21cm. [BX8610.A493] 65-21327 1.50 bds.,
1. Religious education—Text-books for young people—Mormon. I. Title.

REORGANIZED CHURCH OF JESUS CHRIST OF LATTER-DAY SAINTS. DEPT. OF RELIGIOUS EDUCATION. 230.933
Facing today's frontiers: a foundational guide to the theological thinking of older youth, young adults, and adults in the Reorganized Church of Jesus Christ of Latter Day Saints. Edited by the Dept. of Religious Education. [Independence, Mo.] Herald House, 1965. 112 p. 21 cm. [BX8610.A493] 65-21327
1. Religious education — Text-books for young people — Mormon. I. Title.

RICHARDS, Le Grand, Bp., 1886- 230'.9'33
A marvelous work and a wonder / LeGrand Richards. Rev. and enl. ed. Salt Lake City : Deseret Book Co., 1976. xiv, 424 p. ; 18 cm. Includes bibliographical references and index. [BX8635.2.R52 1976] 76-2237 ISBN 0-87747-161-4 pbk. : 1.50
1. Mormons and Mormonism—Doctrinal and controversial works. I. Title.

SMITH, Mildred Nelson. 230'.93'3
The Master's touch; true stories of a seventy's ministry. [Independence, Mo., Herald Pub. House, 1973] 272 p. 21 cm. [BX8678.S55S64] 73-75883 ISBN 0-8309-0091-8 5.95
1. Smith, Delbert Deane, 1922- 2. Reorganized Church of Jesus Christ of Latter Day Saints—Doctrinal and controversial works. I. Title.

SPENCER, Geoffrey F. 230'.9'33
The burning bush : revelation and Scripture in the life of the church / by Geoffrey F. Spencer. Independence, Mo. : Herald Pub. House, [1975] 224 p. : ill. ; 27 cm. Adapted from the author's We have these books. Includes bibliographical references. [BX8672.S67] 74-84762 ISBN 0-8309-0129-9
1. Bible—Study—Text-books. 2. Religious education—Text-books—Reorganized Church of Jesus Christ of Latter-Day Saints. 3. Revelation—Study and teaching. I. Title.

STORIES of insight and inspiration / compiled by Margie Calhoun Jensen. Salt Lake City : Bookcraft, 1976. xiv, 233 p. ; 24 cm. Includes index. [BX8608.S77] 76-5174 ISBN 0-88494-296-1 : 4.95 230'.9'33
1. Church of Jesus Christ of Latter-Day Saints—Collected works. I. Jensen, Margie Calhoun.

TO the glory of God; 230'.93'3
Mormon essays on great issues—environment—commitment—love—peace—youth—man. Contributors: Hugh W. Nibley [and others] Salt Lake City, Deseret Book Co., 1972. xi, 234 p. 24 cm. Includes bibliographical references. [BX8639.A1T6] 72-78244 ISBN 0-87747-475-3 4.95
1. Mormons and Mormonism—Addresses, essays, lectures. I. Nibley, Hugh, 1910-

TURNER, Rodney. 230'.93'3
Woman and the priesthood. Salt Lake City, Deseret Book Co., 1972. 333 p. 24 cm. Includes bibliographical references. [BX8641.T87] 72-90345 ISBN 0-87747-487-7 4.95
1. Women in Mormonism.

UNOPULOS, James J., 1919- 230'.93'3
Reasoning, revelation, and you- Project Temple principles of [BX8635.2.U5] 67-21352
I. Title.

WELLINGTON, Paul A. 230'.9'33
Readings on concepts of Zion, edited by Paul A. Wellington. [Independence, Mo., Herald Pub. House, 1973] 316 p. 21 cm. Includes bibliographical references. [BX8674.W44] 73-81076 ISBN 0-8309-0102-7 7.95
1. Reorganized Church of Jesus Christ of Latter-Day Saints—Doctrinal and controversial works. I. Title. II. Title: Concepts of Zion.

ZOBELL, Albert L comp. 230'.9'33
The joy that endures. Salt Lake City, Deseret Book Co., 1963. 96 p. 16 cm. [BX8608.5.Z62] 63-4967
1. Mormons and Mormonism — Quotations, maxims, etc. I. Title.

ZOBELL, Albert L comp. 230'.9'33
Words of life; continuing moments with the prophets. [Salt Lake City] Deseret Book Co., 1961. 112 p. 16 cm. [BX8608.Z65] 62-1135
1. Mormons and Mormonism. 2. Aphorisms and apothegms. I. Title.

BARNITZ, Harry W. 230.9'4
Existentialism and the new Christianity; a comparative study of existentialism and Swedenborgianism: towards a new universal synthesis, by Harry W. Barnitz. New York, Philosophical Library [1969] xx, 509 p. 23 cm. Includes bibliographical references. [BX8721.2.B3] 69-14353 10.00
1. New Jerusalem Church—Doctrinal and controversial works. I. Title.

KELLER, Helen Adams 230.94
My religion. New York, Avon c.1927, 1960 157p. 17cm. (Bard bk. 7; Avon bk. T-07) .35 pap.,
I. Title.

MAHIN, R. Newton. 230.94
From Swedenborg; an outline of Emanuel Swedenborg's Latin testament. [1st ed.] New York, Greenwich Book Publishers [1959] 120p. 21cm. [BX8711.M32] 59-12046
1. Swedenborg, Emanuel, 1688-1772. I. Title.

MAHIN, R. Newton. 230.94
Palewings... Based on Emanuel Swedenborg's revelation of an internal of the Word. Boston, Meador Pub. Co. [1956] 524p. 21cm. [BX8711.M33] 56-25041
1. Swendenborg, Emanuel, 1688-1772. I. Title.

ODHNER, Hugo Ljungberg, 1891- 230.94
Spirits and men; some essays on the influence of spirits upon men, as described in the writings of Emanuel Swedenbord. Bryn Athyn, Pa., Academy Books Room [1958] 227p. 20cm. [BX8711.O3] 58-48845
1. Swedenborg, Emanuel, 1688-1772. I. Title.

SPALDING, John Howard. 230'.9'4
Introduction to Swedenborg's religious thought / John Howard Spalding. New York : Swedenborg Pub. Association, 1977. 235 p. ; 18 cm. First published in 1916 under title: The kingdom of heaven as seen by Swedenborg; rev. and condensed in 1956 by R. H. Tafel. [BX8721.S692] 77-78682 ISBN 0-87785-121-2 pbk. : 1.50
1. Swedenborg, Emmanuel, 1688-1772. 2. New Jerusalem Church—Doctrinal and controversal works. I. Tafel, Richard H. II. Title.

SWEDENBORG, Emanuel, 1688- 230.9'4
The four doctrines . . . English tr. by John Faulkner Potts. Newly ed. by Alice Spiers Sechrist. New York, Swedenborg Found., 1967. 329p. 18cm. [BX8712.D8 1967] 67-1465 1.00 pap.,
1. New Jerusalem Church—Doctrinal and controversial works. I. Sechrist, Alice Spiers, ed. II. Title.
Contents omitted.

SWEDENBORG, Emanuel, 1688-1772. 230.94
Angelic wisdom concerning the divine love and the divine wisdom. Translation by John C. Ager. New York, Swedenborg Foundation, 1962. xvi, 313 p. 18 cm. On cover: Divine love and wisdom. [BX8712.D4 1962] 63-1052
1. Providence and government of God — Early works to 1800. I. Title. II. Title: Divine love and wisdom.

SWEDENBORG, Emanuel, 1688-1772 230.94
Angelic wisdom concerning the divine love and the divine wisdom. Tr. by John C. Ager. New York, Swedenborg, 1962. xvi, 313p. 18cm. On cover: Divine love and wisdom. 63-1052 .50 pap.,
1. Providence and government of God—Early works to 1800. I. Title. II. Title: Divine love and wisdom.

SWEDENBORG, Emanuel, 1688-1772. 230'.9'4
A compendium of the theological writings of Emanuel Swedenborg / [selected by] Samuel M. Warren. New York : Swedenborg Foundation, 1974. xl, 776 p. ; 23 cm. Reprint of the 1875 ed., with new introd. Includes bibliographical references and index. [BX8711.A7W3 1974] 73-94196 ISBN 0-87785-123-9 : 4.50
1. New Jerusalem Church—Doctrinal and controversial works. I. Warren, Samuel Mills, comp.

SWEDENBORG, Emanuel, 1688-1772. 230.94
A dictionary of correspondence, representatives, and significatives, derived from the Word of the Lord. Extracted from the writings of Emanuel Swedenborg. New York, Swedenborg Foundation, 1962. 453 p. 20 cm. (A Book for Bible readers) "Second photo offset reprint of the thirteenth edition (1931)" Principally an abridgment, by Charles Bolles, of "A new and comprehensive dictionary of correspondence, representatives, and significatives, contained in the World of the Lord . . . Faithfully extracted from all the theological works of the Hon. Emanuel Swedenborg . . . by George Nicholson." [VX8711.A7N4 1962] 62-53179
1. Swedenborg, Emanual, 1688-1772 — Dictionaries, indexes, etc. 2. Correspondence, Doctrine of. I. Nicholson, George, d. 1819. II. Bolles, Charles. 1802-1854. III. Title.

SWEDENBORG, Emanuel, 1688-1772 230.94
A dictionary of correspondence, representatives, and significatives, derived from the Word of the Lord. Extracted from the writings of Emanuel Swedenborg. New York, 150 Fifth, Swedenborg Found. 1962. 453p. 20cm. (Bk. for Bible readers) 62-53179 2.00
1. Correspondence, Dictrine of. 2. Correspondence, Doctrine of. I. Nicholson, George, d. 1819. II. Bolles, Charles, 1802-1854. III. Title.

SWEDENBORG, Emanuel, 1688-1772. 230.9'4
The four doctrines... English translation by John Faulkner Potts. Newly edited by Alice Spiers Sechrist. New York, Swedenborg Foundation, 1967. 329 p. 18 cm. Contents.Contents. -- The doctrine of the Lord for the New Jerusalem. -- The Doctrine of the Sacred Scripture for the New Jerusalem. -- The doctrine of life for the New Jerusalem. -- The doctrine of faith for the New Jerusalem. [BX8712.D8 1967] 67-1465
1. New Jerusalem Church — Doctrinal and controversial works. I. Sechrist, Alice Spiers, ed. II. Title.

SWEDENBORG, Emanuel, 1688-1772. 230'.9'4
The four doctrines : the Lord, Sacred Scripture, life, faith / by Emanuel Swedenborg ; English translation by John Faulkner Potts ; edited by Alice Spiers Sechrist. New York : Swedenborg Foundation, 1976. 328 p. ; 18 cm.

Translation of Doctrina Novae Hierosolymae de Domino, Doctrina Novae Hierosolymae de Scriptura Sacra, Doctrina Novae Hierosolymae de fide, and Doctrina vitae pro Noya Hierosolyma ex praeceptis decalogi. [BX8711.A25 1976] 76-151239 ISBN 0-87785-064-X pbk. : 1.25
1. New Jerusalem Church—Doctrinal and controversial works. 2. Theology—Collected works—18th century. I. Title.

SWEDENBORG, Emanuel, 1688-1772. 230'.94
The four leading doctrines of the New Church, signified by the New Jerusalem in the revelation: being those concerning the Lord, the Sacred Scripture, faith, and life. New York, American Swedenborg Print. and Pub. Society, 1882. [New York, AMS Press, 1971] 247 p. 22 cm. Translations of Doctrina Novae Hierosolymae de Domino, Doctrina Novae Hierosolymae de Scriptura Sacra, Doctrina Novae Hierosolymae de fide, and Doctrina vitae pro Nova Hierosolyma ex praeceptis decalogi. [BX8711.A25 1971] 71-134426 ISBN 0-404-08466-4
1. New Jerusalem Church—Doctrinal and controversial works. 2. Theology—Collected works—18th century. I. Title.

SWEDENBORG, Emanuel, 1688-1772 230.94
The true Christian religion, containing the universal theology of the New Church, foretold by the Lord in Daniel VII. 13, 14; and in Revelation XXI. 1, 2. 2v. Tr. from Latin ed. [by John C. Ager] Standard ed. New York, Swedenborg Found., 1963. 2.v. (588; 510p.) 21cm. 63-1799 ea., 3.50; text ed., ea., 2.50
1. New Jerusalem Church—Doctrinal and controversial works. 2. Theology, Doctrinal. I. Title.

VAN DUSEN, Wilson Miles. 230'.9'4
The presence of other worlds; the psychological/spiritual findings of Emanuel Swedenborg [by] Wilson Van Dusen. New York, Harper & Row [1975, c1974] xv, 240 p., 18 cm. (Perennial Library) Includes bibliographical references. [BX8748.V3] ISBN 0-06-080342-8 1.75 (pbk.)
1. Swedenborg, Emanuel, 1688-1772. I. Title.
L.C. card no. for original ed.: 73-18684

VAN DUSEN, Wilson Miles. 230'.9'4
The presence of other worlds; the psychological/spiritual findings of Emanuel Swedenborg [by] Wilson Van Dusen. [1st ed.] New York, Harper & Row [1974] xv, 240 p. 21 cm. Includes bibliographical references. [BX8748.V3] 73-18684 ISBN 0-06-068826-2 6.95
1. Swedenborg, Emanuel, 1688-1772. I. Title.

WUNSCH, William Frederic, 1882- 230'.9'4
An outline of Swedenborg's teachings : with readings from his theological works / by William F. Wunsch. New York : Swedenborg Pub. Association, [1975] p. cm. Reprint of the 1926 ed. published by New-church Press, New York, under title: An outline of New-church teaching. Includes index. [BX8714.W8 1975] 74-23796 ISBN 0-87785-151-4 pbk. : 3.95
1. New Jerusalem Church. I. Title.

SWEDENBORG, Emanuel, 1688-1772. 230'.9'408
Miscellaneous theological works of Emanuel Swedenborg / translation by John Whitehead. Standard ed. New York : Swedenborg Foundation, [1976] vii, 634 p. ; 22 cm. Contents.Contents.—The New Jerusalem and its heavenly doctrine.—A brief exposition of the doctrine of the new church.—The intercourse between the soul and the body.—The white horse mentioned in the Apocalypse, Chap.XIX.—Appendix to the treatise on The white horse.—The earths in the universe.—The last judgment.—Continuation concerning the last judgment. [BX8711.A25 1976b] 76-46143 ISBN 0-87785-071-2. ISBN 0-87785-070-4 (student)
1. New Jerusalem Church—Doctrinal and controversial works. 2. Theology—Collected works—18th century. I. Title.

BUCHAN-SYDSERFF, Rose Margaret. 230'.9'5
Fundamentally speaking / [by] R. M. Buchan-Sydserff. Woking : The Society for Spreading the Knowledge of True Prayer, 1976. viii, 171 p. ; 24 cm. [BV4832.2.B77] 77-359488 ISBN 0-900678-10-0
1. Meditations. I. Title.

COREY, Arthur. 230.95
Personal introduction to God; with a foreword by Basil Woon. [1st ed.] New York, Exposition Press [1952] 204 p. 23 cm. [BX6997.C65] 52-9237
1. Eddy, Mary (Baker) 1821-1910. 2. Christian Science. 3. Mind and body. I. Title.

EDDY, Mary (Baker) 1821-1910. 230.95
Unity of good. Christian healing. The people's idea of God. Unite du bien. La guerison chretienne. L'idee que les hommes se font de Dieu. [Authorized ed. Boston, Trustees under the will of Mary Baker G. Eddy, 1955] 1v. 20cm. 'Authorized literature of the First Church of Christ, Scientist, in Boston, Massachusetts.' [BX6941.U6 1955] 55-1521
1. Christian Science. I. Title. II. Title: Unity of good. III. Title: Units du bien.

HOLLAND, David. 230.95
The miracle that heals. Miami, Fla., Croydon House [1956] 279p. 21cm. [BX6997.H6] 56-10263
1. Mental healing. I. Title.

ITEMS by and about Mary Baker Eddy, discoverer and founder of Christian Science and author of its textbook: Science and health with key to the Scriptures. Culled from the press (1845 to 1888) With an introd. and appendices. [Providence?] 1948 [stamped: c1961] 240p. 24cm. [BX6995.I 8 1961] 62-27222 230.95
1. Eddy, Mary (Baker) 1821-1910. 2. Christian Science. I. Eddy, Mary (Baker) 1821-1910.

KELLOGG, Samuel Henry, 1839-1899. 230.95
A handbook of comparative religion. Grand Rapids, Eerdmans, 1951 [c1899] viii, 179p. 23cm. [BL85.K] A 53
1. Religions. 2. Religion 3. Christianity and other religions. I. Title. II. Title: Comparative religion.

LAIRD, Margaret. 230.95
Christian Science re-explored; a challenge to original thinking. New York, Published for the Margaret Laird Foundation, Los Angeles, by William-Frederick Press, 1965. x, 262 p. 22 cm. [BX6943.L25] 65-15758
1. Christian Science. I. Title.

LAIRD, Margaret 230.95
Christian Science re-explorrd; a challenge to original thinking. New York, Pub. for the Margaret Laired Found., Los Angeles, William-Frederick [c.]1965. x, 262p. 22cm. [BX6943.L25] 65-15758 6.00
1. Christian Science. I. Title.

LEE, Charles Hamilton, 1883- 230.95
Divine direction or chaos? New York, Philosophical Library [1952] 98p. 21cm. [BX6947.L4] 52-14883
1. Christian Science. I. Title.

MOORE, Irene S. 230'.9'5
Identity : the higher order of science / by Irene S. Moore. Santa Monica : DeVorss, c1974. x, 130 p., [1] leaf of plates ; 24 cm. "Record of talks given at the 1973 classes held in Los Angeles, California." Bibliography: p. 129-130. [BX6943.M67] 74-81338 ISBN 0-87516-192-8 : 5.95
1. Christian Science. I. Title.

NOWELL, Ames. 230.95
Mary Baker Eddy; her revelation of divine egosim. New York, Veritas Institute [c1963] xviii, 236 p. 24 cm. [BX6995.N6] 63-14486
1. Eddy, Mary (Baker) 1821-1910. I. Title.

POPE, Charles Henry, 1841-1918. 230.95
Christian Science theory and practice, by Roger Starcross. Boston, Arakelyan Press, 1908. 164 p. 21 cm. [BX6943.P7] 11-1527
1. Christian Science. I. Title.

SYLVESTER 230.95
What Christian Science means to me--mind-being. New York, Vantage [c.1962] 64p. 21cm. 2.00 bds.,
1. Church of Christ, Scientist. I. Title.

ROSENBLATT, Bernard Abraham, 1886- 230.95694
The American bridge to the Israel commonwealth. New York, Farrar, Straus and Cudahy [1959] 128p. 22cm. [HC497.P2R56] 59-9173
1. Israel—Economic policy. 2. Israel—Pol. & govt. 3. Israel—Civilization—American influences. I. Title.

BRINTON, Howard Haines, 1884- 230'.96
The Quaker doctrine of inward peace, by Howard H. Brinton. Wallingford, Pa., Pendle Hill, 1948 [reprinted 1964] 30 p. 20 cm. (Pendle Hill pamphlet no. 44) [BX7732.B7236 1964] 64-23230
1. Friends, Society of — Doctrinal and controversial works. 2. Peace of mind. I. Title.

BRINTON, Howard Haines, 1884-1973. 230'.9'6
The religious philosophy of Quakerism; the beliefs of Fox, Barclay, and Penn as based on the Gospel of John [by] Howard H. Brinton. Wallingford, Pa., Pendle Hill Publications [1973] xii, 115 p. 22 cm. Contents.Contents.—Light and life in the Fourth Gospel.—The religion of George Fox.—Ethical mysticism in the Society of Friends.—Evolution and the inward light.—Appendix: George Fox and his works.—Bibliography (p. 101)—The published works of Howard H. Brinton. [BX7731.2.B74] 73-80041 3.00
1. Friends, Society of—Doctrinal and controversial works. 2. Fox, George, 1624-1691. 3. Barclay, Robert, 1648-1690. 4. Penn, William, 1644-1718. 5. Bible. N.T. John—Criticism, interpretation, etc. I. Title.

FRIENDS, Society of. Philadelphia Yearly Meeting. 230.96
Faith and practice of the Philadelphia Yearly Meeting of the Religious Society of Friends; a book of Christian discipline, 1955. Philadelphia [1955] iv, 268p. 21cm. 'Index of sources (including authors quoted in the texts)': p.253-256. [BX7731.A5 1955] 56-29677
1. Friends, Society of—Doctrinal and controversial works. I. Title.

HOYLAND, Geoffrey. 230.96
The use of silence. Wallingford, Pa., Pendle Hill [1955?] 24p. 20cm. (A Pendle Hill pamphlet #83) [BX7748.S5H6] 55-9695
1. Friends, Society of—Doctrinal and controversial works. 2. Silence. I. Title.

MARSH, Michael. 230'.9'6
Philosophy of the inner light / Michael Marsh. Wallingford, Pa. : Pendle Hill Publications, c1976. 30 p. ; 19 cm. (Pendle Hill pamphlet ; 209) Bibliography: p. 29-30. [BX7748.I5M37] 76-50674 ISBN 0-87574-209-2 : 0.95
1. Marsh, Michael. 2. Inner Light. I. Title.

SILCOCK, Thomas Henry, 1910- 230'.96
Words & testimonies: the Carey memorial lecture, Baltimore Yearly Meeting, 1971 [by] Thomas H. Silcock. [Wallingford, Pa., Pendle Hill Publications, 1972] 32 p. 20 cm. (Pendle Hill pamphlet, 186) [BJ1031.S48] 72-80097 ISBN 0-87574-186-X 0.70 (pbk.)
1. Friends, Society of—Doctrinal and controversial works. 2. Ethics. I. Title.

STEERE, Douglas Van, 1901- 230.9'6
The hardest journey [by] Douglas V. Steere. [Wallingford, Pa., Pendle Hill Publications, 1969] 30 p. 19 cm. (Pendle Hill pamphlet 163) "Delivered as a lecture on March 5, 1968 ... Whittier College, Whittier, California." [BX7731.2.S7] 70-76226 0.55
1. Friends, Society of—Doctrinal and controversial works. I. Title.

YUNGBLUT, John R. 230'.9'6
Quakerism of the future; mystical prophetic & evangelical [by] John Yungblut. [Wallingford, Pa., Pendle Hill Publications, 1974] 24 p. 20 cm. (Pendle Hill pamphlet, 194) [BX7732.Y85] 74-81830 ISBN 0-87574-194-0 0.70
1. Friends, Society of—Doctrinal and controversial works.

MY personal Pentecost / edited by Roy S. and Martha Koch ; foreword by Kevin Ranaghan. Scottdale, Pa. : Herald Press, c1977. 275 p. : port. ; 20 cm. Includes bibliographical references. [BX8128.C47M9] 77-79229 ISBN 0-8361-1816-2 pbk. : 3.95 230'.9'7
1. Pentecostalism—Mennonites—Addresses, essays, lectures. 2. Mennonites—United States—Biography—Addresses, essays, lectures. I. Koch, Roy S., 1913- II. Koch, Martha.

WALTNER, James H. 230.97
This we believe, by James H. Waltner. Illustrated by Annie Vallotton. Newton, Kan., Faith and Life Press [1968] 230 p. illus. 20 cm. Bibliographical footnotes. [BX8121.2.W3] 68-20281
1. Mennonites—Doctrinal and controversial works. I. Title.

WENGER, John Christian, 1910- 230.97
The doctrines of the Mennonites. Scottdale, Pa., Mennonite Pub. House, 1952 [c195] xii, 163p. port. 24cm. Bibliography: p. 161-163. [BX8121.W44] 56-32548
1. Mennonites—Doctrinal and controversial works. I. Title.

WENGER, John Christian, 1910- 230.97
Introduction to theology; an interpretation of the doctrinal content of Scripture, written to strengthen a childlike faith in Christ. Prepared at the request of the Publishing Committee of Mennonite Publication Board. Scottdale, Pa., Herald Press, 1954. 418p. illus. 24cm. [BT75.W36] 53-9049
1. Theology. Doctrinal. 2. Mennonite Church—Doctrinal and controversial works. I. Title.

BRUDERHOF Communities. 230'.9'7'0924 B
Eberhard Arnold; a testimony of church community from his life and writings. Rifton, N.Y., Plough Pub. House [1973] viii, 107 p. illus. 20 cm. "New edition published ... to commemorate the 90th anniversary of Eberhard Arnold's birth." Contents.Contents.—Arnold, E. and E. Fire song: radiance descend!—Arnold, E. Eberhard Arnold's life and work.—A personal word by Eberhard Arnold.—From lectures and writings by Eberhard Arnold: The character of love. The old creation and the new. The rule of the spirit. Peace and justice. From private property to community. The way to unity. The church community.—From Eberhard Arnold's letters.—Letters from friends.—Songs and poems by Eberhard Arnold: God is bond. Twilight deepening. Thou, Thou! Spirit of Christ. In silence surrounded. The word anew revealed. We pledge the bond now. God is the unity. [BX8129.B68A7 1973] 73-11605 ISBN 0-87486-112-8 3.50
1. Arnold, Eberhard, 1883-1935. I. Arnold, Eberhard, 1883-1935. II. Title.

RIEDEMANN, Peter, 1506-1556. 230.9'7'3
Account of our religion, doctrine, and faith, given by Peter Rideman of the brothers whom men call Hutterians. [2d English ed.] Rifton, N.Y., Plough Pub. House [1970] 298 p. 22 cm. On cover: Confession of faith. Translation of Rechenschaft unsrer Religion, Lehre, und Glaubens. Bibliography: p. 297-298. [BX8129.H8R513 1970] 74-115840 ISBN 8-7486-2027- 5.00
1. Hutterite Brethren—Doctrinal and controversial works. I. Hutterite Brethren. II. Title. III. Title: Confession of faith.

DUNLAVY, John, 1769-1826. 230'.9'8
The manifesto. [1st AMS ed.] New York, AMS Press [1972] vi, 520 p. 22 cm. Reprint of the 1818 ed. [BX9771.D9 1972] 74-134416 ISBN 0-404-08460-5 21.00
1. Stone, Barton Warren, 1772-1844. 2. Shakers. I. Title.

*PIKE, Kermit, comp. 230.98
A guide to Shaker manuscripts in the Library of the Western Reserve Historical Society. With an inventory of its Shaker photographs. Cleveland, Western Reserve Historical Society, 1974. xiii, 159 p. 28 cm. [BX9771] 74-84640 7.50 (pbk.)
1. Shakers. I. Title.
Available from the Society's Publication department 10825 E. Boulevard Cleveland, Ohio 44106

AIKEN, Alfred. 230.99
Lectures on reality. Series 1. New York, Hillier Press [1959] 251p. 21cm. [BF639.A12] 59-44075
1. New Thought. I. Title.

AIKEN, Alfred 230.99
Selected forums on absolute reality, Series I. New York 19, Box 378, Radio City Sta. Hillier Pr., [c.1964] 270p. 22cm. 64-3979 5.50 bds.,
1. New Thought. I. Title.

AUSTIN, Dorothea. 230.99
Of God, by Dorothea. Boston, Christopher Pub. House [1965] 83 p. 21 cm. [BF639.A94] 65-16478
1. New Thought. I. Title.

[AUSTIN, Dorothea] 230.99
Of God, by Dorothea. Boston, Christopher Pub. [c.1965] 83p. 21cm*2.50 [BF639.A94] 65-164788 2.50
1. New Thought. I. Title.

AXUP, Edward J 230.99
The Jehovah Witnesses unmasked; the un-Christian beliefs of this strange cult, and the Bible's eternal answers! [1st ed.] New York, Greenwich Book Publishers [1959] 77p. 21cm. [BX8526.A9] 59-9570
1. Jehovah's Witnesses—Doctrinal and controversial works. I. Title.

BJORNSTAD, James. 230'.9'9
The Moon is not the Son : a close look at the teachings of Rev. Sun Myung Moon and the Unification Church / by James Bjornstad. Minneapolis : Dimension Books, c1976. 125 p. : ill. ; 18 cm. Includes bibliographical references. [BX9750.S4B56] 76-46208 pbk. : 1.75
1. Moon, Sun Myung. 2. Segye Kidokkyo T'ongil Sillyong Hyophoe. I. Title.

BOYER, Harold W. 230.99
The apostolic church and the apostasy; messages on the church in history. Anderson,

Ind., Warner Press [dist. Gospel Trumpet Press c.1960] 79p. 19cm. 60-10186 1.00 pap., *1. Church of God (Anderson, Ind.)—Doctrinal and controversial works. 2. Catholic Church—Doctrinal and controversial works. I. Title.*

BROWN, Charles Ewing, 1883- 230.99
We preach Christ; a handbook of Christian doctrine. Anderson, Ind., Gospel Trumpet Co. [1957] 159p. 22cm. [BX7094.C675B7] 57-30480
1. Church of God (Anderson, Ind.)—Doctrinal and controversial works. 2. Theology, Doctrinal—Popular works. I. Title.

BROWN, Charles Ewing, 1883- 230.99
When souls awaken; an interpretation of radical Christianity. With an introd. by Gene W. Newberry. Anderson, Ind., Gospel Trumpet Co. [1954] 127p. 20cm. [BX7094.C674B7] 54-39720
1. Church of God (Anderson, Ind.)—Doctrinal and controversial works. I. Title.

BUNGER, Fred S. 230.9'9
Going home, by Fred S. Bunger. Philadelphia, Dorrance [1969] xvi, 96 p. 22 cm. [BR126.B79] 79-85744 3.95
I. Title.

CURTIS, Donald. 230'.9'9
The Christ-based teachings / by Donald Curtis. Unity Village, Mo. : Unity Books, c1976. 156 p. ; 20 cm. [BX9890.U5C84] 75-40657
1. Unity School of Christianity. I. Title.

CURTIS, Donald. 230'.9'9
The Christ-based teachings / by Donald Curtis. Unity Village, Mo. : Unity Books, c1976. 156 p. ; 20 cm. [BX9890.U5C84] 75-40657 3.95
1. Unity School of Christianity. I. Title.

EDWARD, John Derek. 230.99
Believe and know. [1st ed.] New York, Vantage Press [1957] 62p. 21cm. [BX9998.E3] 56-12917
I. Title.

ELLIS, Henry Milton, 1891- 230.99
Bible science; the truth and the way. New York, Speller, [1961, c.1960] 626p. Bibl. 60-53417 10.00, lim. ed.
1. Divine Science Church—Doctrinal and controversial works. I. Title.

GODDARD, Neville Lancelot, 1905- 230'.9'9
Immortal man : compilation of lectures / presented by Neville [i.e. N. L. Goddard] ; edited by Marge Broome. Lakemont, Ga. : CSA Press, c1977. 253 p. ; 22 cm. [BF638.G62] 77-81534 ISBN 0-87707-183-7 pbk. : 4.95
1. New Thought. I. Title.

GOLDSMITH, Joel S., 1892- 230'.9'9
Conscious union with God / Joel S. Goldsmith. Secaucus, N.J. : University Books, c1962, 1974 printing. 253 p. ; 21 cm. Includes bibliographical references. [BF639.G5577 1974] 75-307045 ISBN 0-8216-0050-8 : 6.00
1. New Thought. I. Title.

GOLDSMITH, Joel S., 1892- 230'.9'9
Consciousness unfolding / Joel S. Goldsmith. Secaucus, N.J. : University Books, c1962, 1974 printing. 269 p. ; 21 cm. Includes bibliographical references. [BF639.G558 1974] 75-307046 ISBN 0-8216-0043-5 : 6.00
1. New Thought. I. Title.

GOLDSMITH, Joel S., 1892-1964. 230'.9'9
Man was not born to cry / Joel S. Goldsmith ; edited by Lorraine Sinkler. New Hyde Park, N.Y. : University Books, [1974] c1964. x, 210 p. ; 22 cm. [BF639.G567 1974] 75-307212 5.00
1. New Thought. I. Title.

GRIGG, David Henry, 1883- 230.99
Do Jehovah's Witnesses and the Bible agree? [1st ed.] New York, Vantage Press [1958] 250p. 22cm. [BX8526.G7] 58-10656
1. Jehovah's Witnesses—Doctrinal and controversial works. I. Title.

HALL, Kenneth, 1926- 230.99
What do you believe? A discussion for young Christians on some of the principal New Testament doctrines as taught in the Church of God. Anderson, Ind., Gospel Trumpet Co. [1958] 63p. 19cm. [BX7094.C674H3] 58-10529
1. Church of God (Anderson, Ind.)—Doctrinal and controversial works. I. Title.

HALL, Kenneth F 1926- 230.99
What do you believe? A discussion for young Christians on some of the principal New Testament doctrines as taught in the Church of God. Anderson, Ind., Gospel Trumpet Co. [1958] 63 p. 19 cm. [BX7094.C674H3] 58-10529
1. Church of God (Anderson, Ind.)—Doctrinal and controversial works. I. Title.

HOLMES, Ernest Shurtleff. 230.99
A new design for living, by Ernest Holmes and Willis H. Kinnear. Englewood Cliffs, N. J., Prentice-Hall [1959] 236p. 22cm. Includes bibliography. [BF639.H6345] 59-8683
1. New Thought. 2. Peace of mind. I. Kinnear, Willis Hayes, 1907- joint author. II. Title.

JOHNSON, Sarah Eliza, called Saint Sarah, 1913- 230'.9'9
Wilderness to Eden, by Saint Sarah. Philadelphia, Printed by the Patterhannan Print. Co. [1953] 112p. illus. 23cm. [BR1725.J63A3 922] 53-36889
I. Title.

KING, Joseph Hillery(1869- 230.99
From Passover to Pentecost. 3d ed., rev. and enl. Franklin Springs, Ga., Pub. House of the Pentecostal Holiness Church [1955] 208p. 21cm. [BX8795.P25K5 1955] 58-42355
1. Pentecostal Holiness Church—Doctrinal and controversial works. I. Title.

MARTIN, Walter Ralston, 1928- 230.99
Jehovah of the Watchtower; a thorough expose of the important anti-Biblical teachings of Jehovah's Witnesses, by Walter R. Martin and Norman H. Klann. New York, Biblical Truth Pub. Society [1953] 125p. illus. 20cm. Bibliography. [BX8526.M32] 53-12661
1. Jehovah's Witnesses— Doctrinal and controversial works. I. Klann, Norman H., joint author. II. Title.

MARTIN, Walter Ralston, 1928- 230.99
Jehovah's Witnesses. Grand Rapids, Division of Cult Apologetics, Zondervan Pub. House [1957] 64p. 20cm. (The Modern cult library nooklet series) Includes bibliography. [BX8526.M322] 57-44045
1. Jehovah's Witnesses— Doctrinal and controversial works. I. Title.

MOON, Sun Myung. 230'.9'9
New hope; twelve talks. [Washington] Holy Spirit Association for the Unification of World Christianity [1973] xi, 103 p. port. 22 cm. [BR85.M618] 73-88416
1. Theology—Addresses, essays, lectures. I. Title.

NEWBERRY, Gene W 230.99
Primer for young Christians. Anderson, Ind., Warner Press [1955] 112p. 20cm. [BX7094.C674N4] 56-17702
1. Church of God (Anderson, Ind.)—Doctrinal and controversial works. I. Title.

NOYES, John Humphrey, 1811-1886. 230.9'9
The Berean. Male continence. Essay on scientific propagation. New York, Arno Press, 1969. viii, 504, 24, 32 p. 24 cm. (Religion in America) Reprint of the 1847, 1872, and 1875 ed., respectively. [BR85.N68 1969] 74-83431
1. Theology—Addresses, essays, lectures. I. Noyes, John Humphrey, 1811-1886. Male continence. 1969. II. Noyes, John Humphrey, 1811-1886. Essay on scientific propagation. 1969. III. Title. IV. Title: Male continence. V. Title: Essay on scientific propagation.

OLSON, Arnold Theodore. 230.99
This we believe; the background and exposition of the doctrinal statement of the Evangelical Free Church of America. Minneapolis, Free Church Publications [1961] 371p. 21cm. Includes bibliography. [BX7548.Z5O5] 61-18801
1. Evangelical Free Church of America—Doctrinal and controversial works. I. Title.

PALMA, Anthony D. 230'.9'9
Truth : antidote for error / Anthony D. Palma. Springfield, Mo. : Gospel Pub. House, c1977. 128 p. ; 18 cm. (Radiant books) [BX6198.A7P34] 76-52177 ISBN 0-88243-904-9 pbk. : 1.25
1. Assemblies of God, General Council—Doctrinal and controversial works. 2. Cults—United States. I. Title.

PAULK, Earl P 230.99
Your Pentecostal neighbor. [1st ed.] Cleveland, Tenn., Pathway Press, 1958. 237p. 21cm. [BX8795.P25P3] 58-13662
1. Pentecostal churches—Doctrinal and controversial works. I. Title.

PURKISER, W T ed. 230.99
Exploring our Christian faith. W. T. Purkiser, editor [and others] Kansas City, Mo., Beacon Hill Press [1960] 615p. 23cm. Includes bibliography. [BT75.2.P85] 60-10576
1. Theology, Doctrinal. 2. Church of the Nazarene—Doctrinal and controversial works. I. Title.

QUIDAM, Roger D 230.99
The doctrine of Jehovah's Witnesses, a criticism. Enw York, Philosophical Library [1959] 117p. 23cm. In blank verse. [BX8526.Q5] 59-16092
1. Jehovah's Witnesses—Doctrinal and controversial works. I. Title.

RICE, Hillery C 230.99
Tell me about the church; with a foreword by Warren C. Roark. Anderson, Ind., Gospel Trumpet Co. [1956] 112p. 19cm. [BX7094.C674R47] 56-45148
1. Church of God (Anderson, Ind.)—Doctrinal and controversial works. I. Title.

RICE, Hillery C 230.99
Tell me about the church; with a foreword by Warren C. Roark. Anderson, Ind., Gospel Trumpet Co. [1956] 112p. 19cm. [BX7094.C674R47] 56-45148
1. Church of God (Anderson, Ind.)—Doctrinal and controversial works. I. Title.

RIGGS, Ralph M 1895- 230.99
We believe; a comprehensive statement of Christian faith. Springfield, Mo., Gospel Pub. House [1954] 1v. 20cm. (Assemblies of God Cornerstone series, 780) [BX6198.A7R5] 55-24541
1. Assemblies of God, General Council—Doctrinal and controversial works. I. Title.

ROTH, Charles B. 230'.9'9
Mind, the master power / by Charles Roth. Unity Village, Mo. : Unity Books, [1974] 258 p. ; 20 cm. [BX9890.U5R67] 74-186980
1. Unity School of Christianity. I. Title.

SCHNELL, William J 1905- 230.99
Into the light of Christianity; the basic doctrines of the Jehovah's Witnesses in the light of Scripture. Grand Rapids, Baker Book House, 1959. 211p. 23cm. [BX8526.S34] 59-15534
1. Jehovah's Witnesses—Doctrinal and controversial works. I. Title.

SCOTT, Frank Earl, 1899- 230.99
Armageddon and you. [1st ed.] Portland, Or., Metropolitan Press [1968] 184 p. illus. (part col.) 23 cm. Bibliography: p. 170. [BX8526.S37] 68-28928 4.95
1. Jehovah's Witnesses—Doctrinal and controversial works. I. Title.

SHAVER, John Edward. 230.99
The spirit and the living seed. New York, Comet Press Books [1960] 183 p. 21 cm. (A Milestone book) [BF639.S518] 60-676
1. New Thought I. Title.

SHAVER, John Edward 230.99
The spirit and the living seed. v. 2 New York, Comet Press Books [c.]1960. 183p. 21cm. (A Milestone book) Contents.v.2, The spirit and God's man. 60-676 3.00
1. New Thought. I. Title.

SHAVER, John Edward. 230.99
The spirit of Christ within. New York, Comet Press Books, 1960. 178 p. 21 cm. Vol. 3 of the author's projected tetralogy, the 1st of which is The spirit and the living seed, and the 2d, The spirit and God's man. [BF639.S519] 60-50386
1. New Thought. I. Title.

SHAVER, John Edward 230.99
The spirit of Christ within. New York, Comet Press Books [c.]1960. 178p. 21cm. Vol. 3 of the author's projected tetralogy, the 1st of which is The spirit and the living seed, and the 2d, The spirit and God's man. 60-50386 3.00
1. New Thought. I. Title.

SPENCE, Othniel Talmadge, 1926- 230.99
The quest for Christian purity, by O. Talmadge Spence. [1st ed. Richmond?] 1964. xxxiv, 286 p. 24 cm. Bibliography: p. 285-286. [BT767.S6] 64-21996
1. Holiness. 2. Pentecostal Holiness Church—Doctrinal and controversial works. I. Title.

STERNER, R Eugene. 230.99
Toward a Christian fellowship. Anderson, Ind., Warner Press [1957] 112p. 20cm. [BX7094.C674S8] 57-32034
1. Church of God (Anderson, Ind.)—Doctrinal and controversial works. 2. Church. I. Title.

STERNER, R Eugene. 230.99
Toward a Christian fellowship. Anderson, Ind., Warner Press [1957] 112 p. 20 cm. Church of God (Anderson, Ind.) -- Doctrinal and controversial works. [BX7094.C674S8] 57-32
1. Church. I. Title.

SUMNER, Robert Leslie, 1922- 230'.9'9
Armstrongism: the "Worldwide Church of God" examined in the searching light of scripture; (an in-depth study of a false religion) by Robert L. Sumner. Brownsburg, Ind., Biblical Evangelism Press [1974] 424 p. 21 cm. Includes bibliographical references. [BR1725.A77S95] 74-171027 ISBN 0-914012-15-0 5.95
1. Armstrong, Herbert W. 2. Worldwide Church of God. I. Title.

THOMAS, Stan 230'.99
Jehovah's Witnesses, and what they believe. [1st ed.] Grand Rapids, Zondervan [1967] 159p. 23cm. [BX8526.T44] 67-17225 3.95 bds.,
1. Jehovah's Witnesses—Doctrinal and controversial work. I. Title.

WATCH Tower Bible and Tract Society. 230.99
"Let Your name be sanctified." [1st ed. New York, 1961] 382 p. 19 cm. [BX8526.W283] 61-35986
1. Jehovah's Witnesses — Doctrinal and controversial works. I. Title.

WATCH Tower Bible and Tract Society. 230.99
"This means everlasting life." 1st ed. Brooklyn, 1950 317 p. illus. 19 cm. [BX8526.W316] 50-32766
1. Jehovah's Witnesses — Doctrinal and controversial works. I. Title.

WATCH Tower Bible and Tract Society. 230.99
Watch Tower publications index of subjects discussed and Scriptures explained, 1930-1960. [New York, 1961] 380 p. 24 cm. [BX8526.W325] 61-38581
1. Jehovah's Witnesses — Doctrinal and controversial works — Indexes. I. Title.

WATCH Tower Bible and Tract Society of Pennsylvania. 230.9'9
"The nations shall know that I am Jehovah"—how? [1st ed. Brooklyn, Watch Tower Bible and Tract Society of New York, 1971] 412 p. col. illus., col. maps (on lining papers) 19 cm. [BX8526.W366] 74-26854
1. Jehovah's Witnesses—Doctrinal and controversial works. I. Title.

WATCH Tower Bible and Tract Society of Pennsylvania. 230.99
"Things in which it is impossible for God to lie." [1st ed. Brooklyn, Watchtower Bible and Tract Society of New York, 1965] 411 p. illus., maps (on lining papers) 19 cm. [BX8526.W37] 65-6914
1. Jehovah's Witnesses — Doctrinal and controversial works. I. Title.

WILLIAMS, Ernest Swing, 1885- 230.99
Systematic theology. Springfield, Mo., Gospel Pub. House [1954, c1953] 3v. illus. 20cm. [BT75.W53] 54-37091
1. Theology, Doctrinal. 2. Assemblies of God, General Council—Doctrinal and controversial works. I. Title.

WILSON, Ernest Charles, 1896- 230'.9'9
Every good desire [by] Ernest C. Wilson. Boston, G. K. Hall, 1974 [c1973] 226 p. 25 cm. Large print ed. [BX9890.U5W553 1974] 74-4356 ISBN 0-8161-6217-4 7.95 (lib. bdg.)
1. Unity School of Christianity—Doctrinal and controversial works. I. Title.

WILSON, Ernest Charles, 1896- 230'.99
Every good desire [by] Ernest C. Wilson. [1st ed.] New York, Harper & Row [1973] viii, 117 p. 21 cm. Expanded version of the 1948 ed. published by Unity Classics, Los Angeles. [BX9890.U5W553 1973] 73-6322 ISBN 0-06-069440-8 4.95
1. Unity School of Christianity—Doctrinal and controversial works. I. Title.

HOYT, Herman Arthur, 1909- 230.992
Then would my servants fight. Winona Lake, Ind., Brethren Missionary Herald Co. [1956] 115p. 20cm. [BX7829.B64H6] 230.65 56-39520
1. Pacifism. 2. The Brethren Church (Progressive Dunkers)—Doctrinal and controversial works. I. Title.

STUDIES in Christian belief. 230.992
Elgin, Ill., Brethren Press [1958] 279p. 23cm. Includes bibliography. [BX7821.B45] [BX7821.B45] 230.65 58-14602 58-14602
1. Church of the Brethren—Doctrinal and controversial works. 2. Theology, Doctrinal. I. Beahm, William McKinley, 1896- II. Title: Christian belief.

WOODS, Guy N 1908- *230.99 230.66
Woods-Cogdill debate, held in Phillips High School auditorium, Birmingham, Alabama, November 18-23, 1957, between Guy N. Woods, Memphis, Tennessee, and Roy Cogdill, Lufkin, Texas. Nashville, Gospel Advocate Co., 1958. 371 p. illus. 23 cm. [BX7094.C95W63] 58-41141
1. Churches of Christ — Doctrinal and controversial works. I. Cogdill, Roy E. II. Title.

231 God, Trinity, Godhead

ALDER, George. 231
God; a timely consideration of what the Bible says about God and his relationship to you. Cincinnati, Ohio, Standard Pub. [1971] 96 p. 18 cm. (Fountain books) [BT102.A4] 70-164739
1. God.

ALLAN, John Robertson, 1906- 231
The gospel according to science fiction : God was an ancient astronaut, wasn't he? / John Allan. Libertyville, Ill. : Quill Publications, [1976] p. cm. Includes bibliographical references. [BL254.A44 1976] 76-6920 ISBN 0-916608-02-6
1. Bible—Miscellanea. 2. Religion and astronautics. I. Title.

ALTIZER, Thomas J. J. 231
The Altizer-Montgomery dialogue; a chapter in the God is dead controversy. [Chicago, Ill.] Inter-Varsity Press [1967] 96 p. 18 cm. "Dialogue ... February 24, 1967, at Rockefeller Chapel as a part of the University of Chicago Student Government's 75th Anniversary Speakers Program." [BT83.5.A42] 67-5665
1. Death of God theology. I. Montgomery, John Warwick, joint author. II. Title.

ALTIZER, Thomas J. J. 231
The gospel of Christian atheism, by Thomas J. J. Altizer. Philadelphia, Westminster Press [1966] 157 p. 19 cm. [BT83.5.A43] 66-20240
1. Death of God theology. I. Title.

AMES, Edward Remington. 231
Back to Yahweh, an explanation of the philological error which gave rise to the wrong deistic concept. Boston, Christopher Pub. House [1950] xi, 166 p. 21 cm. [BT180.N2A232] 50-4894
1. God—Name. I. Title.

AMES, Edward Remington 231
Who is the Lord? A treatise on rediscovering our God. New York, Exposition Press [c.1960] 185p. 21cm. 60-50110 3.00
1. God—Name. I. Title.

AMES, Edward Remington. 231
Who is the Lord A treatise on rediscovering our God. [1st ed.] New York, Xposition Press [1960] 185p. 21cm. [BT180.N2A245] 60-50110
1. God—Name. I. Title.

ANDERSON, Margaret J. 231
Bill and Betty learn about God. Grand Rapids, Mich., Zondervan [c.1961] 48p. col. illus. 29cm. 1.95 bds.,
1. God (Juvenile literature) I. Title.

ANDERSON, Robert Sir 1841-1918 231
The silence of God. Complete orig. ed. Grand Rapids,Mich., Kregel [1965] xvi, 215p. 20cm. Reissue of work first pub. in 1897 [BR121.A57] 65-16338 3.50
1. Christianity—19th cent. I. Title.

ANGELES, Peter Adam, 1931- 231
The problem of God; a short introduction [by] Peter A. Angeles. Columbus, Ohio, Merrill [1974] xii, 156 p. 23 cm. Bibliography: p. 149-151. [BT102.A53] 73-85469 ISBN 0-675-08887-9 3.95
1. God. I. Title.

ARGYLE, Aubrey William, 1910- 231
God in the New Testament. Philadelphia, Lippincott, 1966 [c.1965] 224p. 21cm. (Knowing Christianity) Consists of Whitley lects. delivered at Cardiff Baptist Coll. and Glasgow Baptist Coll. Bibl. [BT99.A7] 66-13360 2.95 bds.,
1. God—Biblical teaching. I. Title.

ASHER, Hellen Drummond. 231
A child's thought of God; a poem based on Psalm 104. Illustrated by Dorothy Grider. New York, Rand McNally. c1957. unpaged. illus. 20cm. [BT107.A8] 57-7131
1. God—Juvenile literature. I. Title.

ASHER, Hellen Drummond. 231
A child's thought of God; a poem based on Psalm 104. Illustrated by Dorothy Grider. New York, Rand McNally. c1957. unpaged. illus. 20cm. [BT107.A8] 57-7131
1. God—Juvenile literature. I. Title.

AUGUSTINUS, Aurelius, Saint, Bp. of Hippo. 231
The Trinity [by] St. Augustine. Translated by Stephen McKenna. Edited and abridged by Charles Dollen. [Boston] St. Paul Editions [1965] 303 p. 22 cm. [BT110.A813] 64-21602
1. Trinity — Early works to 1800. I. Dollen, Charles, ed. II. Title.

AUGUSTINUS, Aurelius, Saint, Bp. of Hippo. 231
The Trinity. Translated by Stephen McKenna. Washington, Catholic University of America Press [1963] xvii, 539 p. 22 cm. (The Fathers of the church, a new translation, v. 45) Bibliography: p. xvii. [BT110.A813] 63-12482
1. Trinity — Early works to 1800. I. Title. II. Series.

AUGUSTINUS, Aurelius, Saint, Bp. of Hippo 231
The Trinity. Tr. [from Latin] by Stephen McKenna. Washington, D.C., Catholic Univ. [c.1963] xvii, 539p. 22cm. (Fathers of the church, a new translation, v. 45) Bibl. 63-12482 7.95
1. Trinity—Early works to 1800. I. Title. II. Series.

AUGUSTINUS, Aurelius, Saint, Bp. of Hippo 231
The Trinity [by] St. Augustine. Tr. by Stephen McKenna. Ed., abridged by Charles Dollen [Boston] St. Paul Eds. [dist. Daughters of St. Paul, c.1965] 303p. 22cm. [BT110.A813] 64-21602 4.00
1. Trinity—Early works to 1800. I. Dollen, Charles, ed. II. Title.

AULEN, Gustaf Emanuel Hildebrand, Bp., 1879- 231
The drama and the symbols; a book on images of God and the problems they raise, by Gustaf Aulen. Translated by Sydney Linton. [American ed.] Philadelphia, Fortress Press [1970] x, 214 p. 23 cm. Translation of Dramat och symbolerna. [BT102.A913 1970b] 76-124409 6.95
1. God. 2. Symbolism. I. Title.

BAILEY, Kenneth E. 231
God is ... : dialogues on the nature of God for young people / Kenneth E. Bailey. South Pasadena, Calif. : Mandate Press, [1976] p. cm. Bibliography: p. [BT108.B34] 76-15580 ISBN 0-87808-149-6
1. God—Study and teaching. 2. Christian education—Text-books. I. Title.

BAILLIE, John, 1886- 231
Our knowledge of God. New York, Scribner [1959] 263p. 21cm. Includes bibliography. [BT101.B26 1959] 59-1116
1. God (Theory of knowledge) I. Title.

BAILLIE, John, 1886-1960 231
Our knowledge of God. New York, Scribners [1962, c.1959] 263p. (Scribners Lib. SL-57) Bibl. 1.45 pap.,
1. God (Theory of knowledge) I. Title.

BAKER, John Austin. 231
The foolishness of God. Atlanta, J. Knox [1975, c1970] 409 p. 22 cm. Includes bibliographical references. [BT77.B27 1975] 74-3714 ISBN 0-8042-0489-6 9.95
1. Theology, Doctrinal—Popular works. I. Title.

BALL, Virginia. 231
The Godless Christians. Atlanta, Pendulum Books [1966] 190 p. ports. 20 cm. [BT83.5.B3] 66-23719
1. Death of God theology. I. Title.

BARBOTIN, Edmond. 231
The humanity of God / Edmond Barbotin ; translated by Matthew J. O'Connell. Maryknoll, N.Y. : Orbis Books, c1976. p. cm. Translation of Humanite de Dieu. Includes bibliographical references. [BS544.B3713] 76-304 ISBN 0-88344-184-5
1. God—Biblical teaching. I. Title.

BARROSSE, Thomas. 231
God exists; the Biblical record of God's self-revelation. [Notre Dame, Ind.] University of Notre Dame Press. 1963. 79 p. 18 cm. (University theology themes) [BT99.B28] 63-15346
1. God — Biblical teaching. I. Title.

BARROSSE, Thomas 231
God exists; the Biblical record of God's self-revelation. [Notre Dame, Ind.] Univ. of Notre Dame Pr. [c.]1963. 79p. 18cm. (Univ. theology themes) Bibl. 63-15346 1.25 pap.,
1. God—Biblical teaching. I. Title.

BARTHELEMY, Dominique. 231
God and his image: an outline of Biblical theology; translated [from the French] by Dom Aldhelm Dean. London, Dublin (etc.] G. Chapman, 1966. xix. 199 p. 224 cm. 30/- Originally published as Dieu et son image. Paris, Editions du cerf. 1963. Bibliographical footnotes. [BS543.B3713] (B66 66-66713
1. Bible — Theology. I. Title.

BAVINCK, Herman, 1854-1921. 231
The doctrine of God; translated, edited, and outlined by William Hendriksen. Grand Rapids, W. B. Erdmans Pub. Co., 1951. 407 p. 23 cm. Translation of v. 2 of the 3d ed. of the author's Gereformeerde dogmatiek. [BT101.B2743] 52-89
1. God. I. Title.

BELVIN, Agnes Lowry. 231
From garden to city in seven days. New York, Vantage Press [1954] 73p. 22cm. [BT155.B42] 54-10233
1. Covenants (Theology) I. Title.

BENT, Charles N. 231
The death-of-God movement; a study of Gabriel Vahanian, William Hamilton, Paul Van Buren [and] Thomas J. J. Altizer, by Charles N. Bent. Westminster, Md., Paulist Press [1967] viii, 213 p. 21 cm. (Exploration books) Includes bibliographical references. [BT83.5.B4] 67-23604
1. Death of God theology. I. Title.

BERTOCCI, Peter Anthony. 231
Why believe in God? New York, Association Press [1963] 126 p. illus. 16 cm. (A Keen-age reflection book) [BT107.B47] 63-10382
1. God. I. Title.

BERTOCCI, Peter Anthony 231
Why believe in God? New York, Association [c.1963] 126p. illus. 16cm. (Keen-age reflection bk.) 63-10382 .50 pap.,
1. God. I. Title.

BETTS, Gilbert Lee, 1893- 231
The body of God, by Gilbert L. Betts. Boston, Christopher Pub. House [1968] 44 p. 21 cm. [BT102.B42] 68-21462
1. God—Proof, Teleological. 2. Religion and science—1946- I. Title.

BICKERSTETH, Edward Henry, Bp. of Exeter, 1825-1906. 231
The Trinity; Scripture testimony to the one eternal Godhead of the Father, and of the Son, and of the Holy Spirit. Grand Rapids, Kregel Publications, 1959. 182p. 22cm. 'Companion volume to The Holy Spirit.' 'Formerly published under the title, The rock of ages.' [BT111.B6 1959] 59-13770
1. Trinity—Biblical teaching. I. Title. II. Title: Scripture testimony to the one eternal Godhead.

BLAIKIE, Robert J. 231
'Secular Christianity' and God who acts, by Robert J. Blaikie. [1st U.S. ed.] Grand Rapids, Mich., Eerdmans [1970] 256 p. 22 cm. Includes bibliographical references. [BS543.B53 1970] 72-129849 2.95
1. Bible—Theology. 2. Secularism. I. Title.

BLAIKLOCK, E. M. 231
Is it, or isn't it? Why we believe in the existence of God, by E. M. Blaiklock and D. A. Blaiklock. Grand Rapids, Zondervan Pub. House [1968] 83 p. 21 cm. Includes bibliographical references. [BT1102.B5] 68-27470 2.95
1. Apologetics—20th century. 2. God—Proof. I. Blaiklock, David A., joint author. II. Title.

BLAKELY, Hunter Bryson, 1894- 231
I wager on God. Richmond, John Knox Press [1956] 207 p. 21 cm. [BT77.B56] 56-8849
1. Theology, Doctrinal—Popular works. I. Title.

BOHNET, Martin Paul. 231
The mystery of Christ. [1st ed.] New York, Vantage Press [1956] 201p. 21cm. [BR125.B6257] 56-11200
1. Christianity—20th cent. I. Title.

BORSCH, Frederick Houk. 231
God's parable / Frederick Houk Borsch. Philadelphia : Westminster Press, c1975. x, 116 p. ; 19 cm. [BT102.B58 1975] 75-22443 ISBN 0-664-24786-5 pbk. : 3.50
1. Jesus Christ. 2. Bible—Parables. 3. God. I. Title.

BOWIE, Walter Russell 231
Jesus and the Trinity. Nashville, Abingdon Press [c.1960] 160 p. 21 cm. (Bibl. footnotes) 60-10907 2.75
1. Trinity—History of doctrines. I. Title.

BRUMBACK, Carl 231
God in three Persons; a Trinitarian answer to the oneness or Jesus only doctrine concerning the Godhead and water baptism. [Cleveland, Tenn., Pathway Press, c.1959] 192p. (includes bibliography.) 21cm. 59-16846 3.00; 2.00 pap.,
1. Trinity. 2. Pentecostal churches—Doctrinal and controversial works. 3. Baptism. I. Title.

BRUMBACK, Carl, 1917- 231
God in three Persons; a Trinitarian answer to the oneness or 'Jesus only' doctrine concerning the Godhead and water baptism. [1st ed. Cleveland, Tenn., Pathway Press, 1959] 192p. 21cm. Includes bibliography. [BT111.2.B75] 59-16846
1. Trinity. 2. Pentecostal churches—Doctrinal and controversial works. 3. Baptism. I. Title.

BRYAR, William. 231
St. Thomas and the existence of God; three interpretations. Chicago, H. Regnery Co., 1951. 252 p. 22 cm. [BX1749.T6B7] 51-14960
1. Thomas Aquinas, Saint, 1225?-1274. Summa theologica. 2. God—Proof. I. Title.

BUNYAN, John, 1628-1688. 231
The fear of God. Swengel, Pa., Reiner Publications, 1967. 174 p. 19 cm. First published in 1679. [BR75.B77 1967] 67-4585
1. Fear of God. I. Title.

BURROW, Barbara. 231 (j)
God is everywhere. Illustrated by Mary Hamilton. [Kansas City, Mo.] Hallmark Editions [1968] 1 v. (unpaged) col. illus. 16 cm. [BT107.B87] 68-22693 2.00
1. God—Juvenile literature. I. Hamilton, Mary, 1936- illus. II. Title.

BURROW, Barbara. 231
God is everywhere. Illustrated by Mary Hamilton. [Kansas City, Mo.] Hallmark Editions [1968] [46] p. col. illus. 16 cm. A simple description of the omnipresence of God. [BT107.B87] AC 68
1. God. I. Hamilton, Mary, 1936- illus. II. Title.

CAIRNS, David, 1904- 231
God up there? A study in divine transcendence. Philadelphia, Westminster [c.1967] 111p. 19cm. Bibl. [BT124.5.C3 1967b] 68-15906 2.95
1. Transcendence of God. I. Title.

CAIRNS, David, 1904- 231
The image of God in man. New York, Philosophical Library [1953] 255p. 22cm. [BT701.C27] 53-7786
1. Man (Theology) I. Title.

CALHOUN, Robert Lowry, 1896- 231
What is man in Horton Walter Marshall 1895- God Jesus and man -- New York, Association Press [1953] [BT10.H64] 53-7964
I. Title.

CALVIN, Jean, 1509-1564. 231
On God and man; selections from Institutes of the Christian religion. Edited by F. W. Strothmann. New York, F. Ungar Pub. Co. [1956] 54p. 21cm. (Milestones of thought) [BT810.C23] 56-7500
1. Predestination—Early works to 1800. 2. Reformed Church—Doctrinal and controversial works. I. Title.

CANTWELL, Laurence. 231
The theology of the Trinity. Notre Dame, Ind., Fides Publishers [1969] 94 p. 18 cm. (Theology today, no. 4) Bibliography: p. 92-94. [BT111.2.C3] 78-8388 0.95
1. Trinity. I. Title.

CHAFER, Lewis Sperry, 1871- 231
Dispensationalism. Rev. ed. Dallas, Dallas Seminary Press [1951] 108 p. 19 cm. "Second reprint of an article published in Bibliotheca sacra (xciii, 390-449)" [BT155.C45 1951] 51-28817
1. Covenants (Theology) I. Title.

CHESNUT, J. Stanley. 231
The Old Testament understanding of God, by J. Stanley Chesnut. Philadelphia, Westminster Press [1968] 192 p. 21 cm. Bibliography: p. [176]-178. [BT99.C48] 68-10436
1. Bible. O.T.—Theology. 2. God—Biblical teaching. I. Title.

CHRISTENSEN, Otto H., 1898- 231
Getting acquainted with God [by] Otto H. Christensen. Washington, Review and Herald Pub. Association [1970] 128 p. 22 cm. Bibliography: p. 124-128. [BT102.C48] 78-102112
1. God. I. Title.

CHRISTIAN, C. W., comp. 231
Radical theology: phase two; essays in a continuing discussion. Edited by C. W. Christian and Glenn R. Wittig. [1st ed.] Philadelphia, Lippincott [1967] vi, 218 p. 21 cm. Includes bibliographies. [BT83.5.C4] 67-20169
1. Death of God theology. I. Wittig, Glenn R., joint comp. II. Title.

CLOSE, Henry T. 231
Reasons for our faith. Richmond, Va., Knox [c.1962] 103p. 21cm. (Aletheia paperbacks) Bibl. 62-11714 1.45 pap.,
1. God—Proof. I. Title.

CLOSE, HenryT 231
Reasons for our faith. Richmond, John Knox Press [1962] 103p. 21cm. (Aletheia paperbacks) Includes bibliography. [BT102.C55] 62-11714
1. God—Proof. I. Title.

CONGAR, Marie Joseph, 1904- 231
[Secularname:GeorgeYvesCongar]
The mystery of the temple; or, The manner of God's presence to his creatures from Genesis to the Apocalypse, by Yves M. J. Congar. [Tr. by Reginald F. Trevett] Westminster, Md., Newman [1962, c.1958] 322p. 23cm. 62-17188 6.75
1. God—Biblical teaching. 2. Immanence of God. 3. Jerusalem. Temple. I. Title.

COOKE, Bernard J. 231
Beyond Trinity, by Bernard J. Cooke. Milwaukee, Marquette University Press, 1969. 73 p. 19 cm. (The Aquinas lecture, 1969) "[Presented] under the auspices of the Wisconsin-Alpha Chapter of Phi Sigma Tau." Includes bibliographical references. [BT111.2.C63] 70-81373
1. Trinity. I. Title. II. Series.

COTTON, James Harry, 1898- 231
Christian Knowledge of God. New York, Macmillan, 1951. 180 p. 21 cm. (The James Sprunt lectures, 1947) [BT101.C68] 51-11525
1. God (Theory of knowledge) I. Title.

CROSBY, Everett Uberto, 1871- 231
God to me now notes. [Nantucket, Mass., Tetaukimmo Press, 1957] 57 p. 23 cm. [BR124.C7] 57-10877
I. Title.

CRUZ, Nicky. 231
The Magnificent Three / Nicky Cruz with Charles Paul Conn. Old Tappan, N.J. : Revell, c1976. 128 p. ; 21 cm. [BT113.C78] 76-4574 ISBN 0-8007-0788-5 : 4.95
1. Cruz, Nicky. 2. Trinity. I. Conn, Charles Paul, joint author. II. Title.

CUNNINGHAM, Francis L B 231
The indwelling of the Trinity; a historico-doctrinal study of the theory of St. Thomas Aquinas. Dubuque, Priory Press, 1955. 414p. 24cm. (The Aquinas library) Includes bibliography. [BT769.C77] 55-2521
1. Thomas Aquinas, Saint, 1225?-1274. 2. Mystical union. I. Title.

DANIELOU, Jean. 231
Myth and mystery. Translated by P. J. Hepburne-Scott. [1st American ed.] New York, Hawthorn Books [1968] 140 p. 21 cm. (The Twentieth century encyclopedia of Catholicism, v. 8. Section I: Knowledge and faith) Translation of Mythes paiens, mystere chretien. [BT102.D313 1968] 67-14871
1. God. I. Title. II. Series: The Twentieth century encyclopedia of Catholicism, v. 8

†D'ARCY, Martin C. 231
Revelation and love's architecture / Martin C. D'Arcy. Boston : Charles River Books, c1976. 48p. ; 24 cm. [BT113] 76-270990 ISBN 0-89182-010-8 : 8.00
1. Trinity. I. Title.

DAVAR, Ashok. 231
God is. Written and illustrated by Ashok Davar. New York, Paul S. Eriksson [1969] 1 v. (unpaged) illus. 13 x 19 cm. [BT175.D38 1969] 73-93232 2.50
1. God. I. Title.

DEHAAN, Richard W. 231
The living God [by] Richard W. DeHaan. Foreword by Howard F. Sugden. Geand Rapids, Zondervan Pub. House [1967] 192 p. 21 cm. [BT102.D38] 67-17249
1. God. I. Title.

DEHAAN, Richard W. 231
The living God; a ringing declaration of faith! Grand Rapids, Mich., Zondervan Pub. House [1973, c1967] 220 p. 18 cm. [BT102.D38] 67-17249 1.25 (pbk.)
1. God. I. Title.

DEWAN, Wilfrid F 231
The one God. Englewood Cliffs, N.J., Prentice-Hall, 1963. 112 p. illus. 23 cm. (Foundations of Catholic theology series) Includes bibliography. [BT102.D4] 63-9834
1. God. I. Title.

DEWAN, Wilfrid F. 231
The one God. Englewood Cliffs, N. J., Prentice [c.]1963. 112p. illus. 23cm. (Founds. of Catholic theology ser.) Bibl. 63-9834 3.95; 1.50 pap.,
1. God. I. Title.

DILLISTONE, Frederick William, 1903- 231
The Christian faith. Philadelphia, Lippincott [c.1964] 188p. 21cm. (Knowing Christianity) Bibl. 64-23473 2.95 bds.,
1. Christianity—Essence, genius, nature. 2. Christianity—20th cent.—Addresses, essays, lectures. I. Title.

DIRSCHERL, Denis. 231
Speaking of God; essays on belief and unbelief, edited by Denis Dirscherl. Milwaukee, Bruce Pub. Co. [1967] xi, 158 p. 21 cm. Includes bibliographical references. [BT102.A1D5] 67-24538
1. God—Addresses, essays, lectures. 2. Faith—Addresses, essays, lectures. I. Title.

DIX, Gregory, Father. 231
The image and likeness of God. New York, Morehouse-Gorham Co., 1954. 77p. 20cm. [BV4832.D58] 54-8448
1. Meditations. I. Title.

DIX, Gregory, Father. 231
The image and likeness of God. Westminster [London] Dacre Press [1953] 77p. 19cm. [BV4832.D58 1953] 54-27707
1. Meditations. I. Title.

DOSS, Helen (Grigsby) 231
Where can I find God? By Helen Doss. Drawings by Frank Aloise. Nashville, Abingdon Press [1968] [31] p. col. illus. 26 cm. A young boy explains how he knows God exists and how he feels His presence. [BT107.D64] AC 68
1. God. I. Aloise, Frank, illus. II. Title.

DURANDEAUX, Jacques. 231
Living questions to dead Gods. Translated by William Whitman. With an introd. by Gabriel Vahanian. New York, Sheed and Ward [1968] 160 p. 21 cm. Translation of Question vivante a un Dieu mort. Bibliographical references included in "Footnotes" (p. 154-160) [BT102.D8313] 68-13851
1. God. I. Title.

DURRANT, Michael. 231
Theology and intelligibility; an examination of the proposition that God is the last end of rational creatures and the doctrine that God is three persons in one substance (the doctrine of the Holy Trinity). London, Boston; Routledge & K. Paul [1973] xviii, 204 p. 23 cm. (Studies in ethics and the philosophy of religion) Bibliography: p. 198-201. [BT98.D87 1973] 72-96507 ISBN 0-7100-7488-3 £3.75
1. God—History of doctrines. 2. Trinity—History of doctrines. I. Title.

DURRANT, Michael. 231
Theology and intelligibility; an examination of the proposition that God is the last end of rational creatures and the doctrine that God is three persons in one substance (the doctrine of the Holy Trinity). London, Boston; Routledge & K. Paul [1973] xviii, 204 p. 23 cm. (Studies in ethics and the philosophy of religion) Bibliography: p. 198-201. [BT98.D87 1973] 72-96507 ISBN 0-7100-7488-3 11.50
1. God—History of doctrines. 2. Trinity—History of doctrines. I. Title.

EARTH and sky. 231
New York, Paulist Press [1969] [16] p. col. illus. 15 x 18 cm. (Rejoice books) Translation of Terre et ciel. A call to all nature and mankind to bless the Lord for the good things He has placed on earth. [BT107.E1813] 79-7462 0.35
1. God—Juvenile literature.

EBELING, Gerhard, 1912- 231
God and word. [Tr. by James W. Leitch from the German] Philadelphia, Fortress [1967] vii, 53p. 20cm. (Earl lects., 1966) [BT80.E213] 67-14623 1.50 bds.,
1. Theology—Addresses, essays, lectures. I. Title. II. Series.

EDDY, George Sherwood, 1871- 231
Man discovers God [by] Sherwood Eddy. Freeport, N.Y., Books for Libraries Press [1968, c1942] xiv, 270 p. 22 cm. (Essay index reprint series) [BT98.E3 1968] 68-24849
1. God—Knowableness. 2. Theism. I. Title.

*EDWARDS, Charles Thomas. 231
God is good. 1st. ed. [Jericho] N.Y. Exposition [1974] 46 p. 22 cm. [BT102] ISBN 0-682-47870-9 3.50
1. God. I. Title.

EHLERT, Arnold D., comp. 231
A bibliographic history of dispensationalism. Grand Rapids, Mich., Baker Bk., 1965. 110p. 23cm. (BCH bibliographic ser., no.2) First pub. in Bibliotheaca sacra, vol. 101-103, Jan. 1944-Jan. 1946, under the title A bibliography of dispensationalism [BT157.E35] 65-23752 1.50 pap.,
1. Dispensationalism—Abstracts. I. Title. II. Series.

*EKERHOLM, H. E. 231
Hope beyond the darkness. New York, Vantage [1967] 134p. 21cm. 2.95 bds.
I. Title.

ELLER, Vernard. 231
His end up; getting God into the new theology. Nashville, Abingdon Press [1969] 143 p. 22 cm. Bibliographical footnotes. [BT102.E4] 69-18452 3.95
1. God. I. Title.

*ERICKSON, Millard J., ed 231
The living God; readings in Christian theology. Grand Rapids, Baker Book House [1973] 512 p. 22 cm. Includes bibliographical notes. [BT102] ISBN 0-8010-3305-5 7.95 (pbk.)
1. God—Addresses, essays, lectures. I. Title.

FARLEY, Edward 231
The transcendence of God, a study in contemporary philosophical theology. Philadelphia, Westminster Press [c.1960] 255p. 21cm. Bibl.: p.223-244 60-9712 5.00
1. Transcendence of God. I. Title.

FARMER, Herbert H. 231
God and men. Nashville, Abingdon [1961, c.1947] 203p. (Apex bk., G1) 1.25 pap.,
1. God. I. Title.

FARRER, Austin Marsden. 231
God is not dead, by Austin Farrer. New York, Morehouse-Barlow [1966] 127 p. 19 cm. First published in London under title: A science of God? [BT102] 78-4370
1. God. I. Title.

FERRE, Nels Fredrick Solomon, 1908- 231
The Christian understanding of God. [1st ed.] New York, Harper [1951] 277 p. 22 cm. [BT101.F36] 51-11910
1. God. I. Title.

*FITCH, William 231
Guided by God. Chicago, Moody [1968] 61p. illus. 20cm. .95 pap.,
1. Devotional literature. I. Title.

FORTMAN, Edmund J., 1901- 231
The Triune God; a historical study of the doctrine of the Trinity [by] Edmund J. Fortman. Philadelphia, Westminster [1972] xxvi, 382 p. 24 cm. (Theological resources) Bibliography: p. 347-358. [BT109.F67 1972] 75-137395 ISBN 0-664-20917-3 9.95
1. Trinity—History of doctrines. I. Title.

FORTMAN, Edmund J., 1901- 231
The Triune God; a historical study of the doctrine of the Trinity [by] Edmund J. Fortman. Philadelphia, Westminster [1972] xxvi, 382 p. 24 cm. (Theological resources) Bibliography: p. 347-358. [BT109.F67 1972] 73-137395 ISBN 0-664-20917-3 9.95
1. Trinity—History of doctrines. I. Title.

FOSTER, A. Durwood, 1926- 231
The God who loves [by] A. Durwood Foster. New York, Bruce Pub. Co. [1971] 152 p. 18 cm. (Faith and life series) Bibliography: p. 150-152. [BT108.F68] 71-160376 1.95
1. God—Study and teaching. I. Title.

FOX, Edward Seccomb, 1911- 231
Christ is God's middle name; children talk about God [by] Edward S. and Elizabeth H. Fox. Illustrated by Ursula Landshoff. [1st ed.] Garden City, N.Y., Doubleday, 1971. viii, 81 p. illus. 22 cm. [BT102.F66] 72-131076 3.95
1. God. 2. Children—Religious life. I. Fox, Elizabeth H., joint author. II. Title.

GALES, Louis A 1896- 231
My book about God; a first book for little Catholics. Pictures by Hans Helweg. St. Paul, Catechetical Guild Educational Society, c1954. unpaged. illus. 17cm. (First books for little Catholics, FB088) [BT107.G3] 55-18143
1. God—Juvenile literature. I. Title.

GATEWOOD, Otis. 231
There is a God in heaven. Abilene, Tex., Contact, inc. [1970] xiii, 317 p. 24 cm. Bibliography: p. 298-301. [BT102.G34] 74-19031 6.95
1. God. 2. Bible and evolution. I. Title.

GENUYT, F. M. 231
The mystery of God [by] F. M. Genuyt. Translated from the French by John J. Pilch. New York, Desclee Co. [1968] xxii, 149 p. 23 cm. Translation of Le mystere de Dieu. Bibliography: p. [xvii]-xxii. [BT102.G413] 68-54220 4.95
1. God—Knowableness. I. Title.

*GERSTNER, John H. 231
A reconciliation primer. Grand Rapids, Mich., Baker Bk. [c.]1965. 51p. 22cm. .85 pap.,
I. Title.

GIBSON, Roxie E. 231
Hey, God! Where are you? [By] Roxie E. Gibson. Illustrated by James C. Gibson. Nashville, Impact Books [1973] 55 p. illus. 20 cm. Describes in verse a youngster's search for God. [BT107.G5] 73-87145 2.95 (pbk.)
1. God—Juvenile literature. I. Gibson, James C., illus. II. Title.

GLEASON, Robert W 231
The search for God, by Robert W. Gleason. New York, Sheed and Ward [1964] 311 p. 22 cm. Includes bibliographies. [BT102.G57] 64-19904
1. God. I. Title.

GLEASON, Robert W. 231
The search for God, by Robert W. Gleason. New York, Sheed and Ward [1964] 311 p. 22 cm. Includes bibliographies. [BT102.G57] 64-19904
1. God. I. Title.

GLEASON, Robert W. 231
Yahweh, the God of the Old Testament. Englewood Cliffs, N.J., Prentice [c.1964] iv, 124p. 21cm. Bibl. 62-16888 3.95
1. God—Biblical teaching. I. Title.

GLEASON, Robert W 231
Yahweh, the God of the Old Testament. Englewood Cliffs, N.J., Prentice-Hall [1964] iv, 124 p. 21 cm. Bibliography: p. 123-124. [BT99.G55] 62-16888
1. God — Biplical teaching. I. Title.

GOD is everywhere : 231
inspiring writings that reveal His nearness and love / selected by Harold Whaley. Kansas City, Mo. : Hallmark, c1976. 60 p. : ill. ; 24 cm. (Hallmark crown editions) [PN6110.G58G6] 75-13018 ISBN 0-87529-458-8 : 5.00
1. God—Poetry. 2. God—Quotations, maxims, etc. I. Whaley, Harold.

GOLDSMITH, Joel S., 1892- 231
The mystical I [by] Joel S. Goldsmith. Edited by Lorraine Sinkler. [1st ed.] New York, Harper & Row [1971] x, 145 p. 22 cm. [BF639.G5683] 73-149745 4.95
1. New Thought. I. Title.

GOLLWITZER, Helmet 231
The existence of God as confessed by faith, Tr. [from German] by James W. Leitch*Philadelphia, Westminster [c.1965] Philadelphia, Westminster *c.1965* 256p. 23cm. Bibl. [BT102.G643] 65-12514 5.75
I. Title.

GOLLWITZER, Helmut. 231
The existence of God as confessed by faith. Translated by James W. Leitch. Philadelphia, Westminster Press [1965] 256 p. 23 cm. Translation of Die Existenz Gottes im Bekenntnis des Glaubens. Bibliographical references included in footnotes. [BT102.G643] 65-12514
1. God. I. Title.

GRANT, Robert McQueen, 1917- 231
The early Christian doctrine of God [by] Tobert M. Grant. Charlottesville, Univ. Pr. of Va. [1966] vi, 141p. illus. 23cm. (Richard lects. 1965-66) Title. (Series: Richard lectures, University of Virginia, 1965-66) Bibl. [PT98.G68] 66-22845 3.50 bds.,
1. God—History of doctrines. 2. Trinity—History of doctrines. I. Title. II. Series.

GRAY, Donald P. 231
Where is your God? [By] Donald P. Gray. Photos. by Rohn Engh. Dayton, Ohio, G. A. Pflaum [1966] 116 p. illus. 17 cm. (Christian experience series, no. 3) Witness books, 4 Bibliography: p. [122]-123. [BT102.G7] 66-28514
1. God. I. Title.

GREELEY, Andrew M., 1928- 231
Youth asks, does God still speak? By Andrew M. Greeley. Camden, N.J., T. Nelson [1970] 94 p. 21 cm. (Youth forum series [YF 9]) Includes bibliographical references. [BT102.G74] 72-110140 1.50
1. God. 2. Youth—Religious life. I. Title. II. Series.

GUARDINI, Romano, 1885- 231
The living God. Translated by Stanley Godman. [New York] Pantheon [1957] 112p. 21cm. [BT101.G85] 57-7320
1. God. I. Title.

GUARDINI, Romano, 1885- 231
The living God. Tr. by Stanley Godman. Chicago, Regnery [1966,c.1957] 112p. 17cm. (Logos 51L-709) [BT101.G85] 1.25 pap.,
1. God. I. Title.

HAGERTY, Cornelius, 1885- 231
The Holy Trinity / by Cornelius J. Hagerty. North Quincy, Mass. : Christopher Pub. House, c1976. 359 p. : 25 cm. Includes index. Bibliography: p. 347-350. [BT111.2.H34] 73-92102 ISBN 0-8158-0316-8 : 6.95
1. Trinity. I. Title.

HALL, Kenneth F., 1926- 231
On bumping into God [by] Kenneth F. Hall.

Anderson, Ind., Warner Press [1972] iii, 127 p. 19 cm. [BT102.H335] 76-175539 ISBN 0-87162-129-0
1. God. I. Title.

HAMILTON, James Wallace, 1900- 231
Who goes there? What and where is God? [Westwood, N. J.] Revell [1958] 154p. 22cm. [BT101.H24] 58-5343
1. God. I. Title.

HAMILTON, Kenneth 231
God is dead; the anatomy of a slogan. Grand Rapids, Mich., Eerdmans [c.1966] 86p. 21cm. [BT83.5.H3] 66-22945 2.45 pap.,
1. Death of God theology. I. Title.

HANEY, Herbert M. 231
The wrath of God in the former prophets. New York, Vantage Press [c.1960] 87 p. 22 cm. Bibl.: p. 79-87 2.95 bds.,
I. Title.

HARRIS, Erdman, 1898- 231
God's image and man's imagination. New York, Scribner [1959] 236 p. 21 cm. Includes bibliography. [BT102.H35] 59-11438
1. God. I. Title.

HARRIS, F. Donald. 231
The Trinity: is the doctrine biblical? Is it important? By F. Donald Harris and Ronald A. Harris. Neptune, N.J. Loizeaux Brothers [1971] 32 p. 17 cm. [BT113.H33] 77-123613 ISBN 0-87213-310-9 0.50
1. Trinity. I. Harris, Ronald A., joint author. II. Title.

HARTILL, Percy, 1892- 231
The unity of God; a study in Christian monotheism. London, A. R. Mowbray; New York, Morehouse-Gorham [1952] 202p. 23cm. [BT101.H36] 53-18799
1. God. I. Title.

*HARTSHORNE, Charles 231
The divine relativity; a social conception of God. New Haven, Conn., Yale [1964, c.1948] 164p. 21cm. 1.45 pap.,
I. Title.

HAUGH, Richard. 231
Photius and the Carolingians : the Trinitarian controversy / Richard Haugh. Belmont, Mass. : Nordland Pub. Co., [1975] 230 p. ; 23 cm. Includes index. Bibliography: p. 207-214. [BT109.H35] 74-22859 ISBN 0-913124-05-2 : 15.00
1. Photius I, Saint, Patriarch of Constantinople, ca. 820-ca. 891. 2. Trinity—History of doctrines. I. Title.

HAZELTON, Roger, 1909- 231
On proving God; a handbook in Christian conversation. [1st ed.] New York, Harper [1952] 186 p. 22 cm. [BT98.H3] 52-6435
1. God—Proof. I. Title.

HEARN, Florence. 231
I think about God. Pictures by Dorothy Teichman. Nashville, Broadman Press, c1959. unpaged. illus: 21cm. [BT107.H4] 60-5027
1. God—Juvenile literature. I. Title.

HEDLEY, George Percy, 1899- 231
The Holy Trinity; experience and interpretation, by George Hedley. Philadelphia, Fortress [1967] xi, 147p. 18cm. [BT109.H4] 67-16468 2.00 pap.,
1. Trinity —History of doctrines. I. Title.

HEIDE, Florence Parry. 231 E
God and me / written by Florence Parry Heide ; illustrated by Ted Smith. St. Louis : Concordia Pub. House, [1975] [31] p. : col. ill. ; 27 cm. There are many things we cannot see but know are there: the sun at night, the flower in the seed, birds inside their eggs—and so it is with God's presence. [BT107.H44] 75-4627 ISBN 0-570-03437-X : 3.95
1. God—Juvenile literature. I. Smith, Ted, ill. II. Title.

HERDER, Johann Gottfired von, 1744-1803. 231
God, some conversations. A translation, with a critical introd. and notes by Frederick H. Burkhardt. Indianapolis, Bobbs-Merrill [1963? c1940] 247 p. 21 cm. (The Library of liberal arts) "140." Bibliographical references included in "Notes to the transiation" (p. 220-231) Bibliography: p. 233-241. [BT100] 62-20496
1. God. I. Title.

HERMES Trismegistus. 231
The divine pymander, and other writings of Hermes Trismegistus. Translated from the original Greek by John D. Chambers. New York, S. Weiser, 1972. xxiv, 170 p. 21 cm. Reprint of the 1882 ed. published by T. & T. Clark, Edinburgh, under title: The theological and philosophical works of Hermes Trismegistus. Contents.Contents.—Poemandres.—Excerpts from Hermes by Stobaeus.—Notices of Hermes in the Fathers. Includes bibliographical references. [BF1598.H5E5 1972] 70-184564 ISBN 0-87728-193-9 3.50
I. Chambers, John David, 1805-1893, tr. II. Title.

HEWLETT, Henry Charles. 231
The companion of the way. Chicago, Moody Press [1962] 159p. 22cm. [BT128.H4] 62-1315
1. Theophanies. 2. Devotional literature. I. Title.

HILL, Dorothy La Croix. 231
God, help me understand. Illustrated by William A. McCaffery. New York, Abingdon Press [1959] 93p. illus. 24cm. [BT107.H5] 59-1018
1. God—Juvenile literature. I. Title.

HILLIS, Dave. 231
How big is God? / Dave Hillis ; ill. by Nev Sandon. Wheaton, Ill. : Tyndale House Publishers, 1974. 84 p. : ill. ; 18 cm. Answers some commonly asked questions about God with appropriate Bible passages. [BT107.H54] 74-80771 ISBN 0-8423-1510-1 pbk. : 1.25
1. God—Juvenile literature. I. Sandon, Nev., ill. II. Title.

HOHMANN, Harry E 231
Power of God in man by Harry E. Hohmann. San Antonio Naylor Co [1965] 53 p. 20 cm. [BT732.5.H64] 65-20763
1. Faith-cure. I. Title.

HOHMANN, Harry E. 231
Power of God in man. San Antonio, Tex., Naylor [c.1965] 53p. 20cm. [BT732.5.H64] 65-20763 1.95 pap.,
1. Faith-cure. I. Title.

HORTON, Walter M[arshall] 231
The God we trust. Philadelphia, Published for The Cooperative Publication Association by The Judson Press [c.1960] 96p. 19cm. (A cooperative text; Faith for life ser.) 1.00 pap.,
I. Title.

HORTON, Walter Marshall, 1895- 231
God, Jesus, and man; comprising these Hazen book classics: God, by Walter M. Horton. Jesus, by Mary Ely Lyman. What is man? By Robert Lowry Calhoun. New York, Association Press [1953] 1v. (various pagings) 19cm. [BT10.H64] 53-7964
1. God. 2. Jesus Christ—Significance. 3. Man (Theology). I. Lyman, Mary Redington (Ely) 1887- Jesus. II. Calhoun, Robert Lowry, 1896- What is man? III. Title.

HOUGH, Robert Ervin, 1874- 231
The ministry of the glory cloud. New York, Philosophical Library [1955] 145p. 21cm. [BT128.H6] 56-183
1. Theophanies. I. Title.

HUMPHREY, Zephine, 1874- 231
God and company. [1st ed.] New York, Harper [1953] 128p. 20cm. [BT101.H93] 53-8372
1. God. I. Title.

IS God dead? 231
New York, Paulist Press [1966] viii, 181 p. 24 cm. (Concillum theology in the age of renewal: Fundamental theology, v. 16) Bibliographical footnotes. [BL2747.3.I8] 66-25679
1. Atheism — Controversial literature. I. Series. II. Series: Concillum theology in the age of renewal, v. 16

IS God "dead"? 231
A symposium with chapters contributed by Billy Graham [and others. 1st ed.] Grand Rapids, Zondervan Pub. House [1966] 120 p. 21 cm. Contents.Contents.—The graveyard theology: a brief introduction to brash infidelity, by V. C. Grounds.—God is not "dead," by B. Graham.—Who says God is dead? By B. Ramm.—The "Death of God" theology, by B. Ramm.—The death of God: a call to the Church to come alive, by D. Hubbard. [BT83.5.I8] 66-29418
1. Death of God theology.

IS God dead?iNew York, 231
Paulist [1966, i.e. 1967] viii, 181p. 24cm. (Concilium theology in the age of renewal: Fundamental theology, v.16) Bibl. [BL2747.3.18] 66-25679 4.50
1. Atheism— Controversial literature. I. Series: Concilium theology in the age of renewal, v.16

JANSSENS, Alois, 1887-1941 231
The mystery of the Trinity. Fresno, Calif., Acad. Lib. [1962, c.]1954. 168p. 23cm. (Aspect bk.) 1.95 pap.
1. Trinity. I. Title.

JENKINS, Daniel Thomas, 1914- 231
Believing in God. Philadelphia, Westminster Press [1956] 94p. 20cm. (Layman's theological library) [BT101.J45] 56-9576
1. God. 2. Faith. I. Title.

JENKINS, Daniel Thomas, 1914- 231
The Christian belief in God. Philadelphia, Westminster [1964, c.1963] 226p. 23cm. Bibl. 64-13758 4.75
1. God—Proof. I. Title.

JENKINS, David E. 231
Guide to the debate about God, by David E. Jenkins. Philadelphia, Westminister Press [1966] 111 p. 19 cm. (Adventures in faith) Includes bibliographical references. [BT28.J4] 66-13083
1. Theology, Doctrinal—History—20th century. I. Title. II. Title: The debate about God.

JOHANN, Robert O. 231
The pragmatic meaning of God, by Robert O. Johann. Milwaukee, Marquette University Press, 1966. 66 p. 19 cm. (The Aquinas lecture, 1966) Bibliographical footnotes. [BT113.J6] 66-26282
1. God—Addresses, essays, lectures. I. Title. II. Series.

JONES, Mary Alice, 1898- 231
God is good, by Mary Alice Jones in collaboration with Kate Smallwood.tIllustrated by Elizabeth Webbe. Chicago, Rand McNally, c1955. unpaged. illus. 17cm. (A Rand McNally book, 692) [BT107.J6] 55-11977
1. God—Juvenile literature. I. Title.

JONES, Mary Alice, 1898- 231
God speaks to me. Illustrated by Dorothy Grider. Chicago, Rand McNally [1961] 45p. illus. 24cm. Poems. [BT107.J63] 61-12314
1. God—Juvenile literature. I. Title.

JONES, Mary Alice, 1898- 231
Tell me about God. Illus. by Dorothy Grider. A completely new ed. [Chicago] Rand McNally [1967] 71p. illus. (pt. col.) 27cm. [BV1590.J6 1967] 67-15727 2.95 bds.,
1. Religious education—Hoome training. I. Grider, Dorothy, illus. II. Title.

JONES, Mary Alice, 1898- 231
Tell me about God. Illustrated by Dorothy Grider. A completely new ed. [Chicago] Rand McNally [1967] 71 p. illus. (part col.) 27 cm. Mary and Bobby learn through worship, personal relations, nature, and play the factors that make God seem real. [BV1590.J6 1967] AC 67
1. God. I. Grider, Dorothy, illus. II. Title.

JONES, William Ronald. 231
Is God a white racist? A preamble to Black theology, by William R. Jones. [1st ed.] Garden City, N.Y., Anchor Press, 1973. xxii, 239 p. 22 cm. (C. Eric Lincoln series on Black religion) Includes bibliographical references. [BT734.J66] 72-96245 ISBN 0-385-00909-7 7.95
1. Race (Theology) 2. Negroes—Religion. I. Title. II. Series.

JUKES, Andrew John, 1815-1901. 231
The names of God in Holy Scripture. [1st American ed.] Grand Rapids. Kregel Publications [1967] 226 p. 20 cm. "Reproduced complete and unabridged from the first edition published in London, 1888." [BT180.N2J8 1967] 67-28843
1. God—Name. I. Title.

JUKES, Andrew John, 1815-1901. 231
The names of God in Holy Scripture. [1st American ed.] Grand Rapids, Kregel Publications [1967] 226 p. 20 cm "Reproduced complete and unabridged from the first edition published in London, 1888." [BT180.N2J8 1967] 67-28843
1. God—Name—Biblical teaching. I. Title.

JUNGEL, Eberhard. 231
The doctrine of the Trinity : God's being is in becoming / Eberhard Jungel ; [translated by Horton Harris]. Grand Rapids, Mich. : W. B. Eerdmans Pub. Co., 1976. p. cm. Translation of Gottes Sein ist im Werden. Includes bibliographical references and index. [BT101.B2718J813] 76-20794 ISBN 0-8028-1638-X : 4.95
1. Barth, Karl, 1886-1968. 2. God—History of doctrines—20th century. I. Title.

JUNGEL, Eberhard. 231
The doctrine of the Trinity : God's being is in becoming / [by] Eberhard Jungel ; translated [from the German] by Horton Harris. Edinburgh : Scottish Academic Press, 1976. xxi, 110 p. ; 23 cm. (Monograph supplements to the Scottish journal of theology) Translation of Gottes Sein ist im Werden. Includes bibliographical references and index. [BT101.B2718J813 1976b] 77-367479 ISBN 0-7073-0115-7 : £3.25
1. Barth, Karl, 1886-1968. 2. God—History of doctrines—20th century. I. Title. II. Series: Scottish journal of theology. Monograph supplements.

KEE, Alistair, 1937- 231
The way of transcendence: Christian faith without belief in God. Harmondsworth, Penguin, 1971. xxix, 241 p. 19 cm. (Pelican books A1309) Includes bibliographical references. [BT83.7.K4] 70-28820 ISBN 0-14-021309-0 £0.35
1. Secularization (Theology) 2. God—History of doctrines. I. Title.

KELLY, Herbert Hamilton, 1860-1950. 231
The gospel of God. With a memoir by George Every. [London] SCM Press stamped: distributed in U. S. A. by Allenson, Naperville, Ill. [1959?] 151p. illus. 19cm. Includes bibliography. [BR121.2.K4 1959] 59-3371
1. Christianity— Essence, genius, nature. I. Title.

KENNY, John Peter, 1916- 231
The supernatural; medieval theological concepts to modern [by] J. P. Kenny. New York, Alba House [1972] xiv, 150 p. 22 cm. Bibliography: p. [145]-150. [BT745.K45] 72-3575 ISBN 0-8189-0251-5 4.95
1. Supernatural—History of doctrines. I. Title.

KERESZTY, Roch A. 231
God seekers for a new age; from crisis theology to Christian atheism [by] Roch A. Kereszty. Dayton, Ohio, Pflaum Press, 1970. viii, 149 p. 21 cm. (Themes for today) Bibliography: p. 137-141. [BT83.5.K47] 76-93005 2.95
1. Death of God theology. I. Title.

KING, Robert Harlen, 1935- 231
The meaning of God [by] Robert H. King. Philadelphia, Fortress Press [1973] x, 166 p. 24 cm. [BT102.K48] 73-80635 ISBN 0-8006-0257-9 6.95
1. God. I. Title.

KITAMORI, Kazo, 1916- 231
Theology of the pain of God [Tr. from Japanese] Richmond, Va., Knox [c.1965] 183p. 21cm. Bibl. [BT153.S8K513] 65-20544 4.50
1. Suffering of God. I. Title.

KUNG, Hans, 1928- ed. 231
The unknown God? New York, Sheed and Ward [1967, c1966] 158 p. 22 cm. (Theological meditations) Translations of three volumes originally published separately in German. [BT80.K8] 66-22028
1. Theology, Doctrinal—Addresses, essays, lectures. I. Moller, Joseph. Are we searching for God? II. Haag, Herbert. The God of the beginnings and of today. III. Hasenhuttl, Gotthold. Encounter with God. IV. Title.
Contents omitted

KUNG, Hans, 1928- 231
The unknown, God! New York, Sheed and Ward [1967, c1966] 158 p. 22 cm. (Theological meditations) Translations of three volumes originally published separately in German. Contents.CONTENTS. -- Preface, by H. Kung. -- The God of the beginnings and of today, by H. Hang. -- Encounter with God, by G. Hasenhuttl, Notes (p. 1550158) [BT80.K8] 66-22023
1. Theology, Doctrinal — Addresses, essays, lectures. I. Muller, Joseph. Are we searching for God? II. Hand, Herbert. The God of the beginnings and of today. III. Ilasenuhuttl, Gotthold. Encounter with God. IV. Title.

KUNG, Hans, 1928- ed. 231
The unknown God? New York, Sheed and Ward [1967, c1966] 158 p. 22 cm. (Theological meditations) Translations of three volumes originally published separately in German. Contents.Contents.—Preface, by H. Kung.—Are we searching for God? By J. Moller.—The God of the beginnings and of today, by H. Haag.—Encounter with God, by G. Hasenhuttl. Notes (p. 155-158) [BT80.K8] 66-22028
1. Theology, Doctrinal—Addresses, essays, lectures. I. Moller, Joseph. Fragen wir nach Gott? English. 1967. II. Haag, Herbert. Am Morgan der zeit. English. 1967. III. Hasenhuttl, Gotthold. Der unbkannte Gott. english. 1967. IV. Title.

LASCARIS, Andrew. 231
The theology of God. Notre Dame, Ind., Fides Publishers [1973, c1972] 90 p. 19 cm. (Theology today, no. 13) Includes bibliographical references. [BT102.L37 1973] 72-13296 ISBN 0-8190-0540-1 0.95 (pbk.)
1. God. I. Title.

LEIBRECHT, Walter. 231
God and man in the thought of Hamann. Translated by James H. Stam and Martin H. Bertram. Philadelphia, Fortress Press [1966] viii, 216 p. 23 cm. Bibliography: p. 201-208. [BT100.H3L413] 66-11532

1. Hamann, Johann Georg. 1730-1788. 2. God — History of doctrines. 3. Man (Theology) — History of doctrines. I. Title.

LEIBRECHT, Walter 231
God and man in the thought of Hamann. Tr. [from German] by James H. Stam, Martin H. Bertram. Philadelphia, Fortress [c.1966] viii,216p. 23cm. Bibl. [BT100.H3L413] 66-11532 5.00
1. Hamann, Johann Georg, 1730-1788. 2. God—History of doctrines. 3. Man (Theology)—History of doctrines. I. Title.

LICKEY, Arthur E. 231
Where is God? Washington, Review and Herald Pub. Association [1951] 128 p. illus. 16 cm. (Little giant pocket series) [BT101.L49] 51-20625
1. God. I. Title.

LIGHTNER, Robert Paul. 231
The first fundamental: God, by Robert P. Lightner. [1st ed.] Nashville, T. Nelson [1973] 160 p. 21 cm. Bibliography: p. 156. [BT102.L53] 73-6669 5.95
1. God. I. Title.

LOCKYER, Herbert. 231
All the promises of the Bible; a unique compilation and exposition of divine promises in Scripture. Grand Rapids, Zondervan Pub. House [1962] 610p. 25cm. [BT180.P7L6] 62-53110
1. God—Promises. I. Title.

LOCKYER, Herbert Henry John 231
All the promises of the Bible;a unique compilation and exposition of divine promises in Scripture. Grand Rapids, Mich., Zondervan [c.1962] 610p. 25cm. 62-53110 6.95
1. God—Promises. I. Title.

LONERGAN, Bernard J. F. 231
The way to Nicea : the dialectical development of trinitarian theology / Bernard Lonergan ; a translation by Conn O'Donovan of the first part of De Deo Trino. Philadelphia : Westminster Press, c1976. xxxi, 142 p. ; 23 cm. "A translation of pages 17-112, Pars dogmatica, of De Deo Trino, Rome, Gregorian University Press, 1964." Includes bibliographical references and indexes. [BT109.L6613] 76-20792 ISBN 0-664-21340-5 : 9.50
1. Trinity—History of doctrines. 2. Dogma, Development of. 3. Sects. I. Title.

LOVERN, Thomas Y 231
God as I understand Him. Richmond, Garrett & Massie, 1960. 122p. illus. 19cm. [BT102.L6] 60-9008
1. God. I. Title.

LUBAC, Henri de, 1896- 231
The discovery of God. Tr. by Alexander Dru. Chicago, Regnery [1967,c.1960] 212p. 18cm. (Logos, 611-724) Pub. in London in 1960 by Darton, Longman & Todd. First pub. in France by Aubier, Paris, under title Sur les chemins de Dieu. Bibl. [BT101.L733 1960] 1.45 pap.,
1. God. (Theory of knowledge) I. Title.

LUIS DE GRANADA, 1504-1588. 231
Summa of the Christian life, selected texts; translated and adapted by Jordan Aumann. St. Louis, Herder [1954- v. 21cm. (Cross and crown series of spirituality. no. 3 Translation of Obra selecta: una suma de la vida Christiana. [BX2349.L843] 54-10966
1. Christian life—Catholic authors. 2. Catholic Church—Doctrinal and controversial works, Popular. I. Title. II. Series.

MCDONOUGH, William K. 231
The Divine Family; the Trinity and our life in God. New York, Macmillan [c.1963] 178p. 22cm. 63-9235 3.95
1. Trinity. I. Title.

MACGREGOR, Geddes. 231
The sense of absence. [1st ed.] Philadelphia, Lippincott, 1968 [c1967] 158 p. 21 cm. Bibliographical footnotes. [BT102.M24] 68-11130
1. God. I. Title.

MCLARRY, Newman R. 231
His good and perfect will. Nashville, Broadman [c.1965] 62p. 16cm. [BV4501.2.M25] 65-12863 1.25
1. God—Will. I. Title.

MCNAUGHTON, Ruth L 231
Tiny thoughts about God. Illustrated by Faith McNaughton Lowell. Wheaton, Ill., Van Kampen Press, c1951. unpaged. illus. 21 cm. [BT107.M3] 51-6814
1. God—Juvenile literature. I. Title.

MACQUARRIE, John. 231
Thinking about God / John Macquarrie. 1st U.S. ed. New York : Harper & Row, [1975] 238 p. ; 21 cm. Includes bibliographical references and index. [BT102.M274 1975] 74-25704 ISBN 0-06-065367-1 : 8.95
1. God. 2. Theology—Methodology. 3. Theology, Doctrinal—History. I. Title.

MAGAGNA, Anna Marie. 231
My book about God's world. Selected by Blanche Mays from the Authorized King James version of the Bible. Illustrated by Anna Marie Magagna. New York, Grosset & Dunlap, c1962. unpaged illus. 31cm. [BT107.M33] 62-13368
1. God—Juvenile literature. I. Mays, Blanche, ed. II. Title.

MARITAIN, Jacques, 1882- 231
Approaches to God. / Tr. from French by Peter O'Reilly. New York, Macmillan [1965,c.1964] 125p. 18 cm. (MP189) [BT101.M42953] pap.,.95
1. God. (Theory of knowledge) I. Title.

MARITAIN, Jacques, 1882- 231
Approaches to God. Translated from the French by Peter O'Reilly. [1st ed.] New York, Harper [1954] xvi, 128p. 20cm. (World perspectives, v.1) [BT101.M42953] 54-8969
1. God (Theory of knowledge) I. Title. II. Series.

MARITAIN, Jacques, 1882- 231
Approaches to God. Tr. from French by Peter O'Reilly. New York, Collier [1962, c.1954] 125p. 18cm. (AS154V) .95 pap.,
I. Title.

MARITAIN, Jacques, 1882- 231
Man's approach to God. Latrobe, Pa., Archabbey Press [dist. University Publishers, 1961, c.1960] 53p. (Wimmer lecture, 5) 61-2276 2.50
1. God (Theory of knowledge) I. Title.

MARSHALL, Eric, fl.1966- 231
God is a good friend to have. Compiled by Eric Marshall and Stuart Hample. Illustrated by Tony Walton. New York, Simon and Schuster [1969] [64] p. illus. (part col.) 22 cm. [BT102.M33] 71-92193 ISBN 0-671-20400-9 3.50
1. God. 2. Children—Religious life. I. Hample, Stuart E., joint author. II. Watson, Tony, illus. III. Title.

MARXHAUSEN, Joanne. 231
3 in 1 (a picture of God). written by Joanne Marxhausen. Art by Benjamin Marxhausen. St. Louis, Mo., Concordia Pub. House [1973] 47 p. col. illus. 27 cm. Compares the three parts of an apple to the three-in-one concept of God. [BT107.M37] 73-179181 ISBN 0-570-03419-1 3.25
1. God—Juvenile literature. I. Marxhausen, Benjamin, illus. II. Title.

MARXHAUSEN, Joanne. 231
3 in 1 (a picture of God), written by Joanne Marxhausen. Art by Benjamin Marxhausen St. Louis, Mo., Concordia Pub. House [1973] 47 p. col. illus. 27 cm. Compares the three parts of an apple to the three-in-one concept of God. [BT107.M37] 73-179181 ISBN 0-570-03419-1
1. God—Juvenile literature. I. Marxhausen, Benjamin, illus. II. Title.

MAXWELL, C. Mervyn, 1925- 231
Man, what a God! By C. Mervyn Maxwell. Mountain View, Calif., Pacific Press Pub. Association [1970] 63 p. 18 cm. [BT102.M37] 73-140494
1. God. I. Title.

MAZZEI, Alfred Maria. 231
Does God exist? Translated by Daisy Corinne Fornacca. New York, Society of St. Paul [c1956] 292p. 21cm. Includes bibliography. [BT101.M48] 57-4260
1. God—Proof. I. Title.

MAZZEI, Alfredo Maria. 231
Does God exist? Translated by Daisy Corinne Fornacca. New York, Society of St. Paul [c1956] 292p. 21cm. Includes bibliography. [BT101.M48] 57-4260
1. God—Proof. I. Title.

MENARD, William Thompson 231
Living the life eternal. New York, Vantage [c.1961] 47p. 2.00 bds.,
I. Title.

MILTON, John, 1608-1674. 231
Milton on the Son of God and the Holy Spirit : from his treatise, On Christian doctrine / with introd. by Alexander Gordon. Norwood, Pa. : Norwood Editions, 1976. xi, 136 p. ; 23 cm. Reprint of the 1908 ed. published by the British & Foreign Unitarian Association, London. Selected from the 1853 ed. of C. R. Sumner's translation of De doctrina Christiana. [BT115.M53 1976] 76-6564 ISBN 0-8482-0853-6 : 15.00
1. Trinity—Controversial literature. I. Title.

MILTON, John, 1608-1674. 231
Milton on the Son of God and the Holy Spirit, from his Treatise on Christian doctrine. With introd. by Alexander Gordon. [Folcroft, Pa.] Folcroft Library Editions, 1973. xi, 136 p. 24 cm. Reprint of the 1908 ed. published by British and Foreign Unitarian Association, London. [BT115.M53 1973] 73-4827 ISBN 0-8414-2028-9 (lib. bdg.)
1. Trinity—Controversial literature. I. Title.

MITCHELL, James Alexander Hugh, 1939- 231
The God I want [by] Charles Rycroft [and others] Edited, with an introd., by James Mitchell. Indianapolis, Bobbs-Merrill [1967] 192 p. 22 cm. Essays. [BT102.A1M53 1967b] 67-22224
1. God—Addresses, essays, lectures. I. Rycroft, Charles. II. Title.

*MONTGOMERY, John Warwick. 231
How do we know there is a god? and other questions inappropriate in polite society. Minneapolis, Bethany Fellowship [1973] 92 p. 18 cm. (Dimension books) [BT102.] ISBN 0-87123-221-9 0.95 (pbk.)
1. God. I. Title.

MONTGOMERY, John Warwick 231
The 'Is God Dead?' controversy: a philosophical theological critique of the death of God movement Grand Rapids. Zondervan [1966] 66p. 21cm. Bibl. [BT83.5.M6] 66-6559 1.00 pap.,
1. Death of God theology. I. Title.

MONTGOMERY, John Warwick. 231
The 'Is God dead?' controversy; a philosophical-theological critique of the death of God movement. Grand Rapids, Zondervan Pub. House [1966] 66 p. 21 cm. Bibliographical footnotes. [BT83.5.M6] 66-6559
1. Death of God theology. I. Title.

MORRIS, Augustine. 231
The God of the Christians. Westminster [London] Dacre Press [1946] 125 p. 20 cm. [Mirfield books] [BT101.M8] 48-25618
1. God. I. Title.

MOYNIHAN, Anselm. 231
The experience of God's presence. Staten Island, N.Y., Alba House [1967] 96 p. 20 cm. Bibliographical footnotes. [BT102.M66] 67-21424
1. God. I. Title.

MURA, Ernest, 1900- 231
In Him is life. Translated by Angeline Bouchard. St. Louis, B. Herder Book Co. [1956] 226p. 21cm. (Cross and crown series of spirituality, no. 8) Translation of L'humanite vivifiante du Christ. [BX2350.M915] 56-10797
1. Mystical union. 2. Spiritual life—Catholic authors. I. Title.

NEILL, Stephen Charles, Bp. 231
The Christians' God. New York, Association Press [1955] 90p. 20cm. (World Christian books) [T101.N4] 55-7415
1. God. I. Title.

NEILL, Stephen Charles, Bp. 231
The Christians' God. New York, Association Press [1955] 90 p. 20 cm. (World Christian books [1]) [BT101.N4] 55-7415
1. God. I. Title.

NEWBY, J Edwin, 1898- 231
Chart messages on the history and prophecy of the Bible. Berne, Ind., Light and Hope Publications [1951] 168 p. illus. 20 cm. [BT155.N37] 52-17243
1. Covenants (Theology) I. Title.

NICHOLSON, Norman, 1914- 231
H. G. Wells. Denver, A. Swallow [1950] 98 p. 19 cm. (The English novelists) [[PR5776.N]] A52
1. Wells, Herbert George, 1866-1946. I. Title. II. Series: The English novelists (Denver)

NILES, Daniel Thambyrajah. 231
Upon the earth; the mission of God and the missionary enterprise of the churches. New York, McGraw-Hill [1962] 269p. 23cm. (Foundations of the Christian mission; studies in the gospel and the world) [BT165.N5] 62-15292
1. God. 2. Man (Theology) 3. Missions—Theory. I. Title.

NILES, Daniel Thambyrajah. 231
We know in part, by D. T. Niles. Philadelphia, Westminster Press [1964] 158 p. 19 cm. [BT55.R63N5] 64-18685
1. Robinson, John Arthur Thomas, Bp., 1919- Honest in God. I. Title.

NILES, Daniel Thambyrajah 231
We know in part. Philadelphia, Westminster [c.1964] 158p. 19cm. 64-18685 1.95 pap.,
1. Robinson, John Arthur Thomas, Bp., 1919- Honest to God. I. Title.

OCHS, Carol. 231
The myth behind the sex of God : toward a new consciousness—transcending matriarchy and patriarchy / Carol Ochs. Boston : Beacon Press, c1977. xiii, 177 p. ; 21 cm. Includes index. Bibliography: p. 155-169. [BL65.S4O25 1977] 76-48519 ISBN 0-8070-1112-6 : 9.95
1. Sex and religion. 2. Sex (Theology) I. Title.

OGLETREE, Thomas W 231
The death of God controversy [by] Thomas W. Ogletree. Nashville, Abingdon Press [1966] 127 p. 19 cm. Bibliography: p. 123-127. [BT83.5.O4] 66-22914
1. Altizer, Thomas J. J. 2. Hamilton, William, 1924- 3. Van Buren, Paul Mathews, 1924- 4. Death of God theology. I. Title.

OGLETREE, Thomas W. 231
The death of God controversy [by] Thomas W. Ogletree. Nashville, Abingdon [1966] 127p. 19cm. [BT83.5.O4] 66-22914 1.45 pap.,
1. Altizer, Thomas J. J. 2. Hamilton, William, 1924- 3. Van Buren, Paul Matthews, 1924- 4. Death of God theology. I. Title.

ORR, J. Edwin 231
100 question about God. Glendale, iGlendale, Calif. [Gospel Light Pubns., 1966] 216p. 18cm. (Regal bks., GL956) .95 pap.,
I. Title.

OURSLER, Fulton, 1893-1952. 231
Why I know there is a God. [1st ed.] Garden City, N. Y., Doubleday, 1950. 192 p. 21 cm. [BT101.O8] 50-9261
1. God. 2. Apologetics—20th century. 3. Prayer. I. Title.

OXFORD Institute on Methodist Theological Studies, 4th, 1969. 231
The living God. Dow Kirkpatrick, editor. Nashville, Abingdon Press [1971] 206 p. 23 cm. "Prepared under the direction of the World Methodist Council." Includes bibliographical references. [BT102.O94 1969] 77-134248 ISBN 0-687-22340-7 5.95
1. God—Addresses, essays, lectures. I. Kirkpatrick, Dow, ed. II. World Methodist Council. III. Title.

PACKER, James Innall. 231
Knowing God [by] J. I. Packer. Downers Grove, Ill., InterVarsity Press [1973] 256 p. 22 cm. [BT102.P26 1973] 73-81573 ISBN 0-87784-866-1 5.95
1. God. I. Title.

PANIKKAR, Raymond, 1918- 231
The Trinity and the religious experience of man; icon-person-mystery [by] Raimundo Panikkar. New York, Orbis Books [1973] xvi, 82 p. 19 cm. [BT111.2.P36] 73-77329 ISBN 0-88344-495-X 2.95 (pbk.)
1. Trinity. 2. Spirituality. I. Title.

PARKER, Thomas Henry Louis. 231
Calvin's doctrine of the knowledge of God. [Rev. ed.] Grand Rapids, Eerdmans [1959] 128p. 21cm. First published in 1952 under title: The doctrine of the knowledge of God: a study in the theology of John Calvin. Includes bibliography. [BX9418.P34 1959] 59-16294
1. Calvin, Jean, 1509-1564—Theology. 2. God (Theory of knowledge) 3. God—History of doctrines. I. Title. II. Title: Doctrine of the knowledge of God.

PARKES, James William, 1896- 231
God at work in science, politics and human life. New York, Philosophical Library [1952] 180 p. 19 cm. [BL51.P27] 52-12431
1. Religion — Philosophy. 2. Revelation. I. Title.

PATTERSON, Alexander G 231
Following God through the Bible. Boston, Christopher Pub. House [1956] 127p. 21cm. [BT99.P35] 56-2142
1. God—Biblical teaching. I. Title.

PECK, Kathryn (Blackburn) 231
God made this lovely, lovely world. Pictures by Lilli Mathews. Anderson, Ind., Warner Press [dist. Gospel Trumpet Press] [1960] unpaged. col. illus. 23cm. 60-7186 .50 pap.,
1. God—Juvenile literature. I. Title.

PENNINGTON, Chester A. 231
With good reason [by] Chester A. Pennington. Nashville, Abin)don [1967] 157p. 20cm. Bibl. [BT102.P4] 67-14987 2.75
1. God. I. Title.

PEURSEN, Cornelis Anthonie van, 1920- 231
Him again, by Cornelis van Peursen. Translated by Annebeth Macky-Gunning. Richmond, John Knox Press [1969] 71 p. 19 cm. (Chime paperbacks) Translation of Hij is het weer. [BT180.N2P483] 69-17002 1.25
1. God—Name. I. Title.

PHILLIPS, Anthony. 231
God B.C. / Anthony Phillips ; with a foreword by the Bishop of London. Oxford [Eng.] ; New York : Oxford University Press, 1977. xiii, 96 p. ; 21 cm. Includes index. [BS1192.6.P47] 77-357901 ISBN 0-19-213959-2 : 5.50
1. Jesus Christ—Person and offices. 2. Bible. O.T.—Theology. 3. God—Biblical teaching. I. Title.

PHILLIPS, John Bertram, 1906- 231
God our contemporary. New York, Macmillan, 1960. 137 p. 22 cm. [BR121.2.P5] 60-11817
1. Christianity—20th century. I. Title.

PHILLIPS, John Bertram, 1906- 231
Your God is too small. New York, Macmillan [1953] 140 p. 19 cm. [BT101.P48] 52-12744
1. God. I. Title.

PIAULT, Bernard. 231
What is the Trinity? Translated from the French by Rosemary Haughton. [1st ed.] New York, Hawthorn Books [1959] 156p. 21cm. (The Twentieth century encyclopedia of Catholicism. v. 17. Section 2: The basic truths) Translation of Le mystere du Dieu vivant, un et trine. Bibliography: p.156. [BT109.P513] 58-11595
1. Trinity—History of doctrines. 2. Creeds. I. Title. II. Series: The Twentieth century encyclopedia of Catholicism, v. 17

PINK, Arthur Walkington, 1886-1952. 231
Gleanings in the Godhead : [selections] / by Arthur W. Pink ; [compiled by I. C. Herendeen] Chicago : Moody Press, [1975] 247 p. ; 24 cm. [BT102.P53] 75-15760 ISBN 0-8024-2977-7 : 6.95
1. Jesus Christ—Person and offices. 2. God. I. Title.

PINK, Arthur Walkington, 1886-1952. 231
The sovereignty of God. [6th ed.] Swengel, Pa., Bible Truth Depot, 1959[c.1930] 320p. 60-52356 3.75 bds.,
1. Providence and government of God. I. Title.

PITTENGER, William Norman, 1905- 231
The divine triunity / by Norman Pittenger. Philadelphia : United Church Press, c1977. 119 p. ; 22 cm. "A Pilgrim Press book." Bibliography: p. 118-119. [BT111.2.P57] 76-55002 ISBN 0-8298-0330-0 : 5.95
1. Trinity. 2. Process theology. I. Title.

POMERANTZ, Alfred. 231
Of man and God. New York, Philosophical Library [1965] 185 p. 22 cm. [B945.P67O3] 65-10996
1. Monadology. 2. Theology. I. Title.

POMERANTZ, Alfred 231
Of man and God New York, Philosophical [c.1965] 185p. 22cm. [B945.P67O3] 65-10996 4.75
1. Monadology. 2. Theology. I. Title.

POTTHOFF, Harvey H. 231
God and the celebration of life [by] Harvey H. Potthoff. Chicago, Rand McNally [1969] 293 p. 22 cm. Bibliography: p. 277-285. [BT102.P6] 69-16637 6.95
1. God—Knowableness. 2. Christian life—Methodist authors. I. Title.

PRICE, Eugenia. 231
Strictly personal; the advanture of discovering what God is really like. Grand Rapids, Zondervan Pub. House [1960] 180p. 21cm. Includes bibliography. [BT102.P7] 60-10240
1. God. I. Title.

PROTESTANT Episcopal Church in the U. S. A. National Council. Dept. of Christian Education. 231
The wondrous works of God. Illustrated by Symeon Shimin. Greenwich, Conn., Seabury Press [1956] 93p. illus. 22cm. (The Seabury series, R-2) [BT107.P7] 56-7849
1. God—Juvenile literature. I. Title.

PURDY, Alexander Converse, 1890- 231
The reality of God; thoughts on the "death of God" controversy [by] Alexander C. Purdy. [Wallingford, Pa., Pendle Hill, 1967] 32 p. 19 cm. (Pendle Hill pamphlet 154) [BT102.P8] 67-23314
1. God. 2. Christianity—20th century. I. Title.

RAGUIN, Yves, 1912- 231
The depth of God / by Yves Raguin ; translated by Kathleen England. St. Meinard, Ind. : Abbey Press, 1975. xi, 145 p. ; 21 cm. (Religious experience series ; v. 10) Translation of La profondeur de Dieu. Includes bibliographical references. [BT102.R2613] 75-211 ISBN 0-87029-041-X pbk. : 4.95
1. God. I. Title.

RAHNER, Karl, 1904- 231
The Trinity. Translated by Joseph Donceel. [New York] Herder and Herder [1970] 120 p. 21 cm. Translation of Der dreifaltige Gott als transzendenter Urgrund der Heilsgeschichte in Mysterium salutis, v. 2, chapter 5. Includes bibliographical references. [BT111.2.R3] 72-87766 4.95
1. Trinity.

RAMM, Bernard, 1916- 231
Them He glorified; a systematic study of the doctrine of glorification. Grand Rapids, Eerdmans [1963] 148 p. 22 cm. Bibliography: p. 137-138. [BT180.G6R3] 63-17782
1. Glory of God. I. Title.

RAMM, Bernard, 1916- 231
Them He glorified; a systematic study of the doctrine of glorification. Grand Rapids, Mich., Eerdmans [c.1963] 148p. 22cm. Bibl. 63-17782 3.25
1. Glory of God. I. Title.

REES, Paul Stromberg. 231
Stand up in praise to God. Grand Rapids, Eerdmans [1960] 117p. 20cm. (Preaching for today) [BT113.R4] 60-53088
1. Trinity—Sermons. 2. Evangelical Covenant Church of America— Sermons. 3. Sermons, American. I. Title.

RICHARDS, Larry. 231
Is God necessary? Chicago, Moody Press [1969] 160 p. illus. 20 cm. Cover title: Youth asks: Is God necessary? Bibliographical references included in "Footnotes" (p. 159-160) [BT102.R5] 73-80950 1.95
1. God. 2. Youth—Religious life. I. Title.

RICHARDSON, Cyril Charles, 1909- 231
The doctrine of the Trinity. New York, Abingdon Press [1958] 159p. 20cm. Includes bibliography. [BT111.R5] 58-5393
1. Trinity. I. Title.

RINKER, Wilson H. 231
God is. New York, Vantage Press [c.1961] 91p. 2.50 bds.,
I. Title.

ROBERTS, Brigham Henry, 1857-1933. 231
The Mormon doctrine of deity : the Roberts-Van der Donckt discussion, to which is added a discourse, Jesus Christ, the revelation of God : also a collection of authoritative Mormon utterances on the being and nature of God / by B. H. Roberts. Bountiful, Utah : Horizon Publishers, [1976?], c1903. xii, 296 p. ; 23 cm. Reprint of the ed. published by the Deseret news, Salt Lake City. [BX8635.R58 1976] 76-359769 ISBN 0-88290-058-7 : 5.95
1. Mormons and Mormonism—Doctrinal and controversial works. 2. God. I. Van der Donckt, Cyril, 1865- II. Title.

ROBINSON, John Arthur Thomas, Bp., 1919- 231
Exploration into God [by] John A. T. Robinson. Stanford, Calif., Stanford University Press, 1967. vii, 166 p. 23 cm. (The Raymond Fred West memorial lectures, 1966) Bibliographical footnotes. [BT102.R62] 67-26529
1. God. I. Title. II. Series.

ROBINSON, John Arthur Thomas, Bp., 1919- 231
Exploration into God [by] John A. T. Robinson. Stanford, Calif., Stanford University Press, 1967. vii, 166 p. 23 cm. (The Raymond Fred West memorial lectures, 1966) Bibliographical footnotes. [BT102.R62] 67-26529
1. God. I. Title. II. Series.

RYRIE, Charles Caldwell, 1925- 231
Dispensationalism today. Foreword by Frank E. Gaebelein. Chicago, Moody Press [1965] 221 p. 22 cm. Bibliography: p. 213-215. [BT157.R9] 65-14611
1. Dispensationalism. I. Title.

RYRIE, Charles Caldwell, 1925- 231
Dispensationalism today. Foreword by Frank E. Gaebelein. Chicago. Moody [c.1965] 221p. 22cm. Bibl. [BT157.R9] 65-14611 3.95
1. Dispensationalism. I. Title.

SCHOOLLAND, Marian M., 1902- 231
Leading little ones to God; a child's book of Bible teachings. Illus. by Macy Schwarz. Grand Rapids, Mich., Eerdmans [c.1962] 286p. 24cm. 62-11250 3.95
1. God—Juvenile literature. I. Title.

SCHUMM, Robert William 231
God still helps. Foreword by Dr. Charles Ray Goff. New York, Vantage [c.1963] 123p. 21cm. Bibl. 2.75 bds.,
I. Title.

SCHWARZ, Hans, 1939- 231
The search for God : Christianity, atheism, secularism, world religions / Hans Schwarz. Minneapolis : Augsburg Pub. House, [1975] 288 p. ; 23 cm. Includes indexes. Bibliography: p. 262-277. [BT102.S38] 74-14187 ISBN 0-8066-1470-6 : 7.95
1. God. 2. Christianity and other religions. I. Title.

SCOTT, John Martin, 1913- 231
To touch the face of God / John M. Scott. Huntington, Ind. : Our Sunday Visitor, inc., c1975. 144 p. : ill. ; 18 cm. [BT102.S385] 74-25391 ISBN 0-87973-789-1 pbk. : 1.75
1. God. I. Title.

SHINN, Roger Lincoln. 231
Life, death, and destiny. Philadelphia, Westminster Press [1957] 95p. 20cm. (Layman's theological library) [BT101.S583] 57-5764
1. God. I. Title.

SHINN, Roger Lincoln. 231
Life, death, and destiny. Philadelphia, Westminster Press [1957] 95 p. 20 cm. (Laymen's theological library) [BT101.S583] 57-5764
1. God. I. Title.

SILLEM, Edward Augustus 231
Ways of thinking about God; Thomas Aquinas and the modern mind. New York, Sheed [1962, c.1961] 190p. 21cm. 61-14655 3.75 bds.,
1. God—Proof. 2. God—Proof. I. Title.

SIMONSON, Conrad. 231
In search of God. Philadelphia, United Church Press [1974] 223 p. 21 cm. "A Pilgrim Press book." Bibliography: p. 219-223. [BT102.S516] 73-19728 ISBN 0-8298-0256-8 6.95
1. God. I. Title.

SLOYAN, Gerard Stephen, 1919- 231
The three Persons in One God. Englewood Cliffs, N.J., Prentice-Hall [1964] ix, 118 p. illus. 24 cm. (Foundations of Catholic theology series) Bibliography: p. 109-110. [BT109.S55] 63-22046
1. Trinity — History of doctrines. I. Title.

SLOYAN, Gerard Stephen, 1919- 231
The three Persons in One God. Englewood Cliffs, N.J., Prentice [c.1964] ix, 118p. illus. 24cm. (Foundns. of Catholic theology ser.) Bibl. 63-22046 3.95; 1.50 pap.,
1. Trinity—History of doctrines. I. Title.

SMITH, Ronald Gregor. 231
The doctrine of God. Edited and prepared for publication by K. Gregor Smith and A. D. Galloway. Philadelphia, Westminster Press [1970] 192 p. 20 cm. Bibliography: p. 184-186. [BT102.S55 1970b] 79-110726 5.00
1. God. I. Smith, K. Gregor, ed. II. Galloway, Allan Douglas, 1920- ed. III. Title.

SONTAG, Frederick. 231
Divine perfection; possible ideas of God. New York, harper [1962] 158 p. 21 cm. Includes bibliography. [BL205.S65] 62-7301
1. God — History of doctrines. 2. Perfection (Philosophy) I. Title.

SONTAG, Frederick 231
Divine perfection; possible ideas of God. New York, Harper & Row [c.1962] 158p. 21cm. Bibl. 62-7301 3.75 bds.,
1. God—History of doctrines. 2. Perfection (Philosophy) I. Title.

SOPER, David Wesley, 1910- 231
God is inescapable. Philadelphia, Westminister Press [1959] 128 p. 21 cm. Includes bibliography. [BT102.S6] 59-8895
1. God. I. Title.

STAM, Cornelius Richard, 1908- 231
The fundamentals of dispensationalism. Milwaukee, Berean Searchlight [1951] 279 p. illus. 20 cm. [BT155.S7] 51-36437
1. Covenants (Theology) I. Title.

STEENBERGHEN, Fernand van, 1904- 231
Hidden God; how do we know that God exists? Translated by Theodore Crowley. Louvain, Publications universitaires de Louvain; Saint Louis, B. Herder Book Co., 1966. 316 p. 20 cm. Bibliography: p. [309]-310. [BT102.S713] 66-4167
1. God—Proof. I. Title.

STEENBERGHEN, Fernand van, 1904- 231
Hidden God; how do we know that God exists? Tr. by Theodore Crowley. Louvain, Publications universitaires de Louvain: St. Louis B. Herder, 1966. 316p. 20cm. Bibl. [T102.S713] 66-4167 5.50
1. God—Proof. I. Title.

STEVENSON, Herbert F 231
Titles of the tirune God; studies in divine self-revelation. Foreword by Paul S. Rees. [Westwood, N.J.] F. H. Revell Co. [1956] 190 p. 22 cm. [BT180.N2S73 1956] 56-8404
1. God — Name. I. Title.

STEVENSON, Herbert F 231
Titles of the triune God; studies in divine self-revelation. Foreword by Paul S. Rees. [Westwood, N. J.] F. H. Revell Co. [1956] 190p. 22cm. [BT180.N2S73 1956] 56-8404
1. God—Name. I. Title.

*STEWART, James Stuart, 1896- 231
The strong name, by James S. Stewart. Grand Rapids, Baker Book House [1972] viii, 260 p. 20 cm. (James S. Stewart library) First published in Edinburgh as part of the Scholar as preacher series. [BT109] ISBN 0-8010-7975-6 pap., 2.95
1. Trinity—Doctrine—Sermons. I. Title.

STRAUSS, Lehman. 231
The first person; devotional studies on God the Father. [1st ed.] Neptune, N.J., Loizeaux Bros. [1967] 256 p. 20 cm. Bibliographical footnotes. [BV4832.2.S84] 67-20931
1. Devotional literature. 2. God — Attributes. 3. God — Name. I. Title.

STRAUSS, Lehman. 231
The first person; devotional studies on God the Father. [1st ed.] Neptune, N.J., Loizeaux Bros. [1967] 256 p. 20 cm. Bibliographical footnotes. [BV4832.2.S84] 67-20931
1. Devotional literature. 2. God—Attributes. 3. God—Name. I. Title.

SULLIVAN, John Edward. 231
The image of God, the doctrine of St. Augustine and its influence. Dubuque, Iowa, Priory Press [1963] 356 p.. 23 cm. [BT109.S8] 63-12507
1. Trinity. 2. Augustinus, Aurelius, Saint, Bp. of Hippo. I. Title.

SULLIVAN, John Edward 231
The image of God; the doctrine of St. Augustine and its influence. Dubuque, Iowa, Priory Pr. [c.1963] 356p. 23cm. 63-12507 5.00
1. Augustinus, Aurelius, Saint, Bp. of Hippo. 2. Trinity. I. Title.

SWEDENBORG, Emanuel, 1688-1772 231
Angelic wisdom concerning divine love and wisdom. Tr. by John C. Ager. Introd. by Helen Keller. New York Citadel [1965, c.1963] xxiii, 306p. 19cm. (C-189) [BX8712.D6] 65-2713 1.50 pap.,
1. Providence and government of God—Early works to 1800. I. Title.

TERWILLIGER, Robert E 231
Receiving the Word of God. Foreword by Horace W. B. Donegan. New York, Morehouse-Barlow Co., 1960. 147 p. 31 cm. (The Annual Bishop of New York books, 1960) [BT89.T4] 60-6115
1. Bible — Evidences, authority, etc. I. Title.

TERWILLIGER, Robert E. 231
Receiving the Word of God. Foreword by Horace W. B. Donegan. New York, Morehouse-Barlow Co., [c.]1960. 147p. 21cm. (The Annual Bishop of New York books, 1960) 60-6115 2.75 bds.,
1. Bible—Evidences, authority, etc. I. Title.

THANK you. 231
New York, Paulist Press [1969] [16] p. col. illus. 15 x 18 cm. (Rejoice books) Gives thanks to God for all of nature. [BT107.T47] 71-7479 0.35
1. God—Juvenile literature.

THIELICKE, Helmut, 1908- 231
The hidden question of God / by Helmut Thielicke. Grand Rapids, Mich. : Eerdmans, c1976. p. cm. Translation of Die geheime Frage nach Gott. Translated and edited by G. W. Bromiley. [BR85.T4813] 76-44492 ISBN 0-8028-1661-4 pbk. : 3.95
1. Theology—Addresses, essays, lectures. I. Title.

THOMAS, J. M. Lloyd. 231
The veiled being : a comment on Mr. H. G. Wells's "God, the invisible king" / by J. M. Lloyd Thomas. [Folcroft, Pa.] : Folcroft Library Editions, 1974. p. cm. Reprint of the 1917 ed. published by Cornish Bros., Birmingham. [BT101.W43T46 1974] 74-23855 ISBN 0-8414-8512-7 lib.bdg. 4.50
1. Wells, Herbert George, 1866-1946. God, the invisible king. I. Title.

THOMAS AQUINAS, Saint, 1225?-1274. 231
Treatise on God. Texts selected, tr. by James F. Anderson. Englewood Cliffs, N. J., Prentice [c.]1963. 180p. 21cm. 63-16359 2.75 pap.,
1. God. I. Anderson, James Francis, 1910- ed. and tr. II. Title.

THOMPSON, William Hertzog. 231
The fool has said God is dead. Boston, Christopher Pub. House [1966] 102 p. 21 cm. Bibliographical footnotes. [BT1102.T5] 66-28036
1. Apologetics—20th century. I. Title.

TITTMANN, George Fabian. 231
What manner of love; the Bible as the love story of God. New York, Morehouse-Barlow Co. [1959] 183 p. 21 cm. [BT155.T56] 59-13708
1. Covenants (Theology) 2. Love (Theology) I. Title.

TRENT, Robbie, 1894- 231
What is God like? Illus. by Josephine Haskell. New York, Harper [1953] 62p. illus. 23cm. In verse. [BT107.T72] 53-5453
1. God—Juvenile literature. I. Title.

VAN TIL, Cornelius, 1895- 231
Is God dead? Philadelphia, Presbyterian and Reformed Pub. Co., 1966. 43 p. 24 cm. [BT83.5.V3] 68-5482
1. Death of God theology. I. Title.

VAUGHN, Ray. 231
Wallace-Vaughn debate, held at Arvada, Colorado, Septmber 5-7, 1951, between Ray Vaughn and G. K. Wallace. Wire recorded. Longview, Wash., Telegram Sermons Book Co., 1952. 194p. 22cm. [BT113.V3] 53-1093
1. Trinity. 2. Baptism. 3. United Pentecostal Church—Doctrinal and controversial works. 4. Churches of christ—Doctrinal and controversial works. I. Wallace, Gervias Knox, 1906- II. Title.

WARD, Keith, 1938- 231
The concept of God. New York, St. Martin's Press, [1975 c1974] viii, 236 p. 22 cm. Includes bibliographical references and index. [BT102.W33] 74-82271 17.95
1. God—Knowableness. I. Title.

WATSON, Jane (Werner) 1915- 231
My first book about God. Pictures by Eloise Wilkin. New York, Simon and Schuster, 1957. unpaged. illus. 21cm. (A Golden book, 476) [BT107.W27] 57-13589
1. God—Juvenile liferature. I. Title.

WATSON, Jane (Werner) 1915- 231
My first book about God. Pictures by Eloise Wilkin. New York, Simon and Schuster, 1957. unpaged. illus. 21 cm. (A Golden book, 476) [BT107.W27] 57-13589
1. God — Juvenile literature. I. Title.

WATSON, Jane (Werner) 1915- 231
My little golden book about God. Pictures by Eloise Wilkin. New York, Simon and Schuster [1956] unpaged. illus. 21cm. (Little golden book 268) [BT107.W3] 56-58148
1. God—Juvenile literature. I. Title.

WATSON, Jane (Werner) 1915- 231
My little golden book about God. Pictures by Eloise Wilkin. New York, Simon and Schuster [1956] unpaged. illus. 21 cm. (Little golden book 268) [BT107.W3] 56-58148
1. God — Juvenile literature. I. Title.

WATSON, Tom, Jr. 231
The will of my father. Chicago, Moody [c.1963] 153p. 18cm. (Moody pocket bk., 85) .59 pap.,
I. Title.

WHITMAN, Howard Jay, 1914- 231
A reporter in search of God. [1st ed.] Garden City, N. Y., Doubleday, 1953. 320 p. 21 cm. [BT101.W49] 52-13387
1. God. I. Title.

WOLCOTT, Carolyn Muller. 231
God cares for me. Pictures by Lloyd Dotterer. New York, Abingdon Press, 1956. unpaged. illus. 19x22cm. [BT107.W6] 56-14038
1. God—Juvenile literature. I. Title.

WOLCOTT, Carolyn Muller. 231
God cares for me. Pictures by Lloyd Dotterer. New York, Abingdon Press, 1956. unpaged, illus. 19 x 22 cm. [BT107.W6] 56-14038
1. God — Juvenile literature. I. Title.

WOLS-SCHON, Greta 231
Portrait of Yahweh as a young god; or, How to get along with a god you don't necessarily like but can't help loving. [1st ed.] New York, Holt, Rinehart and Winston [1968] 125 p. 22 cm. Bibliography: p. [124]-125. [BT175.W4] 68-14929
1. God. I. Title.

WOODYARD, David O. 231
The opaqueness of God, by David O. Woodyard. Philadelphia, Westminster Press [1970] 160 p. 20 cm. Includes bibliographical references. [BT98.W66] 78-117645 5.50
1. God—History of doctrines—20th century. I. Title.

YOHN, Rick. 231
What every Christian should know about God / Rick Yohn. Irvine, Calif. : Harvest House, c1976. 72 p. : ill. ; 28 cm. [BT108.Y63] 76-20396 ISBN 0-89081-054-0 pbk. : 2.95
1. God—Study and teaching. I. Title.

CAMPBELL, Richard James, 1939- 231'.042
From belief to understanding : a study of Anselm's Proslogion argument on the existence of God / [by] Richard Campbell. Canberra : Faculty of Arts, Australian National University, 1976. 229 p. ; 21 cm. Includes bibliographical references and index. [B765.A83P843 1976] 76-375717 ISBN 0-7081-0142-9
1. Anselm, Saint, Abp. of Canterbury, 1033-1109. Proslogium. 2. God—Proof, Ontalogical. I. Title.

DEVINE, Bob. 231'.042
The helicopter bird / by Bob Devine ; [pictures by Carolyun Bowser] Chicago : Moody Press, c1977. 32 p. : ill. (some col.) ; 21 cm. (God in creation series) Examines phenomena in nature that reflect Christian beliefs. [QH309.2.D48] 76-42207 ISBN 0-8024-3498-3 : 1.25
1. Biology—Addresses, essays, lectures—Juvenile literature. I. Bowser, Carolyn Ewing. II. Title. III. Series.

DEVINE, Bob. 231'.042
The helicopter bird / by Bob Devine ; [pictures by Carolyun Bowser] Chicago : Moody Press, c1977. 32 p. : ill. (some col.) ; 21 cm. (God in creation series) Examines phenomena in nature that reflect Christian beliefs. [QH309.2.D48] 76-42207 ISBN 0-8024-3498-3 : 1.25
1. Biology—Addresses, essays, lectures—Juvenile literature. I. Bowser, Carolyn Ewing. II. Title. III. Series.

DEVINE, Bob. 231'.042
Mr. baggy-skin lizard / by Bob Devine. Chicago : Moody Press, c1977. 32 p. : ill. (some col.) ; 21 cm. (God in creation series) Introduces briefly the characteristics and habits of one reptile and four insects-the chuckwalla lizard, yucca moth, waterboatsman, fig wasp, and bee-relating their activities to Christian principles. [QH309.2.D49] 76-43264 ISBN 0-8024-5671-5 pbk. 1.25
1. Biology—Addresses, essays, lectures—Juvenile literature. 2. Insects—Addresses, essays, lectures—Juvenile literature. 3. Fertilization of plants by insects—Addresses, essays, lectures—Juvenile literature. I. Title. II. Series.

DEVINE, Bob. 231'.042
Mr. baggy-skin lizard / by Bob Devine. Chicago : Moody Press, c1977. 32 p. : ill. (some col.) ; 21 cm. (God in creation series) Introduces briefly the characteristics and habits of one reptile and four insects-the chuckwalla lizard, yucca moth, waterboatsman, fig wasp, and bee-relating their activities to Christian principles. [QH309.2.D49] 76-43264 ISBN 0-8024-5671-5 pbk. 1.25
1. Biology—Addresses, essays, lectures—Juvenile literature. 2. Insects—Addresses, essays, lectures—Juvenile literature. 3. Fertilization of plants by insects—Addresses, essays, lectures—Juvenile literature. I. Title. II. Series.

*KELSEY, Morton. 231.042
Study guide to Encounter with God. Prepared by George E. Trippe and Richard D. Thomson. Minneapolis, Bethany Fellowship, [1975] 40 p. 21 cm. Includes bibliographies. [BT108] ISBN 0-87123-506-4 0.95 (pbk.)
1. God—Biblical teaching. I. Title.

MCLELLAND, Joseph C. 231'.042
God the anonymous : a study in Alexandrian philosophical theology / by Joseph C. McLelland. Cambridge, Mass. : Philadelphia Patristic Foundation : [sole distributors, Greeno, Hadden], 1976[i.e.1977] ix, 209 p. ; 23 cm. (Patristic monograph series ; no. 4) Includes index. Bibliography: p. 179-203. [BT98.M315] 76-27405 ISBN 0-915646-03-X pbk. : 4.50
1. God—Knowableness—History of Doctrines. 2. Transcendence of God. 3. Alexandrian school, Christian. I. Title. II. Series.

MALIK, Charles Habib, 1906- 231'.042
The wonder of being [by] Charles H. Malik. Waco, Tex., Word Books [1974] 150 p. 23 cm. Based on three lectures delivered in Dec. 1969 at Trinity College, Toronto, Canada. Includes bibliographical references. [BT102.M29] 73-85523 4.95
1. Jesus Christ—Person and offices. 2. God—Proof. 3. Apologetics—20th century. I. Title.

PATTERSON, Robert Leet. 231'.042
The conception of God in the philosophy of Aquinas / by Robert Leet Patterson. Merrick, N.Y. : Richwood Pub. Co., [1976,i.e.1977] 508 p. ; 23 cm. Reprint of the 1933 ed. published by Allen & Unwin, London. Includes index. Bibliography: p. [493] [BT100.T4P3 1976] 76-49005 ISBN 0-915172-27-5 : 25.00
1. Thomas Aquinas, Saint, 1225?-1274—Theology. 2. God—History of doctrines. I. Title.

ROWE, William L. 231'.042
The cosmological argument / William L. Rowe. Princeton, N.J. : Princeton University Press, [1975] 273 p. ; 23 cm. Includes bibliographical references and index. [BT102.R69] 74-25628 ISBN 0-691-07210-8 : 13.50
1. God—Proof, Cosmological. I. Title.

ROYAL, Claudia. 231.07
Teaching your child about God. [Westwood, N. J.] Revell [1960] 186p. 21cm. Includes bibliography. [BT108.R65] 60-8458
1. God. 2. Religious education—Home training. I. Title.

ALTIZER, Thomas J. J. comp. 231'.08
Toward a new Christianity: readings in the death of God theology, ed. by Thomas J. J. Altizer. New York, Harcourt [1967] vii, 374p. 23cm. [BT83.5.A47] 67-15337 bBibl. 6.95; 3.95 pap.,
1. Death of God theology—Collections. I. Title.
Contents omitted.

ALTIZER, Thomas J. J., comp. 231'.08
Toward a new Christianity; readings in the death of God theology, edited by Thomas J. J. Altizer. New York, Harcourt, Brace & World [1967] viii, 374 p. 23 cm. [BT83.5.A47] 67-15337
1. Death of God theology — Collections. I. Title.
contents omitted

BURRILL, Donald R., comp. 231'.08
The cosmological arguments; a spectrum of opinion. Edited by Donald R. Burrill. [1st ed.] Garden City, N.Y., Anchor Books, 1967. vi, 302 p. 18 cm. Bibliography: p. [301]-302. Bibliographical footnotes. [BT102.A1B8] 67-21703
1. God—Proof. I. Title.

*ESUS, Hugam E., Jr. 231'.08
Man and gods. New York, Vantage [1968] 43p. 21cm. 2.50 bds.,
1. Death of God theology—Addresses, essays, lectures. I. Title.

KEHOE, Kimball, comp. 231'.08
The theology of God sources. Edited by Kimball Kehoe. New York, Bruce Pub. Co. [1971] xxi, 311 p. 23 cm. (Contemporary theology series) Includes bibliographical references. [BT102.A1K44 1971] 73-143784
1. God—Collections. I. Title.

MURCHLAND, Bernard, comp. 231'.08
The meaning of the death of God; Protestant, Jewish and Catholic scholars explore atheistic theology. Edited and with an introd. by Bernard Murchland. New York, Random House [1967] xv, 265 p. 22 cm. Contents.Contents.—Beyond the death of God, by C. Vahanian.—Variations on the 'death of God' theme in recent theology, by F. T. Trotter.—A philosophical-theological critique of the death of God movement, by J. W. Montgomery.—The Christian and the atheist, by M. Novak—Is God dead? By R. Adolfs.—God-is-dead theology, by E. B. Borowitz.—Taking the death of God seriously, by E. W. Shideler.—The future of God, by R. Hazelton.—From crisis theology to the post-modern world, by J. B. Cobb, Jr.—Religion post mortem dei, by W. O. Fennell.—The myth of God's death, by J. S. Dunne.—What does the slogan mean? By R. M. Brown.—Apocalypse in a casket? By W. L. Moulton.—Deicide, theothanasia, or what do you mean? By J. R. Nelson.—False prophets in the secular city, by D. Miller.—Goodbye, death-of-God, by L. Shiner.—Theology after the 'death of God,' by W. R. Comstock. Includes bibliographical references. [BT83.5.M8] 67-12737
1. Death of God theology—Addresses, essays, lectures. I. Title.

WHY I believe there is a God; 231.082
sixteen essays by Negro clergymen. Introd. by Howard Thurman. Chicago, Johnson [c.]1965. xiii, 120p. 22cm. [BT102.W5] 65-17082 3.95
1. God—Proof—Addresses, essays, lectures. I. Title: Negro clergymen, sixteen essays by.

ARON, Robert, 1898- 231.09
The God of the beginnings. Translated from the French by Frances Frenaye. New York, W. Morrow, 1966. 244 p. 22 cm. Translation of History de Dieu: le Dieu des origines. Bibliography: p. [239]-244. [BT98.A713] 65-20948
1. God — History of doctrines. I. Title.

ARON, Robert, 1898- 231.09
The God the of the beginnings. Tr. from French by Frances Frenaye. New York, Morrow [c.]1966. 244p. 22cm. Bibl. [BT98.A713] 65-20948 5.00
1. God—History of doctrines. I. Title.

FORTMAN, Edmund J., 1901- comp. 231/.09
The theology of God: commentary. Ed. by Edmund J. Fortman. Milwaukee, Bruce [1967,c.1968] x, 368p. 23cm. Contemp. coll. theol. ser. Historical theol. section) Bibl. [BT98.F6] 67-29588 4.50 pap.,
1. God—History of doctrines. I. Title.

*MURRAY, John Courtney 231.09
The problem of God, yesterday and today New Haven, Conn., Yale [1965, c.1964] vii, 121p. 21cm. (St. Thomas More lects., 1; Y-138) [BT98.M8] 1.45 pap.,
I. Title.

NORRIS, Richard Alfred. 231.09
God and world in early Christian theology [by] R. A. Norris, Jr. New York, Seabury Press [1965] x, 177 p. 22 cm. Bibliography: p. 173-177. [BT25.N6] 65-21311
1. Theology, Doctrinal — Hist. — Early church. 2. God — History of doctrines. 3. Creation — History of doctrines. I. Title.

NORRIS, Richard Alfred, Jr. 231.09
God and world in early Christian theology [A study in Justin Martyr, Irenaeus, Tertullian, and Origen] New York, Seabury [c.1965] x, 177p. 22cm. Bibl. [BT25.N6] 65-21311 4.95
1. Theology, Doctrinal—Hist.—Early church. 2. God.—History of doctrines. 3. Creation—History of doctrines. I. Title.

PESCH, Otto Hermann. 231'.09
The God question in Thomas Aquinas and Martin Luther. Translated by Gottfried G. Krodel. Philadelphia, Fortress Press [1972] ix, 38 p. (p. 36-38 advertisement) 20 cm. (Facet books. Historical series (Reformation) 21) First published in Luther, Zeitschrift der Luther-Gesellschaft, v. 41 (1970) Bibliography: p. 34-35. [BT98.P48] 77-171508 ISBN 0-8006-3069-6 1.00
1. Thomas Aquinas, Saint, 1225?-1274—Theology. 2. Luther, Martin, 1483-1546—Theology. 3. God—History of doctrines. I. Title.

MACQUARRIE, John. 231'.09'04
God and secularity. Philadelphia, Westminster Press [1967] 157 p. 21 cm. (New directions in theology today, v. 3) Bibliographical references included in "Notes" (p. [145]-151) [BT28.N47 vol. 3] 67-20391
1. God—History of doctrines—20th century. I. Title. II. Series.

VAHANIAN, Gabriel, 1927- 231.0904
No other god. New York, G. Braziller [1966] xii, 114 p. 21 cm. "References": p. 103-114. [BT28.V3] 66-28591
1. Theology, Doctrinal—History—20th century. 2. Death of God theology. I. Title.

JENSON, Robert W. 231'.0924
God after God; the God of the past and the God of the future, seen in the work of Karl Barth, by Robert Jenson. Indianapolis, Bobbs-Merrill Co. [1969] 218 p. 22 cm. Bibliographical references included in "Notes" (p. 195-211) [BT102.J47] 69-13094 6.00
1. Barth, Karl, 1886-1968. Der Romerbrief. 2. God—History of doctrines—20th century. I. Title.

KENNY, Anthony John Patrick. 231'.0924
The five ways; St. Thomas Aquinas' proofs of God's existence. New York, Schocken Books [1969] 131 p. 23 cm. (Studies in ethics and the philosophy of religion) Bibliography: p. [123]-126. [BT98.K4 1969b] 79-77606 4.95
1. Thomas, Aquinas, Saint, 1225?-1274—Theology. 2. God—Proof. I. Title.

THE Theology of 231'.0924
Altizer: critique and response, edited by John B. Cobb, Jr. Philadelphia, Westminster Press [1970] 269 p. 21 cm. "Bibliography of the works of Thomas J. Altizer": (p. [267]-269) [BT83.5.T47] 79-116529 7.50
1. Altizer, Thomas J. J. 2. Death of God theology. I. Cobb, John B., ed.

WHEAT, Leonard F. 231'.0924
Paul Tillich's dialectical humanism: unmasking the God above God [by] Leonard F. Wheat. Baltimore, Johns Hopkins Press [1970] xiii, 287 p. 24 cm. Includes bibliographical references. [BX4827.T53W5 1970] 74-105365 9.00
1. Tillich, Paul, 1886-1965. I. Title.

DOANE, Pelagie 231.1
God made the world. Philadelphia, Lippincott [c.1960] unpaged. illus. (part col.) 24cm. 60-11356 2.75
1. God—Juvenile literature. I. Title.

GODDARD, Carrie Lou. 231.1
Isn't it a wonder! / Carrie Lou Goddard ; illustrated by Leigh Grant. Nashville : Abingdon Press, c1976. [31] p. : col. ill. ; 21 cm. Examines the many wonders that God has created—the sun, trees, grass, snow, people, and much more. [BS651.G68] 75-15664 ISBN 0-687-19715-5 : 4.25
1. Creation—Juvenile literature. I. Grant, Leigh. II. Title.

HARRELL, Costen Jordan, 231.1
1885-
I believe in God. New York, Abingdon Press [1958] 64p. 20cm. [BT101.H26] 58-5397
1. God. I. Title.

JAGER, Okke. 231'.1
What does God want, anyway? M. E. Osterhaven, translator. Valley Forge [Pa.] Judson Press [1972] 191 p. 23 cm. Translation of Uw wil geschiede. [BV4509.D8J313] 72-75361 ISBN 0-8170-0565-X 6.50
1. God—Will. I. Title.

SPITTLER, Russell P. 231'.1
God the Father / Russell P. Spittler. Springfield, Mo. : Gospel Pub. House, c1976. 126 p. ; 18 cm. (Radiant books) Bibliography: p. 126. [BS544.S65] 76-20888 ISBN 0-88243-898-0 pbk. : 1.25
1. God—Biblical teaching. I. Title.

*COOK, Roselynn 231.107
Exploring God's world. Ed.: Margaret J. Irvin. Illus.: Helen and Bill Hamilton. Designer: William 0 ol. illus. 22x28cm. (LCA vacation church sch. ser.) pap., .50; teacher's guide (to grades 3 & 4) pap., .90
I. Title.

*SMITH, A. Richard 231.107
God and the universe. Ed.: Margaret J. Irvin. Illus.: Roland Shutts. Designer: William C. Kautz. Philadelphia, Lutheran Church Pr. [c.1965] 48p. col. illus. 22x28cm. (LCA vacation church sch. ser.) pap., .50; teacher's guide (to grades 5 & 6) pap., .90
I. Title.

AINSLIE, Peter, 1867-1934. 231'.3
Cultivating the fruit of the Spirit. St. Louis, Bethany Press [1968] 78 p. 21 cm. [BT123.A35] 68-1636
1. Holy Spirit. I. Title.

ALLEN, Charles 231'.3
Livingstone, 1913-
The miracle of the Holy Spirit [by] Charles L. Allen. Old Tappan, N.J., F. H. Revell Co. [1974] 64 p. 19 cm. [BT121.2.A44] 74-10826 ISBN 0-8007-0688-9 2.95
1. Holy Spirit. I. Title.

AMUNDSEN, Wesley. 231'.3
The power of Pentecost. Nashville, Southern Pub. Association [1967] 106 p. 18 cm. [BT123.A4] 67-2107
1. Holy Spirit. I. Title.

ATHANASIUS, Saint, 231'.3
Patriarch of Alexandria, d.373.
The Armenian version of the letters of Athanasius to Bishop Serapion concerning the Holy Spirit. By George A. Egan. Salt Lake City, University of Utah Press, 1968. xvii, 214 p. 25 cm. (Studies and documents, 37) Introductory matter in English; text in English and Armenian. Includes bibliographical references. [BR65.A44373] 76-17651
1. Holy Spirit—Early works to 1800. I. Serapion, Saint, Bp. of Thmuis. II. Egan, George A. III. Title. IV. Series.

AUGSBURGER, Myron S. 231.3
Quench not the Spirit. Scottdale, Pa., Herald Pr. [1962, c.1961] 113p. 62-7330 2.50
1. Holy Spirit. I. Title.

AUGSBURGER, Myron S. 231'.3
Quench not the spirit / Myron S. Augsburger ; introd. by Leighton Ford. Rev. Scottdale, Pa. : Herald Press, 1975. 141 p. ; 18 cm. [BT121.2.A8 1975] 75-313535 ISBN 0-8361-1477-9 pbk. : 1.75
1. Holy Spirit. I. Title.

BARCLAY, William, lecturer 231.3
in the University of Glasgow.
The promise of the Spirit. Philadelphia, Westminster Press [1960] 120p. 20cm. [BT121.2.B3] 60-11200
1. Holy Spirit. I. Title.

BARCLAY, William, lecturer 231.3
in the University of Glasgow.
The promise of the Spirit. Philadelphia, Westminster Press [c.1960] 120p. 20cm. 60-11200 2.50
1. Holy Spirit. I. Title.

BERKHOF, Hendrikus. 231.3
The doctrine of the Holy Spirit. Richmond, John Know Press [1964] 128 p. 21 cm. (The Annie Kinkead Warfield lectures, 1963-1964) Bibliographical references included in "Notes" (p. 122-128) [BT122.B4] 64-16279
1. Holy Spirit — Addresses, essays, lectures. I. Title. II. Series.

BERKHOF, Hendrikus 231.3
The doctrine of the Holy Spirit. Richmond, Va., Knox [c.1964] 128p. 21cm. (Annie Kinkead Warfield lects., 1963-1964) Bibl. 64-16279 3.00
1. Holy Spirit—Addresses, essays, lectures. I. Title. II. Series.

BICKERSTETH, Edward Henry 231.3
The Holy Spirit, His Person and work. 'Companion volume to 'The Trinity.' ' Grand Rapids, Mich., Kregel Publications, 1959. 192p. 22cm. 59-13640 2.95
1. Holy Spirit. I. Title.

*BIEDERWOLF, William 231.3
Edward, 1867-1939.
A help to the study of the holy spirit. 4th edition Grand Rapids, Baker Book House [1974] 127 p. 20 cm. (Notable books on theology) Reprint of the 1903 edition. [BT121.2] ISBN 0-8010-0614-7 1.95 (pbk.)
1. Holy spirit. I. Title.

BISHOP, James R. 231'.3
The spirit of Christ in human relationships [by] James R. Bishop. Grand Rapids, Zondervan Pub. House [1968] 64 p. 21 cm. (A Zondervan paperback) [BT123.B45] 68-22835
1. Holy Spirit. 2. Spirituality. I. Title.

BRANSON, William Henry, 231.3
1887-
The Holy Spirit, His office and work in the world. [2d ed., rev.] Nashville, Southern Pub. Association [1952, c1933] 160p. 20cm. [BT121.B75 1952] 53-16590
1. Holy Spirit. 2. Seventh-Day Adventists—Doctrinal and controversial works. I. Title.

BROOMALL, Wick, 1902- 231.3
The Holy Spirit; a Scriptural study of His person and work. Grand Rapids, Mich., Baker. Bk., 1963 [c.1940] 211p. 21cm. (Christian faith ser.) Bibl. 63-15006 2.95 bds.,
1. Holy Spirit. I. Title.

BROWN, W. Herbert. 231'.3
Pentecostal fire, radiance & love, by W. Herbert Brown. Bryson City, N.C., Southern Bible Testimony, inc. [1973] 256 p. 21 cm. First published in 1967 under title: God's answer. Bibliography: p. 240-245. [BT121.2.B74 1973] 73-11555
1. Holy Spirit—Biblical teaching. I. Title.

BRUNER, Frederick Dale. 231'.3
A theology of the Holy Spirit; the Pentecostal experience and the New Testament witness. Grand Rapids, Eerdmans [1970] 390 p. 24 cm. Bibliography: p. 342-376. [BT121.2.B77] 76-103445 8.95
1. Holy Spirit—Biblical teaching. 2. Pentecostalism. 3. Baptism in the Holy Spirit. I. Title.

CARLSON, G. Raymond. 231'.3
Spiritual dynamics : the Holy Spirit in human experience / G. Raymond Carlson. Springfield, Mo. : Gospel Pub. House, c1976. 125 p. ; 18 cm. (Radiant books) [BT121.2.C255] 76-5633 ISBN 0-88243-894-8 : 1.25
1. Holy Spirit. 2. Christian life—1960- I. Title.

CARTER, Charles Webb, 231'.3
1905-
The person and ministry of the Holy Spirit, a Wesleyan perspective / Charles Webb Carter. Grand Rapids : Baker Book House, 1974. 355 p. ; 23 cm. Includes index. Bibliography: p. 337-350. [BT121.2.C26] 74-75959 ISBN 0-8010-2359-9 : 7.95
1. Holy Spirit. I. Title.

CHAPIAN, Marie. 231'.3
The Holy Spirit and me / written by Marie Chapian ; illustrated by Peter Chapian. Carol Stream, Ill. : Creation House, c1974. [32] p. : ill. (some col.) ; 27 cm. (The Mustard seed library) Brief text and illustrations define the Holy Spirit. [BT121.2.C43] 74-82839 ISBN 0-88419-098-6 : 3.95
1. Holy Spirit—Juvenile literature. I. Chapian, Peter. II. Title.

COCKIN, Frederick Arthur, 231.3
Bp. of Bristol, 1888-
God in action a study in the Holy Spirit. Penguin Books. [dist. New York, Atheneum, c.1961] 184p. (Pelican books, A513) Bibl. 61-2782 .95 pap.,
1. Holy Spirit. I. Title.

CONKLIN, Dorothy Whitney 231.3
The golden oil; the nature and work of the Holy Spirit. Mountain View, Calif., Pacific Press Pub. Association [c.1961] 139p. Bibl. 61-6479 3.00
1. Holy Spirit. I. Title.

CONSULTATION on the Person 231'.3
and Work of the Holy Spirit, Eastern Mennonite College, 1972.
Encounter with the Holy Spirit. Geo. R. Brunk II, editor. Scottdale, Pa., Herald Press, 1972. 244 p. 20 cm. Papers presented at the conference held Jan. 18-21, 1972. Includes bibliographical references. [BT122.C66 1972] 72-2053 ISBN 0-8361-1693-3 3.95
1. Holy Spirit—Addresses, essays, lectures. I. Brunk, George R., ed. II. Title.

CRAMER, Raymond L, 1908- 231.3
The master key. Los Angeles, Cowman Publications [1951] 138 p. 20 cm. Bibliography: p. 137-138. [BT121.C76] 51-22917
1. Holy Spirit. I. Title.

CRISWELL, Wallie A. 231'.3
The baptism, filling & gift of the Holy Spirit, by W. A. Criswell. Grand Rapids, Zondervan Pub. House [1973] 144 p. 18 cm. Includes bibliographical references. [BT123.C74] 73-175531 1.25 (pbk.)
1. Baptism in the Holy Spirit. 2. Gifts, Spiritual. I. Title.

CRISWELL, Wallie A. 231'.3
The Holy Spirit in today's world / W. A. Criswell. 2d ed. Grand Rapids, Mich. : Zondervan Pub. House, 1976, c1966. 242 p. ; 21 cm. [BT122.C85 1976] 76-370720 ISBN pbk. : 3.95
1. Baptists—Sermons. 2. Holy Spirit—Sermons. 3. Sermons, American. I. Title.

*CUMMING, James Elder, D.D. 231.3
Through the eternal spirit: a Bible study on the Holy Spirit. Minneapolis, Bethany Fellowship [c.1965] 203p. 19cm. 1.75 pap.,
I. Title.

DEROSA, Peter. 231'.3
Not I, not I, but the wind that blows through me : about the life of God in the life of men / by Peter DeRosa. Niles, Ill. : Argus Communications, c1975. 150 p. : ill. ; 19 cm. Includes bibliographical references. [BT122.D4 1975] 75-15206 ISBN 0-913592-59-5 : 2.95
1. Holy Spirit—Meditations. I. Title.

DEROSA, Peter. 231'.3
Not I, not I, but the wind that blows through me : about the life of God in the life of men / by Peter DeRosa. Niles, Ill. : Argus Communications, c1975. 150 p. : ill. ; 19 cm. Includes bibliographical references. [BT122.D4 1975] 75-15206 ISBN 0-913592-59-5 pbk. : 2.95
1. Holy Spirit—Meditations. I. Title.

DEWAR, Lindsay 231.3
The Holy Spirit and modern thought; an inquiry into the historical, theological, and psychological aspects of the Christian doctrine of the Holy Spirit. Foreword by Henry P. Van Dusen. New York, Harper [1959, i.e., 1960] xvi, 224p. 22cm. 60-11772 4.50
1. Holy Spirit. I. Title.

DRAKE, Frederick William, 231.3
1869-1930
The Spirit of Glory. [Authorized ed.] New York, Longmans, Green [c.1961] 116p. 61-13442 2.50 bds.,
1. Holy Spirit—Meditations. I. Title.

DUNCAN, George B. 231'.3
The person and work of the Holy Spirit in the life of the believer / George B. Duncan. Atlanta : John Knox Press, 1975, c1973. 86 p. ; 21 cm. Reprint of the ed. published by Lakeland, London. [BT121.2.D86 1975] 74-21900 ISBN 0-8042-0681-3 pbk. : 2.45
1. Holy Spirit. I. Title.

FISON, J E. 231.3
The blessing of the Holy Spirit. London, New York, Longmans, Green [1950] vi, 226 p. 20 cm. [BT121.F5] 50-2573
1. Holy Spirit. I. Title.

FITCH, William. 231'.3
The ministry of the Holy Spirit / William Fitch. Grand Rapids : Zondervan Pub. House, [1974] 304 p. ; 23 cm. Includes indexes. Bibliography: p. 295-297. [BT121.2.F53] 74-11854 7.95
1. Holy Spirit. I. Title.

FORD, Francis Xavier, Bp., 231.3
1892-1952.
Come, Holy Ghost; thoughts on renewing the earth as the kingdom of God. New York, McMullen Books [1953] 113p. 20cm. [BT121.F63] 53-12205
1. Holy Spirit. I. Title.

FORD, Francis Xavier, 231'.3
Bp., 1892-1952.
Come, Holy Spirit / by Francis Xavier Ford. Maryknoll, N.Y. : Orbis Books, 1976, c1953. p. cm. Edition for 1953 published under title: Come, Holy Ghost. [BT121.2.F62 1976] 76-20573 ISBN 0-88344-067-9 : 5.95
1. Holy Spirit. I. Title.

FORD, Josephine 231'.3
Massyngberde.
The spirit & the human person; a meditation, by J. Massingberd Ford. Dayton, Ohio, Pflaum Press, 1969. xiv, 177 p. 22 cm. Includes bibliographical references. [BT121.2.F63] 69-20174 5.95
1. Holy Spirit. I. Title.

FRANKE, Elmer Ellsworth 231.3
The Holy Spirit--the seal of God [3rd ed.] New York 25, Box 87 Cathedral Station People's Christian Bulletin 30p. 19cm. .10 pap.,
I. Title.

FREEMAN, Clifford Wade, 231.3
1906- ed.
The Holy Spirit's ministry; addresses given at the evangelistic conference of the Baptist General Convention of Texas. Grand Rapids, Zondervan Pub. House [1954] 149p. 20cm. [BV3760.F68] 54-12020
1. Evangelistic work—Addresses, essays, lectures. 2. Holy Spirit. I. Title.

*FROOM, Le Roy Edwin. 231.3
La venida del consolador. Rev. ed. Mountain View, Calif., Pacific Press Pub. Assn. [1973, c.1973] 304 p. 18 cm. Translation of The coming of the comforter. [BT122]
1. Holy Spirit—Seventh-Day Adventist authors. I. Title.

FROST, Robert C., 1926- 231'.3
The biology of the Holy Spirit / Robert C. Frost. Old Tappan, N.J. : Revell, [1975] 106 p. : ill. ; 21 cm. [BV4501.2.F77] 75-19260 ISBN 0-8007-0752-4 pbk. : 2.95
1. Christian life—1960- 2. Holy Spirit. I. Title.

GILLQUIST, Peter E. 231'.3
Let's quit fighting about the Holy Spirit [by] Peter E. Gillquist. Grand Rapids, Zondervan Pub. House [1974] 137 p. 21 cm. [BT767.3.G54] 73-22701 3.95; 1.95 (pbk.).
1. Gifts, Spiritual. 2. Holy Spirit. I. Title.

GLEASON, Robert W 231.3
The indwelling Spirit [by] Robert W. Gleason. Staten Island, N.Y., Alba House [1966] 119 p. 22 cm. Includes bibliographical references. [BT121.2.G5] 66-19719
1. Holy Spirit. I. Title.

GLEASON, Robert W. 231.3
The indwelling Spirit. Staten Island. N.Y., Alba [c.1966] 119p. 22cm. Bibl. [BT121.2.G5] 66-19719 3.95
1. Holy Spirit. I. Title.

GORDON, Adoniram Judson, 231.3
1836-1895
The ministry of the Spirit. Introd. by F. B. Meyer. Grand Rapids, Mich., Baker Bk. [1964] xviii, 225p. 20cm. (Religious classics reprint lib.) Bibl. 64-14564 1.50 pap.,
1. Holy Spirit. I. Title.

GREEN, Edward Michael 231'.3
Bankers.
I believe in the Holy Spirit / by Michael Green. Grand Rapids, Mich. : Eerdmans, [1975] 223 p. ; 21 cm. (I believe ; no. 1) Bibliography: p. 219-223. [BT121.2.G72] 74-32121 ISBN 0-8028-1609-6 pbk. : 2.95
1. Holy Spirit. I. Title.

*GUTZKE, Manford G. 231.3
Plain talk about the holy spirit, [by] Manford G. Gutzke. Grand Rapids, Baker Book House, [1974]. 178 p. 21 cm. [BT119] ISBN 0-8010-3676-3. 2.95 (pbk.)
1. Holy Spirit. I. Title.

HAMBLIN, Robert Lee, 1928- 231'.3
The Spirit-filled trauma : a candid plea for Biblical understanding in the matters of the Spirit / Robert L. Hamblin ; foreword by Carl Bates. Nashville : Broadman Press, [1974] 170 p. ; 19 cm. Includes bibliographical references. [BT121.2.H24] 74-78616 ISBN 0-8054-5547-7 pbk. : 3.50
1. Holy Spirit. I. Title.

HARKNESS, Georgia Elma, 231.3
1891
The fellowship of the holy spirit, by George

Harkness. Nashville, Abingdon [1966] 208 p. 21 cm bibl. [bt121.2h33] 66-21188 4.00
1. Holy Spirit Title. I. Title.

HARKNESS, Georgia Elma, 1891- 231.3
The following of the Holy Spirit [by] Georgia Harkness. Nashville, Abingdon Press [1966] 208 p. 21 cm. Bibilographical footnotes. [BT121.2.H33] 66-21188
1. Holy Spirit. I. Title.

HARMS, Paul W F 231.3
Spirit of power, by Paul W. F. Harms. Saint Louis, Concordia Pub. House [1964] 94 p. 19 cm. Bibliography: p. 93-94. [BT121.2.H27] 64-19895
1. Holy Spirit. 2. Christian life — Lutheran authors. I. Title.

HARMS, Paul W. F. 231.3
Spirit of power. St. Louis, Concordia [c.1964] 94p. 19cm. Bibl. 64-19895 1.00 pap.,
1. Holy Spirit. 2. Christian life—Lutheran authors. I. Title.

HARPER, Michael. 231'.3
Walk in the Spirit. Plainfield, N.J., Logos International [1970, c1968] 96 p. 18 cm. Bibliography: p. 95-96. [BV4501.2.H354 1970] 78-135047 ISBN 0-340-02994-3 0.95
1. Spiritual life. 2. Holy Spirit. I. Title.

HAUGHEY, John C. 231'.3
The conspiracy of God; the Holy Spirit in men [by] John C. Haughey. [1st ed.] Garden City, N.Y., Doubleday, 1973. xii, 154 p. 22 cm. [BT121.2.H36] 73-80730 ISBN 0-385-00400-1 4.95
1. Holy Spirit. I. Title.

HAUGHEY, John C. 231.3
The conspiracy of God : the holy spirit in us / John C. Haughey. Garden City, N. Y. : Doubleday [1976c1973] 120p. ; 18 cm. (Image books) [BT121.2.H36] ISBN 0-385-11558-X pbk. : 1.75
1. Holy Spirit. I. Title.
L. C. card no. for original edition: 73-80730.

HENDRY, George Stuart, 1904- 231.3
The Holy Spirit in Christian theology. Philadelphia, Westminster Press [1956] 128p. 21cm. [BT121.H42] 56-7371
1. Holy Spirit. I. Title.

HENDRY, George Stuart, 1904- 231.3
The Holy Spirit in Christian theology, by George S. Hendry. Rev. and enl. ed. Philadelphia, Westminister Press [c1965] 168 p. 21 cm. Bibliographical references included in "Notes" (p. 156-168) [BT121.H42] 64-55310
1. Holy Spirit. I. Title.

HENRY, A. M. 231.3
The Holy Spirit. Translated from the French by J. Lundberg and M. Bell. New York Hawthorn Books [c.1960] 138p. 21cm. (The Twentieth century encyclopedia of Catholicism, v. 18. Section 2: The basic truths) Bibl.: p. 139 60-13835 2.95 half cloth,
1. Holy Spirit. I. Title.

HENRY, Antonin Marcel, 1911- 231.3
The Holy Sprit. Translated from the French by J. Lundberg and M. Bell. [1st ed.] New York, Hawthorn Books [1960] 138p. 21cm. (The Twentieth century encyclopedia of Catholicism, v. 18. Section 2: The basic truths) Includes bibliography. [BT121.2.H413] 60-13835
1. Holy Spirit. I. Title.

HERRING, Ralph A 231.3
God being my helper. Nashville, Broadman Press [1955] 139p. 21cm. [BT121.H47] 55-14629
1. Holy Spirit. I. Title.

HILARIUS, Saint, Bp. of Poitiers, d. 367? 231.3
The Trinity; translated by Stephen McKenna. New York, Fathers of the Church, 1954. xix, 555p. 22cm. (The Fathers of the church, a new translation, v.25) Bibliography: p. xvi-xvii. [BR60.F3H53] 54-14571
1. Trinity—Early works to 1800. 2. Arianism. I. Title. II. Series.

*HILLS, Dick. 231.3
Listen to the spirit as He speaks to youth, by Dick Hills and Don W. Hills. Grand Rapids, Mich., Baker Book House [1973] 98 p. 18 cm. (Baker Book House direction books) [BT121.2] ISBN 0-8010-4080-9 0.95 (pbk.)
1. Holy Spirit. I. Hills, Don W., joint author. II. Title.

HOBBS, Herschel H. 231'.3
The Holy Spirit; believer's guide [by] Herschel H. Hobbs. Nashville, Broadman [1967] 160p. 21cm. Bibl. [BT121.2.H6] 67-17429 3.50
1. Holy Spirit. I. Title.

HORTON, Stanley M. 231'.3
What the Bible says about the Holy Spirit / Stanley M. Horton. Springfield, Mo. : Gospel Pub. House, c1976. 302 p. ; 22 cm. Includes bibliographical references and index. [BS680.H56H67] 75-43154 ISBN 0-88243-640-6 : 7.95. ISBN 0-88243-647-3 pbk. : 4.95
1. Holy Spirit—Biblical teaching. I. Title. II. Title: Holy Spirit.

HUBBARD, David Allan. 231'.3
The Holy Spirit in today's world. Waco, Tex., Word Books [1973] 121 p. 22 cm. [BT122.H8] 73-88737 2.25
1. Holy Spirit—Sermons. 2. Baptists—Sermons. 3. Sermons, American. I. Title.

HUBBARD, David Allen. 231'.3
The Holy Spirit in today's world. Waco, Tex., Word Books [1973] 121 p. 22 cm. [BT122.H8] 73-88737 2.25
1. Holy Spirit—Sermons. 2. Baptists—Sermons. 3. Sermons, American. I. Title.

HUGHES, Ray H 231.3
What is Pentecost? [Cleveland, Tenn., Pathway Press, 1963] 108 p. 19 cm. [BT121.2.H8] 63-14593
1. Pentecost. 2. Holy Spirit. I. Title.

HUGHES, Ray H. 231.3
What is Pentecost? [Cleveland, Tenn., Pathway, c.1963] 108p. 19cm. 63-14593 1.50 pap.,
1. Pentecost. 2. Holy Spirit. I. Title.

HULL, John Howarth Eric. 231'.3
The Holy Spirit in the Acts of the Apostles, by J. H. E. Hull. Cleveland, World Pub. Co. [1968, c1967] 201 p. 23 cm. Bibliography: p. 194-200. [BS2625.2.H8 1968] 67-24476
1. Bible. N.T. Acts—Theology. 2. Holy Spirit—Biblical teaching. I. Title.

HUNT, Earl G., comp. 231'.3
Storms and starlight : bishops' messages on the Holy Spirit / edited by Earl G. Hunt, Jr. Nashville, Tenn. : Tidings, [1974] 117 p. ; 19 cm. Includes bibliographical references. [BT122.H86] 74-14092 pbk. : 1.50
1. Holy Spirit—Addresses, essays, lectures. I. Title.

INTERNATIONAL Lutheran Conference on the Holy Spirit, 1st, Minneapolis, 1972. 231'.3
Jesus, where are you taking us? Messages from the First International Lutheran Conference on the Holy Spirit. Edited by Norris L. Wogen. [1st ed.] Carol Stream, Ill., Creation House [1973] 250 p. 22 cm. [BT123.I57 1972] 72-94921 4.95
1. Baptism in the Holy Spirit—Congresses. I. Wogen, Norris L., ed. II. Title.

JAMES, Maynard G 1902- 231.3
I believe in the Holy Ghost, by Maynard James, Foreword by Norman Grubb. Minneapolis, Bethany Fellowship [1965] 167 p. 21 cm. [BT121.2.J3] 65-6902
1. Holy Spirit. I. Title.

JAMES, Maynard G. 1902- 231.3
I believe in the Holy Ghost. Foreword by Norman Grubb. Minneapolis, Bethany Fellowship [c.1965] 167p. 21cm. [BT121.2.J3] 65-6902 2.95
1. Holy Spirit. I. Title.

JEFFRIES, J Campbell, 1910- 231.3
This same Jesus; the doctrine of the Holy Spirit. New York, Exposition Press [1950] 100 p. 23 cm. [BT121.J4] 50-13554
1. Holy Spirit. I. Title.

JOHNSTON, George, June9,1913- 231'.3
The spirit-paraclete in the Gospel of John. Cambridge [Eng.] University Press, 1970. xii, 192 p. 22 cm. (Society for New Testament studies. Monograph series, 12) Bibliography: p. 172-173. [BS2615.2.J6 1970] 72-98697 75/-($12.50)
1. Bible. N.T. John—Theology. 2. Holy Spirit—Biblical teaching. I. Title. II. Series: Studiorum Novi Testamenti Societas. Monograph series, 12

JONES, James William, 1943- 231'.3
The spirit and the world / James W. Jones. New York : Hawthorn Books, c1975. vii, 158 p. ; 22 cm. Includes index. [BT121.2.J66 1975] 75-2557 ISBN 0-8015-7034-4 : 6.95
1. Holy Spirit. 2. Christian communities. I. Title.

KETCHERSIDE, W. Carl. 231'.3
Heaven help us (the Holy Spirit in your life), by W. Carl Ketcherside. Cincinnati, New Life Books [1974] 176 p. 18 cm. Includes bibliographical references. [BT121.2.K45] 74-77225 ISBN 0-87239-007-1 2.95 (pbk.)
1. Holy Spirit. I. Title.
Division of Standard Publishing.

KILDAHL, John Nathan 231.3
The Holy Spirit and our faith. Revisions by Rolf E. Aaseng and Grace Gabrielsen. Minneapolis, Augsburg Pub. House [c.1937, 1960] ix, 86p. 20cm. 'First printed in 1927 as Misconceptions of the word and work of the Holy Spirit, and . . . later republished as Ten studies on the Holy Spirit. 60-12813 1.00 pap.,
1. Holy Spirit. I. Title.

KILDAHL, John Nathan, 1857- 231.3
The Holy Spirit and our faith. Revision's by Rolf E. Aaseng and Grace Gabrielsen. Minneapolis, Augsburg Pub. House [1960] 86p. 20cm. 'First printed in 1927 as Misconceptions of the word and work of the Holy Spirit, and ... later republished as Ten studies on the Holy Spirit.' [BT121.K5 1960] 60-12813
1. Holy Spirit. I. Title.

KINGHORN, Kenneth C. 231'.3
Fresh wind of the Spirit [by] Kenneth Cain Kinghorn. Nashville, Tenn., Abingdon Press [1975] 128 p. 20 cm. [BT121.2.K525] 74-7415 ISBN 0-687-13495-1 2.95 (pbk.)
1. Holy Spirit. I. Title.

KJESETH, Peter L. 231'.3
The final act; the role of the Holy Spirit in the life of God's people [by] Peter L. Kjeseth. Minneapolis, Augsburg Pub. House [1967] 121 p. 29 cm. (A Tower book) Bibliography: p. 121. [BT121.2.K53] 67-14724
1. Holy Spirit. I. Title.

KJESETH, Peter L. 231'.3
The final act; the role of the Holy Spirit in the life of God's people [by] Peter L. Kjeseth. Minneapolis, Augsburg Pub. House [1967] 121 p. 20 cm. (A Tower book) Bibliography: p. 121. [BT121.2.K53] 67-11724
1. Holy Spirit. I. Title.

LA POTTERIE, Ignace de, 1914- 231'.3
The Christian lives by the Spirit, by Ignace de la Potterie and Stanislaus Lyonnet. Pref. by Yves Congar. [Translated by John Morriss] Staten Island, N.Y., Alba House [1971] xii, 284 p. 22 cm. Translation of La vie selon l'Esprit. Includes bibliographical references. [BT121.2.L2713] 76-140283 ISBN 0-8189-0197-7 6.95
1. Holy Spirit. I. Lyonnet, Stanislas. II. Title.

LEAVELL, Landrum P. 231'.3
God's spirit in you [by] Landrum P. Leavell. Nashville, Tenn., Broadman Press [1974] 125 p. 20 cm. [BT122.L4] 73-89526 ISBN 0-8054-8122-2 1.50
1. Holy Spirit—Sermons. 2. Baptists—Sermons. 3. Sermons, American. I. Title.

LEHMAN, Chester Kindig, 1893- 231.3
The Holy Spirit and the holy life. Scottdale, Pa., Herald Press [1959] 220p. 20cm. (The Conrad Grebel lectures, 1957) Includes bibliography. [BT121.2.L4] 58-14328
1. Holy Spirit. I. Title.

LOGSDON, S Franklin. 231.3
The Lord of the harvest; the manifestation and the ministration of the Holy Spirit. Grand Rapids, Zondervan Pub. House [1954] 153p. 20cm. [BT121.L57] 54-21459
1. Holy Spirit. I. Title.

LUNDWALL, Nels Benjamin, 1884- comp. 231.3
Discourses on the Holy Ghost; also, lectures on faith, as delivered at School of the Prophets at Kirtland, Ohio. Salt Lake City, Bookcraft [1959] 154p. 24cm. [BX8608.L8] 59-37369
1. Mormons and Mormonism—Addresses, essays, lectures. 2. Mormons and Mormonism—Doctrinal and controversial works. 3. Holy Spirit. I. Title.

MCCONKLE, Oscar Walter, 1887- 231.3
The Holy Ghost; a study of the Holy Ghost, according to the standard works of the church. [2d ed.] Salt Lake City, Deseret Book Co., 1952 [i.e.1953, c1944] 321p. 24cm. [BT121.M335 1952] 53-23423
1. Holy Spirit. 2. Mormons and Mormonism—Doctrinal and controversial works. I. Title.

MACLEOD, Donald Malcolm. 231'.3
The doctrine of the Holy Spirit, by Rev. Donald M. Macleod. Inverness, Free Presbyterian Church of Scotland [1967] [2], 16 p. 19 cm. Bibliography: p. 16. [BT121.2.M22] 68-79308 -/6
1. Holy Spirit. I. Title.

MCMAHON, John Thomas, 1893- 231.3
The Gift of God: Come, Holy Spirit. Westminster, Md., Newman Press [1958] 175p. illus. 20cm. [BT121.M413] 58-2229
1. Holy Spirit. I. Title.

MCNAIR, Jim, 1934- 231'.3
Experiencing the Holy Spirit / by Jim McNair. Minneapolis : Bethany Fellowship, c1977. p. cm. Includes index. Bibliography: p. [BT767.3.M33] 77-9262 ISBN 0-87123-135-2 pbk. : 2.95
1. Gifts, Spiritual. 2. Holy Spirit. I. Title.

MAERTENS, Thierry, 1921- 231.3
The breath and spirit of God. Tr. by Robert J. Olsen, Albert J. LaMothe, Jr. Notre Dame, Ind., Fides [c.1964] 166p. 21cm. Bibl. [BT121.2.M253] 64-23515 3.95
1. Holy Spirit. I. Title.

MAERTENS, Thierry, 1921- 231.3
The Spirit of God in Scripture Baltimore, Helicon [1966] 128 p. 18 cm (living word ser.) Tr. ot le souffle et l'espirit de Dieu and l'e spirit quidonne la vie. [bt121.2m253] 66-21188 4.00
1. 1. Holy Spirit. I. Title.

MARMION, Columba, Abbot, 1858-1923. 231.3
The Trinity in our spiritual life; an anthology of the writings of Dom Columba Marmion, compiled by Dom Raymund Thibaut. Westminster, Md., Newman Press, 1953. 284p. 23cm. Translation of Consecration a la Sainte Trinite, texte et commentaire. [BT111.M352] 53-5593
1. Trinity. I. Title.

MARTINEZ, Luis Maria, Abp., 1881-1956. 231.3
The Sanctifier. A translation by Sister M. Aquinas. [1st American ed.] Paterson, N. J., St. Anthony Guild Press [1957] 322p. illus. 24cm. Translation of El espfritu santo. [BT121.M4192] 57-14106
1. Holy Spirit. I. Title.

MATSLER, Bertha Smith. 231.3
The Holy Spirit in power; a course of lessons for Bible classes and home study courses. Boston, Christopher Pub. House [1952] 63 p. 21 cm. [BT121.M46] 52-12802
1. Holy Spirit. I. Title.

MONTAGUE, George T. 231'.3
The Holy Spirit : growth of a Biblical tradition / George T. Montague. New York : Paulist Press, c1976. ix, 374 p. ; 23 cm. (An Exploration book) Includes index. [BS680.H56M66] 76-4691 ISBN 0-8091-1950-1 pbk. : 8.50
1. Holy Spirit—Biblical teaching. I. Title.

MOODY, Dale. 231'.3
Spirit of the living God; the Biblical concepts interpreted in context. Philadelphia, Westminster Press [1968] 239 p. 21 cm. Bibliographical references included in "Notes" (p. 209-219) [BT121.2.M63] 68-11585
1. Holy Spirit—Biblical teaching. I. Title.

MOODY, Dale. 231'.3
Spirit of the living God : what the Bible says about the Spirit / by Dale Moody. Rev. ed. Nashville : Broadman Press, c1976. 241 p. ; 21 cm. Includes bibliographical references and indexes. [BS680.H56M67 1976] 76-29147 ISBN 0-8054-1941-1 pbk. : 3.95
1. Holy Spirit—Biblical teaching. I. Title.

MORRIS, Leon. 231.3
Spirit of the living God. [1st ed.] Chicago, Inter-varsity Press [1960] 102p. 19cm. (Great doctrines of the Bible) Includes bibliography. [BT121.2.M65] 61-868
1. Holy Spirit. I. Title.

MOULE, Handley Carr Glyn, Bp. of Durham, 1841-1920. 231'.3
The person and work of the Holy Spirit / by H. C. G. Moule. Grand Rapids : Kregel Publications, [1977] (Kregel popular commentary series) Reprint of the 1890 ed. published by Hodder and Stoughton, London, under title: Veni Creator. Includes indexes. [BT121.M68 1977] 77-79178 ISBN 0-8254-3220-0 : 5.95
1. Holy Spirit. I. Title.

OATES, Wayne Edward, 1917- 231'.3
The Holy Spirit and contemporary man, by Wayne E. Oates. Grand Rapids, Mich., Baker Book House [1974, c1968] 123 p. 20 cm. (Source books for ministers) Bibliographical references included in "Notes" (p. 117-123). [BT123.o16] 68-11489 ISBN 0-8010-6657-3. 2.45 (pbk.)
1. Holy Spirit. I. Title.

OATES, Wayne Edward, 1917- 231'.3
The Holy Spirit in five worlds: the psychedelic, the nonverbal, the articulate, the new morality, the administrative, by Wayne E. Oates. New York, Association [1968] 123p. 20cm. Bibl. [BT123.O16] 68-11489 3.95

1. Holy Spirit. I. Title.

OATES, Wayne Edward, 1917- 231'.3
The Holy Spirit in five worlds: the psychedelic, the non-verbal, the articulate, the new morality, the administrative, by Wayne E. Oates. New York, Association Press [1968] 123 p. 20 cm. Bibliographical references included in "Notes" (p. 117-123) [BT123.O16] 68-11489
1. Holy Spirit. I. Title.

OCKENGA, Harold John, 1905- 231.3
Power through Pentecost. [1st ed.] Grand Rapids, Erdmans [1959] 128p. 20cm. (Preaching for today) [BT123.O2] 59-2836
1. Holy Spirit. 2. Spirituality. I. Title.

OSGOOD, DeWitt S. 231'.3
Preparing for the latter rain [by] DeWitt S. Osgood. Nashville, Southern Pub. Association [1973] 224 p. 21 cm. [BT121.2.O79] 73-75219 ISBN 0-8127-0070-8 pap. 2.95
1. Holy Spirit. I. Title.

OSGOOD, DeWitt S. 231'.3
The promise of power, by DeWitt S. Osgood. Nashville, Southern Pub. Association [1970] 143 p. 21 cm. [BT121.2.O8] 78-123336
1. Holy Spirit. I. Title.

OWEN, John, 1616-1683. 231.3
The Holy Spirit, His gifts and power; exposition of the Spirit's name, nature, personality, dispensation, operations, and effects. Grand Rapids, Kregel Publications [1960] 356 p. 23 cm. "Originally published ... under title Owen on the Holy Spirit." [BT120.O85] 60-16514
1. Holy Spirit — Early works to 1800. I. Title.

OXFORD Institute on 231'.3
Methodist Theological Studies, 5th, 1973.
The Holy Spirit / edited by Dow Kirkpatrick ; prepared under the direction of the World Methodist Council. Nashville : Tidings, [1974] 242 p. ; 18 cm. Includes bibliographical references. [BT122.O95 1973] 74-83375 pbk. : 2.95
1. Holy Spirit—Addresses, essays, lectures. I. Kirkpatrick, Dow, ed. II. World Methodist Council. III. Title.

PACHE, Rene. 231.3
The person and work of the Holy Spirit; translated by J. D. Emerson. Chicago, Moody Press [c1954] 223p. 22cm. [BT121.P18] 55-688
1. Holy Spirit. I. Title.

PALMA, Anthony D. 231'.3
The Spirit : God in action / Anthony D. Palma. Springfield, Mo. : Gospel Pub. House, [1974] 124 p. ; 19 cm. Bibliography: p. 123-124. [BT121.2.P33] 74-75966 pbk. : 1.25.
1. Holy Spirit. I. Title.

PALMER, Edwin H 231.3
The Holy Spirit. Grand Rapids, Baker Book House, 1958. 174p. 20cm. [BT121.P19] 58-8387
1. Holy Spirit. I. Title.

PALMER, Edwin H. 231'.3
The person and ministry of the Holy Spirit : the traditional Calvinistic perspective / by Edwin H. Palmer. Grand Rapids : Baker Book House, [1974] 196 p. ; 23 cm. Published in 1958 under title: The Holy Spirit. [BT121.2.P35 1974] 74-76250 ISBN 0-8010-6961-0 : 5.95
1. Holy Spirit. I. Title.

*PEARLMAN, Myer. 231.3
Let's meet the Holy Spirit. Springfield, Mo., Gospel Publishing House, [1975 c1935] 64 p. 18 cm. (Radiant books) Originally published as "The heavenly gift." [BT121] ISBN 0-88243-565-5 0.95 (pbk.)
1. Holy Spirit. 2. Gifts, Spiritual. I. Title.

PENTECOST, J Dwight. 231.3
The Divine Comforter: the person and work of the Holy Spirit. [Westwood, N. J.] Revell [1963] 256 p. 21 cm. [BT121.2.P4] 63-7598
1. Holy Spirit I. Title.

PENTECOST, J. Dwight 231.3
The Divine Comforter: the person and work of the Holy Spirit. [Westwood, N.J.] Revell [c.1963] 256p. 21cm. 63-7598
1. Holy Spirit. I. Title.

[PETRELLI, Giuseppe] 231.3
Heavenward: book i, The Holy Spirit; book II, Receiving the kingdom; book III, Partakers of the divine nature. [New York? 1953] 303p. 21cm. [BT121.P38] 53-10088
1. Holy Spirit. I. Title.

PIERCE, Samuel Eyles, 1746- 231.3
1829.
The gospel of the Spirit. Grand Rapids, Eerdmans, 1955. 104p. 23cm. [BT121.P58] 55-3689

1. Holy Sprit. I. Title.

PINK, Arthur Walkington, 231'.3
1886-1952.
The Holy Spirit. Grand Rapids, Baker Book House [1970] 193 p. 23 cm. [BT121.2.P54 1970] 70-107078 4.95
1. Holy Spirit.

PITTENGER, William Norman, 231'.3
1905-
The Holy Spirit, by Norman Pittenger. Philadelphia, United Church Press [1974] 128 p. 22 cm. "A Pilgrim Press book." [BT121.2.P57] 74-10839 ISBN 0-8298-0284-3
1. Holy Spirit.

PONTIFEX, Mark, 1896- 231.3
Belief in the Trinity. New York, Harper [1954] 91p. 19cm. [BT111] 54-12211
1. Trinity. I. Title.

PONTIFEX, Mark, 1896- 231.3
Belief in the Trinity. London, New York, Longmans, Green [1954] 91p. 19cm. [BT111.P78] 54-1712
1. Trinity. I. Title.

POWELL, Sidney Waterbury, 231.3
1889-
Fire on the earth. Nashville, Broadman Press [1963] 171 p. 22 cm. Includes bibliography. [BV3793.P58] 63-8411
1. Evangelicalism. 2. Holy Spirit. I. Title.

POWELL, Sidney Waterbury, 231.3
1889-
Fire on the earth. Nashville, Broadman [c.1963] 171p. 22cm. Bibl. 63-8411 3.50
1. Evangelicalism. 2. Holy Spirit. I. Title.

RAMM, Bernard 231.3
The witness of the Spirit; an essay on the contemporary relevance of the internal witness of the Holy Spirit. Grand Rapids, Mich., Eerdmans [1960, c.1959] 140p. (3p. bibl.) 23cm. 59-14589 3.00
1. Holy Spirit. 2. Authority (Religion) 3. Apologetics—20th cent. I. Title.

RAMM, Bernard L. 1916- 231'.3
Rapping about the Spirit [by] Bernard L. Ramm. Waco, Tex., Word Books [1974] 176 p. 23 cm. Includes bibliographies. [BT121.2.R35] 73-85521 5.95
1. Holy Spirit. I. Title.

RAMSEY, Arthur Michael, 231'.3
Abp. of Canterbury, 1904-
Come Holy Spirit / by Arthur Michael Ramsey, Leon-Joseph Cardinal Suenens ; with sermons by John Maury Allin, Robert E. Terwilliger. New York : Morehouse-Barlow Co., c1976. 104 p. ; 20 cm. [BT122.R25] 74-26351 ISBN 0-8192-1186-9 pbk. : 2.95
1. Holy Spirit—Congresses. I. Suenens, Leon-Joseph, Cardinal, 1904- joint author. II. Allin, John Maury. III. Terwilliger, Robert E. IV. Title.

[RICHARDSON, Albert Ernest] 231.3
1868-
The power-full Christian. Grand Rapids, Zondervan [1961] 144p. 61-19958 1.95; 1.00 bds., pap.,
1. Holy Spirit—Devotional literature. I. Title.

RIGA, Peter J. 231'.3
Gift of the Spirit [by] Peter J. Riga. Notre Dame, Ind., Fides Publishers [1974] p. cm. Includes bibliographical references. [BT121.2.R53] 74-9963 ISBN 0-8190-0603-3 1.50 (pbk.)
1. Holy Spirit. I. Title.

RIMMER, Charles Brandon, 231'.3
1917-
The unpredictable wind : a book on the Holy Spirit / C. Brandon Rimmer and Bill Brown. New York : T. Nelson, [1974] c1972. 115 p. ; 21 cm. [BT121.2.R56 1974] 74-23589 ISBN 0-8407-5578-3
1. Holy Spirit. I. Brown, Bill, 1928- joint author. II. Title.

ROBINSON, William, 1888- 231'.3
Completing the reformation; the doctrine of the priesthood of all believers. Lexington, Ky., College of the Bible, 1955. 70p. 23cm. (The College of the Bible. Spring lectures, 1955) [BT769.R6] 56-783
1. Priesthood, Universal. I. Title. II. Series: Lexington, Ky. College of the Bible. Spring lectures, 1955

RYRIE, Charles Caldwell, 231.3
1925-
The Holy Spirit. Chicago, Moody [1965] 126p. 22cm. (Handbk. of Bible doctrine) Bibl. [BT121.2.R9] 65-14610 1.75
1. Holy Spirit. I. Title.

SANDERS, John Oswald, 231'.3
1902-
The Holy Spirit and His gifts [by] J. Oswald Sanders. [Rev. and enl. ed.] Grand Rapids, Zondervan Pub. House [1970] 155 p. 21 cm. (Contemporary evangelical perspectives) First published in 1940 under title: The Holy Spirit of promise. Bibliography: p. 155. [BT121.S23 1970] 76-120032
1. Holy Spirit. 2. Gifts, Spiritual. I. Title.

*SCOFIELD, Cyrus Ingerson, 231'.3
1843-1921.
A mighty wind, by C. I. Scofield. Grand Rapids, Mich., Baker Book House [1973] 92 p. 18 cm. (Direction Books) [BT122] 0.95 (pbk.)
1. Holy Spirit. I. Title.

SCOFIELD, Cyrus Ingerson. 231.3
1843-1921
Plain papers on the doctrine of the Holy Spirit [Grand Rapids, Mich., Baker Bk., 1966,c.1899] 80p. 20cm. [BT121.S37] 1.50 bds.,
1. Holy Spirit. I. Title.

SCOTT, Ernest Findlay, 231.3
1868-1954.
I believe in the Holy Spirit. New York, Abingdon Press [1958] 92p. 20cm. [BT121.S44] 58-9524
1. Holy Spirit. I. Title.

*SEAMANDS. JOHN T. 231'.3
On tiptoe with joy. Kansas City, Mo., Beacon Hill Pr. [1967] 133p. 20cm. [BW] 2.95
I. Title.

SMAIL, Thomas A., 1928- 231'.3
Reflected glory : the spirit in Christ and Christians / by Thomas A. Smail. 1st American ed. Grand Rapids : Eerdmans, 1976, c1975. 158 p. ; 22 cm. Bibliography: p. 157-158. [BT121.2.S56 1976] 76-968 ISBN 0-8028-3484-1 : 6.95
1. Holy Spirit. I. Title.

SMEATON, George, 1814-1889. 231.3
The doctrine of the Holy Spirit. London, Banner of Truth Trust, 1958; [stamped: distributed by Bible Truth Depot, Swengel, Pa.] 372 p. 22 cm. [BT121.S62 1958] 59-39194
1. Holy Spirit. I. Title.

SMITH, William Edward, 231.3
1881-
The faith of Jesus. Boston, Meador Pub. Co. [1954] 697p. 22cm. [BT115.S56] 55-19726
1. Trinity—Controversial literature. 2. Holy Spirit. I. Title.

SOPER, David Wesley, 1910- 231.3
The spirit is willing. Philadelphia, Westminster Press [1958] 142 p. 21 cm. [BT122.S6] 58-9504
1. Christian life. 2. Holy Spirit. I. Title.

THE Spirit of God in 231'.3
Christian life / contributors, Barnabas Mary Ahern ... [et al.] ; edited by Edward Malatesta. New York : Paulist Press, c1977. v, 149 p. ; 19 cm. (Deus books) Includes bibliographical references. [BT121.2.S565] 77-74585 ISBN 0-8091-2033-X pbk. : 1.95
1. Holy Spirit—Addresses, essays, lectures. 2. Spiritual life—Catholic authors—Addresses, essays, lectures. 3. Glossolalia—Addresses, essays, lectures. I. Ahern, Barnabas M. II. Malatesta, Edward.

*SPURGEON, Charles Haddon, 231'.3
1834-1894.
Twelve sermons on the Holy Spirit, by C. H. Spurgeon. Grand Rapids, Baker Book House [1973] 132 p. 20 cm. (Charles H. Spurgeon library) [BT122] ISBN 0-8010-7983-7 pap., 1.95
1. Holy Spirit—Sermons. I. Title.

STAGG, Frank, 1911- 231'.3
The Holy Spirit today. Nashville, Broadman Press [1973] 93 p. 20 cm. Bibliography: p. 91-93. [BT121.2.S78] 73-85701 ISBN 0-8054-1919-5 1.95 (pbk.)
1. Holy Spirit. I. Title.

STARKEY, Lycurgus Monroe. 231.3
The work of the Holy Spirit, a study in Wesleyan theology. New York, Abingdon Press [1962] 176 p. 23 cm. Bibliography: p. 164-169. [BT119.S75] 62-9996
1. Wesley, John, 1703-1791. 2. Holy Spirit — History of doctrines. I. Title.

STARKEY, Lycurgus Monroe, 231.3
Jr.
The work of the Holy Spirit, a study in Wesleyan theology. Nashville, Abingdon [c.1962] 176p. 23cm. Bibl. 62-9996 3.00
1. Wesley, John, 1703-1791. 2. Holy Spirit—History of doctrines. I. Title.

STOTT, John R. W. 231'.3
Baptism & fullness : the work of the Holy Spirit today / John R. W. Stott. 2d ed. Downers Grove, Ill. : Inter Varsity Press, [1976] 119 p. ; 18 cm. First ed. (c1964) published under title: The baptism and fullness of the Holy Spirit. [BT121.2.S85 1976] 76-21457 ISBN 0-87784-648-0 : 2.25
1. Holy Spirit. I. Title.

STRAUSS, Lehman. 231'.3
Be filled with the Spirit / Lehman Strauss. Grand Rapids, Mich. : Zondervan, c1976. 125 p. ; 18 cm. [BT121.2.S87] 76-11829 pbk. : 1.50
1. Holy Spirit. I. Title.

STRAUSS, Lehman. 231.3
The Third Person; seven devotional studies on the person and work of the Holy Spirit [1st ed.] New York, Loizeaux Bros. [1954] 190p. 20cm. [BT121.S855] 54-42463
1. Holy Spirit. I. Title.

SUENENS, Leon Joseph, 231'.3
Cardinal, 1904-
A new Pentecost? / L. J. Suenens ; translated by Francis Martin. New York : Seabury Press, [1975], c1974. xiii, 239 p. ; 22 cm. "A Crossroad book." Includes bibliographical references. [BT121.2.S9313 1975] 74-30044 ISBN 0-8164-0276-0 : 7.95
1. Holy Spirit. 2. Pentecostalism. I. Title.

TAYLOR, John Vernon, 1914- 231'.3
The go-between God; the Holy Spirit and the Christian mission [by] John V. Taylor. [1st American ed.] Philadelphia, Fortress Press [1973] 246 p. illus. 22 cm. Includes bibliographical references. [BT121.2.T39 1973] 72-89257 ISBN 0-8006-0255-2 5.50
1. Holy Spirit. 2. Mission of the church. I. Title.

THOMAS, William Henry 231.3
Griffith, 1861-1924.
The Holy Spirit of God. [3d ed.] Grand Rapids, Eerdmans, 1955. 303p. 23cm. 'Lectures on the L. P. Stone Foundation, Princeton Theological Seminary, N. J.... 1913.' [BT121.T35 1955] 55-13919
1. Holy Spirit. I. Title.

TORREY, Reuben Archer, 231'.3
1856-1928
The person and work of the Holy Spirit as revealed in the scriptures and in personal experience. Grand Rapids, Mich., Zondervan [1968, c1910] 262p. 21cm. [BT121.T6 1968] 67-14441 3.95
1. Holy Spirit. I. Title.

UNGER, Merrill Frederick, 231.3
1909-
The baptizing work of the Holy Spirit. Wheaton, Ill., Van Kampen Press [1953] 147p. 20cm. [BT123.U5] 54-16312
1. Holy Spirit. I. Title.

VAN DUSEN, Henry Pitney, 231.3
1897-
Spirit, Son, and Father; Christian faith in the light of the Holy Spirit. New York, Scribner [1958] 180 p. 21 cm. (Lectures on the James A. Gray Fund of the Divinity School of Duke University, Durham, North Carolina) Includes bibliography. [BT121.V15] 58-10862
1. Holy Spirit. I. Title.

VAUGHAN, Clement Read, 231'.3
1827-1911.
The gifts of the Holy Spirit to unbelievers and believers / C. R. Vaughan. Edinburgh ; Carlisle, Pa. : Banner of Truth Trust, 1975. 415 p. ; 23 cm. Reprint of the 1894 ed. published in Richmond, Va. [BT121.V2 1975] 75-332678 ISBN 0-85151-222-4 : £2.10
1. Holy Spirit. 2. Gifts, Spiritual. I. Title.

WALKER, Alan, 1911- 231'.3
Breakthrough. rediscovery of the Holy Spirit. Nashville, Abingdon Press [1969] 92 p. 20 cm. [BT121.2.W3] 79-88691 ISBN 0-687-03976-2 2.75
1. Holy Spirit. I. Title.

WALVOORD, John F 231.3
The Holy Spirit; a comprehensive study of the person and work of the Holy Spirit. Wheaton, Ill., Van Kampen Press [1954] 275p. 22cm. A revision of the author's The doctrine of the Holy Spirit. [BT121.W27 1954] 54-2881
1. Holy Spirit. I. Title.

WANSBROUGH, Henry, 1934- 231'.3
The Holy Spirit / Henry Wansbrough. Staten Island, N.Y. : Alba House, 1975, c1973. 90 p. ; 18 cm. (Scripture for meditation ; 9) [BT122.W36 1975] 74-31342 ISBN 0-8189-0314-7 pbk. : 1.95
1. Holy Spirit—Meditations. I. Title. II. Series.

WATKINS, Mamie. 231'.3
The baptism in the Holy Spirit made plain / by Mamie Watkins. Greensburg, Pa. : Manna Christian Outreach, c1975. 128 p. ; 18 cm. [BT123.W34] 75-23401 ISBN 0-8007-8227-5 pbk. : 1.95
1. Baptism in the Holy Spirit. I. Title.

WATSON, David C. K., 1933- 231'.3
One in the spirit, by David C. K. Watson. Old Tappan, N.J., F. H. Revell Co. [1974, c1973] 126 p. 19 cm. Includes bibliographical references. [BT121.2.W37 1974] 73-17498 ISBN 0-8007-0641-2 1.95 (pbk.)
1. Holy Spirit. 2. Pentecostalism. I. Title.

*WIERWILLE, Victor Paul 231'.3
Receiving the Holy Spirit [5th ed. New Knoxville, Ohio, The Way, 1967] 295p. 21cm. 4.95
1. Holy Spirit. I. Title.

WIERWILLE, Victor Paul 231.3
Receiving the Holy Spirit today [4th rev., enl. ed. New Knoxville, Ohio, The Way, 1963, c.1962] 314p. 21cm. 4.95
I. Title.

WILLIAMS, John Rodman. 231'.3
The era of the Spirit, by J. Rodman Williams. Plainfield, N.J., Logos International [1971] 119 p. 21 cm. Includes bibliographical references. [BT119.W55] 71-126170
1. Holy Spirit—History of doctrines. I. Title.

WINDISCH, Hans, 1881-1935. 231'.3
The Spirit-Paraclete in the Fourth Gospel. Translated by James W. Cox. Philadelphia, Fortress Press [1968] xiv, 47 p. 19 cm. (Facet books. Biblical series, 20) Bibliography: p. 39-45. [BS2615.2.W53] 68-12330
1. Bible. N.T. John—Theology. 2. Holy Spirit—Biblical teaching. I. Title. II. Series.

WITH bright wings : 231'.3
a book of the spirit : a collection of texts on the Holy Spirit / compiled by Mary Grace Swift. New York : Paulist Press, c1976. xiii, 246 p. : ill. ; 21 cm. Includes bibliographical references and index. [BT118.W57 1976] 75-44806 ISBN 0-8091-1936-6 pbk. : 5.95
1. Holy Spirit—Collected works. I. Swift, Mary Grace.

WITTY, Robert Gee. 231.3
Power for the church [by] Robert G. Witty. Nashville, Broadman Press [1966] 64 p. 21 cm. Bibliography: p. 63-64. [BT123.W5] 67-12178
1. Holy Spirit. 2. Pentecost. I. Title.

WOOD, Leon James. 231'.3
The Holy Spirit in the Old Testament / Leon J. Wood. Grand Rapids : Zondervan Pub. House, c1976. 160 p. ; 21 cm. (Contemporary evangelical perspectives) Includes indexes. Bibliography: p. 151-154. [BS1199.S69W66] 75-38803 pbk. : 3.95
1. Bible. O.T.—Criticism, interpretation, etc. 2. Holy Spirit—Biblical teaching. I. Title.

*WOODS, Leon P. 231.3
Work of the holy spirit. New York, Carlton [c.1966] 70p. 21cm. (Hearthside bk.) 2.75
I. Title.

WOOLSEY, Raymond H. 231'.3
The Spirit and his church [by] Raymond H. Woolsey. Washington, Review and Herald Pub. Association [1970] 128 p. 22 cm. [BT121.2.W64] 74-90781
1. Holy Spirit. I. Title.

WUNDERLICH, Lorenz 231.3
The half-known God: the Lord and Giver of life. St. Louis, Concordia [c.1963] 117p. 21cm. Bibl. 63-14991 1.95 pap.,
1. Holy Spirit. I. Title.

YOUNG, John Terry, 1929- 231'.3
The spirit within you / J. Terry Young. Nashville : Broadman Press, c1977. 192 p. ; 20 cm. [BT121.2.Y68] 77-368625 ISBN 0-8054-1945-4 : 4.95
1. Holy Spirit. 2. Pentecostalism—Controversial literature. I. Title.

MARMION, Columba Abbot, 231.3081
1858-1923
Fire of love; an anthology of Abbot Marmion's published writings of the Holy Spirit [ed.] by Charles Dollen. St. Louis, B. Herder [1965, c.1964] 124p. 23cm. Bibl. [BT121.2.M28] 65-3557 3.50
1. Holy Spirit. I. Dollen, Charles, ed. II. Title.

WELCH, Claude. 231.3 231
In this name; the doctrine of the Trinity in contemporary theology. New York, Scribner, 1952. 313 p. 22 cm. [BT111.W42] 52-14614
1. Trinity. I. Title.

BROPHY, Donald, comp. 231'.4
Does God punish? Edited by Richard McCarthy. Glen Rock, N.J., Paulist Press [1968] 61 p. 17 cm. Contents.Contents.—Does God punish? By G. Baum.—Suffering and death, by L. Boros.—Forgive us our trespasses, by L. Evely. [BT153.W7B7] 68-57474 0.75
1. God—Wrath. 2. Suffering. I. Baum, Gregory, 1923- Does God punish? 1968. II. Boros, Ladislaus, 1927- Suffering and death. 1968. III. Evely, Louis, 1910- Forgive us our trespasses. 1968. IV. Title.

BURI, Fritz, 1907- 231'.4
How can we still speak responsibly of God? Philadelphia, Fortress Press [1968] viii, 83 p. 22 cm. Translation of Wie konnen wir heute noch verantwortlich von Gott reden? Bibliographical footnotes. [BT102.B813] 68-12329
1. God—Knowableness. I. Title.

CORNWALL, E. Judson. 231'.4
Let us praise [by] E. Judson Cornwall. [1st ed.] Plainfield, N.J., Logos International [1973] 148 p. 21 cm. [BV4817.C65] 73-75957 ISBN 0-88270-039-1 2.50
1. Praise of God. I. Title.

EDWARDS, Francis Henry, 231.4
1897-
All Thy mercies. Independence, Mo., Herald House [c.1962] 213p. 21cm. 62-12900 2.25
1. God—Mercy. I. Title.

ERDMAN, Charles Rosenbury, 231.4
1866-
The spirit of Christ; devotional studies in the doctrine of the Holy Spirit, by Charles R. Erdman. Chicago, Moody [1967] 123p. 17cm. (Colportage lib., 526) First pub. in 1926 [BT121.E7] .39 pap.,
1. Holy Spirit. I. Title.

GOD : 231'.4
what is He like? / Compiled by William F. Kerr. Wheaton, Ill. : Tyndale House Publishers, 1977. 127 p. ; 18 cm. [BT130.G6] 77-77359 ISBN 0-8423-1098-3 pbk. : 1.95
1. God—Attributes—Addresses, essays, lectures. I. Kerr, William F.

GOD of Israel (The); the 231.4
God of Christians, the great themes of scripture [by] J. Giblet [others] Tr. by Kathryn Sullivan. New York, Desclee [c.]1961. 261p. 61-15720 3.95
1. Typology (Theology) 2. Christian life—Catholic authors. I. Giblet, J.

GOD of Israel (The), the 231.4
God of Christians; the great themes of scripture [by] J. Giblet [others] Tr. [from French] by Kathryn Sullivan. Glen Rock, N.J., Paulist [1966, c.1961] vii, 261p. 18cm. (Deus bks) [BS478.G613] .95 pap.,
1. Typology (Theology) 2. Christian life—Catholic authors. I. Giblet, J.

GRABOWSKI, Stanislaus J 231.4
The all-present God; a study in St. Augustine. St. Louis, B. Herder Book Co. [1954] 327p. 23cm. [BT132.A8G7] 53-9108
1. Augustinus, Aurelius, Saint, Bp. of Hippo. 2. God—Omnipresence. 3. God—History of doctrines. I. Title.

HAZELTON, Roger, 1909- 231'.4
Knowing the living God. Valley Forge, Judson Press [1968, c1969] 126 p. 22 cm. [BT102.H38] 69-11679 ISBN 0-8170-0417-3 1.50
1. God—Knowableness. I. Title.

LANGUET DE LA VILLENEUVE DE 231.4
GERGY, Jean Joseph. Abp. of Sens, 1677-1753.
Reflections on confidence in the mercy of God. New ed., rev. Baltimore, F. Lucas, Jr. [c1834] 178p. 15cm. L. C. copy imperfect. [BT153.M4L3 1834] 55-45542
1. God—Mercy. I. Title.

LUBAC, Henri de 231.4
The discovery of God. Translated [from the French] by Alexander Dru. New York, P. J. Kenedy [1960] 212p. 20cm. (b2bl. footnotes) p3.95 60-7786
1. God (Theory of knowledge) I. Title.

*MCCORD, Hugo 231.4
Getting acquainted with God; thirty-five Old Testament descriptions of Deity. Murfreesboro, Tenn., DeHoff Pubns. [c.1965] 58p. 20cm. 1.50 pap.,
I. Title.

MIDDLETON, Robert Lee, 231.4
1894-
The goodness of God. Nashville, Broadman Press [1962] 118p. 21cm. [BT137.M5] 62-9199
1. God.— Goodness. I. Title.

PHILLIPS, Harold L. 231'.4
Knowing the living God, by Harold L. Phillips. Anderson, Ind., Warner Press [1968] 128 p. 19 cm. Bibliographical references included in "Notes and acknowledgments" (p. 125-128) [BT102.P48] 68-58100
1. God—Knowableness. I. Title.

PIKE, Nelson. 231'.4
God and timelessness. New York, Schocken Books [1970] xiv, 192 p. 23 cm. (Studies in ethics and the philosophy of religion) Includes bibliographical references. [BT912.P5 1970b] 74-100988 7.00
1. Eternity. 2. God—Attributes. I. Title.

*PINK, Arthur W. 1886-1952 231.4
The attributes of God. [By] Arthur W. Pink. Grand Rapids, Baker Book House, [1975] 96 p. 22 cm. Includes index of Scriptures quoted. Includes index of Authors quoted. [BL205] ISBN 0-8010-6989-0 2.45 (pbk.)
1. God—Attributes. 2. Providence and Government of God. I. Title.

PINK, Arthur Walkington, 231.4
1886-1952.
The attributes of God; a solemn and blessed contemplation of some of the wondrous and lovely perfections of the divine character. Swengel, Pa., Bible Truth Depot, 1961. 83p. 20cm. [BT130.P5] 61-65718
1. God—Attributes. I. Title.

REDMOND, Howard A. 231.4
The omnipotence of God. Philadelphia, Westminster [c.1964] 192p. 21cm. Bibl. 64-17114 4.50
1. God—Omnipotence. I. Title.

SOPOCKO, Michael. 231.4
God is mercy; translated from the Polish by the Marian Fathers. St. Meinrad, Ind., Grail Publications [1955] 173p. 20cm. 'Litany of the Mercy of God': p. xiii-xv. [BX2187.P6S63] 55-9039
1. Litany of the Mercy of God. 2. Meditations. 3. God—Mercy. I. Title.

SOURCES of Christian 231.4
theology. Westminster, Md., Newman Press, 1955- v. 23cm. Includes bibliographical references. [BX1749.S6] 55-1503
1. Catholic Church—Doctrinal and controversial works. 2. Theology, Doctrinal—Hist.

TRANSCENDENCE. 231'.4
Edited by Herbert W. Richardson and Donald R. Cutler. Boston, Beacon Press [1969] xv, 176 p. 22 cm. Based on papers presented at 2 symposiums sponsored by the Church Society for College Work, Cambridge, Mass., held Dec. 1967 at the Episcopal Theological School, and May 1968 at Endicott House. Includes bibliographical references. [BT124.5.T7] 69-14597 7.50
1. Transcendence of God—Addresses, essays, lectures. I. Richardson, Herbert Warren, ed. II. Cutler, Donald R., ed. III. Church Society for College Work.

WASS, Meldon Clarence, 231.4
1926-
The infinite God and the Summa fratris Alexandri, by Meldon C. Wass. Chicago, Franciscan Herald Press [1964] ix, 101 p. 21 cm. (Quincy College publications) "Forum books." Bibliography: p. 93-97. [BX1749.A62W3] 64-4804
1. Alexander de Hales, d. 1245. Summa theologics. I. Title. II. Series: Quincy, Ill. College. Publications

WASS, Meldon Clarence, 231.4
1926-
The infinite God and the Summa fratris Alexandri. Chicago, Franciscan Herald [1964] ix, 101p. 21cm. (Quincy Coll. pubns., Forum bks.) Bibl. 64-4804 2.25 pap.,
1. Alexander de Hales, d. 1245. Summa theologica. I. Title. II. Series: Quincy, Ill. College. Publications

WATSON, Elizabeth Elaine. 231'.4
Where are you, God? / Elizabeth Elaine Watson ; pictures by Ronald R. Hester. Nashville : Broadman Press, 1977c1976 32 p. : col. ill. ; 24 cm. A little boy wonders where God is and if God watches all his activities. [BT107.W25] 77-362509 ISBN 0-8054-4235-9 bds. : 2.95
1. God—Juvenile literature. I. Hester, Ronald. II. Title.

BAXTER, James Sidlow. 231'.5
Does God still guide? Or, more fully, what are the essentials of guidance and growth in the Christian life? [By] J. Sidlow Baxter. Grand Rapids, Mich., Zondervan Pub. House [1971] 191 p. 23 cm. Reprint of the 1968 ed. [BT135.B35 1971] 71-120047 4.95
1. Providence and government of God. I. Title.

BEERS, Victor Gilbert, 231'.5
1928-
Cats and bats and things like that, and other wonderful things about God's world, by V. Gilbert Beers. Illustrated by Juel Krisvoy. Chicago, Moody Press [1972] [30] p. col. illus. 20 x 26 cm. Describes some of God's gifts in nature, such as the bats' sonar, the changing colors of leaves, and the life contained in a seed. [BT96.2.B43] 72-88038 ISBN 0-8024-1211-4
1. Providence and government of God—Juvenile literature. I. Krisvoy, Juel, illus. II. Title.

BELEW, Pascal P 231.5
The philosophy of providence. Butler, Ind. Higley Press [c1955] 176p. 22cm. [BT135.B38] 56-29678
1. Providence and government of God. I. Title.

BLAMIRES, Harry. 231.5
The will and the way; a study of divine providence and vocation. New York, Macmillan, 1957. 128 p. 22 cm. [BT135.B57] 57-10290
1. Providence and government of God. 2. Vocation. I. Title.

BLAMIRES, Harry 231.5
The will and the way; a study of divine providence and vocation. Greenwich, Conn., Seabury, 1962. 128p. 19cm. 1.50 pap.,
1. Providence and government of God. 2. Vocation. I. Title.

BLAMIRES, Hary. 231.5
The will and the way; a study of divine providence and vocation. New York, Macmillan, c128p. 22cm. [BT135.B57] 57-10290
1. Providence and government of God. 2. Vocation. I. Title.

GOODWIN, Abb L. 231'.5
God's eternal purpose revealed, by Abb L. Goodwin. Rev. ed. Dallas, Crescendo Book Publications [1973] 261 p. illus. 23 cm. [BT96.2.G64 1973] 73-83082 5.95
1. Providence and government of God. I. Title.
Publisher's address: 2580 Gus Thomasson, Dallas, Texas 75228.

HARKNESS, Georgia Elma 231.5
The providence of God. Nashville, Abingdon Press [c.1960] 192p. 23cm. (bibl. footnotes) 60-6932 3.50
1. Providence and government of God. I. Title.

HARKNESS, Georgia Elma, 231.5
1891-
The providence of God. New York, Abingdon Press [1960] 192p. 23cm. Includes bibliography. [BT135.H27] 60-6932
1. Providence and government of God. I. Title.

HAYNES, Carlyle Boynton, 231.5
1882-
On the throne of the world; an analysis of the Bible teaching of the sovereignty of God and His providential supervision of the affairs of men and nations, particularly as it is manifested in the lives of His disciples. Nashville, Southern Pub. Association ['1951] 124 p. 21 cm. [BT135.H33] 52-24898
1. Providence and government of God. 2. Seventh-Day Adventists—Doctrinal and controversial works. I. Title.

HAZELTON, Roger, 1909- 231.5
God's way with man; variations on the theme of providence. New York, Abingdon Press [1956] 204p. 21cm. [BT135.H34] 56-10146
1. Providence and government of God. I. Title.

JOHNSON, Paul Gordon, 231'.5
1931-
Caution—God at work / by Paul G. Johnson. Maryknoll, N.Y. : Orbis Books, [1976] p. cm. Includes bibliographical references. [BT96.2.J63] 75-7781 ISBN 0-88344-052-0
1. Providence and government of God. 2. Theology. I. Title.

JOHNSON, Paul Gordon, 231'.5
1931-
Caution—God at work / Paul G. Johnson. Maryknoll, N.Y. : Orbis Books, c1976. xiv, 137 p. ; 21 cm. Includes bibliographical references. [BT96.2.J63] 75-7781 ISBN 0-88344-052-0 : 3.95
1. Providence and government of God. 2. Theology. I. Title.

KEARNS, Mary Kenneth, comp. 231.5
Divine providence; [anthology. Scranton, Pa., Manus Langan Press, 1959] 112p. illus. 23cm. Includes bibliography. [BT135.K37] 59-14066
1. Providence and government of God. I. Title.

LOCKERBIE, Jeanette W. 231'.5
Just take it from the Lord, brother [by] Jeanette Lockerbie. Old Tappan, N.J., F. H. Revell Co. [1975] 124 p. 21 cm. [BT135.L6] 74-18021 ISBN 0-8007-0698-6 3.95
1. Providence and government of God. 2. Christian life—1960- I. Title.

MATHER, Increase, 1639- 231'.5
1723.
Remarkable providences / Increase Mather.

New York : Arno Press, 1977. p. cm. (International folklore) Reprint of the 1856 ed. published by J. R. Smith, London. [BT135.M34 1977] 77-70610 ISBN 0-405-10107-4 : 18.00
1. Providence and government of God. 2. Legends—New England. I. Title. II. Series.

MEYER, Carl Stamm, 1907- 231'.5
The caring God; perspectives on providence. Edited by Carl S. Meyer and Herbert T. Mayer. St. Louis, Concordia Pub. House [1973] 240 p. 24 cm. Includes bibliographical references. [BT135.M4 1973] 72-91151 ISBN 0-570-03228-8 8.95
1. Providence and government of God. I. Mayer, Herbert T., joint author. II. Title.

OUTLER, Albert Cook, 1908- 231'.5
Who trusts in God; musings on the meaning of providence [by] Albert C. Outler. New York, Oxford University Press, 1968. xvi, 141 p. 21 cm. Bibliographical footnotes. [BT96.2.O8] 68-17616
1. Providence and government of God. I. Title.

POLLARD, William Grosvenor, 1911- 231.5
Chance and providence; God's action in a world governed by scientific law. New York, Scribner [1958] 190 p. 21 cm. [BT135.P6] 58-5722
1. Providence and government of God. 2. Religion and science—1900- I. Title.

SWEDENBORG, Emanuel, 1688-1772 231.5
Angelic wisdom about divine providence. Newly tr. [from Latin] by William Frederic Wunsch. Introd. by Walter M. Horton. New York, Citadel [1964, c.1963] xvii, 419p. 19cm. (C-155) 63-21204 1.95 pap.,
1. Providence and government of God—Early works to 1800. I. Title.

TAYLOR, Jack R. 231'.5
God's miraculous plan of economy / Jack R. Taylor. Nashville : Broadman Press, c1975. 168 p. ; 23 cm. [BT135.T39] 75-27411 ISBN 0-8054-5565-5 : 5.95
1. Providence and government of God. 2. Stewardship, Christian. I. Title.

WARD, Maisie, 1889- ed. 231.5
Be not solicitous; sidelights on the providence of God and the Catholic family. New York, Sheed & Ward, 1953. 254p. 21cm. [BX2351.W3] 53-5194
1. Family—Religious life. 2. Providence and government of God. I. Title.

ALLEN, Diogenes. 231'.6
Finding our father. Atlanta, John Knox Press [1974] 124 p. 21 cm. Includes bibliographical references. [BT102.A43] 73-16917 ISBN 0-8042-0557-4 6.00
1. Jesus Christ—Resurrection. 2. God. 3. Love. 4. Death. I. Title.

ALLER, Catherine. 231.6
The greatest word in the world. Los Angeles, Cowman Publications [c1957] 84p. 18cm. [BT140.A4] 58-20217
1. God—Love. I. Title.

BALTHASAR, Hans Urs von, 1905- 231'.6
Love alone. [New York] Herder and Herder [1969] 124 p. 22 cm. Translation of Glaubhaft ist nur Liebe. Bibliographical footnotes. [BT140.B313 1969] 69-16756 3.95
1. God—Love. 2. Love (Theology) I. Title.

BRIERE, Emile. 231'.6
For uncomplicated Christians; reflections on the power of love. [Boston] St. Paul Editions [1973] 184 p. illus. 22 cm. [BV4639.B79] 73-88166 3.95
1. Love (Theology)—Meditations. I. Title. II. Title: Uncomplicated Christians.

BUCK, Clifford 231.6
The greatest of hese. [Independence, Mo., Herald Pub., 1966] 160p. 21cm. Bibl. [BV4639.B85] 66-28675 2.75
1. Love (Theology). I. Title. II. Title: hese.

CHERVIN, Ronda. 231'.6
Church of love. Liguori, Mo., Liguori Publications [1973] 143 p. 18 cm. [BV4639.C44] 73-78780 1.50 (pbk.)
1. Love (Theology) I. Title.

DELANGHE, Jules A. 231'.6
The philosophy of Jesus: real love, by Jules A. Delanghe. Philadelphia, Dorrance [1973] 141 p. 22 cm. [BV4639.D387] 72-96805 ISBN 0-8059-1821-3 4.95
1. Love (Theology) I. Title.

*DRUMMOND, Henry. 231.6
The greatest thing in the world. Old Tappan,NJ., Revell [1968] 61p.18cm. (Spire bk.) .50 pap.,
I. Title.

FABER, Frederick William, 1814-1863 231.6
The Creator and the creature; or, The wonders of divine love. Pref. by Ronald Chapman. Westminster, Md., Newman Pr. [1961] 356p. (Orchard bks.) 61-16576 3.95
1. God—Worship and love. I. Title.

FORSTER, Roger T. 231'.6
God's strategy in human history [by] Roger T. Forster and V. Paul Marston. Wheaton, Ill., Tyndale House [1974, c1973] viii, 296 p. 21 cm. Includes bibliographical references. [BR115.H5F66 1974] 74-80797 ISBN 0-8467-0032-8 3.95
1. History (Theology) I. Marston, V. Paul, joint author. II. Title.

FRANCOIS de Sales, Saint, Bp. of Geneva, 1567-1622. 231'.6
Treatise on the love of God. Translated into English by Henry Benedict Mackey. With an introd. by the translator. Westport, Conn., Greenwood Press [1971, c1942] xliv, 555 p. 23 cm. Translation of Traite de l'amour de Dieu. [BX2179.F8T74 1971] 71-156190 ISBN 0-8371-6139-8
1. Love (Theology)—Early works to 1800. 2. God—Worship and love. 3. Spiritual life—Catholic authors. I. Title.

*GEE, Donald. 231.6
The fruit of the spirit. Springfield, Mo., Gospel Publishing House, [1975 c1928] 79 p. 18 cm. (Radiant books) [BT130] ISBN 0-88243-501-9 0.95 (pbk.)
1. Pentecostalism. 2. Holy Spirit. I. Title.

GROU, Jean Nicolas, 1731-1803. 231.6
Meditations on the love of God, in the form of a retreat and an instruction on the gift of self to God. With a foreword by Cuthbert Butler. [Translation from the French by the Benedictines of Teignmouth] Westminster, Md., Newman Press [1960] x, 172p. 21cm. (The Orchard books) 60-10717 3.50
1. God—Worship and love. I. Title.

HOWARD, David M. 231'.6
By the power of the Holy Spirit [by] David M. Howard. Downers Grove, Ill., Inter Varsity Press [1973] 172 p. 18 cm. Includes bibliographical references. [BT121.2.H68] 73-83091 ISBN 0-87784-358-9 1.75 (pbk.)
1. Holy Spirit. I. Title.

HUBER, Mathias John, 1901- 231'.6
Love God and do what you please! Translated by C. D. McEnniry from the original Italian of The practice of the love of Jesus Christ, by St. Alphonsus Liguori. Adapted and edited by M. J. Huber. Liguori, No., Liguorian Books [1970] 126 p. 18 cm. [BV4639.H773] 71-116807 1.00
1. Love (Theology) I. Liguori, Alfonso Maria de', Saint, 1696-1787. Pratica di amar Gesu Cristo. II. Title.

JEAN BAPTISTE, Sister. 231.6
Faith in God's love; translated from the French by Mary Paula Williamson and Mary S. Garrity. With a foreword by John Wright. New York, Kenedy [1950] xv, 304 p. 21 cm. [BV4817.J412] 50-12571
1. God—worship and love. 2. God—Love. I. Title.

LACY, Mary Lou. 231'.6
And God wants people. Richmond, John Knox Press [1962] 80p. 21cm. [BV4639.L3] 62-11717
1. Love (Theology) 2. Friendship. I. Title.

LEFEBVRE, Georges, 1908- 231.6
The mystery of God's love. New York, Sheed & Ward [c.1961] 146p. 61-10173 .3.00 bds.,
1. God—Love. 2. God—Worship and love. 3. Love (Theology) I. Title.

MACGREGOR, Geddes. 231'.6
He who lets us be : a theology of love / Geddes MacGregor. New York : Seabury Press, c1975. x, 194 p. ; 22 cm. "A Crossroad book." Includes bibliographical references and index. [BT140.M3] 75-15957 ISBN 0-8164-1202-2 : 8.95
1. God—Love. 2. Incarnation. 3. Theodicy. I. Title. II. Title: A theology of love.

MCINTYRE, John, 1916- 231.6
On the love of God. New York, Harper [1962] 255p. 22cm. [BV4817.M23] 62-11133
1. God—Worship and love. 2. Christian life. I. Title.

MAGEEAN, Robert 231.6
God's infinite love and ours. Fresno, Calif., Academy Library Guild [1959] 183p. 19cm. 59-12595 2.95
1. God—Worship and love. I. Title.

MEGIVERN, James J 231'.6
Concomitance and communion; a study in eucharistic doctrine and practice [by] James J. Megivern. Fribourg, Switzerland, University Press. New York, Herder Book Center, 1963. xxii, 263 p. 24 cm. (Studia Friburgensia, new ser., 33) Thesis -- University of Fribourg. Bibliography: p. [xiii]-xxii. [BV823.M4] 65-6795
1. Lord's Supper — Communion in both elements. 2. Lord's Supper — Hist. I. Title. II. Series.

MOLINIE, Marie Dominique. 231'.6
The struggle of Jacob / by M. D. Molinie ; translated by Lorna Wishaw. New York : Paulist Press, c1977. 129 p. ; 18 cm. (A Deus book) Translation of Le Combat de Jacob. Includes bibliographical references. [BT140.M6513] 77-78216 ISBN 0-8091-2036-4 pbk. : 1.95
1. God—Love. I. Title.

MORANDO, Nazarene. 231'.6
The characteristics of charity. [Boston] St. Paul Editions [1963] 106 p. 19 cm. [BV4639.M59] 63-14589
1. Charity. I. Title.

NYGREN, Anders, Bp., 1890- 231.6
Agape and Eros. Translated by Philip S. Watson. Philadelphia, Westminster Press [1953] 764 p. 22 cm. Translation of Den kristna karlekstanken. Contents.Contents.—pt. 1. A study of the Christian idea of love.—pt. 2. The history of the Christian idea of love. [BV4639.N813] 53-13324
1. Love (Theology) I. Title. II. Title: The Christian idea of love.

NYGREN, Anders, Bp., 1890- 231'.6
Agape and Eros. Translated by Philip S. Watson. New York, Harper & Row [1969] 764 p. 21 cm. (Harper torchbooks. The Library of religion and culture, TB1430) Reprint of the 1953 ed. Translation of Den kristna karlekstanken genom tiderna. Contents.Contents.—A study of the Christian idea of love.—The history of the Christian idea of love. Bibliographical footnotes. [BV4639.N813 1969] 77-3058 4.95 (pbk)
1. Love (Theology) 2. Agape. I. Title.

OUTKA, Gene H. 231'.6
Agape; an ethical analysis, by Gene Outka. New Haven, Yale University Press, 1972. viii, 321 p. 23 cm. (Yale publications in religion, 17) A revision of the author's thesis, Yale University. Includes bibliographical references. [BV4639.O95 1972] 72-88070 ISBN 0-300-01384-1 11.00
1. Agape. 2. Ethics. I. Title. II. Series.

PRUNSKIS, Joseph, 1907- 231'.6
Meile ir laime. Putnam, Conn., Immaculata Press [1958] 248p. illus. 22cm. [BV4639.P7] 58-40621
1. Love (Theology) 2. Happiness. I. Title.

SCHLINK, Basilea. 231'.6
Those who love Him, by M. Basilea Schlink. Translated by Larry Christenson. Grand Rapids, Zondervan Pub. House [1969] 96 p. 21 cm. [BV4639.S3433] 69-11639
1. Love (Theology)—Meditations. I. Title.

SWEDENBORG, Emanuel, 1688-1772. 231'.6
Angelic wisdom concerning the divine love and the divine wisdom / by Emanuel Swedenborg. Standard ed. New York : Swedenborg Foundation, 1976. iii, 293 p. ; 22 cm. Translation of Sapientia angelica de divino amore. Reprint of the ed. published by American Swedenborg Print. and Pub. Society, New York. [BX8712.D4 1976b] 76-46144 ISBN 0-87785-057-7. 0877850569 lib. bdg.
1. God—Love. I. Title.

UNDERHILL, Evelyn, 1875-1941. 231.6
An anthology of the love of God, from the writings of Evelyn Underhill. Edited by Lumsden Barkway and Lucy Menzies. New York, D. McKay Co. [1954] 220p. illus. 21cm. [BT140.U5] 54-2717
1. God—Love. 2. God—Worship and love. 3. Love (Theology) I. Title. II. Title: The love of God.

WHO knows me? 231'.6
New York, Paulist Press [1969] [16] p. col. illus. 15 x 18 cm. (Rejoice books) Translation of Qui me connait? A youngster realizes that though God is invisible he knows us and our thoughts better than family or friends. [BT107.Q513] 77-7459 0.35
1. God—Juvenile literature.

YORK, Raymond. 231'.6
The truth of life is love. [New York] Herder and Herder [1968] xi, 206 p. illus. 22 cm. [BV4639.Y6] 68-24091 4.95
1. Love (Theology) 2. Sex (Theology) I. Title.

ALTHAUS, Paul, 1888- 231.7
The divine command; a new perspective on law and gospel. Translated by Franklin Sherman. Introd. by William H. Lazareth. Philadelphia, Fortress Press [1966] xiii, 50 p. 20 cm. (Facet books. Social ethics series. 9) Translation of Gebot and Gesetz; zum Thema "Gesetz and Evangelum." Bibliography: p. 48. [BT79.A413] 66-10758
1. Law and gospel. I. Title. II. Series.

ALTHAUS, Paul, 1888- 231.7
The divine command; a new perspective on law and gospel. Tr. [from German] by Franklin Sherman Introd. by William H. Lazareth. Philadelphia, Fortress [c.1966] xiii,50p. 20cm. (Facet bks. soc. ethics ser. 9) Bibl. [BT79.A413] 66-10758 .85 pap.,
1. Law and gospel. I. Title. II. Series.

ANDEL, G. K. van. 231'.7
The Christian concept of history in the chronicle of Sulpicius Severus / G. K. van Andel. Amsterdam : Adolf M. Hakkert, 1976. 195 p. ; 22 cm. Includes indexes. Bibliography: p. 169-176. [BR115.H5A47] 77-364625 ISBN 9-02-560722-5
1. Severus, Sulpicius. 2. History (Theology)—History of doctrines. I. Title.

BAUGHMAN, Ray E. 231'.7
The kingdom of God visualized, by Ray E. Baughman. Illustrated by Gerald Schmoyer. Chicago, Moody Press [1972] 286 p. map. 24 cm. Bibliography: p. 277-279. [BT94.B37] 70-181586 ISBN 0-8024-4565-9
1. Kingdom of God. I. Title.

BONHOEFFER, Dietrich, 1906-1945. 231.7
Preface to Bonhoeffer; the man and two of his shorter writings, by John D. Godsey. Philadelphia, Fortress Press [1965] v. 73 p. 20 cm. "Translated from [the author's] Dein Reich komme, edited by Eberhard Bethge ... 1957." [BT94.B6473] 65-13132
1. Kingdom of God. 2. Commandments, Ten. I. Godsey, John D., ed. II. Title.
Contents omitted.

BONHOEFFER, Dietrich, 1906-1945 231.7
Preface to Bonhoeffer; the man and two of his shorter writings, by John D. Godsey [Tr. from German] Philadelphia, Fortress [c.1965] v, 73p. 20cm. [BT94.B6473] 63-13132 2.00
1. Kingdom of God. 2. Commandments, Ten. I. Godsey, John D., ed. II. Title.
Contents omitte4.

BRIGHT, John, 1908- 231.7
The kingdom of God, the Biblical concept and its meaning for the church. Nashville, Abingdon-Cokesbury Press [1953] 288 p. 24 cm. [BT94.B75] 53-8131
1. Kingdom of God—Biblical teaching. I. Title.

BUBER, Martin, 1878-1965. 231'.7
Kingship of God. Translated by Richard Scheimann. [1st American ed] New York, Harper & Row [1967] 228 p. 22 cm. Translation of the 3d, newly enl. ed. of Konigtum Gottes. Bibliographical references included in "Notes" (p. [163]-222) [BT94.B813] 67-14929
1. Kingdom of God. 2. Bible. O.T. — Technology. I. Title.

BUBER, Martin, 1878-1965. 231.7
Kingship of God. trans. by Richard Scheimann. 3d. newly enl. ed. New York, Harper [1973, c.1967] 228 p. 20 cm. (Harper torchbook, TB1717) Translation of Konigtum Gottes. Bibl refs included in "Notes" (p. [163]-222. [BT94.B813] 67-14929 ISBN 0-06-131717-9 pap., 2.45
1. Kingdom of God. 2. Bible—O.T.—Theology. I. Title.

CAMERON, James Munro, 1910- 231.7
Images of authority; a consideration of the concepts of regnum and sacerdotium, by J. M. Cameron. New Haven, Yale University Press, 1966. xii, 81 p. 22 cm. (The Terry lectures, v. 35) Bibliographical footnotes. [BT88.C24] 66-12489
1. Authority (Religion) 2. Church and state—Hist. I. Title. II. Series. III. Series: The Terry lectures, Yale University, v. 35

CAMERON, James Munro, 1910- 231.7
Images of authority; a consideration of the concepts of regnum and sacerdotium. New Haven, Conn., Yale [c.]1966. xii, 81p. 22cm. (Terry lects., v.35) Bibl. [BT88.C24] 66-12489 4.00
1. Authority (Religion) 2. Church and state—Hist. I. Title. II. Series: The Terry lectures, Yale University, v. 35

CENTER for Hermeneutical Studies in Hellenistic and Modern Culture. 231'.7
The transcendence of God in Philo : some possible sources : protocol of the sixteenth colloquy, 20 April 1975 / the Center for Hermeneutical Studies in Hellenistic and Modern Culture, the Graduate Theological

Union & the University of California, Berkeley, California ; John M. Dillon ; W. Wuellner, editor. Berkeley, CA : The Center, c1975. 44 p. ; 21 cm. (Colloquy - the Center for Hermeneutical Studies in Hellenistic and Modern Culture ; nr. 16) Includes bibliographical references. [BT100.C34 1975] 75-38047 ISBN 0-89242-015-4
1. Philo Judaeus. 2. Transcendence of God—History of doctrines. I. Dillon, John M. II. Wuellner, Wilhelm H., 1927- III. Title. IV. Series: Center for Hermeneutical Studies in Hellenistic and Modern Culture. Protocol series of the colloquies ; nr. 16.

A Christian view of history? / Editors, George Marsden, Frank Roberts. Grand Rapids : Eerdmans, [1975] 201 p. ; 22 cm. Includes indexes. Bibliography: p. 181-196. [BR115.H5C55] 75-19419 ISBN 0-8028-1603-7 pbk. : 4.50 231'.7
1. History (Theology)—Addresses, essays, lectures. 2. History (Theology)—History of doctrines—20th century—Addresses, essays, lectures. I. Marsden, George M., 1939- II. Roberts, Frank, 1937-

CLOUD, Fred. 231.7
God's hand in our lives; a study of providence. Nashville, Tidings [c1964] 71 p. 19 cm. Bibliographical footnotes. [BT96.2.C5] 64-7793
1. Providence and government of God. I. Title.

THE Creation : 231'.7
lines from the Old Testament and from Paradise lost by John Milton as told to Adam by the Archangel Raphael / wood engravings by Elfriede Abbe. Manchester Center, Vt. : [s.n.], c1977. [25] p. (on double leaves) : ill. ; 37 cm. "One hundred thirty-five copies ... printed." No. 134. [BS651.C695] 77-370078
1. Bible—Pictures, illustrations, etc. 2. Creation. I. Abbe, Elfriede Martha, 1919- II. Milton, John, 1608-1674. Paradise lost. Books 7-8. 1977. III. Bible. O.T. Genesis. English. Selections. 1977.

†DANKENBRING, William F. 231'.7
The creation book for children / by William F. Dankenbring. Altadena, CA : Triumph Pub. Co., c1976. 56 p. : ill. (some col.) ; 29 cm. Discusses scientific and religious explanations for the creation of the universe and its inhabitants. [BS651.D32] 75-39840 5.95 ISBN 0 ISBN 0-8057-6678-2 lib.bdg. : 7.95
1. Creation—Juvenile literature. I. Title.

DE VRIES, Simon John. 231'.7
Yesterday, today, and tomorrow : time and history in the Old Testament / Simon J. De Vries. Grand Rapids, Mich. : W. B. Eerdmans Pub. Co., [1975] 389 p. ; 24 cm. Includes bibliographical references and indexes. [BS680.T54D48] 74-31322 ISBN 0-8028-3457-4 : 10.95
1. Time (Theology)—Biblical teaching. 2. History (Theology)—Biblical teaching. I. Title.

DUTY, Guy, 1907- 231.7
God's covenants and our time. Minneapolis, Bethany [1965, c.1964] xii, 157p. 19cm. [BT155.D8] 65-1693 1.50 pap.,
1. Covenants (Theology) I. Title.

EVANS, Louis Hadley, 1897- 231.7
The kingdom is yours. Westwood, N. J., Revell [1952] 159 p. 22 cm. [BT94.E8] 52-13028
1. Kingdom of God—Sermons. 2. Presbyterian Church—Sermons. 3. Sermons. American. I. Title.

FORSTER, Roger T. 231'.7
God's strategy in human history [by] Roger T. Forster and V. Paul Marston. Wheaton, Ill., Tyndale House [1974, c1973] viii, 296 p. 21 cm. Includes bibliographical references. [BR115.H5F66 1974] 74-80797 ISBN 0-8423-1080-0 3.95
1. History (Theology) I. Marston, V. Paul, joint author. II. Title.

GILKEY, Langdon Brown, 1919- 231'.7
Reaping the whirlwind : a Christian interpretation of history / Langdon Gilkey. New York : Seabury Press, c1976. ix, 446 p. ; 24 cm. "A Crossroad book." Includes index. Bibliography: p. 434-438. [BR115.H5G54] 76-29738 ISBN 0-8164-0308-2 : 14.95
1. History (Theology) I. Title.

GLUECK, Nelson, 1900- 231'.7
Hesed in the Bible / by Nelson Glueck ; translated by Alfred Gottschalk ; with an introd. by Gerald A. Larue ; edited by Elias L. Epstein. [New York] : Ktav Pub. House, 1975. vii, 107 p. ; 24 cm. Translation of the author's thesis, Jena, 1927, published under title: Das Wort Hesed im alttestamentlichen Sprachgebrauche als menschliche und gottliche Gemeinschaftsgemasse Verhaltungsweise. Reprint of the 1967 ed. published by Hebrew Union College Press, Cincinnati. Bibliography: p. 103-105. [BS525.G653 1975] 75-17689 10.00
1. Bible. O.T.—Theology. 2. Hesed (The word) I. Title.

GRUENLER, Royce Gordon. 231'.7
Jesus, persons, and the kingdom of God. [St. Louis] Bethany Press [1967] 224 p. 23 cm. Includes bibliographies. [BT202.G7] 67-19437
1. Jesus Christ—Person and offices. 2. Kingdom of God. I. Title.

GURENLER, Royce Gordon. 231'.7
Jesus, persons, and the kingdom of God. [St. Louis] Bethany Press [1967] 224 p. 23 cm. Includes bibliographies. [BT202.G7] 67-19437
1. Jesus Christ — Person and offices. 2. Kingdom of God. I. Title.

HAHN, Dietmar. 231.7
Der Begriff des Politischen und der politischen Theologie : Erwagungen zur Reflexion auf die politische Dimension von Theologie / Dietmar Hahn. Hamburg : H. Reich, 1975. 59 p. ; 21 cm. (Evangelische Zeitstimmen ; 76) Includes bibliographical references. [AC30.E83 Nr. 76] [BR115.P7] 261.6 76-451655 ISBN 3-7924-0273-4
1. Christianity and politics. I. Title. II. Series.

HANSON, Richard S. 231'.7
Kingdoms of man and the kingdom of God [by] Richard S. Hanson. Minneapolis, Minn., Augsburg Pub. House [1971] 126 p. 20 cm. [BT94.H33] 75-135231 ISBN 0-8066-1113-8 2.75
1. Kingdom of God. I. Title.

HARKNESS, Georgia Elma, 1891- 231'.7
Understanding the kingdom of God [by] Georgia Harkness. Nashville, Abingdon Press [1974] 175 p. 21 cm. Includes bibliographical references. [BT94.H34] 74-10809 ISBN 0-687-42864-5
1. Kingdom of God. I. Title.

HAZELTON, Roger, 1909- 231'.7
Ascending flame, descending dove : an essay on creative transcendence / by Roger Hazelton. Philadelphia : Westminster Press, [1975] 128 p. ; 19 cm. Includes bibliographical references. [BD362.H38] 75-9649 ISBN 0-664-24767-9 pbk. : 3.75
1. Transcendence (Philosophy) 2. Transcendence of God. I. Title.

HIERS, Richard H. 231'.7
The Kingdom of God in the synoptic tradition [by] Richard H. Hiers. Gainesville, University of Florida Press, 1970. 107 p. 23 cm. (University of Florida humanities monograph no. 33) Includes bibliographical references. [BS2417.K5H5] 70-630982 ISBN 0-8130-0305-9
1. Kingdom of God—Biblical teaching. I. Title. II. Series: Florida. University, Gainesville. University of Florida monographs. Humanities, no. 33

HILLERS, Delbert R. 231'.7
Covenant: the history of a Biblical idea [by] Delbert R. Hillers. Baltimore, Johns Hopkins Press [1969] xii, 194 p. 22 cm. (Seminars in the history of ideas) Includes bibliographical references. [BT155.H62] 69-13539
1. Covenants (Theology) I. Title.

HINES, John Elbridge, Bp., 1910- 231'.7
Thy kingdom come, by John E. Hines. [1st ed.] New York, Morehouse-Barlow, 1967. 123 p. 21 cm. [BX5937.H5T5] 67-12971
1. Protestant Episcopal Church in the U.S.A.—Sermons. 2. Sermons, American. 3. Kingdom of God—Sermons. I. Title.

HISTORY, criticism & faith : 231'.7
four exploratory studies / Gordon J. Wenham ... [et al.] ; edited by Colin Brown. London : Inter-Varsity Press, 1976. 180 p. ; 21 cm. Includes bibliographies and indexes. [BR115.H5H54] 77-354488 ISBN 0-87784-776-2 pbk. : 4.95
1. History (Theology)—Addresses, essays, lectures. I. Wenham, Gordon J. II. Brown, Colin.
Distributed by Inter-Varsity, Ill.

HODGES, Jesse Wilson. 231.7
Christ's kingdom and coming, with an analysis of dispensationalism. Grand Rapids, Eerdmans [1957] 247p. 23cm. Includes bibliography. [BT890.H6] 57-13757
1. Kingdom of God. 2. Second Advent. 3. Covenants (Theology) I. Title.

HOPKINS, Martin K 231.7
God's kingdom in the New testament, by Martin K. Hopkins. Chicago, H. Regnery Co., 1964. xxi, 217 p. illus., col. maps (on lining papers) 25 cm. Bibliography: p. xx-xxv. Includes bibliographical references. [BS2536.H6] 64-66119
1. Bible. N.T — Outlines, syllabl, etc. 2. Kingdom of God. I. Title.

HOPKINS, Martin K 231.7
God's kingdom in the Old Testament, by Martin K. Hopkins. Chicago, H. Regnery Co., 1964. xxvi, 257 p. illus., maps. 25 cm. Bibliography: p. xxiii-xxvi. Includes bibliographical references. [BS1194.H6] 64-17324
1. Bible. O.T. — Outlines, syllabl, etc. 2. Kingdom of God. I. Title.

KETCHERSIDE, W Carl. 231.7
The kingdom of the Messiah; a study of the eternal purpose of God as manifested in the kingdom of His dear Son. St. Louis, Mission Messenger [c1957] 222p. 21cm. [BT94.K45] 58-1591
1. Kingdom of God. I. Title.

KEVAN, Ernest Frederick, 1903- 231.7
The grace of law; a study in Puritan theology, by Ernest F. Kevan. Grand Rapids, Baker Book House, 1965. 294 p. 23 cm. "First published in 1964." "Approved by the University of London for the ... degree of doctor of philosophy." Bibliography: p. [269]-288. [BT96.2.K47 1965] 66-905
1. Law (Theology) 2. Puritans. I. Title.

KEVAN, Ernest Frederick, 1903- 231.7
The grace of law; a study in Puritan theology.iGrand Rapids, Mich., Baker Bk. [c.] 1965. 294p. 23cm. Bibl. [BT96.2.K47] 66-905 4.95
1. Law (Theology) 2. Puritans. I. Title.

*KEVAN, Ernest Frederick, 1903-1965 231.7
The grace of law : a study in Puritan theology / by Ernest F. Kevan. Grand Rapids : Baker Book House, 1976[c1965] 294p. : 22 cm. (Twin brooks series) Includes index. Bibliography:p[269]-288. [BT96.2K47] ISBN 0-8010-5373-0 pbk. : 3.95.
1. Law (Theology) 2. Puritans. I. Title.
L. C. card no. for original ed. 66-905.

KNEVELS, Wilhelm, 1897- 231.7
Euthanasie : Hilfe beim Sterben, Hilfe zum Sterben / Wilhelm Knevels, Franz Bockle, Erich Schmalenberg. Hamburg : H. Reich, 1975. 71 p. ; 21 cm. (Evangelische Zeitstimmen ; 75) Includes bibliographical references. [AC30.E83 Nr. 75] [R726] 128.5 76-453425 ISBN 3-7924-0274-2
1. Euthanasia. I. Bockle, Franz, joint author. II. Schmalenberg, Erich, joint author. III. Title. IV. Series.

LADD, George Eldon 231.7
The gospel of the kingdom; scriptural studies in the kingdom of God. Grand Rapids, Mich., Eerdmans [1959] 143p. 22cm. 59-14591 2.75
1. Kingdom of God. I. Title.

LADD, George Eldon, 1911- 231.7
Crucial questions about the kingdom of God; the sixth annual mid-year lectures of 1952 delivered at Western Conservative Baptist Theological Seminary of Portland, Oregon. Grand Rapids, W. B. Eerdmans Pub. Co., 1952. 193 p. 23 cm. [BT94.L2] 52-14450
1. Kingdom of God. 2. Millennium. I. Title.

LADD, George Eldon, 1911- 231.7
Jesus and the kingdom; the eschatology of Biblical realism. [1st ed.] New York, Harper & Row [1964] xv, 367 p. 22 cm. Bibliography: p. 337-351. [BT94.L23] 64-19498
1. Kingdom of God. I. Title.

LADD, George Eldon, 1911- 231.7
Jesus and the kingdom; the eschatology of Biblical realism. New York, Harper [c.1964] xv, 367p. 22cm. Bibl. 64-19498 5.00
1. Kingdom of God. I. Title.

LADD, George Eldon, 1911- 231'.7
Jesus and the kingdom; the eschatology of Biblical realism. [2d ed.] Waco, Tex., Word Books [1969, c1964] xv, 367 p. 22 cm. Beginning with 1973 ed. published under title: The presence of the future. Bibliography: p. 337-351. [BT94.L23 1969] 73-5863
1. Kingdom of God. I. Title.

LADD, George Eldon, 1911- 231'.7
The presence of the future; the eschatology of biblical realism. Grand Rapids, Mich., Eerdmans Pub. Co. [1974] xiv, 370 p. 21 cm. Editions for 1964-69 published under title: Jesus and the kingdom. Bibliography: p. 341-355. [BT94.L23 1974] 73-11026 ISBN 0-8028-1531-6 4.50
1. Kingdom of God. I. Title.

LEMKE, Arnold E. 231.7
The government of God. New York, Vantage Press [c.1960] 98p. 2.50 bds.,
I. Title.

LUNDSTROM, Gosta, 1905- 231.7
The kingdom of God in the teaching of Jesus; a history of interpretation from the last decades of the nineteenth century to the present day. Translated by Joan Bulman. Richmond. John Knox Press, 1963. xiv, 300 p. 23 cm. "First published in 1947 as a thesis ... Uppsala University." Bibliography: p. 279-296. [BS2417.K5L843] 63-16411
1. Jesus Christ — Teachings. 2. Kingdom of God — History of doctrines. I. Full name: Henning Gosta Lundastrom. II. Title.

MCCLAIN, Alva J. 231.7
The greatness of the kingdom; an inductive study of the kingdom of God. Chicago, Moody [1968,c.1959] 556p. 24cm. Bibl. [BT94.M23] 6.95
1. Kingdom of God. I. Title.

MCCLAIN, Alva J 231.7
The greatness of the kingdom; an inductive study of the kingdom of God as set forth in the Scriptures. Grand Rapids, Zondervan Pub. House [c1959] 556p. 23cm. (Christian theology. 5) Includes bibliography. [BT94.M23] 60-1442
1. Kingdom of God. I. Title.

MAURO, Philip 231.7
The hope of Israel, what is it! [Swengel, Pa., Bible Truth Depot, 1964] 261p. 20cm. 1.95 pap.,
1. Bible—Prophecies. 2. Jews—Restoration. 3. Messiah. 4. Millenium. I. Title.

MAURO, Philip, 1859- 231.7
The gospel of the kingdom, with an examination of modern dispensationalism. Swengel, Pa., Bible Truth Depot [1964] 258p. 20cm. 1.95 pap.,
1. Kingdom of God. 2. Covenants (Theology) I. Title.

METTINGER, Tryggve N. D. 231'.7
King and Messiah : the civil and sacral legitimation of the Israelite kings / N. D. Tryggve Mettinger. Lund : LiberLaromedel/Gleerup, [1976] 342 p. ; 24 cm. (Coniectanea biblica : Old Testament series ; 8) Includes index. Bibliography: p. 312-332. [BS1199.K5M47] 77-360195 ISBN 9-14-004349-5 : kr130.00
1. Kings and rulers—Biblical teaching. I. Title. II. Series.

MORRISON, Gay. 231.7
Law in religion and science. [Hot Springs? Ark.] c1957. 101p. 22cm. [BT96.2.M6] 60-23695
1. Law (Theology) 2. Religion and science—1900- I. Title.

MULLINS, Aloysius. 231.7
A guide to the kingdom; a simple handbook on the parables. With a foreword by Ian Hislop. [Westminster] Md., Newman Press [1963] xxi, 139 p. 22 cm. [BT375.2.M8] 63-25225
1. Jesus Christ — Parables. 2. Kingdom of God. I. Title.

MULLINS, Aloysius 231.7
A guide to the kingdom; a simple handbook on the parables. Foreword by Ian Hislop [Westminster] Md., Newman [c.1963] xxi, 139p. 22cm. 63-25225 3.75
1. Jesus Christ—Parables. 2. Kingdom of God. I. Title.

MUNK, Arthur W 231.7
History and God; clues to His purpose. New York, Ronald Press Co. [1952] 310 p. 21 cm. [BR115.H5M8] 52-6185
1. History — Philosophy. 2. Providence and government of God. I. Title.

NEWMAN, Robert Chapman, 1941- 231'.7
Genesis one & the origin of the Earth / Robert C. Newman & Herman J. Eckelmann, Jr. Downers Grove, Ill. : Intervarsity Press, c1977. 156 p. ; 21 cm. Includes indexes. Bibliography: p. [141]-150. [BS651.N48] 77-72526 ISBN 0-87784-786-X pbk. : 3.95
1. Creation. 2. Bible and science. 3. Cosmogony. 4. Cosmology, Biblical. I. Eckelmann, Herman J., joint author. II. Title.

NIEBUHR, Helmut Richard, 1894-1962. 231.7
The kingdom of God in America. New York, Harper [1959, c1937] 215 p. 21 cm. (Harper torchbooks, TB49) Includes bibliography. [BT94.N5 1959] 59-6647
1. Kingdom of God. 2. United States—Church history. I. Title.

OTTO, Rudolf, 1869-1937. 231.7
The kingdom of God and the Son of Man; a study in the history of religion. Translated from the rev. German ed. by Floyd V. Filson and Bertram Lee- Woolf. New and rev. ed. Boston, Starr King Press [1957] 407p. 22cm.

58A reprint of the substantially revised edition of 1943. [BT94.O73 1957] 57-14100
1. Kingdom of God. 2. Son of Man. I. Title.

PACKER, J. I. 231.7
Evangelism and the sovereignty of God. Chicago, Inter-Varsity Pr. [1961] 126p. (Christian bks. for the modern world) 1.25 pap.,
I. Title.

PANNENBERG, Wolfhart, 1928- 231'.7
Theology and the kingdom of God. Philadelphia, Westminster Press [1969] 143 p. 21 cm. Contents.Contents.—Wolfhart Pannenberg: Profile of a theologian, by R. J. Neuhaus.—Theology and the kingdom of God.—The kingdom of God and the church.—The kingdom of God and the foundation of ethics.—Appearance as the arrival of the future. Bibliographical references included in "Notes to chapter 4" (p. 143) [BT94.P33] 69-12668
1. Kingdom of God. I. Title.

PERRIN, Norman. 231'.7
Jesus and the language of the kingdom : symbol and metaphor in New Testament interpretation / Norman Perrin. Philadelphia : Fortress Press, c1976. xiii, 225 p. ; 24 cm. Includes indexes. Bibliography: p. 209-215. [BT94.P387] 75-13045 ISBN 0-8006-0412-1 : 10.95
1. Jesus Christ—Parables. 2. Kingdom of God. I. Title.

PERRIN, Norman 231.7
The kingdom of God in the teaching of Jesus. Philadelphia, Westminster [c.1963] 215p. 23cm. (New Testament lib.) Bibl. 63-14641 4.50
1. Kingdom of God. 2. Jesus Christ—Teachings. 3. Theology, Doctrinal—Hist.—20th cent. I. Title.

PETERS, George Nathaniel Henry, 1825-1909. 231'.7
The theocratic kingdom of Our Lord Jesus, the Christ, as covenanted in the Old Testament and presented in the New Testament. Pref. by Wilbur M. Smith. Biographical sketch by John H. Stoll. Grand Rapids, Mich., Kregel Publications [1972] 3 v. 24 cm. (Kregel reprint library) "Originally published in 1884." Includes bibliographical references. [BT94.P4 1972] 72-88588 ISBN 0-8254-3502-1 39.95
1. Bible—Prophecies. 2. Kingdom of God. 3. Covenants (Theology) I. Title.

PHILLIPS, Ordis E 1886- 231.7
The kingdom of God. Philadelphia, Hebrew Christian Fellowship [1954] 290p. 21cm. [BT94.P45] 54-37088
1. Kingdom of God. I. Title.

PICO della Mirandola, Giovanni, 1463-1494 231'.7
Heptaplus : or, Discourse on the seven days of creation / Pico della Mirandola ; translated with an introd. and glossary by Jessie Brewer McGaw. New York : Philosophical Library, c1977. x, 128 p. ; 22 cm. Bibliography: p. 127-128. [BS651.P5213] 76-16240 ISBN 0-8022-2189-0 : 7.50
1. Creation. I. Title.

PINK, Arthur W. 231.7
The sovereignty of God; rev. ed. [Dist. Grand Rapids, Mich., Baker Bk., 1962, c.]1961. 160p. 19cm. 1.50 pap.,
I. Title.

RIDDERBOS, Herman N. 231.7
The coming of the kingdom. Tr. by H. de Jongste. Ed. by Raymond O. Zoron. Philadelphia, Presbyterian Reformed [c.]1962. 556p. 22cm. Bibl. 62-15429 8.95
1. Kingdom of God—Biblical teaching. 2. Bible. N. T. Gospels—Theology. I. Title.

RIDDLERBOS, Herman N 231.7
The coming of the kingdom. Translated by H. de Jongste. Edited by Raymond O. Zorn. Philadelphia, Presbyterian and Reformed Pub. Co., 1962. 556 p. 22 cm. [BT94.R413] 62-15429
1. Kingdom of God — Biblical teaching. 2. Bible. N.T. Gospels — Theology. I. Title.

ROPER, David H. 231'.7
The New Covenant in the Old Testament / David H. Roper. Waco, Tex. : Word Books, c1976. 145 p. ; 22 cm. (Discovery books) [BS1199.C6R66] 76-5718 ISBN 0-87680-465-2 : 4.95
1. Covenants (Theology)—Biblical teaching. I. Title.

SALVIANUS, 5thcent. 231.7
On the government of God; a treatise wherin are shown by argument and by examples drawn from the abandoned society of the times the ways of God toward His creatures. Indited by Salvian as a warning and counsel. This 5th century polemic done into English by Eva M. Sanford. New York, Octagon Books, 1966. viii, 241 p. front. 24 cm. (Records of civilization; sources and studies no. 12) Reprint of the 1931 ed. Bibliography: p. 233-234. [BR65.S25 1966] 66-28329
1. Providence and government of God—Early works to 1800. 2. Christian life—Early church, ca. 30-600. 3. Rome—Social conditions. I. Sanford, Eva Matthews, tr. II. Title.

SCHNACKENBURG, Rudolf, 1914- 231.7
God's rule and kingdom. [Translated by John Murray. New York] Herder and Herder [1963] 365 p. 23 cm. Bibliography: p. 358-365. [BT94.S343] 63-12872
1. Kingdom of God. I. Title.

SCHNACKENBURG, Rudolf, 1914- 231'.7
God's rule and kingdom; translated [from the German] by John Murray. 2nd enlarged ed. London, Burns & Oates; New York, Herder and Herder, 1968. 400 p. 22 cm. 50/- (B 68-15512) Translation of Gottes Herrschaft und Reich. Bibliography: p. 377-388. [BT94.S343 1968] 68-133720
1. Kingdom of God. I. Title.

SCHNACKENBURG, Rudolf; 1914- 231.7
God's rule and kingdom [Tr. by John Murray. New York] Herder & Herder [c.1963] 365p. 23cm. Bibl. 63-12872 6.95
1. Kingdom of God. I. Title.

SCHWEITZER, Albert, 1875-1965. 231'.7
The kingdom of God and primitive Christianity. Edited, with an introd. by Ulrich Neuenschwander. Translated by L. A. Garrard. New York, Seabury Press [1968] xiv, 193 p. 22 cm. Translation of Reich Gottes und Christentum. [BT94.S3523 1968] 68-24007 3.95
1. Kingdom of God—Biblical teaching. I. Neuenschwander, Ulrich, ed. II. Title.

SEGRAVES, Kelly L. 231'.7
A double minded man / Kelly L. Segraves. San Diego : Beta Books, c1976. 176 p. ; 22 cm. Bibliography: p. 176. [BS480.S36] 76-2134 ISBN 0-89293-000-4 : 5.95. pbk. : 2.95
1. Bible—Evidences, authority, etc. 2. Bible and science. 3. Creation. I. Title.

SHAW, Leland H 231.7
Membership in the kingdom of God. [1st ed.] New York, Pageant Press [1956] 55p. 21cm. [BT94.S52] 56-11392
1. Kingdom of God. I. Title.

SHAW, Leland H. 231.7
Membership in the kingdom of God. [1st ed.] New York, Pageant Press [1956] 55 p. 21 cm. [BT94.S52] 56-11392
1. Kingdom of God I. Title.

SMITH, Malcolm, 1938- 231'.7
Blood brothers in Christ / Malcolm Smith. Old Tappan, N.J. : F. H. Revell Co., [1975] 159 p. ; 20 cm. [BT155.S6] 74-28018 ISBN 0-8007-0720-6 : 2.45
1. Covenants (Theology) I. Title.

STEPHENS, Julius Harold. 231.7
The churches and the kingdom. Nashville, Broadman Press [1959] 119 p. 20 cm. [BT94.S78] 59-9826
1. Kingdom of God. I. Title.

STOFFEL, Ernest Lee. 231.7
His kingdom is forever. Richmond, John Knox Press [1956] 182p. 21cm. [BT94.S85] 56-7768
1. Kingdom of God. I. Title.

STOFFEL, Ernest Lee. 231.7
His kingdom is forever. Richmond, John Knox Press [1956] 182 p. 21 cm. [BT94.S85] 56-7768
1. Kingdom of God. I. Title.

TRENNUNG von Kirche und Staat? : juristische, theologische und politische Stimmen zu einem alten Problem / Klaus Wegenast ... [et al.] Hamburg : H. Reich Evangelischer Verlag, 1975. 82 p. ; 21 cm. (Evangelische Zeitstimmen ; 74) Includes bibliographical references. [AC30.E83 Nr. 74] [BV631] 201'.1 75-520348 ISBN 3-7924-0272-6 : DM6.00 231.7
1. Church and state—Addresses, essays, lectures. I. Wegenast, Klaus. II. Title. III. Series.

WEATHERLY, Owen Milton. 231.7
The fulfillment of life. Richmond, John Knox Press [1959] 158 p. 21 cm. Includes bibliography. [BT96.2.W4] 59-10516
1. Law (Theology) I. Title.

WEISS, Johannes, 1863-1914. 231'.7
Jesus' proclamation of the kingdom of God. Translated, edited, and with an introd. by Richard Hyde Hiers and David Larrimore Holland. Philadelphia, Fortress Press [1971] xii, 148 p. 19 cm. (Lives of Jesus series) Translation of Die Predigt Jesu vom Reiche Gottes. Bibliography: p. 138-142. [BT94.W3813] 79-135267 ISBN 0-8006-0153-X 3.95
1. Kingdom of God. I. Title.

ZORN, Raymond O 1924- 231.7
Church and kingdom. Philadelphia, Presbyterian and Reformed Pub. Co., 1962. 228 p. 22 cm. (International library of philosophy and theology. Philosophical and historical studies series. [BT94.Z6] 62-15428
1. Kingdom of God. 2. Church. I. Title.

AGNELLET, Michel 231.73
I accept these facts; the Lourdes cures examined [Tr. from French by John Dingle] Foreword by E. B. Strauss. London, M. Parrish [dist. Chester Springs, Pa., Dufour, 1965, c.1958] 153p. illus. 21cm. Bibl. [BT653.A413] 59-31016 3.50 bds.,
1. Lourdes, Notre-Dame de. 2. Miracles. I. Title.

AMBRUST, Arthur 231.73
Do you believe in miracles. Wheaton, Ill., Wheaton Pub. 1966. 143p. 21cm. [BT97.2.A7] 66-29174 3.95
1. Miracles. I. Title.

ARADI, Zsolt. 231.73
The book of miracles. New York, Farrar, Straus [1956] 316p. illus. 22cm. [BT97.A7] 56-11315
1. Miracles. I. Title.

ARADI, Zsolt 231.73
The book of miracles: a fascinating account of the entire panorama of miracles--from the Old and New Testaments to the Apparitions of Our Lady. Derby, Conn., Monarch Bks. [1961, c.1956] 284p. (Monarch human behavior bk., MB509) Bibl. .50 pap.,
1. Miracles. I. Title.

ARMSTRONG, April (Oursler) 231.73
Fatima: pilgrimage to peace [by] April Oursler Armstrong and Martin F. Armstrong, Jr. [1st ed.] Garden City, N. Y., Hanover House [1954] 192p. illus. 22cm. [BT660.F3A73] 54-9853
1. Fatima. Nossa Senhora da. I. Armstrong. Martin F., joint author. II. Title.

BARNES, Kathleen H. 231'.73
What is a miracle? / Kathleen H. Barnes, Virginia H. Pearce ; photos. by Don O. Thorpe. Salt Lake City, Utah : Deseret Book Co., 1975. [32] p. : ill. (some col.) ; 22 cm. (A Book for Latter-day Saint children) A child with a sick mother finds out about many kinds of miracles. [BT97.2.B34] 75-5177 ISBN 0-87747-544-X : 4.95
1. Miracles—Juvenile literature. I. Pearce, Virginia H., joint author. II. Thorpe, Don O. III. Title. IV. Series.

BAXTER, Betty Jean, 1926- 231.73
The Betty Baxter story. [A 1941 miracle of healing as told by herself] Foreword by Oral Roberts. [Elmore? Minn.] D. Heidt [1951] 53 p. illus. 16 cm. [BR115.H4B34] 52-15619
1. Faith cure. I. Title.

BEEVERS, John. 231.73
The Golden Heart; the story of Beauraing. Chicago, H. Regnery Co., 1956 [i. e. 1957] 79p. illus. 19cm. [BT660.B4B4] 57-13600
1. Bearing, Notre-Dame de. I. Title.

BIOT, Rene, 1889- 231.73
The enigma of the stigmata. Translated from the French by P. J. Hepburne-Soctt. [1st ed.] New York, Hawthorn Books [1962] 157 p. 22 cm. (The Twentieth century encyclopedia of Catholicism, v. 57. Section 5: The life of faith) [BV5091.S7B53] 62-21734
1. Stigmatization. I. Title.

BIOT, Rene, 1889- 231.73
The enigma of the stigmata. Tr. from French by P. J. Hepburne-Scott. New York, Hawthorn [c.1962] 157p. 22cm. (Twentieth cent. encyclopedia of Catholicism, v. 57. Sect. 5: The life of faith) Bibl. 62-21734 3.50 bds.,
1. Stigmatization. I. Title.

BLOY, Leon, 1846-1917. 231.73
She who weeps: Our Lady of La Salette; an anthology of Leon Bloy's writings on La Salette, translated and edited with an introd. by Emile La Douceur. Fresno, Calif., Academy Library Guiide, 1956. 167p. illus. 22cm. [BT660.S33B58] 56-14096
1. Salette, Notre-Dame de la. I. Title.

CARREL, Alexis, 1873-1944. 231.73
The voyage to Lourdes; translated from the French by Virgilia Peterson. Pref. by Charles A. Lindbergh. [1st ed.] New York, Harper [1950] viii, 52 p. 20 cm. [BT653.C353] 50-6402
1. Lourdes. I. Title.

THE Catholic digest. 231.73
Jesuit Martyrs' Shrine, Midland. Ontario, in Canada. St. Paul [1959] 64p. illus. 21cm. (Shrines of the world) [BX2321.M5S3] 60-23456
1. Midland, Ont. Martyrs Shrine. I. Title.

THE Catholic digest. 231.73
Marian shrines in the Holyland. St. Paul [1959] 64p. illus. 21cm. (Shrines of the world) [BX2320.C39] 60-23455
1. Shrines—Palestine. I. Title.

THE Catholic digest. 231.73
Shrine of Our Lady of Martyrs, Auriesville in N. Y., U. S. A. St. Paul [1959] 64p. illus. 21cm. (Shrines of the world) [BX2321.A9C3] 60-23454
1. Auriesville, N. Y. Shrine of Our Lady of Martyrs. I. Title.

*COOLEY, Alva Edison. 231.73
The verdict concerning the miracle. New York, Carlton [1968] 63p. 21cm. (Hearthstone bk.) 3.00
1. Miracles. I. Title.

COX, Michael J 231.73
Rain for these roots; the Mother of Grace and the modern world. Milwaukee, Bruce Pub. Co. [1956] 210p. 22cm. [BT650.C6] 56-13331
1. Salette, Notre-Dame de la. 2. Lourdes, Notre-Dame de. 3. Fatima, Nossa Senhora da. I. Title.

CRANSTON, Ruth. 231.73
The miracle of Lourdes. New York, McGraw-Hill [1955] 286p. illus. 21cm. [BT653.C67] 55-9538
1. Lourdes. I. Title.

CRANSTON, Ruth 231.73
The miracle of Lourdes. New York, Popular Lib. [1967,c.1955] 251p. illus. 18cm. (75-1223) [BT653.C67] .75 pap.,
1. Lourdes, Notre-Dame de. I. Title.

DEMAREST, Donald, ed. 231.73
The dark Virgin; the book of Our Lady of Guadalupe, a documentary anthology edited by Donald Demarest & Coley Taylor. [1st ed. Freeport, Me.] C. Taylor [1956] 256p. illus. 25cm. [BT660.G8D4] 54-9611
1. Guadalupe, Nuestra Senora de. I. Taylor, Coley Banks, 1899- joint ed. II. Title.

DICKINSON, John Compton. 231.73
The shrine of Our Lady of Walsingham. Cambridge [Eng.] University Press, 1956. xiii, 150p. 9 plates, plan. 21cm. 'Bibliographical note': p.143-144. [BT660.W3D5] 56-4330
1. Walsingham. Our Lady of. 2. Walsingham Priory. I. Title.

DOOLEY, Lester M, 1898- 231.73
Fatima and you. Notre Dame, Ind., Ave Maria Press [1951] 153 p. 21 cm. Bibliography: p. 151-153. [BT660.F3D6] 51-2817
1. Fatima, Nossa Senhora da. I. Title.

EMERICUS A SANCTO STEPHANO, Father [Secular name: Bernard Josef Barrath] 231.73
The Great and Little One of Prague, by Ludvik Nemec. Philadelphia, P. Reilly Co. [c.1959] 279p. 21cm. (8p. bibl. notes) illus. 59-15897 4.50
1. Infant Jesus of Prague (Statue) I. Nemec, Ludvik, ed. and tr. II. Title.

ERNEST, Brother, 1897- 231.73
Our Lady comes to Banneux. Illus. by Brother Bernard Howard. Notre Dame, Ind., Dujarie Press [1954] 79p. illus. 24cm. [BT660.B28E5] 54-7740
1. Banneux, Onze-Lieve-Vrouw van. I. Title.

ERNEST, Brother, 1897- 231.73
Our Lady comes to Fatima. Illus. by Barbara Smith. Notre Dame, Ind., Dujarie Press [1951] 85 p. illus. 24 cm. [BT660.F3E7] 51-3096
1. Fatima. Nossa Senhora da. I. Title.

ERNEST, Brother, 1897- 231.73
Our Lady comes to La Salette. Illus. by Brother Bernard Howard. Notre Dame, Ind., Dujarie Press [1953] 85p. illus. 24cm. [BT660.S33E7] 53-35198
1. Salette, Notre-Dame de la. I. Title.

ERNEST, Brother, 1897- 231.73
Our Lady comes to Lourdes. Illus. by Laurie McCawley. Notre Dame, Ind., Dujarie Press [1951] 93 p. illus. 24 cm. [BT653.E7] 51-6548
1. Soubirous, Bernadette, Saint, 1844-1879. 2. Lourdes. I. Title.

ERNEST, Brother, 1897- 231.73
A story of Our Lady of Fatima. Pictures by

Carolyn Lee Jagodits. Notre Dame, Ind., Dujarie Press [1957] unpaged. illus. 21cm. [BT660.F3E73] 57-4987
1. F qFatima, Nossa Senhora da. I. Title.

ERNEST, Brother, 1897- 231.73
A story of Our Lady of Guadalupe. Pictures by Carolyn Lee Jagodits. Notre Dame, Ind., Dujarie Press [c1957] unpaged. illus. 21cm. [BT660.G8E72] 57-27078
1. Guadalupe, Nuestra Seffora de. I. Title.

ERNEST, Brother, 1897- 231.73
A story of the Infant Jesus of Prague. Pictures by Joan Marie Roytek. Notre Dame, Ind., Dujarie Press [1956] unpaged. illus. 22cm. [BX2159.C4E7] 56-42840
1. Infant Jesus of Prague (Statue) I. Title.

FLYNN, Maureen, 1900- 231.73
This place called Lourdes. Chicago, H. Regnery Co., 1957. 215p. 22cm. Includes bibliography. [BT653.F6] 57-10268
1. Lourdes, Notre-Dame de. I. Title.

FOX, George, 1624-1691. 231'.73
Book of miracles; edited with an introd. and notes by Henry J. Cadbury. With a foreword by Rufus M. Jones. New York, Octagon Books, 1973. xv, 161 p. illus. 25 cm. Reprint of the 1948 ed. Includes bibliographical references. [BX7748.M5F68 1973] 73-735 ISBN 0-374-92825-8 16.00
1. Friends, Society of. Great Britain. 2. Miracles. 3. Faith-cure. I. Cadbury, Henry Joel, 1883- ed. II. Title.

FRIDRICHSEN, Anton 231'.73
Johnson, 1888-1953.
The problem of miracle in primitive Christianity. Translated [from the French] by Roy A. Harrisville and John S. Hanson. Minneapolis, Augsburg Pub. House [1972] 174 p. 21 cm. Includes bibliographical references. [BT365.F713 1972] 72-176480 ISBN 0-8066-1211-8 5.95
1. Jesus Christ—Miracles. 2. Miracles. 3. Church history—Primitive and early church, ca. 30-600. I. Title.

GABRIELE DI SANTA MARIA 231.73
MADDALENA, Father.
Visions and revelations in the spiritual life. Translated by a Benedictine of Stanbrook Abbey. Westminster, Md., Newman Press, 1950. 123 p. 19 cm. [BV5091.V6G33] 51-8641
1. Visions. I. Title.

GARLAND, George 231'.73
Frederick, comp.
The power of God to heal; all the accounts of healings in the Bible reproduced in their entirety. Compiled by George F. Garland. Mamaroneck, N.Y., Guideform Press, 1973. x, 239 p. 23 cm. [BS680.H4G37] 73-79273 7.95
1. Healing in the Bible. I. Title.

GARLAND, George 231'.73
Frederick, comp.
The power of God to heal; all the accounts of healings in the Bible reproduced in their entirety. Compiled by George F. Garland. Mamaroneck, N.Y., Guideform Press, 1973. x, 239 p. 23 cm. [BS680.H4G37] 73-79273 7.95
1. Healing in the Bible. I. Title.
Publisher's address; 324 B. Mt. Pleasant Ave. Mamaroneck, New York, 10543

GREGORIUS, Bp. of Tours, 231.73
538-594.
Les livres des miracles et autres opuscules de Georges Florent Gregoire, eveque de Tours; 4 v. Revus et collationne-sur de nouveaux manuscrits et traduits pour la Societe de l'histoire de France par H. L. Bordier. Paris, J. Renouard, 1857-1864. New York, Johson Reprint [1965] 4v. (various p.) 22cm. (Societe de L'historie de France. Pubns., no 88, 103, 114, 125) Bibl. [BR65.G58] 65-8103 132.00 120.00 pap.,
1. Miracles—Early works to 1800. 2. Martyrs. 3. Fathers of the church. 4. Church history—Primitive and early church. I. Bordier, Henri Leonard, 1817-1888, ed. and tr. II. Title. III. Series.

GROOT, A de, S.V.D. 231.73
The Bible on miracles, by A. de Groot. Translated by Jos. A. Roessen. De Pere, Wis., St. Norbert Abbey Press, 1966. 112 p. 17 cm. Bibliography: p. [111]-112. [BS680.M5G713] 66-22818
1. Miracles — Biblical teaching. I. Title.

GROOT, A. de. 231.73
The Bible on miracles. Tr. by Jos. A. Roessen. De Pere, Wis. St. Norbert Abbey Pr. c.1966 112 p. 17 cm. Bibl. [BS680.M5G713] 66-22818 .95 pap.,
1. Miracles—Biblical teaching. I. Title.

HABERSHON, Ada Ruth, 1861- 231.73
The study of the miracles. Grand Rapids, Kregel Publications, 1963. 310 p. 23 cm. [BT97.2.H3] 62-19174
1. Miracles. I. Title.

HAFFERT, John Mathias. 231.73
Russia will be converted. Washington, N. J., AMI International Press [1950] 278 p. illus., ports. 21 cm. [BT660.F3H3] 50-58303
1. Fatima, Nossa Senhora da. 2. Russia—Religion—1917- 3. Communism and religion. I. Title.

HUGGETT, Renee. 231.73
The story of Fatima. Illustrated by J. S. Goodall. New York, Roy Publishers [c1959] 78p. illus. 19cm. [BT660.F3H82] 60-6028
1. Fatima. Nossa Senhora da. I. Title.

HUME, Ruth (Fox) 1922- 231.73
Our Lady came to Fatima. Illustrated by Leo Manso. New York, Vision Books [1957] 192p. illus. 22cm. (Vision books, 19) [BT660.F3H83] 57-5195
1. Fatima, Nossa Senhora da. I. Title.

*JONES, Philip Hanson 231.73
Wonders, signs, miracles . . . why not! Tales of a missionary in China. New York, Exposition [1966] 147p. 21cm. (EP44106) 4.00
1. Miracles. I. Title.

KELLER, Ernst, 1929- 231'.73
Miracles in dispute, a continuing debate by Ernst and Marie-Luise Keller. Translated by Margaret Kohl. [1st American ed.] Philadelphia, Fortress Press [1969] 256 p. 23 cm. Translation of Der Streit um die Wunder. Bibliography: p. 253-256. [BT97.2.K413 1969] 70-84557 4.95
1. Miracles. I. Keller, Marie-Luise, 1930- joint author. II. Title.

KENNEDY, John S 231.73
Light on the mountain; the story of La Salette. New York, McMullen Books [1953] 205p. 21cm. [BT660.S33K4] 53-12298
1. Salette, Notre-Dame de la. I. Title.

KENNEDY, John S 231.73
Light on the mountain; the story of La Salette. Garden City, N. Y., Image Books [1986] 197p. 18cm. .A Doubleday image book, D33) [BT660.S33K4 1956] 56-13665
1. Salette. Notre-Dame de la. I. Title.

KENNEDY, John S 231.73
Light on the mountain; the story of La Salette. Garden City, N. Y., Image Books [1956] 197p. 18cm. (A Doubleday image book, D33) [BT660.S33K4 1956] 56-13665
1. Salette, Notre- Dame de la. I. Title.

KRAMER, Helen Mary, 1892- 231.73
When we were there. Rockford, Ill., Bellevue Books [1954] 246p. illus. 23cm. [BX2323.K7] 54-22116
1. Pilgrims and Pilgrimages—Europe. I. Title.

LADOUCEUR, Emile. 231.73
The vision of La Salette: the children speak. New York, Vantage Press [1956] 145p. illus. 21cm. [BT660.S33L3] 56-10542
1. Calvat, Melanie, 1831-1904. 2. Giraud, Maximin, 1835-1875. 3. Salette, Notre-Dame de la. I. Title.

LAWTON, John Stewart 231.73
Miracles and revelation. New York, Association Press [1960] 284p. 23cm. (Lutterworth library) (bibl. notes: p.257-273) 60-6561 6.50
1. Miracles. 2. Revelation. 3. Apologetics—20th cent. I. Title.

LEWIS, Clive Staples, 231.73
1898-
Miracles: a preliminary study. [Abridgment] New York, Association Press [1958] 128p. 16cm. (An Association Press reflection book) [BT97.L432] 58-11529
1. Miracles. I. Title.

LEWIS, Clive Staples, 231.73
1898-
Miracles; a preliminary study. New York, Macmillan [1963, c.1947] 192p. 18cm. (142) .95 pap.,
1. Miracles. I. Title.

MCGRATH, William Cecil, 231.73
1896-
Fatima or world suicide. Scarboro Bluffs, Can., Scarboro Foreign Mission Society [1950] x. 94 p. 20 cm. [BT660.F3M26] 51-4619
1. Fatima, Nossa Senhora da. I. Title.

MARCHI, Joao de. 231.73
The Immaculate Heart, the true story of Our Lady of Fatima; edited by William Fay. New York, Farrar, Straus and Young [1952] 287 p. illus. 21 cm.SFatima, Nossa Senhora da. [BT660.F3M33] 52-13232
I. Title.

MARCHI, Joao de. 231.73
The shepherds of Fatima; retold in English by Elisabeth Cobb. Illustrated by Jeanyee Wong. New York, Sheed & Ward, 1952. 159 p. illus. 20 cm. Translation of La Madonna parlo coal al tre pastorelli. [BT660.F3M343] 52-10607
1. Fatima, Nossa Senhora da. I. Title.

MARTINDALE, Cyril Charlie, 231.73
1879-
The meaning of Fatima. New York Kenedy [c1950] vii, 183 p. 21 cm. [BT660.F3M36] 51-5045
1. Fatima, Nossa Senhora da. I. Title.

MARY Amatora, Sister, 231'.73
1904-
The Queen's heart of gold; the complete story of Our Lady of Beauraing. [4th ed.] New York, Exposition Press [1972] 222, [1] p. illus. 24 cm. (An Exposition-banner book) Bibliography: p. [223] [BT660.B4M3 1972] 78-188443 ISBN 0-682-47467-3 5.00
1. Beauraing, Notre-Dame de. I. Title.

MARY AMATORA, Sister, 231.73
1904-
The Queen's heart of gold; the complete story of Our Lady of Beauraing. [1st ed.] New York, Pageant Press [1957] 214p. illus. 24cm. [BT660.B4M3] 57-59566
1. Beauraing, Notre-Dame de. I. Title.

MEYER, Audrey May. 231.73
Infant King. St. Meinrad, Ind., Grail Publications [1951] 64 p. 20 cm. Includes bibliography. [BX2159.C4M4] 52-6841
1. Infant Jesus of Prague (Statue) I. Title.

MEYERS, Bertrande, Sister. 231.73
Devotedly yours. Westminster, Md., Newman Press, 1951. 400 p. 23 cm. [BX2323.M4] 51-12465
1. Pilgrims and pilgrimages — Rome. 2. Pilgrims and pilgrimages — Palestine. 3. Daughters of Charity of St. Vincent de Paul. I. Title.

MEYERS, Bertrande. 231.73
Devotedly yours. Westminster, Md., Newman Press, 1951. 400p. 23cm. [BX2323.M4] 51-12465
1. Pilgrims and pilgrimages—Rome. 2. Pilgrims and pilgrimages—Palestine. 3. Daughters of Charity of St. Vincentde Paul, Emmitsburg, Md. I. Title.

MIDDLETON, Conyers, 1683- 231'.73
1750.
A free inquiry into the miraculous powers / Conyers Middleton. New York : Garland Pub., 1976. xxxv, 232 p. ; 23 cm. (British philosophers and theologians of the 17th & 18th centuries) Reprint of the 1749 ed. printed for R. Manby and H. S. Cox, London. Includes index. [BT97.A2M58 1976] 75-11235 ISBN 0-8240-1788-9 lib.bdg. : 25.00
1. Miracles—Early works to 1800. I. Title. II. Series.

MONDEN, Louis. 231'.73
Signs and wonders; a study of the miraculous element in religion. Foreword by Avery Dulles. New York, Desclee Co. [1966] xiii, 368 p. 22 cm. Translated from the French version of the author's Het Wonder. Bibliographical footnotes. [BT97.2.M5813] 66-17860
1. Miracles. I. Title.

MOULE, Charles Francis 231.73
Digby, ed.
Miracles; Cambridge studies in their philosophy and history. London, Mowbray [New York, Morehouse, 1966, c.1965] viii, 245p. 23cm. Papers read before the weekly New Testament seminar held at Cambridge Univ. Bibl. [BT97.2] 66-3878 6.95
1. Miracles—Addresses, essays, lectures. I. Title.

NEAME, Alan. 231/.73
The happening at Lourdes; the sociology of the grotto. New York, S. & S. [1968,c. 1967] 323p. illus., ports. 24cm. [BT653.N4] 67-25384 6.95
1. Lourdes, Notre-Dame de. I. Title.

NEMEC, Ludvik. 231.73
The Infant of Prague; the story of the Holy Image and the history of the devotion. New York, Benziger Bros. [1958] 304p. illus. 26cm. Includes bibliography. [BX2159.C4N4] 58-14126
1. Infant Jesus of Prague (Statue) I. Title.

NEWMAN, John Henry, 231'.73
Cardinal, 1801-1890.
Two essays on Biblical and on ecclesiastical miracles. Westminster, Md., Christian Classics, 1969. xi, 400 p. 21 cm. (The works of Cardinal Newman) On spine: Essays on miracles. Bibliographical footnotes. [BT97.N52] 72-4157
1. Miracles. I. Title. II. Title: Essays on miracles.

NORTON, Mabel. 231.73
Eye witness at Fatima. Dublin, C. J. Fallon [1950] 133 p. illus. 22 cm. [BT660.F3N6] 51-40537
1. Fatima, Nossa Senhora da. I. Title.

NOWAK, Andrew Thomas 231.73
Francis.
American ambassadors to Lourdes; the story of St. Bernadette and of G. I. visitors to the Shrine in 1945-1946. [1st ed.] New York, Exposition Press [1955] 514p. 21cm. [BT653.N68] 54-12477
1. Soubirous, Bernadette, Saint, 1844-1879. 2. Lourdes. I. Title.

PELLETIER, Joseph Albert, 231.73
1902-
Fatima, hope of the world. [1st ed.] Worcester, Mass, Washington Press, 1954. 203p. illus. 22cm. 'A sequel to The sun danced at Fatima.' [BT660.F3P38] 55-16796
1. Fatima, Nossa Senhora da. I. Title.

PELLETIER, Joseph Albert, 231.73
1902-
The sun danced at Fatima; a critical story of the apparitions. Worcester, Mass., Caron Press, 1951. 163 p. illus. 22 cm. [BT660.F3P4] 51-12282
1. Fatima, Nossa Senhora da. I. Title.

PELLETIER, Joseph Albert, 231.73
1912-
Fatima, hope of the world. [1st ed.] Worcester, Mass., Washington Press, 1954. 203 p. illus. 22 cm. "A sequel to The sun danced at Fatima." [BT660.F3P38] 55-16796
1. Fatima, Nossa Senhora da. I. Title.

PELLETIER, Joseph Albert, 231.73
1912-
The sun danced at Fatima; a critical story of the apparitions. Worcester, Mass., Caron Press, 1951. 163 p. illus. 22 cm. Sequel: Fatima, hope of the world. [BT660.F3P4] 51-12282
1. Fatima, Nossa Senhora da. I. Title.

SAMMACICCIA, Bruno. 231'.73
The Eucharistic miracle of Lanciano, Italy / by Bruno Sammaciccia ; translated by Anthony E. Burakowski. Trumbull, Conn. : E. J. Kuba, 1976. 102 p. : ill. (some col.) ; 23 cm. Translation of Il miracolo eucaristico di Lanciano. Includes index. Bibliography: p. 100. [BX2225.S2713] 76-18630
1. Lord's Supper—Miracles. 2. Relics and reliquaries—Italy—Lanciano. I. Title.

SHARKEY, Donald C. 1912- 231.73
Our Lady of Beauraing [by] Don Sharkey and Joseph Debergh. Garden City, N.Y., Hanover House, 1958. 239 p. illus. 22 cm. Includes bibliography. [BT660.B4S45] 57-12474
1. Beauraing, Notre-Dame de. I. Debergh, Joseph, joint author. II. Title.

TRENCHARD, John, 1662- 231.73
1723.
Essay on miracles. Edited with an introd. and notes by J. A. R. Seguin. 1st North American ed. Jersey City [N. J.] R. Paxton, 1964. iii, 9 p. 25 cm. (Enlightenment and emancipation series, 1) "Two hundred and fifty copies...no. 32." [BT97.A2T7] 65-3744
1. Miracles — Early works to 1800. I. Sequin, J. A. R., ed. II. Title.

WALSH, William Thomas, 231.73
1891-1949.
Our Lady of Fatima. Introd. by William C. McGrath. Garden City, N.Y., Image Books [1954] 223 p. 19 cm. (Image books, P501) [BT660.F3W33 1954] 54-1799
1. Fatima, Nossa Senhora da.

WARFIELD, Benjamin 231.73
Breckinridge,
Miracles: yesterday and today, true and false [Reissue] Grand Rapids, Mich., Eerdmans [1966] 327p. 23cm. (Thomas Smyth lects. for 1917-1918) Orig. pub. in 1918 under title: Counterfeit miracles. On Spine: Miracles: yesterday and today, real and counterfeit. [BT97.W3] 53-8139 2.25 pap.,
1. Miracles. 2. Faith-cure. I. Title.

WARFIELD, Benjamin 231.73
Breckinridge, 1851-1921.
Miracles: yesterday and today, true and false. Grand Rapids, Eerdmans, 1953. 327 p. 23 cm. (The Thomas Smyth lectures for 1917-1918) "Originally published ... in 1918 under the title: Counterfeit miracles." [BT97.W3 1953] 53-8139
1. Miracles. 2. Faith-cure. I. Title.

WARREN, Mary 231.73
The little boat that almost sank. Illus. by Kveta Rada [St. Louis] Concordia [c.1965] [32]p. col. illus. 21cm. (Arch bks., set 2, no.59-1111) On cover: How Jesus stopped the storm [BS2401.W3] 64-23371 .35 pap.,
1. Stilling of the storm (Miracle)—Juvenile

literature. I. Title. II. Title: How Jesus stopped the storm.

WATSON, Simone. 231.73
The cult of Our Lady of Guadalupe; a historical study. Collegeville, Minn., Liturgical Press [c1964] 87 p. illus. (1 mounted col.) facsims., ports. 24 cm. "Originally submitted to the faculty of St. John's University in partial fulfillment of the requirements for the degree of master of arts of sacred science." Bibliography: p. 83-87. [BT660.G8W3] 66-6567
1. Guadalupe, Nuestra Senora de. I. Title.

WILLIAMS, John Hargreaves Harley, 1901- 231.73
A doctor looks at miracles. New York, Roy Publishers [1960, c.1959] 232p. Includes bibliography. 60-7759 3.75
1. Miracles I. Title.

WINCKLEY, Edward. 231'.73
The Great Healer's prayer. Montesano, Wash. [1971] xiv, 30 p. 16 cm. [BV233.W54] 75-157976 ISBN 0-8111-0409-5
1. Lord's prayer. 2. Faith-cure. I. Title.

WINDEATT, Mary Fabyan, 1910- 231.73
The children of La Salette; illustrated by Gedge Harmon. [St. Meinrad, Ind., 1951] 188 p. illus. 22 cm. "A Grail publication." [BT660.S33W5] 52-221
1. Salette, Notre-Dame de la. I. Title.

BREWER, Ebenezer Cobham, 1810-1897. 231'.73'03
A dictionary of miracles, imitative, realistic, and dogmatic, with illustrations, by E. Cobham Brewer. Philadelphia, Lippincott [1885]. Detroit, Gale Research Co., 1966. xliv, 582 p. illus. 23 cm. "Chief authorities cited in this book": p. [xxiv]-xxv. [BT97.B8 1885a] 66-29783
1. Miracles—Dictionaries. I. Title.

BAILLIE, John, 1886- 231.74
The idea of revelation in recent thought. New York, Columbia [1964, c.1956] 151p. 21cm. (Bampton lects. in Amer., no. 7. 54) Bibl. 1.45 pap.,
1. Revelation. I. Title.

BAILLIE, John, 1886-1960. 231.74
The idea of revelation in recent thought. New York, Columbia University Press, 1956. 151 p. 21 cm. (Bampton lectures in America, no. 7) Includes bibliography. [BT127.B234] 56-8158
1. Revelation. I. Title.

BAKER, John Austin. 231'.74
Prophecy in the Church / [by] John Austin Baker. London : Church Literature Association, 1976. [2], 9 p. ; 21 cm. "This essay was first given as a talk to the Westminster Deanery Chapter on 3 February 1976." [BR115.P8B34] 77-372457 ISBN 0-85191-086-6 : £0.25
1. Prophecy (Christianity)—Addresses, essays, lectures. 2. Prophets—Addresses, essays, lectures. I. Title.

BAVINCK, Herman, 1854-1921. 231.74
The philosophy of revelation. Grand Rapids, Eerdmans, 1953. x, 349p. 23cm. (The Stone lectures for 1908-1909 Princeton Theological Seminary) Bibliographical references included in 'Notes' (p. 317-349: sRevelation. [BT127] 54-6234
I. Title. II. Series: Princeton Theological Seminary. Stone lectures, 1908-9

BEA, Augustin, Cardinal, 1881- 231'.74
The word of God and mankind. Chicago, Franciscan Herald Press [1967] 318 p. 23 cm. Translation of La parola di Dio et l'umanita. Commentary on Constitution on divine revelation of Vatican Council II. Includes bibliographical references. [BX830 1962.A45C772 1967b] 68-17560
1. Vatican Council. 2d, 1962-1965. Constitutio dogmatica de divina revelatione. 2. Revelation. I. Title.

BENDER, Harold Stauffer 231.74
Biblical revelation and inspiration. [Scottdale, Pa., Mennonite Pub. House, c.1959] 20p. 20cm. (Focal pamphlet series, no. 4) 59-15635 .35 pap.,
1. Revelation. 2. Bible—Inspiration. I. Title.

BERKOUWER, Gerrit Cornelis, 1903- 231.74
General revelation. Grand Rapids, W. B. Eerdmans Pub. co., 1955. 336p. 23cm. (His Studies in dogmatics) [BT127.B435] 53-8142
1. Revelation. 2. Theology, Doctrinal. I. Title.

BEVAN, Edwyn Robert, 1870-1943. 231'.74
Sibyls and seers : a survey of some ancient theories of revelation and inspiration / by Edwyn Bevan. Folcroft, Pa. : Folcroft Library Editions, 1976. p. cm. Reprint of the 1928 ed. published by G. Allen & Unwin, London. Includes bibliographical references and index. [BL96.B4 1976] 76-30583 ISBN 0-8414-1750-4 lib. bdg. : 25.00
1. Sibyls. 2. Prophets. 3. Revelation. 4. Inspiration. I. Title.

BRING, Ragnar, 1895- 231.74
How God speaks to us; the dynamics of the living word. Philadelphia, Muhlenberg Press [1962] 120p. 21cm. [BT127.2.B7] 62-15699
1. Revelation. I. Title.

BRING, Ragnar [Anders Ebbe Ragnar Bring] 1895- 231.74
How God speaks to us; the dynamics of the living word. Philadelphia, Muhlenberg [c.1962] 120p. 21cm. 62-15699 2.25
1. Revelation. I. Title.

BUIST, Werner. 231.74
Revelation. Translated by Bruce Vawter. New York, Sheed and Ward [1956] 158 p. 21 cm. Includes bibliographical references. [BT127.1.B813] 65-12200
1. Revelation. I. Title.

BULST, Werner 231.74
Revelation. Tr. [from German] by Bruce Vawter. New York, Sheed [c.1965] 158p. 21cm. Bibl. [BT127.2.B813] 65-12200 3.95
1. Revelation. I. Title.

BUNGER, Fred S. 231'.74
A new light shines out of present darkness, by Fred S. Bunger and Hans N. von Koerber. Philadelphia, Dorrance [1971] xii, 337 p. 22 cm. [BX9998.B85] 77-132428 ISBN 0-8059-1501-X 6.95
1. Revelation—Collections. I. Koerber, Hans Nordewin von, joint author. II. Title.

DORONZO, Emmanuel, 1903- 231'.74
The channels of revelation. Middleburg, Va., Notre Dame Institute Press [1974] vii, 77 p. 22 cm. (His The science of sacred theology for teachers, book 3) Bibliography: p. iv. [BT127.2.D583] 74-76099
1. Revelation. 2. Dogma. 3. Theology, Catholic. I. Title.

DORONZO, Emmanuel, 1903- 231'.74
The channels of revelation. Middleburg, Va., Notre Dame Institute Press [1974] vii, 77 p. 22 cm. (His The science of sacred theology for teachers, book 3) Bibliography: p. iv. [BT127.2.D583] 74-76099 2.00 (pbk.)
1. Revelation. 2. Dogma. 3. Theology, Catholic. I. Title.

DORONZO, Emmanuel, 1903- 231'.74
Revelation. Middleburg, Va., Notre Dame Institute Press [1974] ix, 120 p. 22 cm. (His The science of sacred theology for teachers, book 2) Bibliography: p. iv-v. [BT127.2.D584] 74-76098
1. Revelation.

DORONZO, Emmanuel, 1903- 231'.74
Revelation. Middleburg, Va., Notre Dame Institute Press [1974] ix, 120 p. 22 cm. (His The science of sacred theology for teachers, book 2) Bibliography: p. iv-v. [BT127.2.D584] 74-76098 4.00 (pbk.)
1. Revelation.

DOWNING, Francis Gerald. 231.74
Has Christianity a revelation? [By] F. Gerald Downing. Philadelphia, Westminster Press [c1964] [BT127.2.D6 1964a] 67-12282
1. Revelation. I. Title.

DOWNING, Francis Gerald. 231.74
Has Christianity a revelation? [By] F. Gerald Downing. Philadelphia, Westminster Press [c1964] 315 p. 23 cm. Includes bibliographical references. [BT127.2.D6 1964a] 67-12282
1. Revelation. I. Title.

DULLES, Avery Robert, 1918- 231'.74
Revelation and the quest for unity, by Avery Dulles. With a foreword by Robert McAfee Brown. Washington, Corpus Books [1968] 325 p. 21 cm. Bibliographical references included in "Notes" (p. 284-312) [BT127.2.D8] 68-10450
1. Revelation. 2. Christian union—Catholic Church. 3. Bible and Christian union. I. Title.

DULLES, Avery Robert, 1918- 231'.74
Revelation theology; a history [by] Avery Dulles. [New York] Herder and Herder [1969] 192 p. 22 cm. Bibliography: p. 183-187. [BT126.5.D84] 70-81381 5.95
1. Revelation—History of doctrines. 2. Theology, Catholic—History. I. Title.

DUNNE, John S., 1929- 231'.74
A search for God in time and memory [by] John S. Dunne. [New York] Macmillan [1969] xi, 237 p. 22 cm. Includes bibliographies. [BT102.D8] 69-12645
1. God—Knowableness. I. Title.

FRIES, Heinrich. 231'.74
Revelation. [New York] Herder and Herder [1969] 96 p. 22 cm. (Mysterium salutis) (Series: Feiner, Johannes. Mysterium salutis. English) Translation of Die Offenbarung, originally published in 1965 as p. [159]-234 of Die Grundlagen heilsgeschichtlicher Dogmatik, edited by H. U. von Balthasar. Bibliographical footnotes. [BT127.2.F73] 68-55085 3.95
1. Revelation. I. Series.

HARDINGE, Leslie. 231'.74
Dove of gold, and other signposts of the spirit. Nashville, Southern Pub. Association [1972] 191 p. 21 cm. [BT127.2.H28] 72-80771
1. Revelation. I. Title.

HARRINGTON, Wilfrid J. 231'.74
Vatican II on revelation [by] Wilfrid Harrington and Liam Walsh. Dublin, Chicago, Scepter Books [1967] 191 p. 22 cm. "Constitutio dogmatica de divina revelatione," and its English translation: p. [156]-185. Bibliography: p. [186]-187. [BX830 1962.H36] 76-261381
1. Vatican Council. 2d, 1962-1965. Constitutio dogmatica de divina revelatione. 2. Bible—Study—Catholic Church. 3. Revelation. I. Walsh, Liam. II. Vatican Council. 2d, 1962-65. Constitutio dogmatica de divina revelatione. 1967. III. Vatican Council. 2d, 1962-65. Constitutio dogmatica de divina revelatione. English. 1967. IV. Title.

HATT, Harold E 231.74
Ecountering truth; a new understanding of how revelation, as encounter, yields doctrine by Harold E. Hatt. Nashville, Abingdon [1966] 208 p. 23 cm [bt127.2h3] 66-22197 4.50
1. 1. Revelation Title I. Title.

HATT, Harold E. 231.74
Encountering truth; a new understanding of how revelation, as encounter, yields doctrine, by Harold E. Hatt. Nashville, Abingdon Press [1966] 208 p. 23 cm. Bibliographical footnotes. [BT127.2.H3] 66-22917
1. Revelation. I. Title.

HEWLETT, Henry Charles 231.74
The companion of the way. Chicago, Moody [c.1962] 159p. 22cm. 62-1315 2.75
1. Theophanies. 2. Devotional literature. I. Title.

HYDE, Gordon M. 231'.74
God has spoken / by Gordon M. Hyde. Nashville, Tenn. : Southern Pub. Association, c1976. 94 p. ; 21 cm. Bibliography: p. 93-94. [BT127.2.H9] 75-40913 ISBN 0-8127-0109-7
1. Bible—Evidences, authority, etc. 2. Revelation. I. Title.

JULIANA, anchoret, 1343-1443. 231.74
Revelations of divine love; translated into modern English and with an introduction by Clifton Wolters. Harmondsworth, Penguin, 1966. 213 p. 18 1/2 cm. (Penguin classics, L177) 6/- Bibliography: p. 46. [BV4831.J8] 66-75443
1. Devotional literature. I. Title.

JULIANA, anchoret, 1343-1443. 231'.74
Revelations of divine love / Juliana of Norwich ; translated, with an introd. by M. L. del Mastro. 1st ed. Garden City, N.Y. : Image Books, 1977. 240 p. ; 18 cm. Bibliography: p. [239]-240. [BV4831.J8 1977] 76-52004 ISBN 0-385-12297-7 pbk. : 2.45
1. Devotional literature. I. Del Mastro, M. L. II. Title.

JULIANA, anchoret, 1343-1443. 231'.74
Revelations of divine love / Juliana of Norwich ; translated, with an introd. by M. L. del Mastro. 1st ed. Garden City, N.Y. : Image Books, 1977. 240 p. ; 18 cm. Bibliography: p. [239]-240. [BV4831.J8 1977] 76-52004 ISBN 0-385-12297-7 pbk. : 2.45
1. Devotional literature. I. Del Mastro, M. L. II. Title.

JULIANA, Anchoret, 1343-1443. 231'.74
Revelations of divine love [by] Julian of Norwich. Translated into modern English and with an introd. by Clifton Wolters. [Baltimore] Penguin Books [1966, reissued 1973] 213 p. 18 cm. (Penguin classics, L177) Bibliography: p. 46. [BV4831.J8] 66-7847 ISBN 0-14-044177-8 1.15 (pbk.)
1. Devotional literature. I. Wolters, Clifton, tr. II. Title.

KEAN, Charles Duell, 1910- 231.74
God's Word to His people. Philadelphia, Westminster Press [1956] 187p. 21cm. [BT127.K4] 56-8421
1. Revelation. 2. Bible—Influence. 3. Jews—Election, Doctrine of. I. Title.

KUNTZ, John Kenneth. 231'.74
The self-revelation of God, by J. Kenneth Kuntz. Philadelphia, Westminster Press [1967] 254 p. 24 cm. Bibliography: p. [233]-243. [BT128.K8] 67-10270
1. Theophanies. 2. Revelation. I. Title.

LATOURELLE, Rene. 231.74
Theology of revelation, including a commentary on the constitution "Dei verbum" of Vatican II. Staten Island, N.Y ., Alba House [1966] 508 p. 24 cm. Bibliography: p. [491]-508. [BT126.5.L313] 65-15734
1. Revelation — History of doctrines. 2. Vatican Council. 2d, 1962-1965. Constitutio de divina revelatione. I. Title.

LATOURELLE, Rene 231.74
Theology of revelation, including a commentary on the constitution "Dei verbum' of Vatican II. Staten Island, N. Y., Alba [c.1966] 508p. 24cm. Bibl. [BT126.5.L313] 65-15734 9.50
1. Revelation—History of doctrines. 2. Vatican Council. 2d, 1962-1965. Constitutio de divina revelatione. I. Title.

MCDONALD, Hugh Dermot. 231.74
Ideas of revelation; an historical study, A. D. 1700 to A. D. 1860. London, Macmillan; New York, St. Martin's Press, 1959. 300p. 23cm. [BT126.5.M3] 59-2449
1. Revelation —History of doctrines. I. Title.

MCDONALD, Hugh Dermot 231.74
Theories of revelation; an historical study, 1860-1960. London, G. Allen & Unwin [dist. New York, Humanities, c.]1963. 384p. 22cm. A continuation of the author's Ideas of revelation, 1700-1860. Bibl. 63-4467 7.50
1. Revelation—History of doctrines. I. Title.

MORAN, Gabriel 231.74
Catechesis of revelation. [New York] Herder & Herder [1966] 174p. 22cm. (Studies in relig. educ.) Bibl. [BT127.2.M59] 66-22607 4.50
1. Revelation—Study and teaching. I. Title.

MORAN, Gabriel. 231'.74
The present revelation; the search for religious foundations. [1st ed.] New York Herder and Herder [1972] 318 p. 22 cm. [BT127.2.M597] 72-2307 ISBN 0-07-073787-8 8.95
1. Revelation. 2. Experience (Religion) I. Title.

MORAN, Gabriel. 231.74
Theology of revelation. [New York] Herder and Herder [1966] 223 p. 22 cm. (Studies in religious education) Bibliography: p. 189-201. [BT127.2.M6] 66-16578
1. Revelation. I. Title.

MORRIS, Leon, 1914- 231'.74
I believe in revelation / by Leon Morris. (1st American ed.) Grand Rapids, Mich. : Eerdmans, 1976. 159 p. ; 21 cm. (I believe) Includes bibliographical references. [BT127.2.M64 1976] 75-45349 ISBN 0-8028-1637-1 pbk. : 2.95
1. Revelation. I. Title.

NIEBUHR, Helmut Richard 231.74
The meaning of revelation. New York, Macmillan 1960[c.1941] 196p. (Macmillan paperbacks, 27) 'Contains, with some additions and revisions, the Nathanael W. Taylor lectures given at the Divinity School of Yale University in April, 1940.'—Pref. 1.25 pap.,
1. Revelation. I. Title.

O'COLLINS, Gerald. 231'.74
Foundations of theology. Chicago, Loyola University Press [1971] x, 211 p. 23 cm. Includes bibliographical references. [BT127.2.O28] 70-153756 ISBN 0-8294-0201-2
1. Revelation—Addresses, essays, lectures. 2. Theology—Addresses, essays, lectures. I. Title.

O'COLLINS, Gerald. 231'.74
Theology and revelation. Notre Dame, Ind., Fides Publishers [1968] 96 p. 18 cm. (Theology today, no. 2) Bibliography: p. 95-96. [BT127.2.O3] 79-358 0.95
1. Revelation. I. Title.

ORR, James, 1844-1913. 231'.74
Revelation and inspiration. Grand Rapids, Baker Book House [1969] xii, 224 p. 20 cm. (Twin brooks series) Reprint of the 1910 ed. Bibliography: p. 219. [BT127.O7 1969] 74-100535 2.95
1. Revelation. 2. Inspiration. I. Title.

PANNENBERG, Wolfhart, 1928- 231'.74
Revelation as history. Edited by Wolfhart Pannenberg, in association with Rolf Rendtorff, Trutz Rendtorff, & Ulrich Wilkens. Translated from the German by David

Granskou. New York, Macmillan [1968] x, 181 p. 22 cm. Translation of Offenbarung als Geschichte. Bibliographical footnotes. [BT126.5.P313 1968] 67-20185
1. Revelation—History of doctrines. I. Rendtorff, Rolf, 1925- II. Rendtorff, Trutz. III. Wilkens, Ulrich. IV. Title.

PINK, Arthur Walkington, 231'.74
1886-1952.
The doctrine of revelation / A. W. Pink. Grand Rapids, Mich. : Baker Book House, c1975. 259 p. ; 23 cm. [BT127.2.P56 1975] 74-15575 ISBN 0-8010-6964-5 : 6.95
1. Revelation. I. Title.

RAHNER, Karl, 1904- 231.74
Revelation and tradition [by] Karl Rahner [and] Joseph Ratzinger. [Translated by W. J. O'Hara. New York] Herder and Herder [1966] 78 p. 21 cm. (Quaestiones disputatae, 17) Bibliographical references included in "Notes" (p. 69-78) [BT127.2.R2813 1966a] 66-18747
1. Revelation. 2. Tradition (Theology) I. Ratzinger, Joseph. II. Title.

RAMM, Bernard, 1916- 231.74
Special revelation and the word of God. Grand Rapids, Eerdmans [1961] 220 p. 22 cm. Includes bibliography. [BT127.2.R3] 61-10854
1. Revelation. I. Title.

ROOSEN, P A 231.74
The Bible on revelation, by P. A. Roosen. Translated by F. Vander Heijden. De Pere, Wis., St. Norbert Abbey Press, 1966. 139 p. 17 cm. Translation of De Bijbel over openbaring en overlevering. Bibliography: p. [138]-139. [BT126.R613] 66-22822
1. Revelation — Biblical teaching. I. Title.

ROSENBERG, Leon. 231.74
The various manifestations of the Deity. Los Angeles, American European Bethel Mission [c1961] 250p. 23cm. [BT128.R6] 61-18750
1. Theophanies. I. Title.

SALGUERO, Jose. 231'.74
Biblical revelation : the history of salvation / by J. Salguero ; translated by Judith Suprys. Arlington, Va. : Christian Culture Press, 1976. vii, 202 p. ; 22 cm. Translation of La rivelazione biblica. Includes bibliographical references and index. [BS646.S2313] 76-100100 8.95
1. Revelation—Biblical teaching. 2. Revelation—History of doctrines. I. Title.

SCHILLEBEECKX, Edward 231'.74
Cornelis Florentius Alfons, 1914-
Revelation and theology, by E. Schillebeeckx. Translated by N. D. Smith. New York, Sheed and Ward [1967- "Originally published as parts 1 and 2 of Openbaring en Theologie ... 1964. This translation is based on the second revised edition of 1966." Bibliographical footnotes. [BT127.2.S3313] 67-21907
1. Revelation. 2. Theology, Doctrinal. I. Title.

SCHILLEBEECKX, Edward 231'.74
Cornelis Florentius Alfons, 1914-
Revelation and theology, by E. Schillebeeckx. Translated by N. D. Smith. New York, Sheed and Ward [1967- v. 22 cm. (His Theological soundings) "Originally published as parts 1 and 2 of Openbaring en Theologie ... 1964. This translation is based on the second revised edition of 1966." Bibliographical footnotes. [BT127.2.S3313] 67-21907
1. Revelation. 2. Theology, Doctrinal. I. Title.

SCHILLEBEECKX, Edward 231.74
Cornelius Florentius Alfons, 1914-
Revelation and theology, by E. Schillebeeckx. Tr. by N. D. Smith. New York, Sheed [1968- v. 22cm. (Theological soundings) Orig. pub. as parts 1 & 2 of Openbaringen Theologie . . . 1964. This tr. is based on the second rev. ed. of 1966. Bibl. [BT127.2.S3313] 67-21907 4.95
1. Revelation. 2. Theology, Doctrinal. I. Title.

SCHUTZ, Roger. 231'.74
Revelation, a Protestant view; the Dogmatic Constitution on divine revelation, a commentary, by Roger Schutz and Max Thurian. Pref. by Henri de Lubac. Westminster, Md., Newman Press [1968] v, 104 p. 21 cm. "The dogmatic constitution on divine revelation": p. [81]-102. Bibliography: p. 103-104. [BX830 1962.A45C774] 68-21453
1. Vatican Council, 2d. 1962-1965. Constitutio dogmatica de divina revelatione. 2. Revelation. I. Thurian, Max, joint author. II. Vatican Council, 2d, 1962-1965. Constitutio dogmatica de divina revelatione. English. 1968. III. Title.

SODERBLOM, Nathan, Abp., 231.74
1866-1931.
The nature of revelation. Edited and with an introd. by Edgar M. Carlson. Translated by Frederic E. Pamp. Philadelphia, Fortress Press [1966] vii, 163 p. 21 cm. (Seminar editions) Translation of Uppenbarelsereligion. Bibliographical footnotes. [BT127.S6 1966] 66-23224
1. Revelation. 2. Religion—Philosophy. I. Title.

STOKES, Mack B 231.74
The epic of revelation; an essay in Biblical theology. [1st ed.] New York, McGraw-Hill [1961] 240 p. 22 cm. Includes bibliography. [BT127.2.S8] 61-11655
1. Revelation. I. Title.

TILLEY, Charles J 231.74
Religion with revelation. Boston, Christopher Pub. House, [1963] 323 p. 21 cm. Includes bibliography. [BT127.2.T5] 63-13311
1. Revelation. I. Title.

TILLEY, Charles J., Rev. 231.74
Religion with revelation. Boston, Christopher [c.1963] 323p. 21cm. Bibl. 63-13311 4.75
1. Revelation. I. Title.

VATICAN Council. 2d,1962- 231.74
1965.
De divina revelatione: the dogmatic Constitution on divine revelation of Vatican Council II, Promulgated by Pope Paul VI, November 18, 1965. Commentary and translation by GeorgeH. Tavard. [Study-club ed.] Glen Rock, N.J., Paulist Press, 1966. 94 p. 19 cm. (Vatican II documents) Bibliography: p. 93-94. [BX830 1962.A45C33] 66-19148
1. Revelation. 2. Bible — Study — Catholic Church. I. Tavard, Georges Henri, 1922- II. Title.

VATICAN Council, 2d, 1962- 231.74
1965
De divina releatione the dogmatic constitution on divine revelation of Vatican II, promulgated by Pope Paul VI, November 18, 1965 Glen Rock, N.J. Paulist [c.]1966 94 p. 19 cm (Vatican ii docs.) Commentary and tr. by George H. Tavard [study club. ed.] bibl. [bx8301962.a45c33] 6619148 pap .75
1. Revelation Bible-Study-Catholic Church. I. Title.

VOLKEN, Laurent, 1914- 231.74
Visions, revelations and the church. Tr. [from French] by Edward Gallagher. New York, Kenedy [1963] ix, 292p. 22cm. Bibl. 63-18883 5.50
1. Private revelations. I. Title.

WILSON, Thomas Ernest, 231'.74
1902-
Mystery doctrines of the New Testament : God's sacred secrets / T. Ernest Wilson. 1st ed. Neptune, N.J. : Loizeaux Bros., 1975. 123 p. ; 20 cm. Bibliography: p. 119-123. [BS2545.M87W54] 74-78881 ISBN 0-87213-962-X pbk. : 1.95
1. Bible. N.T.—Criticism, interpretation, etc. 2. Mystery—Biblical teaching. I. Title.

BIEMER, Gunter. 231'.74'0924
Newman on tradition. Translated and edited by Kevin Smyth. [New York] Herder and Herder [1967] xx, 207 p. facsim. 22 cm. Revised version of the original German edition; Uberlieferung und Offenbarung published in 1961. Bibliography: p. 193-203. [BX4705.N5B513 1967b] 66-21076
1. Newman, John Henry, Cardinal, 1801-1890. 2. Tradition (Theology)—History of doctrines. I. Smyth, Kevin, ed. and tr. II. Title.

ARADI, Zsolt. 231.78
The book of miracles. New York, Farrar, Straus [1956] 316p. illus. 22cm. [BT97.A7] 56-11315
1. Miracles. I. Title.

BASS, Clarence B 231.8
Backgrounds to dispensationalism; its historical genesis and ecclesiastical implications. [1st ed.] Grand Rapids, Eerdmans [1960] 184p. 22cm. Includes bibliography. [BT157.B35] 60-12924
1. Dispensationalism. I. Title.

BLACK, Hubert 231.8
Good God! Cry or credo? Nashville. Abingdon [1966] 144p. 20cm. Bibl. [BT160.B5] 66-21967 2.75
1. Theodicy. I. Title.

BRYDEN, James Davenport, 231.8
1900-
God and human suffering. Nashville, Broadman [1965, c.1953] 128p. 20cm. Bibl. [BT732.7.B7] 65-11768 1.95 bds.,
1. Suffering. I. Title.

BRYDEN, James Davenport, 231.8
1900-
Letters to Mark on God's relation to human suffering. [1st ed.] New York, Harper [1953] 150p. 20cm. [BT160.B75] 52-11437
1. Theodicy. 2. Suffering. I. Title.

BUTTRICK, George Arthur, 231.8
1892-
God, pain, and evil. Nashville, Abingdon Press [1966] 272 p. 24 cm. Bibliographical references included in "Notes" (p. 236-259) [BT732.7.B8] 66-16020
1. Suffering. I. Title.

BUTTRICK, George Arthur, 231.8
1892-
God, pain, and evil. Nashville, Abingdon [c.1966] 272p. 24cm. Bibl. [BT732.7.B8] 66-16020 5.95
1. Suffering. I. Title.

CREATIVE suffering: 231'.8
the ripple of hope [by] Alan Paton [and others. Boston] Pilgrim Press [1970] 122 p. ports. 21 cm. [BV4905.2.C7] 79-106559 ISBN 8-298-01529- 2.25
1. Suffering—Addresses, essays, lectures. I. Paton, Alan.

EADE, Alfred Thompson 231.8
The expanded panorama Bible study course. [Westwood, N. J.] Revell [c.1961] 192p. col. illus. 61-13616 3.95
1. Dispensationalism. I. Title.

ELPHINSTONE, Andrew, 1918- 231'.8
1975.
Freedom, suffering and love / [by] Andrew Elphinstone. London : S.C.M. Press, 1976. xii, 147 p. ; 23 cm. [BT160.E45] 77-357905 ISBN 0-334-00502-7 : £4.50
1. Theodicy. 2. Suffering. I. Title.

EVELY, Louis, 1910- 231'.8
Suffering. Translated by Marie-Claude Thompson. [New York] Herder and Herder [1967] 160 p. 21 cm. [BT160.E913] 67-13296
1. Suffering. 2. Theodicy.

EVELY, Louis, 1910- 231'.8
Suffering. Translated by Marie-Claude Thompson. Garden City, N.Y., Doubleday [1974, c1967] 111 p. 18 cm. (Image books). [BT160.E913] ISBN 0-385-02996-9 1.45 (pbk.)
1. Suffering. 2. Theodicy. I. Title.
L.C. card number for original ed.: 67-13296.

FARRER, Austin Marsden 231.8
Love almighty and ills unlimited; an essay on providence and evil, containing the Nathaniel Taylor lectures for 1961. Garden City, N.Y., Doubleday [c.1961] 168p. (Christian faith series) 61-8883 3.50 bds.,
1. Providence and government of God. 2. Theodicy. 3. Good and evil. I. Title.

FITCH, William. 231'.8
God and evil; studies in the mystery of suffering and pain. Grand Rapids, Eerdmans [1967] 183 p. 19 cm. (The Elmore Harris series, no. 1) [BT160.F5] 67-19317
1. Theodicy. 2. Good and evil. 3. Suffering. I. Title. II. Series.

FLOYD, William Edward 231'.8
Gregory.
Clement of Alexandria's treatment of the problem of evil, by W. E. G. Floyd. London, Oxford University Press, 1971. xxiii, 107 p. 23 cm. (Oxford theological monographs) Based on thesis, Oxford, 1968. Bibliography: p. [100] -102. [BJ1401.F58] 70-573660 ISBN 0-19-826707-X £2.10
1. Clemens, Titus Flavius, Alexandrinus. 2. Good and evil. 3. Gnosticism. I. Title.

GALLIGAN, Michael. 231'.8
God and evil / by Michael Galligan. New York : Paulist Press, 1976. vii, 80 p. ; 18 cm. Includes bibliographical references. [BT160.G24 1976] 75-36172 ISBN 0-8091-1925-0 pbk. : 1.65
1. Theodicy. I. Title.

GEACH, Peter Thomas. 231'.8
Providence and evil / Peter Geach. Cambridge [Eng.] ; New York : Cambridge University Press, 1977. xxii, 153 p. ; 21 cm. (Stanton lectures ; 1971-2) Includes bibliographical references and index. [BT160.G3] 76-28005 ISBN 0-521-21477-7 : 12.50
1. Theodicy—Addresses, essays, lectures. I. Title. II. Series.

GEACH, Peter Thomas. 231'.8
Providence and evil / Peter Geach. Cambridge [Eng.] ; New York : Cambridge University Press, 1977. xxii, 153 p. ; 21 cm. (Stanton lectures ; 1971-2) Includes bibliographical references and index. [BT160.G3] 76-28005 ISBN 0-521-21477-7 : 12.50
1. Theodicy—Addresses, essays, lectures. I. Title. II. Series.

GRIFFIN, David, 1939- 231'.8
God, power, and evil : a process theodicy / by David Ray Griffin. Philadelphia : Westminster Press, c1976. p. cm. Includes bibliographical references and index. [BT160.G74] 76-21631 ISBN 0-664-20753-7 : 17.50
1. Theodicy—History of doctrines. 2. Theodicy. 3. Process theology. I. Title.

HEATH, Thomas Richard, 231'.8
1920-
In face of anguish, by Thomas R. Heath. New York, Sheed and Ward [1966] ix, 212 p. 22 cm. Includes bibliographical references. [BT160.H4] 66-22015
1. Theodicy. I. Title.

HICK, John. 231.8
Evil and the God of Love. [1st ed.] New York, Harper & Row [1966] xii, 403 p. 22 cm. Bibliographical footnotes. [BT160.H5] 66-20778
1. Theodicy. I. Title.

HICK, John 231.8
Evil and the God of Love. New York, Harper [c.1966] xii, 403p. 22cm. Bibl. [BT160.H5] 66-20778 6.95
1. Theodicy. I. Title.

HONG, Edna (Hatlestad) 231'.8
1913-
Turn over any stone, by Edna Hong. Designed and illustrated by Don Wallerstedt. Minneapolis, Augsburg Pub. House [1970] 173 p. illus. 24 cm. [BV4909.H64] 77-121966 4.95
1. Suffering. 2. Consolation. I. Title.

KINDRED, Charles Granville, 231.8
1866-1954.
The autobiography of God. Joliet, Ill., Mission Services Association Press [1959] 639p. illus. 25cm. Includes bibliography. [BT157.K5] 59-5170
1. Dispensationalism. I. Title.

KING, Albion Roy, 1895- 231.8
The problem of evil; Christian concepts and the book of Job. New York, Ronald Press Co. [1952] 221 p. 21 cm. [BJ1401.K5] 52-11110
1. Good and evil. 2. Bible. O. T. Job—Theology. I. Title.

KLEMM, Edwin O. 231'.8
Upon request, God in action; the amazing part in the history: United States and China, by Edwin O. Klemm. [1st ed. Saginaw, Mich., 1971] xix, 406 p. illus. 24 cm. [E179.K63] 79-30883 8.80
1. U.S.—History. 2. World War, 1939-1945. 3. China—History—1900- 4. Providence and government of God. I. Title.

LEIBNIZ, Gottfried 231'.8
Wilhelm, von, Freiherr, 1646-1716.
Theodicy, abridged. Edited, abridged, and with an introd. by Diogenes Allen. [Translated by E. M. Huggard] Indianapolis, Bobbs-Merrill, 1966. xx, 176 p. 21 cm. (The Library of liberal arts, 121) Translation of Essais de theodicee sur la bonte de Dieu, la liberte de l'homme et l'origine du mal. Bibliographical references included in "Notes" (p. xvii-xx) [BT160.L4563 1966] 67-4155
1. Theodicy. 2. Theism. 3. Free will and determinism. I. Allen, Diogenes, ed. II. Title.

LEWIS, Clive Staples, 1898- 231.8
The problem of pain. New York, Macmillan [1962, c.1944] 160p. 18cm. (mp 120) .95 pap.,
1. Pain. 2. Good and evil. 3. Providence and government of God. I. Title.

MCGILL, Arthur Chute. 231'.8
Suffering: a test of theological method [by] Arthur C. McGill. Philadelphia, Geneva Press [c1968] 128 p. illus. 21 cm. (Decade books) [BT160.M28] 68-10189
1. Theodicy. 2. Suffering. I. Title.

MADDEN, Edward H. 231'.8
Evil and the concept of God, by Edward H. Madden and Peter H. Hare. Springfield, Ill., [1968] vii, 142 p. 24 cm. (American lecture series. Publication no. 706. A monograph in the Bannerstone division of American lectures in philosophy) Includes bibliographical references. [BT160.M29] 67-27930
1. Theodicy. I. Hare, Peter H., joint author. II. Title.

MARITAIN, Jacques, 1882- 231.8
God and the permission of evil. Tr. by Joseph W. Evans. Milwaukee, Bruce [c.1966] ix,121p. illus. 21cm. (Christian culture and phil. ser.) Bibl. [BT160.M313] 66-17003 3.75
1. Theodicy. I. Title. II. Series.

MASTON, Thomas Bufford, 231'.8
1897-
Suffering, a personal perspective, [by] T. B. Maston, Nashville, Broadman Press [1967] vii, 87 p. 21 cm. [BV4905.2.M3] 68-11848
1. Suffering. I. Title.

MASTON, Thomas Bufford, 231'.8
1897-
Suffering, a personal perspective, [by] T. B. Maston. Nashville. Broadman Press [1967] vii, 87 p. 21 cm. [BV4905.2.M3] 68-11848
1. Suffering. I. Title.

SCHILLING, Sylvester Paul, 1904- 231'.8
God and humar anguish / S. Paul Schilling. Nashville : Abingdon, c1977. 304 p. ; 22 cm. Includes bibliographical references and indexes. [BT160.S33] 77-5857 ISBN 0-687-14909-6 : 11.95
1. Theodicy. 2. Good and evil. I. Title.

SOCKMAN, Ralph Washington, 1889- 231.8
The meaning of suffering. [New York] Woman's Division of Christian Service, Board of Missions, the Methodist Church [1961] 143 p. 20 cm. Includes bibliography. [BV4909.S6] 61-5637
1. Suffering. I. Title.

SOCKMAN, Ralph Washington, 1889- 231.8
The meaning of suffering. Nashville, Abingdon [1962, c.1961] 143p. 21cm. (112) Bibl. 1.25 pap.,
1. Suffering. I. Title.

SONTAG, Frederick. 231'.8
God, why did You do that? Philadelphia, Westminster Press [1970] 172 p. 19 cm. Bibliography: p. 169-172. [BT160.S64] 71-114715
1. Theodicy. I. Title.

TAYLOR, Michael J., comp. 231'.8
The mystery of suffering and death. Michael J. Taylor, editor. Staten Island, N.Y., Alba House [1973] xi, 203 p. 23 cm. [BT732.7.T38] 72-13294 ISBN 0-8189-0263-9 5.95
1. Suffering. 2. Theodicy. 3. Death. I. Title.
Contents omitted.

TAYLOR, Michael J., comp. 231'.8
The mystery of suffering and death. Michael J. Taylor, editor. Garden City, N.Y., Image Books, 1974 [c1973] 228 p. 18 cm. [BT732.7.T38 1974] 74-177305 ISBN 0-385-09556-2 1.75 (pbk.)
1. Suffering. 2. Theodicy. 3. Death. I. Title.
Contents omitted.

TOWNER, Wayne Sibley. 231'.8
How God deals with evil / W. Sibley Towner. Philadelphia : Westminster Press, c1976. p. cm. (Biblical perspectives on current issues) Includes index. Bibliography: p. [BT180.J8T68] 76-24916 ISBN 0-664-24127-1 pbk. : 4.95
1. Judgment of God. 2. Redemption. 3. Theodicy. I. Title. II. Series.

VIEUJEAN, Jean 231.8
Love, suffering, providence. Tr. [from French] by Joan Marie Roth. Westminster, Md., Newman, 1966 [c.1964] xvi, 134p. 21cm. Bibl. [BT732.7.V513] 66-16571 3.50
1. Suffering. I. Title.

WEATHERHEAD, Leslie Dixon, 1893- 231.8
Why do men suffer? Nashville, Abingdon Press [1961, c.1936] 224p. (Apex bks. E 8) 1.25 pap.,
1. Suffering. I. Title.

WENHAM, John William. 231'.8
The goodness of God [by] John W. Wenham. Downers Grove, Ill., InterVarsity Press [1974] 223 p. 21 cm. Includes bibliographical references. [BT160.W45 1974] 74-93141 ISBN 0-87784-764-9 2.95 (pbk.)
1. Theodicy. I. Title.

WENHAM, John William. 231'.8
The goodness of God [by] J. W. Wenham. London, Inter-Varsity Press, 1974. 223 p. 20 cm. Includes bibliographical references and index. [BT160.W45 1974b] 74-174681 ISBN 0-85111-736-8
1. Theodicy. I. Title.
Distributed by Inter-Varsity Press, Downers Grove, Ill. 2.95 (pbk.)

WILDER-SMITH, A. E. 231'.8
The paradox of pain [by] A. E. Wilder Smith. [1st ed.] Wheaton, Ill., H. Shaw Publishers [1971] 132, [1] p. 21 cm. Bibliography: p. 132-[133] [BT732.7.W53] 71-165790 ISBN 0-87788-667-9
1. Suffering. 2. Good and evil. 3. Providence and government of God. I. Title.

*WOODS, B. W. 231'.8
Understanding suffering Grand Rapids, Baker Book House [1974] 176 p. 18 cm. Includes bibliographical references [BT160] ISBN 0-8010-9551-4 2.45 (pbk.)
1. Suffering. 2. Theodigy. I. Title.

232 Jesus Christ & His Family

ADAM, Karl, 1876- 232
The Christ of faith; the Christology of the Church. [Translation from the original German by Joyce Crick. [New York] New American Library [1962, c1957] xi, 408p. (Mentor Omega book. M 430) 'This translation from the original German, Der Christus des Glaubens (Patmos-Verlg) [BT201.A223] 57-5024
1. Jesus sJesus Christ—Person and offices. 2. Jesus Christ—History of Doctrines I. Title.

ADAM, Karl, 1876- 232
Christ our Brother, by Karl Adam. Tr. by Dom Justin McCann. New York, Collier [1962, c.1931, 1959] 128p. 18cm. (AS280) .95 pap.,
1. Jesus Christ—Person and offices. I. McCann, Justin, 1882- tr. II. Title.

AINGER, Geoffrey. 232
Jesus our contemporary. New York, Seabury Press [1967] 128 p. 22 cm. Bibliographical references included in "Notes" (p. [124]-126. [BT202.A35 1967b] 67-21034
1. Jesus Christ—Person and offices. 2. Christianity—20th century. I. Title.

AKHILANANDA, Swami. 232
Hindu view of Christ. Boston, Branden Pr. [1973] 291 p. 22 cm. Originally published in 1949 Bibliography: p. 285-288. [BT303.A43] 72-77209 3.75
1. Jesus Christ—Oriental interpretations. I. Title.

ALDWINCKLE, Russell Foster. 232
More than man : a study in christology / by R. F. Aldwinckle. Grand Rapids : Eerdmans, c1976. 311 p. ; 22 cm. Includes index. Bibliography: p. 294-303. [BT202.A56] 76-876 ISBN 0-8028-3456-6 : 7.95
1. Jesus Christ—Person and offices. 2. Christianity and other religions. I. Title.

ALLEGRA, Gabriele Maria. 232
My conversations with Teilhard de Chardin on the primacy of Christ, Peking, 1942-1945 [by] Gabriel M. Allegra. Translated with an introd. and notes by Bernardino M. Bonansea. Chicago, Franciscan Herald Press [1971] 126 p. 21 cm. Translation of Il primato di Cristo in S. Paolo e in Duns Scoto. Includes bibliographical references. [BT202.A613] 72-129246 ISBN 0-8199-0429-5 3.75
1. Jesus Christ—Primacy. 2. Duns, Joannes, Scotus, 1265?-1308?—Theology. 3. Bible. N.T. Epistles of Paul—Theology. I. Teilhard de Chardin, Pierre. II. Title.

ANDERSON, Roy Allan. 232
The God-Man, his nature and work. Washington, Review and Herald Pub. Association [1970] 160 p. 22 cm. Bibliography: p. 157-160. [BT202.A65] 78-102104
1. Jesus Christ—Person and offices. I. Title.

*ASH, Anthony Lee 232
Prayer [by] Anthony Lee Ash. Austin, Tex., R. B. Sweet [1967] 100p. 21cm. (Living word ser.) .75 pap.,
I. Title.

AUDET, Jean Paul. 232
The Gospel project. Translated by Edmond Bonin. New York, Paulist Press [1969] v, 106 p. 19 cm. (Deus books) Translation of Le projet evangelique de Jesus. Bibliographical footnotes. [BT202.A813] 79-92921 1.25
1. Jesus Christ—Person and offices. 2. Christianity—Early church. I. Title.

AUGSTEIN, Rudolf, 1923- 232
Jesus, Son of Man, / Rudolf Augstein. New York : Urizen Books, [1977] p. cm. Translation of Jesus Menschensohn. Bibliography: p. [BT202.A8413] 76-57698 ISBN 0-916354-63-6 : 12.95
1. Jesus Christ—Person and offices. I. Title.

AUGUSTINUS. AURELIUS, Saint, Bp. of Hippo. 232
Confessions. In the translation of J. G. Pilkington. With an introd. by George N. Shuster and illustrated with paintings by Edy Legrand. New York, Heritage Press [1963] xxx, 206 p. 20 col. plates. 27 cm. [BR65.A6E.5] 64-28
I. Pilkington, Joseph Green, tr. II. Title.

AULEN, Gustaf Emanuel Hildebrand, Bp. 1879- 232
Christus victor; an historical study of the three main types of the idea of atonement. Authorized translation by A. G. Hebert. American ed. New York, Macmillan, 1951. xvi, 163 p. 19 cm. [BT265.A] A52
1. Atonement—Hist. I. Title.

AULEN, Gustaf Emanuel Hildebrand, Bp., 1879- 232
Jesus in contemporary historical research / by Gustaf Aulen ; translated by Ingalill H. Hjelm. Philadelphia : Fortress Press, c1976. viii, 167 p. ; 24 cm. Translation of Jesus i nutida historisk forskning. Includes bibliographical references and index. [BT198.A9313] 75-36451 ISBN 0-8006-0438-5 : 7.95
1. Jesus Christ—History of doctrines—20th century. I. Title.

BABCOCK, Winifred. 232
The Palestinian mystery play. [Winston-Salem, N.C., Harold Institute]; distributed by Dodd, Mead, New York [1971] x, 142 p. 24 cm. "Based on The Shining Stranger by Preston Harold." Includes bibliographical references. [BT295.B13] 71-121986 ISBN 0-396-06201-6 2.95
1. Jesus Christ—Miscellanea. I. Harold, Preston. The Shining Stranger. II. Title.

BAGGARLY, Ioanne D. 232
The Conjugates Christ-Church in the Hexaemeron of Ps.-Anastasius of Sinai : textual foundations and theological context / Ioanne D. Baggarly. Roma : Pontificia Universitas Gregoriana, 1974. 78 p. : ill. ; 24 cm. "Excerpta ex dissertatione ad Lauream in Facultate Theologica Pontificiae Universitatis Gregorianae." [BR65.A343H4833] 74-187876
1. Anastasius Sinaita, Saint, fl. 640-700. Hexaemeron. I. Title.

BAILLIE, Donald Macpherson, 1887-1954 232
God was in Christ; an essay on incarnation and atonement. New York, Scribners [1965, c.1948] 230p. 21cm. (SL 111) [BT201.B13] 1.45 pap.,
1. Jesus Christ—Person and offices. I. Title.

BAILLIE, Donald Macpherson, 1887-1954. 232
God was in Christ; an essay on incarnation and atonement. [New ed.] New York, Scribner, 1955 [c1948] 230p. 22cm. [BT201.B13 1955] 56-1979
1. Jesus Christ—Person and offices. I. Title.

BALLOU, Robert Oleson. 232
The other Jesus; a narrative based on apocryphal stories not included in the Bible. Arr., edited, and with comments by Robert O. Ballou. [1st ed.] Garden City, N.Y., Doubleday, 1972. xix, 213 p. 22 cm. Includes bibliographical references. [BT520.B33] 73-180058 6.95
1. Jesus Christ—Biography—Apocryphal and legendary literature. I. Title.

BAN, Joseph D. 232
Jesus confronts life's issues [by] Joseph D. Ban. Valley Forge [Pa.] Judson Press [1972] 128 p. 22 cm. [BT301.2.B24] 73-182245 ISBN 0-8170-0547-1 1.95
1. Jesus Christ—Biography. I. Title.

BARCLAY, William, lecturer in the University of Glasgow. 232
The mind of Jesus. New York, Harper [1961] 340 p. 22 cm. "Published in Great Britain in two volumes entitled The mind of Jesus and Crucified and crowned." [BT202.B3 1961] 61-7332
1. Jesus Christ—Person and offices. I. Title.

BARNDOLLAR, W. W. 232
Jesus' title to the throne of David; a study in Biblical eschatology. Introd. by F. Walvoord. Findlay, Ohio, Box 28, Dunham Pub. Co., 1963. xii, 151p. geneal. table. 20cm. Bibl. 63-22630 price unreported
1. Jesus Christ—Genealogy. I. Title.

BARRETT, Charles Kingsley. 232
Jesus and the Gospel tradition [by] C. K. Barrett. Philadelphia, Fortress Press, 1968 [c1967] xi, 114 p. 22 cm. Bibliographical footnotes. [BT303.2.B3 1968] 68-10290
1. Jesus Christ—Person and offices. 2. Jesus Christ—Historicity. 3. Bible. N.T. Gospels—Criticism, interpretation, etc. I. Title.

BARTLETT, Clarence, 1895- 232
As a lawyer sees Jesus, a logical analysis of the Scriptural and historical record. [1st ed.] New York, Greenwich Book Publishers [1960] 197p. 21cm. Includes bibliography. [BT303.B26] 60-8074
1. Jesus Christ— Person and offices. 2. Apologetics—20th cent. I. Title.

BARTLEY, Robert F., 1890- 232
The star-studded hoax of Christianity with its allied gods, by Robert F. Bartley. [1st ed.] Toledo, 1966. 237p. 18cm. [BL2775.2.B28] 66-25496 4.95
1. Christianity—Controversial literature. I. Title.
Distributed by the author, 4341 Willys Parkway, Toledo, Ohio, 43612.

BAXTER, James Sidlow. 232
The master theme of the Bible; grateful studies in the comprehensive Saviorhood of Our Lord Jesus Christ [by] J. Sidlow Baxter. Wheaton, Ill., Tyndale House Publishers [1973] 336 p. 22 cm. [BT202.B35] 73-88678 ISBN 0-8423-4185-4 4.95
1. Jesus Christ—Person and offices. 2. Jesus Christ—Crucifixion. 3. Salvation. I. Title.

BEASLEY, Walter J. 232
What think ye of Christ? Being a series of studies on the life and teachings of the Lord Jesus Christ, by Walter J. Beasley. [4th ed.] Melbourne, Australian Institute of Archaeology [1968] 157 p. 19 cm. [BT207.B4 1968] 73-167204
1. Jesus Christ—Person and offices—Study. I. Title.

BERKOUWER, Gerrit Cornelis, 1903- 232
The person of Christ. Translated by John Vriend Grand Rapids, W. B. Eerdmans Pub. Co., 1954. 368p. 23cm. Studies in dogmatics) [BT201.B42] 53-8143
1. Jesus Christ—Person and offices. I. Title.

BERKOUWER, Gerrit Cornelis, 1903- 232
The work of Christ, by G. C. Berkouwer. [Translated by Cornelius Lambregtse] Grand Rapids, W. B. Eerdmans Pub. Co. [1965] 358 p. 23 cm. (His Studies in dogmatics) Bibliographical footnotes. [BT202.B413] 64-22032
1. Jesus Christ. I. Title.

BERKOUWER, Gerrit Cornelis, 1903- 232
The work of Christ [Tr. from Dutch by Cornelius Lambregtse] Grand Rapids, Mich., Eerdmans [c.1965] 358p. 23cm. (His Studies in dogmatics) Bibl. [BT202.B413] 64-22032 7.50
1. Jesus Christ. I. Title.

*BEST, W. E. 232
Studies in the person & work of Jesus Christ [by] W. E. Best. Grand Rapids, Baker Book House, [1975] 129 p. 20 cm. [BS2415] ISBN 0-8010-0644-9 2.95 (pbk.)
1. Jesus Christ—Person and offices. 2. Jesus Christ—Teaching. I. Title.

BIBLE. N.T. Gospels. English. Authorized. Selections. 1976. 232
The life & morals of Jesus Christ of Nazareth / extracted textually from the Gospels of Matthew, Mark, Luke & John by Thomas Jefferson. New York : D. McKay Co., 1976. ix, 191 p. : ill. ; 14 cm. "A biographical sketch of Thomas Jefferson: p. [173]-186. [BT2992.J4 1976] 76-361130 ISBN 0-679-50627-6 : 2.95
1. Jesus Christ—Biography—Sources, Biblical. 2. Jefferson, Thomas, Pres. U.S., 1743-1826. I. Jefferson, Thomas, Pres. U.S., 1743-1826. II. Title.

BLAKE, Eugene Carson, 1906- 232
He is Lord of all. Philadelphia, Westminster Press [1958] 61p. 20cm. [BT295.B57] 58-11140
1. Jesus Christ—Significante. 2. Church. I. Title.

BLIGH, John. 232
Our Divine Master / by John Bligh. Staten Island, N.Y. : Alba House, 1975, c1969. 168 p. ; 19 cm. (Scripture for meditation ; 3) Includes bibliographical references. [BS2415.B56 1975] 74-31345 ISBN 0-8189-0308-2 pbk. : 1.95
1. Jesus Christ—Teachings—Meditations. I. Title. II. Series.

BONHOEFFER, Dietrich, 1906-1945. 232
Christ the center. Introduced by Edwin H. Robertson and translated by John Bowden. [1st ed.] New York, Harper & Row [1966] 125 p. 22 cm. Based on the author's lectures given at the University of Berlin in 1933, which were reconstructed from students' notes by Eberhard Bethge. Translated from the author's Gesammelte Schriften, v. 3, 1960, edited by Bethge. London ed. (Collins) has title: Christology. Bibliographical footnotes. [BT201.B47] 66-15049
1. Jesus Christ—Addresses, essays, lectures. I. Bethge, Eberhard, 1909- II. Title.

BONNEFOY, Jean Francois, 1897- 232
Christ and the cosmos. Translated and edited by Michael D. Meilach. [1st American ed.] Paterson, N. J., St. Anthony Guild Press [1965] xviii, 438 p. 24 cm. Translation of La primaute du Christ seion l'ecriture et la tradition. Includes bibliographical references. [BT202.B613] 65-13686
1. Jesus Christ — Primacy. I. Meiliach, Michael D., ed. and tr. II. Title.

BONNEFOY, Jean Francois, 1897- 232
Christ and the cosmos. Tr. [from French] ed. by Michael D. Meilach [1st Amer. ed.] Paterson, N. J., St. Anthony [c.1965] xviii, 438p. 24cm. Bibl. [BT202.B613] 65-13686 5.95
1. Jesus Christ—Primacy. I. Meilach, Michael D., ed. and tr. II. Title.

BORNKAMM, Gunther. 232
Jesus of Nazareth. Translated by Irene and Fraser McLuskey with James M. Robinson.

New York, Harper [1960] 239 p. 22 cm. [BT301.2.B583 1960a] 61-5256
1. Jesus Christ—Person and offices.

BOWIE, Walter Russell, 1882- 232
I believe in Jesus Christ. Nashville, Abingdon Press [1959] 80p. 20cm. [Know your faith series] [BT205.B63] 59-5207
1. Jesus Christ—Appreciation. 2. Faith. I. Title.

BOWMAN, David J. 232
The Word made flesh. Englewood Cliffs, N. J., Prentice-Hall, 1963. 118 p. 23 cm. (Foundations of Catholic theology series) [BT198.B74] 63-12363
1. Jesus Christ — History of doctrines. I. Title.

BOWMAN, David J. 232
The Word made flesh. Englewood Cliffs, N.J., Prentice [c.]1963. 118p. 23cm. (Founds. of Catholic theology ser.) Bibl. 63-12363 3.95; 1.50 pap.,
1. Jesus Christ—History of doctrines. I. Title.

BOWMAN, John Wick, 1894- 232
Which Jesus? Philadelphia, Westminster Press [1970] 168 p. 19 cm. Bibliography: p. [13]-15. [BT198.B76] 74-100953 ISBN 0-664-24879-9 2.65
1. Jesus Christ—History of doctrines—20th century. I. Title.

*BOYER, A. Leslie 232
Christ is coming. New York, Vantage [c.1965] 48p. 21cm. 2.50 bds.,
I. Title.

BREITIGAM, R. R. 232
The teacher sent from God. Mountain View, Calif., Pacific Press Pub. Association [c.1960] 137p. 19cm. 60-10098 2.00
1. Jesus Christ—Teaching methods. 2. Religious education. 3. Seventh-Day Adventists—Education. I. Title.

BROADUS, John Albert, 1827- 232
1895.
Jesus of Nazareth: I. His personal character. II. His ethical teachings. III. His supernatural works. With pref. by A. T. Robertson. Grand Rapids, Baker Book House, 1962. 105p. 20cm. [BT201.B58 1962] 62-19234
1. Jesus Christ—Person and offices. 2. Jesus Christ —Character. 3. Jesus Christ—Teachings. I. Title.

BRUNNER, Heinrich Emil, 1889- 232
The Mediator, a study of the central doctrine of the Christian faith. Tr. [from German] by Olive Wyon. Philadelphia, Westminster [1965.c.1947] 623p.[1]p. 22cm. The first ed. appeared in 1927; the second ed. was pub. in 1932. The present tr. has been made from the text of the second ed. [BT255.B833] 47-2441 3.25 pap.,
1. Jesus Christ—Person and offices. 2. Atonement. 3. Revelation. I. Wyon, Olive, 1890- tr. II. Title.

BUNYAN, John, 1628-1688. 232
The work of Jesus Christ as an advocate. Swengel, Pa., Reiner Publications, 1968. 143 p. 20 cm. First published in 1688. Reprinted from an ed. of Bunyan's works, published by the American Baptist Publication Society, in 1851. [BT260.B8 1968] 71-1179 1.95
1. Jesus Christ—Priesthood. I. Title.

BURR, William Henry, 1819- 232
1908.
Revelations of Antichrist, concerning Christ and Christianity. New York, Arno Press, 1972 [c1879] xiv, 432 p. 21 cm. (The Atheist viewpoint) [BL2775.B8 1972] 79-161340 ISBN 0-405-03801-1
1. Christianity—Controversial literature. I. Title. II. Series.

BUSHNELL, Horace, 1802-1876. 232
God in Christ. Three discourses, delivered at New Haven, Cambridge, and Andover, with a preliminary dissertation on language. Hartford, Brown and Parsons, 1849. [New York, AMS Press, 1972] 356 p. 23 cm. [BT201.B85 1972] 76-39568 ISBN 0-404-01245-0 12.50
1. Jesus Christ—Person and offices. 2. Atonement. 3. Dogma. 4. Language and languages. I. Title.

CAMBRIDGE. University. 232
Library. MSS. (Oriental 1319)
A Nestorian collection of christological texts, Cambridge University Library ms. Oriental 1319; edited and translated by Luise Abramowski and Alan E. Goodman. Cambridge [Eng.] University Press, 1972- v. 24 cm. (University of Cambridge. Oriental publications, no. 19) Contents.Contents.— — v. 2. Introduction, translation, indexes. Includes bibliographical references. [BT200.C275] 77-130904 ISBN 0-521-08126-2 (v. 2)
1. Jesus Christ—Person and offices—Early works to 1800. I. Abramowski, Luise, ed. II. Goodman, Alan E., ed. III. Title. IV. Series: Cambridge. University. Oriental publications, no. 19.

CANNON, William Ragsdale, 232
1916-
The Redeemer; the work and person of Jesus Christ. New York, Abingdon-Cokesbury Press [1951] 224 p. 22 cm. Bibliographical footnotes. [BT201.C27] 51-10442
1. Jesus Christ—Person and offices. I. Title.

CARMICHAEL, Joel 232
The death of Jesus [New York, Dell, 1967, c.1962] 221p. 18cm. (Laurel ed., 1833) Bibl. .75 pap.,
1. Jesus Christ—Passion. I. Title.

CARTER, Ray Cecil 232
The eternal teacher; a guide to Jesus' teaching methods. New York, Exposition Press [c.1960] 71p. 21cm. (An Exposition-banner book) 60-1538 2.50
1. Jesus Christ—Teaching methods. I. Title.

CARTWRIGHT, Lin Dorwin, 1886- 232
The great commitment; the meaning of the confession of faith. St. Louis, Bethany [c.1962] 144p. 21cm. Bibl. 62-14107 2.50
1. Faith. 2. Jesus Christ—Person and offices. I. Title.

CAYCE, Edgar, 1877-1945. 232
Edgar Cayce's story of Jesus. Selections, arrangement, and comments by Jeffrey Furst. [1st American ed.] New York, Coward-McCann [1969, c1968] 365 p. 22 cm. [BT304.96.C37 1969] 74-88576 5.95
1. Jesus Christ—Spiritualistic interpretations. I. Furst, Jeffrey, ed. II. Title. III. Title: Story of Jesus.

CERFAUX, Lucien, 1883- 232
Christ in the theology of St. Paul. English translation by Geoffrey Webb and Adrian Walker. [New York] Herder and Herder [1959] 559p. 22cm. Includes bibliography. [BS2651.C413 1959a] 58-5989
1. Bible. N. T. Epistles of Paul—Theology. 2. Jesus Christ—Person and offices. I. Title.

CHATHAM, Josiah George, 1914- 232
In the midst stands Jesus; a pastoral introduction to the New Testament [by] Josiah G. Chatham. Staten Island, N.Y., Alba House [1972] vi, 220 p. 22 cm. Bibliography: p. [207] -210. [BS2330.2.C49] 72-3563 ISBN 0-8189-0252-3 4.95
1. Jesus Christ—Biography. 2. Bible. N.T.—Introductions. I. Title.

CHESNUT, Roberta C. 232
Three monophysite christologies : Severus of Antioch, Philoxenus of Mabbug and Jacob of Sarug / by Roberta C. Chesnut. London : Oxford University Press, 1976. 158 p. ; 23 cm. (Oxford theological monographs) Includes index. Bibliography: p. [144]-154. [BT198.C4] 76-375028 ISBN 0-19-826712-6 : 14.75
1. Jesus Christ—History of doctrines—Early church, ca. 30-600. 2. Severus Sozopolitanus, Patriarch of Antioch, d. ca. 536. 3. Philoxenus, Bp. of Hierapolis. 4. Jacob of Serug, 451-521. 5. Monophysites. I. Title. II. Series.
Distributed by oxford, new york Distributed by Oxford, New York

CHITWOOD, Billy J. 232
Meet the real Jesus / Bill Chitwood. Nashville : Broadman Press, 1977, c1976. 128 p. ; 21 cm. [BT202.C49] 76-14631 ISBN 0-8054-8129-X pbk. : 2.50
1. Jesus Christ—Person and offices. I. Title.

CHRISTIAN hope and the 232
Lordship of Christ. Edited by Martin J. Heinecken. Minneapolis, Augsburg Pub. House [1969] ix, 110 p. 22 cm. (The Christian hope series) Includes bibliographical references. [BT270.C47] 70-84810 2.50
1. Jesus Christ—Royal office—Addresses, essays, lectures. I. Heinecken, Martin J.

CHRISTOLOGY and a modern 232
pilgrimage; a discussion with Norman Perrin. Edited by Hans Dieter Betz. [Missoula, Mont.] Society of Biblical Literature, 1971 [reprinted 1973, c1971] vi, 157 p. 22 cm. Published to honor N. Perrin on the occasion of his 50th birthday. Contents.Contents.—Perrin, N. Towards an interpretation of the Gospel of Mark.—Hobbs, E. C. Norman Perrin on methodology in the interpretation of Mark: a critique of "The christology of Mark" and "Toward an interpretation of the Gospel of Mark."—Furnish, V. P. Notes on a pilgrimage: Norman Perrin and New Testament christology.—Epp, E. J. Norman Perrin on the Kingdom of God: an appreciation and an assessment from the perspective of 1970.—Koester, H. The historical Jesus: some comments and thoughts on Norman Perrin's Rediscovering the teaching of Jesus.—Wilder, A. Norman Perrin, What is redaction criticism?—Robinson, J. M. The promise of Bultmann.—Bibliography of the works of Norman Perrin (p. [153]-157) [BS2585.2.C45 1973] 74-181526 ISBN 0-88414-000-8
1. Perrin, Norman—Addresses, essays, lectures. 2. Perrin, Norman—Bibliography. 3. Bible. N.T. Mark—Criticism, interpretation, etc. I. Perrin, Norman. II. Betz, Hans Dieter, ed.

CLASPER, Paul D. 232
New life in Christ, a study of Paul's theology for to-day. New York, Association [1962] 79p. 19cm. (World Christian bks., no. 39, 2d ser.) 62-10269 1.00 pap.,
1. Jesus Christ—Person and offices. 2. Bible. N.T. Epistles of Paul—Theology. I. Title.

COBB, George Thomas, 1875- 232
Modernism vs. Bible Christianity. Dallas [1955] 98p. 21cm. [BT78.C553] 56-18681
1. Modernist-fundamentalist controversy. I. Title.

COBB, John B. 232
Christ in a pluralistic age / by John B. Cobb, Jr. Philadelphia : Westminster Press, [1975] p. cm. Includes bibliographical references and index. [BT202.C62] 74-820 ISBN 0-664-20861-4 : 12.50
1. Jesus Christ—Person and offices. I. Title.

COLE, Clifford A. 232
Jesus the Christ; senior high teacher's manual, course A--October, November, December [Independence, Mo., Herald Pub. House, c.1961] 62p. (T) .40 pap.,
I. Title.

COLEMAN, Robert Emerson, 232
1928-
The mind of the Master / Robert E. Coleman. Old Tappan, N.J. : F. H. Revell Co., c1977. 128 p. ; 21 cm. Includes bibliographical references. [BT202.C63] 77-7351 ISBN 0-8007-0879-2 : 5.95. ISBN 0-8007-0880-6 pbk. : 3.95
1. Jesus Christ—Person and offices. I. Title.

COLLEGE Theology Society. 232
Does Jesus make a difference? Proceedings. Edited by Thomas M. McFadden. New York, Seabury Press [1974] viii, 232 p. 21 cm. "A Crossroad book." "Twelve of those papers originally delivered at the 1973 meeting of the College Theology Society." Includes bibliographical references. [BT202.C64 1974] 73-17902 ISBN 0-8164-1151-4 6.95
1. Jesus Christ—Person and offices—Congresses. I. McFadden, Thomas M., ed. II. Title.

COMBLIN, Joseph, 1923- 232
Jesus of Nazareth : meditations on His humanity / Jose Comblin ; translated by Carl Kabat. Maryknoll, N.Y. : Orbis Books, c1976. 167 p. ; 20 cm. Translation of Jesus de Nazare. [BT306.4.C5913] 75-29580 ISBN 0-88344-231-0 : 5.95
1. Jesus Christ—Meditations. I. Title.

CONGAR, Marie Joseph, 1904- 232
Christ, Our Lady, and the Church; a study in eirenic theology. Translated with an introd. by Henry St. John. Westminster, Md., Newman Press [1957] 103p. 20cm. [BT198.C612] 57-8615
1. Jesus Christ—History of doctrines. 2. Mary, Virgin—Theology. 3. Chalcedon, Council of, 451. I. Title.

CONGAR, Yves Marie Joseph, 232
1904-
Christ, Our Lady, and the Church; a study in eirenic theology. Translated with an introd. by Henry St. John. Westminster, Md., Newman Press [1957] 103 p. 20 cm. [BT198.C612] 57-8615
1. Jesus Christ—History of doctrines. 2. Mary, Virgin—Theology. 3. Chalcedon, Council of, 451. I. Title.

CONZELMANN, Hans. 232
Jesus; the classic article from RGG expanded and updated. Translated by J. Raymond Lord. Edited with an introd. by John Reumann. Philadelphia, Fortress Press [1973] xii, 116 p. 18 cm. "A translation of Jesus Christus, published in [the 3d ed. of] Die Religion in Geschichte und Gegenwart: Handworterbuch fur Theologie und Religionswissenschaft ... vol. 3 (1959)" Bibliography: p. 97-116. [BT202.C6713] 73-79011 ISBN 0-8006-1000-8 2.95
1. Jesus Christ—Person and offices. I. Title.

COOK, Walter L. 232
Youth devotions on the Jesus who was different [by] Walter L. Cook. Nashville, Abingdon Press [1973] 96 p. 16 cm. [BT306.5.C66] 72-6643 ISBN 0-687-47144-3 3.00
1. Jesus Christ—Biography—Devotional literature. 2. Youth—Prayer-books and devotions—English. I. Title.

CRADDOCK, Fred B. 232
The pre-existence of Christ in the New Testament [by] Fred B. Craddock. Nashville, Abingdon Press [1968] 192 p. 21 cm. Bibliographical footnotes. [BT202.C74] 68-11715
1. Jesus Christ—Pre-existence. I. Title.

CULLMANN, Oscar. 232
The Christology of the New Testament. Translated by Shirley C. Guthrie and Charles A. M. Hall. Philadelphia, Westminster Press [1959] 342 p. 24 cm. Includes bibliography. [BT198.C813 1959] 59-10178
1. Jesus Christ—History of doctrines—Early church, ca. 30-600. 2. Jesus Christ—Person and offices. 3. Bible. N.T.—Theology. I. Title.

CULLMANN, Oscar. 232
Jesus and the revolutionaries. Translated from the German by Gareth Putnam. [1st ed.] New York, Harper & Row [1970] xi, 84 p. 22 cm. Includes bibliographical references. [BT202.C8413] 75-124710 3.95
1. Jesus Christ—Person and offices. 2. Zealots (Jewish party) I. Title.

CUTNER, Herbert. 232
Jesus: God, man or myth? An examination of the evidence. New York, Truth Seeker Co. [1950] 298 p. 21 cm. Bibliography: p. 289-292. [BT303.C9] 50-14800
1. Jesus Christ—Historicity. I. Title.

DAHL, Nils Alstrup. 232
The crucified Messiah, and other essays / Nils Alstrup Dahl. Minneapolis : Augsburg Pub. House, [1974] 190 p. ; 22 cm. Includes bibliographical references. [BT450.D33] 74-14189 ISBN 0-8066-1469-2 : 2.95
1. Jesus Christ—Crucifixion. 2. Jesus Christ—Historicity. 3. Bultmann, Rudolf Karl, 1884- Theologie des Neuen Testaments. I. Title.
Contents omitted.

DANIELOU, Jean. 232
Advent; translated by Rosemary Sheed. New York, Sheed and Ward, 1951 ['1950] 181 p. 20 cm. Translation of Le mystere de l'Avent. [BT205.D312 1951] 51-7300
1. Jesus Christ—Person and offices. 2. Christianity and other religions. 3. Missions—Theory. I. Title.

DANIELOU, Jean 232
The advent of salvation: a comparative study of non-Christian religions and Christianity. Tr. [from French] by Rosemary Sheed. Orig. pub. under the title Advent. New York, Paulist Pr. [1962, c.1950] 192p. (Deus bk.) Bibl. .95 pap.,
1. Jesus Christ—Person and offices. 2. Christianity and other religions. 3. Missions—Theory. I. Title.

DANIELOU, Jean. 232
Christ and us. Tr. of Approaches du Christ by Walter Roberts. New York, Sheed & Ward [c.1961] 236p. Bibl. 61-7294 3.95 bds.,
1. Jesus Christ—Person and offices. I. Title.

DANIELOU, Jean 232
The presence of God. A translation [from the French] by Walter Roberts. Baltimore, Helicon Press [1960] 60p. (3p. bibl. notes) 19cm. 59-11463 1.95 bds.,
1. Jesus Christ—Mystical body. I. Title.

DAUGHTERS of St. Paul. 232
I learn about Jesus. Written and illustrated by the Daughters of St. Paul. [1972 i.e. 1973] 144 p. col. illus. 25 cm. Retellings of New Testament stories with related prayers. [BV4870.D33] 72-91979 pap. 2.50
1. Jesus Christ—Biography—Juvenile literature. 2. Children—Prayer-books and devotions—English—1961- I. Title.

DAWE, Donald G. 232
Jesus, Lord for all times / Donald G. Dawe. Atlanta : John Knox Press, [1975] c1974. p. cm. Includes bibliographical references. [BT202.D35 1975] 75-9933 ISBN 0-8042-9066-0 pbk. : 3.95 ISBN 0-8042-9067-9 teacher's ed. : 3.95
1. Jesus Christ—Person and offices. I. Title.

DERK, Francis H. 232
Names and titles of Christ [by] Francis H. Derk. Foreword by Merrill C. Tenney. Minneapolis, Bethany Fellowship, inc. [1969] 164 p. 21 cm. [BT590.N2D45] 70-272167 3.95
1. Jesus Christ—Name. I. Title.

DERK, Francis H. 232
A pocket guide to the names of Christ / Francis H. Derk. [2d ed.]. Minneapolis, Minn. : Bethany Fellowship, [1976, c1969] 164 p. ; 18 cm. (Dimension books) First ed. published under title: Names and titles of Christ. Includes index. [BT590.N2D45 1976] 75-44928 ISBN 0-87123-390-8 pbk. : 1.50
1. Jesus Christ—Name. I. Title. II. Title: The names of Christ.

DESCHNER, John 232
Wesley's Christology, an interpretation. Dallas, Southern Methodist University Press [c.] 1960. ix, 220p. 23cm. (Bibl.: p. 212-214) 60-8676 4.50
1. Wesley, John, 1703-1791. 2. Jesus Christ—History of doctrines. I. Title.

DICKSON, Harley. 232
A special kind of man / Harley Dickson. Waco, Tex. : Word Books, c1975. xiii, 133 p. ; 23 cm. [BT202.D5] 75-10088 ISBN 0-87680-365-6 : 4.95
1. Jesus Christ—Person and offices. I. Title.

DIXON, Jeane. 232
The call to glory; Jeane Dixon speaks of Jesus. New York, Morrow, 1972 [c1971] 192 p. 22 cm. [BF1283.D48A53] 78-187805 4.95
1. Jesus Christ—Person and offices. 2. Prophecies. I. Title.

DIXON, Jeane. 232
The call to glory: Jeane Dixon speaks of Jesus. New York, Bantam [1973, c.1971] 184 p. 18 cm. [BF1283.D48A53] pap., 1.25
1. Jesus Christ—Person and offices. 2. Prophecies. I. Title.

DODD, Charles Harold, 1884- 232
The founder of Christianity [by] C. H. Dodd. [New York] Macmillan [1970] vii, 181 p. 22 cm. Includes bibliographical references. [BT202.D57] 73-90222
1. Jesus Christ—Person and offices. I. Title.

DOUGLASS, Herbert E. 232
Jesus : the benchmark of humanity / by Herbert E. Douglass and Leo Van Dolson. Nashville : Southern Pub. Association, c1977. 128 p. ; 20 cm. [BT202.D59] 76-50968 ISBN 0-8127-0133-X pbk. : 2.95
1. Jesus Christ—Person and offices. I. Van Dolson, Leo R., joint author. II. Title.

DOUGLASS, Herbert E. 232
Jesus : the benchmark of humanity / by Herbert E. Douglass and Leo Van Dolson. Nashville : Southern Pub. Association, c1977. 128 p. ; 20 cm. [BT202.D59] 76-50968 ISBN 0-8127-0133-X pbk. : 2.95
1. Jesus Christ—Person and offices. I. Van Dolson, Leo R., joint author. II. Title.

DOWNING, Francis Gerald. 232
A man for us and a God for us [by] F. Gerald Downing. [American ed.] Philadelphia, Fortress Press [1968] ix, 154 p. 20 cm. Bibliographical references included in "Notes" (p. 142-151) [BT202.D6 1968] 68-19077
1. Jesus Christ—Person and offices. 2. Jesus Christ—Significance. I. Title.

DUNN, James D. G., 1939- 232
Jesus and the spirit : a study of the religious and charismatic experience of Jesus and the first Christians as reflected in the New Testament / by James D. G. Dunn. Philadelphia : Westminster Press, [1975] xii, 515 p. ; 24 cm. Includes indexes. Bibliography: p. [457]-475. [BR110.D86] 75-9802 ISBN 0-664-20804-5 : 19.50
1. Jesus Christ—Spiritual life. 2. Experience (Religion)—History. 3. Spiritual life—History of doctrines. I. Title.

EVANS, David Beecher, 1928- 232
Leontius of Byzantium: an Origenist Christology. Washington, Dumbarton Oaks, Center for Byzantine Studies, trustees for Harvard University; [distributed by J. J. Augustin, Locust Valley, New York] 1970. xiii, 206 p. 25 cm. (Dumbarton Oaks studies, 13) Expanded version of the author's thesis, Harvard Divinity School, 1966. Bibliography: p. 186-194. [BT198.E88 1970] 72-24460 6.00
1. Leontius Byzantinus, ca. 458 — ca. 543. 2. Jesus Christ—History of doctrines—Early church, ca. 30-600. I. Title. II. Series.

EVANS, Illtud. 232
One in Christ. Chicago, Fides Publishers Association [1957] 82p. 19cm. [BX1751.E82] 57-4663
1. Jesus Christ—Mystical body. I. Title.

FARMER, Herbert Henry, 1892- 232
The word of reconciliation [by] H. H. Farmer. Nashville, Abingdon Press [1967, c1966] ix, 105 p. 20 cm. (The Ayer lectures for 1961) Bibliographical footnotes. [BT250.F3] 67-4190
1. Jesus Christ—Person and offices. I. Title. II. Series: The Ayer lectures, 1961

FELDER, Hilarin, Bp. 1867- 232
1951.
Jesus of Nazareth; translated by Berchmans Bittle. Milwaukee, Bruce Pub. Co. [1953] 353p. 23cm. [BT201.F37 1953] 54-87
1. Jesus Christ—Person and offices. I. Title.

FERNAN, John Joseph, 1908- 232
Christ our high priest. [Syracuse? N. Y., 1953] 284p. 24cm. (Theology, a course for college students, v. 2) [BX904.T45 vol.2] 53-2837
1. Jesus Christ—Priesthood. I. Title.

FEUILLET, Andre. 232
The priesthood of Christ and his ministers. Translated by Matthew J. O'Connell. [1st ed.] Garden City, N.Y., Doubleday, 1975. 310 p. 22 cm. Translation of Le sacerdoce du Christ et de ses ministres. Bibliography: p. [286]-294. [BT260.F4813] 74-9446 ISBN 0-385-06009-2 7.95
1. Jesus Christ—Priesthood. 2. Priesthood. I. Title.

FICHTNER, Joseph. 232
Christ, the center of life. Milwaukee, Bruce Pub. Co. [1967, c1968] xi, 158 p. 22 cm. [BT202.F5] 68-13552
1. Jesus Christ—Person and offices. I. Title.

FINLEY, James. 232
Jesus and you : discovering the real Christ / James Finley, Michael Pennock. Notre Dame, Ind. : Ave Maria Press, c1977. 223 p. : ill. ; 24 cm. Bibliography: p. 222-223. [BT207.F56] 77-72283 ISBN 0-87793-130-5 pbk. : 3.50
1. Jesus Christ—Person and offices—Study. 2. Jesus Christ, in fiction, drama, poetry, etc. I. Pennock, Michael, joint author. II. Title.

FISHER, Fred L. 232
Jesus and His teachings; who Jesus is and what He taught as seen through a careful study of the nature, trustworthiness and content of the Synoptic Gospels [by] Fred L. Fisher. Nashville, Broadman Press [1972] 157 p. 22 cm. Includes bibliographical references. [BT202.F58] 74-189502 ISBN 0-8054-1333-2 4.95
1. Jesus Christ—Person and offices. 2. Jesus Christ—Teachings. 3. Bible. N.T. Gospels—Criticism, interpretation, etc. I. Title.

FITZPATRICK, James K. 232
Jesus Christ, before he became a superstar / James K. Fitzpatrick. New Rochelle, N.Y. : Arlington House, c1976. 208 p. ; 23 cm. Includes index. [BT202.F59] 76-8829 ISBN 0-87000-361-5 : 7.95
1. Jesus Christ—Person and offices. 2. Apologetics—20th century. I. Title.

FORD, Douglas William 232
Cleverley.
Why men believe in Jesus Christ. London, Lutterworth Press [1950; label: Chicago, A. R. Allenson] 92p. 19cm. [BR121.F6518] 53-33158
1. Christianity—Essence, genius, nature. I. Title.

FORSYTH, Peter Taylor, 1848- 232
1921.
The person and place of Jesus Christ. London, Independent Press, [label: Chicago, A. R. Allenson, 1951] 357p. 21cm. [BT201.F735] 53-32885
1. Jesus Christ— Person and offices. I. Title.

FORSYTH PETER TAYLOR, 1848- 232
1921
The person and place of Jesus Christ. Grand Rapids, Mich., Eerdmans [1965] 357p. 20cm. [BT201.F735] 2.25 pap.,
1. Jesus Christ—Person and offices. I. Title.

FRANCE, R. T. 232
Jesus and the Old Testament; His application of Old Testament passages to Himself and His mission, by R. T. France. [1st ed. Downers Grove, Ill.] Inter-Varsity Press [1971] 286 p. 23 cm. Revision of the author's thesis, University of Bristol, 1966. Includes bibliographical references. [BT590.O4F7 1971] 78-183849 ISBN 0-87784-954-4 9.95
1. Jesus Christ—Attitude towards the Old Testament. I. Title.

FRANKS, Robert Sleightholme, 232
1871-
The work of Christ; a historical study of Christian doctrine. New York, Nelson [c.1962] 708p. 23cm. (Nelson's lib. of theology) First pub. in 1918 under title: A history of the doctrine of the work of Christ. 62-52924 6.50
1. Jesus Christ—History of doctrines. 2. Redemption—History of doctrines. 3. Theology, Doctrinal—Hist. I. Title.

FREI, Hans W. 232
The identity of Jesus Christ : the hermeneutical bases of dogmatic theology / by Hans W. Frei. Philadelphia : Fortress Press, [1975] xviii, 173 p. ; 24 cm. "First published as 'The mystery of the presence of Jesus Christ' in Crossroads, January, February, March 1967." [BT202.F7 1975] 74-80422 ISBN 0-8006-0292-7 : 8.95
1. Jesus Christ—Person and offices. 2. Identification (Religion) I. Title.

FRUCHTENBAUM, Arnold G. 232
Jesus was a Jew / Arnold Fruchtenbaum. Nashville : Broadman Press, [1974] 156 p. ; 18 cm. Includes bibliographical references. [BT202.F76] 74-75676 ISBN 0-8054-6209-0 pbk. : 2.95
1. Jesus Christ—Person and offices. 2. Jesus Christ—Jewish interpretations. I. Title.

FULLER, Reginald Horace. 232
The foundations of New Testament Christology, by Reginald H. Fuller. New York, Scribner [1965] 268 p. 22 cm. Includes bibliographical references. [BT198.F9] 65-27240
1. Jesus Christ — History of doctrines — Early church. I. Title.

FULLER, Reginald Horace 232
The foundations of New Testament Christology. New York, Scribners [c. 1965] 268p. 22cm. bBibl. [BT198.F9] 65-27240 5.95
1. Jesus Christ—History of doctrines—Early church. I. Title.

FULLER, Reginald Horace. 232
The mission and achievement of Jesus; an examination of the presuppositions of New Testament theology. Chicago, A. R. Allenson [1954] 128p. 22cm. (Studies in Biblical theology, no. 12) [BT201.F79] 55-1548
1. Jesus Christ—Person and offices. I. Title.

GARIEPY, Henry. 232
Portraits of Christ; devotional studies of the names of Jesus. Old Tappan, N.J., Revell [1974] 128 p. 21 cm. [BT590.N2G28] 73-15903 ISBN 0-8007-0644-7 3.95
1. Jesus Christ—Name—Meditations. I. Title.

GARRIGOU-LAGRANGE, Reginald, 232
Father, 1877-
Christ the Savior; a commentary on the third part of St. Thomas Theological summa. Translated by Dom Bede Rose. St. Louis, Herder, 1950. iv, 748 p. 25 cm. Bibliographical footnotes. [BT201.G464] 50-4482
1. Thomas Aquinas, Saint, 1225?-1274. Summa theologica. 2. Jesus Christ—Person and offices. I. Title.

GARRIGOU-LAGRANGE, Reginald, 232
Father, 1877-
our Savior and His love for us; translated by A. Bouchard. St. Louis, Herder, 1951. 398 p. 25 cm. [BT201.G473] 51-7708
1. Jesus Christ—Person and offices. I. Title.

GARTENHAUS, Jacob, 1896- 232
The "Christ-killers" : past and present / by Jacob Gartenhaus. [Chattanooga, Tenn.] : Hebrew Christian Press, c1975. xii, 122 p. ; 24 cm. [BT431.5.G37] 74-20121
1. Jesus Christ—Passion—Role of Jews. 2. Christianity and other religions—Judaism. 3. Judaism—Relations—Christianity. I. Title.

*GILLESE, John Patrick 232
About Advent; essays for Advent. Pulaski, Wis., Franciscan Pubs. [1966] 55p. 19cm. .25 pap.,
I. Title.

GOGARTEN, Friedrich, 1887- 232
1968.
Christ the crisis. [Translated by R. A. Wilson from the German] Richmond, John Knox Press [1970] vi, 308 p. 23 cm. Translation of Jesus Christus, Wende der Welt. [BT202.G5813] 79-107320 ISBN 0-8042-0490-X 7.95
1. Jesus Christ—Person and offices. I. Title.

GOLDSTEIN, Morris. 232
Jesus in the Jewish tradition. New York, Macmillan, 1950. ix, 319 p. 21 cm. "Expansion of a thesis, The record concerning Jesus in rabbinic Judaism, written as a partial requirement for the degree of doctor of Hebrew letters received at the Hebrew Union College of Cincinnati." Bibliography: p. [243]-265. [BM620.G63] 50-10439
1. Jesus Christ—Jewish interpretations. I. Title.

GOODMAN, George 232
Seventy lessons in teaching and preaching Christ. Grand Rapids, Mich., Kregel [1966] 402p. 19cm. 4.50
1. Jesus Christ—Persons and offices. I. Title.

GOULD, Alfred Ernest 232
Jesus, King most wonderful; studies in the sovereignty and saviourhood of Jesus Christ. London, Allen & Unwin [New York, Hillary House, c.1965] 208p. 21cm. Bibl. [BT202.G6] 66-2258 4.00 bds.,
1. Jesus Christ—Person and offices. I. Title.

GRASSO, Domenico, 1917- 232
The problem of Christ. Staten Island, N.Y., Alba House [1969] 288 p. 22 cm. Bibliographical footnotes. [BT202.G684] 76-94699
1. Jesus Christ—Person and offices. 2. Church. I. Title.

GREELEY, Andrew M., 1928- 232
The Jesus myth [by] Andrew M. Greeley. Garden City, N.Y., Doubleday, 1971. 215 p. 22 cm. Includes bibliographical references. [BT202.G687] 75-160882 5.95
1. Jesus Christ—Person and offices. I. Title.

GREELY, Andrew M., 1928- 232
The Jesus myth. Garden City, N.Y., Doubleday, 1973 [c.1971] 198 p. 18 cm. (Image bk., D316) Bibl. refs. [BT202.G687] 75-160882 ISBN 0-385-07865-X pap., 1.25
1. Jesus Christ—Person and offices. I. Title.

GREENE, Oliver B. 232
Our Saviour; the work of our Saviour: past, present, future, by Oliver B. Greene. Greenville, S.C., Gospel Hour [1969] 181 p. 21 cm. [BT202.G69] 77-229960 5.00
1. Jesus Christ—Person and offices. I. Title.

GRIFFIN, David, 1939- 232
A process Christology, by David R. Griffin. Philadelphia, Westminister Press [1973] 273 p. 21 cm. Includes bibliographical references. [BT205.G67] 73-10252 ISBN 0-664-20978-5 10.00
1. Jesus Christ. 2. Process theology. I. Title.

GRILLMEIER, Alois, 1910- 232
Christ in Christian tradition / Aloys Grillmeier ; translated by John Bowden. 2d rev. ed. Atlanta : John Knox Press, [1975- v. ; 24 cm. Includes indexes. Contents.Contents.—v. 1. From the apostolic age to Chalcedon (451) Bibliography: v. 1, p. [569]-579. [BT198.G743 1975] 75-13456 ISBN 0-8042-0492-6 : 22.00
1. Jesus Christ—History of doctrines—Early church, ca. 30-600. I. Title.

GROFF, Warren F. 232
Christ the hope of the future: signals of a promised humanity [by] Warren F. Groff. Grand Rapids, Eerdmans [1971] 145 p. 21 cm. Includes bibliographical references. [BT202.G696] 79-150637 2.45
1. Jesus Christ—Person and offices. 2. Hope. I. Title.

GUILLET, Jacques. 232
The consciousness of Jesus. Translated by Edmond Bonin. New York, Newman Press [1972] 216 p. 23 cm. Translation of Jesus devant sa vie et sa mort. Includes bibliographical references. [BT202.G8313] 72-81573 4.95
1. Jesus Christ—Person and offices. I. Title.

GUILLET, Jacques. 232
The religious experience of Jesus and His Disciples / by Jacques Guillet ; translated by Mary Innocentia Richards. St. Meinrad, Ind. : Abbey Press, 1975. viii, 75 p. ; 21 cm. (Religious experience series ; v. 9) "Translation of the article Jesus, which first appeared in the Dictionnaire de spiritualite, Paris, Beauchesne, 1973, vol. 8, cols. 1065-1109." Bibliography: p. 72-75. [BT303.G8613] 75-210 ISBN 0-87029-044-4 pbk. : 2.95
1. Jesus Christ—Spiritual life. 2. Experience (Religion) I. Title.

GUITTON, Jean. 232
Jesus; the eternal dilemma. [Translated by Donald M. Antoine] Staten Island, N.Y., Alba House [1968, c1967] 342 p. 22 cm. Bibliographical footnotes. [BT201.G933] 68-15384
1. Jesus Christ—Person and offices. I. Title.

GUTHRIE, Donald, 1916- 232
Jesus the Messiah; an illustrated life of Christ. Grand Rapids, Zondervan Pub. House [1972] 386 p. illus. 25 cm. [BT301.2.G86] 74-189588 6.95
1. Jesus Christ—Biography. I. Title.

HAHN, Ferdinand, 1926- 232
The titles of Jesus in Christology; their history in early Christianity. [English translation by Harold Knight and George Ogg] New York, World Pub. Co. [1969] 415 p. 23 cm. (Lutterworth library) Translation of Christologische Hoheitstitel; ihre Geschichte im fruhen Christentum. Based on thesis, Heidelberg, entitled Anfange christologischer Traditionen. Bibliographical footnotes. [BT590.N2H33] 70-77511
1. Jesus Christ—Name. I. Title.

HAMILTON, Neill Quinn. 232
Jesus for a no-God world, by Neill Q. Hamilton. Philadelphia, Westminster Press [1969] 203 p. 21 cm. Includes bibliographies. [BT202.H26] 70-75457 ISBN 6-642-08576-6.50
1. Jesus Christ—Person and offices. 2. Apologetics—20th century. I. Title.

HAROLD, Preston. 232
The Shining Stranger; an unorthodox interpretation of Jesus and His mission. Introd. by Gerald Heard. [New York] Wayfarer Press; distributed by Dodd, Mead, New York [1967] xvii, 443 p. front. 25 cm. Bibliography: p. 395-427. [BT202.H28] 67-20775

1. Jesus Christ—Person and offices. I. Title.

HAROLD, Preston. 232
The Shining Stranger; an unorthodox interpretation of Jesus and His mission. Introductions by Gerald Heard and Winifred Babcock. [3d ed.] [Winston-Salem, N.C., Harold Institute]; distributed by Dodd, Mead, New York [1973] xxxix, 471 p. 25 cm. Bibliography: p. 448-456. [BT202.H28 1973] 73-19480 ISBN 0-396-06931-2 8.50
1. Jesus Christ—Person and offices. I. Title.

HARRINGTON, Jeremy. 232
Jesus: superstar or savior? Edited by Jeremy Harrington. [Cincinnati, St. Anthony Messenger Press, 1972] 132 p. illus. 19 cm. Cover title. [BT202.H29] 72-188255 ISBN 0-912228-06-7 1.00
1. Jesus Christ—Person and offices. I. Title.

HAYES, John Haralson, 1934- 232
Son of God to Super star : twentieth-century interpretations of Jesus / John H. Hayes. Nashville : Abingdon Press, c1976. 255 p. ; 22 cm. Bibliography: p. 249-255. [BT198.H39] 75-30603 ISBN 0-687-39091-5 : 14.95 ISBN 0-687-39092-3
1. Jesus Christ—History of doctrines—20th century. I. Hayes, John Haralson, 1934- II. Title.

HEIM, Karl, 1874- 232
Jesus the Lord: the sovereign authority of Jesus and God's revelation in Christ. Translated [from the German] by D. H. van Daalen. Philadelphia, Muhlenberg Press [1961] x, 192p. Bibls. 61-5286 3.50 bds.,
1. Jesus Christ—Person and offices. I. Title.

HENGEL, Martin. 232
Christ and power / Martin Hengel ; translated by Everett R. Kalin. Philadelphia : Fortress Press, c1977. vii, 82 p. ; 22 cm. Translation of Christus und die Macht. Includes bibliographical references. [BT745.H4613] 76-62608 ISBN 0-8006-1256-6 pbk. : 3.25
1. Jesus Christ—Person and offices. 2. Power (Theology)—History of doctrines. I. Title.

HENGEL, Martin. 232
The Son of God : the origin of Christology and the history of Jewish-Hellenistic religion / Martin Hengel ; [translated by John Bowden from the German]. 1st American ed. Philadelphia : Fortress Press, 1976. xii, 100 p. ; 22 cm. Translation of Der Sohn Gottes. Includes bibliographical references and indexes. [BT198.H4613 1976] 75-37151 ISBN 0-8006-1227-2 pbk. : 3.75
1. Son of God—History of doctrines. 2. Jesus Christ—History of doctrines—Early church, ca. 30-600. I. Title.

HENGEL, Martin. 232
Was Jesus a revolutionist? Translated by William Klassen. Philadelphia, Fortress Press [1971] xviii, 46 p. (p. 45-46 advertisements) 19 cm. (Facet Books. Biblical series, 28) Translation of War Jesus Recolutionar? Includes bibliographical references. [BT202.H4313] 77-157545 ISBN 0-8006-3066-1 1.00
1. Jesus Christ—Person and offices. 2. Revolution (Theology) I. Title.

HENLEY, James Walton, Bp. 232
Jesus Christ is Lord. Nashville, Tidings [1961] 63p. 19cm. [BT270.H4] 61-18714
1. Jesus Christ—Royal office. I. Title.

HENRY, Carl Ferdinand Howard, 1913- ed. 232
Jesus of Nazareth, Saviour and Lord [by] Paul Althaus [and others] Edited by Carl F. H. Henry. Grand Rapids, Eerdmans [1966] viii, 277 p. 24 cm. (Contemporary evangelical thought) Bibliography: p. 265-271. [BT28.H396] 66-18727
1. Theology, Doctrinal—History—20th century. 2. Theology, Doctrinal—Addresses, essays, lectures. I. Title.

HENRY, Philip, 1631-1696. 232
Christ all in all; or, What Christ is made to believers. With a brief memoir of the author. Swengel, Pa., Reiner Publications, 1970. xi, 380 p. 20 cm. Reprint of the 1691 ed. [BT200.H45 1970] 70-261961 3.95
1. Jesus Christ—Person and offices—Sermons. 2. Church of England—Sermons. 3. Sermons, English. I. Title.

HEPPENSTALL, Edward. 232
Our high priest: Jesus Christ in the heavenly sanctuary. Washington, Review and Herald Pub. Association [1972] 254 p. 21 cm. [BT260.H46] 79-164937
1. Jesus Christ—Priesthood. I. Title.

HERIS, Ch V. 232
The mystery of Christ, our Head, Priest and King. Translated by Denis Fahey. Westminster, Md., Newman Press, 1950. 214 p. 23 cm. Bibliography: p. 213-214. [BT201.H4513] 50-12383
1. Jesus Christ—Person and offices. 2. Sacraments—Catholic Church. I. Title.

HERIS, Ch Vincent, 1885- 232
The mystery of Christ, our Head, Priest and King. Translated by Denis Fahey. Westminster, Md., Newman Press, 1950. 214p. 23cm. Bibliography: p. 213-214. [BT201.H4513] 50-12383
1. Jesus Christ—Person and offices. 2. Sacraments—Catholic Church. I. Title.

HEWLETT, Henry Charles. 232
The glories of Our Lord. Foreword by J. C. Tilyard. Chicago, Moody [1962] 128p. 22cm. 62-5535 2.50
1. Jesus Christ—Person and offices. I. Title.

HILL, Rowley. 232
52 sermon outlines on the titles of Our Lord. Grand Rapids, Baker Book House, 1958. 112p. 20cm. [Minister's handbook series] [BT590.N2H5] 58-8386
1. Jesus Christ—Name— Sermons— Outlines. I. Title.

HINSON, E. Genn. 232
Jesus Christ / E. Glenn Hinson. Wilmington, N.C. : Consortium Books, [1977] p. cm. (Faith of our fathers ; v. 1) [BT202.H53] 77-9548 ISBN 0-8434-0620-8 : 9.50
1. Jesus Christ—Person and offices. I. Title. II. Series.

HODGES, Isam B. 232
The eternal architect. New York, Vantage [c.1962] 217p. 21cm. 3.50 bds.,
I. Title.

HODGSON, Peter Crafts, 1934- 232
Jesus - word and presence; an essay in Christology [by] Peter C. Hodgson. Philadelphia, Fortress Press [1971] xiv, 304 p. 23 cm. Includes bibliographical references. [BT202.H57] 70-157538 ISBN 0-8006-0039-8 9.95
1. Jesus Christ—Person and offices. I. Title.

HOFMANS, Flor, 1925-1965. 232
Jesus; who is he? Translated by Mary Foran. Glen Rock, N.J., Newman Press [1968] vii, 342 p. 22 cm. Translation of Het licht van de wereld, v. 3 of the author's Inleiding tot de lezing van het Evangelie. Bibliographical footnotes. [BT202.H58313] 68-31260 6.95
1. Jesus Christ—Person and offices. I. Title.

HOLL, Adolf. 232
Jesus in bad company. Translated from the German by Simon King. New York, Holt, Rinehart and Winston [1973, c1972] 157 p. 22 cm. Translation of Jesus in schlechter Gesellschaft. Includes bibliographical references. [BT202.H5913 1973] 72-78146 ISBN 0-03-001386-0 5.95
1. Jesus Christ—Person and offices. I. Title.

HOLL, Adolf. 232
Jesus in bad company. Translated from the German by Simon King. New York, Avon [1974, c1973] 191 p. 18 cm. (A Discus book) Translation of Jesus in schlecter Gesellschaft Includes bibliographical references. [BT202.H5913 1974] 1.65 (pbk.)
1. Jesus Christ—Person and offices. I. Title.
L.C. card number for original ed.: 72-78146.

HOLMES, George. 232
He is Lord / George Holmes. Springfield, Mo. : Gospel Pub. House, c1977. 128 p. ; 18 cm. (Radiant books) "This book is adapted from Christ, by Frank M. Boyd." [BT202.H593] 77-365591 ISBN 0-88243-902-2 pbk. : 1.25
1. Jesus Christ—Person and offices. I. Boyd, Frank Mathews, 1883- Christ. II. Title.

*HOUSELANDER, Caryll. 232
The reed of God. Garden City, N. Y., Doubleday [1968, c.1944] 153p. 18cm. (Image bk., D245) .95 pap.,
I. Title.

HUFFMAN, Jasper Abraham, 1880- 232
The unique person of Christ. Winona Lake, Ind., Standard Press [1955] 149p. 20cm. [BT201.H83] 55-36987
1. Jesus Christ—Person and offices. I. Title.

HUGHES, Edward James, 1925- 232
The participation of the faithful in the regal and prophetic mission of Christ according to Saint Augustine. Mundelein, Ill., Saint Mary of the Lake Seminary, 1956. 97 p. 23 cm. (Pontificia Facultas Theologica Seminarii Sanctae Mariae ad Lacum. Dissertationes ad lauream, 26) Bibliography: p. 93-97. [BR65.A9H8] 64-36034
1. Augustinus, Aurelius, Saint, Bp. of Hippo—Theology. 2. Jesus Christ—Mystical body. 3. Laity—Catholic Church. I. Title. II. Series: Saint Mary of the Lake Seminary, Mundelein, Ill. Dissertations ad lauream, 26

HUNTER, Archibald Macbride. 232
The work and words of Jesus, by Archibald M. Hunter. Rev. ed. Philadelphia, Westminster Press [1973] 230 p. 22 cm. Includes bibliographical references. [BS2415.H77 1973] 73-7559 ISBN 0-664-24976-0 3.50 (pbk.)
1. Jesus Christ—Teaching. 2. Jesus Christ—Person and offices. I. Title.

INGALLS, Jeremy, 1911- 232
The Galilean way. [1st ed.] New York, Longmans, Green, 1953. 266 p. 22 cm. [BR121.I56] 53-9525
1. Christianity—Essence, genius, nature. I. Title.

ISAAC, Jules, 1877-1963. 232
Jesus and Israel. Edited, and with a foreword, by Claire Huchet Bishop. Translated by Sally Gran. [1st ed.] New York, Holt, Rinehart and Winston [1971] xxiv, 405 p. 24 cm. Translation of Jesus et Israel. Includes bibliographies. [BM620.I713] 69-10236 ISBN 0-03-072550-X 12.50
1. Jesus Christ—Jewish interpretation. 2. Christianity and antisemitism. I. Title.

JARVIS, Frank Washington, 1939- 232
Come and follow; an introduction to Christian discipleship [by] F. Washington Jarvis. New York, Seabury Press [1972] 252 p. 20 cm. [BT301.2.J37] 73-185519 ISBN 0-8164-2072-6 3.95
1. Jesus Christ—Biography. 2. Church history. 3. Sacraments. I. Title.

JENKINS, David E. 232
The glory of man [by] David Jenkins. New York, Scribners [1967] x, 117p. 22cm. (Bampton lects., 1966) [BT202.J38 1967] 67-21343 3.50; 1.95 pap.,
1. Jesus Christ— Person and offices—Addresses, essays, lectures. 2. Man (Theology)— Addresses, essays, lectures. I. Title. II. Series.

JEREMIAS, Joachim, 1900- 232
New Testament theology. New York, Scribner [1971- v. 24 cm. Translation of Neutestamentliche Theologie. Contents.Contents.—[1] The proclamation of Jesus. [BT202.J3913] 70-143936 ISBN 0-684-12363-0(v.1) 10.00 (v. 1)
1. Jesus Christ—Person and offices. I. Title.

JESUS; 232
dialogue with the Saviour, by a monk of the Eastern Church. Tr. [from French] by a monk of the Western Church. New York, Desclee, 1963. 185p. 21cm. 63-10194 3.50
1. Jesus Christ—Meditations. I. A monk of the Eastern Church.

JESUS and the historian. 232
Written in honor of Ernest Cadman Colwell. Edited by F. Thomas Trotter. Philadelphia, Westminster Press [1968] 176 p. 22 cm. Contents.—Ernest Cadman Colwell: an appreciation, by F. T. Trotter.—The Messianic concept in the first book of Samuel, by R. P. Knierim.—Jesus and Qumran, by W. H. Brownlee.—"Can this be the son of David?" by L. R. Fisher.—The Fourth Gospel and the historical Jesus, by E. L. Titus.—Jesus as divine man, by H. D. Betz.—Jesus' parables as God happening, by J. M. Robinson.—Bibliography of Ernest Cadman Colwell, by I. A. Sparks (p. [151]-173) Includes bibliographical references. [BS2395.J43] 68-19190 5.95
1. Colwell, Ernest Cadman, 1901- 2. Bible. N.T.—Addresses, essays, lectures. I. Trotter, Frederick Thomas, 1926- ed. II. Colwell, Ernest Cadman, 1901-

JESUS Christ and human 232
freedom / edited by Edward Schillebeeckx and Bas van Iersel. New York : Herder and Herder, 1974. 159 p. ; 23 cm. (Concilium ; new ser., v. 3, no. 10 (93), Dogma) On cover: The New concilium: religion in the seventies. Includes bibliographical references. [BT202.J426] 73-17908 ISBN 0-8164-2577-9 pbk. : 3.95
1. Jesus Christ—Person and offices. 2. Freedom (Theology) 3. Liberation theology. I. Schillebeeckx, Edward Cornelis Florentius Alfons, 1914- ed. II. Iersel, Bastiaan Martinius Franciscus van, ed. III. Series: Concilium (New York) ; 93.

JOHNSON, Elbert Neil. 232
The Master is here; Jesus' presence in fact and experience. [1st ed.] New York, American Press [1955] 141p. 22cm. [BT205.J6] 55-7998
1. Mystical union. I. Title.

JOHNSON, Lenore, comp. 232
Jesus is ... [1st ed.] New York, Harper & Row [1971] 60 p. illus. (part col.) 18 cm. "Words and drawings of children." Records children's answers to such questions as "Who is Jesus?" "What does Jesus book like?" and "Why was Jesus crucified?" [BT202.J64 1971] 76-150592 1.95
1. Jesus Christ—Person and offices—Juvenile literature. I. Title.

JOHNSON, Robert Clyde. 232
The meaning of Christ. Philadelphia, Westminster Press [1958] 96p. 20cm. (Layman's theological literary) Includes bibliography. [BT205.J64] 58-6120
1. Jesus Christ— Person and offices. I. Title.

JOHNSON, Woodbridge Odlin, 1900- 232
Other Christs; the coming Copernican Christology, by Woodbridge O. Johnson. [1st ed.] New York, Pageant Press International Corp. [1971] 221 p. 21 cm. Includes bibliographical references. [BT220.J58] 70-149065 ISBN 0-8181-0189-X
1. Jesus Christ—Person and offices. 2. Incarnation. 3. Salvation. I. Title.

JONGE, Marinus de, 1925- 232
Jesus: inspiring and disturbing presence. Translated by John E. Steely. Nashville, Abingdon Press [1974] 176 p. 20 cm. Translation of Jezus, inspirator en spelbreker. Includes bibliographical references. [BT202.J6513] 74-10915 ISBN 0-687-19919-0 10.95
1. Jesus Christ—Person and offices—Addresses, essays, lectures. I. Title.
Pbk., 4.95, ISBN 0-687-19920-4.

JURGENSMEIER, Friedrich, 1888-1946. 232
The mystical body of Christ as the basic principle of spiritual life; translated by Harriet G. Strauss. New York, Sheed and Ward, 1954 [i. e. 1955] 379p. 22cm. [BX1751.J82 1955] 55-5674
1. Jesus Christ—Mystical body. 2. Asceticism— Catholic Church. I. Title.

KAPPEN, Sebastian. 232
Jesus and freedom / Sebastian Kappen. Maryknoll, N.Y. : Orbis Books, c1977. viii, 178 p. ; 22 cm. Bibliography: p. 177-178. [BT202.K27] 76-25927 ISBN 0-88344-700-2 : 8.95 ISBN 0-88344-233-7 pbk. : 3.95
1. Jesus Christ—Person and offices. 2. Freedom (Theology) 3. Liberation theology. I. Title.

KAPPEN, Sebastian. 232
Jesus and freedom / Sebastian Kappen. Maryknoll, N.Y. : Orbis Books, c1977. viii, 178 p. ; 22 cm. Bibliography: p. 177-178. [BT202.K27] 76-25927 ISBN 0-88344-700-2 : 8.95 ISBN 0-88344-233-7 pbk. : 3.95
1. Jesus Christ—Person and offices. 2. Freedom (Theology) 3. Liberation theology. I. Title.

KASPER, Walter. 232
Jesus the Christ / Walter Kasper ; [translation by V. Green]. London : Burns & Oates ; New York : Paulist Press, 1976. 289 p. ; 23 cm. Translation of Jesus der Christus. Includes bibliographical references and indexes. [BT202.K313 1976] 76-20021 ISBN 0-8091-0211-0 : 12.95
1. Jesus Christ—Person and offices. I. Title.

KEPLER, Thomas Samuel, 1897- comp. 232
Contemporary thinking about Jesus; an anthology. Compiled by Thomas S. Kepler. New York, Greenwood Press [1969, c1944] 429 p. 23 cm. Bibliography: p. 409-411. [BT199.K4 1969] 78-97314 ISBN 0-8371-2553-7
1. Jesus Christ—Person and offices—Addresses, essays, lectures. 2. Bible. N.T. Gospels—Criticism, interpretations, etc.—Addresses, essays, lectures. I. Title.

KEPLER, Thomas Samuel, 1897- 232
Jesus' spiritual journey--and ours. [1st ed.] Cleveland, World Pub. Co. [1952] 157 p. 21 cm. [BT301.K473] 52-5185
1. Jesus Christ—Biog.—Devotional literature. I. Title.

KIMBALL, Warren Young 232
These are God's sons. Dedham, Mass., 302 Mt. Vernon St., Author, c.1959. 133p. 22cm. 3.50
I. Title.

KING, Alta, 01887-1957. 232
Scripture studies. [1st ed.] New York, Greenwich Book Publishers, 1957. 63p. 21cm. [BT205.K45] 57-11992
1. Jesus Christ—Person and offices. I. Title.

KNOX, John, 1900- 232
Jesus: Lord and Christ; a trilogy comprising: The man Christ Jesus. Christ the Lord, On the meaning of Christ. New York, Harper [1958] 278p. 21cm. [BT201.K57] 58-10367
1. Jesus Christ—Person and offices. I. Title.

KNUTSON, Kent S. 232
His only Son our Lord; ideas about the Christ [by] Kent S. Knutson. Minneapolis, Augsburg Pub. House [1966] viii, 113 p. 20 cm. (A Tower book) Bibliography: p. 113. [BT202.K5] 66-13051
1. Jesus Christ. I. Title.

KNUTSON, Kent S. 232
His only Son our Lord: ideas about the Christ. Minneapolis, Augsburg [c.1966] viii, 113p. 20cm. (Tower bk.) Bibl. [BT202.K5] 66-13051 1.50 pap.,
1. Jesus Christ. I. Title.

KOSSOFF, David, 1919- 232
The book of witnesses. Boston, G. K. Hall, 1972 [c1971] 295 p. 25 cm. Large print ed. [BT301.2.K67 1972] 72-5099 ISBN 0-8161-6041-4 7.95
1. Jesus Christ—Biography. I. Title.

KOYAMA, Kosuke, 1929- 232
No handle on the cross : an Asian meditation on the crucified mind / Kosuke Koyama. Maryknoll, N.Y. : Orbis Books, 1977, c1976. 119 p. ; 22 cm. Includes bibliographical references. [BT202.K65] 76-23160 ISBN 0-88344-338-4 : 7.95 ISBN 0-88344-339-2 pbk. : 3.95
1. Jesus Christ—Person and offices—Addresses, essays, lectures. 2. Christianity—Essence, genius, nature—Addresses, essays, lectures. 3. Christian life—1960- —Addresses, essays, lectures. I. Title.

LANE, Dermot A., 1941- 232
The reality of Jesus : an essay in Christology / Dermot A. Lane. New York : Paulist Press, 1977c1975 180 p. ; 21 cm. (An Exploration book) Includes index. Bibliography: p. 176-177. [BT202.L329 1975b] 77-70635 ISBN 0-8091-2020-8 pbk. : 3.95
1. Jesus Christ—Person and offices. I. Title.

LARSEN, Earnest. 232
Jesus Christ, the gate of power / Earnest Larsen. Canfield, Ohio : Alba Books, 1977,c1976 127 p. : ill. ; 18 cm. [BT202.L36] 76-21589 ISBN 0-8189-1136-0 pbk. : 1.75
1. Jesus Christ—Person and offices. 2. Christian life—Catholic authors. I. Title.

LA TAILLE, Maurice de, 1872-1933. 232
The hypostatic union and created actuation by uncreated act. West Baden Springs, Ind., West Baden College [c1952] 76p. 22cm. (West Baden College. Readings in philosophy and theology) Contains The schoolmen, from The incarnation, edited by C. Lattey, and translations by Cyril Vollert of Actuation creee par Acte incree, and Entretien amical d'Eudoxe et de Palamede sur ea grace d'union. [BT205.L28] 54-2141
1. Jesus Christ—Person and offices. I. Title.

LATIMER-NEEDHAM, Cecil Hugh, 1900-1975. 232
Juggling with Jesus : and His two-thousand-year legacy to mankind / Hugh Latymer de Nedham. 1st ed. Hicksville, N.Y. : Exposition Press, c1977. x, 285 p. ; 22 cm. (An Exposition-university book) Includes bibliographical references. [BT304.95.L37 1977] 76-44900 ISBN 0-682-48651-5 : 10.00
1. Jesus Christ—Rationalistic interpretations. 2. Christianity—Controversial literature. I. Title.

LATOURELLE, Rene, 1918- 232
Christ and the church; signs of salvation. Translated by Sr. Dominic Parker. Staten Island, N.Y., Alba House [1972] viii, 324 p. 22 cm. Translation of Le Christ et l'eglise, signes du salut. Includes bibliographical references. [BT202.L3713] 73-39673 ISBN 0-8189-0241-8 9.50
1. Jesus Christ—Person and offices. 2. Vatican Council. 2d, 1962-1965. 3. Revelation. 4. Church. I. Title.

LEGAUT, Marcel. 232
Meditations of a believer. [1st American ed. Translated by Siegwalt O. Palleske and Suzanne Palleeke] New York, Knopf, 1955 [c1954] 277p. 22cm. [BT309.L453] 54-8758
1. Jesus Christ—Meditations. 2. Christian life. I. Title.

LEHMANN, Johannes, 1929- 232
Rabbi J. Translated by Michael Heron. New York, Stein and Day [1971] 176 p. 25 cm. Translation of Jesus-Report: Protokoll einer Verfalschung. Bibliography: p. 173-176. [BT202.L4313] 70-163348 ISBN 0-8128-1399-5 5.95
1. Jesus Christ—Person and offices. 2. Dead Sea scrolls. I. Title.

LESSING, Erich. 232
Jesus; history and culture of the New Testament, a pictorial narration. [Translated by Stella Musulin, Robert Mahoney, and Angela Zerbe. New York, Herder and Herder, 1971] 292 p. (chiefly col. illus.) 31 cm. Translation of Der Mann aus Galilaa. Includes bibliographical references. [BT301.2.L3713] 76-147032 37.50
1. Jesus Christ—Biography. 2. Jesus Christ—Person and offices. 3. Bible. N.T.—History of contemporary events, etc. 4. Christian art and symbolism. I. Title.

LESSING, Erich. 232
Jesus, Son of God : encounter and confession of faith / by Eugen Weiler and Wolfgang Stadler ; photos. by Erich Lessing ; translated by Matthew J. O'Connell. Chicago : Franciscan Herald Press, 1975. 149 p. : ill. ; 25 cm. Translation of Jesus Gottessohn. [BT202.L45613] 75-8785 ISBN 0-8199-0562-3
1. Jesus Christ—Person and offices. 2. Christian life—1960- I. Weiler, Eugen. II. Stadler, Wolfgang, 1924- III. Title.

LICKEY, Arthur E. 232
Christ forever. Washington, Review and Herald Pub. Association [1951] 122 p. illus. 16 cm. (Little giant pocket series) [BT295.L65] 51-2120
1. Jesus Christ—Devotional literature. I. Title.

LOWE, Marmion L 232
Christ in all the Scriptures. New York, [1954] 130p. illus. 21cm. [BT201.L77] 54-3426
1. Jesus Christ—Person and offices. I. Title.

LUTHER, Martin, 1483-1546. 232
Meditations on the Gospels. Tr., arr. by Roland H. Bainton. Illus. with woodcuts by Virgil Solis. Philadelphia, Westminster [1962] 155p. 24cm. Bibl. 62-7324 3.75
1. Jesus Christ—Biog.—Meditations. I. Bainton, Roland Herbert, 1894- ed. and tr. II. Title.

MCCOLLISTER, John 232
Portraits of the Christ; messages for Lent and Easter. Edited by John C. McCollister. Minneapolis, Augsburg Pub. House [1974] 95 p. illus. 20 cm. [BV4277.M265] 73-88600 ISBN 0-8066-1404-8 2.95
1. Lutheran Church—Sermons. 2. Lenten sermons. 3. Sermons, American. I. Title.

MCDOWELL, Josh. 232
More than a carpenter / Josh McDowell. Wheaton, Ill. : Tyndale House Publishers, 1977. 128 p. ; 18 cm. Includes bibliographical references. [BT202.M27] 76-58135 ISBN 0-8423-4550-7 pbk. : 1.95
1. Jesus Christ—Person and offices. I. Title.

MCINTYRE, John, 1916- 232
The shape of christology. Philadelphia, Westminster [c.1966] 180p. 23cm. Bibl. [BT202.M3] 66-17607 4.50
1. Jesus Christ. I. Title.

MCLEMAN, James. 232
Jesus in our time. Philadelphia, Lippincott [1967] 158 p. 21 cm. [BT303.2.M34] 67-27172
1. Jesus Christ—Historicity. 2. Jesus Christ—Biography—History and criticism. I. Title.

MANSON, Thomas Walter, 1893- 232
Ministry and priesthood: Christ's and ours; two lectures. Richmond, John Knox Press [1958?] 76p. 19cm. Includes bibliography. [BT260.M3 1958] 59-5098
1. Jesus Christ— Priesthood. 2. Priesthood, Universal. I. Title.

MARGERIE, Bertrand de. 232
Christ for the world, the heart of the lamb; a treatise on christology. Translated by Malachy Carroll. Chicago, Franciscan Herald Press [1974, c1973] xxx, 528 p. 22 cm. (IIHJ publication no. 1) Translation of Le Christ pour le monde, which was originally published under title: Cristo para o mundo. Bibliography: p. 513-516. [BT202.M3313 1974] 74-1001 ISBN 0-8199-0460-0 6.95; 3.95 (pbk)
1. Jesus Christ—Person and offices. 2. Jesus Christ—History of doctrines. I. Title. II. Series: International Institute of the Heart of Jesus. IIHJ publication no. 1.

MARSHALL, I. Howard. 232
The origins of New Testament christology / I. Howard Marshall. 1st ed. Downers Grove, Ill. : InterVarsity Press, 1976. 132 p. ; 21 cm. (Issues in contemporary theology) Includes bibliographical references and index. [BT198.M39] 76-21456 ISBN 0-87784-718-5 : 2.95
1. Jesus Christ—History of doctrines—Early church, ca. 30-600. 2. Jesus Christ—History of doctrines—20th century. I. Title. II. Series.

MARSHALL, I. Howard. 232
The work of Christ [by] I. Howard Marshall. Grand Rapids, Zondervan [1970, c1969] 128 p. 21 cm. (Contemporary evangelical perspectives) Bibliography: p. [122] [BT202.M36 1970] 70-106424
1. Jesus Christ—Person and offices. I. Title.

MARTIN, Malachi. 232
Jesus now. [1st ed.] New York, Dutton, 1973. xvii, 317 p. 22 cm. [BT202.M37 1973] 73-8272 ISBN 0-525-13675-4 7.95
1. Jesus Christ—Person and offices. 2. Civilization, Modern—1950- I. Title.

MARXSEN, Willi, 1919- 232
The beginnings of Christology: a study in its problems. Translated by Paul J. Achtemeier. Philadelphia, Fortress Press [1969] xii, 81 p. 20 cm. (Facet books. Biblical series, 22) Translation of Anfangsprobleme der Christologie. Includes bibliographical references. [BT198.M3963] 69-12995 0.85
1. Jesus Christ—History of doctrines—Early church, ca. 30-600. I. Title.

MATTHEWS, Walter Robert, 1881- 232
The problem of Christ in the twentieth century; an essay on the incarnation. London, New York, Oxford University Press, 1950. vii, 88 p. 19 cm. (The Maurice lectures, 1949) [BT201.M33] 51-9230
1. Jesus Christ—Person and offices. I. Title. II. Series: The Frederick Denison Maurice lectures, 1949

MAY, William E., 1928- 232
Christ in contemporary thought [by] William E. May. Dayton, Ohio, Pflaum, 1970. xi, 148 p. 21 cm. (Themes for today) Errata slip inserted. Bibliography: p. 123-127. [BT198.M398] 79-133404
1. Jesus Christ—History of doctrines—20th century. I. Title.

MEILACH, Michael D. 232
Firstborn Son. Chicago, Franciscan Herald [1963] 91p. 18cm. 62-15825 .95 pap.,
1. Jesus Christ—Person and offices. 2. Creation. I. Title.

MEILACH, Michael D. 232
From order to omega [by] Michael D. Meilach. Chicago, Franciscan Herald [1967] 158p. 18cm. First pub. in 1964 under title: The primacy of Christ in doctrine and life. Bibl. [BT250.M4 1967] 67-16083 1.95 pap.,
1. Jesus Christ— Person and offices. 2. Jesus Christ—Primacy. I. Title.

MEILACH, Michael D 232
The primacy of Christ in doctrine and life, by Michael D. Meilach. Chicago, Franciscan Herald Press [1964] xii, 217 p. 21 cm. Bibliographical references included in "Notes" (p. 197-211) Bibliography: p. 213-217. [BT250.M4] 64-24283
1. Jesus Christ — Person and offices. I. Title.

MEILACH, Michael D. 232
The primacy of Christ in doctrine and life. Chicago, Franciscan Herald [c.1964] xii, 217p. 21cm. Bibl. [BT250.M4] 64-24283 4.95
1. Jesus Christ—Person and offices. I. Title.

MELTON, David. 232
This man—Jesus. Written and illustrated by David Melton. New York, McGraw-Hill [1972] 57 p. illus. 28 cm. Presents the adulthood of Jesus from His baptism by John to His Resurrection. [BT302.M43] 72-7240 ISBN 0-07-041442-4 3.95
1. Jesus Christ—Biography—Juvenile literature. I. Title.

MERSCH, Emile, 1890-1940. 232
The theology of the mystical body; translated by Cyril Vollert. St. Louis, Herder, 1951. 663 p. 24 cm. [BX1751.M516] 51-7383
1. Theology, Doctrinal. 2. Catholic Church — Doctrinal and controversial works. 3. Jesus Christ — Mystical body. I. Title.

MEYENDORFF, Jean, 1926- 232
Christ in Eastern Christian thought [by] John Meyendorff. Washington, Corpus Books [1969] ix, 218 p. 21 cm. Translation of Le Christ dans la theologie byzantine. Includes bibliographical references. [BT198.M4313] 78-76472
1. Jesus Christ—History of doctrines. 2. Theology, Eastern Church. I. Title.

MEYENDORFF, Jean, 1926- 232
Christ in Eastern Christian thought / John Meyendorff. [2d ed.] Crestwood, N.Y. : St. Vladimir's Seminary Press, 1975. p. cm. Translation of Le Christ dans la theologie byzantine. Includes bibliographical references and index. [BT198.M4313 1975] 75-31979 ISBN 0-913836-27-3 : 5.95
1. Jesus Christ—History of doctrines. 2. Theology, Eastern Church. I. Title.

MOLTMANN, Jurgen. 232
The crucified God : the cross of Christ as the foundation and criticism of Christian theology / Jurgen Moltmann ; [translated by R. A. Wilson and John Bowden from the German]. 1st U.S. ed. New York : Harper & Row, c1974. 346 p. ; 22 cm. Translation of Der gekreuzigte Gott. Includes bibliographical references and index. [BT202.M5513 1974b] 73-18703 ISBN 0-06-065901-7 : 10.00
1. Jesus Christ—Person and offices. 2. Jesus Christ—Crucifixion. I. Title.

A MONK OF THE EASTERN CHURCH. 232
Jesus; dialogue with the Saviour, by a monk of the Eastern Church. Translated by a monk of the Western Church. New York, Desclee Co., 1963. 185 p. 21 cm. Translation of Jesus, simples regards sur le Sauveur. [BT268.J413] 63-10194
1. Jesus Christ — Meditations. I. Title.

MOONEY, Christopher F., 1925- 232
Teilhard de Chardin and the mystery of Christ. Garden City, N. Y., Doubleday [1968, c.1964] 318p. 18cm. (Image bk. D252) Bibl. [B2430.T374M63] 66-15050 1.35 pap.,
1. Teilhard de Chardin, Pierre. I. Title.

MOONEY, Christopher F 1925- 232
Teilhard de Chardin and the mystery of Christ [by] Christopher F. Mooney. [1st ed.] New York, Harper & Row [1966] 287 p. port. 22 cm. Bibliography: p. 264-277. [B2430.T374M63] 66-15050
1. Teilhard de Chardin, Pierre. I. Title.

MOONEY, Christopher F. 1925- 232
Teilhard de Chardin and the mystery of Christ. New York, Harper [c. 1964-1966] 287p. port. 22cm. Bibl. [B2430.T374M63] 66-15050 6.00
1. Teilhard de Chardin, Pierre. I. Title.

MORE, Paul Elmer, 1846-1937. 232
Christ the Word. New York, Greenwood Press [1969, c1927] vii, 343 p. 23 cm. Bibliographical footnotes. [BT201.M67 1969] 72-88913 ISBN 0-8371-2244-9
1. Jesus Christ—Person and offices. 2. Theology, Doctrinal—History—Early church, ca. 30-600. I. Title.

MORRISON, John A. 1893-1964 232
The person of Jesus Christ. Atlanta, Salvation Army [1966] 64p. 20cm. Bibl. [BT202.M6] 66-17945 2.00
1. Jesus Christ—Person and offices. I. Title.

MORSE, Sidney Levi. 1874- 232
The siege of University City, the Dreyfus case of America, by Sidney Morse ... University City, Saint Louis, Mo., University City publishing company, 1912. xii, 21-772p. incl. front., plates, ports., plans, facsims. 24cm. [PN4899.S27U62] 12-16373
1. Lewis, Edward Gardner, 1869- 2. University City, Mo.—Hist. 3. Postal service—U. S. I. Title.

MORTON, Thomas Ralph. 232
Jesus; man for today [by] T. Ralph Morton. Nashville, Abingdon Press [1970] 168 p. 21 cm. [BT202.M63] 76-109682 ISBN 0-687-20116-0 3.95
1. Jesus Christ—Person and offices. I. Title.

MORTON, Thomas Ralph. 232
Knowing Jesus, by T. Ralph Morton. Philadelphia, Westminster Press [1974] 153 p. 19 cm. Includes bibliographical references. [BT205.M67] 73-16342 ISBN 0-664-24982-5 2.95 (pbk)
1. Jesus Christ—Knowableness. I. Title.

MURPHY, John L 1924- 232
The living Christ. Milwaukee, Bruce Pub. Co. [1952] 228 p. 22 cm. [BT205.M8] 52-1835
1. Jesus Christ — Mystical body. I. Title.

MURPHY, John L 1924- 232
The living Christ. [2d ed.] Milwaukee, Bruce Pub. Co. [1956] 232p. 23cm. [BT205.M8 1956] 56-3535
1. Jesus Christ—Mystical body. I. Title.

*MURRAY, Andrew 232
Jesus Christ: prophet priest. Minneapolis, Bethany [1967] 63p. 19cm. 1.00 pap.,
I. Title.

*MURRAY, Andrew. 232
Jesus Christ—prophet, priest. Minneapolis, Minn., Bethany Fellowship [1973, c.1967] 63 p. 18 cm. (Dimension Books) [BT202] ISBN 0-87123-271-5 pap., 0.75
1. Jesus Christ—Sermons. I. Title.

NEILL, Stephen Charles, Bp. 232
What we know about Jesus [by] Stephen Neill. [1st American ed.] Grand Rapids, Mich., Eerdmans [1972] 84 p. 18 cm. [BT202.N45 1972] 72-75569 ISBN 0-8028-1473-5 1.25
1. Jesus Christ—Person and offices. I. Title.

NILES, Daniel Thambyrajah. 232
Who is this Jesus? [By] D. T. Niles. Nashville, Abingdon Press [1968] 156 p. 21 cm. [BT202.N54] 68-11478
1. Jesus Christ—Person and offices. I. Title.

NOLAN, Albert, 1934- 232
Jesus before Christianity : the gospel of liberation / Albert Nolan. Cape Town : D. Philip, 1976. vii, 159 p. ; 22 cm. Includes index. Bibliography: p. 153-155. [BT202.N64] 76-371272 ISBN 0-949968-60-9. ISBN 0-949968-59-5 pbk.
1. Jesus Christ—Person and offices. I. Title.

OAKMAN, Arthur A. 232
Belief in Christ. Independence, Mo., Herald [1964] 187p. 21cm. Bibl. 64-18778 2.75
1. Jesus Christ—Person and offices. 2. Reorganized Church of Jesus Christ of Latter-Day Saints—Doctrinal and controversial works. I. Title.

OATES, Wayne Edward, 1917- 232
Christ and selfhood. New York, Association [c.1961] 252p. Bibl. 61-14167 4.50 bds.,
1. Jesus Christ—Psychology. 2. Self. 3. Psychology, Religious. I. Title.

OCHS, William Benjamin 232
The Christ-centered life. Mountain View, Calif., Pacific Press Pub. Association [c.1961] 138p. 61-10879 2.50
1. Jesus Christ—Person and offices. I. Title.

O'COLLINS, Gerald. 232
What are they saying about Jesus? / By Gerald O'Collins. New York : Paulist Press, c1977. x, 77 p. ; 18 cm. (A Deus book) Chapters 1-4 reprinted from the Way, v. 16, no. 4, Oct. 1976 and v. 17, no. 1, Jan. 1977 under the titles: Jesus in current theology I and II, respectively. Includes bibliographical references. [BT198.O27] 77-70640 ISBN 0-8091-2017-8 pbk. : 1.75
1. Jesus Christ—History of doctrines—20th century. I. Title.

O'DONOVAN, Leo J., comp. 232
Word and mystery; biblical essays on the person and mission of Christ, edited by Leo J. O'Donovan. Glen Rock, N.J., Newman Press [1968] xiv, 289 p. 21 cm. Bibliographical footnotes. [BT198.O3] 68-31047 3.50
1. Jesus Christ--History of doctrines—Early church. 2. Jesus Christ—Person and offices. 3. Bible. N.T.—Theology. I. Title.

O'GRADY, John F. 232
Jesus, Lord and Christ, by John F. O'Grady. New York, Paulist Press [1973] 152 p. 21 cm. Bibliography: p. 137-148. [BT198.O37] 72-94395 ISBN 0-8091-1765-7 3.95
1. Jesus Christ—History of doctrines—Early church. I. Title.

OLSON, Olaf J. 232
The testimony of Jesus. New York, Carlton [c.1963] 113p. 21cm. (Reflection bk.) 3.00
I. Title.

OXFORD Institute on Methodist Theological Studies. 3d, 1965. 232
The funality of Christ; [papers] Dow Kirkpatrick, ed. Prepd. under the direction of the World Methodist Council. Nashville, Abingdon [1966] 207p. 21cm. Bibl. [BT202.O9 1965] 66-21190 4.15
1. Jesus Christ—Primacy. I. Kirkpatrick, Dow, ed. II. World Methodist Council. III. Title.

PANNENBERG, Wolfhart, 1928- 232
Jesus, God and man. Translated by Lewis L. Wilkins and Duane A. Priebe. Philadelphia, Westminster Press [1968] 415 p. 24 cm. Translation of Grundzuge der Christologie. Bibliographical footnotes. [BT202.P313] 68-12983
1. Jesus Christ—Person and offices. I. Title.

PANNENBERG, Wolfhart, 1928- 232
Jesus, God and man / Wolfhart Pannenberg ; translated by Lewis L. Wilkins and Duane A. Priebe. 2d ed. Philadelphia : Westminster Press, c1977. 427 p. ; 24 cm. Translation of Grundzuge der Christologie. Includes bibliographical references and indexes. [BT202.P313 1977] 76-26478 ISBN 0-664-21289-1 : 12.50
1. Jesus Christ—Person and offices. I. Title.

PATERSON, John H. 232.
The greatness of Christ [by] John H. Paterson. Chicago, Inter-varsity Press [1969, c1962] 121 p. 21 cm. [BT202.P37] 68-54887
1. Jesus Christ—Primacy. I. Title.

PATERSON, John Harris 232
The greatness of Christ. Westwood, N.J., Revell [1963, c.1962] 121p. 21cm. 2.50 bds.,
I. Title.

PAULI, Hertha Ernestine, 1909- j 232
Little town of Bethlehem. Illustrated by Fritz Kredel. [1st ed.] New York, Duell, Sloan and Pearce [1963] 1 v. (unpaged) col. illus., music. 18 cm. Includes Christmas carols in close score. [BT315.2.P3] 63-16847
1. Jesus Christ—Nativity—Juvenile literature. I. Title.

PAULI, Hertha Ernestine, 1909- 232
Little town of Bethlehem. Illus. by Fritz Kredel. New York, Duell [dist. Meredith, c.1963] unpaged. col. illus., music. 18cm. 2.50
1. Jesus Christ—Nativity—Juvenile literature. I. Title.

PAULUS VI, Pope, 1897- 232
Who is Jesus? By Pope Paul VI. Compiled by Daughters of St. Paul. [Boston] St. Paul Editions [1972] 183 p. 18 cm. (Magister books) [BT202.P38] 72-80446 1.25
1. Jesus Christ—Person and offices. 2. Christian life—Catholic authors. I. Daughters of St. Paul. II. Title.

PETERSON, Edward C. 232
To find Jesus. Written by Edward C. Peterson and Barbara Nan Peterson. With illus. by Jim Padgett. Nashville, Abingdon Press [1967] 112 p. illus. (part col.) 26 cm. A biography of Jesus of Nazareth, consisting of what is conjectured scenes that may have occurred. [BT302.P45] AC 67
1. Jesus Christ—Biography. I. Peterson, Barbara Nan, joint author. II. Padgett, Jim, illus. III. Title.

[PETRELLI, Giuseppe] 232
Him--His: part one, Christ Jesus the Lord; part two, In His doctrine; part three, As in heaven; part four, Death and resurrection. [Syracuse? N. Y., 1954] 324p. 21cm. [BT205.P38] 54-11788
1. Jesus Christ—Person and offices. I. Title.

PIERCE, Earle Vaydor, 1869- 232
Ye are my witnesses; an exposition of what has been revealed through God-inspired men concerning the person and work of our Lord, and especially His relationship to humanity through His earthly body, the church. Philadelphia, Judson Press [1954] 272p. 21cm. [BT201.P5] 54-7986
1. Jesus Christ—Person and offices. 2. Church. I. Title.

PIKE, Diane Kennedy. 232
Cosmic unfoldment : the individualizing process as mirrored in the life of Jesus / by Diane Kennedy Pike. San Diego, Ca. : LP Publications, 1976. 99 p. ; 16 cm. [BT304.93.P54] 76-45344 ISBN 0-916192-08-3 pbk. : 3.00
1. Jesus Christ—Miscellanea. I. Title.

PIKE, Diane Kennedy. 232
The wilderness revolt; a new view of the life and death of Jesus based on ideas and notes of the late Bishop James A. Pike [by] Diane Kennedy Pike and R. Scott Kennedy. [1st ed.] Garden City, N.Y., Doubleday, 1972. xxxiii, 385 p. 22 cm. "Quotations from Bishop James A. Pike ... are excerpted and edited from transcripts of a seminar on Christian Origins given in May of 1969 for the Esalen Institute in San Francisco." Bibliography: p. [365]-375. [BT202.P53] 72-171311 7.95
1. Jesus Christ—Person and offices. 2. Qumran community. I. Kennedy, R. Scott, joint author. II. Pike, James Albert, Bp., 1913-1969. III. Title.

PITTENGER, William Norman, 1905- 232
The Word Incarnate; a study of the doctrine of the Person of Christ. [Welwyn, Herts] J. Nisbet [1959] 295p. 23cm. (The Library of constructive theology) Includes bibliography. [BT202.P56 1959] 59-51370
1. Jesus Christ—Person and offices. I. Title.

PITTENGER, William Norman, 1905- 232
The Word incarnate: a study of the doctrine of the person of Christ. New York, Harper [1959] 295 p. 22 cm. (The Library of constructive theology) Includes bibliography. [BT202.P56 1959a] 59-10347
1. Jesus Christ—Person and offices. I. Title.

POLING, Daniel Alfred, 1884- 232
Jesus says to you; His eternal wisdom and its meaning today. New York, McGraw-Hill [1961] 118p. 20cm. [BT306.P6] 60-53354
1. Jesus Christ—Words. I. Title.

*POTTER, Charles Francis 232
The lost years of Jesus revealed. Newly rev. 2d ed. Greenwich, Conn., Fawcett [1965, c.1958, 1962] 160p. 18cm. (Crest bk. d820) .50 pap.,
I. Title.

POTTER, Frederic James 232
Revelation of Jesus and his teachings; as revealed in the Scriptures. New York, Vantage [c.1961] 64p. 2.00 bds.,
I. Title.

†POTTER, Leo Goodwin, 1901- 232
My Bible is Jesus / by Leo Goodwin Potter. Saint Louis : Bethany Press, c1976. 128 p. ; 22 cm. [BT202.P615] 76-12539 ISBN 0-8272-2310-2 pbk. : 3.95
1. Jesus Christ—Person and offices. 2. Jesus Christ—Biography. 3. Christian life—1960- I. Title.

POWELL, John Joseph, 1925- 232
A stranger at your door. Milwaukee, Bruce Pub. Co. [1958] 119p. 23cm. [BX2182.2.P6] 58-13624
1. Jesus Christ—Devotional literature. I. Title.

PREISS, Theo. 232
Life in Christ. Translated by Harold Knight. Chicago, A. R. Allenson [1954] 104p. 22cm. (Studies in Biblical theology, no. 13) 'The English version of selected chapters from La vie en Christ.' [BS2393.P73 1954] 55-1608
1. Bible. N. T.— Addresses, essays, lectures. 2. Bible. N. T.—Theology. I. Title.

PRENTER, Regin, 1907- 232
Luther's theology of the cross. Philadelphia, Fortress Press [1971] viii, 24 p. 20 cm. (Facet books. Historical series, 17) "This study was first published in Lutheran world 6 (1959-1960): 222-233." Bibliography: p. 19-20. [BR333.5.C4P73] 71-152368 1.00
1. Luther, Martin, 1483-1546—Christology. I. Title.

PREUS, Jacob Aall Ottesen, 1920- 232
It is written [by] Jacob A. O. Preus. St. Louis, Concordia Pub. House [1971] 74 p. 23 cm. (Contemporary theology series) [BT590.O4P7] 76-162532 ISBN 0-570-06718-9
1. Jesus Christ—Attitude towards the Old Testament. 2. Bible—Evidences, authority, etc. I. Title.

*PRIME, Derek 232
Tell me about the Lord Jesus Christ. Chicago, Moody [1967, c.1965] 64p. illus. 19cm. (Moody arrows: devotional, no. 18) .50 pap.,
1. Jesus Christ— Person and offices—Juvenile literature. I. Title.

A Pseudo-Epiphanius testimony book / edited and translated by Robert V. Hotchkiss. [Missoula, Mont.] : Society of Biblical Literature, 1974. vii, 82 p. ; 24 cm. (Texts and translations - Society of Biblical Literature ; 4) (Early Christian literature series ; 1) Greek and English on opposite pages. The Greek text combines readings from the 2 available mss.: Codex Athos Iviron 28 and Codex Vaticanus Graecus 790. Includes bibliographical references. [BT200.P84] 74-15203 ISBN 0-88414-043-1 232
1. Jesus Christ—Person and offices. 2. Typology (Theology) I. Epiphanius, Saint, Bp. of Constantia in Cyprus. II. Hotchkiss, Robert V., ed. III. Title. IV. Series. V. Series: Society of Biblical Literature. Texts and translations ; 4.

RAMSAY, William M 232
The Christ of the earliest Christians. Richmond, John Knox Press [1959] 163p. 21 cm. The author's thesis put into shorter and more popular form. Includes bibliography. [BT201.R28 1959] 59-5093
1. Jesus Christ—Person and offices. I. Title.

*RAMSAY, William M. 232
The meaning of Jesus Christ. Illus. by M. Milton Hull. Richmond, Va., CLC Pr. [dist. Knox, c.1964] 199p. 24cm. (Covenant Life Curriculum bk.) 2.95 pap.,
I. Title.

RAWLINSON, Alfred Edward John, Bp. of Derby, 1884- 232
Christ in the Gospels, by A. E. J. Rawlinson. Westport, Conn., Greenwood Press [1970] 128 p. 23 cm. Reprint of the 1944 ed. [BS2555.R36 1970] 77-108846
1. Jesus Christ—Messiahship. 2. Bible. N.T. Gospels—Theology. I. Title.

REHNBORG, C F 1887- 232
Jesus and the new age of faith. [Corona del Mar? Calif.] c1955. 573 l. illus. 29cm. [BR121.R435] 55-58683
1. Christianity—Essence, genius, nature. 2. Jesus Christ—Biog. I. Title.

REID, John Kelman Sutherland. 232
Our life in Christ. Philadelphia, Westminster Press [1963] 148 p. 23 cm. (The Library of history and doctrine) [BV4490.R4] 63-9063
1. Jesus Christ — Person and offices. 2. Spiritual life — History of doctrines. I. Title.

*RICCHIUTI, Paul B. 232
My very best friend by Paul B. Ricchiuti.Illustrated by Howard C. Larkin. Mountain View, Calif., Pacific-Press Pub, Association, 1975. [33]p. col. ill. 23 cm. [BT302] 0.95(pbk)
1. Jesus Christ-juvenile literature I. Title.

RICHARDSON, Alan, 1905- 232
The political Christ. Philadelphia, Westminster Press [1973] 118 p. 22 cm. Includes bibliographical references. [BR115.P7R485] 73-14598 ISBN 0-664-20986-6 4.95
1. Jesus Christ—Person and offices. 2. Christianity and politics—History. I. Title.

RIMMER, Harry, 1890-1952 232
The magnificence of Jesus. Grand Rapids, Mich., Eerdmans [1966.c.1943] 200p. 19cm. (John Laurence Frost memorial lib., v. 6) [BT202.R5] 66-4385 2.00 pap.,
1. Jesus Christ—Person and offices. I. Title. II. Series.

RITSCHL, Dietrich. 232
Memory and hope; an inquiry concerning the presence of Christ. New York, Macmillan [1967] xviii, 237 p. 22 cm. Bibliographical footnotes. [BT202.R57] 67-22732
1. Jesus Christ—Person and offices. I. Title.

ROBINSON, Donald Fay, 1905- 232
Jesus, son of Joseph; a re-examination of the New Testament record Boston, Beacon [c.1964] viii, 216p. 21cm. Bibl. 64-13535 4.95
1. Jesus Christ—Historicity. I. Title.

ROBINSON, Donald Ray, 1905- 232
Jesus, son of Joseph; a re-examination of the New Testament record. Boston, Beacon Press [1964] viii, 216 p. 21 cm. Bibliography: p. 211-212. [BT303.2.R6] 64-13535
1. Jesus Christ — Historicity. I. Title.

ROBINSON, John Arthur Thomas, Bp., 1919- 232
The human face of God, by John A. T. Robinson. Philadelphia, Westminster Press [1973] xii, 269 p. 22 cm. Bibliography: p. [245]-249. [BT202.R59] 73-78 ISBN 0-664-20970-X 7.95
1. Jesus Christ—Person and offices. I. Title.

†ROBINSON, O. Preston, 1903- 232
Christ's eternal gospel : do the Dead Sea scrolls, the pseudepigrapha, and other ancient records challenge or support the Bible? / O. Preston Robinson, Christine H. Robinson. Salt Lake City : Deseret Book Co., 1976. xi, 272 p. : facsim. (on lining papers) ; 24 cm. Includes index. Bibliography: p. 255-259. [BT202.R593] 76-44650 ISBN 0-87747-616-0 : 5.95
1. Jesus Christ—Person and offices. 2. Jesus Christ—Biography—Apocryphal and legendary literature. 3. Christianity—Origin. I. Robinson, Christine Hinckley, joint author. II. Title.

ROLLS, Charles Jubilee, 1887- 232
His glorious name / by Charles J. Rolls. 1st ed. Neptune, N.J. : Loizeaux Brothers, 1975. 255 p. ; 21 cm. (His The names and titles of Jesus Christ ; [5]) [BT590.N2R59] 74-18993 ISBN 0-87213-730-9 : 4.95
1. Jesus Christ—Name. I. Title.

ROLLS, Charles Jubilee, 1887- 232
The indescribable Christ; the names and titles of Jesus Christ. Grand Rapids, Zondervan Pub. House [1953] 215p. 20cm. [BT590.N2R6] 53-37092
1. Jesus Christ—Name. I. Title.

ROLLS, Charles Jubilee, 1887- 232
The name above every name, by Charles J. Rolls. [1st ed.] Neptune, N.J., Loizeaux Bros. [1965] 255 p. 21 cm. [(His The names and titles of Jesus Christ [4]*] [BT590.N2R612] 65-26585
1. Jesus Christ—Name. I. Title.

ROLLS, Charles Jubilee, 1887- 232
The name above every name. Neptune, N. J., Loizeaux [c.1965] 255p. 21cm. (His The names and titles of Jesus Christ, 4) [BT590.N2R612] 65-26585 3.50
1. Jesus Christ—Name. I. Title.

ROLLS, Charles Jubilee, 1887- 232
Time's noblest name. Grand Rapids, Zondervan Pub. House [1958] 217p. 20cm. (His The names and titles of Jesus Christ, 3) [BT590.N2R615] 58-42580
1. Jesus Christ— Name. I. Title.

ROLLS, Charles Jubilee, 1887- 232
The world's greatest name; the names and titles of Jesus Christ. Grand Rapids, Zondervan Pub. House [1956] 185p. 21cm. [BT590.N2R62] 56-39527
1. Jesus Christ—Name. I. Title.

ROSS, Pearl. 232
Jesus the pagan. New York, Philosophical Library [1972] ix, 73 p. 23 cm. [BT301.2.R67] 72-82792 ISBN 0-8022-2097-5 6.00
1. Jesus Christ—Biography. I. Title.

ROUTLEY, Erik. 232
The man for others; an important contribution to the discussions inspired by the book Honest to God. New York, Oxford University Press, 1964. xiv, 107 p. 21 cm. Bibliographical footnotes. [BT202.R63 1964] 64-54536
1. Jesus Christ—Person and offices. I.

Robinson, John Arthur Thomas, Bp., 1919- Honest to God. II. Title.

ROWLINGSON, Donald T 232
Jesus, the religious ultimate. New York, Macmillan, 1961. 138p. 22cm. [BT202.R65] 61-11096
1. Jesus Christ—Person and offices. I. Title.

RUSHING, Richard Ray. 232
Christ, the great deceiver. Boston, Branden Press [1972] 166 p. 22 cm. [BT295.R84] 76-166566 ISBN 0-8283-1325-3 6.95
1. Jesus Christ—Miscellanea. I. Title.

SABOURIN, Leopold. 232
The names and titles of Jesus; themes of Biblical theology. Translated by Maurice Carroll. New York, Macmillan [1967] xviii, 334 p. 21 cm. Includes bibliographical references. [BT590.N2S2] 66-22534
1. Jesus Christ—Name. I. Title.

SANDERS, Jack T. 232
The New Testament Christological hymns; their historical religious background, by Jack T. Sanders. Cambridge [Eng.] University Press, 1971. xi, 162 p. 23 cm. (Society for New Testament Studies. Monograph series, 15) Bibliography: p. 145-147. [BT202.S23] 70-123670 ISBN 0-521-07932-2
1. Jesus Christ—Person and offices. 2. Bible. N.T.—Criticism, interpretation, etc.—History—20th century. I. Title. II. Series: Studiorum Novi Testamenti Societas. Monograph series, 15

SANDERS, John Oswald, 1902- 232
Consider Him / by J. Oswald Sanders. Chicago : Moody Press, c1976. p. cm. Large print ed. [BT306.4.S24 1976] 76-15012 ISBN 0-8024-1613-6 pbk. : 2.95
1. Jesus Christ—Meditations. 2. Sight-saving books. I. Title.

SANDMEL, Samuel. 232
We Jews and Jesus. New York, Oxford University Press, 1965. x, 163 p. 21 cm. Bibliography: p. [154]-158. [BM620.S24] 65-11529
1. Jesus Christ—Jewish interpretations. I. Title.

SANDMEL, Samuel 232
We Jews and Jesus. New York, Oxford [c.] 1965. x, 163p. 21cm. Bibl. [BM620.S24] 65-11529 5.00
1. Jesus Christ—Jewish interpretations. I. Title.

SANDMEL, Samuel. 232
We Jews and Jesus. New York, Oxford University Press [1973] xvi, 163 p. 21 cm. (A Galaxy book) Bibliography: p. [154]-158. [BM620.S24 1973] 72-92778 ISBN 0-19-501676-9 1.95
1. Jesus Christ—Jewish interpretations. I. Title.

SANTUCCI, Luigi. 232
Meeting Jesus; a new way to Christ. Translated from the Italian by Bernard Wall. [New York] Herder and Herder [1971] 222 p. 24 cm. Translation of Volete andarvene anche voi? [BT301.2.S1813] 78-167865 ISBN 0-665-00020-0 7.50
1. Jesus Christ—Biography. I. Title.

SARAYDARIAN, H. 232
Christ, the avatar of sacrificial love / by Haroutiun Saraydarian. Agoura, Calif. : Aquarian Educational Group, [1974] 127 p. ; 27 cm. Includes bibliographical references. [BT304.97.S27] 74-11760
1. Jesus Christ—Theosophical interpretations. I. Title.

SAVARY, Louis M., comp. 232
Jesus: the face of man. Compiled and edited by Louis M. Savary. [1st ed.] New York, Harper & Row [1972] 160 p. illus. 21 cm. "A Collins Associates book." [BT202.S27] 76-175161 2.25
1. Jesus Christ—Person and offices—Collections. 2. Christian life—1960- —Collections. I. Title.

SCAER, David P., 1936- 232
What do you think of Jesus? [By] David P. Scaer. St. Louis, Concordia Pub. House [1973] 114 p. 20 cm. [BT202.S28] 72-97341 ISBN 0-570-03153-2 2.50 (pbk.)
1. Jesus Christ—Appreciation. I. Title.

SCHMELIG, Randolph. 232
Jesus—the man, the Christ / by Randolph Schmelig. Lakemont, Ga. : CSA Press, c1977. 93 p. ; 22 cm. [BT202.S352] 76-47420 ISBN 0-87707-188-8 pbk. : 1.95
1. Jesus Christ—Person and offices. I. Title.

SCHMIDT, Duane A. 232
The late J. C. [by Duane A. Schmidt] Des Moines, Iowa, WH Books, c1972. v, 91 p. illus. 24 cm. Half title: The fifth gospel. [BT295.S36] 72-97231
1. Jesus Christ—Miscellanea. I. Title. II. Title: The fifth gospel.

SCHOONENBERG, Piet J. A. M., 1911- 232
The Christ; a study of the God-man relationship in the whole of creation and in Jesus Christ [by] Piet Schoonenberg. [Translated by Della Couling. New York] Herder and Herder [1971] 191 p. 22 cm. Translation of Hij is een God van mensen. Includes bibliographical references. [BT202.S3613] 74-127874 8.50
1. Jesus Christ—Person and offices. 2. Theology, Doctrinal. I. Title.

SCHULLER, Robert Harold. 232
The greatest possibility thinker that ever lived [by] Robert H. Schuller. Old Tappan, N.J., F. H. Revell Co. [1973] 32 p. 19 cm. [BT202.S375] 73-1196 ISBN 0-8007-0580-7 1.95
1. Jesus Christ—Person and offices. 2. Christian life—1960- I. Title.

SCHWEITZER, Albert, 1875- 232
The mystery of the kingdom of God; the secret of Jesus' messiahship and passion. Tr. [from German]introd by Walter Lowrie. New York, Schocken [1964] 275p. 21cm. (SB78) 64-16462 1.95 pap.,
1. Jesus Christ—Biog. 2. Jesus Christ—Messiahship. 3. Kingdom of God. I. Title.

SCHWEITZER, Albert, 1875-1965. 232
The theology of Albert Schweitzer for Christian inquirers, by E. N. Mozley. With an epilogue by Albert Schweitzer. New York, Macmillan, 1951 [c1950] vii, 117 p. 20 cm. [BR85.S295 1951] 51-1674
1. Jesus Christ—Messiahship. 2. Theology—Collected works—20th century. 3. Eschatology. I. Mozley, Edward Newman, 1875- II. Title.

SCHWEITZER, Albert, 1875-1965. 232
The theology of Albert Schweitzer for Christian inquirers, by E. N. Mozley. With an epilogue by Albert Schweitzer. Westport, Conn., Greenwood Press [1974] vii, 108 p. 20 cm. Reprint of the 1950 ed. published by A. and C. Black, London. [BR85.S295 1974] 73-16630 ISBN 0-8371-7204-7 7.75
1. Schweitzer, Albert, 1875-1965—Theology. 2. Jesus Christ—Messiahship. 3. Eschatology. I. Mozley, Edward Newman, 1875-1950. II. Title.

SCHWEIZER, Eduard [Robert] 232
Lordship and discipleship. [Translated from the German, Naperville, Ill., A. R. Allenson, 1960] 136p. 22cm. (Studies in Biblical theology, no. 28) (bibl. footnotes) 60-1930 2.25 pap.,
1. Jesus Christ—Humiliation. 2. Jesus Christ—Exaltation. I. Title.

SENIOR, Donald. 232
Jesus, a Gospel portrait / by Donald Senior. Dayton, Ohio : Pflaum Pub., 1975. vii, 181 p. : map ; 21 cm. Bibliography: p. 177-181. [BT202.S42] 75-14636 ISBN 0-8278-9003-6 : 3.50
1. Jesus Christ—Person and offices. 2. Bible. N.T. Gospels—Criticism, interpretation, etc. I. Title.

SEYMOUR, Peter S., comp. 232
Portrait of Jesus; the life of Christ in poetry and prose, edited by Peter Seymour. Illustrated with famous paintings and drawings. [Kansas City, Mo.] Hallmark Crown Editions [1973, c1972] 70 p. illus. 25 x 29 cm. [BT301.2.S44] 70-127751 ISBN 0-87529-146-5 8.50
1. Jesus Christ—Biography—Collected works. 2. Jesus Christ—Art. I. Title.

SHEA, John. 232
The challenge of Jesus / by John Shea. Chicago : Thomas More Press, c1975. 191 p. ; 22 cm. Includes bibliographical references. [BT202.S45] 75-324183 ISBN 0-88347-053-5 : 7.50
1. Jesus Christ—Person and offices. I. Title.

SHEED, Francis Joseph, 1897- 232
Christ in the classroom, by F. J. Sheed. London, New York, Sheed and Ward [1973] 96 p. 18 cm. [BT202.S47 1973] 73-952 ISBN 0-8362-0523-5 1.45 (pbk.)
1. Jesus Christ—Person and offices. 2. Christian life—Catholic authors. 3. Religious education. I. Title.

SHEED, Francis Joseph, 1897- 232
What difference does Jesus make? [By] F. J. Sheed. New York, Sheed and Ward [1971] xi, 242 p. 21 cm. [BT202.S5] 76-162382 ISBN 0-8362-1329-7 6.00
1. Jesus Christ—Person and offices. I. Title.

SHILOH, Ailon. 232
Christianity against Jesus : one hundred questions and answers on the tragedy of Christianity / Ailon Shiloh. [Tampa, Fla.] : Shiloh, c1977. viii, 127 p. ; 21 cm. [BR96.S47] 77-71496 ISBN 0-918580-01-3 : 4.95
1. Jesus Christ—Relation to Judaism—Miscellanea. 2. Jesus Christ—Person and offices—Miscellanea. 3. Christianity—Controversial literature—Miscellanea. I. Title.

SLABAUGH, Warren W 1879-1954. 232
The role of the Servant. Elgin, Ill., Brethren Pub. House [1954] 160p. 20cm. [BT205.S62] 54-43033
1. Servant of Jehovah. I. Title.

SLOAN, Harold Paul, 1881- 232
Jesus Christ is Lord; being a series of lectures given in part at the winter convocation of Asbury Seminary and Asbury College, in c) conjunction with the dedication of the Estes Memorial Chapel, January 1954. Louisville, Ky., Pentecostal Pub. Co. [1955] 189p. 20cm. [BT201.S622] 55-32979
1. Jesus Christ—Person and offices. I. Title.

SMART, James D. 232
The quiet revolution; the radical impact of Jesus on men of his time, by James D. Smart. Philadelphia, Westminster Press [1969] 158 p. 21 cm. Bibliographical references included in "Notes" (p. [157]-158) [BS2430.S57] 69-20340 2.95
1. Jesus Christ—Friends and associates. 2. Bible. N.T. Gospels—Criticism, interpretation, etc. I. Title.

SMITH, Joyce Marie. 232
The significance of Jesus / Joyce Marie Smith. Wheaton, Ill. : Tyndale House Publishers, c1976. 61 p. ; 19 cm. (New life Bible studies) [BT207.S63] 76-9370 ISBN 0-8423-5887-0 pbk : 1.25
1. Jesus Christ—Person and offices—Study. I. Title. II. Series.

*SMITH, Wilbur M., 1894- 232
The supernaturalness of Christ; can we still believe in it? [by] Wilbur M. Smith. Grand Rapids, Baker Book House [1974] 231 p. 20 cm. (Notable books on theology) Reprint of the 1940 edition. [BT202] ISBN 0-8010-8020-7 2.95 (pbk.)
1. Jesus Christ—Person and offices. I. Title.

SOLLE, Dorothee. 232
Christ the representative; an essay in theology after the Death of God. [Translated by David Lewis] Philadelphia, Fortress Press [1967] 154 p. 23 cm. Translation of Stellvertretung; ein Kapitel Theologie nach dem Tode Gottes. Bibliography: p. 153-154. [BT254.S613 1967b] 67-19563
1. Jesus Christ—Priesthood. 2. Atonement. I. Title.

SOMMER, Frederick, 1873- 232
God's great secret. Oswego, Kan., Carpenter Press [1951] ix, 278 p. illus. 21 cm. On spine: Drama of the kingdom of Christ. [BT94.S65] 51-2236
1. Kingdom of God. I. Title. II. Title: The drama of the kingdom of Christ.

SPONG, John Shelby. 232
This Hebrew Lord. New York, Seabury Press [1974] xi, 190 p. illus. 22 cm. "A Crossroad book." Bibliography: p. 189-190. [BT301.2.S65] 73-17911 ISBN 0-8164-0254-X 5.95
1. Jesus Christ—Biography. 2. Jesus Christ—Person and offices. I. Title.

STAGES of experience; 232
the year in the church. Translated by J. E. Anderson] Baltimore, Helicon Press [1965] 104 p. 21 cm. "An ecumenical symposium." Translation of Les Etapes de l'an de grace. [BV30.E813] 65-14588
1. Church year — Addresses, essays, lectures;

STAGES of experience; 232
the year in the church. [Tr. from French by J. E. Anderson] Helicon [dist. New York, Taplinger, c.1965] 104p. 21cm. An ecumenical symposium. [BV30.E813] 65-14588 2.75 bds.,
1. Church year—Addresses, essays, lectures. Contents omitted.

STANTON, G. N. 232
Jesus of Nazareth in New Testament preaching / G. N. Stanton. London ; New York : Cambridge University Press, 1974. xi, 207 p. ; 23 cm. (Monograph series - Society for New Testament Studies ; 27) Originally presented as the author's thesis, Cambridge, 1969. Includes bibliographical references and index. [BT198.S69 1974] 73-92782 16.50
1. Jesus Christ—History of doctrines—Early Church, ca. 30-600. 2. Bible. N.T.—Criticism, interpretation, etc. I. Title. II. Series: Studiorum Novi Testamenti Societas. Monograph series ; 27.

STEELE, Algernon Odell, 1900- 232
The questing Christ. New York, Philosophical [1965, c.1964] ix, 197p. 22cm. [BV4501.2.S74] 64-20427 4.50
1. Christian life. 2. Jesus Christ—Devotional literature. I. Title.

STEINHAUSER, Gerhard R. 232
Jesus Christ: heir to the astronauts, by Gerhard R. Steinhauser. [1st American ed.] New York, Abelard-Schuman [1975, c1974] 139 p. illus. 23 cm. Includes bibliographical references. [BT295.S77 1975] 74-9374 ISBN 0-200-04026-X 6.95
1. Jesus Christ—Miscellanea. I. Title.

STOCK, Augustine. 232
Kingdom of heaven; the good tidings of the Gospel. [New York] Herder and Herder [1964] 191 p. 21 cm. Bibliographical references included in "Footnotes" (p. 187-191) [BT821.2.S75] 64-19738
1. Eschatology. 2. Kerygma. 3. Time (Theology) I. Title.

STOCK, Augustine 232
Kingdom of heaven; the good tidings of the Gospel. [New York] Herder & Herder [c.1964] 191p. 21cm. Bibl. 64-19738 3.95
1. Eschatology. 2. Kerygma. 3. Time (Theology) I. Title.

STUBBS, Charles William, Bp. of Truro, 1845-1912. 232
The Christ of English poetry. [Folcroft, Pa.] Folcroft Library Editions, 1973. ix, 216 p. 24 cm. Reprint of the 1906 ed. published by J. M. Dent, London, which was issued as the 1904-1905 Hulsean lectures. Contents.Contents.—lecture 1. Cynewulf.—lecture 2. William Langland.—lecture 3. Shakespeare.—lecture 4. Robert Browning. [BT550.S8 1973] 73-1787 ISBN 0-8414-2621-X (lib. bdg.)
1. Jesus Christ—Poetry. I. Title. II. Series: Hulsean lectures, 1904-1905.

TAVARD, Georges Henri, 1922- 232
Paul Tillich and the Christian message. New York, Scribner [1962] 176 p. 22 cm. [BX4827.T53T3 1962a] 61-7227
1. Tillich, Paul, 1886- 2. Catholic Church — Relations — Protestant churches. 3. Protestant churches — Relations — Catholic Church. I. Title.

TAVARD, Georges Henri, 1922- 232
Paul Tillich and the Christian message. New York, Scribner [1962] 176 p. 22 cm. [BX4827.T53T3 1962a] 61-7227
1. Tillich, Paul, 1886-1965. 2. Catholic Church—Relations—Protestant churches. 3. Protestant churches—Relations—Catholic Church.

TAYLOR, Mason M. 232
On the nature of universal cross-action, by Mason M. Taylor. New York, Dodd, Mead [1966] 70 p. illus. 24 cm. An excerpt from the author's The single reality; a new and unorthodox view of Jesus, His mission and meaning to man, to be published in the fall of 1966. Bibliography: p. 69. [BT205.T3] 66-20508
1. Jesus Christ—Person and offices. 2. Jesus Christ—Significance. I. Title.

TAYLOR, Vincent, 1887- 232
The names of Jesus. New York, St. Martin's Press, 1953. 179p. 22cm. [BT590.N2T3] 53-10573
1. Jesus Christ —Name. I. Title.

TAYLOR, Vincent, 1887- 232
The person of Christ in New Testament teaching. London, Macmillan; New York, St. Martin's Press, 1958. 321 p. 23 cm. Includes bibliography. [BT201.T24] 58-14613
1. Jesus Christ — Person and offices. 2. Bible. N. T. — Theology. I. Title.

TESELLE, Eugene, 1931- 232
Christ in context : divine purpose and human possibility / Eugene TeSelle. Philadelphia : Fortress Press, [1975] xiv, 178 p. ; 24 cm. Includes bibliographical references and index. [BT202.T46] 74-80426 ISBN 0-8006-0282-X : 10.95
1. Jesus Christ—Person and offices. 2. Jesus Christ—History of doctrines. I. Title.

THOMAS, William Henry Griffith, 1861-1924. 232
Christianity is Christ. [4th ed.] Grand Rapids, Eerdmans, 1955. 161p. 23cm. [BT201.T34 1955] 55-3687
1. Jesus Christ—Person and offices. I. Title.

TRAKATELLIS, Demetrius Christ. 232
The pre-existence of Christ in the writings of Justin Martyr / by Demetrius Christ Trakatellis. Missoula, Mont. : Published by Scholars Press for Harvard Theological Review, c1976. xi, 203 p. ; 22 cm. (Harvard

dissertations in religion ; no. 6) Originally presented as the author's thesis, Harvard. Bibliography: p. 185-203. [BT198.T7 1976] 76-44913 ISBN 0-89130-098-8 : 6.00
1. Jesus Christ—Pre-existence—History of doctrines. 2. Justinus Martyr, Saint. I. Title. II. Series.

TROCME, Etienne. 232
Jesus as seen by his contemporaries. Philadelphia, Westminster Press [1973] x, 134 p. 22 cm. Translation of Jesus de Nazareth vu par les temoins de sa vie. Includes bibliographical references. [BT202.T7513] 72-10239 ISBN 0-664-20968-8 4.95
1. Jesus Christ—Person and offices. 2. Jesus Christ—Biography—History and criticism. I. Title.

TROMP, Sebastiaan [Pieter Cornelis] 232
Corpus Christi, quod est ecclesia. Translated by Ann Condit as The body of Christ, which is the church. New York, Vantage Press [c.1960] 239p.bBibl.: p.215-239. 60-11701 3.75 bds.,
1. Church. 2. Jesus Christ—Mystical body. I. Title. II. Title: The body of Christ, which is the church.

TURNBULL, Ralph G. 232
Profile of the Son of Man [by] Ralph G. Turnbull. Grand Rapids, Baker Book House [1969] 160 p. illus. 21 cm. [BT205.T84] 71-101613 3.95
1. Jesus Christ—Person and offices. 2. Jesus Christ—Art. I. Title.

TURNER, Henry Ernest William, 1907- 232
Jesus the Christ / [by] H. E. W. Turner. London : Mowbrays, 1976. ix, 134 p. ; 23 cm. (Mowbrays theological library) Includes index. [BT202.T86 1976] 76-360872 ISBN 0-264-66255-5 : £6.00. ISBN 0-264-66252-0 pbk.
1. Jesus Christ—Person and offices. I. Title.

VAN BUREN, Paul. 232
Christ in our place; the substitutionary character of Calvin's doctrine of reconciliation. Grand Rapids, Eerdmans [1957] 152 p. 23 cm. "[First presented as doctoral dissertation] to the Theological Faculty of the University of Basel." [BT198.V3] 58-14767
1. Calvin, Jean, 1509-1564 — Theology. 2. Jesus Christ — History of doctrines. I. Title.

VAN TIL, Cornelius, 1895- 232
The great debate today. [Nutley, N.J., Presbyterian and Reformed Pub. Co., 1971, c1970] viii, 239 p. 21 cm. Includes bibliographical references. [BT202.V25 1971] 74-133084
1. Jesus Christ—Person and offices. 2. Christianity—Philosophy. 3. Theology, Doctrinal—History—20th century. I. Title.

VATICAN Council. 2d, 1962-1965. 232
The Christ of Vatican II; all in the words of the Second Vatican Council. Compiled by the Daughters of St. Paul. [Boston] St. Paul Editions [1968] 79 p. illus., ports. 22 cm. Also published as part two of the Catechism of modern man. Includes bibliographical references. [BT202.V3 1968] 68-24464 2.00
1. Jesus Christ—Person and offices. I. Daughters of St. Paul. II. Title.

VAWTER, Bruce. 232
This man Jesus; an essay toward a New Testament Christology. [1st ed.] Garden City, N.Y., Doubleday, 1973. 216 p. 22 cm. [BT202.V33] 73-78174 ISBN 0-385-04008-3 5.95
1. Jesus Christ—Person and offices. I. Title.

VERMES, Geza, 1924- 232
Jesus the Jew; a historian's reading of the Gospels. New York, Macmillan [1974, c1973] 286 p. 21 cm. Bibliography: p. [11]-14. [BT202.V45 1974] 73-18516 6.95
1. Jesus Christ—Person and offices. 2. Jesus Christ—Name. I. Title.

VIGEVENO H. S. 232
Jesus the revolution. Glendale Calf, [Gospel light pubns 1966] 199 p. 18 cm (Regal Books 61-954) pap. 95
I. Title.

VINCENT, John J. 232
Secular Christ; a contemporary interpretation of Jesus [by] John J. Vincent. Nashville, Abingdon Press [1968] 240 p. 23 cm. Bibliographical footnotes. [BT202.V5] 68-11475
1. Jesus Christ—Person and offices. I. Title.

WALKER, Thomas, 1881- 232
Jewish views of Jesus; an introduction & an appreciation [by] Thomas T. Walker. New introd. by Seymour Siegel. New York, Arno Press, 1973. 142 p. 21 cm. (The Jewish people: history, religion, literature) Reprint of the 1931 ed. published by G. Allen & Unwin, London. [BM620.W3 1973] 73-2229 ISBN 0-405-05290-1 9.00
1. Jesus Christ—Jewish interpretations. I. Title. II. Series.

*WALLIS, J. L. 232
The good news is true: a newspaperman reports [Birmingham, Ala., 1967] xii, 287p. 24cm. 4.95
I. Title.
Order from Banner Pr., Box 20180, Birmingham, Ala. 35216.

*WALLIS, Reginald. 232
The new sovereignty Minneapolis, Dimension Books [1974] 120 p. 18 cm. [BT301] ISBN 0-87123-391-6 0.95 (pbk.)
1. Jesus Christ—Person and offices. I. Title.

WALVOORD, John F. 232
Jesus Christ our Lord, by John F. Walvoord. Chicago, Moody Press [1969] 318 p. 23 cm. Bibliography: p. [291]-297. [BT202.W33] 70-80941 4.95
1. Jesus Christ—Person and offices. I. Title.

*WARBLER, J.-M. 232
Jesus is born. Story by J.-M. Warbler, Harold Winstone. Pictures by A.-M. Cocagnac. New York, Macmillan, c. 1965, 1966. unpaged. (col. illus.) 20cm. (Dove bks., 15:04567) .59 ., ap.,
I. Title.

WARFIELD, Benjamin Breckinridge, 1851-1921. 232
The Lord of glory : a study of the designations of Our Lord in the New Testament with especial reference to His deity / Benjamin B. Warfield. Grand Rapids : Baker Book House, 1974. 332 p. ; 20 cm. (Notable books on theology) Reprint of the 1907 ed. published by American Tract Society, New York; with a new introd. Includes bibliographical references and indexes. [BT590.N2W2 1974] 76-357110 ISBN 0-8010-9548-4 : 3.95
1. Jesus Christ—Name. 2. Jesus Christ—Divinity. I. Title.

WARFIELD, Benjamin Breckinridge, 1851-1921. 232
The person and work of Christ, edited by Samuel G. Craig. Philadelphia, Presbyterian and Reformed Pub. Co., 1950. xiii, 575 p. port. 24 cm. A selection of articles from the author's collected writings as published by Oxford University Press subsequent to his death. "Other articles on the person and word of Christ": p. xiii. [BT201.W26] 50-2987
1. Jesus Christ — Person and offices. I. Title.

WHEN two great hearts meet / [edited] by E. De Meulder. Allahabad : Allahabad Saint Paul Society, 1976. 246 p., [15] leaves of plates : ill. ; 23 cm. Includes bibliographical footnotes. [BT202.W46] 76-911382 Rs14.00 232
1. Jesus Christ—Person and offices—Addresses, essays, lectures. 2. India—Social conditions—1947- —Addresses, essays, lectures. I. Meulder, E. de.

WHITE, E. G. 232
Vers Jesus [dist. Mountain View, Calif. Inter-American Pubns., c.1961] 126p. illus. 1.00 pap.,
1. Jesus Christ—Person and offices. I. Title.

*WILKERSON, David. 232
Jesus Christ solidrock; the return of Christ [by] David Wilkerson [and others] Grand Rapids, Mich., Zondervan [1973 c.1972] 117 p., photos, 18 cm. [BT202] pap., 0.95
1. Jesus Christ—Second Coming. I. Title.

WIRT, Sherwood Eliot. 232
Jesus power. [1st ed.] New York, Harper & Row [1972] xi, 132 p. 22 cm. Bibliography: p. 125-128. [BT769.W57] 72-78059 ISBN 0-06-069603-6 4.95
1. Power (Theology) I. Title.

YODER, John Howard. 232
The politics of Jesus; vicit Agnus noster [by] John H. Yoder. Grand Rapids, Mich., Eerdmans [1972] 260 p. 21 cm. Includes bibliographical references. [BT202.Y63] 72-77188 ISBN 0-8028-1485-9 3.45
1. Jesus Christ—Person and offices. 2. Social ethics. 3. Pacifism. I. Title.

YOUNG, Andrew, 1885- 232
The poetic Jesus. With six wood engravings by T. R. Williams. [1st U.S. ed.] New York, Harper & Row [1972] 88 p. illus. 22 cm. [BT301.2.Y68 1972b] 72-79467 ISBN 0-06-069731-8 3.95
1. Jesus Christ—Biography. 2. Jesus Christ—Teachings. I. Title.

YUNGBLUT, John R. 232
Rediscovering the Christ [by] John R. Yungblut. New York, Seabury Press [1974] x, 180 p. 22 cm. "A Crossroad book." [BT202.Y92] 74-10810 ISBN 0-8164-1187-5 7.95
1. Jesus Christ—Person and offices. I. Title.

ZAMOYTA, Vincent, comp. 232
The theology of Christ: sources. Milwaukee, Bruce Pub. Co. [1967] xx, 223 p. 23 cm. (Contemporary college theology series. History theology section) Bibliography: p. 217-220. [BT198.Z3] 67-24540
1. Jesus Christ—History of doctrines. I. Title.

KRAMER, Werner R. 1930- 232.014
Christ, Lord, Son of God [by] Werner Kramer. [Translated by Brian Hardy from the German] Naperville, Ill., A. R. Allenson [1966] 237 p. 22 cm. (Studies in Biblical theology, 50) Translation of Christos, Kyrios, Gottessohn. Bibliography: p. 224-228. [BT590.N2] 67-48
1. Jesus Christ — Name. 2. Bible. N. T. Epistles of Paul — Theology. I. Title. II. Series.

KRAMER, Werner R., 1930- 232.014
Christ, Lord, Son of God [by] Werner Kramer. [Translated by Brian Hardy from the German] Naperville, Ill., A. R. Allenson [1966] 237 p. 22 cm. (Studies in Biblical theology, 50) Translation of Christos, Kyrios, Gottessohn. Bibliography: p. 224-228. [BT590.N2] 67-48
1. Jesus Christ—Name. 2. Bible. N.T. Epistles of Paul—Theology. I. Title. II. Series.

LARGE, James. 232.014
Two hundred and eighty tiles and symbols of Christ. Grand Rapids. Basker Book House. 1959. 486p. 23cm. [BT590.N2L3 1959] 60-2162
1. Jesus-Christ—Name. I. Title.

STEEVES, Paul D. 232'.07
The character and work of Jesus Christ; a Bible study for an individual and/or a group, by Paul D. Steeves. [Chicago] Inter-varsity Press [1967] 105 p. 21 cm. Bibliographical footnotes. [BT307.S78] 67-28019
1. Jesus Christ—Biography—Study. I. Title.

CHRIST, faith and history: Cambridge studies in Christology; edited by S. W. Sykes and J. P. Clayton. London, Cambridge University Press, 1972. x, 303 p. 23 cm. Papers presented to a graduate Christology seminar, Cambridge. Includes bibliographical references. [BT202.C5] 70-176257 ISBN 0-521-08451-2 £4.20 232'.08
1. Jesus Christ—Person and offices. I. Sykes, Stephen, ed. II. Clayton, John Powell, ed.

TAPIA, Ralph J., comp. 232'.08
The theology of Christ: commentary; readings in Christology [by] Ralph J. Tapia. New York, Bruce Pub. Co. [1971] ix, 475 p. 23 cm. (Contemporary theology series) Includes bibliographical references. [BT199.T36 1971] 70-87993
1. Jesus Christ—Person and offices—Collections. I. Title.

WHO is Jesus of Nazareth? Dogma. [Glen Rock, N.J.] Paulist [1966, c.1965] viii, 163p. 24cm. (Concilium theol. in the age of renewal, v. 11) Bibl. [BT202.W5] 66-17729 4.50 232.08
1. Jesus Christ—Addresses, essays, lectures. (Series)

TORREY, Reuben Archer, 1856-1928 232.081
The uplifted Christ. Grand Rapids, Mich., Zondervan [c.1965] 104p. 21cm. [BT306.4.T6] 64-22839 2.50 bds.,
1. Jesus Christ—Biog.—Meditations. I. Title.

DOLLEN, Charles, ed. 232.082
Jesus Lord; selected passages on Our Lord from the writings of the fathers, doctors and theologians from the "Fathers of the church" series published by the Catholic University of America Press. [Boston, St. Paul Editions [1964] 283 p.illus. 21 cm. Selections: Extracts, etc.) [BR63.D6] 64-17753
1. Christian literature, Early I. Title.

DOLLEN, Charles, ed. 232.082
Jesus Lord: selected passages on Our Lord from the writings of the fathers. doctors and theologians from the 'Fathers of the church' ser. pub. by the Catholic Univ. of America Pr. [Boston] St. Paul Eds. [dist. Daughters of St. Paul, c. 1964] 283p. illus. 21cm. 64-17753 3.00; 2.00 pap.,
1. Christian literature, Early (Selections: Extracts, etc.) I. Title.

HARDY, Edward Rochie, 1908- ed. 232.082
Christology of the later Fathers, edited by Edward Rochie Hardy, in collaboration with Cyril C. Richardson. Philadelphia, Westminster Press [1954] 400p. 24cm. (The Library of Christian classics, v.3) Includes bibliographies. [BT199.H4] 54-9949
1. Jesus Christ—History of doctrines. 2. Christian literature, Early (Selections: Extracts, etc.) 3. Fathers of the church. I. Title. II. Series: The Library of Christian classics (Philadelphia) v.3

WELCH, Claude, ed. and tr. 232.082
God and Incarnation in mid-nineteenth century German theology: G. Thomasius, I. A. Dorner, A. E. Biedermann. New York, Oxford, 1965. viii, 391p. 24cm. (Lib. of Protestant thought) Bibl. [BT10.W4] 65-18230 7.00
1. Theology—Collections. 2. Theology, Doctrinal—Hist.Germany. 3. Theology, Doctrinal—Hist.—19th. cent. I. Thomasius, Gottfried, 1802-1875. II. Dorner, Isaak August, 1809-1884. III. Biedermann, Aloys Emanuel, 1819-1885. IV. Title. V. Series.

BOUSSET, Wilhelm, 1865-1920. 232'.09
Kyrios Christos; a history of the belief in Christ from the beginnings of Christianity to Irenaeus. Translated by John E. Steely. Nashville, Abingdon Press [1970] 496 p. 24 cm. Includes bibliographical references. [BT198.B713] 73-109684 ISBN 0-687-20983-8 11.00
1. Jesus Christ—History of doctrines—Early church, ca. 30-600. 2. Jesus Christ—Person and offices. I. Title.

JESUS in Christian devotion and contemplation, by Irenee Noye [and others] Translated by Paul J. Oligny. With a pref. by Edward Malatesta. St. Meinrad, Ind., Abbey Press, 1974. xvi, 116 p. 21 cm. (Religious experience series, v. 1) "Translation of the article 'Humanite du Christ (devotion et contemplation)' which first appeared in the Dictionnaire de spiritualite, Paris, Beauchesne, 1969, vol. 8, cols. 1033-1108." Bibliography: p. 114-116. [BT198.H8513] 73-94170 ISBN 0-87029-025-8 3.95 (pbk.) 232'.09
1. Jesus Christ—History of doctrines. I. Noye, Irenee.

PERRIN, Norman. 232'.09
A modern pilgrimage in New Testament christology. Philadelphia, Fortress Press [1974] x, 148 p. 23 cm. Bibliography: p. 133-141. [BT198.P47] 73-88352 ISBN 0-8006-0267-6 6.25
1. Jesus Christ—History of doctrines—Early church, ca. 30-600. I. Title.

ROGERS, Jack Bartlett. 232'.09
Case studies in Christ and salvation / by Jack Rogers, Ross Mackenzie, Louis Weeks. Philadelphia : Westminster Press, c1977. 176 p. ; 23 cm. Includes bibliographies. [BT198.R63] 76-53765 ISBN 0-664-24133-6 pbk. 7.95
1. Jesus Christ—History of doctrines. 2. Salvation—History of doctrines. I. Mackenzie, Ross, 1927- joint author. II. Weeks, Louis, 1941- joint author. III. Title.

SMULDERS, Pieter Frans, 1911- 232'.09
The Fathers on Christology; the development of Christological dogma from the Bible to the great councils, by P. Smulders. Translated by Lucien Roy. De Pere, Wis., St. Norbert Abbey Press, 1968. 160 p. 17 cm. On spine: 2. Includes bibliographical references. [BT198.S6] 68-58125 ISBN 0-8316-1051-4
1. Jesus Christ—History of doctrines—Early church, ca. 30-600. I. Title.

DAHL, Nils Alstrup. 232'.09'01
Jesus in the memory of the early church : essays / by Nils Alstrup Dahl. Minneapolis : Augsburg Pub. House, c1976. 175 p. ; 22 cm. Contents.Contents.—Anamnesis: memory and commemoration in early Christianity.—Form-critical observations on early Christian preaching.—The Passion narrative in Matthew.—The purpose of Mark's gospel.—The story of Abraham in Luke-Acts.—The purpose of Luke-Acts.—The Johannine church and history.—Christ, creation, and the church.—The parables of growth.—The early church and Jesus. Includes bibliographical references. [BS2395.D34] 76-27072 ISBN 0-8066-1561-3 pbk. : 4.95
1. Jesus Christ—History of doctrines—Early church, ca. 30-600—Addresses, essays, lectures. 2. Bible. N.T.—Criticism, interpretation, etc.—Addresses, essays, lectures. I. Title.

MOULE, Charles Francis Digby. 232'.09'015
The origin of Christology / C. F. D. Moule. Cambridge ; New York : Cambridge University Press, 1977. x, 187 p. ; 22 cm. Includes bibliographical references and indexes. [BT198.M68] 76-11087 ISBN 0-521-21290-1 : 12.00
1. Jesus Christ—History of doctrines—Early church, ca. 30-600—Addresses, essays, lectures. I. Title.

POLLARD, T. E. 232'.09'015
Johannine Christology and the early Church [by] T. E. Pollard. London, Cambridge U.P., 1970. xii, 359 p. 23 cm. (Society for New Testament studies. Monograph series, 13) Bibliography: p. 323-335. [BS2615.2.P64 1970] 74-509788 ISBN 0-521-07767-2 6/-/- ($17.50)
1. Jesus Christ—History of doctrines—Early church, ca. 30-600. 2. Bible. N.T. John—Criticism, interpretation, etc.—History. I. Title. II. Series: Studiorum Novi Testamenti Societas. Monograph series, 13

HALE, Robert. 232'.09'04
Christ and the universe: Teilhard de Chardin and the cosmos. Edited by Michael Meilach. Chicago, Franciscan Herald Press [1973] ix, 125 p. 21 cm. Based on the author's thesis. Includes bibliographical references. [BT198.H34 1973] 72-13782 ISBN 0-8199-0449-X 5.50
1. Jesus Christ—History of doctrines—20th century. 2. Teilhard de Chardin, Pierre. I. Title.

HORTON, Thomas Corwin, 232'.092'4
1848-
365 devotions on the names of Our Lord, by T.C. Horton Grand Rapids, Baker Book House, 1965. 191 p. 20 cm. Reprint of work first published in 1925 under title: The wonderful names of our wonderful Lord. [BT590] 66-1048
1. Jesus Christ — Name. I. Title.

KROPF, Richard W., 232'.092'4
1932-
Teilhard, Scripture, and revelation : a study of Teilhard de Chardin's reinterpretation of Pauline themes / Richard W. Knopf. Rutherford : Fairleigh Dickinson University Press, c1975. p. cm. Includes index. Bibliography: p. [BS500.K76 1975] 73-20907 ISBN 0-8386-1481-7 : 18.00
1. Jesus Christ—History of doctrines—20th century. 2. Teilhard de Chardin, Pierre. 3. Bible—Criticism, interpretation, etc.—History—20th century. I. Title.

LARSEN, Beverly. 232'.092'4
Jesus has many names; an alphabetical book for children. Illustrated by Audrey Teeple. Minneapolis, Augsburg Pub. House [1964] [BT590.N2L36] 64-21504
I. Title.

LARSEN, Beverly. 232'.092'4
Jesus has many names; an alphabetical book for children. Illustrated by Audrey Teeple. Minneapolis, Augsburg Pub. House [1964] [23] p. col. illus. 22 cm. [BT590.N2L36] 64-21504
1. Jesus Christ — Name — Juvenile literature. I. Title.

MORSON, John. 232'.092'4
Christ the way; the Christology of Guerric of Igny. [Spencer, Mass.] Cistercian Publications; [distributed by] Consortium Press, Washington, 1973. p. cm. (Cistercian studies series, no. 25) Bibliography: p. [BT198.M66] 74-8591 ISBN 0-87907-825-1
1. Jesus Christ—History of doctrines—Middle Ages, 600-1500. 2. Guerricus, Abbot of Igny, d. ca. 1157. I. Title. II. Series.

SIGGINS, Ian D. 232'.0924
Kingston.
Martin Luther's doctrine of Christ, by Ian D. Kingston Siggins. New Haven, Yale University Press, 1970. x, 331 p. 25 cm. (Yale publications in religion, 14) Bibliography: p. [270]-276. [BR333.5.C4S5 1970] 75-99842 ISBN 0-300-01223-3 10.00
1. Luther, Martin, 1483-1546—Christology. I. Title. II. Series.

BERCOVITCH, Sacvan, comp. 232'.1
Typology and early American literature. [Amherst] University of Massachusetts Press, 1972. 337 p. 24 cm. Includes essays which appeared in Early American literature. Contents.Contents.—Bercovitch, S. Introduction.—Davis, T. M. The traditions of Puritan typology.—Manning, S. Scriptural exegesis and the literary critic.—Rosenmeier, J. "With my owne eyes": William Bradford's Of Plymouth plantation.—Reinitz, R. The separatist background of Roger Williams' argument for religious toleration.—Lowance, M. I., Jr. Cotton Mather's Magnalia and the metaphors of Biblical history.—Reiter, Robert E. Poetry and doctrine in Edward Taylor's Preparatory meditations, series II, 1-30.—Keller, K. "The world slickt up in types": Edward Taylor as a version of Emerson.—Brumm, U. Edward Taylor and the poetic use of religious imagery.—Lowance, M. I., Jr. "Images or shadows of divine things" in the thought of Jonathan Edwards.—Bibliography (p. [245]-337) [BS478.B47] 74-181362 12.00
1. Typology (Theology)—History of doctrines. 2. American literature—Colonial period, ca. 1600-1775—History and criticism. I. Early American literature. II. Title.

BORSCH, Frederick Houk. 232'.1
The Christian and Gnostic Son of Man. Naperville, Ill., A. R. Allenson [1970] 130 p. 22 cm. (Studies in Biblical theology, 2d ser., 14) Includes bibliographical references. [BT232.B58] 77-131585
1. Son of Man. I. Title. II. Series.

BORSCH, Frederick Houk. 232'.1
The Son of Man in myth and history. Philadelphia, Westminster Press [1967] 431 p. 23 cm. (The New Testament library) Revision of the author's thesis, University of Birmingham. Bibliographical footnotes. [BT232.B6 1967] 67-25329
1. Son of Man. I. Title.

BUKSBAZEN, Victor, 1903- 232.1
The Gospel in the feasts of Israel. Philadelphia, Friends of Israel Missionary and Relief Society [1954] 80p. illus. 19cm. [BT225.B8] 54-30703
1. Typology (Theology) 2. Fasts and feasts—Judaism. I. Title.

CALLAWAY, Timothy Walton, 232.1
1874-
Christ in the Old Testament. [1st ed.] New York, Loizeaux Bros. [1950] 190 p. 20 cm. [BT225.C3] 50-10256
1. Typology (Theology) 2. Messiah—Prophecies. 3. Bible. N. T.—Relation to O. T. I. Title.

DENTAN, Robert Claude, 232.1
1907-
The King and His cross, by Robert C. Dentan. New York, Seabury Press [1965] xii, 178 p. 21 cm. [BX5947.H5D4] 65-10305
1. Holy Week. 2. Messiah — Prophecies. I. Title.

DENTAN, Robert Claude, 232.1
1907-
The King and His cross. New York, Seabury [c.1965] xii, 178p. 21cm. [BX5947.H5D4] 65-10305 3.50
1. Holy Week. 2. Messiah—Prophecies. I. Title.

FERRIER, Francis, 1916- 232.1
What is the Incarnation? Tr. from French by Edward Sillem. New York, Hawthorn [c.1962] 174p. 21cm. (Twentieth cent. encycl. of Catholicism, v.24. Sect. 2: Basic truths) Bibl. 62-17117 3.50
1. Incarnation. I. Title.

GUARDINI, Romano, 1885- 232.1
Jesus Christus, meditations; translated from the German by Peter White. Chicago, H. Regnery Co., 1959. 111p. 21cm. Translation of Jesus Christus, geistliches Wort. [BX1756.G85J43] 59-13051
1. Catholic Church—Sermons. 2. Sermons, German—Translations into English. 3. Sermons, English—Translations from German. I. Title.

HAINS, Edmont. 232.1
The Tabernacle. Introd. by Oswald J. Smith. Grard Rapids, Zondervan [1950] 120 p. 20 cm. [BT225.H3] 50-28690
1. Typology (Theology) 2. Tabernacle. I. Title.

HALL, Ona, 1894- 232.1
All the way to Calvary; the story of the Tabernacle in the wilderness and of the Savior and church which it foreshadowed. [1st ed.] New York, Greenwich Book Publishers [c1958] 74p. illus. 21cm. [BT225.H34] 58-59860
1. Typology (Theology) 2. Tabernacle. I. Title.

HARRIS, Ralph W. 232'.1
Pictures of truth : [a look at Old Testament types and their fulfillment in the New Testament] / Ralph W. Harris. Springfield, Mo. : Gospel Pub. House, c1977. 123 p. ; 18 cm. (Radiant books) [BS478.H28] 76-58081 ISBN 0-88243-905-7 pbk. : 1.50
1. Bible. N.T.—Relation to the Old Testament. 2. Typology (Theology) I. Title.

HEINISCH, Paul, 1878-1956. 232'.1
Christ in prophecy. William G. Heidt, translator. [Collegeville, Minn.] Liturgical Press [1956] 179 p. 24 cm. [BT235.H39] 57-2891
1. Messiah — Prophecies. 2. Bible O.T. — Prophecies. 3. Typology (Theology) I. Title.

HENDRY, George Stuart, 232.1
1904-
The gospel of the Incarnation. Philadelphia, Westminster Press [1958] 174p. 21cm. [BT220.H43] 58-5021
1. Incarnation. I. Title.

HERKLOTS, Hugh Gerard 232.1
Gibson, 1903-
The hope of our calling; five Biblical studies. Greenwich, Conn., Seabury Press, 1954. 82p. 19cm. [BT230.H43] 54-4005
1. Jesus Christ—Messiahship. I. Title.

JONES, George Elliott, 232.1
1889-
The pattern, the tebernacle, the Christ. Little Rock, Ark., Baptist Publications Committee [1962] 167p. 21cm. 'Revision and enlargement of Christ revealed in the tabernacle. [BT225.J6 1962] 62-15106
1. Typology (Theology) 2. Tabernacle. I. Title.

JONES, George Elliott, 232.1
1889-
The pattern, the tabernacle, the Christ. Little Rock, Ark., 716 Main St., Baptist Pubns. Comm., c.1962. 167p. 21cm. Rev. and enlargement of Christ revealed in the tabernacle. 62-15106 1.50 pap.,
1. Typology (Theology) 2. Tabernacle. I. Title.

KAC, Arthur W. 232'.1
The Messianic hope : a divine solution for the human problem / by Arthur W. Kac. Grand Rapids, Mich. : Baker Book House, c1975. viii, 355 p. ; 23 cm. (A Canon Press book) Includes bibliographical references and index. [BT230.K3] 75-4483 ISBN 0-8010-5363-3. ISBN 0-8010-5362-5 pbk.
1. Jesus Christ—Messiahship. 2. Messiah. 3. Resurrection. I. Title.

KETCHAM, Robert Thomas, 232.1
1889-
Old Testament pictures of New Testament truth, by Robert T. Ketcham. Des Plaines, Ill., Regular Baptist Press [1965] 249 p. illus. 20 cm. [BS478.K4] 65-23587
1. Typology (Theology) I. Title.

KETCHAM, Robert Thomas, 232.1
1889-
Old Testament pictures of New Testament truth. Des Plaines, Ill., Regular Baptist Pr., 1800 Oakton Blvd. [c.1965] 249p. illus. 20cm. [BS478.K4] 65-23587 2.95
1. Typology (Theology) I. Title.

KRIPKE, Dorothy (Karp) 232.1
Let's talk about God. Pictures by Bobri [pseud.] New York, Behrman House [1953] unpaged. illus. 25cm. [BM610.K7] 53-11529
1. God—Juvenile literature. I. Title.

LOVASIK, Lawrence George, 232.1
1913-
My beloved son. New York, Macmillan [1963] 340 p. 22 cm. [BT202.L6] 63-9598
1. Jesus Christ—Devotional literature. 2. Incarnation. I. Title.

MCDOWELL, Edward Allison, 232.1
1898-
Jesus and His cross. Nashville, Broadman Press [195-, c1944] 216p. 20cm. First published in 1944 under title: Son of Man and Suffering Servant. [BT205.M17] 58-42578
1. Son of Man. 2. Servant of Jehovah. 3. Jesus Christ—Person and offices. I. Title.

THE Myth of God incarnate 232'.1
/ edited by John Hick. 1st ed. Philadelphia : Westminster Press, c1977. xi, 211 p. ; 22 cm. Includes bibliographical references and index. [BT220.M95] 77-9965 ISBN 0-664-24178-6 pbk. : 4.95
1. Incarnation—Addresses, essays, lectures. I. Hick, John.

RIGGAN, George A. 232'.1
Messianic theology and Christian faith, by George A. Riggan. Philadelphia, Westminster Press [1967] 208 p. 21 cm. Bibliographical references included in "Notes" (p. [187]-199) [BM615.R5] 67-19298
1. Jesus Christ—Messiahship. 2. Messiah. I. Title.

SCHILTZER, Albert, 1902- 232.1
Redemptive incarnation; sources and their theological development in the study of Christ. Notre Dame, University of Notre Dame Press [1953] 337p. 23cm. (University religion series) [BT220.S37] 53-12857
1. Incarnation. I. Title.

SCHLITZER, Albert, 1902- 232.1
Redemptive incarnation; sources and their theological development in the study of Christ, [2d ed.] Notre Dame, University of Notre Dame Press [1956] 400p. 24cm. (University religion series) [BT220.S37 1956] 56-10219
1. Incarnation. I. Title.

SCHLITZER, Albert I. 1902- 232.1
Redemptive incarnation: sources and their theological development in the study of Christ. [2d ed.] Notre Dame, University of Notre Dame Press [1956] 100p 21cm.e(University religion series) [BT220.S37 1956] 56-10219
1. Incarnation I. Title.

SCHLITZER, Albert L 1902- 232.1
Redemptive incarnation; sources and their theological development in the study of Christ. Notre Dame, University of Notre Dame Press [1953] 337 p. 23 cm. (University religion series) [BT220.S37] 53-12857
1. Incarnation. I. Title.

SCHLITZER, Albert L 1902- 232.1
Redemptive incarnation; sources and their theological development in the study of Christ. [2d ed.] Notre Dame, University of Notre Dame Press [1956] 400 p. 24 cm. (University religion series) [BT220.S37] 56-10219
1. Incarnation. I. Title.

SKARD, Bjarne. 232.1
The incarnation; a study of the Christology of the Ecumenical creeds. Translated by Herman E. Jorgensen. Minneapolis, Augsburg Pub. House [1960] 184 p. 23 cm. [BT220.S463] 60-6436
1. Incarnation. I. Title.

SKARD, Bjarne 232.1
The incarnation; a study of the Christology of the Ecumenical creeds. Translated by Herman E. Jorgensen. Minneapolis, Augsburg Pub. House [c.1960] 184p. 23cm. 60-6436 3.50
1. Incarnation. I. Title.

SPIELMAN, William Carl, 232.1
1884-
The Messiah story. [1st ed.] New York, Comet Press Books [1955] 73p. 23cm. [BT230.S7] 55-9803
1. Jesus Christ—Messiahship. 2. Messiah. I. Title.

TODT, Heinz Eduard. 232.1
The Son of Man in the synoptic tradition [by] H. D. Todt. [Translated by Dorothea M. Barton] Philadelphia, Westminster Press [1965] 366 p. 23 cm. (The New Testament library) Bibliography: p. [353]-357. [BT232.T613] 65-22392
1. Son of Man. 2. Bible. N. T. Gospels — Criticism, Interpretation, etc. I. Title.

TODT, Heinz Eduard 232.1
The Son of Man in the synoptic tradition. [Tr. from German] by Dorothea M. Barton] Philadelphia, Westminster [c.1965] 366p. 23cm. (New Testament lib.) Bibl. [BT232.T613] 65-22392 8.50
1. Son of Man. 2. Bible. N. T. Gospels—Criticism, interpretation, etc. I. Title.

TORRANCE, Thomas Forsyth, 232'.1
1913-
Space, time and incarnation [by] Thomas F. Torrance. London, New York [etc.] Oxford U.P., 1969. xi, 92 p. 23 cm. Bibliographical footnotes. [BT220.T6] 72-410734 ISBN 0-19-213943-6 25/-
1. Incarnation. 2. Space and time. I. Title.

TRENT, Kenneth E. 232.1
Types of Christ in the Old Testament, a conservative approach to Old Testament typology. Foreword by Jacob Gartenhaus. New York, Exposition Press [c.1960] 123p. illus. 21cm. (An Exposition-Testament book) 60-50188 3.00
1. Typology (Theology) I. Title.

TRENT, Kenneth E 1927- 232.1
Types of Christ in the Old Testament, a conservative approach to Old Testament typology. Foreword by Jacob Gartenhaus. [1st ed.] New York, Exposition Press [1960] 123 p. illus. 21 cm. (An Exposition-Testament book) [BT225.T7] 60-50188
1. Typology (Theology) I. Title.

VOS, Geerhardus, 1862-1949. 232.1
The self-disclosure of Jesus; the modern debate about the Messianic consciousness. Edited and re-written by Johannes G. Vos. [New ed.] Grand Rapids, Eerdmans, 1954. 311p. 23cm. [BT230.V7 1954] 53-8145
1. Jesus Christ—Messiahship. I. Vos, Johannes Geerhardus, ed. II. Title.

WANSBROUGH, Henry, 1934- 232'.1
The Incarnation / Henry Wansbrough. Staten Island, N.Y. : Alba House, 1975, c1973. 110 p. ; 19 cm. (Scripture for meditation ; 10) [BT220.W29 1975] 74-31346 ISBN 0-8189-0315-5 pbk. : 1.95
1. Incarnation—Meditations. I. Title. II. Series.

WINGREN, Gustaf, 1910- 232.1
Man and the incarnation; a study in the Biblical theology of Irenneus. Translated by Ross Mackenzie. Philadelphia, Muhlenberg Press [1959] 233 p. 23 cm. Includes bibliography. [BR65.I64W53 1959] 59-49516
1. Irenaeus, Saint, Bp. of Lyons. I. Title.

WOODHALL, Ralph. 232'.1
The theology of the incarnation. Notre Dame, Ind., Fides Publishers [1968] 95, [1] p. 18 cm. (Theology today, no. 1) Bibliography: p. [96] [BT220.W73] 72-359 0.95
1. Incarnation. I. Title.

WREDE, William, 1859-1906. 232'.1
The messianic secret; translated [from the German] by J. C. G. Greig. Cambridge, J. Clarke, 1971. xxi, 292 p. 23 cm. (Library of

theological translations) Translation of Das Messiasgeheimnis in den Evangelien. Includes bibliographical references. [BT230.W813] 73-161741 ISBN 0-227-67717-X £4.50
1. Jesus Christ—Messiahship. 2. Bible. N.T. Mark—Criticism, interpretation, etc. I. Title.

ZIMMERLI, Walther, 1907- 232.1
The servant of God [by] W. Zimmerli [and] J. Jeremias. Naperville, Ill., A. R. Allenson [1957] 120p. 22cm. (Studies in Biblical theology, no. 20) 'This English translation of the article from Kittel's Theologisches Worterbuch zum NT was drafted by Harold Knight and afterwards completed by the editorial staff of the publisher, with help both from Professor Jeremias and his assistants in Gottingen. First published in ... (Stuttgart 1952)' Bibliography: p. 105-107. [BT235.Z5] 57-21804
1. Servant of Jehovah. I. Jeremias, Joachim, 1900- II. Title. III. Series.

ZIMMERLI, Walther, 1907- 232.1
The servant of God [by] W. Zimmerli [and] J. Jeremias. Naperville, Ill., A. R. Allenson [1957] 120 p. 22 cm. (Studies in Biblical theology, no. 20) "This English translation of the article Haiz Oeov from Kittle's Theologisches Worterbuch zum NT was drafted by Harold Knight and afterwards completed by the editorial staff of the publisher, with help both from Professor Jeremias and his assistants in Gottingen. First published in ... (Stuttgart 1952)" Bibliography: p. 105-107. [BT235.Z5] 57-21804
1. Servant of Jehovah. I. Jeremias, Joachim, 1900- II. Title. III. Series.

BARON, David. 232.12
Rays of Messiah's glory; Christ in the Old Testament. Grand Rapids, Zondervan Pub. House [1955?] 274 p. 20 cm.[Zondervan reprint classic] [BT235.B36] 55-2788
1. Messiah—Prophecies. 2. Jesus Christ—Messiahship. 3. Bible. O. T. — Prophecies. I. Title.

BIBLE. O. T. English. 232.12
Selections. 1960. Knox.
Waiting for Christ, based on the translation of the Old Testament messianic prophecies by Ronald Knox, arranged in a continuous narrative with explanations by Ronald Cox. New York, Sheed and Ward [c.1960] 282p. map. 22cm. 60-11681 3.50 half cloth,
1. Messiah—Prophecies. I. Knox, Ronald Arbuthnott, 1888-1957, tr. II. Cox, Ronald. III. Title.

EDERSHEIM, Alfred, 1825- 232.12
1889.
Prophecy and history in relation to the Messiah. Grand Rapids, Baker Book House, 1955. 391p. 23cm. (The Warburton lectures for 1880-1884) The Baker co-operative reprint library. [BT235] 55-8790
1. Messiah. 2. Prophecies. 3. Bibl. O. T. Pentateuch—Criticism, interpretation, etc. I. Title.

HEINISCH, Paul, 1878- 232.12
Christ in prophecy. William G. Heidt, translator. [Collegeville, Minn.] Liturgical Press [c1956] 279p. 24cm. [BT235.H39] 57-2891
1. Messiah—Prophecies. 2. Bible. O. T.—Prophecies. 3. Typology (Theology) I. Title.

HENGSTENBERG, Ernst 232.12
Wilhelm, 1802-1869.
Christology of the Old Testament, and a commentary on the Messianic predictions. Pref. by Merrill F. Unger. Grand Rapids, Kregel Publications, 1956. 4 v. 23cm. 'This reprint edition is an exact reproduction of the latest British edition printed in 1872-78. Translated from the German by Theod. Meyer and James Martin.' [BT235.H42 1956] 55-9467
1. Messiah—Prophecies. 2. Bible. O. T. — Prophecies. I. Title.

KLIGERMAN, Aaron Judah. 232.12
Messianic prophecy in the Old Testament. Foreword by Wilbur M. Smith. Grand Rapids, Zondervan Pub. House [1957] 155p. 22cm. Includes bibliography. [BT235.K55] 57-37883
1. Messiah—Prophecies. 2. Bible. O. T.—Prophecies. I. Title.

LINDSEY, Hal. 232'.12
The promise / by Hal Lindsey ; illustrated by Norm McGary. Irvine, Calif. : Harvest House, [1974] [100] p. : col. ill. ; 27 cm. Includes bibliographical references. Old Testament prophecies concerning events in the life of the promised Messiah are explained and linked with their fulfillment in the life of Jesus. [BS647.2.L53] 74-18859 ISBN 0-89081-004-4
1. Jesus Christ—Biography—Juvenile literature. 2. Bible—Prophecies—Juvenile literature. I. McGary, Norm, ill. II. Title.

MOWINCKEL, Sigmund Olaf 232.12
Plytt, 1884-
He that cometh. Translated by G. W. Anderson. New York, Abingdon Press [1954?] 258p. 23cm. [BT235] 56-14370
1. Messiah—Prophecies. 2. Jesus Christ—Messiahship. I. Title.

STEDMAN, Ray C. 232'.12
What on earth's going to happen? By Ray C. Stedman. Glendale, Calif., G/L Regal Books [1970] 203 p. 18 cm. [BS647.2.S66] 73-104085 0.95
1. Bible—Prophecies. I. Title.

RINGGREN, Helmer, 1917- 232.125
The Messiah in the Old Testament. Chicago, A. R. Allenson [1956] 71p. 22cm. (Studies in Biblical theology, no. 18) [BT235.R52] 56-14344
1. Messiah—Prophecies. 2. Bible. O. T.—Prophecies. I. Title.

YOUNG, Edward Joseph. 232.127
The messianic prophecies of Daniel. Grand Rapids, Eerdmans, 1954. 88p. 23cm. [BS1556] 54-4435
1. Bible O. T. Daniel—Prophecies. 2. Messiah—Prophecies. I. Title.

ATZBERGER, Leonhard. 232.2
Die Logoslehre des heiligen Athanasius : ihre Gegner u. unmittelbaren Vorlaufer / Leonhard Atzberger. Nachdr. d. Ausg. Munchen, Stahl, 1880. Hildesheim ; New York : Olms, 1975. vii, 246 p. ; 19 cm. Includes bibliographical references. [BT210.A88 1975] 75-522000 ISBN 3-487-05618-6 : DM38.00
1. Jesus Christ—History of doctrines—Early church, ca. 30-600. 2. Athanasius, Saint, Patriarch of Alexandria, d. 373. 3. Logos—History of doctrines. I. Title.

BALTHASAR, Hans Ure von, 232.2
1905-
Word and revelation. [Translated by A. V. Littledale with the cooperation of Alexander Dru. New York] Herder and Herder [1964] 191 p. 22 cm. (His Essays in theology, 1) Translation of Verbum caro. [BT80.B333] 64-19725
1. Theology, Doctrinal—Addresses, essays, lectures. 2. Communication (Theology) I. Title.

BALTHASAR, Hans Urs von, 232.2
1905-
Word and revelation [Tr. by A. V. Littledale with Alexander Dru. New York] Herder & Herder [c.1964] 191p. 22cm. (His Essays in theology, 1) 64-19725 3.95
1. Theology, Doctrinal—Addresses, essays, lectures 2. Communication (Theology) I. Title.

JONES, Alexander, 1906- 232.2
God's living word. New York, Sheed & Ward [1961] 214p. 22cm. [BT210.J62] 61-13039
1. Legos— Addresses. essays, lectures. I. Title.

JONES, Alexander, 1906- 232.2
God's living word. Glen Rock, N.J., Paulist [1965, c.1961] 208p. 18cm. (Deus bks.) [BT210.J62] .95 pap.,
1. Logos—Addresses, essays, lectures. I. Title.

MALONEY, George A., 1924- 232'.2
The cosmic Christ; from Paul to Teilhard [by] George A. Maloney. New York, Sheed and Ward [1968] viii, 309 p. 22 cm. Bibliography: p. 280-291. [BT198.M36] 68-13852 6.95
1. Jesus Christ—History of doctrines. I. Title.

*OLFORD, Stephen F. 232.2
The living word. Chicago, Moody [c.1963] 58p. 20cm. 1.75 bds.,
I. Title.

ERNEST, Brother, 1897- 232.231
Our Lady comes to Guadalupe. Illus. by Brother Bernard Howard. Notre Dame, Ind., Dujarie Press [1953] 93p. illus. 24cm. [BT660.G8E7] 53-3999
1. Gundalupe, Nuestra Sefiora de. I. Title.

AMUNDSEN, Wesley 232.3
Behold the Lamb. Mountain View, Calif., Pacific Pr. Pub. Assn. [c.1961] 107p. 61-15589 2.50
1. Atonement. I. Title.

AMUNDSEN, Wesley. 232.3
Behold' the Lamb. Mountain View, Calif., Pacific Press Pub. Assn. [1961] 107p. 19cm. [BT262.A5] 61-15589
1. Atonement. I. Title.

BARRY, Frank Russell, Bp. 232'.3
of Southwell, 1890-
The Atonement, by F. R. Barry. Philadelphia, Lippincott [1968] 224 p. 21 cm. (Knowing Christianity) Bibliographical references included in "Notes" (p. 193-217) [BT263.B3 1968b] 68-24601 2.95
1. Atonement—History of doctrines. I. Title.

BROWNING, Don S. 232.3
Atonement and psychotherapy, by Don S. Browning, Philadelphia, Westminster [1966] 288p. 21cm. Bibl. [BT265.2.B7] 66-13506 6.00
1. Atonement. I. Title.

CLARK, Theodore R 232.3
Saved by His life; a study of the New Testament doctrine of reconciliation and salvation. New York, Macmillan, 1959. 220p. 22cm. Includes bibliography. [BT265.2.C5] 59-11295
1. Atonement. 2. Salvation. I. Title.

CONNER, Walter Thomas, 232.3
1877-1952.
The cross in the New Testament. Nashville, Broadman Press [1954] 181p. 21cm. [BS2545.A8C6] 54-8022
1. Atonement—Biblical teaching. 2. Bible. N. T.—Theology. I. Title.

CRAWFORD, Thomas Jackson, 232.3
1812-1875.
The doctrine of Holy Scripture respecting the atonement. 4th ed. Grand Rapids, Baker Book House, 1954. x, 538p. 23cm. [Co-operative reprint library] [BT265.C73] 54-11085
1. Atonement. I. Title.

CULPEPPER, Robert H. 232.3
Interpreting the atonement, by Robert H. Culpepper. Grand Rapids, Eerdmans [1966] 170 p. 22 cm. Bibliographical footnotes. [BT265.2.C8] 66-22948
1. Atonement. I. Title.

CURRIN, Beverly Madison. 232'.3
If man is to live; a rediscovery of the meaning of the atonement. Nashville, Abingdon Press [1968, c1969] 174 p. 21 cm. [BT265.2.C85] 69-12011 3.50
1. Atonement. I. Title.

DILLISTONE, Frederick 232'.3
William, 1903-
The Christian understanding of atonement, by F. W. Dillistone. Philadelphia, Westminster Press [1968] 436 p. 23 cm. Bibliography: p. 429-434. [BT265.2.D5] 68-16329
1. Atonement. I. Title.

DILLISTONE, Frederick 232.3
William, 1903-
Jesus Christ and His Cross; studies on the saving work of Christ. Philadelphia, Westminster Press [1953] 143p. 21cm. [BT265.D478] 52-9811
1. Atonement. I. Title.

DIX, Gregory, Father. 232.3
The claim of Jesus Christ. Chicago, Wilcox & Follett Co. [1951] 86 p. 20 cm. (A Cloister Press book) Based on lectures published in England under title: The power and wisdom of God. [BT265.D55 1951] 51-2080
1. Atonement. I. Title.

ELLIS, Eric Kent 232.3
The power of the cross; seven simple considerations on the cross of Christ and the needs of to-day. [New York, Morehouse-Barlow] [1960] 46p. 19cm. 60-1588 .80 pap.,
1. Atonement. I. Title.

*FORSYTH, P. T. 232.3
The cruciality of the Cross. Grand Rapids, Mich., Eerdmans [1965] 104p. 20cm. 1.45 pap.,
I. Title.

GOCKEL, Herman William, 232.3
1906-
The cross and the common man; an everyday religion for everyday people. Saint Louis, Concordia Pub. House [1956, c1955] 155p. 20cm. [BT265.G6] 55-12190
1. Atonement. I. Title.

GRIFFITH, Arthur Leonard, 232.3
1920-
Beneath the cross of Jesus. Nashville, Abingdon [1962, c.1961] 94p. Bibl. 62-1008 1.00 pap.,
1. Atonement. I. Title.

HAUSHALTER, Walter Milton, 232.3
1889-
The mystery of the Cross, as illumined by the great thinkers of the West. Philadelphia, Dorrance [1956] 113p. illus. 20cm. [BT265.H29] 56-6195
1. Atonement. I. Title.

HEIM, Karl, 1874- 232.3
Jesus the world's perfecter; the atonement and the renewal of the world. Tr. [from German] by D. H. van Daalen, Philadelphia, Muhlenberg [1961, c.1959] 234p. 61-10277 3.75 bds.,
I. Title.

HENNESSY, Augustine Paul. 232'.3
The paschal mystery : core grace in the life of the Christian / Augustine Paul Hennessy. Chicago : Franciscan Herald Press, [1976] p. cm. (Synthesis series) [BT775.H37] 76-43245 ISBN 0-8199-0707-3 pbk. : 0.65
1. Redemption. 2. Atonement. 3. Paschal mystery. I. Title.

*HODGE, Archibald 232.3
Alexander, 1823-1886.
The atonement. Grand Rapids, Baker Book House [1974] 440 p. 20 cm. (Notable Books on Theology.) Reprint from the 1907 edition. [BT450] ISBN 0-8010-4097-3 3.95 (pbk.)
1. Atonement. I. Title.

HODGSON, Leonard, 1889- 232.3
The doctrine of the atonement. New York, Scribner, 1951. 159 p. 22 cm. (The Hale lectures, 1950) [BT265.H653 1951a] 51-6326
1. Atonement. I. Title.

HUEGEL, Frederick Julius, 232.3
1889-
The cross through the Scriptures, by F. J. Huegel. Grand Rapids, Zondervan Pub. House [1966] 192 p. 23 cm. [BT453.H85] 65-25948
1. Atonement. I. Title.

HUEGEL, Frederick Julius, 232.3
1889-
The cross through the Scriptures. Grand Rapids, Mich., Zondervan [c. 1966] 192p. 23cm. [BT453.H85] 65-25948 2.95 bds.,
1. Atonement. I. Title.

HUGHES, Thomas Hywel, 1875- 232.3
The Atonement, modern theories of the doctrine. London, Allen & Unwin. Mystic, Conn. 328p. 22cm. Bibl. A50 3.00
1. Atonement. I. Title.

JARRETT-KERR, Martin, 232.3
Father, 1912-
The atonement in our time. New York, Morehouse-Gorham, 1953. 164p. 19cm. 'Published in England as The hope of glory.' [BT265.J35] 53-7755
1. Atonement. I. Title.

KENDALL, Edith Lorna 232.3
A living sacrifice; a study of reparation. Philadelphia, Westminster Press [c.1960] 174p. (Library of history and doctrine) Bibl. 60-10643 4.00
1. Atonement. 2. Sanctification. I. Title. II. Title: Reparation.

KNOX, John, 1900- 232.3
The death of Christ; the Cross in New Testament history and faith. New York, Abingdon Press [1958] 190 p. 21 cm. [BT453.K5] 58-5389
1. Atonement. I. Title.

KUIPER, Rienk Bouke, 1886- 232.3
For whom did Christ die? A study of the divine design of the atonement. Grand Rapids, Eerdmans [1959] 104p. 21cm. [BT267.K8] 58-59779
1. Barth, Karl, 1886- 2. Atonement. 3. Universalism. 4. Arminianism. 5. Calvinism. I. Title.

LANGENSTEIN, Rupert, 1910- 232.3
Behold the man. Milwaukee, Bruce Pub. Co. [1952] 80 p. 20 cm. [BT265.L487] 52-1171
1. Atonement. I. Title.

LIGHTNER, Robert Paul. 232'.3
The death Christ died; a case for unlimited atonement, by Robert P. Lightner. Des Plaines, Ill., Regular Baptist Press [1967] 151 p. · 21 cm. Bibliographical footnotes. [BT267.L54] 67-30992
1. Atonement. I. Title.

MALTBY, William Russell 232.3
Christ and His cross, by W. Russell Maltby. Nashville, Abingdon [1963, c.1936] 128p. 18cm. (Apex bk., N4) 1.00 pap.,
I. Title.

MURRAY, John, 1898- 232.3
Redemption, accomplished and applied. Grand Rapids, W. B. Eerdmans Pub. Co., 1955. 236p. 23cm. [BT775.M8] 55-13972
1. Redemption. I. Title.

NASH, Henry Sylvester, 232.3
1854-1912.
The atoning life. New York, Harper [1950] xii, 112 p. 20 cm. (The Presiding Bishop's book for Lent [1950]) [BT265.N2 1950] 50-5313
1. Atonement. I. Title. II. Series.

NELSON, Clifford Ansgar. 232.3
The cross is the key; a book about the cross for plain, thoughtful people. Rock Island, Ill., Augustana Book Concern [c1954] 196p. 21cm. [BT453.N38] 54-16108
1. Atonement. I. Title.

NICHOLS, James Albert. 232.3
A critique of the theory of vital atonement. [1st ed.] New York, Vantage Press [1955] 94p. 23cm. 'The purpose of this study is to examine

the doctrine of vital atonement as set forth by the late Rev. Clarence H. Hewitt ... in his book, Vital atonement.' [BT265.H48N5] 54-12634
1. Hewitt, Clarence Horace, 1890-1952. Vital atonement. 2. Atonement. 3. Advent Christian Church— Doctrinal and controversial works. I. Title. II. Title: Vital atonement.

OULTON, John Ernest Leonard, 1886- 232.3
The mystery of the cross. Greenwich, Conn., Seabury Press, 1957. 63p. 19cm. 'Lectures... delivered to the students of Lincoln Theological College in Passion Week. 1956.' [BT265] 57-2299
1. Atonement. I. Title.

PAUL, Robert S. 232.3
The atonement and the sacraments; the relation of the atonement to the sacraments of baptism and the Lord's Supper. Nashville, Abingdon Press [c.1960] 396p. 24cm. (bibl. footnotes) 60-5234 6.50
1. Atonement—Hist. 2. Sacraments. I. Title.

PINK, Arthur Walkington, 1886-1952. 232.3
The satisfaction of Christ. Swengel, Pa., Bible Truth Depot, 1955. 313p. 22cm. [BT265.P58] 55-12398
1. Atonement. I. Title.

REINER, Edwin W. 232'.3
The atonement, by Edwin W. Reiner. Nashville, Southern Pub. Association [1971] 255 p. illus. 21 cm. [BT265.2.R43] 74-151003 ISBN 0-8127-0051-1
1. Atonement.

ROGERS, Edward, 1909- 232.3
That they might have life. Pref. by Samuel McCrea Cavert. Great Neck, N. Y., Channel Press [1959] 116p. 21cm. [BT265.2.R6 1959] 59-6805
1. Atonement. I. Title.

RUDISILL, Dorus Paul, 1902- 232'.3
The doctrine of the atonement in Jonathan Edwards and his successors. [1st ed.] New York, Poseidon Books [1971] ix, 143 p. 21 cm. Bibliography: p. 139-143. [BT263.R8] 77-151509 ISBN 0-8181-9998-9 4.95
1. Edwards, Jonathan, 1703-1758. 2. Atonement—History of doctrines. I. Title.

SANDERS, Jim Alvin. 232.3
The Old Testament in the cross. New York, Harper [c.1961] 143p. 61-7348 3.00 bds.,
1. Atonement. 2. Bible. N.T.—Relation to O.T. I. Title.

SODERBLOM, Nathan, Abp., 1866-1931. 232'.3
The death and resurrection of Christ; reflections on the Passion. Translated by A. G. Hebert and Gene J. Lund. Minneapolis, Augsburg Pub. House [1967, c1968] 87 p. 20 cm. "Translation of two chapters of the book Kristi pinas historia." [BT453.S6613] 68-13422
1. Jesus Christ—Crucifixion. 2. Jesus Christ—Resurrection. I. Title.

TAYLOR, John, 1808-1887. 232.3
An examination into and an elucidation of the great principle of the mediation and atonement of Our Lord and Savior Jesus Christ. [1st ed. with concordance. Salt Lake City 1950] 206 p. 24 cm. Cover title: The mediation and atonement. "A concordance of The mediation and atonement, by Peter C. Cariston": . 190-206. [BX8643.B6T3 1950] 50-1763
1. Mormons and Mormonism — Doctrinal and controversial works. 2. Atonement. I. Title. II. Title: The mediation and atonement.

TAYLOR, Vincent, 1887- 232.3
The Cross of Christ; eight public lectures. London, Macmillan; New York, St. Martin's Press, 1956. 108p. 23cm. [BT265.T25] 57-13543
1. Atonement. I. Title.

TAYLOR, Vincent, 1887- 232.3
The Cross of Christ; eight public lectures. London, Macmillan, New York St. Martin's Press 1956. 108 p. 23 cm. [BT265.T25] 57-13543
1. Atonement. I. Title.

THOMAS, George William Curtis. 232.3
The circle and the cross. New York, Abingdon Press [1964] 140 p. 21 cm. Bibliography: p. 137-140. [BT265.2.T5] 64-10441
1. Atonement. I. Title.

THOMAS, George William Curtis 232.3
The circle and the Cross. Nashville, Abingdon [c.1964] 140p. 21cm. Bibl. 64-10441 2.75
1. Atonement. I. Title.

WALKER, Alan. 232.3
The many-sided cross of Jesus. New York, Abingdon Press [1962] 111 p. 20 cm. [BT453.W25] 62-7229
1. Atonement. I. Title.

WALKER, Alan 232.3
The many-sided cross of Jesus. Nashville, Abingdon [c.1962] 111p. 62-7229 2.00
1. Atonement. I. Title.

WILLIAMS, George Huntston 232.3
Anselm; Communion and atonement. Saint Louis, Mo., Concordia Pub. House [c.1960] 72p. 20cm. First printed in Church history, xxvi, (1957) 245--274 . . . It has been slightly enlarged and further documented.' Bibl.: p. 69-72. 60-1023 1.50 pap.,
1. Anselm, Saint, Abp. of Canterbury, 1033-1109. Cur Deus homo. 2. Atonement—Hist. 3. Lord's Supper—Hist. 4. Atonement—Hist. 5. Lord's Supper—Hist. I. Title.

WILLIAMS, George Huntston, 1914- 232.3
Anselm; Communion and atonement. Saint Louis, Concordia Pub. House [1960] 72 p. 20 cm. "First printed in Church history, xxvi (1957), 245-247 ... It has been slightly enlarged and further documented." Includes bibliography. [BT264.A63W5] 60-1023
1. Anselm, Saint. Abp. of Canterbury, 1033-1109. Cur Deus home. 2. Atonement — Hist. 3. Lord's Supper — Hist. I. Title.

WOLF, William J 232.3
No cross, no crown; a study of the atonement. [1st ed.] Garden City, N. Y., Doubleday, 1957. 216p. 22cm. [BT265.W79] 57-5535
1. Atonement. I. Title.

WOLF, William J 232.3
No cross, no crown; a study of the atonement. [1st ed.] Garden City, N.Y., Doubleday, 1957. 216 p. 22 cm. [BT265.W79] 57-5535
1. Atonement. I. Title.

WOLF, William J. 232.3
No cross, no crown; a study of the atonement. Hamden, Conn., Archon Bks. [dist. Shoe String Pr.] 1962 [c.1957] 216p. Bibl. 62-16047 6.00
1. Atonement. I. Title.

ZEIDLER, Clemens H 232'.3
Jesus speaks of his death; a Biblical perspective of the Passion. Minneapolis, T. S. Denison [c1966] 175 p. 22 cm. Bibliographical footnotes. [BT262.Z4] 66-14845
1. Atonement — Biblical teaching. I. Title.

LOEWENICH, Walther von, 1903- 232'.3'0924
Luther's theology of the cross / [by] Walther von Loewenich ; translated [from the German] by Herbert J. A. Bouman. Belfast : Christian Journals Ltd, 1976. 224 p. ; 23 cm. Translation of Luthers theologia crucis. Bibliography: p. 209-215. [BR333.L6313 1976b] 76-376728 ISBN 0-904302-18-0 : £4.00
1. Luther, Martin, 1483-1546—Theology. I. Title.

DALY, Robert J., 1933- 232'.4
The origins of the Christian doctrine of sacrifice / by Robert J. Daly. Philadelphia : Fortress Press, c1977. p. cm. Includes indexes. [BS680.S2D34] 77-78628 ISBN 0-8006-1267-1 : pbk. : 5.95
1. Sacrifice—Biblical teaching. 2. Sacrifice—History of doctrines. I. Title.

*HUEGEL, F. J. 232.4
The cross of Christ--the throne of God. Minneapolis, Bethany [1965] 143p. 19cm. 1.50 pap.,
I. Title.

SMYTH, Frederic Hastings, 1888- 232.4
Sacrifice; a doctrinal homily. New York, Vantage Press [c1953] 149p. illus. 22cm. [BT265.S68] 53-10308
1. Sacrifice. I. Title.

VAUX, Roland de, 1903- 232.4
Studies in Old Testament sacrifice. Cardiff, Univ. of Wales Pr. [Mystic, Conn., Verry, 1966] x, 120p. 23cm. Contains in a somewhat expanded form the Four Elizabeth James lects. given at Univ. Coll. Cardiff, in Oct. 1961. Bibl. [BS1199.S2V3] 65-6513 3.50
1. Sacrifuie—Biblical teaching. 2. Bible. O. T.—Rites and ceremonies. I. Title.

GOLDWIN, Robert A. 1922- ed. 232.41
100 years of emancipation; four essays by Roy Wilkins [others. Chicago] Public Affairs Conf. Center, Univ. of Chic., c.1963. 30cm. 63-2611 apply
1. Negroes—Civil rights. 2. U. S.—Legal status, laws, etc. 3. Emancipation proclamation. I. Wilkins, Roy, 1901- II. Title.

BISER, Eugen 232.5
The light of the Lamb. Tr. by William Kramer. Chicago, H. Regnery Co. [c.]1961. 111p. 61-7024 2.95
1. Jesus Christ—Resurrection. I. Title.

CLARK, Neville. 232'.5
Interpreting the resurrection. Philadelphia, Westminster Press [1967] 128 p. 20 cm. [BT481.C55 1967b] 67-20612
1. Jesus Christ—Resurrection. 2. Resurrection. I. Title.

COLLINS, Thomas P. 232'.5
The risen Christ in the fathers of the church. Prepared and edited with introd. and commentary by Thomas P. Collins. Glen Rock, N.J., Paulist Press [1967] ix, 118 p. 21 cm. (Guide to the Fathers of the church) Bibliography: p. 115. [BT198.C58] 67-23608
1. Jesus Christ—History of doctrines—Early church, ca. 30-600. 2. Jesus Christ—Resurrection. 3. Fathers of the church. I. Title.

FUDGE, Edward. 232'.5
Resurrection! Essays in honor of Homer Hailey. Edited by Edward Fudge. [Athens, Ala.] C.E.I. Pub. Co. [1973] 131 p. port. 23 cm. Includes bibliographies. [BT481.F78] 73-80555 ISBN 0-88407-003-4 4.95
1. Jesus Christ—Resurrection. 2. Hailey, Homer, 1904- 3. Resurrection. I. Hailey, Homer, 1904- II. Title.

FUDGE, Edward. 232'.5
Resurrection! Essays in honor of Homer Hailey. Edited by Edward Fudge. [Athens, Ala.] C.E.I. Pub. Co. [1973] 131 p. port. 23 cm. Includes bibliographies. [BT481.F78] 73-80555 ISBN 0-88407-003-4 4.95
1. Jesus Christ—Resurrection. 2. Hailey, Homer, 1904- 3. Resurrection. I. Hailey, Homer, 1904- II. Title.
Publisher's Address: 1005 Jefferson, Athens, Ala. 35611

FULLER, Daniel P 232.5
Easter faith and history, by Daniel P. Fuller. Grand Rapids, Eerdmans [1965] 279 p. 23 cm. Revision of author's thesis -- Basel. Bibliography: p. [262]-272. [BT481.F8] 64-8577
1. Jesus Christ — Resurrection. 2. Bible. N. T. — Historiography. 3. Jesus Christ — Historicity. I. Title.

FULLER, Daniel P. 232.5
Easter faith and history. Grand Rapids, Mich., Eerdmans [c.1965] 279p. 23cm. Bibl. [BT481.F8] 64-8577 4.95
1. Jesus Christ—Resurrection. 2. Bible. N.T.—Historigoraphy. 3. Jesus Christ—Historicity. I. Title.

THE Gift of Easter / 232'.5
compiled and edited by Floyd Thatcher. Waco, Tex. : Word Books, c1976. 165 p. : ill. ; 23 cm. [BT481.G5] 75-36182 5.95
1. Jesus Christ—Resurrection—Meditations. I. Thatcher, Floyd W.

THE Gift of Easter / 232'.5
compiled and edited by Floyd Thatcher. Waco, Tex. : Word Books, c1976. 165 p. : ill. ; 23 cm. [BT481.G5] 75-36182 5.95
1. Jesus Christ—Resurrection—Meditations. I. Thatcher, Floyd W.

GOPPELT, Leonhard, 1911- 232.5
The Easter message today three essays by Leonhard Goppelt, Helmut Thielicke, Hans-Rudolf MullerSchwefe. Tr. [from German] by Salvator Attanasio, Darrell Likens Guder. Introd. by Markus Barth. New York, Nelson [c.1964] 156p. 21cm. Bibl. 64-17738 2.95
1. Jesus Christ—Resurrection. 2. Easter. I. Title.

HOBBS, Herschel H. 232.5
Messages on the Resurrection. Grand Rapids, Mich., Baker Book House [c.] 1959. 87p. 21cm. 59-15531 1.75 bds.,
1. Jesus Christ—Resurrection—Sermons. 2. Bible. N. T. 1 Corinthians xv—Sermons. 3. Sermons, American. I. Title.

JANSEN, John Frederick. 232'.5
No idle tale. Richmond, John Knox Press [1967] 106 p. 21 cm. Bibliographical references included in "Notes" (p. 93-106) [BT481.J3] 67-25804
1. Jesus Christ—Resurrection. 2. Bible. N.T. Luke XXIV—Commentaries. I. Title.

*JUSTICE, William M. 232'.5
Our visited planet. [First ed.] New York, Vantage [1973] 179 p. 21 cm. [BT481] ISBN 0-533-00735-6 5.95
1. Jesus Christ—Resurrection. I. Title.

KUNNETH, Walter, 1901- 232.5
The theology of the resurrection. [Translated by James W. Leitch] St. Louis, Concordia Pub. House [1965] 302 p. 23 cm. Bibliographical footnotes. [BT480.K833] 65-25571
1. Jesus Christ — Resurrection. I. Title.

KUNNETH, Walter, 1901- 232.5
The theology of the resurrection [Tr. from German by James W. Leitch] St. Louis, Concordia [1966,c.1965] 302p. 23cm. Bibl. [BT480.K833] 65-25571 5.00
1. Jesus Christ—Resurrection. I. Title.

LADD, George Eldon, 1911- 232'.5
I believe in the resurrection of Jesus / by George Eldon Ladd. Grand Rapids : Eerdmans, 1975. 156 p. ; 21 cm. (I believe ; 2) Includes bibliographical references and index. [BT481.L25] 75-14148 ISBN 0-8028-1611-8 pbk. : 2.95
1. Jesus Christ—Resurrection. 2. Resurrection—Biblical teaching. I. Title.

MCLEMAN, James. 232'.5
Resurrection then and now. Philadelphia, Lippincott, 1967 [c1965] 255 p. 21 cm. Bibliography: p. 247-249. [BT431.M3 1967] 67-13304
1. Jesus Christ—Resurrection. I. Title.

MARTELET, Gustave. 232'.5
The risen Christ and the Eucharistic world / Gustave Martelet ; translated by Rene Hague. London : Collins, 1976. 252 p. ; 22 cm. Translation of Resurrection, eucharistie et genese de l'homme. Includes bibliographical references and index. [BT481.M3513] 76-382810 ISBN 0-00-215709-8 : £4.95
1. Jesus Christ—Resurrection. 2. Lord's Supper—Catholic Church. I. Title.

MUMAW, John R 1904- 232.5
The resurrected life, by John R. Mumaw. Scottdale, Pa., Herald Press [1965] 160 p. 20 cm. (The Conrad Grebel lectures, 1964) Bibliographical references included in "Footnotes" (p. 153-160) [BT481.M8] 65-11460
1. Jesus Christ — Resurrection. I. Title.

MUMAW, John R. 1904- 232.5
The resurrected life. Scottdale, Pa., Herald Pr. [c.1965] 160p. 20cm. (Conrad Grebel lects. 1964) Bibl. [BT481.M8] 65-11460 3.50
1. Jesus Christ—Resurrection. I. Title. II. Series.

ORR, James, 1844-1913. 232.5
The resurrection of Jesus. Grand Rapids, Zondervan Pub. House [1965] 292 p. 21 cm. Bibliographical footnotes. [BT480.O75] 65-24409
1. Jesus Christ — Resurrection. I. Title.

PARSONS, Elmer E 232'.5
Witness to the resurrection, by Elmer E. Parsons. Grand Rapids, Baker Book House [1967] 131 p. 20 cm. Bibliography: p. 127-131. [BT481.P3] 67-18189
1. Jesus Christ—Resurrection. I. Title.

PARSONS, Elmer E. 232'.5
Witness to the resurrection, by Elmer E. Parsons. Grand Rapids, Baker Book House [1967] 131 p. 20 cm. Bibliography: p. 127-131. [BT481.P3] 67-18189
1. Jesus Christ—Resurrection. I. Title.

REX, Helmut Herbert, 1913-1967 232'.5
Did Jesus rise from the dead? [by] H. H. Rex. Auckland, B. & J. Paul [1967] 93p. 19cm. Bibl. refs. included in Notes [BT481.R46] 68-96619 1.75 pap.,
1. Jesus Christ—Resurrection. I. Title.
Distributed by Tri-Ocean, San Francisco.

RICHARDS, Hubert John, 1921- 232'.5
The first Easter : what really happened? / [by] Hubert J. Richards. [London] : Collins, 1976. 126 p. ; 18 cm. (Fontana religious) [BT481.R48] 77-356778 ISBN 0-00-624166-2 : £0.65
1. Jesus Christ—Resurrection. I. Title.

ROPER, Albert L. 232.5
Did Jesus rise from the dead? Grand Rapids. Mich., Zondervan [1964, c.1965] 54p. 22cm. [BT481.R58] 65-904 1.95 bds.,
1. Jesus Christ—Resurrection. I. Title. II. Title: A lawyer looks at the evidence. Foreword by Costen J. Ha rrell.

ROYER, W M 232.5
Mystery of the faith; or, A life controlled by the Unseen. [1st ed.] New York, Greenwich Book Publishers [1961, c1959] 55p. 22cm. [BT481.R6 1961] 59-14479
1. Jesus Christ—Resurrection. 2. Faith—Biblical teaching. I. Title.

SELBY, Peter. 232'.5
Look for the living : the corporate nature of resurrection faith / Peter Selby. 1st American ed. Philadelphia : Fortress Press, 1976. viii, 212 p. ; 22 cm. Includes indexes. Bibliography: p. [199]-203. [BT481.S47 1976] 76-15884 ISBN 0-8006-1245-0 pbk. : 5.95

1. Jesus Christ—Resurrection. I. Title.

THE Significance of the 232'.5
message of the resurrection for faith in Jesus Christ [by] Willi Marxsen [and others. Essay I translated by Dorothea M. Barton; the remainder translated by R. A. Wilson] Edited, with an introd., by C. F. D. Moule. Naperville, Ill., A. R. Allenson [1968] v, 142 p. 22 cm. (Studies in Biblical theology. 2d ser., 8) Translation of Die Bedeutung der Auferstehungsbotschaft fur den Glauben an Jesus Christus. Bibliographical footnotes. [BT481.B413 1968b] 68-4917
1. Jesus Christ—Resurrection—Addresses, essays, lectures. I. Marxsen, Willi, 1919- II. Moule, Charles Francis Digby, ed. III. Title. IV. Series.

SIMPSON, William John 232'.5
Sparrow, 1859-1952.
The Resurrection and the Christian faith. Grand Rapids, Zondervan Pub. House [1968] ix, 462 p. 23 cm. Reprint of the 1911 ed., published under the title: The Resurrection and modern thought. Includes bibliographical references. [BT480.S53 1968] 68-13317
1. Jesus Christ—Resurrection. 2. Resurrection. I. Title.

TORRANCE, Thomas Forsyth, 232.5
1913-
Space, time and resurrection / [by] Thomas F. Torrance. Edinburgh : Handsel Press, 1976. xiii, 196 p. ; 23 cm. Includes bibliographical references and index. [BT481.T67 1976b] 77-367706 ISBN 0-905312-00-7 : £5.00
1. Jesus Christ—Resurrection. 2. Jesus Christ—Ascension. 3. Space theology. I. Title.

TULGA, Chester Earl, 1896- 232.5
The case for the resurrection of Jesus Christ. Chicago, Conservative Baptist Fellowship [1951] 59 p. 18 cm. (His Litte books on big subjects) [BT480.T8] 51-36440
1. Jesus Christ — Resurrection. I. Title.

WEATHERHEAD, Leslie Dixon 232.5
The manner of the resurrection in the light of modern science and psychical research. New York, Abingdon Press [1960, c.1959] 92p. 18cm. 60-33 1.00 pap.,
1. Jesus Christ—Resurrection. I. Title.

WEATHERHEAD, Leslie Dixon, 232.5
1893-
The Resurrection and the life. New York, Abingdon-Cokesbury Press [1953, c1948] 60p. 20cm. [BT480.W4] 52-11309
1. Jesus Christ—Resurrection. I. Title.

THOMAS, George Ernest, 232.5081
1907-
The meaning of the Resurrection in Christian experience. Nashville, Tidings, 1908 Grand Ave. [1964] 84p. 19cm. [BT481.T5] 64-25871 .60
1. Jesus Christ—Resurrection—Sermons. 2. Sermons, American. 3. Methodist Church—Sermons. I. Title.

ABRAM, Victor P. 232.6
The restoration of all things. Amherst, N. H., Chestnut Hill Rd. Kingdom Pr., [c.1962] 149p. 21cm. 62-18059 2.00
1. Sandford, Frank W., 1862-1948. 2. Second Advent. I. Title.

ABRAM, Victor P 232.6
The restoration of all things. Amherst, N. H., Kingdom Press [1962] 149p. 21cm. 'The first eleven chapters ... appeared as successive monthly instalments in the Standard during 1951 and 1952.' [BV3785.S18A65] 62-18059
1. Stanford, Frank W., 1862-1948. 2. Second Advent. I. Title.

ALDERMAN, Paul R., Jr. 232.6
God's spotlight on tomorrow; seven sevens concerning the return of Christ. [New York 1019 W. 21 St. Loizeaux Brothers, Inc., 1960] 32p. 20cm. .50 pap.,
I. Title.

ALLEN, Gordon E 1923- 232.6
The second coming of Jesus, with an exposition of the book of Revelation. Goldsboro, N. C., Carolina Print. Co. [1960] 147p. 22cm. [BT886.A4] 60-16977
1. Second Advent. 2. Bible. N. T. Revelation—Commentaries. I. Title.

*ARMERDING, Carl 232.6
Signs of Christ's coming, as son of man. Chicago, Moody [1965] 79p. 18cm. (Compact bks., no. 53. MP29) .29 pap.,
I. Title.

BARKER, Harold P 232.6
Coming twice. New York, Loizeaux Bros. [19--] 159p. 19cm. (Treasury library, no.25) [BT885.B24] 56-26551
1. Second Advent. I. Title.

BERKHOF, Louis, 1873- 232.6
The second coming of Christ. Grand Rapids, W. B. Eerdmans Pub. Co., 1953. 102p. 23cm. [BT885.B42] 53-9734
1. Second Advent. I. Title.

BERKOUWER, Gerrit 232'.6
Cornelis, 1903-
The return of Christ, by G. C. Berkouwer. Grand Rapids, Eerdmans [1972] 477 p. 23 cm. (His Studies in dogmatics) Translation of De wederkomst van Christus. Includes bibliographical references. [BT886.B4513] 72-178664 ISBN 0-8028-3393-4 9.95
1. Second Advent. 2. Eschatology. I. Title.

BLODGETT, Ralph H., 1940- 232'.6
Rapture! : Is it for real? / Ralph Blodgett. Mountain View, Calif. : Pacific Press Pub. Association, c1975. 64 p. : graphs ; 19 cm. Includes index. [BT886.B53] 75-27618
1. Second Advent. I. Title.

CARDEY, Elmer L. 232.6
The countdown of history. Grand Rapids, Mich., Baker Bk. [c.]1962. 198p. 23cm. 62-20455 2.95
1. Second Advent. I. Title.

CRISWELL, Wallie A. 232'.6
Welcome back, Jesus! / W. A. Criswell. Nashville : Broadman Press, c1976. 189 p. ; 21 cm. [BT886.C7] 76-27482 ISBN 0-8054-1939-X : 5.95
1. Second Advent. I. Title.

DE HAAN, Martin Ralph, 232.6
M.D., 1891-
Coming events in prophecy. Grand Rapids, Mich., Zondervan [c.1962] 151p. 62-3002 2.50
1. End of the world. 2. Bible—Prophecies. I. Title.

DOUTY, Norman Franklin, 232.6
1899-
Has Christ's return two stages? [1st ed.] New York, Pageant Press [c1956] 127p. 21cm. Includes bibliography. [BT885.D67] 56-12598
1. Second Advent. I. Title.

*EARLE, Ralph. 232.6
What the Bible says about the second coming. Grand Rapids, Mich., Baker Book House [1973, c1970] 90 p, 18 cm. (Baker book house direction books) Previous editions have title: Behold, I come. Bibliography: p. 89-90 [BT886] ISBN 0-8010-3307-1 0.95 (pbk.)
1. Second Advent. I. Title.

FRASER, Neil McCormick. 232'.6
The gladness of His return; a closer look at the second coming [by] Neil M. Fraser. [1st ed.] Neptune, N.J., Loizeaux Brothers [1967] 127 p. 20 cm. Final vol. in the author's trilogy; the 1st of which is The grandeur of Golgotha; and the 2d of which is The glory of His rising. [BT886.F7] 66-25721
1. Second Advent. I. Title.

HALDEMAN, Isaac Massey, 232.6
1845-1933
Ten sermons on the second coming of Our Lord Jesus Christ, preached in the First Baptist church, New York City, from October 15 to December 17, 1916, by the pastor, I. M. Haldeman. Grand Rapids, Mich., Baker Bk., 1963. 748p. 21cm. 4.95
1. Second advent—Sermons. 2. Baptists—Sermons. 3. Sermons, American. I. Title.

HARRISON, William K. 232.6
Hope triumphant: studies on the rapture of the church, 153p. 22cm. [BT886.H3] 66-9661 2.95
1. Second Advent. I. Title.

HASTINGS, Horace Lorenzo 232.6
The church not in darkness [3rd ed.] New York 25 Box 87 Cathedral Station People's Christian Bulletin, 28p. 19cm. .10 pap.,
I. Title.

HAYNES, Carlyle Boynton, 232.6
1882-
Our Lord's return, by Carlyle B. Haynes. Rev. and reillustrated. Nashville, Southern Pub. Association [1964] 125 p. illus., map. 21 cm. (A Summit book) [BT885.H29 1964] 63-21241
1. Second Advent. I. Title.

HOLLEY, Joseph Winthrop, 232.6
1874-
Regnum montis; Scriptural and historical evidence that the destiny of the South is interwoven with the second coming of Christ. New York, William-Frederick Press, 1954. 112p. illus. 23cm. [BT885.H714] 54-8116
1. Second Advent. 2. Negroes. I. Title.

HOLLEY, Joseph Winthrop, 232.6
1874-
Regnum montis and its contemporary; heralding the second coming of Christ in the decade, 1995-2005, and the end of the world of things material. New York, William-Frederick Press, 1958. 141p. 23cm. [BT885.H713] 57-12740
1. Second Advent. I. Title.

HOLLISTER, Horace Edward. 232.6
"I will come again"--Jesus; the five successive phases of the Advent. A fresh analysis of the Old and New Testament prophetic writings concerning the second coming of Christ the Messiah. Chicago, Society for Bible Re-search, 1950. 319 p. 23 cm. [BT885.H715] 51-20325
1. Second Advent. I. Title.

HUGHES, Archibald, 1905- 232.6
A new heaven and a new earth; an introductory study of the coming of the Lord Jesus Christ and the eternal inheritance. Foreword by C. H. Nash. Philadelphia, Presbyterian and Reformed Pub. Co., 1958. 233p. 22cm. Includes bibliography. [BT885.H864] 58-13254
1. Second Advent. I. Title.

INTERNATIONAL Congress on 232.6
Prophecy, 1st, New York, 1952.
Hastening the day of God; prophetic messages from the International Congress on Prophecy, in Calvary Baptist Church, New York City, November 9-16, 1952. Compiled and edited by John W. Bradbury. Wheaton, Ill., Van Kampen Press [1953] 262p. 22cm. [BT885.I55 1952a] 53-10677
1. Second Advent. I. Bradbury, John W., ed. II. Title.

INTERNATIONAL Congress on 232.6
Prophecy. 2d, New York, 1955.
Understanding the times; prophetic messages delivered at the 2nd International Congress on Prophecy, New York City. Editors: William Culbertson, Herman B. Centz. Grand Rapids, Zondervan Pub. House [1956] 290p. 22cm. 'Produced for American Association for Jewish Evangelism, Winona Lake, Indiana.' [BT885.I55 1955] 57-20452
1. Second Advent. I. Culbertson, William, ed. II. Centz, Herman B., ed. III. Title.

*JONES, Russell Bradley. 232.6
What, where, and when is The Millenium? Grand Rapids, Baker Book House, [1975] 144 p. 20 cm. Includes index. Bibliography: p. 134-135. [BT891] ISBN 0-8010-5058-8 2.95 (pbk.)
1. Jesus Christ. 2. Millennium. 3. Second Advent. I. Title.

KOCH, Kurt E. 232'.6
Day X; the world situation in the light of the second coming of Christ, by Kurt Koch. Grand Rapids, Mich., Kregel Publications [1971?] 128 p. 18 cm. Translation of Tag X. [BT876.K613] 70-160688 ISBN 0-8254-3005-4 0.95
1. End of the world. I. Title.

KRIKORIAN, Meshach Paul, 232'.6
1890-
The Apocalypse of Jesus Christ; an interpretation of Our Saviour's second advent "with power and great glory", by M. P. Krikorian. Philadelphia, Dorrance [1973] 171 p. illus. 22 cm. [BT886.K73] 73-84493 ISBN 0-8059-1906-6 5.00
1. Second Advent. I. Title.

LADD, George Eldon, 1911- 232.6
The blessed hope. Grand Rapids, Eerdmans, 1956. 167p. 23cm. [BT885.L23] 56-10166
1. Second Advent. I. Title.

LADD, George Eldon, 1911- 232.6
Jesus Christ and history. Chicago, Inter-Varsity Press [1963] vii, 62 p. 21 cm. (IVP series in contemporary Christian thought, 5) Bibliography: p. 60-62. [BT886.L3] 63-8556
1. Second Advent. I. Title.

LADD, George Eldon, 1911- 232.6
Jesus Christ and history. Chicago, Inter-Varsity Pr. [c.1963] vii, 62p. 21cm. (IVP ser. in contemporary Christian thought, 5) Bibl. 63-8556 1.25 pap.,
1. Second Advent. I. Title.

LINDSEY, Hal. 232'.6
When is Jesus coming again / by Hal Lindsey and others. Carol Stream, Ill. : Creation House, c1974. 96 p. : ports. ; 18 cm. (New leaf library) Bibliography: p. 83-96. [BT886.L56] 75-3613 ISBN 0-88419-110-9 : 1.45
1. Second Advent—Addresses, essays, lectures. 2. Tribulation (Christian eschatology)—Addresses, essays, lectures. 3. Rapture (Christian eschatology)—Addresses, essays, lectures. I. Title.

LUND, Gerald N. 232'.6
The coming of the Lord [by] Gerald N. Lund. Salt Lake City, Utah, Bookcraft, 1971. xii, 241 p. 24 cm. Includes bibliographical references. [BT886.L85] 79-175135
1. Second Advent. I. Title.

MCKEE, Bill. 232'.6
Orbit of ashes; Jesus is coming! Wheaton, Ill., Tyndale House Publishers [1972] 142 p. 18 cm. [BT886.M33] 72-75965 ISBN 0-8423-4750-X 1.25
1. Second Advent. I. Title.

MANLEY, G. T. 232.6
The return of Jesus Christ. Chicago 101519 N. Astor Inter-Varsity Press [1960] 104p. (bibl. footnotes 19cm. 1.50 pap.,
I. Title.

MAXWELL, Arthur Stanley, 232.6
1896-
The coming King; ten great signs of Christ's return. Mountain View, Calif., Pacific Press Pub. Association [1953] 127p. illus. 20cm. [BT885.M395] 53-8825
1. Second Advent. I. Title.

MAXWELL, Arthur Stanley, 232'.6
1896-
Man the world needs most, by Arthur S. Maxwell. Mountain View, Calif., Pacific Press Pub. Association [1970] 96 p. illus., ports. 18 cm. [BT886.M38] 79-117952
1. Second Advent. I. Title.

MINEAR, Paul Sevier, 1906- 232.6
Christian hope and the Second Coming. Philadelphia, Westminster Press [1954] 220p. 21cm. [BS2545.E7M5] 54-5334
1. Hope—Biblical teaching. 2. Second Advent. I. Title.

MOORE, H. L., Bp. 232'.6
The promise of His coming, by H. L. Moore. Cleveland, Tenn., Bethel Book Publishers [1965] 98 p. 20 cm. [BT886.M63] 225.9 78-207517
1. Church of God of Prophecy—Sermons. 2. Second Advent—Sermons. 3. Sermons, American. I. Title.

MUNHALL, Leander Whitcomb, 232.6
1843-1934.
The Lord's return. [8th ed.] Grand Rapids, Kregel Publications [1962] 224 p. 20 cm. [BT886.M8 1962] 62-13175
1. Second Advent. I. Title.

MUSSNER, Franz. 232.6
Christ and the end of the world; a Biblical study in eschatology. Translated by Maria von Eroes. [Notre Dame, Ind.] University of Notre Dame Press, 1965. 72 p. 18 cm. (Contemporary catechetics series) Translation of Was lehrt Jesus uber das Ende der Welt? [BS2545.E7M83] 65-14737
1. Bibliography: p. 71. 2. Eschatology — Biblical teaching. 3. Jesus Christ — Teachings. 4. Bible. N.T. Mark xiii — Criticism, interpretation, etc. I. Title.

MUSSNER, Franz. 232.6
Christ and the end of the world; a Biblical study in eschatology. Tr. [from German] by Maria von Eroes. [Notre Dame, Ind.] Univ. of Notre Dame Pr. [c.]1965. 71p. 18cm. (Contemp. catechetics ser.) Bibl. [BS2545.E7M83] 65-14737 .95 pap.,
1. Eschatology—Biblical teaching. 2. Jesus Christ—Teachings. 3. Bible. N. T. Mark xiii—Criticism, interpretation, etc. I. Title.

ODLE, Joe T. 232'.6
Is Christ coming soon? [By] Joe T. Odle. Nashville, Broadman Press [1971] xvii, 127 p. 20 cm. (A Broadman inner circle book) [BT886.O3] 74-151622 ISBN 0-8054-8112-5
1. Second Advent. I. Title.

ORCHARD, Richard E. 232'.6
Look who's coming / Richard E. Orchard. Springfield, Mo. : Gospel Pub. House, c1975. 123 p. ; 18 cm. (Radiant books) [BT886.O7] 74-33870 ISBN 0-88243-541-8 pbk. : 1.25
1. Second Advent. I. Title.

PACHE, Rene. 232.6
The return of Jesus Christ; translated by William Sanford LaSor, from a text somewhat abridged by the author. Chicago, Moody Press [1955] 448p. 22cm. [BT885.P15] 55-43714
1. Second Advent. I. Title.

PAYNE, John Barton, 1922- 232.6
The imminent appearing of Christ. Grand Rapids, Mich., Eerdmans [c.1962] 191p. Bibl. 61-10865 3.75
1. Second Advent. I. Title.

RAND, Howard B 1889- 232.6
The hour cometh! By Howard B. Rand. Merrimac, Mass., Destiny Publishers [1966] vii, 280 p. illus. 21 cm. Bibliographical notes. [BT886.R3] 66-16453
1. Second Advent. I. Title.

RAND, Howard B., 1889- 232.6
The hour cometh! Merrimac, Mass., 01860, Destiny Pubs. [c.1966] vii, 0p. 280p. illus. 21cm. Bibl. [BT886.R3] 66-16453 3.75
1. Second Advent. I. Title.

REESE, Alexander, 1881-1969. 232'.6
The approaching advent of Christ / by Alexander Reese. Grand Rapids : Grand Rapids International Publications, 1975. 328 p. ; 23 cm. Reprint of the 1937 ed. published by Marshall, Morgan & Scott, London; with a new pref. Includes bibliographical references and indexes. [BT885.R3 1975] 73-85374 ISBN 0-8254-3610-9 : 5.95
1. Bible—Prophecies. 2. Second Advent. I. Title.

ROBERSON, Lee. 232.6
Some golden daybreak sermons on the second coming of Christ. Wheaton, Ill., Sword of the Lord Publishers [1957] 116p. 21cm. Includes some golden daybreak, hymn with music, by Carl Blackmore. [BT885.R72] 57-41655
1. Second Advent—Sermons. 2. Baptists—Sermons. 3. Sermons, American. I. Title.

ROBINSON, John Arthur Thomas, Bp., 1919- 232.6
Jesus and His coming; the emergence of a doctrine. New York, Abingdon Press [1958, c1957] 192p. 23cm. (William Belden Noble lectures, Harvard University, 1955) [BT885.R724] 58-997
1. Second Advent. I. Title.

ROBINSON, John Arthur Thomas, Bp., 1919- 232.6
Jesus and His coming; the emergence of a doctrine. New York, Abingdon Press [1958, c1957] 192 p. 23 cm. (William Belden Noble lectures, Harvard University, 1955) [BT885.R724] 58-997
1. Second Advent. I. Title.

RUSKIN, Edward V 232.6
The hill of stoning; studies in the predictions about the early return of Jesus, their fulfillment, and related subjects. [1st ed.] New York, Vantage Press [1956] 263p. 21cm. [BT885.R83] 55-11650
1. Second Advent. I. Title.

*SPURGEON C. H. 1834-1892. 232.6
12 sermons on the second coming of Christ / C. H. Spurgeon Grand Rapids : Baker Book House, 1976. 143p. ; 20 cm. (His Library) [BT885] ISBN 0-8010-8066-5 pbk. : 1.95.
1. Second advent. 2. Advent sermons. I. Title.

STANTON, Gerald B 1918- 232.6
Kept from the hour; a systematic study of the rapture in Bible prophecy. Grand Rapids, Zondervan Pub. House, 1956. 820p. 22cm. [BT885.S77] 57-15551
1. Second Advent. I. Title. II. Title: Rapture in Bible prophecy.

*SWAFFORD, Z. W. 232.6
He will come [simple studies of the second coming of Jesus Christ] Little Rock, Ark., Baptist Pubns. [c.1964] 71p. 21cm. .75 pap.,
I. Title.

TORREY, Reuben Archer, 1856-1928 232'.6
The return of the Lord Jesus, by R. A. Torrey. Grand Rapids, Baker Bk. [1966] 142p. 20cm. Collation of Scripture passages on the second coming of Christ for individual study [BT865] 67-2890 2.50
1. Second Advent. 2. Millennium. I. Title.

VINES, Jerry. 232'.6
"I shall return" - Jesus / Jerry Vines. Wheaton, Ill. : Victor Books, c1977. 128 p. ; 18 cm. [BT886.V56] 76-55631 ISBN 0-88207-702-3 pbk. : 1.75
1. Second Advent. 2. Eschatology. I. Title.

WALVOORD, John F 232.6
The return of the Lord. Findlay, Ohio, Dunham Pub. Co. [c1955] 160 p. 20 cm. [BT885.W24] 58-30303
1. Second Advent. I. Title.

WHITE, John Wesley. 232'.6
Re-entry; striking parallels between today's news events and Christ's second coming. Foreword by Billy Graham. Grand Rapids, Mich., Zondervan Pub. House [1970] 164 p. 21 cm. "A series of six sermons given on three Sundays of January 1969 in the Peoples Church, Toronto." [BT886.W48] 75-112868 3.95
1. Second Advent—Sermons. 2. Sermons, English—Canada. I. Title.

WILKERSON, David R. 232'.6
Jesus Christ solid rock; the return of Christ [by] David Wilkerson, with Kathryn Kuhlman [and others] Grand Rapids, Zondervan Pub. House [1973] 117 p. illus. 18 cm. "Zondervan books." [BT886.W53] 73-159523 0.95
1. Second Advent. I. Title.

WOOD, Leon James. 232.6
Is the rapture next? An answer to the question: Will the church escape the tribulation? Grand Rapids, Zondervan Pub. House [1956] 120 p. 20 cm. [BT885.W82] 56-41993
1. Second Advent. I. Title.

WOODS, John Purvis. 232.6
The final invasion of God. Boston, W. A. Wilde Co. [1951] 87 p. 20 cm. [BT885.W85] 51-13848
1. Second Advent. I. Title.

EDDLEMAN, H. Leo, comp. 232.6082
The second coming. Nashville, Broadman [1964, c.1963] 112p. 21cm. 64-10814 2.75 bds.,
1. Second Advent. I. Title.

KUMMEL, Werner Georg, 1905- 232.7
Promise and fulfilment, the eschatological message of Jesus. [Translated by Dorothea M. Barton from the German] Naperville, Ill., A. R. Allenson [1957] 168p. 22cm. (Studies in Biblical theology, no. 23) Bibliographical footnotes. [BS2417.E7K82] 57-3249
1. Jesus Christ—Teachings. 2. Eschatology—Biblical teaching. I. Title. II. Series.

MORRIS, Leon 232.7
The Biblical doctrine of judgment. Grand Rapids, Mich., Erdmans [1961, c.1960] 72p. Bibl. 61-2871 2.00
1. Judgment Day—Biblical teaching. I. Title.

ALTHAUS, Paul, 1888- 232.8
[AugustWilhelmHermannPaulAlthaus]
Fact and faith in the kerygma of today. Translated [from the German] by David Cairns. Philadelphia, Muhlenberg Press [1959 i.e., 1960] 89p. 22cm. Bibl.: p.9-11 60-7473 1.75 bds.,
1. Demythologization. 2. Jesus Christ—Historicity. I. Title.

ANDERSON, Hugh, 1920- 232.8
Jesus and Christian origins; a commentary on modern viewpoints. New York, Oxford University Press, 1964. xii, 368 p. 22 cm. Bibliography: p. 355-360. [BT303.2.A6] 64-10235
1. Jesus Christ — Historicity. 2. Kerygma. 3. Theology, Doctrinal — Hist. — 20th cent. I. Title.

ANDERSON, Hugh, 1920- 232.8
Jesus and Christian origins; a commentary on modern viewpoints. New York, Oxford [c.] 1964. xii, 368p. 22cm. Bibl. 64-10235 ISBN 0235 7.00
1. Jesus Christ—Historicity. 2. Kerygma. 3. Theology, Doctrinal—Hist.—20th cent. I. Title.

BICHLMAIR, Georg, 1890- 232.8
The man Jesus; translated from the German by Mary Horgan. Westminster, Md., Newman Press, 1953. 161p. 22cm. [BT201.B432] 53-11318
1. Jesus Christ—Humanity. I. Title.

BOROS, Ladislaus, 1927- 232'.8
God is with us. Translated by R. A. Wilson. [New York] Herder and Herder [1967] xii, 199 p. 21 cm. Translation of der anwesende Gott. Bibliographical references included in "Notes" (p. [178]-199) [BT218.B613 1967] 67-25878
1. Jesus Christ—Humanity. 2. Jesus Christ—Divinity. I. Title.

BRAATEN, Carl E. 1929- ed. and tr. 232.8
The historical Jesus and the kerygmatic Christ; essays on the new quest of the historical Jesus. Translated and edited by Carl E. Braaten and Roy A. Harrisville. New York, Abingdon Press [1964] 250 p. 22 cm. Bibliographical footnotes. [BT303.2.B7] 64-10679
1. Jesus Christ — Historicity. I. Harrisville, Roy A., joint ed. and tr. II. Title.

BRAATEN, Carl E. 1929- ed. and tr. 232.8
The historical Jesus and the kerygmatic Christ; essays on the new quest of the historical Jesus. Tr. [from German] ed. by Carl E. Braaten, Roy A. Harrisville. Nashville, Abingdon [c.1964] 250p. 22cm. Bibl. 64-10679 5.00
1. Jesus Christ—Historicity. I. Harrisville, Roy A., joint ed. and tr. II. Title.

BROWN, Raymond Edward. 232'.8
Jesus God and man; modern Biblical reflections, by Raymond E. Brown. Milwaukee, Bruce Pub. Co. [1967] xvi, 109 p. 23 cm. (Impact books) Bibliographical footnotes. [BT216.B7] 67-29587
1. Jesus Christ—Divinity. 2. Jesus Christ—Humanity. I. Title.

BROWN, Raymond Edward. 232'.8
Jesus: God and man; modern Biblical reflections, by Raymond E. Brown. Milwaukee, Bruce Pub. Co. [1967] xvi, 109 p. 23 cm. (Impact books) Bibliographical footnotes. [BT216.B7] 67-29587
1. Jesus Christ—Divinity. 2. Jesus Christ—Humanity. I. Title.

BRUCE, Alexander Balmain, 1831-1899. 232.8
The humiliation of Christ in its physical, ethical, and official aspects. Grand Rapids, Eerdmans, 1955. xvi, 455p. 23cm. Bibliographical footnotes. [BT220.B78] 55-14335
1. Jesus Christ—Humiliation. I. Title.

DAWE, Donald G 232.8
The form of a servant; a historical analysis of the kenotic motif. Philadelphia, Westminster Press [1963] 218 p. 21 cm. Bibliographical references included in "Notes" (p. 209-214) [BT220.D36] 64-10064
1. Incarnation. I. Title.

DAWE, Donald G. 232.8
The form of a servant; a historical analysis of the kenotic motif. Philadelphia, Westminster [c.1963] 218p. 21cm. Bibl. 64-10064 4.50
1. Incarnation. I. Title.

DULLES, Avery Robert, 1918- 232.8
Apologetics and the Biblical Christ. Westminster, Md., Newman [c.]1963. xii, 76p. 22cm. (Woodstock papers; occasional essays for theology, no. 6) Bibl. 63-22027 1.50 pap.,
1. Bible—Evidences, authority, etc. 2. Bible. N.T. Gospels—Historiography. 3. Jesus Christ—Historicity. I. Title. II. Series.

FUCHS, Ernst, 1903- 232.8
Studies of the historical Jesus. (Translated by Andrew scobiel) Naperville, Ill., A. R. Allenson [1964] 239 p. 22 cm. (Studies in Biblical theology, no. 42) "Translated ... from the ... [author's] Zur Frage nach dem historichen Jesus (Gesammelte Aufaktxe II) ... (1960)" Bibliographical footnotes. [BT303.2.F813] 65-409
1. Jesus Christ — Historicity. I. Title. II. Series.

FUCHS, Ernst, 1903- 232.8
Studies of the historical Jesus. [Tr. from German by Andrew Scobie] Naperville, Ill., A. R. Allenson [c.1964] 239p. 22cm. (Studies in Biblical theology, no. 42) Bibl. [BT303.2.F813] 65-409 4.50 pap.,
1. Jesus Christ—Historicity. I. Title. II. Series.

GRESHAM, Walter J. 232.8
Evidence of things not seen. New York, Vantage Press [c.1960] 107p. 21cm. 2.75 bds.,
I. Title.

GUITTON, Jean. 232.8
The problem of Jesus; a free-thinker's diary. [Translation by A. Gordon Smith] New York, Kenedy [1955] 289p. 28cm. 'Abridgement of ... [the author's] two volumes, Le probleme de Jesus et les fondements du temoignage chretien and Le probleme de Jesus: divinite et resurrection.; [BT1101.G897] 55-6211
1. Apologetics- 20th cent. 2. Jesus Christ-Divinity. 3. Jesus Christ-Resurrection. I. Title.

KAHLER, Martin, 1835-1912. 232.8
The so-called historical Jesus and the historic, Biblical Christ. Translated, edited, and with an introd. by Carl E. Braaten. Foreword by Paul J. Tillich. Philadelphia, Fortress Press [1964] xiii, 153 p. 21 cm. (Seminar editions) Bibliographical footnotes. [BT303.2.K313] 64-12994
1. Jesus Christ — Historicity. 2. Bible. N.T. — Historiography. I. Title.

KAHLER, Martin, 1835-1912 232.8
The so-called historical Jesus and the historic, Biblical Christ. Tr. [from German] ed., introd. by Carl E. Braaten. Foreword by Paul J. Tillich. Philadelphia, Fortress [c.1964] xiii, 153p. 21cm. (Seminar eds.) Bibl. 64-12994 1.75 pap.,
1. Jesus Christ—Historicity. 2. Bible. N. T.—Historiography. I. Title.

KNOX, John, 1900- 232.8
The church and the reality of Christ. [1st ed.] New York, Harper & Row [1962] 158p. 22cm. Includes bibliographies. [BT303.2.K5] 62-15271
1. Jesus—Historicity. I. Title.

KNOX, John, 1900- 232.8
The church and the reality of Christ. New York, Harper [c.1962] 158p. 32cm. Bibl. 62-15271 3.50 bds.,
1. Jesus Christ—Historicity. I. Title.

KNOX, John, 1900- 232'.8
The humanity and divinity of Christ, a study of pattern in Christology. Cambridge, University P., 1967. x, 118 p. 19 cm. Bibliographical footnotes. [BT218.K5] 67-10349
1. Jesus Christ—Humanity. 2. Jesus Christ—Divinity. I. Title.

LUMIERE ET VIE 232.8
Son and Saviour; the divinity of Jesus Christ in the Scriptures. A symposium by A. Gelin [and others] Translated [from the French] by Anthony Wheaton. Baltimore, Helicon Press, 1960[ ] 151p. 20cm. (Bibl. footnotes) 60-10067 2.95 bds.,
1. Jesus Christ—Divinity. I. Title. II. Title: Jesus, le fls de dieu.

MOEHLMAN, Conrad Henry 232.8
How Jesus became God: an historical study of the life of Jesus to the age of Constantine. New York, Philosophical Library [c.1960] 206p. (4p. bibl.) 23cm. 60-16180 4.75
1. Jesus Christ—History of doctrines—Early church. 2. Jesus Christ—Divinity. I. Title.

MOEHLMAN, Conrad Henry, 1879- 232.8
How Jesus became God; an historical study of the life of Jesus to the age of Constantine. New York, Philosophical Library [1960] 206p. 23cm. Includes bibliography. [BT198.M6] 60-16180
1. Jesus Christ—History of doctrines— Early church. 2. Jesus Christ—Divinity. I. Title.

SCHWEITZER, Albert, 1875- 232.8
The quest of the historical Jesus; a critical study of its progress from Reimarus to Wrede. [Tr. from German by W. Montgomery] Preface by F. C. Burkitt. New York, Macmillan, 1961. 413p. (Macmillan paperbacks, 55) 1.95 pap.,
1. Jesus Christ—Biog.—Hist. & crit. 2. Jesus Christ—Historicity. I. Montgomery, William, 1871-1930, tr. II. Title.

SULLIVAN, Peter 232.8
Christ the answer. [Boston, Daughters of St. Paul, 1964] 262 p. 21 cm. Bibliography: p. 260-262. [BT216.S8] 63-23365
1. Jesus Christ — Divinity — Study and teaching. 2. Christian life — Catholic authors. I. Title.

SULLIVAN, Peter 232.8
Christ the answer [Boston, St. Paul Eds., dist. Daughters of St. Paul, c.1964] 262p. 21cm. Bibl. 63-23365 4.00; 3.00 pap.,
1. Jesus Christ—Divinity—Study and teaching. 2. Christian life—Catholic authors. I. Title.

THEODORETUS, Bp. of Cyrrhus. 232'.8
Eranistes / Theodoret of Cyrus ; critical text and prolegomena by Gerard H. Ettlinger. Oxford : Clarendon Press, 1975. xv, 308 p. ; 23 cm. English or Greek. Includes indexes. Bibliography: p. [xi]-xv. [BT200.T38] 75-320771 ISBN 0-19-826639-1 : 38.50
1. Jesus Christ—Person and offices. I. Ettlinger, Gerard H. II. Title.
Distributed by Oxford University Press, New York.

WAKEFIELD, Elizabeth. 232'.8
James Jays takes a case. Nashville, Southern Pub. Association [1972] 64 p. 19 cm. [BT216.W32] 72-85086
1. Jesus Christ—Divinity. I. Title.

WILLIAMS, Reese F 232.8
The star and door of hope; evidence of the divinity of Christ. New York, William-Frederick Press, 1952. 91p. 24cm. [BT215.W66] 52-10926
1. Jesus Christ—Divinity. I. Title.

WOLF, Herbert C 232.8
Kierkegaard and Bultamnn: the quest of the historical Jesus, by Henry C. Wolf. Minneapolis, Augsburg Pub. House [1965] 100 p. 22 cm. (An Augsburg Publishing House theological monograph) Bibliography: p. 99-100. [BX4827.K5W6] 65-12142
1. Kierkegaard, Soren Aabye, 1813-1855 2. Bultmann, Rudolf Karl, 1884- 3. Jesus Christ — Historicity. I. Title.

WOLF, Herbert C. 232.8
Kierkegaard and Bultmann: the quest of the historical Jesus. Minneapolis, Augsburg [c.1965] 100p. 22cm. (Augsburg theological monograph) Bibl. [BX4827.K5W6] 65-12142 1.95 pap.,
1. Kierkegaard, Soren Aabye, 1813-1855. 2. Bultmann, Rudolf Karl, 1884- 3. Jesus Christ—Historicity. I. Title.

ALLEN, Charles Livingstone, 1913- 232.9
The life of Christ. [Westwood, N. J.] Revell [1962] 157p. 21cm. [BT299.2.A4] 62-17101
1. Jesus Christ—Biog.—Sources, Biblical. I. Bible. N. T. Gospels. English. Paraphrases. 1962. Allen. II. Title.

ALLEN, Charles Livingstone, 1913- 232.9
The life of Christ. [Westwood, N. J.] Revell [c.1962] 157p. 21cm. 62-17101 2.50; 3.95 bds., deluxe ed.,
1. Jesus Christ—Biog.—Sources, Biblical. I.

Bible. N. T. Gospels. English. Paraphrases. 1962. Allen. II. Title.

ALLEN, Hattie Bell (McCracken) 1896- 232.9
As Jesus passed by illustrated by Mariel Wilhoite Turner. [1st ed.] Philadelphia, Winston [1954] 32p. illus. 24cm. (A Silver shield book) [BT302.A4] 53-10715
1. Jesus Christ—Biog.—Juvenile literature. I. Title.

ALLEN, Marion Campbell. 232.9
A voice not our own, by Sam Allen. Valley Forge, [Pa.] Judson Press [1963] 174 p. 21 cm. [BT306.4.A37] 63-9264
1. Jesus Christ — Biog. — Meditations. I. Title.

ALLEN, Marion Campbell 232.9
A voice not our own, by Sam Allen. Valley Forge [Pa.] Judson [c.1963] 174p. 21cm. 63-9264 3.50
1. Jesus Christ—Biog.—Meditations. I. Title.

ALLEN, R Earl. 232.9
Trials, tragedies, & triumphs [by] R. Earl Allen. Westwood, N.J., Revell [1965] 160 p. 21 cm. [BT306.4.A38] 65-10555
1. Jesus Christ — Biog. — Meditations. I. Title.

ALLEN, R. Earl 232.9
Trials, tragedies & triumphs. Westwood, Revell [c.1965] 160p. 21cm. [BT306.4.A38] 65-10555 2.95 bds.,
1. Jesus Christ—Biog.—Meditations. I. Title.

AMBRUZZI, Aloysius 232.9
Jesus: 'yesterday and today, and forever' (Heb. 13:8) Tr. by Gilda Dal Corso. Westminster, Md., Newman [c.]1962. 687p. 17cm. 62-21492 7.50
1. Jesus Christ—Biog.—Meditations. I. Title.

AMBRUZZI, Aloysius. 232.9
Jesus: "yesterday and today, and foreover" (Heb. 13:8) Translated by Gilda Dal Corso. Westminster, Md., Newman Press, 1962. 687 p. 17 cm. [BT306.4.A4] 62-21492
1. Jesus Christ — Biog. — Meditations. I. Title.

AMIOT, Francois. 232.9
The Sources for the life of Christ, by Francois Amiot [and others] Translated from the French by P. J. Hepburne-Scott. [1st ed.] New York, Hawthorn Books [1961] 128 p. 21 cm. (The Twentieth century encyclopedia of Catholicism, v. 67. Section 6: The word of God) [BT305.S613] 62-18501
1. Jesus Christ — Biog. — Sources. I. Title.

ANDERSON, Charles C., 1931- 232.9
Critical quests of Jesus, by Charles C. Anderson. Grand Rapids, Eerdmans [1969] 208 p. 23 cm. Bibliography: p. 201-202. [BT301.9.A49] 69-12312 5.95
1. Jesus Christ—Biography—History and criticism. 2. Jesus Christ—Historicity. I. Title.

ARMSTRONG, April (Oursler) 232.9
Stories from the life of Jesus. Adapted from 'The greateststory ever told' by Fulton Oursler. Illustrated by Jules Gotlieb. Garden City, N. Y., Garden City Books [1955] 256p. illus., 25cm. [BT302.A7] 55-9510
1. Jesus Christ—Biog.—Juvenile literature. I. Title.

AUCLAIR, Marcelle, 1899- 232.9
The little friends of Jesus. Translated from the French. Illustrated by Mary Gehr. Chicago, H. Regnery Co. [1954] 93p. illus. 22cm. Translation of La bonne nouvelle annoncee aux enfants. [BT302] 54-4688
1. Jesus Christ—Biog.—Juvenile literature. I. Title.

BAECHER, Eharlotte Crawford 232.9
A child's life of Jesus. New York, The Paulist Press [c.1959] unpaged illus. (col.) 16cm. .10 pap.,
I. Title.

BARCLAY, William 232.9
Jesus as they saw Him; New Testament interpretations of Jesus. New York, Harper [1963, c.1962] 429p. 22cm. 62-15270 5.00
1. Jesus Christ—History of doctrines—Early Church. I. Title.

*BARCLAY, William 232.9
The life of jesus for everyman. New York, Harper [1966,c.1965] 96p. 21cm. (Chapel bks., CB27F) .95 pap.,
1. Jesus Christ—Biog. I. Title.

BARTON, Bruce 232.9
The Man nobody knows. Bobbs [dist. New York, Macfadden, 1962, c.1962,1952] 133p. 20cm. (Charter bk., 123) 1.35 pap.,
1. Jesus Christ—Character. I. Title.

BARTON, Bruce, 1886- 232.9
The Man and the Book nobody knows. Indianapolis, Bobbs-Merrill [1956] 325 p. 23 cm. A revised ed. of the author's The Man nobody knows and its companion volume, The Book nobody knows. [BT304.B24] 56-9458
1. Jesus Christ—Character. 2. Bible—Criticism, interpretation, etc. I. Title.

BATTENHOUSE, Henry Martin, 1885- 232.9
Christ in the Gospels; an introduction to His life and its meaning. New York, Ronald Press Co. [1952] 339 p. illus. 21 cm. (Series in religion) [BT301.B22] 52-6181
1. Jesus Christ—Biog. 2. Bible. N. T. Gospels—Introductions. I. Title.

BAUMAN, Edward W 232.9
The life and teaching of Jesus. Philadelphia, Westminster Press [1960] 240p. illus. 21cm. Jesus Christ--Biog. Includes bibliography. [BT301.2.B3] 60-7038
1. Jesus Christ—Teachings. I. Title. II. Series.

BEASLEY, Norman. 232.9
This is the promise. [1st ed.] New York, Duell, Sloan and Pearce [1957] 103p. illus. 21cm. [BT301.B255] 57-11056
1. Jesus Christ—Biog.—Devotional literature. I. Title.

BECK, William F. 232.9
The Christ of the Gospels; the life and work of Jesus as told by Matthew, Mark, Luke, and John, presented as one complete story in the language of today, by William F. Beck. Rev. ed. St. Louis, Concordia Pub. House [1968] 231 p. 21 cm. [BT299.2.B4 1968] 68-3591
1. Jesus Christ—Biography—Sources, Biblical. I. Title.

BEEBE, Catherine, 1898- 232.9
The story of Jesus for boys and girls. Pictured by Robb Beebe. Paterson, N.J., St. Anthony Guild Press [1967] 105 p. illus. 23 cm. A life of Christ for Catholic children, from his birth in the manger to his death and ressurection and the founding of His church. [BT302.B32 1967] AC 67
1. Jesus Christ—Biography. I. Beebe, Robb, 1891- illus. II. Title.

BEHM, Bill, 1922- 232.9
The night Jesus was born. St. Louis, Concordia Pub. House [1964] 1 v. (unpaged) illus. (part col.) 27 cm. [BT315.2.B4] 63-23438
1. Jesus Christ — Nativity — Juvenile literature. I. Title.

BERKEMEYER, William C 232.9
Diary of a disciple, a contemporary's portrait of Jesus; devotional reading for forty days. Philadelphia, Muhlenberg Press [c1954] 219p. 16cm. [BV4832.B47] 54-6714
1. Jesus Christ—Biog.—Devotional literature. I. Title.

BERRY, Lora Davis. 232.9
The hidden years, an experience curriculum in religious education. Los Angeles, Commonwealth Press [1952- v. illus. 21 cm. "A revised edition of a thesis originally submitted to ... the University of Wyoming in partial fulfillment of requirements for the degree of master of arts." [BT307.B37] 52-1086
1. Jesus Christ—Biog—Study. I. Title.

BETHUNE-BAKER, James Franklin, 1861- 232.9
Early traditions about Jesus. Abridged and edited by W. Norman Pittenger. Greenwich, Conn., Seabury Press, 1956. 146p. 19cm. [BT305.B42] 56-7968
1. Jesus Christ—Biog.—Sources. 2. Bible. N. T. Gospels—Criticism, interpretation, etc. I. Title.

BETHUNE-BAKER, James Franklin, 1861- 232.9
Early traditions about Jesus. Abridged and edited by W. Norman Pittenger. Greenwich, Conn., Seabury Press, 1956. 146p. 19cm. [BT305.B42] 56-7968
1. Jesus Christ—Biog.—Sources. 2. Bible. N. T. Gospels—Criticism, interpretation, etc. I. Title.

BIBLE. English. Selections. 1954. Douai. 232.9
The story in the Rosary. Text from the Douay-Rheims translation of the Holy Bible selected and illustrated by Katharine Wood. New York, McKay [1954] unpaged. illus. 29 cm. [BX2163.W6] 54-11998
1. Rosary. I. Wood, Katharine Marie, 1910- comp. and illus. II. Title.

BIBLE. N. T. English. Selections. 1955. Authorized. 232.9
The complete sayings of Jesus; the King James version of Christ's own words, without interpolations and divested of the context, excepting the brief portions of the Gospel narratives retained to establish the place, time, or occasion, or a question the reply to which is the Master's own answer. Assembled and arr. in sequence by Arthur Hinds; introd. by Norman Vincent Peale. Philadelphia, Winston [c1955] viii, 279p. map. 15cm. [BT306.H5 1955] 55-1989
1. Jesus Christ—Words. I. Hinds, Arthur. comp. II. Title.

BIBLE N.T. Gospel, English Selection 1966.revisedstandard. j232.9
Gospel for young christians, presented by Harold Winstone. illus. Jacques Lescanff. New York, McGraw [1966] 191 p. col. illus. 16 cm. [bt299.2w5] 6618425 1.95
1. Jesus Christ-biog.-sources. Winstone, Harold ed. ii. title. I. Title.

BIBLE. N. T. Gospels. English. 1952. Confraternity version. 232.9
A life of Christ [by] Aloys Dirksen, together with the four Gospels. New York, Dryden Press [1952] xiii, 338 p. 24 cm. "The four Gospels coustitute the upper section of the book [which is divided in a 'Dutch door arrangement']" Bibliography: p. 325-331. [BT301.D57] 52-11129
1. Jesus Christ—Biog. I. Dirksen, Aloys Herman. II. Title.

BIBLE. N. T. Gospels. English. 1962. Confraternity version. 232.9
A life of Christ, together with the four Gospels [by] Aloys Dirksen. Rev. [i. e. 2d] ed. New York, Holt [c.1952, 1962] xiv, 378p. 24cm. Gospels constitute the upper section of the bk. which is divided in a Dutch door arrangement. Bibl. 62-8479 5.75
1. Jesus Christ—Biog. I. Dirksen, Aloys Herman. II. Title.

BIBLE. N. T. Gospels. English. 1962. Confraternity version. 232.9
A life of Christ, together with the four Gospels [by] Aloys Dirksen. Rev. [i. e. 2d]ed. New York, Holt, Rinehart and Winston [1962] xiv, 378p. 24cm. The Gospels constitute the upper section of the book which is divided in a Dutch door arrangement. Bibliography: p. [365]- 372. [BT301.D57 1962] 62-8479
1. Jusus Christ—Biog. I. Dirksen, Aloys Herman. II. Title.

BIBLE. N. T. Gospels. English. Harmonies. 1951. Authorized. 232.9
In the beginning; a history of the beginning of Christianity as translated in the language of the King James version of the Bible, from the Gospels of Matthew, Mark, Luke, and John. Selected and edited by Charles L. Wooldridge. Philadelphia, Dorrance [1951] 104 p. 20 cm. [BT299.W67] 51-7101
1. Jesus Christ—Biog.—Sources, Biblical. I. Wooldridge. Charles L. ed. II. Title.

BIBLE. N. T. Gospels. English. Harmonies. 1951. Cary. 232.9
The life of Jesus in the words of the four Gospels. Arr. and translated from the Greek text of Wescott [i. e. Westcott] and Hort, by Edward F. Cary. [Poughkeepsie, N. Y., 1951] 224 p. 17 cm. Cover title: The Gospels life of Jesus. Map from dust Jacket Inserted. [BT299.C33] 52-18570
1. Jesus Christ—Biog.—Sources. Biblical. I. Cary, Edward F. tr. II. Title. III. Title: The Gospeis life of Jesus.

BIBLE. N. T. Gospels. English. Harmonies. 1951. Revised standard. 232.9
The Gospel; the unification of the four gospels from the American standard edition of the revised Bible, by Thos. G. Dietz. 1st ed. Grand Rapids, Eerdmans, 1951. xiv, 186 p. 23 cm. [BT299.D54] 51-10561
1. Jesus Christ—Biog.—Sources, Biblical. I. Dietz, Thomas G. II. Title.

BIBLE. N. T. Gospels. English. Harmonies. 1955. Revised standard. 232.9
Behold the son of man; or, The complete Gospel interwoven from the four Gospels, by Thomas U. Fann. Orlando, Fla. [1955] 194p. illus. 21cm. [BT299.F16] 56-44772
1. Jesus Christ—Biog.—Sources, Biblical. I. Fann, Thomas Uriah, 1886- II. Title.

BIBLE. N. T. Gospels. English. Harmonies. 1956. Revised standard. 232.9
The life of Jesus; a consecutive narrative constructed from the Revised standard version New Testament, by John E. Kaltenbach. New York, T. Nelson [1956] 159p. 21cm. [BT299.K3] 56-8840
1. Jesus Christ—Biog.— Sources, Biblical. I. Kaltenbach, John E. II. Title.

BIBLE. N. T. Gospels. English. Harmonies. 1957. Authorized. 232.9
Jesus Christ: the way, the truth, and the life; the four Gospels combined chronologically, the text used being the King James version 1911, the New Testament of Our Lord and Saviour Jesus Christ, translated out of the original Greek, and with the former translations diligently compared and revised, by His Majesty's special command. [Edited by Sarah Norwell Craighill. Lynchburg? Va., 1957] 163p. 24cm. [BT299.C65] 57-4514
1. Jesus Christ—Biog.—Sources, Biblical. I. Craighill, Sarah Norvell., ed. II. Title.

BIBLE. N. T. Gospels. English. Harmonies. 1958. Knox. 232.9
The Gospel story, based on the translation of the four Gospels by Ronald Knox, arranged in a continuous narrative with explanations by Ronald Cox. New York, Sheed and Ward [1958] xiii, 437p. illus., maps. 22cm. [BT299.C6 1958] 58-10553
1. Jesus Christ—Biog.—Sources, Biblical. I. Knox, Ronald Arbuthnott., 1888-1957, tr. II. Cox, Ronald. III. Title.

BIBLE, N. T. Gospels. English Harmonies. 1959. Beck. 232.9
The Christ of the Gospels; the life and work of Jesus as told by Matthew, Mark, Luke, and John, presented as one complete story in the language of today. Saint Louis, Concordia Pub. House [c.1959] xi, 227p. map 21cm. 59-11068 3.00
1. Jesus Christ—Biog.—Sources, Biblical. I. Beck, William F., tr. II. Title.

BIBLE. N.T. Gospels. English. Harmonies. 1960. Authorized. 232.9
The Messiah; the life and ministry of Our Lord and Saviour, Jesus Christ. Compiled and arr. from events contained in the Gospel records according the accounts given by the writers, Matthew, Mark, Luke and John. [1st ed.] New York, Exposition Press [1960] 256p. illus. 21cm. (An Exposition-Testament book) [BT299.2.C55] 60-3753
1. Jesus Christ—Biog.—Sources, Sources, Bibliocal. I. Cissna, William Everett. 1877- ed. II. Title.

BIBLE. N. T. Gospels. English. Harmonies. 1960. Authorized. 232.9
The Messiah; the life and ministry of Our Lord and Saviour Jesus Christ. Compiled and arr. from the facts and events contained in the Gospel records according to the accounts given by the writers. Matthew, Mark, Luke and John. New York, Exposition Press [c.1960] xxviii, 256p. illus. 21cm. (An Exposition-Testament book) 60-3753 4.50
1. Jesus Christ—Biog.—Sources, Biblical. I. Cissna, William Everett, ed. II. Title.

BIBLE. N. T. Gospels. English. Harmonies. 1961. Authorized. 232.9
The four Gospels as one; the life, ministry, and mission of Jesus Christ: an arrangement of the Gospels in narrative form [by] David H. Yarn, Jr. New York, Harper [c.1961] 201p. 61-5269 3.95
1. Jesus Christ—Biog.—Sources, Biblical. I. Yarn, David H. II. Title.

BIBLE. N. T. Gospels. English. Harmonies. 1961. Authorized. 232.9
The four Gospels as one; the ministry, and mission of Jesus Christ: an arrangement of the Gospels York, Harper [1961] 201p. 21cm. [BT299.2.Y3] 61-5269
1. Jesus Christ—Biog.— Sources, Biblical. I. Yarn, David H. II. Title.

BIBLE, N. T. Gospels. English. Harmonies. 1961. Authorized 232.9
The life of Christ as portrayed by the old masters and the words of the Holy Bible. edited by Elizabeth Chamberlayne. New York, Bantam Books [1961] unpaged. illus. 18cm. (A Bantam gallery edition, GDQi [BT299.2.C5] 62-2865
1. Jesus Christ—Biog.—Sources. Biblical. 2. Jesus Christ—Art. I. Chamberlayne, Elizabeth, ed. II. Title.

*BIBLE. N.T. Gospels. English. Harmonies. 1973. Authorized. 232.9
The witnesses; [the eyewitness accounts of the greatest life ever lived, by] Arthur Markve. With an apologetic critique of the Bible, by Ernest O'Neill. Minneapolis, Bethany Fellowship [1973, c.1957] xx, 409 p. 22 cm. Third edition of a work first published in 1957 under the title: A new harmony of the Gospels. [BT299] 62-38849 ISBN 0-87123-393-2 3.95 (pbk.)
1. Jesus Christ—Biography—Sources, Biblical. I. Markve, Arthur. II. O'Neill, Ernest. III. Title.

BIBLE. N. T. Gospels. English. Selections. 1951. Authorized. 232.9
The life of Christ; as told in selections from the New Testament, with wood engravings cut especially for this edition by Bruno Bramanti. New York, Pellegrini & Cudahy [1951] 130 p. illus. 24 cm. "Regular edition" [BT299.P37 1951a] 51-13700
1. Jesus Christ—Biog.—Sources, Biblical. I. Bramanti, Bruno. illus. II. Title.

BIBLE. N. T. Gospels. 232.9
English. Selections. 1951. Authorized.
The life of Christ; as told in selections from the New Testament, with wood engravings cut especially for this edition by Bruno Bramanti. New York, Pellegrini & Cudahy [1951] 130 p. illus. 24 cm. "This edition, signed by the artist, is limited to 150 copies ... No. 126." [BT299.P37] 52-115
1. Jesus Christ—Biog.—Sources, Biblical. I. Bramanti, Bruno. illus. II. Title.

BIBLE. N. T. Gospels. 232.9
English. Selections. 1956. Authorized.
The life of Christ Jesus in Bible language, from the King James Version of the Bible; arr. by Genevieve P. Olson. [San Diego, Calif.] Printed [by] Arts and Crafts Press, c1956. 52p. 19cm. [BT302.O63] 56-36567
1. Jesus Christ—Biog.—Juvenile literature. I. Olson, Genevieve P. II. Title.

BIBLE. N. T. Gospels. 232.9
English. Selections. 1957. Authorised.
Sayings of Jesus. [Westwood, N. J.] Revell [1957] 60p. 17cm. (Revell's inspirational classics) [BT306.R4] 57-12646
1. Jesus Christ—Words. I. Title.

BIBLE. N. T. Gospels. 232.9
English. Selections. 1957. Authorized.
Sayings of Jesus. [Westwood, N. J.] Revell [1957] 60p. 17cm. (Revell's inspirational classics) [BT306.R4] 57-12646
1. Jesus Christ—Words. I. Title.

BIBLE. N.T. Gospels. j232.9
English. Selections. 1966.Revisedstandard.
Gospel for young Christians, presented by Harold Winstone. Illus. by Jacques Lescanff. New York, McGraw-Hill [1966] 191 p. col. illus. 16 cm. [BT299.2.W5] 66-18425
1. Jesus Christ—Biog.—Sources. I. Winstone, Harold, ed. II. Title.

BIRD, Thomas E, 1888- 232.9
A study of the Gospels. With a foreword by the Cardinal Archbishop of Westminster. Westminster, Md., Newman Press. 1950. xiv, 270 p. illus., maps. 19 cm. (Scripture textbooks for Catholicschools, v. 3) Bibliography: p. 261-270. [BT302.B43 1950] 51-5983
1. Jesus Christ—Biog.—Juvenile literature. I. Title. II. Series.

BISHOP, Claire (Huchet) 232.9
Yeshu, called Jesus. Illustrated by Donald Bolognese. New York, Farrar, Straus & Giroux [1966] 97 p. illus. 22 cm. (A Bell book) [BT310.B5] 66-7318
1. Jesus Christ—Childhood—Juvenile literature. I. Title.

BISHOP, Eric Francis Fox. 232.9
Jesus of Palestine; the local background to the Gospel documents. London, Lutterworth Press label: Fair Lawn, N. J., Essential Books [1955:] 328p. 23cm. [BS2555.B533] 55-12646
1. Bible. N. T. Gospels—Criticism, interpretation, etc. 2. Jesus Christ—Biog. 3. Bible. N. T. Gospels—History of contemporary events, etc. I. Title.

BONAVENTURA, Saint, 232.9
Cardinal, 1221- 1274. Spurious and doubtful works.
Meditations on the life of Christ; an illustrated manuscript of the fourteenth century. Paris, Bibliotheque nationale, Ms. Ital., 115. Translated by Isa Ragusa. Completed from the Latin and edited by Isa Ragusa and Rosalie B. Green. Princeton, N. J., Princeton University Press, 1961. xxxvi, 465p. illus. 23cm. (Princeton monographs in art and archaeology, 35) Bibliographical footnotes. [BT300.B7 1961] 61-7411
1. Jesus Christ—Biog.—Meditations. I. Ragusa, Isa, ed. and tr. II. Green, Rosalie B., ed. III. Title. IV. Series.

BONAVENTURA, Saint, 232.9
Cardinal, 1221-1274.
What manner of man? Sermons on Christ by St. Bonaventure. A translation with introd. and commentary by Zachary Hayes. Chicago, Franciscan Herald Press [1974] vi, 135 p. 21 cm. Contents.Contents.—Christ, the one teacher of all.—Sermon II on the nativity of the Lord.—Sermon II on the third Sunday of Advent. Includes bibliographical references. [BT198.B64] 74-1426 ISBN 0-8199-0497-X 4.95
1. Jesus Christ—History of doctrines—Middle Ages, 600-1500. 2. Catholic Church—Sermons. 3. Preaching—History—Middle Ages, 600-1500. 4. Sermons, English—Translations from Latin. 5. Sermons, Latin—Translations into English. I. Hayes, Zachary, ed. II. Title.

BONNIWELL, William Raymond, 232.9
1888-
What think you of Christ? St. Louis, B. Herder Book Co. [c1958] 199p. 21cm. [BT295.B67] 58-14381
1. Jesus Christ—Devotional literature. I. Title.

BOOTH, Edwin Prince, 1898- 232.9
One sovereign life; thoughts on the life of Jesus. New York, Abingdon Press [1965] 144 p. 20 cm. [BT301.2.B56] 65-11074
1. Jesus Christ — Biog. I. Title.

BOOTH, Edwin Prince, 1898- 232.9
One sovereign life; thoughts on the life of Jesus [Nashville] Abingdon [c.1965] 144p. 20cm. [BT301.2.B56] 65-11074 2.50 bds.,
1. Jesus Christ—Biog. I. Title.

BOUGHTON, Willis Arnold, 232.9
1885-
A complete integrated version of the four Gospels for reading and study; a unified narrative in modern English. [1st ed.] New York, Exposition Press [1959] 234p. 21cm. (A Testament book) [BT301.2.B6] 59-16012
1. Jesus Christ—Biog. I. Title.

BOWDEN, Robert J. 232.9
Were you there (Word pictures from the life of Jesus) New York, Pageant [c.1963] 121p. 21cm. 2.75
I. Title.

BOWIE, Walter Russell 232.9
The Master; a life of Jesus Christ. New York Scribner [c.1928-1958] xii, 331p. 21cm. (Scribner lib. SL14) 1.45 pap.,
1. Jesus Christ—Biog. I. Title.

BOWIE, Walter Russell, 232.9
1882-
The Master; a life of Jesus Christ. [Student's ed.] New York, Scribner [1958] 331p. 21cm. [BT301.B725 1958] 58-4169
1. Jesus Christ—Biog. I. Title.

BRACKBERGER, Raymond 232.9
Leopold, 1907-
The history of Jesus Christ, by R. L. Bruckberger. Pref. by Eugene Cardinal Tisserant. Translated from the French by Denver Lindley. New York, Viking Presss [1965] xiv, 462 p. 25 cm. "Reference notes": p. 461-462. [BT301.2.B6963] 64-20684
1. Jesus Christ-Biog. I. Title.

BROWN, Helen (Benjamin) 232.9
Jesus goes to the synagogue. Pictures by William M. Hutchinson. Nashville, Abingdon Press. c.1960. unpaged. illus. 22cm. 60-6811 1.25 bds.,
1. Jesus Christ—Biog.—Juvenile literature. I. Title.

BROWN, Helen (Benjamin) 232.9
1898-
Jesus goes to the synagogue. Pictures by William M. Hutchinson. New York, Abingdon Press, c1960. unpaged. illus. 22cm. [BT309.B757] 60-6811
1. Jesus Christ.—Biog.—Juvenile literature. I. Title.

*BROWN, Parker B. 232.9
He came from Galilee, [by] Parker B. Brown. New York, Hawthorne Books [1974] xii, 164 p. map on front. 22 cm. [BT301.2] 73-1935 ISBN 0-8015-3368-6 6.95
1. Jesus Christ—Biography. I. Title.

BROWNING, Elva Ward, 1904- 232.9
The lighted trail; a children's life of Jesus. [1st ed.] New York, Exposition Press [c1955] 151p. 21cm. [BT302.B67] 55-12460
1. Jesus Christ—Biog.—Juvenile literature. I. Title.

BRUCE, William Franklin, 232.9
1883-
Jesus and youth, His words, thheir ways; light on te pathway of youtgh from the words and ways of Jesus. [1st ed.] New York, Exposition Press [1953] 184p. 21cm. [BS2415.B725] 53-5627
1. Jesus Christ—Teachings. I. Title.

BRUCKBERGER, Raymond 232.9
Leopold, 1907-
he history of Jesus Christ, Pref. by Eugene Cardinal Tisserant. Tr. from French by Denver Lindley. New York, Viking [c.1965] xiv, 462p. 25cm. Bibl. [BT301.2.B6963] 64-20684 8.50
1. Jesus Christ—Biog. I. Title.

BRUMBACK, Robert H 1892- 232.9
Where Jesus walked. Saint Louis, Mission Messenger [1959] 157p. illus. 21cm. [BT301.2.B7] 59-52475
1. Jesus Christ—Biog. I. Title.

BULTMANN, Rudolf Karl 232.9
Jesus and the Word. Translated [from the German] by Louise Pettibone Smith and Erminie Huntress Lantero. New York, Scribner [c.1934, 1958] x, 226p. 21cm. (Scribner lib. SL 16) 1.25 pap.,
1. Jesus Christ—Teachings. 2. Dialectical theology. I. Title.

BULTMANN, Rudolf Karl, 232.9
1884-
Jesus and the Word. Translated by Louise Pettibone Smith [and] Erminie Huntress Lantero. [Student's ed.] New York, Scribner [1958] 226 p. 21 cm. Translation of Jesus. [BS2415.B732 1958] 58-4390
1. Jesus Christ—Teachings. 2. Dialectical theology. I. Title.

BURT, Olive (Woolley) 1894- 232.9
They knew Jesus; verses and pictures about some of the people who knew Jesus. Pictures by William Heyer. Anderson, Ind., Warner Press [1959] unpaged. illus. 23cm. [BT302.B83] 59-6240
1. Jesus Chirst—Biog.—Juvenile literature. I. Title.

CARMODY, James M., comp. 232.9
Christ and his mission; Christology and soteriology, edited with commentary by James M. Carmody and Thomas E. Clarke. Westminster, Md., Newman Press, 1966. xli, 328 p. 23 cm. (Sources of Christian theology, v. 3) Includes bibliographical references. [BX1747.5.S6 vol. 3] 77-7692 6.75
1. Jesus Christ—History of doctrines. I. Clarke, Thomas E., joint comp. II. Title. III. Series.

CARRINGTON, Philip, Abp., 232.9
1892-
Our Lord and Saviour, His life and teachings. Greenwich, Conn., Seabury Press, 1958. 138p. 20cm. [BT301.C33] 58-14563
1. Jesus Christ—Biog. I. Title.

CASE, Shirley Jackson, 232.9
1872-1947.
Jesus; a new biography. New York, AMS Press, [1969] ix, 452 p. 23 cm. Reprint of the 1927 ed. Bibliographical footnotes. [BT301.C36 1969] 70-95149
1. Jesus Christ—Biography. I. Title.

CASE, Shirley Jackson, 232.9
1872-1947.
Jesus; a new biography. New York, Greenwood Press [1968, c1927] ix, 452 p. 23 cm. Bibliographical footnotes. [BT301.C36 1968] 68-57594
1. Jesus Christ—Biography. I. Title.

*CASSELS, Louis. 232.9
This fellow Jesus. Anderson, Ind. Warner Press [1973] 93 p. 18 cm. [BT302] ISBN 0-87162-149-5 0.95 (pbk)
1. Jesus Christ—Biography. I. Title.

CHILDS, Ann Taylor. 232.9
Parables to the point. Philadelphia, Westminster Press [1963] 106 p. 19 cm. [BT375.2.C5] 63-7493
1. Jesus Christ—Parables. I. Title.

CHRIST and spirit in the 232.9
New Testament. Edited by Barnabas Lindars and Stephen S. Smalley in honour of Charles Francis Digby Moule. Cambridge [Eng.] University Press, 1973. xviii, 440 p. port. 24 cm. English, French, or German. Includes bibliographical references. [BT198.C43] 72-91367 ISBN 0-521-20148-9 £8.30 ($25.00 U.S.)
1. Jesus Christ—History of doctrines—Early church, 600-1500—Addresses, essays, lectures. 2. Moule, Charles Francis Digby. 3. Holy Spirit—Biblical teaching—Addresses, essays, lectures. I. Lindars, Barnabas, ed. II. Smalley, Stephen S., ed. III. Moule, Charles Francis Digby.
Distributed by Cambridge University Press, New York; 23.50.

CHRISTOPHER, Beth 232.9
This beautiful one (a fantasia of the Christ life). New York, Pageant Press [c.1960] 73p. 21cm. 2.50
I. Title.

CHUTE, Marchette Gaylord, 232.9
1909-
Jesus of Israel. [1st ed.] New York, Dutton, 1961. 116p. 21cm. [BT302.C56] 61-8429
1. Jesus Christ—Biog.—Juvenile literature. I. Title.

CLARK, Glenn, 1882- 232.9
'Come, follow me.' [1st ed.] Saint Paul, Macalester Park Pub. Co. [c1952] 206p. 21cm. [BT302.C57] 53-2294
1. Jesus Christ—Biog.—Juvenile literature. I. Title.

CLOW, William MacCallum, 232.9
1853-1930.
The secret of the Lord. Grand Rapids, Baker Book House, 1955. 353p. 20cm. 'A series of addresses on the sayings and doings of Jesus during the days of a religious retreat.' [BX9178] 55-10436
1. Jesus Christ—Biog.— Sermons. 2. Sermons, English—Scotland. I. Title.

COLINA, Tessa. 232.9
Bible stories about Jesus. Cincinnati, Standard Pub. Co. [1954] 160p. illus. 21cm. [BT302.C6] 54-4784
1. Jesus Christ—Biog.—Juvenile literature. I. Title.

COLTON, Clarence Eugene, 232.9
1914-
Expository studies in the life of Christ: His early days. Introd. by W. A. Criswell. Grand Rapids, Zondervan Pub. House [1957] 116p. 20cm. [BT310.C6] 57-4729
1. Jesus Christ—Biog.—Early life. I. Title.

COLWELL, Ernest Cadman 232.9
1901-
Jesus and the Gospel. New York, Oxford University Press, 1963. 76 p. 19 cm. (The Cole lectures for 1962 at Vanderbilt University) Includes bibliography. [BT303.2.C6] 63-11917
1. Jesus Christ — Historicity. I. Title.

COLWELL, Ernest Cadman, 232.9
1901-
Jesus and the Gospel. New York, Oxford [c.] 1963. 76p. 19cm. (Cole lects. for 1962 at Vanderbilt Univ.) Bibl. 63-11917 2.75 bds.,
1. Jesus Christ—Historicity. I. Title.

CONNICK, C. Milo 232.9
Jesus: the man the mission, and the message. Englewood Cliffs, N.J., Prentice [c.]1963. 462p. illus. 24cm. Bibl. 63-10450 9.25
1. Jesus Christ—Biog. I. Title.

COOKE, Greville. 232.9
The Light of the World; a reconstruction and interpretation of the life of Christ. Indianapolis, Bobbs-Merrill [1950] 470 p. maps (on lining papers) 23 cm. [BT301.C765 1950] 50-5766
1. Jesus Christ—Biog. I. Title.

CRAIG, Samuel G 1874- 232.9
Jesus of yesterday and today. Philadelphia, Presbyterian and Reformed Pub. Co., 1956. 186p. 21cm. [BT201.C82] 56-8575
1. Jesus Christ—Person and offices. I. Title.

CRANFORD, Clarence William, 232.9
1906-
Taught by the Master. Nashville, Tenn., Broadman Press [1956] 122p. 21cm. [BT590.T5C7] 56-10284
1. Jesus Christ—Teaching methods. I. Title.

CRAWFORD, Mary 232.9
Who is this? A life of Jesus taken from the four Gospels. With illus. by Antony Lewis and pref. by J. B. Phillips. Westminster [London] Faith Press[dist. New York, Morehouse-Barlow, 1959, i.e. 1960] 93p. illus. (col.). map (col.) 24cm. 2.10 bds.,
1. Jesus Christ—Biog.—Juvenile literature. I. Title.

CROSS, Colin. 232.9
Who was Jesus? [1st American ed.] New York, Atheneum, 1970. 230 p. 22 cm. Bibliography: p. [229]-230. [BT301.2.C75 1970] 79-124431 5.95
1. Jesus Christ—Biography. 2. Church history—Primitive and early church, ca. 30-600. I. Title.

CROWE, Charles M 232.9
The years of Our Lord. Nashville, Abingdon Press [c1955] 155p. 21cm. [BX8333.C78Y4] 55-5398
1. Jesus Christ—Biog.—Sermons. 2. Methodist Church—Sermons. 3. Sermons, American. I. Title.

CROWELL, Grace (Noll) 1877- 232.9
Come see a Man. New York, Abingdon Press [1956] 125p. 18cm. Prose and poems. [BV4832.C733] 56-11409
1. Jesus Christ—Biog—Meditations. I. Title.

CROWELL, Grace (Noll) 1877- 232.9
Come see a Man. Nashville, Abingdon [1964, c.1956] 125p. 18cm. (Apex bk.) .95 pap.,
1. Jesus Christ—Biog.—Meditations. I. Title.

DALLAS, Harriet (Hughes). 232.9
Our friend from Bethlehem. New York, Vantage Press [1951] 326 p. 23 cm. [BS2416.D3] 51-12057
1. Jesus Christ—Teachings—Juvenile literature. I. Title.

DANIEL-ROPS, Henry, 1901- 232.9
The Book of Life; the story of the New Testament. Translated by Donal O'Kelly. Illustrated by Fritz Kredel. New York, P. J. Kenedy [1956] 154p. illus. 25cm. Translation of L'Evangile de mes filleuls. [BS2401.D312] 56-8935
1. Bible. N. T.—History of Biblical events. I. Title.

DANIEL-ROPS, Henry, 1901- 232.9
Jesus and His times. [New rev. Catholic ed.]

New York, Dutton, 1956. 479p. illus. 22cm. Translated from the French by Ruby Millar. [BT301.D2213 1956] 56-8299
1. Jesus Christ—Biog. I. Title.

DANIEL-ROPS, Henry, 1901- 232.9
Jesus and His times; translated from the French by Ruby Millar. [1st ed.] New York, Dutton, 1954. 615p. 22cm. Translation of Jesus en Son temps. [BT301.D2213] 53-6095
1. Jesus Christ—Biog. I. Title.

DANIEL-ROPS, Henry, 1901- 232.9
The life of our Lord, by Henri Daniel-Rops. Translated from the French by J. R. Foster. [1st ed.] New York, Hawthorn Books [1964] 175 p. maps. 22 cm. (The Twentieth century encyclopedia of Catholicism, v. 68. Section 6: The word of God.) Translation of Histoire du Christ-Jesus. Bibliography: p. [174]-175. [BT301.2D313] 64-25385
1. Jesus Christ — Biog. I. Title. II. Series. III. Series: The twentieth century encyclopedia of Catholicism, v. 68

DAVIES, John Gordon, 1919- 232.9
Holy Week: a short history. Richmond, John Knox Press [1963] 82 p. illus. 22 cm. (Ecumenical studies in worship, no. 11) Includes bibliographies. [BV90.D3] 63-8698
1. Holy Week — Hist. I. Title.

DAVIES, John Gordon, 1919- 232.9
Holy Week; a short history. Richmond, Va., Knox [c.1963] 82p.illus. 22cm. (Ecumenical studies in worship, no. 11) Bibl. 63-8698 1.75 pap.,
1. Holy Week—Hist. I. Title.

DAVIS, Sadie Holcombe. 232.9
Jesus, once a child. Nashville, Broadman Press, c1954. unpaged. illus. 25cm. (Little treasure series, 7) [BT302.D25] 54-42579
1. Jesus Christ.-Biog.—Juvenile literature. I. Title.

DEANE, Anthony Charles, 1870- 232.9
The world Christ knew; the social, personal and political conditions of His time. [1st American ed. East Lansing] Michigan State College Press, 1953. 119p. 22cm. [BT303.D24 1953] 53-3410
1. Jesus Christ—Biog. 2. Bible. N. T. Gospets—History of contemporary events. etc. I. Title.

DEANE, Anthony Charles, 1870- 232.9
The world Christ knew; the social, personal and political conditions of His time, by Anthony C. Deane [2d rev. ed.] London, Eyre Spottiswoode [dist. Chester Springs, Pa., Dufour, 1964] 116p. 19cm. First pub. February, 1944, reprinted April, 1944. 2.50 bds.,
1. Jesus Christ—Biog. 2. Bible. N.T. Gospels—History of contemporary events, etc. 3. Bible—History of contemporary events, etc.—N.T. Gospels. I. Title.

DE PINA, Albert. 232.9
The Galilean; a life of Christ. Hollywood, House-Warven, 1951. 250 p. illus. 24 cm. [BT309.D43 1951] 51-13625
1. Jesus Christ—Fiction. I. Title.

DE SANTIS, Zerlina. 232.9 (j)
A child's story of the baby who changed the world. Illustrated by Sue. [Boston] St. Paul Editions [1968] 45 p. illus. (part col.) 22 cm. [BT302.D4] 74-232 0.35
1. Jesus Christ—Biography—Juvenile literature. I. Title.

DE SANTIS, Zerlina. 232.9
A child's story of the baby who changed the world. Illustrated by Sue. [Boston] St. Paul Editions [1968] 45 p. illus. (part col.) 22 cm. The birth, life, and death of the One who changed the world and religion. [BT302.D4] AC 68
I. Sue, illus. II. Title.

DESHLER, G Byron. 232.9
Finding the truth about God; a personal study of Christ's revelation of God as portrayed in the four Gospels [by] G. Byron Deshler. Nashville, Tidings [c1964] 192 p. 21 cm. [BT306.5.D4] 64-66434
1. Jesus Christ — Biog. — Devotional literature. I. Title.

DOANE, Pelagie, 1906- 232.9
The boy Jesus. New York, H. Z. Walck, 1954 [i.e. 1963?] 54 p. col. illus. 26 cm. Catholic ed. [BT320.D6 1963] 63-21355
1. Jesus Christ — Childhood — Juvenile literature. I. Title.

DOANE, Pelagie, 1906- 232.9
The boy Jesus. New York, Oxford University Press, 1954. 54p. illus. 26cm. [Oxford books for boys and girls] Catholiced. [BT325.D6 1954] 54-4914
1. jesus Christ—Childhood—Juvenile literature. I. Title.

DOUGHERTY, Robert Lee. 232.9
Jesus the pioneer; the Christ of the Gospels. Boston, Christopher Pub. House [1952] 136 p. 21 cm. [BT301.D64] 52-11974
1. Jesus Christ—Biog. I. Title.

EDERSHEIM, Alfred, 1825-1889. 232.9
Jesus the Messiah; being an abridged edition of The life and times of Jesus the Messiah. Grand Rapids, W. B. Eerdmans Pub. Co., 1954. 645p. 23cm. [BT301] 54-1763
1. Jesus Christ—Biog. I. Title.

EDWARDS, Richard Alan. 232.9
The sign of Jonah in the theology of the Evangelists and Q. London, S.C.M. Press, 1971. xi, 122 p. 22 cm. (Studies in Biblical theology. 2d series, 18) Bibliography: p.[111]-117. [BS2555.2.E33 1971b] 72-189247 ISBN 0-334-01499-9
1. Bible. N.T. Gospels—Criticism, interpretation, etc. 2. Sign of Jonah. 3. Q document (Biblical criticism) I. Title. II. Series.
Available from Allenson, 9.95, ISBN 0-8401-4068-1, pap. 7.45, ISBN 0-8401-3068-6

EIKAMP, Arthur R. 232.9
Jesus Christ; a study of the Gospels. Anderson, Ind., Warner [c.1963] 176p. 22cm. 63-20427 2.95 bds.,
1. Jesus Christ—Biog. I. Title.

ELY, Virginia, 1899- 232.9
Your hand in His. Westwood, N.J., F. H. Revell Co. [1966] 126 p. 21 cm. [BT306.5.E4] 66-12434
1. Jesus Christ — Devotional literature. I. Title.

ELY, Virginia, 1899- 232.9
Your hand in His. Westwood, N.J., Revell [c.1966] 126p. 21cm. [BT306.5.E4] 66-12434 2.95 bds.,
1. Jesus Christ—Devotional literature. I. Title.

ENSLIN, Morton Scott, 1897- 232.9
The Prophet from Nazareth. New York, McGraw-Hill [c.1961] 221p. Bibl. 60-53348 4.95
1. Jesus Christ—Biog. I. Title.

ENSLIN, Morton Scott, 1897- 232.9
The prophet from Nazareth. New York, Schocken Books [1968, c1961] xiv, 221 p. 21 cm. Bibliography: p. 219-221. [BT303.E55 1968] 68-27322 5.00 (cloth)
1. Jesus Christ—Biography. I. Title.

EWING, Upton Clary. 232.9
The Essene Christ; a recovery of the historical Jesus and the doctrines of primitive Christianity. New York, Philosophical Lib. [c.1961] 438p. illus. 61-10608 5.75
1. Jesus Christ—Biog.—Hist. & crit. I. Title.

FALLON, Patrick 232.9
The life of Jesus [Staten Island, N.Y.] St. Paul Pubns. [dist. Alba, c.1963] xiv, 173p. col. illus., map. 25cm. 63-22938 4.50
1. Jesus Christ—Biog.—Juvenile literature. I. Title.

FARRELL, Melvin L 232.9
Getting to know Christ [by] Melvin L. Farrell. Milwaukee, Bruce Pub. Co. [1965] x, 221 p. 21 cm. "Originally comprised lessons for a high school religion course and were published weekly by Hi-Time Publishers, inc., Milwaukee." [BT307.F26] 65-25657
1. Jesus Christ — Biog. — Study. I. Title.

FARRELL, Melvin L. 232.9
Getting to know Christ. Milwaukee, Bruce. [c.1965] Orig. comprising lessons for a high school religion course and were pub. weekly by HiTime Publishers, inc., Milwaukee. [BT307.F26] 65-25657 2.50 pap.,
1. Jesus Christ—Biog.—Study. I. , 221p. 21cm. II. Title.

FARRELL, Walter, 1902-1951. 232.9
Only Son. New York, Sheed and Ward, 1953. 244p. 22cm. [BT301.F25] 53-12118
1. Jesus Christ—Biog. I. Title.

FENNER, Mabel B 232.9
Stories of Jesus; illustrated by Ralph Pallen Coleman. Philadelphia, Muhlenberg Press [1952] unpaged. illus. 23cm. [BT302.F4] 52-14242
1. Jesus Christ—Biog.—Juvenile literature. I. Title.

FERNAN, John J, 1908- 232.9
Christ as Prophet and King. [Syracuse? N. Y., 1952] [Syracuse? N. Y., 1952] xviii, 309 p. 24 cm. (Theology, a course for college students, v. 1) [BX904.T45 vol. 1] 52-4097
1. Bible. N. T.—Introductions. 2. Jesus Christ—Biog. I. Title. II. Title: Christ as Prophet and King.

FERNAN, John Joseph, 1908- 232.9
Christ as prophet and king. [Syracuse? N. Y., 1952] xviii, 309p. 24cm. (Theology, a course for college students, v. 1) [BX904.T45 vol. 1] 52-4097
1. Bible. N. T.—Introductions. 2. Jesus Christ—Biog. I. Title.

FERRIS, Theodore Parker, 1908- 232.9
The story of Jesus. New York, Oxford University Press, 1953. 123p. 20cm. [BT301.F33] 53-9186
1. Jesus Christ—Biog. I. Title.

FIELD, Frank McCoy. 232.9
Where Jesus walked; through the Holy Land with the Master. New York, Exposition Press [1951] 243 p. illus., port. 28 cm. Bibliography: p. [237]-238. [BT301.F4] 51-11711
1. Jesus Christ—Biog. 2. Jesus Christ—Journeys. I. Title.

FILMER, Edmund. 232.9
The story of Jesus, told by Edmund Filmer, with pictures by A. W. Lacey and S. W. Donnison. Wheaton, Ill., Van Kampen Press [1954] 182p. illus. 26cm. [BT302] 54-12923
1. Jesus Christ—Biog—Juvenile literature. I. Title.

FINEGAN, Jack, 1908- 232.9
Jesus, history and you. Richmond, John Knox Press [1964] 144 p. 21 cm. Bibliography: p. 141-144. [BT301.2.F54] 64-15174
1. Jesus Christ — Biog. 2. Jesus Christ — Historicity. I. Title.

FINEGAN, Jack, 1908- 232.9
Jesus, history, and you. Richmond, Va. Knox [c.1964] 144p. 21cm. Bibl. 64-15174 1.95 pap.,
1. Jesus Christ—Biog. 2. Jesus Christ—Historicity. I. Title.

FINEGAN, Jack, 1908- 232.9
Rediscovering Jesus. New York, Association Press [c1952] 176p. 21cm. [BT201.F55] 52-11606
1. Jesus Christ—Person and offices. I. Title.

FLEMING, Sandford, 1888- 232.9
Where Jesus walked; journeys with Jesus in the land He loved. With a foreword by Ralph E. Knudsen. [1st ed.] Philadelphia, Judson Press [1953] 208p. illus. 21cm. [BT590.J7F5] 53-5345
1. Jesus Christ— Journeys. I. Title.

FLOOD, Edmund. 232.9
Jesus and his contemporaries. Glen Rock, N.J., Paulist Press [1968] v, 85 p. 18 cm. (Deus books) [BT301.2.F57] 68-54403 0.95
1. Jesus Christ—Biography. I. Title.

FOSDICK, Harry Emerson, 1878- 232.9
The Man from Nazareth, as his contemporaries saw Him. New York, Harper [1965, c.1949] 282p. 22cm. 277p. 20cm. (Harper Chapelbks., CB8) Bibl. [BT303.F62] 1.65 pap.,
1. Jesus Christ—Biog. I. Title.

FOSDICK, Harry Emerson, 1878- 232.9
Meditations from the Manhood of the Master. New York, Association Press [1966] 128 p. 16 cm. [BT304.F7 1966] 66-15747
1. Jesus Christ — Character. 2. Jesus Christ — Devotional literature. I. Title.

FOSTER, Rupert Clinton, 1888- 232.9
Studies in the life of Chirst. Cincinnati, F.L. Rowe, 1938-68. 3v. 20 cm. Vol. 2-3 have imprint: Grand Rapids, Baker Book House. Contents.Early period.--The middle period. The final week. [BT301.F6] 62-13483
1. Jesus Christ—Biog. I. Title.

FOSTER, Rupert Clinton, 1888- 232.9
Studies in the life of Christ; v.3. Grand Rapids, Mich., Baker Bk. [c.]1962. 345p. 22cm. Contents.v.3. The final week. 38-15166 4.50
1. Jesus Christ—Biog. I. Title.

FOUARD, Constant Henri, 1837-1904. 232.9
The life of Christ. New York, Guild Press; distributed by Golden Press [c.1954, 1960] 415p. 17cm. (An Angelus book) 60-4875 .95 bds.,
1. Jesus Christ—Biog. I. Title.

FRASER, Edith 232.9
A boy hears about Jesus. Illus. by Kurt Werth. Nashville, Abingdon [1967, c. 1965] 95p. illus. 25cm. First pub. in Gt. Britain in 1961 under title: David John hears about Jesus. [BT302.F68] 65-10720 2.95
1. Jesus Christ—Biog.— Juvenile literature. I. Title.

FRASER, Edith, 1903- 232.9
A boy hears about Jesus. Illus. by Kurt Werth. Nashville, Abingdon [c.1961, 1965] 94p. illus. (pt. col.) 25cm. First pub. in Gt. Britain in 1961 under title: David John hears about Jesus. [BT302.F68] 65-10720 2.95
1. Jesus Christ—Biog.—Juvenile literature. I. Title.

GALES, Louis A 1896- 232.9
A first life of Christ for little Catholics, in the words of Mary, the Mother of Jesus; the story is about her Son, who is also the Son of God. Pictures by Bruno Frost. St. Paul, Catechetical Guild Educational Society [1952] unpaged. illus. 17cm. [BT302.G2] 53-23426
1. Jesus Christ—Biog.—Juvenile literature. I. Title.

GALOT, Jean. 232.9
The heart of Christ; translated by John Chapin. Westminster, Md., Newman Press, 1955. 295p. 21cm. [BV4833.G255] 55-7050
1. Jesus Christ—Devotional literature. I. Title.

GIORDANI, Igino, 1894- 232.9
Christ, hope of the world. Tr. by Clelia Maranzana [Boston] St. Paul Eds. [dist. Daughters of St. Paul, c.1964] 470p. col. illus. 24cm. 63-13898 7.00; 5.00 pap.,
1. Jesus Christ—Biog. I. Title.

GIORDANI, Igino, 1894- 232.9
Christ, hope of the world. Translated by Clelia Maranzana. [Boston] St. Paul Editions [1964] 470 p. col. illus. 24 cm. [BT301.2.G5] 63-13898
1. Jesus Christ — Blog. I. Title.

GOGUEL, Maurice 232.9
Jesus and the origins of Christianity. Translated by Olive Wyon, with an introd. by C. Leslie Mitton. New York, Harper [c.1960] 2v.; xv, 590p. Includes bibliography. 21cm. (Harper torchbooks, TB65, 66 The Cloister library.) 60-5490 v.1, 1.35 v.2, 1.85 pap.,
1. Jesus Christ—Biog. 2. Church history—Primitive and early church. I. Title.

GOGUEL, Maurice, 1880- 232.9
The life of Jesus, by Maurice Goguel. Tr. [from French] by Olive Wyon. New York, Barnes & Noble [1963] A tr. of the 1st vol. of a trilogy entitled Jesus et les origines du christianisme; the 2d vol. has title: The birth of Christianity. Bibl. 7.00
1. Jesus Christ—Biog. I. Wyon, Olive, 1890- tr. II. Title.

GOODSPEED, Edgar Johnson, 1871-1962 232.9
A life of Jesus. Large type ed. New York, Watts [1967, c.1950] 248p. 29cm. (Keith Jennison bk.) [BT301.G73] 6.95
1. Jesus Christ—Biog. I. Title.

GOODSPEED, Edgar Johnson, 1871-1962. 232.9
A life of Jesus. [1st ed.] New York, Harper [1950] 248 p. maps (on lining papers) 22 cm. [BT301.G73] 50-10789
1. Jesus Christ—Biography.

GOUDGE, Elizabeth, 1900- 232.9
God so loved the world. New York, Coward-McCann [1951] 311 p. 22 cm. [BT301.G77] 51-10022
1. Jesus Christ—Biography. I. Title.

GRAFE, Loyola, 1893- 232.9
What did Christ say? By Loyola & Louis M. Grafe. [1st ed.] Los Angeles, Grafe & Grafe [1954] 386p. 22cm. [BT306.G7] 54-37561
1. Jesus Christ—Words. I. Grafe, Louis Michael, 1892- joint author. II. Title.

GRAHAM, Eleanor, 1896- 232.9
The Story of Jesus, Illus. by Brian Wildsmith. Penguin [dist. New York, Atheneum, 1961, c.1959] 264 p. illus. map. (Puffin bks., PS135) 61-66128 .95, pap.
1. Jesus Christ—Biog. I. Title.

GRANDMAISON, Leonce de [Septime Leonce de Grandmaison] 1868-1927 232.9
Jesus Christ. Pref. by Jean Danielou. New York, Sheed and Ward [c.1961] 266p. 61-7286 4.50
1. Jesus Christ—Biog. I. Title.

GRANT, Robert McQueen, 1917- 232.9
The earliest lives of Jesus. New York, Harper [c.1961] ix, 134p. Bibl. 61-17602 3.50 bds.,
1. Jesus Christ—History of doctrines—Early church. 2. Bible. N. T. Gospels—Criticism, interpretation, etc.—Hist. 3. Origenes. I. Title.

GRAY, Ernest Alfred 232.9
The fifth testament. New York, Barnes

[c.1961] 159p. (Wonderful world book) 61-8564 2.95
1. Jesus Christ—Juvenile fiction. I. Title.

GREEN, Doyle L 232.9
He that liveth; the story of Jesus Christ the Son of God. Salt Lake City, Deseret Book Co., 1953. 229p. illus. 22cm. [BT301.2.G7] 59-21541
1. Jesus Christ—Biog. I. Title.

GRILLMEIER, Alois, 1910- 232.9
Christ in Christian tradition. Tr. [from German] by J. S. Bowden. New York, Sheed [1965] 258p. 22cm. Bibl. [BT198.G743] 65-12205 8.50
1. Jesus Christ—History of doctrines—Early church. I. Title.
Contents omitted.

GUARDINI, Romano, 1885- 232.9
The humanity of Christ; contributions to a psychology of Jesus. Translated from the German by Ronald Walls. New York, Pantheon Books [1964] xxiv, 146 p. 22 cm. Translation of Die menschliche Wirklichkeit des Herrn. [BT218.G813] 64-11806
1. Jesus Christ — Humanity. I. Title.

GUARDINI, Romano, 1885- 232.9
The humanity of Christ; contributions to a psychology of Jesus. Tr. from German by Ronald Walls. New York, Pantheon [c.1958, 1964] xxiv, 146p. 22cm. 64-11806 4.95 bds.,
1. Jesus Christ—Humanity. I. Title.

GUARDINI, Romano, 1885- 232.9
The Lord. [Translated from the German by Elinor Castendyk Briefs] Chicago, Regnery, 1954. xi, 535 p. 24 cm. [BT301.G914] 54-11830
1. Jesus Christ—Biography. I. Title.

GUIGNEBERT, Charles Alfred Honore, 1867- 232.9
Jesus; translated from the French by S. H. Hooke. New York, University Books [1956] xii, 563p. 22cm. Bibliography: p. 539-553. [BT301.G9472 1956] 56-7837
1. Jesus Christ—Biog. 2. Jesus Christ—Teachings. I. Title.

GUILLET, Jacques 232.9
Jesus Christ yesterday and today; introduction to Biblical spirituality. Tr. [from French] by John Duggan. Chicago, Franciscan Herald [1965, c.1964] x. 243p. 23cm. [BT304.2.G813] 65-18948 5.95 bds.,
1. Jesus Christ—Example. 2. Spritual life—Biblical teaching. I. Title.

HAMILTON, Edith, 1867- 232.9
Witness to the truth; Christ and his interpreters. New York, Norton [1957] 230p. 22cm. [BT304.H23 1957] 57-7138
1. Jesus Christ—Character. I. Title.

HAMILTON, Edith, 1867- 232.9
Witness to the truth; Christ and his interpreters. New York, Norton [1962, c.1948, 1957] 230p. 20cm. (Norton lib. N113) 1.25 pap.,
1. Jesus Christ—Character. I. Title.

HAMILTON, Edith, 1867-1963. 232.9
Witness to the truth; Christ and his interpreters. New York, Norton [1957] 230 p. 22 cm. [BT304.H23 1957] 57-7138
1. Jesus Christ—Character. I. Title.

HARINGTON, Joy. 232.9
Jesus of Nazareth. [1st American ed.] Garden City, N. Y., Doubleday, 1957. 192p. illus. 25cm. [BT309.H314 1957] 57-11421
1. Jesus Christ—Fiction. I. Title.

HARINGTON, Joy. 232.9
Jesus of Nazareth. [1st American ed.] Garden City, N. Y., Doubleday, 1957. 192p. illus. 25cm. [BT309.H314 1957] 57-11421
1. Jesus Christ—Fiction. I. Title.

*HAYES, Wanda 232.9
My Jesus book; stories. Illus. by Frances Hook [Cincinnati, Ohio, Standard Pub. Co., 1964. c.1963] unpaged. col. illus. 31cm. (3046) cover title. 1.50 bds.,
I. Title.

HEINEMANN, Thea. 232.9
Stories of Jesus. Illustrated by Don Bolognese. Designed by Walter Brooks. Racine, Wis., Whitman Pub. Division, Western Pub. Co. [1968] 223 p. col. illus. 27 cm. (The Whitman library of giant books) Retellings of fifty Bible stories about Jesus from the time of His birth to His ascension. [BT302.H44 1968] AC 68
1. Jesus Crist—Biography. I. Bolognese, Don, illus. II. Title.

HENRY, Antonin Marcel, 1911- 232.9
The triumph of Christ; the Word made flesh. Notre Dame, Ind., Fides [1962, c.1958] 159p. (Fides dome bk., D14) 'Reprinted from The historical and mystical Christ, vol. V, Theology library.' Bibl. 62-1618 .95 pap.,
1. Jesus Christ—Biog. 2. Eschatology. I. Title.

HERGET, John Francis, 1873- 232.9
Behold the Man; highlights in the life of Jesus. Cincinnati [1950] 105 p. 21 cm. [BT303.H54] 51-621
1. Jesus Christ—Biog.—Meditations. I. Title.

HIGHTOWER, Ted. 232.9
The gospel according to Jesus. [Westwood, N. J.] Revell [1957] 160p. 22cm. [BS2415.H5] 57-9964
1. Jesus Christ—Teachings. 2. Christianity—Essence, genius, nature. I. Title.

HILL, Dave. 232.9
The most wonderful King; Luke 19:28-24:43 and John 12:12-20:31 for children. Illustrated by Betty Wind. St. Louis, Concordia Pub. House [1968] [32] p. col. illus. 21 cm. (Arch books) Briefly tells in rhyme of the death and resurrection of Jesus Christ. [BT302.H5] AC 68
1. Jesus Christ—Biography. I. Wind, Betty, illus. II. Title.

HOFFMANN, Hans Peter 1929- j 232.9
Children's life of Jesus. Illus. by Johannes Gruger. Text by Hans Hoffmann. [Translated by Rosemarie McManus] Baltimore Helicon [c1966] 1 v. (unpaged) col. illus. 35 cm. Translation of Bilder fur Kinder aus dem Leben Jesu. [BT302.H6813] 67-2593
1. Jesus Christ — Biog. — Juvenile literature. I. Gruger, Johannes, 1906- illus. II. Title.

HOLLAND, Cornelius Joseph, 1873- 232.9
The divine story; a short life of Our Blessed Lord for youth. Illustrated by Gedge Harmon. St. Meinrad, Ind. [1954] 173p. illus. 22cm. 'A Grail publication.' [BT302.H7 1954] 54-11550
1. Jesus Christ—Biog.—Juvenile literature. I. Title.

HOLLIS, William Slater. 232.9
The character of Christ; a narrative presentation of the life and teachings of Jesus, with supporting Scriptures. [1st ed.] New York Exposition Press [1962] 175 p. 24 cm. (An Exposition-Testament book) [BT304.H58] 62-14064
1. Jesus Christ — Character. I. Title.

HORNE, Herman Harrell, 1874-1946 232.9
Jesus, the master teacher. Foreword by Milford F. Henkel [Reprint ed.] Grand Rapids, Mich., Kregel, 1964. 212p. 22cm. Bibl. 64-16634 3.50
1. Jesus Christ—Teaching methods. I. Title.

HUG, Fritz. 232.9
The story of Our Lord, by Fritz and Margaret Hug. New York, Random House, 1961. unpaged. illus. 26x36cm. [BT302.H8653 1961] 61-11728
1. Jesus Christ—Biog.—Juvenile literature. I. Title.

HUNT, Marigold. 232.9
A life of Our Lord. Drawings by Rus Anderson. [Rev. ed.] New York, Sheed & Ward [1959] 191p. illus. 21cm. First published in 1939 under title: A life of Our Lord for children. [BT302.H87 1959] 59-6386
1. Jesus Christ—Biog.— Juvenile literature. I. Title.

IRVIN, Donald F. 232.9
The life of Jesus. Illus. by Ralph Pallen Coleman. Philadelphia, Muhlenberg Press [1951] 219 p. col. illus. 24 cm. [BT302.I 7] 51-11111
1. Jesus Christ—Biog.—Juvenile literature. I. Title.

JAHSMANN, Allan Hart. 232.9
It's all about Jesus : a book of devotional readings—to be read by older children—to be read to young children / Allan Hart Jahsmann ; ill. by Art Kirchhoff. St. Louis : Concordia Pub. House, [1975] 157 p. : ill. ; 23 cm. Stories from the life of Jesus with supplemental devotions for each. [BT302.J25] 74-21233 ISBN 0-570-03025-0 : 4.95 ISBN 0-570-03031-5 pbk. : 2.95
1. Jesus Christ—Biography—Juvenile literature. 2. Children—Prayer-books and devotions—English—1961- I. Kirchhoff, Art, ill. II. Title.

JESUS; a dialogue with the Saviour, by a monk of the Eastern Church. Tr. [from French] by a monk of the Western Church. Glen Rock, N. J., Paulist [1965] 157p. 18cm. (Deus bks.) [BT268.J413] 65-1496 .95 232.9
1. Jesus Christ—Meditations. I. A monk of the Eastern Church.

**JESUS stills the storm* 232.9
[Tr. from Dutch] Minneapolis, Augsburg, 1968. 1v. (unpaged) col. illus. 20x20cm. 1.50

JOHNSON, Hunter L 1882- 232.9
The natural government of mankind: in the human body, its statutes are written. New York, Comet Press Books [1956] 388p. 21cm. [BS2415.J57] 56-7548
1. Jesus Christ— Teachings. I. Title.

JOHNSON, Sherman Elbridge, 1908- 232.9
Jesus in His homeland. New York, Scribner [1957] 182p. 22cm. Includes bibliography. [BT303.J63] 57-10565
1. Jesus Christ—Biog. I. Title.

JONES, Claude C 1879- 232.9
The teaching methods of the Master. St. Louis, Bethany Press [1957] 144p. 21cm. Includes bibliography. [BT590.T5J6] 57-13120
1. Jesus Christ—Teaching methods. I. Title.

JONES, Mary Alice, 1898- 232.9
The baby Jesus. Illustrated by Elizabeth Webbe. Chicago, Rand McNally [1965, c1961] 1 v. (unpaged) col. illus. 26 cm. [BT315.2.J6 1965] 64-15251
1. Jesus Christ—Nativity—Juvenile literature. I. Title.

JONES, Mary Alice, 1898- 232.9
His name was Jesus. Illustrated by Rafaello Busoni. Chicago, Rand McNally [1950] 208 p. illus. 24 cm. [BT302.J586] 50-10331
1. Jesus Christ—Biog.—Juvenile literature. I. Title.

JONES, Mary Alice, 1898- 232.9
My first book about Jesus; illustrated by Robert Hatch Ed. of 1953. Chicago, Rand McNally, c1953. unpaged. illus. 33cm. (A Rand McNally book-elf giant) [BT302.J589] 53-7230
1. Jesus Christ—Biog.—Juvenile literature. I. Title.

JONES, Mary Alice, 1898- 232.9
Tell me about Jesus. Illustrated by Dorothy Grider. A completely new ed. [Chicago] Rand McNally [1967] 71 p. illus. (part col.) 27 cm. Out of situations arising in their everyday life, parents teach their two children basic facts about Jesus, His life, and His message. [BT302.J593 1967] AC 67
1. Jesus Christ. I. Grider, Dorothy, illus. II. Title.

KELLER, Hippolyt. 232.9
No greater life; the story of Jesus of Nazareth. Translated by Kathryn Sullivan. New York, Catholic Book Pub. Co. [1954] 239p. illus. 20cm. Translation of Leben Jesu dem Volke erzahit. [BT301.K433] 56-425
1. Jesus Christ—Biog. I. Title.

KLAUSNER, Joseph Gedaliah, 1874-1958 232.9
Jesus of Nazareth; His life, times, and teaching. Tr. from Hebrew by Herbert Danby. Boston, Beacon [1964, c.1925] 434p. 21cm. (BP 185) 2.75 pap.,
1. Jesus Christ—Biog. I. Danby, Herbert, 1889- tr. II. Title.

KOMROFF, Manuel, 1890- 232.9
His great journey; the most beautiful story in the world told anew. New York [1953] 159p. 17cm. (A Lion book, 128) [BT301.K74] 53-2405
1. Jesus Christ—Biog. I. Title.

KOMROFF, Manuel, 1890- 232.9
His great journey. New York, Pyramid Books [1961, c.1953, 1956] 160p. (G608) .35 pap.,
1. Jesus Christ—Biog. I. Title.

KOMROFF, Manuel, 1890- ed. 232.9
Jesus through the centuries, his figure and teachings as reflected in the minds 0f many men. New York, Sloane [1953] 607 p. 22 cm. [BT205.K63] 53-5465
1. Jesus Christ—Appreciation. I. Title.

KOMROFF, Manuel, 1890- 232.9
The story of Jesus. Drawings by Steele Savage. Philadelphia, Winston [c1955] 154p. illus. 23cm. [BT301.K75] 55-5294
1. Jesus Christ—Biog. I. Title.

KOPP, Clemens, 1886- 232.9
The holy places of the Gospels. [Translated by Ronald Walls. New York] Herder and Herder, [1963] 424 p. illus. 23 cm. [BT303.9.K65 1963a] 63-8233
1. Jesus Christ — Journeys. 2. Bible. N. T. Gospels — Geography. 3. Palestine — Descr & trav. I. Title.

KOPP, Clemens, 1886- 232.9
The holy places of the Gospels. [Tr. from German by Ronald Walls. New York Herder & Herder [c.1963] 424p. illus., maps. 23cm. Bibl. 63-8322 8.50
1. Jesus Christ—Journeys. 2. Bible. N.T. Gospels—Geography. 3. Palestine—Descr.& trav. I. Title.

KORFKER, Dena, 1908- 232.9
The story of Jesus for boys and girls illustrated by Lou Mahacek. Grand Rapids, Zondervan Pub. House [1954] unpaged. illus. 24cm. [BT302.K6] 55-247
1. Jesus Christ— Biog.—Juvenile literature. I. Title.

KRAMER, Janice. 232.9
The Baby born in a stable: Luke 2:1-18 for children. Illustrated by Dorse Lampher. St. Louis, Concordia Pub. House [1965] 1 v. (unpaged) col. illus. 21 cm. (Arch books) [BT315.2.K7] 65-15145
1. Jesus Christ — Nativity — Juvenile literature. I. Title.

LAFFERTY, John Parks, 1873-1954. 232.9
Impressive inquiries; a study of questions by Christ, to Christ, about Christ, in the Gospels and the Acts. [1st ed.] New York, Exposition Press [1956] 100p. 21cm. [BS2415.A2L3] 55-12468
1. Jesus Christ—Teachings. 2. Jesus Christ—Person and offices. I. Title.

LAFFERTY, John Parks, 1873-1954. 232.9
Impressive inquiries; a study of questions by Christ, to Christ, about Christ, in the Gospels and the Acts. [1st ed.] New York, Exposition Press [1956] 100 p. 21cm. [BS2415.A2L3] 55-12468
1. Jesus Christ—Teachings. 2. Jesus Christ—Person and offices. I. Title.

LAKE, Gerard. 232.9
Our Lord; an elementary life of Christ. Westminster, Md., Newman Press, 1952. 123p. illus. 19cm. [BT301.L173] 52-8958
1. Jesus Christ—Biog. I. Title.

*LARSEN, Beverly 232.9
Jesus has many names; an alphabet book for children. Illus. by Audrey Reeple. Minneapolis, Augsburg [c.1964] unpaged. illus. (pt. col.) 22cm. 1.00 pap.,
I. Title.

LAUBACH, Frank Charles, 1884- 232.9
The autobiography of Jesus, edited by Frank C. Laubach. [1st ed.] New York, Harper & Row [1962] 192 p. 22 cm. Written in the first person, following the sequence used in harmonies of the Gospels, based on Edgar J. Goodspeed's translation. Published in 1956 under title: The greatest life. [BT301.L26 1962] 62-14578
1. Jesus Christ — Biog. I. Title.

LAUBACH, Frank Charles, 1884- 232.9
The autobiography of Jesus, ed. by Frank C. Laubach. New York, Harper [c.1962] 192p. 22cm. Written in the first person, following the sequence used in harmonies of the Gospels, based on Edgar J. Goodspeed's translation. Pub. in 1956 under title: The greatest life. 62-14578 3.00; 1.50 bds., pap.,
1. Jesus Christ—Biog. I. Title.

LAUBACH, Frank Charles, 1884- 232.9
The greatest life; Jesus tells his story. [Westwood, N. J.] Revell [1956] 192p. 21cm. Written as Jesus' autobiography, following the sequence used in harmonies of the Gospels, based on Edgar J. Goodspeed's translation. [BT301.L26] 56-7438
1. JesusChrist—Biog. I. Title.

LAUBACH, Frank Charles, 1884- 232.9
The greatest life; Jesus tells his story. [Westwood, N. J.] Revell [1956] 192p. 21cm. 'Written as Jesus' autobiography, following the sequence used in harmonles of the Gospels, based on Edgar J. Goodspeed's translation. [BT301.L26] 56-7438
1. Jesus Christ—Biog. I. Title.

*LAVIN, Pat Carey. 232.9
Jesus died for me. Notre Dame, Ind., Dujarie, 1968. 1v. (unpaged) illus. 21cm. 2.00
1. Jesus Christ—Biog.—Juvenile literature. I. Title.

LAYMON, Charles M. 232.9
Christ in the New Testament. New York, Abingdon Press [1958] 256 p. 24 cm. Includes bibliography. [BT301.L274] 58-9520
1. Jesus Christ. I. Title.

LAYMON, Charles M 232.9
The life and teachings of Jesus. New York, Abingdon Press [c1955] 336p. illus. 24cm. Includes bibliographies. [BT301.L275] 55-5053
1. Jesus Christ—Biog. 2. Jesus Christ—Teachings. I. Title.

LAYMON, Charles M. 232.9
The life and teachings of Jesus. Rev. ed. Nashville, Abingdon [c.1955, 1962] 336p. map. 24cm. Bibl. 62-7439 4.50
1. Jesus Christ—Biog. 2. Jesus Christ—Teachings. I. Title.

LAYMON, Charles M 232.9
Luke's portrait of Christ. [New York] Woman's Division of Christian Service, Board of Missions, Methodist Church [1959] 162 p. 19 cm. Includes bibliography. [BT301.2.L3] 59-8319
1. Jesus Christ — Biog. 2. Bible. N. T. Luke — Criticism, interpretation, etc. I. Title.

LAYMON, Charles M. 232.9
Luke's portrait of Christ. Nashville, Abingdon Press [c.1959] x, 162 p. 19 cm. map (Bibl.: p. 159-162 & bibl. footnotes) 1.00 pap.,
1. Jesus Christ-Biog. 2. Bible. N.T. Luke—Criticism, interpretation, etc. I. Title.

LAYMON, Charles M 232.9
Lukes's portrait of Christ. [New York] Woman's Division of Christian Service, Board of Missions, Methodist Church [1959] 162p. 19cm. Includes bibliography. [BT301.2.L3] 59-8319
1. Jesus Christ—Biog. 2. Bible. N. T. Luke—Criticism, interpretation, etc. I. Title.

LEVY, Rosalie Marie, 1889- 232.9
Jusus, the Divine Master. [Derby, N. Y.] Daughters of St. Paul, Apostolate of the Press [1953?] 363p. illus. 22cm. [BT301.2.L4] 59-24944
1. Jesus Christ —Biog.—Devotional literature. I. Title.

LEWIS, Harve Spencer, 1883-1939. 232.9
The mystical life of Jesus. [10th ed.] San Jose, Calif., Supreme Grand Lodge of AMORC [1953] 236p. illus. 20cm. (Rosicrucian library. v. 3) [BF1623.R7R65 vol. 3, 1953] 54-20988
1. Jesus Christ—Rosicrucian interpretations. I. Title.

LILLIE, William 232.9
Jesus, then and now. Philadelphia, Westminster [1965, c.1964] 87p. 19cm. Bibl. [BT303.2.L5] 65-11613 1.25 pap.,
1. Jesus Christ—Historicity. I. Title.

LINDSAY, Gordon. comp. 232.9
Amazing discoveries in the words of Jesus. Shreveport, La., Voice of Healing Pub. Co., '1951. 119 p. 31 cm. [BT306.L54] 52-18344
1. Jesus Christ—Words. 2. Bible. N. T. Gospels—Indexes, Topical. I. Title.

LOCKWOOD, Myna 232.9
The life of Our Lord. Pictures by Zac Zaccardi. New York, Guild. [dist. Golden] c.1963. 30p. col. illus. 29cm. 63-25079 1.95 bds.,
1. Jesus Christ—Biog.—Juvenile literature. I. Title.

LONDON. Vita et Pax Convent School. j232.9
Children's Lent and Easter, written and illustrated by Vita et Pax, Benedictine Nuns of Cockfosters, London. Baltimore, Helicon [1965] 1 v. (unpaged) col. illus. 21 cm. [BT400.L6] 65-16730
1. Jesus Christ — Passion — Juvenile literature. 2. Jesus Christ — Resurrection — Juvenile literature. I. Title.

LONDON. Vita et Pax Convent School 232.9
Children's Lent and Easter, written, illus. by Vita et Pax, Benedictine Nuns of Cockfosters, London. Helicon [dist. New York, Taplinger, c.1965] iv. (unpaged) col. illus. 21cm. [BT400.L6] 65-16730 2.50 bds.,
1. Jesus Christ—Passion—Juvenile literature. 2. Jesus Christ—Resurrection—Juvenile literature. I. Title.

LOTZ, Benjamin, 1901- 232.9
Life and of Christ. Philadelphia, Muhlenberg Press [1957] 96p. illus. 18cm. [BT307.L6] 57-3245
1. Jesus Christ—Biog.—Study. I. Title.

LOTZ, Benjamin, 1901- 232.9
Life and work of Christ. Philadelphia, Muhlenberg Press [1957] 96p. illus. 18cm. [BT307.L6] 57-3245
1. Jesus Christ—Biog.—Study. I. Title.

LOVASIK, Lawrence George, 1913- 232.9
Praying the Gospels; meditations in prayer on the life of Christ according to the four Evangelists. New York, Macmillan, 1953. 333p. 22cm. [BX2182.L6] 53-12999
1. Jesus Christ—Biog.—Devotional literature. I. Title.

LUDWIG, Emil, 1881-1948. 232.9
The Son of Man. Foreword by Charles Francis Potter. Cover painting by Max Wieczorek. Authorized rev. ed. Greenwich, Conn., Fawcett Publications [1957] 190p. 18cm. (A Premier book, d55) [BT301.L8 1957] 58-147
1. Jesus Christ—Biog. I. Title.

LUDWIG, Emil, 1881-1948 232.9
The Son of Man. Newly rev. ed. Greenwich, Conn., Fawcett [1962, c.1928, 1957] 190p. 18cm. (Premier bk., d55) .50 pap.,
1. Jesus Christ—Biog. I. Title.

MACARTNEY, Clarence Edward Noble, 1879-1957. 232.9
Twelve great questions about Chirst. Grand Rapids, Baker Book House, 1956. 221p. 20cm. [BT201] 56-11838
1. Jesus Christ—Person and offices. 2. sPresbyterian Church—Sermons. 3. Sermons, American. I. Title.

MACARTNEY, Clarence Edward Noble, 1879-1957. 232.9
Twelve great questions about Christ. Grand Rapids, Baker Book House, 1956. 221p. 20cm. [BT201] 56-11838
1. Jesus Christ—Person and offices. 2. Presbyterian Church—Sermons. 3. Sermons, American. I. Title.

MACARTNEY, Clarence Edward Noble, 1879-1957. 232.9
What Jesus really taught. New York, Abingdon Press [1958] 176p. 20cm. [BS2415.M22] 58-7433
1. Jesus Christ—Teachings. I. Title.

MCBIRNEY, Allegra 232.9
Jesus, friend of boys and girls, a book to lead little children to an understanding and love of the names and titles of Our Lord. Grand Rapids, Mich., Zondervan [c.1960] 29p. illus. 26cm. .50 pap.,
I. Title.

MCBIRNIE, William Steuart, 1920- 232.9
Preaching on the life of Christ; sermons on the epochs in the life of Christ. Introd. by W. A. Criswell. Grand Rapids, Zondervan Pub. House [1958] 118p. 21cm. [BT301.M14] 58-42575
1. Jesus Christ—Biog.—Sermons. 2. Baptists—Sermons. 3. Sermons, American. I. Title.

MCCASLAND, Selby Vernon, 18961 232.9
The pioneers of our faith; a new life of Jesus. New York, McGraw [c.1964] x, 210p. 22cm. Bibl. 63-23047 4.95 bds.,
1. Jesus Christ—Biog. I. Title.

MCGRATTY, Arthur R, 1909- 232.9
The Sacred Heart yesterday and today; with a supplement containing prayers and devotions to the Sacred Heart. New York, Benziger, 1951. xiv. 306 p. col. front. 21 cm. Bibliography: p. 300-302. [BX2157.M25] 264 51-4497
1. Sacred Heart, Devotion to. I. Title.

MACKAY, John Alexander. 1889- 232.9
His life and our life; the life of Christ and the life in Christ. Philadelphia, Westminster [c.1964] 80p. 19cm. 64-13757 1.45 pap.,
1. Jesus Christ—Biog.—Devotional literature. 2. Christian life. I. Title.

MCLAREN, Robert Bruce 232.9
What's special about Jesus? New York, Association [c.1963] 126p. 16cm. (Keen-age reflection bk.) 63-10381 .50 pap.,
1. Jesus Christ—Biog.—Devotional literature. I. Title.

MADDEN, Richard C 232.9
Father Madden's life of Christ. Milwaukee, Bruce [1960] 161p. illus. 23cm. [BT302.M23] 60-10205
1. Jesus Christ— Biog.—Juvenile literature. I. Title.

MANSON, Thomas Walter, 1893- 232.9
The beginning of the gospel. London, New York, Oxford University Press, 1950. 113. [3] p. 20 cm. (A Primer of Christianity, pt. 1) Bibliography: p. [115] [BT301.M198] 50-12102
1. Jesus Christ—Biog. I. Title. II. Series.

MANSON, Thomas Walter, 1893- 232.9
The Servant-Messiah; a study of the public ministry of Jesus. [New York] Cambridge, 1961[ ] 103p. 1.25 pap.,
1. Jesus Christ—Messiahship. I. Title.

MANSON, Thomas Walter, 1893-1958 232.9
The teaching of Jesus; studies of its form and content, by T. W. Manson. [New York] Cambridge [1963] 351p. 20cm. 1.95 pap.,
1. Jesus Christ—Teachings. 2. Bible. N. T. Gospels—Theology. I. Title.

MARC, Paul, abbe. 232.9
Gospel gems, meditations; translated from the French by Joseph A. Fredatte, with pref. by John J Wright. New York, F. Pustet Co., 1950. xiv, 226 p. 20 cm. Translation of Pages d'gvangile. [BX2183.M282] 50-21392
1. Jesus Christ—Blog.—Meditations. I. Title.

MARTIN, Ira Jay, 1911- 232.9
The faith of Jesus; a study for inquiring Christians. [1st ed.] New York, Exposition Press [1956] 210p. 21cm. (An Exposition--university book) [BT205.M364] 56-8718
1. Jesus Christ—Person and offices. I. Title.

MARTIN, Jex 232.9
The words of Our Lord; the story of Christ's life, with special emphasis on the words He spoke. Catholic Pr. [dist. New York, Grosset, 1962, c.1957, 1961] 304p. illus. (pt. col.) 16cm. 62-1067 2.95
1. JesusChrist—Biog. 2. Jesus Christ—Biog. I. Title.

MARTINDALE, Cyril Charlie, 1879- 232.9
Can Christ help me? Westminster, Md., Newman Press, 1950. 205 p. 18 cm. [BT205.M37] 51-1025
1. Jesus Christ—Significance. 2. Apologetics—20th cent. I. Title.

MARTINDALE, Cyril Charlie, 1879- 232.9
New Testament stories, Illustrated by Herbert B. Oliver. St. Louis, Herder Book Co. [1954?] 140p. illus. 21cm. [BS2401.M3] 54-3864
1. Bible stories, English—N. T. I. Title.

MARTINEZ, Luis Maria, Abp., 1881-1956. 232.9
Only Jesus. Translated from the Spanish by Mary St. Daniel. St. Louis, B. Herder Book Co. [1962] 283p. 21cm. (Cross and crown series of spirituality, no. 22) Translation of Jesus. [BT306.39.M313] 62-15404
1. Jesus Christ—Devotional literature. I. Title.

MARTIN VON COCHEM Father, 1634-1712. 232.9
Life of Christ. Adapted by Bonaventure Hammer. New York, Benziger Bros., 1897. 314p. illus. 20cm. [BT7300.M34] 38-13618
1. Jesus Christ—Biog.—Early works to 1800. I. Title.

MARTIN VON COCHEM, Father, 1634?-1712. 232.9
Our Redeemer: a series of meditations drawn from the study of the life of Christ and His ever glorious mother Mary. English arrangement by Frances M. Kemp. New York, A. Eichler, c1890. x, 1148p. illus. 33cm. [BT300.M35] 1-3228
1. Jesus Christ—Biog.—Early works to 1800. 2. Jesus Christ—Biog.—Meditations. 3. Mary. Virin—Meditations. 4. Devotional exercises. I. Title.

MARY ELEANOR, Mother, 1903- 232.9
Jesus. son of David. Illustrated by George Pollard. Milwaukee, Bruce Pub. Co. [1955] 224p. illus. 23cm. [BT301.M278] 55-7864
1. Jesus Christ—Biog. I. Title.

MAURIAC, Francois 232.9
The Son of Man. Translated [from the French] by Bernard Murchland. Cleveland, World Pub. Co. [c.1960] 158p. 22cm. 60-5803 3.00 bds.,
1. Jesus Christ—Influence. I. Title.

MAURIAC, Francois, 1885- 232.9
Life of Jesus. Translated by Julie Kernan; illustrated by George Buday. New York, D. McKay Co. [1951,c1937] 258 p. illus. 21 cm. [BT301.M342 1951] 51-12093
1. Jesus Christ—Biog I. Title.

MAURIAC, Francois, 1885- 232.9
Life of Jesus. Tr. [from French] by Julie Kernan. New York, Avon [1961, c.1937] 224p. illus. (G1058) .50 pap.,
1. Jesus Christ—Biog. I. Title.

MAURIAC, Francois, 1885- 232.9
The Son of Man. Translated by Bernard Murchland. [1st ed.] Cleveland, World Pub. Co. [c1960] 158p. 22cm. [BT205.M413] 60-5803
1. Jesus Christ—Influence. I. Title.

MAUS, Cynthia Pearl, 1880- 232.9
Christ and the fine arts; an anthology of pictures, poetry, music, and stories centering in the life of Christ. Rev. and enl. ed. New York, Harper [1959] 813p. illus. 24cm. Includes bibliography. [BT199.M3 1959] 59-5221
1. Jesus Christ—Art. 2. Jesus Christ—Biog. 3. Jesus Christ—Poetry. I. Title.

*MAXWELL, Arthur S. 232.9
Les belles histoires de la Bible, plus de quatre cents histoires reparties en dix volumes couvrant la Bible entiere de la Genese a l'Apocalypse; v. 7. Eds. Inter. Americaines Eds. Inter-Americaines [dist. Washington, D.C., Review & Herald, 1964, c.1956] 191p. col. illus. 26cm. Contents.v.7. Jesus l'Incomparable. price unreported
I. Title.

MESCHLER, Moritz, 1830-1912. 232.9
The life of Our Lord Jesus Christ in meditations. translated by Sister Mary Margaret. 5th [i.e. 8th] ed. St. Louis, Herder, 1950. 2 v. maps, plan. 22 cm. [BT301.M53] 50-1304
1. Jesus Christ — Biog. I. Title.

METCALF, Walter 232.9
The amazing man of Galilee. New York, Pageant [c.1961] 121p. p2.50
I. Title.

MILLER, T Franklin. 232.9
Life and teachings of Jesus. [Rev. ed.] Anderson, Ind., Warner Press [1959] 124p. 19cm. [BT307.M58 1959] 59-13465
1. Jesus Christ—Biog.—Study. I. Title.

MITCHELL, Curtis. 232.9
The birth of Christ. Garden City, N.Y. [Doubleday, 1963] 64 p. illus. 21 cm. (Know your Bible program) [BT315.2.M5] 63-3082
1. Jesus Christ — Nativity — Juvenile literature. I. Title.

MITCHELL, Curtis. 232.9
Jesus spreads His Gospel. Garden City, N. Y. [Doubleday, c1961] 64p. illus. 21cm. (Know your Bible program) [BT302.M62] 62-1009
1. Jesus Christ—Biog.— Juvenile literature. I. Title.

A MONK OF THE EASTERN CHURCH. 232.9
Jesus; a dialogue with the Saviour, by a monk of the Eastern Church. Translated by a monk of the Western Church. Glen Rock, N.J., Paulist Press [1965] 157 p. 18 cm. (Deus books) Translation of Jesus, simples regards sur le Sauveur. [BT268.J413 1965] 65-1496
1. Jesus Christ — Meditations. I. Title.

MOORE, Hight C, 1871-1957. 232.9
From Bethlehem to Olivet. Nashville, Convention Press [1960, c1934] 119p. illus. 19cm. [BT307.M817 1960] 59-9312
1. Jesus Christ—Biog.—Study. I. Title.

MOORE, Thomas Hendrick, 1898- 232.9
The Eternal Shepherd. New York, Apostleship of Prayer, 1952-55. 4v. 19cm. [BX2182M642] 52-10793
1. Jesus Christ—Biog.—Meditations. I. Title.

MOORE, Thomas Hendrick, 1898- 232.9
The Eternal Shepherd. New York, Apostleship of Prayer, 1952. 82 p. 19 cm. "First series." -- Dust jacket. Jesus Christ -- Biog. -- Meditations. [BX2182.M642] 52-10793
I. Title.

MORE, Paul Elmer, 1864-1937. 232.9
The Christ of the New Testament. New York, Greenwood Press [1969, c1924] ix, 294 p. 23 cm. Bibliographical footnotes. [BT301.M6 1969] 79-88912
1. Jesus Christ—Biography. 2. Bible. N.T.—Criticism, interpretation, etc. I. Title.

MORGAN, George Campbell, D.D. 1863-1945. 232.9
Discipleship. [New ed., rev.] Westwood, N.J., Revell [1962] 90p. (Campbell Morgan pocket lib.) 62-1874 .95 pap.,
1. Jesus Christ—Example. I. Title.

MORGAN, Richard. 232.9
The Christ of the Cross; dare Christians follow him. New York, R. R. Smith, 1950. 285 p. 24 cm. [BT301.M73] 50-11109
1. Jesus Christ — Biog. 2. Christianity — 20th cent. I. Title.

MORRIS, Leon. 232.9
The Lord from heaven; a study of the New Testament teaching on the diety and humanity of Jesus Christ. Grand Rapids, Thrdmans [1958] 112p. 20cm. (A Pathway book) [BT2M69] 58-13514
1. Christ—Person and offices. I. Title.

MUIR, Augustus, 1892- 232.9
The story of Jesus; illustrated by Eric Winter and Eric Wade. New York, Greystone Press [1954] 128p. illus. 25cm. [BT302.M9] 54-11489
1. Jesus Christ—Biog.— Juvenile literature. I. Title.

NEELEY, Deta Petersen. 232.9
Jesus of Nazareth, by Deta Petersen Neeley and Nathan Glen Neeley. Salt Lake City, Printed by Deseret News Press, 1956. 174p.

illus. 20cm. (A Child's story of the New Testament, v.1) [BT302.N35] 57-19522
1. Jesus Christ—Biog. —Juvenile literature. I. Neeley, Nathan Glen, joint author. II. Title.

NEIL, William, 1909- 232.9
The life and teaching of Jesus. Philadelphia, Lippincott [c.1965] 190p. 21cm. (Knowing Christianity) [BT301.2.N4] 65-14897 2.95 bds.,
1. Jesus Christ. I. Title.

NEILL, Stephen Charles, Bp. 232.9
Who is Jesus Christ? New York, Association Press [1957] 92p. 20cm. (World Christian books) [BT201.N4 1957] 57-6880
1. Jesus Christ—Person and offices. I. Title.

NEUBERT, Emile Nicolas, 232.9
1878-
The soul of Jesus contemplated in union with Mary. Pref. by John Julian Weber. Translated by Sylvester P. Juergens. Milwaukee, Bruce Pub. Co. [1963] 202 p. 23 cm. [BT304.N413] 63-10932
1. Jesus Christ — Character. I. Title.

NEUBERT, Emile Nicolas, 232.9
1878-
The soul of Jesus contemplated in union with Mary. Pref. by John Julian Weber. Tr. [from French] by Sylvester P. Juergens. Milwaukee, Bruce [c.1963] 202p. 23cm. 63-10932 3.95
1. Jesus Christ—Character. I. Title.

NILES, Daniel T 232.9
Living with the gospel. New York, Association Press [1957] 92p. 20cm. (World [BT301.N5] 57-11614
I. Title.

NILES, Daniel Thambyrajah. 232.9
Living with the Gospel. New York, Association Press [1957] 92p. 20cm. (World Christian books) [BT301.N5 1957a] 57-11614
1. Jesus Christ-Biog. I. Title.

NORRIS, Richard Alfred. 232.9
Manhood and Christ; a study in the Christology of Theodore of Mopsuestia. Oxford, Clarendon Press, 1963. xv, 274 p. 23 cm. Based on thesis, Oxford University. Bibliography: p. [263]-269. [BR1720.T35N6] 63-2531
1. Theodorus, Bp. of Mopsuestia, d. ca. 428. 2. Jesus Christ — History of doctrines. I. Title.

NORRIS, Richard Alfred, Jr. 232.9
Manhood and Christ; a study in the Christology of Theodore of Mopsuestia. Oxford, Clarendon Pr. [New York, Oxford, c.] 1963. xv, 274p. 23cm. Bibl. 63-2531 6.10
1. Theodorus, Bp of Mopsuestia, d. ca. 428. 2. Jesus Christ—History of doctrines. I. Title.

NORTHCOTT, William Cecil, 232.9
1902-
The greatest gift; picture stories of Jesus [by] Mary Miller [pseud.] With Harold Copping pictures. Westwood, N. J., Revell [1954] 126p. illus., 26cm. [BS2401] 54-12603
1. Bible stories, English—N.T. I. Title.

NOUET, Jacques, 1605-1680. 232.9
Meditations on the life of Our Lord, for every day in the year. [New and rev. ed.] Westminister [sic] Md., Newman Press, 1956. 450p. 19cm. [BX2183.N63 1956] 56-14111
1. Jesus Christ—Meditations. I. Title.

O'BRIEN, John Anthony, 232.9
1893-
The life of Christ. New York, J. J. Crawley [1957] 623p. illus. 22cm. [BT301.O18] 57-2585
1. Jesus Christ—Biog. I. Title.

O'CONNELL, John P ed. 232.9
The life of Christ; Our Lord's life, with lessons in His own words for our life today. Edited by John P. O'Connell and Jex Martin. Chicago, Catholic Press [c1954] 304p. illus. 18cm. [BT301.O25] 55-1054
1. Jesus Christ—Biog.—Devotional literature. I. Martin, Jex, joint ed. II. Title.

O'MAHONY, James Edward, 232.9
1897-
Jesus the Saviour, by Father James. Westminster, Md., Newman Press, 1956. 145p. 24cm. [BX2182O45] 56-9136
1. Jesus Christ—Biog.—Devotional literature. I. Title.

O'MAHONY, James Edward, 232.9
1897-
Jesus the Saviour, by Father James. Westminster, Md., Newman Press, 1956. 145p. 21cm. [BX2182.O45] 56-9136
1. Jesus Christ—Biog.—Devotional literature. I. Title.

O'NEALL, Kelly. 232.9
I have called you friends. Saint Louis, Bethany Press [1954] 160p. 20cm. [BS2430.O5] 54-8126
1. Jesus Christ—Friends and associates. I. Title.

O'RAHILLY, Alfred, 1884- 232.9
Gospel cmeditations. With a foreword by M. C. D'Arcy. Baltimore, Helicon Press [c1958] 286p. illus. 23cm. [BT301.2.O7] 58-13222
1. Jesus Christ—Biog.—Meditations. I. Title.

ORSSER, Gladys. 232.9
Our Friend of Galilee. Illustrated by James Converse. Mountain View, Calif., Pacific Press Pub. Association [1962] 138p. illus. 28cm. [BT302.R7] 62-13530
1. Jesus Christ—Biog.— Juvenile literature. I. Title.

OUR blessed Lord. 232.9
Charlotte, N.C. Catholic Bible House [1964] viii, 287p. illus. (pt. col.) col. maps. 24cm. Contributions by various authors and artists. Sold as set with 'Famous Foreunners of Christ,' [BT302.O78] 64-57122 24.95
1. Jesus Christ—Biog.—Juvenile literature.

OURSLER, Fulton, 1893- 232.9
The greatest story ever told; a tale of the greatest life ever lived. Garden City, N. Y., Doubleday [1961, c.1949] 350p. (Image bk., 121) .95 pap.,
1. Jesus Christ—Biog. I. Title.

OURSLER, Fulton, 1893-1952. 232.9
A child's life of Jesus. Pictures by Elinore Blaisdell. new York, F. Watts, c1951. [42] p. illus. (part col.) 23 cm. [BT302.O83] 51-9893
1. Jesus Christ—Biography—Juvenile literature. I. Title.

OURSLER, Fulton, 1893-1952. 232.9
The greatest story ever told; a tale of the greatest life ever lived. Paintings by Kenneth Riley. [1st illustrated ed.] Garden City, N.Y., Doubleday, 1950. xvii, 332 p. col. plates. 27 cm. [BT301.O85 1950] 50-11671
1. Jesus Christ—Biography. I. Title.

PAGE, Kirby, 1890- 232.9
The creative revolution of Jesus, then and now. La Habra, Calif., [1950] 62 p. 28 cm. [BS2415.P3] 50-21385
1. Jesus Christ — Teachings. 2. Church and social problems. I. Title.

PALLASCIO-MORIN, Ernest. 232.9
The immortal profile. Translated by Ella-Marie Cooper. Chicago, Franciscan Herald Press [c1957] 166p. 19cm. Translation of Jesus passait. [BT301.P153] 58-8689
1. Jesus Christ—Biog. I. Title.

PARK, Charles Edwards, 232.9
1873-
The way of Jesus. Boston, Starr King Press; distributed by the Beacon Press [1956] 109p. 21cm. [BT304.P27] 56-34997
1. Jesus Christ—Character. I. Title.

PAUL, Leslie Allen, 1905- 232.9
Son of Man, the life of Christ. New York, Dutton [c.]1961. 287p. illus. Bibl. 61-12484 4.00
1. Jesus Christ—Biog. 2. Jews—Hist.—586 B. C.—70 A. D. I. Title.

PAUL, Leslie Allen, 1905- 232.9
Son of Man, the life of Christ. [1st ed.] New York, Dutton, 1961. 287p. illus. 21cm. Includes bibliography. [BT301.2.P35 1961a] 61-12484
1. Jesus Christ— Biog. 2. Jews—Hist.—586 B. C.-70 A.D. I. Title.

PEARSON, Roy Messer, 1914- 232.9
The hard commands of Jesus. New York, Abingdon Press [1957] 125p. 21cm. [BT306.P38] 57-6120
1. Jesus Christ—Words. I. Title.

PESCH, Christian, 1853- 232.9
1925.
Our best Friend, translated by Bernard A. Hausmann from the German. Milwaukee, Bruce Pub. Co. [1953] 220p. 23cm. [BX2157.P35 1953] 53-2238
1. Sacred Heart, Devotion to. I. Title.

PIERCE, William Dwight, 232.9
1881-
Jesus, interpreter of the eternal; a dramatic arrangement of the Gospels and Apocryphal data as one coordinated story. [1st ed.] New York, Pageant Press [1957] ix, 565p. 24cm. Bibliographical references included in 'Footnotes.' [BT301.P633] 57-9967
1. Jesus Christ—Biog. I. Title.

PIERCE, William Dwight, 232.9
1881-
Jesus, interpreter of the eternal; a dramatic arrangement of the Gospels and Apocryphal data as one coordinated story. [1st ed.] New York, Pageant Press [1957] ix, 565p. 24cm. Bibliographical references included in 'Footnotes.' [BT301.P633] 57-9937
1. Jesus Christ—Biog. I. Title.

PITTENGER, William Norman, 232.9
1905-
The life of Jesus Christ, by W. Norman Pittenger. New York, F. Watts [1968] x, 115 p. 22 cm. (Immortals of philosophy and religion) Bibliography: p. 109-111. [BT301.2.P5] 68-22144 3.95
1. Jesus Christ—Biography.

POLACK, Albert Isaac, 1892- 232.9
Jesus in the background of history, by A.I. Polack and W.W. Simpson. New York, R.M. McBride Co. [1959] 160p. illus. 23cm. [BT301.P67 1959] 59-8872
1. Jesus Christ—Biog. 2. Jesus Christ—Teachings. 3. Jesus Christ—Significance. I. Simpson, William Wynn, joint author. II. Title.

POLING, Daniel Alfred, 232.9
1884-
He came from Galilee, [by]Daniel A. Poling. [Rev] New York, Harper & Row [1965] viii, 246 p. 20 cm. First ed. published in 1931 under title: Between two worlds. [BT301.P68] 65-15393
1. Jesus Christ—Biog. I. Title.

POLING, Daniel Alfred, 232.9
1884-
He came from Galilee [Rev.] New York, Harper [c.1931-1965] viii, 246p. 20cm. First ed. pub. in 1931 under title: Between two worlds. [BT301.P68] 65-15393 3.75
1. Jesus Christ—Biog. I. Title.

POTEAT, Edwin McNeill, 232.9
1892-
Jesus' belief in man. New York, Abingdon Press [1956] 159p. 21cm. [BS2417.M25P6] 56-8743
1. Man (Theology)—Biblical teaching. 2. Jesus Christ—Teachings. I. Title.

POTEAT, Edwin McNeill, 232.9
1892-
Jesus'belief in man. New York, Abingdon Press [1956] 159p. 21cm. [BS2417.M25P6] 56-8743
1. Man (Theology)—Biblical teaching. 2. Jesus Christ—Teachings. I. Title.

POWELL, F. Ellsworth 232.9
Knothole glimpses of glory, or miraculous manifestations of heavenly glory from Bethlehem to the city of gold. [Minneapolis 22, 4500 W. Bway., Minn., Osterhus Pub. House, c.1963] 264p. 20cm. 3.50; 2.50 pap.,
I. Title.

PRAT, Ferdinand, 1857-1938. 232.9
Jesus Christ; His life, His teaching, and His work. Translated from the 16th French ed. [by] John J. Heenan. Milwaukee, Bruce [1950] 2 v. 23 cm. (Science and culture series) Full name: Antoine Ferdinand Prat. Bibliographical footnotes. [BT301.P6852] 50-58219
1. Jesus Christ — Biog. I. Title.

PRAT, Ferdinand [Antoine 232.9
Ferdinand Prat] 1857-1938
Jesus Christ; His life, His teaching, and His work; 2v. in 1. Tr. from the 16th French ed. [by] John J. Heenan. Milwaukee, Bruce [1963, c.1950] 2v. in 1. 568p. map (pt. col. on endpapers) 23cm. Bibl. 10.00
1. Jesus Christ—Biog. I. Title.

PUTNEY, Max C 1893- 232.9
The man of Galilee; a new life of Jesus. [1st ed.] New York, Exposition Press [1955] 274p. 21cm. (A Banner book) Includes bibliography. [BT301.P88] 55 10300
1. Jesus Christ—Biog. I. Title.

RADIUS, Marianne 232.9 (j)
Catherine (Vos)
God with us; a life of Jesus for young readers, by Marianne Radius. Linoleum cuts by Frederick J. Ashby. Grand Rapids, Eerdmans Pub. Co. [1966] 286 p. illus., col. map (on lining papers) 24 cm. [BT302.R13] 66-28496
1. Jesus Christ—Biography—Juvenile literature. I. Title.

RADIUS, Marianne Catherine 232.9
(Vos)
God with us; a life of Jesus for young readers, by Marianne Radius. Linoleum cuts by Frederick J. Ashby. Grand Rapids, Eerdmans Pub. Co. [1966] 286 p. illus., col. map (on lining papers) 24 cm. The story of Jesus retold from the New Testament with the author's comments. [BT302.R13] AC 67
1. Jesus Christ—Biography. I. Ashby, Frederick J., illus. II. Title.

RADIUS, Mariannwe. 232.9
Ninety story sermons for children's church / Marianne Radius ; linoleum cuts by Frederick J. Ashby. Grand Rapids : Baker Book House, 1976c1966. 286p. : ill. ; 22 c. Formerly published as : God with us. [BT302.R13] ISBN 0-8010-7641-2 bpk. : 3.95
1. Jesus Christ-Biog-Juvenile. I. Title.
L.C. card no. for 1966 Eerdmans ed: 66-28496.

RAEMERS, Sidney Albert, 232.9
1892-
A teen-ager's life of Christ. Foreword by John T. Smith. Illus. by M. Cerezo-Barredo. New York, 51 Chambers St. Helios Bks., [1964] 218p. illus., map. 22cm. 64-21286 4.95
1. Jesus Christ—Biog.—Juvenile literature. I. Title.

RAMSAY, DeVere Maxwell. 232.9
God's Son; a book of stories about Jesus for young children, by DeVere Ramsay. Illustrated by Rita Endhoven. Grand Rapids, W. B. Eerdmans Pub. Co. [1964] 48 p. illus. 27 cm. [BT302.R17] 64-8582
1. Jesus Christ — Biog. — Juvenile literature. I. Endhoven, Rita, illus. II. Title.

RAMSAY, DeVere Maxwell 232.9
God's Son; a book of stories about Jesus for young children. Illus. by Rita Endhoven. Grand Rapids, Mich., Eerdmans [c.1964] 48p. illus. 27cm. [BT302.R17] 64-8582 1.95
1. Jesus Christ—Biog.—Juvenile literature. I. Endhoven, Rita, illus. II. Title.

RAMSEY, Joyce Sikes. 232.9
Ye are my friends; a simple study of the life and teachings of Jesus. [Jacksonville? Fla., 1956] 329p. 25cm. [BT301.R354] 56-38677
1. Jesus Christ—Biog. I. Title.

RANKIN, John Chambers 232.9
A believer's life of Christ. Natick, Mass., W. A. Wilde Co. [c.1960] 210p. 21cm. 60-15263 3.50
1. Jesus Christ—Biog. I. Title.

RANKIN, John Chambers, 232.9
1888-
A believer's life of Christ. Natick, Mass., W. A. Wilde Co. [1960] 210p. 21cm. [BT301.2.R3] 60-15263
1. Jesus Christ.—Biog. I. Title.

RICCIOTTI, Giuseppe, 1890- 232.9
Life of Jchrist; translated by Alba I. Zizzamia. Abridged and edited by Aloysius Croft. Popular ed. Milwaukee, Bruce Pub. Co. [1952] 402 p. illus. 22 cm. [BT301.R4815 1952] 52-14174
1. Jesus Chirst — Biog. I. Title.

ROBINSON, Ella May (White) 232.9
1882-
When Jesus was here. Nashville, Southern Pub. Association [1951] 240 p. illus. 21 cm. [BT302.R63] 52-17419
1. Jesus Christ — Biog. — Juvenile literature. I. Title.

ROBINSON, James McConkey, 232.9
1924-
A new quest of the historical Jesus. Naperville, Ill., A. R. Allenson [1959] 128p. 22cm. (Studies in Biblical theology, no. 25) Bibliographical footnotes. [BT303.R59] 59-1300
1. Bultmann, Rudolf Karl, 1884- 2. Jesus Christ—Historicity. 3. Demythologization. I. Title. II. Series.

ROLLINS, Wallace Eugene, 232.9
1870-
Jesus and His ministry, by Wallace Eugene Rollins and Marion Benedict Rollins. Greenwich, Conn., Seabury Press, 1954. 299p. 22cm. [BT301.R73] 54-13076
1. Jesus Christ—Biog. I. Rollins,Marion Josephine (Benedict) 1896- joint author. II. Title.

ROSSER, Gladys 232.9
Our friend of Galilee. Illus. by James Converse. Mountain View, Calif., Pac. Pr. Pub. [c.1962] 138p. illus. 23cm. 62-13530 3.00
1. Jesus Christ—Biog.—Juvenile literature. I. Title.

ROWLINGSON, Donald T. 232.9
The Gospel-perspective on Jesus Christ, by Donald T. Rowlingson. Philadelphia, Westminster Press [1968] 221 p. 21 cm. Bibliographical references included in "Notes" (p. [199]-214) [BT297.R68] 68-22646 6.95
1. Jesus Christ—Biography—Sources. 2. Bible. N.T. Gospels—Criticism, interpretation, etc. I. Title.

*ROYAL 232.9
A textbook on character; v.1. New York, Pageant [c.1964] 349p. 21cm. Contents.v.1. The miracle of perfection. 5.00
I. Title.

RUEF, John Samuel. 232.9
The Gospels and the teachings of Jesus; an introduction for laymen [by] John S. Ruef. New York, Seabury Press [1967] 144 p. 21

cm. (A Seabury paperback) [BS2415.R8] 67-10846
1. Jesus Christ—Teachings. I. Title.

RUFIE, Frederick Charles. 232.9
Immanuel; the story of the living Christ, the Lord of the church. Boston, Christopher Pub. House [1954] 192p. 21cm. [BT301.R8] 54-486
1. Jesus Christ— Biog. I. Title.

SAINT Bonaventura, Cardinal 232.9
Meditations on the life of Christ; an illustrated manuscript of the fourteenth century. Paris, Bibliotheque nationale, Ms. Ital., 115. Tr. by Isa Ragusa. Completed from Latin, ed. by Isa Ragusa, Rosalie B. Green. Princeton, N. J., Princeton [c.]1961. xxxvi, 465p. illus. (Princeton monographs in art and archaeology, 35) Bibl. 61-7411 15.00
1. Jesus Christ—Biog.—Meditations. I. Ragusa, Isa, ed. and tr. II. Green, Rosalie B., ed. III. Title. IV. Series.

SAUNDERSON, Henry Hallam, 232.9
1871-
His Word was with power. Boston, Beacon Press [1952] 248 p. 22 cm. [BT301.S336] 52-7867
1. Jesus Christ — Biog. I. Title.

SAVAGE, Carol. 232.9
The Lord Jesus. Illustrated by Gil Miret. Greenwich, Conn., Seabury Press [1962] 70p. illus. 21cm. Prepared for the Department of christian Education of the National Council of the Protestant Episcopal Church...as part of the church's teaching for closely graded church schools.' [BT302.S255] 62-15055
1. Jesus Christ —Biog.—Juvenile literature. I. Title.

*SAXTON, E. E. 232.9
The life of Jesus in rhythmic writing. Illus. by Arthur R. Askue. New York, Pageant [c.1965] 33p. illus. 29cm. 2.75
I. Title.

SCHLINK, Edmund, 1903- 232.9
The Victor speaks. Translated by Paul F. Koehneke. Sant Louis, Concordia Pub. House [1958] 126p. 20cm. Translation of Der Erhonte spricht. [BT306.S353] 57-13395
1. Jesus Christ—Words. I. Title.

SCHOEN, Max, 1888- 232.9
The man Jesus was. [1st ed.] New York, Knopf, 1950. xii, 271 p. 20 cm. [BT304.S44 1950] 50-8980
1. Jesus Christ — Character. I. Title.

SCHONFIELD, Hugh Joseph, 232.9
1901-
The Passover plot new light on the history of Jesus. New York, Bantam [1967, c.1965] 278p. 18cm. (N3341) [BM620.S36] .95 pap.,
1. Jesus Christ—Jewish interpretations. I. Title.

SCHONFIELD, Hugh Joseph, 232.9
1901-
The Passover plot; new light on the history of Jesus [by] Hugh J. Schonfield. [New York] B. Geis Associates; distributed by Random House [1966, 1965] 287 p. 22 cm. [BT301.2.S3 1966] 66-22755
1. Jesus Christ—Jewish interpretations. 2. Jesus Christ—Passion—Role of Jews. I. Title.

SCHWEIZER, Eduard, 1913- 232.9
Jesus. Translated by David E. Green. Richmond, John Knox Press [1971] viii, 200 p. 22 cm. Translation of Jesus Christus im vielfaltigen Zeugnis des Neuen Testaments. Includes bibliographical references. [BT202.S38213 1971] 76-107322 ISBN 0-8042-0330-X 7.50
1. Jesus Christ—Person and offices. I. Title.

SCRIVEN, Gerard F 1920- 232.9
1949.
While angels watch; the life of Jesus our King. Illus. by Fausto Conti. St. Paul, Catechetical Guild Educational Society [1953] 192p. illus. 24cm. [BT302.S26] 54-15630
1. Jesus Christ—Biog.—Juvenile literature. I. Title.

SEBOLDT, Roland H. A. 232.9 (j)
God's son on earth. [Text by Roland Seboldt. Illus. by Marianne Bellenhaus. St. Louis, Concordia Pub. House, 1968] 1 v. (unpaged) col. illus. 23 x 30 cm. Cover title. Translation and adaptation of Gottes Sohn auf Erden by Eleanore Beck and Gabrielle Miller. [BT302.S29] 68-13366
1. Jesus Christ—Biography—Juvenile literature. I. Bellenhaus, Marianne, illus. II. Beck, Eleanore. Gottes Sohn auf Erden. III. Title.

SEBOLT, Roland H A j232.9
God's son on earth. [Text by Roland Sebolt. Illus. by Marianne Bellenhaus. St. Louis, Concordia Pub. House, 1968] 1 v. (unpaged) col. illus. 23 x 30 cm. Cover title. Translation and adaptation of Gottes Sohn auf Erden by Eleanore Beck and Gabrielle Miller. [BT302.S29] 68-13366
1. Jesus Christ—Biog.—Juvenile literature. I. Bellenhaus, Marianne, illus. II. Beck, Eleanore. Gottes Sohn auf Erden. III. Title.

SEBOLT, Roland H. A. 232.9
God's son on earth. [Text by Roland Sebolt. Illus. by Marianne Bellenhaus. St. Louis, Concordia Pub. House, 1968 [30] p. col. illus. 23 x 30 cm. Cover title. Translation and adaptation of Gottes Sohn auf Erden by Eleanore Beck and Gabrielle Miller. A brief retelling of the major events in Jesus' life, from birth to death and resurrection. [BT302.S29] AC 68
1. Jesus Christ—Biography. I. Bellenhaus, Marianne, illus. II. Beck, Eleanor. Gottes Sohn auf Erden. III. Title.

SEVENTH DAY ADVENTISTS. 232.9
GENERAL CONFERENCE. DEPT. OF EDUCATION.
Day by day with Jesus; Bible stories for grades 5 and 6. Illustrated by Helen Torrey. [Teacher's ed.] Mountain View, Calif., Mountain View Pub. Assn. [1951] 269, 319 p. illus. (part col.) maps. 21 cm. "Series IIIa, even year." The main work, also issued separately, is preceded by "Teacher's guide and key for Day by day with Jesus," with special t.p. [BT302.S45 1951a] 51-8861
1. Jesus Christ — Biog. — Juvenile literature. 2. Jesus Christ — Biog. — Study. I. Title.

SHEED, Francis Joseph, 232.9
1897-
To know Christ Jesus. New York, Sheed [c.1962] 377p. 22cm. 62-15273 5.00 bds.,
1. Jesus Christ—Biog. I. Title.

SHEEN, Fulton John, Bp. 232.9
Life of Christ. New York, Popular Library [1960, c.1958] xiii, 546p. 18cm. (Popular special W700) .75 pap.,
1. Jesus Christ—Biog. I. Title.

SHEEN, Fulton John, 1895- 232.9
The eternal Galilean. Garden City, N.Y., Garden City Pub. Co. [1950, c1934] 280 p. 21 cm. [BT301.S418 1950] 51-1976
1. Jesus Christ—Biog. I. Title.

SHEEN, Fulton John, Bp., 232.9
1895-
The life of Christ. New York, Maca Magazine Corp., c1954 126p. illus. 24 cm [BT301.S4182] 54-1587
1. Jesus Christ—Biog. I. Title.

SHEEN, Fulton John, Bp., 232.9
1895-
Life of Christ. [1st ed.] New York, McGraw-Hill [1958] 559 p. 24 cm. [BT301.S4183] 58-13889
1. Jesus Christ—Biography.

SHEEN, Fulton John, Bp., 232.9
1895-
Life of Christ : complete and unabridged / Fulton J. Sheen. Garden City, N.Y. : Image Books, 1977. 476 p. ; 21 cm. Reprint of the 1958 ed. published by McGraw-Hill, New York. Includes index. [BT301.2.S464 1977] 77-81295 ISBN 0-385-13220-4 : pbk. : 3.95
1. Jesus Christ—Biography. 2. Christian biography—Palestine. I. Title.

SHILTON, Lance R. 232.9
The Word made flesh. Grand Rapids, Mich., Zondervan [c.1963] 120p. 21cm. 63-1183 2.50
1. Sermons, Australian. I. Title.

SINCLAIR, Upton Beall, 232.9
1878-
A personal Jesus; portrait and interpretation. New York, Evans Pub. Co. [1952] ix, 228 p. 22 cm. [BT301.S42] 52-13861
1. Jesus Christ—Biog. I. Title.

SINGH, Surjit. 232.9
Christology and personality. Foreword by Nels F. S. Ferre. Philadelphia, Westminster Press [1961] 206 p. 21 cm. "Revision of a monograph originally published in India under the title: Preface to personality ... 1952." Includes bibliography. [BT212.S5 1961] 61-6102
1. Radhakrishnan, Sir Sarvepalli, 1888- 2. Jesus Christ — Person and offices. 3. Man (Theology) I. Title.

SINGH, Surjit 232.9
Christology and personality. Foreword by Nels F. S. Ferre. Philadelphia, Westminster Pr. [c.1961] 206p. Bibl. 61-6102 4.50
1. Radhakrishnan, Sarvepalli, Sir 1888- 2. Jesus Christ—Person and offices. 3. Man (Theology) I. Title.

SLAUGHTER, Frank Gill, 232.9
1908-
The crown and the cross; the life of Christ. [1st ed.] Cleveland, World Pub. Co. [1959] 446 p. 22 cm. [BT309.S62] 59-5924
1. Jesus Christ—Biography—Fiction. I. Title.

SLOYAN, Gerard Stephan, 232.9
1919-
Christ the Lord. Garden City, N. Y., Doubleday [1965, c.1962] 195p. 18cm. (Echo bk., E6) [BT301.2.S57] .75 pap.,
1. Jesus Christ—Biog. I. Title.

SLOYAN, Gerard Stephen, 232.9
1919-
Christ the Lord. [New York] Herder and Herder [1962] 238 p. illus. 21 cm. [BT301.2.S57] 62-17231
1. Jesus Christ — Biog. I. Title.

SLOYAN, Gerard Stephen, 232.9
1919-
Christ the Lord. [New York] Herder & Herder [c.1962] 238p. illus. 21cm. 62-17231 4.50
1. Jesus Christ—Biog. I. Title.

SMALLWOOD, Kate. 232.9
I think about Jesus. Pictures by Esther Friend. Chicago, Rand McNally, 1958. unpaged. illus. 20 cm. [BT302.S555] 58-11617
1. Jesus Christ — Biog. — Juvenile literature. I. Title.

SMALLWOOD, Kate. j 232.9
I think about Jesus. Pictures by Esther Friend. Chicago, Rand McNally [1964 c1958] 1 v. (unpaged) col. illus. 32 cm. [BT302.S555 1964] 64-17037
1. Jesus Christ — Biog. — Juvenile literature. I. Friend, Esther, illus. II. Title.

SMITH, Roy Lemon, 1887- 232.9
Toward an understanding of the carpenter's son. Nashville, Tidings [1960] 80 p. 19 cm. [BT301.2.S6] 60-53552
1. Jesus Christ — Biog. I. Title.

SMITH, Wistaria 232.9
Jesus shall have pre-eminence. New York, Comet Press [c.]1960 170p. 21cm. 3.50
I. Title.

SMITHER, Ethel Lisle. 232.9
Stories of Jesus; illustrated by Kurt Wiese. Nashville, Abingdon Press [1954] 80p. illus. 21cm. [BT302.S574] 54-8460
1. Jesus Christ— Biog.—Juvenile literature. I. Title.

SMYTH, John Paterson, 232.9
d.1932
A people's life of Christ. [54th ed.] Westwood, N.J., Revell [1963?] 365 p. 20 cm. [[BT301]] 63-6847 CD
1. Jesus Christ — Biog. I. Title.

SNYDER, Russell Dewey, 232.9
1898-
Jesus: his mission and teachings. Arthur H. Getz, editor. Philadelphia, Muhlenberg Press [1959] 142 p. illus. 20 cm. Includes bibliography. [BT307.S7] 59-499
1. Jesus Christ — Biog. — Study. I. Title.

SOCKMAN, Ralph Washington, j232.9
1889-
The Easter story for children [by] Ralph W. Sockman. Illustrated by Gordon Laite. New York, Abingdon Press [1966] 1 v. (unpaged) col. illus. 23 cm. [BT302.S63 1966] 66-10566
1. Jesus Christ—Biog.—Juvenile literatures. 2. Easter—Juvenile literatures. I. Laite, Gordon, illus. II. Title.

SOCKMAN, Ralph Washington, 232.9
1889-
The Easter story for children. Illus. by Gordon Laite. Nashville, Abingdon [c.1957,1966] 1v. (unpaged) col. illus. 23cm. [BT302.S63] 66-10566 2.25
1. Easter—Juvenile literature. 2. Jesus Christ—Biog.—Juvenile literature. I. Laite, Gordon, illus. II. Title.

SOCKMAN, Ralph Washington, 232.9
1889-
The paradoxes of Jesus. New York, Abingdon Press [c1936] 264 p. 21 cm. (Apex books, D4) Includes bibliography. [BT590.P3S6 1936a] 59-16378
1. Paradoxes. 2. Jesus Christ — Teachings. I. Title.

SOPER, David Wesley, 1910- 232.9
You have met Christ. Philadelphia, Westminster Press [1957] 142p. 21cm. [BT303. 67] 57.6034
1. Jesus Christ—Influence. 2. Christian life. I. Title.

SOPER, David Wesley, 1910- 232.9
You have met Christ. Philadelphia, Westminster Press [1957] 142 p. 21 cm. [BT303.S67] 57-6034
1. Jesus Christ — Influence. 2. Christian life. I. Title.

SOPER, David Wesley, 1910- 232.9
You have met Christ. Philadelphia, Westminster Press [1957] 142p. 21cm. [BT303. 67] 57.6034
1. Jesus Christ—Influence. 2. Christian life. I. Title.

SOURCES for the life of 232.9
Christ (The) by Francois Amiot [others] Tr. from French by P. J. Hepburne-Scott. New York, Hawthorn [c.1962] 128p. 21cm. (Twentieth cent. ency. of Catholicism, v.67. Section 6: The word of God) 62-18501 3.50 bds.,
1. Jesus Christ—Biog.—Sources. I. Amiot, Francois.

STALKER, James: 1848-1927. 232.9
Christ, our example, formerly published as Imago Christi. Grand Rapids, Zondervan Pub. House [1960] 332 p. 21 cm. "Reprinted from the nineteenth edition released by Hodder and Stoughton, London, in 1908." [BT304.2S75 1960] 61-578
1. Jesus Christ — Example. 2. Jesus Christ — Ethics. I. Title.

STALKER, James, 1848-1927. 232.9
Christ, our example, formerly published as Imago Christi. Grand Rapids, Zondervan Pub. House [1960] 332p. bBibl. 61-578 2.95 bds.,
1. Jesus Christ—Example. 2. Jesus Christ—Ethics. I. Title.

STAMM, Frederick Keller, 232.9
1883-
One fine hour. [1st ed.] New York, Harper [c1954] 176p. 22cm. [BT205.S84] 53-10978
1. Jesus Christ—Significance. I. Title.

STAUFFER, Ethelbert, 1902- 232.9
Jesus and His story. Translated from the German by Richard and Clara Winston. [1st American ed.] New York, Knopf, 1960 [c1959]. 243 p. illus. 22 cm. Translation of Jesus; Gestalt and Geschichte. Includes bibliography. [BT301.2S683] 59-15321
1. Jeses Christ — Biog. I. Title.

STAUFFER, Ethelbert, 1902- 232.9
Jesus and His story. Translated from the German by Richard and Clara Winston. [1st American ed.] New York, Knopf, 1960 [c1959] 243 p. illus. 22 cm. Translation of Jesus: Gestalt und Geschicte. Includes bibliography. [BT301.2.S683] 59-15321
1. Jesus Christ—Biography. I. Title.

STEINMANN, Jean.
The life of Jesus. Translated from the French by Peter Green. [1st ed.] Boston, Little, Brown [1963] xi, 240 p. map. 21 cm. Bibliographical references included in "Notes": p. [233]-234. [BT301.2.S6913] 63-17426
1. Jesus Christ—Biography.

STERN, Gladys Bronwyn, j232.9
1890-
The personality of Jesus. Garden City, N.Y. [1961] 64 p. illus. 24 cm. (The Catholic know-your-Bible program) [BT304.S82] 61-1259
1. Jesus Christ — Character — Juvenile literature. I. Title.

STEVENSON, Herbert F. 232.9
The road to the Cross. Introd. by Paul S. Rees. [Westwood, N.J.] Revell [1964, c.1962] 128p. 21cm. 64-968 2.95 bds.,
1. Jesus Christ—Biog.—Devotional literature. 2. Jesus Christ—Passion—Devotional literature. I. Title.

STEWART, James Stuart, 232.9
1896-
The life and teaching of Jesus Christ. New York, Abingdon Press [195-?] 192p. 19cm. [BT301.S643] 57-4515
1. Jesus Christ—Biog. 2. Jesus Christ—Teachings. I. Title.

STEWART, James Stuart, 232.9
1896-
The life and teaching of Jesus Christ. New York, Abingdon Press [195- ?] 192 p. 19 cm. [BT301.S643] 57-4515
1. Jesus Christ — Biog. 2. Jesus Christ — Teachings. I. Title.

STOKE, John H 232.9
A man called Jesus. [1st ed.] New York, Vantage Press [1959] 231 p. illus. 21 cm. [BT301.2.S7] 59-56453
1. Jesus Christ — Biog. I. Title.

STOKE, John H. 232.9
A man called Jesus. New York, Vantage Press [c.1959] 231p. illus. 21cm. 59-65453 3.50 bds.,
1. Jesus Christ—Biog. I. Title.

*STONE, Betty E. 232.9
Here begins the Gospel, a reading book; selections from the New English Bible. Philadelphia, United Church [1964, c.1963] 86p. illus. 22cm. 1.50 pap.,
I. Title.

STOOPS, John Dashiell, 1873- 232.9
The kingdom of Jesus. New York, Philosophical Library [1951] xxiv, 172 p. 21 cm. [BS2417.S7S78] 51-11445
1. Jesus Christ — Teachings. 2. Sociology, Christian. I. Title.

SWANK, Calvin Peter, 1880- 232.9
The Lord of Life; an account of the life and teachings of the Savior for students of high school age. [1st ed.] New York, Greenwich Book Publishers [1957] 112p. 21cm. [BT307.S89] 57-9028
1. Jesus Christ— Biog.—Study. I. Title.

SWANK, Calvin Peter, 1880- 232.9
The Lord of Life; an account of the life and teachings of the Savior for students of high school age. [1st ed.] New York, Greenwich Book Publishers [1957] 112 p. 21 cm. [BT307.S89] 57-9028
1. Jesus Christ—Biog.—Study. I. Title.

TANNER, Jacob, 1865- 232.9
The personality we have missed; studies in the life of Jesus. Minneapolis, Augsburg Pub. House [c1954] 76p. 22cm. [BT304.T3] 55-14056
1. Jesus Christ—Character. I. Title.

TAYLOR, Mendell. 232.9
Every day with Jesus; a day-by-day devotional book of the life, teachings, and interviews of Jesus. Grand Rapids, Eerdmans [1961] 237 p. 23 cm. [BT309.T28] 61-18337
1. Jesus Christ — Meditations. I. Title.

TAYLOR, Mendell 232.9
Every day with Jesus; a day-by-day devotional book of the life, teachings, and interviews of Jesus. Grand Rapids, Mich., Eerdmans [c.1961] 237p. 61-18337 3.65
1. Jesus Christ—Meditations. I. Title.

TAYLOR, Vincent, 1887- 232.9
The life and ministry of Jesus. Nashville, Abingdon Press [c1955] 240p. 23cm. A revision and enlargement of the author's The life and ministry of Jesus, published in 1951 in the Interpreter's Bible, v. 7. [BT301.T28 1955] 55-5055
1. Jesus Christ —Biog. I. Title.

*TAYLOR, Willard H. 232.9
The story of our Saviour. Kansas City, Mo., Beacon Hill Pr. [c.1963] 138p.19cm. Bibl. 1.25 pap.,
I. Title.

TESTER, Sylvia 232.9
Flannelgraph stories [2v.] Art by James E. Seward. Cincinnati, Ohio, Standard Pub., c.1963. [2v.] unpaged (chiefly illus.) 31cm. (Redi-Cut pict-o-graph, 2230; 2240) Contents.[v.1] Jesus is born.--[v.2] Jesus lives. 1.50 ea.,
I. Title.

THEODORE, John T 232.9
Who was Jesus? A historical analysis of the misinterpretations of His life and teachings. [1st ed.] New York, Exposition Press [1961] 233 p. 21 cm. (An Exposition-testament book) [BT301.9.T5] 62-16026
1. Jesus Christ — Biog. — Hist. & crit. 2. Jesus Christ — Humanity. I. Title.

THEODORE, John T., Rev., D.D. 232.9
Who was Jesus? A historical analysis of the misinterpretations of His life and teachings. New York, Exposition [c.1961] 233p. (Exposition-testament bk.) 62-16026 4.00
1. Jesus Christ—Biog.—Hist. & crit. 2. Jesus Christ—Humanity. I. Title.

THOME DE JESUS, Father, 1529-1582 232.9
The sufferings of Our Lord Jesus Christ. Edited by Edward Gallagher. [Translated from the Portuguese] Westminster, Md., Newman Press [1960] xvi, 584p. 18cm. 60-50812 5.75
1. Jesus Christ—Biog.—Early works to 1800. I. Title.

THOME DE JESUS, Father, 1529?-1582. 232.9
The sufferings of Our Lord Jesus Christ. Edited by Edward Gallagher. Westminster, Md., Newman Press [1960] 584 p. 18 cm. Translation of Trabalhos de Jesus. [BT300.T412] 60-50812
1. Jesus Christ — Biog. — Early works to 1800. I. Title.

THOMPSON, Ernest Trice, 1894- 232.9
Jesus and citizenship. Richmond, John Knox Press [1957, c1956] 86 p. 21 cm. Includes bibliogrpahy. [BS2415.T48] 56-13456
1. Jesus Christ — Teachings. I. Title.

TILDEN, Elwyn E 232.9
Toward understanding Jesus. Englewood Cliffs, N. J., Prentice-Hall, 1956. 289p. 22cm. [BT301.T5] 56-9147
1. Jesus Christ—Biog. 2. Jesus Christ—Teachings. I. Title.

TILDEN, Elwyn E 232.9
Toward understanding Jesus. Englewood Cliffs, N.J., Prentice-Hall, 1956. 289 p. 22 cm. [BT301.T5] 56-9147
1. Jesus Christ—Biog. 2. Jesus Christ—Teachings. I. Title.

TONDINI Melgari, Amelia. 232.9
Our Lord's life: His story in reverent words and original paintings. Translated from the Italian by Joy Mary Terruzzi. With original paintings by Irina Kessler. [1st American ed.] New York, Hawthorne Books [1960] 167 p. illus. 28 cm. Translation of Io sono la vita. [BT301.2.T613 1960] 60-10123
1. Jesus Christ — Biog. 2. Bible. N. T. Gospels — History of Biblical events. 3. Bible. N. T. Gospels — Pictures, illustrations, etc. I. Kessler, Irina, illus. II. Title.

TONDINI MELGARI, Amelia 232.9
Our Lord's life: His story in reverent words and original paintings. Translated from the Italian by Joy Mary Terruzzi. With original paintings by Irina Kessler. New York, Hawthorn Books [c.1960] 167p. col. illus. 28cm. 60-10123 6.95 bds.,
1. Jesus Christ—Biog. 2. Bible. N. T. Gospels—History of Biblical events. 3. Bible. N. T. Gospels—Pictures, Illustrations, etc. I. Kessler, Irina, illus. II. Title.

TOTTEN, Charles Adiel Lewis, 1851-1908. 232.9
The gospel of history; an interwoven harmony of Matthew, Mark, Luke, and John, with their collaterals, jointly and severally re-translated and con-solidated word-by-word into one composite truth ... Merrimac, Mass., Destiny Publishers [1972] xxvi, 470 p. 20 cm. Reprint of the 1900 ed., which was issued as ser. 7, no. 25-26 of Our race. [BT299.T58 1972] 72-80391
1. Jesus Christ—Biography—Sources, Biblical. I. Title. II. Series: Our race, ser. 7, no. 25-26.

TREMAINE, Guy Everton. 232.9
The prayer life of Jesus; a devotional study of the prayer life of Jesus consisting of forty essays with Scripture references and a prelude and postlude. Philadelphia, Dorrance [1954] 160p. illus. 20cm. [BV210.T63] 54-6759
1. Prayer. 2. Jesus Christ—Prayers. I. Title.

TRENT, Robbie, 1894- j232.9
The life of Jesus; student's book. Nashville, Broadman Press [1965] 96 p. illus. (part. col.) maps. 21 cm. 192 p. maps 21 cm. (The Weekday Bible study series) "For use with 9 and 10-year-olds: may by adapted for other ages" Teachers book [by] Robbie Trent [and] Harriett H. Maffett, Nashville, Broadman Press[1965] [BT302.T69] 65-12862
1. Jesus Christ — Biog. — Juvenile literature. 2. Jesus Christ — Biog. — Study and teaching. I. Maffett, Harriett, H., joint author. II. Title.

TRENT, Robbie, 1894- 232.9
The life of Jesus; student's book. Nashville, Broadman [c.1965] 96p. illus. (pt. col.) maps. 21cm. (,weekday Bible study ser.) For use with 9- and 10-year-olds; may be adapted for other ages. [BT302.T69] 65-12862 pap., 1.00; teacher's ed., 2.75
1. Jesus Christ—Biog.—Juvenile literature. 2. Jesus Christ—Biog.—Study and teaching. I. Title.

TRENT, Robbie, 1894- 232.9
Stories of Jesus; illustrated by Paul Frame. Racine, Wis., Whitman Pub. Co., c1954. unpaged. illus. 21cm. (A Cozy-corner book) [BT302.T73 1954] 55-17419
1. Jesus Christ—Biog. —Juvenile literature. I. Title.

TRENT, Robbie, 1894- 232.9
They saw Jesus. Nashville, Broadman Press, c1952. unpaged. illus. 25cm. [BT302.T74] 53-5813
1. Jesus Christ —Biog.—Juvenile literature. I. Title.

TRUEBLOOD, David Elton, 1900- 232.9
The humor of Christ. [1st ed.] New York, Harper & Row [c1964] 127 p. 22 cm. Bibliographical footnotes. [BT590.H8T7] 64-10756
1. Jesus Christ — Humor. I. Title.

TRUEBLOOD, David Elton, 1900- 232.9
The humor of Christ. New York, Harper [c.1964] 127p. 22cm. Bibl. 64-10756 2.50
1. Jesus Christ—Humor. I. Title.

TRUEBLOOD, David Elton, 1900- 232.9
The Lord's prayers, by Elton Trueblood. [1st ed.] New York, Harper & Row [1965] 128 p. 21 cm. Bibliographical footnotes. [BV229.T7] 65-10706
1. Jesus Christ — Prayers. I. Title.

TRUEBLOOD, David Elton, 1900- 232.9
The Lord's prayers. New York, Harper [c.1965] 128p. 21cm. Bibl. [BV229.T7] 65-10706 2.50
1. Jesus Christ—Prayers. I. Title.

TURNBULL, Ralph G 232.9
The pathway to the cross. Grand Rapids, Baker Book House, 1959. 126 p. 20 cm. Sequel to The seven words from the cross. [BT453.T8] 59-15536
1. Jesus Christ — Passion — Meditations. I. Title.

TURNBULL, Ralph G. 232.9
The pathway to the cross. Grand Rapids, Baker Book House [c.]1959. 126p. 20cm. 59-15536 2.00
1. Jesus Christ—Passion—Meditations. I. Title.

VOS, Howard Frederic, 1925- 232.9
The life of Our Divine Lord. Grand Rapids, Zondervan Pub. House [1956] 223 p. illus. 22 cm. Includes bibliography. [BT301.V67] 58-4624
1. Jesus Christ — Biog. I. Title.

VOS, Howard Frederic, 1925- 232.9
The life of Our Lord [orig. title: The life of Our Divine Lord] Chicago, Moody [1965, c.1958] 255p. illus. 17cm. (43) Bibl. [BT301.V67] .89 pap.,
1. Jesus Christ—Biog. I. Title.

WADSWORTH, Ernest M 232.9
My Good Shepherd, by Ernest M. Wadsworth, and others; illustrated by JoAnne Cameron. Chicago, Moody Press [c1951] 160 p. illus. 21 cm. [BT302.W14] 52-6734
1. Jesus Christ — Biog. — Juvenile literature. I. Title.

WALSH, Chad, 1914- j232.9
The personality of Jesus. Garden City, N.Y. [1961] 64 p. illus. 21 cm. (Know your Bible program) [BT304.W36] 61-4257
1. Jesus Christ — Character — Juvenile literature. I. Title.

WAND, John William Charles, Bp. of London, 1885- 232.9
The life of Jesus Christ. New York, Morehouse- Gorham [1955] 208p. 21cm. [BT301.W24 1955a] 55-10000
1. Jesus Christ—Biog. I. Title.

WEATHERHEAD, Leslie Dixon, 1893- 232.9
Over His own signature: a devotional study of Christ's pictures of Himself, and of their relevance to our lives today. New York, Abingdon Press [1956, c1955] 155 p. 21 cm. [BT306.W37] 56-5374
1. Jesus Christ — Words — Sermons. I. Title.

WEATHERHEAD, Leslie Dixon, 1893- 232.9
Over His own signature; a devotional study of Christ's pictures of Himself, and of their relevance to our lives today. New York, Abingdon Press [1956, c1955] 155 p. 21 cm. [BT306.W37 1956] 56-5374
1. Jesus Christ—Words—Sermons. I. Title.

WHISTON, Charles Francis, 1900- 232.9
The ministry of Jesus; a devotional study. Boston, Pilgrim Press [1951] xiii, 153 p. 20 cm. [BT309.W39] 51-2684
1. Jesus Christ—Meditations. I. Title.

WHITE, Ellen Gould (Harmon) 1827-1915. 232.9
The desire of ages; the conflict of the ages illustrated in the life of Christ. Mountain View, Calif, Pacific Press Pub. Association [1953, c1940] 885p. illus. 23cm. [BT301.W43 1953] 54-21719
1. Jesus Christ—Biog. I. Title.

WHITE, Ellen Gould (Harmon) 1827-1915 232.9
The desire of ages; the conflict of the ages illustrated in the life of Christ. Spot illus. by James L. Converse [New ed.] Mountain View, Calif., Pacific Pr. Pub. [1964, c.1898, 1940] x, 804p. col. illus. 26cm. [BT301.W43] 65-1019 14.50; 15.50 deluxe ed.,
1. Jesus Christ. I. Title.

WHITE, Reginald E. 232.9
The Stranger of Galilee; meditations on the life of Our Lord. Grand Rapids. Mich., Eerdmans [c.1960] 203p. 22cm. 60-10096 3.50 half cloth,
1. Jesus Christ—Biog.—Meditations. I. Title.

WHITE, Reginald E O 232.9
The Stranger of Galilee; meditations on the life of Our Lord. [1st ed.] Grand Rapids, Eerdmans [1960] 203 p. 22 cm. [BT306.4.W5] 60-10096
1. Jesus Christ — Biog. — Meditations. I. Title.

WHITE, Reginald E. O. 232.9
The stranger of galilee. Meditations on the life of our lord. New Canaan, Conn., Keats Publishing [1975, c1960] 203 p., 20 cm. (A Pivot family reader) [BT306.4.W5] 2.25 (pbk.)
1. Jesus Christ—Biog.—Meditations. I. Title.
L.C. card no. for original ed.: 60-10096.

WHITEHOUSE, Elizabeth Scott, 1893- 232.9
Jesus, friend and teacher; a cooperative weekday text for boys and girls of grades five and six. Teacher's book. [Philadelphia, Westminster Press, 1957] 192 p. 20 cm. (The Cooperative series texts for weekday religious education classes and released-time religious education instruction) [BT302.W55] 57-5977
1. Jesus Christ — Biog. — Study. I. Title.

WIEAND, Albert Cassel, 1871- 232.9
The gospel of prayer, its practice and psychology as revealed in the life and teachings of Jesus. Grand Rapids, W. B. Eerdmans Pub. Co., 1953. 245p. 23cm. [BV215.W47] 248 53-9295
1. Prayer. I. Title.

WILSON, Lawrence Ray, 1896- 232.9
The triumphant Jesus. [Bartlesville? Okla., 1952] 265 p. 20 cm. [BT301.W498] 52-44004
1. Jesus Christ—Biog. I. Title.

WISE, Charles C. 232.9
Windows on the Master [by] Charles C. Wise, Jr. Nashville, Abingdon Press [1968] 143 p. 21 cm. Poems. [BT306.4.W55] 68-25365 3.00
1. Jesus Christ—Biography—Meditations. I. Title.

WITSELL, William Postell, 1874- 232.9
Jesus Christ, the light of the world. Boston, Christopher Pub. House [1953] 125p. 21cm. [BT205.W54] 54-9096
1. Jesus Christ—Influence. I. Title.

WOLCOTT, Carolyn Muller. 232.9
Jesus goes to the market place. Pictures by Mary Young. New York, Abingdon [1963] unpaged. illus. 21 cm. [BT302.W72] 63-7974
1. Jesus Christ — Childhood — Juvenile literature. I. Title.

WOLCOTT, Carolyn Muller 232.9
Jesus goes to the market place. Pictures by Mary Young. Nashville, Abingdon [c.1963] unpaged. illus. 21cm. 63-7974 1.25
1. Jesus Christ—Childhood—Juvenile literature. I. Title.

ZAHRNT, Heinz, 1915- 232.9
The historical Jesus. Translated from the German by J. S. Bowden. New York, Harper & Row [1963] 159 p. 22 cm. Translation of Es begann mit Jesus von Nazareth. [BT303.2.Z313] 63-12164
1. Jesus Christ — Historicity. I. Title.

ZAHRNT, Heinz, 1915- 232.9
The historical Jesus. Tr. from German by J. S. Bowden. New York, Harper [c.1960, 1963] 159p. 22cm. Bibl. 63-12164 3.50 bds.,
1. Jesus Christ—Historicity. I. Title.

EVANS, David, 1933- 232.9'002'07
The good book, by Matthew, Mark, Luke, and John, as told to David Evans. Drawings by Sherman. Los Angeles, Price/Stern/Sloan [1972] [39] l. illus. 17 x 19 cm. Cartoons. [BT308.E95] 73-186697 ISBN 0-8431-0129-6 2.00
1. Jesus Christ—Cartoons, satire, etc. I. Sherman, illus. II. Title.

EVANS, David, 1933- 232.9'002'07
The good book, by Matthew, Mark, Luke, and John, as told to David Evans. Drawings by Sherman. Los Angeles, Price/Stern/Sloan [1972] [39] l. illus. 17 x 19 cm. Cartoons. [BT308.E95] 73-186697 ISBN 0-8431-0129-6 Pap. $2.00
1. Jesus Christ—Cartoons, satire, etc. I. Sherman, illus. II. Title.

FISCHER, Michael Hadwin, 1875- 232.90076
The story of Jesus, with suggestions for further study; a text for classes in Christian training schools, by M. Hadwin Fischer ... Philadelphia, Pa., The United Lutheran publication house [c1924] 174 p. incl. front., illus. (maps) diagrs. 20 1/2 cm. "For further study" at end of each chapter. [BT307.F5] 24-5834
1. Jesus Christ — Biog. — Study. I. Title.

TORREY, Reuben Archer, 1856-1928 232.90076
Studies in the life and teachings of our Lord. Grand Rapids, Mich., Baker Bk., 1966[c.1909] 346p. 21cm. [BT307] 66-3846 3.95
1. Jesus Christ—Biog.—Outlines, syllabi, etc. I. Title.

ANDERSON, Hugh, 1920- comp. 232.9'009
Jesus. Englewood Cliffs, N.J., Prentice-Hall [1967] vii, 182 p. 21 cm. (Great lives observed) A Spectrum book. Includes bibliographical references. [BT301.9.A5] 67-28396
1. Jesus Christ—Biog.—Hist. & crit. I. Title.

ADCOCK, Roger. 232.9'01
Stories of Jesus. Rev. by Elsiebeth McDaniel. Illustrated by Gordon King. Wheaton, Ill., Scripture Press Publications, 1971. 77 p. col. illus. 32 cm. London ed. published in 1969 under title: Story of Jesus. Retells Bible stories tracing the events of Jesus' life. [BT302.A26 1971] 70-151699 ISBN 0-361-01210-1
1. Jesus Christ—Biography—Juvenile literature. 2. Jesus Christ—Parables—Juvenile literature. I. McDaniel, Elsiebeth. II. King, Gordon, fl. 1971- illus. III. Title.

ANOINTED Music & Publishing Co. 232.9'01 B
Walk with Jesus : the unabridged version / by the Anointed Music & Publishing Co., inc. [Meriden, Conn. : TAMPCO, 1975- v. : ill. ; 28 cm. Cover title. Vol. 1 consists of the abridged version of the story of Walk with Jesus, the chronological recorded events in the life of the Lord Jesus Christ, the epilogue, why did Jesus walk? and the unabridged version of the story of Walk with Jesus. [BT299.2.A56 1975] 76-359612
1. Jesus Christ—Biography—Sources, Biblical. 2. Jesus Christ—Chronology. 3. Bible. N.T.—Paraphrases, English. I. Title.

ARMSTRONG, Garner Ted. 232.9'01 B
The real Jesus / Garner Ted Armstrong. Kansas City, Mo. : Sheed Andrews and McMeel, [1977] p. cm. [BT306.5.A69] 77-20002 ISBN 0-8362-0727-0 : 9.95
1. Jesus Christ—Biography—Devotional literature. 2. Christian biography—Palestine. I. Title.

BARCLAY, William, lecturer in the University of Glasgow. 232.9'01 B
Jesus of Nazareth / William Barclay ; based on the film directed by Franco Zefirelli, from the script by Anthony Burgess, Suso Cecchi d'Amico and Franco Zefirelli ; photos. by Paul Ronald. London ; Cleveland : Collins, 1977. 285 p. : col. ill. ; 26 cm. [BT301.2.B25] 77-365179 ISBN 0-00-250653-X : 14.95
1. Jesus Christ—Biography. 2. Christian biography—Palestine. I. Zefirelli, Franco. II. Burgess, Anthony, 1917- III. Cecchi d'Amico, Suso. IV. Jesus of Nazareth.

BARNETT, Walter, 1933- 232.9'01 B
Jesus, the story of His life : a modern retelling based on the Gospels / Walter Barnett. Chicago : Nelson-Hall, 1976 c1975 x, 273 p. ; 23 cm. Includes index. [BT301.2.B28] 75-28260 ISBN 0-88229-308-7 : 6.95
1. Jesus Christ—Biography. I. Title.

*BAUGHMAN, Ray E. 232.9'01
The life of Christ visualized. Illus. by Bryan Lee Baughman. Chicago, Moody [1968] 256p. illus. 17cm. (Moody giants, no. 54) .89 pap.,
1. Jesus Christ—Biog. I. Title.

BIBLE. N.T. Gospels. English. Today's English. Selections. 1973. 232.9'01
His story; a chronological account of the life of Jesus from Good news for modern man. Compiled by John Calvin Reid. Waco, Tex., Word Books [1973] 233 p. illus. 18 cm. (A Word paperback) [BT299.2.R44 1973] 73-84605 1.35
1. Jesus Christ—Biography—Sources, Biblical. I. Reid, John Calvin, 1901- II. Title.

BIBLE. N.T. Gospels. Polyglot. Selections. 1904. 232.9'01 B
The life and morals of Jesus of Nazareth : extracted textually from the Gospels in Greek, Latin, French, and English / by Thomas Jefferson ; with an introd. [by Cyrus Adler]. Folcroft, Pa. : Folcroft Library Editions, 1976. p. cm. Reprint of the 1904 ed. published by the Govt. Print. Off., Washington, which was issued as Document no. 755, House of Representatives, 58th Congress, 2d session. [BS2549.J3 1976] 76-17582 ISBN 0-8414-5323-3 lib. bdg. : 25.00
1. Jesus Christ—Biography—Sources, Biblical. 2. Jesus Christ—Teachings. I. Jefferson, Thomas, President U.S., 1743-1826. II. Bible. N.T. Gospels. Polyglot. Selections. 1976. III. Title. IV. Series: United States. 58th Congress, 2d session, 1903-1904. House. Document ; no. 755.

BISHOP, John, 1908- 232.9'01
Seeing Jesus today; a portrait of Jesus the man. Valley Forge [Pa.] Judson Press [1973, c1969] 158 p. 20 cm. [BT306.3.B56 1973] 72-6302 ISBN 0-8170-0575-7 pap 2.50
1. Jesus Christ—Biography—Sermons. 2. Methodist Church—Sermons. 3. Sermons, American. I. Title.

BOROS, Ladislaus, 1927- 232.9'01
Meditations. Translated by David Smith. Garden City, N.Y., Doubleday, 1974 [c1973] 114 p. 22 cm. Translation of Weinachtsmeditationen. [BT315.2.B613 1974] 73-22785 ISBN 0-385-06367-9 5.95
1. Jesus Christ—Nativity—Meditations. I. Title.

BOSLEY, Harold Augustus, 1907- 232.9'01
The deeds of Christ [by] Harold A. Bosley. Nashville, Abingdon Press [1969] 176 p. 20 cm. [BT306.4.B57] 69-12017 3.50
1. Jesus Christ—Biography—Meditations. I. Title.

BUSHELL, Gerard, 1915- 232.9'01
Jesus: where it all began, by Gerald [i.e. Gerard] Bushell. Photography by David Harris. General editor, Mordecai Raanan. New York, Abelard-Schuman [1975] 223 p. illus. (part col.) 28 cm. Adaptation of In the footsteps of Jesus, by W. E. Pax. Details the life of Jesus using historical and literary allusions and photographs of the Holy Land. [BT301.2.P382B87 1975] 74-9373 ISBN 0-200-00144-2 8.95
1. Jesus Christ—Biography. 2. Palestine—Description and travel—Views. 3. Shrines—Palestine. I. Pax, Wolfgang E. In the footsteps of Jesus. II. Harris, David, fl. 1967- illus. III. Title.

CARDWELL-HILL, Henry. 232.9'01
The-me: an imaginary auto-biography of Jesus Christ, recorded by H. Cardwell-Hill. London, Regency P., [1966]. 84 p. 19 cm. 12/6 (B67-1079) [BT301.2C318] 67-96472
1. Jesus Christ—Biog. I. Title.

CARTLEDGE, Samuel Antoine, 1903- 232.9'01
Jesus of fact and faith; studies in the life of Christ, by Samuel A. Cartledge. Grand Rapids, Eerdmands [1968] 160 p. 22 cm. Bibliographical footnotes. [BT301.9.C37] 68-56120 4.50
1. Jesus Christ—Biography—History and criticism. I. Title.

CASSELS, Louis. 232.9'01
The real Jesus, how he lived and what he taught. [1st ed.] Garden City, N.Y., Doubleday, 1968. xii, 131 p. 22 cm. Bibliography: p. [129]-131. [BT301.2.C38] 68-10563
1. Jesus Christ—Biography. 2. Jesus Christ—Teachings. I. Title.

CHARRAT, Andre 232.901
The life of Christ for teenagers. Tr. by S. G. A. Luff. Notre Dame, Ind., Fides [1965] x, 146p. illus. 22cm. (Fides paperback textbook, 7) [BT302.C473] 65-13803 1.95
1. Jesus Christ—Biog.—Juvenile literature. I. Title.

CHENEY, Johnston M. 232.9'01
The life of Christ in stereo; the four gospels combined as one, by Johnston M. Cheney. Edited by Stanley A. Ellisen. Foreword by Earl D. Radmacher. Portland, Or., Western Baptist Seminary Press [1969] xviii, 273 p. 22 cm. Bibliography: p. 266. [BT299.2.C52] 74-84672 2.95
1. Jesus Christ—Biography—Sources, Biblical. I. Ellisen, Stanley A., ed. II. Title.

COLBY, Jean (Poindexter) 1908- 232.9'01
Jesus and the world. Illustrated by Jane Paton. 1st American ed. New York, Hastings House, 1968. [26] p. illus. (part col.) 26 cm. Bibliography: p. [26] Describes simply the life of Christ emphasizing His crucifixion and the importance of His teachings to civilization. [BT302.C58 1968] 68-25569 3.75
1. Jesus Christ—Biography—Juvenile literature. I. Paton, Jane, illus. II. Title.

COLTON, Ann Ree. 232.9'01
The Jesus story. [1st ed.] Glendale, Calif., ARC Pub. Co. [1969] 396 p. 23 cm. [BT304.93.C6] 71-1491 7.95
1. Jesus Christ—Biography. 2. Jesus Christ—Miscellanea. I. Title.

COMSTOCK, Jim F. 232.9'01 B
Good news : the life of Jesus reported in newspaper style / by Jim Comstock ; [photos. by William C. Rogers]. McLean, Va. : EPM Publications, c1974. [48] p. : ill. ; 44 cm. [BT301.2.C57] 74-22829 ISBN 0-914440-06-3 : 6.95 ($7.95 Can)
1. Jesus Christ—Biography. I. Title.

CONGAR, Yves Marie Joseph, 1904- 232.9'01
Jesus Christ [by] Yves Congar. Translated by Luke O'Neill. [New York] Herder and Herder [1966] 223 p. 22 cm. Bibliographical footnotes. [BT306.4.C613] 66-16946
1. Jesus Christ—Meditations. I. Title.

CONNICK, C. Milo. 232.9'01
Jesus: the man, the mission, and the message [by] C. Milo Connick. 2d ed. Englewood Cliffs, N.J., Prentice-Hall [1974] xiv, 464 p. illus. 24 cm. Bibliography: p. 425-439. [BT301.2.C6 1974] 74-6264 ISBN 0-13-509521-2 12.95
1. Jesus Christ—Biography. I. Title.

CONWAY, Charles Abbott. 232.9'01
The Vita Christi of Ludolph of Saxony and late medieval devotion centred on the incarnation : a descriptive analysis / by Charles Abbott Conway. Salzburg : Institut fur Englische Sprache und Literatur, Universitat Salzburg, 1976, c1975. i, 153 p. ; 21 cm. (Analecta Cartusiana ; 34) Thesis—University of Toronto. Bibliography: p. 150-153. [BT300.L83C66] 76-478406 S515.00
1. Ludolphus de Saxonia, 14th cent. Vita Christi. 2. Jesus Christ—Biography—Early works to 1800. 3. Christian biography—Palestine. I. Title. II. Series.

CORNELL, George W. 232.9'01
Behold the Man : people, politics, and events surrounding the life of Jesus / by George Cornell. Waco, Tex. : Word Books, [1974] 206 p. ; 23 cm. [BT301.2.C64] 74-78044 5.95
1. Jesus Christ—Biography. I. Title.

COUGAR, Marie Joseph, 1904. 232.901
Jesus Christ [by] Yves Cougar Tr [from French] by Luke O'Neill [New York] Herder & Herder [c.1966] 223 p. 22 cm bibl. [fbt306.4c613] 66-16946 4.95
I. Title.

COUNTS, Bill. 232.9'01 B
Once a carpenter / Bill Counts. Irvine, Calif. : Harvest House Publishers, [1975] xiii, 255 p. ; 21 cm. [BT301.2.C66] 74-32568 ISBN 0-89081-008-7 pbk. : 2.95
1. Jesus Christ—Biography. I. Title.

CRAVERI, Marcello, 1914- 232.9'01
The life of Jesus. Translated by Charles Lam Markmann. New York, Grove Press [1967] xii, 520 p. illus. 24 cm. Bibliography: p. 479-505. [BT301.2.C713] 66-30412
1. Jesus Christ—Biography. I. Title.

CULVER, Robert Duncan. 232.9'01 B
The life of Christ / Robert Duncan Culver. Grand Rapids, Mich. : Baker Book House, c1976. 304 p. : ill. ; 23 cm. Includes bibliographical references and indexes. [BT301.2.C84] 76-17967 ISBN 0-8010-2379-3 : 8.95
1. Jesus Christ—Biography. 2. Christian biography—Palestine. I. Title.

DANIEL-ROPS, Henry, 1901- 232.901
The life of our Lord [by] Henri Daniel-Rops. Translated from the French by J. R. Foster. Illus. by Charles Keeping. [Deluxe illustrated ed.] New York, Hawthorn Books [1965] 191 p. col. illus., maps. 24 cm. Translation of Histoire du Christ-Jesus. [BT301.2.D313 1965] 65-14642
1. Jesus Christ — Biog. I. Keeping, Charles, illus. II. Title.

DELL'ISOLA, Frank. 232.9'01 B
The good news about Jesus : the New Testament in Today's English version / edited and rearranged in a continuous narrative by Frank Dell'Isola. 3d ed. Philadelphia : A. J. Holman Co., [1975] 335 p. ; 21 cm. [BT299.2.D43 1975] 75-4579 ISBN 0-87981-043-2 : 6.95
1. Jesus Christ—Biography—Sources, Biblical. I. Title.

DISCUSSIONS on the life of Jesus Christ; 232.9'01 twelve studies for students who want to know more about the person and work of Jesus Christ. [Rev. ed.] Chicago, Inter-varsity Press [1967. c1962] 54 p. 18 cm. On cover: An Inter-varsity guide for Bible discussions. [BT307.D57 1967] 67-29347
1. Jesus Christ—Biog.—Study.

EDWARDS, David Lawrence. 232.9'01
Today's story of Jesus / abridged by David L. Lawrence from Good news Bible in Today's English version ; illustrated by Guido Bertello. Cleveland : Collins World, 1976. p. cm. [BT299.2.E35 1976] 76-42223 ISBN 0-529-05331-4 : 6.95
1. Jesus Christ—Biography—Sources, Biblical. 2. Christian biography—Palestine. I. Bertello. II. Bible. N.T. English. Today's English. III. Title.

EGERMEIER, Elsie Emilie, 1890- 232.901
Picture-story life of Jesus. Story revisions by Arlene S. Hall. Anderson, Ind., Warner [1966,c.1965]c127p. col. illus. 25cm. Adapted from Egermeier's Bible story book. Previous eds. pub. under title: Picturestory life of Christ. [BT302.E35] 65-14972 2.95
1. Jesus Christ—Biog—Juvenile literature. 2. Bible stories, English—N. T. Gospels. I. Hall, Arlene Stevens. II. Title.

ELLIOTT, Andrew. 232.9'01
A Geordie life of Jesus. Newcastle upon Tyne, Graham, 1974. 32 p. illus. 22 cm. [BT301.2.E4] 74-177024 ISBN 0-85983-031-4 £0.30
1. Jesus Christ—Biography. I. Title.

ELLIOTT, Graeme Maurice. 232.9'01 B
The psychic life of Jesus / by G. Maurice Elliott. New York : Gordon Press, 1974. 168 p. ; 24 cm. Originally published in 1938 by Psychic Press, London. [BT304.96.E44 1974] 74-20331 ISBN 0-87968-185-3 : 29.95
1. Jesus Christ—Spiritualistic interpretations. I. Title.

EMERSON, William A., 1923- 232.9'01 B
The Jesus story [by] William A. Emerson, Jr. [1st ed.] New York, Harper & Row [1971] 132 p. 21 cm. [BT301.2.E45] 70-148432 4.95
1. Jesus Christ—Biography. I. Title.

EWING, Upton Clary. 232.9'01
The martyred Jew; an expository treatise on the life and the death of the historical Jesus. Coral Gables, Fla., Library of Humane Literature [1967] vii, 95 p. 22 cm. Bibliography: p. 89-90. [BT301.2.E9] 66-30198
1. Jesus Christ — Biog. I. Title.

FARRAR, Frederic William, 1831-1903 232.901
The life of Christ [New] illus. ed. Cleveland, World [1965, c.1913] xvii, 427p. col. illus. 21cm. [BT301.F2] 65-23377 6.50
1. Jesus Christ—Biog. I. Title.

FLUSSER, David Gustav. 232.9'01
Jesus [by] David Flusser. Translated by Ronald Walls. [New York] Herder and Herder [1969] 159 p. illus. 22 cm. Translation of Jesus in Selbstzeugnissen und Bilddokumenten. Bibliography: p. 153-157. [BT303.F61213] 73-81781 4.95
1. Jesus Christ—Biography. 2. Bible. N.T. Gospels—Antiquities. I. Title.

GEORGE, Bill. 232.9'01 B
His story : the life of Christ / Bill George. Cleveland, Tenn. : Pathway Press, c1977. 132 p. ; 18 cm. Bibliography: p. 131-132. [BT301.2.G4] 76-53630 ISBN 0-87148-406-4 pbk. : 2.50
1. Jesus Christ—Biography. 2. Christian biography—Palestine. I. Title.

GEORGE, Bill. 232.9'01 B
His story : the life of Christ / Bill George. Cleveland, Tenn. : Pathway Press, c1977. 132 p. ; 18 cm. Bibliography: p. 131-132. [BT301.2.G4] 76-53630 ISBN 0-87148-406-4 pbk. : 2.50
1. Jesus Christ—Biography. 2. Christian biography—Palestine. I. Title.

GOGUEL, Maurice, 1880-1955. 232.9'01 B
The life of Jesus / by Maurice Goguel ; translated by Olive Wyon. New York : AMS Press, [1976] p. cm. Translation of the 1st v. of a trilogy entitled Jesus et les origines du christianisme; the 2d v. has title: The birth of Christianity. Reprint of the 1933 ed. published by Macmillan, New York. Includes index. Bibliography: p. [BT301.G65 1976] 75-41114 ISBN 0-404-14546-9 : 32.50
1. Jesus Christ—Biography. 2. Bible. N.T.—Biography. I. Title.

THE Gospel message of Jesus Christ : 232.9'01 arranges all the language in the four Gospels of Matthew, Mark, Luke, John into one consecutive narrative / [compiled] by Talma L. Smith. Rev. ed. New York : Vantage Press, c1976. 251, viii, iv p. ; 26 cm. Includes indexes. [BT299.2.G67 1976] 76-373114 ISBN 0-533-02030-1 : 12.50
1. Jesus Christ—Biography—Sources, Biblical. 2. Christian biography—Palestine. I. Smith, Talma L.

GOYEN, William. 232.9'01
A book of Jesus. [1st ed.] Garden City, N.Y., Doubleday, 1973. 143 p. 18 cm. [BT301.2.G6] 72-84915 ISBN 0-385-05979-5 4.95
1. Jesus Christ—Biography.

GOYEN, William. 232.9'01
A book of Jesus. [New York] New American

Library [1974, c1973] 128 p. 18 cm. (A Signet book) [BT301.2.G6] 1.25 (pbk.)
1. Jesus Christ—Biography. I. Title.
L.C. card for original ed.: 72-84915.

GRAHAM, Eleanor, 1896- 232.9'01
The story of Jesus; illustrated by Brian Wildsmith. Revised ed. Harmondsworth, Penguin, 1971. 206 p. illus., map. 18 cm. (Puffin books) [BT301.2.G67 1971] 72-181112 ISBN 0-14-030135-6 £0.25
1. Jesus Christ—Biography. I. Title.

GRANT, Michael, 1914- 232.9'01 B
Jesus : an historian's review of the Gospels / Michael Grant. New York : Scribner, c1977. 261 p. : maps ; 25 cm. Includes index. Bibliography: p. 251. [BT301.2.G68 1977b] 77-70218 ISBN 0-684-14889-7 : 12.50
1. Jesus Christ—Biography. 2. Christian biography—Palestine. I. Title.

GRANT, Michael, 1914- 232.9'01 B
Jesus : an historian's review of the Gospels / Michael Grant. New York : Scribner, c1977. 261 p. : maps ; 25 cm. Includes index. Bibliography: p. 251. [BT301.2.G68 1977b] 77-70218 ISBN 0-684-14889-7 : 12.50
1. Jesus Christ—Biography. 2. Christian biography—Palestine. I. Title.

GUTHRIE, Donald, 1916- 232.9'01
A shorter life of Christ. Grand Rapids, Zondervan Pub. House [1970] 186 p. 21 cm. (Contemporary evangelical perspectives) Bibliography: p. 181-186. [BT301.2.G88] 71-120039
1. Jesus Christ—Biography. I. Title.

GUTMAN, Ernest M. 232.9'01
The Hebrew-Christians, by Ernest M. Gutman. Philadelphia, Dorrance [1973] 216 p. map. 22 cm. Bibliography: p. 212. [BT301.2.G9] 72-96178 ISBN 0-8059-1813-2 5.95
1. Jesus Christ—Biography. I. Title.

HANSER, Richard. 232.9'01
Jesus: what manner of man is this? New York, Simon and Schuster [1972] 191 p. 22 cm. Traces the life and death of Jesus, His effect on world history, and, briefly, the reviving interest in Him found in today's "Jesus movement." [BT302.H24] 72-82219 ISBN 0-671-65200-1 4.95
1. Jesus Christ—Biography—Juvenile literature. I. Title.

HARRISON, Everett 232.9'01
Falconer, 1902-
A short life of Christ, by Everett F. Harrison. Grand Rapids, W. B. Eerdmans [1968] 288 p. 23 cm. Includes bibliographies. [BT301.2.H3] 68-30985 5.95
1. Jesus Christ—Biography. I. Title.

HOBBS, Herschel H 232.901
The life and times of Jesus; a contemporary approach [by] Herschel H. Hobbs. Grand Rapids, Zondervan Pub. House [1966] 218 p. col. map. 23 cm. [BT301.2H6] 65-25953
1. Jesus Christ — Biog. I. Title.

HOBBS, Herschel H. 232.901
The life and times of Jesus; a contemporary approach. Grand Rapids, Mich., Zondervan [c.1966] 218p. col. map. 23cm. [BT301.2H6] 65-25953 3.50
1. Jesus Christ— Biog. I. Title.

HOEHNER, Harold W. 232.9'01
Chronological aspects of the life of Christ / by Harold W. Hoehner. Grand Rapids : Zondervan Pub. House, c1977. p. cm. Includes index. Bibliography: p. [BT303.H58] 76-30350 pbk. : 2.95
1. Jesus Christ—Chronology. I. Title.

[HOLBACH, Paul Henri 232.9'01
Thiry, baron d'] 1723-1789.
Ecce homo! : or, A critical inquiry into the history of Jesus of Nazareth, being a rational analysis of the Gospels / [translated by George Houston]. New York : Gordon Press, 1976. p. cm. Translation of Histoire critique de Jesus Christ. Reprint of the 1st American ed., rev. and corr., of 1827, printed for the proprietors of the Philosophical library, New York, which was issued as no. 1 of the Philosophical library. [BT300.H74 1976] 73-8281 ISBN 0-87968-077-6 lib.bdg. : 34.95
1. Jesus Christ—Biography—Early works to 1800. I. Title. II. Series: The Philosophical library ; no. 1.

HOTH, Iva. 232.9'01
Jesus; Matthew-John. Script by Iva Hoth. Illus. by Andre Le Blanc. Bible editor: C. Elvan Olmstead. Elgin, Il., D. C. Cook Pub. Co. [1973] 158 p. illus. 18 cm. (Her The picture Bible for all ages, v. 5) [BT302.H83] 73-78172 ISBN 0-912692-17-0 0.95 (pbk.)
1. Jesus Christ—Biography—Juvenile literature. I. Title.

JACOBS, William J. 232.9'01 B
Jesus / by William Jacobs. N[ew] Y[ork] : Paulist Press, c1977. vii, 124 p. ; 18 cm. (Emmaus books) [BT301.2.J3] 76-24439 ISBN 0-8091-1986-2 pbk. : 1.45
1. Jesus Christ—Biography. 2. Christian biography—Palestine. I. Title.

JACOBS, William J. 232.9'01 B
Jesus / by William Jacobs. N[ew] Y[ork] : Paulist Press, c1977. vii, 124 p. ; 18 cm. (Emmaus books) [BT301.2.J3] 76-24439 ISBN 0-8091-1986-2 pbk. : 1.45
1. Jesus Christ—Biography. 2. Christian biography—Palestine. I. Title.

JEREMIAS, Joachim, 1900- 232.9'01
The prayers of Jesus. Naperville, Ill., A. R. Allenson [1967] 124 p. 22 cm. (Studies in Biblical theology, 2d ser. 6) Selections translated from Abba: Studien zur neutestamentlichen Theologie und Zeitgeschichte. Bibliographical footnotes. [BV229.J4 1967b] 68-131
1. Jesus Christ—Prayers. 2. Lord's prayer. I. Title. II. Series.

JESUS : 232.9'01
the four Gospels, Matthew, Mark, Luke, and John, combined in one narrative and rendered in modern English. Boston : G. K. Hall, 1975, c1973. xxviii, 351 p. : map ; 25 cm. Large print ed. Includes index. [BT299.2.J47 1975] 75-5681 ISBN 0-8161-6275-1 lib.bdg. : 9.95
1. Jesus Christ—Biography—Sources, Biblical. 2. Sight-saving books.

JESUS, our Friend. 232.9'01 B
Valley Forge, Pa. : Judson Press, c1976. 47 p. : col. ill. ; 22 cm. Traces the life of Jesus Christ through a retelling of twenty stories from the New Testament. [BS2401.J44] 75-42379 ISBN 0-8170-0713-X : 1.50
1. Jesus Christ—Biography—Juvenile literature. 2. Bible stories, English—N.T. Gospels.

JESUS; the four Gospels, 232.9'01
Matthew, Mark, Luke and John, combined in one narrative and rendered in modern English. [Editorial committee: Charles B. Templeton and others]. New York, Pocket Books [1975, c1974] 240 p. map. 18 cm. [BT299.2.J47] 73-20754 ISBN 0-671-78888-4
1. Jesus Christ—Biography—Sources, Biblical.

KALLAS, James G. 232.9'01
Jesus and the power of Satan, by James Kallas. Philadelphia, Westminster Press [1968] 215 p. 21 cm. Bibliographical footnotes. [BT301.2.K34] 68-10364
1. Jesus Christ—Biography. 2. Bible. N.T. Gospels—Theology. 3. Devil—Biblical teaching. 4. Bible. N.T. Gospels—Theology. I. Title.

KELLER, Weldon 232.9'01 B
Phillip, 1920-
Rabboni ... which is to say master / W. Phillip Keller. Old Tappan, N.J. : Revell, c1977. 320 p. ; 24 cm. [BT301.2.K44] 77-24304 ISBN 0-8007-0882-2 : 8.95
1. Jesus Christ—Biography. 2. Christian biography—Palestine. I. Title.

KELLER, Weldon 232.9'01 B
Phillip, 1920-
Rabboni ... which is to say master / W. Phillip Keller. Old Tappan, N.J. : Revell, c1977. 320 p. ; 24 cm. [BT301.2.K44] 77-24304 ISBN 0-8007-0882-2 : 8.95
1. Jesus Christ—Biography. 2. Christian biography—Palestine. I. Title.

LAMSA, George 232.9'01
Mamishisho, 1893-
The man from Galilee; a life of Jesus [by] George M. Lamsa. [1st ed.] Garden City, N.Y., Doubleday, 1970. xv, 293 p. 22 cm. [BT301.2.L24] 73-78702 5.95
1. Jesus Christ—Biography. I. Title.

LEVIN, Simon S. 232.9'01
Jesus alias Christ; a theological detection [by] Simon S. Levin. New York, Philosophical Library [1969] 136 p. 22 cm. Bibliographical footnotes. [BT301.2.L38] 71-81814 5.50
1. Jesus Christ—Biography.

LONGFORD, Frank 232.9'01 B
Pakenham, 7th Earl of, 1905-
Jesus : a life of Christ / by Lord Longford ; illustrated by Richard Cuffari. Garden City, N.Y. : Doubleday, 1975. 184, [3] p. : ill. ; 22 cm. First ed. published in 1974 under title: The life of Jesus Christ. Bibliography: p. [187] [BT301.2.L6 1975] 74-12698 ISBN 0-385-07008-X : 5.95
1. Jesus Christ—Biography. I. Title.

MOORE, Sebastian, 1917- 232.9'01
No exit. Glen Rock, N.J., Newman Press [1968] 151 p. 21 cm. [BT450.M6 1968] 68-31257
1. Jesus Christ—Crucifixion. 2. Atonement. I. Title.

NOTOVICH, Nikolai, 232.9'01
1858-
The unknown life of Jesus Christ / by the discoverer of the manuscript, Nicholas Notovich ; translated by J. H. Connelly and L. Landsberg. New York : Gordon Press, [1974] p. cm. Translation of La vie inconnue. Reprint of the 1890 ed. published by R. F. Fenno, New York, which was issued as v. 1, no. 185, of the Globe library. [BT520.N6813 1974] 73-11500 ISBN 0-87968-073-3
1. Jesus Christ—Biography—Apocryphal and legendary literature. I. Title. II. Series: Globe library ; v. 1, no. 185.

O'BRIEN, Isidore, 232.9'01 B
1895-1953.
The life of Christ / Isidore O'Brien. 5th ed. [Boston] : St. Paul Editions, [1975] 612 p., [8] leaves of plates : ill. ; 22 cm. Includes bibliographical references and index. [BT307.O35 1975] 75-5719 7.95 pbk. : 6.95
1. Jesus Christ—Biography—Study. I. Title.

PAX, Wolfgang E. 232.9'01
In the footsteps of Jesus [by] Wolfgang E. Pax. New York, Putnam [1970] 231 p. illus. (part col.), map (on lining papers) 29 cm. Bibliography: p. 229-231. [BT301.2.P38 1970] 78-90908 15.00
1. Jesus Christ—Biography. 2. Palestine—Description and travel—Views. 3. Shrines—Palestine. I. Title.

PEALE, Norman Vincent, 232.901
1898-
Jesus Nazareth; a dramatic interpretation of His life from Bethlehem to Calvary. Englewood Cliffs, N.J. Prentice c.1966 1v. (unpaged) 32cm. (Inspirational bk. serv. bk.) [BT301.2P4] 66-18471 3.95 bds.,
1. Jesus Christ—Biog. I. Title.

PEALE, Norman Vincent, 232.901
1898-
Jesus of Nazareth; a dramatic interpretation of His life from Bethlehem to Calvary. Englewood Cliffs, N. J., Prentice-Hall [1966] 1 v. (unpaged) 32 cm. (An Inspirational book service book) [BT301.2.P4] 66-18471
1. Jesus Christ—Biog. I. Title.

PEALE, Norman Vincent, 232.9'01
1898-
The story of Jesus / Norman Vincent Peale ; illustrated by Robert Fujitani. Norwalk, Conn. : C. R. Gibson, c1976. 88 p. : ill. ; 21 cm. [BT301.2.P43] 75-36009 ISBN 0-8378-1797-8 : 4.50
1. Jesus Christ—Biography. I. Fujitani, Robert. II. Title.

PHILLIPS, Wendell, 232.9'01 B
1921-
An explorer's life of Jesus / by Wendell Phillips. New York : Two Continents Pub. Group, [1975] p. cm. Includes bibliographical references and index. [BT301.2.P476] 75-11181 ISBN 0-8467-0072-7 : 20.00
1. Jesus Christ—Biography. 2. Bible. N.T. Gospels—Criticism, interpretation, etc. I. Title.

PHILLIPS, Wendell, 232.9'01 B
1921-
A popular life of Jesus / Wendell Phillips. New York : Two Continents Pub. Group, [1975] p. cm. An abridged version of the author's An explorer's life of Jesus. Includes index. [BT301.2.P477] 75-11183 ISBN 0-8467-0073-5 : 9.95
1. Jesus Christ—Biography. 2. Bible. N.T. Gospels—Criticism, interpretation, etc. I. Title.

RAPPOPORT, Angelo 232.9'01
Solomon, 1871-1950.
Mediaeval legends of Christ / A. S. Rappoport. Folcroft, Pa. : Folcroft Library Editions, 1976. p. cm. Reprint of the 1st ed. published in 1934 by I. Nicholson and Watson, London. Includes index. Bibliography: p. [BT520.R3 1976] 76-15555 ISBN 0-8414-7346-3 lib. bdg. : 30.00
1. Jesus Christ—Biography—Apocryphal and legendary literature. I. Title.

REIMARUS, Hermann 232.9'01
Samuel, 1694-1768.
Fragments. Edited by Charles H. Talbert. Translated by Ralph S. Fraser. Philadelphia, Fortress Press [1970] x, 279 p. 19 cm. (Lives of Jesus series) Translation of part of the author's unpublished Apologie; oder, Schutzschrift fur die vernunftigen Verehrer Gottes. "Hermann Samuel Reimarus and his Apology, by David Friedrich Strauss. [section symbol] 38": p. 44-57. Bibliography: p. [273]-[274] [BT198.R4132] 74-127527 4.95
1. Jesus Christ—History of doctrines—18th century. I. Talbert, Charles H., ed. II. Strauss, David Friedrich, 1808-1874. Hermann Samuel Reimarus und seine Schutzschrift fur die vernunftigen Verehrer Gottes. Section 38. English. 1970.

REUMANN, John Henry 232.9'01
Paul.
Jesus in the church's Gospels; modern scholarship and the earliest sources [by] John Reumann. Philadelphia, Fortress Press [1968] xviii, 539 p. 23 cm. Includes bibliographical references. [BT301.2.R4] 68-10983
1. Jesus Christ—Biography. I. Title.

*RICHARDS, Jean H. 232.901
Stories of Jesus. Racine, Wisc., Golden Press [1974] [24] p. illus. 21 cm. (A little Golden book) [BT302] 0.49
1. Jesus Christ—Biography—Juvenile literature. 2. Jesus Christ—Parables—Juvenile literature. I. Title.

ROBBINS, Ray F., 1915- 232.9'01
The life and ministry of our Lord [by] Ray F. Robbins. Nashville, Tenn., Convention Press [1970] ix, 211 p. illus., maps. 21 cm. (Bible survey series, v. 6) Bibliography: p. 202-204. [BT301.2.R6] 70-110607
1. Jesus Christ—Biography. I. Title. II. Series.

*ROBERTSON, A. T. 232.901
Epochs in the life of Jesus; a study of development and struggle in the Messiah's work [by] A. T. Robertson. Grand Rapids, Baker Book House, [1974]. ix, 192 p. 20 cm. [BT307] ISBN 0-8010-7624-2. 2.95 (pbk.)
1. Jesus Christ—Biography. 2. Jesus Christ—Historicity. I. Title.

ROBERTSON, Archibald 232.9'01
Thomas, 1863-1934.
Epochs in the life of Jesus : a study of development and struggle in the Messiah's work / A. T. Robertson. Nashville : Broadman Press, 1974. ix, 192 p. ; 20 cm. (A. T. Robertson library) Reprint of the 1907 ed. published by Scribner, New York. Includes index. [BT301.R59 1974] 74-193286 ISBN 0-8054-1347-2 pbk. : 2.95
1. Jesus Christ—Biography. I. Title.

RUSSELL, Josiah Cox, 232.9'01
1900-
Jesus of Nazareth, by Josiah C. Russell. [1st ed. New York] Pageant Press [1967] 130 p. 21 cm. [BT301.2.R8] 67-5686
1. Jesus Christ—Biography. I. Title.

SAKLATVALA, Beram. 232.9'01 B
The rebel king : the story of Christ as seen against the historical conflict between the Roman Empire and Judaism / by Henry Marsh [i.e. B. Saklatvala]. New York : Coward, McCann & Geoghegan, [1975] xi, 222 p. ; 22 cm. Bibliography: p. 221-222. [BT301.2.S14] 74-30594 ISBN 0-698-10663-6 : 7.95
1. Jesus Christ—Biography. 2. Bible. N.T. Gospels—History of contemporary events, etc. I. Title.

SALSTRAND, George A. 232.9'01 B
E., 1908-
What Jesus began : the life and ministry of Christ / George A. E. Salstrand. Nashville : Broadman Press, c1976. 180 p. : ill. ; 21 cm. [BT301.2.S163] 75-20694 ISBN 0-8054-1356-1 : 4.95
1. Jesus Christ—Biography. I. Title.

SAUNDERS, Ernest W. 232.9'01
Jesus in the Gospels [by] Ernest W. Saunders. Englewood Cliffs, N.J., Prentice-Hall [1967] xii, 324 p. illus., map (on lining papers) 22 cm. Bibliographical footnotes. [BT301.2.S2] 67-10316
1. Jesus Christ—Biography. I. Title.

SCHLEIERMACHER, 232.9'01 B
Friedrich Ernst Daniel, 1768-1834.
The life of Jesus / by Friedrich Schleiermacher ; edited and with an introd. by Jack C. Verheyden ; translated by S. Maclean Gilmour. Philadelphia : Fortress Press, c1975. lxii, 481 p. ; 22 cm. (Lives of Jesus series) Translation of Das Leben Jesu. Bibliography: p. lxi-lxii. [BT301.S3613 1975] 72-87056 ISBN 0-8006-1272-8 : 14.95
1. Jesus Christ—Biography. I. Title.

SMITH, Morton, 1915- 232.9'01
Jesus the magician / Morton Smith. 1st ed. New York : Harper and Row, c1977. p. cm. Includes indexes. Bibliography: p. [BT304.93.S63 1977] 77-14518 ISBN 0-06-067412-1 : 12.95
1. Jesus Christ—Miscellanea. I. Title.

A Son is given. 232.9'01
Edited by Virginia Sutch. Based on God so loved the world by Adeline Hill Ostwalt. [Atlanta, John Knox Press [1974] 127 p. col. illus. 21 cm. A record of the significant events in the life of Christ as noted in the writings of Luke. [BT302.S64 1974] 73-9599 ISBN 0-8042-9507-7
1. Jesus Christ—Biography—Juvenile

literature. I. Sutch, Virginia, ed. II. Ostwalt, Adeline Hill. God so loved the world.

STORIES of Jesus. 232.9'01 B
Adapted from the Jerusalem Bible. Illustrated by Eric de Saussure. Philadelphia, Fortress Press [1973, c1968] 62 p. illus. (part col.) 23 cm. [BT301.2.S73 1973] 72-92183 ISBN 0-8006-0164-5 1.95
1. Jesus Christ—Biography. I. Saussure, Eric de, illus.

STRAUSS, David Friedrich, 1808-1874. 232.9'01
The Christ of faith and the Jesus of history : a critique of Schleiermacher's Life and Jesus / by David Friedrich Strauss ; translated, edited, and with an introduction by Leander E. Keck. Philadelphia : Fortress Press, c1977. cxii, 169 p. ; 19 cm. (Lives of Jesus series) Translation of Der Christus des Glaubens und der Jesus der Geschichte. Bibliography: p. cvii-cxii. [BT301.S363S813] 75-37152 ISBN 0-8006-1273-6 pbk. : 9.95
1. Schleiermacher, Friedrich Ernst Daniel, 1768-1834. Das Leben Jesu. 2. Jesus Christ—Biography. I. Title.

STRAUSS, David Friedrich, 1808-1874. 232.9'01
The life of Jesus, critically examined. Translated from the 4th German ed. by Marian Evans. New York, C. Blanchard, 1860. St. Clair Shores, Mich., Scholarly Press, 1970. 2 v. (901 p.) port. 23 cm. Bibliographical footnotes. [BT301.S72 1970] 74-107193
1. Jesus Christ—Biography. I. Title.

STRAUSS, David Friedrich, 1808-1874. 232.9'01
The life of Jesus, critically examined. Edited and with an introd. by Peter C. Hodgson. Translated from the 4th German ed. by George Eliot. Philadelphia, Fortress Press [1973, c1972] lviii, 39-812 p. 22 cm. (Lives of Jesus series) Bibliography: p. 803-812. [BT301.S72 1973] 72-75655 ISBN 0-8006-1271-X 12.00
1. Jesus Christ—Biography. I. Title.

TAYLOR, Kenneth Nathaniel. 232.9'01
The life of Christ; a pictorial essay from The living Bible. [Photography by Alan (Wim) Auceps] Wheaton, Ill., Tyndale House Publishers [1974] 1 v. (unpaged) col. illus. 27 cm. [BT299.2.T272 1974] 73-92956 ISBN 0-8423-2215-9
1. Jesus Christ—Biography—Sources, Biblical. I. Auceps, Alan, illus. II. Title.

TAYLOR, Kenneth Nathaniel. 232.9'01
The living story of Jesus: Matthew, Mark, Luke. John. Glendale, Calif., G/L Regal [1967] 1 v. (unpaged) illus. (pt. col.), col. map. 27cm. [BT299.2.T28] 67-30247 4.95 bds.,
1. Jesus Christ—Biog.—Sources, Biblical. I. Title.

TAYLOR, Kenneth Nathaniel. 232.9'01
The man Jesus. Glendale, Calif., G/L Regal Books [1967] 273 p. 18 cm. Text from Living Gospels by Kenneth N. Taylor. [BT299.2.T3 1967] 67-27444
1. Jesus Christ—Biography—Sources, Biblical. I. Title.

TENNANT, Charles Roger 232.901
Christ encountered; a short life of Jesus. New York, Seabury [1966,c. 1961] v, 135p. 21cm. (Seabury paperbacks, SP25) [BT301.2.T4] 66-1386 1.45 pap.,
1. Jesus Christ—Biog. I. Title.

TRAPP, Maria Augusta. 232.9'01 B
When the King was carpenter / by Maria von Trapp. Harrison, Ark. : New Leaf Press, c1976. 141 p. ; 18 cm. Includes bibliographical references. [BT301.2.T7] 75-46021 ISBN 0-89221-018-4 : 1.95
1. Jesus Christ—Biography. 2. Christian biography—Palestine. I. Title.

TREASURE, Geoff. 232.9'01
The most unforgettable character you'll ever meet / Geoff Treasure. Chicago : Moody Press, 1977, c1973. 156 p. ; 19 cm. "Moody paperback edition." [BT301.2.T73] 77-4416 ISBN 0-8024-5625-1 pbk. : 1.50
1. Jesus Christ—Biography. 2. Bible. N.T. Mark—Criticism, interpretation, etc. 3. Christian biography—Palestine. I. Title.

VAN VECHTEN, Schuyler, comp. 232.9'01
The Bethlehem star; children's newspaper reports of the life of Jesus. Created by Schuyler Van Vechten, Jr., and fifty-two children. New York, Walker [1972] [60] p. 27 cm. Reconstructs the events of Jesus' life in the form of newspaper reports, editorials, letters, and advertisements. [BT302.V36 1972] 70-183923 ISBN 0-8027-6097-X 4.95

1. Jesus Christ—Biography—Juvenile literature. I. Title.

VOS, Howard Frederic, 1925- 232.9'01 B
Beginnings in the life of Christ / by Howard F. Vos. Rev. ed. Chicago : Moody Press, [1975] p. cm. First ed. published in 1958 under title: The life of Our Divine Lord. Includes index. Bibliography: p. [BT301.2.V63 1975] 75-11981 ISBN 0-8024-0608-4 pbk : 2.95
1. Jesus Christ—Biography. I. Title.

WHO is this man Jesus? 232.901
: the complete life of Jesus from the living Bible. New York : Bantam Books ,1976 c1966. viii, 215 p. : ill., maps ; 18 cm. Includes index. [BT299.2] ISBN 0-553-07911-5 pbk. : 1.50
1. Jesus Christ—Biography—Sources, Biblical.

*WHYTE, Alexander 232.901
The walk, conversation and character of Jesus Christ Our Lord. Grand Rapids, Baker Book House, [1975] 340 p. 23 cm. (Religious heritage library) [BT301] ISBN 0-8010-9568-9 7.95
1. Jesus Christ—Biography. I. Title.

CHAMBERLAIN, Eugene. 232.9'01'024054 B
Jesus : God's Son, Savior, Lord / Eugene Chamberlain ; illustrated by James Padgett. Nashville : Broadman Press, c1976. 47 p. : col. ill. ; 24 cm. (Biblearn series) Discusses the life and teachings of Jesus Christ. [BT302.C45] 76-382763 ISBN 0-8054-4226-X : 3.95
1. Jesus Christ—Biography—Juvenile literature. 2. Christian biography—Palestine—Juvenile literature. I. Padgett, James. II. Title.

TAYLOR, Kenneth Nathaniel. 232.9'01'08
The greatest life ever lived; selections [by] Kenneth N. Taylor. Wheaton, Ill., Tyndale House Publishers [1969] 59 p. illus. 20 cm. (Heritage edition) [BT306.5.T3] 70-75245
1. Jesus Christ—Biography—Devotional literature. I. Title.

MANN, Christopher Stephen. 232.9'012 B
The man for all time [by] C. S. Mann. New York, Morehouse-Barlow [1971] 126 p. maps. 19 cm. [BT301.2.M26] 75-161567 ISBN 0-8192-1127-3
1. Jesus Christ—Biography. I. Title.

BOSLEY, Harold Augustus, 1907- 232.9'03
The character of Christ [by] Harold A. Bosley. Nashville, Abingdon Press [1967] 143 p. 20 cm. [BT304.B62] 67-22163
1. Jesus Christ—Character. I. Title.

HARRINGTON, Donald Szantho. 232.903
As we remember Him. Boston, Beacon Press [1965] xi, 111 p. 24 cm. [BT306.3.H3] 65-20785
1. Jesus Christ — Biog. — Sermons. 2. Sermons, American. 3. Unitarian churches — Sermons. I. Title.

HARRINGTON, Donald Szantho 232.903
As we remember Him. Boston, Beacon [c.1965] xi, 111p. 24cm. [BT306.3.H3] 65-20785 4.95 bds.,
1. Jesus Christ—Biog.—Sermons. 2. Sermons, American. 3. Unitarian churches—Sermons. I. Title.

MORRISON, Mary (Chase). 232.9'03
Jesus: man and master [by] Mary C. Morrison. [1st ed.] Cleveland, World [1968] 119p. 21cm. [BT304.M62] 67-24757 3.95
1. Jesus Christ—Character I. Title.

TORREY, reuben archer, 1856-1928 232.903
The real Christ. Grand Rapids mich., Zondervan [1966] 157 p. 21 cm [bt304] -65 2.95
1. 1. Jesus Christ—character. I. Title.

TORREY, Reuben Archer, 1856-1928. 232.903
The real Christ... Grand Rapids, Zondervan Pub. House [1966] 157 p. 21 cm. [BT304] 65-25950
1. Jesus Christ — Character. I. Title.

DEWEY, Bradley R. 232.9'03'0924
The new obedience; Kierkegaard on imitating Christ [by] Bradley R. Dewey. Foreword by Paul L. Holmer. Washington, Corpus Books, [1968] xxviii, 247 p. 21 cm. Bibliography: p. 229-242. [BT304.2.D4] 68-27862 7.50
1. Jesus Christ—Example. 2. Kierkegaard, Soren Aabye, 1813-1855. I. Title.

HIGGINS, Angus John Brockhurst 232.904
Jesus and the Son of Man, by A. J. B. Higgins. Philadelphia, Fortress [1965, c.1964] 223p. 23cm. Bibl. [BT232.H5] 65-21083 4.25
1. Son of Man. I. Title.

HEINZ, Susanna Wilder. 232.907
"Who do men say that I am?" A study of Jesus. Boston, Beacon Press [1965] vii, 176 p. illus., geneal. table. 24 cm. ([The Beacon series in religious education]) Bibliography: p. 174-176. [BT307.H45] 65-12
1. Jesus Christ — Biog. — Study and teaching. I. Title.

HEINZ, Susanna Wilder 232.907
'Who do men say that I am?' A study of Jesus. Boston, Beacon [c.1965] vii, 176p. illus., geneal. table. 24cm. (Beacon ser. in religious educ.) Bibl. [BT307.H45] 65-12240 4.95
1. Jesus Christ—Biog.—Study and teaching. I. Title.

*FRASER, T. Layton 232.9076
The life and philosophy of Christ [3d. ed., rev.] Grand Rapids, Mich., Eerdmans [1965, c.1961] 308p. 24cm. Bibl. 3.75
I. Title.

ANDERSON, Charles C., 1931- 232.9'08
The historical Jesus; a continuing quest, by Charles C. Anderson. Grand Rapids, Eerdmans [1972] 271 p. 21 cm. Bibliography: p. 259-264. [BT301.9.A493] 71-184697 ISBN 0-8028-1441-7 3.95
1. Jesus Christ—Biography—History and criticism. 2. Jesus Christ—Historicity. I. Title.

BARKATULLAH, Qazi Muhammad. 232.9'08
Jesus, Son of Mary: fallacy and factuality. Philadelphia, Dorrance [1973] 127 p. 22 cm. Includes bibliographical references. [BT303.2.B276] 73-77630 ISBN 0-8059-1857-4 4.95
1. Jesus Christ—Historicity. 2. Jesus Christ—Biography—History and criticism. I. Title.

BETZ, Otto. 232.9'08
What do we know about Jesus? Philadelphia, Westminster Press [1968] 126 p. 19 cm. Translation of Was wissen wir von Jesus? Bibliographical footnotes. [BT303.2.B413 1968] 68-18938
1. Jesus Christ—Historicity. 2. Jesus Christ—Biography—Sources. I. Title.

BROWN, Parker B. 232.9'08
He came from Galilee / Parker B. Brown. New York : Hawthorn Books, [1974] xii, 164 p. : map ; 22 cm. Includes index. [BS2555.5.B78 1974] 73-19385 ISBN 0-8015-3368-6 : 6.95
1. Jesus Christ—Biography. 2. Bible. N.T. Gospels—History of contemporary events, etc. I. Title.

BRUCE, Frederick Fyvie, 1910- 232.9'08
Jesus and Christian origins outside the New Testament, by F. F. Bruce. Grand Rapids, Eerdmans [1974] 215 p. 20 cm. Bibliography: p. 205-206. [BT297.B74 1974] 74-2012 ISBN 0-8028-1575-8 3.45
1. Jesus Christ—Biography—Sources. 2. Christianity—Origin. I. Title.

DREWS, Arthur Christian Heinrich, 1865-1935. 232.9'08
The witnesses to the historicity of Jesus. [Translated by Joseph McCabe] New York, Arno Press, 1972. xii, 319 p. 23 cm. (The Atheist viewpoint) Reprint of the 1912 ed. "An abbreviated and amended version ... of ... the second part of The Christ-myth." Includes bibliographical references. [BT303.2.D753 1972] 70-161327 ISBN 0-405-03811-9
1. Jesus Christ—Historicity. 2. Bible. N.T.—Criticism, interpretation, etc. I. Title. II. Series.

HIERS, Richard H. 232.9'08
The historical Jesus and the kingdom of God; present and future in the message and ministry of Jesus [by] Richard H. Hiers. Gainesville, University of Florida Press, 1973. viii, 128 p. 23 cm. (University of Florida humanities monograph no. 38) Includes bibliographical references. [BS2417.E7H53] 73-2623 ISBN 0-8130-0386-5
1. Jesus Christ—Teachings. 2. Jesus Christ—Historicity. 3. Eschatology—Biblical teaching. I. Title. II. Series: Florida. University, Gainesville. University of Florida monographs. Humanities, no. 38.

JERVELL, Jacob 232.908
The continuing search for the historical Jesus. Tr. by Harris E. Kaasa. Minneapolis, Augsburg [c.1965] 106p. 21cm. Bibl. [BT303.2.J433] 65-22841 3.00
1. Jesus Christ—Historicity. I. Title.

KECK, Leander E. 232.9'08
A future for the historical Jesus; the place of Jesus in preaching and theology [by] Leander E. Keck. Nashville, Abingdon Press [1971] 271 p. 23 cm. Includes bibliographical references. [BT303.2.K43] 70-148073 ISBN 0-687-13883-3 6.50
1. Jesus Christ—Historicity. I. Title.

LEON-DUFOUR, Xavier. 232.9'08
The Gospels and the Jesus of history. Translated and edited by John McHugh. New York, Desclee Co. [1967, c1968] 288 p. 22 cm. Translation of Les Evangiles et l'histoire de Jesus. Bibliography: p. 277-280. [BT303.2.L413 1968b] 67-17676 5.75
1. Jesus Christ—Biography—Sources. 2. Jesus Christ—Historicity. I. Title.

MCARTHUR, Harvey K., comp. 232.9'08
In search of the historical Jesus. Edited by Harvey K. McArthur. New York, Scribner [1969] xiii, 284 p. 24 cm. (Scribner source books in religion) Bibliography: p. 281-284. [BT303.2.M28] 69-11956
1. Jesus Christ—Historicity. 2. Jesus Christ—Biography—History and criticism. I. Title.

MCARTHUR, Harvey K. 232.908
The quest through the centuries; the search for the historical Jesus. Philadelphia, Fortress [c.1966] xi, 173p. 22cm. Includes a list of 16th century Gospel harmonies. [BT303.2.M3] 66-14243 3.75
1. Jesus Christ—Historicity. I. Title.

MARSHALL, I. Howard. 232.9'08
I believe in the historical Jesus / by I. Howard Marshall. 1st American ed. Grand Rapids : Eerdmans, 1977. 253 p. ; 21 cm. Bibliography: p. [251]-253. [BT303.2.M38 1977] 77-2224 ISBN 0-8028-1691-6 : 2.95
1. Jesus Christ—Historicity. I. Title.

MITTON, C. Leslie. 232.9'08
Jesus: the fact behind the faith, by C. Leslie Mitton. Grand Rapids, Eerdmans [1974] 152 p. 21 cm. Bibliography: p. 152. [BT303.2.M57] 73-20193 ISBN 0-8028-1563-4 2.95 (pbk.)
1. Jesus Christ—Historicity. I. Title.

PETER, James 232.908
Finding the historical Jesus; a statement of the principles involved. New York, Harper [1966,c.1965] 222p. 21cm. Bibl. [BT303.2.P47] 66-10231 4.50 bds.,
1. Jesus Christ—Historicity. I. Title.

SCHWEITZER, Albert, 1875-1965. 232.9'08
The quest of the historical Jesus; a critical study of its progress from Reimarus to Wrede. [With a new] introd. by James M. Robinson. [Translated by W. Montgomery] New York, Macmillan [1968] xxxiii, 413 p. 21 cm. (Macmillan paperbacks) Reprint of the 1910 ed. Translation of Von Reimarus zu Wrede. Bibliography: p. 405-413. [BT303.S42 1968] 68-29509 2.95
1. Jesus Christ—Biography—History and criticism. 2. Jesus Christ—Historicity. I. Montgomery, William, 1871-1930, tr. II. Robinson, James McConkey, 1924- III. Title.

†ALBERIONE, Giacomo Guiseppe, 1884-1971. 232.91
Mary, Queen of Apostles / by James Alberione ; translated and updated in the light of Vatican II by a team of Daughters of St. Paul. 2d ed. Boston : St. Paul Editions, c1976. 301 p. : ill. ; 22 cm. Translation of Maria, Regina degli Apostoli. [BT638.A413 1976] 76-10323 4.00 pbk. : 3.00
1. Mary, Virgin. I. Title.

ASHE, Geoffrey. 232.91
The virgin / Geoffrey Ashe. London : Routledge & Paul, 1976. vi, 261 p. ; 23 cm. Includes index. Bibliography: p. 251-254. [BT645.A85] 76-364472 ISBN 0-7100-8342-4 : 11.25
1. Mary, Virgin—Cultus. 2. Women in religion. I. Title.
Distributed by Routledge & Kegan Paul, Boston

BENKO, Stephen, 1924- 232.91
Protestants, Catholics, and Mary. Valley Forge [Pa.] Judson Press [1968] 160 p. 23 cm. Bibliography: p. 145-155. [BT613.B44] 68-28074 5.75
1. Mary, Virgin—Theology. 2. Mary, Virgin, and Christian union. I. Title.

*BOUYER, Louis 232.91
The seat of wisdom; an essay on the place of the Virgin Mary in Christian theology. Tr. [from French] by A. V. Littledale. Chicago, Regnery [1965] 212p. 18cm. (Logos bk., L704) 1.45 pap.,
I. Title.

BRAUN, Francois Marie, 1893- 232.91
Mother of God's people, by F. M. Braun. [Translator: John Clarke] Staten Island, N.Y., Alba House [1967] 181 p. 22 cm. Translation of La Mere des fideles. Bibliographical footnotes. [BT611.B713] 67-24919
1. Mary, Virgin—Biblical teaching. 2. Bible. N.T. Johannine literature—Theology. I. Title.

CATHOLIC Church. National Conference of Catholic Bishops. 232.91
Behold your mother, woman of faith; a pastoral letter on the Blessed Virgin Mary, November 21, 1973. Washington, Publications Office, United States Catholic Conference, 1973. v, 65 p. 22 cm. Bibliography: p. 59. [BT602.C39 1973] 73-179289
1. Mary, Virgin. I. Title.

CRANNY, Titus F., 1921- 232.91
Is Mary relevant? A commentary on chapter 8 of Lumen gentium. The Constitution on the Church from Vatican Council II [by] Titus Cranny. [1st ed.] New York, Exposition Press [1970] 183 p. 22 cm. (An Exposition-testament book) [BT638.C69] 72-126366 6.00
1. Mary, Virgin—Theology. I. Vatican Council, 2d, 1962-1965. Constitutio dogmatica de ecclesia. Chapter 8. English. 1970. II. Title.

DE SATGE, John. 232.91
Down to Earth : the new Protestant vision of the Virgin Mary / John de Satge. 1st American ed. [Wilmington, N.C.] : Consortium Books, 1976. ix, 162 p. ; 22 cm. Includes bibliographical references and indexes. [BT602.D47 1976] 76-19776 ISBN 0-8434-0607-0 : 12.00
1. Mary, Virgin. I. Title.

DE SATGE, John. 232.91
Mary and the Christian gospel / [by] John de Satge. London : S.P.C.K., 1976. x, 162 p. ; 22 cm. Includes bibliographical references and indexes. [BT602.D49] 77-353990 ISBN 0-281-02926-1 : £3.25
1. Mary, Virgin. I. Title.

DONLEAVY, Al. 232.91
The counter-revolution for peace : words of warning and love from the Virgin Mary / by Al DonLeavy. Roslyn Heights, N.Y. : Libra Publishers, c1976. xvi, 128 p. : ill. ; 22 cm. [BT650.D59] 76-16324 5.00
1. Mary, Virgin—Apparitions and miracles (Modern) 2. Mary, Virgin—Shrines. I. Title.

FORTUNAT, Father. 232.91
Marija v skrivnosti Kristusa in Cerkve. Lemont, Ill., Ave Maria [1965] 128 p. 19 cm. [BX2160.F6] 66-58037
1. Mary, Virgin — Meditations. I. Title.

FOX, Robert Joseph, 1927- 232.91
The Marian catechism / Robert J. Fox. Huntington, Ind. : Our Sunday Visitor, inc., c1976. 128 p. ; 18 cm. [BT602.F69] 75-45756 ISBN 0-87973-766-2 pbk. : 1.95
1. Mary, Virgin—Miscellanea. I. Title.

GALOT, Jean. 232.91
Full of grace. Translated and adapted by Paul Barrett. Westminster, Md., Newman Press, 1965. x, 192 p. 20 cm. [BX2160.G313] 65-21738
1. Mary, Vrgin — Meditations. I. Title.

GALOT, Jean 232.91
Full of grace. Tr. [from French] adapted by Paul Barrett. Westminster, Md., Newman [c.] 1965. x, 192p. 20cm. [BX2160.G313] 65-21738 3.50
1. Mary, Virgin—Meditations. I. Title.

GIORDANI, Igino, 1894- 232.91
Mary of Nazareth. Tr. by Clelia Maranzana and Mary PaulaWilliamson. [Boston] St. Paul Eds. [dist. Daughters of St. Paul, c.1965] xix, 181p. plates 24cm. [BT601.G47] 65-24079 5.00; 4.00 pap.,
1. Mary, Virgin. I. Title.

THE Glories of 232.91
Czestochowa and Jasna Gora. 3d ed. Webster, Mass., Our Lady of Czestochowa Foundation, 1959. 155 p. 20 cm. "Translated, edited, and compiled by the Polish Roman Catholic clergy of the Diocese of Worcester, Massachusetts." [BT660.C9G5 1959] 72-403
1. Czestochowa, Poland. Klasztor Paulinow. 2. Czestochowa, Our Lady of. I. Our Lady of Czestochowa Foundation.

GREELEY, Andrew M., 1928- 232.91
The Mary myth : the femininity of God / Andrew M. Greeley. New York : Seabury Press, 1977. p. cm. "A Crossroad book." [BT613.G73] 76-53545 ISBN 0-8164-0333-3 : 12.95
1. Mary, Virgin—Theology. 2. Femininity of God. I. Title.

GREELEY, Andrew M., 1928- 232.91
The Mary myth : the femininity of God / Andrew M. Greeley. New York : Seabury Press, 1977. p. cm. "A Crossroad book." [BT613.G73] 76-53545 ISBN 0-8164-0333-3 : 12.95
1. Mary, Virgin—Theology. 2. Femininity of God. I. Title.

GRIPKEY, Mary Vincentine, Sister, 1908- 232.91
The Blessed Virgin Mary as mediatrix. New York, AMS Press [1969, c1938] x, 238 p. 22 cm. (Catholic University of America. Studies in Romance languages and literatures, v. 17) Originally presented as the author's thesis, Catholic University of America, under the title: The Blessed Virgin Mary as mediatrix in the Latin and Old French legend prior to the fourteenth century. Bibliography: p. 223-231. [BT640.G7 1969] 72-94166
1. Mary, Virgin—Mediation. 2. Mary, Virgin—Legends. I. Title. II. Series.

HARAN, John P. 232.91
Mary, Mother of God [by] John P. Haran. Huntington, Ind., Our Sunday Visitor, inc. [1973] xi, 146 p. 21 cm. Includes bibliographical references. [BT645.H35] 73-84689 ISBN 0-87973-846-4
1. Mary, Virgin—Cultus. I. Title.

HAWKINS, Henry, 1572(ca)-1646,supposedauthor 232.91
Partheneia sacra, by H. A., 1633. Introd. by Iain Fletcher. Aldington [Eng.] Hand & Flower Pr. [Chester Springs, Pa., Dufour, 1966] xxiv, 286p. illus., facsim. 23cm. Also attributed to Herbert Aston. Cf. introd. [BX2160.A2] 66-2304 17.50
1. Mary, Virgin—Prayer-books and devotions—English. 2. Mary, Virgin—Symbolism. I. A., H. II. Aston, Herbert, 1614-1689, supposed author. III. Fletcher, Iain. IV. Title.

HIGGINS, Paul Lambourne. 232.91
Mother of all. Minneapolis, T. S. Denison [1969] 132 p. illus. 23 cm. Bibliography: p. 125-132. [BT645.H47] 73-8719 4.00
1. Mary, Virgin—Cultus. I. Title.

JOANNES DE RUPELLA ca.1190-1245. 232.91
Eleven Marian sermons [by] John de La Rochelle. Edited by Kilian F. Lynch. St. Bonaventure, N.Y., Franciscan Institute, 1961. xxiv, 103 p. 24 cm. (Franciscan Institute publications. Text series, no. 12) Includes bibliographical references. [BT608.J6] 73-253541
1. Mary, Virgin—Sermons. 2. Catholic Church—Sermons. 3. Sermons, Latin. I. Lynch, Kilian F., ed. II. Title. III. Series: St. Bonaventure University, St. Bonaventure, N.Y. Franciscan Institute. Text series, no. 12

LAURENTIN, Rene 232.91
The question of Mary. Tr. from French by I. G. Pidoux. Pref. by Hilda Graer. Techny, Ill., Divine Word [1967]c.1965] u76p. 21cm. Bibl. [BT602.L313] 1.85 pap.,
1. Mary, Virgin. I. Title.

LAURENTIN, Rene. 232.91
The question of Mary. Translated from the French by I.G. Pidoux. Pref. by Hilda Graef. [1st ed.] New York, Holt, Rinehart and Winston [1965] 161 p. 21 cm. Bibliographical references included in "Notes" (p. 149-161) [BT602.L313] 65-12075
1. Mary, Virgin. I. Title.

†LEBLANC, Mary Francis. 232.91
Cause of our joy / Mary Francis LeBlanc ; illustrated by Mary Anthony Martin. [Boston] : St. Paul Editions, c1976. 172 p. : ill. ; 22 cm. [BT650.L45] 74-79803 4.00
1. Mary, Virgin—Apparitions and miracles (Modern) I. Martin, Mary Anthony. II. Title.

LONG, Valentine. 232.91
The Mother of God / by Valentine Long. Chicago : Franciscan Herald Press, [1976] p. cm. [BT602.L65] 76-22515 ISBN 0-8199-0619-0 : 6.95
1. Mary, Virgin. 2. Mary, Virgin—Apparitions and miracles (Modern) I. Title.

MCHUGH, John. 232.91
The mother of Jesus in the New Testament / John McHugh. Garden City, N.Y. : Doubleday, 1975. xiviii, 510 p. ; 22 cm. Includes indexes. Bibliography: p. 475-498. [BT611.M3 1975b] 74-33652 ISBN 0-385-04748-7 : 12.50
1. Mary, Virgin—Biblical teaching. I. Title.

NOONE, Patricia. 232.91
Mary for today / by Patricia Noone. Chicago : T. More Press, c1977. 180 p. ; 22 cm. Includes bibliographical references. [BT602.N66] 77-153382 ISBN 0-88347-078-0 : 8.95
1. Mary, Virgin. I. Title.

OBERMAN, Heiko Augustinus. 232.91
The Virgin Mary in evangelical perspective, by Heiko A. Oberman. With an introd. by Thomas F. O'Meara. Philadelphia, Fortress Press [1971] xvi, 38 p. 19 cm. (Facet books. Historical series, 20 (Medieval)) Bibliography: p. 33. [BT602.O23] 70-157546 ISBN 0-8006-3067-X 1.00
1. Mary, Virgin. I. Title.

O'MEARA, Thomas A 232.91
Mary in Protestant and Catholic theology [by] Thomas A. O'Meara. New York, Sheed and Ward [1966] 376 p. 22 cm. Bibliography: p. 355-370. [BT610.O4] 64-13573
1. Mary, Virgin — History of doctrines. 2. Protestant churches — Relations — Catholic Church. 3. Catholic Church — Relations — Protestant churches. I. Title.

O'MEARA, Thomas A. 232.91
Mary in Protestant and Catholic theology. New York, Sheed [c.1966] 376p. 22cm. Bibl. [BT610.04] 64-13573 7.50
1. Mary, Virgin—History of doctrines. 2. Protestant churches— Relations—Catholic Church. 3. Catholic Church—Relations—Protestant churches. I. Title.

RINALDI, Bonaventura. 232.91
Mary of Nazareth, myth of history? Translated by Mary F. Ingoldsby. Westminster, Md., Newman Press, 1966 [c1962] xvii, 228 p. 23 cm. Includes bibliographical references. [BT602.R513] 66-16576
1. Mary, Virgin. I. Title.

RUETHER, Rosemary Radford. 232.91
Mary, the feminine face of the Church / by Rosemary Radford Ruether. 1st ed. Philadelphia : Westminster Press, c1977. 106 p. : port. ; 21 cm. [BT602.R83] 77-7652 ISBN 0-664-24759-8 pbk. : 3.65
1. Mary, Virgin. I. Title.

SCHEETZ, Leo A., 1896- 232.91
Mary, Tree of Life and Our Hope [by] Father Leo A. Scheetz. [1st ed.] New York, Exposition Press [1971] 215 p. 21 cm. (An Exposition-testament book) [BT613.S35] 76-164868 ISBN 0-682-47331-6 4.00
1. Mary, Virgin—Theology. I. Title.

SHEEN, Fulton John, 1895- 232.91
The world's first love Fulton J. Sheen. Garden City, N. Y. : Doubleday [1976c1952] 237p. ; 18 cm. (Image books) [BT602.S53] ISBN 0-385-11559-8 pbk. : 1.95
1. Mary, Virgin. I. Title.
L. C. card no. for original edition: 52-6554.

VAN HOOF, Mary Ann, 1909- 232.91
Revelations and messages as given through Mary Ann Van Hoof at Necedah, Wisconsin, 1950-1970. [Necedah, Wis., For My God and My Country, inc., 1971] lxx, 634 p. illus., ports. 19 cm. "The contents of the first edition of the Revelations and message book was compiled and edited by Myrtle Sommers ... The additional work since Myrtle's death has been carried on by other dedicated workers." [BT660.N4V35 1971] 77-25776
1. Necedah, Wis. Queen of the Holy Rosary Mediatrix of Peace Shrine. I. Sommers, Myrtle, ed. II. Title.

VOLLERT, Cyril O., 1901- 232.91
A theology of Mary [New York] Herder & Herder [c.1965] 253p. 22cm. (Saint Mary's theology ser., 3) Bibl. [BT613.V6] 64-19740 5.50
1. Mary, Virgin—Theology. I. Title.

WARNER, Marina, 1946- 232.91
Alone of all her sex : the myth and the cult of the Virgin Mary / Marina Warner. 1st American ed. New York : Knopf : distributed by Random House, 1976. xxv, 400, xix p., [20] leaves of plates : ill. ; 25 cm. Includes index. Bibliography: p. 395-400. [BT602.W37 1976] 76-13682 ISBN 0-394-49913-1 (Knopf) : 15.00
1. Mary, Virgin. I. Title.

MASCALL, Eric Lionell, 1905- ed. 232.9108
The Blessed Virgin Mary; essays by Anglican writers, ed. by E. L. Mascall, H. S. Box. [London] Darton, Longman & Todd [1963] v, 131p. 23cm. Imprint covered by label: New York, Hilary House [BT597.M33] 66-9179 4.50 bds.,
1. Mary, Virgin—Addresses, essays, lectures. I. Box, Hubert Stanley, 1904- joint ed. II. Title.

BONNEFOY, Jean Francois. 232.91'1
The immaculate conception in the divine plan. Translated from the French by Michael D. Meilach. Paterson, N.J., St. Anthony Guild Press [1967] xviii, 75 p. 24 cm. Translation of L'Immaculee dans le plan divin. Bibliographical references included in "Notes" (p. 63-75) [BT620.B58] 67-4189
1. Immaculate Conception—History of doctrines. I. Title.

BONNEFOY, Jean Francois, 1897- 232.91'1
The immaculate conception in the divine plan. Translated from the French by Michael D. Meilach. Paterson, N. J., St. Anthony Guild Press [1967] xviii, 75 p. 24 cm. Translation of L Immaculee dans le plan divin. Bibliographical references included in "Notes" (p. 63-75) [BT620.B58] 67-4189
1. Immaculate Conception—History of doctrines. I. Title.

BROWN, Raymond Edward. 232.91'1
The virginal conception and bodily resurrection of Jesus, by Raymond E. Brown. New York, Paulist Press [1973] viii, 136 p. 21 cm. Includes bibliographical references. [BT620.B76] 72-97399 ISBN 0-8091-1768-1 pap. 2.25
1. Jesus Christ—Resurrection. 2. Immaculate Conception. I. Title.

BIRCH, w. Grayson. 232.913
Mary and the virgin birth error, by W. Grayson Birch. Berne, Ind., Publishers Print. House [1966] 284 p. illus. 23 cm. Bibliographical footnotes. [BT317.B53] 65-28187
1. Virgin birth. I. Title.

LAWLOR, George L. 232.9'13
Almah—virgin or young woman? By George L. Lawlor. Des Plaines, Ill., Regular Baptist Press [1973] 124 p. 18 cm. Bibliography: p. 119-124. [BT317.L38] 73-76072 1.50
1. Virgin birth. 2. 'Almah (The Hebrew word) I. Title.

STANFORD, Ray. 232.91'6
Fatima prophecy; days of darkness, promise of light. [Austin, Tex.] Association for the Understanding of Man [1972] 194 p. illus. 23 cm. Bibliography: p. [187]-188. [BF1311.M42S7] 72-86078 6.95
1. Mary, Virgin—Apparitions and miracles (Modern) 2. Spirit writings. I. Title.

WINDEATT, Mary Fabyan, 1910- 232.91'6
The children of Fatima. [Rev.] St. Meinrad, Ind., Abbey Press, 1973 [c1948] ix, 179 p. illus. 18 cm. [BT660.F3W5 1973] 73-160628 2.00
1. Fatima, Nossa Senhira da. I. Title.

ARON, Robert, 1898- 232.92
The Jewish Jesus. Translated by Agnes H. Forsyth and Anne-Marie de Commaille and in collaboration with Horace T. Allen, Jr. Maryknoll, N.Y., Orbis Books [1971] viii, 183 p. 22 cm. Translation of Ainsi priait Jesus enfant. [BT310.A7313] 73-151181
1. Jesus Christ—Biography—Early life. I. Title.

BIBLE. N. T. Gospels. English. Selections. 1952? Authorized. 232.92
The story of the Nativity in wood engravings; the text taken from the King James version of the Holy Bible. Wood engravings by Boyd Hanna. Mount Vernon, N. Y., Peter Pauper Press [1952?] [59] p. illus. 18 cm. "From the first and second chapters of St. Luke, and the second chapter of St. Matthew." [BT315.H27] 52-43438
1. Jesus Christ—Nativity—Texts. 2. Jesus Christ—Art. I. Hanna, Boyd. illus. II. Title.

BISHOP, James Alonzo, 1907- 232.9'2
The day Christ was born / Jim Bishop. p. New York : Harper & Row, [1977] c1960. p. cm. [BT315.2.B53 1977] 77-10021 ISBN 0-06-060785-8 : pbk. : 1.95
1. Jesus Christ—Nativity. 2. Christian biography—Palestine. I. Title.

BRANLEY, Franklyn Mansfield, 1915- 232.92
The Christmas sky, by Franklyn M. Branley. Illus. by Blair Lent. New York, Crowell [1966] *v. (unpaged) col. illus. 24cm. [BT315.2.B67] 66-7687 3.75
1. Star of Bethlehem—Juvenile literature. I. Lent, Blair, illus. II. Title.

BRYANT, Al, 1926- 232.92
Little boy Jesus. Grand Rapids, Zondervan Pub. House [1955] unpaged. illus. 21cm. (A Zondervan story-picture book) [BT320.B7] 56-25039
1. Jesus Christ—Childhood. I. Title.

CAEDMON, Father. 232.92
How Jesus came. [Saint Paul, North Central Pub. Co., 1959] unpaged. illus. 25cm. [BT315.C3] 60-19008
1. Jesus Christ—Nativity —Juvenile literature. I. Title.

CAEDMON, Father 232.92
How Jesus came. Baltimore, Md., Helicon Press [1960, c.1959] unpaged col. illus.25cm. 2.95 bds.,
1. Jesus Christ—Nativity—Juvenile literature. I. Title.

DANIELOU, Jean. 232.92
The infancy narratives. Translated by Rosemary Sheed. [New York] Herder and Herder [1968] 126 p. 21 cm. Translation of Les Evangiles de l'enfance. [BT310.D313] 68-55083 3.95
1. Jesus Christ—Biography—Early life. I. Title.

DILLARD, Pauline (Hargis) 232.92
1916-
My book about Jesus [by] Polly Hargis Dillard. Pictures by Anne R. Kasey. Nashville, Broadman Press [1968] 32 p. col. illus. 21 cm. An easy to read story of Christ's birth, his early years, and his teachings. [BT302.D55] AC 68
I. Kasey, Anne R., illus. II. Title.

EDWARDS, Annette, pseud. 232.92
The story of the Christ child. Illus. by Pranas Lape. New York, Wonder Books, c1953. unpaged. illus. 21cm. (Wonder books, 587) [BT315.D3] 53-39548
1. Jesus Christ— Nativity—Juvenile literature. I. Title.

ELDON, Magdalen. 232.92
The childhood of Jesus, by Magdalen Eldon and Frances Phipps. New York, D. McKay Co. [1953] 96p. illus. 26cm. [BT320.E4] 53-11366
1. Jesus Christ—Childhood. I. Phipps, Frances, joint author. II. Title.

FITCH, Florence Mary, 232.92
1875-1959.
The child Jesus; illustrated by Leonard Weisgard. New York, Lothrop, Lee and Shepard Co., c1955. 1 v. (unpaged) illus. 27 cm. [BT320.F5] 55-10438
1. Jesus Christ—Childhood. I. Title.

GODDARD, Carrie Lou. 232.92
Jesus goes to school. Pictures by Doris Stolberg. Nashville, Abingdon Press, c1654. unpaged. illus. 21cm. [BT302.G54] 54-11704
1. Jesus Christ—Childhood—Juvenile literature. I. Title.

HORTON, Adey, 1912- 232.92
The child Jesus / Adey Horton. New York : Dial Press, 1975. 207 p. : ill. (some col.) ; 27 cm. Includes index. Bibliography: p. 200-201. [BT320.H67] 75-11922 ISBN 0-8037-5379-9 : 17.50
1. Jesus Christ—Childhood. I. Title.

JESUS is born. 232.92 (j)
Minneapolis, Augsburg Pub. House [1967] [26] p. col. illus. 20 cm. Nativity story for young children, illustrated by de Kort. [BT315.2.J48] 68-1827
1. Jesus Christ—Nativity—Juvenile literature.

JESUS is born. 232.92
Minneapolis, Augsburg Pub. House [1967] [26] p. col. illus. 20 cm. Illustrated by de Kort. An illustrated retelling of the nativity story, from Joseph and Mary's leaving on a trip to Bethlehem to the arrival of the wise men with their gifts. [BT315.2.J48] AC 68
1. Jesus Christ—Nativity. I. Kort, de, illus.

JONES, Elizabeth Orton, 232.92
1910-
How far is it to Bethlehem? Boston, Horn Book, 1955. 38 p. illus. 18 cm. Describes a nativty play presented by crippled children at a rehabilitation center, telling how each participant achieved a small miracle as he sought to overcome physical disability and perform his role. [PN3157.J6] AC 68
1. Plays—Presentation, etc. 2. Christmas plays. 3. Handicapped. I. Title.

JONES, Mary Alice, 1898- 232.92
Stories of the Christ child; illustrated by Eleanor Corwin. Chicago, Rand McNally, c1953. unpaged. illus. 21cm. (A Rand McNally book-elf book, 484) [BT302.J59 1953] 53-34336
1. Jesus Christ—Childhood—Juvenile literature. I. Title.

JONES, Mary Alice, 1898- j232.92
Stories of the Christ child. Illustrated by Eleanor Corwin. Chicago, Rand McNally [1964] c1953. 1 v. (unpaged) col. illus. 33 cm. (A Rand McNally giant book) [BT302.J59 1964] 64-17038
1. Jesus Christ—Childhood—Juvenile literature. I. Corwin, Eleanor, illus. II. Title.

KENT, Herbert Harold. 232.92
The house of Christmas, by H. Harold Kent. Grand Rapids, Eerdmans [1964] 123 p. 21 cm. [BT315.2.K4] 64-22020
1. Jesus Christ — Nativity. I. Title.

KENT, Herbert Harold 232.92
The house of Christmas. Grand Rapids, Mich., Eerdmans [c.1964] 123p. 21cm. 64-22020 2.95 bds.,
1. Jesus Christ—Nativity. I. Title.

LINES, Kathleen. 232.92
Once in royal David's city; a picture book of the Nativity, retold from the Gospels by Kathleen Lines & drawn by Harold Jones. [New York] Watts [1956] unpaged. illus. 26cm. [BT315] 56-10071
1. Jesus Christ—Nativity—Juvenile literature. I. Jones, Harold, illus. II. Title.

LONDON. Vita et Pax j232.92
Convent School.
Children's Advent and Christmas, written and illustrated by Vita et Pax, Benedictine Nuns of Cockfosters. Baltimore, Helicon [1966] 1 v. (unpaged) col. illus. 21 cm. [BT315.2.L6] 66-31765
1. Jesus Christ — Nativity — Juvenile literature. I. Title.

LONDON Vita et Pax Convent 232.92
School
Children's Advent and Christmas, written, illus. by Vita et Pax, Benedictine Nuns of Cockfosters. Baltimore, Helicon [1966] 1v. (unpaged) col. illus. 21cm. [BT315.2.L6] 66-31765 2.50 bds.,
1. Jesus Christ—Nativity—Juvenile literature. I. Title.
Available from Taplinger in Enw York.

MARSHALL, Peter, 1902- 232.92
1949.
Let's keep Christmas. [A sermon] Introd. by Catherine Marshall; illus. by Barbara Cooney. New York, McGraw-Hill, c1953. unpaged. illus. 17 cm. [BV4257.M37] 53-10628
1. Christmas sermons. I. Title.

MUNOWITZ, Ken. 232.9'2
Happy birthday, baby Jesus / pictures by Ken Munowitz ; text by Charles L. Mee, Jr. 1st ed. New York : Harper & Row, c1976. [32] p. : ill. ; 21 x 26 cm. Retells the story of the birth of Jesus Christ in pictures and easy-to-read text. [BT315.2.M86 1976] 76-3831 ISBN 0-06-024162-4 : 4.95. ISBN 0-06-024163-2 lib. bdg. : 4.79
1. Jesus Christ—Nativity—Juvenile literature. I. Mee, Charles L. II. Title.

NORTH, Sterling, 1906- 232.92
The birthday of little Jesus; illustrated by Valenti Angelo. [1st ed.] New York, Grosset & Dunlap [1952] unpaged. illus. 28 cm. [BT315.N65] 52-4667
1. Jesus Christ — Nativity — Juvenile literature. I. Title.

PAULI, Hertha Ernestine, 232.92
1909-
Christmas and the saints. Illustrated by Rus Anderson. New York, Farrar, Straus and Cudahy [1956] 190 p. illus. 22 cm. (Vision books, 16) [BX4658.P3] 56-11060
1. Saints—Juvenile literature. 2. Christmas.

RICE, John R., 1895- 232.92
I love Christmas; Christmas messages. Wheaton, Ill., Sword of the Lord Publishers [1955] 144p. 21cm. [BV4257.R5] 56-16594
1. Christmas sermons. 2. Baptists—Sermons. 3. Sermons, American. I. Title.

SMITH, Betty 232.92
Baby Jesus. Illus. by Cicely Steed. Philadelphia, Westminster [1963, c.1962] 32p. illus. (pt. col.) 21cm. (Stories of Jesus, bk. 1) .75 bds.,
1. Jesus Christ—Nativity—Juvenile literature. I. Title.

SMITH, Betty 232.92
The boy Jesus. Illus. by Cicely Steed. Philadelphia, Westminster [1963, c.1962] 32p. illus. (pt. col.) 21cm. (Stories of Jesus, bk. 2) .75 bds.,
1. Jesus Christ—Biog.—Juvenile literature. I. Title.

STOLEE, Ingeborg B 1907- 232.92
The Christmas promise, as told by Ingeborg Stolee; illustrated by Dorothy Divers. Minneapolis, Augsburg Pub. House [1952] Unpaged. illus. 22 cm. [BT315.S8] 52-41241
1. Jesus Christ — Nativity. I. Title.

TAYLOR, Florence Marian 232.92
(Tompkins) 1892-
A boy once lived in Nazareth, by Florence M. Taylor. Illustrated by Len Ebert. New York, H. Z. Walck [1969] [38] p. col. illus. 22 x 26 cm. Life and customs in Biblical Nazareth are presented in a description of the childhood of Jesus. [BT320.T37] 69-10730 3.75
1. Jesus Christ—Childhood—Juvenile literature. I. Ebert, Len, illus. II. Title.

TIPPETT, James Sterling, 232.92
1885-
Jesus lights the Sabbath lamp. Pictures by Doris Stolberg. Nashville, Abingdon-Cokesbury Press, c1953. unpaged. illus. 22cm. [BT302.T56] 53-2550
1. Jesus Christ—Childhood—Juvenile literature. I. Title.

TRENT, Robbie, 1894- 232.92
Jesus' first trip. Pictures by Beatrice Darwin. Nashville, Broadman Press, c.1961. unpaged. illus. (part col.) 61-5065 1.00; .60 bds.,
1. Jesus Christ—Nativity—Juvenile literature. I. Title.

ADAIR, James R. 1923-ed. 232.921
Teen with a future. Grand Rapids, mich., baker bk. [c.]1965 83 p. illus. port. 21 cm [bv45.31.2a3] 248 65-25476 bds. 1.95
1. Youth—religious life. I. Title.

ALLEN, Charles 232.9'21
Livingstone, 1913-
Christmas / Charles L. Allen and Charles L. Wallis. Old Tappan, N.J. : F. H. Revell, c1977. 158 p. ; 21 cm. Contents.Contents.—Christmas in our hearts.—Candle, star, and Christmas tree.—When Christmas came to Bethlehem. [BV45.A53 1977] 77-22979 ISBN 0-8007-0874-1 : 6.95
1. Jesus Christ—Nativity—Devotional literature. 2. Christmas. 3. Christmas—Meditations. I. Wallis, Charles Langworthy, 1921- joint author. II. Title.

ALLEN, Charles 232.921
Livingstone, 1913-
Christmas in our hearts, by Charles L. Allen and Charles L. Wallis. [Westwood, N.J.] Revell [1957] 64p. 17cm. [BV45.A55] 57-11325
1. Christmas. I. Wallis, Charles Langworthy, 1921- joint author. II. Title.

ALLEN, Charles 232.921
Livingstone, 1913-
Christmas in our hearts, by Charles L. Allen and Charles L. Wallis. [Westwood, N.J.] Revell [1957] 64p. 17cm. [BV45.A55] 57-11325
1. Christmas. I. Wallis, Charles Langworthy, 1921- joint author. II. Title.

ALLEN, Charles 232.921
Livingstone, 1913-
When Christmas came to Bethlehem [by] Charles L. Allen [and] Charles L. Wallis. [Westwood, N.J.] Revell,[1963] 64 p. 20 cm. [BT315.2.A] 63-17112
1. Jesus Christ — Nativity — Devotional literature. 2. Christmas — Meditations. I. Wallis, Charles Langworthy, 1921- joint author. II. Title.

ALLEN, Charles 232.921
Livingstone, 1913-
When Christmas came to Bethlehem [by] Charles L. Allen, Charles L. Wallis. [Westwood, N. J.] Revell [c.1963] 64p. 20cm. 63-17112 1.50 bds.,
1. Jesus Christ—Nativity—Devotional literature. 2. Christmas—Meditations. I. Wallis, Charles Langworthy, 1921- joint author. II. Title.

BEHM, Bill, 1922- 232.921
The night Jesus was born. St. Louis, Concordia [c.1964] 1v. (unpaged) illus. (pt. col.) 27cm. 63-23438 1.25 bds.,
1. Jesus Christ—Nativity—Juvenile literature. I. Title.

BIBLE. N. T. Gospels. 232.921
English. Selections. 1960. Authorized.
The first Christmas; from the Gospels according to Saint Luke and Saint Matthew. Illustrated with etchings by Barbara Neustadt. New York, Crowell [c.1960] unpaged. col. illus. 25cm. 60-9161 2.75
1. Jesus Christ—Nativity—Texts. I. Neustadt, Barbara, illus. II. Title.

BIBLE. N. T. Gospels. 232.921
English. Selections. 1960. Authorized.
The first Christmas; from the Gospels according to Saint Luke and Saint Matthew. Illustrated with techings by Barbara Neustadt. New York, Crowell [1960] unpaged. illus. 25cm. [BT315.A3 1960] 60-9161
1. Jesus Christ—Nativity—Texts. I. Neustadt, Barbara, illus. II. Title.

BIBLE. N.T. Gospels. 232.921
English. Selections. 1966. Authorized.
The Christmas story from the Gospels of Matthew & Luke. Edited by Marguerite Northrup. [New York] Metropolitan Museum of Art; distributed by New York Graphic Society, Greenwich, Conn. [1966] 32 p. illus. (part col.) 28 cm. Bibliography: p. 32. [BT315.A3] 65-23504
1. Jesus Christ—Nativity—Texts. I. Northrup, Marguerite, ed. II. New York. Metropolitan Museum of Art. III. Title.

BIBLE, N.T. Gospels. 232.921
English. Selections. 1966. Authorized
The Christmas story from the Gospels of Matthew & Luke. Ed. by Marguerite Northrup. [New York] Metropolitan Mus. of Art; dist. by New York Graphic, Greenwich, Conn. [1966] 32p. illus. (pt. col.) 28cm. Bibl. [BT315.A3 1966] 65-23504 3.75
1. Jesus Christ—Nativity—Texts. I. Northrup, Marguerite, ed. II. New York. Metropolitan Museum of Art. III. Title.

BLIGH, John. 232.9'21
The infancy narratives / by John Bligh. Staten Island, N.Y. : Alba House, 1975, c1968. 110 p. ; 19 cm. (Scripture for meditation ; 1) [BT315.2.B54 1975] 74-31348 ISBN 0-8189-0306-6 pbk. : 1.95
1. Jesus Christ—Nativity—Meditations. 2. Jesus Christ—Childhood—Meditations. I. Title. II. Series.

BLYTHE, LeGette, 1900- 232.9'21
When was Jesus born? / By LeGette Blythe. Charlotte, N.C. : Charlotte Pub., 1974. 40 p. : ill. (some col.) ; 21 cm. [BT318.B56] 75-24050 ISBN 0-914998-00-5
1. Jesus Christ—Date of birth—Juvenile literature. I. Title.

BOSLOOPER, Thomas David, 232.921
1923-
The virgin birth. Philadelphia, Westminster Press [1962] 272 p. 24 cm. [BT317.2.B6] 62-7941
1. Virgin birth.

BOWDEN, William Sheldon. 232.921
Why Jesus came; or, Christmas the year 'round. [Evansville, Wis., 1955] 121p. 21cm. [BV45.B68] 55-42626
1. Christmas. I. Title.

BRENNAN, Gerald Thomas, 232.921
1898-
When Jesus came. Pictures by George Pollard. Milwaukee, Bruce Pub. Co. [1956] unpaged. illus. 21cm. (Christian child's stories, 12) [BT315.B7] 56-14486
1. Jesus Christ—Nativity. I. Title.

BROWN, Handel H 232.921
A recipe for a merry Christmas. Grand Rapids, Eerdmans [1960] 89p. 23cm. [GT4985.B73] 60-53093
1. Christmas. I. Title.

BROWN, Handel H 232.921
When Jesus came. Grand Rapids, Eerdmans [c1963] 160 p. 22 cm. [BT315.2.B7] 63-22536
1. Jesus Christ — Nativity. I. Title.

BROWN, Handel H. 232.921
When Jesus came. Grand Rapids, Mich., Eerdmans [c.1963] 160p. 22cm. 63-22536 3.00
1. Jesus Christ—Nativity. I. Title.

CAMPENHAUSEN, Hans, 232.921
Freiherr von, 1903-
The virgin birth in the theology of the ancient church. [Translated by Frank Clarke] Naperville, Ill., A. R. Allenson [1964] 92 p. 22 cm. (Studies in historical theology, 2) Bibliographical footnotes. [BT317.C3] 64-55217
1. Virgin birth—History of doctrines. I. Title. II. Series.

CAMPENHAUSEN, Hans, 232.921
Freiherr von, 1903-
The virgin birth in the theology of the ancient church [Tr. by Frank Clarke] Naperville, Ill., A. R. Allenson [c.1964] 92p. 22cm. (Studies in hist. theology,, 2) Bibl. 64-55217 2.75 pap.,
1. Virgin birth—History of doctrines. I. Title. II. Series.

CHRISTMAS chimes. 232.921
Blair, Neb., Lutheran Pub. House. v. illus. (part col., mounted) 23-41cm. annual. Published 19 by the Young People's Luther League (called 19 -33 the Central Committee of Luther League of the Danish Evangelical Lutheran Church of America (called 19 United Danish Evangelical Lutheran Church in America (varies slightly)); 19 by the Luther League of the United Evangelical Lutheran Church. [BV45.C57] 31-1385
1. Christmas—Yearbooks. I. Danish Evangelical Lutheran Church of America. Young People's Luther League. II. United Evangelical Lutheran Church. Luther League.

CROFT, aloysius, ed. 232.921
The mystery of Christmas. Milwaukee, Bruce Pub. Co. [1956] 95 p. illus. 24 cm. [BT315.C68] 56-13197
1. Jesus Christ—Nativity. I. Title.

CUSHING, Richard James, 232.921
Cardinal, 1895-
Christ in Bethlehem; Christ in the Eucharist. [Boston] [Daughters of St. Paul, 1960] 188p. (St. Paul eds.) 60-536159 3.00; 2.00 pap.,
1. Jesus Christ—Nativity—Meditations. 2. Lord's Supper—Meditations. I. Title.

DORSEY, Leslie. 232.921
Once upon a Christmas. [Colorado Springs] Taylor Museum, Colorado Springs Fine Arts Center [196-?] 1 v (unpaged) illus. (part col.) 36 cm. Cover title: A Victorian Christmas album. [GT4985.D6] 66-6117

1. Christmas. I. Title. II. Title: A Victorian Christmas album.

DORSEY, Leslie. 232.921
Once upon a Christmas. [Colorado Springs] Taylor Museum, Colorado Springs Fine Arts Center [196-?] 1 v (unpaged) illus. (part col.) 36 cm. Cover title: A Victorian Christmas album. [GT4985.D6] 66-6117
1. Christmas. I. Title. II. Title: A Victorian Christmas album.

EDMAN, Victor Raymond, 1900- 232.921
Wiser than they thought. Wheaton, Ill., Scripture Press [c.1960] 142p. 61-424 2.50 bds.,
1. Jesus Christ—Nativity. I. Title.

GEBHARD, Anna Laura 232.921
Come to Christmas! A family book of preparation, by Anna Laura Gebhard and Edward Gebhard. Illustrated by Frances Johnston. Nashville, Abingdon Press [c.1960] unpaged. (Bibl.) illus. (col.) 23cm. .75 pap.,
I. Title.

*GERLINGER, Lorena. 232.92'1
Baby Jesus. Illustrated by Evelyn Martin. [Camden, Me., 1972, i.e., 1973] 1 v. (unpaged) col. illus. 24 cm. [BT315.2] 4.95
1. Jesus Christ—Nativity—Juvenile literature. I. Title.
Available from the author, 41 Pearl St., Camden, Me. 04843.

GRAHAM, Lorenz B. 232.92'1
Every man heart lay down, by Lorenz Graham. Pictures by Colleen Browning. New York, Crowell [1970, c1946] [47] p. illus. (part col.) 22 cm. Originally published in the author's How God fix Jonah. The story of the Nativity told in the speech patterns and images of African people newly acquainted with the English language. [BT315.2.G7] 75-109899 3.75
1. Jesus Christ—Nativity—Juvenile literature. I. Browning, Colleen, illus. II. Title.

GROMACKI, Robert Glenn. 232.9'21
The virgin birth: doctrine of deity. Nashville, T. Nelson [1974] 202 p. 21 cm. Bibliography: p. 199-202. [BT317.G75] 74-12250 3.50 (pbk.).
1. Virgin birth. I. Title.

GROVES, Wayne. 232.921
There was no virgin birth, thus, Jesus Christ is not the Son of God.[1st ed.] New York, Vantage Press [1962] 60p. 21cm. [BT218.G7] 62-4813
1. Christianity—Controversial literature. 2. Jesus Christ—Humanity. I. Title.

GROVES, Wayne 232.921
There was no virgin birth thus Jesus Christ is not the Son of God. New York, Vantage [c.1962] 60p. 21cm. 2.00 bds.,
I. Title.

GUDNASON, Kay. 232.921
David's son is born; a week of Christmas meditations from the Gospels and the Psalms. Los Angeles, Cowman Publications [1958] 85p. 17cm. [BV45.G8] 58-4455
1. Christmas—Meditations. I. Title.

HANKE, Howard A 232.921
The validity of the virgin birth. Grand Rapids, Mich., Zondervan Pub. House [1963] 121 p. 21 cm. Bibliography: p. 117-118. [BT317.H34] 63-20390
1. Virgin birth. I. Title.

HANKE, Howard A. 232.921
The validity of the virgin birth. Grand Rapids, Mich., Zondervan [c.1963] 121p. 21cm. Bibl. 63-20390 2.50 bds.,
1. Virgin birth. I. Title.

HOFFMANN, Felix. 232.9'21
The story of Christmas : a picture book / retold and illustrated by Felix Hoffmann. 1st American ed. New York : Atheneum, 1975. [32] p. : col. ill. ; 22 cm. "A Margaret K. McElderry book." [BT315.2H6 1975] 75-6921 ISBN 0-689-50031-9 lib.bdg. : 6.95
1. Jesus Christ—Nativity—Juvenile literature. I. Title.

HOLZER HANS W., 1920- 232.92'1
Star in the east, by Hans Holzer. Illus. by Catherine Buxhoeveden. [1st ed.] New York, Harper & Row [1968] 124 p. illus. 22 cm. [BT315.2.H64] 68-29564 4.95
1. Jesus Christ—Nativity. 2. Christmas. I. Title.

HOOPER, Van B 1897- 232.921
Christmas around the world. Milwaukee, Ideals Pub. Co., 1958. unpaged. illus. 28cm. [GT4985.H58] 58-46533
1. Christmas. I. Title.

JACKSON, Kathryn, 1907- 232.9'21
The story of Christmas; concept created ... [and] story adapted by Kathryn Jackson. Illustrated by Augie Napoli. New York, Golden Press, [1973] [29] p. col. illus. 25 cm. Cover title: The story of Christmas with its own Advent calendar. The events surrounding the birth of Jesus Christ are told in segments that correspond with each day of Advent. [BT315.2.J3] 73-78812 3.95
1. Jesus Christ—Nativity—Juvenile literature. I. Napoli, Augie, illus. II. Title.

KASUYA, Masahiro. 232.9'21 E
The way Christmas came, by Masahiro Kasuya. English text by Chieko Funakoshi. Edited by Mildred Schell. Valley Forge, Pa., Judson Press, 1973, c1972. [23] p. col. illus. 22 x 30 cm. Translation of Kurisumasu. An account of the birth of Jesus. [BT315.2.K313] 72-13014 ISBN 0-8170-0593-5 3.95
1. Jesus Christ—Nativity—Juvenile literature. I. Funakoshi, Chieko. II. Title.

KEEPING, Charles. 232.92'1
The Christmas story. New York, Watts, 1969, c1968. [24] p. col. illus. 28 cm. An illustrated retelling of the nativity of Christ. [BT315.2.K36 1969] 69-12596 3.95
1. Jesus Christ—Nativity—Juvenile literature. I. Title.

KNIGHT, William Allen, 1863- 232.921
The story of the manger. Boston, W. A. Wilde Co. [1954] 52p. illus. 20cm. [BT315.K65] 54-9505
1. Jesus Christ—Nativity. I. Title.

KRAMER, Janice 232.921
The Baby born in a stable: Luke 2:1-18 for children. Illus. by Dorse Lampher. St. Louis, Concordia, c.1965. lv. (unpaged) col. illus. 21cm. (Arch bk., set 2, no. 59-1118) [BT315.2.K7] 65-15145 .35 pap.,
1. Jesus Christ—Nativity—Juvenile literature. I. Title.

LLOYD, Mary Edna. 232.921
Jesus, the little new baby. Pictures by Grace Paull. New York, Abingdon-Cokesbury Press, c1951. unpaged. illus. 21 cm. [BT315.L57] 51-12137
1. Jesus Christ—Nativity—Juvenile literature. I. Title.

LUTHER, Martin, 1483-1546. 232.921
The Martin Luther Christmas book, with celebrated wood-cuts by his contemporaries. Translated and arr. by Roland H. Bainton. Philadelphia, Muhlenberg Press [1959, c1958] 74p. illus. 25cm. Extracts from the author's sermons. [BT315.L8 1959] 59-2930
1. Jesus Christ—Nativity. I. Bainton, Roland Herbert, 1894- ed. and tr. II. Title.

MCCALL, Yvonne Holloway. 232.9'21
The man who didn't have time : the Christmas story for children / written by Yvonne Holloway McCall ; illustrated by Betty Wind. St. Louis : Concordia Pub. House, 1977c1976 p. cm. (Arch books ; ser. 14) Recounts the birth of Jesus emphasizing how the inkeeper's preoccupation with his own life and worries prevented his involvement with the glory of God's gift to man. [BT315.2.M24] 76-28023 ISBN 0-570-06112-1 pbk. : 0.59
1. Jesus Christ—Nativity—Juvenile literature. I. Wind, Betty. II. Title.

MACHEN, John Gresham, D.D., 1881-1937 232.921
The virgin birth of Christ. Grand Rapids, Mich., Baker Bk., 1965[c.1930] x,415p. 22cm. [BT317] 66-839 2.95 pap.,
1. Virgin birth. I. Title.

MAIER, Paul L. 232.92'1
First Christmas; the true and unfamiliar story in words and pictures [by] Paul L. Maier. [1st ed.] New York, Harper & Row [1971] 125 p. illus. (part col.) 22 cm. Includes bibliographical references. [BT315.2.M3 1971] 76-163162 ISBN 0-06-065396-5 4.95
1. Jesus Christ—Nativity. I. Title.

MASON, Miriam Evangeline, 1899- 232.921
The baby Jesus. Illustrated by Johannes Troyer. New York, Macmillan, 1959. 58p. illus. 21cm. [BT315.M38] 59-13094
1. Jesus Christ—Nativity—Juvenile literature. I. Title.

MEEK, Pauline Palmer. 232.92'1
When joy came; the story of the first Christmas. Illustrated by Shannon Stirnweis. New York, Golden Press [1971] [25] p. col. illus. 32 cm. (A Big golden book) An illustrated retelling of the birth of Jesus. [BT315.2.M38] 77-27407 1.00
I. Stirnweis, Shannon, illus. II. Title.

MELVIN, Frank J 232.921
Mary and Christian life. New York, Macmillan, 1958. 99p. 22cm. [BT601.M37] 58-8153
1. Mary, Virgin. I. Title.

*MIGUENS, Manuel. 232.92'1
The Virgin birth; an evaluation of scriptual evidence. Westminster, M.D., Christian Classics, 1975. iv, 169 p. 22 cm. Includes bibliographical references and scripture index. [BT317] 7.95 (pbk.)
1. Virgin Birth. 2. Mary, Virgin. 3. Immaculate Conception. I. Title.

MORRIS, Leon 232.921
The story of the Christ Child; a devotional study of the Nativity stories in St.Luke and St. Matthew. Grand Rapids, Mich., Eerdmans 1961 [ ] 128p. 61-19348 2.50 bds.,
1. Jesus Christ—Nativity—Devotional literature. I. Title.

OAKLEY, Helen McKelvey. 232.921
An alphabet of Christmas words, selected by Helen McKelvey Oakley from the Oxford English dictionary. New York, Oxford University Press, 1966. 1 v. (unpaged) illus. 16 cm. Cover title: A B C D, an alphabet of Christmas words. [GT4985.O3] 66-27549
1. Christmas — Dictionaries. I. Murry, Sir James August Henry, 1837-1915, ed.The oxford English dictionary. II. Title.

O'SHEA, Denis. 232.921
The first Christmas. Milwaukee, Bruce Pub. Co. [1952] 160 p. 22 cm. [BT315.O8] 52-4716
1. Jesus Christ—Nativity. I. Title.

PEALE, Norman Vincent, 1898- 232.921
The coming of the King; the story of the Nativity. Illustrated by William Moyers. Englewood Cliffs, N. J., Prentice-Hall [1956] unpaged. illus. 23cm. [BT315.P4] 56-9774
1. Jesus Christ—Nativity. I. Title.

PITT, Harriett Philmus. 232.921
Land of two Christmases. Illus. by Erwin Schachner. New York, Oxford University Press, 1965. 1 v. (unpaged) col. illus. 16 cm. (The Typophiles Monograph no. 79) Includes Puerto Rican Christmas carols (tunes with words) [GT4985.P5] 65-28180
1. Christmas—Puerto Rico. I. Schachner, Erwin, illus. II. Title. III. Series: The Typophiles, New York. Typophile monographs, no. 79

POTTEBAUM, Gerard A. 232.921
The story of Christmas. Illus. by Robert Strobridge. Dayton, Ohio, 38 W. 5th St., Geo. A. Pflaum, c.1963. unpaged. col. illus. 18cm. (Little people's paperbacks, LPP5) .35 pap.,
I. Title.

POWELL, Gordon George, 1911- 232.921
The innkeeper of Bethlehem; or, Why Jesus Christ was born in a stable, Illustrated by Charles Raymond. [Westwood, N. J.,] Revell [1960] 28p. illus. (part col.) 17cm. 60-51232 1.50 bds.,
1. Jesus Christ—Fiction. I. Title. II. Title: Why Jesus Christ was born in a stable.

POWELL, Gordon George, 1911- 232.921
The shepherd of Bethlehem. Illus. by John Robinson. [Westwood, N.J.] Revell [1961] 32p. col. illus. 61-16204 1.50 bds.,
1. Jesus Christ—Nativity. I. Title.

RAYMOND, Father, 1903- 232.921
Love does such things; God's Christmas gift to man. Milwaukee, Bruce Pub. Co. [1955] 129p. illus. 24cm. [BT315.R28] 55-11516
1. Jesus Christ—Nativity—Meditations. I. Title.

RIEDEL, Margaret. 232.9'21
The Christmas story : a chronology of events concerning the birth of Jesus Christ / [by Margaret Riedel]. [Tampa, Fla. : Bay Area Bible Studies, c1974] 55 p. : ill. ; 25 cm. Uses excerpts from the Bible to relate the events surrounding the birth of Christ. [BT315.2.R48] 74-19786 2.50
1. Jesus Christ—Nativity—Juvenile literature. I. Title.

ROGERS, Roy, 1912- 232.921
My favorite Christmas story [by] Roy Rogers, with Frank S. Mead. [Westwood, N. J.] Revell [1960] 64p. 20cm. [BT315.2.R6] 60-13095
1. Jesus Christ— Nativity—Juvenile literature. I. Title.

ROGERS, Roy [Name originally: Leonard Franklin Slye] 232.921
My favorite Christmas story [by] Roy Rogers, with Frank S. Mead. [Westwood, N. J.] Revell [c.1960] 64p. 20cm. 60-13095 1.50 bds.,
1. Jesus Christ—Nativity—Juvenile literature. I. Title.

SAYERS, Dorothy Leigh 232.921
The days of Christ's coming. Illustrated by Fritz Wegner. New York, Harper [c.1960] unpaged. col. illus. 19cm. 60-50259 1.50 half cloth,
1. Jesus Christ—Nativity—Juvenile literature. I. Title.

SAYERS, Dorothy Leigh, 1893-1957. 232.921
The days of Christ's coming. Illustrated by Fritz Wegner. New York, Harper [1960] unpaged. illus. 19cm. [BT315.2.S3] 60-50259
1. Jesus Christ—Nativity— Juvenile literature. I. Title.

UNITED Evangelical Lutheran Church. Luther League. 232.921
Christmas chimes. Blair, Neb., Lutheran Pub. House. v, illus. (part col. mounted) 23-41 cm. annual. Issued 19 by the Luther League (called 19 -33, Central Committee of Young People's Leagues; 1934- Central Committee of Luther Leagues, 19 Young People's Luther League) of the United Evangelical Luthern Church (called 19 the United Danish Evangelical Luthern Church in America) [BV45.C57] 31-1385
1. Christmas — Yearbooks. I. Title.

VAART SMIT, H W van der. 232.921
Born in Bethelehem; Christmas as it really was. Translated from the German by Thomas R. Milligan. Baltimore, Helicon [1963] v. 148 p. 22 cm. [BT315.2.V313] 63-19399
1. Jesus Christ — Nativity. I. Title.

VAART SMIT, H W van der. 232.921
Born in Bethlehem; Christmas as it really was [by] H. W. van der Vaart Smit. Translated from the German by Thomas R. Milligan. Baltimore, Helicon [1966] v. 148 p. 22 cm. Bibliographical footnotes. [BT315.2.V313] 66-7313
1. Jesus Christ — Nativity. I. Title.

VAART SMIT. H. W. VAN DER 232.921
Born in Bethlehem; Christmas as it really was. Tr. from German by Thomas R. Milligan. Helicon [dist. New York, Taplinger, c.1963] v, 148p. 22cm. 63-19399 3.50 bds.,
1. Jesus Christ—Nativity. I. Title.

WATSON, Jane (Werner) 1915- 232.921
The Christmas story, told by Jane Werner. Pictures by Eloise Wilkin. New York, Simon and Schuster [1952] unpaged. illus. 21cm. (The Little golden library, 158) [BT315.W35] 52-12287
1. Jesus Christ—Nativity—Juvenile literature. I. Title.

WATSON, Jane (Werner) 1915- 232.921
The little golden Christmas manger. Pictures by Steffie Lerch. New York, Simon and Schuster [1953] unpaged. illus. 21cm. (A Little golden book, 176) Cover title: The little golden cut-out Christmas manger. [BT315.W36] 54-1175
1. Jesus Christ—Nativity— Juvenile literature. I. Title. II. Title: Christmas manger. III. Title: The little golden cut-out Christmas manger.

WERNER, Jane, 1915- 232.921
The Christmas story, told by Jane Werner. Pictures by Eloise Wilkin. New York, Simon and Schuster [1952] unpaged. illus. 21 cm. (The Little golden library, 158) [BT315.W42] 52-12287
1. Jesus Christ — Nativity — Juvenile literature. I. Title.

BLACKWOOD, Andrew Watterson, 1915- 232.922
When God came down. Grand Rapids, Baker Book House, 1955. 71p. 20cm. [BX9178.B662W5] 55-10435
1. Presbyterian Church—Sermons. 2. Sermons, American. 3. Incarnation. I. Title.

ARON, Robert, 1898- 232.927
Jesus of Nazareth: the hidden years. Translated from the French by Frances Frenaye. New York, Morrow, 1962 [c1961] 253 p. 22 cm. Translation of Les annees obscures de Jesus. [BT330.A713 1962] 62-7721
1. Jesus Christ—Education. I. Title.

FITCH, Florence Mary, 1875-1959. 232.92'9
Young Jesus asks questions. New York, Lothrop, Lee & Shepard [1970] 64 p. 25 cm. Describes how the thinking of the boy Jesus Christ may have been influenced by the philosophies of his time. [BT320.F53] 79-101473 3.75
1. Jesus Christ—Childhood—Juvenile literature. I. Title.

BIRCH, W Grayson. 232.93
Veritas and the Virgin; or, Jesus, the Son of God and the children of Joseph and Mary.

[Berne, Ind., Berne Witness, inc., c1960] 264p. illus. 23cm. [BT313.B5] 61-21876
1. Jesus Christ—Brethren. 2. Mary, Virgin—History of doctrines. I. Title.

BRUCE, Janet 232.93
The life of the Blessed Virgin Mary. Pictures by Emile Probst. New York, Herder & Herder [1965] iv. (unpaged) col. illus. 19cm. (Men of God, 2) [BT607.B7] 65-13485 1.50 bds.,
1. Mary, Virgin—Juvenile literature. I. Probst, Emile, illus. II. Title. III. Series.

DOESWYCK, Peter J 1907- 232.93
Roman customs and practices, their origin and development. Long Beach, Calif., Knights of Christ [1963] 179 p. 21 cm. (His History of dogma, v. 4) Bibliography: p. 159-167. [BX1765.2.D627] 63-8583
1. Catholic Church — Doctrinal and controversial works — Protestant authors. I. Title.

GEARON, Patrick J. 232.93
Chats with Our Lady for boys and girls. Downers Grove, Ill., Carmelite [1962] 147p. illus. 19cm. 2.00 bds.,
I. Title.

GEARON, Patrick J., D.D. 232.93
Chats with Our Lady for children. Downers Grove, Ill., Cass Ave. No. at Route 66 Carmelite Third Order Pr., [1962] 49p. 19cm. .50 pap.,
I. Title.

*GEARON, Patrick J. 232.93
The litany of Our Lady for boys and girls. Chicago, Carmelite Third Order Pr. [1964] 99p. 19cm. 1.25
I. Title.

*GEARON, Patrick J. 232.93
The Litany of Our Lady for children. Downers Grove, Ill., Cass Ave. N. at Rt. 66 The Carmelite Third Order Pr., [1964] 49p. col. illus. 18cm. .50 pap.,
I. Title.

GEARON, Patrick J., D.D. 232.93
St. Anne for children. Downers Grove, Ill., Cass Ave. N. at Route 66. Carmelite Third Order Pr., [1962] 71p. 19cm. .75 pap.,
I. Title.

GRIFFIN, Nancy Hearn, 1873- 232.93
Legends of St. Anne and Mary, the Mother of Jesus (Scriptural and legendary) [Pasadena? Calif.] c1952. 112p. illus. 23cm. [BX1765.G8] 53-17032
1. Anne, Saint, Mother of the Virgin Mary. 2. Mary, Virgin. 3. Catholic Church—Doctrinal and controversial works—Protestant authors. I. Title.

MATHEWS, Stanley G ed. 232.93
The Promised Woman; an anthology of the Immaculate Conception. St. Meinrad, Ind., Grail [1954] 316p. 22cm. (The Marian library series) [BT620.M3] [BT620.M3] 232.1 54-9405 54-94051
1. Immaculate Conception. I. Title.

O'CONNOR, Edward Dennis, ed. 232.93
The dogma of the Immaculate Conception: History and significance. [Notre Dame, Ind.] University of Notre Dame Press, 1958. 645p. illus: 24cm. Includes bibliography. [BT620.O26] [BT620.O26] 232.1 56-9806 56-9806
1. Immaculate Conception. I. Title.

O'GORMAN, Walter Ernest Rupert, 1903- 232.93
Church, state, and Rome, by W. E. R. O'Gorman. Glendale, Calif., 1963. 128 p. 21 cm. [BX1765.2.O35] 66-4487
1. Catholic Church — Doctrinal and controversial works. I. Title.

PLASSMANN, Thomas Bernard, 1879- 232.93
The radiant crown of glory; the story of the dogma of the Immaculate Conception. New York, Benziger Bros. [1954] 258p. 21cm. [BT620.P54] [BT620.P54] 232.1 55-150 55-150
1. Immaculate Conception. I. Title.

SAVAGE, Alma Helen, 1900- 232.93
The Holy Family. Pictures by Gertrude Elliott Espenscheid. New York, Guild Press; distributed by Golden Press [1961] unpaged. illus. 20cm. (A Read-with-me book) [BT313.S3] 61-1943
1. Jesus Christ—Family—Juvenile literature. I. Title.

SLAVES of the Immaculate Heart of Mary. 232.93
The Holy family: Jesus, Mary, and Joseph. Still River [Mass., 1963] 120 p. col. illus., col. map. 24 cm. [BT313.S55] 63-22475
1. Jesus Christ — Family. I. Title.

STROMWALL, Mary W. 232.93
The life of Our Lady. Pictures by Sheilah Beckett. New York, Guild [dist. Golden] c.1963. 30p. col. illus. 29cm. 1.95 bds.,
I. Title.

WELLS, Herbert George, 1866-1946. 232.93
Crux ansata; an indictment of the Roman Catholic Church. New York, Freethought Press Association [c1953] 160p. port. 19cm. The appendix carries the report of an interview with Mr. Wells by Mr. John Rowland originally published in the Literary guide, London, in March 1944. [BX1765.W] A54
1. Catholic Church—Doctrinal and controversial works—Miscellaneous authors. I. Title.

WILSON, Lawrence Ray, 1896- 232.93
Roman Catholicism: facts or fabrications? [by] L. R. Williamson. Nashville, Freedom Press [c1965] xii, 198 p. 21 cm. Bibliography: p. 195-198. [BX1765.2.W55] 65-24974
1. Catholic Church — Doctrinal and controversial works — Protestant authors. I. Title.

ALASTRUEY SANCHEZ, Gregorio. 232.931
The Blessed Virgin Mary. Translated by M. Janet La Giglia. [St. Louis] B. Herder Book Co. [1963- v. 24 cm. Translation of Tratado de la Virgen Santisima. Includes bibliography. [BT602.A383] 63-12532
1. Mary, Virgin—Theology. I. Title.

ALASTRUEY SANCHEZ, Gregorio 232.931
The Blessed Virgin Mary; v.2. Tr. [from Spanish] by M. Janet La Giglia [St. Louis] B. Herder [c.1964] v. 24cm. Bibl. 63-12532 6.00
1. Mary, Virgin—Theology. I. Title.

ALBERIONE, Giacomo Giuseppe, 1884- 232.931
Glories and virtues of Mary, by J. Alberione. Translation by Hilda Calabro. [Boston?] St. Paul Editions [c1958] 251p. illus. 22cm. [BT602.A113] 59-28193
1. Mary, Virgin. I. Title.

ALBERIONE, Giacomo Giuseppe, 1884- 232.931
Mary, hope of the world, by James Alberione. Translation by Hilda Calabro. [Boston?] St. Paul Editions [c1958] 218p. illus. 22cm. [BT605.2.A113] 59-28503
1. Mary, Virgin—Biog. I. Title.

ALBERIONE, Giacomo Giuseppe, 1884- 232.931
Mary, mother and model; feasts of Mary, by James Alberione. Translation by Hilda Calabro. [Boston?] St. Paul Editions [c1958] 237p. illus. 22cm. [BT645.5.A413] 59-28525
1. Mary. Virgin—Feasts. I. Title.

ALBERIONE. GIACOMO GIUSEPPE, 1884- 232.931
Mary, Queen of the Apostles, by James Alberione. Translated by a Daughter of St. Paul. [Derby? N. Y.] Apostolate of the Press [c1956] 346p. illus. 22cm. [BT638.A413] 59-28488
1. Mary, Virgin. I. Title.

AMERICAN ecclesiastical review. 232.931
Studies in praise of Our Blessed Mother; selections from the American ecclesiastical review. Edited by Joseph Clifford Fenton and Edmond Darvil Benard. Washington, Catholic University of America Press, 1952. xi, 280p. 23cm. Bibliographical footnotes. [BT597.A5] A53
1. Mary, Virgin. I. Fenton, Joseph Clifford, 1906- ed. II. Benard, Edmond Darvil, 1914- ed. III. Title.

ARADI, Zsolt. 232.931
Shrines to Our Lady around the world. New York, Farrar, Straus and Young [1954] 213 p. illus. 27 cm. [BX2320.A7] 54-10580
1. Shrines. I. Title.

ATTWATER, Donald, 1892- 232.931
A dictionary of Mary. New York, Kenedy [1956] viii, 312p. 24cm. [BT599.A9] 56-10460
1. Mary, Virgin—Dictionaries. I. Title.

BAECHER, Charlotte Crawford 232.931
A child's life of Mary. New York, Paulist Press [c.1959] unpaged illus. col. 16cm. .10 pap.,
I. Title.

BAINVEL, Jean Vincent, 1858-1937. 232.931
And the light shines in the darkness; a way of life through Mary. Translated by John J. Sullivan. New York, Benziger Bros [1953] 239p. 21cm. Translation of Le saint coeur de Marie. [BX2160.3.B253] 53-9641
1. Sacred Heart of Mary, Devotion to. I. Title.

BAIRD, Mary Julian. 232.931
Our Lady of the Forest; a book of Mary names. Milwaukee, BrucePub. Co. [1957] 140p. 23cm. [BT670.T5B3] 57-9130
1. Mary, Virgin—Titles. I. Title.

BARBIERI, Albert, Rev. 232.931
Mary, Star of the Sea. Tr. by Hilda Calabro. [Boston] St. Paul [dist. Daughters of St. Paul, c.1962] 162p. illus. 21cm. 62-18503 3.00; 2.00 pap.,
1. Mary, Virgin—Meditations. I. Title.

BEEBE, Catherine, 1898- 232.931
The story of Mary, the mother of Jesus. Illustrated by Robb Beebe. Milwaukee, Bruce [1950] ix, 147 p. illus. 23 cm. [BT607.B36] 50-13526
1. Mary, Virgin. I. Title.

BEEVERS, John. 232.931
The sun her mantle. Westminster, Md., Newman Press, 1953. 228p. illus. 22cm. [BT650] 53-2990
1. Mary, Virgin—Apparitions and miracles (Modern) I. Title.

BERNARD, Rogatien, 1888- 232.931
The mystery of Mary. Translated by M. A. Bouchard. St. Louis, Herder [1960] 304p. 21cm. (Cross and crown series of spirituality, no. 16) Includes bibliography. [BT613.B453] 60-14099
1. Mary, Virgin—Theology. I. Title.

BISKUPEK, Aloysius, 1884- 232.931
Our Lady's litany: readings and reflections. Milwaukee, Bruce Pub. Co. [1954] 166p. 21cm. [BT670.T5B5] 54-7548
1. Mary, Virgin—Titles. 2. Litany of Loreto. I. Title.

BONNET, Leon, 1888- 232.931
Our Lady speaks; thoughts on her litany. Translated by Leonard J. Doyle. St. Meinrad, Ind., Grail [1954] 283p. 22cm. Translation of O Vierge Marie. [BT670.T5B613] 54-11419
1. Litany of Loreto. 2. Mary, Virgin—Titles. I. Title.

BOUYER, Louis, 1913- 232.931
The seat of wisdom; an essay on the place of the Virgin Mary in Christian theology. Tr. by A. V. Littledale. [New York] Pantheon [1962, c.1960] 212p. Bibl. 59-11962 4.50
1. Mary, Virgin—Theology. I. Title.

BOYD, Beverly Mary, ed. 232.931
The Middle English miracles of the Virgin, by Beverly Boyd. San Marino, Calif., Huntington Library, 1964. xviii, 148 p. plates. 24 cm. (Huntington Library publications) Bibliographical footnotes. [BT609.B67] 63-13992
1. Mary, Virgin — Poetry. 2. Mary, Virgin, in literature. 3. Mary, Virgin — Legends. I. Title. II. Series: Henry E. Huntington Library and Art Gallery, San Marino, Calif. Huntington Library publications

BREEN, Stephen. 232.931
Recent apparitions of the blessed Virgin Mary. New York, Scapular Press, 1952. 356 p. 22 cm. [BT650.B67] 52-41871
1. Mary, Virgin—Apparitions and miracles (Modern) I. Title.

BREEN, Stephen. 232.931
Recent apparitions of the blessed Virgin Mary. New York, Scapular Apostolate [1953] 168p. 18cm. (Lumen books, 527) [BT650.B67 1953] 54-30270
1. Mary, Virgin— Apparitions and miracles (Modern) I. Title.

BROSCHART, Charles B 232.931
Call her Blessed. Staten Island, N. Y., Society of St. Paul [c1961] 278p. 21cm. [BT645.B8] 61-15618
1. Mary, Virgin—Cultus. I. Title.

BROWN, Beverly Holladay, 1912- 232.931
The life of Mary as seen by the mystics;) compiled from the revelations of St. Elizabeth of Schoenau, St. Bridget of Sweden, Ven. Mother Mary of Agreda, Sister Anna Catherine Emmerich, by Raphael Brown [pseud.] Foreword by Edward A. Ryan. Milwaukee, Bruce [1951] 292 p. 21 cm. [BT605.B74] 51-7221
1. Mary, Virgin. I. Title.

BROWN, Beverly Holliday, 1912- ed. and tr. 232.931
Our Lady and Saint Francis; all the earliest texts, compiled and translated by Raphael Brown [pseud.] Chicago, Franciscan Herald Press [1954] x, 80p. 16cm. (His St. Francis texts, no. 1) 'Presents all the texts [on the life of St. Francis] which refer...to the Blessed Virgin.' Bibliography: p. 78-80. [BX4700.F6B76 no.1] 54-2916
1. Mary, Virgin—Cultus. I. Francesco d'Assisi, Saint, 1188-1226. II. Title.

BUKSBAZEN, Victor, 1903- 232.931
Miriam, the virgin of Nazareth. Philadelphia, Spearhead Pr. [1963] 239p. 22cm. 63-15246 apply
1. Mary, Virgin. I. Title.

BURGHARDT, Walter J 232.931
The testimony of the Patristic Age concerning Mary's death. Westminster, Md., Newman Press, 1957. viii, 59p. 22cm. (Woodstock papers: occasional essays for theology, no. 2) 'A slightly revised version of the article which appeared under the same name in Marian studies 8 (1957) 58-99.' Bibliographical references included in 'Notes' (p. 43-56) [BT630.B8] 57-14815
1. Mary, Virgin—Assumption. I. Title. II. Series.

BURKE, Anselm, 1924- 232.931
Mary in history, in faith, and in devotion. New York, Scapular Press, 1956. 262p. 22cm. [BT601.B79] 57-3120
1. Mary, Virgin. I. Title.

BURKE, Anselm, 1924- 232.931
Mary in history, in faith, and in devotion. New York, Scapular Press, 1956. 262p. 22cm. [BT601.B79] 57-3120
I. Title.

BURKE, Thomas J M 1920- ed. 232.931
Mary and modern man. New York, America Press, 1954. 231p. 22cm. [BT597.B8] 54-13249
1. Mary, Virgin. I. Title.

CAROL, Juniper B 1911- 232.931
Fundamentals of Mariology. New York, Benziger Bros. [19560 203p. 21cm. [BT613.C3] 56-33588
1. Mary, Virgin—Theology. I. Title.

CAROL, Juniper B 1911- ed. 232.931
Mariology. Milwaukee, Bruce Pub. Co. [c1955-61] 3v. 23cm. Bibliographical footnotes. [BT597.C25] 55-6959
1. Mary, Virgin. I. Title.

CAROL, Juniper B., 1911- ed. 232.931
Mariology. v.3. Milwaukee, Bruce [c.1961] 456p. Bibl. 55-6959 9.50
I. Title.

CATHOLIC Church. Pope. 232.931
Mary and the popes; five great Marian letters, edited by Thomas J. M. Burke. New York, America Press, 1954. 107p. 20cm. Includes bibliographical references. [BT597.C27] 54-10984
1. Mary, Virgin. I. Burke, Thomas J. M., ed. II. Title.

CATHOLIC Church. Pope. 232.931
Our Lady. Selected and arr. by the Benedictine monks of Solesmes. Translated by the Daughters of St. Paul. [Boston] St. Paul Editions [1961] 591p. 19cm. (Papal teachings) [BT597.C29] 61-14934
1. Mary, Virgin—Papal documents. I. Solesmes, France. Saint-Pierre (Benedictine abbey) II. Title.

CATHOLIC Church. Pope. 232.931
Papal documents on Mary, compiled and arr. by William J. Doheny and Joseph P. Kelly. Milwaukee, Bruce Pub. Co. [1954] x, 270p. 23cm. Bibliographical footnotes. [BT597.C3] 54-7737
1. Mary, Virgin. I. Dhoeny, William Joseph, 1898- ed. II. Kelly, Joseph Patrick, 1902- ed. III. Title.

CATHOLIC Church. Pope. 232.931
The popes speak of Mary, 1854-1954; papal pronouncements on the Blessed Virgin Mary, compiled and edited by Vincent A. Yzermans. Saint Cloud, Minn., 1954. 156p. 27cm. [BT597.C32] 54-30268
1. Mary, Virgin. I. Ysermans, Vincent Arthur, 1925- ed. II. Title.

CATHOLIC Church. Pope, 1939-1958 (Pius XII) 232.931
Four Marian encyclicals and the apostolic constitution Munificentissimus Deus. With discussion club outlines by Gerald C. Treacy. Introd. by William F. Hogan. Edited by Edward R. Lawler. New York, Raulist Press [c1959] 158p. 19cm. Includes bibliography. [BT598.C3] 60-465
1. Mary, Virgin—Papal documents. I. Title.

CUSHING, Richard James, Cardinal 232.931
Mary. [Boston] St. Paul Eds. [dist. Daughters of St. Paul, c.1963] 152p. 22cm. 63-17866 2.50; 1.50 pap.,
1. Mary, Virgin—Sermons. 2. Catholic Church—Sermons. 3. Sermons, American. I. Title.

CUSHING, Richard James, Cardinal 232.931
Mary. [Boston, Daughters of St. Paul, 1960] 152p. 22cm. (St. Paul Editions) 60-50065 2.50; 1.50 pap.,
1. Mary, Virgin—Sermons. 2. Catholic Church—Sermons. 3. Sermons, American. I. Title.

CUSHING, Richard James, Cardinal, 1895- 232.931
Mary. [Boston] St. Paul Editions [1963] 152 p. 22 cm. [BT608.C85] 63-17866
1. Mary, Virgin — Sermons. 2. Catholic Church — Sermons. 3. Sermons, American. I. Title.

DANIEL-ROPS, Henry [Real name: Henry Jules Charles Petiot] 232.931
The book of Mary. Translated from the French by Alastair Guinan. New York, Hawthorn Books [c.1960] 224p. 24cm. (bibl. note: p. 215-218) illus. (part col.)p4.95 60-5895
1. Mary, Virgin. I. Bible N. T. Gospels. English. Selections. 1960. II. Bible. N. T. Apocryphal books. Gospels. English. Selection. 1960 III. Title.

BIBLE. N. T. Gospels. English. Selections. 1960. 232.931
The book of Mary. Tr. from French by Alastair Guinan. Garden City, N. Y., Doubleday [1963, c.1960] 189p. 18cm. (Image bk., D158) Bibl. .75 pap.,
1. Mary, Virgin. I. Bible. N.T. Apocryphal books. Gospels. English. Selections. 1960. II. Title.

DEMPSEY, Martin, 1904- 232.931
In praise of Our Lady; with a novena to Our Lady of Fatima. New York, Wagner [1950] vi, 225 p. 21 cm. [BT645.D36] 50-4613
1. Fatima, Nossa Senhora da. 2. Mary, Virgin—Cultus. I. Title.

DOLLEN, Charles, ed. and tr. 232.931
A voice said Ave! Selected passages on Our Lady from the writings of the fathers, doctors and theologians; free translations. [Boston] St. Paul Editions [1963] 229 p. illus. 22 cm. Includes bibliography. [BT601.D55] 63-18346
1. Mary, Virgin — History of doctrines — Early church. 2. Mary, Virgin — Sermons. 3. Christian lietarture. Early (Selections: Extracts, etc) I. Title.

DOLLEN, Charles, ed. and tr. 232.931
A voice said Ave! Selected passages on Our Lady from the writings of the fathers, doctors and theologians; free trs. [Boston] St. Paul Eds. [dist. Daughters of St. Paul, c.1963] 229p. illus. 22cm. Bibl. 63-18346 3.00; 2.00 pap.,
1. Mary, Virgin—History of doctrines—Early church. 2. Christian literature, Early (Selections: Extracts, etc.) 3. Mary, Virgin—Sermons. I. Title.

DONOVAN, Mary Annice. 232.931
The mission of Mary. Milwaukee, Bruce Pub. Co. [1963] 131 p. 22 cm. [BT638.D6] 63-10765
1. Mary, Virgin — Theology. I. Title.

DONOVAN, Mary Annice, Sister. 232.931
The mission of Mary. Milwaukee, Bruce [c.1963] 131p. 22cm. 63-10765 3.25
1. Mary, Virgin—Theology. I. Title.

DORCY, Mary Jean, 1914- 232.931
Fount of our joy; Madonna legends for dramatization. Westminster, Md., Newman Press, 1955. 125p. illus. 22cm. [BT609.D6] 55-7048
1. Mary, Virgin—Drama. I. Title.

DORCY, Mary Jean, 1914- 232.931
Shrines of Our Lady. Illustrated by Johannes Troyer. New York, Sheed & Ward [1956] 160p. illus. 21cm. [BT650.D6] 56-9531
1. Shrines. I. Title.

DUHR, Joseph. 232.931
The glorious Assumption of the Mother of God; translated by John Manning Fraunces. New York, P. J. Kenedy ['1950] 153 p. 19 cm. [BT630.D813] 51-5806
1. Mary, Virgin—Assumption. I. Title.

ERNEST, Brother, 1897- 232.931
Our Lady comes to Beauraing. Illustrated by Rena Bianucci. Notre Dame, Ind., Dujarie Press [1954] 85p. illus. 24cm. [BT660.B4E7] 54-30265
1. Beauraing, Notre-Dame de. I. Title.

ERNEST, Brother, 1897- 232.931
Our Lady comes to Pontmain. Illus. by Brother Etienne Cooper. Notre Dame, Ind., Dujarie Press [1954] 86p. illus. 24cm. [BT660.P7E7] 54-43125
1. Pontmain, Notre-Dame de. I. Title.

ERNEST, Brother, 1897- 232.931
Your mother and mine; a story of the Blessed Virgin. Illus. by Albert Kern. Notre Dame, Ind., Dujarie Press [1954] 85p. illus. 24cm. [BT605.E7] 54-3701
1. Mary, Virgin—Biog. I. Title.

FABER, Frederick William, 1814-1863. 232.931
The foot of the cross; or, The sorrows of Mary. New ed. Philadelphia, P. Reilly Co. [1956] 406p. 24cm. [BX2161.5.S6F2 1956] 57-2960
1. Sorrows of the Blessed Virgin Mary, Devotion to. I. Title.

FRANCISCANS. Province of the Assumption of the Blessed Virgin Mary. 232.931
Tribute to Mary; papers presented to the provincial Marian congress of the Assumption Province of Franciscans on the occasion of the Marian Year. Edited by Theodore Zaremba. Pulaski, Wis., Franciscan Printery, 1955. 199p. illus. 22cm. Some of the papers are in Polish. Includes bibliographies. [BT597.F7] 57-36858
1. Mary, Virgin—Addresses, essays, lectures. I. Zaremba, Theodore Anthony, ed. II. Title.

GALOT, Jean 232.931
Mary in the Gospel. Tr. [from French] by Sister Maria Constance. Westminster, Md., Newman, 1965 [c.1964] viii, 231p. 22cm. Bibl. [BT611.G313] 63-12258 4.50
1. Mary, Virgin—Biblical teaching. I. Title.

GAROFALO, Salvatore 232.931
Mary in the Bible. Tr. [from Italian] by Thomas J. Tobin. Milwaukee, Bruce [c.1961] 106p. 61-174367 3.00
1. Mary, Virgin—Biog. I. Title.

GEARON, Patrick J. 232.931
Chats with Our Lady. Chicago, Carmelite Third Order Pr. [1961] 200p. 2.00
I. Title.

GEARON, Patrick J. 232.931
Our Lady for boys & girls. Chicago, Carmelite Third Order Press [1960] 164p. 19cm. 60-807 2.00 bds.,
1. Mary, Virgin—Juvenile literature. I. Title.

GILLETT, Henry Martin, 1902- 232.931
Famous shrines of Our Lady. With a foreword by the Apostolic Delegate of England. Westminster, Md., Newman Press, 19 v. plates. 20cm. Bibliography: v.2, p. 277-284. [BT650.G52] 54-14504
1. Shahrines. 2. Mary, Virgin— Oultus. I. Title.

[GOETTEN, Henry] 1900- ed. 232.931
Mary, God's masterpiece. [1st ed.] New York, Perpetual Help Press [1954] 64p. col. illus. 22cm. 'Text taken from New Catholic edition of the Holy Bible, the Dally missal, and the Roman braviiary.' [BT601.G63] 54-27854
1. Mary, Virgin. 2. Mary, Virgin—Art. I. Title.

GRAEF, Hilda C 232.931
The devotion to Our Lady. [1st ed.] New York, Hawthorn Books [1963] 108 p. 22 cm. (The Twentieth century encyclopedia of Catholicism, v. 45. Section 4: The means of redemption) "Publication 106." Includes bibliography. [BT645.G68] 63-17333
1. Mary, Virgin — Cultus — Hist. I. Title.

GRAEF, Hilda C. 232.931
The devotion to Our Lady. New York, Hawthorn [c.1963] 108p. 22cm. (Twentieth cent. encyclopedia of Catholicism, v.45. Section 4: The means of redemption; pubn. 106) Bibl. 63-17333 3.50
1. Mary, Virgin—Cultus—Hist. I. Title.

GRAEF, Hilda C. 232.931
Mary; a history of doctrine and devotion; v.1. New York, Sheed [1964, c.1963] 371p. illus. 22cm. Contents.v.1. From the beginnings to the eve of the Reformation. Bibl. 64-13565 5.95
1. Mary, Virgin—History of doctrines. I. Title.

GRIGNON, de Montfort, Louis Marie, Saint, 1673-1716. 232.931
True devotion to the Blessed Virgin. Foreword by Frank Duff. [Tr. from French by Malachy Gerard Carroll] Staten Island, N. Y., Alba [1963, c.1962] xvi, 204p. 20cm. 63-12679 2.50
1. Mary, Virgin—Cultus. I. Title.

GUITTON, Jean. 232.931
The Virgin Mary; translated by A. Gordon Smith. New York, Kenedy [1952] 190 p. 21 cm. London ed. (Burns, Oates) has title: The Blessed Virgin. [BT601.G813 1952a] 52-9718
1. Mary, Virgin. I. Title.

HEPPLER, Richard Leo. 232.931
'Thou art all fair'; thoughts on Our Lady. Paterson, N.J., St. Anthony Guild Press [1959] 34p. 18cm. 59-65224 .20 pap.,
1. Mary, Virgin. I. Title.

HINNEBUSCH, Paul. 232.931
Sword of sorrow. Chicago, Franciscan Herald Press [1964] 68 p. 21 cm. Bibliographical footnotes. [BX2160.2.H5] 64-24288
1. Mary, Virgin — Meditations. I. Title.

HINNEBUSCH, Paul 232.931
Sword of sorrow. Chicago, Franciscan Herald [c.1964] 68p. 21cm. Bibl. [BT2160.2.H5] 64-24288 1.50 pap.,
1. Mary, Virgin—Meditations. I. Title.

HOPHAN, Otto. 232.931
Mary, Our Most Blessed Lady. Translated by Berchmans Bittle. Milwaukee, Bruce Pub. Co. [1959] 374p. 24cm. Includes bibliography. [BT602.H613] 59-10217
1. Mary, Virgin. I. Title.

*JABLONSKI, Edward 232.931
Mary, Mother of Jesus. Derby, Conn., Monarch [c.1964] 159p. 18cm. (Monarch select bk. K72) .50 pap.,
I. Title.

JOURNET, Charles. 232.931
Notre-Dame des sept douleurs. St.-Maurice (Suisse) L'Oeuvre St.-Augustin, 1955. 110p. 18cm. [BT601.J] A 55
1. Sorrows of the Blessed Virgin Mary, Devotion to. I. Title.

KEYES, Frances Parkinson (Wheeler) 1885- 232.931
The grace of Guadalupe. New York, J. Messner [1953] 182p. illus. 22cm. [BT660.G8K4 1953] 53-10507
1. Guadalupe, Nuestra Seflora de. I. Title.

KLAVER, Richard. 232.931
The Litany of Loreto. St. Louis, B. Herder Book Co. [1954] 227p. 21cm. [BT670.T5K55] 54-8389
1. Mary, Virgin—Titles. 2. Litany of Loreto. I. Title.

LANCASHIRE, A 232.931
Born of the Virgin Mary. London, Faith Press; New York, Morehouse-Barlow [1962] 144 p. illus. 19 cm. (Studies in Christian faith and practice, 3) [BT602] A63
1. Mary, Virgin — Theology. I. Title.

LANCASHIRE, A. 232.931
Born of the Virgin Mary. London, Faith Pr.; New York, Morehouse [1963, c.1962] 144p. illus. 19cm. (Studies in Christian faith and practice, 3) A63 2.10 pap.,
1. Mary, Virgin—Theology. I. Title.

LIGUORI, Alfonso Maria de', Saint, 1696-1787. 232.931
The glories of Mary. Tr. from Italian. Helicon[dist. New york, Taplinger, c.1962] 196p. 23cm. (His Ascetical works, v.1.) 62-21258 3.95 bds.,
1. Mary, Virgin—Early works to 1800. I. Title.

LIGUORI, Alfonso Maria de', Saint, 1696-1787 232.931
The glories of Mary; pt.2. Tr. from Italian. Baltimore, Helicon [c.1963] 228p. 23cm. (His Ascetical works, v.2; pt.2, Sermons and meditations) 62-21258 3.95
1. Mary, Virgin—Early works to 1800. I. Title.

LIGUORI, Alfonso Maris de', Saint, 1696-1787. 232.931
The glories of Mays. Translated from the Italian. Baltimore, Helicon Press [1962-63] 2 v. 23 cm. (His Ascetical works, v. 1-2) [BT600.L722] 62-21258
1. Mvry, Virgin — Early works to 1800. I. Liguori, Alfonso Maria de', Saint, 1696-1787. II. Title.

LOVASIK, Lawrence George, 1913- 232.931
Our Lady in Catholic life. New York, Macmillan, 1957. 409p. 22cm. [BT645.5.L7] 57-7500
1. Mary, Virgin—Feasts. 2. Mary, Virgin—Titles. I. Title.

LOVASIK, Lawrence George, 1913- 232.931
Our Lady in Catholic life. New York, Macmillan, 1957. 409p. 22cm. [BT645.5.L70] 57-7500
1. Mary, Virgin—Feasts. 2. Mary, Virgin—Titles. I. Title.

LYONS, Mark J 232.931
Mary and the priest; meditations. Milwaukee, Bruce Pub. Co. [1963] 233 p. 23 cm. [BT602.L9] 63-8948
1. Mary, Virgin — Meditations. 2. Catholic Church — Clergy. 3. Meditations. I. Title.

LYONS, Mark J. 232.931
Mary and the priest; meditations. Milwaukee, Bruce [c.1963] 233p. 23cm. 63-8948 4.75
1. Mary, Virgin—Meditations. 2. Catholic Church—Clergy. 3. Meditations. I. Title.

MCLOUGHLIN, William A 232.931
The holy years of Mary; edited by Joseph G. Cox. [1st ed.] Philadelphia, Winston [1954] 114p. illus. 24cm. [BT605.M22] 54-7893
1. Mary, Virgin—Biog. I. Title.

MCNALLY, James J 232.931
Litany at Nazareth. New York, J. F. Wagner [1958] 246p. 21cm. [BT608.M2] 58-47872
1. Mary, Virgin—Sermons. 2. Catholic Church—Sermons. 3. Sermons, American. I. Title.

MCNALLY, James J 232.931
Make way for Mary; with a foreword by Christopher J. Weldon. New York, J. F. Wagner [c1950] 272 p. 21 cm. [BT601.M26] 51-2141
1. Mary, Virgin. I. Title.

MCNAMARA, Kevin, ed. 232.931
Mother of the Redeemer, aspects of doctrine and devotion; lectures of Maynooth Union summer school. New York, Sheed & Ward, 1960. xiii, 258p. 22cm. (2p. bibl. and bibl. footnotes) 60-7308 4.00
1. Mary, Virgin—Addresses essays, lectures. I. Maynooth, Ire. St. Patrick's College. II. Title.

MARIAN era (The) 232.931
v.5, 1964. Chicago, Pub. by Franciscan Herald for the Franciscan Natl. Marian Commn. c.1964. 128p. illus. (pt. col.) 29cm. annual. Bibl. 60-12982 4.95
1. Mary, Virgin—Yearbooks. I. Franciscan National Marian Commission.

MARIAN era (The) 232.931
v.1, 1960 Chicago [Published by Franciscan Herald Press for the Franciscan National Marian Commission] c.1960. 128p. illus. (part col.) 29cm. annual. 60-12982 4.95 bds.,
1. Mary, Virgin—Yearbooks. I. Franciscan National Marian Commission.

MARNAS, Melanie. 232.931
My Lady Miriam. Translated and adapted from the French by Sidney A. Raemers. Westminster, Md., Newman Press, 1958. 244p. 21cm. 'Originally published in France ... as Myriam.' [BT605.M333] 58-11455
1. Mary, Virgin—Biog. I. Title.

MARTORANA, Maria 232.931
Thread of gold. New York, Pageant [c.1962] 60p. 21cm. 2.50
I. Title.

MARY the mirror. 232.931
By a Carthusian. Tr. from French by a Monk of Parkminster. Springfield, Ill., Templegate [1963] 96p. 15cm. 1.25

MARY AMATORA, Sister, 1904- 232.931
The Queen's way; or, To Jesus through Mary. [Chicago, J. S. Paluch Co., 1954] 185p. 18cm. (Lumen books, 528) A simplified edition of St. Louis de Montfort's . . . True devotion to the Blessed Virgin. [BT645.M3] 54-31945
1. Mary, Virgin—Cultus. I. Grignon de Montfort, Louis Marie, Saint 1673-1716. Treatise on the true devotion to the Blessed Virgin Mary. II. Title. III. Title: To Jesus through Mary.

MARY ST. PAUL, Sister. 232.931
Hail Mary for little Catholics. Pictures by Steffie Lerch. St. Paul, Catechetical Guild Educational Society, c1953. unpaged. illus. 17cm. (First books for little Catholics) [BT607.M33] 54-21711
1. Mary, Virgin—Juvenile literature. I. Title.

MATHEWS, Stanley G ed. 232.931
Queen of the Universe; an anthology on the Assumption and Queenship of Mary. Saint Meinrad, Ind., Grail Publications [1957] xiv, 258p. 22cm. (The Marian Library series) Bibliographical footnotes. [BT630.M3] 57-8327
1. Mary, Virgin—Assumption. 2. Mary, Virgin—Queenship. I. Title. II. Series.

MIEGGE, Giovanni. 232.931
The Virgin Mary; the Roman Catholic Marian doctrine. Translated from the Italian by Waldo Smith; with a foreword by John A. Mackay. Philadelphia, Westminster Press [1955] 196p. 23cm. [BT613.M53] 56-5884
1. Mary, Virgin—Titles. 2. Mary, Virgin—Theology. I. Title.

MOST, William George, 1914- 232.931
Mary in our life 3d ed. New York, P. J. Kenedy [1959] 332p. 21cm. [BT640.M6 1959] 59-65087
1. Mary, Virgin—Mediation. 2. Mary, Virgin—Cultus. I. Title.

MOST, William George, 1914- 232.931
Mary in our life. New York, P. J.Kenedy [1954] xviii, 328p. 21cm. Includes bibliographies. [BT640.M6] 54-6530
1. Mary, Virgin—Mediation. 2. Mary, Virgin—Cultus. I. Title.

MURPHY, John F 1922- 232.931
Mary's Immaculate Heart; the meaning of the devotion to the Immaculate Heart of Mary. Milwaukee, Bruce [1951] xiii, 127 p. 20 cm. Bibliography: p. 121-127. [BX2160.3.M8] 51-2735
1. Sacred Heart of Mary, Devotion to. I. Title.

NEUBERT, Emile Nicolas, 1878- 232.931
Life of union with Mary. Translated from the 3d French ed., La vie d'union a Marie, by Sylvester P. Juergens. Milwaukee, Bruce Pub. Co. [1959] 255p. 23cm. [BX2160.N4373] 59-10216
1. Mary, Virgin Meditations. I. Title.

NEUBERT, Emile Nicolas, 1878- 232.931
Mary in doctrine. Milwaukee, Bruce [1954] 257p. 23cm. Translation of Marie dans le dogme. [BT613.N43] 54-10949
1. Mary, Virgin—Theology. I. Title.

NEWMAN, John Henry, Cardinal, 1801-1890. 232.931
The new Eve. Oxford, Newman Bookshop 1952 96p. 19cm. on label: Westminster, Md., Newman Press [BT601.N43] 52-13430
1. Mary Virgin. I. Title.

NUGENT, Francis Edward, comp. 232.931
'Fairest star of all'; a little treasury of Mariology. Paterson, N. J., St. Anthony Guild Press, 1956. 59p. 22cm. [BT597.N8] 56-14391
1. Mary, Virgin. I. Title.

O'CARROLL, Michael. 232.931
Mediatress of all graces. Westminster, Md., Newman Press [1958] 308p. 23cm. Includes bibliography. [BT640.O28] 58-59411
1. Mary. Virgin—Mediation. I. Title.

O'CONNOR, Edward D ed. 232.931
The mystery of the woman; essays on the Mother of God, sponsored by the Dept. of Theology, University of Notre Dame. Notre Dame, Ind., University of Notre Dame Press [1956] 150p. illus. 20cm. [BT613.O25] 55-9517
1. Mary, Virgin—Theology. I. Title.

O'CONNOR, Edward Dennis, ed. 232.931
The mystery of the woman; essays on the Mother of God, sponsored by the Dept. of Theology, University of Notre Dame. Notre Dame, Ind., University of Notre Dame Press [1956] 150p. illus: 20cm. [BT613.O25] 55-9517
1. Mary, Virgin—Theology. I. Title.

OLIVER, Father. 232.931
The failing wine; Mary, Seat of Wisdom. Westminster, Md., Newman Press, 1954. 153p. 23cm. [BT601.O39] 54-12451
1. Mary, Virgin. I. Title.

OLIVER, Father. 232.931
Fair as the moon; Mary, purest of creatures. Westminster, Md., Newman Press, 1950. 235 p. front. 23 cm. [BT601.O4] 50-3969
1. Mary, Virgin. I. Title.

O'REILLY, James P 1913- 232.931
The story of La Salette; Mary's apparition, its history and sequels. Chicago, J. S. Paluch Co. [1953] 167p. illus. 18cm. (Lumen books, 526) [BT660.S33O7] 54-30228
1. Salette, Notre Dame de la. I. Title.

PALMER, Paul F 232.931
Mary in the documents of the church; with a word to the reader by Gerald G. Walsh. Westminster, Md., Newman Press, 1952. 129 p. 21 cm. [BT610.P3] 52-7507
1. Mary, Virgin — History of doctrines. I. Title.

PANNULLO-PARNOFIELLO, Louise. 232.931
Change the world through Mary, by Louise Parnell [pseud.] Great Notch, N. J., Notch Pub. House [1958] 113p. illus. 23cm. [BT645.P3] 58-8566
1. Mary, Virgin—Cultus. 2. Mary, Virgin—Apparitions and miracles (Modern) I. Title.

PARISH, Helen Rand. 232.931
Our Lady of Guadalupe. Illustrated by Jean Charlot. New York, Viking Press, 1955. 48 p. illus. 26 cm. [BT660.G8P3] 55-1055
1. Guadalupe, Nuestra Senora de.

PATSCH, Joseph, 1881- 232.931
Our Lady in the Gospels. [Translation by Basil Wrighton] Westminster, Md., Newman Press [1958] 231p. illus. 22cm. Translation of Maria, die Mutter des Herrn. [BT605.P313] 58-59413
1. Mary, Virgin—Biog. I. Title.

PHILIPON, Marie Michel, 1898- 232.931
The Mother of God; translated by John A. Otto. Westminster, Md., Newman Press, 1953. 154p. 20cm. Translation of Le vral visage de Notre-Dame. [BT601.P472] 53-7492
1. Mary, Virgin—Theology. I. Title.

PHILIPPE, Paul, 1905- 232.931
The Blessed Virgin and the priesthood. Translated from the French by Dorothy Cole. Chicago, H. Regnery Co., 1955. 82p. 19cm. [BT601] 55-6976
1. Mary, Virgin. 2. Clergy—Religious life. I. Title.

PIAT, Stephane Joseph, 1899- 232.931
Our Lady of the Smile and St. Therese of the Child Jesus. Translated by Michael Collins. Chicago, Franciscan Herald Press [1954] 134p. illus. 17cm. [BT601] 54-14577
1. Mary, Virgin. 2. Therese, Saint, 1873-1897. I. Title.

POLLOI, Ch 232.931
A retreat with Our Lady; a study in the theological and cardinal virtues. Westminster, Md, Newman Press, 1956. 169p. 15cm. [BX2160.P6] 56-9816
1. Mary. Virgin— Meditations. 2. Virtues. 3. Cardinal virtues. I. Title.

POTTER, Mary, Mother, 1847-1913. 232.931
To Jesus through Mary; spiritual exercises for consecrating one's self to Mary. New York, Catholic Book Pub. Co. [1952] 256p. illus. 16cm. Previous ed. published under title: Spiritual exercises of Mary. [BX2182.P67 1952] 53-606
1. Spiritual exercises. I. Title.

RAHNER, Karl, 1904- 232.931
Mary. Mother of the Lord: theological meditations. [Translated by W. J. O'Hara. New York] Herder and Herder [1963] 106 p. 21 cm. [BT613.R553] 63-8324
1. Mary, Virgin—Theology. I. Title.

RAHNER, Karl, 1904- 232.931
Mary. Mother of the Lord: theological meditations. [Tr. from German by W. J. O'Hara. New York] Herder & Herder [c.1963] 106p. 21cm. 63-8324 2.95
1. Mary, Virgin— Theology. I. Title.

RAYMOND, Father, 1903- 232.931
God, a woman, and the way. Illustrated by John Andrews. Milwaukee, Bruce Pub. Co. [1955] 169p. illus. 23cm. [BX2161.5.S6R3] 55-7112
1. Sorrows of the Blessed Virgin Mary, Devotion to. I. Title.

RESCH, Peter Anthony, 1895- 232.931
A life of Mary, co-redemptrix. Milwaukee, Bruce Pub. Co. [1954] 96p. 20cm. [BT605.R4] 54-2419
1. Mary, Virgin—Biog. I. Title.

ROBERTSON, Archibald Thomas, 1863-1934 232.931
The mother of Jesus; her problems and her glory. Grand Rapids, Mich., Baker Bk. 1963. 71p. 20cm. 63-20108 1.75
1. Mary, Virgin. I. Title.

ST. John's University, New York. Mariological Institute, 1958. 232.931
The Mariological Institute lectures. Jamaica, N. Y., St. John's University Press, 1959. 85 p. front. (St. John's University studies. Theological series, 1) Includes bibliographical references. [BT613.S34] 63-681
1. Mary. Virgin—Addresses, essays, lectures. I. Title. II. Series.
Contents ommitted

SCHILLEBEECKX, Edward Cornelis Florentius Alfons, 1914- 232.931
Mary, mother of the redemption, by E. Schillebeeckx. Translated by N. D. Smith. New York, Sheed and Ward [1964] xvi, 175 p. 22 cm. "This translation is based on the third revised Dutch edition with further revisions and additions." Bibliograpical footnotes. [BT613.S373] 64-19913
1. Mary, Virgin—Theology. I. Title.

SCHILLEBEECKX, Edward Cornelis Florentius Alfons, 1914- 232.931
Mary, mother of the redemption. Tr. [from Dutch] by N. D. Smith. New York, Sheed [c.1964] xvi, 175p. 22cm. Tr. is based on the 3d rev. Dutch ed. with further revs. and additions. Bibl. 64-19913 3.95
1. Mary, Virgin—Theology. I. Title.

SCHMID, Mark Joseph, 1901- 232.931
Mary, full of grace. Staten Island 14, N.Y., 2187 Victory Blvd. St. Paul publications, [1961, c.1960] 176p. 60-14930 3.00
1. Mary, Virgin. I. Title.

SCHORSCH, Alexander Peter, 1882- 232.931
Our Lord and Our Lady; Jesus associated Mary with Him in our redemption, by Alexander P. Schorsch and M. Dolores Schorsch. Illustrated by Pauline B. Adams. New York, Philosophical Library [c1957] 179p. illus. 22cm. Includes bibliography. [BT640.S28] 58-335
1. Mary, Virgin—Co-redemption. I. Schorsch, Dolores, 1896- joint author. II. Title.

SEBOLDT, Roland H A 232.931
Christ or Mary? The coredemption of Mary in contemporary Roman Catholic theology. Saint Louis, Concordia Pub. House [1963] 60 p. 18 cm. [BT640.S4] 63-2688
1. Mary, Virgin—Coredemption. 2. Catholic Church—Doctrinal and controversial works—Protestant authors. I. Title.

SEBOLDT, Roland H. A. 232.931
Christ or Mary? The coredemption of Mary in contemporary Roman Catholic theology. St. Louis, Concordia [c.1963] 60p. 18cm. 63-2688 .50 pap.,
1. Mary, Virgin—Coredemption. 2. Catholic Church—Doctrinal and controversial works—Protestant authors. I. Title.

SEMMELROTH, Otto. 232.931
Mary, archetype of the church. Translated by Maria von Eroes and John Devlin. Introd. by Jaroslav Pelikan. New York, Sheed and Ward [1963] xiv, 175 p. 21 cm. Translation of Urbild der Kirche. Includes bibliographical references. [BT613.S413] 63-8547
1. Mary, Virgin—Theology. I. Title.

SEMMELROTH, Otto 232.931
Mary, archetype of the church. Tr. [from German] by Maria von Eroes, John Devlin. Introd. by Jaroslav Pelikan. New York, Sheed [c.1963] xiv, 175p. 21cm. Bibl. 63-8547 3.95
1. Mary, Virgin—Theology. I. Title.

SHARKEY, Donald C 1912- 232.931
The Woman shall conquer; the story of the Blessed Virgin in the modern world. Milwaukee, Bruce Pub. Co. [1954] 306p. 22cm. [BT601.S46 1954] 54-2773
1. Mary, Virgin. I. Title.

SHARKEY, Donald C 1912- 232.931
The Woman shall conquer; the story of the Blessed Virgin in the modern world. Milwaukee, Bruce Pub. Co. [1952] 306 p. 22 cm. Includes bibliography. [BT601.S46] 52-11560
1. Mary, Virgin. I. Title.

SHARKEY, Donald C., 1912- 232.931
The Woman shall conquer; the story of the Blessed Virgin in the modern world. New York, All Saints Pr. [1961, c.1954] 258p. (AS209) .50 pap.,
1. Mary, Virgin. I. Title.

SHEEN, Fulton John, Bp., 1895- 232.931
The world's first love. New York, McGraw-Hill [1952] 285 p. 21 cm. [BT601.S53] 52-6554
1. Mary, Virgin. I. Title.

SLAVES of the Immaculate Heart of Mary. 232.931
The Mother of God. Cambridge [Mass.] 1956. 123p. illus. 22cm. [BT601.S57] 56-12751
1. Mary, Virgin. I. Title.

SLAVES of the Immaculate Heart of Mary. 232.931
The Mother of God. Cambridge [Mass.] 1956. 123 p. illus. 22 cm. [BT601.S57] 56-12751
1. Mary, Virgin. I. Title.

SMITH, George Duncan, 1893- 232.931
Mary's part in our redemption. [Rev. ed.] New York, Kenedy, 1954. 191p. 20cm. [BT601] 54-6532
1. Mary, Virgin—Theology. I. Title.

SPEYR, Adrienne von. 232.931
The Handmaid of the Lord. Translated by Alexander Dry. New York, D. McKay Co. [1955] 186p. 21cm. [BT605.S615] 55-14892
1. Mary, Virgin—Biog. I. Title.

STRATER, Paul. 232.931
The heart of Mary, sacrificial altar of Christ's love. Translated by Mother Mary Aloysi Kiener. New York, F. Pustet Co., 1957. 170p. 22cm. [BX2160.3.S8] 57-31387
1. Sacred Heart of Mary, Devotion to. I. Title.

STRATER, Paul. 232.931
The heart of Mary, sacrificial altar of Christs' love, Translated by Mother Mary Aloysi Kiener. New York, F. Pustet Co., 1957. 170 p. 22 cm. [BX2160.3.S8] 57-31387
1. Sacred Heart of Mary, Devotion to. I. Title.

SUENENS, Leon Joseph, Cardinal, 1904- 232.931
Mary the Mother of God. Translated from the French by a nun of Stanbrook Abbey. [1st American ed.] New York, Hawthorn Books [1959] 139 p. 22 cm. (The Twentieth century encyclopedia of Catholicism, v. 44. Section 4: The means of redemption) Translation of Quelle est Celle-ci? [BT613.S913] 59-12168
1. Mary, Virgin—Theology. I. Title.

THOMAS A KEMPIS, 1380-1471. 232.931
In praise of the Blessed Virgin Mary; translated by Robert E. Patterson. Milwaukee, Bruce Pub. Co. [1956] 52p. 18cm. Translation of discourses 21 through 24 of Sermones and novicios. [BT608.T52] 56-8198
1. Mary, Virgin—Sermons. 2. Catholic Church—Sermons. 3. Sermons, Latin—Translations into English. 4. Sermons, English—Translations from Latin. I. Title.

THOMAS A KEMPIS, 1380-1471. 232.931
In praise of the Blessed Virgin Mary; translated by Robert E. Patterson. Milwaukee, Bruce Pub. Co. [1956] 52 p. 18 cm. Translation of discourses 21 through 24 of Sermones and novicios. [BT608.T52] 56-8198
1. Mary, Virgin — Sermons. 2. Catholic Church — Sermons. 3. Sermons, Latin — Translations into English. 4. Sermons, English — Translations from Latin. I. Title.

THURIAN, Max 232.931
Mary, mother of all Christians [Tr. from French by Neville B. Cryer. New York] Herder & Herder [1964, c.1962, 1963] 204p. 23cm. Bibl. 64-13681 4.75
1. Mary, Virgin—Biblical teaching. I. Title.

VANDEUR, Eugene, 1875- 232.931
Hail Mary; translated by John H. Collins. Westminster, Md., Newman Press, 1954. 135p. 24cm. Translation of Je vous salue Marie. [BX2175.A8V34] 54-12083
1. Ave Maria. 2. Mary, Virgin—Meditations. I. Title.

VANN, Gerald, 1906- 232.931
The seven swords; with eight reproductions from the paintings of El Greco. [New York] Sheed and Ward, 1953. 82p. illus. 23cm. [BX2161.5.S6V3 1953] 53-5195
1. Sorrows of the Blessed Virgin Mary, Devotion to. I. Title.

WALTON, Mary Ethel 232.931
The woman God loved. New York, Pageant [c.1962] 192p. 3.50
1. Mary, Virgin—Biog. I. Title.

WEIGER, Josef 232.931
Mary, mother of faith. Tr. by Ruth M. Bethel. Spec. introd. to the Eng. tr. by Romano Guardini. Garden City, N.Y., Doubleday [1962, c.1959] 267p. 18cm. (Image bk., D148) .85 pap.,
1. Mary, Virgin. I. Title.

WILLAM, Franz Michel, 1894- 232.931
The Rosary: its history and meaning. Translated by Edwin Kaiser. New York, Benziger Bros. [1953] 216p. 21cm. Translation of Die Geschichte und Gebetsschule des Rosenkranzes. [BX2163.W513] 53-1421
1. Rosary. I. Title.

WILLAM, Franz Michel, 1894- 232.931
The Rosary in daily life; translated by Edwin Kaiser. New York, Benziger Bros. [1953] 238p. 21cm. Translation of Der Rosenkranz und das Menschenleben. [BX2163.W5312] 54-188
1. Rosary. I. Title.

WORKSHOP on Our Lady in Education, University of Dayton, 1958. 232.931
Our Lady in education; the proceedings of the Workshop on Our Lady in Education, conducted at the University of Dayton, Dayton, Ohio, from June 11 to June 18, 1958, in commemoration of the 100th anniversary of the Lourdes apparitions. Edited by Louis J. Faerber. Dayton, Marian Library, University of Dayton, 1958. 208 p. illus. 24 cm. [BT608.7.W6 1958] 58-59761

1. Mary, Virgin, and education. I. Faerber, Louis Joseph, 1909- ed. II. Title.

BEHRINGER, William. 232.9315
Mary and the Beatitudes. Staten Island, N.Y., Alba House [1964] 128 p. 19 cm. Bibliographical footnotes. [BT602.B4] 63-12678
1. Mary. Virgin — Titles. 2. Beatitudes. I. Title.

BEHRINGER, William 232.9315
Mary and the Beatitudes. Staten Island, N. Y., Alba [c.1964] 128p. 19cm. Bibl. 63-12678 2.25
1. Mary, Virgin—Titles. 2. Beatitudes. I. Title.

CRANNY, Titus F 1921- 232.9316
Our Lady and reunion; an essay on the role of the Blessed Virgin Mary, queen and mother of the world, in uniting all mankind with God. Garrison, N.Y., Chair of Unity Apostolate [c1962] 176 p. illus. 22 cm. [BT638.C7] 62-21829
1. 1. Mary Virgin, and Christian union. I. Title.

CASSIDY, Joseph L 232.9317
Mexico, land of Mary's wonders. Paterson, N. J., St. Anthony Guild Press [1958] 192p. illus. 24cm. Includes bibliography. [BT645.C35] 59-183
1. Mary, Virgin—Cultus— Mexico. 2. Shrines—Mexico. I. Title.

THE Catholic digest. 232.9317
Notre Dame de la Salette in France. St. Paul [1959] 64p. illus. 21cm. (Shrines of the world) [BT660.S33S3] 60-23457
1. Salette, Notre-Dame de la. I. Title.

THE Catholic digest. 232.9317
Our Lady of Einsiedeln in Switzerland. St. Paul [1958] 64p. illus. 21cm. (Shrines of the world) [BX2659.E4C3] 59-17820
1. Einsiedeln, Switzerland (Benedictine abbey) 2. Einsiedeln, Switzerland—Descr. I. Title.

CONNOR, Edward 232.9317
Recent apparitions of Our Lady. Fresno, Calif., Academy Guild Press [c.1960] xvii, 99p. (bibl.) illus. 22cm. 59-12594 2.95
1. Mary, Virgin—Apparitions and miracles (Modern) I. Title.

DELANEY, John J. ed. 232.9317
A woman clothed with the sun: eight great appearances of Our Lady in modern times. Garden City, N.Y. Doubleday [1961, c.1960] 274p. (Image bk. D118) .85 pap.,
1. Mary, Virgin—Apparitions and miracles (Modern) I. Title.

DELANEY, John J., ed. 232.9317
A woman clothed with the sun: eight great appearances of Our Lady in modern times. Illus. by Paul Galdone. Garden City, N.Y., Hanover House [c.1960] 240p. illus. 22cm. 60-5922 3.95
1. Mary, Virgin—Apparitions and miracles (Modern) I. Title.

DE MONTFORT, Odile 232.9317
Ordeal at Lourdes; the new discoveries [by] Odile De Montfort and John O'Meara. [New York, Taplinger Publishing Co.] [1959, i.e.1960] 126p. illus. 19cm. 60-16143 2.00 pap.,
1. Lourdes. I. O'Meara, John, II. Title.

DEUTSCH, Bernard Francis, 1925- 232.9317
Our Lady of Ephesus [by] Bernard F. Deutsch. Milwaukee, Bruce Pub. Co. [1965] xiii, 171 p. illus., plan. 22 cm. Bibliography: p. 165-171. [BT660.E6D4] 65-17607
1 Mary, Virgin — Homes. 2. Ephesus. Panaya Kapulu. I. Title.

DEUTSCH, Bernard Francis, 1925- 232.9317
Our Lady of Ephesus. Milwaukee, Bruce [c.1965] xiii, 171p. illus., plan. 22cm. Bibl. [BT660.E6D4] 65-17607 4.50
1. Ephesus. Panaya Kapulu. 2. Mary, Virgin—Homes. I. Title.

DOOLEY, Lester M., Rev., 1898- 232.9317
That motherly Mother of Guadalupe. [Boston] St. Paul Ed. [dist. Daughters of St. Paul, c.1962] 74p. illus., map. 21cm. 62-20702 1.50; 1.00 pap.,
1. Guadalupe, Nuestra Senora de. I. Title.

FORD, Lauren [Julia Lauren Ford] 232.9317
Our Lady's book. Pictures and words by Lauren Ford. New York, Dodd [c.1962] 269p. illus. (pt. col.) 61-15978 4.50
1. Mary, Virgin—Apparitions and miracles (Modern) I. Title.

GALLERY, John Ireland 232.9317
Mary, vs. Lucifer; the apparitions of Our Lady, 1531-1933. Milwaukee, Bruce Pub. Co. [c.1960] x, 176p. (bibl. footnotes) 23cm. 60-7346 3.75
1. Mary, Virgin—Apparitions and miracles, Modern. I. Title.

HUNERMANN, Wilhelm. 232.9317
Miracle at Fatima; translated from the German by Isabel and Florence McHugh. New York, P. J. Kenedy [1959] 214p. illus. 21cm. Translation of Der Himmel ist starker als wir. [BT660.F3H813] 59-13900
1. Fatima, Nossa Senhora da. I. Title.

LEIES, Herbert F 232.9317
Mother for a new world: Our Lady of Guadalupe, by Herbert F. Leies. Westminister, Md., Newman Press, 1964. xi, 425 p. col. front. 22 cm. Bibliography: p. 417-425. [BT660.G8L44] 64-66034
1. Guadalupe, Nuestra Senora de. I. Title.

LEIES, Herbert F. 232.9317
Mother for a new world: Our Lady of Guadalupe. Westminster, Md., Newman. [c.] 1964. xi, 425p. col. front. 22cm. Bibl. [BT660.G8L44] 64-66034 5.95
1. Guadalupe, Nuestra Senora de. I. Title.

LOCHET, Louis 232.9317
Apparitions of Our Lady, their place in the life of the Church. [Translation by John Dingle. New York] Herder and Herder [1960] ix, 127p. 19cm. 59-14946 2.95
1. Mary, Virgin—Apparitions and miracles (Modern) I. Title.

MARY AMATORA, Sister, 1904- 232.9317
The Queen's heart of gold; the complete story of Our Lady of Beauraing. Fresno, Calif., Acad. Guild [1964, c.1957] 214p. illus. 24cm. 3.95; 1.95 pap.,
1. Beauraing, Notre-Dame de. I. Title.

MARY AMATORA, Sister, 1904- 232.9317
The Queen's portrait; the story of Guadalupe. [Fresno, Calif., Academy Guild Press, 1961] 119p. illus. 27cm. Includes bibliography. [BT660.G8M33] 59-11965
1. Guadalupe, Nuestra Senora de. I. Title.

MARY AMATORA, Sister, 1904- 232.9317
The rose tree; life of Mother Marie Rose Durocher (1811-1849) foundress of the Sisters of the Holy Names of Jesus and Mary. Milwaukee, Bruce [c.1961] 125p. illus. 61-17408 2.50
1. Marie Rose, Mother, 1811-1849—Juvenile literature. I. Title.

PROUTY, Amy 232.9317
Mexican shrines; a pearl for the Lovely Lady. Philadelphia, Dorrance [c.1960] 28p. illus. 60-53142 2.75
1. Shrines—Mexico. I. Title.

ROBERTO, Brother, 1927- 232.9317
The forgotten Madonna; a story of Our Lady of Prompt Succor. Notre Dame, Ind., Dujarie Press [1959] 143p. illus. 22cm. [BT660.P8R6] 59-2781
1. Prompt Succor, Our Lady of. I. Title.

ROBERTO, Brother, 1927- 232.9317
Our Lady comes to New Orleans. Illus. by Thekla Ofria. Notre Dame, Ind., Dujarie Press [1957] 95p. illus. 24cm. [BT660.P8R62] 59-2745
1. Prompt Succor, Our Lady of. I. Title.

WEST, Donald James. 232.9317
Eleven Lourdes miracles. [New York] Helix Press [1957] 134 p. 23 cm. Includes bibliography. [BT653.W4 1957a] 57-14975
1. Lourdes, Notre-Dame de. 2. Miracles. I. Title.

BURDEN, Shirley 232.9317084
Behold thy Mother. Garden City, N.Y., Doubleday 1965 [c.1963] 93p. (chiefly illus.) 29cm. [BT653.B87] 65-10235 7.50
1. Lourdes—Descr.—Views. I. Title.

ANDREW, Marguerite [Sister M. Marguerite Andrew] 232.9318
Journal for Mary. Boston, Christopher Pub. House [c.1960] 227p. illus. 21cm. 60-9031 4.00
1. Mary, Virgin. I. Title.

COLLINS, John H 232.9318
Hail, holy Queen; reflections on a well-known prayer. [Boston] St.Paul Editions [c1963] 69 p. col. illus. 22 cm. [BV469.S3C6] 63-22754
1. Salve Regina. I. Title.

COLLINS, John H. 232.9318
Hail, holy Queen; reflections on a well-known prayer. [Boston] St. Paul Eds. [c.1963] 69p. col. illus. 22cm. 63-22754 2.00; 1.00 pap.,
1. Salve Regina. I. Title.

GEARON, Patrick J. 232.9318
The imitation of Mary. With a pref. by Archbishop Carboni. Chicago, [6415] Woodlawn Ave. Carmelite Third Order Press [1960] 167p. 19cm. 60-809 2.00 bds.,
1. Mary, Virgin. I. Title.

GEARON, Patrick J. 232.9318
In praise of Mary; an explanation of the Hail Mary, the Angelus, the Hail Holy Queen, the Magnificat. [dist. Downers Grove, Ill., Aylesford, Madden at Route 66, The Carmelite Third Order Press, 1961] 186p. 2.50
I. Title.

GEARON, Patrick J. 232.9318
The litany of Our Lady. With a pref. from J. D. Simonds. Chicago, Carmelite Third Order Press] [1960] x, 237p. 19cm. 60-808 2.50 bds.,
1. Mary, Virgin—Titles. I. Title.

MARY save us, 232.9318
prayers written by Lithuanian prisoners in Northern Siberia; tr. by Kestutis A. Trimakas. New York, Paulist Press [c.1960] 71p. facsims. 15cm. .50 pap.,

MONTH with Mary (A) 232.9318
by a Carthusian. Tr. from French by a monk of Parkminster. Springfield, Ill., Templegate [1965, c.1964] xii, 126p. 18cm. [BX2161M6273] 65-3339 3.50 bds.,
1. Mary, Virgin—May devotions. I. A Carthusian.

RAHNER, Hugo, 1900- 232.9318
Our Lady and the church. Translated by Sebastian Bullough. [New York] Pantheon Books [1961] 131p. 21cm. Translation of Maria und die Kirche. [BX2160.2.R313] 58-13487
1. Mary, Virgin—Meditations. I. Title.

VAN Zeller, Hubert, 1905- 232.9318
Our Lady in other words, a presentation for beginners. Springfield, Ill., Templegate [1963] 92 p. 20 cm. [In other words series] Secular name: Claude Van Zeller. [BX2175.A8V36] 63-3366
1. Ave Maria. 2. Mary, Virgin — Meditations. I. Title.

VAN ZELLER, Hubert [Secular name: Claude Van Zeller] 1905- 232.9318
Our Lady in other words, a presentation for beginners. Springfield, Ill., Templegate [c.1963] 92p. 20cm. (In other words ser.) 63-3366 2.95
1. Ave Maria. 2. Mary, Virgin—Meditations. I. Title.

MCCARRAN, Mary L. 232.9319
The life of Mary in legend and art, according to the Apocryphal and Canonical Gospels. Illustrated with reproductions of well known masterpieces. New York, Vantage Press [c.1960] 80p. illus. 60-11705 2.95
1. Mary, Virgin—Art. 2. Mary, Virgin—Legends. I. Title.

ERNEST, Brother, 1897- 232.932
A story of Saint Joseph. Pictures by Carolyn Lee Jagodits. Notre Dame, Ind., Dujarie Press [1957] unpaged. illus. 21cm. [BS2458.E7] 57-4988
1. Joseph, Saint. I. Title.

FILAS, Francis Lad, 1915- 232.932
Joseph: the man closest to Jesus; the complete life, theology and devotional history of St. Joseph. [Boston] St. Paul Editions [1962] 677 p. 22 cm. Includes bibliography. [BT690.F47] 62-22009
1. Joseph, Saint Theology. I. Title.

FILAS, Francis Lad, 1915- 232.932
Joseph and Jesus; a theological study of their relationship. Milwaukee, Bruce Pub. Co. [1952] 179 p. 23 cm. Includes bibliography. [BT690.F48] 52-2821
1. Joseph, Saint. 2. Jesus Christ—Person and offices. I. Title.

FILAS, Francis Lad, 1915- 232.932
Joseph Most Just; theological questions about St. Joseph. Milwaukee, Bruce Pub. Co. [1956] 141p. 23cm. [BT690.F49] 56-9643
1. Joseph, Saint. I. Title.

FILAS, Francis Lad, 1915- 232.932
Joseph: the man closest to Jesus; the complete life, theology and devotional history of St. Joseph. [Boston] St. Paul Eds. [dist. Daughters of St. Paul. c.1962] 677p. 22cm. Bibl. 62-22009 6.50; 5.50 pap.,
1. Joseph, Saint—Theology. I. Title.

FILAS, Francis Lad, 1915- 232.93'2
St. Joseph after Vatican II; conciliar implications regarding St. Joseph and his inclusion in the Roman canon [by] Francis L. Filas. Staten Island, N.Y., Alba House [1969] 168 p. 22 cm. Includes bibliographical references. [BT690.F518] 69-15852 3.95
1. Joseph, Saint—Theology. 2. Vatican Council. 2d, 1962-1965. I. Title.

FILAS, Francis Lad, 1915- 232.932
St. Joseph and daily Christian living; reflections on his life and devotion. New York, Macmillan [1962] 223p. 18cm. (118) 1.45 pap.,
1. Joseph, Saint. I. Title.

FLECK, Raymond, 1927- 232.932
Good Saint Joseph. Illus. by Carolyn Lee Jagodits. Notre Dame, Ind., Dujarie Press [1957] 95p. illus. 24cm. [BS2458.F5] 57-59235
1. Joseph, Saint. I. Title.

GASNIER, Henri Michel 232.932
Joseph the silent. Tr. from French by Jane Wynne Saul. New York, Kenedy [c.1962] 192p. illus. 61-14293 4.50
1. Joseph, Saint. I. Title.

GASNIER, Henri Michel 232.932
Joseph the silent. Tr. from French by Jane Wynne Saul. Glen Rock, N.J., Paulist Pr. [1963, c.1962] 158p. 18cm. (Deus bks.) Bibl. 63-20219 .95 pap.,
1. Joseph, Saint. I. Title.

ISACSSON, Alfred, ed. 232.932
The praises of Saint Joseph. New York, Scapular Press [1961] 94p. 23cm. (The Marian forum, v. 1) [BT690.I8] 61-15732
1. Joseph, Saint. 2. Monstic and religious life of women. I. Title. II. Series.

JOSEPH, Emily, Sister, comp. 232.932
Joseph son of David. Paterson, N.J., St. Anthony's Guild, c.1961. 97p. 1.50; .75 pap.,
I. Title.

LEVY, Rosalie Marie, 1889- 232.932
Joseph, the just man. [Derby, N. Y., Daughters of St. Paul, Apostolate of the Press [c1955] 285p. 22cm. [BS2458.L46] 59-23942
1. Joseph, Saint. I. Title.

LLAMERA, Boniface 232.932
Saint Joseph. Tr. [from Spanish] by Sister Mary Elizabeth. St. Louis, B. Herder [c.1962] 316p. Bibl. 62-10506 5.50
1. Joseph, Saint. I. Title.

MUELLER, Joseph, 1863- 232.932
The fatherhood of St. Joseph. Translated by Athanasius Dengler. St. Louis, Herder, 1952. 238 p. 21 cm. Translation of Der heillge Joseph. [BT690.M813] 52-19915
1. Joseph, Saint. I. Title.

RONDET, Henri, 1898- 232.932
Saint Joseph. Translated and edited by Donald Attwater. New York, P. J. Kenedy [1956] 243p. illus. 21cm. [BS2458.R63] 56-6430
1. Joseph, Saint. I. Title.

SHEED, Wilfrid. 232.932
Joseph. Drawings by Rafaello Busoni. New York, Sheed & Ward [1958] unpaged. illus. 21 cm (A Patron saint book) [BS2458.S45] 58-10560
1. Joseph, Saint. I. Title.

ZELLER, Renee C T 232.932
The book of Joseph. Translated from the French by Salvator Attanasio. [1st ed.] New York, Hawthorn Books [1963] 224 p. illus. 24 cm. Translation of Joseph le charpentier. Includes bibliography. [BS2458.Z413] 63-8018
1. Joseph, Saint. I. Title.

ZELLER, Renee C. T. 232.932
The book of Joseph. Tr. from French by Salvator Attanasio. New York, Hawthorn [c.1963] 224p. col. illus. 24cm. 63-8018 4.95
1. Joseph, Saint. I. Title.

*GEARON, Patrick J. 232.933
Chats with St. Anne. Chicago, The Carmelite Third Order Pr. [1964] 122p. illus. 19cm. 1.25 bds.,
I. Title.

GEARON, Patrick J., D.D., 1890- 232.933
St. Anne, the Mother of Mary. Chicago, Carmelite Third Order Pr. [1961] 172p. illus. 61-66178 2.00 bds.,
1. Anne, Saint, Mother of the Virgin Mary. I. Title.

KEYES, Frances Parkinson (Wheeler) 1885- 232.933
St. Anne, grandmother of Our Saviour. New, rev. ed. New York, Hawthorn [c.1955, 1962] 188p. illus. 26cm. Bibl. 62-8390 5.95
1. Anne, Saint, Mother of the Virgin Mary. I. Title.

KEYES, Frances Parkinson (Wheeler) 1885- 232.933
St. Anne, grandmother of Our Saviour. New and rev. ed. New York, Hawthorn Books [1962] 188p. illus. 26cm. Includes bibliography. [BT685.K4 1962] 62-8390
1. Anne, Saint, Mother of the Virgin Mary. I. Title.

KEYES, Francis Parkinson Wheeler, 1885-1970. 232.933
St. Anne, grandmother of Our Saviour. New York, Messner [1955] 189 p. illus. 26 cm. [BT685.K4] 55-10544
1. Anne, Saint, Mother of the Virgin Mary.

RICHARDSON, Mary Kathleen, 1903- 232.933
Anne. Drawings by Salem Tamer. New York, Sheed & Ward [1960] unpaged. illus. 21cm. (A Patron saint book) [BT685.R5] 60-11678
1. Anne, Saint, Mother of the Virgin Mary—Juvenile literature. I. Title.

DANIELOU, Jean 232.94
The work of John the Baptist. [Tr. from French by Joseph A. Horn] Baltimore, Helicon [1966] 148p. 22cm. Tr. of Jean-Baptiste, temoin de l'Agneau. [BS2456.D313] 66-17079 3.95 bds.,
1. John the Baptist. I. Title.
Available from Taplinger, New York

MATTHEWS, Robert J. 232.9'4 B
A burning light: the life and ministry of John the Baptist [by] Robert J. Matthews. [Provo, Utah] Brigham Young University Press [1972] xviii, 125 p. map. 24 cm. Bibliography: p. 113-115. [BS2456.M34] 71-186683 ISBN 0-8425-1470-8
1. John the Baptist. I. Title.

BAILEY, James H., 1934- 232.9'5
The miracles of Jesus for today / James H. Bailey. Nashville : Abingdon, c1977. 127 p. ; 19 cm. [BT366.B33] 76-51202 ISBN 0-687-27070-7 pbk. : 3.95
1. Jesus Christ—Miracles—Sermons. 2. Methodist Church—Sermons. 3. Sermons, American. I. Title.

BARCLAY, William, lecturer in the University of Glasgow. 232.9'5
And he had compassion / William Barclay. Rev. ed. Valley Forge [Pa.] : Judson Press, [1976] p. cm. Published in 1955 under title: And he had compassion on them. Bibliography: p. [BT366.B36 1976] 75-28099 ISBN 0-8170-0686-9 : 4.95
1. Jesus Christ—Miracles. I. Title.

BARKER, William Pierson. 232.95
As Matthew saw the Master [by] William P. Barker. Westwood, N.J., F. H. Revell Co. [1964] 154 p. 21 cm. [BS2575.4.B3] 64-20185
1. Bible. N. T. Matthew — Devotional literature. 2. Jesus Chirst — Biog. — Devotional literature. I. Title.

BARKER, William Pierson 232.95
As Matthew saw the Master. Westwood, N.J., Revell [c.1964] 154p. 21cm. 64-20185 2.95 bds.,
1. Bible. N. T. Matthew—Devotional literature. 2. Jesus Christ—Biog.—Devotional literature. I. Title.

BECK, Hubert F. 232.9'5
Into the wilderness : dialogue meditations on the temptations of Jesus / by Hubert F. Beck and Robert L. Otterstad. Philadelphia : Fortress Press, [1974] c1975. vi, 90 p. ; 22 cm. Includes index. [BT355.B4] 74-80417 ISBN 0-8006-1082-2 pbk. : 2.75
1. Jesus Christ—Temptation. 2. Temptation. I. Otterstad, Robert L., joint author. II. Title.

BOWKER, John Westerdale. 232.9'5
Jesus and the Pharisees [by] John Bowker. Cambridge [Eng.] University Press, 1973. 192 p. 23 cm. Bibliography: p. [180]-181. [BM175.P4B69] 72-87439 ISBN 0-521-20055-5
1. Jesus Christ—Trial. 2. Pharisees. 3. Rabbinical literature—Translations into English. I. Title.
Distributed by Cambridge University Press, N.Y. 13.50

BRUCE, Alexander Balmain, 1831-1899. 232.95
The training of the twelve. Grand Rapids, Kregel Publications [1971] xiv, 552 p. 23 cm. (Kregel reprint library) Includes bibliographical references. [BS2440.B7 1971] 73-129738 6.95
1. Apostles. I. Title.

BRUCE, Alexander Balmain, 1831-1899 232.95
The training of the twelve; or, Passages out of the Gospels, exhibiting the twelve disciples of Jesus under discipline for the apostleship. 3d ed. [3d ed.] Grand Rapids, Mich., Zondervan [1963] xvi, 539p. 23cm. Bibl. 63-2074 6.95
1. Apostles. I. Title. II. Title: Passages out of the Gospels.

COLEMAN, Robert Emerson, 1928- 232.95
The master plan of evangelism [by] Robert E. Coleman. Introd. by Paul S. Rees. Westwood, N.J., F. H. Revell Co. [1964] 126 p. 19 cm. Bibliographical footnotes. [BT590.E8C6 1964] 64-23345
1. Jesus Christ — Evangelistic methods. I. Title.

COLEMAN, Robert Emerson, 1928- 232.95
The master plan of evangelism. Introd. by Paul S. Rees. Westwood, N.J., Revell [c.1963, 1964] 126p. 19cm. Bibl. 64-23345 2.95; 1.00 pap.,
1. Jesus Christ—Evangelistic methods. I. Title.

DALMAN, Gustaf Hermann, 1855-1941. 232.95
Jesus-Jeshua, studies in the Gospels. Authorised translation by Paul P. Levertoff. New York, Ktav Pub. House, 1971. xii, 256 p. 24 cm. Reprint of the 1929 ed. Includes bibliographical references. [BS2555.D3 1971] 77-149608 ISBN 0-87068-154-0
1. Jesus Christ—Words. 2. Jesus Christ—Language. 3. Bible. N.T. Gospels—Criticism, interpretation, etc. I. Title.

FAIRWEATHER, Eugene Rathbone. 232.95
The meaning and message of Lent. [1st ed.] New York, Harper [1962] 159 p. 20 cm. [BV85.F3] 62-7284
1. Lent. I. Title.

FARRER, Austin Marsden 232.95
The triple victory; Christ's temptations according to Saint Matthew. Foreword by the Archbishop of Canterbury. London, Faith Pr.; New York, Morehouse [c.1965] 96p. 19cm. (Archbishop of Canterbury's Lent bks., 1965) Title. (Series: The Archbishop of Canterbury's Lent book, 1965) [BT355.F29] 65-936 1.75 pap.,
1. Jesus Christ—Temptation. 2. Bible. N. T. Matthew iv, 1-11—Criticism, interpretation, etc. I. Title. II. Series.

FERRIS, Theodore Parker, 1908- 232.95
What Jesus did. New York, Oxford University Press, 1963. 131 p. 20 cm. [BT306.4.F4] 63-11918
1. Jesus Christ—Biog.—Meditations. I. Title.

FERRIS, Theodore Parker, 1908- 232.95
What Jesus did. New York, Oxford [c.] 1963. 131p. 20cm. 63-11918 3.25
1. Jesus Christ—Biog.—Meditations. I. Title.

*GRIFFITH, Leonard 232.95
Encounters with Christ; the personal ministry of Jesus [1st Amer. ed.] New York. Harper [1966.c.1965] 158p. 21cm. (Chapel Bks.-CB29) First pub. in England in 1965 under title The crucial encounter. 1.45 pap.,
1. Jesus Christ—Ministry. I. Title.

HILDE, Reuben. 232.9'5
In the manner of Jesus / by Reuben Hilde. Mountain View, Calif. : Pacific Press Pub. Association, c1977. 143 p. ; 22 cm. (Dimension ; 127) Bibliography: p. 143. [BV4319.H54] 76-14727 pbk. : 2.95
1. Jesus Christ—Teaching methods. 2. Communication (Theology) 3. Witness bearing (Christianity) I. Title.

HOBBS, Herschel H. 232.95
Who is this? Nashville, Broadman Press [1952] 190 p. 20 cm. [BT201.H575] 52-10244
1. Jesus Christ—Person and offices. 2. Baptists—Sermons. 3. Sermons, American. I. Title.

LEE, Frederick. 232.95
Thoughts of Jesus. Washington, Review and Herald Pub. Association [1952] 128 p. 20 cm. [BV4832.L38] 52-38626
1. Jesus Christ—Biog.—Devotional literature. I. Title.

RAVENHILL, Leonard 232.95
Tried and transfigured. Minneapolis, Bethany Fellowship [1963] 144p. 20cm. 63-4213 apply
1. Jesus Christ—Temptation. 2. Jesus Christ—Transfiguration. I. Title.

SCHWEITZER, Albert, 1875-1965. 232.95
The mystery of the Kingdom of God; the secret of Jesus' messiahship and passion. Translated with an introd. by Walter Lowrie. New York, Macmillan, 1950. xv, 174 p. 21 cm. Translation of the 2d part of Das Abendmahl. [BT340.S5 1950] 50-6882
1. Jesus Christ—Biography. 2. Jesus Christ—Messiahship. 3. Kingdom of God. I. Title.

SCOTT, Ernest Findlay, 1868- 232.95
The crisis in the life of Jesus; the cleansing of the temple and its significance. New York, Scribner, 1952. 152 p. 21 cm. [BT303.S43] 52-12810
1. Jesus Christ — Biog. 2. Jesus Christ — Messiahship. I. Title.

SMITH, Betty 232.95
Stories Jesus told. Illus. by Cicely Steed. Philadelphia, Westminster [1963, c.1962] 32p. illus. (pt. col.) 21cm. (Stories of Jesus, bk. 3) .75 bds.,
1. Jesus Christ—Teachings—Juvenile literature. I. Title.

THIELICKE, Helmut, 1908- 232.95
Between God and Satan. Translated by C. C. Barber. [1st ed.] Grand Rapids, Eerdmans [1958] 84 p. 23 cm. Translation of Zwischen Gott and Satan, first published under title: Jesus Christus am Scheidewege. [BT355.T513 1958] 59-10213
1. Jesus Christ — Temptation. I. Title.

THOMAS, George Ernest, 1907- 232.95
Jesus and discipleship. Nashville, Methodist Evangelistic Materials [1961] 78 p. 19 cm. [BT304.2.T5] 61-13210
1. Jesus Christ — Example. I. Title.

THOMAS, George Ernest, 1907- 232.95
Jesus and discipleship. Nashville, Methodist Evangelistic Materials [c.1961] 78p. 61-13210 .50 pap.,
1. Jesus Christ—Example. I. Title.

VANDERLIP, George. 232.95
Jesus, teacher and Lord. Valley Forge [Pa.] Judson Press [1964] 127 p. map. 20 cm. Bibliography: p. 126-127. [BT306.5.V3] 64-15795
1. Jesus Christ — Biog. — Devotional literature. I. Title.

VANDERLIP, George 232.95
Jesus, teacher and Lord. Valley Forge [Pa.] Judson c.1964 127p.map. 20cm. Bibl. 64-15795 1.50 pap.,
1. Jesus Christ—Biog.—Devotional literature. I. Title.

WALKER, Alan. 232.95
How Jesus helped people. New York, Abingdon Press [1964] 158 p. 20 cm. Jesus Christ--Friends and associates. [BS2431.W3] 64-21128
1. Methodist Church—Sermons. 2. Sermons, English—Australia. I. Title.

WALKER, Alan 232.95
How Jesus helped people. Nashville, Abingdon [c.1964] 158p. 20cm. 64-21128 2.75
1. Jesus Christ—Friends and associates 2. Methodist Church—Sermons. 3. Sermons, English—Australia. I. Title.

WAND, John William Charles, Bp. of London, 1885- 232.95'
Transfiguration, by J. W. C. Wand foreword by the Abp. of Canterbury. London, Faith Pr. 1967. 92p. 19cm. [BT410.W3] 67-74302 2.00 pap.,
1. Jesus Christ—Transfiguration. I. Title.
American distributor: Morehouse-Barlow, New York.

WHITE, Ellen Gould (Harmon), 1827-1915. 232.9'5
Confrontation. Washington, Review & Herald Pub. Association [1971] 93 p. 18 cm. Originally published under title: Redemption: or, The temptation of Christ in the wilderness. [BT355.W66 1971] 78-166143
1. Jesus Christ—Temptation. 2. Christian life—Seventh-Day Adventist authors. I. Title.

WOODSON, Leslie H., 1929- 232.9'5
Many signs, one son / Leslie H. Woodson. Chicago : Moody Press, 1975, c1970. 256 p. ; 18 cm. Includes bibliographical references. [BT366.W66 1975] 74-15356 ISBN 0-8024-5180-2 pbk. : 1.50
1. Jesus Christ—Miracles. I. Title.

BIRCH, John Joseph, 1894- 232.952
The temptation or, Christ at the crossroads. [1st ed.] New York, Bookman Associates [c1957] 136p. 23cm. [BT355.B5] 58-255
1. Jesus Christ— Temptation. I. Title.

HANSON, James H 232.952
Through temptation; a series of messages based on Genesis 3 and Matthew 4. Minneapolis, Augsburg Pub. House [1959] 79p. 20cm. [BT725.H2] 59-6984
1. Temptation. 2. Jesus Christ—Temptation. I. Title.

VANN, Gerald, 1906- 232.952
The temptations of Christ, by Gerald Vann and P. K. Meagher. New York, Sheed and Ward [1958, c1957] 126 p. 22 cm. [BT355.V3] 58-5877
1. Jesus Christ — Temptation. I. Meagher, Paul K. joint author. II. Title.

BAIRD, Joseph Arthur. 232.954
The justice of God in the teaching of Jesus. Philadelphia, Westminster Press [1963] 283 p. 24 cm. [BS2415.B32] 62-17787
1. Jesus Christ—Teachings. 2. God—Biblical teaching. I. Title.

BAIRD, Joseph Arthur 232.954
The justice of God in the teaching of Jesus. Philadelphia, Westminster [c.1963] 283p. 24cm. Bibl. 62-17787 6.50
1. Jesus Christ—Teachings. 2. God—Biblical teaching. I. Title.

BALDWIN, Stanley C. 232.9'54
What did Jesus say about that? / Stanley C. Baldwin. Wheaton, Ill. : Victor Books, c1975. 156 p. ; 21 cm. (An Input book) [BS2415.B333] 74-28510 ISBN 0-88207-718-X pbk. : 1.95
1. Jesus Christ—Teachings. I. Title.

BIBLE. English. Selections. 1959. Authorized. 232.954
This He believed; the religion of Jesus of Nazareth as revealed by readings from the Old and New Testaments and other sources. Selected and arr. with comments by Robert O. Ballou. With decorations by Valenti Angelo. New York, Viking Press [1959] 80p. illus. 24cm. [BS2415.A2B3] 59-12455
1. Jesus Christ—Teachings. I. Ballou, Robert Oleson, 1892- ed. II. Title.

BIBLE. N.T. English. Revised standard. Selections. 1970. 232.95'4
What Jesus said about it; all the words of Jesus in the New Testament arranged according to subjects [by] Henry Koestline. New York, New American Library [1970] 175 p. 18 cm. (A Mentor book, MQ977) [BS2261.K6] 72-100556 0.95
1. Jesus Christ—Words. I. Koestline, Henry. II. Title.

BIBLE. N.T. English. Selections. 1969. 232.95'4
Quotations from Chairman Jesus, by David Kirk. With a foreword by Daniel Berrigan. Springfield, Ill., Templegate Publishers [1969] 191 p. 15 cm. Chiefly selections from the New Testament. [BT306.K5] 71-98154 1.95
1. Jesus Christ—Works. I. Kirk, David, 1935- ed. II. Title.

BIBLE. N.T. English. Selections. 1974. 232.9'54
Commandments & promises of Jesus Christ. [Compiled by] David Wilkerson. Glendale, Calif., G/L Regal Reflections [1974, c1973] 63 p. illus. 16 cm. [BS2415.A2W54] 73-87283 ISBN 0-8307-0273-3 1.00 (pbk.)
1. Jesus Christ—Teachings. I. Wilkerson, David R., comp. II. Title.

BIBLE. N.T. Gospels. English. New International. Selections. 1976. 232.9'54
A pocket guide to the sayings of Jesus : [compiled from the New International version of the New Testament] / Bryce D. Bartruff ; [photos by Georgia Waddington]. Minneapolis : Bethany Fellowship, c1976. 188 p. : ill. ; 18 cm. (Dimension books) [BS2415.A2B35] 76-2256 ISBN 0-87123-461-0 pbk. : 1.95
1. Jesus Christ—Teachings. I. Bartruff, Bryce D. II. Title. III. Title: The sayings of Jesus.

BIBLE. N.T. Gospels. English. Revised Standard. Selections. 1973. 232.9'54
The wisdom of Jesus. St. Louis [Published by Pyramid Publications for] Concordia Pub. House [1973, c1971] 63 p. 18 cm. [BS2415.A2 1973] 73-78849 ISBN 0-570-03163-X 0.75 (pbk.)
1. Jesus Christ—Teachings. I. Title.

BIBLE, N. T. Gospels. English Selection. 1967. Revised Standard. 232.95'4
Sayings of Jesus, by Edward Dumbauld. Scottdale, Pa., Herald Pr. [1967] 196p. 20cm. [BS2415.A2Bd] 67-15989 3.75; 2.00 pap.,
1. Jesus Christ—Teachings. I. Dumbauld, Edward, 1905- ed. II. Title.

BIBLE. N.T. Gospels. English. Selections. 1963. Knox. 232.954
Behold the Lamb of God, aspects of Our Lord's personality from the Gospels. Chosen by Robert Murrary. New York, Sheed & Ward [1963] 142 p. 21 cm. "Quotations ... taken from the New Testament in the translation of Monsignor Ronald Knox." [BS2415.A2M8] 63-10494
1. Jesus Christ—Person and offices. I. Murray,.Robert, 1925- comp. II. Knox, Ronald Arbuthnott, 1888-1957, tr. III. Title.

BIBLE. N. T. Gospels. English. Selections. 1963. Knox. 232.954
Behold the Lamb of God, aspects of Our

Lord's personality from the Gospels. Chosen by Robert Murray. New York, Sheed [c.1963] 142p. 21cm. Quotations taken from the New Testament in the translation of Monsignor Ronald Knox. 63-10494 3.00 bds.,
1. Jesus Christ—Person and offices. I. Murray, Robert, 1925- comp. II. Knox, Ronald Arbuthnott, 1888-1957, tr. III. Title.

BIBLE. N.T. Gospels. 232.95'4
English. Selections. 1967. Revised Standard *Sayings of Jesus,* by Edward Dumbauld. Scottdale, Pa., Herald Press [1967] 196 p. 20 cm. [BS2415.A2D8] 67-15989
1. Jesus Christ—Teachings. I. Dumbauld, Edward, 1905- ed. II. Title.

BIBLE, N.T. Gospels. 232.95'4
English. Selections. 1967. Authorized. *The sayings of Jesus. Selected by Kenneth Seeman Giniger. Illustrated by Eugene Karlin.* New York, Golden Press [1967] 62 p. illus. 17 cm. (Golden library of faith & inspiration) "A Giniger book." [BS2415.A2G5] 67-13734
1. Jesus Christ—Words. I. Giniger, Kenneth Seeman, 1919- ed. II. Title.

BIBLE. N. T. Gospels. 232.95'4
English. Selections. 1967. Authorized *The sayings of Jesus.* Selected by Kenneth Seeman Giniger. Illus. by Eugene Karlin. New York, Golden Pr. [1967] 62p. illus. 17cm. (Golden lib. of faith inspiration) A Giniger bk. [BS2415.A2G5] 67-13734 1.00 bds.,
1. Jesus Christ—Words. I. Giniger, Kenneth Seeman, 1919- ed. II. Title.

BOSLEY, Harold Augustus, 232.954
1907-
He spoke to them in parables. [1st ed.] New York, Harper & Row [1963] 184 p. 22 cm. [BT375.2.B6] 63-12050
1. Jesus Christ—Parables—Sermons. 2. Methodist Church—Sermons. 3. Sermons, American. I. Title.

BOWMAN, John Wick, 1894- 232.954
Jesus' teaching in its environment. Richmond, John Knox Press [1963] 120 p. 21 cm. [BS2415.B6] 63-12076
1. Jesus Christ — Teachings. I. Title.

BOWMAN. JOHN WICK, 1894- 232.954
Jesus' teaching in its environment. Richmond. Va., John Knox [c.1963] 120p. 21cm. Bibl. 63-12076 1.75 pap.,
1. Jesus Christ—Teachings. I. Title.

BRANSCOMB, [Bennett] 232.954
Harvie
The message of Jesus; a survey of the teaching of Jesus contained in the Synoptic Gospels. Rev. by Ernest W. Saunders. Nashville, Abingdon Press [c.1954, 1960] 184p. (bibl. footnotes) 19cm. 60-12069 1.50 pap.,
1. Jesus Christ—Teachings. 2. Bible. N.T. Gospels—Theology. I. Title.

BRANSCOMB, Bennett 232.954
Harvie, 1894-
The message of Jesus; a survey of the teaching of Jesus contained in the Synoptic Gospels. Rev. by Ernest W. Saunders. Henry M. Bullock, general editor. New York, Abingdon Press [1960] 184p. 19cm. [BS2415.B67 1960] 60-12069
1. Jesus Christ—Teachings. 2. Bible. N. T. Gospels—Theology. I. Title.

BRETT, Gilbert James 232.954
The words of Jesus, as recorded in the Authorized, King James version of the Holy Bible; comprising the words of Jesus with authoritative adaptations of the Bible text of which they are a part. Arranged and chronicled by Gilbert James Brett. Edited by Melbourne I. Feltman. Consolidated Bk. Pubs. [dist. New York, Grosset, 1962, c.1943,1961] xxvii, 291p. illus. (pt. col.) 16cm. 62-2833 2.95
1. Jesus Christ—Words. 2. Bible. N. T. English. Selections. 1961. Authorized. I. Title.

BUTTERWORTH, Eric. 232.95'4
Discover the power within you. [1st ed.] New York, Harper & Row [1968] xi, 239 p. 22 cm. Bibliographical references included in "Notes" (p. 235-239) [BS2415.B87] 68-17583
1. Jesus Christ—Teachings. I. Title.

CAEMMERER, Richard 232.95'4
Rudolph, 1904-
Earth with heaven; an essay in sayings of Jesus [by] Richard R. Caemmerer, Sr. St. Louis, Concordia Pub. House [1969] 124 p. 21 cm. Bibliographical references included in "The interested reader" (p. 115-117) [BS2415.C32] 69-13724 2.75
1. Jesus Christ—Teachings. 2. Jesus Christ—Person and offices. I. Title.

CARVER, William Owen, 232.954
1868-1954
The self-interpretation of Jesus. Nashville, Broadman Press [1961] 181p. (Broadman star bks.) 60-51583 1.25 pap.,
1. Jesus Christ—Teachings. I. Title.

CLOWER, Joseph B 232.954
The church in the thought of Jesus. Richard, John Knox Press [c1959] 160p. 21cm. Includes bibliography. [BS2417.C53C5] 60-9290
1. Jesus Christ—Teachings. 2. Church—Foundation. I. Title.

CRAMER, Raymond L., 1908- 232.954
The psychology of Jesus and mental health. Grand Rapids, Mich., Zondervan [1965, c.1959] 257p. 21cm. (Cowan Pubn.) Bibl. [BT590.P9C7] 1.50 pap.,
1. Jesus Christ—Psychology. I. Title.

DAUGHTERS of St. Paul. 232.95'4
The teachings and miracles of Jesus. Illustrated by G. B. Conti. [Boston] St. Paul Editions [1970] 128 p. illus. 25 cm. A simple retelling of the teachings and miracles of Jesus Christ. Questions follow each chapter. [BS2416.D35] 76-118182
1. Jesus Christ—Teachings—Juvenile literature. 2. Jesus Christ—Miracles—Juvenile literature. I. Conti, G. B., illus. II. Title.

FAUCETT, Lawrence 232.9'54
William.
Seeking Jesus in his teachings, illustrated by drawings of great artists. Arranged by Lawrence W. Faucett. [2d ed. San Marcos, Calif., 1966, c1962] 88, 6 p. illus. 28 cm. "A source book of the sayings of Jesus in the Gospels for comparison with similar teachings in other great scriptures." [BS2415.A2F3] 66-9835
1. Jesus Christ—Teachings. 2. Jesus Christ—Art. I. Title.

GARRISON, R. Benjamin. 232.9'54
Seven questions Jesus asked [by] R. Benjamin Garrison. Nashville, Abingdon Press [1975] 94 p. 19 cm. Includes bibliographical references. [BT306.G33] 74-19266 ISBN 0-687-38194-0 2.75 (pbk.)
1. Jesus Christ—Words—Meditations. I. Title.

GWYNNE, John Harold, 232.954
1899-
Christ's word to this age. Grand Rapids, Mich., Eerdmans [1965, c.1964] 145p. 21cm. [BS2415.G9] 64-8907 3.00 bds.,
1. Jesus Christ—Teachings. I. Title.

HARRINGTON, Wilfrid J. 232.9'54
Christ and life / by Wilfrid Harrington. Chicago : Franciscan Herald Press, [1975] p. cm. Bibliography: p. [BS2415.H28] 75-12510 ISBN 0-8199-0571-2 : 7.95
1. Jesus Christ—Teachings. 2. Christian life—Catholic authors. I. Title.

HIERS, Richard H. 232.95'4
Jesus and ethics; four interpretations, by Richard H. Hiers. Philadelphia, Westminster Press [1968] 208 p. 22 cm. Based on the author's thesis, "The teaching of Jesus in Christian ethical theory as interpreted by New Testament scholarship," Yale, 1961. Bibliographical references included in "Notes" (p. [169]-200) [BS2417.E8H47] 68-22644 6.50
1. Jesus Christ—Ethics. 2. Christian ethics—Comparative studies. I. Title.

HOLLAND, David. 232.95'4
If Jesus came back to earth. Miami, Croydon House [1968] x, 395 p. 21 cm. [BS2415.H58] 68-31578 7.95
1. Jesus Christ—Teachings. I. Title.

I am the way : 232.9'54
the loving words of Jesus / [selected by Kitty McDonald Clevenger]. Kansas City, Mo. : Hallmark Cards, c1975. [48] p. : col. ill. ; 24 cm. (Hallmark crown editions) [BT306.I2] 74-78839 ISBN 0-87529-394-8 : 5.00
1. Jesus Christ—Words. I. Clevenger, Kitty McDonald. II. Bible. N.T. Gospels. English. Authorized. Selections. 1975.

†INMAN, W. Richard. 232.9'54
A message from heaven and things to think about / by W. Richard Inman. [Sunnyvale, CA] : Inman, c1976. iv, 134 p. ; 18 cm. Imprint from label mounted on p. [2] of cover. [BS2415.A2I55] 76-18436 2.95
1. Jesus Christ—Teaching. 2. Private revelations. I. Title.

LAYMON, Charles M. 232.954
The teachings of Jesus for evangelism. Nashville, Methodist Evangelistic Materials [c.1961] 93p. Bibl. 61-11567 .50 pap.,
1. Jesus Christ—Teachings. 2. Evangelistic work. I. Title.

LEE, Jung Young. 232.9'54
Patterns of inner process : the rediscovery of Jesus' teachings in the I ching and Preston Harold / Jung Young Lee. 1st ed. Secaucus, N.J. : Citadel Press, c1976. p. cm. Includes bibliographical references. [PL2464.Z6L38] 76-8858 ISBN 0-8065-0528-1 pbk. : 5.95
1. Jesus Christ—Teachings. 2. Harold, Preston. 3. I ching. 4. Self (Philosophy) I. Title.

LEVER, Katherine, 1916- 232.954
The Perfect Teacher. New York, Seabury Press [1964] 129 p. 22 cm. [BT590.T;L44] 64-19621
1. Jesus Christ — Teaching methods. I. Title.

LEVER, Katherine, 1916- 232.954
The Perfect Teacher. New York, Seabury [c.1964] 129p. 22cm. 64-19621 3.50
1. Jesus Christ—Teaching methods. I. Title.

LIGHTNER, Robert Paul. 232.9'54
The Saviour and the Scriptures, by Robert P. Lightner. Philadelphia, Presbyterian and Reformed Pub. Co., 1970 [c1966] v, 170 p. 22 cm. Includes bibliographical references. [BT590.O4L5 1970] 65-27480 2.50
1. Jesus Christ—Attitude towards the Old Testament. 2. Bible—Criticism, interpretation, etc.—History—20th century. I. Title.

LOCKYER, Herbert. 232.9'54
Everything Jesus taught / Herbert Lockyer. 1st ed. New York : Harper & Row, c1976. 5 v. ; 18 cm. (Harper jubilee books ; HJ 19-23) Contents.Contents.—v. 1. Everything Jesus taught about Himself, God, the Holy Spirit, the Scriptures.—v. 2. Everything Jesus taught about man, sin, repentance, forgiveness, salvation, righteousness.—v. 3. Everything Jesus taught about faith, humility, money, prayer, the Sabbath, sickness, and death.—v. 4. Everything Jesus taught about love, marriage and divorce, women and children.—v. 5. Everything Jesus taught about angels, Heaven, Satan, Hell, the Kingdom, the Second Coming. Includes bibliographies. [BS2415.L6] 75-36738 ISBN 0-06-065260-8 (v. 1) : 1.95 per vol.
1. Jesus Christ—Teachings. I. Title.

*LOHKAMP, Nicholas 232.9'54
The commandments and the new morality Cincinnati, St. Anthony Messenger Pr. [1974] lx., 172 p. 18 cm. [BS2415] ISBN 0-912228-11-3 1.85 (pbk.)
1. Jesus Christ—Teachings. I. Title.

MCCLELLAN, Albert 232.9'54
The hard sayings of Jesus / Albert McClellan. Nashville : Broadman Press, [1975] 135 p. ; 20 cm. Includes bibliographical references. [BT306.M28] 73-83827 ISBN 0-8054-1340-5 : 3.95
1. Jesus Christ—Words—Meditations. I. Title.

MANSON, Thomas Walter, 232.954
1893-1958.
Ethics and the Gospel. New York, Scribner [1961, c1960] 109 p. 21 cm. [BS2417.E8M3] 61-7225
1. Jesus Christ—Ethics. 2. Christian ethics. I. Title.

MARCH, William J. 232.954
Christian belief and Christian practice. Grand Rapids, Mich., Eerdmans [c.1964] 219 p. 23 cm. 63-22535 3.50
1. Jesus Christ—Teachings. 2. Jesus Christ—Biog. Devotional literature. I. Title.

MINEAR, Paul Sevier, 232.9'54
1906-
Commands of Christ [by] Paul S. Minear. Nashville, Abingdon Press [1972] 190 p. 23 cm. Includes bibliographical references. [BS2415.M53] 72-2926 ISBN 0-687-09113-6 4.95
1. Jesus Christ—Teachings. I. Title.

MONTEFIORE, Claude 232.9'54
Joseph Goldsmid, 1858-1938.
Some elements of the religious teaching of Jesus, according to the Synoptic Gospels. New York, Arno Press, 1973. xii, 171 p. 21 cm. (The Jewish people: history, religion, literature) Reprint of the 1910 ed. published by Macmillan, London, in series: Jowett lectures. Includes bibliographical references. [BS2415.M58 1973] 73-2223 ISBN 0-405-05285-5 10.00
1. Jesus Christ—Teachings. I. Title. II. Series. III. Series: Jowett lectures, 1910.

NEIL, William, 1909- 232.9'54
The difficult sayings of Jesus / by William Neil. Grand Rapids : Eerdmans, [1975] viii, 105 p. ; 22 cm. [BT306.N4 1975] 75-14059 ISBN 0-8028-3467-1 4.95
1. Jesus Christ—Words. I. Title.

PALMER, Lloyd. 232.95'4
On this rock. New York, Philosophical Library [1967, c1966] xx, 307 p. 23 cm. Includes bibliographical references. [BS2415.P33] 66-20217
1. Jesus Christ—Teachings. I. Title.

PALMER, Lloyd. 232.95'4
On this rock. New York, Philosophical Library [1967, c1966] xx, 307 p. 23 cm. Includes bibliographical references. [BS2415.P33] 66-20217
1. Jesus Christ—Teachings. I. Title.

PELZ, Werner. 232.954
God is no more, by Werner and Lotte Pelz. With a foreword by Edward Carpenter. Philadelphia, Lippincott, 1964. 160 p. 21 cm. [BT306.P39 1964] 64-11808
1. Jesus Christ—Words. I. Pelz, Lotte, joint author. II. Title.

PERRIN, Norman. 232.9'54
Rediscovering the teaching of Jesus / Norman Perrin. New York : Harper & Row, 1976. 272 p. ; 21 cm. Includes indexes. Bibliography: p. [249]-266. [BS2415.P4 1976] 76-363301 ISBN 0-06-066493-2 : 4.95
1. Jesus Christ—Teachings. I. Title.

PERRIN, Norman. 232.95'4
Rediscovering the teaching of Jesus. [1st ed.] New York, Harper & Row [1967] 272 p. 22 cm. "Annotated bibliographies": p. [249]-266. [BS2415.P4] 67-11510
1. Jesus Christ—Teachings. I. Bible. N.T. English. Selections. 1967. Revised standard. II. Title.

POWELL, Gordon George, 232.954
1911-
Difficult sayings of Jesus. [Westwood, N. J.] Revell [1963, c.1962] 119p. 21cm. London ed. (Hodder & Stoughton) has title: New solutions to difficult sayings of Jesus. 63-2231 3.00
1. Jesus Christ—Words. I. Title.

RAGSDALE, Ray W. 232.95'4
Foundation for reconciliation: the Beatitudes, by Ray W. Ragsdale. Nashville, Tidings [1969] 70 p. 19 cm. (A Tidings study book) Cover title: Foundations for reconciliation: the Beatitudes. Bibliographical footnotes. [BT382.R3] 70-92793
1. Beatitudes. I. Beatitudes. II. Title. III. Title: Foundations for reconciliation: the Beatitudes.

RAGSDALE, Ray W 232.954
What Jesus proclaimed: sermonic interpretations of the basic teachings of Jesus [by] Ray W. Ragsdale. Nashville, Abingdon Press [1967] 159 p. 21 cm. [BS2415.R3] 67-11006
1. Jesus Christ—Teachings—Sermons. 2. Sermons, American. 3. Methodist Church—Sermons. I. Title.

RAGSDALE, Ray W. 232.954
What Jesus proclaimed; sermonic interpretations of the basic teachings of Jesus [by] Ray W. Ragsdale. Nashville, Abingdon Press [1967] 159 p. 21 cm. [BS2415.R3] 67-11006
1. Jesus Christ—Teachings—Sermons. 2. Methodist Church—Sermons. 3. Sermons, American. I. Title.

RATZLAFF, Lydia Nelson. 232.954
Jesus said... St. Paul, Bruce Pub. Co. [1963] 355 p. col. illus. 24 cm. "Concordant index": p. 295-355. [BT306.R35] 63-20369
1. Jesus Christ—Words. 2. Jesus Christ—Teachings. I. Title.

RIGA, Peter J. 232.95'4
Be sons of your father [by] Peter J. Riga. [Staten Island, N.Y., Alba House, 1969] xv, 126 p. 20 cm. [BT380.2.R5] 75-77648 3.95
1. Sermon on the Mount. I. Title.

RUPERT, Hoover 232.954
And Jesus said . . . The Master's answers to human needs. Nashville, Abingdon Press [c.1960] 143p. 21cm. 60-9202 2.00
1. Jesus Christ—Words. I. Title.

RUPERT, Hoover 232.954
And Jesus said... The Master's answers to human needs. New York, Abingdon Press [1960] 143p. 21cm. [BT306.R78] 60-9202
1. Jesus Christ—Words. I. Title.

SALLAWAY, George H 232.954
Follow me: be human, by George H. Sallaway. Baltimore, Helicon [1966] 174 p. 21 cm. [BT306.5.S3] 66-17081
1. Jesus Christ—Biog.—Devotional literature. I. Title.

SALLAWAY, George H. 232.954
Follow me: be human. Taplinger, 1966] Helicon dist. New York, Taplinger, 1966 Helicon[dist. New York.] 174p. 21cm. [BT306.5.S3] 66-17081 4.50 bds.,
1. Jesus Christ—Biog.—Devotional literature. I. Title.

SANFORD, John A. 232.95'4
The kingdom within; a study of the inner meaning of Jesus' sayings [by] John A. Sanford. [1st ed.] Philadelphia, Lippincott [1970] 226 p. 22 cm. Bibliography: p. 220-221. [BT306.S33] 77-105548 4.95
1. Jesus Christ—Words. 2. Christianity—Psychology. I. Title.

SOCKMAN, Ralph Washington, 1889- 232.954
Whom Christ commended. New York, Abingdon Press [1963] 141 p. 21 cm. [BS2415.S64] 63-11381
1. Jesus Christ—Teachings. I. Title.

SOCKMAN, Ralph Washington, 1889- 232.954
Whom Christ commended. Nashville, Abingdon [c.1963] 141p. 21cm. 63-11381 2.50
1. Jesus Christ—Teachings. I. Title.

STRAWSON, William. 232.954
Jesus and the future life; a study in the Synoptic Gospels. Philadelphia, Westminster Press [1959] 250 p. 22 cm. (The Fernley-Hartley lecture, 1959) Includes bibliography. [BS2417.F7S75 1959] 60-5617
1. Jesus Christ — Teachings. 2. Future life — Biblical teaching. I. Title.

STRAWSON, William 232.954
Jesus and the future life; a study in the Synoptic Gospels. Philadelphia, Westminster Press [1959, i.e., 1960] xii, 250p. (3p. bibl.) 23cm. (The Fernley-Hartley lecture, 1959) 60-5617 3.95
1. Jesus Christ—Teachings. 2. Future life—Biblical teaching. I. Title.

STRUTHERS, Alice Ball 232.954
The word and the way; following the Master teacher to the triumphant life. New York, Exposition [c.1961] 180p. (Exposition-Banner bk.) Bibl. 4.00
I. Title.

TOLSTOI, Lev Nikolaevich, graf, 1828-1910. 232.954
The kingdom of God is within you; or, Christianity not as a mystical teaching but as a new concept of life. Tr. from Russian by Leo Wiener. Introd. by Kenneth Rexroth. [New York] Noonday Press [dist. Farrar, Straus and Cudahy, 1961, c.1905-1961] 380p. 61-10575 4.50; 1.95 pap.,
1. Christianity—19th cent. 2. Evil, Non-resistance to. I. Title.

TOLSTOI, Lev Nikolaevich, graf, 1828-1910. 232.954
The kingdom of God is within you; or, Christianity not as a mystical teaching but as a new concept of life. Translated from the Russian by Leo Wiener. Introd. by Kenneth Rexroth. [New York] Noonday Press [1961] 380 p. 21 cm. [BR125.T683 1961] 61-10575
1. Christianity — 19th cent. 2. Evil, Non-resistance to. I. Title.

TROCME, Andre, 1901-1971. 232.9'54
Jesus and the nonviolent revolution. Translated by Michael H. Shank and Marlin E. Miller. With introd. by Marlin E. Miller. Scottdale, Pa., Herald Press, 1973. 211 p. 22 cm. (The Christian peace shelf) Includes bibliographical references. [BS2417.P2T7613] 73-9934 ISBN 0-8361-1719-0 9.95
1. Jesus Christ—Person and offices. 2. Nonviolence—Biblical teaching. I. Title.

WASSIL, Aly, 1930- 232.954
The wisdom of Christ. [1st ed.] New York, Harper & Row [1965] xv, 224 p. 22 cm. [BT540.W36] 65-15396
1. Jesus Christ—Islamic interpretations. 2. Jesus Christ in literature. I. Title.

WESTON, Sidney A. 232.954
Jesus and the problems of life. Boston [16 Ashbrtn. Pl.], Whittemore Assocs., [rev. ed., c.1961] 110p. .75 pap.,
I. Title.

BALDWIN, Harry Anderson 232.95407
101 outline studies on questions asked and answered by Our Lord. Grand Rapids, Mich., Baker Bk., 1965. 126p. 20cm. (Minister's handbk. ser.) Orig. pub. by Revell in 1938 under title: Asked and answered [BS2415] 66-1049 1.95 bds.,
1. Jesus Christ—Teachings. I. Title.

CAMPBELL, Paul Omar. 232.957
'That they may be one.' Mountain View, Calif., Pacific Press Pub. Association [1953] 160p. 21cm. [BX6121.6.C3] 53-10776
1. Lord's Supper—Seventh-Day Adventists. I. Title.

(COLLINS,) John H. 232.957
The greater love; meditations on the Blessed Sacrament. [Boston] St. Paul Editions [c.1959] 75p. 21cm. 60-101 1.50; 1.00 pap.,
1. Lord's Supper—Meditations. I. Title.

JAUBERT, Annie 232.957
The date of the Last Supper. [Tr. from French by Isaac Rafferty] Staten Island, N. Y., Alba [c.1965] 171p. 21cm. Bibl. [BT414.J313] 65-17975 3.50
1. Jesus Christ—Passion. 2. Jesus Christ—Chronology. 3. Lord's Supper. I. Title. II. Title: Last Supper.

JEREMIAS, Joachim, 1900- 232.957
The eucharistic words of Jesus. [Translated by Norman Perrin from the German 3d ed.] New York, Scribner [1966] 278 p. 24 cm. [BT420.J415 1966] 66-18846
1. Last Supper. I. Title.

MCKELVIE, Martha Groves. 232.95'7
The quest. Illus. by Evelyn F. Haines. Philadelphia, Franklin Pub. [c.1967] ix, 99p. illus. 24cm. [BS2400.M25] 67-28629 4.50
1. Grail. I. Title.

MCKELVIE, Martha Groves. 232.95'7
The quest. Illustrated by Evelyn F. Haines. Philadelphia, Franklin Pub. Co. [c1967] ix, 99 p. illus. 24 cm. [BS2400.M25] 67-28629
1. Grail. I. Title.

RADCLIFFE, Lynn James. 232.957
With Christ in the Upper Room. New York, Abingdon Press [1960] 80p. 20cm. [BT420.R3] 60-5475
1. Lord's Supper. I. Title.

BADHAM, Leslie Stephen Ronald. 232.958
Love speaks from the Cross; thoughts on the seven words. Nashville, Abingdon Press [c1955] 64p. 19cm. [BT455.B2] 55-5044
1. Jesus Christ—Seven last words. I. Title.

BELLARMINO, Roberto Francesco Romolo, Saint, 1542-1621. 232.958
The seven words spoken by Christ on the cross, from the Latin of Saint Robert Bellarmine. New ed. Westminster, Md., Carroll Press, 1950. xv, 235 p. 19 cm. [BT455.B] A 51
1. Jesus Christ—Seven last words. 2. Jesus Christ—Passion. I. Title.

BLACKWOOD, Andrew Watterson, 1915- 232.958
The voice from the Cross; sermons on the seven words from the Cross. [1st ed.] Grand Rapids, Mich., Baker Book House, 1955. 71p. 20cm. [BT455.B55] 55-6504
1. Jesus Christ—Seven last words. 2. Presbyterian Church—Sermons. 3. Sermons, American. I. Title.

BONNELL, John Sutherland, 1893- 232.958
He speaks from the cross; the seven last words [by] John Sutherland Bonnell [and others. Bonnell [and others. Westwood, N.J.] Revell [1963] 126 p. 21 cm. [BT456.H4] 63-7595
1. Jesus Christ — Seven last words. I. Title.

BROWN, Robert R 232.958
The miracle of the cross; the story of the centurion. [Westwood, N. J.] F. H. Revell Co. [c1954] 124p. 20cm. [BT455.B75] 54-5436
1. Jesus Christ—Seven last words. I. Title.

BROWN, Robert Raymond, Bp., 1910- 232.958
The miracle of the cross; the story of the centurion. [Westwood, N. J.] Revell [1954] 124p. 20cm. [BT455.B75] 54-5436
1. Jesus Christ—Seven last words. I. Title.

CHAPPELL, Clovis Gillham, 1882- 232.958
The seven words. New York, Abingdon-Cokesbury Press [1952] 78 p. 20 cm. [BT455.C414] 51-14681
1. Jesus Christ—Seven last words. 2. Methodist Church—Sermons. 3. Sermons, American. I. Title.

DAWLEY, Powel Mills, 1907- 232.958
The words of life; addresses for Good Friday on the words of Christ on the cross. New York, Oxford University Press, 1950. 95 p. (Incl. cover) 19 cm. [BT455.D36] 50-6263
1. Jesus Christ—Seven last words. 2. Good Friday sermons. 3. Protestant Episcopal Church in the U. S. A.—Sermons. 4. Sermons, American. I. Title.

DAY, Gardiner Mumford, 1900- 232.958
Christ speaks from the Cross. Greenwich, Conn., Seabury Press, 1956. 148p. 20cm. [BT455.D38] 55-8744
1. Jesus Christ—Seven last words. I. Title.

DIX, Gregory, Father. 232.958
God's way with man; addresses for the Three Hours. With a foreword by the Bishop of Durham. Westminster [London] Dacre Press [1954]*76p. 18cm. First published in 1953 under title: Power of God. [BT455.D58 1954] 55-43962
1. Jesus Christ—Seven last words. I. Title.

DIX, Gregory, Father. 232.958
Power of God; addresses for the Three Hours given at the Church of the Resurrection, New York, 1951. New York, Morehouse-Gorham Co., 1953. 96p. 19cm. [BT455.D58] 53-1368
1. Jesus Christ—Seven last words. I. Title.

FORD, William Herschel, 1900- 232.958
Seven simple sermons on the Saviour's last words. Introd. by W. A. Criswell. Grand Rapids, Zondervan Pub. House [1953] 89p. 20cm. [BT455.F63] 53-22455
1. Jesus Christ—Seven last words. I. Title.

FOSBROKE, Hughell E W 232.958
By means of death; Good Friday meditations. Foreword by Henry Knox Sherrill. Greenwich, Conn., Seabury Press [c1956] 93p. 20cm. [BT455.F65] 56-12474
1. Jesus Christ— Seven last words. I. Title.

GONZALEZ, Francisco Jose, 1905-1949. 232.958
He reigns from the cross; thoughts on the Passion. Translated from the Spanish by Adele Marie Lemon Foreword by James Francis Cardinal McIntyre. [Boston] St. Paul Editions [1963] 117 p. illus. 19 cm. [BT456.G613] 63-13897
1. Jesus Christ — Seven last words. I. Title.

GONZALEZ, Francisco Jose, 1905-1949 232.958
He reigns from the cross; thoughts on the Passion. Tr. from Spanish by Adele Marie Lemon. Foreword by James Francis Cardinal McIntyre. [Boston] St. Paul Eds. [dist. Daughters of St. Paul, c.1963] 117p. illus. 19cm. 63-13897 2.00; 1.00 pap.,
1. Jesus Christ—Seven last words. I. Title.

HAGEMAN, Howard G. 232.958
We call this Friday good. Philadelphia, Muhlenberg Press [c.1961] 83p. illus. 61-5303 1.50 half cloth,
1. Jesus Christ—Seven last words. I. Title.

HE speaks from the cross; 232.958
the seven last words [by] John Sutherland Bonnell [others. Westwood, N.J.] Revell [c.1963] 126p. 21cm. 63-7595 3.00 bds.,
1. Jesus Christ—Seven last words. I. Bonnell, John Sutherland, 1893-

HOBBS, Herschel H 232.958
The crucial words from Calvary. Grand Rapids, Baker Book House, 1958. 103p. 20cm. [BT455.H58] 58-59823
1. Jesus Christ— Seven last words. I. Title.

HOLT, John Agee 232.958
The seven words. Grand Rapids, Mich., Baker Bk. House, 1961. 95p. 61-17547 1.50
1. Jesus Christ—Seven last words. 2. Baptists—Sermons. 3. Sermons, American. I. Title.

HUGGENVIK, Theodore, 1889- 232.958
Victory by the cross: Lenten mediations. Minneapolis, Augsburg Pub. House [1954] 118p. 21cm. [BT455.H78] 54-654
1. Jesus Christ—Seven last words. 2. Apostles' Creed— Meditations. 3. Indifferentism (Religion) I. Title.

JACOB, William Ungoed 232.958
Meditation on the seven words. New York, Morehouse-Barlow Co. [1960] 50p. 19cm. 60-1439 .80 pap.,
1. Jesus Christ—Seven last words. I. Title.

JONES, Russell Bradley, 1894- 232.958
Gold from Golgotha. Grand Rapids, Baker Book House, 1957 [c1945] 96p. 20cm. [BT455.J6 1957] 57-14771
1. Jesus Christ—Seven last words. 2. Baptists—Sermons. 3. Sermons, American. I. Title.

KEAN, Charles Duell, 1910- 232.958
The inward cross. Philadelphia, Westminster Press [1952] 61 p. 21 cm. [BT453.K36] 51-14921
1. Jesus Christ—Passion—Devotional literature. 2. Jesus Christ—Seven last words. I. Title.

KLEIN, Walter Conrad, 1904- 232.958
The dying Lord. New York, Morehouse-Barlow Co. [1963] 80 p. 18 cm. Jesus Christ -- Seven last words. [BT456.K5] 63-12113
I. Title.

KLEIN, Walter Conrad, Very Rev. 1904- 232.958
The dying Lord. New York, Morehouse [c.1963] 80p. 18cm. 63-12113 1.25 pap.,
1. Jesus Christ—Seven last words. I. Title.

*LINDSAY, S. B. 232.958
The three hours' vigil. New York, Vantage [c.1965] 57p. 21cm. 2.50 bds.,
I. Title.

LOANE, Marcus L., Bp. 232.958
The voice of the Cross. Grand Rapids, Mich., Zondervan [1963] 127p. 22cm. This bk., pts. of which first appeared in 1944 under the title of Vox Crucis, has been rev. 63-23894 2.50
1. Jesus Christ—Seven last words. I. Title.

MCELROY, John Alexander 232.958
Living with the seven words; daily devotions for Lent. Nashville, Abingdon Press [c.1961] 128p. 61-5196 2.00 bds.,
1. Jesus Christ—Seven last words. I. Title.

MARNEY, Carlyle, 1916- 232.958
He became like us; the words of identification. [Nashville] Abingdon [c.1964] 80p. illus. 20cm. 64-10603 1.75
1. Jesus Christ—Seven last words. I. Title.

MUSA, Thomas, 1927- 232.958
The words from the cross. Rock Island, Ill., Augustana [c.1962] 45p. illus., map. 62-8283 1.00 pap.,
1. Jesus Christ—Seven last words. 2. Lutheran Church—Sermons. 3. Sermons, American. I. Title.

RENGERS, Christopher. 232.958
Words from the Cross. Milwaukee, Bruce Pub. Co. [1958] 66p. 20cm. [BT455.R38] 58-7668
1. Jesus Christ—Seven last words. I. Title.

RICARD, Olfert Herman 232.958
Seven times He spoke. Translated from Danish by Bernhard H. J. Habel. Minneapolis, Augsburg Pub. House [c.1960] x, 82p. 20cm. 60-6441 1.75 pap.,
1. Jesus Christ—Seven last words. I. Title.

RICARD, Olfert Herman, 1872-1929. 232.958
Seven times He spoke. Translated from Danish by Bernhard H. J. Habel. Minneapolis, Augsburg Pub. House [1960] 82p. 20cm. [BT455.R513] 60-6441
1. Jesus Christ—Seven last words. I. Title.

SANDERCOCK, Kenneth L. 232.958
The battle of the cross. New York, Morehouse-Barlow Co. [c.1960] 61p. 18cm. 60-6203 1.25 pap.,
1. Jesus Christ—Seven last words. I. Title.

SERMONS and outlines on 232.958
the seven words, by F. W. Robertson and others. Grand Rapids, Baker Book House, 1953. Prose and poetry. [BT455.S38] 53-545
1. Jesus Christ—Seven last words. I. Robertson, Frederick William, 1816-1853.

SHEEN, Fulton John, Bp., 1895- 232.958
Calvary and the mass; a missal companion. Garden City, N. Y., Garden City Books [1953, c1936] 94p. 21cm. [BT455.S44 1953] 53-1800
1. Jesus Christ—Seven last words. 2. Mass. I. Title.

SHEEN, Fulton John, Bp., 1895- 232.958
The rainbow of sorrow. Garden City, N. Y., Garden City Books [1953, c1938] 94p. 20cm. [BT455.S444 1953] 53-29147
1. Jesus Christ—Seven last works. I. Title.

SHEEN, Fulton John, Bp., 1895- 232.958
The seven last words. Garden City, N.Y., Garden City Books [1952, c1933] 63 p. 20 cm. [BT455.S45 1952] 52-2225
1. Jesus Christ—Seven last words. I. Title.

SHEEN, Fulton John, Bp., 1895- 232.958
Victory over vice. Garden City, N. Y., Garden City Books [1953, c1939] 96p. 20cm. [BT455.S46 1953] 54-482
1. Jesus Christ— Seven Last words. 2. Sin. 3. Catholic Church—Sermons. 4. Sermons, American. I. Title.

SPURGEON, Charles Haddon, 1834-1892. 232.958
Christ's words from the cross. Grand Rapids, Mich., Zondervan [c.1961] 120p. 62-932 1.95 bds.,
1. Jesus Christ—Seven last words. I. Title.

THOMAS, George Ernest, 1907- 232.958
Daily meditations on the seven last words. New York, Abingdon Press [1959] 143 p. 20 cm. [BT455.T47] 59-5214
1. Jesus Christ — Seven last words. I. Title.

THOMAS, George Ernest, 1907- 232.958
Daily meditations on the seven last words. New York, Abingdon Press [1959] 143 p. 20 cm. [BT455.T47] 59-5214
1. Jesus Christ—Seven last words. I. Title.

TODD, Galbraith Hall. 232.958
Seven words of love. [1st ed.] Grand Rapids, Baker Book House, 1955. 71p. 21cm. Sermons. [BT455.T6] 55-12068
1. Jesus Christ—Seven last words. 2. Presbyterian Church—Sermons. 3. Sermons, American. I. Title.

TODD, Galbraith Hall. 232.958
Seven words of love. [1st ed.] Grand Rapids, Baker Bk. [1968,c.1955] 71p. 20cm. (Preaching helps ser) Sermons. [BT455.T6] 55-12068 1.50 pap.,
1. Jesus Christ—Seven last words. 2. Presbyterian Church—Sermons. 3. Sermons, American. I. Title.

TURNBULL, Ralph G 232.958
The seven words from the cross. [1st ed.] Grand Rapids Baker Book House, 1956. 53p. 21cm. [BT455.T8] 56-13227
1. Jesus Christ—Seven last words. 2. Presbyterian Church— Sermons. 3. Sermons, American. I. Title.

TURNBULL, Ralph G 232.958
The seven words from the cross. [1st ed.] Grand Rapids, Baker Book House, 1956. 53 p. 21 cm. [BT455.T8] 56-13227
1. Jesus Christ — Seven last words. 2. Presbyterian Church — Sermons. 3. Sermons, American. I. Title.

WALLACE, Ronald S 232.958
Words of triumph: the words from the Cross and their application today. Illustrated by Mary Alice Bahler. Richmond, John Knox Press [1964] 95 p. illus. 21 cm. Bibliographical references included in "Notes" (p. 95) [BT456.W3] 64-10646
1. Jesus Christ — Seven last words. I. Title.

WALLACE, Ronald S. 232.958
Words of triumph: the words from the Cross and their application today. Illus. by Mary Alice Bahler. Richmond, Va., Knox [c.1964] 95p. illus. 21cm. Bibl. 64-10646 2.50
1. Jesus Christ—Seven last words. I. Title.

WRIGHT, John Joseph, Bp., 1909- 232.958
Words in pain; conferences on the seven last words of Christ. Notre Dame, Ind., Fides Publishers [1961] 93 p. illus. 19 cm. [BT456.W7] 61-10367
1. Jesus Christ — Seven last words. 2. Catholic Church — Sermons. I. Title.

WRIGHT, John Joseph, Bp., 1909- 232.958
Words in pain; conferences on the seven last words of Christ. Notre Dame, Ind., Fides [c.1961] 93p. illus. 61-10367 2.95 bds.,
1. Jesus Christ—Seven last words. 2. Catholic Church—Sermons. I. Title.

ALBERIONE, Giacomo Giuseppe, 1884- 232.96
The paschal mystery and Christian living [by] James Alberione. Translated by the Daughters of St. Paul. [Boston] St. Paul Editions [1968] 187 p. illus. 20 cm. [BT431.A413] 68-28102
1. Jesus Christ—Passion—Meditations. I. Title.

BAUMGAERTNER, John H. 232.96
The bitter road; a Lenten journey with the suffering Christ from Bethlehem to Calvary and the Garden [by] John H. Baumgaertner. St. Louis, Concordia Pub. House [1968, c1969] 104 p. 20 cm. [BT431.B3 1969] 68-54219 1.95
1. Jesus Christ—Passion. I. Title.

BENOIT, Pierre, Aug.3,1906- 232.96
The passion and Resurrection of Jesus Christ. Translated by Benet Weatherhead. New York, Herder and Herder [1969] x, 342 p. 22 cm. Translation of Passion et resurrection du Seigneur. [BT431.B413] 75-87748 ISBN 0-232-48110-5 9.50
1. Jesus Christ—Passion. 2. Jesus Christ—Resurrection. I. Title.

BESSER, Wilhelm Friedrich, 1816-1864. 232.96
The passion story, a devotional study of the sufferings of Christ; translated by J. Melvin Moe. Minneap0lis, Augsburg Pub. House [c1953] 328p. 22cm. Translation of Die Leidensgeachichte nach den [BT430.B493] 53-151
1. Evangelisten. 2. Jesus Christ—Passion—Devotional literature. I. Title.

BIBLE. N.T. Gospels. English. Selections. 1967. Authorized. 232.96
The Easter story from the Gospels. Edited by Marguerite Northrup. [New York] Metropolitan Museum of art distributed by New York Graphic Society, [New York] Metropolitan Museum of art distributed by New York Graphic Society, Greenwich, Conn. [1967] Greenwich, Conn. [1967] 40 p. illus. (part col.) 28 cm. The illustrations are from the collections of the Metropolitan Museum of Art. [BT414.N6] 66-29796
1. Jesus Christ—Biog.—Passion week. 2. Jesus Christ—Art. I. I. Northrup, Marguerite, ed. II. Northrup, Marguerite, ed. III. New York. Metropolitan Museum of Art. IV. II. New York. Metropolitan Museum of Art. V. Title.

BIBLE. N.T. Gospels. English. Selections. 1967. Authorized. 232.96
The Easter story from the Gospels. Edited by Marguerite Northrup. [New York] Metropolitan Museum of Art; distributed by New York Graphic Society, Greenwich, Conn. [1967] 40 p. illus. (part col.) 28 cm. The illustrations are from the collections of the Metropolitan Museum of Art. [BT414.N6 1967] 66-29796
1. Jesus Christ—Biography—Passion week. 2. Jesus Christ—Art. I. Northrup, Marguerite, ed. II. New York. Metropolitan Museum of Art. III. Title.

BISHOP, Hugh, 1907- 232.96
The Passion drama. New York, Morehouse-Gorham Co., 1956. 61p. 19cm. 'Talks . . . broadcast in the Home Service of the B. B. C. in Holy Week, 1955.' [BT430.B53 1956] 56-6510
1. Jesus Christ—Passion. I. British Broadcasting Corporation. II. Title.

BISKUPEK, Aloysius, 1884-1955. 232.96
Our Saviour's last night and day. Milwaukee, Bruce Pub. Co. [1957] 78p. 21cm. [BT430.B55] 57-8313
1. Jesus Christ—Passion. I. Title.

BISKUPEK, Aloysius, 1884-1955. 232.96
Our Saviour's last night and day. Milwaukee, Bruce Pub. Co. [1957] 78p. 21cm. [BT430.B55] 57-8313
1. Jesus Christ—Passion. I. Title.

BOESE, Homer H. 232.96
The miracles of Golgotha. Grand Rapids, Mich., Baker Bk. [c.1963] 143p. 21cm. Bibl. 63-21465 2.95
1. Jesus Christ—Passion. I. Title.

BORIES, Marcel. 232.96
Life through the cross; meditation on the Way of the Cross based on the seven sacraments. Translated by Kathryn Sullivan. New York, Desclee [1954?] 111p. 19cm. Translation of Ma vie par la croix. [BX2040] 56-3536
1. Stations of the Cross. 2. Sacraments—Catholic Church. I. Title.

BRODRICK, James, 1891- 232.96
The sufferings and glory of Jesus. Westminster, Md., Newman Bookshop [1958] 71p. 19cm. [BT430.B79] 59-859
1. Jesus Christ—Passion—Devotional literature. I. Title.

BUETOW, Harold A 232.96
To Calvary with Christ. Milwaukee, Bruce Pub. Co. [1960] 136p. illus. 20cm. [BX2040.B76] 60-7392
1. Stations of the Cross. I. Title.

BUNCH, Taylor Grant. 232.96
Memorials of Calvary. Washington, Review and Herald Pub. Association [1962] 190 p. 22 cm. [BT431.B8] 62-9141
1. Jesus Christ — Passion. I. Title.

CARMICHAEL, Joel 232.96
The death of Jesus. New York, Macmillan [1963, c.1962] 275p. illus. 22cm. Bibl. 62-16646 4.95
1. Jesus Christ—Passion. I. Title.

CARTER, Ray Cecil. 232.96
The royal way of the cross. [Philadelphia] Fortress Press [1963] 98 p. 20 cm. [BT453.C3] 63-7902
1. Jesus Christ — Passion — Meditations. I. Title.

CARTER, Ray Cecil 232.96
The royal way of the cross. [Philadelphia] Fortress Pr. [c.1963] 98p. 20cm. 63-7902 2.00 bds.,
1. Jesus Christ—Passion—Meditations. I. Title.

CHARMOT, Francois [Marie] 232.96
From Gethsemani to Calvary. Translated from the French by Richard H. Brenan. Westminster, Md., Newman Press [1959] 71p. 18cm. 60-521 1.50 pap.,
1. Jesus Christ—Passion—Meditations. I. Title.

CHRISTIE, Christie Rev. 232.96
Significance of the Passion. [dist.] Taplinger Pub. Co. 47p. 19cm. (More books) .50
I. Title.

CLOW, William MacCallum, 1853-1930. 232.96
The day of the cross a course of sermons on the men and women and some of the notable things of the Day of the Crucifixion of Jesus. Rev. and enl. ed. Grand Rapids, Baker Book House, 1955. 383p. 20cm. A reprint of the 1909 edition published by Hodder and Stoughton.' [BX7233.C684D3 1955] 55-6505
1. Jesus Christ—Passion—Sermons. 2. Sermons, English—Scotland. I. Title.

COLTHARP, Bruce R. 232.9'6
When they crucified our Lord / Bruce R. Coltharp. Nashville : Broadman Press, [1974] 77 p. ; 18 cm. [BT431.C64] 74-81762 ISBN 0-8054-1929-2 pbk. : 1.50
1. Jesus Christ—Passion—Sermons. 2. Baptists—Sermons. 3. Sermons, American. 4. Dialogue sermons. I. Title.

CONNIFF, James C G 232.96
The story of Easter, by James C. G. Conniff in consultation with Paul Bussard. New York, Dauntless Books [1956] unpaged. illus. 28cm. [BT430.C555] 56-6718
1. Jesus Christ—Biog.—Passion week. I. Title.

CROCK, Clement Henry, 1890- 232.96
Christ's darkest hours; or, The characters of the Passion. New York, Society of Saint Paul [1956] 139 p. illus. 21 cm. [BT430.C584] 57-2367
1. Jesus Christ—Passion—Devotional literature. I. Title.

DICKINSON, Clarence Heber, 1899- 232.96
Seven days & the seven words. Toronto, Ryerson Press [1952] 54p. 21cm. [BT430.D48] 53-32888
1. Jesus Christ—Biog.—Passion Week. 2. Jesus Christ—Seven last words. I. Title.

DODD, Charles Harold, 1884- 232.96
Benefits of His passion. New York, Abingdon Press [1956?] 62p. 16cm. [BT453] 56-5184
1. Jesus Christ—Passion—Devotional literature. I. Title.

DUNPHY, Hubert M. 232.96
In blood-burnt footsteps. Paterson, N.J., St. Anthony's Guild [c.1960] xvi, 84p. illus. 16cm. .50
I. Title.

EDWARDS, Richard Alan. 232.96
The sign of Jonah in the theology of the Evangelists and Q. Naperville, Ill., A. R. Allenson [1971?] viii, 122 p. 22 cm. (Studies in Biblical theology, 2d ser., 18) Bibliography: p. [111]-117. [BS2555.2.E33] 74-153931 ISBN 0-8401-3068-6
1. Bible. N.T. Gospels—Criticism, interpretation, etc. 2. Sign of Jonah. I. Title. II. Series.

ELDERSVELD, Peter H. 232.96
Sharing His suffering. Grand Rapids, Mich., Eerdmans [c.1961] 99p. 61-17396 2.50 bds.,
1. Jesus Christ—Passion—Meditations. I. Title.

ELSNER, Paul J. 232.96
By Thy holy cross; considerations on the Stations of the Cross. Milwaukee, Bruce [1950] 69 p. 19 cm. [BX2040.E55] 50-6411
1. Stations of the Cross. I. Title.

GIROD, Gordon H 232.96
The words and wonders of the Cross. Grand Rapids, Baker Book House, 1962. 154 p. 21 cm. [BT431.G5] 62-21705
1. Jesus Christ — Passion — Sermons. 2. Reformed Church in America — Sermons 3. Sermons, American. I. Title.

GIROD, Gordon H. 232.96
The words and wonders of the Cross. Grand Rapids, Mich., Baker, 1962. 154p. 21cm. 62-21705 2.50
1. Jesus Christ—Passion—Sermons. 2. Reformed Church in America—Sermons. 3. Sermons, American. I. Title.

GOLLWITZER, Helmut 232.96
The dying and living Lord. [Translated from the German by Olive Wyon] Philadelphia, Muhlenberg Press [1960] 123p. 19cm. 59-65320 1.25 pap.,
1. Jesus Christ—Passion—Meditations. I. Title.

GOODIER, Archbishop 232.96
Fifty meditations on the Passion. Springfield, Ill., Templegate [1963] 50p. 15cm. 1.25
I. Title.

GORMAN, Ralph 232.96
The last hours of Jesus. New York, Sheed & Ward [c.1960] 277p. map 22cm. 60-7307 2.50
1. Jesus Christ—Biog.—Passion Week. I. Title.

GORMAN, Ralph. 232.9'6
The trial of Christ; a reappraisal. Huntington, Ind., Our Sunday Visitor [1972] 200 p. 21 cm. [BT431.G67] 70-189319 ISBN 0-87973-811-1 2.95
1. Jesus Christ—Passion. I. Title.

GRAHAM, Eric, Eric Bp. of Brechin, 1888- 232.96
Waymarks of the Passion. Foreword by the Bishop of London. [New York] Longmans [c1961] 85p. 61-2279 1.75; .95 pap.,
1. Jesus Christ—Biog.—Passion Week. I. Title.

GRANT, Frederick Clifton, 1891- 232.96
Christ's victory and ours, a book for Good Friday & Easter. New York, Macmillan, 1950. 85 p. front. 20 cm. [BX5937.G7C5] 50-5696
1. Jesus Christ—Seven last words. 2. Good Friday sermons. 3. Easter—Sermons. 4. Protestant Episcopal Church in the U.S.A.—Sermons. 5. Sermons, American. I. Title.

GRANT, James Ralph, 1908- 232.96
The way of the cross. Grand Rapids, Mich., Baker Bk., 1963. 173p. 20cm. 63-10844 2.95 bds.,
1. Jesus Christ—Passion—Sermons. 2. Baptist—Sermons. 3. Sermons, American. I. Title.

HANSON, E Kenneth. 232.96
The Savior's suffering; sermons on the Passion symbols. Illustrated by Bert Baumann. Minneapolis, Augsburg Pub. House [1964] 79 p. illus. 20 cm. [BT431.H24] 64-13442
1. Jesus Christ — Passion — Sermons. 2. Sermons, American. 3. Lutheran Church — Sermons. I. Title.

HANSON, E. Kenneth 232.96
The Savior's suffering; sermons on the Passion symbols. Illus. by Bert Baumann. Minneapolis, Augsburg [c.1964] 79p. illus. 20cm. 64-13442 1.75 pap.,
1. Jesus Christ—Passion—Sermons. 2. Sermons, American. 3. Lutheran Church—Sermons. I. Title.

HARTMANN, Helen Louise. 232.96
Journey of love; the Way of the Cross through the eyes of a mother, by Helen Louise Hartmann and Janice Brickey. Paterson, N.J., St. Anthony Guild Press [1960] 99p. illus. 16cm. [BX2040.H27] 60-14147
1. Stations of the Cross I. Brickey, Janice, Joint author. II. Title.

HAYNES, Robert Talmadge. 232.96
Christ's eternal invitation. Art: Robert A. Stratton. Richmond, John Knox Press [1963] 62 p. illus. 21 cm. [BT431.H3] 63-7778
1. Jesus Christ — Passion — Meditations. I. Title.

HAYNES, Robert Talmadge, Jr. 232.96
Christ's eternal invitation, Art: Robert A. Stratton. Richmond, Knox [c.1963] 62p. illus. 21cm. 63-7778 2.00
1. Jesus Christ—Passion—Meditations. I. Title.

HEINS, Lester F. 232.96
They were there . . . when they crucified my Lord. Illus. by Paul Kinnear. Minneapolis, Augsburg [c.1963] 79p. illus. 20cm. 62-21817 1.75 pap.,
1. Jesus Christ—Passion—Devotional literature. I. Title.

HOEKSEMA, Herman. 232.96
Man of sorrows. Grand Rapids, Eerdmans, 1956. 129p. 23cm. [BT430.H6] 56-13719
1. Jesus Christ—Passion—Devotional literature 2. Servant of Jehovah. I. Title.

HOUSELANDER, Frances Caryll. 232.96
The way of the cross; written and illustrated by Caryll Houselander. New York, Sheed & Ward, 1955. 173p. illus. 20cm. [BX2040.H68] 55-7479
1. Stations of the Cross. I. Title.

HURM, Ken. 232.9'6
Breakthrough; Christ's journey for everyman. Illus. by Mary Therese Fraize. St. Meinrad, Ind., Abbey Press, 1974. x, 101 p. illus. 21 cm. (A Priority edition) [BT431.H87] 73-94165 ISBN 0-87029-019-3 2.95 (pbk.)
1. Jesus Christ—Passion—Meditations. I. Title.

JONES, George Curtis, 1911- 232.96
I met a man; imagined remembrances of Jesus [by] G. Curtis Jones. Waco, Tex., Word Books [1971] 133 p. 23 cm. Contents.Contents.—Obed and the colt.—Menahem and the guest room.—Judas Iscariot.—Simon called Peter.—Caiaphas the High Priest.—Pontius Pilate.—Claudia Procula.—Barabbas who was released.—Simon the cross-bearer.—Cleopas the new disciple. [BT431.J64] 74-144366 3.95
1. Jesus Christ—Passion. I. Title.

JONES, Robert Franklin, 1911- 232.96
Seven words to the cross. Richmond, Va., John Knox Press [1961] 92p. 21cm. [BT453.J58] 61-7593

1. Jesus Christ—Passion—Devotional literature. I. Title.

KIETZELL, Fritz von. 232.96
Behold the Lamb of God. Translated from the German [by Ernest Gast and Eugene P. Vedder, Sr. Sunbury, Pa., Believers Bookshelf [1969] vi, 116 p. 21 cm. Translation of Der erfullte Ausgang. [BT431.K513] 75-103706
1. Jesus Christ—Passion—Meditations. I. Title.

KRUMMACHER, Friedrich Wilhelm, 1796-1868 232.96
The suffering Saviour; meditations on the last days of Christ. Biog. introd. by Wilbur M. Smith. Chicago, Moody [1966, c.1947] xxvii, 444p. 22cm. (Half-title: Wycliffe ser. of Christian classics) Reissue, with minor revs., of Samuel Jackson's Eng. tr.; first pub. in 1856. Bibl. [BT430.K78] 47-2985 4.95
1. Jesus Christ—Passion—Devotional literature. I. Jackson, Samuel, of Tulse Hill, tr. II. Title.

KUYPER, Abraham, 1837-1920. 232.96
The death and resurrection of Christ; messages for Good Friday and Easter. Tr. from Dutch by Henry Zylstra. Grand Rapids, Mich. Zondervan Pub. House [c.1960] 150p. 61-676 2.50
1. Good Friday sermons. 2. Easter—Sermons. 3. Sermons, Dutch—Translations into English. 4. Sermons, English—Translations from Dutch. I. Title.

LARSEN, Herman Astrup, 1915- 232.96
By man rejected. Minneapolis, Augsburg Pub. House [1953] 197p. 21cm. [BT430.L28] 53-6105
1. Jesus Christ—Passion—Meditations. I. Title.

LIEFELD, Theodore S., 1910- 232.96
According to the Scriptures: New Testament views of the Passion. Minneapolis, Augsburg [c.1962] 70p. 62-9090 1.50 pap.,
1. Jesus Christ—Passion—Devotional literature. I. Title.

LOANE, Marcus L. 232.96
Life through the cross, by Marcus Loane. Grand Rapids, Zondervan Pub. House [1966] 300 p. 23 cm. The 4 chapters were previously published separately. Contents.Contents.—The Man of Sorrows.—The crown of thorns.—The Prince of Life.—Then came Jesus.—Bibliography (p. 299-300) [BT431.L58] 66-22048
1. Jesus Christ—Passion. I. Title.

LOCKYER, Herbert. 232.96
The week that changed the world. Grand Rapids, Zondervan Pub. House [1968] 128 p. 21 cm. [BT414.L6] 68-12946
1. Jesus Christ—Biography—Passion Week. I. Title.

LOGSDON, S Franklin. 232.96
Lingering at Calvary. Chicago, Moody Press [1956] 160p. 22cm. [BT453.L6] 56-2919
1. Jesus Christ— Passion—Sermons. 2. Sermons, American. I. Title.

LOHSE, Eduard, 1924- 232.96
History of the suffering and death of Jesus Christ. Translated by Martin O. Dietrich. Philadelphia, Fortress Press [1967] 120 p. 23 cm. Bibliographical footnotes. [BT431.L6413] 67-11112
1. Jesus Christ—Passion. 2. Bible. N.T. Gospels—Criticism, interpretation, etc. I. Title.

LORD, Daniel Aloysius, 1888- 232.96
His passion forever. Milwaukee, Bruce [1951] xl, 135 p. 22 cm. [BT430.L65] 51-2118
1. Jesus Christ—Passion—Devotional literature. I. Title.

LORD, Daniel Aloysius, 1888- 232.96
His passion forever. New York, All Saints [1962, c.1951] 144p. 17cm. (AS228) .50 pap.,
1. Jesus Christ—Passion—Devotional literature. I. Title.

LUDWIG, Charles, 1918- 232.96
At the cross. Anderson, Ind., Warner Press [1961] 80p. illus. 19cm. [BT431.L8] 61-9721
1. Jesus Christ—Passion—Meditations. I. Title.

LUDWIG, Charles Shelton, 1918- 232.96
At the cross. Anderson, Ind., Warner Press [dist. Gospel Trumpet Press, c.1961] 80p. illus. 61-9721 1.25 pap.,
1. Jesus Christ—Passion—Meditations. I. Title.

LUTHER, Martin, 1483-1546. 232.96
Sermons on the Passion of Christ. Translated from the German by E. Smid and J. T. Isensee. Rock Island, Ill., Augustana Press [1956] vii, 223p. 21cm. Translation of Passion oder Historie vom Leiden Christi Jesu, unoere Hellands. [BT430.L873] 56-13633
1. Jesus Christ—Passion— Sermons. 2. Lutheran Church—Sermons. 3. Sermons, German—Translations into English. 4. Sermons, English—Translations from German. I. Title.

LUTHER, Martin, 1483-1546. 232.96
Sermons on the Passion of Christ. Translated from the German by E. Smid and J. T. Isensee. Rock Island, Ill., Augustana Press [1956] vii, 223p. 21cm. Translation of Passion oder Historie vom Leiden Christi Jesu, unsers Hellands. [BT430.L873] 56-13633
1. Jesus Christ—Passion—Sermons. 2. Lutheran Church— Sermons. 3. Sermons, German—Translations into English. 4. Sermons, English —Translations from German. I. Title.

MCKNIGHT, Felix R 232.96
The Easter story, as retold by Felix R. McKnight. [1st ed.] New York, Holt [1953] 31p. illus. 22cm. [BT414.M22] 53-5503
1. Jesus Christ—Passion— Juvenile literature. I. Title.

MAIER, Paul L. 232.9'6
First Easter; the true and unfamiliar story in words and pictures [by] Paul L. Maier. [1st ed.] New York, Harper & Row [1973] 128 p. illus. 22 cm. [BT414.M3 1973] 72-81346 ISBN 0-06-065397-3 4.95
1. Jesus Christ—Biography—Passion Week. I. Title.

MARMION, Columba Abbot [secular name: Joseph Marmion] 232.96
The Way of the Cross, its efficacy and practice. Translated from the French by a nun of Tyburn Convent. St. Louis, B. Herder [1960] 39p. 17cm. 60-2685 .85 pap.,
1. Stations of the Cross. I. Title.

MARSHALL, Peter, 1902-1949. 232.96
The first Easter. Edited and with an introd. by Catherine Marshall. With illus. by William Hofmann. [1st ed.] New York, McGraw-Hill [1959] 137 p. illus. 22 cm. [BT430.M295] 59-7315
1. Jesus Christ—Passion. I. Title.

MARY MADELINE, Sister. 232.96
In the shadow of the cross. [1st ed.] New York, Vantage Press [1960, c1959] 64p. 22cm. [BT453.M38] 60-578
1. Jesus Christ—Passion—Devotional literature. I. Title.

MEAD, Jude. 232.96
The hours of the Passion. Wood engravings by Bruno Bramanti. Milwaukee, Bruce Pub. Co. [c1956] 145p. illus. 23cm. [BT430.M36] 56-6947
1. Jesus Christ—Passion—Meditations. I. Title.

MEAD, Jude. 232.96
The plaints of the Passion, meditations on the reproaches of the Good Friday liturgy. Milwaukee, Bruce Pub. Co. [1958] 133p. 23cm. [BT453.M4] 58-6898
1. Jesus Christ—Passion— Devotional literature. I. Title.

MEGINNISS, Ben A 232.96
The third hour; meditations on the cross. New York, Morehouse-Gorham Co., 1958. 68p. 19cm. [BT430.M38] 58-5784
1. Jesus Christ—Passion—Meditations. I. Title.

MILLER, Calvin. 232.96
Once upon a tree; devotional essays on the cross. Grand Rapids, Baker Book House [1967] 127 p. 23 cm. Bibliographical footnotes. [BT453.M5] 67-18187
1. Jesus Christ—Crucifixion. I. Title.

NEUHAUSLER, Engelbert. 232.96
The sacred way; Biblical meditations on the Passion of Christ. Translated [from the German] by Gregory J. Roettger. Baltimore, Helicon Press, [c.]1960. 128p. 21cm. 60-10793 2.95 bds.,
1. Jesus Christ—Passion—Meditations. I. Title.

OLSSON, Karl A 232.96
Passion, [1st ed.] New York, Harper & Row [1963] 124 p. 20 cm. Bibliographical footnotes. [BT431.O4] 63-10964
1. Jesus Christ — Passion — Devotional literature. I. Title.

OLSSON, Karl A. 232.96
Passion. New York, Harper [c.1963] 124p. 20cm. Bibl. 63-10964 2.75 bds.,
1. Jesus Christ—Passion—Devotional literature. I. Title.

PATRICK, Johnstone G 232.96
The rainbow and the Resurrection; meditations for Lent, the seven last words, Good Friday, and Easter. Grand Rapids, Zondervan Pub. House [1962] 150 p. 21 cm. [BT431.P3] 63-351
1. Jesus Christ—Passion—Meditations. 2. Jesus Christ—Resurrection—Meditations. I. Title.

PATRICK, Johnstone G. 232.96
The rainbow and the Resurrection; meditations for Lent, the seven last words, Good Friday, and Easter. Grand Rapids, Mich. Zondervan [c.1962] 159p. 21cm. 63-351 2.95 bds.,
1. Jesus Christ—Passion—Meditations. 2. Jesus Christ—Resurrection—Meditations. I. Title.

PURVIANCE, Albert E. 232.96
The other side of Calvary: how we are involved in the Crucifixion--and what we can do about it. New York, Exposition Press [c.1960] 80p. (Exposition Testament) 2.50
I. Title.

RAHNER, Karl, 1904- 232.96
Watch and pray with me. Translated by William V. Dych. New York, Herder and Herder [1966] 63 p. 22 cm. Translation of Hellige Stunde und Passionsandacht. [BT453.R313] 66-13068
1. Jesus Christ—Passion—Meditations. 2. Jesus Christ—Seven last words. I. Title.

RAHNER, Karl, 1904- 232.96
Watch and pray with me. Tr. [from German] by William V. Dych. New York, Herder & Herder Quill [c.1966] 72p. 21cm. [PS3535.A846S6] 66-18432 3.00
1. Jesus Christ—Passion—Meditations. 2. Jesus Christ—Seven last words. I. Title.

*REICH, Wilhelm, 1897-1957. 232.96
The murder of Christ; volume one of the emotional plague of mankind. New York, Pocket Books [1976 c1953] 302 p. 18 cm. [BT453] 1.95 (pbk.)
1. Jesus Christ—Rationalistic interpretations. 2. Jesus Christ—Passion. I. Title.
L.C. card no. of 1966 Farrar, Straus and Giroux edition: 67-64728.

RIGA, Peter J. 232.96
The redeeming Christ [by] Peter J. Riga. Washington, Corpus Books [1969] x, 124 p. 21 cm. Bibliography: p. 123-124. [BT431.R48] 79-83514
1. Jesus Christ—Passion. 2. Jesus Christ—Resurrection. I. Title.

ROONEY, Gerard Jerome, 1908- 232.96
The mystery of Calvary. New York, Macmillan, 1959. 131p. 22cm. [BT430.R74] 59-6979
1. Jesus Christ— Passion—Devotional literature. I. Title.

ROZENDAAL, Henry T., Rev. 232.96
Shadow and light. New York, Vantage [c.1962] 126p. 21cm. 3.50
I. Title.

RUCKSTUHL, Eugen 232.96
Chronology of the last days of Jesus; a critical study. Tr. from German by Victor J. Drapela. New York, Desclee [1965] x, 143p. 22cm. Bibl. [BT414.R813] 65-25985 3.95
1. Jesus Christ—Passion. 2. Jesus Christ—Chronology. I. Title.

SANGSTER, William Edwin, 1900- 232.96
They met at Calvary: were you there? Nashville, Abingdon Press [1956] 111p. 20cm. [BT453.S3 1956a] 56-8744
1. Jesus Christ—Passion. 2. Atonement. I. Title.

SANGSTER, William Edwin, 1900-1960. 232.96
They met at Calvary were you there...? [by] W. E. Sangster. Grand Rapids, Baker Book House [1975 c1956] 111 p. 20 cm. (W. E. Sangster Library) [BT453.S3] 56-8744 ISBN 0-8010-8057-6 2.50 (pbk.)
1. Jesus Christ—Passion. 2. Atonement. I. Title.

SANQSTER, William Edwin, 1900- 232.96
They met at Calvary: were you there? Nashville, Abingdon Press [1956] 111p. 20cm. [BT453.S3 1956a] 56-8744
1. Jesus Christ—Passion. 2. Atonement. I. Title.

SCHLINK, Basilea. 232.9'6
Behold His love. [1st American ed.] Minneapolis, Bethany Fellowship [1974, c1973] 140 p. illus. 18 cm. (Dimension books) [BT431.S28 1974] 74-174402 ISBN 0-87123-039-9 1.45 (pbk.).
1. Jesus Christ—Passion—Meditations. I. Title.

SCHULTZ, John Ahern. 232.9'6
Prelude to victory : an instructional commentary on the trial and crucifixion of Jesus Christ / by John Ahern Schultz. Ambler, Pa. : Trinity Press, [1975] 76 p. : ill. ; 28 cm. Cover title. Bibliography: p. 76. [BT431.S34] 74-84323 ISBN 0-912046-10-4 pbk. : 5.95
1. Jesus Christ—Passion. I. Title.

SESSIONS, Will. 232.96
Week of the cross. St. Louis, Bethany Press [1960] 96 p. 21 cm. [BT414.S45] 60-6227
1. Jesus Christ — Biog. — Passion Week. I. Title.

SESSIONS, Will 232.96
Week of the cross. St. Louis, Bethany Press [c.1960] 96p. 21cm. 60-6227 2.00 bds.,
1. Jesus Christ—Biog.—Passion Week. I. Title.

SHEEN, Fulton John, Bp., 1895- 232.96
Characters of the passion. Garden City, N. Y., Garden City Books [1953, c1947] 95p. 21cm. [BT430.S47 1953] 53-1797
1. Jesus Christ—Passion. 2. Bible. N. T. Gospels—Biog. I. Title.

SHEEN, Fulton John, Bp., 1895- 232.96
The way of the cross. Garden City, N.Y., Garden City Books [1956? c1932] unpaged. illus. 13 cm. [BX2040] 56-286
1. Stations of the Cross. I. Title.

SHEEN, Fulton John, Bp., 1895- 232.96
The way of the cross. Garden City, N. Y., Garden City Books [1956? c1932] unpaged. illus. 13cm. [BX2040] 56-286
1. Stations of the Cross. I. Title.

SOUTHWELL, Robert, Saint, 1561?-1595. 232.9'6
Marie Magdalens funeral teares (1591) / by Robert Southwell. A facsim. reproduction / with an introd. by Vincent B. Leitch. Delmar, N.Y. : Scholars' Facsimiles & Reprints, 1975 c1974. 68 p. ; 21 cm. Reprint of the ed. printed by J. W. for G. C., London. [BT430.S64 1591a] 74-22099 ISBN 0-8201-1144-9 : 10.00
1. Jesus Christ—Passion. 2. Mary Magdalene, Saint. I. Title.

SPECTER, Ruth Rachel. 232.96
On what day did Christ die? A day-by-day account of events in Jesus Christ's last week on earth. Foreword by P. A. Gaglardi. (1st ed.) New York, Exposition Press (c1958) 86 p. illus. 21 cm. Includes bibliographies. [BT414.S6] 60-1452
1. Jesus Christ — Biog. — Passion Week. I. Title.

SPECTER, Ruth Rachel 232.96
On what day did Christ die? A day-by-day account of events in Jesus Christ's last week on earth. Foreword by P. A. Gaglardi. New York, Exposition Press [c.1959] 86 p. foldout diagr. 21 cm. (Bibl.) 60-1452 3.00
1. Jesus Christ—Biog.—Passion Week. I. Title.

*SPURGEON, C. H. 232.96
The passion and death of Christ. Grand Rapids, Mich., Eerdmans [1965] 152p. 20cm. 1.45 pap.,
I. Title.

STEINHAEUSER, Albert Theodore William 1876-1924 232.96
The man of sorrows; a book of Lenten devotions on the passion of Our Lord. Minneapolis, Augsburg [1964, c.1925] x, 293p. 20cm. 51-30534 1.95 pap.,
1. Jesus Christ—Passion—Meditations. 2. Lent—Prayer-books and devotions—English. I. Title.

STREUFERT, Paul William, 1903- 232.96
King ever glorious; the story of Holy Week. Saint Louis, Concordia Pub. House [1955] 112p. 19cm. [BV4298.S87] 55-6437
1. Holy-Week sermons. 2. Lutheran Church—Sermons. 3. Sermons, American. I. Title.

TARGET, George William. 232.96
Watch with me; spiritual exercises toward learning the lesson of penitence and humiliation at the foot of the cross. Philadelphia, Westminster Press [1961] 95 p. 19 cm. [BV4813.T35] 62-17396
1. Meditation. 2. Jesus Christ — Passion — Meditations. I. Title.

TARGET, George William 232.96
Watch with me; spiritual exercises toward learning the lesson penitence and humiliation at the foot of the cross. Philadelphia, Westminster [1963, c.1961] 95p. 19cm. 62-17396 1.65 pap.,
1. Meditation. 2. Jesus Christ—Passion—Meditations. I. Title.

THOLUCK, August, 1799- 1877. 232.96
Light from the cross; with a biographical introd. by J. C. Macaulay. Chcago, Moody Press, 1952. 293 p. 23 cm. (The Wycliffe series of Christian classics) "Translator's preface" signed: R. L. B. [i. e. Robert Christopher Lundin Brown] Full name: Friedrich August Gottreu Tholuck. [BT430.T4] 52-2780
1. Jesus Christ — Passion — Sermons. 2. Sermons, English — Translations from German. 3. Sermons, German — Translations into English. I. Title.

TODD, Galbraith Hall. 232.96
Culture and the cross. Grand Rapids, Baker Book House, 1959. 111 p. 21 cm. [BV4253.T65] 59-15535
1. Sermons, American. I. Title.

TODD, Galbraith Hall 232.96
Culture and the cross. Grand Rapids, Mich., Baker Book House, [c.]1959. 111p. 21cm. 59-15535 2.00
1. Sermons, American. I. Title.

VAN ZELLER, Hubert, 1905- 232.96
Approach to Calvary. New York, Sheed and Ward [1961] 128 p. illus. 10 cm. Secular name: Calude Van Zeller. [BX2040.V3] 61-7282
1. Stations of the Cross. I. Title. II. Series.

VAN ZELLER, Hubert, 1905- 232.96
[Secularname:ClaudeVanZeller]
Approach to Calvary. New York, Sheed and Ward [c.1961] 128p. illus. 61-7282 2.95 half cloth,
1. Stations of the Cross. I. Title.

VEUTHEY, Leon. 232.96
The Way of the Cross. Translated by Theodoric Kernel. Chicago, Franciscan Herald Press [c1956] 106p. illus. 20cm. (Franciscan spirituality, no.3) [BX2040.V42] 57-1029
1. Stations of the Cross. I. Title.

VEUTHEY, Leon. 232.96
The Way of the Cross. Translated by Theodoric Kernel. Chicago, Franciscan Herald Press [c1956] 106 p. illus. 20 cm. (Franciscan spirituality, no. 8) [BX2040.V42] 57-1029
1. Stations of the Cross. I. Title.

WANSBROUGH, Henry, 1934- 232.9'6
The passion / Henry Wansbrough. Staten Island, N.Y. : Alba House, 1975, c1972. 111 p. ; 19 cm. (Scripture for meditation ; 7) [BT431.W36 1975] 74-31341 ISBN 0-8189-0312-0 pbk. : 1.95
1. Jesus Christ—Passion—Meditations. I. Title. II. Series.

WHITE, Reginald E O 232.96
Beneath the cross of Jesus; meditations on the Passion of Our Lord. [1st ed.] Grand Rapids, Eerdmans [1959] 159 p. 22 cm. [BT453.W5] 59-14587
1. Jesus Christ — Passion — Meditations. I. Title.

WHITE, Reginald E. O. 232.96
Beneath the cross of Jesus; meditations on the Passion of Our Lord. Grand Rapids, Mich., Eerdmans [c.1959] 159p. 22cm. 59-14578 3.00
1. Jesus Christ—Passion—Meditations. I. Title.

WHITE, Reginald E. O. 232.96
Beneath the cross of Jesus. Meditations on the passion of our lord. New Canaan, Conn., Keats Publishing [1975, c1959] 159 p., 20 cm. [BT453.W5] 2.25 (pbk.)
1. Jesus Christ—Passion—Meditations. I. Title.

WILLIAMS, Clayton Edgar 232.96
The dark road to triumph; Passion Week sermons from a Paris pulpit, including meditations on the seven words from the cross. Foreword by Ralph W. Sockman. New York, Crowell [1960] xviii, 110p. 21cm. 60-8256 2.75
1. Jesus Christ—Passion—Sermons. 2. Jesus Christ—Seven last words. I. Title.

WILSON, Ernest Charles, 1896- 232.96
The week that changed the world [by] Ernest C. Wilson. Lee's Summit, Mo., Unity Books [1968] 212 p. 20 cm. [BT414.W54] 68-15193
1. Jesus Christ—Biography—Passion Week. I. Title.

WILSON, William Riley. 232.96
The execution of Jesus; a judicial, literary, and historical investigation. New York, Scribner [1970] x, 243 p. 22 cm. Bibliography: p. 227-240. [BT431.W48] 70-123334 7.95
1. Jesus Christ—Passion. I. Title.

WYON, Olive, 1890- 232.96
Consider Him; three meditations on the Passion story. New York, Abingdon Press [1957, c1956] 64 p. 16 cm. [BT430.W9 1957] 57-5081
1. Jesus Christ — Passion — Meditations. I. Title.

WYON, Olive, 1890- 232.96
The grace of the Passion. Philadelphia, Fortress [1965, c.1959] x, 69p. 18cm. Bibl. [BT431.W9] 65-13405 1.50 pap.,
1. Jesus Christ—Passion—Meditations. I. Title.

FLETCHER, Howard A. 232.961
Saint Judas Iscariot. Introd. by Ananda Bhavanani. New York, Vantage Press [c.1961] 144p. 61-4041 3.00
I. Title.

GARTNER, Bertil Edgar, 1924- 232.96'1
Iscariot, by Bertil Gartner. Translated by Victor I. Gruhn. Philadelphia, Fortress Press [1971] xvii, 46 p. 20 cm. (Facet books. Biblical series, 29) "Translation from the German of ... 'Judas Iskariot,' an essay which appeared in Die ratselhaften Termini Nazoraer und Iskariot (Horae Soederblomianae ... 4) A Swedish version ... appeared in Svensk exegetisk arsbok 21 [1956]: 50-81." Bibliography: p. 40-45. [BS2460.J8G2413] 73-157544 ISBN 0-8006-3065-3 1.00
1. Judas Iscariot. I. Title.

BLINZLER, Josef, 1910- 232.962
The trial of Jesus; the Jewish and Roman proceedings against Jesus Christ described and assessed from the oldest accounts by Josef Blinzler. Translated from the 2d rev. and enl. ed. by Isabel and Florence McHugh. Westminster, Md., Newman Press, 1959. 312 p. illus. 23 cm. Includes bibliography. [BT440.B613] 59-10400
1. Jesus Christ—Trial. I. Title.

BLINZLER, Joseph. 232.962
The trial of Jesus; the Jewish and Roman proceedings against Jesus Christ described and assessed from the oldest accounts by Josef Blinzler. Translated from the 2d rev. and Nl. ed. by Isabel and Florence McHugh. Westminster, Md. Newman Press, 1959. 312p. illus. 23cm. Includes bibliography. [BT44o.B613] 59-10400
1. Jesus Christ—Trial. I. Title.

BRANDON, Samuel George Frederick. 232.96'2
The trial of Jesus of Nazareth [by] S. G. F. Brandon. New York, Stein and Day [1968] 223 p. illus. 23 cm. (Historic trials series) Bibliography: p. [204]-210. [BT440.B7 1968] 68-9206 6.95
1. Jesus Christ—Trial. I. Title.

CHANDLER, Walter Marion, 1867-1935. 232.962
The trial of Jesus from a lawyer's standpoint. [Complete reprint ed.] Atlanta, Harrison Co. [1956] 2v. in 1. Illus. 25cm. Bibliography: v. 2. p. 383-387. [BT440.C4 1956] 56-38467
1. Jesus Christ—Trial. I. Title.

CHANDLER, Walter Marion, 1867-1935. 232.9'62
The trial of Jesus from a lawyer's standpoint / by Walter M. Chandler ; ill. by William M. McLane. Illustrated ed. Norcross, Ga. : Harrison Co., c1976. 2 v. in 1 : ill. ; 27 cm. Includes index. Bibliography: v. 2, p. [191]-193. [BT440.C4 1976] 77-356039
1. Jesus Christ—Trial. I. Title.

COHN, Haim Hermann, 1911- 232.96'2
The trial and death of Jesus, by Haim Cohn. [1st U.S. ed.] New York, Harper & Row [1971] xxiv, 419 p. 22 cm. (A Cass Canfield book) Based in part on the author's Mishpato u-moto shel Yeshu ha-notsri (romanized form) Bibliography: p. 393-411. [BT440.C642 1971] 75-123922 ISBN 0-06-010818-5 12.50
1. Jesus Christ—Trial. 2. Jesus Christ—Crucifixion. I. Title.

GALLAGHER, Augustine F. 232.96'2
Jewish and Roman acquittal, by A. F. Gallagher. [Cleveland, Printed by Gates Legal Pub. Co., 1967] 50 p. 24 cm. Cover title. [BT440.G34] 71-15909
1. Jesus Christ—Trial. I. Title.

JUEL, Donald. 232.9'62
Messiah and temple : the trial of Jesus in the Gospel of Mark / by Donald Juel. Missoula, Mont. : Published by Scholars Press for the Society of Biblical Literature, c1977. 223 p. ; 22 cm. (Dissertation series - Society of Biblical Literature ; no. 31) Bibliography: p. 217-223. [BT440.J8] 76-46397 ISBN 0-89130-120-8 : 4.50
1. Jesus Christ—Trial. 2. Bible. N.T. Mark—Criticism, interpretation, etc. I. Society of Biblical Literature. II. Title. III. Series: Society of Biblical Literature. Dissertation series ; no. 31.

SLOYAN, Gerard Stephen, 1919- 232.9'62
Jesus on trial; the development of the Passion narratives and their historical and ecumenical implications. Edited, with an introd., by John Reumann. Philadelphia, Fortress Press [1973] xix, 156 p. 18 cm. Bibliography: p. 135-149. [BT440.S56] 73-79040 ISBN 0-8006-1033-4 3.75
1. Jesus Christ—Trial. 2. Jesus Christ—Passion—Role of Jews. I. Title.

STALKER, James, 1848- 1927. 232.96'2
The trial and death of Jesus Christ; a devotional history of Our Lord's passion. Grand Rapids, Zondervan Pub. House [1970] 185 p. 21 cm. Includes bibliographical references. [BT430.S7 1970] 79-20314
1. Jesus Christ—Trial. 2. Jesus Christ—Crucifixion. I. Title.

THE Trial of Jesus. 232.96'2
Cambridge studies in honour of C. F. D. Moule. Edited by Ernest Bammel. Naperville, Ill., A. R. Allenson [1970] xiii, 177 p. 22 cm. (Studies in Biblical theology, 2d ser., 13) Contents.Contents.—The Israel-idea in the Passion narratives, by P. Richardson.—Ex illa itaque die consilium fecerunt ..., by E. Bammel.—John 11.50, by M. Barker.—The problem of the historicity of the Sanhedrin trial, by D. R. Catchpole.—Peter's curse, by H. Merkel.—The charge of blasphemy at Jesus' trial before the Sanhedrin, by J. C. O'Neill.—Why Pilate? By J. E. Allen.—Why did Pilate hand Jesus over to Antipas? By H. W. Hoehner.—The cry of the centurion - a cry of defeat, by J. Pobee.—The trial of Jesus in Jewish tradition, by W. Horbury.—The ego-proclamation in Gnostic sources, by G. W. MacRae.—Nothing more negative ... a concluding unscientific postscript to historical research on the trial of Jesus, by R. Morgan.—The Jewish punishment of stoning in the New Testament period, by J. Blinzler.—Crucifixion as a punishment in Palestine, by E. Bammel. Includes bibliographical references. [BT440.T75] 73-131584
1. Jesus Christ—Trial—Addresses, essays, lectures. I. Moule, Charles Francis Digby. II. Bammel, Ernst, ed. III. Title. IV. Series.

WINGO, Earl L. 232.962
The illegal trial of Jesus [Bobbs. Dist. New York, Macfadden, 1962, c.1954] 142p. 21cm. (Charter bks. 120) 1.45 pap.,
1. Jesus Christ—Trial. I. Title.

WINTER, Paul, writer on religion. 232.9'62
On the trial of Jesus / by Paul Winter. 2d ed. / rev. and edited by T. A. Burkill and Geza Vermes. Berlin ; New York : De Gruyter, 1974. xxii, 225 p. ; 24 cm. (Studia Judaica, Forschungen zur Wissenschaft des Judentums ; Bd. 1) Includes index. Bibliography: p. [209]-217. [BT440.W74 1974] 73-94226 ISBN 3-11-002283-4 : 21.40
1. Jesus Christ—Trial. I. Burkill, T. Alec, ed. II. Vermes, Geza, ed. III. Title. IV. Series.

ZEITLIN, Solomon, 1892- 232.962
Who crucified Jesus? [4th ed.] New York, Bloch Pub. Co. [1964] xxii, 250 p. 21 cm. Bibliography: p. 226-227. [BM620.Z4] 64-7855
1. Jesus Christ — Crucifixion. 2. Jesus Christ — Jewish interpretations. I. Title.

ZEITLIN, Solomon, 1892- 232.962
Who crucified Jesus? [4th ed.] New York, Bloch [c.1964] xxii, 250p. 22cm. Bibl. 64-7855 4.50
1. Jesus Christ—Crucifixion. 2. Jesus Christ—Jewish interpretations. I. Title.

BALTHASAR, Hans Urs von, 1905- 232.96'3
The way of the cross. Drawings by Joseph Hegenbarth. Translated by Rodelinde Albrecht and Maureen Sullivan. [New York] Herder and Herder [1969] 30 p. illus. 20 cm. Translation of Der Kreuzweg der St-Hedwigs Kathedrale in Berlin. [BX2040.B313 1969b] 69-17500 2.50
1. Stations of the Cross. I. Title.

BARBET, Pierre. 232.963
A doctor at Calvary; the Passion of Our Lord Jesus Christ as Described by a surgeon. Translated by the Earl of Wicklow. New York, P. J. Kenedy [1953?] 178p. illus. 22cm. [BT450.B32] 54-5015
1. Jesus Christ—Crucifixion. 2. Jesus Christ—Passion. 3. Holy Shroud. I. Title.

BARBET, Pierre, M.D. 232.963
A doctor at Calvary; the Passion of Our Lord Jesus Christ as described by a surgeon. Tr. by the Earl of Wicklow. Garden City, N.Y., Doubleday, 1963] 213p. illus. 17cm. (Image bk., D155) .85 pap.,
1. Jesus Christ—Crucifixion. 2. Jesus Christ.—Passion. 3. Holy Shroud. I. Title.

BISHOP, James Alonzo, 1907- 232.9'63
The day Christ died / Jim Bishop. New York : Harper & Row, [1977] c1957. p. cm. Bibliography: p. [BT450.B54 1977] 77-10020 ISBN 0-06-060786-6 : pbk. : 1.95
1. Jesus Christ—Crucifixion. 2. Christian biography—Palestine. I. Title.

BRIDGER, Gordon Frederick. 232.9'63
A day that changed the world / Gordon Bridger. Downers Grove, Ill. : Intervarsity Press, 1975. 96 p. ; 18 cm. Includes bibliographies. [BT450.B7] 75-7246 ISBN 0-87784-483-6 pbk. : 1.95
1. Jesus Christ—Crucifixion. 2. Jesus Christ—Person and offices. I. Title.

CHRIST is victor / 232.9'63
by W. Glynn Evans, ed[itor]. Valley Forge, Pa. : Judson Press, [1977] p. cm. [BT268.C46] 77-79774 ISBN 0-8170-0756-3 pbk. : 3.95
1. Jesus Christ—Crucifixion—Sermons. 2. Jesus Christ—Resurrection—Sermons. I. Evans, William Glynn.

COFFIN, Henry Sloane, 1877-1954. 232.963
The meaning of the Cross. With a new pref. by James T. Cleland. New York, Scribner [1959] 164p. 20cm. [BT453.C58 1959] 59-8077
1. Jesus Christ—Passion—Devotional literature. 2. Atonement. I. Title.

THE Crucifixion, 232.9'63
by an eye witness. [7th ed. Las Vegas, Nev., J. M. Harvey, c1971] iii, 107 p. 19 cm. (Supplemental harmonic series, v. 4) Published also under titles, "Important historical disclosures about the real manner of the death of Jesus," Allegheny, Pa., 1880; "The crucifixion and the resurrection of Jesus, by an eye-witness," Los Angeles, 1919. German ed. published in Leipzig, 1849; French ed., under title, "La mort de Jesus," Paris, 1863. [BT520.I6 1971] 70-186124
1. Jesus Christ—Crucifixion—Apocryphal and legendary literature. 2. Jesus Christ—Resurrection—Apocryphal and legendary literature. 3. Essenes. I. An eye witness.

HAMMES, John A 232.963
To help you follow the way of the Cross; brief meditations drawn from the Scriptures. Milwaukee, Bruce Pub. Co. [1964] vi, 120 p. 16 cm. [BX2040.H26] 64-13748
1. Stations of the Cross. I. Title.

HAMMES, John A. 232.963
To help you follow the way of the Cross: brief meditations drawn from the Scriptures. Milwaukee, Bruce [c.1964] vi, 120p. 16cm. 64-13748 1.50 pap.,
1. Stations of the Cross. I. Title.

HARDINGE, Leslie 232.963
These watched Him die. Washington, Review & Herald [1966] 128p. 22cm. [BT450.H26] 66-19415 3.95
1. Jesus Christ—Crucifixion. I. Title.

HUSAYN, Muhammad Kamil, 1901- 232.963
City of wrong; a Friday in Jerusalem [by] M. Kamel Ilussein. Tr. from Arabic, introd., by Kenneth Cragg. New York, Seabury [1966, c.1959] xxv, 225p. 21cm. (SP28) [BP172.H813 1966] 66-22992 1.95 pap.,
1. Jesus Christ—Islamic interpretations. I. Title.

JONES, Russell Bradley, 1894- 232.963
Calvary attitudes. Grand Rapids, Baker Book House, 1958. 80p. 20cm. [BV4277.J6] 58-11761
1. Lenten sermons. 2. Baptists—Sermons. 3. Sermons, American. I. Title.

KNUTSON, Kent S. 232.96'3
God's drama in seven acts; meditations on the words of Christ from the cross, by Kent S. Knutson. Minneapolis, Augsburg Pub. House [1970] 48 p. 20 cm. Bibliography: p. 48. [BT456.K58] 77-101104 1.00
1. Jesus Christ—Seven last words—Sermons. 2. Lutheran Church—Sermons. 3. Sermons, American. I. Title.

THE Language of the cross / edited by Aelred Lacomara. Chicago : Franciscan Herald Press, c1977. vii, 149 p. ; 21 cm. [BT431.L37] 76-43287 ISBN 0-8199-0617-4 : 6.95 232.9'63
1. Jesus Christ—Passion—Addresses, essays, lectures. 2. Suffering—Addresses, essays, lectures. I. Lacomara, Aelred.

MOORE, Paul L. 232.963
Seven words of men around the Cross. New York, Abingdon Press [1963] 94 p. 20 cm. [BT453.M75] 63-7766
1. Jesus Christ — Crucifixion. I. Title.

MOORE, Paul L. 232.963
Seven words of men around the Cross. Nashville, Abingdon [c.1963] 94p. 20cm. 63-7766 2.00
1. Jesus Christ—Crucifixion. I. Title.

NELSON, Carl Ellis, 1916- 232.9'63
Just the greatest [by] Carl Nelson. Cartoons by Joe DeVelasco. Downers Grove, Ill., Intervarsity Press [1972] 96 p. illus. 18 cm. [BT450.N45 1972] 72-184953 ISBN 0-87784-543-3
1. Jesus Christ—Crucifixion. I. Title.

O'COLLINS, Gerald. 232.9'63
The Calvary Christ / Gerald O'Collins. Philadelphia : Westminster Press, c1977. xii, 124 p. ; 22 cm. Includes index. Bibliography: p. [121]. [BT450.O25] 76-54973 ISBN 0-664-24801-2 : 4.95
1. Jesus Christ—Crucifixion. I. Title.

RICE, John R 1895- 232.963
Watching Jesus die; 10 sermons on the Crucifixion of Christ. Wheaton, Ill., Sword of the Lord Publishers [c1956] 246p. 21cm. [BT430.R53] 57-22942
1. Jesus Christ—Passion—Sermons. 2. Baptists—Sermons. 3. Sermons, American. I. Title.

RICE, John R 1895- 232.963
Watching Jesus die, 10 sermons on the Crucifixion of Christ Wheaton, Ill., Sword of the Lord Publishers [c1956] 246p. 21cm. [BT430.R53] 57-22942
1. Jesus Christ—Passion— Sermons. 2. Baptists—Sermons. 3. Sermons, American. I. Title.

SANFORD, Agnes Mary (White) 232.96'3
Twice seven words, by Agnes Sanford. Plainfield, N.J., Iogos International [1971] 101 p. 22 cm. [BT306.S327] 78-161660 ISBN 0-912106-16-6 2.95
1. Jesus Christ—Words—Meditations. I. Title.

SHEEN, Fulton John, Bp., 1895- 232.963
Seven words to the cross. Garden City, N. Y., Garden City Books [1953, c1944] 94p. 20cm. [BT453.S47 1953] 53-1787
1. Jesus Christ—Crucifixion. I. Title.

SMITH, Wilbur Moorehead, 1894- comp. 232.963
Great sermons on the death of Christ by celebrated preachers; with biographical sketches and bibliographies. Compiled Wilbur M. Smith. Natick, Mass., W. A. Wilde Co. [1965] 244 p. 22 cm. Includes bibliographies. [BT431.S6] 65-12941
1. Jesus Christ — Passion — Sermons. 2. Sermons, English. I. Title.

URBANO, Paul. 232.9'63
The marks of the nails. St. Paul, Minn., Yellow Bird Division, Economic Information, inc. [1973] vii, 111 p. 22 cm. Includes bibliographical references. [BX5937.U7M37] 73-90039 ISBN 0-913514-04-7 3.50
1. Protestant Episcopal Church in the U.S.A.—Sermons. 2. Jesus Christ—Seven last words—Sermons. 3. Sermons, American. I. Title.

WEBSTER, Douglas 232.963
In debt to Christ; a study in the meaning of the Cross. Philadelphia, Fortress [1964] 158p. col. front. 18cm. Bibl. 64-10650 1.75 pap.,
1. Jesus Christ—Passion—Devotional literature. 2. Christian life—Anglican authors. I. Title.

WHITE, Jesse Eugene, 1926- 232.96'3
The drama of the cross, by J. Eugene White. Grand Rapids, Baker Book House [1968] 111 p. 21 cm. [BT431.W45] 68-31476 2.95
1. Jesus Christ—Passion—Sermons. 2. Baptists—Sermons. 3. Sermons, American. I. Title.

BABBAGE, Stuart Barton. 232.9630922
The light of the Cross; a look at the persons who stood at the Cross, by S. Barton Babbage. Grand Rapids, Zondervan Pub. House [1966] 183 p. 23 cm. Bibliographical footnotes. [BS2430.B25] 66-18950
1. Bible. N.T.—Biography. I. Title.

BAXTER, Kathleen Mary. 232.96'35
And I look for the Resurrection [by] Kay M. Baxter. Nashville, Abingdon Press [1968] 64 p. 23 cm. [BT456.B37] 68-11711
1. Jesus Christ—Seven last words—Sermons. I. Title.

BENKO, Stephen, 1924- 232.96'35
My Lord speaks. Valley Forge [Pa.] Judson Press [1970] 128 p. 20 cm. Includes bibliographical references. [BT456.B45] 68-20433 2.50
1. Jesus Christ—Seven last words. I. Title.

BININGER, Clem E. 232.96'35
The seven last words of Christ, by Clem E. Bininger. Grand Rapids, Baker Book House [1969] 109 p. 21 cm. [BT456.B55] 71-98138 2.95
1. Jesus Christ—Seven last words—Sermons. 2. Presbyterian Church—Sermons. 3. Sermons, American. I. Title.

GRITTER, George 232.9635
Listening to God on Calvary; messages on the seven words from the cross. Grand Rapids, Mich., Baker Bk. [c.]1965. 143p. 21cm. [BT456.G7] 65-25477 2.50 bds.,
1. Jesus Christ— Seven last words—Sermons. I. Title.

HOYER, Richard O. 232.96/35
The word from the cross [by] Richard O. Hoyer. Saint Louis, Concordia [c.1968] 96p. 19cm. [BT456.H65] 68-11894 1.95 pap.,
1. Jesus Christ—Seven last words—Sermons. 2. Sermons, American. 3. Lutheran Church—Sermons. I. Title.

LOCKYER, Herbert. 232.9'635
Seven words of love / Herbert Lockyer. Waco, Tex. : Word Books, [1975] 168 p. 23 cm. Bibliography: p. 167-168. [BT456.L63] 74-28719 5.95
1. Jesus Christ—Seven last words. I. Title.

POOVEY, William Arthur, 1913- 232.96'35
Cross words; sermons and dramas for Lent, by W. A. Poovey. Minneapolis, Augsburg Pub. House [1967, c1968] 111 p. 20 cm. [BT456.P6] 68-13421
1. Jesus Christ—Seven last words—Sermons. 2. Jesus Christ—Seven last words—Drama. I. Title.

STRAUSS, Lehman. 232.9635
The day God died. Grand Rapids, Zondervan Pub. House [1966, c1965] 112 p. 23 cm. Bibliography: p. 111. [BT456.S7] 65-25947
1. Jesus Christ — Seven last words — Sermons. 2. Baptists — Sermons. 3. Sermons, American. I. Title.

STRAUSS, Lehman 232.9635
The day God died. Grand Rapids, Mich., Zondervan [1966, c.1965] 112p. 23cm. Bibl. [BT456.S7] 65-25947 2.50 bds.,
1. Jesus Christ—Seven last words—Sermons. 2. Baptists— Sermons. 3. Sermons, American. I. Title.

BULST, Werner. 232.966
The Shroud of Turin. Translated by Stephen McKenna and James J. Galvin, in co-operation with the Holy Shroud Guild, Esopus, New York. Milwaukee, Bruce Pub. Co. [c1957] 167p. illus. 23cm. [BT587.S4B812] 57-6317
1. Holy Shroud. I. Title.

CHESHIRE, Geoffrey Leonard, 1917- 232.966
Pilgrimage to the Shroud. With a foreword by His Grace the Archbishop of Birmingham. New York, McGraw-Hill [c1956] 74p. illus. 20cm. [BT587.S4C45 1956a] 57-7227
1. Woollam, Josephine, 1944 or 5- 2. Holy Shroud. I. Title.

WALSH, John Evangelist, 1927- 232.966
The Shroud. Garden City, N.Y. Doubleday [1965, c.1963] 160p. illus., ports. 18cm. (Echo bk., E12) Bibl. .85 pap.,
1. Holy Shroud. I. Title.

WALSH, John Evangelist, 1927- 232.966
The Shroud. New York, Random House [1963] xiv, 202 p. illus., ports. 22 cm. Includes bibliographical references. [BT587.S4W3] 63-16850
1. Holy Shroud.

WILCOX, Robert K. 232.9'66
Shroud / Robert K. Wilcox. New York : Macmillan, c1977. x, 180 p. : ill. ; 21 cm. Includes index. Bibliography : p. 174-176. [BT587.S4W5] 77-4960 ISBN 0-02-628510-X : 10.95
1. Holy Shroud. I. Title.

WUENSCHEL, Edward A 232.966
Self-portrait of Christ, the Holy Shroud of Turin. Esopus, N. Y., Holy Shroud Guild, 1954. 128p. illus. 23cm. [BT587.S4W8] 54-27378
1. Holy Shroud. I. Title.

BARNHOUSE, Donald Grey, 1895- 232.97
The cross through the open tomb. Grand Rapids, Mich., Eerdmans [c.1961] 152p. 60-53513 3.00 bds.,
1. Jesus Christ—Resurrection. I. Title.

BOWDEN, Joan Chase. 232.9'7
Something wonderful happened : the first Easter for beginning readers : Matthew 28:1-10, for children Mark 16:1-11, Luke 24:1-12, John 20:1-18 / by Joan Chase Bowden ; illustrated by Aline Cunningham. St. Louis : Concordia Pub. House, c1977. [46] p. : col. ill. ; 23 cm. (I can read a Bible story) Relates the events of the Resurrection. [BT481.B65] 77-6325 ISBN 0-570-07324-3 : 3.95. ISBN 0-570-07318-9 pbk. : 1.95
1. Jesus Christ—Resurrection—Juvenile literature. I. Cunningham, Aline. II. Title.

CHAPPELL, Wallace D. 232.9'7
When Jesus rose [by] Wallace D. Chappell. Nashville, Broadman Press [1972] 127 p. 21 cm. [BT485.C5] 72-90034 ISBN 0-8054-2218-8 3.95
1. Jesus Christ—Resurrection—Sermons. 2. Methodist Church—Sermons. 3. Sermons, American. I. Title.

COMBLIN, Joseph, 1923- 232.97
The resurrection in the plan of salvation. Translated by Sister David Mary. Notre Dame, Ind., Fides Publishers [1966] 176 p. 20 cm. Translation of La resurrection de Jesus-Christ. Bibliographical reference included in "Notes" (p. 176) [BT481.C613] 65-24102
1. Jesus Christ—Resurrection. 2. Salvation. I. Title.

DURRWELL, F. X. 232.97
The resurrection, a Biblical study. Translated [from the French] by Rosemary Sheed, and with an introd. by Charles Davis. New York, Sheed and Ward [c.1960] 371p. 60-15679 6.00
1. Redemption. 2. Jesus Christ—Resurrection I. Title.

ELLIS, Eric Kent. 232.97
The power of His resurrection. London, Faith Press; New York, Morehouse-Barlow [1962] 95 p. 19 cm. (Studies in Christian faith and practice, 4) [[BT481]] A 63
1. Jesus Christ — Resurrection. I. Title.

ELLIS, Eric Kent 232.97
The power of His resurrection. London, Faith Pr.; New York, Morehouse [1963, c.1962] 95p. 19cm. (Studies in Christian faith and practice, 4) A63 1.20 pap.,
1. Jesus Christ—Resurrection. I. Title.

ELSON, Edward Lee Roy 232.97
And still He speaks, the words of the risen Christ. Westwood, N.J. Revell [c.1960] 127p. 21cm. (bibl.) 60-8453 2.50
1. Jesus Christ—Forty days. 2. Jesus Christ—Words. I. Title.

EVELY, Louis, 1910- 232.97
Joy. Translated by Brian and Marie-Claude Thompson. [New York] Herder and Herder [1968] 96 p. 21 cm. Translation of Le chemin de joie. [BT481.E913] 68-12016
1. Jesus Christ—Resurrection—Meditations. 2. Jesus Christ—Resurrection—Meditations. I. Title.

EVELY, Louis, 1910- 232.97
Joy. Translated by Brian and Marie-Claude Thompson. Garden City, N.Y., Doubleday [1974, c1968] 119 p. 18 cm. (Image books.) [BT481.E913] ISBN 0-385-02971-3 1.45 (pbk.)
1. Jesus Christ—Resurrection—Meditations. I. Title.
L.C. card number for original ed.: 68-12016.

FLOOD, Edmund. 232.9'7
The resurrection. New York, Paulist Press [1973] v, 55 p. 17 cm. Includes bibliographical references. [BT481.F54] 73-81107 ISBN 0-8091-1774-6 0.75 (pbk.)
1. Jesus Christ—Resurrection. I. Title.

FLYNN, Leslie B 232.97
Day of resurrection [by] Leslie B. Flynn. Nashville, Broadman Press [1965] 96 p. 20 cm. [BT481.F55] 65-10339
1. Jesus Christ — Resurrection — Meditations. I. Title.

FLYNN, Leslie B. 232.97
Day of resurrection. Nashville, Broadman [c.1965] 96p. 20cm. [BT481.F55] 65-10339 2.00 bds.,
1. Jesus Christ—Resurrection—Meditations. I. Title.

FLYNN, Leslie B. 232.97
Day of resurrection [by] Leslie B. Flynn. Grand Rapids, Baker Book House [1974, c1965] 96 p. 20 cm. [BT481.F55] ISBN 0-8010-3467-1 1.95 (pbk.)
1. Jesus Christ—Resurrection—Meditations. I. Title.
L.C. card no. for original ed.: 65-10339

FRASER, Neil McCormick 232.97
The glory of His rising; a closer look at the Resurrection. Neptune, N.J., Loizeaux [c.1963] 127p. 20cm. 63-13778 2.50 bds.,
1. Jesus Christ—Resurrection. I. Title.

FULLER, Reginald Horace. 232.97
The formation of the Resurrection narratives [by] Reginald H. Fuller. New York, Macmillan [1971] xiv, 225 p. 22 cm. Includes bibliographical references. [BT481.F84] 77-123140 2.95
1. Jesus Christ—Resurrection—Biblical teaching. I. Title.

GAULT, Clarence W 232.97
Indebted to Christ's resurrection. [1st ed.] New York, Pageant Press [1956] 237 p. illus. 21 cm. [BT485.G3] 56-9750
1. Jesus Christ—Forty days. I. Title.

GREEN, Edward Michael Bankes. 232.97
Man alive! [by] Michael Green. Chicago, Inter-Varsity Press [1968] 96 p. 18 cm. [BT481.G74 1968] 68-28326
1. Jesus Christ—Resurrection. I. Title.

*GUTZKE, Manford George 232.97
Plain talk on the Resurrection. Grand Rapids, Baker Book House [1974] 73 p. 20 cm. [BT481] ISBN 0-8010-3684-4 1.95 (pbk.)
1. Jesus Christ—Resurrection. I. Title.

KEPLER, Thomas Samuel, 1897- 232.97
The meaning and mystery of the Resurrection. New York, Association Press [1963] 188 p. 20 cm. [BT481.K4] 63-8882
1. Jesus Christ — Resurrection. I. Title.

KEPLER, Thomas Samuel, 1897- 232.97
The meaning and mystery of the Resurrection. New York, Association [c.1963] 188p. 20cm. 63-8882 4.50
1. Jesus Christ—Resurrection. I. Title.

KING, Geoffrey R 232.97
The forty days; studies in the last six weeks of our Lord's earthly life, from Calvary and Easter to the Ascension, by Geoffrey R. King. [1st American ed.] Grand Rapids, W.B. Eerdmans Pub. Co. [1962] 105 p. 20 cm. [BT485.K5 1962] 62-21378
1. Jesus Christ—Forty days. I. Title.

KING, Geoffrey R. 232.97
The forty days. Grand Rapids, Mich., Eerdmans [1962, c.1949] 105p. 20cm. 2.00
I. Title.

LAMPE, Geoffrey William Hugo. 232.97
The resurrection; a dialogue, by G. W. H. Lampe and D. M. Mackinnon. Edited by William Purcell. Philadelphia, Westminster Press [1967, c1966] 112 p. 19 cm. [BT481.L3 1967] 67-12284
1. Jesus Christ—Resurrection. I. MacKinnon, Donald MacKenzie, 1913- II. Purcell, William Ernest, 1909- ed. III. Title.

LARSON, Douglas J. 232.9'7
My gift from Jesus, written by Douglas J. Larson. Illustrated by Gary Kapp. Salt Lake City, Bookcraft, 1972. [24] p. col. illus. 30 cm. When his grandfather dies, a little boy learns about the Christian principle of life after death. [BT902.L37] 72-89013
1. Jesus Christ—Resurrection—Juvenile literature. 2. Future life—Juvenile literature. I. Kapp, Gary, illus. II. Title.

LEON-DUFOUR, Xavier. 232.9'7
Resurrection and the message of Easter. Translated by R. N. Wilson. New York, Holt, Rinehart and Winston [1975, c1974] xxii, 330 p. 22 cm. Translation of Resurrection de Jesus et message pascal. Bibliography: p. [275]-284. [BT481.L4513 1975] 73-16861 ISBN 0-03-012456-5 : 9.95
1. Jesus Christ—Resurrection. I. Title.

LLOYD, Mary Edna 232.97
Glad Easter day. Pictures by June Goldsborough. Nashville, Abingdon Press [1961] unpaged. illus. (part col.) 61-5094 1.25 bds.,
1. Jesus Christ—Resurrection—Juvenile literature. I. Title.

LOANE, Marcus L. 232.97
Our risen Lord, by Marcus L. Loane. Foreword by L. L. Morris. Grand Rapids, Zondervan Pub. House [1968, c1965] 119 p. 21 cm. Bibliography: p. 113. [BT485.L6] 68-10519
1. Jesus Christ—Forty days. I. Title.

MCGEE, John Vernon, 1904- 232.97
The empty tomb; proof of life after death, by J. Vernon McGee. Glendale, Calif., Regal Books [1968] 128 p. 18 cm. [BT481.M29] 68-26385
1. Jesus Christ—Resurrection. I. Title.

MARTIN, James 232.97
The empty tomb; the disappearance of Jesus as related in the letters of Caiaphas, the High

Priest. New York, Harper [c.1960] 93p. 22cm. 60-8135 2.50 half cloth,
1. Jesus Christ—Fiction. 2. Bible, N. T. Acts—History of Biblical events—Fiction. I. Title.

MARTIN, James, 1921- 232.97
Did Jesus rise from the dead? New York, Association Press [1956] 91p. 20cm. (World Christian books) [BT480.M3 1956a] 56-6458
1. Jesus Christ—Resurrection. I. Title.

MARTIN, James, 1921- 232.97
The empty tomb; the disappearance of Jesus as related in the letters of Caiaphas, the High Priest. New York, Harper [1960] 93p. 22cm. 'Published in Great Britain under the title of Letters of Calaphas to Annas.' [BT309.M345 1960] 60-8135
1. Jesus Christ—Fiction. 2. Bible. N. T. Acts—History of Biblical events—Fiction. I. Title.

MARXSEN, Willi, 1919- 232.97
The resurrection of Jesus of Nazareth. [Translated by Margaret Kohl from the German. 1st American ed.] Philadelphia, Fortress Press [1970] 191 p. 22 cm. Translation of Die Auferstehung Jesu von Nazareth. [BT481.M3713] 76-120083 2.95
1. Jesus Christ—Resurrection. I. Title.

MINEAR, Paul Sevier, 232.9'7
1906-
To die and to live : Christ's resurrection and Christian vocation / Paul S. Minear. New York : Seabury Press, 1977. p. cm. "A Crossroad book." Includes bibliographical references and index. [BT481.M56] 77-8238 ISBN 0-8164-0340-6 : 8.95
1. Jesus Christ—Resurrection. 2. Vocation. I. Title.

NIEBUHR, Richard R 232.97
Resurrection and historical reason a study of theological method. New York, Scribner [1957] viii, 184p. 22cm. Based on thesis, Yale University. Bibliographical footnotes. [BT480.N54] 57-12063
1. Jesus Christ—Resurrection. I. Title.

NIEBUHR, Richard R 232.97
Resurrection and historical reason; a study of theological method. New York, Scribner [1957] viii, 184p. 22cm. Based on thesis, Yale University. Bibliographical footnotes. [BT480.N54] 57-12063
1. Jesus Christ—Resurrection. I. Title.

O'COLLINS, Gerald. 232.9'7
The resurrection of Jesus Christ. Valley Forge, Pa., Judson Press, 1973. xiv, 142 p. 22 cm. Bibliography: p. [139]-140. [BT481.O34 1973] 73-2613 ISBN 0-8170-0614-1
1. Jesus Christ—Resurrection. I. Title.

PERRIN, Norman. 232.9'7
The Resurrection according to Matthew, Mark, and Luke / Norman Perrin. Philadelphia : Fortress Press, c1977. x, 85 p. ; 19 cm. Includes bibliographical references. [BT481.P48] 76-47913 ISBN 0-8006-1248-5 pbk. : 2.95
1. Jesus Christ—Resurrection—Biblical teaching. 2. Bible. N.T. Gospels—Criticism, interpretation, etc. I. Title.

RISS, Richard. 232.9'7
The evidence for the resurrection of Jesus Christ : legal, historical, and eyewitness evidence for the resurrection! / Richard Riss. Minneapolis : Bethany Fellowship, c1977. 106 p. ; 18 cm. [BT481.R52] 76-50978 ISBN 0-87123-134-4 pbk. : 1.95
1. Jesus Christ—Resurrection. I. Title.

[ROSS, Albert Henry] 1881- 232.97
Who moved the stone? [By] Frank Morison [pseud.] New York, Barnes & Noble [1962] 192p. 21cm. (Univ. paperback, UP-24) 62-13524 1.25 pap.,
1. Jesus Christ—Resurrection. I. Title.

ROSS, Albert Henry, 1881- 232.9'7
Who moved the stone? / Frank Morison [i.e. A. H. Ross] Grand Rapids : Zondervan Pub. House, [1977] 193 p. ; 18 cm. Reprint of the 1930 ed. published by Faber and Faber, London. [BT480.R6 1977] 76-26084 ISBN 0-571-03259-1 pbk. : 2.45
1. Jesus Christ—Resurrection. I. Title.

SMITH, Wilbur Moorehead, 232.97
1894- ed.
Great sermons on the Resurrection of Christ, by celebrated preachers. Bibliographical sketches, bibliographies. Natick, Mass., W. A. Wilde [c.1964] 289p. 21cm. Bibl. 64-16628 4.50
1. Jesus Christ—Resurrection—Sermons. 2. Sermons, English. 3. Easter—Sermons. I. Title.

SMITH, Wilbur Moorehead, 232.97
1894- ed.
Great sermons on the Resurrection of Christ, by celebrated preachers. With bibliographical sketches and bibliographies. Natick, Mass., W. A. Wilde Co. [1964] 289 p. 21 cm. Includes bibliographies. [BV4259.S55] 64-16628
1. Jesus Christ — Resurrection — Sermons. 2. Sermons, English. 3. Easter — Sermons. I. Title.

STEPHENSON, William, 1882- 232.97
comp.
Days of joy; thoughts for all times. Westminster, Md., Newman Press, 1955. 176p. 18cm. [BT485.S8] 55-8639
1. Jesus Christ—Forty days. I. Title.

TATHAM, C. Ernest 232.97
He lives! Seven studies of the Resurrection appearances of the Lord Jesus Christ. Foreword by H. G. Lockett. Chicago, Moody [1963] 80p. 20cm. 1.95
I. Title.

TENNEY, Merrill Chapin, 232.97
1904-.
The reality of the Resurrection. [1st ed.] New York, Harper & Row [1963] 221 p. 22 cm. Includes bibliography. [BT481.T4] 63-10507
1. Jesus Christ — Resurrection. I. Title.

TENNEY, Merrill Chapin, 232.97
1904-
The reality of the Resurrection. New York, Harper [c.1963] 221p. 22cm. Bibl. 63-10507 4.00 bds.,
1. Jesus Christ—Resurrection. I. Title.

TORRANCE, Thomas Forsyth, 232.9'7
1913-
Space, time, and resurrection / by Thomas F. Torrance. Grand Rapids : Eerdmans, [1977] p. cm. Includes bibliographical references and index. [BT481.T67] 76-19069 ISBN 0-8028-3488-4 pbk. : 4.95
1. Jesus Christ—Resurrection. 2. Jesus Christ—Ascension. 3. Space theology. I. Title.

WANSBROUGH, Henry, 1934- 232.9'7
The resurrection / Henry Wansbrough. Staten Island, N.Y. : Alba House, 1975, c1972. 109 p. ; 19 cm. (Scripture for meditation ; 8) [BT481.W36 1975] 74-31343 ISBN 0-8189-0313-9 pbk. : 1.95
1. Jesus Christ—Resurrection—Meditations. I. Title. II. Series.

WHITSON, Robley Edward. 232.9'7
The Resurrection Christ: community as interperson. New York, Alba House [1973] p. [BT481.W46] 73-15958 5.95
1. Jesus Christ—Resurrection. 2. Church. I. Title.

WUELLNER, Bernard. 232.97
Graces of the risen Christ, Designs by Frank Kacmarcik. Milwaukee, Bruce Pub. Co. [1960] 138 p. 24 cm. Includes bibliography. [BT485.W8] 60-8242
1. Jesus Christ — Forty days. I. Title.

YARNOLD, Greville Dennis. 232.97
Risen indeed; studies in the Lord's resurrection. New York, Oxford University Press, 1959. 134 p. 19 cm. [BT480.Y3 1959] 59-827
1. Jesus Christ — Resurrection. 2. Jesus Christ — Forty days. I. Title.

THEISZ, George Elmer. 232.971
The eight first words of the risen Saviour, John 20-21. Chicago, Moody Press [1950] 124 p. 19 cm. [BT485.T46] 50-2072
1. Jesus Christ — Forty days. 2. Jesus Christ — Words. I. Title.

BRUMBACK, Carl. 232.972
Accent on the Ascension! Springfield, Mo., Gospel Pub. House [1955] 151p. illus. 20cm. [BT500.B7] 56-25038
1. Jesus Christ Ascension. I. Title.

GAER, Joseph, 1897- 232.99
The lore of the New Testament. [1st ed.] Boston, Little, Brown [1952] xi, 371 p. 23 cm. "Basic sources": p. [319]-322. "Reading list with notes": p. [347]-357. [BT520.G3] 52-9075
1. Jesus Christ—Blog.—Apocryphal and legendary literature. 2. Apostles—Legends. I. Title.

PANNEEL, Henry. 232.99
Witnesses of the Gospel. Translated by Paul A. Barrett. St. Louis, B. Herder Book Co. [1960] 192p. 21cm. [BT309.P253] 60-10238
1. Jesus Christ—Fiction. I. Title.

ROTH, Samuel, 1803- 232.99
My friend Yeshea. Decorations by Chester Kalm. New York 13, 446 Broadway Pub. for Friends of Mishillim by by Bridgehead Bks., [c.1961] 628p. 61-9588 10.00
1. Jesus Christ—Miscellanea. I. Title.

ROTH, Samuel, 1893- 232.99
My friend Yeshea. Decorations by Chester Kalm. New York, Published for the Friends of Mishillim by Bridgehead Books [1961] 628p. illus. 24cm. [BT304.93.R65] 61-9588
1. Jesus Christ—Miscellanea. I. Title.

CARHART, Alfreda (Post) 232.991
Wonderful Jesus; a book of poems. With illus. by Chinese artists. Boston, Bruce Humphries [c1954] unpaged. illus. 31cm. [PS3505.A698W6] 55-500
1. Jesus Christ— Poetry. I. Title.

THE life of Christ in 232.991
poetry; a selection from Christ in poetry, which was compiled and edited by Thomas Curtis Clark and Hazel Clark. New York, Association Press [c1957] 126p. 16cm. (An Association Press reflection book) [PN6110.J4C56] 821.082 57-5495
1. Jesus Christ—Poetry. I. Clark, Hazel Davis, ed.

THOMAS, Joan Gale. 232.991
If Jesus came to my house. New York, Lothrop, Lee & Shepard [c1951] unpaged. illus. 21 cm. [BV4715.T5] 51-14698
1. Golden rule. I. Title.

THORNLEY, Gwendella, ed. 232.991
How beautiful upon the mountains; an anthology of poetry about Jesus. [Logan, Utah, 1954] 66p. 24cm. (Utah State Agricultural College. Monograph series, v. 2, no. 1) [PN6110.J4T5] 54-62339
1. Jesus Christ—Poetry. I. Title. II. Series: Utah. Agricultural College, Logan. Monograph series, v. 2, no. 1

WHITMAN, John Pratt. 232.991
He grew in wisdom; with foreword by Henry J. Cadbury. Illus. by the author. Boston, Christopher Pub. House [1955] 188p. illus. 21cm. [PS3545.H757H4] 811.5 55-36315
1. Jesus Christ—Poetry. I. Title.

MILLER, Franklin [232.991] 811.5
Hoyt, 1875-
Poems of Jesus the Christ. New York, Exposition Press [1950] 53 p. 23 cm. [PS3525.I5383P6] 50-9232
1. Jesus Christ — Poetry. I. Title.

SPENCE, Walter, [232.991]811.5
1867-
Lyrics of Jesus, and other poems. Boston, B. Humphries [c1951] 109 p. 20 cm. [PS3537.P443L9] 52-8715
1. Jesus Christ — Poetry. I. Title.

LOVELACE, Delos Wheeler, 232.993
1894-1967.
Journey to Bethlehem; illustrated by Valenti Angelo. New York, Crowell [1953] 215 p. 21 cm. [BT560.L68] 53-8434
1. Jesus Christ—Fiction. I. Title.

MILLER, Randolph Crump, 232.993
1910-
I remember Jesus. Greenwich, Conn., Seabury Press, 1958. 96p. 20cm. [BT309.M63] 58-12004
1. Jesus Christ—Fiction. I. Title.

233 Man

ALBERIONE, Giacomo Giuseppe, 233
1884-
Fundamentals of Christian sociology. [Boston] St. Paul Editions [1962] 183p. 22cm. [BT738.A4] 61-17985
1. Sociology, Christian (Catholic) I. Title.

ALBERIONE, Giacomo Giuseppe, 233
1884-
Fundamentals of Christian sociology. [Boston] St. Paul Eds. [dist. Daughters of St. Paul, c.1962] 183p. 22cm. 61-17985 2.50; 1.50 pap.,
1. Sociology, Christian (Catholic) I. Title.

ALTER, Karl Joseph, Bp. 233
The mind of an archbishop; a study of man's essential relationship to God, church, country. and fellow man, as expressed in the writings of the Most Rev. Karl J. Alter ... archbishop of Cincinnati. Foreword: Paul F. Leibold. Editor: Maurice E. Reardon. Golden jubilee ed. [Cincinnati, Archdiocese of Cincinnati distributor: St. Anthony's Guild, Paterson, N. J., c.1960] xix, 406p. illus. (front. port.) 24cm. 60-50193 6.00
1. Catholic Church—Doctrinal and controversial works. I. Title.

ALTER, Karl Joseph, Bp., 233
1885-
The mind of an archbishop; a study of man's essential relationship to God, church, country, and fellow man. as expressed in the writings of the Most Rev. Karl J. Alter ... archbishop of Cincinnati. Foreword: Paul F. Leibold. Editor: Maurice E. Reardon. Golden Jubilee ed. [Cincinnati, Archdiocese of Cincinnati; distributor: St. Anthony's Guild, Paterson, N. J., 1960] 406p. illus. 24cm. [BX1751.2.A45] 60-50193
1. Catholic Church—Doctrinal and controversial works. I. Title.

AVERILL, Lloyd James, 1923- 233
Between faith and unfaith, by Lloyd J. Richmond. Knox [1968] 87p. 21 cm. Bibl. [BR121.2.A9] 67-19135 1.75 pap.,
1. Christianity—20th cent. I. verill. II. Title.

BABBAGE, Stuart Barton. 233
Man in nature and in grace. Grand Rapids, Eerdmans [1957] 125p. 19cm. (A Pathway book) [BT701.B2] 57-9773
1. Man (Theology) I. Title.

BAILEY, Derrick Sherwin, 233
1910-
Sexual relation in Christian thought. New York, Harper [1959] 312p. 22cm. London ed. (Longmans) has title: The man-woman relation in Christian thought. [BT708.B3 1959a] 59-10326
1. Sex and religion. I. Title.

BAKER, Wesley C. 233
Believer in hell [by] Wesley C. Baker. Philadelphia, Westminster Press [1968] 144 p. 22 cm. [BR110.B28] 68-24676 4.75
1. Christianity—Psychology. 2. Depression, Mental. I. Title.

BALLOU, Adin, 1803-1890. 233
Christian non-resistance in all its important bearings. Appendix by William S. Heywood. New York, Da Capo Press, 1970. xv, 278 p. ports. 23 cm. (Civil liberties in American history) Reprint of the 1910 ed. [BT736.6.B34 1970] 70-121104
1. Evil, Non-resistance to. 2. Christian ethics. 3. War and religion. I. Title. II. Series.

BALTHASAR, Hans Urs von, 233
1905-
A theological anthropology. New Yrok, Sheed and Ward [1968, c1967] x, 341 p. 22 cm. Translation of Das Ganze im Fragment. Includes bibliographical references. [BR115.H5B283] 67-29289
1. History (Theology) 2. Man (Theology) I. Title.

BARRY, Freedom 233
I do; spiritual awakening through individual endeavor. New York, Vantage [c.1963] 61p. 21 cm. 3.00 bds.,
I. Title.

BERKOUWER, Gerrit Cornelis, 233
1903-
Man: the image of God. [Translated by Dirk W. Jellema] Grand Rapids, Eerdmans [1962] Bibliographical footnotes. [BT701.2.B413] 60-12643
1. Man (Theology)—Biblical teaching. I. Title.

BERKOUWER, Gerrit Cornelis, 233
1903-
Man: the image of God. [Tr. by Dirk W. Jellema] Grand Rapids, Mich. Eerdmans [c.1962] 376p. 23cm. (His Studies in dogmatics) Bibl. 60-12643 6.00
1. Man (Theology)—Biblical teaching. I. Title.

BOROS, Ladislaus, 1927- 233
Hidden God. Translated by Erika Young. New York, Seabury Press [1973] 126 p. 22 cm. (A Continuum book) Translation of Der gute Mensch und sein Gott. Includes bibliographical references. [BT701.2.B59713] 72-3939 ISBN 0-8164-1042-9 5.95
1. Man (Theology) I. Title.

BOROS, Ladislaus, 1927- 233
In time of temptation. Translated by Simon and Erika Young. [New York] Herder and Herder [1968] 112 p. 21 cm. Translation of In der Versuchung. [BT725.B6313 1968b] 68-55983 3.95
1. Temptation. 2. Perfection (Catholic) I. Title.

BRAATEN, Carl E., 1929- 233
The living temple : a practical theology of the body and the foods of the earth / Carl E. Braaten & LaVonne Braaten. 1st ed. New York : Harper & Row, c1976. xiii, 94 p. ; 21 cm. Includes bibliographies. [BT741.2.B7 1976] 75-36746 ISBN 0-06-061044-1 pbk. : 2.95
1. Body, Human (in religion, folk-lore, etc.) 2. Man (Theology) 3. Food. 4. Hygiene. I. Braaten, LaVonne, joint author. II. Title.

BRAME, Isaiah Jefferson 233
Man's divine nature, the trinity of God, Christ, and man. New York, Exposition Press [c.1960] 109p. 22cm. (An Exposition-Testament book) 60-3850 3.00
1. Man (Theology) I. Title.

BRAME, Isaiah Jefferson, 233
1893-
Man's divine nature, the trinity of God, Christ, and man. [1st ed.] New York, Exposition Press [1960] 109p. 22cm. (An Exposition- Testament book) [BT701.2.B7] 60-3850
1. Man (Theology) I. Title.

BRANDON, Samuel George Frederick. 233
Man and his destiny in the great religions; an historical and comparative study containing the Wilde lectures in natural and comparative religion delivered in the University of Oxford, 1954-1957. [Toronto] University of Toronto Press [1962] xiv, 442p. 23cm. Bibliography: p. 386-413. [BT703.B7] 62-52779
1. Man (Theology)—Comparative studies. I. Title.

BRETSCHER, Paul G. 233
Cain, come home! / by Paul G. Bretscher ; [original art concepts by Joel Paul Bretscher]. St. Louis : Clayton Pub. House, c1976. xvi, 140 p. : ill. ; 23 cm. Includes index. [BT731.B73] 76-1810 ISBN 0-915644-05-3 pbk. : 4.25
1. Alienation (Theology) 2. Reconciliation. I. Title.

*BUSCH, Fred W. 233
The case against original sin; Minerva presents a diploma to Eve. New York, Pageant [c.1964] 124p. 22cm. 2.75
I. Title.

CAEMMERER, Richard Rudolph, 1904- 233
God's great plan for you. St. Louis, Concordia Pub. House [c.]1961. 90p. 61-11239 2.00
1. Man (Theology) I. Title.

CATHOLIC Church. Liturgy and ritual. Martyrology. Dominican. English. 233
The martyrology of the Sacred Order of Frairs Preachers. Translated by W. R. Bonniwell. Published with the approbation of T. S. McDermott, O. P., vicar general of the Order of Preachers. Westminster, Md., Newman Press, 1955. xv, 283p. 24cm. [BX2049.D6M3 1955] 55-8660
I. Bonniwell, William Raymond, 1888- tr. II. Catholic Church. Liturgy and ritual. Dominican. III. Catholic Church. Liturgy and ritual. English. IV. Title.

CHEMNITZ, Martin, 1522-1586. 233
The doctrine of man in classical Lutheran theology. Ed. by Herman A. Preus, Edmund Smits, Tr. from the works of Martin Chemnitz, Johann Gerhard by Mario Colacci [others] Minneapolis, Augsburg [c.1962] 245p. 23cm. Bibl. 62-9097 5.00
1. Man (theology)—Early works to 1800. 2. Sin—Early works to 1800. 3. Lutheran Church—Doctrinal and controversial works. I. Gerhard, Johann, 1582-1637. II. Preus, Herman Amberg, 1896- ed. III. Smits, Edmund, ed. IV. Colacci, Mario, tr. V. Title.

COLLEGE Theology Society. 233
To be a man; [proceedings. Edited by] George Devine. Englewood Cliffs, N.J., Prentice-Hall [1969] viii, 151 p. 22 cm. Proceedings of the national convention of the College Theology Society, held in San Francisco, 1968. Bibliographical footnotes. [BV1610.C586] 69-20489 ISBN 1-392-29639-
1. Universities and colleges—Religion—Societies, etc. 2. Theology—Study and teaching—Societies, etc. 3. Man (Theology)—Addresses, essays, lectures. I. Devine, George, 1941- ed. II. Title.

CONFERENCE on Theology and Body, Emory University, 1973. 233
Theology and body. Edited by John Y. Fenton. Philadelphia, Westminster Press [1974] 157 p. 21 cm. Sponsored by Columbia Theological Seminary, Emory University, and the Interdenominational Theological Center. Includes bibliographical references. [BT702.C66 1973] 74-13404 ISBN 0-664-20712-X
1. Man (Theology)—Congresses. I. Fenton, John Y., ed. II. Columbia Theological Seminary, Decatur, Ga. III. Emory University, Atlanta. IV. Interdenominational Theological Center, Atlanta. V. Title.

COOPER, David Lipscomb, 1886- 233
Man, his creation, fall, redemption, and glorification. (Chapter one, revised and enlarged) Los Angeles, Biblical Research Society ['1950] xi, 164 p. 21 cm. Bibliography: p. 164. [BT751.C753 1950] 51-3637
1. Salvation. 2. Bible. N. T. Hebrews I-II—Commentaries. I. Title.

CRONAN, Edward Paul, 1913- 233
The dignity of the human person. With a foreword by Francis Cardinal Spellman. New York, Philosophical Library [1955] 207 p. 23cm. Issued also in the microprint form, as thesis Catholic University of America, under title: The dignity of a human person. [BD431.C87 1955] 55-14491
1. Man. I. Title.

D'ARCY, Martin Cyril, 1888- 233
Humanism and Christianity [by] Martin C. D'Arcy. New York, World Pub. Co. [1969] xix, 226 p. 22 cm. (Perspectives in humanism) "An NAL book." Bibliographical footnotes. [BR128.H8D3] 69-10749 6.50
1. Christianity and religious humanism. 2. Secularism. I. Title. II. Series.

D'ARCY, Martin Cyril, 1888- 233
No absent God; the relations between God and the self. [1st ed.] [New York] Harper & Row [1962] 157 p. 22 cm. (Religious perspectives, v. 6) [BT701.2.D3] 62-14574
1. Man (Theology) I. Title.

ECREMENT, Lloyd L. 233
Man, the Bible, and destiny; what is man, what does he know about himself and the Bible, where is he going, and what can he do about it? Grand Rapids, Mich., Eerdmans [c.1961] 109p. 61-16128 2.50
1. Man (Theology)—Biblical teaching. 2. Resurrection—Biblical teaching. I. Title.

EICHRODT, Walther, 1890- 233
Man in the Old Testament; translated by K. and R. Gregor Smith. Chicago, H. Regnery Co., 1951. 83 p. 22 cm. (Studies in Biblical theology, no. 4) [BS1199.M2E53] 52-6869
1. Man (Theology)—Biblical teaching. 2. Bible. O. T.—Theology. I. Title. II. Series.

FICHTNER, Joseph. 233
Theological anthropology; the science of man in his relations to God. [Notre Dame, Ind.] University of Notre Dame Press, 1963. 100 p. 18 cm. (University theology themes) [BT703.F5] 63-15345
1. Man (Theology) I. Title.

FICHTNER, Joseph 233
Theological anthropology; the science of man in his relations to God. [Notre Dame, Ind.] Univ. of Notre Dame Pr. [c.]1963. 100p. 18cm. (Univ. theology themes) Bibl. 63-15345 1.25 pap.,
1. Man (Theology) I. Title.

*FINE, Herbert J. 233
Tomorrow is ours. New York, Vantage [1968] 51p. 21cm. 2.75 bds.,
1. Theology, Doctrinal—Popular works. I. Title.

FOX, Douglas A., 1927- 233
Buddhism, Christianity, and the future of man, by Douglas A. Fox. Philadelphia, Westminster Press [1972] 190 p. 22 cm. Bibliography: p. [185]-186. [BT702.F68] 70-189123 ISBN 0-664-20937-8 6.95
1. Man (Theology) 2. Man (Buddhism) I. Title.

FRAINE, Jean de. 233
Adam and the family of man. Translated by Daniel Raible. Staten Island, N.Y., Alba House [1965] 287 p. 22 cm. Translation of Adam et son lignage. Bibliography: p. [277-287. [BT701.2.F653] 65-15729
1. Man (Theology) — Biblical teaching. 2. Race. 3. Sociology, Biblical. I. Title.

FRAINE, Jean de 233
Adam and the family of man. Tr. [from French] by Daniel Raible. Staten Island, N.Y., Alba [c.1965] 287p. 22cm. Bibl. [BT701.2.F653] 65-15729 4.95
1. Man (Theology)—Biblical teaching. 2. Race. 3. Sociology, Biblical. I. Title.

FRAINE, Jean de. 233
The Bible and the origin of man. [2d ed.] Staten Island, N. Y., Alba [1967] 85p. 22cm. Tr. from the rev. Dutch ed. De Bijbel en het ontstaan van de mens. [BS661.F713 1967] 67-15497 2.50
1. Man (Theology) I. Title.

FRAINE, Jean de 233
The Bible and the origin of man [Tr. from Dutch] New York, Desclee [c.]1962. 85p. 61-15718 2.50
1. Man (Theology) I. Title.

GELIN, Albert. 233
The concept of man in the Bible. David M. Murphy, translator. Staten Island, N.Y., Alba House [1968] 165 p. 22 cm. Translation of L'homme selon la Bible. Includes bibliographical references. [BT701.2.G413] 68-17767 3.95
1. Man (Theology)—Biblical teaching. I. Title.

GHOLSON, Edward. 233
The philosophy of ignorance. Boston, Christopher [1951] 170 p. 21 cm. [BF437.G5] 51-3751
1. Inefficiency, Intellectual. 2. Knowledge, Theory of. I. Title.

GOODYKOONTZ, Harry G. 233
The persons we teach. Philadelphia, Westminster [1965] 187p. 21cm. Bibl. [BT701.2.G6] 65-12515 4.50
1. Man (Theology) 2. Pastoral psychology. I. Title.

GUARDINI, Romano, 1885- 233
Freedom, grace, and destiny; three chapters in the interpretation of existence. Translated by John Murray. [New York] Pantheon Books [1961] 384p. 21cm. [BR100.G7713] 61-7450
1. Christianity—Philosophy. 2. Freedom (Theology) 3. Grace (Theology) 4. Fate and fatalism. I. Title.

GUARDINI, Romano, 1885- 233
Freedom, grace, and destiny; three chapters in the interpretation of existence. Tr. [from German] by John Murray. Chicago, Regnery [1965, c.1961] 251p. 17cm. [Logos bk., L705) [BR100.G7713] 1.45 pap.,
1. Christianity—Philosophy. 2. Freedom (Theology) 3. Grace (Theology) 4. Fate and fatalism. I. Title.

GUARDINI, Romano, 1885- 233
The world and the person. Translated by Stella Lange. Chicago, H. Regnery Co. [1965] ix, 226 p. 21 cm. Includes bibliographical references. [BT701.G813] 65-26910
1. Man (Theology) I. Title.

GUARDINI, Romano, 1885- 233
The world and the person. Tr. [from German] by Stella Lange. Chicago, Regnery [c. 1939,1965] ix, 226p. 21cm. Bibl. [BT701.G813] 65-26910 4.95
1. Man (Theology) I. Title.

GUARDINI, Romano, 1885-1968. 233
Freedom, grace, and destiny : three chapters in the interpretation of existence / Romano Guardini ; translated by John Murray. Westport, Conn. : Greenwood Press, 1975, c1961. 251 p. ; 21 cm. Translation of Freiheit, Gnade, Schicksal. Reprint of the ed. published by Pantheon Books, New York. Includes bibliographical references. [BR100.G7713 1975] 75-8786 ISBN 0-8371-8111-9 : 13.25
1. Christianity—Philosophy. 2. Freedom (Theology) 3. Grace (Theology) 4. Fate and fatalism. I. Title.

GUNDRY, Robert Horton. 233
Soma in biblical theology : with emphasis on Pauline anthropology / Robert H. Gundry. Cambridge ; New York : Cambridge University Press, 1976. xii, 266 p. ; 22 cm. (Monograph series - Society for New Testament Studies ; 29) Includes indexes. Bibliography: p. 245-252. [BS2655.M3G78] 75-22975 ISBN 0-521-20788-6 : 25.00
1. Bible. N.T. Epistles of Paul—Theology. 2. Man (Theology)—Biblical teaching. 3. Soma (The Greek word) I. Title. II. Series: Studiorum Novi Testamenti Societas. Monograph series ; 29.

HAGIN, Kenneth E., 1917- 233
The woman question / Kenneth E. Hagin. Greensburg, Pa. : Manna Christian Outreach, c1975. 93 p. ; 18 cm. [BS680.W7H33] 75-10513 ISBN 0-8007-8214-3 pbk. : 1.50
1. Woman (Theology)—Biblical teaching. I. Title.

HAMILTON, William, 1924- 233
The Christian man. Philadelphia, Westminster Press [1956] 93p. 20cm. (Layman's theological library) [BT701.H19] 56-8666
1. Man (Theology) I. Title.

HARNED, David Baily. 233
Images for self recognition : the Christian as player, sufferer, and vandal / David Baily Harned. New York : Seabury Press, c1977. p. cm. "A crossroad book." Includes bibliographical references. [BT701.2.H28] 76-30642 ISBN 0-8164-0334-1 : 12.95
1. Man (Theology) 2. Self.

HARRIS, Robert Laird. 233
Man—God's eternal creation; Old Testament teaching on man and his culture, by R. Laird Harris. Chicago, Moody Press [1971] 190 p. 22 cm. Bibliography: p. 188-190. [BS661.H37] 70-143471 4.95
1. Man (Theology)—Biblical teaching. 2. Sociology, Biblical. I. Title.

HAUGHTON, Rosemary. 233
On trying to be human. Springfield, Ill., Templegate, 1966. 199 p. 23 cm. [BT701.2.H3] 66-28201
1. Man (Theology) I. Title.

HEIDE, Florence Parry. 233
You and me / written by Florence Parry Heide ; illustrated by Ted Smith. St. Louis : Concordia, [1975] [32] p. : col. ill. ; 27 cm. Explores the concept of each person's being a separate individual whose thoughts make him different from anyone else. [BJ1631.H4] 75-4539 ISBN 0-570-03436-1 : 3.95
1. Children—Conduct of life. 2. Individuality—Juvenile literature. I. Smith, Ted, ill. II. Title.

HILL, Carl Richard. 233
Between two worlds : an approach to ministry / by Carl Richard Hill, Jr. Limited 1st ed. [Atlanta] : Research in Religion Program, Center for Research in Social Change, Emory University, 1976. viii, 40 p. ; 28 cm. (Research in religion series ; no. 2) Bibliography: p. 40. [BT703.H54] 76-4276
1. Booker T. Washington Junior High School. 2. Man (Theology) 3. Sociology, Christian. I. Title. II. Series.

HOLLAND, Jack H., 1922- 233
Man's victorious spirit; how to release the victory within you, by Jack H. Holland. Monterey, Calif., Hudson-Cohan Pub. Co., 1971. 127 p. 23 cm. [BV4501.2.H54] 76-179668 ISBN 0-87852-001-5 2.95
1. Spirituality. I. Title.

HOUGH, Lynn Harold, 1877- 233
The dignity of man. New York, Abingdon-Cokesbury Press [1950] 143 p. 19 cm. [BR121.H6419] 50-14250
1. Christianity—Essence, genius, nature. I. Title.

HOWARD, Richard E., 1919- 233
Newness of life : a study in the thought of Paul / by Richard E. Howard. Kansas City, Mo. : Beacon Hill Press of Kansas City, [1975] 266 p. ; 23 cm. Includes index. Bibliography: p. 241-242. [BS2655.M3H68] 74-33561 ISBN 0-8341-0353-2 : 5.95
1. Bible. N.T. Epistles of Paul—Theology. 2. Man (Theology)—Biblical teaching. 3. Conversion—Biblical teaching. I. Title.

IERSEL, Bastiaan Martinus Franciscus van. 233
The Bible on the temptations of man, by B. van Iersel. Translated by F. Vander Heijden. De Pere, Wis., St. Norbert Abbey Press, 1966. 88 p. 17 cm. [BT725.I 313] 66-16991
1. Temptation — Biblical teaching. I. Title.

IERSEL, Bastiaan Martinus Franciscus van. 233
The Bible on the temptations of man. Tr. by F. Vander Heijden. De Pere, Wis., St. Norbert Abbey Pr. [c.] 1966. 88p. 17cm. [BT725.I313] 66-16991 .95 pap.,
1. Temptation—Biblical teaching. I. Title.

INNOCENTIUS III, Pope, 1160or61-1216. 233
On the misery of the human condition. De miseria humane conditionis. Donald R. Howard, editor. Translated by Margaret Mary Dietz. Indianapolis, Bobbs-Merrill 1969. xliii, 92 p. 21 cm. (The Library of liberal arts, 132) Bibliography: p. 91-92. [BT700.I513] 69-13633 2.25
1. Man (Theology) 2. Christian ethics—Catholic authors. I. Howard, Donald Roy, 1927- ed. II. Title.

JABAY, Earl. 233
The god-players. [1st ed.] Grand Rapids, Mich., Zondervan Pub. House [1969] 151 p. illus. 23 cm. Bibliographical footnotes. [BT701.2.J3] 69-11637 3.95
1. Man (Theology) 2. Salvation. I. Title.

JABAY, Earl. 233
The kingdom of self. Plainfield, N.J., Logos International [1974] ix, 159 p. illus. 21 cm. [BT701.2.J33] 73-89494 ISBN 0-88270-068-5 2.50
1. Man (Theology) 2. Kingdom of God. I. Title.

JENKINS, David E. 233
What is man? [By] David Jenkins. Valley Forge, Judson Press [1971, c1970] 125 p. 19 cm. Bibliography: p. 125. [BD450.J4] 79-132998 ISBN 0-8170-0516-1 1.95
1. Man. I. Title.

JOHNSON, Melvin Edward, 1897- 233
The image and likeness of God, as the origin and destiny of man. [Minneapolis] c1954. 224p. 23cm. [BT703.J6] 55-168423
1. Man (Theology) 2. Eschatology. I. Title.

JONES, George Curtis, 1911- 233
Strongly tempted, by G. Curtis Jones. Cleveland, World Pub. Co. [1968] x, 150 p. 21 cm. Bibliography: p. 144-150. [BT725.J6] 68-26841 4.50
1. Temptation. I. Title.

JOY, Donald Marvin. 233
The Holy Spirit and you [by] Donald M. Joy. New York, Abingdon Press [1965] 160 p. 20 cm. [BV4501.2.J68] 65-10810
1. Christian life — Methodist authors. 2. Holy Spirit. I. Title.

JOY, Donald Marvin 233
The Holy Spirit and you. Nashville, Tenn., Abingdon [c.1965] 160p. 20cm. [BV4501.2.J68] 65-10810 2.75 bds.,
1. Christian life—Methodist authors. 2. Holy Spirit. I. Title.

KAVANAUGH, James J. 233
Man in search of God, by James J.

Kavanaugh. New York, Paulist Press [1967] 109 p. illus. 19 cm. (Deus books) [BT77.K26] 67-23600
1. Theology, Doctrinal—Popular works. I. Title.

KEEN, Sam. 233
Apology for wonder. New York, Harper [1973, c.1969] 218 p. 20 cm. Bibl. refs. included in "Notes" (p. 213-218) [BT701.2.K4] 69-17017 pap., 1.95
1. Awe. 2. Man (Theology) I. Title.

KELLER, Mary E 233
Blueprint and structure; thoughts concerning man growing out of a study of symbols found in the first chapter of Genesis. [1st ed.] New York, Pageant Press [1957] 193p. 21cm. [BT701.K4] 57-9930
1. Man (Theology) 2. Creation. I. Title.

KEZYS, Algimantas. 233
Sventoji auka. [Fotografija: Algimantas Kezys. Maldu vertimas: Bruno Markaitis. Dailininkas Algirdas Kurkauskas] Chicago, Jesuit Fathers of Della Strada, 1965. 92 p. illus. 24 cm. [BX2230.K47] 67-32341
1. Mass — Pictures, illustrations, etc. I. Title.

KING, Martin Luther. 233
The measure of a man. Philadelphia, Pilgrim Press [1968] 64 p. illus., ports. 16 cm. [BT703.K5 1968] 68-8357 2.95
1. Man (Theology) I. Title.

KUMMEL, Werner Georg, 1905- 233
Man in the New Testament. Translated by John J. Vincent. Rev. and enl. ed. Philadelphia, Westminister Press [1963] 100 p. 19 cm. Translation of Das Bild Des Menschen im Neuen Testament. Includes bibliography. [BT701.2.K813] 63-10420
1. Man (Theology) — Biblical teaching. I. Title.

KUMMEL, Werner Georg, 1905- 233
Man in the New Testament. Tr. by John J. Vincent. Rev., enl. ed. Philadelphia, Westminster [c.1963] 100p. 19cm. Bibl. 63-10420 2.95
1. Man (Theology)—Biblical teaching. I. Title.

LANGE, Joseph. 233
A Christian understanding of existence. Westminister, Md., Newman Press, 1965. xi, 214 p. 23 cm. [BX2350.2.L25] 65-24592
1. Christian life — Catholic authors. 2. Christianity — Philosophy. I. Title.

LANGE, Joseph 233
A Christian understanding of existence Westminister, Md., Newman [c.]1965. xi, 214p. 23cm. [BX2350.2.L25] 65-24592 4.50
1. Christian life—Catholic authors. 2. Christinity— philosphy. I. Title.

*LANTERMAN, Wilmer D. 233
Will man live again? The Name whereby we are saved. New York, Carlton [1967] 69p. 21cm. 2.00
I. Title.

LARSON, Douglas J. 233
I am a child of God. Written by Douglas J. Larson. Illustrated by Gary Kapp. Salt Lake City, Bookcraft, 1971. [23] p. illus. 29 cm. In discussing the arrival of the new baby brother, Mother explains that all human beings exist spiritually in heaven before being born on earth. [BT695.L37] 74-169747
1. Creation—Juvenile literature. I. Kapp, Gary, illus. II. Title.

LEE, Francis Nigel. 233
The origin and destiny of man. [Nutley, N.J.] Presbyterian and Reformed Pub. Co., 1974. vi, 119 p. 21 cm. (Coronation series, 1) Includes bibliographical references. [BT701.2.L39] 74-81509 2.95
1. Man (Theology) I. Title.

LEE, Jung Young. 233
The I: a Christian concept of man. New York, Philosophical Library [1971] 146 p. 23 cm. Includes bibliographical references. [BT701.2.L4] 70-150100 ISBN 0-8022-2052-5 5.95
1. Man (Theology) I. Title.

LEFEVRE, Perry D 233
Man: six modern interpretations [by] Perry LeFevre. Philadelphia, Geneva Press [c1968] 128 p. 21 cm. (Decade books) Bibliographical references included in "Notes" (p. 122-127) [BT701.2.L42] 67-18728
1. Man (Theology) I. Title.

LE TROCQUER, Rene. 233
What is man? Translated from the French by Eric Earn haw Smith. [1st ed.] New York, Hawthorn Books [1961] 124p. 21cm. (Twentieth century encyclopedia of Catholicism, v. 31. Section 3: The nature of man) Translation of Homme, qui suis-je? Includes bibliography. [BT701.2.L453] 61-9458
1. Man (Theology) I. Title.

LE TROQUER, Rene 233
What is man? Tr. from French by Eric Earnshaw Smith. New York, Hawthorn Books [c.1961] 124p. (Twentieth century encyclopedia of Catholicism, v.31. Section 3: The nature of man) Bibl. 61-9458 3.50 bds.,
1. Man (Theology) I. Title.

LIGNEE, Hubert 233
The living temple. Baltimore, Helicon [1966] 107p. 18cm. (Living word ser., 5) Tr. of Le temple nouveau. [BS680.T4L523] 66-9663 1.25 pap.,
1. Temple of God. I. Title.
Available from Taplinger, New York.

LITTLEFAIR, Duncan Elliot, 1912- 233
The glory within you: modern man and the spirit, by Duncan E. Littlefair. Philadelphia, Westminster Press [1973] 218 p. 22 cm. Includes bibliographical references. [BV4501.2.L56] 72-8972 ISBN 0-664-20960-2
1. Spirituality. I. Title.

LLOYD-JONES, David Martyn. 233
Truth unchanged, unchanging. New York, Revell [1950] 96 p. 20 cm. (Jonathan Blanchard Lectures, 1st ser.) [ET701.L7] 50-6981
1. Man (Theology) I. Title. II. Series.

LOGANBILL, Evangeline E. 233
Man's divinity. New York, Pageant Press [c.1960] 111p. 21cm. 3.00
I. Title.

MCLELLAND, Joseph C. 233
The clown and the crocodile [by] Joseph C. McLelland. Richmond, John Knox Press [1970] 158 p. 21 cm. Bibliography: p. [153]-158. [BD431.M29] 70-93829 2.95
1. Life. 2. Festivals. 3. Mythology. I. Title.

MADSEN, Truman G. 233
Eternal man, by Truman G. Madsen. Salt Lake City, Deseret Book Co., 1966. 80 p. illus. 24 cm. Bibliographical footnotes. [BT701.2.M3] 66-26092
1. Man (Theology) I. Title.

MAN in a new society. 233
Edited by Franz Bockle. [New York] Herder and Herder [1972] 156 p. 23 cm. (Concilium, religion in the seventies. Moral theology, v. 75) Includes bibliographical references. [BT701.2.M34] 70-185751 2.95
1. Man (Theology)—Addresses, essays, lectures. 2. Christian ethics—Addresses, essays, lectures. I. Bockle, Franz, ed. II. Series: Concilium: theology in the age of renewal, v. 75.

MASCALL, Eric Lionel, 1905- 233
The importance of being human some aspects of the Christian doctrine of man. New York, Columbia University Press, 1958. 118p. 21cm. (Bampton lectures in America, no. 11) Includes bibliography. [BT701.M36] 58-13109
1. Man (Theology) I. Title.

MASCALL, Eric Lionell, 1905- 233
The importance of being human; some aspects of the Christian doctrine of man, by E. L. Mascall. Westport, Conn., Greenwood Press [1974, c1958] vi, 118 p. 22 cm. Reprint of the ed. published by Columbia University Press, New York, which was issued as no. 11 of Bampton lectures in America. Bibliography: p. [115]-118. [BT701.2.M365 1974] 74-12849 ISBN 0-8371-7761-8
1. Man (Theology) I. Title. II. Series: Bampton lectures in America, no. 11.

MASCALL, Eric Lionell, 1905- 233
The importance of being human; some aspects of the Christian doctrine of man, by E. L. Mascall. Westport, Conn., Greenwood Press [1974, c1958] vi, 118 p. 22 cm. Reprint of the ed. published by Columbia University Press, New York, which was issued as no. 11 of Bampton lectures in America. Bibliography: p. [115]-118. [BT701.2.M365 1974] 74-12849 ISBN 0-8371-7761-8 8.00
1. Man (Theology) I. Title. II. Series: Bampton lectures in America, no. 11.

MEAGHER, Robert E. 233
Personalities and powers; a theology of personal becoming [by] Robert E. Meagher. [New York] Herder and Herder [1968] 142 p. 21 cm. Bibliographical footnotes. [BT701.2.M4] 68-26999 3.50
1. Man (Theology) 2. Identification (Religion) I. Title.

MOLIN, Lennart, 1944- 233
Hearts and structures : about man and society out of an American theological material / Lennart Molin. [Stockholm] : Gummesson, 1976. 212 p. ; 19 cm. Bibliography: p. 203-212. [BT701.2.M555] 77-366778 ISBN 9-17-070487-2 : kr40.00
1. Niebuhr, Reinhold, 1892-1971. 2. Niebuhr, Helmut Richard, 1894-1962. 3. Gustafson, James M. 4. Lehmann, Paul Louis, 1906- 5. Man (Theology)—History of doctrines—20th century. 6. Sociology, Christian—History. 7. Christian ethics—History. I. Title.

MOLL, Willi 233
The Christian image of woman. Tr. by Elisabeth Reinecke, Paul C. Bailey. Notre Dame, Ind., Fides [1967] 168p. 20cm. Tr. of Die dreifache Antwort der Liebe. Bibl. [BT704.M613] 66-30592 2.95 pap.,
1. Woman (Theology) I. Title.

MOLL, Willi. 233
The Christian image of woman. Translated by Elisabeth Reinecke and Paul C. Bailey. Notre Dame, Ind., Fides Publishers [1967] 168 p. 20 cm. Translation of Die drelfache Antwort der Liebe. Bibliography: p. 165. [BT704.M613] 66-30592
1. Woman (Theology) I. Title.

MOLTMANN, Jurgen. 233
Human identity in Christian faith : lectures delivered by Jurgen Moltmann at Stanford University for the Raymond Fred West memorial lectures on immortality, human conduct, and human destiny, March 1974. [Stanford, Calif.] : Board of Trustees of the Leland Stanford Junior University, c1976. iii, 26 p. ; 29 cm. (The Raymond Fred West memorial lectures ; 1974) [BT703.M6] 76-362768
1. Jesus Christ—Person and offices—Addresses, essays, lectures. 2. Man (Theology)—Addresses, essays, lectures. I. Title. II. Series.

MOLTMANN, Jurgen. 233
Man : Christian anthropology in the conflicts of the present / Jurgen Moltmann ; translated by John Sturdy. Philadelphia : Fortress Press, [1974] xi, 124 p. ; 20 cm. Translation of Mensch. Includes bibliographical references. [BT701.2.M5613] 73-88350 ISBN 0-8006-1066-0 pbk. : 3.25
1. Man (Theology) I. Title.

MOONEY, Christopher F., 1925- 233
Man without tears : soundings for a Christian anthropology / Christopher F. Mooney. 1st ed. New York : Harper & Row, [1975] vii, 148 p. ; 22 cm. Includes bibliographical references. [BT701.2.M57 1975] 74-25705 ISBN 0-06-065921-1 : 7.95
1. Man (Theology) I. Title.

MORGAN, Richard. 233
The Biblical theology of sacrifice. Nashville, Printed by Parthenon Press [1969] 85 p. 24 cm. [BS680.S2M6] 72-100635 2.00
1. Sacrifice—Biblical teaching. I. Title.

MORK, Wulstan. 233
The Biblical meaning of man. Milwaukee, Bruce Pub. Co. [1967] xi, 168 p. 22 cm. (Impact books) Includes bibliographical references. [BT701.2.M58] 67-21898
1. Man (Theology)—Biblical teaching. I. Title.

MOULE, Charles Francis Digby. 233
Man and nature in the New Testament; some reflections on Biblical ecology, by C. F. D. Moule. Philadelphia, Fortress Press [1967] xviii, 27 p. 19 cm. (Facet books. Biblical series, 17) First published in 1964. Bibliography: p. 23-24. Bibliographical footnotes. [BT701.2.M6 1967] 67-10504
1. Man (Theology)—Biblical teaching. 2. Image of God. I. Title. II. Series.

MOUROUX, Jean 233
The meaning of man. Tr. [from French] by A. H. G. Downes. Garden City, N. Y., Doubleday [1961, c.1948] 278p. (Image bk., D122) Bibl. .85 pap.,
I. Title.

MUMFORD, Bob. 233
The purpose of temptation. Old Tappan, N.J., Revell [1973] 156 p. illus. 21 cm. "Adapted from the popular tape series: The purpose and principle of temptation." [BT725.M85] 73-15622 ISBN 0-8007-0633-1 2.95
1. Temptation. I. Title.

MURPHY, Carol R. 233
Man: the broken image [by] Carol R. Murphy. [Wallingford, Pa., Pendle Hill Publications, 1968] 24 p. 20 cm. (Pendle Hill pamphlet 158) [BT703.M88] 68-30960
1. Man (Theology) I. Title.

MURRAY, John Courtney, ed. 233
Freedom and man. [Contributors] Hans Kung [and others] New York, P. J. Kenedy [1965] 217 p. 22 cm. (A Wisdom and discovery book) Bibliographical footnotes. [BV741.M87] 65-23957
1. Liberty of conscience. I. Kung, Hans, 1928- II. Title.

NEILL, Stephan Charles, Bp. 233
Man in God's purpose. New York, Association Press [1961] 79p. (World Christian books, no. 36, 2d ser.) First published in 1960 under title: What is man? 61-7469 1.00 pap.,
1. Man (Theology) I. Title.

NEILL, Thomas Patrick, 1915- 233
Religion and culture; the Christian idea of man in contemporary society. Milwaukee, Bruce [1952] 102 p. 20 cm. (The Gabriel Richard lecture, 1951) "Co-sponsored by the National Catholic Educational Association and De Paul University." Bibliographical references included in "Notes" (p. 75-102) [BT701.N44] 52-4009
1. Man (Theology) 2. Civilization, Modern. I. Title. II. Series.

NEMESSZEGHY, Ervin. 233
The theology of evolution, by Ervin Nemesszeghy and John Russell. Notre Dame, Ind., Fides Publishers [1972, c1971] 96 p. 19 cm. (Theology today, no. 6) Bibliography: p. 92-93. [BT712.N45] 73-160592 ISBN 0-85342-291-5
1. Evolution and Christianity. I. Russell, John Leonard, joint author. II. Title.

NICHOLLS, William. ed. 233
Conflicting images of man. New York, Seabury [1967] vii, 231p. 18cm. Bibl. [BT701.2.N5] 64-19627 4.95; 2.25 pap.,
1. Man (Theology)—Addresses, essays, lectures. I. Title.

NICHOLLS, William, ed. 233
Conflicting images of man. New York, Seabury Press [1966] vii, 231 p. 22 cm. Bibliographical references included in "Notes": p. 221-229. [BT701.2.N5] 64-19627
1. Man (Theology)—Addresses, essays, lectures. I. Title.

NIEBUHR, Reinhold, 1892- 233
The nature and destiny of man; a Christian interpretation. New York, Scribner [1964] 2 v. 21 cm. (Gifford lectures) The Scribner library, SL97-98. Contents.Contents. -- v. 1. Human nature. -- v. 2. Human destiny. Bibliographical footnotes. [BT701.N5214] 65-5034
1. Man (Theology) I. Title. II. Series.

*NIEBUHR, Reinhold, 1892- 233
The nature and destiny of man, a Christian interpretation [2v.] New York, Scribners [c.1941-1964] 2v. (305; 328p.) 21cm. (Gifford lects., 1939; SL97; SL98) Contents.v.1. Human nature.--v.2. Human destiny. Bibl. 1.65 pap., ea.,
1. Man (Theology) I. Title.

NIEBUHR, Reinhold, 1892- 233
The self and the dramas of history. New York, Scribner, 1955. ix, 246p. 21cm. Bibliographical footnotes. [BT701.N53] 55-7197
1. Man (Theology) 2. Self. 3. Christianity and politics. 4. Sociology, Christian. I. Title.

NORTH, Robert Grady, 1916- 233
Teilhard and the creation of the soul. Introd. by Karl Rahner. Milwaukee, Bruce [1967] xiv, 317p. 23cm. (St. Louis Univ. (Saint Marys) theol. studies. 5) Index of Teilhard writings: p. 308-317. Bibl. [B2430.T374N6] 67-15250 7.95
1. Teilhard de Chardin, Pierre. 2. Soul. I. Title. II. Series.

O'CONNELL, Robert J. 233
St. Augustine's early theory of man, A.D. 386-391 [by] Robert J. O'Connell. Cambridge, Mass., Belknap Press of Harvard University Press, 1968. xviii, 301 p. 24 cm. Based on the author's thesis, Sorbonne. Bibliographical footnotes. [BR65.A9O28] 68-21981 10.00
1. Augustinus, Aurelius, Saint, Bp. of Hippo—Anthropology. 2. Man (Theology)—History of doctrines. I. Title.

O'GRADY, John F. 233
Christian anthropology : a meaning for human life / John F. O'Grady. New York : Paulist Press, c1976. viii, 231 p. ; 21 cm. Bibliography: p. 217-231. [BT701.2.O33] 75-32307 ISBN 0-8091-1907-2 pbk. : 4.95
1. Man (Theology) I. Title.

OWEN, Derwyn Randolph Grier. 233
Body and soul; a study on the Christian view of man. Philadelphia, Westminster Press [1956] 239p. 21cm. [BT701.O85] 56-7369
1. Man (Theology) I. Title.

OWN, Derwyn Randolph Grier. 233
Body and soul; a study on the Christian view of man. Philadelphia, Westminster Press [1956] 239p. 21cm. [BT701.O85] 56-7369
1. Man (Theology) I. Title.

PANNENBERG, Wolfhart, 1928- / 233
Human nature, election, and history / by Wolfhart Pannenberg. 1st ed. Philadelphia : Westminster Press, c1977. p. cm. [BT701.2.P34] 77-22026 ISBN 0-664-24145-X pbk. : 4.95

1. Man (Christian theology) 2. Kingdom of God. 3. Church and the world. 4. Election (Theology)—History of doctrines. 5. History (Theology) I. Title.

PELZ, Lotte. 233
True deceivers, by Lotte and Werner Pelz. Philadelphia, Westminster Press [1966] 254 p. 21 cm. [BT701.2.P4 1966a] 67-10275
1. Man (Theology) I. Pelz, Werner, joint author. II. Title.

PHIPPS, William E., 1930- 233
Recovering Biblical sensuousness / by William E. Phipps. Philadelphia : Westminster Press, [1975] 192 p. ; 22 cm. Includes bibliographical references and index. [BS680.E4P47] 75-22348 ISBN 0-664-20805-3 : 7.95
1. Emotions—Biblical teaching. 2. Sex and religion. 3. Senses and sensation. I. Title.

PIERIK, Marie, 1884- 233
Dramatic and symbolic elements in Gregorian chant. New York, Desclee Co. 1963. 136 p. facsim., music. 22 cm. [ML3082.P525] 63-20670
1. Chants (Plain,Gregorian, etc.)—Hist. & crit. I. Title.

PITTENGER, William Norman, 233
1905-
The Christian understanding of human nature. Philadelphia, Westminster Press [1964] 190 p. 21 cm. Bibliographical references included in "Notes" (p. [187]-190) [BT701.2.P48] 64-10065
1. Man (Theology) I. Title.

RAHNER, Hugo. 1900- 233
Man at plav. [Tr. by Brian Battershaw. Edward Quinn. New York] Herder & Herder [1967, c.1965] xiv, 105p. 22cm. Tr. of Der Spielende Mensch. Bibl. [BT745.R313] 67-141475 3.50
1. Play. 2. Man (Theology) 3. Recreation. I. Title.

RAHNER, Karl, 1904 233
Hominisation; the evolutionary origin of man as a theological problem. [Tr. [from German] by W. T. O'Hara] [New York] Herder & Herder [1966, c.1965] 119, [1]p. 22cm. (Quaestiones disputatae, 13) Bibl. [BT701.2.R313] 66-944 2.50 pap.,
1. Man (Theology) 2. Evolution. I. Title.

RAVITCH, Norman, comp. 233
Christian man. Belmont, Calif., Wadsworth Pub. Co. [1973] x, 266 p. 23 cm. (Images of Western man, 2) [BR53.R37] 72-89431 ISBN 0-534-00228-5
1. Christian literature. I. Title.

RAYBURN, John 233
Gregorian chant; a history of the controversy concerning its rhythm. New York, 1964. xiv, 90 p. 23 cm. Bibliography: p. 69-82. Bibliographical footnotes. [ML3082.R36] 65-722
1. Chants (Plain, Gregorian, etc.) — Hist. & crit. 2. Musical meter and rhythm. I. Title.

RAYBURN, John. 233
Gregorian chant rhythm; a history of the controversy concerning its interpretation. New York, 1961. 171l. 30cm. Bibliography: leaves [147]-168. [ML3082.R35] 61-30511
1. Chants (Plain, Gregorian, etc.)—Hist. & crit. 2. Musical meter and rhythm. I. Title.

RAYMOND, Father, 1903- 233
You. Milwaukee, Bruce Pub. Co. [1957] 301p. 24cm. [BT701.R19] 57-134
1. Man (Theology) I. Title.

RELIGIOUS Education 233
Association.
What is the nature of man? Images of man in our American culture [by] Kenneth Boulding [and others] Philadelphia, Christian Education Press [1959] 209p. 22cm. Papers either prepared as a basis for study prior to the association's 1957 convention or read at that convention. [BT701.2.R4] 59-7324
1. Man (Theology) 2. Man. I. Boulding, Kenneth Ewart, 1910- II. Title.

ROBERTSON, Edwin Hanton. 233
Man's estimate of man. Richmond, John Knox Press [1958] 125 p. 19 cm. Includes bibliography. [BT701.R58] 58-6940
1. Man (Theology). I. Title.

SAUER, Erich. 233
The king of the earth; the nobility of man according to the Bible and science. Grand Rapids, Eerdmans [1962] 256p. 23cm. Translated by Michael Bolister. [BT701.2.S263] 62-52471
1. Man (Theology) I. Title.

SAUER, Erich Ernst 233
The King of the earth; the mobility of man according to the Bible and science. Grand Rapids, Mich., Eerdmans [c.1962] 256p. 23cm. Tr. by Michael Bolister. 62-52471 3.95
1. Man (Theology) I. Title.

SCHARLEMANN, Martin Henry, 233
1910-
Healing and redemption [by] Martin H. Scharlemann. [St. Louis] Concordia Pub. House [1965] 122 p. 21 cm. Bibliography: p. 115-122. [BT732.4.S3] 65-18457
1. Faith-cure. I. Title.

SCHARLEMANN, Martin Henry, 233
1910-
Healing and redemption [St. Louis] Concordia [c.1965] 122p. 21cm. Bibl. [BT732.4S3] 65-18457 1.95 pap.,
1. Faith-cure. I. Title.

SCHEFFCZYK, Leo, 1920- 233
Man's search for himself; modern and Biblical images. New York, Sheed and Ward [1966] 176 p. 21 cm. Translation of Der moderne Mensch vor dem biblischen Menschenbild. Bibliography: p. [171]-176. [BT701.2.S283] 66-22026
1. Man (Theology) I. Title.

SCHMIDT, Karl Theodore, 1909- 233
Rediscovering the natural in Protestant theology. Minneapolis, Augsburg [c.1962] 91p. 22cm. (Augsburg theological monograph) Bibl. 62-12928 1.65 pap.,
1. Man (Theology) 2. Love (Theology) I. Title.

SHARKEY, Owen, 1917- 233
The mystery of man : an anthropologic study / by Owen Sharkey. Philadelphia : Franklin Pub. Co., [1975] vi, 189 p. ; 24 cm. Includes index. Bibliography: p. 182-185. [BT701.2.S47] 74-29012 ISBN 0-87133-046-6 : 10.95
1. Man (Theology) I. Title.

SHEDD, Russell Philip, 1929- 233
Man in community; a study of St. Paul's application of Old Testament and early Jewish conceptions of human solidarity. Grand Rapids, Mich., Eerdmans [1964] xiii, 200p. 22cm. Bibl. 63-20688 1.95 pap.,
1. Bible. N.T. Epistles of Paul—Criticism interpretation, etc. 2. Man (Theology)—Biblical teaching. 3. Church—Biblical teaching. I. Title.

SHINN, Roger Lincoln. 233
Man: the new humanism. Philadelphia, Westminster Press [1968] 207 p. 21 cm. (New directions in theology today, v. 6) Bibliographical references included in "Notes" (p. [183]-200) [BT28.N47 vol. 6] 68-12256
1. Man (Theology) 2. Humanism. I. Title. II. Series.

SIIRALA, Aarne. 233
Divine humanness. Translated by T. A. Kantonen. Philadelphia, Fortress Press [1970] vi, 186 p. 23 cm. Translation of Jumalallinen in himillisyys. Bibliography: p. 171-179. [BT701.2.S5513] 70-99460 6.50
1. Luther, Martin, 1483-1546—Anthropology. 2. Erasmus, Desiderius, d. 1536. 3. Man (Theology) I. Title.

SIIRALA, Aarne. 233
The voice of illness; a study in therapy and prophecy. Foreword by Paul Tillich. Introd. by Gotthard Booth. Philadelphia, Fortress Press [1964] x, 214 p. 22 cm. Bibliography: p. 199-207. [BT732.S5] 64-10647
1. Medicine and religion. 2. Pastoral medicine. 3. Psychiatry and religion. 4. Psychotherapy. I. Title.

SIIRALA, Aarne 233
The voice of illness; a study in therapy and prophecy. Foreword by Paul Tillich. Introd. by Gotthard Booth. Philadelphia, Fortress [c.1964] x, 214p. 22cm. Bibl. 64-10647 4.50
1. Medicine and religion. 2. Pastoral medicine. 3. Psychiatry and religion. 4. Psychotherapy. I. Title.

SMITH, Ronald Gregor. 233
The new man: Christianity and man's coming of age. London, SCM Press [1956] 120 p. 23 cm. (The Alexander Love lectures, 1955) [BT701.S57] 56-2753
1. Man (Theology) I. Title.

SMITH, Ronald Gregor. 233
The whole man; studies in Christian anthropology. Philadelphia, Westminster Press [1969] 159 p. 21 cm. "Published in Great Britain under the title: The free man." Bibliographical footnotes. [BT703.S6 1969] 69-14819 2.45
1. Man (Theology)—Addresses, essays, lectures. 2. Secularism. I. Title.

STACEY, Walter David. 233
The Pauline view of man in relation to its Judaic and Hellenistic background. London, Macmillan; New York, St. Martin's Press, 1956. 233p. 23cm. [BS2655.M3S73] 56-4824
1. Man (Theology) 2. Bible. N.T. Epistles of Paul—Theology. I. Title.

STAGG, Frank, 1911- 233
Polarities of man's existence in Biblical perspective. Philadelphia, Westminster Press [1973] 220 p. 22 cm. Bibliography: p. [207]-212. [BT701.2.S68] 73-8812 ISBN 0-664-20976-9 7.50
1. Man (Theology) I. Title.

STAMM, Frederick Keller, 233
1883-
I believe in man. New York. Abingdon Press [1959] 77 p. 20 cm. [Know your faith series] [BT701.2.S7] 59-7249
1. Man (Theology) I. Title.

STAMM, Frederick Keller, 233
1883-
I believe in man. New York, Abingdon Press [1959] 77 p. 20 cm. (Know your faith series) [BT701.2.S7] 59-7249
1. Man (Theology) I. Title.

STEDMAN, Ray C. 233
Understanding man / Ray C. Stedman. Waco : Word Books, c1975. 154 p. ; 21 cm. (Discovery books) [BT701.2.S74] 75-18257 ISBN 0-87680-433-4 : 4.95 ISBN 0-87680-984-0 pbk. :
1. Man (Theology) I. Title.

STEVENSON, Wilfred S 233
In God's image. New York, Vantage Press [1954] 61p. 22cm. [BT703.S8] 54-8367
1. Man (Theology) I. Title.

TAYLOR, Louis H 233
The new creation; a study of the Pauline doctrines of creation, innocence, sin, and redemption. [1st ed.] New York Pageant Press [1958] 141 p. 24 cm. Includes bibliography. [BX2655.M3T3] 59-95
1. Man (Theology) — Biblical teaching. 2. Creation. 3. Bible. N. T. Epistles of Paul — Theology. I. Title.

TEILHARD de Chardin, Pierre. 233
On suffering / Pierre Teilhard de Chardin. 1st U.S. ed. New York : Harper & Row, [1974?] 120 p. ; 15 cm. Translation of Sur la souffrance. [BV4909.T4413 1974] 75-18606 ISBN 0-06-068211-6
1. Suffering. I. Title.

THOMAS AQUINAS, Saint, 1225?- 233
1274.
Treatise on man. Translated by James F. Anderson. Englewood Cliffs, N.J., Prentice-Hall, 1962. xiv, 178 p. 21 cm. Selections from the Summa theologica. Bibliographical footnotes. [BT700.T513 1962] 62-7450
1. Man (Theology) — History of doctrines. 2. Thomas Aquinas, Saint — Anthropology. I. Title.

THOMAS AQUINAS, Saint, 1225?- 233
1274
Treatise on man. Tr. by James F. Anderson. Englewood Cliffs, N.J., Prentice-Hall [c.]1962. xiv, 178p. Bibl. 62-7450 2.75 pap.,
1. Man (Theology)—History of doctrines. 2. Thomas Aquinas, Saint—Anthropology. I. Title.

TORRANCE, Thomas Forsyth, 233
1913-
Calvin's doctrine of man. [New ed.] Grand Rapids, Eerdmans [1957] 183p. 23cm. Bibliographical footnotes. [BX9418.T67 1957] 57-9771
1. Man (Theology)—History of doctrines. 2. Calvin, Jean, 1509-1564—Anthropology. I. Title.

TORRANCE, Thomas Forsyth, 233
1913-
Calvin's doctrine of man. [New ed.] Grand Rapids, Eerdmans [1957] 183 p. 23 cm. Bibliographical footnotes. [BX9418.T67 1957] 57-9771
1. Calvin, Jean, 1509-1564 — Anthropology. 2. Man (Theology) — History of doctrines. I. Title.

TORRANCE, Thomas Forsyth, 233
1913-
Calvin's doctrine of man / by T. F. Torrance. Westport, Conn. : Greenwood Press, 1977. 183 p. ; 23 cm. Reprint of the 1957 new ed. published by Eerdmans, Grand Rapids. Includes bibliographical references. [BX9418.T67 1977] 77-5615 ISBN 0-8371-9639-6 lib.bdg. : 13.00
1. Calvin, Jean, 1509-1564—Anthropology. 2. Man (Theology)—History of doctrines. I. Title.

TOURNIER, P. 233
To resist or to surrender? Tr. by John S. Gilmour. Richmond, Va., Knox [1967, c.1964] 63p. 19cm. (Chime paperbacks) The German orig. ed. was pub. under title: Sich Durchsetzen order [i.e. oder] Nachgeben [BL53.T663] 1.00 pap.,
1. Psychology, Religious. 2. Christian ethics. 3. Social interaction. I. Title.

TOURNIER, Paul. 233
The whole person in a broken world. Translated by John and Helen Doberstein. [1st ed.] New York, Harper & Row [1964] 180 p. illus. 22 cm. Translation of Desharmonie de la vie moderne. Bibliography: p. 171-175. [BL53.T643] 64-14377
1. Psychology, Religious. I. Title.

VAGAGGINI, Cipriano, 1909- 233
The flesh, instrument of salvation; a theology of the human body. Staten Island, N.Y., Alba House [1969] 152 p. 22 cm. Translation of Caro salutis est cardo. Bibliographical footnotes. [BT701.2.V313] 69-15856 3.95
1. Catholic Church. Liturgy and ritual. 2. Man (Theology)—History of doctrines. I. Title.

VAN KAAM, Adrian L., 1920- 233
Personality fulfillment in the spiritual life. by Adrian Van Kaam. [1st Amer. ed.] Wilkes-Barre, Pa., Dimension Bks. [1966] 191p. 21cm. [BX2350.2.V27 1966] 66-17195 3.95
1. Spritual life—Catholic authors. I. Title.

VERDUIN, Leonard. 233
Somewhat less than God; the Biblical view of man. Grand Rapids, Eerdmans [1970] 168 p. 22 cm. [BT701.2.V45] 75-103450 2.95
1. Man (Theology)—Biblical teaching. I. Title.

VICKERS, Douglas. 233
Man in the maelstrom of modern thought : an essay in theological perspective / by Douglas Vickers. [Nutley, N.J.] : Presbyterian and Reformed Pub. Co., 1975. ix, 192 p. ; 21 cm. Includes bibliographical references. [BT701.2.V5] 75-322974 4.95
1. Man (Theology) I. Title.

VOGEL, Arthur Anton. 233
The Christian person. New York, Seabury Press, 1963. 124 p. 20 cm. Includes bibliography. [BT701.2.V6] 64-16284
1. Man (Theology) 2. Psychology, Religious. I. Title.

VOGEL, Arthur Anton 233
The Christian person. New York, Seabury [c.] 1963. 124p. 20cm. Bibl. 63-16284 3.50 bds.,
1. Man (Theology) 2. Psychology, Religious. I. Title.

VON HILDEBRAND, Dietrich, 233
1889-
Man and woman. Chicago, Franciscan Herald Press [1966] 103 p. 21 cm. [BT708.V6] 65-25840
1. Sex. 2. Love (Theology) I. Title.

WALLACE, Edwin Ross, 1866- 233
What think ye of man? [n.p., 1954?] 55p. 19cm. [BT703.W3] 54-31527
1. Man (Theology) I. Title.

WEBB, Clement Charles Julian, 233
1865-1954.
God and personality. Freeport, N.Y., Books for Libraries Press [1971] 281 p. 23 cm. (Gifford lectures, 1918-19) Reprint of the 1919 ed. Includes bibliographical references. [BT101.W2 1971] 76-164632 ISBN 0-8369-5916-7
1. God. 2. Personality. I. Title. II. Series.

WILKIN, Vincent. 233
The image of God in sex. New York, Sheed & Ward, 1955. 88p. illus. 20cm. [BT708.W5] 55-14070
1. Sex and religion. I. Title.

WINGREN, Gustaf, 1910- 233
Creation and law. Translated by Ross Mackenzie. [American ed.] Philadelphia, Muhlenberg Press [1961] 210 p. 23 cm. Includes bibliography. [BT701.2.W513] 61-10276
1. Man (Theology) 2. Law and gospel. I. Title.

WINGREN, Gustaf Fredrick, 233
1910-
Creation and law. Tr. [from Swedish] by Ross Mackenzie. Philadelphia, Muhlenberg [c.1958, 1961] 210p. Bibl. 61-10276 4.00
1. Man (Theology) 2. Law and gospel. I. Title.

WOLFF, Hans Walter. 233
Anthropology of the Old Testament / Hans Walter Wolff ; [translated by Margaret Kohl from the German]. Philadelphia : Fortress Press, c1974. x, 293 p. ; 23 cm. Rev. translation of Anthropologie des Alten Testaments. Includes indexes. Bibliography: p. [256]-270. [BS1199.M2W6413 1974] 74-21591 ISBN 0-8006-0298-6 : 14.95
1. Bible. O.T.—Criticism, interpretation, etc. 2. Man (Theology)—Biblical teaching. I. Title.

WOLFF, Richard, 1927- 233
The meaning of loneliness. Wheaton, Ill., Key

Publishers [1970] 132 p. 22 cm. Includes bibliographical references. [BV4911.W6] 77-103929 3.95
1. Loneliness. I. Title.

WRIGHT, John Stafford. 233
Man in the process of time; a Christian assessment of the powers and functions of human personality. Grand Rapids, Eerdmans, 1956. 192p. 23cm. Published in Great Britain under the title: What is man?' [BT701] 56-14016
1. Man (Theology) I. Title.

WRIGHT, John Stafford. 233
Mind, man, and the spirits; man's desperate search for meaning in intellectualism, mysticism, and the occult, by J. Stafford Wright. Grand Rapids, Mich., Zondervan Pub. House [1972, c1968] 190 p. 18 cm. (Zondervan books) Previously published under title: What is man? Bibliography: p. 188. [BT701.2.W7 1972] 73-156240 ISBN 0-85364-010-6 0.95
1. Man (Theology) I. Title.

ZAEHNER, Robert Charles. 233
Matter and spirit: their convergence in eastern religions, Marx, and Teilhard de Chardin. New York, Harper & Row [1963] 210 p. 22 cm. (Religious perspectives, v. 8) "First published in Great Britain under the title: The convergent spirit: towards a dialectics of religion." [BT701.2.Z3] 63-7614
1. Man (Theology) 2. Dialectical theology. I. Title.

ZAEHNER, Robert Charles 233
Matter and spirit: their convergence in eastern religions, Marx, and Teilhard de Chardin. New York, Harper [c.1963] 210p. 22cm. (Religious perspectives, v.8) First pub. in Great Britain under the title: The convergent spirit: towards a dialectics of religion. Bibl. 63-7614 4.50
1. Man (Theology) 2. Dialectical theology. I. Title.

*MONRO, Margaret T. 233.06
Enjoying the wisdom books. Foreword by Brendan McGrath. Chicago, Regnery [1967, c.1963] 111p. 18cm. (Lagos 61L-725) 1.45 pap.,
I. Title.

ARE you nobody? 233.08
[By] Paul Tournier [and others] Pref. by Kyle Haselden. Richmond, John Knox Press [1966] 77 p. 19 cm. (Chime paperbacks) [BT701.2.A67] 66-21649
1. Man (Theology)—Addresses, essays, lectures. 2. Psychology, Religious—Addresses, essays, lectures. I. Tournier, Paul.

MAN before God: 233.'.08
toward a theology of man; readings in theology [by] Juan Alfaro [others] Foreword by Ronald E. Murphy. Comp. at the Canisianum, Innsbruck. [Eds.: Denis Burkhard, others. Tr.: Donald Becker, others] New York, Kenedy [1966] xiv, 241p. 22cm. [BT703.M33] 66-26485 4.95
1. Man(Theology)—Addresses, essays, lectures. I. Alfaro Jimenez, Juan. II. Burkhard, Denis, ed.
Contents omitted.

VERNON, Percy L. 233.081
Man, the creature of three worlds. Francestown, N.H., Jones Co. [1965, c.1964] 116p. 21cm. [BT732.V4] 64-25362 3.00
1. Man (Theology)—Addresses, essays, lectures. I. Title.

A Christian 233'.09
anthropology, by Joseph Goetz [and others] Translated by Mary Innocentia Richards. With a pref. by Robert Faricy. St. Meinrad, Ind., Abbey Press, 1974. xv, 92 p. 21 cm. (Religious experience series, v. 2) "Translation of the articles 'Homme' and 'Homme interieur' which first appeared in the Dictionnaire de spiritualite, Paris, Beauchesne, 1969, vol. 7, cols. 617-650 and 650-674 respectively." Bibliography: p. 91-92. [BT701.2.H6513] 73-94171 ISBN 0-87029-026-6 3.95 (pbk.)
1. Man (Theology)—History of doctrines. I. Goetz, Joseph.

COLE, William Grahman, 233.0904
1917-
The restless quest of modern man. New York, Oxford, 1966. vi, 110p. 21cm. Bibl. [BR121.2.C6] 66-22260 3.50
1. Christianity—20th cent. I. Title.

DONNELLY, John 233'.092'4
Patrick.
Calvinism and Scholasticism in Vermigli's doctrine of man and grace / John Patrick Donnelly. Leiden : Brill, 1976. x, 235 p. ; 25 cm. (Studies in medieval and Reformation thought ; v. 18) Includes indexes. "Appendix: Peter Martyr's Library": p. 211-217. [BT701.2.D64] 76-363864 fl 68.00
1. Vermigli, Pietro Martire, 1499-1562. 2. Man (Theology)—History of doctrines. I. Title. II. Series.

WHITE, William Luther, 233'.0924
1931-
The image of man in C. S. Lewis. Nashville, Abingdon Press [1969] 239 p. 25 cm. Based on the author's thesis, Northwestern University. Bibliography: p. 223-235. [BT701.2.W46] 76-84722 ISBN 0-687-18673-0 5.95
1. Lewis, Clive Staples, 1898-1963. 2. Man (Theology)—History of doctrine—20th century. I. Title.

*BONHOEFFER, Dietrich 233.1
Creation and fall; a theological interpretation of Genesis 1-3 [Tr. from German by John C. Fletcher. and] Temptation [Tr. from German by Kathleen Downham] New York, Macmillan [1965, c.1959] 128p. 18cm. .95 pap.,
I. Title.

FITZPATRICK, Edmund J. 233.1
The sin of Adam in the writings of Saint Thomas Aquinas. Mundelein, Ill., Saint Mary of the Lake Seminary, 1950. 179 p. 23 cm. (Pontificia Facultas Theologica, Seminaril Sanctae Mariae ad Lacum. Dissertationes ad lauream, 20) Bibliography: p. 173-179. [BX1749.T7F5] 51-4893
1. Thomas Aquinas, Saint, 1225?-1274. 2. Fall of man—History of doctrines. I. Title. II. Series: St. Mary of the Lake Seminary, Mundelein, Ill. Dissertationes ad lauream, 20

KOHN, Jacob, 1881- 233.1
Evolution as revelation. New York, Philosophical [c.1963] 171p. 22cm. Bibl. 62-15032 3.75
1. Creation. 2. Evolution. 3. Religion and science—1946- I. Title.

MESTERS, Carlos. 233'.1
Eden, golden age or goad to action? / Carlos Mesters ; translated by Patrick J. Leonard. Maryknoll, N.Y. : Orbis Books, [1974] x, 126 p. ; 22 cm. Translation of Paraiso terrestre. Bibliography : p. 125-126. [BS1237.M4713] 74-78453 ISBN 0-88344-103-9 : 4.95
1. Eden. 2. Fall of man. 3. Sin, Original. I. Title.

MUCKENHIRN, Charles 233.1
Borromeo, Sister.
The image of God in creation. Englewood Cliffs, N.J., Prentice-Hall, 1963. 113 p. 24 cm. (Foundations of Catholic theology series) [BT695.M8] 63-13302
1. Creation. 2. Man (Theology) I. Title.

MUCKENHIRN, Charles 233.1
Borromeo, Sister
The image of God in creation. Englewood Cliffs, N. J., Prentice [c.]1963. 113p. 24cm. (Founds, of Catholic theology ser.) 63-13302 3.95; 1.50 pap.,
1. Creation. 2. Man (Theology) I. Title.

POTTEBAUM, Gerard A. 233.1
God made the world. Illus. by Robert Strobridge. Dayton, Ohio, 38 W. 5th St., Geo. A. Pflaum, c.1963. unpaged. col. illus. 18cm. (Little people's paperbacks, LPP1) .35 pap.,
I. Title.

WESTERMANN, Claus. 233'.1
Creation / Claus Westermann : translated by John J. Scullion. Philadelphia : Fortress Press, [1974] 123 p. ; 20 cm. Translation of Schopfung. [BT695.W4813] 74-75730 ISBN 0-8006-1072-5 pbk. : 3.25 3.25
1. Creation.

YOUNG, Norman James. 233'.1
Creator, creation and faith / [by] Norman Young. London : Collins, 1976. 3-219 p. ; 22 cm. Includes bibliographical references and index. [BT695.Y68 1976b] 76-377640 ISBN 0-00-215140-5 : £3.50
1. Creation. I. Title.

BUTTERWORTH, Robert. 233'.11
The theology of creation. Notre Dame, Ind., Fides Publishers [1969] 91 p. 18 cm. (Theology today, no. 5) Bibliography: p. 91. [BT695.B8] 71-8389 0.95
1. Creation. I. Title.

OVERMAN, Richard H. 233.11
Evolution and the Christian doctrine of creation; a Whiteheadian interpretation, by Richard H. Overman. Philadelphia, Westminster [1967] 301p. 21cm. Bibl. [BT695.O8] 67-15089 7.50 bds.,
1. Whitehead, Alfred North, 1861-1947. 2. Evolution. 3. Creation. I. Title.

OVERMAN, Richard H 233'.11
Evolution and the Christian doctrine of creation; a Whiteheadian interpretation, by Richard H. Overman. Philadelphia, Westminster Press [1967] 301 p. 21 cm. Bibliographical footnotes. [BT695.O8] 67-15089
1. Whitehead, Alfred North, 1861-1947. 2. Evolution. 3. Creation. I. Title.

SCHEFFCZYK, Leo, 1920- 233'.11
Creation and providence. Translated by Richard Strachan. [New York] Herder and Herder [1970] ix, 252 p. 22 cm. (The Herder history of dogma) Translation of Schopfung und Vorsehung. Includes bibliographies. [BT695.S2813 1970b] 68-9677 9.50
1. Creation—History of doctrines. I. Title.

BRUMER, William T 233.14
Children of the Devil; a fresh investigation of the fall of man and original sin, by William T. Bruner. New York, Philosophical Library [1966] xix, 311 p. 21 cm. Bibliography: p. 298-299. [BT720.B78] 65-21756
1. Sin, Original. 2. Fall of man. I. Title.

BRUNER, William T. 233.14
Childern of the Devil; a fresh investigation of the fall of man and original sin. New York, Philosophical [c.1966] xix, 311p. 21cm. Bibl [BT720.B78] 65-21756 5.95
1. Sin, Original. 2. Fall of man. I. Title.

DE ROSA, Peter. 233'.14
Christ and original sin. Milwaukee, Bruce Pub. Co. [1967] xi, 138 p. 22 cm. (Impact books) Bibliographical footnotes. [BT720.D45] 67-19791
1. Jesus Christ — Person and offices. 2. Sin, Original. I. Title.

DE ROSA, Peter. 233'.14
Christ and original sin. Milwaukee, Bruce Pub. Co. [1967] xi, 138 p. 22 cm. (Impact books) Bibliographical footnotes. [BT720.D45] 67-19791
1. Jesus Christ—Person and offices. 2. Sin, Original. I. Title.

DUBARLE, A. M. 233.14
The Biblical doctrine of original sin. Tr. [from French] by E. M. Stewart. New York, Herder & Herder [1965, c.1964] 245p. 21cm. Bibl. [BT720.D7813] 64-20437 4.95 bds.,
1. Sin, Original—Biblical teaching. I. Title.

DUBARLE, Andre Marie, 233.14
1910-
The Biblical doctrine of original sin [by] A. M. Dubarle. Translated by E. M. Stewart. New York, Herder and Herder [1965, c1964] 245 p. 21 cm. Translation of Le peche originel dans l'Ecriture. Bibliographical footnotes. [BT720.D7813] 64-20437
1. Sin, Original — Biblical teaching. I. Title.

HAAG, Herbert, 1915- 233'.14
Is original sin in Scripture? Translated by Dorothy Thompson. With an introd. by Bruce Vawter. New York, Sheed and Ward [1969] 127 p. 21 cm. Translation of Biblische Schopfungslehre und kirchliche Erbsundenlehre. Bibliographical references included in "Notes" (p. 109-127) [BT710.H1313] 69-16995 3.95
1. Sin, Original. 2. Fall of man. I. Title.

HEMINGER, Carl 233.14
The sin of Adam and Eye. New York, Vantage Press [c.1960] 141p. 22cm. 3.00 bds.,
I. Title.

HUTCHINSON, George P. 233'.14
The problem of original sin in American Presbyterian theology, by George P. Hutchinson. [Nutley, N.J.] Presbyterian and Reformed Pub. Co., 1972. x, 119 p. 23 cm. (An International library of philosophy and theology: Biblical and theological studies) Bibliography: p. 117-119. [BT720.H87] 77-190463 2.95
1. Sin, Original—History of doctrines. 2. Theology, Presbyterian—United States. I. Title. II. Series: International library of philosophy and theology: Biblical and theological studies series.

MURRAY, John, 1898- 233.14
The imputation of Adam's sin. Grand Rapids, Eerdmans [1959] 95p. 20cm. Includes bibliography. [BT720.M78] 59-10078
1. Sin, Original. I. Title.

POTTEBAUM, Gerard A. 233.14
They disobeyed. Illus. by Robert Strobridge. Dayton, Ohio; 38 W. 5th St., Geo. A. Pflaum, c.1963. unpaged. col. illus. 18cm. (Little people's paperbacks, LPP3) .35 pap.,
I. Title.

RONDET, Henri, 1898- 233'.14
Original sin: the patristic and theological background. Translated from the French by Cajetan Finegan. Staten Island, N.Y., Alba House [1972] 282 p. 22 cm. Translation of Le peche originel dans la tradition patristique et theologique. Includes bibliographical references. [BT720.R6413] 72-1792 ISBN 0-8189-0249-3 4.95
1. Sin, Original—History of doctrines. I. Title.

SMITH, Hilrie Shelton, 233.14
1893-
Changing conceptions of original sin; a study in American theology since 1750. New York, Scribner, 1955. 242p. 22cm. [BT720.S5] 55-9682
1. Sin, Original—History of doctrines. 2. Theology, Doctrinal—Hist.—U. S. I. Title.

TENNANT, Frederick 233'.14
Robert, 1866-1957.
The sources of the doctrines of the fall and original sin. New York, Schocken Books [1968] xvi, 363 p. 22 cm. Reprint of the 1903 ed., with the 1946 introd. by M. F. Thelen. Bibliographical footnotes. [BT710.T4 1968] 68-27323
1. Fall of man. 2. Sin. I. Title.

TROOSTER, Stephanus 233'.14
Gerardus Maria, 1915-
Evolution and the doctrine of original sin, by S. Trooster. Translated by John A. Ter Haar. Glen Rock, N.J., Newman Press [1968] v, 138 p. 21 cm. Translation of Evolutie in de erfzondeleer. Bibliographical footnotes. [BT720.T713] 68-24814 4.95
1. Sin, Original. I. Title.

YARNOLD, Edward. 233'.14
The theology of original sin. Notre Dame, Ind., Fides Publishers [1971] 95 p. 18 cm. (Theology today, no. 28) Bibliography: p. 92-93. [BT720.Y37] 72-185902 ISBN 0-85342-278-8
1. Sin, Original. I. Title.

BERKOUWER, Gerrit 233'.2
Cornelis, 1903-
Sin, by G. C. Berkouwer. [Translated by Philip C. Holtrop] Grand Rapids, Eerdmans [1971] 599 p. 23 cm. (His Studies in dogmatics) Translation of De Zonde, originally published in 2 v. Includes bibliographical references. [BT715.B4513] 73-27796 9.95
1. Sin.

CHERBONNIER, Edmond La 233.2
Beaume, 1918-
Hardness of heart; a contemporary interpretation of the doctrine of sin. [1st ed.] Garden City, N. Y., Doubleday, 1955. 188p. 22cm. (Christian faith series) [BT701.C47] 55-5500
1. Sin. I. Title.

FARRELL, Walter, 1902-1951 233.2
Sin. New York, Sheed and Ward [1960] 94p. (Canterbury books) 'From [the author's] A companion to the Summan, vol. II.' 60-51669 .75 pap.,
1. Sin. I. Title.

FERRE, Nels Fredrick 233.2
Solomon, 1908-
Evil and the Christian faith, by Nels F. S. Ferre. Freeport, N.Y., Books for Libraries Press [1971, c1947] xi, 173 p. 23 cm. (Essay index reprint series) Original ed. issued as v. 2 of the author's Reason and the Christian faith. Includes bibliographical references. [BJ1401.F4 1971] 71-134075 ISBN 0-8369-2393-6
1. Good and evil. 2. Christianity—Essence, genius, nature. I. Title.

*JANSSENS, Paul Mary, Sr. 233'.2
Things go better with peace. [by] Paul Mary Janssens [and] Pauletta Overbeck. Notre Dame, Ind. Fides Publishers [1973] 122 p. 20 cm. [BT715.] ISBN 0-8190-0480-4. 1.50 (pbk.)
1. Sin. I. Overbeck, Pauletta, Sr. II. Title.

KRUMM, John McGill, 1913- 233.2
The art of being a sinner [by] John M. Krumm. New York, Seabury [c.1967] 128p. 22cm. Bibl. [BT715.K7] 67-10844 3.50 bds.,
1. Sin. 2. Salvation—Popular works. I. Title.

KRUMM, John McGill, 1913- 233.2
The art of being a sinner [by] John M. Krumm. New York, Seabury Press [c1967] 128 p. 22 cm. Bibliographical references included in "Notes" (p. 125-128) [BT715.K7] 67-10844
1. Sin. 2. Salvation — Popular works. I. Title.

LITTLEFAIR, Duncan E., 233'.2
1912-
Sin comes of age / by Duncan E. Littlefair. Philadelphia : Westminster Press, [1975] 191 p. ; 22 cm. Includes bibliographical references and index. [BV4625.L54] 75-23277 ISBN 0-664-20807-X : 6.50
1. Sin. 2. Good and evil. 3. Sins. 4. Salvation. I. Title.

MALY, Eugene H. 233'.2
Sin; Biblical perspectives, by Eugene H. Maly. Dayton, Ohio, Pflaum/Standard [1973] viii, 110 p. 21 cm. Includes bibliographical references. [BT715.M277] 73-79518 ISBN 0-8278-0006-1 1.95 (pbk.)
1. Sin.

MENNINGER, Karl, 1893- 233'.2
Whatever became of sin? New York, Hawthorn Books [1973] viii, 242 p. 25 cm. Includes bibliographical references. [BV4625.M46] 72-7776 7.95
1. Sin. I. Title.

OLSSON, Karl A. 233.2
Seven sins and seven virtues. New York, Harper [c.1959, 1962] 126p. 62-7297 2.75 bds.,
1. Deadly sins. 2. Virtues. I. Title.

PALACHOVSKY, V. 233.2
Sin in the Orthodox Church, by V. Palachovsky. And in the Protestant churches, by C. Vogel. [Tr. from French by Charles Schaldenbrand] New York, Desclee [1966] 106p. 22cm. 66-11142 3.50
1. Sin—History of doctrines. 2. Orthodox Eastern Church—Relations—Protestant Churches. 3. Protestant churches—Relations—Relations—Orthodox Estern Church. I. Vogel, Cyrille. II. Title.

PASTORAL treatment of 233'.2
sin, by P. Delhaye [and others. Translation from the French by Charles Schaldenbrand, Firmin O'Sullivan and Eugene Desmarchelier] New York, Desclee [1968] 319 p. 22 cm. Bibliographical footnotes. [BT715.P3713 1968] 68-25350 7.50
1. Sin. I. Delhaye, Philippe.

PETIT, Francois, O. Pream. 233.2
The problem of evil; translated from the French by Christopher Williams, [1st ed.] New York, Hawthorn Books [1959] 141p. 22cm. (The Twentieth century encyclopedia of Catholicism, v. 20. Section 2: The basic truths) Includes bibliography. [BJ1402.P413] 59-12166
1. Good and evil. 2. Suffering. I. Title. II. Series.

PINK, Arthur Walkington, 233'.2
1886-1952.
Gleanings from the Scriptures; man's total depravity. Chicago, Moody Press [1970, c1969] 347 p. 24 cm. [BT720.P53] 73-80942 5.95
1. Sin, Original. 2. Man (Theology) I. Title.

REGNIER, Jerome, 1918- 233.2
What is sin? Translated from the French by Una Morrissy. Westminster, Md., Newman Press [1961* 125p. 18cm. Translation of La sens du peche. [BT715.R413] 61-66766
1. Sin. I. Title.

RICE, John R., 1895- 233.2
When a Christian sins. Wheaton, Ill., Sword of the Lord Publishers [1954] 134p. 21cm. [BT715.R47] 55-16793
1. Sin. I. Title.

RICoUR, Paul. 233'.2
The symbolism of evil. Translated from the French by Emerson Buchanan. [1st ed.] New York, Harper & Row [1967] xv, 357 p. 22 cm. (Religious perspectives, v. 17) Translation of La symbolique du mal, the 2d pt. of Finitude et culpabilite, which was published as v. 2 of the author's Philosophie de la volonte. Bibliographical footnotes. [BT715.R48] 67-11506
1. Sin. 2. Good and evil. I. Title. II. Series.

ROBERSON, Lee. 233.2
5 ancient sins. Wheaton, Ill., Sword of the Lord Publishers [1954] 74p. 21cm. [BV4625.R58] 55-16567
1. Sin—Sermons. 2. Baptists—Sermons. 3. Sermons, American. I. Title.

ROGERS, William Henry, 233.2
1901-
There shall be no peace. Burlington, N. D. [1955] 86p. 20cm. [BT715.R616] 55-41734
1. Sin. I. Title.

RONDET, Henri, 1898- 233.2
The theology of sin. Translated by Royce W. Hughes. Notre Dame, Ind., Fides Publishers Association [1960] 131p. 20cm. (Themes of theology) Translation of Notes sur la theologie du peche. Includes bibliography. [BT715.R613] 60-15437
1. Sin. I. Title.

SCHOONENBERG, Peter, 1911- 233.2
Man and sin; a theological view [by] Piet Schoonenberg. Tr. by Joseph Donceel. Chicago, Regnery [1968.c.1965] ix, 205p. 17cm. (71L-730) Tr. of De macht der zonde. Bibl. [BT715.S333] 65-23519 1.75 pap.,
1. Sin. I. Title.

SCHOONENBERG, Peter, 1911- 233.2
Man and sin; a theological view [by] Piet Schoonenberg. Translated by Joseph Donceel. [Notre Dame, Ind.,] University of Notre Dame Press, 1965. ix, 205 p. 21 cm. Translation of De macht der zonde. Bibliographical footnotes. [BT715.S333] 65-23519
1. Sin. I. Title.

SELLERS, James Earl 233.2
When trouble comes; a Christian view of evil, sin, and suffering. Nashville, Abingdon Press [c.1960] 128p. 20cm. 60-5476 2.00 bds.,
1. Suffering. I. Title.

SINS of the day, 233.2
[1st ed.] London, New York, Longmans, Green [1959] 75 p. 18 cm. [BV4625.S5] 59-8177
1. Sins.

WEBB, Lance. 233.2
Conquering the seven deadly sins. New York, Abingdon Press [1955] 224p. 23cm. [BV4625.W42] 55-6768
1. Sin, Mortal. I. Title.

WEBB, Lance 233.2
Conquering the seven deadly sins. Nashville, Abingdon [1965, c.1955] 224p. 21cm. (Apex bks., V5) [BV4625.W42] 55-6768 1.25 pap.,
1. Sin, Mortal. I. Title.

*WEDGE, Florence 233.2
What are temptations? Pulaski, Wis., Franciscan Pubs. [1966, c.1965] 56p. 19cm. .25 pap.,
I. Title.

FINNEY, Charles 233.208
Grandison, 1792-1875.
The guilt of sin; evangelistic messages. Grand Rapids, Kregel Publications [1965] 124 p. 20 cm. (The Charles G. Finney memorial library: Evangelistic sermon series) "Selected from Sermons on the way of salvation." [BV3797.F53] 65-25845
1. Sin — Sermons. 2. Evangelistic sermons. 3. Sermons, American. I. Title.

FINNEY, Charles 233.208
Grandison, 1792-1875
The guilt of sin; evangelistic messages. Grand Rapids, Mich., Kregel [c.1965] 124p. 20cm. (Charles G. Finney memorial lib.: Evangelistic sermon ser.) Selected from Sermons on the way of salvation [BV3797.F53] 65-25845 2.50
1. Sin—Sermons. 2. Evangelistic sermons. 3. Sermons, American. I. Title.

TAYLOR, Michael J., 233'.2'08
comp.
The mystery of sin and forgiveness. Michael J. Taylor, editor. Contributors: Paul Anciaux [and others] Staten Island, N.Y., Alba House [1971] xiv, 285 p. 21 cm. Contents.Contents.—Introduction, by M. J. Taylor.—The mystery of sin: The sense of sin in the modern world, by R. O'Connell. Missing the mark, by B. Vawter. Towards a Biblical catechesis of the Decalogue, by P. Tremblay. Sin and community in the New Testament, by J. Murphy-O'Connor. The reality of sin; a theological and pastoral critique, by K. F. O'Shea.—The mystery of forgiveness: The sacrament of penance; an historical outline, by M.-B. Carra de Vaux Saint-Cyr. The ecclesial dimension of penance, by P. Anciaux. Confession: psychology is not enough, by L. Monden. Confession as a means of self-improvement, by J. F. Filella. Communal penance; a liturgical commentary and catechesis, by G.-M. Nissim.—Mystery of original sin: New thinking on original sin, by J. P. Mackey. Evolution and original sin, by P. Smulders. Original sin and man's situation, by P. Schoonenberg. A catechesis on original sin, by M. van Caster. Bibliography: p. [279]-281. [BT715.T25] 70-140284 ISBN 0-8189-0198-5 3.95
1. Sin—Addresses, essays, lectures. 2. Forgiveness of sin—Addresses, essays, lectures. 3. Sin, Original—Addresses, essays, lectures.

SIN 233.2082
[by] Marc Oraison [others] Tr. by Bernard Murchland, Raymond Meyerpeter. Introd. by Bernard Murchland. New York, Macmillan, 1962 [c.1959-1962] 177p. 22cm. 61-151621 4.50
1. Sin. 2. Sin—Psychology. I. Oraison, Marc. II. Murchland, Bernard, ed. and tr.

BLOOMFIELD, Morton 233.21
Wilfred, 1913-
The seven deadly sins; an introduction to the history of a religious concept, with special reference to medieval English literature. [East Lansing] Michigan State College Press, 1952. xiv, 482 p. front. 24 cm. ([Michigan. State College of Agriculture and Applied Science, East Lansing] Studies in language and literature) Bibliography: p. [257]-306. [BV4625.B55] 52-4902
1. Sin, Mortal. 2. Anglo-Saxon literature—Hist. & crit. 3. English literature—Early English (1100-1500)—Hist. & crit. I. Title. II. Series.

GRAHAM, William Franklin, 233.21
1918-
The 7 deadly sins Grand Rapids, Zondervan Pub. House [c1955] 113p. 21cm. [BV4626.G7] 56-4172
1. Deadly sins. I. Title.

PIKE, James Albert, Bp., 233.21
1913-
Man in the middle: conversations of a tempted soul with two voices on the seven deadly sins, by James A. Pike and Howard A. Johnson. Greenwich, Conn., Seabury Press, 1956. 118p. 20cm. [BV4626.P5] 56-7970
1. Deadly sins. I. Johnson, Howard Albert, 1915- joint author. II. Title.

THE Sunday times, London. 233.21
The seven deadly sins [by] Angus Wilson [and others] Special foreword by Ian Fleming. Introd. by Raymond Mortimer. New York, Morrow [1962] 87 p. illus. 23 cm. A series of essays from the Sunday times. [BV4626.S86] 62-52537
1. Deadly sins I. Wilson, Angus. II. Title.

THE Sunday times, London. 233.21
The seven deadly sins [by] Angus Wilson [and others] Special foreword by Ian Fleming. Introd. by Raymond Mortimer. New York, Morrow [1962] 87 p. illus. 23 cm. A series of essays from the Sunday times. [BV4626.S86] 62-52537
1. Deadly sins. I. Wilson, Angus.

WARMATH, William Walter. 233'.21
Seven problems of the spirit in conflict and their solution. Waco, Tex., Word Books [1970] 112 p. 21 cm. Bibliography: p. 111-112. [BV4626.W3 1970] 77-91945 2.95
1. Deadly sins—Sermons. 2. Baptists—Sermons. 3. Sermons, American. I. Title.

WHITLOW, Brian. 233.21
Hurdles to heaven. [1st ed.] New York, Harper & Row [c1963] 155 p. 20 cm. [BV4626.W5] 63-7611
1. Deadly sins. I. Title.

WHITLOW, Brian 233.21
Hurdles to heaven. New York, Harper [c.1963] 155p. 20cm. 63-7611 3.00 bds.,
1. Deadly sins. I. Title.

HARING, Bernhard, 1912- 233'.22
Sin in the secular age [by] Bernard Haring. [1st ed.] Garden City, N.J., Doubleday, 1974. 215 p. 22 cm. Includes bibliographical references. [BT715.H25] 73-10539 ISBN 0-385-09017-X 5.95
1. Sin. I. Title.

BALY, Denis 233.4
The cause of freedom. Greenwich, Conn., Seabury [c.1962] 63p. illus. 21cm. (Senior-high-sch. unit) .75 pap.,
I. Title.

LAWLOR, Monica Mary 233.4
Personal responsibility. New York, Hawthorn [c.1963] 142, [1]p. diagrs. 21cm. (20th cent. ency. of Catholicism. v.33. Section 3: The nature of man) Bibl. 63-20565 3.50 bds.,
1. Man (Theology) I. Title. II. Series: The Twentieth century encyclopedia of Catholicism, v.33

WARLICK, Harold G. 233'.4
Liberation from guilt / Harold G. Warlick, Jr. [Nashville] : Broadman Press, 1977c1976 128 p. ; 20 cm. Includes bibliographical references. [BJ1471.5.W37] 76-27480 ISBN 0-8054-5246-X pbk. : 2.50
1. Guilt. I. Title.

AUGUSTINUS, Aurelius, 233.5
Saint, Bp. of Hippo.
The greatness of the soul [and] The teacher; translated and annotated by Joseph M. Colleran. Westminster, Md., Newman Press, 1950. 255 p. 22 cm. (Ancient Christian writers. The works of the Fathers in translation, no. 9) Bibliographical references included in "Notes" (p. [187]-239) [BR60.A35 no. 9] 50-6436
1. Soul. 2. Knowledge, Theory of (Religion) 3. Signs and symbols. 4. Inner light. I. Title. II. Title: The teacher. III. Series.

BEATTIE, Nathaniel, 1889- 233.5
The heart of things; some striking analogies from modern medical science. Westwood, N. J., Revell [1961] 119p. 20cm. [BT732.B38] 61-65843
1. Medicine and religion. I. Title.

MCGINN, Bernard, 1937 233'.5
comp.
Three treatises on man; a Cistercian anthropology. Edited by Bernard McGinn. [Spencer, Mass.] Cistercian Publications; [distributed by] Consortium Press, Washington, 1974 [c1972] p. cm. (Cistercian Fathers series, no. 24) Includes bibliographical references. [BT743.M25] 74-8679 ISBN 0-87907-024-2 10.95
1. Soul—Addresses, essays, lectures. 2. Man (Theology)—Addresses, essays, lectures. I. Guillaume de Saint-Thierry, 1085 (ca.)-1148. De natura corporis et animae. English. 1974. II. Isaac of Stella, d. 1169. Epistola de anima. English. 1974. III. Alcherus, of Clairvaux, 12th cent. De anima et spiritu. English. 1974. IV. Title. V. Title: Treatise on the spirit and the soul.
Contents omitted.

MCGINN, Bernard, 1937- 233'.5
comp.
Three treatises on man; a Cistercian anthropology. Edited by Bernard McGinn. [Spencer, Mass.] Cistercian Publications; [distributed by] Consortium Press, Washington, 1974 [c1972] p. cm. (Cistercian Fathers series, no. 24) Contents.Contents.—McGinn, B. Introduction.—William of St. thierry. The nature of the body and soul. Translated by B. Clark.—The letter of Isaac of Stella on the soul. Translated by B. McGinn.—Treatise on the spirit and the soul. Translated by E. Leiva and St. Benedicta Ward. Includes bibliographical references. [BT743.M25] 74-8679 ISBN 0-87907-024-2 10.95
1. Soul—Addresses, essays, lectures. 2. Man (Theology)—Addresses, essays, lectures. I. Guillaume de Saint-Thierry, 1085 (ca.)-1148. De natura corporis et animae. English. 1974. II. Isaac of Stella, d. 1169. Epistola de anima. English. 1974. III. Alcherus, of Clairvaux, 12th cent. De anima et spiritu. English. 1974. IV. Title. V. Title: Treatise on the spirit and the soul.

*PATTON, Walter S. 233.5
Soul surgery. New York, Vantage [c.1964] 47p. 21cm. 2.00 bds.,
I. Title.

WETZEL, Elizabeth (Saylor) 233.5
1868-
Showers of blessing. Philadelphia, Soul Scientist [1952] 300 p. 21 cm. [BT743.W42] 52-4213
1. Soul. I. Title.

*WOOD, A. Skevington 233.5
Life by the spirit (formerly pub. as Paul's Pentecost) Grand Rapids, Mich., Zondervan [1964, c.1963] 144p. 21cm. 2.50
I. Title.

BURNS, Norman T. 233'.5'09
Christian mortalism from Tyndale to Milton [by] Norman T. Burns. Cambridge, Harvard University Press, 1972. 222 p. 24 cm. A revision of the author's thesis, University of Michigan. Bibliography: p. [203]-213. [BT741.2.B87 1972] 72-75406 ISBN 0-674-12875-3 10.00
1. Soul—History of doctrines. 2. Immortality—History of doctrines. I. Title.

MILLER, Alexander, 1908- 233.6
The man in the mirror; studies in the Christian understanding of selfhood. [1st ed.] Garden City, N. Y., Doubleday, 1958. 186p. 22cm. (The William Belden Noble lectures, 1957) Christian faith series. Includes bibliography. [BR123.M53] 58-10031
1. Christianity—Addresses, essays, lectures. I. Title.

AUGUSTINUS, Aurelius, 233.7
Saint, Bp. of Hippo.
On free choice of the will [by] Saint Augustine. Translated by Anna S. Benjamin and L. H. Hackstaff. With an introd. by L. H. Hackstaff. Indianapolis, Bobbs-Merrill [1964] xxxi, 162 p. 21 cm. (The Library of liberal arts) "150" Bibliography: p. xxxi. [BR65.A6643] 63-16932
1. Free will and determinism. 2. Good and evil. I. Benjamin, Anna S., tr II. Hackstaff, L. H., tr. III. Title.

CONN, Charles W. 233.7
Why men go back; studies in defection and devotion, by Charles W. Conn. Foreword by Wade H. Horton. [1st ed.] Cleveland, Tenn., Pathway Pr. [1966] 136p. 22cm. [BV4501.2.C66] 65-21953 2.50
1. Christian life. I. Title.

DIETRICH, Suzanne de 233.7
Free men; meditations on the Bible today. Tr. introd. by Olive Wyon. Philadelphia, Westminster [1964, c.1961] 127p. 20cm. 61-5654 1.25 pap.,
1. Freedom (Theology) I. Title.

DIETRICH, Suzanne de 233.7
Free men; meditations on the Bible today. Tr. [from French and] introd. by Olive Wyon. Philadelphia, Westminster Press [c.1961] 127p. 61-5654 2.75
1. Freedom (Theology) I. Title.

FISK, Samuel. 233'.7
Divine sovereignty and human freedom. [1st ed.] Neptune, N.J., Loizeaux Bros. [1973] 175 p. 21 cm. On spine: Seeing both sides ... Divine sovereignty and human freedom. Bibliography: p. 155-164. [BJ1461.F5] 73-81550 ISBN 0-87213-165-3 3.95
1. Free will and determinism. I. Title. II. Title: Seeing both sides ... Divine sovereignty and human freedom.

FISK, Samuel. 233'.7
Divine sovereignty and human freedom. [1st ed.] Neptune, N.J., Loizeaux Bros. [1973] 175 p. 21 cm. On spine: Seeing both sides ... Divine sovereignty and human freedom. Bibliography: p. 155-164. [BJ1461.F5] 73-81550 ISBN 0-87213-165-3 3.95
1. Free will and determinism. I. Title. II. Title: Seeing both sides ... Divine sovereignty and human freedom.

HOFMANN, Hans F., 1923- 233'.7
Discovering freedom, by Hans Hofmann. Boston, Beacon Press [1969] 100 p. 21 cm. [BT810.2.H6] 70-86345 6.00
1. Freedom (Theology) I. Title.

MICHELS, Florence. 233'.7
Faces of freedom. Westminster, Md., Newman Press [1968] vi, 106 p. 21 cm. Includes bibliographies. [BT810.2.M5] 68-16665
1. Freedom (Theology) I. Title.

MIEGGE, Giovanni. 233.7
Religious liberty. New York, Association Press [1957] 94p. 20cm. (World Christian books) [BV741.M5] 57-6882
1. Religious liberty. I. Title.

PAOLI, Arturo. 233'.7
Freedom to be free. Translated by Charles Underhill Quinn. [Maryknoll, N.Y., Orbis Books, 1973] viii, 303 p. 23 cm. Translation of Dialogo della liberazione. [BT810.2.P313] 72-93340 ISBN 0-88344-142-X 7.95
1. Freedom (Theology) I. Title.

*PATTON, Walter S. 233.7
You are the master. New York, Vantage [1964, c.1963] 60p. 21cm. 2.00 bds.,
I. Title.

RATHWICK, Clyde W. 233'.7
Plan or purpose, by Clyde W. Rathwick. Philadelphia, Dorrance [1967] 57p. 20cm. [BT701.2.R37] 67-20528 2.50
1. Man (Theology) I. Title.

SMITH, Gerard. 233.7
Freedom in Molina. Chicago, Loyola University Press [1966] x, 230 p. 24 cm. Bibliography: p. 227-230. [BX4705.M598S6] 67-616
1. Molina, Luis de, 1535-1600. 2. Freedom (Theology)—History of doctrines. I. Title.

SMITH, Macklin, 1944- 233'.7
Prudentius' Psychomachia : a reexamination / Macklin Smith. Princeton, N.J. : Princeton University Press, c1976. xii, 310 p. ; 23 cm. Includes bibliographical references and index. [BR65.P783S6] 75-29436 ISBN 0-691-06299-4 : 17.50
1. Prudentius Clemens, Aurelius. Psychomachia. I. Title.

TOURNIER, Paul. 233.7
To resist or to surrender? Translated by John S. Gilmour. Richmond, John Knox Press [1964] 63 p. 21 cm. Translation of Tenir tete ou ceder. [BL53.T663] 64-16284
1. Psychology, Religious. 2. Christian ethics. 3. Social interaction. I. Title.

LINDSLEY, James Elliott. 233.749
A history of Saint Peter's Church, Morristown, New Jersey. Morristown? 1952 102 p. illus. 21 cm. [BX5980.M67S3] 52-31358
1. Morristown, N.J. St. Peter's Church. I. Title.

234 Salvation (Soteriology)

ALLEN, Hattie Bell (McCracken), 1896- 234
Jesus saves. Drawings by Mariel Wilhoite Turner. Nashville, Broadman Press [1951] 107 p. illus. 19 cm. Includes hymns, with music. [BT751.A55] 51-3529
1. Salvation—Study and teaching. 2. Religious education—Text. books for adolescents—Baptist. I. Title.

ANDERSON, Robert, Sir 1841-1918. 234
The gospel and its ministry, a handbook of evangelical truth. 17th ed. Grand Rapids, Kregel Publications, 1956. 213p. 20cm. [BT751.A6 1956] 55-8176
1. Salvation. I. Title.

BATES, Maurice L. 234
Saved forever. [By] Maurice L. Bates. Nashville, Broadman Press [1968] 63 p. 19 cm. [BT753.B33] 68-26917
1. Salvation—Popular works. I. Title.

BAXTER, James Sidlow. 234
God so loved; an expository series on the theology and evangel of the best-known text in the Bible. Grand Rapids, Zondervan Pub. House [1960] 206p. 23cm. First published in London in 1949 under title: The best word ever. [BT753.B35 1960] 60-50189
1. Salcation—Sermons. 2. Baptists—Sermons. 3. Sermons, English. I. Title.

BEALL, James Lee. 234
Laying the foundation / James Lee Beall, Marjorie Barber. Plainfield, N.J. : Logos International, c1976. xvii, 389 p. ; 21 cm. [BT753.B39] 76-42084 ISBN 0-88270-198-3 pbk. : 4.95
1. Salvation—Miscellanea. I. Barber, Marjorie, joint author. II. Title.

BLOESCH, Donald G., 1928- 234
The Christian life and salvation, by Donald G. Bloesch. Grand Rapids, W. B. Eerdmans Pub. Co. [1967] 164 p. 23 cm. Bibliographical footnotes. Bibliographical references included in "Explanatory notes" (p. 141-153) [BT751.2.B5] 66-27406
1. Salvation. I. Title.

BLOESCH, Donald G., 1928- 234
Jesus is victor! : Karl Barth's doctrine of salvation / Donald G. Bloesch. Nashville : Abingdon, c1976. 176 p. ; 19 cm. Includes bibliographical references and index. [BT751.2.B54] 76-14360 ISBN 0-687-20225-6 pbk. : 5.95
1. Barth, Karl, 1886-1968. 2. Salvation—History of doctrines. I. Title.

BROOKES, James Hall, 1830-1897 234
The way made plain [an ancient classic rev., adapted for modern use] by James H. Brookes. D. D. Grand Rapids. Mich., Baker Bk. [1967, c.1937] 305p. 19cm. [BT751.B86 1937] 3.50
1. Salvation. 2. Evangelistic work. 3. Sunday-schools. 4. Bible. N. T. Romans x, 1-13—Criticism, interpretation, etc. I. Title.

BUCKLER, Henry Reginald, 1840- 234
The perfection of man by charity. St. Louis, Herder [1954] 235p. 23cm. [BX2350.5] 54-14435
1. Perfection—Catholic authors. I. Title.

CAMPBELL, Robert Edward, 1924- 234
Catholic theology and the human race. [Maryknoll, N. Y.] Maryknoll Publications [1956?] 54p. 24cm. (World horizon reports, report no. 17) Includes bibliography. [BT755.C3] 58-22513
1. Salvation outside the Catholic Church. I. Title.

CHAFER, Lewis Sperry, 1871-1952. 234
Salvation. Grand Rapids, Zondervan Pub. House [1972, c1917] ix, 149 p. 21 cm. "A Dunham publication." [BT751.C5 1972] 73-150623 3.50
1. Salvation.

CITRON, Bernhard, 1905- 234
New birth; a study of the evangelical doctrine of conversion in the Protestant Fathers. With a pref. by Hugh Watt. Edinburgh, University Press, 1951. xvi, 214p. 23cm. (Edinburgh University publications; theology. no. 1) Bibliography: p. 203-207. [BT790.C5] 54-19256
1. Regeneration (Theology) I. Title. II. Series: Edinburgh. University. Edinurgh University publications: theology, no. 1

CLARK, Will C 1896- 234
The path the failure of the faith doctrine and the awakening of self-knowledge through grace. New York, William-Frederick Press, 1956. 212p. illus. 22cm. [BR126.C58] 56-5567
I. Title.

CLARKE, Catherine Goddard. 234
Gate of heaven. Boston, Ravengate Press, 1952 ['1951] 141 p. 20 cm. [BT755.C58 1951a] 52-7634
1. Salvation outside the Catholic Church. 2. St. Benedict Center, Cambridge, Mass. 3. Catholic Church—Doctrinal and controversial works—Miscellaneous authors. I. Title.

CLARKE, Catherine Goddard. 234
Gate of Heaven. Cambridge, Mass., Saint Benedict Center [1951] 145 p. 19 cm. [BT755.C58] 52-349
1. Salvation outside the Catholic Church. 2. St. Benedict Center. Cambridge, Mass 3. Catholic Church—Doctrinal and controversial works—Miscellaneous authors. I. Title.

CLARKE, Catherine Goddard. 234
The Loyolas and the Cabots, the story of the Boston heresy case. Boston, Ravengate Press, 1950. xi, 301 p. 21 cm. [BT755.C6] 50-8321
1. Salvation. 2. St. Benedict Center, Cambridge, Mass. 3. Catholic Church—Doctrinal and controversial works—Miscellaneous authors. I. Title.

COLIN, Louis, 1884- 234
Striving for perfection; the fundamental obligation of the religious state. Translated from the French by Kathryn Day Wyatt. Westminster, Md., Newman Press [c1956] 272p. 22cm. Translation of Tendance a la perfection. [BX2350.5.C63] 55-12403
1. Perfection—Catholic authors. I. Title.

COMPTON, W. H. comp. 234
Salvation sermon outlines. [Westwood, N. J.] Revell Co. [c.1961] 64p. (Revell's sermon outline ser.) 61-9247 1.00 pap.,
1. Salvation—Sermons—Outlines. I. Title.

CONGAR, Marie Joseph,
[Secular name: Georges Yves Congar] 1904-
The wide world my parish; salvation and its problems [by] Yves Congar. Tr. [from French] by Donald Attwater. Baltimore, Helicon Pr. [c.1961] 188p. Bibl. 61-14675 4.50 bds.,
1. Salvation outside the Catholic Church. I. Title.

CONGAR, Yves Marie Joseph, 1904- 234
The wide world my parish; salvation and its problems [by] Yves Congar. Translated by Donald Attwater. Baltimore, Helicon Press [1961] 188 p. 21 cm. [BT755.C653] 61-14675
1. Salvation outside the Catholic Church. I. Title.

COTTRELL, Jack. 234
Being good enough isn't good enough : God's wonderful grace / by Jack Cottrell. Cincinnati : New Life Books, c1976. 96 p. ; 18 cm. [BT751.2.C67] 75-44590 ISBN 0-87239-060-8
1. Salvation—Popular works. 2. Justificaton—Popular works. I. Title.

CROSBY, Michael, 1940- 234
The call and the answer. [Chicago] Franciscan Herald Press [1969] xiv, 165 p. 21 cm. Bibliographical references included in "Notes" (p. 159-165) [BX2350.2.C73] 79-94559 4.95
1. Vocation—Biblical teaching. I. Title.

CULLMANN, Oscar. 234
Salvation in history. [English translation drafted by Sidney G. Sowers and afterwards completed by the editorial staff of the SCM Press. 1st American ed.] New York, Harper & Row [1967] 352 p. 22 cm. Translation of Heil als Geschichte. Bibliographical footnotes. [BR115.H5C83 1967b] 67-21545
1. History (Theology) I. Title.

CUTTING, George. 234
Light for anxious souls in some of their difficulties, by Geo. Cutting. New York, Loizeaux Bros. [1954?] 90 p. 19 cm. [BT753.C88] 75-304255
1. Salvation. 2. Christian life. I. Title.

CYGON, Joseph R 1887-- 234
Journey towards self-realization; an interpretation of the Christian Gospels in relation to certain psychological and metaphysical aspects of soul regeneration. San Gabriel, Calif., Willing Pub. Co. [1955] 267p. 21cm. Includes bibliography. [BJ1470.C9] 55-28235
1. Self-realization. 2. Bible. N. T. Gospels—Criticism, interpretation, etc. I. Title.

DART, John Lovering Campbell. 234
God's plan of salvation. London, Faith Press; New York, Morehouse-Gorham [1952] 129 p. 19 cm. [BT751.D3] 52-8881
1. Salvation. I. Title.

*DEETER, Walter Wells. 234
Eternal life, how attained, how and where served. New York, Vantage [1968] 65p. 21 cm. 2.50
I. Title.

DE ROPP, Robert S. 234
Science and salvation, a scientific appraisal of religion's central theme. New York St. Martin's [c.1962] 308p. 22cm. Bibl. 62-11103 5.00
1. Salvation—Comparative studies. 2. Religion and science—1946- I. Title.

DE ROSA, Peter. 234
God our Savior; a study of the atonement. Milwaukee, Bruce Pub. Co. [1967] ix, 230 p. 22 cm. (Impact books) Bibliographical footnotes. [BT751.2.D4] 67-28213
1. Salvation—Popular works. I. Title.

DE ROSA, Peter. 234
God our Saviour; a study of the atonement. Milwaukee, Bruce Pub. Co. [1967] ix, 230 p. 22 cm. (Impact books) Bibliographical footnotes. [BT751.2.D4] 67-28213
1. Salvation — Popular works. I. Title.

DICKIE, Edgar Primrose, 1897- 234
God is light; studies in revelation and personal conviction. New York, Scribner, 1954. 261p. 23cm. [BT751] 54-8545
1. Salvation. 2. Revelation. I. Title.

DOUTY, Norman Franklin, 1899- 234
Union with Christ [by] Norman F. Douty. Swengel, Pa., Reiner Publications, 1973. 274 p. 23 cm. [BT751.2.D68] 73-160672 7.95
1. Salvation. I. Title.

DOUTY, Norman Franklin, 1899- 234
Union with Christ [by] Norman F. Douty. Swengel, Pa., Reiner Publications, 1973. 274 p. 23 cm. [BT751.2.D68] 73-160672 7.95
1. Salvation. I. Title.

DOYLE, Charles Hugo. 234
In pursuit of perfection; conferences for religious. 214p. 21cm. [BX2350.5.D6] 56-1029
1. Perfection—Catholic authors. I. Title. II. Title: Tarrytown, N. Y.,

DUKEHART, Claude Henry, 1917- 234
State of perfection and the secular priest; a theological study. St. Meinrad, Ind. [1952] x, 186 p. 23 cm. "A Grail publication." Issued also as thesis, Catholic University of America, in microcardform. Bibliography: p. 174-180. [BX1912.D883] 52-4011
1. Perfection—Catholic authors. 2. Clergy—Religious life. 3. Clergy (Canon law) I. Title.

DUN, Angus, Bp., 1892- 234
The Saving Person. [1st ed.] New York, Harper [1957] 127p. 20cm. [BT751.D85] 56-12065
1. Salvation. I. Title.

DUTY, Guy, 1907- 234
If ye continue. Minneapolis, Bethany Fellowship [1966] 186 p. 21 cm. Bibliographical footnotes. [BT751.2.D8] 66-3086
1. Salvation. I. Title.

DUTY, Guy, 1907- 234
If ye continue. Minneapolis, Bethany Fellowship [c.1966] 186p. 21cm. Bibl. [PT751.2.D8] 66-3086 2.95
1. Salvation. I. Title.

EBELING, Gerhard, 1912- 234
The nature of faith. Tr. by Ronald Gregor Smith. Philadelphia, Fortress [1967, c.1961] 191p. 18cm. Tr. of Das Wesen des christlichen Glaubens. [BT771.2.F213 1962] 2.25 pap.,
1. Faith. I. Title.

EDWARDS, Walter Ross, 1910- 234
Have you been saved? [By] W. Ross Edwards. Nashville, Broadman Press [1973] 128 p. 21 cm. [BT751.2.E35] 73-78215 ISBN 0-8054-8121-4
1. Salvation. I. Title.

EMERSON, James Gordon, Jr. 1926- 234
The dynamics of forgiveness. Philadelphia, Westminster [c.1964] 203p. 21cm. Bibl. 64-15856 5.00
1. Forgiveness of sin. I. Title.

EMINYAN, Maurice, 1922- 234
The theology of salvation. [Boston] St. Paul Editions [dist. Daughters of St. Paul, c.1960] 233p. Bibl. 60-53304 4.00; 3.00 pap.,
1. Salvation outside the Catholic Church. I. Title.

FABER, Frederick William 234
The Precious Blood: The price of our salvation. New ed. Philadelphia, P. Reilly Co. [1959] 278 p. 24 cm. 59-16917 3.95
1. Salvation. 2. Precious Blood, Devotion to. I. Title.

FAHS, Sophia Blanche (Lyon) 1876- 234
The old story of salvation. Boston, Starr King Press; distributed by the Beacon Press [1955] 191p. illus. 25cm. [BT751.F3] 55-9360
1. Salvation. I. Title.

FEE, Zephyrus Roy, 1890- 234
The divine plan of man's salvation. Dallas, Wilkinson Pub. Co. [1952] 104 p. illus. 18 cm. [BX8333.F35D5] 52-33961
1. Methodist Church—Sermons. 2. Sermons, American. I. Title.

FEENEY, Leonard, 1897- 234
Bread of life. Cambridge, Mass., Saint Benedict Center, 1952. 204p. illus. 19cm. [BT755.F4] 53-15579
1. Salvation. 2. Salvation outside the Catholic Church. I. Title.

FEUERBACH, Ludwig Andreas, 1804-1872. 234
The essence of faith according to Luther [by] Ludwig Feuerbach. Translated by Melvin Cherno. [1st American ed.] New York, Harper & Row [1967] 127 p. 21 cm. (The Library of religion and culture) Translation of Das Wesen des Glauben im Sinne Luthers. [B2971.W45E5] 67-21547
1. Luther, Martin, 1483-1546. 2. Faith. 3. Christianity—Essence, genius, nature. I. Title.

FLEW, Robert Newton, 1886- 234
The idea of perfection in Christian theology; an historical study of the Christian ideal for the present life, by R. Newton Flew. Oxford, Clarendon Press, 1968. xv, 422 p. 23 cm. Bibliographical footnotes. [BT766.F5 1968] 68-121493 ISBN 0-19-826620-0
1. Perfection—History of doctrines. I. Title.

FRAZEE, Willmonte Doniphan, 1906- 234
Ransom and reunion through the sanctuary / W. D. Frazee. Nashville : Southern Pub. Association, c1977. 124 p. ; 20 cm. [BX6154.F67] 77-76135 ISBN 0-8127-0138-0 pbk. : 3.95
1. Seventh-Day Adventists—Doctrinal and controversial works. 2. Sanctuary doctrine (Seventh-Day Adventists) I. Title.

FRAZEE, Willmonte Doniphan, 1906- 234
Ransom and reunion through the sanctuary / W. D. Frazee. Nashville : Southern Pub. Association, c1977. 124 p. ; 20 cm. [BX6154.F67] 77-76135 ISBN 0-8127-0138-0 pbk. : 3.95
1. Seventh-Day Adventists—Doctrinal and controversial works. 2. Sanctuary doctrine (Seventh-Day Adventists) I. Title.

GARRETT, Willis Edward. 234
The life that wins; salvation sermonettes. [1st ed.] New York, Exposition Press [1954] 56p. 21cm. [BT753.G3] 54-10336
1. Salvation—Sermons. 2. Presbyterian Church—Sermons. 3. Sermons, American. I. Title.

GARTH, John Goodall, 1871- 234
The little Gospel, a popular study of John 3: 16. [Charlotte? N. C., 1952] 158 p. 24 cm. [BT751.G25] 52-24897
1. Salvation. 2. Bible. N. T. John III, 16—Criticism, interpretation, etc. I. Title.

GERSTNER, John H. 234
Steps to salvation; the evangelistic message of Jonathan Edwards. Philadelphia, Westminster Press [c.1959] 192p. 22cm. 60-5118 3.95
1. Edwards, Jonathan, 1703-1758. 2. Preaching—Hist.—U.S. I. Title.

*GORRIE, Ron 234
Man's greatest question; precisely how good does a man have to be before God will let him pass into heaven.? New York, Exposition [c.1965] 225p. 22cm. 4.00
I. Title.

GRACE unlimited / 234
edited by Clark H. Pinnock. Minneapolis : Bethany Fellowship, inc., [1975] p. cm. Includes bibliographical references. [BT761.2.G7] 75-22161 ISBN 0-87123-185-9 pbk. : 4.95
1. Grace (Theology)—Addresses, essays, lectures. 2. Salvation—Addresses, essays, lectures. I. Pinnock, Clark H., 1937-

*GRAHAM, William Franklin, 1918- 234
Peace with God. by Billy Graham. Westwood, N.J., Revell [1968,c.1953] 248p. 16cm. (Spire bks.) .50 pap.,
I. Title.

GREATHOUSE, Josephine A. 234
Calvary life insurance. Santa Monica, Calif., Wesco Publications [1951] 210 p. illus. 24 cm. [BT751.G67] 51-38722
1. Salvation—Popular works. I. Title.

GREEN, Edward Michael Bankes 234
The meaning of salvation. Philadelphia, Westminster [1966,c.1965] 255p. 23cm. Bibl. [BT751.2.G67] 66-11090 4.50
1. Salvation. I. Title.

GREENSTOCK, David L. 234
Be ye perfect. St. Louis, Herder, 1952. 362 p. 21 cm. [BX2350.5.G7] 52-9323
1. Perfection—Catholic authors. I. Title.

GRITZMACHER, Victor J. 234
Out of the night; the way of salvation. Anderson, Ind., Warner Press [dist. Gospel Trumpet Press, c.1961] 160p. 61-7027 2.95
1. Salvation. I. Title.

GROMACKI, Robert Glenn. 234
Salvation is forever. Chicago, Moody Press [1973] 188 p. 22 cm. [BT751.2.G74] 73-7331 ISBN 0-8024-7506-X 2.50
1. Salvation. I. Title.

HAMMEL, W. W., 1900- 234
How shall we escape if we neglect... so great salvation; a scriptural study with poems and chart [by] W. W. Hammel. [1st ed.] Cleveland, Tenn., Pathway Press [1972] 95 p. 21 cm. [BT751.2.H28] 72-86758
1. Salvation. I. Title. II. Title: So great salvation.

HARTMAN, A Lincoln. 234
The gospel according to the Scriptures; unique outline method of Bible study. A Course of study comprising twenty-three lessons or examinations, which may be competed in from three to five months. [Rev. ed.] Boston, Christopher Pub. House [1952] 86 p. illus. 21 cm. [BT753.H29] 52-4541
1. Salvation—Popular works. I. Title.

HASTINGS. H. L. 234
Will all men be saved? New York 25, Box 87, Cathedral Station, People's Christian Bulletin, 1960. 22p. .25 pap.,
I. Title.

HEGRE, Theodore A 234
Three aspects of the Cross. Minneapolis, Bethany Fellowship Press [c1960] 276p. illus. 20cm. [BT751.2.H4] 61-45612
1. Salvation—Popular works. 2. Perfection. I. Title.

HEPPENSTALL, Edward. 234
Salvation unlimited; perspectives in righteousness by faith. Washington, Review and Herald Pub. Association [1974] 256 p. 21 cm. Bibliography: p. 255-256. [BT751.2.H46] 73-91425 6.95
1. Salvation. I. Title.

HILTON, Walter d.1396. 234
The scale of perfection. Translated into modern English, with an introd. and notes, by Gerard Sitwell. Westminster, Md., Newman Press [1953] xx, 316p. 20cm. (The Orchard books) [BV4831.H5 1953] 54-356
1. Devotional literature. 2. Perfection—Catholic authors. I. Sitwell, Gerard, ed. and tr. II. Title.

HILTON, Walter, d.1396. 234
The scale of perfection / by Walter Hilton ; abridged and presented by Illtyd Trethowan ; [translated by Leo Sherley-Price]. New abridged ed. St. Meinrad, In. : Abbey Press, 1975. x, 148 p. ; 20 cm. (A Priority edition) "The text is from The Ladder of perfection, Penguin (1957)." [BV4831.H5 1975] 75-19926 ISBN 0-87029-055-X pbk. : 3.95
1. Devotional literature. 2. Perfection (Catholic) I. Trethowan, Illtyd, 1907- II. Title.

HORNE, Charles M. 234
Salvation, by Charles M. Horne. Chicago, Moody Press [1971] 128 p. illus. 22 cm. (A Handbook of Bible doctrine) Includes bibliographies. [BT751.2.H67] 72-143477 1.95
1. Salvation.

HOYT, Herman Arthur, 1909- 234
The new birth. Findlay, Ohio, Dunham Pub. Co. [c1961] 122p. 20cm. [BT790.H85] 62-4946
1. Regeneration (Theology) I. Title.

JAEGHER, Paul de. 234
One with Jesus; or, The life of identification with Christ. Translated from the French. [New enl. ed.] Westminster, Md., Newman Press, 1956. 59p. 21cm. Translation of La vie d'identification au Christ Jesus. [BT769.J313] 57-59535
1. Mystical union. I. Title.

JOHNSON, Early Ashby, 1917- 234
Saved, from what? By E. Ashby Johnson. Richmond, Va., Knox [1966] 79p. 19cm. (Chime paperbacks) [BT751.2.J6] 66-11687 1.00 pap.,
1. Salvation—Popular works. I. Title.

JOHNSON, Edward H. 234
For a time like this; studies on salvation today and mission today [by] E. H. Johnson. New York, Friendship Press [1973] 128 p. 21 cm. Includes bibliographical references. [BT751.2.J63] 73-3087 ISBN 0-377-03001-5 pap. 1.95
1. Salvation. 2. Missions. I. Title.

KAISER, Edwin G., 1893- 234
The everlasting covenant; theology of the Precious Blood [by] Edwin G. Kaiser. Carthagena, Ohio, Messenger Press [1968] x, 303 p. illus. 23 cm. Includes bibliographical references. [BT751.2.K3] 68-6134
1. Salvation. 2. Atonement. 3. Precious Blood, Devotion to. I. Title.

KEAN, Charles Duell, 1910- 234
Christ in our hearts. New York, Abingdon [1957] 109p. 20cm. Bibliographical references included in 'Notes' (p. 107-109) [BT751] 56-10148
1. Salvation—Popular works. I. Title.

KEVAN, Ernest Frederick, 1903- 234
Salvation. Grand Rapids, Baker Book House, 1963. 130 p. 21 cm. (Christian faith series) [TB751.2.K4] 63-13774
1. Salvation. I. Title.

KEVAN, Ernest Frederick, 1903- 234
Salvation. Grand Rapids, Mich., Baker Bk. [c.] 1963. 130p. 21cm. (Christian faith ser.) Bibl. 63-13774 2.50 bds.,
1. Salvation. I. Title.

KILLINGER, John. 234
The salvation tree. [1st ed.] New York, Harper & Row [1973] xxii, 169 p. 22 cm. Includes bibliographical references. [BT751.2.K54 1973] 72-11357 ISBN 0-06-064583-0 5.95
1. Salvation. 2. Christianity—20th century. I. Title.

KILLINGER, John. 234
The saving image: redemption in contemporary preaching, edited by John Killinger. Nashville, Tidings [1974] 95 p. 19 cm. [BV3797.A1K54] 73-86375 1.25 (pbk.)
1. Evangelistic sermons. 2. Sermons, American. I. Title.

KLASSEN, William. 234
The forgiving community. Philadelphia, Westminister Press [1966] 253 p. 21 cm. Bibliography: p. [247]-253. [BT795.K55] 66-10141
1. Forgiveness of sin. I. Title.

KLASSEN, William 234
The forgiving community. Philadelphia, Westminster [c.1966] 253p. 21cm. Bibl. [BT795.K55] 66-1014 6.00
1. Forgiveness of sin. I. Title.

KRAMER, Paul Stevens, 1895- 234
The doctrine of our salvation; an introduction to the theology of atonement, of the church, and of the sacraments. New York, Exposition Press [1951] 165 p. 22 cm. Bibliography: p. [163]-165. [BT751.K73] 51-4896
1. Salvation. 2. Protestant Episcopal Church in the U. S. A.—Doctrinal and controversial works. I. Title.

KROLL, Woodrow Michael, 1944- 234
It will be worth it all : a study in the believer's rewards / by Woodrow Michael Kroll. Neptune, N.J. : Loizeaux Bros., [1977] p. cm. [BT940.K76] 76-30438 ISBN 0-87213-475-X
1. Reward (Theology) 2. Salvation. I. Title.

KUIPER, Herman. 234
By grace alone; a study in soteriology. Grand Rapids, Eerdmans, 1955. 165p. 23cm. [BT751.K8] 55-13836
1. Salvation. I. Title.

LAPSLEY, James N. 234
Salvation and health; the interlocking processes of life, by James N. Lapsley. Philadelphia, Westminster Press [1972] 174 p. 21 cm. Includes bibliographical references. [BT732.L33] 79-188383 ISBN 0-664-20936-X
1. Salvation. 2. Hygiene. 3. Mental hygiene. I. Title.

LASSITER, Perry. 234
Once saved ... always saved / Perry Lassiter. Nashville : Broadman Press, [1975] 96 p. ; 18 cm. Includes bibliographical references. [BT768.L37] 74-15289 ISBN 0-8054-1931-4 pbk. : 1.50
1. Perseverance (Theology) I. Title.

LINEBERRY, John, 1926- 234
Salvation is of the Lord; topical and word studies in the plan of salvation, its need, meaning, source, blessing, and assurance. Foreword by Kenneth S. Wuest. Grand Rapids, Zondervan Pub. House [1959] 96p. 20cm. [BT751.2.L5] 59-38172
1. Salvation. I. Title.

LLOYD-JONES, David Martyn. 234
The plight of man and the power of God [by] D. Martyn Lloyd-Jones. [2d ed.] Grand Rapids, W. B. Eerdmans Publ. Co. [1966] 93 p. 21 cm. Reprint of the 1945 ed. [BT751.L55 1966] 66-18724
1. Salvation. I. Title.

LLOYD-JONES, David Martyn 234
The plight of man and the power of God [by] D. Martyn Lloyd-Jones [2d ed.] Grand Rapids, Mich., Eerdmans [1966] 93p. 21cm. Reprint of the 1945 London ed. [BT751.L55 8] 66-18724 2.50 bds.,
1. Salvation. I. Title.

LOMBARDI, Riccardo. 234
The salvation of the unbeliever. [Translation from the Italian by Dorothy M. White] Westminster, Md., Newman Press [1956] 376p. 23cm. [BT755.L62] 56-11424
1. Salvation outside the Catholic Church. I. Title.

*LUCK, G. Coleman 234
What it means to be saved. Chicago, Moody [c.1963] 64p. 18cm. (Moody compact bk., 49) .29 pap.,
I. Title.

MCDONOUGH, Thomas M. 234
The law and the gospel in Luther; a study of Martin Luther's confessional writings. [New York] Oxford [c.]1963. 180p. 23cm. (Oxford theological monographs) Bibl. 63-51261 4.80
1. Luther, Martin—Theology. I. Title. II. Series.

MACGUIRE, Meade. 234
Lambs among wolves. Nashville, Southern Pub. Association [1957] 136p. 18cm. [BT751.M254] 57-29530
1. Salvation—Popular works. I. Title.

MCKINLEY, O. Glenn. 234
Where two creeds meet; a Biblical evaluation of Calvinism and Arminianism. Kansas City, Mo., Beacon Hill Press [1959] 124p. 20cm. [BX6195.M3] 59-9813
1. Arminianism. 2. Calvinism. I. Title.

MACON, Leon Meertief, 1908- 234
Salvation in a scientific age. Grand Rapids, Zondervan Pub. House [1955] 121p. 21cm. [BT751.M26] 55-39576
1. Salvation. I. Title.

MARCHBANKS, John B., 1914- 234
Great doctrines relating to salvation, by John B. Marchbanks. Neptune, N.J., Loizeaux Bros. [1970] 96 p. 21 cm. [BT753.M29] 73-123612 1.50
1. Salvation—Addresses, essays, lectures. I. Title.

MARSHALL, I. Howard. 234
Kept by the power of God : a study of perseverance and falling away / I. Howard Marshall. [2d ed.] Minneapolis : Bethany Fellowship, [1974] c1969. 281 p. ; 22 cm. Based on thesis, University of Aberdeen, 1963. Includes indexes. Bibliography: p. 259. [BT768.M34 1974] 74-23996 ISBN 0-87123-304-5 : 3.95
1. Perseverance (Theology) I. Title.

*MARTIN, Harold S. 234
Simple messages on Romans, by Harold S. Martin. Elgin, Ill., Brethren Press, [1974] 123 p. 21 cm. [BT751] 3.95
1. Salvation. 2. Theology. I. Title.

MAST, Russell L. 234
Lost and found. Scottdale, Pa., Herald [c.1963] 102p. 20cm. 63-7537 2.50
1. Salvation—Sermons. 2. Bible. N. T. Luke xv—Sermons. 3. Mennonite Church—Sermons. 4. Sermons, American. I. Title.

MAURIER, Henri. 234
The other covenant; a theology of paganism. Translated by Charles McGrath. Glen Rock, N.J., Newman Press [1968] xiii, 268 p. 21 cm. Translation of Essai d'une theologie du paganisme. Bibliographical footnotes. [BT759.M313] 68-55400 4.95
1. Paganism. 2. Salvation outside the church. I. Title.

MAXWELL, L E 234
Crowded to Christ. Grand Rapids, Eerdmans, 1950. 354 p. 22 cm. [BT751.M4] 50-14781
1. Salvation. I. Title.

MAXWELL, L. E. 234
Crowded to Christ. Grand Rapids, Mich., Eerdmans [1965, c.1950] 354p. 22cm. [BT751.M4] 2.25 pap.,
1. Salvation. I. Title.

MEADE, Russell J. 234
Handbook on deliverance, by Russell J. Meade. Carol Stream, Ill., Creation House [1973] ix, 182 p. 19 cm. (New leaf library) Earlier ed. published under title: Victory over demonism today. [BT981.M4 1973] 73-81495 ISBN 0-88419-052-8 1.45 (pbk.)
1. Devil. 2. Demonology. I. Title.

MORANDO, Nazarene 234
The characteristics of charity [Boston] St. Paul Eds. [dist. Daughters of St. Paul, c.1963] 106p. 19cm. 63-14589 2.00; 1.00 pap.,
1. Charity. I. Title.

MORRIS, Frederick M 234
Power to save. Greenwich, Conn., Seabury Press, 1960. 64p. 21cm. [BT751.2.M6] 60-5885
1. Salvation. I. Title.

MUMAW, John R. 234
Assurance of salvation. Scottdale, Pa., Herald

Press, 1950. xii, 138 p. 21 cm. An expansion of the author's Christian assurance. Bibliography: p. 137-138. [BT785.M8] 51-15088
1. Assurance (Theology) I. Title.

NEWBIGIN, James Edward Lesslie, Bp. 234
Sin and salvation. Philadelphia, Westminster Press [1957] 128p. 20cm. [BT751] 57-5901
1. Salvation—Popular works. I. Title.

NEWBIGIN, James Edward Lesslie, Bp. 234
Sin and salvation. Philadelphia, Westminster Press [1937] 128p. 20cm. [BT751] 57-5901
1. Salvation—Popular works. I. Title.

NUNEZ C., Emilio Antonio. 234
Caminos de renovacion / Emilio Antonio Nunez C. Grand Rapids, Mich. : Editado por Publicaciones Portavoz Evangelico para Outreach Publications, c1975. 218 p. ; 18 cm. Includes bibliographical references. [BT751.2.N86] 76-459912 ISBN 8-439-94101-3
1. Salvation. 2. Church renewal. I. Title.

PAXSON, Ruth. 234
War in your heart. Chicago, Moody Press [1952] 180 p. 20 cm. [BT751.P35] 52-44403
1. Salvation — Popular works. I. Title.

PENTECOST, J. Dwight. 234
Things which become sound doctrine [by] J. Dwight Pentecost. Grand Rapids, Zondervan [1970, c1965] 159 p. 21 cm. [BV4501.2.P4 1970] 74-120045 0.95
1. Christian life—1960- 2. Theology, Doctrinal—Popular works. I. Title.

PERRIN, Joseph Marie, 1905- 234
Christian perfection and married life. Translated by P.D.Gilbert. Westminister, Md., Newman Press, 1958. 92p. 19cm. [BX2350.5.P413] 58-14896
1. Perfection—Catholic authors. 2. Marriage—Catholic Church. I. Title.

PETERS, John Leland. 234
Christian perfection and American Methodism. New York, Abingdon Press [1956] 252p. 23cm. [BT766.P43] 56-7764
1. Perfection—History of doctrines. 2. Methodist Church in the U. S. I. Title.

PFURTNER, Stephanus 234
Luther and Aquinas on salvation. Tr. [from German] by Edward Quinn. Introd. by Jaroslav Pelikan. New York, Sheed [1965, c.1964] 160p. 21cm. Bibl. [BT752.P453] 65-12206 3.50
1. Luther, Martin, 1483-1546—Theology. 2. Thomas Aquinas, Saint, 1225?-1274—Theology. 3. Salvation—History of doctrines. 4. Assurance (Theology)—History of doctrines. I. Title.

PINK, Arthur Walkington, 1886-1952. 234
The doctrine of salvation / A. W. Pink. Grand Rapids, Mich. : Baker Book House, c1975. 164 p. ; 24 cm. [BT751.2.P53] 75-18228 ISBN 0-8010-6980-7 : 5.95
1. Salvation. I. Title.

PINK, Arthur Walkington, 1886-1952. 234
The doctrine of salvation / A.W. Pink. Grand Rapids, Mich. : Baker Book House, 1977,c1975. 169p. ; 22 cm. Includes indexes. [BT751.2P53] ISBN 0-8010-7026-0 pbk. : 2.95
1. Salvation. I. Title.
L.C. card no. for hardcover ed.: 75-18228.

*PINK, Arthur Walkington 1886-1952 234
Eternal security [by] Arthur W. Pink. Grand Rapids, Guardian Press, [1974] 126 p. 21 cm. [BT751] ISBN 0-89086-001-7 2.95 (pbk.)
1. Salvation. I. Title.
Distributed by Baker Book House, Grand Rapids, Michigan

POWERS, Joseph M., 1926- 234
Spirit and sacrament; the humanizing experience, by Joseph M. Powers. New York, Seabury Press [1973] x, 211 p. 22 cm. (A Continuum book) [BT77.P7] 72-10566 ISBN 0-8164-1121-2 6.95
1. Theology, Doctrinal—Popular works. 2. Life. I. Title.

PROSPER, Tiro, Aquitanus, 234
Saint. Spurious and doubtful works.
The call of all nations; translated and annotated by P. de Letter. Westminster, Md., Newman Press, 1952. 234 p. 23 cm. (Ancient Christian writers; the works of the Fathers in translation, no. 14) Variously ascribed to St. Prosper, St. Ambrose, and St. Leo the Great. Translation of De vocatione omnium gentium. Bibliographical references included in "Notes" (p. [155]-219) [BR60.A35 no. 14] 52-9014
1. Salvation outside the Catholic Church. 2. Semi-Pelagianism. I. Ambrosius, Saint, Bp. of Milan. Spurious and doubtful works. The call of all nations. II. Leo I, the Great, Saint, Pope, d. 461. Spurious and doubtful works. The call of all nations. III. Letter, Prudentius de, ed. and tr. IV. Title. V. Title: De vocatione omnium gentium. VI. Series.

PURKISER, W T 234
Sanctification and its synonyms; studies in the Biblical theology of holiness. Kansas City, Mo., Beacon Hill Press [c1961] 96p. 20cm. (Aycock lectures, 1959) Includes bibliography. [BT766.P9] 61-5118
1. Perfection—Biblical teaching. 2. Church of the Nazarene— Doctrinal and controversial works. I. Title.

PURKISER, W T 234
Security: the false and the true. Kansas City, Mo., Beacon Hill Press [1956] 64p. 20cm. [BT785.P8] 56-2146
1. Assurance (Theology) I. Title.

RALL, Harris Franklin, 1870- 234
Religion as salvation. Nashville, Abingdon-Cokesbury Press [1953] 254p. 24cm. [BT751.R25] 53-5400
1. Salvation. I. Title.

RECONCILIATION and hope; 234
New Testament essays on atonement and eschatology presented to L. L. Morris on his 60th birthday. Edited by Robert Banks. [1st American ed.] Grand Rapids, W. B. Eerdmans Pub. Co. [1975, c1974] 317 p. port. 22 cm. [BS2395.R4] 74-5370
1. Marris, Leon. 2. Marris, Leon—Bibliography. 3. Bible. N.T.—Addresses, essays, lectures. I. Banks, Robert J., ed. II. Morris, Leon.

RETIF, Andre 234
The salvation of the gentiles and the prophets, by A. Retif, P. Lamarche. Baltimore, Helicon [1966] 120p. 18cm. (Living word ser., 4) Tr. of Le salut des nations. [BS1199.P34R43] 66-9678 1.25 pap.,
1. Bibl. O. T.—Theology. 2. Salvation—Biblical teaching 3. Universalism. I. Lamarche, P., joint author. II. Title.
Available from Taplinger in New York.

RICE, John R., 1895- 234
A know- so salvation. Wheaton, Ill., Sword of the Lord Publishers [1953] 187p. 21cm. [BT751.R49] 53-30193
1. Salvation. I. Title.

ROPER, Anita, 1908- 234
The anonymous Christian. Translated by Joseph Donceel. With an afterword: The anonymous Christian according to Karl Rahner, by Klaus Riesenhuber. New York, Sheed and Ward [1966] ix, 179 p. 22 cm. Bibliographical references for the afterword included in "Notes" (p. 172-179) [BT759.R613] 66-12269
1. Salvation outside the church. I. Title.

ROYER, W M 234
The mystery of God; or, There is a spiritual body. [1st ed.] New York, Greenwich Book Publishers [c1958] 54p. 21cm. [BT751.2.R6] 58-14372
1. Salvation. I. Title.

ROYO MARIN, Antonio 234
The theology of Christian perfection [by] Antonio Royo, Jordan Aumann. [Tr. from Spanish, adapted by Jordan Aumann] Dubuque, Iowa, Priory Pr. [1962] 692p. 25cm. 62-17314 10.95
1. Perfection (Catholic) I. Aumann, Jordan. II. Title.

RUST, Eric Charles. 234
Salvation history; a Biblical interpretation. Richmond, John Knox Press [1962] 325 p. 21 cm. [BT751.2.R8] 62-19459
1. Salvation—Biblical teaching. 2. Eschatology—Biblical teaching. I. Title.

RUST, Eric Charles 234
Salvation history; a Biblical interpretation. Richmond, Knox [c.1962] 325p. 21cm. Bibl. 62-19459 6.00
1. Salvation—Biblical teaching. 2. Eschatology—Biblical teaching. I. Title.

SAUER, Erich. 234
From eternity to eternity, an outline of the divine purposes' translated by G. H. Lang. Grand Rapids, Eerdmans, 1954. 207p. illus. 23cm. Translation of Der gottliche Erlosungsplan von Ewigkeit su Ewigkeit. [BT751.S273] 54-4153
1. Salvation. I. Title.

SAWYER, John F. A. 234
Semantics in Biblical research; new methods of defining Hebrew words for salvation [by] John F. A. Sawyer. Naperville, Ill., A. R. Allenson [1972] xii, 146 p. 22 cm. (Studies in Biblical theology, 2d ser., 24) "Revised version of a thesis submitted to the Faculty of Divinity in the University of Edinburgh in 1968 under the title, Language about salvation." Bibliography: p. [130]-136. [BT752.S28 1972] 72-75901 ISBN 0-8401-3074-0
1. Bible. O.T.—Language, style. 2. Salvation—Biblical teaching. 3. Ysh' (Hebrew root) I. Title. II. Series.

SCHLEIERMACHER, Friedrich 234
The Christian faith [2v. Introd. to this ed. by Richard R. Niebuhr. Tr. from German. Ed. by H. R. MacKintosh, J. S. Stewart] New York, Harper [c.1963] 2v. (xxiv, 354; viii, 406p.) (Harper torchbk.; Cloister Lib., TB-108, TB-109) Pub. orig. in Edinburgh in 1928. 2.25 ea., pap.,
I. Title.

SHAMON, Albert J. 234
First steps to sanctity. Westminster, Md., Newman Press, 1958. 128 p. 23 cm. [BX2350.52.S5] 58-11028
1. Purgative way to perfection. I. Title.

SHULER, John Lewis, 1887- 234
Give your guilt away, by J. L. Shuler. Mountain View, Calif., Pacific Press Pub. Association [1972] 62 p. 19 cm. [BT753.S53] 72-79605
1. Salvation—Popular works. I. Title.

SIWEL, Hplour, 1940- 234
Society in rebellion. Philadelphia, Dorrance [1973] 22 p. 22 cm. [BT751.2.S54] 73-78155 ISBN 0-8059-1862-0 2.95
1. Salvation—Popular works. I. Title.

SMEDES, Lewis B. 234
All things made new; a theology of man's union with Christ, by Lewis B. Smedes. Grand Rapids, Eerdmans [1970] 272 p. 23 cm. Includes bibliographical references. [BT205.S64] 67-31668 6.95
1. Jesus Christ—Person and offices. 2. Bible. N.T. Epistles of Paul—Theology. 3. Man (Theology) I. Title.

SMITH, William Edward, 1881- 234
How to be saved; miscellaneous writings. Boston, Meador Pub. Co. [1950] 622 p. 21 cm. [BT751.S67] 50-10773
1. Salvation. I. Title.

SOVIK, Arne. 234
Salvation today. Foreword by Philip Potter. Minneapolis, Augsburg Pub. House [1973] 112 p. 20 cm. [BT751.2.S6] 73-78252 ISBN 0-8066-1318-1 2.95
1. Salvation. I. Title.

STOCK, Augustine. 234
Lamb of God, the promise and fulfillment of salvation. [New York] Herder & Herder [1963] 175p. 21cm. 63-9554 3.95
1. Salvation. I. Title.

STOCK, Augustine. 234
The way in the wilderness; Exodus, wilderness, and Moses themes in Old Testament and New. Collegeville, Minn., Liturgical Press [1969] xii, 156 p. 23 cm. Bibliographical footnotes. [BS680.E9S86] 72-13548 4.75
1. Moses. 2. Exodus, The—Biblical teaching. I. Title.

*SZOPKO, Emey J. 234
Jesus: his mission on earth; a book of salvation. New York, Carlton [1968] 84p. 21cm. (Hearthstone bk.) 2.75
1. Salvation. I. Title.

TELFER, William 234
The forgiveness of sins; an essay in the history of Christian doctrine and practice. Philadelphia, Muhlenberg Press [1960] 154p. 20cm. 60-3096 2.75
1. Forgiveness of sin—History of doctrines. I. Title.

TELFER, William, 1886- 234
The forgiveness of sins; an essay in the history of Christian doctrine and practice. Philadelphia, Muhlenberg Press [1960, c1959] 154 p. 20 cm. [BT795.T4] 60-3096
1. Forgiveness of sin — History of doctrines. I. Title.

TURNER, John Clyde, 1878- 234
Soul-winning doctrines. [Rev. ed.] Nashville, Convention Press [1955, c1943] 116 p. 19 cm. [BT77.T8] 58-11353
1. Theology, Doctrinal — Popular works. I. Title.

VERKUYL, Johannes. 234
The message of liberation in our age, by J. Verkuyl. Translated by Dale Cooper. Grand Rapids, Mich., W. B. Eerdmans Pub. Co. [1972] 110 p. 21 cm. Translation of De boodschap der bevrijding in deze tijd. [BT751.2.V4413 1972] 75-180786 ISBN 0-8028-1437-9 2.45
1. Salvation. I. Title.

WESLEY, John, 1703-1791. 234
Christian perfection, as believed and taught by John Wesley; edited and with an introd. by Thomas S. Kepler. Cleveland, World Pub. Co. [1954] xviii, 144p. 17cm. (World devotional classics) [BT766.W515 1954] 52-8445
1. Perfection. I. Title.

WHITE, Ellen Gould (Harmon) 1827-1915. 234
Love unlimited: combining Steps to Christ, and Thoughts from the Mount of Blessing. Mountain View, Calif., Pacific Press Pub. Association [c1958] 313 p. illus. 18 cm. [BX6111.W513] 59-6403
1. Salvation. 2. Sermon on the Mount. I. Title.

WIDMER, R. Rubin. 234
Jesus, the light of the world; a study of contemporary views, by R. Rubin Widmer. Nashville, Southern Pub. Association [1967] 142 p. 22 cm. Bibliography: p. 135-142. [BT759.W5] 67-28845
1. Salvation outside the church. I. Title.

WILLETS, Alfred 234
What the New Testament says about forgiveness. Foreword by J. B. Phillips. New York, Association [c.1964] 127p. 15cm. (Reflection bk.) 64-12562 .50 pap.,
1. Forgiveness of sin—Biblical teaching. I. Title.

WILLETTS, Alfred. 234
What the New Testament says about forgiveness. With a foreword by J. B. Phillips. New York, Association Press [1964] 127 p. 15 cm. (A Reflection book) [BT795.W54] 64-12562
1. Forgiveness of sin — Biblical teaching. I. Title.

WORDSWORTH, Ephraim Edward 1887- 234
Steps to heaven. Kansas City, Mo., Beacon Hill Press [1955] 103p. 19cm. [HF753] 55-14618
1. Salvation—Popular works. I. Title.

*WOYCHUCK, N. A. 234
The incomparable salvation. St. Louis, Mo., Miracle Pr. [1968,c.1967] 112p. 20cm. 1.75 bds.,
1. Salvation—Popular works. I. Title.
Publisher's address: 5410 Kerth Rd., St. Louis, Mo. 63128.

ZIMMERLI, Walther, 1907- 234
Man and his hope in the Old Testament. Naperville, Ill., A. R. Allenson [1971?] 174 p. 22 cm. (Studies in Biblical theology, 2d ser., 20) Translation of Der Mensch und seine Hoffnung im Alten Testament. Includes bibliographical references. [BS1199.H65Z513] 70-161528
1. Hope—Biblical teaching. I. Title. II. Series.

RANDALL, John Herman, 1899- 234'.01
Hellenistic ways of deliverance and the making of the Christian synthesis. New York, Columbia University Press, 1970. ix, 242 p. 21 cm. [BR128.G8R395] 74-137339 7.95
1. Christianity and other religions—Greek. 2. Christianity—Philosophy—History. 3. Philosophy, Ancient. I. Title.

FRELIGH, Harold Meredith, 1891- 234.0202
Newborn; a basic handbook on salvation for personal or group study [by] Harold M. Freligh. Minneapolis, Bethany Fellowship [1975 c1962] 123 p. 18 cm. [BT751.2F7] 75-5444 ISBN 0-87123-120-4 1.25 (pbk.)
1. Salvation. I. Title.

CHICK, Jack T. 234'.02'07
The battle, by Jack T. Chick. Chino, Calif., Chick Publications [1972] 96 p. illus. 13 cm. [BT753.C48] 72-84847 1.25
1. Salvation—Caricatures and cartoons. I. Title.

MURRMAN, Warren Daniel. 234'.092'4
The significance of the human nature of Christ and the Sacraments for salvation according to William Estius. Latrobe, Pa., Saint Vincent Archabbey, c1970. xvii, 259 p. 23 cm. Inaug. Diss.—Munich, 1967. Includes bibliographical references. [BT198.M87] 74-158340
1. Jesus Christ—History and doctrines—17th century. 2. Estius, Guilielmus, 1542-1613. 3. Salvation—History of doctrines. 4. Sacraments—History of doctrines. I. Title.

REYMOND, Robert L. 234'.0924
Barth's soteriology [by] Robert L. Reymond. Philadelphia, Presbyterian and Reformed Pub. Co., 1967. 41 p. 23 cm. (International library of philosophy and theology: Biblical and theological studies series) Bibliographical references included in "Notes" (p. 39-41) [BX4827.B3R47] 67-26019
1. Barth, Karl, 1886- I. Title. II. Series.

BALES, James D., 1915- 234'.1
Pat Boone and the gift of tongues [by] James D. Bales. Searcy, Ark., 1970. 378 p. 22 cm. Bibliography: p. 377-378. [BL54.B35] 70-275946
1. Boone, Charles Eugene. 2. Glossolalia. 3. Gifts, Spiritual. I. Title.

BARTON, Levi Elder, 1870- 234.1
Amazing grace. Boston, Christopher Pub. House [1954] 213p. 21cm. [BT761.B3] 54-11045
1. Grace (Theology)—Sermons. 2. Baptists—Sermons. 3. Sermons, American. I. Title.

BAXTER, James Sidlow. 234'.1
Christian holiness restudied and restated / J. Sidlow Baxter. Grand Rapids : Zondervan Pub. House, c1977. 206 p. ; 23 cm. Contents.Contents.—A new call to holiness.—His deeper work in us.—Our high calling. [BT765.B34] 76-52939 ISBN 0-310-20600-6 : 12.95
1. Sanctification. 2. Holiness. 3. Holiness—Biblical teaching. I. Title.

BENNETT, Dennis J. 234'.1
The Holy Spirit and you; a study-guide to the spirit-filled life [by] Dennis and Rita Bennett. Plainfield, N.J., Logos International [1971] 224 p. 21 cm. Includes bibliographical references. [BT123.B37] 71-140673 ISBN 0-912106-14-X 4.95
1. Baptism in the Holy Spirit. 2. Gifts, Spiritual. I. Bennett, Rita, joint author. II. Title.

BISHOP, George Sayles, 1836-1914. 234.1
The doctrines of grace, and kindred themes. Grand Rapids, Baker Book House, 1954. 509p. 21cm. [BT761.B5 1954] 54-2721
1. Grace (Theology)—Sermons. 2. Reformed Church—Sermons. 3. Sermons, American. I. Title.

BITTLINGER, Arnold, 1928- 234'.1
Gifts and ministries. Introd. by Kilian McDonnell. [Translated from the German by Clara K. Dyck] Grand Rapids, W. B. Eerdmans Pub. Co. [1973] 109 p. 21 cm. Includes bibliographical references. [BT767.3.B53] 72-96403 ISBN 0-8028-1497-2 1.95 (pbk.)
1. Gifts, Spiritual. I. Title.

BOOTH, Abraham 234.1
The reign of grace, from its rise to its consummation. Introd. essay by Thomas Chalmers. Swengel, Pa., Bible Truth [1963] 291p. 19cm. 1.95 pap.,
I. Title.

BRENNAN, Robert Edward, 1897- 234.1
The seven horns of the lamb; a study of the gifts based on Saint Thomas Aquinas. Milwaukee, Bruce Pub. Co. [1966] ix, 169 p. 22 cm. Bibliography: p. 167-169. [BT767.3.B7] 66-17940
1. Thomas Aquinas, Saint, 1225?-1274 — Ethics. 2. Gifts, Spiritual. I. Title.

BRENNAN, Robert Edward, 1897- 234.1
The seven horns of the lamb; a study of the gifts based on Saint Thomas Aquinas. Milwaukee, Bruce [c.1966] ix, 169p. 22cm. Bibl. [BT767.3.B7] 66-17940 4.95
1. Thomas Aquinas, Saint, 1225?-1274—Ethics. 2. Gifts, Spiritual. I. Title.

BRIDGE, Donald. 234'.1
Spiritual gifts & the church [by] Donald Bridge [and] David Phypers. Downers Grove, Ill., InterVarsity Press [1974, c1973] 160 p. 18 cm. Includes bibliographical references. [BT767.3.B74 1974] 73-89303 ISBN 0-87784-672-3 1.75 (pbk.).
1. Gifts, Spiritual. I. Phypers, David, joint author. II. Title.

BUNYAN, John, 1628-1688. 234'.1
A holy life; the beauty of Christianity. Swengel, Pa., Reiner Publications, 1968. 123 p. 19 cm. First published in 1684. Reprinted from an ed. of Bunyan's works, published by the American Baptist Publication Society, circa 1851. [BT767.B9 1968] 73-1296 1.75
1. Holiness. I. Title.

BUNYAN, John, 1628-1688. 234'.1
Saved by grace. Swengel, Pa., Reiner Publications, 1967. 73 p. 19 cm. Original t.p. reads: A selection from the Works of that eminent servant of Christ, John Bunyan ... consisting of thirteen discourses, and his Grace abounding to the Chief of sinners. Selected by Isaac Beeman. Volume 1. London, Printed by T. Bensley; published by J. Eedes ... 1827. [BT760.B83] 67-9415
1. Grace (Theology)—Early works to 1800. I. Title.

BURDICK, Donald W. 234'.1
Tongues, to speak or not to speak / by Donald W. Burdick. Chicago : Moody Press, [1969], 1974 printing. 94 p. ; 22 cm. (Moody evangelical focus) Bibliography: p. 90-94. [BL54.B8] 76-80940 ISBN 0-8024-8795-5
1. Glossolalia. I. Title.

CHANTRY, Walter J., 1938- 234'.1
Signs of the apostles : observations on Pentecostalism old and new / Walter J. Chantry. 2d rev. ed. Edinburgh ; Carlisle, Pa. : Banner of Truth Trust, 1976. viii, 147 p. ; 18 cm. Bibliography: p. 147. [BR1644.C42 1976] 77-366357 £0.60
1. Pentecostalism. I. Title.

CHAPIAN, Marie. 234'.1
I learn about the gifts of the Holy Spirit / written by Marie Chapian ; illustrated by Peter Chapian. Carol Stream, Ill. : Creation House, [1975] c1974 [30] p. : ill. (some col.) ; 27 cm. (The Mustard seed library) Brief text and illustrations list some of the gifts of the Holy Spirit given by God. [BT767.3.C45] 74-18151 ISBN 0-88419-099-4 : 3.95
1. Gifts, Spiritual—Juvenile literature. I. Chapian, Peter. II. Title.

A Charismatic reader. 234'.1
New York, Religious Book Club [1974] 281, 160, 162, 138 p. illus. 22 cm. Includes bibliographies. [BR110.C43] 74-81757 8.95
1. Pulkingham, W. Graham. 2. Church of the Redeemer, Houston, Tex. 3. Experience (Religion) 4. Theology, Doctrinal—History. 5. Pentecostalism 6. Glossolalia—Addresses, essays, lectures. I. Religious Book Club.
Contents omitted.

CHRISTENSON, Laurence. 234'.1
The charismatic renewal among Lutherans : a pastoral and theological perspective / Larry Christenson. [Minneapolis] : Lutheran Charismatic Renewal Services : distributed by Bethany Fellowship, c1976. 160 p. ; 21 cm. Bibliography: p. [141]-151. [BX8065.5.C47] 76-377263 pbk. : 2.95
1. Pentecostalism—Lutheran Church. I. Title.

COOKE, Joseph R. 234'.1
Free for the taking : the life-changing power of grace / Joseph R. Cooke. Old Tappan, N.J. : F. H. Revell Co., [1975] 190 p. ; 21 cm. [BT761.2.C64] 75-14057 ISBN 0-8007-0731-1 : 4.95
1. Grace (Theology) I. Title.

COTE, Richard G., 1934- 234'.1
Universal grace : myth or reality? / Richard G. Cote. Maryknoll, N.Y. : Orbis Books, c1977. 172 p. ; 19 cm. [BT761.2.C66] 77-5570 ISBN 0-88344-521-2 : 4.95
1. Grace (Theology) I. Title.

CROWTHER, Duane S 234.1
Gifts of the spirit [by] Duane S. Crowther. Salt Lake City, Bookcraft [1965?] xi, 352 p. 24 cm. [BT767.3.C7] 65-29176
1. Gifts, Spiritual. I. Title.

CULVERHOUSE, Cecil. 234.1
No strings attached: insights into the means of grace. Richmond, John Knox Press [1966] 120 p. 21 cm. Bibliography: p. 119-120 [BT761.2.C8] 66-12594
1. Grace (Theology) I. Title.

CULVERHOUSE, Cecil 234.1
No strings attached; insights into the means of grace. Richmond, Va., Knox [c.1966] 120p. 21cm. Bibl. [BT761.2.C8] 66-12594 1.95 pap.,
1. Grace (Theology) I. Title.

DAANE, James. 234.1
A theology of grace; an inquiry into and evaluation of Dr. C. Van Til's doctrine of common grace. Grand Rapids, W. B. Eerdmans Pub. Co., 1954. 159p. 23cm. [BT761.D22] 54-10940
1. Grace (Theology) 2. Van Til, Cornelius, 1895— Common grace. 3. Christian Reformed Church—Doctrinal and controversial works. I. Title.

DE HAAN, Martin Ralph, 1891- 234.1
Law or grace, by M. R. De Haan. Grand Rapids, Zondervan Pub. House [1965] 182 p. 20 cm. [BT96.2.D4] 64-8842
1. Law (Theology) 2. Grace (Theology) I. Title.

DE HAAN, Martin Ralph, M.D., 1891- 234.1
Law or grace. Grand Rapids, Mich., Zondervan [c.1965] 182p. 20cm. [BT96.2.D4] 64-8842 2.50 bds.,
1. Law (Theology) 2. Grace (Theology) I. Title.

DILLOW, Joseph. 234'.1
Speaking in tongues / Joseph Dillow. Grand Rapids : Zondervan Pub. House, [1975] 191 p. ; 18 cm. Includes bibliographical references. [BL54.D54] 74-25334 pbk. : 1.75
1. Glossolalia. I. Title.

DITMANSON, Harold H. 234'.1
Grace in experience and theology / Harold H. Ditmanson. Minneapolis : Augsburg Pub. House, c1977. 296 p. ; 23 cm. Includes bibliographical references and indexes. [BT761.2.D56] 77-72447 ISBN 0-8066-1587-7 : 9.95
1. Grace (Theology)—Addresses, essays, lectures. 2. Reconciliation—Addresses, essays, lectures. I. Title.

DRAPER, Maurice L. 234'.1
The gifts and fruit of the spirit, by Maurice L. Draper. [Independence, Mo., Herald Pub. House, 1969] 174 p. 21 cm. Includes bibliographical references. [BT769.D7] 76-78621
1. Gifts, Spiritual. I. Title.

DUNN, James D. G., 1939- 234'.1
Baptism in the Holy Spirit : a re-examination of the New Testament teaching on the gift of the Spirit in relation to pentecostalism today / James D. G. Dunn. Philadelphia : Westminster Press, 1977,c1970. vii, 248 p. ; 22 cm. Includes bibliographical references and indexes. [BS680.H56D86 1970] 77-3995 ISBN 0-664-24140-9 pbk. : 6.95
1. Baptism in the Holy Spirit—Biblical teaching. I. Title.

DUNN, James D. G., 1939- 234'.1
Baptism in the Holy Spirit : a re-examination of the New Testament teaching on the gift of the Spirit in relation to pentecostalism today / James D. G. Dunn. Philadelphia : Westminster Press, 1977,c1970. vii, 248 p. ; 22 cm. Includes bibliographical references and indexes. [BS680.H56D86 1970] 77-3995 ISBN 0-664-24140-9 pbk. : 6.95
1. Baptism in the Holy Spirit—Biblical teaching. I. Title.

DUNN, James D. G., 1939- 234'.1
Baptism in the Holy Spirit; a re-examination of the New Testament teaching on the gift of the Spirit in relation to pentecostalism today [by] James D. G. Dunn. Naperville, Ill., A. R. Allenson [1970] vii, 248 p. 22 cm. (Studies in Biblical theology, 2d ser., 15) "A revised form of the [author's] thesis ... 1968." Bibliographical footnotes. [BT123.D8 1970] 70-131586
1. Baptism in the Holy Spirit—Biblical teaching. I. Title. II. Series.

EASTWOOD, Charles Cyril, 1916- 234.1
The royal priesthood of the faithful; an investigation of the doctrine from Biblical times to the Reformation. Minneapolis, Augsburg Pub. House [1963] 264 p. 23 cm. Bibliography: p. 251-255. [BT767.5.E32 1963] 63-16595
1. Priesthood, Universal. I. Title.

EASTWOOD, Cyril 234.1
The royal priesthood of the faithful; an investigation of the doctrine from Biblical times to the Reformation. Minneapolis, Augsburg [c.1963] 264p. 23cm. Bibl. 63-16595 4.50
1. Priesthood, Universal. I. Title.

EDWARDS, Jonathan, 1703-1758. 234'.1
Treatise on grace, and other posthumously published writings; edited with an introduction by Paul Helm. Cambridge, James Clarke, 1971. ii-x, 131 p. 23 cm. Contents.Contents.—Treatise on grace.—Observations concerning the Trinity and the Covenent of the Redemption.—An essay on the Trinity. [BT760.E38] 72-193962 ISBN 0-227-67739-0 £1.50
1. Grace (Theology) 2. Trinity. I. Title.

ENSLEY, Eddie. 234'.1
Sounds of wonder : speaking in tongues in the Catholic tradition / by Eddie Ensley. New York : Paulist Press, c1977. xiv, 140 p. ; 18 cm. Includes bibliographical references. [BL54.E57] 77-70456 ISBN 0-8091-1883-1 : 2.95
1. Glossolalia—History. 2. Ecstasy. 3. Pentecostalism—Catholic Church—History. I. Title.

ERVIN, Howard M. 234'.1
"These are not drunken as ye suppose" (Acts 2:15) by Howard M. Ervin. [1st ed.] Plainfield, N.J., Logos International [1968] x, 241 p. 22 cm. Bibliography: p. 235-241. [BT767.3.E7] 68-22448 5.95
1. Gifts, Spiritual. 2. Holy Spirit. I. Title.

ERVIN, Howard M. 234'.1
This which ye see and hear, by Howard M. Ervin. Plainfield, N.J., Logos International [1972] 112 p. 21 cm. [BX8763.E78] 79-186153 ISBN 0-912106-27-1 1.95
1. Pentecostalism. I. Title.

FLYNN, Leslie B. 234'.1
19 gifts of the spirit: Which do you have? Are you using them? [By Leslie B. Flynn. Wheaton, Ill., Victor Books [1974] 204 p. 21 cm. (An input book) [BT767.3.F57] 73-91027 ISBN 0-88207-701-5 1.95
1. Gifts, Spiritual. I. Title.

FLYNN, Leslie B. 234'.1
19 gifts of the spirit: Which do you have? Are you using them? [By] Leslie B. Flynn. Wheaton, Ill., Victor Books [1974] 204 p. 21 cm. (An input book) [BT767.3.F57] 73-91027 ISBN 0-88207-701-5 1.95 (pbk.)
1. Gifts, Spiritual. I. Title.

FORD, William Herschel, 1900- 234'.1
Simple sermons on grace and glory / W. Herschel Ford. Grand Rapids : Zondervan Pub. House, c1977. p. cm. [BX6333.F568S488] 77-24412 ISBN 0-310-24751-9 pbk. : 2.95
1. Baptists—Sermons. 2. Sermons—American. I. Title.

FORD, William Herschel, 1900- 234'.1
Simple sermons on grace and glory / W. Herschel Ford. Grand Rapids : Zondervan Pub. House, c1977. p. cm. [BX6333.F568S488] 77-24412 ISBN 0-310-24751-9 pbk. : 2.95
1. Baptists—Sermons. 2. Sermons—American. I. Title.

FORTMAN, Edmund J 1901- ed. 234.1
The theology of man and grace; commentary; readings in the theology of grace [edited by] Edmund J. Fortman. Milwaukee, Bruce Pub. Co. [1966] xii, 409 p. 23 cm. (Contemporary college theology series. Historical theology section) Bibliographical footnotes. [BT761.2.F6] 66-19970
1. Grace — History of doctrines. I. Title.

FORTMAN, Edmund J., 1901- ed. 234.1
The theology of man and grace; commentary; readings in the theology of grace. Milwaukee, Bruce [c.1966] xii, 409p. 23cm. (Contemp. coll. theol. ser. Hist. theol. sect.) Bibl. [BT761.2.F6] 66-19970 3.95 pap.,
1. Grace—History of doctrines. I. Title.

FOSTER, K. Neill. 234'.1
Help! I believe in tongues : a third view of the charismatic phenomenon / K. Neill Foster. Minneapolis : Bethany Fellowship, c1975. 160 p. ; 21 cm. Includes bibliographical references. [BL54.F67] 75-2518 ISBN 0-87123-211-1 pbk. : 2.45
1. Glossolalia. 2. Gifts, Spiritual. I. Title.

FRANSEN, Piet Frans. 234.1
Divine grace and man [by] Peter Fransen. Translated from the Flemish by Georges Dupont. Rev. ed. [New York] New American Library [1965] xvi, 207 p. 18 cm. (A Mentor-Omega book, MT604) [BT761.2.F713 1965] 65-3743
1. Grace (Theology) I. Title.

FRANSEN, Piet Frans 234.1
Divine grace and man. [Tr. from Dutch by Georges Dupont] New York, Desclee [c.]1962. 117p. 22cm. 61-15719 2.25
1. Grace (Theology) I. Title.

FRANSEN, Piet Frans 234.1
Divine grace and man. Tr. Flemish by Georges Dupont. [New York] New Amer. Lib. [c.1962, 1965] 207p. 18cm. (Mentor-Omega MT604) [BT761.2.F713] .75 pap.,
1. Grace (Theology) I. Title.

FRANSEN, Piet Frans. 234'.1
The new life of grace [by] Peter Fransen. Translated from the Flemish by Georges Dupont. Foreword by John MacQuarrie. [New York] Desclee Co. 1969. x, 369 p. 22 cm. "English translation of ... De Genade: werkelijkheid en leven." Bibliography: p. [353]-369. [BT761.2.F7313 1969b] 69-20373 8.50
1. Grace (Theology) I. Title.

FRANSEN, Piet Frans. 234'.1
The new life of grace [by] Peter Fransen. Foreword by John Macquarrie. [Translated by Georges Dupont. New York] Herder and Herder [1972, c1969] x, 369 p. 21 cm. Translation of De Genade: werkelijkheid en leven. Bibliography: p. [353]-369. [BT761.2.F7313 1972] 72-178788 ISBN 0-665-00017-0 4.95
1. Grace (Theology) I. Title.

GARDINER, George E. 234'.1
The Corinthian catastrophe / George E. Gardiner. Grand Rapids, MI : Kregel Publications, [1974] 56 p. ; 18 cm. [BX8763.G37] 74-75106 ISBN 0-8254-2708-8 pbk. : 0.95

1. Pentecostalism—Controversial literature. I. Title.

GARRIGOU-LAGRANGE, Reginald, 1877- 234.1
The theological virtues. Translated by Thomas a Kempis Reilly. St. Louis, Herder [1965-] v. 24 cm. Contents.v. 1. On faith; a commentary on St. Thomas' Theological summa, IaIIaa qq. 62, 65, 68: IIaIIaa qq. 1-16. Bibliographical footnotes. [BV4635.G313] 64-8560
1. Thomas Aquinas, Saint, 1225?-1274 — Ethics. 2. Theological virtures. I. Title.

GARRIGOU-LAGRANGE, Reginald, 1877- 234.1
The theological virtues [v.1] Tr. [from Latin] by Thomas a Kempis Reilly. St. Louis, Herder [c.1965] 480p. 24cm. Bibl. Contents.v.1. On faith; a commentary on St. Thomas's Theological summa, IaIIae, qq. 62, 65, 68: IIaIIae, qq. 1-16. [BV4635.G313] 64-8560 8.50
1. Theological virtues. 2. Thomas Aquinas, Saint, 1225?-1274—Ethics. I. Title.

GLEASON, Robert W. 234.1
Grace. New York, Sheed & Ward [c.1962] 240p. Bibl. 61-11796 3.95 bds.,
1. Grace (Theology) I. Title.

HARNED, David Baily. 234'.1
Grace and common life. [1st American ed.] Charlottesville, University Press of Virginia [1971] xvi, 150 p. 23 cm. Includes bibliographical references. [BT761.2.H37 1971] 70-171486 ISBN 0-8139-0379-3
1. Grace (Theology) I. Title.

*HILL, Stephen. 234.'1
Healing is yours? Harrison, Ark. : New Leaf Press [1976] 112p. ; 22 cm. [BT732.5] 75-45836 ISBN 0-89221-014-1 pbk. : 2.95
1. Faith-cure. I. Title.

*HILLIS, Don W., comp. 234'.1
Is the whole body a tongue.? edited by Don W. Hillis Grand Rapids, Baker Book, [1974] 109 p. 20 cm. Bibliography: p. 111. [BL54] ISBN 0-8010-4110-4 2.95 (pbk.)
1. Glossolalia. I. Title.

HOEKEMA, Anthony A., 1913- 234'.1
Holy Spirit baptism, by Anthony A. Hoekema. Grand Rapids, Eerdmans [1972] 101 p. 21 cm. Bibliography: p. 94-95. [BT123.H63] 79-184699 ISBN 0-8028-1436-0 1.95
1. Baptism in the Holy Spirit. I. Title.

HONG, Edna (Hatlestad) 1913- 234'.1
The gayety of grace [by] Edna Hong. Minneapolis, Augsburg Pub. House [1972] 122 p. 18 cm. [BT761.2.H65] 77-176484 ISBN 0-8066-1213-4 3.95
1. Grace (Theology) I. Title.

HUGHES, Philip Edgcumbe 234.1
But for the grace of God; divine initiative and human need. Philadelphia, Westminster [1965, c.1964] 94p. 19cm. (Christian found.) Bibl. [BT761.2.H8] 65-16839 1.25 pap.,
1. Grace (Theology) I. Title.

JENSEN, Richard A. 234'.1
Touched by the Spirit : one man's struggle to understand his experience of the Holy Spirit / Richard A. Jensen. Minneapolis : Augsburg Pub. House, [1975] 160 p. ; 20 cm. "Prepared under the auspices of the Division for Life and Mission in the Congregation and the Board of Publication of the American Lutheran Church ... by Robert W. Ellison." Inserted in pocket of main work. Bibliography: p. [8] [BT767.3.J46] 75-2838 0.10
1. Gifts, Spiritual. I. Ellison, Robert W. II. American Lutheran Church (1961-). Division for Life and Mission in the Congregation. III. American Lutheran Church (1961-). Board of Publication. IV. Title.

JOURNET, Charles 234.1
The meaning of grace. [Translated into English by A. V. Littledale] New York, P. J. Kenedy [1960] 127p. 60-14732 3.50 bds.,
1. Grace (Theology) I. Title.

JOURNET, Charles 234.1
The meaning of grace, with study-club questions. [Tr. by A. V. Littledale] New York, Paulist Pr. [c.1960, 1962] 158p. 18cm. (Deus Bks) .95 pap.,
1. Grace (Theology) I. Title.

JOYCE, George Hayward, 1864-1943. 234.1
The Catholic doctrine of grace. Westminster, Md., Newman Press, 1950. xiv, 267 p. 20 cm. [BT761.J6] 51-1228
1. Grace (Theology) I. Title.

JURIEU, Pierre, 1637-1713. 234'.1
Traite de la nature et de la grace. Dans l'appendice: Jugement sur les methodes rigides et relachees d'expliquer la providence et la grace. Hildesheim, New York, G. Olms, 1973. 419, 113 p. 16 cm. "Nachdruck der Ausgaben Utrecht 1687 und 1688." [BT760.J87 1973] 74-163266 ISBN 3-487-04911-2
1. Grace (Theology)—Early works to 1800. 2. Nature (Theology) 3. Providence and government of God. I. Title. II. Title: Jugement sur les methodes rigides et relachees d'expliquer la providence et la grace.

KERR, John Stevens. 234'.1
The fire flares anew; a look at the new Pentecostalism. Philadelphia, Fortress Press [1974] 107 p. illus. 18 cm. [BX8763.K47] 73-89061 ISBN 0-8006-1074-1 2.95 (pbk.)
1. Pentecostalism. I. Title.

KILDAHL, John P. 234'.1
The psychology of speaking in tongues, by John P. Kildahl. [1st ed.] New York, Harper & Row [1972] xi, 110 p. 22 cm. Bibliography: p. 87-106. [BL54.K53] 74-178011 4.95
1. Glossolalia—Psychology. I. Title.

KINGHORN, Kenneth C. 234'.1
Gifts of the spirit / Kenneth Cain Kinghorn. Nashville : Abingdon Press, [1976] p. cm. Includes index. [BT767.3.K56] 75-22268 ISBN 0-687-14695-X pbk. : 3.25
1. Gifts, Spiritual. I. Title.

KNIGHT, George Angus Fulton, 1909- 234.1
Law and grace; must a Christian keep the Law of Moses? Philadelphia, Westminster [c.1962] 128p. 19cm. Bibl. 62-8837 2.50
1. Law and gospel. 2. Grace (Theology) I. Title.

LARSEN, Earnest. 234'.1
Holiness / by Earnest Larsen. New York : Paulist Press, [1975] 106 p. : ill. ; 18 cm. (Deus books) [BT767.L34] 75-8165 ISBN 0-8091-1877-7 pbk. : 1.45
1. Holiness. I. Title.

LOWE, Harry William. 234'.1
Redeeming grace; a doctrinal and devotional study of salvation by grace through faith, by Harry W. Lowe. Mountain View, Calif., Pacific Press Pub. Association [1968] 208 p. 22 cm. Bibliography: p. [205]-208. [BT761.2.L6] 68-28764
1. Grace (Theology) 2. Salvation. I. Title.

MACGORMAN, Jack W. 234'.1
The gifts of the spirit [by] Jack W. MacGorman. Nashville, Broadman Press [1974] 124 p. 21 cm. Includes bibliographical references. [BT767.3.M32] 73-85700 ISBN 0-8054-1341-3 3.95
1. Gifts, Spiritual. I. Title.

MCRAE, William J. 234'.1
The dynamics of spiritual gifts / by William J. McRae. Grand Rapids, Mich. : Zondervan Pub. House, c1976. 141 p. : ill. ; 18 cm. Bibliography : p. 141. [BT767.3.M34] 75-37838 pbk. : 1.75
1. Gifts, Spiritual. I. Title.

MARTIN, Ira Jay, 1911- 234'.1
Glossolalia, the gift of tongues; a bibliography [by] Ira J. Martin, III. [Cleveland, Tenn.] Pathway Press [1970] 72 p. 21 cm. [Z7798.M36] 76-107042
1. Glossolalia—Bibliography. I. Title.

MEISSNER, William W. 234.1
Foundations for a psychology of grace, by William W. Meissner. Glen Rock, N.J., Paulist [1966] vii, 246p. 21cm. Includes selections from the works of William James, others. Bibl. [BT761.2.M4] 66-21896 2.95 pap.,
1. Psychology, Religious. 2. Grace (Theology) I. Title.

MEYER, Charles Robert, 1920- 234'.1
A contemporary theology of grace, by Charles R. Meyer. Staten Island, N.Y., Alba House [1971] vi, 250 p. 22 cm. Bibliography: p. [239]-244. [BT761.2.M47] 70-158567 ISBN 0-8189-0202-7 6.95
1. Grace (Theology) I. Title.

MIKOLASKI, Samuel J. 234.1
The grace of god, by Samuel J. Mikolaski. Grand Rapids, Eerdmans [1966] 108p. 21cm. Bibl. [BT761.2.M5] 65-18091 1.65 pap.,
1. Grace (Theology). I. Title.

MONTAGUE, George T. 234'.1
The Spirit and his gifts; the Biblical background of Spirit-baptism, tongue-speaking, and prophecy, by George T. Montague. New York, Paulist Press [1974] v, 66 p. 18 cm. (Paulist Press/Deus books) Based on a paper presented by the author at a meeting of the Catholic Biblical Association at Immaculate Conception Seminary, Douglaston, N.Y., entitled: Baptism in the Spirit and speaking in tongues: an appraisal. Includes bibliographical references. [BT123.M58] 74-77425 ISBN 0-8091-1829-7 0.95 (pbk.).
1. Baptism in the Holy Spirit. 2. Glossolalia. 3. Prophecy (Christianity) I. Title.

MURPHY, Edward F., 1929- 234'.1
Spiritual gifts and the great commission / Edward F. Murphy. South Pasadena, Calif. : Mandate Press, [1975] xv, 352 p. ; 23 cm. Includes index. Bibliography: p. 337-345. [BT767.3.M87] 75-15740 ISBN 0-87808-144-5 pbk. : 5.95
1. Gifts, Spiritual. 2. Mission of the church. I. Title.

MURRAY, Andrew. 234'.1
Divine healing : a series of addresses and a personal testimony / by Andrew Murray. Plainfield, N.J. : Logos International, c1974. vii, 192 p. ; 18 cm. [BT732.5.M86 1974] 74-77087 ISBN 0-88270-080-4 pbk. : 1.25
1. Faith-cure. I. Title.

MURRAY, Andrew, 1828-1917. 234'.1
The full blessing of Pentecost; the one thing needful. Plainfield, N.J., Logos International [1974?] 153 p. 18 cm. (A Logos classic) First published in 1908. [BT121.M85 1974] 73-84205 1.25 (pbk.).
1. Holy Spirit. I. Title.

MYERS, Jacob Martin, 1904- 234'.1
Grace and torah / by J. M. Myers. Philadelphia : Fortress Press, [1975] x, 86 p. ; 22 cm. Based on lectures delivered at the Winebrenner Theological Seminary in 1973. Includes bibliographical references. [BS680.G7M93] 74-26343 ISBN 0-8006-1099-7 pbk. : 2.95
1. Grace (Theology)—Biblical teaching. 2. Law and gospel. I. Title.

NCNAIR, Jim, 1934- 234'.1
Love and gifts / by Jim McNair. Minneapolis : Bethany Fellowship, c1976. p. cm. Includes bibliographical references. [BS2545.G47M3] 76-6555 ISBN 0-87123-328-2 : 2.95
1. Gifts, Spiritual—Biblical teaching. 2. Love (Theology)—Biblical teaching. I. Title.

NEIGHBOUR, Ralph Webster, 1929- 234'.1
This gift is mine [by] Ralph W. Neighbour, Jr. Nashville, Broadman Press [1974] 122 p. 19 cm. [BT767.3.N44] 73-93907 ISBN 0-8054-5223-0 1.95
1. Gifts, Spiritual. I. Title.

NICOLAS, Jean Herve. 234.1
The mystery of God's grace, by J. H. Nicolas. Dubuque, Iowa, Priory Press [c1960] 132 p. 19 cm. Translation of Le mystere de la grace. [BT761.2.N513] 64-22905
1. Grace (Theology) I. Title.

O'DRISCOLL, J. A. 234.1
The Holy Spirit and the art of living. St. Louis, B. Herder Book Co. [1959, i.e.1960] 127p. 21cm. (12p. bibl. notes) 60-2656 2.35
1. Gifts, Spiritual. I. Title.

O'ROURKE, Edward W. 234'.1
Gift of gifts / by Edward W. O'Rourke. New York : Paulist Press, c1977. iii, 124 p. : ill. ; 19 cm. (A Deus book) Includes index. Bibliography: p. 118-119. [BT121.2.O69] 77-74580 ISBN 0-8091-2025-9 pbk. : 1.95
1. Holy Spirit. 2. Christian life—Catholic authors. I. Title.

PARSONS, Martin. 234'.1
The call to holiness : spirituality in a secular age / Martin Parsons. 1st American ed. Grand Rapids : Eerdmans, 1975, c1974. 95, [1] p. ; 18 cm. Bibliography: p. [96] [BT767.P27 1975] 74-26988 ISBN 0-8028-1600-2 pbk. : 1.65
1. Holiness. I. Title.

PERFECTION : 234'.1
the impossible possibility / by Herbert E. Douglass ... [et al.]. Nashville : Southern Pub. Association, [1975] 200 p. : ports. ; 22 cm. (Anvil series) [BT766.P42] 75-10350 ISBN 0-8127-0097-X
1. Perfection—Addresses, essays, lectures. 2. Seventh-Day Adventists—Doctrinal and controversial works—Addresses, essays, lectures. I. Douglass, Herbert E.

PETTIT, Norman. 234.1
The heart prepared; grace and conversion in Puritan spiritual life. New Haven, Yale University Press, 1966. ix, 252 p. 23 cm. (Yale publications in American studies 11) "Originally undertaken as a doctoral dissertation ... Yale University." Bibliography: p. [223]-235. [BX9322.P4 1966] 66-21530
1. Theology, Puritan. 2. Grace (Theology)—History of doctrines. 3. Conversion—Histroy of doctrines. I. Title. II. Series.

PINK, Arthur Walkington, 1886-1952. 234'.1
The doctrines of election and justification / A. W. Pink. Grand Rapids : Baker Book House, c1974. 252 p. ; 23 cm. [BT810.2.P5 1974] 75-306319 ISBN 0-8010-6969-6 : 6.95
1. Election (Theology) 2. Justification. I. Title.

ROBERTSON, John J. 234'.1
Tongues : what you should know about glossolalia / by John J. Robertson. Mountain View, Calif. : Pacific Press Pub. Association, c1977. 58 p. ; 19 cm. [BS2545.G63R62] 76-6618 pbk. : 0.75
1. Seventh-Day Adventists—Doctrinal and controversial works. 2. Glossolalia—Biblical teaching. I. Title.

RONDET, Henri, 1898- 234'.1
The grace of Christ; a brief history of the theology of grace. Tr., ed. by Tad W. Guzie. Westminster, Md., Newman [1967] Westminster, Md., Newman [1967] xxii, xxii, 426p. 22cm. Tr. of Gratia Christi. Bibl. [BT761.R5713] 66-28935 8.95
1. Grace (Theology)—History of doctrines. I. Title.

RYRIE, Charles Caldwell, 1925- 234.1
The grace of God. Chicago, Moody Press [1963] 126 p. 22 cm. [BT761.2.R9] 63-5624
1. Grace (Theology) I. Title.

RYRIE, Charles Caldwell, 1925- 234.1
The grace of God. Chicago, Moody [c.1963] 126p. 22cm. 63-5624 2.50
1. Grace (Theology) I. Title.

SATTERFIELD, Carroll E. 234'.1
Two actual currents in the Thomistic analysis of faith / Carroll E. Satterfield. Baltimore : Satterfield, 1975. 227, [7] p. ; 23 cm. Includes index. Bibliography: p. [229]-[234] [BT761.2.S25] 75-22531
1. Grace (Theology)—History of doctrines. 2. Faith and reason—History of doctrines. I. Title.

SCHEEBEN, Matthias Joseph, 1835-1888. 234.1
Nature and grace; translated by Cyril Vollert. St. Louis, B. Herder Book Co. [1954] 361p. 21cm. [BT761.S335] 54-7471
1. Grace (Theology) 2. Catholic Church—Doctrinal and controversial works—Catholic authors. I. Title.

*SEAMANDS, John T. 234'.1
On tiptoe with joy. Grand Rapids, Mich., Baker Book House [1973] 123 p. 18 cm. Reprint of 1967 ed. published by Beacon Hill Press of Kansas City. [BT123] ISBN 0-8010-7989-6 0.95 (pbk.)
1. Baptism in the Holy Spirit. I. Title.

SEYER, Herman D. 234'.1
The stewardship of spiritual gifts : a study of First Corinthians, chapters twelve, thirteen, and fourteen, and the charismatic movement / by Herman D. Seyer. Madison, Wis. : Published for Herman D. Seyer by Fleetwood Art Studios, [1974] 103 p. ; 22 cm. [BS2675.2.S47] 74-18872 2.95
1. Bible. N.T. 1 Corinthians. XII-XIV—Criticism, interpretation, etc. 2. Pentecostalism. 3. Holy Spirit. I. Title.

SITTLER, Joseph. 234'.1
Essays on nature and grace. Philadelphia, Fortress Press [1972] 134 p. 21 cm. Contents.Contents.—The emergence of a theme.—Grace in the Scriptures.—Some crucial moments in ecumenical Christology.—Grace in post-Reformation culture.—Grace and a sense for the world.—Christian theology and the environment. Includes bibliographical references. [BT761.2.S58] 76-171505 ISBN 0-8006-0070-3 4.95
1. Grace (Theology) 2. Nature (Theology) I. Title.

SMITH, Charles Russell, 1935- 234'.1
Tongues in Biblical perspective; a summary of Biblical conclusions concerning tongues, by Charles R. Smith. [2d ed., rev.] Winona Lake, Ind., BMH Books [1973] 141 p. illus. 21 cm. Bibliography: p. 136-141. [BL54.S59 1973] 73-180230 2.25
1. Glossolalia. I. Title.

STEPHENS, Julius Harold. 234.1
Surpassing grace. Nashville, Broadman Press [1957] 104p. 20cm. [BT85.S8] 57-6329
1. Law and gospel. I. Title.

STEPHENS, Julius Harold. 234.1
Surpassing grace. Nashville, Broadman Press [1957] 104 p. 20 cm. [BT85.S8] 57-6329
1. Law and gospel. I. Title.

STEVENS, Gregory. 234.1
The life of grace. Englewood Cliffs, N.J., Prentice-Hall, 1963. 118 p. 24 cm. (Foundations of Catholic theology series) Includes bibliography. [BT761.2.S77] 63-11810
1. Grace (Theology) I. Title.

STILES, Jack E. 234'.1
The gift of the Holy Spirit. Old Tappan, N.J., Revell [1971] 127 p. 21 cm. [BT121.2.S84] 79-165287 ISBN 0-8007-0478-9 3.95
1. Holy Spirit. 2. Glossolalia. I. Title.

STINNETTE, Charles Roy, 1914- 234.1
Grace and the searching of our heart. New York, Association Press [1962] 192 p. 20 cm. [BT761.2.S8] 62-9378
1. Grace (Theology) 2. Christianity — Psychology. I. Title.

STINNETTE, Charles Roy, 1914- 234.1
Grace and the searching of our heart. New York, Association [c.1962] 192p. 20cm. 62-9378 4.00
1. Grace (Theology) 2. Christianity—Psychology. I. Title.

*STROMBECK, J.F. 234.1
Shall never perish. Chicago, Moody [1966] 127p. 17cm. (Colportage lib.,) .39 pap.,
I. Title.

TATHAM, C. Ernest. 234'.1
Let the tide come in! / C. Ernest Tatham. Carol Stream, Ill. : Creation House, c1976. 150 p. ; 22 cm. Includes bibliographical references. [BT767.3.T37] 76-16290 ISBN 0-88419-005-6 pbk. : 2.95
1. Gifts, Spiritual. I. Title.

TAYLOR, Jesse Paul, Bp., 1895- 234'.1
Holiness, the finished foundation. Winona Lake, Ind., Light and Life Press [1963] 216 p. 28 cm. [BT765.T3] 63-35498
1. Santification. I. Title.

THOMAS, James David, 1910- 234'.1
The Biblical doctrine of grace / by J. D. Thomas. Abilene, Tex. : Biblical Research Press, c1977. vii, 80 p., [1] fold. leaf of plates : ill. ; 22 cm. (The Way of life series ; no. 111) Includes bibliographical references. [BT761.2.T48] 76-56472 ISBN 0-89112-111-0 pbk. : 1.95
1. Grace (Theology) I. Title.

TORRANCE, Thomas Forsyth, 1913- 234.1
The doctrine of grace in the Apostolic Fathers. [1st American ed.] Grand Rapids, Eerdmans [1959] vii, 150 p. 23 cm. Bibliography: p. 142-145. [BR60.A65T6] 59-10212
1. Apostolic Fathers. 2. Grace (Theology) — History of doctrines — Early church. I. Title.

TUGWELL, Simon. 234'.1
Did you receive the Spirit? New York, Paulist Press [1972] 143 p. 19 cm. (Deus books) Includes bibliographical references. [BX2350.T76 1972b] 72-93023 ISBN 0-8091-1760-6 1.25
1. Pentecostalism. I. Title.

TUTTLE, Robert G., 1941- 234'.1
The partakers; Holy Spirit power for persevering Christians [by] Robert G. Tuttle, Jr. Nashville, Abingdon Press [1974] 142 p. 20 cm. Includes bibliographical references. [BT121.2.T87] 74-9561 ISBN 0-687-30109-2 4.95
1. Holy Spirit. I. Title.

UNGER, Merrill Frederick, 1909- 234'.1
The baptism and gifts of the Holy Spirit, by Merrill F. Unger. Chicago, Moody Press [1974] 189 p. 22 cm. Bibliography: p. 181-189. [BT123.U49] 74-2931 ISBN 0-8024-0467-7 2.95 (pbk.).
1. Baptism in the Holy Spirit. I. Title.

VAN TIL, Cornelius, 1895- 234'.1
The sovereignty of grace; an appraisal of G. C. Berkouwer's view of Dordt. [Philadelphia] Presbyterian and Reformed Pub. Co., 1969. 110 p. 21 cm. Includes bibliographical references. [BX9478.V35] 73-190462
1. Dort, Synod of, 1618-1619. 2. Berkouwer, Gerrit Cornelis, 1903- 3. Grace (Theology)—History of doctrines. I. Title.

VOGEL, Arthur Anton. 234.1
The gift of grace; an adult reading and discussion course. Prepared for the Adult Division, Dept. of Christian Education, the Protestant Episcopal Church. Greenwich, Conn., Seabury Press, 1958. 78 p. 21 cm. [BX5049.V6] 58-11507
1. Grace (Theology) — Study and teaching. 2. Religious education — Text-books for adults — Anglican. I. Title.

VOIGT, Robert J. 234'.1
Go to the mountain : an insight into charismatic renewal / by Robert J. Voigt; with a foreword by Larry Christenson. St. Meinrad, IN : Abbey Press, 1975. xi, 143 p. ; 21 cm. (A Priority edition) Bibliography: p. 141-143. [BX2350.57.V64] 75-205 ISBN 0-87029-040-1 pbk. : 2.95
1. Pentecostalism. I. Title.

WALSH, Vincent M. 234'.1
A key to charismatic renewal in the Catholic Church / by Vincent M. Walsh. St. Meinrad, Ind. : Abbey Press, 1974. xi, 286 p. ; 20 cm. (A Priority edition) Bibliography: p. 285-286. [BX2350.57.W34] 74-82238 ISBN 0-87029-033-9 : 4.95
1. Pentecostalism. I. Title.

WATSON, Philip Saville, 1909- 234.1
The concept of grace; essays on the way of divine love in human life. Philadelphia, Muhlenberg Press [1959] 116 p. 21 cm. [BT761.2.W35] 59-4476
1. Grace (Theology) I. Title.

WELLS, Bob. 234'.1
All the Bible says about tongues / Bob Wells. Denver : Accent Books, c1977. 128 p. ; 18 cm. [BS2545.G63W44] 76-50298 ISBN 0-916406-69-5 pbk. : 1.75
1. Glossolalia—Biblical teaching. I. Title.

WHAT the Spirit is saying to the churches : essays / by Krister Stendahl ... [et al.] ; edited by Theodore Runyon. New York : Hawthorn Books, c1975. viii, 142 p. ; 21 cm. Includes bibliographical references. [BX8762.A2A5 1975] 75-2563 ISBN 0-8015-8546-5 : 3.95 234'.1
1. Pentecostalism—Congresses. 2. Holy Spirit—Congresses. I. Stendahl, Krister. II. Runyon, Theodore.

WIERWILLE, Victor Paul. 234'.1
Receiving the Holy Spirit today. [6th ed.] New Knoxville, Ohio, American Christian Press [1972] xi, 358 p. 22 cm. Includes bibliographical references. [BT121.2.W53 1972] 73-176282 ISBN 0-910068-00-3 5.95
1. Bible. N.T. Acts—Criticism, interpretation, etc. 2. Bible. N.T. 1 Corinthians XII-XIV—Criticism, interpretation, etc. 3. Holy Spirit. 4. Gifts, Spiritual. I. Title.

YOHN, Rick. 234'.1
Discover your spiritual gift and use it. Wheaton, Ill., Tyndale House [1974] 154 p. 22 cm. Bibliography: p. 154. [BT767.3.Y63] 74-80798 ISBN 0-8423-0667-6 3.95
1. Gifts, Spiritual. I. Title.

BERTOCCI, Peter Anthony. 234.115
Free will, responsibility, and grace. New York, Abingdon Press [1957] 110p. 20cm. [BT810.B47] 57-8352
1. Free will and determinism. 2. Responsibility. 3. Grace (Theology) I. Title.

BERTOCCI, Peter Anthony. 234.115
Free will, responsibility, and grace. New York, Abingdon Press [1957] 110p. 20cm. [BT810.B47] 57-8352
1. Free will and determinism. 2. Responsibility. 3. Grace (Theology) I. Title.

FARRELL, Walter, 1902-1951. 234.15
Swift victory; essays on the gifts of the Holy Spirit, by Walter Farrell and Dominic Hughes. New York, Sheed and Ward [1955] 211p. 22cm. [BT769.F3] 55-9444
1. Gifts, Spiritual. I. Hughes, Dominic, 1918- joint author. II. Title.

GARDELL, Ambroise, Father, 1859-1931. 234.15
The Holy Spirit in Christian life. St. Louis, Herder, 1954. 158p. 20cm. '[These] studies ... served as the theme of a retreat given in 1933 to the Little Nursing Sisters of the Poor, of the Dominican. Third Order at Beaune.' [BT769.G35] 54-9750
1. Gifts, Spiritual. 2. Christian life—Catholic authors. I. Title.

WOOLLEN, C J 234.15
The twelve fruits. New York, J. F. Wagner [c1950] viii, 181 p. 21 cm. [BT769.W6] 51-2186
1. Gifts, Spiritual. 2. Virtue. 3. Holy Spirit — Meditations. I. Title.

BARNES, Kathleen H. 234'.16
Sacrament time, by Kathleen H. Barnes [and] Virginia H. Pearce. Photos. by Don O. Thorpe. Salt Lake City, Deseret Book Co., 1973. [32] p. illus. 22 cm. "A book for LDS children." Brief text, photographs, and Bible verses help convey the significance of the sacrament in the Church of Jesus Christ of Latter-day Saints. [BV4571.2.B37] 73-89224 ISBN 0-87747-513-X 3.95
1. Children—Religious life. I. Pearce, Virginia H., joint author. II. Thorpe, Don O., illus. III. Title.

CHAMPLIN, Joseph M. 234'.16
The sacraments in a world of change [by] Joseph M. Champlin. Notre Dame, Ind., Ave Maria Press [1973] 141 p. 21 cm. An outgrowth of the author's syndicated column, Workship and the world, in the NC News Service Know your faith series. [BX2200.C38] 73-83347 ISBN 0-87793-085-6 1.65 (pbk.)
1. Sacraments—Catholic Church. I. Title.

GOODRICH, William Lloyd. 234'.16
Black rubric 1965; sermons on the Anglican view of the new liturgy, [1st ed. Washinton, St. James' Parish, [1965] xi, 64 p. 23 cm. 200 copies printed. Bibliography: p. 63-64. [BX5940.G6] 67-7336
1. Protestant Episcopal Church in the U.S.A. Liturgy and ritual — Sermons. 2. Sermons, American. 3. Protestant Episcopal Church in the U.S.A. — Sermons. I. Title. II. Title: Sermons on the Anglican view of the new liturgy.

HARING, Bernhard, 1912- 234'.16
The sacraments in a secular age : a vision in depth on sacramentality and its impact on moral life / [by] Bernhard Haring. Slough : St. Paul Publications, 1976. [8], 253 p. ; 21 cm. Includes index. Bibliography: p. 246-247. [BX2200.H24] 76-374949 ISBN 0-85439-122-3 : £3.50
1. Jesus Christ—Person and offices. 2. Sacraments—Catholic Church. 3. Church. I. Title.

HELLWIG, Monika. 234'.16
The meaning of the sacraments. Foreword by Robert W. Hovda. Dayton, Ohio, Pflaum/Standard, 1972. ix, 102 p. 21 cm. Bibliography: p. 101-102. [BV800.H45] 78-178840 1.50
1. Sacraments. I. Title.

HINES, John M. 234'.16
By water and the Holy Spirit; new concepts of baptism, confirmation, and communion [by] John M. Hines. Foreword by Alfred R. Shands. New York, Seabury Press [1973] 95 p. 21 cm. "A Crossroad book." [BX5940.H5] 74-155336 ISBN 0-8164-5703-4 2.95 (pbk.).
1. Protestant Episcopal Church in the U.S.A. Liturgy and ritual. 2. Baptism—Anglican Communion. 3. Confirmation—Anglican Communion. 4. Lord's Supper—Anglican Communion. 5. Children—Religious life. I. Title.

HOLIFIELD, E. Brooks. 234'.16
The covenant sealed : the development of Puritan sacramental theology in old and New England, 1570-1720 / E. Brooks Holifield. New Haven : Yale University Press, 1974. xi, 248 p. ; 25 cm. Includes index. Bibliography: p. 233-242. [BV800.H64] 73-92695 ISBN 0-300-01733-2 : 12.50
1. Sacraments—History of doctrines. 2. Puritans. I. Title.

RAHNER, Karl, 1904- 234'.16
Meditations on the Sacraments / Karl Rahner. New York : Seabury Press, c1977. p. cm. Translation of Die siebenfaltige Gabe. "A Crossroad book." [BX2200.R3313] 76-52938 ISBN 0-8164-0344-9 : 7.95
1. Sacraments—Catholic Church—Meditations. I. Title.

RIGA, Peter J. 234'.16
Sign and symbol of the invisible God: essays on the sacraments today [by] Peter J. Riga. Notre Dame, Ind., Fides Publishers [1971] v, 89 p. 18 cm. (A Fides dome book, D-79) Includes bibliographies. [BX2200.R53] 72-166155 ISBN 0-8190-0495-2 1.25
1. Sacraments—Catholic church. I. Title.

ROGERS, Elizabeth Frances, 1892- 234'.16'09
Peter Lombard and the sacramental system / Elizabeth Frances Rogers. Merrick, N.Y. : Richwood Pub. Co., 1976. 250 p. ; 24 cm. Reprint of the 1917 ed. published in New York. Originally presented as the author's thesis, Columbia University, 1917. Vita. Bibliography: p. 247-250. [BX2200.R6 1976] 76-20688 ISBN 0-915172-22-4 lib.bdg. : 18.50
1. Petrus Lombardus, Bp of Paris, 12th cent. 2. Sacraments—History of doctrines. I. Title.

PAYNE, John Barton, 1931- 234'.16'0924
Erasmus: his theology of the sacraments [by] John B. Payne. [Richmond, Va., John Knox Press, 1970] 341 p. 21 cm. (Research in theology) A revision of the author's thesis, Harvard University, 1966. Bibliography: p. [338]-341. [BV800.P38 1970] 70-82938
1. Erasmus, Desiderius, d. 1536. 2. Sacraments—History of doctrines. 3. Theology, Doctrinal—History—16th century. I. Title.

ARNDT, Elmer J. F. 234'.16'1
The font and the table, by Elmer J. F. Arndt. Richmond, John Knox Press [1967] 88 p. 22 cm. (Ecumenical studies in worship, no. 16) Bibliographical footnotes. [BV811.2.A7] 67-15296
1. Baptism. I. Title. II. Series.

BRAND, Eugene, 1931- 234'.161
Baptism : a pastoral perspective / Eugene L. Brand. Minneapolis : Augsburg Pub. House, [1975] 127 p. ; 20 cm. [BX8073.5.B7] 75-2827 ISBN 0-8066-1472-2 pbk. : 3.50
1. Baptism—Lutheran Church. I. Title.

CONANT, Thomas Jefferson, 1802-1891. 234'.161
The meaning and use of baptizein / by Thomas Jefferson Conant. Grand Rapids : Kregel Publications, c1977. 192 p. ; 23 cm. First published in 1860 by the American Bible Union, New York, under title: The meaning and use of baptizein, philologically and historically investigated, for the American Bible Union. Chiefly English and Greek or Latin. [BV811.5.C66 1977] 76-16231 ISBN 0-8254-2319-8 : 4.95
1. Baptism—Terminology. 2. Baptism—Baptists. 3. Baptizein (The Greek word) I. Title.

ELLER, Vernard. 234'.161
In place of sacraments; a study of Baptism and the Lord's Supper. Grand Rapids, Mich., Eerdmans [1972] 144 p. 21 cm. [BV800.E46] 72-75570 ISBN 0-8028-1476-X 2.95
1. Sacraments. 2. Baptism. 3. Lord's Supper. I. Title.

GANOCZY, Alexandre. 234'.161
Becoming Christian / by Alexander Ganoczy ; translated by John G. Lynch. New York : Paulist Press, c1976. v, 113 p. ; 19 cm. Translation of Devenir chretien. Includes bibliographical references. [BX2205.G3513] 76-23530 ISBN 0-8091-1980-3 pbk. : 1.95
1. Baptism—Catholic Church. I. Title.

MARTY, Martin E., 1928- 234'.161
Baptism / by Martin E. Marty. Philadelphia : Fortress Press, 1977, c1962. 63 p. ; 19 cm. [BV811.2.M3 1977] 77-78635 ISBN 0-8006-1317-1 pbk. : 1.50
1. Baptism. I. Title.

MOUROUX, Jean. 234'.161
From baptism to the act of faith. Translation by Sister M. Elizabeth and Sister M. Johnice. Introd. by Bernard J. Cooke. Boston, Allyn and Bacon, 1964. viii, 56 p. illus. 21 cm. [BX2205.M613] 64-2691
1. Baptism — Catholic Church. 2. Religious education of children. I. Title.

ONE baptism for the remission of sins. Edited by Paul C. Empie and William W. Baum. [New York] U.S.A. National Committee, Lutheran World Federation [1966] 87 p. 20 cm. (Lutherans and Catholics in dialogue, 2) Summary statements by participants in the 2d of a series of ongoing theological discussions between Lutheran and Roman Catholic theologians. The meeting was held at the Center for Continuing Education, University of Chicago, Feb. 11-13, 1966. Includes bibliographical references. [BV811.2.O53] 73-172052 234'.161
1. Lutheran Church—Relations—Catholic Church. 2. Catholic Church—Relations—Lutheran Church. 3. Baptism. I. Empie, Paul C., ed. II. Baum, William W., ed. III. Chicago. University. Center for Continuing Education. IV. Title. V. Series.

PARDEE, William H., 1913- 234'.161
Baptism, its importance, its subjects, its mode / William H. Pardee. Schaumburg, Ill. : Regular Baptist Press, c1977. 61 p. ; 21 cm. Includes bibliographical references. [BV811.2.P33] 77-24969 ISBN 0-87227-015-7 pbk. : 1.50
1. Baptism—Baptists. I. Title.

SCHLINK, Edmund, 1903- 234'.161
The doctrine of baptism. Translated by Herbert J. A. Bouman. Saint Louis, Concordia Pub. House [1972] 228 p. 24 cm. Translation of Die Lehre von der Taufe. Includes bibliographical references. [BV811.2.S3513] 78-159794 ISBN 0-570-03217-2
1. Baptism. I. Title.

SCHMEMANN, Alexander, 1921- 234'.161
Of water and the spirit : a liturgical study of baptism / Alexander Schmemann. Crestwood, N.Y. : St. Vladimir's Seminary Press, 1974. p. cm. Bibliography: p. [BX378.B3S35] 74-30061 ISBN 0-913836-10-9 : 4.50
1. Baptism—Orthodox Eastern Church. I. Title.

SKELLY, Andrew Maria, 1855- 234'.161
The sacraments and the commandments: discourses on various occasions, by the Rev. A. M. Skelly, O. P. St. Louis, Mo. and London, B. Herder book co., 1929. vi, 306 p. 19 1/2 cm. [BX2200.S5] 29-20812

1. Sacraments — Catholic church. 2. Commandments, Ten — Sermons. I. Title.

NASH, Robert. 234'.1612
I didn't ask to be baptized. Dublin, Irish Messenger Office, 1971. 27 p. 17 cm. [BX2205.N37] 72-189129 ISBN 0-901335-20-7 £0.05
1. Baptism—Catholic Church. I. Title.

NEWMAN, Albert Henry, 1852-1933. 234'.1612
A history of anti-pedobaptism, from the rise of pedo baptism to A.D. 1609. Philadelphia, American Baptist Publication Society, 1897. [New York, AMS Press, 1973] xi, 414 p. 23 cm. Bibliography: p. 395-406. [BV813.N48 1973] 71-144664 ISBN 0-404-04686-X 12.75
1. Infant baptism—History.

LUMPKIN, William Latane. 234'.1613
Meditations on Christian baptism / William L. Lumpkin. Nashville : Broadman Press, c1976. 76 p. ; 19 cm. Includes bibliographical references. [BV811.2.L85] 76-4372 ISBN 0-8054-1938-1 : 2.50
1. Baptism. I. Title.

ANTEKEIER, Charles. 234'.162
Confirmation: the power of the Spirit; a charismatic preparation program for youth, their parents, and sponsors [by] Charles Antekeier, Janet K. Vandagriff [and] Van Vandagriff. Notre Dame, Ind., Ave Maria Press [1972] 128 p. illus. 22 cm. [BX2210.A75] 72-89623 ISBN 0-87793-049-X 2.25
1. Confirmation—Instruction and study. 2. Holy Spirit. I. Vandagriff, Janet K., joint author. II. Vandagriff, Van, joint author. III. Title.

HAAS, LaVerne. 234'.162
Personal Pentecost; the meaning of confirmation. St. Meinrad, Ind., Abbey Press, 1973. xi, 108 p. 21 cm. (A Priority edition) Bibliography: p. 107-108. [BV815.H26] 72-90054 1.95
1. Confirmation. I. Title.

HOLMES, Urban Tigner, 1930- 234'.162
Confirmation : the celebration of maturity in Christ / Urban T. Holmes III. New York : Seabury Press, [1975] xii, 98 p. ; 21 cm. "A Crossroad book." Includes bibliographical references. [BV815.H6] 75-15879 ISBN 0-8164-2589-2 : 3.95
1. Confirmation. I. Title.

*HUGHES, Philip Edgcumbe. 234.162
Confirmation in the church today. Grand Rapids, Mich., W. B. Eerdmans [1973] 56 p. 22 cm. Includes bibliographical references. [BV800] ISBN 0-8028-1538-3 1.45 (pbk.)
1. Holy Communion. I. Title.

MILNER, Austin P., 1935- 234'.162
The theology of confirmation, by Austin P. Milner. Notre Dame, Ind., Fides Publishers [1972, c1971] 127 p. 19 cm. (Theology today, no. 26) Includes bibliographical references. [BX2210.M52] 73-159126 ISBN 0-85342-292-3
1. Confirmation—Catholic Church. I. Title.

NATIONAL Lutheran Council. Division of Welfare. 234'.162
Directory of Lutheran agencies and institutions. [New York] v. 23 cm. [BX8074.B4N3] 64-4323
1. Lutheran Church — Charities — Direct. I. Title.

NATIONAL Lutheran Social Welfare Conference. 234'.162
Lutheran health and welfare directory. 1959- New York. v. 23 cm. annual. Issued by the National Lutheran Social Welfare Conference (called 1959 the Lutheran Welfare Conference in America) Supersedes the conference's Proceedings. Title varies: 1959- Lutheran health and welfare annual. [BX8074.B4L8] 64-1247
1. Lutheran Church — Charities — Direct. I. Title. II. Title: Lutheran health and welfare annual.

REMEMBER your confirmation. 234'.162
Saint Louis : Concordia Pub. House, c1977. [48] p. ; 18 cm. Includes thoughts, prayers, scripture, and songs that relate to confirmation. [BV815.R4] 76-58001 ISBN 0-570-03751-4 pbk. : 1.50
1. Confirmation—Prayer-books and devotions—English—Juvenile literature. I. Concordia Publishing House, St. Louis.

SMITH, Michael H. 234'.162
Preparing for Confirmation [by] Michael H. Smith and Mary Kay Persse. Notre Dame, Ind., Ave Maria Press [1972] 77 p. illus. 21 cm. [BX2210.S59] 72-92730 ISBN 0-87793-050-3 1.25
1. Confirmation—Instruction and study. I. Persse, Mary Kay, joint author. II. Title.

ANDERSON, Stanley Edwin. 234'.163
The First Communion, by Stanley E. Anderson. Texarkana, Ark.-Tex., Bogard Press [1973] 159 p. 20 cm. [BV825.2.A8] 72-97329
1. Lord's Supper. I. Title.

CHAMPLIN, Joseph M. 234'.163
The Mass in a world of change [by] Joseph M. Champlin. Notre Dame, Ind., Ave Maria Press [1973] 142 p. 21 cm. An outgowth of the author's syndicated column, Worship and the world, in the NC News Service Know your faith series. [BX2230.2.C47] 73-83348 ISBN 0-87793-084-8 1.65 (pbk.)
1. Mass—Celebration. I. Title.

COCHRANE, Arthur C. 234'.163
Eating and drinking with Jesus; an ethical and Biblical inquiry, by Arthur C. Cochrane. Philadelphia, Westminster Press [1974] 208 p. 21 cm. Bibliography: p. [187]-197. [BV823.C58] 73-22364 ISBN 0-664-20865-7 9.00
1. Lord's Supper—Biblical teaching. 2. Food in the Bible. 3. Drinking in the Bible. I. Title.

COOKE, Bernard J. 234'.16'3
The Eucharist; mystery of a friendship, by Bernard Cooke. Edited by Matthew Eussen from a series of lectures. Dayton, Ohio, G. A. Pflaum, 1969. 127 p. illus. 18 cm. (Witness books, CI6) (Christian identity series.) Bibliography: p. 123. [BX2215.2.C6] 70-97040 0.95
1. Lord's Supper—Catholic Church. I. Title.

DEISS, Lucien. 234'.163
It's the Lord's Supper : the Eucharist of Christians / by Lucien Deiss ; translated by Edmond Bonin. New York : Paulist Press, c1976. vi, 157 p. ; 21 cm. Translation of La Cene du Seigneur. Includes bibliographical references. [BX2215.2.D4213] 76-12649 ISBN 0-8091-1954-4 pbk. : 4.95
1. Lord's Supper—Catholic Church. I. Title.

THE Eucharist in ecumenical dialogue 234'.163
/ Kenan B. Osborne ... [et al.] ; edited by Leonard Swidler ; pref. by William W. Baum. New York : Paulist Press, c1976. v, 154 p. ; 23 cm. Includes bibliographical references. [BX9.5.S2E82] 76-374248 ISBN 0-8091-1953-6 pbk. : 2.95
1. Lord's Supper and Christian union—Addresses, essays, lectures. I. Osborne, Kenan B. II. Swidler, Leonard J.

GUZIE, Tad W. 234'.163
Jesus and the Eucharist [by] Tad W. Guzie. New York, Paulist Press [1974] 161 p. 22 cm. Includes bibliographical references. [BV825.2.G89] 73-90069 ISBN 0-8091-0186-6 5.95
1. Jesus Christ—Person and offices. 2. Lord's Supper. I. Title.

HELLWIG, Monika. 234'.163
The Eucharist and the hunger of the world / Monika K. Hellwig. New York : Paulist Press, c1976. v, 90 p. ; 19 cm. Includes bibliographical references. [BX2215.2.H38] 76-18050 ISBN 0-8091-1958-7 pbk. : 1.65
1. Lord's Supper—Catholic Church. I. Title.

HOLMES, Urban Tigner, 1930- 234'.163
Young children and the Eucharist [by] Urban T. Holmes III. New York, Seabury Press [1972] 123 p. 21 cm. Includes bibliographical references. [BV828.H63] 72-86972 ISBN 0-8164-5700-X Pap. 2.50
1. Lord's Supper. 2. Children—Religious life. I. Title.

†LIVING and growing through the Eucharist 234'.163
/ compiled by Daughters of St. Paul. Boston : St. Paul Editions, c1976. p. cm. [BX2215.A1L58] 76-26698 5.95 pbk. : 4.95
1. Lord's Supper—Catholic Church—Papal documents. I. Daughters of St. Paul.

LUSSIER, Ernest, 1911- 234'.163
The Eucharist : the bread of life / Ernest Lussier. New York : Alba House, c1977. xxii, 247 p. ; 22 cm. Bibliography: p. 247. [BX2215.2.L85] 77-3035 ISBN 0-8189-0349-X : 5.95
1. Lord's Supper—Catholic Church. I. Title.

LUSSIER, Ernest, 1911- 234'.163
Getting to know the Eucharist. New York, Alba House [1974] xiii, 190 p. 22 cm. [BX2215.2.L87] 74-3236 ISBN 0-8189-0289-2 4.95
1. Lord's Supper—Catholic Church. I. Title.

LUSSIER, Ernest, 1911- 234'.163
Living the Eucharistic mystery / Ernest Lussier. New York : Alba House, [1976] p. cm. [BX2215.2.L88] 75-22027 ISBN 0-8189-0322-8 : 5.95
1. Lord's Supper—Catholic Church. I. Title.

LUTHERAN Church-- Missouri Synod. Districts. Brazil. 234'.163
Synodal-Bericht. St. Louis. v. 20-23 cm. Issued 190 by the district under the synod's earlier name: Deutsche Evangelisch-Lutherische Synode von Missouri, Ohio und Andern Staaten [BX8063.B77L8] 51-31300
I. Title.

LUTHERANS and Catholics in dialogue, I-III 234'.163
/ edited by Paul C. Empie and T. Austin Murphy. Minneapolis : Augsburg Pub. House, [1974?] 36, 87, 200 p. ; 20 cm. Papers and summary statements for meetings sponsored jointly by the Bishops' Committee for Ecumenical and Interreligious Affairs and the U.S.A. National Committee of the Lutheran World Federation, and held in various cities in 1965, 1966, and 1967. Reissue of the first three volumes of a series published under the same title by the U.S.A. National Committee of the Lutheran World Federation. Includes bibliographical references. [BX8063.7.C3L87] 74-187921 ISBN 0-8066-1451-X pbk. : 2.95
1. Catholic Church—Relations—Lutheran Church—Congresses. 2. Lutheran Church—Relations—Catholic Church—Congresses. 3. Nicene Creed—Congresses. 4. Baptism—Congresses. 5. Lord's Supper—Congresses. I. Empie, Paul C., ed. II. Murphy, Thomas Austin, 1911- ed. III. Catholic Church. National Conference of Catholic Bishops. Bishops' Committee for Ecumenical and Interreligious Affairs. IV. Lutheran World Federation. U.S.A. National Committee.
Contents omitted.

MAYNARD, Lee Carter, comp. 234'.163
Memories of the Master; 90 communion meditations. Cincinnati, Standard Pub. [1973] 96 p. 16 cm. [BV826.5.M39] 72-95182 2.25
1. Lord's Supper—Meditations. I. Title.

PITTENGER, William Norman, 1905- 234'.163
Life as Eucharist, by Norman Pittenger. Grand Rapids, Mich., Eerdmans [1973] 104 p. 21 cm. Based on lectures given in Amarillo, Tex., Mar., 1972. [BV825.2.P57] 73-7765 ISBN 0-8028-1542-1 1.95 (pbk.)
1. Lord's Supper. I. Title.

ZOLLINGER, Camma Larsen. 234'.163
Sacrament. Illustrated by William Kuhre. Salt Lake City, Bookcraft [1973] [24] p. col. illus. 31 cm. Discusses the sacrament in the Mormon church as a reminder of the friendship and love of Jesus. [BX8655.A1Z64] 73-88613
1. Sacraments—Mormons and Mormonism—Juvenile literature. I. Kuhre, William, illus. II. Title.

BUCHANAN, Colin Ogilvie. 234'.163'0924
What did Cranmer think he was doing? / by Colin Buchanan. Bramcote : Grove Books, 1976. 32 p. : ill. ; 22 cm. (Grove liturgical study ; no. 7 ISSN 0306-0608s) [BV823.B79] t77-359984 ISBN 0-901710-98-9 : £0.65
1. Cranmer, Thomas, Abp. of Canterbury, 1489-1556. 2. Lord's Supper—History. I. Title.

ACHTEMEIER, Elizabeth Rice, 1926- 234'.165
The committed marriage / Elizabeth Achtemeier. Philadelphia : Westminster Press, c1976. 224 p. ; 21 cm. (Biblical perspectives on current issues) Includes index. Bibliography: p. [219] [BV835.A25] 76-7611 ISBN 0-664-24754-7 4.95
1. Marriage. I. Title. II. Series.

ARNOLD, Heini, 1913- 234'.165
In the image of God : marriage and chastity in Christian life / by Heini Arnold. Rifton, N.Y. : Plough Pub. House, c1977. xv, 168 p. : 19 cm. Bibliography: p. 167-168. [BV835.A76] 76-53542 ISBN 0-87486-169-1 pbk. : 2.00
1. Marriage. I. Title.

BARNES, Kathleen H. 234'.165
Forever and ever : a book for LDS children about temple marriage / by Kathleen H. Barnes, Virginia H. Pearce ; photos. by Don O. Thorpe. Salt Lake City : Deseret Book Co., 1975. [30] p. : ill. ; 22 cm. Brief text, photographs, and scripture help convey the significance of temple marriage in the Church of Jesus Christ of Latter Day Saints. [BX8641.B3] 75-28899 ISBN 0-87747-603-9
1. Marriage—Church of Jesus Christ of Latter Day Saints—Juvenile literature. I. Pearce, Virginia H., joint author. II. Thorpe, Don O. III. Title.

ENGELSMA, David. 234'.165
Marriage : the mystery of Christ and the church / by David Engelsma. Grand Rapids, Mich. : Reformed Free Pub. Association : distributed by Kregel Publications, c1975. 112 p. ; 21 cm. [BV835.E53] 74-31902 ISBN 0-8254-2519-0 : 3.50
1. Marriage. I. Title.

GERKE, Leonard F. 1911- 234.165
Christian marriage, a permanent sacrament, by Leonard F. Gerke. Washington, Catholic Univ. 1965. xi, 171p. 23cm. (Catholic Univ. of Amer. Studies in sacred theol., 2d. ser., no. 161) Title. (Series Catholic University of America. School of Sacred Theology. Studies in sacred theology, 2d. ser., no. 191) Thesis--Catholic Univ. of Amer. Vita. Bibl. [BX2250.G44] 66-8650 3.00 pap.,
1. Marriage—Catholic Church. I. Title. II. Series.

JOHNSON, James Turner. 234'.16'5
A society ordained by God; English Puritan marriage doctrine in the first half of the seventeenth century. Nashville, Abingdon Press [1970] 219 p. 23 cm. (Studies in Christian ethics series) A revision of the author's thesis, Princeton University, 1968. Bibliography: p. 209-216. [BT706.J64 1970] 77-124759
1. Marriage—Puritans. I. Title.

KELLEHER, Stephen Joseph, 1915- 234'.165
Divorce and remarriage for Catholics? [By] Stephen J. Kelleher. [1st ed.] Garden City, N.Y., Doubleday, 1973. 192 p. 22 cm. [BX2250.K34] 72-89322 5.95
1. Marriage—Catholic Church. 2. Divorce. I. Title.

KELLEHER, Stephen Joseph, 1915- 234.165
Divorce and remarriage for Catholics / Stephen J. Kelleher. Garden City, N. Y. : Doubleday [1976] 160p. ; 18 cm. (Image books) [BX2250K34] ISBN 0-385-11371-4 pbk. : 1.75
1. Marriage-Catholic Church. 2. Divorce. I. Title.
L. C. card no. for original edition: 72-89322.

MCHUGH, James T. 234'.165
Marriage in the light of Vatican II. James T. McHugh, editor. [1st ed.] Washington, Family Life Bureau, 1968. vii, 144 p. 18 cm. Includes bibliographical references. [BX2250.M19] 68-9687 1.25 (pbk)
1. Marriage—Catholic Church—Addresses, essays, lectures. I. Title.

MONTSERRAT Torrents, Josep. 234'.16'5
The abandoned spouse. Translated and edited by Gary MacEoin. Milwaukee, Bruce Pub. Co. [1969] viii, 196 p. 21 cm. Translation of Matrimonio, divorcio, separacion. Bibliography: p. 190-191. [BX2250.M57] 73-77153
1. Marriage—Catholic Church. 2. Remarriage. I. Title.

NIMETH, Albert J. 234'.165
Of course I love you; [by] Albert J. Nimeth. [Chicago, Franciscan Herald Press, 1973] 126 p. illus. 19 cm. [BX2250.N5] 73-12194 ISBN 0-8199-0466-X 7.95
1. Marriage—Catholic Church. I. Title.

BASSET, Bernard. 234'.166
Guilty, O Lord; yes, I still go to confession. [1st ed. in the United States of America] Garden City, N.Y., Doubleday, 1975 [c1974] 118 p. 22 cm. British ed. published under title: Guilty, my Lord. Includes bibliographical references. [BX2265.2.B323 1975] 74-9475 ISBN 0-385-02531-9 5.95
1. Confession. I. Title.

BUCKLEY, Francis J. 234'.166
"I confess"; the sacrament of Penance today [by] Francis J. Buckley. Notre Dame, Ind., Ave Maria Press [1972] 95 p. illus. 21 cm. Bibliography: p. 95. [BX2260.B8] 72-80971 ISBN 0-87793-048-1 1.25
1. Penance. 2. Confession. I. Title.

KELLY, George Anthony, 1916- 234'.166
The sacrament of penance and reconciliation / [George A. Kelly]. Chicago : Franciscan Herald Press, c1975. 55 p. ; 18 cm. (Synthesis series) Includes bibliographical references. [BX2260.K4] 75-35596 ISBN 0-8199-0701-4 : 0.65
1. Penance. 2. Sociology, Christian (Catholic) I. Title.

†THE Sacrament of penance in our time 234'.166
/ edited by George A. Kelley. Boston : St. Paul Editions, c1976. 165 p. ; 21 cm. Includes bibliographical references and index. [BX2260.S23] 76-18719 4.00 pbk. : 3.00
1. Penance—Addresses, essays, lectures. I. Kelly, George Anthony, 1916-

TENTLER, Thomas N., 1932- 234'.166
Sin and confession on the eve of the Reformation / Thomas N. Tentler. Princeton, N.J. : Princeton University Press, c1977. xxiv, 395 p. ; 25 cm. Includes index. Bibliography: p. 371-389. [BV840.T43] 76-3022 ISBN 0-691-07219-1 : 25.00
1. Penance—History. I. Title.

*ALDRICH, Willard M. 234.2
The battle for your Faith, by Dr. Willard M. Aldrich. Portland, Or., Multnomah Press, [1975] 158 p. 22 cm. [BV4637] 3.50 (pbk.)
1. Faith. 2. Christian life—1960- I. Title.

ALLEN, Charles Livingstone, 1913- 234'.2
The miracle of hope [by] Charles L. Allen. Old Tappan, N.J., Revell [1973] 64 p. 19 cm. [BV4638.A56] 73-9812 2.95
1. Hope—Meditations. I. Title.

AUGUSTINUS, Aurelius, Saint, Bp. of Hippo. 234.2
Saint Augustine's De fide rerum quae non videntur: a critical text and translation [sic] with introd. and commentary by Sister Mary Francis McDonald. Washington, Catholic University of America Press, 1950. xvi, 147 p. diagrs. 23 cm. (The Catholic University of America. Patristic studies, v. 84) The editor's thesis--Catholic University of America. "Select bibliography": p. xiii-xvi. [BR65.A657 1950] A 50
I. McDonald, Mary Francis, Sister, 1920- ed. and tr. II. Title. III. Series.

BARS, Henry, 1911- 234.2
The assent of faith. Translated by Ronald Halstead. Baltimore, Helicon Press, 1960 [c1959] 215p. 19cm. Includes bibliography. [BT774.B313] 59-11461
1. Belief and doubt. 2. Faith. I. Title.

BARS, Henry, 1911- 234.2
Faith, hope and charity. Translated from the French by P. J. Hepburne Scott. [1st ed.] New York, Hawthorn Books [1961] 143p. 21cm. (The Twentieth century encyclopedia of Catholicism, v. 27. Section 2: The basic truths) Translation of Trois vertus-clef. Includes bibliography. [BV4635.B313] 61-12988
1. Faith. 2. Hope. 3. Charity. I. Title.

BAUMAN, Bert. 234'.2
The healing of the soul / Bert Bauman. Minneapolis : Bethany Fellowship, c1975. 64 p. ; 18 cm. (Dimension books) [BV4637.B34] 75-5445 ISBN 0-87123-223-5 pbk. : 0.95
1. Faith. 2. Christian life—1960- I. Title.

BAVINCK, Johan Herman, 1895- 234.2
Faith and its difficulties. Translated from the Dutch by M. B. Eerdmans, Sr. Grand Rapids, Eerdmans [1959] 85p. 21cm. 'The pieces ... are taken from the symposium Het geloof en zijn moeilijkheden, by J. H. Bavinck, J. de Groot, and M. J. A. de Vrijer.' [BT771.2.B313] 59-8745
1. Faith. I. Title.

BELGUM, David 234.2
Why did it happen to me? Christian answers to questions about faith and health. Minneapolis, Augsburg Pub. House [c.1960] 110p. 20cm. 60-14166 1.25 pap.,
1. Medicine and religion. I. Title.

BELGUM, David Roudolph, 1922- 234.2
Why did it happen to me? Christian answers to questions about faith and health. Minneapolis, Augsburg Pub. House [1960] 110p. 20cm. [BT732.B4] 60-14166
1. Medicine and religion. I. Title.

BENDALL, Kent. 234.2
Exploring the logic of faith: a dialogue on the relation of modern philosophy to Christian faith, by Kent Bendall and Frederick Ferre. New York, Association Press [1962] 219p. 21cm. (A Haddam House book) [BT771.2.B4] 62-17296
1. Faith. 2. Philosophy and religion. I. Ferre, Frederick, joint author. II. Title.

BESNARD, Albert Marie. 234'.2
Faith: its life and growth [by] A. M. Besnard. Translated by Paul Joseph Oligny. Westminster, Md., Newman Press [1967] vi, 198 p. 22 cm. Translation of Vie et combats de la foi. Bibliographical footnotes. [BT771.2.B4613] 67-23606
1. Faith. I. Title.

BIXLER, Julius Seelye, 1894- 234.2
A faith that fulfills. [1st ed.] New York, Harper [1951] 122 p. 20 cm. [BR121.B52] 51-10833
1. Christianity—20th cent. I. Title.

BIXLER, Julius Seelye, 1894- 234'.2
A faith that fulfills. Westport, Conn., Greenwood Press [1971, c1951] 122 p. 23 cm. [BR121.2.B465 1971] 74-138100 ISBN 0-8371-5676-9
1. Christianity—20th century. I. Title.

BLIGH, John. 234'.2
Faith and revelation / by John Bligh. Staten Island, N.Y. : Alba House, 1975, c1972. 115 p. ; 19 cm. (Scripture for meditation ; 6) [BV4637.B54 1975] 74-31319 ISBN 0-8189-0311-2 pbk. : 1.95
1. Faith—Meditations. 2. Revelation—Meditations. I. Title. II. Series.

*BRONSTEIN, David. 234.2
Everyday spiritual perception. Philadelphia, Dorrance [1968] 67p. 21cm. 3.00
1. Faith. I. Title.

BROWN, Robert McAfee, 1920- 234'.2
Is faith obsolete? Philadelphia, Westminster Press [1974] 157 p. 22 cm. Includes bibliographical references. [BV4637.B8] 74-13420 ISBN 0-664-20715-4 5.95
1. Faith. I. Title.

BRUNNER, Heinrich Emil, 1889- 234.2
Faith, hope, and love. Philadelphia, Westminster Press [1956] 79p. 20cm. (The Earl lectures, 1955) [BV4635.B7] 56-7370
1. Faith. 2. Hope. 3. Love (Theology) I. Title.

BUNYAN, John, 1628-1688. 234'.2
Israel's hope encouraged; or, What hope is and how it is distinguished from faith. Swengel, Pa., Reiner Publications, 1968. 126 p. 19 cm. Reprint of the 1852 ed. published in v. 6, Consoling works, of The practical works of John Bunyan. [BS1199.H65B8 1968] 70-1863 1.75
1. Bible. O.T. Psalms cxxx, 7—Criticism, interpretation, etc. 2. Hope—Biblical teaching. I. Title.

BUSENBENDER, Wilfrid, 1907- 234.2
An opportunity for faith. Translated from the German by Salvator Attanasio. Chicago, H. Regnery Co., 1963. 155 p. 21 cm. Translation of Die Welt als Chance des Glaubens. Bibliographical references included in "Notes ..." (p. 153-155) [BR121.2.B843] 63-12896
1. Christianity — 20th cent. I. Title.

BUSENBENDER, Wilfrid, 1907- 234.2
An opportunity for faith. Tr. from German by Salvator Attanasio. Chicago, Regnery [c.]1963. 155p. 21cm. Bibl. 63-12896 5.00
1. Christianity—20th cent. I. Title.

CAPPS, Walter H. 234'.2
Hope against hope : Molton [i.e. Moltmann] to Merton in one decade / Walter Holton Capps. Philadelphia : Fortress Press, c1976. xxiii, 167 p. ; 20 cm. Includes bibliographical references. [BV4638.C27] 75-36456 ISBN 0-8006-0436-9 : 4.75
1. Moltmann, Jurgen. 2. Merton, Thomas, 1915-1968. 3. Hope—History of doctrines. I. Title.

CHENU, Marie Dominique, 1895- 234'.2
Faith and theology [by] M. D. Chenu. Translated by Denis Hickey. Dublin, Gill [1968] viii, 227 p. 22 cm. Translation of La parole de Dieu. Bibliographical footnotes. [BT771.2.C4813 1968b] 72-229959 35/-
1. Faith. 2. Communication (Theology) I. Title.

CHENU, Marie Dominique, 1895- 234'.2
Faith and theology [by] M. D. Chenu. Translated by Denis Hickey. [1st American ed.] New York, Macmillan [1968] viii, 227 p. 23 cm. Translation of La parole de Dieu. Bibliographical footnotes. [BT771.2.C4813 1968] 67-10873
1. Faith. 2. Communication (Theology) I. Title.

CIRNE-LIMA, Carlos. 234.2
Personal faith, a metaphysical inquiry. Translated by G. Richard Dimler. [New York] Herder and Herder [1965] 206 p. 21 cm. Bibliographical footnotes. [BT771.2C513] 64-19726
1. Faith. I. Title.

CIRNE-LIMA, Carlos 234.2
Personal faith, a metaphysical inquiry. Tr. [from German by G. Richard Dimler. [New York] Herder & Herder [c.1965] 206p. 21cm. Bibl. [BT771.2.C513] 64-19726 4.50
1. Faith. I. Title.

COLE, Clifford Adair, 1915- 234.2
Faith for new frontiers. Independence, Mo., Herald House [1956] 156p. 21cm. [BX8674.C6] 56-12023
1. Reorganized Church of Jesus Christ of Latter-Day Saints—Dectrinal and controversial works. 2. Faith. I. Title.

COLLINS, Earl L 234.2
As of a mustard seed. New York, Vantage Press [1955, c1954] 78p. 23cm. [BT771.C65] 54-11882
1. Faith. 2. God —Promises. I. Title.

CONFERENCE on Hope and the Future of Man, New York, 1971. 234'.2
Hope and the future of man. Ewert H. Cousins, editor. Philadelphia, Fortress Press [1972] xii, 148 p. 21 cm. Sponsored by the American Teilhard de Chardin Association, and others. Includes bibliographical references. [BV4638.C58 1971] 72-75647 ISBN 0-8006-0540-3 3.95
1. Hope—Addresses, essays, lectures. I. Cousins, Ewert H., ed. II. American Teilhard de Chardin Association. III. Title.

COOKE, Bernard J. 234.2
Formation of faith. Chicago Loyola [c.]1965. 107p. 23cm. (Loyola pastoral ser.) Consists of the slightly modified text of a ser. of television programs planned anc executed by the Archdiocese of Chic. School Bd. and Marquette Univ., with study aids developed by Sister Francis Borgia and a committee of the Religion Teachers Assn. of Chic. Bibl. [BV4637.C6] 65-27619 2.00 pap.,
1. Faith—Study and teaching. 2. Religious education—Textbooks—Catholic. I. Chicago (Archdiocese) School Board. II. Marquette University, Milwaukee. III. Title.

COVENTRY, John. 234'.2
The theology of faith. Notre Dame, Ind., Fides Publishers [1968] 93 p. 18 cm. (Theology today, no. 3) Bibliography: p. 93. [BT771.2.C64] 70-326 0.95
1. Faith. I. Title.

DAY, Albert Edward, 1884- 234.2
Dialogue and destiny. New York, Harper [c.1961] 192p. Bibl. 61-12839 3.50 bds.,
1. Faith. I. Title.

EBELING, Gerhard, 1912- 234.2
The nature of faith. Tr. [from German] by Ronald Gregor Smith. Philadelphia, Muhlenberg Pr. [1962, c.1959, 1961] 191p. 62-7194 3.00
1. Faith. I. Title.

*EDMAN, V. Raymond. 234.2
Look unto the hills. Chicago, Moody [1968] 61p. illus. 21cm. (Devotionals) .95 pap.,
1. Faith. I. Title.

ELLUL, Jacques, 1912- 234'.2
Hope in time of abandonment. Translated by C. Edward Hopkin. New York, Seabury Press [1973] xiii, 306 p. 22 cm. Translation of l'Esperance oubliee. [BV4638.E4413] 72-81025 ISBN 0-8164-0247-7 8.95
1. Hope. 2. Civilization, Modern—1950- I. Title.

FAITH in the face of doubt, 234'.2
edited by John P. Keating. New York, Paulist Press [1968] x, 176 p. 19 cm. (Deus books) "A series of eight talks given at the Catholic Student Center at the University of California at Berkeley." [BT771.2.F26] 68-31051 1.45
1. Faith—Addresses, essays, lectures. I. Keating, John P., comp.

FERRE, Nels Fredrick Solomon, 1908- 234'.2
Faith and reason, by Nels F. S. Ferre. Freeport, N.Y., Books for Libraries Press [1971, c1946] xii, 251 p. 23 cm. (Essay index reprint series) "Originally published as volume 1 of Reason and the Christian faith." Includes bibliographical references. [BT50.F4 1971] 78-142626 ISBN 0-8369-2392-8
1. Faith and reason.

FERRE, Nels Fredrick Solomon, 1908- 234.2
The finality of faith, and Christianity among the world religions. [1st ed.] New York, Harper & Row [1963] 115 p. 20 cm. [BT771.2.F4] 63-10749
1. Faith. 2. Christianity and other religions. I. Title.

FERRE, Nels Fredrick Solomon, 1908- 234.2
The finality of faith, and Christianity among the world religions. New York, Harper [c.1963] 115p. 20cm. 63-10749 2.75 bds.,
1. Faith. 2. Christianity and other religions. I. Title.

FRANKE, Carol W 1928- 234.2
I do believe because . . . A testament of faith in the Bible from creation to consummation. [1st ed.] New York, Exposition Press [1955] 148p. 21cm. [BT772.F7] 55-10294
1. Faith. I. Title.

FRAZIER, Claude Albee, 1920- 234'.2
What faith has meant to me / edited by Claude A. Frazier. Philadelphia : Westminster Press, [1975] 171 p. ; 20 cm. [BV4637.F69] 75-2054 ISBN 0-664-24825-X pbk. : 4.95
1. Faith. 2. Witness bearing (Christianity) I. Title.

FRIES, Heinrich. 234'.2
Faith under challenge. Translated by William D. Seidensticker. [New York] Herder and Herder [1969] 207 p. 22 cm. Translation of Herausgeforderter Glaube. Bibliographical footnotes. [BT771.2.F6713] 74-92317 5.95
1. Faith. 2. Apologetics—20th century. I. Title.

GALOT, Jean. 234'.2
The mystery of Christian hope / Jean Galot ; translated by M. Angeline Bouchard. New York : Alba House, c1977. vi, 141 p. ; 22 cm. Translation of Le mystere de l'esperance. Includes bibliographical references. [BV4638.G3413] 77-1222 ISBN 0-8189-0346-5 : 4.95
1. Hope. I. Title.

GALOT, Jean. 234'.2
The mystery of Christian hope / Jean Galot ; translated by M. Angeline Bouchard. New York : Alba House, c1977. vi, 141 p. ; 22 cm. Translation of Le mystere de l'esperance. Includes bibliographical references. [BV4638.G3413] 77-1222 ISBN 0-8189-0346-5 : 4.95
1. Hope. I. Title.

GOODENOUGH, Erwin Ramsdell, 1893- 234.2
Toward a mature faith. New York, Prentice-Hall [1955] 180 p. 22 cm. [BR121.G57] 55-6264
1. Christianity—Essence, genius, nature. I. Title.

GUINNESS, Os. 234'.2
In two minds : the dilemma of doubt & how to resolve it / Os Guinness. Downers Grove, Ill. : InterVarsity Press, c1976. 302 p. ; 21 cm. Includes bibliographical references. [BT771.2.G84] 75-21456 ISBN 0-87784-771-1 : 4.95
1. Faith. I. Title.

HARING, Bernhard, 1912- 234'.2
Hope is the remedy [by] Bernard Haring. Garden City, NY., Doubleday [1973, c.1972] 160 p. 18 cm. (Image Book, D323) [BV4638.H3] 72-76165 ISBN 0-385-03889-5 1.25 (pbk.)
1. Hope. I. Title.

HARBUCK, Don B. 234'.2
The dynamics of belief [by] Don B. Harbuck. Nashville, Broadman Press [1969] 121 p. 19 cm. Includes bibliographical references. [BV4637.H37] 75-84502
1. Faith. I. Title.

HARING, Bernhard, 1912- 234'.2
Faith and morality in the secular age, by Bernard Haring. [1st ed.] Garden City, N.Y., Doubleday, 1973. 237 p. 22 cm. [BL2747.8.H33] 73-79876 ISBN 0-385-03837-2 6.95
1. Secularism. 2. Religion and culture. 3. Faith. 4. Prayer. I. Title.

HAUGHTON, Rosemary. 234'.2
Act of love. Philadelphia, Lippincott [1969, c1968] 191 p. 23 cm. [BT771.2.H36 1969] 69-13274 4.50
1. Faith. 2. Conversion. 3. Love (Theology) I. Title.

HERMANN, Ingo, 1932- 234.2
The experience of faith; a contribution to the biblicotheological dialogue. Foreword by John L. McKenzie. Translated by Daniel Coogan. New York, P. J. Kenedy [1966] vii, 119 p. 22 cm. Transition of Das Experiment unit dem Glauben. Includes bibliographical references. [BT771.2.H413] 66-25141
1. Faith. I. Title.

HERMANN, Ingo, 1932- 234.2
The experience of faith; a contribution to the biblico-theological dialogue. Foreword by John L. McKenzie. Translated by Daniel Coogan. New York, P. J. Kenedy [1966] vii, 119 p. 22 cm. Translation of Das Experiment mit dem Glauben. Includes bibliographical references. [BT771.2.H413] 66-25141
1. Faith. I. Title.

HOLBROOK, Clyde A 234.2
Faith and community, a Christian existential approach. [1st ed.] New York, Harper [1959] 159p. 22cm. Includes bibliography. [BT771.2.H6] 59-7153
1. Faith. 2. Christianity—Philosophy. I. Title.

HOLLAND, Henry Scott, 1847-1918 234.2
Fibres of faith. Introd. by B. M. G. Reardon.

London, S. P. C. K. [dist. Greenwich, Conn., Seabury, c.1962] 105p. 19cm. 63-591 1.25 pap.,
1. Faith. I. Title.

HOLMER, Paul L. 234'.2
Youth considers doubt and frustration, by Paul L. Holmer. Camden, N.J., T. Nelson [1967] 96 p. illus. 21 cm. (Youth forum series) [BT771.2.H65] 65-22018
1. Faith. I. Title. II. Series.

HULME, William Edward, 1920- 234'.2
Am I losing my faith? [By] William E. Hulme. Philadelphia, Fortress Press [1971] vii, 56 p. 19 cm. (Pocket counsel books) Includes bibliographical references. [BV4637.H8] 71-133035 1.50
1. Faith. 2. Belief and doubt. I. Title.

JOLY, Eugene, 1901- 234.2
What is faith? Translated from the French by Illtyd Trethowan. [1st ed.] New York, Hawthorn Books [1958] 144p. 21cm. (The Twentieth century encyclopedia of Catholicism, v. 6. Section 1: Knowledge and faith) Translation of Qu'est-ce que croire? Includes bibliography. [BT771.J613] 58-11592
1. Faith. I. Title.

KANELLOPOULOS, Panagiotes 1902. 234.2
A scent to Faith [by] Panayotis Kanellopoulos Tr. from Greek, introd. by Mary P. Giano. New York, Exposition [c.1966 101 p. 22 cm (exposition-univ. bk). consist of the 5th, 7th &, 9th chapters rewritten from christianity in our times. [bt825.k3131] 66-17922 4.00
1. 1. Death. Suffering. Faith. I. Title.

KAZEE, Buell H. 234.2
Faith is the victory. Grand Rapids, Eerdmans, 1951. 181 p. 21 cm. [BT771.K3] 51-9750
1. Faith. I. Title.

KENELLOPOULOS, Panagiotes, 1902- 234.2
Ascent to faith [by] Panayotis Kanellopoulos. Translated from the Greek and with an introd. by Mary P. Gianos. [1st ed.] New York, Exposition Press [1966] 101 p. 22 cm. (An Exposition-university book) Consists of the 5th, 7th and 9th chapters, rewritten, from Christianity in our times. [BT825.K313] 66-17922
1. Death. 2. Suffering. 3. Faith. I. Title.

KENNEDY, Eugene C. 234'.2
Believing [by] Eugene C. Kennedy. [1st ed.] Garden City, N.Y., Doubleday, 1974. 216 p. 22 cm. [BV4637.K43] 73-79681 ISBN 0-385-07496-4 5.95
1. Faith. I. Title.

KENNEDY, Eugene C. 234'.2
Believing / Eugene C. Kennedy. Garden City, N.Y. : Image Books, 1977c1974. 237p. ; 18 cm. (A Doubleday Image Book) [BV463.K43] pbk. : 1.95
1. Faith. I. Title.
L.C. card no. for 1974 Doubleday ed.:73-79681.

KENNEDY, Eugene C. 234'.2
Believing / Eugene C. Kennedy. Garden City, N.Y. : Image Books, 1977c1974. 237p. ; 18 cm. (A Doubleday Image Book) [BV463.K43] pbk. : 1.95
1. Faith. I. Title.
L.C. card no. for 1974 Doubleday ed.:73-79681.

*KETTNER, Elmer A. 234.2
What do I believe? A personal and group Bible study guide on the essence of the Christian faith and ways of presenting it to the unconverted [st. Louis, Concordia, 1966] 93p. 19cm. 1.00 pap.,
1. Faith. I. Title.

LADRIERE, Jean. 234'.2
Language and belief. Translated by Garrett Barden. [American ed. Notre Dame, Ind.] University of Notre Dame Press [1972] 204 p. 22 cm. Translation of L'articulation du sens. Includes bibliographical references. [BL65.L2L3313 1972] 72-3506 ISBN 0-268-00479-X 10.95
1. Religion and language. 2. Science—Language. I. Title.

LAZARETH, William Henry, 1928- 234.2
Man: in whose image. Philadelphia, Muhlenberg [c.1961] 54p. (Fortress bk.) 61-13581 1.00 bds.,
1. Christian life. I. Title.

LINDSEY, Hal. 234'.2
The terminal generation / by Hal Lindsey with C. C. Carlson. Old Tappan, N.J. : Revell, c1976. 192 p. ; 24 cm. Includes bibliographical references. [BV4638.L56] 76-14925 ISBN 0-8007-0794-X : 6.95. ISBN 0-8007-0795-8 pbk. : 3.95
1. Hope. I. Carlson, Carole C., joint author. II. Title.

LYNCH, William F., 1908- 234'.2
Images of faith; an exploration of the ironic imagination [by] William F. Lynch. Notre Dame [Ind.] University of Notre Dame Press [1973] x, 184 p. 22 cm. Includes bibliographical references. [BV4637.L94] 73-11560 ISBN 0-268-00515-X 6.95
1. Faith. I. Title.

LYNCH, William F., 1908- 234'.2
Images of hope; imagination as healer of the hopeless [by] William F. Lynch. Notre Dame [Ind.] University of Notre Dame Press [1974, c1965] 319 p. 21 cm. Reprint of the ed. published by Helicon, Baltimore. Bibliography: p. 309-319. [BD216.L9 1974] 73-20418 ISBN 0-268-00536-2 8.95
1. Hope. I. Title.
Pbk. 2.95, ISBN 0-268-00537-0.

MCCAULEY, MichaelF. 234'.2
A contemporary meditation on doubting / by Michael F. McCauley. Chicago : Thomas More Press, c1976. 115 p. ; 21 cm. (Contemporary meditations) [BV4637.M23] 76-378091 ISBN 0-88347-060-8 pbk. : 2.95
1. Belief and doubt—Meditations. 2. Faith—Meditations. I. Title.

MACGREGOR, Geddes. 234.2
Christian doubt. London, New York, Longmans, Green [1951] 160p. 20cm. [BT774.M32] 52-6699
1. Belief and doubt. I. Title.

MACLAREN, Elizabeth. 234'.2
The nature of belief / [by] Elizabeth Maclaren. London : Sheldon Press, 1976. [1], viii, 118 p. ; 20 cm. (Issues in religious studies) Includes bibliographies and index. [BT771.2.M233 1976b] 76-382252 ISBN 0-85969-052-0 : £1.60
1. Faith. I. Title.

MACLAREN, Elizabeth. 234'.2
The nature of belief / Elizabeth Maclaren. New York : Hawthorn Books, 1976. 117 p. ; 21 cm. (Issues in religious studies) Includes bibliographical references and index. [BT771.2.M233 1976] 75-31371 ISBN 0-8015-5336-9 pbk. : 3.50
1. Faith. I. Title.

*MACNEVINS, Harold A., 1897- 234'.2
Faith in God is the victory. New York, Vantage [1973] 74 p. 21 cm. [BV4637] ISBN 0-533-00583-3 3.00
1. Faith. 2. God—Proof. I. Title.

MELAND, Bernard Eugene, 1899- 234.2
Faith and culture. New York, Oxford University Press, 1953. 229p. 21cm. [BT771.M45] 53-9189
1. Faith. 2. Culture. I. Title.

MICHALSON, Carl 234.2
The rationality of faith; an historical critique of the theological reason. New York, Scribners [1963] 160p. 22cm. 63-8674 3.50
1. Faith. I. Title.

MILLER, Samuel Howard, 1900- 234'.2
Man the believer; [essays, by] Samuel H. Miller. Nashville, Abingdon Press [1968] 144 p. 20 cm. [BT771.2.M53] 68-11471
1. Faith—Psychology. 2. Man (Theology) I. Title.

MOHLER, James A. 234'.2
Dimensions of faith: yesterday and today [by] James A. Mohler. Chicago, Loyola University Press [1969] xvi, 213 p. 23 cm. Bibliography: p. 183-202. [BT771.2.M593] 69-13120
1. Faith—History of doctrines. I. Title.

MONDEN, Louis. 234'.2
Faith; can man still believe? Translated by Joseph Donceel. New York, Sheed & Ward [1970] vii, 243 p. 22 cm. Includes bibliographical references. [BT771.2.M595] 72-101545 5.95
1. Faith. 2. Revelation. 3. Apologetics—20th century. I. Title.

MOULE, Charles Francis Digby. 234.2
The meaning of hope: a Biblical exposition with concordance. Philadelphia, Fortress Press [1963] vii, 72 p. 19 cm. (Facet books. Biblical series, 5) Bibliography: p. 56-57. [BV4638.M6] 63-17881
1. Hope — Biblical teaching. I. Title. II. Series.

MOULE, Charles Francis Digby 234.2
The meaning of hope: a Biblical exposition with concordance. Philadelphia, Fortress [c.1963] vii, 72p. 19cm. (Facet bks. Biblical ser., 5) Bibl. 63-17881 .75 pap.,
1. Hope—Biblical teaching. I. Title. II. Series.

MOUROUX, Jean 234.2
I believe; the personal structure of faith. Translated [from the French] by Michael Turner. New York, Sheed and Ward [1959, i.e., 1960] 109p. (bibl. and bibl. footnotes) 19cm. 60-16021 2.75 bds.,
I. Title.

O'CONNOR, Edward Dennis 234.2
Faith in the Synoptic Gospels; a problem in the correlation of Scripture and theology. [Notre Dame, Ind.] Univ. of Notre Dame Press [c.]1961. 164p. Bibl. 61-10847 5.00 pap.,
1. Faith—Biblical teaching. 2. Bible, N. T. Gospels—Criticism, interpretation, etc. I. Title.

OLIVIER, Bernard. 234.2
Christian hope. Translated by Paul Barrett. Westminster, Md., Newman Press, 1963. 140 p. 21 cm. Includes bibliography. [BV4638.O413] 63-12233
1. Hope. I. Title.

OLIVIER, Bernard 234.2
Christian hope. Tr. by Paul Barrett. Westminster. Md., Newman [c.]1963. 140p. 21cm. Bibl. 63-12233 2.95
1. Hope. I. Title.

PARDUE, Austin, Bp., 1899- 234.2
The single eye. New York, Morehouse-Gorham, 1957. 133p. 20cm. [BT772.P3] 57-6429
1. Faith. 2. Prayer. I. Title.

PEASE, Norval F. 234'.2
The faith that saves [by] Norval F. Pease. [Washington, Review and Herald Pub. Association, c1969] 64 p. 18 cm. Cover title. [BT772.P38] 76-128408
1. Seventh-Day Adventists—Doctrinal and controversial works. 2. Faith. I. Title.

PENELHUM, Terence, 1929- 234'.2
Problems of religious knowledge. [New York] Herder and Herder [1972, c1971] ix, 186 p. 22 cm. (Philosophy of religion series) Bibliography: p. 175-184. [BV4637.P45 1972] 78-171519 7.95
1. Faith. 2. Evidence. 3. God—Proof. 4. Religion—Philosophy. I. Title.

*PIKE, James A. 234.2
A time for Christian candor. New York, Harper [c.1964] 1v. 24cm. 3.50
I. Title.

PROTESTANT Episcopal Church in the U. S. A. National Council. Dept. of Christian Education. 234.2
Belief and behavior; leaders guide: senior high school, course 1. Greenwich, Conn., Seabury Press [1958] 115p. illus. 28cm. (The Seabury series, T-10) Includes bibliography. [BT772.P88] 58-9265
1. Faith—Juvenile literature. I. Title.

RABUT, Olivier A. 234'.2
Faith and doubt, by Olivier A. Rabut. Translated by Bonnie and William Whitman. New York, Sheed and Ward [1967] 119 p. 21 cm. Translation of La verification religieuse. Includes bibliographical references. [BT40.R313] 67-29288
1. Knowledge, Theory of (Religion) 2. Faith. I. Title.

RAHNER, Karl, 1904- 234.2
On the theology of death. [Translated by Charles H. Henkey. New York] Herder and Herder [1961] 127p. 22cm. (Quaestiones disputatae, 2) [BT825.R313] 61-11443
1. Death. 2. Martyrdom. I. Title.

RATZINGER, Joseph. 234'.2
Faith and the future. [Chicago] Franciscan Herald Press [1971] xii, 112 p. 22 cm. Translation of Glaube und Zukunft. Includes bibliographical references. [BT772.R3513] 79-155850 ISBN 0-8199-0427-9 4.95
1. Faith—Addresses, essays, lectures. 2. Christianity—20th century—Addresses, essays, lectures. I. Title.

REDDING, David A. 234'.2
God is up to something [by] David A. Redding. Waco, Tex., Word Books [1972] 164 p. 23 cm. Includes bibliographical references. [BV4638.R43] 72-84169 4.95
1. Hope. I. Title.

REDHEAD, John A 234.2
Learning to have faith. Nashville, Abingdon Press [1955] 128p. 20cm. [BT771.R4] 55-5736
1. Faith—Sermons. 2. Presbyterian Church—Sermons. 3. Sermons, American. I. Title.

RHEA, Carolyn 234.2
Such is my confidence. New York, Grosset [c.1961] 81p. 16cm. 61-19284 1.50 pap.,
1. Faith. I. Title.

ROGERS, Dale Evans. 234.2
To my son: faith at our house. [Westwood, N. J.] Revell [1957] 142p. 22cm. The author's letters to her son Tom. [BR1725.R63A4] 57-6856
I. Fox, Thomas Frederick. II. Title.

ROMAINE, William, 1714-1795. 234'.2
The life, walk and triumph of faith, by William Romaine; with an account of his life and work by Peter Toon. Cambridge, James Clarke, 1970. xxv, 413 p. 23 cm. Includes bibliographical references. [BV4500.R63 1970] 75-853080 ISBN 0-227-67744-7 30/-
1. Christian life. I. Title.

*SANDERS, J. Oswald 234.2
Mighty faith. Chicago, Moody [c.1964] 58p. 18cm. (Moody compact bks., no.48) .29 pap.,
I. Title.

SARNO, Ronald A. 234'.2
The story of hope: the nation, the man, the kingdom [by] Ronald A. Sarno. Liguori, Mo., Liguori Publications [1972] 256 p. 18 cm. Bibliography: p. 235-239. [BS511.2.S27] 72-75145 2.00
1. Jesus Christ—Person and offices. 2. Bible—Criticism, interpretation, etc. 3. Church. 4. Hope. I. Title.

SKOVGAARD-PETERSEN, Carl Axel, 1866- 234.2
Faith and certainty. Translated from the Danish by A. W. Kjellstrand. Rock Island, Ill., Augustana Press [1957] 62p. 19cm. [BT771.S5552] 57-7759
1. Faith. 2. Assurance (Theology) I. Title.

SKOVGAARD-PETERSEN, Carl Axel, 1866- 234.2
Faith and certainty. Translated from the Danish by A. W. Kjellstrand. Rock Island, Ill., Augustana Press [1957] 62 p. 19 cm. [BT771.S5552] 57-7759
1. Faith. 2. Assurance (Theology) I. Title.

SLOAN, Harold Paul, 1881- 234.2
Faith is the victory. Philadelphia, Methodist Book Room, 1950. 118 p. 20 cm. [BT771.S557] 50-8669
1. Faith. I. Title.

SMITH, Bradford, 1909-1964. 234.2
Dear gift of life; a man's encounter with death. Foreword by Mark Van Doren. [Wallingford, Pa., Pendle Hill Publications, 1965] 38 p. 19 cm. (Pendle Hill pamphlet, 142) Verse and prose. [BT825.S6] 65-24496
1. Death. 2. Death — Poetry. I. Title.

SMITH, Wilfred Cantwell, 1916- 234'.2
Belief and history / Wilfred Cantwell. Charlottesville : University Press of Virginia, 1977. vi, 136 p. ; 24 cm. (Richard lectures for 1974-75, University of Virginia) Includes bibliographical references and indexes. [BV4637.S558] 76-50587 ISBN 0-8139-0670-9 : 12.50
1. Faith—Addresses, essays, lectures. 2. Belief and doubt—Addresses, essays, lectures. 3. Religion and language—Addresses, essays, lectures. I. Title. II. Series: Richard lectures, University of Virginia ; 1974-75.

SPINKS, George Stephens 234.2
The fundamentals of religious belief. London, Hodder and Stoughton[dist. Mystic, Conn., L. Verry, 1944, c.1961] 223p. 22cm. Bibl. 64-9786 4.00
1. Faith. 2. Belief and doubt. I. Title.

STANLEY, David Michael, 1914- 234'.2
Faith and religious life; a New Testament perspective, by David M. Stanley. New York, Paulist Press [1971] v, 90 p. 21 cm. "Originally given as a series of lectures ... during November, 1970." Includes bibliographical references. [BT772.S7] 73-155846 1.50
1. Faith. 2. Prayer. 3. Monastic and religious life. I. Title.

TILLICH, Apul, 1886- 234.2
Dynamics of faith. New York, Harper [1958, c1957] 134 p. 20 cm. (Harper torchbooks, TB42) [BT771.T54 1958] 58-10150
1. Faith. I. Title.

TILLICH, Paul, 1886- 234.2
Dynamics of faith. Planned and edited by Ruth Nanda Anshen. [1st ed.] New York, Harper [1956, c1957] xix, 127 p. 20 cm. (World perspectives, v. 10) [BT771.T54] 56-12231
1. Faith. I. Title. II. Series.

TILLICH, Paul, 1886-1965. 234.2
Dynamics of faith. New York, Harper [1958,

c1957] 134 p. 20 cm. (Harper torchbooks, TB42) [BT771.T54 1958] 58-10150
1. Faith. I. Title.

TILLICH, Paul, 1886-1965. 234.2
Dynamics of faith. Planned and edited by Ruth Nanda Anshen. [1st ed.] New York, Harper [1956, c1957] xix, 127 p. 20 cm. (World perspectives, v. 10) [BT771.T54] 56-12231
1. Faith. I. Title.

WAGERS, Herndon 234.2
Christian faith and philosophical inquiry. Lexington, Ky., College of the Bible, 1961. 80p. (Coll. of the Bible spring lectures, 1959) 61-66146 1.50 pap.,
1. Philosophy and religion. 2. Christianity—Philosophy. I. Title.

WALTER, Eugen, 1906- 234'.2
The faith that saves [by] Eugene Walter. Translated by Elisabeth Reinecke and Paul C. Bailey. Notre Dame, Ind., Fides Publishers [1968] 127 p. 18 cm. (A Fides dome book, D-62) Translation of Vom heilbringenden Glauben. [BT771.2.W2713] 68-57406 0.95
1. Faith. I. Title.

WARE, Sarah Pollard. 234.2
Faith makes the difference. [1st ed.] New York, Greenwich Book Publishers [1955] 63p. 21cm. [BT772.W26] 55-8767
1. Faith. I. Title.

WATKINS, William Turner, Bp., 1895- 234.2
The nature and meaning of Christian faith; a theological approach to depth evangelism. Nashville, Tidings [1960] 76 p. 19 cm. [B1771.2.W3] 60-15986
1. Faith. I. Title.

WILLIAMS, Rheinallt Nantlais. 234'.2
Faith, facts, history, science, and how they fit together. [1st American ed.] Wheaton, Ill., Tyndale House Publishers [1974, c1973] 140 p. 21 cm. First published in 1973 under title: Faith facing facts. Bibliography: p. 135. [BT1102.W54 1974] 73-93969 ISBN 0-8423-0839-3 1.95 (pbk.)
1. Apologetics—20th century. 2. Faith. I. Title.

WOODS, David F., 1909- comp. 234'.2
The flame of faith. Compiled by David F. Woods. New York, World Pub. Co. [1970] 45 p. 21 cm. [BV4637.W64 1970] 70-131165
1. Faith—Quotations, maxims, etc. I. Title.

WOODYARD, David O. 234'.2
Beyond cynicism; the practice of hope, by David O. Woodyard. Philadelphia, Westminster Press [1972] 112 p. 21 cm. Includes bibliographical references. [BV4638.W66] 75-190504 ISBN 0-664-20942-4
1. Hope. I. Title.

TOWARD a theology of Christian faith; 234'.2'08 readings in theology [by] Avery Dulles [and others] Prepared at the Canisianum, Innsbruck, by Michael Mooney [and others] New York, P. J. Kenedy [1968] ix, 344 p. 22 cm. Bibliographical footnotes. [BT771.2.T6] 68-22875
1. Faith—Addresses, essays, lectures. I. Dulles, Avery Robert, 1918- II. Mooney, Michael, comp. III. Title.

HEANEY, John J., ed. 234.2082
Faith, reason, and the Gospels; a selection of modern thought on faith and the Gospels. Westminster, Md., Newman Pr. [c.]1961. 327p. Bibl. 61-8964 4.95; 1.95 pap.,
1. Faith. 2. Reason. 3. Bible. N. T. Gospels—Evidences, authority, etc. I. Title.

BAKER, Albert Edward, 1884- 234'.2'0922
Prophets for a day of judgment, by A. E. Baker. With an introd. by the Archbishop of Canterbury. Freeport, N.Y., Books for Libraries Press [1969, c1944] viii, 95 p. 23 cm. (Essay index reprint series) Contents.Contents.—Jeremiah.—St. Augustine of Hippo.—The Lady Julian of Norwich.—Dostoevsky.—The gospel for a day of judgment. [BT771.B328 1969] 72-90605
1. Belief and doubt. 2. Faith. I. Title.

BURKE, Thomas Patrick, 1934- 234'.2'0924
Faith and the human person; an investigation of the thought of Scheeben [by] Patrick Burke. Chicago, John XXIII Institute [1968] xi, 176 p. 23 cm. Includes bibliographical references. [BX1751.S257B8] 68-9724
1. Scheeben, Matthias Joseph, 1835-1888. 2. Faith—History of doctrines. I. Title.

FEY, William R., 1942- 234'.2'0924
Faith and doubt : the unfolding of Newman's thought on certainty / by William R. Fey ; with a pref. by Charles Stephen Dessain. Shepherdstown, W.Va. : Patmos Press, 1976. xix, 229 p. ; 23 cm. Includes index. Bibliography: p. 203-213. [BT50.F45] 75-38101 ISBN 0-915762-02-1 : 16.95
1. Newman, John Henry, Cardinal, 1801-1890. 2. Faith and reason. 3. Belief and doubt. I. Title.

HACKER, Paul, 1913- 234'.2'0924
The ego in faith; Martin Luther and the origin of anthropocentric religion. [Chicago] Franciscan Herald Press [1970] xvi, 146 p. 21 cm. "A condensed recast by the author of his work Das Ich im Glauben bei Martin Luther." Includes bibliographical references. [BR333.2.H3132] 70-85506 ISBN 0-8199-0406-6 6.50
1. Luther, Martin, 1483-1546—Theology. I. Title.

MOHLER, James A. 234'.2'0924
The beginning of eternal life; the dynamic faith of Thomas Aquinas; origins and interpretation [by] James A. Mohler. New York, Philosophical Lib. [1968] 144p. 22cm. Bibl. [BT771.2.M59] 67-27267 4.95
1. Thomas Aquinas. Saint, 1225?-1274—Theology. 2. Faith—History of doctrines. I. Title.

NEWMAN, John Henry, Cardinal, 1801-1890. 234'.2'0924
The theological papers of John Henry Newman on faith and certainty / selected and edited by J. Derek Holmes ; partly prepared for publication by Hugo M. de Achaval ; with a note of introd. by Charles Stephen Dessain. Oxford [Eng.] : Clarendon Press, 1976. xv, 170 p. ; 25 cm. Includes bibliographical references and indexes. [BV4635.N48 1976] 76-358306 ISBN 0-19-920071-8 : 15.95
1. Faith—Collected works. 2. Knowledge, Theory of (Religion)—Collected works. 3. Christianity—Philosophy—Collected works. I. Holmes, J. Derek. II. De Achaval, Hugo M. III. Title.
Distributed by Oxford University Press N.Y.

ACHTEMEIER, Paul J 234'.3
To save all people; a study of the record of God's redemptive acts in Deuteronomy and Matthew [by] Paul J. and Elizabeth Achtemeier. Boston, United Church Press [1967] 154 p. 21 cm. [BT775.A23] 67-19499
1. Redemption—Biblical teaching. 2. Bible. O. T. Deuteronomy—Study—Outlines, syllabi, etc. 3. Bible. N.T. Matthew—Study—Outlines, syllabi, etc. I. Achtemeier, Elizabeth Rice, 1926-joint author. II. Title.

CASTER, Marcel van. 234.3
The redemption; a personalist view. Translated by Eileen O'Gorman and Olga Guedatarian. Glen Rock, N.J., Paulist Press [1965] 155 p. 18 cm. (Deus books, T895H) Translation of La redemption situee dans une perspective personnaliste. Bibliographical footnotes. [BT775.C373] 65-26793
1. Redemption. I. Title.

CASTER, Marcel van 234.3
The redemption; a personalist view. Tr. [from French] by Eileen O'Gorman, Olga Guedatarian. Glen Rock, N.J., Paulist [c.1965] 155p. 18cm. (Deus bks., T895H) Bibl. [BT775.C373] 65-26793 .95 pap.,
1. Redemption. I. Title.

CHAPMAN, Clifford Thomas. 234.3
The conflict of the kingdoms; the Christian message of salvation, its history and significance. London, New York, Hutchinson's University Library, 1951. 144p. 19cm. (Hutchinson's university library: Christian religion) Includes bibliography. [BT751.2.C5] 60-40636
1. Salvation. I. Title.

DOUTY, Norman Franklin, 1899- 234'.3
The death of Christ; a treatise which answers the question: "Did Christ die only for the elect?" [By] Norman F. Douty. Swengel, Pa., Reiner Publications, 1972. 120 p. 23 cm. Includes bibliographical references. [BT775.D68] 73-153887 3.95
1. Redemption. 2. Election (Theology) I. Title.

DURRWELL, F. X. 234'.3
The mystery of Christ and the apostolate [by] F. X. Durrwell. Translated by Edward Quinn. London, New York, Sheed and Ward [1972] x, 180 p. 21 cm. Translation of Le mystere pascal, source de l'apostolat, chapters 1-8. [BV601.2.D8713 1972] 72-1482 ISBN 0-7220-7210-4
1. Apostolate (Theology) 2. Paschal mystery. I. Title.

FISHER, Fred L. 234.3
The purpose of God and the Christian life. Philadelphia, Westminster [1963, c.1962] 189p. 21cm. Bibl. 62-14174 3.75
1. Redemption. 2. Salvation. 3. Election (Theology) I. Title.

GALLOWAY, Allan Douglas, 1920- 234.3
The cosmic Christ. New York, Harper [1951] 274 p. 22 cm. [BT775.G3 1951a] 52-4212
1. Redemption. I. Title.

HOGAN, William F 1920- 234.3
Christ's redemptive sacrifice. Englewood Cliffs, N.J. Prentice-Hall [1963] 118 p. illus. 23 cm. (Foundation of Catholic theology series) Includes bibliography. [B5263.H6] 63-17628
1. Redemption — History of doctrines. 2. Atonement — Hist. I. Title.

HOGAN, William F., 1920- 234.3
Christ's redemptive sacrifice. Englewood Cliffs, N.J., Prentice [c.1963] 118p. illus. 23cm. (Found. of Catholic theology ser.) Bibl. 63-17628 3.95; 1.50 pap.,
1. Redemption—History of doctrines. 2. Atonement—Hist. I. Title.

HOOKER, Thomas, 1586-1647. 234'.3
The application of redemption by the effectual work of the word and spirit of Christ, for the bringing home of lost sinners to God / Thomas Hooker New York : Arno Press, 1972. 451 [i.e. 431] p. ; 23 cm. (Research library of colonial Americana) Reprint of the 1657 ed. printed by P. Cole, London. [BT775.H75] 70-141111
1. Redemption. I. Title. II. Series.

HOOKER, Thomas, 1586-1647. 234.3
Redemption: three sermons, 1637-1656; facsimile reproductions With an introd. by Everett H. Emerson Gainesville, Fla., Scholars' Facsimiles & Reprints, 1956. xvi, 139p. facsims. 23cm. [BT775.H77 1938a] 56-9145
1. Redemption —Early works to 1800. I. Title.
Contents omitted.

HOOKER, Thomas, 1586-1647. 234.3
Redemption: three sermons, 1637-1656; facsimile reproductions, With an introd. by Everett H. Emerson Gainesville, Fla., Scholars' Facsimiles & Reprints, 1956. xvi, 139p. facsims. 23cm. [BT775.H77 1638a] 56-9145
1. Redemption —Early works to 1800. I. Title.
Contents omitted.

HULSBOSCH, A. 1912- 234'.3
The Bible on conversion, by A. Hulsbosch. Translated by F. Vander Heijden. De Pere, Wis., St. Norbert Abbey Press, 1966. 101, [2] p. 17 cm. Translation of De Bijbel over bekering. Bibliography: p. [103] [BT780.H813] 66-22820
1. Conversion—Biblical teaching. I. Title.

LEFEBVRE, Gaspar 234.3
Redemption through the blood of Jesus. Translated [from the French] by Edward A. Maziarz. Westminster, Md., Newman Press, [c.] 1960. xiv, 233p. illus. 23cm. 59-14811 4.00
1. Redemption. I. Title.

LEFEBVRE, Gaspar, 1880- 234.3
Redemption through the blood of Jesus. Translated by Edward A. Maziarz. Westminster, Md., Newman Press, 1960. 233p. 23cm. [BT775.L513] 59-14811
1. Redemption. I. Title.

OLESEN, Albert H. 234.3
The golden chain; or, The process of redemption. Mountain View, Calif., Pacific Press Pub. Association [c.1960] 103p. 23cm. 60-10105 3.00
1. Salvation—Popular works. I. Title.

PHILIPPE DE LA TRINITE, Father. 234.3
What is redemption? Translated from the French by Anthony Armstrong. [1st ed.] New York, Hawthorn Books [1961] 151p. 21cm. (Twentieth century encyclopedia of Cathllcism, v. 25. Section 2: The basic truths) Translation of La redemption par le sang. Includes bibliographies. [BT775.P533] 61-17220
1. Redemption. I. Title.

POTTEBAUM, Gerard A. 234.3
God's big promise. Illus. by Robert Strobridge. Dayton, Ohio, 38 W. 5th St., Geo. A. Pflaum, c.1963. unpaged, col. illus. 18cm. (Little people's paperbacks, LPP4) .35 pap.,
I. Title.

RICHARD, Louis, 1880-1956. 234.3
The mystery of the redemption. With a foreword by Frank B. Norris. [Translated from the French by Joseph Horn] Baltimore, Helicon [1966] 358 p. 21 cm. Translation of Le mystere de la redemption, which was first published under the title, Le dogme de la redemption. Bibliography: p. 353-356. [BT775.R4713] 65-24129
1. Redemption. I. Title.

RICHARD, Louis, 1880-1956 234.3
The mystery of the redemption. Foreword by Frank B. Norris. [Tr. from French by Joseph Horn] Helicon [dist. New York, Taplinger, c.1966] 358p. 21cm. Bibl. [BT775.R4713] 65-24129 5.95 bds.,
1. Redemption. I. Title.

RUTENBER, Culbert Gerow, 1909- 234.3
The reconciling gospel. Philadelphia, Judson Press [1960] Philadelphia, Judson Press [1960] 183p. 19cm. 27p. 19cm. Includes bibliography. [BT265.2.R8] 60-13367
1. Atonement. I. Ban, Joseph D. II. Title. III. Title: —Leader's guide, by Joseph D. Ban and Harvey G. Cox.

SHEETS, John R., comp. 234'.3
The theology of the atonement; readings in soteriology. Edited by John R. Sheets. Englewood Cliffs, N.J., Prentice-Hall [1967] vi, 233 p. 22 cm. Bibliography: p. 230-233. Bibliographical footnotes. [BT775.S45] 67-15180
1. Redemption. 2. Atonement. 3. Salvation. I. Title.

SHERRILL, Lewis Joseph, 1892- 234.3
Guilt and redemption. Rev. ed. Richmond, John Knox Press [c1957] 255 p. illus. 21 cm. [BT775.S47 1957] 56-13378
1. Redemption. 2. Guilt. I. Title.

SHERRILL, Lewis Joseph, 1892- 234.3
Guilt and redemption [reissue of] rev. ed. Richmond, Knox [1963, c.1945, 1957] 255p. illus. 21cm. 2.00 pap.,
1. Redemption. 2. Guilt. I. Title.

WAHLSTROM, Eric Herbert. 234.3
God who redeems; perspectives in Biblical theology. Philadelphia. Muhlenberg Press [1962] 198 p. 22 cm. [BT775.W17] 62-15701
1. Redemption — Biblical teaching. I. Title.

WAHLSTROM, Eric Herbert. 234.3
God who redeems; perspectives in Biblical theology. Philadelphia, Muhlenberg [c.1962] 198p. 22cm. 62-15701 4.00
1. Redemption—Biblical teaching. I. Title.

WARD, Wayne E 234.3
The drama of redemption [by] Wayne E. Ward. Nashville, Broadman Press [1966] 128 p. 20 cm. Bible -- History of Biblical events. [BS635.2.W3] 66-26221
I. Title.

WARD, Wayne E. 234.3
The drama of redemption [by] Wayne E. Ward. Nashville, Broadman [1966] 128p. 20cm. [BS635.2.W3] 66-26221 1.50 pap.,
1. Bible—History of Biblical events. I. Title.

WHALE, John Seldon, 1896- 234.3
Victor and victim; the Christian doctrine of redemption. [New York] Cambridge University Press, 1960[ ] 172p. Bibl. notes. 60-16320 3.75
1. Redemption. I. Title.

WILKIN, Vincent 234.3
From limbo to heaven; an essay on the economy of the redemption. Pref. by Maurice Bevenot. New York, Sheed & Ward [c.1961] 145p. 61-11799 3.00 bds.,
1. Redemption. I. Title.

WILKIN, Vincent. 234.3
From limbo to heaven; an essay on the economy of the redemption. With a pref. by Maurice Bevenot. New York, Sheed and Ward [1961] Brooklyn [1958] 145 p. 20 cm. 154 p. illus. 22 cm. [BT775.W68] [PE1128.W725] 428.24 61-11709 58-7703
1. Redemption. 2. English language — Textbooks for foreigners. I. Wilkins, C D II. Title. III. Title: Let us speak English;

WILLEMS, Boniface A., 1926- 234'.3
The reality of redemption [by] Boniface A. Willems. [New York] Herder and Herder [1970] 128 p. 23 cm. Translation of Verlossing in kerk en wereld. Includes bibliographical references. [BT775.W6913] 78-105366 4.95
1. Redemption. I. Title.

MCNABB VINCENT JOSEPH, 1868-1943. 234.354
Faith and Prayer. Westminster, Md., Newman Press, 1953. 215p. 23cm. Part 1 was first published in 1905 under title: Oxford conferences on faith; pt. 2 in 1903 under title: Oxford conferences on prayer. [BT771.M235]
1. Faith. 2. Prayer. I. Title.

BAILLIE, John, 1886-1960. 234.4
Baptism and conversion; [lectures] New York, Scribner [1963] 121 p. 20 cm. Bibliographical footnotes. [BT790.B3 1963] 63-17936

1. Regeneration (Theology) 2. Conversion—History of doctrines. 3. Conversion—Psychology. I. Title.

CRICHLOW, Cyril A 1889- 234.4
The new birth; a handbook of Scriptu[r]al documentation. [1st ed.] New York, Pageant Press [1956] 143 p. 21 cm. [BT790.C7] 56-11348
1. Regeneration (Theology) I. Title.

ELVY, Cora. 234.4
The light of God, lost and found; a message of the second birth. New York, Exposition Press [1952] 71 p. 21 cm. [BT790.E4] 52-6086
1. Regeneration (Theology) I. Title.

GODWIN, Johnnie C. 234'.4
What it means to be born again / Johnnie C. Godwin. Nashville : Broadman Press, 1977, c1976. 138 p. ; 19 cm. Includes bibliographical references. [BT790.G57] 76-44039 ISBN 0-8054-1944-6 pbk. : 2.50
1. Regeneration (Theology) I. Title.

GRAHAM, William Franklin, 1918- 234'.4
How to be born again / by Billy Graham. Waco, Tex. : Word Books, c1977. 187 p. ; 23 cm. Includes bibliographical references. [BT790.G66] 77-76057 ISBN 0-8499-0017-4 : 6.95
1. Regeneration (Theology)—Popular works. 2. Salvation—Popular works. I. Title.

GRAHAM, William Franklin, 1918- 234'.4
How to be born again / by Billy Graham. Waco, Tex. : Word Books, c1977. 187 p. ; 23 cm. Includes bibliographical references. [BT790.G66] 77-76057 ISBN 0-8499-0017-4 : 6.95
1. Regeneration (Theology)—Popular works. 2. Salvation—Popular works. I. Title.

*HALLESBY, O. 234.4
Infant baptism and adult conversion. Tr. from Norwegian by Clarence J. Carlsen. Minneapolis, Augsburg [c.1964] 108p. 20cm. 2.00 pap.,
I. Title.

ANTONII, Metropolitan of Kiev and Galich, 1863-1936. 234'.5
Confession : a series of lectures on the mystery of repentance / by Metropolitan Antony (Khrapovitsky) ; translated from the Russian by Christopher Birchall. Jordanville, N.Y. : Holy Trinity Monastery, 1975. 112 p. : port. ; 24 cm. [BX378.C6A5713] 74-29537 ISBN 0-88465-005-7
1. Confession—Orthodox Eastern Church—Addresses, essays, lectures. 2. Sins—Addresses, essays, lectures. I. Title.

ASHCRAFT, Morris. 234'.5
The forgiveness of sins. Nashville, Tenn., Broadman Press [1972] 128 p. 20 cm. Bibliography: p. 127-128. [BT795.A84] 77-189500 ISBN 0-8054-8113-3
1. Forgiveness of sin.

*AUGSBURGER, David. 234'.5
The freedom of forgiveness; 70 x 7. Chicago, Moody Pr. [1973, c.1970] 128 p. 18 cm. (Moody pocket books) Includes bibliographical notes. [BT795] ISBN 0-8024-2875-4 0.75 (pbk.)
1. Forgiveness of sin. I. Title. II. Title: Seventy by seven.

BRANDT, Leslie F. 234'.5
Can I forgive God? By Leslie F. Brandt. Saint Louis, Concordia Pub. House [1970] 78 p. illus. 20 cm. [BT795.B7] 74 113077
1. Forgiveness of sin. I. Title.

EVANS, Colleen Townsend. 234'.5
Start loving : the miracle of forgiving / Colleen Townsend Evans. Boston : G. K. Hall, 1977, c1976. 162 p. ; 25 cm. Large print ed. [BJ1476.E9 1977] 77-3421 ISBN 0-8161-6476-2 lib.bdg. : 8.95
1. Forgiveness. 2. Forgiveness of sin. 3. Large type books. I. Title.

EVANS, Colleen Townsend. 234'.5
Start loving : the miracle of forgiving / by Colleen Townsend Evans. 1st ed. Garden City, N.Y. : Doubleday, 1976. 119 p. ; 22 cm. [BJ1476.E9 1976b] 74-18883 ISBN 0-385-03955-7 : 4.95
1. Forgiveness. 2. Forgiveness of sin. I. Title.

EVANS, Colleen Townsend. 234'.5
Start loving : the miracle of forgiving / Colleen Townsend Evans. Boston : G. K. Hall, 1977, c1976. 162 p. ; 25 cm. Large print ed. [BJ1476.E9 1977] 77-3421 ISBN 0-8161-6476-2 lib.bdg. : 8.95
1. Forgiveness. 2. Forgiveness of sin. 3. Large type books. I. Title.

IRONSIDE, Henry Allan, 1876-1951 234.5
Except ye repent. Grand Rapids, Mich., Zondervan [1963, c.1937] 191p. 21cm. Reprinted by special arrangement with the Amer. Tract Soc. 63-17745 2.50 bds.,
1. Repentance. I. Title.

KIMBALL, Spencer W., 1895- 234'.5
The miracle of forgiveness [by] Spencer W. Kimball. Salt Lake City, Bookcraft, 1969. xii, 376 p. port. 24 cm. Bibliographical footnotes. [BT795.K5] 67-30389
1. Forgiveness of sin. 2. Forgiveness. I. Title.

MANASSES, pseud. 234.5
Go in peace. New York, Macmillan, 1959. 116p. 19cm. [BX5149.C6M35] 59-8375
1. Confession. I. Title.

MORRISON, Mary Chase. 234'.5
Re-conciliation : the hidden hyphen / by Mary Morrison. Wallingford, Pa. : Pendle Hill Publications, 1974. 24 p. ; 19 cm. (Pendle Hill pamphlet ; 198 ISSN 0031-4250) [BV4509.5.M67] 74-24007 ISBN 0-87574-198-3 : 0.95
1. Reconciliation. I. Title.

ROGNESS, Alvin N., 1906- 234'.5
Forgiveness & confession; the keys to renewal, by Alvin N. Rogness. Minneapolis, Augsburg Pub. House [1970] 58 p. illus. 20 cm. [BT795.R6] 75-121960 1.50
1. Forgiveness. 2. Confession. I. Title.

SACRAMENTAL reconciliation. Edited by Edward Schillebeeckx. [New York] Herder and Herder [1971] 156 p. 23 cm. (Concilium: religion in the seventies, v. 61. Dogma) Includes bibliographical references. [BV4509.5.S24] 76-129760 2.95 234'.5
1. Reconciliation—Addresses, essays, lectures. 2. Penance—Addresses, essays, lectures. I. Schillebeeckx, Edward Cornelis Florentius Alfons, 1914- ed. II. Series: Concilium (New York) v. 61

SCHLINK, Basilea. 234'.5
Repentance—the joy-filled life [by] M. Basilea Schlink. Translated by Harriet Corbin with Sigrid Langer. Grand Rapids, Zondervan [1968] 63 p. 21 cm. [BT800.S33] 68-56090
1. Repentance. I. Title.

SEYMOUR, Richard A. 234'.5
All about repentance [by] Richard A. Seymour. Hollywood, Fla., Harvest House Publishers [1974] 180 p. 18 cm. Bibliography: p. 167-171. [BT800.S47] 74-81381 1.50
1. Repentance. I. Title.

STUHLMUELLER, Carroll. 234'.5
Reconciliation : a Biblical call / by Carroll Stuhlmueller. Chicago : Franciscan Herald Press, [1975] p. cm. (Herald Biblical booklets) Bibliography: p. [BS680.R28S8] 74-34059 ISBN 0-8199-0522-4 pbk. : 0.95
1. Reconciliation—Biblical teaching. I. Title.

UNDERWOOD, Joseph B. 234'.5
New persons in an old world : adventures in reconciliation in many lands / Joseph B. Underwood. Nashville : Broadman Press, c1976. 127 p. ; 21 cm. [BV4509.5.U5] 75-39447 ISBN 0-8054-8510-4 pbk. : 2.50
1. Reconciliation. I. Title.

UPDIKE, L. Wayne. 234.5
Whosoever repenteth; a series of lectures delivered to the Melchisedec priesthood of Independence, Missouri, January 6-11, 1957. [Independence, Mo.] Herald House [c1957] 111 p. illus. 21 cm. [BX8674.U62] 57-14408
1. Repentance. 2. Reorganized Church of Jesus Christ of Latter-Day Saints — Doctrinal and controversial works. I. Title.

WIGHT, Fred Hartley, 1899- 234.5
If my people; repentance and revival. Butler, Ind., Higley Press, 1959. 148 p. 23 cm. [BT800.W46] 60-45
1. Repentance. 2. Revivals. I. Title.

DAUGHTERS of St. Paul. 234.608
Obedience, the greatest freedom, in the words of Alberione [and others. Boston] St. Paul Editions [1966] 363 p. 22 cm. [BX2435.D27] 66-28123
1. Obedience — Collections. I. Title.

.DAUGHTERS of St.Paul 234.608
Obedience, the greatest freedom, in the words of Albereone [others. Boston St. Paul Eds. 1966 363p. 22cm. [BX2435.D27] 66-28123 4.00; 3.00 pap.,
1. Obedience—Collections. I. Title.

BARTH, Markus. 234'.7
Justification; Pauline texts interpreted in the light of the Old and New Testaments. Translated by A. M. Woodruff III. Grand Rapids, Mich., Eerdmans [1971] 90 p. 21 cm. Translation of Rechtfertigung. Bibliography: p. 7-9. [BS2655.J8B3713] 70-162028 1.95
1. Bible. N.T. Epistles of Paul—Theology. 2. Justification—Biblical teaching. I. Title.

BERKOUWER, Gerrit Cornelis, 1903- 234.7
Faith and justification. [Translated by Lewis B. Smedes] Grand Rapids, W. B. Eerdmans Pub. Co., 1954. 207p. 23cm. (His Studies in dogmatics) [BT764.B4] 54-6170
1. Justification. 2. Faith. I. Title.

BUCHANAN, James, 1804-1870. 234.7
The doctrine of justification; an outline of its history in the church and of its exposition from Scripture. Grand Rapids, Baker Book House, 1955. 514p. 23cm. (Cunningham lectures, 2d ser.) Theological reprint library. 'Reprinted from the 1867 printing by T. and T. Clark, Edinburgh.' sJustification. [BT764.B8] 55-1819
I. Title.

*BUNYAN, John, 1628-1688 234.7
Justification by an imputed righteousness. Swengel, Pa., Reiner Pubns. [1967] 89p. 18cm. 1.50 pap.,
I. Title.

COX, David. 234.7
Jung and St. Paul; a study of the doctrine of justification by faith and its relation to the concept of individuation. New York, Association Press [1959] 357 p. 21 cm. Includes bibliography. [BF173.J85C63] 59-6834
1. Jung, Carl Gustav, 1875-1961. 2. Justification. 3. Christianity—Psychology. I. Title.

CRABTREE, Arthur Bamford, 1910- 234.7
The restored relationship, a study in justification and reconciliation. Valley Forge, Pa., Judson [c.1963] 208p. 23cm. (W. T. Whitley lect. for 1961) Bibl. 62-19230 5.00 bds.,
1. Justification—History of doctrines. I. Title.

CROSBY, John F 234'.7
From religion to grace; the doctrine of justification by grace through faith. Interpreted for laymen [by] John F. Crosby. Nashville, Abingdon Press [1967] 126 p. 20 cm. Bibliographical references included in "Notes" (p. 121-124) [BT764.2.C4] 67-22164
1. Jusitification I. Title.

CROSBY, John F. 234'.7
From religion to grace; the doctrine of justification by grace through faith. Interpreted for laymen [by] John F. Crosby. Nashville, Abingdon Press [1967] 126 p. 20 cm. Bibliographical references included in "Notes" (p. 121-124) [BT764.2.C74] 67-22164
1. Justification. I. Title.

DANTINE, Wilhelm. 234'.7
Justification of the ungodly. Translators: Eric W. Gritsch and Ruth C. Gritsch. Saint Louis, Concordia Pub. House [1968] 173 p. 24 cm. Translation of Die Gerechtmachung des Gottlosen. Bibliography: p. 170-173. [BT764.2.D313] 68-31561 5.95
1. Justification. I. Title.

HORDERN, William. 234'.7
Living by grace / by William Hordern. Philadelphia : Westminster, [1975] 208 p. ; 22 cm. Includes bibliographical references and index. [BT764.2.H66] 75-6548 ISBN 0-664-24763-6 pbk. : 3.95
1. Justification. I. Title.

HORN, Robert Millen. 234'.7
Go free! / Robert M. Horn. Downers Grove, Ill. : InterVarsity Press, c1976. 128 p. ; 18 cm. Includes bibliographical references. [BT764.2.H668 1976] 76-4736 ISBN 0-87784-644-8 pbk. : 2.25
1. Justification. I. Title.

KUBO, Sakae, 1926- 234'.7
Acquitted! : Message from the cross / by Sakae Kubo. Mountain View, Calif. : Pacific Press Pub. Association, c1975. 63 p. ; 19 cm. [BT764.2.K78] 74-28685 pbk. : 0.60
1. Justification. I. Title.

KUNG, Hans, 1928- 234.7
Justification; the doctrine of Karl Barth and a Catholic reflection. With a letter by Karl Barth. Translated from the German by Thomas Collins, Edmund E. Tolk, and David Granskou. New York, Nelson [1964] xxvi, 332 p. 22 cm. Bibliography: p. 303-321. [BT764.2.K813] 64-25285
1. Barth, Karl, 1886- 2. Justification — History of doctrines. I. Title.

KUNG, Hans, 1928- 234.7
Justification; the doctrine of Karl Barth and a Catholic reflection. With a letter by Karl Barth. Tr. from German by Thomas Collins, Edmund E. Tolk, David Granskou. New York, Nelson [1964] xxvi, 332p. 22cm. Bibl. 64-25285 7.00
1. Barth, Karl, 1886- 2. Justification—History of doctrines. I. Title.

MILLER, Alexander, 1908- 234.7
The renewal of man; a twentieth century essay on justification by faith. [1st ed.] Garden City, N. Y., Doubleday, 1955. 184p. 22cm. (Christian faith series) [BT764.M5] 55-5296
1. Justification. I. Title.

MIZHER, N. S. 234.7
The message of Galatians. Nashville, Southern Pub. [c.1964] 125p. 18cm. 64-55965 2.00
1. Bible. N.T. Galatians—Addresses, essays, lectures. 2. Seventh-Day Adventists—Doctrinal and controversial works. I. Title.

MIZHER, N S 234.7
The message of Galatians, by N. S. Mizher. Nashville, Southern Pub. Association [1964] 125 p. 18 cm. [BS2685.5.M5] 64-55965
1. Bible. N.T. Galatians — Addresses, essays, lectures. 2. Seventh-Day Adventists — Doctrinal and controversial works. I. Title.

NEWMAN, John Henry, Cardinal, 1801-1890. 234.7
Lecture on the doctrine of justification. Westminster, Md., 21157, Christian Classics [205 Willis St.] 1966. xvi, 404 p 21 cm. (his works) reprint of 1900 ed. [[bt764.2n4-1966]] 66-20433 8.00
1. Justification Title. I. Title.

NEWMAN, John Henry, Cardinal, 1801-1890. 234.7
Lectures on the doctrine of justification. Westminster, Md., Christian Classics, 1966. xvi, 404 p. 21 cm. (His Works) Reprint of the 1900 ed. [BT764.2.N4] 66-20433
1. Justification. I. Title.

PEASE, Norval F 234.7
By faith alone. Mountain View, Calif., Pacific Press Pub. Association [1962] xiii, 248p. 23cm. Bibliography: p. xiii. [BT764.2.P4] 62-13528
1. Justification. I. Title.

RITSCHL, Albrecht Benjamin, 1822-1889. 234'.7
The Christian doctrine of justification and reconciliation; the positive development of the doctrine. English translation edited by H. R. Mackintosh and A. B. Macaulay. Clifton, N.J., Reference Book Publishers, 1966. xii, 673 p. 23 cm. (Library of religious and philosophical thought) On cover: Library of religious and philosophical thought. Translation of the 3d vol. of Die Christliche Lehre von der Rechtfertigung und Versohnung. Bibliographical footnotes. [BT764.R513] 65-27052
1. Justification. 2. Forgiveness of sin. I. Mackintosh, Hugh Ross, 1870-1936, ed. II. Macaulay, Alexander Beith, ed. III. Title.

SHAW, Joseph M. 234.7
If God be for us; a study in the meaning of justification [by] Joseph M. Shaw. Minneapolis, Augsburg [1966] 120p. 20cm. (Tower bk) 'Footnotes': p. 117-120. [BT764.2.S5] 66-8428 1.50 pap.,
1. Justification. I. Title.

WADE, Thomas Jefferson. 234.7
God's remedy for the world's tragedy; a study in practical religion. New York, Exposition Press [1951] 131 p. 23 cm. [BT674.W3] 51-13285
1. Justification. 2. Sanctification. 3. Christian life. I. Title.

ZIESLER, J. A. 234'.7
The meaning of righteousness in Paul; a linguistic and theological enquiry [by] J. A. Ziesler. Cambridge [Eng.] University Press, 1972. xii, 254 p. 23 cm. (Society for New Testament Studies. Monograph series, 20) Bibliography: p. 217-230. [BS2655.J8Z53] 75-164455 ISBN 0-521-08316-8
1. Bible. N.T. Epistles of Paul—Theology. 2. Justification—Biblical teaching. I. Title. II. Series: Studiorum Novi Testamenti Societas. Monograph series, 20.

HAGGLUND, Bengt, 1920- 234'.7'0924
The background of Luther's doctrine of justification in late medieval theology. Philadelphia, Fortress Press [1971] viii, 40 p. 20 cm. (Facet books. Historical series, 18) "This study was first published in Lutheran world 8 (1961): 24-46." Bibliography: p. 35-36. [BR333.2.H32] 78-152367 ISBN 0-8006-3063-7 1.00
1. Luther, Martin, 1483-1546—Theology. 2. Justification—History of doctrines. I. Title.

LEAVER, Robin A. 234'.7'0924
Luther on justification [by] Robin A. Leaver. St. Louis, Concordia Pub. House [1975] 84 p.

21 cm. Includes bibliographical references. [BR333.5.J8L4 1975] 74-17035 ISBN 0-570-03188-5 3.95
1. Luther, Martin, 1483-1546—Theology. 2. Justification—History of doctrines. I. Title.

SHERIDAN, Thomas L., 1926- 234'.7'0924
Newman on justification; a theological biography, by Thomas L. Sheridan. Staten Island, N.Y., Alba [1967] 265p. 22cm. Bibl. [BX4705.N5S4] 67-21427 6.50
1. Newman, John Henry, Cardinal, 1801-1890. 2. Justification—History of doctrines. I. Title.

ATKINSON, Joseph Baines. 234.8
The beauty of holiness. New York, Philosophical Library [1953] 160p. 19cm. [BT767.A8] 53-8377
1. Holiness. I. Title.

BARKER, John H J 234.8
This is the will of God; a study in the doctrine of entire sanctification as a definite experience. Winona Lake, Ind., Light and Life Press [1956] 110p. 20cm. [BT767.B277 1956] 56-45081
1. Holiness. I. Title.

BAXTER, James Sidlow. 234'.8
A new call to holiness; a restudy and restatement of New Testament teaching concerning Christian sanctification [by] J. Sidlow Baxter. Grand Rapids, Zondervan Pub. House [1973] 257 p. 21 cm. [BT765.B35 1973] 73-13058 2.95 (pbk.)
1. Sanctification. 2. Holiness. I. Title.

BAXTER, James Sidlow. 234'.8
Our high calling : a series of devotional and practical studies in the New Testament doctrine of personal sanctification / J. Sidlow Baxter. Grand Rapids, Mich. : Zondervan Pub. House, 1975, c1967. 206 p. ; 21 cm. [BT765.B36 1975] 75-323761 pbk. : 2.95
1. Sanctification. I. Title.

BOURDEAU, Daniel T. 234'.8
Sanctification; or, Living holiness, by D. T. Bourdeau. Battle Creek, Mich., Steam Press, 1864. [Nashville, Tenn., Printed by Southern Pub. Association, 1970] 144 p. 21 cm. [BT767.B68 1970] 74-19705
1. Sanctification. 2. Holiness. 3. Sabbath. I. Title: Living holiness.

BRESSON, Bernard L. 234.8
Studies in ecstasy [by] Bernard L. Bresson. [1st ed.] New York, Vantage Press [1966] 127 p. 21 cm. Includes bibliographies. [BT767.3.B73] 66-25875
1. Gifts, Spiritual—History of doctrines. I. Title.

CHEVIGNARD, Bernard Marie. 234'.8
Reconciled with God, by B. M. Chevignard. Translated by Angele Demand. New York, Sheed and Ward [1967] vii, 212 p. 22 cm. Translation of Reconcilies avec Dieu. [BX2350.5.C4813] 67-21906
1. Spiritual life—Catholic authors. 2. Perfection (Catholic) I. Title.

GAURDINI, Ramano, 1885 234.8
The saints in daily christian life. Philadelphia, Chilton [c.1966] 110 p. illus 21 cm project of dimension bks. [bx2350.2.68] 66-17193 2.95
1. 1. santification. christian life-catholic author. I. Title.

GEIGER, Kenneth, comp. 234.8
Further insights into holiness; nineteen leading Wesleyan scholars present various phases of holiness thinking. Kansas City, Mo., Beacon Hill Press [1963] 349 p. 20 cm. [BT767.G34] 63-13779
1. Holiness — Addresses, essays, lectures. I. Title.

GEIGER, Kenneth, comp. 234.8
Further insights into holiness; nineteen leading Wesleyan scholars present various phases of holiness thinking. Kansas City, Mo., Beacon Hill [c.1963] 349p. 20cm. 63-13779 3.50
1. Holiness—Addresses, essays, lectures. I. Title.

GRAY, Joseph. 234.8
The double cure, and other holiness sermons. Kansas City, Mo., Beacon Hill Press [1953] 142p. 20cm. [BX8699.N3] 53-10430
1. Holiness—Sermons. 2. Church of the Nazarene—Sermons. 3. Sermons, American. I. Title.

GUARDINI, Romano, 1885- 234.8
The saints in daily Christian life. Philadelphia, Chilton Books [1966] 110 p. illus. 21 cm. "A project of Dimension Books." [BX2350.2.G8] 66-17193
1. Sanctification. 2. Christian life—Catholic authors. I. Title.

HULME, William Edward, 1920- 234.8
The dynamics of sanctification [by] William E. Hulme. Minneapolis, Augsburg Pub. House [1966] iv. 194 p. 22 cm. Bibliographical footnotes. [BT765.H84] 66-13052
1. Sanctification. I. Title.

HULME, William Edward, 1920- 234.8
The dynamics of sanctification. Minneapolis, Augsburg [c.1966] iv, 194p. 22cm. Bibl. [BT765.H84] 66-13052 4.75
1. Sanctification. I. Title.

IRONSIDE, Henry Allan, 1876-1951. 234.8
Holiness, the false and the true. New York, Loizeaux Bros. [1953] 142p. 20cm. [BT767.I67] 54-32507
1. Holiness. I. Title.

JONES, O. R. 234.8
The concept of holiness. New York, Macmillan [1962, c.]1961. 200p. 23cm. 62-16095 3.75
1. Holiness. I. Title.

MCCUMBER, W. E. 234.8
Our sanctifying God. Kansas City, Mo., Beacon Hill Press [1956] 124p. 20cm. [BT765.M23] 57-1206
1. Sanctification. I. Title.

MARSHALL, Walter, 1628-1680. 234.8
The gospel-mystery of sanctification. Grand Rapids, Zondervan Pub. House [1954] viii, 264p. 23cm. Includes Marshall's sermon, The doctrine of justification opened and applied. [BT765.M3 1954] 55-14089
1. Sanctification— Early works to 1800. I. Title.

MURRAY, Andrew, 1828-1917 234.8
Holy in Christ: thoughts on the calling of God's children to be holy as He is holy. Grand Rapids, Mich., Zondervan [1962] 280p. 18cm. 62-53071 2.50
1. Holiness. I. Title.

PIERSON, Arthur Tappan, 1837-1911. 234.8
Vital union with Christ. Grand Rapids, Mich., Zondervan [1961] 120p. 'Formerly published as: Shall we continue to sin?' 61-19957 1.95; 1.00 bds., pap.,
1. Mystical union. I. Title.

*PINK, Arthur W. 234.8
The doctrine of sanctification. Swengel, Pa., Reiner, 1966. 206p. 21cm. 1.95 pap.,
I. Title.

PINK, Arthur Walkington, 1886-1952. 234.8
The doctrine of sanctification. Grand Rapids. Baker Book House, 1955. 206p. 22cm. [BT765.P5] 55-8587
1. Sanctification. I. Title.

PINK, Arthur Walkington, 1886-1952. 234.8
The doctrine of sanctification [by] Arthur W. Pink. Swengel, Pa., Reiner Publications, 1966. 206 p. 21 cm. [BT765.P5 1966] 67-1476
1. Sanctification. I. Title.

PRICE, Walter K. 234'.8
Channels for power; [how Christians today can know the power of the Holy Spirit in daily living. By Walter K. Price. Nashville, Broadman Press [1966] 63 p. 21 cm. Bibliography: p. 62-63. [BT765.P86] 67-12174
1. Sanctification. I. Title.

PRIOR, Kenneth Francis William 234.8
The way of holiness; the Christian doctrine of sanctification, by Kenneth F. W. Prior. Chicago, Inter-Varsity [1967] 128p. 19cm. (Great doctrines of the Bible) Bibl. [BT765.P7 1967b] 67-27067 1.50 pap.,
1. Sanctification. I. Title.

PRIOR, Kenneth Francis William. 234'.8
The way of holiness: the Christian doctrine of sanctification, by the Rev. Kenneth F. W. Prior. 128 p. 18 1/2 cm. (Great doctrines of the Bible) 6/- (B67-8934) [BT765.P7] 67-90498
1. Sanctification. I. Inter-Varsity Fellowship of Evangelical Unions. II. Title. III. Title: London,

PURKISER, W T 234.8
Conflicting concepts of holiness; some current issues in the doctrine of sanctification. Kansas City, Mo., Beacon Hill Press [1953] 110p. 20cm. [BT767.P87] 54-1308
1. Holiness. 2. Church of the Nazarene—Doctrinal and controversial works. I. Title.

ROLDAN, Alejandro, 1910- 234'.8
Personality types and holiness, by Alexander Roldan. Tr. by Gregory McCaskey. Staten Island, N.Y., Alba [1968] 384p. illus. 22cm. (Mental health ser. [8]) Tr. of Introduction a la ascetica diferencial. Bibl. [BX2350.7.R613] 67-16844 6.50
1. Spiritual direction. 2. Perfection (Catholic) 3. Personality. 4. Psychology, Religious. I. Title.

RYLE, John Charles, Bp. of Liverpool, 1816-1900 234.8
Holiness: its nature, hindrances, difficulties, and roots. Foreword by D. Martyn Lloyd-Jones. Grand Rapids, Mich., Kregel [1962] 333p. 22cm. A62 3.95
1. Holiness. I. Title.

TAYLOR, Jesse Paul, Bp., 1895- 234.8
Holiness, the finished foundation. Winona Lake, Ind., Light &Life Pr. [c.1963] 216p. 23cm. 63-35498 2.95; 1.95 pap.,
1. Sanctification I. Title.

TRESE, Leo John, 1902- 234.8
You are called to greatness [by] Leo J. Trese. Notre Dame, Ind., Fides Publisher [1964] 153 p. 21 cm. [BX2350.2.T72] 64-16496
1. Spiritual life — Catholic authors. I. Title.

VAN Zeller, Hubert, 1905- 234.8
Sanctity in other words; presentation for beginners. Springfield, Ill., Templegate [1963] 94 p. 20 cm. [In other words series] [BX2350.2.V3] 63-1969
1. Sanctification. I. Title.

VAN ZELLER, Hubert [Secular name: Claude Van Zeller] 1905- 234.8
Sanctity in other words; a presentation for beginners. Springfield, Ill., Templegate [c.1963] 94p. 20cm. (In other words ser.) 63-1969 2.95
1. Sanctification. I. Title.

WESLEY, John, 1703-1791. 234'.8
Christian perfection; selections, edited by David A. MacLennan. New York, World Pub. Co. [1969] 63 p. 17 cm. (World inspirational books) [BT766.W522 1969] 71-90925 1.25
1. Perfection. I. Title.

WINCHESTER, Olive May, 1880-1947. 234.8
Crisis experiences in the Greek New Testament; an investigation of the evidence for the definite, miraculous experiences of regeneration and sanctification as found in the Greek New Testament, especially in the figures emphasized and in the use of the aorist tense. Edited throughout, with final chapter and appendix, by Ross E. Price. Kanss City, Mo., Beacon Hill Press, 193)053. 110p. 20cm. Includes bibliography. [BT765.W53] 53-11007
1. Sanctification. 2. Regeneration (Theology) 3. Greek language. Biblical—Tense. I. Title.

GEIGER, Kenneth, comp. 234.8082
Insights into holiness; discussions of holiness by fifteen leading scholars of the Wesleyan persuasion. Kansas City, Mo., Beacon Hill [c.1962] 294p. 20cm. Fifteen papers of the seminars on holiness doctrine, sponsored by the Natl. Holiness Assn., presented in 1961 at various colleges and seminaries. Bibl. 62-14842 3.50
1. Holiness. I. Title.

BERKOUWER, Gerrit Cornelis 234.9
Divine election. [Translated by Hugo Bekker from the Dutch] Grand Rapids, Mich., Eerdmans [1960] 336p. (bibl. footnotes) 23cm. (His Studies in dogmatics) 58-7568 4.50
1. Election (Theology) I. Title.

BERKOUWER, Gerrit Cornelis, 1903- 234.9
Faith and perseverance. [Translated by Robert D. Knudsen from the Dutch] Grand Rapids, Eerdmans [1958] 256p. 23cm. (His Studies in dogmatics) Includes bibliography. [BT68.B413] 57-11583
1. Perseverance (Theology) 2. Reformed Church—Doctrinal and controversial works. I. Title.

BOYLE, Joseph M., 1942- 234'.9
Free choice : a self-referential argument / Joseph M. Boyle, Jr., Germain Grisez, Olaf Tollefsen. Notre Dame, Ind. : University of Notre Dame Press, c1976. p. cm. Includes bibliographical references and index. [BJ1461.B684] 76-645 ISBN 0-268-00940-6 : 15.95
1. Free will and determinism. I. Grisez, Germain Gabriel, 1929- joint author. II. Tollefsen, Olaf, 1944- joint author. III. Title.

BUIS, Harry. 234.9
Historic Protestantism and predestination. Philadelphia, Presbyterian and Reformed Pub. Co. [c1958] 142p. 21cm. Includes bibliography. [BT810.B8] 58-59920
1. Predestination—History of doctrines. I. Title.

CLARK, Gordon Haddon. 234'.9
Biblical predestination, by Gordon H. Clark. Nutley, N.J., Presbyterian and Reformed Pub. Co., 1969. 155 p. 21 cm. (An International library of philosophy and theology. Biblical and theological studies) [BS680.P65C57] 74-92699
1. Predestination—Biblical teaching. I. Title. II. Series.

EDWARDS, Jonathan, 1703-1758. 234.9
Freedom of the will. Edited by Paul Ramsey. New Haven, Yale University Press, 1957. xii, 494 p. port., facsim. 24 cm. (His Works, v. 1) First published in 1754 under title: A careful and strict enquiry into the modern prevailing notions of that freedom of will, which is supposed to be essential to moral agency, vertue and vice, reward and punishment, praise and blame. "Remarks on the Essays on the principles of morality and natural religion": p. 453-465. [BX7117.E3 1957 vol. 1] 57-6875
1. Kames, Henry Home, Lord, 1696-1782. Essays on the principles of morality and natural religion. 2. Free will and determinism. I. Title.

EDWARDS, Jonathan, 1703-1758. 234'.9
Freedom of will. Edited, with an introd. by Arnold S. Kaufman and William K. Frankena. Indianapolis, Bobbs-Merrill [1969] xl, 269 p. 21 cm. (The Library of liberal arts) First ed., 1754, has title: A careful and strict enquiry into the modern prevailing notions of that freedom of will, which is supposed to be essential to moral agency, vertue and vice, reward and punishment, praise and blame. Includes bibliographical references. [BJ1461.E3 1969] 68-22202 2.45 (pbk)
1. Kames, Henry Home, Lord, 1696-1782. Essays on the principles of morality and natural religion. 2. Free will and determinism. I. Kaufman, Arnold Saul, 1927- ed. II. Frankena, William K., ed. III. Title.

EDWARDS, Jonathan, 1745-1801. 234'.9
A dissertation concerning liberty & necessity; containing remarks on the essays of Dr. Samuel West, and on the writings of several other authors, on those subjects. New York, B. Franklin Reprints [1974] 234 p. 23 cm. (Burt Franklin research & source works series. Philosophy & religious history monographs, 140) Reprint of the 1797 ed. printed by L. Worcester at Worcester. [BJ1461.E32 1974] 73-21786 ISBN 0-8337-1003-6 15.00
1. West, Samuel, 1730-1807. Essays on liberty and necessity. 2. Free will and determinism. I. Title.

ERASMUS, Desiderius, d.1536. 234.9
Discourse on free will [by] Erasmus [and] Luther. Translated and edited by Ernst F. Winter. New York, Ungar [1961] xiii, 138 p. 20 cm. (Milestones of thought in the history of ideas, M114) Contents.Contents.—Erasmus: The free will.—Luther: The bondage of the will. [BT810.E63] 60-53363
1. Free will and determinism. I. Erasmus, Desiderius, d. 1536. The free will. II. Luther, Martin, 1483-1546. The bondage of the will. III. Title. IV. Series.

FARRELLY, Mark John. 234.9
Predestination, grace, and free will, by Dom M. John Farrelly. Westminster, Md., Newman Press, 1964. xiv, 317 p. 24 cm. Originally written as the author's thesis, Catholic University of America, under title: Predestination and grace: a re-examination in the light of modern Biblical and philosophical developments. Bibliographical footnotes. [BT810.2.F3] 64-15405
1. Predestination. 2. Free will and determinism. I. Title.

FARRELLY, Mark John 234.9
Predestination, grace, and free will. Westminster, Md., Newman [c.]1964. xiv, 317p. 24cm. Bibl. 64-15405 6.95
1. Predestination. 2. Free will and determinism. I. Title.

FOREMAN, Kenneth Joseph, 1891- 234.9
God's will and ours; an introduction to the problem of freedom, foreordination and faith. [1st ed.] Richmond, Outlook Publishers [1954] 63p. 19cm. [BT810.F6] 54-10449
1. Predestination. I. Title.

GREEN, Edward Michael Bankes. 234'.9
Jesus spells freedom [by] Michael Green. Downers Grove, Ill., Inter-Varsity Press [1973, c1972] 128 p. 18 cm. [BT810.2.G73 1973] 72-96068 ISBN 0-87784-353-8 1.50
1. Jesus Christ—Person and offices. 2.

Freedom (Theology) 3. Christian life—1960- I. Title.

GUARDINI, Romano, 1885- 234.9
The focus of freedom. Translated by Gregory Roettger. Baltimore, Helicon [1966] 160 p. 22 cm. "Originally published ... under the titles Der heilige Franziskus (1951), Vom Sinn der Gemeinschaft (1950), Vom Sinn der Schwermut (1949), and Lebendiger Geist (1950)." [BT810.G813] 65-15038
1. Freedom (Theology)—Addresses, essays, lectures. I. Title.

GUARDINI, Romano, 1885- 234.9
The focus of freedom. Translated by Gregory Roettger. Baltimore, Helicon [1966] 160 p. 22 cm. "Originally published ... under the titles Der heilige Franziskus (1951), Vom Sinn der Gemienschaft (1950), Vom Sinn der Schwermut (1949), and Lebendiger Geist (1950)." [BT810.G813] 65-15038
1. Freedom (Theology) — Addresses, essays, lectures. I. Title.

GUARDINI, Romano, 1885- 234.9
1968.
The focus of freedom. Translated by Gregory Roettger. Baltimore, Helicon [1966] 160 p. 22 cm. "Originally published ... under the titles Der heilige Franziskus (1951), Vom Sinn der Gemeinschaft (1950), Vom Sinn der Schwermut (1949), and Lebendiger Geist (1950)" [BT810.G813] 65-15038
1. Freedom (Theology)—Addresses, essays, lectures. I. Title.

HAGEMAN, Howard G. 234.9
Predestination. Philadelphia, Fortress [c.1963] 74p. 20cm. (Fortress bk.) 63-12533 1.00 bds.,
1. Predestination. I. Title.

HAUSMANN, William John. 234'.9
Karl Barth's doctrine of election. New York, Philosophical Library [1969] 103 p. 23 cm. Thesis (M.A.)—Drew University. Bibliography: p. 100-103. [BT810.2.H38] 74-81812 4.95
1. Barth, Karl, 1886-1968. 2. Election (Theology) I. Title.

LUTHER and Erasmus: Free 234'.9
will and salvation. Philadelphia, Westminster Press [1969] xiv, 348 p. 24 cm. (The Library of Christian classics, v. 17) "Erasmus: De libero arbitrio, translated and edited by E. Gordon Rupp, in collaboration with A. N. Marlow": p. [33]-97. "Luther: De servo arbitrio, translated and edited by Philip S. Watson, in collaboration with B. Drewery": p. [99]-334. [BJ1461.L8] 76-79870 7.50
1. Free will and determinism. I. Rupp, Ernest Gordon, tr. II. Watson, Philip Saville, 1909- tr. III. Luther, Martin, 1483-1546. De servo arbitrio. IV. Erasmus, Desiderius, d. 1536. De libero arbitrio diatribe. V. Title. VI. Series.

LUTHER, Martin, 1483-1546. 234.9
Martin Luther on the bondage of the will. A new translation of De servo arbitrio (1525) Martin Luther's reply to Erasmus of Rotterdam, by J. I. Packer and O. R. Johnston. [Westwood, N. J.] Revell [1957] 322p. 21cm. [BJ1460.L8 1957a] 58-8660
1. Free will and determinism. 2. Erasmus, Desiderius, d. 1536. Hyperaspistes diatribe. I. Title.

LUTZ, Charles P. 234'.9
You mean I have a choice? [By] Charles P. Lutz. Minneapolis, Augsburg Pub. House [1971] 127 p. 20 cm. Includes bibliographical references. [BJ1461.L84] 78-158998 ISBN 0-8066-1131-6
1. Will. I. Title.

MAURY, Pierre 234.9
Predestination, and other papers. [Translated by Edwin Hudson from the French] With a memoir 23cm. 60-6369 2.50
1. Predestination. 2. Christmas sermons. I. Title.

MAURY, Pierre, 1890-1956. 234.9
Predestination, and other papers. [Translated by Edwin Hudson from the French] With a memoir by Robert Mackie, and a foreword by Karl Barth. Richmond, John Knox Press [1960] 109p. 23cm. [BT810.M423 1960] 60-6369
1. Predestination. 2. Christmas sermons. I. Title.

OCKHAM, William, 234'.9
d.ca.1349.
Predestination, God's foreknowledge, and future contingents. Translated with an introd., notes, and appendices by Marilyn McCord Adams [and] Norman Kretzmann. New York, Appleton-Century-Crofts [1969] ix, 136 p. 21 cm. (Century philosophy sourcebooks) Translation of Tractatus de praedestinatione et de praescientia Die et de futuris contigentibus. Bibliography: p. 115-128. [B765.O33T73] 69-19995 ISBN 0-390-67500-8
1. Predestination—Early works to 1800. 2. Logic—Early works to 1800. I. Adams, Marilyn McCord, ed. II. Kretzmann, Norman, ed. III. Title.

SHANK, Robert, 1918- 234'.9
Elect in the Son; a study of the doctrine of election. Introd. by William W. Adams. Springfield, Mo., Westcott Publishers [1970] 242 p. 23 cm. Bibliography: p. 235-237. [BT810.2.S5] 74-114957 4.95
1. Election (Theology) I. Title.

THORNWELL, James Henley, 234.9
1812-1862.
Election and reprobation. Philadelphia, Presbyterian and Reformed Pub. Co., 1961. 97 p. 23 cm. (Biblical and theological studies) International library of philosophy and theology. [BT810.T48 1961] 61-11745
1. Predestination. 2. Election (Theology) I. Title.

VERGHESE, Paul. 234'.9
The freedom of man; an inquiry into some roots of the tension between freedom and authority in our society, by T. Paul Verghese. Philadelphia, Westminster Press [1972] 157 p. 22 cm. Includes bibliographical references. [BT810.2.V47] 73-176081 ISBN 0-664-20928-9 6.95
1. Freedom (Theology) 2. Authority. I. Title.

WRIGHT, H. Elliott, 1937- 234'.9
Go free, by Elliott Wright. New York, Friendship Press [1973] 96 p. 21 cm. Includes bibliographical references. [BS680.J8W75] 73-4785 ISBN 0-377-03011-2 pap 1.75
1. Justice—Biblical teaching. 2. Freedom (Theology)—Biblical teaching. 3. God—Biblical teaching. I. Title.

WYNKOOP, Mildred Bangs. 234'.9
Foundations of Wesleyan-Arminian theology. Kansas City, Mo., Beacon Hill Press [1967] 128 p. 20 cm. Bibliography: p. 127. [BX6195.W9] 72-13635
1. Arminianism. I. Title.

235 Spiritual Beings

BERKHOF, H 235
Christ and the powers. Translated from the Dutch by John Howard Yoder. Scottdale, Pa., Herald Press [1962] 62p. 20cm. [BT962.B413] 62-13713
1. Spirits. 2. Bible. N. T.—Theology. I. Title.

BERKHOF, H. 235
Christ and the powers. Tr. from Dutch by John Howard Yoder. Scottdale, Pa., Herald [c.1962] 62p. 20cm. 62-13713 1.25 pap.,
1. Spirits. 2. Bible, N.T.—Theology. I. Title.

BERKHOF, Hendrikus. 235
Christ and the powers. Translated from the Dutch by John Howard Yoder. Scottdale, Pa., Herald Press [1962] 62 p. 20 cm. [BT962.B413] 62-13713
1. Spirits. Bible. N.T. — Theology. I. Title.

BRUNO de Jesus-Marie, Father 235
ed. Etudes caramelitaines.
Satan. London and New York, Sheed and Ward [1951] 506 p. illus. 23 cm. "Based upon a volume of the series ... Etudes carmelitaines, published in French ... under the editorship of Pere Bruno de Jesus-Marie, O.C.D." "Translated by Malachy Carroll [and others]" Bibliographical footnotes. [BT980.S32] 51-8781
1. Devil. 2. Devil — Art. 3. Devil in literature. I. Title.

COUSINS, Mary 235
Do you know about angels? Pictures by Patricia Revell. New York, Kenedy, 1965. 127p. illus. 23cm. [BT966.2.C6] 64-66438 2.95
1. Angels—Juvenile literature. I. Title.

EIMER, Robert. 235
Tilted haloes. Milwaukee, Bruce Pub. Co. [1964] xv, 126 p. 21 cm. Bibliographical footnotes. [BX4661.E5] 64-15487
1. Saints. 2. Wit and humor. I. Title.

*HALDEMAN, I. M. 235.
Can the dead communicate with the living? / I. M. Haldeman. Grand Rapids : Baker Book House, 1976. 138p. ; 18 cm. (Direction books) [BT962] ISBN 0-8010-4141-4 pbk. : 1.25.
1. Spiritualism. I. Title.

KELLY, Bernard J. 235
God, man and Satan; Satan the adversary in theology and life. Westminster, Md., Newman Press [1950] 102 p. 19 cm. "Completes the chapter on Satan in my earlier work, Thy Kingdom come, published in 1942." [BT980.K37] 51-9757
1. Devil. I. Kelly, Bernard J. II. Title. III. Title: Thy Kingdom come.

LAMIRANDE, Emilien. 235
The communion of saints. Translated from the French by A. Manson. [1st ed.] New York, Hawthorn Books [1963] 154 p. 21 cm. (The twentieth century encyclopedia of Catholicism, v. 26. Section 2: The basic truths) [BT972.L313] 63-10986
1. Communion of saints. I. Title.

LAMIRANDE, Emilien 235
The communion of saints Tr. from French by A. Manson. New York, Hawthorn [c.1963] 154p. 21cm. (Twentieth cent. ency. of Catholicism, v.26. Section 2: The basic truths) Bibl. 63-10986 3.50 bds.,
1. Communion of saints. I. Title.

MORRISS, Frank. j 235
Saints for the small. Illustrated by Robert Poppert. Milwaukee, Bruce Pub. Co. [1964] 112 p. illus. 22 cm. [BX4658.M64] 64-23894
1. Saints — Juvenile literature. I. Title.

MORRISS, Frank 235
Saints for the small. Illus. by Robert Poppert. Milwaukee, Bruce [c.1964] 112p. illus. 22cm. 64-23894 2.50
1. Saints—Juvenile literature. I. Title.

ROBINSON, William, 1888- 235
The devil and God. New York, Abingdon-Cokesbury Press [1945] 125p. 20cm. [BT980.R57 1945a] 46-4024
1. Devil. 2. Sin. 3. Good and evil. I. Title.

ROUGEMONT, Denis de, 1906- 235
The Devil's share; an essay on the diabolic in modern society. Translated from the French by Haakon Chevalier. New York, Meridian Books, 1956 [c1944] 221p. 19cm. (Meridian books, M21) [BT980] 56-6569
1. Devil. 2. Civilization. 3. Culture. I. Title.

STRAUSS, Lehman. 235
Demons, yes—but thank God for good angels / Lehman Strauss. Neptune, N.J. : Loizeaux Brothers, c1976. 121 p. ; 19 cm. [BT981.S77] 75-38804 ISBN 0-87213-831-3 pbk. : 1.95
1. Devil. 2. Angels. I. Title.

TAILLEPIED, Noel, 1540-1589. 235
A treatise of ghosts; being the Psichologie, or Treatise upon apparitions and spirits ... Written in French by Noel Taillepied, and translated into English, with an introd. and commentary by Montague Summers. London, Fortune Press. Ann Arbor, Mich., Gryphon Books, 1971. xix, 263 p. 22 cm. Reprint of the 1933 ed. Translation of Psichologie; ou Traite de l'apparition des esprits. Includes bibliographical references. [BF1445.T23 1971] 71-162520
1. Apparitions. I. Title.

WOOD, Katharine Marie, 1910- j235
Angels of God, story and pictures by Katharine Wood. New York, P. J. Kenedy [1963] unpaged. illus. 29 cm. [BT966.2.W6] 63-11332
1. Angels — Juvenile literature. I. Title.

WOOD, Katharine Marie, 1910- 235
Angels of God, story, pictures by Katharine Wood. New York, Kenedy [c.1963] unpaged. col. illus. 29cm. 63-11332 2.50
1. Angels—Juvenile literature. I. Title.

GRENOBLE, Universite. 235.01
Ecole d'ete de physique theorique, Les Houches
Hautes energies en astrophysique. High energy astrophysics. Lectures delivered at Les Houches during the 1966 session of the Summer School of Theoretical Physics, with a grant from NATO. Edite par C. DeWitt, E. Schatzman [et] P. Veron. New York, Gordon & Breach [1967- v. illus. 24cm. Text in English. Bibl. [QB464.G7] 67-6412 12.50; 8.50 pap.,
1. Nuclear astrophysics—Congresses. I. DeWitt, Cecile M. ed. II. Veron, P. ed. III. Schatzman, Evry. ed. IV. Title. V. Title: High energy astrophysics.

BROWN, Beverly Holladay, 235.2
1912-
Mary communes with the saints, by Raphael Brown [pseud.] St. Meinrad, Ind. [1955] 147p. illus. 20cm. (A Grall publication) [BX4657.B76] 55-9130
1. Saints. 2. Mary, Virgin—Apparitions and miracles (Modern) I. Title.

BROWNSON, Orestes Augustus, 235.2
1803-1876
Saint-worship [and] The worship of Mary. Ed., abridged by Thomas R. Ryan. Paterson, N.J., St. Anthony Guild [c.1963] ix, 122p. 23cm. 63-18551 2.50
1. Saints—Cultus. 2. Mary, Virgin—Cultus. I. Ryan, Thomas Richard, 1898- ed. II. Title. III. Title: The worship of Mary.

BROWNSON, Orestes Augustus, 235.2
1803-1876
Saint-worship[and] The worship of Mary, Edited and abridged by Thomas R. Ryan. Paterson, N.J., St. Anthony Guild Press [1963] ix, 122 p. 23 cm. [BX2333.B76] 63-18551
1. Saints — Cultus. 2. Mary, Virgin — Cultus. I. Ryan, Thomas Richard, 1898- ed. II. Title. III. Title: The worship of Mary.

DELEHAYE, Hippolyte, 1859- 235.2
1941
The legends of the saints; an introduction to hagiography, from the French of H. Delehaye. Introd. by Richard J. Schoeck. Tr. by V. M. Crawford. [Notre Dame, Ind.] Univ. of Notre Dame Pr., 1961 [c.1907, 1961] 241p. (Notre Dame pubns., NDP7) Bibl. 61-14879 1.95 pap.,
1. Hagiography. I. Title.

DELEHAYE, Hippolyte, 1859- 235.2
1941.
The legends of the saints. With a memoir of the author, by Paul Peeters. Translated by Donald Attwater. New York, Fordham University Press, 1962. xx, 252 p. 23 cm. Translation of Les legends hagiographiques. "Bibliography of scientific works by Hippolyte Delehaye": p. 229-244. [BX4662.D343 1962] 61-18761
1. Christian hagiography. I. Title.

DENSMORE, Warren I., Rev. 235.2
Heroes of Heaven, by Rev. & Mrs. Warren I. Densmore. New York, 347 Madison Ave., Amer. Church Pubns., c.1961. unpaged. illus. 28cm. 1.00 pap.,
I. Title.

DOUILLET, Jacques Marie 235.2
Joseph
What is a saint? Tr. from French by Donald Attwater. New York, Paulist Pr. [1963, c.1958] 115p. 19cm. (Deus bks.) Bibl. .95 pap.,
1. Saints. 2. Saints—Cultus. I. Title.

EMERY, Pierre Yves 235.2
The communion of saints; tr. [from French] by D.J. and M. Watson. [London, Faith Pr., 1966] xiii, 7-256p. 23cm. Orig. pub. as L'unite des croyantsau ciel et sur la terre. Taize,Presses de Taize, 1962. Bibl. [BT972.E413] 66-78144 10.00 bds.,
1. Communion of saints I. Title.
Available from Morehouse New York

LAVELLE, Louis, 1883-1951. 235.2
Four saints. With an introd. by Illtyd Trethowan. [Translation by Dorothea O'Sullivan. Notre Dame, Ind.] University of Notre Dame Press [c1963] xiv, 113 p. 18 cm. [BT765.L313 1963] 64-78
1. Sanctification. 2. Saints. I. Title.

LAVELLE, Louis, 1883-1951 235.2
Four saints. Introd. by Illtyd Trethowan [Tr. from French by Dorothea O'Sullivan. Notre Dame, Ind.] Univ. of Notre Dame Pr. [c.1963] xiv, 113p. 18cm. (ndp 33) 64-78 1.25 pap.,
1. Sanctification. 2. Saints. I. Title.

LECKIE, Robert. 235.2
These are my heroes; a study of the saints. New York, Random House [1964] 177 p. 22 cm. Bibliography: p. 175-177. [BX4655.2.L4] 64-20039
1. Saints. I. Title.

MCGINLEY, Phyllis, 1905- 235'.2
Saint-watching. Garden City, N.Y., Doubleday, 1974 [c1969] 239 p. 18 cm. (Image books.) [BR1710.M23] ISBN 0-385-09537-6 1.75 (pbk.)
1. Saints. 2. Heroes. I. Title.
L.C. card number for original ed.: 79-83242.

MARSH, George Perkins, 235'.2
1801-1882.
Mediaeval and modern saints and miracles. New York, Harper & Row [1969] 307 p. 22 cm. (J. & J. Harper editions) Reprint of the 1876 ed. Bibliography: p. [7]-9. [BX1765.M277 1969] 71-81865
1. Catholic Church—Doctrinal and controversial works—Protestant authors. 2. Miracles—Controversial literature. 3. Saints. I. Title.

MOLINARI, Paolo, 1912- 235.2
Saints: their place in the church, by Paul Molinari. Pref. by Cardinal Larraona. Translated by Dominic Maruca. New York. Sheed and Ward [1965] xv, 240 p. 22 cm. Translation of I santi e il loro culto. Bibliographical references included in "Notes" (p. 176-233) [BN2325.M613] 65-20853
1. Saints. 2. Saints — Cultus. I. Title.

MOLINARI, Paolo, 1912- 235.2
Saints: their place in the church, by Paul Molinari. Pref. by Cardinal Larraona. Tr. [from Italian] by Dominic Maruca. New York, Sheed [c.1965] xv, 240p. 22cm. Bibl. [BX2325.M613] 65-20853 5.50
1. Saints. 2. Saints—Cultus. I. Title.

SANGSTER, William Edwin, 1900- 235.2
The pure in heart; a study in Christian sanctity. Nashville, Abingdon Press [1954] 254p. 23cm. (The Cato lecture of 1954) [BR1710.S35] 54-13191
1. Saints. 2. Holiness. 3. Piety. I. Title.

SHEPPARD, Lancelot Capel, 1906- 235'.2
The saints who never were, by Lancelot Sheppard. Dayton, Ohio, Pflaum Press [1969] xi, 170 p. 22 cm. "A Giniger book." Bibliography: p. 169-170. [BX4662.S53] 70-93009 5.95
1. Christian hagiography. 2. Bollandists. I. Title.

SMITH, Charles Merrill. 235'.2'0207
When the saints go marching out. Illustrated by Robert Osborn. [1st ed.] Garden City, N.Y., Doubleday, 1969. xi, 225 p. illus. 22 cm. [BR153.S58] 69-15883 4.95
1. Christian saints—Anecdotes, facetiae, satire, etc. I. Title.

THE Book of saints; 235.203
a dictionary of persons canonized or beatified by the Catholic Church. Compiled by the Benedictine monks of St. Augustine's Abbey, Ramsgate. 5th ed., entirely rev. and re-set. New York, Crowell [1966] xii, 740 p. 24 cm. [BX4655.B6 1966] 66-22140
1. Saints—Dictionaries. I. St. Augustine's Abbey, Ramsgate, Eng.

BOOK of saints (The); 235.203
a dictionary of persons canonized or beatified by the Catholic Church. Comp. by the Benedictine monks of St. Augustine's Abbey, Ramsgate. 5th ed., entirely rev., re-set. New York, Crowell [1966] xii, 740p. 24cm. [BX4655.B6 1966] 66-22140 8.95
1. Saints—Dictionaries. I. St. Augustine's Abbey, Ramsgate, Eng.

ALBERSTON, Clinton, comp. 235'.2'0922
Anglo-Saxon saints and heroes [ed., tr. by] Clinton Albertson. [Bronx, N.Y.] Fordham [1967] xv, 347p. illus. 24cm. Bibl. [BX4659.G7A5] 67-16652 7.50
1. Saints, English. I. Title.
Contents omitted.

ALBERTSON, Clinton, comp. 235.20922
Anglo-Sazon saints and heroes [ed., tr. by] Clinton Albertson. [Bronx, N.Y.] Fordham [1967] xv, 347p. illus. 24cm. Bibl. [BX4659.G7A5] 67-16652 7.50
1. Saints, English. I. Title.
Contents omitted.

ATTWATER, Donald, 1892- 235.20922
The Penguin dictionary of saints [Magnolia, Mass., P. Smith, 1967, c.1965] 362p. 19cm. (Penguin ref. bk., R30 rebound) [BX4655.8.A8] 3.50
1. Saints—Dictionaries. I. Title. II. Title: Dictionry of saints.

ATTWATER, Donald, 1892- 235.20922
The Penguin dictionary of saints. Baltimore, Penguin Books [1965] 362 p. 19 cm. (Penguin reference books, R30) [BX4655.8.A8] 65-5009
1. Saints—Dictionaries. I. Title. II. Title: Dictionary of saints.

ATTWATER, Donald, 2)1892- 235.20922
The Penguin dictionary of saints [Magnolia, Mass., P. Smith, 1967, c.1965] 362p. 19cm. (Penguin ref. bk., R30 rebound) [BX4655.8.A8] 3.50
1. Saints—Dictionaries. I. Title. II. Title: Dictionary of saints.

BUTLER, Alban, 1711-1773. 235.20922
Lives of the saints. Edited, rev., and supplemented by Herbert Thurston and Donald Attwater. Complete ed. [New York. P. J. Kenedy, 1965, c1963] 4 v. 24 cm. Includes bibliographies. [BX4654.B8] 67-5269
1. Saints. 2. Devotional calendars. I. Thurston, Herbert, 1856-1939. II. Attwater, Donald, 1892- III. Title.

THE Encyclopedia of Catholic saints. 235.20922
[1st American ed.] Philadelphia, Chilton Books [1966] 12 v. col. illus. 20 cm. Arranged according to dates of the saints' feast days. Based on Les saints de tous les jours. "A project of Dimension Books." [BX4655.2.E5 1966] 66-28561
1. Christian saints. 2. Christian saints—Calendar. I. Les Saints de tous les jours. II. Title.

BOROS, Ladislaus, 1927- 235'.3
Angels and men / [by] Ladislaus Boros ; illustrated by Max von Moos ; translated [from the German] by John Maxwell. London : Search Press, 1976. 128 p. : ill. ; 22 cm. Translation of Engel und Menschen. [BT966.2.B613 1976] 77-359487 ISBN 0-85532-375-2 : £2.25
1. Angels. I. Moos, Max von, 1903- II. Title.

DANIELOU, Jean. 235.3
The angels and their mission; according to the fathers of the church. Translated from the French by David Heimann. Westminister, Md., Newman Press [1957] 118p. 21cm. [BT966.D312] 56-11414
1. Angeles—History of doctrines. I. Title.

*DANIELOU, Jean 235.3
The Angels and their mission: according to the Fathers of the Church / by Jean Danielou ; trans. from the French by David Heimann. Westminster, Md. : Christian Classics, 1976 c1957. x, 118 p. ; 21 cm. Includes bibliographical references and index. [BT966.D312] pbk. : 5.45
1. Angels—History of doctrines. I. Title.
L.C. card no. for 1957 Newman ed.: 56-11414.

EVANS, Irwin Henry, 1862- 235.3
The ministry of angels. Rev.ed. Mountain View, Calif., Pacific Press Pub. Association [1953] 303p. 18cm. (Christian home library) [BT966.E9 1953] 53-8826
1. Angels. I. Title.

GRAHAM, William Franklin, 1918- 235'.3
Angels : God's secret agents / Billy Graham. 1st ed. Garden City, N.Y. : Doubleday, 1975. xii, 175 p. ; 22 cm. [BT966.2.G7] 75-16814 ISBN 0-385-11307-2 : 4.95
1. Angels. I. Title.

GRAHAM, William Franklin, 1918- 235'.3
Angels. : God's secret agents / Billy Graham. 1st ed. New York : Pocket Books, 1977,c1975. 188p. ; 18 cm. (A Kangaroo Book) [BT966.2G7] ISBN 0-671-80755-2 pbk. : 1.75
1. Angels. I. Title.
L.C. card no. for 1975 Doubleday edition:75-16814

GRAHAM, William Franklin, 1918- 235'.3
Angels. : God's secret agents / Billy Graham. 1st ed. New York : Pocket Books, 1977,c1975. 188p. ; 18 cm. (A Kangaroo Book) [BT966.2G7] ISBN 0-671-80755-2 pbk. : 1.75
1. Angels. I. Title.
L.C. card no. for 1975 Doubleday edition:75-16814

GRAHAM, William Franklin, 1918- 235'.3
Angels, God's secret agents / Billy Graham. Boston : G. K. Hall, 1976, c1975. p. cm. Large print ed. [BT966.2.G7 1976] 76-4911 ISBN 0-8161-6367-7
1. Angels. 2. Sight-saving books. I. Title.

HILL, Mary V., 1941- 235'.3
Angel children: those who die before accountability [by] Mary V. Hill. Bountiful, Utah, Horizon Publishers [1973] viii, 70 p. 2 ports. 22 cm. Bibliography: p. 61-64. [BV4907.H5] 73-75397 ISBN 0-88290-017-X 2.95
1. Hill, Stephen Davis, May 4-Aug. 14, 1971. 2. Children—Death and future state. I. Title.

HUNT, Marigold. 235.3
A book of angels. Illus. by Johannes Troyer. New York, Sheed & Ward [1958] 182p. illus. 20cm. [BT966.H78] 58-5878
1. Angels. I. Title.

JOPPIE, A S 1906- 235.3
The ministry of angels. Grand Rapids, Baker Book House, 1953. 97p. 20cm. [BT966.J6] 54-27381
1. Angels. I. Title.

JOPPIE, A. S., 1906- 235.3
The ministry of angels. Grand Rapids, Mich., Baker Bk. [1963, c.1953] 97p.20cm. 1.25 pap.,
1. Angels. I. Title.

LEAVELL, Landrum P. 235'.3
Angels, angels, angels [by] Landrum P. Leavell. Nashville, Broadman Press [1973] 96 p. 20 cm. [BT966.2.L34] 73-75627 ISBN 0-8054-2222-6 1.95 (pbk.)
1. Angels. I. Title.

LINTON, John, 1888- 235.3
I believe in angels. Grand Rapids, W. B. Eerdmans Pub. Co., 1952. 85p. 21cm. [BT966.L54] 53-5903
1. Angels. I. Title.

LONG, Valentine. 235'.3
The angels in religion and art. Paterson, N.J., St. Anthony Guild Press [1970] vii, 214 p. 20 cm. Includes bibliographical references. [BT966.2.L65] 73-117712
1. Angels. I. Title.

MCCONKIE, Oscar Walter, 1887- 235'.3
Angels / Oscar W. McConkie, Jr. Salt Lake City : Deseret Book Co., [1976]c1975. 136 p. ; 24 cm. Includes index. Bibliography: p. [131]-132. [BT966.2.M27] 75-29505 ISBN 0-87747-572-5 : 5.95
1. Angels. 2. Mormons and Mormonism—Doctrinal and controversial works. I. Title.

MCCONKIE, Oscar Walter, 1887- 235'.3
Angels / Oscar W. McConkie, Jr. Salt Lake City : Deseret Book Co., c1975. 136 p. ; 24 cm. Includes index. Bibliography: p. [131]-132. [BT966.2.M27] 75-29505 ISBN 0-87747-572-5
1. Angels. 2. Mormons and Mormonism—Doctrinal and controversial works. I. Title.

MARITAIN, Jacques 235.3
The sin of the angel; an essay on a re-interpretation of some Thomistic positions. Translated [from the French] by William L. Rossner. Westminister, Md., Newman Press [c.]1959 106p. 21cm. 59-14806 3.00
1. Angels. 2. Thomas Aquinas, Saint—Theology. I. Title.

MARITAIN, Jacques, 1882- 235.3
The sin of the angel; an essay on a re-interpretation of some Thomistic positions. Translated by William L. Rossner. Westminister, Md., Newman Press, 1959. 106p. 21cm. [BT966.M283] 59-14806
1. Angels. 2. Thomas Aquinas, Saint—Theology. I. Title.

MILLER, C. Leslie. 235'.3
All about angels; the other side of the spirit world [by] C. Leslie Miller. Glendale, Calif., G/L Regal Books [1973] 128 p. 18 cm. Bibliography: p. 127-128. [BT966.2.M45] 73-82096 ISBN 0-8307-0257-1 1.25 (pbk.)
1. Angels. I. Title.

MORRILL, Madge (Haines) 235.3
Angel stories of the Bible. Mountain View, Calif., Pacific Press Pub. Association [1956] 130p. illus. 21cm. [BT966.M63] 56-9489
1. Angels. I. Title.

MOULD, Daphne Desiree Charlotte Pochin. 235.3
Angels of God: their rightful place in the modern world. New York, Devin-Adair, 1963. 177 p. 21 cm. Includes bibliography. [BT966.2.M6] 63-12106
1. Angels. I. Title.

MOULD, Daphne Desiree Charlotte Pochin 235.3
Angels of God: their rightful place in the modern world. New York, Devin-Adair [c.] 1963. 177p. 21cm. Bibl. 63-12106 3.95
1. Angels. I. Title.

PALMER, Tobias. 235'.3
An angel in my house / Tobias Palmer ; illustrated by Betty Eming. Notre Dame, Ind. : Ave Maria Press, c1975. 62 p. : ill. ; 19 cm. [BT966.2.P27] 75-22990 ISBN 0-87793-103-8 pbk. : 1.95
1. Angels. I. Title.

PARENTE, Pascal P 1890- 235.3
The angels. St. Meinrad, Ind., Grail Publications [1958] 158p. 22cm. Includes bibliography. [BT966.P27] 58-1725
1. Angels. I. Title.

PARENTE, Pascal P 1890- 235.3
Beyond space. New York, St. Paul Publications [c1961] 160p. 21cm. [BT966.2.P3] 61-15619
1. Angels. I. Title.

PETERSON, Erik, 1890-1960. 235.3
The angels and the liturgy [by] Eric Petersson. Translated by Ronald Walls. [New York] Herder and Herder [1964] xi, 71 p. 23 cm. Translation of Das Buch von den Engein. Bibliographical references included in "Notes" (p. 51-71) [BT966.P4813] 63-18158
1. Angels—Cultus. I. Title.

PETERSON, Erik, 1890-1960 235.3
The angels and the liturgy. Tr. [from German] by Ronald Walls. [New York] Herder & Herder [c.1964] xi, 71p. 23cm. Bibl. 63-18158 2.95 bds.,
1. Angels—Cultus. I. Title.

REGAMEY, Raymond, 1900- 235.3
What is an angel? Translated from the French by Dom Mark Pontifex. [1st ed.] New York, Hawthorn Books [1960] 126p. 21cm. (Twentieth century encyclopedia of Catholicism, v. 47. Section 4: The means of redemption) Translation of Les anges au ciel et parmi nous. Includes bibliography. [BT966.2.R413] 60-7124
1. Angels. I. Title.

REGAMY, Raymond [Father Pie Regamey] 235.3
What is an angel? Translated from the French by Dom Mark Pontifex. New York, Hawthorn Books [c.1960] 126p. Includes bibliography. 21cm. (Twentieth century encyclopedia of Catholicism, v.47. Section 4: The means of redemption) 60-7124 2.95 bds.,
1. Angels. I. Title.

STROMWALL, Mary W 235.3
My guardian angel; a first book for little Catholics. Pictures by Adele Werber. St. Paul, Catechetical Guild Educational Society, c1954. unpaged. illus. 17cm. (First books for little Catholics. FB 089) [BX2371.S8] 55-21992
1. Angels— Juvenile literature. I. Title.

VAN DER HART, Rob. 235'.3
The theology of angels and devils. Notre Dame, Ind., Fides Publishers [1973, c1972] p. (Theology today, no. 36) Bibliography: p. [BT966.2.V35 1973] 72-13297 ISBN 0-8190-0575-4 Pap. 0.95
1. Angels. 2. Demonology. I. Title.

WARD, Theodora (Van Wagenen) 1890- 235'.3
Men and angels. New York, Viking Press [1969] xiv, 241 p. illus. 22 cm. Bibliography: p. 229-233. [BT966.2.W35 1969] 75-83233 7.50
1. Angels. I. Title.

DAVIDSON, Gustav, 1895- 235'.3'03
A dictionary of angels, including the fallen angels. New York, Free Press [1967] xxxii, 387 p. illus. 26 cm. Bibliography: p. 363-387. [BL477.D3] 66-19757
1. Angels—Dictionaries. I. Title.

ANDERSON, Kenneth, 1917- 235'.4
Satan's angels : a personal warning / Ken Anderson. Nashville : T. Nelson, [1975] 153 p. ; 21 cm. [BF1548.A5] 75-5598 ISBN 0-8407-5595-3 pbk. : 3.50
1. Anderson, Kenneth, 1917- 2. Devil. 3. Demonology. I. Title.

BARNHOUSE, Donald Grey, 1895-1960. 235.4
The invisible war. Grand Rapids, Zondervan Pub. House [1965] 288 p. 23 cm. [BT981.B3] 64-8847
1. Devil. I. Title.

BARNHOUSE, Donald Grey, 1895-1960 235.4
The invisible war. Grand Rapids, Mich., Zondervan [c.1965] 288p. 23cm. [BT981.B3] 64-8847 4.95
1. Devil. I. Title.

[BLACKSTONE, William E.] 1841- 235.4
Satan, his kingdom and its overthrow, by W. E. B. [pseud. Westwood. N.J.] Revell 54p. diagrs. 20cm. (Revell's pop. religious ser., 257) 0-4001 1.50 bds.,
1. Devil. I. Title.

BRUNO de Jesus-Marie, Father, ed. Etudes carmelitaines. *235.4
Satan. New York, Sheed & Ward, 1952 [c1951] xxv, 506 p. illus. 22 cm. "Based upon a volume of the series ... Etudes carmelitaines, published in French ... under the editorship of Pere Bruno de Jesus-Marie, O.C.D." Translated by Malachy Carroll, and others. Bibliographical footnotes. [BT980.S32 1952] 52-1245
1. Devil. 2. Devil — Art. 3. Devil in literature. I. Title.

*BUNYAN, John 235.4
The ruin of antichrist. Swengel, Pa., Reiner Pubns., 1966. 112p. 20cm. 1.50 pap.,
I. Title.

CANNON, H. Brevoort, 1905- 235'.4
The falling angels : a myth in "demontia" / by H. Brevoort Cannon ; illustrated by Joseph Stannard. 1st ed. New York : Vantage Press, c1976. xvi, 155 p. : ill. ; 21 cm. Includes bibliographical references. [BT981.C36] 76-366131 ISBN 0-533-01948-6 : 6.50
1. Devil. 2. Civilization, Modern—20th century. I. Title.

CLASON, Clyde B. 235.4
I am Lucifer; confessions of the Devil as dictated to Clyde B. Clason. Philadelphia, Muhlenberg Press [c.1960] 254p. 23cm. Bibl.: p.252-254. 60-6185 3.50
1. Devil—Fiction. I. Title.

CULLETON, Richard Gerald, 1902-1950. 235.4
The reign of Antichrist. Fresno, Calif. [Academy Duplicating Service, 1951. 224p. illus. 23cm. Includes bibliography. [BT985.C8] 56-47451
1. Antichrist. I. Title.

DEMON possession : 235'.4
a medical, historical, anthropological, and theological symposium : papers presented at the University of Notre Dame, January 8-11, 1975, under the auspices of the Christian Medical Society / edited by John Warwick Montgomery. Minneapolis : Bethany Fellowship, [1975] p. cm. Includes indexes. Bibliography: p. [BF1501.D45] 75-19313 ISBN 0-87123-102-6 pbk. : 3.95
1. Demonology—Congresses. I. Montgomery, John Warwick. II. Christian Medical Society.

THE Devil, you say? : 235'.4
perspectives on demons and the occult / John Allen Chalk ... [et al.]. Austin, Tex. : Sweet Pub. Co., [1974] 159 p. ; 21 cm. Includes bibliographical references. [BF1531.D48] 74-6758 ISBN 0-8344-0083-9
1. Demonology. 2. Occult sciences. I. Chalk, John Allen, 1937-

THE Devil, you say? : 235'.4
perspectives on demons and the occult / John Allen Chalk ... [et al.]. Austin, Tex. : Sweet Pub. Co., [1974] 159 p. ; 21 cm. Includes bibliographical references. [BF1531.D48] 74-6758 ISBN 0-8344-0083-9 pbk. : 2.95.
1. Demonology. 2. Occult sciences. I. Chalk, John Allen, 1937-

DISGUISES of the demonic 235'.4
: contemporary perspectives on the power of evil / edited by Alan M. Olson. New York : Association Press, [1975] 159 p. ; 22 cm. Some of the essays are based on the Lowell Institute lectures for 1973 at the Boston University School of Theology. Includes bibliographical references. [BT981.D57] 74-31321 ISBN 0-8096-1896-6 : 5.95
1. Devil. 2. Demonology. 3. Good and evil. I. Olson, Alan M., ed.

FARRELL, Walter, 1902-1951. 235.4
The Devil, by Walter Farrell, Bernard Leeming, and others. New York, Sheed and Ward [1957] 94p. 18cm. (Canterbury books) [BT980.F3] 57-4662
1. Devil. 2. Demoniac possession. I. Leeming. Bernard. II. Title.

FISHWICK, Marshall William 235.4
Faust revisited; some thoughts on Satan. New York; Seabury [c.]1963. viii, 182p. 22cm. Bibl. 63-19452 3.95 bds.,
1. Devil. 2. U.S.—Moral conditions. I. Title.

FISHWICK, Marshall William. 235.4
Faust revisted; some thoughts on Satan. New York, Seabury Press, 1963. viii, 182 p. 22 cm. "Bibliographical note": p. 179-182. [BT981.F5] 63-19452
1. Devil. 2. U.S. — Moral conditions. I. Title.

GUAZZO, Francesco Maria. 235'.4
Compendium maleficarum. [Edited with notes by Montague Summers. Translated by E. A. Ashwin] New York, Barnes & Noble [1970] xxi, 206 p. illus. 27 cm. Facsimile of the 1929 ed. Includes bibliographical references. [BF1520.G813 1970] 71-18470
1. Demonology. 2. Witchcraft. 3. Exorcism. I. Summers, Montague, 1880-1948, ed. II. Title.

KELLY, Henry Ansgar, 1934- 235'.4
The Devil, demonology, and witchcraft; the development of Christian beliefs in evil spirits. Garden City, N.Y., Doubleday, 1968. vi, 137 p. 22 cm. (A Scott & Collins book) Bibliographical footnotes. [BT975.K42] 68-24838 4.95
1. Demonology. I. Title.

KELLY, Henry Ansgar, 1934- 235'.4
The Devil, demonology, and witchcraft; the development of Christian beliefs in evil spirits. Rev. ed. Garden City, N.Y., Doubleday [1974] 142 p. 21 cm. Includes bibliographical references. [BT975.K42 1974] 74-5917 ISBN 0-385-09551-1 2.95 (pbk.)
1. Demonology. I. Title.

MORGAN, Richard. 235.4
The plight of God, as told in Bible story. Rindge, N. H., R. R. Smith, 1955. 206p. 25cm. [BT980.M6] 54-10321
1. Devil. I. Title.

PAPINI, Giovanni, 1881- 235.4
The Devil; translated from the Italian by Adrienne Foulke. [1st ed.] New York, Dutton, 1954. 246p. 21cm. Appendix (p. 223-246): The Devil's temptation, a play for radio, in three acts. [BT980.P314] 54-9304
1. Devil. I. Title.

RHODES, Henry Taylor 235'.4
Fowkes, 1892-
The satanic mass; a sociological and criminological study. London, New York, Rider [1954] 232p. illus. 22cm. Includes bibliography. [BF1548.R5] 54-41984
1. Devil-worship. 2. Demonology. I. Title.

RICHARDSON, Carl. 235'.4
Exorcism: New Testament style! Old Tappan, N.J., F. H. Revell Co. [1974] 128 p. 18 cm. (Spire books) [BT981.R45] 74-14911 ISBN 0-8007-8171-6 1.25
1. Devil. 2. Demonology. 3. Occult sciences. 4. Exorcism. I. Title.

UNGER, Merrill Frederick, *235.4
1909-
Biblical demonolegy; a study of the spiritual forces behind the present world unrest. Wheaton, Ill., Van Kampen Press [1952] 250 p. 22 cm. Includes bibliography. [BT975.U5] 52-29312
1. Demonology. I. Title.

UNGER, Merrill Frederick, 235.4
1909-
Biblical demonology; a study of the spiritual forces behind the present world unrest. [5th ed.] Wheaton, Ill., Scripture [1963, c.1952] 250p. 22cm. Bibl. 63-1433 4.00
1. Demonology. I. Title.

UNGER, Merrill Frederick, 235'.4
1909-
What demons can do to saints / by Merrill F. Unger. Chicago : Moody Press, c1977. p. cm. Bibliography: p. [BT975.U54] 77-685 ISBN 0-8024-9381-5 : 6.95
1. Demonology. 2. Demoniac possession. I. Title.

WALL, James Charles. 235'.4
Devils, by J. Charles Wall. London, Methuen [1904]. Detroit, Singing Tree Press, 1968. x, 152 p. illus. 21 cm. [BT980.W2 1968] 69-16798
1. Devil.

WOOLF, Mildred E. 235.4
The origin of Satan and his work in the world. Dallas, Tex., Royal [c.1962] 139p. 21cm. 3.50
I. Title.

LARSON, Bob. 235'.4'098
Babylon reborn / Bob Larson. Carol Stream, Ill. : Creation House, 1977, c1976. 111 p. : ill. ; 22 cm. [BF1517.L29L37] 76-22307 ISBN 0-88419-006-4 pbk. : 2.95
1. Demonology, Latin American. 2. Cults—Latin America. 3. Devil. I. Title.

ANSHEN, Ruth Nanda. 235'.47
The reality of the devil: evil in man. [New York, Dell; 1974, c1972] xviii, 142 p. illus. 21 cm. (A Delta book) [BT981.A57] 2.45 (pbk.)
1. Devil. 2. Good and evil. I. Title.
L.C. card number for original ed.: 72-78057.

ANSHEN, Ruth Nanda. 235'.47
The reality of the devil: evil in man. [1st ed.] New York, Harper & Row [1972] xviii, 142 p. illus. 22 cm. [BT981.A57] 72-78057 ISBN 0-06-060242-2 6.95
1. Devil. 2. Good and evil. I. Title.

BOUNDS, Edward McKendree, 235.47
1835-1913
Satan: his personality, power, and overthrow. Grand Rapids, Mich., Baker Bk., 1963. 157p. 20cm. 64-158 2.95
1. Devil. I. Title.

CRISTIANI, Leon, 1879- 235.47
Evidence of Satan in the modern world. [New York] Avon [1975, c1963] 250 p. 18 cm. [BT981.C713] 62-9278 ISBN 0-380-00413-5 1.50 (pbk.)
1. Devil. I. Title.

CRUZ, Nicky. 235'.47
Satan on the loose. Old Tappan, N.J., F. H. Revell Co. [1973] 158 p. 22 cm. [BT981.C76] 73-1125 ISBN 0-8007 0574 2 3.95
1. Cruz, Nicky. 2. Devil. 3. Demonology. I. Title.

DEHAAN, Richard W. 235'.47
Satan, satanism, and witchcraft, by Richard W. Dehaan with Herbert Vander Lught. Grand Rapids, Mich., Zondervan Pub. House [1972] 125 p. 18 cm. (Zondervan books) Bibliography: p. 123-125. [BT981.D44] 72-81786 0.95 (pbk.)
1. Devil. 2. Christianity and occult sciences. I. Vander Lught, Herbert, joint author. II. Title.

ELWOOD, Roger. 235'.47
Prince of Darkness. Illustrated with renderings, assorted woodcuts and with engravings by Gustav Dore. Norwalk, Conn., C. R. Gibson Co. [1974] [54] p. illus. 21 cm. [BT981.E48] 73-86688 ISBN 0-8378-1751-X
1. Devil. I. Title.

HALL, Frederic Thomas, 235'.47
d.1885.
The pedigree of the Devil. New York, B. Blom, 1971. xv, 256 p. illus. 21 cm. Reprint of the 1883 ed. Includes bibliographical references. [BT980.H17 1971] 76-173108
1. Demonology. 2. Devil. I. Title.

HUEGEL, Frederick Julius, 235'.47
1889-
The mystery of iniquity; keys to victorious Christian living [by] F. J. Huegel. Minneapolis, Bethany Fellowship [1968] 116 p. 20 cm. [BT981.H8] 68-4492
1. Devil. I. Title.

JENNINGS, Frederick 235'.47
Charles, 1847-1948.
Satan, his person, work, place, and destiny / by F. C. Jennings. Neptune, N.J. : Loizeaux Bros., 1975. 254 p. ; 19 cm. Includes bibliographical references. [BT981.J46 1975] 75-321802 ISBN 0-87213-422-9 pbk. : 2.50
1. Devil. I. Title.

KALLAS, James G. 235'.47
The real Satan : from Biblical times to the present / James Kallas. Minneapolis : Augsburg Pub. House, [1975] 111 p. ; 20 cm. [BT981.K34] 74-14184 ISBN 0-8066-1466-8 : 2.95
1. Jesus Christ—Person and offices. 2. Devil. I. Title.

KLEINSCHMIDT, Gladys J., 235'.47
1904-
Challenger of the most high God / by G. J. Kleinschmidt. [s.l. : s.n.], c1976 ([South Pasadena, Calif.] : William Carey Library) p. cm. Includes index. Bibliography: p. [BT981.K57] 76-29069 9.95
1. Devil. 2. Demonology. 3. Good and evil. I. Title.

KLUGER, Rivkah Scharf, 235.47
1907-
Satan in the Old Testament. Tr. by Hildegard Nagel. Evanston, Northwestern, 1967. (Studies in Jungian thought) xvii, 173p. 22cm. Tr. of the author's thesis, Zurich, 1948, pub. under title: Die Gestalt des Satans im Alten Testament. Pub. also as part III of C.G. Jung's Symbolik des Geistes. Bibl. [BS1199.D4K5] 67-15935 5.50
1. Devil—Biblical teaching. I. Jung, Carl Gustav, 1875-1961. Symbolik des Geistes. II. Title.

KLUGER, Rivkah Scharf, 235'.47
1907-
Satan in the Old Testament. Translated by Hildegard Nagel. Evanston Northwestern University Press, 1967. xvii, 173 p. 22 cm. (Studies in Jungian thought) Translation of the author's thesis, Zurich, 1948, published under title: Die Gestalt des Satans im Alten Testament. Published also as part III of C. G. Jung's Symbolik des Geistes. Bibliographical footnotes. [BS1199.D4K5] 67-15935
1. Devil—Biblical teaching. I. Jung, Carl Gustav, 1875-1961. Symbolik des Geistes. II. Title.

LANGTON, Edward, 1886- 235'.47
Satan, a portrait; a study of the character of Satan through all the ages. [Folcroft, Pa.] Folcroft Library Editions, 1974. 128 p. illus. 26 cm. Reprint of the 1945 ed. published by Skeffington, London. Includes bibliographical references. [BT980.L3 1974] 74-2434 ISBN 0-8414-5716-6 (lib. bdg.)
1. Devil. I. Title.

LINDSEY, Hal. 235'.47
Satan is alive and well on planet earth, by Hal Lindsey with C. C. Carlson. Grand Rapids, Zondervan Pub. House [1972] 255 p. 22 cm. Includes bibliographical references. [BT981.L56] 72-85564 4.95
1. Devil. 2. Christianity and occult sciences. 3. Christianity and psychical research. I. Title.

PENTECOST, J. Dwight. 235'.47
Your adversary, the Devil [by] J. Dwight Pentecost. Grand Rapids, Zondervan [1969] 191 p. 23 cm. [BT981.P46] 77-95037 4.95
1. Devil. I. Title.

PETERSON, Robert. 235'.47
Trail of the serpent : the story of Satan told in the Bible, from the fall to the lake of fire / Robert L. Peterson. New Canaan, Conn. : Keats Pub., 1976, i.e.1977 176 p. ; 18 cm. (A Pivot original) Bibliography: p. 175-179. [BS680.D56P47] 76-21438 ISBN 0-87983-130-8 pbk. : 1.95
1. Devil—Biblical teaching. I. Title.

SANDERS, John Oswald, 235'.47
1902-
Satan is no myth / J. Oswald Sanders. Chicago : Moody Press, [1975] 141 p. ; 22 cm. Includes bibliographical references. [BT981.S26] 74-15358 ISBN 0-8024-7525-6 : 1.50
1. Devil. I. Title.

TATFORD, Frederick A., 235'.47
1901-
Satan, the Prince of Darkness / by Fredk. A. Tatford. Grand Rapids, Mich. : Kregel Publications, [1974] 118 p. ; 18 cm. [BT981.T37] 74-82808 ISBN 0-8254-3807-1 : 1.95
1. Devil. I. Title.

WHITE, John Wesley. 235'.47
The devil : what the Scriptures teach about him / John Wesley White. Wheaton, Ill. : Tyndale House Publishers, 1977. 192 p. ; 22 cm. [BS680.D56W47] 76-58130 ISBN 0-8423-0663-3 4.95
1. Devil—Biblical teaching. I. Title.

*ADAMS, Jay E. 235.5
Coping with counseling crises : first aid for Christian crises / Jay E. Adams. Grand Rapids : Baker Book House, 1976. v, 90p. : music ; 22 cm. [BV4012.2] ISBN 0-8010-0112-9 pbk. : 1.95
1. Pastoral counseling. I. Title.

DICKS, Russell Leslie, 235.5
1906-
Principles and practice of pastoral care. Philadelphia, Fortress [1966,c.1963] 143p. 21cm. (Successful pastoral counseling ser.) bBibl. 1.50 pap.,
1. Pastoral counsling. I. Title.

DICKS, Russell Leslie, 235.5
1906-
Principles and practices of pastoral care. Englewood Cliffs, N.J., Prentice [c.1963] 143p. 21cm. (Successful pastoral counseling ser.) Bibl. 63-8623 2.95 bds.,
1. Pastoral counseling. I. Title.

REORGANIZED Church of Jesus 235.5
Christ of Latter Day Saints. Worship Committee.
Manual of marriage. Independence, Mo., Herald House, 1971. 131 p. 18 cm. (Pastor's reference library) [HQ10.R44] 79-162861 ISBN 0-8309-0049-7
1. Marriage counseling. I. Title.

236 Eschatology

ADAMS, Jay Edward. 236
Realized millennialism; a study in Biblical eschatology. St. Louis. 1959. 87p. Illus. 19cm. [BT821.2.A3] 59-13014
1. Eschatology. I. Title.

AGARD-NATO Specialists' 236
Meeting, Sint-Genesius-Rode, Belgium, 1962.
The high temperature aspects of hypersonic flow; proceedings. Oxford, New York, Published for and on behalf of Advisory Group for Aeronautical Research and Development, North Atlantic Treaty Organization by Pergamon Press, 1963. xiv, 786 p. illus., diagrs. 26 cm. (AGARDograph 68) "Sponsored by the Fluid Dynamics Panel of AGARD." English and French. Includes bibliographics. [TL500.N6 no. 68] 63-17827
1. Aerodynamics, Hypersonic—Congresses. 2. Aerothermodynamics—Congresses. 3. High temperatures—Congress. I. Nelson, Iwlbur Clifton, 1913— ed. II. North Atlantic Treaty Organization, Advisory Group for Aeronautics Research and Development. Fluid dynamics Panel. III. Title. IV. Series.

ALBERIONE, Giacomo Giuseppe, 236
1884-
The last things, by James Alberione. Translated by the Daughters of St. Paul. [Boston?] St. Paul Editions [1964] 357 p. 19 cm. [BT823.A413] 64-17751
1. Death—Meditations. 2. Eschatology I. Title.

[ALBERIONE, Giacomo Giuseppe] 236
1884-
The last things, by James Alberione. Tr. by the Daughters of St. Paul [Boston] St. Paul Eds. [dist. Daughters of St. Paul, c.1964] 357p. 19cm. 64-17751 3.50; 2.50 pap.,
1. Death—Meditations. 2. Eschatology. I. Title.

ALLEN, Edgar Leonard. 236
Freedom in God; a guide to the thought of Nicholas Berdyaev, by E. L. Allen. [Folcroft, Pa.] Folcroft Library Editions, 1973. 43 p. 24 cm. Reprint of the ed. published by Hodder & Stoughton, London. Bibliography: p. [44] [B4238.B44A7 1973] 73-5751 ISBN 0-8414-1740-7 4.50 (lib. ed.)
1. Berdiaev, Nikolai Aleksandrovich, 1874-1948. I. Title.

†ALLNUTT, Frank. 236
Antichrist : after The Omen / Frank Allnutt. Old Tappan, N.J. : F. H. Revell Co., c1976. 154 p. ; 18 cm. (Spire books) [BT985.A38] 76-45802 ISBN 0-8007-8285-2 pbk. : 1.75
1. Bible—Prophecies. 2. The Omen. [Motion picture] 3. Antichrist. I. Title.

ARENDZEN, John Peter, 1873- 236
What becomes of the dead? A study of eschatology. [2d ed.] New York, Sheed &

Ward, 1951. 279 p. 20 cm. [BT821.A67 1951] 51-9704
1. Eschatology. I. Title.

BADHAM, Paul. 236
Christian beliefs about life after death / [by] Paul Badham. London : Macmillan, 1976. viii, 174 p. ; 23 cm. (Library of philosophy and religion) Includes index. [BT902.B3 1976b] 77-360732 ISBN 0-333-19769-0 : £8.95
1. Future life. I. Title.

BADHAM, Paul. 236
Christian beliefs about life after death / Paul Badham. New York : Barnes & Noble Books, 1976. 174 p. ; 23 cm. (Library of philosophy and religion) Includes bibliographical references and indexes. [BT902.B3 1976] 75-43224 ISBN 0-06-490280-3 : 17.00
1. Future life. I. Title.

BAKER, Nelson B 236
What is the world coming to? A study for laymen of the last things, by Nelson B. Baker. Philadelphia, Westminster Press [1965] 157 p. 21 cm. Bibliographical references included in "Notes" (p. [155]-157) [BT821.2.B3] 65-14039
1. Eschatology. I. Title.

BAKER, Nelson B. 236
What is the world coming to? A study for laymen of the last things. Philadelphia, Westminster [c.1965] 157p. 21cm. Bibl. [BT821.2.B3] 65-14039 2.25 pap.,
1. Eschatology. I. Title.

BARNEY, Kenneth D. 236
Preparing for the storm / Kenneth D. Barney. Springfield, Mo. : Gospel Pub. House, [1975] 96 p. ; 18 cm. (Radiant books) [BV4253.B35] 74-21021 pbk. : 1.25
1. Sermons, American. I. Title.

BARRETT, George West. 236
Dialogue on destiny, by George W. Barrett and J. V. Langmead Casserley. Greenwich, Conn, Seabury Press, 1955. 96p. 19cm. [BT821.B24] 56-901
1. Eschatology. I. Casserley, Julian Victor Langmead, 1909- joint author. II. Title.

BERKHOF, Hendrikus. 236
Well-founded hope. Richmond, John Knox Press [1969] 107 p. 21 cm. Bibliographical references included in "Notes" (p. [101]-107) [BT823.B44] 69-13272 3.25
1. Eschatology—Addresses, essays, lectures. I. Title.

BLOOMFIELD, Arthur Edward, 1895- 236
How to recognize the Antichrist / Arthur E. Bloomfield. Minneapolis : Bethany Fellowship, c1975. 153 p. : ill. ; 21 cm. [BT985.B55] 75-29424 ISBN 0-87123-225-1 pbk. : 2.45
1. Antichrist. I. Title.

BOETTNER, Loraine. 236
Immortality. Grand Rapids, Eerdmans, 1956. 159p. 23cm. [BT821.B6] 56-14056
1. Eschatology. I. Title.

BRAATEN, Carl E., 1929- 236
Christ and counter-Christ; apocalyptic themes in theology and culture [by] Carl E. Braaten. Philadelphia, Fortress Press [1971, c1972] viii, 152 p. 22 cm. Includes bibliographical references. [BT823.B68] 76-171493 ISBN 0-8006-0120-3 3.50
1. Eschatology—Addresses, essays, lectures. 2. Theology—Addresses, essays, lectures. I. Title.

BRAATEN, Carl E., 1929- 236
Eschatology and ethics; essays on the theology and ethics of the Kingdom of God [by] Carl E. Braaten. Minneapolis, Augsburg Pub. House [1974] 192 p. 22 cm. Includes bibliographical references. [BT823.B684] 74-77674 3.95
1. Eschatology—Addresses, essays, lectures. 2. Christian ethics—Lutheran authors—Addresses, essays, lectures. I. Title.

BRAATEN, Carl E., 1929- 236
The future of God; the revolutionary dynamics of hope [by] Carl E. Braaten. [1st ed.] New York, Harper & Row [1969] 186 p. 21 cm. Bibliographical references included in "Notes" (p. [167]-181) [BT75.2.B68] 69-17024 5.95
1. Theology, Doctrinal. 2. Eschatology. 3. Hope. 4. Revolution (Theology) I. Title.

BRANSON, Gene N. 236
Joy beyond sorrow. Boston, Christopher [c.1962] 54p. 21cm. 62-9712 2.00
1. Eschatology. I. Title.

BROWNE, Frederic Zollicoffer, 1878- 236
Visible glory ... [1st ed.] New York, Greenwich Book Publishers [c1957] 133p. 21cm. [BT875.B78] 57-14596
1. End of the world. I. Title.

BRUNNER, Heinrich Emil, 1889- 236
Eternal hope; translated by Harold Knight. Philadelphia, Westminster Press [1954] 232p. 23cm. Translation of Das Ewige als Zukunft und Gegenwart. Bibliographical references included in 'Notes' (p. 221-232) [BT821.B733 1954] 54-3507
1. Eschatology. I. Title.

BRUNNER, Heinrich Emil, 1889-1966. 236
Eternal hope. Translated by Harold Knight. Westport, Conn., Greenwood Press [1972] 232 p. 22 cm. Reprint of the 1954 ed. Translation of Das Ewige als Zukunft und Gegenwart. Includes bibliographical references. [BT821.D733 1972] 72-6930 ISBN 0-8371-6508-3
1. Eschatology. I. Title.

*BUNYAN, John 236
Visions of heaven and hell. Swengel, Pa., Reiner Pubns., 1966. 63p. 20cm. .75 pap.,
I. Title.

*CHAIJ, Fernando 236
Preparacion para la crisis final; recopilacion y comentarios de pasajes de la Biblia y el espiritu de profecia. Apendice de M. E. Loewen. Prologo prep. por A. L. White. Mountain View, Calif., Pacific Pr.1350 Villa St. [c.1966] 160p. 22cm. (Publicaciones interamericanas) 1.00 pap.,
I. Title.

CHAIJ, Fernando. 236
Preparation for the final crisis; a compilation of passages from the Bible and the spirit of prophecy, with comments by Fernando Chaij. With an appendix by M. E. Loewen. [1st ed.] Mountain View, Calif., Pacific Press Pub. Association [1966] 189 p. illus. 22 cm. Includes quotations from the writings of Ellen G. White. [BX6154.C42] 66-29118
1. Seventh-Day Adventists—Doctrinal and controversial works. I. White, Ellen Gould (Harmon) 1827-1915. II. Title.

CHARLES, Robert Henry, 1855-1931. 236
Eschatology, the doctrine of a future life in Israel, Judaism, and Christianity; a critical history. Introd. by George Wesley Buchanan. New York, Schocken Books [1963] 482 p. 21 cm. (Schocken paperbacks, SB49) First edition published in 1899 under title: A critical history of the doctrine of a future life in Israel, in Judaism, and in Christianity. [BT821.C45 1963] 63-10991
1. Eschatology—Biblical teaching.

COLBY, James Adams. 236
God's in His heaven--but all's not well with the world. With biographical glossary of names used. Boston, House of Edinboro [1950] 223 p. 21 cm. [BT875.C65] 51-21150
1. End of the world. I. Title.

COX, William Edward, 1923- 236
Biblical studies in final things, by William E. Cox. Philadelphia, Presbyterian & Reformed Pub. Co., 1967 [c1966] xiv, 226 p. 22 cm. Bibliography: p. 223-226. [BT821.2.C6] 67-11794
1. Eschatology—Biblical teaching. I. Title.

CRAFTS, Glenn Alty 236
Life is forever. Nashville, Abingdon [c.1963] 93p. 20cm. 63-11377 2.00 bds.,
1. Eschatology—Sermons. 2. Sermons, American. 3. Methodist Church—Sermons. I. Title.

CROWLEY, Dale 236
The soon coming of Our Lord. New York, Loizeaux Bros. [c.1958, 1960] 176p. 61-2020 2.50 bds.,
1. End of the world. I. Title.

*CUNNINGHAM, Sam L. 236
Beware of these days, light your lamps. New York, Exposition [c.1964] 333p. 21cm. (EP42116) 4.00
I. Title.

DAVIES, William David, 1911- 236
The Gospel and the land; early Christianity and Jewish territorial doctrine, by W. D. Davies. Berkeley, University of California Press [1974] xiv, 521 p. illus. 24 cm. Bibliography: p. 439-471. [BS2545.P43D38] 72-82228 ISBN 0-520-02278-5 15.00
1. Palestine in the Bible. 2. Palestine in Judaism. I. Title.

DE HAAN, Martin Ralph, 1891- 236
The days of Noah and their prophetic message for today. Grand Rapids, Zondervan Pub. House [1963] 184 p. 20 cm. [BT876.D39] 63-6012
1. End of the world. 2. Bible — Prophecies. I. Title.

DE HAAN, Martin Ralph, 1891- 236
The days of Noah and their prophetic message for today. Grand Rapids, Mich., Zondervan [c.1963] 184p. 20cm. 63-6012 2.50
1. End of the world. 2. Bible—Prophecies. I. Title.

EDWARDS, David Lawrence. 236
The last things now [by] David L. Edwards. Valley Forge [Pa.] Judson Press [1970, c1969] 128 p. 19 cm. Inlcudes bibliographical references. [BT902.E3 1970] 76-121056 1.95
1. Future life. I. Title.

ELERT, Werner, 1885-1954. 236
Last things / Werner Elert ; translated by Martin Bertram ; edited by Rudolph F. Norden. St. Louis : Concordia Pub. House, [1974] 56 p. ; 23 cm. Exerpted and translated from Der Christliche Glaube. [BT823.E42] 74-4914 ISBN 0-570-03181-8 pbk. : 2.50
1. Eschatology. I. Elert, Werner, 1885-1954. Der christliche Glaube. II. Title.

ELLIS, Edward Earle. 236
Eschatology in Luke, by E. Earle Ellis. Philadelphia, Fortress Press [1972] xvi, 29 p. 20 cm. (Facet books. Biblical series, 30) "Revision of a paper entitled 'The function of eschatology in the Gospel of Luke,' read at the Journees bibliques, at the University of Louvain, Belgium, August 21-23, 1968." Bibliography: p. 21-25. [BS2545.E7E43] 72-75649 ISBN 0-8006-3070-X 1.00
1. Bible. N.T. Luke—Criticism, interpretation, etc. 2. Eschatology—Biblical teaching. I. Title.

ERB, Paul, 1894- 236
The alpha and the omega; a restatement of the Christian hope in Christ's coming. Scottdale, Pa., Herald Press [1955] 153 p. 20 cm. (The Conrad Grebel lectures, 1955) [BT821.E7] 55-10561
1. Eschatology. I. Title.

FACKRE, Gabriel J. 236
The rainbow sign; Christian futurity [by] Gabriel Fackre. Grand Rapids, Mich., W. B. Eerdmans Pub. Co. [1969] viii, 151 p. 23 cm. [BV4638.F3] 72-7794 4.50
1. Hope. I. Title.

FISON, J E 236
The Christian hope; the presence and the parousia. London, New York, Longmans, Green, 1954. Bibliographic footnotes. [BT821.F5] 54-963
1. Eschatology. I. Title.

FORD, William Herschel, 1900- 236
Simple sermons on prophetic themes, by W. Herschel Ford. Grand Rapids, Zondervan Pub. House [1968] 122 p. 22 cm. [BT823.F6] 68-27461 2.95
1. Eschatology—Sermons. 2. Sermons, American. I. Title.

FRANKLIN, Eric, 1929- 236
Christ the Lord : a study in the purpose and theology of Luke-Acts / Eric Franklin. Philadelphia : Westminster Press, c1975. 241 p. ; 23 cm. Includes indexes. Bibliography: p. [219]-224. [BS2589.F7] 75-28162 ISBN 0-664-20809-6 : 10.00
1. Luke, Saint. 2. Bible. N.T. Luke and Acts—Theology. 3. Eschatology—Biblical teaching. I. Title.

THE Future of hope; 236
theology as eschatology [by] Jurgen Moltmann with Harvey Cox [and others] Edited by Frederick Herzog. [New York] Herder and Herder [1970] x, 166 p. 22 cm. "Result of the April 4-6, 1968 Duke consultation on the task of theology today." Sponsored by the Duke Divinity School. Includes bibliographical references. [BT823.F85] 79-110793 5.95
1. Eschatology—Addresses, essays, lectures. 2. Hope—Addresses, essays, lectures. I. Moltmann, Jurgen. II. Herzog, Frederick, ed. III. Duke University, Durham, N.C. Divinity School.

GARRIGOU-LAGRANGE, Reginald, Father, 1877- 236
Life everlasting; translated by Patrick Cummins. St. Louis, Herder, 1952. 274 p. 24 cm. Translation of Lieternelle vie et la profondeur de l'ame. [BT821.G313] 52-11306
1. Eschatology. I. Title.

GROMACKI, Robert Glenn. 236
Are these the last days? Old Tappan, N.J., Revell Co. [1969, c1970] 190 p. 21 cm. [BS647.2.G76] 73-96250 4.50
1. Bible—Prophecies. 2. Second Advent. I. Title.

GUARDINI, Romano, 1885- 236
The last things: concerning death, purification after death, resurrection, judgment, and eternity. Translated by Charlotte E. Forsyth and Grace B. Branham. [New York] Pantheon [1954] 118p. 21cm. [BT821.G82] 54-7069
1. Eschatology. I. Title.

GULLEY, Norman R. 236
Final events on planet Earth / by Norman R. Gulley. Nashville : Southern Pub. Association, c1977. 124 p. ; 20 cm. Includes bibliographical references. [BT821.2.G84] 77-24206 ISBN 0-8127-0144-5 pbk. : 2.95
1. Eschatology. I. Title.

HANCOCK, Harry N 236
And after this? An interpretation of the Christian belief in life after death. [1st ed.] New York, Longmans, Green [1954] 115p. 20cm. [BT820.H3] 54-13146
1. Eschatology. I. Title.

HANSON, Paul D. 236
The dawn of apocalyptic / by Paul D. Hanson. Philadelphia : Fortress Press, [1975] xii, 426 p. ; 24 cm. Includes indexes. Bibliography: p. 417-419. [BS646.H35] 74-76933 ISBN 0-8006-0285-4 : 14.95
1. Bible. O.T. Isaiah LVI-LXVI—Commentaries. 2. Bible. O.T. Zechariah IX-XIV—Commentaries. 3. Apocalyptic literature. 4. Zadokites. I. Title.

HARRIS, Victor, 1910- 236
All coherence gone; a study of the seventeenth century controversy over disorder and decay in the universe. [1st ed.], new impression. London, Cass, 1966: [New York, Barnes & Noble] x, 255p. 23cm. Bibl. [BT875.H32 1966] 68-74761 7.50
1. Goodman, Godfrey, Bp. of Gloucester, 1583-1656. 2. Hakewill, George, 1578-1649. 3. End of the world. 4. Philosophy, English—17th cent. I. Title.

HAYNES, Carlyle Boynton, 1882- 236
Life, death, and immortality. Nashville, Southern Pub. Association [1952] 408 p. 18 cm. (Christian home library) [BT821.H415] 52-36204
1. Eschatology. 2. Seventh-Day Adventists—Doctrinal and controversial works. I. Title.

HAYNES, Carlyle Boynton, 1882- 236
The other side of death. Rev. and reillustrated. By Carlyle B. Haynes. Nashville, Southern Pub. Association [1964] 128 p. illus. 21 cm. (A Summit book) [BT821.2.H3] 63-21244
1. Eschatology. I. Title.

HAYNES, Carlyle Boynton, 1882- 236
The other side of death. Rev., reillus. Nashville, Southern Pub. Assn. [c.1944, 1964] 128p. illus. 21cm. (Summit bk.) [BT821.2.H3] 63-21244 price unreported pap.,
1. Eschatology. I. Title.

HEALER, Carl T., 1925- 236
The quiet revolutionary, by Carl T. Healer. Philadelphia, Dorrance [1971] ix, 40 p. 22 cm. Includes bibliographical references. Analyzes the motives, problems, and expectations of the twelve disciples. [BV4832.2.H37] 76-159685 ISBN 0-8059-1577-X 2.50

1. Meditations. I. Title.

HEINECKEN, Martin J. 236
Beginning and end of the world. Philadelphia, Muhlenberg Press [c.1960] ix, 62p. diagrs. 20cm. (A Fortress book) 60-3805 1.00 bds.,
1. Creation. 2. End of the world. I. Title.

HENDRIKSEN, William, 1900- 236
Lectures on the last things. Grand Rapids, Baker Book House, 1951. 65 p. 21 cm. [BT821.H44] 51-5700
1. Eschatology. I. Title.

*HESBURGH, Theodore M. 236
The humane imperative a challenge for the year 2000 [by] Theodore M. Hesburgh. Preface by Kingman Brewster. New Haven, Yale University Press, 1974 xi., 115 p. 21 cm. (The Dwight Horrington Terry Foundation Lectures on Religion in the Light of Science and Philosophy) [BT821] 74-79381 ISBN 0-300-01787-1 5.95
1. Eschatology. I. Title.

HILL, John Edward 236
Christopher, 1912-
Antichrist in seventeenth-century England: the Riddell memorial lectures, forty-first series, delivered at the University of Newcastle upon Tyne on 3, 4 and 5 November 1969, by Christopher Hill. London, New York, Oxford University Press, 1971. x, 201 p. 19 cm. (University of Newcastle upon Tyne. Publications) (Riddell memorial lectures, 41st series) Includes bibliographical references. [BR757.H54] 70-28701 ISBN 0-19-713911-6 £1.50
1. Antichrist—History of doctrines. 2. Religious thought—England. 3. Religious thought—17th century. I. Title. II. Series.

HOYT, Herman Arthur, 1909- 236
The end times [by] Herman A. Hoyt. Chicago, Moody Press [1969] 256 p. 23 cm. Bibliography: p. 244-249. [BT821.2.H68] 79-13504 4.95
1. Eschatology—Biblical teaching. I. Title.

KANTONEN, Taito Almar, 1900- 236
Life after death. Philadelphia, Muhlenberg Press [1962] 54p. 19cm. (A Fortress book) [BT823.K3] 62-8205
1. Eschatology. I. Title.

KEE, Howard Clark. 236
The renewal of hope. New York, Association Press [1959] 190p. 20cm. (A Haddam House book) Includes bibliography. [BT821.2.K4] 59-6836
1. Eschatology. 2. Hope. 3. Church and social problems. I. Title.

KELBER, Werner H. 236
The kingdom in Mark; a new place and a new time [by] Werner H. Kelber. Philadelphia, Fortress Press [1974] xii, 173 p. 24 cm. Based on the author's thesis, University of Chicago, 1970. Bibliography: p. 151-162. [BS2585.2.K44] 73-88353 ISBN 0-8006-0268-4 8.50
1. Bible. N.T. Mark I-XIII—Criticism, interpretation, etc. 2. Kingdom of God—Biblical teaching. I. Title.

KIK, Jacob Marcellus, 1903- 236
The eschatology of victory, by J. Marcellus Kik. With an introd. by Rousas John Rushdoony. [Nutley, N.J.] Presbyterian and Reformed Pub. Co., 1971. ix, 268 p. 21 cm. Contents.Contents.—Historic reformed eschatology.—Matthew twenty-four: an exposition.—Revelation twenty: an exposition. Includes bibliographical references. [BS2545.E7K54] 77-173817
1. Bible. N.T. Matthew XXIV—Criticism, interpretation, etc. 2. Bible. N.T. Revelation XX—Criticism, interpretation, etc. 3. Millennialism. 4. Eschatology—Biblical teaching. I. Title.

KIMBALL, Warren Young 236
The lake of fire, and consummation. Dedham, Mass., 302 Mt. Vernon St., Author c.1959 52p. 22cm. 1.00 pap.,
I. Title.

KING, Archibald Milroy, 1875- 236
Life's eternal drama, the only pathway to peace; theology and facts coordinated to produce the strangest and most important true story ever written. 2 illus. of the 4 horse-men and their significance. Boston, Christopher Pub. House [1950] 104 p. illus. 21 cm. [BT823.K5 1950] 51-3221
1. Eschatology—Miscellanea. I. Title.

KIRBAN, Salem. 236
Guide to survival. Huntingdon Valley, Pa. [1968] 278 p. illus. 22 cm. Bibliography: p. 276-277. [BT876.K5] 68-57811 1.95
1. Bible—Prophecies. 2. End of the world. I. Title.

LAST things; 236
a symposium of prophetic messages. Edited by H. Leo Eddleman. Grand Rapids, Zondervan Pub. House [1969] 160 p. 21 cm. Includes bibliographical references. [BT823.L33] 76-81057 3.95
1. Eschatology—Addresses, essays, lectures. I. Eddleman, H. Leo, ed.

THE Last things; 236
essays presented by his students to Dr. W. B. West, Jr., upon the occasion of his sixty-fifth birthday. Jack P. Lewis, editor. Austin, Tex., Sweet Pub. Co. [1972] xi, 168 p. port. 22 cm. "Bibliography of W. B. West, Jr.": p. vii. [BT823.L333] 75-188165 ISBN 0-8344-0076-6
1. Eschatology—Addresses, essays, lectures. I. West, W. B., 1907- II. Lewis, Jack Pearl, 1919- ed.

MCKEATING, Henry. 236
God and the future / Henry McKeating. Valley Forge, Pa. : Judson Press, 1975, c1974. 94 p. ; 22 cm. [BT821.2.M29 1975] 74-17844 ISBN 0-8170-0661-3 : 3.50
1. Eschatology. I. Title.

MACPHERSON, Dave. 236
The incredible cover-up : the true story on the pre-trib rapture / by Dave MacPherson. Rev. and combined ed. Plainfield, N.J. : Logos International, c1975. xiii, 162 p., [2] leaves of plates : ill. ; 21 cm. Combines The unbelievable pre-trib origin and The late great pre-trib rapture, both written by the author and originally published in 1973 and 1974 respectively. Bibliography: p. [158]-162. [BT887.M3 1975] 75-25171 ISBN 0-88270-143-6 : 5.95. pbk. : 2.95
1. Rapture (Christian eschatology) 2. Tribulation (Christian eschatology) I. Title.

MACPHERSON, Ian, 1912- 236
God's plan for this planet / Ian Macpherson. Springfield, Mo. : Gospel Pub. House, c1977. 91 p. ; 18 cm. (Radiant books) [BS680.E8M32] 76-51001 ISBN 0-88243-517-5 pbk. : 1.25
1. Bible—Prophecies. 2. Eschatology—Biblical teaching. I. Title.

MAXWELL, Arthur S. 236
Time running out: new evidence of approaching climax. Mountain View, Calif., Pac. Pr. Pub. [c.1963] 116p. illus. 18cm. .25 pap.,
I. Title.

MAXWELL, Arthur Stanley, 236
1896-
This is the end! by Arthur S. Maxwell. Mountain View, Calif., Pacific Press Pub. Association [c1967] 96 p. illus. 18 cm. [BT876.M28] 67-26303
1. End of the world. I. Title.

*MAXWELL, Arturo S. 236
El tiempo se acaba, nuevas evidencias de que nox acercamos al momento crucial de la historia Spanish. Mountain View, Calif., Pac. Pr. Pub., c.1964] 128p. illus. 22cm. [in Spanish.] 1.25 pap.,
I. Title.

MOLTMANN, Jurgen. 236
Theology of hope; on the ground and the implications of a Christian eschatology. [1st U.S. ed.] New York, Harper & Row [1967] 342 p. 22 cm. Translation of Theologie der Hoffnung. Bibliographical footnotes. [BT821.2.M6313 1967b] 67-21550
1. Hope. 2. Eschatology. I. Title.

MOLTMANN, Jurgen 236
Theology of hope; the ground and the implications of a christian eschatology [trans. by James W. Leitch from the German] New York, Harper & Row [1975 c1967] 342 p. 20 cm. Originally published as Theologieder Hoffnung. 5th. ed. Munich, Kaiser, 1965. Includes index. Includes bibliographical reference [BT821.2M6313] ISBN 0-06-065904-1 4.95 (pbk.)
1. Hope. 2. Eschatology. I. Title.
L.C. card no. for original edition: 67-21550.

MOODY, Dale. 236
The hope of glory. Grand Rapids, W. B. Eerdmans Pub. Co. [1964] 300 p. 23 cm. Bibliographical footnotes. [BT821.2.M65] 62-21367
1. Eschatology. I. Title.

MOODY, Dale 236
The hope of glory. Grand Rapids, Mich., Eerdmans [c.1964] 300p. 23cm. Bibl. 62-21367 4.95
1. Eschatology. I. Title.

MURRAY, Ralph L. 236
The Biblical shape of hope [by] Ralph L. Murray. Nashville, Broadman Press [1971] 95 p. 19 cm. Includes bibliographical references. [BV4638.M84] 79-143283 ISBN 0-8054-1122-4
1. Hope. I. Title.

NIETZSCHE, Friedrich Wilhelm, 236
1844-1900.
The Antichrist. New York, Arno Press, 1972. 60 p. 24 cm. (The Atheist viewpoint) Reprint of the 1930 ed. [B3313.A8E5 1972] 70-161338 ISBN 0-405-03799-6
1. Christianity—Controversial literature. I. Title. II. Series.

OBER, Douglas. 236
The great world crisis. Wheaton, Ill., Van Kampen Press [1950] 141 p. 20 cm. [BT875.O2] 50-2411
1. End of the world. 2. Jews—Restoration. 3. Bible—Prophecies. I. Title.

OLSEN, Benjamin David. 236
The veil was rent and I saw ... Richmond, Calif., Trump of God Pub. Co. [1969] 188 p. illus. 22 cm. [BT821.2.O47] 79-13520
1. Eschatology. I. Title.

PEEL, Malcolm Lee. 236
The Epistle to Rheginos; a Valentinian letter on the resurrection; introduction, translation, analysis, and exposition. Philadelphia, Westminster Press [1969] xv, 208 p. 23 cm. (The New Testament library) Based on the author's thesis, Yale. Bibliography: p. [181]-183. [BT870.P4 1969] 70-89686 ISBN 0-664-20877-0 10.00
1. Resurrection—Early works to 1800. 2. Eschatology—Early works to 1800. 3. Gnosticism. I. Treatise concerning the resurrection. II. Title.

PELIKAN, Jaroslav, 1923- 236
The shape of death; life, death, and immortality in the early fathers. New York, Abingdon Press [1961] 128p. 20cm. [BT821.2.P4] 61-5197
1. Eschatology—History of doctrines. 2. Death. 3. Immortality. 4. Fathers of the church. I. Title.

PELIKAN, Jaroslav Jan 236
1923-
The shape of death; life, death, and immortality in the early fathers. New York, Abingdon [1967] 128p. 19cm. [BT821.2.P4] 61-5197 1.25 pap.,
1. Eschatology—History of doctrines. 2. Death. 3. Immortality. 4. Fathers of the church. I. Title.

PELIKAN, Jaroslav Jan, 1923- 236
The shape of death; life, death, and immortality in the early fathers. New York, Abingdon Press [1961] 128 p. 20 cm. [BT821.2.P4] 61-5197
1. Eschatology—History of doctrines. 2. Death. 3. Immortality. 4. Fathers of the church. I. Title.

PELIKAN, Jaroslav Jan, 1923- 236
The shape of death; life, death, and immortality in the early fathers. New York, Abingdon [1967] 128p. 19cm. [BT821.2.P4] 61-5197 1.25 pap.,
1. Eschatology—History of doctrines. 2. Death. 3. Immortality. 4. Fathers of the church. I. Title.

PERKINS, James Scudday. 236
Experiencing reincarnation / James S. Perkins ; pen drawings by author. Wheaton, Ill. : Theosophical Pub. House, c1977. ix, 192 p. : ill. ; 21 cm. (A Quest book) Includes index. Bibliography: p. 187-189. [BL515.P465] 77-5249 ISBN 0-8356-0500-0 pbk. : 3.95
1. Reincarnation. I. Title.

*PETERSEN, Bill 236
The last days of man / Bill Petersen New York : Warner ,1977 190 p. ; 18 cm. [BS680.E8] ISBN 0-446-59708-2 pbk. : 1.75
1. Eschatology—Biblical teaching. I. Title.

PETRY, Ray C, 1903- 236
Christian eschatology and social thought; a historical essay on the social implications of some selected aspects in Christian eschatology to A. D. 1500. New York, Abingdon Press [c1956] 415p. 24cm. Bibliography: p. 381-396. [BT821.P45] 56-5372
1. Eschatology—History of doctrines. 2. Sociology, Christian—Early church. 3. Sociology, Christian—Middle Ages. I. Title.

PHILLIPS, Ordis E 1886- 236
Birth pangs of a new age. [2d ed.] Philadelphia, Hebrew Christian Fellowship [1955] 163p. 21cm. [BT875.P45 1955] 55-57987
1. End of the world. I. Title.

PLUEGER, Aaron Luther, 1926- 236
Things to come for planet Earth : what the Bible says about the last times / Aaron Luther Plueger. St. Louis : Concordia Pub. House, c1977. 96 p. : ill. ; 21 cm. Includes bibliographical references. [BS680.E8P58] 77-23598 ISBN 0-570-03762-X pbk. : 2.95
1. Bible—Prophecies. 2. Eschatology—Biblical teaching. I. Title.

POHLE, Joseph, 1852-1922. 236
Eschatology; or, The Catholic doctrine of the last things; a dogmatic treatise. Authorized English version with some abridgment and additional references, by Arthur Preuss. Westport, Conn., Greenwood Press [1971] 164 p. 23 cm. Reprint of the 1917 ed., which was originally published as v. 7 of the author's Lehrbuch der Dogmatik in sieben Buchern. Includes bibliographical references. [BT821.P6413 1971] 72-109823 ISBN 0-8371-4314-4
1. Eschatology.

PRICE, Walter K. 236
The coming antichrist, by Walter K. Price. Chicago, Moody Press [1974] 240 p. 22 cm. Bibliography: p. 224-231. [BT985.P7] 73-15088 ISBN 0-8024-1602-0 4.95
1. Antiochus IV, Epiphanes, King of Syria, d. 164 B.C. 2. Antichrist. I. Title.

THE Problem of eschatology. 236
Edited by Edward Schillebeeckx [and] Boniface Willems. New York, Paulist Press [1969] viii, 167 p. 24 cm. (Concilium: theology in the age of renewal. Dogma, v. 41) Bibliographical footnotes. [BT823.P7] 79-76195 4.50
1. Eschatology—Addresses, essays, lectures. I. Schillebeeckx, Edward Cornelis Florentius Alfons, 1914- ed. II. Willems, Boniface A., 1926- ed. III. Series: Concilium (New York) v. 41

QUISTORP, Heinrich. 236
Calvin's doctrine of the last things. Translated by Harold Knight. Richmond, John Knox Press [1955] 200p. 22cm. Translation of Die letxten Dinge im Zeugnis Calvins. [BX9418.Q52 1955] 56-1188
1. Calvin, Jean, 1509-1564. 2. Eschatology—History of doctrines I. Title.

ROBERSON, Lee. 236
Death. . . and after! Wheaton, Ill., Sword of the Lord Publishers [c1954] 96p. 21cm. [BT823.R5] 55-20573
1. Eschatology—Sermons. 2. Baptists—Sermons. 3. Sermons, American. I. Title.

ROBINSON, John Arthur Thomas, Bp., 1919- 236
In the end, God [by] John A. T. Robinson. [1st ed.] New York, Harper & Row [1968] xii, 148 p. 21 cm. (Religious perspectives, v. 20) Bibliography: p. 141-146. [BT821.2.R6 1968] 68-17582
1. Eschatology. I. Title. II. Series.

RYRIE, Charles Caldwell, 1925- 236
The living end / Charles Caldwell Ryrie. Old Tappan, N.J. : Revell, c1976. p. cm. [BS647.2.R93] 76-4772 ISBN 0-8007-0799-0 : 4.95
1. Bible—Prophecies. I. Title.

SCHWARZ, Hans, 1939- 236
On the way to the future; a Christian view of eschatology in the light of current trends in religion, philosophy, and science. Minneapolis, Augsburg Pub. House [1972] 254 p. 23 cm. Bibliography: p. 230-240. [BT821.2.S355] 78-176479 ISBN 0-8066-1208-8 6.95
1. Eschatology. I. Title.

SEYMOUR, St. John Drelincourt. 236
Irish visions of the other-world; a contribution to the study of mediaeval visions, by St. John D. Seymour. New York, Lemma Pub. Co. [1973] p. cm. Reprint of the 1930 ed. published by Society for Promoting Christian Knowledge, London. Bibliography: p. [BT833.S4 1973] 72-87987 ISBN 0-87696-055-7 12.50
1. Visions. 2. Eschatology—History of doctrines. I. Title.

SHIRES, Henry M. 236
The eschatology of Paul in the light of modern scholarship. Philadelphia, Westminster [c.1966] 287p. 21cm. bBibl. [BS2655.E7S5] 66-10339 6.95
1. Bible. N.T. Epistles of Paul—Theology. I. Title.

SHIRES, Henry M 236
The eschatology of Paul in the light of modern scholarship, by Henry M. Shires. Philadelphia, Westminster Press [1966] 287 p. 21 cm. Bibliography: p. [265]-273. [BS2655.E7S5] 66-10339
1. Bible. N. T. Epistles of Paul—Theology. I. Title.

SIEKMANN, Theodore C 236
Come the end; instructions for young people on the last things. New York, J. F. Wagner [1951] 131 p. 21 cm. [BT821.S5] 51-28815
1. Eschatology. I. Title.

SIMCOX, Carroll Eugene, 1912- 236
Is death the end? The Christian answer. Greenwich, Conn., Seabury Press, 1959. 96 p. 20 cm. Includes bibliography. [BT821.1.S5] 59-9963
1. Eschatology. I. Title.

SIMPSON, Michael. 236
The theology of death and eternal life. Notre Dame, Ind., Fides [1971] 95 p. 19 cm. (Theology today, no. 42) Cover title: Death and eternal life. Bibliography: p. 95. [BT821.2.S52] 74-30784 ISBN 0-85342-259-1 0.95
1. Eschatology. 2. Death. 3. Future life. I. Title. II. Title: Death and eternal life.

SMITH, Chuck, 1927- 236
The soon to be revealed Antichrist : [Bible exposition] / by Chuck Smith. Costa Mesa, Calif. : Maranatha Evangelical Association, c1976. 46 p. ; 18 cm. [BT985.S57] 76-7450 0.95
1. Bible—Prophecies. 2. Antichrist. I. Title.

SMITH, Wilbur Moorehead, 1894- 236
You can know the future [by] Wilbur M. Smith. Glendale, Calif., G/L Regal Books [1971] 118 p. 18 cm. [BS647.2.S62] 75-169845 ISBN 0-8307-0110-9 1.25
1. Bible—Prophecies. 2. Eschatology—Biblical teaching. I. Title.

STAM, Cornelius Richard, 1908- 236
Man, his nature and destiny. Chicago, Berean Bible Society [1961] 219 p. 20 cm. [BT821.2S.7] 61-4437
1. Eschatology. I. Title.

STAM, Cornelius Richard, 1908- 236
Man, his nature and destiny. Chicago 35, 7609 W. Belmont Ave. Berean Bible Society, [c.1961] 219p. 61-4437 3.00
1. Eschatology. I. Title.

STRAUSS, Lehman. 236
The end of this present world. Grand Rapids, Zondervan [1968,c.1967] 133p. 23cm. Bibl. [BS647.2.S68] 67-22683 3.95 bds.,
1. Bible—Prophecies. I. Title.

SUMMERS, Ray. 236
The life beyond. Nashville, Broadman Press [1959] 233 p. 22 cm. Includes bibliography. [BT821.2.S8] 59-5863
1. Eschatology. I. Title.

TENNYSON, Elwell Thomas, 1899- 236
The time of the end. Jefferson City, Mo., Harvest Publishers [c1951] 328 p. 24 cm. [BT875.T34] 52-680
1. End of the world. I. Title.

THOMPSON, Claude H 236
Theology of the kerygma; a study in primitive preaching. Englewood Cliffs, N.J., Prentice-Hall, 1962. 174 p. 22 cm. [BS2545.E7T5] 62-15838
1. Eschatology — Biblical teaching. 2. Preaching — Hist. — Early church. 3. Bible. N.T. — Theology. I. Title.

THOMPSON, Claude H. 236
Theology of the kerygma; a study in primitive preaching. Englewood Cliffs, N.J., Prentice [c.] 1962. 174p. 22cm. 62-15838 5.35
1. Eschatology—Biblical teaching. 2. Preaching—Hist.—Early church. 3. Bible. N.T.—Theology. I. Title.

TOMBLER, John W. 236
The raptured : a Catholic view of the latter days and the Second Coming / John W. Tombler and Hubert J. Funk. East Orange, N.J. : Trumpet Press, c1977. viii, 179 p. ; 23 cm. [BT887.T65] 77-80110 ISBN 0-918952-01-8 : 4.95
1. Rapture (Christian eschatology) I. Funk, Hubert J., joint author. II. Title.

TOON, Peter, 1939- 236
Puritans, the Millennium and the future of Israel: Puritan eschatology, 1600 to 1660: a collection of essays; edited by Peter Toon with contributions by B. S. Capp [and others] Cambridge, James Clarke, 1970. 157 p. 23 cm. Includes bibliographical references. [BT819.5.T65] 70-858762 £1.35
1. Eschatology—History of doctrines—Addresses, essays, lectures. 2. Millennium—History of doctrines—Addresses, essays, lectures. 3. Puritans—England—Addresses, essays, lectures. I. Capp, B. S. II. Title.

WARD, Harry E 1888- 236
Christ's theory and resurrection power. [1st ed.] New York, Greenwich Book Publishers, 1957. 77 p. 22 cm. [BT875.W27] 57-9274
1. End of the world. I. Title.

WARD, William B. 236
After death, what? By William B. Ward. Richmond, John Knox Press [1965] 95 p. 19 cm. (Chime paperbacks) [BT823.W3] 65-10754
1. Eschatology — Addresses, essays, lectures. I. Title.

WARD, William B. 236
After death, what? Richmond, Va., Knox [c.1965] 95p. 19cm. (Chime paperbacks) [BT823.W3] 65-10754 1.00 pap.,
1. Eschatology—Addresses, essays, lectures. I. Title.

WAUGH, Raymond A. 236
America educates for Antichrist : pungent words on America's educational plight / by Raymond A. Waugh, Sr. Ashland, Ky. : Economy Printers, c1977. vi, 47 p. ; 21 cm. [BT985.W36] 77-77671
1. Antichrist. 2. United States—Moral conditions. 3. Sin. I. Title.

WICKLOW, William Cecil James Philip John Paul Howard, 8th earl of, ed. 236
Life after death, an anthology. Westminster, Md., Newman Press [1959] 117p. 19cm. 60-16004 2.75
1. Eschatology. I. Title.

WILCOX, Llewellyn A 236
Now is the time. Escondido, Calif., Outdoor Pictures [1962, c1961] 279 p. 22 cm. [BX6154.W556] 62-19003
1. Eschatology. 2. Seventh-Day Adventists Doctrinal and controversial works. I. Title.

WILCOX, Llewellyn A. 236
Now is the time, by Llewellyn A. Wilcox. Rev. ed. Escondido, Calif., Outdoor Pictures [1966] 279 p. 22 cm. [BX6154.W556 1966] 66-19548
1. Seventh-Day Adventists—Doctrinal and controversial works. 2. Eschatology. I. Title.

WILDER, Amos Niven, 1895- 236
Eschatology and ethics in the teaching of Jesus, Rev.ed. New York, Harper [1950] 223 p. 21 cm. Bibliography: p. 215-219. [BS2417.E7W5] 50-6434
1. Jesus Christ—Teachings. 2. Eschatology—Biblical teaching. 3. Kingdom of God—Biblical teaching. 4. Jesus Christ—Ethics. I. Title.

WILLIS, Charles DuBois. 236
End of days, 1971-2001 : an eschatological study / Charles D. Willis. 1st ed. New York : Exposition Press, [1972] 121 p. : ill. ; 21 cm. Bibliography: p. [118]-121. [BS647.2.W5] 75-305286 ISBN 0-682-47385-5 : 7.50
1. Bible—Prophecies. 2. Eschatology. I. Title.

WILLMINGTON, H. L. 236
The King is coming; an outline study of the last days [by] H. L. Willmington. With a foreword by Jerry Falwell. Wheaton, Ill., Tyndale House Publishers [1973] 236 p. 22 cm. Includes bibliographical references. [BS680.E8W54] 73-81006 ISBN 0-8423-2085-7
1. Eschatology—Biblical teaching. I. Title.

WINKLHOFER, Alois, 1907- 236
The coming of His Kingdom; a theology of the last things. [Tr. from German by A. V. Littledale. New York] Herder & Herder [1963] 253p. 22cm. 62-20156 4.95
1. Eschatology. I. Title.

CARGAS, Harry J., comp. 236'.08
Death and hope, edited by Harry J. Cargas and Ann White. New York, Corpus Books [1971, c1970] 138 p. 21 cm. Includes bibliographical references. [BT825.C37] 79-102777 7.50
1. Death—Addresses, essays, lectures. 2. Hope—Addresses, essays, lectures. I. White, Ann, joint comp. II. Title.

GOLDBRUNNER, Josef, ed. 236.08
The dimension of future in our faith. Ed. by Josef Goldbrunner. Tr. by Sister M. Veronica Riedl. [Notre Dame] Univ. of Notre Dame Pr., 1966. 137p. 18cm. (Contemporary catechetics ser.) Tr. of Der Zukunftsbezug in der Verkundigung. Bibl. [BT821.2.G6413] 66-14633 1.25
1. Eschatology—Addresses, essays,lectures. I. Title.

GOLDBRUNNER, Josef, ed. 236.08
The dimension of future in our faith. Edited by Josef Goldbrunner. Translated by Sister M. Veronica Riedl. Notre Dame, University of Notre Dame Press, 1966. 137 p. 18 cm. (Contemporary catechetics series) Translation of Der Zukunftsbezug in der Verkundigung. Bibliographical footnotes. [BT821.2.G6413] 66-14633
1. Eschatology — Addresses, Essays, lectures. I. Title.

CROWDER, Wilbur S 236.088
Up to infinity. New York, Commet Press Books [1955, c1954] 88p. 23cm. [BF1999.C74] 55-825
I. Title.

PELIKAN, Jaroslav Jan, 1923- 236.09
The finality of Jesus Christ in an age of universal history; a dilemma of the third century, by Jaroslav Pelikan. Richmond, Va., Knox [1966, c.1965] 71p. 22cm. (Ecumenical studies in hist., no. 3) bBibl. [BR115.H5P4] 66-12354 1.75 pap.,
1. History (Theology) 2. Eschatology History of doctrines. I. Title. II. Series.

ROWELL, Geoffrey. 236'.09'034
Hell and the Victorians; a study of the nineteenth-century theological controversies concerning eternal punishment and the future life. Oxford, Clarendon Press, 1974. xii, 242 p. 23 cm. Bibliography: p. [222]-234. [BT819.5.R68] 74-174598 ISBN 0-19-826638-3
1. Eschatology—History of doctrines—19th century. 2. Great Britain—Religion—19th century. I. Title.
Distributed by Oxford University Press, New York; 15.75.

CALIAN, Carnegie Samuel. 236'.0924
Berdyaev's philosophy of hope; a contribution to Marxist-Christian dialogue, by C. S. Calian. Minneapolis, Augsburg Pub. House [1969, c1968] 134 p. 22 cm. First published in 1965 under title: The significance of eschatology in the thoughts of Nicolas Berdyaev. Bibliography: p. [126]-132. [B4238.B44C33 1969] 69-14183 2.50
1. Berdiaev, Nikolai Aleksandrovich, 1874-1948. 2. Eschatology—History of doctrines. I. Title.

ALLEN, R. Earl 236.1
Christian comfort [three messages of consolation for the difficulties of life] Nashville, Broadman [c.1965] 44p. 22cm. [BV4905.2.A43] 65-19547 1.50 bds.,
1. Consolation—Sermons. 2. Baptists—Sermons. 3. Sermons, American. I. Title.

ASQUITH, Glenn H. 236'.1
Death is all right [by] Glenn H. Asquith. Nashville, Abingdon Press [1970] 64 p. 18 cm. [BT825.A76] 79-124746 2.50
1. Death—Meditations. I. Title.

BAYLY, Joseph T. 236'.1
The view from a hearse; [a christian view of death, by] Joseph Bayly. Elgin, Ill., D. C. Cook Pub. Co. [1969] 95 p. 18 cm. [BT825.B38] 70-87318 0.95
1. Death. I. Title.

BAYLY, Joseph T. 236'.1
The view from a hearse [by] Joseph Bayly. [Rev. and expanded ed.] Elgin, Il[l.] D. C. Cook Pub. Co. [1973] 122 p. 18 cm. Bibliography: p. 122. [BT825.B38 1973] 73-168241 ISBN 0-912692-01-4 1.25
1. Death. I. Title.

BELGUM, David Rudolph, 1922- 236.1
His death and ours; meditations on death based on the seven last words. Minneapolis, Augsburg Pub. House [1958] 65p. 20cm. [BT825.B4] 58-6617
1. Death—Meditations. 2. Jesus Christ—Seven last words. I. Title.

BELGUM, David Rudolph, 1922- 236.1
His death and ours; meditations on death based on the seven last words. Minneapolis, Augsburg Pub. House [1958] 65 p. 20 cm. [BT825.B4] 58-6617
1. Death — Meditations. 2. Jesus Christ — Seven last words. I. Title.

BOROS, Ladislaus, 1927- 236.1
The mystery of death. [Translation by Gregory Bainbridge. New York] Herder and Herder [1965] x, 201 p. 21 cm. Bibliographical references included in "Notes" (p. 171-201) [BT825.B563] 65-13489
1. Death. I. Title.

BOROS, Ladislaus, 1927- 236.1
The mystery of death [Tr. from German by Gregory Bainbridge. New York] Herder & Herder [c.1965] x, 201p. 21cm. Bibl. [BT825.B563] 65-13489 4.50
1. Death. I. Title.

BROOKS, D. P. 236'.1
Dealing with death—a Christian perspective [by] D. P. Brooks. Nashville, Broadman Press [1974] 126 p. 21 cm. Includes bibliographical references. [BT825.B74] 73-85697 ISBN 0-8054-8229-6 1.50 (pbk.)
1. Death. I. Title.

DEATH—JESUS made it all different / edited by Miriam G. Moran. New Canaan, Conn. : Keats Pub., 1977. 140 p. ; 18 cm. (A Pivot family reader) (A Pivot book) [BT825.D38] 76-58768 1.95 236'.1
1. Death—Addresses, essays, lectures. 2. Consolation—Addresses, essays, lectures. I. Moran, Miriam G.

DONNE, John, 1572-1631. 236'.1
Deaths duell : a sermon delivered before King Charles I in the beginning of Lent 1630/1 / by John Donne ; edited with a postscript by Geoffrey Keynes. Boston : D. R. Godine, 1973. 54 p., 5 leaves of plates : ill. ; 28 cm. Includes bibliographical references. [BT825.D68 1973] 72-75133 ISBN 0-87923-050-9 : 12.00. ISBN 0-87923-051-7 de luxe : 40.00
1. Church of England—Sermons. 2. Death—Sermons. 3. Sermons, English. I. Title.

DOSS, Richard W. 236'.1
The last enemy; a Christian understanding of death [by] Richard W. Doss. [1st ed.] New York, Harper & Row [1974] xiv, 104 p. 21 cm. Includes bibliographical references. [BT825.D697 1974] 73-18700 ISBN 0-06-061980-5 4.95
1. Death. I. Title.

DOTY, William Lodewick, 1919- 236'.1
Where is your victory? Death as a dynamic theme of Christian spirituality, by William L. Doty. Paterson, N.J., St. Anthony Guild Press [1970] ix, 190 p. 21 cm. [BT825.D7] 72-97815 2.50
1. Death. I. Title.

DUNN, Paul H. 236'.1
The birth that we call death / Paul H. Dunn, Richard M. Eyre. Salt Lake City : Bookcraft, c1976. 72 p. ; 24 cm. [BT825.D79] 76-5170 ISBN 0-88494-297-X : 3.50
1. Death. 2. Future life. I. Eyre, Richard M., joint author. II. Title.

ERASMUS, Desiderius, d.1536. 236'.1
The dyaloge called Funus; a translation of Erasmus's colloquy (1534) & A very pleasaunt & fruitful diologe called the Epicure; Gerrard's translation of Erasmus's colloquy (1545). Edited by Robert R. Allen. [Chicago] Published for the Newberry Library by the University of Chicago Press [1969] 114 p. illus., facsims. 24 cm. (The publications of the Renaissance Text Society, v. 3) The text of The dyaloge called Funus is based on the British Museum's copy. The text of A very pleasaunt & fruitful diologe called the Epicure (STC 10460) is based on the editor's thesis (Harvard, 1963) which was based on copies of the text in the Folger and Harvard University Libraries. Includes bibliographical references. [PA8509.F8E5] 79-92771 ISBN 0-226-21483-4
1. Death—Early works to 1800. I. Allen, Robert R., 1933- ed. II. Erasmus, Desiderius, d. 1536. Colloquia. Epicureus. English. 1969. III. Title. IV. Series: Renaissance English Text Society. Publications, v. 3

GATCH, Milton McC. 236'.1
Death; meaning and mortality in Christian thought and contemporary culture [by] Milton McC. Gatch. New York, Seabury Press [1969] viii, 216 p. 22 cm. Bibliographical references included in "Notes" (p. 188-209) [BT825.G35] 69-13541 5.95
1. Death. 2. Immortality—History of doctrines. 3. Resurrection—History of doctrines. I. Title.

GREENSTOCK, David L 236.1
Death: the glorious adventure. Westminster, Md., Newman Press [1956] 112p. 19cm. [BT825.G68] 56-14063
1. Death. I. Title.

GREENSTOCK, David L 236.1
Death: the glorious adventure. Westminster, Md., Newman Press [1956] 112p. 19cm. [BT825.G68] 56-14063
1. Death. I. Title.

GRUBER, Otto. 236.1
When I die. [1st ed.] New York, Vantage Press [c1955] 68p. 21cm. [BT825.G7] 55-11667
1. Death. I. Title.

HERHOLD, Robert M. 236'.1
Learning to die, learning to live / Robert M. Herhold. Philadelphia : Fortress Press, c1976. 96 p. : ill. ; 19 cm. [BT825.H44] 76-7861 ISBN 0-8006-1232-9 : 2.95
1. Death. I. Title.

HOLDEN, Douglas T., 1936- 236'.1
Death shall have no dominion; a New Testament study [by] Douglas T. Holden. St. Louis, Bethany Press [1971] 190 p. 23 cm. Bibliography: p. 189-190. [BS2545.D45H65] 79-127851 ISBN 0-8272-0610-0 4.95
1. Death—Biblical teaching. I. Title.

IRISH, Jerry A., 1936- 236'.1
A boy thirteen : reflections on death / Jerry A. Irish. Philadelphia : Westminster Press, [1975] 62 p. ; 21 cm. Includes bibliographical references. [BT825.I74] 74-22318 ISBN 0-664-20720-0
1. Death. I. Title.

JUNGEL, Eberhard. 236'.1
Death, the riddle and the mystery / Eberhard Jungel ; translated by Iain and Ute Nicol. Philadelphia : Westminster Press, [1975] c1974. viii, 141 p. ; 21 cm. Translation of Tod. Includes bibliographical references. [BT825.J8413 1975] 74-28021 ISBN 0-664-20821-5 : 6.95
1. Death. I. Title.

KANTONEN, Taito Almar, 1900- 236.1
Life after death. Philadelphia, Muhlenberg [c.1962] 54p. (Fortress bk.). 62-8205 1.00 bds.,
1. Eschatology. I. Title.

KLOPFENSTEIN, Janette. 236'.1
Tell me about death, Mommy / Janette Klopfenstein ; introd. by J. Lorne Peachey. Scottdale, Pa. : Herald Press, c1977. 110 p. ; 18 cm. [BT825.K55] 77-76989 ISBN 0-8361-1821-9 : 1.75
1. Death. 2. Children and death. I. Title.

LYMAN, Mary Redington (Ely) 236.1
Death and the Christian answer. [Wallingford, Pa., Pendle Hill, 1960] 16p. Includes bibliography. 19cm. (Pendle Hill pamphlet 107) 60-9784 .35 pap.,
1. Death. I. Title.

MCGEACHY, D. P. 236.1
A matter of life and death, by D. P. McGeachy, iii. Richmond, Knox [1966] 80p. 19cm. (Chime paperbacks) bBibl. [BT825.M18] 66-11604 1.00 pap.,
1. Death. I. Title.

MADDEN, Myron C. 236'.1
Raise the dead! / Myron C. Madden. Waco, Tex. : Word Books, [1975] 118 p. ; 21 cm. Includes bibliographical references. [BT825.M275] 74-27483 4.95
1. Death. I. Title.

MARXHAUSEN, Joanne. 236'.1
If I should die, if I should live / written by Joanne Marxhausen ; art by Benjamin Marxhausen. St. Louis : Concordia Pub. House, [1975] [48] p. : col. ill. ; 27 cm. Examines death from the perspective of the Christian who looks forward to everlasting life. [BT825.M34] 75-11648 ISBN 0-570-03440-X : 4.95
1. Death—Juvenile literature. I. Marxhausen, Benjamin. II. Title.

MILLER, Randolph Crump, 1910- 236'.1
Live until you die. Philadelphia, United Church Press [1973] 157 p. 22 cm. "A Pilgrim Press book." Includes bibliographical references. [BT825.M5] 73-8657 ISBN 0-8298-0253-3 5.95
1. Death. I. Title.

MILLS, Liston O., comp. 236'.1
Perspectives on death. Liston O. Mills, editor. Nashville, Abingdon Press [1969] 288 p. 23 cm. Essays by L. H. Silberman and others originally presented as lectures at Vanderbilt University in 1967. Bibliographical footnotes. [BD444.M5] 69-19742 6.50
1. Death—Addresses, essays, lectures. I. Title.

OCHS, Robert, 1930- 236'.1
The death in every now. New York, Sheed and Ward [1969] 159 p. 21 cm. Bibliography: p. 158-159. [BT825.O25] 69-19253 4.25
1. Rahner, Karl, 1904- Schriften zur Theologie. 2. Death. I. Title.

PARVILLEZ, Alphonse de 236.1
Joy in the face of death. Tr. [from French] by Pierre de Fontnouvelle. New York, Desclee, 1963. vii, 253p. 21cm. Bibl. 63-15200 3.95
1. Consolation. 2. Death. I. Title.

PERRET, Andre. 236.1
Toward our Father's house. Translated R.N.Albright. St. Louis, Herder [1959] 118p. 21cm. [BT825.P42] 59-7586
1. Death. I. Title.

PERRET, Andre S 236.1
Toward our Father's house. Translated by R. N. Albright. St. Louis, Herder [1959] 118 p. 21 cm. [BT825.P42] 59-7586
1. Death. I. Title.

PREACHING about death : 236'.1
eighteen sermons dealing with the experience of death from the Christian perspective / edited by Alton M. Motter. Philadelphia : Fortress Press, [1975] vii, 86 p. ; 22 cm. Includes bibliographical references. [BT825.P73] 74-26336 ISBN 0-8006-1098-9 pbk. : 2.95
1. Death—Sermons. 2. Sermons, American. I. Motter, Alton M.

RAHNER, Karl, 1904- 236.1
On the theology of death. [Tr. from German by Charles H. Henkey. New York] Herder & Herder [c.1961] 127p. (Quaestiones disputatae, 2) 61-11443 2.25 pap.,
I. Title.

RUANE, Gerald P. 236'.1
Birth to birth : the life-death mystery / Gerald P. Ruane ; photo editor, M. Gerarda. New York : Alba House, c1976. viii, 96 p. : ill. ; 21 cm. [BT825.R76] 75-40300 ISBN 0-8189-0326-0 pbk. : 2.95
1. Death. 2. Life. 3. Consolation. I. Title.

SCHMITT, Abraham. 236'.1
Dialogue with death / Abraham Schmitt. Waco, Tex. : Word Books, c1976. 132 p. ; 23 cm. [BT825.S328] 76-1731 ISBN 0-87680-454-7 : 5.95
1. Death. I. Title.

STARENKO, Ronald C. 236'.1
God, grass, and grace; a theology of death [by] Ronald C. Starenko. St. Louis, Concordia Pub. House [1975] 80 p. 21 cm. Bibliography: p. 78-80. [BT825.S78] 74-18244 ISBN 0-570-03198-2 2.50 (pbk.)
1. Death. I. Title.

*STUTZMAN, D. J. 236.1
The language of the death bed [Rev. ed.] LaGrange, Ind. 46761, Pathway Pub. Corp. [1965,c.1958] xii, 211p. 23cm. 3.00 bds.,
I. Title.

THIELICKE, Helmut, 1908- 236'.1
Death and life. Translated by Edward H. Schroeder. Philadelphia, Fortress Press [1970] xxvi, 230 p. 23 cm. Translation of Tod und Leben, Studien zur christlichen Anthropologie. Includes bibliographical references. [BT825.T4713] 75-117978 7.50
1. Death. I. Title.

VAN Zeller, Hubert, 1905- 236.1
Death in other words; a presentation for beginners. Springfield, Ill., Templegate [c1963] 96 p. 20 cm. ([His In other words series]) [BT825.V3] 63-23647
1. Death. I. Title. II. Series.

VAN ZELLER, Hubert, 1905- 236.1
Death in other words; a presentation for beginners. Springfield, Ill., Templegate [c.1963] 96p. 20cm. (His In other words ser.) 63-23647 2.95
1. Death. I. Title.

WATTS, Richard G., 1934- 236'.1
Straight talk about death with young people / by Richard G. Watts. Philadelphia : Westminster Press, [1975] 92 p. : ill. ; 19 cm. Includes bibliographical references. [BT825.W33] 75-12551 ISBN 0-664-24765-2 pbk. : 2.95
1. Death—Juvenile literature. I. Title.

WHITAKER, O'Kelley. 236'.1
Sister death / O'Kelley Whitaker. New York : Morehouse-Barlow, c1974. 110 p. ; 21 cm. Bibliography: p. 105-109. [BT825.W48] 74-80381 ISBN 0-8192-1182-6 pbk. : 4.50
1. Death. I. Title.

FARGUES, Marie 236.107
The child and the mystery of death. Tr. by Sister Gertrude. With discussion questions. Glen Rock, N.J., Paulist [1966] 96p. 19cm. (Deus bks.) [BT825.F2413] 66-22056 .75 pap.,
1. Death—Study and teaching. 2. Children and death. I. Title.

ALDWINCKLE, Russell Foster. 236'.2
Death in the secular city; life after death in contemporary theology and philosophy, by Russell Aldwinckle. Grand Rapids, Eerdmans [1974, c1972] 194 p. 21 cm. Bibliography: p. 185-189. [BT825.A36 1974] 74-757 ISBN 0-8028-1574-X 3.95 (pbk.)
1. Death. 2. Future life. I. Title.

ALGER, William Rounseville, 1822-1905. 236'.2
The destiny of the soul; a critical history of the doctrine of a future life. 10th ed., with six new chapters. New York, Greenwood Press, 1968 [c1878] 2 v. (xi, 1008 p.) 23 cm. First published under title: A critical history of the doctrine of a future life. "The literature of the doctrine of a future life ... by Ezra Abbot": v. 2, p. [771]-1008. [BT901.A3 1968] 68-19263
1. Future life—History of doctrines. 2. Future life—Bibliography. I. Abbot, Ezra, 1819-1884. The literature of the doctrine of a future life. II. Title.

BEDFORD, Sidney McHenry. 236.2
When eternity dawns, by Sidney M. Bedford, Sr. Boston, Christopher Pub. House [1966] 120 p. 21 cm. Bibliographical references included in "Acknowledgements" (p. 117-120) [BT902.B4] 66-23209
1. Future life. I. Title.

BEDFORD, Sidney McHenry 236.2
When eternity dawns. Boston, Christopher Pub. House [c.1966] 120p. 21cm. Bibl. [BT902.B4] 66-23209 3.00
1. Future life. I. Title.

CARTER, James Everard, 1906- 236'.2
What is to come? / James E. Carter. Nashville : Broadman Press, c1975. 153 p. ; 18 cm. Includes bibliographical references. [BT902.C37] 75-2929 ISBN 0-8054-1933-0 pbk. : 1.95
1. Future life. 2. Eschatology. I. Title.

CROWTHER, Duane S. 236'.2
Life everlasting [by] Duane S. Crowther. Salt Lake City, Bookcraft [1967] xix, 399 p. port. 24 cm. Bibliography: p. 371-373. [BX8635.2.C73] 67-25433
1. Mormons and Mormonism—Doctrinal and controversial works. 2. Future life. I. Title.

FERBER, Adolph C. 236'.2
We are immortal / A. C. Ferber. 1st ed. Hicksville, N.Y. : Exposition Press, [1975] 143 p. ; 22 cm. (An Exposition-testament book) Includes excerpts from the works of E. Swedenborg and others. Includes bibliographical references. [BX8711.F47] 75-319949 ISBN 0-682-48288-9 : 7.00
1. Swedenborg, Emanuel, 1688-1772. 2. Future life—History of doctrines. I. Title.

FORD, William Herschel, 1900- 236'.2
Simple sermons on heaven, hell, and judgment, by W. Herschel Ford. Grand Rapids, Zondervan Pub. House [1969] 108 p. 21 cm. [BT823.F58] 69-11642 2.95
1. Eschatology—Sermons. 2. Baptists—Sermons. 3. Sermons, American. I. Title.

FORTMAN, Edmund J., 1901- 236'.2
Everlasting life after death / E. J. Fortman. New York : Alba House, c1976. xviii, 333 p. ; 22 cm. Bibliography: p. [323]-333. [BT902.F67] 76-41186 ISBN 0-8189-0333-3 : 6.95
1. Future life. I. Title.

GLASKIN, Gerald M., 1924- 236'.2
Windows of the mind: discovering your past and future lives through massage and mental exercise [by] G. M. Glaskin. New York, Delacorte Press [1974] 268 p. 22 cm. [BL515.G55] 73-19760 6.95
1. Reincarnation. I. Title.

GREELEY, Andrew M., 1928- 236'.2
Death & beyond / by Andrew Greeley. Chicago : Thomas More Press, c1976. 144 p. ; 22 cm. Includes bibliographical references. [BT902.G73] 76-356229 ISBN 0-88347-062-4 : 7.95
1. Future life. 2. Death. I. Title.

HODGKINSON, Frank Cyril. 236'.2
After our pilgrimage; what the Bible says about life after death [by] F. C. Hodgkinson. Valley Forge, Judson Press [1971, c1970] 96 p. 18 cm. [BS2417.F7H6 1971] 75-140962 ISBN 0-8170-0513-7 1.50
1. Future life—Biblical teaching. I. Title.

HOLL, Adolf. 236'.2
Death and the Devil / Adolf Holl ; translated by Matthew J. O'Connell. New York : Seabury Press, c1976. p. cm. Translation of Tod und Teufel. "A Crossroad book." Includes bibliographical references. [BD444.H5913] 76-13207 ISBN 0-8164-0313-9 : 8.95
1. Death. 2. Devil. I. Title.

HOWE, Quincy, 1934- 236'.2
Reincarnation for the Christian. Philadelphia, Westminster Press [1974] 112 p. 21 cm. Bibliography: p. [109]-112. [BL515.H65] 73-19758 ISBN 0-664-20996-3 4.95
1. Reincarnation. I. Title.

IN after days : 236'.2
thoughts on the future life / by W. D. Howells ... [et al.]. New York : Arno Press, 1977c1910 232 p., [8] leaves of plates : ill. ; 23 cm. (The Literature of death and dying) Reprint of the ed. published by Harper, New York. [BT899.I5 1977] 76-19576 ISBN 0-405-09574-0 : 18.00
1. Future life—Addresses, essays, lectures. I. Howells, William Dean, 1837-1920. II. Series.

THE Journey to the other world 236'.2
/ edited by H. R. Ellis Davidson. Ipswich : Published by D. S. Brewer and Rowman and Littlefield, Totowa, N.J., for the Folklore Society, 1975. 149 p. ; 23 cm. (Mistletoe books ; no. 2) Papers, given at a conference at the University of Exeter in April 1971, and sponsored by the Dept. of History and the London Folklore Society. Includes bibliographical references. [BL535.J68 1975] 74-22305 ISBN 0-87471-613-6 : 8.00
1. Future life. I. Davidson, Hilda Roderick Ellis, ed. II. Exeter, Eng. University. Dept. of History. III. Folk-lore Society, London. IV. Series: Folk-lore Society, London. Publications ; no. 2

KINGSLAKE, Brian, 1907- 236'.2
The Aqueduct papers; twenty interviews with an angel concerning life after death. North Qunicy, Mass., Christopher Pub. House [1970] 197 p. port. 22 cm. [BX8729.F8K5] 70-116035 4.95
1. New Jerusalem Church—Doctrinal and controversial works. 2. Future life. I. Title.

LOCKYER, Herbert. 236.2
Death and the life hereafter. Grand Rapids, Baker Book House [1975] 110 p. 18 cm. [BL535.L6] ISBN 0-8010-5551-2 1.25 (pbk.)
1. Heaven. 2. Future life. 3. Eschatology. I. Title.
L.C. card no. for original edition: 68-6204.

*MACARTHUR, Jack. 236.2
Exploring the next world. Foreword by Louis T. Talbot. Minneapolis, Minn., Bethany Fellowship [1973? c.1967] iv, 164 p. 18 cm. (Dimension Books) [BL535] ISBN 0-87123-124-7 1.25 (pbk.)
1. Future life. 2. Death. I. Title.

MACHOVEC, Frank J. 236'.2
Life after death : the chances, the choices / by

Frank J. MacHovec. Mount Vernon, N.Y. : Peter Pauper Press, c1975. 64 p. ; 20 cm. [BL535.M24] 75-327697 1.95
1. Future life. I. Title.

MAN'S destiny in 236'.2
eternity [by] Arthur H. Compton [and others] Freeport, N.Y., Books for Libraries Press [1970, c1949] vi, 238 p. 23 cm. (Essay index reprint series.) (The Garvin lectures) Contents.Contents.—Preface, by F. L. Windolph.—A modern concept of God, by A. H. Compton.—The immortality of man, by J. Maritain.—The idea of God in the mind of man, by M. Royden.—Psychical research and the life beyond death, by H. Hart.—Religion and modern knowledge, by R. Niebuhr.—Immortality in the light of science and philosophy, by W. E. Hocking.—"To whom shall ye liken God?" By C. E. Park.—Man's destiny in eternity, by W. L. Sperry.—The idea of God as affected by modern knowledge, by F. S. C. Northrop. Includes bibliographical references. [BT101.A1M3 1970] 75-117821 ISBN 0-8369-1762-6
1. God—Addresses, essays, lectures. 2. Immortality—Addresses, essays, lectures. 3. Religion and science—1946- —Addresses, essays, lectures. I. Compton, Arthur Holly, 1892-1962. II. Title. III. Series.

MOODY, Raymond A. 236'.2
Life after life / Raymond A. Moody, Jr. Harrisburg, Pa. : Stackpole Books, 1976. p. cm. [BL535.M64] 75-37963 ISBN 0-8117-0946-9 : 5.95
1. Future life—Case studies. 2. Death—Case studies. I. Title.

MOODY, Raymond A. 236'.2
Life after life : the investigation of a phenomenon, survival of bodily death / Raymond A. Moody, Jr. ; with a foreword by Elizabeth Kubler-Ross. Boston : G. K. Hall, 1977, c1975. xviii, 245 p. ; 25 cm. Large print ed. [BL535.M64 1977] 77-3218 ISBN 0-8161-6472-X lib.bdg. : 10.95
1. Future life—Case studies. 2. Death—Case studies. 3. Large type books. I. Title.

MOTYER, J. A. 236.2
After death; a sure and certain hope? Philadelphia, Westminster [1966, c.1965] 95p. 19cm. (Christian founds.) Bibl. [BT902.M67] 66-10324 1.25 pap.,
1. Future life. I. Title.

PANNETON, Georges. 236.2
Heaven or hell. Translated by Ann M. C. Forster. Westminster, Md., Newman Press, 1965. x, 360 p. 24 cm. Bibliography: p. 341-346. [BT832.P313] 65-23767
1. Heaven. 2. Hell. I. Title.

PANNETON, Georges 236.2
Heaven or hell. Tr. [from French] by Ann M. C. Forster. Westminster, Md., Newman [c.] 1965. x, 360p. 24cm. Bibl. [BT832.P313] 65-23767 6.95
1. Heaven. 2. Hell. I. Title.

PENDLETON, Charles 236'.2
Rittenhouse.
Space and extense in the spiritual world. Bryn Althyn, Pa., 1962. 66 p. 23 cm. [BX8711.P4] 63-36811
1. Swedenborg, Emanuel, 1688-1772. 2. Space and time. I. Title.

PETTYJOHN, Marie Louise. 236'.2
One immortal being / by Marie Louise Pettyjohn. New York : Philosophical Library, c1975. 117 p., [1] leaf of plates : ill. ; 22 cm. [BL515.P47] 75-7966 ISBN 0-8022-2168-8 : 8.75
1. Reincarnation. I. Title.

SCHLINK, Basilea. 236'.2
What comes after death? : the reality of heaven and hell / [by] Basilea Schlink ; [translated from the German]. London : Lakeland, 1976. 121 p. ; 18 cm. Translation of Holle, Himmel, Wirklichkeiten. Includes bibliographical references. [BT902.S3413] 76-378396 ISBN 0-551-00750-8 : £0.60
1. Future life. 2. Heaven. I. Title.

STOVER, Ross Harrison, 236'.2
1888-
What do we know about life after death? [By] Ross H. Stover. Grand Rapids, Zondervan Pub. House [1969] 96 p. 21 cm. (A Zondervan paperback) [BT901.S76 1969] 75-81062 0.95
1. Future life. I. Title.

STUDER, Gerald C. 236'.2
After death, what? / Gerald C. Studer ; introd. by Paul Erb. Scotdale, Pa. : Herald Press, c1976. 183 p. ; 18 cm. Includes bibliographical references and index. [BT902.S78] 75-38074 ISBN 0-8361-1792-1 pbk. : 1.95
1. Future life. I. Title.

*SWEDENBORG, Emanuel 236'.2
Heaven and its wonders and Hell, from Things seena nd heard. New York, Swedenborg Found., 1967. xvi, 496p. 18cm. First pub. in Latin, London, 1758. 1st English tr. pub. in U.S.A. in 1852. Introd. to the present ed. is taken from the Everyman lib. ed. of Swedenborg's Heaven and Hell. 1.00 pap.,
1. Heaven. 2. Hell. I. Title.

SWEDENBORG, Emanuel, 1688- 236'.2
1772.
Heaven and hell / Emanuel Swedenborg ; translated by George F. Dole. New York : Pillar Books, 1976. 426 p. ; 18 cm. Translation of De coelo et ejus mirabilibus. [BX8712.H5 1976] 75-21132 ISBN 0-89129-110-5 pbk. : 1.95
1. Heaven. 2. Hell. 3. Future life—Early works to 1800. I. Dole, George F. II. Title.

WEATHERHEAD, Leslie Dixon, 236'.2
1893-
Life begins at death [by] Leslie D. Weatherhead; replies to questions put to him by Norman French. Nashville, Abingdon Press [1970, c1969] 80 p. 19 cm. [BT904.W37] 73-97570 ISBN 0-687-21805-5 1.25
1. Future life—Miscellanea. I. French, Norman. II. Title.

WEISS, Jess E., comp. 236.2
The vestibule, edited and written by Jess E. Weiss. New York, Pocket Books [1974, c1972] 142 p. 18 cm. [BL535.W4] ISBN 0-671-78451-X 1.25 (pbk.)
1. Future life. 2. Death. I. Title.
L.C. card number for original edition: 72-78506. Contents omitted.

WEISS, Jess E., comp. 236'.2
The vestibule, by Jess E. Weiss. [1st ed.] Port Washington, N.Y., Ashley Books [1972] 128 p. 23 cm. Contents.—Rickenbacker, E. V. The Atlanta crash.—Jenkins, B. I was an atheist, until I died, as told to J. E. Weiss.—Sampson, M. C. When the curtains of death parted.—Ruopp, J. P. The window of heaven.—Ross, E. K. The experience of death.—Swedenborg, E. Heaven and hell.—Ritchie, G. G. Return from tomorrow.—Keller, H. My religion.—Snell, D. How it feels to die.—Trine, R. W. Character-building thought power.—Huffine, E. L. I watched myself die.—Goldsmith, J. Infinite way letters.—MacMillan, R. L. and Brown, K. W. G. Cardiac arrest remembered.—Lamsa, G. M. And the scroll opened.—Weiss, J. E. Death, where is thy sting. [BL535.W4] 72-78506 ISBN 0-87949-004-7 5.95
1. Future life. 2. Death. I. Title.

WHERE are the dead? 236'.2
Plainview, N.Y., Books for Libraries Press [1974] p. cm. (The Collected works of Arnold Bennett) Reprint of the 1928 ed. published by Cassell, London. [BT904.W48 1974] 74-17034 ISBN 0-518-19168-0
1. Future life—Addresses, essays, lectures. 2. Immortality—Addresses, essays, lectures.

WIERWILLE, Victor Paul. 236'.2
Are the dead alive now? Old Greenwich, Conn., Devin-Adair Co. [1971] 123 p. 21 cm. [BT902.W54] 74-179279 4.95
1. Future life. I. Title.

WINTER, David Brian. 236'.2
Hereafter: what happens after death? [By] David Winter. Wheaton, Ill., Shaw Publishers [1973, c1972] 91 p. illus. 18 cm. Includes bibliographical references. [BT902.W56 1973] 72-94097 ISBN 0-87788-341-6 1.25
1. Future life. I. Title.

FECHNER, Gustav Theodor, 236'.22
1801-1887.
The little book of life after death / by Gustav Theodor Fechner ; translated from the German by Mary C. Wadsworth. New York : Arno Press, 1977 [c1904] xxviii, 108 p. ; 21 cm. (The Literature of death and dying) Translation of Das Buchlein vom Leben nach dem Tode. Reprint of the ed. published by Little, Brown, Boston. [BT921.F2313 1977] 76-19570 ISBN 0-405-09565-1 lib.bdg. 12.00
1. Immortality. I. Title. II. Series.

FECHNER, Gustav Theodor, 236'.22
1801-1887.
The little book of life after death / by Gustav Theodor Fechner ; translated from the German by Mary C. Wadsworth. New York : Arno Press, 1977 [c1904] xxviii, 108 p. ; 21 cm. (The Literature of death and dying) Translation of Das Buchlein vom Leben nach dem Tode. Reprint of the ed. published by Little, Brown, Boston. [BT921.F2313 1977] 76-19570 ISBN 0-405-09565-1 lib.bdg. 12.00
1. Immortality. I. Title. II. Series.

GUERINI, Edmund W 1925- 236'.22
Evolution in the afterlife; the extended concepts of Pierre Teilhard de Chardin, by Edmund W. Guerini. [1st ed.] New York, Exposition Press [1967] 80 p. 21 cm. [BD423.G8] 67-29055
1. Immortality. I. Teilhard de Chardin, Pierre. II. Title.

GUERINI, Edmund W., 1925- 236'.22
Evolution in the afterlife; the extended concepts of Pierre Teilhard de Chardin, by Edmund W. Guerini. [1st ed.] New York, Exposition Press [1967] 80 p. 21 cm. [BD423.G8] 67-29055
1. Teilhard de Chardin, Pierre. 2. Immortality. I. Title.

JAMES, William, 1842- 236'.22
1910.
Human immortality : two supposed objections to the doctrine / by William James. Folcroft, Pa. : Folcroft Library Editions, 1977. p. cm. Reprint of the 1898 ed. published by Houghton, Mifflin, Boston, which was issued as the Ingersoll lecture of 1898. [BT921.2.J35 1977] 77-7140 ISBN 0-8414-5261-X lib. bdg. : 8.50
1. Immortality—Controversial literature. I. Title. II. Series: The Ingersoll lecture, Harvard University ; 1898.

JAMES, William, 1842- 236'.22
1910.
Human immortality : two supposed objections to the doctrine / by William James. Folcroft, Pa. : Folcroft Library Editions, 1977. p. cm. Reprint of the 1898 ed. published by Houghton, Mifflin, Boston, which was issued as the Ingersoll lecture of 1898. [BT921.2.J35 1977] 77-7140 ISBN 0-8414-5261-X lib. bdg. : 8.50
1. Immortality—Controversial literature. I. Title. II. Series: The Ingersoll lecture, Harvard University ; 1898.

MATTHEWS, Walter Robert, 236.22
1881-
The hope of immortality, by W. R. Matthews. [1st Amer. ed.] New York, Morehouse [1966] 76. [1]p. 19cm. Bibl. [BT921] 66-31344 2.75 bds.,
1. Immortality. I. Title.

OSLER, William, Sir, 236'.22
bart., 1849-1919.
Science and immortality / by William Osler. New York : Arno Press, 1977. 54 p. ; 21 cm. (The Literature of death and dying) Reprint of the 1904 ed. published by Houghton, Mifflin, Boston, and issued as the Ingersoll lecture, 1904. Includes bibliographical references. [BT921.O8 1977] 76-19586 ISBN 0-405-09581-3 : 10.00
1. Immortality—Addresses, essays, lectures. I. Title. II. Series. III. Series: The Ingersoll lecture, Harvard University, 1904.

PENELHUM, Terence, 1929- 236'.22
comp.
Immortality. Belmont, Calif., Wadsworth Pub. Co. [1973] 162 p. 21 cm. (Basic problems in philosophy series) Contents.Contents.—Geach, P. Immortality.—Price, H. H. Survival and the idea of "another world."—St. Paul. The resurrection of Christ and the resurrection of men. Cullmann, O. Immortality of the soul or resurrection of the dead?—Hick, J. Theology and verification.—St. Thomas Aquinas.—Price, H. H. The problem of life after death.—Flew, A. The question of survival.—Hick, J. Towards a Christian theology of death.—Bibliography (p. 159-162) [BL530.P43] 73-88463 ISBN 0-534-00333-8
1. Immortality. 2. Resurrection. 3. Future life. I. Title.

REICHENBACH, Bruce R. 236'.22
Is man the Phoenix? : A study of immortality / by Bruce R. Reichenbach. Grand Rapids : Eerdmans, c1977. p. cm. Includes index. [BT921.2.R44] 77-12148 ISBN 0-8028-1714-9 pbk. : 5.95
1. Immortality. 2. Future life. I. Title.

ROYCE, Josiah, 1855-1916. 236'.22
The conception of immortality. New York, Greenwood Press, 1968 [c1900] 91 p. 19 cm. (The Ingersoll lecture, 1899) Bibliographical references included in "Notes" (p. [81]-91) [BT921.R65 1968] 68-19293
1. Immortality—Addresses, essays, lectures. 2. Individuality. I. Title. II. Series: The Ingersoll lecture, Harvard University

SWIFT, Montgomery. 236'.22
Love-love / Montgomery Swift. LaSalle, Que. : Delta Can Press, c1972. 63 p. ; 18 cm. [BL530.S87] 75-305391 ISBN 0-919162-39-8
1. Immortality. I. Title.

WALTER ROBERT, 1881- 236.22
The hope of immortality, by W. R. Matthews. [1st Amer. ed.] New York, Morehouse [1966] 76. [1]p. 19cm. Bibl. [BT921] 66-31344 2.75 bds.,
1. Immortality. I. Title.

WARD, Elizabeth Stuart 236'.22
(Phelps) 1844-1911.
The struggle for immortality. Freeport, N.Y., Books for Libraries Press [1973] p. (Essay index reprint series) Reprint of the 1889 ed. published by Houghton, Mifflin, Boston. Contents.Contents.—What is a fact?—Is God good?—What does revelation reveal?—The struggle for immortality.—The Christianity of Christ.—The psychical opportunity.—The psychical wave. [BT921.W3 1973] 73-5706 ISBN 0-518-10121-5
1. Immortality. I. Title.

MOURANT, John 236'.22'0924
Arthur, 1903-
Augustine on immortality [by] John A. Mourant. [Villanova, Pa., Augustinian Institute, Villanova University, c1969] 138 p. 20 cm. (The Saint Augustine lecture series: Saint Augustine and the Augustinian tradition, 1968) Includes bibliographical references. [BR65.A9M65] 71-90917 4.00
1. Augustinus, Aurelius, Saint, Bp. of Hippo—Theology. 2. Immortality—History of doctrines. 3. Resurrection—Sermons. 4. Sermons, Latin—Translations into English. 5. Sermons, English—Translations from Latin. I. Title. II. Series.

FROOM, LeRoy Edwin, 236.2309
1890-
The conditionalist faith of our fathers; the conflict of the ages over the nature and destiny of man; v.2. Washington, D.C., Review & Herald [1965] 1v. illus. (pt. col.) ports. 24cm. Bibl. [BT930.F7] 64-17664 15.00
1. Annihilationism—Hist. I. Title.

BOUNDS, Edward McKendree, 236.24
1835-1913.
Heaven: a place, a city, a home. Grand Rapids, Baker Book House [1966] 151 p. 20 cm. Reprint of work first published in 1921. [BT846.B64 1966] 66-31500
1. Heaven. I. Title.

*COTHRAN, J. Guy 236.24
The Christian's home in glory. New York, Exposition [c.1965] 78p. 22cm. 3.00
I. Title.

*DIETEL, Mary Holder 236.24
Who wants to play a harp? Nashville, Southern Pub. [c.1965] 101p. 21cm. 2.95 bds.,
I. Title.

GREENE, Oliver B. 236'.24
Heaven, and other sermons, by Oliver B. Greene. Greenville, S.C., Gospel Hour [1969] 200 p. 21 cm. [BT846.2.G7] 70-10312 5.00
1. Heaven—Sermons. 2. Sermons, American. I. Title.

LOCKYER, Herbert. 236'.24
The Gospel of the life beyond. Westwood, N.J., Revell [1968, c1967] 110 p. 19 cm. [BT846.2.L6] 68-6204
1. Heaven. I. Title.

SCHOONHOVEN, Calvin 236.24
Robert.
The wrath of heaven. Grand Rapids, W. B. Eerdmans Pub. Co. [1966] 187 p. 21 cm. Bibliography: p. 167-174. [BT846.2.S3] 65-18100
1. Heaven. 2. Wrath of God. I. Title.

SCHOONHOVEN, Calvin Robert 236.24
The wrath of heaven. Grand Rapids, Mich., Eerdmans [c.1966] 187p. 21cm. Bibl. [BT846.2.S3] 65-18100 2.45 pap.,
1. Heaven. 2. Wrath of god. I. Title.

TRAVIS, Arthur E. 236'.24
Where on earth is heaven? [By] Arthur E. Travis. Nashville, Broadman Press [1974] 158 p. 21 cm. [BT846.2.T7] 74-78967 ISBN 0-8054-1928-4 4.95
1. Heaven. I. Title.

*UHRIG, Gilbert R. 236.24
The journey beyond. New York, Exposition [1966] 53p. 21cm. 3.00
I. Title.

MAYLE, Peter. 236'.24'024054
Will I go to heaven? / By Peter Mayle. New York : Corwin Books, c1976. [40] p. : ill. ; 27 cm. Answers questions about heaven, who is likely to go there, and what it might be like. [BT849.M39] 76-1190 ISBN 0-498-01983-7 : 7.95
1. Heaven—Juvenile literature. I. Title.

BRYSON, Harold T. 236'.25
Yes, Virginia, there is a hell / Harold T. Bryson. Nashville : Broadman Press, c1975. 147, [3] p. ; 19 cm. Includes bibliographical references. [BT836.2.B79] 74-33001 ISBN 0-8054-1932-2 pbk. : 1.95
1. Hell. I. Title.

GREENE, Oliver B. 236'.25
Hell, by Oliver B. Greene. Greenville, S.C., Gospel Hour [1969] 179 p. 21 cm. [BT836.2.G74] 77-13541 5.00

1. Hell—Sermons. 2. Sermons, American. I. Title.

HOLLANDER, P. Scott. 236'.25
The stellar almanac : a history and tour guide of the Infernal Kingdom of Hades / written by P. Scott Hollander ; illustrated by John T. Swanson, II. 1st ed. Lakemont, Ga. : Tarnhelm Press, 1974. ix, 317 p. : ill. ; 26 cm. Bibliography: p. 307-316. [BL545.H64] 73-94036 ISBN 0-87707-137-3 : 5.95
1. Hell—Miscellanea. I. Title.

KELLEY, P. J. 236'.25
So high the price, by P. J. Kelly. [Boston] St. Paul Editions [1968] 85 p. 20 cm. [BT836.2.K4] 68-28104
1. Hell. I. Title.

KELLY, P J 236'.25
So high the price, by P.J. Kelly [Boston] st. Paul Editions [1968] 85 p. 20 cm. [BT836.2K4] 68-28104
1. Hell. I. Title.

PAINE, Lauran. 236'.25
The hierarchy of hell. New York, Hippocrene Books [1972] 190 p. illus. 23 cm. Bibliography: p. [183]-184. [BT836.2.P24] 72-81243 ISBN 0-88254-018-1 6.95
1. Hell. 2. Devil. I. Title.

WOODSON, Leslie H., 1929- 236'.25
Hell and salvation [by] Leslie H. Woodson. Old Tappan, N.J., F. H. Revell Co. [1973] 128 p. 21 cm. Bibliography: p. 119-124. [BT836.2.W6] 72-10942 ISBN 0-8007-0581-5 3.95
1. Hell. I. Title.

AUNE, Kenneth E. 236'.3
God, history, and the end of the world, by Kenneth E. Aune. [1st ed. Savage, Minn., Invictus Enterprise Co., c1971] 290 p. illus. 24 cm. [BS647.2.A9] 79-190371 7.95
1. Bible—Prophecies. I. Title.

*BARKUN, Michael. 236'.3
Disaster and the millennium New Haven, Yale University Press, 1974. x, 246 p. 21 cm. Includes bibliographical references. [BT891] 73-86884 ISBN 0-300-01725-1 10.00
1. Millenium. I. Title.

BOETTNER, Loraine. 236.3
The millennium. Philadelphia, Presbyterian and Reformed Pub. Co., 1958 [c1957] 380p. 22cm. Includes bibliography. [BT890.B63] 57-12170
1. Millennium. I. Title.

BUXTON, Clyne W. 236'.3
What about tomorrow? [By] Clyne W. Buxton. Cleveland, Tenn., Pathway Press [1974] 144 p. 19 cm. Bibliography: p. 143-144. [BS647.2.B83] 73-90815 ISBN 0-87148-903-1 1.75 (pbk.).
1. Bible—Prophecies. I. Title.

CHAMBERLIN, Eric Russell. 236'.3
Antichrist and the millenium, [by] E. R. Chamberlin. [1st ed.] New York, Saturday Review Press [1975] xii, 244 p. 22 cm. Bibliography: p. 232-235. [BT891.C43 1975] 74-19323 ISBN 0-8415-0356-7 12.50
1. Millennialism—History. I. Title.

COX, William Edward, 1923- 236.3
Amillennialism today, by William E. Cox. Philadelphia, Presbyterian and Reformed Pub. Co., 1966. vii, 143 p. 22 cm. Bibliography: p. 141-143. [BT891.C58] 66-28450
1. Millennium. I. Title.

COX, William Edward, 1923- 236.3
An examination of dispensationalism. Philadelphia, Presbyterian & Reformed. 1963 61p. 23cm. Bibl. 62-21165 apply
1. Dispensationalism. I. Title.

CULVER, Robert D. 236.3
Daniel and the latter days. Chicago, Moody [1965, c.1954] 224p. 22cm. Bibl. 3.50
1. Millennium. 2. Bible. O. T. Daniel—Prophecies. I. Title.

DUTY, Guy, 1907- 236'.3
Escape from the coming tribulation : how to be prepared for the last great crisis of history / Guy Duty. Minneapolis : Bethany Fellowship, [1975] 157 p. ; 21 cm. Bibliography: p. [154]-157. [BT888.D87] 75-17979 ISBN 0-87123-131-X : 2.45
1. Tribulation (Christian eschatology) I. Title.

EVANS, Robert Llewelyn. 236.3
Christ and the nations. Alhambra, Calif. [1950] 113 p. 20 cm. [BT890.E9] 50-32948
1. Millennium. I. Title.

FEINBERG, Charles Lee. 236.3
Premillennialism or amillennialism? The premillennial and amillennial systems of Biblical interpretation analyzed and compared. 2d and enl. ed. Wheaton, Ill., Van Kampen Press [c1954] 354p. 22cm. [BT885.F 1954] 55-5433
1. Millennium. I. Title.

*GROOM, M.S. 236.3
The millennium; Christ's thousand-year reign. New York, Exposition [1966] 73p. 22cm. 4.50
I. Title.

HOPKINS, Samuel, 1721-1803. 236'.3
A treatise on the millennium. New York, Arno Press, 1972. 158 p. 23 cm. (Religion in America, series II) Reprint of the 1793 ed., which was issued in the author's The system of doctrines contained in divine revelation explained and defended. [BT890.H65 1972] 70-38450 ISBN 0-405-04070-9
1. Millennium.

HURST, William D., d.1968. 236'.3
Hooks in their jaws; a premillennial study of Bible prophecy. [1st ed.] New York, Exposition Press [1969, c1968] 95 p. 22 cm. [BT891.H8 1969] 76-11071 4.50
1. Millennium. 2. End of the world. I. Title.

KRAUS, Clyde Norman. 236.3
Dispensationalism in America: its rise and development. Richmond, John Knox Press [1958] 156p. 22cm. [BT157.K7] 58-10510
1. Dispensationalism. I. Title.

LAHAYE, Tim F. 236'.3
The beginning of the end, by Tim LaHaye. Wheaton, Ill., Tyndale House Publishers [1972] 173 p. illus. 22 cm. Includes bibliographical references. [BT876.L3] 72-75010 ISBN 0-8423-0105-4 3.95
1. End of the world. I. Title.

MCCONNER, John E., 1893- 236'.3
Armageddon, when & where? / by John E. McConner. Philadelphia : Dorrance, [1974] 51 p. ; 22 cm. [BS647.2.M16] 74-79087 ISBN 0-8059-2032-3 : 4.00
1. Bible—Prophecies. I. Title.

THE Meaning of the millennium : four views / with contributions by George Eldon Ladd ... [et al.] ; edited by Robert G. Clouse. Downers Grove, Ill. : InterVarsity Press, c1977. 223 p. ; 21 cm. Bibliography: p. [217]-220. [BT891.M4] 77-151882 ISBN 0-87784-794-0 pbk. : 4.25 236'.3
1. Millennium—Addresses, essays, lectures. 2. Eschatology—Addresses, essays, lectures. I. Ladd, George Eldon, 1911- II. Clouse, Robert G., 1931-

NEAL, Charles McKendre, 1878- 236'.3
Neal-Wallace discussion on the thousand years reign of Christ : conducted at Winchester, Kentucky, January 2 to 6, 1933 / stenographically reported by Chas. A. Ford. Extended ed. Fort Worth, Tex. : F. E. Wallace Jr. Publications, c1976. 411 p. : ill. ; 24 cm. [BT890.N4 1976] 76-374434
1. Millennium. 2. Second Advent. I. Wallace, Foy Esco, 1896- II. Ford, Charles A. III. Title.

ODLE, Joe T. 236'.3
The coming of the King [by] Joe T. Odle. Nashville, Tenn., Broadman Press [1974] 128 p. 18 cm. [BT886.O29] 73-91612 ISBN 0-8054-1926-8 1.95 (pbk.)
1. Second Advent. I. Title.

OTIS, George. 236'.3
Millennium man / by George Otis. 1st ed. Van Nuys, Calif. : Bible Voice, inc., c1974. 150 p. ; 22 cm. [BT891.O87] 75-312392 5.95
1. Millennium. I. Title.

RUBERT, Nettie E 236.3
The only possible road to peace; God's true plan as shown in the Bible. New York, Exposition Press [1952] 70 p. 21 cm. [BT890.R8] 52-6773
1. Millennium. 2. Peace. I. Title.

RYRIE, Charles Caldwell, 1925- 236.3
The basis of the premillennial faith. [1st ed.] New York, Loizeau0 Bros. [1953] 160p. 0cm. 'Originally presented to . . [Dallas Theological Seminary] as a doctoral dissertation.' [BT885.R9] 53-13552
1. Millennium. I. Title.

SKINNER, Floyd L 1900- 236.3
The millennial myth; a logical study in prophetic truth. [1st ed.] New York, Exposition Press [1958] 93 p. 21 cm. [BT890.S58] 58-14882
1. Millennium. I. Title.

THOMPSON, C. A. 236.3
Is there a millennium? A churchman's denial of the millennial theory. New York, Exposition Press [c.1960] 55p. 21cm. 60-1037 2.50
1. Millennium. I. Title.

THOMPSON, C A 1870- 236.3
Is there a millennium? A churchman's denial of the millennial theory. [1st ed.] New York, Exposition Press [1960] 55 p. 21 cm. [BT890.T5] 60-1037
1. Millennium. I. Title.

THRUPP, Sylvia Lettice, 1903- ed. 236'.3
Millennial dreams in action; studies in revolutionary religious movements, edited by Sylvia L. Thrupp. New York, Schocken Books [1970] 229 p. 21 cm. "This volume is the outcome of a conference held at the University of Chicago on April 8th and 9th, 1960 ... Some of the papers were made available in draft form beforehand but since have been revised; others were not written until after the conference." Includes bibliographical references. [BT891.T5 1970] 70-107614 6.50
1. Millennium. I. Title.

WALLACE, Foy Esco, 1896- 236.3
God's prophetic word; a series of addresses delivered in the Music Hall in Houston, Texas, January 21-28, 1945, exposing modern millennial theories. [Rev. ed.] Oklahoma City, Foy E. Wallace, Jr., Publications [1960] 573 p. illus. 24 cm. [BT890.W16 1960] 60-42657
1. Millennium. 2. Churches of Christ — Doctrinal and controversial works. I. Title.

WALVOORD, John F. 236'.3
Armageddon : oil and the Middle East crisis ; what the Bible says about the future of the Middle East and the end of Western civilization / John F. Walvoord with John E. Walvoord. Grand Rapids : Zondervan Pub. House, 1974. 207 p. : ill. ; 18 cm. [BS647.2.W27] 74-4946 pbk. : 1.75
1. Bible—Prophecies. 2. Near East—Politics and government—Miscellanea. I. Walvoord, John E., joint author. II. Title.

WALVOORD, John F 236.3
The millennial kingdom. Findlay, Ohio, Dunham Pub. Co. [1959] 373 p. 22 cm. Includes bibliography. [BT891.W3] 60-35409
1. Millennium. I. Title.

WALVOORD, John F 236.3
The rapture question. Findlay, Ohio, Dunham Pub. Co. [c1957] 204 p. 21 cm. [BT885.W23] 58-1052
1. Millennium. I. Title.

WEINSTEIN, Donald, 1926- 236'.3
Savonarola and Florence; prophecy and patriotism in the Renaissance. Princeton, N.J., Princeton University Press, 1970. viii, 399 p. illus., port. 25 cm. Includes bibliographical references. [DG737.97.W4] 76-113013 13.50
1. Savonarola, Girolamo Maria Francesco Matteo, 1452-1498. 2. Florence—History—Prophecies. 3. Millennialism—Italy—Florence. I. Title.

ARENDZEN, John Peter 236.5
Purgatory and heaven. New York, Sheed and Ward [1960] 96p. 18cm. (Canterbury books) 'From What becomes of the dead?' 60-7317 .75 pap.,
1. Purgatory. 2. Heaven. I. Title.

HUBERT, Father, O.F.M. Cap. 236'.5
The mystery of purgatory / Father Hubert. Chicago : Franciscan Herald Press, [1975] p. cm. Includes bibliographical references. [BT842.H8] 74-28028 ISBN 0-8199-0559-3
1. Purgatory. I. Title.

DYER, George J 1927- 236.7
Limbo: unsettled question. Foreword by Robert W. Gleason. New York, Sheed and Ward [1964] xii, 196 p. 22 cm. Bibliographical references included in "Notes" (p. 183-196) [BT860.D9] 64-16121
1. Limbo. I. Title.

DYER, George J., 1927- 236.7
Limbo: unsettled question. Foreword by Robert W. Gleason. New York, Sheed [c.1964] xii, 196p. 22cm. Bibl. 64-16121 3.95
1. Limbo. I. Title.

BOURGY, Paul. 236.8
The resurrection of Christ and of Christians. Translated by Raymond E. Marieb. Dubuque, Iowa, Priory Press [1963] 88 p. 19 cm. [BT481.B613] 63-3810
1. Jesus Christ — Resurrection. 2. Eschatology. I. Title.

BOURGY, Paul 236.8
The resurrection of Christ and of Christians. Tr. [from French] by Raymond E. Marieb. Dubuque, Iowa, Priory [c.1963] 88p. 19cm. 63-3810 .95 pap.,
1. Jesus Christ—Resurrection. 2. Eschatology. I. Title.

WILLIAMS, Harry Abbot. 236'.8
True resurrection [by] H. A. Williams. New York, Holt, Rinehart and Winston [1972] x, 182 p. 22 cm. Includes bibliographical references. [BT872.W53] 72-78108 ISBN 0-03-091994-0 6.95
1. Resurrection. I. Title.

WILLIAMS, Harry Abbott. 236'.8
True resurrection. New York, Harper & Row [1974, c1972] x, 182 p. 20 cm. (Colophon books, CN332) [BT872.W53] ISBN 0-06-090332-5 2.45 (pbk.)
1. Resurrection. I. Title.
L.C. card no. for the hardbound edition: 72-78108.

WOOLSEY, Raymond H. 236'.8
The secret of the rapture / Raymond H. Woolsey. Washington : Review and Herald Pub. Association, [1975] 64 p. ; 19 cm. Bibliography: p. 64. [BT887.W66] 75-9364
1. Rapture (Christian eschatology) I. Title.

CORNELIS, Humbert, 1915- 236.8082
The resurrection of the body, by H. Cornelis [others] Tr. [from French] by Sister M. Joselyn. Notre Dame. Ind., Fides [c.1964] 278p. 20cm. (Themes of theology) 64-16497 4.50
1. Resurrection—Addresses, essays, lectures. I. Title.

MARTIN, James Perry 236.9
The last Judgment: in Protestant theology from orthodoxy to Ritschl. Grand Rapids, Mich., Eerdmans [c.1963] xvi, 214p. 23cm. Bibl. 62-21371 4.00
1. Judgment Day. 2. Eschatology—History of doctrines. 3. Protestantism. I. Title.

SMITH, Chuck, 1927- 236'.9
Snatched away! / Chuck Smith. Costa Mesa, Calif. : Maranatha Evangelical Association of Calvary Chapel, c1976. 70 p. ; 18 cm. [BT887.S6] 76-26645 ISBN 0-89337-004-5 pbk. : 1.25
1. Bible—Prophecies. 2. Rapture (Christian eschatology) 3. Tribulation (Christian eschatology) 4. Second Advent. I. Title.

WALVOORD, John F. 236'.9
The blessed hope and the tribulation : a Biblical and historical study of posttribulationism / by John F. Walvoord. Grand Rapids : Zondervan Pub. House, c1976. 167, [9] p. ; 21 cm. (Contemporary evangelical perspectives) Includes indexes. Bibliography: p. [1-5] [BT888.W34] 76-13467 pbk. : 3.95
1. Tribulation (Christian eschatology) 2. Rapture (Christian eschatology) 3. Second Advent. I. Title.

WILKERSON, David R. 236'.9
The vision / David Wilkerson. New York : Pillar Books, 1975, c1974. 143 p. ; 18 cm. [BV5091.R4W54] 73-21088 ISBN 0-89129-088-5 pbk. : 1.50
1. Bible—Prophecies. 2. Prophecies. 3. Visions. I. Title.

237 Future Life

ABBOTT, Vera 237
Billy; a boy comes home [Westwood, N. J.] Revell [c.1963] 62p. 18cm. 63-17106 2.50 bds.,
1. Children—Death and future state. I. Title.

BARBER, Lora Ella. 237
Life goes on. Los Angeles, Wetzel Pub. Co. [1954] 174p. 21cm. [BT904.B3] 53-7357
1. Future life. I. Title.

BECQUE, Maurice. 237
Life after death, by Maurice Becque and Louis Becque. Translated from the French by P. J. Hepburne-Scott. [1st ed.] New York, Hawthorn Books [1960] 125p. 21cm. (The Twentieth century encyclopedia of Catholicism, v. 28, Section 2: The basic truths) Translation of Je ressusciterai. Includes bibliography. [BL535.B373] 60-13833
1. Future life. I. Becque, Louis, joint author. II. Title.

CAMPBELL, Roberick, 1883- 237
Israel and the new convenant. Philadelphia, Presbuterian and Reformed Pub. Co., 1954. 336p. 23cm. [BT155.C35] 54-8387
1. Covenants (Theology) 2. Eschatology. I. Title.

DAY, Gwynn McLendon 237
The joy beyond. Grand Rapids, Mich., Baker Book House [c.]1960. 70p. 22cm. .75 pap.,
I. Title.

HENDRIKSEN, William, 1900- 237
The Bible on the life hereafter. Grand Rapids, Baker Book House, 1959. 222p. 20cm. [BT912.H45] 59-8339
1. Future life. I. Title.

JENSENIUS, Bertram. 237
Calling on eternity; a candid report on the

hereafter. [1st ed.] New York, Pageant Press [1956] 80p. 21cm. [BT824.J4] 56-9453
I. Title.

KERR, Clarence W. 237
They live forever, our Christian dead. Los Angeles, Cowman Publications [1952] 114 p. 20 cm. [BT901.K34] 52-64333
1. Future life. I. Title. II. Title: Our Christian dead.

KERR, Clarence Ware, 1893- 237
They live forever, our Christian dead. Los Angeles, Cowman Publications [1952] 114p. 20cm. [BT901.K34] 52-64333
1. Future life. I. Title. II. Title: Our Christian dead.

*MANN, Stella Terrill 237
Beyond the darkness: three reasons why I believe we live after death; a report on personal experiences which sent me on a journey of questions concerning what happens after death, and some of the answers I found. New York, Dodd [c.1965] 178p. 21cm. 3.50
I. Title.

PACHE, Rene. 237
The future life. Translated by Helen I. Needham. Chicago, Moody Press [1962] 376p. 22cm. [BT902.P313] 62-2570
1. Future life. I. Title.

PARK, Olga 237
Between time and eternity. New York, Vantage Press [c.1960] 105p. 21cm. 2.75 bds.,
I. Title.

STAUDINGER, Josef 237
Life hereafter [1st Amer. ed.] Tr. from German by John J. Coyne. Westminster, Md., Newman [1964] vi, 278p. 22cm. Bibl. 64-54834 5.50
1. Future life. I. Title.

SWEDENBORG, Emanuel, 1688-1772 237
Heaven and its wonders, and hell. Tr. [from Latin] by John C. Ager. Introd. by Helen Keller. New York, Citadel [1965, c.1963] xvi, 496p. 19cm. [BX8712.H5] 65-2890 1.95 pap.,
1. Heaven. 2. Hell. 3. Future life—Early works to 1800. I. Ager, John Curtis, 1835-1913, tr. II. Title.

WATTS, Isaac, 1674-1748. 237
The world to come. [Discourses] With a biographical sketch of Dr. Watts by S. Maxwell Coder. Chicago, Moody Press, 1954. 448p. 23cm. (The Wycliffe series of Christian classics) [BT900.W3 1954] 55-18139
1. Future life—Early works to 1800. 2. Funeral sermons. 3. Future punishment—Early works to 1800 I. Title.

WINSOR, Laura Ellen. 237
My journey beyond. [2d ed.] San Francisco, A. G. Winsor [1955] 75p. illus. 20cm. [BT904.W5 1955] 55-28055
1. Future life. I. Title.

BONNELL, John Sutherland, 1893- 237.2
I believe in immortality. New York, Abingdon Press [1959] 96p. 20cm. [BT921.2.B6] 59-5206
1. Immortality. I. Title.

HOLMES, Ernest Shurtleff 237.2
You will live forever. New York, Dodd, Mead [c.]1960. 124p. 20cm. 60-15010 3.50
1. New Thought. I. Title.

KNOX, John 237.2
Christ and the hope of glory Nashville, Abingdon Press [c.1960] 63p. 18cm. 60-12073 1.00 bds.,
1. Immortality. 2. Hope. I. Title.

KNOX, John, 1900- 237.2
Christ and the hope of glory. New York, Abingdon Press [1960] 63p. 18cm. [BT921.2.K55] 60-12073
1. Immortality. 2. Hope. I. Title.

LAMONT, Corliss, 1902- 237.2
The illusion of immoratality. 2d ed. New York, Philosophical Library [1950] xvii, 316 p. illus. 22 cm. (The Humanist bookshelf) Bibliography: p. 302-308. [BT921.L167 1950] 50-7748
1. Immortality. I. Title.

LAMONT, Corliss, 1902- 237.2
The illusion of immortality. 3d ed. New York, Philosophical Library [1959] 303p. illus. 20cm. (The Humanist bookshelf) [BT921.L167 1959] 59-16215
1. Immortality. I. Title.

MOORE, Clifford Herschel, 1866-1931. 237.2
Ancient beliefs in the immortality of the soul, with some account of their influence on later views. New York, Cooper Square Publishers, 1963. xi, 188 p. 19 cm. (Our debt to Greece and Rome) Bibliographical references included in "Notes" (p. 171-183) Bibliography: p. 184-188. [BL530.M6 1963] 63-10283
1. Immortality. I. Title. II. Series.

MOYLE, Frank W 237.2
Our undying self. London, New York, Longmans, Green [1958] 122p. 19cm. [BT921.2.M6] 59-777
1. Immortality. I. Title.

SALIT, Charles R 237.2
Man in search of immortality. New York, Philosophical Library [1958] 185p. 22cm. Includes bibliography. [BD421.S32] 58-14923
1. Immortality. I. Title.

SANDERS, Adam Achad, 1889- 237.2
Man and immortality: a religion for men and women able and willing to think. [1st ed.] New York, Pageant Press [1956] 89p. 21cm. [BD421.S35] 56-13253
1. Immortality. I. Title.

WOOD, Edward Cope. 237.2
Death -- the gateway to life; evidences of personal immortality. Introd. by Harold Paul Sloan. [1st ed.] New York, Exposition Press [1958] 102 p. illus. 21 cm. [BT921.2W6] 58-4023
1. Immortality. I. Title.

CLARK, Hazel Davis, comp. 237.2082
Evidence of eternity, a treasury of testimony on immortality. New York, Association Press [1960] 126p. 16cm. (An Association Press reflection book) 'Selected from The golden book of immortality, which was compiled and edited by Thomas Curtis Clark and Hazel Davis Clark.' [BT919.C53] 60-6567
1. Immortality. I. Title.

CLARK, Thomas Curtis, 1877-1953, comp. 237.2082
The golden book of immortality; a treasury of testimony, compiled and edited by Thomas Curtis Clark and Hazel Davis Clark. New York, Association Press [1954] 232p. 20cm. [BT919.C55] 54-8447
1. Immortality. I. Clark, Hazel Davis, joint comp. II. Title.

BAXTER, Richard, 1615-1691. 237.4
The saints' everlasting rest. [Westsood, N. J.] Revell [1962] x, 157p. port., facsims. 21cm. Abridgement by John T. Wilkinson. [BV4831.B4W5] 62-2903
1. Devotional literature. I. Wilkinson, John Thomas 1893- ed. II. Title.

BONNELL, John Sutherland, 1893- 237.4
Heaven and hell, a present-day Christian interpretation. New York, Abingdon Press [c1956] 62p. 20cm. [BT832.B6] 56-5369
1. Heaven. Hell. I. Title.

COOK, Robert Dane. 237.4
The Heavenly City, a devotional exposition of the Christian hope. Dallas, Mathis, Van Nort [1953] 163p. 20cm. [BT846.C65] 53-11917
1. Heaven. I. Title.

JONES, Mary Alice, 1893- 237.4
Tell me about heaven. Illustrated by Marjorie Cooper. Chicago, Rand McNally [1956] 70p. illus. 27cm. [BT849.J6] 56-6054
1. Heaven. I. Title.

JONES, Mary Alice, 1898- 237.4
Tell me about heaven. Illustrated by Marjorie Cooper. Chicago, Rand McNally [1956] 70 p. illus. 27 cm. [BT849.J6] 56-6054
1. Heaven. I. Title.

LOSSKY, Vladimir, 1903- 237.4
The vision of God. Tr. [from French] by Asheleigh Moorhouse. Pref. by John Meyendorff. London, Faith Pr.; Clayton, Wis. Rte. 1, Box 17, Amer. Orthodox Pr. [1964, c.1963] 139p. 23cm. (Lib. of orthodox theology, no. 2) Bibl. 64-2895 4.50 bds.,
1. Beatific vision—History of doctrines. 2. God—History of doctrines. 3. God (Theory of knowledge) I. Title. II. Series.

MCCARTHY, J P 237.4
Heaven. New York, P. J. Kenedy [1958] 143p. 19cm. [BT846.2.M3 1958] 58-12717
1. Heaven. I. Title.

MASCALL, Eric Lionel, 1905- 237.4
Grace and glory. Pref. by the Archbishop of York. New York, Morehouse--Barlow Co. [1961] 90p. 20cm. [BT846.2.M35] 61-8743
1. Heaven. I. Title.

SCHILDER, Klas, 1890- 237.4
Heaven, what is it? Translated and condensed, by Marian M. Schoolland. Grand Rapids, Eerdmans, 1950. 118p. 20cm. [BT846.S33] 80-866
1. Heaven. I. Title.

SIMON, Ulrich E 237.4
Heaven in the Christian tradition. New York, Harper [1958] 310 p. illus. 22 cm. [BT846.2.S5 1958] 58-12932
1. Heaven I. Title.

SWEDENBORG, Emanuel, 1688-1772 237.4
Heaven and its wonders, and hell, from things heard and seen, by Emanuel Swedenborg. First published in Latin London, 1758. Standard ed. New York, Swedenborg Found., 1962. 496p. 18cm. .50 pap.,
1. Heaven. 2. Hell. 3. Future life. I. Title.

WALKER, Daniel Pickering. 237.5
The decline of hell; seventeenth-century discussions of eternal torment, by D. P. Walker. [Chicago] University of Chicago Press [1964] vii, 272 p. 22 cm. Bibliographical footnotes. [BT836.2.W3] 64-19849
1. Hell—History of doctrines. I. Title.

WALKER, Daniel Pickering 237.5
The decline of hell; seventeenth-century discussions of eternal torment [Chicago] Univ. of Chic. Pr. [c.1964] vii, 272p. 22cm. Bibl. 64-19849 5.95
1. Hell—History of doctrines. I. Title.

MUNSEY, William Elbert, 1833-1877. 237.6
Eternal retribution. [1st ed.] Wheaton, Ill., Sword of the Lord Publishers [1951] 128 p. 21 cm. [BT821.M8] 51-37197
1. Eschatology — Sermons. 2. Methodist Church — Sermons. 3. Sermons, American. I. Title.

BUIS, Harry. 237.7
The doctrine of eternal punishment. Philadelphia, Presbyterian and Reformed Pub. Co. [1957] 148p. 21cm. [BT836.B88] 57-8808
1. Future punishment. I. Title.

238 Creeds & Confessions Of Faith

*BABIN, Pierre 238
Teaching religion to adolescents [by] Pierre Babin, J. P. Bagot. New York, Sadlier [1967] 99p. 21cm. Tr. and adaptation from French of two works by Pierre Babin & J. P. Bagot. 2.66 pap.,
1. Religious education. I. Bagot, J. P., joint author. II. Title.

BAKER, Henry clergyman 238
Christian doctrine for beginners. Grand Rapids, Baker Book House, 1954. unpaged. 18cm. [BT1031.B28] 54-12458
1. Catechisms, English. I. Title.

BLAIR, Harold Arthur. 238
A creed before the creeds. London, New York, Longmans, Green [1955] 173p. 22cm. [BT990.B55] 56-528
1. Creeds—Hist. & crit. I. Title.

BOELTER, Francis W. 238
The covenant people of God, by Francis W. Boelter. Nashville, Tidings [1971] 94 p. 19 cm. Includes bibliographies. [BS680.C67B6] 79-171885
1. Covenants (Theology)—Biblical teaching. I. Title.

CASTER, Marcel van. 238
God's word today; principles, methods, and examples of catechesis. New York, Benziger Bros., 1966. 144 p. 22 cm. 66-23491
1. Religious education. I. Title.

CHASE, Loring D. 238
Words of faith; a resource and discussion book for youth [by] Loring D. Chase. Illustrated by Micaela Myers. Boston, United Church Press [1968] 92 p. illus. 22 cm. (Confirmation education series) "Part of the United Church curriculum, prepared and published by the Division of Christian Education and the Division of Publication of the United Church Board for Homeland Ministries." [BX9884.A3C49] 68-10038
1. United Church of Christ—Catechisms and creeds. 2. Religious education—Text-books for young people—United Church of Christ. I. United Church Board for Homeland Ministries. Division of Christian Education. II. United Church Board for Homeland Ministries. Division of Publication. III. Title.

*CONWAY, Thomas D. 238
Forming catechists; an introduction to CCD teaching by Thomas D. Conway, Eileen E. Anderson. Contributing ed.: Anthony T. Prete. New York Sadlier [1966] 116p. 21cm. 1.50 pap.,
I. Title.

DANKER, Frederick W. 238
Creeds in the Bible [by] Frederick W. Danker. St. Louis, Concordia Pub. House [1966] 64 p. 19 cm. (Biblical monographs) Bibliography: p. 64. [BT990.D3] 66-29454
1. Creeds—History and criticism. I. Title.

EVANS, Robert F. 238
Making sense of the creeds. New York, Association Press [1964] 124 p. 16 cm. (A Reflection book) [BT990.E9] 64-11422
1. Creeds. I. Title.

EVANS, Robert F. 238
Making sense of the creeds. New York, Association [c.1964] 124p. 16cm. (Reflection bk. ABA/NACS 23) 64-11422 .50 pap.,
1. Creeds. I. Title.

FARRER, Austin 238
Lord I believe; suggestions for turning the Creed into prayer. 2d. ed., rev., enl. London, S.P.C.K. [dist. Greenwich, Conn., Seabury] 1962 [c.1958] 95p. 18cm. 1.00 pap.,
I. Title.

FUHRMANN, Paul Traugott, 1903- 238
An introduction to the great creeds of the church. Phildelphia, Westminster Press [c.1960] 144p. 21cm. Bibl. notes: p.127-139. 60-10003 3.00
1. Creeds. I. Title.

GALLAGHER, Joseph Vincent, 1923- 238
A parish catechumenate; materials and format for adult catechesis, by Joseph V. Gallagher. Westminster, Md., Newman Press [1967] vii, 183 p. 22 cm. Includes bibliographies. [BX930.G3] 67-18461
1. Religious education—Text-books for adults—Catholic Church. I. Title.

†GENTILE, Ernest B. 238
Charismatic catechism / by Ernest B. Gentile. Harrison, Ark. : New Leaf Press, 1976,1977 199 p. : ill. ; 21 cm. Includes index. [BT1031.2.G46] 76-22255 ISBN 0-89221-025-7 pbk. : 2.95
1. Catechisms, English. I. Title.

GERRISH, Brian Albert, 1931- ed. 238
The faith of Christendom; a source book of creeds and confessions. Cleveland, World [c.1963] 371p. 19cm. (Meridian Bks.; Living age bk., LA40) Bibl. 63-12322 1.95 pap.,
1. Creeds. I. Title.

GERRISH, Brian Albert, 1931- ed. 238
The faith of Christendom; a source book of creeds and confessions [Gloucester, Mass., P. Smith, 1964, c.1963] 371p. 19cm. (Meridian Living age bk., LA40 rebound) Bibl. 4.00
1. Creeds. I. Title.

GUIDE to the Revised 238
Baltimore catechism for first communion: according to the St. Paul Catechism of Christian Doctrine, First Communion, by the Daughters of St. Paul. [Boston] St. Paul Eds. [Dist. Daughters of St. Paul [c.1962] 135p. 22cm. 1.50; 1.00 pap.,

GUINAN, Michael D. 238
Covenant in the Old Testament / by Michael D. Guinan ; Robert J. Karris, general editor. Chicago : Franciscan Herald Press, [1975] p. cm. (Herald Biblical booklet) [BS1199.C6G84] 74-31128 ISBN 0-8199-0520-8 pbk. : 0.95
1. Covenants (Theology)—Biblical teaching. I. Title.

HARDON, John A. 238
The spirit and origins of American Protestantism; a source book in its creeds [by] John A. Hardon. Dayton, Ohio, Pflaum Press, 1968. xvi, 516 p. 24 cm. Companion volume to the author's The Protestant churches of America, rev. ed. [BT990.H18] 68-21241 9.75
1. Creeds—Collections. 2. Sects—United States. 3. Protestant churches—United States. I. Title.

HELLWIG, Monika. 238
The Christian creeds: a faith to live by. Foreword by Alfred M. McBride. Dayton, Ohio, Pflaum/Standard Pub. [1973] 96 p. 21 cm. Includes bibliographies. [BT990.H35] 72-97917 ISBN 0-8278-9057-5 1.50
1. Creeds. I. Title.

JOCZ, Jakob. 238
The Covenant; a theology of human destiny. Grand Rapids, Eerdmans [1968] 320 p. 23 cm.

Bibliography: p. 299-305. [BS680.C67J6] 67-13984 6.95
1. Covenants (Theology)—Biblical teaching. I. Title.

KETCHERSIDE, W. Carl. 238
The death of the custodian : the case of the missing tutor / by W. Carl Ketcherside. Cincinnati : New Life Books, c1976. 152 p. ; 18 cm. [BT155.K37] 75-32003 ISBN 0-87239-035-7 pbk. : 2.95
1. Covenants (Theology) 2. Law (Theology) 3. Grace (Theology) I. Title.
Distributed by Standard Pub., Cincinnati, Ohio

*LITTLE, Sara 238
The language of the Christian community. Illus. by Bruce Smith, Doyle Robinson. Richmond, Va., CLC Pr. [dist. Knox, 1966, c.1965] 224p. illus. (pt. col.) 24cm. Bibl. 2.95 pap.,
I. Title.

LUTHER, Martin, 1483-1546. 238
An explanation of Dr. Martin Luther's Small catechism. Mankato, Minn., Lutheran Synod Book Co. [1966] 270 p. illus. 22 cm. "Work of a number of pastors of the Evangelical Lutheran Synod." Translation of Catechismus, Kleiner. [BX8070.L72L83] 68-2957
1. Lutheran Church—Catechisms and creeds—English. I. Title.

LUTHER, Martin, 1483-1546. 238
An explanation of Dr. Martin Luther's Small catechism. Mankato, Minn., Lutheran Synod Book Co. [1966] 270 p. illus. 22 cm. "Work of a number of pastors of the Evangelical Lutheran Synod." Translation of Catechismus, Kleiner. [BX8070.L72L83] 68-2957
1. Lutheran Church—Catechisms and creeds—English. I. Title.

MCCARTHY, Dennis J. 238
Old Testament covenant: a survey of current opinions [by] Dennis J. McCarthy. Richmond, John Knox Press [1972] viii, 112 p. 22 cm. (Growing points in theology) Translation of Der Gottesbund im Alten Testament. Bibliography: p. [90]-108. [BS1199.C6M313 1972] 71-37117 ISBN 0-8042-0020-3 3.95
1. Covenants (Theology)—Biblical teaching. I. Title.

MEHL, Paul F 238
Classic creeds & living faith: creeds as a compass for trusting, an adult resource book, by Paul F. Mehl. Boston, United Church Press [c1964] 123 p. illus. 21 cm. [BT990.M38] 64-19467
1. Creeds. I. Title.

MILTON, John Peterson, 1897- 238
God's covenant of blessing. Rock Island, Ill., Augustana Pr. [c.1961] 234p. Bibl. 61-17513 3.95
1. Covenants (Theology) I. Title.

MONTREAL (Ecclesiasti cal 238
Province) Office catechistique provincial.
Come to the Father series. [Pupils text. New York, Paulist Press, 1966- v. col. illus. 22 cm. Title from p. [4] of cover of y. 1. "English version of the cathechism...written by the Office catechistique provincial, Montreal, Canada." Commentaries on doctrinal themes according to the catechetical program of Come to the Father series. grades 1 and 2- New York, Paulist Press [1967- v. 21 cm. Contents.- grade Come to the Father.--grade Celebrate God's mighty deeds. Includes bibliograaphies. BX930.V42 [BX930.V4] 66-24234
1. Religious education—Text-books for children—Catholic. I. Title.

NIJMEGEN, Netherlands. Hoger 238
Katechetisch Instituut.
A New catechism: Catholic faith for adults; [translated from the Dutch by Kevin Smyth] London, Burns & Oates; New York, Herder and Herder, 1967. xviii, 510 p. 21 1/2 cm. (B67-21055) Originally published as De nieuwe katechismus. Hilversum, Brand, 1966. [BX1966.D8N53] 67-29673
1. Catholic Church—Catechisms and creeds—Dutch. I. Title.

NIJMEGEN, Netherlands. Hoger 238
Katechetisch Instituut.
A New catechism: Catholic faith for adults. [Translation by Kevin Smyth. New York] Herder and Herder [1967] xviii, 510 p. 21 cm. Translation of De nieuwe katechismus. [BX1966.D8N6213 1967b] 68-3626
1. Catholic Church—Catechisms and creeds—Dutch. I. Title.

AN Otomi catechism. 238
[Introd. by Gillett G. Griffin] Princeton [N.J.; Printed by the Meriden Gravure Co., Meriden, Conn.] 1968. [21], 51 p. illus. "Published under the sponsorship of the Friends of the Princeton University Library." Includes a facsimile (51 p.) of an early 19th century Testerian MS. in native picture writing, containing in addition to the catechism, the Ave Maria, the Credo, Articles of faith, the Ten commandments, and various practical instructions. The MS. was given to Princeton in 1949 by Robert Garrett. [PM4149.O8] 68-8966
1. Catholic Church—Catechisms and creeds—Otomi. 2. Otomi language—Texts. I. Griffin, Gillett Good, 1928- II. Princeton University. Library. Friends of the Princeton University Library.

PIERINI, Franco, S.S.P. 238
Catechism of Vatican II. Staten Island, N.Y., Alba House [1967] 260 p. 20 cm. Translation of Catechismo del Concilio vaticano II. [BX1961.P513] 68-1104
1. Catholic Church—Catechisms and creeds—English. 2. Vatican Council. 2d, 1962-1965. I. Title.

PIERINI, Franco. 238
Catechism of Vatican II Staten Island, N. Y., Alba House [1967] 260 p. 20 cm. Translation of Catechismo del Concillo vaticano II. [BX1961.P513] 68-1104
1. Catholic Church—Catechisms and creeds—English. 2. Vatican Council. 2d, 1962-1965. I. Title.

PINK, Arthur Walkington, 238
1886-1952.
The divine covenants [by] A. W. Pink. Grand Rapids, Baker Book House [1973] 317 p. 23 cm. [BS680.C67P56 1973] 73-75022 ISBN 0-8010-6938-6 6.95
1. Covenants (Theology)—Biblical teaching. I. Title.

ROUTLEY, Erik. 238
Creeds and confessions: from the Reformation to the modern church. Philadelphia, Westminster Press [1963, c1962] 158 p. 20 cm. Bibliography: p. [156]-158. [BT990.R6 1963] 63-7214
1. Creeds—Comparative studies. 2. Protestant churches—Catechisms and creeds. I. Title.

RUNIA, Klaas. 238
I believe in God; current questions and the creeds. [1st ed.] Chicago, Inter-Varsity Press [1963] 77 p. 22 cm. (IVP series in contemporary Christian thought, 6) Bibliographical references included in footnotes. [BT990.R8] 63-25420
1. Creeds. I. Title.

SCRIPTURE and confession; 238
a book about confessions old and new. Edited by John H. Skilton. [Nutley, N.J.] Presbyterian and Reformed Pub. Co., 1973. ix, 273 p. 21 cm. Includes bibliographical references. [BT990.S46] 73-78290 4.95
1. Creeds. I. Skilton, John H., ed.

SPYKMAN, Gordon J. 238
Never on your own; a course of study on the Heidelberg catechism and compendium. Written by Gordon J. Spykman. Illus. by Robin Jensen. Grand Rapids, Board of Publications of the Christian Reformed Church [1969] 202 p. illus. 24 cm. [BX9428.S67] 70-19342
1. Heidelberg catechism. I. Title.

STARK, Lawrence. 238
Physiology of the visual control system, by Lawrence Stark. Carl Kupfer, and Laurence R. Young. Springfield, Va., For sale by the Clearinghouse for Federal Scientific and Technical Information [1965] v. 88 p. illus. 27 cm. (NASA contractor report, NASA CR-238) "Prepared under contract no. NAS2-1328 by Biosystems, inc., Cambridge, Mass., for National Aeronautics and Space Administration." Includes bibliographies. [TL521.3.C6A3] 65-61790
1. Eye—Movements. 2. Vision. I. Kupfer, Carl, 1928- joint author. II. Young, Laurence R., joint author. III. Biosystems, inc., Cambridge, Mass. IV. U.S. National Aeronautics and Space Administration. V. Title. VI. Series: U.S. National Aeronautics and Space Administration. NASA contractor report CR-238

SWANSTON, Hamish F. G., 1933- 238
A language for madness : the abuse and the use of Christian creeds / Hamish F. G. Swanston. Assen : Van Gorcum, 1976. 154 p. ; 23 cm. Includes bibliographical references and index. [BT990.S93] 77-352565 ISBN 9-02-321426-9
1. Creeds. I. Title.

VATICAN Council. 2d, 1962- 238
1965.
The catechism of modern man; all in the words of Vatican II. Compiled by a group of priest specialists of the Roman province of the Society of St. Paul. Editing of the English ed., addition of the latest implementing documents, arrangement and documentation for study and discussion, topic index, and bibliographical lists, by the Daughters of St. Paul. [Boston] St. Paul Editions [1967] 533 p. 21 cm. National Catholic Welfare Conference translation. Includes bibliograhies. [Bx830 1962.A517] 67-31725
1. Catholic Church—Doctrinal and controversial works, 2. Religious education—Text-books for adults—Catholic. I. Pious Society of St. Paul. II. Daughters of St. Paul. III. Title.

VATICAN Council. 2d, 1962- 238
1965.
The catechism of modern man; all in the words of Vatican II and related documents. Compiled and edited by a team of Daughters of St. Paul. [Boston] St. Paul Editions [1968] 771 p. 22 cm. Includes bibliographies. [BX830 1962.A5172] 68-4643
1. Catholic Church—Doctrinal and controversial works. 2. Religious education—Text-books for adults—Catholic. I. Daughters of St. Paul. II. Title.

VATICAN Council. 2d, 1962- 238
1965.
The catechism of modern man; all in the words of Vatican II and related documents. Compiled and edited by a team of Daughters of St. Paul. [Boston] St. Paul Editions [1968] 803 p. 22 cm. Includes bibliographical references. [BX830 1962.A5172 1968b] 78-627 5.95
1. Catholic Church—Doctrinal and controversial works. 2. Religious education—Text-books for adults—Catholic. I. Daughters of St. Paul. II. Title.

VATICAN Council. 2d, 1962- 238
1965.
The catechism of modern man; all in the words of Vatican II. Compiled by a group of priest specialists of the Roman province of the Society of St. Paul. Editing of the English edition, addition of the latest implementing documents, arrangement and documentation for study and discussion, topic index, and bibliographical lists, by the Daughters of St. Paul. [Boston] St. Paul Editions [1967] 533 p. 21 cm. National Catholic Welfare Conference translation. Includes bibliographies. [BX830 1962.A517] 67-31725
1. Catholic Church—Doctrinal and controversial works. 2. Religious education—Text-books for adults—Catholic. I. Pious Society of St. Paul. II. Daughters of St. Paul. III. Title.

LEITH, John H ed. 238.062
Creeds of the churches; a reader in Christian doctrine from the Bible to the present. [1st ed.] Garden City, N.Y., Anchor Books, 1963. 589 p. 18 cm. (Anchor, A312) [BT990.A1L4] 63-10439
1. Theology — Collections. 2. Creeds — Collections. I. Title.

MEHL, Paul F. 238.07
Classic Christian creeds; a course-book for leaders of adults. by Paul F. Mehl. Boston, United Church Press [c1964] 122 p. illus. 21 cm. Bibliography: p. 120-122. [BT990.M37] 64-19466
1. Creeds — Study and teaching I. Title.

LEITH, John H., ed. 238'.08
Creeds of the churches; a reader in Christian doctrine, from the Bible to the present. Edited by John H. Leith. Rev. ed. Richmond, Va., John Knox Press [1973] x, 597 p. 19 cm. [BT990.A1L4 1973] 73-5346 ISBN 0-8042-0515-9 3.95
1. Creeds—Collections. 2. Theology—Collections. I. Title.

SCHAFF, Philip, 1819-1893 238.08
The creeds of Christeddom, with a history and critical notes. 4th ed. rev. enlarged. Grand Rapids Mich., Baker Bk., 1966]c.1877-1919] 966 p. 23cm. (Biblotheca symbolica ecclesiae universalis, v.3) [BT990.S4] 5-6772
1. Creeds—Collections. I. Title. II. Title: Bibliotheca symbolica ecclesiae universalis.
Contains omitted.

LEITH, John H., ed. 238.082
Creeds of the churches; a reader in Christian doctrine from the Bible to the present. Chicago, Aldine [c.1963] 589p. 22cm. 7.50
1. Theology—Collections. 2. Creeds—Collections. I. Title.

LEITH, John H., ed. 238.082
Creeds of the churches; a reader in Christian doctrine from the Bible to the present. Garden City, N. Y., Doubleday [c.]1963. 589p. 18cm. (Anchor bk., A312) 63-10439 1.95 pap.,
1. Theology—Collections. 2. Creeds—Collections. I. Title.

*AUGUSTINUS, Aurelius, 238.1
Saint, Bp. of Hippo
The first catechetical instruction (De catechizandis rudibus) Tr., annotated by Joseph P. Christopher. Chicago, Regnery [1966] 169p. 18cm. (Logos 6L714) Bibl. 1.25 pap.,
I. Title.

BEDIER, Mary Juliana, 238.1
Sister, 1896-
I believe, a first book on the Apostles' Creed for little Catholics; illustrated by E. Joseph Dreany. St. Paul, Catechetical Guild Educational Society, c1953] unpaged. illus 17cm. (First books for little Catholica) [BT993.B38] 54-21713
1. Apostles Creed—Juvenile literature. I. Title.

GYLDENVAND, Lily M, 1917- 238.1
What am I saying? A devotional approach to the Apostles' Creed. Minneapolis, Augsburg Pub. House [1952] 68 p. 20 cm. [BT993.G86] 52-27703
1. Apostles' Creed. I. Title.

ILEANA, Princess of 238.1
Rumania, 1908-
Meditations on the Nicene creed. New York, Morehouse-Gorham Co. [1958] 144p. 18cm. [BT999.I4] 58-5310
1. Nicene creed. I. Title.

KELLY, John Norman 238'.1
Davidson.
Early Christian creeds [by] J. N. D. Kelly. 3d ed. New York, D. McKay Co. [1972] xi, 446 p. 23 cm. Bibliography: p. x. [BT990.K4 1972b] 72-172064 17.50
1. Creeds. I. Title.

NEUFELD, Vernon H. 238.1
The earliest Christian confessions. Grand Rapids, Mich., Eerdmans [1964,c.1963] xiii, 166p. 25cm. (New Testament tools & studies, v.5) Bibl. 64-2096 4.00
1. Creeds—Hist. & crit. 2. Bible. N.T.—Theology. I. Title. II. Series.

RUFINUS Tyrannius, 238.1
Aquileiensis, 345 (ca.)-410.
A commentary on the Apostles' Creed. Translated and annotated by J. N. D. Kelly. Westminster, Md., Newman Press, 1955. 166p. 23cm. (Ancient Christian writers; the works of the Fathers in translation, no. 20) Translation of Commentarius in symbolum apostolorum (otherwise described as Expositio symboll apostolorum) ; based on the Latin text of D. Vallarsi. [BR60.A35 no. 20] 55-7040
1. Apostles' Creed. I. Title. II. Series.

RUSHDOONY, Rousas John. 238'.1
The foundations of social order; studies in the creeds and councils of the early church. [Nutley, N.J.] Presbyterian and Reformed Pub. Co., 1968. 232 p. 21 cm. Includes bibliographical references. [BT990.R84] 68-25836
1. Creeds, Ecumenical—History and criticism. 2. Councils and synods, Ecumenical. I. Title.

SHAMON, Albert J 238.1
Treasure untold; reflections on the Apostles' Creed. Westminster, Md., Newman Press, 1955. 222p. 23cm. [BT993.S45] 55-7049
1. Apostles' Creed. I. Title.

SOCKMAN, Ralph Washington, 238.1
1889-
How to believe; the questions that challenge man's faith answered in the light of the Creed. Nashville, Abingdon [1965, c.1953] 224p. 22cm. (Apex bks., V2) [BR121.S695] 1.50 pap.,
1. Christianity—Essences, genius, nature. 2. Apostle's Creed. 3. Faith. I. Title.

SOCKMAN, Ralph Washington, 238.1
1889-
How to believe; the questions that challenge man's faith answered in the light of the Apostles' Creed. [1st ed.] Garden City, N.Y., Doubleday, 1953. 224 p. 22 cm. [BR121.S695] 53-5281
1. Christianity—Essence, genius, nature. 2. Apostles' Creed. 3. Faith. I. Title.

ABBEY, Merrill R 238.11
Creed of our hope. Nashville, Abingdon Press [1954] 109p. 18cm. [BT993.A18] 54-10202
1. Apostles Creed. I. Title.

BARCLAY, William, 238'.11
lecturer in the University of Glasgow.
The Apostles Creed for everyman. [1st American ed.] New York, Harper & Row [1967] 384 p. 21 cm. London ed. (Collins) has title: The plain man looks at the Apostles' Creed. [BT993.2.B25 1967] 67-14928
1. Apostles' Creed. I. Title.

BARR, O. Sydney. 238.11
From the Apostles' faith to the Apostles' Creed [by] O. Sydney Barr. New York, Oxford University Press, 1964. viii, 232 p. 21 cm. Bibliography: p. 221-223. [BT993.2.B3] 64-20263
1. Apostles' Creed. I. Title.

BARTH, Karl, 1886- 238.11
Credo. With a foreword by Robert McAfee Brown. New York, Scribner [1962] 203 p. 21 cm. (The Scribner library, SL72) Translated by J. Strathearn McNab. [BT993.B32 1962] 62-6954
1. Apostles' creed. I. Title.

BARTH, Karl, 1886- 238.11
The faith of the Church; a commentary on the Apostle's Creed according to Calvin's Catechism. Edited by Jean-Louis Leuba. Translated by Gabriel Vahanian. New York, Meridian Books [1958] 188p. 18cm. (Living age books, LA22) Translation of La confession de foi de l'Eglise. Bibliography: p. 175-188. [BT993.B273] 58-11930
1. Apostles' Creed. 2. Calvin, Jean, 1509-1564. Catechisme. I. Title. II. Series.

BEACH, Walter Raymond. 238'.11
The Creed that changed the world. Mountain View, Calif., Pacific Press Pub. Association [1971] 189 p. illus. (part col.) 23 cm. [BT993.2.B37] 68-9424
1. Apostles' Creed. I. Title.

BENKO, Stephen, 1924- 238.11
The meaning of sanctorum communio [Tr. from German by David L. Scheidt] Naperville, Ill., A. R. Allenson [1964] 152p. 22cm. (Studies in hist. theology, 3) Bibl. 64-55292 3.85 pap.,
1. Communion of saints—History of doctrines. 2. Forgiveness of sin—History of doctrines. I. Title. II. Series.

BETHUNE-BAKER, James Franklin, 1861- 238.11
The faith of the Apostles' Creed. Abridged and edited by W. Norman Pittenger. Greenwich, Conn., Seabury Press, 1955. 95p. 19cm. [BT993] 55-11547
1. Apostles' Creed. I. Title.

BRUCE, Michael 238.11
No empty creed. New York, Seabury [1966, c.1964] 143p. 21cm. (Seabury paperback) [BT993.2.B7] 66-4589 1.45 pap.,
1. Apostles' Creed. I. Title.

BRUNNER, Heinrich Emil, 1889- 238.11
I believe in the living God; sermons on the Apostles' Creed. Translated [from the German] and edited by John Holden. Philadelphia, Westminster Press [1960, c.1961] 160p. 20cm. 60-10347 3.00
1. Apostles' Creed—Sermons. 2. Sermons, German—Translations into English. 3. Sermons, English—Translations from German. I. Title.

CHILCOTE, Thomas F. 238'.11
Quest for meaning; conversations on the Apostles' creed [by] Thomas F. Chilcote. [Nashville, Tenn.] Upper Room [1972] 64 p. 19 cm. [BT993.2.C48] 75-184470 1.25
1. Apostles' Creed—Meditations. I. Title.

CLAUDEL, Paul, 1868-1955. 238.11
I believe in God, a meditation on the Apostles' Creed. Edited by Agnees du Sarment. Translated by Helen Weaver. Introd. by Henri de Lubac. [1st ed.] New York, Holt, Rinehart and Winston [1963] 318 p. 24 cm. [BT993.2.C513] 63-11868
1. Apostles' Creed—Meditations. I. Title.

COME, Arnold B. 238.11
An introduction to Barth's Dogmatics for preachers. Philadelphia, Westminster Press [1963] 251 p. 21 cm. [BT993.B36C6] 62-17065
1. Barth, Karl, 1886- Die Kirchliche Dogmatik. 2. Preaching. Doctrinal—Introductions.

DAY, Gardiner Mumford, 1900- 238.11
The Apostles' Creed; an interpretation for today. New York, Scribner [1963] xiii, 174 p. 21 cm. Bibliography: p. 169. [BT993.2.D35] 63-19030
1. Apostles' Creed.

EVELY, Louis, 1910- 238'.11
Credo. Translated by Rosemary Sheed. [American ed.] Notre Dame, Ind., Fides [1967] ix, 179 p. 21 cm. [BT993.E913 1967] 67-24810
1. Apostles' Creed. I. Title.

GRIBBIN, Raymond. 238.11
Listen, my children; talks on the Creed and the Commandments. Westminster, Md., Newman Press, 1954. 116p. 23cm. [BT993.G75] 54-12079
1. Apostles' Creed. 2. Commandments, Ten. 3. Commandments of the church. I. Title.

GRIBBIN, Raymond William. 238.11
Listen, my children; talks on the Creed and the Commandments. Westminster, Md., Newman Press, 1954. 116p. 23cm. [BT993.G75] 54-12079
1. Apostles' Creed. 2. Commandments, Ten. 3. Commandments of the church. I. Title.

HURLEY, Wilfred Geoffrey. 1895- 238.11
The Creed of a Catholic. [Boston] St. Paul Eds. [dist., Daughters of St. Paul, 1965] 153p. 22cm. [BT993.2.H8] 64-21603 3.00 2.00 pap.,
1. Apostles' Creed. I. Title.

JOHNSON, Cliff Ross, 1916- 238.11
Every moment an Easter [by] Cliff R. Johnson. [1st ed. Alexandria? Va., Privately published for the members and friends of Westminster Presbyterian Church, Alexandria, Virginia, c1962] 125 p. 24 cm. [BT993.2.J6] 62-22272
1. Apostles' Creed — Sermons. 2. Presbyterian Church — Sermons. 3. Sermons, American. I. Title.

JOINVILLE, Jean, sire de, 1224?-1317? 238.11
Text and iconography for Joinville's Credo, by Lionel J. Friedman. Cambridge, Mass., Mediaeval Academy of America, 1958. 82p. illus. 26cm. (Mediaeval Academy of America. Publication no. 68) Bibliographical footnotes. [BT992.J7 1958] 58-7918
1. Apostles Creed—Early works to 1800. I. Friedman, Licenel J. II. Title. III. Title: Credo. IV. Title: Li romans as ymages des poinz de nostre foi. V. Series.
Contents omitted.

MCDERMOTT, Timothy S. 238'.11
Beyond questions and answers; the creed for today's Catholic [by] Timothy S. McDermott. [New York] Herder and Herder [1968] 173 p. 21 cm. [BT993.2.M3] 68-19353
1. Apostles' Creed. I. Title.

MOUBARAC, Youakim 238.11
I believe in God. by Yves Moubarac. Notre Dame, Ind., Fides [1966. c.1965] xiv, 136p. 21cm. (Saint Severin ser. for adult Christians, v.1; es Fides paperback textbks., PBT-17) Orig. pub. in France in 1963. [BT993.2.M613] 66-3236 1.75 pap.,
1. Apostles' Creed. I. Title.

A New look at the Apostles' creed. 238'.11
Edited by Gerhard Rein. Minneapolis, Augsburg Pub. House [1969] 87 p. 19 cm. Title on spine: The Apostles' creed. Translation of Das Glaubensbekenntnis, which originated as a radio series broadcast by the South German Radio (Suddeutscher Rundfunk) in the spring of 1967 under the title: In defence of thinking (Pladoyer fur Denken) [BT993.2.G5513] 72-75401
1. Apostles' Creed. I. Rein, Gerhard, 1936- ed. II. Title: In defence of thinking. III. Title: Pladoyer fur Denken.

PANNENBERG, Wolfhart, 1928- 238'.11
The Apostles' Creed in the light of today's questions. [Translated from the German by Margaret Kohl] Philadelphia, Westminster Press [1972] viii, 178 p. 22 cm. Translation of Das Glaubensbekenntnis, ausgelegt und verantwortet vor den Fragen der Gegenwart. [BT993.2.P3513] 72-5767 ISBN 0-664-20947-5 5.95
1. Apostles' Creed. I. Title.

REDDING, David A. 238'.11
The faith of our fathers, by David A. Redding. Grand Rapids, Eerdmans [1971] 96 p. 18 cm. (An Eerdmans evangelical paperback) [BT993.2.R38] 73-132033 1.25
1. Apostles' Creed. I. Title.

ROSS, John A 238.11
This we believe; meditations on the Apostles' creed [by] John A. Ross. Nashville, Abingdon Press [1966] 143 p. 20 cm. [BT993.2.R6] 66-15001
1. Apostles' Creed. I. Title.

ROSS, John A. 238.11
This we believe; meditations on the Apostles' creed. Nashville, Abingdon [c.1966] 143p. 20cm. [BT993.2.R6] 66-15001 2.75
1. Apostles' Creed. I. Title.

SHIDELER, Mary (McDermott) 238'.11
A creed for a Christian skeptic. Grand Rapids, Eerdmans [1968] 167 p. 23 cm. Bibliographical references included in "Notes" (p. 163-164) [BT993.2.S5] 67-28377
1. Apostles' Creed. I. Title.

SMART, James D 238.11
The creed in Christian teaching. Philadelphia, Westminster Press [1962] 238 p. 21 cm. [BT993.2.S6] 62-7508
1. Apostles' Creed — Study and teaching. 2. Religious education. I. Title.

SMART, James D. 238.11
The creed in Christian teaching. Philadelphia, Westminster [c.1962] 238p. 21cm. 62-7508 4.50
1. Apostles' Creed—Study and teaching. 2. Religious education. I. Title.

SMITH, Dana Prom. 238'.11
An old creed for a new day / by Dana Prom Smith. Philadelphia : Fortress Press, [1975] x, 134 p. ; 19 cm. [BT993.2.S64] 74-26331 ISBN 0-8006-1093-8 pbk. : 3.50
1. Apostles' Creed. I. Title.

THIELICKE, Helmut, 1908- 238'.11
I believe; the Christian's creed. Translated by John W. Doberstein and H. George Anderson. Philadelphia, Fortress Press [1968] xvi, 256 p. 22 cm. Translation of Ich glaube. Das Bekenntnis der Christen. Bibliographical footnotes. [BT993.2.T543] 68-23991 2.50
1. Apostles' Creed. 2. Theology, Doctrinal—Popular works. I. Title.

WIERSMA, J T 238.11
The Apostles' Creed interpreted in words and pictures, by J. T. Wiersma and J. W. Schulte Nordholt. Translated by Henriette Breebaart. Philadelphia, Westminster Press [1961] 137 p. illus. 22 cm. Translated of Ais ziende den onzienlijke. [BT993.2.W513] 61-6797
1. Apostles' Creed — Meditations. 2. Apostles' Creed — Pictures, illustrations, etc. I. Schulte Nordholt, J. W., 1920- joint author. II. Title.

WIERSMA, J. T. 238.11
The Apostles' Creed interpreted in words and pictures. by J. T. Wiersma, J. W. Schulte, Nordholt. Tr. [from Dutch] by Henriette Breebaart. Philadlpehia. Westminster Press [c.1961] 137p. illus. 61-6797 1.65 pap.,
1. Apostles' Creed—Meditations. 2. Apostles' Creed—Pictures, illustrations, etc. I. Schulte Nordholt, J. W., 1920- joint author. II. Title.

DUBOSE, Henry Wade 238.1107
We believe; a study of the Apostles' Creed. Richmond, Va., John Knox [1961,c.1946-1960] 79p. (Aletheia paperback) 1.25 pap.,
1. Apostles' Creed—Study and teaching. I. Title.

RUPP, Ernest Gordon. 238.11081
Last things first; four lectures on belief in the communion of saints, the forgiveness of sins, the resurrection of the body, and the life everlasting, by Gordon Rupp. Philadelphia, Fortress Press [1964] 83 p. 20 cm. Bibliography: p. 83. [BT993.2.R8] 64-18952
1. Communion of saints—Addresses, essays, lectures. 2. Forgiveness of sin—Addresses, essays, lectures. 3. Resurrection—Addresses, essays, lectures. 4. Future life—Addresses, essays, lectures. I. Title.

RUPP, Ernest Gordon 238.11081
Last things first; four lectures on belief in the communion of saints, the forgiveness of sins, the resurrection of the body, and the life everlasting. Philadelphia, Fortress [c.1964] 83p. 20cm. Bibl. 64-18952 2.00 bds.,
1. Communion of saints—Addresses, essays, lectures. 2. Forgiveness of sin—Addresses, essays, lectures. 3. Resurrection—Addresses, essays, lectures. 4. Future life—Addresses, essays, lectures. I. Title. II. Title: Life everlasting.

WADDAMS, Herbert Montague. 238.14
Believing. New York, Morehouse-Gorham [1958] 98 p. 19 cm. [BT999.W3] 58-2241
1. Nicene Creed. 2. Creeds — Subscription. I. Title.

BASSET, Bernard. 238'.142
And would you believe it! : Thoughts about the Creed / Bernard Basset. 1st ed. Garden City, N.Y. : Doubleday, 1976. 120 p. ; 22 cm. Includes bibliographical references. [BT999.B37] 76-3920 ISBN 0-385-12164-4 : 5.95
1. Nicene Creed. I. Title.

BASSET, Bernard. 238'.142
And would you believe it? : the story of the Nicene Creed / [by] Bernard Basset. London : Sheed and Ward, 1976. [5], 106 p. ; 21 cm. Includes bibliographical references. [BT999.B37 1976b] 76-378881 ISBN 0-7220-7601-0 : £2.95
1. Nicene Creed. I. Title.

FORELL, George Wolfgang. 238.142
Understanding the Nicene Creed, by George W. Forell. Philadelphia, Fortress Press [c1965] v. 122 p. 20 cm. [BT999.F6] 65-13407
1. Nicene Creed. I. Title.

FORELL, George Wolfgang 238.142
Understanding the Nicene Creed. Philadelphia, Fortress [c.1965] v*22p. 20cm. [BT999.F6] 65-13407 2.50
1. Nicene Creed. I. Title.

KELLY, John Norman Davidson 238.144
The Athanasian Creed. New York, Harper [1965, c.1964] x, 140p. 22cm. (Paddock lects., 1962-3) Bibl. [BT995.K4] 65-10237 3.00
1. Athanasian Creed. I. Title. II. Series.

CALLINICOS, Constantine N 238.19
The Greek Orthodox catechism; a manual of instruction on faith, morals, and worship. New York, Published under the auspices of Greek Archdiocese of No. and So. America, 1953. 119p. illus. 20cm. [BX735.C3] 53-39559
1. Orthodox Eastern Church, Greek, in the U. S.—Catechisms and creeds—English. I. Title.

NOLI, Fan Stylian, Abp., 1882- ed. and tr. 238.19
Eastern Orthodox catechism. Boston, Albanian Orthodox Church in America, 1954. 162p. 19cm. Based on the Catechism in Russian by Meteopolitan Phllaret, Moscow, 1840. [BX345.N6] 55-16568
1. Orthodox Eastern Church—Catechisms and creeds—English. I. Filaret, Metropolitan of Moscow, 1782-1867. II. Albanian Orthodox Church in America. III. Title.

ORTHODOX Eastern Church. 238.19
Liturgy and ritual. Euchologion. English.
An abridged Euchologion, compiled and edited by David F. Abramtsov. Philadelphia, Orthodox Catholic Literature Association, 1954. 119p. illus. 16cm. [BX360.A5A2] 55-16788
I. Abramtsov. David Feodor, 1924- ed. II. Title. III. Title: Euchologion.

ALBERIONE, Giacomo Giuseppe, 1884- 238'.2
Catechism for adults, by James Alberione. New Vatican II ed. updated by the Daughters of St. Paul. [Boston] St. Paul Editions [1971] 253 p. 18 cm. (Magister books) First published in 1961 under title: Introduction to Christian doctrine. Bibliography: p. 242-247. [BX1961.A6 1971] 75-160578 1.25
1. Catholic Church—Catechisms and creeds—English. I. Daughters of St. Paul. II. Title.

ALBERIONE, Giacomo Giuseppe, 1884- 238.2
Introduction to Christian doctrine. by James Alberione. [Boston] St. Paul Editions [1961] 87p. 22cm. [BX1961.A6] 62-8917
1. Catholic Church Catechisms and creeds—English. I. Title.

AN American Catholic catechism / [edited by George J. Dyer]. 238'.2
New York : Seabury Press, [1975] xii, 308 p. ; 22 cm. "A Crossroad book." Includes index. [BX1751.2.A795] 75-7786 ISBN 0-8164-1196-4 : 10.00 ISBN 0-8164-2588-4 pbk. : 4.95
1. Catholic Church—Doctrinal and controversial works. 2. Theology, Catholic. I. Dyer, George J., 1927-

BALTIMORE catechism. 238.2
A catechism of Christian doctrine. Rev. ed. of the Baltimore catechism no. 2. [Paterson, N. J., St. Anthony Guild Press, 1954] xiv, 128 p. 18 cm. [BX1961.B26 no.2 1954] 55-16781
1. Catholic Church—Catechisms and creeds—English., I. Title.

BALTIMORE catechism. 238.2
A catechism of Christian doctrine; prepared and jenjoined by order of the Third Plenary Council of Baltimore (in accordance with the new canon law No. 3. Suplemented by Thomas L. Kinkead. New York, Benziger Bros. [1952] 314 p. 16 cm. (Kinkead's Baltimore series of catechisms) ' 'Published by ecclesiastical authority.' [BX1961.B26 no.3 1952] 54-27855
1. Catholic Church—Catechisms and creeds—English. I. Kinkead, Thomas L. II. Title.

BALTIMORE catechism. 238.2
The Catholic faith; an official edition of the revised Baltimore catechism no. 3,confraternity of Christian Doctrine edition. With supplenentary material and explanatory charts and illus. prepared by John A. O'Brien. Notre Dame, Ind., Ave Maria Press [1955] vi, 281 p. illus. 19 cm. [BX1961.B26 no.3 1955] 56-572
1. Catholic Church—Catechisms and creeds—English. I. O'Brien, John Anthony, 1893- II. Title.

BALTIMORE catechism. 238.2
Father Connell's The new Baltimore catechism no. 3; being the text of the official revised edition, 1941, of the Baltimore catechism no. 2, amplifild with supplemental questions, answer, and a glossary by Francis J. Connell.Enriched with study helps and exercises by Thomas A. Chapman. The Father Kinkead memorial ed. New York, Benziger Bros. [c1954] 376 p. illus. 20 cm. [bX1961.B26 no.3 1954] 54-3108
1. Catholic Church—Catechisms and creeds—English. I. Connell, Francis Jeremiah, 1888- II. Title.

BALTIMORE catechism. 238.2
The new Confraternity edition, revised Baltimore catechism no. 3. The text of the official revised edition, 1949, with summarizations of doctrine and study helps, by Francis J. Connell. New York, Benzinger Bros. [c1954] 320 p. 21 cm. [BX1961.B26 no.3 1954a] 54-30700
1. Catholic Church—Catechisma and creeds—English. I. Connell, Francis Jeremiah, 1888- II. Title.

BALTIMORE catechism. 238.2
This we believe: by this we live. Rev. ed. of the Baltimore catechism no. 3. [Paterson, N. J., St. Anthony Guild Press, 1954] xiv, 426 p. 18 cm. 'Catechism no. 2, revised edition of the Baltimore catechism, with supplementary statements and quotations from Holy Scripture.' [BX1961.B26 no.3 1954b] 54-13268
1. Catholic Church—Catechisms and creeds—English. I. Title.

BALTIMORE catechism. 238.2
The "visualized" Baltimore catechism no. 2. Official reved.,ed.,illustrated, explained, applied by Ferdinand Richard. Hudson, N. H., Trinity Guild ['1950- v. illus. 21 cm. Contents.v. 1. The Creed. [BX1961.B26 no.2 1950] 51-22916
1. Catholic Church—Catechisms and creeds—English. I. Richard. Ferdinand, 1910- II. Title.

BALTIMORE catechnism. 238.2
First communion catechism. New rev. ed. [by] Michael A. McGuire [and] Sr. Annunziata. Study helps and exercises by Sr. Mary Michael. New York, Benziger Bros. [1962] 60p. illus. 21cm. Text prepared from the rev. ed. of the Baltimore catechism. [BX1961.B263 1962] 61-8924
1. Catholic Church — Catechisms and creeds — English. 2. First communion— Instruction and study. I. McGuire, Michael Augustine, 1899- II. Annunziata, Sister. III. Title.

BATTIMORE catechism 238.2
First communion catechism. New rev. ed. [by] Michael A. McGuire, Sr. Annunziata. Study helps and exercises by Sr. Mary Michael. New York, Benziger Bros. [1962] 60p. illus. 21cm. Text prepared from the rev. ed. of the Baltimore catechism. 61-8924 41
1. Catholic Church—Catechisms and creeds—English. 2. First communion—Instruction and study. I. McGuire, Michael Augustine, 1899- II. Annunziata, Sister. III. Title.

CASTER, Marcel van 238.2
Theme of cathechesis [tr. by Olga Guedatarian. New York, Herder & Herder, 1966. 207 p. 22 cm. Tr. of dieu nous parle. 2. Themes de la cathechesis [bv14712.c3213] 66-10377 4.95
1. Religious education. Title. I. Title.

CASTER, Marcel van. 238.2
Themes of catechesis. [Translation by Olga Guedatarian. New York] Herder and Herder [1966] 207 p. 22 cm. Translation of Dieu nous parie. 2. Themes de la catechese. [BV1471.2.C3213] 66-13077
1. Religious education. I. Title.

A Catholic catechism. 238.2
[1st ed. New York] Herder and Herder [1959] 414p. 18cm. 'Based on the original German version of 'Katholischer Katechismus der Bistumer Deutschlands' [BX1961.K25 1959a] 59-8303
1. Catholic Church—Catechisms and creeds—English.

A Catholic catechism. 238.2
[New York] Herder and Herder [1957] 447p. illus. 21cm. 'Based on the original German version of 'Katholischer Katechismus der Bistilmer Deutschlands.' ' [BX1961.K25 1957a] 57-14730
1. Catholic Church—Catechisms and Creeds—English.

A Catholic catechism. 238.2
[Popular ed. New York] Herder and Herder [1959] 455p. illus. 21cm. 'Based on the original German version of 'Katholischer Katechismus der Bistumer Deutschlands.' [BX1961.K25 1959] 59-7605
1. Catholic Church—Catechisms and creeds—English.

A Catholic catechism. 238.2
[Popular ed. New York] Herder and Herder [1958] 447p. illus. 21cm. 'Based on the original German version of 'Katholischer Katechismus der Bistumer Deutschlands. [BX1961.K25 1958a] 58-11752
1. Catholic Church— Catechisms and creeds—English.

CATHOLIC catechism. 238'.2
Grades five and six. Huntington, Ind., Our Sunday Visitor, inc. [1971] x, 262 p. col. illus. 19 cm. A rev. ed. for use in North America of a work originally issued as "Book one" in 1962 for use in the Catholic schools of Australia by the Australian hierarchy. [BX930.C34 1971] 71-27774
1. Religious education—Text-books for adolescents—Catholic.

CATHOLIC catechism. 238'.2
Grades seven and eight. Huntington, Ind., Our Sunday Visitor, inc. [1971] xii, 356 p. col. illus. 19 cm. A rev. ed. for use in North America of a work originally issued as "Book two" in 1963 for use in the Catholic schools of Australia by the Australian hierarchy. [BX930.C342 1971] 76-27743
1. Religious education—Text-books for young people—Catholic.

A Catholic catechism 1. 238.2
[New York] Herder and Herder [1961] 3v. illus. 19cm. 'Based upon The way and the life by Father Desmond A. D Abreo... and is an adaptation for children of the method and lesson-form structure of 'A Catholic catechism." [BX1961.C4 1961] 61-14073
1. Catholic Church— Catechisms and creeds—English.

A Catholic catechism 2. 238.2
[School ed. New York] Herder and Herder [1961] 3v, illus. 19cm. 'Original edition: Katholischer Katechismus der Bistumer Deutschlands." [BX1961.K25 1961] 61-8662
1. Catholic Church—Catechisms and creeds—English.

CATHOLIC Church. 238'.2
Catechism of the Council of Trent for parish priests, issued by order of Pope Pius V. Translated into English with notes, by John A. McHugh and Charles J. Callan. South Bend, Ind., Marian Publications [1972] lv, 589 p. 21 cm. Reprint of the 1923 ed., with a new appendix. [BX1958.E5 1972] 72-195914
1. Catholic Church—Catechisms and creeds—English. I. McHugh, John Ambrose, 1880-1950, tr. II. Callan, Charles Jerome, 1877-1962, tr. III. [Catechismus Romanus. English] IV. Title.

COLLINS, Joseph Burns, 238.2
1897-
Teaching religion, an introduction to catechetics; a textbook for the training of teachers of religion. Milwaukee, Bruce Pub. Co. [1953] 422p. 24cm. [BX1968.C65] 53-2626
1. Catechetics—Catholic Church. I. Title.

COUDREAU, Francois. 238'.2
Basic catechetical prespectives. Paramus, N.J., Paulist Press [1970] v, 167 p. 18 cm. (Deus books) [BX926.C6] 75-100006 1.95
1. Catechetics—Catholic Church. I. Title.

*DAUGHTERS of St. Paul 238.2
Christ lives in me; grade 2. Prep. by the Daughters of St. Paul under the direction of Rev. James Alberione, following the Concentric method and the Kerygmatic approach to Catechetics [Boston] St. Paul Catechetical Ctr. [dist. Daughters of St. Paul, c.1965] Richmond, Va., Author [c.1965] 60p. illus. (pt. col.) 21cm. 336p. 21cm. (St. Paul way, truth, and life ser. 2) Ea. lesson contains Sacred scripture; catechism; liturgy. With teacher's gd., and activity sheets. [BX9183.P7] 238.5 65-3898 2.10 pap., set, n3 1.50 pap.,
1. Presbyterian Church—Catechisms and creeds. I. Presbyterian Church in the U.S. General Assembly. II. Westminster Assembly of Divines. The Confession of Faith. III. Westminster Assembly of Divines. Larger catechism. IV. Westminster Assembly of Divines. Shorter catechism. V. Title. VI. Title: The Confession of Faith of the Presbyterian Church in the United States;

DAUGHTERS of St. Paul. 238'.2
The faith we live by, by a team of Daughters of St. Paul. [Boston] St. Paul Editions [1969] 395 p. illus. 24 cm. [BX1751.2.D34] 68-59044
1. Catholic Church—Doctrinal and controversial works—Catholic authors. I. Title.

DAUGHTERS OF ST. PAUL 238.2
Guide to the Revised Baltimore Catechism for grades 7, 8; according to the text: St. Paul Catechism of Christian Doctrine for grades 7, 8. Boston, Daughters of St. Paul [c.1959] 444p. 22cm. (St. Paul eds.) 3.50; 2.50 pap.,
I. Title.

FISCHER, Hubert, ed. 238.2
An introduction to A Catholic catechism: its concepts, usage, and aims. With a pref. by Josef Andreas Jungmann; introd. by Clifford Howell. [New York] Herder and Herder [1960] xiv, 169p. 21cm. 'Translation by Bernard Adkins . . . based on the third German edition of 'Einfuhrung in den neuen Katechismus,' published by Herder, Freiburg, 1955.' 60-4221 2.50 pap.,
1. A Catholic catechism. 2. Catechetics—Catholic Church. I. Title.

GALLAGHER, Joseph Vincent, 238'.2
1923-
To be a Catholic; a catechism for today, by Joseph V. Gallagher. New York, Paulist Press [1970] vii, 83 p. 19 cm. [BX1961.G26] 73-137884 0.50
1. Catholic Church—Catechisms and creeds—English. I. Title.

GESU, Remo di, Brother 238.2
The active method: review lessons on the Catechism. Tr. by B. Edwin. St. Paul 2, Minn., Catechetical Guild Educational Society [c.1961] 191p. illus. 1.50 pap.,
I. Title.

GOLDBRUNNER, Josef. 238.2
Teaching the Catholic catechism with the religion workbook; Volume II, The Church and the Sacraments. [Translation by Bernard Adkins. New York] Herder and Herder [c. 1959] 111p. illus. 18cm. 59-65039 1.65 pap.,
1. Catechetics—Catholic Church. I. Title.

GOLDBRUNNER, Josef 238.2
Teaching the Catholic catechism with the religion workbook. v. 3. [Tr. from German by Bernard Adkins. New York] Herder and Herder [1961, c.1960] v.3. 144p. illus. Contents.v.3: Life in accordance with God's commandments. 59-65039 1.65 pap.,
1. Catechetics—Catholic Church. I. Title.

HOFINGER, Johannes. 238.2
The art of teaching Christian doctrin; the good news and its proclamation. [Notre Dame, Ind.] University of Notre Dame Press [1957] 278p. 24cm. [BX1968.H58] 57-11224
1. Catechetics—Catholic Church. I. Title.

HOFINGER, Johannes. 238.2
The art of teaching Christian doctrine; the good news and its proclamation. [Notre Dame, Ind.] University of Notre Dame Press [1957] 278p. 24cm. [BX1968.H58] 57-11224
1. Catechetics—Catholic Church. I. Title.

HOFINGER, Johannes 238.2
The art of teaching Christian doctrine; the good news and its proclamation. [2d] rev., enl. ed. Notre Dame, Ind., Univ. of Notre Dame Pr. [1962] 290p. illus. 24cm. Bibl. 62-10620 4.95
1. Catechetics—Catholic Church. I. Title.

HOFINGER, Johannes 238.2
Imparting the Christian message; from The art of teaching Christian doctrine. Notre Dame, Ind., Univ. of Notre Dame Pr. [c.]1961 119p. (NDP 9) (T) 1.75 pap.,
I. Title.

INTERNATIONAL Study Week on 238.2
Missionary Catechetics, Eichstatt, 1960.
Teaching all nations; a symposium on modern catechetics. Edited by Johannes Hofinger. English version rev. and partly translated by Clifford Howell. [New York] Herder and Herder [1961] xvi, 421p. illus. 23cm. 'Original edition, 'Katechetik heute." Bibliographical footnotes. [BX1968.I63 1960a] 61-9372
1. Catechetics— Catholic Church. I. Hofinger, Johannes, ed. II. Title.

JUNGMANN, Josef Andreas, 238.2
1889-
Handing on the faith; a manual of catechetics. [Translated and rev. by A. N. Fuerst, with supplementary material for Great Britain by J. D. Crichton. New York] Herder and Herder [1959] xiv, 445p. 23cm. Translation of Katechetik. Includes bibliographical references. [BX1968.J813 1959] 59-10748
1. Catechetics—Catholic Church. I. Title.

LIVING faith (The); 238.2
a Catholic catechism [New York] Herder & Herder [c.1959-1962] 345p. illus. 19cm. Popular ed. of 'A Catholic catechism.' 62-15663 1.50 pap.,
1. Catholic Church—Catechisms and creeds—English. I. Title: A Catholic catechism.

LIVING my religion 238.2
series; a textbook for use in the lower grades, containing questions and answers of The new Baltimore first communion catechism, official revised Confraternity edition, with text explanations. Illus. and cover design by Jo Polseno. Newly rev. ed. by the School Sisters of Notre Dame, Milwaukee, Wisconsin, under the direction of Edmund J. Goebel. [New York, Benziger Bros., 1960- v. illus. 22cm. Contents.book 1. Living in God's love, by W. R. Kelly and Sisister Mary Imelda, in association with M. A. Schumacher. [BX1961.L52] 60-14608
1. Baltimore catechism. 2. Catholic Church—Catechisms and ereeds—English. I. School Sisters of Notre Dame, Milwaukee.

LOVASIK, Lawrence George, 238.2
1913-
Catechism in stories. Rev. ed. Milwaukee, Bruce Pub. Co. [1956] 294p. 20cm. [BX1961.B265L6 1956] 56-59251
1. Baltimore catechims. 2. Homilectical illustrations I. Title.

LOVASIK, Lawrence George, 238.2
1913-
Cathecism in stories. Milwaukee, Bruce Pub. Co. [1954] xviii, 294p. 20cm. [BX1961.B265L6] 54-14933
1. Baltimore catechism. 2. Homiletical illustrations. I. Title.

LOVASIK, Lawrence George, 238.2
1913-
Cathecism in stories. Rev. ed. Milwaukee, Bruce Pub. Co. [1956] 294p. 20cm. [bX1961.B265L6 1956] 56-59251
1. Baltimore catechism. 2. Homiletical illustrations. I. Title.

MORROW, Louis La Ravoire, 238.2
Bp., 1892-
My Catholic faith; a manual of religion. New and rev. ed.] Kenosha, Wis, My Mission House [1963] 430 p. illus. 27 cm. [BX1961.M67 1963] 64-327
1. Catholic Church — Catechisms and creeds — English. I. Title.

NIJMEGEN, Netherlands. 238'.2
Hoger Katechetisch Instituut.
A new catechism; Catholic faith for adults, with supplement. [Translation by Kevin Smyth. New York] Herder and Herder [1969] xviii, 574 p. 21 cm. Translation of De nieuwe katechismus. [BX1966.D8N6213 1969] 74-8249 6.95
1. Catholic Church—Catechisms and creeds—Dutch. I. Title.

PEDRO de Cordoba, 1460- 238'.2
1525.
Christian doctrine for the instruction and information of the Indians. Introd. and translation by Sterling A. Stoudemire. Coral Gables, Fla., University of Miami Press [1970] 152 p. 22 cm. Translation of Doctrina cristiana para instruccion y informacion de los indios. Bibliography: p. [143]-152. [BX1965.P3613] 79-121681 ISBN 0-87024-159-1 5.95
1. Catholic Church—Catechisms and creeds—Spanish. I. Title.

ST. Paul catechism of 238.2
Christian doctrine, grades vii, viii, catechism and answers from the revised ed. of the Baltimore catechism, no.2. Prepared and illustrated by the daughters of St. Paul [Boston, Daughters of St. Paul, c.1955, 1959] 64p. col. illus. 19cm. (St. Paul eds.) .60 pap.,

SCHOOL Sisters of Notre 238.2
Dame, Milwaukee.
Living my religion series... Newly rev. ed. by the School Sisters of Notre Dame, Milwaukee, under the direction of Edmund J. Goebel. [New York, Benziger Bros., 1960-62 8 v. illus. 23 cm. These textbooks for the lower, middle, and upper grades contain questions and answers of The new Baltimore first communion catechism and The new Baltimore catechism no. 1 and no. 2, Official rev. Confraternity editions, with text explanations. [BX1961.L52] 60-14608
1. Religious education — Textbooks for children — Catholic. 2. Baltimore catechism. I. Title.

SPIRAGO, Franz, 1862- 238.2
The catechism explained. Translated by Richard F. Clarke, Completely new and rev. ed. by Anthony N. Fuerst. New York, Benziger Bros, [1961] 458 p 27 cm. Includes bibliography. [BX1968.S75] 61-8925
1. Catechetics — Catholic Church. I. Fuerst, Anthony Norman, 1904- ed. II. Title.

*SPURGEON, Charles 238.2
H.tSpurgeon's catechism, With proofs. Comp. by Charles H. Spurgeon from the Assembly's Shorter Catechism Martin, 1483-1546
The Lithuanian catechism of Baltramiejus Vilentas (1579). and the Baptist Catechism. Chicago, Moody [1966] 61p. 14cm. (Acorn booklets) rice unreported.
I. Title.

TOWNSEND, Anne B 238.2
Chapel talks for school and camp. Greenwich, Conn., Seabury Press, 1961. 128 p. 22 cm. [BV4310.T6] 61-11315
1. Youth — Religious life. 2. Sermons, American. I. Title.

TRESE, Leo John 238.2
The faith explained. Chicago, Fides Publishers Association [1959] 564p. 20cm. 59-7820 2.50 pap.,
1. Baltimore catechism. 2. Religious education—Text-books for adults—Catholic. 3. Catholic Church—Doctrinal and controversial works, Popular. I. Title.

TRESE, Leo John, 1902- 238.2
The faith explained. Chicago, Fides Publishers Association [1959] 564 p. 21 cm. "Published ... originally by the Confraternity of Christian Doctrine in a series of six discussion club booklets under the general title of This we believe." "Commentary on the official Catholic catechism for adults, the Baltimore catechism number 3." -- Dust jacket. [BX1961.B265T7] 59-7820
1. Baltimore catechism. 2. Religious education — Text-books for adults — Catholic. 3. Catholic Church — Doctrinal and controversial works, Popular. I. Title.

VIANNEY, Jean Baptiste Marie, Saint, 1786-1859. 238.2
The Cure of Ars to his people; instructions on the catechism, explanations and exhortations. St. Meinrad, Ind. [1951] 139 p. 18 cm. "Grail publication." [BX1968.V5] 51-36439
1. Catechetical sermons. I. Title.

KEAN, Charles Duell, 1910- 238.3
The meaning of the quadrilateral. New York, Seabury Press [c1963] 56 p. 21 cm. Bibliography: p. 54-56. [BX5939.K4] 63-25956
1. Protestant Episcopal Church in the U.S.A. — Catechisms and creeds. I. Title.

KEAN, Charles Duell, 1910- 238.3
The meaning of the quadrilateral. New York, Seabury [c.1963] 56p. 21cm. Bibl. 63-25956 .65 pap.,
1. Protestant Episcopal Church in the U. S. A.—Catechisms and creeds. I. Title.

NOWELL, Alexander, 1507?-1602. 238'.3
A catechisme : or, First instruction and learning of Christian religion (1570) / by Alexander Nowell ; translated by Thomas Norton ; a facsim. reproduction, with an introd. by Frank V. Occhiogrosso. Delmar, N.Y. : Scholars' Facsimiles & Reprints, 1975. 79 p. ; 21 cm. Photoreprint of the ed. printed by J. Daye, London. Includes bibliographical references. [BX5139.N6 1975] 74-23570 ISBN 0-8201-1143-0 lib.bdg. : 10.00
1. Church of England—Catechisms and creeds. I. Title.

OBERLY, Henry Harrison, 1841-1914. 238.3
Lessons on the prayer book catechism: for the use of children, by the Rev. H. H. Oberly ... 1st- series ... New York, J. Pott & co. [1896-] v. 17 cm. Contents.-- 1st ser. Doctrine. -- 3d ser. Worship: pt. 2. The sacraments. [BX5939.O28] 0-935
1. Protestant Episcopal church in the U.S.A. Catechism. 2. Protestant Episcopal church in the U.S.A. — Catechisms and creeds — English. 3. Sacraments — Anglican Communion. I. Title.

OLDHAM, George Ashton, Bp., 1877- 238.3
The catechism today; instructions on the church catechism. 2d ed. New York, Morehouse-Gorham, 1954. 143p. 19cm. [BX5139.O55 1954] 54-8666
1. Church of England. Catechism. 2. Protestant Episcopal Church in the U. S. A. Catechism. I. Title.

OLDHAM, George Ashton, Bp., 1887- 238.3
The catechism today; primary principles of the faith. Greenwich, Conn., Seabury Press, 1961 [c1956] 143 p. 19 cm. [BX5139.O55] 61-9109
1. Protestant Episcopal Church in the U.S.A. Catechism. I. Title.

OLDHAM, George Ashton. Rt. Rev., Bp., 1887- 238.3
The catechism today; primary principles of the faith. Greenwich, Conn., Seabury Press, 1961[c.1929, 1956] 141p. 61-9109 1.75 pap.,
1. Protestant Church in the U. S. A. Catechism. I. Title.

RANDALL, Edwin Jarvis, Bp. 238.3
The church catechism and the living Word. [New York] Parthenon Press [1954] 88p. 16cm. [BX5939.R3] 55-18972
1. Protestant Episcopal Church in the U. S. A. Catechism. I. Title.

ALLBECK, Willard Dow, 1898- 238.41
Studies in the Lutheran confessions. Philadelphia, Muhlenberg Press [1952] 305p. 24cm. Includes bibliography. [BX8068.A75] 52-14123
1. Lutheran Church. Book of concord. I. Title.

ALLBECK, Willard Dow, 1898- 238'.4'1
Studies in the Lutheran confessions. [Rev.] Philadelphia, Fortress Press [1968] xi, 318 p. 21 cm. Bibliography: p. 305-307. [BX8068.A75 1968] 68-11139
1. Lutheran Church. Book of concord. I. Title.

DISCORD, dialogue, and concord : studies in the Lutheran Reformation's Formula of concord / edited by Lewis W. Spitz and Wenzel Lohff. Philadelphia : Fortress Press, [1977] p. cm. [BX8069.4.D57] 77-78644 ISBN 0-8006-0511-X : 9.95 238'.4'1
1. Lutheran Church. Formula of concord—Addresses, essays, lectures. I. Spitz, Lewis William, 1922- II. Lohff, Wenzel.

FORELL, George Wolfgang. 238'.4'1
The Augsburg confession; a contemporary commentary, by George W. Forell. Minneapolis, Augsburg Pub. House [1968] 112 p. 22 cm. "A revision of articles that appeared originally in The Lutheran, vol. 5, nos. 1-26 ... 1967." [BX8069.F6] 68-25798 1.95
1. Augsburg confession. I. Title.

GIRGENSOHN, Herbert, 1887- 238.41
Teaching Luther's Catechism. Translated [from the German] by John W. Doberstein. Philadelphia, Muhlenberg Press [c.1960] 310p. 59-8463 3.00
1. Luther, Martin. Catechismus, Kleiner. 2. Luther, Martin. Catechismus, Kleiner. I. Title.

IRVIN, Donald F. 238.41
Learning the way; a catechetical guidebook for youth. Arthur H. Getz, editor. Prepared under the auspices of the Parish and Church School Board of the United Lutheran Church in America. Philadelphia, United Lutheran Publication House ['1951] 208 p. illus. 22 cm. [BX8070.L72 I 7] 52-1626
1. Lutheran Church—Catechisms and creeds—English. I. Luther, Martin. II. Title. III. Title: The small catechism.

IRVIN, Donald F. 238.41
Teaching the way; a pastor's guide for catechetical instruction. Arthur H. Getz, editor. Prepared under the auspices of the Enatish and Church School Board of the United Lutheran Church in America. Philadelphia, United Lutheran Publication House ['1951] 144 p. 22 cm. "Companion book to ... [the author's] Learning the way." [BX8070.L8 I 7] 52-1499
1. Catechetics—Lutheran Church. I. Title.

JOELSSON, A G. 238.41
A boy meets Luther; translated from the Swedish by Ruth Jacobson Ullberg. Illus. by Edvin K. Holmer. Rock Island, Ill., Augustana Book Concern [1950] 293 p. illus. 21 cm. "A translation of ... Sven l Tallbacken hos Martin Luther." [BX8070.L8J62] 50-2209
1. Luther, Martin. Catechismus, Kleiner. 2. Luther, Martin, 1483-1546. I. Title.

[KELLER, Paull F] 238.41
Studies in Lutheran doctrine. [Minneapolis, Sacred Design Associates, 1959] 121p. illus. 28cm. [BX8074.C7K4] 59-13231
1. Confirmation—Instruction and study. 2. Lutheran Church—Catechisms and creeds—English. I. Title.

KLUG, Eugene F. 238'.4'1
Getting into the Formula of Concord : a history and digest of the Formula : historical notes and discussion questions / by Eugene F. Klug; translation of the Epitome by Otto F. Stahlke. St. Louis : Concordia Pub. House, c1977. 120 p. ; 23 cm. [BX8069.4.K58] 76-28382 ISBN 0-570-03742-5 pbk. : 1.95
1. Lutheran Church. Formula of concord. I. Stahlke, Otto F., joint author. II. Title.

KOEHNEKE, Martin L 238.41
God and I. Saint Louis, Concordia Pub. House [1956] 55p. 23cm. [BX8070.K65] 55-12192
1. Lutheran Church—Catechisms and creeds—English. I. Title.

LACKMANN, Max. 238.41
The Augsburg Confession and Catholic unity. [Translation by Walter R. Bouman. New York] Herder and Herder [1963] 159 p. 21 cm. Translation of Katholische Einheit und Augsburger Konfession. [BX8069.L313] 63-9560
1. Augsburg Confession. 2. Creeds — Comparative studies. 3. Christian union. I. Title.

LACKMANN, Max 238.41
The Augsburg Confession and Catholic unity. [Tr. from German by Walter R. Bouman. New York] Herder & Herder [c.1963] 159p. 21cm. Bibl. 63-9560 4.50
1. Augsburg Confession. 2. Creeds—Comparative studies. 3. Christian union. I. Title.

LUTHER, 1483-1546 238.41
The Lithuanian catechism of Baltramiejus Vilentas (1579). Ed. by Gordon B. Ford. Jr. 3d rev. ed. Louisville, Ky., Pyramid Pr., c.1964-1966. xxv, 77, 78, 1. 29cm. Facsim. of the 1579 Konigsberg ed. In Gothic type with Lithuanian transcription. Orig. t. p. reads: Enchiridion, Cathechismas maszas . . . workischku lieszuwiu paraschits per Martina Luthera . . . ant lietuwischka . . . perguldita per Baltramieju Willentha . . . Ischspaustas Karalauczui per J. Osterbergera 1579. [BX8070.L727A21579c] 66-57008 36.00
1. Lutheran Church—Catechisms and creeds—Lithuanian. I. Vilentas. Baltramiejus. 1525 (ca.)—1587,tr. II. Ford, Gordon B., ed. III. Title. IV. Title: Enchiridion, Catechismas maszas.

LUTHER, Martin 238.41
The small catechism: a handbook of basic Christian instruction for the family and the congregation, in contemporary English. Philadelphia, Fortress [1963, c.1960] 61p. illus. 17cm. (UE833) .50 pap.,
I. Title.

LUTHER, Martin, 1483-1546. 238.41
An explanation of Luther's Small catechism; a handbook for catechetical instruction, by Joseph Stump. 2d rev. ed. Philadelphia, Muhlenberg Press [1960] 146p. 18cm. [BX8070.L72S75 1960] 60-51204
1. Lutheran Church—Catechisms and creeds—English. I. Stump, Joseph, 1866- II. Title.

LUTHER, Martin, 1483-1546. 238.41
Growing in Christ; an exposition of Luther's Small catechism; illustrated by George Kuhasz and Harry Tillson. Saint Louis, Concordia Pub. House [1953] 296p. illus. 21cm. [BX8070.L72A3 1953] 53-3802
1. Lutheran Church—Catechisms and creeds—English. I. Title.

LUTHER, Martin, 1483-1546. 238.41
Large catechism. Translated by Robert H. Fischer. Philadelphia, Muhlenberg Press [c1959] 105p. 23cm. 'Taken from the Book of Concord, translated and edited by Theodore G. Tappert.' [BX8070.L62F5] 61-3802
1. Lutheran Church—Catechisms and creeds—English. I. Title.

LUTHER, Martin, 1483-1546 238.41
The Lithuanian catechism of Baltramiejus Vilentas, 1579. Ed. by Gordon B. Ford, Jr. 2d, rev. ed. Louisville, Ky., Pyramid Pr. [1965] v, 75, 78 l. 28cm. Facsim, of the 1579 Konigsberg ed. In Gothic type with Lithuanian trancription. Orig. t. p. reads: Enchiridion, Catechismas maszas . . . wokischku lieszuwiu paraschits per Martina Luthera . . . antlietuwischka . . . perguldita per Baltramieju Willentha . . . Ischspaustas Karalauczui per J. Osterbergera, 1579 [BX8070.L727A2 1579b] 66-3380 20.00
1. Lutheran Church—Catechisms and creeds—Lithuanian. I. Vilentas, Baltramiejus, 1525 (ca.)—1587, tr. II. Ford, Gordon B., ed. III. Title. IV. Title: Enchiridion, Cathechismas maszas.

LUTHER, Martin, 1483-1546. 238'.41
The small catechism, in contemporary English. Illustrated by Gerd Wilk. Philadelphia, Fortress Press [1967] 59 p. col. illus. 21 cm. Translation of Catechismus kleiner. [BX8070.L72A3 1967] 67-8579
1. Lutheran Church—Catechisms and creeds—English. I. Title.

LUTHER, Martin, 1483-1546. 238.41
Small catechism with explanation. Rev. under the direction of the Board of Parish Education by authority of the Augustana Evangelical Lutheran Church. Rock Island, Ill., Augustana Press [1957] 98p. illus. 22cm. [BX8070.L72A3 1957] 57-7760
1. Lutheran Church—Catechisms and creeds—English. I. Title.

LUTHERAN Church. Book of Concord. 238.41
The Book of Concord; the confessions of the Evangelical Lutheran Church. Translated and edited by Theodore G. Tappert in collaboration with Jaroslav Pelikan, Robert H. Fischer [and] Arthur C. Piepkorn. Philadelphia, Muhlenberg Press [1959] vii, 717p. 23cm. [BX8068.A3 1959] 59-11369
1. Lutheran Church—Catechisms and creeds. I. Tappert, Theodore, Gerhardt, 1904- ed. and tr. II. Title.

LUTHERAN Church. Book of concord 238.41
Historical introductions to the Book of concord [by] F. Bente. St. Louis, Concordia Pub. House [1965] 266 p. 24 cm. Reprint of Historical introductions to the symbolic books of the Evangelical Lutheran Church, contained in Lutheran Church. Book of concord. Concordia triglotta. St. Louis, Concordia Pub. House, 1921. [BX8068.A3 1964] 66-1126
1. Lutheran Church — Catechisms and creeds. I. Bente, Friedrich, 1858-1930. II. Title.

MEYER, R Z 238.41
This faith is mine; meditations for youth on Luther's Catechism. Saint Louis, Concordia Pub. House [1960] 135p. 20cm. [BX8070.L8M4] 60-1822
1. Luther, Martin. Catechismus, Kleiner—Meditations. 2. Youth—Prayer-books and devotions—English. I. Title.

PEDERSON, Carl O 238.41
The story of God's kingdom; a first year confirmation book. Minneapolis, Augsburg Pub. House [1954] 112p. illus. 22cm. [BX8070.P4] 54-4603
1. Lutheran Church—Catechisms and creeds—English. I. Title.

SCHLINK, Edmund, 1903- 238.41
Theology of the Lutheran confessions. Translated by Paul F. Koehneke and Herbert J. A. Bouman. Philadelphia, Muhlenberg Press [1961] 353 p. 23 cm. [BX8065.S283] 61-6757
1. Luthern Church—Doctrinal and controversial works. 2. Luthern Church. Book of Concord. I. Title.

SCHLINK, Edmund, 1903- 238'.4'1
Theology of the Lutheran confessions / by Edmund Schlink ; translated by Paul F. Koehneke and Herbert J. A. Bouman. Philadelphia : Fortress Press, 1975, c1961. xxix, 353 p. ; 22 cm. Translation of Theologie der lutherischen Bekenntnisschriften. Originally published by Muhlenberg Press, Philadelphia. Includes index. Bibliography: p. 318-344. [BX8065.S283 1975] 75-324004 ISBN 0-8006-1883-1 : 5.95
1. Lutheran Church—Doctrinal and controversial works. 2. Lutheran Church. Book of Concord. I. Title.

SCHMIDT, John, 1905- 238.41
The Lutheran confessions: their value and meaning. Arthur H. Getz, editor. Philadelphia, Muhlenberg Press [1957, c1956] 108p. illus. 18cm. [BX8068.A1S35] 67-1229
1. Lutheran Church—Catechisms and creeds. I. Title.

FAGERBERG, Holsten. 238'.4'109
A new look at the Lutheran confessions (1529-1537) Translated [from the Swedish manuscript] by Gene J. Lund. St. Louis, Concordia [1972] 320 p. 24 cm. German translation has title: Die Theologie der lutherischen Bekenntnisschriften von 1529 bis 1537. Bibliography: p. [307]-320. [BR333.2.F313] 71-179376 ISBN 0-570-03223-7
1. Luther, Martin, 1483-1546—Theology. 2. Melanchthon, Philipp, 1497-1560. 3. Lutheran Church—Catechisms and creeds—History and criticism. I. Title.

BARTH, Karl, 1886- 238.42
The Heidelberg catechism for today. Translated by Shirley C. Guthrie, Jr. Richmond, John Knox Press [1964] 141 p. 21 cm. Contents.CONTENTS. -- I. Christian doctrine according to the Heldelberg catechism. -- II. Introduction to the Heldelberg catechism. [BX9428.B313] 64-11811
1. Heldelberg catechism. I. Title.

BARTH, Karl, 1886- 238.42
The Heidelberg catechism for today. Tr. [from German] by Shirley C. Guthrie, Jr. Richmond, Va., Knox [c.1964] 141p. 21cm. Contents.I. Christian doctrine according to the Heidelberg catechism.--II. Introduction to the Heidelberg catechism. 64-11811 2.00 pap.,
1. Heidelberg catechism. I. Title.

COCHRANE, Arthur C ed 238.42
Reformed confessions of the 16th century, edited, with historical introductions, by Arthur C. Cochrane Philadelphia, Westminster Press [1966] 336 p. 23 cm. [BX9428.A1C6] 66-13084
1. Reformed Church — Catechisms and creeds — Collections. I. Title.

COCHRANE, Arthur C. ed. 238.42
Reformed confessions of the 16th century, ed., with hist. introds., by Arthur C. Cochrane Philadelphia, Westminster [c.1966] 336p. 23cm. [BX9428.A1C6] 66-13084 3.50 pap.,
1. Reformed Church—Catechisms and creeds—Collections. I. Title.

COURVOISIER, Jaques 238.42
Zwingli, a Reformed theologian. Richmond, Va., Knox [c.1963] 101p. 21cm. (Annie Kinkead Warfield lects., 1961) Bibl. 63-8064 1.75 pap.,
1. Zwingli, Ulrich, 1484-1531. I. Title. II. Series.

ESSAYS on the Heidelberg catechism [by] Bard Thompson [others] Philadelphia, United Church [c.1963] 192p. 23cm. Most of the essays were delivered as lects. at the Annual Convocation of Lancaster Theological Seminary in January 1963. Bibl. 63-21522 3.50 pap., 238.42
1. Heidelberg catechism. I. Thompson, Bard, 1925-

HOEKSEMA, Herman. 238.42
The Heidelberg catechism (an exposition) The triple knowledge. Grand Rapids, W. B. Eerdmans Pub. Co., 19 v. 21cm. Contents.v. 4. The Lord of Glory.--v. 5. Abundant mercy.--v. 6. Baptized into Christ.--v. 7. Eating and drinking Christ.--v. 8. Love the Lord thy God.--v. 9. Love thy neighbor for God's sake.--v. 10. The perfect prayer. [BX9428.H6] 47-26500
1. Heidelberg catechism. I. Title.

MASSELINK, Edward J. 238.42
The Heidelberg story. Grand Rapids, Mich., Baker Bk., 1964. 121p. illus., ports. 23cm. 64-56196 price unreported
1. Heidelberg catechism. I. Title.

THOMPSON, Bard, 1925- 238.42
Essays on the Heidelberg catechism [by] Bard Thompson [and others] Philadelphia, United Church Press [1963] 192 p. 23 cm. "Most of the essays ... were delivered as lectures at the Annual Convocation of Lancaster Theological Seminary in January 1963." Bibliographical references included in "Author's notes" (p. 181-192) [BS9428.E75] 63-21522
1. Heidelberg catechism. I. Title.

TORRANCE, Thomas Forsyth, 1913- ed. and tr. 238.42
The school of faith; the catechisms of the Reformed Church. Translated and edited with an introd. by Thomas F. Torrance. New York, Harper [1959] cxxvi, 208 p. 20 cm. Contents.The larger catechisms: Calvin's Geneva catechism, 1541. The Heidelberg catechism, 1563. Craig's catechism, 1581. The new catechism, 1644. The larger catechism, 1648. -- The shorter catechisms: The little catechism, 1556. -- Craig's short catechism, 1592. A catechism for young children 1641. The shorter catechism, 1648. The Latin catechism, 1595. [BX9428.A1T613] 59-10932
1. Reformed Church — Catechisms and creeds — Collections. 2. Church of Scotland — Catechisms and creeds — Collections. I. Title.

URSINUS, Zacharias, 1534-1583. 238.42
Commentary on the Heidelberg catechism. Translated from the original Latin by G. W. Williard. Grand Rapids, Eerdmans, 1954. xxxviii, 659p. 23cm. Reproduction of the 2d American ed. of the theological lectures of Ursinus printed at Columbus in 1852, based on the Latin ed. published in 1616, the most complete of the David Pareus editions. [BX9428.U7 1954] 54-1602
1. Heldelberg catechism. I. Title.

CLARK, Gordon Haddon. 238.5
What do Presbyterians believe? The Westminster Confession; yesterday and today [by] Gordon H. Clark. With an introd. by John R. Richardson. Philadelphia, Presbyterian and Reformed Pub. Co., 1965. xiv, 284 p. 23 cm. First published in 1956 under title: What Presbyterians believe. Bibliographical footnotes. [BX9183.C63] 65-27481
1. Westminster Assembly of Divines. The Confession of Faith. 2. Presbyterian Church — Catechisms and creeds. I. Title. II. Title: The Westminster Confession; yesterday and today.

CLARK, Gordon Haddon. 238.5
What Presbyterians believe. With an introd. by John R. Richardson. Philadelphia, Presbyterian and Reformed Pub. Co., 1956. 130p. 23cm. [BX9183.C63] 56-8576
1. Westminster Assembly of Divines. The Confession of Faith. 2. Presbyterian Church-Catechisms and creeds. I. Title.

HEIDELBERG CATECHISM. ENGLISH 238.5
The Heidelberg catechism. 400th anniversary ed., 1563-1963. [Tr. from orig. German and Latin texts by Allen O. Miller, M. Eugene Osterhaven] Philadelphia, United Church [c.1962] 127p. 17cm. 62-20891 1.00 pap.,
1. Reformed Church—Catechisms and creeds—English. I. Title.

HENDRY, George Stuart, 238.5
The Westminster Confession for today; a contemporary interpretation. Richmond, John Knox Press [c.1960] 253p. 21cm. 60-6283 2.00
1. Westminster Assembly of Divines. The Confession of Faith. I. Title.

HENDRY, George Stuart, 1904- 238.5
The Westminster Confession for today; a contemporary interpretation. Richmond, John Knox Press [1960] 253p. 21cm. [BX9183.H4] 60-6283
1. Westminster Assembly of Divines. The Confession of Faith. I. Title.

PRESBYTERIAN Church in the U.S. General Assembly. 238.5
The Confession of Faith of the Presbyterian Church in the United States; together with the Larger catechism and the Shorter catechism, declared by the General Assembly at Augusta, Georgia. December 1861. With amendments that were enacted by the General Assemblies of 1886, 1939, 1942, 1944, 1959, and 1963. [Rev. ed. with amendments] Richmond, Printed by the Board of Christian Education [1965] 336 p. 21 cm. [BX9183.P7] 65-3898
1. Presbyterian Church—Catechisms and creeds. I. Westminster Assembly of Divines. The Confession of Faith. II. Westminster Assembly of Divines. Larger catechism. III. Westminister Assembly of Divines. Shorter Catechism. IV. Title.

WESTMINSTER ASSEMBLY OF DIVINES. 238.5
A harmony of the Westminster Presbyterian standards, with explanatory notes, by James Benjamin Green. Richmond, John Knox Press [1951] 231 p. 28 cm. [BX9183.A38] 51-2866
1. Presbyterian Church—Catechisms and creeds—English. I. Green, James Benjamin, 1871- II. Title. III. Title: Westminster Presbyterian standards.

WILLIAMSON, Gerald Irvin, 1925- 238.5
The Westminster Confession of Faith, for study classes [Grand Rapids, Mich., Baker bk. 1965, c.1964] vi, 309p. 26cm. [BX9183.W5] 5.00 pap.,
1. Westminster Assembly of Divines. The Confession of Faith. I. Title.

LEITH, John H. 238'.5'1
Assembly at Westminster; reformed theology in the making [by] John H. Leith. Richmond, Va., John Knox Press [1973] 127 p. facsim. 21 cm. Bibliography: p. [125]-127. [BX9183.L44] 72-11162 ISBN 0-8042-0885-9 3.95 (pbk.)
1. Westminster Assembly of Divines. 2. Westminster confession of faith. I. Title.

DOWEY, Edward A. 238'.5'131
A commentary on the Confession of 1967 and an introduction to The book of confessions, by Edward A. Dowey, Jr. Philadelphia, Westminster Press [1968] 273 p. 21 cm. "The Confession of 1967": p. 13-25. [BX8955.D68] 68-27690 2.65
1. United Presbyterian Church in the U.S.A.—Catechisms and creeds. 2. United Presbyterian Church in the U.S.A.—Doctrinal and controversial works. I. United Presbyterian Church in the U.S.A. Confession of 1967. 1968 II. Title.

MILES, O. Thomas. 238'.5'131
Crisis and creed; a contemporary statement of faith [by] O. Thomas Miles. Grand Rapids, Eerdmans [1968] 82 p. 20 cm. Bibliographical footnotes. [BX9183.M5] 68-20586
1. United Presbyterian Church in the U.S.A.—Catechisms and creeds. 2. United Presbyterian Church in the U.S.A.—Doctrinal and controversial works. I. Title.

ROGERS, Jack Bartlett. 238'.5'131
Scripture in the Westminster Confession; a problem of historical interpretation for American Presbyterianism. Grand Rapids, W. B. Eerdmans, 1967. x, 475 p. 25 cm. Errata slip inserted. Bibliography: p. 457-475. [BX9183.R6] 67-2316
1. Westminster confession of faith. I. Title.

UNITED Presbyterian Church in the U.S.A. General Assembly. 238'.5'131
The proposed Book of confessions of the United Presbyterian Church in the United States of America. Philadelphia, 1966. 186 p. 23 cm. [BX8955.A27] 567
1. United Presbyterian Church in the U.S.A. — Catechisms and creeds. I. Title.

VAN TIL, Cornelius, 1895- 238'.5'132
The confession of 1967, its theological background and ecumenical significance Philadelphia, Presbyterian and Reformed Pub. Co., 1967. vi, 128 p. 23 cm. Bibliographical references included in "Publisher's note" (p. v-vi) [BX9183.V3] 66-30704
1. United Presbyterian Church in the U.S.A.—Catechisms and creeds. 2. United Presbyterian Church in the U.S.A.—Doctrinal and controversial works. I. Title.

PRESBYTERIAN Church in the U.S. 238'.5'133
A declaration of faith / The Presbyterian Church in the United States. Atlanta : The Church, c1977. 29 p. ; 26 cm. Cover title. [BX8965.P73 1977] 77-154197 0.65
1. Presbyterian Church in the U.S.—Catechisms and creeds. I. Title.

LEITH, John H. 238'.5'2
Assembly at Westminster; reformed theology in the making [by] John H. Leith. Richmond, Va., John Knox Press [1973] 127 p. facsim. 21 cm. Bibliography: p. [125]-127. [BX9183.L44] 72-11162 ISBN 0-8042-0885-9 3.95 (pbk.)
1. Westminster Assembly of Divines. 2. Westminster confession of faith. I. Title.

BRUGGINK, Donald J ed. 238.57
Guilt, grace, and gratitude; a commentary on the Heidelberg catechism, commemorating its 400th anniversary. New York, Half Moon Press [1963] 226 p. 23 cm. The nine articles in this commentary are written by scholars of the Reformed Church in America, as the church's tribute to the catechism. "The translation of the Heidelberg catechism used in this publication is the 400th anniversary edition of the Heldelberg catechism translated from original German and Latin texts by Alien O. Miller and M. Eugene Osterhaven." [BX9428.B7] 63-17779
1. Heidelberg catechism. I. Heidelberg catechism. English. II. Reformed Church in America. III. Title.

BRUGGINK, Donald J., ed. 238.57
Guilt, grace, and gratitude; a commentary on the Heidelberg catechism, commemorating its 400th anniversary. New York, Half Moon Pr. [dist. Grand Rapids, Mich., Eerdmans, c.1963] 226p. 23cm. The nine articles in this commentary are written by scholars of the Reformed Church in America, as the church's tribute to the catechism. The translation of the Heidelberg catechism used in this pubn. is the 400th anniversary ed. of the Heidelberg catechism translated from orignal German and Latin texts by Allen O. Millar, M. Eugene Osterhaven. 63-17779 3.50
1. Heidelberg catechism. I. Heidelberg catechism. English. II. Reformed Church in America. III. Title.

AUSTIN, Arthur, 1911- 238'.5'732
The family book of favorite hymns, illustrated by George Louden, Jr. New York, Funk & Wagnalls, 1950. 176 p. illus. 29 cm. With music. [M2117.A9F3] 50-10293
1. Hymns. English. I. Title.

REFORMED Church in America. 238'.5'732
Our song of hope : a provisional confession of faith of the Reformed Church in America ; with commentary and appendixes by Eugene P. Heideman. Grand Rapids : Eerdmans, [1975] c1974. vi, 90 p. ; 21 cm. [M2124.R26O8] 74-28219 ISBN 0-8028-1604-5 pbk. : 2.95
1. Reformed Church in America—Hymns. 2. Reformed Church in America—Catechisms and creeds—English. 3. Hymns, English. I. Heideman, Eugene P., ed. II. Title.

SANKEY, Ira David, 1840-1908, ed. 238'.5'732
Sacred songs no. 2, compiled and arr. for use in gospel meetings. Sunday schools, prayer meetings, and other religious services, by Ira D. Sankey, James McGranahan, and Geo. C. Stebbins. New York, Biglow & Main Co. [1900] 159 p. 14 cm. "Words only." [BV459.S22] 0-1743
1. Hymns, English. I. McGranahan, James, 1840-1907, joint ed. II. Stebbins, George Coles, 1846-1945, joint ed. III. Title.

WALKER, Williston, 1860-1922, ed. 238.58
The creeds and platforms of Congregationalism. With an introd. by Douglas Horton. Boston, Pilgrim Press [1960] xvi, 604 p. 22 cm. Bibliographical footnotes. [BX7236.W3 1960] 60-14698
1. Congregational churches — Catechisms and creeds. I. Title.

WALKER, Williston, 1860-1922, ed. 238.58
The creeds and platforms of Congregationalism. With an introd. by Douglas Horton. Boston, Pilgrim Press [c.1960] xvi, 604p. 22cm Bibl. footnotes. 60-14698 2.45 pap.,
1. Congregational churches—Catechisms and creeds. I. Title.

WILLARD, Samuel, 1640-1707. 238'.5'8
A compleat body of divinity. New York, Johnson Reprint Corp., 1969 [c1968] xii, iv, 914, [1] p. 31 cm. (Series in American studies) Reprint of the 1726 ed., with a new introd. by Edward M. Griffin. "A catalogue of the author's works": p. [915] Bibliography: p. xii. [BX9184.A5W55 1969] 68-30728
1. Westminster Assembly of Divines. Shorter catechism. 2. Congregational churches—Doctrinal and controversial works. 3. Sermons, American. I. Title. II. Series.

LUMPKIN, William Latane. 238.6
Baptist confessions of faith. Chicago, Judson Press [c.1959] 430p. 22cm. (bibl. footnotes) illus. 59-7945 6.00
1. Baptists—Catechisms and creeds. I. Title.

HEIDELBERG catechism. English. 238.85
The Heidelberg catechism with commentary. 400th anniversary ed., 1563-1963. Philadelphia, United Church Press [1963] 224 p. 23 cm. "This ... edition of the Heidelberg catechism is a translation from original German and Latin texts by Allen O. Miller and M. Eugene Osterhaven. The commentary is a translation by Allen O. Miller ... from Le cathechisme de Heidelberg, by And[r]e Pery." [BX9428.A3] 63-1098
1. Reformed Chruch — Catechisms and creeds — English. I. Pery, Andre. Le cathechisme de Heidelberg. II. Title.

HEIDELBERG catechism. English. 238.85
The Heidelberg catechism with commentary. 400th anniversary ed., 1563-1963. Philadelphia, United Church [c.1962, 1963] 224p. 23cm. This ed. of the Heidelberg catechism is a tr. from orig. German and Latin texts by Allen O. Miller and M. Eugene Osterhaven. 63-10981 3.00 pap.,
1. Reformed Church—Catechisms and creeds—English. I. Pery, Andre. Le cathechisme de Heidelberg. II. Title.

SPERRY, Sidney Branton, 1895- 238.93
Doctrine and covenants compendium. Salt Lake City, Bookcraft 1960. 779 p. 24 cm. Includes bibliography. [BX8628.S7] 60-52227
1. Smith, Joseph, 1805-1844. Doctrine and covenants. I. Title.

TRIPP, Robert M., comp. 238'.9'3
Oaths, covenants & promises: their meaning to Latter-day Saints. Compiled by Robert M. Tripp. Salt Lake City, Utah, Bookcraft [1973] x, 230 p. 24 cm. Includes bibliographical references. [BX8656.T74] 73-83989 4.50
1. Covenants (Church polity) 2. Christian life—Mormon authors. I. Title.

239 Apologetics & Polemics

ALEXANDER, Anthony F 239
College apologetics. Chicago, H. Regnery Co. [1954] 246p. 22cm. [BX1751.A46] 54-37085
1. Catholic Church—Apologetic works. 2. Apologetics—20th cent. I. Title.

ALLEN, Clifton J., 1901- 239
Affirmations of our faith [by] Clifton J. Allen. Nashville, Tenn., Broadman Press [1972] 128 p. 21 cm. (A Broadman inner circle book) Includes bibliographical references. [BT1102.A39] 72-79164 ISBN 0-8054-8115-X
1. Apologetics—20th century. I. Title.

ALLEN, Diogenes. 239
The reasonableness of faith; a philosophical essay on the grounds for religious beliefs. Foreword by Gene Fontinell. Washington, Corpus Books [1968] xx, 140 p. 21 cm. Bibliography: p. 119-133. [BT1102.A4] 68-9032 4.95
1. Apologetics—20th century. 2. Philosophy and religion. I. Title.

BACKLUND, Jonas Oscar, 1875- 239
Our questioning age; does Christianity have the answers? Chicago, Moody Press [1950] 128 p. 18 cm. (Colportage library, 195) [BT1105.B25] 50-7579
1. Apologetics—20th cent. I. Title.

BARBOTIN, Edmond. 239
Faith for today. Translated by Matthew J. O'Connell. Maryknoll, N.Y., Orbis Books [1974] 195 p. illus. 20 cm. Translation of Croire. Includes bibliographical references. [BT1102.B2313] 73-85155 ISBN 0-88344-125-X 3.95
1. Apologetics—20th century. 2. Faith. I. Title.

BARCLAY, Oliver R. 239
Reasons for faith / Oliver R. Barclay. Downers Grove, Ill. : InterVarsity Press, 1974. 142, [1] p. ; 18 cm. Bibliography: p. [143] [BT1102.B24] 74-14304 ISBN 0-87784-764-9 : 2.25
1. Apologetics—20th century. I. Title.

BARNHOUSE, Donald, 1927- 239
Is anybody up there? : Santa Claus, flying saucers, and God / Donald Barnhouse. New York : The Seabury Press, 1977. p. cm. "A Crossroad book." [BT1102.B26] 76-51734 ISBN 0-8164-0305-8 : 6.95
1. Apologetics—20th century. I. Title.

BARRY, Frank Russell, Bp. of Southwell, 1890- 239
Questioning Christian faith. New York, Seabury [1966, c.1965] 192p. 21cm. (Seabury paperback, SP23) [BT1102.B3] 66-4803 1.65 pap.,
1. Apologetics—20th cent. I. Title.

BARTLEY, Robert F., 1890- 239
The star-studded hoax of Christianity with its allied gods, by Robert F. Bartley. [Rev. 2d ed.] Detroit, Harlo, 1969. 287 p. 23 cm. [BL2775.2.B28 1969] 68-59511 5.95
1. Christianity—Controversial literature. I. Title.

BAXTER, Batsell Barrett, 1916- 239
I believe because ...; a study of the evidence supporting Christian faith. Grand Rapids, Baker Book House Co. [1971] 284 p. 22 cm. Bibliography: p. 281-284. [BT1102.B32] 75-172297 ISBN 0-8010-0549-3 3.95 (pbk)
1. Apologetics—20th century. I. Title.

BLAMIRES, Harry. 239
The Kirkbride conversations; six dialogues of the Christian faith. New York, Morehouse-Gorham, 1958. 167p. 19cm. [BT1101.B543] 58-10765
1. Apologetics—20th cent. I. Title.

BLONDEL, Maurice, 1861-1949. 239
The letter on apologetics, and History and dogma. Texts presented and translated by Alexander Dru and Illtyd Trethowan. [1st ed.] New York, Holt, Rinehart and Winston [1965, c1964] 301 p. port. 22 cm. Translation of Lettre sur les exigences de la pensee contemporaine en matiere d'apologetique et sur la methode de la philosophie dans l'etude du probleme reliqieux, and Historie et dogme. Bibliography: p. [289]-293. [B2430.B584L43] 65-12073
1. Philosophy and religion. 2. Apologetics—Methodology. 3. Tradition (Theology) 4. History—Philosophy. I. Dru, Alexander, ed. and tr. II. Trethowan, Illtyd, 1907- ed. and tr. III. Blondel, Maurice, 1861-1949. History and dogma. IV. Title.

BLOOM, Anthony, 1914- 239
God and man / Anthony Bloom. New York : Paulist Press, [1975] c1971. 125 p. ; 19 cm. [BT1102.B55 1975] 75-34845 ISBN 0-8091-1923-4
1. Apologetics—20th century. I. Title.

BRUCE, Frederick Fyvie, 1910- 239
The defence of the Gospel in the New Testament. GrandRapids, Eerdmans [1959] 105p. 19cm. (The Calvin Foundation lectures, 1958) A Pathway book. [BS2397.B7] 59-6950
1. Bible, N. T.—Theology. 2. Apologetics—Early church. I. Title.

BRUCE, Frederick Fyvie, 1910- 239
The defence of the Gospel in the New Testament / F. F. Bruce. Rev. ed. Grand Rapids : Eerdmans, c1977. p. cm. Includes bibliographical references and index. [BS2397.B7 1977] 77-22827 ISBN 0-8028-1024-1 pbk. : 2.95
1. Bible. N.T.—Theology. 2. Apologetics—Early church, ca. 30-600. I. Title.

BRYANT, Alice Franklin. 239
Religion for the hardheaded. [New York] Dodd, Mead [1953] 116 p. 20 cm. [BT1101.B87] 53-10255
1. Apologetics—20th century. I. Title.

BUSHNELL, Horace, 1802-1876. 239
Nature and the supernatural, as together constituting the one system of God. 3d ed. New York, Scribner, 1858. [New York, AMS Press, 1973] 528 p. 19 cm. [BT1101.B97 1973] 70-39569 ISBN 0-404-01246-9 25.00
1. Apologetics—19th century. 2. Natural theology. 3. Supernatural. I. Title.

CARNELL, Edward John, 1919- 239
Christian commitment. an apologetic. New York, Macmillan, 1957. 314p. 22cm. [BT1101.C278] 57-8099
1. Apologetics—20th cent. I. Title.

CARNELL, Edward John, 1919- 239
The kingdom of love and the pride of life. Grand Rapids, Eerdmans [c.1960] 164p. Bibl. 60-53086 3.50
1. Apologetics—20th cent. 2. Love (Theology) I. Title.

CASS, John Aloysius, 1889- 239
Quest of certainty; a modern irenicon. Paterson, N. J., St. Anthony Guild Press, 1950. v, 210 p. 24 cm. [BT1210.C35] 51-2188
1. Apologetics—20th cent. 2. Skepticism—Controversial literature. I. Title.

CASSERLEY, Julian Victor Langmead, 1909- 239
Apologetics and evangelism. Philadelphia, Westminster Press [1962] 186p. 21cm. (Westminster studies in Christian communication) [BT1101.C33] 62-12645
1. Apologetics—20th cent. I. Title.

CHAPMAN, Colin Gilbert. 239
Christianity on trial / Colin Chapman. American ed. Wheaton, Ill. : Tyndale House, 1975, c1972-1974. xiii, 594 p. : ill. ; 23 cm. Originally published in 3 v. by Lion Publishing, Berkhamsted, Eng. Includes bibliographical references and index. [BT1102.C43 1975] 74-19644 ISBN 0-8423-0246-8 : 7.95
1. Apologetics—20th century. I. Title.
Contents omitted

CHESTERTON, Gilbert Keith, 1874-1936. 239
Orthodoxy. Westport, Conn., Greenwood Press [1974, c1908] 299 p. 22 cm. Reprint of the ed. published by John Lane Co., New York. [BR121.C5 1974] 74-2837 ISBN 0-8371-7438-4 13.50
1. Apologetics—20th century. I. Title.

CHRISTIANITY for the tough-minded; essays in support of an intellectually defensible religious commitment. Edited, with introd. and preliminary essay on God's existence by John Warwick Montgomery. Minneapolis, Bethany Fellowship [1973] 296 p. illus. 22 cm. Includes bibliographical references. [BT1105.C55] 73-4842 ISBN 0-87123-076-3 3.95 239
1. Apologetics—20th century—Addresses, essays, lectures. I. Montgomery, John Warwick, ed.

CHURCH, Virginia Woodson Frame, 1880- 239
The adventure of finding God. New York, Abingdon-Cokesbury Press [1950] 160 p. 16 cm. "References": p. 157-160. [BT1101.C53] 50-8026
1. Apologetics—20th century. I. Title.

CLARK, Gordon Haddon. 239
A Christian view of men and things; the Payton lectures delivered in condensed form at the Fuller Theological Seminary, Pasadena, 1951. Grand Rapids, W. B. Eerdmans Pub. Co., 1952. 325 p. 23 cm. [BT1210.C57] 52-12821
1. Apologetics—20th cent. 2. Theism. I. Title.

DE SIANO, Frank. 239
Searching for sense : the logic of Catholic belief / Frank De Siano. N[ew] Y[ork] : Paulist Press, c1975. 189 p. ; 18 cm. (Deus books) [BX1752.D47] 75-23155 ISBN 0-8091-1886-6 pbk. : 1.95
1. Catholic Church—Apologetic works. I. Title. II. Title: The logic of Catholic belief.

DOLAN, Henry Thomas 239
The divine dimension. New York, Morehouse-Barlow Co. [c.1961] 231p. Bibl. 61-5516 4.00
1. Apologetics—20th cent. I. Title.

EDDISON, John. 239
Who died why? [1st ed.] Wheaton, Ill., H. Shaw Publishers [1971] 95 p. illus. 21 cm. [BT1102.E24] 79-165792 ISBN 0-87788-920-1
1. Apologetics—20th century. I. Title.

FITZGERALD, Ernest A. 239
You can believe / Ernest A. Fitzgerald. Nashville : Abingdon Press, [1975] 126 p. ; 19 cm. [BT1102.F46] 74-34281 ISBN 0-687-46710-1 pbk. : 3.25
1. Apologetics—20th century. I. Title.

GEISLER, Norman L. 239
Christian apologetics / Norman Geisler. Grand Rapids : Baker Book House, c1976. 393 p. ; 24 cm. Includes index. Bibliography: p. 379-390. [BT1102.G43] 76-24706 ISBN 0-8010-3704-2 : 9.95
1. Apologetics—20th century. I. Title.

GERSTNER, John H. 239
Reasons for faith. New York, Harper [[c.1960] x, 245 p. 22 cm. (3p. bibl.) 60-5294 4.00, half cloth
1. Apologetics—20th cent. I. Title.

GORMAN, Robert. 239
Catholic apologetical literature in the United States (1784-1858). Washington, Catholic University of America Press, 1939. [New York, AMS Press, 1974] x, 192 p. 23 cm. Reprint of the author's thesis, Catholic University of America, 1939, which was issued as v. 28 of the Catholic University of America. Studies in American church history. "Apologetical publications": p. 165-181. [BX1406.G6 1974] 73-3582 ISBN 0-404-57778-4 9.00
1. Catholic Church in the United States. 2. Catholic Church—Bio-bibliography. 3. Catholic literature—History and criticism. I. Title. II. Series: Catholic University of America. Studies in American church history, v. 28.

THE Grace of God in the Gospel [by] John Cheeseman [and others. London, Carlisle, Pa.] Banner of Truth Trust [1972] 141 p. 19 cm. Bibliography: p. 139-141. [BT1102.G68] 72-169864 £0.30 239
1. Apologetics—20th century. I. Cheeseman, John.

GRIFFITH, Arthur Leonard, 1920- 239
Barriers to Christian belief, [1st ed.] New York, Harper & Row [c1962] 191 p. 22 cm. [BT1102.G75] 63-7605
1. Apologetics — 20th cent. I. Title.

GUITTON, Jean. 239
The church and the gospel. [Translation by Emma Craufurd] Chicago, H. Renery Co., 1961. 288p. 23cm. [BX1752.G813 1961] 61-65664
1. Catholic Church—Apologetic works. I. Title.

GUITTON, Jean Marie Pierre 239
The church and the gospel. [Tr. from French by Emma Craufurd] Chicago, Regnery, 1961 [c.1959,1961] 288 p. 61-65664 6.50
1. Catholic Church—Apologetic works. I. Title.

GUTTERIDGE, Don J. 239
The defense rests its case / Don J. Gutteridge, Jr. Nashville : Broadman Press, c1975. 96 p. ; 19 cm. Bibliography: p. 83-85. [BT1102.G88] 75-27409 ISBN 0-8054-5560-4 pbk. : 2.25
1. Apologetics—20th century. I. Title.

HAENTZSCHEL, Adolph Theodore Esaias. 239
The great paradox. St. Louis, Concordia Pub. House [1959] 156p. 22cm. Includes bibliography. [BT1200.H2] k9-9567
1. Apologetics—20th cent. I. Title.

HAENTZSCHEL, Adolph Theodore Esaias. 239
How about Christianity? St. Louis, Concordia Pub. House, 1961. 117p. 19cm. Includes bibliography. [BT1102.H25 1961] 61-11241
1. Apologetics—20th cent. I. Title.

HAMILTON, Floyd Eugene, 1890- 239
The basis of Christian faith; a modern defense of the Christian religion. Rev. and enl. ed. New York, Harper & Row [1964] xv. 364 p. daigr. 22 cm. Bibliography: p. 331-353. [BT1101.H27] 64-10367
1. Apologetics—20th cent. I. Title.

HAMILTON, Floyd Eugene, 1890- 239
The basis of Christian faith; a modern defense of the Christian religion. Rev., enl. ed. New York, Harper [c.1927-1964] xv, 364p. diagr. 22cm. Bibl. 64-10367 5.00
1. Apologetics—20th cent. I. Title.

HANFT, Frank William. 239
You can believe; a lawyer's brief for Christianity. [1st ed.] Indianapolis, Bobbs-Merrill [1952] 187 p. 21 cm. [BT1210.H318] 52-10275
1. Apologetics—20th cent. 2. Atheism—Controversial literature. I. Title.

HANSON, Richard Patrick Crosland. 239
Mystery and imagination : reflections on Christianity / R. P. C. Hanson. London : SPCK, 1976. xii, 113 p. ; 20 cm. [BT1105.H34] 76-378099 ISBN 0-281-02934-2 : £2.25
1. Apologetics—20th century—Addresses, essays, lectures. I. Title.

HENRY, Carl Ferdinand Howard, 1913- 239
The drift of Western thought. Grand Rapids, Eerdmans, 1951. 164 p. 21 cm. (The W. B. Riley memorial lectures, 1951) Bibliographical footnotes. [BT1101.H518] 51-4098
1. Apologetics—20th cent. 2. Religious thought. I. Title. II. Series.

HIERONYMUS, Saint. 239
Saint Jerome, dogmatic and polemical works. Translated by John N. Hritzu. Washington, Catholic University of America Press [1965] xix, 410 p. 22 cm. (The Fathers of the church, a new translation, v. 53) Bibliographical footnotes. [BR60.F3H52] 65-20802
1. Theology — Collected works — Early church. I. Hritzu, John Nicholas, tr. II. Title. III. Series.

HIERONYMUS, Saint 239
Saint Jerome, dogmatic and polemical works. Tr. by John N. Hritzu. Washington, D.C., Catholic Univ. [c.1965] xix, 410p. 22cm. (Fathers of the church, a new tr., v.53) Bibl. [BR60.F3H52] 65-20802 7.55
1. Theology—Collected works—Early church. I. Hritzu John Nicholas tr. (Series) II. Title.

HIGMAN, Francis M 239
The style of John Calvin in his French polemical treatises, by Francis M. Higman. London, Oxford U. P., 1967. viii, 191 p. 221 cm. (Oxford modern languages and literature monographs) 42/- (B 67-23907) "Revised version of a thesis presented for the degree of Bachelor of Letters at Oxford in 1964." Bibliography: p. [177]-182. [BX9418.H5] 67-114882
1. Calvin, Jean, 1509-1564—Language. 2. Apologetics—Hist. I. Title.

HIGMAN, Francis M. 239
The style of John Calvin in his French polemical treatises. by Francis M. Higman. London, Oxford Univ. Pr., 1967. viii, 191p. 22 cm. (Oxford modern languages and literature monographs) Rev. version of a thesis presented for the degree of Bachelor of Letters at Oxford in 1964. Bibl. [BX9418.H5] 67-114882 6.70
1. Calvin, Jean, 1509-1564—Language. 2. Apologetics—Hist. I. Title.
Available from the publisher's New York office.

HILLIS, Dick. 239
Is there really only one way? / Dick Hillis. Santa Ana, Calif. : Vision House, [1974] 117 p. : ill. ; 18 cm. [BT1102.H53] 74-75877 ISBN 0-88449-005-X pbk. : 1.25
1. Apologetics—20th century. I. Title.

HONG, Howard, 1912- 239
This world and the church; studies in secularism. Minneapolis, Augsburg Pub. House [1955] 143p. 22cm. 'Lectures delivered at the 1952 mid-wint convocation, Luther Theological Seminary, St. Faul, Minnesota'. [BT1210.H56] 55-7121
1. Secularism—Controversial literature. 2. Apologetics—20th cent. I. Title.

HONG, Howard Vincent, 1912- 239
This world and the church; studies in secularism. Minneapolis, Augsburg Pub. House [1955] 143 p. 22 cm. "Lectures delivered at the 1952 mid-winter convocation, Luther Theological Seminary, St. Paul. Minnesota." [BT1210.H56] 55-7121
1. Secularism—Controversial literature. 2. Apologetics—20th cent. I. Title.

*HOOKER, Arlie J. 239
Dear Agnos : a defense of Christianity / Arlie J. Hoover. Grand Rapids : Baker Book House, c1976. 274p. ; 23 cm. [BT1102] 7.95
1. Apologetics-20th century. I. Title.

HOOVER, Arlie J. 239
Dear Agnos : a defense of Christianity / Arlie J. Hoover. Grand Rapids, : Baker Book House, 1977c1976 274 p. ; 23 cm. Includes bibliographical references. [BT1102.H65] 76-151827 ISBN 0-8010-4156-2 pbk. : 7.95
1. Apologetics—20th century. I. Title.

HOWARD, Thomas. 239
Once upon a time, God ... [1st ed.] Philadelphia, A. J. Holman Co. [1974] 114 p. 22 cm. [BT1102.H68] 73-22213 ISBN 0-87981-032-7 3.95
1. Apologetics—20th century. I. Title.

HUBERT, Marie Louise, Sister. 239
Pascal's unfinished Apology; a study of his plan. Port Washington, N.Y., Kennikat Press [1973, c1952] ix, 165 p. 23 cm. Original ed. issued as 2d ser., 3 of Yale Romanic studies. A revision of the author's thesis, Yale University. Bibliography: p. 150-159. [B1901.P44H8 1973] 70-153272 ISBN 0-8046-1699-X 9.75
1. Pascal, Blaise, 1623-1662. Pensees. 2. Catholic Church—Doctrinal and controversial works—Catholic authors. 3. Apologetics—17th century. I. Title. II. Series: Yale Romanic studies, 2d ser., 3.

HUDNUT, Robert K. 239
A thinking man and the Christ, by Robert K. Hudnut. Philadelphia, Fortress Press [1971] viii, 120 p. 18 cm. [BT1102.H8] 74-157539 ISBN 0-8006-0100-9 2.50
1. Apologetics—20th century. I. Title.

INGRAM, Kenneth, 1882- 239
Is Christianity credible? A plain guide for intelligent inquirers. London, Faith Press; New York, Morehouse-Barlow [1963] 166 p. 19 cm. [BT1102.I 6] 64-2357
1. Apologetics — 20th cent. I. Title.

INGRAM, Kenneth, 1882- 239
Is Christianity credible? A plain guide for intelligent inquirers. London, Faith Pr.; New York, Morehouse [1964, c.1963] 166p. 19cm. 64-2357 2.50 pap.,
1. Apologetics—20th cent. I. Title.

KNOX, John, 1900- 239
Limits of unbelief. New York, Seabury Press [1970] 128 p. 21 cm. (A Seabury paperback, SP 65) Includes bibliographical references. [BT1102.K53] 72-11141
1. Apologetics—20th century. 2. Faith. I. Title.

KNOX, Ronald Arbuthnott, 1888- 239
The hidden stream. New York, Sheed & Ward, 1953. 248p. 21cm. [BX1751.K692] 53-5196
1. Catholic Church—Apologetic works. I. Title.

KNOX, Ronald Arbuthnott, 1888- 239
The hidden stream. Garden City, N.Y., Doubleday [1964, c.1953] 197p. 18cm. (Image bk., D178) .75 pap.,
1. Catholic Church—Apologetic works. I. Title.

KOENIG, Richard Edwin. 239
If God is God; conversations on faith, doubt, freedom, and love. Saint Louis, Concordia Pub. House [1969] 100 p. 21 cm. Bibliographical references included in "Notes" (p. 97-100) [BT1102.K6 1969] 77-89878 1.50
1. Apologetics—20th century. I. Title.

KUNG, Hans, 1928- 239
On being a Christian / Hans Kung ; translated by Edward Quinn. Garden City, N.Y. : Doubleday, c1976. 720 p. ; 24 cm. Translation of Christ sein. Includes bibliographical references and index. [BT1102.K8313] 75-36597 ISBN 0-385-02712-5 : 12.95
1. Apologetics—20th century. 2. Theology. I. Title.

LANGFORD, Norman F 1914- 239
Barriers to belief. Philadelphia, Westminster Press [1958] 96p. 20cm. (Layman's theological library) [BT1101.L27] 58-6121
1. Apologetics—20th cent. I. Title.

LEWIS, Gordon Russell, 1926- 239
Testing Christianity's truth-claims : approaches to Christian apologetics / Gordon R. Lewis. Chicago : Moody Press, c1976. 347 p. ; 24 cm. Includes bibliographical references. [BT1106.L44] 75-38501 ISBN 0-8024-8595-2 : 8.95
1. Apologetics—History—20th century. I. Title.

LILLY, William Samuel, 1840-1919. 239
The great enigma. Freeport, N.Y., Books for Libraries Press [1973] p. (Essay index reprint series) Reprint of the 1892 ed. published by D. Appleton, New York. [BT1210.L5 1973] 73-5625 ISBN 0-518-10114-2
1. Apologetics—19th century. 2. Religion and science—1860-1899. 3. Agnosticism—Controversial literature. 4. Rationalism—Controversial literature. I. Title.

LINDEN, James V 239
The fundamentals of religion, by James V. Linden and William T. Costello. Chicago, Loyola University Press, 1956. 344p. 21cm. [BT1107.L5] 56-8512
1. Apologetics. 2. Catholic Church—Apologetic works. I. Costello, William T., joint author. II. Title.

LUBAC, Henri de, 1896- 239
The drama of atheist humanism; tr. by Edith M. Riley. Cleveland, World [1963, c.1950] 253p. 21cm. (Meridian bk., M165) 1.95 pap.,
1. Atheism—Controversial literature. 2. Apologetics—20th cent. I. Title.

LUBAC, Henri de, 1896- 239
The drama of atheist humanism. Tr. by Edith M. Riley [Gloucester, Mass., P. Smith, 1964, c.1950] x, 253p. ports. 21cm. (Meridian bk. rebound) 4.00
1. Atheism—Controversial literature. 2. Apologetics—20th cent. I. Title.

MACINTYRE, Alasdair C 239
Difficulties in Christian belief. New York, Philosophical Library [1960, c1959] 126p. 20cm. [BT1102.M26] 60-2895
1. Apologetics—20th cent. I. Title.

MARTIN, James Alfred, 1917- 239
Fact, fiction, & faith. New York, Oxford University Press, 1960. 186p. 21cm. [BT1102.M34] 61-5478
1. Apologetics—20th cent. I. Title.

MAXWELL, Arthur Graham, 1921- 239
Can God be trusted? / By A. Graham Maxwell. Nashville : Southern Pub. Association, [1977] p. cm. [BT102.M365] 77-10550 ISBN 0-8127-0155-0 pbk. : 1.00
1. God. 2. Apologetics—20th century. I. Title.

MICKLEM, Nathaniel, 1888- 239
Ultimate questions. Nashville, Abingdon Press [c1955] 136p. 23cm. [BT1101.M62] 55-5054
1. Apologetics —20th cent. I. Title.

MILLER, Libuse Lukas. 239
The Christian and the world of unbelief. New York, Abingdon Press [c1957] 240p. 24cm. [BT1200.M5] 57-5078
1. Apologetics—20th cent. I. Title.

MILLER, Randolph Crump, 1910- 239
Religion makes sense. Chicago, Wilcox & Follett [1950] iii, 308 p. 21 cm. [BT1101.M655] 50-6456
1. Apologetics — 20th cent. 2. Church. I. Title.

MILLER, Randolph Crump, 1910- 239
This we can believe / Randolph Crump Miller. New York : Hawthorn Books, c1976. xiii, 200 p. ; 22 cm. Includes index. Bibliography: p. 185-190. [BT1102.M55 1976] 75-31369 ISBN 0-8015-8572-4 : 6.95
1. Apologetics—20th century. 2. Theology, Doctrinal. I. Title.

MOLLEGEN, Albert T 239
Christianity and modern man; the crisis of secularism. [1st ed.*4 Indianapolis, Bobbs-Merrill [1961] 160p. 22cm. [BT1210.M616] 61-7895
1. Secularism— Controversial literature. 2. Apologetics—20th cent. I. Title.

MOLLEGEN, Albert T. 239
Christianity and modern man the crisis of secularism. Indianapolis, Bobbs-Merrill [c.1961] 160p. 61-7895 3.50
1. Secularism—Controversial literature. 2. Apologetics—20th cent. I. Title.

MONTIZAMBERT, Eric St. Lucian Percy, 1888- 239
This we believe! A brief study of the foundations of faith. New York, Morehouse-Gorham Co., 1951. xiv, 142 p. 20 cm. Bibliography: p. 141-142. [BT1101.M7382] 51-9433
1. Apologetics—20th cent. I. Title.

MORNAY, Philippe de, seigneur du Plessis-Marly, called Du Plessis-Mornay, 1549-1623. 239
A woorke concerning the trewnesse of the Christian religion / by Philippe de Mornay ; translated by Sir Philip Sidney and Arthur Golding. A facsimile reproduction / with an introd. by F. J. Sypher. Delmar, N.Y. : Scholars' Facsimiles & Reprints, 1976. xix, 641 p. : port. ; 21 cm. Translation of De la verite de la religion chrestienne. Photoreprint ed. of work originally imprinted in 1587 by G. Robinson for T. Cadman at London. [BT1100.M6513 1976] 75-45384 ISBN 0-8201-1166-X lib.bdg. : 52.00
1. Apologetics—16th century. I. Sidney, Philip, Sir, 1554-1586. II. Golding, Arthur, 1536-1606. III. Title.

MORRIS, Henry Madison, 1918- 239
Many infallible proofs : practical and useful evidences of Christianity / by Henry M. Morris. San Diego, Calif. : Creation-Life Publishers, [1974] ii, 381 p. ; 21 cm. Includes bibliographies and indexes. [BT1102.M67] 74-81484 ISBN 0-89051-006-7 5.95 ISBN 0-89051-005-9 pbk. : 4.95
1. Bible—Evidences, authority, etc. 2. Apologetics—20th century. I. Title.

MORRIS, Thomas V. 239
Francis Schaeffer's apologetics : a critique / by Thomas V. Morris. Chicago : Moody Press, c1976 128 p. ; 22 cm. Bibliography: p. 126-128. [BT1102.M69] 75-43866 ISBN 0-8024-2873-8 pbk. : 2.50
1. Schaeffer, Francis August. 2. Apologetics—20th century. I. Title.

MUNK, Arthur W 239
Perplexing problems of religion. St. Louis, Bethany Press [1954] 176p. 23cm. [BT1101.M82] 54-37558
1. Apologetics—20th cent. I. Title.

MYTH, allegory, and gospel; 239
an interpretation of J. R. R. Tolkien, C. S. Lewis, G. K. Chesterton [and] Charles Williams, by Edmund Fuller [and others] Minneapolis, Bethany Fellowship, inc. [1974] 159 p. facsim. 22 cm. Based on a lecture series held 1969-70, and sponsored by the Departments of Theology and English at DePaul University and the Division of Philosophy and Religion of the DePaul College. Includes bibliographical references. [BT1102.M93] 74-1358 ISBN 0-87123-357-6 4.95
1. Chesterton, Gilbert Keith, 1874-1936. 2. Lewis, Clive Staples, 1898-1963. 3. Tolkien, John Ronald Reuel, 1892- 4. Williams, Charles, 1886-1945. 5. Apologetics—20th century. I. Fuller, Edmund, 1914-
Pbk. 2.95; ISBN 0-87123-358-4.

NORTON, Andrews, 1786-1853. 239
A discourse on the latest form of infidelity; delivered at the request of the "Association of the Alumni of the Cambridge Theological School," on the 19th of July, 1839, with notes. Port Washington, N.Y., Kennikat Press [1971] 64 p. 22 cm. (Kennikat Press scholarly reprints. Series on literary America in the nineteenth century) Reprint of the 1839 ed. [BT1101.N82 1971] 71-122660
1. Apologetics—19th century. I. Title.

O'BRIEN, John Anthony, 1893- 239
Truths men live by, a philosophy of religion and life. New York, Macmillan, 1961 [c.1946] 423 p. (Macmillan paperbacks, 52) Bibl. 1.95 pap.,
1. Apologetics—20th cent. 2. Religion and science—1900- 3. Christianity—Philosophy. I. Title.

OLDHAM, Lewis T. 239
Is there really a God? By Lewis T. Oldham. Valuable assistance rendered by W. L. Oliphant and George A. Klingman. Murfreesboro, Tenn., DeHoff Publications [1965] 121 p. 20 cm. "A series of lectures given by the author in the Tung Shan Gong and Maan Fuk Road Churces of Christ, Canton, China, during the months of March and April, 1931." [BR1102.O4] 65-20978
1. Apologetics — 20th cent. I. Title.

OLDHAM, Lewis T. 239
Is there really a God? [With] assistance of W. L. Oliphant, George A. Klingman. Murfreesboro, Tenn., DeHoff Pubns., 749 N. W. Broad St. [c.1965] 121p. 20cm. Ser. of lects. given by the author in the Tung Shan Fong and Maan Fuk Road Churches of Christ, Canton, China, during the months of March and April, 1931. [BT1102.04] 65-20978 2.25 pap.,
1. Apologetics—20th cent. I. Title.

O'MALLEY, William J. 239
The roots of unbelief : in defense of everything / by William J. O'Malley. New York : Paulist Press/Deus Book c1976. 89 p. ; 18. cm. [BT1105.O45] 75-34840 ISBN 0-8091-1915-3 pbk. : 1.65
1. Apologetics—20th century. I. Title.

ORR, James Edwin, 1912- 239
The faith that persuades / J. Edwin Orr. 1st ed. New York : Harper & Row, c1977. p. cm. (A Harper jubilee book original ; HJ 30) Bibliography: p. [BT1102.O77] 76-62924 ISBN 0-06-066939-X pbk. : 3.95
1. Apologetics—20th century. 2. Religion and science—1946- 3. Religion—Philosophy. I. Title.

OTWELL, John H 239
Ground to stand on. New York, Oxford University Press, 1957. 232p. 22cm. [BT1101.O87] 57-5771
1. Apologetics—20th cent. I. Title.

PASCAL, Blaise, 1623-1662. 239
The Pensees, translated with an introd. by J. M. Cohen. Baltimore, Penguin Books [1961] 287p. 19cm. (The Penguin classics, L110) [B1901.P43C6 1961] 61-2561
1. Apologetics—17cent. 2. Catholic Church—Doctrinal and controversial works—Catholic authors. I. Title.

PASCAL, Blaise, 1623-1662. 239
Pensees, with an English translation, brief notes and introd. by H. F. Stewart. [New York] Pantheon Books [1950] xxiv, 543 p. 23 cm. [B1901.P4 1950] 50-10042
1. Apologetics — 17th cent. 2. Catholic Church — Doctrinal and controversial works — Catholic authors. I. Title.

PASCAL, Blaise, 1623-1662. 239
Pensees. Garden City, N. Y., Doubleday, 1961. 270p. 19cm. (Collection internationale, F7) 'Nous reprodulsons le texte des Pensees d'apres l'edition etablie par Leon Brunschvicg.' [B1901.P4 1961] 61-3274
1. Apologetics—17th cent. 2. Catholic Church—Doctrinal and controversial works—Catholic authors. I. Title.

PASCAL, Blaise, 1623-1662. 239
Pensees, translated with an introd. by Martin Turnell. New York, Harper [1962] 447 p. 22 cm. Bibliographical footnotes. [B1901.P43T8] 62-11134
1. Apologetics—17th cent. 2. Catholic Church—Doctrinal and controversial works—Catholic authors. I. Turnell, Martin, tr.

PASCAL, Blaise, 1623-1662. 239
Pensees; translated [from the French] with an introduction by A. J. Krailsheimer. Harmondsworth, Penguin, 1966. 359 p. 18 cm. (Penguin classics) [B1901.P43K7 1966] 66-72858
1. Apologetics—17th century. 2. Catholic Church—Doctrinal and controversial works—Catholic authors. I. Title.

PASCAL, Blaise, 1623-1662 239
The Pensees, tr. [from French] with introd. by J. M. Cohen. Baltimore, Penguin Books [dist. New York, Atheneum Press., c.1961] 287p. (Penguin classics, L110) 61-2561 1.25 pap.,
1. Apologetics—17cent. 2. Catholic Church—Doctrinal and controversial works—Catholic authors. I. Cohen, John Michael, tr. II. Title.

PASCAL, Blaise, 1623-1662. 239
Pensees; notes on religion and other subjects, ed. with introd. and notes by Louis Lafuma. Tr. [from French] by John Warrington. New York, Dutton [1961, c.1960] xviii, 289p. (Everyman's library, 874. Theology & philosophy) 61-1354 1.95
1. Apologetics—17th cent. 2. Catholic Church—Doctrinal and controversial works—Catholic authors. 3. Jesuits. 4. Port Royal. 5. Jansenists. I. Title.

PASCAL, Blaise, 1623-1662 239
Thoughts [Tr. from French. Gloucester, Mass., Peter Smith, 1961] 320p. (Dolphin bks., C231 rebound) 3.01
1. Apologetics—17th cent. 2. Catholic Church—Doctrinal and controversial works—Catholic authors. I. Title.

PASCAL, Blaise, 1623-1662. 239
Thoughts. Garden City, N. Y., Doubleday [1961?] 320 p. 19 cm. (Dolphin books, C231) [B1901.P43D6] 61-3681
1. Apologetics—17th cent. 2. Catholic Church—Doctrinal and controversial works—Catholic authors.

PENNINGTON, Chester A. 239
Christian counter culture [by] Chester A. Pennington. Nashville, Abingdon Press [1973] 143 p. 20 cm. Includes bibliographical references. [BT1102.P37] 72-13776 ISBN 0-687-07063-5 3.75
1. Apologetics—20th century. I. Title.

PHILLIPS, Ordis E 1886- 239
'I know whom I have believed'; a work on Christian evidences. Philadelphia, Hebrew Christian Fellowship [1957] 319p. 21cm. [BT1101.P45] 57-49206
1. Apologetics—20th cent. I. Title.

PIERHAL, Armand, 1897- 239
The living God; translated from the French by Wilhelmina Guerard. [1st ed.] New York, Harper [1950] 118 p. 20 cm. Translation of v. 1 of the author's Science sans conscience. [BT1101.P523] 50-5499
1. Apologetics — 20th cent. I. Title.

PIKE, James Albert 239
Roadblocks to faith; the believer answers the skeptic [by] James A. Pike, John McG. Krumm. Foreword by Horace W. B. Donegan. New York, Collier [1963, c.1954] 126p. 12cm. (AS502) Bibl. .95 pap.,
1. Apologetics—20th cent. I. Krumm, John McGill, 1913— joint author. II. Title.

PIKE, James Albert, 1913- 239
Roadblocks to faith, by James A. Pike and John McG. Krumm. Foreword by Horace W. B. Donegan. New York, Morehouse-Gorham Co., 1954. 144p. 21cm. (Bishop of New York books, 1954) [BT1105.P46] 54-7335
1. Apologetics—20th cent. I. Krumm, john McGill, 1913- joint author. II. Title.

PITTENGER, William Norman, 1905- 239
Rethinking the Christian message. Greenwich, Conn., Seabury Press, 1956. 147p. 22cm. [BT1101.P6] 56-7972
1. Apologetics—20th cent. 2. Christianity—Essence, genius, nature. I. Title.

PITTENGER, William Norman, 1905- 239
Tomorrow's faith today; essays on rethinking the Christian message toward a new modernism. [1st ed.] New York, Exposition Press [1956] 68p. 21cm. (An Exposition-Testament book) [BT1101.P62] 56-10975
1. Apologetics—20th cent. I. Title.

POOVEY, William Arthur, 1913- 239
Problems that plague the saints. Columbus, Ohio, Wartburg Press [1950] 184 p. 20 cm. [BT1101.P7] 50-12692
1. Apologetics — 20th cent. I. Title.

RAHNER, Karl, 1904- 239
Do you believe in God? Translated by Richard Strachan. New York, Newman Press [1969] vii, 114 p. 22 cm. Translation of Glaubst du an Gott? [BT1102.R3313] 70-77644 3.95
1. Apologetics—20th century. I. Title.

RAMM, Bernard, 1916- 239
Protestant Christian evidences, a textbook of the evidences of the truthfulness of the Christian faith for conservative Protestants. Chicago, Moody Press, 1953. 252p. 22cm. [BT1101.R16] 53-13454
1. Apologetics—20th cent. I. Title.

RAMM, Bernard, 1916- 239
Types of apologetic systems, an introductory study to the Christian philosophy of religion. Wheaton, Ill., Van Kampen Press [1953] 239p. 22cm. [BT1106.R25] 53-7199
1. Apologetics—Hist. 2. Religion—Philosophy. I. Title.

RAMM, Bernard, 1916- 239
Varieties of Christian apologetics. [Rev. ed.] Grand Rapids, Baker Book House, 1961. 190p. 23cm. A revision of Types of apologetic systems. Includes bibliography. [BT1106.R25 1961] 61-17550
1. Apologetics—Hist. 2. Religion—Philosophy. I. Title.

RAMM, Bernard L., 1916- 239
The God who makes a difference; a Christian appeal to reason, by Bernard L. Ramm. Waco, Tex., Word Books [1972] 160 p. 23 cm. Includes bibliographies. [BT1102.R37] 70-188071 5.95

1. Apologetics—20th century. 2. God—Proof. 3. Good and evil. I. Title.

READ, David Haxton Carswell. 239
Overheard [by] David H. C. Read. Nashville, Abingdon Press [1971] 141 p. 19 cm. Talks first presented on the National radio pulpit, produced by NBC radio in association with the Broadcasting and Film Commission of the National Council of Churches. [BT1105.R38] 78-136052 ISBN 6-87299-365- 1.95
1. Apologetics—20th century—Addresses, essays, lectures. I. National radio pulpit. II. Title.

REID, Albert Clayton, 1894- 239
Man and Christ. With a foreword by Frank S. Hickman. Durham, N. C., Duke University Press, 1954. 90p. 22cm. Lectures. [BT1220.R4] 54-11676
1. Apologetics—20th cent. 2. Religion and science—1900- I. Title.

RIMMER, Charles Brandon, 1917- 239
Religion in shreds [by] C. Brandon Rimmer. [With revisions] Carol Stream, Ill., Creation House [1973] 71 p. 18 cm. (New leaf library) Originally published in 1970 under title: The needle's eye. [BT1105.R49 1970] 73-82861 ISBN 0-88419-046-3 1.25 (pbk.)
1. Apologetics—20th century. I. Title.

RUMKE, Henricus Cornelius, 1893- 239
The psychology of unbelief; character and temperament in relation to unbelief. Tr. from the Dutch by M. H. C. Willems. New York, Sheed [1962] 80p. 18cm. (Canterbury Bks.) .75 pap.,
1. Skepticism. 2. Character. 3. Apologetics—20th cent. I. Title.

SCHAEFFER, Francis August. 239
The God who is there; speaking historic Christianity into the twentieth century [by] Francis A. Schaeffer. Chicago, Inter-varsity Press [1968] 191 p. 21 cm. Bibliographical references included in "Notes" (p. 181-187) [BT1102.S3 1968b] 68-29304
1. Apologetics—20th century. 2. Christianity—20th century. I. Title.

SCHLINK, Basilea. 239
Escaping the web of deception / M. Basilea Schlink. 2d English ed. Darmstadt-Eberstadt : Evangelical Sisterhood of Mary, 1976. 60 p. ; 19 cm. Translation of Im Sog der Verfuhrung unserer Zeit. Includes bibliographical references. [BT1105.S3613 1976] 76-379911 ISBN 3-87209-618-4
1. Apologetics—20th century. 2. Deception. I. Title.

SEGRAVES, Kelly L. 239
Sons of God return / Kelly L. Segraves. New York : Pyramid Books, 1975. 191 p. ; 18 cm. Bibliography: p. [187]-191. [TL789.S32] 75-4464 ISBN 0-515-03682-X pbk. : 1.50
1. Bible—Miscellanea. 2. Flying saucers (in religion, folk-lore, etc.) I. Title.

SEYMOUR, Richard A. 239
Religion : who needs it? / By Richard A. Seymour. Chicago : Moody Press, c1977. p. cm. [BT1105.S46] 77-8661 ISBN 0-8024-7191-9 pbk. : 1.25
1. Apologetics—20th century—Addresses, essays, lectures. I. Title.

SHEEN, Fulton John, Bp., 1895- 239
Peace of soul. [Garden City Books reprint ed.] Garden City, N.Y., Garden City Books [1951, c1949] 292 p. 21 cm. [BT1200.S5 1951] 52-1058
1. Apologetics—20th cent. 2. Catholic Church—Apologetic works. 3. Conversion. I. Title.

SHRADER, Wesley. 239
The long arm of God. [1st ed.] New York, American Press, 1955. 105p. 22cm. [BT1101.S546] 55-11592
1. Apologetics—20th cent. I. Title.

*SMITH, Wilbur M. 239
Therefore, stand christian apologetics [by] Wilbur M. Smith Grand Rapids, Baker Book House [1974] xxiv., 614 p. 22 cm. [BT1101] ISBN 0-8010-8036-3 5.95 (pbk.)
1. Apologetics—20th Century. I. Title.

SOPER, Edmund Davison, 1876- 239
The inevitable choice: Vedanta philosophy or Christian gospel. New York, Abingdon Press [c1957] 192p. 21cm. [BT1235.H5S6] 57-5080
1. Apologetics—20th cent. 2. Vedanta. 3. Christianity and other religions—Handulism. 4. Hinduism—Relations—Christianity. I. Title.

SOPER, Edmund Davison, 1876- 239
The inevitable choice: Vedanta philosophy or Christian gospel. New York, Abingdon Press [c1957] 192 p. 21 cm. [BT1235.H5S6] 57-5080
1. Apologetics — 20th cent. 2. Vedanta. 3. Christianity and other religions — Hinduism. 4. Hinduism — Relations — Christianity. I. Title.

TAYLOR, David Bruce. 239
Elements of Christian belief, by D. B. Taylor. Philadelphia, Westminster Press [1969, c1966] xxiii, 170 p. 19 cm. [BT1102.T3 1969] 69-11137 2.45 (pbk)
1. Apologetics—20th century. I. Title.

THOMAS, Fred W., 1931- 239
Kingdom of darkness, by F. W. Thomas. Plainfield, N.J., Logos International [1973] xi, 158 p. 21 cm. Includes bibliographical references. [BF1411.T45] 73-75958 ISBN 0-88270-041-3 1.95
1. Occult sciences. 2. Spiritualism. I. Title.

THOMAS Aquinas, Saint, 1225?-1274. 239
Summa contra gentiles / Saint Thomas Aquinas. Notre Dame [Ind.] : University of Notre Dame Press, 1975, c1955-1957- v. ; 21 cm. Reprint of the ed. published by Hanover House, Garden City, N.Y., under title: On the truth of the Catholic faith. Contents.Contents.—book 1. God, translated, with an introd. and notes, by A. C. Pegis.—book 2. Creation, translated, with an introd. and notes, by J. F. Anderson.—book 3. Providence, translated, with an introd. and notes, by V. J. Bourke. 2 v.—book 4. Salvation, translated, with an introd. and notes, by C. J. O'Neil. Includes bibliographical references and indexes. [BX1749.T4 1975] 75-19883
1. Apologetics—Middle Ages, 600-1500. I. Title.

TITTMANN, George Fabian. 239
Whispers from the dust; inquiries of an agnostic believer [by] George F. Tittmann. Berkeley, Calif., T. Didymus Press, 1971. vi, 140 p. 22 cm. Includes bibliographical references. [BT1102.T58] 70-174184 2.95
1. Apologetics—20th century. I. Title.

TYRRELL, Francis Martin, 1916- 239
Man: believer and unbeliever [by] Francis M. Tyrrell. Staten Island, N.Y., Alba House [1974] xi, 415 p. 21 cm. Includes bibliographies. [BT1102.T9] 73-20055 ISBN 0-8189-0283-3 5.95 (pbk.)
1. Apologetics—20th century. I. Title.

UNGER, Merrill Frederick, 1909- 239
God is waiting to meet you / by Merrill F. Unger ; with Zola Levitt. Chicago : Moody Press, [1975] 159 p. ; 18 cm. Includes bibliographical references. [BT1102.U53] 75-14099 ISBN 0-8024-3021-X : 1.50
1. Apologetics—20th century. I. Levitt, Zola, joint author. II. Title.

VAN TIL, Cornelius, 1895- 239
A Christian theory of knowledge. [Philadelphia] Presbyterian and Reformed Pub. Co. [1969] 390 p. 23 cm. Includes bibliographical references. [BT1102.V3] 76-76781 6.50
1. Apologetics—20th century. 2. Theology, Reformed Church. I. Title.

WEIR, Wilbert Walter, 1882- 239
How real is religion? [1st ed.] New York, Vantage Press [1956] 268p. 21cm. [BT1101.W35] 56-10545
1. Apologetics—20th cent. I. Title.

WEIR, Wilbert Walter, 1882- 239
How real is religion? [1st ed.] New York, Vantage Press [1956] 268 p. 21 cm. [BT1101.W35] 56-10345
1. Apologetics — 20th cent. I. Title.

WOOD, Barry, 1940- 239
Questions non-Christians ask / Barry Wood. Old Tappan, N.J. : Revell, c1977. 160 p. ; 21 cm. Includes bibliographies and index. [BT1102.W65] 77-6280 ISBN 0-8007-0873-3 pbk. : 3.95
1. Apologetics—20th century. I. Title.

DULLES, Avery Robert, 1918- 239'.009
A history of apologetics [by] Avery Dulles. New York, Corpus [1971] xix, 307 p. 24 cm. (Theological resources) Bibliography: p. 277-289. [BT1106.D85 1971] 74-107039 ISBN 0-664-20911-4 9.95
1. Apologetics—History. I. Title.

REID, John Kelman Sutherland. 239'.009
Christian apologetics, by J. K. S. Reid. [1st U.S. ed.] Grand Rapids, Eerdmans [1970, c1969] 224 p. 21 cm. Bibliography: p. 211-212. [BT1106.R4 1970] 71-127632
1. Apologetics—History. I. Title.

PINEAS, Rainer, 1930- 239'.009'031
Thomas More and Tudor polemics. Bloomington, Indiana University Press [1968] xi, 262 p. 24 cm. Contents.Contents.—Lutheran controversy.—William Tyndale.—Robert Barnes.—Simon Fish.—John Frith.—Christopher Saint-German. Bibliography: p. 223-232. [BT1106.P5] 68-14610
1. More, Thomas, Saint, Sir, 1478-1535. 2. Apologetics—History—16th century. I. Title.

PASCAL, Blaise, 1623-1662. 239'.009'032
Pensees. With an English translation, brief notes and introd. by H. F. Stewart. New York, Modern Library [1967] xxiv, 545 p. 19 cm. (Modern Library college editions, T 81) Bibliographical references included in "Notes" (p. [511]-539) [B1901.P4 1967] 67-6009
1. Catholic Church—Doctrinal and controversial works—Catholic authors. 2. Apologetics—17th century. I. Stewart, Hugh Fraser, 1863-1948, ed. II. Title.

AUGSBURGER, Myron S. 239'.009'04
Faith for a secular world, by Myron S. Augsburger. Waco, Tex., Word Books [1968] 96 p. 21 cm. [BT1102.A9] 68-31104 2.95
1. Apologetics—20th century. I. Title.

BARDSLEY, Cuthbert, Bp., 1907- 239'.009'04
Him we declare, by Cuthbert Bardsley and William Purcell. Waco, Tex., Word Books [1968, c1967] vi, 145 p. 19 cm. Bibliographical footnotes. [BT1211.B3 1968] 68-31105 3.95
1. Apologetics—20th century. I. Purcell, William Ernest, 1909- joint author. II. Title.

BELL, Bernard Iddings, 1886- ed. 239'.009'04
Affirmations, by a group of American Anglo-Catholics, clerical and lay. Freeport, N.Y., Books for Libraries Press [1968] ix, 171 p. 22 cm. (Essay index reprint series) Reprint of the 1938 ed. Contents.Contents.—Foreword, by J. D. Perry.—The pertinency of the Christian faith, by B. I. Bell.—Christianity or chaos, by W. A. Orton.—The church and modern thought, by W. M. Urban.—Dogma, science and poetry, by F. A. Pottle.—The church in a day of crisis, by T. O. Wedel.—Revisions, by F. Gavin.—To religion through beauty, by R. A. Cram. Bibliographical footnotes. [BT1095.B4 1968] 68-16906
1. Apologetics—20th century. I. Title.

BOUILLARD, Henri. 239'.009'04
The logic of the faith. New York, Sheed [1967] 185p. 21cm. Bibl. [BT1102.B613 1967] 67-18012 4.00
1. Apologetics—20th cent. 2. Theology, Doctrinal—Hist.—20th cent. I. Title.

BOUILLARD, Henri. 239'.009'04
The logic of the faith. New York, Sheed and Ward [1967] 185 p. 21 cm. Bibliographical footnotes. [BT1102.B613] 67-18012
1. Apologetics — 20th cent. 2. Theology, Doctrinal — Hist. — 20th cent. I. Title.

BOUILLARD, Henri. 239'.009'04
The logic of the faith. Dublin, Gill [1967] 185 p. 22 cm. (Logos books) "Originally published as Logique de la foi." Bibliographical footnotes. [BT1102.B613 1967b] 67-8054
1. Apologetics—20th century. 2. Theology, Doctrinal—History—20th century. I. Title.

CRISWELL, Wallie A. 239'.009'04
Look up, brother! The buoyant assertion of what's right with us [by] W. A. Criswell. Nashville, Broadman Press [1970] 143 p. 21 cm. [BT1102.C7] 71-95416 3.50
1. Apologetics—20th century. I. Title.

GARRISON, R. Benjamin. 239'.009'04
Creeds in collision [by] R. Benjamin Garrison. Nashville, Abingdon Press [1967] 111 p. 20 cm., Bibliographical footnotes. [BT1102.G33] 67-14982
1. Apologetics — 20th cent. I. Title.

GARRISON, R. Benjamin 239.00904
Creeds in collison [by] R. Benjamin Garrison. Nashville, Abingdon [1967] 111p. 20cm. Bibl. [BT1102.G33] 67-14982 2.50 bds.,
1. Apologetics—20th cent. I. Title.

HARTMAN, Olov. 239'.009'04
Earthly things; essays. Translated, with an introd., by Eric J. Sharpe. Grand Rapids, Eerdmans [1968] 235 p. 21 cm. [BT1102.H34] 68-28851 5.95
1. Apologetics—20th century. I. Title.

HICK, John. 239'.009'04
Christianity at the centre. [New York] Herder and Herder [1970] 124 p. 21 cm. Bibliography: p. 119. [BT1102.H5 1970] 75-110792 3.95
1. Apologetics—20th century. I. Title.

JACKSON, Warren W. 239'.009'04
The New Testament in the contemporary world [by] Warren W. Jackson. New York, Seabury [1968] iv, 154p. illus. 21cm. [BJ1102.J3] 67-13314 2.50 pap.,
1. Apologetics—20th cent. I. Title.

KAVANAUGH, James J. 239'.009'04
The struggle of the unbeliever [by] James J. Kavanaugh. New York, Trident Press [1968, c1967] xiii, 207 p. 25 cm. Bibliography: p. 199-207. [BT1102.K3] 68-22569
1. Apologetics—20th century. I. Title.

LITTLE, Paul E. 239'.009'04
Know why you believe [by] Paul E. Little. Wheaton, Ill., Scripture Press Publications [1967] 96 p. 22 cm. Bibliographical footnotes. [DT1102.L5] 67-12231
1. Apologetics — 20th cent. I. Title.

LITTLE, Paul E. 239'.009'04
Know why you believe, by Paul E. Little. [Rev. ed.] Chicago, Inter-Varsity Press [1968] ii, 110 p. 21 cm. Bibliography: p. 109-110. Bibliographical footnotes. [BT1102.L5 1968] 68-8267
1. Apologetics—20th century. I. Title.

LITTLE. PAUL E. 239.00904
Know why you believe [by] Paul E. Little. Wheaton, Ill., Scripture Pr. Pubns. [1967] 96p. 22cm. Bibl. [BT1102.L5] 67-12231 1.25 pap.,
1. Apologetics—20th cent. I. Title.

MCDORMAND, Thomas Bruce. 239.00904
The Christian must have an answer. Nashville, Broadman Press [1959] 112p. 21cm. Includes bibliography. [BT1102.M23] 59-9686
1. Apologetics—20th cent. I. Title.

TRUEBLOOD, David Elton, 1900- 239'.009'04
A place to stand [by] Elton Trueblood. [1st ed.] New York, Harper & Row [1968, c1969] 128 p. 22 cm. Bibliographical footnotes. [BT1102.T7] 69-10474 2.95
1. Apologetics—20th century. I. Title.

WHITNEY, Harold J. 239'.009'04
The new "myth"-ology; an exposure of popular theological "myths" [by] Harold J. Whitney. Nutley, N.J., Presbyterian and Reformed Pub. Co., 1969. 180 p. 21 cm. Bibliography: p. 178-180. [BT1102.W48] 77-81506 2.50
1. Apologetics—20th century. 2. Theology—20th century. I. Title.

BLOESCH, Donald G., 1928- 239'.00922
The Christian witness in a secular age; an evaluation of nine contemporary theologians, by Donald G. Bloesch. Minneapolis, Augsburg Pub. House [1968] 160 p. 22 cm. Contents.Contents.—Introduction: the secularization of Western culture.—Reappraising the Christian witness.—Karl Barth.—Emil Brunner.—Rudolf Bultmann.—Reinhold Niebuhr.—Paul Tillich.—Dietrich Bonhoeffer.—John Robinson.—Harvey Cox.—Thomas Altizer.—Beyond apologetics: a restatement of the Christian witness.—Notes (p. 137-151) [BT1106.B55] 68-25803 2.95
1. Apologetics—History—20th century. 2. Theology, Doctrinal—History—20th century. 3. Theologians. I. Title.

CUNNINGHAM, Richard B. 239'.00924
C. S. Lewis, defender of the faith, by Richard B. Cunningham. Philadelphia, Westminster Press [1967] 223 p. 21 cm. Bibliography [of works by C. S. Lewis]: p. [219]-223. Bibliographical references included in "Notes" (p. [207]-217) [BX5199.L53C8] 67-19299
1. Lewis, Clive Staples, 1898- 2. Apologetics—20th century.

OBJECTIONS to Christian belief 239.082
[by] D. M. MacKinnon [others] Introd. by A. R. Vidler. Philadelphia, Lippincott, 1964[c.1963] 111p. 20cm. Course of lectures given in Cambridge in Feb. 1963 under the auspices of the Divinity Faculty. 64-15408 2.50
1. Apologetics—20th cent.—Addresses, essays, lectures. I. MacKinnon, Donald MacKenzie, 1913- II. Cambridge, University. Board of the Faculty of Divinity.
Contents omitted.

ASPECTS of religious 239'.1
propaganda in Judaism and early Christianity / Elisabeth Schussler Fiorenza, editor. Notre Dame, Ind. : University of Notre Dame Press, c1975. p. cm. "Essays ... originally delivered as lectures in a series on Apologetics and mission in Judaism and early Christianity."

Includes index. [BT1110.A84] 74-27890 ISBN 0-268-00578-8 : 12.95
1. Apologetics—Early church, ca. 30-600—Addresses, essays, lectures. 2. Heroes—Addresses, essays, lectures. 3. Magic—History—Addresses, essays, lectures. 4. Miracles—History—Addresses, essays, lectures. 5. Judaism—History—Post-exilic period, 586 B.C.-210 A.D.—Addresses, essays, lectures. I. Fiorenza, Elisabeth Schussler, 1938-

ATHENAGORAS. 2d cent. 239.1
Embassy for the Christians. The resurrection of the dead. Translated and annotated by Joseph Hugh Crehan. Westminster, Md., Newman Press, 1956. 193p. 23cm. (Ancient Christian writers; the works of the Fathers in translation, no. 23) Bibliographical references included in 'Notes' (p.[117]-182) [BR60.A35 no.23] 56-11421
1. Apologetics—Early church. 2. Resurrection—Early works to 1800. I. Athenagoras, 2d cent. The resurrection of the dead. II. Title. III. Title: The resurrection of the dead. IV. Series.

ATHENAGORAS, 2d cent. 239'.1
Legatio and De Resurrectione. Edited and translated by William R. Schoedel. Oxford, Clarendon Press, 1972. xxxviii, 156 p. 21 cm. (Oxford early Christian texts) Greek text with English translation of Presveia peri Christianon and Peri anastaseos nekron. Bibliography: p. [xxxvii]-xxxviii. [BT1116.A84 1972] 72-196405 ISBN 0-19-826808-4 £2.50
1. Apologetics—Early church, ca. 30-600. 2. Resurrection—Early works to 1800. I. Schoedel, William R., ed. II. Athenagoras, 2d cent. Peri anastaseos nekron. English and Greek. 1972. III. Title. IV. Series.

AUGUSTINUS, Aurelius, 239.1
Saint, Bp. of Hippo.
The city of God: translated by Demetrius B. Zema and Gerald G. Walsh, with an introd. by Etienne Gilson. New York, Fathers of the Church, inc., 1950- v. 22 cm. (Writings of Saint Augustine, v. 6 The Fathers of the Church. a new translation, v. 8 [BR60.F3A8 vol. 6, etc.] 239.3 52-9414
1. Kingdom of God. 2. Apologetics—Early church. I. Title.

AUGUSTINUS, Aurelius, 239.1
Saint, Bp. of Hippo.
The city of God; an abridged version from the translation by Gerald G. Walsh [and others] With a condensation of the original foreword by Etienne Gilson. Edited, with an introd., by Vernon J. Bourke. Garden City, N. Y., Image Books [1958] 551p. 19cm. (A Doubleday image book, D59) Bibliographical footnotes. [BR65.A642 1958] 1958] 239.3 58-5717
1. Kingdom of God. 2. Apologetics—Early church. I. Title.

AUGUSTINUS, Aurelius, 239.1
Saint, Bp. of Hippo.
The city of God against the pagans. With an English translation by George E. McCracken. Cambridge, Harvard University Press, 1957- v. 17cm. (The Loeb classical library. Latin authors. [411]) Latin and English. 'Bibliographical note': v. 1, p. lxxxiii-lxxxix. [PA6156.A82] 239.3 A57
1. Kingdom of God. 2. Apologetics—Early church. I. McCracken, George Englert, 1904- ed. and tr. II. Title. III. Series.

AUGUSTINUS, Aurelius, 239.1
Saint, Bp. of Hippo.
De civiate Dei. Selections with notes and vocabulary by William G. Most. A textbook for colleges, universities and seminaries. 2d ed., rev. and enl. Washington, Catholic Education Press, 1956. 261p. 23cm. Bibliography: p. 22-28. [BR65.A642 1956] 239.3 57-25842
I. Most, William George, 914- ed. II. Title.

AUGUSTINUS, Aurelius, 239.1
Saint, Bp. of Hippo.
De civitate Dei Selections with notes and vocabulary by William G. Most. A textbook for colleges, universities and seminaries 2d ed., rev. and enl. Washington, Catholic Education Press, 1956. 261p. 23cm. Bibliography: p. 22-28. [BR65.A642 1956] 239.3 57-25842
I. Most, William George, 1914- ed. II. Title.

AUGUSTINUS, Aurelius, 239.1
Saint, Bp. of Hippo.
On the two cities: selections from The city of God, edited by F. W. Strothmann. New York, F. Ungar Pub. Co. [1957] 127p. 21cm. (Milestones of thought) [BR65A642 1957] [BR65A642 1957] 239.3 57-13344 57-13344
1. Kingdom of God. 2. Apologetics—Early church. I. Strothmann, Friedrich Willielm, 1904- ed. II. Title.

AUGUSTINUS, Aurelius, 239.1
Saint. Bp. of Hippo.
The city of God against the pagans. v.4. English tr. by George E. McCracken. Cambridge, Harvard [1966] 581p. 18cm. (Loeb classical lib. Latin authors. 411) Latin and English. English. English tr. by Philip Levine [PA6156.A82] A57 4.00
1. Kingdom of God. 2. Apologetics—Early church. I. McCracken. George Englert, 1904- ed. and tr. II. Title. III. Series.
Contents omitted.

TERTULLIANUS, Quintus 239'.1
Septimius Florens.
Adversus Marcionem; edited and translated by Ernest Evans. Oxford, Clarendon Press, 1972. 2 v. 21 cm. (Oxford early Christian texts) Latin text, parallel English translation. Contents.Contents.—v. [1]: Books I-III.—v. [2] : Books IV-V. Bibliography: v. 1, p. xxii-xxiii. [BT1116.T4 1972] 72-183204 ISBN 0-19-826807-6 £8.00
1. Marcion, of Sinope, 2d century. 2. Apologetics—Early church, ca. 30-600. I. Evans, Ernest, 1889- tr. II. Title.

VERSEFELD, *239.1 239.2
Marthinus.
A guide to The city of God. London, New York, Sheed and Ward [1958] 141 p. 21 cm. Includes bibliography. [BR65.A65V43] 58-13982
1. Augustinus, Aurelius, Saint, Bp. of Hippe. De civitate Dei. I. Title.

VERSFELD, Marthinus. *239.1 239.3
A guide to The city of God. New York, Sheed & Ward [1958] 141 p. 21 cm. [BR65.A65V43] 58-10556
1. Augustinus, Aurelius, Saint, Bp. of Hippo. De civitate Dei. I. Title.

JUSTINUS, Martyr, Saint 239.2
Selections from Justin Martyr's Dialogue with Trypho, a Jew. Tr., ed. by R. P. C. Hanson. New York, Association [1964] 80p. 19cm. (World Christian bks., no. 49. 3d ser.) [BR65] 64-57268 1.25 pap.,
1. Trypho, Judaeus. I. Hanson, Richard Patrick Crosland, ed. and trans. II. Title.

AUGUSTINUS, Aurelius, 239.3
Saint, Bp. of Hippo.
City of God. Abridged and translated by J. W. C. Wand. London, Oxford University Press, 1963. xxiii, 428 p. 19 cm. [BR65.A642] 63-25888
1. Kingdom of God. 2. Apologetics — Early church. I. Wand, John William Charles, Bp. of London, 1885- ed. and tr. II. Title.

AUGUSTINUS, Aurelius, 239.3
Saint, Bp. of Hippo.
City of God. Abridged, tr. by J.W.C. Wand. [New York] Oxford [c.]1963. xxiii, 428p. 19cm. 63-25888 3.40
1. Kingdom of God. 2. Apologetics—Early church. I. Wand, John William Charles, Bp. of London, 1885- ed. and tr. II. Title.

AUGUSTINUS, Aurelius, 239.3
Saint, Bp. of Hippo.
The city of God against the pagans. Cambridge, Harvard University Press, 1957-72. 7 v. 17 cm. (The Loeb classical library. Latin authors) Latin and English on opposite pages. Contents.Contents.—1. Books 1-3, translated by G. E. McCracken.—2. Books 4-7, translated by W. M. Green.—3. Books 8-11, translated by D. S. Wiesen.—4. Books 12-15, translated by P. Levine.—5. Book 16-book 18, chapters 1-35, translated by E. M. Sanford and W. M. Green.—6. Book 18, chapter 36-book 20, translated by W. C. Greene.—7. Books 21-22, translated by W. M. Green, and an index to City of God by W. M. Green. Bibliography: v. 1, p. lxxxiii-lxxxix. [PA6156.A82] 73-155442
1. Kingdom of God. 2. Apologetics—Early church, ca. 30-600. I. Title. II. Series.

AUGUSTINUS, Aurelius, 239.3
Saint, Bp. of Hippo.
The city of God, books VII-XVI. Translated by Gerald G. Walsh and Grace Monahan Washington, Catholic University of America Press [1963, c1952] 567 p. 22 cm. (Writings of Saint Augustine, v. 7) The Fathers of the church, a new translation, v. 14. [[BR65.A]] 83-19613
1. Walsh, Gerald Groveland, 1892-1952, tr. I. Monahan, Grace, tr. II. Title. III. Series: The Fathers of the church, a new translation, v. 14

AUGUSTINUS, Aurelius, 239'.3
Saint, Bp. of Hippo.
Concerning the city of God against the pagans. A new translation by Henry Bettenson, with an introd. by David Knowles. Harmondsworth, Penguin Books [1972] 1097 p. 20 cm. (Pelican classics) Translation of De civitate Dei. Includes bibliographical references. [BR65.A64E5 1972] 72-197308
1. Kingdom of God. 2. Apologetics—Early church, ca. 30-600. I. Bettenson, Henry Scowcroft, tr. II. Title. III. Title: City of God against the pagans.

AUGUSTINUS, Aurelius, Bp. 239'.3
of Hippo.
Concerning the City of God against the pagans. A new translation by Henry Bettenson, with an introd. by David Knowles. [Baltimore] Penguin [1972] li, 1097 p. 20 cm. (Pelican classics) Translation of De civitate Dei. Includes bibliographical references. [BR65.A64E5 1972] 72-197308 ISBN 0-14-040022-2 pap., 3.95
1. Kingdom of God. 2. Apologetics—Early church. I. Bettenson, Henry Scowcroft, tr. II. Title. III. Title: City of God against the pagans.

AUGUSTINUS, Aurelius, 239.3
Saint, Bp. of Hippo.
The city of God; translated by Marcus Dods. With an introd. by Thomas Merton. New York, Modern Library [1950] xv, 892 p. 21. (The Modern library of the world's best books. Modern library giants [74]) "Books IV, XVII, and XVIII translated by the Rev. George Wilson. Books V, VI, VII, and VIII by the Rev. J. J. Smith." [BR65.A64E5 1950] 50-8294
1. Kingdom of God. 2. Apologetics—Early Church. I. Title.

DALEY, Leo Charles. 239.3
The works of St. Augustine, by Leo C. Daley. New York, Distributed by Monarch Press [1965] 89 p. 22 cm. (Monarch notes and study guides, 537-1) Cover title: The City of God and the Confessions of Saint Augustine. Bibliography: p. 89. 66-27750
1. Augustinus, Aurelius, Saint, bp. of Hippo. I. Title.

FIRMICUS Maternus, Julius. 239'.3
Firmicus Maternus: the error of the pagan religions. Translated and annotated by Clarence A. Forbes. New York, Newman Press, 1970. v, 251 p. 22 cm. (Ancient Christian writers, the works of the Fathers in translation, no. 37) Translation of De errore profanarum religionum. Bibliography: p. 123-128. [BR60.A35 no. 37] 70-118037 8.95
1. Apologetics—Early church, ca. 30-600. 2. Paganism. I. Forbes, Clarence Allen, 1901- II. Title. III. Title: The error of the pagan religions. IV. Series.

FUCHS, Harald. 239'.3
Augustin und der antike Friedensgedanke. With a new introd. for the Garland ed. by Walter F. Bense. New York, Garland Pub., 1973. 26, 258 p. 22 cm. (The Garland library of war and peace) Originally presented as the author's thesis, Berlin, 1925. Reprint of the 1926 ed., issued as Heft 3 of Neue philologische Untersuchungen. Bibliography: p. 20-26. [BR65.A65F8 1973] 72-147669 ISBN 0-8240-0337-3 15.00
1. Augustinus, Aurelius, Saint, Bp. of Hippo. De civitate Dei. 2. Peace. I. Title. II. Series. III. Series: Neue philologische Untersuchungen, Heft 3.

O'MEARA, John Joseph 239.3
Charter of Christendom; the significance of the City of God. New York, Macmillan [c.]1961. 120p. (St. Augustine lecture ser.: St. Augustine and the Augustinian tradition, 1961) Bibl. 61-15186 2.50
1. Augustinus, Aurelius, Saint, Bp. of Hippo. De civitate Dei. I. Title.

ORIGENES 239.3
Contra Celsum. Tr., d., introd., notes by Henry Chadwick [New York] Cambridge. 1965.cx1.530p. illus. 26cm. First pub. in 1953. Bibl. [BT1116.O7E5] 66-199 18.50
1. Celsus, Platonic philosopher, fl. 180. I. Chadwick, Henry, 1920- ed. and tr. II. Title.

WALKER, Daniel 239'.3'09
Pickering.
The ancient theology; studies in Christian Platonism from the fifteenth to the eighteenth century [by] D. P. Walker. Ithaca, N.Y., Cornell University Press [1972] 276 p. 23 cm. Includes bibliographical references. [BT1106.W3 1972] 72-3841 ISBN 0-8014-0749-4 14.50
1. Apologetics—History. 2. Christianity—Philosophy. 3. Platonists. I. Title.

GERSTNER, John H. 239.4
A predestination primer. Grand Rapids, Baker Book House [c.]1960. 51p. 22cm. 60-2958 .85 pap.,
1. Predestination. I. Title.

ALLISON, Christopher 239.7
FitzSimons, 1927-
Guilt, anger, and God; the patterns of our discontents. New York, Seabury Press [1971, c1972] xi, 164 p. 22 cm. Bibliography: p. 160-164. [BT1102.A42] 71-163970 4.50
1. Apologetics—20th century. I. Title.

ALLISON, Christopher 239'.7
FitzSimons, 1927-
Guilt, anger, and God; the patterns of our discontents [by] C. FitzSimons Allison. New York, Seabury Press [1974, c1972] xi, 164 p. 21 cm. "A Crossroad book." Includes bibliographical references. [BT1102.A42 1974] 73-21665 2.95
1. Apologetics—20th century. I. Title.

BALES, James D, 1915- 239.7
Atheism's faith and fruits. Boston, W. A. Wilde Co. [1951] 176 p. 20 cm. [BT1210.B34] 51-13918
1. Atheism—Controversial literature. 2. Apologetics—20th cent. I. Title.

CASSELS, Louis. 239'.7
The reality of God. [1st ed.] Garden City, N.Y., Doubleday, 1971. viii, 112 p. 22 cm. Bibliography: p. [109]-112. [BT1102.C327] 71-150879 4.95
1. Apologetics—20th century. I. Title.

A Concordance to Pascal's 239'.7
Pensees / edited by Hugh M. Davidson and Pierre H. Dube. Ithaca : Cornell University Press, 1975. ix, 1476 p. ; 25 cm. (The Cornell concordances) [B1900.A16C65] 75-16808 ISBN 0-8014-0972-1 : 27.50
1. Pascal, Blaise, 1623-1662—Concordances. I. Pascal, Blaise, 1623-1662. Pensees. II. Davidson, Hugh McCullough, 1918- III. Dube, Pierre H. IV. Series.

MILLER, Calvin. 239'.7
A thirst for meaning in the face of skepticism and doubt. Grand Rapids, Zondervan Pub. House [1973] 128 p. 22 cm. Includes bibliographical references. [BT1102.M54] 73-2656 3.95
1. Apologetics—20th century. I. Title.

PASCAL, Blaise, 1623-1662. 239.7
Pensees, with an English translation, brief notes, and introduction, by H. F. Stewart New York, Pantheon Books [1965] xxiv, 545 p. 22 cm. Text in French and English. Bibliographical references included in "Notes" (p. [511]-539) [B1901.P4] 65-11079
1. Apologetics—17th cent. 2. Catholic Church—Doctrinal and controversial works—Catholic authors. I. Stewart, Hugh Fraser, 1863- ed. II. Title.

PASCAL, Blaise, 1623-1662. 239.7
Pensees; thoughts on religion and other subjects. Translated by William Finlayson Trotter. Edited and with an introd. and notes by H. S. Thayer; co-edited by Elisabeth B. Thayer. New York, Washington Square Press [1965] xxix, 338 p. 18 cm. Bibliographical references included in "Notes" (p. [287]-[326]) [B1901.P43T68] 65-9381
1. Apologetics—17th cent. 2. Catholic Church—Doctrinal and controversial works—Catholic authors. I. Thayer, Horace Standish, 1923- ed. II. Thayer, Elisabeth B., ed. III. Title.

PASCAL, Blaise, 1623-1662 239.7
Pensees; tr. [from French], introduction by A. J. Krailsheimer. Harmondsworth, Penguin, 1966. 359p. 18cm. (Penguin classics) (Series no. L171) [B1901. P43K7 1966] 66-72858 1.65 pap.,
1. Apologetics—17th cent. 2. Catholic Church—Doctrinal and controversial works—Catholic authors. I. Title.
Available from publisher's Baltimore office

PASCAL, Blaise, 1623-1662. 239'.7
Les pensees. Translated by Martin Turnell. Illustrated by Ismar David. Bloomfield, Conn., Printed for the members of the Limited Editions Club, 1971 [c1962] xix, 184 p. illus. 30 cm. Includes bibliographical references. [B1901.P43T8 1971] 72-176806
1. Catholic Church—Doctrinal and controversial works—Catholic authors. 2.

Apologetics—17th century. I. Turnell, Martin, tr. II. Title.

PASCAL, Blaise, 1623-1662. 239.7
Selections from the Thoughts. Translated and edited by Arthur H. Beattie. New York, Appleton-Century-Crofts[1965] xvii, 124 p. 28 cm. (Crofts classics) Bibliohraphy: p. 123-124. [B1901.P43B4] 65-12901
1. Apologetics—17th cent. 2. Catholic Church—Doctrinal and controversial works—Catholic authors. I. Beattle, Arthur Henry, ed. and tr. II. Title.

PASCAL BLAISE, 1623-1662 239.7
Selections from the Thoughts. Tr., ed. by Arthur H. Beattie. New York, Appleton [c.1965] xvii, 124p. 28cm. (Crofts classics) Bibl. [B1901.P43B4] 65-12901 .50 pap.,
1. Apologetics—17th cent. 2. Catholic Church—Doctrinal and controversial works—Catholic authors. I. Beattie, Arthur Henry, ed. and tr. II. Title.

ROSS, John Elliot, 1884-1946. 239'.7
Truths to live by. Freeport, N.Y., Books for Libraries Press [1972, c1929] x, 246 p. 23 cm. (Essay index reprint series) [BT1101.R78 1972] 72-37834 ISBN 0-8369-2622-6
1. Apologetics—20th century. I. Title.

SOPER, David Wesley, 1910- 239.7
Epistle to the skeptics. New York, Association Press [c1956] 109p. 21cm. [BT1210.S67] 56-6444
1. Skepticism—Controversial literature. 2. Apologetics—20th cent. I. Title.

SOPER, David Wesley, 1910- 239.7
Epistle to the skeptics. New York, Association Press [c1956] 109 p. 21 cm. [BT1210.S67] 56-6444
1. Skepticism — Controversial literature. 2. Apologetics — 20th cent. I. Title.

SPROUL, Robert Charles, 1939- 239'.7
The psychology of atheism, by R. C. Sproul. Minneapolis, Bethany Fellowship [1974] 166 p. 21 cm. Includes bibliographical references. [BT1102.S6] 74-13762 ISBN 0-87123-459-9 2.25 (pbk.)
1. Apologetics—20th century. 2. Theism. 3. Atheism. I. Title.

TOPLISS, Patricia 239.7
The rhetoric of Pascal: a study of his art of persuasion in the 'Provinciales' and the 'Pensees.' Leicester, Leicester Univ. Pr., 1966. 342p. 23cm. Bibl. [PQ1876.P3P74] 66-78161 8.50
1. Pascal, Blaise, 1623-1662. Les provincials. 2. Pascal, Blaise, 1623-1662. Pensees. I. Title.
American distributor: Humanities, New York.

WURMBRAND, Richard. 239'.7
My answer to the Moscow atheists / Richard Wurmbrand. New Rochelle, N.Y. : Arlington House, 1975. 192 p. ; 21 cm. First published in 1975 under title: The answer to Moscow's Bible. [BR128.A8W87 1975] 76-50015 ISBN 0-87000-372-0 : 7.95
1. Christianity and atheism. 2. Sputnik ateista. 3. Atheism. 4. Religions. I. Title.

CASAUBON, Meric, 1599-1671. 239'.8
A letter of Meric Casaubon to Peter du Moulin concerning natural experimental philosophie (1669) and Of credulity and incredulity (1668, 1670) / by Meric Casaubon ; with an introd. by David G. Lougee. Delmar, N.Y. : Scholars' Facsimiles & Reprints, 1976. 600 p. in various pagings : port. ; 21 cm. Reprint of: A letter of Meric Casaubon to Peter du Moulin, published in 1669 by W. Morden, Cambridge; Of credulity and incredulity in things natural, civil and divine, published in 1668 by T. Garthwait, London; Of credulity and incredulity in things divine & spiritual, printed in 1670 by T. N. for S. Lownds, London. [BT1100.C24 1976] 76-47045 ISBN 0-8201-1284-4 : 48.00
1. Epicurus. 2. Apologetics—17th century. 3. Witchcraft. 4. Supernatural. I. Du Moulin, Pierre, 1601-1684. II. Casaubon, Meric, 1599-1671. Of Credulity and incredulity in things natural, civil and divine. 1976. III. Casaubon, Meric, 1599-1671. Of credulity and incredulity in things divine & spiritual. 1976. IV. Title: A letter of Meric Casaubon to Peter du Moulin concerning natural experimental philosophie.

DE WOHL, Louis, 1903- 239.8
Adam, Eve, and the ape. Occasionally illustrated by the author. Chicago, H. Regnery Co., 1960. 118 p. illus. 22 cm. Essays. [BT1102.D4] 60-6637
1. Apologetics—20th cent. I. Title.

GLEGG, Gordon Lindsay. 239'.8
A scientist and his faith [by] Gordon L. Glegg. Foreword by Billy Graham. Grand Rapids, Zondervan Pub. House [1969] 59 p. 21 cm. First published in 1961 under title: The Christ of science. [BT1105.G56 1969] 69-11661
1. Apologetics—20th century. I. Title.

HAINES, Perry Franklin, Rev. 239.8
Christian evidences; or, God reveals Himself to man. Natick, Mass., W. A. Wilde Co. [c.1959] 184p. 21cm. 59-14832 2.95 bds.,
1. Apologetics—20th cent. I. Title.

HAINES, Perry Franklin, 1889- 239.8
Christian evidences; or, God reveals Himself to man. Natick, Mass., W. A. Wilde Co. [1959] 184p. 22cm. [BT1102.H3] 59-14832
1. Apologetics—20th cent. I. Title.

MASCALL, Eric Lionel, 1905- 239.8
The Christian universe [by] E. L. Mascall. New York, Morehouse [1966] 174p. 22cm. (Boyle lects. 1965) Bibl. [BT1102.M36 1966] 66-7066 4.25 bds.,
1. Apologetics —20th cent. I. Title. II. Series.

ANDERSON, Edward W 239.9
Where do we go from here? Seattle [1960] 135p. 22cm. Includes bibliography. [BT1215] 60-3452
1. Communism—U. S. 2. Apologetics—20th cent. I. Title.

ANDERSON, Edward W. 239.9
Where do we go from here? Seattle, 2111 E. 102nd Author, [c.1960] 135p. 22cm. (Bibl. footnotes) 60-3452 1.50 pap.,
1. Communism—U. S. 2. Apologetics—20th cent. I. Title.

BANGS, Carl Oliver, 1922- 239'.9
The Communist encounter; [vital Christianity is the only adequate answer] Kansas City, Mo., Beacon Hill Press [1963] 94 p. 20 cm. [HX536.B258] 62-22160
1. Communism and religion. I. Title.

BARNABAS, pseud. 239.9
Christian witness in communist China. New York, Morehouse-Gorham [1951] 79 p. 22 cm. [BR1285.B3] 51-12957
1. China—Church history. 2. Apologetics—20th cent. 3. Communism and religion. 4. Communism—China. I. Title.

BROWNLOW, Leroy, 1914- 239'.9
Bible vs. Communism. Fort Worth, Tex., Brownlow Publications [1961] 180p. illus. 21cm. [HX536.B83] 61-39194
1. Communism and religion. I. Title.

CADE, James O. 239.9
Communism vs. Christianity; a twentieth century Christian manifesto. San Antonio, Tex., Naylor [c.1964] viii, 112p. 22cm. 63-22563 2.95
1. Communism and religion. I. Title.

ETERNAL thoughts from Christ the teacher [Ed. by] Richard Cardinal Cushing. [Boston] St. Paul Eds. [dist. Daughters of St. Paul, c.1961] [2v.] 349 335p. 61-18863 3.00 2.00 ea., pap., ea., 239.9
1. Jesus Christ—Biog.—Meditations. I. Cushing, Richard James, Cardinal, 1895- ed.

FERRIS, Helen. 239.9
The Christian church in Communist China, by Helen Ferris under the direction of Theodore H. E. Chen. Advance ed. [n. p.] 1952. 1441. 28cm. (Studies in Chinese communism, ser. 2, no. 5) Cover title. Bibliographical footnotes. [BR1285.F4 1952] 56-45138
1. Church and state in China. 2. China—Religion. I. Title. II. Series.

GEREN, Paul Francis, 1913- 239'.9
Christians confront communism. Nashville, Convention Press [1962] 149 p. 19 cm. Includes bibliography. [HX536.G4] 62-11753
1. Communism and religion. 2. Communism—Study and teaching. I. Title.

HOCKIN, Katharine. 239.9
Servants of God in People's China. New York, Friendship Press [1962] 127p. 19cm. [BR1285.H6] 62-7861
1. Christians in China. I. Title.

HORDERN, William. 239.9
Christianity, communism, and history. Nashville, Abingdon Press [1954] 174 p. 21 cm. [BT1240.H6] 54-7029
1. Apologetics—20th century. 2. History—Philosophy. 3. Communism. 4. Sects. I. Title.

IONESCU, Petre Gogoneatza, 1906- 239.9
The Kremlin and the church. [2d ed. Detroit, Distributed by S. J. Bloch Pub. Co., 1953] 80p. 22cm. 'First published in condensed form in the Romanian language entitled 'Was Christ a Communist? July, 1950.' [BT1240.I58 1953] 53-27732
1. Apologetics—20th cent. 2. Communism. I. Title.

LEE, Francis Nigel. 239'.9
Communism versus creation. Nutley, N.J., Craig Press, 1969. xii, 252 p. 21 cm. (University series: historical studies) Includes bibliographical references. [HX536.L563] 77-75003
1. Communism and Christianity. 2. Creation. I. Title.

LESLIE, Kenneth, 1892- 239'.9
Christ, church, and communism. [Gravenhurst, Ontario, Northern Book House; distributed by World Books, New York, 1962] 39 p. 23 cm. Cover title. [HX536.L62] 70-219163
1. Communism and Christianity. I. Title.

MORRIS, Max, 1928- 239'.9
How to win over communism. Grand Rapids, Mich., Zondervan Pub. House [1962] 63p. 21cm. [HX536.M64] 62-5633
1. Communism and religion. 2. Communism. I. Title.

NATIONAL Council of the Churches of Christ in the United States of America. Division of Foreign Missions. Committee on World Literacy and Christian Literature. 239'.9
A Christian's handbook on communism. [3d ed., rev. and enl. New York] Committee on World Literacy and Christian Literature [1962] vi, 86 p. 22 cm. [HX536.C38 1962] 66-43692
1. Communism and religion. I. Title.

O'BRIEN, John Anthony, 1893- 239.9
Jesus spreads His Gospel. Garden City, N. Y. [Doubleday, 1962] 64p. illus. 21cm. (The Catholic know-your-bible program) [BT301.O28] 62-1010
1. Jesus Christ—Biog.—Juvenile literature. I. Title.

STEVENS, Paul M 239.9
The ultimate weapon -- Christianity; the case for a foreign policy of militant Christianity. New York, Nelson [1961] 158 p. 21 cm. [BT1215.S75] 61-7748
1. Apologetics — 20th cent. 2. Communism. I. Title.

STEVENS, Paul M. 239.9
The ultimate weapon--Christianity; the case for a foreign policy of militant Christianity. New York, Nelson [c.1961] 158p. 61-7748 3.95
1. Apologetics—20th cent. 2. Communism. I. Title.

TOMASIC, Dinko Antun, 1902- 239.9
The problem of unity of world communism, by Dinko A. Tomasic. Milwaukee, Marquette University, Slavic Institute, 1962. 31 p. 23 cm. (Marquette University. Slavic Institute. Papers, no. 16) Bibliographical footnotes. [HX518.S8T6] 68-4002
1. Communist strategy. 2. Communist countries—Politics and government. 3. Russia—Relations (general) with China. 4. China—Relations (general) with Russia. I. Title. II. Series: Marquette University, Milwaukee. Slavic Institute. Papers, no. 16

VOOBUS, Arthur. 239'.9
The communist menace, the present chaos, and our Christian responsibility. [2d ed.] New York, ETSE [1957] 116 p. 22 cm. [HX536.V59 1957] 60-23283
1. Communism and religion. I. Title.

VOOBUS, Arthur. 239'.9
The Communist menace, the present chaos, and our christian responsibility. New York, Estonian Theological Society in Exile, 1955. 64 p. 25 cm. (Papers of the Estonian Theological Society in Exile, popular series, 1) Bibliographical footnotes. [HX536.V59] 58-49619
1. Communism and religion. I. Title. II. Series: Ecsti Usuteadlaste Selts Paguluses. Tolmetused: populaarteadusiik seeria, 1

WALLACE, Lillian Parker, 1890- 239.9
Leo XIII and the rise of socialism. [Durham, N.C.] Duke University Press, 1966. viii, 464 p. port. 23 cm. Bibliography: p. [415]-433. [BX1374.W3] 66-16033
1. Leo XIII, Pope, 1810-1906. 2. Socialism and Catholic Church. I. Title.

WALLACE, Lillian Parker, 1890- 239.9
Leo XIII and the rise of socialism [Durham. N.C.] Duke [c.]1966. viii.464p. port. 23cm. Bibl. [BX1374.W3] 66-16033
1. Leo XIII Pope, 1810-1903. 2. Socialism and Catholic Church. I. Title.

240 CHRISTIAN MORAL & DEVOTIONAL THEOLOGY

*ALMA MARIE, Sister 240
Preparing for Confirmation, by Sister Alma Marie, Sister Helen Clare. New York, Sadlier [c.1964] 64p. illus. 21cm. (On our way ser.) .52 pap.,
I. Title.

ARMES, Sybil (Leonard) 240
Devotions for dynamic living. Westwood, N.J., Revell [1967] 126 p. 21 cm. [BV4832.2.A72] 67-11062
1. Devotional literature. I. Title.

BERTRAM, Robert w. ed. 240
Theology in the life of the church. Philadelphia, Fortress Press [1963] v 282 p. 22 cm. Symposium planned by the Conference of Lutheran Professors of Theology. Includes bibliographical references. [BT78.B48] 63-7905
1. Theology, Practical — Congresses. I. Conferences of Lutheran Professors of Theology. II. Title.

BERTRAM, Robert W., ed. 240
Theology in the life of the church. Philadelphia, Fortress Pr. [c.1963] v. 282p. 22cm. Bibl. 63-7905 5.00
1. Theology, Practical—Congresses. I. Conference of Lutheran Professors of Theology. II. Title.

CARTER, Edward, 1929- 240
Spirituality for modern man. Notre Dame, Ind., Fides Publishers [1971] ix, 208 p. 21 cm. Includes bibliographical references. [BX2350.2.C363] 71-142907 ISBN 0-8190-0080-9 6.50
1. Spiritual life—Catholic authors. I. Title.

CROSBY, John F 240
Witness for Christ, by John F. Crosby. Philadelphia, Westminster Press [1965] 96 p. 19 cm. Bibliography: p. [95]-96. [BV4520.C7] 65-12520
1. Witness bearing (Christianity) I. Title.

CROSBY, John F. 240
Witness for Christ. Philadelphia, Westminster [c.1965] 96p. 19cm. Bibl. [BV4520.C7] 65-12520 1.45 pap.,
1. Witness bearing (Christianity) I. Title.

*GILLESE, John Patrick 240
The challenge of suffering. Pulaski, Wis., Franciscan [c.1964] 71p. 19cm. .35 pap.,
I. Title.

KILLINGER, John. 240
For God's sake, be human. Waco, Tex., Word Books [1970] 153 p. 23 cm. [BV4501.2.K49] 77-111961 3.95
1. Christian life—1960- I. Title.

MARTIN, Hugh, 1890- 240
Great Christian books. Freeport, N.Y., Books for Libraries Press [1971, c1945] 128 p. facsims. 23 cm. (Essay index reprint series)

Includes bibliographical references. [BR117.M3 1971] 77-142666 ISBN 0-8369-2242-5
1. Christian literature—History and criticism. I. Title.

MURRAY, Andrew, 1828-1917 240
Be perfect! A message from the Father in heaven to His children on earth; Meditations. Minneapolis, Bethany [c.1965] 171p. 19cm. [BT766.M78] 1.50 pap.,
1. Perfection. I. Title.

MURRAY, Andrew, 1828-1917. 240
Be perfect; "Be perfect as your Heavenly Father is perfect": a devotional study of Christ's Command. Minneapolis, Minn., Bethany Fellowship [1973, c.1966] 171 p. 18 cm. (Dimension Books) [BT766.M78] ISBN 0-87123-031-3 pap., 1.25
1. Perfection. I. Title.

*OBERG, Ernest. 240
Vision of god. New York, Vantage Press, [1974] 69 p. 21 cm. [BV4821] ISBN 0-533-01004-7 3.95
1. Devotional literature. 2. Theology. I. Title.

RYAN, Mary Perkins, 1915- 240
Through death to life. Dayton, Ohio, Pflaum [1965] 125p. illus. 17cm. (Christian experience ser., no. 1; Witness bks., 2) Bibl. [BX2350.2.R9] 65-28084 price unreported
1. Death. 2. Consolation. 3. Christian life—Catholic authors. I. Title.

SCHNEIDER, Louis, 1915- 240
Popular religion; inspirational books in America, by Louis Schneider and Sanford M. Dornbusch. [Chicago] University of Chicago Press [1958] xi, 173p. 24cm. Includes bibliographical references. [BV4818.S36] 58-11958
1. Devotional literature—Hist. & crit. 2. Religion and sociology. 3. U. S.—Religion. I. Dornbusch, Sanford M., joint author. II. Title.

SEVRE, Leif 240.5
The story of the Upper room: 30th anniversary, March--April 1935--1965 [Planned and produced by Earle H. MacLeod. Supervised by the ed.: J. Manning Potts. Nashville, Upper Room, 1965] 96p. illus. (pt. col.) col. map (on lining papers) ports. (pt. col.) 29cm. [BV4800] 65-23640 1.00 bds.,
1. The Upper room. 2. Methodist Church (United States)—Period.—Hist. I. Potts, James Manning, 1895- ed. II. MacLeod, Earl Henry. III. Title.

*ALMA MARIE, Sister 240.7
Preparing for confirmation: confirmation course, teacher's guide and key, by Sister Alma Marie, Sister Helen Clare. New York, Sadlier [c.1964] 80p. 28cm. .25 pap.,
I. Title.

SPIRITUALITY in church and 240.8
world. New York, Paulist Press [1965] viii, 166 p. 24 cm. (Concilium theology in the age of renewal: Spirituality, v. 9) Includes bibliographical references. [BX2350.2.S63] 65-28868
1. Christian life — Catholic authors. 2. Laity — Catholic Church. 3. Christianity — 20th cent. — Addresses, essays, lectures. I. Series: Concilium theology in the age of renewal, v. 9

SPIRITUALITY in church and 240.8
world. New York, Paulist [c.1965] viii, 166p. 24cm. (Concilium theology in the age of renewal: Spirituality, v.9) Bible. [BX2350.2.S63] 65-28868 4.50
1. Christian life—Catholic authors. 2. Laity—Catholic Church. 3. Christianity—20th cent.—Addresses, essays, lectures. I. Series: Concilium theology in the age of renewal, v.9

*LEWIS, Clive Staples, 240.81
1898-
The weight of glory, and other addresses. Grand Rapids, Mich., Eerdmans [1965, c.1949] 66p. 20cm. First pub. in England under title: Transposition and other addresses. 1.00 pap.,
I. Title.

BLACKBURN, Emmeline 240.82
Alethea, 1910- ed.
A treasury of the Kingdom; an anthology compiled by E. A. Blackburn and others. New York, Oxford University Press, 1954. 280p. 20cm. [BR53.B55] 54-10012
1. Religious literature (Selections: Extracts, etc.) 2. Religious poetry. I. Title.

LUNDQUIST, Amos Theodore, 240.82
1896- comp.
Inspiration for today; readings for church and home. Rock Island, Ill., Augustana Book Concern [1950] xi, 244 p. 20 cm. Verse and prose. [PN6071.R4L8] 50-58178
1. Religious literature (Selections: Extracts, etc.) I. Title.

241 Moral Theology

ABAILARD, Pierre, 1079-1142. 241
Abailard's Ethics / translated with an introd. by J. Ramsay McCallum ; foreword by Kenneth E. Kirk. Merrick, N.Y. : Richwood Pub. Co., [1976] p. cm. Reprint of the 1935 ed. published by Basil Blackwell, Oxford. Includes index. Bibliography: p. [BJ255.A25E8413 1976] 76-39931 ISBN 0-915172-08-9 lib.bdg. : 12.50
1. Christian ethics. I. McCallum, James Ramsay. II. Title.

ALLISON, Christopher Fitz 241
Simmons, 1927-
Fear, love, and worship New York, Seabury, [1965,c1962] 144p. 21 cm. (SP17) [BV10.2.A4] 62-7473 1.45pap.,
1. Worship. 2. Fear. I. Title.

ALLISON, Christopher 241
FitzSimons, 1927-
Fear, love and worship. Greenwich, Conn., Seabury [c.1962] 143p. 62-7473 2.75 bds.,
1. Worship. 2. Fear. I. Title.

ALLISON, Christopher 241
FitzSimons, 1927-
Fear, love, and worship. Greenwich, Conn., Seabury Press [1962] 143p. 20cm. [BV10.2.A4] 62-7473
1. Worship. 2. Fear. I. Title.

AQUINAS Institute of 241
Philosophy and Theology. Institute of Spiritual Theology
Sex, love, & the life of the spirit. Augustine Rock, ed. Chicago, Priory Pr. [c.1966] xii, 236p. 23cm. (Its Special lects., v.1, 1965) Bibl. [BT708.A7] 66-17485 5.00
1. Sex (Theology) I. Rock, Augustine, ed. II. Title. III. Series.

BAELZ, Peter. 241
Ethics and belief / Peter Baelz. New York : Seabury Press, 1977. 117 p. ; 21 cm. (Issues in religious studies) "A Crossroad book." Includes index. Bibliography: p. 114-115. [BJ47.B33 1977] 76-15425 ISBN 0-8164-1229-4 pbk. : 3.95
1. Religion and ethics. I. Title.

BAKER, Wesley C. 241
The open end of Christian morals, by Wesley C. Baker. Philadelphia, Westminister [1967] 170p. 21cm. [BJ1251.B27] 67-15087 2.25 pap.,
1. Christian ethics—Presbyterian authors. I. Title.

BARR, O. Sydney. 241
The Christian new morality; a Biblical study of situation ethics [by] O. Sydney Barr. New York, Oxford University Press, 1969. x, 118 p. 22 cm. Bibliography: p. 117-118. [BJ1251.B344] 69-17758 4.00
1. Situation ethics. I. Title.

BARRETT, Edward John Boyd, 241
1883-
Life begins with love. Milwaukee, Bruce Pub. Co. [1952] 114 p. 21 cm. [BV4639.B34] 52-3971
1. Love (Theology) I. Title.

BARTH, Karl, 1886-1968. 241
On marriage. Philadelphia, Fortress Press [1968] v, 56 p. 19 cm. (Facet books. Social ethics series, 17) Translation of pt. 4 of v. III, Die Lehre von der Schopfung, of the author's Die kirchliche Dogmatik. Bibliography: p. 54. [BT706.B313] 68-11462
1. Marriage. I. Title. II. Series.

BATTISTA, O. A. 241
How love can change your life. Pulaski, Wisconsin, Franciscan Publishers, [c.]1960. 47p. 19cm. .25 pap.,
I. Title.

*BAXTER, Batsell Barrett. 241
America; its not too late. Grand Rapids, Baker Book House [1974] 121 p. 18 cm. [BJ1251] ISBN 0-8010-0622-8 0.95 (pbk.)
1. Christian ethics. I. Title.

BEACH, Waldo, ed. 241
Christian ethics; sources of the living tradition. Edited with introductions by Waldo Beach and H. Richard Niebuhr. [2d ed.] New York, Ronald Press Co. [1973] ix, 550 p. 22 cm. Includes bibliographies. [BJ1201.B4 1973] 72-91122 8.00
1. Christian ethics—History—Sources. I. Niebuhr, Helmut Richard, 1894-1962, joint ed. II. Title.

BECK, Frank B. 241
Questions on worldliness, what about--television, smoking. dancing, the theater, the lodge, gambling. Grand Rapids, Michigan, Zondervan [c.1960] 32p. 20cm. .35 pap.,
I. Title.

BECKER, Edwin L. 241
Responding to God's call [by] Edwin L. Becker. Illus. by Don Kueker. St. Louis, Bethany Press [1970] 128 p. col. illus. 22 cm. Includes bibliographical references. [BJ1251.B38] 75-98399 1.75
1. Christian ethics. I. Title.

BENNETT, John Coleman, 1902- 241
The radical imperative : from theology to social ethics / by John C. Bennett. Philadelphia : Westminster Press, [1975] 208 p. ; 22 cm. Includes bibliographical references. [BJ1251.B43] 75-15538 ISBN 0-664-20824-X : 8.50 ISBN 0-664-24769-5 pbk. : 4.50 pbk.
1. Christian ethics. 2. Social ethics. I. Title.

BERTSCHE, Leopold. 241
The life of love; meditations on the love of God. Translated by Frank Albert. Westminster, Md., Newman Press, 1964. xii, 193 p. illus. 15 cm. [BX2184.B463] 63-12238
1. Love (Theology) — Meditations. I. Title.

BERTSCHE, Leopold 241
The life of love; meditations on the love of God. Tr. by Frank Albert. Westminster, Md., Newman [c.]1964. xii, 193p. illus. 15cm. 63-12238 3.50
1. Love (Theology)—Meditations. I. Title.

BIRCH, Bruce C. 241
Bible and ethics in the Christian life / Bruce C. Birch, Larry L. Rasmussen. Minneapolis : Augsburg Pub. House, c1976. 221 p. : 21 cm. Bibliography: p. 217-221. [BS680.E84B57] 76-3856 ISBN 0-8066-1542-7 : 8.95.
1. Bible—Ethics. 2. Christian ethics. I. Rasmussen, Larry L., joint author. II. Title.

BLENKINSOPP, Joseph, 1927- 241
Sexuality and the Christian tradition. Dayton, Ohio, Pflaum Press, 1969. xi, 127 p. 21 cm. (Themes for today) Bibliographical footnotes. [HQ63.B5] 79-93011 2.95
1. Sex and religion. 2. Sex (Theology) I. Title.

BOCKLE, Franz. 241
Fundamental concepts of moral theology. Translated by William Jerman. New York, Paulist Press [1968] v. 111 p. 21 cm. (Exploration books) Translation of Grundbegriffe der moral. Bibliography: p. 111. [BX1758.2.B5713] 68-16668
1. Christin ethics—Catholic authors. I. Title.

BOCKLE, Franz. 241
Fundamental concepts of moral theology. Translated by William Jerman. New York, Paulist Press [1968] v, 111 p. 21 cm. (Exploration books) Translation of Grundbegriffe der Moral. Bibliography: p. 111. [BX1758.2.B5713] 68-16668
1. Christian ethics—Catholic authors. I. Title.

BOCKLE, Franz. 241
Law and conscience. Translated by M. James Donnelly. New York, Sheed and Ward [1966] 139 p. 21 cm. Bibliographical references included in "Footnotes" (p. [133]-139) [BJ1200.B613] 66-22009
1. Christian ethics — Catholic authors. 2. Law and gospel. 3. Catholic Church — Relations — Protestant churches. 4. Protestant churches — Relations — Catholic Church. I. Title.

BOCKLE, Franz 241
Law and conscience. Tr. by M. James Donnelly. New York, Sheed [1966] 139p. 21cm. Bibl. [BJ1200.B613] 66-22009 3.75
1. Christian ethics—Catholic authors. 2. Law and gospel. 3. Catholic Church—Relations—Protestant churches. 4. Protestant churches—Relations—Catholic Church. I. Title.

BOCKLE, Franz, ed. 241
Moral problems and Christian personalism. [Editor: Franz Bockle] New York, Paulist Press [1965] viii, 183 p. 24 cm. (Concillum theology in the age of renewal: Moral theology, v. 5) Bibliographical footnotes. [BJ1251.M63] 65-24045
1. Christian ethics — Catholic authors. I. Title. II. Series: Concillum theology in the age of renewal, v. 5

BOGGS, Wade H 241
All ye who labor; a Christian interpretation of daily work. Richmond, John Knox Press [1961] 288p. 21cm. Includes bibliography. [BV4740.B6] 61-13480
1. Vocation. I. Title.

BOOZER, Jack 241
Faith to act; an essay on the meaning of Christian existence [by] Jack Boozer, William A. Beardslee. Nashville, Abingdon [1967] 272p. 23cm. Bibl. [BJ1251,B6] 67-22763 5.75
1. Christian ethics. I. Beardslee, William A., joint author. II. Title.

BOOZER, Jack. 241
Faith to act; an essay on the meaning of Christian existence [by] Jack Boozer & William A. Beardslee. Nashville, Abingdon Press [1967] 272 p. 23 cm. Bibliographical footnotes. [BJ1251.B6] 67-22763
!. Christian ethics. I. Beardslee, William A., joint author. II. Title.

BOURDEAU, Francois. 241
Introduction to the law of Christ [by] F. Bourdeau [and] A. Danet. Pref. by Bernard Haring. [Translated by Edward Gallagher. Staten Island, N. Y., Alba House, 1966] 242 p. 22 cm. Bibliographical footnotes. [BJ1249.B613] 66-16471
1. Christian ethics — Catholic authors. I. Danet, Armand, joint author. II. Title. III. Title: The law of Christ.

BOURDEAU, Francois 241
Introduction to the law of Christ [by] F. Bourdeau, A. Danet. Pref. by Bernard Haring [Tr. from French by Edward Gallagher. Staten Island, N.Y., Alba, c.1966] 242p. 22cm. Bibl. [BJ1249.B613] 66-16471 3.95
1. Christian ethics—Catholic authors. I. Danet, Armand, joint author. II. Title. III. Title: The law of Christ.

*BOYER, Rev. Leland J. 241
God's law of love; teacher's manual. by Rev. Leland J. Boyer, Rev. Dominic Bebek, William J. Reedy. Advisory comm.: Rt. Rev. Msgr. John K. Clarke [others] New York, Sadlier [c.1963] 187 p. illus. (pt. col.) (pt. col.) (Confraternity high sch. ser., bk. 3) 1.25, pap., plastic bdg.
I. Bebek, Dominic, joint author. II. Title.

BRETHREN. 241
Second thoughts on the new morality. Bristol, Evangelical Christian Literature [1966] 64 p. 20 cm. 5/6 (B 67-3759) Papers presented at a conference in Swanwick, 1965. Includes bibliographies. [BJ1191.B7] 68-134380
1. Christian ethics—Addresses, essays, lectures. I. Title.

BROWN, S. Spencer N. 241
Christian answers to teenage sex questions, by S. Spencer N. Brown. [1st ed.] Atlanta, Hallux [1970] vi, 198 p. 24 cm. (A Genesis Press book) Bibliography: p. 195-198. Answers from a Christian viewpoint the questions teenagers ask about sex and love. [HQ63.B74] 79-123355 ISBN 0-87667-061-3 4.95
1. Sexual ethics—Juvenile literature. 2. Sex and religion—Juvenile literature. I. Title.

BURGESS, Cale Kight, 1891- 241
The greatest of these is love. Raleigh, N. C., Brotherhood Press [1953] 245p. 21cm. [BV4639.B87] 53-36466
1. Love (Theology) I. Title.

BUTZER, Martin, 1491-1551. 241
Instruction in Christian love, 1523; translated by Paul Traugott Fuhrmann, with introd. and notes Richmond, John Knox Press [1952] 68 p. port. 20 cm. Translation of Das ym selbs niemat/sonder anderea leben soll, vnd wie der mensch dahyn kummen mog. [BV4500.B863] 52-11491
1. Christian life. I. Title.

CALLAHAN, Sidney Cornelia. 241
Beyond birth control; the Christian experience of sex. New York, Sheed and Ward [1968] 248 p. 21 cm. Includes bibliographical references. [BT708.C3] 68-13848
1. Sex (Theology) 2. Marriage. I. Title.

CALVIN, Jean, 1509-1564. 241
Golden booklet of the true Christian life; a modern translation from the French and the Latin, edited by Henry J. van Andel. Grand Rapids, Baker Book House, 1952. 98 p. 16 cm. [BV4500.C313] 52-36167
1. Christian life. I. Title.

CALVIN, Jean, 1509-1564. 241
Golden booklet of the true Christian life. A modern translation from the French and the Latin by Henry J. Van Andel. Grand Rapids, Baker Book House, 1955 [c1952] 98p. 16cm. Translation of De vita hominis Christiani. [BV4500.C313 1955] 55-12085
1. Christian life. I. Title.

CANICE, Father. 241
Humility; the foundation of the spiritual life, with a pref. by Very Rev. Dr. James. Westminster, Md., Newman Press, 1951. 93 p. 20 cm. [BV4647.H8C3] 52-897
1. Humility. I. Title.

CARLSON, Sebastian. 241
The virtue of humility. Dubuque, W. C. Brown Co. [c1952] xiii, 144p. 23cm. (Dominican Fathers, Province of St. Albert the Great. The Aquinas library. Doctrinal studies, 1) Bibliography: p. 137-139. [BV4647.H8C32] 53-1678
1. Humility. I. Title. II. Series: Dominicans. Province of St. Albert the Great. Doctrinal studies, 1

CARPENTER, Edward Frederick, 1910- 241
Common sense about Christian ethics. New York, Macmillan, 1962[c.1961] 174p. (Common sense ser.) 62-9276 2.95
1. Christian ethics. I. Title.

CARTER, Del. 241
Good news for Grimy Gulch / by Del Carter ; based on the Tumbleweeds comic strip by Tom K. Ryan. Valley Forge, PA : Judson Press, c1977. [64] p. : ill. ; 22 cm. [BJ1275.C35 1977] 76-48545 ISBN 0-8170-0736-9 pbk. : 1.50
1. Christian ethics. I. Ryan, Tom K. II. Title.

CATHOLIC Church. Pope. 241
The human body. Selected and arr. by the monks of Solesmes. [Boston] St. Paul Editions [1960] 394, 51p. 20cm. (Papal teachings) Includes bibliography. [BT701.2.C313] 60-4698
1. Man (Theology)—Papal documents. 2. Body, Human—Papal documents. 3. Medicine and religion—Papal documents. I. Solesmes, France. Saint-Pierre (Benedictine abbey) II. Title.

CATTAUI DE MENASCE, Giovanni, 1904- 241
The dynamics of morality [by] C. G. de Menasce. Translated by Bernard Bommarito. New York, Sheed and Ward [1961] 353p. 22cm. Translation of Saggi di analisl dell'atto morale. Includes bibliography. [BX1758.2.C313] 61-11792
1. Christian ethics—Catholic authors. I. Title.

CHAUNCEY, George A., 1927- 241
Decisions! Decisions! [By] George A. Chauncey. Cartoons by Jim Crane. Richmond, John Knox Press [1972] 127 p. illus. 19 cm. (Christian ethics for modern man) (Chime paperbacks) Bibliography: p. [126]-127. [BJ1251.C476] 73-161841 ISBN 0-8042-9090-3 1.00
1. Christian ethics. I. Title.

CHEEVER, George Barrell, 1807-1890. 241
The guilt of slavery and the crime of slaveholding, demonstrated from the Hebrew and Greek scriptures. New York, Negro Universities Press [1969] viii, 472 p. 23 cm. Reprint of the 1860 ed. Bibliographical footnotes. [E449.C512 1969] 69-16586
1. Bible—Criticism, interpretation, etc. 2. Slavery in the United States—Controversial literature—1860. I. Title.

COLE, Stephen, pseud. 241
The hell of it; a devil's guide to tempting Americans. Garden City, N.Y., Doubleday, [c.]1960. 95p. 22cm. 60-8858 1.95
1. Sins. I. Title.

COLIN, Louis 241
Love one another. Translated from the French by Fergus Murphy. Westminster, Md., Newman Press, 1960. xiii, 325p. 21cm. (bibl. footnotes) 60-8654 4.25
1. Love (Theology) 2. Charity. 3. Christian life—Catholic authors. 4. Catholic action. I. Title.

COLIN, Louis, 1884- 241
Love the Lord the God. Translated from the French by Donald Attwater. Westminster, Md., Newman Press [c1956] 240p. 21cm. Translation of Caritas. [BV4639.C582] 56-11418
1. Love (Theology) I. Title.

CONGAR, Yves Marie Joseph, 1904- 241
Lay people in the church; a study for a theology of laity [by] Yves M. J. Congar. Translated by Donald Attwater. [2d] rev. ed., with additions by the author. Westminster, Md., Newman Press, 1965. xxi, 408 p. 22 cm. 612 262.15 65-28804rev Translation of Jalons pour une theologie du laicat. Bibliographical footnotes. [BX1920.]
1. Catholic Church. 2. Laity—Catholic Church. 3. Priesthood, Universal. 4. Catholic action. I. Title.

CONNELL, Francis Jeremiah, 1888- 241
Outlines of moral theology. Milwaukee, Bruce [1953] 247p. 23cm. [BX1758.C6] 53-3554
1. Christian ethics—Catholic authors. I. Title.

COTTRELL, Georgia Wright. 241
Burning bushes. Washington, Review and Herald Pub. Association [1956] 219p. 21cm. [BV4520.C67] 56-58664
1. Ability. 2. Duty. I. Title.

COX, Harvey Gallagher, comp. 241
The situation ethics debate, edited with an introd. by Harvey Cox. Philadelphia, Westminster Press [1968] 285 p. 19 cm. Bibliography: p. [273]-285. [BJ1251.F55C6] 68-11991
1. Fletcher, Joseph Francis, 1905- Situation ethics. 2. Situation ethics. I. Title.

CRESPY, Georges. 241
Marriage and Christian tradition [by] George Crespy, Paul Evdokimov [and] Christian Duquoc. Translated by Agnes Cunningham. Techny, Ill., Divine Word Publications [1968] ix, 178 p. 18 cm. (Churches in dialogue) Translation of Le mariage. Bibliographical footnotes. [BT706.C683] 68-8360 1.95
1. Marriage. I. Evdokimoff, Paul. II. Duquoc, Christian. III. Title.

CUDWORTH, Ralph, 1617-1688. 241
A treatise concerning eternal and immutable morality / Ralph Cudworth. New York : Garland Pub., 1976. p. cm. (British philosophers and theologians of the 17th and 18th centuries ; no. 17) Reprint of the 1731 ed. printed for J. and J. Knapton, London. [BJ1241.C8 1976] 75-11214 ISBN 08240-1768-4 lib.bdg. : 25.00
1. Christian ethics. I. Title. II. Series.

CURRAN, Charles E. 241
Absolutes in moral theology? Edited by Charles E. Curran. Washington, Corpus Books [1968] 320 p. 21 cm. Bibliographical references included in "Notes" (p. 261-312) [BX1758.2.C8] 68-10448
1. Christian ethics—Catholic authors. I. Title.

CURRAN, Charles E. 241
Catholic moral theology in dialogue [by] Charles E. Curran. Notre Dame, Ind., Fides Publishers [1972] ix, 270 p. 21 cm. Includes bibliographical references. [BX1758.2.C817] 71-172639 ISBN 0-8190-0572-X 6.50
1. Christian ethics—Catholic authors. I. Title.

CURRAN, Charles E. 241
Contemporary problems in moral theology [by] Charles E. Curran. Notre Dame, Ind., Fides Publishers [1970] 272 p. 21 cm. Includes bibliographies. [BX1758.2.C82] 76-104749 6.50
1. Christian ethics—Catholic authors—Addresses, essays, lectures. I. Title.

CURRAN, Charles E. 241
A new look at Christian morality; Christian morality today, II [by] Charles E. Curran. Notre Dame, Ind., Fides Publishers [1968] viii, 249 p. 21 cm. Includes bibliographical references. [BJ1249.C82] 71-33 5.95
1. Christian ethics—Catholic authors. I. Title. II. Title: Christian morality today, II.

CURRAN, Charles E. 241
New perspectives in moral theology [by] Charles E. Curran. Notre Dame, Ind., Fides Publishers [1974] ix, 284 p. 21 cm. Includes bibliographical references. [BX1758.2.C825] 74-940 ISBN 0-8190-0602-5 8.50
1. Christian ethics—Catholic authors. 2. Social ethics. I. Title.

CURRAN, Charles E. 241
New perspectives in moral theology / Charles E. Curran. Notre Dame, [Ind.] : University of Notre Dame Press, 1976, c1974. ix, 284 p. ; 21 cm. Reprint of the ed. published by Fides Publishers, Notre Dame, Ind. Includes bibliographical references and index. [BX1758.2.C825 1976] 76-13206 ISBN 0-268-01449-3 10.95 ISBN 0-268-01450-7 pbk. : 3.95
1. Christian ethics—Catholic authors. 2. Social ethics. I. Title.

CURRAN, Charles E. 241
Ongoing revision : studies in moral theology / by Charles E. Curran. Notre Dame, Ind. : Fides Publishers, [1975] p. cm. Includes bibliographical references. [BX1758.2.C83] 75-28450 ISBN 0-8190-0612-2 : 10.95
1. Christian ethics—Catholic authors—Addresses, essays, lectures. I. Title.

CUTTAZ, Francois Joseph 241
Fraternal charity, its theology and its application. [Tr. from French by Malachy Gerard Carroll] Staten Island, N.Y., Alba [1964, c.1962] xi, 279p. 19cm. 63-21604 4.95
1. Charity. I. Title.

DALY, Cahal B. 241
Morals, law, and life, by Cahal B. Daly. Chicago, Scepter [1966] 228p. 19cm. Bibl. 66-21148 2.95; .95 pap.,
1. Williams, Glanville Llewelyn, 1911- The sanctity of life and the criminal law. 2. Sex and law. I. Title.

DANIEL-ROPS, Henry [Henry Jules Charles Petiot] 241
Of human love. Notre Dame, Ind., Fides Publishers [1960] 58p. 18cm. 60-722 .75 pap.,
1. Love (Theology)—Biblical teaching. I. Title.

D'ARCY, Eric, 1924- 241
Conscience and its right to freedom. New York, Sheed & Ward [1962, c.1961] 277p. Bibl. 62-9104 3.50 bds.,
1. Conscience. 2. Liberty of conscience. 3. Christian ethics—Catholic authors. I. Title.

DEFERRARI, Teresa Mary. 241
The problem of charity for self; a study of the doctrine and its presentation to college students. [Boston] St. Paul Editions [1962] 205 p. 22 cm. [BV4639.D38 1962a] 62-20471
1. Self-love (Theology) I. Title.

DEFERRARI, Teresa Mary 241
The problem of charity for self; a study of the doctrine and its presentation to college students. [Boston] St. Paul Eds. [dist. Daughters of St. Paul, c.1962] 205p. 22cm. 62-20471 3.50; 2.50 pap.,
1. Self-love (Theology) I. Title.

DE WOLF, Lotan Harold, 1905- 241
Responsible freedom; guidelines to Christian action [by] L. Harold DeWolf. [1st ed.] New York, Harper & Row [1971] xii, 366 p. 24 cm. Includes bibliographical references. [BJ1251.D44] 79-126034 10.00
1. Christian ethics—Methodist authors. I. Title.

DRINKWATER, Francis Harold, 1886- 241
Birth control and natural law; [four essays] by F. H. Drinkwater. Baltimore, Helicon [1965] 93 p. 20 cm. Appendices (p. 69-84): 1. Four speeches in the third session of Vatican II. -- 2. Address to the Second Vatican on the subject of the problems of the family. [HQ766.3.D7] 65-20509
1. Birth control — Religious aspects. I. Title.

DUNPHY, William. 241
The new morality; continuity and discontinuity, edited by William Dunphy. [New York] Herder and Herder [1967] 192 p. 22 cm. Bibliographical footnotes. [BJ1249.D8] 67-27735
1. Christian ethics—Catholic authors. 2. Ethics, Modern—20th cent. I. Title.

DUNPHY, William. 241
The new morality; continuity and discontinuity, edited by William Dumphy. [New York] Herder and Herder [1967] 192 p. 22 cm. Bibliographical footnotes. [BJ1249.D8] 67-27735
1. Christian ethics—Catholic authors. 2. Ethics, Modern—20th century. I. Title.

DUTY, Guy, 1907- 241
Divorce & remarriage. Minneapolis, Bethany Fellowship [1967] 153 p. 21 cm. [HQ824.D8] 68-2481
1. Divorce—Biblical teaching. I. Title.

DUTY, Guy, 1907- 241
Divorce & remarriage. Minneapolis, Bethany Fellowship [1967] 153 p. 21 cm. [HQ824.D8] 68-2481
1. Divorce—Biblical teaching. I. Title.

EDWARDS, Jonathan 241
Religious affections Edited by John E. Smith. New Haven, Yale University Press [c.]1959. 526p. facsim. 24cm. (His Works, v.2) (Bibliographical footnotes.) 59-12702 7.50
1. Emotions—Early works to 1850. I. Title.

ELLER, Vernard. 241
The promise: ethics in the kingdom of God. [1st ed.] Garden City, N.Y., Doubleday, 1970. 223 p. 22 cm. Bibliographical footnotes. [BJ1251.E38] 79-89116 5.95
1. Christian ethics. I. Title.

ELLUL, Jacques. 241
The ethics of freedom / by Jacques Ellul ; translated and edited by Geoffrey W. Bromiley. Grand Rapids : Eerdmans, c1976. 517 p. ; 25 cm. Translations of Ethique de la liberte. Includes bibliographical references and indexes. [BT1462.E4413] 75-31592 ISBN 0-8028-3472-8 : 12.95
1. Liberty. 2. Free will and determinism. 3. Freedom (Theology) I. Title.

ELLUL, Jacques. 241
To will & to do; an ethical research for Christians. Translated by C. Edward Hopkin. Philadelphia, Pilgrim Press [1969] viii, 310 p. 22 cm. Translation of Le vouloir et le faire; recherches ethiques pour les chretiens. Bibliographical references included in "Notes" (p. 268-310) [BJ1251.E413] 70-91166 10.00
1. Christian ethics. I. Title.

ENGEMANN, Antonellus. 241
The new song; faith, hope, and charity in Franciscan spirituatiy. Translated from the German by Isabel and Florence McHugh. Chicago, Franciscan Herald Press [1964] ix, 140 p. 21 cm. Bibliographical references included in "Notes" (p. 129-136) [BV4635.E513] 64-14255
1. Theological virtues. 2. Franciscans. I. Title.

ENGEMANN, Antonellus 241
The new song; faith, hope, and charity in Franciscan spirituality. Tr. from German by Isabel and Florence McHugh. Chicago, Franciscan Herald [c.1964] ix, 140p. 21cm. Bibl. 64-14255 3.50
1. Theological virtues. 2. Franciscans. I. Title.

ERICKSON, Millard. 241
Relativism in contemporary Christian ethics [by] Millard J. Erickson. Grand Rapids, Baker Book House [1974] xiii, 170 p. 22 cm. Bibliography: p. 155-163. [BJ1012.E72] 74-174440 ISBN 0-8010-3315-2 3.95 (pbk.).
1. Ethics. I. Title.

ETHELRED, Saint, 1109?-1166. 241
The mirror of charity; the Speculum caritatis of St. Aelred of Rievaulx. Tr., arr. by Geoffrey Webb, Adrian Walker. Introd., notes. London, A. R. Mowbray [dist. Chester Springs, Pa., Dufour 1963, c.1962] xv, 159p. 21cm. 63-3925 5.00
1. Love (Theology) I. Webb, Geoffrey, tr. II. Walker, Adrian, tr. III. Title.

ETHICS of decision; 241
an introduction to Christian ethics. Philadelphia, Muhlenberg Press [1955] 158p. 20cm. [BJ1251.F6] [BJ1251.F6] 171.1 55-7767 55-7767
1. Christian ethics. 2. Commandments, Ten. I. Forell, George Wolfgang.

EVERDING, H. Edward. 241
Decision making and the Bible / H. Edward Everding, Jr. & Dana W. Wilbanks. Valley Forge, Pa. : Judson Press, [1975] 160 p. ; 22 cm. Includes bibliographies and indexes. [BJ1468.5.E92] 75-11656 ISBN 0-8170-0656-7 pbk. : 5.95
1. Bible—Ethics. 2. Decision-making (Ethics) I. Wilbanks, Dana W., joint author. II. Title.

EWBANK, Walter F. 241
Morality without law, by Walter F. Ewbank. New York, World Pub. Co. [1969] 150 p. 21 cm. Bibliographical footnotes. [BJ1251.E87] 68-26839 4.50
1. Christian ethics. I. Title.

FINNEY, Charles G. 241
Attributes of love: a section from Lectures on systematic theology. Minneapolis, Minn., 6820 Auto Club Rd. Bethany Fellowship, [1963] 136p. 19cm. 1.50 pap.,
I. Title.

FLETCHER, Joseph Francis, 1905- 241
Moral responsibility: situation ethics at work, by Joseph Fletcher. Philadelphia, Westminster [1967] 256p. 19cm. Bibl. [BJ1251.F52] 67-14515 3.95; 1.95 pap.,
1. Christian ethics—Anglican authors. 2. Situation ethics. I. Title.

FORD, John Cuthbert, 1902- 241
Contemporary moral theology, by John C. Ford and Gerald Kelly. Westminster, Md., Newman Press, 1958-63. 2 v. 23 cm. Includes bibliographies. [BX1758.F65] 58-7530
1. Christian ethics — Catholic authors. 2. Marriage — Catholic Church. I. Kelly, Gerald A., joint author. II. Title.

FORD, John Cuthbert, 1902- 241
Contemporary moral theology, v.2 by John C. Ford, Gerald Kelly. Westminster, Md., Newman Pr. [c.1963] 474p. 23cm. Bibl. 58-7530 7.50
1. Christian ethics—Catholic authors. I. Kelly, Gerald A., joint author. II. Title.

FURFEY, Paul Hanly, 1896- 241
The morality gap. New York, Macmillan [1968, c1969] x, 150 p. 22 cm. Includes bibliographical references. [BJ1249.F8] 68-28292
1. Christian ethics—Catholic authors. 2. Social ethics. I. Title.

GAFFNEY, James. 241
Moral questions / by James Gaffney. New York : Paulist Press, c1974. 147 p. ; 18 cm. (Deus books) Includes bibliographical references. [BX1758.2.G32] 74-30536 ISBN 0-8091-1870-X pbk. : 1.65
1. Christian ethics—Catholic authors. I. Title.

GENNARO, Camillus. 241
Faith, hope, love. Translated by Bruno Cocuzzi and Matthias Montgomery. Milwaukee, Spiritual Life Press, 1965. 150 p. 19 cm. (The Way, v. 2) Bibliographical footnotes. [BV4635.G413] 64-66113
1. Theological virtues. I. Title.

GENNARO, Camillus 241
Faith, hope, love. Tr. by Bruno Cocuzzi, Matthias Montgomery. Milwaukee, Spiritual Life Pr., 1223 S. 45 St. [c.]1965. 150p. 19cm. (The Way, v.2.) Bibl. [BV4635.G413] 64-66113 1.75 pap.,
1. Theological virtues. I. Title.

GIBSON, Alexander Boyce, 1900- 241
The challenge of perfection; a study in Christian ethics, by A. Boyce Gibson. Melbourne, Aldersgate Press [1968?] 32 p. 18 cm. [BJ1225.G52] 79-490311 unpriced
1. Christian ethics. 2. Perfection—Biblical teaching. I. Title.

GILLELMAN, Gerard 241
The primacy of charity in moral theology. Translated from the 2d French ed. by William F. Ryan and Andre Vachon. Westminster, Md., Newman Press [c.] 1959. xxviii, 420p. 23cm. (9p. bibl.) 59-14798 5.50
1. Love (Theology) 2. Christian ethics—Catholic authors. 3. Thomas Aquinas, Saint—Ethics. I. Title.

GILLON, Louis Bertrand, 1901- 241
Christ & moral theology, by Louis B. Gillon. [Translated by Cornelius Williams] Staten Island, N. Y., Alba House [1967] 144 p. 20 cm. Translation of Cristo e la teologia morale. Bibliographical footnotes. [BX1758.2.G513] 68-17764
1. Christian ethics—Catholic authors. I. Title.

GILLON, Louis Bertrand, 1901- 241
Christ & moral theology, by Louis B. Gillon. [Translated by Cornelius Williams] Staten Island, N.Y., Alba House [1967] 144 p. 20 cm. Translation of Cristo e la teologia morale. Bibliographical footnotes. [BX1758.2.G513] 68-17764
1. Christian ethics—Catholic authors. I. Title.

GINEVER, Violet, 1910- 241
The twelve commandments. London, S.P.C.K. [dist. Greenwich, Conn., Seabury, c.1962] 120p. 19cm. (Seraph) 63-346 1.25 pap.,
1. Commandments, Ten. 2. Summary of the Law (Theology) I. Title.

GUARDINI, Romano, 1885- 241
The word of God on faith, hope and charity. Translated by Stella Lange. Chicago, H. Regnery Co., 1963. 113 p. 21 cm. Translation of Drei Schriftauslegungen. [BV4635.G813] 63-12895
1. Theological virtues — Biblical teaching. I. Title.

GUARDINI, Romano, 1885- 241
The word of God on faith, hope and charity. Tr. [from German] by Stella Lange. Chicago, Regnery [c.]1963. 113p. 21cm. 63-12895 3.25 bds.,
1. Theological virtues—Biblical teaching. I. Title.

GUDER, Eileen L. 241
Living in both worlds [by] Eileen Guder. [1st ed.] Grand Rapids, Zondervan Pub. House [1968] 186 p. 23 cm. [BT382.G8] 68-27457 3.95
1. Beatitudes—Meditations. 2. Christian ethics. I. Title.

GUDER, Eileen L. 241
The many faces of friendship [by] Eileen L. Guder. Waco, Tex., Word Books [1969] 139 p. 23 cm. [BJ1533.F8G8] 72-96290 3.95
1. Friendship. I. Title.

GUSTAFSON, James M. 241
Can ethics be Christian? An inquiry [by] James M. Gustafson. Chicago, University of Chicago Press [1975] p. cm. Includes bibliographical references. [BJ1251.G86] 74-11622 ISBN 0-226-31103-1 8.95
1. Christian ethics. I. Title.

GUSTAFSON, James M. 241
Christ and the moral life [by] James M. Gustafson. [1st ed.] New York, Harper & Row [1968] xi, 275 p. 22 cm. Bibliographical footnotes. [BJ1251.G87] 68-29556 8.00
1. Jesus Christ—Significance. 2. Jesus Christ—Ethics. 3. Christian ethics. I. Title.

GUSTAFSON, James M. 241
Christian ethics and the community [by] James M. Gustafson. Philadelphia [Pilgrim Press, 1971] 224 p. 22 cm. Includes bibliographical references. [BJ1251.G875] 70-163660 ISBN 0-8298-0207-X 7.95
1. Christian ethics—Addresses, essays, lectures. I. Title.

GUSTAFSON, James M. 241
The church as moral decision-maker [by] James M. Gustafson. Philadelphia, Pilgrim Press [1970] 163 p. 22 cm. Includes bibliographical references. [BT738.G85] 74-124454 5.95
1. Sociology, Christian. 2. Church. 3. Christian ethics. I. Title.

GUSTAFSON, James M. 241
Theology and Christian ethics [by] James M. Gustafson. Philadelphia, United Church Press [1974] 315 p. 22 cm. "A Pilgrim Press book." Includes bibliographical references. [BJ1251.G88] 74-510 ISBN 0-8298-0270-3 8.95
1. Christian ethics—Addresses, essays, lectures. I. Title.
Contents omitted.

HADEN, Lila Carpenter. 241
Bits of truth; essays of love and faith according to the teachings of the Church of Latter-Day Saints, by Aunt Lila [pseud. 1st ed.] New York, Greenwich Book Publishers [1961] 114p. 21cm. [BX8638.H25] 61-10886
1. Mormons and Mormonism. I. Title.

HANSON, Oscar Conrad, 1908- 241
March to win. Minneapolis, Bible Banner Press [1952] 99p. 21cm. [BV4501.H2775] 52-67721
1. Christianlife. I. Title.

HARING, Bernhard, 1912- 241
The law of Christ; moral theology for priests and laity. Tr. by Edwin G. Kaiser. Westminster, Md., Newman, 1966. v. 24cm. Contents.v.3. Special moral theology. Bibl. [BX1758.2.H313] 60-14826 12.00
1. Christian ethics—Catholic authors. I. Title.

HARING, Bernard, 1912- 241
Christian renewal in a changing world. Tr. by M. Lucidia Haring. [Rev. ed.] Garden City, N.Y., Doubleday [1968,c.1964] 433p. 18cm. (Image bk. D244) [BX2350.2.H313] 65-12896 1.45 pap.,
1. Christian life—Catholic authors. I. Title.

HARING, Bernhard, 1912- 241
Christian renewal in a changing world [Tr. by M. Lucidia Haring. Rev. ed.] New York, Desclee [c.1964] xxi, 480p. 22cm. [BX2350.2.H313] 65-12896 6.75
1. Christian life—Catholic authors. I. Title.

HARING, Bernhard, 1912- 241
Christian renewal in the changing world [by] Bernhard Haring. [Translated by M. Lucidia Haring. Rev. ed.] New York, Desclee Co. [c1964] xxi, 480 p. 22 cm. Translation of Christ in einer neuen Welt. [BX2350.2.H313 1964] 65-12896
1. Christian life — Catholic authors. I. Title.

HARING, Bernhard, 1912- 241
The law of Christ; moral theology for priests and laity. Tr. [from German] by Edwin G. Kaiser. Westminster, Md., Newman [c.]1963. 573p. 24cm. Bibl. 8.50
1. Christian ethics—Catholic authors. I. Title.

HARING, Bernhard, 1912- 241
Road to relevance [by] Bernhard Haring. Translated by Hilda Graef. [Staten Island, N.Y., Alba House, 1970] vii, 127 p. 22 cm. Translation of Moralverkundigung nach dem Konzil. Includes bibliographical references. [BX1758.2.H3183] 79-110592 3.95
1. Christian ethics—Catholic authors. I. Title.

HARING, Bernhard, 1912- 241
What does Christ want? [By] Bernhard Haring. Staten Island, N.Y., Alba House [1968] 234 p. 19 cm. Bibliography: p. [233]-234. [BX1758.2.H33] 68-15383
1. Christian ethics—Catholic authors. I. Title.

HART, Levi, 1738--1808. 241
A Christian minister described, and distinguished from a pleaser of men. In a discourse, Galatians I, 10, at the ordination of the Reverend Abiel Holmes. Addressed to the reverend clergy of Connecticut, at their convention in New-Haven, September 15, 1785, the day following the public commencement. New-Haven, Printed by Meigs & Dana, 1787. 56p. 21cm. [BX7233.H2666C5] 56-51646
1. Holmes, Abiel, 1763-1837. 2. Ordination sermons. I. Title.

HAUERWAS, Stanley, 1940- 241
Character and the Christian life : a study in theological ethics / by Stanley Hauerwas. San Antonio : Trinity University Press, [1975] x, 239 p. ; 24 cm. (Trinity University monograph series in religion ; v. 3) Based on the author's thesis, Yale University. Includes bibliographical references and index. [BJ1521.H355] 74-78095 ISBN 0-911536-55-8 : 8.00
1. Character. 2. Christian ethics. I. Title. II. Series: Trinity University, San Antonio. Monograph series in religion ; v. 3.

HAUERWAS, Stanley, 1940- 241
Truthfulness and tragedy : further investigations in Christian ethics / Stanley Hauerwas with Richard Bondi and David B. Burrell. Notre Dame, Ind. : University of Notre Dame Press, c1977. xii, 251 p. ; 24 cm. Includes bibliographical references and index. [BJ1251.H33] 76-30425 ISBN 0-268-01831-6 : 12.95. ISBN 0-268-01832-4 pbk. : 5.95
1. Christian ethics—Addresses, essays, lectures. 2. Social ethics—Addresses, essays, lectures. I. Bondi, Richard, joint author. II. Burrell, David B., joint author. III. Title.

HAUERWAS, Stanley, 1940- 241
Vision and virtue; essays in Christian ethical reflection. Notre Dame, Ind., Fides Publishers [1974] ix, 264 p. 22 cm. Includes bibliographical references. [BJ1241.H38] 74-9712 ISBN 0-8190-0485-5 5.00
1. Christian ethics—Addresses, essays, lectures. I. Title.

HEMINGWAY, Leslie. 241
The modern world and self-control, by L. Hemingway. [Melbourne] Polding Press [1968] xiv, 241 p. 21 cm. Bibliographical footnotes. [HQ766.3.H4] 75-396350 unpriced
1. Birth control—Religious aspects. I. Title.

HENRY, Matthew, 1662-1714. 241
The quest for meekness and quietness of spirit. Grand Rapids, Eerdmans, 1955. 144p. 23cm. Previously published under title: A discourse on meekness and quietness of spirit. [BV4647.H8H4 1955] 55-1056
1. Humility. I. Title.

HIS servants speak : 241
statements by Latter-day Saint leaders on contemporary topics / R. Clayton Brough, [compiler]. Bountiful, Utah : Horizon Publishers, c1975. 298 p. ; 24 cm. Includes index. Bibliography: p. 279-283. [BX8635.2.H57] 75-17101 ISBN 0-88290-054-4 : 6.95
1. Church of Jesus Christ of Latter-Day Saints—Doctrinal and controversial works. I. Brough, Robert Clayton.

HORMANN, Karl 241
An introduction to moral theology. Tr. [from German] by Edward Quinn. Westminster, Md., Newman [1962, c.1961] 283p. Bibl. 62-603 4.95
1. Christian ethics—Catholic authors. I. Title.

HOWE, Reuel L., 1905- 241
Herein is love; a study of the Biblical doctrine of love in its bearing on personality, parenthood, teaching, and all other human relationships. Chicago, Judson [c.1961] 116p. 61-11105 3.00; 1.50 pap.,
1. Love (Theology) I. Title.

HOYT, Robert G., comp. 241
The birth control debate, edited with a commentary by Robert G. Hoyt. Kansas City, Mo., National Catholic reporter [1968] 224 p. 18 cm. (NCR paperback) Consists chiefly of material first published in the National Catholic reporter. Bibliographical footnotes. [HQ766.3.H67] 68-59370 2.25
1. Birth control—Religious aspects. I. National Catholic reporter. II. Title.

HUGEL, Friedrich, Freiherr von, 1852-1925. 241
Spiritual counsel and letters. Edited with an introductory essay by Douglas V. Steere. New York, Harper & Row [1964] viii, 184 p. 22 cm. [BX2350.H82] 64-10754
1. Spiritual life—Catholic authors. I. Title.

HUGEL, Friedrich, Freiherr von, 1852-1925 241
Spiritual counsel and letters. Ed., introd. essay by Douglas V. Steere. New York, Harper [c.1964] viii, 184p. 22cm. 64-10754 5.00
1. Spiritual life—Catholic authors. I. Title.

HUNTER, J. F. G. 241
A code of life to health, wealth, happiness. New York, Greenwich Book Publishers [1960, c.1959] 33p. 22cm. 59-13629 2.00
1. Conduct of life. I. Title.

HUTCHISON, Owen. 241
Christian love in everyday living. Philadelphia, Westminster Press [1955] 94p. 20cm. [BV4639.H87] 55-7706
1. Love (Theology) I. Title.

INSTITUTE in Basic Youth Conflicts. 241
Character sketches from the pages of Scripture, illustrated in the world of nature / Institute in Basic Youth Conflicts, Inc. 1st ed. [Oak Brook, Ill.] : The Institute, 1976. 382 p. : ill. (some col.) ; 32 cm. Includes indexes. Discusses Christian character traits illustrated in the Bible and nature. [BJ1261.I57 1976] 76-3050 ISBN 0-916888-01-0
1. Bible—Juvenile literature. 2. Christian ethics—Juvenile literature. 3. Animals, Habits and behavior of—Juvenile literature. 4. Zoology—Miscellanea—Juvenile literature. I. Title: Character sketches from the pages of Scripture ...

JAUNCEY, James H. 241
The two great commandments. Nashville, The Upper Room [c.1962] 64p. p.35 pap.,
I. Title.

JOHNSON, Paul Emanuel, 1898- 241
Christian love. New York, Abingdon-Cokesbury Press [1951] 240 p. 24 cm. Bibliographical footnotes. [BV4639.J56] 50-11007
1. Love. 2. Love (Theology) I. Title.

JONES, Elizabeth Brown 241
When you need a special story for boys and girls in church and home. Anderson, Ind., Warner Press [dist. Gospel Trumpet Press] [c.1959] 128p. 21cm. 59-13466 2.00 bds.,
I. Title.

JONES, Elizabeth Brown 1907- 241
When you need a special story for boys and girls in church and home. Anderson, Ind., Warner Press [1959] 128p. 21cm. Prose and verse. [BV4571.J572] 59-13466
I. Title.

JONES, Major J., 1919- 241
Christian ethics for Black theology [by] Major J. Jones. Nashville, Abingdon Press [1974] 205 p. 20 cm. Bibliography: p. 201-205. [BJ1251.J63] 74-8680 ISBN 0-687-07208-5 4.50 (pbk.)
1. Christian ethics. 2. Negroes—Religion. I. Title.

JONSEN, Albert R. 241
Responsibility in modern religious ethics, by Albert R. Jonsen. Foreword by James M. Gustafson. Washington, Corpus Books [1968] xiv, 249 p. 21 cm. Includes bibliographical references. [BJ1451.J57] 68-25761 6.95
1. Responsibility. 2. Christian ethics. I. Title.

JUDGE, Thomas Augustine, 1865-1933. 241
Sparks of faith, selected and compiled from the writings of Father Judge by Lawrence Brediger. Westminster, Md., Newman Press, 1961. 74p. illus. 15cm. [BV4637.J8] 61-16563
1. Fath. I. Title.

KAGAWA, Toyohiko, 1888- 241
Love, the law of life; with foreward [sic] by Allen Hunter, afterword by Glenn Clark. [1st ed.] St. Paul, Macalester Park Pub. Co. [1951] 95 p. 17 cm. "Revision of ... the original edition in English." [BV4639.K3 1951] 51-35225
1. Love (Theology) I. Title.

KANE, John A 241
The school of virtue. [1st ed.] New York, Pageant Press [1954, c1953] 168p. 21cm. [BV4630.K3] 53-11795
1. Virtue. I. Title.

KAUFMAN, Gordon D. 241
The context of decision; a theological analysis. Nashville, Abingdon Press [c.1961] 126p. 61-8410 2.50
1. Christian ethics. I. Title.

KEELING, Michael. 241
Morals in a free society. New York, Seabury Press [1968] 157 p. 23 cm. Bibliography: p. [151]-154. [BJ1241.K4 1968] 68-11557
1. Christian ethics. I. Title.

KELLEY, Carl Franklin, 1914- 241
The spirit of love, based on the teachings of St. Francois de Sales. [1ste ed.] New York, Harper [1951] xii, 287 p. 22 cm. Bibliography: p. 277-279. [BX4700.F85K4] 51-9229
1. Francois de Sales, Saint, Bp. of Geneva, 1567-1622. 2. Love (Theology) I. Title.

KENNEDY, Eugene C. 241
A sense of life, a sense of sin / Eugene Kennedy. 1st ed. Garden City, N.Y. : Doubleday, 1975. 191 p. ; 22 cm. [BJ1012.K43] 74-25110 ISBN 0-385-09538-4 : 6.95
1. Ethics. 2. Sin. I. Title.

KERNS, Joseph E. 241
How does God teach us morals? By Joseph E. Kearns. Glen Rock, N.J., Paulist Press [1969] v, 57 p. 17 cm. [BX1758.2.K4] 69-18370 0.75
1. Christian ethics—Catholic authors. I. Title.

KIENER, Mary Aloysi, 1882- 241
'Hearts shall be enlightened'; reflections for

the examination of conscience. New York, F. Pustet Co., 1955. 179p. 16cm. [BX2377.K5] 55-3890
1. Conscience, Examination of. I. Title.

KIENER, Mary Aloysi, Mother, 1882- 241
This is the victory! With foreword by Joseph Kreuter. New York, F. Pustet Co., 1952. 216 p. 20 cm. [BX2350.K52] 52-3531
1. Christian life—Catholic authors. I. Title.

KINGREY, David W. 241
*Now is tomorrow : crucial questions for space-age Christians / by David W. Kingrey and Marion F. Baumgardner. Richmond, Ind. : Friends United Press, c1975. xiv, 91 p. : ill. ; 21 cm. [BJ59.K55] 75-34946 3.45
1. Technology and ethics. 2. Religion and science—1946- I. Baumgardner, Marion F., joint author. II. Title.

KINSELLA, Nivard 241
Unprofitable servants; conferences on humility. Westminster, Md., Newman Press [1961c.] 1960[ ] 105p. 19cm. 61-1446 3.00
1. Humility. I. Title.

KNIGHT, Margaret Kennedy, 1903- 241
Honest to man : Christian ethics re-examined / Margaret Knight. Buffalo, N.Y. : Prometheus Books, 1974. ix, 213 p. : 21 cm. Includes bibliographical references and index. [BL2775.2.K53 1974] 74-194695 ISBN 0-87975-029-4
1. Christianity—Controversial literature. I. Title.

KNIGHT, Margaret, Kennedy. 1903- 241
Honest to man: Christian ethics re-examined. Buffalo, N.Y. Prometheus Books, [1975 c1974] ix, 213 p. 21 cm. Includes bibliographical references and index. [BL2775.2.K53] ISBN 0-87975-029-4 10.95
1. Christianity—Controversial literature. I. Title.
L.C. card no. for original edition: 74-194695

*KOOPMAN, Leroy. 241
Beauty care for the tongue. Grand Rapids, Mich., Zondervan, [1974, c1972] 99 p. 18 cm. [BJ1360] 0.95 (pbk.)
1. Humanistic ethics. I. Title.

KOSTYU, Frank A 241
Pathways to personal contentment; how to live 7 days a week. Englewood Cliffs, N.J., Prentice-Hall [1960] 191p. 24cm. [BV4647.C7K6] 60-16626
1. Contentment. I. Title.

KOSTYU, Frank A. 241
Pathways to personal contentment; how to live 7 days a week. Englewood Cliffs, N.J., Prentice-Hall [1961, c.1960] 191p. 60-16626 4.95
1. Contentment. I. Title.

LANZA, Antonio 241
Principles of moral theology, by Antonio Lanza, Pietro Palazzini. Tr. [from Italian] by W. J. Collins. [Boston] St. Paul Eds. [dist. Daughters of St. Paul, c.1961] 254p. Contents.v. 1. General moral theology. Bibl. 60-53616 4.00; 3.00 pap.,
1. Christian ethics—Catholic authors. I. Palazzini, Pietro, 1912- joint author. II. Title.

LARGE, John Ellis. 241
Think on these things. [1st ed.] New York, Harper [c1954] 127p. 20cm. [BR121.L335] 53-10972
1. Christianity— 20th cent. I. Title.

LEBRET, Louis Joseph, 1897- 241
An examination of conscience for modern Catholics, by L. J. Lebret and Theodore [i. e. Thomas] Suavet. Translated into English by Bernard B. Gilligan. [1st ed.] New York, Longmans, Green, 1961. 168p. 29cm. Translation of Rajeunir l'examen de conscience. [BX2377.L413 1961] 61-14222
1. Conscience, Examination of. I. Suavet, Thomas, joint author. II. Title.

LEBRET, Louis Joseph, 1897- 241
An examination of conscience for modern Catholics, by L.-J. Lebret and Theodore [i. e. Thomas] Suavet. Tr. from French by Bernard B. Gilligan. New York, Longmans [c.]1961. 168p. 61-14222 3.75; 2.45 bds., pap.,
1. Conscience, Examination of. I. Suavet, Thomas, joint author. II. Title.

LEE, Luther, 1800-1889. 241
Slavery examined in the light of the Bible. Syracuse, N.Y., Wesleyan Methodist Book Room, 1855; Detroit, Negro History Press [1969] 185 p. 22 cm. [E449.L47 1969] 76-92434
1. Slavery in the United States—Controversial literature—1855. I. Title.

*LEONARD, B. G. 241
Except . . . for fornication. New York, Carlton [c.1966] 61p. 21cm. (Reflection bk.) 2.00
I. Title.

LEWIS, Clive Staples, 1898-1963. 241
The four loves. New York, Harcourt, Brace [1960] 192 p. 21 cm. [BV4639.L45 1960a] 60-10920
1. Love. 2. Love (Theology) I. Title.

*LINDSELL, Harold. 241
The world, the flesh, and the devil. Washington D.C. Canon Press [1973] xiv. 227 p. 22 cm. [BJ1275] ISBN 0-913686-04-2 4.95
1. Christian ethics. I. Title.

LOIZEAUX, A. S. 241
Christian joy. New York, Loizeaux Brothers, Inc. [1959] 32p. 19cm. .30 pap.,
I. Title.

LONG, Edward Le Roy. 241
Conscience and compromise: an approach to Protestant casuistry. Philadelphia, Westminster Press [c1954] 166p. 21cm. [BV4611.L6] 54-5280
1. Casuistry. I. Title.

LONG, Edward Le Roy 241
A survey of Christian ethics. New York, Oxford Univ. Pr., 1967. viii, 342p. 24cm. Bibl. [BJ1201.L6] 67-12388 6.50; 4.75 text ed.,
1. Christian ethics. I. Title.

LONG, Edward Le Roy. 241
A survey of Christian ethics. New York, Oxford University Press, 1967. viii, 342 p. 24 cm. Bibliographical references included in "Notes" (p. 315-335) [BJ1201.L6] 67-12388
1. Christian ethics. I. Title.

LOVASIK, Lawrence George, 1913- 241
Kindness. New York, Macmillan [c.1962] 334p. 22cm. 62-17337 4.50
1. Charity. 2. Kindness. I. Title.

LOVE and society : 241
essays and epics and Paul Ramsey / [edited by] James T. Johnson, David Smith. Missoula, Mont. : Scholars Press, [1975] p. cm. (AAR studies in religious ethics) Contents.—Smith, D. H. Paul Ramsey, love and killing.—Evans, D. Paul Ramsey on exceptionless moral rules.—Curran, C. E. Paul Ramsey and traditional Roman Catholic natural law theory.—Camenisch, P. F. Paul Ramsey's task, some methodological clarifications and questions.—Johnson, J. T. Morality and force in statecraft.—Walters, L. Historical applications of the just war theory.—Little, D. The structure of justification in the political ethics of Paul Ramsey.—O'Brien, W. V. Morality and war, the contribution of Paul Ramsey.—Outka, G. Social justice and equal access to health care.—McCormick, R. A. Proxy consent in the experimentation situation.—May, W. F. Attitudes toward the newly dead.—Bibliography of Paul Ramsey's works (p.) Includes bibliographies. [BJ1251.L68] 74-19665 ISBN 0-88420-123-6
1. Ramsey, Paul. 2. Ramsey, Paul—Bibliography. 3. Christian ethics—Addresses, essays, lectures. 4. Social ethics—Addresses, essays, lectures. I. Johnson, James Turner, ed. II. Smith, David H., 1939- ed. III. Series: American Academy of Religion. AAR studies in religious ethics.

LOVE and violence. 241
[Translations by George Lamb] New York, Sheed and Ward, 1954. 260p. illus. 22cm. Based upon the 1946 volume of the series uetudes carmelltaines,' Amour et violence, published ... under the editorship of Pere Bruno de Jesus-Marie, o. c. D.' [BV4639.A533] 54-11142
1. Love (Theology) I. Bruno de Jesus-Marie, Father, ed.

LUDER, William Fay, 1910- 241
A new approach to sex. Boston, Farnsworth Books, [1966] xx, 103 p. front. 18 cm. [HQ31.L8754]
1. Sexual ethics. I. Title.

LUDER, William Fay, 1910- 241
A new approach to sex. Boston, Mass., 02210, Farnsworth Bks. [44 Farnsworth St., c.1966] xx, 103p. front. 18cm. [HQ31.L8754] 66-18176 1.85., .85, pap.,
1. Sexual ethics. I. Title.

MCCABE, Herbert, 1926- 241
What is ethics all about? Washington, Corpus Books [1969] viii, 215 p. 19 cm. Includes bibliographical references. [BX1758.2.M3] 70-77348 3.95
1. Christian ethics—Catholic authors. I. Title.

MCCLAIN, Dayton E 241
The sin of omission. Philadelphia, Dorrance [1959] 78p. 20cm. [BV4625.M3] 59-5749
1. Sin. I. Title.

MCDERMOTT, Irene. 241
Enter the temple called Beautiful. Los Angeles, DeVorss [1969] 187 p. 24 cm. [BJ1581.2.M24] 78-79230
1. Conduct of life. 2. Self-realization. I. Title.

MCDONAGH, Enda. 241
Gift and call : towards a Christian theology of morality / Enda McDonagh. Dublin : Gi-l and Macmillan, 1975. ix, 182 p. ; 21 cm. Includes bibliographical references. [BJ1251.M26] 75-320766 ISBN 0-7171-0642-X : £4.75
1. Christian ethics. 2. Theology, Doctrinal. I. Title.

MCDONAGH, Enda. 241
Gift and call : towards a Christian theology of morality / Enda McDonagh. St. Meinrad, Ind. : Abbey Press, 1975. ix, 182 p. ; 21 cm. (A Priority edition) Includes bibliographical references. [BJ1251.M26 1975b] 75-19921 ISBN 0-87029-048-7 : 3.95
1. Christian ethics. 2. Theology, Doctrinal. I. Title.

MCELLHENNEY, John. 241
Cutting the monkey-rope. Valley Forge [Pa.] Judson Press [1973] 126 p. 22 cm. Includes bibliographical references. [BJ1533.H9M3] 73-2550 ISBN 0-8170-0581-1 2.50
1. Life. 2. Abortion. 3. Euthanasia. I. Title.

MCELLIGOTT, C. J. 241
The crown of life; a study of perseverance [St. Louis] B. Herder [c.1963] xiv, 268p. 22cm. Bibl. 63-23155 4.50
1. Perseverance (Theology) I. Title.

MCGARRIGLE, Francis Joseph, 1888- 241
The two commandments of Christ. Milwaukee, Bruce Pub. Co. [1962] 198 p. 23 cm. [BV4714.M3] 62-16839
1. Summary of the Law (Theology) I. Title.

MCLAREN, Robert Bruce. 241
All to the good: a guide to Christian ethics [by] Robert B. McLaren and Homer D. McLaren. With a foreword by D. Elton Trueblood. New York, World Pub. Co. [1969] xv, 203 p. 21 cm. Bibliographical references included in "Notes" (p. 185-197) [BJ1251.M27 1969] 69-15078 5.95
1. Christian ethics. I. McLaren, Homer D., 1887- joint author. II. Title.

MACQUARRIE, John. 241
3 issues in ethics. [1st ed. New York, Harper & Row [1970] 157 p. 22 cm. Includes bibliographical references. [BJ1251.M28 1970] 73-109057 4.95
1. Christian ethics. I. Title.

MARCH, Walter William Seymour 241
Ground of the heart; a commentary of the General thanksgiving. Foreword by the Archbishop of Canterbury. London, Faith Pr.; New York, Morehouse [c.1963] 119p. 19cm. A63 1.25 pap.,
1. Gratitude. I. Title.

MARCK, W. H. M. van der. 241
Toward a Christian ethic; a renewal in moral theology, by W. H. M. van der Marck. Translated by Denis J. Barrett. Westminster, Md., Newman Press [1967] vi, 170 p. 22 cm. Translation of Het Christus-geheim in de menselijke samenleving. Bibliographical footnotes. [BX1758.2.M3413] 67-28699
1. Christian ethics—Catholic authors. I. Title.

MARNEY, Carlyle, 1916- 241
Structures of prejudice. New York, Abingdon Press [1961] 256p. 24cm. Includes bibliography. [BF575.P9M3] 61-8411
1. Prejudices and antipathies. I. Title.

MARY ST. PAUL Sister 241
Good manners in God's house. Pictures by Brinton Turkle. New York, Guild Press; distributed by Golden Press [1960] c.1959 unpaged. illus. (col.) 17cm. (A First book for little Catholics; A Catechetical Guild book.) 60-279 .25 bds.,
1. Etiquette for children and youth. 2. Church etiquette. I. Title.

MASON, William V. 241
Corrupt the young; a Communist plan [by] William V. Mason. [Springfield, Mo., Fellowship Publications, 1969] 48 p. illus. 19 cm. "Footnotes": p. 45-48. [BJ1661.M37] 77-12150
1. Youth—Conduct of life. I. Title.

MAY, William E., 1928- 241
Becoming human : an invitation to Christian ethics / William E. May. Dayton, Ohio : Pflaum Pub., [1975] viii, 147 p. ; 21 cm. Bibliography: p. 143-147. [BJ1251.M44] 74-82489 ISBN 0-8278-0002-9 pbk. : 4.65
1. Christian ethics. I. Title.

MEHL, Roger. 241
Catholic ethics and Protestant ethics. Translated by James H. Farley. Philadelphia, Westminster Press [1971] 126 p. 21 cm. (The Warfield lectures, Princeton Theological Seminary, 1968) Translation of Ethique catholique et ethique protestante. Includes bibliographical references. [BJ1252.M413] 73-141511 ISBN 0-664-20903-3 4.95
1. Christian ethics. I. Title. II. Series: The Annie Kinkead Warfield lectures, 1968

MENASCE, C. G. de 241
The dynamics of morality. Tr. [from Italian] by Bernard Bommarito, New York, Sheed & Ward [c.1961] 353p. Bibl. 61-11792 6.00 bds.,
1. Christian ethics—Catholic authors. I. Title.

MENENDEZ, Josefa, Sister, 1890-1923. 241
Christ's appeal for love to His humble servant Josefa Menendez, translated by L. Keppel. Newman Press 1951 176p. illus. 19cm. 'A revised, abridged edition of [the author's] The way of divine love.' Translation of Un liamamiento al amor. [BV5082.M42 1951] 53-26456
1. Mysticism—Catholic Church. 2. Love (Theology) I. Title.

MENENDEZ, Josefa, 1890-1923. 241
The way of divine love; or, The message of the Sacred Heart to the world, and a short biography of His messenger, Sister Josefa Menendez, coadjutrix sister of the Society of the Sacred Heart of Jesus, 1890-1923. Westminster, Md., Newman Press [1956] 504p. illus. 22cm. 'Translation of Un Hamamiento al amor. [BV5082.M415 1956] 57-1484
1. Mysticism—Catholic Church. 2. Love (Theology) I. Title.

METHODIUS, Saint, Bp. of Olympus, d.ca.311. 241
The symposium; a treatise on chastity. Translated and annotated by Herbert Musurillo. Westminster, Md., Newman Press, 1958. vi, 249p. 23cm. (Ancient Christian writers; the works of the Fathers in translation, no.27) Translation of Symposium decem virginum. Bibliographical references included in 'Notes' (p.[163]-239) [BR60.A35 no.27] 58-7775
1. Chastity. I. Musurillo, Herbert Anthony, ed. and tr. II. Title. III. Series.

MEYNERS, Robert, 1922- 241
Solomon's sword : clarifying values in the church / Robert Meyners & Claire Wooster. Nashville : Abingdon, c1977. 144 p. ; 20 cm. Includes bibliographies. [BJ1468.5.M49] 77-9391 ISBN 0-687-39050-8 pbk. : 4.95
1. Decision-making (Ethics) 2. Values. 3. Church work. I. Wooster, Claire, 1942- joint author. II. Title.

MILHAVEN, John Giles, 1927- 241
Toward a new Catholic morality. Garden City, N.Y., Doubleday, 1970. 240 p. 22 cm. Includes bibliographical references. [BX1758.2.M53] 77-116235 5.95
1. Christian ethics—Catholic authors—Addresses, essays, lectures. I. Title.

*MITCHELL, Joseph 241
Applied Christianity, recorded by Joseph Mitchell. New York, Vantage [1967] 293p. 21cm. 4.50 bds.,
I. Title.

MOLLENKOTT, Virginia R. 241
In search of balance [by] Virginia R. Mollenkott. Waco, Tex., Word Books [1969] 151 p. 23 cm. Includes bibliographies. [BJ1251.M58] 73-91936 3.95
1. Christian ethics. I. Title.

MONDEN, Louis. 241
Sin, liberty, and law. Translated by Joseph Donceel. New York, Sheed and Ward [1965] x, 181 p. 21 cm. Translation of Vernieuwd geweten. "Bibliographical notes": p. [171]-178. [BJ1231.M613] 65-20857
1. Christian ethics—Catholic authors. 2. Pastoral theology—Catholic Church. I. Title.

MORAL problems and Christian personalism 241
[Ed.: Franz Bockel] New York, Paulist [c.1965] viii, 183p. 24cm. (Concilium theology in the age of renewal: Moral theology, v.5) Bibl. [BJ1251.M63] 65-24045 4.50
1. Christian ethics—Catholic authors. I. Bockle, Franz, ed. (Series: Concilium theology in the age of renewal, v.5)

MORALS, law, and authority; 241
sources and attitudes in the church. Edited by J. P. Mackey. Dayton, Ohio, Pflaum Press, 1969. xv, 154 p. 22 cm. Bibliographical footnotes. [BX1758.2.M63] 79-93003 4.95
1. Christian ethics—Catholic authors—Addresses, essays, lectures. I. Mackey, James Patrick, ed.

MORGAN, Richard. 241
Famine of righteous vision. Nashville, Printed by the Parthenon Press [1965] 102 p. 24 cm. [BR121.2.M63] 64-66426
1. Christianity — 20th cent. I. Title.

MORGAN, Richard 241
Famine of righteous vision. Nashville, Parthenon Pr. [dist. Methodist Pub. House. c.1965] 102p. 24cm. [BR121.2.M63] 64-66426 3.00
1. Christianity—20th cent. I. Title.

MORTIMER, Robert Cecil, Bp. of Exeter, 1902- 241
The elements of moral theology. New York, Harper [1960] 236p. 22cm. [BV4612.M6] 60-15272
1. Christian ethics—Anglican authors. I. Title.

MOW, Anna B. 241
The secret of married love; a Christian approach [by] Anna B. Mow. [1st ed.] Philadelphia, Lippincott [1970] 156 p. 21 cm. Bibliography: p. 149-156. [BT706.M68] 76-110649 3.95
1. Marriage. 2. Love. I. Title.

MUELDER, Walter George, 1907- 241
Moral law in Christian social ethics [by] Walter G. Muelder. Richmond, John Knox Press [1966] 189 p. 21 cm. Bibliography: p. [185]-189. [BJ1251.M8] 66-15972
1. Christian ethics. 2. Social ethics. I. Title. II. Title: Christian social ethics.

MUELDER, Walter George, 1907- 241
Moral law in Christian social ethics [by] Walter G. Muelder. Richmond, Knox [1966] 189p. 21cm. Bibl. [BJ1251.M8] 66-15972 5.00
1. Christian ethics. 2. Social ethics. I. Title. II. Title: Christian social ethics.

MURPHY, Francis Xavier, 1914- 241
Moral teaching in the primitive church, by Francis X. Murphy. Glen Rock, N.J., Paulist Press [1968] vi, 118 p. 21 cm. (Guide to the Fathers of the church, 4) [BR195.C5M87] 68-16664 2.50
1. Christian life—Early church, ca. 30-600. 2. Christian literature. I. Title.

MURPHY, John F 1922- 241
The virtues on parade. Milwaukee, Bruce Pub. Co. [1959] 144p. 23cm. [BV4630.M8] 59-7946
1. Virtues. I. Title.

MURRAN, George. 241
There is a place for God in business; spiritual guide for business. [1st ed.] New York, Pageant Press [1956] 176p. 22cm. [BV4596.B8M8] 56-13128
1. Business ethics. 2. Christian ethics. I. Title.

MYERS, T Cecil. 241
Thunder on the mountain [by] T. Cecil Myers. New York, Abingdon Press [1965] 176 p. 20 cm. "Sermons on the Ten commandments." [BV4655.M9] 65-13147
1. Commandments, Ten — Sermons. I. Title.

MYERS, T. Cecil 241
Thunder on the mountain. Nashville, Abingdon [c.1965] 176p. 20cm. Sermons on the Ten commandments [BV4655.M9] 65-13147 3.00
1. Commandments, Ten—Sermons. I. Title.

NEILL, Stephen Charles, Bp. 241
The Christian character. New York, Association Press [c1955] 92p. 20cm. (World Christian books) [BV4600.N4] 55-9116
1. Christian ethics. 2. Virtue. I. Title.

NEILL, Stephen Charles, Bp. 241
The difference in being a Christian. New York, Association Press [1960, c.1955] 125p. 16cm. (An Association Press reflection book) 60-6566 .50 pap.,
1. Christian ethics. 2. Virtues. I. Title.

NELSON, James Bruce. 241
Moral nexus; ethics of Christian identity and community by James B. Nelson. Philadelphia, Westminster Press [1971] 255 p. 22 cm. Includes bibliographical references. [BJ1251.N38] 72-159475 ISBN 0-664-20913-0 7.95
1. Christian ethics. I. Title.

NELSON, James Bruce. 241
The responsible Christian; a churchly ethics for worldly people, by James B. Nelson. Boston, United Church Press [1969] 127 p. illus. 21 cm. Bibliography: p. [10]-11. [BJ1275.N4] 69-10386
1. Ethical problems. 2. Responsibility. I. Title.

THE New American 241
revolution; moral, student, and theological. Andrew J. Buehner, editor. St. Louis, Lutheran Academy for Scholarship [1968] 89 p. 21 cm. Three plenary session papers, presented at the sixth university staff assembly in Chicago, 1966; sponsored by the Lutheran Academy for Scholarship and the Commission on College and University Work of the Lutheran Church—Missouri Synod. Bibliographical footnotes. [BJ1251.N45] 68-7220
1. Christian ethics. 2. Students—Political activity. 3. Sociology, Christian. I. Buehner, Andrew J., ed. II. Lutheran Academy for Scholarship. III. Lutheran Church—Missouri Synod. Commission on College and University Work.

*NIELSEN, Kai. 241
Ethics without God. [Buffalo, New York] Prometheus Books [1973] 103 p. 20 cm. (The humanist library) Includes bibliographical references. [BJ1275] ISBN 0-87975-014-6 7.95
1. Christian ethics. I. Title.
Pbk. 2.95, ISBN 0-87975-019-7

NOONAN, John Thomas, 1926- 241
The church and contraception; the issues at stake, by John T. Noonan, Jr. New York, Paulist Press [1967] vii, 84 p. 18 cm. (Deus books) Bibliographical footnotes. [HQ766.3.N57] 67-27543
1. Birth control—Religious aspects. I. Title.

OLSON, Charles, 1886- 241
It pays to praise spiritual praise. [1st ed.] New York, Pageant Press [1957] 63p. 21cm. [BV4520.O4] 58-293
1. Praise. I. Title.

O'NEIL, Robert P. 241
Sexuality and moral responsibility, by Robert P. O'Neil and Michael A. Donovan. Foreword by Gregory Baum. Washington, Corpus Books [1968] xii, 154 p. 21 cm. Includes bibliographical references. [BJ1249.O65] 68-18713 4.95
1. Christian ethics—Catholic authors. 2. Sexual ethics. I. Donovan, Michael A., joint author. II. Title.

O'NEILL, David P 241
About loving [by] David P. O'Neill. Dayton, Ohio, G. A. Pflaum [1966] 123 p. illus. 17 cm. (Christian experience series, no. 2) Witness books, no. 3. Bibliography: p. 121-123. [BV4639.O6] 66-18515
1. Love (Theology) I. Title.

O'NEILL, David P. 241
About loving. Dayton, Ohio 45402, Pflaum, 38 W. 5th St. [c.1966] 123p. illus. 17cm. (Christian experience ser., no.2; Witness bks., no.3) Bibl. [BV4639.O6] 66-18515 .75 pap.,
1. Love (Theology) I. Title.

ORAISON, Marc 241
Learning to love; frank advice for young Catholics. Tr. [from French] by Andre Humbert [1st Eng. lang. ed.] New York, Hawthorn [c.1965] 143p. illus. 21cm. Bibl. [HQ35.O73] 65-12400 3.95
1. Sex. 2. Adolescence. I. Title.

ORAISON, Marc. 241
Morality for our time. Translated by Nels Challe. [1st ed.] Garden City, N.Y., Doubleday, 1968. 140 p. 22 cm. Translation of Une morale pour notre temps. [BJ1249.O713] 68-11922
1. Christian ethics—Catholic authors. I. Title.

ORR, William W 241
The Christian and amusements. Chicago, Moody Press [1960] 158p. 19cm. (Moody pocket books, 51) [BV4597.O7] 60-25435
1. Amusements—Moral and religious aspects. I. Title.

OSBORN, Eric Francis. 241
Ethical patterns in early Christian thought / Eric Osborn. Cambridge ; New York : Cambridge University Press, 1976 viii, 252 p. ; 24 cm. Includes indexes. Bibliography: p. [221]-227. [BJ1212.O8] 75-10040 ISBN 0-521-20835-1 : 2.00
1. Christian ethics—Early church, ca. 30-600. I. Title.

OUTKA, Gene H. 241
Norm and context in Christian ethics, edited by Gene H. Outka [and] Paul Ramsey. Frederick S. Carney [and others, contributors] New York, Scribner [1968] x, 419 p. 24 cm. Bibliographical footnotes. [BJ1251.O8] 68-17352 7.95
1. Christian ethics—Addresses, essays, lectures. I. Ramsey, Paul, joint author. II. Carney, Frederick Smith, 1924- III. Title.

PAULUS VI, Pope. 1897- 241
The Christian in the material world, by Giovanni Battista Cardinal Montini. [Translated by Michael M. McManus. 1st ed.] Baltimore, Helicon Press [1964, c1963] 71 p. 20 cm. Translation of Il Cristiano e il benessere temporale. [BV4647.P6P313] 64-14666
1. Poverty (Virtue) 2. Charity. I. Title.

PAULUS VI, Pope, 1897- 241
The Christian in the material world, by Giovanni Battista Cardinal Montini [Tr. from Italian by Michael M. McManus] Helicon [dist. New York, Taplinger, 1964, c.1963] 71p. 20cm. 64-14666 1.95
1. Poverty (Virtue) 2. Charity. I. Title.

PERRIN, Joseph Marie, 1905- 241
The gospel of joy. Translated by P. D. Gilbert. Westminster, Md., Newman Press [1957] 129p. 19cm. [BX2183.P4] 57-13866
1. Joy and sorrow. 2. Beatitudes. I. Title.

PETERSEN, Mark E. 241
Our moral challenge. Salt Lake City, Deseret, 1965. 150p. illus. 24cm. [BJ1581.2.P48] 65-28411 price unreported
1. Conduct of life. I. Title.

PIEPER, Josef, 1904- 241
The four cardinal virtues: Prudence, Justice, Fortitude, Temperance. [Translated by Richard and Clara Winston and others. 1st ed.] New York, Harcourt, Brace & World [1965] xiii, 206 p. 21 cm. "A Helen and Kurt Wolff book."Translations of four studies previously published separately under titles: Traktat uber die Klugheit, Uber die Gerechtigkeit, Vom Sinn der Tapferkeit, and Zucht und Mass. [BV4645.P513] 65-14713
1. Cardinal virtues. I. Title.

PIEPER, Josef, 1904- 241
The four cardinal virtues: Prudence, Justice, Fortitude, Temperance [Tr. from German by Richard and Clara Winston, others] New York, Harcourt [c.1954-1965] xiii, 206p. 21cm. (Helen and Kurt Wolff bk.) [BV4645.P513] 65-14713 4.50
1. Cardinal virtues. I. Title.

PIEPER, Josef, 1904- 241
Justice; translated by Lawrence E. Lynch. [New York] Pantheon Books [1955] 121p. illus. 21cm. Translation of Uber die Gerechtigkeit. [BV4647.J8P53] 55-5546
1. Justice (Virtue) I. Title.

PIKE, James Albert, Bp., 1913-1969. 241
You & the new morality; 74 cases [by] James A. Pike. New York, Harper & Row [1967] viii, 147 p. 21 cm. Includes bibliographical references. [BJ1251.P53] 67-14935
1. Situation ethics. 2. Christian ethics—Anglican authors. I. Title.

PITTENGER, William Norman, 1905- 241
Making sexuality human [by] W. Norman Pittenger. Philadelphia, Pilgrim Press [1970] 96 p. 22 cm. [BT708.P56] 79-126862 3.95
1. Sex (Theology) I. Title.

POWELL, Enoch John, 1912- 241
No easy answers [by] Enoch Powell. New York, Seabury Press [1974, c1973] 135 p. 22 cm. "A Crossroad book." [BJ1251.P68 1974] 73-17906 ISBN 0-8164-0251-5 6.95
1. Christian ethics. 2. Social ethics. I. Title.

PRICE, Eugenia. 241
Never a dull moment; honest questions by teen agers, with honest answers by Eugenia Price. Grand Rapids, Zondervan Pub. House [1955] 121p. 20cm. [BR96.P7] 55-13639
1. Questions and answers—Theology. I. Title.

PRUMMER, Dominicus M 1866-1931. 241
Handbook of moral theology. Translated from the Latin by Gerald W. Shelton. Edited for American usage by John Gavin Nolan. New York, P. J. Kenedy [1957] 496p. 18cm. [BX1758.P7] 55-9737
1. Christian ethics—Catholic authors. I. Title.

PURCELL, William Ernest, 1909- 241
The plain man looks at himself; a book about self-examination for the ordinary Christian. Philadelphia, Fortress [1964, c.1960] 128p. 18cm. 64-18150 1.50 pap.,
1. Christian life—Anglican authors. I. Title.

RAMM, Bernard L., 1916- 241
The right, the good & the happy; the Christian in a world of distorted values, by Bernard L. Ramm. Waco, Tex., Word Books [1971] 188 p. 23 cm. Bibliography: p. 183-188. [BJ1251.R25] 70-144362 5.95
1. Christian ethics—Baptist authors. 2. Social ethics. I. Title.

RAMSEY, Paul. 241
Deeds and rules in Christian ethics. New York, Scribner [1967] viii, 245 p. 24 cm. Bibliographical footnotes. [BJ1251.R28] 67-21332
1. Christian ethics. I. Title.

RAMSEYER, Lloyd L 241
The more excellent way [by] Lloyd L. Ramseyer. Newton, Kan., Faith and Life Press [1965] 122 p. 21 cm. [BV4639.R3] 65-20481
1. Charity. I. Title.

RAMSEYER, Lloyd L. 241
The more excellent way. Newton, Kan., Faith & Life [c.1965] 122p. 20cm. [BV4639.R3] 65-20481 2.75
1. Charity. I. Title.

RANSIL, Bernard Jerome, 1929- 241
Abortion, by Bernard J. Ransil. Paramus, N.J., Paulist Press [1969] vi, 121 p. 19 cm. (Deus books) Bibliographical references included in "Notes" (p. 118-119) "Selected bibliograpphy": p. 120-121. [HQ767.R33] 70-92628 1.25
1. Abortion—Religious aspects. I. Title.

*RAUSCHENBUSCH, Walter, 1861-1918 241
Christianity and the social crisis. New York, Harper [1964, c.1920] 1v. 21cm. (Universal Lib.; Torchbk TB-3059) 2.25 pap.,
I. Title.

RAUSCHENBUSCH, Walter, 1861-1918 241
Christianity and the social crisis. Ed. by Robert D. Cross [Gloucester, Mass., P. Smith, 1965, c.1964] xxv, 429p. (Harper torchbk., TB3059, Univ. lib. rebound) First pub. in 1907. 4.25
I. Title.

RAYMOND, Irving Woodworth, 1898- 241
The teaching of the early church on the use of wine and strong drink. New York, AMS Press [1970] 170 p. 23 cm. (Studies in history, economics and public law, no. 286) Reprint of the 1927 ed. Originally presented as the author's thesis, Columbia, 1927. Bibliography: p. 156-164. [HV5186.R3 1970] 79-120207 ISBN 0-404-51286-0
1. Temperance. 2. Christian ethics—Early church, ca. 30-600. I. Title. II. Series: Columbia studies in the social sciences 286

RAYNOLDS, Robert, 1902- 241
The choice to love. [1st ed.] New York, Harper [1959] 192p. 22cm. Essays. [HQ33.R3] 59-103380
1. Love. I. Title.

READ, David Haxton Carswell. 241
Christian ethics, by David H. C. Read. Philadelphia, Lippincott, 1969 [c1968] 127 p. 21 cm. (Knowing Christianity) [BJ1251.R38] 69-16962 2.45
1. Christian ethics.

REDDING, David A. 241
The new immorality [by] David A. Redding. Westwood, N.J., F.H. Revell Co. [1967] 156 p. 21 cm. [BJ1251.R39] 67-14775
1. Christian ethics. I. Title.

REDDING, David A. 241
The new immorality [by] David A. Redding. Westwood, N.J., Revell [1967] 156p. 21cm. [BJ1251.R39] 67-14775 3.50 bds.,
1. Christian ethics. I. Title.

REHWINKEL, Alfred Martin, 1887- 241
The voice of conscience. Saint Louis, Concordia Pub. House [1956] 189p. 21cm. [BV4615.R4] 56-9538
1. Conscience. I. Title.

REID, Gaines S 1890- 241
The church and the layman: man' s duty to God: a plea for positive and dynamic support of the Christian church. Foreword by George W. Baber. [1st ed.] New York, Exposition Press [1959] 86p. 21cm. [BV4525.R43] 59-3720
1. Laity. I. Title.

RIDENOUR, Fritz. 241
It all depends; a comparison of Situation ethics and the Playboy philosophy with what the Bible teaches about morality. Illustrated by Joyce Thimsen. Research by Georgiana Walker. Glendale, Calif., G/L Regal Books [1969] 234 p. illus. 18 cm. Includes bibliographical references. [BJ1251.R5] 68-8388
1. Fletcher, Joseph Francis, 1905- Situation ethics. 2. Playboy. 3. Christian ethics. I. Title.

RILEY, Willard D 241
Widsom in Ethiopia 1st ed. New York, Vantage Press [1959] 66p. 22cm. [BR563.N4R54] 59-3659
1. Negroes— Religion. I. Title.

RILEY, William Bell, 1861-1947. 241
God's seven abominations, by W. B. Riley and Robert G. Lee. Wheaton, Ill., Van Kampen Press [c1954] 80p. 20cm. [BV4625.R5] 55-14164
1. Sin. I. Lee, Robert Greene, 1886- II. Title.

RIQUET, Michel. 241
Christian charity in action. Translated from the French by P. J. Hepburne-Scott. [1st ed.] New York, Hawthorn Books [1961] 171p.

21cm. (Twentieth century encyclopedia of Catholicism, v. 105. Section 9: The church in the modern world) Translation of La charite du Christ en action, des origines a saint Vincent de Paul. Includes bibliography. [BV4639.R553] 61-18917
1. Charity. 2. Christian giving. I. Title.

ROBINSON, Norman Hamilton Galloway, 1912- 241
The groundwork of Christian ethics [by] N. H. G. Robinson. Grand Rapids, Mich., Eerdmans [1972, c1971] 336 p. 23 cm. [BJ1251.R64 1972] 72-77180 ISBN 0-8028-3420-5 7.95
1. Christian ethics. I. Title.

ROY, Rustum, 1924- 241
Honest sex [by] Rustum and Della Roy. [New York] New American Library [1968] 209 p. illus. 21 cm. Bibliography: p. 187-199. [HQ31.R86] 68-18258
1. Sexual ethics. I. Roy, Della, joint author. II. Title.

RYRIE, Charles Caldwell, 1925- 241
You mean the Bible teaches that ... / Charles Caldwell Ryrie. Chicago : Moody Press, [1974] 127 p. ; 19 cm. Includes bibliographical references. [BS680.E84R9] 74-15331 1.95
1. Bible—Ethics. I. Title.

SALM, Celestine Luke, ed. 241
Readings in Biblical morality [edited by] C. Luke Salm. Englewood Cliffs, N. J., Prentice-Hall [1967] ix, 148 p. 22 cm. Includes bibliographical references. [BJ1249.S3] 67-10317
1. Christian ethics—Catholic authors. I. Title.

SALM, Celestine Luke, ed. 241
Readings in Biblical morality [edited by] C. Luke Salm. Englewood Cliffs, N.J., Prentice-Hall [1967] ix, 148 p. 22 cm. Includes bibliographical references. [BJ1249.S3] 67-10317
1. Christian ethics—Catholic authors. I. Title.

SCHERLING, A R 241
Scherling-Bailey debate, held in Vancouver, Wash., July 20-23, 1953, between A. R. Scherling ... and J. C. Bailey ... Tape recorded. 1st ed. Longview, Wash., Telegram Book Co., 1954. 180p. illus. 21cm. [BV4615.S35] 56-26570
1. Conscience. I. Bailey, John Carlos. II. Title.

SELLERS, James Earl. 241
Theological ethics [by] James Sellers. New York, Macmillan [1966] xi, 210 p. 21 cm. Includes bibliographical references. [BJ1251.S4] 66-14213
1. Christian ethics. I. Title.

SELLERS, James Earl. 241
Theological ethics [by] James Sellers. New York, Macmillan [1966] xi, 210 p. 21 cm. Includes bibliographical references. [BJ1251.S4] 66-14213
1. Christian ethics. I. Title.

SHANNON, William Henry, 1917- 241
The lively debate; response to Humanae vitae, by William H. Shannon. New York, Sheed & Ward [1970] viii, 216 p. 21 cm. (A Search book) Bibliography: p. [204]-209. [HQ766.3.S53] 75-101551 3.95
1. Birth control—Religious aspects. I. Catholic Church. Pope, 1963- (Paulus VI) Humanae vitae. II. Title.

SHEEDY, Charles Edmund. 241
The Christian virtues; a book on moral theology for college studentsand lay readers. [2d ed.] Notre Dame, Ind., University of Notre Dame Press [1956, c1951] xi, 369p. 24cm. (University religion series. Texts in theology for the layman) (university religion series) Bibliography: p.360-361. [BX1758] 55-8274
1. Virtues. 2. Christian ethics— Catholic authors. I. Title. II. Series.

SHEEDY, Charles Edmund. 241
The Christian virtues; a book on moral theology for college students and lay readers. [2d ed.] Notre Dame, Inc., University of Notre Dame Press [1956, c1951] xi, 369 p. 24 cm. (University religion series. Texts in theology for the layman) Bibliography: p. 360-361. [BX1758] 55-8274
1. Virtues. 2. Christian ethics — Catholic authors. I. Title. II. Series: University religion series

SHEEN, Fulton J. 241
The power of love. Garden City, N.Y., Doubleday [1968, c. 1965] 118p. 18cm (.Image bk., D235) [BV4639.S52] .75 pap.,
1. Love (Theology) I. Title.

SHEEN, Fulton John, Bp., 1895- 241
The moral universe; a preface to Christian living, by Fulton J. Sheen. Freeport, N. Y., Books for Libraries Press [1967] vii, 170 p. 22 cm. (Essay index reprint series) [BJ1249.S43 1967] 67-28766
1. Christian ethics—Catholic authors. 2. Catholic Church—Apologetic works. I. Title.

SHEEN, Fulton John, Bp., 1895- 241
The moral universe; a preface to Christian living, by Fulton J. Sheen. Freeport, N.Y., Books for Libraries Press [1967] vii, 170 p. 22 cm. (Essay index reprint series) [BJ1249.S43 1967] 67-28766
1. Catholic Church—Apologetic works. 2. Christian ethics—Catholic authors. I. Title.

SHEEN, Fulton John, Bp., 1895- 241
The power of love [by] Fulton J. Sheen. New York, Simon and Schuster [1965] 157 p. 16 cm. [BV4639.S52 1965] 65-15027
1. Love (Theology) I. Title.

SHEEN, Fulton John, Bp., 1895- 241
The power of love [Edw York, Maco c.1964] 96p. illus. 24cm. (M52) 64-55268 .60 pap.,
1. Love (Theology) I. Title.

SHEEN, Fulton John, Bp., 1895- 241
The power of love [by] Fulton J. Sheen. New York, Simon and Schuster [1965] 157 p. 16 cm. [BV4639.S52 1965] 65-15027
1. Love (Theology) I. Title.

SLUYTER, John Bennett, 1884- 241
Man, the character animal: discussions on the primacy of personal character. New York, Exposition Press [c.1960] 130p. 3.00
I. Title.

THE Social message of the gospels. 241 Edited by Franz Bockle. New York, Paulist Press [1968] viii, 180 p. 24 cm. (Councilium: theology in the age of renewal. Moral theology, v. 35) Includes articles translated from several languages by various persons. Contents.Contents.—Preface, by F. Bockle.—Articles: Empirical social study and ethics, by W. Korff. What does a non-Christian expect of the church in matters of social morality, by R. Garaudy. Social cybernetics as a permanent function of the church, by C. Wagner. World trade and international cooperation for development, by A. Ferrer. How can the church provide guidelines in social ethics? by P. Herder-Dorneich. Races and minorities: a matter of conscience by J. Musulin. The modern sexual revolution, by G. Struck. Prudence and moral change, by F. Furger.—Bibliographical survey: Strength and weakness of the declaration on the Jews, by J.-P. Lichtenberg.—Documentation Concilium: Peace through revolution, by Concilium General Secretariat and H. Gross-Mayr. Bibliographical footnotes. [HM216.S56] 68-31249
1. Social ethics—Addresses, essays, lectures. I. Bockle, Franz, ed. II. Series: Concilium (New York) v. 35

SOCKMAN, Ralph Washington, 1889- 241
Man's first love; the great commandment. [1st ed.] Garden City, N.Y., Doubleday, 1958. 211 p. 22 cm. [BV4817.S6] 58-7370
1. God — Worship and love. I. Title.

SOLLE, Dorothee. 241
Beyond mere obedience; reflections on a Christian ethic for the future. Translated by Lawrence W. Denef. Minneapolis, Augsburg Pub. House [1970] 85 p. 20 cm. Translation of Phantasie und Gehorsam. Includes bibliographical references. [BJ1459.S5713] 70-121967
1. Obedience. 2. Christian ethics. I. Title.

SPICQ, Ceslaus, 1901- 241
Charity and liberty in the New Testament. [Translated by Francis V. Manning] Staten Island, N.Y., Alba House [1965] 112 p. 20 cm. [BV4639.S673] 65-19409
1. Love (Theology) I. Title.

SPICQ, Ceslaus, 1901- 241
Charity and liberty in the New Testament [Tr. by Francis V. Manning] Staten Island, N.Y., Alba [c.1965] 112p. 20cm. [BV4639.S673] 65-19409 2.95
1. Love (Theology) I. Title.

STARKEY, Lycurgus Monroe. 241
James Bond's world of values [by] Lycurgus M. Starkey, Jr. Nashville, Abingdon Press [1966] 96 p. 19 cm. Bibliographical footnotes. [BJ1251.S813] 67-11015
1. Fleming, Ian, 1908-1964. 2. Methodist Church—Sermons. 3. Christian ethics—Methodist authors. 4. Sermons, American. I. Title.

STEARNS, Bill. 241
Anybody here know right from wrong? / Bill Stearns. Wheaton, Ill. : Victor Books, c1976. 94 p. ; 18 cm. [BJ1251.S814] 75-31310 ISBN 0-88207-724-4 pbk. : 1.25
1. Christian ethics. I. Title.

STEINKE, Peter L. 241
Right, wrong, or what? By Peter L. Steinke. St. Louis, Concordia Pub. House [1970] 85, [1] p. illus. 21 cm. (Perspective, 10) Bibliography: p. 85-[86] A compilation of the opinions of young people between the ages of fifteen and twenty on sexual ethics. [HQ35.S83] 73-114729
1. Sexual ethics for youth. I. Title.

STOTTS, Jack L 241
Believing, deciding, acting [by] Jack L. Stotts. Philadelphia, Geneva Press [c1968] 126 p. 21 cm. (Decade books) [BJ1251.S87] 68-10437
1. Christian ethics. I. Title.

STRINGFELLOW, William. 241
Free in obedience. New York, Seabury Press, 1964. 128 p. 20 cm. [BT77.S745] 64-10142
1. Theology, Doctrinal — Popular works. I. Title.

STRINGFELLOW, William 241
Free in obedience. New York, Seabury [1967, c.1964] 128p. 21cm. (SP30) Cover title: Free in obedience; the Radical Christian life. 1.45 pap.,
1. Perseverance (Theology) I. Title.

STUART, Moses, 1780-1852. 241
Conscience and the constitution; with remarks on the recent speech of the Hon. Daniel Webster in the Senate of the United States on the subject of slavery. New York, Negro Universities Press [1969] 119 p. 23 cm. Reprint of the 1850 ed. [E449.S929 1969b] 77-97441
1. Webster, Daniel, 1782-1852. Speech ... on Mr. Clay's resolution ... March 7, 1850. 2. Slavery in the United States—Controversial literature—1850. I. Title.

STUART, Moses, 1780-1852. 241
Conscience and the Constitution; with remarks on the recent speech of the Hon. Daniel Webster in the Senate of the United States on the subject of slavery. Boston, Crocker & Brewster, 1850. Miami, Fla., Mnemosyne Pub. Co. [1969] 119 p. 23 cm. [E449.S929 1969] 70-83951
1. Webster, Daniel, 1782-1852. Speech ... on Mr. Clay's resolution ... March 7, 1850. 2. Slavery in the United States—Controversial literature—1850. I. Title.

SUENENS, Leon Joseph, Cardinal, 1904- 241
Love and control; the contemporary-problem. [Translation by George J. Robinson] Westminister, Md., Newman Press [1961] 200 p. 20 cm. Translation of Un probleme crucial: amour et maitrise de sol. [HQ766.S8783] 61-4170
1. Birth control—Religious aspects. I. Title.

SUENENS, Leon Joseph, Bp., 1904- 241
Love and control; the contemporary problem. Tr. [from French] by George J. Robinson. Westminster, Md., Newman Press [c.1961] 200p. 61-4170 3.25
1. Birth control—Religious aspects. I. Title.

SULLIVAN, John J 241
The Commandment of love; the first and greatest of the Commandments explained according to the teaching of St. Thomas Aquinas. [1st ed.] New York, Vantage Press [1957, c1956] 138p. 21cm. [BV4639.S8] 56-12192
1. Love (Theology) 2. Thomas Aquinas, Saint—Theology. I. Title.

SULLIVAN, John J 241
The Commandment of love; the first and greatest of the Commandments explained according to the teaching of St. Thomas Aquinas. [1st ed.] New York,Vantage Press [1957, c1956] 138 p. 21 cm. [BV4639.S8] 56-12192
1. Love (Theology) 2. Thomas Aquinas, Saint—Theology. I. Title.

SWYHART, Barbara Ann DeMartino. 241
Bioethical decision-making : releasing religion from the spiritual / by Barbara Ann DeMartino Swyhart. Philadelphia : Fortress Press, c1975. x, 130 p. ; 23 cm. Includes bibliographical references. [BJ1188.S9] 75-13040 ISBN 0-8006-0418-0 : 6.50
1. Religious ethics. 2. Bioethics. 3. Abortion—Religious aspects. I. Title.

TANNER, Obert Clark, 1904- 241
Christ's ideals for living. For the Sunday schools of the Church of Jesus Christ of Latter-Day Saints. Salt Lake City, Desert Sunday School Union Board [1954, c1955] 468p. illus. 23cm. [BX8610.T33] 55-21974
1. Christian life—Study and teaching. 2. Christian life—Mormon authors. I. Church of Jesus Christ of Latter-Day Saints. Deseret Sunday School Union. II. Title.

THIELICKE, Helmut, 1908- 241
Theological ethics. Edited by William H. Lazareth. Philadelphia, Fortress Press [1966- v. 24 cm. "An abridgment and translation of Theologische Ethik." Contents.Contents.—v. 1. Foundations.—v. 2. Politics. Bibliographical footnotes. [BJ1253.T513] 66-17343
1. Christian ethics. 2. Christianity and politics. I. Lazareth, William Henry, 1928- ed. II. Title.

THOMAS AQUINAS, Saint, 1225?-1274. 241
On charity (De caritate) Translated from the Latin, with an introd. by Lottie H. Kendzierski. Milwaukee, Marquette University Press, 1960. 115 p. 23 cm. (Mediaeval philosophical texts in translation, no. 10) Bibliography: p. 110-112. [BV4639.T523] 59-8110
1. Love (Theology) I. Title. II. Series.

THOMAS AQUINAS, Saint 241
On charity (De caritate) Translated from the Latin, with an introd., by Lottie H. Kendzierski. Milwaukee, Marquette University Press [c.] 1960. 115 p. 23 cm. (Mediaeval philosophical texts in translation, no. 10) Bibliography: p. 110-112. 59-8110 apply
1. Love (Theology). I. Title. II. Series.

TILLICH, Paul, 1886-1965. 241
Love, power, and justice; ontological analyses and ethical applications. Given as Firth lectures in Nottingham, England, and as Sprunt lectures in Richmond, Virginia. New York, Oxford University Press, 1954. 127 p. 20 cm. [BV4633.T5] 54-6522
1. Love. 2. Power (Philosophy) 3. Justice. I. Title.

TILLICH, Paul [Johannes Oskar] 241
Love, power, and justice; ontological analyses and ethical applications. Given as Firth lectures in Nottingham, England, and as Sprunt lectures in Richmond, Virginia. New York, Oxford University Press, 1960 [c.1954]. 127 p. 20 cm. (Galaxy bk. GB38) .95, pap.
1. Love. 2. Power (philosophy). 3. Justice. I. Title.

TILLICH, Paul [Johannes Oskar] 1886- 241
Love, power, and justice: ontological analyses and ethical applications. [Gloucester, Mass., Peter Smith] 1960. 127p. (Galaxy bk. rebound in cloth) 3.00
1. Love. 2. Power (Philosophy) 3. Justice. I. Title.

TILLMANN, Fritz, 1874- 241
The Master calls; a handbook of Christian living. Translated by Gregory J. Roettger. Baltimore, Helicon Press, 1960 [i.e. 1961] 355 p. 24 cm. [BX1758.2.T513 1961] 60-15489
1. Christian ethics—Catholic authors. I. Title.

TILLMANN, Fritz, 1874- 241
The Master calls; a handbook of Christian living. Trans. [from German] by Gregory J. Roettger. Baltimore, Helicon Press, 1960 c.1961 355p. 60-15489 5.00
1. Christian ethics—Catholic authors. I. Title.

TOEWS, Abraham Peter, 1899- 241
The problem of Mennonite ethics. Grand Rapids, Eerdmans [1963] xii, 277 p. 23 cm. Bibliography: p. 256-268. [BJ1251.T6] 60-53095
1. Christian ethics — Mennonite authors. I. Title.

TOEWS, Abraham Peter, 1899- 241
The problem of Mennonite ethics. Grand Rapids, Eerdmans [c.1963] xii, 277p. 23cm. Bibl. 60-53095 5.50
1. Christian ethics—Mennonite authors. I. Title.

TOURVILLE, Henri de 241
Letters of direction; thoughts on the spiritual life from the letters of the Abbe de Tourville.[Translated from the French by Lucy Menzies]. With an introd. by Evelyn Underhill. New York, Crowell [1959] 111p. 16cm. 59-65387 1.00 pap.,
1. Spiritual life—Catholic authors. I. Title.

TOURVILLE, Henri de, 1842-1903. 241
Letters of direction; thoughts on the spiritual life from the letters of the Abbe de Tourville. With an introd. by Evelyn Underhill. New York, Crowell [1959] 111 p. 16 cm. "Extracts [translated from] Plete confiante." [BX2350.T633] 59-65387
1. Spiritual life — Catholic authors. I. Title.

TURKEL, Roma Rudd 241
Church is for the birds [about people who

scoff at religion]. New York, Paulist Press [c.1959] unpaged illus. (col.) 16cm. .10 pap., *I. Title.*

UNDERSTANDING the signs of the times. 241
Edited by Franz Bockle. New York, Paulist Press [1967] viii, 168 p. 24 cm. (Concilium. Moral theology, v. 25) Contents.Contents.—Preface, by F. Bockle.—Does the New Testament provide principles for modern moral theology? By J. Blank.—Toward a morality based on the meaning of history: the condition and renewal of moral theology, by I. Lobo.—The natural law and statute law: a lawyer's view, by P. Benenson.—Beyond natural law and positivism, by Heinz—orst Schrey.—Reflections on the virtue of truthfulness, by S. Kutz.—Communications media at the service of "good morals", by L. Hamelin.—Secularism and Christian ethics; some types and symptoms, by C. van Ouwerkerk.—Signs of the times, by M. C. Vanhengel and J. Peters.—Confessing the faith in Asia today, by M. Chen.—Pastoral work in Amsterdam, by M. van Hulten. Bibliographical footnotes. [BX1758.2.U5] 67-25694
1. Christian ethics—Catholic authors. I. Bockle, Franz, ed. II. Title: Moral theology. III. Series: Concilium (New York) v. 25.

VOGEL, Max 241
I speak again: Christ to the clergy of all denominations and to all the people, as interpreted by Max Fogel. New York, Exposition [c.1962] 40p. 2.50
I. Title.

VON HILDEBRAND, Dietrich, 1889- 241
The art of living, by Dietrich von Hildebrand and Alice von Hildebrand. Chicago, Franciscan Herald Press [1965] 119 p. 21 cm. [BX2350.2.V6] 65-16673
1. Christian life—Catholic authors. I. Von Hildebrand, Alice M. (Jourdain) II. Title.

VON HILDEBRAND, Dietrich, 1889- 241
The art of living, by Diedrich von Hildebrand, Alice von Hildebrand. Chicago, Regnery [1967, c.1965] 119p. 18cm. (Logos, 71 L-726) [BX2350.2.V6] 1.25 pap.,
1. Christian life—Catholic authors. I. Von Hildebrand, Aiice M. (Jourdain) II. Title.

VON HILDEBRAND, Dietrich, 1889- 241
The art of living, by Dietrich von Hildebrand, Alice von Hildebrand. Chicago, Franciscan Herald [c.1965] 119p. 21cm. [BX2350.2.V6] 65-16673 3.95 bds.,
1. Christian life—Catholic authors. I. Von Hildebrand, Alice M. (Jourdain). II. Title.

VON HILDEBRAND, Dietrich, 1889- 241
In defense of purity; an analysis of the Catholic ideals of purity and virginity. Baltimore, Helicon Press [1962] viii, 142 p. 23 cm. Translation of Reinbeit and Jungfraulichkeit. Bibliographical footnotes. [BV4647.C5V62 1962] 62-17094
1. Chastity. 2. Sex and religion. 3. Virginity. I. Title.

VON HILDEBRAND, Dietrich, 1889- 241
In defense of purity; an analysis of the Catholic ideals of purity and virginity. Chicago, Franciscan Herald Press [1970] viii, 142 p. 21 cm. [BV4647.C5V62 1970] 75-10185
1. Chastity. 2. Sex and religion. 3. Virginity. I. Title.

VON HILDEBRAND, Dietrich, 1889- 241
In defense of purity; an analysis of the Catholic ideals of purityand virginity. [Tr. from German] Helicon [dist. New York, Taplinger, c.1962] viii, 142p. 23cm. Bibl. 62-17094 3.50
1. Chastity. 2. Sex and religion. 3. Virginity. I. Title.

VON HILDEBRAND, Dietrich, 1889- 241
Morality and situation ethics, by Dietrich and Alice Von Hildebrand. Pref. by Bernard Haring. Chicago, Franciscan Herald [1966] xi, 191p. 21cm. Bibl. [BJ1249.V63] 66-25648 4.50
1. Christian ethics—Catholic authors. 2. Situation ethics. 3. Mystique of sin. I. Von Hildebrand, Alice M. (Jourdain) joint author. II. Title.

WADDAMS, Herbert Montague. 241
A new introduction to moral theology. New York, Seabury [1965, c.1964] 240p. 21cm. (SP22) Bibl. [BV4612.W3] 65-22258 2.25 pap.,
1. Christian ethics—Anglican authors. I. Title.

WAGNER, Oscar Walter, 1903- 241
Brotherhood in our apartment-size world. Boston, United Church [1964] 75p. illus. 21cm. (A13RB) Bibl. 64-14503 .75 pap.,
1. Brotherliness. I. Title.

WALKER, Granville T. 241
The greatest of these. St. Louis, Bethany [c.1963] 112p. 23cm. Bibl. 63-17873 2.50
1. Charity. I. Title.

WARD, Keith, 1938- 241
The divine image : the foundations of Christian morality / Keith Ward. London : SPCK, 1976. ix, 115 p. ; 23 cm. Bibliography: p. 113-115. [BJ1251.W238] 76-374288 ISBN 0-281-02935-0 : £3.50
1. Christian ethnics. I. Title.

WASSMER, Thomas A., 1916- 241
Christian ethics for today [by] Thomas A. Wassmer. Milwaukee, Bruce Pub. Co. [1969] xv, 240 p. 23 cm. (Contemporary college theology series) "Select bibliography in Christian ethics": p. 233-234. Bibliographical footnotes. [BX1758.2.W3] 69-17477
1. Christian ethics—Catholic authors. I. Title.

WEDGE, Florence 241
When you get up in the morning. Pulaski, Wisc., Franciscan Pubs. [c.1963] 55p. 19cm. (When ser.) .25 pap.,
I. Title.

WESSLER, Martin F. 241
Christian view of sex education; a manual for church leaders, by Martin F. Wessler. St. Louis, Concordia Pub House [1967] 87 p. 23 cm. (Concordia sex education series, book 6) Bibliography: p. 79-83. "Films, filmstrips, slides, and tapes": p. 83-85. [BT708.W4] 67-24875
1. Sex(Theology) 2. Sex instruction. I. Title.

WEST, Richard F. 241
Christian decision and action; a resource and discussion book for youth [by] Richard F. West. Illustrated by Don Herzbach. Boston, United Church Press [1968] 76 p. illus. 22 cm. (Confirmation education series) "Part of the United Church curriculum, prepared and published by the Division of Christian Education and the Division of Publication of the United Church Board for Homeland Ministries." [BJ1261.W43] 68-10036
1. Christian ethics. 2. Religious education—Text-books for young people—United Church of Christ. I. United Church Board for Homeland Ministries. Division of Christian Education. II. United Church Board for Homeland Ministries. Division of Publication. III. Title.

WESTERMARCK, Edward Alexander, 1862-1939. 241
Christianity and morals. by Edward Westermarck. Freeport, N.Y., Books for Libraries Press [1969] xiii, 427 p. 23 cm. (Essay index reprint series) Reprint of the 1939 ed. Bibliographical footnotes. [BJ1251.W47 1969] 78-80406
1. Christian ethics. I. Title.

WHITE, Ernest, 1887- 241
Marriage and the Bible. Nashville, Broadman Press [1965] ix, 149 p. 21 cm. Bibliographical references includes in "Notes" (p. 144-149) [BS680.M35W43] 65-15598
1. Marriage — Biblical teaching. 2. Sex in the Bible. I. Title.

WHITE, Ernest, 1887- 241
Marriage and the Bible. Nashville, Broadman [c.1965] xi, 149p. 21cm. Bibl. [BS680.M35W43] 65-15598 3.50 bds.,
1. Marriage—Biblical teaching. 2. Sex in the Bible. I. Title.

•WIER, Frank 241
What about sex? by Frank and Leslie Wier. New York, Friendship [1967] 63p. 16cm. (Questions for Christians, no. 12)pbBibl. .65 pap.,
1. SX I. Wier, Leslie, joint II. Title. III. Series.

WOGAMAN, J. Philip. 241
A Christian method of moral judgment / J. Philip Wogaman. Philadelphia : Westminster Press, c1976. xi, 270 p. ; 21 cm. Includes bibliographical references and index. [BJ1251.W58 1976] 76-40108 ISBN 0-664-24134-4 : 12.95
1. Christian ethics. I. Title.

WOOD, Frederic C. 241
Sex and the new morality, by Frederic C. Wood, Jr. New York, Association Press [1968] 157 p. 21 cm. Bibliographical references included in "Notes" (p. 151-157) [HQ31.W797] 68-17779 2.25
1. Sexual ethics. 2. Situation ethics. I. Title.

WOOD, Wilford C ed. 241
Joseph Smith begins his work. Salt Lake City? 1958- v. illus., ports., map, facsims. 24 cm. Contents.-- v. 1. Book of Mormon. [BX8621.W6] 58-2314
1. Smith, Joseph, 1805-1844. 2. Mormons and Mormonism. I. Title.

WOODS, George Frederick. 241
A defence of theological ethics, by G. F. Woods. Cambridge [Eng.] University Press, 1966. vii, 135 p. 19 cm. (Hulsean lectures, 1964) Bibliography: p. 133-134. [BJ1251.W6] 66-11032
1. Christian ethics. I. Title. II. Series.

WOODS, George Frederick 241
A defence of theological ethics. [New York] Cambridge [c.] 1966. vii, 135p. 19cm. (Hulsean lects., 1964) Bibl. [BJ1251.W6] 66-11032 4.50
1. Christian ethics. I. Title. II. Series.

YODER, John Howard. 241
Karl Barth and the problem of war, [by] John H. Yoder. Nashville, Abingdon Press [1970] 141 p. 23 cm. (Studies in Christian ethics series) Includes bibliographical references. [BX4827.B3Y6 1970] 71-124760 ISBN 0-687-20724-X 2.95
1. Barth, Karl, 1886-1968. 2. War and religion. I. Title.

ZIEMKE, Donald C 241
Love for the neighbor in Luther's theology: the development of his thought, 1512-1529. Minneapolis, Augsburg Pub. House [1963] 108 p. 22 cm. (An Augsburg theological monograph) Bibliography: p. 95-104. [BR333.5.C4Z5] 63-16607
1. Luther, Martin, 1483-1546. 2. Charity. I. Title.

ZIEMKE, Donald C. 241
Love for the neighbor in Luther's theology: the development of his thought, 1512-1529. Minneapolis, Augsburg [c.1963] 108p. 22cm. (Augsburg theological monograph) Bibl. 63-16607 1.95 pap.,
1. Luther, Martin, 1483-1546. 2. Charity. I. Title.

SCHALLER, Jean Pierre. 241'.01'9
Our emotions and the moral act. [Translated by M. Angeline Bouchard] Staten Island, N.Y., Alba House [1968] 199 p. 22 cm. (Mental health series, 11) Translation of Morale et affectivite. Bibliographical footnotes. [BJ1249.S3513] 68-55035 4.95
1. Christian ethics—Catholic authors. 2. Emotions. I. Title.

CARROLL, James. 241'.02
A terrible beauty; conversions in prayer, politics, and imagination. New York, Newman Press [1973] 190 p. 20 cm. [BX2350.2.C338] 72-97400 ISBN 0-8091-0182-3 4.50
1. Christian life—Catholic authors. 2. Conversion. I. Title.

BAKER'S dictionary of Christian ethics. 241'.03
Carl F. H. Henry, editor. Grand Rapids, Baker Book House [1973] xxv, 726 p. 25 cm. [BJ1199.B34] 73-83488 ISBN 0-8010-4079-5 16.95
1. Christian ethics—Dictionaries. 2. Social ethics—Dictionaries. I. Henry, Carl Ferdinand Howard, 1913- ed. II. Baker Book House.

MACQUARRIE, John. 241'.03
Dictionary of Christian ethics, edited by John Macquarrie. Philadelphia, Westminster Press [1967] viii, 366 p. 26 cm. Includes bibliographical references. [BJ63.M3] 67-17412
1. Christian ethics—Dictionaries. 2. Ethics—Dictionaries. I. Title.

ROBERTI, Francesco 241.03
Dictionary of moral theology. Comp. under the direction of Francesco Cardinal Roberti. Ed. under the direction of Dietro Palazzini. Tr. from 2d Italian ed. under the direction of Henry J. Yannone. Westminster, Md., Newman [c.1962] xxxix, 1352 p. 24 cm. Bibl. 60-14828 25.00, bxd.
1. Christian ethics—Dictionaries. I. Title.

ABAILARD, Pierre, 1079-1142. 241'.04'2
Peter Abelard's Ethics: an edition with introduction, English translation and notes by D. E. Luscombe. Oxford, Clarendon Press, 1971. lxi, 144 p. facsim. 22 cm. (Oxford medieval texts) Abailard's text in English and Latin. Includes bibliographical references. [B765.A23E82 1971] 70-885574 ISBN 0-19-822217-3 £4.00
1. Christian ethics. I. Luscombe, David Edward, ed. II. Title. III. Series.

CARTER, Edward, 1929- 241'.04'2
The spirit is present; themes on Christian spirituality. Canfield, Ohio, Alba Books [1973] v, 130 p. 18 cm. [BX2350.2.C362] 72-9577 1.25 (pbk.)
1. Spiritual life—Catholic authors. I. Title.

CURRAN, Charles E. 241'.04'2
Absolutes in moral theology? / Edited by Charles E. Curran. Westport, Conn. : Greenwood Press, 1975, c1968. 320 p. ; 23 cm. Reprint of the ed. published by Corpus Books, Washington. Includes bibliographical references and index. [BX1758.2.C8 1975] 75-3988 ISBN 0-8371-7450-3
1. Christian ethics—Catholic authors—Addresses, essays, lectures. I. Title.

CURRAN, Charles E. 241'.04'2
Absolutes in moral theology? / Edited by Charles E. Curran. Westport, Conn. : Greenwood Press, 1975, c1968. 320 p. ; 23 cm. Reprint of the ed. published by Corpus Books, Washington. Includes bibliographical references and index. [BX1758.2.C8 1975] 75-3988 ISBN 0-8371-7450-3 lib.bdg. : 16.00
1. Christian ethics—Catholic authors—Addresses, essays, lectures. I. Title.

CURRAN, Charles E. 241'.04'2
Catholic moral theology in dialogue / Charles E. Curran. Notre Dame [Ind.] : University of Notre Dame Press, 1976, c1972. 270 p. ; 21 cm. Reprint of the ed. published by Fides Publishers, Notre Dame, Ind. Includes bibliographical references and index. [BX1758.2.C817 1976] 76-14906 ISBN 0-268-00716-0 10.95 ISBN 0-268-00717-9 pbk. : 3.95
1. Christian ethics—Catholic authors. I. Title.

CURRAN, Charles E. 241'.04'2
Themes in fundamental moral theology / Charles E. Curran. Notre Dame : University of Notre Dame Press, c1977. p. cm. [BJ1249.C84] 76-51614 ISBN 0-268-01833-2 : 11.95. ISBN 0-268-01834-0 pbk. : 4.95
1. Christian ethics—Catholic authors—Addresses, essays, lectures. I. Title.

CURRAN, Charles E. 241'.04'2
Themes in fundamental moral theology / Charles E. Curran. Notre Dame : University of Notre Dame Press, c1977. p. cm. [BJ1249.C84] 76-51614 ISBN 0-268-01833-2 : 11.95. ISBN 0-268-01834-0 pbk. : 4.95
1. Christian ethics—Catholic authors—Addresses, essays, lectures. I. Title.

DEDEK, John F., 1929- 241'.04'2
Titius and Bertha ride again : contemporary moral cases / John F. Dedek. New York : Sheed and Ward, [1974] 160 p. ; 21 cm. Bibliography: p. 155-160. [BX1758.2.D39] 74-1532 ISBN 0-8362-0570-7 : 5.95. ISBN 0-8362-0580-4 pbk. : 2.45
1. Casuistry. I. Title.

DRANE, James F. 241'.04'2
Religion and ethics / by James F. Drane. New York : Paulist Press, c1976. x, 107 p. ; 19 cm. (Topics in moral argument) (Paulist Press/Deus book) Includes bibliographical references. [BJ1249.D72] 76-45935 ISBN 0-8091-1992-7 pbk. : 1.95
1. Christian ethics—Catholic authors. I. Title.

FAUSSET, Hugh I'Anson, 1895- 241'.04'2
John Donne; a study in discord. New York, Russell & Russell [1967] 318 p. ports. 21 cm. Reprint of the 1924 ed. [PR2248.F3 1967] 67-28776
1. Donne, John, 1572-1631.

FINLEY, James. 241'.04'2
Christian morality & you : right & wrong in an age of freedom / James Finley, Michael Pennock. Notre Dame, Ind. : Ave Maria Press, c1976. 191 p. : ill. ; 23 cm. [BX1758.2.F55] 76-15218 ISBN 0-87793-112-7 : 3.50
1. Christian ethics—Catholic authors. I. Pennock, Michael, joint author. II. Title.

HARING, Bernhard, 1912- 241'.04'2
Morality is for persons [by] Bernhard Haring. New York, Farrar, Straus and Giroux [1971] x, 214 p. 22 cm. Includes bibliographical references. [BX1758.2.H316] 79-154861 ISBN 0-374-21253-8 6.95
1. Christian ethics—Catholic authors. 2. Personalism. 3. Natural law. I. Title.

JACOBS, William J. 241'.04'2
Caricatures & Christians, by William Jacobs. Dayton, Ohio, Pflaum/Standard [1973] 96 p. 17 cm. (Christian experience series. Witness book, 18) [BX2350.2.J26] 72-97596 ISBN 0-8278-2125-5 0.95
1. Christian life—Catholic authors. I. Title.

JACOBS, William J. 241'.04'2
Caricatures & Christians, by William Jacobs. Dayton, Ohio, Pflaum/Standard [1973] 96 p. 17 cm. (Christian experience series. Witness book, 18) [BX2350.2.J26] 72-97596 ISBN 0-8278-2125-5 0.95 (pbk.)
1. Christian life—Catholic authors. I. Title.

JACOBS, William J. 241'.04'2
What's right now? By William J. Jacobs. New York, Paulist Press [1971] 70 p. 17 cm. [BJ1249.J32] 70-160512 0.75

1. Christian ethics—Catholic authors. I. Title.

LOHKAMP, Nicholas. 241'.04'2
What's happening to morality? [Cincinnati, St. Anthony Messenger Press, 1971] v, 114 p. illus. 19 cm. [BX1758.2.L63] 76-151400 ISBN 0-912228-02-4 0.95
1. Christian ethics—Catholic authors. I. Title.

REGAN, George M. 241'.042
New trends in moral theology: a survey of fundamental moral themes, by George M. Regan. New York, Newman Press [1971] vi, 213 p. 21 cm. Includes bibliographies. [BX1758.2.R4 1971] 72-171102 3.75
1. Christian ethics—Catholic authors. I. Title.

VAN DER POEL, Cornelius J., 1921- 241'.04'2
The search for human values, by Cornelius J. van der Poel. New York, Newman Press [1971] viii, 186 p. 22 cm. Includes bibliographical references. [BJ1249.V295] 75-161445 4.95
1. Christian ethics—Catholic authors. I. Title.

BARCLAY, William, lecturer in the University of Glasgow. 241'.04'3
Ethics in a permissive society. [1st U.S. ed.] New York, Harper & Row [1971] 223 p. 22 cm. Based on the television series, Jesus today: the Christian ethic in the twentieth century. Bibliography: p. 217-223. [BJ1251.B32 1971b] 70-175157 ISBN 0-06-060415-8 4.95
1. Christian ethics. I. Title.

STRINGFELLOW, William. 241'.04'3
An ethic for Christians and other aliens in a strange land. Waco, Tex., Word Books [1973] 156 p. 23 cm. [BJ1251.S88] 73-84048 5.95
1. Christian ethics—Anglican authors. 2. Social ethics. 3. United States—Moral conditions. I. Title.

STOB, Henry, 1908- 241'.04'57
Essays on moral themes / by Henry Stob Grand Rapids : Eerdmans, c1977. p. cm. [BJ1251.S86] 77-16258 ISBN 0-8028-1708-4 pbk. : 5. 95
1. Christian ethics—Reformed authors—Addresses, essays, lectures. I. Title.

SIMMONS, Billy. 241'.04'61
Resplendent themes; meditations on the Christian life, by Billy E. Simmons. [Dallas, Crescendo Book Publications, c1971] 70 p. 22 cm. [BV4501.2.S47] 73-81145 1.95
1. Christian life—Baptist authors. I. Title.

POTTER, C. Burtt. 241'.04'6132
Baptists: the passionate people [by] C. Burtt Potter, Jr. Nashville, Broadman Press [1973] 128 p. 21 cm. Includes bibliographical references. [BX6207.A48P67] 72-94400 ISBN 0-8054-8802-2 1.50 (pbk.)
1. Southern Baptist Convention. I. Title.

BOYER, Leland 241.07
The life of faith; bk.4, by Leland J. Boyer, William J. Reedy. New York, Sadlier [c.1964] 176p. illus. (pt. col.) 28cm. (Confraternity high sch. ser.; 634) pap., 1.60; teacher's manual and key, pap., 1.67
I. Title.

WAGNER, Oscar Walter, 1903- 241.07
Levels of brotherhood; a coursebook for adults. Philadelphia, United Church [1964] 60p. illus. 21cm. Bibl. 64-14504 .75
1. Sociology, Christian—Study and teaching. 2. Brotherliness—Study and teaching. 3. Brotherliness—Study and teaching. I. Title.

WESTERHOFF, John H. 241'.07
Values for tomorrow's children; an alternative future for education in the church, by John H. Westerhoff III. Philadelphia, Pilgrim Press [1970] xii, 116 p. 22 cm. Bibliography: p. 115-116. [BV1471.2.W47] 72-125961 ISBN 0-8298-0179-0 4.95
1. Christian education. I. Title.

CONNELL, Francis Jermiah, 1888- 241.076
More answers to today's moral problems. Ed. by Eugene J. Weitzel. Washington, D.C., Catholic Univ. [c.1965] xiii, 249p. 23cm. Bibl. [BX1758.2.C647] 65-16255 4.95
1. Questions and answers—Theology. 2. Christian ethics—Catholic authors. 3. Casuistry. I. Title.

RAMSEY, Ian T., ed. 241.08
Christian ethics and contemporary philosophy, ed. by Ian T. Ramsey. New York, Macmillan [1966] 399p. 23cm. Bibl. [BJ1251.R27] 66-16926 7.95
1. Christian ethics—Addresses, essays, lectures. I. Title.

ROBINSON, John Arthur Thomas, Bp. 1919- 241'.08
Christian freedom in a permissive society [by] John A. T. Robinson. Philadelphia, Westminster Press [1970] xi, 244 p. 21 cm. Includes bibliographical references. [BJ1251.R62 1970b] 75-110149 2.95
1. Christian ethics—Anglican authors. 2. Freedom (Theology) I. Title.

RYAN, Mary Perkins, 1915- comp. 241'.08
Toward moral maturity; religious education and the formation of conscience, by Daniel C. Maguire [and others] Glen Rock, N.J., Paulist Press [1968] vi, 153 p. 19 cm. (Deus books) Articles from the Living light. Includes bibliographical references. [BX1759.R9] 68-31046
1. Christian ethics—Study and teaching. 2. Christian ethics—Catholic authors. I. Maguire, Daniel C. II. The Living light. III. Title.

VANN, Gerald, 1906-1963. 241.08
Moral dilemmas. [1st ed.] Garden City, N.Y., Doubleday, 1965. 214 p. 22 cm. Essays. Bibliographical footnotes. [BX2350.2.V34 1965a] 65-24685
1. Christian life — Catholic authors. 2. Pastoral counseling. I. Title.

VANN, Gerald, 1906-1963. 241.08
Moral dilemmas. Garden City, N. Y., Doubleday [c.]1965. 214p. 22cm. Bibl. [BX2350.2.V34] 65-24685 4.50
1. Christian life—Catholic authors. 2. Pastoral counseling. I. Title.

HASELBARTH, Hans. 241'.096
Christian ethics in the African context / Hans Haselbarth. Ibadan : Daystar Press, 1976. viii, 233 p. ; 21 cm. [BJ1251.H324] 77-365213 ISBN 9-7812-2115-1. ISBN 9-7812-2116-X pbk.
1. Christian ethics. 2. Social ethics. 3. Africa, Sub-Saharan—Moral conditions. 4. Africa, Sub-Saharan—Social conditions. I. Title.

CONSCIENCE in today's world. 241'.1
Edited by Jeremy Harrington. [Cincinnati, St. Anthony Messenger Press, 1970] xi, 114 p. illus. 19 cm. Includes bibliographical references. [BJ1471.C58] 72-132546 ISBN 0-912228-01-6 0.95
1. Conscience—Addresses, essays, lectures. I. Harrington, Jeremy, ed.

DELHAYE, Philippe. 241'.1
The Christian conscience. Translated from the French by Charles Underhill Quinn. New York, Desclee Co. [1968?] 277 p. 23 cm. Translation of La conscience morale du chretien. Includes bibliographical references. [BV4615.D413] 68-31195 4.95
1. Conscience. I. Title.

DONNELLY, John, comp. 241'.1
Conscience. John Donnelly & Leonard Lyons, ed[itor]s. Staten Island, N.Y., Alba House [1973] x, 249 p. 21 cm. Includes bibliographical references. [BJ1471.D66] 72-6720 ISBN 0-8189-0259-0 4.95
1. Conscience. I. Lyons, Leonard, joint comp. II. Title.

FRANCE, Malcolm Norris, 1928- 241'.1
The paradox of guilt; a Christian study of the relief of self-hatred [by] Malcolm France. Philadelphia, United Church Press [1968, c1967] 127, [1] p. 21 cm. Bibliographical references included in "Notes": p. 127-[128] [BJ1471.5.F7 1968] 67-28405
1. Guilt. 2. Conscience. I. Title.

KUNG, Hans, 1928- 241.1
Freedom today Translated by Cecily Hastings. New York, Sheed and Ward [1966] xiii, 176 p. 22 cm. (Theological meditations) [BV741.K8] 65-20861
1. Liberty of conscience. I. Title.

KUNG, Hans, 1928- 241.1
Freedom today. Tr. [from German] by Cecily Hastings. New York, Sheed [c.1965.c.1966] xiii, 176p. 22cm. (Theol. meditations) [BV741.K8] 65-20861 3.95
1. Liberty of conscience. I. Title.

LAPLACE, Jean, S.J. 241'.1
Preparing for spiritual direction. Translated by John C. Guinness. Chicago, Franciscan Herald Press [1975] 192 p. 22 cm. Translation of La direction de conscience. Reprint of the 1967 ed. published by Herder & Herder, New York, under title: The direction of conscience. [BX2350.7.L3213 1975] 74-17135 ISBN 0-8199-0550-X 6.95
1. Spiritual direction. I. Title.

MCKEATING, Henry. 241'.1
Living with guilt. Valley Forge [Pa.] Judson Press [1970, c1969] 125 p. 19 cm. Bibliography: p. 125. [BJ1471.5.M27] 71-133000 ISBN 0-8170-0515-3 1.95
1. Guilt. 2. Christian life—Methodist authors. I. Title.

MOUNT, Eric. 241'.1
Conscience and responsibility. Richmond, Va., John Knox Press [1969] 191 p. 21 cm. Includes bibliographical references. [BJ1471.M68] 76-82937 4.95
1. Conscience. I. Title.

NELSON, Carl Ellis, 1916- comp. 241'.1
Conscience: theological and psychological perspectives, edited by C. Ellis Nelson. New York, Newman Press [1973] xi, 353 p. 23 cm. Contents.Contents.—Theological perspectives: Ricoeur, P. Guilt, ethics, and religion. Lehmann, P. The decline and fall of conscience. Tillich, P. A conscience above moralism. Tillich, P. The nature of a liberating conscience. Schar, H. Protestant problems with conscience. Rudin, J. A Catholic view of conscience. Dulles, A. R. Conscience and church authority. Mortimer, R. C. An Anglo-Catholic view of conscience. Curran, C. E. The Christian conscience today. Cousins, E. H. The mature Christian conscience. Macquarrie, J. The struggle of conscience for authentic selfhood. Glaser, J. W. Conscience and superego; a key distinction.—Psychological perspectives: Sanford, N. Elements of personality. Zilboorg, G. Superego and conscience. Buber, M. Guilt and guilt feelings. Pattison, E. M. The development of moral values in children. McCarthy, D. The development of the normal conscience. Sears, R., Macoby, E., and Levin, H. How conscience is formed. Bettelheim, B. Personality formation in the kibbutz. Josselyn, I. M. Changes in conscience during adolescence. Keniston, K. The struggle of conscience in youth. Includes bibliographies. [BV4615.N44] 73-75245 ISBN 0-8091-1767-3 5.95 (pbk.)
1. Conscience. I. Title.
Contents Omitted.

O'FLAHERTY, V. M. 241.1
How to cure scruples [by] V. M. O'Flaherty. Milwaukee, Bruce [1966] x, 108p. 17cm. Bibl. [BX1759.5.S4033] 66-25043 2.75
1. Scruples. I. Title.

BANKS, Robert J. 241'.2
Jesus and the law in the synoptic tradition / Robert Banks. Cambridge, Eng. ; New York : Cambridge University Press, [1975] x, 310 p. ; 22 cm. (Monograph series - Society for New Testament Studies ; 28) A revision of the author's thesis, Cambridge, 1969. Includes indexes. Bibliography: p. 264-280. [BT590.J34B36 1975] 75-7215 ISBN 0-521-20789-4 : 24.50
1. Jesus Christ—Attitude towards Jewish law. 2. Law (Theology)—Biblical teaching. 3. Jewish law. I. Title. II. Series: Studiorum Novi Testamenti Societas. Monograph series ; 28.

IANNUCCI, Remo Joseph, 1914- 241.3
The treatment of the capital sins and the Decalogue in the German sermons of Berthold von Regensburg. New York, AMS Press [1970, c1942] xvii, 128 p. 23 cm. (Catholic University of America. Studies in German, v. 17) Originally presented as the author's thesis, Catholic University of America, 1942. Bibliography: p. 117-123. [BV4208.G3I3 1970] 70-140024 ISBN 0-404-50237-7
1. Berthold von Regensburg, d. 1272. 2. Preaching—History—Germany. 3. Commandments, Ten. 4. Deadly sins. I. Title. II. Series.

LOCKYER, Herbert. 241.3
The sins of saints; scriptural unfolding of victorious living, by Herbert G. Lockyer. Neptune, N.J., Loizeaux Bros. [1970] 255 p. 20 cm. [BV4625.L57] 75-108378 3.50
1. Sins. 2. Christian life—1960- I. Title.

MCCRACKEN, Robert James 241.3
What is sin? What is virtue? New York, Harper [c.1966] 94p. 22cm. Bibl. [BV4626.M32] 66-15043 2.95 bds.,
1. Deadly sins. 2. Cardinal virtues. I. Title.

MARTIN, William Benjamin James. 241.3
Little foxes that spoil the vines [by] W. B. J. Martin. Nashville, Abingdon Press [1968] 127 p. 20 cm. [BV4625.M34] 68-17448
1. Sins. I. Title.

MAY, William F. 241.3
A catalogue of author sins; a contemporary examination of christian conscience, by William F. May [1st ed.] New York, Holt [1967] ix, 208p. 22cm. Bibl. [BV4625.M38] 66-13494 4.95
1. Sins. I. Title.

THE Sunday times, London. 241.3
The seven deadly sins [by] Angus Wilson [and others]. Special foreword by Ian Fleming. Introd. by Raymond Mortimer. Freeport, N.Y., Books for Libraries Press [1970, c1962] xvi, 87 p. illus. 23 cm. (Essay index reprint series) [BV4626.S86 1970] 75-117848
1. Deadly sins. I. Wilson, Angus. II. Title.

*WEDGE, Florence 241.3
Envious? Who, me? Pulaski, Wis., Franciscan Pubs. [1967] 60p. 19cm. .25 pap.,
I. Title.

WENZEL, Siegfried 241.3
The sin of sloth; acedia in medieval thought and literature. Chapel Hill, Univ. of N. C. Pr. [1967] x, 269p. 24cm. Bibl. [BV4627.S65W43] 67-17027 7.50
1. Laziness. I. Title. II. Title: Acedia in medieval thought and literature.

ANDERSEN, Richard, 1931- 241'.4
The love formula : living in forgiveness / Richard Andersen. St. Louis : Concordia Pub. House, [1974] 163 p. ; 21 cm. Includes bibliographical references. [BJ1476.A5] 73-20721 ISBN 0-570-03182-6 pbk. : 2.50
1. Forgiveness. I. Title.

BALLOU, Adin, 1803-1890. 241'.4
Christian non-resistance in all its important bearings, illustrated and defended, together with A discourse on Christian non-resistance in extreme cases, and Christian non-resistance defended against Rev. Henry Ward Beecher, by Adin Ballou, and Non-resistance, a critical review of Adin Ballou's Christian non-resistance, by C. H. With an introd. for the Garland ed. by Larry Gara. New York, Garland Pub., 1972. 12, xv, 278, 32, 20, 87-113 p. 22 cm. (The Garland library of war and peace) Reprint of 3 works by the author originally published in 1910, 1860, and 1862, respectively, and Non-resistance by C. H. originally published in the Christian examiner, v. 44, Jan. 1848. [BT736.6.B34 1972] 77-147697 ISBN 0-8240-0225-3 14.50
1. Evil, Non-resistance to. 2. Christian ethics. 3. War and religion. I. Ballou, Adin, 1803-1890. A discourse on Christian non-resistance in extreme cases. 1972. II. Ballou, Adin, Christian non-resistance defended against Rev. Henry Ward Beecher. 1972. Christian non-resistance defended against Rev. Henry Ward Beecher. 1972. III. Title. IV. Series.

BECKER, Wilhard. 241.4
Love in action. Translated by Susan Wiesman. Foreword by Rosalind Rinker. [1st ed.] Grand Rapids, Mich., Zondervan Pub. House [1969] 135 p. 21 cm. Translation of Angriff der Liebe. [BV4639.B413] 69-11651 3.95
1. Love (Theology) I. Title.

BIGELOW, John, 1817-1911. 241.4
Toleration and other essays and studies; posthumous. With an introd. by Glenn Frank. Freeport, N.Y., Books for Libraries Press [1969] xii, 162 p. port. 23 cm. (Essay index reprint series) Reprint of the 1927 ed. Contents.Contents.—Toleration.—The unfailing moral standard.—What is charity?—Poverty and riches. [BR85.B58 1969] 78-84298
1. Christianity—Addresses, essays, lectures. 2. Toleration. I. Title.

BOROS, Ladislaus, 1927- 241.4
Living in hope; future perspectives in Christian thought. Translated by W. J. O'Hara. [New York] Herder and Herder [1970, c1969] 127 p. 21 cm. Translation of Aus der Hoffnung leben. [BV4638.B5813] 75-105404 4.50
1. Hope. I. Title.

BOROS, Ladislaus, 1927- 241.4
Meeting God in man. Translated by William Glen-Doepel. [New York] Herder and Herder [1968] xi, 142 p. 21 cm. Translation of Im Menschen Gott begegnen. [BV4630.B613 1968b] 68-55082 4.50
1. Virtues. I. Title.

BOUILLOC, Jean. 241.4
The hope that is in us. Edited by Jean Bouilloc. Translated by Sister Gertrude. Glen Rock, N.J., Newman Press [1968] ix, 145 p. 22 cm. Translation of L'esperance qui est en vous. "The outlines for reflection presented in this book have their origin in a number of doctrinal courses that were given during the formation sessions organized by Catholic Action for Health and Welfare during the summer of 1963." [BV4638.B613] 68-57472 5.95
1. Hope. I. Title.

BUGGE, John M., 1941- 241'.4
Virginitas : an essay in the history of a medieval ideal / by John Bugge. The Hague : Martinus Nijhoff, 1975,i.e.1976 viii, 168 p. ; 24 cm. (Archives internationales d'histoire des idees : Series minor ; 17) Includes index. Bibliography: p. [155]-163. [BV4647.C5B84] 75-510872 ISBN 90-247-1695-0 pbk. 11.25
1. Virginity. I. Title. II. Series.
Distributed by Humanities

CAVIT, Marshal. 241.4
The will of my Father; messages on the relationship between holiness and missions. Newberg, Or., Barclay Press [1968] vi, 115 p. 23 cm. [BT767.C36] 67-29648 2.50
1. Holiness—Sermons. 2. Missions—Sermons. 3. Sermons, American. I. Title.

CHRISTIAN hope and the future of humanity. Edited by Franklin Sherman. Minneapolis, Augsburg Pub. House [1969] 94 p. 22 cm. (Christian hope series) Contents.Contents.—The phenomenology of hope, by C. E. Braaten.—Non-Christian eschatologies, by M. E. Marty.—The church and the proximate goals of history: a sociological view, by K. H. Hertz.—The church and the proximate goals of history: a theological perspective, by F. Sherman. Bibliographical references included in "Notes" (p. 91-94) [BV4638.C48] 70-95768 2.50 241.4
1. Hope. 2. Eschatology. 3. Sociology, Christian. 4. Kingdom of God. I. Sherman, Franklin, ed.

DESBUQUOIS, Gustave, 1869-1959 241.4
Charity. Tr. from French by Kathleen Pond. Notre Dame, Ind., Fides [1965] 140p. 19cm. (Fides dome bks., D-46) [BV4639.D42] 65-5825 2.95; .95 pap.,
1. Charity. I. Title.

DRUMMOND, Henry, 1851-1897. 241.4
The greatest thing in the world. Edited by David A. MacLennan. New York, World Pub. Co. [1969] 63 p. 17 cm. (World inspirational books) [BV4639.D7 1969] 77-80438 1.25
1. Love (Theology) I. Title.

ELLIS, John Tracy, 1905- 241.4
A commitment to truth. Latrobe, Pa., Archabbey Press [c1966] vii, 93 p. 20 cm. (Wimmer lecture 19) Bibliographical references included in "Notes" (p. 79-88) [BR1610.E55] 66-18697
1. Toleration. 2. Truth. I. Title. II. Series.

FITCH, Robert Elliot, 1902- 241.4
Of love and of suffering; preface to Christian ethics for heathen philosophers, by Robert E. Fitch, with a postscript for heathen theologians. Philadelphia, Westminster Press [1970] 176 p. 19 cm. [BV4639.F56] 73-115821 2.75
1. Love (Theology) 2. Christian Ethics. I. Title.

FORD, Josephine Massingberd. 241.4
A trilogy on wisdom and celibacy [by] J. Massingberd Ford. Notre Dame, Univ. of Notre Dame Pr., 1967. xv, 256p. 22cm. (Cardinal O'Hara ser., v. 4) Bibl. [BV4647.C5F6] 67-22988 7.95
1. Celibacy. 2. Virginity. I. Title. II. Series.

FORD, Josephine Massingberd. 241.4
A trilogy on wisdom and celibacy [by] J. Massingberd Ford. Notre Dame, University of Notre Dame Press, 1967. xv, 256 p. 22 cm. (The Cardinal O'Hara series, v.4) Bibliography: p. 234-245. [BV4647.C5F6] 67-22988
1. Celibacy. 2. Virginity. I. Title. II. Series.

FRANZMANN, Martin H. 241.4
Grace under pressure; the way of meekness in ecumenical relations [by] Martin H. Franzmann, F. Dean Lueking. [St. Louis] Concordia [1966] vii, 105p. 21cm. (Witnessing church ser.) Bibl. [BV4647.M3F7] 66-25512 1.95 pap.,
1. Meekness. 2. Ecumenical movement. I. Lueking, Frederick Dean, 1928- joint author. II. Title.

THE Future of hope; 241.4
[essays by Bloch, Fackenheim, Moltmann, Metz, Capps] Edited by Walter H. Capps. Philadelphia, Fortress Press [1970] vi, 154 p. 18 cm. Papers from a symposium on "The future of hope" sponsored by the Department and Institute of Religious Studies of the University of California, Santa Barbara together with a speech: Man as possibility, by Ernst Bloch. Includes bibliographical references. [BV4638.F84] 77-96862
1. Hope—Addresses, essays, lectures. I. Capps, Walter H., ed.

GEACH, Peter Thomas. 241'.4
The virtues / Peter Geach. Cambridge : Cambridge University Press, 1977. xxxv, 173 p. ; 21 cm. (The Stanton lectures ; 1973-4) Includes index. [BV4630.G4] 76-19628 ISBN 0-521-21350-9 : 21.50
1. Virtues—Addresses, essays, lectures. I. Title. II. Series.

GEACH, Peter Thomas. 241'.4
The virtues / Peter Geach. Cambridge : Cambridge University Press, 1977. xxxv, 173 p. ; 21 cm. (The Stanton lectures ; 1973-4) Includes index. [BV4630.G4] 76-19628 ISBN 0-521-21350-9 : 21.50
1. Virtues—Addresses, essays, lectures. I. Title. II. Series.

GUARDINI, Romano, 1885- 241.4
The virtues: on forms of moral life. Translated by Stella Lange. Chicago, Il. Regnery Co., [1967] vii, 163 p. 21 cm. Translation of Tugenden: Meditationen uber Gestalten sittlichen Lebens. [BV4630.G813] 67-28495
1. Virtues. I. Title.

GUARDINI, Romano, 1885-1968. 241.4
The virtues; on forms of moral life. Translated by Stella Lange. Chicago, H. Regnery Co., [1967] vii, 163 p. 21 cm. Translation of Tugenden: Meditationen uber Gestalten sittlichen Lebens. [BV4630.G813] 67-28495
1. Virtues.

HARNED, David Baily. 241'.4
Faith and virtue. Philadelphia, United Church Press [1973] 190 p. 22 cm. "A Pilgrim Press book." Includes bibliographical references. [BV4630.H37] 73-5686 ISBN 0-8298-0250-9 6.95
1. Virtue. 2. Virtues. 3. Christian ethics. I. Title.

HERIS, Charles Vincent, 1885- 241.4
Perfection and charity [by] C. V. Heris. Translated by Lillian M. McCarthy. St. Louis, Herder, 1969. vii, 118 p. 18 cm. (An Intex selection) Bibliographical footnotes. [BX2350.5.H413] 70-83698 1.35
1. Perfection (Catholic) I. Title.

HERIS, Charles Vincent, 1885- 241.4
Spirituality of love, by Charles V. Heris. Translated by David Martin. St. Louis, B. Herder Book Co. [1965] 243 p. 21 cm. [BV4639.H413] 65-24372
1. Love (Theology) 2. Spiritual life — Catholic authors. I. Title.

HERIS, Charles Vincent, 1885- 241.4
Spirituality of love. Tr. [from French] by David Martin. St. Louis, B. Herder [c.1965] 243p. 21cm. (Cross and crown ser. of spirituality, no. 31) [BV4639.H413] 65-24372 4.95
1. Love (Theology) 2. Spiritual life—Catholic authors. I. Title. II. Series.

KERKEN, Liberius vander, 1910- 241.4
Loneliness and love [by] L. vander Kerken. Tr., foreword by J. Donceel. New York, Sheed [1967] xv, 142p. 21cm. Tr. of Menselijke liefde en vriendschap. Bibl. [BV4639.K413] 67-14817 3.75
1. Love (Theology) I. Title.

KERKEN, Liberius vander, 1910- 241.4
Loneliness and love [by] L. vander Kerken. Translated with a foreword by J. Donceel. New York, Sheed & Ward [1967] xv, 142 p. 21 cm. Translation of Menselijke liefde en vriendschap. Bibliographical references included in "Notes" (p. 141-142) [BV4639.K413] 67-14817
1. Love (Theology) I. Title.

MENSCHING, Gustav, 1901- 241'.4
Tolerance and truth in religion. Translated by H.-J. Klimkeit. Augm. in collaboration with the author. University, University of Alabama Press [1971] xii, 207 p. 22 cm. Translation of Toleranz und Wahrheit in der Religion. Bibliography: p. [196]-200. [BR1610.M413] 79-169495 ISBN 0-8173-6701-2 8.00
1. Toleration. I. Title.

METZ, Johannes Baptist, 1928- 241.4
Poverty of spirit. Translated by John Drury. Glen Rock, N.J., Newman Press [1968] 53 p. 19 cm. Translation of Armut im Geiste. [BV4647.P6M43] 68-31045
1. Poverty (Virtue) I. Title.

MURRAY, Robert Henry, 1874-1947. 241'.4
Erasmus & Luther: their attitude to toleration, by Robert H. Murray. New York, B. Franklin [1972] xxiii, 503 p. ports. 23 cm. (Burt Franklin research and source works series. Philosophy and religious history monographs 91) Includes bibliographies. [BR350.E7M8 1972] 70-183697 ISBN 0-8337-4297-3 25.00
1. Erasmus, Desiderius, d. 1536. 2. Luther, Martin, 1483-1546. 3. Toleration. 4. Reformation. I. Title.

RIVEST, Michael W. 241.4
Love to death [by] Michael W. Rivest. North Quincy, Mass., Christopher Pub. House [1969] 55 p. 20 cm. [BV4639.R58] 76-91804
1. Love (Theology) I. Title.

TERBOVICH, John B 241.4
The faces of love [by] John B. Terbovich [1st ed.] Garden City, N.Y., Doubleday, 1966. 167 p. 22 cm. [BV4639.T43] 66-11759
1. Charity. I. Title.

TERBOVICH, John B. 241.4
The faces of love. Garden City, N. Y., Doubleday [c.]1966. 167p. 22cm. [BV4639.T43] 66-11759 3.95
1. Charity. I. Title.

THOMAS AQUINAS, Saint 1225?-1274 241.4
Treatise on the virtues. Tr. by John A. Oesterle. Englewood Cliffs, N. J., Prentice [c.1966] xvii, 171p. 21cm. Bibl. [BV4630.T473] 66-18262 2.95 pap.,
1. Virtue. I. Oesterle, John A., tr. II. Title.

THOMAS AQUINAS, Saint, 1225?-1274. 241.4
Treatise on the virtues. Translated by John A. Oesterle. Englewood Cliffs, N.J., Prentice-Hall [1966] xvii, 171 p. 21 cm. Bibliographical footnotes. [BV4630.T473 1966] 66-18262
1. Virtue. I. Oesterle, John A., tr. II. Title.

THOMPSON, Hugo W., 1900- 241.4
Love-justice, by Hugo W. Thompson. North Quincy, Mass., Christopher Pub. House [1970] 256 p. 21 cm. Includes bibliographical references. [BV4639.T52354] 78-112342 6.95
1. Love (Theology) 2. Justice (Virtue) 3. Christian ethics. I. Title.

TRAHERNE, Thomas, d.1674 241.4
Christian ethicks. General introd. commentary by Carol L. Marks. Textual introd., commentary by George Robert Guffey. Ithaca, N. Y., Cornell Univ. Pr. [1968] 1xii, 391p. 24cm. (Cornell studies in English, v. 43) The critical old-spelling text of this ed. was established after a collation of six copies of the 1675 ed. Based on doctoral dissertations written at the Universities of Wisconsin (Marks) and Illinois (Guffey) Bibl. [BV4630.T7 1968] 66-20015 10.00
1. Virtues. I. Marks, Carol L. II. Guffey, George Robert. III. Title. IV. Series: Cornell Univeristy. Cornell studies in English, v. 43)

*WEDGE, Florence 241.4
What is humility? Pulaski, Wis., Franciscan Pubs. [1967] 56p. 19cm. .25 pap.,
I. Title.

WEHRLI, Eugene S. 241.4
The shape of hope [by] Eugene S. Wehrli. Boston, United Church Press [1968] 137 p. illus. 21 cm. Includes bibliographical references. [BV4638.W37] 68-28246
1. Bible. O.T. Ezekiel—Criticism, interpretation, etc. 2. Bible. N.T. Revelation—Criticism, interpretation, etc. 3. Hope—Biblical teaching. I. Title.

WILLIAMS, Daniel Day, 1910- 241.4
The spirit and the forms of love. [1st U.S. ed.] New York, Harper & Row [1968] ix, 306 p. 22 cm. Based on lectures at the General Council of the Congregational Christian Churches in Claremont, California, in 1952 and the Nathaniel W. Taylor lectures at the Yale Divinity School in 1953. Bibliographical footnotes. [BV4639.W484 1968] 68-29561 6.50
1. Love (Theology) I. Title.

*HARDIE, Katherine Johnson 241.5
The people of God [by] Katherine Johnson Hardie, Barbara Ann Hornby. Illus. by Eleanor Mill. Richmond, Va., CLC Pr., 1966. 32p. col. illus. 22cm. 1.45 bds.,
1. Christian life—Juvenile literature. I. Title.
Young readers. Available from Knox.

*HAUGHTON, Rosemary 241.5
The holiness of sex, Abbey Pr. [dist. New York, Guild, c.1965] 96p. 17cm. (Marriage paperback lib., 20015) .50 pap.,
I. Title.

HODGSON, Leonard, 1889- 241.5
Sex and Christian freedom, an enquiry. New York, Seabury Press [1967] 127 p. 22 cm. Bibliographical footnotes. [HQ63.H577 1967b] 67-21832
1. Sex and religion. 2. Sexual ethics. I. Title.

PRATER, Arnold. 241'.5
The divine transplant. Waco, Tex., Word Books [1973] 123 p. 21 cm. Includes bibliographical references. [BV4501.2.P65] 72-96362 2.95
1. Christian life—Methodist authors. I. Title.

PRIOR, Kenneth Francis William 241.5
God and mammon; the Christian mastery of money. Philadelphia, Westminster [1966,c.1965] 95p. 19cm. (Christian founds.) Bibl. [BR115.E3P7] 66-10325 1.25 pap.,
1. Christianity and economics. 2. Wealth, Ethics of. I. Title.

SMITH, Harmon L., 1930- comp. 241.5
The Christian and his decisions; an introduction to Christian ethics [by] Harmon L. Smith [and] Louis W. Hodges. Nashville, Abingdon Press [1969] 328 p. 26 cm. Bibliographical footnotes. [BJ1191.S57] 76-84714 7.95
1. Christian ethics—Collections. I. Hodges, Louis W., 1933- joint comp. II. Title.

*TAYLOR, Gerald J., M.D. 241.5
Adolescent freedom and responsibility: a guide to sexual maturity. New York, Exposition [c.1965] 68p. illus. 21cm. (Exposition-banner bk.) 3.50
I. Title.

POSPISHIL, Victor J. 241.5'1
Divorce and remarriage; towards a new Catholic teaching [by] Victor J. Pospishil. [New York] Herder & Herder [1967] 217p. 22cm. Bibl. [BX2254.P6] 67-17624 4.95
1. Divorce. 2. Remarriage. I. Title.

ALLEN, Charles Livingstone, 1913- 241.52
The Ten commandments; an interpretation. [Westwood, N.J.] Revell [1965] 64p. col. illus. 20cm. From the author's 'God's psychiatry.' [BV4655.A4] 65-9578 2.00
1. Commandments, Ten. I. Title.

BARCLAY, William, lecturer in the University of Glasgow. 241.5'2
The old law & the new law. Philadelphia, Westminster Press [1972] vi, 121 p. 19 cm. [BV4655.B377] 72-1412 ISBN 0-664-24958-2 1.95
1. Commandments, Ten. 2. Sermon on the Mount. I. Title.

BARCLAY, William. 241.5'2
The Ten Commandments for today / William Barclay. Grand Rapids ; Eerdmans, 1977. 220p. ; 18 cm. [BV4655.B378] ISBN 0-8028-1666-5 pbk. : 1.95
1. Commandments, Ten. I. Title.
L.C. card no. for 1973 Harper and Row ed.: 73-18673.

BARCLAY, William, lecturer in the University of Glasgow. 241.5'2
The Ten Commandments for today. [1st U.S. ed.] New York, Harper & Row [1974, c1973] 205 p. 21 cm. [BV4655.B378 1973b] 73-18673 ISBN 0-06-060416-6 5.95
1. Commandments, Ten. I. Title.

BROKKE, Harold J. 241.5'2
Ten steps to the good life / Harold J. Brokke. 3d ed. Minneapolis : Bethany Fellowship, 1976. 151 p. ; 18 cm. (Dimension books) First-2d editions published under title: The law is holy. [BV4655.B7 1976] 75-44926 ISBN 0-87123-332-0 pbk. : 1.50
1. Commandments, Ten. I. Title.

COTTRELL, Jack. 241.5'2
His way. Cincinnati, Standard Pub. [1973] 96 p. 18 cm. (Fountain books) [BV4655.C64] 77-180749
1. Commandments, Ten. 2. Christian life—1960- I. Title.

*DEANE, John 241.52
Love's imperative; a meditation on the Ten Commandments. Chicago, Moody [c.1965] 61p. illus. 21cm. Cover title: Devotionals: Love's imperatives. 1.00 pap.,
I. Title.

DIVES and pauper. 241.5'2
A facsim. reproduction of the Pynson ed. of 1493 with an introd. and index by Franois J. Sheerhan. Delmar, N.Y., Scholars' Facsimiles & Reprints, 1973. p. A facsim. of the ed. published in London, before 1900 attributed to H. Parker. Includes bibliographical references. [BV4655.D56 1493a] 73-17391 ISBN 0-8201-1111-2 35.00
1. Commandments, Ten—Early works to 1800. I. Parker, Henry, d. 1470. II. Title.

DIVES and pauper. 241.5'2
Dives and pauper. A facsim. reproduction of the Pynson ed. of 1493 with an introd. and index by Francis J. Sheeran. Delmar, N.Y., Scholars' Facsimiles & Reprints, 1973. xxxiii, 497 p. 23 cm. S.T.C. no. 19212. A facsim. of the ed. published in London, before 1900 attributed to H. Parker. Bibliography: p. 489-490. [BV4655.D56 1493a] 73-17391 ISBN 0-8201-1111-2
1. Commandments, Ten—Early works to 1800. I. Parker, Henry, d. 1470.

FARKAS, Jozsef. 241.5'2
Bench marks. Translated by John R. Bodo. Richmond, John Knox Press [1969] 112 p. 21 cm. [BV4655.F23] 69-12847 ISBN 8-04-220204- 3.50
1. Commandments, Ten. I. Title.

FLYNN, Leslie B. 241.5'2
Now a word from Our Creator / Leslie B. Flynn. Wheaton, Ill. : Victor Books, c1976. 144 p. ; 21 cm. [BV4655.F55] 75-36901 ISBN 0-88207-728-7 : 2.25
1. Commandments, Ten. I. Title.

FLYNN, Leslie B. 241.5'2
Now a word from Our Creator / Leslie B. Flynn. Wheaton, Ill. : Victor Books, c1976. 144 p. ; 21 cm. [BV4655.F55] 75-36901 ISBN 0-88207-728-7 pbk. : 2.25
1. Commandments, Ten. I. Title.

GREELEY, Andrew M., 1928- 241.5'2
The Sinai myth. Garden City, N.Y., Image Books 1975, [c1972] 196 p., 18 cm. [BV4655.G67] ISBN 0-385-08824-8 1.75 (pbk.)
1. Commandments, Ten. I. Title.

GREELEY, Andrew M., 1928- 241.5'2
The Sinai myth [by] Andrew M. Greeley. [1st ed.] Garden City, N.Y., Doubleday, 1972. 216 p. 22 cm. Includes bibliographical references. [BV4655.G67] 72-79390 ISBN 0-385-01468-6 5.95
1. Commandments, Ten. I. Title.

HENNIG, Kurt, 1910- 241.5'2
God's basic law; the Ten commandments for the man of today. Translated by George Williams. Philadelphia, Fortress Press [1969] x, 245 p. 22 cm. Translation of Das Grundgesetz Gottes. [BV4655.H3813] 69-14619
1. Commandments, Ten. I. Title.

JOHNSON, Alan F. 241.5'2
God speaks to an X-rated society: are the Ten commandments still valid? Edited by Alan F. Johnson. Chicago, Moody Press [1973] 95 p. 22 cm. Includes bibliographical references. [BV4655.J63] 72-95024 ISBN 0-8024-3023-6 1.50 (pbk.)
1. Commandments, Ten. I. Title.

LEMON, Cal. 241.5'2
God, you've got to be kidding. Carol Stream, Ill., Creation House [1974] 110 p. 18 cm. (New leaf library) [BV4655.L35 1974] 73-81983 ISBN 0-88419-049-8 1.25 (pbk.)
1. Commandments, Ten—Sermons. 2. Universities and colleges—Sermons. 3. Sermons, American. I. Title.

*PINK, Arthur W. 1886-1952. 241.52
The Ten Commandments / Arthur W. Pink. Rev. ed. Grand Rapids : Baker Book House, 1976. 79p. ; 21 cm. [BS1285.3] ISBN 0-8010-7006-6 pbk. : 2.45.
1. Commandments, Ten. I. Title.

*REYNOLDS, Leroy N. 241.52
In God's defense; a study of the ten commandments, [by] Leroy N. Reynolds. First edition. [Jericho] New York, Exposition Press, [1974] 109 p. 22 cm. [BV4655] ISBN 0-682-47874-1 5.00
1. Commandments, Ten. 2. Bible—Devotional literature. I. Title.

SHARMAN, Sydney. 241.5'2
Psychiatry, the Ten Commandments, and you. New York, Dodd, Mead [1974, c1967] 158 p. 21 cm. Originally published under title: The Ten Commandments and the psychiatrist. [RA790.S47 1974] 74-98 ISBN 0-396-06949-5 5.95
1. Mental hygiene. 2. Commandments, Ten. I. Title.

SPONG, John Shelby. 241.5'2
The living commandments / John Shelby Spong. New York : Seabury Press, 1977. x, 129 p. ; 22 cm. "A Crossroad book." [BV4655.S66] 77-8344 ISBN 0-8164-0356-2 : 6.95
1. Commandments, Ten—Addresses, essays, lectures. I. Title.

WALLACE, Ronald S 241.52
The Ten commandments; a study of ethical freedom [by] Ronald S. Wallace. Grand Rapids, Eerdmans [1965] xiv, 181 p. 23 cm. [BV4655.W273] 65-5753
1. Commandments, Ten. I. Title.

WALLACE, Ronald S. 241.52
The Ten commandments; a study of ethical freedom. Grand Rapids, Mich., Eerdmans [c.1965] xiv, 181p. 23cm. [BV4655.W273] 65-5753 3.95
1. Commandments, Ten. I. Title.

WILLIAMS, Jay G., 1932- 241.5'2
Ten words of freedom; an introduction to the faith of Israel, by Jay G. Williams. Philadelphia, Fortress Press [1971] xii, 226 p. 21 cm. Includes bibliographical references. [BS1285.2.W54] 75-139344 ISBN 0-8006-0131-9 4.95
1. Bible. O.T.—Theology. 2. Commandments, Ten. I. Title.

OSBORNE, William. 241.5'7
Man's responsibility; an ecumenical study. New York, Philosophical Lib. [1968] 258p. 22cm. Bibl.: p. 238-258. [BV4740.O8] 67-29201 6.00
1. Vocation. I. Title.

POSPISHIL, Victor J. 241.57
Divorce and remarriage; towards a new Catholic teaching [by] Victor J. Pospishil. [New York] Herder and Herder [1967] 217 p. 22 cm. Bibliography: p. 205-211. [BX2254.P6] 67-17624
1. Divorce 2. Remarriage. I. Title.

WEBER, Leonhard Maria. 241.57
On marriage, sex, and virginity [by] Leonhard M. Weber. [Translated by Rosaleen Brennan. New York] Herder and Herder [1966] 144 p. 22 cm. (Quaestiones disputatae, 16) A translation of Mysterium magnum. Bibliographical references included in "Notes" (p. 112-144) [BT706.W413 1966] 66-10596
1. Marriage — Catholic Church. 2. Sex (Theology) I. Title.

CURRAN, Charles E. 241'.6
Issues in sexual and medical ethics / Charles E. Curran. Notre Dame, Ind. : University of Notre Dame Press, c1978. p. cm. [BX1759.C85] 77-89767 ISBN 0-268-01141-9 : 9.95
1. Christian ethics—Catholic authors—Addresses, essays, lectures. 2. Sexual ethics—Addresses, essays, lectures. 3. Medical ethics—Addresses, essays, lectures. 4. Sociology, Christian (Catholic)—Addresses, essays, lectures. I. Title.

CURRAN, Charles E. 241'.6'2
Politics, medicine, and Christian ethics; a dialogue with Paul Ramsey [by] Charles E. Curran. Philadelphia, Fortress Press [1973] viii, 228 p. 24 cm. Includes bibliographical references. [BR115.P7C83] 72-91521 ISBN 0-8006-0500-4 6.95
1. Ramsey, Paul. 2. Christianity and politics. 3. War and religion. 4. Medical ethics. 5. Human genetics. I. Title.

CHURCH Peace Mission. 241.6'24
Church Peace Mission pamphlet. 1- Washington, 1963- v. 21 cm. Vol. 1 is a reissue; first published in 1950. [BT736.4.C5] 65-5754
1. Peace (Theology) I. Title.

FRANCK, Sebastian, 1499-1542. 241.6'24
Krieg Buchlin des Friedes / Sebastian Franck. Hildesheim ; New York : G. Olms, 1975. 307 leaves ; 15 cm. Reprint of the 1550 ed. by C. Jacob, Frankfurt. [BT736.4.F68 1975] 75-507198 ISBN 3-487-05381-0
1. Peace (Theology) 2. War and religion. 3. Alcoholism. I. Title.

METHODIST Church (United States) Commission to Study the Christian Faith and War in the Nuclear Age. 241.6'24
The Christian faith and war in the nuclear age. New York, Abingdon Press [1963] 108 p. 19 cm. Bibliography: p. 107-108. Bibliographical footnotes. [BT736.2.M43] 261 63-22301
1. War and religion. 2. Christianity and international affairs. I. Title.

SMITH, William Kyle. 241.6'24
Calvin's ethics of war; a documentary study. Annapolis [Published for Westminster Foundation of Annapolis by] Academic Fellowship, 1972. vii, 166 p. 23 cm. Bibliography: p. 165-166. [BT736.2.S55] 72-88871
1. Calvin, Jean, 1509-1564—Ethics. 2. War and religion—History of doctrines. I. Title.

WAR and Christian ethics / edited by Arthur F. Holmes. Grand Rapids : Baker Book House, c1975. 356 p. ; 22 cm. "A Canon Press book." Includes bibliographical references and index. [BT736.2.W34] 75-14602 ISBN 0-8010-4138-4 : 7.95 241'.6'24
1. War and religion—Addresses, essays, lectures. I. Holmes, Arthur Frank, 1924-

BOSLER, Raymond T. 241'.6'3
What they ask about marriage / Raymond T. Bosler. Notre Dame, Ind. : Ave Maria Press, [1975] 285 p. ; 21 cm. [BX2250.B639] 75-11019 ISBN 0-87793-096-1 : 3.50
1. Marriage—Catholic Church. I. Title.

SMITH, Bob, 1914- 241'.6'3
Love story ... the real thing / by Bob Smith. Waco, Tex. : Word Books, c1975. 97 p. ; 21 cm. (Discovery books) [BV835.S57 1975] 75-17111 pbk. : 2.95
1. Marriage. I. Title.

FARR, Alfred Derek. 241'.6'42
God, blood and society [by] A. D. Farr. Aberdeen, Impulse Publications Ltd, 1972. 119, [8] p. illus., ports. 23 cm. [RM171.F37] 72-305959 ISBN 0-901311-18-9 £2.50
1. Blood—Transfusion—Moral and religious aspects. 2. Blood—Transfusion—Social aspects. I. Title.

MALL, E. Jane, 1920- 241'.6'43
A mother's gifts : a book of praise and inspiration / E. Jane Mall, drawings by Billie Jean Osborne. Nashville : Abingdon Press, c1976. 62 p. : ill. ; 20 cm. [BV283.M7M33] 75-33082 ISBN 0-687-27249-1 : 3.50
1. Mothers—Prayer-books and devotions—English. I. Title.

NORTHBROOKE, John, fl.1568-1579. 241'.6'5
A treatise. With a pref. for the Garland ed. by Arthur Freeman. New York, Garland Pub., 1974. 7, 148 p. 18 cm. (The English stage: attack and defense, 1577-1730) Reprint of the 1577? ed. published in London. Original t.p. reads: Spiritus est vicarius Christi in terra. A treatise wherein dicing, dauncing, vaine playes, or enterluds, with other idle pastimes, &c., commonly used on the Sabboth day, are reproued by the authoritie of the word of God and auntient writers ... At London, Imprinted for H. Bynneman for George Byshop. [BV4597.N6 1974] 72-170401 ISBN 0-8240-0584-8 22.00
1. Amusements—Moral and religious aspects. 2. Theater—Moral and religious aspects. 3. Dice. 4. Dancing—Early works to 1800. I. Title. II. Series.

NORTHBROOKE, John, fl.1568-1579. 241'.6'5
A treatise against dicing, dancing, plays, and interludes. With other idle pastimes. From the earliest edition, about A.D. 1577. With an introd. and notes. London, Reprinted for the Shakespeare Society, 1843. [New York, AMS Press, 1971] xx, 188 p. 23 cm. Reprint of the London ed. published between 1577-79. Original t.p. reads: Spiritus est vicarius Christi in terra. A treatise wherein dicing, dauncing, vaine playes, or enterluds, with other idle pastimes, &c., commonly used on the Sabboth day, are reproued by the authoritie of the word of God and auntient writers ... At London, Imprinted by H. Bynneman for George Byshop. [BV4597.N62] 77-149667 ISBN 0-404-04793-9
1. Amusements—Moral and religious aspects. 2. Theater—Moral and religious aspects. 3. Dice. 4. Dancing—Early works to 1800. I. Title.

BLACKWELL, Elizabeth, 1821-1910. 241'.6'6
Essays in medical sociology. New York, Arno Press, 1972. 2 v. in 1. 22 cm. (Medicine & society in America) Reprint of the 1902 ed. Includes bibliographical references. [HQ32.B55 1972] 73-180555 ISBN 0-405-03935-2
1. Sexual ethics. 2. Prostitution. 3. Social medicine. I. Title. II. Series.

CATHOLIC Church. Congregatio pro Doctrina Fidei. 241.6'6
Declaration on certain questions concerning sexual ethics / Sacred Congregation for the Doctrine of the Faith ; [translated from the Latin]. London : Catholic Truth Society, [1976] 21 p. ; 19 cm. "Do 486." Includes bibliographical references. [HQ32.C39 1976] 76-368339 ISBN 0-85183-159-1 : £0.15
1. Catholic Church. Congregatio pro Doctrina Fide. 2. Sexual ethics. 3. Christian ethics. I. Title.

DEDEK, John F., 1929- 241.6'6
Contemporary sexual morality, by John F. Dedek. New York, Sheed and Ward [1971] x, 170 p. 20 cm. Bibliography: p. 163-170. [HQ32.D43] 79-152319 ISBN 0-8362-1159-6 5.95
1. Sexual ethics. I. Title.

FOX, Robert Joseph, 1927- 241'.6'6
Charity, morality, sex, and young people / Robert J. Fox. Huntington, Ind. : Our Sunday Visitor, inc., [1975] 173 p. ; 18 cm. [BT708.F69] 74-21889 ISBN 0-87973-763-8 pbk. : 1.95
1. Sex (Theology) 2. Youth—Conduct of life. I. Title.

*FRANKL, George. 241.66
The failure of the sexual revolution. London, Kahn & Averill [1975 c1974] 190 p. 22 cm. Includes index. Bibliography: p. 186-190. [HQ31] ISBN 0-900707-35-6
1. Sexual ethics. I. Title.
Distributed by Humanities Press for 6.95.

GUINDON, Andre, 1933- 241'.6'6
The sexual language : an essay in moral theology / Andre Guindon. [Toronto] : University of Ottawa Press, 1976. x, 476 p. ; 21 cm. Bibliography: p. [441]-476. [HQ31.G943] 77-371039 ISBN 0-7766-0050-8
1. Sexual ethics. 2. Christian ethics. I. Title.

THE Right to birth : 241'.6'6
some Christian views on abortion / edited by Eugene Fairweather and Ian Gentles. Toronto : Anglican Book Centre, c1976. 76 p. ; 21 cm. Includes bibliographical references. [HQ767.5.C2R54] 77-366581 ISBN 0-919030-14-9
1. Abortion—Canada—Addresses, essays, lectures. 2. Abortion—Religious aspects. I. Fairweather, Eugene Rathbone. II. Gentles, Ian.

RINZEMA, J. 241'.6'6
The sexual revolution; challenge and response, by J. Rinzema. Translated by Lewis B. Smedes. Grand Rapids, Eerdmans [1974] 107 p. 20 cm. Includes bibliographical references. [HQ31.R6213] 73-14712 ISBN 0-8028-1545-6 2.45 (pbk.)
1. Sexual ethics. I. Title.

SMALL, Dwight Hervey. 241'.6'6
Christian: celebrate your sexuality; a fresh, positive approach to understanding and fulfilling sexuality. Old Tappan, N.J., Revell [1974] 221 p. 21 cm. Includes bibliographical references. [BT708.S6] 74-11161 ISBN 0-8007-0661-7 5.95
1. Sex (Theology) I. Title.

TAYLOR, Michael J., comp. 241'.6'6
Sex: thoughts for contemporary Christians. Edited by Michael J. Taylor. Garden City, N.Y., Doubleday, 1973 [c.1972] 240 p. 18 cm. (Image Book, D324) Bibliography: p. [237]-240. [HQ32.T36] 70-171400 ISBN 0-385-03893-3 1.45 (pbk.)
1. Sexual ethics—Addresses, essays, lectures. I. Title.

TROBISCH, Walter. 241.6'6
My beautiful feeling : correspondence with Ilona / Walter & Ingrid Trobisch. Downers Grove, Ill. : InterVarsity Press, 1976. 123 p. ; 18 cm. Translation of Mein schones Gefuhl. Includes bibliographical references. [HQ71.T8613] 76-21459 ISBN 0-87784-577-8 pbk. : 2.25
1. Masturbation. 2. Sexual ethics. I. Trobisch, Ingrid Hult, joint author. II. Title.

WILLIAMS, Tom M. 241'.6'6
See no evil : Christian attitudes toward sex in art and entertainment / T. M. Williams. Grand Rapids, Mich. : Zondervan Pub. House, c1976. 102, [1] p. ; 18 cm. "Zondervan books." Bibliography: p. [103] [BV4597.6.W54] 75-21125 pbk. : 1.50
1. Pornography. 2. Sex in the arts—Moral and religious aspects. 3. Censorship. I. Title.

*HICKEY, Marilyn. 241.'6'65
In the shadow of Gomer. Harrison, Ark. : New Leaf Press [1976]c1975. 82p. ; 21 cm. [BT708] 75-32006 ISBN 0-89221-009-5 pbk. : 2.50
1. Sex (Theology) 2. Prostitution. I. Title.

HAUGHEY, John C. 241'.6'7
Should anyone say forever? : On making, keeping, and breaking commitments / John C. Haughey. 1st ed. Garden City, N.Y. : Doubleday, 1975. 166 p. ; 22 cm. [BF619.H37] 74-12690 ISBN 0-385-09754-9 : 6.95
1. Commitment (Psychology) I. Title.

DELAFIELD, D. A. 241'.6'74
What's in your clothes closet? / D. A. Delafield. Washington : Review and Herald Pub. Association, c1974. 94 p. ; 21 cm. Includes bibliographical references. [BX6154.D38] 74-78482 2.50
1. Seventh-Day Adventists—Doctrinal and controversial works. 2. Clothing and dress—Moral and religious aspects. I. Title.

MARY Francis, Mother, 1921- 241'.6'76
But I have called you friends. Chicago, Franciscan Herald Press [1974] vii, 84 p. 22 cm. "Essays or conferences on friendship which originally appeared in the Cord." [BJ1533.F8M33] 74-8351 ISBN 0-8199-0500-3 4.50
1. Friendship—Addresses, essays, lectures. I. Title.

LUSSIER, Ernest, 1911- 241'.6'77
God is love : according to St. John / Ernest Lussier. New York : Alba House, c1977. xvi, 207 p. ; 22 cm. [BS2601.L85] 76-57254 ISBN 0-8189-0339-2 : 5.95
1. Bible. N.T. Johannine literature—Theology. 2. Love (Theology)—Biblical teaching. 3. Holy Spirit—Biblical teaching. I. Title.

TAVARD, George Henri, 1922- 241'.6'77
A way of love / George H. Tavard. Maryknoll, N.Y. : Orbis Books, c1977. xi, 160 p. ; 22 cm. Includes bibliographical references. [BV4639.T29] 76-22542 ISBN 0-88344-700-2 : 6.95

1. Love (Theology) I. Title.

LINZEY, Andrew. 241'.6'93
Animal rights : a Christian assessment of man's treatment of animals / [by] Andrew Linzey. London : S.C.M. Press, 1976. viii, 120 p. ; 22 cm. Bibliography: p. 117-120. [HV4708.L56] 76-367556 ISBN 0-334-00034-3 : £2.25
1. Animals, Treatment of. I. Title.

*BAJEMA, Clifford E. 241'.6'97
Abortion and the meaning of personhood/ Clifford E. Bajema. Grand Rapids: Baker Book House, 1976 c1974. 114 p.; 18 cm. (Direction books.) Includes bibliographical references and index. [HQ767] pbk.: 1.25
1. Abortion—Religious aspects. I. Title.

CLARK, Robert Edward David. 241'.6'97
Does the Bible teach pacifism? / [by] Robert E. D. Clark ; foreword by J. Stafford Wright. [New Malden] : Fellowship of Reconciliation, 1976. [1], 70 p. ; 21 cm. Cover title. Includes index. Bibliography: p. [1] [BT736.2.C57] 76-378740 ISBN 0-900368-30-6 : £0.80
1. War and religion. 2. War—Biblical teaching. 3. Pacifism. I. Title.

KLOTZ, John William. 241'.6'97
A Christian view of abortion [by] John W. Klotz. St. Louis, Concordia Pub. House [1973] 56 p. 23 cm. (Contemporary theology series) Includes bibliographical references. [HQ767.K56] 73-80316 ISBN 0-570-06721-9 1.95 (pbk.)
1. Abortion—Religious aspects. 2. Abortion, Therapeutic. I. Title.

SULLIVAN, Shaun J. 241'.6'97
Killing in defense of private property : the development of a Roman Catholic moral teaching, thirteenth to eighteenth centuries / by Shaun J. Sullivan. Missoula, Mont. : Published by Scholars Press for the American Academy of Religion, c1976. x, 234 p. ; 22 cm. (Dissertation series - American Academy of Religion ; no. 15) Originally presented as the author's thesis, Graduate Theological Union, 1973. Bibliography: p. 221-234. [LAW] 75-38843 ISBN 0-89130-067-8 pbk. : 4.50
1. Justifiable homicide. 2. Right of property—Moral and religious aspects. 3. Christian ethics—Catholic authors—History. I. Title. II. Series: American Academy of Religion. Dissertation series — American Academy of Religion ; no. 15.

EDWARDS, George R. 241'.6'98
Jesus and the politics of violence [by] George R. Edwards. [1st ed.] New York, Harper & Row [1972] vi, 186 p. 22 cm. Bibliography: p. 157-169. [BT736.15.E3] 70-183635 ISBN 0-06-062124-9 5.95
1. Jesus Christ—Person and offices. 2. Violence—Moral and religious aspects. I. Title.

DIMENSIONS of spirituality. 241.6'9'9
Edited by Christian Duquoc. [New York] Herder and Herder [1970] 158 p. 23 cm. (Concilium: theology in the age of renewal. Spirituality, v. 59) Includes bibliographical references. [BV4638.D54] 78-129758 2.95
1. Hope—Addresses, essays, lectures. I. Duquoc, Christian, ed. II. Series: Concilium (New York) v. 59

GOSPEL poverty : 241'.6'99
essays in biblical theology / A. George ... [et al.] ; pref. by C. Koser ; translated and with a pref. by Michael D. Guinan. Chicago : Franciscan Herald Press, [1976] p. cm. Translation of La Pauvrete evangelique. Papers presented at a symposium on poverty held in Rome, June 23-25, 1970. Includes bibliographical references. [BS680.P47P3813] 76-44548 ISBN 0-8199-0610-7 : 6.95
1. Poverty (Virtue)—Biblical teaching—Addresses, essays, lectures. I. George, Augustin.

JONES, Major J., 1919- 241'.6'99
Black awareness: a theology of hope [by] Major J. Jones. Nashville, Abingdon Press [1971] 143 p. 19 cm. Includes bibliographical references. [BR563.N4J64] 77-148067 ISBN 0-687-03585-6
1. Negroes—Religion. 2. Negroes—Race identity. I. Title.

MAYEROFF, Milton, 1925- 241'.6'99
On caring. [1st U.S. ed.] New York, Harper & Row [1971] xxii, 63 p. 22 cm. (World perspectives, v. 43) [BV4639.M36 1971] 71-144183 4.95
1. Charity. I. Title.

MAYEROFF, Milton, 1925- 241'.6'99
On caring. New York, Barnes & Noble [1974, c1971] 74 p. 21 cm. (World perspectives) [BV4639.M36 1974] ISBN 0-06-464003-5 1.50 (pbk.)
1. Charity. I. Title.

L.C. card no. for hardbound ed.: 71-144183

242 Devotional Literature

AEGIDIUS of Assisi, d. 1262 242
Golden words; the sayings of Brother Giles of Assisi. With a biog. by Nello Vian. Tr. from Italian by Ivo O'Sullivan. Chicago, Franciscan Herald [1966] 159p. 21cm. Bibl. [BV4830.A38] 66-18854 3.95, bds.,
1. Devotional literature. I. Title.

AGORA Inc. 242
Buy me, by the men of Agora. Sioux Falls, S.D., Agora Pub. Co. [1971] [53] p. illus., group port. 19 cm. [BJ1595.A34] 78-147787
1. Conduct of life. I. Title.

ALBERIONE, Giacomo Giuseppe, 1884- 242
Lest we forget, by James Alberione. [Boston] St. Paul Editions [1967] 252 p. 19 cm. [BX2170.D5A5] 65-29135
1. Prayers for the dead—November devotions. I. Title.

ALBERIONE, Giacomo Giuseppe, 1884-1971. 242
J. Alberione: thoughts; fragments of apostolic spirituality from his writings and talks. [Prepared by the Center of Pauline Spirituality. Presentation and introductory notes by John Roatta. English translation by Aloysius Milella. Boston] St. Paul Editions [1974] 193 p. port. 22 cm. Bibliography: p. 11-[13] [BX2350.2.A38] 74-163643 3.00
1. Christian life—Catholic authors. I. Centro paolino di spiritualita. II. Title. III. Title: Thoughts.

ALBERIONE, Giacomo Giuseppe, 1884-1971. 242
Meditation notes on Paul the Apostle, model of the spiritual life. [Translated by Aloysius Milella. Boston] St. Paul Editions [1972] 100 p. facsims. 20 cm. [BS2506.A4 1972] 72-83471 2.00
1. Paul, Saint, apostle—Meditations. 2. Spiritual exercises. I. Title.

ALBIOL ESTAPE, Enrique. 242
Spirit of joy, by Henry Albiol. Translated from the Spanish and edited by B. T. Buckley. Westminster, Md., Newman Press [1956] 173p. 20cm. Translation of the author's "Soliloquios' which have been appearing in several Spanish magazines.' [BX2186.A4] 56-11431
1. Meditations. 2. Joy and sorrow. I. Title.

ALLEN, Charles Livingstone, 1913- 242
Healing words. Westwood, N. J., Revell [c.1961] 159p. 61-13619 2.50 bds.,
I. Title.

ALLEN, Charles Livingstone, 1913- 242
Healing words. Westwood, N. J., F. H. Revell Co. [1961] 159p. 21cm. [BV4908.5.A4] 61-13619
1. Peace of mind. I. Title.

ALLEN, Charles Livingstone, 1913- 242
The Sermon on the Mount [by] Charles L. Allen. Westwood, N.J., Revell [1966] 187 p. 21 cm. [BT380.2.A63] 66-21902
1. Sermon on the Mount. I. Title.

ALLSHORN, Florence, 1887-1950. 242
Notebooks. Selected and arr. by a member of St. Julian's Community. Napcrville, Ill., SCM Book Club [1957] 127 p. 19 cm. (RBC edition, no. 120) [BV4832.A46] 58-3033
1. Devotional literature.

*ALNEY 242
Treasures shared; the original manuscript from typewriter and pen of the author. Miami, Fla., Venus Pubns., P.O. Box 4892 [c.1965] 168p. illus., port. 23cm. 4.75
I. Title.

AMEN, Carol. 242
Hyacinths to feed the soul / by Carol Amen. Nashville : Southern Pub. Association, [1975] 62 p. ; 19 cm. (Better living series) [BV4832.2.A45] 74-33850 ISBN 0-8127-0094-5 pbk. : 0.60
1. Meditations. I. Title.

ANDERSEN, Richard, 1931- 242
Loving in forgiveness; devotions for celebrating another year of marriage. [St. Louis, Mo., Concordia Pub. House, 1973] 32 p. 22 x 9 cm. [BV4596.M3A5] 73-174100 ISBN 0-570-03142-7
1. Married people—Prayer-books and devotions—English. I. Title.

ANDERSON, Godfrey Tryggve, 1909- 242
Walk God's battlefield, by Godfrey T. Anderson. Nashville, Tenn., Southern Pub. Association [1971] 160 p. 21 cm. [BV4832.2.A58] 75-150112 ISBN 0-8127-0041-4
1. Meditations. I. Title.

ANDERSON, Robert Emory, 1919- 242
Sentence sermons, by Robert E. Anderson. Philadelphia, Dorrance [1972] 80 p. 22 cm. [BV4832.2.A62] 72-82882 ISBN 0-8059-1728-4 3.95
1. Meditations. I. Title.

ANDERSON, Stuart LeRoy. 242
A faith to live by. New York, Oxford University Press, 1959. 115p. 20cm. [BV4832.2.A63] 60-5098
1. Meditations. I. Title.

ANDREWES, Lancelot, Bp. of Winchester, 1555-1626. 242
Private devotions. Edited and with an introd. by Thomas S. Kepler. [1st ed.] Cleveland, World Pub. Co. [1956] 208p. 16cm. (World devotional classics) [BV4830.A652 1956] 56-9258
1. Devotional exercises. I. Title.

*ANDREWS, Ernest C. 242
Fifty new devotional programs. Grand Rapids, Mich., Baker Book House [1973] 126 p. 19 cm. [BV4832] ISBN 0-8010-0055-6 pap., 1.50.
1. Devotional literature (Selections: Extracts, etc.) I. Title.

ANDREWS, Lancelot, Bp. of Winchester, 1555-1626. 242
The private devotions of Lancelot Andrewes; preses privatae. Tr. with introd. and notes by F. E. Brightman, and including 'Lancelot Andrewes' (1926) by T. S. Eliot. Meridian Books [dist. Cleveland, World Pub. Co. 1961] 392p. (Living age bk. LA32) 1.65 pap.,
1. Devotional exercises. I. Title.

ANDROSS, Matilda Ericson 242
Alone with God. Illus. by James Converse. Mountain View, Calif., Pacific Pr. Assn. [c.1929, 1961] 80p. .50 pap.,
I. Title.

ANGELL, James W. 242
Yes is a world / James W. Angell. Waco, Tex. : Word Books, [1974] 132 p. ; 23 cm. Issued in a case. Includes bibliographical references. [BV4501.2.A54] 74-82653 4.95
1. Meditations. I. Title.

ANONYMOUS. 242
The soul delight, by Anonymous. Boston, Christopher Pub. House [1961] 91 p. 21 cm. Mediations, poems, etc. [BV4832.2.S65] 61-15191
1. Meditations. 2. Conduct of life. 3. Love. I. Title.

APPLEBY, Rosalee (Mills) 1895- 242
White wings of splendor. Nashville [Broadman c.1962] 112p. 20cm. 62-9195 1.95
1. Devotional literature. I. Title.

APPLEBY, Rosalee (Mills) 1895- 242
White wings of splendor. Nashville, Broadman Press [1962] 112p. 20cm. [BV4832.2.A67] 62-9195
1. Devotional literature. I. Title.

THE Apron-pocket book of meditation and prayer. 242
Greenwich, Conn., Seabury Press, 1958. 89p. 17cm. [BV4844.A6] 58-9229
1. Women—Prayer-books and devotions English.

ARMOR, Reginald Cavin, 1903- 242
The magic of love [by] Reginald C. Armor. New York, Dodd, Mead [1967] xxi, 161 p. 21 cm. [BV4639.A7] 67-14304
1. Love. 2. Love (Theology)—Meditations. I. Title.

ARMSTRONG, Richard G. 242
Now is the time [by] Richard Armstrong. New York, The Christophers [1970] xiii, 365 p. 17 cm. [BV4811.A734] 78-28056 0.95
1. Devotional calendars. I. Title.

ARNDT, Johann, 1555-1621. 242
Devotions and prayers, Selected and translated by John Joseph Stoudt. Grand Rapids, Baker Book House, 1958. 111p. 16cm. [BV4834.A743] 59-446
1. Lutheran Church—Prayer-books and devotions—English. I. Title.

ARNOLD, Eberhard, 1883-1935. 242
The heavens are opened, by Eberhard and Emmy Arnold and Heini Arnold. [Translated from the German and edited by the Society of Brothers] Rifton, N.Y., Plough Pub. House [1974] xi, 180 p. illus. 22 cm. Consists chiefly of excerpts from the works of Eberhard Arnold. Includes bibliographical references. [BV4832.2.A725 1974] 73-20715 ISBN 0-87486-113-6 4.95
1. Meditations. I. Arnold, Emmy. II. Arnold, Heini, 1913- III. Bruderhof Communities. IV. Title.

ASQUITH, Glenn H. 242
Footprints in the sand / by Glenn H. Asquith. Valley Forge, Pa. : Judson Press, [1975] p. cm. [BV4832.2.A748] 75-12188 ISBN 0-8170-0676-1 pbk. : 2.95
1. Meditations. I. Title.

ASQUITH, Glenn H. 242
God in my day [by] Glenn H. Asquith. Nashville, Abingdon Press [1967] 159 p. 20 cm. [BV4832.2.A75] 67-22170
1. Meditations. I. Title.

AUGUSTINUS, Aurelius, Saint, Bp. of Hippo. 242
Confessions. Translated by Edward B. Pusey; introd. by Harold C. Gardiner. New York, Pocket Books [1952, '1951] 301 p. 17 cm. (Collector's edition, 26) [BR65.A6E5 1952] 51-39975
I. Title.

AUGUSTINUS, Aurelius, Saint, Bp. of Hippo. 242
Confessions. A new translation by Rex Warner. [New York] New American Library [1963] xv. 351 p. 18 cm. (A Mentor-Omega book) "MT490." Bibliography: p. 351. [BR65.A6E5] 63-11920
1. Warner, Rex, 1905- tr. I. Title.

AUGUSTINUS, Aurelius, Saint, Bp. of Hippo. 242
Confessions. Translated with an introd. and notes by E. B. Pusey. New York, Dutton, 1950. xxviii, 382 p. 19 cm. (Everyman's library. Philosophy and theology. 200A) Bibliography: p. [v] [BR65.A6E5 1950] 50-7331
I. Title.

AUGUSTINUS, Aurelius, Saint, Bp. of Hippo. 242
Confessions; translated by Vernon J. Bourke. New York, Fathers of the Church, inc., 1953. xxxii, 481p. 22cm. (Writings of Saint Augustine, v. 5) The Fathers of the church, a new translation, v. 21. Bibliography: p.xviii-xx. [BR60.F3A8 vol.5] 54-24
I. Title.

AUGUSTINUS, Aurelius, Saint, Bp. of Hippo. 242
Confessions. Translated by Vernon J. Bourke. Washington. Catholic University of America Press [1966, c1953] xxxii, 481 p. 22 cm. (Writings of Saint Augustine, v. 5) The Fathers of the church, a new translation, v. 21. Bibliography: p. xviii-xx. [BR60.F3A8218] 66-20310
I. Title. II. Series: The Fathers of the church, a new translation, v. 21

AUGUSTINUS, Aurelius, Saint, Bp. of Hippo 242
Confessions. Tr. with introd. by R. S. Pine-Coffin. Penguin[dist. New York, Atheneum, c.1961] 346p. (Penguin classic, L114) 1.25 pap.,
I. Pine-Coffin, R.S., tr. II. Title.

AUGUSTINUS, Aurelius, Saint, Bp. of Hippo 242
Confessions. New tr. by Rex Warner. [New York] New Amer. Lib. [c.1963] xv, 351p. 18cm. (Mentor-Omega bk. MT 490) Bibl. 63-11920 .75 pap.,
I. Warner, Rex, 1905- tr. II. Title.

AUGUSTINUS, Aurelius, Saint, Bp. of Hippo. 242
Confessions. Translated with an introd. by R. S. Pine-Coffin. Baltimore, Penguin Books [1961] 346p. 18cm. (The Penguin classics, L114) Bibliographical footnotes. [BR65.A6E5 1961] 61-66334
I. Title.

AUGUSTINUS, Aurelius, Saint, Bp. of Hippo. 242
Confessions. In the transl. of J. G. Pilkington. Introd. by George N. Shuster; illus. with paintings by Edy Legrand. New York, Heritage [dist. New York, Dial, c.1963] xxx, 296p. 20 col. plates. 27cm. 64-28 6.95
I. Pilkington, Joseph Green, tr. II. Title.

AUGUSTINUS, Aurelius, Saint, Bp. of Hippo. 242
The confessions. [Translated by Edward Bouverie Pusey] The city of God. [Translated by Marcus Dods] On Christian doctrine. [Translated by J. F. [i.e. J.] Shaw] Chicago, Encyclopedia Britannica [1955, c1952] x, 698 p. 25 cm. (Great books of the Western World,

v. 18) Bibliographical footnotes. [AC1.G72 vol. 18] 55-10327
1. Theology—Collected works—Early church, ca. 30-600. I. Pusey, Edward Bouverie, 1800-1882, tr. II. Dods, Marcus, 1786-1838, tr. III. Shaw, James Johnston, 1845-1910, tr. IV. Augustinus, Aurelius, Saint, Bp. of Hippo. The city of God. 1955. V. Augustinus, Aurelius, Saint, Bp. of Hippo. On Christian doctrine. 1955. VI. Title: The city of God.

AUGUSTINUS, Aurelius, Saint, Pp. of Hippo. 242
Confessions and Enchiridion, newly translated and edited by Albert C. Outler. Philadelphia, Westminster Press [1955] 423p. 24cm. (The Library of Christian classics, v. 7) Bibliography: p.413-416. [BR65.A6E5 1955] 55-5021
1. Theology—Early church. I. Augustinus, Aurelius. Saint, Bp. of Hippo. II. Outler, Albert Cook, 1908- ed. and tr. III. Title. IV. Series: The Library of Christian classics (Philadelphia) v. 7

AUGUSTINUS, Aurelius, Saint, Bp. of Hippo. 242
Confessions; in thirteen books. A new English translation from the original Latin, edited by J. M. Lelen. [Complete ed.] New York, Catholic Book Pub. Co. [1952] 384p. col. front. 21cm. [BR65.A6E5 1952a] 53-580
I. Title.

AUGUSTINUS, Aurelius, Saint, Bp. of Hippo 242
The confessions of St. Augustine. Tr. by Edward B. Pusey. New York, Collier Bks. [1962] 255p. (HS8) .65 pap.,
I. Title.

AUGUSTINUS, Aurelius, Saint, Bp. of Hippo. Spurious and doubtful works. 242
Little book of contemplation; edited and rev. into modern English by Joseph Whittkofski. New York, Morehouse-Gorham, 1950. 101 p. 16 cm. With facsimile reproduction of the t. p. of the edition of 1577: S.Avgvstines Manuell, or litle booke of the Contemplation of Christ. or of Gods worde ... At London, Printed by Iohn Daye ... 1577. [BX2179.A8E5 1950] 50-10895
1. Spiritual life. I. Title.

AUGUSTINUS, Aurelius, Saint, Bp. of Hippo 242
The confessions of Saint Augustine. Tr. by Edward B. Pusey. 0 xiv, 338p. 19cm. (Modern lib. coll. eds., T72) [BR65.A6E50] 2.45 pap.,
I. Title.

AUGUSTINUS, Aurelius, Saint Bp. of Hippo. 242
The confessions of St. Augustine. Translated, with an introd. and notes, by John K. Ryan. [1st ed.] Garden City, N. Y., Image Books [1960] 429 p. 18 cm. (A Doubleday image book, D101) Bibliography: p. [425]-426. [BR65.A6E5 1960] 60-13725
I. Ryan, John Kenneth, 1897- ed. and tr.

AUGUSTINUS, Aurelius, Saint, Bp. of Hippo. 242
Confessions. Translated by Vernon J. Bourke. Washington, Catholic University of America Press [1966, c1953] xxxii, 481 p. 22 cm. (Writings of Saint Augustine, v. 5) The Fathers of the church, a new translation, v. 21. Bibliography: p. xviii-xx. [BR60.F3A8218] 66-20310
I. Series: The Fathers of the church, a new translation, v. 21

AUSTIN, Elva M. 242
The potter's shop, by Alice Glen [pseud.] Decorations by Iris Johnson. Washington, Review and Herald [1952] 94 p. illus. 18 cm. [BV4832.A8] 52-41518
1. Providence and government of God—Devotional literature. I. Title.

AUSTIN, Orval H 242
Come as you are. New York, Abingdon Press [c1956] 110p. 30cm. [BV4332.A83] 56-5368
1. Meditations. I. Title.

AUSTIN, Orval H. 242
Come as you are Nashville, Abingdon [1966,c.1956] 110p. 19cm. [BV4832.A83] 56-5368 .95 pap.,
1. Meditations. I. Title.

AVERY, William S. 242
Desk drawer devotions. Philadelphia, Fortress [1965, c.1964] v, 90p. 18cm. [BV4832.2.A9] 65-10508 1.50 bds.,
1. Devotional exercises. I. Title.

BACH, Marcus, 1906- 242
What's right with the world. Englewood Cliffs, N.J., Prentice-Hall [1973] 176 p. 22 cm. [BV4832.2.B25] 73-9623 ISBN 0-13-955096-8 5.95
1. Meditations. I. Title.

BAIRD, P. J., ed. 242
From out of the West, messages from Western pulpits. Stockton, Calif., Lantern Pr., 1962. 156p. illus. 21cm. 3.50
I. Title.

BAKER, John Austin. 242
Travels in Oudamovia / [by] John Austin Baker ; foreword by the Archbishop of Canterbury. Leighton Buzzard : Faith Press, 1976. 80 p. ; 19 cm. [BV4832.2.B26] 76-380901 ISBN 0-7164-0435-4 : £0.90
1. Meditations. I. Title.

BALLOU, Benedict, 1901- 242
"Whom my soul loveth"; monthly holy hour reflections and prayers for priests and religious. Paterson, N. J., St. Anthony Guild Press, 1950. xi, 304 p. 17 cm. [BX2159.H7B3] 51-20288
1. Holy Hour. 2. Clergy—Religious life. I. Title.

BANIGAN, Sharon (Church) 1912- comp. 242
Hear our grace, selected, illus. by Sharon Banigan. Chicago, Follett [1966] 44p. col. illus. 29x14cm. [BV264.B3 1966] 66-15914 1.00 bds.,
1. Children—Prayer-books and devotions. 2. Grace at meals. I. Title.

BARON, Samuel Halevi, ed. 242
Children's devotions; illustrated by Friedel Dzubas. New York, Bookman Associates [1954] 105p. illus. i2cm. [BM666.B3] 55-362
1. Children—Prayer books and devotions—English. 2. Jews -prayer-books and devotions— English. I. Title.

*BARRETT, Ethel 242
'Sometimes I feel like a blob.' Glendale, Calif., 91205, Gospel Light Pubns. [725 E. Colorado, Box 1591]c.1965. 190p. illus. 18cm. (Regal bks., PB-1) 1.00 pap.,
I. Title.

BARSTOW, Robbins Wolcott. 242
Parables from the sea. With sketches by Ruth Rhoads Lepper. Penobscot, Me., Traversity Press [1959] 67p. illus. 20cm. [BV4832.2.B3] 59-15571
1. Devotional literature. I. Title.

BARTH, Karl, 1886-1968. 242
Action in waiting, by Karl Barth on Christoph Blumhardt; including Joy in the Lord, by Christoph Blumhardt. [Edited and translated from the German by the Society of Brothers] Rifton, N.Y., Plough Pub. House, 1969. vii, 69 p. 20 cm. Translation of Auf das Reich Gottes warten, by K. Barth and Freude im Herrn, by C. Blumhardt. Bibliography: p. vii. [BX8080.B614B33] 75-90295 2.50
1. Blumhardt, Christoph, 1842-1919. I. Bruderhof Communities. II. Blumhardt, Christoph, 1842-1919. Joy in the Lord. III. Title.

BASSET, Elizabeth, comp. 242
Love is my meaning; an anthology of assurance. Atlanta, John Knox Press [1974, c1973] 272 p. 23 cm. [BV4801.B28 1974] 74-3708 ISBN 0-8042-2300-9 5.95
1. Devotional literature. I. Title.

BATH, V. C. 242
The Lord's Prayer in daily life. Chicago, 3930 N. Cicero Ave. Thoughts That Inspire Pub. Co., [1962, c.1960] 111p. 16cm. 2.00; deluxe ed., 2.50; pap., 1.00, plastic bdg.
I. Title.

BAUR, Benedikt, 1877- 242
Saints of the missal. Translated by Raymond Meyerpeter. St. Louis, Herder [1958] 2 v. 20cm. 'Translation of volume IV of Werde Licht.' [BX2170.C55B314] 58-7061
1. Church year—Meditations. 2. Saints. I. Title.

BAXTER, James Sidlow 242
His part and ours; devotional gathering round the Scripture usage of the possessive pronoun "my". Grand Rapids, Mich., Zondervan Pub. House [c.1960] 191 p. 22 cm. 60-50192 2.95
1. Devotional literature. 2. God—Promises. I. Title.

BAXTER, Richard, 1615-1691. 242
Devotions and prayers Compiled and edited by Leonard T. Grant. Grand Rapids, Baker Book House, 1964 [1966] 119 p. 16 cm. [BV4831.B37] 64-25820
1. Devotional exercises. I. Grant, Leonard T., ed. II. Title.

BAXTER, Richard, 1615-1691 242
Devotions and prayers. Comp., ed. by Leonard T. Grant. Grand Rapids, Mich., Baker Bk. [c.1966] 119p. 16cm. [BV4831.B37] 64-25820 1.00 pap.,
1. Devotional excercises. I. Grant, Leonard T., ed. II. Title.

BAYLY, Joseph T. 242
Out of my mind [by] Joseph Bayly. Wheaton, Ill., Tyndale House Publishers [1970] 192 p. 22 cm. Editorials from the magazines His and Eternity. [BV4832.2.B36] 79-123292 ISBN 0-8423-4790-9 3.50
1. Meditations. I. Title.

BEAMAN, Joyce Proctor. 242
Bloom where you are planted / Joyce Proctor Beaman. Durham, N.C. : Moore Pub. Co., c1975. 160 p. ; 23 cm. [BV4501.2.B388] 75-34645 ISBN 0-87716-060-0 : 4.95
1. Christian life—1960- I. Title.

BEERS, Victor Gilbert, 1928- 242
Joy is ...; how to discover the prayerful presence of joy in our daily lives [by] V. Gilbert Beers. Old Tappan, N.J., F. H. Revell Co. [1974] 128 p. 21 cm. [BV4905.2.B35] 74-9780 ISBN 0-8007-0677-3 3.95
1. Joy—Meditations. I. Title.

BEL Geddes, Joan. 242
To Barbara with love; prayers and reflections by a believer for a skeptic. [1st ed.] Garden City, N.Y., Doubleday, 1974. xiv, 151 p. 22 cm. [BV260.B37] 73-14039 ISBN 0-385-09614-3 4.95
1. Prayers. 2. Meditations. I. Title.

BELL, L. Nelson, 1894- 242
While men slept, by L. Nelson Bell. [1st ed.] Garden City, N.Y., Doubleday, 1970. xii, 247 p. 22 cm. "Based on the columns Dr. Bell wrote for the magazine 'Christianity today.'"—Dust jacket. [BV4832.2.B39] 76-100041 4.95
1. Meditations. I. Title.

BELL, Roy E 242
Help in time of trouble, and other dial-a-prayer meditations [by] Roy E. Bell. Charlotte [N.C.] Anderson Press [1964] 192 p. 25 cm. [BV4832.2.B42] 64-8159
1. Devotional exercises. I. Title. II. Title: Dial-a-prayer meditations.

BENNETT, Dink. 242
Living reflections / by Dink Bennett. [Cincinnati : Standard Pub. Co., 1975] [48] p. : ill. ; 20 cm. [BV4832.2.B43] 75-3948 ISBN 0-87239-042-X : 2.95
1. Meditations. 2. Prayers. I. Title.

BENNETT, Dink. 242
Moments with my Master / by Dink Bennett. Cincinnati : Standard Pub. Co., c1975. [48] p. : ill. ; 20 cm. [BV4832.2.B433] 75-3949 ISBN 0-87239-043-8 : 2.95
1. Meditations. I. Title.

BENTON, Josephine Moffett. 242
Gift of a golden string. Philadelphia, United Church Press [1963] 255 p. 21 cm. Includes bibliography. [BV4801.B4] 63-12578
1. Devotional literature. I. Title.

BENTON, Josephine Moffett 242
Gift of a golden string. Philadelphia, United Church [c.1963] 255p. 21cm. Bibl. 63-12578 3.95 bds.,
1. Devotional literature. I. Title.

BERG, Marina de, 1926- 242
Vigil in the sun. [1st ed.] Garden City, N. Y., Doubleday, 1962. 138p. 22cm. [BX2182.2.B4] 62-11319
1. Meditations. 2. Monastic and religious life of women. I. Title.

BERG, Marina de, 1926- 242
Vigil in the sun. Garden City, N.Y., Doubleday [c.] 1962. 138p. 22cm. 62-11319 3.50
1. Meditations. 2. Monastic and religious life of women. I. Title.

BERNEKING, William 242
Echoes from the past, with emphasis on matters of church. [1st ed.] New York, Greenwich Book Publishers [1961] 154p. 21cm. [BV4832.2.B45] 61-12204
1. Devotional literature. I. Title.

BERNEKING, William 242
Echoes from the past, with emphasis on matters of church. New York, Greenwich [c.1961] 154p. 61-12204 2.95
1. Devotional literature. I. Title.

BERRIGAN, Daniel. 242
A book of parables / Daniel Berrigan. New York : Seabury Press, 1977. p. cm. "A Crossroad book." [BS1151.5.B47] 76-53537 ISBN 0-8164-0328-7 : 7.95
1. Bible. O.T.—Meditations. I. Title.

BERRY, Mabel Macena (Pennington) 1907- 242
The pathway upward, by Mrs. W. J. Berry. Elon College N. C., Primitive Baptist Pub. House [1957] 207p. 20cm. Verse and prose. [BV4832.B48] 58-16285
1. Devotional literature. I. Title.

BIBLE. English. Revised standard. Selections. 1975. 242
Christianica : the basic teachings of the Christian faith arranged for prayer and meditation. 1st ed. Chicago : Christianica Center, 1975. 144 p. : ill. ; 15 cm. [BS391.2 1975] 74-13005 ISBN 0-911346-02-3
I. Title.

BLACKSTOCK, John W. 242
Moments of meditation [by] John W. Blackstock. Independence, Mo., Herald Pub. House [1965] 75 p. 16 cm. [BV4805.B48] 65-14289
1. Devotional literature (Selections: Extracts, etc.) I. Title.

BLACKSTOCK, John W. 242
Moments of meditation. Independence, Mo., Herald Pub. [c.1965] 75p. 16cm. [BV4805.B48] 65-14289 1.25 bds.,
1. Devotional literature (Selections: Extracts, etc.) I. Title.

BLACKWOOD, Andrew Watterson, 1915- 242
We need you here, Lord; prayers from the city [by] Andrew W. Blackwood, Jr. Grand Rapids, Mich., Baker Book House [1969] 124 p. illus. 23 cm. [BV245.B57] 73-82127 3.95
1. Prayers. I. Title.

BLEIDORN, Eugene F ed. 242
Start thinking of God. Cover and drawings by Doe. O'Connell. Milwaukee, Bruce Pub. Co. [1958] 61p. 18cm. [BX2182.B57] 58-6895
1. Meditations. I. Title.

BLESSITT, Arthur. 242
Forty days at the cross. Nashville, Broadman Press [1972, c1971] 96 p. 19 cm. (Broadman books) [BV4832.2.B54] 75-178057 ISBN 0-8054-5128-5 1.95
1. Devotional exercises. I. Title.

BLOOM, Anthony, 1914- 242
Meditations on a theme: a spiritual journey, by Metropolitan Anthony (Archbishop Anthony Bloom). London, Oxford, Mowbrays, 1972. [9] , 125 p. 19 cm. [BX382.B56] 72-195708 ISBN 0-264-64571-5 £0.60
1. Spiritual life—Orthodox Eastern authors. I. Title.

BOCKELMAN, Eleanor 242
Bread for her day. Columbus, Ohio, Wartburg Press [1958] 70p. 20cm. [BV4501.B673] 58-11790
1. Christian life. I. Title.

BOLDING, Amy. 242
Fingertip devotions. Grand Rapids, Baker Book House [1970] 102 p. 21 cm. [BV4832.2.B58] 79-115635 2.50
1. Devotional exercises. I. Title.

BOLDING, Amy. 242
Inspiring fingertip devotions. Grand Rapids, Mich., Baker Book House [1971] 104 p. 20 cm. "A companion to ... Fingertip devotions."—Dust jacket. [BV4832.2.B584] 75-175832 ISBN 0-8010-0558-2 2.50
1. Devotional exercises. I. Title.

BOLDING, Amy 242
Please give a devotion. Grand Rapids, Mich., Baker Bk. [c.]1963. 99p. 20cm. 63-19524 1.95
1. Devotional literature. I. Title.

BOLDING, Amy. 242
Please give a devotion for active teens. Grand Rapids, Baker Books [1974, c1969] 96 p. 18 cm. (Direction books) Originally published under title: Please give a devotion for juniors. [BV4832.2.B58] 77-88243 ISBN 0-8010-0620-1. 0.95 (pbk.)
1. Devotional exercises. I. Title.

*BOLDING, Amy 242
Please give a devotion for church groups Grand Rapids, Baker Book House [1974] 105 p. 20 cm. [BV4801] ISBN 0-8010-0623-6 1.95
1. Devotional literature. I. Title.

BOLDING, Amy. 242
Please give a devotion of gladness. Grand Rapids, Baker Book House, 1965. 108 p. 21 cm. [BV4832.2.B615] 65-25478
1. Devotional exercises. I. Title.

BOLDING, Amy 242
Please give a devotion of gladness. Grand

Rapids, Mich., Baker Bk. [c.]1965. 108p. 21cm. [BV4832.2.B615] 65-25478 1.95 bds.,
1. Devotional exercises. I. Title.

BOLOGNE, Charles Damian, 1911- 242
My friends, the senses; translated by Jane Howes. Foreword by Gerald Vann. New York, P. J. Kenedy [1953] 206p. 21cm. [BF233.B642] 53-11511
1. Senses and sensation. I. Title.

BOLT, Peter, 1925- 242
A way of loving. [Nashville] Upper Room [1973] 104 p. 20 cm. [BS2675.4.B64] 73-86798 1.25
1. Bible. N.T. 1 Corinthians XIII—Devotional literature. I. Title.

BONTRAGER, John Kenneth 242
Sea rations. Nashville, Upper Room [c.1964] 88p. illus. 19cm. 64-14855 .50 pap.,
1. Worship programs. I. Title.

BOONE, Charles Eugene. 242
Dr. Balaam's talking mule / [Pat Boone]. 1st ed. Van Nuys, Calif. : Bible Voice, [1974] 156 p. ; 22 cm. (Son-rise books) [BV4832.2.B625] 74-189470 5.95
1. Meditations. 2. Christian life—1960- I. Title.

BOONE, Charles Eugene. 242
My brother's keeper? = Original title, Dr. Balaam's talking mule / Pat Boone. New York : Pillar Books, 1975, c1974. 159 p. ; 18 cm. [BV4832.2.B625 1975] 75-7829 ISBN 0-89129-028-1 pbk. : 1.75
1. Meditations. 2. Christian life—1960- I. Title.

BOROS, Ladislaus, 1927- 242
We are future. [Translated by W. J. O'Hara. New York] Herder and Herder [1970] 175 p. 21 cm. Translation of Wir sind Zukunft. [BV4638.B58413] 71-110077 4.95
1. Hope—Meditations. I. Title.

BOROS, Ladislaus, 1927- 242
We are future. Translated by W. J. O'Hara Garden City, New York, Doubleday [1973, c.1970] 158 p. 18 cm. (Image Book, D326) Translation of Wir Sind Zukunft. [BV4638.B58413] ISBN 0-385-05423-8 1.45 (pbk.)
1. Hope—Meditations. I. Title.
L.C. card no. for hardbound edition: 71-110077.

*BOUNDS, Edward M. 242
The necessity of prayer / Edward M. Bounds. Grand Rapids : Baker Book House, 1976. 144p. ; 18 cm. (Direction books) [BV210.2] ISBN 0-8010-0659-7 pbk. : 1.45.
1. Prayer. I. Title.

BOWIE, Walter Russell, 1882- 242
Christ be with me; daily meditations and personal prayers. New York, Abingdon Press [1958] 137p. 16cm. [BV4832.B724] 58-5395
1. Meditations. I. Title.

BOWIE, Walter Russell, 1882- 242
Christ be with me; daily meditations and personal prayers. Nashville, Abingdon [1965, c.1958] 137p. 16cm. (Apex bks., T1) [BV4832.B724] .69 pap.,
1. Meditations. I. Title.

BOWMAN, Clarice Marguerette, 1910- 242
Resources for worship. New York, Association Press [1961] 383p. 20cm. Includes bibliography. [BV10.2.B65] 61-8181
1. Worship. 2. Prayers. I. Title.

BOWMAN, Clarice Margurette, 1910- 242
Resources for worship. New York, Association Press [c.1961] 383p. Bibl. 61-8181 4.95 bds.,
1. Worship. 2. Prayers. I. Title.

BOYD, Malcolm, 1923- 242
The alleluia affair / Malcolm Boyd. Waco, Tex. : Word Books, [1975] [139] p. : ill. ; 24 cm. [BV4832.2.B67] 74-27474 5.95.
1. Meditations. I. Title.

BRACHER, Marjory Louise, comp. 242
Family prayers. Philadelphia, Muhlenberg Press [1962] 89p. 15cm. [BV255.B68] 62-8200
1. Family—Prayer-books and devotions—English. I. Title.

BRANDT, Catharine. 242
Praise God for this new day : second thoughts for busy women / Catharine Brandt ; ill. by Audrey Teeple. Minneapolis : Augsburg Pub. House, [1975] 128 p. : ill. ; 20 cm. [BV4832.2.B69] 75-2831 ISBN 0-8066-1477-3 : 2.95
1. Meditations. I. Teeple, Audrey. II. Title.

BRANDT, Leslie F. 242
Great God, here I am [by] Leslie F. Brandt. Saint Louis, Concordia Pub. House [1968, c1967] 96 p. 21 cm. On cover: Today's man talks with God. A collection of devotions and brief prayers based on Bible text. [BV4832.2.B7] 69-13112 1.95
1. Devotional literature. I. Title.

BREIG, Joseph Anthony, 1905- 242
God in our house, reflections on the Gospels or Epistles for Sundays and some of the feasts. New York, America Press [1949] xvii, 156p. 21cm. 'A compilation from the weekly column The Word in the national Catholic weekly review, America.' [BX2170.C55B75] 50-5121
1. Church year—Meditations. I. Title.

BRENNEMAN, Helen Good. 242
Meditations for the new mother, a devotional book for the new mother during the first month following the birth of her baby. Drawings by Esther Rose Graber. Scottdale, Pa., Herald Press, 1953. 78p. illus. 28cm. [BV4847.B7] 53-7585
1. Mothers—Prayer-books and devotions—English. I. Title.

BRETON, Valentin Marie, 1877- 242
In Christ's company. Translated from the French by Michael D. Meilach. Chicago, Franciscan Herald Press [1962] 79p. 18cm. (New Herald paperbacks) Translation of De l'imitation du Christ a l'ecole de Saint Francois. [BX2188.F7B73] 61-18902
1. Meditations. 2. Franciscans. I. Title.

BRETON, Valentin Marie 1877- 242
In Christ's company. Tr. from French by Michael D. Meilach. Chicago, Franciscan Herrald [c.1962] 79p. 18cm. (New Herald paperbacks) 61-18902 .95 pap.,
1. Meditations. 2. Franciscans. I. Title.

BRETT, Laurence, comp. 242
In the presence of my Father; prayers from the Bible, translated and compiled by Laurence Brett. Baltimore, Helicon [1968] 224 p. 21 cm. [BV228.B7] 67-13788 4.95
1. Bible—Prayers. I. Title.

BRISTOL, Lee Hastings, 1923- 242
The big picnic, and other meals in the New Testament / by Lee Hastings Bristol, Jr. Atlanta : John Knox Press, c1975. 79 p. ; 24 cm. Includes hymns with music. [BS2545.D56B74] 75-13455 ISBN 0-8042-2286-X : 4.95
1. Dinners and dining in the Bible. 2. Devotional exercises. I. Title.

BRO, Margueritte (Harmon) 1894- 242
Today makes a difference! An everyday book of prayer. Camden, [N.J.] T. Nelson [1970] xiv, 210 p. 19 cm. [BV4832.2.B74] 78-127071 2.95
1. Devotional literature. I. Title.

BROKERING, Herbert F. 242
Uncovered feelings; out-loud words on seventy-one happenings [by] Herbert F. Brokering. Philadelphia, Fortress Press [1969] 95 p. illus. 15 x 24 cm. [PS3552.R63U5] 69-14625 3.95
I. Title.

BROOKE, Avery. 242
As never before / words by Avery Brooke ; photos. by Alex Darrow and the students of the Wykeham-Gunnery Schools. Noroton, Conn. : Vineyard Books, c1976. 46 p. : ill. ; 25 cm. [BV4832.2.B744] 76-375550 ISBN 0-913886-05-X : 5.95
1. Meditations. I. Darrow, Alex.

BROU, Alexandre, 1862- 242
The Ignatian way to God; translated from the French of Alexandre Brou by William J. Young. Milwaukee, Bruce Pub. Co. [1952] 156 p. 22 cm. Translation of La spiritualite de Saint Ignace. Includes bibliography. [BX2179.L8B743] 52-2739
1. Loyola, Ignacio de, Saint, 1491-1556. 2. Spiritual exercises. 3. Spiritual life—Catholic authors. I. Title.

BROWN, Bob W. 242
How can we get Lily Rose to settle down? : The thoughts, tears, prayers, frustrations, and victories of a people-hearted pastor / Bob W. Brown. [Nashville] : Impact Books, [1975] 167 p. ; 23 cm. [BV4832.2.B747] 75-4160 ISBN 0-914850-28-8 : 3.95
1. Meditations. I. Title.

BROWN, Stephen James Meredith, 1881- 242
Alone with God; meditations for a retreat. New York City, Wagner [1956] 310p. 21cm. [BX2375.B77] 56-3334
1. Retreats. 2. Meditations. I. Title.

BROX, Gertrude V 1916-1954. 242
Thou didst say unto me . . . Pages from the devotional diary of Gertrude V. Brox, collected and edited by Ada P. Stearns. Philadelphia, Judson Press [1955] 64p. illus. 18cm. [BV4832.B8] 55-7854
1. Devotional literature. I. Title.

BUCKINGHAM, James. 242
Some gall—and other reflections on life ... Waco, Tex., Word Books [1970] 148 p. 23 cm. [BV4832.2.B78] 71-135352 3.95
1. Devotional literature. I. Title.

BUECHNER, Frederick, 1926- 242
The hungering dark. New York, Seabury Press [1968, c1969] 125 p. 22 cm. [BV4832.2.B8] 68-29987 3.95
1. Meditations. I. Title.

BUEGE, William A. 242
Vacationing with a purpose; meditations for vacationers. St. Louis, Concordia [c.1962] 63p. illus. (pt. col.) 15cm. .10 pap.,
I. Title.

BUNYAN, John, 1628-1688. 242
The spiritual riches of John Bunyan, edited and with an introd. by Thomas S. Kepler. [1st ed.] Cleveland, World Pub. Co. [1952] xxv, 352p. 16cm. (World devotional classics) [BR75.B863] 52-10321
1. Devotional literature (Selections: Extracts, etc.) I. Title.

BURNS, Betty. 242
With God as thy companion. Nashville, Broadman Press [1965] 64 p. 22 cm. Biblical quotations, prayers, and hymns. [BV4805.B8] 65-12866
1. Devotional literature (Selections: Extracts, etc.) I. Title.

BURNS, Betty 242
With God as thy companion. Nashville, Broadman [c.1965] 64p. 22cm. Biblical quotations, prayers, hymns. [BV4805.B8] 65-12866 2.00 bds.,
1. Devotional literature (Selections: Extracts, etc.) I. Title.

BURTON, Joe Wright, 1907- comp. 242
Light from above. Joe W. Burton: compiler. Nashville, Broadman Press [1968] 127 p. 21 cm. Articles reprinted from the periodical Home life. [BV4801.B8] 68-20669 2.75
1. Devotional literature. I. Home life, Nashville. II. Title.

CALDWELL, Turner A. 242
The splendor of life. New York, Exposition [c.1963] 56p. 21cm. 2.50
I. Title.

CALVIN, Jean, 1509-1564. 242
Devotions and prayers. Compiled by Charles E. Edwards. Grand Rapids, Baker Book House, 1954. 120p. 16cm. 'Originally published under the title Scripture texts, with expositions and sentence prayers from Calvin's Commentaries on the minor prophets.' [BV262] 54-10083
1. Prayers. I. Title.

CARGAS, Harry J. 242
Encountering myself : contemporary Christian meditations / Harry James Cargas. New York : Seabury Press, 1977. p. cm. "A Crossroad book." [BV4832.2.C266] 76-56519 ISBN 0-8164-0372-4 : 6.95
1. Meditations. I. Title.

CARLSON, Betty. 242
No one's perfect / by Betty Carlson ; with ill. also by the author. Westchester, Ill. : Good News Publishers, c1976. 192 p. : ill. ; 21 cm. [BV4832.2.C2696] 76-17669 ISBN 0-89107-143-1 : 3.50
1. Meditations. I. Title.

CARLSON, Betty. 242
A song and a prayer. Grand Rapids, Mich., Baker Book House [1970] 100 p. 20 cm. [BV4832.2.C27] 73-115639 1.95
1. Meditations. I. Title.

A Carmelite nun. 242
World without end, by a Carmelita nun. Westminster, Md., Newman Press, 1951. 196 p. 18 cm. [BX2182.W6] 51-35586
1. Devotional literature. I. Title.

CARR, Jo. 242
Living on tiptoe; devotions for families with children. [Nashville] Upper Room [1972] 104 p. 22 cm. [BV255.C28] 72-77613 1.25
1. Family—Prayer-books and devotions—English. I. Title.

CARRETTO, Carlo. 242
The God who comes. Translated by Rose Mary Hancock. Maryknoll, N.Y., Orbis Books [1974] xxi, 232 p. 20 cm. Translation of Il Dio che viene. [BX2185.C3213] 73-89358 ISBN 0-88344-164-0 4.95
1. Meditations. I. Title.

CARRETTO, Carlo. 242
Letters from the desert. Translated by Rose Mary Hancock. With a foreword by Ivan Illich. Maryknoll, N.Y., Orbis Books [1972] xxi, 146 p. illus. 19 cm. Translation of Lettere dal deserto. [BX2185.C3413] 72-85791 3.95
1. Meditations. I. Title.

CARRETTO, Carlo. 242
Love is for living / by Carlo Carretto ; translated by Jeremy Moiser. Maryknoll, N.Y. : Orbis Books, 1977. 158 p. ; 21 cm. Translation of Cio che conta e amare. Reprint of the 1976 ed. published by Darton, Longman and Todd, London. [BS495.5.C3413 1977] 76-49878 ISBN 0-88344-291-4 : 6.95
1. Bible—Meditations. I. Title.

CARROLL, James. 242
Tender of wishes; the prayers of a young priest. Paramus, N.J., Newman Press [1969] 138 p. illus. 23 cm. [BV245.C35] 73-92219 1.75
1. Prayers. I. Title.

CARROLL, James. 242
Wonder and worship. Paramus, N.J., Newman Press, 1970. 142 p. illus. 23 cm. [BX2182.2.C34] 70-133469 1.75
1. Devotional exercises. I. Title.

CARSON, David M., 1922- 242
From the study window [by] David M. Carson. Pittsburgh, National Reform Association, 1971. vii, 120 p. 21 cm. [BV4832.2.C276] 75-157085
1. Meditations. I. Title.

CARTER, Edward, 1929- 242
Everyday and its possibilities. St. Meinrad, Ind., Abbey Press, 1973. viii, 144 p. 21 cm. (A Priority edition) Includes bibliographical references. [BX2182.2.C35] 73-85337 2.95
1. Meditations. I. Title.

†CARTER, Edward, 1929- 242
The Jesus experience / Edward Carter. Canfield, Ohio : Alba Books, c1976. 107 p. : ill. ; 18 cm. Includes bibliographical references. [BX2182.2.C353] 76-6701 ISBN 0-8189-1131-X pbk. : 1.75
1. Meditations. I. Title.

CARTER, Edward, 1929- 242
Now is the time / by Edward Carter. Canfield, Ohio : Alba Books, [1975] 127 p. ; 18 cm. [BX2182.2.C354] 74-27609 1.45
1. Meditations. I. Title.

CARTER, John M., 1911- 242
The second cross [by] John M. Carter. Nashville, Broadman Press [1969] 128 p. 21 cm. Includes bibliographies. [BV4832.2.C28] 69-14366
1. Devotional literature. I. Title.

CASEY, Lawrence B. 242
The heart remembers, too / by Lawrence B. Casey. New York : Paulist Press, c1976. x, 182 p. ; 18 cm. (Deus books) [BX2182.2.C357] 76-45933 ISBN 0-8091-1997-8 pbk. : 1.95
1. Meditations. I. Title.

CATERINA DA SIENA, Saint, 1347-1380. 242
The orcherd of Syon; edited from the early manuscripts of Phyllis Hodgson and Gabriel M. Liegey. London, New York [etc.] Published for the Early English Text Society by the Oxford U. P., 1966- v. front. (facsims.) 22 1/2 cm. (Early English Text Society. [Publications. Original series] no. 258) v. 1:84/ (v. 1:B 66-19173) "The orcherd is an early fifteenth-century translation of the work perhaps now best known as The dialogue of St. Catherine of Siena." Contents.CONTENTS. -- v. 1. Text. [PR1119.A2 no. 258] 67-74981
1. Mysticism — Middle Ages. I. Hodgson, Phyllis, ed. II. Liegey, Gabriel Michael, 1904- ed. III. Title.

CHAMPION, Richard G. 242
Go on singing : how to find joyful living from the Psalms / Richard G. Champion. Springfield, Mo. : Gospel Pub. House, c1976. 125 p. ; 18 cm. (Radiant books) [BS1430.4.C47] 76-20889 ISBN 0-88243-895-6 pbk. : 1.25
1. Bible. O.T. Psalms—Meditations. 2. Christian life—1960- I. Title.

CHANEY, Robert Galen, 1913- 242
The inner way. Los Angeles, De Vorss [1962] 149p. 22cm. [BV4813.C5] 62-52927
1. Meditation. I. Title.

CHANNELS of challenge 242
[by] Maxie D. Dunnam. New York, Abingdon Press [1965] 144 p. 21 cm. [BV4832.2.D8] 65-15231
1. Meditations.

CHAPMAN, Joseph I. 242
First things first ; What are our Christian priorities? / by Joseph I. Chapman. Valley Forge, Pa. : Judson Press, [1975] 96 p. ; 22 cm. [BV4832.2.C523] 74-22523 ISBN 0-8170-0649-4 : 2.50
1. Meditations. I. Title.

CHAPMAN, Rex. 242
A kind of praying. Philadelphia, Westminster Press [1971, c1970] 121 p. 21 cm. Bibliography: p. 117. [BT306.4.C48 1971] 76-159476 ISBN 0-664-24934-5 1.95
1. Jesus Christ—Meditations. 2. Prayers. I. Title.

CHARLES, Pierre 242
The prayer of all things, [New York] Herder & Herder [1964, c.1962] viii, 210p. 21cm. 64-10921 3.95
1. Meditations. I. Title.

CHARLTON, David W 242
By these things men live; meditations. [1st ed.] New York, Greenwich Book Publishers, 1957. 63p. 22cm. [BV4832.C487] 57-7316
1. Meditations. I. Title.

CHARMOT, Francois. 242
In retreat with the Sacred Heart; translated by Sister Maria Constance. Westminster, Md., Newman Press, 1956. 221p. 24cm. In verse. [BX2157.C553] 56-9985
1. Sacred Heart, Devotion to. I. Title.

CHAUTARD, Jean Baptiste, 242
1858-1935.
The soul of the apostolate. Translated, and with an introd., by Thomas Merton. Garden City, N. Y., Image Books [1961] 270p. 18cm. (A Doubleday image book, D124) [BX2183.C5 1961] 31-19283
1. Spiritual life—Catholic authors. I. Title.

CHAUTARD, Jean Baptiste 242
[Secular name: Auguste Philogene Gustave Chautard] 1858-1935.
The soul of the apostolate. Tr. with an introd. by Thomas Merton. Garden City, N.Y., Image Books [dist. Doubleday, c.1946, 1961] 270p. (Doubleday image bk., D124) 61-19283 .85 pap.,
1. Spiritual life—Catholic authors. I. Title.

CHENEY, Lois A. 242
God is no fool [by] Lois A. Cheney. Nashville, Abingdon Press [1969] 176 p. 21 cm. [BV4832.2.C524] 77-84709 3.75
1. Meditations. I. Title.

CHESHAM, Sallie. 242
Today is yours. Edited by Sallie Chesham. Waco, Tex., Word Books [1972] 104 p. 20 cm. [BV4832.2.C528] 72-93390 3.50
1. Devotional exercises. I. Title.

CHINMOY. 242
The Supreme and his four children; five spiritual dictionaries [by] Sri Chinmoy. New York, Fleet Press Corp. [1973] 60 p. 22 cm. [BL624.C475] 72-188849 ISBN 0-8303-0121-6 3.00
1. Meditations. I. Title.

CHRISTENSEN, Bernhard 242
Marinus, 1901-
The inward pilgrimage : spiritual classics from Augustine to Bonhoeffer / Bernhard Christensen. Minneapolis : Augsburg Pub. House, c1976. 176 p. ; 22 cm. Includes bibliographical references. [Br117.C47] 75-22725 ISBN 0-8066-1510-9 pbk. : 3.50
1. Christian literature—History and criticism. I. Title.

CHRISTOPHER, 1950- 242
Our new age : (words for the people) / Christopher. 1st paperback ed. Louisville, Ky. : World Light Publications, 1977. 77 p. : ill. ; 22 cm. [BL624.C48 1977] 77-72309 ISBN 0-916940-01-2 pbk. : 2.95
1. Meditations. I. Title.

CHRISTOPHER, 1950- 242
Slanted to ladies / Christopher. 1st paperback ed. Louisville, Ky. : World Light Publications, 1976. 47 p. ; 22 cm. [BL624.C49] 76-6234 ISBN 0-916940-00-4 : 2.95
1. Meditations. I. Title.

CHURCH, Virginia Woodson 242
Frame, 1880-
To meet the day [by] Virginia Church and Francis C. Ellis. Nashville, Abingdon-Cokesbury Press [1953] 128 p. 20 cm. [BV4850.C55] 53-5393
1. Youth—Prayer-books and devotions—English. I. Ellis, Francis C., joint author. II. Title.

CLARK, Leslie Savage. Mrs. 242
With all thy heart devotional vignettes of Bible, poetry,and prayer. Nashville, Broadman Press [1957] 80p. 20cm. [BV4832.C58] 57-10108
1. Devotional exercises. I. Title.

CLARK, Mrs. Leslie Savage. 242
With all thy heart; devotional vignettes of Bible, poetry, and prayer. Nashville, Broadman Press [1957] 80p. 20cm. [BV4832.C58] 57-10108
1. Devotional exercises. I. Title.

CLEVELAND, Earl E. 242
Free at last [by] E. E. Cleveland. Washington, Review and Herald Pub. Association [1970] 447 p. col. illus., col. ports. 26 cm. [BX6123.C55] 70-97596
1. Seventh-Day Adventists—Sermons. 2. Sermons, American. I. Title.

CLINARD, Turner Norman. 242
Words in season / by Turner N. Clinard. Nashville : Tidings, [1974] viii, 101 p. ; 19 cm. [BV4832.2.C548] 74-80893 2.45
1. Meditations. I. Title.

CLINTON, Keneth. 242
Shrines of God. Natick, Mass., W. A. Wilde Co. [1960] 127p. 20cm. [BV4832.2.C55] 60-8217
1. Devotional literature. I. Title.

CLINTON, Kenneth. 242
Let's pray about it; a book of daily evotions for all who seek the love and guidance of our Heavenly Father 1st. ed. New York, American Press [c1957] 104p. 21cm. [BV4832.C6223] 57-14420
1. Devotional exercises. I. Title.

CLINTON, Kenneth 242
Shrines of God. Natick, Mass., W. A. Wilde Co. [c.1960] 127p. 20cm. 60-8217 2.00 bds.,
1. Devotional literature. I. Title.

COFFIN, Henry Sloane, 1877- 242
Joy in believing; selections from the spoken and written words and the prayers of Henry Sloane Coffin, edited by Walter Russell Bowie. New York, Scribner [1956] 248p. 20cm. [BV4832.C6225] 56-10345
1. Devotional literature. I. Title.

COGGAN, Frederick Donald, 242
1909-
Christ and our crises / F. Donald Coggan. Waco, Tex. : Word Books, [1975] 52 p. ; 21 cm. Meditations based on a series of talks delivered at St. Bartholomew's, New York City, 1974. [BV4832.2.C59] 74-27475 ISBN pbk. : 2.95
1. Meditations. I. Title.

COLLINS, John H 242
Soul of Christ; meditations on the Anima Christi. Westminster, Md., Newman Press, 1956. 122p. 24cm. [BX2175.A5C6] 56-7640
1. Anima Christi—Meditations. I. Title.

CONGDON, Ruth. 242
God breaks in. Plainfield, N.J., Logos International [1968] 127 p. 21 cm. [BV4832.2.C6] 68-57712 3.75
1. Meditations. I. Title.

CONNERS, Kenneth Wray. 242
Who's in charge here? Valley Forge [Pa.] Judson Press [1973] 124 p. 22 cm. "Guidelines for Christian living." [BV4832.2.C63] 73-6609 ISBN 0-8170-0601-X 2.95 (pbk.)
1. Meditations. I. Title.

CONNOLLY, Donald, comp. 242
A voice for the heart; the Imitation of Christ and An introduction to the devout life for all Christians. Translated and edited by Donald Connolly. [1st ed.] New York, Vantage Press [1972] 168 p. 21 cm. "Certain sections are now outdated ... Such passages have been eliminated from both books." [BV4821.C65] 72-197451 ISBN 0-533-00361-X 5.95
1. Meditations. I. Francois de Sales, Saint, Bp. of Geneva, 1567-1622. Introduction a la vie devote. English. Selections. 1972. II. Imitatio Christi. English. Selections. 1972. III. Title

CONSIDINE, Daniel 242
Delight in the Lord; notes of spiritual direction and exhortations. Springfield, Ill., Templegate [1963] 58p. 15cm. 1.25
I. Title.

COOGAN, Aloysius F. 242
Forty steps to Easter; with a pref. by Francis Cardinal Spellman. Milwaukee, Bruce Pub. Co. [1952] 141 p. 21 cm. [BX2170.L4C6] 52-7956
1. Lent—Prayer-books and devotions—English. I. Title.

COOK, Walter L. 242
Youth meditations [by] Walter L. Cook. Nashville, Abingdon Press [1970] 96 p. 16 cm. [BV4531.2.C58] 72-98898 2.50
1. Youth—Prayer-books and devotions. I. Title.

COON, Glenn A. 242
Lovely lord of the Lord's day / Glenn and Ethel Coon. Mountain View, Calif. : Pacific Press Pub. Association, c1976. 192 p. ; 22 cm. Includes bibliographical references. [BV4832.2.C64] 75-46423 pbk. : 3.95
1. Meditations. 2. Prayer groups. I. Coon, Ethel, joint author. II. Title.

COONEY, Barbara, 1917- illus j242
A Little prayer, with pictures by Barbara Cooney. New York, Hastings House [1967] 1 v. (unpaged) col. illus. 13 x 15 cm. [BV265.L53 1967] 67-27101
1. Children — Prayer-books and devotions. I. Title.

CORBISHLEY, Thomas, tr. 242
The spiritual exercises of Saint Ignatius. A new translation by Thomas Corbishley. New York, P. J. Kenedy [1963] 124 p. 18 cm. [The Silver treasury series] [BX2179.L7E5 1963] 63-12296
1. Spiritual exercises I. Title.

COURTOIS, Gaston 242
Fruitful activity; spiritual conferences for educators. Tr. [from French] by Sister Helen Madeleine. Westminister, Md., Newman [c.] 1962. 140p. 21cm. 62-17189 3.00
1. Spiritual life—Catholic authors. I. Title.

COWMAN, Charles E. Mrs. 242
Streams in the desert: v.2. From the files and unpublished writings of Mrs. Charles E. Cowman. Grand Rapids, Zondervan [1966] unpaged. 18cm. (Cowman pubn.) 2.95
I. Title.

COWMAN, Lettie (Burd) 1870- 242
Handfuls of purpose, by Mrs. Charles E. Cowman. Los Angeles, Cowman Publications [1955] 139p. 20cm. [BV4832.C638] 56-202
1. Devotional literature. I. Title.

CRANFORD, Mary Poole. 242
From my window; to shut-ins all over the world. New York, Pageant Press [1953] 146p. illus. 21cm. Essays. [BV4585.C7] 53-12317
1. Sick—Prayer-books and devotions—English. I. Title.

CRAVNER, William Charles. 242
God's Heartbreak Hill. [1st ed.] New York, Vantage Press [1957] 75p. illus. 21cm. [BV4832.C714] 56-14380
1. Devotional literature. I. Title.

CRAVNER, William Charles. 242
A life in my hands. [1st ed.] New York, Vantage Press [1957] 68p. illus. 21cm. [BV4832.C72] 56-12315
1. Devotional literature. I. Title.

CRAVNER, William Charles. 242
Treasures of darkness. [1st ed.] New York, Vantage Press [1957] 80p. illus. 21cm. [BV4832.C725] 56-12774
1. Devotional literature. I. Title.

CRAWLEY-BOEVEY, Mateo, 1875- 242
1960.
Father Mateo speaks to priests on priestly perfection. Tr. from French by Francis Larkin. Westminster, Md., Newman Press [c.]1960. 258p. 60-14830 3.75
1. Clergy—Religious life. 2. Retreats—Addresses, essays, lectures. I. Title.

CROUCH, Austin. 242
The bright side of death. Nashville, Broadman Press [1951] 32 p. 19 cm. Bibliography: p. 32. [BV4905.C695] 51-25524
1. Consolation. 2. Death. I. Title.

CROWELL, Grace (Noll) 242
Vital possessions. Nashville, Abingdon Press [c.1960] 108p. 18cm. 60-10908 1.50 bds.,
1. Devotional exercises. I. Title.

CROWELL, Grace (Noll), 1877- 242
Meditations; devotions for women. Nashville, Abingdon-Cokesbury Press [1951] 128 p. 18 cm. [BV4844.C7] 51-10747
1. Women—Prayer-books and devotions—English. I. Title.

CROWELL, Grace (Noll), 1877- 242
Moments of devotion; meditations and verse. Nashville, Abingdon-Cokesbury Press ['1953] 144 p. 18 cm. [BV4832.C735] 52-11308
1. Devotional exercises. I. Title.

CROWELL, Grace (Noll) 1877- 242
Proofs of His presence. Nashville, Abingdon [1965, c.1958] 110p. 18cm. (Apex bks., T3) [BV4832.C737] .69 pap.,
1. Meditations. I. Title.

CROWELL, Grace (Noll) 1877- 242
Riches of the kingdom. Nashville, Abingdon Press [1954] 126p. 18cm. Prose and poems. [BV4844.C72] 54-7028
1. Women—Prayer-books and devotions—English. I. Title.

CROWLEY, Mary C. 242
Be somebody ... God doesn't take time to make a nobody [by] Mary Crowley. [Dallas, Crescendo Book Publications, 1974] 63 p. 12 cm. [BV4832.2.C76] 73-92309
1. Meditations. I. Title.

CROWLEY, Mary C. 242
Moments with Mary, by Mary C. Crowley. With an introd. by W. A. Criswell. Dallas [Crescendo Book Publications, 1973] 115 p. 20 cm. [BV4832.2.C77] 73-81147
1. Meditations. I. Title.

CUNNEEN, Sally. 242
A contemporary meditation on the everyday God / by Sally Cunneen. Chicago : Thomas More Press, c1976. 128 p. ; 21 cm. (Contemporary meditations) [BX2182.2.C84] 76-378089 ISBN 0-88347-061-6 pbk. : 2.95
1. Meditations. I. Title.

CUNNINGHAM, Mabel E. 242
The hour has come; messages from the spirit of God about a new order to save mankind, as interpreted by Mabel E. Cunningham. New York, Exposition [c.1962] 90p. 21cm. 3.00
I. Title.

†CURTIS, Donald. 242
Master meditations / by Donald Curtis. Lakemont, Ga. : CSA Press, c1976 237 p. ; 21 cm. [BX9890.U5C86] 76-47422 ISBN 0-87707-185-3 pbk. : 3.25
1. Unity School of Christianity. 2. Meditations. I. Title.

CURTIS, Lindsay R. 242
Talks for a Sunday morn / Lindsay R. Curtis. Salt Lake City : Bookcraft, 1976. viii, 120 p. ; 24 cm. [BV4832.2.C86] 76-22311 ISBN 0-88494-303-8 pbk. : 3.50
1. Meditations. I. Title.

CUSHING, Richard, Cardinal 242
Holy hour meditations. [Boston, Daughters of St. Paul, c.1961] 66p. 14cm. .15 pap.,
I. Title.

CUSHING, Richard James, 242
Cardinal
Meditations for religious. [Boston] St. Paul Editions [dist. Daughters of St. Paul] [1959] 270p. 22cm. 60-148 3.00; 2.00 pap.,
1. Monastic and religious life. 2. Meditations. I. Title.

CUSHMAN, Ralph Spaulding, 242
Bp., 1879-
Meditations and verse on living in two worlds. New York, Abingdon-Cokesbury Press [1952] 94 p. 18 cm. [BV4832.C773] 52-5735
1. Meditations. I. Title.

CUSHMAN, Ralph Spaulding, 242
Bp., 1879-- comp.
The pocket book of hope. Nashville, Upper Room [c1953] 126p. 12cm. [BV4832.C777] 57-43691
1. Devotional literature. 2. Hope. I. Title.

CUSHMAN, Ralph Spaulding, 242
bp., 1879-
Practicing the presence; a quest for God. Nashville, Abingdon [1966, c.1936, 1964] 202p. 18cm. [BV4832.C78] 36-20232 .95 pap.,
1. Devotional exercises. I. Title.

CUSHMAN, Ralph Spaulding, 242
1879-
Spiritual hilltops, a book of devotion. Nashville, Tenn., Abingdon Press [1961, c.1960] 159p. (Apex bks. F5) .69 pap.,
1. Devotional exercises. I. Title.

CUSHMAN, Ralph Spaulding, 242
Bp., 1879-- comp.
Ye shall receive power; a pocket book of power for church members [by] Ralph Spaulding Cushman and Robert Earl Cushman. Nashville, Upper Room [c1951] 127p. 12cm. [BV4832.C82] 57-43692
1. Devotional literature. I. Cushman, Robert Earl, joint comp. II. Title.

DAEHLIN, Marlene. 242
Hearts aglow. San Antonio, Naylor Co. [1968] xi, 88 p. illus. 20 cm. [BV260.D23] 68-25398 3.50
1. Prayers. I. Title.

DAEHLIN, Marlene. 242
Hearts aglow. [Enl. and rev. ed.] San Antonio, Naylor Co. [1969] xi, 92 p. illus. 20 cm. [BV260.D23 1969] 75-110662 3.50
1. Prayers. I. Title.

D'ARCY, Martin Cyril, 1888- 242
Facing the people, by Martin D'Arcy. [1st American ed.] Wilkes-Barre, Pa., Dimension Books [1968] 140 p. 20 cm. [BX2182.2.D33 1968] 68-13730
1. Meditations. I. Title.

D'ARCY, Martin Cyril, 1888- 242
Of God and man; thoughts on faith and morals, by Martin C. D'Arcy. Wilkes-Barre, Pa., Dimension Books [1964] 173 p. 20 cm. [BX2350.2D36] 64-55293
1. Christian life — Catholic authors. I. Title.

DARIES, Frederick Reinhard, 1894- ed. 242
With God and friends each day; a book of devotions and a record of friendships for every day of the year. Indianapolis [1951] 382 p. 18 cm. [BV4810.D28 1951] 51-37199
1. Devotional exercises. 2. Calendars. I. Title.

DAUGHERTY, Myra (Mills). 242
Beauty for ashes. [Nocona? Tex., 1951] 55 p. 21 cm. [BV4832.D315] 52-17630
1. Devotional literature. I. Title.

DAVIS, Charles 242
English spiritual writers. Foreword by Cardinal Godfrey. New York, Sheed & Ward [1962, c.1961] 233p. Bibl. 62-9110 3.50 bds.,
1. Devotional literature—Hist. & crit. 2. English literature—Catholic authors—Hist. & crit. I. Title.

DAVIS, Jean Reynolds. 242
To God with love. [1st ed.] New York, Harper & Row [1968] ix, 147 p. 22 cm. [BV4832.2.D37] 68-29562 3.95
1. Devotional literature. I. Title.

DAY, Dorothy, 1897- 242
Meditations. Selected & arr. by Stanley Vishnewski. Drawings by Rita Corbin. New York, Newman Press [1970] 81 p. 24 cm. [BX2182.2.D36] 73-133570 3.95
1. Meditations.

DAY, Gwynn McLendon 242
Gleams of glory. Nashville, Broadman [1964] 127p. 20cm. 64-18273 1.50
1. Devotional exercises. I. Title.

DAY with Jesus (A), 242
by a monk of the Eastern Church. Tr. [from 2d French ed.] by a monk of the Western Church. New York, Desclee [1964] 109p. 21cm. 64-23931 2.50
1. Jesus Christ—Biog.—Meditations. I. A monk of the Eastern Church. II. A monk of the Western Church, tr.

DEAN, Herschel B. 242
Bible quotes & comments / by H. B. Dean ; cover art by John Ham. Cincinnati : Standard Pub., 1975, c1968. 96 p. ; 18 cm. (Fountain books) [BV4832.2.D39 1975] 74-28727 ISBN 0-87239-040-3 pbk. : 1.50
1. Meditations. I. Bible. English. Authorized. Selections. 1975. II. Title.

†DEAN, Herschel B. 242
Gleanings from God's word / by H. B. Dean ; cover art by Tom Greene. Cincinnati : Standard Pub., c1976. 96 p. ; 19 cm. (Fountain books) [BS491.5.D4] 75-39488 ISBN 0-87239-090-X pbk. : 1.50
1. Bible—Meditations. I. Title.

DEAN, Herschel B. 242
More Bible quotes & comments / by H. B. Dean ; cover art by John Ham. Cincinnati : Standard Pub., 1975. 96 p. ; 18 cm. (Fountain books) Selected from the author's newspaper column, Bible digest. [BV4832.2.D394] 74-28726 pbk. : 1.50
1. Meditations. I. Bible. English. Authorized. Selections. 1975. II. Title. III. Title: Bible quotes & comments.

DECHANET, Jean Marie. 242
Christian yoga. [Translation by Roland Hindmarsh] New York, Harper [1960] 196 p. illus. 22 cm. Translation of La vole du silence. [BV4813.D373 1960] 60-8142
1. Meditation. I. Title.

DECISION. 242
The quiet corner; a devotional treasury from the pages of Decision magazine, edited by Sherwood Eliot Wirt. Westwood, N.J., F. H. Revell Co., [1965] x, 116 p. 20 cm. [BV4805.D4] 65-23621
1. Devotional literature (Selections: Extracts, etc) I. Wirt, Sherwood Elliot, ed. II. Title.

DECISION 242
The quiet corner; a devotional treasury from the pages of Decision magazine, ed. by Sherwood Eliot Writ. Westwood, N.J., Revell [c.1965] x, 116p. 20cm. [BV4805.D4] 65-23621 2.50 bds.,
1. Devotional literature (Selections: Extracts, etc.) I. Wirt, Sherwood Eliot, ed. II. Title.

DECKER, James Arthur, 1917- 242
What will you have? By James A. Decker. Unity Village, Mo., Unity Books [1973] 159 p. 20 cm. [BV4832.2.D42] 73-80292 3.95
1. Meditations. I. Title.

*DEJONG, Benjamin R. 242
God's promise for today [by] Benjamin R. DeJong. Grand Rapids, Baker Book House [1974, c1951] lv. (unpaged) 18 cm. [BV4832] ISBN 0-8010-2834-5. 1.45 (pbk.)
1. Meditations. I. Title.

DELAFIELD, D A, 1913- 242
Just for today; practical meditations on the Christian's life. Washington, Review and Herald Pub. Association [1950] 382 p. 16 cm. [BV4832.D34] 50-38879
1. Devotional exercises. 2. Calendars. I. Title.

DELAFIELD, D A 1913- 242
Life at its best. Illus. by Pauline Billings. Washington, Review and Herald Pub. Assn. [1954, c1953] 126p. illus. 18cm. [BV4832.D344] 54-8245
1. Devotional literature. I. Title.

DELP, Alfred 242
Prison meditations. Introd. by Thomas Merton. [Tr. from German] New York, Macmillan [1966, c.1963] xxvi, 166p. 18cm. [BX4705.D422A53] 63-9557 1.25 pap.,
I. Title.

DELP, Alfred. 242
Prison meditations. With an introd. by Thomas Merton. [New York] Herder and Herder [1963] 193 p. 21 cm. Translation of Im Angesicht des Todes. [BX4705.D422A53] 63-9557
I. Title.

DEMAREST, Victoria Booth-Clibborn. 242
Alive and running : devotions for active people / Victoria Booth Demarest. Waco, Tex. : Word Books, c1976. 152 p. ; 23 cm. [BV4832.2.D44] 76-150529 ISBN 0-87680-482-2 : 5.95
1. Devotional exercises. I. Title.

DEPREE, Gordon. 242
Faces of God [by] Gordon and Gladis DePree. [1st ed.] New York, Harper & Row [1974] 120 p. 24 cm. [BV4832.2.D45 1974] 73-18707 ISBN 0-06-061881-7 5.95
1. Meditations. I. DePree, Gladys Lenore, 1933- joint author. II. Title.

DE ROBECK, Nesta, comp. 242
Praise the Lord, an anthology. Chicago, Franciscan Herald Press [1967] vii, 161 p. 22 cm. [BV4801.D38] 67-28206
1. Devotional literature. 2. God—Worship and love. I. Title.

DESBUQUOIS, Gustave, 1869-1959 242
Hope. Tr. by Kathleen Pond. Notre Dame, Ind., Fides [1966, c.1965] 202p. 18cm. (Fides dome bk. D-50) [BV4638.D413] 65-18122 1.25 pap.,
1. Hope—Meditations. I. Title.

DESBUQUOIS, Gustave, 1869-1959. 242
Hope, Translated by Kathleen Pond. Notre Dame, Ind., Fides Publishers [1966, c1965] 202 p. 18 cm. (A Fides dome book, D-50) [BV4638.D413] 65-18122
1. Hope — Meditations. I. Title.

DESBUQUOIT, Achille M 242
How to meditate. Translated and arr. by G. Protopapas. Milwaukee, Bruce Pub. Co. [1955] 75p. 19cm. [BV4813.D412] 55-7861
1. Meditation. I. Title.

DEVEREUX, Christina Anne, 1898- 242
Come and see; meditations for an eight day retreat, according to the "Spiritual exercises of St. Ignatius." Milwaukee, Bruce [1951] 119 p. 20 cm. [BX2182.D4] 51-8682
1. Loyola. Ignacio de, Saint, 1491-1556. Exercitia spiritualia. 2. Spiritual exercises. I. Title.

DILLARD, Annie. 242
Holy the firm / Annie Dillard. 1st ed. New York : Harper & Row, c1977. 76 p. ; 21 cm. [BV4832.2.D54 1977] 77-6883 ISBN 0-06-010528-3 : 7.50
1. Meditations. I. Title.

DOHERTY, Edward Joseph, 1890- 242
I cover God. Milwaukee, Bruce [c.1962] 207p. 22cm. 62-15225 3.75
1. Devotional literature. I. Title.

DONNE, John, 1572-1631. 242
Devotions upon emergent occasions, by John Donne. Edited by John Sparrow. With a bibliographical note by Geoffrey Keynes. Cambridge [Eng.] University Press, 1923. [Folcroft, Pa.] Folcroft Library Editions, 1972. Bibliography: p. [BV4831.D6 1972] 72-10115 ISBN 0-8414-0650-2 (lib. bdg.)
1. Meditations. I. Sparrow, John Hanbury Angus, 1906- ed. II. Title.

DOTY, William Lodewick, 1919- 242
Waiting for the Lord : meditation themes / by William L. Doty. New York : Alba House, c1977. x, 170 p. ; 22 cm. [BX2182.2.D64] 76-45384 ISBN 0-8189-0338-4 : 4.95
1. Meditations. I. Title.

DOTY, William Lodewick, 1919- 242
Waiting for the Lord : meditation themes / by William L. Doty. New York : Alba House, c1977. x, 170 p. ; 22 cm. [BX2182.2.D64] 76-45384 ISBN 0-8189-0338-4 : 4.95
1. Meditations. I. Title.

DOWD, John C. 242
You cannot hold back the dawn; faith and love in a new dimension [by] John C. Dowd. [Boston] St. Paul Editions [1974] 293 p. 21 cm. [BX2182.2.D66] 74-75619 4.95
1. Meditations. I. Title.

DRAKEFORD, John W. 242
A proverb a day keeps the troubles away / John W. Drakeford. Nashville : Broadman Press, c1976. 136 p. ; 19 cm. [BS1465.4.D7] 76-368302 ISBN 0-8054-5143-9 : 2.50
1. Bible. O.T. Proverbs—Meditations. I. Title.

DRESCHER, John M. 242
Follow me; Christian discipleship for today, by John M. Drescher. Scottdale, Pa., Herald Press [1971] 175 p. port. 21 cm. [BV4832.2.D73] 78-153967 ISBN 0-8361-1637-2 3.95
1. Meditations. I. Title.

DRESCHER, John M. 242
Spirit fruit [by] John M. Drescher. Scottdale, Pa., Herald Press, 1974. 351 p. port. 23 cm. Bibliography: p. 348-350. [BV4832.2.D74] 73-21660 ISBN 0-8361-1730-1 5.95
1. Meditations. I. Title.

DRESCHER, John M. 242
Spirit fruit [by] John M. Drescher. Scottdale, Pa., Herald Press, 1974. 351 p. port. 23 cm. Bibliography: p. 348-350. [BV4832.2.D74] 73-21660 ISBN 0-8361-1730-1 5.95
1. Meditations. I. Title.

DUE, Lucille Stroud 242
Look to this day. New York, Vantage [1962, c.1961] 94p. illus. (pt. col.) 17cm. 2.50 bds.,
I. Title.

*DUNCAN, George. 242
Living the Christian life. Chicago, Moody [1968] 127p. 17cm. .50 pap.,
I. Title.

DUNLAP, Emma Wysor. 242
For your pilgrimage. Richmond, John Knox Press [1950] 109 p. 21 cm. [BV4832.D77] 50-8009
1. Devotional exercises. I. Title.

DUNNAM, Maxie D 242
Channels of challenge [by] Maxie D. Dunnam. New York, Abingdon Press [1965] 144 p. 21 cm. [BV4832.2.D8] 65-15231
1. Meditations. I. Title.

DUNNAM, Maxie D. 242
Channels of challenge. Nashville, Abingdon [c.1965] 144p. 21cm. [BV4832.2.D8] 65-15231 2.75 bds.,
1. Meditations. I. Title.

DUNNAM, Maxie D 242
Direction and destiny [by] Maxie D. Dunnam. Nashville, Abingdon Press [1967] 144 p. 21 cm. [BV4501.2.D77] 67-11005
1. Christian life — Methodist authors. 2. Meditations. I. Title.

DUNNAM, Maxie D. 242
Direction and destiny [by] Maxie D. Dunnam. Nashville, Abingdon [c.1967] 144p. 21cm. [BV4501.2.D77] 67-11005 2.75 bds.,
1. Christian life—Methodist authors. 2. Meditations. I. Title.

*DUNSTAN, J. Leslie 242
Jesus the Christ. Illus. by Larry Channing. Philadelphia, United Church Pr. [1964, c.1963] 128p. illus. (pt. col.) 21cm. Bibl. 2.25 pap.,
I. Title.

DUX, Victor L 1903- 242
What the world needs, by Victor L. Dux. [Boston] St. Paul Editions [1968] 192 p. 22 cm. [BV4832. D85] 67-31068
1. Meditations. I. Title.

DUX, Victor L., 1903- 242
What the world needs, by Victor L. Dux, [Boston] St. Paul Eds. [1968] 192p. 22cm. [BV4832.2.D85] 67-31068 3.00; 2.00 pap.
1. Meditations. I. Title.

EBINGER, Warren R. 242
Parables for a new creation, by Warren R. Ebinger. [Nashville] The Upper Room [1973] 72 p. illus. 20 cm. [BV4832.2.E24] 73-88067 1.00
1. Meditations. I. Title.

EDENS, David, 1926- 242
Making the most of family worship [by] David and Virginia Edens. Anderson, Ind., Warner Press [1972, c1968] 128 p. 19 cm. Includes bibliographical references. [BV200.E3 1972] 72-1777 ISBN 0-87162-138-X
1. Family—Religious life. 2. Family—Prayer-books and devotions—English. I. Edens, Virginia, joint author. II. Title.

*EDMAN, V. Raymond 242
In step with God. Chicago, Moody [c.1965] 62p. illus. 21cm. Cover title: Devotional: In step with God. .95 pap.,
I. Title.

*EDMAN, V. Raymond 242
Windows in heaven. Chicago, Moody [1967] 61p. illus. 22cm. .95 pap.,
1. Devotional exercises. I. Title.

EDMAN, Victor Raymond, 1900- 242
The delights of life. Wheaton, Ill., Van Kampen Press [1954] 268p. 16cm. [BV4832.E36] 54-11370
1. Devotional literature. I. Title.

EDMAN, Victor Raymond, 1900- 242
Just why? A little book to help find the answer to one of life's most perplexing problems--why? Often this question is asked in the Bible and here are the explanations given in the Scriptures. Wheaton, Ill., Scripture Press [c1956] 88p. 18cm. [BV4832.E365] 57-28020
1. Devotional exercises. 2. Questions and answers—Theology. I. Title.

EDMAN, Victor Raymond, 1900- 242
Out of my life; lessons learned from the Scriptures on the presence of God with His own, and on the promises made by the Most High. Grand Rapids, Mich., Zondervan Pub. House [c.1961] 224p. 61-11609 3.50
1. Devotional literature. I. Title.

EDMAN, Victor Raymond, 1900- 242
Sweeter than honey: a little book of deep and personal devotion to the Saviour, with poems from John Oxenham's Bees in amber. and meditations from Bible references to honey. Chicago. Scripture Press [1956] 88p. 18cm. [BV4832.E37] 56-34614
1. Devotional exercises. I. Title.

EDMAN, Victor Raymond, 1900- 242
Then and there! The touch of the eternal upon human hearts, by V. Raymond Edman. Grand Rapids, Zondervan Pub. House [1964] 224 p. illus. 23 cm. [BS483.5.E32] 64-22837
1. Bible — Devotional literature. I. Title.

EDMAN, Victor Raymond, 1900- 242
Then and there! The touch of the eternal upon human hearts. Grand Rapids, Mich., Zondervan [c.1964] 224p. illus. 23cm. [BS483.5.E32] 64-22837 3.95 bds.,
1. Bible—Devotional literature. I. Title.

EDMONDS, Henry Morris, 1878- 242
Beginning the day. New York, Abingdon-Cokesbury Press [1951] unpaged. 18 cm. [BV245.E3] 51-14216
1. Prayers. 2. Calendars. I. Title.

EDWARDS, Charlotte Walrath. 242
View through your picture window : five minutes a day with Charlotte Edwards. New York : Hawthorn Books, c1975. 124 p. ; 22 cm. [BV4832.2.E34 1975] 74-33592 ISBN 0-8015-8314-4 : 5.95
1. Meditations. I. Title.

EDWARDS, David L. 242
God's cross in our world. Philadelphia, Westminister [c.1963] 151p. 19cm. 1.45 pap.,
I. Title.

EGAN, Harvey D. 242
The spiritual exercises and the Ignatian mystical horizon Harvey D. Egan, foreword by Karl Rahner. St. Louis : Institute of Jesuit Sources ,1976. xx, 178p. ; 23 cm. (Study aids on Jesuit topics, no. 5) Includes indexes. Bibliograhy: pp. 163-170. [BX2179.L8E33] 76-5742 ISBN 0-912422-18-1 smyth sewn : 7.00 ISBN 0-912422-14-9 pbk. : 6.00
1. Loyola, Ignacio de, Saint, 1491-1556. 2. Exercitia spiritualia. 3. Spiritual exercises. I. Title.

ELEFSIADES, Juna (Carey) 242
On life's highway. [1st ed.] New York, Vantage Press [1956] 82p. 21cm. [BV4832.E46] 56-6837
1. Devotional literature. I. Title.

ELLIOTT, George P., comp. 242
Syracuse poems, 1966-67, selected, and with a foreword by George P. Elliott. Syracuse, N.Y., Dept. of English, Syracuse University [1967] vii, 18 p. 24 cm. [PS508.C6E4] 67-18848
1. College verse—Syracuse University. I. Syracuse University. Dept. of English. II. Title.

ELLIOTT, Hubert A ed. 242
Bible words that guide me. New York, Grosset & Dunlap [1963] 248 p. ports. 22 cm. [BV4832.2.E36] 63-12936
1. Devotional literature. I. Title.

ELLIOTT, Hubert A., ed. 242
Bible words that guide me. New York, Grosset [c.1963] 248p. ports. 22cm. 63-12936 5.95, 3.95 bxd.; bds.,
1. Devotional literature. I. Title.

ELMER, Myrtie Louise, 1874- 242
1960
Conversations with God; the devotional journals of Myrtie L. Elmer, begun in her seventy-eighth year and continued until her death at the age of eighty-five. Comp., ed., introd. by Raymond E. Gibson. Grand Rapids, Mich., Eerdmans [c.1962] 70p. 23cm. front port. 62-13404 2.50
1. Devotional literature. I. Title.

ELSON, Edward Lee Roy, 1906- 242
One moment with God. [1st ed.] Garden City, N. Y., Doubleday [1951] 192 p. 13 cm. [BV4832.E57] 51-14394
1. Devotional exercises. 2. Calendars. I. Title.

ELY, Virginia 242
Devotion, for personal and group worship. [Westwood, N. J.] Revell [c.1960] 128p. 21cm. 60-13098 2.50 bds.,
1. Devotional literature. I. Title.

ELY, Virginia, 1899- 242
Adoration, devotions for personal and group worship. New York, F. H. Revell Co. [1951] 174 p. 21 cm. [BV4832.E58] 51-11791
1. Devotional literature. I. Title.

EMERSON, James Gordon, 1926- 242
The Bible and democracy / by James G. Emerson, Jr. Denver, Colo. : Emerson Communication Corp., c1976. vi, 100 p. : port. ; 23 cm. [BS1235.4.E43] 76-11395 3.50
1. Bible. O.T. Genesis—Meditations. 2. Bible. N.T. Matthew—Meditations. 3. Democracy—Meditations. I. Title.

EMMONS, Helen Keith Boulware. 242
The mature heart. Nashville, Abingdon-Cokesbury Press [1953] 160p. 26cm. [BV4832.E65] 53-5394
1. Meditations. I. Title.

ENGSTROM, Barbie, 1937- 242
Faith to see : photographs and reflections / by Barbie Engstrom. 1st ed. Bryn Mawr, Pa. : Kurios Press, c1974. [64] p. : ill. (some col.) ; 23 cm. "An original to see book." "Limited to 100 copies, signed by the author." [BV4832.2.E53] 74-25540
1. Meditations. I. Title.

EPPINGA, Jacob D. 242
Of cabbages & kings, by Jacob D. Eppinga. Grand Rapids, Zondervan Pub. House [1974] 190 p. 21 cm. "The majority of this material was previously published in the column 'Of cabbages and kings' Jacob D. Eppinga in the Banner." [BV4832.2.E66] 73-13067 1.95 (pbk.)
1. Meditations. I. Title.

ESCRIBANO, Eugenio. 242
The priest at prayer. Translated from the Spanish by B. T. Buckley. Westminster, Md., Newman Press [1954] 584p. illus. 18cm. Translation of v.1 of Meditaciones sacerdotales. [BX2186.E65] 54-4930
1. Meditations. 2. Clergy—Religious life. I. Title.

ESTEVE, Sirio. 242
The experience; a celebration of being. Photos. by James L. McGuire. [1st ed.] New York, Random House [1974] 159 p. illus. 24 cm. [BV4832.2.E8 1974] 72-11425 ISBN 0-394-48322-7 4.95
1. Meditations. I. Title.

EVANS, Glenn. 242
Life is like that / Glenn "Tex" Evans. Nashville : Tidings, [1975] xii, 74 p. ; 19 cm. [BV4832.2.E87] 74-82282
1. Evans, Glenn. 2. Meditations. I. Title.

EVANS, Richard Louis, 1906- 242
Faith, peace, and purpose [by] Richard L. Evans. Cleveland, World Pub. Co. [1966] xiv, 242 p. 21 cm. Twelfth vol. of selections from the author's "spoken word" which accompanies the CBS Sunday broadcast of sacred music by the Tabernacle Choir in Salt Lake City. [BX8639.E8F32] 66-25880
1. Mormons and Mormonism—Addresses, essays, lectures. I. Title.

EVELY, Louis, 1910- 242
In His presence. Translated by J. F. Stevenson. Garden City, N.Y., Image Books [1974, c1970] 115 p. 18 cm. Translation of Dieu et le prochain. [BX2183.E8613 1974] 74-181515 ISBN 0-385-06002-5 1.45 (pbk.).
1. Meditations. I. Title.

EVELY, Louis, 1910- 242
Rejoice! Gospel meditations. Translated by J. F. Bernard. [1st ed.] Garden City, N.Y., Doubleday, 1974. 189 p. 22 cm. Translation from Meditations d'Evangiles. [BS2555.4.E9413 1974] 74-6796 ISBN 0-385-05994-9 5.95
1. Bible. N.T. Gospels—Meditations. I. Title.

EVELYN, John, 1620-1706. 242
A devotionarie book of John Evelyn of Wotton, 1620-1706. Now first published with an introd. by Walter Frere. London, J. Murray. [Folcroft, Pa.] Folcroft Library Editions, 1973. p. Reprint of the 1936 ed. [BX5149.C5E8 1973] 73-3159 ISBN 0-8414-1903-5
1. Lord's Supper—Prayer-books and devotions—English. I. Title.

EVELYN, John, 1620-1706. 242
A devotionarie book of John Evelyn of Wotton, 1620-1706. Now first published with an introd. by Walter Frere. London, J. Murray. [Folcroft, Pa.] Folcroft Library Editions, 1973. p. Reprint of the 1936 ed. [BX5149.C5E8 1973] 73-3159 ISBN 0-8414-1903-5 10.00
1. Lord's Supper—Prayer-books and devotions—English. I. Title.

FANCHER, Wilda. 242
I have heard the rainbow / 'Wilda Fancher. Nashville : Broadman Press, c1976. 128 p. ; 20 cm. [BV4832.2.F36] 75-39141 3.95
1. Meditations. I. Title.

FENELON, Francois de Salignac 242
de la Mothe, Abp., 1651-1715.
Meditations and devotions from the writings of Francois de Salignac de la Mothe Fenelon, Archbishop of Cambrai. Selected and translated by Elizabeth C. Fenn. New York, Morehouse-Gorham Co., 1952. 143p. 19cm. [BX2183.F4F44] 52-13196
1. Devotional exercises. I. Title.

FERLITA, Ernest. 242
The way of the river / by Ernest Ferlita. New York : Paulist Press, c1977. vii, 120 p. : maps ; 19 cm. (A Deus book) Includes bibliographical references. [BS2555.4.F46] 76-45675 ISBN 0-8091-2009-7 pbk. : 1.95
1. Bible. N.T. Gospels—Meditations. I. Title.

FINKBEINER, John. 242
The Lord is . . . [Portland?Or., 1953] 86p. 21cm. [BV4832.F53] 54-21693
1. Devotional literature. I. Title.

FLEMING, David L., 1934- 242
A contemporary reading of The spiritual exercises : a companion to St. Ignatius' text / David L. Fleming. Experimental ed. St. Louis : Institute of Jesuit Sources, 1976. xv, 91 p. ; 23 cm. (Study aids on Jesuit topics ; no. 2) [BX2179.L8F56] 76-2125 ISBN 0-912422-11-4 : 2.00
1. Loyola, Ignacio de, Saint, 1491-1556. Exercitia spiritualia. 2. Spiritual exercises. I. Loyola, Ignacio de, Saint, 1491-1556. Exercitia spiritualia. II. Title. III. Series.

FOERSTER, Norman, 1887- ed. 242
Eight American writers, an anthology of American literature. Norman Foerster & Robert P. Falk, general editors. [Contributing editors]: Floyd Stovall [and others. 1st ed.] New York, Norton [c1963] xvi, 1610 p. 22 cm. Contents.Edgar Allan Poe. -- Ralph Waldo Emerson. -- Henry David Thoreau. -- Nathaniel Hawthorne. -- Herman Melville. -- Walt Whitman. -- Samuel L. Clemens. -- Henry James. Bibliography: p. 1589-1605. [PS535.F6] 62-20920
1. American literature — 19th cent. I. Falk, Robert P., 1914- joint ed. II. Title.

FOOTE, Arthur, 1911- 242
Taking down the defenses / Arthur Foote. Boston : Beacon Press, [1976], c1972. p. cm. Reprint of the ed. published by Essex Pub. Co., Essex Junction, Vt. [BV4832.2.F62 1976] 76-7743 ISBN 0-8070-1117-7 pbk. : 3.95
1. Meditations. I. Title.

FOOTE, Gaston, 1902- 242
Footnotes; sidewalk semonettes for saints and sinners. [Westwood, N.J.] Revell [1956] 124p. 20cm. [BV4832.F59] 56-7439
1. Devotional literature. I. Title.

FOOTE, Gaston, 1902- 242
How God helps. Nashville, Abingdon Press [1966] 128 p. 21 cm. [BV4832.2.F6] 66-14991
1. Devotional literature. I. Title.

FOOTE, Gaston, 1902- 242
How God helps. Nashville, Abingdon [c.1966] 128p. 21cm. [BV4832.2.F6] 66-14991 2.75 bds.,
1. Devotional literature. I. Title.

FORD, William Herschel, 1900- 242
Simple sermons on prayer, by W. Herschel Ford. Grand Rapids, Zondervan Pub. House [1969] 88 p. 21 cm. [BV213.F67] 72-95017 2.95
1. Prayer—Sermons. 2. Baptists—Sermons. 3. Sermons, American. I. Title.

FOREMAN, Kenneth Joseph, 242
1891-
Candles on the glacier; warm thoughts for a cold world, being fables and fantasies about faith for the modern mind. New York, Association Press [1956] 184p. 21cm. [BV4832.F594] 56-10657
1. Devotional literature. I. Title.

FRANCOIS DE SALES, Saint, 242
Bp. of Geneva.
Introduction to the devout life, by St. Francis de Sales. Newly translated [from the French] by Michael Day. Westminster, Md., Newman Press [1959, i.e., 1960] 261p. 17cm. flex. cl., 2.00
I. Title.

FRANCOIS DE SALES, Saint, 242
Bp. of Geneva, 1567-1622.
A diary of meditations. Cuthbert Smith, editor. Chicago, H. Regnery Co., 1957. 227p. 22cm. First published in London in 1948 under title: A year with St. Francis of Sales. [BX2178.F7 1957] 57-10265
1. Devotional calendars. I. Smith, Cuthbert, ed. II. Title.

FRANCOIS DE SALES, Saint, 242
Bp. of Geneva, 1567-1622.
Introduction to a devout life; edited with an introd. by Thomas S. Kepler. [1st ed.] Cleveland, World Pub. Co. [1952] 352 p. 16 cm. (World devotional classics) [BX2179.F8 I 54 1952a] 52-5187
1. Meditations. I. Kepler, Thomas Samuel, 1897- ed. II. Title.

FRANCOIS DE SALES, Saint, 242
Bp. of Geneva, 1567-1622.
Introduction to the devout life. Newly translated by Michael Day. Westmiinster, Md., Newman Press [1956] x, 261p. 21cm. [BX2179.F8I54 1956] 56-44100
1. Meditations. I. Day, Michael, tr. II. Title.

FRANCOIS DE SALES, Saint, 242
Bp. of Geneva, 1567-1622.
Introduction to the devout life; translated and edited by John K. Ryan. Garden City, N. Y., Image Books [1955, c1950] 314p. 18cm. (A Doubleday image book, D13) [BX2179] 55-802
1. Meditations. I. Title. II. Title: The devout life.

FRANCOIS DE SALES, Saint, 242
Bp. of Geneva, 1567-1622.
Introduction to the devout life; translated and edited by John K. Ryan, with an introd. by Douglas V. Steere. New York, Harper [1952] xxxi, 255 p. 22 cm. Bibliographical references included in "Notes" (p. 231-251) [BX2179.F8 I 54 1952] 52-10233
1. Meditations. I. Ryan, John Kenneth, 1897- ed. and tr. II. Title. III. Title: The devout life.

FRANCOIS DE SALES, Saint Bp. 242
of Geneva, 1567-1622.
Introduction to the devout life. Tr. [from French] by Michael Day. New York, Dutton [1961] 261p. (Everyman's lib., 324) 61-65003 1.95
1. Meditations. I. Day, Michael, tr. II. Title.

FRANCOIS DE SALES, Saint, 242
Bp. of Geneva, 1567-1622.
Letters from a saint; the great Christian guide to peace of mind and soul. Edited by George T. Eggleston. [1st ed.] New York, Holt [1957] 125p. 20cm. Extracts from L'introduction a la vie devote. [BX2179.F81545 1957] 57-10416
1. Meditations. I. Title.

FRANCOIS DE SALES, Saint, 242
Bp. of Geneva, 1567-1622.
The love of God, a treatise. Tr. introd. by Vincent Kerns. Westminster, Md., Newman [1963, c.1962] 561p. 20cm. (Orchard bks.) 63-2668 5.95
1. Love (Theology)—Early works to 1800. 2. God—Worship and love. 3. Spiritual life—Catholic authors. I. Title.

FRANCOIS DE SALES, Saint, 242
Bp. of Geneva, 1567-1622.
On the love of God. Translated with an introd and notes by John K. Ryan [1st ed.] Garden City, N.Y., Image Books [1963] 2 v. 18 cm. (A Doubleday image book) Translation of Traite de l'amour de Dieu. "D164A-B." Bibliography: v. 2, p. [351]-352. [BX2179.F8T74 1963] 63-16638
1. Love (Theology) — Early works to 1800. 2. God — Worship and love. 3. Spiritual love — Catholic authors. I. Title.

FRANCOIS DE SALES, Saint, 242
Bp. of Geneva, 1567-1622.
On the love of God; 2v. Tr. introd., notes by John K. Ryan. Garden City, N. Y., Doubleday [c.1963] 2v. (314; 350p.) Doubleday image bk.; D164A-B) Bibl. 63-16638 .95 pap., ea.,
1. Love (Theology)—Early works to 1800. 2. God—Worship and love. 3. Spiritual life—Catholic authors. I. Title.

FRANCOIS DE SALES, Saint Bp. 242
of Geneva, 1567-1622.
Spiritual conferences. Tr. from the Annecy text of 1895 under the supervision of Abbot Gasquet, Canon Mackey. Westminster, Md., Newman, 1962. lxxi, 406p. 19cm. 62-4748 3.95
1. Spiritual life—Catholic authors. I. Title.

FRANCOIS DE SALES, Saint, 242
Bp. of Geneva, 1567-1622.
The spiritual directory of Saint Francis de Sales for people living in the world. With a commentary by Joseph E. Woods. Westminster, Md., Newman Press, [c.]1959 124p. illus. 13cm. 59-15886 2.00 flex. lea. cl.,
1. Spiritual life—Catholic authors. I. Woods, Joseph E. II. Title.

FRANCOIS DE SALES, Saint, 242
Bp. of Geneva, 1567-1622.
Spiritual maxims; edited and with an introd. by C. F. Kelley. [1st ed.] New York, Harper [1953] 191p. 14cm. [BX2178.F68] 53-6418
1. Maxims. I. Title.

FRANCOIS DE SALES, Saint, 242
Bp. of Geneva, 1567-1622.
Spiritual maxims; edited, and with an introd. by C. F. Kelley. London, New York, Longmans, Green [1954] 191p. 17cm. [BX2178.F68 1954] 54-4285
1. Maxims. I. Title.

FRANKE, Hermann, 1908- 242
Lent and Easter; the church's spring. Translated by the Benedictines of St. John's Abbey, Collegeville, Minnesota. Westminster, Md., Newman Press, 1955 [c1939] 95p. illus. 20cm. [BV85.F64] 55-7043
1. Lent. 2. Easter. I. Title.

FRANKLIN, Jessie Merle. 242
A song about forever things. Nashville, Broadman Press [1974] 127 p. 20 cm. [BV4832.2.F63] 73-93904 ISBN 0-8054-8234-2 1.50 (pbk.)
1. Devotional literature. I. Title.

FRANTZ, George Arthur. 242
Book of mercies. [1st ed.] Indianapolis, Bobbs-Merrill [1952] 128 p. 20 cm. [BV4832.F66] 52-10692
1. Devotional literature. I. Title.

FRAZIER, Claude Albee, 1920- 242
Devotionals by a physician, by Claude A. Frazier. With forewords by Billy Graham, Charles A. Trentham, and Theron D. Price. Springfield, Ill., C. C. Thomas [1970] xix, 201 p. 24 cm. [BS483.5.F75] 71-100423
1. Bible—Devotional literature. I. Title.

FREEMAN, James Dillet. 242
A case for believing. [1st ed.] Garden City, N.Y., Doubleday, 1972. viii, 152 p. 22 cm. [BV4832.2.F64] 72-111164 4.95
1. Meditations. I. Title.

FREEMAN, James Dillet. 242
Look with eyes of love. Illustrated by Betty Fraser. [1st ed.] Garden City, N.Y., Doubleday, 1969. vi, 86 p. illus. 22 cm. [BJ1581.2.F7] 69-15887 3.95
1. Conduct of life. I. Title.

FREER, Harold Freer 242
Christian disciplines; meditations for prayer classes. New York, Pageant Press [c.1960] 266p. Bibl. 3.50
I. Title.

FREER, Harold Wiley. 242
Two or three together; a manual for prayer groups, by Harold Wiley Freer and Francis B. Hall. [1st ed.] New York, Harper [1954] 187p. 22cm. [BV4832.F692] 54-5849
1. Devotional exercises. I. Hall, Francis B., joint author. II. Title.

FRENCH, Marion Flood. 242
Silver Saturdays. Nashville, Abingdon Press [1966] 96 p. 18 cm. 44 meditations. [BV4832.2.F65] 66-15727
1. Meditations. I. Title.

FRENCH, Marion Flood 242
Silver Saturdays. Nashville, Abingdon [c.1966] 96p. 18cm. 44 meditations. [BV4832.2.F65] 66-15727 2.00 bds.,
1. Meditations. I. Title.

FRENCH, Mary Montague 242
(Billings) comp.
Thoughts and meditations from the notebooks

of Mary M. Billings French. Compiled and edited by Anna V. Rice. New York, c1955. 53p. illus. 24cm. [BV4805.F7] 55-25499
1. Devotional literature (Selections: Extracts, etc.) I. Title.

FRIDY, Wallace. 242
Adults at worship. New York, Abingdon Press [1959] 128 p. 16 cm. [BV4832.2.F7] 59-8195
1. Devotional exercises. I. Title.

FRIDY, Wallace. 242
Devotions for adult groups. New York, Abingdon Press [1956] 127p. 16cm. [BV4832.F6938] 56-10144
1. Devotional exercises. 2. Worship programs. I. Title.

FRIDY, Wallace. 242
Devotions for personal and group renewal. Nashville, Abingdon Press [1969] 144 p. 18 cm. [BV4832.2.F712] 78-86162 2.75
1. Devotional exercises. I. Title.

FRIDY, Wallace. 242
A light unto my path. New York, Abingdon-Cokesbury Press [1953] 128p. 16cm. [BV4832.F6943] 53-10008
1. Devotional exercises. I. Title.

FROHNE, Marydel D j 242
Christians together, by Marydel D. And Victor M. Forhne. Illustrated by Eric Von Schmidt. Boston, United Church Press [1964] v. 90 p. col. illus. 23 cm. "Part of the United Church curriculum, prepared and published by the Division of Christian Education and the Division of Publication of the United Church Board for Homeland Ministries." "A hymn to read or sing, O praise ye the Lord" with keyboard acc. (p. 32) [BV85.F67] 64-19470
1. United Church of Christ — Prayer-books and devotions. 2. Lent-Prayer-books and devotions — English. 3. Children — Prayer-books and devotions — 1961- I. Frohne, Victor M. joint author. II. United Church Board for Homeland Ministries. Division of Christian Education. III. United Church Board for Homeland Ministries. Division of Publications. IV. Title.

FROHNE, Victor M., joint author. j 242
Christians togethers, by Marydel D. and Victor M. Forhne. Boston, United Church Press [1964] v. 90 p. col. illus. 23 cm. "Part of the United Church curriculum, prepared and published by the Division of Christian Education and the Division of Publication of the United Church Board for Homeland Ministries." "A hymn to read or sing, O praise ye the Lord" with keyboard acc. (p. 32) [BV85.F67] 64-19470
1. United Church of Christ — Prayer-books and devotions. 2. Lent-Prayer-books and devotions — English. 3. Children — Prayer-books and devotions — 1961- I. United Church Board for Homeland Ministries. Division of II. Title. III. Title: Christians together,

FULTON, Mary Beth. 242
Highways of worship; uniting the worship of God with life's daily experiences. Philadelphia, Judson Press [1955] 95p. 21cm. [BV4832.F8] 55-8803
1. Meditations. 2. Worship programs. I. Title.

GARDNER, Edmund Garratt, 1869-1935, comp. 242
The cell of self-knowledge: seven early English mystical treatises printed by Henry Pepwell in 1521, edited with an introd. and notes by Edmund G. Gardner. New York, Cooper Square Publishers, 1966. xxvii, 134 p. front. 17 cm. (The Medieval library) "Pepwells volume has been made the basis of the present edition of these seven treatises; but in each case, the text has been completely revises." [BV4805.G3 1966] 66-25702
1. Devotional literature. I. Pepwell, Henry, d. 1540. II. Title.

GARDNER, Edmund Garratt, 1869-1935, comp. 242
The cell of self-knowledge: seven early English mystical treatises printed by Henry Pepwell in 1521. edited with an introd. and notes by Edmund G. Gardner. New York, Cooper Square Publishers, 1966. xxvii, 134 p. front. 17 cm. (The Medieval library) "Pepwell's volume has been made the basis of the present edition of these seven treatises; but, in each case, the text has been completely revised." [BV4805.G3 1966] 66-25702
1. Devotional literature. I. Pepwell, Henry, d. 1540. II. Title.

GARESCHE, Edward Francis, 1876- 242
Your stay in the hospital; thoughts of information, cheer, consolation and encouragement for the sick, especially in hospitals. New York, Vista Maria Press [1951] 112 p. 19 cm. Published in 1925 under title: The patient's book. [BX2170.S5G3 1951] 51-28823
1. Sick. 2. Sick—Prayer-books and devotions—English. 3. Catholic Church—Prayer-books and devotions—English. I. Title.

GARNER, James Herbert. 242
Just a half-a-minute. Battle Creek, Mich. [c1957] 117p. 23cm. Short messages previously presented and recorded on an automatic telephone device. [BV4832.G336] 57-22937
1. Devotional exercises. I. Title.

GATES, Carl M 242
Faith for daily living. South Pasedena, Calif., Onconta Congretional Church (United Church of Christ) 1963. 122 p. illus. 23 cm. [BV4832.2.G3] 63-16987
1. Devotional literature. I. Title.

GEIB, Richard W. 242
Complete with commas, by Richard W. Geib. Illus. by Keith Bratton. St. Louis, Bethany Press [1968] [64] p. illus. 21 cm. [BV4832.2.G44] 68-55948
1. Meditations. I. Title.

GEIER, Woodrow Augustus. 242
A wayfarer's book of devotion [by] Woodrow A. Geier. Nashville, Abingdon Press [1973] 124 p. 21 cm. [BV4832.2.G445] 72-7411 ISBN 0-687-44215-X 2.95
1. Meditations. I. Title.

GEMME, Mike. 242
Song of love / Mike Gemme. Wheaton, Ill. : Victor Books, c1975. 64 p. ; 20 cm. [BS1485.4.G45] 75-17169 ISBN 0-88207-806-2 : 2.95
1. Bible. O.T. Song of Solomon—Meditations. 2. Marriage—Meditations. I. Title.

GEMME, Mike. 242
Song of love / Mike Gemme. Wheaton, Ill. : Victor Books, c1975. 64 p. ; 20 cm. [BS1485.4.G45] 75-17169 ISBN 0-88207-806-2 : 2.95
1. Bible. O.T. Song of Solomon—Meditations. 2. Marriage—Meditations. I. Title.

GENESIS and the Christian life; 242 daily devotions and Bible studies. [Edited by Betty Pershing] Glendale, Calif., G/L Regal Books [1970] 138 p. 18 cm. Cover title: Studies in Genesis and the Christian life. [BV4832.2.G46] 73-112034 0.95
1. Devotional exercises. I. Pershing, Betty, ed. II. Title: Studies in Genesis and the Christian life.

GIBBONEY, Charles H. 242
Worth thinking about : 60 pointed reflections / by Charles H. Gibboney. Saint Louis : Bethany Press, c1976. p. cm. [BV4832.2.G5] 76-43073 ISBN 0-8272-4210-7 : 3.95
1. Meditations. I. Title.

GILE, Louisa Boyd. 242
My book of personal devotions. New York, Morehouse-Gorham Co. [1953] 96p. illus. 19cm. Includes bibliography. [BV4832.G53] 53-13016
1. Devotional literature. I. Title.

GINIGER, Kenneth Seeman, 1919- ed. 242
The compact treasury of inspiration. [1st ed.] New York Hawthorn Books [1955] 301 p. illus. 20 cm. [PS507.G53] 55-6604
1. American literature. 2. English literature. I. Title. II. Title: Treasury of inspiration.

GIUDICE, Liliane, 1913- 242
The gift of retirement. Translated by David E. Green. Richmond, Va., John Knox Press [1973] 64 p. 21 cm. Translation of Der Tag der Pensionierung. [BV4580.G5813] 73-5344 ISBN 0-8042-2070-0 3.95
1. Aged—Prayer-books and devotions—English. I. Title.

GIUDICE, Liliane, 1913- 242
The gift of retirement. Translated by David E. Green. Richmond, Va., John Knox Press [1973] 64 p. 21 cm. Translation of Der Tag der Pensionierung. [BV4580.G5813] 73-5344 ISBN 0-8042-2070-0 3.95
1. Aged—Prayer-books and devotions—English. I. Title.

GLOBUS, Alfred R. 242
Veritism. [1st ed. Long Island City, N.Y., Distributed by the Veritism Foundation, 1968?] 2 v. in 1. 24 cm. [BV4832.2.G54] 79-274615
1. Meditations. I. Veritism Foundation. II. Title.

GOCKEL, Herman William, 1906- 242
Answer to anxiety. St. Louis, Concordia [c.1961] 179p. 61-13455 3.00
1. Peace of mind. I. Title.

GOCKEL, Herman William, 1906- 242
Give your life a lift; devotions in the form of modern parables [by] Herman W. Gockel. St. Louis, Concordia Pub. House [1968] 161 p. 21 cm. [BV4832.2.G57] 68-20262
1. Devotional exercises. I. Title.

GOLDMAN, June Parker. 242
To touch the sky. Nashville, Abingdon Press [1969] 144 p. 21 cm. [BV4832.2.G62] 70-84723 2.95
1. Meditations. I. Title.

GOODSELL, Fred Field, 1880- 242
Reflections based on the Bible,'Fenelon [and] a Statement of Christian faith. Milford, N.H. Hunter Press, 1964 115 p. 24 cm. "Statement of Christian faith": p. [108] Contents.CONTENTS. -- Through the Bible book by book. -- On reading Fenelon's Christian perfection. -- On pondering the Statement of faith approved by the United Church of Christ. [BS483.5G6] 64-25798
1. Fenelon, Francois-de Sallignac de La Mothe, Abp. 1651-1715. Instructions et avis. 2. Bible — Devotional Literature. 3. United Church of Christ, Statement of faith. I. United Church of Christ. Statement of faith. II. Title.

GORDON, Arthur. 242
A touch of wonder : a book to help people stay in love with life / Arthur Gordon. Old Tappan, N.J. : F. H. Revell Co., [1974] 251 p. ; 21 cm. [BV4832.2.G63] 74-23794 6.95 ISBN 0-8007-0695-1 :
1. Meditations. I. Title.

GORDON, Samuel Dickey, 1859-1936 242
Quiet talks on prayer, by S. D. Gordon. Westwood, N. J., Revell [1967] 159p. 18cm. (Spire bk.) [BV210.G65] .60 pap.,
1. Prayer. I. Title.

GORDON, Samuel Dickey, 1859-1936. 242
The treasury of quiet talks, selections. Westwood, N. J., Revell ['1951] 251 p. 21 cm. [BV4832.G683] 51-14858
1. Devotional literature. I. Title.

GRANDMAISON, Leonce de [Septime Leonce de Grandmaison] 1868-1927 242
Tongues of fire. Tr. [from French] by M. Angeline Bouchard. Notre Dame. Ind., Fides [1965, c.1961] 214p. 20cm. (Spire bk.,) [BX2375.B673] 61-17234 1.95 pap.,
1. Retreats. 2. Meditations. I. Title.

GRAVES, Richard W. 242
Saints and silhouettes; musings and meditations of an editor. Pittsburgh, Board of Christian Education of the United Presbyterian Church of North America, 1951. 152 p. 21 cm. [BV4832.G783] 52-17418
1. Devotional literature. I. Title.

GREAT phrases of the Christian language; 242 a devotional book [by] Roger L. Shinn [and others] Philadelphia, United Church Press [1958] 121p. 20cm. [BV4805.G68] 58-10540
1. Devotional literature. I. Shinn, Roger Lincoln.

GRIFFIN, Robert, 1925- 242
I never said I didn't love you / by Robert Griffin. New York : Paulist Press, c1977. 119 p. ; 19 cm. (Emmaus books) [BX2182.2.G74] 76-24442 ISBN 0-8091-1989-7 pbk. : 1.45
1. Griffin, Robert, 1925- 2. Meditations. I. Title.

GRIFFIN, Robert, 1925- 242
I never said I didn't love you / by Robert Griffin. New York : Paulist Press, c1977. 119 p. ; 19 cm. (Emmaus books) [BX2182.2.G74] 76-24442 ISBN 0-8091-1989-7 pbk. : 1.45
1. Griffin, Robert, 1925- 2. Meditations. I. Title.

GRIFFITH, Arthur Leonard, 1920- 242
God and His People, the renewal of the church. Nashville, Abingdon [1961, c.1960] 84p. 61-65540 1.00
1. Church. 2. Meditations. I. Title.

GRISEZ, Wanda R. 242
Cadence : the song of love / Wanda R. Grisez. [St. Petersburg, Fla. : Valkyrie Press, c1976] 141 p. ; 18 cm. [BV4832.2.G67] 76-562 ISBN 0-912760-18-4 : 5.00
1. Meditations. I. Title.

*GRUMAN, Lawrence L. 242
Members one of another. Illus. by Nathan Goldstein. Philadelphia, United Church Pr. [c.1964] 60p. illus. 21cm. (MHI-3) 1.15 pap.,
I. Title.

GUARDINI, Romana 242
The way of the Cross [Tr. from German] Woodcuts by Michael Biggs. Chicago, Scepter Pubs. [1963] 77p. illus. 18cm. (Scepter-Prow ser.) .95 pap.,
I. Title.

GUILLAUME DE SAINT-THIERRY, 1085(ca.)-1148? 242
The meditations of William of St. Thierry. Meditativae orationes. Translated from the Latin by a religious of C. S. M. V. With an introd. and notes. New York, Harper [1954] 108p. 20cm. [BX2180.G79] 54-12741
1. Meditations. I. Title.

GUNN, John R. 242
Good morning, Lord : devotions on the hope of glory / John R. Gunn. Grand Rapids : Baker Book House, c1977. 80 p. ; 19 cm. Consists of selections from the author's newspaper column, Short sermon for today, published by the Fort Wayne journal gazette. [BV4832.2.G77] 77-151327 ISBN 0-8010-3706-9 : 2.45
1. Meditations. I. Title.

GUSTAVSON, Eric J. 242
God's hand I see; vacation meditations. Rock Island, Ill., Augustana [c.1962] 104p. illus. 62-10420 2.00 pap.,
1. Meditations. I. Title.

GWYNNE, John Harold, 1899- 242
The chariots of God; weekly devotional meditations of deliverance. [1st ed.] Cleveland, World Pub. Co. [c1955] 120p. 21cm. [GV4832.G9] 55-5280
1. Meditations. I. Title.

GYLDENVAND, Lily M 1917- 242
Of all things. [Essays] Minneapolis, Augsburg Pub. House [1956*C117p. 20cm. 117p. 20cm. [BV4832.G93] 56-7250
1. Devotional literature. I. Title.

GYLDENVAND, Lily M 1917- 242
So you're only human. Minneapolis, Augsburg Pub. House [1957] 118p. 16cm. [BV4832.G94] 57-14795
1. Devotional literature. I. Title.

HACKMAN, Ruth Y. 242
All things and stuff [by] Ruth Y. Hackman. Westwood, N.J., F. H. Revell Co. [1967] 127 p. 21 cm. [BV4832.2.H22] 67-22569
1. Meditations. I. Title.

HALL, Bennie Caroline. ed. 242
The spiritual diary, a day-by-day inspirational guide. [New ed.] New York, Austin-Phelps, 1951. unpaged. 20 cm. [BV4810.H224 1951] 51-13322
1. Devotional exercises. 2. Calendars. I. Title.

HALL, Ennen Reaves. 242
Gifts from the Bible. Drawings by Ismar David. [1st ed.] New York, Harper & Row [1968] 114 p. illus. 27 cm. [BS483.5.H27] 68-11734
1. Bible—Meditations. I. Title.

HALLMARK, Erma Elder. 242
Here in this house / Erma Hallmark. Atlanta : John Knox Press, [1975] vii, 118 p. ; 21 cm. [BV4832.2.H26] 74-3716 ISBN 0-8042-2320-3 : 4.95
1. Meditations. I. Title.

HALTNER, Robert E 242
Moments with Jesus; a Christ-centered volume of weekly meditations for the entire year, by Robert E. Haltner. Boston, Christopher Pub. House [c1965] 278 p. 21 cm. [BV4832.2.H27] 64-8590
1. Meditations. 2. Devotional calendars—Lutheran Church. I. Title.

HALTNER, Robert E. 242
Moments with Jesus; a Christ-centered volume of weekly meditations for the entire year, Boston, Christopher Pub. [c.1965] 278p. 21cm. [BV4832.2.H27] 64-8590 3.95 bds.,
1. Meditations. 2. Devotional calendars—Lutheran Church. I. Title.

HANCOCK, Harry N 242
Red letter days; a series of meditations on the holy days of the Christian year. London, New York, Longmans, Green [1956] 156p. 18cm. [BV4832.H34 1956] 56-3195
1. Church year— Meditations. I. Title.

HANEY, Thomas R. 242
Gather up the fragments, by T. R. Haney. New York, Sheed and Ward [1971] vi, 148 p. illus. 21 cm. [BX2182.2.H35] 72-162381 ISBN 0-8362-1196-0 4.95
1. Meditations. I. Title.

HARBAUGH, Henry, 1817-1867. 242
The golden censer; devotions for young Christians. Philadelphia, Christian Education Press [1954] 203p. 18cm. [BV4834.H267] 54-12384
1. Devotiooal exercises. 2. Reformed Church in the United States—Prayer-books and devotions—English. I. Title.

HARDON, John A 242
All my liberty; theology of the Spiritual exercises. Westminster, Md., Newman Press, 1959. 207p. 22cm. Includes bibliography. [BX2179.L8H3] 59-10405
1. Loyola, Ignacio de, Saint. 1491-1556. Exercitia spiritualia. I. Title.

HARING, Bernhard, 1912- 242
Celebrating joy. [Translated by Edward Quinn. New York] Herder and Herder [1970] 86 p. 21 cm. Translation of Die Freude verkunden. [BX2184.H2713] 78-110790 4.50
1. Meditations. I. Title.

HARKNESS, Georgia Elma, 1891- 242
Grace abounding [by] Georgia Harkness. Nashville, Abingdon Press [1969] 192 p. 21 cm. [BV4832.2.H315] 74-84719 3.75
1. Devotional exercises. I. Title.

*HARRELL, Costen J. 242
Friends of God. Nashville, Abingdon [1967, c.1958] 158p. 16cm. (Apex bks., AA4) 1.25 pap.,
1. Devotional literature. I. Title.

HARRELL, Costen Jordan, 1885- 242
Walking with God. 2d ed. Nashville, Abingdon [1962, c.1928] 186p. 16cm. (Apex bks., J4) 62-3916 .95 pap.,
1. Devotional exercises. I. Title.

HARRELL, Costen Jordan, 1885- 242
The wonders of His grace [by] Costen J. Harrell. Nashville, Abingdon [1966] 126p. 18cm. [BV4832.2.H32] 66-19808 2.50 bds.,
1. Devotional literature. I. Title.

HARRELL, Irene Burk. 242
Lo, I am with you; prayersteps to faith. Plainfield, N.J., Logos International [1970] xiv, 108 p. 21 cm. [BT732.5.H37] 78-109243 ISBN 9-12-106077- 3.95
1. Faith-cure. I. Title.

HARRELL, Irene Burk. 242
Muddy sneakers and other family hassles [by] Irene Burk Harrell and Tommy, Alice, Dino, Susan, 'Guerite, and Maria. Nashville, Abingdon Press [1974] 108 p. illus. 21 cm. [BV255.H34] 73-15575 ISBN 0-687-27295-5 3.50
1. Family—Prayer-books and devotions—English. I. Title.

HARRELL, Irene Burk. 242
Security blankets family size [by] Irene Harrell. Waco, Tex., Word Books [1973] 139 p. 23 cm. [BV4832.2.H324] 73-76258 3.95
1. Meditations. I. Title.

HARRELL, Irene Burk. 242
Super prayerables : to add a glow to your life / Irene Burk Harrell. Los Angeles : Acton House, c1977. x, 103 p. ; 23 cm. [BV4832.2.H3242] 77-152206 0-89202 ISBN pbk. : 3.95
1. Meditations. I. Title.

HARRIS, Frederick Brown, 1883- 242
Spires of the spirit. New York, Abingdon-Cokesbury Press [1952] 174 p. 20 cm. [BV4832.H378] 52-5382
1. Devotional literature. I. Title.

HARRIS, Frederick Brown, 1883-1970. 242
Senate prayers and Spires of the spirit. Edited by J. D. Phelan. St. Louis, Bethany Press [1970] 175 p. 23 cm. [BV280.H34] 75-137366 ISBN 0-8272-3412-0 4.95
1. Legislative bodies—Chaplains' prayers. 2. Meditations. I. Title.

HARRISON, Margaret Wynne. 242
Angels then and now / by Margaret Wynne Harrison. Fort Worth, Tex. : Branch-Smith, [1975] xiv, 73 p. : ill. ; 23 cm. [PS3558.A6714A82] 75-2691 ISBN 0-87706-061-4 : 5.95
I. Title.

HARRISVILLE, Roy A. 242
Play on your harp : meditations on Biblical themes / Roy A. Harrisville. Minneapolis : Augsburg Pub. House, [1975] 112 p. ; 20 cm. [BS483.5.H29] 74-14188 ISBN 0-8066-1471-4 : 2.95
1. Bible—Meditations. I. Title.

*HARTLEY, William. 242
In the beginning God; jottings from Genesis. Grand Rapids, Baker Book House, [1975] 110 p. 18 cm. [BV4811] ISBN 0-8010-4132-5 1.45 (pbk.)
1. Bible—Meditations—O.T. I. Title.

HARTMAN, Marvin J 242
'He restoreth my soul' thoughts for meditation. Anderson, Ind., Warner Press [1957] 96p. 16cm. [BV4832.H42] 57-4520
1. Devotional exercises. I. Title.

HASKIN, Dorothy (Clark) 1905- 242
God in my family, by Dorothy C. Haskin. Anderson, Ind., Warner Press [1970] 95 p. 21 cm. [BV255.H36] 75-123007
1. Family—Prayer-books and devotions. I. Title.

HASKIN, Dorothy (Clark) 1905- 242
God in my kitchen; fifty-two thoughts for homemakers. Anderson, Ind., Warner Press [1958] 96p. 21cm. [BV4832.H415] 58-6418
1. Devotional exercises. I. Title.

HASKIN, Dorothy (Clark) 1905- comp. 242
Meditations from around the world [comp. by Dorothy C. Haskin] Anderson, Ind., Warner Pr. [1966] 96p. illus., ports. 21cm. Cover title: Open my eyes; meditations from around the world. [BV4805.H33] 66-23606 2.00, pap, plastic bdg. 2.00, pap., plastic bdg.
1. Devotional exercises. 2. Devotional exercises. I. round the world. II. Title. III. Title: Open my eyes.

HASTINGS, Robert J. 242
Devotional talks on everyday objects [by] Robert J. Hastings. Nashville, Broadman Press [1968] viii, 136 p. 21 cm. [BV4832.2.H334] 68-26919 3.25
1. Devotional exercises. I. Title.

HASTINGS, Robert J. 242
Letters from home : vignettes of truth in everyday experiences / Robert J. Hastings. Nashville : Broadman Press, c1976. 96 p. ; 18 cm. [BV4832.2.H3343] 75-35394 ISBN 0-8054-5140-4 : 2.75
1. Meditations. I. Title.

HAVNER, Vance, 1901- 242
By the way; meditations of a Christian pilgrim. New York, Revell [1950] 89 p. 20 cm. [BV4832.H49512] 50-4953
1. Devotional literature. I. Title.

HAVNER, Vance, 1901- 242
It is toward evening. Westwood, N.J., Revell [1968] 127 p. 20 cm. [BV4832.2.H335] 68-17090
1. Devotional literature. I. Title.

HAVNER, Vance, 1901- 242
Jesus only; devotional meditations. [Old Tappan, N.J.] F. H. Revell Co. [1969] 127 p. 20 cm. [BX6333.H345J4 1969] 76-2370 3.50
1. Baptists—Sermons. 2. Sermons, American. I. Title.

HAVNER, Vance, 1901- 242
Living in kingdom come. Westwood, N. J., Revell [1967] 128p. 20cm. [BV4832.2.H336] 67-14777 2.95 bds.,
1. Devotional literature. I. Title.

HAVNER, Vance, 1901- 242
Peace in the valley. [Westwood, N. J.] F. H. Revell Co. [1962] 124p. 17cm. [BV4832.2.H34] 62-17106
1. Devotional literature. I. Title.

HAVNER, Vance, 1901- 242
Rest for the weary. [Westwood, N. J.] Revell [1956] 154p. 17cm. [BV4832.H4993] 56-7441
1. Devotional literature. I. Title.

HAVNER, Vance, 1901- 242
Seasonings. Old Tappan, N.J., Revell [1970] 127 p. 20 cm. [BV4832.2.H35] 78-123064 3.50
1. Meditations. I. Title.

HAVNER, Vance, 1901- 242
Song at twilight. Old Tappan, N.J., F. H. Revell [1974, c1973] 128 p. 19 cm. [BV4832.2.H353 1974] 73-16423 ISBN 0-8007-0635-8 3.95
1. Meditations. I. Title.

HAVNER, Vance Houston, 1901- 242
Peace in the valley. [Westwood, N.J.] Revell [c.1962] 124p. 17cm. 62-17106 2.50
1. Devotional literature. I. Title.

HEFFNER, Christine Fleming. 242
Parables for the present / Christine Fleming Heffner. New York : Hawthorn Books, [1974] xii, 129 p. ; 22 cm. [BV4832.2.H39 1974] 73-14234 4.95
1. Meditations. I. Title.

HEFFNER, Christine Fleming. 242
The Way of Light; illustrated by Gedge Harmon. New York, Morehouse-Gorham Co., 1954. 100p. illus. 21cm. [BV4832.H54] 54-9441
1. Devotional literature. I. Title.

HEFLEY, James C. 242
Thinkables; meditations for people who mean it [by] James C. Hefley. Old Tappan, N.J., Revell [1970] 158 p. 22 cm. [BV4832.2.H4] 77-96251 3.95
1. Meditations. I. Title.

HELVERSON, Ralph N 242
Speak to the earth; a devotional manual. [Boston, Starr King Press, 1955] 63p. 16cm. [BV4832.H563] 55-11328
1. Devotional exercises. I. Title.

HEMBREE, Charles R. 242
Pocket of pebbles; inspirational thoughts on the fruits of the spirit. [by] Charles R. Hembree. Grand Rapids, Baker Book House [1969] 128 p. 20 cm. [BT769.H4] 71-97508 2.95
1. Gifts, Spiritual. I. Title.

HEMBREE, Charles R. 242
Voice of the turtledove [by] Charles R. Hembree. Grand Rapids, Mich., Baker Book House [1971] 140 p. 21 cm. [BV4832.2.H42] 79-149847 ISBN 0-8010-4015-9 2.95
1. Meditations. I. Title.

HERRING, Ralph A. 242
The cycle of prayer [by] Ralph A. Herring. Nashville, Brodman [1966] 80p. 21cm. [BV210.2H43] 67-12170 2.50 bds.,
1. Prayer. I. Title.

HERRON, Orley R. 242
Input/output; some thoughts for today, by Orley R. Herron and Betty Alexander. Chicago, Moody Press [1970] 126 p. 18 cm. [BV4832.2.H44] 75-123153 2.95
1. Meditations. I. Alexander, Betty, joint author. II. Title.

HERZBERGER, Frederik William, 1859-1930. 24.2
Family altar; brief daily devotions based on selected Scripture texts Rev. by Harry N. Huxhold. Rev. [i.e. 3d] ed. Saint Louis, Concordia Pub. House, 1964. v. 382 p. 24 cm. [BV255.H47] 63-23487
1. Family — Prayer-books and devotions — English. 2. Lutheran Church — Prayer-books and devotions — English. 3. Devotional calendar — Lutheran Church. I. Title.

HETTICH, Blaise, comp. 242
Prayer starters from the Bible for every mood [compiled] by Blaise Hettich. St. Meinrad, Ind., Abbey Press, 1972. vii, 87 p. illus. 18 cm. (A Priority edition) [BV228.H46] 72-89196 3.95
1. Bible—Prayers. I. Title.

HEWITT, Mary Elizabeth (Moore) b. 1807, ed. 242
Laurel leaves; a chaplet woven by the friends of the late Mrs. Osgood. New York, Lamport, Blakeman & Law, 1854. 347p. illus. 24cm. 'Originally published as 'The memorial.'' 'Frances Sargent Osgood,' by R. W. Griswold: p. 13-30. [PS535.H4 1854] 10-20231
1. Osgood, Frances Sargent (Locke) 1811-1850. I. Griswold, Rufus Wilmot, 1815-1857. II. Title.

HICKS, Beulah Kay. 242
Organ notes of dawn; a book of simple beauty. Ideas for devotions, comfort for the bewildered, inspiration to the young. San Antonio, Naylor [1950] 169 p. 20 cm. [BV4832.H59] 50-6828
1. Devotional literature. I. Title.

HIESBERGER, Jean Marie. 242
You have given us today; a photo/meditation book. With photos by John Glaser. Design by William Kautz. New York, Paulist Press [1973] 63 p. illus. 18 cm. [BX2182.2.H53] 72-93025 ISBN 0-8091-1750-9 1.50 (pbk.)
1. Meditations. 2. Prayers. I. Title.

HILLMAN, Ruth Estelyn, 1925- 242
Four-letter words that are good / by Ruth E. Hillman. Cincinnati : Standard Pub., [1974] 96 p. ; 18 cm. (Fountain books) [BV4832.2.H55] 74-77027 ISBN 0-87239-016-0 pbk. : 1.50
1. Meditations. I. Title.

HINNEBUSCH, Paul. 242
Dynamic contemplation; inner life for modern man. New York, Sheed and Ward [1970] xviii, 300 p. 22 cm. Includes bibliographical references. [BV5091.C7H5] 78-106154 6.50
1. Contemplation. I. Title.

HOBBS, Herschel H. 242
Showers of blessings [by] Herschel H. Hobbs. Grand Rapids, Mich., Baker Book House [1973] 122 p. 20 cm. [BT382.H62] 72-97560 ISBN 0-8010-4070-1 2.95
1. Beatitudes—Meditations. 2. Meditations. I. Title.

HOES, Jack. 242
I speak, as heard by Jack Hoes. [Hilo, Hawaii, I Speak Press, 1972] 1 v. (unpaged) 14 cm. [BV4832.2.H62] 74-152418
1. Meditations. I. Title.

HOFFER, Gertrude (Schafer) 242
Glimpses of God meditative essays. [1st ed.] New York, Pageant Press [1957] 105p. 21cm. [BV4832.H6] 57-
1. Devotional literature. I. Title.

HOFFMANN, Oswald C. J. 242
Hurry home where you belong [by] Oswald C. J. Hoffmann. St. Louis, Concordia Pub. House [1970] 98 p. 20 cm. [BX8066.H583H85] 76-113868
1. Lutheran Church—Sermons. 2. Sermons, American. I. Title.

HOFFMANN, Oswald C J 242
Life crucified. Grand Rapids, Eerdmans [1959] 125p. 22cm. [BV4832.2.H6] 59-6956
1. Devotional literature. I. Title.

HOGAN, Bernice. 242
Listen for a rainbow. Westwood, N.J. Revell [1965] 108 p. 21 cm. [BV4832.2.H63] 65-14799
1. Devotional exercises. I. Title.

HOGAN, Bernice 242
Listen for a rainbow. Westwood, N. J., Revell [c.1965] 108p. 21cm. [BV4832.2.H63] 65-14799 2.50 bds.,
1. Devotional exercises. I. Title.

HOLLIS, Marcia. 242
Down to earth; thoughts on God and gardening. New York, Seabury Press [1971] 144 p. 21 cm. [BV4501.2.H56] 77-131952 3.95
1. Christian life—Anglican authors. I. Title.

HOLMES, Marjorie, 1910- 242
How can I find you, God? / Marjorie Holmes ; illustrated by Betty Fraser. 1st ed. Garden City, N.Y. : Doubleday, 1975. 202 p. : ill. ; 22 cm. [BV4832.2.H636] 74-25107 ISBN 0-385-04437-2 : 5.95
1. Meditations. I. Title.

HOLTERMANN, Carla. 242
Days aglow. Old Tappan, N.J., F. H. Revell Co. [1970] 123 p. 21 cm. [BV4832.2.H638] 74-123063
1. Meditations. I. Title.

HOLTERMANN, Carla. 242
Trustful living. Old Tappan, N.J., Revell [1969] 64 p. 17 cm. [BV4832.2.H64] 69-20147 1.50
1. Meditations. I. Title.

HONEYCUTT, Roy Lee. 242
Crisis and response [by] Roy L. Honeycutt. New York, Abingdon Press [1965] 176 p. 21 cm. Bibliography: p. 168-171. [BS483.5.H6] 65-10549
1. Bible. O.T. — Meditations. I. Title.

HONEYCUTT, Roy Lee 242
Crisis and response [Nashville] Abingdon [c.1965] 176p. 21cm. Bibl. [BS483.5.H6] 65-10549 3.50
1. Bible. O.T.—Meditations. I. Title.

HONG, Edna (Hatlestad), 1913- 242
Clues to the kingdom; a mystery. Book design and illus. by Ollie Jacobson Jensen. Minneapolis, Augsburg Pub. House [1968] 93 p. illus. 21 cm. [BV4832.2.H65] 68-13423
1. Devotional literature. I. Title.

HOOD, C Azella. 242
Guidance for the new age; inspirational essays and advice, recorded by C. Azella Hood. [1st ed.] New York, Exposition Press [1957] 68p. 21cm. [BV4832] 57-4086
1. Devotional literature. I. Title.

HOPKINS, Mary, 1941- 242
Celebrating family prayer services / Mary Hopkins. New York : Paulist Press, c1975. x, 153 p. : ill. ; 28 cm. [BX2170.F3H66] 75-30486 ISBN 0-8091-1893-9 : 7.95
1. Catholic Church—Prayer-books and devotions—English. 2. Family—Prayer-books and devotions—English. I. Title.

HORTIN, Paul. 242
Something for everybody; smorgasbord for the varied hungers of the spirit. Illustrated by Jack Hamm [1st ed.] Anderson, S.C., Droke House [1968] 127 p. illus. 23 cm. $2.95 On cover: Something for everybody; the inspiration of Paul Hortin. [BV4832.2.H66] 68-28778
1. Devotional literature. I. Title. II. Title: Smorgasbord for the varied hungers of the spirit.

HORTIN, Paul. 242
Something for everybody; smorgasbord for the varied hungers of the spirit. Illustrated by Jack Hamm [1st ed.] Anderson, S.C., Droke House [1968] 127 p. illus. 23 cm. On cover: Something for everybody; the inspiration of Paul Hortin. [BV4832.2.H66] 68-28778 2.95
1. Devotional literature. I. Title. II. Title: Smorgasbord for the varied hungers of the spirit.

HOUSELANDER, Frances Caryll. 242
The risen Christ. New York, Sheed and Ward [1958] 111p. 20cm. [BX2182.H68] 58-5883
1. Devotional literature. I. Title.

HOWARD, John Gordon, 1899- 242
Small windows on a big world [by] J. Gordon Howard. Nashville, Abingdon Press [1969] 112 p. 20 cm. [BV4832.2.H667] 69-12020 2.95
1. Meditations. I. Title.

HOWELL, Clinton Talmage, 1913- 242
Design for living [by] Clinton T. Howell. New York, Grosset & Dunlap [1970] 138 p. 29 cm. [BJ1581.2.H67] 72-120425 5.95
1. Conduct of life. I. Title.

HUBBARD, David Allan. 242
More psalms for all seasons / by David Allan Hubbard. Grand Rapids : Eerdmans, [1975] 96 p. ; 18 cm. [BS1430.4.H8] 74-32469 ISBN 0-8028-1596-0 pbk. : 1.50
1. Bible. O.T. Psalms—Meditations. I. Title.

HUSS, John Ervin, 1910- 242
Pause for power; devotional thoughts for men and women. Introd. by Herschel H. Hobbs. Grand Rapids, Zondervan Pub. House [1957] 137p. 21cm. [BV4832.H9] 57-31386
1. Devotional exercises. I. Title.

HUSS, John Ervin, 1910- 242
Pause for power; devotional thoughts for men and women. I trod. by herschel H. Hobbs. Grand Rapids, Zondervan Pub. House [1957] 137p. 21cm. [BV4832.H9] 57-31386
1. Devotional exercises. I. Title.

HUTCHESON, Lena Edwards. 242
Food for thought day by day; a treasury of religious inspiration. New York, Exposition Press [1950] 234 p. 23 cm. [BV4810.H79] 50-9039
1. Devotional exercises. 2. Calendars. I. Title. II. Title: A treasury of religious inspiration.

HUTSON, Joan. 242
Heal my heart O Lord / Joan Hutson. Notre Dame, Ind. : Ave Maria Press, c1976. 109 p. ; 21 cm. [BV4832.2.H78] 75-30493 ISBN 0-87793-106-2 pbk. : 2.25
1. Meditations. I. Title.

HUTSON, Joan. 242
The wind has many faces; a book of minute meditations. St. Meinrad, Ind., Abbey Press, 1974. [105] p. 21 cm. (A Priority edition) [BV4832.2.H8] 74-78724 ISBN 0-87029-031-2 3.95
1. Meditations. I. Title.

HUXHOLD, Harry N. comp. j 242
Adventures with God. Compiled by Harry N. Huxhold. Illustrated by Arthur Kirchhoff. St. Louis, Concordia Pub. House [1966] viii, 230 p. illus. 24 cm. [BV4870.H8] 66-15551
1. Children — Prayer-books and devotions — 1961- . I. Title.

HUXHOLD, Harry N., comp. 242
Adventures with God. Comp. by Harry N. Huxhold. Illus. by Arthur Kirchhoff. St. Louis, Concordia [c.1966] viii, 230p. illus. 24cm. [BV4870.H8] 66-15551 3.50
1. Children—Prayer-books and devotions—1961- I. Title.

HUXHOLD, Harry N. 242
Power for the church in the midst of chaos [by] Harry N. Huxhold. St. Louis, Concordia Pub. House [1973] 95 p. 20 cm. [BV4832.2.H83] 73-82078 ISBN 0-570-03160-5 1.95 (pbk.)
1. Meditations. I. Title.

HUXHOLD, Harry N. 242
What is the question; discovering the meaning of life from recent novels and ancient Scriptures [by] Harry N. Huxhold. Saint Louis, Concordia Pub. House [1968] 91 p. 25 cm. [BV4832.2.H84] 68-19991
1. Devotional literature. I. Title.

ICE, Orva Lee. 242
A candle for the dark. New York, Abingdon Press [1955] 128p. 20cm. Essays. [BV4832.I3] 55-8610
1. Devotional literature. I. Title.

IDOL, Vera. 242
Paths of shining light. New York, Abingdon Press [1956] 111p. illus. 24cm. [BV4832.I33] 56-6355
1. Devotional literature. I. Title.

IKERMAN, Ruth C. 242
Calendar of faith and flowers [by] Ruth C. Ikerman. Nashville, Abingdon Press [1970] 106 p. illus. 16 cm. [QK84.I37] 75-134242 3.25
1. Flowers. 2. Flower arrangement. I. Title.

IKERMAN, Ruth C. 242
Devotional programs about people and places. Nashville, Abingdon Press [c.1947-1960] 158p. 16cm. 60-5473 2.00 bds.,
1. Worship programs. 2. Woman—Religious life. I. Title.

IKERMAN, Ruth C 242
Devotional programs for every month. New York, Abingdon Press [1957] 128p. 16cm. [BV4832.I38] 57-6117
1. Devotional exercises. I. Title.

IKERMAN, Ruth C. 242
Devotional thoughts from the Holy Land [by] Ruth C. Ikerman. Nashville, Abingdon Press [1968] 110 p. 21 cm. [BV4832.2.I38] 68-17453
1. Meditations. I. Title.

IKERMAN, Ruth C. 242
The disciplined heart [by] Ruth C. Ikerman. New York, Abingdon Press [1964] 143 p. 21 cm. [BV4832.I 39] 64-19347
1. Devotional exercises. I. Title.

IKERMAN, Ruth C. 242
The disciplined heart. Nashville, Abingdon [c.1964] 143p. 21cm. 64-19347 2.25 bds.,
I. Title.

IKERMAN, Ruth C. 242
Meditations for bird lovers [by] Ruth C. Ikerman. Nashville, Abingdon Press [1972] 108 p. 16 cm. [QL795.B57I53] 71-186825 ISBN 0-687-24081-6 3.00
1. Birds—Legends and stories. 2. Bird watching. 3. Meditations. I. Title.

IKERMAN, Ruth C. 242
On morning trails [by] Ruth C. Ikerman. Nashville, Abingdon Press [1974] 127 p. 16 cm. [BV4832.2.I39] 73-18469 ISBN 0-687-28853-3 3.95
1. Meditations. I. Title.

IKIN, Alice Graham, 1895- 242
Bay windows into eternity; glimpses into unseen. Foreword by J. B. Phillips. New York, Macmillan, 1961. 117 p. 20 cm. [BV4501.2.I4 1961] 61-13308
1. Spiritual life. I. Title.

*IMITATIO Christi. English. 242
Of the imitation of Christ; [four books by] Thomas a Kempis. New Canaan, Conn., Keats Pub. Co. [1973] [x] 226 p. 18 cm. (Pivot family reader) [BV4821.A1] 0.95 (pbk)
I. Title.

INSTITUTE on Contemporary Thought and the Spiritual Exercises of St. Ignatius of Loyola, Loyola University, Chicago, 1962. 242
Proceedings, July 23-27, 1962. Directed by Robert F. Harvanek. Chicago, 1963. iii, 88 p. 23 cm. "Conducted by Loyola University." Cover title: Contemporary thought and the Spiritual exercises of St. Ignatius Loyola. Includes bibliographies. [BX2179.L8. I 5] 64-3334
1. Loyola, Ignacio de, Saint, 1491-1556. Exercitia spiritualia — Congress. I. Harvanek, Robert F., ed. II. Loyola University, Chicago. III. Title. IV. Title: Contemporary thought and the Spiritual exercises of St. Ignatius Loyola.

INTO the woods, and other favorite verses, compiled by Daughters of St. Paul. [Boston] St. Paul Editions [1973] 91 p. illus. 21 cm. [BX2177.I57] 73-89937 4.95 (pbk.). 242
1. Devotional literature. I. Daughters of St. Paul.

IRKEPMAN, Ruth C 242
Devotional programs for the changing seasons. New York, Abingdon Press [1958] 158p. 16cm. [BV199.W614] 58-10459
1. Worship programs. 2. Women—Religious life. I. Title.

IVERSEN, John Orville. 242
Perspectives for everyday living. Nashville, Southern Pub. Association [1971] 63 p. 18 cm. (Better living series) [BV4832.2.I87] 70-166996
1. Meditations. I. Title.

IVERSON, Sylva F. 242
Releasing the power within; a book on the positive mind of Christ within the believer, by Sylva F. Iverson. Rev., enl. ed. [Portland, 1969] 126 p. illus. 22 cm. [BV4832.2.I9 1969] 70-9837
1. Meditations. I. Title.

JACOBS, Margaret [Branch] (Moore) 242
Roses every day. Grand Rapids, Eerdmans [c.1959] 119p. 23cm. 59-14586 3.50
1. Devotional literature. I. Title.

JACOBS, Margaret Branch (Moore) 1901- 242
Roses every day. Grand Rapids, Eerdmans [c1959] 119p. 23cm. [BV4832.2.J3] 59-14586
1. Devotional literature. I. Title.

*JACOBS, Margaret Moore 242
My master has a garden. Grand Rapids, Mich., Eerdmans [1965, c.1964] 96p. 23cm. 3.50 bds.,
I. Title.

JAEGHER, Paul de. 242
The virtue of love; meditations. New York, Kenedy [1955] 176p. 22cm. [BX2182.J33] 55-6518
1. Love (Theology) —Meditations. I. Title.

JAMES, Bruno Scott. 242
Seeking God. [1st ed.] New York, Harper [1960] 128p. 14cm. [BX2350.2.J3] 60-15269
1. Spiritual life—Catholic authors. I. Title.

JARRETT, Bede, 1881-1934. 242
Living temples. Westminster, Md., Newman Press, 1956. 103p. illus. 17cm. [BX2182.J36] 56-14229
1. Devotional literature. I. Title.

JEAN Marie, Sister, O.S.B. 242
He knows how you feel. Liguori, Mo., Liguorian Pamphlets & Books [1971] 87 p. illus. 18 cm. [BV4832.2.J4] 75-160054 1.50
1. Meditations—Pictorial works. I. Title.

JOHNSON, Eola. 242
Beloved disciples. [Anderson, Ind.] Warner Press [1973] 95 p. 19 cm. [BS2615.4.J64] 73-4539 ISBN 0-87162-154-1
1. Bible. N.T. John—Meditations. I. Title.

JOHNSON, Eola. 242
Beloved disciples. [Anderson, Ind.] Warner Press [1973] 95 p. 19 cm. [BS2165.4.J64] 73-4539 ISBN 0-87162-154-1 1.95 (pbk.)
1. Bible. N.T. John—Meditations. I. Title.

JOHNSON, Gustaf F 242
From a shepherd's heart; brief meditations. Minneapolis, Free Church Publications [c1960] 108p. 23cm. [BV4832.2.J6] 61-21265
1. Meditations. I. Title.

JOHNSON, Joe, 1933- comp. 242
A field of diamonds / compiled by Joseph S. Johnson ; drawings by Phyllis Jolly. Nashville, Tenn. : Broadman Press, [1974] 191 p. : ill. ; 29 cm. Includes index. [BV4801.J63] 73-87067 ISBN 0-8054-5133-1 : 5.95
1. Devotional literature—Collected works. I. Title.

*JOHNSON, Ruth I. 242
Daily devotions for juniors; no. 3. Chicago, Moody [1967] 64p. 19cm. (Moody arrows: devotional, no. 21) .50 pap.,
1. Devotional literature—Juvenile. I. Title.

JOHNSON, Ruth I. 242
Daily devotions for juniors, no. 2. Chicago, Moody [c.1965] 64p. 19cm. .50 pap.,
I. Title.

JOHNSTON, Dorothy Grunbock 242
Pete and Penny know and grow; delightful devotional readings for boys and girls 5 to 9 years old [reissue] Wheaton, Ill., Scripture [1963, c.1957] 191p. illus. 23cm. 2.95 bds.,
1. Children—Prayer-books and devotions—English. I. Title.

JOHNSTON, Dorothy Grunbock. 242
Pete and Penny play and pray; delightful devotional readings for boys and girls. Chicago, Scripture Press [1954] 189p. illus. 23cm. [BV4870.J57] 54-41454
1. Children— Prayer-books and devotions—English. I. Title.

JOHNSTON, Minton C. 242
The noise in the sky [by] Minton C. Johnston. Nashville, Abingdon Press [1968] 111 p. 18 cm. [BV4832.2.J62] 68-25361 2.50
1. Meditations. I. Title.

JONES, Anna May. 242
Think on these things and live : a devotional handbook for spiritual guidance, meditation, and reference / Anna May Jones. 1st ed. Portland, Or. : Jones, 1976. viii, 82 p. : port. ; 22 cm. Includes index. Bibliography: p. 79. [BV4832.2.J63] 76-21039 3.95
1. Meditations. I. Title.

JONES, Anna May. 242
Think on these things and live : a devotional handbook for spiritual guidance, meditation, and reference / Anna May Jones. 1st ed. Portland, Or. : Jones, 1976. viii, 82 p. : port. ; 22 cm. Includes index. Bibliography: p. 79. [BV4832.2.J63] 76-21039 3.95
1. Meditations. I. Title.

JONES, Bob, 1911- 242
Showers upon the grass; a companion volume to As the small rain. Grand Rapids, Zondervan [1951] 185 p. 20 cm. [BV4832.J433] 51-4101
1. Devotional literature. I. Title.

JONES, Christopher William. 242
Look around, pilgrim. Milwaukee, Bruce Pub. Co. [1968] ix, 107 p. 22 cm. [BX2182.2.J6] 68-55279
1. Meditations. I. Title.

JONES, Eli Stanley, 1884- 242
Christian maturity. New York, Abingdon Press [1957] 364p. 16cm. [BV4832.J454] 57-10274
1. Devotional exercises. I. Title.

JONES, Eli Stanley, 1884- 242
How to be a transformed person. New York, Abingdon-Cokesbury Press [1951] 364 p. 16 cm. [BV4832.J46] 51-14737
1. Devotional exercises. I. Title.

JONES, Elizabeth Brown, 1907- 242
God loves me; devotional thoughts for boys and girls. Anderson, Ind., Warner Press [1954] unpaged. illus. 28cm. [BV4870.J58] 54-43038
1. Children—Prayer-books and devotions—English. I. Title.

JONES, Elizabeth Brown, 1907- 242
God plans for happy families; devotional thoughts for children. Anderson, Ind., Warner Press [1955] unpaged. illus. 28cm. [BV4870.J59] 56-17703
1. Children— Prayer-books and devotions—English. I. Title.

JONES, Elizabeth Brown. 1907- 242
God's loving-kindness; a book of devotional readings for children. Illus. by Ruby Kampschroeder. Kansas City, Mo., Beacon Hill Press [1948] 94p. illus. 22cm. [BV4870.J6] 48-3976
1. Children—Prayer-books and devotions—English. I. Title.

JONES, Mary Alice, 1898- 242
Prayers for little children, and suggestions to father and mothers for teaching their children to pray, edited by Mary Alice Jones. Illustrated by Suzanne Bruce. Abridged ed. Chicago, Rand McNally, 1964, c1949. 1 v. (unpaged) col. illus. 27 cm. [BV265.J613 1964] 64-15256
1. Children—Prayer-books and devotions. I. Title.

JONES, Ruby A 242
The searching wind, by Ruby A. Jones. Illustrated by Edith Lacy. Anderson, Ind., Warner Press [1964] 112 p. illus. 19 cm. [BT4832.2.J65] 64-14752
1. Devotional literature. I. Title.

JONES, Ruby A. 242
The searching wind. Illus. by Edith Lacy. Anderson, Ind., Warner [c.1964] 112p. illus. 19cm. 64-14752 2.50
1. Devotional literature. I. Title.

JONES, William McKendrey. 242
A guide to living power / by William M. Jones. Atlanta : John Knox Press, [1975] 120 p. ; 21 cm. [BV4509.5.J66] 74-19969 ISBN 0-8042-1105-1 : 3.95
1. Spiritual exercises. 2. Mental discipline. I. Title.

*JOSEPH, Stephen M. 242
Daily meditations: your guide to inner happiness [New York] Bantam [1968] 96p. 14cm. (Bantam mini-bk., FX4301) .50 pap.,
1. Devotional literature. 2. Meditations. I. Title.

JOWETT, John Henry, 1864-1923. 242
The best of John Henry Jowett. Edited with an introd. by Gerald Kennedy. Freeport, N.Y., Books for Libraries Press [1971, c1948] xix, 167 p. 23 cm. (Biography index reprint series) Includes bibliographical references. [BV4832.J59 1971] 79-179729 ISBN 0-8369-8097-2
1. Devotional literature. I. Kennedy, Gerald Hamilton, Bp., 1907- ed.

*JOWETT, John Henry, 1864-1923. 242
Life in the heights; studies in the epistles [by] J. H. Jowett. [Introduction by Ralph G. Turnbull] Grand Rapids, Mich., Baker Book House [1973 c1925] 266 p. 19 cm. (Minister's Paperback Library) [BV4832] ISBN 0-8010-5020-0 pap., 2.95
1. Devotional literature (Selections: Extracts, etc.) I. Title.

JUAN de la Cruz, Saint, 1542-1591. 242
The voice of the spirit : the spirituality of St. John of the Cross / edited and introduced by Elizabeth Hamilton. Huntington, IN : Our Sunday Visitor, 1977c1976 127, [1] p. ; 21 cm. Bibliography: p. [128] [BX2349.J8513 1976b] 76-53609 ISBN 0-87973-686-0 pbk. : 2.95
1. Spiritual life—Catholic authors. 2. Meditations. I. Hamilton, Elizabeth, 1906- II. Title.

JUAN de la Cruz, Saint, 1542-1591. 242
The voice of the Spirit : the spirituality of St. John of the Cross / edited and introduced by Elizabeth Hamilton. London : Darton, Longman and Todd, 1976. 128 p. ; 19 cm.

Consists of an introd. and selection of texts from the prose writings of St. John of the Cross [translated from the Spanish by the editor] as well as some of the better known poems. Bibliography: p. [128] [BX2349.J8513] 76-379874 ISBN 0-232-51349-X : £1.20
1. Spiritual life—Catholic authors. 2. Meditations. I. Hamilton, Elizabeth, 1906- II. Title.

JUAN de la Cruz, Saint, 1542-1591. 242
The voice of the spirit : the spirituality of St. John of the Cross / edited and introduced by Elizabeth Hamilton. Huntington, IN : Our Sunday Visitor, 1977c1976 127, [1] p. ; 21 cm. Bibliography: p. [128] [BX2349.J8513 1976b] 76-53609 ISBN 0-87973-686-0 pbk. : 2.95
1. Spiritual life—Catholic authors. 2. Meditations. I. Hamilton, Elizabeth, 1906- II. Title.

JULIANA, anchoret, 1343-1443. 242
A revelation of love / [by] Julian of Norwich ; edited by Marion Glasscoe. [Exeter] : University of Exeter, 1976. xviii, 111 p. ; 21 cm. (Exeter medieval English texts) Middle English text, modern English introd. and notes. Text of the revelations as found in BM Sloane manuscript no. 2499. Includes index. Bibliography: p. xviii. [BV4831.J8 1976] 77-373917 ISBN 0-85989-061-9 : £1.00
1. Devotional literature. I. Glasscoe, Marion. II. Title. III. Series.

JULIANA, anchoret, 1343-1443. 242
The revelations of divine love of Julian of Norwich. Translated by James Walsh. New York, Harper [c1961] xix, 210p. 20cm. 'This ... edition represents a collation of Paris and Sloane [manuscripts]' [BV4831.J8 1961] 62-4645
1. Devotional literature. I. Walsh, James, 1920- tr. II. Title.

JULIANA, anchoret, 1343-1443. 242
The revelations of divine love of Julian of Norwich. Tr. by James Walsh. New York, Harper & Row [1962, c.1961] xix, 210 p. 20 cm. 62-4645 4.50, bds.
1. Devotional literature. I. Walsh, James, 1920- tr. II. Title.

JULIANA, anchoret, 1343-1443. 242
Revelations of divine love shewed to a devout ankress, by name Julian of Norwich. Edited from the mss. by Roger Hudleston, with an introd. by the same. [2d ed.] Westminster, Md., Newman Press [1952] xxxviii, 178 p. 20cm. (The Orchard books [11] 'In the present edition the text has been based upon ms. Sloane 2499.' [BV4831.J8 1952] 52-14306
1. Devotional literature. I. Hudleston, Gilbert Roger, 1874- ed. II. Title. III. Series.

KAGAWA, Toyohiko, 1888- 242
Meditations. Translated by Jiro Takenaka. [1st ed.] New York, Harper [1950] 101 p. 20 cm. [BV4839.J3K3] 50-13754
1. Meditations. I. Title.

KANABAY, Donald. 242
Prayers for the self-sufficient; the negative approach to God [by] Don Kanabay. Chicago, Regnery [1968] vi, 39 p. 22 cm. [BL2777.P7K3] 68-31465 1.95
1. Prayers. I. Title.

KATES, Frederick Ward, 1910- comp. 242
Moments with the devotional masters. Nashville 5, 1908 Grand Ave. Upper Room, [c.1961] 96p. 16cm. 60-53492 .75
1. Devotional literature (Selections: Extracts, etc.) I. Title.

KATES, Frederick Ward, 1910- 242
The use of life. [1st ed.] New York, Harper [c1953] 143p. 20cm. [BV4832.K23] 52-11440
1. Devotional literature. I. Title.

KEATING, Joseph Ignatius, 1865-1939. 242
Retreat notes. Compiled and edited by Philip Caraman. Westminster, Md., Newman Press, 1953. 129p. 19cm. [BX2182.K38] 53-5584
1. Meditations. I. Title.

KEEN, Sam. 242
Beginnings without end / Sam Keen. 1st ed. New York : Harper & Row, c1975. p. cm. [BR1725.K4A33 1975] 75-9321 ISBN 0-06-064259-9 : 5.95
1. Keen, Sam. 2. Meditations. I. Title.

KEIGHTON, Robert Elwood, 1896- 242
Lamps for the journey. Nashville, Abingdon [c.1961] 80p. Bibl. 61-10813 1.75 bds.,
1. Devotional literature. I. Title.

KELLER, James [Gregory] 242
Three minutes a day (second series) New York, Permabooks (dist. Pocket Bks.) [1960, c.1959] xii, 365p. 17cm. (Permabooks M4162) .35 pap.,
1. Catholic Church—Prayer-books and devotions—English. 2. Calendars. I. Title.

KELLER, James Gregory, 1900- 242
It's your day; a Christopher thought for every day of the year. Garden City, N. Y., Hanover House, 1958. 365p. 20cm. [BX2182.2.K4] 58-12300
1. Devotional calendars—Catholic Church. I. Title.

KELLER, James Gregory, 1900- 242
One moment please! Christopher daily guides to better living. [1st ed.] Garden City, N. Y., Doubleday, 1950. xiii, 365 p. 20 cm. [BV4832.K429] 50-10141
1. Devotional exercises. 2. Calendars. I. Title.

KELLER, James Gregory, 1900- 242
Three minutes a day; Christopher thoughts for daily living. Garden City, N. Y., Doubleday, 1951. xi, 333 p. 13 cm. [BX2110.K34 1951] 51-1802
1. Catholic Church—Prayer-books and devotions—English. 2. Calendars. I. Title.

KELLER, James Gregory, 1900- 242
Three minutes a day; Christopher thoughts for daily living. Garden City, N. Y., Permabooks [1951] xvi, 365 p. 17 cm. (Permabooks, P 105) [BX2110.K34 1951a] 51-32283
1. Catholic Church—Prayer-books and devotions—English. 2. Calendars. I. Title.

*KELLER, W. Phillip 242
As a tree grows. Chicago, Moody [1966] 61p. illus. 22cm. Cover title: Devotionals: As a tree grows. price unreported
I. Title.

KELLEY, Erma W 242
Channels of Thy peace; meditations on a prayer of Francis of Assisi. New York, Abingdon Press [1958] 111p. 18cm. Authorship of prayer uncertain. Cf. J. Meyer. The words of Saint Francis. 1952. [BV4832.K4294] 58-8123
1. Meditations. I. Title.

KELLY, Thomas Raymond, 1893-1941 242
The eternal promise [by] Thomas Kelly. [1st ed.] New York, Harper [1966] 124p. 20cm. [BV4832.K4297] 66-11485 2.99
1. Devotional literature. 2. Christian life—Friend authors I. Title.

KENNEDY, Eugene C. 242
A time for being human / Eugene Kennedy. Chicago : Thomas More Press, c1977. 239 p. ; 25 cm. [BX2182.2.K427] 77-153979 ISBN 0-88347-077-2 pbk. : 9.95
1. Meditations. I. Title.

KENNEDY, Eugene C. 242
A time for being human / Eugene Kennedy. Chicago : Thomas More Press, c1977. 239 p. ; 25 cm. [BX2182.2.K427] 77-153979 ISBN 0-88347-077-2 pbk. : 9.95
1. Meditations. I. Title.

KENSETH, Arnold. 242
Sabbaths, sacraments, and seasons; a collection of meditations, prayers, and canticles. Philadelphia, Pilgrim Press [1969] 160 p. illus. 27 cm. Poems. [BV4832.2.K43] 71-96298 6.95
1. Meditations. 2. Prayers. I. Title.

KEPLER, Thomas Samuel 242
Leaves from a spiritual notebook. Nashville, Abingdon Press [c.1960] 304p. 25cm. 60-10910 5.50
*1. Devotional literature *Selections: Extracts, etc.) 2. Prayers. I. Title.*

KEPLER, Thomas Samuel, 1897- 242
A journey into faith. Nashville, Abingdon Press [c1954] 160p. 20cm. [BV4832.K442] 53-11341
1. Meditations. 2. Theology, Doctrinal—Popular works. I. Title.

KEPLER, Thomas Samuel, 1897- 242
Leaves from a spiritual notebook. New York, Abingdon Press [1960] 301p. 25cm. [BV4832.K45] 60-10910
1. Devotional literature (Selections: Extracts, etc.) 2. Prayers. I. Title.

KEPLER, Thomas Samuel, 1897- comp. 242
Pathways to spiritual power; a pocket devotional guide for spiritual living. [1st ed.] Cleveland, World Pub. Co. [1952] 138 p. 13 cm. [BV4805.K4] 52-8421
1. Devotional exercises. I. Title.

KEPLER, Thomas Samuel, 1897- 242
A spiritual journey with Paul. Nashville, Abingdon-Cokesbury Press [1953] 157p. 20cm. [BV4832.K445] 52-12421
1. Paul, Saint, apostle. 2. Meditations. I. Title.

KETTNER, Elmer A. 242
Living with my Lord; a Christian growth study guide. St. Louis, Concordia [c.1961] 76p. p1.00 pap.,
I. Title.

KEYSOR, Charles W. 242
Living unafraid / Charles W. Keysor. Elgin, Ill. : D. C. Cook Pub. Co., c1975. 157, [1] p. ; 18 cm. Bibliography: p. [158] [BS1430.4.K49] 75-892 ISBN 0-912692-61-8 : 1.50
1. Bible. O.T. Psalms—Meditations. 2. Christian life—1960- I. Title.

KEYSOR, Charles W. 242
Living unafraid / Charles W. Keysor. Elgin, Ill. : D. C. Cook Pub. Co., c1975. 157, [1] p. ; 18 cm. Bibliography: p. [158] [BS1430.4.K49] 75-892 ISBN 0-912692-61-8 pbk. : 1.50
1. Bible. O.T. Psalms—Meditations. 2. Christian life—1960- I. Title.

KIERKEGAARD, Soren Aabye, 1813-1855. 242
Meditations. Translated and edited by T. H. Croxall. Philadelphia, Westminster Press [1955] 165p. 21cm. [BV4836.K515] 55-8596
1. Meditations. I. Title.

KILLIAN, Ida F. 242
Message of the shells, by Ida F. Killian. Anderson, Ind., Warner Press [1973] 79 p. illus. 21 cm. [BV4832.2.K5] 73-4849 ISBN 0-87162-155-X
1. Meditations. I. Title.

KING, Frankie Jackson 242
Sitting at His feet. San Antonio, Naylor Co. [c.1960] 83p. 22cm. 60-7917 2.95
1. Meditations. I. Title.

KINGSLAKE, Brian, 1907- 242
"For heaven's sake!" Forty-six variations on the theme: how to react to the conditions of life on earth in such a way as to prepare oneself for life in the Kingdom of Heaven. North Quincy, Mass., Christopher Pub. House [1974] 321 p. 21 cm. [BV4832.2.K54] 74-75163 2.00
1. Meditations. I. Title.

KLEINHANS, Theodore J 242
Talking with God. St. Louis, Concordia Pub. House [1962] 108p. 19cm. [BV4832.2.K56] 60-11415
1. Devotional literature. I. Title.

KNAUF, Ethel. 242
I have learned. Philadelphia, Dorrance [1969] xii, 160 p. 22 cm. [BV4832.2.K58] 75-82027 3.95
1. Meditations. I. Title.

KNOX, Ronald Arbuthnott, 1888-1957. 242
Lightning meditations. New York, Sheed and Ward [1959] 164p. 21cm. [BX2182.2.K57] 59-12090
1. Meditations. I. Title.

KOHN, Harold E. 242
Adventure in insight, by Harold E. John. Illus. by the author. Grand Rapids. Eerdmans [1967] 159p. illus. 21cm. [BV4832.2.K59] 67-3113 3.50
1. Devotional literature. I. Title.

KOHN, Harold E. 242
Best wishes for common days and special days, by Harold E. Kohn. Illustrated by the author. Grand Rapids, Eerdmans [1969] 171 p. illus. 24 cm. [BV4832.2.K593] 75-78026 4.95
1. Meditations. I. Title.

KOHN, Harold E. 242
Evergreen things [by] Harold E. Kohn. [Nashville, Tenn., Tidings, 1973] 79 p. illus. 19 cm. [BV4832.2.K594] 73-86377 1.00 (pbk.)
1. Meditations. I. Title.

KOHN, Harold E. 242
Nearby, by Harold E. Kohn. Nashville, Tenn., Tidings, [1970] 79 p. illus. 19 cm. [BV4832.2.K595] 71-134363 1.00
1. Meditations. I. Title.

KOHN, Harold E 242
Pathways to understanding; outdoor adventures in meditation. Illustrated with forty-five line drawings by the author. Grand Rapids, W. B. Eerdmans Pub. Co. [1958] 196p. illus. 23cm. [BV4832.K62] 58-7573
1. Devotional literature. I. Title.

KOHN, Harold E. 242
Small wonders, by Harold E. Kohn. Nashville, Tenn., Tidings [1969] 88 p. illus. 19 cm. [BV4832.2.K597] 78-103030
1. Meditations. I. Title.

KOHN, Harold E 242
Thoughts afield; meditations through the seasons. Illustrated with 63 drawings by the author. Grand Rapids, Eerdmans [1959] 171p. illus. 24cm. [BV4832.2.K6] 59-8749
1. Meditations. 2. Seasons. I. Title.

KOHN, Harold E. 242
Where heaven and earth meet / Harold E. Kohn. Nashville : Tidings, c1975. vii, 72 p. : ill. ; 19 cm. Includes bibliographical references. [BV4832.2.K63] 75-3636
1. Meditations. I. Title.

KOLLER, Charles W 1886- 242
Tents toward the sunrise; sixty-six timely messages, devotional, inspirational. [1st ed.] Philadelphia, Judson Press [1953] 152p. 20cm. [BV4832.K63] 53-11491
1. Devotional exercises. I. Title.

KOLLER,Charles W 1896- 242
Tents toward the sunrise; sixty-six timely messages, devotional, inspirational. [1st ed.] Philadelphia, Judson Press [1953] 152 p. 20 cm. [BV4832.K63] 53-11491
1. Devotional exercises. I. Title.

KONIG, Franz, Cardinal, 1905- 242
The hour is now / Franz Cardinal Konig ; translated by Herbert W. Richardson. [1st ed.] New York : Harper & Row, [1975] vi, 124 p. ; 20 cm. Translation of Die Stunde der Welt. [BX2184.K6313 1975] 74-4642 ISBN 0-06-064772-8 : 5.95
1. Meditations. I. Title.

KOOIMAN, Helen W. 242
Please pray for the cabbages; pint-sized parables for grown-ups, by Helen W. Kooiman. Westwood, N.J., Revell [1967] 123p. 21cm. [BV4832.2.K66] 67-14780 2.95 bds.,
1. Devotional literature. 2. Children—Religious life. I. Title.

KRASS, Elizabeth, comp. 242
Something greater than us. [Los Angeles] Stanyan Books [1970] [57] p. col. illus. 20 cm. (A Stanyan book, 23) [PN6084.R3K7] 70-20550 ISBN 0-394-46814-7 3.00
1. God—Quotations, maxims, etc. I. Title.

KRETZMANN, Otto Paul, 1901- 242
Hosanna in the whirlwind; devotional readings for times of change [by] O. P. Kretzmann. Saint Louis, Concordia Pub. House [1969] 95 p. 20 cm. [BV4832.2.K7] 69-12765 3.00
1. Devotional literature. I. Title.

KREYCHE, Robert J., 1920- 242
The making of a saint; a guide to the spiritual life [by] Robert J. Kreyche. Staten Island, N.Y., Alba House [1973] x, 218 p. illus. 21 cm. Bibliography: p. 211-213. [BX2182.2.K73] 73-7531 ISBN 0-8189-0276-0 3.95
1. Devotional exercises. I. Title.

KUBO, Sakae, 1926- 242
Calculated goodness / by Sakae Kubo. Nashville : Southern Pub. Association, [1974] 128 p. ; 22 cm. (Anvil series) [BV4832.2.K78] 74-82291 ISBN 0-8127-0083-X : 3.95
1. Meditations. I. Title.

KUHLMANN, Edward, 1882- 242
Choosing our memories. Columbus, Ohio, Wartburg Press [1954] 188p. 20cm. [BV4832.K8] 54-30263
1. Devotional literature. I. Title.

KUNTZ, Kenneth A 242
The pilgrim. St. Louis, Bethany Press [1957] 96p. 17cm. [BV4832.K85] 57-12725
1. Meditations. I. Title.

KUNTZ, Kenneth A. 242
The pioneer. St. Louis, Bethany Press [c.1960] 96p. 17cm. 60-6226 1.75
1. Meditations. I. Title.

KUYPER, Abraham, 1837-1920. 242
Near to God. [Tr. from Dutch by John Hendrik de Vries] Grand Rapids, Mich., Eerdmans [c.1961] 108p. 61-10859 2.00
1. Meditations. I. Title.

LA AOGSALLE, Jean Baptiste de, Saint, 1651-1719. 242
Meditations. Edited by W. J. Battersby. London, New York, Longmans, Green [1953] xxxii, 481p. illus., ports. 23cm. Bibliographical footnotes. [BX2182.L28] 55-19730
1. Church year—Meditations. I. Battersby, William John, ed. II. Title.

LAMB, Elizabeth Searle. 242
Today and every day. Unity Village, Mo., Unity Books [1970] 190 p. 20 cm. Poems and prose. [BV4832.2.L3] 73-120121 ISBN 8-7159-1391-
1. Devotional exercises. I. Title.

LANDORF, Joyce. 242
For these fragile times / Joyce Landorf. Wheaton, Ill. : Victor Books, c1975. 64 p. ; 19 cm. Selections from the author's column, I've been thinking, which appears in Power for living. [BV4832.2.L315] 75-6209 ISBN 0-88207-805-4 : pbk. : 2.95

1. Meditations. I. Title.

LANGE, Ernst. 242
Ten great freedoms. Translated by David T. Priestley. Downers Grove, Ill., Inter-Varsity Press [1970] [59] p. illus. 21 cm. Translation of Die zehn grossen Freiheiten. [BV4655.L2513] 76-90744
1. Commandments, Ten—Meditations. I. Title.

LANGEVIN, Jean Marie. 242
A pale but ... splendid morning. Huntington, Ind., Our Sunday Visitor [1974] 192 p. 18 cm. [BX2182.2.L27] 73-89574 ISBN 0-87973-779-4 2.95 (pbk.)
1. Meditations. I. Title.

LANYON, Walter Clemow, 1887- 242
The eyes of the blind. [New York] Inspiration House [c1959] 220p. 21cm. [BF639.L205 1959] 60-32791
1. New Thought. I. Title.

LANZA del Vasto, Joseph Jean, 1901- 242
Make straight the way of the Lord; an anthology of the philosophical writings of Lanza del Vasto. Translated from the French by Jean Sidgwick. [1st ed.] New York, Knopf; [distributed by Random House] 1974. xii, 254 p. 22 cm. [BV4832.2.L3213 1974] 74-7739 ISBN 0-394-49387-7 7.95
1. Meditations. I. Title.

LARKIN, Francis. 242
Enthronement of the Sacred Heart. [2d rev. augm. ed.] New York, Guild Press; distrubuted by Golden Press [1960] 416p. illus. 17cm. (Angelus books) Includes bibliography. [BX2157.L33 1960] 60-4950
1. Sacred Heart, Devotion to. 2. Sacred Heart of Mary, Devotion to. I. Crawley-Boevey, Mateo, 1875- II. Title.

LARKIN, Francis 242
Enthronement of the sacred heart. [2d rev. angm. ed.] New York, Guild Press; distributed by Golden Press [c.1956, 1960] 416p. (Angelus books) Bibl.: 60-4950 .408-412 front. 17cm. .95 bds.,
1. Crawley-Boevey, Mateo, 1875- 2. Sacred Heart, Devotion. 3. Sacred Heart of Mary, Devotion to. I. Title.

LARSEN, Earnest. 242
Week of fire. [Paramus, N.J., Pastoral Educational Services, Special Projects Division, Paulist Press, 1973] 96 p. illus. 29 cm. [BX2182.2.L29] 72-93751 ISBN 0-8091-8755-8 4.95
1. Meditations. I. Title.

LARSEN, Earnest. 242
Where and how. [Liguori, Mo.] Liguorian Pamphlets and Books [1969] 80 p. illus. 28 cm. Cover title. [BX2182.2.L3] 76-107093 1.75
1. Meditations. I. Title.

LARSON, Muriel. 242
How to give a devotion; with suggested outlines. Grand Rapids, Baker Book House [1967] 107 p. 21 cm. [BV4235.D4L3] 67-26189
1. Devotional exercises—Handbooks, manuals, etc. I. Title.

LASH, William Quinlan, 1905- 242
The Temple of God's Wounds, by Will Quinlan [pseud.] New York, Morehouse-Gorham, 1951. 118 p. 19 cm. [BV4817.L3] 51-9644
1. God—Worship and love. I. Title.

LASSITER, Lelia Boring. 242
The Christian life; devotional messages for day-to-day Christian living. [1st ed.] New York, Greenwich Book Publishers [1956] 94p. 22cm. [BV4832.L355] 56-10303
1. Meditations. 2. Christian life. I. Title.

LAUBACH, Frank Charles, 1884- 242
Christ liveth in me, and Game with minutes. [Westwood, N.J.] Revell [c.1961] 64p. 61-9241 1.00 bds.,
1. Mystical union. 2. Christian life. I. Title.

LAUTERBACH, William Albert, 1903- 242
Heaven bound / William A. Lauterbach. St. Louis : Concordia Pub. House, [1975] 127 p. ; 29 cm. Large print ed. Includes index. [BV4580.L36] 74-34277 ISBN 0-570-03028-5 pbk. : 3.95
1. Aged—Prayer-books and devotions—English. 2. Hope—Meditations. 3. Sight-saving books. I. Title.

LAVENDER, John Allan. 242
Faithlifters. Valley Forge [Pa.] Judson Press [1969] 1 v. (unpaged) 20 cm. [BV4832.2.L35] 77-75184 2.50
1. Devotional literature. I. Title.

LAVENDER, Lucille. 242
Struggles of a sinner-saint. [Nashville] Upper Room [1973] 72 p. 18 cm. [BV4832.2.L36] 73-84031 1.00
1. Meditations. I. Title.

LAW, William, 1686-1761. 242
Christian perfection / by William Law ; edited and abridged by Erwin Paul Rudolph. 1st ed. Carol Stream, Ill. : Creation House, 1975. 145 p. ; 21 cm. Originally published in 1726 under title: A practical treatise upon Christian perfection. Includes bibliographical references. [BV4831.L355 1975] 74-29649 ISBN 0-88419-108-7 pbk. : 2.95
1. Devotional literature. 2. Perfection. I. Rudolph, Erwin Paul, 1916- II. Title.

LAWRENCE, Emeric Anthony, 1908- 242
Meditating the Gospels. Collegeville, Minn., Liturgical Press [1957] 460p. 22cm. [BX2170.C55L3] 57-3222
I. Title.

LE Sage, Wilfred, 1907- 242
The shepherd of my sout; meditations for all [by] Wilfred Le Sage. Staten Island, N.Y., Alba House [1967] 262 p. 19 cm. [BX2182.2.S3] 66-27533
1. Meditations. 2. Spritual exercises. I. Title.

LE BAR, Lois Emogene, 1907- 242
Family devotions with school-age children; creative guidelines for Christian parents [by] Lois E. Le Bar. Old Tappan, N.J., F. H. Revell Co. [1973] 253 p. illus. 23 cm. [BV255.L37] 73-5525 ISBN 0-8007-0593-9 7.50
1. Family—Prayer-books and devotions—English. I. Title.
Pbk. 3.95; ISBN 0-8007-0594-7.

LEBUFFE, Francis Peter, 1885-1954. 242
My changeless friend / by Francis P. LeBuffe ; adapted by Catharine Hughes. Updated ed. New York : Arena Lettres, [1974] vii, 116 p. ; 18 cm. "Original edition published in 1949 by Apostleship of Prayer." [BX2182.L36 1974] 73-94410 ISBN 0-88479-950-6 pbk. : 1.45
1. Meditations. I. Hughes, Catharine, 1935- II. Title.

LEE, G. Avery. 242
The roads to God [by] G. Avery Lee. Nashville, Tenn., Broadman Press [1969] 128 p. 20 cm. Includes bibliographical references. [BV4832.2.L4] 69-17886
1. Devotional literature. I. Title.

LEESTMA, Harold F. 242
More than a spectator / by Harold F. Leestma. Glendale, Calif. : G/L Regal Books, [1974] [61] p. : ill. ; 18 cm. "Meditations." [BV4832.2.L42] 74-82676 ISBN 0-8307-0302-0 pbk. : 2.00
1. Meditations. I. Title.

LEFEBVRE, Georges, 1908- 242
The well-springs of prayer [Tr. from French by Kathleen Pond.] NewYork 7, 280 Broadway, Desclee Co., 1961[c.1960] 79p. 61-7440 1.75
1. Prayer. I. Title.

LEHNER, Francis C., tr. 242
Mental prayer and modern life, a symposium; translated by Francis C. Lehner. With a pref. by Walter Farrell. New York, P. J. Kenedy [1950] xi, 202 p. 21 cm. "Translated from L'Oralson (Cahlers de la vie spirituelle)" Contents.Contents. -- Historical considerations: Mental prayer in the Catholic tradition, by P. Phillippe. -- Theological considerations: Method in prayer, by R. Rouquette. The virtues and gifts in prayer, by A. Pie. -- Practical considerations: Making one's life a prayer, by J. M. Perrin. Liturgy and lay life, by M. D. The Old Testament is a book of prayer, by P. M. de la Croix. Putting the Gospel in our midst, by a directress of J. I. C. F. Bibliographical references included in "Notes" (p. 186-202) [BV4813.O613] 50-2547
1. Meditation. I. Title.

LERCARO, Giacomo, Cardinal, 1891- 242
Methods of mental prayer. [Translation from the original Italian by T. F. Lindsay] Westminster, Md., Newman Press [1957] 308p. 23cm. Includes bibliography. [BV4813.L412] 57-8614
1. Meditation. I. Title.

LE SAGE, Wilfred, 1907- 242
The shepherd of my soul; meditations for all. Staten Island, N.Y., Alba House [1967] 262 p. 19 cm. [BX2182.2.S3] 66-27533
1. Meditations. 2. Spiritual exercises. I. Title.

LETOURNEAU, R. G., Mrs. 242
Recipes for living / Mrs. R. G. LeTourneau, with N. Stjernstrom. Grand Rapids, Mich. : Zondervan Pub. House, [1974] 122 p. : ill. ; 26 cm. [BV4832.2.L46] 73-2663 5.95
1. LeTourneau, R. G., Mrs. 2. Meditations. 3. Cookery. I. Stjernstrom, N., joint author. II. Title.

LIBERMANN, Francois Marie Paul [Name orig.: Jacob Libermann] 1802-1852 242
The spiritual letters of the Venerable Francis Libermann. Ed., tr. by Walter van de Putte, James Collery. Pittsburgh, Duquesne Univ. Pr. [1965, c.1964] xii, 420p. illus. 22cm. (Duquesne studies. Spiritan ser., v.8) Contents.v.4. Letters to clergy and religious (Nos. 76 to 184) [BX4705.L62A4] 62-12768 5.25
1. Spiritual life—Catholic authors. I. Title.

LIBERMANN, Francois Marie Paul [Name orig. Jacob Libermann] 1802-1852 242
The spiritual letters of the Venerable Francis Libermann; v.5. Ed., tr. by Walter Van de Putte. Pittsburgh, Duquesne Univ. Pr. [c.]1966. 336p. illus. 22cm. (Duquesne studies. Spirtan ser., v.9) Contents.v.5. Letters to clergy and religious (Nos. 185-274.) [BX4705.L62A4] 62-12768 5.00
1. Spiritual life—Catholic authors. I. Title.

LIGUORI, Alfonso Maria de', Saint, 1-. 242
How to converse continually and familiarly with God. Translated by L. X. Aubin. [Boston?] St. Paul Editions [1663] 75 p. 20 cm. [BV4813.L513] 63-13908
1. Meditation. I. Title.

LIGUORI, Alfonso Maria de', Saint, 1696-1787. 242
How to converse continually and familiarly with God. Tr. by L. X. Aubin. [Boston] St. Paul Eds. [dist. Daughters of St. Paul, c.1963] 75p. 20cm. 63-13908 1.00; .50 pap.,
1. Meditation. I. Title.

LIGUORI, Alfonso Maria de', Saint, 1696-1787. 242
The passion of Jesus Christ, by St. Alphonsus Maria de Iguori. Translated from the Italian. Baltimore, Helicon [1965] xii, 230 p. 22 cm. (His Ascetical works, v. 3) [BT430.L533] 65-2753
1. Jesus Christ — Passion — Devotional literature. I. Title.

LIGUORI, Alfonso Maria de', Saint, 1696-1787 242
The Passion of Jesus Christ. Tro fromItalian. Helicon [dist. New York, Taplinger, c.1965] xii, 230p. 22cm. (His Ascetical works, v. 3) [BT430.L533] 65-3753 4.95
1. JesusChrist—Passion—Devotional literature. I. Title.

LILJE, Hanns, 1899- 242
Messages from God's Word; tr. [from German] by Walter G. Tillmanns. Minneapolis, Augsburg [c.1961] 196p. 61-13884 3.95
1. Meditations. I. Title.

*LINDEMANN, Henry 242
God's silent preachers reflections on nature. New York, Exposition [c.194] 125p. 22cm. 3.50
I. Title.

LIOTTA, Matthew Alexis, 1886- 242
Thoughts. [1st ed.] New York, Vantage Press [1959, c1958] 143p. 21cm. [BX2350.2.L5] 58-14026
1. Christian life—Catholic authors. I. Title.

LISTER, Lincoln Ulysses 242
Consciousness of God, an introduction to spiritual life thrugh meditation. New York Exposition Press [c.1959] 71 p. 21 cm. (Bibl.) 2.50
I. Title.

A Little prayer, 242 (j)
with pictures by Barbara Cooney. New York, Hastings House [1967] 1 v. (unpaged) col. illus. 13 x 15 cm. [BV265.L53 1967] 67-27101
1. Children—Prayer-books and devotions. I. Cooney, Barbara, 1917- illus.

LIVINGSTON, Ruth Hull 242
Come unto me. New York, Vantage Press [c.1960] 48p. 2.00 bds.,
I. Title.

*LOCKERBIE, Jeanette. 242
Salt in my kitchen. Chicago, Moody [1967] 128p. 15cm. (M30-7500) 1.00 pap.,
I. Title.

LOCKHART, Mary E. 242
Living vistas [by] Mary E. Lockhart. Nashville, Abingdon Press [1971] 112 p. illus. 21 cm. [BV4832.2.L56] 73-148074 ISBN 0-687-22442-X 3.25
1. Meditations. I. Title.

LONG, Haniel, 1888- 242
A letter to St. Augustine after re-reading his Confessions. New York, Duell, Sloan and Pearce [1950] 245 p. 20 cm. [BR65.A9L63] 50-5220
1. Augustinus, Aurelius, Saint, Bp. of Hippo. I. Title.

LONG, Mildred. 242
Listen to the silence; meditations. Los Angeles, DeVorss [1970] 95 p. 21 cm. Poems. [BV4832.2.L58] 79-117412
1. Meditations. I. Title.

LONG, Valentine. 242
Whatever comes to mind. Paterson, N.J., Saint Anthony Guild Press [1966] viii, 292 p. 21 cm. [BX2182.2.L6] 65-27068
1. Devotional literature. I. Title.

LONG, Valentine 242
Whatever comes to mind. Paterson, N. J., St. Anthony Guild [c.1966] viii, 292p. 21cm. [BX2182.2.L6] 65-27068 4.00
1. Devotional literature. I. Title.

LOYOLA, Ignacio de, Saint, 1491-1556. 242
The spiritual exercises of St. Ignatius. A new translation based on studies in the language of the autograph, by Louis J. Puhl. Westminster, Md., Newman Press, 1951. xiii, 216 p. 20 cm. [BX2179.L7E5 1951] 51-10438
1. Spiritual exercises. I. Title.

LOYOLA, Ignacio de, Saint, 1491-1556. 242
The spiritual exercises of Saint Ignatius. A new translation by Thomas Corbishley. New York, P. J. Kenedy [1963] 124 p. 18 cm. [The Silver treasury series] [BX2179.L7E5 1963] 63-12296
1. Spiritual exercises I. Corbishley, Thomas, tr. II. Title.

LOYOLA, Ignacio de, Saint, 1491-1556. 242
The spiritual exercises of St. Ignatius. Translated by Anthony Mottola. Introd. by Robert W. Gleason. [1st ed.] Garden City, N.Y., Image Books [1964] 200 p. 18 cm. (An Image book original) "D 170." [BX2179.L7E5 1964] 64-12784
1. Spiritual exercises. I. Mottola, Anthony, tr. II. Title.

LOYOLA, Ignacio de, Saint, 1491-1556 242
The spiritual exercises of Saint Ignatius. New tr. by Thomas Corbishley. New York, Kenedy [c.1963] 124p. 18cm. (Silver treasury ser.) 63-12296 2.95
1. Spiritual exercises. I. Corbishley, Thomas, tr II. Title.

LOYOLA, Ignacio de, Saint, 1491-1556 242
The spiritual exercises of St. Ignatius. Tr. by Anthony Mottola. Introd. by Robert W. Gleason. Garden City, N.Y., Doubleday [c.1964] 200p. 18cm. (Image bk. org. D170) 64-12784 .85 pap.,
1. Spiritual exercises. I. Mottola, Anthony, tr. II. Title.

LUBICH, Chiara, 1920- 242
It's a whole new scene. [Translated by Sharry Silvi] New York, New City Press [1970] 67 p. 18 cm. Translation of Detti Gen. [BX2185.L7813] 78-133629 0.65
1. Meditations. I. Title.

LUBICH, Chiara, 1920- 242
A little "harmless" manifesto. [Translated from the Italian by Sharry Silvi] New York, New City Press [1973] 52 p. 18 cm. [BX2182.2.L813] 72-97595 0.75 (pbk.)
1. Meditations. I. Title.

LUBICH, Chiara, 1920- 242
Stirrings of unity [Long Island City, N.Y.] New City Pr. [1964] 93p. 19cm. 64-24944 price unreported
1. Christian life—Catholic authors. I. Title.

LUCCOCK, Halford Edward, 1885- 242
Out of this world. Nashville, Tidings [1959] 48p. 17cm. [BV4832.2.L8] 59-15766
1. Devotional literature. I. Title.

LUNGER, Alberta (Huff) 242
Roadside tables. St. Louis, Bethany Press [1961, c.1960] 112p. 60-53143 2.45
1. Devotional literature. I. Title.

LUTHER, Martin, 1483-1546. 242
Day by day we magnify Thee; daily meditations from Luther's writings arranged according to the year of the church, compiled and translated by Margarete Steiner and Percy Scott. Philadelphia, Muhlenberg Press, 1950. viii, 437 p. 20 cm. [BR331.E5S8 1950] 50-6016
1. Devotional exercises. I. Title.

LUTHER, Martin, 1483-1546. 242
Devotions and prayers; selected and translated [from the standard German texts] by Andrew Kosten. Grand Rapids, Baker Book House, 1956. 111p. 16cm. [BV260.L8] 56-7581
1. Lutheran Church—Prayer-books and devotions—English. I. Kosten. Andrew, ed. and tr. II. Title.

LUTZE, Karl E. 242
Forgive our forgettings, Lord! Reflections on gifts and promises [by] Karl E. Lutze. St. Louis, Concordia Pub. House [1972] 94 p. illus. 21 cm. [BV245.L87] 72-81921 pap. 1.50
1. Prayers. I. Title.

LYNCH, John W 242
Hourglass: stories of a measured year. New York, Macmillan, 1952. 172 p. 21 cm. [BX2182.L77] 52-766
1. Devotional literature. I. Title.

LYON, Quinter Marcellus 242
Meditations from world religions. Nashville. Abingdon [1966, c.1960] xi, 234p. 19cm. (Apex bks., W3-175) First pub. in 1960 by Harper under title Quiet strength from world religions. Bibl. [BL560.L9] 1.75 pap.,
1. Meditations. I. Title.

LYON, Quinter Marcellus 242
Quiet strength from world religions. New York, Harper [c.1960] xi, 234p. 20cm. (Bibl.: p.223-232) 60-7957 3.75
1. Meditations. I. Title.

LYONS, Mark J 242
Getting to know Mary, by Mark J. Lyons. Milwaukee, Bruce Pub. Co. [1965] vi, 130 p. 21 cm. [BX2160.2.L9] 65-23746
1. Mary Virgin — Meditations. I. Title.

LYONS, Mark J. 242
Getting to know Mary. Milwaukee, Bruce [c.1965] vi, 130p. 21cm. [BX2160.2.L9] 65-23746 1.95 pap.,
1. Mary, Virgin—Meditations. I. Title.

MCCALL, Oswald Walter Samuel, 1885- 242
The hand of God. Enl. ed. New York, Harper [1957] 180p. illus. 22cm. [BV4832.M14 1957] 57-6198
1. Devotional literature. I. Title.

MCCORRY, Vincent P., 1909- 242
The Gospel of now [by] Vincent P. McCorry. [New York] Herder and Herder [1968] 159 p. 21 cm. [BX2170.C55M32] 68-55087
1. Church year—Meditations. I. Title.

MCDANIEL, Audrey. 242
Garden of hope; inspirational thoughts and verses. Floral motifs by Hazel Hoffman. [Norwalk, Conn., C. R. Gibson]; distributed by Doubleday [New York, 1967, c1966] 40 p. illus. (part col.) 21 cm. [BV4832.2.M17] 66-21558
1. Devotional literature. I. Title.

MCDANIEL, Audrey. 242
God is there; sacred thoughts and verses. Floral designs by Hazel Hoffmann. [Norwalk, Conn.] Gibson [1969] 40 p. illus. (part col.) 21 cm. [BV4832.2.M173] 69-16105
1. Devotional literature. I. Title.

• 242
Golden nuggets of wisdom, compiled by Paul S. McElroy, with illustrations by Stanley Clough. Mount Vernon, N.Y., Peter Pauper Press [1974] 62 p. illus. 20 cm. [BV4801] 1.95
1. Devotional literature. I. Title.

MCELROY, Paul Simpson, 1902- 242
Moments of meditation. Mount Vernon, N. Y., Peter Pauper Press [c.1961] unpaged. 61-2030 1.00 bds.,
1. Meditations. I. Title.

MCELROY, Paul Simpson, 1902- 242
Quiet thoughts. Illus. by Stanley Clough. Mount Vernon, N.Y., Peter Pauper [c.1964] 60p. illus. 19cm. 64-2946 1.00 bds.,
1. Devotional literature. I. Title.

MCGAVRAN, Grace Winifred. 242
All through the year; a devotional reader for boys and girls.Decorations by Ruth W. Rogers. St. Louis, Bethany Press [1958] 126p. illus. 23cm. [BV4870.M15] 58-9109
1. Children—Prayer-books and devotions—English. I. Title.

MCKEE, Bill, 1919- 242
Life after birth; practical exercises for spiritual growth. Wheaton, Ill., Tyndale House [1973] 95 p. 19 cm. [BV4832.2.M197 1973] 72-97659 ISBN 0-8423-2190-X 0.95 (pbk.)
1. Devotional exercises. I. Title.

MCKEE, Bill, 1919- 242
Life after birth; practical exercises for spiritual growth. Wheaton, Ill., Tyndale House [1973] 95 p. 19 cm. [BV4832.2.M197 1973] 72-97659 ISBN 0-8423-2190-X
1. Devotional exercises. I. Title.

MCKINNEY, Donald, 1909- 242
Joy begins with you / Donald McKinney. Nashville : Abingdon Press, [1975] 95 p. ; 20 cm. [BV4832.2.M199] 74-20523 ISBN 0-687-20647-2: 3.95.
1. Joy—Meditations. I. Title.

MACLENNAN, David Alexander, 1903- 242
Making the most of your best. Philadelphia, Westminster Press [1958] 183p. 21cm. [BV4832.M2785] 58-8053
1. Meditations. I. Title.

MACLEOD, Earle Henry. 242
Moments for everyone, one by one, by Earle H. MacLeod. Grand Rapids, Mich., Zondervan Pub. House [1969] 93 p. 18 cm. [BV4832.2.M2] 76-95034 2.50
1. Meditations. I. Title.

MCMAHON, Edwin M., 1930- 242
The in-between; evolution in Christian faith, by Edwin M. McMahon and Peter A. Campbell. New York, Sheed and Ward [1969] 189 p. 21 cm. [BX2350.2.M264] 69-16990 4.95
1. Spiritual life—Catholic authors. I. Campbell, Peter A., 1935- joint author. II. Title.

MCMAHON, Edwin M., 1930- 242
Please touch [by] Edwin M. McMahon [and] Peter A. Campbell. [New York] Sheed and Ward [1969] 46 p. illus. 28 cm. (A Search book) [BV4832.2.M22] 70-82598 2.95
1. Meditations. I. Campbell, Peter A., 1935- joint author. II. Title.

MCMENAMY, Francis Xavier, 1872-1949. 242
Eight-day retreat; based on the Spiritual exercises of St. Ignatius. Edited by William J. Grace. Milwaukee, Bruce Pub. Co. [1956] 218p. 22cm. [BX2179.L8M3] 56-9645
1. Loyola, Igacio de, Saint, 1491-1556. Exercitia spiritualia. 2. Spiritual exercises. I. Title.

MCNABB, Vincent Joseph, 1868-1943. 242
Stars of comfort; retreat conferences. Chicago, H. Regnery Co. [1958] 149p. 19cm. [BX2182.M318] 58-14540
1. Meditations. I. Title.

MCNEIL, Jesse Jai. 242
As thy days so thy strength. Grand Rapids, Eerdmans [1960] 167p. 23cm. [BV4832.M23] 60-10090
1. Devotional exercises. I. Title.

MCNEIL, Jesse Jai. 242
Moments in His Presence. Grand Rapids, Eerdmans [1962] x, 98p. 21cm. [BT306.4.M3] 62-13400
1. Jesus Christ—Biog.—Meditations. I. Title.

MCQUARY, Rodney L. 242
Ponderings, by Rodney L. McQuary. [1st ed.] Friday Harbor, Wash., Long House Printcrafters [1973] 121 p. 23 cm. [BV4832.2.M234] 73-77118
1. Meditations. I. Title.

MCSORLEY, Joseph, 1874- 242
Meditations for everyman; v.2. New York, Paulist Pr. [c.1948, 1963] 213p. 18cm. (Deus bk.) Contents.v.2. Pentecost to Advent. .95 pap.,
1. Church year—Meditations. I. Title.

MCSORLEY, Joseph, 1874- 242
Think and pray; prayers for use during retreat or holy hour or private devotions. New York, Paulist Pr. [1962, c.1936] 159p. (Deus bks.) .95 pap.,
1. Meditations. 2. Retreats. 3. Holy hour. I. Title.

MAGANA, Jose. 242
A strategy for liberation : notes for orienting the Exercises toward Utopia / by Jose Magana ; translated from the Spanish by Mary Angela Roduit. 1st ed. Jersey City, N.J. : Program to Adapt the Spiritual Exercises, [1974] xxx, 183 p. ; 21 cm. Bibliography: p. 169-183. [BX2179.L8M325] 74-195220
1. Loyola, Ignacio de, Saint, 1491-1556. Exercitia spiritualia. I. Title.

*MAGDALENE 242
A modern Magdalene, by "Magdalene" [New York] Warner Paperback Library [1975] 155 p. 18 cm. [BV4832] 1.25 (pbk.)
1. Devotional literature. I. Title.

*MAINPRIZE, Donald Charles 242
Good morning, lord meditations for teacher Grand Rapids, Baker Book House, [1974] lv. (unpaged) 19 cm. [BV4832] ISBN 0-8010-5959-3 1.95
1. Teachers—Prayer book and devotions I. Title.

MALANIA, Fae, 1919- 242
The quantity of a hazel nut. [1st ed.] New York, Knopf, 1968. 152 p. 22 cm. [BX2182.2.M28] 67-22217
1. Devotional literature. I. Title.

MANTON, Joseph E., 1904- 242
Give God equal time! / Joseph Manton. Huntington, Ind. : Our Sunday Visitor, c1977. 254 p. ; 21 cm. [BX2182.2.M29] 76-52620 ISBN 0-87973-747-6 pbk. : 3.95
1. Meditations. I. Title.

MANTON, Joseph E., 1904- 242
Straws from the crib. Foreword by Richard Cardinal Cushing [Boston] St. Paul Eds. [dist. Daughters of St. Paul, c.1964] 566p. 22cm. [BX1756.M2924S7] 64-7925 5.95; 4.95 pap.,
1. Catholic Church—Sermons. 2. Sermons, American. I. Title.

MARCH, William H 242
Look up and lift up. Grand Rapids, Eerdmans [1959] 120p. 23cm. [BV4832.2.M28] 59-12937
1. Meditations. I. Title.

MARMION, Columba Abbot 242
[Secular name: Joseph Marmion] 1858-1923
The structure of God's plan, being the first part of Christ the life of the soul. Tr. from French by a nun of Tyburn Convent. Introd. by Cardinal Godfrey. St. Louis, B. Herder [1963] 160p. 19cm. 63-5917 1.95 pap.,
1. Meditations. I. Title. II. Title: Christ the life of the soul.

MARSHALL, William Renwick, 1905- 242
Eternity shut in a span. [1st ed.] New York, Pageant Press [1959] 75p. 21cm. [BV4832.2.M3] 59-11708
1. Devotional literature. I. Title.

*MARTIN, Paul 242
Good morning, lord devotions for young people Grand Rapids, Baker Book House [1974 c1971] 64 p. 19 cm. [BV4832] ISBN 0-8010-5958-5 1.95 (pbk.)
1. Youth—Prayer books and devotions. I. Title.

MARY Teresa, Sister, O.P. 242
Prayers at mealtime. New York, Paulist Press [1972] 60 p. 17 cm. [BV283.G7M37] 72-91457 ISBN 0-8091-1745-2 0.75 (pbk.)
1. Grace at meals. 2. Prayers. I. Title.

[MARY MILDRED, Sister] 1876- 242
The heart of the King, by a Sister of Mercy. [n.p.] St. Paul Editions [c1956] 140p. 20cm. [BX2157.M27] 59-25206
1. Sacred Heart, Devotion to. I. Title.

MARY ROSAMOND, Sister, O. P. 242
Miniature missiles for heaven's sake. With a foreword by Maurice B. Walsh. Illustrated by Joseph Swan. [New York] St. Paul Publications [1960] 144p. illus. 20cm. [BX2182.2.M3] 60-8946
1. Meditations. I. Title.

MASON, David E 242
Now then; [essays] Nashville, Broadman Press [1957] 96p. 21cm. [BV4832.M3355] 57-6330
1. Devotional literature. I. Title.

MASON, David E 242
Now then; [essays] Nashville, Broadman Press [1957] 96p. 21cm. [BV4832.M3355] 57-6330
1. Devotional literature. I. Title.

MATHESON, George, 1842-1906 242
Devotional selection. Comp., ed. by Andrew Kosten. Nashville, Abingdon [c.1962] 95p. 62-7228 2.00
1. Meditations. I. Kosten, Andrew, ed. II. Title.

MATHESON, George, 1842-1906. 242
Devotional selections. Compiled and edited by Andrew Kosten. New York, Abingdon Press [1962 95p. 18cm. [BV4832.M3358] 62-7228
1. Meditations. I. Kosten, Andrew, ed. II. Title.

MAXWELL, Neal A. 242
"For the power is in them ... " Mormon musings [by] Neal A. Maxwell. Salt Lake City, Deseret Book Co., 1970. 63 p. 23 cm. [BV4832.2.M36] 70-120731 2.95
1. Meditations. I. Title.

MEAD, J. Earl. 242
With God in the garden [by] J. Earl Mead. Nashville, Broadman Press [1968] 78 p. 19 cm. [BV4832.2.M38] 68-20681
1. Devotional literature. I. Title.

MEADERS, Margaret S. 242
Soul soliloquy, by Margaret S. Meaders. Brooklyn, N.Y., T. Gaus' Sons [1974] 54 p. 23 cm. [BV4501.2.M44] 73-92861
1. Meditations. I. Title.

MEDITATIONS on the church, 242
based on the Constitution on the church. Introd. by John J. Wright. [New York] Herder and Herder [1967] 192 p. 22 cm. [BX830 1962.A45C88] 67-19758
1. Church. I. Wright, John Joseph, Cardinal, 1909- II. Vatican Council. 2d, 1962-1965. Constitutio dogmatica de ecclesia.

MEDITATIONS on the Litany of 242
the Sacred Heart. Baltimore, Md., Reparation Society of the Immaculate Heart of Mary [1967] vi, 198 p. 18 cm. "These meditations first appeared serially in Fatima findings between January, 1957 and March 1967." [BX2158.M46] 67-27287
1. Litany of the Sacred Heart—Meditations. I. Fatima findings.

*MELINE, Virginia 242
Available aid. Illus. by Eva E. Meline. New York, Vantage [1966] 95p. 21cm. 2.75
I. Title.

MERCHANT, Jane. 242
Every good gift. Nashville, Abingdon Press [1968] 96 p. illus. 18 cm. [BV4832.2.M39] 68-25359 2.50
1. Meditations. I. Title.

MERCHANT, Jane. 242
The greatest of these... [Poems and prayers] Nashville, Abingdon Press [1954] 96p. 16cm. [BV4832.M42] 54-9197
1. Devotional exercises. I. Title.

MERCHANT, Jane. 242
An green pastures. New York, Abingdon Press [1959] 110p. 16cm. Verse and prose. [BV4832.2.M4] 59-8199
1. Devotional exercises. I. Title.

MERCHANT, Jane. 242
Think about these things. New York, Abingdon Press [1956] 96p. 16cm. Meditations in poetry and prayer, with selections from the Bible. [BV260.M38] 56-8742
1. Prayers. I. Title.

MEREDITH, Ronald R 242
The Twenty-third psalm; a meditation by Ronald R. Meredith. Design and illus. by Bill Hunter. New York, Abingdon Press [1965] 1 v. (unpaged) col. illus. 19 cm. [BS1450 23d.M35] 65-20372
1. Bible. O. T. Psalms xxiii — Meditations. I. Title.

MEREDITH, Ronald R. 242
The Twenty-third psalm; a meditation. Design, illus. by Bill Hunter. Nashville, Abingdon [c.1965] 1 v. (unpaged) col. illus. 19cm. [BS1450 23d.M35] 65-20372 1.50
1. Bible. O.T. Psalms XXIII—Meditations. I. Title.

MERTON, Thomas 242
The new man. New York, Farrar [1962, c.1961] 248p. 62-7168 3.50 bds.,
1. Spiritual life—Catholic authors. I. Title.

MERTON, Thomas 242
Thoughts in solitude. [New York, Dell 1961, c.1956, 1958] 160p. (Chapel bk. F132) .50 pap.,
1. Spiritual life—Meditations and comtemplations. I. Title.

MERTON, Thomas, 1915- 242
The ascent to truth. [1st ed.] New York, Harcourt Brace [1951] x, 342 p. 22 cm. Name in religion: Louis, Father. Bibliography: p. [336]-342. [BV5091.C7M4] 51-12819
1. Contemplation. I. Title.

MERTON, Thomas, 1915- 242
Thoughts in solitude. New York, Farrar, Straus & Cudahy [1958] 124p. 21cm. [BX2350.M543] 58-8817
1. Spiritual life—Catholic authors. 2. Solitude. I. Title.

MERTON, Thomas, 1915- [Name in religion: Father Louis] 242
Thoughts in solitude. Garden City, N.Y., Doubleday [1968, c.1958] 120p. 18cm. (Image bk., D247) .85 pap.,
1. Spiritual life—Catholic authors. 2. Solitude. I. Title.

*MERTON, Thomas [Name in religion, Father Louis] 1915- 242
The new man [New York] New Amer. Lib. [1963, c.1961] 141p. 18cm. (Mentor-omega bk., MP548) .60 pap.,
1. Spiritual life—Catholic authors. I. Title.

MERTON. Thomas [Name in religion: Father Louis] 1915- 242
New seeds of contemplation. [Norfolk, Conn.] New Directions [1962, c.1961] 297p. 61-17869 4.50

1. Spiritual life—Catholic authors. I. Title.

MESSNER, Nancy Shingler. 242
Patterns of thinking [by] Nancy Shingler Messner [and] Gerald Messner. Belmont, Calif., Wadsworth Pub. Co. [1968] 339 p. illus. 23 cm. [PE1417.M48] 68-12960
1. College readers. 2. English language—Rhetoric. I. Messner, Gerald, joint author. II. Title.

METALLIDES, Constantine L 242
Happiness through victory. [1st ed.] New York, Vantage Press [1957] 150p. 21cm. [BV4832.M436] 56-12836
1. Devotional literature. I. Title.

MEYER, Frederick Brotherton, 1847-1929. 242
My daily prayer; a short supplication for every day in the year. [Westwood, N. J.] Revell [1957] 63p. 17cm. (Revell's inspirational classics) [BV260.M4 1957] 57-12366
1. Prayers. 2. Devotional calendars. I. Title.

MICHELINO. 242
The keys to truth : a guide to your inner self / by Michelino. New York : Philosophical Library, 1977c1976 90 p. ; 22 cm. [BV4832.2.M46] 76-47834 ISBN 0-8022-2194-7 : 5.00
1. Meditations. I. Title.

MIDDLETON, Robert Lee, 1894- 242
The gift of love / R. L. Middleton. Nashville : Broadman Press, c1976. 124 p. ; 21 cm. Includes bibliographical references. [BV4832.2.M468] 76-2241 ISBN 0-8054-5145-5 : 3.95
1. Meditations. I. Title.

MIDDLETON, Robert Lee, 1894- 242
My cup runneth over. Nashville, Broadman Press [1960] 115p. 21cm. [BV4832.2.M47] 60-5631
1. Devotional literature. I. Title.

MIDDLETON, Robert Lee, 1894- 242
Take time! Messages of spiritual refreshment. Nashville, Abingdon [1964, c.1949] 128p. 18cm. (Apex bks., Q5) .95 pap.,
1. Devotional literature. I. Title.

MIDDLETON, Robert Lee, 1894- 242
Thinking about God; devotional mediations ... Nashville, Broadman Press [1955] 119p. 21cm. [BV4832.M465] 55-14880
1. Devotional literature. I. Title.

MILLS, Flossie E 242
From earth to sky; a book of devotional readings. [1st ed.] New York, Greenwich Book Publishers [1959] 63p. 21cm. [BV4832.2.M5] 59-7988
1. Devotional literature. I. Title.

MIRROR of the heart. 242
Author unknown. A translation of the Norwegian Menneskets hjertes speil, published 1900. Translated by Edward C. Eid. [Minneapolis] Hauge Lutheran Inner Mission Federation; purchase from R. P. Haakonson. Moorhead, Minn. [1959] 62p. illus. 23cm. [BV4836.M413] 60-25733
1. Devotional literature. I. Eid, Edward C., tr.

MITSON, Eileen Nora. 242
The innermost room / Eileen Mitson. 1st ed. Chappaqua, N.Y. : Christian Herald Books, c1976. 126 p. ; 22 cm. [BV4832.2.M53 1976] 76-16593 ISBN 0-915684-10-1 : 4.95
1. Meditations. 2. Christian life—Baptist authors. I. Title.

MOFFATT, John Edward, 1894- 242
Minute meditations. Milwaukee. Bruce Pub. Co. [c1958] 146p. 21cm. [BX2182.2.M6] 59-356
1. Meditations. I. Title.

MOFFATT, John Edward, 1894- 242
Stirring the embers; brief readings and meditations for religious. Milwaukee, Bruce Pub. Co. [1952] 137 p. 20 cm. [BX2182.M57] 52-2840
1. Meditations. I. Title.

MOLTON, Warren Lane. 242
Bruised reeds. Photos. by David Mark Breed. Valley Forge [Pa.] Judson Press [1970] 112 p. illus. 21 cm. [BV245.M58] 70-103391 2.50
1. Prayers. I. Breed, David Mark, illus. II. Title.

MONK of Farne (The); 242
the meditations of a fourteenth century monk, ed., introd. by Hugh Farmer. Tr. [from Latin] by a Benedictine of Stanbrook. Baltimore, Helicon [c.1961] vii, 155p. illus. (Benedictine studies [1]) Bibl. 61-19349 3.95
1. Meditations. I. Farmer, Hugh, ed. II. Series.

MONKA, Paul. 242
Meditations in uni verse. Illustrated by Gertrude Halpern. [1st ed. New York, Harper & Row, 1969] [96] p. col. illus. 14 x 20 cm. [BV4832.2.M56] 74-85050 3.95
1. Meditations. I. Title.

MONTGOMERY, Robert, 1923- 242
Get high on yourself : get on to life / by Robert Montgomery. St. Meinrad, IN : Abbey Press, 1976 [c1975] 71 p. : ill. ; 25 x 12 cm. [BV4832.2.M564 1976] 75-39420 pbk. : 1.95
1. Meditations. I. Title.

MOODY, Dwight Lyman, 1837-1899. 242
One thousand and one thoughts from my library. Grand Rapids, Baker Book House [1974] 396 p. 21 cm. Reprint of the 1898 ed. published by the F. H. Revell Co. [BV4801.M6 1974] 74-167259 ISBN 0-8010-5951-8 5.95
1. Meditations. I. Title.

MOODY, Dwight Lyman, 1837-1899. 242
The wit and wisdom of D. L. Moody / compiled and edited by Stanley and Patricia Gundry. Chicago : Moody Press, [1974] 78 p. : ill. ; 22 cm. Includes bibliographical references and index. [BV4832.M553] 74-15332 ISBN 0-8024-9568-0 pbk. : 1.95
1. Meditations. I. Title.

MOORE, Jack L., 1920- 242
From a listening heart / Jack L. Moore. 1st ed. Garden City, N.Y. : Doubleday, 1975. viii, 179 p. ; 22 cm. [BV4832.2.M567] 74-31517 ISBN 0-385-08422-6 : 6.95
1. Meditations. I. Title.

MOORE, Mary Hunter. 242
Down nature's paths. [Meditations] Nashville, Southern Pub. Association [1953] 143p. 20cm. [BV4832.M555] 54-21717
1. Devotional literature. I. Title.

MOORE, Sebastian, 1917- 242
Before the deluge [by] Sebastian Moore and Anselm Hurt. New York, Newman Press [1968] 124 p. 23 cm. [BX2182.2.M63 1968] 68-57109 3.95
1. Meditations. I. Hurt, Anselm, 1932- joint author. II. Title.

MOORE, Thomas Hendrick, 1898- 242
The risen dead. New York, McMullen Books [1951] 185 p. 21 cm. [BX2182.M644] 51-10915
1. Meditations. I. Title.

MOORE, Walter Lane, 1905- 242
Courage and confidence from the Bible, by Walter L. Mmore and the staff of the Christian herald. Foreword by Daniel A. Poling [1st ed.] New York, Prentice-Hall [1951] xviii, 365 p. 20 cm. [BV4832.M556] 51-1024
1. Devotional exercises. 2. Calendars. I. Christian herald (New York, 1878-) II. Title.

MOORE, Walter Lane, 1905- 242
Courage and confidence from the Bible, by Walter L. Moore and the staff of the Christian herald. Foreword by Daniel A. Poling. A staff of the Christian herald. Foreword by Daniel A. Poling. A [New York] New American Library [1951] 175 p. 19 cm. (A Signet book, 862) [BV4832.M556] 51-3099
1. Devotional exercises. 2. Calendars. I. Christian herald (New York, 1878-) II. Title.

MORE, Thomas, Sir Saint, 1478-1535. 242
Dialogue of comfort against tribulation. London, New York, Sheed and Ward [1951] vii, 262 p. 20 cm. [BV4904.M] 51-10669
1. Consolation. I. Title.

MORGAN, Beatrice Payne 242
Seventh dimension: a potpourri of meditations for the Christian today. Chicago, Adams, c.1963. 52p. 18cm. 1.25 pap.,
I. Title.

MORGAN, Elise (Nevins) 1876- 242
Communion. 2d ed. enl. Wellesley Hills, Mass., Elisian Guild [c1967] ix, 117 p. 14 cm. (Her The meditation series) [BV4832.2.M58] 67-18961
1. Devotional literature. I. Title.

MORGAN, Elise (Nevins) 1876- 242
That we may be willing to receive. 2d ed., enl. Wellesley Hills, Mass., Elisian Guild [1965, c1966] xii, 116 p. 14 cm. (Her The meditation series) [BV4832.2.M59 1966] 65-28116 2.50
1. Meditations. I. Title.

MORRISON, John Arch, 1893- 242
As I was thinking, by John A. Morrison. Anderson, Ind., Warner Press [1964] 96 p. 20 cm. [BV4832.2.M6] 64-12622
1. Devotional literature. I. Morrison, John Arch, 1893- II. Title.

MORRISON, John Arch, 1893- 242
As I was thinking. Anderson, Ind., Warner [c.1964] 96p. 20cm. 64-12622 1.25 pap.,
1. Devotional literature. I. Title.

MORTIMORE, Olive. 242
Out of abundance. [Independence, Mo., Herald Pub. House, 1971] 41 p. 16 cm. [BV4832.2.M63] 75-157452 ISBN 0-8309-0048-9
1. Meditations. I. Title.

MOSER, Lawrence E. 242
Home celebrations; studies in American pastoral liturgy, by Lawrence E. Moser. Paramus, N.J., Newman Press [1970] vi, 166 p. 22 cm. [BX2170.F3M68] 72-133298 4.95
1. Catholic Church—Prayer-books and devotions. 2. Family—Prayer-books and devotions. I. Title.

MOSS, Sidney Phil, 1917- comp. 242
Readings for Composition by logic. [Compiled by] Sidney P. Moss. Belmont, Calif., Wadsworth Pub. Co. [1968] x, 243 p. 22 cm. [PE1417.M64] 68-13722
1. College readers. I. Moss, Sidney Phil, 1917- Composition by logic. II. Title.

MULLEN, Thomas James, 1934- 242
Birthdays, holidays, and other disasters [by] Thomas Mullen. Nashville, Abingdon Press [1971] 144 p. 20 cm. [BV4832.2.M85] 75-158669 ISBN 0-687-03557-0 2.75
1. Meditations. I. Title.

MUNRO, Bertha. 242
Strength for today. Companion volume to Truth for today. Kansas City, Mo., Beacon Hill Press [1954] 384p. 22cm. [BV4832.M854] 54-4588
1. Devotional calendars. I. Title.

*MURRAY, Andrew 242
Like Christ. Minneapolis, Dimension Books [1974] 231 p. 18 cm. [BV4832] 1.45 (pbk.)
1. Devotional literature. 2. Meditations. I. Title.

MURRAY, Mary Grace, ed. 242
The D'Youville anthology. 1st- . . . 1960- Buffalo, D'Youville College. v. 24 cm. "The prose and poetry of New York State high school students," 1960- Editor: 1960- M.G. Murray. [PS508.S4D9] 60-13008
1. School prose. 2. School verse. I. D'Youville College, Buffalo. II. Title.

MURRAY, Mary Grace, ed. 242
The D'Youville anthology. 1st- . . . 1960- Buffalo, D'Youville College. v. 24 cm. "The prose and poetry of New York State high school students," 1960- Editor: 1960- M.G. Murray. [PS508.S4D9] 60-13008
1. School prose. 2. School verse. I. D'Youville College, Buffalo. II. Title.

MURRAY, Ralph L 242
The other dimension; meditations on the disciples' prayer [by] Ralph L. Murray. Nashville, Broadman Press [c1966] 96 p. 20 cm. "Notes" (bibliographica): p. 95-96. [BV230.M9] 66-10666
1. Lord's prayer. I. Title.

MURRAY, Ralph L. 242
The other dimension; meditations on the disciples' prayer. Nashville, Broadman [c.1966] 96p. 20cm. Bibl. [BV230.M9] 66-10666 2.00 bds.,
1. Lord's prayer. I. Title.

*MURRAY, Rev, Andrew 242
The new life; words of God for young disciples of Christ. Tr. from Dutch by Rev. J. P. Lilley. Minneapolis, Bethany Pr. [1966, c.1965] 254p. 19cm. 1.95 pap.,
I. Title.

NASH, Robert. 242
Ideals to live by; a guide to the spiritual exercises of St. Ignatius Loyola. New York, Benziger Bros. [1959] 179p. 21cm. [BX2179.L8N3] 59-12545
1. Loyola, Ignacio de, Saint, 1491-1556. Exercitia spiritualia. I. Title.

NASH, Robert. 242
The seminarian at his prie-dieu. Westminster, Md., Newman Press, 1951. 312 p. 23 cm. [BX903.N3] 52-6323
1. Seminarians — Religious life. I. Title.

NEAL, Effie C. 242
Nuggets of gold, a devotional guide. New York, Carlton [c.1960] 60p. 21cm. (Reflection bk.) 1.50
I. Title.

NEAL, Lucille A 242
Like a tree planted, [1st ed.] New York, Pageant Press [1955] 133p. 21cm. [BV4832.N27] 55-11413
1. Meditations. I. Title.

NELSON, Clifford Ansgar. 242
With hearts uplifted; [meditations on nuggets of Scripture] Rock Island, Ill., Augustana Press [1956] 200p. 22cm. [BV4832.N34] 56-11913
1. Meditations. I. Title.

NELSON, Ruth Youngdahl. 242
You can make a difference. Minneapolis, Minn., Augsburg Pub. House [1974] 128 p. 20 cm. [BV4832.2.N4] 74-77678 ISBN 0-8066-1429-3 2.95
1. Meditations. I. Title.

NEWTON, Joseph Fort, 1876-1950. 242
Everyday religious living. New York, Abingdon-Cokesbury Press [1951] 256 p. 16 cm. [BV4253.N42] 51-14229
1. Sermons, American. I. Title.

NEWTON, Joseph Fort, 1876-1950. 242
Everyday religious living. Abingdon [1962, c.1951] 256p. (Apex bks., J6) .95 pap.,
1. Sermons, American I. Title.

NOONAN, Hugh. 242
Companion to the clams / by Hugh Noonan ; illustrated by Phero Thomas. Chicago : Franciscan Herald Press, [1977] p. cm. [BX2182.2.N65] 77-14193 ISBN 0-8199-0680-8 pbk. : 4.95
1. Meditations. I. Title.

NOONAN, Hugh. 242
Listen, the clams are talking. Photos by Emery Tang. Chicago, Franciscan Herald Press [1973] v, 58 p. illus. 27 cm. [BX2182.2.N66] 73-12092 ISBN 0-8199-0469-4 7.95
1. Meditations. I. Title.

NORBORG, Kaut, 1897- ed. 242
With Gode and His mercy; meditations for the days of the church year, by sixty pastors of the Church of Sweden. Translated from the Swedish by Arthur O. Hjelm. Rock Island, Ill., Augustana Press [1958] 592 p. 20 cm. Translation of Dagar komma, dagar flykta, edited by Knut Norborg. [BV4836.D273] 58-7175
1. Church year — Meditations. 2. Lutheran Church — Prayer-books and devotions — English. I. Hjelm, Arthur O., tr. II. Title.

NORRIS, Judy. 242
Have you seen my father? / by Judy Norris. Cincinnati, Ohio : New Life Books, [1975] 96 p. ; 18 cm. [BS483.5.N67] 74-28723 ISBN 0-87239-030-6 pbk. : 1.50
1. Bible—Meditations. I. Title.

NORRIS, Judy. 242
Lord, I'm glad You know the way. Cincinnati, Standard Pub. [1973] 96 p. illus. 18 cm. (Fountain books) [BV4832.2.N6] 73-79471
1. Meditations. I. Title.

NOUWEN, Henri J. M. 242
Out of solitude; three meditations on the Christian life, by Henri J. M. Nouwen. Photography by Ron P. van den Bosch. Notre Dame, Ind., Ave Maria Press [1974] 63 p. illus. 20 cm. "These mediations were first given as sermons at 'Battell,' The United Church of Christ at Yale University." [BX2182.2.N67] 74-176325 ISBN 0-87793-071-6 3.50
1. Meditations. I. Title.
Pbk. 1.75; ISBN 0-87793-072-4.

NUGENT, Francis Edward, comp. 242
A spiritual reader. Westminster, Md., Newman Press, 1953. 210p. 21cm. [BX2177.N8] 53-10461
1. Devotional literature. 2. Spiritual life—Catholic authors. I. Title.

NUNN, William Curtis, 1908- 242
Peace unto you, by Will Curtis. New York, Grosset & Dunlap [1970] viii, 116 p. 17 cm. (The Family inspirational library) [BV4832.2.N8] 70-105940 1.95
1. Meditations. I. Title.

NYSTEDT, Olle. 242
Fast falls the eventide, words for devotion and contemplation. Translated by Clifford Ansgar Nelson. Rock Island, Ill., Augustana Press [1956] 96p. 22cm. [BV4580.N9] 56-11914
1. Aged—Prayer-books and devotions—English. I. Title.

OAKESHOTT, Walter Fraser, 1903- 242
The sword of the spirit; a meditative and devotional anthology. Boston, Beacon Press, 1952. 197 p. 20 cm. (Selections: Extracts, etc.) [BV4801.O2] 52-7343
1. Devotional literature. I. Title.

O'BRIEN, Bartholomew J 242
Spurs to meditation. Milwaukee, Bruce Pub. Co. [1955] 116p. 17cm. [BV4813.O2] 55-7866
1. Meditation. I. Title.

O'BRIEN, Hary Corita, 1906- 242
Footnotes and headlines, a play-pray book [by] Sister Corita. New York, Herder and Herder [1967] 50 p. illus. (part col.) 27 cm. [BV4832.2.O2] 67-27568
1. Meditations. I. Title.

O'BRIEN, Isidore, 1895-1953. 242
Seven baskets; [essays] Paterson, N. J., St. Anthony Guild Press, 1955 [c1951] 175p. 20cm. [BX2182] 56-518
1. Devotional literature. I. Title.

O'BRIEN, May Corita, 1906- 242
Footnotes and headlines, a play-pray book [by] Sister Corita. New York, Herder and Herder [1967] 50 p. illus. (part col.) 27 cm. [BV4832.2.O2] 67-27568
1. Meditations. I. Title.

OCHS, William Benjamin. 242
In the morning; daily meditations on Christ and His truth. Washington, Review and Herald [1951] 368 p. 16 cm. [BV4832.O3] 51-31775
1. Devotional exercises. 2. Seventh-Day Adventists—Prayer-books and devotions—English. 3. Calendars. I. Title.

OCHSENRIDER, Robert. 242
Celebration; becoming whole persons in a fractured society. Nashville, Tidings [1971] 30 p. illus. 19 cm. [BV4832.2.O25] 78-155701
1. Meditations. I. Title.

O'CONNOR, Elizabeth. 242
Our many selves. [1st ed.] New York, Harper & Row [1971] xxi, 201 p. 22 cm. Bibliography: p. [199]-201. [BV4801.O23 1971] 78-124699 4.95
1. Devotional exercises. I. Title.

OLSON, Harry E., 1934- 242
Monday morning Christianity / Harry E. Olson, Jr. ; foreword by Tom Landry. Minneapolis : Augsburg Pub. House, [1975] 128 p. ; 20 cm. [BS491.5.O47] 75-2833 ISBN 0-8066-1478-1 : 2.95
1. Bible—Meditations. I. Title.

OLSSON, Karl A 242
Things common and preferred Christian perspectives. Minneapolis, Augsburg Pub. House [1959] 181p. 21cm. [BR115.C5O5] 59-6680
1. Civilization, Christian. I. Title.

O'REILLY, James D. 242
Renewal and reconciliation; reflections for a Holy Year [by] James D. O'Reilly. [Chicago, Franciscan Herald Press, 1974] 31 p. 18 cm. (Synthesis series) [BX2182.2.O73] 74-12115 0.65 (pbk.)
1. Meditations. 2. Holy Year, 1975. I. Title.

OSENBERG, Hans Dieter. 242
Zeit die uns bleibt : Meditationen im Alltag / Hans Dieter Osenberg. Hamburg : Furche-Verlag, c1975. 128 p. ; 18 cm. (Stundenbucher : Bd. 122) [BV4834.O8] 75-511834 ISBN 3-7730-0253-X
1. Meditations. I. Title.

OSENDE, Victorino, 1879- 242
Fruits of contemplation; translated by a Dominican Sister of the Perpetual Rosary, Milwaukee, Wisconsin. St. Louis, B. Herder Book Co., 1953. 338p. 21cm. (Cross and crown series of spirituality) Translation of Contemplata: momentos misticos. [BV5091.C7O82] 53-10673
1. Contemplation. I. Title.

OURSLER, Grace (Perkins) 242
When sorrow comes [by] Grace Perkins Oursler and April Armstrong [1st ed.] Garden City, N.Y., Doubleday, 1950. 155 p. 20 cm. [BV4905.O8] 50-9870
1. Consolation. I. Armstrong, April (Oursler) joint author. II. Title.

OUTLAW, Nell (Warren) 242
This is the day; devotional thoughts on the special days in the year. Grand Rapids, Zondervan Pub. House [1957] 149p. 22cm. [BV4832O8] 57-38375
1. Devotional literature. I. Title.

PADDOCK, Charles Lee, 1891- 242
Whistle stops; two-minute meditations. Drawings by Robert Kutsch. Mountain View, Calif., Pacific Press Pub. Association [1955] 58p. illus. 19cm. [BV4832.P23] 55-3265
1. Meditations. I. Title.

PAGANSKI, Donald J. 242
40 objects lessons, by Donald J. Poganski. St. Louis, Concordia Pub. House [1973] 160 p. illus. 19 cm. "Sermonettes." Bibliography: p. 160. [BV4832.2.P59] 72-86233 ISBN 0-570-03148-6 1.95 (pbk.)
1. Meditations. 2. Religious education—Audio-visual aids. I. Title.

PAGE, Kirby, 1890- 242
Living joyously; an anthology of devotional readings for 365 days. New York, Rinehart [1950] xi, 380 p. 20 cm. [BV4832.P315] 50-9722
1. Devotional exercises. I. Title.

PALLOTTI, Vincenzo, Saint, 1795-1850. 242
Spiritual thoughts and aspirations of St. Vincent Pallotti. Translated and edited under the supervision of Flavian Bonifazi. Baltimore, Pallottine Fathers Press, 1964. xix, 227 p. 21 cm. [BX4700.P23A33] 64-8852
I. Bonifazi, Flavian, ed. and tr. II. Title.

PAONE, Anthony J 1913- 242
My life with Christ. [1st ed.] Garden City, N. Y., Doubleday [1962] 310p. 22cm. esus Christ--Biog.--Meditations. [BT306.4.P3] 62-17359
I. Title. II. Series.

PAONE, Anthony J., 1913- 242
My life with Christ. Garden City, N.Y., Doubleday [c.1962] 310p. 22cm. 62-17359 4.50
1. Jesus Christ—Biog. Meditations. I. Title.

PARADIS, Adrian A 242
Grow in grace [by] Adrian A. and Grace D. Paradis. New York, Abingdon Press [1958] 128p. 20cm. [BV4832.P345] 58-9522
1. Devotional calendars. I. Paradis, Grace D., joint author. II. Title.

PARET, Barbara, 1926- 242
Just You and me, God. Richmond, John Knox Press [1973] 63 p. illus. 20 cm. [BV4832.2.P32] 73-5351 3.25
1. Devotional exercises. I. Title.

PARISH, Karl E. 242
I hear St. Francis singing. Meditations. New York, Exposition Press, [c.1960] 41p. 21cm. (Exposition-Testament book) 2.50
1. Title.

PARR, Robert H. 242
Sparrow among the eagles / by Robert H. Parr. Nashville : Southern Publishing Association, c1975. 96 p. ; 21 cm. (A Crown book) [BV4832.2.P325] 75-18150 ISBN 0-8127-0101-1
1. Meditations. I. Title.

PARSCH, Pius, 1884- 242
Seasons of grace. Tr. by H. E. Winstone. [New York] Herder & Herder [c.1963] 369p. 23cm. 63-8323 5.00
1. Church year—Meditations. I. Title.

PARSONS, Charles H 242
The doctor-merchant, his inspirational letters. [1st ed.] NewYork, Exposition Press [1956] 125p. illus: 24cm. [BV4832.P357] 57-13515
1. Devotional literature. I. Title.

PARSONS, Charles H 242
The doctor-merchant, his inspirational letters. [1st ed.] New York, Exposition Press [1956] 125p. illus. 24cm. [BV4832.P357] 57-13515
1. Devotional literature. I. Title.

PATON, Alan. 242
Instrument of thy peace. New York, Seabury [1968] 124p. 22cm. [BV4832.2.P33] 68-11857 3.50
1. Meditations. I. Title.

PAWELZIK, Fritz, comp. 242
I lie on my mat and pray; prayers by young Africans. Illustrated by Georg Lemke. Translated by Robbins Strong. New York, Friendship Press [1964] 63 p. illus. 20 cm. A collection originally translated into German by Fritz Pawelzik and published in Wuppertal. [BV245.P34] 64-20103
1. Prayers. I. Title.

PEARCE, J. Winston. 242
The light on the Lord's face [by] J. Winston Pearce. Nashville, Broadman Press [1970] 128 p. 20 cm. (A Broadman book) Contents.Contents.—The light on the Lord's face.—The river and the oak.—"The heart is a lonely hunter."—"An 'de walls come tumblin' down."—My favorite things.—Make no more giants, God.—What are your boundaries?—Lantern in my hand.—Thank God a man can grow.—A heart fixed to give.—Home for Christmas (Christmas theme).—On making covenants (New Year's theme).—Mark the earth with a cross (Good Friday theme).—Lazarus laughed (Easter theme).—"What's in a name?" [BX6333.P4L5] 72-117298
1. Baptists—Sermons. 2. Sermons, American. I. Title.

PEARSON, Roy Messer, 1914- 242
Seeking and finding God. New York, Abingdon Press [1958] 112p. 18cm. [BV4832.P377] 58-9523
1. Devotional exercises. I. Title.

PEASE, Dorothy Wells, ed. 242
Inspiration under the sky. New York, Abingdon Press [1963] 140 p. 18 cm. [BV4801.P39] 63-11379
1. Devotional literature (Selections: extracts, etc.) I. Title.

PEASE, Dorothy Wells, ed. 242
Inspiration under the sky. Nashville, Abingdon [c.1963] 140p. 18cm. 63-11379 2.00
1. Devotional literature (Selections: extracts, etc.) I. Title.

PEASE, Dorothy Wells, ed. 242
Meditations under the sky. New York, Abingdon Press [1957] 143p. 16cm. [BV4801.P4] 57-7097
1. Devotional literature (Selections: Extracts, etc.) I. Title.

PEASE, Norval F. 242
Think on these things [by] Norval F. Pease. Washington, Review and Herald Pub. Association [1969] 376 p. 21 cm. [BV4811.P35] 74-81307
1. Devotional calendars—Seventh-Day Adventists. I. Title.

PEETERS, Louis, 1868-1937. 242
An Ignatian approach to divine union. Translated by Hillard L. Brozowski. Milwaukee, Bruce Pub. Co. [1956] 114p. 22cm. [BX2179.L8P39] 56-9647
1. Loyola(Ignacio de, Saint, 1491-1556. Exercitia spiritualia. 2. Spiritual exercises. I. Title.

PEIRCE, Francis X 242
Ponder slowly; outlined meditations. Westminster, Md., Newman Press, 1957. 323p. 23cm. [BX2182.P4] 57-11827
1. Meditations. I. Title.

PENMAN, Archibald. 242
The prayer-telephone; daily devotional poems for the months of January and February to begin your New Year by offering a 'direct wire' to God's love and grace. [1st ed.] New York, Greenwich Book Publishers [1958, c1957] 59p. 21cm. [BV4832.P386] 57-14664
1. Devotional calendars. I. Title.

PENNINGTON, Chester A. 242
The Word among us [by] Chester A. Pennington. Philadelphia, United Church Press [1973] 125 p. front. 24 cm. "A Pilgrim Press book." Poems. [BT380.2.P36] 73-8503 ISBN 0-8298-0259-2 4.95
1. Sermon on the Mount—Meditations. 2. Lord's prayer—Meditations. I. Title.

PENTECOST, Dorothy Harrison. 242
My pursuit of peace. Chicago, Moody Press [1962] 253p. 22cm. [BV4908.5.P45] 62-52075
1. Peace of mind. I. Title.

PETERMAN, Ruth. 242
My world was too small. Wheaton, Ill., Tyndale House Publishers [1974] 126 p. 18 cm. [BV4501.2.P426] 74-79608 ISBN 0-8423-4658-9 1.45 (pbk.).
1. Meditations. I. Title.

PETERS, William A. M. 242
The spiritual exercises of St. Ignatius; exposition and interpretation, by William A. M. Peters. Jersey City, Program to Adapt the Spiritual Exercises [1968] xv, 204 p. 23 cm. Bibliographical references included in "Notes" (p. 182-197) [BX2179.L8P44] 68-16158
1. Loyola, Ignacio de, Saint, 1491-1556. Exercitia spiritualia. I. Title.

PETERSON, Russell Arthur, 1922- 242
How love will help. Boston, Meador Pub. Co. [1953] 96p. 21cm. [BV4832.P45] 53-2949
1. Devotional literature. I. Title.

PETTY, Jo, comp. 242
Promises and premises. Designed by Gordon G. Brown. [Norwalk, Conn.] C. R. Gibson Co. [1972, c1962] 86 p. 21 cm. Brief passages from the King James version of the Bible (some paraphrased) arranged by topic. [BS491.5.P47] 73-183644 ISBN 0-8378-1791-9 3.50
1. Bible—Devotional literature. I. Title.

PHILIPPE, Marie Dominique. 242
The worship of God; translated from the French by Mark Pontifex. [1st ed.] New York, Hawthorn Books [1959] 142p. 21cm. (The Twentieth century encyclopedia of Catholicism, v. 16. Section 2: The Basic truths) Translation of Un seul Dieu tu adoreras. Includes bibliography. [BV4817.P513] 59-12167
1. God—Worship and love. I. Title.

PHIPPS, Jerome Kenton. 242
My word put God first / by Jerome Kenton Phipps. Parsons, W. Va. : McClain Print Co., 1975. xvii, 95 p. : port. ; 22 cm. [BV4832.2.P5] 74-15997 ISBN 0-87012-196-0 : 3.00
1. Meditations. I. Title.

PIERSON, Robert H. 242
Heart to heart [by] R. H. Pierson. Washington, Review and Herald Pub. Association [1970] 159 p. 22 cm. [BV4832.2.P52] 70-113041
1. Meditations. I. Title.

*PINK, Arthur W. 242
Comfort for christians / Arthur W. Pink. Grand Rapids : Baker Book House, c1976 112 p. ; 24 cm. Large print edition. [BV4817] ISBN 0-8010-6999-8 pbk. : 3.95
1. Devotional literature. 2. Christian life. I. Title.

PIPPIN, Frank Johnson, 1906- 242
In the night His song. Boston, Christopher Pub. House [1956] 169p. illus. 21cm. [BV4832.P56] 57-16731
1. Devotional literature. I. Title.

POPE, Robert H. 242
A gift of doubt; struggles with Christian faith and uncertainty [by] Robert H. Pope. Englewood Cliffs, N.J., Prentice-Hall [1971] 143 p. 22 cm. [BV4501.2.P556 1971] 70-158192 ISBN 0-13-354878-3 4.95
1. Christian life—1960- I. Title.

POTTS, James Manning, 1895- ed. 242
Listening to the saints; a collection of meditations from the devotional masters. Nashville, The Upper room [1962] 239 p. 20 cm. "Compiled from the Upper room series entitled 'Living selections from the great devotional classics.'" [BV4801.P6] 62-20472
1. Devotional literature (Selections: extracts, etc.) I. Title.

POTTS, James Manning, 1895- ed. 242
Listening to the saints; a collection of meditations from the devotional masters. Nashville, Upper Room [c.1962] 239p. 20cm. 62-20472 1.00
1. Devotional literature (Selections: extracts, etc.) I. Title.

POWELL, George C., 1920- 242
Portraits of Christ / George C. Powell. Philadelphia : Dorrance, [1974] 142 p. ; 22 cm. [BX2182.2.P59] 74-75409 ISBN 0-8059-2006-4 : 6.95
1. Meditations. I. Title.

†*PRECIOUS promises* / 242
Joseph S. Johnson, compiler. Nashville : Broadman Press, c1976. 96 p. : ill. ; 20 cm. [BV4832.2.P66] 76-8561 ISBN 0-8054-5146-3 pbk. : 3.25
1. Meditations. 2. God—Promises—Meditations. I. Johnson, Joe, 1933-

PRICE, Carl E. 242
Trails and turnpikes [by] Carl E. Price. Illus. by William Loechel. Nashville, Abingdon Press [1969] 128 p. illus. 12 x 18 cm. "Meditations." [BV4832.2.P67] 69-18445 ISBN 6-87424-445- 2.75
1. Meditations. I. Title.

PRICE, Eugenia. 242
Just as I am. [1st ed.] Philadelphia, Lippincott [1968] 184 p. 21 cm. [BV4832.2.P7] 68-11375
1. Devotional literature. I. Title.

PRICHARD, Lucette Marguerite (Hutton) 1887- 242
Restless hearts and the pressure of God's spirit. [New York] B. Wheelwright [1951, c1950] 109 p. 22 cm. [BV4832.P6895] 51-9448
1. Devotional literature. I. Title.

A priest. 242
The Treasury of devotion; a manual of prayers, compiled by a priest and edited by T. T. Carter. New [i.e. 9th] ed., rev. by Robert Petitpierre. London, New York, Longmans, Green [1957] 205 p. 18 cm. (The Inner life series) [BV4832.T68] 58-14572
1. Devotional exercises. I. Carter, Thomas Thellusson, 1808-1901, ed. II. Petitpierre, Robert. III. Title.

PRIESTER, Gertrude Ann. 242
Let's talk about God; devotions for families with young children. Illustrated by R. O. Fry. Philadelphia, Westminster Press [1967] 271 p. illus. 23 cm. Bibliography: p. [269]-271. A collection of Christian commentaries for family worship. [BV4870.P7] AC 67
1. Prayer-books and devotions. I. Fry, R. O., illus. II. Title.

PROCHNOW, Herbert Victor, 1897- 242
Inspirational thoughts on the Beatitudes [by] Herbert V. Prochnow. Grand Rapids, Baker Book House [1970] 76 p. 16 cm. [BT382.P697] 76-115645 ISBN 8-01-068541-
1. Beatitudes—Meditations. I. Title.

PROCHNOW, Herbert Victor, 1897- 242
Inspirational thoughts on the Lord's Prayer [by] Herbert V. Prochnow. Grand Rapids, Mich., Baker Book House [1970] 74 p. 16 cm. [BV233.P74] 72-115644
1. Lord's prayer—Meditations. I. Title.

PROCHNOW, Herbert Victor, 1897- 242
Inspirational thoughts on the Ten commandments [by] Herbert V. Prochnow. Grand Rapids, Baker Book House [1970] 88 p. 15 cm. [BV4655.P69] 79-115643
1. Commandments, Ten—Meditations. I. Title.

PROCUNIER, Edwin R 242
A knife to thy throat, and nine other one-act plays. Agincourt, Book Society of Canada [1962] vi, 217 p. illus., diagrs. 21cm. [PR6066.R6K5] 63-47569
I. Title.

PROKOP, Phyllis Stillwell 242
Conversations with giants. St. Louis, Concordia [1965, c.1964] 99p. 15cm. [BS572.P7] 64-7928 1.50
1. Bible—Biog.—Devotional literature. I. Title.

PSALMS of Thistleonia; 242
a book of private & public devotions consisting of meditations, aspirations, prayers, thanksgivings & praise, written by one pilgrim on behalf of fellow travelers. [Detroit? 1968] xvi, 314 p. illus. 26 cm. [BX2182.2.P7] 68-16131
1. Meditations.

PUENTE, Luis de la, 1554-1624. 242
God's friendship; selections from the Meditations of the venerable servant of God, Luis de la Puente; translated and supplemented by John M. Thill. Milwaukee, Bruce Pub. Co. [1951] 215 p. 23 cm. [BX2186.P813] 51-8680
1. Meditations. I. Title.

PURDUE, William J 242
You and God; meditations on some of the great and familiar chapters of the Bible. [1st ed.] New York, Exposition Press [1953] 54p. 21cm. [BV4832.P84] 53-5634
1. Meditations. I. Title.

PUTZ, Louis J 242
The Lord's Day. Notre Dame, Ind., Fides Publishers [1963] 234 p. 23 cm. [BX2170.C55P8] 63-12047
1. Church year—Meditations. I. Title.

PUTZ, Louis J. 242
The Lord's Day. Notre Dame, Ind., Fides [c.1963] 234p. 23cm. 63-12047 3.95 bds.,
1. Church year—Meditations. I. Title.

QUIERY, William H., 1926- 242
Facing God [by] William H. Quiery. Foreword by Bernard J. Cooke. New York, Sheed [1967] xii, 211p. 22cm. Bibl. [BV4813.Q5] 67-13760 4.95
1. Meditation. 2. Contemplation. I. Title.

QUIERY, William H., 1926- 242
Facing God [by] William H. Quiery. With a foreword by Bernard J. Cooke. New York, Sheed and Ward [1967] xii, 211 p. 22 cm. Bibliographical footnotes. [BV4813.Q5] 67-13760
1. Meditation. Contemplation. I. Title.

QUOIST, Michel. 242
I've met Jesus Christ. Translated by J. F. Bernard. Garden City, N.Y. Image Books, 1975. 156 p., 18 cm. [BX2183.Q5713] ISBN 0-385-02802-4 1.45 (pbk.)
1. Meditations. 2. Prayers. I. Title.
L.C. card no. for original edition: 73-79643.

RADER, Ralph Wilson, 1930- ed. 242
Essays; an analytic reader. [Edited by] Melvin Rader [and] Sheldon Sacks. Boston, Little, Brown [1964] xvii, 657 p. 25 cm. [PE1417.R24] 64-17099
1. English language—Rhetoric. 2. College readers. I. Sacks, Sheldon, 1930- joint ed. II. Title.

RAHNER, Karl 242
Encounters with silence. Translated [from the German] by James M. Demske. Westminster, Md., Newman Press [c.]1960. 87p. 21cm. 60-10721 1.95
1. Devotional literature. I. Title.

RAHNER, Karl, 1904- 242
Spiritual exercises. Translated by Kenneth Baker. [New York] Herder and Herder [1965] 287 p. 22 cm. Translation of Betrachtungen zum ignatianischen Exerzitienbuch. [BX2179.L8R33] 65-21949
1. Loyola, Ignacio de, Saint, 1491-1556. Exercitia spiritualia. 2. Spiritual exercises. 3. Retreats.

RAINES, Robert Arnold, ed. 242
Creative brooding [edited] by Robert A. Raines New York, Macmillan [1966] 126 p. 18 cm. [BV4801.R3] 66-13975
1. Devotional literature. I. Title.

RAINES, Robert Arnold, ed: 242
Creative brooding. New York, Macmillan [c.1966] 126p. 18cm. [BV4801.R3] 66-13975 2.95
1. Devotional literature. I. Title.

RAINES, Robert Arnold. 242
Soundings [by] Robert A. Raines. [1st ed.] New York, Harper & Row [1970]. 144 p. 22 cm. [BV4832.2.R23] 73-85066 3.95
1. Devotional literature. I. Title.

RAND, Howard B., 1889- 242
Gems of truth, by Howard B. Rand. Merrimac, Mass., Destiny Publishers [1968] vii, 192 p. 21 cm. Articles originally published in Destiny magazine. [BV4832.2.R25] 68-57766
1. Meditations. I. Title.

THE Rand McNally book of favorite prayers and stories. 242 (j)
Chicago, Rand McNally [1966] 96 p. col. illus. 32 cm. Each story has special t. p. Contents.Contents.—My prayer book, by M. Clemens.—My Bible book, by J. Walker.—God is good, by M. A. Jones.—I think of Jesus, by K. Smallwood. [BV265.R27] 66-8945
1. Children—Prayer-books and devotions—1961- I. Title: Favorite prayers and stories.

RAND Mcnally book of favorite prayers and stories. (The) 242
Chicago, Rand McNally [1966] 96p. col. illus. 32cm. Ea. story has special t.p. [BV265.R27] 66-8945 2.95 bds.,
1. Children—Prayer-books and devotions—1961- I. Title: Favorite prayers and stories.
Contents omitted.

RAVN, Karen. 242
Little seeds of wisdom / by Karen Ravn ; illustrated by Sue Tague and Becky Farley. Kansas City, Mo. : Hallmark, c1975. [32] p. : col. ill. ; 12 cm. (Hallmark editions) [BV4832.2.R34] 74-21916 ISBN 0-87529-437-5 : 2.00
1. Meditations. I. Tague, Susan Lipsey. II. Farley, Becky. III. Title.

REARDON, David M. 242
Meditations on Scripture texts : from the writings of David M. Reardon. Brooklyn, N.Y. : T. Gaus Sons, c1976. 125 p. ; 22 cm. [BV4832.2.R37] 76-708
1. Meditations. I. Title.

REDDING, David A. 242
If I could pray again / David A. Redding. New rev. ed. Millbrae, Calif. : Celestial Arts, 1975. p. cm. Includes index. [BV245.R4 1975] 75-9084 ISBN 0-89087-060-8 pbk. : 3.95
1. Prayers. I. Title.

REES, Melvin E. 242
God's plan for social security [by] Melvin E. Rees. Mountain View, Calif., Pacific Press Pub. Association [1970] 63 p. illus. 19 cm. [BV4832.2.R38] 73-125337
1. Meditations. I. Title.

REES, Wilbur E. 242
$3.00 worth of God [by Wilbur E. Rees. Illus. by Paul Edwards. Valley Forge [Pa.] Judson Press [1971] 94 p. illus. 17 cm. [BV4832.2.R384] 77-151044 ISBN 0-8170-0505-6 2.95
1. Meditations. I. Title.

REID, Frances P 242
Thy word in my heart. With an introd. by Elizabeth Yates. Minneapolis, Augsburg Pub. House [1962] 135 p. 21 cm. Meditations. [BV4832.2.R4] 62-12927
1. Meditations. I. Title.

REID, Frances P. 242
Thy word in my heart. Introd. by Elizabeth Yates. Minneapolis, Augsburg [c.1962] 135p. 21cm. 62-12927 2.50
1. Meditations. I. Title.

*REINER, D. E. 242
Jesus never fails. Nashville, Southern Pub. [c.1964] 72p. 19cm. .60 pap.,
I. Title.

RENDALL, Norline. 242
Just a taste of honey / by Norline Rendall. Chicago : Moody Press, [1975] 128 p. ; 16 cm. [BV4832.2.R43] 74-15359 ISBN 0-8024-4494-6 pbk. : 1.25
1. Meditations. I. Title.

REYNER, John Hereward. 242
A philosophy of delight / by J. H. Reyner. London : Watkins, 1976. vii, 66 p. ; 21 cm. [BV4832.2.R44] 77-362657 ISBN 0-7224-0144-2 : £2.00
1. Meditations. I. Title.

RHEA, Carolyn 242
My heart kneels too. New York, Grosset [c.1965] 113p. 17cm. (Family inspirational lib., 1665) [BV245.R5] 65-16921 1.50 bds.,
1. Prayers. I. Title.

RHEA, Ralph. 242
The good word; inspiration for joy and fulfillment in our daily lives. [Kansas City, Mo., Hallmark Cards, 1974, c1973] 60 p. col. illus. 20 cm. (Hallmark editions) [BV4832.2.R45 1974] 72-96870 ISBN 0-87529-341-7 3.00
1. Meditations. I. Title.

RHEA, Ralph. 242
The word is ... / Ralph Rhea. New York : Hawthorn Books, [1975] 128 p., [2] leaves of plates : col. ill. ; 22 cm. [BV4832.2.R47 1975] 74-22922 ISBN 0-8015-8818-9 : 4.95
1. Meditations. I. Title.

RILLING, John William, 1906- 242
A table before me : daily devotions from Luke's Gospel / John W. Rilling. Philadelphia : Fortress Press, c1977. iv, 60 p. ; 19 cm. [BS2595.4.R55] 76-7859 ISBN 0-8006-1230-2 pbk. : 1.95
1. Bible. N.T. Luke—Meditations. I. Title.

*RISTOW, Cecil Frederic. 242
Windows on the world of truth; meditations on the meaning of life. 1st ed. New York, Vantage [1974] 186 p. 22 cm. [BV4832.2] ISBN 0-533-01045-4 4.50
1. Devotional exercises. I. Title.

RIVERS, Clarence Joseph. 242
Reflections. Designer: William Schickel & Associates. New York, Herder and Herder [1970] 95 p. illus. 21 cm. [BX2182.2.R55] 77-122328 5.50
1. Meditations. I. Title.

ROBERTS, William. 242
At the door knocking / William Roberts. [Dayton, Ohio] : Pflaum Pub., 1975. vii, 108 p. : ill. ; 21 cm. [BV4832.2.R56] 74-82488 ISBN 0-8278-9002-8 pbk. : 2.50
1. Meditations. I. Title.

ROBERTSON, Josephine. 242
Meditations on garden themes. New York, Abingdon Press [1959] 112p. 16cm. [BV4832.2.R6] 59-12785
1. Meditations. I. Title.

*ROBINSON, Haddon W. 242
Psalm twenty-three, a devotional. Chicago, Moody [1968] 61p. illus. 21cm. pap., price unreported
1. Devotional literature. I. Title.

ROBINSON, Haddon W. 242
Psalm twenty-three : a devotional / by Haddon W. Robinson. Large print ed. Chicago : Moody Press, 1976, c1968. 127 p. : ill. ; 21 cm. [BS1450.23d.R6 1976] 76-21233 2.95
1. Bible. O.T. Psalms XXIII—Meditations. 2. Sight-saving books.

ROBINSON, William Eason 242
On spiritual reading: a short practical guide. New York, Morehouse [c.1962] 57p. 19cm. (Star bk.) Bibl. 1.00 pap.,
I. Title.

ROCHE, Jean Baptiste 242
The Blessed Virgin's silence [Tr. from French] Pref. by John W. Lynch [1st Amer. ed.] Wilkes-Barre, Pa., Dimension Bks. [1965] 102p. 20cm. [BX2160.2.R613] 65-25565 3.00
1. Mary, Virgin—Meditations. I. Title.

ROGERS, Dale Evans. 242
Christmas is always. [Westwood, N. J.] Revell [1958] 61p. illus. 17cm. [BV45.R6] 58-13765
1. Christmas. I. Title.

ROGERS, Harold, 1907- 242
Live coals. Nashville, Tidings [1969] 72 p. 19 cm. "Personal reflections." [BV4832.2.R62] 75-78558
1. Meditations. I. Title.

ROGERS, Harold, 1907- 242
Rocks and rills. Illustrated by Harold Bales. Nashville, Tidings [1971] 87 p. illus. 18 cm. [BV4832.2.R624] 71-160191
1. Meditations. I. Title.

ROGERS, William F. 1909- 242
Ye shall be comforted. Philadelphia, Westminster Press [1950] 89 p. 20 cm. (The Westminster pastoral aid books) [BV4905.R57] 50-3146
1. Consolation. I. Title.

ROGERS, William F. 1909- 242
Ye shall be comforted, [by] William F. Rogers. Philadelphia, Westminster Press, [1975 c1950] 89 p. 19 cm. [BV4905.R57] ISBN 0-664-24776-8 1.95 (pbk.)
1. Consolation. I. Title.
L.C. card no. for original ed.: 50-3146.

ROGERS, William Fred, 1909- 242
Ye shall be comforted. Philadelphia, Westminster Press [1950] 89p. 20cm. (The Westminster pastoral aid books) [BV4905.R57] 50-3146
1. Consolation. I. Title.

ROGNESS, Alvin N., 1906- 242
Bridges to hope / Alvin N. Rogness. Minneapolis : Augsburg Pub. House, [1975] 96 p. ; 20 cm. [BV4832.2.R628] 74-14182 ISBN 0-8066-1464-1 pbk. : 1.95
1. Meditations. I. Title.

ROGNESS, Alvin N., 1906- 242
Captured by mystery; devotional readings. Minneapolis, Augsburg [c.1966] ix, 147p. 21cm. [BV4832.2.R63] 66-22562 3.50
1. Devotional literature. I. Title.

ROGNESS, Alvin N., 1906- 242
Signs of hope in the thunder of spring, by Alvin N. Rogness. Art by Don Wallerstedt. Minneapolis, Augsburg Pub. House [1971] 89 p. illus. 21 cm. [BV4832.2.R635] 73-159009 ISBN 0-8066-1132-4 3.50
1. Meditations. I. Title.

ROGNESS, Alvin N., 1906- 242
The touch of his love; devotions for every season [by] Alvin N. Rogness. Minneapolis, Augsburg Pub. House [1973, c1974] 111 p. 20 cm. [BV4832.2.R636 1974] 73-88602 ISBN 0-8066-1405-6 2.95
1. Devotional exercises. I. Title.

ROGUET, A M 1906- 242
Bread and the word; meditations on the liturgy, by A. M. Roguet. translated by Joseph Donceel. New York, Macmillan [1966] xix, 231 p. 21 cm. Translation of Notre fol. in vie sacramentelle, notre sacrifice. Bibliography: p. [221] [BX2170.C55R613] 66-21161
1. Church year—Meditations. I. Title.

ROGUET, A. M. 1906- 242
Bread and the word; meditations on the liturgy. Tr. [from French] by Joseph Donceel. New York, Macmillan [c.1963, 1966] xix, 231p. 21cm. Bibl. [BX2170.C55R613] 66-21161 5.95
1. Church year—Meditations. I. Title.

ROHRBACH, Peter Thomas. 242
Conversation with Christ; an introduction to mental prayer. Chicago, Fides Publishers Association [1956] 171p. 21cm. [BV4813.R57] 56-11626
1. Meditation. I. Title.

ROLLE, Richard, of Hampole, 1290?-1349. 242
The Incendium amoris of Richard Rolle of Hampole, edited by Margaret Deanesly. [Folcroft, Pa.] Folcroft Library Editions, 1974. p. cm. Reprint of the 1915 ed. published at the University Press, Manchester, which was issued as no. 26 of the Publications of the University of Manchester, Historical series; and as no. 97 of the University of Manchester publications. [BX2180.R6 1974] 74-9872 45.00
1. Devotional literature. I. Deanesly, Margaret, ed. II. Title. III. Series: Victoria University of Manchester. Publications. Historical series, no. 26. IV. Series: Victoria University of Manchester. Publications, no. 97.

ROPER, Anita, 1908- 242
The fifteenth station. With an epilogue by Karl Rahner. Translated by M. Dolores Sablone. [New York] Herder and Herder [1967] 108 p. 22 cm. Translation of Die 14 Stationen im Leben des NN. [BV2040.R613] 67-22226
1. Stations of the Cross. I. Title.

ROSENBERGER, Harleigh M. 242
Thoughts along the road [by] Harleigh M. Rosenberger. Valley Forge [Pa.] Judson [1966] 126p. 21cm. [BV4832.2.R66] 66-22520 3.50 bds.,
1. Devotional literature. I. Title.

ROSSI, Giovanni, of Assisi. 242
This way to God. [Translated from the Italian by J. A. Abbo and T. A. Opdenaker] Morristown, N. J., Villa Walsh Press [c1954] 287p. 14cm. Translation of Breviario Cristiano. [BX2185.R62] 54-13039
1. Devotional literature. I. Title.

ROUTH, Freda Karsin 242
My beloved, my friend. Philadelphia, Dorrance [c.1962] 46p. 20cm. 62-20706 2.50
1. Meditations. I. Title.

ROWE, Lois. 242
On call; daily devotional readings for nurses. Chicago, Inter-varsity Press [1958] unpaged. 22cm. [BV4832.R76] 58-7316

1. Devotional calendars. 2. Nurses and nursing. I. Title.

ROWELL, Eugene 242
Skylines. New York, Vantage [c.1962] 79p. 21cm. 2.50 bds.,
I. Title.

RULER, Arnold Albert van 242
God's Son and God's world; sixteen meditations on the person of Christ and the psalm of nature. Translated from the Dutch by Lewis B. Smedes Grand Rapids, Eerdmans [c.1960] 79p. 22cm. 59-14592 2.00
1. Meditation. I. Title.

RULER, Arnold Albert van, 1908- 242
God's Son and God's world; sixteen meditations on the person of Christ and the psalm of nature. Translated from the Dutch by Lewis B. Smedes. [1st ed.] Grand Rapids, Eerdmans [1960] 79p. 21cm. Translation of Vertrouw en geniet. [BV4839.D8R813] 59-14592
1. Meditations. I. Title.

RUNES, Dagobert David, 1902- 242
Letters to my God. New York, Philosophical Library [1958] 58p. 21cm. [B945.R83L39] 58-14857
I. Title.

RUSSELL, Solveig Paulson 242
1, 2, 3, and more. Illus. by Don Pallarito. St. Louis, Concordia, c.1966. 1v. (unpaged) col. illus. 27cm. [BV4870.R8] 66-18230 1.25 bds.,
1. Children—Prayer-books and devotions—English. I. Pallarito, Don, illus. II. Title.

RYAN, Mary Perkins, 1915- 242
Psalms '70: a new approach to old prayers. Design: Wm. Schickel & Assoc. Dayton, Ohio, Pflaum Press, 1969. 109 p. illus. 13 cm. [BV210.2.R9] 73-93007 2.75
1. Bible. O.T. Psalms—Liturgical use. 2. Prayer. I. Title.

SAINT JURE, Jean Baptiste de, 1588-1657. 242
The secret of peace and happiness, by Father Jean Baptiste Saint-Jure and Blessed Claude de la Colombiere. Translated by Paul Garvin. Staten Island, N. Y., St. Paul Publications [c1961] 139p. 16cm. 'Extracts from Blessed Claude de la Colombiere and Ther Jean Baptiste Saint-Jure. --Dust jacket. [BX2183.S283] 61-15620
1. Spiritual life— Catholic authors. I. Colombiere, Claude de la, 1641-1682. II. Title.

SANDLER, Lena. 242
Wisdom of the Eternal 1st ed. Miami Beach, Fla. [1958] 269p. 23cm. [BR126.S215] 58-1135
I. Title.

SANDLIN, John Lewis. 242
Moments with the Master. [Westwood, N. J.] Revell [1961] 128p. 17cm. [BV4832.2.S27] 61-9242
1. Devotional literature. I. Title.

SAURO, Joan. 242
Man in-between : a celebration of waiting / text and photos. by Joan Sauro. St. Meinrad, Ind. : Abbey Press, 1974. ix, 100 p. : ill. ; 15 x 23 cm. (A Priority edition) [BX2182.2.S33] 74-82239 pbk. : 3.95
1. Meditations. I. Title.

SAVARY, Louis M., comp. 242
Cycles: the first year. Reflections for the Sundays of the year. Edited by Louis M. Savary. New York, Regina Press, 1971. 267 p. illus. 21 cm. [BV4812.A1S28] 72-87358 2.95
1. Church year—Prayer-books and devotions—English. I. Title.

SAVARY, Louis M., comp. 242
Finding God. Compiled by Louis M. Savary and Thomas J. O'Connor. New York, Newman Press, 1971. 191 p. illus. 21 cm. [BV4805.S28] 73-133467 2.95
1. Meditations. I. O'Connor, Thomas Joseph, 1909- joint comp. II. Title.

SAYERS, Dorothy Leigh, 1893-1957. 242
A matter of eternity. Selections from the writings of Dorothy L. Sayers. Chosen and introduced by Rosamond Kent Sprague. Grand Rapids, Mich., Eerdmans [1973] 139 p. 23 cm. [BV4832.2.S275] 72-94648 ISBN 0-8028-1515-4 4.50
1. Meditations. I. Title.

SCHAEFFER, Francis August. 242
Everybody can know, by Francis and Edith Schaeffer. Illustrated by Franky A. Schaeffer, V. Wheaton, Ill., Tyndale House Publishers [1974, c1973] xi, 403 p. illus. 22 cm. [BV4832.2.S277 1974] 73-87127 ISBN 0-8423-0785-0
1. Meditations. I. Schaeffer, Edith, joint author. II. Title.

SCHERZER, Carl J 242
Followers of the way. Philadelphia, Christian Education Press [c1955] 120p. 22cm. [BV4832.S347] 55-6521
1. Meditations. I. Title.

SCHLESSELMAN, Robert H 242
Dear Father in heaven; prayers for boys and girls, written and compiled by Robert H. Schlesselman and Luella Spitzack Ahrens. Saint Louis, Concordia Pub. House [1963] 52 p. illus. 18 cm. [BV4870.S4] 62-19956
1. Children—Prayer-books and devotions—1961- I. Ahrens, Luella Spitzack, joint author. II. Title.

*SCHLINK, Basilea. 242
Behold His love. [First American ed.] Minneapolis, Bethany Fellowship [1974, c1973] 140 p. 18 cm. (A Dimension book) [BV4832] ISBN 0-87123-039-9. 1.45 (pbk.)
1. Meditations. I. Title.

SCHMIECHEN, Samuel John. 242
Wonder in God's wilderness. Illustrated by Abigail Bahnemann. Minneapolis, Augsburg Pub. House [1967] vii, 135 p. illus. 22 cm. [BV4832.2.S28] 67-11722
1. Meditations.

SCHMITZ, Charles Henry 242
Security from above; Biblical thoughts on ultimate values. Nashville, Abingdon [c.1966] 144p. 21cm. [BV4832.2.S29] 66-10851 2.50 bds.,
1. Devotional literature. I. Title.

SCHMITZ, Charles Henry. 242
Security from above; Biblical thoughts on ultimate values [by] Charles H. Schmitz. New York, Abingdon Press [1966] 144 p. 21 cm. [BV4832.2.S29] 66-10851
1. Devotional literature. I. Title.

SCHMITZ, Charles Henry. 242
Windows toward God. New York, Abingdon-Cokesbury Press [1950] 192 p. illus. 18 cm. [BV4832.S37] 50-9536
1. Devotional exercises. I. Title.

SCHMITZ, Charles Henry 242
Windows toward God. [Nashville] Abingdon [1963, c.1950] 192p. illus. 18cm. (Apex bk., M7) .95 pap.,
1. Devotional exercises. I. Title.

SCHNACKENBURG, Rudolf, 1914- 242
Belief in the New Testament / Rudolf Schnackenburg ; translated by Jeremy Moiser. New York : Paulist Press, [1974] x, 118 p. ; 18 cm. (Deus books) Translation of Glaubensimpulse aus dem Neuen Testament. [BX2184.S2813] 74-14023 ISBN 0-8091-1847-5 pbk. : 1.45
1. Meditations. I. Title.

SCHOOLLAND, Marian M 1902- 242
When I consider -- With 40 illus. by Reynold H. Weidenaar Grand Rapids, Eerdmans, 1956. 124p. illus. 23cm. [BV4832.S38] 56-12135
1. Nature— Religious interpretations. I. Title.

SCHOOLLAND, Marian M 1902- 242
When I consider ... With 40 illus. by Reynold H. Weidenaar. Grand Rapids, Eerdmans, 1956. 124p. illus. 23cm. [BV4832.S38] 56-12135
1. Nature—Religious interpretation. I. Title.

SCOTT, Jane, 1894- 242
My adventures with God. Foreword:,Billy Graham. [New York] Nelson [1964] 139p. 21cm. (Thistle bk.) 64-25988 2.00 bds.,
1. Devotional literature. I. Title.

SCOTT, John, 1921- comp. 242
Treasured volume of prayers; an anthology collected by John Scott. New York, Oak Tree Press [1970] 155 p. 22 cm. [BV245.S36] 76-104722
1. Prayers. I. Title.

SCRAGG, Walter. 242
Run this race; a daily devotional and inspirational guide for early-teens and near-teens. Washington, Review and Herald Pub. Association [1969] 367 p. 21 cm. (A Junior devotional) A scripture and devotional commentary for each day of the year. [BV4850.S35] 73-81304
1. Youth—Prayer-books and devotions. 2. Devotional calendars—Seventh-Day Adventists. I. Title.

SEALS, B V 242
Beside the Shepherd's tent; brief, warm devotions; helps for the hungry in heart. Kansas City, Mo., Beacon Hill Press [1956] 79p. 19cm. [BV4832] 56-2198
1. Devotional literature. I. Title.

SEBOLDT, Roland H A 242
The joy of living, in health and suffering, in success and failure, in every time of life, by Roland Seboldt. St. Louis, Concordia Pub. House [1965] 83 p. 5 cm. [BV4501.2.S37] 65-17536
1. Christian life. 2. Joy and sorrow. I. Title.

SEBOLDT, Roland H. A. 242
The joy of living, in health and suffering, in success and failure, in every time of life. St. Louis, Concordia [c.1965] 83p. 5cm. [BV4501.2.S37] 65-17536 1.50
1. Christian life. 2. Joy and sorrow. I. Title.

THE Secret place. 242
Help in troubled times; meditations from The Secret place based on actual life experiences. Compiled and edited by Bruce E. Mills. Valley Forge [Pa.] Judson Press [1962] 256p. 20cm. [BV4805.S4] 62-14079
1. Meditations. I. Mills, Bruce E., ed. II. Title.

SECRET place (The) 242
Help in troubled times; meditations from The Secret place based on actual life experiences. Comp., ed. by Bruce E. Mills. Valley Forge [Pa.] Judson [c.1962] 256p. 20cm. 62-14079 3.50
1. Meditations. I. Mills, Bruce E., ed. II. Title.

SEELIGER, Wes. 242
One inch from the fence, written and illustrated. Atlanta, Forum House [1973] 160 p. illus. 23 cm. [BV4832.2.S39] 72-97821 ISBN 0-913618-07-1 5.25
1. Meditations. I. Title.

SEERVELD, Calvin. 242
Take hold of God and pull: moments in a college chapel; translations of Scripture with accompanying meditations. Paintings by Mary Steenland. [Palos Heights, Ill.] Trinity Pennyasheet Press [1966] 173 p. 4 col. illus. 23 cm. [BS491.5.S4] 66-24940
1. Bible—Meditations. 2. Devotional exercises. I. Title.

SEERVELD, Calvin 242
Take hold of God and pull: moments in a college chapel; translations of Scripture with accompanying meditations. Paintings by Mary Steenland. [Palos Heights, Ill.] Trinity Pennyasheet Pr. [dist. Trinity Christian Coll. Bk. Store, c.1966] 173p. 4 col. illus. 23cm. [BS491.5.S4] 66-24940 2.50 pap.,
1. Bible—Meditations. 2. Devotional exercises. I. Title.

SEQUOIA. 242
[Stanford, Calif., Associated Students of Stanford University] v. in illus. 24cm. 3 no. a year. [PS508.C6S48] 61-40841
1. College prose—Stanford University. 2. College verse— Stanford University. I. Stanford University. Associated Students.

SERTILLANGES, Antonin Gilbert, 1863- 242
Recollection; translated by the Dominican nuns of Corpus Christi Monastery, Menlo Park, Calif. New York, McMullen Books, 1950. 235 p. 21 cm. Name in religion: Dalmatius Sertillanges. [BX2183.S452] 51-857
1. Meditations. I. Title.

SERTILLANGES, Antonin Gilbert, 1863-1948. 242
Kinships; translated by the Dominican nuns of Corpus Christi Monastery, Menlo Park, Calif. New York, McMullen Books, 1952. 234p. 21cm. [BX2183.S443] 52-8879
1. Devotional literature. I. Title.

SERTILLANGES, Antonin Gilbert, 1863-1948. 242
Rectitude; translated by the Dominican Nuns, Corpus Christi Monastery, Menlo Park, Calif. New York, McMullen Books, 1953. 244p. 21cm. Translation of Devoirs. [BX2183.S453] 53-7694
1. Meditations. I. Title.

SEVENTEEN 242
New York, Macmillan [c.1965] 224p. illus. 20cm. [BV4801.S38] 65-14989 4.95
1. Devotional literature (Selections: Extracts, etc.) I. Title: he Seventeen book of prayer

SEVENTEEN. 242
The Seventeen book of prayer [an anthology of inspirational prose and poetry by the editors of Seventeen magazine] New York, Macmillan [1965] 224 p. illus. 20 cm. [BV4801.S38] 65-14989
1. Devotional literature. I. Title.

SHAW, Henry B., Rt. Rev. Msgr. 242
Approaches to the true church. Derby, N.Y., St. Paul Pubns., Queen of Apostles Seminary [1962] 84p. 18cm. .80 pap.,
I. Title.

SHEDD, Charlie W. 242
Time for all things; meditations on the Christian management of time. New York, Abingdon Press, [1962] 96 p. 18 cm. [BV4832.2.S5] 62-11522
1. Meditations. I. Title.

SHEDD, Charlie W. 242
Time for all things; meditations on the Christian management of time. Nashville, Abingdon [c.1962] 96p. 18cm. 62-11522 2.00 bds.,
1. Meditations. I. Title.

SHEED, Francis Joseph, 1897- 242
Our hearts are restless : the prayer of St. Augustine / F. J. Sheed ; photos. by Catharine Hughes. New York : Seabury Press, c1976. 95 p. : ill. ; 23 cm. "A Crossroad book." [BR1720.A9S53] 76-20197 ISBN 0-8164-2127-7 : 4.95
1. Augustinus, Aurelius, Saint, Bp. of Hippo. 2. Christian saints—Hippo, Algeria—Biography. 3. Hippo, Algeria—Biography. 4. Prayer—History. I. Hughes, Catharine, 1935- II. Title.

SHEEN, Fulton John, Bp., 1895- 242
God love you [1st ed.] Garden City, N. Y., Garden City Books [1955] 188p. 22cm. [BX2182.S47] 55-14788
1. Devotional literature e(Selections: Extracts, etc.) I. Title.

SHEEN, Fulton John, Bp., 1895- 242
God love you, the best of Fulton J. Sheen Bishop Sheen selects a treasury of his own guideposts to peace of mind and soul. [New York, Maco Magazine Corp., 1955] 95p. illus. 24cm. (Selections: Extracts, etc.) [BX2182.S48] 55-25500
1. Decotional literature I. Title.

*SHELLEY, Bruce. 242
Let's face it. Chicago, Moody [1968] 127p. 18cm. (MB3-530) Bibl. .50 pap.,
I. Title.

SHEPARD, Royal F 242
Seeking the mind of Christ; a book of spiritual exercises. Nashville, Abingdon Press [1964] 95 p. 19 cm. [BV4832.2S52] 64-10106
1. Meditations. I. Title.

SHEPARD, Royal F., Jr. 242
Seeking the mind of Christ; a book of spiritual exercises. Nashville, Abingdon [c.1964] 95p. 19cm. 64-10106 2.00
1. Meditations. I. Title.

[SHERMAN, Thomas] 242
Divine breathings; or, A pious soul thirsting after Christ in a hundred pathetical meditations. London, Pickering New York, Dodd, Mead, 1879. xi, 150p. 92mm. Pref. signed: W. J. Leftie. Reprint, with reproduction of original t. p., of the 15th ed., published in 1775 with pref. by Christopher Perin. [BV4831.S43 1879] 54-45571
1. Devotional literature. I. Title.

SHOEMAKER, Helen (Smith) 242
Prayer is action. New York, Morehouse-Barlow Co. [1969] 128 p. 21 cm. Bibliography: p. 125-128. [BV210.2.S52] 70-88122
1. Prayer. I. Title.

SHULER, John Lewis, 1887- 242
Link of love, by J. L. Shuler. Mountain View, Calif., Pacific Press Pub. Association [1971] 64 p. 18 cm. [BV4832.2.S523] 72-154294
1. Meditations. I. Title.

SIEKMANN, T. C., Rev. 242
Modern reflections. Derby, N.Y., St. Paul Pubns. [dist.] St. Paul Bk. Ctr., Queen of Apostles Seminary [1962] 147p. 19cm. 1.00 pap.,
I. Title.

*SIKKING, Sue. 242
Beyond a miracle. Lee's Summit, Mo., Unity Books [1973]. 104 p. 20 cm. [BV4832.2] 72-92063
1. Devotional literature. I. Title.

SIKKING, Sue. 242
Only believe : how to live in the empire of love / by Sue Sikking. Unity Village, Mo. : Unity Books, c1976. 153 p. ; 20 cm. [BV4832.2.S5238] 76-4558 3.95
1. Meditations. I. Title.

SILL, Sterling W. 242
The keys of the kingdom [by] Sterling W. Sill. Salt Lake City, Bookcraft, 1972. x, 334 p. port. 24 cm. [BV4832.2.S524] 72-85927
1. Meditations. I. Title.

SILL, Sterling W. 242
The strength of great possessions [by] Sterling W. Sill. Salt Lake City, Bookcraft, 1970. xi, 339 p. port. 24 cm. [BV4832.2.S525] 78-138282
1. Meditations. I. Title.

SIMCOX, Carroll Eugene, 1912- 242
The promises of God, an exercise in Biblical thinking. New York, Morehouse-Gorham Co., 1958. 176 p. 21 cm. [BV4832.S119] 58-5340
1. Meditations I. Title.

SITWELL, Gerard 242
Spiritual writers of the Middle Ages. New York, Hawthorn [c.1961] 144p. (Twentieth century encyclopedia of Catholicism, v.40. Sec. 4: The means of redemption) Bibl. 61-15610 3.50 bds.,
1. Devotional literature—Hist. & crit. I. Title.

SIZOO, Joseph Richard, 1884- 242
Still we can hope; assurances that give meaning to life [by] Joseph R. Sizoo. Nashville, Abingdon Press [1966] 158 p. 20 cm. [BV4832.2.S53] 66-14995
1. Devotional literature. I. Title.

SIZOO, Joseph Richard, 1884- 242
Still we can hope; assurances that give meaning to life. Nashville, Abingdon [c.1966] 158p. 20cm. [BV4832.2.S53] 66-14995 3.00
1. Devotional literature. I. Title.

SMAGULA, Billie J. 242
Inspirational think-it-overs, by Billie J. Smagula. San Antonio, Naylor Co. [1970] ix, 27 p. 20 cm. [BV4832.2.S536] 75-129646 3.95
1. Meditations. I. Title.

SMITH, Bradford, 1909- 242
Meditation: the inward art. Philadelphia, Lippincott [c.1962, 1963] 224p. 21cm. 63-14633 3.95 bds.,
1. Meditation. I. Title.

SMITH, Bradford, 1909-1964 242
Mediation: the inward art. [1st ed.] Philadelphia, Lippincott [1963] 224 p. 21 cm. [BV4813.S55] 63-14633
1. Meditation. I. Title.

SMITH, Bradford, 1909-1964. 242
Meditation: the inward art. [1st ed.] Philadelphia, Lippincott [1968,c.1963] 224p. 21cm. (LP6) [BV4813.S55] 63-14633 1.95 pap.,
1. Meditation. I. Title.

SMITH, Don Ian. 242
By the River of No Return. Illustrated by David Dawson. Nashville, Abingdon Press [1967] 111 p. illus. 20 cm. Autobiographical. [BV4832.2.S545] 67-14991
1. Meditations. I. Title.

SMITH, Herbert F. 242
God day by day [by] Herbert F. Smith. Huntington, Ind., Our Sunday Visitor, inc. [1973] 191 p. 20 cm. [BX2182.2.S6] 73-84545 ISBN 0-87973-866-9
1. Meditations. I. Title.

SMITH, Jean Louise. 242
Take more joy / Jean Louise Smith. Winona, Minn. : St. Mary's College Press, [1974] 102 p. : ill. (some col.) ; 21 cm. [BV4832.2.S548] 73-87023 ISBN 0-88489-054-6 : 4.95
1. Meditations. I. Title.

SMITH, Leslie R. 1904- 242
Four keys to prayer. St. Louis, Bethany Press [1962] 128 p. 17 cm. [BV4832.2.S55] 62-17919
1. Meditations. I. Title.

SMITH, Leslie R., 1904- 242
Four keys to prayer. St. Louis, Bethany [c.1962] 128p. 17cm. 62-17919 1.95
1. Meditations. I. Title.

SMITH, Roy Lemon, 1887- 242
New light from old lamps. Nashville, Abingdon [1966, c.1953] 252p 19cm. [BV4832.S635] 52-11319 1.25 pap.,
1. Devotional literature. I. Title.

SMITH, Roy Lemon, 1887-1963. 242
Tales I have told twice. New York, Abingdon Press [1964] 127 p. 20 cm. [BX8495.S59A3] 64-16151
1. Homiletical illustrations. I. Title.

SMITH, Roy Lemon, 1887-1963 242
Tales I have told twice. Nashville, Abingdon [c.1964] 127p. 20cm. 64-16151 2.25 bds.,
1. Homiletical illustrations. I. Title.

SMUCKER, Jesse N 242
Look to your faith. Newton, Kan., Faith and Life Press [1963] 111 p. 20 cm. [BV4832.S56] 63-3227
1. Devotional literature. I. Title.

SMUCKER, Jesse N. 242
Look to your faith. Newton, Kan., Faith & Life Pr. [c.1963] 111p. 20cm. 63-3227 2.50
1. Devotional literature. I. Title.

SMYLIE, Theodore S. 242
Taking stock; help for daily living. Richmond, Va., Knox [c.1965] 128p. 21cm. [BV4832.2.S564] 65-22562 1.75 pap.,
1. Meditations. I. Title.

SMYLIE, Theodore S 242
Taking stock help for daily living, by Theodore S. Smylie. Richmond, John Knox Press [1965] 128 p. 21 cm. [BV4832.2S564] 65-22562
1. Meditations. I. Title.

SNOWDEN, Rita Frances. 242
"Arts of His ways"; a book of devotions. Philadelphia, Muhlenberg Press [1958] 78 p. illus. 20 cm. [BV4832.2.S57] 59-23129
1. Devotional exercises. I. Title.

SNOWDEN, Rita Frances. 242
Psalms in the midst of life. Philadelphia, Fortress Press [1963] 124 p. illus. 18 cm. First published in London under title: Sung in our hearts. [BV4832.2.S58 1963] 63-13875
1. Meditations. I. Title.

SNOWDEN, Rita Frances 242
Psalms in the midst of life. Philadelphia, Fortress [c.1963] 124p. illus. 18cm. First pub. in London under title: Sung in our hearts. 63-13875 1.25 pap.,
1. Meditations. I. Title.

SNOWDEN, Rita Frances. 242
Seven days of the week. Philadelphia, Muhlenberg Press [1958] 129 p. illus. 19 cm. [BV4832.S737] 58-3430
1. Devotional literature. I. Title.

SNOWDEN, Rita Frances. 242
The time of our lives [by] Rita F. Snowden. Nashville, Abingdon Press [1966] 208 p. 18 cm. [BV4832.2.S59] 66-15002
1. Devotional exercises. I. Title.

SNOWDEN, Rita Frances 242
The time of our lives. Nashville, Abingdon [c.1966] 208p. 18cm. [BV4832.2.S59] 66-15002 2.75
1. Devotional exercises. I. Title.

SNOWDEN, Rita Frances. 242
"White the candle burn..."; a book of devotions. London, Epworth Press [label:Chicago, A.R.Allenson, 1950] 95p. illus. 19cm. [BV4832.S742] 53-32863
1. Devotional exercises. I. Title.

SOCKMAN, Ralph Washington, 1889- 242
A lift for living. New York, Abingdon Press [1956] 144p. 20cm. [BV4832.S746] 56-13464
1. Devotional literature. I. Title.

SOCKMAN, Ralph Washington, 1889- 242
A lift for living. New York, Abingdon Press [1956] 144 p. 20 cm. [BV4832.S746] 56-13464
1. Devotional literature. I. Title.

SONTAG, Peter J 242
Meditations for every day. Milwaukee, Bruce [1951] w v. 23 cm. (Science and culture series) Contents.For the first half of the liturgical year from Advent to Trinity Sunday. -- Suited especially for second half of liturgical year from Trinity Sunday to Advent. [BX2182.S65] 51-3634
1. Church year — Meditations. I. Title.

SOUL Delight (The); 242
this is a collection of shared thoughts born of the inspiration that is the calm possession of those who know a daily, an hourly walk and talk with the One Great Eternal Spirit of the universe. By Anonymous. Boston, Christopher Pub. House [c.1961] 91p. 2.50 bds.,

SPEAKMAN, Frederick B 242
God and Jack Wilson [by] Frederick B. Speakman. Westwood, N.J., Revell [1965] 125 p. 21 cm. [BV4832.2.S69] 65-23619
1. Devotional literature. I. Title.

SPETTER, Matthew Ies 242
To deny the night: reflections on life and essence. Photography by Bruce Wolff. [New York] Fieldston Press, 1969. 41 p. illus. 28 cm. [BV4832.2.S72] 73-89850 5.95
1. Meditations. I. Title.

*SPURGEON, C. H. 242
Spurgeon's devotional bible; selected passages from the Word of God with running comments. [by] C. H. Spurgeon. Grand Rapids, Baker Book House [1974] 784 p. 24 cm. [BV4832] ISBN 0-8010-8043-6 9.95
1. Devotional literature. I. Title.

SRI Ram, Nilakanta. 242
Thoughts for aspirants. Compiled from notes and writings of N. Sri Ram. Wheaton, Ill., Theosophical Pub. House [1972] vi, 145 p. 16 cm. (A Quest book) (A Quest miniature) [BP565.S515T48 1972] 73-152060 ISBN 0-8356-0431-4 1.00 (pbk.)
1. Theosophy. I. Title.

STANLEY, David Michael, 1914- 242
A modern scriptural approach to the Spiritual exercises [by] David M. Stanley. Chicago, Institute of Jesuit Sources, 1967. xvi, 358 p. 24 cm. Bibliography: p. 331-334. [BX2179.L8S7] 67-25219
1. Loyola, Ignacio de, Saint, 1491-1556. Exercitia spiritualia. 2. Spiritual exercises. 3. Mediations. 4. Retreats. I. Title.

STAUDINGER, Josef. 242
Holiness of the priesthood; meditations and readings for priests. Translated from the German by John J. Coyne. Westminster, Md., Newman Press [1957?] 546 p. 17 cm. [BX2184.S683] 58-8750
1. Meditations. 2. Clergy — Religious life. I. Title.

STEERE, Douglas Van, 1901- 242
On being present where you are [by] Douglas V. Steere. [Wallingford, Pa., Pendle Hill Publications, c1967] 36 p. 19 cm. (Pendle Hill pamphlet 151.) (The James Backhouse lecture, 1967) [BV4510.2.S7] 67-12913
1. Devotional literature. I. Title. II. Series.

STEINGRAEBER, John. 242
Love is prayer, prayer is love. Selected writings of St. Alphonsus, adapted for moderns by John Steingraeber. Liguori, Mo., Liguori Publications [1973] 191 p. 18 cm. [BV213.S7] 72-97592 1.50 (pbk.)
1. Jesus Christ—Meditations. 2. Mary, Virgin. 3. Prayer. 4. Christian life—Catholic authors. I. Liguori, Alfonso Maria de', Saint, 1696-1787. II. Title.

STETLER, Roy Herben, 1890- 242
God was there. Rock Island, Ill., Augustana Press [1956] 127 p. 18 cm. [BV4832.S816] 56-10135
1. Devotional literature. I. Title.

STETLER, Roy Herben, 1890- 242
Good was there. Rock Island, Ill., Augustana Press [1956] 127p. 18cm. [BV482.S816] 56-10135
1. Devotional literature. I. Title.

STETLER, Roy Herben, 1890- 242
Good was there. Rock Island, Ill., Augustana Press [1956] 127p. 18cm. [BV482.S816] 56-10135
1. Devotional literature. I. Title.

STETLER, Roy Herben, 1890- 242
In the strangest places ... God. Harrisburg, A., Printed by the Evangelical Press [1953] 127p. 18cm. [BV4832.S817] 53-39862
1. Devotional literature. I. Title.

STEVENS, Paul M. 242
Gathered gold / Paul M. Stevens. Waco, Tex. : Word Books, c1975. 126 p. : ill. ; 24 cm. [BV4832.2.S78] 75-19894 4.95
1. Meditations. I. Title.

STEVENSON, Dwight Eshelman, 1906- 242
A way in the wilderness; Holy Land meditations, by Dwight E. Stevenson. St. Louis, Bethany Press [1968] 128 p. 21 cm. Bibliographical footnotes. [DS107.4.S73] 68-4561
1. Palestine—Description and travel. 2. Meditations. I. Title. II. Title: Holy Land meditations.

STEWART, James Alexander, 1910- ed. 242
Still waters, a book of daily devitional mediations. Philadelphia, Revival Literature [1962] 369 p. illus. 19 cm. [BV4810.S72] 62-3809
1. Devotional calendars. I. Title.

STODDARD, William S. 242
Pebbles of truth / William S. Stoddard. Elgin, Ill. : David C. Cook Pub. Co., c1975. 122 p. : ill. ; 18 cm. [BV4832.2.S83] 74-25299 ISBN 0-912692-54-5 : 1.25
1. Meditations. I. Title.

STORER, James Wilson. 242
These historic Scriptures; meditations upon the Bible texts used by our Presidents, from Lincoln to Truman, at their inaugurations. Portrait drawings of the Presideents by T. Victor Hall. Nashville, Broadman Press [1952] 136 p. illus. 21 cm. [BR516.S86] 52-7244
1. Presidents — U.S. — Religion. I. Title.

STORIES that strengthen / 242
compiled by Lucy Gertsch Thomson. Salt Lake City, Utah : Bookcraft, 1975. 58 p. ; 24 cm. [BJ1597.S76] 75-15083 ISBN 0-88494-281-3 : 2.95
1. Conduct of life. I. Thomson, Lucy Gertsch.

STRIETELMEIER, John H. 242
Off-key praises; second thoughts on Scripture texts [by] John Strietelmeier. [St. Louis] Concordia Pub. House [1968] 77 p. illus. 19 cm. [BV4832.2.S86] 68-13893
1. Meditations. I. Title.

STRONG, Patience. 242
The morning watch; a thought for every day of the year. [1st ed.] New York, Dutton, 1951. 192 p. 20 cm. [BV4832.S8736] 51-7937
1. Devotional exercises. 2. Calendars. I. Title.

STRONG, Patience. 242
Wayside glory. [1st ed.] New York, Dutton, 1950. 64 p. 17 cm. [BV4832.S874] 50-9731
1. Devotional literature. I. Title.

STUBER, Stanley Irvin, 1903- ed. 242
Basic Christian writings: compiled and edited by Stanley I. Stuber from his full-length book, The Christian reader. New York, Association Press [1957] 127 p. 16 cm. (An Association Press reflection book) [BV801.S86] 57-5493
1. Devotional literature (Selections: Extracts, etc.) I. Title.

STUBER, Stanley Irving, 1903- ed. 242
Basic Christian writings; compiled and edited by Stanley I. Stuber from his full-length book, The Christian reader. New York, Association Press [c1957] 127p. 16cm. (An Association Press reflection book) [BV4801.S86] 57-5493
1. Devotional literature (Selections: Extracts, etc.) I. Title.

STUBER, Stanley Irving, 1903- ed. 242
The Christian reader; inspirational and devotional classics. New York, Association Press [c1952] 514p. 21cm. [BV4801.S85] 52-12148
1. Devotional literature (Selections: Extracts, etc.) I. Title.

STULL, Ruth. 242
Gardens and gleanings; along life's way. Chicago, Moody Press [1958] 192 p. 22 cm. [BV4832.S8765] 58-4742
1. Devotional literature. I. Title.

SUECHTING, August G ed. 242
Thine forever; daily devotions following Luther's Small catechism, collated and edited by August G. Suechting. Columbus, Ohio, Wartburg Press [1950] 383 p. 16 cm. [BV4832.S877] 50-3397
1. Devotional exercises. 2. Lutheran Church — Prayer-books and devotions — English. 3. Calendars. I. Luther, Martin, Catechismus, Kleiner. II. Title.

SULLIVAN, James L. 242
Reach out! [By] James L. Sullivan. Compiled by Gomer R. Lesch. Nashville, Broadman Press [1970] 128 p. 20 cm. (A Broadman inner circle book) A collection of essays written for Facts and trends, the monthly publication of the Sunday School Board, Southern Baptist Convention. [BV4832.2.S88] 77-113217
1. Meditations. I. Facts and trends. II. Title.

SULLIVAN, Leon Howard, 1922- 242
Philosophy of a giant; quotations. Compiled and edited by Edna C. Wells. Philadelphia, Progressive Ventures Printers [1973] 72 p. illus. 14 x 22 cm. On cover: Meditation. Bibliography: p. 70-71. [BX6455.S84A5] 73-76352
1. Sullivan, Leon Howard, 1922- —Quotations. I. Title. II. Title: Meditation.

SULLIVAN, Walter J. 242
Thoughts for troubled times. New York, Paulist Pr. [c.1961] 128p. (Deus bks.) 61-17237 .75 pap.,
1. Devotional literature. I. Title.

SULLIVAN, William Laurence, 1872-1935. 242
The flaming spirit; mediations and prayers. Edited by Max F. Daskam. With an introd. by Gerald H. Kennedy. New York, Abingdon Press [1961] 143 p. 20 cm. [BV4832.S88] 61-13192
1. Mediations. I. Title.

SULLIVAN, William Laurence, 1872-1935 242
The flaming spirit; meditations and prayers. Ed. by Max F. Daskam. Introd. by Gerald H. Kennedy. Nashville, Abingdon [c.1961] 143p. 61-13192 3.00
1. Meditations. I. Title.

SULZBERGER, Cyrus Leo, 1912- 242
Go gentle into the night / C. L. Sulzberger. Englewood Cliffs, N.J. : Prentice-Hall, c1976. 152 p. ; 22 cm. Includes index. [BL560.S94] 75-42344 ISBN 0-13-357293-5 : 6.95
1. Sulzberger, Cyrus Leo, 1912- 2. Prayer. 3. Prayers. 4. Religion. 5. Death. I. Title.

SWEETING, George, 1924- 242
And the greatest of these: the power of Christian love. Westwood, N.J., Revell [1968] 128 p. 21 cm. [BV4639.S84] 68-11368

1. Love (Theology)—Meditations. I. Title. II. Title: The power of Christian love.

TALMAGE, James Edward, 1862- 242
1933.
The parables of James E. Talmage. Compiled by Albert L. Zobell, Jr. Salt Lake City, Deseret Book Co., 1973. v, 71 p. 18 cm. [BV4832.2.T34] 73-77367 ISBN 0-87747-495-8 2.95
1. Meditations.

TANKSLEY, Perry. 242
Reach out and touch. Old Tappan, N.J., F. H. Revell [1974] 24 p. 27 cm. [BV4832.2.T35] 73-22344 ISBN 0-8007-0663-3 1.95
1. Devotional literature. I. Title.

TANKSLEY, Perry. 242
We're in this thing together. Old Tappan, N.J., F. H. Revell [1974] 80 p. 21 cm. [BV4832.2.T353] 73-22359 ISBN 0-8007-0664-1 3.95
1. Devotional literature. I. Title.

TASSELL, Paul 242
The infinite skills of the infallible Scriptures. New York, Carlton [c.1963] 49p. 21cm. (Reflection bk.) 1.95
I. Title.

TEHOLOGIA deutsch. 242
Theologia Germanica; the way to a sinless life, edited by Thomas S. Kepler. [1st ed.] Cleveland, World Pub. Co. [1952] 192 p. 16 cm. (World devotional classics) [BV4834.T47] 52-5188
1. Christian life — Middle Ages. 2. Mysticism — Germany. I. Kepler, Thomas Samuel, 1897- ed. II. Title.

TEMPLE, William, Abp. of 242
Canterbury, 1881-1944.
Daily readings. Compiled by Hugh C. Warner. New York, Macmillan, 1950. 279 p. port. 21 cm. Bibliography: p. 271. [BX5037.T4] 50-6632
1. Calendars. I. Title.

TERESA, Mother, 1910- 242
A gift for God / Mother Teresa of Calcutta. 1st U.S. edition. New York : Harper & Row, c1975. 87 p. ; 15 cm. [BX2182.2.T39 1975] 76-351372 ISBN 0-06-060660-6 : 3.95
1. Meditations. I. Title.

TERRA, Russell G. 242
On the way : thoughts for pilgrims / by Russell G. Terra. Boston : St. Paul Editions, [1975] p. cm. [BX2182.2.T43] 75-25531
1. Meditations. I. Title.

THEY speak by silences, 242
by a Carthusian. Translated from the French by a monk of Parkminster. London, New York, Longmans, Green [1955] 137p. 18cm. Translation of Silence cartusien, and Voix cartusienne. [BX3303.S53] 56-58312
1. Carthusians. 2. Spiritual life—Catholic authors. I. A Carthusian.

THOMAS, Martha (Horton) 1919- 242
A string of pearls; beautiful poems and meditations for daily reading, pointing the way to the truly Christian life. [1st ed.] New York, Greenwich Book Publishers [c1957] 74 p. 21 cm. [BV4832.T48] 57-13099
1. Meditations. I. Title.

THOMPSON, Blanche Jennings, 242
1887-
All day with God. Milwaukee, Bruce Pub. Co. [1962] 186 p. illus. 15 cm. [BX2110.T5 1962] 62-4262
1. Catholic Church — Prayer-books and devotions — English. I. Title.

THURMAN, Howard, 1899- 242
The centering moment. [1st ed.] New York, Harper & Row [1969] 125 p. 21 cm. [BV4832.2.T525] 69-10479 3.95
1. Devotional literature. I. Title.

THURMAN, Howard, 1899- 242
Deep is the hunger; meditations for apostles of sensitiveness. [1st ed.] New York, Harper [1951] x, 212 p. 22 cm. An expansion of the author's Meditations for apostles of sensitiveness, published in 1948. [BV4832.T558] 51-9391
1. Devotional literature. I. Title. II. Title: Meditations for apostles of sensitiveness.

THURMAN, Howard, 1899- 242
Deep is the hunger; meditations for apostles of sensitiveness. Richmond, Indiana, Friends United Press [1973] p. Reprint of the 1951 ed. published by Harper, New York, which was an expansion of the author's Meditations for apostles of sensitiveness, published in 1948. [BV4832.T558 1973] 73-16023 ISBN 0-913408-10-7 2.75 (pbk)
1. Devotional literature. I. Title. II. Title: Meditations for apostles of sensitiveness.

THURMAN, Howard, 1899- 242
Disciplines of the spirit. [1st. ed.] New York, Harper & Row, [1963] 127 p. 22 cm. [BV4832.2.T527] 63-17716
1. Devotional literature. I. Title.

THURMAN, Howard, 1899- 242
Disciplines of the spirit. New York, Harper [c.1963] 127p. 22cm. 63-17716 3.00
1. Devotional literature. I. Title.

THURMAN, Howard, 1899- 242
The inward journey. [1st ed.] New York, Harper [1961] 155 p. 22 cm. [BV4832.2.T53] 61-12833
1. Devotional literature. I. Title.

THURMAN, Howard, 1899- 242
The inward journey. New York, Harper [c.1961] 155p. 61-12833 3.00 bds.,
1. Devotional literature. I. Title.

THURMAN, Howard, 1899- 242
Meditations of the heart. [1st ed.] New York, Harper [1953] 216p. 22cm. [BV4832.T57] 53-10980
1. Devotional literature. I. Title.

THURMAN, Howard, 1899- 242
Meditations of the heart / by Howard Thurman. Richmond, Ind. : Friends United Press, 1976, c1973. p. cm. Reprint of the 1953 ed. published by Harper & Row, New York. [BV4832.T55 1976] 76-18287 ISBN 0-913408-25-5 pbk. : 3.45
1. Devotional literature. I. Title.

TIERNEY, Mary E. 242
All the miracles we hope for; a Paulist photo/meditation book, by Mary E. Tierney. With photos by John Glaser. Designed by William Kautz. New York, Paulist Press [1973] 63 p. illus. 19 cm. [BX2182.2.T53] 72-93026 ISBN 0-8091-1751-7 1.50 (pbk.)
1. Meditations. I. Title.

TIPPETT, Harry Moyle, 1891- 242
Radiant horizons. Illus. by Stanley Dunlap, Jr. Washington, Review and Herald Pub. Assn. [1956] 128p. illus. 18cm. [BV4832.T5813] 56-58425
1. Devotional literature. I. Title.

TIPPETT, Harry Moyle, 1891- 242
Radiant horizons. Illus. by Stanley Dunlap, Jr. Washington, Review and Herald Pub. Assn. [1956] 128 p. illus. 18 cm. [BV4832.T5813] 56-58425
1. Devotional literature. I. Title.

TONER, Helen L 242
The quest for personal poise. St. Louis, Bethany Press [1954] 79p. 18cm. [BV4832.T64] 54-38568
1. Meditations. I. Title.

TONNE, Arthur J., Rt. Rev. 242
Msgr.
Five-minute parish talks. [Emporia, Kans., Didde, c.1962] 60p. 23cm. 1.50 pap.,
I. Title.

TORREY, Reuben Archer, 1856- 242
1928.
The power of prayer and the prayer of power. Grand Rapids, Zondervan Pub. House [1972, c1924] 191 p. 18 cm. (Zondervan books) [BV210.T6 1972] 74-156243 1.25 (pbk)
1. Prayer. I. Title.

TOWNSEND, Zella. 242
Whisperings in the silence; meditations of Zella Townsend. Santa Monica, Calif., DeVorss [1972, c1971] 96 p. 21 cm. [BV4832.2.T68 1972] 79-184743 ISBN 0-87516-121-9
1. Meditations. I. Title.

TRAHERNE, Thomas, d.1674. 242
Centuries. Introd. by John Farrar. New York, Harper [1960] 228 p. 21 cm. First published in 1908 under title: Centuries of meditations. [BV4831.T7] 60-15275
1. Devotional literature. I. Title.

TRAHERNE, Thomas, d.1674 242
Centuries. Introd. by John Farrar. New York, Harper [c.1960] x, 228p. 21cm. First published in 1908 under title: Centuries of meditations. 60-15275 3.50
1. Devotional literature. I. Title.

TRAHERNE, Thomas, d.1674. 242
Centuries, poems, and thanksgivings. Edited by H. M. Margoliouth. Oxford, Clarendon Press, 1958. 2 v. facsims. 23 cm. [BV4831.T72] 58-4245
1. Devotional literature. I. Margoliouth, Herschel Maurice, 1887- ed. II. Title.

TRAHERNE, Thomas, d.1674. 242
Poems, Centuries and three Thanksgivings; edited by Anne Ridler. London, Oxford U. P., 1966. xviii, 427 p. 22 1/2 cm. [Oxford Standard authors series] [BV4831.T72] 66-70162
1. Devotional literature. I. Ridler, Anne (Bradley) 1912- ed. II. Title.

TRAHERNE, Thomas, d.1674 242
Poems, Centuries and three Thanksgivings ed. by Anne Ridler. [New York] Oxford [c.]1966. xviii, 427p. 23cm. (Oxford Standard authors ser.) [BV4831.T72] 66-70162 7.00
1. Devotional literature. I. Ridler, Anne (Bradley) 1912- ed. II. Title.

TREASURES of silver / 242
compiled by Jo Petty. Norwalk, Conn. : C. R. Gibson Co., c1977. 85 p. ; 21 cm. [BV4805.T73] 76-52082 ISBN 0-8378-1768-4 : 3.95
1. Devotional literature. I. Petty, Jo.

TRIMBLE, John Thomas, 1934- 242
Silver in the Psalms / J. Thomas Trimble. Nashville : Broadman Press, c1976. 138 p. ; 20 cm. Includes index. [BS1430.4.T74] 75-35396 ISBN 0-8054-5139-0 : 4.95
1. Bible. O.T. Psalms—Devotional literature. I. Title.

TROUT, Jessie M 242
Like a watered garden. Drawings by Alice Rist Langford. St. Louis, Bethany Press [1954] 144p. illus. 22cm. [BV4832.T73] 54-43039
1. Devotional exercises. I. Title.

TRUEBLOOD, David Elton, 1900- 242
The meditations of Elton Trueblood / edited by Stephen R. Sebert and W. Gordon Ross. 1st ed. New York : Harper & Row, c1975. p. cm. [BV4832.2.T78 1975] 75-9340 ISBN 0-06-068671-5 : 5.95
1. Meditations. 2. Yokefellow Movement. I. Title.

TURNER, Dorothy Banker. 242
Crown of life; a collection of inspirational articles. Claremont, Calif., Creative Press, 1955. 55p. 22cm. [BV4832.T82] 55-8568
1. Devotional literature. I. Title.

TYSON, M. Dewey. 242
Love is for living / M. Dewey Tyson. Nashville : Upper Room, c1975. 61 p. : ill. ; 14 x 23 cm. [BV4832.2.T9] 75-21089 1.75
1. Meditations. I. Title.

UNGER, Merrill Frederick 242
Stop existing and start living. Grand Rapids, Mich., Eerdmans [c.1959] 131p. 22cm. 59-14579 2.50
1. Devotional literature. I. Title.

UNGER, Merrill Frederick, 242
1909-
The God-filled life. Grand Rapids, Zondervan Pub. House [1959] 155 p. 21 cm. [BV4832.2.U48] 59-16866
1. Devotional literature. I. Title.

UNGER, Merrill Frederick, 242
1909-
Stop existing and start living, [1st ed.] Grand Rapids, Eerdmans [1959] 131 p. 22 cm. [BV4832.2.U49] 59-14579
1. Devotional literature. I. Title.

VANDEMAN, George E. 242
Hammers in the fire, and what wore the hammers out, by George E. Vandeman. Mountain View, Calif., Pacific Press Pub. Association [1971] 96 p. 19 cm. [BV4832.2.V35] 79-154293
1. Meditations. I. Title.

VANDEMAN, George E. 242
Is anybody driving? / George Vandeman. Mountain View, Calif. : Pacific Press Pub. Association, c1975. 96 p. ; 19 cm. [BV4832.2.V36] 75-11469 pbk. : 0.60
1. Meditations. I. Title.

VANDEN Berg, William Ernest, 242
1916-
Devotions for church groups, by William E. Vanden Berg. Grand Rapids, Baker Book House [1966] 126 p. 20 cm. [BX9527.V3] 67-2210
1. Reformed Church in America—Sermons. 2. Sermons, American. I. Title.

VANDEN BERG, William E 242
Devotions for church groups, by William E. Vanden Berg. Grand Rapids, Baker Book House [1966] 126 p. 20 cm. [BX9527.V3] 67-2210
1. Reformed Church in America — Sermons. 2. Sermons, American. I. Title.

VANDEUR, Eugene, 1875- 242
Pledge of glory; meditations on the Eucharist and the Trinity. Translated from the French by the Dominican Nuns of Corpus Christi Monastery, Menlo Park, Calif. Westminster, Md., Newman Press, 1958. 238 p. 21 cm. Translation of A la Trinite par l'Hostie. [BV5082.E6V273] 57-11831
1. Elisabeth de la Trinite, Sister, 1880-1906. Priere. 2. Lord's Supper — Meditations. 3. Trinity. 4. Mysticism — Catholic Church. I. Title.

VANDEUR, Eugene, 1875- 242
Trinity whom I adore, meditations. Prayer of Sister Elizabeth of the Trinity, Carmelite, with a commentary by Eugene Vandeur. Enl., completed, 1931. Translated from the French by the Dominican Nuns, Corpus Christi Monastery, Menlo Park, Calif. New York, F. Pustet Co., 1953. 163p. 16cm. Translation of O mon Dieu, Trinite que j'adore. [BV5082.E6V32] 54-19591
1. Elizabeth de la Trinite, Sister 1880-1906. Prayer. I. Title.

VAN LINDEN, Philip. 242
The Gospel of St. Mark : read and pray: daily Bible readings, with comments, reflections, prayers, one page a day for three months by Philip Van Linden. Chicago : Franciscan Herald Press, c1976. 96 p. ; 18 cm. (Read and pray ; no. 4) [BS2585.V28] 76-46627 ISBN 0-8199-0630-1 : 0.95
1. Bible. N.T. Mark—Devotional literature. I. Title. II. Series.

VAN NUYS, Roscoe Golden, 242
1881-
The whole man: body, mind, spirit, by Roscoe Van Nuys. New York, Philosophical Library [1971] 134 p. 22 cm. [BL50.V3] 77-145467 ISBN 0-8022-2050-9 5.95
1. Meditations. I. Title.

VAN ZELLER, Hubert, 1905 242
Moments of light. Springfield, Ill., Templegate [1963] xi, 196p. 17cm. (Golden lib.) 63-25560 3.50
1. Spiritual life—Catholic authors. I. Title.

VAN ZELLER, Hubert, 1905- 242
More ideas for prayer; 200 suggestions. Springfield, Ill., Templegate [1967] 160 p. 24 cm. [BX2182.2.V3] 67-1357
1. Meditations. 2. Christian life—Catholic authors. I. Title.

VAUGHN, Ruth. 242
Even when I cry / Ruth Vaughn. Chicago : Moody Press, [1975] 94 p. ; 22 cm. [BV4832.2.V38] 75-14258 ISBN 0-8024-2389-2 pbk. : 1.95
1. Meditations. I. Title.

VIGEVENO, H. S. 242
Day brighteners / H. S. Vigeveno. Santa Ana, Calif. : Vision House Publishers, c1976. 192 p. ; 21 cm. [BS2665.4.V53] 76-12184 ISBN 0-88449-020-3 : 2.95
1. Bible. N.T. Romans—Meditations. I. Title.

VIGEVENO, H. S. 242
The early church speaks to us; daily devotion and Bible studies, by H. S. Vigeveno. Glendale, Calif., G/L Regal Books [1970] 166 p. 18 cm. [BV4811.V5] 76-104083 ISBN 8-307-00609-
1. Devotional calendars. I. Title.

VINCENT DE PAUL, Saint, 1581- 242
1660.
A thought from St. Vincent de Paul for each day of the year. Translated from the French by Frances M. Kemp. New York, Cincinnati [etc.] Benziger brothers [c1888] 141 p. incl. front. 13 1/2 cm. (On cover: Words of the saints. [v. 5]) [BX2178.W6 vol. 5] 32-18166
1. Devotional calendars — Catholic Church. I. Title.

VINCENTIANS. WESTERN PROVINCE 242
OF THE U.S.A.
Annual retreat mediations. [St. Louis, 1959] 117 p. 20 cm. [BX3770.A42] 60-23643
1. Meditations. I. Title.

VINING, Elizabeth Gray, 1902- 242
The world in tune. [1st ed.] New York, Published in association with Pendle Hill by Harper [1954] 124 p. 19 cm. [BV4832.V53] 54-9007
1. Devotional literature. I. Title.

VOILLAUME, Rene. 242
The truth will make you free : letters to the Little Brothers / [by] Rene Voillaume ; [translated from the French by Jeremy Moiser] . London : Darton, Longman and Todd, 1976. vii, 152 p. ; 22 cm. Translation of Voyants de Dieu dans la cite which was published as v. 4 of the author's Lettres aux fraternites. Includes bibliographical references. [BX2182.2.V6A413 1976] 77-359983 ISBN 0-232-51358-9 : £2.25
1. Meditations. I. Little Brothers of Jesus. II. Title.

VONK, Idalee Wolf, 1913- 242
The will of the wind; inspirational thoughts on Christian virtues [by] Idalee W. Vonk. Grand Rapids, Baker Book House [1969] 79 p. illus. 20 cm. [BV4832.2.V6] 69-15664

1. Meditations. I. Title.

*WAGNER, Estry G. 242
Might-mystery-mercy by Estry G. Wagner. New York, Vantage [1974] 61 p. 22 cm. [BV4832.2] ISBN 0-533-00863-8 3.75
1. Devotional exercises. I. Title.

WAGONER, Walter D. 242
Say a good word for Jesus, by Walter D. Wagoner. Philadelphia, United Church Press [1973] 128 p. 22 cm. "A Pilgrim Press book." Includes bibliographical references. [BV4832.2.W32] 73-9674 ISBN 0-8298-0257-6 4.95
1. Meditations. I. Title.

WALKER, Granville T. 242
Go placidly amid the noise and haste; meditations on the "desiderata," by Granville T. Walker. Fort Worth, Texas Christian University Press, 1973. 103 p. 23 cm. (Texas Christian University monographs in religion, no. 2) Includes bibliographical references. [BX7327.W28G6] 73-78070 3.50
1. Disciples of Christ—Sermons. 2. Sermons, American. I. Title. II. Series: Texas Christian Univeristy, Fort Worth. Monographs in religion, no. 2.

WALKER, Harold Blake. 242
Heart of the Christian year; daily "Living faith" meditations from Advent through Easter. [1st ed.] New York, Harper [1961] 152 p. 21 cm. [BV4812.W3] 61-12837
1. Church year — Meditations. I. Title.

WALLACE, Archer, 1884- 242
The autograph of God. New York, Macmillan, 1952. 150 p. 21 cm. [BV4832.W23] 52-12453
1. Meditations. I. Title.

WALLACE, W J 242
Meditations for five Saturdays devotion; spiritual reflections for public and private use. [1st ed.] New York, Exposition Press [1955] 83p. 21cm. [BX2163.W25] 55-10307
1. Rosary—Meditations. I. Title.

WALLIS, Charles Langworthy, 1921- comp. 242
Holy Holy Land; a devotional anthology, edited by Charles L. Wallis. Photos. by Archie Lieberman. [1st ed.] New York, Harper & Row [1969] 224 p. illus. 29 cm. [BS483.5.W3] 79-85046
1. Bible—Meditations. 2. Bible—Devotional literature. 3. Religious poetry. I. Lieberman, Archie, illus. II. Title.

WALLIS, Charles Langworthy, 1921- ed. 242
Words of life; a religious and inspirational album containing 1100 quotations from the minds and hearts of writers of twenty centuries and illustrated by scenes of the Holy Land. Edited by Charles L. Wallis. [1st ed.] New York, Harper & Row [1966] vii, 248 p. illus. 30 cm. [BV4801.W3] 66-13616
1. Devotional iliterature (Selections: Extracts, etc.) I. Title.

WALLIS, Charles Langworthy, 1921- ed. 242
Words of life; a religious and inspirational album containing 1100 quotations from the minds and hearts of writers of twenty centuries and illustrated by scenes of the Holy Land. New York, Harper [c.1966] vii, 248p. illus. 30cm. [BV4801.W3] 66-13616 4.95; 8.50; bds., presentation ed., deluxe ed.,
1. Devotional literature (Selections: Extracts, etc.) I. Title.

WALSH, Chad, 1914- 242
Behold the glory. [1st ed.] New York, Harper [c1956] 156p. 20cm. [BV4332.W27] 55-11486
1. Devotional literature. I. Title.

WALSH, Chad, 1914- 242
Behold the glory. [1st ed.] New York, Harper [c1956] 156 p. 20 cm. [BV4832.W27] 55-11486
1. Devotional literature. I. Title.

WALSH, Mary Rosamond. 242
Miniature missiles for heaven's sake, by Sister Mary Rosamond. With a foreword by Maurice B. Walsh. Illustrated by Joseph Swan. [New York] St. Paul Publications [1960] 144 p. illus. 20 cm. [BX2182.2W34] 60-8946
1. Meditations. I. Title.

WALSH, Vincent M. 242
Preparing newcomers for life in the Spirit / Vincent M. Walsh. St. Meinrad, IN. : Abbey Press, 1976. p. cm. [BX2182.2.W35] 76-7442 ISBN 0-87029-061-4 : 1.95
1. Devotional exercises. 2. Pentecostalism. I. Title. II. Title: Life in the Spirit.

WARD, Arthur Sterling, ed. 242
Strength for service to God and country; daily devotional messages for those in the services. Rev. ed., edited by Arthur Sterling Ward. New York, Abingdon-Cokesbury Press [1950] 1 v. (unpaged) 14 cm. "Based on the World War II edition edited by Norman E. Nygaard." [BV4588.S87 1950] 51-9195
1. Soldiers — Religious life. I. Title.

WARD, Clara Mills. 242
Consider ... interpretations of selected scriptural texts. [1st ed.] New York, Exposition Press [1956] 86 p. 21 cm. Chiefly essays written as a weekly feature column "Consider ... " for the Metropolis news, Metropolis, Illinois, and a collection of maxims "Coffee grounds." [BR115.H4W36] 56-8722
1. Mental healing. I. Title.

WARD, Clara Mills. 242
Consider ... interpretations of selected scriptural texts. [1st ed.] New York, Exposition Press [1956] 86p. 21cm. Chiefly essays written as a weekly feature column 'Consider ...' for the Metropolis news, Metropolis, Illinois, and a collection of maxims 'Coffee grounds.' [BR115.H4W36] 56-8722
1. Mental healing. I. Title.

WARD, Marjory Goldfinch. 242
This costly fragrance. Nashville, Broadman Press [1971] 59 p. 20 cm. [BV4832.2.W37] 74-128855 ISBN 0-8054-5149-8 2.50
1. Devotional exercises. I. Title.

WARD, William Arthur, 1921- 242
Fountains of faith; the words of William Arthur Ward. [1st ed.] Anderson, S.C., Droke House [1970] 82 p. 23 cm. [BJ1548.W35] 77-118205
1. Conduct of life—Quotations, maxims, etc. I. Title.

WEATHERHEAD, Leslie Dixon, 1893- 242
Time for God, by Leslie D. Weatherhead. Nashville, Abingdon Press [1968, c1967] 143 p. 22 cm. [BV4832.2.W42 1968] 68-11716
1. Meditations. I. Title.

WEDEL, Alton F. 242
Chin up, and other devotional preludes to praise [by] Alton F. Wedel. St. Louis, Concordia Pub. House [1969] 95 p. 19 cm. [BV4832.2.W434 1969] 76-77281 1.95 (pbk)
1. Meditations. I. Title.

WEEKLEY, James, 1939- 242
Making love a family affair; family meditations on Christian themes. Nashville, Abingdon Press [1973, c1974] 142 p. 20 cm. [BV255.W39] 73-8730 ISBN 0-687-23040-3 3.95
1. Family—Prayer-books and devotions—English. I. Title.

WEITZNER, Emil. 242
Humanist meditations and paraphrases. New York, Random House [1965] xi, 243 p. 22 cm. [PS3545.W4915H8] 65-18107
I. Title.

WEITZNER, Emil 242
Humanist meditations and paraphrases. New York, Random [c.1965] xi, 243p. 22cm. [PS3545.W4915H8] 65-18107 5.00
I. Title.

WELLBORN, Grace (Pleasant) 242
Devotionals on flowers of the Bible. Illus. by David E. Carrell. Grand Rapids, Baker Bk. [1967] 128p. illus. 20cm. A companion to the author's Devotionals on trees of the Bible. [BV4832.W44] 67-18201 2.95
1. Devotional literature. 2. Bible—Natural history. I. Title.

WELLBORN, Grace (Pleasant) 242
Devotionals on trees of the Bible. Grand Rapids. Baker Bk. [1966] 109, [2] p. illus. 20cm. Bibl. [BV4832.W45] 66-25397 2.50
1. Devotional literature. 2. Bible—Natural history. I. Title.

WERSELL, Thomas W. 242
Spiritual thoughts and prayers [by] Thomas W. Wersell. Philadelphia, Fortress Press [1974] 76 p. 18 cm. [BV245.W395] 74-76920 ISBN 0-8006-1305-8 1.95 (pbk.).
1. Prayers. 2. Meditations. I. Title.

WESBERRY, James Pickett. 242
Meditations for happy Christians [by] James P. Wesberry. Nashville, Tenn., Broadman Press [1973] 126 p. 20 cm. [BV4832.2.W466] 72-90035 ISBN 0-8054-5521-3 3.50
1. Meditations. I. Title.

WESTFALL, Tom. 242
What does God want with a dead dog. Yuma, Colo., Pioneer Press [1973] 133 p. 21 cm. "A Your Life publication." Excerpted from the author's newspaper column "Your faith and mine". [BV4832.2.W473] 72-96025 1.95
1. Meditations. I. Title.

WHALEY, Catrina Parrott 242
Share my meditations; living devotions for personal and group use. Grand Rapids. Baker Bk. [1967] 116p. 21cm. [BV4832.2.W48] 67-17263 2.50
1. Meditations. I. Title.

WHALEY, Catrina Parrott. 242
Share my meditations; living devotions for personal and group use. Grand Rapids, Baker Book House [1967] 116 p. 21 cm. [BV4832.2.W48] 67-17263
1. Meditations. I. Title.

WHEATCROFT, Anita. 242
Preface for parents; counsels for the expectant mother and father. Foreword by Dora P. Chaplin. Illustrated by Berit Homstead. Greenwich, Conn., Seabury Press, 1955. 95p. illus. 20cm. [BV4847.W46] 55-8741
1. Mothers—Prayer-books and devotions—English. I. Title.

WHEELER, Joseph Clyde. 242
Light for dark days. St. Louis, Bethany Press [1961] 124 p. 17 cm. [BV4908.5.W48] 61-11932
1. Peace of mind. I. Title.

WHEELER, Joseph Clyde 242
Light for dark days. St. Louis, Bethany [c.1961] 124p. 61-11932 1.95
1. Peace of mind. I. Title.

WHELAN, Basil, 1896- 242
Happiness with God. St. Louis, Herder [1959] 149 p. 20 cm. [BX2350.2.W5 1959] 59-2323
1. Spiritual life — Catholic authors. I. Title.

WHEN fires burn; 242
insights into the devotional life. Edited by Wilson O. Weldon. Nashville, The Upper room [1969] 70 p. 19 cm. [BV4813.W5] 72-81640
1. Meditation. I. Weldon, Wilson O., ed. II. The Upper room.

WHITE, Helen Constance, 1896- 242
The Tudor books of private devotion. [Madison] University of Wisconsin Press [1951] 284 p. facsims. 24 cm. Bibliography: p. [251]-255. [BV4818.W48] 51-62475
1. Devotional literature—Hist. & crit. 2. Religious literature, English—Hist. & crit. I. Title.

WHITERIG, John, d. 1371, supposed author. 242
The monk of Farne; the meditations of a fourteenth century monk, edited and introduced by Hugh Farmer. Translated by a Benedictine of Stanbrook. [1st American ed.] Baltimore, Helicon Press [1961] vii, 155 p. illus. 22 cm. (The Benedictine studies [1]) Includes bibliographical references. [BX2181.W513 1961] 61-19349
1. Meditations. I. Farmer, Hugh, ed. II. Title. III. Series.

WHITMAN, Virginia. 242
Kindle a blaze for Christ. Nashville, Broadman Press [c1962] 72 p. 20 cm. [BV4832.2.W53] 63-7339
1. Devotional literature. I. Title.

WHITMAN, Virginia 242
Kindle a blaze for Christ. Nashville, Broadman [c.1962] 72p. 20cm. 63-7339 1.50 pap.,
1. Devotional literature. I. Title.

WHITTIER, A. Gerald 242
Christian meditations. New York, Carlton Press [dist. Comet, c.]1961. 178p. (Reflection book) 3.00
1. Meditations. I. Title.

†WIERSBE, Warren W. 242
His name is Wonderful / by Warren W. Wiersbe. Wheaton, Ill. : Tyndale House, 1976. 101 p. : ill. ; 20 cm. [BV4832.2.W536] 76-42116 ISBN 0-8423-1435-0 : 3.95.
1. Meditations. I. Title.

WIERSBE, Warren W. 242
Thoughts for men on the move; strength for the journey, by Warren W. Wiersbe. Chicago, Moody Press [1970] 128 p. 18 cm. [BV4832.2.W537] 73-123158 2.95
1. Meditations. I. Title.

WILKIN, Eloise (Burns) 242
Song of praise [Illus. by] Eloise Wilkin. New York, American Heritage Press, 1970. [26] p. col. illus. 20 cm. The text is a paraphrase of selections from the Old Testament apocryphal book, The song of the three children. Praises God for the many things He created. [BT107.W5] 70-95733 2.95
1. God—Juvenile literature. I. Title.

WILLIAMS, Charles, 1886-1945, comp. 242
The new Christian year; chosen by Charles Williams. London, New York, Oxford University Press [1958] 281 p. 18 cm. [BV4810.W47 1958] 58-1166
1. Church year — Prayer-books and devotions — English. 2. Religious literature (Selections: Extracts, etc.) I. Title.

WILLIAMS, Loyd Elmo. 242
Fireside chats, by Loyd E. Williams. San Antonio, Naylor Co. [1970] xi, 160 p. 22 cm. [BV4832.2.W555] 74-114705 5.95
1. Meditations. I. Title.

WILLISTON, Mary Denny, comp. 242
Where and how to find God; a selection of quotations carefully arranged to suggest the answers. New York, R.R. Smith, 1951. 118 p. 22 cm. [BV4805.W55] 51-10091
1. Devotional literature (Selections: extracts, etc.) I. Title.

WILSON, Jesse Rodman, 1892- 242
Light in a dark world. Grand Rapids, Grand Rapids International Publications; distributed by Kregel's, 1957. 80 p. illus. 23 cm. [BV4832.W487] 57-14956
1. Devotional literature. I. Title.

WILSON, Oliver G. 242
Boundless horizons; meditations on the Christian life. Grand Rapids, Zondervan Pub. House [1960] 111 p. 20 cm. [[BV4832.2.W58]] 60-2995
1. Devotional literature. I. Title.

WILSON, Oliver G. 242
Boundless horizons; meditations on the Christian life. Marion, Ind., Wesley Press [1960] 111 p. illus. 20 cm. [BV4832.2.W58 1960a] 60-42652
1. Devotional literature. I. Title.

WILSON, Oliver G. 242
Boundless horizons; meditations on the Christian life. Grand Rapids, Mich., Zondervan Pub. House [c.1960] 111p. 20cm. 60-2995 2.00
1. Devotional literature. I. Title.

WOLCOTT, Leonard T 242
Meditations on Ephesians [by] Leonard T. Wolcott. New York, Abingdon Press [1965] 184 p. 23 cm. Bibliographical references included in "Notes" (p. 183-184) [BS2695.4.W6] 65-21975
1. Bible. N. T. Ephesians — Meditations. I. Title.

WOLCOTT, Leonard T. 242
Meditations on Ephesians. Nashville, Abingdon [c.]1965. 184p. 23cm. Bibl. [BS2695.4.W6] 65-21975 2.95
1. Bible. N. T. Ephesians—Meditations. I. Title.

WOOD, June Smallwood. 242
A workable faith / June Smallwood Wood. New York : Philosophical Library, [1974] 99 p. ; 22 cm. [BV4832.2.W66] 74-80277 ISBN 0-8022-2152-1 : 6.00
1. Meditations. I. Title.

WOOD, Nettie Wyatt, Rev. 242
The mystery of life. New York, Vantage [c.1963] 93p. 21cm. 2.75
I. Title.

WOODALL, William Live, 1908- 242
100 devotions for boys and girls. New York, Association Press [1957] 122 p. 20 cm. [BV4870.W6] 57-11599
1. Children — Prayer-books and devotions — English. I. Title.

WOODALL, William Love, 1908- 242
100 devotions for boys and girls. New York, Association Press [1957] 122p. 20cm. [BV4870.W6] 57-11599
1. Children—Prayer-books and devotions—English. I. Title.

WRIGHT, Richardson Little, 1887- 242
A book of days for Christians. [1st ed.] Philadelphia, Lippincott [1951] 223 p. 20 cm. [BV4832.W72] 51-11195
1. Devotional exercises. I. Title.

WRIGHT, Robert Roy. 242
Seven themes from the Gospel of John; a devotional guide. New York, Abingdon Press [1964] 124 p. 20 cm. [BV4832.W724] 64-12959
1. Meditations. I. Title.

WRIGHT, Robert Roy 242
Seven themes from the Gospel of John; a devotional guide. Nashville, Abingdon [c.1964] 124p. 20cm. 64-12959 2.25
1. Meditations. I. Title.

YATES, Elizabeth, 1905- 242
A book of hours / Elizabeth Yates ; art by Carol Aymar Armstrong. Noroton, Conn. : Vineyard Books ; New York : distributed to the trade by Seabury Press, c1976. 64 p. : ill. ;

22 cm. Includes bibliographical references. [BV4832.2.Y3] 76-383908 ISBN 0-913886-07-6 : 5.95 ISBN 0-913886-06-8 pbk : 2.95
1. Devotional exercises. I. Title.

YATES, Miles Lowell, 1890-1956. 242
The King in His beauty. Foreword by Lawrence Rose. Greenwich, Conn., Seabury Press, 1957. 91p. 20cm. [BV4832.Y3] 57-10128
1. Devotional literature. 2. Devotion. I. Title.

YATES, Miles Lowell, 1890-1956. 242
The King in His beauty. Foreword by Lawrence Rose. Greenwich, Conn., Seabury Press, 1957. 91 p. 20 cm. [BV4832.Y3] 57-10128
1. Devotional literature. 2. Devotion. I. Title.

*YONGE, Charlotte Mary, 1823-1901. 242
Gold dust, by Charlotte M. Yonge. [New Canaan, Conn.] [Keats Pub. Co.] [1973] xiv, 96 p. 18 cm. "A translation from a collection of devotional thoughts published in France under the title of Paillettes d'Or, and first published in/1880." [BV4832] 0.95 (pbk)
1. Devotional exercises. I. Title.

YOUNG, Loren. 242
Sprint for the sun. Waco, Tex., Word Books [1969] 90 p. 22 cm. [BV4832.2.Y6] 69-20223
1. Meditations. I. Title.

YOUNG, Samuel, 1901- 242
God makes a difference. Kansas City, Mo., Beacon Hill Press [1954] 128p. 20cm. [BV4832] 54-3148
1. Devotional literature. I. Title.

YOUNGDAHL, Reuben K 1911- 242
Going God's way. Rock Island, Ill., Augustana Book Concern [1951] 366 p. 20 cm. [BV4832.Y6] 51-14594
1. Devotional exercises. 2. Calendars. I. Title.

ZEARFOSS, Robert Newell, 1914- 242
Call to reflection [by] Robert N. Zearfoss. Valley Forge [Pa.] Judson Press [1966] 126 p. 20 cm. [BV4832.2.Z4] 66-25623
1. Meditations. I. Title.

ZEARFOSS, Robert Newell, 1914- 242
With wonder in your soul. [1st ed.] Cleveland, World Pub. Co. [1958] 149 p. 21 cm. [BV4832.Z4 1958] 58-9404
1. Meditations. I. Title.

ZELLER, Harry K. 242
Free to be, free to give. Elgin, Ill., Brethren Press [1974] 156 p. port. 21 cm. [BX7827.Z4F7] 74-5487 ISBN 0-87178-295-2 4.95
1. Church of the Brethren—Sermons. 2. Sermons, American. 3. Meditations. I. Title.

BRO, Harmon Hartzell, 1919- 242'.01'9
Dreams in the life of prayer: the approach of Edgar Cayce. [1st ed.] New York, Harper & Row [1970] 156 p. 22 cm. [BF1091.B68 1970] 72-85055 4.95
1. Cayce, Edgar, 1877-1945. 2. Dreams. 3. Spiritual life. I. Title.

BACHELDER, Louise, comp. 242'.08
Golden words of faith, hope & love. Illus. by Chrystal Corcos. Mount Vernon, N.Y., Peter Pauper Press [1969] 62 p. col. illus. 20 cm. [PN6081.B15] 75-5771 1.25
1. Quotations, English. I. Title.

*HARDIE, Katherine Johnson 242.08
Praise God! Hymns, prayers, and Bible passages selected for boys, girls, their families and friends. Illus. by Mary Alice Bahler. Richmond, Va., CLC Pr. 1966. 32p. illus. (pt. col.) 22cm. 1.45 bds.,
1. Prayers—Collections—Juvenile literature. I. Title.
Young readers. Available from Knox.

JONES, John Gordon, 1901- 242'.08
A man with a book in his hand, an introduction to the classics of the devotional literature of the seventeenth century, and to the men who wrote them [by] J. Gordon Jones. Toronto, Ontario, J. Gordon Jones, 1967. 196 p. 20 cm. Includes bibliographical references. [BV4818.J6] 79-414042 unpriced
1. Devotional literature—History and criticism. I. Title.

LOCKYER, Herbert. 242'.08 s
Bible-centered devotions on fulfillment and splendor / Herbert Lockyer. 1st ed. New York : Harper & Row, c1977. p. cm. (His Seasons of the Lord ; v. 3) (Harper jubilee books ; HJG 3) [BS483.5.L6 vol. 3] 242'.3 76-55756 ISBN 0-06-065267-5 pbk. : 3.95
1. Bible—Meditations. I. Title.

LOCKYER, Herbert. 242'.08 s
Bible-centered devotions on purity and hope / Herbert Lockyer. 1st ed. New York : Harper & Row, c1977. p. cm. (His Seasons of the Lord ; v. 1) (Harper jubilee books : HJG 1) [BS483.5 vol. 1] 234'.2 76-55823 ISBN 0-06-065265-9 pbk. : 3.95
1. Bible—Meditations. I. Title.

LOCKYER, Herbert. 242'.08 s
Bible-centered devotions on resurrection and glory / Herbert Lockyer. 1st ed. New York : Harper & Row, c1977. p. cm. (His Seasons of the Lord ; v. 2) (Harper jubilee books ; HJG 2) [BS483.5.L6 vol. 2] 232.9'7 76-55755 ISBN 0-06-065266-7 pbk. : 3.95
1. Bible—Meditations. I. Title.

LOCKYER, Herbert. 242'.08 s
Bible-centered devotions on silence and remembrance / Herbert Lockyer. 1st ed. New York : Harper & Row, c1977. p. cm. (His Seasons of the Lord ; v. 4) (Harper jubilee books ; HJG 4) [BS483.5.L6 vol. 4] 242'.4 76-56075 ISBN 0-06-065268-3 pbk. : 3.95
1. Bible—Meditations. I. Title.

LOCKYER, Herbert. 242'.08
Seasons of the Lord / Herbert Lockyer. 1st ed. New York : Harper & Row, c1977. p. cm. (Harper jubilee books ; HJG 1-4) Contents.Contents.—v. 1. Bible-centered devotions on purity and hope.—v. 2. Bible-centered devotions on resurrection and glory.—v. 3. Bible-centered devotions on fulfillment and splendor.—v. 4. Bible-centered devotions on silence and remembrance. [BS483.5.L6] 76-9998 ISBN pbk. : 3.95 per vol.
1. Bible—Meditations—Collected works. I. Title.

ROBERTS, John Richard. 242.08
A critical anthology of English recusant devotional prose, 1558-1603, by John R. Roberts. Pittsburgh, Duquesne University Press, 1966. x, 322 p. 27 cm. (Duquesne studies. Philological series 7) Bibliography: p. 320-322. [BX2177.R6] 65-13006
1. Devotional literature. 2. Catholics in England. I. Title. II. Series.

ROBERTS, John Richard. 242.08
A critical anthology of English recusant devotional prose, 1558-1603, by John R. Roberts. Pittsburgh, Duquesne University Press, 1966. x, 322 p. 27 cm. (Duquesne studies. Philological series, 7) Bibliography: p. 320-322. [BX2177.R6] 65-13006
1. Devotional literature (Selections: Extracts, etc.) 2. Catholics in England. I. Title. II. Series.

WAGNER, Ruth H., comp. 242'.08
For I am with you. Written and compiled by Ruth H. Wagner. Illustrated by Marvin Besunder. Norwalk, Conn., Gibson Co. [1969] [41] p. illus. 21 cm. [BV4801.W28] 69-16104
1. Devotional literature. I. Title.

BRYAN, G McLeod, ed. 242.082
In His likeness; forty selections on the imitation of Christ through the centuries. Richmond, John Knox Press [1959] 192p. 20cm. Includes bibliography. [BV4805.B76] 59-10455
I. Title.

THE Craft of dying; 242'.09
a study in the literary tradition of the Ars moriendi in England. [Edited] by Nancy Lee Beaty. New Haven, Yale University Press, 1970. xii, 299 p. 23 cm. (Yale studies in English, 175) A revision of the editor's thesis, Yale. Contents.Contents.—The Ars moriendi: Wellspring of the tradition.—The Waye of dyenge well: A humanistic "crafte".—The sicke mannes salve: A Calvinistic "crafte".—Parsons, Bunny, and the counter-reformation "crafte".—The Holy dying: Artistic climax of the tradition.—Bibliography (p. 271-281) [BV4818.C7 1970] 76-115365 ISBN 0-300-01336-1 10.00
1. Devotional literature—History and criticism. I. Beaty, Nancy Lee, ed. II. Title. III. Series.

HALL, Thor, 1927- 242'.09'04
A theology of Christian devotion; its role in the modern religious setting. [Nashville, Tenn.] Upper Room [1969] x, 93 p. 20 cm. [BV4501.2.H265] 74-85803
1. Christian life—1960- 2. Devotion. 3. Christianity—20th century. I. Title.

*ACKER, Julius W., ed. 242.1
A thought for today. New ed. [St. Louis] Concordia [1966] iv. (unpaged) 11cm. 1.95
I. Title.

ALBRIGHT, Bliss, comp. 242.1
The treasury of inspirational classics. Westwood, N. J., Revell [1966] 188p. 26cm. [BV4805.A54] 66-21900 3.95 bds.,
1. Devotional literature (Selections: Extracts, etc.) I. Title.

Contents omitted.

AMES, Kenneth John. 242'.1
The religious language of Thomas Traherne's Centuries / by Kenneth John Ames. New York : Revisionist Press, 1977. p. cm. Bibliography: p. [BV4831.T73A54] 77-4000 ISBN 0-87700-260-6 lib.bdg. : 39.95
1. Traherne, Thomas, d. 1674. Centuries of meditations. 2. Devotional literature. I. Title.

ANGELA, of Foligno, 1248?-1309. 242'.1
The book of divine consolation of the Blessed Angela of Foligno. Translated from the Italian by Mary G. Steegmann. Introd. by Algar Thorold. New York, Cooper Square Publishes, 1966. xiiv, 265 p. illus., facsims. 17 cm. (The Medieval library) Translation of Liber de vera fidelium experientia. [BV5080.A52 1966] 66-30731
1. Mysticism—Middle Ages. I. Steegmann, Mary G., tr. II. Thorold, Algar Labouchere, 1866-1936. III. Title.

ANGELA, of Foligno, 1248?-1309. 242'.1
The book of divine consolation of the Blessed Angela of Foligno. Translated from the Italian by Mary G. Steegmann. Introd. by Algar Thorold. New York, Cooper Square Publishers, 1966. xliv, 265 p. illus., facsims. 17 cm. (The Medieval library) Translation of Liber de vera fidelium experientia. [BV5080.A52 1966] 66-30731
1. Mysticism—Middle Ages. I. Steegmann, Mary G., tr. II. Thorold, Algar Labouchere, 1866-1936. III. Title.

AUGUSTINUS, Aurelius, Saint, Bp. of Hippo. 242/.1
The confessions of St. Augustine. Introd. by Georges A. Barrois. Grand Rapids, Zondervan [1967] 295p. 19cm. (Great religious bks. ser.) [BR65.A6E5 1967] 67-17248 2.95 bds.,
I. Title.

AUGUSTINUS, Aurelius, Saint, Bp. of Hippo. 242'.1
The confessions of Saint Augustine; selections, edited by David A. MacLennan. New York, World Pub. Co. [1969] 63 p. 17 cm. (World inspirational books) [BR65.A6E53 1969] 75-90926 1.25
I. Title.

AUGUSTINUS, Aurelius, Saint, Bp. of Hippo. 242'.1
Love song; Augustine's Confessions for modern man [translated and abridged by] Sherwood Eliot Wirt. [1st ed.] New York, Harper & Row [1971] xvi, 143 p. 22 cm. [BR65.A6E55 1971] 77-148434 4.95
I. Wirt, Sherwood Eliot, ed. II. Title.

COSIN, John, bp. of Durham, 1594-1672 242'.1
A collection of private devotions; ed. by P. G. Stanwood with Daniel O'Connor. London, Oxford Univ. Pr., 1967. iv, 371p. front. (port.), 2 plates (facsims.), col. tables. 23cm. Orig. pub., London, 1627. [BX5145.A55C64 1967] 68-76791 12.00
1. Church of England—Prayer-books and devotions. I. Stanwood, P. G. ed. II. O'Connor, Daniel. III. Title.
Available from the publisher's New York office.

DAUGHTERS of St. Paul. 242.1
Christ is here; the life of the Daughters of St. Paul reflected in pictures and prose. [Boston] St. Paul Editions [1964] [87] p. illus., map, ports. 28 cm. [BX4334.D3] 64-21601
1. Daughters of St. Paul. I. Title.

DE MONTMORENCY, James Edward Geoffrey, 1866-1934. 242'.1
Thomas a Kempis; his age and book. Port Washington, N.Y., Kennikat Press [1970] xxiii, 312 p. facsims. 22 cm. "First published in 1906." Contents.Contents.—Introduction.—List of manuscripts of the treatise "De imitatione Christi" in English libraries.—List of other manuscripts cited.—List of printed editions of the treatise "De imitatione Christi" cited.—The age of Thomas a Kempis.—Some fifteenth century manuscripts and editions of the Imitation.—Master Walter Hilton and the authorship of the Imitation.—The structure of the Imitation.—The content of the Imitation.—Appendix I. "De meditatione cordis," by Jean le Charlier de Gerson, chancellor of Paris.—Appendix II. Extract from the "Garden of roses," by Thomas a Kempis. [BV4829.D4 1970] 73-103183
1. Thomas a Kempis, 1380-1471. 2. Imitatio Christi. I. Gerson, Joannes, 1363-1429. De meditatione cordis.

FRANCOIS de Sales, Saint, Bp. of Geneva, 1567-1622. 242.1
Introduction to the devout life [by] St. Francis de Sales. Newly translated with an introd. and notes by John K. Ryan. [2d ed., rev.] New York, Harper & Row [1966] 258 p. 21 cm. (Harper torchbooks. The cathedral library, TB316) Bibliographical references included in "Notes to the text" (p. 240-255) [BX2179.F8154 1966] 66-8844
1. Meditations. I. Ryan, John Kenneth, 1897- ed. and tr. II. Title. III. Title: The devout life.

IMITATIO Christi. English 242'.1
The imitation of Christ [by] Thomas a Kempis. Introd. by Paul M. Bechtel. Grand Rapids, Mich., Zondervan House [1967] 227p. 19cm. (Great religious bks.) [BV4821.A1 1967] 67-17246 2.95 bds.,
I. Title.

IMITATIO Christi. English. 242.1
The imitation of Christ, by Thomas a Kempis. The full text of the autograph manuscript of A. D. 1441 translated into modern English by Edgar Daplyn. New York, Sheed & Ward, 1950. 184 p. 18 cm. [BV4821.A1 1950] 50-7625
I. Title.

IMITATIO Christi. English. 242.1
The imitation of Christ. Edited with an introd. by Thomas S. Kepler. [1st ed.] Cleveland, World Pub. Co. [1952] 287 p. 16 cm. (World devotional classics) [BV4821.A1 1952] 52-5186
I. Kepler, Thomas Samuel, 1897- ed. II. Title.

IMITATIO Christi. English. 242.1
The imitation of Christ [by] Thomas a Kempis. A modern version based on the English translation made by Richard Whitford around the year 1530. Edited with introd. by Harold C. Gardiner. Garden City, N. Y., Image Books [1955] 236p. 10cm. (A Doubleday image book, D17) [BV4821.A1 1955] 55-9752
I. Gardiner Harold Charles, 1904- ed. II. Title.

IMITATIO Christi. English. 242.1
The imitation of Christ [by] Thomas a Kempis. A modern version based on the English translation made by Richard Whitford around the year 1530; edited with introd. by Harold C. Gardiner. Garden City, N. Y., Hanover House [1955] 236p. 20cm. [BV4821.A1 1955a] 55-8729
I. Whytford, Richard, fl. 1495-1555? tr. II. Gardiner, Harold Charles, 1904- ed. III. Title.

IMITATIO Christi. English. 242.1
The imitation of Christ, by Gerard Zerbolt of Zutphen (1367-1398) teacher of Thomas a Kempis. Translated for the first time and edited by Albert Hyma. Grand Rapids, Eerdmans, 1950. 116 p. 14 cm. Book 1 only: translated from an original version now the property of the Gymnasium at Eutin, Germany. [BV4821.A1 1950a] 50-9094
I. Zerbolt, Gerard, 1367-1398, supposed author. II. Title.

IMITATIO Christi. English. 242.1
The imitation of Christ, in four books, by Thomas A. Kempis. Tr. by Daughters of St. Paul [Boston, St. Paul Eds., dist. Daughters of St. Paul, c.1962] 445p. (front. port.) 14cm. 62-15656 2.00; 1.00 pap.,
1. Daughters of St. Paul I. Title.

IMITATIO Christi. English 242.1
The imitation of Christ, by Thomas a Kempis. Tr. from Latin into Modern English [by] Aloysius Croft, Harry F. Bolton. Milwaukee, Bruce [c.1962] xiii, 257p. 18cm. 62-51531 2.00
I. Croft, Aloysius, tr. II. Bolton, Harry F., tr. III. Title.

IMITATIO Christi. English. 242.1
The imitation of Christ, by Thomas a Kempis. Translated by Ronald Knox and Michael Oakley. New York, Sheed and Ward [1960, c.1959] 217p. 20cm. 60-73052 2.50 half cloth,
I. Knox, Ronald Arbuthnott, 1888-1957, tr. II. Oakley, Michael, tr. III. Title.

IMITATIO Christi. English. 242'.1
Imitation of Christ, by Thomas a Kempis. Translated from the original Latin, rendered into modern English, by Albert J. Nevins. Huntington, Ind., Our Sunday Visitor [1973] 224 p. illus. 11 x 14 cm. On cover: For Protestant followers of Jesus. [BV4821.A1 1973] 73-82653 ISBN 0-87973-780-8 1.50 (pbk.)
I. Thomas a Kempis, 1380-1471.

IMITATIO Christi. English. 242.1
The Imitation of Christ. / [by] Thomas a' Kempis ; a modern version based on the English translation made by Richard Whitford arount the year 1530 ; edited with introd. by Harold C. Gardiner. Garden City, N.Y. : Doubleday, 1976c1955. 213p. ; 22 cm. [BV4821.A1] ISBN 0-385-12313-2 : 6.95
I. Kempis, Thomas a'. II. Whitford, Richard, 1495-1555? tr. III. Gardiner, Harold Charles, 1904- ed. IV. Title.
L.C. card no. for original ed. 55-9752.

IMITATIO Christi. English. 242.1
The imitation of Christ, in four books, by Thomas A. [i.e.a] Kempis. Translation by the Daughters of St. Paul. [Boston, St. Paul Editions [1962] 445 p. front. 14 cm. [BV4821.A1 1962] 62-15656
I. Daughters of St. Paul. II. Title.

IMITATIO Christi. English. 242.1
Meditations from the following of Christ of Thomas a Kempis. Arr. from an old translation, by Ivah May Navaro. Illus. by Caroline Williams. [Burlington, Ky.] Penandhoe Press, 1954. 98p. illus. 16cm. [BV4821.N3] 54-39719
I. Navaro, Ivah May, 1906- ed. II. Title.

IMITATIO Christi. English. 242.1
My Imitation of Christ [by] Thomas a Kempis. Rev. translation. Brooklyn, Confraternity of the Precious Blood [1954] 474p. illus. 14cm. [BV4821.A1 1954a] 54-43123
I. Confraternity of the Percious Blood. II. Title. III. Title: Imitation of Christ.

IMITATIO Christi. English. 242.1
Of the imitation of Christ, in four books by Thomas a Kempis. Translated by Justin McCann. Westminster, Md., Newman Press [1952] xvi, 262p. 16cm. [BV4821.A1 1952a] 53-1631
I. McCann, Justin, 1882- tr. II. Title.

IMITATIO Christi. English. 242.1
Of the imitation of Christ; in four books by Thomas a Kempis. Translated by Justin McCann. [New York] New American Library [1957] x, 189p. 18cm. (N. A. L. Mentor books, MD193) A Mentor religious classic. [BV4821.A1 1957] 57-44043
I. McCann, Justin, 1882- tr. II. Title.

IMITATIO Christi. English. 242.1
Of the imitation of Christ; in four books by Thomas a Kempis. Translated by Justin McCann. [New York] New American Library [1957] x, 189p. 18cm. (N. A. L. Mentor books, MD196) A Mentor religious classic. [BV4821.A1 1957] 57-44043
I. McCann, Justin, 1882- tr. II. Title.

IMITATIO Christi. English. 242.1
Of the imitation of Christ; selections [by] Thomas a Kempis. [Westwood, N. J.] Revell [c.1963] 63p. 17cm. (Revell inspirational classic) 63-17118 1.00 bds.,
I. Title.

IMITATIO Christi. English 242.1
Of the imitation of Christ; in four books by Thomas a Kempis. Tr. by Justin McCann. [New York] New Amer. Lib. [1962, c.1957] x, 189p. 18cm. (Mentor. Omega bk., MT467) .75 pap.,
I. McCann, Justin, 1882- tr. II. Title.

IMITATIO Christi. English. 242'.1
Thoughts of the Imitation of Christ from the words of Thomas a Kempis. Selected by Herbert B. Greenhouse. Decorated by Ahza Cohen. New York, Golden Pr. [1967] 63p. 16cm. (Golden lib. of faith & inspiration) Giniger bk. [BV4821.G7] 67-13733 1.00 bds.,
I. Greenhouse, Herbert B., comp. II. Title.

IMITATIO Christi. English. 242'.1
Selections.
The imitation of Christ, by Thomas a Kempis. Selections, edited by David A. MacLennan. New York, World Pub. Co. [1969] 63 p. 17 cm. (World inspirational books) [BV4821.I45 1969] 79-80441 1.25
I. Thomas a Kempis, 1380-1471. II. MacLennan, David Alexander, 1903- comp.

IMITATIO CHRISTI. ENGLISH. 242.1
The imitation of Christ, in four books, by Thomas A. Kempis. Translation by the Daughters of St. Paul. [Boston] St. Paul Editions [1962] 445p. front. 14cm. [BV4821.A1 1962] 62-15656
I. Daughters of St. Paul. II. Title.

IMITATIO CHRISTI. ENGLISH. 242.1
Of the imitation of Christ; selections [by] Thomas a Kempis. New York Pyramid [1966, c.1963] 63p. 17cm. (Little inspiration classic. LP 7) [BV4821.K42] .35 pap.,
I. Title.

*KEMPIS, Thomas A. 242.1
The imitation of Christ. Tr. by Richard Whitford. Springfield, Ill., Templegate [1964] 283p. 15cm. (Temple bk.) 1.25 pap.,
I. Title.

*MCKENZIE, E. C. 242.1
1600 squibs and quips for church bulletins and bulletin boards. Grand Rapids, Mich., Baker Bk. [c.1966] 72p. 22cm. 1.00 pap.,
I. Title.

MARGERIE, Bertrand de. 242'.1
Theological retreat : with some Ignatian spiritual exercises / Bertrand de Margerie ; translated by A. Owen. Chicago : Franciscan Herald Press, c1976. xxix, 333 p. ; 24 cm. Includes indexes. Bibliography: p. 309-311. [BX2179.L8M33] 76-50929 ISBN 0-8199-0656-5 : 10.95
1. Loyola, Ignacio de, Saint, 1491-1556. Exercitia spiritualia. 2. Spiritual exercises. I. Title.

MEYER, Wendelin, 1882- 242.1
Living the interior life; v.2. Tr. from German by Colman J. O'Donovan. Westminster, Md., Newman Press, [1961, c.]1960 189p. 58-8749 3.75
1. Imitatio Christi. 2. Monastic and religious life of women. I. Title.

MORE, Thomas, Sir, Saint, 242'.1
1478-1535.
A dialogue of comfort against tribulation / St. Thomas More ; edited with introd. and notes by Frank Manley. New Haven : Yale University Press, 1977. p. cm. (The Yale edition of the works of St. Thomas More : Selected works) "Published by the St. Thomas More Project, Yale University." Includes index. Bibliography: p. [BV4904.M62 1977] 77-9938 ISBN 0-300-02082-1 : 22.50 ISBN 0-300-02185-2 pbk. : 6.95
1. Consolation. I. Manley, Frank. II. Title.

MORE, Thomas, Saint, Sir 242.1
1478-1535
A dialogue of comfort against tribulation. Ed. for modern readers, introd. & notes, by Leland Miles. Bloomington, Ind. Univ. Pr. [1966, c.1965] xxxi, 269p. illus., ports. 20cm. (Midland bk., MB80) [BV4904.M62] 65-19701 2.65 pap.,
1. Consolation. I. Miles, Leland, ed. II. Title.

O'CONNELL, Robert J. 242'.1
St. Augustine's Confessions; the Odyssey of soul [by] Robert J. O'Connell. Cambridge, Mass, Belknap Press of Harvard University Press, 1969. xiii, 200 p. 24 cm. Includes bibliographical references. [BR65.A9O26] 69-12731 6.50
1. Augustinus, Aurelius, Saint, Bp. of Hippo. Confessiones. I. Title.

PEERS, Edgar Allison. 242'.1
Behind that wall; an introduction to some classics of the interior life. Freeport, N.Y., Books for Libraries Press [1969, c1948] 181 p. 23 cm. (Essay index reprint series) Contents.Contents.—Introduction: Behind that wall.—St. Augustine: The city of God.—St. Bernard: The book of the love of God.—Ramon Lull: The book of the lover and the beloved.—The imitation of Christ.—Jan van Ruysbroeck: The seven steps of the ladder of spiritual love.—The cloud of unknowing.—St. Ignatius of Loyola: Spiritual exercises.—St. Peter of Alcantara: The golden treatise of mental prayer.—St. Teresa of Jesus: The interior castle.—St. John of the Cross: Songs of the soul.—St. Francis of Sales: Introduction to the devout life.—Jeremy Taylor: Holy living.—Henry Vaughan: The flint flashing fire.—Thomas Traherne: Poems. Includes bibliographies. [BV4818.P4 1969] 72-90672
I. Title.

PISAN, Christine de, 242.1
ca.1363-ca.1431.
Les sept psaumes allegorises. A critical ed. from the Brussels and Paris manuscripts, by Ruth Ringland Rains. Washington, Catholic University of America Press [1965] ix. 181 p. geneal. table. 28 cm. Introductory material in English; the author's text written in 1409 in Old French, includes O. F. translation of the 7 penitential Psalms. "The Brussels manuscript (Bib. roy. 10987) has been used as the basic text, except where the Paris reading (B. n. nouv. acq. fr. 4792) is obviously superior." Bibliography: p. 170-179 [BS1445.P4P55] 65-17049
1. Penitential Psalms. I. Rains, Ruth Rea Ringland, 1927- ed. II. Bible. O. T. Psalms. French (Old French) Selections. 1965. Pisan. III. Title.

PISAN, Christine de, ca. 242.1
1363-ca. 1431
Les sept psaumes allegorises. A critical ed. from the Brussels and Paris manuscripts, by Ruth Ringland Rains. Washington. D.C., Catholic Univ. of Amer. Pr. [c.1965] ix, 181p. geneal. table. 28cm. Introd. material in English; the author's text written in 1409 in Old French, includes O.F. tr. of the 7 penitential Psalms. The Brussels ms. (Bib. roy. 10987) has been used as the basic text, except where the Paris reading (B. n. nouv. acq. fr. 4792) is obviously superior. Bibl. [BS1445.P4P55] 65-17049 5.00 pap.,
1. Penitential Psalms. I. Rains, Ruth Rea Ringland, 1927- ed. II. Bible. O.T. Psalms. French (Old French) Selections. 1965. Pisan. III. Title.

ROLLE, Richard, of 242'.1
Hampole, 1290?-1349.
The fire of love; translated [from the Latin] into modern English with an introduction by Clifton Wolters. Harmondsworth, Penguin, 1972. 192 p. 19 cm. (The Penguin classics) Translation of Incendium amoris. [BX2180.R613 1972] 72-190574 ISBN 0-14-044256-1 £0.35 ($1.65 U.S.)
1. Devotional literature. I. Wolters, Clifton, tr. II. Title.

SMITH, Don Ian, 1918- 242'.1
Sagebrush seed / Don Ian Smith. Nashville : Abingdon, c1977. 111 p. : ill. ; 20 cm. [BT695.5.S64] 77-4347 ISBN 0-687-36746-8 : 5.95
1. Nature (Theology)—Mediations. I. Title.

SMITH, Preserved, 1880- 242'.1
1941.
Luther's table talk; a critical study. New York, AMS Press [1970, c1907] 135 p. 23 cm. (Columbia University studies in the social sciences, 69) Originally presented as the author's thesis, Columbia University, 1907. Bibliography: p. 111-135. [BR332.T5S6 1970] 78-127457 ISBN 0-404-51069-8
1. Luther, Martin, 1483-1546. Tischreden. I. Title. II. Series: Columbia studies in the social sciences, 69

STREEBING, Cecilian, 242'.1
Brother, 1912-
Devout humanism as a style: St. Francois de Sales' Introduction a la vie devote. New York, AMS Press [1970, c1954] x, 165 p. 23 cm. (Catholic University of America. Studies in Romance languages and literatures, v. 50) Originally presented as the author's thesis, Catholic University of America, 1954. Bibliography: p. 157-161. [BX2179.F8I7 1970] 70-128930 ISBN 0-404-50350-0
1. Francois de Sales, Saint, Bp. of Geneva, 1567-1622. Introduction a la vie devote. 2. Humanism. I. Title. II. Series.

YULE, George Udny, 1871- 242'.1
1951.
The statistical study of literary vocabulary. [Hamden, Conn.] Archon Books, 1968. viii, 306 p. illus. 25 cm. Reprint of the 1944 ed. Includes bibliographies. [BV4829.Y8 1968] 68-8027 ISBN 0-208-00689-3
1. Thomas A Kempis, 1380-1471. 2. Gerson, Joannes, 1363-1429. 3. Gerson, Joannes, 1363-1429. 4. Imitatio Christi. 5. Imitatio Christi. I. Title.

HARKNESS, Georgia 242'.1'09015
Elma, 1891-
A devotional treasury from the early church, compiled by Georgia Harkness. Nashville, Abingdon Press [1968] 160 p. 21 cm. Bibliography: p. 157-160. [BV4801.H25] 68-17436
1. Devotional literature. 2. Christian literature, Early. I. Title.

ACKER, Julius William. 242.2
A thought for today, edited by Julius W. Acker. New ed. [St. Louis] Concordia [1966] 1 v. (unpaged) 11 cm. [BV4832.2.A3 1966] 66-22198
1. Meditations. I. Title.

ADLER, Denise Rinker. 242'.2
The morning star : God's gift for daily living / Denise Rinker Adler ; edited by Rosalind Rinker. Waco, Tex. : Word Books, [1974] 130 p. ; 23 cm. [BV4832.2.A35] 74-82652 4.95
1. Meditations. I. Title.

ALLEN, James, 1864-1912. 242.2
Morning and evening thoughts. With illus. by Maggie Jarvis. Mount Vernon, N.Y., Peter Pauper Press [1966] 60 p. col. illus. 19 cm. [BV4832.A44] 67-264
1. Devotional exercises. I. Title.

ANGRISANI, Giuseppe, Bp., 242.2
1894-
Daily breviary meditations; meditations for every day on the Scriptural lessons of the Roman breviary, in accordance with the encyclical 'Divino afflante.' Translated by Joseph A. McMullin; introd. by Joseph A. Nelson; letter of recommendation by G. B. Montini. New York, Benziger Bros. [1954] 4v. 16cm. Translation of In matitutinis meditabor in te. [BX2180.A58] 55-487
1. Church year—Meditations. 2. Catholic Church. Liturgy and ritual. Breviary. I. Title.

APPLETON, George 242.2
Daily prayer and praise; morning and evening prayers for a month. New York, Association [1963] unpaged. 19cm. (World Christian bks., 2d ser., no. 41) 63-3223 1.00 pap.,
1. Devotional calendars. 2. Prayers. I. Title.

ARMSTRONG, Richard G. 242.2
Make your life worthwhile, by Richard Armstrong. New York, Trident Press [1970] 375 p. 22 cm. Contents.Contents.—Consists of daily meditations for a calendar year. [BV4811.A73] 76-124598 7.50
1. Devotional calendars—Catholic Church. I. Title.

ARNOLD, Emmy, comp. 242.2
Inner words for every day of the year. Woodcrest, Rifton, N.Y., Plough Pub. House [1963] 188 p. 15 cm. [BV4810.A7] 63-1398
1. Devotional calendars. I. Title.

ARNOLD, Emmy, comp. 242.2
Inner words for every day of the year. Woodcrest, Rifton, N.Y., Plough [c.1963] 188p. 15cm. 63-1398 3.00
1. Devotional calendars. I. Title.

ARNOLD, Emmy, comp. 242.2
Inner words for every day of the year. Rifton, N.Y., Plough Pub. House [1971, c1963] 185 p. 15 cm. [BV4810.A7 1971] 77-164915 ISBN 0-87486-101-2 2.25
1. Devotional calendars. I. Title.

ARNOLD, Emmy, comp. 242'.2
Innere Worte fur jeden Tag des Jahres / ausgewahlt und angeordnet von Emmy Arnold. Rifton, N.Y. : Plough Pub. House, c1976. p. cm. Issued also in English under title: Inner words for every day of the year. "Aus den Schriften von Eberhard Arnold, Johann Christoph Blumhardt, Christoph Blumhardt, Dietrich Bonhoeffer, Bodelschwingh und anderen." [BV4810.A715] 76-10987 ISBN 0-87486-166-7
1. Devotional calendars. I. Title.

AVANCINI, Nicolaus, 1611- 242.2
1686.
The life and teaching of Our Lord Jesus Christ. Taken from theGospels and arranged for daily meditation. Tr. from Latin by B. E. Kenworthy-Browne. Pref. by the Abbot of Ampleforth. New York, Kenedy [1962, c.1961] xxxi. 554p. col. front. [Silver treasury ser.] 61-15563 4.95
1. Jesus Christ—Biog.—Meditations. 2. Devotional calendars. I. Kenworthy-Browne, B. E., tr. II. Title.

AVERY, William S ed. 242.2
Devotions for every day. Philadelphia, Muhlenberg Press [1961] 365p. 18cm. [BV4832.A86] 61-13579
1. Devotional calendars—Lutheran Church. I. Title.

AVERY, William S., ed. 242.2
Devotions for everyday. Philadelphia, Muhlenberg [c.1961] 365p. 61-13579 2.50 bds.,
1. Devotional calendars—Lutheran Church. I. Title.

BACCI, Antonio, 1885- 242.2
Meditations for each day. Tr. [from Italian] by DesmondWilliams, Brian Power. Westminster, Md., Newman, 1965. vii, 688p. 19cm. [BV4811.B313] 63-12251 8.50
1. Devotional calendars—Catholic Church. I. Title.

BAILLIE, John, 1886- ed. 242.2
A diary of readings; being an anthology of pages suited to engage serious thought, one for every day of the year, gathered from the wisdom of many centuries. New York, Scribner, 1955. 385p. 20cm. [BV4832.B18] 55-7196
1. Devotional exercises. I. Title.

BARCLAY, William, 242'.2
lecturer in the University of Glasgow.
Daily celebration; devotional readings for every day of the year. Edited by Denis Duncan. Waco, Tex., Word Books [1973, c1971] 316 p. 24 cm. Readings originally appeared in British weekly, 1957-1970. [BV4811.B32 1973] 77-175724 ISBN 0-340-14990-6 4.95
1. Devotional calendars. I. Title.

BARCLAY, William 242.2
A guide to daily prayer. New York, Harper [c.1962] 160p. 20cm. 62-11473 3.00
1. Devotional calendars. I. Title. II. Title: Daily prayer.

BARCLAY, William, lecturer 242.2
in the University of Glasgow.
A guide to daily prayer. [1st ed.] New York, Harper & Row [1962] 160p. 20cm. [BV4811.B33] 62-11473
1. Devotional calendars. I. Title. II. Title: Daily prayer.

BARCLAY, William, 242.2.
lecturer in the University of Glasgow.
A guide to daily prayer. New York, Harper & Row [1974, c1962] 160 p. 21 cm. [BV4811.B33] ISBN 0-06-060401-8. 1.95 (pbk.)
1. Devotional calendars. I. Title. II. Title: Daily prayer.
L.C. card number for original ed.: 62-11473.

BARCLAY, William, 242'.2
lecturer in the University of Glasgow.
Marching on : daily readings for younger people / William Barclay ; edited by Denis Duncan. Philadelphia : Westminster Press, [1975] c1974. 223 p. ; 20 cm. Companion volume to the author's Marching orders. Daily readings for six months, with suggested additional Bible readings, present the philosophies of Christian writer William Barclay. [BV4850.B28 1975] 74-30053 ISBN 0-664-24827-6 pbk. : 3.95
1. Youth—Prayer-books and devotions—English. I. Duncan, Denis, ed. II. Title.

BARCLAY, William, 242'.2
lecturer in the University of Glasgow.
Marching orders : daily readings for younger people / William Barclay ; edited by Denis Duncan. Philadelphia : Westminster Press, [1975] c1973. 192 p. ; 20 cm. Daily readings for six months, with suggested additional Bible readings, present the philosophies of Christian writer William Barclay. [BV4850.B29 1975] 74-26601 ISBN 0-664-24826-8
1. Youth—Prayer-books and devotions—English. I. Duncan, Denis, ed. II. Title.

BARCLAY, William L. 242'.2
By His Spirit [by] William L. Barclay. Washington, Review and Herald Pub. Association [1972] 375 p. 21 cm. [BV4811.B333] 70-190578
1. Devotional calendars. I. Title.

BASH, Ewald 242.2
Seven days; worship for twentieth-century man. Saint Louis, Concordia [c.1966] 101p. 15cm. [BV4832.2.B33] 66-20536 1.50
1. Meditations. I. Title.

BAXTER, James Sidlow. 242.2
Awake, my heart; daily devotional and expository studies in-brief, based on a variety of Bible truths, and covering one complete year. Grand Rapids, Zondervan Pub. House [1960] 384p. 22cm. [BV4811.B35] 60-50191
1. Devotional calendars. I. Title.

BEACH, Walter Raymond. 242.2
Light from God's lamp. Washington, Review and Herald [1960] 367p. 16cm. [BV4811.B4] 60-9408
1. Devotional calendars—Seventh-Day Adventists. I. Title.

BELL, Alvin Eugene, 1882- 242.2
Today's good news, reported by Matthew, Mark, Luke, and John; devotions for every day of the year. Philadelphia, Muhlenberg Press [1953] 374p. 16cm. [BV4832.B44] 53-12651
1. Devotional exercises. I. Title.

BERGH, Henry T 242.2
Upward trails, a junior devotional. Washington, review and Herald Pub. Association [1963] 358 p. 21 cm. [BV4811.B47] 63-19762
1. Devotional calendars — Seventh-Day Adventists. I. Title.

BERGH, Henry T. 242.2
Upward trails, a junior devotional. Washington, D.C., Review & Herald [c.1963] 358p. 21cm. 63-19762 3.00
1. Devotional calendars—Seventh-Day Adventists. I. Title.

BIBLE. English. Jerusalem 242'.2
Bible. Selections. 1972.
Daily devotions from the Jerusalem Bible. Compiled by Vivian Symons. [1st U.S. ed.] New York, Harper & Row [1972, c1970] 226 p. 19 cm. [BS391.2.S97 1972] 70-183390 ISBN 0-06-067815-1 4.95
I. Symons, Vivian, 1913- comp. II. Title.

BIBLE. English. New 242'.2
Berkeley version. Selections. 1972.
This day. Edited by James W. Reapsome. Grand Rapids, Zondervan Pub. House [1972] 1 v. (unpaged) 18 cm. A daily devotional book consisting of Scriptures selections from the Modern language Bible (New Berkeley version) [BS390.R4] 72-83877 3.95
1. Devotional calendars. I. Reapsome, James W., ed. II. Title.

BIBLE. English. Revised 242'.2
Standard. Selections. 1972.
Every day; Bible readings for each day of the year. Philadelphia, A. J. Holman [1972, c1971] 1 v. (unpaged) 18 cm. [BS390.H47 1972] 72-4169 ISBN 0-87981-015-7
1. Devotional calendars. I. Title.

BIBLE. English. Selections. 242.2
1963.
The daily reading for school and home; passages from the Bible, comp. by G. W. Briggs. Baltimore, Penguin [1963] 282p. 19cm. (Pelican bks., A602) 63-4017 .95 pap.,
1. Devotional calendars. I. Briggs, George Wallace, 1875-1959, comp. II. Title.

BIBLE. N.T. English. 242.2
Paraphrases. 1967. Taylor.
Living words for today; a Bible reading for each day of the year, taken from the living New Testament, paraphrased by Kenneth N. Taylor. [Don W. Hillis, compiler] Wheaton, Ill., Tyndale House [1967] 366 p. 20 cm. [BS2261.T3] 67-28430
1. Devotional calendars. I. Taylor, Kenneth Nathaniel. II. Hillis, Don W., comp. III. Bible. N.T. English. Selections. 1967. Taylor. IV. Title.

BIBLE. N.T. Gospels. 242.2
English. Harmonies. 1955. Confraternity version
The daily Gospel; Gospel text taken from the New Testament of our Lord and Savior Jesus Christ--a revision of the Challoner-Rheims version, under the patronage of the Episcopal Committee of the Confraternity of Christian Doctrine. With reflections compiled by John E. Robaldo, translated by a Daughter of St. Paul. [Derby, N. Y] Daughters of St. Paul, Apostolate of the Press [c1955] 495p. illus. 22cm. 'The harmonization of the Gospel text follows especially that of Reverned Szczepanski, S. J. The texts of the Fathers and Doctors of the Church were taken from Reverend G. Bellino's 'Jesus Christ in the Sacred Scriptures, in the Fathers and the Doctors.' [BT299.2.R6] 59-24938
1. Jesus Christ—Biog.— Medittions. 2. Devotional calendars—Catholic Church. I. Confraternity of Christian Doctrine. II. Robaldo, John E., comp. III. Title.

BLUMHARDT, Christoph, 1842- 242.2
1919.
Evening prayers for every day of the year. Rifton, N.Y., Plough Pub. House [1971] xiii, 234 p. 15 cm. Translation of Abendgebete fur alle Tage des Jahres. [BV245.B5813 1971] 73-141948 ISBN 0-87486-204-3 2.95
1. Prayers. I. Title.

BOLDING, Amy. 242.2
Day by day with Amy Bolding. Grand Rapids, Baker Book House [1968] 314 p. 23 cm. [BV4811.B57] 68-29785 4.95
1. Devotional calendars—Baptists. I. Title.

*BOYD, Malcolm. 242.2
Free to live, free to die. [New York,] New Amer. Lib., [1968,c.1967] 128p. 18cm. (Signet bk., T3426) [BV4832.2.B68] .75 pap.,
1. Meditations. I. Title.

BOYD, Malcolm, 1923- 242.2
Book of days. New York, Random House [1968] 215 p. 21 cm. [BV4811.B63] 68-14524
1. Devotional calendars. I. Title.

BOYD, Malcolm, 1923- 242.2
Free to live, free to die. [1st ed.] New York, Holt, Rinehart and Winston [1967] 114 p. 21 cm. [BV4832.2.B68] 67-12905
1. Meditations. I. Title.

BOYD, Malcolm, 1923- 242.2
Free to live, free to die. [1st ed.] New York, Holt, Rinehart and Winston [1967] 114 p. 21 cm. [BV4832.2.B68] 67-12905
1. Meditations. I. Title.

BRINK, Frederick Wright, 242.2
1912-
God speaks. Philadelphia, Westminster Press [1954] 96p. 16cm. [BV4832.B758] 54-5652
1. Devotional exercises. I. Title.

BRYANT, Al, 1926- comp. 242.2
Climbing the heights; daily devotions. Grand Rapids, Zondervan Pub. House [1956] 382p. 20cm. [BV4810.B77] 56-41989
1. Devotional calendars. I. Title.

CALVIN, Jean, 1509-1564. 242.2
Thine is my heart; devotional readings from the writings of John Calvin. Compiled by John H. Romminga. Grand Rapids, Zondervan Pub. House [c1958] unpaged. 20cm. [BX9420.A32K7] 59-29214
1. Devotional calenders—Reformed Church. I. Title.

CASSELS, Louis, comp. 242'.2
Preludes to prayer; 365 daily meditations. Nashville, Abingdon Press [1974] 189 p. 21 cm. [BV4810.C34] 74-180342 ISBN 0-687-33916-2 3.95
1. Devotional calendars. I. Title.

CAVERT, Walter Dudley 242.2
Ours is the faith. Nashville, Abingdon Press [c.1960] 256 p. 16 cm. 'References': p. 255-256. 60-9195 2.00
1. Devotional calendars—Presbyterian Church. I. Title.

CAVERT, Walter Dudley, 242.2
1891-
Ours is the faith. New York, Abingdon Press [1960] 256p. 16cm. [BV4832.2.C3] 60-9195
1. Devotional calendars—Presbyterian Church. I. Title.

CHALLONER, Richard, Bp., 242.2
1691-1781.
A daily thought; compiled from Richard Challoner's Meditations, by V. Guazzelli. Westminster, Md., Newman Press [1958?] 184p. illus. 17cm. [BX2182.2.C5] 59-2068
1. Devotional calendars—Catholic Church. I. Title.

CHAMBERLAIN, Elsie 242.2
Calm delight. Garden City, N.Y., Doubleday, [c.]1960. 142p. 18cm. 59-11582 2.50 half cloth,
1. Devotional exercises. I. Title.

CHAMBERLAIN, Elsle. 242.2
Calm delight. [1st ed.] Gardan City, N. Y., Doubleday, 1960. 142p. 18cm. [BV4832.2.C5] 59-11582
1. Devotional exercises. I. Title.

CHAMBERS, Oswald, 1874- 242'.2
1917.
Daily thoughts for disciples / from Oswald Chambers. Grand Rapids : Zondervan Pub. House, c1976. 251 p. ; 22 cm. Includes index. [BV4811.C45 1976] 76-41387 ISBN 0-551-05543-X : 6.95 ISBN 0-914264-20-6 pbk. : 5.00
1. Devotional calendars. I. Title.

CHAMBERS, Oswald, 1874- 242.2
1917.
Still higher for His Highest; devotional selections for every day. Grand Rapids, Mich., Zondervan Pub. House [1970] 192 p. 19 cm. [BV4832.2.C514] 75-120048 2.95
1. Devotional calendars. I. Title.

*CLAGGETT, Ralph P. 242.2
Jesus speaks, by Ralph P. Claggett. Pacific Grove, Calif., Boxwood Press [1973] 160 p. 18 cm. "A daily devotional book." [BV4811] ISBN 0-910286-28-0 2.50 (pbk)
1. Devotional calanders. 2. Meditations. I. Title.
Publisher's address: 183 Ocean View Blvd., Pacific Grove, CA 93950

CLARK, Glenn, 1882- 242.2
Windows of heaven; graphic editing and all photos. unless otherwise stated by Lucien Aigner. New York, Harper [1954] 188p. illus. 24cm. [BV4832.C55] 54-8940
1. Meditations. I. Title.

CLARK, Miles Morton, 1920- 242.2
ed.
My God and I; meditations to deepen the spiritual life. St. Paul. Macalester Park Pub. Co. [1950] 96 p. 16 cm. [BV4805.C6] 52-31356
1. Meditations. I. Title.

CLEVELAND, Earl E. 242.2
Come unto me, by E. E. Cleveland. Washington, Review and Herald [1968] 367 p. 21 cm. "This book is published in collaboration with the Missionary Volunteer Department [General Conference of Seventh Day Adventists] as an enrichment of the Morning watch devotional plan." [BV4811.C58] 68-18740
1. Devotional calendars—Seventh-Day Adventists. I. Title.

CLIMBING higher : 242'.2
mountaintop meditations for each day of the year / compiled by Al Bryant. Minneapolis : Bethany Fellowship, c1977. p. cm. [BV4810.C535] 77-24978 ISBN 0-87123-052-6 : 6.95. ISBN 0-87123-054-2 pbk. : 3.95
1. Devotional calendars. I. Bryant, Al, 1926-

CLOUGH, Charlotte Marvin, 242.2
ed.
Partners in prayer; a family book of devotion. Garden City, N. Y., Doubleady [1953] 256p. 22cm. [BV255.C66] 53-10645
1. Family—Prayer-books and devotions—English. I. Title.

COLTON, Ann Ree. 242.2
Precepts for the young. Glendale, Calif., Arc Pub. Co. [c1959] 66 p. 20 cm. [BV4571.2.C6] 68-335
1. Children—Religious life. I. Title.

COWMAN, Lettie (Burd) 1870- 242.2
comp.
Traveling toward sunrise. Los Angeles, Cowman Publications, 1952. 254p. 20cm. 'Companion volume to Streams in the desert.' [BV4810.C62] 53-15581
1. Devotional calendars. I. Title.

COX, Anna Grace, 1870-1950. 242.2
Help thou my want: devotions of a deaconess in her growth in grace; meditations, compiled by Theodora C. Cox. New York, Comet Press Books [1955] 218p. 22cm. [BV4832.C647] 55-8509
1. Devotional calendars—Protestant Episcopal Church. I. Title.

CROWE, Charles M 242.2
The best of the Sanctuary. New York, Abingdon Press [1963] 112 p. 18 cm. Devotional readings selected from yearly issues of the Sanctuary from 1949 through 1962. [BV4811.C7] 63-7478
1. Devotional calendars — Methodist Church. I. Title.

CROWE, Charles M. 242.2
The best of the Sanctuary. Nashville, Abingdon [c.1963] 112p. 18cm. 63-7478 2.25
1. Devotional calendars—Methodist Church. I. Title.

DAILY guidance: 242.2
selected readings from the Old and New Testament scriptures. Grand Rapids, Mich., Zondervan [1964] unpaged 14cm. 2.00

DAVIS, Thomas A. 242.2
Preludes to prayer, by Thomas A. Davis. Washington, Review & Herald [1966] 378p. 16cm. [BV4811.D3] 66-20308 3.00; 3.75, deluxe ed.,
1. Devotional calendars—Seventh-Day Adventists. I. Title.

*DAVIS, Thomas A. 242.2
Preludios para la oracion. Libro de meditaciones matinales para 1967. Mountain View, Calif., Pacific Pub. [1966] 367p. 18cm. (Publicaciones interamerianas) 2.50 bds.,
I. Title.

A Day at a time. 242'.2
Minneapolis : CompCare Publications, c1976. ca. 350 p. ; 15 cm. [BV4810.D33] 76-55448
1. Devotional calendars.

DEAL, William S 242.2
Daily Christian living. Grand Rapids, Mich., Baker Book House, 1962. unpaged. 16 cm. [BV4811.D36] 62-22195
1. Devotional calendars. I. Title.

DEAL, William S. 242.2
Daily Christian living. Grand Rapids, Mich., Baker Bk. [c.]1962. unpaged. 16cm. 62-22195 1.00 pap.,
1. Devotional calendars. I. Title.

DE HAAN, Martin Ralph, 242.2
1891-
Bread for each day; 365 devotional meditations, by M. R. De Haan, Henry G. Bosch. Grand Rapids, Mich., Zondervan [c.1962] unpaged. 20cm. Companion volume to the authors' Our daily bread. 62-51268 3.00
1. Devotional calendars. I. Bosch, Henry Gerard, 1914- II. Title.

DEPREE, Gladys Lenore, 242.2
1933-
A blade of grass; a book of daily devotions, by Gladys and Gordon DePree. Grand Rapids, Zondervan Pub. House [1967] 189 p. 23 cm. [BV4810.D42] 65-19504
1. Devotional calendars—Reformed Church authors. I. DePree, Gordon, joint author. II. Title.

DOMINICAN Sisters. 242.2
Congregation of the Most Holy Rosary, Adrian, Mich.
Liturgical meditations for the entire year 2v. Rev. ed. St. Louis, Herder [1961, c.1949, 1961] 492p. 475p.) Contents.v.1. From Advent to the Ascension v.2. From the Ascension to Advent. 61-8060 12.00 2v.,
1. Church year—Meditations. I. Title.

DOUGLASS, Earl Leroy, 1888- 242.2
The Douglass devotional [by] Earl L. Douglass. New York, M. Evans; distributed in association with Lippincott, Philadelphia [1964] 385 p. 19 cm. [BV4811.D6] 64-20783
1. Devotional calendars. I. Title.

DOUGLASS, Earl Leroy, 1888- 242.2
The Douglass devotional. M. Evans, dist. Philadelphia, Lippincott [c.1964] 385p. 19cm. 64-20783 2.95
1. Devotional calendars. I. Title.

DRAPER, Edythe, comp. 242'.2
Living light: daily light in today's language, compiled by Edythe Draper; selections from the The living Bible, paraphrased, by Kenneth N. Taylor. Wheaton, Ill., Tyndale House [1972] 1 v. (unpaged) 19 cm. [BS390.D73] 72-75963 ISBN 0-8423-2651-0
1. Devotional calendars. I. Taylor, Kenneth Nathaniel. The living Bible, paraphrased. II. Title.

*DRUMMOND, Henry, 1851- 242'.2
1897.
A thought for every day, from Henry Drummond. Ed. by John Birkbeck. Old Tappan, N.J., [Pyramid Publications] [1974,

c1972] 125 p. 18 cm. (A Spire book.) [BV4810] 0.95 (pbk.)
1. Devotional calendars. I. Title.
L.C. card no. for original ed.: 72-10938.

EAVEY, Charles Benton, 1889- 242.2
Each day. Chicago, Moody Press [1956] 373p. 15cm. [BV4832.E29] 57-474
1. Devotional exercises. I. Title.

EDWARDS, Roselyn. 242'.2
Start here; directions for young Christians. Washington, Review and Herald Pub. Association [1972] 367 p. 21 cm. [BV4811.E3] 72-78421
1. Devotional calendars. 2. Youth—Prayer-books and devotions—English. I. Title.

ELY, Virinia, 1899- ed. 242.2
A time a part; daily devotions for young people. [Westwood, N. J.] Revell [1957] 188 p. 22 cm. [BV4850.E4] 57-11324
1. Devotional calendars. 2. Youth—Prayer-books and devotions—English. I. Title.

ERICKSON, Melvin E. 242.2
In tune with God; a junior devotional, by Melvin E. Erickson. Washington, Review & Herald [1966] 448p. 21cm. [BV4811.E7] 66-19414 3.75
1. Devotational calendars—Seventh-Day Adventists. I. Title.

ESTEB, Adlai Albert 242.2
Morning manna. Daily meditations based on selected texts from Genesis to Revelation, following progressively the MV Bible year reading plan of twenty-three chapters each week. Washington, D.C., Review & Herald Pub. [1963, c.1962] 383p. 16cm. 62-14171 2.50
1. Devotional calendars—Seventh Day Adventists. I. Title.

ESTEB, Adlai Albert. 242'.2
Straight ahead; a book to help young people along the way [by] Adlai A. Esteb. Washington, Review and Herald Pub. Association [1974] 378 p. 21 cm. [BV4850.E87] 73-89469 3.95
1. Youth—Prayer-books and devotions—English. 2. Devotional calendars—Seventh-Day Adventists. I. Title.

EVERYDAY, five minutes with God. Compiled by William S. Cannon. Nashville, Broadman Press [1969] 157 p. 21 cm. [BV4810.E83] 69-17891 3.50 242.2
1. Devotional calendars. I. Cannon, William S., comp.

FEDER, Jose. 242'.2
Prayer for each day. New York, Paulist Press [1974] 312 p. illus. 14 cm. Translation of Prieres du jour. [BV4811.F3513] 73-88905 ISBN 0-8091-1814-9 3.95
1. Devotional calendars—Catholic Church. I. Title.

FOELSCH, Charles Berend, 1891- ed. and comp. 242.2
The new day's worship; meditations for every day of the year, edited and compiled by Charles B. Foelsch. Philadelphia, Fortress Press [1966] v, 386 p. 18 cm. [BV4810.F62] 66-26027
1. Devotional calendars—Lutheran Church. I. Title.

FOOTE, Arthur, 1911- 242.2
Taking down the defenses; a lenten manual for 1954. [Boston, Beacon Press, 1954] 58p. 16cm. [BV85.F62] 54-6658
1. Lent—Prayer-books and devotions—English. I. Title.

FOSDICK, Harry Emerson, 1878- 242.2
The meaning of being a Christian, by Harry Emerson Fosdick. [Meditations] from his three famous books about the meaning of faith, prayer, and service: 365 selections for the Christian who wants to be. New York, Association Press [1964] 384 p. 22 cm. [BV4811.F6] 64-10880
1. Devotional calendars. I. Title.

FOSDICK, Harry Emerson, 1878- 242.2
The meaning of being a Christian, by Harry Emerson Fosdick [Meditations] from his three famous books about the meaning of faith, prayer, and service: 365 selections for the Christian who wants to be. New York, Association [c.1964] 384p. 22cm. 64-10880 4.95
1. Devotional calendars. I. Title.

FREMANTLE, Anne (Jackson) 1909- ed. 242.2
Christian conversation; Catholic thought for every day of the year. New York, Stephen Daye Press [1953] unpaged. illus. 25cm. [BX2177.F7] 53-11132
1. Devotional calendars—Catholic Church. I. Title.

FRIDY, Wallace. 242.2
A lamp unto my feet; guidance for every day. New York, Abingdon-Cokesbury Press [1952] 128 p. 16 cm. [BV4832.F694] 52-11316
1. Devotional exercises. I. Title.

GABRIELE DI SANTA MARIA MADDALENA, Father. 242.2
Divine intimacy; meditations on the interior life for every day of the year. Tr. from the 7th Italian ed. by the Discalced Carmelite Nuns of Boston. New York, Desclee [1964] xxviii, 1227p. illus. 19cm. [BX2170.C55G33] 64-24532 8.75
1. Church year—Meditations. I. Title.

GABRIELE DI SANTA MARIA MADDALENA Father. 242.2
Divine intimacy; meditations on the interior life for every day of the year [by] Father Gabriel of St. Mary Magdalen. Translated from the 7th Italian ed. by the Discalced Carmelite Nuns of Boston. New York, Desclee Co. [1964] xxviii, 1227 p. illus. 19 cm. [BX2170.C55G33] 64-24532
1. Church year — Meditations. I. Title.

GABRIELE DI SANTA MARIA MADDALENA Father. 242.2
Divine intimacy; meditations on the interior life for everyday of the year [by] Father Gabriel of St. Mary Magdalen. Translated from the 7th Italian ed. by the Discalced Carmelite Nuns of Boston. New York, Desclee Co. [1964] xxviii, 1227 p. illus. 19 cm. [BX2170.C55G33] 64-24532
1. Church year — Meditations. I. Title.

*GAEBELEIN, Frank E. 242.2
From day to day; a message from the Bible for each day of the year, by Frank E. Gaebelein. Grand Rapids, Baker Book House [1975] 195 p. 21 cm. (Canon Press Book) Includes index. [BS390] ISBN 0-8010-3701-8 6.95.
1. Devotional calendars. I. Title.
Pbk. 2.95; ISBN: 0-8010-3699-2.

GAEBELEIN, Frank Ely, 1899- 242.2
Looking unto Him; a message for each day [New ed.] Grand Rapids, Mich., Zondervan [1961, c.1941] 208p. 61-15818 3.00
1. Devotional calendars. I. Title.

GO quickly and tell. 242'.2
Edited by Janet Sugioka. St. Louis, Bethany Press [1973] 208 p. illus. 19 cm. [BV4810.G53] 73-15628 ISBN 0-8272-1215-1 2.95 (pbk.)
1. Devotional calendars. I. Sugioka, Janet, 1913- ed.

GOUDGE, Elizabeth, 1900- comp. 242.2
A diary of prayer. [1st American ed.] New York, Coward-McCann [1966] 377 p. 23 cm. [BV4810.G63 1966] 66-20151
1. Devotional calendars. I. Title.

GRAEF, Richard, 1899- 242.2
Christ my friend; meditations for daily use. Tr. from German by John J. Coyne. Helicon[dist. New York, Taplinger, 1963] 223p. 19cm. 62-11184 3.50
1. Jesus Christ—Biog.—Meditations. I. Title.

GRAINGE, Julia. 242.2
Gathered gold. New York, Dodd, Mead, 1956. 232p. 18cm. 'A devotional diary.'--Dust jacket. [BV4832.G782] 56-6289
1. Devotional literature. I. Title.

GUTZKE, Manford George. 242.2
A look at the book; daily devotions and studies in the Bible and what it says about itself. Glendale, Calif., G/L Regal Books [1969] 148 p. 18 cm. "Books for further study": p. 147-148. [BV4811.G8] 69-16632
1. Bible—Devotional literature. 2. Devotional calendars. I. Title.

GUTZKE, Manford George. 242.2
Wanderers, slaves & kings; daily devotions and Bible studies. Glendale, Calif., G/L Regal Books [1969] 168 p. 18 cm. "Books for further study": p. 167-168. [BV4811.G83] 71-78549
1. Bible. O.T.—Devotional literature. 2. Devotional calendar. I. Title.

HADLEY, Hazel (Mason) 242.2
Behold God's love; devotional readings for a year for junior high young people. Richmond, Published for the Cooperative Publication Association by John Knox Press [1957] 239p. 21cm. [BV4850.H25] 57-11748
1. Youth—Prayer- books and devotions—English. 2. Devotional calendars. I. Title.

HAGEN, John Milton, 1892- 242.2
I am in iambics [by] Jo'n Milton Hagen. New York, A. S. Barnes [1965] 79 p. 22 cm. "Rhymed daily calendar of Bible verses." [BV4811.H24] 65-14112
1. Devotional calendars. I. Title.

HAGEN, John Milton, 1892- 242.2
I am in iambics [by] Jo'n Milton Hagen. New York, A. S. Barnes [c.1965] 79p. 22cm. Rhymed daily calendar of Bible verses. [BV4811.H24] 65-14112 4.50
1. Devotional calendars. I. Title. II. Title: Iambics.

HALVERSON, Richard C. 242'.2
A day at a time : devotions for men / Richard Halverson. Grand Rapids, Mich. : Zondervan Pub. House, [1974] 256 p. ; 18 cm. [BV4843.H29] 74-11851
1. Men—Prayer-books and devotions—English. I. Title.

HANSON, Virginia, comp. 242'.2
Gifts of the lotus; a book of daily meditations. Wheaton, Ill., Theosophical Pub. House [1974] x, 191 p. 15 cm. (A Quest book) Includes bibliographical references. [BL624.H3] 74-5130 ISBN 0-8356-0450-0 1.50 (pbk.).
1. Devotional calendars. I. Title.

HARDINGE, Miriam. 242.2
Begin today with God; a junior devotional. Washington, Review and Herald [1961] 346p. 20cm. [BV4850.H33] 61-15580
1. Devotional calendars. 2. Youth—Prayer-books and devotions— English. I. Title.

HARE, Eric B 242.2
Make God first; joyful moments with the junior Bible year, by Eric B. Hare. Washington, Review and Herald Pub. Association [1964] 400 p. 21 cm. (A Junior devotional) [BV4811.H27] 64-17656
1. Devotional calendars. I. Title.

HARE, Eric B. 242.2
Make God first; joyful moments with the junior Bible year. Washington, D.C., Review & Herald [c.1964] 400p. 21cm. (Junior devotional) [BV4811.H27] 64-17656 3.00
1. Devotional calendars. I. Title.

HARKNESS, Georgia Elma, 1891- 242.2
Be still and know. Nashville, Abingdon-Cokesbury Press [1953] 96p. 17cm. [BV4832.H357] 53-8133
1. Devotional exercises. I. Title.

HARKNESS, Georgia Elma, 1891- 242.2
The Bible speaks to daily needs. New York, Abingdon Press [1959] 94p. 18cm. [BV4832.2.H3] 59-8196
1. Devotaional exercises. I. Title.

HASH, John A. 242'.2
Bible-light on life's pathway / John A. Hash. Nashville : Action Press : distributed to the book trade by T. Nelson, c1977. 318 p. : ill. ; 22 cm. [BS390.H37] 76-151436 ISBN 0-8407-9502-5 pbk. : 3.95
1. Bible—Criticism, interpretation, etc. 2. Devotional calendars. I. Title.

HAVERGAL, Frances Ridley, 1836-1879 242.2
Opened treasures. Comp. by William J. Pell. New York, Loizeaux [1962] 1v. (front. port.) 22cm. 62-21063 3.25
1. Devotional exercises. I. Title.

HAVNER, Vance, 1901- 242'.2
All the days / Vance Havner. Old Tappan, N.J. : F. H. Revell Co., c1976. 189 p. ; 21 cm. [BV4811.H295] 76-16281 ISBN 0-8007-0812-1 : 5.95
1. Devotional calendars. I. Title.

HAVNER, Vance, 1901- 242.2
Day by day. [Westwood, N. J.] F. H. Revell Co. [1953] 272p. 17cm. [BV4832.H497] 54-5430
1. Devotional calendars. I. Title.

HAVNER, Vance, 1901- 242.2
Truth for each day; meditations for every day of the year. [Westsood, N. J.] Revell [1960] 270p. 17cm. [BV4811.H3] 60-13091
1. Devotional calendars. I. Title.

HAVNER, Vance [Houston] 242.2
Truth for each day; meditations for every day of the year. [Westwood, N. J.] Revell [c.1960] 270p. 17cm. 60-13091 2.95 half cloth.
1. Devotional calendars. I. Title.

HAYES, Edward L. 242.2
Words to live by, by Edward L. Hayes. Chicago, Moody Press [1968] 254 p. 18 cm. [BS2615.4.H3] 68-26409 3.50
1. Bible. N.T. John—Devotional literature. 2. Devotional calendars. I. Title.

HEGLAND, Martin, 1880- 242.2
Thus saith the Lord; daily devotional readings from the Old Testament. A book for devotions with a Scripture selection and a prayer for every day of the year. Minneapolis, Augsburg Pub. House [1955] 500p. 18cm. [BV4832.H549] 55-7120
1. Devotional calendars—Lutheran Church. I. Title.

*HEMBREE, Charles R. 242.2
Good morning, Lord; five-minute devotions [by] Charles R. Hembree. Grand Rapids, Mich., Baker Book House [1973] 64 p. 19 cm. (Good morning, Lord series) [BV4832.2] ISBN 0-8010-4075-2 1.95 (pbk.)
1. Devotional exercises. I. Title.

HEMBREE, Charles R. 242.2
Good morning, Lord; devotions for everyday living [by] Charles R. Hembree. Grand Rapids, Mich., Baker Book House [1971] [64] p. 19 cm. [BV4832.2.H417] 75-164376 ISBN 0-8010-4020-5
1. Devotional exercises. I. Title.

*HEMBREE, Charles R. 242.2
Know and grow; devotions through the Bibl [by] Charles R. Hembree. Grand Rapids, Baker Book House, [1975] 95 p. 18 cm. (Direction books) [BV4832.2] ISBN 0-8010-4106-6 1.25 (pbk.)
1. Meditations. I. Title.

HENRY, Matthew, 1662-1714. 242.2
Moments of meditation from Matthew Henry; 366 daily devotions gleanedfrom the greatest devotional commentary of all time. Comp. and ed. by Fredna W. Bennett. Grand Rapids, Mich., Zondervan [c.1963] 1v. (unpaged) 23cm. 63-15743 3.95
1. Devotional calendars. I. Bennett, Fredna W., ed. II. Title.

HEPPENSTALL, Edward. 242'.2
In touch with God / Edward Heppenstall. Washington : Review and Herald Pub. Association, c1975. 374 p. ; 21 cm. "Published in collaboration with the Youth Department as an enrichment of the Morning watch devotional plan." [BV4811.H44] 74-29819
1. Devotional calendars—Seventh-Day Adventists. I. Title.

HERZBERGER, Frederik William, 1859-1930 242.2
Family altar; brief daily devotions based on selected Scripture texts. Rev. by Harry N. Huxhold. Rev. [i.e. 3d] ed. St. Louis, Concordia [c.]1964. v, 382p. 24cm. 63-23487 4.95 bds.,
1. Family—Prayer-books and devotions—English. 2. Lutheran Church—Prayer-books and devotions—English. 3. Devotional calendars—Lutheran Church. I. Title.

HEUBACH, Paul C 242.2
This is life. Washington, Review and Herald [1957] 367p. 16cm. [BV4832.H575] 57-44914
1. Devotional calendars—Seventh-Day Adventists. I. Title.

HEYRMAN, Jules, 1885- 242.2
Alone with God; meditations for every day. Staten Island, N.Y., Alba House [1961?] 2 v. 21 cm. [BX2170.C55H493] 63-14571
1. Church year — Meditations. I. Title.

HEYRMAN, Jules, 1885- 242.2
Alone with God, meditations for every day [2v.] Staten Island, N.Y., Alba [c.1963] 2v. (562; 538p.) 21cm. 63-14571 5.00; 10.00, ea., set, bxd.
1. Church year—Meditations. I. Title.

HIBMA, J. E. 242.2
A spiritual idea for the day, by J. E. Hibma. [1st ed.] New York, Greenwich Book Pub. [c1966] 217 p. 21 cm. [BV4811.H5] 66-20443
1. Devotional calendars — Reformed Church. I. Title.

*HOFINGER, Johannes. 242.2
Our message is Christ the more outstanding elements of the Christian message [by] Johannes Hofinger. Notre Dome, In Fides 1974 x, 125 p. 22 cm. Bibliography: p. 119-120. [BX2177] 0-8190-0498-7 3.50 (pbk.)
1. Devotional literature—Catholic church. I. Title.

THE Home altar. 242.2
Home altar treasures; selection from the Home altar, 1940-1957. Edited by Daniel Nystrom. Rock Island, Ill., Augustana Press [1960] 397p. 20cm. [BV4811.H6] 60-16827
1. Devotional calendars—Lutheran Church. I. Nystrom, Daniel, 1886- ed. II. Title.

HOME Altar (The) 242.2
Home Altar treasures; selection from the Home Altar, 1940-1957. Edited by Daniel Nystrom. Rock Island, Ill., Augustana Press [c.1960] 397p. 60-16827 3.00
1. Devotional calendars—Lutheran Church. I. Nystrom, Daniel, 1886- ed. II. Title.

HOME life (Nashville) 242.2
Altar fires for family worship; a daily devotional guide compiled from Home life.

Edited by Joe W. Burton. Nashville, Broadman Press [1955] 373p. 21cm. [BV4810.H6] 55-13660
1. Devotional calendars—Baptists. I. Burton, Joe Wright, 1907- ed. II. Title.

HORTON, Thomas Corvin, 1848- 242.2
365 devotions on the names of Our Lord. Grand Rapids, Mich., Baker Bk., 1965. 191p. 20cm. [BT5901] 66-1048 ISBN CD 2.95
1. Jesus Christ—name. I. Title.

HOUSE, Anne W. ed. 242.2
The day book of meditations; meditations for every day of the Christian year. Greenwich, Conn., Seabury [c.]1962. unpaged. 18cm. 62-14954 2.75 bds.,
1. Devotional calendars. 2. Meditations. I. Title.

HOUSE, Anne W ed. 242.2
The day book of meditions; meditations for every day of the Christian year. Greenwich, Conn., Seabury Press, 1962. unpaged. 18cm. 'A companion volume to The day book of the Bible.'SDevotional calendars. [BV4811.H65] 62-14954
1. Meditations. I. Title.

HOUSE, Anne W., ed. 242.2
The day book of the Bible; devotions for every day of the Christian year. Greenwich, Conn., Seabury [c.]1962. unpaged. 18cm. 62-14955 2.75 bds.,
1. Devotional calendars. I. Title.

IKERMAN, Ruth C. 242.2
Golden words for every day [by] Ruth C. Ikerman. Nashville, Abingdon Press [1969] 239 p. 16 cm. [BV4811.I38] 69-18457 2.95
1. Devotional calendars. I. Title.

IN touch; selections from 242'.2
Living light. Wheaton, Ill., Tyndale House [1973] 1 v. (unpaged) illus. 18 cm. [BV4850.I5] 73-80923 ISBN 0-8423-1710-4 1.95
1. Youth—Prayer-books and devotions—English. 2. Devotional calendars. I. The Living light.

JEPSON, Sarah Anne. 242.2
Dawn of devotion. Chicago, Moody Press [1961] 560p. 18cm. [BV4811.J45] 61-59758
1. Devotional calendars. I. Title.

JEPSON, Sarah Anne. 242.2
Show me thy glory. Chicago, Moody Press [1965] 576 p. 18 cm. [BV4811.J47] 65-29742
1. Devotional calendars — Presbyterian Church. I. Title.

JEPSON, Sarah Anne 242.2
Show me thy glory. Chicago, Moody [c.1965] 576p. 18cm. [BV4811.J47] 65-29742 3.95
1. Devotional calendars—Presbyterian Church. I. Title.

JOANNES XXIII Pope, 1881-1963 242.2
Pope John: daily readings. Edited by Vincent A. Yzermans. New York, Morehouse-Barlow [1968] 120 p. 22 cm. Excerpts selected and translated from Pope John's speeches and letters. Bibliography: p. 113-117. [BX2170.L4J6] 68-16115
1. Lent—Prayer-books and devotions. I. Yzermans, Vincent Arthur, 1925- comp.

JOANNES XXIII Pope, 1881-1963. 242.2
Prayers and devotions from Pope John XXIII; selected passages from his writings and speeches arranged for every day of the year. Edited and introduced by John P. Donnelly, with a pref. by Loris Capovilla. Translated by Dorothy White. [1st American ed.] New York] Published in association with Grosset & Dunlap [1967] 315, [3] p. 19 cm. "A Giniger book." Translation of Il breviario di Papa Giovanni. Bibliography: p. [317]-[318] [BX2185.J613 1967] 66-19503
1. Devotional calendars—Catholic Church. I. Title.

JONES, Eli Stanley, 1884- 242.2
Growing spiritually. Nashville, Abingdon-Cokesbury Press [1953] 364 p. 16 cm. [BV4832.J457] 53-11338
1. Devotional exercises. I. Title.

JONES, Eli Stanley, 1884- 242.2
In Christ. New York, Abingdon Press [1961] 380 p. 16 cm. [BV4832.2.J64] 61-8409
1. Devotional exercises. I. Title.

JONES, Eli Stanley, 1884- 242.2
Mastery: the art of mastering life. New York, Abingdon Press [1955] 364p. 16 cm. [BV4832.J465] 55-9140
1. Devotional exercises. I. Title.

JONES, Eli Stanley, 1884- 242.2
The Word became flesh. New York, Abingdon Press [1963] 382 p. illus. 16 cm. [BV4811.J6] 63-9936
1. Devotional calendars. I. Title.

JONES, Eli Stanley, 1884- 242.2
The Word became flesh. Nashville, Abingdon Pr. [c.1963] 382p. illus. 16cm. 63-9936 2.50
1. Devotional calendars. I. Title.

JUST for today; 242.2
comp., tr. from the writings of St. Theresa of Lisieux with selections from the Imitation of Christ, by a Benedictine of Stanbrook, Worcester. Introd. by Ronald Knox. Springfield, Ill., Templegate [1963] viii, 242p. 17cm. (Golden lib.) 63-25559 3.50
1. Devotional calendars—Catholic Church. I. Therese, Saint, 1873-1897. II. Imitatio Christi. English. III. A Benedictine of Stanbrook, comp. and tr.

KARRIS, Robert J. 242'.2 s
The Gospel of Luke, by Robert J. Karris. Chicago, Franciscan Herald Press [1974] 96 p. 18 cm. (Read and pray, no. 2) [BS2595.4.K37] 226'.4'06 74-12219 ISBN 0-8199-0626-3 0.95 (pbk.)
1. Bible. N.T. Luke—Devotional literature. I. Title. II. Series.

KELLER, James 242.2
Three minutes a day, v.6. New York, 16 E. 48 St. The Christophers, [c.1963] 365p. 17cm. .50 pap.,
I. Title.

KELLER, James Gregory, 1900- 242.2
Stop, look and live; a story for each day of the year to bring out the power within you. A new Christopher book. [1st ed.] Garden City, N. Y., Hanover House, 1954. 365 p. 20 cm. [BX2182.K4] 54-9585
1. Devotional calendars—Catholic Church. I. Title.

KELLER, James Gregory, 1900- 242.2
A day at a time; a Christopher thought for each day of the year. Garden City, N. Y., Hanover House, 1957. 365p. 20cm. [BV4832.K426] 57-13078
1. Devotional calendars. I. Title.

KELLER, James Gregory, 1900- 242.2
Give us this day; a Christopher thought for each day of the year. Garden City,N. Y., Hanover House, 1956. 365p. 19cm. [BV4832.K427] 56-9837
1. Devotional calendars. I. Title.

KELLER, James Gregory, 1900- 242.2
Just for today; a Christopher thought for every day of the year. Garden City, N. Y., Doubleday, 1952. 365 p. 20 cm. [BV4832.K428] 52-11784
1. Devotional calendars. I. Title.

KELLER, James Gregory, 1900- 242.2
Make each day count; a Christopher thought for every day of the year. Garden City, N. Y., Hanover House, 1955. 366p. 19cm. [BX2182.K395] 55-9987
1. Devotional calendars— Catholic Church. I. Title.

KELLOW, Norman B. 242.2
Daily will I praise Thee: 366 devotions based on the Psalms from the amplified Bible [by] Norman B. Kellow. Westwood, N.J., Revell [1966] 383p. 20cm. [BV4811.K4] 66-21901 3.50 bds.,
1. Devotional calendars. 2. Bible. O.T. Psalms—Devotional literature. I. Title.

KEMPER, Inez, comp. 242.2
The doorway to heaven. Grand Rapids, Baker Book House, 1958. 153p. 20cm. [BV4801.K38] 58-124234
1. Devotional exercises. I. Title.

KENNEDY, Eugene C. 242'.2
The joy of being human : reflections for every day of the year / by Eugene Kennedy. Chicago : Thomas More Press, [1974] 256 p. ; 23 x 25 cm. [BV4810.K45] 74-187923 ISBN 0-88347-043-8 : 12.95
1. Devotional calendars. I. Title.

KENNEDY, Eugene C. 242.2
The joy of being human : reflections for everyday of the year / by Eugene Kennedy. Garden City, N. Y. : Doubleday [1976c1974] 355p. ; 18 cm. (Image books) [BV4811K45] ISBN 0-385-00943-7 pbk. : 1.95
1. Devotional calendars. I. Title.
L. C. card no. for original edition: 74-187923.

KNIGHT, Walter Brown. 242.2
Just for today, by Walter B. Knight. Grand Rapids, Eerdmans [1965] 349 p. 23 cm. [BV4811.K6] 64-8578
1. Devotional calendars. I. Title.

KNIGHT, Walter Brown 242.2
Just for today. Grand Rapids, Mich., Eerdmans [c.1965] 349p. 23cm. [BV4811.K6] 64-8578 4.25
1. Devotional calendars. I. Title.

LARSON, Bruce. 242'.2
Thirty days to a new you / Bruce Larson ; edited by Hazel Larson. Grand Rapids : Zondervan, [1974] 175 p. ; 18 cm. [BV4832.2.L33] 74-4963 3.95
1. Devotional exercises. I. Title.

LEONBERGER, Elinor Ann. 242.2
Moments of meditation. Philadelphia, Dorrance [1970] ix, 115 p. 22 cm. "Biblical quotations are from the King James Version of the Old and New Testaments." [BV4811.L46] 70-104750 3.95
1. Devotional calendars—Lutheran Church. I. Title.

LINDSELL, Harold, 1913- 242.2
The morning altar; daily devotions for the year. [Westwood, N. J. Revell [1956] 255p. 20cm. [BV4832.L53] 56-10893
1. Devotional calendars. I. Title.

LINDSELL, Harold, 1913- 242.2
The morning alter daily devotions for the year. [Westwood, N. J.] Revell [1956] 255p. 20cm. [BV4832.L53] 56-10893
1. Devotional calendars. I. Title.

LINDSELL, Harold, 1913- 242.2
My daily quiet time; daily devotions for the year. Grand Rapids, Zondervan Pub. House [1969] 255 p. 21 cm. (A Zondervan paperback) 1956 ed. publishd under title: The morning altar. [BV4811.L54 1969] 72-95033 0.95
1. Devotional calendars. I. Title.

LINTZ, Harry McCormick. 242.2
Strength for each day; a book of daily devotional meditations. Grand Rapids, [BV4832.2.L5] 59-31015
I. Title.

LITTLE, William Herbert, 1876- 242.2
A verse a day poetic meditations based on Scripture verses. [1st ed.] New York, Vantage Press [1957] 367p. 21cm. [BV4832.L54] 56-12324
1. Devotional calendars. I. Title.

LONG, Samuel Burman, 1883- 242.2
Calendar of love: brief daily devotional readings that show the development of the principle of righteousness with the Trinity of love which is the love of God, respect for the self and love toward all people. by S. Burman Long. Boston, Christopher Pub. House [1967] 236 p. 21 cm. [BV4811.L6] 67-13545
1. Devotional calendars. 2. Love (Theology]-Meditations. I. Title.

LONG, Samuel Burman, 1883- 242.2
Calendar of love Brief daily devotional readings that show the development of the principle of righteousness with the Trinity of love which is the love of God, respect for the self and love toward all people, by S. Burman Long. Boston, Christopher Pub. House [1967] 236p. 21cm. [BV4811.L6] 67-13545 4.00
1. Devotional calendars. 2. Love (Theology)—Meditations. I. Title.

LUCCOCK, Halford Edward 242.2
365 windows. [Nashville] Abingdon Press [c.1955-1960] 239p. 16cm. 60-5232 2.00
1. Devotional calendars. I. Title.

LUCCOCK, Halford Edward, 1885- 242.2
Never forget to live. Nashville, Abingdon Press [c.1956-1961] 238p. 16cm. 61-5557 2.00
1. Devotional calendars. I. Title.

LUCCOCK, Halford Edward, 1885- 242.2
365 windows New York, Abingdon Press [1960] 239p. 16cm. [BV4811.L8] 60-5232
1. Devotional calendars. I. Title.

LUCCOCK, Robert Edward, 1915- 242.2
Putting life on center; brief meditations for the prompting of daily personal devotion [by] Robert E. Luccock. New York, Abingdon Press [1964] 235 p. 15 cm. [BV4811.L82 1964] 64-21133
1. Devotional calendars. I. Title.

LUCCOCK, Robert Edward, 1915- 242.2
Putting life on center; brief meditations for the prompting of daily personal devotion, Nashville, Abingdon [c.1961-1964] 235p. 16cm. 64-21133 2.75
1. Devotional calendars. I. Title.

LUNDQUIST, Amos Theodore, 1896- 242.2
Lives that glorify God; daily biographical meditations. Rock Island, Ill., Augustana Book Concern [1953] 374p. 20cm. [BV4832.L75] 53-11094
1. Devotional calendars—Lutheran Church. I. Title.

MCCANN, Edna. 242'.2
The heritage book, 1977 / Edna McCann. Don Mills, Ont. : Collier Macmillan Canada, c1976. ca. 250 p., [16] leaves of plates : col. ill. ; 19 cm. [BV4810.M33] 77-352515 ISBN 0-02-976670-2
1. Devotional calendars. I. Title.

MCCULLOH, Gerald O., ed. 242.2
The Upper room companion; a devotional manaual for ministers, theological students, and other church workers. Nashville, The Upper room [1959] 336p. 19cm. [BV4810.M32] 59-15166
1. Devotional calendars—Methodist Church. I. The Upper room. II. Title.

MCGRANN, Albert P 242.2
In Him we live; the good word for today. Milwaukee, Bruce Pub. Co. [c1956] 365p. 18cm. [BX2182.M2] 56-6190
1. Devotional exercises. I. Title.

MACGREGOR, Geddes. 242.2
So help me God; a calendar of quick prayers for half-skeptics. New York, Morehouse-Barlow Co. [1970] 95 p. 19 cm. [BV245.M44] 72-97263 ISBN 0-8192-1104-4
1. Prayers. I. Title.

MCSORLEY, Joseph, 1874- 242.2
Meditations for everyman. New York, Paulist Pr. [c.1948, 1962] 207p. 19cm. (Deus bk.) Contents.v. 1. contents—Advent to Pentecost. .95 pap.,
1. Church year—Meditations. I. Title.

MARMION, Columba, Abbot, 1858-1923. 242.2
Words of life; on the margin of the missal. Edited by Dom Thibaut; translated by Mother M. St. Thomas. St. Louis, Herder, 1952. 487p. 16cm. [BX2183] 54-3777
I. Title.

MERTON, Thomas, 1915-1968. 242'.2
Day unto day : a year in the meditations of Thomas Merton / selected and edited by Thomas P. McDonnell ; with ill. by Thomas Merton. Garden City, N.Y. : Doubleday, 1975. p. cm. [BV4811.M43 1975] 74-33683 ISBN 0-385-08683-0
1. Devotional calendars—Catholic Church. I. McDonnell, Thomas P. II. Title.

MILLER, Keith. 242.2
Habitation of dragons; a book of hope about living as a Christian. Waco, Tex., Word Books [1970] 188 p. 23 cm. Includes bibliographical references. [BV4501.M5872] 72-123009 4.95
1. Christian life—1960- I. Title.

MOODY, Dwight Lyman, 1837-1899. 242.2
Daily meditations: a living daily message from the words of Dwight L. Moody. Selected by Emma Moody Fitt. Grand Rapids, Baker Book House, 1964. 234 p. 20 cm. First published in 1900 under title: The D. L. Moody year book. [BV3797.M7Y4 1964] 64-8602
1. Devotional calendars. I. Fitt, Emma (Moody) ed. II. Title.

MOREAU, Basile Antoine Marie, 1799-1873. 242.2
Daily meditations compiled by Sister M. Monica from the writings of Basil Anthony Moreau; supplemented by materials in accordance with his spirit drawn from various other sources Milwaukee, Bruce Press [1958] 885p. 18cm. (Catholic life publications) [BX2183.M55] 58-3768
1. Devotional calendars—Catholic Church. I. Title.

MORRIS, James Kenneth, 1896- 242.2
My strength and my shield, daily meditations. Nashville, Abingdon [c.1963] 144p. 21cm. 63-16376 2.50
1. Collects—Meditations. 2. Devotional calendars. I. Title.

MORRIS, James Kenneth, 1896- 242.2
My strength and my shield, daily meditations. New York, Abingdon Press [1963] 144 p. 21 cm. [BX5944.C7M6] 63-16376
1. Collects — Meditations. 2. Devotional calendars. I. Title.

MURDOCH, William Gordon 242.2
Christ is our victory; daily meditations on great texts from the Book of Books. Washington, D.C., Review & Herald [1965]

373p. 16cm. [BV4811.M77] 65-18671 2.75; 3.50 deluxe ed.,
1. Devotional calendars—Seventh-Day Adventists. I. Title.

MURRAY, Andrew, 1828-1917. 242.2
Day-by-day with Andrew Murray, comp. by M. J. Shepperson. Foreword by Armin R. Gesswein. Grand Rapids, Mich., Zondervan [c.1961] 119p. 62-933 1.95 bds.,
1. Devotional calendars. I. Shepperson, Mary Johnson, comp. II. Title.

MURRY, Andrew, 1828-1917. 242.2
Day-by-day with Andrew Murray, compiled by M. J. Shepperson. Foreword by Armin R. Gesswein. Grand Rapids, Zondervan Pub. House [1961] 119p. 18cm. First published in 1899 under title: Andrew Murray yearbook. [BV4811.M8 1961] 62-933
1. Devotional calendars. I. Shepperson, Mary Johnson, comp. II. Title.

NELSON, Ruth Youngdahl. 242.2
God's song in my heart; daily devotions for women. Rock Island, Ill., Augustana Press [1957] 418p. 22cm. Includes hymns with music. [BV4832.N345] 56-11912
1. Women—Prayer-books and devotions—English. 2. Lutheran Church— Prayer-books and devotions—English. I. Title.

NILES, Daniel T 242.2
For to-day; a series of daily Bible studies for a whole year. Philadelphia, Muhlenberg Press [1955] 442p. 19cm. [BV4832] 55-4181
1. Devotional calendars. I. Title.

NYGAARD, Norman Eugene, 242.2
1897- comp.
Power for today; a devotional guide for every day of the year, comp. by Norman E. Nygaard. Grand Rapids, Mich., Zondervan [1966, c.1965] 1v. (unpaged) 21cm. [BV4810.N86] 65-24406 3.95 bds.,
1. Devotional calendars—Presbyterian Church. I. Title.

NYSTEDT, Olle. 242.2
At dawn of day; a thought for each day of the church year, translated by P. O. Bersell. Hymns selected by Daniel Nystrom. Rock Island, Ill., Augustana Press [1955] 397p. 20cm. [BV4836.N915] 55-57263
1. Church year—Prayer-books and devotions—English. 2. Lutheran Church—Prayer-books and devotions—English. I. Title.

OSMUNSON, Robert Lee. 242.2
With God you win; a daily devotional and inspirational guide for early-teens and near-teens. Washington, Review and Herald Pub. Association [1968] 375 p. 21 cm. (A Junior devotional) [BV4811.O8] 68-22290
1. Devotional calendars—Seventh-Day Adventists. 2. Youth—Prayer-books and devotions. I. Title.

PALMS, Roger C. 242'.2
God's promises for you / Roger C. Palms. Old Tappan, N.J. : F. H. Revell Co., c1977. p. cm. [BV4832.2.P316] 77-9413 ISBN 0-8007-0888-1 : pbk. : 3.95
1. Meditations. I. Title.

PAONE, Anthony J 1913- 242.2
My daily bread; a summary of the spiritual life, simplified and arranged for daily reading, reflection, and prayer. Brooklyn, Confraternity of the Precious Blood, 1954. viii, 439p. 14cm. [BX2350.P28] 54-43119
1. Spiritual life—Catholic authors. 2. Meditations. I. Title.

PATHWAYS of prayer 242.2
a book of daily devotions for youth. [By Clement W. De Chant and others] Philadelphia, Christian Education Press [1953] 384p. illus: 17cm. [BV4805.P38] 53-9922
1. Devotional calendars. I. Christian Education Press, Philadelphia.

PETERSON, Wilferd Arlan, 242'.2
1900-
The art of living, day by day; three hundred and sixty-five thoughts, ideas, ideals, experiences, adventures, inspirations, to enrich your life, by Wilferd A. Peterson. New York, Simon and Schuster [1972] 411 p. 22 cm. [BV4811.P39] 72-83633 ISBN 0-671-21343-1 10.00
1. Devotional calendars. I. Title.

*PHILLIPS, J. B. 242.2
For this day, 365 meditations by J. B. Phillips Waco, Texas, Word Books [1975 c1974] 255 p. 22 cm. [BV4811] ISBN 0-340-19232-1 5.95
1. Devotional calendars. I. Duncan, Denis, ed. II. Title.

PHIPPS, Burton H 242.2
Day unto day: spiritual meditations for each day, revealing God in nature. Washington, Review and Herald Pub. Association [1954] 381p. 16cm. [BV4832.P53] 54-39045
1. Devotional calendars—Seventh-Day Adventists. I. Title.

PIERSON, Delavan Leonard, 242.2
1867-1938, comp.
For each new day, selected and arranged by Delavan L. Pierson. Grand Rapids, Baker Book House [1966] 388 p. 18 cm. [BV4810.P49 1966] 67-2821
1. Devotional calendars. I. Title.

PIERSON, Robert H. 242'.2
Faith triumphant [by] Robert H. Pierson. Washington, Review and Herald Pub. Association [1974] 371 p. 21 cm. [BV4811.P48] 73-91426 3.95
1. Devotional calendars—Seventh-Day Adventists. I. Title.

PORTALS of prayer. 242.2
Meditations from Portals of prayer. [Special 20th anniversary ed.] Saint Louis, Concordia Pub. House [c1957] 379p. 17cm. [BV4810.P56 1957] 56-12418
1. Devotional calendars— Lutheran Church. I. Title.

PRICE, Eugenia. 242.2
Share my pleasant stones every day for a year. [1st ed.] Grand Rapids, Zondervan Pub. House [cu957] 384p. 21cm. [BV4832.P6886] 58-20235
1. Devotional calendars. I. Title.

A Private devotional diary 242'.2
/ edited by John Birkbeck. Atlanta : John Knox Press, c1975. 188 p. ; 23 cm. Includes index. [BV4810.P64] 75-13465 ISBN 0-8042-2511-7 : 5.95
1. Devotional calendars. I. Birkbeck, John, 1908-

PROKOP, Phyllis Stillwell. 242'.2
Your day-by-day heavenscope / Phyllis S. Prokop, with Anita M. Parks and Chloris M. Johnson. Nashville : Broadman Press, c1975. 160 p. ; 18 cm. [BV4810.P66] 75-8323 ISBN 0-8054-5137-4 pbk. : 2.50
1. Devotional calendars. I. Parks, Anita M., joint author. II. Johnson, Chloris M., joint author. III. Title.

RAMSEY, Arthur Michael, 242'.2
Abp. of Canterbury, 1904-
Through the year with Michael Ramsey : devotional readings for every day / edited by Margaret Duggan. 1st American ed. Grand Rapids : Eerdmans, [1977, c1975] 253 p. ; 24 cm. [BV4811.R28 1976] 76-49556 ISBN 0-8028-3494-9 : 6.95
1. Devotional calendars—Church of England. I. Duggan, Margaret. II. Title.

RANDOLPH, Lois Christian. 242.2
Come up higher; a junior devotional. Washington, Review and Herald Pub. Association [1967] 461 p. 22 cm. "Published in collaboration with the Missionary Volunteer Department as an enrichment of the Morning Watch devotional plan." [BV4811.R3] 67-19714
1. Devotional calendars—Seventh-Day Adventists. I. Title.

RANDOLPH, Lois Christian. 242'.2
Target-Heaven; a daily devotional and inspirational guide designed for early-teens, near-teens, their parents, and all who feel themselves young. Washington, Review and Herald Pub. Association [1973] 371 p. 21 cm. (Directions for young Christians) "This book is published in collaboration with the Missionary Volunteer Department as an enrichment of the Morning Watch devotional plan." [BV4811.R33] 73-83098
1. Devotional calendars. 2. Youth—Prayer-books and devotions—English. I. Title.

RASKAS, Bernard S 242.2
Heart of wisdom; a thought for each day of the Jewish year. New York, Burning Bush Press [1962] 372p. 19cm. [BM724.R3] 62-18076
1. Devotional calendars—Jews. I. Title.

READ and pray; 242'.2
daily Bible readings, with comments, reflections, prayers, one page a day, for three months. Robert J. Karris, general editor. Chicago, Franciscan Herald Press [1974] p. cm. [BS390.R38] 74-11197
1. Devotional calendars. I. Karris, Robert J., ed.

READ, Leonard Edward, 242'.2
1898- comp.
The free man's almanac, compiled by Leonard E. Read. Irvington-on-Hudson, N.Y., Foundation for Economic Education, 1974. vi, 376 p. 17 cm. [BV4810.R33] 74-174427 ISBN 0-910614-51-2 5.00
1. Devotional calendars. I. Title.

RHOADES, Winfred, 1872- 242.2
comp.
To know God better. New York, Harper [1958] 210p. 18cm. [BV4805.R5] 57-9890
1. Devotional exercises. I. Title.

RICH, Elaine Sommers, 1926- 242.2
ed.
Breaking bread together. Scottdale, Pa., Herald Press [1958] 391p. 18cm. [BV4810.R48] 58-10304
1. Devotional calendars—Mennonites. 2. Women—Prayer-books and devotions—English. I. Title.

RICHARDS, Harold Marshall 242.2
Sylvester, 1894-
The promises of God; the morning watch texts with a devotional reading for each day. Washington, D. C., Review and Herald [1956] 367p. 16cm. [BV4832.R436] 56-4580
1. Devotional calendars. I. Title.

RICHARDS, Harold Marshall 242.2
Sylvester, 1894-
The promises of God; the morning watch texts with a devotional reading for each day. Washington, D. C., Review and Herald [1956] 367p. 16cm. [BV4832.R436] 56-4580
1. Devotional calendars. I. Title.

ROBERTSON, Josephine. 242.2
Living with love; thoughts for forty days. New York, Abingdon Press [1963] 95 p. 18 cm. [BV4832.2.R59] 63-16377
1. Meditations. I. Title.

ROBERTSON, Josephine 242.2
Living with love; thoughts for forty days. Nashville, Abingdon [c.1962, 1963] 95p. 18cm. 63-16377 2.00 bds.,
1. Meditations. I. Title.

ROBINSON, Virgil E. 242.2
Reach out; a daily devotional and inspirational guide for early-teens and near-teens, by Virgil E. Robinson. Washington, Review and Herald Pub. Association [1970] 367 p. 21 cm. [BV4850.R63] 70-121416
1. Youth—Prayer-books and devotions. 2. Devotional calendars—Seventh-Day Adventists. I. Title.

RUSSELL, Arthur James, ed. 242.2
A treasury of devotion. [Edited by A. J. Russell] A special omnibus ed. of the world-famous devotional diaries, God calling, and God at eventide. [1st omnibus ed.] New York, Dodd, Mead, 1966 [i. e. 1967] 2 v. in 1. 14 cm. Each vol. also has individual t. p. [BV4810.R83] 67-1278
1. Devotional calendars. I. Title. II. Title: God calling. III. Title: God at eventide.

RUSSELL, Arthur James, ed. 242.2
A treasury of devotion. [Edited by A. J. Russell] A special omnibus ed. of the world-famous devotional diaries, God calling, and God at eventide. [1st omnibus ed.] New York, Dodd, Mead, 1966 [i.e. 1967] 2 v. in 1. 14 cm. Each vol. also has individual t.p. [BV4810.R83] 67-1278
1. Devotional calendars. I. Title. II. Title: God calling. III. Title: God at eventide.

†SAINT and thought for 242'.2
every day / profiles of saints by the Daughters of St. Paul ; thoughts by James Alberione. Boston, Mass. : St. Paul Editions, c1976. 315 p. : ill. ; 19 cm. [BV4811.S18] 76-53946 3.95 pbk. : 2.95
1. Devotional calendars—Catholic Church. 2. Christian saints—Calendar. 3. Christian saints—Biography. I. Alberione, Giacomo Giuseppe, 1884-1971. II. Daughters of St. Paul.

*SALLEE, Lynn. 242. '2
Coffee-time prayers. Grand Rapids : Baker Book House, 1976. 64p. : ill. ; 20 cm. [BV283.M7] ISBN 0-8010-8083-5 : 2.95.
1. Prayers I. Title.

SANGSTER, William Edwin, 242.2
1900-1960
Daily readings from W. E. Sangster; ed. by Frank Cumbers. London, Epworth Pr., 1966. [7] 368p. 20cm. [BV4811.S2] 66-66878 3.95 bds.,
1. Devotional calendars—Methodist Church. I. Cumbers, Frank Henry, ed. II. Title.
American distributor: Revell, Westwood, N. J.

SANGSTER, William Edwin, 242.2
1900-1960.
Daily readings from W. E. Sangster. Edited by Frank Cumbers. [Westwood, N.J.] F. H. Revell Co. [1966] 368 p. 19 cm. [BV4811.S2 1966] 67-8799
1. Devotional calendars—Methodist Church. I. Cumbers, Frank Henry, ed. II. Title.

SCHNEIDER, Frieda Johnetta 242.2
My devotional diary. Grand Rapids, Eerdmans [c.1959] 95p. 23cm. 59-15640 1.50 bds.,
1. Devotional exercises. I. Title.

SCHNEIDER, Frieda Johnetta, 242.2
1911-
My devotional diary. Grand Rapids, Eerdmans [c1959] 95p. 23cm. [BV4832.2.S3] 59-15640
1. Devotional exercises. I. Title.

SCHREINER, Samuel Jonathan. 242.2
What a layman believes; a book of daily devotions [by] Samuel J. Schreiner. Nashville, Broadman Press [1967] 128 p. 20 cm. [BV4811.S364] 67-12179
1. Devotional calendars—Baptists. I. Title.

SEAMANDS, John T. 242'.2
Power for the day : 108 meditations from Mathew / John T. Seamands. Nashville : Abingdon, c1976. 112 p. ; 20 cm. [BS2575.4.S39] 75-45044 ISBN 0-687-33265-6 pbk. : 3.50
1. Bible. N.T. Matthew—Devotional literature. 2. Devotional calendars. I. Title.

SENIOR, Donald. 242'.2 s
Gospel of St. Matthew. Chicago, Franciscan Herald Press [1974] 96 p. 18 cm. (Read and pray, no. 1) [BS2575.4.S45] 226'.2'06 74-11196 ISBN 0-8199-0625-5 0.95
1. Bible. N.T. Matthew—Devotional literature. I. Title. II. Series.

*SERIG, Beverly. 242'.2
Daily bread; a devotional guide for every day of the year, edited by Beverly Serig. Independence, Mo., Herald Pub. House, 1973. 1 v. (unpaged) 17 cm. [BV4810] ISBN 0-8309-0078-0 4.50
1. Devotional calendars. I. Title.

SERIG, Beverly. 242'.2
Daily bread; a devotional guide for every day of the year. Edited by Beverly Serig. Independence, Mo., Herald Pub. House, 1974 [c1973] 1 v. (unpaged) 18 cm. [BV4810.S36 1974] 74-161764 ISBN 0-8309-0104-3 2.00
1. Devotional calendars—Reorganized Church of Latter-Day Saints. I. Title.

SHEPHERD, J. Barrie. 242'.2
Diary of daily prayer / J. Barrie Shepherd. Minneapolis : Augsburg Pub. House, [1975] 127 p. ; 18 cm. [BV245.S5] 74-14176 ISBN 0-8066-1459-5 pbk. : 2.95
1. Prayers. I. Title.

SHILLONG, Eric W. 242'.2
Guiding thoughts to success and achievement : for students each day of the year / by Eric W. Shillong. Philadelphia : Dorrance, [1974] 462 p. ; 24 cm. Includes bibliographical references and index. [BV4531.2.S54] 73-91540 ISBN 0-8059-1972-4 : 10.00
1. Students—Prayer-books and devotions—English. 2. Devotional calendars. I. Title.

SISTERS of Charity of Saint 242.2
Elizabeth, Convent Station, N.J.
Daily missal meditations; meditations for every day of the year based on the liturgy of the Mass. New York, Benziger Bros. [1959-] v.18 cm. Contents.v. 1.Winter. [BX2015.S5] 60-17894
1. Catholic Church. Liturgy and ritual. Missal. I. Title.

SISTERS of Charity of Saint 242.2
Elizabeth, Convent Station, N.J.
Daily missal meditations; meditations for every day of the year based on the liturgy of the Mass. New York, Benziger Bros. [1959-62] 4 v. 18 cm. Contents.Contents -- v. 1. Winter. -- v. 2. Spring. -- v. 3. Summer. -- v. 4. Autumn. [BX2170.C55S53] 60-17894
1. Church year — Meditations. I. Title.

SMITH, Paul B. 242.2
Daily gospel, evangelistic meditations by every day of the year. Grand Rapids, Mich., Zondervan [c.1963] unpaged. 18cm. 63-15732 1.95 bds.,
1. Devotional calendars. I. Title.

SMITH, Paul B 242.2
Daily gospel, evangelistic meditations for every day of the year. Grand Rapids, Zondervan Pub. House [1963] 1 v. (unpaged) 18 cm. [BV4811.S4] 63-15732
1. Devotional calendars. I. Title.

SNOWDEN, Rita Frances. 242.2
Today; a book of devotions. London, Epworth Press [label: Chicago A. R. Allenson, 1952] 96p. illus. 19cm. [BV4832.S74] 53-32869
1. Devotional exercises. I. Title.

SOPER, Eunice. 242.2
God is my friend; a junior devotional. Washington, Review and Herald Pub. Association [1965] 448 p. 20 cm. [BV4811.S6] 65-24500
1. Devotional calendars—Seventh-Day Adventists. I. Title.

SPIRITUAL diary; 242.2
selected sayings and examples of saints. [Boston] St. Paul Ed. [dist. Daughters of St. Paul, c.1962] 266p. 19cm. 62-18504 3.00; 2.00 pap.,
1. Devotional calendars—Catholic Church.

SPRAY, Pauline. 242'.2
Daily delights; devotional meditations for women. Grand Rapids, Zondervan Pub. House [1968] 1 v. (unpaged) 23 cm. [BV4811.S64] 68-27458 4.95
1. Devotional calendars. I. Title.

STAMM, Mildred. 242.2
Meditation moments for women. Grand Rapids, Zondervan Pub. House [1967] 1 v., (unpaged) 22 cm. [BV4811.S8] 67-22690
1. Devotional calendars. 2. Women—Religious life. I. Title.

STEWART, James Alexander, 242.2
1910-
Pastures of tender grass, daily inspirational readings. Philadelphia, Revival Literature [1962] 458 p. 19 cm. "Companion volume to [the author's] Still waters." [BV4810.S719] 63-624
1. Devotional calendars. I. Title.

STOREY, William George, 242.2
1923ed
Days of the Lord, ed by William G. Storey. New York Herder & Herder [c.1965] 219 p. 19 cm Contents.il winter [br2170.c55d3] 65.21941 3.95
1. Church year—Meditations. Devotional calender. I. Title.

STOREY, William George, 242.2
1923- ed.
Days of the Lord, edited by William G. Storey. [New York] Herder and Herder [1965- v. 19 cm. Contents.Winter. [BX2170.C55D3] 65-21941
1. Church year — Meditations. 2. Devotional calendars. I. Title.

SUECHTING, August G., ed. 242'.2
Thine forever : daily devotions following Luther's Small catechism / collated and edited by August G. Suechting. Minneapolis : Augsburg Pub. House, 1975, c1950. 383 p. ; 15 cm. Originally published by Wartburg Press, Columbus, Ohio. Includes index. [BV4832.2.S87 1975] 75-6245 ISBN 0-8066-1491-9 : 3.75
1. Devotional calendars—Lutheran Church. I. Luther, Martin, 1483-1546. Catechismus, Kleiner. II. Title.

SWOR, Chester E. 242.2
To enrich each day [by] Chester E. Swor and Jerry Merriman. Old Tappan, N.J., F. H. Revell Co. [1969] 351 p. 18 cm. [BV4810.S88] 70-85313
1. Devotional calendars. I. Merriman, Jerry, joint author. II. Title.

TABER, Gladys (Bagg) 1899- 242.2
Another path. [1st ed.] Philadelphia, Lippincott [1963] 139 p. 20 cm. Full name: Gladys Leona (Bagg) Taber. [BV4905.2.T3] 63-17678
1. Consolation. I. Title.

TAYLOR, Florence Marian 242'.2
Tompkins, 1892-
In the morning, bread : devotions for the new day / Florence M. Taylor. New Canaan, Conn. : Keats Pub., c1976. xix, 391 p. ; 24 cm. Includes bibliographical references and indexes. [BV4810.T38] 76-2983 ISBN 0-87983-121-9 : 8.95
1. Devotional calendars. I. Title.

TAYLOR, Kenneth Nathaniel. 242'.2
My living counselor : daily readings from The living Bible. Wheaton, Ill. : H. Shaw Publishers, c1976. ca. 650 p. : ill. ; 18 cm. [BS390.T38] 76-43126 ISBN 0-87788-573-7 : 4.95
1. Devotional calendars. I. Title.

TEN BOOM, Corrie. 242'.2
Each new day / Corrie ten Boom. Old Tappan, N.J. : Revell, [1977] p. cm. [BV4811.R4] 77-12780 ISBN 0-8007-0894-6 : 7.95
1. Devotional calendars. I. Title.

THOMAS, George Ernest 242.2
Personal power through the spiritual disciplines. Nashville, Abingdon Press [c.1960] 127p. 20cm. 60-12074 2.00 bds.,
1. Devotional exercises. I. Title.

THOMAS, George Ernest, 242.2
1907-
Personal power through the spiritual disciplines. New York, Abingdon Press [1960] 127 p. 20 cm. [BV4832.2.T5] 60-12074
1. Devotional exercises. I. Title.

THOMPSON, Ken, 1926- 242'.2
Bless this desk : prayers 9 to 5 / Ken Thompson. Nashville : Abingdon Press, c1976. 76 p. ; 21 cm. [BV245.T43] 75-33818 ISBN 0-687-33599-X : 3.95
1. Prayers. I. Title.

TILESTON, Mary Wilder 242'.2
(Foote) 1843-1934, ed.
Daily strength for daily needs. Special introd. by William J. Petersen. New Canaan, Conn., Keats Pub. [1973] 378 p. 18 cm. (A Pivot family reader) [BV4810.T5 1973] 73-80030 1.25 (pbk.)
1. Devotional calendars. I. Title.

TORREY, Reuben Archer, 242.2
1856-1928
Daily meditations; a thought, a meditation, and a related scripture passage, for every day in the year, comp., ed. by A. Chester Mann [pseud.] Grand Rapids, Mich. Baker Bk., 1963. 160p. 21cm. First pub. in 1929 under title: The R. A. Torrey yearbook. 63-22971 2.50
1. Devotional calendars. I. Roberts, Phillip Ilott, 1872-1938, comp. II. Title.

TRENT, Robbie, 1894- 242.2
Daily discoveries. [1st ed.] New York, Harper [1955] 151p. 20cm. Devotional readings. [BV4870.T7] 55-11484
1. Children—Prayer-books and devotions—English. I. Title.

TUCKER, James A. 242'.2
Windows on God's world : glimpses of the Creator through His handiwork / James A. Tucker. Washington : Review and Herald Pub. Association, c1975. 372 p. ; 21 cm. "Published by the Youth Department of Missionary Volunteers and an enrichment of the Morning watch devotional plan." [BV4850.T8] 74-29820
1. Youth—Prayer-books and devotions—English. 2. Devotional calendars—Seventh-Day Adventists. I. Title.

TWO Listeners. 242.2
God calling; a devotional classic, by the Two Listeners. Edited by A. J. Russell. [1st large print ed.] New York, Dodd, Mead [1968] 197 p. 28 cm. [BV4810] 68-4861
1. Devotional calendars. I. Russell, Arthur James, ed. II. Title.

THE Upper room. 242.2
The Upper room disciplines; a devotional manual for ministers, theological students, and other church workers. Introd. by Gerald O. McCulloh. Nashville [1962, c1961] 372 p. 19 cm. [BV4810.U6] 62-8162
1. Devotional calendars — Methodist Church. 2. Clergy — Prayer-books and devotions — English. I. Title.

UPPER Room disciplines 242.2
(The), 1963 a devotional manual for ministers, theological students, and other church workers. Nashville, Upper Room [c.1962] 373p. 19cm. annual 63-7844 1.00 pap.,
1. Devotional calendars—Methodist Church. I. The Upper room.

UPPER Room disciplines 242.2
(The) 1965. A devotional manual for ministers, theological students, and otherchurch workers. Ed. by Sulon G. Ferree. Foreword by David A. MacLennan. Nashville, Upper Room [c.1964] 375p. 17cm. annual. 63-7844 1.00 pap.,
1. Devotional calendars—Methodist Church. I. The Upper Room. II. MacLennan, David A., ed.

UPPER Room (The) 242.2
The Upper room disciplines 1962; a devotional manual for ministers, theological students and other church workers. Introd. by Gerald O. McCulloh. Nashville 5 1908 Grand Ave. [Author] [c.1961] 372p. 62-8162 1.00 pap.,
1. Devotional calendars—Methodist Church. 2. Clergy—Prayerbooks and devotions—English. I. Title.

VERCRUYSSE, Bruno, 1797- 242.2
1880.
New practical meditations for every day in the year, on the life of our Lord Jesus Christ; chiefly intended for the use of religious communities ... The only complete English translation, published with approbation and under the direction of the author. New ed. New York, Benziger Bros. [1954] 2v. illus. 19cm. [BX2183.V5 1954] 54-1886
1. Meditations. I. Title.

VIEROW, Duain W., 1935- 242'.2
On the move with the Master : a daily devotional guide on world mission / Duain W. Vierow. South Pasadena, Calif. : William Carey Library, c1977. viii, 166 p. : ill. ; 22 cm. Includes index. [BV2070.V53] 76-57679 ISBN 0-87808-155-0 : 4.95
1. Missions—Meditations. I. Title.

WALKER, Harold Blake. 242.2
Inspirational thoughts for every day. New York, Hawthorn Books [1970] ix, 368 p. 24 cm. [BV4811.W3 1970] 70-102012 6.95
1. Devotional calendars—Presbyterian Church. I. Title.

*WARNER, Hugh C., comp. 242.2
Daily readings from William Temple. Ed., abridged by William Wand. Nashville, Abingdon [1965] 189p. 18cm. (Apex Bks., V-4) 1.45 pap.,
I. Title.

WEATHERHEAD, Leslie Dixon, 242'.2
1893-
Daily readings from the works of Leslie D. Weatherhead. Selected by Frank Cumbers. Nashville, Abingdon Press [1969, c1968] 367 p. 20 cm. [BV4811.W4 1969] 70-2828 3.50
1. Devotional calendars. I. Cumbers, Frank Henry, comp. II. Title.

WEATHERHEAD, Leslie Dixon, 242.2
1893-
A private house of prayer. New York, Abingdon Press [1958] 267 p. 21 cm. [BV4832.2.W4] 59-7251
1. Devotional exercises. I. Title.

WHITE, Anne S. 242'.2
Dayspring [by] Anne S. White. Plainfield, N.J., Logos International [1971] 180 p. 21 cm. [BV4811.W45] 71-160700 ISBN 0-912106-21-2 1.95
1. Devotional calendars. I. Title.

WHITE, Anne S. 242'.2
Healing devotions : daily meditations and prayers based on scriptures and hymns / by Anne S. White. New York : Morehouse-Barlow Co., [1975] vi, 138 p. ; 21 cm. [BV4811.W455] 75-5218 ISBN 0-8192-1192-3 pbk. : 3.25
1. Devotional calendars. I. Title.

*WHITE, Elena G. De 242.2
Ayuda en la vida cotidiana. Mountain View, Calif., Pacific Pr. Pub. Assn. [c.1966] 60p. 19cm. .30 pap.,
I. Title.

*WHITE, Ellen G. 242.2
Conseils pour la vie quotidienne. Mountain View, Calif., Pacific Pr. Pub. Assn. [c.1966] 60p. 19cm. (Pubns. Inter-Americaines) .30 pap.,
I. Title.

WHITE, Ellen Gould (Harmon) 242.2
1827-1915.
Conflict and courage. Compiled from the writings of Ellen G. White. Washington, Review and Herald [1970] 381 p. 21 cm. [BV4811.W47] 71-129227
1. Devotional calendars. I. Title.

WHITE, Ellen Gould 242'.2
(Harmon) 1827-1915.
God's amazing grace. Compiled from the writings of Ellen G. White. Washington, Review and Herald Pub. Association [1973] 383 p. 21 cm. [BV4811.W477 1973] 73-83097
1. Devotional calendars—Seventh-Day Adventists. I. Title.

WHITE, Ellen Gould (Harmon) 242.2
1827-1915.
In heavenly places; the morning watch texts with appropriate selections compiled from the writings of Ellen G. White. Washington, Review and Herald [1967] 382 p. 21 cm. "Compiled largely from unpublished and out-of-print Spirit of prophecy materials." [BV4811.W48] 67-19711
1. Devotional calendars—Seventh-Day Adventists. I. Title.

WHITE, Ellen Gould *242.2
(Harmon) 1827-1915.
My life today; the morning watch texts with appropriate selections from the writings of Ellen G. White. Washington, D.C., Review and Herald [1952] 377 p. 16 cm. [BV4832.W4518] 52-4342
1. Devotional exercises. 2. Calendars. I. Title.

WHITE, Ellen Gould (Harmon) 242.2
1827-1915.
Sons and daughters of God; the mornign watch texts with appropriate selections from the writings of Ellen G. White. Washington, Review and Herald [1955] 283p. 16cm. [BV4832.W4523] 56-19285
1. Devotional calendars— Seventh-Day Adventists. I. Title.

WHITE, Ellen Gould (Harmon) 242.2
1827-1915.
That I may know Him; the morning watch texts with appropriate selections, compiled from the writings of Ellen G. White. Washington, Review and Herald [1964] 382 p. 16 cm. [BV4811.W5] 64-17650
1. Devotional calendars. I. Title.

WHITE, Ellen Gould (Harmon) 242.2
1827-1915.
That I may know Him; the morning watch texts with appropriate selections, comp. from the writings of Ellen G. White. Washington, D.C., Review & Herald [c.1964] 382p. 16cm. [BV4811.W5] 64-17650 2.50
1. Devotional calendars. I. Title.

WHITE, Reginald E. O. 242.2
Five minutes with the Master; a year's meditations in the company of Christ. Grand Rapids, Mich., Eerdmans [1966, c.1965] 372p. 17cm. [BV4811.W57] 65-25195 3.95
1. Devotional calendars. I. Title.

WILSON, Hazel Thorne. 242.2
Strength for living; a diary of daily devotions. New York, Abingdon Press [1960] 80 p. 21 cm. [BV4832.2.W56] 60-9204
1. Devotional exercies. I. Title.

WILSON, Hazel Thorne 242.2
Strength for living; a diary of daily devotions. Nashville, Abingdon Press [c.1960] 80p. 21cm. 60-9204 1.50 bds.,
1. Devotional exercises. I. Title.

WOOD, Kenneth H 242.2
Meditations for moderns; three-minute devotional readings for daily inspiration. Washington, Review and Herald Pub. Association [1963] 381 p. 16 cm. [BV4811.W66] 63-18400
1. Devotional calendars — Seventh-Day Adventists. I. Title.

WOOD, Kenneth H. 242.2
Meditations for moderns; three-minute devotional readings for daily inspiration. Washington, D.C., Review & Herald [c.1963] 381p. 16cm. 63-18400 2.50
1. Devotional calendars—Seventh-Day Adventists. I. Title.

WOODALL, William Love, 242.2
1908-
Devotions for boys and girls. Illus. by Politzer. New York, Association Press [1953] 64p. illus. 20cm. [BV265.W8] 53-13180
1. Children—Prayer-books and devotions—English. I. Title.

WURMBRAND, Richard. 242'.2
Reaching toward the heights : book of daily devotions / by Richard Wurmbrand. Grand Rapids : Zondervan Pub. House, c1977. ca. 250 p. ; 21 cm. [BV4811.W87] 77-4488 4.95
1. Devotional calendars. I. Title.

YOUNG, Valentine. 242.2
Daily meditations for seminarians. Chicago, Franciscan Herald Press [c1960] 337 p. illus. 16 cm. [BX2182.2.Y6] 60-11993
1. Seminarians — Meditations. I. Title.

YOUNG, Valentine 242.2
Daily meditations for seminarians. Chicago, Franciscan Herald Press [c.1960] 337p. front. 60-11993 1.75 pap.,
1. Seminarians—Meditations. I. Title.

YOUNGDAHL, Reuben K 1911- 242.2
Live today. Rock Island, Ill., Augustanta Press [1959] 366 p. 20 cm. [BV4811.Y65] 59-14544
1. Devotional calendars — Lutheran Church. I. Title.

YOUNGDAHL, Reuben K 1911- 242.2
o follow the Master in the pathway of glorious living. Minneapolis, T. S. Denison [1953] 378p. 22cm. [BV4832.Y63] 53-12543
1. Devotional calendars—Lutheran Church. I. Title.

YOUNGDAHL, Reuben K 1911- 242.2
This is God's day. Rock Island, Ill., Augustana Press [1956] 366p. 21cm. [BV4832.Y65] 56-10136
1. Devotional calendars—Lutheran Church. I. Title.

YOUNGDAHL, Reuben K 1911- 242.2
This is God's day. Rock Island, Ill. Augustana Press [1956] 366 p. 21 cm. [BV4832.Y65] 56-10136
1. Devotional calendars — Lutheran Church. I. Title.

YOUNGDAHL, Reuben K 1911- 242.2
This is God's world. Rock Island, Ill., Augustana Press [1961] 365 p. 20 cm. [BV4811.Y66] 61-17515
1. Devotional calendars. 2. Travel. I. Title.

YOUNGDAHL, Reuben K. 1911- 242.2
This is God's world. Rock Island, Ill., Augustana [c.1961] 365p. 61-17515 3.00
1. Devotional calendars. 2. Travel. I. Title.

YOUNGDAHL, Reuben K 1911- 242.2
ed.
Today; meditations for every day of the year, edited and compiled by Reuben K. Youngdahl.

Philadelphia, Fortress Press [1965] vi, 394 p. 18 cm. [BV4811.Y67] 65-25434
1. Devotional calendars — Lutheran Church. I. Title.

YOUNGDAHL, Reuben K., 1911- ed. 242.2
Today; meditations for every day of the year. Philadelphia, Fortress [c.1965] vi, 394p. 18cm. [BV4811.Y67] 65-25434 3.50
1. Devotional calendars—Lutheran Church. I. Title.

YOUNGS, Robert W. 242.2
Renewing your faith day by day; based on the Christian Herald Daily meditations, with a supplement for special days. Garden City, N.Y., Doubleday, 1965 [c.1963-1965] viii, 198p. 22cm. [BV4811.Y68] 65-11051 3.95
1. Devotional calendars—Presbyterian Church. I. Title.

ABBEY, Merrill R. 242.3
The shape of the gospel; interpreting the Bible through the Christian year [by] Merrill R. Abbey. Nashville, Abingdon Press [1970] 352 p. 24 cm. "The Bible readings used here follow the lectionary of the United Methodist Church, adopted in 1964." Includes bibliographical references. [BV30.A23] 78-124751 9.50
1. Church year—Meditations. I. United Methodist Church (United States) II. Title.

AMIOT, Francois. 242.3
From Scripture to prayer; daily readings on the Gospels and St. Paul. [Translated by Norah Smaridge] Staten Island, N.Y., Alba House [1967] 2 v. 23 cm. Translation of 365 Meditations sur les evangiles et S. Paul. Contents.Contents.—v. 1. Advent to Pentecost.—v. 2. Pentecost to Advent. [BS2650.4.A4513] 67-21426
1. Bible N.T. Epistles of Paul—Meditations. I. Title.

ANDREWS, Ernest C. 242.3
Fifty devotional programs. Grand Rapids, Mich., Baker Bk. [c.1966] 108p. 20cm. 1.50 pap.,
I. Title.

BAILLIE, John Launcelot. 242.3
Meditation in flowers: a flower festival guide (without illustrations) or a book for the bedside table (with illustrations); designed for private meditation on themes of the church's year, by John L. Baillie. Dorchester (Dorset), Clarius Publications, 1967. 80 p. 38 plates, illus. (some col.) 20 cm. 21/- [BV30.B26 1967] 68-107874
1. Church year—Meditation. 2. Flower arrangement in churches. I. Title.

BAILLIE, John Launcelot. 242.3
Meditation in flowers; a flower festival guide (without illustrations or a book for the bedside table (with illustrations); designed for private meditation on themes of the church's year, by John L. Baillie. Dorchester (Dorset), Clarius Publications, 1967. 80 p. 38 plates, illus. (some col.) 20 cm. [BV30.B26 1967] 68-107874 21/-
1. Church year—Meditations. 2. Flower arrangement in churches. I. Title.

BARTH, Karl, 1886- 242.3
Selected prayers. Tr. [from German] by Keith R. Crim. Richmond, Va., Knox [c.1965] 72p. 19cm. (Chime paperbacks) [BV250.B37] 65-10144 1.00 pap.,
1. Pastoral prayers. I. Title.

BAUR, Benedikt, 1877- 242.3
The light of the world; translated by Edward Malone. St. Louis, Herder, 1952- v. 25 cm. Translation of Werde Lichti [BX2170.C55B313] 52-4010
1. Church year—Meditations. I. Title.

BAUR, Benedikt, 1877- 242.3
The light of the world; liturgical meditations for the weekdays and Sundays of the ecclesiastical year. Translated by Edward Malone. Rev. ed. St. Louis, Herder [1958-59] 3 v. 25cm. Translation of Werdelicht! [BX2170.C55B315] 58-13571
1. Church year—Meditations. I. Title.

BAYNE, Stephen Fielding, Bp., 1908- 242.3
In the sight of the Lord; eight meditations for Lent. [1st ed.] New York, Harper [1958] 150 p. 22 cm. [BV85.B37] 58-5190
1. Lent—Prayer-books and devotions—English. I. Title.

BECK, Victor Emanuel 1894- 242.3
A book of Advent, with daily devotions, by Victor E. Beck and Paul M. Lindberg. Illus. by Don Wallerstedt. Rock Island, Ill., Augustana press [1958] 147p. illus. 20cm. [BV40.B4] 58-13378
1. Advent. I. Lindberg, Paul M., joint author. II. Title.

BERRY, Joan P. 242.3
For everything a season, by Joan P. Berry. Illustrated by Barbara A. Williams. Philadelphia, Fortress Press [1971] 55 p. illus. 18 cm. [BV30.B47] 76-157534 ISBN 0-8006-0101-7 1.50
1. Church year—Meditations. I. Title.

BERSELL, Peter Olof Immanuel, 1882- 242.3
Christmas voices; Christmas meditations and reveries. Rock Island, Ill., Augustana Book Concern [1954] 83p. illus. 22cm. [BV4257.B45] 54-38571
1. Christmas sermons. 2. Lutheran Church—Sermons. 3. Sermons, American. I. Title.

BIBLE. N.T. John. Greek. 1962. 242.3
Family 13 (the Ferrar group) the text according to John, by Jacob Geerlings Salt Lake City, University of Utah Press, 1962. viii, 111 p. Facsims. 25 cm. (Studies and documents, 21) [BS2615.2.G4] 63-3454
1. Bible. N.T. John—Criticism, Textual. I. Geerlings, Jacob. II. Title. III. Series.

BOULTWOOD, Alban. 242.3
Alive to God; meditations for everyman. Baltimore, Helicon [1964] 180 p. 23 cm. (Benedictine studies, 7) [BX2182.2.B6] 63-12092
1. Meditations. I. Title. II. Series: The benedictine studies, 7

BOULTWOOD, Alban 242.3
Alive to God; meditations for everyman. Helicon [dist. New York, Taplinger, c.1964] 180p. 23cm. (Benedictine studies, 7) 63-12092 4.50
1. Meditations. I. Title. II. Series: The Benedictine studies, 7

BOULTWOOD, Alban. 242.3
Into his splendid light. With a foreword by Eugene J. McCarthy. New York, Sheed and Ward [1968] xiii, 238 p. 22 cm. (American Benedictine Academy studies) [BX2170.C55B68] 68-13843
1. Church year—Meditations. I. Title. II. Series: American Benedictine Academy, Latrobe, Pa. Studies

COOGAN, Aloysius F 242.3
Spiritual steps to Christmas. Milwaukee, Bruce Pub. Co. [1953] 116p. 21cm. [BV40.C6] 53-13251
1. Advent. 2. Christmas. I. Title.

COUGHLAN, Peter, comp. 242'.3
A Christian's prayer book; poems, psalms, and prayers for the church's year. Edited by Peter Coughlan, Ronald C. D. Jasper [and] Teresa Rodrigues. Chicago, Franciscan Herald Press [1972] x, 374 p. 18 cm. [BX2170.C55C646 1972] 72-9357 ISBN 0-8199-0447-3 2.95
1. Church year—Prayer-books and devotions—English. I. Jasper, Ronald Claud Dudley, joint comp. II. Rodrigues, Teresa, O.S.B., joint comp. III. Title.

CULLY, Kendig Brubaker. 242.3
Two sensons: Advent and Lent, by Kendig Brubaker Cully and Iris V. Cully. [1st ed.] Indianapolis, Bobbs-Merrill [1954] 159p. 20cm. [BV40.C8] 54-6056
1. Advent — Prayer-books and devotions — English. 2. Lent — Prayer-books and devotions—English. I. Cully, Iris V., joint author. II. Title.

DALTON, Frederick Thomas, 1855- 242.3
The authenticity, character, and purpose of the Fourth Gospel. Oxford, J. Parker, 1879. 59 p. 22 cm. (The Ellerton prize essay. 1879) [BS2615.D26] 57-52873
1. Bibl. N. T. John—Criticism, interpretation, etc. I. Title.

DODD, Charles Harold, 1884- 242.3
Historical tradition in the Fourth Gospel. Cambridge [Eng.] University Press, 1963. xii, 453 p. 25 cm. [BS2615.52D6] 63-23896
1. Bible. N. T. John — Criticism, interpretation, etc. I. Title.

DOTY, William Lodewick, 1919- 242.3
One season following another; a cycle of faith [by] William L. Doty. Chicago, Franciscan Herald Press [1968] 141 p. 21 cm. [BX2170.C55D66] 68-54394 4.50
1. Church year—Meditations. I. Title.

DOYLE, Charles Hugo. 242.3
Reflections on the Passion. Milwaukee, Bruce Pub. Co. [1957] 88p. 18cm. [BX2170.L4D6] 57-6320
1. Lent—Prayer-books and devotions—English. I. Title.

EDWIN, B. 242.3
Retreat conferences for religious. Milwaukee, Bruce [1964] 150p. 22cm. 64-24742 price unreported
1. Retreats for members of religious orders. I. Title.

EMERSON, Laura S., comp. 242.3
Effective readings for special days and occasions. Grand Rapids, Mich., Zondervan Pub. House [c.1961] 118p. 61-29013 1.95 bds.,
1. Devotional literature. I. Title.

FEHREN, Henry. 242.3
God spoke one word. New York, Kenedy [1967] 212 p. 22 cm. [BX1756.F37G6] 67-26802
1. Church year sermons. 2. Sermons, American. 3. Catholic Church—Sermons. I. Title.

FEHREN, Henry. 242.3
God spoke one word. New York, Kenedy [1967] 212 p. 22 cm. [BX1756.F37G6] 67-26802
1. Catholic Church—Sermons. 2. Church year sermons. 3. Sermons, American. I. Title.

FIELD, Laurence N 242.3
Journey to Easter; a book of daily meditations for Lent. Minneapolis, Augsburg Pub. House [1957] 152p. 21cm. [BV85.F5] 57-7475
1. Lent—Prayer-books and devotions—English. I. Title.

GEARON, Patrick J., 1890- 242.3
Rest a while retreat talks. Pref. from Kilian Healy. Chicago, 6415 Woodlawn Ave. Carmelite Third Order Pr., [1963] 315p. 19cm. 63-6663 3.50 bds.,
1. Retreats for members of religious orders. I. Title.

GLESSNER, Chloe Holt. 242'.3
Holiday devotionals / by Chloe Holt Glessner. San Antonio : Naylor Co., c1976. vii, 45 p. ; 20 cm. [BV4897.A1G55] 76-1020 ISBN 0-8111-0600-4 : 3.95. ISBN 0-8111-0609-8 pbk. : 2.95
1. Holidays—Prayer-books and devotions—English. I. Title.

GLESSNER, Chloe Holt. 242'.3
Holiday devotionals / by Chloe Holt Glessner. San Antonio : Naylor Co., c1976. vii, 45 p. ; 20 cm. [BV4897.A1G55] 76-1020 ISBN 0-8111-0600-4 : 3.95. ISBN 0-8111-0609-8 pbk. : 2.95
1. Holidays—Prayer-books and devotions—English. I. Title.

HEDLEY, John Cuthbert, Bp., 1837-1915. 242.3
A retreat; thirty-three discourses with meditations for the use of the clergy, religious, and others. [16th ed.] Westminster, Md., Newman Press [1951] 266 p. 22 cm. [BX2182.H352 1951] 51-13721
1. Meditations. I. Title.

HOGAN, Joseph F 1910- 242.3
A do-it- yourself retreat; how to bring out the real good in you. Chicago, Loyola University Press [c1961] 274p. illus. 19cm. [BX2376.5.H6] 61-15688
1. Retreats—Addresses, essays, lectures. I. Title.

HOLLAND, Kenneth J ed. 242.3
Those Sabbath hours, compiled by Kenneth J. Holland. Nashville, Southern Pub. Association [1966] 214 p. 26 cm. [BV4801.H64] 64-15622
1. Devotional literature. 2. Sabbath. I. Title.

HOLLAND, Kenneth J., ed. 242.3
Those Sabbath hours. Nashville, Southern Pub. [c.1966] 214p. 26cm. [BV4801.H64] 64-15622 6.95 bds.,
1. Devotional literature. 2. Sabbath. I. Title.

JOHNSON, Ruth I. 242.3
Devotional programs for special days and occasions; a program for every month of the year. Grand Rapids, Mich., Zondervan [c.1961] 63p. 1.00 pap.,
1. Church year—Meditations. I. Title.

KENNEDY, James William, 1905- 242.3
Holy Island, a Lenten pilgrimage. Foreword by Horace W. B. Donegan. New York, Morehouse-Gorham, 1958. 160p. illus. 21cm. (The Annual Bishop of New York books, 1958) [BV85.K4] 58-5782
1. Lent-Prayer-books and devotions— English. 2. Holy Island. I. Title.

KENNEDY, James William, 1905- 242.3
Meditations in His presence; a devotional companion to the Church year. Foreword by Massey H. Shepherd, Jr. Greenwich, Conn., Seabury Press, 1954. 245p. 22cm. [BV4832.K436] 54-7517
1. Church year—Meditations. I. Title.

KNOX, Ronald Arbuthnott, 1888- 242.3
A retreat for lay people. New York, Sheed and Ward, 1955. 258p. 21cm. [BX2182.K58] 269 55-7477
1. Meditations. 2. Retreats. I. Title.

KNOX, Ronald Arbuthnott, 1888- 242.3
A retreat for lay people. New York, Paulist Pr. [1963, c.1955] 256p. 18cm. (Deus Bk.) .95 pap.,
1. Meditations. 2. Retreats. I. Title.

KNOX, Ronald Arbuthnott, 1888-1957. 242.3
The layman and his conscience: a retreat. New York, Sheed & Ward [1961] 218p. 21cm. [BX2375.K5] 61-11797
1. Retreats—Addresses, essays, lectures. I. Title.

KRAMER, A. T. 242.3
Brosamlein von des Herrn Tisch; Andachten fur die Sonn- und Festtage des Kirchenjahres. St. Louis, Concordia [c.1961] 275p. 60-53150 4.50
1. Church year—Meditations. I. Title.

L'ENGLE, Madeleine. 242'.3
The irrational season / Madeleine L'Engle. New York : Seabury Press, c1977. 215 p. ; 22 cm. "A Crossroad book." [BV30.L46] 76-46944 ISBN 0-8164-0324-4 : 8.95
1. Church year—Meditations. I. Title.

LUNDIN, Jack W. 242.3
Celebrations for special days and occasions, by Jack W. Lundin. Illustrated by Josephine Mulhearn. [1st ed.] New York, Harper & Row [1971] xi, 98 p. illus. 22 cm. [BV255.L85] 70-148443 ISBN 0-06-065313-2 3.95
1. Family—Prayer-books and devotions—English. I. Title.

MAERTENS, Marlene. 242.3
God for all seasons. Philadelphia, Westminster Press [1969] 160 p. 21 cm. [BV30.M23] 74-83529 2.45
1. Church year—Meditations. I. Title.

MARTINEZ, Luis Maria, Abp., 1881-1956. 242.3
Liturgical preludes. Translated from the Spanish by Sister Mary St. Daniel. Philadelphia, P. Reilly Co. [c1961] 224p. 23cm. [BX2170.C55M343] 61-18859
1. Church year—Meditations. I. Title.

MARTINI, Prosdocimus, 1893- 242.3
Be ye renewed; an eight-day retreat for missionary priests. Translated from the Latin by Valerian Schott. Chicago, Franciscan Herald Press [c1956] 473p. 19cm. [BX2375.M272] 269 57-1697
1. Retreats. I. Title.

OGILVIE, Lloyd John. 242'.3
The cup of wonder : a communion meditations / by Lloyd John Ogilvie. Wheaton, Ill. : Tyndale House Publishers, 1976. 141 p. ; 20 cm. [BV825.2.O36] 76-8684 ISBN 0-8423-0490-8 : 4.95
1. Lord's Supper—Meditations. I. Title.

PARDUE, Austin, Bp., 1899- *242.3
Create and make new. [1st ed.] New York, Harper [1952] 128 p. 20 cm. [BV85.P32] 51-11947
1. Lent. 2. Christian life. 3. Sanctification. I. Title.

PAWLIKOWSKI, John. 242.3
Epistle homilies. Milwaukee, Bruce Pub. Co. [1966] xiv, 127 p. 22 cm. The text of the Epistles is reproduced with permission of the Confraternity of Christian Doctrine. The commentaries were first published in Novena notes magazine. [BX1756.P39E6] 66-25269
1. Catholic Church—Sermons. 2. Sermons, American. 3. Church year sermons. I. Bible. N. T. Epistles. English. Selections. 1966. Confraternity version. II. Title.

PAWLIKOWSKI, John 242.3
Epistle homilies. Milwaukee, Bruce [1966] xiv, 127p. 23cm. Text of the Epistles is reproduced with permission of the Confraternity of Christian Doctrine. Commentaries were first pub. in Novena Notes magazine. [BX1756.P39E6] 66-25269 3.95
1. Catholic Church—Sermons. 2. Sermons, American. 3. Church year sermons. I. Bible. N.T. Epistles. English. Selections. 1966. Confraternity version. II. Title.

PEARSON, Lawrence W *242.3
The carillon; foreword by Stephen F. Bayne, Jr. New York, Morehouse-Gorham Co., 1952. 136 p. 19 cm. Essays. [BV4832.P374] 52-14557
1. Meditations. I. Title.

PETRELLI, Giuseppe] 242.3
Eoce Homo: part one, Another King; part two,

Another Priest; part three, Another Prophet; part four, Behold the Man. [Syracuse? N. Y., 1962] 356p. 21cm. In English. [BT306.4.P4] 62-19911
1. Jesus Christ—Meditations. I. Title.

PFARR, Anthony J. 242'.3
Seek His face; short meditations for Sundays and some feast days, based on readings from the Lectionary, by Anthony J. Pfarr. [Boston] St. Paul Editions [1973] 268 p. 22 cm. [BX2170.C55P43] 73-86211 4.95
1. Church year—Meditations. I. Title.

PORTER, Jean Kelleher. 242.3
Halo for a housewife; a retreat at home. Milwaukee, Bruce Pub. Co. [1962] 136p. 22cm. [BX2353.P6] 62-12430
1. Woman—Religious life. I. Title.

QUINN, Alexander James, 242.3
1932-
Thoughts for our times; sermon outlines for Sundays and holydays [by] A. James Quinn and James A. Griffin. Staten Island, N.Y., Alba House, 1969. xviii, 126 p. 22 cm. [BX2170.C55Q5] 79-107233 1.95
1. Church year—Meditations. I. Griffin, James A., joint author. II. Title.

RAHNER, Karl, 1904- 242.3
The eternal year. Translated by John Shea. Baltimore, Helicon [1964] 144 p. 22 cm. Translation of Kleines Kirchenjahr. [BX2170.C55R33] 64-20233
1. Church year. I. Title.

RAHNER, Karl, 1904- 242.3
The eternal year. Tr. [from German] by John Shea. Helicon [dist. New York, Taplinger, c.1964] 144p. 22cm. 64-20233 3.50 bds.,
1. Church year. I. Title.

RAHNER, Karl, 1904- 242.3
Everyday faith. [Translated by W. J. O'Hara. New York] Herder and Herder [1968] 217 p. 22 cm. Translation of Glaube, der die Erde liebt. Bibliography: p. [215]-217. [BX2170.C55R353 1968b] 68-6375 4.95
1. Church year—Meditations. I. Title.

RAHNER KARL, 1904- 242.3
Everyday faith; [tr. from German] by W. J. O'Hara. London, Burns & Oates, New York, Herder & Herder, 1968. 3-217p. 21cm. Tr. of Glaube, der die Erde liebt. Bibl. [BX2170.C55R353 1968] 67-25881 4.95
1. Church year-Meditations. I. Title.

RANDALL, Edwin Jarvis, Bp. 242.3
A year of good cheer. [Nashville] Parthenon Press [c1959] 286p. 20cm. [BV4832.2.R3] 60-22702
1. Church year—Meditations. I. Title.

RENARD, Alexandre Charles, 242'.3
1906-
Growth in Christ through the Gospels, by Alexandre Renard. Translated by Sister Gertrude. Glen Rock, N.J., Paulist Press [1966] 160 p. 19 cm. (Deus books) Translation of Prieres de simplicite, avec les evangiles des dimanches et fetes. [BX2170.C55R43] 66-22050
1. Church year—Meditations. I. Title.

SACRED and secular : 242'.3
a companion / compiled by Adam Fox and Gareth and Georgina Keene. Grand Rapids : Eerdmans Pub. Co., [1975] xv, 336 p. : ill. ; 20 cm. Includes index. [BV4812.A1S2 1975] 75-20224 ISBN 0-8028-3469-8 : 7.95
1. Church year—Prayer-books and devotions—English. I. Fox, Adam, 1883- II. Keene, Gareth, 1944- III. Keene, Georgina, 1948-

SCHERER, Paul [Ehrman] 242.3
1892-
Love is a spendthrift; meditations for the Christian year. NewYork, Harper [c.1961] 230p. 61-5268 3.75
1. Church year—Meditations. I. Title.

SHILTON, Lance R 242.3
The Word made flesh. Grand Rapids, Zondervan Pub. House [1963] 120 p. 21 cm. [BV4253.S65] 63-1183
1. Sermons, Australian. I. Title.

STEVENS, Edouard 242.3
From the housetops: a pastor speaks to adults, by Edouard Stevens. Tr. by Mary Ilford. Introd. by Gerard S. Sloyan. Glen Rock,N.J., Paulist [1967, c.1965] 196p. 18cm. (Deus bks.) [BX2170.C5sS73] 1.25 pap.,
1. Church year—Meditations. 2. Church bulletins. I. Title.

STEVENS, Edouard. 242.3
From the housetops; a pastor speaks to adults. Translated by Mary Ilford. Introd. by Gerald S. Sloyan. [1st ed.] New York, Holt, Rinehart and Winston [1965] 197 p. 22 cm. Translation of Pastorale d'un cure de compagne. [BX2170.C55S73] 65-22446
1. Church year — Meditations. 2. Church bulletins. I. Title.

STOREY, William George, 242.3
1923- ed.
Days of the Lord, edited by William G. Storey. [New York] Herder and Herder [1965-66] 3 v. 19 cm. Contents.-- 1. Winter. -- 2. Spring. -- e. Summer and Fall. [BX2170.C55S78] 65-21941
1. Church year — Meditations. 2. Devotional calendars. I. Title.

STRASSER, Bernard 242.3
The dews of Tabor; light and strength for our every day. Foreword by Martin B. Hellriegel New York, Exposition Press [c.1960] 207p. 21cm. (An Exposition-Testament book) 60-3849 4.00
1. Devotional calendars—Catholic Church. I. Title.

STRASSER, Bernard, 1895- 242.3
The dews of Tabor; light and strength for our every day. Foreword by Martin B. Hellriegel. [1st ed.] New York, Exposition Press [1960] 207 p. 21 cm. (An Exposition-Testament book) [BX2182.2.S7] 60-3849
1. Devotional calendars — Catholic Church. I. Title.

STUART, Janet Erskine, 242.3
1857-1914.
Prayer in faith; thoughts for liturgical seasons and feasts. Compiled from the spiritual notes and occasional verses of Janet Erskine Stuart. Edited by L. Keppel, with a foreword by W. F. Brown. Westminster, Md., Newman Press [1951] 277p. 19cm. [BX2170.C55S8 1951] 52-10928
1. Church year—Meditations. I. Title.

WAND, John William Charles, 242.3
Bp. of London, 1885-
Seven steps to heaven. London, New York, Longmans, Green [1956] 99p. 17cm. [BV85.W34] 56-4749
1. Lent—Prayer-books and devotions—English. I. Title.

WAND, John William *242.3
Charles, Bp. of London, 1885-
Seven steps to heaven. London, New York, Longmans, Green [1956] 99 p. 17 cm. [BV85.W34] 56-4749
1. Lent — Prayer-books and devotions — English. I. Title.

WEEK end with God; 242.3
the authentic account of a forty-eight hour period spent at a typical retreat house for men. Recorded with candid photos. [By] Hugh Morley and John Jewell. New York, D. McKay Co. [c1953] 80p. illus. 26cm. [BX2375.M6] 269 53-13299
1. Retreat. I. Morley, Hugh M II. Jewell, John, joint author.

WHEELER, Francis L. 242.3
The days of our life. Edited for American readers by A. Pierce Middleton. New York, Morehouse-Barlow, 1959. 202 p. 20 cm. "An American edition of Think on these things published in England in 1959." [BV4832.2.W5 1959a] 59-15373
1. Devotional literature. 2. Church year. I. Title.

WHEELER, Francis L. 242.3
The days of our life. Edited for American readers by A. Pierce Middleton. New York, Morehouse-Barlow, [c.]1959 xv, 202p. 20cm. 59-15373 2.70 bds.,
1. Devotional literature. 2. Church year. I. Title.

WILDER, Lesley 242.3
The Christian year; meditations of great days and seasons. New York, Collier [1963, c.1961] 157p. 18cm. (AS 509) Orig. pub. under title, The great days and seasons. Bibl. .95 pap.,
1. Devotional calendars. I. Title.

WILDER, Lesley. 242.3
The great days and seasons; meditations for the Christian year. Greenwich, Conn., Seabury Press, 1961. 150 p. 22 cm. [BV4812.W5] 61-12985
1. Devotional calendars. I. Title.

WILDER, Lesley 242.3
The great days and seasons; meditations for the Christian year. Greenwich, Conn., Seabury [c.]1961. 150p. 61-12985 3.50 bds,
1. Devotional calendars. I. Title.

WRIGHT, Richardson Little, 242.3
1887-
A sower went forth. New York, Morehouse-Gorham Co., 1953. 95p. 19cm. [BV85.W72] 53-20854
1. Lent—Prayer-books and devotions—English. I. Title.

ZODIATES, Spyros 242.3
Was Christ God? An exposition of John I-1-18 from the original Greek text, by Spiros Zodhiates. Grand Rapids. Eerdmans [c.1966] ix, 350p. 21cm. Orig. broadcast on New Testament Light radio program & pub. in twelve bklets. [BS2615.3.Z6] 226 66-31308 3.95
1. Bible. N.T. John I. 1-18—Commentaries. I. New Testament light (Radio Program) II. Title.

ALLEN, R. Earl. 242.3'3
Sign of the star [by] R. Earl Allen. Nashville, Broadman Press [1968] 126 p. 20 cm. [BV45.A57] 68-20664
1. Christmas—Meditations. I. Title.

ANDERSON, Raymond. 242.33
The Jesse tree; the heritage of Jesus in stories and symbols of Advent for the family, by Raymond and Georgene Anderson. Philadelphia, Fortress Press [1966] 63 p. col. illus. 19 cm. [BV40.A5] 66-24857
1. Advent — Prayer-books and devotions — English. I. Anderson, Georgene, joint author. II. Title.

ANDERSON, Raymond 242.33
The Jesse tree; the heritage of Jesus in stories and symbols of Advent for the family, by Raymond & Georgene Anderson. Philadelphia, Fortress [c.1966] 63p. col. illus. 19cm. [BV40.A5] 66-24857 1.95, pap.,
1. Advent—Prayer-books and devotions—English. I. Anderson, Georgene, joint author. II. Title.

ARNOLD, Eberhard, 1883- 242.33
1935.
When the time was fulfilled; on Advent and Christmas. Talks and writings by Eberhard Arnold [and others. Edited and translated from the German at the Society of Brothers, Rifton, N.Y.] Rifton, N.Y., Plough Pub. House, 1965. xxvii, 220 p. 20 cm. [BV40.A7] 65-17599
1. Advent. 2. Christmas. 3. Bruderhof Communities — Collections. I. Title.

ARNOLD, Eberhard, 1883- 242.33
1935
When the time was fulfilled; on Advent and Christma. Talks and writings by Eberhard Arnold [others. Ed. and tr. from German at the Soc. of Brothers, Rifton, N.Y.] Rifton, N.Y., Plough [c.]1965. xxvii, 220p. 20cm. [BV40.A7] 65-17599 4.00
1. Advent. 2. Christmas. 3. Bruderhof Communities—Collections. I. Title.

BECK, Victor Emanuel, 242.33
1894-
A book of Christmas and Epiphany, with daily devotions, by Victor E. Beck and Paul M. Lindberg. Illus. by Don Wallerstedt. Rock Island, Ill., Augustana Press [1961] 229p. illus. 21cm. [BV45.B38] 61-17514
1. Christmas. 2. Epiphany. I. Lindberg, Paul M., joint author. II. Title.

BOHRS, Mary Ann. 242'.33
Getting ready for Christmas / Mary Ann Bohrs. Valley Forge, Pa. : Judson Press, [1976] p. cm. A reading, a suggestion for a psalm and hymn, a prayer thought, and a question to think about for each of twenty-two days during the christmas season. [BV45.B59] 76-14930 pbk. : 2.95
1. Christmas—Prayer-books and devotions—English—Juvenile literature. I. Title.

BOONE, Charles Eugene 242.33
The real Christmas [by] Pat Boone. [Westwood, N. J.] Revell [c.1961] 62p. 61-17105 1.50 bds.,
1. Christmas. I. Title.

BOONE, Charles Eugene. 242'.33
The real Christmas [by] Pat Boone. Old Tappan, N.J., F. H. Revell Co. [1972] 63 p. 20 cm. [BV45.B63 1972] 72-6299 ISBN 0-8007-0546-7 2.95
1. Christmas. I. Title.

CELEBRATE while we wait 242'.33
: family devotional resources for Advent and Christmas too / The Schroeder family, Ted, Linda, Christopher, Joel, and Mark. St. Louis : Concordia Pub. House, c1977. 62 p., [1] leaf of plates : ill. ; 28 cm. Devotional readings for each day of Advent with prayers and suggestions for family-involvement activities. [BV40.C43] 77-8587 ISBN 0-570-03052-8 pbk. : 2.95
1. Advent—Prayer-books and devotions—English. 2. Christmas—Prayer-books and devotions—English. 3. Family—Prayer-books and devotions—English. I. Schroeder, Ted, 1937-

COWLEY, Patrick, 1904- 242.33
Advent: its liturgical significance. London, Faith Press; New York, Morehouse-Barlow Co. [1960] 88 p. Includes bibl. 60-51086 1.20 pap.,
1. Advent. I. Title.

CUSHING, Richard James, 242.33
Cardinal, 1895-!!!!
Lent with Christ. [Boston] St. Paul Editions, [1964] 139 p. 19 cm. [BX2170.L4C79] 64-18224
1. Lent — Prayer-books and devotions — English. I. Title.

DALY, Lowrie John. 242.33
Meditations from Advent to Lent, by Lowrie J. Daly and Mary Virgene Daly. With an introd. by Cardinal Ritter. New York, Sheed and Ward [1966] xiii, 236 p. 22 cm. [BX2170.C55D3] 66-22010
1. Church year—Meditations. I. Daly, Mary Virgene, joint author. II. Title.

DARIAN, Mujana. 242'.33
Thoughts to take home: from the three cycles of Advent readings. Chicago, Franciscan Herald Press [1972] ix, 97 p. 21 cm. [BX2170.A4D3] 72-6223 ISBN 0-8199-0446-5 1.95
1. Advent—Meditations. I. Title.

GIBSON, Roxie E. 242'.33
Hey, God: What is Christmas? [By] Roxie E. Gibson. Printed and illustrated by James C. Gibson. Nashville, Impact Books [1973] 62 p. illus. 20 cm. A youngster discusses with God his search for the true meaning of Christmas. [BV45.G48] 73-89188 2.95 (pbk.)
1. Christmas—Juvenile literature. I. Gibson, James C., illus. II. Title.

HARTMAN, Olov. 242.3'3
The birth of God. Translated from the Swedish by Gene J. Lund. Philadelphia, Fortress Press [1969] xvii, 156 p. 19 cm. Translation of passages from various books by O. Hartman. [BV40.H36] 75-84537 2.75 (pbk)
1. Advent—Meditations. 2. Christmas—Meditations. I. Title.

HAYMAN, Carol Bessent. 242'.33
What is Christmas? : [poems and prose] / by Carol Bessent Hayman. Nashville : Tidings, [1974] 56 p. : ill. ; 13 x 19 cm. [BV45.H37] 74-80896 pbk. : 1.35
1. Christmas—Meditations. I. Title.

KOHN, Harold E. 242.3'3
Seeing stars, by Harold Kohn. Nashville, Tenn., Tidings [1971] 77 p. illus. 19 cm. [BV45.K75] 71-182396 1.00
1. Christmas—Meditations. 2. Meditations. I. Title.

*LIEBKNECHT, Henrietta. 242.33
The stranger and other stories [Louisville, Ky., 1968] 140p. 18cm. 3.50; 2.50 pap.,
1. Christmas—Meditations. I. Title.
Order from the author, 415 Trinity Towers, Louisville, Ky. 40202.

METZ, Johannes Baptist, 242.3'3
1928-
The advent of God. Translated by John Drury. [New York] Newman Press [1970] 1 v. (unpaged) illus. 18 cm. [BX2182.2.M45] 74-135760
1. Meditations. I. Title.

MIDDLETON, Robert Lee, 242.33
1894-
God so loved, He gave. Nashville Broadman [c.1965] 126p. 20cm. [BV45.M46] 65-23046 1.50
1. Christmas—Prayer-books and devotions—English. I. Title.

MIDDLETON, Robert Lee, 242.33
1894-
God so loved, He gave. Nashville, Broadman [1967, c.1965] 127p. 21cm. [BV45.M46] 65-23046 2.50
1. Christmas—Prayer-books and devotions—English. I. Title.

MILLER, Charles Edward, 242'.33
1929-
Until He comes; reflections and commentaries on the new liturgical readings for the weekdays of Advent. Reflections by Charles E. Miller; commentaries by John A. Grindel. Staten Island, N.Y., Alba House [1972] x, 94 p. 21 cm. [BX2170.A4M5] 72-8565 ISBN 0-8189-0255-8 2.50
1. Advent—Meditations. I. Grindel, John A. II. Title.

MOORE, Grace. 242'.33
The Advent of women / by Grace Moore. Valley Forge, Pa. : Judson Press, [1975] p. cm. [BV4844.M6] 75-12189 ISBN 0-8170-0691-5 pbk. : 1.00
1. Women—Prayer-books and devotions—English. 2. Advent—Prayer-books and devotions—English. I. Title.

*MUELLER, Charles S. 242.33
The Christian family prepares for Christmas; daily devotions for the Advent season. Special projects by Diane Dieterich. Pencil sketches by Mary Beth Gaitskill. St. Louis, Concordia [c.1965] 63p. illus. 28cm. price unreported. pap.,
I. Title.

*NYBERG, Dennis. 242.33
Advent: a calendar of devotions nineteen sixty-eight Nashville, Abingdon [1968] 62p. 14cm. pap., price unreported.
1. Advent—Prayer. borks and devotions. 2. Christmas—Prayer-works and devotions. I. Title.

PIPPIN, Frank Johnson, 1906- 242.33
The Christmas light and the Easter hope. Decorations by Donald Bologhese. New York, Crowell [1959] 88p. 20cm. [BV45.P55] 60-6236
1. Christmas. 2. Easter. I. Title.

POOVEY, William Arthur, 1913- 242'.33
The days before Christmas : how your family can prepare for the coming of Jesus / W. A. Poovey ; ill. by Audrey Teeple. Minneapolis : Augsburg Pub. House, [1975] 128 p. : ill. ; 20 cm. [BV40.P66] 75-2835 ISBN 0-8066-1480-3 pbk. : 2.95
1. Advent. 2. Advent—Meditations. I. Title.

RAMM, Charles A. 242.33
Meditations on the mystery of Christmas. Edited by Catherine Marie Lilly. Woodblocks by M. Joanne Cullimore. Palo Alto, Calif., Pacific Books [c.1959] 76p. illus. 22cm. 59-15709 3.00
1. Christmas. I. Title.

RAMM, Charles A 1863-1951. 242.33
Meditations on the mystery of Christmas. Edited by Catherine Marie Lilly. Woodblocks by M. Joanne Cullimore. Palo Alto, Calif., Pacific Books [1959] 76p. illus. 22cm. [BV45.R3] 59-15709
1. Christmas. I. Title.

RENARD, Alexandre Charles, 1906- 242.33
Growth in Christ through the Gospels, by Alexandre Renard Translated by Sister Gertrude. Glen Rock, N. J., Paulist Press [1966] 160 p. 19 cm. (Deus books) Translation of Prieres de simplicite, avec les evangiles des dimanches et fetes. [BX2170.C55R43] 66-22050
1. Church year—Meditations. I. Title.

RONGIONE, Louis A. 242'.33
Reform and rejoice; daily homily/meditation - themes for Advent [by] Louis A. Rongione. New York, Alba House [1974] x, 144 p. 21 cm. [BX2170.A4R66] 74-8989 ISBN 0-8189-0294-9
1. Advent—Meditations. I. Title.

SMITH, Dana Prom. 242'.33
Reflections on the light of God : meditations and prayers for Advent and Christmas based on the prologue to the Gospel of John / Dana Prom Smith ; [sketches by Marilyn Barr]. Corte Madera, Calif. : Omega Books, c1976. 121 p. : ill. ; 22 cm. Includes bibliographical references. [BS2615.4.S63] 76-42602 ISBN 0-89353-018-2 pbk. : 4.00
1. Bible. N.T. John I, 1-18—Meditations. 2. Advent—Prayer-books and devotions—English. 3. Christmas—Prayer-books and devotions—English. I. Title.

TEN BOOM, Corrie. 242'.33
Corrie's Christmas memories / Corrie ten Boom. Old Tappan, N.J. : F. H. Revell Co., c1976. p. cm. [BV45.T43] 76-17649 ISBN 0-8007-0822-9 : 3.95
1. Christmas. I. Title.
Contents omitted

TERRA, Russell. 242'.33
The coming God : daily homily/meditation themes for Advent / Russell G. Terra. New York : Alba House, c1976. xii, 123 p. : ill. ; 21 cm. [BX2170.A4T47] 76-12413 ISBN 0-8189-0331-7 pbk. : 3.75
1. Advent—Meditations. I. Title.

THURMAN, Howard, 1899- 242'.33
The mood of Christmas. [1st ed.] New York, Harper & Row [1973] xii, 127 p. 24 cm. Includes selections from the author's previous works. [BV45.T46] 73-6332 ISBN 0-06-068051-2 4.95
1. Christmas—Meditations. I. Title.

TIETJEN, Mary Louise. 242'.33
The Bethlehem tree : a family Advent resource book / Mary Louise Tietjen. New York : Paulist Press, c1976. 132 p. : ill. ; 18 cm. Bibliography: p. 130-132. Presents Advent activities and devotions that prepare Christian families for Christmas. [BV40.T53] 76-9364 ISBN 0-8091-1949-8 pbk. : 3.95
1. Advent. I. Title.

WATT, J. Robert 242.33
The stars of Christmas. [Nashville, Abingdon c.1963] 79p. 20cm. 63-14597 2.50
1. Advent—Meditations. I. Title.

WEST, Edward N. 242.33
The far-spent night. Greenwich, Conn., Seabury Press, 1960. 128 p. 20 cm. [BV40.W44] 60-11087
1. Advent — Meditations. I. Title.

WEST, Edward N. 242.33
The far-spent night. Greenwich, Conn., Seabury Press [c.]1960. 128p. 20cm. 60-11087 2.50 bds.,
1. Advent—Meditations. I. Title.

ABBOTT, Eric Symes, 1906- 242.34
The compassion of God and the passion of Christ; a scriptural meditation for the weeks of Lent. With a foreward by the Bishop of London. New York, D. McKay Co., [1963] 96 p. 17 cm. [BV85.A2 1963] 63-10491
1. Lent — Prayer-books and devotions — English. I. Title.

ABBOTT, Eric Symes, 1906- 242.34
The compassion of God and the passion of Christ; a scriptural meditation for the weeks of Lents. Foreword by the Bishop of London. New York, McKay [c.1963] 96p. 17cm. 63-10491 .95 pap.,
1. Lent—Prayer-books and devotions—English. I. Title.

BARRETT, George West 242.34
Key words for Lent. Greenwich, Conn., Seabury [c.1963] 133p. 20cm. 63-8079 2.75 bds.,
1. Lent—Prayerbooks and devotions—English. I. Title.

BARRETT, George West. 242.34
Key words of Lent. Greenwich, Conn., Seabury Press [c1963] 133 p. 20 cm. [BV85.B34] 63-8079
1. Lent — Prayerbooks and devotions — English. I. Title.

BECK, Victor Emanuel, 1894- 242.34
A book of Lent, with daily devotions, by Victor E. Beck and Paul M. Lindberg. Illus. by Don Wallerstedt. Philadelphia, Fortress Press [1963] 197 p. illus. 21 cm. [BV85.B38] 62-20741
1. Lent — Prayer books and devotions — English I. Lindberg, Paul M., joint author. II. Title.

BECK, Victor Emanuel, 1894- 242.34
A book of Lent, with daily devotions, by Victor E. Beck, Paul M. Lindberg. Illus. by Don Wallerstedt. Philadelphia, Fortress [c.1963] 197p. 21cm. 62-20741 3.25
1. Lent—Prayer-books and devotions—English. I. Lindberg, Paul M., joint author. II. Title.

CASSELS, Louis. 242'.34
A feast for a time of fasting; Meditations for Lent. Nashville, Abingdon Press [1973] 95 p. illus. 20 cm. [BV85.C36] 72-5547 ISBN 0-687-12878-1 2.95
1. Lent—Prayer-books and devotions—English. I. Title.

*CHABANEL, Mother M. 242.34
Gospel initiations for Lent. Introd. by Gregory Baum. Glen Rock, N.J., Paulist Pr. [c.1965] 104p. 18cm. .75 pap.,
I. Title.

CROWE, Charles M. 242.34
The sanctuary: daily devotional readings for Lent. [Nashville, Abingdon Press, c.1961] 44p 15cm. .10 pap.,
1. Meditations for religious occasions—Lent. I. Title.

CUSHING, Richard James, Cardinal, 1895- 242.34
Along with Christ, by Richard Cardinal Cushing. [Boston] St. Paul Editions [1965] 115 p. illus. 19 cm. [BX2170.L4C78] 65-17553
1. Lent — Prayer-books and devotions. 2. Stations of the Cross. I. Title.

CUSHING, Richard James, Cardinal, 1895- 242.34
Along with Christ. [Boston] St.Paul Eds. [dist. Daughters of St. Paul, c.1965] 115p. illus. 19cm. [BX2170.L4C78] 65-17553 2.00; 1.00 pap.,
1. Lent—Prayer-books and devotions. 2. Stations of the Cross. I. Title.

CUSHING, Richard James, Cardinal, 1895- 242.34
A time for remembering [by] Richard Cardinal Cushing Boston] St. Paul Eds. [1966] 111p. 19cm. Orig. appeared as daily messages in the author's 'Just a minute' coloumn of the Boston traveler, during Lent, 1965 [BX2170.L4C82] 66-19617 2.00
1. Lent—Prayer-books and devotions. I. The Boston traveler. II. Title.
Available from the Daughters of St. Paul.

DARIAN, Mujana. 242'.34
Thoughts to take home for Lent; from the three cycles of Lenten readings. Chicago, Franciscan Herald Press [1973] ix, 162 p. 20 cm. [BX2170.L4D37] 73-2619 ISBN 0-8199-0452-X 2.75
1. Lent—Prayer-books and devotions—English. I. Title.

FORD, Josephine Massyngberde. 242.3'4
We are Easter people; a commentery for the time of resurrection [by] J. Massingberd Ford and Ralph A. Keifer. [New York] Herder and Herder [1970] 250 p. 22 cm. Bibliography: p. 238-244. [BX2170.L4F67] 73-110789 6.50
1. Lent—Prayer-books and devotions—English. 2. Easter—Prayer-books and devotions—English. I. Keifer, Ralph A., joint author. II. Title.

FRYHLING, Paul P. 242.34
Steps to crucifixion. Grand Rapids, Mich., Zondervan [c.1961] 117p. (Lenten ser.) 1.95 bds.,
I. Title.

GREENSTOCK, David L 242.34
Lenten meditations. Milwaukee, Bruce Pub. Co. [c1960] 155 p. 19 cm. [[BX2170.L4]] 64-9512 CD
1. Lent — Prayer-books and devotions — English. I. Title.

GRIFFIN, James A. 242'.34
Sackcloth and ashes : liturgical reflections for Lenten weekdays / James A. Griffin. New York : Alba House, c1976. iv, 74 p. ; 21 cm. [BX2170.L4G74 1976] 76-44463 ISBN 0-8189-0325-2 pbk. : 2.95
1. Lent—Prayer-books and devotions—English. I. Title.

HAMMARBERG, Melvin A 242.34
My body broken; a book for Lent. Philadelphia, Fortress Press [1963] 138 p. 20 cm. [BV85.H316] 62-20740
1. Lent—Prayer-books and devotions—English. I. Title.

HAMMARBERG, Melvin A. 242.34
My body broken; a book for Lent. Philadelphia, Fortress [c.1963] 138p. 20cm. Bibl. 62-20740 1.75 pap.,
1. Lent—Prayer-books and devotions—English. I. Title.

HARTMAN, Olov. 242.3'4
The crucified answer. Translated by Gene L. Lund. Philadelphia, Fortress Press [1967] xiv, 201 p. 19 cm. Translation of passages from the author's books originally written in Swedish. [BV85.H378] 67-10983
1. Lent—Prayer-books and devotions. I. Title.

HATCHETT, Marion J. 242.3'4
Lenten prayers for everyman, edited by Marion J. Hatchett. Pref. by Arthur Lichtenberger. Introd. by Sister Sylvia Mary. New York, Morehouse-Barlow Co. [1967] 109 p. 19 cm. [BV85.H39] 67-2676
1. Lent—Prayer-books and devotions. I. Title.

HEAD, David 242.34
Seek a city saint [1st Amer. ed.] New York, Macmillan [1965, c.1964] 128p. 20cm. [BV85.H48] 65-17312 2.95
1. Lent Prayer books and devotions—English. I. Title.

HERBST, Charles M 242.34
A daily thought for Lent. Milwaukee, Bruce Pub. Co. [1960] 90p. 20cm. [BV85.H525] 60-8231
1. Lent—Prayer-books and devotions—English. I. Title.

HERBST, Charles M. 242.3'4
The liturgy of the word in Lent, by Charles M. Herbst. Milwaukee, Bruce Pub. Co. [1967, c1968] viii, 116 p. 22 cm. [BV4277.H39] 68-15912
1. Catholic Church—Sermons. 2. Lenten sermons. 3. Sermons, American. I. Title.

JOHNSON, Theodore E. 242.34
God in the hands of man. Rock Island, Ill., Augustana [1961, c.1962] 74p. 62-8282 1.65 pap.,
1. Lent—Prayer-books and devotions—English. I. Title.

LICHTENBERGER, Arthur, comp. 242.34
The way of renewal; meditations for the forty days of Lent. Greenwich, Conn., Seabury Press, [c.]1960. 64p. 21cm. 60-5818 apply pap.,
1. Lent—Prayer-books and devotions—English. I. Title.

LONNING, Per. 242.34
Pathways of the Passion; daily meditations for the Lenten season, Translated by J. Melvin Moe. Minneapolis, Augsburg Pub. House. [c1965] xi, 148 p. 21 cm. Translation of part 1 of Vandring gjennom fasten. [BT431.L613] 65-12133
1. Jesus Christ — Passion — Meditations. I. Title.

LONNING, Per 242.34
Pathways of the Passion; daily meditations for the Lenten season. Tr. by J. Melvin Moe. Minneapolis, Augsburg [c.1965] xi, 148p. 21cm. [BT431.L613] 65-12133 3.50
1. Jesus Christ—Passion—Meditations. I. Title.

MCCARTHY, Joseph, 1934- 242'.34
Papal bulls and english muffins: meditation for everyday in Lent [by] Joe McCarthy. New York, Paulist Press [1974] vi, 118 p. 18 cm. (Deus books) [BX2170.L4M32] 73-91372 ISBN 0-8091-1812-2 1.25 (pbk.).
1. Lent—Prayer-books and devotions—English. I. Title.

MANNING, Michael, 1940- 242'.34
Pardon my Lenten smile! : Daily homily-meditation themes for Lent / Michael Manning. New York : Alba House, c1976. viii, 130 p. ; 21 cm. [BX2170.L4M36] 75-37881 ISBN 0-8189-0325-2 pbk. : 2.95
1. Lent—Meditations. I. Title.

MILLER, Charles Edward, 1929- 242.3'4
Repentance and renewal; reflections on the new liturgical readings for the weekdays of Lent [by] Charles E. Miller [and] John A. Grindel. Staten Island, N.Y., Alba House [1971] 130 p. 21 cm. [BV4277.M5] 70-148679 ISBN 0-8189-0212-4 2.50
1. Catholic Church—Sermons. 2. Lenten sermons. 3. Sermons, American. I. Grindel, John A., joint author. II. Title.

PARVEY, Constance F. 242'.34
Come Lord Jesus, come quickly : Lenten meditations / Constance F. Parvey. Philadelphia : Fortress Press, c1976. vii, 87 p. ; 20 cm. [BV85.P325] 75-13044 ISBN 0-8006-1212-4 pbk. : 2.75
1. Lent—Prayer-books and devotions—English. I. Title.

POLAERT, Andre 242.3'4
Lord, show us your face: reflections for every day during Lent. Tr. by Anthony Buono. New York, Paulist [1967] ix, 149p. 19cm. (Deus bks.) Tr. of Careme. route de Paques [BX2170.L4P613] 67-15723 .95 pap.,
1. Lent—Prayer-books and devotions. I. Title.

POLAERT, Andre. 242.3'4
Lord, show us your face: reflections for every day during Lent. Translated by Anthony Buono. New York, Paulist Press [1967] ix, 149 p. 19 cm (Deus books) Translation of Careme, route de Paques. [BX2170.L4P613] 67-15723
1. Lent—Prayer-books and devotions. I. Title.

POOVEY, William Arthur, 1913- 242'.34
The days before Easter / W. A. Poovey. Minneapolis : Augsburg Pub. House, c1977. 128 p. ; 20 cm. [BV85.P577] 76-27074 ISBN 0-8066-1557-5 pbk. : 2.95
1. Lent. 2. Lent—Prayer-books and devotions—English. I. Title.

POOVEY, William Arthur, 1913- 242.3'4
What did Jesus do? Meditations and dramas for Lent, by W. A. Poovey. Minneapolis, Augsburg Pub. House [1968, c1969] 128 p. 20 cm. [BV85.P578] 69-14180 2.25
1. Lent—Prayer-books and devotions. 2. Easter—Drama. I. Title.

REMEMBER man; 242.3'4
a Lenten coffee table reader for people who seldom find time for Lenten reading, compiled and designed by Charles E. Jones. Notre Dame, Ind., Ave Maria Press [1971] 89 p. illus. 18 x 23 cm. [BX2170.L4R4] 79-149591 ISBN 0-87793-032-5 3.95
1. Lent—Prayer-books and devotions. I. Jones, Charles Edward, 1926- ed.

SHERLEY-PRICE, Leo 242.34
Lent with Mother Julian. Readings from her 'Revelations of Divine Love. New York, Morehouse [c.1962] 69p. 5.00 pap.,
I. Title.

SHINN, Roger Lincoln. 242.34
Moments of truth; a devotional book for Lent. Philadelphia, United Church Press [1964] 112 p. illus. 19 cm. [BV85.S5] 64-14138

1. Lent—Prayer-books and devotions—English. I. Title.

SHINN, Roger Lincoln 242.34
Moments of truth; a devotional book for Lent. Philadelphia, United Church [c.1964] 112p. illus. 19cm. 64-14138 1.45 pap.,
1. Lent—Prayer-books and devotions—English. I. Title.

SMITH, Frederick Augustus 242.34
The multiphase cross; a group of Lenten meditations. New York, Greenwich Book Publishers [c.1960] 59p. 21cm. 60-7814 2.50
1. Lent—Prayer-books and devotions—English. I. Title.

SMITH, Frederick Augustus, 242.34
1897-
The multiphase cross; a group of Lenten meditations. [1st ed.] New York, Greenwich Book Publishers [1960] 59 p. 21 cm. [BV85.S615] 60-7814
1. Lent — Prayer-books and devotions — English. I. Title.

TEMPLE, William, Abp. of 242.34
Canterbury, 1881-1944.
Lent with William Temple; selections from his writings, edited by G. P. Mallick Belshaw. New York, Morehouse-Barlow Co. [1966] 110 p. 19 cm. Bibliography: p. 110. [BV85.T4] 66-1830
1. Lent — Prayer-books and devotions. I. Belshaw, G. P. Mellick, ed. II. Title.

TEMPLE, William, Abp. of 242.34
Canterbury, 1881-1944
Lent with William Temple; selections from his writings, ed. by G. P. Mellick Belshaw. New York, Morehouse [c.1966] 110p. 19cm. Bibl. [BV85.T4] 66-1830 1.95 pap.,
1. Lent—Prayer-books and devotions. I. Belshaw, G. P. Mellick, ed. II. Title.

TERRIEN, Samuel L., 1911- 242.3'4
The power to bring forth; daily meditations for Lent [by] Samuel L. Terrien. Philadelphia, Fortress Press [1968] 182 p. 18 cm. (A Fortress paperback original) Bibliography: p. 178-182. [BV85.T42] 68-11704
1. Lent—Prayer-books and devotions. I. Title.

UNDERHILL, Evelyn, 1875- 242.34
1951
Lent with Evelyn Underhill; selections from her writings. Ed. by G. P. Mellick Belshaw. New York, Morehouse, 1964. 105p. 19cm. 64-582 1.75 pap.,
1. Lent—Prayer-books and devotions—English. I. Title.

WARREN, Matthew M 242.34
The slow of heart. [1st ed.] New York, Harper [1959] 124 p. 20 cm. [BV85.W36] 59-5547
1. Lent — Prayer-books and devotions — English. I. Title.

*WEDGE, Florence. 242.3'4
The new look of Lent. Pulaski, Wis., Franciscan Pubs. [1968] 62p. 19cm. Cover title: The new lok of Lent: penance. .35 pap.,
1. Lent—Meditations. I. Title.

WESLEY, John, 1703-1791. 242.34
Lent with John Wesley; selections from his writings, edited by Gordon S. Wakefield. With a foreword by J. W. C. Wand. New York, Morehouse-Barlow [1965] 106 p. 19 cm. [BV85.W39] 65-1850
1. Lent — Prayer-books and devotions — English. I. Wakefield, Gordon Stevens, ed. II. Title.

WESLEY, John, 1703-1791 242.34
Lent with John Wesley; selections from his writings, ed. by Gordon S. Wakefield. Foreword by J. W. C. Wand. New York, Morehouse-Barlow [c.1965] 106p. 19cm. [BV85.W39] 65-1850 1.75 pap.,
1. Lent—Prayer-books and devotions—English. I. Wakefield, Gordon Stevens, ed. II. Title.

*WROBLEWSKI, Sergius. 242.3'4
Growth in Christ; readings for Lent. Pulaski, Wis., Franciscan Pubs. [1968] 80p. 19cm. .50 pap.,
1. Lent—Prayer-books and devotions. I. Title.

CLARKSON, E. Margaret 242.35
The wondrous cross; meditations on the Cross of Christ. Chicago, Moody [c.1966] 63p. illus. (pt. col.) 21cm. .95 pap.,
I. Title.

CLELAND, James T 242.35
He died as He lived; meditations on the seven words from the Cross [by] James T. Cleland. New York, Abingdon Press [1966] 79 p. 21 cm. [BT456.C55] 66-11058
1. Jesus Christ — Seven last words — Sermons. 2. Sermons, American. I. Title.

CLELAND, James T. 242.35
He died as He lived; meditations on the seven words from the Cross. Nashville, Abingdon [c.1966] 79p. 21cm. [BT456.C55] 66-11058 2.00
1. Jesus Christ—Seven last words—Sermons. 2. Sermons, American. I. Title.

ELPHINSTONE-FYFFE, John M. 242.35
Three hours, a new form of the Good Friday service. New York, Oxford Univ. Press [c.] 1961[ ] 61-2333 2.00
I. Title.

HAUSHALTER, Walter 242.3'5
Milton, 1889-
The crucifixion of superiority, by Walter M. Haushalter. Philadelphia. Dorrance [1967] 51p. 20cm. [BV95.H3] 66-28861 2.50
1. Good Friday sermons. 2. Jesus Christ—Passion—Sermons. I. Title.

MOULE, Charles Francis 242'.35
Digby.
The energy of God : talks about the meaning of Holy Week / [by] C. F. D. Moule. London : British Broadcasting Corporation, 1976. 30 p. ; 21 cm. "Professor Moule's talks were broadcast on Radio 4 and have been edited slightly for publication." [BT431.M69] 77-354248 ISBN 0-563-17101-4 : £0.55
1. Jesus Christ—Passion—Addresses, essays, lectures. I. Title.

NEWHOUSE, Flower Arlene 242.35
(Sechler) 1909-
The drama of incarnation [2d ed.] Escondido, Calif., Christward Pubns., Box 1628, 92026 [1965, c.1948] 82p. illus. 25cm. [BT414.N4] 65-4088 2.50
1. Holy Week—Meditations. 2. Christward Ministry. I. Title.

SMITH, Bernie, 1920- 242.3'5
Journey to Calvary. Grand Rapids, Baker Bk. [1967, c.1966] 88p. 21cm. [BT431.S58] 67-15766 1.95
1. Jesus Christ—Passion—Devotional literature. I. Title.

TARGET, George William. 242.3'5
We, the crucifiers, by G. W. Target. Grand Rapids, W. B. Eerdmans [1969, c1964] 159 p. 19 cm. [BT431.T3 1969] 69-12320 1.95
1. Jesus Christ—Passion—Meditations. 2. Christianity—20th century. I. Title.

WILLIAMS, Harry Abbott 242.35
God's wisdom in Christ's cross. New York, Morehouse-Barlow Co. [1960] 48p. 19cm. 60-1417 .80 pap.,
1. Holy-Week sermons. 2. Sermons, English. I. Title.

WISE, Charles C 242.35
Windows on the Passion [by] Charles C. Wise, Jr. Nashville, Abingdon Press [1967] 143 p. 21 cm. [BT431.W5] 67-11007
1. Jesus Christ — Passion — Meditations. I. Title.

WISE, Charles C. 242.35
Windows on the Passion [by] Charles C. Wise, Jr. Nashville, Abingdon Press [1967] 143 p. 21 cm. [BT431.W5] 67-11007
1. Jesus Christ—Passion—Meditations. I. Title.

WOODSON, Leslie H., 1929- 242.3'5
Eight days of glory; reflections on Holy Week. Grand Rapids, Mich., Baker Book House [1972, c.1971] 134 p. 19 cm. Includes bibliographical references. [BV4298.W66] ISBN 0-8010-9532-8 pap., 1.95
1. Holy Week sermons. 2. Methodist Church—Sermons. 3. Sermons, American. I. Title.
L.C. card no. for original edition: 76-140906.

YZERMANS, Vincent Arthur, 242.35
1925-
Death and resurrection; meditations on Holy Week from the Church Fathers, with Scripture readings from the Revised standard version. Foreword by Peter W. Bartholome, Bishop of St. Cloud. Collegeville, Minn., Liturgical Press, St. John's Abbey [1963] 92 p. illus. 24 cm. [BX2170.H6Y9] 63-3044
1. Holy Week — Meditations. I. Bible. N.T. English. Selections. 1963. Revised standard. II. Title.

YZERMANS, Vincent Arthur, 242.35
1925-
Death and resurrection; meditations on Holy Week from the Church Fathers, with Scripture readings from the Revised standard version. Foreword by Peter W. Bartholome, Bishop of St. Cloud. Collegeville, Minn., St. John's Abbey Liturgical Pr., [c.1963] 92p. illus. 24cm. 63-3044 2.00
1. Holy Week—Meditations. I. Bible. N. T. English. Selections. 1963. Revised standard. II. Title.

LINDBERG, Paul M 242.36
A book of Easter, with daily devotions, by Paul M. Lindberg. Illus. by Don Wallerstedt. Philadelphia, Fortress Press [1965] 192 p. illus. 20 cm. [BV55.L5] 65-10708
1. Easter — Prayer-books and devotions. I. Title.

LINDBERG, Paul M. 242.36
A book of Easter, with daily devotions. Illus. by Don Wallerstedt. Philadelphia, Fortress [c.1965] 192p. illus. 20cm. [BV55.L5] 65-10708 3.75
1. Easter—Prayer-books and devotions. I. Title.

LONG, Simon Peter, 1860- 242.36
1929.
The wounded Word; a brief meditation on the seven sayings of Christ on the cross, by S. P. Long. Grand Rapids, Mich., Baker Book House [1966, c1904] 87 p. 20 cm. [BT455.L8 1966] 66-31820
1. Jesus Christ—Seven last words. I. Title.

BREWSTER, H. Pomeroy, 242'.37
d.1906.
Saints and festivals of the Christian church. New York, F. A. Stokes Co. Detroit, Gale Research Co., 1974. xiv, 558 p. illus. 22 cm. "A considerable part of the matter presented in the following pages was printed [as] a series of articles in the Union and advertiser of Rochester, N.Y." Reprint of the 1904 ed. [BR1710.B7 1974] 73-159896 ISBN 0-8103-3992-7 17.50
1. Christian saints—Calendar. 2. Fasts and feasts. I. Title.

*FOLEY, Leonard, ed. 242'.37
Saint of the day. Cincinnati, St. Anthony Messenger Press [1974] 161 p. illus. 18 cm. Includes index Contents.Contents: Vol. 1: January-June [BR1710] ISBN 0-912228-16-4 1.95 (pbk.)
1. Saints—Calendar. 2. Christian saints—Calendar. I. Title.

ABNEY, Beth Mobley. 242'.4
Thanksgiving every week / by Beth Mobley Abney. Athens, Ga. : Abney, c1975. 123 p. : ill. ; 23 cm. Includes bibliographical references. [BX8495.A37A37] 75-25469
1. Abney, Beth Mobley. 2. Meditations. I. Title.

ALLEN, Charles Livingstone, 242.4
1913-
When you lose a loved one. [Westwood, N. J.] F. H. Revell Co. [1959] 61p. 20cm. [BV4905.2.A4] 59-5495
1. Consolation. I. Title.

ALLEN, R. Earl. 242.4
Strength from shadows [by] R. Earl Allen. Nashville, Broadman Press [1967] 112 p. 21 cm. [BV4905.2.A45] 67-19395
1. Consolation. I. Title.

ANDERSON, Colena M. 242'.4
Joy beyond grief / by Colena M. Anderson. Grand Rapids : Zondervan Pub. House, [1974] 80 p. : ill. ; 22 cm. Includes bibliographical references. [BV4905.2.A52] 74-1612 4.95
1. Consolation. I. Title.

ANGELL, James W. 242'.4
O Susan! By James W. Angell. Anderson, Ind., Warner Press [1973] 125 p. 22 cm. Includes bibliographical references. [BV4907.A53] 73-5678 ISBN 0-87162-158-4 3.95
1. Consolation. I. Title.

BAKER, Pat A., 1931- 242'.4
In this moment / Pat A. Baker. Nashville : Abingdon, c1977. 94 p. ; 20 cm. [BV4832.2.B27] 76-28802 ISBN 0-687-19445-8 : 4.95
1. Meditations. I. Title.

BARCLAY, William. lecturer 242.4
in the University of Glasgow.
Prayers for help and healing. [1st U.S. ed.] New York, Harper [1968] 124p. 18cm. [BV270.B3 1968] 68-29568 3.50
1. Sick—Prayer-books and devotions. I. Title.

BARCLAY, William, lecturer 242.4
in the University of Glasgow.
Prayers for help and healing. New York, Harper & Row [1975, c1968] 124 p. 18 cm. [BV270.B3] 68-29568 ISBN 0-06-060481-6 1.75 (pbk.)
1. Sick—Prayer-books and devotions. I. Title.

BENTON, Josephine Moffett. 242.4
A door ajar. Philadelphia, United Church Press [1965] 127 p. 21 cm. "Sources and acknowledgments": p. 125-127. [BV4905.2.B4] 65-16442
1. Consolation. 2. Death. I. Title.

BERNER, Carl W. 242'.4
Why me, Lord? Meaning and comfort in times of trouble [by] Carl W. Berner. Minneapolis, Augsburg Pub. House [1973] 112 p. 20 cm. [BV4905.2.B43] 73-78267 ISBN 0-8066-1331-9 2.50 (pbk.)
1. Consolation. I. Title.

BISHOP, Bette, comp. 242.4
I will lift up mine eyes; inspiring words of comfort and hope. Illustrated by Paula Krekovich. [Kansas City, Mo.] Hallmark Editions [1968] 60 p. illus. 20 cm. [BV4900.B5] 68-23460 2.50
1. Consolation. I. Title.

BJORGE, James R. 242'.4
And heaven and nature sing / James R. Bjorge. St. Louis : Concordia Pub. House, c1977. 96 p. : col. ill. ; 26 cm. [BV4832.2.B52] 76-30407 ISBN 0-570-03047-1 pbk. : 3.95
1. Meditations. 2. Sight-saving books. I. Title.

BOLDING, Amy. 242.4
Kind words for sad hearts, for times of bereavement. Grand Rapids, Baker Book House [1967] 132 p. 21 cm. [BV4905.2.B64] 67-18172
1. Consolation. I. Title.

BOYD, Malcolm, 1923- 242'.4
The lover. Waco, Tex., Word Books [1972] 176 p. 23 cm. [BV4832.2.B683] 72-84155 4.95
1. Meditations. I. Title.

BRACHER, Marjory Louise 242.4
The anchor of hope; meditations for the seriously ill. Philadelphia, Fortress [c.1964] 63p. 15cm. Alternate pages blank. 64-18149 1.25 bds.,
1. Sick—Prayer-books and devotions—English. I. Title.

BRANDT, Catharine. 242'.4
Flowers for the living / Catharine Brandt. Minneapolis : Augsburg Pub. House, c1977. 96 p. : ill. ; 20 cm. Bibliography: p. 95-96. [BV4908.B69] 77-72449 ISBN 0-8066-1585-0 pbk. : 2.95
1. Widows—Prayer-books and devotions—English. I. Title.

BRENNEMAN, Helen Good. 242.4
My comforters; a book of daily inspiration for those who are ill. Scottdale, Pa., Herald Press [1966] 80 p. illus., port. 27 cm. [BV4910.B74] 66-13156
1. Sick — Prayer-books and devotions. I. Title.

BRENNEMAN, Helen Good 242.4
My comforters; a book of daily inspiration for those who are ill. Scottdale, Pa., Herald Pr. [c.1966] 80p. illus., port. 27cm. [BV4910.B74] 66-13156 1.50 pap.,
1. Sick—Prayer-books and devotions. I. Title.

BROWN, Henry Clifton. 242.4
A search for strength, by H. C. Brown, Jr. Waco, Tex., Word Books [1967] 126 p. 20 cm. [BV4905.2.B7] 67-30168
1. Consolidation. I. Title.

BUNYAN, John, 1628-1688 242.4
Heart's ease for heart trouble. Ed., introd. by N. A. Woychuk. St. Louis, Miracle Pr., 1963. 96p. illus. 20cm. 63-4736 apply
1. Consolidation—Early works to 1800. I. Title.

BURTON, Alma P., 1913- 242.4
comp.
For they shall be comforted, by Alma P. and Clea M. Burton. Salt Lake City, Utah, Deseret Bk. Co., 1964. 106p. 20cm. [BV4900.B85] 64-57119 1.75
1. Consolation—Collections. I. Burton, Clea M., joint comp. II. Title.

CAMPION, Albert E comp. 242.4
Prayers for Christian healing. New York, Morehouse-Gorham [1958] 96p. 18cm. [BV270.C2] 58-11445
1. Sick—Prayer-books and devotions—English. I. Title.

CHAKOUR, Charles M., 1929- 242'.4
Brief funeral meditations [by] Charles M. Chakour. Nashville, Abingdon Press [1971] 96 p. 20 cm. [BV199.F8C45] 70-134246 ISBN 0-687-03980-0 2.95
1. Funeral service. 2. Death—Meditations. I. Title.

CHAPMAN, Ian M. 242'.4
Do a loving thing / Ian M. Chapman. Valley Forge, Pa. : Judson Press, c1977. 63 p., [4] leaves ; 22 cm. Includes bibliographical references. [BS2675.4.C46] 76-48750 ISBN 0-8170-0717-2 pbk. : 2.75
1. Bible. N.T. 1 Corinthians XIII—Meditations. 2. Love (Theology)—Meditations. I. Title.

CHURCH, Leslie Frederic, 242'.4
1886-
Knight of the burning heart; the story of John Wesley. New York, Abingdon-Cokesbury

Press [1953] 185 p. 19cm. [BX8495.W5C] A53
1. Wesley, john,1703-1791. I. Title.

CLARKSON, Edith Margaret, 1915- 242'.4
Grace grows best in winter : help for those who must suffer / by Margaret Clarkson. Grand Rapids : Zondervan Pub. House, [1975] c1972. p. cm. Large print ed. [BV4909.C56 1975] 75-25997 4.95
1. Suffering. 2. Sight-saving books. I. Title.

CLERK, N. W. [pseud.] 242.4
A grief observed. Greenwich, Conn., Seabury, 1963 [c.1961] 60p.22cm. 63-10447 2.00 bds.,
1. Consolation. I. Title.

CLIFFORD, Joan. 242'.4
The young John Wesley; illustrated by Arthur Roberts. London, Parrish; New York, Roy Publishers [1966] 126 p. illus. 20 1/2 cm. 12/6 [BX8495.W5C56 1966] 67-72555
1. Wesley, John, 1703-1791 — Juvenile literature. I. Title.

*CORNILS, Stanley P. 242.4
Managing grief wisely. Grand Rapids, Mich., Baker Bk. [1967] 51p. 21cm. Bibl. .85 pap.,
1. Grief—Consolation. I. Title.

CRUMPLER, Frank H. 242'.4
God is near; bedside companion of inspiration and strength [by] Frank H. Crumpler. Old Tappan, N.J., F. H. Revell [1973] 63 p. 19 cm. [BV4910.C78] 73-1707 ISBN 0-8007-0589-0 2.50
1. Sick—Prayer-books and devotions—English. I. Title.

DAWSON, Louise Susie (Dewey) 1895- 242'.4
Vital faith. Foreword by W. S. Kendall. Seattle, Printed by L. & H. Print. Co. [1962] 61 p. illus., ports., music. 28 cm. [BX8495.D35D3] 64-28485
1. Dawson, Franklin Raymond, 1894-1960. I. Title.

DE LACZAY, Etti. 242'.4
Loneliness. New York, Hawthorn Books [1972] 64 p. illus. 21 cm. [BV4911.D43] 73-39247 1.25 ($1.45 Can)
1. Loneliness.

DIBDEN, Jean T. 242'.4
God within : another listener / Jean T. Dibden. Old Tappan, N.J. : Revell, c1977. p. cm. (Spire books) [BV4832.2.D5] 77-9564 ISBN 0-8007-8306-9 pbk. : 1.50
1. Meditations. I. Title.

DICKS, Russell Leslie, 1906- 242.4
And peace at the last; a study of death, the unreconciled subject of our times, by Russell L. Dicks and Thomas S. Kepler. Philadelphia, Westminster Press [1953] 94p. 20cm. (The Westminster pastoral aid books) [BT825.D5] 53-6651
1. Death. I. Kepler, Thomas Samuel, 1897- joint author. II. Title.

DILDAY, Russell H. 242'.4
You can overcome discouragement / Russell H. Dilday, Jr. Nashville : Broadman Press, c1977. 127 p. ; 20 cm. [BV4905.2.D47] 76-24063 ISBN 0-8054-5247-8 pbk. : 2.50
1. Consolation. 2. Devotional literature. I. Title.

DOERFFLER, Alfred, 1884- 242'.4
The burden made light / Alfred Doerffler. St. Louis : Concordia Pub. House, [1975] p. cm. [BV4910.D6] 74-34213 ISBN 0-570-03026-9 pbk. : 3.95
1. Sick—Prayer-books and devotions—English. I. Title.

DOERFFLER, Alfred, 1884- 242'.4
The yoke made easy / Alfred Doerffler. St. Louis : Concordia Pub. House, [1975] p. cm. Large print ed. [BV4910.D63 1975] 75-2344 ISBN 0-570-03027-7 pbk. : 3.95
1. Sick—Prayer-books and devotions—English. 2. Meditations. 3. Sight-saving books. I. Title.

DOHERTY, Edward Joseph, 1890-1975. 242'.4
Psalms of a sinner / by Eddie Doherty ; with a foreword by Catherine de Hueck Doherty. St. Meinrad, IN : Abbey Press, 1976. x, 138 p. : ill. ; 21 cm. [BV4832.2.D63 1976] 76-226 ISBN 0-87029-058-4 pbk. : 2.95
1. Meditations. I. Title.

*DRAKOS, Theodore Soter. 242.4
How to pray for Vietnam. New York, 1968. 48p. 11cm. 1.00 pap.,
1. Vietnam—Prayers. I. Title.
Order from the author, 102-01 Ascan Avenue, Forest Hills New York, 11375.

EAGLESON, Hodge MacIlvain, 1895- 242.4
A handful of certainties. Boston, Christopher Pub. House [1966] 108p. 21cm. [BV4907E2] 66-19215 2.50
1. Children—Death and future state. 2. Consolation. I. Title.

ERDAHL, Lowell O. 242'.4
The lonely house / Lowell O. Erdahl. Nashville : Abingdon, c1977. 112 p. ; 20 cm. [BV4905.2.E73] 77-1907 ISBN 0-687-22589-2 : 5.95
1. Consolation. I. Title.

ERDAHL, Lowell O. 242'.4
The lonely house / Lowell O. Erdahl. Nashville : Abingdon, c1977. 112 p. ; 20 cm. [BV4905.2.E73] 77-1907 ISBN 0-687-22589-2 : 5.95
1. Consolation. I. Title.

EVANS, C. Stephen. 242'.4
Despair; a moment or a way of life? [By] C. Stephen Evans. Downers Grove, Ill., Inter-varsity Press [1971] 135 p. 18 cm. Includes bibliographical references. [BJ1488.E9] 78-169906 ISBN 0-87784-699-5
1. Despair. 2. Hope.

FALEY, Roland James. 242'.4
The cup of grief : biblical reflections on sin, suffering, and death / Roland J. Faley. New York : Alba House, c1977. ix, 159 p. ; 21 cm. Includes bibliographical references. [BS680.G6F34] 77-6839 ISBN 0-8189-0352-X : 4.95
1. Good and evil—Biblical teaching. 2. Theodicy. I. Title.

FALEY, Roland James. 242'.4
The cup of grief : biblical reflections on sin, suffering, and death / Roland J. Faley. New York : Alba House, c1977. ix, 159 p. ; 21 cm. Includes bibliographical references. [BS680.G6F34] 77-6839 ISBN 0-8189-0352-X : 4.95
1. Good and evil—Biblical teaching. 2. Theodicy. I. Title.

*FLEECE, Isabel 242.4
Not by accident. Introd. by Stephen F. Olford. Chicago, Moody [c.1964] 72p. 19cm. 1.00 pap.,
I. Title.

FLINT, Cort R. 242.4
Grief's slow wisdom, by Cort R. Flint. [1st ed.] Anderson, S. C., Droke House; dist. by Grosset New York [1967] 56p. 20cm. Bibl. [BV4905.2.F65] 67-13266 2.00 bds.,
1. Consolation. I. Title.

FOLLIET, Joseph. 242.4
Invitation to joy. Translated by Edmond Bonin. Glen Rock, N.J., Newman Press [1968] 117 p. 21 cm. [BV4905.2.F613] 68-55582 4.50
1. Joy. I. Bonin, Edmond, tr. II. Title.

FULLER, Dorothy Mason, comp. 242'.4
Light in hours of darkness; readings for the grief-stricken, selected and arranged by Dorothy Mason Fuller. Nashville, Abingdon Press [1971] 78 p. illus. 27 cm. [BV4900.F83] 77-162456 ISBN 0-687-22013-0
1. Consolation—Collections. I. Title.

GALLOWAY, Dale E. 242'.4
Dream a new dream : how to rebuild a broken life / Dale E. Galloway. Wheaton, Ill. : Tyndale House Publishers, c1975. 128 p. ; 22 cm. Includes bibliographical references. [BV4905.2.G3] 75-7222 ISBN 0-8423-0675-7 : 4.95
1. Galloway, Dale E. 2. Consolation. I. Title.

GALLOWAY, Dale E. 242'.4
Dream a new dream : how to rebuild a broken life / Dale E. Galloway. Wheaton, Ill. : Tyndale House Publishers, c1975. 128 p. ; 22 cm. Includes bibliographical references. [BV4905.2.G3] 75-7222 ISBN 0-8423-0675-7 : 4.95
1. Galloway, Dale E. 2. Consolation. I. Title.

GILLET, Lev. 242'.4
In Thy presence / by Lev Gillet. Crestwood, N.Y. : St. Vladimir's Seminary Press, 1977. p. cm. [BX383.G54 1977] 77-1040 ISBN 0-913836-34-6 pbk. : 2.95
1. Meditations. I. Title.

GILLET, Lev. 242'.4
In Thy presence / by Lev Gillet. Crestwood, N.Y. : St. Vladimir's Seminary Press, 1977. p. cm. [BX383.G54 1977] 77-1040 ISBN 0-913836-34-6 pbk. : 2.95
1. Meditations. I. Title.

GIUDICE, Liliane, 1913- 242'.4
Alone until tomorrow. [Translated by David E. Green] Atlanta, John Knox Press [1974] 64 p. 21 cm. Translation of Ohne meinen Mann. [BF575.G7G5813] 73-16912 ISBN 0-8042-1982-6 3.95
1. Bereavement—Personal narratives. I. Title.

GOCKEL, Herman William, 1906- 242.4
My Father's world. by Herman W. Gockel. St. Louis. Concordia [1967, c.1966] xi. 64p. 15cm. [BV4832.2.G58] 67-13291 1.50
1. Devotional literature. I. Title.

GOCKEL, Herman William, 1906- 242.4
My Father's world, by Herman W. Gockel. St. Louis, Concordia Pub. House [1967, c1966] xi, 64 p. 15 cm. [BV4832.2.G58] 67-13291
1. Devotional literature. I. Title.

GOODRICH, Robert E., Jr. 242.4
On the other side of sorrow. Nashville, Abingdon [c.1955-1962] 31p. 18cm. 1.00 bds.,
I. Title.

GOULOOZE, William, 1903-1955. 242.4
Glory awaits me. Memorial ed. Grand Rapids, Baker Book House, 1956. 112p. 20cm. [BV4905.G635] 56-7008
1. Consolation. I. Title.

GRANTHAM, Rudolph E. 242'.4
The healing relationship, by Rudolph E. Grantham. [Nashville] The Upper Room [1972] 79 p. 18 cm. [BV4910.G7] 72-81154 1.00
1. Sick—Prayer-books and devotions—English. I. Title.

GRAVES, Charles B., 1926- 242'.4
When tragedy strikes / Charles B. Graves, Jr. Chicago : Moody Press, 1976, c1972. 111 p. ; 18 cm. [BV4905.2.G7 1976] 75-29016 ISBN 0-8024-9429-3 pbk. : 1.25
1. Consolation. I. Title.

GREENBERG, Sidney, 1917- ed. 242.4
A treasury of comfort. New York, Crown Publishers [1954] 277p. 22cm. Verae and prose. [BV4900.G68] 54-11178
1. Consolation. I. Title.

GREENBERG, Sidney, 1917- ed. 242.4
A treasury of comfort. 1967 ed. Hollywood, Calif., Wilshire [1967, c.1954] 277p. 21cm. Verse and prose [BV4900.G68] 2.00 pap.,
1. Consolation. I. Title.

GREENBERG, Sidney, 1917- ed. 242'.4
A treasury of comfort : consolation, hope, and guidance for the bereaved / edited by Sidney Greenberg. Expanded and rev. ed. New York : Hartmore House, c1975. x, 310 p. ; 22 cm. [BV4900.G68 1975] 74-32508 ISBN 0-87677-022-7 : 7.95
1. Consolation—Collected works. I. Title.

GROLLMAN, Earl A. 242'.4
Living when a loved one has died / Earl A. Grollman. Boston : Beacon Press, c1977. xi, 115 p. : ill. ; 21 cm. [BJ1487.G73] 76-48508 ISBN 0-8070-2740-5 7.95
1. Grief. 2. Consolation. I. Title.

GROLLMAN, Earl A. 242'.4
Living when a loved one has died / Earl A. Grollman. Boston : Beacon Press, c1977. xi, 115 p. : ill. ; 21 cm. [BJ1487.G73] 76-48508 ISBN 0-8070-2740-5 7.95
1. Grief. 2. Consolation. I. Title.

*HALVERSON, Richard C. 242'.4
Perspective devotional thoughts for men. Grand Rapids, Mich., Zondervan [1973, c.1957] 203 p. 18 cm. [BV4832.2] 0.95 (pbk)
1. Devotional exercises. I. Title.

HARRITY, Michael. 242'.4
Thoughts on suffering, sorrow, and death. Huntington, Ind., Our Sunday Visitor [1973] 96 p. 18 cm. [BT732.7.H3] 73-86976 ISBN 0-87973-812-X
1. Suffering. 2. Meditations. I. Title.

HAVEN, Robert Marshall, 1926- 242.4
Look at us, Lord. Photos. by James R. Finney. Design by Nancy R. Bozeman. Nashville, Abingdon Press [1969] [96] p. illus. 24 cm. [BV245.H34] 69-19736 4.95
1. Prayers. I. Finney, James R., illus. II. Title.

HAVNER, Vance, 1901- 242'.4
Though I walk through the valley. Old Tappan, N.J., F. H. Revell [1974] 128 p. port. 21 cm. [BV4905.2.H38] 74-1404 ISBN 0-8007-0654-4 3.95
1. Havner, Vance, 1901- 2. Consolation. I. Title.

HEUBACH, Paul 242.4
The problem of human suffering. Washington, D.C., Review and Hearld [c.1963] 49p. 14cm. .15 pap.,
1. Consolation. I. Title.

HOBBS, Herschel H 242.4
When the rain falls: comfort for troubled hearts, by Herschel H. Hobbs. Grand Rapids, Baker Book House [1967] 89 p. 21 cm. [BV4905.2.H58] 67-26188
1. Consolation. I. Title.

HOBBS, Herschel H. 242.4
When the rain falls; comfort for troubled hearts, by Herschel H. Hobbs. Grand Rapids, Baker Book House [1967] 89 p. 21 cm. [BV4905.2.H58] 67-26188
1. Consolation. I. Title.

HOFFMAN, Dona, 1932- 242'.4
Yes, Lord / Dona Hoffman. St. Louis : Concordia Pub. House, [1975] p. cm. Includes correspondence between the author and Paul G. Bretscher. [BV4909.H6] 74-30867 ISBN 0-570-03195-8 pbk. : 3.95
1. Hoffman, Dona, 1932- 2. Bretscher, Paul G. 3. Suffering. 4. Consolation. I. Bretscher, Paul G. II. Title.

HOLMES, Marjorie, 1910- 242'.4
Beauty in your own backyard / Marjorie Holmes ; photos. by Elizabeth P. Welsh. McLean, Va. : EPM Publications, c1976. 128 p. : ill. ; 24 cm. [BV4832.2.H635] 76-28719 ISBN 0-914440-15-2 : 12.95
1. Meditations. I. Welsh, Elizabeth P. II. Title.

HORNE, Hugh R 242.4
Light in the dark valleys. Grand Rapids, Eerdmans [1958] 121p. 23cm. [BV4905.2.H6] 58-59781
1. Consolation. I. Title.

HOSMER, John Wesley. 242.4
The immortal hope; meditations for those who mourn. Boston, Christopher Pub. House [1955] 128p. 21cm. [BV4905.H66] 55-37388
1. Consolation. I. Title.

HUNT, Gladys M. 242'.4
The Christian way of death, by Gladys Hunt. Grand Rapids, Mich., Zondervan Pub. House [1971] 117 p. 21 cm. (A Zondervan "reflections" book) [BT825.H86] 77-133362 3.50
1. Death. I. Title.

HUNT, Ruth. 242'.4
Sparrow on the house top : reaching beyond loneliness to true peace and joy / by Ruth Hunt. Old Tappan, N.J. : F. H. Revell Co., c1976. p. cm. [BS571.H793] 76-18182 ISBN 0-8007-0814-8 ; 5.95
1. Bible—Biography. 2. Loneliness. I. Title.

HUOT, Patricia W., comp. 242'.4
The Lord is my shepherd. Compiled by Patricia W. Huot. New York, World Pub. Co. [1970] 45 p. 21 cm. Verse and prose. [PN6084.C57H8 1970] 71-131160
1. Quotations, English. 2. Consolation. I. Title.

IKERMAN, Ruth C. 242'.4
A little book of comfort / Ruth C. Ikerman. Nashville : Abingdon, c1976. 79 p. ; 21 cm. [BV4905.2.I38] 75-34421 ISBN 0-687-22145-5 : 3.95
1. Consolation. 2. Bereavement. I. Title.

IN quietness and confidence : a book of devotions / compiled by V. Raymond Edman. Wheaton, Ill. : Victor Books, c1976. 64 p. : ill. ; 20 cm. [BV4832.2.I5 1976] 76-18625 ISBN 0-88207-809-7 pbk. : 2.95 242'.4
1. Devotional literature. I. Edman, Victor Raymond, 1900-1967.

JACKSON, Edgar Newman. 242.4
The Christian funeral; its meaning, its purpose, and its modern practice [by] Edgar N. Jackson. [1st ed.] New York, Channel Press [1966] viii, 184 p. 21 cm. [BV199.F8J3] 66-25968
1. Funeral service. 2. Death. I. Title.

JACKSON, Edgar Newman. 242'.4
The many faces of grief / Edgar N. Jackson. Nashville : Abingdon, c1977. 174 p. ; 23 cm. [BJ1487.J29 1977] 77-4363 ISBN 0-687-23203-1 : 7.95
1. Grief. I. Title.

JACKSON, Edgar Newman. 242'.4
The many faces of grief / Edgar N. Jackson. Nashville : Abingdon, c1977. 174 p. ; 23 cm. [BJ1487.J29 1977] 77-4363 ISBN 0-687-23203-1 : 7.95
1. Grief. I. Title.

JENSEN, Kai, Bp., 1899- 242.4
The hollow of His hand: devotions for times of adversity. Tr. [from Danish] by Bernhard H. J. Habel. Minneapolis, Augsburg [c.1963] 128p. 21cm. 62-20844 2.75
1. Consolation. I. Title.

JENSEN, Kai, Bp., 1899- 242.4
In the hollow of His hand: devotions for times of adversity; Translated by Bernhard H. J. Habel. Minneapolis, Augsburg Pub. House [1963] 128 p. 21 cm. Translation of Alt staar i Guds faderhaand. [BV4905.2.J413] 62-20844
1. Consolation. I. Title.

KARO, Nancy. 242'.4
Adventure in dying / by Nancy Karo, with Alvera Mickelsen. Chicago : Moody Press, c1976. 223 p. ; 22 cm. [BT993.2.K37] 76-809 ISBN 0-8024-0141-4 pbk. : 3.50
1. Karo, Lindon. 2. Apostles' Creed—Sermons. 3. Baptists—Sermons. 4. Sermons, American. 5. Cancer patients—Biography. 6. Baptists—Clergy—Biography. 7. Clergy—United States—Biography. I. Mickelsen, Alvera, joint author. II. Title.

KELLETT, Arnold, ed. 242.4
Prayers for patients; a collection of prayers for those who are ill or in need. Westwood, N. J., F. H. Revell Co. [c1964] 111 p. 17 cm. "Notes on sources and authors": p. 100-111. [BV270.K4] 66-4555
1. Sick — Prayer-books and devotions. I. Title.

KEMPER, Inez, comp. 242.4
In touch with heaven. Grand Rapids, Eerdmans [1964] 252 p. 23 cm. [BV4801.K39] 63-17780
1. Devotional literature (Selections: Extracts, etc.) I. Title.

KEMPER, Inez, comp. 242.4
In touch with heaven. Grand Rapids, Mich., Eerdmans [c.1964] 252p. 23cm. 63-17780 3.50
1. Devotional literature (Selections: Extracts, etc.) I. Title.

KENNEDY, Jessie (Harper) 242.4
The Lord shall preserve, and Treasures out of the darkness. Berne, Ind., Printed by Light and Hope Publications [1954] 192p. illus. 20cm. Poetry and prose. [BV4905.K44] 55-18970
1. Consolation. I. Title. II. Title: Treasures out of the darkness.

KENNEDY, John S 242.4
The common cross. New York, McMullen Books [1954] 141p. 20cm. [BX2373.S5K4] 54-7090
1. Suffering. I. Title.

KING, Audrey R., comp. 242.4
Words of consolation. Selected by Audrey R. King. Illustrated by Sheilah Beckett. New York, Golden Press [1968] 64 p. illus. 17 cm. (The Golden library of faith & inspiration) "A Giniger book." [BV4900.K45] 68-17170
1. Consolation. I. Title.

KIRKLAND, Bryant M. 242.4
Home before dark [by] Bryant M. Kirkland. New York, Abingdon Press [1965] 157 p. 21 cm. [BV4905.2.K5] 65-15972
1. Death — Meditations. 2. Consolation. I. Title.

KIRKLAND, Bryant M. 242.4
Home before dark. Nashville, Abingdon [c.1965] 157p. 21cm. [BV4905.2.K5] 65-15972 2.75
1. Death—Meditations. 2. Consolation. I. Title.

KOHN, Harold E 242.4
Feeling low? Illustrated with 40 line drawings by the author. [1st ed.] Grand Rapids, W. B. Eerdmans Pub. Co., 1955. 160p. illus. 28cm. [BV4905.K64] 55-14342
1. Consolation. I. Title.

KOHN, Harold E. 242.4
Wide horizons; a book of faith for the sick, by Harold E. Kohn. Nashville, Tidings [1970?] 42 p. illus. 22 x 9 cm. [BV4910.K64] 70-128172
1. Sick—Prayer-books and devotions. I. Title.

KUTSCHER, Austin H., comp. 242'.4
Religion and bereavement; counsel for the physician, advice for the bereaved, thoughts for the clergyman. Edited by Austin H. Kutscher, Lillian G. Kutscher and with 33 contributing clergymen and 40 contributing consultants. New York, Health Sciences Pub. Corp., 1972. xiii, 224 p. 24 cm. [BV4905.2.K86] 74-187977 ISBN 0-88238-515-1 12.50
1. Consolation—Addresses, essays, lectures. 2. Grief—Addresses, essays, lectures. I. Kutscher, Lillian G., joint comp. II. Title.

LAUTERBACH, William Albert, 242.4
1903-
He cares for me. St. Louis, Concordia Pub. House [1957] 152p. 19cm. [BV4909.L3] 57-1655
1. Affliction. 2. Sick—Prayer-books and devotions—English. I. Title.

LAUTERBACH, William 242'.4
August, 1903-
Look down from above : prayers at the sickbed / William A. Lauterbach. St. Louis : Concordia Pub. House, c1977. 32 p. ; 16 cm. [BV270.L35] 77-5897 ISBN 0-570-03051-X pbk. : 0.95
1. Sick—Prayer-books and devotions—English. I. Title.

LAUTHERBACH, William 242.4
Albert, 1903-
He cares for me. St. Louis, Concordia Pub. House [1957] 152p. 19cm. [BV4909.L3] 57-1655
1. Affliction. 2. Sick—Prayer-books and devotions— English. I. Title.

LEWIS, Clive Staples, 1898- 242.4
1963.
A grief observed [by] N. W. Clerk [Pseud.] Greenwich, Conn., Seabury Press, 1963 [c1961] 60 p. 22 cm. [BV4905.2.L4] 63-10447
1. Consolation. I. Title.

LEWIS, Clive Staples, 1898- 242.4
1963.
A grief observed [by] C. S. Lewis. Afterword by Chad Walsh. New York, Bantam [1976 c1961] 151 p. 18 cm. [BV4905.2L4] 1.95 (pbk.)
1. Consolation. I. Title.
L.C. card no. of 1963 Seabury Press edition: 63-10447

LILES, Lester R comp. 242.4
Streams of healing; a book of comfort. [Westwood, N. J.] Revell [1958] 160p. 21cm. [BV4910.L5] 58-11019
1. Sick—Prayer-books and devotions—English. I. Title.

LIND, Robert W 242'.4
From the ground up; the story of 'Brother Van,' Montant pioneer minister, 1848-1919. [n. p., Treasure State Pub. Co., 1961] 182p. illus. 20cm. Includes bibliography. [BX8495.V2L5] 61-59891
1. Van Orsdel, William Wesley, 1848-1919. I. Title.

LOVETTE, Roger, 1935- 242'.4
Journey toward joy / Roger Lovette. Valley Forge, Pa. : Judson Press, c1977. 96 p. ; 22 cm. Includes bibliographical references. [BS2705.4.L68] 76-48745 ISBN 0-8170-0642-7 pbk. : 2.95
1. Bible. N.T. Philippians—Meditations. I. Title.

LUTHER, Martin, 1483-1546. 242.4
Letters of spiritual counsel. Edited and translated by Theodore G. Tappert. Philadelphia, Westminster Press [1955] 367 p. 24 cm. (The Library of Christian classics, v. 18) Bibliography: p. 350-353. [BR331.E5T3] 55-7705
1. Consolation. I. Tappert, Theodore Gerhardt, 1904- ed. and tr. II. Title. III. Series: The Library of Christian classics (Philadelphia) v. 18

MCELROY, Paul Simpson, 242.4
1902- comp.
Words of comfort. Edited by Paul S. McElroy. Illustrated by Vee Guthrie. Mount Vernon, N.Y., Peter Pauper Press [1968] 61 p. col. illus. 19 cm. [BV4900.M27] 68-3690
1. Consolation—Collections. I. Title.

†MCHUGH, Patrick J. 242'.4
Meditating the Sunday Gospels / by P. J. McHugh. Boston : St. Paul Editions, c1976- v. ; 22 cm. Contents.Contents.— —v. 2. B cycle. [BS2565.M3] 75-44262 3.50 pbk. : 2.50
1. Bible. N.T. Epistles and Gospels, Liturgical—Meditations. 2. Church year—Meditations. I. Title.

MCKINNEY, Donald, 1909- 242'.4
Living with joy / Donald McKinney. Nashville : Abingdon, c1976. 96 p. ; 20 cm. [BV4832.2.M1994] 76-8203 ISBN 0-687-22375-X : 4.95
1. Meditations. I. Title.

MCLARRY, Newman R 242.4
When shadows fall. Nashville, Broadman Press [1960] 60p. 16cm. [BV4909.M3] 60-9534
1. Suffering. I. Title.

MASTON, Thomas Bufford, 242'.4
1897-
God speaks through suffering / T. B. Maston. Waco, Tex. : Word Books, c1977. 95 p. ; 21 cm. [BV4909.M38] 77-76349 ISBN 0-8499-2802-8 pbk. : 3.25
1. Suffering. 2. Consolation. I. Title.

MAY, Edward C. 242.4
I was sick and You visited me; a book of prayers, by Edward C. May. Minneapolis, Augsburg Pub. House [1968] 127 p. 21 cm. [BV270.M33] 68-13425
1. Sick—Prayer-books and devotions. I. Title.

MAYFIELD, L. H. 242.4
Behind the clouds--light; meditations for the sick and distressed. Nashville, Tenn., Abingdon [c.1965] 63p. illus. 20cm. [BV4910.M3] 65-938 1.50 bds.,
1. Sick—Prayer-books and devotions—English. I. Title.

METHODISM'S Aldersgate 242'.4
heritage, by four Wesleyan scholars. Nashville, Methodist Evangelistic Materials [1964] 62 p. 19 cm. [BX8495.W5M48] 64-17883
1. Wesley, John, 1703-1791. 2. Methodism — Addresses, essays, lectures.

MEYER, Frederick 242'.4
Brotherton, 1847-1929.
Peace, perfect peace; a portion for the sorrowing [by] F. B. Meyer. Old Tappan, N.J., Revell [1970] 63 p. 17 cm. [BV4905.2.M4] 77-103614
1. Consolation. I. Title.

MIELKE, Arthur W. 242'.4
Through the valley / Arthur W. Mielke. New York : Association Press, c1976. xi, 112 p. ; 19 cm. Bibliography: p. 111-112. [BV4905.2.M5] 76-10353 ISBN 0-8096-1917-2 pbk. : 4.95
1. Mielke, Arthur W. 2. Grief. 3. Consolation. I. Title.

MIELKE, Arthur W. 242'.4
Through the valley / Arthur W. Mielke. New York : Avon, 1977,c1976. 125p. ; 18 cm. Bibliography:p.124-125. [BV4905.2.M5] ISBN 0-380-01759-8 pbk. : 1.25
1. Mielke, Arthur W. 2. Grief. 3. Consolation. I. Title.
L.C. card no. for c1975 Association Press ed.:76-10353.

MINCHIN, Gerald H., 1901- 242.4
Bow in the cloud [by] Gerald H. Minchin. Washington, Review and Herald Pub. Association [1968] 160 p. 21 cm. Bibliography: p. 159-60. Bibliographical footnotes. [BV4909.M5] 68-18367
1. Suffering. I. Title.

MITSON, Eileen Nora. 242.4
Beyond the shadows [by] Eileen N. Mitson. Foreword by Dale Evans Rogers. Grand Rapids, Zondervan Pub. House [1969, c1968] 127 p. 21 cm. [BV4907.M54 1969] 73-81067
1. Consolation. 2. Leukemia—Personal narratives. I. Title.

MONTGOMERY, Herbert. 242'.4
Beyond sorrow : reflections on death and grief / by Herb & Mary Montgomery ; [photos. by Herb & Mary Montgomery]. Minneapolis : Winston Press, c1977. 62 p. : ill. ; 22 cm. [BV4905.2.M64] 77-78260 ISBN 0-03-022961-8 pbk. : 4.95
1. Consolation. 2. Grief. I. Montgomery, Mary Ann, 1931- joint author. II. Title.

MORAL, Herbert Renard, 242.4
1901-
How to have better health through prayer. Noroton, Conn., Life-Study Fellowship [1955] 190p. 21cm. [BV4585.M6] 55-58701
1. Sick—Prayer-books and devotions—English. I. Title.

MULLEN, Thomas James, 242'.4
1934-
Where 2 or 3 are gathered together, someone spills his milk [by] Tom Muller. Waco, Tex., Word Books [1973] 126 p. 23 cm. [BV4832.2.M86] 72-96355 3.95
1. Meditations. I. Title.

MULLEN, Thomas James, 242'.4
1934-
Where 2 or 3 are gathered together, someone spills his milk [by] Tom Mullen. Waco, Tex., Word Books [1973] 126 p. 23 cm. [BV4832.2.M86] 72-96355 3.95
1. Meditations. I. Title.

MURPHY, Carol R. 242'.4
The valley of the shadow, by Carol R. Murphy. [Wallingford, Pa., Pendle Hill Publications, 1972] 24 p. 19 cm. (Pendle Hill pamphlet 184) [BT825.M87] 72-80095 ISBN 0-87574-184-3 0.70
1. Death. I. Title.

NALL, Torney Otto, 1900- 242.4
The Bible when you need it most; Scriptural selections and personal meditations. New York, Association Press [1958] 127p. 16cm. (An Association Press reflection book) [BV4905.N25] 58-6473
1. Consolation. I. Title.

NEFF, Merlin L 242.4
Triumphant in suffering. Mountain View, Calif., Pacific Press Pub. Association [1954] 120p. 21cm. [BV4596.A3N4] 54-10676
1. Suffering. I. Title.

NEVER alone / 242'.4
words and compiled by Ruth Harley ; designed and illustrated by Kathy Travers. Norwalk, Conn. : C. R. Gibson Co., c1976. 56 p. : ill. ; 21 cm. [BV4911.N48] 75-16041 ISBN 0-8378-1756-0 : 3.95
1. Loneliness. 2. Consolation. 3. Hymns, English. I. Harley, Ruth W., 1919-

NOW is eternity : 242'.4
words / by Johann Christoph Blumhardt and Christoph Friedrich Blumhardt ; [translated from the German by the Society of Brothers ; chosen by Alo Munch]. Rifton, N.Y. : Plough Pub. House, c1976. 31 leaves ; 22 cm. Translation of Jetzt ist Ewigkeit. [BV4834.J4713] 76-10251 ISBN 0-87486-209-4 : 2.25 pbk. : 1.25
1. Meditations. I. Blumhardt, Johann Christoph, 1805-1880. II. Blumhardt, Christoph, 1842-1919. III. Munch, Alo.

OTTERSTAD, Robert L. 242.4
They came to a place; meditations on human suffering. Minneapolis, Augsburg [c.1962] 47p. 21cm. 62-9091 1.25
1. Suffering. I. Title.

OZMENT, Robert Varnell, 242.4
1927-
Putting life together again [by] Robert V. Ozment. Westwood, N.J., F. H. Revell Co. [1965] 124 p. 21 cm. [BV4905.2.O89] 65-23618
1. Consolation. I. Title.

OZMENT, Robert Varnell, 242.4
1927-
Putting life together again. Westwood, N.J., Revell [c.1965] 124p. 21cm. [BV4905.2.O89] 65-23618 2.50 bds.,
1. Consolation. I. Title.

OZMENT, Robert Varnell, 242.4
1927-
There's always hope [by] Robert V. Ozment. Westwood, N.J., F. H. Revell Co. [1964] 64 p. 20 cm. [BV4905.2.O9] 64-25009
1. Consolation. I. Title.

OZMENT, Robert Varnell, 242.4
1927-
There's always hope. Westwood, N.J., Revell [c.1964] 64p. 20cm. [BV4905.2.O9] 64-25009 2.00 bds.,
1. Consolation. I. Title.

OZMENT, Robert Varnell, 242.4
1927-
When sorrow comes [by] Robert V. Ozment. Waco, Tex., Word Books [1970] 91 p. 20 cm. [BV4905.2.O93 1970] 78-111964
1. Consolation. I. Title.

PEALE, Norman Vincent, 242.4
1898-
The healing of sorrow. Inspirational Book Serv.; dist. Garden City, N.Y., Doubleday [c.1966] 96p. 21cm. [BV4905.2.P37] 66-19658 2.95 bds.,
1. Consolation. I. Title.

PEALE, Norman Vincent, 242.4
1898-
The healing of sorrow. Pawling, N. Y., Inspirational Book Service; distributed to the book trade by Doubleday, Garden City, N. Y. [1966] 96 p. 21 cm. [BV4905.2.P37] 66-19658
1. Consolation. I. Title.

PIKE, Diane Kennedy. 242'.4
Life is victorious! : How to grow through grief : a personal experience / Diane Kennedy Pike. New York : Simon and Schuster, c1976. 209 p., [4] leaves of plates : ill. ; 23 cm. [BR1725.P54A34] 76-17328 ISBN 0-671-22335-6 : 7.95
1. Pike, Diane Kennedy. 2. Pike, James Albert, Bp., 1913-1969. 3. Grief. I. Title.

PIKE, Diane Kennedy. 242'.4
Life is victorious!: How to grow through grief : a personal experience / Diane Kennedy Pike. New York : Pocket Books, 1977,c1976. 238p. : ill. ; 18 cm. (A Kangaroo Book) [BR1725.P54A34] ISBN 0-671-81241-6 pbk. : 1.95
1. Pike, Diane Kennedy. 2. Pike, James Albert, Bp. 1913-1969. 3. Grief. I. Title.
L.C. card no. for 1976 Simon & schuster ed.:76-17328.

PINK, Arthur Walkington, 242.4
1886-1952
Comfort for Christians. Swengel, Pa., Bible Truth [c.]1962. 121p. 19cm. 52-14667 1.50 pap.,
1. Consolation. I. Title.

POWER, P. B. 242'.4
A book of comfort for those in sickness / P. B. Power. Edinburgh ; Carlisle, Pa. : Banner of Truth Trust, 1974. 100 p. ; 19 cm. [BV4910.P68] 75-322816 ISBN 0-85151-203-8 : £0.40

1. Sick—Prayer-books and devotions—English. 2. Consolation. I. Title.

PUGSLEY, Clement H. 242.4
In sorrow's lone hour. Foreword by Leslie D. Weatherhead. Nashville, Abingdon [1964, c.1963] 93p. 18cm. 64-14619 1.75 bds.,
1. Consolation. I. Title.

*PURKISER, W. T. 242'.4
When you get to the end of yourself. Grand Rapids, Mich., Baker Book House [1973] 91 p. 18 cm. (Direction Books) Bibliographical footnotes. [BV4900] ISBN 0-8010-6931-9 pap., 0.95
1. Consolation. I. Title.

READ, Ralph Harlow, 1903- 242.4
In time of trouble; a guide to deep and abiding faith in God. [1st ed.] New York, American Press [1958] 135p. 21cm. [BV4909.R4] 58-11036
1. Affliction. I. Title.

RHEA, Carolyn. 242.4
Healing in His wings. New York, Grosset & Dunlap [1968] 95 p. 17 cm. (The Family inspirational library) [BV4909.R5] 68-31348 1.95
1. Suffering. 2. Consolation. I. Title.

RICH, Charles. 242'.4
Reflections from an inner eye / by Charles Rich. Huntington, Ind. : Our Sunday Visitor, c1977. 152 p. ; 21 cm. [BX2182.2.R49] 76-51953 ISBN 0-87973-751-4 pbk. : 3.95
1. Meditations. I. Title.

RIESS, Walter 242.4
Prayers for a time of crisis. St. Louis, Concordia [c.1966] 71p. 15cm. [BV260.R5] 66-16628 1.50
1. Lutheran Church—Prayer-books and devotions—English. I. Title.

ROBERTSON, Josephine. 242'.4
Garden meditations / Josephine Robertson ; ill. by Billie Jean Osborne. Nashville : Abingdon, c1977. 111 p. : ill. ; 21 cm. [BT695.5.R62] 77-23316 ISBN 0-687-14000-5 : 5.95
1. Nature (Theology)—Meditations. 2. Gardening—Meditations. I. Title.

ROGERS, William Fred, 1909- 242'.4
Ye shall be comforted / William F. Rogers. Philadelphia : Westminster Press, c1950. 92 p. ; 19 cm. [BV4905.R57 1950b] 76-355561 ISBN 0-664-24776-8 : 1.95
1. Consolation. I. Title.

ROSE, Ada (Campbell) 1901- 242'.4
Acquainted with grief. Philadelphia, Westminster Press [1972] 96 p. 20 cm. [BV4905.2.R67] 72-1408 ISBN 0-664-20949-1 4.50
1. Consolation. I. Title.

RUDOLPH, Erwin Paul, 1916- 242'.4
Good-by, my son. Grand Rapids, Zondervan Pub. House [1971] 150 p. facsims., port. 22 cm. [BV4905.2.R83] 72-153463 3.95
1. Rudolph, Erwin Paul, 1947-1969. 2. Consolation. I. Title.

RUDOLPH, Erwin Paul, 1916- 242.4
Good-by, my son. Grand Rapids, Zondervan [1975 c1971] 150 p. 17 cm. [BV4905.2] 1.50 (pbk.)
1. Rudolph, Erwin Paul, 1947-1969. 2. Consolation. I. Title.
L.C. card number for original edition: 72-153463.

SALLS, Betty Ruth. 242'.4
Death is no dead end. Chicago, Moody Press [1972] 125 p. 22 cm. [BV4905.2.S23] 77-175495 ISBN 0-8024-2075-3 2.95
1. Consolation. I. Title.

SCHEUER, Garry A. 242'.4
God in our lives / by Garry A. Scheuer, Jr. Norwalk, Conn. : C.R. Gibson Co., c1976. 88 p. ; 22 cm. [BV4832.2.S278] 74-83782 ISBN 0-8378-1772-2 : 3.95
1. Meditations. I. Title.

SCHOOLEY, Frank Budd, 1905- 242'.4
Spiritual traveler / by Frank Budd Schooley. [Dallas? Pa.] : Schooley, 1976. 319 p. : ill. ; 24 cm. Includes index. [F159.D14S36] 76-365508
1. Schooley, Frank Budd, 1905- 2. Dallas, Pa.—History—Miscellanea. 3. Meditations. I. Title.

SCHOONOVER, Melvin E. 242'.4
Letters to Polly; on the gift of affliction [by] Melvin E. Schoonover. Grand Rapids, Mich., Eerdmans [1971] 106 p. 23 cm. [BV4905.2.S33] 76-144049 3.95
1. Consolation. 2. Affliction. I. Title.

SCHULTZ, Harold Peters. 242.4
Strength and power, a book for the sick. Philadelphia, Christian Education Press [1956] 90p. 20cm. Poems and prose. [BV4910.S35] 56-8237
1. Sick—Prayer-books and devotions—English. I. Title.

SCHULTZ, Harold Peters. 242.4
Strength and power, a book for the sick. Philadelphia, Christian Education Press [1956] 90p. 20cm. Poems and prose. [BV4910.S35] 56-8237
1. Sick—Prayers-books and devotions—English. I. Title.

SEGLER, Franklin M. 242'.4
A pailful of stars; gleams of hope for a time of despair, by Franklin M. Segler. Nashville, Tenn., Broadman Press [1972] xii, 127 p. 21 cm. Includes bibliographical references. [BV4832.2.S4] 75-178065 ISBN 0-8054-8224-5
1. Devotional exercises. I. Title.

SELF, William L. 242'.4
Survival kit for the stranded : helps for those who hurt / William L. Self, with Carolyn Self. Nashville : Broadman Press, [1975] 141 p. ; 21 cm. [BV4905.2.S44] 74-16850 4.95
1. Consolation. I. Self, Carolyn, joint author. II. Title.

SHORB, Wil, 1938- 242'.4
It's your day. Nashville, Abingdon Press [1973] 128 p. 21 cm. Bibliography: p. 127-128. [BV4832.2.S522] 73-5778 ISBN 0-687-19764-3 2.95
1. Meditations. I. Title.

SHORT, Ruth Gordon. 242'.4
Affectionately yours, John Wesley. Illustrated by Jim Padgett. Nashville, Southern Pub. Association [1963] 298 p. illus. 21 cm. Bibliography: p. 297-298. [BX8495.W5S46] 63-12812
1. Wesley, John, 1703-1791. I. Title.

SIBLEY, Celestine. 242'.4
Small blessings / Celestine Sibley ; ill. by Mona Mark. 1st ed. Garden City, N.Y. : Doubleday, 1977. vi, 184 p. ; 22 cm. [BV4832.2.S5233] 76-42394 ISBN 0-385-12318-3 : 6.95
1. Meditations. I. Title.

SLADEN, Kathleen 242.4
While you're sick, Illus. by Mary Alice Bahler. Richmond, Va., Knox [1966, c.1965] 63p. illus. 21cm. First pub. in 1965 in Ontario, Canada under title: When we are sick. [BV4910.5.S55] 66-13306 1.95 bds.,
1. Sick children—Prayer-books and devotions. I. Title.

SNOWDEN, John Baptist, 1801-1885. 242'.4
The autobiography of Rev. John Baptist Snowden. Edited by his son, Thomas Baptist Snowden. [n.p.] 1900. 88 p. ports. 18 cm. "Family tree": leaf inserted [BX8495.S642A3] 67-40929
I. Snowden, Thomas Baptist, ed. II. Title.

SOUTHWELL, Robert, 1561-1595 242.4
An epistle of comfort to the reverend priests, and to the honourable, worshipful, and other of the lay sort, restrained in durance for the Catholic faith. Ed. by Margaret Waugh. Foreword by Philip Caraman. Chicago, Loyola Univ. Pr. [1966] xxii, 256p. 21cm. (Orchards bks.) [BV4904.S6 1966] 66-22384 5.00
1. Consolation—Early works to 1800. I. Title.

STARENKO, Ronald C. 242.4
It's time to live, by Ronald C. Starenko. St. Louis, Concordia Pub. House [1969] 81 p. illus. 20 cm. [BV4905.2.S7] 69-18865 2.50
1. Consolation. I. Title.

STAUDERMAN, Albert P. 242.4
Earth has no sorrow; courage and comfort for those who mourn. Philadelphia, Muhlenberg Press [1955] 52p. 17cm. [BV4905.S75] 55-7764
1. Consolation. I. Title.

STAUDERMAN, Albert P. 242.4
Earth has no sorrow; courage and comfort for those who mourn. Philadelphia, Muhlenberg Press [1955] 52p. 17cm. [BV4905.S75] 55-7764
1. Consolation. I. Title.

STRAUSS, Lehman. 242.4
Certainties for today; comforting truths for dark days. [1st ed.] New York, Loizeaux Bros. [1956] 182p. 20cm. [BV4905.S82] 56-38244
1. Consolation. 2. Christian life. I. Title.

STRAUSS, Lehman. *242.4
Certainties for today; comforting truths for dark days. [1st ed.] New York, Loizeaux Bros. [1956] 182 p. 20 cm. [BV4905.S82] 56-38244
1. Consolation. 2. Christian life. I. Title.

STRENGTH for the soul : 242'.4
wisdom from past and present / selected and arr. by Dorothy Mason Fuller. Philadelphia : Fortress Press, c1975. x, 118 p. ; 24 cm. Includes bibliographical references. [BV4832.2.S85] 75-13037 ISBN 0-8006-0417-2 : 5.95
1. Meditations. I. Fuller, Dorothy Mason.

TABER, Gladys Leona (Bagg) 1899- 242.4
Another path. Philadelphia, Lippincott [c.1963] 139p. 20cm. 63-17678 2.95 bds.,
1. Consolation. I. Title.

TAYLOR, June Filkin, 1938- 242'.4
But for our grief : how comfort comes / June Filkin Taylor. 1st ed. Philadelphia : A. J. Holman Co., c1977. 129 p. ; 22 cm. Includes bibliographical references. [BJ1487.T375] 77-3345 ISBN 0-87981-078-5 pbk. : 3.45
1. Taylor, June Filkin, 1938- 2. Grief. 3. Consolation. I. Title.

TEN BOOM, Corrie. 242'.4
He cares, He comforts / Corrie ten Boom. Old Tappan, N.J. : F.H. Revell, c1977. 95 p. ; 20 cm. (Her Jesus is victor) [BV4905.2.T46] 77-8260 ISBN 0-8007-0891-1 : 3.95
1. Consolation. I. Title.

TURNER, George Allen. 242'.4
The vision which transforms; is Christian perfection scriptural? Kansas City, Mo., Beacon Hill Press [1964] 348 p. 23 cm. "A through revision under ... new title' of the author's thesis, first published in 1952 under title: The more excellent way; the MS. Thesis (Harvard University) has title: A comparative study of the Biblical and Wesleyan ideas of perfection. Bibliography: p. 329-345. [BX8495.W5T67 1964] 64-18588
1. Wesley, John, 1703-1791. 2. Perfection — History of doctrines. I. Title.

UNTERMEYER, Louis, 1885- comp. 242.4
Lift up your heart. New York, Golden Pr. [1968] 1 v. (unpaged) col. illus. 13cm. (Golden thought bk) [BV4900.U5] 67-10499 1.25
1. Consolation. I. Title.

UPDIKE, L. Wayne. 242'.4
Ministry to the bereaved, by L. Wayne Updike. Independence, Mo., Herald Pub. House, 1973. 112 p. 16 cm. Pages 110-112 blank for "Notes." [BV4905.2.U6] 73-80212 ISBN 0-8309-0101-9 2.95
1. Consolation. I. Title.

*VAN Dalfsen, Patricia. 242.4
Good morning, Lord: devotions for shut-ins. Grand Rapids : Baker Book House, 1976. 48, [5]p. ; 19 cm. (The good morning Lord series) [BV4910] ISBN 0-8010-9264-7 : 2.45.
1. Sick-Prayer-books and devotions-English 2. Suffering. I. Title.

WALLACE, Archer, 1884- 242.4
In grateful remembrance. New York, Abingdon Press [1955] 128p. 20cm. [BV4905.W22] 55-6767
1. Consolation. I. Title.

WARD, Alice Armstrong. 242.4
I remain unvanquished [by] Alice Armstrong Ward with A. Dudley Ward. Nashville, Abingdon Press [1970] 175 p. 22 cm. [BV4905.2.W37] 76-112887 5.00
1. Consolation. I. Ward, Alfred Dudley, 1914- joint author. II. Title.

WARD, William B 242.4
The Divine Physician; devotions for the sick. [2d ed.] Richmond, John Knox Press [1957] [68] p. 18 cm. [BV4910.W3 1957] 57-4113
1. Sick — Prayer-books and devotions — English. I. Title.

WARD, William B 242.4
The Divine Physician; devotions for the sick. Richmond, John Knox Press [1953] unpaged. 16cm. [BV4585.W28] 53-11762
1. Sick—Prayer-books and devotions—English. I. Title.

WARD, William B 242.4
The Divine Physician; devotions for the sick. [2d ed.] Richmond. John Knox Press [1957] [68]p. 18cm. [BV4910.W3 1957] 57-4113
1. Sick—Prayer-books and devotions—English. I. Title.

WARREN, Meta (Hullihen) 242.4
It is always spring! Philadelphia, Dorrance [1955] 164p. 20cm. 'Forty-two religious and inspirational articles.'--Dust jacket. [PS3545.A7473I7] 54-12869
I. Title.

WATT, J Robert. *242.4
Let not your heart be troubled; comfort for the bereaved. Nashville, Abingdon Press [1957] 125 p. 20 cm. [BV4905.W34] 57-6123
1. Consolation. I. Title.

WEDGE, Florence 242.4
When your cross is heavy. Pulaski, Wis., Franciscan Pubs. [c.1963] 62p. 19cm. (When ser.) .25 pap.,
I. Title.

WESCHE, Percival A 242'.4
Henry Clay Morrison; crusador saint. [Berne, Ind., Herald Press, c1963] 208 p. 21 cm. Imprint on mounted label. Bibliographical references included in "Footnotes" (p. 206-208) [BX8495.M68W4] 64-1036
1. Morrison, Henry Clay, 1857-1942. I. Title.

WESLEY, John, 1703-1791. 242'.4
John Wesley's Journal; as abridged by Nehemiah Curnock. New York, Philosophical Library [1951] viii, 433 p. 19 cm. [[BX8495.W5A]] A51
I. Curnock, Nehemiah, 1840-1915, ed. II. Title.

WESLEY, John, 1703-1791. 242'.4
The journal of John Wesley; with an introd. by Hugh Price Hughes, appreciation of the journal by Augustine Birrell. Edited by Percy Livingstone Parker. Chicago, Moody Press, 1951. 438 p. 21 cm. (The Tyndale series of great biographies) [[BX8495.W5A]] A 52
I. Title. II. Series.

WESTBERG, Grange E. 242.4
Good grief; a constructive approach to the problem of loss. Rock Island, Ill., Augustana [c.1962] 57p. 16cm. 'Based on a chapter from [the author's] Minister and doctor meet.' 62-10419 1.00 pap.,
1. Consolation. I. Title.

WHITE, Helen Chappell. 242.4
With wings as eagles. Introd. by Ralph W. Sockman. New York, Rinehart [1953] 246 p. 20 cm. [BD444.W46] 52-12109
1. Death. I. Title.

WHITE, Henry E., Jr. 242.4
Look for the stars. Boston, Christopher Pub. [c.1963] 61p. 21cm. 63-17180 2.50
1. Consolation. I. Title.

WHITEHOUSE, Elizabeth Scott, 1893- 242.4
My window world [by] Elizabeth S. Whitehoues [sic] Valley Forge [Pa.] Judson Press [1969] 127 p. 17 cm. [BV4832.2.W52] 69-16385 2.50
1. Meditations. I. Title.

WILSON, Leland. 242'.4
Living with wonder / Leland Wilson. Waco, Tex. : Word Books, c1976. 128 p. ; 21 cm. [BV4832.2.W57] 76-19543 ISBN 0-87680-839-9 pbk. : 3.25
1. Wilson, Leland. 2. Meditations. I. Title.

WINGS of joy / 242'.4
[compiled by] Joan Winmill Brown. Old Tappan, N.J. : F. H. Revell Co., c1977. p. cm. Includes index. [BV4900.W58] 77-16686 ISBN 0-8007-0877-6 : 7.95
1. Consolation—Addresses, essays, lectures. I. Brown, Joan Winmill.

WISLoFF, Fredrik, 1904- 242'.4
On our Father's knee; devotions for times of illness. Minneapolis, Augsburg Pub. House [1973, c1966] 137 p. 15 cm. Translation of Pa var Herres fang. [BV4910.W5613] 72-90264 ISBN 0-8066-1309-2 1.95 (pbk.)
1. Sick—Prayer-books and devotions—English. 2. Consolation. I. Title.

WOODS, Bobby W. 242.4
God's answer to anxiety [by] B. W. Woods. Nashville, Broadman Press [1968] 127 p. 20 cm. Bibliographical references included in "Notes" (p. 124-127) [BV4908.5.W66] 68-20687
1. Peace of mind. I. Title.

WORDS of silver and gold 242'.4
/ [compiled by] Jo Petty. Old Tappan, N.J. : Revell, c1977. 143 p. ; 21 cm. [BV4832.2.W67] 77-23121 ISBN 0-8007-0867-9 : 5.95
1. Meditations. I. Petty, Jo.

WRIGLEY, Louise Scott. 242.4
Pocketful of sun. [Independence, Mo., Herald Pub. House, 1969] 76 p. col. illus. 16 cm. [BJ1581.2.W7] 70-80873
1. Conduct of life. I. Title.

YATES, Elizabeth, 1905- 242.4
Up the golden stair. [1st ed.] New York, Dutton, 1966. 64 p. 24 cm. [BV4905.2.Y3] 66-11548
1. Consolation. I. Title.

STRINGFELLOW, William 242.42
Instead of death. New York, Seabury [c.1963] 72p. 21cm. .95 pap.,
I. Title.

BEHNKE, Charles A 1891- 242.6
New frontiers for spiritual living; devotions for people who are growing spiritually with the years. Saint Louis, Concordia Pub. House [1959] 108p. 21cm. [BV4580.B43] 59-10978
1. Aged—Prayer-books and devotions—English. 2. Lutheran Church—Prayer-books and devotions—English. I. Title.

BOLDING, Amy. 242.'6
Please give a devotion-for all occasions. Grand Rapids, Baker Book House [1967] 121 p. 20 cm. [BV4832.2.B612] 67-26187
1. Devotional exercises. I. Title.

[BRANSIET, Philippe] 1792-1874. 242.6
As stars for all eternity; meditations for teachers. Rev. by Brother Francis Patrick [for] the Brothers of the Christian Schools. Milwaukee, Bruce Pub. Co. [1959] 255p. 18cm. 'Abridged and revised edition of Considerations for Christian teachers.' [BX2373.T4B7] 59-13017
1. Teachers— Meditations. I. Francis Patrick, Brother, 1884- ed. II. Brothers of the Christian Schools. III. Title.

BRANSIET, Philippe; secular name: Mathieu Bransiet 242.6
As stars for all eternity; meditations for teachers. Rev. by Brother Francis Patrick [for] the Brothers of the Christian Schools. Milwaukee, Bruce Pub. Co. [c.1959] xiv, 255p. 18cm. 59-13017 3.75
1. Teachers—Meditations. I. Francis Patrick, Brother, 1884- ed. II. Brothers of the Christian Schools. III. Title.

BRENNEMAN, Helen Good. 242'.6
Meditations for the expectant mother; a book of inspiration for the lady-in-waiting. Drawings by Esther Rose Graber. Scottdale, Pa., Herald Press [1968] 80 p. illus. 27 cm. "Acknowledgments" (bibliographical): p. 77-78. [BV4847.B69] 68-12025
1. Mothers—Prayer-books and devotions. I. Title.

CAMPBELL, Ralph. 242.6
Alive in Christ; meditations for young people. Westminster, Md., Newman Press, 1959. 321p. 23cm. [X2182.2.C3] 59-10402
1. Meditations, . 2. Youth—Religious life. I. Title.

CEGIELKA, Francis A. 242.6
Three hearts; Felician meditations. Milwaukee, Bruce [1964] 2 v. 18 cm. (Catholic life publications) [BX2060.F4C4] 64-17329
1. Felician Sisters of the Order of St. Francis — Prayer-books and devotions. 2. Church year — Meditations. I. Title.

COURTOIS, Gaston 242.6
Before His face, v. 1., meditations for priests and religious. [Tr. from French. New York] Herder and Herder [c.1961] 348p. 61-8837 6.50
1. Clergy—Religious life. 2. Meditations. I. Title.

DENT, Barbara. 242.6
Open me the gates, meditations of a convert. Staten Island, N.Y., Alba House [1963] 310 p. 21 cm. [BX2182.2.D4] 63-12675
1. Meditations. 2. Converts, Catholic. I. Title.

DENT, Barbara 242.6
Open me the gates, meditations of a convert. Staten Island, N. Y., Alba [c.1963] 310p. 21cm. 63-12675 3.95
1. Meditations. 2. Converts, Catholic. I. Title.

DUBAY, Thomas 242.6
Dawn of a consecration meditations for young Sisters [Boston] St. Paul Eds. [dist. Daughters of St. Paul, 1964] 460p. 19cm. 64-21599 4.00; 3.00 pap.,
1. Monastic and religious life of women. 2. Meditations. 3. Church year—Meditations. I. Title.

*GEARON, Patrick J. 242.6
'I have chosen you': retreat talks for priests. Chicago, Carmelite Third Order Pr. [1964] 210p. 19cm. 2.50
I. Title.

GOLDSMITH, Joel S. 242.6
The art of spiritual healing. New York, Harper [c.1959] 190p. 20cm. 59-14532 3.00 bds.,
1. New Thought I. Title.

HABIG, Marion Alphonse, 1901- 242.6
Tertiary's companion. Chicago, Franciscan Herald Press [1961] 324p. illus. 13cm. [BX2050.F7H25] 61-17421
1. Franciscans—Prayer-books and devotions—English. 2. Franciscans. Third Order. I. Title.

HASKIN, Dorothy (Clarks) 1905- 242'.6'
Devotions from around the world for women, by Dorothy C. Haskin. Grand Rapids, Zondervan [1967] 92p. illus., ports. 21cm. [BV4844.H3] 67-17227 price unreported. pap.,
1. Women—Prayer-books and devotions. I. Title.

HEIN, Lucille E. 242'.6
We talk with God; devotions for holy days, holidays, special days, every day, for use in families and groups with children twelve and younger [by] Lucille E. Hein. Philadelphia, Fortress Press [1968] 122 p. 18 cm. [BV255.H43] 68-16263
1. Family—Prayer-books and devotions. I. Title.

JOHNSON, Edythe J 242.6
Peace, poise, power; meditations for women based on the Gospel of Luke. Rock Island, Ill., Augustana Press [1959] 424p. 21cm. [BS2595.4.J6] 59-7597
1. Bible. N. T. Luke— Meditations. 2. Women—Prayer-books and devotions—English. 3. Devotional calendars—Lutheran Church. I. Title.

KANE, H. Victor. 242'.6
Devotions for dieters [by] H. Victor Kane. Valley Forge, Judson Press [1967] 95 p. 16 cm. [BV4805.K25] 67-22216
1. Diet—Meditations. I. Title.

KANE, H. Victor. 242'6
Devotions for dieters, by H. Victor Kane. New York, Family Library [1973, c1967] 64 p. 18 cm. [BV4805.K25] 0.95 (pbk)
1. Diet—Meditations I. Title.
LC card no. for orig. ed. 67-22216.

KLAUSLER, Alfred P 242.6
90 meditations for youth St. Louis, Concordia Pub. House [1959] 90p. 19cm. [BV4850.K55] 59-11121
1. Youth—Prayer-books and devotions—English. 2. Lutheran Church—Prayer-books and devotions—English. I. Title.

*LOCKERBIE, Jeannette W. 242.6
Designed for duty; devotional readings [for nurses] Chicago, Moody [c.1964] 128p. 16cm. 1.00 pap.,
I. Title.

NASH, Robert 242.6
Wisdom I ask. Westminster, Md., Newman [1965, c.1964] viii, 342p. 22cm. [BX2182.N33] 65-3453 4.95
1. Meditations. 2. Clergy—Religious life. I. Title.

RIHN, Roy J. 242.6
The priestly amen. by Roy Rhin [sic] New York, Sheed [c.1965] x, 180p. 22cm. [BX1912.5.R46] 65-12202 3.95
1. Retreats for clergy. 2. Catholic Church—Clergy—Religious life. I. Title.

SYVERUD, Genevieve Wold. 242.6
This is my song of songs; devotions for church choirs. Minneapolis, Augsburg Pub. House [1966] 80 p. illus. 20 cm. Bibliography: p. [8] [BV290.S95] 66-22557
1. Lutheran Church — Prayer-books and devotions — English. 2. Religion and music. I. Title.

SYVERUD, Genevieve Wold 242.6
This is my song of songs; devotions for church choirs. Minneapolis, Augsburg [c.1966] 80p. illus. 20cm. Bibl. [BV290.S95] 66-22557 1.50 pap.,
1. Lutheran Church—Prayer-books and devotions—English. 2. Religion and music. I. Title.

TIBBETTS, Norris L 242.6
Talks with men. New York, Association Press [1958] 96 p. 20 cm. [BV4832.T575] 58-11528
1. Meditations. I. Title.

WEIKL, Ludwig. 242.6
"Stir up the fire" considerations on the priesthood. Translated from the German by Isabel and Florence McHugh. Milwaukee, Bruce Pub. Co. [1959] 233 p. 21 cm. [BX1912.W383] 58-12815
1. Clergy — Religiour life. 2. Meditations. I. Title.

WOLTER, Martin. 242.6
The voice of your Father. Chicago, Franciscan Herald Press [1959] 400 p; 16 cm. [BX2050.F7W62] 59-14707
1. Franciscans — Prayer-books and devotions — English. 2. Church year — Prayer-books and devotions — English. I. Title.

BARNES, Kathleen H. 242'.6'2
Testimony / by Kathleen H. Barnes, Virginia H. Pearce ; photos. by Don O. Thorpe. Salt Lake City, Utah : Deseret Book Co., 1974. [32] p. : ill. ; 22 cm. (A Book for Latter-day Saint children) The analogy of an apple seed is used to explain the meaning of testimony in the Church of Jesus Christ of Latter-Day Saints. [BV4870.B28] 74-80585 ISBN 0-87747-525-3 pbk. : 4.95
1. Children—Prayer-books and devotions—English—1961- 2. Religious education—Text-books for children—Mormon. I. Pearce, Virginia H., joint author. II. Title. III. Series.

BUROW, Daniel R. 242'.6'2
I meet God through the strangest people; 110 devotions for the 9 to 13 generation [by] Daniel R. Burow. Illustrated by Betty Wind. Saint Louis, Concordia Pub. House [1970] 206 p. illus. 24 cm. [BV4870.B77] 77-98299
1. Children—Prayer-books and devotions—English—1961- I. Title.

COLEMAN, William L. 242'.6'2
Counting stars / by William L. Coleman. Minneapolis : Bethany Fellowship, c1976. p. cm. Links Scripture, scientific information about nature, and a meditative thought regarding the wonders of God in nature. [BV4870.C63] 76-28973 ISBN 0-87123-055-0 pbk. : 1.95
1. Children—Prayer-books and devotions—English. I. Title.

*FIELD, Rachel. 242.6'2
Prayer for a child. Pictures by Elizabeth Orton Jones. New York, Collier Books [1973, c.1944] 1 v. (unpaged) Col. illus. 23 cm. (Collier juvenile paperbacks) [BV4850] pap.,
1. Children—Prayer-books and devotions. I. Title.

*GEARON, Patrick J. 242.62
Chats with St. Anne for children. [Downers Grove, Ill.] Carmelite Third Order Pr., Aylesford [1965] 64p. illus. 19cm. .75 pap.,
I. Title.

GESCH, Roy G. 242'.6'2
God's world through young eyes [by] Roy G. Gesch. Drawings by Edward Q. Luhmann. St. Louis, Concordia Pub. House [1969] 160 p. illus. 24 cm. A collection of 104 readings, prayers, and stories drawn from and applicable to the lives of young people. [BV4870.G4] 69-13111 3.95
1. Children—Prayer-books and devotions—1961- I. Luhmann, Edward Q., illus. II. Title.

GIBSON, Roxie E. 242'.6'2
Hey, God! Hurry! / By Roxie E. Gibson ; printed & illustrated by James C. Gibson. [Dallas] : Crescendo Publications, c1976. 48 p. : ill. ; 19 cm. A youngster talks to God about the ability to cope with the pressure and fast pace of life. [BV4870.G46] 76-16464 ISBN 0-89038-030-9 pbk. : 2.95
1. Children—Prayer-books and devotions—English. I. Gibson, James C. II. Title.

GOLISCH, John 242'.6'2
It's time to talk to God, by John and Joan Golisch. Minneapolis, Augsburg Pub. House [1965] 1 v. (unpaged) col. illus. 22 x 28 cm. [BV212.G6] 65-12139
1. Prayer — Juvenile literature. I. Golisch, Joan, joint author. II. Title.

GOOD night. 242'.6'2
New York, Paulist Press [1969] [16] p. col. illus. 15 x 18 cm. (Rejoice books) Before going to bed a little boy asks Jesus to bless his family, friends, and all the people in the world. [BV4870.G65] 71-7460 0.35
1. Children—Prayer-books and devotions—English—1961-

HEIN, Lucille E. 242'.6'2
I can make my own prayers [by] Lucille E. Hein. Illustrated by Joan Orfe. Valley Forge, Judson Press [1971] 31 p. col. illus. 25 cm. Discusses God's presence in the world and encourages the reader to make up his own prayers. [BV212.H4] 72-154026 ISBN 0-8170-0528-5 2.95
1. Prayer—Juvenile literature. I. Orfe, Joan, illus. II. Title.

HUGHES, William Jacoway, 1932- 242'.6'2
Bible hero devotions for boys and girls, by William J. Hughes. New York, Association Press [1966] 126 p. 20 cm. [BV4870.H75] 66-20474
1. Children—Prayer-books and devotions. I. Title.

LARSON, Muriel. 242'.6'2
Devotions for children. Grand Rapids, Baker Book House [1969] 117 p. 21 cm. [BV4870.L35] 69-16931 2.95
1. Children—Prayer-books and devotions—English—1961- I. Title.

*MILES, Mary Lillian 242.62
Quiet moments with God [2v.] Chicago, Moody [c.1963] 2 v. (177; 175p.) 16cm. 1.00 pap., ea.
I. Title.

PRIESTER, Gertrude Ann. 242'.6'2
Let's talk about God; devotions for families with young children. Illustrated by R. O. Fry. Philadelphia, Westminster Press [1967] 271 p. illus. 23 cm. Bibliography: p. [269]-271. [BV4870.P7] 67-11494
1. Children—Prayer-books and devotions. 2. Family—Prayer-books and devotions. I. Title.

SCHREIVOGEL, Paul A. 242'.6'2
Small prayers for small children about big and little things, by Paul A. Schreivogel. Illustrated by George Ellen Holmgren. Minneapolis, Augsburg Pub. House [1971] [32] p. col. illus. 27 cm. Brief prayers about everyday things in a child's life—morning, water, friends, pain, the seasons, television, and other topics. [BV4870.S43] 76-135226 ISBN 0-8066-1109-X 3.50
1. Children—Prayer-books and devotions. I. Holmgren, George Ellen, illus. II. Title.

SLADEN, Kathleen. 242'.6'2
Are you in the picture? Nashville, Abingdon Press [1973] 80 p. illus. 24 cm. The reader is invited to step into various paintings and art objects for interpretation and religious guidance. [BV4870.S55] 78-186615 ISBN 0-687-01713-0 3.50
1. Children—Prayer-books and devotions—English. I. Title.

SPEERSTRA, Karen. 242'.6'2
Let's go Jesus / written by Karen Speerstra ; illustrated by Fred Stout. St. Louis : Concordia Pub. House, c1977. [63] p. : ill. ; 23 cm. Conservation-prayers with Jesus which deal with such common events of a child's life as going to the hospital, planting a garden, taking piano lessons, and flying a kite. [BV4870.S66] 77-24030 ISBN 0-570-03468-X pbk. : 2.50
1. Children—Prayer-books and devotions—English. I. Stout, Fred. II. Title.

STARDUST book of prayers. 242'.6'2
Illus. by Stina Nagel. Norwalk, Conn., C. R. Gibson Co. [1969] [24] p. illus. (part col.) 19 cm. (Stardust books) Illustrated collection of short prayers for daily use. [BV265.S75] 69-12373 1.95
1. Children—Prayer-books and devotions. I. Nagel, Stina, 1918- illus. II. Title: Book of prayers.

*VAL, Sue 242.6'2
I think about God; two stories about my day. Why? Pictures by Christiane Cassan. Racine, Wis. Golden Press 1974 c1965 1 v. (unpaged) col. illus. 21 cm. (A little golden book) Also bound in this volume; I do my best, by Norah Smaridge. Pictures by Trina Hyman. [BV4850] 0.49
1. Children—Prayer-books and devotions. I. Title.

WALLACE, Betty Dollar. 242'.6'2
Children's prayers, praises & pledges : beautiful prayers and poems of praise for individual, family, and public worship / Betty Dollar Wallace. Denver : World Press, c1976. 96 p. : ill. ; 22 cm. A collection of prayers for everyday activities, mealtime, special occasions, and friends. [BV4870.W28] 77-352947 4.95
1. Children—Prayer-books and devotions—English. I. Title.

*WHITE, Mary Michaels 242.6'2
A book of God's gifts. I sing a song of praise. Adapted from Psalm 103. Pictures by Idellette Bordigoni. Racine, Wis. Golden Press 1974, c1972. 1 v. (unpaged) col. illus. 21 cm. (A little golden book) Also bound in this volume; a book of God's gifts, by Ruth Hannon. Pictures by Rick Schreter. [BV4850] 0.49
1. Children—Prayer-books and devotions. I. Title.

AHRENS, Herman C., comp. 242'.6'3
Tune in, edited by Herman C. Ahrens, Jr. Philadelphia, Pilgrim Press [1968] 93 p. illus. 21 cm. A collection of prayers from Youth magazine. [BV283.Y6A4] 68-54031 2.95
1. Youth—Prayer-books and devotions. I. Youth (Philadelphia) II. Title.

BARCLAY, William lecturer in the University of Glasgow 242.63
Epilogues and prayers. New York, Abingdon Press [1964, c1963] 227 p. 23 cm. [BV29.B33] 64-10678
1. Worship programs. I. Title.

BARCLAY, William 242.63
Epilogues and prayers [Nashville] Abingdon [1964, c.1963] 227p. 23cm. 64-10678 3.25
1. Worship programs. I. Title.

BENNETT, Marian, comp. 242'.6'3
What do I do now, Lord? Cincinnati, Ohio, Standard Pub. [1973] 96 p. illus. 18 cm. [BV4850.B46] 73-79468
1. Youth—Prayer-books and devotions—English. I. Title.

BOLDING, Amy 242.63
Please give a devotion for young people. Grand Rapids, Baker Bk. [1966] 121p. 20cm. [BV4832.2.B613] 66-25395 1.95
1. Devotional exercises. I. Title.

BRYANT, Al, ed. 242.63
Devotional programs for young adults. Grand Rapids, Michigan, Zondervan [c.1960] 63p. 20cm. 1.50 pap.,
I. Title.

BRYANT, Al, 1926- comp. 242.63
Time out; daily devotions for young people, compiled and written by Al Bryant. Grand Rapids, Zondervan Pub. House [1961] unpaged. 18cm. [BV4850.B74] 61-3105
1. Devotional calendars. 2. Youth—Prayer-books and devotions—English. I. Title.

BRYANT, Al [Thomas Alton Bryant] 1926- comp. 242.63
Time out; daily devotions for young people, comp. and written by Al Bryant. Grand Rapids, Zondervan Pub. House [c.1961] unpaged. 61-3105 1.95 bds.,
1. Devotional calendars. 2. Youth—Prayer-books and devotions—English. I. Title.

CALDWELL, Louis O. 242'.6'3
Good morning, Lord; devotions for college students [by] Louis O. Caldwell. Grand Rapids, Mich., Baker Book House [1971] [64] p. 19 cm. [BV4531.2.C3] 78-164374 ISBN 0-8010-2324-6
1. College students—Prayer-books and devotions—English. I. Title.

COOK, Walter L. 242'.6'3
Christian friendship; youth devotions that lead to action [by] Walter L. Cook. Nashville, Abingdon Press [1967] 108 p. 16 cm. [BV4850.C57] 67-22171
1. Youth—Prayer-books and devotions. I. Title.

COOK, Walter L. 242.63
Daily life devotions for youth. New York, Association [c.1965] 128p. 15cm. [BV4850.C58] 65-11081 1.95 bds.,
1. Youth—Prayer-books and devotions—English I. Title.

COOK, Walter L. 242'.6'3
Devotional thoughts for youth [by] Walter L. Cook. Nashville, Abingdon Press [1975] 92 p. 16 cm. Quotations from the Bible are followed by explanations of their application in everyday life. [BV4850.C585] 74-14607 ISBN 0-687-10600-1 4.50
1. Youth—Prayer-books and devotions—English. I. Title.

COOK, Walter L. 242.63
Meeting the test; a book of devotions for young people. Nashville, Abingdon Press [c.1960] 112p. 16cm. 60-6929 1.75 bds.,
1. Youth—Prayer-books and devotions—English. I. Title.

COOK, Walter L. 242.63
365 meditations for teen-agers, based on the sayings of Jesus. New York, Abingdon Press [1964] 222 p. 16 cm. [BV4850.C63] 64-10104
1. Youth—Prayer-books and devotions. 2. Devotional calendars. I. Title.

COUCH, Helen F. 242.63
Devotions for young teens [by] Helen F. Couch and Sam S. Barefield. New York, Abingdon Press [1965] 111 p. 18 cm. Bibliography: p. 111. [BV4850.C66] 65-11076
1. Youth—Prayer-books and devotions. I. Barefield, Sam S., joint author. II. Title.

*DANTUMA, Angelyn Grace 242.63
This is life! devotional readings for students. Chicago, Moody [c.1965] 128p. 16cm. (Meditations in the Proverbs) 1.00 pap.,
I. Title.

DRESCHER, Sandra. 242'.6'3
Just between God & me / Sandra Drescher. Grand Rapids : Zondervan Pub. House, c1977. a. 250 p. ; 18 cm. Includes a meditation, Scripture verse, and short prayer for every day of the year. [BV4850.D73] 76-51295 ISBN 0-310-23940-0 : 5.95 ISBN 0-310-23941-9 pbk. : 2.95
1. Youth—Prayer-books and devotions—English. I. Title.

DRESCHER, Sandra. 242'.6'3
Just between God & me / Sandra Drescher. Grand Rapids : Zondervan Pub. House, c1977. a. 250 p. ; 18 cm. Includes a meditation, Scripture verse, and short prayer for every day of the year. [BV4850.D73] 76-51295 ISBN 0-310-23940-0 : 5.95 ISBN 0-310-23941-9 pbk. : 2.95
1. Youth—Prayer-books and devotions—English. I. Title.

EMSWILER, Thomas Neufer. 242'.6'3
Love is a magic penny : meditations for junior highs / Tom Neufer Emswiler. Nashville : Abingdon, c1977. 111 p. : ill. ; 19 cm. A collection of meditations for daily life, special occasions, and holidays. [BV4850.E48] 76-44384 ISBN 0-687-22815-8 pbk. :
1. Youth—Prayer-books and devotions—English. I. Title.

FITZGERALD, Lawrence P 242.63
Just a minute! A pocketbook meditation guide for youth. Anderson, Ind., Warner Press [1963] 64 p. 14 cm. [BV4805.F5] 63-10216
1. Meditations. I. Title.

FITZGERALD, Lawrence P. 242.63
Just a minute! A pocketbook meditation guide for youth. Anderson, Ind., Warner [c.1963] 64p. 14cm. 63-10216 .65 pap.,
1. Meditations. I. Title.

GESCH, Roy G. 242'.6'3
Help! I'm in college [by] Roy G. Gesch. St. Louis, Concordia Pub. House [1969] 136 p. 18 cm. Poems. [BV4850.G4] 70-77282 1.95
1. College students—Prayer-books and devotions—English. I. Title.

GIESSLER, Phillip B. 242'.6'3
Christian love: campus style; chats with collegians Nathan and Nancy [by] Phillip B. Giessler. Cleveland, Dillon Liederbach [1974- v. 21 cm. Contents.Contents.—[1] Their first year: semester I. [BV4531.2.G53] 73-94079 ISBN 0-913228-12-5 (v. 1) 4.95 (v. 1)
1. College students—Prayer-books and devotions—English. I. Title.

HURON, Rod. 242'.6'3
Do you know who you are? : Youth devotions for the computer age / Rod Huron ; [computer symbology in collaboration with Joe Shelley]. Cincinnati : Standard Pub., c1976. 96 p. : ill. ; 18 cm. (Fountain books) Contains forty-six devotions focusing on building a personal relationship with God and dealing with problems of everyday life. [BV4850.H87] 75-38226 ISBN 0-87239-089-6
1. Youth—Prayer-books and devotions—English. I. Title.

KLEINHANS, Theodore J. 242'.6'3
Scoutways to God; thoughts, words and deeds, by Theodore J. Kleinhans. Philadelphia, Fortress [1967] ix, 101p. 18cm. [BV4541. K5.] 67-17403 1.50 pap.,
1. Boy Scouts—Prayer-books and devotions. 2. Girl Scouts—Prayer-books and devotions. I. Title.

KLEINHANS, Theodore J. 242'.6'3
Scoutways to God; thoughts, words, and deeds, by Theodore J. Kleinhans. Philadelphia, Fortress Press [1967] ix, 101 p. 18 cm. [BV4541.2.K5] 67-17403
1. Boy Scouts — Prayer-books and devotions. 2. Girl Scouts — Prayer-books and devotions. I. Title.

LEHMAN, Celia. 242'.6'3
My best friend is God. Cincinnati, Standard Pub. [1973] 96 p. illus. 18 cm. (Fountain books) [BV4832.2.L43] 73-79469
1. Meditations. I. Title.

MEDITATIONS for college students, by Donald Deffner [and others] St. Louis, Concordia Pub. House [1961] 152p. 20cm. [BV4850.M4] 61-11242 242.63
1. Students—Prayer-books and devotions—English. I. Deffner, Donald.

*MILES, Mary Lillian 242.63
God speaks to me; devotions for juniors and early teens, Chicago, Moody [c.1965] 128p. 15cm. (MP100) 1.00 pap.,
I. Title.

REDDER, Ronald M. 242'.6'3
Perforated mood-swing book [by] Ronald M. Redder. St. Louis, Concordia Pub. House [1972] 79 p. illus. 23 cm. In verse. [BV4850.R4] 76-186644 ISBN 0-570-03134-6
1. Youth—Prayer-books and devotions—English. I. Title.

ALLEMAN, Herbert Christian, 1868-1953. 242.632
Prayers for boys. [Rev. ed. Camden, N.J., T. Nelson [1966] 64 p. 16 cm. [BV283.B7A6] 66-14195
1. Boys — Prayer-books and devotions. I. Title.

HALVERSON, Richard C. 242'.6'32
Manhood with meaning; the God principle [by] Richard Halverson. Grand Rapids, Mich., Zondervan Pub. House [1972] 120 p. 18 cm. [BV4843.H32] 74-189762 0.95
1. Men—Prayer-books and devotions—English. I. Title.

IKERMAN, Ruth C. 242'.6'32
Prayers of a homemaker [by] Ruth C. Ikerman. Nashville, Abingdon Press [1966] 72 p. 12 cm. [BV283.M7I4] 66-28024
1. Mothers—Prayer-books and devotions—English. I. Title.

INGZEL, Marjorie, comp. 242.632
Table graces for the family. London, New York, T. Nelson [1964] 64 p. 16 cm. [BV283.G7 I 6] 64-13997
1. Grace at meals. I. Title.

KRUTZA, William J. 242'.6'32
Dynamic devotionals for men [by] William J. Krutza. Grand Rapids, Mich., Baker Book House [1970] 96 p. 20 cm. [BV4843.K73] 70-138832 ISBN 0-8010-5306-4
1. Men—Prayer-books and devotions—English. I. Title.

PETER Pauper Press, Mount Vernon, N.Y. 242.632
Prayers for peace. Illustrated by Ruth McCrea. Mount Vernon, N.Y. [1962] 60 p. illus. 19 cm. [BV283.P4P4] 62-53635
1. Prayers for peace. I. Title.

SIMMONS, Patricia A. 242'.6'32
Guess what, God! / Patricia A. Simmons. Nashville. : Broadman Press, 1977, c1976. 64 p. ; 20 cm. [[BV283.B7S5]] 75-22974 ISBN 0-8054-4413-0 : 2.95
1. Boys—Prayer-books and devotions—English. I. Title.

BARKMAN, Alma. 242'.6'33
Sunny-side up / by Alma Barkman. Chicago : Moody Press, c1977. p. cm. [BV4844.B34] 77-7048 ISBN 0-8024-8431-X pbk. : 1.50
1. Women—Prayer-books and devotions—English. I. Title.

BURROW, Barbara. 242'.6'33
We planted miracles today, Lord; a mother's meditations and prayers. Illustrated by Lilian Weytjens. [Kansas City, Mo., Hallmark Cards, 1973] 1 v. (unpaged) col. illus. 16 cm. (Hallmark editions) [BV283.M7B87] 72-75046 ISBN 0-87529-289-5 2.00
1. Mothers—Prayer-books and devotions—English. I. Title.

MURPHY, Mary Maloney. 242'.6'33
Creating; reflections during pregnancy. New York, Paulist Press [1974] 53 p. illus. 18 cm. [BV283.M7M87] 73-90086 ISBN 0-8091-1815-7 1.50 (pbk.)
1. Mothers—Prayer-books and devotions—English. I. Title.

PELGER, Lucy J. 242'.6'33
Living for a living Lord; devotions for women's groups [by] Lucy J. Pelger. St. Louis. Concordia [1967] 97p. 22cm. [BV4844.P4] 67-14080 2.95
1. Women—Prayer-books and devotions. I. Title.

PELGER, Lucy J 242'.6'33
Living for a living Lord; devotions for women's groups [by] Lucy J. Pelger. St. Souis, Concordia Pub. House [1967] 97 p. 22 cm. [BV4844.P4] 67-14080
1. Women—Prayer books and devotions. I. Title.

RUSSELL, Frances, 1913- 242'.6'33
Seek and find. Toronto, J.M.Dent 1954 104p. 23cm. [BV4860.R8 1954] 55-18062
1. Girls—Prayer-books and devotions—English. I. Title.

SHAFFER, Wilma L. 242'.6'33
Proverbs and programs for women, "a proverb for every problem," by Wilma L. Shaffer. Cincinnati, Standard Pub. [1972] 112 p. 22 cm. [BV4844.S5] 72-75097
1. Bible. O.T. Proverbs—Devotional literature. 2. Women—Prayer-books and devotions—English. I. Title.

SIMMONS, Patricia A. 242'.6'33
Between you and me, God : [meditations for growing girls] / Patricia A. Simmons. Nashville : Broadman Press, [1974] 64 p. ; 20 cm. An eleven-year-old girl takes her problems to God in prayer. Gives a scripture in answer to each prayer. [BV4860.S56] 74-79486 ISBN 0-8054-4412-2 pbk. : 2.50
1. Girls—Prayer-books and devotions—English. I. Title.

WILLIAMSON, Norma. 242'.6'33
Please get off the seesaw slowly / Norma Williamson. Old Tappan, N.J. : F. H. Revell Co., [1975] 127 p. ; 21 cm. [BJ1610.W54] 75-4999 ISBN 0-8007-0738-9: 4.95
1. Women—Conduct of life. 2. Women—Religious life. I. Title.

ABERNETHY, Jean (Beaven) 1912- ed. 242.64
Meditations for women, by Edith Lovejoy Pierce, [others] Introd. by Dorothy Canfield Fisher. Nashville, Abingdon Press [1961, c.1947] 378p. 16cm. (Apex bk. F I) .69 pap.,
1. Women—Prayer-books and devotions—English. I. Pierce, Edith Lovejoy, 1904- II. Title.

BOWMAN, Mary D. 242'.6'4
Love, honor and ...? [By] Mary D. Bowman. With illus. by Bill Bryant. Old Tappan, N.J., F. H. Revell Co. [1970] 63 p. illus. (part col.) 16 x 21 cm. [BV835.B67] 71-123065 ISBN 0-8007-0401-0 3.50
1. Marriage. I. Title.

CARLSON, Betty. 242.64
Living above; inspirational devotions for women's groups. Grand Rapids, Zondervan Pub. House [1964] 120 p. 21 cm. [BV4527.C27] 64-22828
1. Devotional literature. 2. Woman—Religious life. I. Title.

CARLSON, Betty 242.64
Living above; inspirational devotions for women's groups. Grand Rapids, Mich., Zondervan [c.1964] 120p. 21cm. [BV4527.C27] 64-22828 2.50 bds.,
1. Devotional literature. 2. Woman—Religious life. I. Title.

CROWELL, Grace (Noll) 1877- 242.64
Riches of the kingdom. Nashville, Abingdon Press [1961, c.1954] 126p. (Apex bk., F4) .69 pap.,
1. Women—Prayer-books and devotions—English I. Title.

DRESCHER, John M. 242'.6'4
Meditations for the newly married, by John M. Drescher. Scottdale, Pa., Herald Press [1969] 141 p. 23 cm. Bibliography: p. 139. [BV4596.M3D7] 69-10835 4.00
1. Married people—Prayer-books and devotions—English. I. Title.

FRENCH, Marion Flood 242.64
Gingham joys. Nashville, Abingdon [c.1962] 96p. 62-7226 1.50 bds.,
I. Title.

FRIDY, Wallace. 242.64
Meditations for adults. New York, Abingdon Press [1965] 143 p. 18 cm. [BV4832.2.F715] 65-20362
1. Devotional exercises. 2. Meditations. I. Title.

FRIDY, Wallace 242.64
Meditations for adults. Nashville Abingdon [c.1965] 143p. 18cm. [BV4832.2.F715] 65-20362 2.00 bds.,
1. Devotional exercises. 2. Meditations. I. Title.

GARRISON, Webb B. 242'.6'4
Devotions for the middle years, by Webb Garrison. [Nashville] The Upper Room [1974] 64 p. 20 cm. [BV4579.5.G37] 74-75223 1.00
1. Middle age—Prayer-books and devotions—English. I. Title.

HASKIN, Dorothy (Clark) 1905- 242.64
God in my home, thoughts for homemakers. Anderson, Ind., Warner Press [1964] 95 p. port. 21 cm. [BV4832.2.H33] 64-10943
1. Devotional literature. 2. Women — Religious life. I. Title.

HASKIN, Dorothy (Clark) 1905- 242.64
God in my home, thoughts for homemakers. Anderson, Ind., Warner [c.1964] 95p. port. 21cm. 64-10943 1.50, plastic bdg., bxd.
1. Devotional literature. 2. Women—Religious life. I. Title.

HOGAN, Bernice 242.64
Grains of sand. Nashville, Abingdon [c.1961] 128p. 16cm. 61-13195 2.00 bds.,
1. Women—Prayer-books and devotions—English. I. Title.

HUXHOLD, Harry N. 242.64
Magnificat: devotions for the new mother. St. Louis, Concordia [c.1961] 60p. .50 pap.,
1. Devotional literature. 2. Motherhood—Devotional literature. I. Title.

JACOBS, J. Vernon 242.64
24 messages for men. Cincinnati, Ohio, Standard Pub. Co. [c.1961] 128p. 1.50 pap.,
I. Title.

LANGFORD, Alec J., 1926- 242'.6'4
Meditations and devotions for adults / Alec J. Langford. Nashville : Abingdon, c1976. 112 p. ; 16 cm. [BV4832.2.L317] 76-223 ISBN 0-687-24090-5 : 4.95
1. Meditations. I. Title.

MCQUADE, James J 242.64
How to give the spiritual exercises of St. Ignatius to lay apostles. Chicago, Loyola University Press, 1962. 94p. 24cm. [BX2179.L8M32] 61-18210
1. Loyola, Ignacio de, Saint, 1491-1556.

Exercitia spiritualia. 2. Spiritual exercises. I. Title.

PARROTT, Lora Lee 242.64
Devotional programs for women's groups; no.3. Grand Rapids, Mich., Zondervan [c.1961] 60p. 1.00 pap.,
1. Meditations for women's groups. I. Title.

PRICE, Eugenia. 242.64
God speaks to women today. Grand Rapids, Zondervan Pub. House, 1964. 256 p. 24 cm. Bibliography: p. 256. [BV4527.P7] 63-9315
1. Woman—Religious life. I. Title.

SHAFFER, Wilma L. 242.64
Devotions and dialogs for women: serenity of the soul. Cincinnati, Ohio, Standard Pub. Co. [c.1961] 123p. 1.50, pap., plastic binding
1. Devotional literature. I. Title.

WALLACE, Helen Kingsbury 242.64
Meditations on New Testament symbols; devotions for women. [Westwood, N. J.] Revell [c.1962] 127p. 21cm. 62-17104 2.50 bds.,
1. Christian art and symbolism. 2. Bible. N. T.—Meditations. I. Title.

FATHERS are special / 242'.6'42
compiler, William Hall Preston ; illustrator, Bill McPheeters ; foreword, James L. Sullivan. Nashville : Broadman Press, c1977. 96 p. : ill. ; 20 cm. [BV4846.F37] 76-39715 ISBN 0-8054-5622-8 pbk. : 3.95
1. Fathers—Prayer-books and devotions—English. I. Preston, William Hall.

FATHERS are special / 242'.6'42
compiler, William Hall Preston ; illustrator, Bill McPheeters ; foreword, James L. Sullivan. Nashville : Broadman Press, c1977. 96 p. : ill. ; 20 cm. [BV4846.F37] 76-39715 ISBN 0-8054-5622-8 pbk. : 3.95
1. Fathers—Prayer-books and devotions—English. I. Preston, William Hall.

HALVERSON, Richard C. 242'.6'42
Perspective; devotional thoughts for men, by Richard C. Halverson. Grand Rapids, Mich., Zondervan Pub. House [1973, c1957] 203 p. 18 cm. [BV4843.H33 1973] 74-155349 0.95 (pbk.)
1. Men—Prayer-books and devotions—English. I. Title.

KOOIMAN, Gladys. 242'.6'42
When death takes a father. Grand Rapids, Mich., Baker Book House [1974, c.1968] 171 p. illus. 18 cm. (Direction Books) [BV4908.K6] 68-31473 ISBN 0-8010-5341-2 1.25 (pbk.)
1. Death. 2. Consolation. I. Title.

KRUTZA, William J. 242'.6'42
Devotionals for modern men, by William J. Krutza. Grand Rapids, Baker Book House [1968] 79 p. 20 cm. [BV4843.K7] 68-31474
1. Men—Prayerbooks and devotions. I. Title.

ANDERSON, Evelyn 242'.6'43
McCullough.
Devotionals for today's women. Grand Rapids, Mich., Baker Book House [1969] 79 p. 21 cm. [BV4844.A49] 75-101614
1. Women—Prayer-books and devotions. I. Title.

ANDERSON, Evelyn 242'.6'43
McCullough.
Good morning, Lord; devotions for women [by] Evelyn Anderson. Grand Rapids, Mich., Baker Book House [1971] 60 p. 19 cm. [BV4844.A493] 74-164373 ISBN 0-8010-0023-8
1. Women—Prayer-books and devotions—English. I. Title.

ANDERSON, Evelyn 242'.6'43
McCullough.
Only a woman. Grand Rapids, Baker Book House [1969] 79 p. illus. 20 cm. [BV4844.A5] 69-15663
1. Women—Prayer-books and devotions—English. I. Title.

BOWMAN,Mary D. 242.643
Hey, Mom! Illus. by Don Sampson. Westwood, N.J., Revel [c.1965] 31p. col. illus. 19cm. [BV4847.B6] 65-23622 2.00
1. Mothers—Religious life. I. Title.

BRANSON, Mary Kinney. 242'.6'43
A woman's place / Mary Kinney Branson. Denver : Accent Books, c1975. 160 p. : ill. ; 18 cm. [BV4844.B7] 75-40909 ISBN 0-916406-14-8 pbk. : 1.95
1. Women—Prayer-books and devotions—English. I. Title.

CARLSON, Betty. 242'.6'43
Happiness is ...; devotional talks for women's groups. Grand Rapids, Zondervan Pub. House [1972, c1971] 61 p. 21 cm. [BV4527.C268] 75-146564
1. Devotional literature. 2. Woman—Religious life. I. Title.

CARR, Jo. 242.643
Too busy not to pray; a homemaker talks with God [by] Jo Carr & Imogene Sorley. Nashville, Abingdon Press [1966] 112 p. 21 cm. [BV4844.C35] 66-10853
1. Women — Prayer-books and devotions. I. Sorley,Imogene, joint author. II. Title.

CARR, Jo 242.643
Too busy not to pray; a homemaker talks with God [by] Jo Carr, Imogene Sorley. Nashville, Abingdon [c.1966] 112p. 21cm. [BV4844.C35] 66-10853 2.50
1. Women—Prayer-books and devotions. I. Sorley, Imogene, joint author. II. Title.

DAVIDSON, Clarissa 242'.6'43
Start.
Look here, Lord; meditations for today's woman, by Clarissa Start. Illustrated by Audrey F. Teeple. Minneapolis, Augsburg Pub. House [1972] 128 p. illus. 21 cm. [BV4844.D38] 72-78550 ISBN 0-8066-1218-5 3.50
1. Women—Prayer-books and devotions—English. I. Title.

DROUIN, Francis M., 242'.6'43
1901-
The sounding solitude; meditations for religious women [by] Francis M. Drouin. Staten Island, N.Y., Alba House [1971] ix, 156 p. 22 cm. Includes bibliographical references. [BX4214.D75] 72-148682 ISBN 0-8189-0204-3 3.95
1. Meditations. I. Title.

FROST, Marie. 242'.6'43
Mother's meditations. Wheaton, Ill., Tyndale House Publishers [1969, c1968] 59 p. illus. 20 cm. (Heritage edition) [BV283.M7F76] 68-56397
1. Mothers—Prayer-books and devotions. I. Title.

GLAZIER, Donna L. 242'.6'43
Heaven help me; devotions for young mothers, by Donna L. Glazier. Minneapolis, Augsburg Pub. House [1970] vii, 139 p. 23 cm. [BV283.M7G55] 75-101109 3.95
1. Mothers—Prayer-books and devotions—English. I. Title.

GOODRICH, Donna Clark. 242'.6'43
Brighten the corner, and 45 other women's devotions. Cincinnati, Standard Pub. [1972] 96 p. illus. 18 cm. (Fountain books) [BV4844.G66] 72-82086
1. Women—Prayer-books and devotions—English. I. Title.

GRAFF, Mab. 242'.6'43
God loves my kitchen best / Mab Graff. Grand Rapids : Zondervan Pub. House, c1977. 206 p. ; 18 cm. [BV4844.G7] 77-5618 ISBN 0-310-35612-1 pbk. : 1.95
1. Wives—Prayer-books and devotions—English. I. Title.

GRAFF, Mab. 242'.6'43
God loves my kitchen best / Mab Graff. Grand Rapids : Zondervan Pub. House, c1977. 206 p. ; 18 cm. [BV4844.G7] 77-5618 ISBN 0-310-35612-1 pbk. : 1.95
1. Wives—Prayer-books and devotions—English. I. Title.

HARRELL, Irene B. 242'.6'43
Praverables meditations of a homemaker, by Irene B. Harrell. Waco. Tex.. Word Bks. [1967] 101p. 21cm. [BV4832.2.H523] 67-17828 2.95
1. Meditations 2. Women—Prayer-books and devotions. I. Title.

HARRELL, Irene B 242'6'43
Prayerables; meditations of a homemaker, by Irene B. Harrell. Waco, Tex., Word Books [1967] 101 p. 21 cm. [BV4832.2.H323] 67-17828
1. Meditations. 2. Women — Prayer-books and devotions. I. Title.

HARRELL, Irene Burk. 242'.6'43
Ordinary days with an extraordinary God; prayerables II, by Irene Harrell. Waco, Tex., Word Books [1973, c.1971] 125 p. 18 cm. (A Word pbk., 90036) [BV283.M7H37] 72-144360 0.95 (pbk.)
1. Mothers—Peayerbooks and devotions—English. I. Title. II. Title: Prayerables II.

HOLMES, Deborah Aydt, 242'.6'43
1949-
Survival prayers for young mothers / by Deborah Aydt Holmes. Atlanta : John Knox Press, c1977. 111 p. ; 21 cm. [BV4847.H55] 76-12390 ISBN 0-8042-2195-2 : 4.95
1. Mothers—Prayer-books and devotions—English. I. Title.

HOLMES, Deborah Aydt, 242'.6'43
1949-
Survival prayers for young mothers / by Deborah Aydt Holmes. Atlanta : John Knox Press, c1977. 111 p. ; 21 cm. [BV4847.H55] 76-12390 ISBN 0-8042-2195-2 : 4.95
1. Mothers—Prayer-books and devotions—English. I. Title.

HOLMES, Marjorie, 1910- 242.643
As tall as my heart; a mother's measure of love. New York, Bantam Books, [1975] 117 p. 18 cm. [BV283.M7H46] 1.25 (pbk.)
1. Mothers—Prayer-books and devotions—English. I. Title.
L.C. card no. for original edition: 74-75733

HOLMES, Marjorie, 1910- 242'.6'43
As tall as my heart; a mother's measure of love. McLean, Va., EFM Publications; distributed by Hawthorn Books [New York] 1974. 120 p. illus. 23 cm. (A Love and laughter book) [BV283.M7H64] 74-75733 ISBN 0-914440-03-9 4.95
1. Mothers—Prayer-books and devotions—English. I. Title.

HOLMES, Marjorie, 1910- 242'.6'43
Hold me up a little longer, Lord / Marjorie Holmes ; illustrated by Patricia Mighell. 1st ed. Garden City, N.Y. : Doubleday, 1977. 120 p. : ill. ; 22 cm. [BV4844.H628] 76-42338 ISBN 0-385-12403-1 : 5.95
1. Women—Prayer-books and devotions—English. I. Title.

HOLMES, Marjorie, 1910- 242'.6'43
I've got to talk to somebody, God; a woman's conversations with God. [1st ed.] Garden City, N.Y., Doubleday, 1969. xviii, 121 p. illus. 22 cm. [BV4844.H63] 69-10938 3.95
1. Women—Prayer-books and devotions. I. Title.

IKERMAN, Ruth C. 242.643
Women's programs for special occasions [by] Ruth C. Ikerman. Nashville, Abingdon Press [1966] 159 p. 16 cm. [BV4844.I 4] 66-15003
1. Women — Prayer-books and devotions — English. I. Title.

IKERMAN, Ruth C. 242.643
Women's programs for special occasions. Nashville, Abingdon [c.1966] 159p. 16cm. [BV4844.I4] 66-15003 2.25 bds.,
1. Women—Prayer-books and devotions—English. I. Title.

KOOIMAN, Gladys. 242.6'43
When death takes a father. Grand Rapids, Baker Bk. [1968] 171p. illus. 21cm. [BV4908.K6] 68-31473 3.95 bds.,
1. Death. 2. Consolation. I. Title.

KOOIMAN, Helen W 242.643
Joyfully expectant; meditations before baby comes [by] Helen W. Kooiman. Westwood, N.J., F. H. Revell Co. [1966] 121 p. 21 cm. [BV4529.K6] 66-21898
1. Mothers — Religious life. I. Title.

KOOIMAN, Helen W. 242.643
Joyfully expectant; meditations before baby comes. Westwood, N.J., Revell [c.1966] 121p. 21cm. [BV4529.K6] 66-21898 2.95
1. Mothers—Religious life. I. Title.

LARSON, Muriel. 242'.6'43
Devotions for women's groups. Grand Rapids, Baker Book House [1967] 105 p. 21 cm. [BV4527.L35] 67-2217
1. Women—Prayer-books and devotions. I. Title.

MICHAEL, Phyllis C. 242'.6'43
Is my head on straight? : Meditations for women / Phyllis C. Michael. Waco, Tex. : Word Books, c1976. 120 p. : ill. ; 21 cm. [BV4844.M45] 75-19912 pbk. : 3.50
1. Women—Prayer-books and devotions—English. I. Title.

NORRIS, Judy. 242'.6'43
Flowers of inspiration in God's garden. Cincinnati, Standard Pub. [1972] 95 p. illus. 18 cm. (Fountain books, 2271) [BV4844.N67] 73-190359
1. Women—Prayer-books and devotions—English. I. Title.

SNOWDEN, Rita Frances. 242'.6'43
A woman's book of prayers [by] Rita F. Snowden. Foreword by William Barclay. [1st American ed.] New York, Association Press [1969, c1968] 128 p. 19 cm. [BV4844.S6 1969] 69-18850
1. Women—Prayer-books and devotions—English. I. Title.

WHALEY, Catrina Parrott. 242.643
Share my devotions; living devotions for women for personal and group use. Grand Rapids, Baker Book House, 1965. 120 p. 20 cm. [BV4844.W5] 65-27516
1. Women — Prayer-books and devotions. I. Title.

WHALEY, Catrina Parrott 242.643
Share my devotions; living devotions for women for personal and group use. Grand Rapids, Mich., Baker Bk. [c.]1965. 120p. 20cm. [BV4844.W5] 65-27516 1.95
1. Women—Prayer-books and devotions. I. Title.

ASQUITH, Glenn H 242.65
Lively may I walk; devotions for the golden years. New York, Abingdon Press [1960] 123p. 22cm. [BV4580.A8] 60-9193
1. Aged—Prayer-books and devotions—English. I. Title.

ASQUITH, Glenn H. 242.65
Lively may I walk; devotions for the golden years. Nashville, Abingdon Press [c.1960] 123p. 22cm. 60-9193 2.00 bds.,
1. Aged—Prayer-books and devotions—English. I. Title.

ASQUITH, Glenn H. 242'.6'5
The person I am [by] Glenn H. Asquith. Nashville, Abingdon Press [1969] 144 p. 21 cm. [BV4501.2.A78] 69-18449 3.00
1. Christian life. I. Title.

BEHNKE, Charles A 1891- 242.65
Today and tomorrow; devotions for people who are growing with the years. by Charles W. [i.e. Charles A.] Behnke. Saint Louis, Concordia Pub. House [1965] viii, 120 p. 22 cm. [BV4580.B44] 65-26491
1. Aged — Religious life. I. Title. II. Title: Devotions for people who are growing with the years.

BEHNKE, Charles A., 1891- 242.65
Today and tomorrow; devotions for people who are growing with the years. St. Louis, Concordia [c.1965] viii, 120p. 22cm. [BV4580.B44] 65-26491 2.95
1. Aged—Religious life. I. Title. II. Title: Devotions for people who are growing with the years.

BRANDT, Catharine. 242'.6'5
You're only old once / Catharine Brandt ; illustrated by Audrey Teeple. Minneapolis : Augsburg Pub. House, c1977. 126 p. : ill. ; 22 cm. "Large print." [BV4580.B68] 76-27085 ISBN 0-8066-1570-2 pbk. : 3.95
1. Aged—Prayer-books and devotions—English. 2. Large type books. I. Title.

BUHRIG, Wanda Maria. 242'.6'5
We older people. [Translated by Kathleen M. S. Easton] Valley Forge [Pa.] Judson Press [1971, c1969] 62 p. 20 cm. Translation of Erfulltes Alter. [BV4580.B8413 1971] 77-124992 1.50
1. Aged—Prayer-books and devotions. I. Title.

COCHARD, Thomas S. 242'.6'5
The beloved community, America! / By Thomas S. Cochard. Boston : Branden Press, [1974] 229 p. ; 23 cm. Essays. [BV4832.2.C58] 73-92509 ISBN 0-8283-1539-6 : 10.00
1. Meditations. 2. National characteristics, American. I. Title.

EGGERS, William T. 242'.6'5
Space of joy, by William T. Eggers. St. Louis, Concordia Pub. House [1968] 222 p. 22 cm. [BV4580.E32] 68-31070 4.95
1. Aged—Prayer-books and devotions. I. Title.

FIELD, Laurence N. 242'.6'5
Rainbows; reflections for the evening of life, by Laurence N. Field. Minneapolis, Augsburg Pub. House [1970] ix, 134 p. illus. 22 cm. [BV4580.F5] 74-101114 3.75
1. Aged—Prayer-books and devotions—English. I. Title.

KEENE, Milton Henry 242'.6'5
1912-
Patterns for mature living / Milton Henry Keene. Nashville : Abingdon, c1976. 112 p. ; 23 cm. [BV4580.K43] 76-27093 4.95
1. Aged—Prayer-books and devotions—English. I. Title.

LANG, Paul H. D. 242'.6'5
The golden days / Paul H. D. Lang. St. Louis : Concordia Pub. House, c1976. p. cm. Large print ed. [BS483.5.L36 1976] 75-43871 pbk. : 3.95
1. Bible—Meditations. 2. Aged—Prayer-books and devotions—English. 3. Sight-saving books. I. Title.

LEWIS, Alvin G. 242'.6'5
Teach me, Lord : devotions on basic Christian teachings / Alvin G. Lewis. Minneapolis : Augsburg Pub. House, c1976. 159 p. ; 22 cm. Large print ed. [BV4580.L49 1976] 76-3879 ISBN 0-8066-1535-4 : 4.50
1. Aged—Prayer-books and devotions—English. 2. Sight-saving books. I. Title.

LUNDE, Johan, Bp., 1866- 1938 242'.6'5
Light at eventide; devotions for the autumn years. Tr. by Palmer Loken. Minneapolis, Minn., Augsburg [1967] 172p. 22cm. Tr. of Sondagsbok for eldre. [BV4580.L8] 67-11726 3.95
1. Aged—Prayer-books and devotions. I. Title.

LUNDE, Johan, Bp., 1866- 1938. 242'.6'5
Light at eventide; devotions for the autumn years. Translated by Palmer Loken. Minneapolis, Minn., Augusburg Pub. House [1967] 172 p. 22 cm. Translation of Sondagsbok for eldre. [BV4580.L8] 67-11726
1. Aged — Prayer-books and devotions. I. Title.

*MCCREARY, W. Burgess 242.65
With the passing seasons; meditations for the mature years. Anderson, Ind., Warner, c.1965. 96p. 21cm. 1.50, pap., plastic bdg., bxd.
1. Church year—Meditations. I. Title.

ROBERTSON, Josephine. 242'.6'5
Meditations for the later years. Drawings by Giorgetta Bell McRee. Nashville, Abingdon Press [1974] 80 p. illus. 21 cm. [BV4580.R57] 73-19935 ISBN 0-687-24099-9 3.50
1. Aged—Prayer-books and devotions—English. I. Title.

ROBERTSON, Josephine 242.65
Saying yes to life as we grow older. Nashville, Abingdon [1966] 144p. 21cm. [BV4501.2.R615] 66-21191 2.75
1. Christian life. 2. Aged—Religious life. I. Title.

SCHEIDT, David L. 242'.6'5
The best is yet to be / by Kurt Rommel ; translated and adapted by David L. Scheidt. Philadelphia : Fortress Press, [1975] 77 p. : ill. ; 22 cm. Free translation of Das Alter, die hohe Zeit des Lebens. [BV4580.S29513] 74-26327 ISBN 0-8006-1096-2 pbk. : 2.95
1. Aged—Prayer-books and devotions—English. I. Rommel, Kurt. Das Alter, die hohe Zeit des Lebens. II. Title.

SWANSON, D. Verner 242.65
Life's crowing years; a book of inspiration, by D. Verner Swanson. Philadelphia, Fortress [1966] 122p. 23cm. Bibl. [BV4580.S9] 66-24861 3.50
1. Aged—Prayer-books and devotions. I. Title.

WISLoFF, Hans Edvard, 1902-1969. 242'.6'5
Safe in His arms; devotions for the autumn years, by H. E. Wisloff. Translated by Joel M. Njus. Minneapolis, Augsburg Pub. House [1969] 94 p. 27 cm. Translation of Trygg tross alt. [BV4580.W5413] 69-14185 3.95
1. Aged—Prayer-books and devotions. I. Title.

BOROS, Ladislaus, 1927- 242.66
Pain and providence. Tr. by Edward Quinn. Baltimore, Helicon [1966] 131p. 21cm. Tr. of Erlostes Dasein: theologische Betrachtungen. [BT732.7.B613] 66-26629 3.50 bds.,
1. Suffering. I. Title.
Available from Taplinger, New York

BOROS, Ladislaus, 1927- 242'.6'6
Pain and Providence / by Ladislaus Boros ; translated by Edward Quinn. New York : Seabury Press, [1975] 1972. p. cm. Translation of Erlostes Dasein: theologische Betrachtungen. "A Crossroad book." [BT732.7.B613 1975] 74-26563 ISBN 0-8164-2110-2 pbk. : 2.95
1. Suffering. I. Title.

COFFEY, John W. 242'.6'8
God is my pilot; meditations for Christian servicemen and veterans, by John W. Coffey, Jr. Nashville, T. Nelson [1973] 88 p. illus. 19 cm. [BV4588.C57] 73-6933 2.50
1. Armed forces—Prayer-books and devotions—English. I. Title.

FITZGERALD, Lawrence P 242.68
The serviceman at prayer, by Lawrence P. Fitzgerald. Nashville, Upper Room [1966] 95 p. 13 cm. [BV273.F5] 66-16858
1. Armed Forces — Prayer-books and devotions — English. I. Title.

FITZGERALD, Lawrence P. 242.68
The serviceman at prayer. Nashville, Upper Room [c.1966] 95p. 13cm. [BV273.F5] 66-16858 1.00
1. Armed Forces—Prayer-books and devotions—English. I. Title.

HACKMAN, Jenny. 242'.6'8
Jenny's prayer diary. Old Tappan, N.J., F. H. Revell Co. [1971] 128 p. 19 cm. [BV245.H22] 70-160275 ISBN 0-8007-0469-X
1. Prayers. I. Title.

*LOCKERBIE, Jeanette W. 242.68
Daily assignment, devotional readings for teachers. Chicago, Moody [c.1966] 127p. 15cm. 1.00 pap.,
I. Title.

PARSONS, William Edward, 1936- 242'.6'8
Meditations for servicemen [by] William E. Parsons, Jr. Nashville, Abingdon Press [1967] 160 p. 18 cm. [BV4588.P3] 67-14986
1. Armed Forces—Prayer-books and devotions. I. Title.

PARSONS, William Edward, 1936- 242'.6'8
Meditations for servicemen [by] William E. Parsons, Jr. Nashville, Abingdon [1967] 160p. 18cm. [BV4588.P3] 67-14986 2.50
1. Armed Forces—Prayer-books and devotions. I. Title.

STRENGTH for service to God and country. 242'.6'8 Edited by Lawrence P. Fitzgerald. Nashville, Abingdon Press [1969] 1 v. (unpaged) 13 cm. [BV4588.S86] 71-84710
1. Armed Forces—Prayer-books and devotions—English. I. Fitzgerald, Lawrence P., ed.

WARNER, Wayne E. 242'.6'8
Good morning, Lord; devotions for servicemen [by] Wayne E. Warner. Grand Rapids, Mich., Baker Book House [1971] 64 p. 19 cm. Bibliography: p. 64. [BV4588.W34] 71-164375 ISBN 0-8010-9520-4
1. Armed Forces—Prayer-books and devotions—English. I. Title.

CHAMPLIN, Joseph M. 242'.6'82
Together in peace for children / Joseph M. Champlin and Brian A. Haggerty. Notre Dame, Ind. : Ave Maria Press, c1976. 72 p. : ill. (some col.) ; 22 cm. [BX2150.C578] 76-26348 ISBN 0-87793-119-4 pbk. : 1.35
1. Children—Prayer-books and devotions—English. 2. Penance—Juvenile literature. I. Haggerty, Brian A., joint author. II. Title.

*MOORE, Cora 242.69
Inspiring devotional programs for women's groups; v.2. Grand Rapids, Mich., Zondervan [1967] v. 21cm. 1.25 pap.,
I. Title.

*MOORE, Cora. 242.69
Inspiring devotional programs for women's groups; v.3. Grand Rapids. Mich., Zondervan [1968] v. 20cm. 1.00 pap.,
I. Title.

*MOORE, Cora 242.69
Inspiring devotional programs for women's groups; complete devotional programs for every month of the year. Grand Rapids, Mich., Zondervan [c.1966] 64p. 21cm. 1.00 pap.,
I. Title.

PATT, Richard W. 242'.6'9
Psallite : devotions and prayers for church choir singers : based on the Gospels, series C, from The church year calendar and lectionary / by Richard W. Patt. St. Louis : Concordia Pub. House, c1976. 80 p. ; 21 cm. [BV4596.C48P37] 76-47672 ISBN 0-570-03748-4 pbk. : 2.00
1. Choirs (Music)—Prayer-books and devotions—English. I. Title.

CHURCH year book; 242'.6'92
directory and general information of Catholic churches, schools, institutions, societies, etc., in the City of Chicago, Illinois. [Chicago] v. illus. 30cm. [BX1418.C4C47] 56-48899
1. Catholic Church in Chicago—Yearbooks.

CHURCH year book; 242'.6'92
directory and general information of Catholic churches, schools, institutions, societies, etc., in the City of Chicago, Illinois. [Chicago] v. illus. 30 cm. [BX1418.C4C47] 56-48899
1. Catholic Church in Chicago—Yearbooks.

COURTOIS, Gaston 242.692
You who are sent; prayers for the apostolate. [Tr. from French by Sister David Mary. New York] Herder & Herder [c.1966] 126p. 21cm. [BX1912.5.C6193] 66-13076 2.95
1. Meditations. 2. Clergy—Religious life. I. Title.

HERR, Vincent V 242'.6'92
Screening candidates for the priesthood and religious life [by] Vincent V. Herr [and others] Chicago, Loyola University Press [1964] vii, 203 p. illus. 24 cm. Includes bibliographies. [bX2380.H44] 68-1770
1. Vocation (in religious orders, congregations, etc.) I. Title.

PASH, Joseph J 242'.6'92
History of the Immaculate Conception Parish in the Colville Valley [Colville, Wash.] 1962. 67 p. illus. 22 cm. [BX1418.C7P3] 63-303
1. Colville, Wash. Immaculate Conception Church. I. Title.

RAHNER, Karl, 1904- 242'.6'92
Mission and grace; essays in pastoral theology. Tranlated by Cecily Hastings. London, New York, Sheed and Ward [1963-66] 3 v. 18 cm. (Stagbooks) vol. 2 translated by Cecily Hastings and Richard Strachan. Includes bibliographies. [BX1913.R3132] 66-2860
1. Pastoral theology—Catholic Church. I. Title.

RAHNER, Karl, 1904- 242'.6'92
The priesthood. Translated by Edward Quinn. [New York] Herder and Herder [1973] vi, 281 p. 22 cm. Translation of Einubung priesterlicher Existenz. [BX2184.R2813 1973] 72-94304 ISBN 0-07-073791-6 8.95
1. Catholic Church—Clergy. 2. Meditations. I. Title.

RIEGERT, Berard M 242'.6'92
The obligation of following a religious vocation, a study of theological opinion from the seventeenth to the nineteenth centuries. Washington, Catholic University of America Press, 1962. xiii, 168 p. 23 cm. (Catholic University of America. Studies in sacred theology, 2d ser., no. 136) Thesis -- Catholic University of America. Bibliography: p. 159-166. [BX2380.R5] 64-328
1. Vocation (in religious orders, congregations, etc.) — History of doctrines. I. Title. II. Series. III. Series: Catholic University of America. School of Sacred Theology. Studies in sacred theology, 2d ser., no. 136

DALY, Lowrie John 242.694
Meditation for educators, by Lowrie J. Daly, Mary Virgene Daly. Introd. by Paul C. Reinert. New York, Sheed [c.1965] 176p. 21cm. [BX2373.T4D3] 65-20865 3.95
1. Teachers—Meditations. I. Daly, Mary Virgene, joint author. II. Title.

DALY, Lowrie John. 242.694
Meditations for educators, by Lowrie J. Daly and Mary Virgene Daly. With an introd. by Paul C. Reinert. New York, Sheed and Ward [1965] 176 p. 21 cm. [BX2373.T4D3] 65-20865
1. Teachers — Meditations. I. Daly, Mary Virgene, joint author. II. Title.

MERTON, Thomas, 1915- 1968. 242'.6'94
Contemplative prayer. [New York] Herder and Herder [1969] 144 p. 21 cm. Bibliographical footnotes. [BV4813.M43] 74-87761 4.50
1. Meditation. 2. Prayer. I. Title.

*BAYNE H. RAYMOND. 242.7
Before the offering : mini-messages on giving / Raymond Bayne. Grand Rapids : Baker Book House c1976. 130p. ; 22 cm. [BV4812.B] ISBN 0-8010-0660-0 pbk. : 1.95
1. Meditations. I. Title.

SJOGREN, Per-Olof, 1919- 242'.72
The Jesus prayer = Lord Jesus Christ, Son of God, have mercy upon me / [by Per-Olof Sjogren ; translation by Sydney Linton]. 1st American ed. Philadelphia : Fortress Press, 1975. 96 p. ; 18 cm. Translation of Jesusbonen. Includes bibliographical references. [BT590.J28S5613 1975] 75-18789 ISBN 0-8006-1216-7 pbk. : 2.50
1. Jesus prayer. I. Title.

STRUCHEN, Jeanette. 242.7'2
Thank God for the red, white, and black. [1st ed.] Philadelphia, J. B. Lippincott Co. [1970] 57 p. 19 cm. [BV245.S843] 75-105550
1. Prayers. I. Title.

CARTWRIGHT, Colbert S., 1924- 242'.722
The Lord's prayer comes alive [by] Colbert S. Cartwright. St. Louis, Bethany Press [1973] p. Includes bibliographical references. [BV230.C225] 73-2816 ISBN 0-8272-2112-6
1. Lord's prayer. I. Lord's prayer. 1973. II. Title.
Publishers address: 2640 Pine Blvd., St. Louis, Mo. 63166.

EBELING, Gerhard, 1912- 242.722
On prayer; nine sermons. [Translated by James W. Leitch] Introd. by David James Randolph. Philadelphia, Fortress Press [1966] ix, 145 p. 18 cm. (The Preacher's paperback library, 6) [BV230.E2313] 66-17341
1. Lord's prayer—Sermons. 2. Sermons, German—Translations into English. I. Title.

EBELING, Gerhard, 1912- 242.722
On prayer; nine sermons. [Tr. from German by James W. Leitch] Introd. by David James Randolph. Philadelphia, Fortress [c.1966] ix, 145p. 18cm. (Preacher's paperback lib., 6) [BV230.E2313] 66-17341 2.00 pap.,
1. Lord's prayer—Sermons. 2. Sermons, German—Translations into English. I. Title.

EVELY, Louis, 1910- 242'.722
We dare to say Our Father. [Translated by James Langdale. New York] Herder and Herder [1965] 128 p. 22 cm. Translation of Notre Pere—aux sources de notre fraternite. [BV230.E853 1965b] 64-21428
1. Lord's prayer. I. Title.

LESSMANN, Paul G. 242.722
The Lord's prayer and the Lord's Passion; Lenten sermons, by Paul G. Lessmann. St. Louis, Concordia [1966, c.1965] 109p. 19cm. [BV230.L43] 66-12154 1.75 pap.,
1. Lord's prayer—Sermons. 2. Jesus Christ—Passion—Sermons. 3. Lenten sermons. I. Title.

LETCHFORD, Peter. 242'.722
Help! I don't know how to pray. Amen / by Peter Letchford. 1st ed. Nashville : Impact Books, c1976. 146 p. ; 21 cm. [BV230.L435] 76-29332 4.95
1. Lord's prayer—Sermons. 2. Sermons, American. I. Title.

LOHMEYER, Ernst, 1890- 1946 242.722
'Our Father'; an introduction to the Lord's prayer. Tr. by John Bowden. New York, Harper [1966, c.1965] 320p. 22cm. London ed. (Collins) has title: The Lord's prayer. Bibl. [BV230.L5513] 66-10228 4.95
1. Lord's prayer. I. Title.

*PRIME, Derek 242.722
Tell me about the Lord's Prayer. Chicago, Moody [1967, c.1965] 64p. illus. 19cm. (Moody arrows: devotional, no. 20) .50 pap.,
1. Lord's Prayer—Study and teaching—Juvenile literature. I. Title.

WELDON, Wilson O. 242.7'22
Our Father; discoveries in the Lord's prayer, by Wilson O. Weldon. Nashville, Tenn., Upper Room [1968] 64 p. 20 cm. Originally published in 1966 under title: Discoveries in the Lord's prayer. [BV230.W37 1968] 68-26902
1. Lord's prayer. I. Title.

PATON, Alan. 242'.726
Instrument of Thy peace : the Prayer of St. Francis / Alan Paton ; photos. by Ray Ellis. New York : Seabury Press, c1975. 128 p. : ill. ; 23 cm. "A Crossroad book." [BV284.F7P37 1975] 75-13522 ISBN 0-8164-2596-5 : 4.95
1. Prayer of St. Francis—Meditations. I. Title.

BRICKEY, Janice. 242'.742
The triumphant way; rosary meditations. Foreword by Patrick J. Peyton. Pictures by Fra Angelico. St. Louis, Herder [1962] 95p. illus. 18cm. [BX2163.B68] 61-18371
1. Rosary—Meditations. I. Title.

HABIG, Marion Alphonse, 1901- 242'.742
The Franciscan crown / by Marion A. Habig. Chicago : Franciscan Herald Press, c1976. p. cm. [BX2163.H3] 76-10670 ISBN 0-8199-0605-0 : 2.50
1. Franciscan crown. 2. Rosary—History. I. Title.

HARRINGTON, Wilfrid J. 242'.742
The Rosary : a Gospel prayer / W. J. Harrington. Canfield, Ohio : Alba Books, c1975. xii, 146 p. : ill. ; 18 cm. Bibliography: p. [145]-146. [BX2163.H34] 75-44676 ISBN 0-8189-1129-8 pbk. : 1.65
1. Rosary. I. Title.

SCRIPTURAL Rosary Center. 242'.742
Scriptural Rosary; a modern version of the way the Rosary was once prayed throughout Western Europe in the late Middle Ages. Chicago [1963, c1961] 80 p. col. illus. 13 cm. [BX2163.S37] 64-66463
1. Rosary—Meditations. I. Title.

SLAVES of the Immaculate Heart of Mary. 242'.742
Hail Mary, full of grace. Still River [Mass., 1972] 116 p. illus. 21 cm. [BX2163.S6 1972] 72-93984
1. Rosary. I. Title.

WALLS, Ronald. 242'.742
The glory of Israel; scriptural background on the mysteries of the Rosary. Huntington, Ind., Our Sunday Visitor [1972] 94 p. illus. 21 cm. [BT303.W26] 72-75088 ISBN 0-87973-813-8 1.95
1. Catholic Church—Sermons. 2. Mysteries of the Rosary—Sermons. 3. Sermons, English—Scotland. I. Title.

WARD, Joseph Neville. 242'.742
Five for sorrow, ten for joy; a consideration of the Rosary [by] J. Neville Ward. Garden City, N.Y., Image Books, 1974 [c1971] 197 p. 18 cm. [BX2163.W29 1974] 74-3378 ISBN 0-385-09544-9 1.45 (pbk.).
1. Rosary. 2. Christian life—Methodist authors. I. Title.

*WARD, Joseph Neville 242.742
Five for sorrow, ten for joy; a consideration of

the rosary, [by] J. Neville Ward. Garden City, N.Y., Doubleday, 1974 197 p. 18 cm. (Image books) [BX2310.R7] ISBN 0-385-09544-9 1.45 (pbk.)
1. Devotional literature. 2. Rosary. 3. Mary, Virgin. I. Title.
L.C. card number for original ed.: 72-86579

WARD, Joseph Neville. 242'.742
Five for sorrow, ten for joy; a consideration of the Rosary [by] J. Neville Ward. [1st ed.] Garden City, N.Y., Doubleday, 1973 [c1971] 164 p. 22 cm. Includes bibliographical references. [BX2163.W29 1973] 72-96263 ISBN 0-385-03805-4 4.95
1. Rosary. 2. Christian life—Methodist authors. I. Title.

*WEDGE, Florence 242.7'42
Rediscovering the Rosary. Pulaski, Wis., Franciscan Pubs. [1967] 62p. 19cm. .25 pap.,
I. Title.

AASENG, Rolf E. 242.8
God is great, God is good; devotions for families, by Rolf E. Aaseng. Designed and illustrated by Don Wallerstedt. Minneapolis, Augsburg Pub. House [1971, c1972] 125 p. illus. 23 cm. [BV255.A18] 75-176470 ISBN 0-8066-1200-2 3.95
1. Family—Prayer-books and devotions—English. I. Title.

ALDERMAN, Joy. 242'.8
Renewed in strength. Valley Forge [Pa.] Judson Press [1975] [28] p. illus. 18 cm. Prayers. [BV245.A38] 74-18108 ISBN 0-8170-0660-5 1.00 (pbk.)
1. Prayers. I. Title.

ARMSTRONG, Richard G. 242'.8
Christopher prayers for today [by] Richard Armstrong. Introd. by James Keller. New York, Paulist Press [1972] 64 p. illus. 17 cm. [BV245.A74] 72-86745 ISBN 0-8091-1735-5 0.75 (pbk.)
1. Prayers. I. Title.

BANIGAN, Sharon (Church) j 242.8
1912- comp.
Graces for children, selected and illustrated by Sharon Banigan. Chicago, Follet Pub. Co. [1966] 44 p. col. illus. 29 x 14 cm. [BV265.B27] 66-15915
1. Children — Prayer-books and devotions — 1961- 2. Grace at meals. I. Title.

BANIGAN, Sharon (Church) 242.8
1912- comp.
Graces for children, selected, illus. by Sharon Banigan. Chicago, Follett [c.1966] 44p. col. illus. 29x14cm. [BV265.B27] 66-15915 1.00 bds.,
1. Children—Prayer-books and devotions—1961- 2. Grace at meals. I. Title.

BANIGAN, Sharon (Church) j 242.8
1912- comp.
Hear our prayer. Illustrated by Helen Page. Prayers selected by Sharon Stearns. Chicago, Follett Pub. Co. [1966] 44 p. col. illus. 29 x 14 cm. [BV265.B32] 66-15919
1. Children — Prayer-books and devotions I. Title.

BANIGAN, Sharon (Church) 242.8
1912- comp.
Hear our prayer. Illus. by Helen Page. Prayers selected by Sharon Stearns. Chicago, Follett [c.1966] 44p. col. illus. 29x14cm. [BV265.B32] 66-15919 1.00 bds.,
1. Children—Prayer-books and devotions. I. Title.

BANIGAN, Sharon (Church) 242.8
1912- comp.
Prayers for children. Illus. by Helen Page. Prayers selected by Sharon Banigan, Jessie Corrigan Pegis. Chicago, Follett [c.1966] 44p. col. illus. 29x14cm. [BV265.B35] 66-15918 1.00 bds.,
1. Children—Prayer-books and devotions—1961- I. Pegis, Jessie Corrigan, joint comp. II. Title.

BEIMFOHR, Herman N 242.8
Prayers for today [by] Herman N. Beimfohr. Westwood, N.J., F. H. Revell Co. [1967] 128 p. 17 cm. [BV245.B54] 67-22567
1. Prayers. I. Title.

BEIMFOHR, Herman N. 242.8
Prayers for today [by] Herman N. Beimfohr. Westwood, N.J., F. H. Revell Co. [1967] 128 p. 17 cm. [BV245.B54] 67-22567
1. Prayers. I. Title.

BERG, Roger J. 242'.8
The roses are grinning / by Roger Berg. Corona Del Mar, Calif. : Emerson House Publishers, c1974. 142 p. ; 23 cm. [BV245.B544] 74-32585
1. Prayers. I. Title.

BERTHIER, Rene. 242'.8 s
Prayers for everyday life / Rene Berthier, Jean Puyo, Paul Gilles Trebossen ; [translated by Jerome J. DuCharme]. Notre Dame, Ind. : Fides Publishers, [1974] vii, 86 p. ; 20 cm. (Contemporary prayer ; v. 2) Includes indexes. [BV246.L5813 vol. 2] 242'.8 74-194398
1. Prayers. I. Puyo, Jean, joint author. II. Trebossen, Paul Gilles, joint author. III. Title. IV. Series: Livre de la priere. English. vol. 2.

BIBLE. English. Selections. 242.8
1967. Authorized.
Prayers from the Bible, selected by Hilda Noel Schroetter. Illustrated by Martin Silverman. New York, Golden Press [1967] 64 p. illus. 16 cm. (The Golden library of faith & inspiration) "A Giniger book." [BV228.S3] 67-13732
1. Bible—Prayers. I. Schroetter, Hilda (Noel), comp. II. Title.

BIBLE. English. Selections. 242.8
1967. Authorized
Prayers from the Bible, selected by Hilda Noel Schroetter. Illus. by Martin Silverman. New York, Golden [1967] 64p. illus. 16cm. (Golden lib. of faith & inspiration) A Giniger bk. [BV228.S3] 67-13732 1.00 bds.,
1. Bible—Pravers. I. Schroetter, Hilda (Noel), comp. II. Title.

BISHOP, Bette. comp. 242.8
A child's prayers; beautiful prayers for every occasion. Color illus. by Vivian Smith. [Kansas City, Mo., Hallmark Eds., 1968] 60p. col. illus. 20cm. [BV265.B57] 67-21534 2.50
1. Children—Prayer-books and devotions. I. Title.

BISHOP, Bette, comp. 242.8
A child's prayers; beautiful prayers for every occasion. With color illus. by Vivian Smith. [Kansas City, Mo., Hallmark Editions, 1968] 60 p. col. illus. 20 cm. Seventy-eight prayers in verse for loved ones, meals, and special occasions, as well as morning and evening prayers. [BV265.B57] AC 68
1. Prayer-books and devotions. I. Smith, Vivian, illus. II. Title.

BOYD, Malcolm 242.8
Are you running with me, Jesus? Prayers by Malcolm Boyd. [New York] Avon [1967, c.1965] 158p. 18cm. (VS17) [BV425.B63] .75 pap.,
1. Prayers. I. Title.

BOYD, Malcolm. 242.8
Are You running with me, Jesus? Prayers. [1st ed.] New York, Holt, Rinehart and Winston [1965] 119 p. 21 cm. The personal prayers of a modern Episcopalian priest who believes that prayer is a direct response, offered freely by an individual man thinking as he usually speaks, and that prayer concerns the everyday events and concerns of man. Organized by topics, such as racial freedom, the campus, films, and sexual freedom. [BV245.B63] AC 68
1. Prayers. I. Title.

BOYD, Malcolm, 1923- 242.8
Are Your running with me, Jesus? Prayers. [1st ed.] New York, Holt, Rinehart and Winston [1965] 119 p. 21 cm. [BV245.B63] 65-22473
1. Prayers. I. Title.

BOYD, Malcolm, 1923- 242'.8
When in the course of human events [by] Malcolm Boyd and Paul Conrad. [New York] Sheed and Ward [1973] 155 p. illus. 23 cm. Prayers. [BV245.B636] 73-11507 ISBN 0-8362-0558-8 5.95
1. Prayers. 2. Editorial cartoons—United States. I. Conrad, Paul, 1924- illus. II. Title.

BRANDT, Leslie F. 242'.8
Book of Christian prayer [by] Leslie F. Brandt. Minneapolis, Augsburg Pub. House [1974] 96 p. 18 cm. [BV245.B638] 73-88603 ISBN 0-8066-1406-4 1.95 (pbk.)
1. Prayers. I. Title.

BRANDT, Leslie F. 242.8
Good Lord, where are You? Prayers for the 20th century based on the Psalms [by] Leslie F. Brandt. St. Louis, Concordia [1967] 66p. 21cm. [BS1424.B7] 67-17974 1.75
I. Bible. O. T. Psalms. English. paraghrases. 1967. II. Title.

BRANDT, Leslie F. 242'.8
Growing together : prayers for married people / Leslie and Edith Brandt. Minneapolis, Minn. : Augsburg Pub. House, 1975. 96 p. ; 20 cm. [BV4596.M3B7] 75-2830 ISBN 0-8066-1476-5 pbk. : 2.50
1. Married people—Prayer-books and devotions—English. I. Brandt, Edith, joint author. II. Title.

BROKERING, Herbert F. 242.8
Lord, be with, by Herbert Brokering. Saint Louis, Concordia Pub. House [1969] 155 p. facsims. 22 cm. [BV245.B67] 74-88060 1.95
1. Prayers. I. Title.

BROOKE, Avery. 242'.8
Plain prayers for a complicated world / by Avery Brooke ; illustrated by Ronald Kuriloff. New York : Reader's Digest Press : distributed by Crowell, 1975. 95 p. : ill. ; 22 cm. [BV245.B673 1975] 75-10614 ISBN 0-88349-060-9 : 4.95 ISBN 0-88349-061-7 pbk. : 2.95
1. Prayers. I. Title.

BROWN, Annice Harris, 242'.8
1897-
Thank you, Lord, for little things. Illustrated by Eleanor Troth Lewis. Richmond, John Knox Press [1973] 39 p. illus. 16 cm. Poems. [BV245.B674] 72-11166 ISBN 0-8042-2580-X 2.95
1. Prayers. I. Title.

CAMPBELL, Ernest T. 242'.8
Where cross the crowded ways: prayers of a city pastor [by] Ernest T. Campbell. New York, Association Press [1973] 96 p. 22 cm. [BV245.C26] 73-9792 ISBN 0-8096-1861-3 2.95
1. Prayers. I. Title.

CARR, Jo. 242'.8
Mockingbirds and angel songs & other prayers / Jo Carr and Imogene Sorley. Nashville : Abingdon Press, [1975] 109 p. ; 21 cm. [BV245.C324] 75-11847 ISBN 0-687-27099-5 : 3.50
1. Prayers. I. Sorley, Imogene, joint author. II. Title.

CARR, Jo. 242'.8
Plum jelly and stained glass & other prayers [by] Jo Carr & Imogene Sorley. Nashville [Tenn.] Abingdon Press [1973] 110 p. 21 cm. [BV245.C325] 72-14163 ISBN 0-687-31659-6 2.75
1. Prayers. I. Sorley, Imogene, joint author. II. Title.

CLOUD, Fred, comp. 242.8
Prayers for reconciliation. [Nashville, Tenn.] Upper Room [1970] 87 p. 13 cm. [BV245.C54] 71-103397
1. Prayers. I. Title.

CLOUD, Fred, ed. 242.8
A traveler's prayer book. Nashville, Upper Room [1965] 93p. illus. 13cm. [BV283.T7C6] 65-23851 1.00 pap.,
1. Travelers—Prayer-books and devotions. I. Title.

COBURN, John B. 242'.8
A diary of prayers, personal and public / by John B. Coburn. Philadelphia : Westminster Press, [1975] 155 p. ; 21 cm. [BV245.C55] 75-12824 pbk. : 4.95
1. Prayers. I. Title.

CONTEMPORARY prayer / 242'.8
Thierry Maertens ... [et al. ; translated by Jerome J. DuCharme]. Notre Dame, Ind. : Fides Publishers, [1974] 2 v. ; 20 cm. Translation of 1-v. work: Livre de la priere. [BV246.L5813] 74-194400 ISBN 0-8190-0446-4(v.1) pbk. : 2.95
1. Prayers. I. Maertens, Thierry, 1921-

COURTNEY, Star L. 242'.8
Now is too soon [by] Star L. Courtney. Old Tappan, N.J., F. H. Revell [1974] 64 p. illus. 19 cm. [BV283.M7C68] 73-22358 ISBN 0-8007-0652-8 2.95
1. Mothers—Prayer-books and devotions—English. 2. Parent and child. I. Title.

CRAGG, Kenneth, comp. 242.8
Alive to God: Muslim and Christian prayer; compiled with an introductory essay by the author. London, New York, Oxford U.P., 1970. xiv, 194 p. 20 cm. Bibliography: p. 173-183. [BL560.C7 1970] 72-525790 ISBN 1-921322-02- 30/-
1. Prayer—Comparative studies. 2. Prayers. 3. Islamic prayers. I. Title.

CUNNINGHAM, Gail Harano. 242'.8
The little book of prayer : with inspiration from the Psalms / by Gail Harano Cunningham ; illustrated by Linda Welty. Kansas City, Mo. : Hallmark, c1975. [32] p. : ill. (some col.) ; 11 cm. (Hallmark editions) [BV245.C83 1975] 74-21915 ISBN 0-87529-435-9 : 2.00
1. Prayers. I. Welty, Linda. II. Bible. O.T. Psalms. English. Revised Standard. Selections. 1975. III. Title.

CUNNINGHAM, Gail Harano. 242'.8
The little book of prayer, with inspiration from the Psalms. Selected and written by Gail Harano Cunningham. Illustrated by Linda Welty. [Kansas City, Mo., Hallmark, 1974] [48] p. col. illus. 16 cm. (Hallmark editions) [BV245.C83] 73-78223 ISBN 0-87529-348-4 2.50
1. Prayers. I. Welty, Linda, illus. II. Bible. O.T. Psalms. English. Revised Standard. Selections. 1974. III. Title.

DEANE, Elisabeth, comp. 242.8
Gift of prayer; a selection of prayers designed to make the burdens lighter and the hours less lonely. Mount Vernon, N.Y., Peter Pauper Press [1971] 62 p. 17 cm. (Gifts of gold) [BV245.D4] 79-25081 1.95
1. Prayers. I. Title.

DRESCHER, John M. 242.8
Heartbeats; emerging from encounters in prayer [by] John M. Drescher. Grand Rapids, Zondervan Pub. House [1970] 158 p. 21 cm. [BV245.D73] 71-106443 3.50
1. Prayers. I. Title.

DUBAY, Thomas. 242'.8
Pilgrims pray. New York, Alba House [1974] vi, 272 p. 22 cm. Includes bibliographical references. [BV210.2.D76] 74-533 ISBN 0-8189-0286-8 4.95
1. Prayer. I. Title.

DUFFICY, Edward. 242'.8
Family prayer. New York, Paulist Press [1973] vii, 68 p. illus. 17 cm. [BV255.D8] 73-82651 ISBN 0-8091-1785-1 0.95 (pbk.)
1. Family—Prayer-books and devotions—English. I. Title.

FERGUSON, Robert R. 242.8
Prayers offered at daily sessions of the Assembly [by] Robert R. Ferguson, chaplain of the Assembly. [Sacramento, 1966] 94 p. port. 15 cm. Cover title: Assembly prayers, 1966. At head of title: California Legislature, 1966 regular (budget) session, 1966 first extraordinary session, 1966 second extraordinary session. [BV280.F46] 73-631097
1. Legislative bodies—Chaplains' prayers. I. California. Legislature. Assembly. II. Title. III. Title: Assembly prayers, 1966.

FIRST graces. 242.8
Illustrated by Tasha Tudor. New York, H. Z. Walck, 1955 [i.e. 1959] 47 p. illus. 14 cm. Twenty-one short graces, including several for meals, and ones for the New Year, Easter, springtime, school, the Fourth of July, United Nations Day, Thanksgiving, and Christmas. [BV265.F54 1959] AC 68
1. Prayer books and devotions. 2. Grace at meals. I. Tudor, Tasha, illus.

FIRST prayers. 242.8
Illustrated by Tasha Tudor. [New York] H. Z. Walck [1959, c1952] 48 p. illus. 14 cm. Catholic edition. Twenty-six prayers for Catholic children, including ones for morning and evening, graces, and such familiar ones as The Lord's Prayer or the Twenty-Second Psalm. [BX2150.F56 1959] AC 68
1. Catholic Church—Prayer books and devotions. 2. Prayer books and devotions. I. Tudor, Tasha, illus.

FORD, Agnes Gibbs, comp. 242.8
Prayers for everyone. Illus. by Joyce D. May. Grand Rapids, Baker Book House [1967] 94 p. illus. 23 cm. [BV245.F65] 67-18175
1. Prayers. I. Title.

FRANKE, Merle G. 242'.8
New life and other joys; prayers for today, by Merle G. Franke. Philadelphia, Fortress Press [1974] 127 p. illus. 22 cm. [BV245.F675] 73-88342 ISBN 0-8006-0263-3 4.95
1. Prayers. I. Title.

FRIDY, Wallace. 242'.8
Everyday prayers for all sorts of needs. Nashville, Abingdon Press [1974] 112 p. 16 cm. [BV245.F695] 73-14745 ISBN 0-687-12332-1 3.50
1. Prayers. I. Title.

GARDEN of prayer / 242'.8
[Ray Schafer, compiler ; Pat Pratt, designer ; Cathy Stanton, illustrator]. Santa Ana, CA. : Vision House, c1976. 85 p. : ill. ; 22 cm. [BV245.G35] 75-42851 ISBN 0-88449-052-1
1. Prayers. I. Schafer, Ray.

GARDEN of prayer / 242'.8
[Ray Schafer, compiler ; Pat Pratt, designer ; Cathy Stanton, illustrator]. Santa Ana, CA. : Vision House, c1976. 85 p. : ill. ; 22 cm. [BV245.G35] 75-42851 ISBN 0-88449-052-1
1. Prayers. I. Schafer, Ray.

GESCH, Roy G. 242.8
On active duty; meditations for the serviceman [by] Roy G. Gesch. St. Louis, Concordia Pub. House [1967] 88 p. 16 cm. [BV4588.G4] 67-12419
1. Armed Forces—Prayer-books and devotions. I. Title.

GRAFTON, Thomas H. 242.8
Make meaningful these passing years; prayers, by Thomas H. Grafton on the campus of Mary Baldwin College. [1st ed.] Staunton, Va.,

Alumnae Association, Mary Baldwin College [1968] 80 p. 20 cm. [BV283.C7G7] 68-21671
1. Universities and colleges—Prayers. I. Mary Baldwin College, Staunton, Va. II. Title.

GRIOLET, Pierre. 242'.8
You call us together. Translated by Edmond Bonin. New York, Paulist Press [1973] x, 198 p. 23 cm. Poems. Translation of Tu viens nous rassembler. [BV245.G6813] 73-82650 ISBN 0-8091-1783-5 3.95 (pbk.)
1. Prayers. I. Title.

HANEY, Thomas R. 242'.8
That nothing may be wasted, by T. R. Haney. New York, Sheed and Ward [1972] ix, 170 p. 21 cm. [BV245.H27] 72-5842 ISBN 0-8362-0501-4 5.95
1. Prayers. I. Title.

HERZEL, Catherine B., comp. 242.8
Prayers of the people of God, by Catherine Herzel. Philadelphia, Fortress Press [1967] 90 p. 18 cm. [BV245.H4] 67-19038
1. Prayers. I. Title.

HOLLINGS, Michael. 242'.8
It's me, O Lord! New prayers for every day, by Michael Hollings and Etta Gullick. Illustrated by Paul Shuttleworth. [1st ed.] Garden City, N.Y., Doubleday, 1973. 159 p. illus. 22 cm. [BV245.H57 1973] 73-79069 ISBN 0-385-04141-1 4.95
1. Prayers. I. Gullick, Etta, joint author. II. Title.

*HOLLINGS, Michael. 242'.8
The one who listens; a book of prayers [compiled by] Michael Hollings & Etta Gullick. New York, Morehouse-Barlow [1973? c.1971] ix, 194 p. 18 cm. [BV245] ISBN 0-8192-4037-0 pap., 2.75
1. Prayers. I. Gullick, Etta, joint comp. II. Title.

*HOTSINPILLER, Stanley T. 242.8
Cluster of church prayers. New York, Carlton [1966] 254p. 22cm. (Hearthstone bk.) 3.50
I. Title.

HUXHOLD, Harry N. 242.8
Great prayers; devotions on prayers in the Bible [by] Harry N. Huxhold. Saint Louis, Concordia Pub. House [1968] 104 p. 19 cm. [BV228.H83] 68-11555
1. Bible—Prayers. I. Title.

JERPHAGNON, Lucien, 1921- 242'.8
Prayers for impossible days / Paul Geres [i.e. L. Jerphagnon] ; [translated by Ingalill H. Hjelm]. Philadelphia : Fortress Press, c1976. vi, 58 p. ; 17 cm. A translation of selections from the author's Prieres pour les jours intenables. [BV260.J35213] 75-36442 ISBN 0-8006-1214-0 pbk. : 1.95
1. Prayers. I. Title.

KLAUSLER, Alfred P. 242'.8
The journalist's prayer book; prayers by prominent writers, editors, and newsmen. Edited by Alfred P. Klausler and John De Mott. Minneapolis, Augsburg Pub. House [1972] 112 p. 20 cm. [BV283.J6K53] 72-78564 ISBN 0-8066-1231-2 2.50
1. Journalists—Prayer-books and devotions—English. I. De Mott, John, 1923- joint author. II. Title.

LARSSON, Flora. 242'.8
Between you & me, Lord : prayer-conversations with God / Flora Larsson. Wheaton, Ill. : H. Shaw Publishers, 1976, c1975. 105 p. : ill. ; 18 cm. [BV245.L27] 76-1341 ISBN 0-87788-062-X pbk. : 1.45
1. Prayers. I. Title.

LAW, Virginia W., comp. 242'.8
Come on, let's pray! Prayers for personal and family worship. Compiled by Virginia Law. Edited by Ronald Patterson. [Nashville] Upper Room [1973] 96 p. 16 cm. [BV245.L33] 72-96026
1. Prayers. I. Title.

LAZ, Medard. 242'.8
Lift up my spirit, Lord! / By Medard Laz. N[ew] Y[ork] : Paulist Press, c1977. vi, 89 p. ; 18 cm. (Emmaus books) [BV245.L36] 76-24444 ISBN 0-8091-1991-9 pbk. : 1.45
1. Prayers. I. Title.

MCELROY, Paul Simpson, 1902- comp. 242.8
Prayers and graces of thanksgiving. With illus. by Stanley Clough. Mount Vernon, N.Y., Peter Pauper Press [1966] 62 p. illus. 19 cm. [BV245.M43] 67-2283
1. Prayers. 2. Grace at meals. I. Title.

MAERTENS, Thierry, 1921- 242'.8 s
Prayers in community / Thierry Maertens, Marguerite DeBilde ; [translated by Jerome J. DuCharme]. Notre Dame, Ind. : Fides Publishers, [1974] x, 145 p. ; 20 cm. (Contemporary prayer ; v. 1) [BV246.L5813 vol. 1] 264'.13 74-194397 ISBN 0-8190-0446-4 : 2.95
1. Prayers. I. DeBilde, Marguerite, joint author. II. Title. III. Series: Livre de la priere. English. ; vol. 1.

MARTIN, Francis A. 242'.8
Prayers from where you are / Francis A. Martin. Waco, Tex. : Word Books, [1975] 96 p. : ill. ; 23 cm. [BV245.M482] 75-10084 2.95
1. Prayers. I. Title.

MEAD, Frank Spencer, 1898- 242'.8
Talking with God : prayers for today / edited by Frank S. Mead. 1st ed. Philadelphia : A. J. Holman Co., c1976. 96 p. ; 19 cm. [BV245.T26] 75-37620 ISBN 0-87981-052-1 : 3.95
1. Prayers. I. Mead, Frank Spencer, 1898- II. Title.

MILES, O. Thomas 242.8
Dialogues with God; prayers for day-to-day living, by O. Thomas Miles. Grand Rapids, Eerdmans [1966] 185p. 21cm. [BV245.M49] 66-22947 2.25
1. Prayers. I. Title.

MORE prayers. 242.8 (j)
Illustrated by Tasha Tudor. New York, H. Z. Walck, 1967. 38 p. illus. (part col.) 14 cm. [BV265.M66] 67-19929
1. Children—Prayer-books and devotions. I. Tudor, Tasha, illus.

OOSTERHUIS, Huub. 242.8
Your word is near; contemporary Christian prayers. Translated by N. D. Smith. Westminster, Md., Newman Press [1968] xii, 152 p. 22 cm. Translation of Bid om vrede. [BV260.O613] 68-20848
1. Prayers. I. Title.

ORTMAYER, Roger. 242'.8
Sing and pray and shout hurray! New York, Friendship Press [1974] 64 p. illus. 21 cm. Bibliography: p. 64. [BV198.O77] 74-3074 ISBN 0-377-00004-3 2.75 (pbk.).
1. Worship programs. 2. Prayers. I. Title.

A Pocketful of prayers for today's needs, moods, and circumstances / 242'.8
edited by Ralph L. Woods. New York : Pillar Books, 1976. 126 p. ; 18 cm. [BV245.P64] 76-16661 ISBN 0-89129-217-9 pbk. : 1.50
1. Prayers. I. Woods, Ralph Louis, 1904-

PRAYERS for all seasons / 242'.8
edited by Paul S. McElroy ; with decorations by Ruth McCrea. Mount Vernon, N.Y. : Peter Pauper Press, [1975] 62 p. : ill. ; 20 cm. [BV245.P83] 75-307242 1.95
1. Prayers. I. McElroy, Paul Simpson, 1902-

PRAYERS for everyone : 242'.8
anthology compiled over thirty years / [by] Pat Lawlor. Melbourne : Hawthorn Press, 1975. 66 p. ; 22 cm. [BV245.P84] 75-317079 ISBN 0-7256-0117-5
1. Prayers. I. Lawlor, Patrick Anthony.

PRAYERS of faith / 242'.8
edited by Richard Newman. Boston : G. K. Hall, 1976. xxi, 165 p. : ill. ; 24 cm. Large print ed. [BV245.P86 1976] 76-7386 ISBN 0-8161-6368-5 lib.bdg. : 8.95
1. Prayers. 2. Sight-saving books. I. Newman, Richard.

PUNGENT prayers / 242'.8
[edited] by Phil E. Pierce. Nashville : Abingdon, c1977. 124 p. : ill. ; 19 cm. [BV245.P93] 77-4936 ISBN 0-687-34909-5 pbk. : 3.95
1. Prayers. I. Pierce, Phil E., 1912-

*QUOIST, Michel. 242.8
I've met Jesus Christ. Translated by J. F. Bernard. [1st ed.] Garden City, New York, Doubleday, 1973. 168 p. 22 cm. Originally published in France under the title: Jesus-Christ ma donne rendez-vous. [BV229] 73-79643 ISBN 0-385-06462-4 4.95.
1. Meditation. 2. Prayer. 3. Christian life—1960- I. Title.

RAUSCHENBUSCH, Walter, 1861-1918. 242'.8
For God and the people : prayers of the social awakening / by Walter Rauschenbusch. Folcroft, Pa. : Folcroft Library Editions, 1977. p. cm. Originally published in 1910 also under title: Prayers of the social awakening. Reprint of the 1910 ed. published by the Pilgrim Press, Boston. [BV245.R35 1977] 77-8615 ISBN 0-8414-7332-3 lib. bdg. : 10.00
1. Prayers. I. Title.

ROBISON, Charles D. 242.8
Look deeply; prayers and photos., by Charles D. Robison. Valley Forge [Pa.] Judson Press [1971] 1 v. (unpaged) illus. 26 cm. [BV245.R6] 77-144084 ISBN 0-8170-0511-0
1. Prayers. I. Title.

ROUNER, Arthur Acy. 242.8
Someone's praying, Lord [by] Arthur A. Rouner, Jr. With a foreword by James S. Stewart. Englewood Cliffs, N.J., Prentice-Hall [1970] xiii, 257 p. 25 cm. [BV245.R68] 74-105716 7.95
1. Prayers. I. Title.

SANBORN, Ruth. 242.8
Do you hear me, God? [by] Ruth and Arthayer Sanborn. Valley Forge [Pa.] Judson Press [1968] 80 p. 20 cm. [BV260.S29] 68-13605
1. Prayers. I. Sanborn, Arthayer, joint author. II. Title.

SANDLIN, John Lewis. 242.8
A boy's book of prayers. Westwood, N.J., Revell [1966] 64 p. 17 cm. Prayers for all occasions especially written for young boys. [BV283.B7S2] AC 67
1. Prayer-books and devotions. I. Title.

SANDLIN, John Lewis. 242.8
A girl's book of prayers. Westwood, N.J., F. H. Revell [1966] 63 p. 17 cm. Prayers for various occasions especially written for young girls. [BV283.G5S2] AC 67
1. Prayer-books and devotions. I. Title.

SCHULLER, Robert Harold. 242'.8
Positive prayers for power-filled living / Robert H. Schuller. New York : Hawthorn Books, c1976. ix, 117 p. ; 22 cm. [BV245.S33 1976] 75-20901 ISBN 0-8015-5950-2 : 4.95
1. Prayers. I. Title.

SCUDDER, Delton Levis, 1906- 242'.8
A larger view; Delton L. Scudder's prayers and addresses. Edited by Austin B. Creel. Gainsville, University of Florida Foundation, 1973. xii, 131 p. 24 cm. [BV245.S38] 74-159912
1. Prayers. 2. Memorial service. I. Title.

SPRINGSTEEN, Anne. 242.8
It's me, O Lord. St. Louis, Concordia Pub. House [1970] 71 p. illus. 16 cm. Poems. [BV245.S63] 75-128866
1. Prayers. I. Title.

SPRINGSTEEN, Anne. 242.8
It's me, O Lord. photography by Edward Bock III. St. Louis, Concordia [1975] 47 p. ill. 14 cm. by 21 cm. [BV245.S63] 75-8467 ISBN 0-570-03242-3 3.95.
1. Prayers. I. Title.

STARKEY, Lycurgus Monroe, ed. 242.8
Prayers of the modern era, edited by Lycurgus M. Starkey, Jr. Nashville, Upper room [1966] 80 p. 15 cm. [BV245.S65] 66-28997
1. Prayers. I. The Upper room. II. Title.

STARKEY, Lycurgus Monroe, ed. 242.8
Prayers of the modern era, ed. by Lycurgus M. Starkey, Jr. Nashville, Upper Room [1966] 80p. 15cm. [BV245.S65] 66-28997 1.00 bds.,
1. Prayers. I. The Upper room. II. Title.

STRUCHEN, Jeanette. 242.8
Prayers to pray wherever you are. [1st ed.] Philadelphia, Lippincott [1969] 64 p. 19 cm. [BV245.S83] 69-14498 2.50
1. Prayers. I. Title.

TALEC, Pierre. 242'.8
Bread in the desert. Translated by Edmond Bonin. New York, Newman Press [1973] vi, 216 p. 23 cm. Translation of Un grand desir. [BV246.T3313] 72-95650 ISBN 0-8091-0178-5 5.95
1. Prayers. I. Title
pap. 3.95; ISBN 0-8091-1763-0.

TANGHE, Omer, 1928- 242.8
Prayers from life. Translated from the Flemish by Annalies Nieuwenhuis. New York, P. J. Kenedy [1968] xii, 156 p. 21 cm. Translation of Wonderen vraag ik U niet. [BV260.T313] 68-22878
1. Prayers. I. Title.

TENGBOM, Mildred. 242'.8
Table prayers : new prayers, old favorites, songs & responses / Mildred Tengbom. Minneapolis : Augsburg Pub. House, c1977. 128 p. ; 18 cm. Contains music. [BV283.G7T4] 77-72451 ISBN 0-8066-1594-X pbk. : 1.95
1. Grace at meals. I. Title.

TIBBETTS, Orlando L. 242'.8
More sidewalk prayers [by] Orlando L. Tibbetts. Valley Forge [Pa.] Judson Press [1973] 96 p. 22 cm. [BV245.T46] 72-11222 ISBN 0-8170-0590-0 pap. 1.95
1. Prayers. 2. Prayer. I. Title.

TIBBETTS, Orlando L. 242.8
Sidewalk prayers [by] Orlando L. Tibbetts. Valley Forge [Pa.] Judson Press [1971] 94 p. 22 cm. [BV245.T47] 71-139501 ISBN 0-8170-0489-0 1.95
1. Prayers. I. Title.

VAN DYKE, Vonda Kay. 242'.8
Your love is here [by] Vonda Van Dyke. [1st ed.] Garden City, N.Y., Doubleday, 1974. viii, 117 p. illus. 22 cm. [BV245.V36] 74-3699 ISBN 0-385-09539-2 4.95
1. Prayers. I. Title.

WALKER, Michael, 1932- 242.8
Hear me, Lord; prayers from life. [1st ed.] Old Tappan, N.J., Revell [1971, c1969] 128 p. illus. 20 cm. [BV245.W27 1971] 76-138260 ISBN 0-8007-0438-X
1. Prayers. I. Title.

WEGENER, William E., comp. 242.8
Prayers for Protestants [Philadelphia] Fortress [1966, c.1946-1965] vi, 122p. 12cm. Bibl. [BV245.W36] 66-10158 1.95
1. Prayers. I. Title.

WEISHEIT, Eldon. 242.8
Excuse me, Sir ... St. Louis, Concordia Pub. House [1971] 117 p. 20 cm. Poems. [BV245.W38] 78-139996 ISBN 0-570-03009-9
1. Prayers. I. Title.

WEST, Herbert B. 242'.8
Stay with me Lord: a man's prayers [by] Herbert B. West. New York, Seabury Press [1974] 127 p. 21 cm. "A Crossroad book." [BV245.W44] 73-17914 ISBN 0-8164-0255-8 4.95
1. Prayers. I. Title.

WILSON, Alton H. 242'.8
Lord, it's me again / Alton H. Wilson. 1st ed. Garden City, N.Y. : Doubleday, 1975. 102 p. ; 22 cm. [BV245.W49] 74-22842 ISBN 0-385-09626-7 : 5.95
1. Prayers. I. Title.

WILSON, Bruce M. 242'.8
I'm glad you called [by] Bruce M. Wilson. [Jesup, Ga., Printed by Sentinel Press, c1973] 1 v. (unpaged) 19 cm. [BV245.W5] 74-168200
1. Prayers. I. Title.

WIRT, Winola Wells 242.8
Interludes in a woman's day. Introd. by Mrs. Billy Graham. Chicago, Moody [1964] 160p. 22cm. [BV4832.2.W59] 65-855 2.95
1. Devotional literature. 2. Woman—Religious life. I. Title.

ZDENEK, Marilee. 242'.8
God is a verb! / Words by Marilee Zdenek ; action by Marge Champion. Waco, Tex. : Word Books, [1974] 91 p. : ill. ; 19 x 22 cm. [BV245.Z34] 74-82663 5.95
1. Prayers. I. Champion, Marge Belcher, ill. II. Title.

ANSELM, Saint, Abp. of Canterbury, 1033-1109. 242'.802
The prayers and meditations of St. Anselm; translated [from the Latin] and with an introduction by Sister Benedicta Ward; with a foreword by R. W. Southern. Harmondsworth, Penguin, 1973. 287 p. 18 cm. (Penguin classics) [BV245.A5] 73-178518 ISBN 0-14-044278-2 £0.60
1. Prayers. 2. Meditations. I. Ward, Benedicta, tr. II. Title.

ARIAS, Juan. 242'.802
Prayer without frills / by Juan Arias ; translated by Paul Barrett. St. Meinrad, Ind. : Abbey Press, 1974. viii, 196 p. ; 20 cm. (A Priority edition) Translation of Preghiera nuda. [BV245.A7] 74-83340 ISBN 0-87029-037-1 : 3.95
1. Prayers. I. Title.

BREAULT, William. 242'.802
Power & weakness; a book of honest prayers. [Boston] St. Paul Editions [1973] 119 p. illus. 20 cm. [BV245.B64] 73-86209 3.95
1. Prayers. I. Title.

CASSIDY, Norma Cronin, comp. 242'.802
Favorite novenas and prayers. New York, Paulist Press [1972] x, 134 p. 18 cm. (Paulist Press/Deus books) [BX2170.N7C27] 72-91456 ISBN 0-8091-1761-4
1. Novenas. 2. Prayers. I. Title.

CHALET, Francois. 242.8'02
Cries from the heart, by Francois Chalet. Translated by Mary Ilford. New York, Sheed and Ward [1968] 156 p. 21 cm. Includes excerpts from the Jerusalem Bible and from the Holy Bible, translated by R. Knox. Translation of Cris d'hommes. [BS1424.C513] 68-13840
1. Bible. O.T. Psalms—Paraphrases, English. I. Bible. O. T. Psalms. English. Selections. 1968. II. Title.

COME aside and rest awhile : a book of family prayer / edited by 242'.802

Joseph C. Kelly ; illustrated by Colleen Kelly Spellecy. N[ew] Y[ork] : Paulist Press, 1976, c1977. vii, 112 p. : ill. ; 18 cm. (Emmaus books) [BX2130.C65] 76-24441 ISBN 0-8091-1988-9 pbk. : 1.45
1. Catholic Church—Prayer-books and devotions—English. I. Kelly, Joseph G.

COOKE, Terence James, 1921- comp. 242'.802
Prayers for today. Compiled by Terence Cardinal Cooke. New York, Macmillan [1971] xxii, 261 p. 16 cm. [BX1981.C63] 74-180294
1. Catholic Church—Prayer-books and devotions—English. I. Title.

FOX, Robert Joseph, 1927- 242'.802
A Catholic prayer book, for every Catholic, for every day. Written and compiled by Robert J. Fox. Rev. and enl. ed. Huntington, Ind., Our Sunday Visitor, inc. [1974] 128 p. 14 cm. [BX2130.F68] 74-75133 ISBN 0-87973-771-9
1. Catholic Church—Prayer-books and devotions—English. I. Title.

FRANCESCO d'Assisi, Saint, 1182-1226. 242'.802
Heaven on earth : inspirational writings of Saint Francis of Assisi / illustrated by Noreen Bonker. Kansas City, Mo. : Hallmark, c1975. [48] p. : col. ill. ; 11 x 16 cm. (Hallmark editions) [BV245.F67 1975] 74-83541 ISBN 0-87529-402-2 : 3.00
1. Prayers. 2. Meditations. I. Bonker, Noreen. II. Title.

FRANCESCO d'Assisi, Saint, 1182-1226. 242'.802
Heaven on earth; the inspirational writings of Saint Francis of Assisi, selected by Karen Hill. Illustrated by Noreen Bonker. [Kansas City, Mo., Hallmark Cards, 1973] [48] p. illus. 16 cm. (Hallmark editions) [BV245.F67] 72-84373 ISBN 0-87529-322-0 2.50
1. Prayers. 2. Meditations. I. Title.

MARY Loretta, Sister, A.P.B. 242.8'02
My thing. Liguori, Mo., Liguorian Pamphlets and Books [1970] 95 p. illus. 18 cm. Poem. [BV245.M483] 75-130661 1.50
1. Prayers. I. Title.

MOONEY, Patrick. 242'.802
Praise to the Lord of the morning! : Three prayer experiences / Patrick Mooney ; with photography by the author. Notre Dame, Ind. : Ave Maria Press, c1976. 127 p. : ill. ; 21 cm. [BV260.M64] 76-16673 ISBN 0-87793-116-X pbk. : 2.95
1. Prayers. I. Title.

CASTLE, Robert W. 242.8'03
Prayers from the burned-out city [by] Robert W. Castle, Jr. New York, Sheed and Ward [1968] 126 p. 21 cm. [BR124.C38] 68-9371 3.95
1. Church and social problems. 2. Christianity—20th century. I. Title.

CHURCH Service League of the Diocese of Massachusetts. 242'.803
Prayers for the Church Service League of the Diocese of Massachusetts. 7th ed. rev. and enl. Boston [Riverside Press] 1952. 146 p. 18 cm. [BV245.C46 1952] 75-313520
1. Prayers. I. Title.

DE CANDOLE, Henry. 242.8'03
Re-shaping the liturgy; an invitation to a parish enquiry [by] Henry De Candole and Arthur Couratin. [2d ed.] Westminster [Eng.] Church Information Office [1965] vi, 62 p. 22 cm. [BX5145.A63D4 1965] 68-3905
1. Church of England. Book of common prayer. Communion service. I. Couratin, Arthur Hubert, 1902- joint author. II. Title.

MORE contemporary prayers; prayers on fifty-two themes, by Anthony Coates [and others] Edited by Caryl Micklem. [1st U.S. ed.] Grand Rapids, Eerdmans [1970] ix, 117 p. 22 cm. [BV245.M595] 79-127634 3.50 242.8'03
1. Prayers. I. Micklem, Caryl, ed. II. Coates, Anthony.

**PRAYER BOOK for the Armed Forces (A).* 1967. Pub. for the Bishop for the Armed Forces, the Episcopal Church. New York, Seabury [1967] 168p. music. 15cm. 2.50 242.8'03
1. Prayer-books and devotions—Episcopal. 2. Armed Forces—Prayer-books and devotions—Episcopal.

LUTHER, Martin, 1483-1546 242.8'04'1
Luther's prayers. Ed. by Herbert F. Brokering. Minneapolis, Augsburg [1967] 120p. 17cm. [BV260.L76] 67-25366 3.00
1. Prayers, 2. Lutheran Church—Prayer-books and devotions. I. Brokering, Herbert F., ed. II. Title.

LUTHER, Martin, 1483-1546. 242.8'04'1
Luther's prayers. Edited by Herbert F. Brokering. Minneapolis, Augsburg Pub. House [1967] 120 p. 17 cm. [BV260.L76] 67-25366
1. Prayers. 2. Lutheran Church — Prayer-books and devotions. I. Brokering, Herbert F., ed. II. Title.

LUTHERAN book of prayer. Saint Louis, Concordia Pub. House [1970] 203 p. 15 cm. [BV245.L82 1970] 76-119916 242.8'04'1
1. Lutheran Church—Prayer-books and devotions—English.

SEAMAN, William R 242.8'04'1
Daily prayer for family and private use, by William R. Seaman. Philadelphia, Fortress Press [1967] vi, 57 p. 18 cm. [BX8067.P7S4] 67-31233
1. Lutheran Church—Prayer-books and devotions. 2. Prayers. I. Title.

SEAMAN, William R. 242.8'04'1
Daily prayer for family and private use, by William R. Seaman. Philadelphia, Fortress Press [1967] vi, 57 p. 18 cm. [BX8067.P7S4] 67-31233
1. Lutheran Church—Prayer-books and devotions. 2. Prayers. I. Title.

FIEDLER, Lois. 242.8'05'1
The many faces of love. Westwood, N.J., Revell [1968] 127 p. 21 cm. [BV260.F5] 68-17089
1. Prayers. 2. Meditations. I. Title.

WONG, Richard. 242.8'05'834
Prayers from an island. Pref. by J. Akuhead Pupule. Richmond, John Knox Press [1968] 79 p. 21 cm. First delivered daily on J. A. Pupule's radio program over Radio Station KGMB, Honolulu. [BV245.W6] 68-25014 3.00
1. Prayers. I. Title.

BUSH, Roger. 242.8'07
Prayers for pagans. Dayton, Ohio, Pflaum Press, 1969 [c1968] vii, 63 p. illus. 21 cm. Poems. [BV245.B685 1969] 75-93002 1.50
1. Prayers. I. Title.

PARROTT, Bob W 242.8'07
A man talks with God, by Bob W. Parrott. [1st ed.] Dallas, Printed by Southern Methodist University Print. Dept. [1967] xi, 66 p. 20 cm. [BV260.P33] 67-30888
1. Prayers. I. Title.

PARROTT, Bob W. 242.8'07
A man talks with God, by Bob W. Parrott. [1st ed.] Dallas, Printed by Southern Methodist University Print. Dept. [1967] xi, 66 p. 20 cm. [BV260.P33] 67-30888
1. Prayers. I. Title.

STRUCHEN, Jeanette. 242.8'07
Prayers to pray without really trying. [1st ed.] Philadelphia, Lippincott [1967] New York, Friendship Press [1966] 62 p. 19 cm. 32 p. illus. 26 cm. [BV245.S84] [HC110.P6S84] 339.46 67-16922 66-5820
1. Prayers. 2. Poverty. 3. Poor — U.S. I. Struchen, Jeanette. II. Title. III. Title: This is the puzzle of poverty.

STRUCHEN, Jeanette. 242.8'07
Prayers to pray without really trying. [1st ed.] Philadelphia, Lippincott [1967] 62 p. 19 cm. [BV245.S84] 67-16922
1. Prayers. I. Title.

AASENG, Rolf E. 242'.82
Jesus loves me, this I know; devotions for families with children, by Rolf E. Aaseng. Designed and illustrated by Don Wallerstedt. Minneapolis, Augsburg Pub. House [1973] 144 p. illus. 23 cm. Devotions on various subjects include a meditation, brief Bible reading, questions for discussion, and suggestions for projects. [BV4870.A23] 72-90253 ISBN 0-8066-1300-9 3.95
1. Children—Prayer-books and devotions—English. 2. Family—Prayer-books and devotions—English. I. Wallerstedt, Don, illus. II. Title.

ANGELA, Sister, O.S.B., 1941- 242'.82
God and a mouse; a festival of reflective jubilation. Illustrated by DeGrazia. Words by Sister M. Angela. San Diego, Calif., Benedictine Sisters [1972] 12, [39] p. illus. (part col.) 17 cm. A little mouse talks to God in a series of prayers. [BV4870.A374] 72-84198 3.50
1. Children—Prayer-books and devotions—English—1961- I. DeGrazia, Ted Ettore, 1909- illus. II. Title.

ARONIN, Ben, 1904- 242.82
Daily prayers for children. Illustrated by Haig and Regina Shekerjian. [1st ed.] New York, Citadel Press [1966] 127 p. col. illus. 21 cm. [BV265.A7] 66-24224
1. Children—Prayer-books and devotions. 2. Devotional calendars. I. Title.

BARTLETT, Robert Merrill, 1898- 242.8'2
A boy's book of prayers. Boston, Pilgrim Press [1971? c1930] v, 58 p. 16 cm. [BV283.B7B3 1971] 74-30603
1. Boys—Prayer-books and devotions—English. I. Title.

†COOK, Walter L. 242'.82
Table prayers for children / by Walter L. Cook ; [cover and ill. by Joni Fredman]. St. Louis, Mo. : Bethany Press, c1976. 61 p. : ill. ; 16 x 18 cm. A collection of mealtime graces and prayers that express real concerns and appreciation of true blessings. [BV283.G7C63] 76-54155 2.95
1. Grace at meals—Juvenile literature. 2. Children—Prayer-books and devotions—English. I. Fredman, Joni. II. Title.

THE Golden Treasury of prayers for boys and girls / selected by Esther Wilkin ; illustrated by Eloise Wilkin. New York : Golden Press, [1975] 45 p. : col. ill. ; 32 cm. Contains prayers for children from many religions and varied parts of the world. [BV4870.G6] 74-15598 ISBN 0-307-13744-9 : 3.95 242'.82
1. Children—Prayer-books and devotions—English. I. Wilkin, Esther Burns. II. Wilkin, Eloise Burns.

JOHNSON, Lois Walfrid. 242'.82
Hello, God! : Prayers for small children / written by Lois Walfrid Johnson ; and illustrated by Judy Swanson. Minneapolis, Minn. : Augsburg Pub. House, [1975] [32] p. : col. ill. ; 27 cm. [BV4870.J54] 75-4157 ISBN 0-8066-1482-X : 4.95
1. Children—Prayer-books and devotions—English—1961- I. Swanson, Judy. II. Title.

KAUFMAN, William Irving, 1922- comp. 242.8'2
UNICEF book of children's prayers, compiled and with photos. by William I. Kaufman. Prepared for English-reading children by Rosamond V. P. Kaufman [and] Joan Gilbert Van Poznak. [Harrisburg, Pa.] Stackpole Books [1970] 95 p. illus. 24 cm. (His Children's favorites around the world) Fifty-one prayers and devotional poems from all over the world. Illustrated with photographs of children from many countries. [BV4870.K38] 74-110477
1. Children—Prayer-books and devotions—1961- I. Kaufman, Rosamond V. P. II. Van Poznak, Joan Gilbert. III. Title.

L'ENGLE, Madeleine. 242'.82
Everyday prayers / by Madeleine L'Engle ; ill. by Lucile Butel. New York : Morehouse-Barlow Co., c1974. [38] p. : col. ill. ; 15 cm. Translation of Prieres pour tous les jours. A collection of prayers for every occasion. [BV4870.L4413] 75-323059 ISBN 0-8192-1154-0
1. Children—Prayer-books and devotions—English. I. Butel, Lucile. II. Title.

MOLAN, Dorothy Lennon. 242.8'2
Thank you, God, by Dorothy L. Molan. Illustrated by Ginger Tootill. Valley Forge [Pa.] Judson Press [1969] [24] p. illus. (part col.) 21 cm. Relates various events and situations in a day and gives in rhyme prayers a child might offer regarding them. [BV4870.M57] 69-18151 ISBN 8-17-004255- (pbk.)
1. Children—Prayer-books and devotions—1961- I. Tootill, Ginger, illus. II. Title.

NORTHCOTT, William Cecil, 1902- comp. 242'.82
Children's prayers and praises. Chosen by Mary Miller. Illustrated by Esme Eve. [1st U.S. ed.] Minneapolis, Augsburg Pub. House [1972, c1971] [32] p. col. illus. 23 cm. Traditional and original prayers for morning and evening, holidays, the seasons, and other occasions. [BV4870.N67 1972] 77-189649 ISBN 0-8066-1215-0
1. Children—Prayer-books and devotions—English—1961- I. Eve, Esme, illus. II. Title.

PIKE, Morris D., 1928- 242'.82
All our days—laugh & praise [by] Morris D. Pike. Illustrated by Karen Tureck. New York, Friendship Press [1974] 48 p. illus. 26 cm. A collection of reprinted and original prayers, poems, litanies, and hymns which can be used to understand the Christian worship heritage as well as discover new forms of worship. [BV4870.P54] 74-838 ISBN 0-377-00007-8 1.95 (pbk.)
1. Children—Prayer-books and devotions—English. I. Tureck, Karen, illus. II. Title.

PRAYERS to grow by. 242'.82
1st American ed. Chappaqua, N.Y. : Christian Herald Books, 1977. 93 p. : ill. (some col.) ; 25 cm. Old and new prayers relating to children's experiences. [BV265.P764 1977] 76-41630 ISBN 0-915684-12-8 : 6.95
1. Prayers—Juvenile literature.

SANDLIN, John Lewis. 242.82
A boy's book of prayers. Westwood, N.J., Revell [1966] 64 p. 17 cm. [BV283.B7S2] 66-28003
1. Boys—Prayer-books and devotions. I. Title.

SANDLIN, John Lewis 242.82
A boy's book of prayers. Westwood, N.J., Revell [1966] 64p. 17cm. [BV283.B7S2] 66-28003 1.00 bds.,
1. Boys—Prayer-books and devotions. I. Title.

SANDLIN, John Lewis. 242.82
A girl's book of prayers. Westwood, N.J., F. H. Revell [1966] 63 p. 17 cm. [BV283.G5S2] 66-28004
1. Girls—Prayer-books and devotions. I. Title.

WALLACE, Betty Dollar. 242.8'2
Prayers for mother & child; beautiful prayers and inspirations for all occasions. Nashville, Impact Books [1970] 80 p. 15 cm. [BV245.W28] 78-141645 1.95
1. Prayers. I. Title.

WHITE, Dorothy Margaret. 242.8'2
Early will I seek thee. Philadelphia, Dorrance [c1966] 86 p. 21 cm. [BV4870.W5] 66-27486
1. Children — Prayer-books and devotions. I. Title.

WHITE, Dorothy Margaret 242.8'2
Early will I seek thee. Philadelphia. Dorrance [c.1966] 86p. 21cm. [BV4870.W5] 66-27486 3.00
1. Children—Prayer-books and devotions I. Title.

WIMBERLY, Vera L. 242'.82
Please listen, God! / Vera L. Wimberly. St. Louis : Concordia Pub. House, c1977. p. cm. A selection of simple prayers accompanied by notes to help parents and teachers teach young children to pray. [BV212.W5] 77-8892 ISBN 0-570-03467-1 pbk. : 2.50
1. Prayer—Juvenile literature. I. Title.

WORTMAN, Arthur, comp. 242.8'2
Father, we thank Thee; simple and beautiful prayers for young children. Illustrated by Sue Tague. [Kansas City, Mo.] Hallmark Children's Editions [1970] [23] p. col. illus. 18 cm. Traditional and modern prayers for children. Traditional and modern prayers for children. [BV4870.W67] 72-102159 ISBN 0-87529-053-1 2.50
1. Children—Prayer-books and devotions. I. Tague, Sue, illus. II. Title.

BARCLAY, William, lecturer in the University of Glasgow. 242.83
Prayers for young people. [1st ed.] New York, Harper & Row [1967, c1963] 128 p. 18 cm. Pages 122-128, blank for "Your favorite prayers." [BV4850.B3 1967] 67-10711
1. Youth—Prayer-books and devotions. I. Title.

BURKE, Carl F. 242.8'3
Treat me cool, Lord; prayers, devotions, litanies, as prepared by some of God's bad-tempered angels with busted halos, with the help of Carl F. Burke. New York, Association Press [1968] 128 p. 18 cm. [BV283.Y6B8] 68-11493
1. Youth—Prayer-books and devotions. 2. Youth—Religious life. I. Title.

FOX, Robert Joseph, 1927- 242'.83
A prayer book for young Catholics / Robert J. Fox. Huntington, IN : Our Sunday Visitor, c1977. 168 p. : ill. ; 16 cm. A collection of prayers and devotions including prayers for school, special occasions, and the Church year. [BX2150.F69] 76-47869 ISBN 0-87973-638-0 : 2.95 pbk. : 1.95
1. Children—Prayer-books and devotions—English. 2. Youth—Prayer-books and devotions—English. I. Title.

FOX, Robert Joseph, 1927- 242'.83
A prayer book for young Catholics / Robert J. Fox. Huntington, IN : Our Sunday Visitor, c1977. 168 p. : ill. ; 16 cm. A collection of prayers and devotions including prayers for school, special occasions, and the Church year. [BX2150.F69] 76-47869 ISBN 0-87973-638-0 : 2.95 pbk. : 1.95
1. Children—Prayer-books and devotions—English. 2. Youth—Prayer-books and devotions—English. I. Title.

HABEL, Norman C. 242.8'3
Interrobang; a bunch of unanswered prayers and unlimited shouts, by Norman C. Habel. Illus. by Patrick Mason. Philadelphia, Fortress Press [1969] 96 p. illus. (part col.) 22 cm. (Open 2) [BV283.Y6H27] 72-84555 1.95

1. Youth—Prayer-books and devotions—English. I. Title.

HEYER, Robert J., comp. 242.8'3
Discovery in prayer [by] Robert J. Heyer [and] Richard J. Payne. Photographed by Edward Rice. New York, Paulist Press [1969] 144 p. illus. 21 cm. [BV210.2.H47] 78-104882
1. Prayer. 2. Prayers. 3. Meditations. I. Payne, Richard J., joint comp. II. Title.

SANDLIN, John Lewis. 242.83
A book of prayers for youth. Westwood, N. J., F. H. Revell Co. [1966] 120 p. 17 cm. [BV4850.S3] 66-17049
1. Youth—Prayer-books and devotions. I. Title.

SANDLIN, John Lewis 242.83
A book of prayers for youth. Westwood, N. J., Revell [c.1966] 120p. 17cm. [BV4850.S3] 66-17049 2.50 bds.,
1. Youth—Prayer-books and devotions. I. Title.

STRUCHEN, Jeanette. 242.8'3
Zapped by Jesus. Photos. by Richard Lerner. [1st ed.] Philadelphia, Holman [1972] 91 p. illus. 24 cm. Conversational prayers of young people who have turned from drugs to God. Appropriate quotations from Scripture and a photograph of each individual accompany the conversations. [BV245.S846] 73-38739 ISBN 0-87981-004-1 (pbk) 2.95
1. Prayers. I. Title.

WELDON, Wilson O., comp. 242'.8'3
Break thru; youth devotions, reflections on life in prayers, poems, and readings. Compiled by Wilson O. Weldon. [Nashville, The Upper Room, 1972] 96 p. illus. 15 x 20 cm. [BV4805.W4] 74-183568
1. Devotional literature. I. Title.

WITT, Elmer N. 242'.8'3
Help it all make sense, Lord! By Elmer N. Witt; drawings by Jim Cummins. St. Louis, Concordia Pub. House [1972] 117 p. illus. 20 cm. [BV283.Y6W49] 72-85147
1. Youth—Prayer-books and devotions—English. 2. Prayers. I. Title.

HEARN, Raymond. 242.8'3'2
Modern psalms by boys; illustrated by Anne Netherwood, with a foreword by the Most Reverend and Right. Hon. F. D. Coggan. London, University of London P. [1966] 62 p. front., illus. 22 1/2 cm. (B 66-8266) [BV283.H4] 67-109451
1. Boys—Prayer-books and devotions. I. Title.

HOLMES, Marjorie, 1910- 242'.83'3
Nobody else will listen; a girl's conversations with God. [1st ed.] Garden City, N.Y., Doubleday, 1973. ix, 133 p. 22 cm. A collection of prayers touching on important matters in an adolescent girl's life. [BV4860.H64] 72-84919 ISBN 0-385-04458-5 3.95
1. Girls—Prayer-books and devotions—English. I. Title.

HOLMES, Marjorie, 1910- 242'.83'3
Nobody else will listen; a girl's conversations with God. New York, Bantam Books [1974, c1973] viii, 135 p. 18 cm. A collection of prayers touching on important matters in an adolescent girl's life. [BV4860.H64] 1.25 (pbk.)
1. Girls—Prayer-books and devotions—English. I. Title.
L.C. card number for original ed.: 72-84919.

JOHNSON, Lois. 242'.83'3
Just a minute, Lord. Designed and illustrated by David Koechel. Minneapolis, Augsburg Pub. House [1973] 96 p. illus. 20 cm. [BV4860.J63] 73-78265 ISBN 0-8066-1329-7 1.95 (pbk.)
1. Girls—Prayer-books and devotions—English. I. Title.

MATTISON, Judith N. 242'.83'3
Who will listen to me? / Judith Mattison ; art by Judy Swanson. Minneapolis : Augsburg Pub. House, c1977. 95 p. : ill. ; 20 cm. Seventy-one conversational prayers concerning everyday problems of high school girls. [BV4860.M37] 77-72450 ISBN 0-8066-1596-6 pbk. : 2.95
1. Girls—Prayer-books and devotions—English. I. Title.

SCOVIL, Elisabeth Robinson, 1849- 242.833
Prayers for girls. [Rev. ed. Camden, N.J.] T. Nelson [c1966*C64 p. 17 cm. 64 p. 17 cm. [BV283.G5S4 1966] 66-14194
1. Girls—Prayer-books and devotions. I. Title.

SANDLIN, John Lewis. 242.8'4
Prayers for parents who care. Old Tappan, N.J., Revell [1970] 128 p. 17 cm. [BV4845.S25] 74-112455 2.95
1. Married people—Prayer-books and devotions—English. I. Title.

BUEGE, William A. 242.842
The Lord's men: meditations for men in the world of work [by]William A. Buege. St. Louis, Concordia [1966] 90p. 19cm. [BV4843.B8] 66-27384 2.50
1. Men—Prayer-books and devotions. I. Title.

BUEGE, William A. 242.842
The Lord's men: meditations for men in the world of work [by] William A. Buege. Saint Louis, Concordia Pub. House [1966] 90 p. 19 cm. [BV4843.B8] 66-27384
1. Men—Prayer-books and devotions—English. I. Title.

GESCH, Roy G. 242.8'42
A husband prays, by Roy G. Gesch. St. Louis, Concordia Pub. House [1968] 104 p. 19 cm. [BV283.H8G4] 68-22574
1. Husbands—Prayer-books and devotions. I. Title.

GESCH, Roy G. 242.8'4'2
Man at prayer [by] Roy Gesch. St. Louis, Concordia Pub. House [1970] 113 p. 19 cm. [BV245.G45] 79-108884
1. Prayers. I. Title.

GESCH, Dorothy K. 242.8'43
Make me aware, Lord [by] Dorothy K. Gesch. Minneapolis, Augsburg Pub. House [1971] 91 p. illus. 21 cm. Free verse prayers for today's woman. [BV4844.G44] 75-135215 ISBN 0-8066-1102-2 3.50
1. Women—Prayer-books and devotions. I. Title.

GESCH, Roy G. 242.8'43
A wife prays, by Roy G. Gesch. St. Louis, Concordia Pub. House [1968] 104 p. 19 cm. [BV283.W6G4] 68-22575
1. Wives—Prayer-books and devotions. I. Title.

HOLMES, Marjorie, 1910- 242.8'43
Who am I, God? Illustrated by Betty Fraser. [1st ed.] Garden City, N.Y., Doubleday, 1971. x, 176 p. illus. 22 cm. [BV4844.H64] 77-139035 3.95
1. Women—Prayer-books and devotions. I. Title.

MATTISON, Judith N. 242'.8'43
Prayers from a mother's heart / Judith Mattison ; ill. by Audrey Teeple. Minneapolis : Augsburg Pub. House, [1975] 95 p. : ill. ; 20 cm. [BV283.M7M37] 74-14177 ISBN 0-8066-1460-9 pbk. : 2.95
1. Mothers—Prayer-books and devotions—English. I. Teeple, Audrey. II. Title.

RUSSELL, Grace. 242.8'43
Rings and things; thoughts of a man's wife. Illustrated by Gordon Haug. [Nashville] Upper Room [1970] 88 p. illus. 20 cm. [BV4844.R88] 77-115830
1. Women—Prayer-books and devotions—English. I. Title.

DAUGHDRILL, Jim. 242'.8'8
Man-talk; prayers for the man at work. [1st ed.] New York, Harper & Row [1972] vii, 120 p. 19 cm. [BV4596.B8D38] 72-78048 ISBN 0-06-061698-9
1. Businessmen—Prayer-books and devotions—English. I. Title.

GESCH, Roy G. 242.8'8
Parents pray [by] Roy G. Gesch. St. Louis, Concordia Pub. House [1968] 120 p. illus. 19 cm. [BV4845.G4] 68-30807 3.00
1. Devotional literature. I. Title.

MARSHALL, Peter, 1902-1949. 242.8'8
Peter Marshall's lasting prayers, with encouragement to prayer in the drawings of Jack Hamm. [1st ed.] Anderson, S.C., Droke House Publishers; distributed by Grosset & Dunlap, New York [1969] 1 v. (unpaged) illus. 24 cm. [BV280.M32] 69-14345
1. Legislative bodies—Chaplains' prayers. I. Title.

SANDLIN, John Lewis 242.8'8
Prayers for servicemen. Westwood. N.J., Revell [1967] 63p. 12cm. [BV4588.S24] 67-22573 1.00
1. Armed Forces—Prayer-books and devotions—English. I. Title.

SANDLIN, John Lewis. 242.8'8
Prayers for servicemen. Westwood, N. J., F. H. Revell Co. [1967] 63 p. 12 cm. [BV4588.S24] 67-22573
1. Armed Forces—Prayer-books and devotions—English. I. Title.

VANNORSDALL, John W. 242.8'8
Campus prayers for the '70s [by] John W. Vannorsdall. Philadelphia, Fortress Press [1970] x, 118 p. 18 cm. [BV283.C7V35] 70-101425 2.50
1. Universities and colleges—Prayers. I. Title.

*LAPP, Rhoda Snadeo. 242.888
Devotionals for nurses. Grand Rapids, Baker Book House [1974] 63 p. 20 cm. (An Ultra book) [BV4596.N8] ISBN 0-8010-5539-3 2.95
1. Devotional literature. I. Title.

ANDREWES, Lancelot, Bp. of Winchester, 1555-1626. 242.8'9'2
The private devotions of Lancelot Andrewes; Selections, edited by David A. McLennan. New York, World Pub. Co. [1969] 62 p. 17 cm. (World inspirational books) Translation of Preces privatae. [BV4830.A653 1969] 79-90927 1.25
1. Devotional exercises. I. Title.

CURRIE, David M., 1918- 242'.89'2
Come, let us worship God : a handbook of prayers for leaders of worship / by David M. Currie. Philadelphia : Westminster Press, c1977. p. cm. [BV250.C87] 77-6808 ISBN 0-664-24757-1 pbk. : 4.25
1. Pastoral prayers. I. Title.

CURRIE, David M., 1918- 242'.89'2
Come let us worship God : a handbook of prayers for leaders of worship / by David M. Currie. Philadelphia : Westminster Press, c1977. p. cm. [BV250.C87] 77-6808 ISBN 0-664-24757-1 pbk. : 4.25
1. Pastoral prayers. I. Title.

243 Evangelistic Writings For Individuals

ARCHIBALD, Arthur Crawley, 1878- 243
This is our gospel. Nashville, Broadman Press [1959] 135p. 21cm. [BV3797.A68] 59-9693
1. Evangelistic sermons. 2. Baptists—Sermons. 3. Sermons, American. I. Title.

AUTREY, C. E. 243
Evangelistic sermons. Grand Rapids, Mich., Zondervan [c.1962] 108p. Bibl. 1.95 bds.,
1. Evangelistic work. I. Title.

*BAILLIE, John. 243
Invitation to pilgrimage. Grand Rapids : Baker Book House, 1976c 1942. 134p. ; 20cm. (Ministers paperback library) Includes index [BV3797] ISBN 0-8010-0654-6 pbk. : 2.95.
1. Evangelistic work 2. Faith I. Title.

BLACKWOOD, Andrew Watterson, 1882- ed. 243
Evangelical sermons of our day; thirty-seven foremost examples of Bible preaching, compiled and edited with special annotations. New York, Harper [1959] 383p. 21cm. [BV3797.B54] 59-10752
1. Evangelistic sermons. I. Title.

BLACKWOOD, Andrew Watterson, 1882- ed. 243
Special-day sermons for Evangelicals; thirty-eight representative examples of Bible preaching on red-letter days of the Christian year and the calendar year, comp., ed., special annotations by Andrew W. Blackwood. Great Neck, N.Y., Channel Pr. [c.1961] 448p. Bibl. 61-17037 4.95 bds.,
1. Evangelistic sermons. 2. Church year sermons. I. Title.

BLACKWOOD, Andrew Watterson, 1882- ed. 243
Special-day sermons for Evangelicals; thirty-eight representative examples of Bible preaching on red-letter days of the Christian year and the calendar year, compiled and edited with special annotations by Andrew W. Blackwood. Great Neck, N. Y., Channel Press [1961] 448p. 21cm. Includes bibliography. [BV3797.A1B5] 61-17037
1. Evangelistic sermons. 2. Church year sermons. I. Title.

CARTER, Charles Webb, 1905- 243
Road to revival. Butler, Ind., Higley Press [1959] 152p. 23cm. [BV3797.C248] 59-48870
1. Evangelistic sermons. 2. Methodist Church—Sermons. 3. Sermons, American. I. Title.

COLE, Earl 243
Is the door open? New York, Carlton [dist. Comet, c.1961] 82p. front. port. 2.75
I. Title.

COUSINS, Oliver A. 243
Into the mind of God. New York, Carlton [c.1963] 378p. 21cm. (Reflection bk.) 5.00
I. Title.

DE KOCK, Gertrude 243
Read and live; talks given by Gertrude de Kock [dist. San Antonio, Texas, Naylor, 1963] 238p. 19cm. pap., gratis
I. Title.

DE LONG, Russell Victor, 1901- ed. 243
Evangelistic sermons by great evangelists. Introduction by Bishop Arthur J. Moore. Grand Rapids, Mich., Zondervan Pub. House [1956] 183p. 20cm. [BV3797.A1D4] 56-38681
1. Evangelistic sermons. 2. Sermons, American. I. Title.

EVANGELISM in action through 243
Christ-centered messages; twelve evangelistic sermons by C. Wade Freeman, Frank Weeden, C. B. Jackson [and] Jesse Yelvington, members of the staff of the Baptist General Convention of Texas. Wheaton, Ill., Van Kampen Press [1951] 112 p. ports. 20 cm. [BV3797.A1E8] 51-1343
1. Evangelistic sermons. 2. Baptists—Sermons. 3. Sermons, American. I. Freeman, Clifford Wade, 1906- II. Baptists. Texas, General Convention.

FERRE, Nels Frederick Solomon, 1908- 243
The sun and the umbrella. [1st ed.] New York, Harper [1953] 156p. 20cm. [BR121.F547] 53-8368
1. Christianity—Essence, genius, nature. I. Title.

FERRE, Nels Fredrick Solomon, 1908- 243
The sun and the umbrella [1st ed.] New York, Harper [1953] 156 p. 20 cm. [BR121.F547] 53-8368
1. Christianity—Essence, genius, nature. I. Title.

FISHER, Gary. 243
Satan's been cross since Calvary / by Gary Fisher ; with Robert L. McGrath. New York : Hawthorn Books, [1974] xii, 147 p. : 21 cm. [BV3797.F548] 73-9310 3.95
1. Evangelistic sermons. I. Title.

FISHER, Wilfred, 1914-- 243
Winning men to Christ. Under auspices of the Kentucky Mountain Holiness Association. [Vancleve? Ky., 1954] 100p. 20cm. [BV4253.F46] 54-37270
1. Sermons, American. I. Title.

FREEMAN, Clifford Wade, 1906- 243
Deeper life for you. Grand Rapids, Zondervan Pub. House [1963] 95 p. 21 cm. [BV3797.F69] 63-17753
1. Evangelistic sermons. 2. Sermons, America. 3. Baptists — Sermons. I. Title.

FREEMAN, Clifford Wade, 1906- 243
Deeper life for you. Grand Rapids, Mich., Zondervan [c.1963] 95p. 21cm. 63-17753 2.50 bds.,
1. Evangelistic sermons. 2. Sermons, American. 3. Baptists—Sermons. I. Title.

FULLER, David Otis, 1903- ed. 243
Valiant for the truth; a treasury of evangelical writings. Introductions by Henry W. Coray. New York, McGraw-Hill [c.1961] 460p. 61-9768 7.95 bds.,
1. Evangelicalism. I. Title.

GIVE this man place / 243
by Billy Graham, and associates. Minneapolis : World Wide Publications, [1973] 143 p. ; 18 cm. (Decision books) Contents.Contents.—Gustafson, R. W. Give this man place.—Graham, B. Our rock.—Wilson, G. Sure and certain hope.—Bell, R. S. Man in the galaxies.—Ford L. He is able.—Barrows, C. The great shepherd.—Abdul-Hagg, A. In Him was life.—Jones, H. O. The burning heart.—Wilson, T. W. There is a remedy.—Bell, L. N. The blood of Christ.—White, J. W. Be ready!—Dienert, M. There came to Him a woman.—Nelson, V. B. Immortality.—Brownville, G. The signature of hope.—Little, P. The man God uses.—Ferm, R. O. Grasping the Bible's authority. [BV3797.A1G57] 73-84957 1.45
1. Evangelistic sermons. 2. Sermons, American. I. Graham, William Franklin, 1918-

*GOODWIN, W. R. 243
The great world and people. New York, Vantage [c.1965] 55p. 21cm. 2.50 bds.,
I. Title.

GRAHAM, William Franklin, 1918- 243
The wit and wisdom of Billy Graham. Edited and compiled by Bill Adler. New York, Random House [1967] 165 p. 22 cm. [BV3797.G675] 66-21481
I. Adler, Bill, ed. II. Title.

GRAHAM, William Franklin, 1918- 243
World aflame. by Billy Graham. New York, Pocket Bks. [1966, c.1965] xvi, 224p. 18cm. (Cardinal ed., 75146) [BV3797.G676] .75 pap.,
1. Christianity—20th cent.—Addresses, essays, lectures. I. Title.

GRAHAM, William Franklin, 1918- 243
World aflame [by] Billy Graham. [1st ed.]

Garden City, N.Y., Doubleday, 1965. xvii, 267 p. 22 cm. Bibliographical references included in "Notes" (p. [265]-267) [BV3797.G676] 65-24684
1. Christianity—20th century—Addresses, essays, lectures. I. Title.

GREENE, Oliver B. 243
Evangelistic messages. Grand Rapids. Mich., Baker Bk. [c.]1962. 145p. 21cm. 62-19663 2.50 bds.,
1. Evangelistic sermons. 2. Sermons, American. I. Title.

GREENE, Oliver B 243
Gospel hour sermons. Grand Rapids, Baker Book House, 1963. 132 p. 21 cm. [BV3797.G683] 63-20013
1. Evangelistic sermons. 2. Sermons, American. I. Title.

GREENE, Oliver B. 243
Gospel hour sermons. Grand Rapids, Mich., Baker Bk., [c.]1963. 132p. 21cm. 63-20013 2.95 bds.,
1. Evangelistic sermons. 2. Sermons, American. I. Title.

HOBBS, Herschel H 243
New Testament evangelism: the eternal purpose. Nashville, Convention Press [1960] 130p. 19cm. 'Church study course for teaching and training ... number 0107 in category 1, section A.' [BV3795.H58] 60-14371
1. Evangelistic work—Study and teaching. I. Title.

*HYLES, Jack 243
Let's hear Jack Hyles: burning messages for the saved and unsaved. Murfreesboro, Tenn., Sword of the Lord Pubs. [c.1964] 226p. 21cm. 2.75 bds.,
I. Title.

IRONSIDE, Henry Allan, 1876-1951. 243
Care for God's fruit-trees, and other messages. [Rev. ed.] New York, Loizeaux Bros. [1945] 156p. 20cm. [BV3797.I68 1945] 56-56274
1. Evangelistic sermons. 2. Sermons, American. I. Title.

KUIPER, Rienk Bouke, 1886- 243
God-centered evangelism; a presentation of the Scriptural theology of evangelism. Grand Rapids, Baker Book House, 1961. 216p. 23cm. [BV3790.K8] 61-18264
1. Evangelistic work. I. Title.

KUIPER, Rienk. Bouke, 1886- 243
God-centered evangelism; a presentation of the Scriptural theology of evangelism, by R. B. Kuiper. Grand Rapids, Baker Book House [1975 c1961] 216 p. 22 cm. (Twin brooks series) [BV3790.K8] 61-18264 ISBN 0-8010-5360-9 3.95 (pbk.)
1. Evangelistic work. I. Title. II. Series.

LAWRENCE, John Benjamin, 1873- 243
Kindling for revival fires. New York, Revell [1950] 187 p. 21 cm. [BV3797.L36] 50-4783
1. Evangelistic sermons. 2. Baptists—Sermons. 3. Sermons, American. I. Title.

LINTON, John, 1888- 243
Household salvation, and other sermons. Wheaton, Ill., Sword of the Lord Publishers [1950] 126 p. 21 cm. [BV3797.L5] 51-19202
1. Evangelistic sermons. 2. Sermons, American. I. Title.

LOWRY, Oscar 243
Scripture memorizing for successful soul-winning. abridged. Grand Rapids, Mich., Zondervan, 1962 [c.1932, 1934] 140p. 21cm. 1.00 pap.,
I. Title.

MCDERMOTT, Andrew W., comp. 243
Revival sermon outlines. [Westwood, N. J.] Revell [c.1960] 64p. 21cm. (Revell's sermon outline series) 60-8459 1.00 pap.,
1. Evangelistic sermons—Outlines. I. Title.

MARTINEZ, Angel 243
Crying in the chapel, and other messages. Grand Rapids, Mich., Zondervan [c.1961] 117p. 1.95 bds.,
I. Title.

*MEARS, George 243
The word of God. New York, Vantage [c.1965] 100p. 21cm. 2.50 bds.,
I. Title.

MOORE, Waylon B 243
New Testament follow-up for pastors and laymen, How to conserve, mature, and multiply the converts. Grand Rapids, Eerdmans [1963] 192 p. illus. 21 cm. Includes bibliography. [BV3793.M6] 63-5667
1. Evangelistic work. I. Title.

MOORE, Waylon B. 243
New Testament follow-up for pastors and laymen, how to conserve, mature, and multiply the converts. Grand Rapids, Mich., Eerdmans [c.1963] 192p. illus. 21cm. Bibl. 63-5667 1.95 pap.,
1. Evangelistic work. I. Title.

OLFORD, Stephen F. 243
Heart-cry for revival; expository sermons on revival. [Westwood, N.J.] Revell [c.1962] 128p. 20cm. 62-10738 2.50
1. Revivals. I. Title.

OLFORD, Stephen F. 243
The secret of soul-winning. Chicago, Moody [c.1963] 124p. 20cm. 2.50
I. Title.

OUTLER, Albert Cook, 1908- 243
Evangelism in the Wesleyan spirit [by] Albert C. Outler. Nashville, Tenn., Tidings [1971] 109 p. 19 cm. [BV3795.O94] 72-171886
1. Wesley, John, 1703-1791—Addresses, essays, lectures. 2. Evangelistic work—Addresses, essays, lectures. I. Title.

PLETT, C. J. J. M. M. 243
Satan's headquarters exposed. New York, Vantage [1962, c.1961] 116p. 2.75 bds.,
I. Title.

REVIVAL sermons and outlines, by J. H. Jowett, F. B. Meyer, Charles H. Spurgeon, others. Grand Rapids, Mich., Baker Bk., 1963. 104p. 20cm. (Minister's handbk. ser.) 63-14312 1.95 bds., 243
1. Evangelistic sermons. 2. Sermons—Outlines. I. Jowett, John Henry, 1864-1923.

RICE, John R., 1895- 243
The gospel that has saved 16,000 souls, by John R. Rice. Murfreesboro, Tenn., Sword of the Lord [1974] 291 p. 21 cm. [BV3797.R436] 74-76917 3.95
1. Evangelistic sermons. 2. Baptists—Sermons. 3. Sermons, American. I. Title.

RICE, William Henry, 1912- 243
The heavyweight champion who lost his title, and other sermons. Wheaton, Ill., Sword of the Lord Publishers [1950] 128 p. 21 cm. [BV3797.R4452] 50-3602
1. Evangelistic sermons. 2. Sermons, American. I. Title.

ROBERTS, Oral. 243
The fourth man. Rev. ed. Tulsa, Okla., Summit Book Co., 1960. 124p. 16cm. First ed. published in 1951 under title: The 4th man, and other famous sermons. [BV3797.R38 1960] 60-22708
1. Evangelistic sermons. 2. Pentecostal Holiness Church—Sermons. I. Title.

ROSELL, Mervin E 243
Revival: God's plan for today. Wheaton, Ill., Van Kampen Press [c1951] 60 p. 20 cm. [BV3790.R66] 52-22289
1. Evangelistic works. I. Title.

*SCHOFIELD, Joseph A. Jr. 243
Favorite object talks, by Joseph A. Schofield. Grand Rapids, Mich, Baker Book House [1973, c1951] 144 p. 20 cm. (Object Lesson series) [BV4307.S7] ISBN 0-8010-8017-7 1.50 (pbk.)
1. Sermon stories. I. Title.

SELLERS, James Earl. 243
The outsider and the word of God; a study in Christian communication. New York, Abingdon Press [1961] 240p. 23cm. [BV3790.S154] 61-8444
1. Evangelistic work. I. Title.

SHOEMAKER, Samuel Moor 243
With the Holy Spirit and with fire. New York, Harper [c.1960] 127p. 22cm. 60-8136 2.50
1. Evangelistic work. 2. Holy Spirit. I. Title.

SHOEMAKER, Samuel Moor, 1893- 243
With the Holy Spirit and with fire. [1st ed.] New York, Harper [1960] 127 p. 22 cm. [BV3703.S46] 60-8136
1. Evangelistic work. 2. Holy Spirit. I. Title.

SPARKS, Jacob B., 1886- 243
Things which don't happen every day. Grand Rapids, Eerdmaus [1958] 216 p. 23 cm. [BV3785.S68A3] 58-59782
1. Evangelists — Correspondence, reminiscences, etc. I. Title.

SPURGEON, Charles Haddon 243
Evangelistic sermons. Selected and edited by Chas. T. Cook. Grand Rapids, Mich., Zondervan Pub. House [1959 i.e. 1960] 256p. 23cm. (Library of Spurgeon's sermons, v.8) 60-2686 2.95
1. Evangelistic sermons. 2. Sermons, English. I. Title.

SPURGEON, Charles Haddon, 1834-1892 243
The soul winner: how to lead sinners to the Saviour [Foreword by Helmut Thielicke] Grand Rapids, Mich., Eerdmans [c.1963] 319p. 19cm. 1.75 pap.,
1. Evangelistic work. I. Title.

TORREY, Reuben Archer, 1856-1928. 243
Soul-winning sermons. [Westwood, N.J.] Revell [1956-60] 2 v. (485 p.) 22 cm. [BV3797T585] 56-8503
1. Evangelistic sermons. 2. Congregational churches — Sermons. 3. Sermons, American. I. Title.

TRENT, John Scott. 243
Evangelistic entreaties; revival messages and methods. Grand Rapids, Zondervan Pub. House [1959] 120 p. 20 cm. [BV3797.T7] 59-41033
1. Evangelistic sermons. 2. Baptists — Sermons. 3. Sermons, American. I. Title.

VERSTEEG, Robert John 243
The gracious calling of the Lord. Nashville, Abingdon Press [1960] 142p. 20cm. (bibl. footnotes)p2.50 bds., 60-10913
1. Evangelistic work. I. Title.

VICK G BEAUCHAMP. 243
Soul-winning sermons. Introd. by John W. Rawlings. Grand Rapids, Zondervan Pub. House [1958] 104 p. 20 cm. [BV3797.V5] 58-4942
1. Evangelistic sermons. 2. Baptists — Sermons. 3. Sermons, American. I. Title.

WASHBURN, Alphonso V 243
Outreach for the unreached. Nashville, Convention Press [1960] 150 p. illus. 19 cm. "Church study course for teaching and training ... number 1726 in category 17, section A." [BV1523.E9W3] 60-12434
1. Evangelistic work. 2. Sunday schools. I. Title.

WHITE, Douglas Malcolm, 1909- 243
Holy ground; expositions from Exodus. Grand Rapids, Mich., Baker Bk., 1962. 144p. (Evangelical pulpit lib.) 62-12669 2.50
1. Bible, O.T. Exodus—Sermons. 2. Evangelistic sermons. 3. Baptists—Sermons. 4. Sermons, American. I. Title.

WILLIAMS, Jerome Oscar, 1885- 243
Evangelistic sermons hotline Nashville, Broadman ss [c1951] c165 p. 20 cm. [BV3797.W48] 52-6
1. Evangelistic sermons—Ou lines. I. Title.

WINN, Douglas. 243
Rebuilding revival gates. [1st ed.] Wheaton, Ill., Sword of the Lord Publishers [1951] 124 p. 21 cm. [BV3797.W557] 51-36024
1. Evangelistic sermons. I. Title.

*WOODRUM, Lon 243
The rebellious planet. Grand Rapids, Mich. Zondervan [c.1965] 93p. 21cm. (6900 ser.) .69 pap.,
I. Title.

FULLER, David Otis, 1903- ed. 243.08
Valiant for the truth; a treasury of evangelical writings. Introductions by Henry W. Coray. Philadelphia, Lippincott [c1961] xi, 460 p. 24 cm. [BR1646.F8] 66-31590
1. Evangelicalism — Collections. I. Title.

FULLER, David Otis, 1903- ed. 243.08
Valiant for the truth; a treasury of evangelical writings. Introductions by Henry W. Coray. Philadelphia, Lippincott [c1961] xi, 460 p. 24 cm. [BR1646.F8] 66-31590
1. Evangelicalism — Collections. I. Title.

FULLER, David Otis, 1903- ed. 243.08
Valiant for the truth; a treasury of evangelical writings. Introd. by Henry W. Coray. Philadelphia, Lippincott [1967, c.1961] xi, 460p. 24cm. [BR1646.F8] 66-31590 5.95 bds.,
1. Evangelicalism—Collections. I. Title.

MCDONALD, Erwin Lawrence, ed. 243.08
The church proclaiming and witnessing; messages, by W. A. Criswell, others. Ed. by Erwin L. McDonnald. Grand Rapids, Mich., Baker Bk. [c.1966] 135p. 20cm. [BV3790.M227] 66-6399 2.50
1. Evangelistic work—Addresses, essays, lectures. I. Criswell, Wallie A. II. Title.

*WALLIS, Charles Langworthy, 1921- ed 243.082
88 evangelistic sermons edited by Charles L. Wallis Grand Rapids, Baker Book [1975] 242 p. 20 cm. [BV3795] 64-14374 ISBN 0-8010-9554-9 2.95 (pbk.)
1. Evangelistic sermons. 2. Sermons, American. I. Title.

WALLIS, Charles Langworthy, 1921- ed. 243.082
88 evangelistic sermons. Introd. by Charles L. Allen. [1st ed.] New York, Harper & Row [1964] viii, 242 p. 22 cm. (The New anvil library) "Sources": p. 233-234. [BV3797.A1W3] 64-14374
1. Evangelistic sermons. 2. Sermons, American. I. Title.

GRAHAM, William Franklin, 1918- 243.0924
The quotable Billy Graham. Compiled and edited by Cort R. Flint and the staff of Quote. [1st ed.] Anderson, S. C., Droke House [1966] 258 p. 20 cm. [BV3797.G674] 66-25566
I. Title.

GRAHAM WILLIAM FRANKLIN. 1918- 243.0924
The quotable Billy Graham. Comp. ed. by Cort R. Flint, the staff of Quote. [1st ed.] Anderson. S. C. Droke House [1966] 258p. 20cm. [BV3797.G674] 66-25566 5.95
I. Title.

VIEUJEAN, Jean. 243.4
Your other self. Translated from the French by Richard E. Cross. Westminster, Md., Newman Press, 1959. 165 p. 23 cm. [VB4630.V513] 58-11459
1. Love (Theology) I. Title.

BELLER, Herbert N. 243'.73'04 s
Unrelated debt-financed income / by Herbert N. Beller ; Leonard L. Silverstein, chief editor. Washington : Tax Management, c1976- 1 v. ; 28 cm. (Tax management portfolios ; 339) This portfolio revises and supersedes 257 T.M., Unrelated debt-financed income by K. C. Eliasberg and S. A. Arenberg. Loose-leaf for updating. Includes bibliography. [KF6289.A1T35 no. 339] [KF6449] 343'.73'052 77-150838
1. Charitable uses, trusts, and foundations—Taxation—United States. I. Eliasberg, Kenneth C. Unrelated debt-financed income. II. Title. III. Series.

244 Stories Allegories Satires

APPLEGARTH, Margaret Tyson, 1886- 244
Men as trees walking. [1st ed.] New York, Harper [1952] 282 p. 22 cm. Stories. [BV4515.A5] 52-8458
1. Christian life—Stories. I. Title.

APPLEGARTH, Margaret Tyson, 1886- 244
Moment by moment. [Stories] New York, Harper [1955] 236p. 22cm. [BV4515.A52] 54-8933
1. Christian life—Stories. I. Title.

ARMENIAN Church Youth Organization of America. 244
Annual assembly; [booklet] [New York] v. illus., ports. 25cm. [BV1280.A7A7] 57-34189
I. Title.

ARMENIAN Church Youth Organization of America. 244
Annual assembly; [booklet] [New York] v. illus., ports. 25cm. [BV1280.A7A7] 57-34189
I. Title.

BOURNE, Emma (Guest) 1882- 244
A story of the good sand. Dallas, Story Book Press [1953] 46p. 20cm. [BV4571.B59] 53-39542
I. Title.

BREIG, Joseph Anthony, 1905- 244
Under my hat. [Sketches] New York, McMullen Books [c1954] 189p. 21cm. [BX2350.B657] 54-12241
1. Christian life—Catholic authors. I. Title.

CHRISTIAN herald (New York, 1878- 244
Golden moments of religious inspiration; a treasury of faith from the Christian herald. Edited by Ruth M. Elmquist. Foreword by Daniel A. Poling. New York, Mc-Graw-Hill [1954] 303p. 21cm. [BV4801.C45] 54-11265
1. Devotional literature. I. Elmquist, Ruth M., ed. II. Title.

DYER, Delbert, 1903- 244
Satan's secret service; true, life experiences. Kansas City, Kan., Wonder House, 1953. 106p. illus. 18cm. [BV4501.D9] 53-39547
1. Christian life. I. Title.

ELVY, Cora. 244
The apple is my symbol. [1st ed.] New York, Pageant Press [1957] 114p. 21cm. [BR126.E53] 57-8304
I. Title.

EMERSON, Laura S comp. 244
Twenty-five inspiring readings; religious stories for oral reading. Kansas City, Mo., Beacon Hill Press [1952] 156 p. 19 cm. [BV4801.E66] 52-102573
1. Devotional literature. I. Title.

GARRISON, Maxine. 244
The Angel spreads her wings. [Westwood, N. J.] Revell [1956] 159 p. 22 cm. [BR1715.R6R65] 55-8762
1. Rogers, Dale Evans Angel unaware. 2. Rogers, Robin Elizabeth, 1950-1952. 3. Rogers, Roy, 1911- I. Title.

GAYLORD, Harding W. 244
Mr. Bradford gets around; stories of a Christian about town. Philadelphia, Muhlenberg Press [1952] 97 p. 20 cm. [BV4515.G3] 52-7992
1. Christian life—Stories. I. Title.

GORE, Russell Daniel. 244
An auto ride to heaven; a Christian travelogue. Traverse City, Mich. [1951?] 112 p. illus. 21 cm. [BV4515.G6] 51-28347
1. Christian life. I. Title.

JONES, Elizabeth Brown, 1907- 244
When you need a story. Kansas City, Mo., Beacon Hill Press [1953] 128p. 20cm. [BV4571.J573] 53-10434
1. Children's stories. I. Title.

KNIGHT, Alice Marie (Neighbour) 1901- 244
1001 stories for children and children's workers. Grand Rapids, Eerdmans, 1952. 287p. 24cm. [BV4571.K6] 52-10811
1. Christian life—Stories. 2. Homiletical illustrations. I. Title.

LEWIS, Clive Staples, 1898-1963. 244
The screwtape letters & Screwtape proposes a toast. New York, Macmillan, 1962 [c1961] 172 p. 18 cm. (Macmillan paperbacks, MP108) [BR125.L67 1962] 62-16314
1. Christianity—20th century. I. Title. II. Title: Screwtape proposes a toast.

LUTHER, Martin, 1483-1546. 244
The table talk of Martin Luther, edited with an introd. by Thomas S. Kepler. [1st American ed.] New York, World Pub. Co. [1952] xxiii, 345p. 16cm. (World devotional classics) Based on the English translation of William Hazlitt.' [BR332.T4H3 1952] 52-10322
1. Table-talk. I. Title.

PALMER, Kenyon Alexander, 1871-1952. 244
Kenyon Palmer's scrapbook; compilation of Christian experiences in his work with the Gideons. Chicago, Gideons International [1952] 80p. 20cm. [BV1280.G4P3] 54-24795
1. Gideons International. I. Title.

PRESTON, Virgie Viola (Vail) 1890- 244
Divine names and attributes of animals, birds, fish, insects, and creeping things. New York, Vantage Press [c1953] 115p. 23cm. [BR126.P67] 53-6776
I. Title.

ROGERS, Dale Evans. 244
Angel unaware. [Westwood, N. J.] Revell [1953] 63 p. 20 cm. [BR1715.R6R6] 53-7446
1. Rogers, Robin Elizabeth, 1950-1952. I. Title.

ROGERS, Dale Evans [Orig. name: Frances Octavia Smith] 244
Angel unaware. New York, Pyramid [1963, c.1953] 64p. 18cm. (R826) .50 pap.,
1. Rogers, Robin Elizabeth, 1950-1952. I. Title.

SNOWDEN, Rita Frances. 244
'Listen children!' True stories and object talks. London. Epworth Press [labl: Chicago, A. R. Allenson, 1952] 128p. 19cm. [BV4571.S57] 53-33368
I. Title.

SNOWDEN, Rita Frances. 244
Story-time again. London, Epworth Press [labl: Chicago. A. R. Allenson, 1951] 127p. 19cm. [BV4571.S58] 53-33369
I. Title.

STORIES of the Restoration, 244
a collection of true stories for children. [Independence, Mo.] Herald House, 1953. 240p. 21cm. [BV4571.S75] 53-31995
1. Children's stories. 2. Reorganized Church of Jesus Christ of Latter-Day Saints.

THE story of the Three Kings: 244
Melchior, Balthasar, and Jaspar, which originally was written by John of Hildesheim in the fourteenth century and is now retold by Margaret B. Freeman. New York, Metropolitan Museum of Art, 1955. 80p. illus. 26cm. 'The illustrations and the general format are from Leben heiligen Drei Konigen in the Pierpont Morgan Library.' Bibliography: p. 74-75. [PA8360.J6A72] 879.3 55-12148
1. Magi. Legend. I. Joannes, of Hildesheim, d. 1375. II. Freeman, Margaret Barss, 1905- III. Title: The Three Kings.

TIERNEY, William L 244
Victory at the cost of purification of his soul. Boston, Christopher Pub. House [1955] 55p. 21cm. [BX1755.T5] 55-13502
1. Catholic Church. I. Title.

PRICE, Walter K. 244'.5'07
In the final days / by Walter K. Price. Chicago : Moody Press, c1977. 192 p. ; 22 cm. Bibliography: p. 183-192. [BS1555.2.P74] 76-58907 ISBN 0-8024-4059-2 : 5.95
1. Bible. O.T. Daniel XI—Criticism, interpretation, etc. I. Title.

245 Hymns Without Music

**ANALECTA Hymnica Medii* 245
Aevi; v.1-55. New York, Johnson Reprint [1964] 55v. (various p.) Contents.v.1-55. 1886-1922. 1,050.00 set; 18.50 ea., pap.

BARROWS, Cliff, ed. 245
Crusade hymn stories. Edited by Cliff Barrows. With hymn studies and personal stories by Billy Graham and the crusade musicians. Chicago, Hope Pub. Co., 1967. 160 p. 22 cm. $3.50 [BV315.C78] 68-7265
1. Hymns, English—Hist. & crit. 2. Revivals—Hymns. I. Graham, William Franklin, 1918- II. Title.

CRUSADE hymn stories. 245
Edited by Cliff Barrows. With hymn studies and personal stories by Billy Graham and the crusade musicians. Chicago, Hope Pub. Co., 1967. 160 p. 22 cm. [BV315.C78] 68-7265 3.50
1. Hymns, English—History and criticism. 2. Revivals—Hymns. I. Barrows, Cliff, ed. II. Graham, William Franklin, 1918-

EGGE, Mandus A., ed. 245
Hymns; how to sing them. Edited by Mandus A. Egge and Janet Moede. Minneapolis, Augsburg Pub. House [1966] 110 p. illus. 22 cm. "Prepared under the auspices of the Commission on Worship and Church Music, the American Lutheran Church." [BV311.E35] 66-26801
1. Hymns—Study and teaching. 2. Hymns, English—History and criticism. I. Moede, Janet, joint ed. II. American Lutheran Church (1961-) Commission on Worship and Church Music. III. Title.

EMURIAN, Ernest K. 245
Hymn festivals. Natick, Mass., W. A. Wilde [c.1961] 126p. 61-17633 2.95 bds.,
1. Hymn festivals. I. Title.

EMURIAN, Ernest K 245
Sing the wondrous story. Natick, Mass., W. A. Wilde Co., [1963] 148 p. 22 cm. [BV311.E55] 63-22167
1. Hymns, English — Hist. & crit. I. Title.

FIRST hymns. 245
Illustrated by Brenda Meredith Seymour. New York, H. Z. Walck, 1968 [c1967] 40 p. illus. (part col.) 14 cm. The words of seventeen hymns for children, including All Things Bright and Beautiful, There is a Green Hill Far Away, and Jesus, Friend of Little Children. [BV353.F5] AC 68
1. Hymns. I. Seymour, Brenda Meredith, illus.

GOODENOUGH, Caroline Louisa Leonard, 1856- 245
High lights on hymnists and their hymns [by] Caroline Leonard Goodenough. Rochester, Mass., c1931. [New York, AMS Press, 1974] 505 p. 23 cm. [BV310.G6 1974] 72-1626 ISBN 0-404-08310-2 20.00
1. Hymns—History and criticism. 2. Hymn writers. 3. Hymns—Indexes. I. Title.

KEITH, Edmond D 245
Hymns we sing [by] Edmond D. Keith and Gaye L. McGlothlen. Nashville, Tenn., Convention Press [1960] xii, 124p. 22cm. Includes hymns with music. 'Church study course for teaching and training [of the Sunday School Board of the Southern Baptist Convention] This book is number 1986 in category 19, section C.' [ML3160.K4] 61-13989
1. Baptists—Hymns—Hist. & crit. 2. Hymns, English—Hist. & crit. I. McGlothlen, Gaye L., joint author. II. Southern Baptist Convention. Sunday School Board. III. Title.

KEITH, Edmond D 245
Know your hymns [by] Edmond D. Keith and Gaye L. McGlothen. Nashville, Convention Press [1962] xii, 132p. 22cm. Includes hymns in close score. 'Church study course [of the Sunday School Board of the Southern Baptist Convention] This book is number 1920 in category 19, section for adults and young people.' [ML3160.K43] 62-16109
1. Baptists—Hymns—Hist. & crit. 2. Hymns, English— Hist. & Crit. I. McClothen, Gaye L., joint author. II. Southern Baptist Convention. Sunday School Board. III. Title.

KEITH, Edmond D 245
Know your hymns [by] Edmond D. Keith and Gaye L. McGlothlen. Nashville, Convention Press [1962-66] 2 v. 22 cm. Includes hymns in close score. Vols. 2 by Edmond D. Keith and Joseph F. Green. "Church study course [of the Sunday School Board of the Southern Baptist Convention] This book is number 1920 [and number 1926] in category 19, section for adults and young people." [ML3160.K43] 62-16109
1. Baptists — Hymns — Hist. & crit. 2. Hymns, English — Hist. & crit. I. McGlothlen, Gaye L joint author. II. Green, Joseph Franklin, 1924- joint author. III. Southern Baptist Convention. Sunday School Boar' IV. Title.

KONKEL, Wilbur. 245
Next hymn, please; a delightful quest for hymn-stories. New York, Carlton Press [1963] 176 p. illus. 21 cm. (A Reflection book) [BV312.K6] 64-159
1. Hymns, English — Addresses, essays, lectures. 2. Hymn writers. I. Title.

LOVELACE, Austin Cole. 245
The anatomy of hymnody [by] Austin C. Lovelace. New York, Abingdon Press [1965] 112 p. music. 20 cm. Bibliographical footnotes. [BV335.L6] 65-10550
1. Hymns — Metrics and rhythmics. I. Title.

LOVELACE, Austin Cole 245
The anatomy of hymnody. Nashville, Abingdon [c.1965] 112p. music. 20cm. Bibl. [BV335.L6] 65-10550 2.75 bds.,
1. Hymns—Metrics and rhythmics. I. Title.

NORTHCOTT, William Cecil, 1902- 245
Hymns in Christian worship; the use of hymns in the life of the church. Richmond, Va., Knox [1965] 83p. 22cm. (Ecumenical studies in worship, no. 13) [BV310.N6] 65-10264 1.75 pap.,
1. Hymns, English—Hist. & crit. I. Title. II. Series.

RATLIFF, Foster. 245
The new Baptist song book, 1971; a collection of good hymns, songs and ballads. Lookout, Ky. [1971, c1957] 151 p. 16 cm. [BV380.R37] 72-196425
1. Baptists—Hymns. 2. Hymns, English. I. Title.

REST, Friedrich, 1913- 245
The cross in hymns. Valley Forge, Pa., Judson Press [1969] 110 p. 23 cm. Includes hymns in close score. Bibliographical references included in "Notes" (p. 109-110) [BT453.R4] 69-16392 3.95
1. Jesus Christ—Crucifixion. 2. Hymns—History and criticism. I. Title.

RIZK, Helen Salem. 245
Stories of the Christian hymns. Drawings by William Duncan. Boston, Whittemore Associates [1964] 62 p. illus. 19 cm. [BV311.R5] 64-56251
1. Hymns, English — Juvenile literature. I. Title.

RIZK, Helen Salem 245
Stories of the Christian hymns. Drawings by William Duncan. Boston, Whittemore [c.1964] 62p. illus. 19cm. 64-56251 .60 pap.,
1. Hymns, English—Juvenile literature. I. Title.

ROMANUS MELODUS, Saint, fl.500 245
Melodi cantica [v.1.] ed. by Paul Maas, C. A. Trypanis. Oxford, Clarendon Pr. [dist. New York, Oxford, c.]1963. 546p. 23cm. Text in Greek. Contents.[v.1] Cantica genuina. Bibl. 63-24135 20.20
1. Hymns, Greek. I. Mass, Paul, 1880- ed. II. Trypanes, Konstantinos Athanasiou, ed. III. Title.

RONANDER, Albert C. 245
Guide to the Pilgrim hymnal [by] Albert C. Ronander [and] Ethel K. Porter. Philadelphia, United Church Press [1966] xxiv, 456 p. 22 cm. Includes music (principally unacc. melodies) Bibliography: p. 425-427. [ML3162.R65] 65-26448
1. United Church of Christ. Pilgrim hymnal. 2. United Church of Christ—Hymns—History and criticism. 3. Hymns—History and criticism. 4. Hymns—Dictionaries. I. Porter, Ethel K., joint author. II. Title. III. Title: Pilgrim hymnal.

ROUTLEY, Erik. 245
Hymns today and tomorrow. New York, Abingdon Press [1964] 205 p. 24 cm. [BV310.R69] 64-21135
1. Hymns, English—History and criticism.

JULIAN, John, 1839-1913. 245.03
A dictionary of hymnology, setting forth the origin and history of Christian hymns of all ages and nations. New York, Dover Publications [1957] 2 v. (xviii, 1768 p.) 25 cm. Bibliography: p. [xvii]-xviii. [BV305.J8 1957] 58-416
1. Hymns—Dictionaries. 2. Hymns—Indexes. I. Title.

REID, William Watkins 245.06273
Sing with spirit and understanding, the story of the Hymn Society of America. New York, 475 Riverside Dr., Hymn Soc. of America, [c.1962] 85p. front. port. 23cm. 62-53130 1.00 pap.,
1. Hymn Society of America I. Title.

BENSON, Louis FitzGerald, 1833-1930. 245.09
The hymnody of the Christian church. Richmond, John Knox Press [1956] 310p. 21cm. [BV310] 56-11827
1. Hymns—Hist. and crit. I. Title.

BENSON, Louis FitzGerald, 1855-1930. 245.09
The hymnody of the Christian church. Richmond. John Knox Press [1956] 310p. 21cm. [BV310] 56-11827
1. Hymns—Hist. and crit. I. Title.

EMURIAN, Ernest K 245.09
Famous stories of inspiring hymns. Boston, W. A. Wilde Co. [1956] 185p. 21cm. [BV315.E48] 56-10727
1. Hymns—Hist. & crit. I. Title.

EMURIAN, Ernest K. 245.09
Famous stories of inspiring hymns [by] Ernest K. Emurian. Grand Rapids, Baker Book House [1975, c1956] 185 p. 20 cm. (Interlude books) [BV315.E48] 56-10727 ISBN 0-8010-3317-9 2.95 (pbk.)
1. Hymns—History and criticism. I. Title.

ENGLAND, Martha Winburn. 245'.09
Hymns unbidden; Donne, Herbert, Blake, Emily Dickinson, and the hymnographers, by Martha Winburn England and John Sparrow. [New York] New York Public Library, 1966. vii, 153 p. illus., facsims., plate. 26 cm. Bibliographical footnotes. [BV310.E5] 66-28617
1. Hymns—History & criticism. 2. Hymns, English. I. Sparrow, John Hanbury Angus, 1906- joint author. II. Title.

HERZEL, Catherine B. 245.09
To Thee we sing, by Catherine and Frank Herzel. Philadelphia, Muhlenberg Press, 1946. 254 p. 20 cm. [BV310.H45] 46-4981
1. Hymns — Hist. & crit. I. Herzel, Frank Benton, joint author. II. Title.

KEITH, Edmond D 245.09
Christian hymnody. Nashville, Convention Press [1956] 147p. 19cm. [ML3186.K35] 56-14018
1. Hymns—Hist. & crit. 2. Church music—Hist. & crit. I. Title.

PATRICK, Millar 245.09
The story of the church's song. Rev. for Amer. use by James Rawlings Sydnor. Richmond, Va., Knox [c.1962] 208p. 21cm. Bibl. 62-11775 3.75
1. Hymns—Hist. & crit. 2. Church music—U. S.—Hist. & crit. I. Sydnor, James Rawlings, ed. II. Title.

PFATTEICHER, Helen Emma. 245.09
In every corner sing. Philadelphia, Muhlenberg Press [1954] 214p. 20cm. [BV310.P4] 54-7588
1. Hymns—Hist. & crit. I. Title.

RYDEN, Ernest Edwin. 245.09
The story of Christian hymnody. Rock Island, Ill., Augustana Press [1959] xiv, 670p. illus. 24cm. 'A revision and enlargement of the author's 'The story of our hymns,' first published in 1930.' Bibliography: p. 669-670. [BV310.R9 1959] 59-9242
1. Hymns—Hist. & crit. I. Title. II. Title: Christian hymnody.

THOMSON, Ronald William. 245'.0922
Who's who of hymn writers [by] Ronald W. Thomson. London, Epworth Pr., 1967. [7] 104p. 23cm. Bibl. [BV325.T5] 67-107975 3.50
1. Hymn writers. I. Title.
Distributed by Verry, Mystic, Conn.

BENSON, Louis FitzGerald, 1855-1930 245.0942
The English hymn: its development and use in worship. Richmond, Knox [1962, c.1915] 624p. illus. 24cm. 62-13877 6.50

1. Hymns, English—Hist. & crit. I. Title.

THE American Lutheran Church (1961-) 245.2
Selected hymns in large type. Minneapolis, Augsburg Pub. House [1964] 96 p. 27 cm. "The hymns and the collect have been selected from the Service book and hymnal [of the Lutheran Church in America] by permission of the Commission on the Liturgy and Hymnal." [BV410.S42] 64-4838
1. Hymns, English. 2. Lutheran Church—Hymns. I. Title. II. Title: Hymns in large type.

BAILEY, Albert Edward, 1871- 245.2
The gospel in hymns; backgrounds and interpretations. New York, Scribner, 1950. xx, 600 p. illus., ports. 25 cm. "Selected bibliography": p. 579-583. [BV312.B3] 50-6256
1. Hymns, English—Hist. & crit. I. Title.

BONNER, Clint. 245.2
Ahymn is born. Illustrated by Charles E. Smith. Nashville, Broadman Press [1959] 160p. illus. 22cm. [BV310.B65 1959] 59-9694
1. Hymns—Hist. crit. I. Title.

BRITISH Broadcasting Corporation. 245.2
The BBC hymn book. London, New York, Oxford University Press, 1951. 1 v. (unpaged) 19 cm. Without the music. [BV350.B75] 52-28960
1. Hymns, English. I. Title.

CHRISTIAN Science Publishing Society. 245.2
Concordance to Christian science hymnal and hymnal notes. Boston [1961] 377p. 22cm. Includes bibliography. [BV390.C5 1961] 61-19434
1. Church of Christ, Scientist. Hymnal. I. Title.

CHRISTIAN Science Publishing Society. 245'.2
Concordance to Christian science hymnal and hymnal notes. Boston [1967] 377 p. 22 cm. Bibliography: p. [168] [BV390.C5 1967] 68-1651
1. Church of Christ, Scientist. Hymnal. I. Title.

CLARK, Wille Thorburn, 1868- 245.2
Hymns that endure. Nashville, Broadman [1961, c.1952] 168p. (Broadman Starbks.) 1.25 pap.,
1. Hymns—Hist. & crit. 2. Hymns, English—Hist. & crit. I. Title.

COMPENDICUS book of godly and spiritual songs, (A) commonly known as 'The guiude and godlieballatis,' reprinted from the ed. of 1567. [ed., introd., notes by A. F. Mitchell. Edinburgh, Printed for the Society by W. Blackwood 1897; New York, Johnson Reprint, 1966 2 p. 1., [iii]-cxxvi, [22]-338p. facsims. 22cm. (Half-title: The Scottish text society. [Pubns. 39]) Scottish hymns and versions of Psalms, ascribed to John Wedderburn, and his brothers James and Robert; many based on German or Swiss orig. Facsims. of t.p.'s of the eds. of 1578, 1600 and 1621, and 2 ps. of the ed. of 1507. Appendix III contains tunes from German Gesangbuch 1524, 1570, and Coverdale's 'Goostly Psalms. [PR8633.S4 no. 39] 23.00 245.2
1. Hymns, Scottish. 2. Hymns, Scottish—Hist. & crit. 3. Hymns, German—Translations into Scottish I. Wedderburn, John, 1500?-1556, supposed author. II. Wedderburn, James, 1495?-1553, supposed author. III. Wedderburn, Robert, ca.1510-ca. 1557, supposed author. IV. Mitchell, Alexander Ferrier, 1822-1899, ed. V. Title: The gude and godlie ballatis.
Contents omitted.

DAVES, Michael 245.2
Famous hymns and their writers. [Westwood, N.J.] Revell [c.1962] 128p. 21cm. 62-17105 2.50
1. Hymns, English—Addresses, essays, lectures. I. Title.

EMURIAN, Ernest K 245.2
Living stories of famous hymns. Boston, W. A. Wilde Co. [1955] 144p. 21cm. [BV315.E5] 55-9054
1. Hymns—Hist. & crit. I. Title.

EMURIAN, Ernest K. 245.2
Sing the wondrous story. Natick, Mass., W. A. Wilde Co. [c.1963] 148p. 22cm. 63-22167 2.50
1. Hymns, English—Hist. & crit. I. Title.

FOOTE, Henry Wilder, 1875- 245.2
Three centuries of American hymnody. Hamden, Conn., Shoe String, 1961[c.1940] x, 418p. facsim. 61-4914 8.50
1. Hymns, English—Hist & crit. 2. Church music—U.S.—Hist. & crit. 3. Psalmody. I. Title.

FOOTE, Henry Wilder, 1875- 245'.2
Three centuries of American hymnody. [Hamden, Conn.] Archon Books, 1968 [c1940] x, 418, [23] p. facsim. 23 cm. "With a new appendix, Recent American hymnody, reprinted ... from the Papers of the Hymn Society, vol. XVII, 1952": p. [419]-[441] Bibliography: p. [441] [ML3111.F6T4 1968] 68-15615
1. Hymns, English—History and criticism. 2. Church music—United States—History and criticism. 3. Psalmody. I. Foote, Henry Wilder, 1875- Recent American hymnody. II. Title.

GEALY, Fred Daniel. 245'.2
Companion to the Hymnal; a handbook to the 1964 Methodist hymnal. [Texts: Fred D. Gealy. Tunes: Austin C. Lovelace. Biographies: Carlton R. Young. General editor: Emory Stevens Bucke] Nashville, Abingdon Press [1970] 766 p. 23 cm. Bibliography: p. 723-726. [ML3170.G4] 76-98899 10.00
1. Methodist Church—Hymns—History and criticism. 2. Hymns, English—History and criticism. 3. Biography. I. Lovelace, Austin Cole, joint author. II. Young, Carlton R., joint author. III. The Methodist hymnal. 1964. IV. Title.

HARVEY, Robert, 1884- 245.2
Best-loved hymn stories. Grand Rapids, Zondervan Pub. House [1963] 160 p. 21 cm. [BV312.H35] 63-2667
1. Hymns, English — Hist. & crit. I. Title.

HARVEY, Robert, 1884- 245.2
Best-loved hymn stories. Grand Rapids, Mich., Zondervan [c.1963] 160p. 21cm. 63-2667 2.50 bds.,
1. Hymns, English—Hist. & crit. I. Title.

*KONKEL, Wilbur. 245'.2
Stories of children's hymns; intriguing stories behind great Christian songs for children. [3d ed.] Minneapolis, Bethany Fellowship [1967] 51p. 19cm. 1.00 pap.,
I. Title.

KONKEL, Wilbur. 245'.2
Stories of childrens hymns; intriguing stories behind great Christian songs for children. [3d ed.] Minneapolis, Bethany Fellowship [1967] 51 p. illus., port. 19 cm. Contents.Contents.—Children of the Heavenly King.—Jesus loves even me.—There is a happy land.—Something more than gold.—There is a green hill far away.—All the things bright and beautiful.—Dare to be a Daniel.—Stand up for Jesus.—Hast thou not known?—Jesus is our shepherd.—Yield not to temptation.—"Oh, give me Samuel's heart!"—My God, my Father, while I stray.—Who would true valour see?—Saviour, like a shepherd lead us!—Gentle Jesus, Meek and mild.—Be a little star and shine. [BV311.K65 1967] 77-15684
1. Hymns, English—History and criticism. I. Title.

KRONKEL, Wilbur 245.2
Next hymn, please; a delightful quest for hymn stories. New York, Carlton [c.1963] 176p. 21cm. (Reflection bk.) 2.50
1. Hymns—English. I. Title.

NORTHCOTT, William Cecil, 1902- 245.2
Hymns we love; stories of the hundred most popular hymns. Philadelphia, Westminster Press [1955] 168p. 19cm. [BV315.N67] 55-7813
1. Hymns—Hist. & crit. 2. Hymns, English—Hit. & crit. I. Title.

PRICE, Carl Fowler, 1881- 245.2
One hundred and one hymn stories. Nashville, Abingdon [1962, c.1951] 112p. 18cm. (Apex bks., J7) 62-3404 .69 pap.,
1. Hymns, English—Hist. & crit. I. Title.

QUINN, Eugene F 245'.2
A hymnal concordance. Compiled by Eugene F. Quinn. Louisville, Ky., Personalized Printing [1966] 1 v. (unpaged) 22 cm. [BV380.Q5] 68-1083
1. Sims, W. Hines, comp. The Baptist hymnal. 2. Hymns, English—Indexes. I. Title.

QUINN, Eugene F. 245'.2
A hymnal concordance. Compiled by Eugene F. Quinn. Louisville, Ky., Personalized Printing [1966] 1 v. (unpaged) 22 cm. [BV380.Q5] 68-1083
1. Sims, Walter Hines, comp. The Baptist hymnal. 2. Hymns, English—Indexes. I. Title.

REID, William Watkins. 245.2
My God is there, controlling, and other hymns and poems. New York, Hymn Society of America [1965] 1 v. (unpaged) 24 cm. Hymns, English. [BV459.R42] 66-4632
I. Title.

REYNOLDS, William Jensen. 245.2
Hymns of our faith; a handbook for the Baptist hymnal. Nashville, Broadman Press [1964] xxxvi, 452 p. music. 23 cm. Bibliographical footnotes. [BV313.R4] 64-14049
1. Hymns, English — Hist. & crit. 2. Baptists — Hymns — Hist. & crit. 3. Hymn writers. 4. Southern Baptist Convention. Sunday School Board. Baptist hymnal. I. Title.

REYNOLDS, William Jensen 245.2
Hymns of our faith; a handbook for the Baptist hymnal. Nashville, Broadman [c.1964] xxxvi, 452p. music. 23cm. Bibl. 64-14049 6.00
1. Hymns, English—Hist. & crit. 2. Baptists—Hymns—Hist. & crit. 3. Hymn writers. 4. Southern Baptist Convention. Sunday School Board. Baptist hymnal. I. Title.

ROUTLEY, Erik. 245.2
Hymns and human life. New York, Philosophical Library [1953, c1952] 346p. 22cm. [BV310.R68 1953] 53-9649
1. Hymns—Hist. & crit. 2. Hymns, English — Hist. & crit. I. Title.

ROUTLEY, Erik 245.2
Hymns and human life [2d ed.] Grand Rapids, Mich., Eerdmans [1966] 346p. 23cm. [BV310.R6 1953] 3.95
1. Hymns—Hist. & crit. 2. Hymns, English—Hist. & crit I. Title.

ROUTLEY, Erik. 245'.2
Hymns and the faith. [1st U.S.A. ed.] Grand Rapids, W. B. Eerdmans Pub. Co. [1968] xii, 311 p. 23 cm. [BV312.R68 1968] 68-20583
1. Hymns, English—History and criticism. I. Title.

SAINT BONAVENTURA, Cardinal 1221-1274. 245.2
Hymn to the cross. [Translated by Jose de Vinck] Paterson, N. J., St. Anthony Guild Press [c.1960] [14]p. 23cm. 60-51162 .25 pap.,
I. Title.

SANFORD, Don, comp. 245.2
Popular hymn stories. Grand Rapids, Zondervan Pub. House [1957] 92p. 21cm. [BV315.S28] 58-20234
1. Hymns, English—Hist. & crit. I. Title.

SELECTED hymns in large type. Minneapolis, Augsburg [c.1964] 96p. 27cm. Hymns and the collect have been selected from the Service book and humnal of the Lutheran Church in Amer. by permission of the Comm. on the Liturgy and Hymnal. 64-4838 2.00 245.2
1. Hymns, English. 2. Lutheran Church—Hymns. I. The American Lutheran Church (1961-) II. Title: Hymns in large type.

STATLER, Ruth Beeghly, 1906- 245.2
Handbook on Brethren hymns [by] Ruth B. Statler and Nevin W. Fisher. Elgin, Ill., Brethren Press [1959] 93 p. 21 cm. [BV403.G4S8] 59-16708
1. Church of the Brethren. Hymnal. 2. Church of the Brethren — Hymns — Hist. & crit. 3. Hymns, English — Hist. & crit. I. Fisher, Nevin Wishard, 1900- joint author. II. Church of the Brethren. The Brethren hymnal. III. Title.

TIPPETT, Harry Moyle, 1891- 245.2
Treasured themes from familiar hymns. Illustrated by Harry Baerg. Washington, Review and Herald Pub. Association [1959] 128 p. illus. 18 cm. [BV312.T5] 60-19010
1. Hymns, English—Hist. & crit. I. Title.

DEARMER, Percy, 1867-1936. 245.203
The parson's handbook; practical directions for parsons and others according to the Anglican use, as set forth in the Book of common prayer, on the basis of the twelfth edition. Rev. and rewritten by Cyril E. Pocknee. 13th ed. London, New York, Oxford University Press, 1965. xx. 192 p. illus. 19 cm. Bibliography: p. [183] -- 187. [BX5141.D38 1965] 65-29557
1. Church of England. Liturgy and ritual. 2. Pastoral theology — Anglican communion — Handbooks, manuals, etc. 3. Church vestments. I. Pocknee, Cyril Edward, ed. II. Title.

LAMBURN, Edward Cyril Russell. 245.203
Anglican services; a book concerning ritual and ceremonial in the Anglican Communion, by E.C.R. Lamburn. 2d ed. London, W. Knott, 1963. 370 p. 23 cm. [BX5141.L27] 67-33361
1. Church of England. Liturgy and ritual. I. Title.

LAMBURN, Edward Cyril Russell. 245.203
Anglican services; a book concerning ritual and ceremonial in the Anglican Communion, by E.C.R. Lamburn. 2d ed. London, W. Knott, 1963. 370 p. 23 cm. [BX5141.L27] 67-33361
1. Church of England. Liturgy and ritual. I. Title.

MCDORMAND, Thomas Bruce 245.203
Judson concordance to hymns [by] Thomas B. McDormand, Frederic S. Crossman. Valley Forge, Pa., ludson [c.1965,54 375p. 25cm. [BV305.M3] 65-15009 7.50
1. Hymns, English—Concordances. I. Crossman, Frederic S., joint author. II. Title. III. Title: Concordance to hymns.

POCKNEE, Cyril Edward. 245.203
The French diocesan hymns and their melodies. [1st ed.] London, Faith Press; New York, Morehouse-Gorham [1954] vi, 162p. 19cm. (Alcuin Club. Tracts, 29) 'A translation of those hymns that have passed into Anglican hymn books, together full Latin text.'--British national bibliography. 1954. With plainsong notation. Corrigenda slip inserted. Includes bibliographical references. [BX5141.A1A65 vol. 20] A56
1. Church of England—Hymns. 2. Hymns, Latin. 3. Hymns, English—Translations from Latin. 4. Hymns, Latin—Translations into English. I. Title. II. Series.

SHANDS, Alfred Rives, 1928- 245.203
The liturgical movement and the local church. Naperville, Ill., Allenson [1959] 126 p. 19 cm. (Religious Book Club edition, 129) Bibliography: p. 119-124. [BX5141.S45] 62-1937
1. Liturgical movement — Anglican Communion. I. Title.

HASERODT, E V 245.2041
Concordance to The Lutheran hymnal. Saint Louis, Mo., Concordia Pub. House [1956] vii, 682p. 22cm. [BV410.H35] 55-6435
1. The Lutheran hymnal. 2. Hymns, English—Concordances. 3. Lutheran Church—Hymns—Concordances. I. Title.

LIVING hymns of Charles Wesley. The singing saint [by] Bishop Leslie R. Marston. Hymns that are immortal [by] Bishop W. T. Hogue. Hymn poems [by] Charles Wesley. [Winona Lake, Ind.] Light and Life Press, c1957. 61p. illus. 16cm. [PR3763.W4L5] 57-42019 245.207
I. Wesley, Charles, 1707-1788.

LIVING hymns of Charles Wesley. The singing saint [by] Bishop Leslie R. Marston. Hymns that are immortal [by] Bishop W. T. Hogue. Hynn Poems [by] Charles Wesley. [Winona Lake, Ind.] Light and Life Press, c1957. 64p. illus. 16cm. [PR3763.W4L5] 57-42019 245.207
I. Wesley, Charles, 1707-1788.

CHEVILLE, Roy Arthur, 1897- 245.2093
They sang of the Restoration; stories of Latter Day Saint hymns. [Independence, Mo., Herald Pub. House, 1955] 267p. 21cm. [BV420.A1C4] 55-5413
1. Mormons and Mormonism—Hymns—Hist. & crit. I. Title.

WEDDLE, Franklyn S 245.2093
How to use the hymnal. Independence, Mo., Herald House [1956] 96p. 22cm. [BV420.A1W4] 56-12877
1. Reorganized Church of Jesus Christ of Latter-Day Saints—Hymns— Hist. & crit. I. Title.

WEDDLE, Franklyn S 245.2093
How to use the hymnal. Independence, Mo., Herald House [1956] 96 p. 22 cm. [BV420.A1W4] 56-12877
1. Reorganized Church of Jesus Christ of Latter-Day Saints — Hymns — Hist. & crit. I. Title.

BANKS, Louis Albert, 1855-1933. 245'.21
Immortal hymns and their story ... With ports. and illus. by Norval Jordan. [Boston] Milford House [1974] p. cm. Reprint of the 1898 ed. published by Burrows Bros. Co., Cleveland. [BV315.B3 1974] 73-20093 ISBN 0-87821-258-2 25.00
1. Hymns—History and criticism. I. Title.

METZ, Lois (Lunt) 245'.21
Hop, skip, and sing; a collection of twenty-five songs and rhythms based on the interests and activities of children. Minneapolis, T. S. Denison [c1959] 87 p. 29 cm. With piano acc. Includes instructions for movement. [M1993.M59H7] 59-1033
1. Singing games. 2. Children's songs. I. Title.

WATTS, Isaac, 1674-1748. 245'.21
Divine songs : in easy language for the use of children / by Isaac Watts; introd. by Elizabeth McEachern Wells; drawings by Leone Bowers Hamilton. Fairfax, Va. : Thoburn Press, 1975. xiv, 81 p. : ill. ; 22 cm. [PR3763.W2A65 1975] 75-593

1. Children's songs—Texts. 2. Hymns, English—Texts. I. Title.

WATTS, Isaac, 1674-1748. 245'.21
Divine songs attempted in easy language for the use of children; with an introduction and bibliography by J. H. P. Pafford. London, Oxford University Press, 1971. xiii, 338 p.; illus., music, port. 18 cm. (Juvenile library) Reprint of 1st ed., originally published in London, Lawrence, 1715; and of an illustrated ed., originally published, Derby, Mozley, [ca 1840] Includes original pagings. Bibliography: p. 275-330. [PR3763.W2A65 1971] 72-176904 £2.00
1. Children's songs. 2. Hymns, English. I. Pafford, John Henry Pyle. II. Title.

WELLER, Katharine J 245'.21
We sing to God, by Katharine J. Weller. Minneapolis, Augsburg Pub. House, 1964- v. 28 cm. "Reprinted from Steps, a church paper for young Lutherans." Contents.CONTENTS. -- [v. 1. Advent to Whitsunday] -- v. 2. Trinity season. Includes settings of the hymns in close score. [BV353.W4] 64-21501
1. Hymns, English. 2. Lutheran Church — Hymns. I. Title.

FISHER, Nevin Wishard, 245.265
1900-
The history of Brethren hymnbooks; a historical, critical, and comparative study of the hymnbooks of the Church of the Brethren. With an introd. by Desmond W. Bittinger. Bridgewater, Va., Beacon Publishers, 1950. 153 p. 28 cm. "Annotated bibliography": p. 142-145. [ML3178.B7F5] 50-13133
1. Church of the Brethren—Hymns—Hist. & crit. I. Title.

UNITED Lutheran Church in 245.3
America. Committee on German Interests.
Evangelisches Liederbuch fur Gemeinde, Schule, Haus. Philadelphia, United Lutheran Publication House [1960] 32, [70] p. 19 cm. [BV481.L8A5] 60-25226
I. Hymns, German. II. Title.

HEWITT, Theodore 245'.31'0924 B
Brown, 1881-
Paul Gerhardt as a hymn writer and his influence on English hymnody / by Theodore Brown Hewitt. St. Louis : Concordia Pub. House, c1976. p. cm. "Second edition." Originally presented as the author's thesis, Yale, 1917. Reprint of the 1918 ed. published by Yale University Press, New Haven; with new afterword and updated bibliography. Includes index. Bibliography: p. [BV330.G4H4 1976] 76-13913 ISBN 0-570-01313-5 : 5.95
1. Gerhardt, Paulus, 1607-1676. 2. Hymns, English—History and criticism. 3. Literature, Comparative—German and English. 4. Literature, Comparative—English and German. I. Title.

FRANCESCO D'ASSISI, Saint, 245.5
1182-1226.
Song of the sun, from the Canticle of the sun, by St. Francis of Assisi; illustrated by Elizabeth Orton Jones. [Text from the translation by Matthew Arnold] New York, Macmillan, 1952. unpaged. illus. 23 cm. [BV469.F7A43] 52-14483
I. Title.

PRESTON, Floyd W., 1923- 24550
BALGOL programs and geologic application for single and double Fourier series using IBM 7090/7094 computers, by Floyd W. Preston and John W. Harbaugh. Lawrence, State Geological Survey, University of Kansas, 1965. 72 p. illus., maps. 28 cm. (Kansas. State Geological Survey. Special distribution publication, 24) Cover title. Bibliography: p. 70-71. [QE113.A33no.] 66-64169 .75
1. Geology—Computer programs. I. Harbaugh, John Warvelle, 1926-, joint author. II. Title. III. Series.

JUAN DE LA CRUZ, Saint, 245.6
1542-1591.
Spiritual canticle. 3d rev. ed. Translated, edited, and with an introd. by E. Allison Peers from the critical ed. of P. Silverio de Santa Teresa. Garden City, N. Y., Image Books [1961] 520p. 18cm. (A Doubleday image book, D110) [BV5080.J773 1961] 61-1028
1. Mystical union. I. Title.

MESSENGER, Ruth Ellis, 245.7
1884-
The medieval Latin hymn. Washington, Capital Press [1953] x, 138p. 25cm. Bibliography: p. 123-134. [BV468.M46] 53-859
1. Hymns, Latin—Hist. & crit. 2. Sequences (Liturgy) I. Title.

CATHOLIC Church. Liturgy 245.702
and ritual. Hymnary.
Hymns of the Roman liturgy, by Joseph Connelly. Westminster, Md., Newman Press [1957] xxiii, 263p. 26cm. Hymns in Latin with English translations and notes. Without music. Bibliography: p. xi-xii. [BV468.C4 1957] 57-6438
1. Hymns, Latin. I. Connelly, Joseph, ed. and tr. II. Catholic Church. Liturgy and ritual. Hymnary. English. III. Title.

MESSENGER, Ruth Ellis, 245'.7'09
1884-
Ethical teachings in the Latin hymns of medieval England with special reference to the seven deadly sins and the seven principle virtues New York, AMS Press, 1967. 210 p. 23 cm. Reprint of the 1930 ed., which was first issued as thesis, Columbia University. Bibliography: p. 195-200. [BV468] 68-854
1. Hymns, Latin—Hist. & crit. 2. Catholic Church—Hymns. 3. Catholic Church in England. 4. Christian ethics—Middle Ages. I. Title.

MESSENGER, Ruth Ellis, 245'.7'09
1884-
Ethical teachings in the Latin hymns of medieval England, with special reference to the seven deadly sins and the seven principal virtues. New York, AMS Press, 1967. 210 p. 23 cm. Reprint of the 1930 ed., which was first issued as thesis, Columbia University. Bibliography: p. 195-200. [BV468] 68-854
1. Catholic Church—Hymns. 2. Catholic Church in England. 3. Hymns, Latin—History and criticism. 4. Christian ethics—Middle Ages, 600-1500. I. Title.

246 Art In Christianity

ANASTOS, Milton Vasil, 1909- 246
The immutability of Christ and Justinian's condemnation of Theodore of Mopsuestia. (In Dumbarton Oaks papers. Cambridge, Mass., 1951. 30 cm. no. 6, p. [123]-160) Bibliographical footnotes. [N5970.D8 no. 6] 52-1151
1. Jesus Christ—Person and offices. 2. Theodorus, Bp. of Mopsuestia, d. ca. 428. 3. Justinianus I, Emperor of the East. 483?-565. I. Title. II. Series: Dumbarton Oaks papers, no. 6, p. [123]-160

BRANDON, Samuel George 246
Frederick.
Man and God in art and ritual; a study of iconography, architecture and ritual action as primary evidence of religious belief and practice [by] S. G. F. Brandon. New York, Scribner [1974] p. Bibliography: p. [N72.R4B72] 73-1358 ISBN 0-684-13657-0 20.00
1. Art and religion. 2. Ritual. I. Title.

COPE, Gilbert Frederick 246
Symbolism in the Bible and the church. New York, Philosophical Library [1959] 287p. 23cm. (bibl. footbotes)illus. 59-65286 10.00
1. Symbolism. I. Title.

DAVES, Michael 246
Meditations on early Christian symbols. Nashville, Abingdon [c.1964] 159p. illus. 20cm. 64-10600 2.75
1. Meditations. I. Title.

DAVES, Michael. 246 (j)
Young readers book of Christian symbolism. Illustrated by Gordon Laite. Nashville, Abingdon Press [1967] 128 p. col. illus. 29 cm. [BV150.D35] 67-2817
1. Christian art and symbolism—Juvenile literature. I. Laite, Gordon, illus. II. Title.

DILLISTONE, Frederick 246
William, 1903-
Christianity and symbolism. Philadelphia, Westminster Press [1955] 320p. 22cm. [BL600.D5] 55-8598
1. Signs and symbols. 2. Symbolism. 3. Sacraments. I. Title.

DURANTIS, Gulielmus, Bp. of 246
Mende, ca.1237-1296.
The symbolism of churches and church ornaments: a translation of the first book of the Rationale divinorum officiorum. With an introductory essay, notes, and illus. by John Mason Neale and Benjamin Webb. Leeds, T. W. Green, 1843. [New York, AMS Press, 1973] cxxxv, 252 p. 23 cm. Includes bibliographical references. [BV150.D8 1973] 71-173017 ISBN 0-404-04653-3 18.00
1. Christian art and symbolism. 2. Church architecture. 3. Symbolism in architecture. I. Title.

DVORNIK, Francis 1893- 246
Emperors, popes, and general councils. (In Dumbarton Oaks papers. Cambridge, Mass., 1951. 30 cm. no. 6, p. [1]-23) Bibliographical footnotes. [N5970.D8 no. 6] 52-1153
1. Councils and synods. I. Title. II. Series: Dumbarton Oaks papers. no. 6. p. [1]-23

GARSIDE, Charles. 246
Zwingli and the arts. New Haven, Yale University Press, 1966. xiv, 190 p. 25 cm. (Yale historical publications. Miscellany 83) Revision of thesis, Yale University. "Bibliographical note": p. 185-186. [BR345.G3 1966] 66-12496
1. Zwingli, Ulrich, 1484-1531. 2. Church decoration and ornament. 3. Music in churches. 4. Worship — Hist. I. Title. II. Series.

GARSIDE, Charles 246
Zwingli and the arts. New Haven, Conn., Yale [c.] 1966. xiv, 190p. 25cm. (Yale hist. pubns. Miscellany 83) Bibl. [BR345.G3] 66-12496 7.50
1. Zwingli, Ulrich, 1484-1531. 2. Church decoration and ornament. 3. Music in churches. 4. Worship—Hist. I. Title. II. Series.

GOBLET d'Alviella, Eugene 246
Felicien Albert, comte, 1846-1925.
The migration of symbols. With an introd. by Sir George Birdwood. New York, B. Franklin [1972] xxiii, 277 p. illus. 23 cm. (Burt Franklin: research & source works series. Art history & reference series, 36) Reprint of the 1894 ed. [BL603.G6 1972] 76-154638 ISBN 0-8337-0762-0
1. Symbolism. I. Title.

GOBLET D'ALVIELLA, Eugene 246
Feliclen Albert, comts, 1846-1925.
The migration of symbols. With an introd. by Sir George Birdwood. New York, University Books [1956] 277p. illus. 22cm. 'A faithful reproduction of the whole of the original as published at Westminster in 1894.' [BL603.G6 1956] 56-7828
1. Symbolism. I. Title.

HAGEMANN, Gerard, 1922- j 246
Child of many wonders; a story of the Divine Infant, Jesus of Prague. Illustrated by Carolyn Jagodits. Notre Dame, Ind., Dujarie Press, 1964. 95 p. illus. 24 cm. [BX2159.C4H3] 65-853
1. Infant Jesus of Prague (Statute) — Juvenile literature. I. Title.

HAGEMANN, Gerard, 1922- 246
Child of many wonders; a story of the Divine Infant, Jesus of Prague. Illus. by Carolyn Jagodits. Notre Dame, Ind., 46556, Dujare Pr. [c.]1964. 95p. illus. 24cm. [BX2159.C4H3] 65-853 2.25
1. Infant Jesus of Prague (Statue)—Juvenile literature. I. Title.

KERR, James S. 246
Come and see the symbols of my church. Illus. by Helen Huntington. Minneapolis, Augsburg Pub. House [c.1960] 31p. illus. (part col.) 29cm. 61-7001 1.95 bds.,
1. Christian art and symbolism—Juvenile literature. I. Title.

KNAPP, Justina, Sister, 1863- 246
Christian symbols and how to use them [by] M. A. Justina Knapp. Milwaukee, Bruce Pub. Co. Detroit, Gale Research Co., 1974. xii, 164 p. illus. 22 cm. Reprint of the 1935 ed. Bibliography: p. 159-160. [BV150.K6 1974] 74-8172 ISBN 0-8103-4050-X 12.00
1. Christian art and symbolism. I. Title.

MCGEE, Ratha Doyle 246
Symbols, signposts of devotion. Illus. by Bodo Jose Weber, Ernest A. Pickup. Rev. Nashville, Upper Room [c.1956, 1962] 116p. col. illus. 20cm. 62-21157 1.00
1. Christian art and symbolism. I. Title.

MAY, Rollo, ed. 246
Symbolism in religion and literature. New York, G. Braziller, 1960. 253 p. 22 cm. Six of the nine "essays ... were originally published in Daedalus, the journal of the American Academy of Arts and Sciences, in the issue devoted to 'Symbolism in religion and literature' (vol. 87, no. 3)" [BL600.M35] 59-8842
1. Symbolism. 2. Symbolism in literature. I. Title.

MOREY, Charles Rufus, 1877- 246
1955.
Christian art. New York, Norton [1958, c1935] 120p. illus. 21cm. (The Norton library) [N7832.M66 1958] 58-11664
1. Christian art and symbolism. I. Title.

NATHAN, Walter Ludwig, 1905- 246
1961.
Art and the message of the church. Philadelphia, Westminster Press [1961] 208p. illus. 21cm. (Westminster studies in Christian communication) Includes bibliography. [N7831.N3] 61-7258
1. Christian art and symbolism. I. Title.

NEVOTNY, Louise (Miller) 246
1889-
Worship in art and music; complete programs based on great paintings and favorite hymns. Grand Rapids, Zondervan Pub. House [c1959] 89p. illus. 20cm. [BV198.N6] 60-225
1. Worship programs. I. Title.

NOVOTNY, Louise [Virgie] 246
(Miller)
Worship in art and music; complete programs based on great paintings and favorite hymns. Grand Rapids, Zondervan Pub. House [c.1959] 89p. illus. 20cm. 60-225 2.00 bds.,
1. Worship programs. I. Title.

OSTROGORSKI, Georgije. 246
Byzantine cities in the early Middle Ages. (In Dumbarton Oaks papers. Cambridge, Mass. 30 cm. no. 13 (1959) p. [45]-66) Bibliographical footnotes. [N5970.D8] A 65
1. Cities and towns — Byzantine Empire. I. Title.

PITT-RIVERS, George Henry 246
Lane Fox, 1890-
The riddle of the 'Labarum' and the origin of Christian symbols, [by] George Pitt-Rivers. London, Allen & Unwin, 1966. 93p. col. front., illus. 22cm. Bibl. [BV168.C4P5] 66-74110 6.50
1. Chi Rho symbol. 2. Christian art and symbolism. I. Title.
American distributor: Hillary House, New York.

POST, Willard Ellwood. 246
Saints, signs, and symbols. Illustrated by the author. Foreword by Edward N. West. New York, Morehouse-Barlow Co. [1962] 80p. illus. 20cm. [BV150.P6] 62-19257
1. Christian art and symbolism. I. Title.

POST, Willard Ellwood. 246
Saints, signs, and symbols / W. Ellwood Post ; illustrated and revised by the author ; foreword by Edward N. West. 2d ed. New York : Morehouse-Barlow Co., 1974. 96 p. : ill. ; 24 cm. Includes index. [BV150.P6 1974] 74-191738 ISBN 0-8192-1171-0 : 3.95
1. Christian art and symbolism. I. Title.

REST, Friedrich 246
Our Christian symbols; illustrated by Harold Minton. Philadelphia, Christian Education Press [c.1954] 86p. illus. 23cm. (pocket ed.) .75 pap.,
1. Christian art and symbolism. I. Title.

REST, Friedrich, 1913- 246
Our Christian symbols; illustrated by Harold Minton. Philadelphia, Christian Education Press [1954] 86 p. illus. 23 cm. [BV150.R4] 53-9923
1. Christian art and symbolism. I. Title.

SCOTT, Nathan A. 246
The wild prayer of longing; poetry and the sacred [by] Nathan A. Scott, Jr. New Haven, Yale University Press, 1971. xix, 124 p. 23 cm. Includes bibliographical references. [BL65.C8S36 1971] 72-140538 ISBN 0-300-01389-2 6.75
1. Roethke, Theodore, 1908-1963. 2. Religion and culture. 3. Holy, The. 4. Religion and poetry. I. Title.

SEARS, Fern. 246
Let me speak! The language of Christian symbols. Illus. by Lucille Vitatoe. Kansas City, Mo., Brown-White-Lowell Press, 1953. 59p. illus. 23cm. [BV150.S4] 54-7699
1. Christian art and symbolism. I. Title.

SEASOLTZ, R Kevin. 246
The house of God; sacred art and church architecture. [New York] Herder and Herder [1963] 272 p. diagrs. 21 cm. Bibliography: p. [251]-267. [NA4820.S4] 63-18161
1. Churches, Catholic. 2. Church architecture. 3. Christian art and symbolism. I. Title.

SEASOLTZ, R. Kevin 246
The house of God; sacred and church architecture. [New York] Herder & Herder [c.1963] 272p. diagrs. 21cm. Bibl. 63-18161 4.95
1. Churches, Catholic. 2. Church architecture. 3. Christian art and symbolism. I. Title.

STILLWELL, Richard, 1899- 246
Houses of Antioch. In Dumbarton Oaks papers. Cambridge, Mass. 30 cm. no. 15 (1961) p. [45]-57. plates) Bibliographical footnotes. [N5970.D8 no. 15] A65
1. Architecture, Domestic — Antioch. I. Title.

UNDERWOOD, Paul Atkins, 1902- 246
Fourth preliminary report on the restoration of the frescoes in the Kariye Camii at Istanbul by the Bysantine Institute, 1957-1958 [by] Paul A. Underwood. Cambridge, Mass. 30 cm. no. 13 (1959) p. [185]-212. plates) (In Dumbarton Oaks papers. Bibliographical footnotes. [N5970.D8 no. 13] A65
1. Istanbul. Kariye Camii. I. Byzantine Institute of America. II. Title.

UNDERWOOD, Paul Atkins, 1902- 246
The mosaics of Hagia Sophia at Istanbul, the portrait of the Emperor Alexander; a report on

work done by the Byzantine Institute in 1959 and 1960[by] Paul A. Underwood and Ernest J. W. Hawkins. Cambridge, Mass. 30 cm. no. 15 (1961) p. [187]-217. illus., plates) (In Dumbarton Oaks papers. Bibliographical footnotes. [N5970.D8 no. 15] A65
1. Alexander the Great, 356-323 v. c. 3. Mosaics. 2. Istanbul. Ayasofya Muxesi. I. Bysantine Institute of America. II. Hawkins, Enrest J. W., joint author. III. Title.

VAN TREECK, Carl. 246
Symbols in the church [by] Carl Van Treeck and Aloysius Croft. [2d ed.] Milwaukee, Bruce Pub. Co. [c1960] 111 p. illus. 24 cm. [N7830.V3] 61-494
1. Christian art and symbolism. I. Croft, Aloysius, joint author. II. Title.

VASILIEV, Alexander Alexandrovich, 1867- 246
Hugh Capet of France and Byzantium. Cambridge, Mass, 1951. 30 cm. no. 6, p. [227] -251 In Dumbartrn Oaks papers. Bibliographical footnotes. [N5970.DS no. 6] 52-1149
1. Hugues Capet, King of France, d. 906. 2. France — For. rel. — Byzantine Empire. 3. Byzantine Empire — For. rel. — France. I. Title. II. Series: Dumbarton Oaks papers, no. 6, p. [227]-251

VASILIEV, Alexander Alexandrovich, 1867- 246
The second Russian attack on Constantinople. Cambridge, Mass. 1951. 30 cm. no. 6, p. [161] -225) (In Dumbarton Oaks papers. Bibliographical footnotes. [N5970.DS no. 6] 52-1150
1. Oleg. Grand Duke of Kiev, d. 912. 2. Istanbul — Hist. 3. Varangians in the Byzantine Empire. I. Title. II. Series: Dumbarton Oaks papers, no. 6. p. [161]-225

VOGT, Von Ogden 246
Art & religion. With a new preface and epilogue by the author. Boston, Beacon Press [c.1921-1960] xv, 269p. 20cm. (Beacon ser. in liberal religion, LR 5) Bibl. footnotes. illus. 1.75 pap.,
1. Art and religion. 2. Church. 3. Church architecture. 4. Christian art and symbolism. 5. Liturgies. I. Title.

VOGT, Von Ogden, 1879- 246
Art & religion. With a new pref. and epilogue by the author. [Rev ed.] Boston, Beacon Press [1960] 269 p. illus. 21 cm. (Beacon series in liberal religion, LR5) [BV150.V6 1960] 61-479
1. Art and religion. 2. Church. 3. Church architecture. 4. Christian art and symbolism. I. Title.

VOIGT, Robert J 246
Symbols in Christian art. Somerset, Ohio, Rosary Pfess [1950] 52 p. illus. 18 cm. [N7740.V58] 50-746
1. Symbolism in art. I. Title.

WHITTEMORE, Carroll E., ed. 246
My first book of Christian symbols illus. by William Duncan. Boston, [16Ashbrtn. Pl. Whittemore Assocs. 1961] unpaged. illus. .60 pap.,
I. Title.

WINZEN, Damasus. 246
Symbols of Christ: the Old Testament, the New Testament. Drawings by William V. Cladek. New York, P. J. Kenedy [1955] 103p. illus. 20cm. [BV150.W52] 55-9738
1. Christian art and symbolism. I. Title.

FRITZ, Dorothy B. 246.07
The use of symbolism in Christian education. Philadelphia, Westminster [c.1961] 64p. illus. Bibl. 61-8294 1.45 pap.,
1. Christian art and symbolism—Study and teaching. I. Title. II. Title: Symbolism in Christian education.

FRITZ, Dorothy Bertolet. 246.07
The use of symbolism in Christian education. Philadelphia, Westminster Press [1961] 64 p. illus. 23 cm. Includes bibliography. [BV150.F7] 61-8294
1. Christian art and symbolism — Study and teaching. I. Title. II. Title: Symbolism in Christian education.

DANIELOU, Jean. 246.2
Primitive Christian symbols. Translated by Donald Attwater. Baltimore, Helicon Press [1964] xvi, 151 p. illus. 22 cm. Bibliographical footnotes. [BV155.D313] 64-12383
1. Christian art and symbolism. I. Title.

DANIELOU, Jean 246.2
Primitive Christian symbols. Tr.[from French] by Donald Attwater. Helicon [dist. New York, Taplinger, c.1961,1964] xvi, 151p. illus. 22cm. Bibl. 64-12383 3.95 bds.,
1. Christian art and symbolism. I. Title.

ALEXANDER, Paul Julius, 1910- 246.3
The Patriarch Nicephorus of Constantinople; ecclesiastical policy and image worship in the Byzantine Empire. Oxford, Clarendon Press, 1958. xii, 287p. facsim. 22cm. Bibliography: p.[266]-280. [BR238.A4] 58-1693
1. Nicephorus, Saint, Patriarch of Constantinople. 2. Iconoclasm. I. Title.

TENAZAS, Rosa C. 246.3
The Santo Nino of Cebu [by] Rosa C. P. Tenazas. Manila, Catholic Trade School: foreign dist. by the Cellar Bk. Shop, Detroit, 1965. vii, 122p. illus. 23cm. (San Carlos pubns. Ser. A. Humanities, no. 4) On verso of t.p.: 'Series A: Humanities, number 5. [BX2159.C4T4] 66-6769 3.25 pap.,
1. Santo Nino Jesus de Cebu (Statue) I. Title. II. Series.

GALAVARIS, George. 246'.5
Bread and the liturgy; the symbolism of early Christian and Byzantine bread stamps. Madison, University of Wisconsin Press, 1970. xvii, 235 p. illus. 25 cm. Includes bibliographical references. [BV825.52.G34] 75-98120 10.00
1. Bread stamps (Liturgical objects) I. Title.

GRIFFITH, Helen Stuart 246.5
The sign language of our faith: learning to read the message of Christian symbols. Illus. by the author. Grand Rapids, Eerdmans [1966] 96p. illus. 20cm. Bibl. [BV150.G7 1966] 67-13972 1.95 pap.,
1. Christian art and symbolism. I. Title.

WILKINS, Eithne. 246'.5
The rose-garden game; a tradition of beads and flowers. [New York] Herder and Herder [1969] 239 p. illus. (part col.) 24 cm. (An Azimuth book) Includes bibliographical references. [BX2310.R7W5 1969] 70-87776 7.50
1. Rosary. 2. Rosary in art. I. Title.

CHILD, Heather. 246'.55
Christian symbols, ancient and modern: a handbook for students [by] Heather Child and Dorothy Colles. New York, Scribner [1972, c1971] xxi, 270 p. illus. 26 cm. Bibliography: p. 256-259. [BV150.C53 1972] 72-2769 ISBN 0-684-13093-9 17.50
1. Christian art and symbolism. I. Colles, Dorothy, joint author. II. Title.

MELLINKOFF, Ruth. 246'.55
The horned Moses in medieval art and thought. Berkeley, University of California Press, 1970. xix, 210 p. 130 illus. 27 cm. (California studies in the history of art, 14) Bibliography: p. 185-201. [BL604.H6M44] 77-85450 ISBN 0-520-01705-6 16.50
1. Moses—Art. 2. Horns (in religion, folk-lore, etc.) I. Title. II. Series.

REEVES, Marjorie. 246'.55
The Figurae of Joachim of Fiore, by Marjorie Reeves and Beatrice Hirsch-Reich. Oxford, Clarendon Press, 1972. [xxiii], 350 p. illus. 24 cm. (Oxford-Warburg studies) Bibliography: p. [xix]-[xxi] [BV150.J63R4] 73-162381 ISBN 0-19-920038-6 £10.00
1. Joachim, Abbot of Fiore, 1132 (ca.)-1202. Liber figurarum. 2. Symbolism. 3. Trinity—Early works to 1800. 4. History (Theology) I. Hirsch-Reich, Beatrice. II. Title. III. Series.

WOLFE, Betty. 246'.55
The banner book / written and illustrated by Betty Wolfe. New York : Morehouse-Barlow Co., [1974] 64 p. : ill. ; 23 cm. [BV168.F5W64] 74-80378 5.95
1. Church pennants. I. Title.

THE Anglo-Saxon cross. 246'.558
Hamden, Conn. : Archon Books, 1977. 282 p. : ill. ; 23 cm. Reprint of the 1904 ed. of W. O. Steven's The cross in the life and literature of the Anglo-Saxons, and of the 1914 ed. of A. S. Cook's Some accounts of the Bewcastle Cross between the years 1607 and 1861, published by H. Holt, New York, which were issued as v. 22 and 50, respectively, of the Yale studies in English; with new prefaces. [BV160.A53 1977] 76-23238 ISBN 0-208-01555-8 : 15.00
1. Crosses. 2. Anglo-Saxon literature—Hisotry and criticism. 3. Bewcastle cross. I. Stevens, William Oliver, 1878-1955. The cross in the life and literature of the Anglo-Saxons. 1977. II. Cook, Albert Stanburrough, 1853-1927. Some accounts of the Bewcastle Cross between the years 1607 and 1861. 1977. III. Series: Yale studies in English ; 22 [etc.].

BENSON, George Willard. 246'.558
The cross, its history & symbolism : an account of the symbol more universal in its use and more important in its significance than any other in the world / by George Willard Benson. New York : Hacker Art Books, 1976. 196 p., [17] leaves of plates : ill. ; 25 cm. Reprint of the 1934 ed. priv. print. in Buffalo, N.Y. [BV160.B4 1976] 73-88643 ISBN 0-87817-149-5 : 17.50
1. Crosses. 2. Christian art and symbolism. I. Title.

*CHAPPELL, Clovis G. 246.558
Faces about the cross [by] Clovis G. Chappell. Grand Rapids, Baker Book House, [1974, c1969] 217 p. 19 cm. [BT465] 2.95 (pbk.)
1. Holy cross. I. Title.

POCKNEE, Cyril Edward 246.6
The Christian altar in history and today. London, A. R. Mowbray; Westminster, Md., Canterbury Pr. [c.1963] 112p. illus. (pt. col.) 26cm. Bibl. 64-1983 4.95
1. Altars. I. Title.

REINHOLD, Hans Ansgar, 1897- 246.6
Liturgy and art [by] H. A. Reinhold. [1st ed.] New York, Harper & Row [1966] 105 p. plates. 22 cm. (Religious perspectives, v. 16) [BV150.R37] 66-20797
1. Christian art and symbolism. I. Title. II. Series.

STAFFORD, Thomas Albert, 1885- 246.6
Within the chancel. Illustrated by the author. New York, Abingdon Press [1955] 92p. illus. 24cm. [BV150.S76] 55-6766
1. Christian art and symbolism. I. Title.

WETZLER, Robert P. 1932- 246.6
Seasons & symbols; a handbook on the church year, by Robert P. Wetzler and Helen Huntington. Illus. by Helen Huntington. Minneapolis, Augsburg Pub. House [1962] 108 p. illus. 22 cm. Includes bibliography. [BV150.W42] 62-9094
1. Christian art and symbolism. I. Huntington, Helen, 1933- joint author. II. Title.

WETZLER, Robert P., 1932- 246.6
Seasons & symbols; a handbook on the church year, by Robert P. Wetzler, Helen Huntington. Illus. by Helen Huntington. Minneapolis, Augsburg [c.1962] 108p. illus. Bibl. 62-9094 1.95 pap.,
1. Christian art and symbolism. I. Huntington, Helen, 1933- joint author. II. Title.

BACKMAN, Eugene Louis, 1883- 246.7
Religious dance in the Christian church and in popular medicine. Tr. [from Swedish] by E. Classen. London, Allen & Unwin[dist. Mystic, Conn., Verry, 1964] xii, 364p. illus., ports., fold. map. 25cm. Bibl. 52-12781 7.50
1. Dancing (in religion, folk-lore, etc.) I. Title.

BACKMAN, Eugene Louis, 1883- 246'.7
Religious dances in the Christian church and in popular medicine / E. Louis Backman ; translated by E. Classen. Westport, Conn. : Greenwood Press, 1977. p. cm. Translation of Den religiosa dansen inom kristen kyrka och folkmedicin. Reprint of the 1952 ed. published by Allen & Unwin, London. Includes index. Bibliography: p. [BL605.B213 1977] 77-8069 ISBN 0-8371-9678-7 : 28.00
1. Dancing (in religion, folk-lore, etc.) I. Title.

FISK, Margaret (Palmer), 1908- 246.7
The art of the rhythmic choir; worship through symbolic movement. Illus. by Lois-Louise Hines. [1st ed.] New York, Harper [1950] xi, 205 p. illus. 22 cm. Bibliography: p. 195-205. [BL605.F5] 50-9694
1. Dancing (in religion, folklore, etc.) I. Title. II. Title: The rhythmic choir.

FISK, Margaret (Palmer) 1908-- 246.7
Look up and live. [1st ed.] Saint Paul, Macalester Park Pub. Co. [1953] 97p. illus. 29cm. [BL605.F52] 54-36207
1. Dancing (in religion, folk-lore, etc.) I. Title.

PRAYER meeting talks and outlines by David Thomas, Charles Simeon, Charles H. Spurgeon, F. B. Meyer. others. Grand Rapids, Baker Bk. [1968,c.1954] 96p. 21cm. (Minister's handbk. ser.) [BV285.P82] 54-3030 1.50 pap., 246.7
1. Prayer-meetings. I. Thomas, David, minister.

TAYLOR, Margaret Fisk. 246.7
The art of the rhythmic choir; worship through symbolic movement, by Margaret Palmer Fisk. Illus. by Lois-Louise Hines. [1st ed.] New York, Harper [1950] xi, 205 p. illus. 22 cm. Bibliography: p. 203-205. [GV1783.5.T28] 50-9694
1. Religious dance, Modern. I. Title. II. Title: The rhythmic choir.

TAYLOR, Margaret Fisk. 246.7
Look up and live, by Margaret Palmer Fisk. [1st ed.] Saint Paul, Macalester Park Pub. Co. [1953] 97, [2] p. illus. 29 cm. Includes hymns, with music. Bibliography: p. [99] [GV1783.T38] 54-36207
1. Religious dance, Modern. I. Title.

TAYLOR, Margaret Fisk. 246'.7
A time to dance; symbolic movement in worship. Philadelphia, United Church Press [1967] 180 p. illus., facsims. 21 cm. Bibliography: p. 177-180. [GV1783.5.T3] 67-21103
1. Religious dance, Modern. I. Title.

TAYLOR, Margaret Fisk. 246'.7
A time to dance; symbolic movement in worship. Philadelphia, United Church Press [1967] 180 p. illus., facsims. 21 cm. Bibliography: p. 177-180. [GV1783.5.T3] 67-21103
1. Religious dance, Modern. I. Title.

DE CHARMS, George, 1889- 246'.9
The tabernacle of Israel. [1st ed.] New York, Pageant Press International Corp. [1969] 293 p. illus. (part col.) 21 cm. [BM654.D37] 77-76583 7.95
1. Tabernacle. I. Title.

HUFF, Russell J. 1936- 246.9
Come build my church; the story of Our Lady of Guadalupe, by Russell J. Huff. Illus. by Carolvn Lee Jagodits. Notre Dame, Ind., Dujarie [1966] 93p. illus. 24cm. [BT660.G8H8] 66-22271 2.25
1. Guadalupe, Nuestra Senora de. 2. Gustavo A. Madero, Mexico. Basilica de Santa Maria de Guadalupe. I. Title.

JALABERT, Henri, 1913- 246.9
Lebanon: the land and the lady [by] Joseph Goudard, Henri Jalabert. Tr. by Eugene P. Burns. Beirut, Catholic Press; Chicago, Loyola Univ. Pr. [1966] 364p. illus., map., 3 col. plates. 32cm. Tr. of the author's La Sainte Vierge au Liban; a new study, based on the work by J. Goudard, first pub. in 1908 under the same title. Map inserted at beginning of text. bBibl. [BT652.L4J3] 66-6108 14.00
1. Mary, Virgin—Shrines—Lebanon. I. Goudard, Joseph, 1873-1951. La Sainte Vierge au Liban. II. Title.

LOOKING to the future : 246'.9
papers read at an international symposium on prospects for worship, religious architecture and socio-religious studies, 1976 / editor J. G. Davies. [Birmingham] : University of Birmingham, Institute for the Study of Worship and Religious Architecture, [1976] [6] , 171 p. : map ; 30 cm. Includes bibliographical references. [NA4605.L66] 77-369107 ISBN 0-7044-0234-3 : £1.35
1. Liturgy and architecture—Addresses, essays, lectures. 2. Christian art and symbolism—Addresses, essays, lectures. 3. Worship—Addresses, essays, lectures. I. Davies, John Gordon, 1919- II. Birmingham, Eng. University. Institute for the Study of Worship and Religious Architecture.

NARBUTAS, Titas. 246'.9
Marian shrines of the Americas. [1st ed.] New York, Vantage Press [1968] 144 p. illus. 21 cm. Bibliography: p. 143-144. [BT652.A5N3] 68-5955 3.50
1. Mary, Virgin—Shrines—America. I. Title.

NEAME, Alan. 246'.9
The happening at Lourdes; the sociology of the grotto. New York, Simon and Schuster [1968, c1967] 323 p. illus., ports. 24 cm. [BT653.N4] 67-25384
1. Lourdes, Notre-Dame de. I. Title.

LAFFINEUR, M., 1897- 246'.9'0946351
Star on the mountain, by M. Laffineur [and] M. T. le Pelletier. Translated by Service de traduction Champlain, ENR [and] Shelia Laffan Lacouture. Newtonville, N.Y., Our Lady of Mount Carmel of Garabandal, inc. [1967, c1968] xi, 284 p. illus. 21 cm. Translation of L'Etoile dans la montagne. [BT660.S343L313] 68-28493
1. San Sebastian de Garabandal. I. Le Pelletier, M. T., 1901- joint author. II. Title.

MURPHY, Walter Thomas, 1915- 246'.9'0973
Famous American churches and shrines. Walter T. Murphy, editor. Catholic ed. Bloomfield Hills, Mich., Walmur Pub. Co. [1968] 119 p. illus. 18 cm. [BX4600.M85] 68-28363 4.95
1. Shrines—United States. 2. Churches—United States. I. Title.

WEDDA, John. 246.90974
New England worships; 100 drawings of churches and temples with accompanying text. New York, Random House [1965] 1 v. (unpaged) illus. 28 cm. [BR530.W4] 65-21218
1. Churches — New England. I. Title.

WEDDA, John 246.90974
New England worships; 100 drawings of

churches and temples with accompanying text. New York, Random [c.1965] iv. (unpaged) illus. 28cm. [BR530.W4] 65-21218 7.95
1. Churches—New England. I. Title.

247 Church Furnishings & Related

DELDERFIELD, Eric R. 247
A guide to church furniture, by Eric R. Delderfield. New York, Taplinger [1967, c1966] 157p. illus. 21cm. Bibl. [NA5050.D4 1967] 67-14049 5.00 bds.,
1. Church furniture. I. Title.

DELDERFIELD, Eric R. 247
A guide to church furniture, by Eric R. Delderfield. New York, Taplinger Pub. Co. [1967, 1966] 157 p. illus. 21 cm. Bibliography: p. [149]-150. [NA5050.D4 1967] 67-14049
1. Church furniture. I. Title.

HOEFLER, Richard Carl. 247
Designed for worship; a study of the furniture, vessels, linens, paraments, and vestments of worship. Illus. by author. [Columbia, S.C., State Print. Co., c1963] viii, 77 p. illus., plans 28 cm. [NA5050.H6] 64-4499
1. Church furniture. 2. Church vestments. I. Title.

KUTZ, LeRoy. 247
The chancel: why, what, how? By LeRoy and Marie Kutz. Illus. by George Malick. Philadelphia, Christian Education Press [1960] 54p. illus. 22cm. Includes bibliography. [BV195.K8] 60-3851
1. Altar gilds. I. Kutz, Marie, joint author. II. Title.

KUTZ, LeRoy. 247
The chancel: why, what, how? By LeRoy and Marie Kutz. Illus. by George Malick. Philadelphia, Christian Education Press [c.1960] 54p. (Bibl.) illus. 60-3851 1.00 pap.,
1. Altar guilds. I. Kutz, Marie, joint author. II. Title.

LANG, Paul H D 247
What an altar guild should know [by] Paul H. D. Lang. Saint Louis, Concordia Pub. House [1964] 130 p. illus. 29 cm. Bibliography: p. 126-128. [BV195.L3] 64-56866
1. Altar guilds. I. Title.

LESAGE, Robert 247
Vestments and church furniture. Translated from the French by Fergus Murphy. New York, Hawthorn Books [c.1960] 152p. 21cm. (The Twentieth century encyclopedia of Catholicism. 114. Section 10: The worship of the church) (bibl.) 60-8783 2.95 half cloth,
1. Catholic Church. Liturgy and ritual. 2. Christian art and symbolism. 3. Church vestments. I. Title.

LESAGE, Robert, 1891- 247
Vestments and church furniture. Translated from the French by Fergus Murphy. New York, Hawthorn Books [1960] 152p. 21cm. (The Twentieth century encyclopedia of Catholicism, 114. Section 10: The worship of the church) Includes bibliography. [BX1970.L4183] 60-8783
1. Catholic Church. Liturgy and ritual. 2. Christianart and symbolism. 3. Church vestments. I. Title.

PERRY, Edith (Weir) 1875- 247
An altar guild manual. 3d ed. New York, Morehouse-Barlow Co. [1969, c1934] 72 p. illus. 18 cm. [BX5975.P45 1969] 78-16609
1. Altar gilds. I. Title.

SCOTFORD, John Ryland, 1888- 247
How to decorate your church. [Westwood, N. J.] Revell [1962] 61p. (Revell's better church ser.) 62-8413 1.00 pap.,
1. Church decoration and ornament. 2. Church furniture. I. Title.

WILSON, Winefride. 247
Modern Christian art. [1st ed.] New York, Hawthorn Books [1965] 175 p. illus. 22 cm. (The Twentieth century encyclopedia of Catholicism, v. 123. Section 12: Catholicism and the arts) Bibliography: p. [174]-175. [N7831.W5 1965] 65-13399
1. Christian art and symbolism. 2. Art and religion. 3. Art — Hist. — 19th cent. 4. Art — Hist. — 20th cent. I. Title. II. Series: The Twentieth century encyclopedia of Catholicism, v. 123

WILSON, Winefride 247
Modern Christian art. New York, Hawthorn [c.1965] 175p. illus. 22cm. atholicism, v.123. Section 12: Catholicism and the arts) bBibl. (Twentieth cent. ency. of Title (Series: The Twentieth century encyclopedia of Catholicism, v.123) [N7831.W5] 65-13399 3.50
1. Christian art and symbolism. 2. Art and religion. 3. Art—Hist.—19th cent. 4. Art—Hist.—20th cent. I. Title. II. Series.

BARRERE, Albert Marie Victor. 247.09
A dictionary of slang, jargon & cant, embracing English, American, and Anglo-Indian slang, pidgin English, tinker's jargon, and other irregular phraseology. Comp., ed. by Albert Barrere, Charles G. Leland. New introd. by Eric Partridge. Detroit, Galo 1967. 2v. 23cm. T.ps. include orig. imprint: [London] Ballantyne Press. 1889-90. [PE3721.B32] 66-27828 36.00 set,
1. English language—Slang—Dictionaries. I. Leland, Charles Godfrey, 1824-1903, joint author. II. Title.

BOCKELMAN, Eleanor. 247.7
A practical guide for altar guilds. Illustrated by Thelma Bush. Minneapolis, Augsburg Pub. Hose [1962] 63p. illus. 20cm. [BV195.B6] 62-16939
1. Altar silds. I. Title.

DIGGS, Dorothy C 247.7
A working manual for altar guilds. New York, Morehouse-Gorham [1957] 127p. illus. 19cm. [BX5975.D5] 57-6108
1. Altar gilds. I. Title.

DIGGS, Dorothy C. 247'.7
A working manual for altar guilds, by Dorothy C. Diggs. [2d] rev. ed. New York, Morehouse-Barlow Co. [1968] 128 p. illus. 19 cm. [BX5975.D5 1968] 73-3511
1. Altar gilds. I. Title.

HALL, Kathryn Evangeline, 1924- 247.7
The papal tiara. [Palm Beach? Fla.] '1952. 74 l. 34 plates. 28 cm. Bibliography: leaves [66]-74. [CR4480.H25] 52-40960
1. Tiara, Papal. I. Title.

IRELAND, Marion P. 247.7
Textile art in the Church; vestments, paraments, and hangings in contemporary worship, art, and architecture [by] Marion P. Ireland. Nashville, Abingdon Press [1971] 283 p. illus., col. plates. 36 cm. Bibliography: p. 271-275. [NK8810.I7] 70-139750 ISBN 0-687-41363-X 27.50
1. Christian art and symbolism. 2. Textile fabrics. 3. Art, Modern—20th century. I. Title.

NORRIS, Herbert. 247.7
Church vestments, their origin & development. Illustrated with 8 pages of photos. and with 8 colour plates, and black & white drawings by the author. New York, Dutton [1950] xv, 190 p. illus. (part col.) 26 cm. Bibliography: p. xiii-xiv. [BV167.N67] 50-6481
1. Church vestments. I. Title.

PIEPKORN, Arthur Carl, 1907- 247.7
The survival of the historic vestments in the Lutheran Church after 1555. Saint Louis, School for Graduate Studies, Concordia Seminary, 1956. 122p. 22cm. (Concordia Seminary. School for Graduate Studies. Graduate study no. 1) Errata slip inserted. Includes bibliographical references. [BV167.P5] 56-10006
1. Church vestments. 2. Lutheran Church. Liturgy and ritual. I. Title. II. Series: Concordia Theological Seminary, St. Louis. School for Graduate Studies. Graduate study no. 1

PIEPKORN, Arthur Carl, 1907- 247.7
The survival of the historic vestments in the Lutheran Church after 1555. 2d ed. Saint Louis, School for Graduate Studies, Concordia Seminary, 1958. 149p. 22cm. (Concordia Seminary. School for Graduate Studies. Graduate study no. 1) Errata slip inserted. Includes bibliographical references. [BV167.P5 1958] 58-13829
1. Church vestments. 2. Lutheran Church. Liturgy and ritual. I. Title. II. Series: Concordia Theological Seminary, St. Louis. School for Graduate Studies. Graduate study no. 1

PIEPKORN, Arthur Carl, 1907- 247.7
The survival of the historic vestments in the Lutheran Church lifter 1555. Saint Louis, School for Graduate Studies, Concordia Seminary, 1956. 122p. 22cm. (Concordia Seminary. School for Graduate Studies. Graduate study no. 1) Errata slip inserted. Includes bibliographical references. [BV167.P5] 56-10006
1. Church vestments. 2. Lutheran Church. Liturgy and ritual. I. Title. II. Series: Concordia Theological Seminary, St. Louis. School for Graduate Studies. Graduate study no. 1

POCKNEE, Cyril Edward 247.7
Liturgical vesture, its origins and development. Westminster, Md., Canterbury Pr. [c.1961] 57p. illus. 26cm. Bibl. 61-16277 3.95
1. Church vestments. I. Title.

POCKNEE, Cyril Edward. 247.7
Liturgical vesture, its origins and development. Westminster, Md., Canterbury Press [1961] 57p. illus. 26cm. Includes bibliography. [BV167.P6 1961] 61-16277
1. Church vestments. I. Title.

RUOSS, George Martin. 247.7
An altar guild workbook, prepared for Lutheran churches [by] G. Martin Ruoss. [3d ed.] York, Pa., Kyle Print. Co. [1953] 137p. illus. 28cm. Includes bibliography. [BV195.R8 1953] 54-39716
1. Altar gilds. I. Title.

WALSH, Louise M 247.7
Manual for altar societies. Milwaukee, Bruce Pub. Co. [1960] 97 p. illus. 17 cm. [BV195.W3] 60-12651
1. Altar gilds. I. Title.

WEINSTEIN, Jack B. 247'.73'203
Reform of Federal court rule-making procedures / Jack B. Weinstein. [Great Neck? N.Y.] : Weinstein, c1976. 309 leaves in various foliations ; 28 cm. Includes bibliographical references. [KF8840.W4] 76-371702
1. Court rules—United States. 2. Court administration—United States. I. Title.

JOHNSON, John Sevier, 1899- 247.9
The rosary in action. With a foreword by Robert W. Barron. St. Louis, Herder [1954] 271p. 21cm. [BX2163.J57] 54-8388
1. Rosary. I. Title.

MILLER, Madeleine (Sweeney) 1890- 247.9
A treasury of the cross. Photos. by J. Lane Miller, drawings by Claire Valentine. New York, Harper [1956] 240p. illus. 22cm. [BV160.M5] 56-7027
1. Cross and crosses. I. Title.

MILLER, Madeleine (Sweeny) 1890- 247.9
A treasury of the cross. Photos. by J. Lane Miller, drawings by Claire Valentine. New York, Harper [1956] 240 p. illus. 22 cm. [BV160.M5] 56-7027
1. Crosses. I. Title.

SHAW, James Gerard. 247.9
The story of the rosary. Milwaukee, Bruce [1954] 175p. 21cm. [BX2310.R7S47] 54-9337
1. Rosary. I. Title.

GUENON, Rene 247.92
Symbolism of the cross. Tr. by Angus Macnab. London, Luzac [Mystic, Conn., Verry, 1965] xiv, 134p. 22cm. Bibl. [BL604.C7G83] 65-8464 5.00
1. Crosses. 2. Symbolism. I. Title.

LALIBERTE, Norman. 247.92
The history of the cross [by] Norman Laliberte and Edward N. West. New York, Macmillan, 1960. 72 p. illus. 31 cm. Includes bibliography. [BV160.L3] 59-8171
1. Cross and crosses. I. West, Edward N., joint author.

**STATIONS of the Cross for children.* 247.92
Written, illus. by the Daughters of St. Paul. Boston, St. Paul Eds. [dist. Daughters of St. Paul, c.1965] 30p. illus. (pt. col.) 18cm. .15 pap.,

TROYER, Johannes. 247.92
The cross as symbol & ornament; collected, drawn, and described by Johannes Troyer. Philadelphia, Westminster Press [1961] 126 p. illus. (part col.) 27 cm. [BV160.T65] 61-8766
1. Crosses. 2. Christian art and symbolism. I. Title.

TROYER, Johannes 247.92
The cross as symbol & ornament; collected, drawn, described by Johannes Troyer. Philadelphia, Westminster [c.1961] 126p. illus. (part col.) 27cm. 61-8766 4.50
1. Crosses. 2. Christian art and symbolism. I. Title.

248 Personal Religion

ADAMS, Theodore Floyd, 1898- 248
Making the most of what life brings. [1st ed.] New York, Harper [1957] 145p. 22cm. [BV4501.A36] 57-10531
1. Christian life. I. Title.

ADAMS, Theodore Floyd, 1898- 248
Making the most of what life brings. [1st ed.] New York, Harper [1957] 145p. 22cm. [BV4501.A36] 57-10531
1. Christian life. I. Title.

ALEXANDER, Archibald, 1874- 248
Feathers on the moor. Freeport, N.Y., Books for Libraries Press [1967] 220 p. 19 cm. (Essay index reprint series) Reprint of the 1928 ed. [BR85.A36 1967] 67-22050
1. Christianity—Addresses, essays, lectures. 2. Christian life. I. Title.

ALLEN, Charles Livingstone, 1913- 248
The Charles L. Allen treasury. Edited by Charles L. Wallis. Old Tappan, N.J., Revell [1970] 191 p. 22 cm. [BV4501.2.A395] 72-123068 4.95
1. Christian life—Methodist authors. I. Title.

ALLEN, Charles Livingstone, 1913- 248
God's psychiatry: the Twenty-third psalm, the Ten commandments, the Lord's prayer, the Beatitudes. [Westwood, N.J.] F. H. Revell Co. [1953] 159 p. 22 cm. [BV4501.A5164] 53-12523
1. Christian life. I. Title.

ALLEN, Charles Livingstone, 1913- 248
In quest of God's power. [1st ed.] Westwood, N. J., F. H. Revell Co. [1952] 191 p. 22 cm. [BV4501.A5166] 52-13269
1. Christian life. I. Title.

ALLEN, Charles Livingstone, 1913- 248
Roads to radiant living. New York, Revell [1951] 157 p. 22 cm. Articles which originally appeared in the author's column in the Atlanta journal-constitution. [BV4501.A5168] 51-10238
1. Christian life. I. The Atlanta journal-constitution. II. Title.

AMABEL DU COEUR DE JESUS, Mother. 248
To love and to suffer; the gifts of the Holy Ghost in St. Therese of the Child Jesus. Translated by a Discalced Carmelite. Westminster, Md., Newman Press, 1953. 158p. 20cm. [BX4700.T5A74] 53-6251
1. Therese, Saint, 1873-1897. 2. Gifts, Spiritual. I. Title.

AMICK, Lon Gilbert, 1920- 248
The divine journey; a guide to spiritual understanding, by Lon Amick. Illustrated by Arthur Kraft. Philadelphia, Dorrance [1968] 78 p. illus. 21 cm. [BV4501.2.A45] 68-14765
1. Spiritual life. I. Title.

*ANDERSON, J. Keith 248
The three telltale allegories by J. Keith Anderson 1st. ed. New York, Vantage, 1974 168 p. 22 cm. [BV4515] ISBN 0-533-01326-7 5.95
1. Christian life. I. Title.

ANDERSON, Thomas, 1899- 248
Estate of glory. Atlanta, Tupper and Love, 1951. 104 p. 26 cm. [BV4501.A657] 51-14458
1. Christian life. I. Title.

ANDREW, Father, 1869-1946. 248
Love's fulfilment; an anthology from the writings of Father Andrew. Edited by Kathleen E. Burne. With an introd. by Bishop Lumsden Barkway. London, A. R. Mowbray; New York, Morehouse-Gorham Co. [1957] 192p. 21cm. [BV4501.A66] 57-14180
1. Spiritual life. I. Title.

ANDREW, Father, 1869-1946. 248
Love's fulfilment; an anthology from the writings of Father Andrew. Edited by Kathleen E. Burne. With an introd. by Bishop Lumsden Barkway. London, A. R. Mowbray; New York, Morehouse-Gorham Co. [1957] 192p. 21cm. [BV4501.A66] 57-14180
1. Spiritual life. I. Title.

ANDREWES, Lancelot, Bp. of Winchester, 1555-1626. 248
The private devotions of Lancelot Andrewes. Translated from the Greek and arr. anew by John Henry Newman. New York, Abingdon-Cokesbury Press [1950] xii, 146 p. 16 cm. A photographic reproduction from the limited ed. of 1807 which was entitled: The devotions of Bishop Andrewes. [BV264.G8A5 1950] 49-50200
1. Devotional exercises. I. Newman, John Henry, Cardinal, 1801-1890, tr. II. Title.

ANGELL, James W. 248
Put your arms around the city [by] James W. Angell. Old Tappan, N.J., Revell [1970] 188 p. 21 cm. [BR115.C45A5] 79-123067 4.95
1. Cities and towns—Religious life. I. Title.

ANGRISANI, Giuseppe, Bp., 1894- 248
It is you I beckon; a book of spiritual inspiration for seminarians, based on the exhotation Menti nostrae of Pope Pius XII. Translated by Joseph A. McMullin. New York, Benziger Bros. [1957] 337p. 20cm. [BX903.A5] 57-31394
1. Seminarians—Religious life. I. Title.

APPLEBY, Rosalee Mills 248
Flaming fagots. Nashville, Tenn., Broadman

Press [1960c.1943] 252p. (Broadman starbooks) Essays 1.50 pap.,
1. Christian life. I. Title.

ARBAUGH, George Bartholomew, 1905- 248
Growth of a Christian. Philadelphia, Muhlenberg Press [1953] 143p. illus. 20 cm. [B v4501.A736] 53-10156
1. Christian liffe. 2. Character. I. Title.

ARNOLD, Eberhard, 1883- 248 s
The experience of God and his peace : a guide into the heart and soul of the Bible / by Eberhard Arnold. Rifton, N.Y. : Plough Pub. House, 1975. x p., p. 189-315 ; 20 cm. (His Inner land ; v. 3) Translation of chapters 6-7 of Innenland. [BV4495.A7413 vol. 3] [BV4503] 248 75-9720 ISBN 0-87486-155-1 : 4.50
1. Spiritual life. 2. God. I. Title.

ARNOLD, Eberhard, 1883-1935. 248
Inner land : a guide into the heart and soul of the Bible / by Eberhard Arnold. Rifton, N.Y. : Plough Pub. House, 1975. p. cm. Includes index. [BV4495.A7413 1975] 74-30356 ISBN 0-87486-152-7 : 15.00
1. Christian life. I. Title.

ARNOLD, Eberhard, 1883-1935. 248
Inner land: a guide into the heart and soul of the Bible. Rifton, N.Y., Plough Pub. House, 1974- p. cm. Translation of Innenland: ein Wegweiser in die Seele der Bibel. Contents.Contents.—v. 1. The inner life. [BV4495.A7413] 74-18433 ISBN 0-87486-178-0 (v. 1)
1. Spiritual life—Collected works. I. Title.

ARNOLD, Eberhard, 1883-1935. 248 s
Light and fire and The Holy Spirit / by Eberhard Arnold. Rifton, N.Y. : Plough Pub. House, 1975. p. cm. (His Inner land ; v.4) "Translated from the 1936 edition of Innenland." [BV4495.A7413 vol. 4] [BT121.2] 248'.2 75-16303 ISBN 0-87486-156-X : 4.50
1. Holy Spirit. 2. Light and darkness (in religion, folk-lore, etc.) 3. Fire (in religion, folk-lore, etc.) I. Title.

ARNOLD, Eberhard, 1883-1935. 248 s
The Living Word / by Eberhard Arnold. Rifton, N.Y. : Plough Pub. House, c1975. xv p., p. 441-576 ; 19 cm. (His Inner land ; v. 5) "Translated from the 1936 ed. of Innenland. Includes index. [BV4495.A7413 vol. 5] [BV4503] 248'.42 75-33241 ISBN 0-87486-157-8
1. Spiritual life. I. Title.

ARNOLD, Eberhard, 1883-1935. 248 s
The struggle of the conscience / by Eberhard Arnold. Rifton, N.Y. : Plough Pub. House, 1975. (His Inner land ; v. 2) Translation of chapters 4-5 of Innenland. [BV4495.A7413 vol. 2] [BV4503] 248 75-1335 ISBN 0-87486-154-3 : 4.25
1. Spiritual life. I. Title.

AUGSBURGER, Myron S. 248
Plus living; meditations on discipleship and grace. Grand Rapids, Mich., Zondervan [c.1963] 59p. 21cm. 1.00 pap.,
I. Title.

AUMANN, Jordan. 248
Christian spirituality East & West [by] Jordan Aumann, Thomas Hopko [and] Donald G. Bloesch. Chicago, Priory Press [1968] 203 p. 23 cm. (Institute of Spirituality. Special lectures, v. 3, 1967) Includes bibliographical references. [BV4509.5.A9] 68-29598 5.95
1. Spirituality. I. Hopko, Thomas. II. Bloesch, Donald G., 1928- III. Title. IV. Series.

AUSTIN, Lou, 1891- 248
You are greater than you know. Winchester, Va., Partnership Foundation [1955] 206p. 22cm. [BJ1611.2.A8] 55-43371
1. Success. 2. Christian life. I. Title.

BABSON, Roger Ward, 1875- 248
Before making important decisions, and why I love gardens . Rev. ed. Philadelphia, Lippincott, 1957. 85p. illus. 20cm. [BV4501.B22 1957] 57-59217
1. Christian life. I. Title.

BACH, T. J. 248
Called to action. Grand Rapids, Mich. Baker Bk. [1963, c.1949] 124p. 19cm. Orig. pub. under title: God's challenge for today. 1.00 pap.,
I. Title.

BAILEY, Faith Coxe. 248
You have a talent, don't bury it! Chicago, Moody Press [1956] 128p. 19cm. [BV4740.B25] 57-2701
1. Vocation. 2. Vocational guidance. I. Title.

BAILLIE, John, 1886-1960. 248
Christian devotion; addresses. London, Oxford University Press, 1962. 88 p. 20 cm. [BV4501.2.B3] 63-2947
1. Sermons, English. 2. Christian life—Presbyterian authors. I. Title.

BAKER, Augustine, Father, 1575-1641. 248
Holy wisdom; or, Directions for the prayer of contemplation extracted out of more than forty treatises by the Ven. Father F. Augustine Baker. Methodically digested by R. F. Serenus Cressy and now edited from the Douay ed. of 1557 by the Right Rev. Abbot Sweeney. New York, Harper [1950?] xxvi, 667 p. 19 cm. First ed. published in 1657 under title: Sancta sophia. Or, Directions for the prayer of contemplation. [BV5030.B3 1950] 49-9933
1. Asceticism—Catholic Church. I. Cressy, Serenus, Father, 1605-1674. II. Title.

BAKER, Gladys. 248
I had to know. New York, Appleton-Century-Crofts [1951] viii. 309 p. 21 cm. [BX4668.B25] 51-11270
1. Converts. Catholic. I. Title.

BARBER, Walter Lanier. 248
Show me the way to go home, by Red Barber. Philadelphia, Westminster Press [1971] 192 p. 22 cm. [BX5995.B373A3] 72-150993 ISBN 0-664-20901-7 4.95
I. Title.

BARETT, Ethel. 248
Don't look now. Glendale, Calif., G/L Regal Books [1968] 207 p. illus. 18 cm. [BV4501.2.B384] 68-25807
1. Christian life. 2. Interpersonal relations. I. Title.

BARNARD, Floy Merwyn. 248
Christian witnessing. Nashville, Convention Press [1959] 111p. 19cm. [BV4520.B35] 59-9683
1. Witness bearing (Christianity) I. Title.

BARNETTE, Henlee H. 248
Has God called you? [By] Henlee Barnette. Nashville, Broadman Press [1969] 128 p. 21 cm. (A Broadman inner circle book) Includes bibliographies. [BV4740.B32] 69-17896
1. Vocation. I. Title.

BARRETT, Ethel. 248
Don't look now. Glendale, Calif., G/L Regal Books [1968] 207 p. illus. 18 cm. [BV4501.2.B384] 68-25807
1. Christian life. 2. Interpersonal relations. I. Title.

BARTSCH, Peter H. 248
My honest conviction. New York, Carlton [c.1963] 64p. 21cm. (Reflection Bk.) 2.00
I. Title.

BASSET, Bernard. 248
The noonday devil; spiritual support in middle age. Garden City, N.Y., Doubleday, 1968,c.1964] 160p. 18cm. (Image bk., D237) Bibl. [BX2350.2.B34 1964] .95 pap.,
1. Christian life—Catholic authors. 2. Middle age. I. Title.

BATLEY, Ernest Lawson. 248
The preacher of the law and testimony: the second book of the principalians. [1st ed.] New York, Exposition Press [1954, c1953] 174p. 21cm. [BR126.B33] 53-11253
I. Title. II. Title: Principalians.

BAUGHMAN, John Lee. 248
Polarity in our desires / John Lee Baughman. New York : Church of the Truth, c1976. 22 p. ; 16 cm. Cover title. [BV4501.2.B3845] 76-364791 1.00
1. Christian life—1960- 2. Polarity (Philosophy) 3. Desire. I. Title.

BAUR, Benedikt, 1877- 248
In silence with God. Translated from the 4th German ed. by Elisabethe Corathiel- Noonan. Chicago, H. Regnery Co., 1955. 157p. 22cm. [BX2350] 57-2506
1. Spiritual life—Catholic authors. I. Title.

BAYLY, Joseph. 248
The gospel blimp. New York, Pyramid [1968, c.1960] 64p. 18cm. (R1746) [BV3795.B36] 269 .50 pap.,
1. Evangelical work. I. Title.

BAYLY, Joseph T. 248
I saw Gooley fly; and other stories [by] Joseph Bayly. Old Tappan, N.J., Revell [1968] 127 p. 20 cm. Edition for 1973 published under title: How silently, how silently, and other stories. [BV4515.2.B37] 68-28433 2.95
1. Christian life—Stories. I. Title.

BAYNE, Stephen Fielding, Bp., 1908- 248
Christian living. With the assistance of the Authors'Committee of the Dept. of Christian Education of the Protestant Episcopal Church. Greenwich, Conn., Seabury Press, 1957. 341p. 22cm. (The Church's teaching, v. 5) Includes bibliography. [BV4511.B3] 57-5739
1. Christian life—Study and teaching. I. Title.

BAYNE, Stephen Fielding, Bp., 1908- 248
Christian living. With the assitance of the Authors' Committee of the Dept. of Christian Education of the Protestant Episcopal Church. Greenwich, Conn., Seabury Press, 1957. 341 p. 22 cm. (The Church's teaching, v. 5) Includes bibliography. [BV4511.B3] 57-5739
1. Christian life—Study and teaching. I. Title.

BECKELHYMER, Hunter. 248
Meeting life on higher levels. Nashville, Abingdon Press [1956] 96p. 20cm. [BV4501.B416] 56-10142
1. Christian life. I. Title.

BEHANNA, Gertrude Florence (Ingram) 248
The late Liz; the autobiography of an ex-pagan, by Elizabeth Burns. New York, Appleton-Century-Crofts [1957] 342 p. 22 cm. [BV4935.B4A3] 57-7207
1. Converts. I. Title.

BELDEN, Albert David, 1883- 248
The practice of prayer. New York, Harper [1954?] 96p. 20cm. [BV210] 54-3658
1. Prayer. I. Title.

BELORGEY, Godefroid. 248
The practice of mental prayer. With foreword by M. Eugene Boylan. Translated from the French. Westminster, Md., Newman Press, 1952. 184 p. 19 cm. [BV4813.B413] 52-8543
1. Meditation. I. Title.

BENNETT, John Godolphin, 1897- 248
A spiritual psychology [London] Hodder & Stoughton [dist. Mystic Conn., Verry [1965, c.1964] 256p. 22cm. Bibl. [BP605.B376] 65-3270 6.00
1. Psychology, Religious. I. Title.

BERNER, Carl W. 248
The power of pure stewardship [by] Carl W. Berner, Sr. St. Louis, Concordia Pub. House [1970] 125 p. illus. 21 cm. [BV772.B38] 77-126536
1. Stewardship, Christian. I. Title.

BERTHOLD, Fred, 1922- 248
The fear of God; the role of anxiety in contemporary thought. New York, Harper [1959] 158p. 20cm. Includes bibliography. [BR110.B45] 59-10329
1. Fear of God. 2. Anxiety. 3. Psychology, Religious. I. Title.

*BERWITT, Elaine 248
Turn on to life the best is yet to be Hicksville, N.Y. Exposition Press, 1974 56 p. 21 cm. [BV4515.2] ISBN 0-682-48039-8 3.50
1. Christian life. I. Title.

BIETZ, Arthur Leo. 248
The "know-how" of Christian living. Mountain View, Calif., Pacific Press Pub. Association [1951] 177 p. 21 cm. [BV4501.B54] 51-14676
1. Christian life. I. Title.

BIETZ, Arthur Leo. 248
Pulling life together; a source book for physicians, ministers, teachers, and laymen. Mountain View, Calif., Pacific Press Pub. Association [1952] 238p. illus. 20cm. [BV4501.B5417] 52-14716
1. Christian life. I. Title.

BIETZ, Arthur Leo. 248
Truths for eternity. Nashville, Southern Pub. Association [1952] 140 p. illus. 21 cm. [BV4501.B542] 52-28107
1. Christian life. I. Title.

BLACKMAR, Mary K. 248
Conversations on the edge of eternity [by] Mary K. Blackmar, set down by Bruce Gould. Foreword by George Gallup. New York, Morrow [c.]1965. ix, 150p. port. 20cm. [BV4501.2.B55] 65-11490 3.50 bds.,
1. Christian life—Friend authors. I. Gould, Bruce. II. Title.

BLOCKER, Simon, 1881- 248
The secret of radiant Christian living. Grand Rapids, W. B. Eerdmans Pub. Co. [1957] 111p. 23cm. [BV4501.B629] 57-13035
1. Christian life. I. Title.

BLOESCH, Donald G., 1928- 248
The crisis of piety; essays towards a theology of the Christian life, by Donald G. Bloesch. Grand Rapids, W. B. Eerdmans Pub. Co. [1968] 168 p. 23 cm. Bibliographical footnotes. [BV4501.2.B56] 68-16255
1. Christian life. 2. Spiritual life. I. Title.

BLOIS, Louis de, 1506-1566. 248
A book of spiritual instruction (Institutio spiritualis) Translated from the Latin by Bertrand A. Wilberforce; edited by a Benedictine of Stanbrook Abbey. [Rev. ed.] Westminster, Md., Newman Press [1955] xxvi, 143p. 20cm. (The Orchard books) [BV5080.B484 1955] 55-8651
1. Mysticism—Catholic Church. I. Title. II. Title: Spiritual Instruction. III. Series.

BLYTH, Robert Bayne. 248
Letters to my congregation; being some commonplace comments on Christian convictions. [1st ed.] New York, Vantage Press [1956] 156p. 21cm. [BV4501.B64] 56-5818
1. Christian life. I. Title.

BOLT, David Langstone, 1927- 248
Of heaven and hope [by] David Bolt. New York, John Day Co. [1965] 128 p. 22 cm. Bibliographical references included in "Notes" (p. [127]-128) [BT60.B6] 65-13749
1. Christianity — Essence, genius, nature. I. Title.

BOLT, David Langstone, 1927- 248
Of heaven and hope. New York, John Day [c.1965] 128p. 22cm. Bibl. [BT60.B6] 65-13749 3.75
1. Christianity—Essence, genius, nature. I. Title.

BONAVENTURA, Saint, Cardinal, 1221-1274. 248
The enkindling of love, also called The triple way. Adapted from the original, edited and arr. by William I. Joffe. Paterson, N. J., Saint Anthony Guild Press, 1956. xiv, 71p. 19cm. [BX2350.B6382] 56-14359
1. Spiritual life—Catholic authors. I. Title. II. Title: The triple way.

BONHOEFFER, Dietrich, 1906-1945. 248
Life together. Translated, and with an introd., by John W. Doberstein. [1st ed.] New York, Harper [1954] 122 p. 20 cm. [BF4503.B622] 54-5848
1. Christian life. I. Title.

BOONE, Charles Eugene. 248
A new song [by] Pat Boone. [1st ed.] Carol Stream, Ill., Creation House [1970] 192 p. ports. 23 cm. [ML420.B7A3] 75-131441 4.95
I. Title.

BOYD, Gwen, 1905- 248
Ask the Master; reflections on the Christian faith in everyday living. [1st ed.] New York, Greenwich Book Publishers [1956] 142p. 21cm. [BR125.B698] 56-9968
I. Title.

BRABY, Lois. 248
Hear ye Him! Illustrated by Jill Lind. Independence, Mo., Herald House, 1963. 70 p. illus. 21 cm. [BV4515.2.B7] 63-14393
1. Christian life — Stories. I. Title.

BRABY, Lois 248
Hear ye Him! Illus. by Jill Lind. Independence, Mo., Herald House [c.]1963 70p. col. illus. 21cm. 63-14393 1.50 bds.,
1. Christian life—Stories. I. Title.

BRANDT, Henry R. 248
The struggle for peace. Wheaton, Ill., Scripture [c.1965] 79p. illus. 21cm. Bibl. [BV4908.B7] 65-11930 1.00 pap.,
1. Peace of mind. I. Title.

BRATTGARD, Helge, 1920- 248
God's stewards; a theological study of the principles and practices of stewardship. Translated by Gene J. Lund. Minneapolis, Augsburg Pub. House [c1963] 248 p. 23 cm. Full name: Heige Axel Kristian Brattgard. Bibliography: p. 241-248. [BV772.B68] 63-16594
1. Stewardship, Christian. I. Title.

BRATTGARD, Helge Arel Kristian, 1920- 248
God's stewards; a theological study of the principles and practices of stewardship. Tr. by Gene J. Lund.
I. Title.

BREIG, Joseph Anthony, 1905- 248
A halo for father. Milwaukee, Bruce Pub. Co. [1953] 127p. 21cm. [BX2352.B7] 53-2814
1. Fathers—Religious life. I. Title.

BREIG, Joseph Anthony, 1905- 248
My pants when I die. New York, McMullen Books [1952] 159p. 21cm. [BX2350.B655] 52-11320
1. Christian life—Catholic authors. I. Title.

BREITHAUPT, Gerald O 248
Why? Questions and answers on the Christian faith. 2d ed. New York, Greenwich Book

Publishers, 1957 [i. e. 1958] 67p. 21cm. [BR121.B63 1958] 57-10513
1. Christianity—Essence, genius, nature. I. Title.

BRENNAN, Gerald Thomas, 1898- 1962. 248
Father Brennan's favorite stories [by] Gerald T. Brennan. Milwaukee, Bruce Pub. Co. [1964] vi, 168 p. 23 cm. [BX1756.Z9B725] 64-24368
1. Children's sermons. 2. Sermons, American. 3. Catholic Church — Sermons. I. Title.

BRENNAN, Gerald Thomas, 1898- 1962 248
Father Brennan's favorite stories. Milwaukee, Bruce [c.1964] vi, 168p. 23cm. 64-24368 3.00
1. Children's sermons. 2. Sermons. American. 3. Catholic Church—Sermons. I. Title.

*BRIDGET, Lorraine. 248
Editorial subjects and viewpoints of life. New York, Vantage [1968] 85p. 21cm. 2.75
I. Title.

BRISCOE, D. Stuart. 248
Living dangerously, by D. Stuart Briscoe. Grand Rapids, Zondervan Pub. House [1968] 132 p. 21 cm. [BV4501.2.B74] 68-55322
1. Christian life. I. Title.

BRISTER, C. W. 248
Dealing with doubt [by] C. W. Brister. Nashville, Broadman Press [1970] 127 p. 20 cm. Includes bibliographical references. [BT1102.B67] 72-113213
1. Apologetics—20th century. 2. Faith. I. Title.

BRITT, Bertha Marie. 248
Ashes of tomorrow. Philadelphia, Dorrance [1955] 94p. 20cm. Prose and poems. [PS3503.R5765A7] 55-7594
I. Title.

BRONSTEIN, David. 248
Everyday spiritual perception. Philadelphia Dorrance [1968] 67p. 21cm. [BV4501.2.B764] 67-30760 3.00
1. Christian life. I. Title.

BROOKS, Clara M. 248
The climber, a series of stories for boys and girls. Springfield, Mo., Gospel Pub. House ['1951] 159 p. illus. 20 cm. [BV4571.B645] 52-64335
1. Children—Religious life. I. Title.

BROWN, Hugh B 248
The abundant life, by Hugh B. Brown. Salt Lake City, Bookcraft [1965] 371 p. 24 cm. [BX8635.2.B7] 65-29175
1. Mormons and Mormonism — Doctrinal and controversial works. I. Title.

BROWNLOW, Leroy, 1914- 248
Some "do's" and "don'ts" for the Christian; studies in better living. Fort Worth, Tex., L. Brownlow Publications [1951] 166 p. 20 cm. [BV4501.B7557] 51-26523
1. Christian life. I. Title.

BRUCKBERGER, Raymond Leopold, 1907- 248
The secret ways of prayer, by R. L. Bruckberger. Wilkes-Barre, Pa., Dimension Books [1964] 95 p. 30 cm. (The Carmel series on Christina life, v. 3) Translation of Rejoindre Dieu. [BX2350.B753] 64-19474
1. Christian life — Catholic authors. (Series) I. Title. II. Series.

*BRUCKBERGER, Raymond Leopold, 1907- 248
The secret ways of prayer. Glen Rock, N.J., Paulist [1965, c.1964] 86p. 18cm. (Deus bk.) .75 pap.,
I. Title.

BRUCKBERGER, Raymond Leopold, 1907- 248
The secret ways of prayer [Tr. from French by Salvator Attanasio] Wilkes Barre, Pa., Dimension Bks. [c.1964] 95p. 30cm. (Carmel ser. on Christian life, v.3) 64-19474 2.95 bds.,
1. Christian life—Catholic authors. I. Title. II. Series.

BRUNTON, Paul, 1898- 248
The secret path; a technique of spiritual self-discovery for the modern world. New York, Dutton, 1958 [c1935] 128p. 19cm. (A Dutton everyman paperback, D29) [BL624] 58-59641
1. Spiritual life. I. Title.

BUNCH, Taylor Grant. 248
The armor of righteousness. Nashville, Southern Pub. Association [1957] 96p. 18cm. [BV4501.B7724] 57-40145
1. Christian life. I. Title.

BUNCH, Taylor Grant. 248
Secrets of godly living. Washington. Review and Herald Pub. Association [1953] 125p. 20cm. [BV4501.B7725] 53-29139
1. Christian life. I. Title.

BURKHART, Roy Abram, 1895- 248
The secret of life. [1st ed.] New York, Harper [1950] 118 p. 20 cm. Bibliography: p. 114-118. [BV4501.B776] 50-9514
1. Christian life. I. Title.

BURNS, Elizabeth. 248
The late Liz [the autobiography of an expagan] New York, Popular Lib. [1968, c. 1957] 283p. 18cm. (75-1266) [BV4935. B8A3] .75 pap.,
1. Converts. I. Title.

BURNS, Elizabeth. 248
The late Liz; the autobiography of an ex-pagan. New York, Appleton-Century-Crofts [1957] 342 p. 22 cm. [BV4935.B8A3] 57-7207
1. Converts. I. Title.

BURTON, Jack Robert. 248
Transport of delight / [by] Jack Burton. London : S.C.M. Press, 1976. viii, 200 p. : ill. ; 23 cm. [BX8495.B89A37] 77-353519 ISBN 0-334-01682-7 : £2.50
1. Burton, Jack Robert. 2. Methodist Church—Clergy—Biography. 3. Clergy—England—Biography. I. Title.

BURTON, Naomi. 248
More than sentinels. [1st ed.] Garden City, N. Y., Doubleday, 1964. 346 p. 22 cm. Autobiographical. [BX4705.B945A3] 64-19288
I. Title.

BUTT, Howard. 248
The velvet covered brick; Christian leadership in an age of rebellion. [1st ed.] New York, Harper & Row [1973] xii, 186 p. 21 cm. Includes bibliographical references. [BV652.1.B87 1974] 72-11352 ISBN 0-06-061258-4 5.95
1. Christian leadership. I. Title.

CAILLIET, Emile, 1894- 248
Alone at high noon; reflections on the solitary life. Grand Rapids, Zondervan Pub. House [1971] 94 p. 21 cm. (A Zondervan "reflections" book) [BJ1499.S6C3] 74-133356 2.95
1. Solitude. I. Title.

CAILLIET, Emile, 1894- 248
Journey into light. Grand Rapids, Zondervan Pub. House [1968] 117 p. 23 cm. [BV4501.2.C23] 68-12954
1. Spiritual life. I. Title.

CALHOUN, Robert Lowry, 1896- 248
God and the day's work; Christian vocation in an unchristian world. New York, Association Press [1957] 128p. 16cm. (An Association Press reflection book) [BV4740.C3 1957] 57-11605
1. Vocation. I. Title.

CALLAN, Charles Jerome, 1877- 248
Spiritual riches of the Rosary mysteries, by Charles J. Callan and John F. McConnell. New York, J. F. Wagner [c1957] 106p. illus. 21cm. [BX2163.C32] 58-1174
1. Rosary. I. McConnell, John F., joint author. II. Title.

CALLENS, L J 248
Our search for God [by] L. J. Callens. Translated by David Martin. [St. Louis] Herder [1964] ix, 141 p. 21 cm. (Cross and crown series of spirituality, no. 27) Translation of Le mystere de notre intimite avec Dieu. Bibliographical footnotes. [BX2350.5.C313] 64-18771
1. Spiritual life—Catholic authors. I. Title.

CALLENS, L. J. 248
Our search for God. Tr. [from French] by David Martin [St. Louis] B.Herder [c.1964] ix, 141p. 21cm. (Cross and crown ser. of spirituality, no. 27) Bibl. 64-18771 3.25 bds.,
1. Spiritual life—Catholic authors. I. Title.

CALVIN, Jean, 1509-1564. 248
The piety of John Calvin; an anthology illustrative of the spirituality of the reformer of Geneva. Selected, translated, and edited by Ford Lewis Battles. Pittsburgh, Pittsburgh Theological Seminary, 1969. vii, 190 p. 23 cm. [BX9420.A32B3] 71-2831
1. Reformed Church—Collected works. 2. Theology—Collected works—16th century. I. Battles, Ford Lewis, ed. II. Title.

CAMPBELL, Dortch, 1880-1953. 248
Break those fetters of fear. New York, J. Felsberg, 1954. 166p. 23cm. [BV4637.C33] 54-34237
1. Trust in God. 2. Fear. I. Title.

CAMPBELL, Raymond Kenneth, 1909- 248
The Christian home; some thoughts and gleanings, by R. K. Campbell. [4th ed.] Sunbury, Pa., Believers Bookshelf [1972] vii, 65 p. 21 cm. [BV4526.2.C25 1972] 72-166451 2.25
1. Family—Religious life. I. Title.

CAMUS, Jean Pierre, Bp., 1584-1652. [248]
The spirit of St. Francois de Sales; edited and newly translated,and with an introd. by C. F. Kelley. New York, Harper [1952] xxxi, 249 p. 22 cm. (p. 235-249) Bibliographical references included in "Notes" [BX2183.C36] 242 52-5457
1. Devotional literature. 2. Christian life—Catholic authors. I. Francois de Sales, Saint, Bp. of Geneva, 1567-1622. II. Title.

CAPRIO, Betsy. 248
Experiments in growth, spiritual growth, that is / by Betsy Caprio. Notre Dame, Ind. : Ave Maria Press, c1976. 255 p. : ill. ; 28 cm. Includes bibliographical references and index. [BX930.C26] 76-22268 ISBN 0-87793-114-3 : 5.95
1. Christian education—Text-books—Catholic. I. Title.

CARPENTIER, Rene. 248
Life in the City of God; an introduction to the religious life. Translated by John Joyce. A completely recast ed. of A catechism of the vows. New York, Benziger Bros. [1959] 192p. 22cm. Translation of Temoins de la cite de Dieu. [BX2437.C283] 59-9802
1. Vows. 2. Vows (Canon law) I. Title.

CARR, Sidney Eugene, 1903- 248
Religion in and on the job. Foreword by Eugene Carson Blake. New York, Coward McCann [1957, c1956] 128p. 20cm. [BV4593.C3] 57-7056
1. Christian life. I. Title.

CARRE, Ambrosius Maris, 1908- 248
Hope or despair. Translated by Rene Hague. New York, P. J. Kenedy [1955?] 119p. 22cm. [BV4638.C3] 55-9735
1. Hope. 2. Despair. I. Title.

CASAUBON, Meric, 1599-1671. 248
A treatise concerning enthusiasme (1655). A facsim. reproduction of the 2d ed. of 1656, with an introd. by Paul J. Korshin. Gainesville, Fla., Scholars' Facsimiles & Reprints, 1970. xxv, 297 p. 23 cm. Original t.p. has imprint: London, Printed by Roger Daniel, and are to be sold by Thomas Johnson, 1656. "Reproduced from a copy owned by Harry R. Warfel." [BR112.C3 1970] 77-119864
1. Enthusiasm. I. Title.

CASH, Grace, 1915- 248
Blueprint for abundant living; 20 guides to happiness. New York, Exposition Press [1952] 104 p. 22 cm. [BV4501.C345] 52-6768
1. Christian life. I. Title.

CAUSSADE, Jean Pierre de, d.1751. 248
Abandonment; or, Absolute surrender to divine providence, posthumous work of J. P. de Caussade. Rev. and corr. by H. Ramiere. Translated from the 8th French ed. by Ella McMahon. New York, Benziger Bros. [1952] 192 p. 16 cm. [BV5080.C3 1952] 52-4982
1. Mysticism—Catholic Church. 2. Spiritual life—Catholic authors. I. Title. II. Title: Absolute surrender to divine providence.

CAYRE, Fulbert. 248
The vital Christian; translated by Robert C. Healey. Introd, by Daniel-Rops. New York, Kenedy [1951] xiv, 137 p. 20 cm. [BX2350.C39] 51-9793
1. Christian life—Catholic authors. I. Title.

CECIL, Lord Martin, 1909- 248
Being where you are. New Canaan, Conn., Keats Pub. [1974] 204 p. 18 cm. (A Pivot original) [BP605.E4C42] 73-93652 1.50 (pbk.).
I. Title.

*CETI, Tau 248
Wisdom. New York, Carlton [c.1964] 93p. 22cm. 3.00
I. Title.

CHADWICK, Owen, ed. 248
Western asceticism; selected translations, with introductions and notes. Philadelphia, Westminster Press [1958] 368 p. 24 cm. (The Library of Christian classics, v. 12) Contents.—The sayings of the Fathers.—The conferences of Cassian.—The rule of Saint Benedict. Bibliography: p. 361-362. [BV5017.C5 1958] 58-8713
1. Asceticism. I. Title. II. Series.

CHALMERS, Allan Knight, 1897- 248
That revolutionary--Christ. New York, Scribner [1957] 152p. 21cm. [BV4501.C349] 57-10563
1. Christian life. I. Title.

CHANEY, Robert Galen 248
The inner way. Los Angeles, DeVorss 'c.1962] 149p. 22cm. 3.50
I. Title.

CHANGEY, Eugene 248
All souls are mine. New York, Comet Press Books, [c.]1959. 111p. 21cm. (A Reflection book) 60-520 2.75
I. Title.

CHAPMAN, Raymond 248
The loneliness of man. Philadelphia, Fortress [1964, c.1963] vi, 170p. 18cm. Bibl. 63-19548 1.70 pap.,
1. Loneliness. I. Title.

CHARDON, Louis, 1595-1651. 248
The cross of Jesus. Translated by Richard T. Murphy. St. Louis, Herder [1957- v. 21cm. (Cross and crown series of spirituality, no. 9 [BX2350.C422] 57-9133
1. Spiritual life—Catholic authors. I. Title.

CHRISTENSEN, Bernhard Marinus, 1901- 248
He who has no sword; the meaning of contemporary Christian witness, by Bernhard Christensen. Minneapolis, T. S. Denison [1964] 160 p. 22 cm. Bibliography: p.157-160. [BR123.C57] 64-8372
1. Christianity — 20th cent. — Addresses, essays, lectures. I. Title.

CHRISTENSEN, Bernhard Marinus, 1901- 248
He who has no sword; the meaning of contemporary Christian witness. Minneapolis, Denison [c.1964] 160p. 22cm. Bibl. 64-8372 3.00
1. Christianity—20th cent.—Addresses, essays, lectures. I. Title.

CHRISTIAN asceticism and modern man. 248 Translated by Walter Mitchell and the Carisbrooke Dominicans. New York, Philosophical Library [1955] 262p. 23cm. [BV5032] 57-2469
1. Asceticism. I. Mitchell, Walter, tr.

CHRISTIAN, Dorothy E (White) 248
ABC's in the Bible. Washington, Review and Herald Pub. Association [1953] 60p. illus. 25cm. [BV4571.C532] 53-39558
I. Title.

CHRISTUS (PARIS) 248
Finding God in all things; essays in Ignatian spirituality selected from Christus. Translated by William J. Young. Chicago, H. Regnery Co., 1958. 276p. 21cm. (The Library of living Catholic thought) [BX2350.A1C45] 58-12411
1. Loyola, Ignacio de, Saint, 1491-1556. 2. Spiritual life —Catholic authors. I. Young, William John, 1885- tr. II. Title.

*CLARK, Cline 248
The Bronze age God in the space age; how to establish vital contact with God. New York, Exposition [c.1965] 43p. 21cm. (EP43041) 2.75
I. Title.

CLARK, Glenn, 1882- 248
God's reach. [1st ed.] St. Paul, Macalester Park Pub. Co. ['1951] 223 p. 21 cm. [BV4501.C622] 52-3163
1. Christian life. I. Title.

CLARK, Glenn, 1882- 248
The soul's sincere desire. Silver anniversary ed. Boston, Little, Brown, 1950 ['1925] 113 p. 20 cm. [BV210.C55 1950] 50-13727
1. Prayer. I. Title.

CLEMENS, Titus Flavius, Alexandrinus. 248
Christ the educator; translated by Simon P. Wood. New York, Fathers of the Church, inc., 1954. xxiii, 309 p. 22 cm. (The Fathers of the church, a new translation, v. 23) Translation of Paedagogus. Bibliography: p. xix. [BR60.F3C54] 54-2226
1. Christian life—Early church. I. Title. II. Series.

CLIFFE, Albert D 248
Lessons in successful living; practical faith in practice. [New & rev. ed.] New York, Prentice-Hall [1953] 142p. 21cm. Previous editions published under title: Lessons in living. [BV4501.C645 1953] 53-9625
1. Christian life. I. Title.

CLIFFE, Albert E. 248
Lessons in living; practical faith in practice. Rev. and enl. ed. Drexel Hill, Pa., Bell Pub. Co. [1952] 152 p. 20 cm. [BV4501.C645 1952] 52-31354
1. Christian life. I. Title.

CLIFFE, Albert E. 248
Let go and let God; steps in victorious living. [1st ed.] New York, Prentice-Hall [1951] 176 p. 22 cm. [BV4501.C646] 51-8275
1. Christian life. I. Title.

THE cloud of unknowing, and other treatises, 248 by an English mystic of the fourteenth century; with a commentary on the

Cloud by Father Augustine Baker;edited by Justin McCann. [6th and rev. ed.] Westminster, Md., Newman Press [1952] xxix, 220p. 20cm. (The Orchard books) [BV5080.C5 1952] [BV5080.C5 1952] 149.3 52-14308 52-14308
1. Mysticism—Middle Ages. I. Cloud of unknowing. II. Baker, Augustine, Father, 1575-1641. III. McCann, Justin, 1882- ed. IV. Dionysius Areopagita. De mystica theologia. V. Title: A book of contemplation. VI. Series.
Contents omitted.

COAKLEY, Mary Lewis, 1907- 248
Fitting God into the picture. Milwaukee, Bruce [1950] ix, 223 p. 21 cm. [BX2350.C475] 50-6080
1. Christian life—Catholic authors. I. Title.

COCHRAN, Leonard Hill. 248
Man at his best. Nashville, Abingdon Press [1957] 174p. 21cm. [BV4501.C657] 57-7095
1. Christian life. I. Title.

[COFFMAN, Roxanna] 1895- 248
When we walk with the Lord, by a Christian pilgrim. New York, Vantage Press [1954] 110p. 23cm. [BV4501.C666] 54-4809
1. Criristian life. I. Title.

COLE, Martin L 248
Living with yourself. Boston, Christopher Pub. House [1956] 60p. 21cm. [BV4501.C68] 56-38469
1. Christian life. I. Title.

CONDRE, Bertha, 1871- 248
A way to peace, health, and power; studies for the inner life. [Special ed.] Boston, Score and Script, inc. [1956] 233p. 21cm. [BV4501.C713 1956] 56-44896
1. Christian life. I. Title.

CONFESSIONS. 248
Compiled and edited by W. Scott Palmer [pseud.] With an introd. by Evelyn Underhill. New York, Harper [1954] 188p. 14cm. [BV5080.B65E5 1954] [BV5080.B65E5 1954] 149.3 53-10976 53-10976
1. Mysticism. I. Bohme, Jakob, 1575-1624.

CONN, Howard James. 248
The hope that sets men free. [1st ed.] New York, Harper [1954] 192 p. 22 cm. [BV4638.C6] 54-9653
1. Hope.

COOPER, W. Norman. 248
Finding your self, by W. Norman Cooper. Santa Monica, Calif., DeVorss [1974] 88 p. 21 cm. [BL53.C655] 74-78511 ISBN 0-87516-183-9
1. Psychology, Religious. I. Title.

COOPER, W. Norman. 248
Finding your self, by W. Norman Cooper. Santa Monica, Calif., DeVorss [1974] 88 p. 21 cm. [BL53.C655] 74-78511 ISBN 0-87516-183-9 3.00 (pbk.)
1. Psychology, Religious. I. Title.

CORSON, Fred Pierce, 1896- 248
Pattern for successful living. [1st ed.] Philadelphia, Winston [1953] 148p. 21cm. [BV4501.C724] 52-12903
1. Christian life. I. Title.

COUSINS, Mary 248
Tell me about prayer. Illus. by Thelma Lambert. New York, Kenedy [c.1963] 127p. illus. 23cm. 62-22116 2.95 bds.,
1. Prayer-Juvenile literature. I. Title.

COVINGTON, G. Edwin. 248
What they believe; a survey of religious faith among groups of college students. New York, Philosophical Library [1956] 109p. 24cm. [BT85.C6] 56-3294
1. Students—Religious life. 2. Theology, Doctrinal. I. Title.

COWAN, William Hardy. 248
Freedom versus slavery. New York, Exposition Press [1950] 61 p. 22 cm. [BR125.C817] 50-11468
1. Christianity—20th cent. I. Title.

COWLES, S. Macon. 248
Living the incarnation; a coursebook for adults, by S. Macon Cowles, Jr. Boston, United Church Press [1967] 60 p. 21 cm. Bibliography: p. 59-60. [BV4511.C6] 67-10051
1. Christian life—Study and teaching. I. Title.

CRANFORD, Clarence William, 1906- 248
The overflowing life. Nashville, Broadman Press [1964] 128 p. 20 cm. Bibliographical references included in "Notes" (p. 125-128) [BV4501.2.C72] 64-12409
1. Christian life. I. Title.

CRANFORD, Clarence William, 1906- 248
The overflowing life. Nashville, Broadman [c.1964] 128p. 20cm. Bibl. 64-12409 1.50 bds.,
1. Christian life. I. Title.

*CRAVNER, William Charles 248
God's ultimate victory. New York, Vantage [c.1964] 112p. 21cm. 2.75 bds.,
I. Title.

CRIST, Evamae Barton. 248 B
Take this house / Evamae Barton Crist ; introd. by Frances Hunter. Scottdale, Pa. : Herald Press, c1977. 141 p. : ill. ; 18 cm. [BV4470.C7] 77-151776 ISBN 0-8361-1817-0 pbk. : 1.95
1. Crist, Evamae Barton. 2. Church work with refugees. 3. Christian biography—Pennsylvania. 4. Refugees—Pennsylvania. 5. Refugees—Vietnam. 6. Vietnamese Conflict, 1961-1975—Refugees. I. Title.

CROCK, Clement Henry 248
Paths to eternal glory this is your life. [Boston] St. Paul Editions [dist. Daughters of St. Paul] [c.1960] 210p. 22cm. 60-4699 3.00; 2.00 pap.,
1. Vocation. I. Title.

CROCK, Clement Henry, 1890- 248
No cross, no crown; or, Through suffering to eternal glory. New York, Society of Saint Paul [1955] 174 p. 21 cm. 'New and revised edition.'--Dust jacket. [BV4905.C693 1955] 57-3097
1. Suffering. I. Title.

*CROMER, Grace E. 248
The invisibles and I [by] Grace E. Cromer Hicksville, N.Y., Exposition, [1974] 44 p. 21 cm. [BV4515] ISBN 0-682-48079-7 4.00
1. Christian life. I. Title.

CRONK, Walter. 248
The golden light. Los Angeles, DeVorse [1964] 196 p. illus. 24 cm. [BV5095.C7A3] 64-15645
1. Mysticism. I. Title.

CRONK, Walter Lt. Col. 248
The golden light. Los Angeles, DeVorss [c.1964] 196p. illus. 24cm. 64-15645 4.95
1. Misticism. I. Title.

CROSSLEY, Robert. 248
We want to live. [1st ed.] Chicago, Inter-Varsity Press [1967] 95 p. 18 cm. [BT60.C7] 67-21859
1. Christianity—Essence, genius, nature. 2. Christian life. I. Title.

CROWE, Charles M. 248
On living with yourself. New York, Abingdon-Cokesbury Press [1952] 192 p. 20 cm. [BV4501.C813] 52-5734
1. Christian life. I. Title.

CROWE, John H 248
You can master life. New York, Prentice-Hall [1954] 160p. 21cm. [BV4501.C814] 54-5669
1. Christian life. 2. Psychology, Applied. I. Title.

CROWELL, Grace (Noll), 1877- 248
A child kneels to pray. [Twenty-six prayer poems] Illus. by Lee Mero. Minneapolis, Augsburg Pub. House [1950] 33 p. illus. 19 cm. [BV265.C74] 50-10745
1. Children—Prayer-books and devotions—English. I. Title.

CROWSTON, C C 248
Yon motley crowd, including My conversion. New York, Loizeaux Bros. [1953?] 94p. 19cm. (Treasury of truth. no. 177) [BV4930.C75] 53-28739
1. Converts. I. Title.

CURRIN, Beverly Madison. 248
Decision in crisis; a call for personal commitment to Christ in our age of anxiety. [1st ed.] New York, Greenwich Book Publishers, 1956. 80p. 21cm. [BR121.C92] 56-8066
1. Christianity—Essence, genius, nature. I. Title.

CUSKELLY, Eugene James 248
A heart to know thee; a practical summa of the spiritual life. Glen Rock, N.J., Paulist [1967, c.1963] 317p. 19cm. (Deus Bks.) Bibl. 1.45 pap.,
1. Spiritual life—Catholic authors. I. Title.

CUSKELLY, Eugene James. 248
A heart to know thee; a practical summa of the spiritual life. Westminster, Md., Newman Press, 1963. xvii, 317 p. 23 cm. Bibliographical references included in "Notes." [BX2350.5.C8] 63-12243
1. Spiritual life — Catholic authors. I. Title.

CUSKELLY, Eugene James 248
Heart to know thee; a practical summa of the spiritual life. Westminster, Md., Newman [c.] 1963. xvii, 317p. 23cm. Bibl. 63-12243 5.50
1. Spiritual life—Catholic authors. I. Title.

CUSTER, Dan 248
Know thyself. Lakewood, N.J., 112 2nd St. G. S. Rand, [1962, c.1952] 79p. 21cm. 1.00 pap.,
1. Devotional literature. I. Title.

CUTTAZ, Francois Joseph. 248
Children of God; or, The love of the Father. Translated by M. Angeline Bouchard. Notre Dame, Ind., Fides [1963] viii, 391 p. 23 cm. "A continuation of [the author's] Our life of grace." [BV4817.C813] 63-21254
1. God—Worship and love. 2. Spiritual life—Catholic authors. I. Title. II. Title: The love of the Father.

DAILY, Starr, pseud. 248
God's answer to juvenile delinquency. [1st ed.] St. Paul, Macalester Park Pub. Co. [1953] 155p. 21cm. [BV4637.D3] 54-35840
1. Juvenile delinquency. 2. Trust in God. I. Title.

DAILY, Starr pseud. 248
This is the life; with a foreword by Glenn Clark. [1st ed.] New York, Harper [1952] 189p. 22cm. [BV4501.D23] 52-13054
1. Christian life. I. Title.

DAILY, Starr, pseud. 248
Through valleys to victories. [1st ed.] Garden City, N. Y., Doubleday, 1952. 220 p. 22 cm. [BS1450 23d.D3] 52-7533
1. Bible. O. T. Psalms. XXIII—Criticism, interpretation, etc. I. Title.

DAILY, Starr, pseud. 248
You can. Los Angeles, G. & J. Pub. Co. [1956] 138p. 20cm. Includes bibliographies. [BV4501.D24] 56-57273
1. Christian life. I. Title.

DALY, James Jeremiah, 1872- 248
The road to peace, by James J. Daly. [Milwaukee] Bruce Pub. Co. [1936] Freeport, N.Y., Books for Libraries Press [1970] x, 191 p. 23 cm. (Essay index reprint series) Contents.—Sweetness and light.—The spiritual person.—The supernatural life.—The note of sanctity.—Prayer.—Devotion.—The self-invited Guest.—The priest.—The angels.—The kingdom of Christ.—The two standards.—The three classes of men.—Outstretched caressingly.—Amenities of the road.—Courtesies of the road.—Love's fear.—The souls of purgatory.—The world assails heaven.—The body assails heaven.—Visio pacis.—All saints. [BX2350.D3 1970] 78-107691
1. Christian life—Catholic authors. I. Title.

DARCY-BERUBE, Francoise. 248
To be a parent; a Christian renewal program for parents of young children [by] Francoise Darcy-Berube [and] John Paul Berube. New York, Paulist Press [1973] 162 p. illus. 28 cm. [BX2352.D37] 73-83912 ISBN 0-8091-1784-3 5.95
1. Family—Religious life. 2. Parent and child. 3. Religious education of children. I. Berube, John Paul, joint author. II. Title.

DAVIDSON, Charles Theodore, Bp., 1905- 248
Light in our dwellings. Cleveland, Tenn., White Wing Pub. House & Press [1952] 250p. 20cm. [BV4501.D29] 53-17038
1. Christian life. I. Title.

DAVIES, Elam. 248
This side of Eden. Westwood, N.J., F. H. Revell Co. [1964] 127 p. 21 cm. [BR123.D335] 64-20186
1. Christianity — Addresses, essays, lectures. 2. Christian life — Presbyterian authors. I. Title.

DAVIES, Elam 248
This side of Eden. Westwood, N.J., Revell [c.1964] 127p. 21cm. 64-20186 2.95 bds.,
1. Christianity—(Addresses, essays, lectures. 2. Christian life—Presbyterian authors. I. Title.

DAVIS, Creath. 248
Beyond this God cannot go. Foreword by Keith Miller. Grand Rapids, Mich., Zondervan Pub. House [1971] 148 p. 22 cm. Includes bibliographical references. [BV4501.2.D37] 79-146565 3.95
1. Christian life—Baptist authors. I. Title.

DAVIS, Denver Jackson, 1915- 248
Across the pastor's desk; problems and questions faced by ourpeople in these troubled times. With an introd. by Norman Vincent Peale. Philadelphia, Dorrance [1954] 187p. 20cm. [BR96.D3] 54-8892
1. Questions and answers-Theology. I. Title.

DAVIS, Mona. 248
Seek first the Kingdom; an essay on the teachings of Jesus Christ. [1st ed.] New York, Exposition Press [1955] 156p. 21cm. [BV4501.D3135] 55-8205
1. Christian life. I. Title.

DAVIS, Robert Clarence, 1907- 248
Alive unto God. New York, Vantage Press [1954] 95p. 23cm. [BV4501.D314] 53-12132
1. Christian life. I. Title.

DAWSON, Joseph Martin, 1879- 248
The liberation of life. Nashville, Broadman Press ['1950] 90 p. 20 cm. Bibliographical footnotes. [BV740.D3] 51-9469
1. Liberty. I. Title.

DAY, Gwynn McLendon. 248
Path of the dawning light. Nashville, Broadman Press [1952] 124 p. 20 cm. [BV4501.D343] 52-12134
1. Christian life. I. Title.

DEAL, Haskell Robert. 248
The kingdom of God is now; an essay on Christian living. [1st ed.] New York, Exposition Press [1955] 128p. 21cm. Includes bibliography. [BT94.D4] 55-12281
1. Kingdom of God. I. Title.

DEAL, William S 248
The victorious life; a guide book for victorious living. Grand Rapids, Eerdmans, 1954. 159p. 20cm. [BV4501.D347] 54-11047
1. Christian life. I. Title.

DEAN, Robert James, 1932- 248
God's big little words / Robert J. Dean. Nashville : Broadman Press, c1975. 126 p. ; 21 cm. Includes bibliographical references. [BS680.L5D4] 74-82583 ISBN 0-8054-8124-9 : 1.95
1. Life—Biblical teaching. 2. Love (Theology)—Biblical teaching. 3. Hope—Biblical teaching. 4. Joy—Biblical teaching. 5. Peace (Theology)—Biblical teaching. I. Title.

DEHAU, Pierre Thomas, 1870- 248
The living water; translated from the French by Dominic Ross. Westminster, Md., Newman Press, 1957. 134p. 20cm. Translation of Des fleuves d'eau vive. [BX2350.D372] 57-13828
1. Christian life—Catholic authors. I. Title.

DE LA BEDOYERE, Michael, 1900- 248
Living Christianity; with a foreword by T. D. Roberts. New York, D. McKay Co. [1954] 200p. 21cm. [BX2350.D382 1954] 55-324
1. Christian life—Catholic authors. I. Title.

DELAFIELD, D A 1913- 248
Choice stories, by D. A. Delafield. Illustrated by Jim Padgett. Nashville, Southern Pub. Association [1965] 188 p. illus. 19 cm. [BV4515.2.D44] 64-18875
1. Christian life — Stories. I. Title.

DELAFIELD, D. A., 1913- 248
Choice stories. Illus. by Jim Padgett. Nashville, Southern Pub. Assn. [c.1965] 188p. illus. 19cm. [BV4515.2.D44] 64-18875 3.50 bds.,
1. Christian life—Stories. I. Title.

DELAFIELD, D A 1913- 248
Life of power. [Essays] Illus. by Stanley Dunlap. Washington, Review and Herald Pub. Assn. [1955] 127p. illus. 18cm. [BV4501.D43] 55-59116
1. Christian life. I. Title.

DELAGE, Augustin, 1877- 248
Living in God, by Robert de Langeac (Fr. Delage, priest of St. Sulpice) With an introd. by Francois de Sainte-Marie. English translation by P. Moloney. Westminster, Md., Newman Press [1953] 117p. 17cm. Translation of La vie cachee en Dieu. [BX2350.D383] 53-3142
1. Spiritual life—Catholic authors. I. Title.

DE LONG, Russell Victor, 1901- 248
The game of life; specifications for character engineering, by Russell V. De Long and Mendell Taylor. [1st ed.] Grand Rapids, Eerdmans, 1954. 89p. 23cm. [BV4630.D4] 54-14528
1. Virtue. 2. Youth—Religious life. I. Taylor, Mendell, joint author. II. Title.

DEMAREST, Victoria Booth 248
Shade of his hand; a book of consolation. Grand Rapids, Mich., Zondervan [1962, c.1944] 87p. 21cm. 1.00 pap.,
I. Title.

DEMPSEY, Martin, 1904- 248
People and the Blessed Sacrament. New York, Sentinel Press [1950] 95 p. 18 cm. [BX2350.D39] 51-393
1. Christian life—Catholic authors. I. Title.

DEVAS, Francis. 248
The law of love; the spiritual teaching of Francis Devas, S. J.; edited with an introd. by

Philip Caraman. New York, P. J. Kenedy [1954] 155 p. 20 cm. [BX2350.D47] 54-6529
1. Spiritual life—Catholic authors. I. Caraman, Phillip, 1911- ed. II. Title.

DICKSON, Louis Klaer, 1890- 248
Portals to power. Mountain View, Calif., Pacific Press Pub. Association [1957] 144p. 19cm. [BV4501.D56] 57-7778
1. Christian life. 2. Seventh-Day Adventists—Doctrinal and controversial works. I. Title.

DIEHL, Thomas, ed. 248
Teaching the devotion to the Sacred Heart. Editors: Thomas Diehl [and] John Hardon. Chicago, Loyola University Press, 1963. 242 p. 24 cm. [BX2157.D5] 63-3368
1. Sacred Heart, Devotion to — Study and teaching. I. Harden, John A., joint ed. II. Title.

DIEHL, Thomas, ed. 248
Teaching the devotion to the Sacred Heart. Eds.: Thomas Diehl, John Hardon. Chicago, Loyola [c.]1963. 242p. 24cm. Bibl. 63-3368 4.00
1. Sacred Heart, Devotion to—Study and teaching. I. Hardon, John A., joint ed. II. Title.

DIMENSIONS of the future; 248
the spirituality of Teilhard de Chardin. Edited by Marvin Kessler and Bernard Brown. Washington, Corpus Books [1968] viii, 216 p. 21 cm. Bibliographical references included in "Notes" (p. 189-207) [B2430.T374D5] 68-25584 5.95
1. Teilhard de Chardin, Pierre. I. Kessler, Marvin, ed. II. Brown, Bernard, 1936- ed.

DION, Philip E 248
Keys to the third floor; how to live religious life. New York, J.F. Wagner ,531953] 188p. 21cm. [BX2350.D52] 53-3841
1. Spiritual life—Catholic authors. I. Title.

DITZEN, Lowell Russell. 248
Personal security through faith. With an introd. by Ralph W. Sockman. [1st ed.] New York, Holt [1954] 243 p. 22 cm. [BV4637.D5] 54-5446
1. Trust in God. 2. Security (Psychology) I. Title.

DITZEN, Lowell Russell. 248
You are never alone. [1st ed.] New York, Holt [1956] 253p. 22cm. [BV4911.D5] 56-6459
1. Loneliness. I. Title.

DOHEN, Dorothy. 248
Vocation to love. Foreword by Leo Trese. New York, Sheed & Ward, 1950. ix, 169 p. 20 cm. [BX2350.D53] 50-10436
1. Christian life—Catholic authors. 2. Love (Theology) I. Title.

DOHERTY, Catherine de Hueck, 1900- 248
Not without parables : stories of yesterday, today, and eternity / Catherine de Hueck Doherty. Notre Dame, Ind. : Ave Maria Press, c1977. 187 p. : ill. ; 21 cm. [BV4515.2.D63] 76-50488 ISBN 0-87793-127-5 pbk. : 3.50
1. Christian life—Stories. I. Title.

DOHERTY, Catherine de Hueck, 1900- 248
Not without parables : stories of yesterday, today, and eternity / Catherine de Hueck Doherty. Notre Dame, Ind. : Ave Maria Press, c1977. 187 p. : ill. ; 21 cm. [BV4515.2.D63] 76-50488 ISBN 0-87793-127-5 pbk. : 3.50
1. Christian life—Stories. I. Title.

DOING, Robert Burns, 1904- 248
Three who dance together, by Robert B. Doing. Waco, Tex., Word Books [1970] 143 p. 23 cm. Includes bibliographical references. [BV4501.2.D62] 74-128445 3.95
1. Christian life—Anglican authors. I. Title.

A Dominican tertiary. 248
Simple rosary meditations, by a Dominican tertiary. Westminster, Md., Newman Press [1951] 164 p. 17 cm. [BX2163.S52] 52-928
1. Rosary—Meditations. I. Title.

DONOHUE, John, 1917- 248
Christian maturity. New York, P. J. Kenedy [1955] 214p. 21cm. [BX2350.D57] 55-6519
1. Christian life—Catholic authors. I. Title.

DOTY, William Lodewick, 1919- 248
The on-going pilgrimage; process, psychodynamics and personal presence in the spiritual life, by William L. Doty. Staten Island, N.Y., Alba House [1970] vi, 179 p. 22 cm. [BX2350.2.D649] 78-117200 4.95
1. Spiritual life—Catholic authors. I. Title.

DOTY, William Lodewick, 1919- 248
Stories for discussion. New York, J. F. Wagner ['1951] 168 p. 21 cm. [BX2350.D58] 51-14934
1. Christian life—Stories. 2. Christian life—Catholic authors. I. Title.

DOW, Robert Arthur. 248
Learning through encounter. Valley Forge [Pa.] Judson Press [1971] 174 p. illus. 22 cm. (Experiential education in the church) Includes bibliographical references. [BV652.2.D69] 75-133001 ISBN 0-8170-0510-2 3.50
1. Church group work. 2. Pastoral counseling. I. Title.

DRUMMOND, Henry, 1851-1897. 248
The changed life, an address. [Westwood, N. J.,] F. H. Revell Co. [1954] 55p. 20cm. [BV4501.D68 1954] 54-13153
1. Christian life. I. Title.

DRUMMOND, Henry, 1851-1897. 248
The changed life. [Westwood, N. J.] Revell [1956] 64p. 17cm. (Revell's inspirational classics) [BV4501] 56-12980
1. Christian life. I. Title.

DRUMMOND, Henry, 1851-1897. 248
The greatest thing.) in the world. [Westwood, N. J.] Revell [1956] 63p. 17cm. (Revell's inspirational classics) [BV4639] 56-12981
1. Love (Theology) I. Title.

DRUMMOND, Henry, 1851-1897 248
The greatest thing in the world.. New York, Pyramid [1966] 63p. 17cm. (Little inspriation classics, LP1) [BV4639] .35 pap.,
1. Love (Theology) I. Title.

DRUMMOND, Henry, 1851-1897. 248
The greatest thing in the world [by] Henry Drummond. The song of our Syrian guest [by] William Allen Knight. The practice of the presence of God [by] Brother Lawrence. New Canaan, Conn., Keats Pub. [1973] 113 p. 18 cm. (A Pivot family reader) (Inspiration three, v. 2) [BV4639.D7 1973] 74-156284 1.25
1. Bible. O.T. Psalms XXIII—Criticism, interpretation, etc. 2. Love (Theology) 3. Christian life—Catholic authors. I. Knight, William Allen, 1863- The song of our Syrian guest. 1973. II. Herman, Nicolas, 1611-1691. La pratique de la presence de Dieu. English. 1973. III. Title. IV. Series.

DUFFEY, Felix D, 1903- 248
Psychiatry and asceticism. St. Louis, Herder, 1950. 132 p. 21 cm. [BV5031.D8] 50-777
1. Asceticism—Catholic Church. 2. Psychistry. 3. Psychology, Pastoral. I. Title.

DUNCOMBE, David C. 248
The shape of the Christian life [by] David C. Duncombe. Nashville, Abingdon Press [1969] 208 p. 23 cm. Bibliography: p. 191-197. [BV4501.2.D76] 70-84718
1. Christian life. 2. Psychology, Religious. I. Title.

[DUNFORD, Katherine] 1920- 248
The journal of an ordinary pilgrim Philadelphia, Westminster Press [1954] 133p. 20cm. [BV4501.D82] 53-11669
1. Christian life. I. Title.

DUNNINGTON, Lewis Le Roy, 1890- 248
Power to become. New York, Macmillan, 1956. 233p. 20cm. [BV4501.D837] 56-7298
1. Christian life. I. Title.

DURBIN, B. Paul. 248
Everlasting goodwill and glory; outlines for Christian living. [1st ed.] New York, Greenwich Book Publishers [1963] 130 p. 22 cm. [BV4501.2.D8] 63-14394
1. Christian life—Methodist authors. I. Title.

DURBIN, B. Paul. 248
Everlasting goodwill and glory; outlines for Christian living. [1st ed.] New York, Greenwich Book Publishers [1963] 130 p. 22 cm. [BV4501.2.D8] 63-14394
1. Christian life—Methodist authors. I. Title.

DYCK, Cornelius J. 248
They gave themselves; lessons in Christian stewardship, Newton, Kan., Faith and Life Pr., 724 Main [1965] 111, [1]p. 17cm. Bibl. [BV772.D9] 64-8699 .40 pap.,
1. Stewardship, Christian. I. Title.

DYE, Harold Eldon, 1907- 248
The weaver. Nashville, Broadman Press [1952] 143 p. 21 cm. [BV4501.D88] 52-10101
1. Christian life. I. Title.

ECKHART, Meister, d. 1327. 248
Meister Eckhart speaks; a collection of the teachings of the famous German mystic, with an introd. by Otto Karrer. Translated from the German by Elizabeth Strakosch. New York, Philosophical Library [1957] 72p. 19cm. [BV5080.E45E57] 57-14137
1. Mysticism—Middle Ages. I. Title.

EDMAN, Victor Raymond, 1900- 248
Storms and starlight. Wheaton, Ill., Van Kampen Press [1951] 240 p. 20 cm. [BV4501.E32] 51-13941
1. Christian life. I. Title.

EILUL, Jacques. 248
The presence of the Kingdom. Translated by Olive Wyon. Philadelphia, Westminster Press [1951] 153 p. 20 cm. [BV4501.E588] 52-13180
1. Christian life. 2. Church and social problems. I. Title.

ELLARD, Gerald, 1894- 248
Service, by Gerald Ellard and Sister M. Anne Burns. Illus. by Vinton R. Boecher. Chicago, Loyola University Press, 1951. Chicago, Loyola University Press, 1955. 316p. 24cm. 373p. illus. 21cm. (Religion essentials series, book 4) [BX2355.E4] 51-7879
1. Christian life—Catholic authors. 2. Youth—Religious life. I. Schmidt, Austin Guildford, 1883- II. Title. III. Title: — Teacher's manual,

ELLISON, John Malcus, 1889- 248
Tensions and destiny. Richmond, John Knox Press, 1953. 135 p. 21 cm. [BV4501.2.E38] 53-8461
1. Christian life. I. Title.

ELLISON, John Malcus, 1892- 248
Tensions and destiny. Richmond, John Knox Press, 1953. 135p. 21cm. [BV4501.E5875] 53-8461
I. Christian life. II. Title.

ENGQUIST, Richard, comp. 248
Is anyone for real? Introd. by Gert Behanna. Waco, Tex., Word Books [1971] 132 p. 23 cm. [BV4501.2.E58 1971] 70-134936 3.95
1. Christian life—Addresses, essays, lectures. I. Title.

*ENSLEY, Francis Gerald 248
Persons can change. Nashville, Abingdon [1964, c.1963] 127p. 20cm. 1.00
I. Title.

ERPESTAD, Emil, 1912- 248
Ten studies in prayer. Minneapolis, Augsburg Pub. House [1951] 89 p. 20 cm. (Ten-week teacher-training course books) "Published under the auspices of the Board of Christian Educationof the Evangelical Lutheran Church." [BV215.E7] 51-4502
1. Prayer. I. Title.

ESCH, Ludwig, 1883- 248
New life in Christ. Translated by W. T. Swain. Westminster,Md., Newman Press, 1957. 294p. 22cm. [BX2350.E712] 57-11841
1. Christian life—Catholic authors. I. Title.

ESCRIVA, Jose Maria. 248
Holy rosary. [1st American ed.] Chicago, Scepter, 1953. 157p. illus. 16cm. [BX2163.E813] 53-29341
1. Rosary. I. Title.

ESCRIVA, Jose Maria. 248
The way. Foreword by Samuel Cardinal Stritch, Archbishop of Chicago. Chicago, Scepter, 1954. 256p. 16cm. [BX2350.E74 1954a] 55-19727
1. Spiritual life—Catholic authors. I. Title.

ESCRIVA, Jose Maria [Jose Maria Escriva de Balaguer Albos] 248
The way. New York, All Saints [1963, c.1954, 1962] 268p. 17cm. (AS702) .75 pap.,
1. Spiritual life—Catholic authors. I. Title.

ESSAYS on guidance; 248
a His reader, by Joseph Bayly and others. Chicago, Inter-Varsity Press [1968] 103 p. illus. 22 cm. A collection of articles that had originally appeared in His magazine. [BV4740.B38] 68-57742
1. Vocation. I. Bayly, Joseph T. II. His.

ETTINGER, Cecil R. 248
Thy will be done; a continuing study in the Christian ethic with emphasis on the nature of sacrifice [Independence, Mo., Herald Pub., 1967] 71p. 22cm. A study course for women; the year's emphasis: Women search for an understanding of sacrifice. At foot of t.p.: Reorganized Church of Jesus Christ of Latter Day Saints. .85 pap.,
I. Title.

EVANS, Robert Llewelyn. 248
Christ, the Divine Comforter. Alhambra, Calif. [1951] 94 p. 21 cm. [BV4905.E8] 51-38721
1. Consolation. I. Title.

FABER, Frederick William, 1814-1863. 248
All for Jesus; edited and rev. by Maurice V. Shean. Westminster, Md., Newman Press, 1956. 254p. 23cm. [BX2182.F2 1956] 56-9995
1. Spiritual life—Catholic authors I. Title.

FAGAL, William A. 248
By faith I live. Nashville, Southern Pub. [c.1965] 192p. 21cm. (Summit bk.) [BV4515.2.F3] 65-28488 1.00 pap.,
1. Christian life—Stories. I. Title.

FARAH, Charles. 248
How to rear a happy Christian family. Chicago, Moody Press [c1953] 125p. 18cm. (Colportage library, 247) [BV4526.F25] 54-1174
1. Family—Religious life. I. Title.

FARGO, Gail B. 248
Talks to truth searchers with answers to puzzling "why" questions [by] Gail B. Fargo. New York, Philosophical Library [1974] 56 p. 23 cm. Bibliography: p. 55-56. [BF645.F28] 74-75082 ISBN 0-8022-2106-8 4.75
1. New Thought. I. Title.

FEE, Zephyrus Roy, 1890- 248
Self-encouragement. Dallas, Wilkinson Pub. Co. [1952] 318 p. illus. 20 cm. [BV4501.F37] 52-42360
1. Christian life. I. Title.

FENELON, Francois de Salignac de La Mothe-, Abp., 1651-1715. 248
Letters and reflections; edited and with an introd. by Thomas S. Kepler. [1st ed.] Cleveland, World Pub. Co. [c1955] 172p. 16cm. (World devotional classics) [BX2183.F4K4] 55-5276
1. Christian life—Catholic authors. I. Title.

FENELON, Francois de Salignac de La Mothe-, Abp., 1651-1715. 248
Letters to men and women. Selected with an introd. by Derek Stanford. Westminster, Md., Newman Press, 1957. 208p. port. 22cm. 'Selection ... made from the English text of H. L. Sidney Lear.' Bibliographical footnotes. [BX2183.F4L64] 57-11812
1. Christian life—Catholic authors. I. Stanford, Derek, ed. II. Title.

FERGUSON, Rowena. 248
Youth and the Christian community. Nashville, Abingdon Press [1954] 140p. 19cm. [BV4531.F4] 54-11091
1. Youth—Religious life. 2. Church work with youth. I. Title.

FERRE, Nels Fredrick Solomon, 1908- 248
Making religion real. [1st ed.] New York, Harper [1955] 157p. 20cm. [BV4501.F378] 55-6784
1. Christian life. I. Title.

FERRE, Nels Fredrick Solomon, 1908- 248
Strengthening the spiritual life. [1st ed.] New York, Harper [1951] 63 p. 20 cm. [BV4501.F38] 51-10175
1. Spiritual life. I. Title.

FERWERDA, Floris, 1871- 248
Jesus only. [1st ed.] New York, Vantage Press [1955] 142p. 21cm. Includes bibliography. [BR121.F548] 54-13141
1. Christianity—20th cent. I. Title.

FIFLELD, James W 248
The single path. Englewood Cliffs, N. J., Prentice-Hall [1957] 237p. 22cm. [BV4501.F44] 57-13152
1. Christian life. I. Title.

FINEGAN, Jack, 1908- 248
Clear of the brooding cloud. Nashville, Abingdon-Cokesbury Press [1953] 176p. 20cm. [BV4501.F445] 53-6349
1. Christian life. I. Title.

FINEGAN, Jack, 1908- 248
The orbits of life. Saint Louis, Bethany Press [1954] 160p. 20cm. [BR121.F568] 54-2692
1. Christianity—20th cent. 2. Christian life. I. Title.

FIRST prayers; 248
illustrated by Tasha Tudor. [New York] Oxford University Press [1952] 48 p. illus. 14 cm. [Oxford books for boys and girls] Catholic edition. [BX2150.F56] 52-4340
1. Children—Prayer-books and devoticns—English. 2. Catholic Church—Prayer-books and devotions—English. I. Tudor, Tasha. illus.

FISCHER, Joseph Golznig 248
The world of life. New York, Vantage Press [c.1960] 213p. 22cm. 3.75 bds.,
I. Title.

FISHER, C. William 248
Don't park here! Nashville, Abingdon [c.1962] 158p. 21cm. 62-16253 3.00
1. Suffering. 2. Conduct of life. 3. Biography. I. Title.

FITZGERALD, Lawrence P 248
Military service and you. Philadelphia JudsonPress 1956 96p. illus. 19cm. Includes bibliography. [BV4588.F57] 57-17599
1. Soldiers— Religious life. 2. Military service, Compulsory—U. S. I. Title.

FLOREEN, Harold. 248
Pictures of the Way; some principles of the Christian life presented largely through illustrations. Rock Island, Ill., Augustana Book

Concern [1952] 167 p. 20 cm. [BV4501.F623] 52-42358
1. Christian life. I. Title.

FOERSTER, Friedrich Wilhelm, 1869- 248
Christ and the human life. [Translated from the German by Daniel F. Coogan, Jr.] New York, Philosophical Library [1953] 333p. 24cm. [BV4503.F612] 53-7908
1. Christian life. I. Title.

FOOTE, Gaston, 1902- 248
Living in four dimensions. [Westwood, N. J.] F. H. Revell Co. [1953] 160p. 22cm. [BV4501.F624] 53-10524
1. Christian life. 2. Emotions. 3. Psychology, Applied. I. Title.

FORD, William Herschel, 1900- 248
Simple sermons for time and eternity, by W. Herschel Ford. Grand Rapids, Zondervan Pub. House [1964] 120 p. 21 cm. [BX6333.F568S484] 64-15559
1. Baptists—Sermons. 2. Sermons, American. I. Title.

FORD, William Herschel, 1900- 248
Simple sermons for time and eternity. Grand Rapids, Mich., Zondervan [c.1964] 120p. 21cm. [BX6333.F568S484] 64-15559 1.95 bds.,
1. Baptists—Sermons. 2. Sermons, American. I. Title.

FOREMAN, Kenneth Joseph, 1891- 248
Identification: human and divine. Richmond, John Knox Press [1963] 160 p. 21 cm. (The Annie Kinkead Warfield lectures, 1962-1963) Includes bibliographies. [BV4509.5.F6] 63-9002
1. Identification (Religion) I. Title.

FOREMAN, Kenneth Joseph, 1891- 248
Identification: human and divine. Richmond, Va., Knox [c.1963] 160p. 21cm. (Annie Kinkead Warfield lects., 1962-1963) Bibl. 63-9002 3.50
1. Identification (Religion) I. Title.

FORSYTH, Peter Taylor, 1848-1921. 248
The cure of souls; an anthology of P. T. Forsyth's practical writings, with an appraisement by Harry Escott. [Rev. and enl. ed.] Grand Rapids, W. B. Eerdmans Pub. Co. [1971, c1970] xxii, 128 p. 19 cm. First ed. published in 1948 under title: Peter Taylor Forsyth: director of souls. Includes bibliographical references. [BR85.F593 1971] 74-142905 ISBN 0-04-248008-6
1. Theology—Collected works—20th century. 2. Congregational churches—Collected works. I. Escott, Harry, ed. II. Title.

FOSDICK, Harry Emerson, 1878-1969. 248
A faith for tough times. [1st ed.] New York, Harper [1952] 128 p. 20 cm. [BR123.F64] 52-8471
1. Christianity—Addresses, essays, lectures. I. Title.

FOSTER, Constance J 248
Launching your spiritual power in the space age [by] Constance Foster. Foreword by Norman Vincent Peale. [New York] C. & R. Anthony [1964] 148 p. 22 cm. (A Master publication) [BV4501.2.F64] 65-3489
1. Christian life. I. Title.

FOSTER, Constance J. 248
Launching your spiritual power in the space age. Foreword by Norman Vincent Peale [New York] C. & R Anthony, 300 Park Ave. S. [1965, c.1964] 148p. 22cm. (Master pubn.) [BV4501.2.F64] 65-3489 3.00 bds.,sChristian life.
I. Title.

FOUCAULD, Charles Eugene Vicomtede 1858-1916. 248
Spiritual autobiography of Charles de Foucauld. Edited and annotated by Jean-Francois Six. Translated from the French by J. Holland Smith. New York, P. J. Kenedy [1961] x, 214 p. 22 cm. [BX4705.F65A3] 64-21850
I. Six, Jean Francois, ed. II. Title.

FOUCAULD, Charles Eugene, vicomte de, 1858-1916 248
Spiritual autobiography of Charles de Foucauld. Ed., annotated by Jean-Francois Six. Tr. from French by J. Holland Smith. New York, Kenedy [c.1964] x, 214p. 22cm. 64-21850 4.95
I. Six, Jean Francois, ed. II. Title.

FOULSTON, Pauline Hekard 248
Lifts for living, a book of practical psychology and spiritual aids for everyday living. New York, Vantage [c.1963] 42p. 21cm. 2.00
I. Title.

FRANKE, Carol W., 1928- 248
How to stay alive all your life, by C. W. Franke. Grand Rapids, Zondervan [1967] 135p. 23cm. [BV4501.2.F72] 248 3.95
1. Christian life—Evangelical United Brethren authors. I. Title.

FRASER, Jean M 248
A ship sets sail. New York, Friendship Press [1953] 94p. 19cm. [BR481.F7] 53-9351
1. Christianity— 20th cent. 2. Youth—Religious life. 3. World Conference of Christian Youth. 3d, Travancore, 1952. I. Title.

*FRENCH, Fannie. 248
God was, God is, God shall be. New York, Vantage [1967] 202p. illus., music. 21cm. 3.95 bds.,
I. Title.

FRITZ, Dorothy B 248
The spiritual growth of children. Philadelphia, Board of Christian Education of the Presbyterian Church in the United States of America [1957] 67p. 23cm. Includes bibliography. [BV1590.F7] 57-5094
1. Children—Religious life. 2. Religious education—Home training. I. Title.

FRITZ, Dorothy Bertolet. 248
The spiritual growth of children. Philadelphia, Board of Christian Education of the Presbyterian Church in the United States of America [1957] 67 p. 23 cm. Includes bibliography. [BV1590.F7] 57-5094
1. Children — Religious life. 2. Religious education — Home training. I. Title.

GAGERN, Friedrich Ernst, Freiherr von. 248
The meaning of life and marriage; translated from the German by Meyrick Booth. Westminster, Md., Newman Press, 1954. 252p. 23cm. Translation of Selbstbesinnning und Wandlung and Glickliche Ehe. [BX2350.G17] 54-11781
1. Christian life—Catholic authors. 2. Psychology, Applied. 3. Marriage. I. Title.

GAITHER, Gloria. 248
Because He lives / Gloria Gaither. Old Tappan, N.J. : F. H. Revell Co., 1977. 202 p. ; 22 cm. [ML420.G13A3] 77-10336 ISBN 0-8007-0881-4 : 5.95
1. Gaither, Gloria. 2. Gospel musicians—United States—Biography. 3. Christian biography—United States. I. Title.

GAITHER, Gloria. 248
Because He lives / Gloria Gaither. Old Tappan, N.J. : F. H. Revell Co., 1977. 202 p. ; 22 cm. [ML420.G13A3] 77-10336 ISBN 0-8007-0881-4 : 5.95
1. Gaither, Gloria. 2. Gospel musicians—United States—Biography. 3. Christian biography—United States. I. Title.

GARDNER, John Edward, 1917- 248
Personal religious disciplines, by John E. Gardner. Grand Rapids, W. B. Eerdmans Pub. Co. [1966] 134 p. 21 cm. Bibliography: p. 134. [BV5027.G3] 65-25188
1. Asceticism. I. Title.

GARDNER, John Edward, 1917- 248
Personal religious disciplines. Grand Rapids, Mich., Eerdmans [c.1966] 134p. 21cm.bBibl. [BV5027.G3] 65-25188 3.00
1. Asceticism. I. Title.

GARRIGOU-LAGRANGE, Reginald, Father, 1877- 248
The three ways of the spiritual life; from the French. Westminster, Md., Newman Press, 1950. xii, 112 p. 19 cm. [BX2350.G336 1950] 51-5839
1. Spiritual life—Catholic authors. I. Title.

GATLIN, Dana. 248
Prayer changes things. Lee's Summit, Mo., Unity School of Christianity, 1951. 186 p. 17 cm. [BV210.G35] 52-25950
1. Prayer. 2. Unity School of Christianity—Doctrinal and controversial works. I. Title.

GEANEY, Dennis J 248
You are not your own. Chicago, Fides Publishers [1954] 178p. 21cm. [BX2348.G4] 54-10890
1. Catholic action. I. Title.

GEISSLER, Eugene S. 248
There is a season; a search for meaning [by] Eugene S. Geissler. Introd. by John S. Dunne. Art by Sarah Geissler. Notre Dame, Ind., Ave Maria Press [1969] 164 p. illus. 21 cm. [BX4705.G415A3] 69-17337 4.50
I. Title.

GIBB, Robert E 248
Armed for crisis; a coursebook for leaders of adults [by] Robert E. Gibb. Boston, United Church Press [c1965] 124 p. illus., ports. 21 cm. Includes bibilographical references. [BX9884.A3G5] 65-14277
1. Religious education — Text-books for adults — United Church of Christ. I. Title.

GILKEY, James Gordon, 1889- 248
Here is help for you. New York, Macmillan, 1951. 164 p. 20 cm. [BV4501.G5156] 51-14304
1. Christian life. I. Title.

GILLIS, James Martin, 1876- 248
So near is God; essays on the spiritual life. New York, Scribner, 1953. 210p. 21cm. [BX2350.G485] 53-8785
1. Spiritual life—Catholic authors. I. Title.

GILMORE, G Don. 248
Everything is yours. New York, Abingdon Press [1964] 128 p. 20 cm. [BV4501.2.G52] 64-16148
1. Christian life — Methodist authors. I. Title.

GILMORE, G. Don 248
Everything is yours. Nashville, Abingdon [c.1964] 128p. 20cm. 64-16148 2.50 bds.,
1. Christian life—Methodist authors. I. Title.

GLADDEN, Washington, 1836-1918. 248
Ruling ideas of the present age. Boston, Houghton, Mifflin, 1895. New York, Johnson Reprint Corp., 1971. iv, 299 p. 19 cm. (Series in American studies) [BR121.G5 1971] 78-155109
1. Christian life. 2. Social ethics. I. Title.

GOLDBRUNNER, Josef. 248
Holiness is wholeness. [New York] Pantheon [1955] 63p. 22cm. Translation, by Stanley Goodman, of Heiligkeit und Gesundheit. [BX2350.G643] 55-8183
1. Christian life— Catholic authors. 2. Psychology, Pastoral. I. Title.

GOLDSMITH, Joel S 1892- 248
The contemplative life. New York, Julian Press, 1963. 209 p. 22 cm. [BF639.G5584] 63-12486
1. New Thought. I. Title.

GOLDSMITH, Joel S. 1892- 248
The contemplative life. New York, Julian [c.] 1963. 209p. 22cm. 63-12486 4.50
1. New Thought. I. Title.

GOLLAND TRINDADE, Henrique Heitor, Bp., 1897- 248
Recollection the soul of action. Translated by Conall O'Leary from the Portuguese. [1st ed.] Paterson, N. J., St. Anthony Guild Press [1957] 166p. illus: 20cm. [BX2350.6.G6] 57-39769
1. Recollection (Theology) I. Title.

GOOD business. 248
Prayer in the market place; a collection from Good business. Lee's Summit, Mo., Unity School of Christianity, 1950. 188 p. 17 cm. [BV210.G58] 51-30189
1. Prayer. 2. Unity School of Christianity—Doctrinal and controversial works. I. Title.

GORDON, Adoniram Judson, 1836-1895. 248
In Christ or, The believer's union with his Lord. Grand Rapids, Baker Book House, 1964. 209 p. 20 cm. "Reprinted from the edition issued in 1872." Bibliographical references included in "Notes" (p. [208]-209) [BT769.G6 1964] 64-14563
1. Mystical union. I. Title.

GORDON, Adoniram Judson, 1836-1895 248
In Christ: or, The believer's union with his Lord. Grand Rapids, Mich., Baker Bk. [c.] 1964. 209p. 20cm. Bibl. 64-14563 2.95
1. Mystical union. I. Title.

GORNITZKA, Odd. 248
Living witnesses; studies in personal evangelism. Rev. by Rolf E. Aaseng. Minneapolis, Augsburg Pub. House [1965] viii, 87 p. 20 cm. Revision of the author's Ten studies in personal evangelism. Leader's manual, by Rolf E. Aaseng, Minneapolis, Augsburg Pub. House [1965] [BV3795.G6] 65-22835
1. Evangelisitc work — Addresses, essays, lectures. I. Aaseng, Rolf E. II. Title.

GORNITZKA, Odd 248
Living witnesses; studies in personal evangelism. Rev. by Rolf E. Aaseng. Minneapolis, Augsburg [c.1965] viii, 87p. 20cm. Rev. of the author's Ten studies in personal evangelism. [BV3795.G6] 65-22835 1.50 pap.,
1. Evangelistic work—Addresses, essays, lectures. I. Aaseng, Rolf E. II. Title.

GOSS, Edgar M 248
Man at his best; the key to happiness and success. Kansas City, Mo., Burton Pub. Co. [c1953] 160p. 21cm. [BR121.G68] 55-22577
1. Christianity—Essence, genius, nature. I. Title.

GOULD, William Blair. 248
The worldly Christian; Bonhoeffer on discipleship. Philadelphia, Fortress Press [1967] xviii, 94 p. 18 cm. (A Fortress paperback original) Bibliography: p. 89-94. [BX4827.B57G6] 67-19039
1. Bonhoeffer, Dietrich, 1906-1945. 2. Christian life. I. Title.

GOULOOZE, William, 1903- 248
Blessings of suffering. Grand Rapids, Baker Book House, 1954. 173 p. 20 cm. [BV4905.G63] 51-5370
1. Suffering. I. Title.

GOULOOZE, William, 1903-1955. 248
Grace for today. Grand Rapids, Baker Book House, 1957. 114p. 21cm. [BV4905.G636] 57-9383
1. Suffering. I. Title.

GOULOOZE, William, 1903-1955. 248
My second valley. Grand Rapids, Baker Book House, 1955 [c1953] 170p. 21cm. [BV4905.G638] 57-2583
1. Suffering. I. Title.

GRAEF, Hilda C. 248
God in our daily life. Westminster, Md., Newman Press, 1951. 225 p. 23 cm. [BX2350.G6818] 51-14937
1. Christian life—Catholic authors. I. Title.

GRAEF, Richard, 1899- 248
Lord, teach us how to pray; translated from the German of Richard Graf by Sister Mary Hildegard Windecker. New York, F. Pustet Co., 1952. 193 p. 20 cm. [BV210.G6963] 52-38624
1. Prayer. I. Title.

GRAEFF, Grace M. 248
House not made with hands, by Grace M. Graeff. New York, Philosophical Library [1966] 54 p. 22 cm. [BJ1581.2.G67] 66-22002
1. Conduct of life. I. Title.

GRANDMAISON, Leonce de, 1868-1927. 248
Come Holy Spirit, meditations for apostles. Translated by Joseph O'Connell. Chicago, Fides Publishers Association [1956] 117p. 21cm. Translation of Ecrits spirituels, v. 3: Dernieres retraites et triduums. [BX2350.G745] 56-2752
1. Spiritual life—Catholic authors. I. Title.

GRANDMAISON, Leonce de, 1868-1927. 248
We and the Holy Spirit, talks to laymen; the spiritual writings of Leonce de Grandmaison. Translated by Angeline Bouchard. Chicago, Fides Publishers [1953] 223p. 21cm. Translation of Ecrits spirituels, v. 1. [BX2350.G743] 53-20711
1. Spiritual life—Catholic authors. I. Title.

GRANT, Vernon W. 248
The roots of religious doubt and the search for security [by] Vernon W. Grant. New York, Seabury Press [1974] 243 p. 22 cm. "A Crossroad book." Includes bibliographical references. [BL51.G724] 74-9779 ISBN 0-8164-1165-4
1. Religion—Philosophy. 2. Belief and doubt. I. Title.

GRASHOFF, Raphael. 248
The joys, sorrows, and glories of the Rosary. St. Meinrad, Ind., Grail [1954] 173p. 14cm. [BX2163.G7] 54-37564
1. Rosary. I. Title.

GREEN, Joseph Franklin, 1924- 248
The Bible's secret of full happiness [by] Joseph F. Green. Nashville, Broadman Press [1970] 154 p. 21 cm. [BV4501.2.G745] 72-127197 3.95
1. Christian life—Baptist authors. I. Title.

GREENWAY, Leonard, 1907- 248
Talks to teeners; chapel talks delivered during morning devotions at the Christian High School, Grand Rapids, Michigan. Grand Rapids, Zondervan Pub. House [1952] 58p. 21cm. [BV4531.G68] 53-16583
1. Youth—Religious life. I. Title.

GRIMAL, Julius Leo, 1867-1953. 248
The three stages of the spiritual life under the inspiration of Jesus. Translated under the direction of Joseph Buckley. Milwaukee, Bruce Pub. Co. [1956] 3v. 20cm. [BX2350.G765] 56-7737
1. Spiritual life— Catholic authors. I. Title.

GRISINGER, George F., M.D. 248
A modern prophet speaks. New York, Carlton [c.1963] 58p. 21cm. 2.00

I. Title.

GRITTER, George. 248
The quest for holiness; or, The development of spiritual life. [1st ed.] Grand Rapids, W. B. Eerdmans Pub. Co., 1955. 78p. 23cm. Includes bibliography. [BV4501.G778] 55-1149
1. Spiritual life. I. Title. II. Title: The development of spiritual.

GROU, Jean Nicolas, 1731- 248
1803.
Manual for interior souls. Newly edited and introduced by Donal O'Sullivan. New ed. Westminster, Md., Newman Press [1955] 273p. 20cm. [BV4833.G7 1955] 56-902
1. Spiritual life. I. Title.

GROU, Jean Nicolas, 1731- 248
1803.
Marks of true devotion, with the Christian sanctified by the Lord's prayer. Newly translated and edited by a Monk of Parkminster. Springfield, Ill., Templegate [1962] 165 p. 18 cm. [BV4815.G7 1962] 63-3270
1. Devotion. I. Title.

GROU, Nicolas., S. J., 1731- 248
1803
Marks of true devotion, with the Christian sanctified by the Lord's prayer. Newly tr. [from French], ed. by a Monk of Parkminister. Springfield, Ill., Templegate [1963] 165p. 18cm. Bibl. 63-3270 3.50
1. Devotion. I. Title.

GUARDINI, Romano, 1885- 248
The rosary of Our Lady. Translated by H. von Schuecking. New York, Kenedy [1955] 94p. illus. 20cm. [BX2163.G8] 55-6637
1. Rosary. I. Title.

GUELLUY, Robert. 248
Christian commitment to God and to the world. Translated from the 3d French ed. by M. Angeline Bouchard. New York, Desclee Co., 1965. 178 p. 22 cm. Translation of Vie de fol et taches terrestres. [BX2350.2.G813] 65-15994
1. Christian life — Catholic authors. 2. Vocation. I. Title.

GUELLUY, Robert 248
Christian commitment to God and to the world. Tr. from the 3d French ed. by M. Angeline Bouchard. New York, Desclee, 1965. 178p. 22cm. [BX2350.2.G813] 65-15944 3.95
1. Christian life—Catholic authors. 2. Vocation. I. Title.

GUIBERT, Joseph de. 248
The theology of the spiritual life; translated by Paul Barrett. New York, Sheed and Ward, 1953. 382p. 22cm. Translation of Theologia spiritualis, ascetica et mystica. [BX2350.G7913] 53-9804
1. Spirituality. 2. Asceticism—Catholic Church. 3. Mysticism—Catholic Church. I. Title.

GUIDEPOSTS. 248
Faith made them champions, edited by Norman Vincent Peale. Carmel, N. Y., Guideposts Associates [1954] 270 p. illus. 22 cm. [BV4495.G87] 54-14412
1. Christian life. I. Peale, Norman Vincent, 1898- ed. II. Title.

GUIDEPOSTS. 248
The Guideposts anthology, edited by Norman Vincent Peale. Pawling, N. Y., Guideposts Associate [1953] 333 p. 22 cm. [BV4515.G83] 53-3462
1. Christian life—Stories. 2. Prayers. I. Peale, Norman Vincent, 1898 ed. II. Title.

GUIDEPOSTS. 248
Guideposts to a stronger faith, edited by Norman Vincent Peale. Carmel, N. Y., Guideposts Associates [1959] 308p. 22cm. [BV4908.5.G83] 59-4153
1. Peace of mind. 2. Christian biography. I. Peale, Norman Vincent, ed. II. Title.

GUIDEPOSTS. 248
Unlock your faith-power, edited by Norman Vincent Peale. Carmel, N. Y., Guideposts Associates [1957] 307p. 22cm. 'Seventy-five articles from Guideposts magazine.' [BV4495.G93] 57-1144
1. Christian life. I. Peale, Norman Vincent, 1898- ed. II. Title.

GULLIXSON, Thaddeus Frank, 248
1882-
Christ for a world like this. Minneapolis, Augsburg Pub. House [1955] 114p. 21cm. [BV4501.G83] 55-7119
1. Christian life. I. Title.

HABEL, Bernhard H J, 1890- 248
Snapshots. Minneapolis, Augsburg Pub. House [1950] 167 p. 21 cm. Essays. [BX8054.H3] 50-13816
1. Evangelical Lutheran Church—Addresses, essays, lectures. I. Title.

HAGGAI, John Edmund. 248
How to win over worry; a practical formula for victorious living. Grand Rapids, Zondervan Pub. House [1959] 179p. 21cm. [BV4908.5.H3] 59-4286
1. Peace of mind. I. Title.

HAGGAI, John Edmund 248
How to win over worry; a practical formula for successful living. New York, Pyramid [1967, c. 1959] 157p. 18cm. (X1674) [BV4908.5.H3] .60 pap.,
1. Peace of mind. I. Title.

HALE, Joe, 1935- 248
Christ matters! [Nashville, Tenn., Tidings, 1971] 87 p. 19 cm. Includes bibliographical references. [BV4501.2.H263] 77-147950 1.00
1. Christian life—Methodist authors. 2. Christianity—20th century. I. Title.

HALEY, Joseph Edmund. 248
Accent on purity; guide for sex education. [4th ed.] Chicago, Fides Publishers [1957, c1948] 130p. illus. 21cm. Includes bibliography. [BV4647.C5H3 1957] 57-7962
1. Chastity. I. Title.

HALVORSON, John V. 248
The ages in tension [by] John V. Halvorson. Minneapolis, Augsburg Pub. House [1970] 87 p. 20 cm. Includes bibliographical references. [BR115.H5H35] 70-121964
1. History (Theology)—Biblical teaching. I. Title.

HAMILTON, James Wallace, 248
1900-
Serendipity [by] J. Wallace Hamilton. Westwood, N.J., Revell [1965] 187 p. 21 cm. [BV4501.2.H29] 65-14280
1. Christian life. 2. Serendipity. I. Title.

HAMILTON, James Wallace 1900- 248
Serendipity. Westwood, N.J., Revell [c.1965] 187p. 21cm. [BV4501.2.H29] 65-14280 3.95 bds.,
1. Christian life. 2. Serendipity. I. Title.

HAMILTON, Lulu (Snyder). 248
Our children and God, by Mrs. Clarence H. Hamilton. [1st ed.] Indianapolis, Bobbs-Merrill [1952] 218 p. 21 cm. [BV4529.H3] 52-5805
1. Children—Religious life. 2. Religious education—Home training. I. Title.

HAMM, Jack. 248
Drawing toward God; the art and inspiration of Jack Hamm. [1st ed.] Anderson, S.C., Droke House; distributed by Grosset & Dunlap, New York [1968] 111 p. illus. 24 cm. [BV4515.H31315] 68-16896
1. Christian life—Pictures, illustrations, etc. I. Title.

HAMM, Jack. 248
The living scriptures; religious drawings. Grand Rapids, Kregel Publications, 1958. 127p. (cheifly illus.) 23cm. [BV4515.H3133] 58-13703
1. Christian life— Pictures, illustrations, etc. I. Title.

HANCOCK, Laurice Hicks. 248
Prayer in every day living. Dallas, Story Book Press [1950] 71 p. 20 cm. [BV210.H344] 50-4256
1. Prayer. I. Title.

HANNUM, John A. 248
Living goals for everyone; achieving insight through self-development. New York, Exposition [c.1963] 78p. 21cm. 3.00
I. Title.

HANSON, Cscar Conrad, 1908- 248
Live to win. Minneapolis, Augsburg Pub. House [1949] 145p. 21cm. [BV4531.H22] 49-7758
1. Youth —Religious life. I. Title.

HANSON, Melvin B 248
Present your bodies. Springfield, Mo., Gospal Pub. House, c1955. 167p. 20cm. [BV4501.H2773] 56-17687
1. Christian life. I. Title.

HANSON, Oscar Conrad, 1908- 248
At your best. Minneapolis, Augsburgh Pub. House [c1956] 98p. 21cm. [BV4501.H2774] 56-7246
1. Christian life. I. Title.

HARDY, G. B. 248
Countdown: a time to choose, Chicago, Moody [1963] 79p. 19cm. 1.00 pap.,
I. Title.

*HARDY, G. B. 248
Countdown: a time to choose, Chicago, Moody [1968] 96p. 18cm. .60 pap.,
I. Title.

HARDY, Ray Morton. 248
High adventure. San Gabriel, Calif., Willing Pub. Co. [1954] 112p. 21cm. [BF639.H435] 54-43975
1. New Thought. I. Title.

HARKNESS, Georgia Elma, 1891- 248
The religious life; comprising these Hazen book classics: Religious living, by Georgia Harkness. Prayer and worship, by Douglas V. Steere. Christians in an unchristian society, by Ernest Fremont Tittle. New York, Association Press [1953] 1v. (various pagings) 19cm. [BV4495.H25] 53-7970
1. Christian life. 2. Prayer. 3. Worship. 4. Sociology, Christian. I. Steere, Douglas Van, 1901- Prayer and worship. II. Title. III. Title: Ernest Fremont, 1885-1949. Christians in an unchristian society.

HARKNESS, Georgia Elma, 1891- 248
Religious living; a revision of the classic Hazen book on religion. New York, Association Press [c1957] 126p. 16cm. (An Association Press reflection book) Includes bibliography. [BV4501.H2785 1957] 57-5496
1. Christian life. I. Title.

HARPER, Redd. 248
I walk the glory road. [Westwood, N. J.] F. H. Revell Co. [1957] 157p. illus. 22cm. [BV4935.H35A3] 57-9962
1. Converts. I. Title.

HARRIS, Marquis Lafayette, 248
1907-
Life can be meaningful. Boston, Christopher [1951] 195 p. 21 cm. [BV4501.H284] 51-4686
1. Christian life. I. Title.

HARRIS, Pierce. 248
Spiritual revolution. [1st ed.] Garden City, N. Y., Doubleday, 1952. 191 p. 20 cm. [BR525.H35] 52-10400
1. U. S.—Religion. 2. Civilization, Christian. I. Title.

HARRISON, Marie (Lemoine) 248
1880
God's good will. Narberth, Pa., Livingston Pub. Co., 1965. x, 102 p. 21 cm. Bibliographical footnotes. [BV4501.2.H36] 65-19376
1. Christian life. I. Title.

HARRISON, Marie (Lemoine) 248
1880-
God's good will. Narberth, Pa., Livingston [c.] 1965. x, 102p. 21cm. Bibl. [BV4501.2.H36] 65-19376 2.50
1. Christian life. I. Title.

HARRISON, Martin. 248
Credo; a practical guide to the Catholic faith [1st American ed.] Chicago, H. Regnery Co., 1954. 369p. 22cm. First published in England in 1947 under title: The everyday Catholic. [BX1754.H37 1954] 53-13012
1. Catholic Church—Doctrinal and controversial works, Popular. 2. Christian life—Catholic authors. I. Title.

HARRISON, Martin, 1884- 248
Credo; a practical guide to the Catholic faith. [1st American ed.] Chicago, H. Regnery Co., 1954. 369p. 22cm. First published in England in 1947 under title: The everyday Catholic. [BX1754.H37 1954] 53-13012
1. Catholic Church—Doctrinal and controversial works, Popular. 2. Christian life—Catholic authors. I. Title.

HART, Hornell Norris, 1888- 248
Your share of God; spiritual power for life fulfillment. Englewood Cliffs, N. J., Prentice-Hall, 1958. 216 p. illus. 24 cm. [BV4501.H327] 58-10642
1. Christian life. I. Title.

HASKIN, Dorothy (Clark), 248
1905-
Your questions answered. Chicago, Moody Press [1952] 128 p. 17 cm. (Colportage library, 223) [BR96.H34] 52-4343
1. Questions and answers—Theology. I. Title.

HAWKES, Ernest William, 1883- 248
Paths of peace. [1st ed.] New York, Exposition Press [1952] 166 p. 22 cm. [BV4580.H3] 52-9819
1. Old age—Religious life. I. Title.

HEFLEY, James C. 248
God on the gridiron [by] James C. Hefley. Grand Rapids, Zondervan Pub. House [1973] 141 p. ports. 18 cm. [BV4596.A8H39] 73-2662 1.25 (pbk.)
1. Athletes—Religious life. 2. Christian life—Stories. I. Title.

HEICK, Otto William. 248
Guide to Christian living. Philadelphia, Muhlenberg Press [1954] 229p. 20cm. [BV4501.H425] 54-9181
1. Christian life. 2. Christian ethics. I. Title. II. Title: Christian living.

HEIGES, Donald R. 248
The Christian's calling. Philadelphia, Muhlenberg [1962, c.1958] 114p. 18cm. Bibl. 1.00 pap.,
1. Vocation. I. Title.

HEINECKEN, Martin J 248
The moment before God. Philadelphia, Muhlenberg Press [1956] 386p. illus. 24cm. [BX4827.K5H4] 56-5642
1. Kierkegaard, Soren Aabye, 1813-1855. I. Title.

HENRY, Iona. 248
Triumph over tragedy [by] Iona Henry with Frank S. Mead. [Westwood, N. J.] F. H. Revell Co. [1957] 125p. 20cm. Autobiograhical. [BV4905.H4] 57-6852
1. Consolation. 2. Providence and government of God. I. Mead, Frank Spencer, 1898- II. Title.

HERCUS, John 248
Pages from God's case-book. Chicago, Inter-Varsity [c.1962] 142p. 18cm. 1.25 pap.,
I. Title.

HERHOLD, Robert M. 248
Funny, you don't look Christian, by Robert M. Herhold. With an afterword by William Robert Miller. Illus. by Roy Doty. New York, Weybright and Talley [1969] xi, 116 p. illus. 22 cm. [BV4517.H43 1969] 69-10603 3.95
1. Christian life—Stories. I. Doty, Roy, 1922- illus. II. Title.

HERMAN, Nicolas, 1611-1691-. 248
The practice of the presence of God, being conversations and letters of Nicholas Herman of Lorraine, Brother Lawrence. Translated from the French. [Westwood, N. J.] Revell [1958] 64p. 17cm. (A Revell inspirational classic) [BX2349.H42 1958] 58-10227
1. Christian life—Catholic authors. I. Title.

HERMAN, Nicolas, 1611-1691. 248
The practice of the presence of God, being conversations and letters of Nicholas Herman of Lorraine, Brother Lawrence. Tr. from French. New York, Pyramid [1966, c.1958] 64p. 17cm. (Little inspiration classic, LP14) [BX2349.H42 1958] .35 pap.,
1. Christian life—Catholic authors. I. Title.

HERSHBERGER, Merlin. 248
The endless quest. New York, Exposition Press [1951] 60 p. 22 cm. [BV4501.H44] 51-4500
1. Christian life. I. Title.

HIGHBAUGH, Irma, 1891- 248
We grow in the family; a study guide for family living. New York, Agricultural Missions, 1953. 215p. 23cm. [BV4526.H5] 53-34344
1. Family—Religious life. I. Title.

HINNEBUSCH, Paul. 248
Like the Word; to the Trinity through Christ. St. Louis, B. Herder Book Co. [1965] vi, 266 p. 21 cm. (Cross and crown series of spirituality, no. 29) Bibliographical footnotes. [BX2350.5.H56] 65-17849
1. Spiritual life — Catholic authors. I. Title. II. Series.

HINNEBUSCH PAUL 248
Like the word; to the Trinity through Christ St. Louis, B. Herder [c.1965] vi, 266p. 21cm. (Cross & crown ser. of spirtiuality, no. 29) Bibl. [BX2350.5.H56] 65-17849 4.50 bds.,
1, Spirtual life—Catholic authors. I. Title. II. Series.

HISTORY of Christian 248
spirituality; v.1 [by] Louis Bouyer [others. New York, Desclee, 1964, c.1963] v. 23cm. Contents.v.1. The spirituality of the New Testament and the fathers, by L. Bouyer. Bibl. 63-16487 9.50
1. Spiritual life—History of doctrines. I. Bouyer, Louis, 1913-

HOFFMAN, Hazel Ward. 248
Greater happiness. Philadelphia, Dorrance [1958] 104p. 20cm. [BV4501.H53433] 58-6875
1. Christian life. 2. Happiness. I. Title.

HOFRENNING, James B comp. 248
His hand upon me. Minneapolis, Augsburg Pub. House [1955] 127p. 20cm. Religious experiences of young people. [BV4495.H6] 55-7118
1. Christian life. I. Title.

HOLCOMB, Carlysle Henry. 248
Clearing the passageways. Dallas, Story Book Press [1951] 220 p. 20 cm. [BV4501.H53437] 51-14115
1. Christian life. I. Title.

HOLT, Turner Hamilton. 248
Life's convictions. [1st ed.] New York, Vantage Press [1956] 95p. 21cm. [BV4501.H53442] 56-5537
1. Christian life. I. Title.

HOLTERMANN, Carla. 248
Paths to happier living. Rock Island, Ill., Augustana Book Concern [1950] 63 p. 20 cm. [BV4501.H53443] 51-861
1. Christian life. I. Title.

HOLTERMANN, Carla. 248
Paths to peace. Minneapolis, Bible Banner Press [1956] 64p. 20cm. [BV4501.H53444] 56-44099
1. Christian life. I. Title.

HOPE, Mary. 248
Towards evening. New York, Sheed and Ward [1955] 178p. 21cm. [BX2372.H6] 55-9447
1. Aged—Religious life. I. Title.

THE How-to book : 248
loving God, loving others / edited by Jan P. Dennis. Westchester, Ill. : Good News Publishers, c1976. 153 p. ; 21 cm. [BV4501.2.H615] 76-17671 ISBN 0-89107-145-8 : 2.95
1. Christian life—1960- —Addresses, essays, lectures. I. Dennis, Jan P.
Contents omitted

HOWARD, Philip Eugene. 248
Bible light on daily life; editorial notes from the Sunday school times. Wheaton, Ill., Van Kampen Press [1951] 211 p. 20 cm. [BV4501.H5678] 51-12155
1. Christian life. I. Title.

HOWARD, Philip Eugene, 1898- 248
New every morning [by] Philip E. Howard, Jr. Illus. by James Howard. Introd. by Frank E. Gaebelein. [1st ed.] Grand Rapids, Mich., Zondervan Pub. House [1969] 187 p. illus. 21 cm. "Adapted from [the author's] Editorial notes in the Sunday school times." [BV4501.2.H63] 69-11650 3.95
1. Christian life—Addresses, essays, lectures. I. Title.

HOWE, Reuel L., 1905- 248
Man's need and God's action. Foreword by Theodore O. Wedel. Greenwich, Conn., Seabury Press, 1953. 159 p. 22 cm. [BR121.H68] 53-13368
1. Christianity—Essence, genius, nature. I. Title.

HUDNUT, Robert K. 248
A sensitive man and the Christ, by Robert K. Hudnut. Philadelphia, Fortress Press [1971] xii, 110 p. 18 cm. Includes bibliographical references. [BV4501.2.H74] 72-135268 2.50
1. Christian life—Presbyterian authors. 2. Emotions. I. Title.

HUDSON, Robert Lofton. 248
Growing a Christian personality. Nashville, Broadman Press [1956, c1955] 121p. 21cm. [BV4501.H722 1956] 56-3477
1. Christian life—Study and teaching. I. Title.

HUDSON, Robert Lofton. 248
The religion of a mature person. Nashville, Broadman Press [1952] 136 p. 20 cm. [BV4501.H723] 52-10136
1. Christian life. I. Title.

HUDSON, Robert Lofton. 248
Taproots for tall souls. Nashville, Broadman Press [1954] 148p. 21cm. [BV4501.H724] 54-10556
1. Christian life. 2. Psychology, Applied. I. Title.

HUEGEL, Frederick Julius, 248
1889-
Forever triumphant. Grand Rapids, Zondervan Pub. House [1955] 86p. 21cm. [BV4501.H7244] 55-39573
1. Christian life. I. Title.

HUEGEL, Frederick Julius, 248
1889-
Forever triumphant [by] F. J. Huegel. Minneapolis, Minn., Bethany Fellowship [1973, c.1955] 96 p. 18 cm. (Dimension Books) [BV4501.H7244] ISBN 0-87123-155-7 pap., 0.95
1. Christian life. I. Title.
L.C. card no. for 1955 edition: 55-39563.

HUGHES, Clarissa 248
The world today. New York, Carlton [c.1963] 67p. 21cm. (Reflection bk.) 2.00
I. Title.

HUMBERT, Russell J. 248
A man and his God; spiritual vitamins for men. New York, Abingdon-Cokesbury Press [1952] 124 p. 20 cm. [BV4501.H74] 52-5378
1. Christian life—Addresses, essays, lectures. I. Title.

HUNT, Dave. 248 B
Confessions of a heretic. Plainfield, N.J., Logos International, 1972. vi, 216 p. 21 cm. [BR1725.H8A3] 72-76590 ISBN 0-912106-28-X 4.95
1. Hunt, Dave. I. Title.

HUNTER, John Edward, 1909- 248
.
Limiting God; an analysis of Christian failure, with the sure answer for success, by John E. Hunter. Grand Rapids, Zondervan Pub. House [1966] 159 p. 22 cm. [BV4501.2.H85] 66-22554
1. Christian life. I. Title.

HUNTER, John Edward, 1909- 248
Limiting God; an analysis of Christian failure, with the sure answer for success. Grand Rapids, Mich. Zondervan [c.1966] 159p. 22cm. [BV4501.2.H85] 66-22554 2.50 bds.,
1. Christian life. I. Title.

HURLEY, Wilfred Geoffrey, 248
1895-.
Catholic devotional life, by Wilfred G. Hurley. [Boston] St. Paul Editions [1965] 148 p. 21 cm. [BX2350.2.H8] 65-17555
1. Spiritual life — Catholic authors. I. Title.

HURLEY, Wilfred Geoffrey, 248
1895-
Catholic devotional life [Boston] St. Paul Eds. [dist. Daughters of St. Paul c.1965] 148p. 21cm. [BX2350.H8] 65-17555 3.00;2.00 pap.,
1. Spiritual life—Catholic authors. I. Title.

HUSSLEIN, Joseph Casper, 248
1873-1952.
Channels of devotion. Milwaukee, Bruce Pub. Co. [1953] 221p. 23cm. [BV4815.H8] 53-2289
1. Devotion. I. Title.

HUYGHE, Gerard, Bp., 1909- 248
.
Growth in the Holy Spirit. Translated by Isabel and Florence McHugh. Westminister, Md., Newman Press, 1966. xiii, 200 p. 22 cm. First published under title: Conduits par l'Esprit. Bibliographical footnotes. [BX2350.5.H813] 66-17358
1. Spiritual life — Catholic authors. 2. Faith. I. Title.

HUYGHE, Gerard, Bp., 1909- 248
Growth in the Holy Spirit. Tr. [from French] by Isabel and Florence McHugh. Westminster, Md., Newman Pr. [c.]1966. xiii, 200p. 22cm. Bibl. [BX2350.5.H813] 66-17358 4.50
1. Spiritual life—Catholic authors. 2. Faith. I. Title.

ICE, Orva Lee. 248
Tomorrow is yours. Nashville, Abingdon-Cokesbury Press [1953] 153p. 20cm. [BV4310.I25] 52-11317
1. Youth— Religious life. 2. Baptists—Sermons. 3. Sermons, American. I. Title.

IKIN, Alice Graham, 1895- 248
Life, faith, and prayer. With an introductory note by Leslie D. Weatherhead. New York, Oxford University Press, 1954. 127p. 20cm. [BR110.I45] 54-6909
1. Christianity— Psychology. 2. Psychology, Pastoral. 3. Psychology, Applied. I. Title.

IKIN, Alice Graham, 1895- 248
Victory over suffering; glimpses into a mystery. Foreword by J. B. Philips. Introd. by Edward Ely. Great Neck, N. Y., Channel Press [1961] 144p. 21cm. [BV4909.I4 1961] 61-7572
1. Suffering. I. Title.

INESON, George, 1914- 248
Community journey. London, New York, Sheed and Ward [1956] 199p. illus. 21cm. [BX4668.I5 1956] 56-3887
1. Converts, Catholic. I. Title.

IRWIN, John Capps, 1896- 248
On being a Christian. Henry M. Bullock, general editor. New York, Abingdon Press [1958] 140p. 18cm. [BR121.I7] 58-1694
1. Christianity—Essence, genius, nature. 2. Christian life—Study and teaching. I. Title.

JABAY, Earl. 248
Search for identity; a view of authentic Christian living. Grand Rapids, Zondervan Pub. House [1967] 150 p. 22 cm. [BV4501.2.J3] 66-13693
1. Christian life. 2. Personality. I. Title.

JACKAWAY, Clarice M 248
The tapestry of life, a devotional guidebook, [1st ed.] New York, Exposition Press [1955] 160p. 21cm. [BV4501.J25] 55-9402
1. Christian life. I. Title.

*JACKSON, M. Violet 248
Spiritual truth . . . spiritual law. New York, Carlton [1967] 195p. 21cm. (Hearthstone bk.) 3.50
I. Title.

JACOBS, Margaret Branch 248
(Moore) 1901-
Happiness always. [Grand Rapids? 1957] 121p. 23cm. [BR1725.J32A35] 57-28031
I. Title.

JACOBS, Margaret Branch 248
(Moore), 1901-
The secret of a happy life. [Rock Island? Ill., 1952] 112 p. illus. 21 cm. [BR1725.J32A3] 52-8872
I. Title.

JACOBS, William Charles. 248
The catechism of life. Boston, Christopher Pub. House [1953] 90p. 21cm. [BR125.J2] 54-19598
1. Christianity—20th cent. 2. Questions and answers—Theology. I. Title.

JAMES, Ava Leach. 248
Devotions for juniors. Grand Rapids, Zondervan Pub. House [1955] 154p. 20cm. [BV4870.J3] 56-17701
1. Children—Prayer-books and devotions—English. I. Title.

JAMES, Ava Leach. 248
More devotions for juniors. Grand Rapids, Zondervan Pub. House [c1956] 152p. 20cm. [BV4870.J32] 57-23345
1. Children—Prayer-books and devotions—English. I. Title. II. Title: Devotions for juniors.

JAN VAN RUYSBROECK, 1293- 248
1381.
The spiritual espousals. Translated from the Dutch with an introd. by Eric Colledge. New York, Harper [1953] 195p. 21cm. (Classics of the contemplative life) [BV5080.J5273 1953] 149.3 53-1009
1. Mysticism—Middle Ages. I. Title.

JARMAN, W Maxey. 248
A businessman looks at the Bible [by] W. Maxey Jarman. Westwood, N.J., F. H. Revell Co. [1965] 159 p. 21 cm. [BV4596.B8J3] 65-14795
1. Businessmen—Religious life. I. Title.

JARMAN, W. Maxey 248
A businessman looks at the Bible. Westwood, N.J., Revell [c.1965] 159p. 21cm. [BV4596.B8J3] 65-14795 2.95 bds.,
1. Businessmen—Religious life. I. Title.

JAUNCEY, James H 248
This faith we live by; practical insights into the real meaning of Christian living. Grand Rapids, Zondervan Pub. House [1961] 157p. 21cm. [BV4501.2.J35] 61-1587
1. Christian life. I. Title.

JAUNCEY, James H 248
This power within; the Holy Spirit in action in the life of the Christian. Grand Rapids, Zondervan Pub. House [c1963] 115 p. 21 cm. [BV4501.2.J36] 63-15747
1. Christian life. I. Title.

JAUNCEY, James H. 248
This power within; the Holy Spirit in action in the life of the Christian. Grand Rapids, Mich., Zondervan [c.1963] 115p. 21cm. 63-15747 1.95
1. Christian life. I. Title.

JOANNES, Climacus, Saint, 248
6th cent.
The ladder of divine ascent. Translated by Archimandrite Lazarus Moore. With an introd. by M. Heppell. New York, Harper [1959] 270p. illus. 21cm. (Classics of the contemplative life) Errata leaf inserted. Bibliographical footnotes. [BX382.J613 1959a] 59-10331
1. Spiritual life—Orthodox Eastern authors. I. Title.

JOHN, Mike. 248
Think spiritually. [1st ed.] New York, Exposition Press [1954] 148p. 21cm. [BV4501.J49] 54-7046
1. Christian life. I. Title.

*JOHNSON, Carl G., Comp. 248
More story-telling programs. Grand Rapids, Mich., Baker Bk. [1966] 112p. 20cm. 1.50
I. Title.

JOHNSON, Mel. 248
Tips for teens. Grand Rapids, Zondervan Pub. House [c1956] 62p. illus. 20cm. [BV4531.J59] 57-2403
1. Youth—Religious life. I. Title.

JOHNSON, Orien. 248
Becoming transformed; [guidebook for personal renewal] Valley Forge, Pa., Judson Press [1973] 126 p. 22 cm. [BV4832.2.J615] 73-2546 ISBN 0-8170-0607-9 2.50
1. Christian life—1960- I. Title.

JOHNSTON, Fran. 248
Please don't strike that match; a young mother in today's world faces the fires of adversity. Grand Rapids, Mich., Zondervan Pub. House [1970] 133 p. 21 cm. Autobiographical. [BR1725.J64A33] 79-120049 3.50
I. Title.

JOHNSTON, William, 1925- 248
Christian Zen. [1st ed.] New York, Harper & Row [1971] viii, 109 p. 22 cm. [BR128.B8J64 1971] 77-149746 ISBN 0-06-064194-0 4.95
1. Christianity and other religions—Zen Buddhism. 2. Zen Buddhism—Relations—Christianity. I. Title.

JOHNSTON, William, 1925- 248
Christian Zen. New York, Harper & Row [1974, c1971] viii, 109 p. 18 cm. (A Colophon book) [BR128.B8J64 1974] ISBN 0-06-090368-6. 2.25 (pbk.)
1. Christianity and other religions—Zen Buddhism. 2. Zen Buddhism—Relations—Christianity. I. Title.
L.C. card number for original ed.: 77-149746.

JONES, Eli Stanley, 1884- 248
Conversion. New York, Abingdon Press [1959] 253 p. 20 cm. [BT780.J65] 59-10362
1. Conversion.

JONES, Elizabeth Brown, 1907- 248
Round about me; devotional thoughts for little folks. Anderson, Ind., Warner Press [1953] unpaged. illus. 29cm. [BV4870.J63] 53-12394
1. Children— Prayer-books and devotions—English. I. Title.

JONES, Elizabeth Brown, 1907- 248
Together with God; guidance for the Christian home when children are six to eight. Kansas City, Mo., Beacon Hill Press [1952] 158p. illus. 19cm. (Christian home series) [BV4571.J57] 52-11166
1. Children—Religious life. I. Title.

JONES, G Curtis. 248
What are you doing? St. Louis, Bethany Press [1956] 160p. 21cm. [BV4501.J5793] 56-6555
1. Christian life. I. Title.

JONES, Mary Alice, 1898- 248
The Lord's prayer; comments. Illus. by Dorothy Grider. Chicago, Rand McNally [c.1964] 45p. illus. (pt. col.) 24cm. 64-17446 2.00
1. Lord's prayer—Juvenile literature. I. Title.

JONES, Mary Alice, 1898- j248
Tell me about God's plan for me. Illustrated by Dorothy Grider. Chicago, Rand McNally [1965] 70 p. illus. (part col.) 27 cm. [BV4571.2.J64] 65-22218
1. Children—Religious life. I. Grider, Dorothy, illus. II. Title.

JONES, Mary Alice, 1898- 248
Tell me about God's plan for me. Illus. by Dorothy Grider. Chicago, Rand McNally [c.1965] 70p. illus. (pt. col.) 27cm. [BV4571.2.J64] 65-22218 2.95
1. Children—Religious life. I. Grider, Dorothy, illus. II. Title.

JONES, William Hubert, 1923- 248
Guide to Greetings! For teachers and leaders of preinduction discussion groups. Washington, National Catholic Community Service [1953] 128p. 22cm. [BV4457.J65] 54-27853
1. Soldiers—Religious life. 2. Discussions. I. O'Donnell, Thomas J. Greetings! II. Title. III. Title: Greetings. IV. Title: Pre-induction discussion groups.

JORDAN, Gerald Ray, 1896- 248
Beyond despair; when religion becomes real. New York, Macmillan, 1955. 166p. 21cm. [BV4501.J66] 55-14241
1. Spiritual life. I. Title.

JORDAN, William C 248
Practicing Christian psychology. [1st ed.] New York, Vantage Press [1958] 151p. illus. 21cm. [BR121.J666] 58-10658
1. Christianity—20th cent. I. Title.

JUD, Gerald John. 248
The shape of crisis and tragedy; an adult resource book [by] Gerald J. Jud. Boston, United Church Press [c1965] 124 p. illus. 21 cm. [BT732.7.J8] 65-14278
1. Suffering. I. Title.

KAVANAUGH, James J. 248
A journal for renewal, by James J. Kavanaugh. New York, Paulist [1967] x, 150p. 18cm. (Deus bks.) [BX2350.2.K3] 67-17790 .95 pap.,
1. Christian life—Stories. 2. Pastoral theology—Anecdotes, facetiae, satire, etc. I. Title.

KEAN, Charles Duell, 1910- 248
Making sense out of life. Philadelphia, Westminster Press [1954] 156p. 21cm. [BR121.K32] 54-9446

1. Christianity—Essence, genius, nature. I. Title.

KELLER, Helen 248
My religion. New York, Swedenborg Found. [1962] 208p. 18cm. 1.00
I. Title.

KELLER, James Gregory, 1900- 248
You can change the world! The Christopher approach. Garden City, N. Y., Halcyon House [1950, '1948] xx, 387 p. 21 cm. [BV4501.K4242 1950] 50-3344
1. Christian life. I. Title.

KELLER, James Gregory, 1900- 248
You can change the world! The Christopher approach. Garden City, N. Y., Permabooks [1951, '1948] 364 p. 17 cm. (Permabooks, [BV4501.K4242 1951] 52-22286
1. Christian life. I. Title.

KELPIEN, Lottie Stout. 248
Heart first. New York, Vantage Press [1954] 94p. 23cm. [BV4501.K42424] 54-9634
1. Christian life. I. Title.

KEMP, Charles F., 1912- 248
Prayer-based growth groups [by] Charles F. Kemp. Nashville, Abingdon Press [1974] 128 p. 20 cm. Bibliography: p. 122-128. [BV652.2.K45] 74-11174 ISBN 0-687-33369-5 2.95 (pbk.).
1. Church group work. 2. Prayers. I. Title.

KEMP, Mabel Duncan. 248
The you you want to be. St. Paul, Macalester Park Pub. Co. [1952] 155p. 22cm. [BV4501.K42428] 53-29146
1. Christian life. I. Title.

KEMPIN, Albert J, 1900- 248
How to live a Christian life; helps for converts. Anderson, Ind., Gospel Trumpet Co. [1950] 78 p. 19 cm. [BV4501.K4243] 50-35071
1. Christian life. I. Title.

KENNEDY, Gerald Hamilton, Bp., 1907- 248
The lion and the lamb; paradoxes of the Christian faith. New York, Abingdon-Cokesbury Press [1950] 233 p. 21 cm. [BR121.K343] 50-7627
1. Christianity—Essence, genius, nature. 2. Paradoxes. I. Title.

KEPLER, Thomas Samuel, 1897- 248
Religion for vital living. 1st ed. Cleveland, World Pub. Co. [1953] 113p. 21cm. [BV4501.K4248] 53-6634
1. Christian life. I. Title.

KERIGAN, Florence. 248
Inspirational talks for women's groups. Cincinnati, Standard Pub. Co. ['1951] 124 p. 19 cm. [BV4309.K4] 52-8283
1. Woman—Religious life. I. Title.

KEVAN, Ernest Frederick, 1903- 248
Going on in the Christian faith [by] Ernest F. Kevan. Grand Rapids, Baker Book House, 1964. 142 p. 20 cm. [BV4501.2.K48 1964] 64-23174
1. Christian life. 2. Conversion. I. Title.

KEYES, Frances Parkinson (Wheeler) 1885- 248
Along a little way. Introd. by Francis Beauchesne Thornton. New, rev. ed. New York, Hawthorn [c.1940, 1962] 126p. 19cm. 62-9033 2.50
1. Converts, Catholic. I. Title.

KIERKEGAARD, Sooren Aabye, 1813-1855. 248
Edifying discourses, a selection. Edited with an introd. by Paul L. Holmer. Translated by David F. and Lillian Marvin Swenson. New York, Harper [1958] 265 p. 21 cm. (Harper torchbooks, TB32) Contents.Contents.—The expectation of faith.—Every good and perfect thing is from above.—Love shall cover a multitude of sins.—The Lord gave and the Lord hath taken away, blessed by the name of the Lord.—Remember now thy Creator in the days of thy youth.—The expectation of an eternal happiness.—Man's need of God constitutes his highest perfection.—Love conquers all.—The narrowness is the way.—The glory of our common humanity.—The unchangeableness of God. [BV4505.K46 1958] 58-7107
1. Spiritual life. I. Title.

KIERKEGAARD, Soren Aabye, 1813-1855 248
Edifying discourses [2v.] Tr. from Danish by David F. Swenson, Lillian Marvin Swenson. Minneapolis, Augsburg [c.1943-1962] 2v. (239;253p.) 22cm. 62-53676 1.75 pap., ea.,
1. Spiritual life. I. Title.

KIERKEGAARD, Soren Aabye, 1813-1855. 248
For self-examination and Judge for yourselves! And three discourses, 1851, by Soren Kierkegaard: tr. by Walter Lowrie. Princeton, Princeton [1968] vii p., 5 1., [9]-243p. 21 cm. (115) First pub. in Great Britain, 1941. Reprinted by offset in the U.S.A., 1944. [BR100.K] A44 2.45 pap.,
1. Religion—Philosophy. 2. Lutheran church—Sermons. 3. Sermons, Danish—Translations into English. 4. Sermons, English—Translations from Danish. I. Lowrie, Walter, 1868- tr. II. Title. III. Title: Judge for yourselves!

KIERKEGAARD, Soren Aabye, 1813-1855. 248
The gospel of our sufferings; Christian discoures, being the third part of Edifying discourses in a different vein. published in 1847 at Copenhagen. Tr. from Danish by A. S. Aldworth. W. S. Ferrie. Grand Rapids, Mich., Eerdmans [1964] 150p. 20cm. 64-22016 1.45 pap.,
1. Spiritual life. 2. Affiction. I. Title.

KIERKEGAARD, Soren Aabye, 1813-1855. 248
Works of love; some Christian reflections in the form of discourses. Translated by Howard and Edna Hong. New York, Harper [1962] 383 p. 22 cm. [BV4505.K42 1962] 62-7293
1. Spiritual life. I. Title.

KIERKEGAARD, Soren Aabye, 1813-1855 248
Works of love; some Christian reflections in the form of discourses. Tr. by Howard and Edna Hong. Pref. by R. Gregor Smith. New York, Harper [1964, c.1962] 378p. 21cm. (Harper torchbks., TB122. Cloister lib.) Bibl. 64-7445 1.85 pap.,
1. Spiritual life. I. Title.

KIERKEGAARD, Soren Aabye, 1813-1855 248
Works of love; some Christian reflections in the form of discourses. Tr. by Howard and Edna Hong. Preface by R. Gregor Smith [Gloucester, Mass., P. Smith, 1965, c.1962] 378p. 21cm. (Harper torchbk., TB122. Cloister lib. rebound) Bibl. [BV4505] 3.85
1. Spiritual life. I. Title.

KING, William Peter, 1871- 248
How shall we meet troble? Nashville, Tenn., Parthenon Press [1953] 79p. 20cm. 'Companion volume to [the author's] The search for happiness.' Includes bibliography. [BV4596.A3K5] 53-37088
1. Affliction. I. Title.

KINNIBURGH, L B. 248
Lessons on the life of St. Paul. New York, Vantage Press [1952] 67 p. 22 cm. [BR126.K54] 52-9687
I. Title.

KLAUSLER, Alfred P 248
Christ and your job; a study in Christian vocation. Saint Louis, Mo., Concordia Pub. House [c1956] 145p. 19cm. Includes bibliography. [BV4740.K54] 56-9537
1. Vocation. I. Title.

KLEISER, Roy Hagan, 1883- 248
How to find the good life. New Orleans, Pelican Pub. Co. [1956] 103p. 22cm. [BV4501.K56] 56-45156
1. Christian I. Title.

KNAPP, Ida C. 248
Myself the challenger. New York, Island Press Cooperative [1952] 80 p. 22 cm. [BV5082.K6] 149.3 52-7187
1. Mysticism. I. Title.

KNOCK, Arthur Wilhelm, 1885- 248
Who's who in you; a short study of the old and new natures. [1st ed.] Minneapolis, Distributed by Bible Banner Press [1957] 97p. 20cm. [BV4511.K5] 57-13846
1. Christian life—Study and teaching. I. Title.

KNOTT, Luella (Pugh), 1871- 248
Keys to Christian living. Boston, W. A. Wilde Co. [1951] 248 p. 21 cm. [BV4501.K593] 51-14498
1. Christian life. I. Title.

KORFKER, Dena, 1908- 248
My Bible ABC book. Grand Rapids, Zondervan Pub. House [1952] 62 p. illus. 25 cm. [BV4870.K6] 52-42359
1. Children—Prayer-books and devotions—English. I. Title.

KRAMER, William Albert, 1900- 248
Living for Christ, a guide for the newly confirmed. Saint Louis, Concordia Pub. House [1952] 97 p. 14 cm. [BX8074.C7K7] 52-25951
1. Confirmation. 2. Youth—Religious life. I. Title.

KREML, Anne Lee. 248
Guidelines for parents. Lee's Summit, Mo., Unity Books [1967] 192 p. 20 cm. [BV4526.2K7] 67-11541
1. Family — Religious life. I. Title.

KREML, Anne Lee. 248
Guidelines for parents. Lee's Summit, Mo., Unity Books [1967] 192 p. 20 cm. [BV4526.2.K7] 67-11541
1. Family—Religious life. I. Title.

KROMMINGA, John H 1918- 248
You shall be my witnesses; a challenge to bashful Christians. Grand Rapids, Eerdmans, 1954. 84p. 23cm. [BV4520.K7] 54-4136
1. Witness bearing (Christianity) I. Title.

KUHLMANN, Edward, 1882- 248
Marks of distinction. Columbus, Ohio, Wartburg Press [1958] 161p. 20cm. [BV4501.K794] 58-11793
1. Christian life. I. Title.

KUHN, Isobel 248
Precious things of the lasting hills. Chicago, Moody [c.1963] 64p. 18cm. (China Inland Mission bk.; Compact bk., 42) .29 pap.,
I. Title.

KUNG, Hans, 1928- comp. 248
Life in the Spirit. New York, Sheed and Ward [1968] 157 p. 22 cm. (Theological meditations) Contents.Contents.—The one priesthood, by K. H. Schelkle.—Changes in Christian spirituality, by T. Sartory.—Celibacy, by M. Pfliegler. Bibliographical footnotes. [BX2350.2.K8] 68-14539
1. Spiritual life—Catholic authors. 2. Celibacy. I. Schelkle, Karl Hermann. Ihr alle seid Geistliche. English. 1965. II. Sartory, Thomas A. Wander christlicher Spiritualitat. English. 1968. III. Pfliegler, Michael, 1891- Der Zolibat. English. 1968. IV. Title.

*KVANDE, Carol 248
God speaks in daily work; summer bk., by Carol Kvande, Donna Paulson. Drawings by William K. Plummer. Gustav K. Wiencke, ed. Philadelphia, Lutheran Church Pr. [c.1965] 63p. illus. 21cm. (LCA Sunday church sch. ser.) .60 pap.,
I. Title.

LA Vie spirituelle. 248
Mystery and mysticism [by] A. Ple [and others] New York, Philosophical Library [1956] v. 137p. 22cm. First published in French as a special issue of La Vie spirituelle. Bibliographical footnotes. [BV5072.V5 1956a] [BV5072.V5 1956a] 149.3 56-4331 56-4331
1. Mysticism. I. Pie, Albert. II. Title.
Contents omitted.

LACY, Mary Lou. 248
A woman wants God. Richmond, John Knox Press [1959] 80p. 22cm. [BV4527.L25] 59-5120
1. Woman Religious life. I. Title.

LAMB, Clyde Kern, 1895- 248
The challenge to you. New York, B. Wheelwright Co., 1950. 159 p. port. 22 cm. [BR121.L3] 50-7934
1. Christianity—20th cent. I. Title.

LANE, Carlie. 248
I walk a joyful road [Introd. by Dale Evans Rogers] Westwood, N.J., F. Revell [1967] 110 p. 21 cm. [BV4935.L3] 67-22571
I. Title.

LANGENSTEIN, Rupert, 1910- 248
The constant cross. Milwaukee, Bruce Pub. Co. [1954] 109p. 23cm. [BX2350.L26] 54-8556
1. Christian life—Catholic authors. 2. Christianity in literature. I. Title.

LAREDO, Bernardino de, 1482-1545? 248
The ascent of Mount Sion, being the third book of the treatise of that name translated with an introduction and notes by E. Allison Peers. New York, Harper [1952] 275 p. 21 cm. (Classics of the contemplative life) [BV5080.L263 1952a] 52-4612
1. Mysticism. I. Title.

LARGE, John Ellis. 248
God is able: how to gain wholeness of life. Englewood Cliffs, N.J., Prentice-Hall [1963] 172 p. 21 cm. [BT732.5.L3] 63-11801
1. Faith-cure. I. Title.

LARGE, John Ellis 248
God is able: how to gain wholeness of life. Englewood Cliffs, N.J., Prentice [c.1963] 172p. 21cm. 63-11801 3.95
1. Faith-cure. I. Title.

LARSON, Bruce. 248
No longer strangers. Waco Tex., Word Books [1971] 145 p. 23 cm. [BV4501.2.L327] 74-146675 4.95
1. Christian life—Presbyterian authors. I. Title.

LARSON, Doris Linell. 248
Dear Lord; prayers for young people. Rock Island, Ill., Augustana Book Concern [1950] x, 102 p. illus. 19 cm. [BV283.Y6L3] 50-58275
1. Youth—Prayer-books and devotions—English. I. Title.

LASKY, William, 1921- 248
Tell it on the mountain / by William R. Lasky, with James F. Scheer. New York : Pocket Books, 1977,c1976. 257,[8]p. : ill. ; 18 cm. (A Kangaroo Book) [BV4935.L32A34] pbk. : 1.95
1. Lasky, William R., 1921- 2. Conversion. I. Scheer, James F., joint author. II. Title.
LC. card no. for 1976 Doubleday ed.:76-2998.

LASKY, William., 1921- 248
Tell it on the mountain / by William R. Lasky, with James F. Scheer. 1st ed. Garden City, N.Y. : Doubleday, 1976. viii, 271 p., [4] leaves of plates : ill. ; 22 cm. Autobiography. [BV4935.L32A34] 76-2998 ISBN 0-385-11366-8 : 7.95
1. Lasky, William R., 1921- 2. Conversion. I. Scheer, James F., joint author. II. Title.

LAUBACH, Frank Charles, 1884- 248
Channels of spiritual power. [Westwood, N. J.] Revell [1954] 186p. 21cm. [BV4501.L4] 54-9684
1. Christian life. I. Title.

LAUFERTY, Lilian, 1887- 248
God keeps an open house. [1st ed.] Indianapolis, Bobbs-Merrill [1952] 246 p. 21 cm. [BV4501.L4124] 52-6642
1. Christian life. I. Title.

LAW, William, 1686-1761. 248
The life of Christian devotion; devotional selections from the works of William Law. Ed. and introd. by Mary Cooper Robb. Nashville, Abingdon Press [c.1961] 158p. 61-8413 3.00
1. Devotional literature. I. Title.

LAW, William, 1686-1761. 248
A serious call to a devout and holy life. Edited and abridged for the modern reader by John W. Meister and others. With a foreword by D. Elton Trueblood. Philadelphia, Westminster Press [1955] 158p. 21cm. [BV4500.L3 1955] 55-5330
1. Christian life. I. Title.

LAWSON, William, S. J. 248
For goodness' sake, an informal treatise on being good. New York, Sheed and Ward, 1951. 184 p. 19 cm. [BX2350.L37] 51-9714
1. Christian life—Catholic authors. I. Title.

LAWSON, William, 1904- 248
For goodness' sake, an informal treatise on being good. New York, Sheed and Ward, 1951. 184p. 19cm. [BX2350.L37] 51-2714
1. Christian life—Catholic authors. I. Title.

LAWSON, William, 1904- 248
Person to person, a recipe for living. London, New York, Longmans, Green [1958, c1957] 234p. 19cm. Includes bibliography. [BX2350.L38] 58-899
1. Christian life—Catholic authors. 2. Interpersonal relations. I. Title.

LAZARETH, William Henry, 1928- 248
Man: in whose image. Philadelphia, Muhlenberg Press [1961] 54p. 19cm. (A Fortress book) [BV4501.2.L37] 61-13581
1. Christian life. I. Title.

LEAHY, J Kenneth. 248
As the eagle; the spiritual writings of Mother Butler, R. S. H. M., foundress of Marymount, by a Carmelite pilgrim. New York, P. J. Kenedy [c1954] 206p. 21cm. [BX2350.B882L4] 54-11236
1. Butler, Marie Joseph, Mother, 1860-1940. 2. Spiritual life—Catholic authors. I. Title.

LE BAR, Mary Evelyn, 1910- 248
Living in God's family; for boys and girls who know the Savior. Wheaton, Ill., Scripture Press, c1957. 34p. illus. 23x27cm. [BV4571.L4] 58-40622
1. Children—Religious life. I. Title.

LECLERQ, Jacques, 1891- 248
Approaches to the cross. Tr. from French by the Earl of Wicklow. New York, Macmillan, 1963. 115p. 20cm. 63-5310 2.50 bds.,
1. Suffering. I. Title.

LEE, Frederick. 248
Thoughts of peace. Washington, Review and Herald Pub. Association [1950] 95 p. 20 cm. [BV4647.P35L4] 50-4999
1. Peace (Theology) I. Title.

LESLIE, Robert Campbell, 1917- 248
Sharing groups in the Church; an invitation to

involvement [by] Robert C. Leslie. Nashville, Abingdon Press [1971] 221 p. 20 cm. Bibliography: p. 212-213. [BV652.2.L45] 79-138277 ISBN 0-687-38346-3 2.95
1. Church group work. I. Title.

LEUTY, Joseph D 1909- 248
In God we trust; everyday essays on life and philosophy. [1st ed.] New York, Exposition Press [1956] 84p. 21cm. [BV4637.L46] 56-12680
1. Trust in God. I. Title.

LEVI, Anthony 248
Religion in practice; an outline of Christian religious teaching in the light of the religious relevance of humane standards of conduct. [1st ed.] New York, Harper [1966] xii, 208p. 22cm. Bibl. [BR121.2.L4 1966] 66-20791 6.00
1. Christianity—Essence, genius, nature. I. Title.

LEWIS, Alice Hudson. 248
Always an answer. New York, Friendship Press [1958] 86p. illus. 21cm. Includes bibliography. [BV4531.L37] 58-7039
1. Christian life—Stories. 2. Youth—Religious life. I. Title.

LEWIS, Clive Staples, 1898- 248
Surprised by joy; the shape of my early life. [1st American ed.] New York, Harcourt, Brace [1956, c1955] 238p. 22cm. [BV4935.L43A3 1956] 56-5329
1. Converts. I. Title.

LEWIS, Clive Staples, 1898- 248
1963
Surprised by joy; the shape of my early life. [1st Amer. ed.] New York, Harcourt, [1967, c.1955] 238p. 22cm. [BV4935.L43A3 1956] 1.65 pap.,
1. Converts. I. Title.

LEWIS, Clive Staples, 1898- 248
1963.
Surprised by joy; the shape of my early life. [1st American ed.] New York, Harcourt, Bruce [1956, c1955] 238 p. 22 cm. [BV4935.L43A3 1956] 56-5329
1. Converts, Anglican. I. Title.

LEWIS, Norman 248
'Go ye' means you! and other missionary messages. Introd. by Rev. Albert D. Helser. Chicago, Moody [1963, c.1962] 128p. 17cm. (Colportage lib., 497) .39 pap.,
I. Title.

LIN, Yutang, 1895- 248
From pagan to Christian. New York, Avon [1962, c.1959] 224p. 16cm. (S-109) .60 pap.,
1. Converts. I. Title.

LIN, Yutang, 1895- 248
From pagan to Christian. [1st ed.] Cleveland, World Pub. Co. [1959] 251 p. illus. 22 cm. [BV4935.L5A3] 59-11534
1. Converts. I. Title.

LINK, Bessie A 248
Truth is everybody's business. Brooklyn, G. J. Rickard [1958] 100p. 22cm. [BT50.L55] 58-13152
I. Title.

LINK, Helen Kendall, 1911- 248
Our Father; thoughts and prayers for children. Illus. by Harold Minton. Philadelphia, Christian Education Press [1952] 96 p. illus. 23 cm. [BV4571.L52] 52-29137
1. Children—Religious life. I. Title.

LINTZ, Harry McCormick. 248
Obligations of Christians to one another. Wheaton, Ill., Van Kampen Press [1951] 61 p. 20 cm. [BV4501.L48] 51-8687
1. Christian life. I. Title.

LIPTAK, David Q., Rev. 248
All about fast and abstinence. New York, Paulist Press [1960] 32p. 19cm. .15 pap.,
I. Title.

LLOYD, Marjorie Lewis. 248
Flickering desire. Washington, Review and Herald [1953] 95p. 21cm. [BV4531.L47] 54-1210
1. Youth—religious life. I. Title.

LOCHET, Louis. 248
Son of the Church. Translated by Albert J. LaMothe, Jr. Chicago, Fides Publishers Association [1956] 255p. 21cm. [BX1751.L8313] 56-11628
1. Catholic Church. 2. Christian life—Catholic authors. I. Title.

*LONG, Mildred Withers 248
The naked church. New York, Vantage [c.1966] 199p. 21cm. Bibl. 3.95
I. Title.

LONG, Nat G 248
Goal posts; talks to young people on building a sound, successful life in today's troubled world. Atlanta, Tupper & Love [1953] 162p. 22cm. [BV4531.L555] 53-1532
1. Youth—Religious life. I. Title.

LONSDALE, Kathleen (Yardley) 248
1903-
I believe... by Kathleen Lonsdale. Cambridge [Eng.] University Press, 1964. 56 p. 19 cm. [Arthur Stanley Eddington memorial lecture, 18) Delivered 6 November 1964. Bibliography: p. 58. [BX7795.L65A3] 65-588
1. Religion and science — 1946- I. Title. II. Series.

LONSDALE KATHLEEN (YARDLEY) 248
1903-
I believe . . . [New York] Cambridge [c.]1964. 56p. 19 cm. (Arthur Stanley Eddington memorial lect. 18) Bibl. [BX7795.L65A3] 65-588 .95 pap.,
1. Religion and science—1946- I. Title. II. Series.

LOUTTIT, Henry Irving, Bp., 248
1903-
Fear not. Foreword by Austin Pardue. Greenwich, Conn., Seabury Press, 1954. 65p. 20cm. Includes bibliography. [BV4637.L66] 54-9582
1. Trust in God. 2. Fear. I. Title.

LOVASIK, Lawrence George, 248
1913-
Stepping stones to sanctity; practical hints for religious and lay people. New York, Macmillan, 1951. 151 p. 21 cm. [BX2350.L7] 51-10213
1. Christian life—Catholic authors. I. Title.

LOVASIK, Lawrence George, 248
1913-
Stepping stones to sanctity; practical hints for religious and lay people. New York, Macmillan, 1951. 151p. 21cm. [BX2350.L7] 51-10213
1. Christian life—Catholic authors. I. Title.

LOWE, Arnold Hilmar, 1888- 248
Power for life's living. [1st ed.] New York, Harper [1954] 190p. 22cm. [BV4501.L6] 54-6898
1. Christian life. I. Title.

LUCCOCK, Halford Edward, 248
1885-
Living without gloves; more letters of Simeon Stylites [pseud.] New York, Oxford University Press, 1957. 181p. 20cm. [BR125.L873] 57-10385
1. Christianity—Addresses, essays, lectures. I. Title.

LUNDQUIST, Amos Theodore, 248
1896-
God, my exceeding joy. Rock Island, Ill., Augustana Press [1956] 145p. 21cm. [BV4501.L853] 56-13849
1. Christian life. I. Title.

MACARTNEY, Clarence Edward 248
Noble, 1879-1957
Wrestlers with God; prayers of the Old Testament. Grand Rapids, Mich., Baker Bk. 1963[c.1958] 207p. 20cm. (Evangelical pulpit lib.) 63-12029 2.95
1. Bible—Prayers. 2. Bible. O. T.—Biog. I. Title.

MCCLAIN, Roy O 248
This way, please; facing life's crossroads. [Westwood, N.J.] Revell [1957] 217p. 22cm. [BV4501.M158] 57-13150
1. Christian life. I. Title.

MCCONNELL, Dorothy Frances 248
Guide to three spiritual classics: Christian perfection, by Francois Fenelon. Christian perfection, by John Wesley. The spiritual life, by Evelyn Underhill. For use with the text Teachings toward Christian perfection, by Olive Wyon. New York, Woman's Div. of Christian Serv., Bd. of Missions, Methodist Church [1963] 68 p. 20 cm. Bibl. 63-14252 apply
1. Fenelon, Francois de Salignac de La Mothe-, Abp., 1651-1715. Instructions et avis. 2. Wesley, John, 1703-1791. Christian perfection. 3. Underhill, Evelyn, 1875-1941. The spiritual life. 4. Spiritual life—Outlines, syllabi, etc. I. Title.

MCDANIEL, Mabel C. 248
God's great plan of salvation. New York, Pageant [c.1963] 164p. 21cm. 2.50
I. Title.

MCDANIELS, Geraldine 248
God is the answer [2d ed] New York, Vantage 1966 c.1962,1965 118 p. 21 cm bds. 2.50
I. Title.

MCDONALD, Claude C. 248
There's comfort in His love [by] Claude C. McDonald, Jr. Old Tappan, N.J., Revell [1970] 160 p. 21 cm. [BV45011.2.M226] 70-123062 3.95
1. Christian life—Disciples of Christ authors. 2. Consolation. I. Title.

MCDONNELL, Kilian. 248
The restless Christian. New York, Sheed and Ward [1957] 183p. 21cm. [BX2350.M143] 57-10183
1. Christian life—Catholic author. I. Title.

MCDONNELL, Killan. 248
Nothing but Christ; a Benedictine approach to lay spirituality. [St. Meinrad, Ind.,]Grail [1953] 185p. 21cm. [BX2350.M14] 53-12934
1. Spiritual life—Catholic authors. I. Title.

MCEACHERN, Ted. 248
Being there for others. Nashville, Abingdon Press [1967] 158 p. illus. 19 cm. Bibliography: p. 157-158. [BV4501.2.M23] 67-24330
1. Stewardship, Christian. 2. Christian life—Methodist authors. I. Title.

*MCELVANY, Harold. 248
Are Americans a chosen people? New York, Vantage [1968] 80p. 20cm. 2.50 bds.,
I. Title.

MCGRADE, Francis. 248
The Rosary for little Catholics; illustrated by Bruno Frost. St. Paul, Catechetical Guild Educational Society, c1952. unpaged. illus. 17cm. [BX2163.M26] 53-15935
1. Rosary—Juvenile literature. I. Title.

MCSORLEY, Joseph, 1874- 248
Common sense. Milwaukee, Bruce Pub. Co. [1957] 136p. 21cm. [BX2350.M213] 57-12563
1. Christian life— Catholic authors. I. Title.

MAGUIRE, John David 248
The dance of the pilgrim; a Christian style of life for today. New York, Association [1967] 128p. 18cm. Originated as a set of lects. . . . delivered . . . at the 73rd annual Northfield, Mass. Conf. for Girls. June 17-23, 1966. Bibl. [BT60.M3] 67-14587 3.50; 1.75 pap.,
1. Christianity—Essence, genius, nature. I. Title.

MANN, Stella Terrill. 248
Change your life through faith and work! New York, Dodd, Mead [1953] 152p. 20cm. [BV4637.M3] 52-14113
1. Trust in God. I. Title.

MANN, Stella Terrill. 248
How to analyze and overcome your fears. New York, Dodd, Mead [1962] 179p. 21cm. [BV4908.5.M33] 61-15984
1. Peace of mind. I. Title.

MANN, Stella Terrill 248
How to analyze and overcome your fears. New York [Apollo Eds., 1965, c.1962] vii, 179p. 20cm. (A113) [BV4908.5.M33] 1.50 pap.,
1. Peace of mind. I. Title.

MARIE DE LA TRINITE, Sister, 248
1901-1942.
The spiritual legacy of Sister Mary of the Holy Trinity, Poor Clare of Jerusalem (1901-1942) Edited by Silvere van den Broek; translated from the French. Westminster, Md., Newman Press, 1950. 364 p. illus., port. 19 cm. Secular name: Louisa Jacques. [BV5082.M342] 50-4895
1. Mysticism. I. Broek, Silvere van den, 1880-1949, ed. II. Title.

MARITAIN, Jacques 248
Liturgy and contemplation [by] Jacques and Raissa Maritain. Translated from the French by Joseph W. Evans. New York, P. J. Kenedy [c.1960] 96p. 21cm. (bibl. footnotes) 60-7788 2.95
1. Contemplation. 2. Catholic Church. Liturgy and ritual. I. Maritain, Raissa, joint author. II. Title.

MARITAIN, Jacques, 1882- 248
Liturgy and contemplation [by] Jacques and Raissa Maritain. Translated from the French by Joseph W. Evans. New York, P. J. Kenedy [1960] 96p. 21cm. Includes bibliography. [BV5091.C7M313] 60-7788
1. Contemplation. 2. Catholic Church. Liturgy and ritual. I. Maritain, Raissa, joint author. II. Title.

MARTIN, William Ivan, 1916- 248
Thank you, God, by Bill and Bernard Martin in collaboration with Mary Amams. Kansas City, Mo., Tell-Well Press, c1952. unpaged. illus. 27cm. [BV265.M32] 53-2189
1. Children—Prayer-books and devotions—English. I. Martin, Bernard Herman, 1912- joint author. II. Title.

MARVIN, Dwight, 1880- 248
The faith I found; a layman looks at religion. New York, Crowell [c1954] 149p. 20cm. [BR121.M418] 54-5529
1. Christianity—20th cent. I. Title.

MARY, pseud. 248
All that you are. Los Angeles, DeVorss [1959] 210p. 22cm. [BX639.M36] 60-616
1. New Thought. 2. Reincarnation. I. Title.

MARY, pseud. 248
All that you are. Los Angeles, DeVorss [c.1959] 210p. 22cm. 60-616 3.50
1. New Thought. 2. Reincarnation. I. Title.

MASHECK, Charles L. 248
You and others ed. by Philip R. Hoh. Illus. by Noel G. Miles, Jr. Philadelphia, Lutheran Church Pr. 1966. 103 p. (LCA sunday sch. ser) pap. 1.00 teacher's ed. pap. 1.25
I. Title.

MASTON, Thomas Bufford, 1897- 248
Right or wrong? Nashville, Broadman Press [1955] 146p. 21cm. [BV4531.M29] 55-14633
1. Youth—Religious life. 2. Christian ethics. I. Title.

MATTHEWS, John Vincent, 1895- 248
The life that is grace. Westminster, Md., Newman Press, 1953. 196p. 23cm. [BX2350.M38] 53-7493
1. Christian life—Catholic authors. I. Title.

MAVES, Paul B. 248
The best is yet to be. Philadelphia, Westminster Press [1951] 96 p. 20 cm. (The Westminster pastoral aid books) [BV4580.M35] 51-9868
1. Old age. I. Title.

MAXIMUS Confessor, Saint, 580 248
(ca.)- 662.
The ascetic life. The four centuries on charity. Translated and annotated by Polycarp Sherwood. Westminster, Md., Newman Press, 1955. viii, 284p. 23cm. (Ancient Christian writers; the works of the Fathers in translation. no. 21) Bibliography: p. 211-213. [BR60.A35 no. 21] 55-8642
1. Asceticism—Early church. I. Maximus Confessor, Saint, 580 (ca.)-662. The four centuries on charity. II. Title. III. Title: The four centuries on charity. IV. Series.

MAXWELL, L E 248
Abandoned to Christ. [1st ed.] Grand Rapids, Eerdmans, 1955. 248p. 22cm. [BV4501.M4613] 55-13725
1. Christian life. I. Title.

*MAYNARD, Aurora 248
The inner guidance. New York, Vantage [c.1965] 116p. 21cm. 2.75 bds.,
I. Title.

MEABON, Vera Van Eman, 1893- 248
Life and you; a memoir but also a commentary on life. Falconer, N.Y., c1951. 222 p. 22 cm. [BR121.M45] 52-17424
1. Christianity — 20th cent. I. Title.

MEARS, Henrietta Cornelia, 248
1890-
431 quotes from the notes of Henrietta C. Mears. Compiled by Eleanor L. Doan. Glendale, Calif., G/L Regal Books [1970] 104 p. 18 cm. [BV4513.M4 1970] 72-134583 1.25
1. Christian life—Quotations, maxims, etc. I. Title.

MENZIES, Robert. 248
Fight the good fight; studies in the Christian life. Nashville, Abingdon-Cokesbury Press [1953, label 1949] 173p. 20cm. [BV4501.M4625] 52-11313
1. Christian life. I. Title.

MERRELL, James L. 248
They live their faith; portraits of men and women with a mission, by James L. Merrell. St. Louis, Bethany Press [1965] 143 p. 20 cm. [BX7341.M46] 65-12290
1. Disciples of Christ — Biog. I. Title.

MERRELL, James L. 248
They live their faith; portraits of men and women with a mission, by James L. Merrell. St. Louis, Bethany [c.1965] 143p. 20cm. [BX7341.M46] 65-12290 1.50 pap.,
1. Disciples of Christ—Biog. I. Title.

MERTON, Thomas, 1915- 248
No man is an island. New York, Doubleday [1967,c.1955] 197p. 18cm. (Image bk., D231) [BX2350.M535] .95 pap.,
1. Spiritual life—Catholic authors. I. Title.

MERTON, Thomas, 1915-1968. 248
No man is an island. [1st ed.] New York, Harcourt, Brace [1955] 264 p. 22 cm. [BX2350.M535] 55-7420
1. Spiritual life—Catholic authors. I. Title.

MESERVE, Harry C 248
No peace of mind. [1st ed.] New York, Harcourt, Brace [1958] 181p. 21cm. [BV4908.5.M4] 58-10902

1. Peace of mind. I. Title.

MEYER, Bernard F 1891- 248
Lend me your hands. Chicago, Fides Publishers [1955] 293p. 21cm. [BX2348.M38] 55-7898
1. Catholic action. I. Title.

MICHAEL, Chester P. 248
The new day of Christianity [by] Chester P. Michael. Baltimore, Helicon [1965] 189 p. 21 cm. [BX2350.5.M5] 65-15042
1. Spiritual life — Catholic authors. I. Title.

MICHAEL, Chester P. 248
The new day of Christianity. Helicon[dist. New York, Taplinger, c.1965] 189p. 21cm. [BX2350.5.M5] 65-15042 4.50 bds.,
1. Spiritual life—Catholic authors. I. Title.

MIDDLETON, Robert Lee, 1894- 248
Don't disappoint God! Challenging you to live more abundantly. Nashville, Broadman Press [1951] 174 p. 21 cm. [BV4531.M463] 51-13803
1. Youth — Religious life. I. Title.

MILES, Mary Lillian. 248
Quiet moments with God. Winona Lake, Ind., Light and Life Press [1957] unpaged. 23cm. [BV4870.M5] 57-41494
1. Children—Prayer-books and devotions—English. I. Title.

MILHOUSE, Paul William, 1910- 248
Doorways to spiritual living. [Dayton? Ohio, 1950] 158 p. 20 cm. [BV4501.M513] 50-29277
1. Spiritual life. I. Title.

MILLER, Harvey N 248
Good cheer. Shawnee, Printed by Oklahoma Baptist University Press [c1950] 170 p. 20 cm. Essays and poems. [BV4501.M537] 51-21145
1. Christian life. I. Title.

MILLER, Keith. 248
The taste of new wine. Waco, Tex., Word Books [1966, c1965] 116 p. 21 cm. Sequel: A second touch. [BR1725.M45A5] 65-9347
I. Title.

MILLER, Osborne Theodore, comp. 248
The path of prayer, an anthology. Foreword by William E. Wilson. New York, Harper [1954] 159p. 21cm. [BV205] 54-8467
1. Prayer. I. Title.

MILLER, Randolph Crump, 1910- 248
Be not anxious. Greenwich, Conn., Seabury Press, 1957. 237p. 22cm. [BV4501.M5875] 57-5736
1. Chiistian life. 2. Anxiety. I. Title.

MILLER, Samuel Howard, 1900- 248
The life of the soul [1st ed.] New York, Harper [1951] 158 p. 20 cm. [BV4501.M59] 51-12236
1. Christian life. I. Title.

MILLER KEITH 248
The taste of new wine. Waco, Tex., World Bks. [c.1965] 116p. 21cm. [BR1725.M45T3] 65-9347 2.50
I. Title.

MINDSZENTY, Jozsef, Cardinal, 1892- 248
The face of the Heavenly Mother. New York, Philosophical Library [1951] 150 p. 22 cm. Translation, by Charles Donahue, of Mutter in Gottes Augen, originally published in Hungarian as v. 2 of Az edesanya. Name originally: Jozsef Pehm. [BX2353.M553] 51-14179
1. Mothers. I. Title.

MOFFATT, John Edward, 1894- 248
Ave Maria; thoughts on the mysteries of the holy rosary. Milwaukee, Bruce Pub. Co. [1957] 64p. 18cm. [BX2163.M55 1957] 57-543
1. Rosary. I. Title.

MONSMA, John Clover, ed. 248
This I believe about Jesus Christ; the personal testimonies of leading Americans. [Westwood, N. J.] F. H. Revell Co. [c1955] 189p. 21cm. [BV4520.M58] 55-5389
1. Witness bearing (Christianity) I. Title.

MONTGOMERY, Saphronia Geodwin. 248
The Christian woman, a religious miscellany. [1st ed.] New York, Exposition Press [c1954] 58p. 21cm. [BV4527.M6] 54-12284
1. Woman Religious life. 2. Church work—Addresses, essays, lectures. I. Title.

MOON, Floyce (Orr) j248
A horse named Amber [by] Floyce Moon. [Teacher's ed.] Nashville, Convention Press [1965] ix, 97 p. illus. 19 cm. "Helps for the teacher": [(15] p.) bound between p. 46-47. [BV772.M54] 65-15603
1. Stewardship, Christian — Juvenile literature. I. Title.

MOORE, Elton E 1912- 248
God's little crumbs. [1st ed.] New York, Greenwich Book Publishers [1964] 54 p. 21 cm. [BV4501.2.M577] 61-15100
1. Christian life. I. Title.

MOORE, J. Phillips, 1895- 248
Let not your heart be troubled. New York, Vantage Press [1951, c1950] 75 p. 23 cm. [BV4501.M752] 51-10082
1. Christian life. I. Title.

MOORE, Thomas Hendrick, 1898- 248
The morning offering. New York, Apostleship of Prayer, 1952. 162 p. 21 cm. [BV210.M755] 52-8062
1. Prayer. 2. Apostleship of prayer. I. Title.

MOORE, Thomas Verner, 1877- 248
Heroic sanctity and insanity; an introduction to the spiritual life and mental hygiene. New York, Grune & Stratton, 1959. 243p. 23cm. Includes bibliography. [BX2350.2.M64] 59-7827
1. Spiritual life—Catholic authors. 2. Psychiatry and religion. I. Title.

MOORE, Thomas Verner, 1877- 248
The life of man with God. [1st ed.] New York, Harcourt, Brace [1956] 402p. 22cm. [BX2350.M73] 56-7919
1. Spiritual life—Catholic authors. I. Title.

MOORE, Thomas Verner [name in religion: Father Pablo Maria] 1877- 248
Heroic sanctity and insanity; an introduction to the spiritual life and mental hygiene. New York, Grune [1964, c.1959] 243p. 23cm. Bibl. 59-7827 5.00
1. Spiritual life—Catholic authors. 2. Psychiatry and religion. I. Title.

MORGAN, Dewi. ed. 248
They became Anglicans; the story of sixteen converts and why they chose the Anglican Communion. With an introd. by the Bishop of Peterborough. New York, Morehouse-Barlow Co. [1959] ix, 177p. 20cm. 60-879 2.25 bds.,
1. Converts. Anglican. I. Title.

MOUROUX, Jean. 248
The Christian experience; an introduction to a theology. Translated by George Lamb. New York, Sheed and Ward, 1954. 370p. 22cm. [BX2350.M763] 54-11143
1. Christian life— Catholic authors. 2. Experience (Religion) I. Title.

MUDGE, Lewis Seymour. 248
In His service; the Servant Lord and His servant people. Philadelphia, Westminster Press [1959] 176 p. 21 cm. [BR121.2.M8] 59-10282
1. Christianity—Essence, genius, nature. 2. Presbyterian Church—Doctrinal and controversial works. I. Title.

MUEDEKING, George H 248
Emotional problems and the Bible.. Philadelphia, Muhlenberg Press [c1956] 188p. 20cm. [BV4012.M76] 55-11317
1. Psychology, Pastoral. I. Title.

MUELLER, Francis John, 1894- 248
The faith in action. Milwaukee, Bruce [1952] 164 p. 22 cm. [BX2350.M794] 52-3905
1. Christian life — Catholic authors. I. Title.

MUGGERIDGE, Malcolm, 1903- 248
Jesus rediscovered. Garden City, N.Y., Doubleday, 1969. xvi, 217 p. 22 cm. [BR85.M77] 71-86888 5.95
1. Christianity—Addresses, essays, lectures. I. Title.

MULLINS, Eustace Clarence, 1923- 248
My life in Christ, by Eustace Mullins. Staunton, Va., Faith and Service Books, Aryan League of America [1968] 90 p. 22 cm. [CT275.M723A3] 68-25403
I. Title.

MURPHY, John L 1924- 248
In the image of Christ. Milwaukee, Bruce [1954] 169p. 23cm. [BV4501.M795I5] 54-9868
1. Christian life —Catholic authors. I. Title.

MURRAY, Andrew, 1828-1917. 248
The treasury of Andrew Murray. Introd. by Ralph G. Turnbull. Westwood, N.J., F. H. Revell Co. [1952] 255 p. 21 cm. [BV4501.M8T65] 52-4966
1. Spiritual life. I. Title.

MURRAY, John, 1915- 248
The daily life of the Christian. New York, Philosophical Library [1955] 127p. 20cm. [BV4501.M815D3 1955] 55-14496
1. Christian life. I. Title.

NASH, Gerald R. 248
Investment, the miracle offering, by Gerald R. Nash, Lois M. Parker. Mountain View, Calif., Pacific Pr. [c.1965] xii, 146p. illus. 22cm. [BV772.N3] 65-21139 3.25
1. Stewardship, Christian. I. Parker, Lois M., joint author. II. Title.

NASH, Gerald R. 248
Investment, the miracle offering, by Gerald R. Nash and Lois M. Parker. Mountain View, Calif., Pacific Press Pub. Association [1965] xii, 146 p. illus. 22 cm. [BV772.N3] 65-21139
1. Stewardship, Christian. I. Parker, Lois M, joint author. II. Title.

NASH, Robert. 248
Living your faith. [1st American ed.] New York, Prentice-Hall [1951] 311 p. 22 cm. "Originally published [1949] in Ireland under the title: Is life worthwhile?" [BX2350.N28] 51-1977
1. Christian life — Catholic authors. I. Title.

NASH, Robert 248
Living your faith. New York A Catechetical Guild book published by Guild Press. Inc. Dist. by Golden Press, [1959, c.1951] 415p. 17cm. (1175) .50 pap.,
1. Christian life—Catholic authors. I. Title.

NAVONE, John J. 248
Communicating Christ / [by] John Navone. Slough : St Paul Publications, 1976. viii, 239 p. ; 21 cm. Includes bibliographical references and indexes. [BV4319.N38] 77-350367 ISBN 0-85439-127-4 : £3.50
1. Communication (Theology) I. Title.

NAYLOR, Charles Wesley, 1874-1950. 248
The secret of the singing heart. Rev. and abridged. Anderson, Ind., Warner Press [1954] 127p. 20cm. [BV4501.N28 1954] 54-37087
1. Christian life. I. Title.

NAYLOR, Charles Wesley, 1874-1950. 248
The secret of the singing heart [by] C. W. Naylor. [Rev. and abridged ed.] Anderson, Ind., Warner Press [1974, c.1954] 126 p. 18 cm. (Portal Books) [BV4501.N28] 54-37087 1.25 (pbk.)
1. Christian life. I. Title.

NEE, Watchman. 248
The normal Christian church life. [Rev. ed.] Washington, International Students Press [c1962] 128 p. 22 cm. [BV4501.2.N4 1962] 67-4661
1. Christian life. I. Title.

*NELSON, Ruby 248
The door of everything. Los Angeles, DeVorss [c.1963] 180p. 17cm. 3.00
I. Title.

NELSON, Ruth Youngdahl. 248
Where Jesus walks. Minneapolis, Augsburg Pub. House [1966] xi, 144 p. 21 cm. [BV4501.2.N45] 66-22558
1. Christian life. I. Title.

NELSON, Ruth Youngdahl. 248
The woman beautiful; ten programs for women's organizations. Rock Island, Ill., Augustana Book Concern [1954] 96p. 20cm. [BV199.W6N4] 56-2291
1. Worship programs. 2. Woman—Religious life. I. Title.

NEWBIGIN, James Edward Lesslie, Bp. 248
Journey into joy [by] Lesslie Newbigin. [1st American ed.] Grand Rapids, Eerdmans [1973, c1972] 125 p. 18 cm. (An Eerdmans evangelical paperback) [BV4501.2.N53 1973] 73-76339 1.95
1. Christian life—1960- I. Title.

NEWMAN, John Henry, Cardinal, 1801-1890 248
Reflections on God and self. Ed. by Lawrence F. Barmann [New York] Herder & Herder [1965] 60p. 19cm. [BX2350.5.N4] 63-18156 1.75 bds.,
1. Spiritual life—Catholic authors. I. Title.

NEWTON, Percy John. 248
The road to happiness, and other essays. Boston, Chapman & Grimes [1955] 153p. illus. 22cm. [BV4501.N46] 54-7551
1. Christian life. I. Title.

NIEBOER, Joe. 248
How to be a happy Christian. North East, Pa., Our Daily Walk Publishers [1956, c1955] 175p. 20cm. [BV4501.N48] 56-28910
1. Christian life. I. Title.

NIEBOER, Joe. 248
One another; or, How to get along with other Christians. Erie, Pa., Our Daily Walk Publishers [1953] 155p. 21cm. [BV4501.N5] 54-21287
1. Christian life. I. Title. II. Title: How to get along with other Christians.

NOUWEN, Henri J. M. 248
The living reminder : service and prayer in memory of Jesus Christ / Henri J. M. Nouwen. New York : Seabury Press, 1977. p. cm. "A Crossroad book." [BV4011.6.N68] 76-52738 ISBN 0-8164-1219-7 : 5.95
1. Clergy—Religious life. I. Title.

NYSTROM, Daniel, 1886- ed. 248
When we pray; prayers for worship in the home and for private devotions. Rock Island, Ill., Augustana Book Concern [1950] xxiii, 261 p. 19 cm. [BV4801.N9] 50-11467
1. Devotional exercises. 2. Lutheran Church—Prayer-books and devotions—English. I. Title.

OATES, Wayne Edward, 1917- 248
Anxiety in Christian experience. Philadelphia, Westminster Press [1955] 156p. 21cm. [BR110.O22] 55-8184
1. Anxiety. 2. Christianity—Psychology. I. Title.

O'BRIEN, John Anthony, 1893- ed. 248
Roads to Rome; the intimate personal stories of convert. to the Catholic faith. New York, Macmillan, 1954. 255p. 22cm. [BX4668.O252] 54-9380
1. Converts, Catholic. I. Title.

O'BRIEN, John Anthony, 1893- ed. 248
Where dwellest thou? intimate personal stories of twelve converts to the Catholic faith New York, Gilbert Press; distributed by J. Messner [c1956] 188p. 22cm. [BX4668.A1O25] 56-6793
1. Converts, Catholic. I. Title.

O'BRIEN, John Anthony, 1893- ed. 248
Where dwellest thou? Intimate personal stories of twelve converts to the Catholic faith. New York, Gilbert Press; distributed by J. Messner [c1956] 188p. 22cm. [BX4668.A1O25] 56-6793
1. Converts, Catholic. I. Title.

OCHS, Daniel A 1890- 248
Life's realities, by D. A. Ochs. Nashville, Southern Pub. Association [1965] 191 p. 19 cm. [BV4501.2.O28] 65-18529
1. Christian life. I. Title.

OCHS, Daniel A., 1890- 248
Life's realities. Nashville, Southern pub. [c.1965] 191p. 19cm. [BV4501.2.O28] 65-18529 3.50
1. Christian life. I. Title.

OCHS, William Benjamin. 248
Happiness in Christian living. Nashville, Southern Pub. Association [1957] 208p., 21cm. [BV4501.O2] 57-3626
1. Christian life. I. Title.

O'COLLINS, Gerald. 248
Man and his new hopes. [New York] Herder and Herder [1969] 180 p. 21 cm. Bibliographical footnotes. [BV4638.O25] 78-87762 5.50
1. Hope. I. Title.

O'CONNER, Clarence H 248
Messianic intelligence. [1st ed.] New York, Pageant Press [c1955] 174p. 21cm. [BR125.O16] 55-12522
I. Title.

ODDO, Gilbert Lawrence, ed. 248
These came home; the odyssey of fifteen converts. With a prefatory note by John J. Wright, Bishop of Worcester. Milwaukee, Bruce Pub. Co. [1954] 179p. 21c4. [BX4668.O3] 54-9336
1. Converts, Catholic. I. Title.

ODELL, Jack. 248
Not the righteous! Adapted from Pacific Garden Mission's radio series, 'Unshackled.' [Westwood, N. J.] F. H. Revell Co. [1955] 158p. 22cm. [BV4930.O3] 55-9843
1. Converts. 2. Pacific Garden Mission, Chicago. I. Unshackled (Radio program) II. Title.

OESTERREICHER, John M 1904- 248
Walls are crumbling; seven Jewish philosophers discover Christ. Foreword by Jacques Maritain. New York, Devin-Adair, 1952. 393p. illus. 23cm. [BV2623.A1O3] 52-9554
1. Jews—Converts to Christianity. I. Title.

OESTERREICHER, John M., 1904- 248
Walls are crumbling seven Jewish philosophers discover Christ. Foreword by Jacques Maritain. New York, Devin-Adair, 1952. 393 p. illus. 23 cm. [BV2623.A1O3] 52-9554
1. Jews—Converts to Christianity. I. Title.

O'FLAHERTY, Vincent M. 248
"Who ... me?" A study in identification by seeking the will of God, by V. M. O'Flaherty. Chicago, Franciscan Herald Press [1974] 107 p. 21 cm. Bibliography: p. 105-107. [BV4509.5.O34] 74-10851 ISBN 0-8199-0540-2 4.95
1. Loyola, Ignacio de, Saint, 1491-1556. Exercitia spiritualia. 2. Identification (Religion) 3. God—Will. I. Title.

OLDHAM, Dale. 248
Living close to God. Anderson, Ind., Warner Press [1957] 176p. 21cm. [BV4501.O49] 57-13922
1. Christian life. I. Title.

OLMSTED, David Lockwood, 1926- 248
The pacemakers; the story of six conversions to Christianity from the Acts of the Apostles. Minneapolis, Board of Publications, Evangelical Free Church of America, [1957] 159 p. 22 cm. [BV4932.O4] 57-20300
1. Conversion — Biblical teaching. 2. Bible. N. T. Acts — Biog. I. Title.

OLSON, Arnold Theodore. 248
The pacemakers the story of six conversions to Christianity from the Acts of the Apostles. Minneapolis, Minn., Board of Publications, Evangelical Free Church of America [1957] 159p. 22cm. [BV4932O4] 57-20300
1. Conversion—Biblical teaching. 2. Bible. N. T. Acts—Biog. I. Title.

O'MAHONY, James Edward, Father, 1897- 248
The secret of holiness. Westminster, Md., Newman Press, 1952. 178 p. 21 cm. [BX2350.O52] 52-8548
1. Christian life—Catholic authors. 2. Holiness. I. Title.

ORR, James Edwin, 1912- 248
Hte inside story of the Hollywood Christian Group. Introd. by Tim Spencer. Grand Rapids Zondervan Pub. House [1956] 134p. illus. 20cm. [BV4930.O7] 55-42017
1. Hollywood Christian Group. 2. Converts. 3. Actors, American. 4. Actresses, American. I. Title.

ORTIZ, Juan Carlos, 1934- 248
Call to discipleship / by Juan Carlos Ortiz, as told to Jamie Buckingham. Plainfield, N.J. : Logos International, [1975] xiv, 136 p. ; 21 cm. [BV4501.2.O724] 75-7476 ISBN 0-88270-130-4. ISBN 0-88270-122-3 pbk. : 3.50
1. Christian life—1960- I. Buckingham, Jamie. II. Title.

OSENDE, Victorino, 1879- 248
Pathways of love; translated by a Dominican sister of the Perpetual Rosary, Milwaukee, Wisconsin. St. Louis, B. Herder Book Co. [1958] 268p. 21cm. (Cross and crown series of spirituality, no. 12) Translation of Las grandes etapas de la vida espiritual. [BV5082.O753] 58-13828
1. Mysticism. I. Title.

OUTLAW, Nell (Warren) 248
For love, for life; the presence of Christ in human experience. Westwood, N.J., Revell [1952] 160 p. 24 cm. [BV4501.O784] 52-8877
1. Christian life. I. Title.

OVERDUIN, Jacobus, 1902- 248
Adventures of a deserter, by Jan Overduin. [Translated, by Harry Van Dyke from the Dutch ed.] Grand Rapids, W. B. Eerdmans Pub. Co. [1965] 153 p. 23 cm. [BS580.J55O93] 65-18098
1. Jonah, the prophet. I. Title.

OVERDUIN, Jacobus, 1902- 248
Adventures of a deserter, by Jan Overduin. [Tr. by Harry Van Dyke from the Dutch ed.] Grand Rapids, Mich., Eerdmans [c.1964, 1965] 153p. 23cm. [BS580.J55O93] 65-18098 3.50
1. Jonah, the prophet. I. Title.

PADDOCK, Charles Lee, 1891- 248
Byways. Mountain View, Calif., Pacific Press Pub. Association [1953] 87p. 19cm. [BV4515.P18] 53-6429
1. Christian life—Stories. I. Title.

PADDOCK, Charles Lee, 1891- 248
Highways to happiness. Washington, Review and Herald Pub. Association [1950] 384 p. illus. (part col.) 22 cm. [BX6154.P25] 50-13911
1. Seventh-Day-Adventists — Doctrinal and controversial works. I. Title.

PADGETT, Nora 248
My money helps. Pictures by Maggie Dugan. Nashville, Broadman c.1964. [32]p. illus. (pt. col.) 21cm. 64-10812 .60; 1.00 bds., lib. ed.,
1. Christian giving—Juvenile literature. I. Title.

PADOVANO, Anthony T. 248
Belief in human life [by] Anthony T. Padovano. [Paramus, N.J., Pastoral Educational Services, National Catholic Reading Distributors, 1969] 96 p. illus. (part col.) 29 cm. Caption title. "Human life in our day; pastoral letter of the American bishops": p. 83-95. [BV4501.2.P25] 75-96134
1. Christian life. I. Title.

PADOVANO, Anthony T. 248
Dawn without darkness [by] Anthony T. Padovano. [Paramus, N.J., Pastoral Educational Services, 1971] 92 p. illus. (part col.) 28 cm. [BX2350.2.P25] 77-140085
1. Christian life—Catholic authors. I. Title.

PAPPAS, Andreas S 248
Man and his world. New York, Vantage Press [c1953] 96p. illus. 23cm. [BR126.P24] 53-10302
I. Title.

PARDUE, Austin, Bp., 1899- 248
'A right judgment in all things.' Foreword by Lauriston L. Scaife. Greenwich, Conn., Seabury Press, 1954. 236p. 22cm. [BV4501.P263] 54-2359
1. Christian life. I. Title.

PARENTE, Pascal P 1890- 248
The ascetical life. Rev. ed. St. Louis, Herder [1955] 280p. 22cm. Includes bibliography. [BV5031.P3 1955] 55-9247
1. Asceticism—Catholic Church. I. Title.

PARENTE, Pascal P 1890- 248
Spiritual direction. St. Meinrad, Ind. [1950] vi, 109 p. 21 cm. "Grall publication." Bibliography: p. [107]-109. [BX2350.P29] 50-12987
1. Spiritual life — Catholic authors. I. Title.

PARKER, William R 248
Prayer can change your life; experiments and techniques in prayer therapy, by William R. Parker and Elaine St. Johns Dare. Englewood Cliffs, N. J., Prentice-Hall [1957] 270p. 22cm. [BV220.P24] 57-6777
1. Prayer. I. Dare, Elaine St. Johns, joint author. II. Title.

*PARKER, William R. 248
Prayer can change your life, by William R. Parker and Elaine St. Johns. New York, Pocket Books [1974, c1957] 253 p. 18 cm. [BV220.P24] 57-6777 ISBN 0-671-78372-6 1.25 (pbk.)
1. Psychology, Religious. I. St. Johns, Elaine, joint author. II. Title.

PARKER, William R. 248
Prayer can change your life; experiments and techniques in prayer theraphy by William R. Parker and Elaine St. Johns. New York, Cornerstone Library [1974, c1957] 224 p. 21 cm. [BV220.P24] 1.95 (pbk.)
I. St. Johns, Elaine, joint author. II. Title.
L.C. card number for hardbound ed.: 57-6777.

PARRISH, Mary Virginia, 1911- 248
Then comes the joy / Mary Virginia Parrish. Nashville: Abingdon, [c1977] 128 p. ; 19 cm. [BV4501.2.P352] 76-44383 ISBN 0-687-41439-3
1. Christian life—1960- I. Title.

*PARROTT, Leslie. 248
Trying to live like a Christian in a world that doesn't understand. Grand Rapids, Mich., Baker Book House [1973] 79 p. 18 cm. (Direction Books) [BF149] ISBN 0-8010-6948-3 0.95 (pbk.)
1. Christian life. I. Title.

PARROTT, Leslie, 1922- 248
The art of happy Christian living; the principles and practices of Christian living. Grand Rapids, Zondervan Pub. House [1955] 120p. 20cm. [BV4501.P266] 55-14092
1. Christian life. I. Title.

PATEY, Edward Henry. 248
Christian life-style / by Edward H. Patey. London : Mowbrays, 1976. 126 p. ; 19 cm. Includes bibliographical references. [BV4501.2.P353] 76-364407 ISBN 0-264-66232-6 : £0.80
1. Christian life—Anglican authors. I. Title.

PEALE, Norman Vincent, 1898- 248
The amazing results of positive thinking. Englewood Cliffs, N. J., Prentice- Hall [1959] 280p. 21cm. [BV4908.5.P4] 59-14147
1. Peace of mind. I. Title.

PEALE, Norman, Vincent, 1898- 248
The amazing results of positive thinking. Greenwich, Conn., Fawcett [1965, c.1959] 223p. 18p. (Crest bk., R792) [BV4908.5.P4] .60 pap.,
1. Peace of mind. I. Title.

*PEALE, Norman Vincent. 1898- 248
A guide to confident living. Greenwich, Conn., Fawcett [1963, c.1948] 192p. 18cm. (Crest bk., R667) .60 pap.,
1. Christian life. 2. Success. I. Title.

PEALE, Norman Vincent, 1898- 248
Inspiring messages for daily living. Englewood Cliffs, N. J., Prentice-Hall [1955] 208 p. 21 cm. [BV4501.P423] 55-11010
1. Christian life. I. Title.

PEALE, Norman Vincent, 1898- 248
The power of positive thinking. New York, Prentice-Hall [1952] 276 p. 21 cm. [BF636.P37] 52-10833
1. Psychology, Applied. I. Title.

PEALE, Norman Vincent, 1898- 248
The power of positive thinking. by Robert Todd, Greenwich, Conn., Fawcett [1963, c.1952] 223p. 18cm. (Crest bk., R608) .60 pap.,
1. Psychology, Applied. I. Title.

PEALE, Norman Vincent, 1898- 248
The power of positive thinking. Designed by Gene Galasso. Norwalk, Conn., C. R. Gibson Co. [1970, c1956] 105 p. 22 cm. "Especially condensed for this Gift Edition." [BF637.P3P42 1970] 75-130444 ISBN 0-8378-1786-2 3.50
1. Peace of mind. I. Title.

PEALE, Norman Vincent, 1898- 248
The power of positive thinking for young people. Illus. by Robert Todd. New York, Prentice-Hall [1954] 214 p. illus. 21 cm. Abridged ed. of the author's The power of positive thinking. [BF636.P38] 54-11547
1. Psychology, Applied. I. Title.

PEALE, Norman Vincent, 1898- 248
Stay alive all your life. Englewood Cliffs, N. J., Prentice-Hall [1957] 300p. 21cm. [BF636.P39] 57-6179
1. Psychology, Applied. I. Title.

PEALE, Norman Vincent, 1898- 248
Stay alive all your life. Greenwich, Conn., Fawcett [1968,c.1957] 256p. 18cm. (Crest bk., T1143) [BF636.P39] .75 pap.,
1. Psychology, Applied. I. Title.

PEALE, Norman Vincent, 1898- 248
Stay alive all your life. Greenwich, Conn., Fawcett [1964, c.1957] 256p. 18cm. (Crest R712) .60 pap.,
1. Psychology, Applied. I. Title.

PEALE, Norman Vincent, 1898- 248
You can win. Garden City, N.Y., Permabooks [1950 c1938] 188 p. 17 cm. (Permabooks, P 97) [BV4501.P425 1950] 51-18540
1. Christian life. 2. Success. I. Title.

PEARSON, Roy Messer, 1914- 248
Here's a faith for you. Nashville, Abingdon-Cokesbury Press [c1953] 155p. 20cm. [BV4501.P44] 52-11312
1. Christian life. I. Title.

PEARSON, Roy Messer, 1914- 248
This do--and live. Nashville, Abingdon Press [1954] 124p. 20cm. [BV4501.P445] 54-5942
1. Christian life. I. Title.

PECK, Kathryn (Blackburn) 1904- 248
In favor with God and man; guidance for the Christian home when children are nine to eleven. Kansas City, Mo., Beacon Hill Press [1952] 154p. illus. 19cm. (Christian home series) [BV4571.P4] 52-11227
1. Children—Religious life. I. Title.

PENTECOST, J. Dwight. 248
Design for discipleship [by] J. Dwight Pentecost. Grand Rapids, Zondervan Pub. House [1971] 130 p. 23 cm. [BV4501.2.P385] 75-134628 3.95
1. Christian life—1960- 2. Sermons, American. I. Title.

PEPLER, Conrad, 1908- 248
The English religious heritage. St. Louis, Herder [1958] 444p. 23cm. Originally published in The life of the spirit. [BV5077.G7P4] 58-3295
1. Mysticism—Gt. Brit. I. Title.

PERKINS, Faith. 248
Meet more people, have more fun. New York, Putnam [1957] 192p. 20cm. [BV4911.P4] 57-11715
1. Loneliness. I. Title.

PERKINS, Faith. 248
Meet more people, have more fun. New York, Putnam [1957] 192p. 20cm. [BV4911.P4] 57-11715
1. Loneliness. I. Title.

PERO 248
The last revelation of the Piscean Age. New York, Vantage. [c.1966] 47p. illus. 20cm. 2.50 bds.,
I. Title.

PERRET, Andre S 248
Holiness of life [by] A. S. Perret. Translated by Lillian M. McCarthy. St. Louis. Herder [1964] 166 p. 24 cm. (Cross and crown series of spirituality, no. 28) Translation of La vie santifiee. Bibliographical footnotes. [BX2350.5.P383] 64-7635
1. Spiritual life—Catholic authors. I. Title. II. Series.

PERRET, Andre S. 248
Holiness of life. Tr. [from French] by Lillian M. McCarthy. St. Louis, B. Herder [c.1964] 166p. 21cm. (Cross and crown ser. of spirituality, no. 28) [BX2350.5.P383] 64-7635 3.25 bds.,
1. Spiritual life—Catholic authors. I. Title. II. Series.

PERRIN, Joseph Marie, 1905- 248
Virginity. Translated by Katherine Gordon. Westminster, Md., Newman Press [1956] 161p. 19cm. [BV4647.C5P42] 56-9994
1. Virginity. I. Title.

PETRY, Ray C, 1903- ed. 248
Late medieval mysticism. Philadelphia, Westminster Press [1957] 424p. 24cm. (The Library of Christian classics, v. 13) [BV5072.P4] 149.3 57-5092
1. Mysticism—Middle Ages. I. Title.

PETRY, Ray C., 1903- ed. 248
Late medieval mysticism. Philadelphia, Westminister Press [1957] 424 p. 24 cm. (The Library of Christian classics, v. 13) [BV5072.P4] 149.3 57-5092
1. Mysticism—Middle ages. I. Title.

PETTY, Jo, comp. 248
Wings of silver. Norwalk, Conn., C. R. Gibson Co. [1967] 89 p. illus. 21 cm. [BV4360.P47] 67-21924
1. Virtues. I. Title.

PETTY, Jo, comp. 248
Wings of silver. Norwalk, Conn., C. R. Gibson Co. [1967] 89 p. illus. 21 cm. [BV4360.P47] 67-21924
1. Virtues. I. Title.

PHILIPON, Marie Michel, Father. 248
The eternal purpose; translated by John A. Otto. Westminster, Md., Newman Press, 1952. 112 p. 20 cm. [BX2350.P433] 52-7509
1. Spiritual life — Catholic authors. 2. Eternity. I. Title.

PHILIPON, Marie Michel, 1898- 248
The eternal purpose; translated by John A. Otto. Westminster, Md., Newman Press, 1952. 112p. 20cm. [BX2350.P433] 52-7509
1. Spiritual life—Catholic authors. 2. Eternity. I. Title.

PHILLIPS, John Bertram, 1906- 248
Is God at home? New York, Abingdon Press [1957] 109p. 18cm. [BV4832.P52] 57-8334
1. Devotional literature. I. Title.

PHILLIPS, John Bertram, 1906- 248
Making men whole. New York, Macmillan, 1953 [c1952] 73p. 22cm. [BR121.P516 1953] 53-12213
1. Christianity—20th cent. I. Title.

PIAT, Stephane Joseph, 1899- 248
Principles and paradoxes of the militant life; translated by James Meyer. Chicago, Franciscan Herald Press [1953] 199p. 20cm. [BX2350.P44] 53-30887
1. Christian life—Catholic authors. I. Title.

PICCARDA, pseud. 248
The veil of the heart. Franciscan letters of a secular missionary. From the Italian of Piccarda, translated by Clelia Maranzana. Translation edited by Frances Laughlin. Paterson, N. J., St. Anthony Guild Press [1959] 243p. illus. 19cm. 'These letters were written, from November 1945 through December 1949, by a member of a Franciscan secular institute to a young friend, Donatella.' [BX2350.2.P513] 59-3097
1. Franciscans. 2. Spiritual life—Catholic authors. I. Donatella, pseud. II. Title.

PIEPER, Josef, 1904- 248
Happiness and contemplation. Translated by Richard and Clara Winston. [New York] Pantheon [1958] 124 p. 21 cm. Includes bibliography. [BV5091.C7P513] 58-7204
1. Contemplation. 2. Happiness.

PIETRO DAMIANI, Saint 248
Selected writings on the spiritual life. Translated, with an introd., by Patricia McNulty. New York, Harper [1960] 187p. 21cm. (Classics of the contemplative life) Bibliography: p. 182-184 60-16035 5.00
1. Spiritual Life—Catholic authors. I. McNulty, Patricia, II. Title.

PIKE, James Albert, 1913- 248
Beyond anxiety; the Christian answer to fear, frustration. guilt, indecision, inhibition, loneliness, despair. New York, Scribners [1962, c.1953] 149p. 21cm. (SL74) 1.25 pap.,
1. Psychology, Pastoral. 2. Christian ethics. I. Title.

PIKE, James Albert, Bp., 248
1913-1969.
Beyond anxiety; the Christian answer to fear, frustration, guilt, indecision, inhibition, loneliness, despair. New York, Scribner, 1953. 149 p. 22 cm. [BV4012.P53] 53-12237
1. Psychology, Pastoral. 2. Christian ethics. I. Title.

PINK, Arthur W. 248
Spiritual growth : growth in grace, or Christian Progress / by Arthur W. Pink. Grand Rapids : Baker Book House, c1976. 200p. ; 22 cm. Includes index. [BV4501.2] ISBN 0-8010-6862-2 pbk. : 3.95
1. Spritual life. I. Title.
L.C. card no. for original ed. 77-139863.

PINK, Arthur Walkington, 248
1886-1952.
Spiritual growth; growth in grace, or Christian progress. Grand Rapids, Mich., Baker Book House [1971] 193 p. 23 cm. [BV4501.2.P553 1971] 77-139863 ISBN 0-8010-6862-2 4.95
1. Spiritual life. I. Title.

PIPER, Otto A., 01891- 248
The Christian meaning of money. Englewood Cliffs, N. J., Prentice [c.1965] xii, 116p. 21cm. (Lib. of Christian stewardship, LCS-3) Bibl. [BV772.P53] 65-16594 2.95; 1.50 pap.,
1. Stewardship, Christian. 2. Wealth, Ethics of. I. Title.

PIPER, Otto A 1891- 248
The Christian meaning of money, by Otto A. Piper. Englewood Cliffs, N J., Prentice-Hall [1965] xii, 116 p. 21 cm. (Library of Christian stewardship, LCS-3) Bibliographical footnotes. [BV772.P53] 65-16594
1. Stewardship, Christian 2. Wealth, Ethics of. I. Title.

PITT, James E. 248
Adventures in brotherhood. New York, Farrar, Straus [1955] 242 p. 22 cm. [BV4647.B7P5] 55-72132
1. Brotherliness. I. Title.

PLAQUEVENT, Jean. 248
Jesus and I; conversations between Jesus and any child who wants to talk to Him. Translated by Emma Craufurd; illus. by Mary Taylor. London, New York, Sheed and Ward, 1950. 92 p. illus. 21 cm. [BX2371.P55] 50-2208
1. Children — Religious life. I. Title.

PLAQUEVENT, Jean. 248
Jesus and I; conversation between Jesus and any child who wants to talk to Him. Translated by Emma Craufurd; illus. by Mary Taylor. New York, Sheed and Ward, 1950. 92 p. illus. 21 cm. Translation of L'Imitation du petit Jesus. [BX2371.P55 1950a] 50-11937
1. Children — Religious life. I. Title.

PLUS, Raoul, 1882- 248
Christ in our time. [Translation by Elizabeth Belloc] Westminster, Md., Newman Press [1953] 105p. 19cm. Translation of Comment presenter le Christ a sotre temps. [BX2350.P5272] 53-13453
1. Christian life—Catholic authors. I. Title.

PLUS, Raoul, 1882- 248
Inward peace. [Translation by Helen Ramsbotham] Westminster, Md., Newman Press [1956] ix, 131p. 19cm. Bibliographical footnotes. [BX2350.P5282] 56-7081
1. Spiritual life—Catholic authors. I. Title.

PLUS, Raoul, 1882- 248
Living with God. With prefatory letter by Cardinal Mercier. Westminster, Md., Newman Press, 1950. xvi, 93 p. 16 cm. [BX2350.P563] 50-8377
1. Christian life — Catholic authors. I. Title.

PLUS, Raoul, 1882- 248
The path to the heights. Westminster, Md., Newman Press [1954] 128p. 20cm. 'Translation from the original French, Le chemin de la grandeur ... made by Wilfrid B. Kane.' [BX2350.P523] 54-3276
1. Spiritual life—Catholic authors. I. Title.

PLUS, Raoul, 1882- 248
Some rare virtues. Translated from the French by Sister Mary Edgar Meyer. Westminster, Md., Newman Press, 1950. vi, 213 p. 16 cm. [BV4630.P613] 50-8813
1. Virtue. I. Title.

POURRAT, Pierre, 1871- 248
Christian spirituality. Westminster, Md., Newman Press, 1953-55. 4v. 21cm. Vol. 1 translated by W. H. Mitchell and S. P. Jacques; v.2, by S. P. Jacques: v. 3, by W. H. Mitchell; v. 4, by D. Attwater. Contents.v. 1. From the time of Our Lord till the dawn of the Middle Ages.--v.2. In the Middle Ages.--v.3-4. Later developments. Bibliographical footnotes. [BV5021.P62] 53-5585
1. Asceticism. 2. Mysticism—Hist. 3. Monasticism and religious orders. I. Title.

POWELL, Oliver. 248
Household of power; the task and testing of the church in our time. Boston, United Church Press [1962] 114p. 22cm. (A Pilgrim Press publication) [BV4501.2.P59] 62-18361
1. Theology, Practical. 2. Christian life. I. Title.

POWERS, Thomas E 248
First questions on the life of the Spirit. [1st ed.] New York, Harper [1959] 241p. 22cm. Includes bibliography. [BV4501.2.P6] 59-7159
1. Spiritual life. I. Title.

PRAPTR, Arnold 248
You can have joy. Grand Rapids, Mich., Zondervan [c.1965] 120p. 21cm. [BJ1481.P7] 64-8840 2.95 bds.,
1. Joy and sorrow. I. Title.

PRATER, Arnold. 248
More parables from life. Grand Rapids, Mich., Zondervan Pub. House [1969] 119 p. illus. 22 cm. [BV4515.2.P7] 69-11649 2.95
1. Christian life—Stories. I. Title.

PRATER, Arnold. 248
You can have joy! Grand Rapids, Zondervan Pub. House [1965] 120 p. 21 cm. [BJ1481.P7] 64-8840
1. Joy and sorrow. I. Title.

PRICE, Eugenia. 248
The burden is light! The autobiography of a transformed pagan who took God at His word. [Westwood, N. J.] F. H. Revell Co. [c1955] 221p. illus. 22cm. [BV4935.P75A32] 55-5388
1. Converts. I. Title.

PRICE, Eugenia. 248
Discoveries made from living my new life. Introd. by Paul S. Rees. Grand Rapids, Zondervan Pub. House [1953] 119 p. 21 cm. [BV4935.P75A3] 53-3655
1. Converts. 2. Christian life. I. Title.

PRICE, Eugenia. 248
Early will I seek Thee, journal of a heart that longed and found. [Westwood, N. J.] F. H. Revell Co. [1956] 185p. 22cm. [BV4935.P75A35] 56-10894
1. Converts. I. Title.

PRICE, Eugenia. 248
Early will I seek Thee, journal of a heart that longed and found. [Westwood, N. J.] F: H. Revell Co. [1956] 185p. 22cm. [BV4935.P75A35] 56-10894
1. Converts. I. Title.

PRICE, Eugenia. 248
No pat answers. Grand Rapids, Zondervan Pub. House [1972] 145 p. 23 cm. [BV4501.2.P695] 72-83880 3.95
1. Christian life—1960- I. Title.

PRICE, Eugenia. 248
Unshackled; stories of transformed lives, adapted from 'Unshackled' radio broadcasts: stories from Pacific Garden Mission. Radio scripts by Eugenia Price. Book revision by Faith Coxe Bailey. [2d ed., rev.] Chicago, Moody Press [1953] 159p. 22cm. [BV4930.P7 1953] 53-2953
1. Converts. I. Balley, Faith Coxe. II. Unshackled (Radio program) III. Title.

*PRICE, Fannie 248
Turn your problems to achievement. New York, Carlton [c.1964] 67p. 21cm. 2.00
I. Title.

PRIEBE, Kenneth, comp. 248
The call to youth, by Lutheran youth leaders. Minneapolis, Augsburg Pub. House [1952] 131 p. 21 cm. [BV4531.P683] 52-9408
1. Youth-Religious life. I. Title.

PROPHET, Mark. 248
Climb the highest mountain; the everlasting Gospel, by Mark and Elizabeth Prophet. [1st ed.] Colorado Springs, Summit Lighthouse [1972- v. illus. 23 cm. Includes bibliographical references. [BF1999.P76] 72-175101
I. Prophet, Elizabeth, joint author. II. Title.

PROPHET, Mark. 248
Studies in alchemy / by Saint Germain. Colorado : Summit Lighthouse, c1974. 92 p., [1] leaf of plates : col. ports ; 21 cm. (Alchemy series ; v. 1) "The instruction set forth ... was given to Mark L. Prophet by the Ascended Master Saint Germain." [BF1311.S25P76] 75-321272
1. Spirit writings. I. Saint-Germain, comte de, d. 1784? II. Title.

THE Protestant year. 1955- 248
New York, Hawthorn Books. v. 24cm. 'Prepared by the editors of the Christian herald.' [BV4810.P7] 55-15751
1. Devotional calendars. I. Christian herald (New York. 1878-)

PROUDFOOT, Merrill. 248
Suffering: a Christian understanding. Philadelphia, Westminster Press[1964] 194 p. 21 cm. [BS2655.S8P7] 64-23954
1. Suffering—Biblical teaching. 2. Bible. N.T. Epistles of Paul—Criticism, interpretation, etc. I. Title.

PROUDFOOT, Merrill 248
Suffering: a Christian understanding. Philadelphia, Westminster [c.1964] 194p. 21cm. 64-23954 5.00
1. Suffering—Biblical teaching. 2. Bible. N.T. Epistles of Paul—Criticism, interpretation, etc. I. Title.

RAHNER, Karl, 1904- 248
Christian at the crossroads. New York : Seabury Press [1976c1975] 95p. ; 2! cm. (Crossroad book) [BR85.R237] 75-29634 ISBN 0-8164-1204-9 : 5.95
1. Theology-Addresses, essays, lectures. 2. Monastic and religious life-Addresses, essays, lectures. I. Title.

RALPH, John Robertson. 248
The happy bondage. [1st ed.] New York, Vantage Press [1956] 64p. 21cm. [BR123.R28] 56-10559
1. Christianity —Addresses, essays, lectures. I. Title.

RALPH, John Robertson. 248
The happy bondage. [1st ed.] New York, Vantage Press [1956] 64p. 21cm. [BR123.R28] 56-10559
1. Christianity—Addresses, essays, lectures. I. Title.

RAMIGE, Eldon Albert, 1894- 248
The things that really matter. Boston, Christopher Pub. House [1950] 199 p. 21 cm. [BV4501.R25] 50-2493
1. Christian life. I. Title.

RAYBURN, Robert Gibson, 1915- 248
Fight the good fight; lessons from the Korean War. [Pasadena, Calif.] Covenant College Press [1956] 108p. 21cm. [BV4501.R38] 56-25040
1. Christian life. 2. Korean War, 1950-1953—Religious aspects. I. Title.

RAYMOND, Father, 1903- 248
God goes to murderer's row. Milwaukee, Bruce Pub. Co. [1951] 211 p. illus. 21 cm. [HV6248.P38R3] 51-14888
1. Penney, Thomas C., 1909 or 10-1943. I. Title.

REDHEAD, John A 248
Letting God help you. New York, Abingdon Press [1957] 125p. 20cm. [BV4501.R385] 57-11014
1. Christian life. I. Title.

*REES, Jean A. 248
Saints at work. Grand Rapids, Mich., Zondervan [1964, c.1958] 121p. illus. 21cm. 1.25 pap.,
I. Title.

REGAMEY, Raymond, 1900- 248
The cross and the Christian; translated by Angeline Bouchard. St. Louis, B. Herder Book Co. [1954] 177p. 21cm. (Cross and crown series of spirituality, no. 2) Translation of La croix du Christ et celle du chretien. [BX2373.S5R413] 54-7327
1. Suffering. 2. Atonement. 3. Christian life—Catholic authors. I. Title.

REID, Clyde H. 248
The return to faith; finding God in the unconscious [by] Clyde Reid. Illustrated by Dan Marshall. [1st ed.] New York, Harper & Row [1974] xii, 106 p. illus. 21 cm. Includes bibliographical references. [BL53.R36] 73-18426 ISBN 0-06-066822-9 4.95
1. Experience (Religion) 2. Psychology, Religious. I. Title.

REID, Clyde H ed. 248
Why I belong, by Clyde H. Reid. Illustrated by Robert J. Hanson. Boston, United Church Press [c1964] 92 p. illus., ports. 22 cm. "Part of the United Church Curriculum, prepared and published by the Division of Christian Education and the Division of Publication of the United Church Board for Homeland Ministries." [BR1703.R4] 64-19461
1. Christian biography. I. United Church Board for Homeland Ministries. Division of Christian Education. II. United Church Board for Homeland Ministries. Division of Publication. III. Title.

REID, Marie L 1884- 248
Pedigreed souls. [1st ed.] New York, Greenwich Book Publishers [1958] 90p. 21cm. [BV4501.R418] 58-9987
1. Christian life. I. Title.

REIN, Remus C 1905- 248
Adventures in Christian stewardship. Saint Louis, Mo., Concordia Pub. House [c1955] 100p. illus. 22cm. [BV772.R4] 55-11139
1. Stewardship, Christian. I. Title.

REIQUAM, Oleen T. 248
Golden straws and chaff in the wind; a positive approach to the Bible message, by Oleen T. Reiquam. New York, William-Frederick Press, 1971. 43 p. 20 cm. [BV4501.2.R44] 77-146212 2.00
1. Christian life—1960- I. Title.

RENOUF, Robert W 248
A leader's guide. New York, Morehouse-Barlow Co. [1963] 112 p. 21 cm. "For use with The privilege of teaching, by Dora Chaplin." [BV1533.R4] 64-1962
1. Religious education — Teacher training. I. Chaplin, Dora P. The privilege of teaching. II. Title.

RIBBLE, Arthur Le Baron, 248
1904-
The curate; illustrated by the author. Boyce, Va., Printed by the Carr Pub. Co. [1951] 1 v. (unpaged) illus. 23 cm. [BV4510.R38] 51-29676
1. Christian life. I. Title.

RICCARDO. 248
Be wise as serpents / by Riccardo. Chicago : Richard Jarrett Institute, [1975] 108 p. ; 23 cm. [BV4501.2.R49] 74-28578
1. Christian life—1960- 2. Art—Philosophy. I. Title.

RICE, M Leslie. 248
Light for life's tunnels. Washington, Review and Herald Pub. Association [1950] 93 p. 20 cm. [BV4501.R5318] 50-31156
1. Christian life. I. Title.

RICHARD OF ST. VICTOR d.1173 248
Selected writings on contemplation. Tr. [from Latin] introd. notes by Clare Kirchberger. London, Faber & Faber [Mystic, Conn., Verry, 1966] 269p. 21cm. (Classics of the contemplative life) Bibl. [BV5091.C7R5] A58 5.00
1. Contemplation. I. Kirchberger, Clare. II. Title.

RICHTMYER, Bernice D 248
Straws in the wind. [1st ed.] New York, Vantage Press [1955] 98p. 22cm. Essays. [BV4501.R535] 55-8625
1. Christian life. I. Title.

RIEKE, Marcus. 248
From plight to power, by Marcus Rieke and Gordon Huffman. Columbus, Ohio, Wartburg Press [1951] 139 p. illus. 20 cm. [BV4447.R47] 52-16998
1. Church work with youth. 2. Youth — Religious life. I. Title.

RIESS, Oswald. 248
The secret of beautiful living. [St. Louis, Concordia Pub. House, 1953] 134p. 19cm. [BV4501.R428] 53-2269
1. Christian life. I. Title.

RIESS, Walter. 248
Teen-ager, Christ is for you. Saint Louis, Mo., Concordia Pub. House [1958, c1957] 83p. illus. 19cm. [BV4531.R53] 57-59570
1. Youth—Religious life. I. Title.

RINKER, Rosalind. 248
The years that count; a book that lets young people think for themselves. Grand Rapids, Zondervan Pub. House [1958] 118p. 20cm. [BV4531.2.R5] 58-4706
1. Youth—Religious life. I. Title.

RISCHE, Henry. 248
When the lights are low; guidelines to heart's ease. Saint Louis, Concordia Pub. House [c1957] 238p. 23cm. [BV4501.R56] 56-8254
1. Christian life. I. Title.

ROBB, Edmund W. 248
Prisons of the world [by] Edmund W. Robb. [1st ed.] Abilene, Tex., Evangelical Publishers [1971] 101 p. 22 cm. [BV3797.R55] 79-164701
1. Methodist Church—Sermons. 2. Evangelistic sermons. 3. Sermons, American. I. Title.

ROBERTS, Guy L 248
The way of life. New York, Comet Press Books [1956] 120p. 21cm. [BV4501.R57] 56-10401

1. Christian life. 2. Christianity—Essence, genius, nature. I. Title.

ROBERTS, Oral, ed. 248
God's formula for success and prosperity, edited by Oral Roberts and G. H. Montgomery. Tulsa, Okla., 1956. 158p. 20cm. [BJ1611.2.R57] 56-8450
1. Success. 2. Christian life. I. Montgomery, G. H. joint ed. II. Title.

ROBERTS, Oral. 248
God's formula for success and prosperity, edited by the editorial staff, Abundant life magazine. Rev. ed. Tulsa, Okla., Abundant Life Publications, 1966. 128 p. 20 cm. First ed., by O. Roberts and G. H. Montgomery, published in 1956. [BJ1611.2.R57] 66-15958
1. Success. 2. Christian life. I. Montgomery, G. H., joint author. II. Abundant life magazine. III. Title.

ROBINSON, George Livingstone, 248
1864-
Why I am a Christian. New York, Abelard Press [1952] 128p. 23cm. [BR121.R565] 52-14895
1. Christianity—Essence, genius, nature. I. Title.

ROBINSON, George Livinstone, 248
1864-
Live out your years [1st ed.] New York, Abelard Press [1951] 114 p. 24 cm. [BV4580.R6] 51-14801
1. Old age — Religious life. I. Title.

ROBISON, James, 1943- 248
7 ways I can better serve the Lord. Nashville, Broadman Press [1971] 128 p. illus., ports. 20 cm. [BV4501.2.R618] 70-157385 ISBN 0-8054-5212-5 3.50
1. Christian life—Baptist authors. I. Title.

RODENMAYER, Robert N 248
Thanks be to God. [1st ed.] New York, Harper [1960] 126p. 20cm. [BV4647.G8R6] 59-5223
1. Gratitude. 2. Protestant Episcopal Church in the U. S. A. Book of common prayer. A general thanksgiving. I. Title.

RODENMAYER, Robert N.N. 248
Thanks be to God. New York, Harper [c.1960] 126p. 20cm. 59-5223 2.50 bds.,
1. Gratitude. 2. Protestant Episcopal Church in the U.S.A. Book of common prayer. A general thanks-giving. I. Title.

ROGER, Brother. 248
So easy to love. London, New York, Longmans, Green [1958, c1957] 101p. 17cm. (The Inner life series) [BX2350.R658] 58-1027
1. Christian life—Catholic authors. I. Title.

ROGERS, Dale Evans. 248
My spiritual diary. [Westwood, N.J.] F. H. Revell Co. [1955] 144 p. 22 cm. [BR1725.R63A3] 55-5390
I. Title.

ROGERS, Dale Evans. 248
Salute to Sandy. Westwood, N. J., F. H. Revell Co. [1967] 117 p. illus., ports. 20 cm. [BR1725.R63A32] 67-19296
1. Rogers, Sandy. I. Title.

ROGERS, Paula 248
With deep grown roots. New York, Vantage Press [c.1959] 129p. 21cm. 2.95 bds.,
I. Title.

ROMANOWSKI, Henry J. 1920- 248
The unholy three. Milwaukees, Bruce [1950] xiii, 160 p. 23 cm. [BX2350.R67] 50-6948
1. Christian life — Catholic authors. I. Title.

RONSIN, F X 248
A wakeners of souls; addressed to parents, educators, civic and military leaders. Translated from the French by Eugenia Logan. New York, Society of St. Paul [c1957] 304p. 22cm. [BX2350.R6743] 58-1678
1. Christian life—Catholic authors. I. Title.

ROONEY, Richard L 248
The adventures of an angel; illustrated by P. N. Stavroulakis. Notre Dame, Ind., Ave Maria Press [1953] 164p. illus. 22cm. [BX2350.R678] 53-5946
1. Christian life— Catholic authors. I. Title.

ROSAGE, David E., Rev. 248
Letters to an altar boy. Drawings by Laura Herber Trezona. Milwaukee, Bruce [c.1963] 79p. illus. 20cm. .95 pap.,
I. Title.

ROSELL, Mervin E 248
How to live with yourself. Wheaton, Ill., Van Kampen Press [1951] 77 p. 20 cm. [BV4501.R637] 52-88
1. Christian life. I. Title.

ROSENFIELD, Joe. 248
Have no fear, [1st ed.] New York, Citadel Press [1959] 102p. illus. 21cm. [BV4908.5.R6] 59-11133
1. Peace of mind. 2. Happiness exchange (Radio program) I. Title.

ROSENTHAL, George David, 248
1881-1938.
Sins of the saints. [Rev. ed.] New York, Morehouse-Gorham Co., 1958. 164p. 19cm. [BV4625.R6 1958] 58-13713
1. Sins. 2. Christian ethics—Anglican authors. I. Title.

ROUTLEY, Erik. 248
The gift of conversion. Philadelphia, Muhlenberg Press [1958] 144p. 22cm. Includes bibliography. [BT780.R67] 58-634
1. Conversion. I. Title.

ROWLAND, Stanley J. 248
Hurt and healing; modern writers speak [by] Stanley J. Rowland, Jr. New York, Friendship Press [1969] 96 p. 19 cm. Includes bibliographies. [BL53.R65] 68-57231 1.50
1. Psychology, Religious—Case studies. I. Title.

RUPERT, Hoover, ed. 248
Your life counts; messages for youth. New York, Abingdon-Cokesbury Press [1950] 157 p. 20 cm. [BV4310.R78] 50-7460
1. Youth—Religious life. I. Title.

RUSSELL, William Henry, 1895- 248
Teaching the Christian virtues. Milwaukee, Bruce Pub. Co. [1952] 200p. 23cm. [BV4630.R85] 53-148
1. Virtue. 2. Christian ethics—Study and teaching. I. Title.

ST. PAUL, George A 248
Here and hereafter. Westminster, Md., Newman Press, 1956. 299p. 24cm. [BX2350.S15] 56-9839
1. Christian life— Catholic authors. I. Title.

ST. PAUL, George A. 248
Here and hereafter. [Reissue] Chicago, Loyola [1963, c.1956] 299p. 24cm. (Loyola request reprint) 4.50
1. Christian life—Catholic authors. I. Title.

*SANDERS, J. Oswald 248
Cultivation of Christian character. Chicago, Moody [c.1965] 128p. 17cm. (Colportage lib. 513) .39 pap.,
I. Title.

SANDERS, J Oswald. 248
A spiritual clinic; a suggestive diagnosis and prescription for problems in Christian life and service. Chicago, Moody Press [1958] 160p. 22cm. [BV4501.2.S2] 58-4740
1. Christian life. I. Title.

SANDERS, John Oswald, 1902- 248
A spiritual clinic; a suggestive diagnosis and prescription for problems in Christian life and service. Chicago, Moody Press [1958] 160 p. 22 cm. [BV4501.2.S2] 58-4740
1. Christian life. I. Title.

SANDERS, Stephen, 1919- 248
To him who conquers. [1st ed.] Garden City, N.Y., Doubleday, 1970. 209 p. 22 cm. [BJ1581.2.S23] 73-111183 4.95
I. Title.

SANFORD, Agnes Mary (White) 248
Let's believe. Illus. by Ted Sanford. New York, Religious Book Dept., Harper [1954] 119p. illus. 23cm. [BT772.S3] 54-5854
1. Faith—Juvenile literature. I. Title.

SANGSTER, William Edwin, 248
1900-
The secret of radiant life. New York, Abingdon Press [1957] 219p. 23cm. [BV4501.S364 1957a] 57-9789
1. Christian life. I. Title.

SAUER, Erich. 248
In the arena of faith; a call to a consecrated life. Grand Rapids, Eerdmans, 1955. 188p. 23cm. [BV4501.S368] 55-3688
1. Christian life. 2. Bible. N. T. Hebrews XII—Criticism, interpretation, etc. I. Title.

*SAUL, John Allen 248
These gracious golden years; reflections and meditations from the eighth decade of my life. New York, Exposition [1965, c.1958, 1964] 79p. 22cm. [EP42122] 2.50
I. Title.

SCANLAN, Michael. 248
Inner healing. New York, Paulist Press [1974] vi, 85 p. 21 cm. Bibliography: p. 83-85. [BT732.5.S24] 74-81901 ISBN 0-8091-1846-7 2.25
1. Faith-cure. I. Title.

SCHACHTEL, Hyman Judah, 1907- 248
The life you want to live. [1st ed.] New York, Dutton, 1956. 224 p. 21 cm. [BJ1581.2.S33] 56-8327
1. Conduct of life. I. Title.

SCHACHTEL, Hyman Judah, 1907- 248
The life you want to tive. [1st ed.] New York, Dutton, 1956. 224p. 21cm. [BJ1581.2.S33] 56-8327
1. Conduct of life. I. Title.

SCHLOSSER, Felix. 248
Forms of Christian life. Translated by R. A. Wilson. Milwaukee, Bruce Pub. Co. [1969] 96 p. 21 cm. [BV4740.S313] 69-20476
1. Vocation. I. Title.

SCHNEIDER, Frieda Johnetta, 248
1911-
Affliction worketh. Grand Rapids, Mich, W. B. Eerdmans Pub. Co., 1956. 131p. 23cm. [BV4909.S37] 57-372
1. Affliction. I. Title.

[SCHUEMACHER, Simone] 248
Your way. Translated from the French by a sister of Notre Dame de Namur. Milwaukee, Bruce Pub. Co. [1955] 78p. 17cm. [BX2163.S333] 56-968
1. Rosary. I. Julie du St. Esprit. Sister, 1808- tr. II. Title.

SCHUETTE, Walter Erwin. 248
Letters Jesus might write. [1st ed.] New York, Vantage Press [1956] 136p. 21cm. [BV4501.S3827] 56-6856
1. Christian life. I. Title.

SCHUETTE, Walter Erwin. 248
Letters Jesus might write. [1st ed.] New York, Vantage Press [1956] 136p. 21cm. [BV4501.S3827] 56-6856
1. Christian life. I. Title.

SCHULLER, Robert Harold 248
Your future is your friend; an inspirational pilgrimage through the Twenty-third Psalm. Grand Rapids, Mich., Eerdmans [c.1964] 98p. 22cm. [BS1450.23d.S3] 64-22023 2.50 bds.,
1. Bible. O. T. Psalms XXIII—Devotional literature. I. Title.

SCHULZ, Florence. 248
Friends and neighbors; a resource book for ministering to primary and junior boys and girls in inner-city areas. Boston, Published for the Cooperative Publication Association [by] Pilgrim Press [1962] 118p. 23cm. (The Cooperative vacation church school texts) [BV1585.S33] 62-21605
1. Vacation schools, Religions. 2. Church work with children. I. Title.

SCHWENCKFELD, Caspar, 1490?- 248
1561.
The piety of Caspar Schwenckfeld. [Compiled by] Edward J. Furcha with the collaboration of Ford Lewis Battles. Pittsburgh, Pittsburgh Theological Seminary [1969] 123 p. 23 cm. Cover title. [BV4500.S25] 71-263287
1. Christian life—Schwenkfelder authors. 2. Prayers. 3. Worship. I. Furcha, Edward J., comp. II. Battles, Ford Lewis, comp. III. Title.

SCHWERTNER, Thomas Maria, 248
1883-1933.
The rosary, a social remedy. 2d ed. prepared by Vincent M. Martin. Milwaukee, Bruce [1952] 137 p. 21 cm. (Science and culture series) [BX2163.S35 1952] 52-2365
1. Rosary. I. Title.

SCOTT, John Martin, 1913- 248
Phenomena of our universe : mysteries that influence our lives / John M. Scott. Huntington, Ind. : Our Sunday Visitor, c1976. 136 p. : ill. ; 18 cm. [BT127.5.S35] 75-28977 ISBN 0-87973-797-2 pbk. : 1.75
1. Mystery. 2. Supernatural. I. Title.

SCOUGAL, Henry, 1650-1678. 248
The life of God in the soul of man / Henry Scougal ; edited, with a historical introd., by Winthrop S. Hudson. Minneapolis : Bethany Fellowship, 1976, c1946. 95 p. ; 18 cm. (Dimension books) (Classics of devotion series) Reprint of the ed. published by Westminster Press, Philadelphia. [BV4500.S3 1976] 76-27560 ISBN 0-87123-326-6 pbk. : 1.50
1. Christian life. I. Title. II. Series.

SECULARIZATION and 248
spirituality. Edited by Christian Duquoc. New York, Paulist Press, [1969] viii, 179 p. 24 cm. (Concilium: theology in the age of renewal. Spirituality, v. 49) On spine: Spirituality and secularization. Bibliographical footnotes. [BV4501.2.S373] 76-103390 4.50
1. Spiritual life—Addresses, essays, lectures. 2. Secularism—Addresses, essays, lectures. I. Duquoc, Christian, ed. II. Title: Spirituality and secularization. III. Series: Concilium (New York) v. 49

SELKIRK, Thomas Mann. 248
A fortune for your thoughts. New York, Exposition Press [c1950] 40 p. 23 cm. [BF171.S4] 51-9277
1. Mind and body. I. Title.

SELVEY, Virginia F 248
And my high tower. [1st ed.] Garden City, N.Y., Doubleday, 1951. 160 p. 20 cm. Autobiographical [BR1725.S43A3] 51-10826
I. Title.

SHEEHY, Maurice Stephen, 248
1898-
Head over heels; a guide for the better self. New York, Farrar, Straus and Young [1951] 178 p. 21 cm. [BX2350.S47] 51-11771
1. Christian life—Catholic authors. I. Title.

SHEEN, Fulton John, Bp., 248
1895-
The choice; the sacred or profane life. [New York, Dell, 1963, c.1954-1957] 240p. illus. 17cm. (Life is worth living ser.; Chapel Bk. 1270) .50 pap.,
I. Title.

SHEEN, Fulton John, Bp., 248
1895-
Life is worth living. Illus. by Dik Browne. Garden City, N. Y., Garden City Books [1955, c1953] 180p. 22cm. Transcribed from tape recordings of the author's television talks.sCatholic Church--Addresses, essays, lectures. [BX890.S533] 55-3406
I. Life is worth living (Television program) II. Title.

SHEEN, Fulton John, Bp., 248
1895-
Life is worth living [first and second series] Illus. by Dik Browne. Garden City, N. Y., Garden City Books [1955 c1953] 284p. illus. 22cm. 'Transcribed from tape recordings of the author's television talks. [BX890] 56-519
1. Catholic Church—Addresses, essays, lectures. 2. Life is worth living (Television program) I. Title.

SHEEN, Fulton John, Bp., 248
1895-
Life is worth living. Illus. by Dik Browne. New York, McGraw-Hill [1953- 4 v. illus. 21 cm. Series 3 has title: Thinking life through. Transcribed from tape recordings of the author's television talks. [BX890.S53] 53-11650
1. Catholic Church—Addresses, essays, lectures. I. Life is worth living (Television program) II. Title. III. Title: Thinking life through

SHEEN, Fulton John, 1895- 248
The life of all living; the philosophy of life. Garden City, N.Y., Garden City Books [1951, c1929] ix, 236 p. 21 cm. [BX2350.S48 1951] 51-5200
1. Life. 2. Christian life. I. Title.

SHEEN, Fulton John, 1895- 248
Lift up your heart. New York, McGraw-Hill [1950] 308 p. 21 cm. [BX2350.S49] 50-14249
1. Christian life—Catholic authors. I. Title.

SHEEN, Fulton John, Bp., 248
1895-
Lift up your heart. Garden City, N. Y., Image Books [1955, c1950] 270p. 19cm. (A Doubleday image book, D9) [BX2350.S49 1955] 55-39163
1. Christian life—Catholic authors. I. Title.

SHEEN, Fulton John, Bp., 248
1895-
Lift up your heart. [Garden City books reprint ed.] Garden City, N.Y., Garden City Books [1952, c1950] 308 p. 21 cm. [BX2350.S49 1952] 52-4259
1. Christian life—Catholic authors. I. Title.

SHEEN, Fulton John, Bp., 248
1895-
Love one another. Garden City, N. Y., Garden City Books [1953, c1944] 160p. 21cm. [BV4639.S5 1953] 53-1818
1. Love (Theology) 2. Friendship. I. Title.

SHEEN, Fulton, John, Bp., 248
1895-
Science, psychiatry and religion. [New York, Dell, 1962, c.1954-1957] 190p. 16cm. (7858) From the Life is worth living television ser. .50 pap.,
I. Title.

SHEEN, Fulton John, Bp., 248
1895-
Thoughts for daily living. [1st ed.] Garden City, N. Y., Garden City Books [c1956] 190p. 22cm. [BX2350.S52] 56-1030
1. Christian life—Catholic authors. I. Title.

SHEEN, Fulton John, Bp., 248
1895-
Thoughts for daily living. [1st ed.] Garden

City, N.Y., Garden City Books [c1956] 190 p. 22 cm. [BX2350.S52] 56-1030
1. Christian life — Catholic authors. I. Title.

SHEEN, Fulton John, Bp., 1895- 248
Way to happiness. Greenwich, Conn., Fawcett [1968,c.1954] 175p. 18cm. (Crest bk., R1083) [BX2350.S53] .60 pap.,
1. Christian life—Catholic authors. I. Title.

SHEEN, Fulton John, Bp., 1895- 248
Way to happiness. Garden City, N.Y., Garden City Books [1954] 192 p. 22 cm. [BX2350.S53 1954] 54-7278
1. Christian life—Catholic authors. I. Title.

SHEEN, Fulton John, Bp., 1895- 248
Way to happy living. [New York, Maco Magazine Corp., 1955] 96p. illus. 24cm. (Maco, 35) [BX2350.S535] 55-13617
1. Christian life—Catholic authors. I. Title.

SHEEN, Fulton John, Bp., 1895- 248
Way to inner peace. New York, Maco Magazine Corp. [1954] 95p. illus. 24cm. [BX2350.S54 1954] 54-12564
1. Christian life—Catholic authors. I. Title.

SHEEN, Fulton John, Bp., 1895- 248
Way to inner peace. Garden City, N.Y., Garden City Books [1955] 188 p. 22 cm. [BX2350.S54] 55-14292
1. Christian life—Catholic authors. I. Title.

SHEEN FULTON JOHN, Bp., 1895- 248
Way to happiness. New York, Maco Magazine Corp., [1953] 95p. illus. 24cm. [BX2350.S53] 53-4105
1. Christian life—Catholic authors. I. Title.

SHELDON, Dorothy, comp. 248
The big treasure book of prayers and grace; illustrated by Pelagie Doane. New York, Grosset & Dunlap, c1956. unpaged. illus. 34cm. (Big treasure books) First published in 1951 under title: Prayers and graces. [BV265.S5 1956] 56-3480
1. Children—Prayer-books and devotions—English. I. Title.

SHELDON, Dorothy, comp. 248
The big treasure book of prayers and graces; illustrated by Pelagie Doane. New York. Grosset & Dunlap. c1956. unpaged. illus. 31 cm. (Big treasure books) First published in 1951 under title: Prayers and graces. [BV265.S5 1956] 56-3480
1. Children — Prayer books and devotions — English I. Title.

SHERRILL, Lewis Joseph, 1892- 248
The struggle of the soul. New York, Macmillan, 1951. viii, 155 p. 21 cm. (The Smyth lectures, 1930) Bibliographical references included in "Notes" (p. 153-155) [BV4501.S467] 51-10464
1. Christian life. I. Title. II. Series: Thomas Smyth lectures, Columbia Theological Seminary, Decatur, Ga., 1950

SHERRILL, Lewis Joseph, 1892- 248
The struggle of the soul. New York, Macmillan [1963, c.1951] 233p. 18cm. (Smyth lects., 1950 Macmillan paperbacks, 127) Bibl. 1.45 pap.,
1. Christian life. I. Title. II. Series: Thomas Smyth lectures, Columbia Theological Seminary Decatur, Ga., 1950

SHEVCHUK, Tetiana 248
Born of the spirit, by Tania Kroiter Bishop. New York, Philosophical Library [1968] 80 p. 22 cm. [BV4510.2.S3] 68-13394
1. Spiritual life. I. Title.

SHIDELER, Mary (McDermott) 248
Consciousness of battle; an interim report on a theological journey. Grand Rapids, Mich., Eerdmans [1970] 200 p. 23 cm. Bibliography: p. 199-200. [BX5995.S346A3] 69-12318 5.95
I. Title.

SHLEMON, Barbara Leahy. 248
Healing prayer / Barbara Leahy Shlemon ; foreword by Francis MacNutt. Notre Dame, Ind. : Ave Maria Press, c1976. 85 p. ; 18 cm. [BT732.5.S53] 75-36056 ISBN 0-87793-108-9: 1.75
1. Faith-cure. 2. Prayer. I. Title.

SHOEMAKER, Samuel Moor, 1893- 248
By the power of God. [1st ed.] New York, Harper [1954] 158p. 20cm. [BV4501.S474] 54-9654
1. Spiritual life. 2. Evangelistic work. I. Title.

SHOEMAKER, Samuel Moor, 1893- ed. 248
Faith at work. [1st ed.] New York,Hawthorn Books [1958] 318 p. 24 cm. [BV4915.S416] 58-5624
1. Conversion. I. Title.

SHOEMAKER, Samuel Moor, 1893- 248
How to become a Christian. [1st ed.] New York, Harper [1953] 158p. 20cm. [BV4915.S42] 53-5451
1. Conversion. 2. Christian life. I. Title.

SIGSWORTH, John Wilkins, 1915- , comp. 248
"How I found God's will for my life"; fifteen personal testimonies from choice Christian servants. Grant Rapids, Zondervan Pub. House [1960] 63 p. 20 cm. [BV4740.S55] 60-4131
1. Vocation. I. Title.

SIMCOX, Carroll Eugene, 1912- 248
Living the love of God; reflections upon the knowledge and love of God, by Carroll E. Simcox. New York, Morehouse-Barlow [1965] 141 p. 21 cm. Bibliographical references included in "Acknowledgments" (p. 139-141) [BV4501.2.S46] 65-27002
1. Christian life—Anglican authors. 2. God—Worship and love. 3. God—Knowableness. I. Title. II. Title: Reflections upon the knowledge and love of God.

SIMCOX, Carroll Eugene, 1912- 248
Living the love of God; reflections upon the knowledge and love of God. New York, Morehouse [c.1965] 141p 21cm. Bibl. [BV4501.2.S46] 65-27002 3.75 bds.,
1. Christian life—Anglican authors. 2. God—Worship and love. 3. God—Knowableness. I. Title. II. Title: Reflections upon the knowledge and love of God.

SIMON, Ann, comp. 248
Heads bowed together; worship resources on reconciliation. Drawings by Maggie Jarvis. New York, Friendship [1966] 94p. illus. 20cm. [BV4805.S5] 66-11128 1.50 pap.,
1. Devotional literature (Selections: Extracts, etc.) I. Title.

SIMON, Raphael M., 1909- 248
The glory of Thy people; the story of a conversion. Pref. by Fulton J. J Sheen. New York. Macmillan, 1961 [c.1948] 139p. (Macmillan paperback, 80) 1.10 pap.,
1. Converts, Catholic. 2. Jews—Converts to Christianity. I. Title.

SLEETH, Ronald Eugene. 248
Which way to God? [By] Ronald E. Sleeth. Nashville, Abingdon Press [1968] 126 p. 20 cm. Bibliographical references included in "Notes" (p. 123-126) [BR110.S55] 68-11474
1. Experience (Religion) 2. Christianity—Psychology. I. Title.

SMITH, Alson Jesse. 248
Live all your life. Chicago, H. Regnery, 1955. 219 p. 22 cm. [BV4010.S545] 55-11493
1. Theology, Pastoral. 2. Psychology, Applied. I. Title.

SMITH, Barbara (Hawkins) 248
22 devotional talks Westwood, N.J., F. H. Revell Co., [1965] 122 p. 21 cm. [BV4832.2.S54] 65-14797
1. Devotional exercises. I. Title.

SMITH, Barbara (Hawkins) 248
22 devotional talks. Westwood, N.J. Revell [c.1965] 122p. 21cm. [BV4832.2.S54] 65-14797 2.50 bds.,
1. Devotional exercises. I. Title.

SMITH, Hannah (Whitall) 1832-1911. 248
The Christian's secret of a happy life. Westwood, N.J., Revell [1952] 248 p. 21 cm. [BV4501.S649] 52-3506
1. Christian life. 2. Faith. I. Title.

*SMITH, Robert Ora 248
Life and the Bible. New York, Pageant [c.1964] 209p. 21cm. 3.00
I. Title.

SMITH, Ronald Gregor. 248
Still point, an essay in living, by Ronald Maxwell [pseud.] London, Nisbet [1943] 74 p. 20 cm. [BV4501.S688] 44-26459
1. Spiritual life. 2. Clergy — Religious life. I. Title.

SMITH, Roy Lemon, 1887- 248
Don't kid yourself! New York, Abingdon Press [1957] 126p. 20cm. [BV4501.S689] 57-5280
1. Christian life. 2. Slang. I. Title.

SMITH, Roy Lemon, 1887- 248
Don't kid yourself! New York, Abingdon Press [1957] 126 p. 20 cm. [BV4501.S689] 57-5280
1. Christian life. 2. Slang. I. Title.

SMITH, Wade Cothran, 1869- 248
The Little Jetts youth talks. Boston, W. A. Wilde Co. [1953] 192p. illus. 21cm. [BV4541.S47] 53-6181
1. Boys—Religious life. I. Title.

SOCKMAN, Ralph Washington, 1889- 248
The whole armor of God. Nashville, Abingdon Press [c1955] 78p. illus. 20cm. [BV4501.S739] 55-6075
1. Christian life. I. Title.

SOUTHARD, Samuel. 248
Conversion and Christian character. Nashville, Broadman Press [1965] 127 p. 20 cm. Bibliographical footnotes. [BV4501.2.S65] 65-15600
1. Christian life—Baptist authors. I. Title.

SOUTHARD, Samuel 248
Conversion and Christian character. Nashville, Broadman [c.1965] 127p. 20cm. Bibl. [BV4501.2.S65] 65-15600 1.50 bds.,
1. Christian life—Baptist authors. I. Title.

SPARKS, Enid. 248 (j)
Through the week with Jesus. Illustrated by Jim Padgett. Nashville, Southern Pub. Association [1968] 128 p. illus. 22 cm. [BV4515.2.S6] 68-3129
1. Christian life—Stories. 2. Christian life—Seventh-Day Adventist authors. I. Title.

SPAUGH, Herbert, 1896- 248
Everyday counsel for everday living. [Charlotte, N.C.] 1951- v. port. 19 cm. [BV4501.S7395] 51-3473
1. Christian life. I. Title.

SPEERS, Wallace Carter, 1896- ed. 248
What on earth are you doing? With an introd. by Elton Trueblood. New York Harper [1951] 158 p. 22 cm. [BR123.S74] 51-12791
1. Christianity — Addresses, essays, lectures. 2. Laity. I. Title.

SPELLER, Jon P. 248
Seed money in action; working the law of tenfold return. New York, Speller [1965] 87p. 18cm. Based on Seed money, by J. Hoshor, pub. in 1960. [BV772.S68] 65-26790 2.50; 1.00 pap.,
1. Christian giving. I. Hoshor, John. Seed money. II. Title. III. Title: Tenfold return.

**SPRINGS of consolation;* 248
Epicurus, Kierkegaard, Michelangelo, Shakespeare, Turgenev. New York, Herder Bk. Ctr., 1968. 1v. (unapged) col. illus. 13cm. 1.50 bds., wire bdg.

SPURGEON, Charles Haddon, 1834-1892 248
According to promise; or, The Lord's method of dealing with his chosen people. Grand Rapids, Mich., Baker Bk., 1964, 128p. 19cm. Reprinted from the 1890 ed. 64-14565 1.25 pap.,
1. Baptists—Sermons. 2. Sermons, English. I. Title. II. Title: The Lord's method of dealing with his chosen people.

SPURGEON, Charles Haddon, 1834-1892 248
Twelve sermons on holiness. Swengel, Pa., Reiner Pubs. 1965., 152p. 20cm. [BX6333.S6T8] 65-29723 1.50 pap.,
1. Holiness—Sermons. 2. Baptists—Sermons. 3. Sermons, English. I. Title.

STACKEL, Robert W 248
The awakened heart; ways of cultivating the devotional life of young people, a study book, Edited by Gustav K. Wiencke. Philadelphia, Muhlenberg Press [1951] 96 p. 19 cm. [BV4531.S73] 51-13001
1. Youth — Religious life. I. Title.

STANNARD, William H 248
My Christian responsibility. Boston, Christopher Pub. House [1950] 70 p. 21 cm. [BV4520.S67] 50-3498
1. Duty. 2. Christian life. I. Title.

STAPLETON, Ruth Carter. 248
The experience of inner healing / Ruth Carter Stapleton. Waco, Tex. : Word Books, c1977. 213 p. ; 23 cm. Includes bibliographical references. [BT732.5.S74] 76-56479 ISBN 0-87680-507-1 : 7.95
1. Faith-cure. 2. Psychology, Religious. I. Title.

STAPLETON, Ruth Carter. 248
The gift of inner healing / Ruth Carter Stapleton. Waco, Tex. : Word Books, c1976. 115 p. : port. ; 23 cm. Includes bibliographical references. [BT732.5.S75] 75-36180 4.95
1. Faith-cure. I. Title.

STAPLETON, Ruth Carter. 248
The gift of inner healing / [by] Ruth Carter Stapleton. New York : Bantam Books, 1977,c1976. 113p. ; 18 cm. Includes bibliographical references. [BT732.5S75] ISBN 0-553-10291-5 pbk. : 1.75
1. Faith-cure. I. Title.
L.C. card no. for 1976 Word Books ed.: 75-36180.

STARKIE, Walter Fitzwilliam, 1894- 248
The road to Santiago; pilgrims of St. James. New York, Dutton, 1957. x, 339 p. illus., map, music. 22 cm. Bibliographical footnotes. [BX2321.S3S68] A 58
1. James, Saint, Apostle. 2. Santiago de Compostela. 3. Pilgrimages—Spain. 4. Spain—Description and travel. I. Title.

STEUART, Robert Henry Joseph, 1874-1948. 248
Spiritual teaching of Father Steuart, s.j. Notes of his retreats and conferences collected and arr. by Katharine Kendall. With an introd. by H. P. C. Lyons. Westminster, Md., Newman Press [1952] 148 p. 22 cm. [BX2350.S65] 52-4526
1. Spiritual life — Catholic authors. I. Title.

STEUART, Robert Henry Joseph, 1874-1948. 248
The two voices; spiritual conferences of R. H. J. Steuart, S. J. Edited, with a memoir, by C. C. Martindale. Westminster, Md., Newman Press [1952] 274p. 22cm. [BX2350.S68] 52-14313
1. Spiritual life—Catholic authors. 2. Prayer. I. Title.

STEWART, Ora (Pate) 1910- 248
A letter to my daughter. Salt Lake City, Bookcraft [c1956] 160p. 17cm. [BV4451.S8] 57-31081
1. Young women—Religious life. I. Title.

STILLMAN, Peter 248
That happy feeling of 'Thank you.' Illus. by Judy Stane. Norwalk, Conn., Gibson Co. [c.1964] 1v. (unpaged) col. illus. 19cm. 64-16631 1.95
1. Gratitude—Juvenile literature. I. Title.

STILLMAN, Peter. 248
That happy feeling of "Thank you." Illus. by Judy Stang. Norwalk, Conn., C. R. Gibson Co. [1964] 1 v. (unpaged) col. illus. 19 cm. [BV4647.G8S8] 64-16631
1. Gratitude — Juvenile literature. I. Title.

STINNETTE, Charles Roy, 1914- 248
Faith, freedom, and selfhood; a study in personal dynamics. Greenwich, Conn., Seabury Press, 1959. 239 p. 22 cm. Includes bibliography. [BR110.S73] 59-9805
1. Christianity — Sychology. 2. Liberty. I. Title.

STRINGFELLOW, William. 248
A second birthday. [1st ed.] Garden City, N.Y., Doubleday, 1970. 203 p. 22 cm. [BT732.7.S75] 75-116256 5.95
1. Suffering. 2. Faith-cure. I. Title.

*SULLIVAN, Daniel A. 248
Our bad, our good, our God [by] Daniel A. Sullivan. [1st. ed.] Hicksville, N.Y. Exposition Press [1974] 80 p. 22 cm. [BR110] ISBN 0-682-48000-2 4.50
1. Spiritual life. 2. Christian life. I. Title.

SWISHER, Rolla O 248
That church in your life. Anderson, Ind., Warner Press [1958] 96 p. 21 cm. [BV4501.2.S9] 58-13720
1. Christian life — Study and teaching. I. Title.

SWOR, Chester E 248
Very truly yours. Nashville, Broadman Press [1954] 163p. 21cm. [BV4501.S86] 54-12425
1. Christian life. I. Title.

TAYLOR, Harry Milton. 248
Faith must be lived; prescriptions in Christian psychology. [1st ed.] New York, Harper [1951] 188 p. 22 cm. [BR110.T3] 51-11958
1. Christianity — Psychology. 2. Emotions. I. Title.

TAYLOR, Herbert John, 1893- 248
God has a plan for you [by] Herbert J. Taylor with Robert Walker. Old Tappan, N.J., Revell [1968] 128 p. 21 cm. [BR1725.T28A3] 68-28440 3.50
1. Christian life. 2. Success. I. Walker, Robert, 1912- II. Title.

TAYLOR, Jeremy, Bp. of Down and Connor, 1613-1667. 248
The rule and exercise of holy living, by Jeremy Taylor. Abridged with a pref. by Anne Lamb. Foreword by Henry Chadwick. [1st U.S. ed.] New York, Harper & Row, [1970] xvii, 173 p. 22 cm. [BV4500.T3 1970] 76-141658 4.95
1. Christian life. I. Lamb, Anne. II. Title. III. Title: Holy living.

TAYLOR, Jeremy, Bp. of Down and Connor, 1613-1667. 248
The rule and exercises of holy living. Edited and with an introd. by Thomas S. Kepler. [1st ed.] Cleveland, World Pub. Co. [1956] xxiv. 293p. 16cm. (World devotional classics) [BV4500.T3 1956] 56-9257
1. Christian life. I. Title. II. Title: Holy living.

TAYLOR, Jeremy, Bp. of Down and Connor, 1613-1667. 248
The rule and exercises of holy living. Edited and with an introd. by Thomas S. Kepler. [1st ed.] Cleveland, World Pub. Co. [1956] xxiv, 293 p. 16 cm. (World devotional classics) [BV4500.T3 1956] 56-9257
1. Christian life. I. Title. II. Title: Holy living.

TAYLOR, Kenneth Nathaniel. 248
I see what God wants me to know. Chicago, Moody Press [1955] unpaged. illus. 29cm. [BV4571.T36] 55-2746
1. Children—Religious life. I. Title.

TAYLOR, Richard Shelley, 1912- 248
The disciplined life. Kansas City, Mo., Beacon Hill Press [1962] 102 p. 20 cm. [BV4501.2.T3] 62-7123
1. Christian life. I. Title.

TERESA, Saint, 1515-1582. 248
The collected works of St. Teresa of Avila / translated by Kieran Kavanaugh and Otilio Rodriguez. Washington : Institute of Carmelite Studies, 1976- v. ; 22 cm. Contents.Contents.—v. 1. The book of her life. Spiritual testimonies. Soliloquies. Includes bibliographical references and index. [BX890.T353 1976] 75-31305 ISBN 0-9600876-2-1 : 4.95
1. Catholic Church—Collected works. 2. Theology—Collected works—16th century.

*TERESA OF AVILA, St., 1515-82 248
The way of perfection. Tr. [from Spanish] ed. by E. Allison Peers. From the critical ed. of P. Silverio De Santa Teresa, C.D. Garden City, N.Y., Doubleday [1964] 280p. 18cm. (Image bk. D 176) .85 pap.,
I. Title.

*THATCH, Harrell G. 248
God gets in the way of a sailor. Foreword by O. Hobart Mowrer. New York, Exposition [c.1964] 266p. 21cm. (EP42077) 4.50
I. Title.

THOMAS Aquinas, Saint, 1225?-1274. 248
The religious state; the episcopate and the priestly office. A translation of the minor work of the Saint, On the perfection of the spiritual life. Edited with prefatory notice by Father Proctor. Westminster, Md., Newman Press, 1950. viii, 166 p. 20 cm. [BX2350.5.T52] 50-12499
1. Perfection — Catholic Church. 2. Clergy — Religious life. 3. Bishops. I. Title.

THOMAS, George Ernest, 1907- 248
Disciplines of the spiritual life. New York, Published for the Cooperative Publication Association by Abingdon Press [1963] 96 p. 19 cm. (Faith for life series) [BV5031.2.T5] 63-23648
1. Spiritual life. I. Title.

THOMAS, George Ernest, 1907- 248
Faith can master fear. New York, Revell [1950] 160 p. 21 cm. Bibliographical references: p. 159-160. [BV4012.T5] 50-10876
1. Psychology, Pastoral. 2. Fear. I. Title.

THOMAS, George Ernest, 1907- 248
Spiritual life in the New Testament. [Westwood, N. J.] Revell [1955] 160p. 21cm. [BR195.C5T5] 55-8761
1. Christian life—Early church. I. Title.

THOMAS, George Finger, 1899- 248
Poetry, religion and the spiritual life. Houston, Elsevier Press, 1951. (The Rockwell lectures, the Rice Institute, Houston) [BV4501.T46] 52-5649
1. 113 p. 21 cm. 2. Spiritual life. I. Title.

THOMAS, George Finger, 1899- 248
Poetry, religion and the spiritual life. [New York, Amer. Elsevier, 1963] 113p. 21cm. 2.75 bds.,
1. Spiritual life. I. Title.

THOMAS, Winburn T ed. 248
Stewardship in mission [edited] by Winburn T. Thomas. Authors: Elmer J. F. Arndt [and others] Englewood Cliffs, N.J., Prentice-Hall [1964] xiv, 114 p. 21 cm. (Library of Christian stewardship, LCS-2) Bibliographical footnotes. [BV772.T48] 64-20978
1. Stewardship, Christian. I. Title.

THOMAS, Winburn T., ed. 248
Stewardship in mission [ed.] by Winburn T. Thomas. Authors: Elmer J. F. Arndt [others] Englewood Cliffs, N.J., Prentice [c.1964] xiv, 114p. 21cm. (Lib. of Christian stewardship, LCS-2) Bibl. 64-20978 2.75; 1.50 pap.,
1. Stewardship, Christian. I. Title.

THOMPSON, Olive Ross 248
That His word will live. New York, Philosophical Lib. [1966] 69p. 21cm. [BV4501.2.T52] 65-26683 3.50
1. Christian life. I. Title.

THOMPSON, Thomas K ed. 248
Stewardship illustration, edited by T. K. Thompson. Englewood Cliffs, N.J., Prentice-Hall [1965] xvi, 112 p. 21 cm. (Library of Christian stewardship, v. 4) [BV772.T49] 65-16587
1. Stewardship, Christian. I. Title.

THOMPSON, Thomas K., ed. 248
Stewardship illustrations. Englewood Cliffs, N.J., Prentice [c.1965] xvi, 112p. 21cm. (Lib. of Christian stewardship, v.4) [BV772.T49] 65-16587 2.95; 1.50 pap.,
1. Stewardship, Christian. I. Title.

THOMPSON, Thomas K ed. 248
Stewardship in contemporary life, edited by T. K. Thompson. New York, Association Press [1965] 190 p. 21 cm. Contents.CONTENTS. -- Motives for giving in the New Testament, by T. M. Taylor. -- Corporate stewardship, by J. C. McLelland. -- The ethics of promotion, by J. M. Gustafson. -- The denominational structure, by S. P. Austin. Includes bibliographical references. [BV772.T47] 65-11094
1. Stewardship, Christian. I. Title.

THOMPSON, Thomas K., ed. 248
Stewardship in contemporary life. New York, Association [c.1965] 190p. 21cm. Bibl. [BV772.T47] 65-11094 4.95; 1.95 pap.,
1. Stewardship, Christian. I. Title.
Contents omitted.,

THOMSON, Lucy Gertsch, comp. 248
Stories that live; [a collection of inspirational, character-building stories] Salt Lake City, Deseret Book Co. [1956] 129p. 16cm. [BJ1597.T5] 57-557
1. Conduct of life. I. Title.

THOMSON, Lucy Gertsch, comp. 248
Stories that live; [a collection of inspirational, character-building stories] Salt Lake City, Deseret Book Co. [1956] 120 p. 16 cm. [BJ1597.T5] 57-557
1. Conduct of life. I. Title.

THURMAN, Howard, 1899- 248
The creative encounter; an interpretation of religion and the social witness. [1st ed.] New York, Harper [1954] 153p. 20cm. 'The substance ... Ohil Wesleyan University in March, 1954.' [BR110.T48] 54-11664
1. Experience (Religion)
** *08
sReligion. I. Title.

THURMAN, Howard, 1899- 248
The creative encounter; an interpretation of religion and the social witness. Richmond, Ind., Friends United Press [1972, c1954] 153 p. 21 cm. [BR110.T48 1972] 72-12773 ISBN 0-913408-07-7 pap. 1.95
1. Experience (Religion) 2. Religion. I. Title.

TIPPETT, Harry Moyle, 1891- 248
Who waits in faith. Washington, Review and Herald Pub. Assn. [1951] 128 p. 20 cm. [BV4637.T56] 52-15009
1. Trust in God. I. Title.

TITTMANN, George Fabian. 248
Is religion enough? The challenge of the Gospel. Greenwich, Conn., Seabury Press, 1962. 177 p. 22 cm. [BV4501.2.T57] 62-17082
1. Spiritual life. I. Title.

TITTMANN, George Fabian 248
Is religion enough? The challenge of the Gospel. Greenwich, Conn., Seabury [c.]1962. 177p. 22cm. 62-17082 4.00
1. Spiritual life. I. Title.

TODD, John Murray. 248
We are men; a book for the Christian layman. London, New York, Sheed & Ward [1955] 194p. 20cm. [BX1920.T6 1955] 55-2554
1. Laity. 2. Christian life—Catholic authors. I. Title.

TONER, Helen L 248
Little prayers for personal poise. St. Louis, Bethany Press [1953] 64p. 18cm. [BV260.T65] 53-36753
1. Prayers. I. Title.

*TORREY, R. A. 248
The baptism with the Holy Spirit. Minneapolis, Bethany [1965] 50p. 15cm. .25 pap.,
I. Title.

TOURNIER, Paul. 248
Guilt and grace ; The meaning of persons ; The person reborn ; To understand each other / Paul Tournier. New York : Iverson [i.e. Iversen]-Norman, 1977. 795 p. in various pagings ; 22 cm. On spine: The best of Paul Tournier. Reprint of the works published between 1957 and 1967 by Harper & Row, New York and John Knox Press, Richmond. Includes bibliographical references and indexes. [BJ1471.5.T5913] 77-152051 ISBN 0-8010-8837-2 : 14.95
1. Guilt. 2. Grace (Theology) 3. Personality. 4. Pastoral psychology. 5. Marriage. I. Title. II. Title: The best of Paul Tournier.
Publisher's address : 175 5th Ave., New York, N.Y. 10010

TOURNIER, Paul 248
The person reborn. Tr. by Edwin Hudson. [1st ed.] New York, Harper [1966] vi, 248p. 22cm. Tr. of Technique et foi. [BV4502.T613] 66-20787 4.50
1. Christian life. 2. Pastoral Psychology. I. Title.

TOZER, Aiden Wilson, 1897- 248
The divine conquest. Introd. by William L. Culbertson. New York, Revell [1950] 128 p. 20 cm. [BV4501.T755] 50-10877
1. Spriitual life. I. Title.

TOZER, Aiden Wilson, 1897- 248
The root of the righteous. Harrisburg, Pa., Christian Publications [1955] 160 p. 20 cm. [BR123.T67] 55-39562
1. Christianity—Addresses, essays, lectures. I. Title.

TRESE, Leo John 248
More than many sparrows. 2nd ed. Notre Dame, Ind., Fides [1960, c.1958] 128p. 18cm. (Dome bk.) .95 pap.,
1. Christian life—Catholic authors. I. Title.

TRESE, Leo John, 1902- 248
More than many sparrows. Chicago, Fides [1958] 137 p. 21 cm. [BX2350.T68] 58-9652
1. Christian life — Catholic authors. I. Title.

TREVINO, Jose Guadalupe, 1889- 248
Rules for the spiritual life. Translated by Benjamin B. Hunt. Milwaukee, Bruce Pub. Co. [1956] 179p. 23cm. [BX2350.T713] 56-7046
1. Spiritual life—Catholic authors. I. Title.

TREVINO, Jose Guadalupe, 1889- 248
Rules for the spiritual life. Translated by Benjamin B. Hunt. Milwaukee, Bruce Pub. Co. [1956] 179 p. 23 cm. [BX2350.T713] 56-7046
1. Spiritual life — Catholic authors. I. Title.

TRUEBLOOD, David Elton, 1900- 248
The predicament of modern man. by D. Elton Trueblood . . . New York. London, Harper [1967.c.1944] ix p.. 1 1., 105p. 20cm. (Chapel bk., CB37) [BR479.T7] 44-7058 .95 pap.,
1. Christianity—20th cent. 2. Reconstruction (1939-1945) 3. Civilization. I. Title.

TURNAGE, Mac N., 1927- 248
People, families & God : a study guide for participants / by Mac N. and Anne Shaw Turnage. Atlanta : John Knox Press, c1976. 79 p. ; 28 cm. Bibliography: p. 5. [BV4526.2.T87] 76-12400 ISBN 0-8042-9077-6 pbk. : 5.95
1. Family—Religious life—Study and teaching. I. Turnage, Anne Shaw, 1927- joint author. II. Title.

TURNBULL, Bob. 248
Will the old Bob Turnbull please drop dead? Elgin, Ill., D. C. Cook Pub. Co. [1970] 93 p. 18 cm. [BV4501.2.T85] 72-113867 0.95
1. Christian life—1960- I. Title.

TURNBULL, Ralph G. 248
Basic Christian beliefs. Grand Rapids, Mich., Baker Bk. [c.]1962. 91p. 22cm. (Bible companion ser. for lesson and sermon preparation) 1.00 pap.,
I. Title.

TURNER, Dorothy Banker. 248
How to gain health, happiness, prosperity; a collection of inspirational pieces. Claremont, Calif., Creative Press, 1955. 56p. 22cm. [BV4501.T88] 55-8567
1. Christian life. I. Title.

TURNER, Pearl Iva. 248
Living the more abundant life. Boston, Christopher Pub. House [1954] 72p. 21cm. [BV4510.T78] 55-21991
I. Title.

UNDERHILL, Evelyn 248
The golden sequence; a fourfold study of the spiritual life. New York, Harper [1960, c.1933] 123p. 21cm. (Harper Torchbooks/The Cloister Library TB 68) 1.25 pap.,
1. Spiritual life. 2. Mysticism. 3. Prayer. I. Title.

UNDERHILL, Evelyn, 1875-1941. 248
Mixed pasture; twelve essays and addresses. Freeport, N.Y., Books for Libraries Press [1968] xi, 233 p. 22 cm. (Essay index reprint series) Reprint of the 1933 ed. Contents.Contents.—The philosophy of contemplation (Counsell memorial lecture,1930).—What is sanctity?—Spiritual life.—Some implicits of Christian social reform.—The will of the voice.—The Christian basis of social action.—The ideals of the ministry of women.—The spiritual significance of the Oxford Movement.—St. Francis and Franciscan spirituality (Walter Seton memorial lecture, 1933)—Richard the hermit.—Walter Hilton.—Finite and infinite: a study of the philosophy of Baron Friedrich von Hugel.—Additional note: Baron von Hugel as a spiritual teacher. [BV4501.U52 1968] 68-8501
1. Spiritual life. 2. Mysticism. I. Title.

UNDERHILL, Evelyn, 1875-1941. 248
The spiritual life. New York, Harper [1963?] 127, [1] p. 14 cm. "Books on the spiritual life": p. 127-[128] [BV4501] 63-6840
1. Spiritual life. I. Title.

UNGER, Merrill Frederick, 1909- 248
Pathways to power. Grand Rapids, Zondervan Pub. House [c1953] 160p. 20cm. [BV4832.U5] 54-718
1. Devotional literature. I. Title.

VAN Zeller, Hubert, 1905- 248
Suffering in other words; a presentation for beginners. Springfield, Ill., Templegate [1964] 96 p. 20 cm. 96 p. 20 cm. (His[In other words series]) (His [In other words series]) [BT732.7.V3] 65-3298
1. Suffering. I. Title.

VAN Zeller, Hubert, 1905- 248
The will of God in other words; a presentation for beginners. Springfield, Ill., Templegate [1964] 124 p. 20 cm. (His [In other words series]) [BX2350.2.V32] 65-2835
1. Christian life — Catholic authors. 2. God — Will. I. Title.

VAN BAALEN, Jan Karel, 1890- 248
If thou shall confess. Grand Rapids, Eerdmans [1962] 65 p. 18 cm. [BV4501.2.V3] 62-13402
1. Christian life. I. Title.

VAN DUSEN, Henry Pitney, 1897- 248
Life's meaning: the why and how of Christian living. New York, Association Press, 1951. 244 p. 21 cm. "A Haddam House book." [BV4531.V3] 51-13621
1. Youth — Religious life. I. Title.

VAN KAAM, Adrian L., 1920- 248
Religion and personality [by] Adrian van Kaam. Englewood Cliffs, N.J., Prentice-Hall [1964] viii, 170 p. 21 cm. Bibliography: p. 161-163. [BX2350.V15] 64-15831
1. Psychology, Religious. 2. Personality. 3. Spiritual life—Catholic authors. I. Title.

VANN, Gerald, 1906- 248
The paradise tree; on living the symbols of the church. New York, Sheed and Ward [1959] 820 p. 22 cm. Includes bibliography. [BV5083.V3] 59-8236
1. Mysticism — Catholic Church. 2. Sacraments — Catholic Church. 3. Symbolism. I. Title.

VANN, Gerald, 1906- 248
The water and the fire. New York, Sheed and Ward [1954] 187p. 22cm. [BX2350.V18 1954] 54-6139
1. Christian life—Catholic authors. I. Title.

VAN WOERDAN, Peter. 248
In the secret place, a story of the Dutch underground. Wheaton, Ill., Van Kampen Press [1954] 64p. 20cm. [BR1725.V3A3] 54-1749
1. World War, 1939-1945— Personal narratives, Dutch. I. Title.

VAN ZELLER, Dom Hubert 248
Famine of spirit. Springfield, Ill., Templegate [1964] 194p. 18cm. 3.50
I. Title.

VAN ZELLER, Hubert, 1905- 248
The inner search. New York, Sheed and Ward [1957] 230p. 21cm. [BX2350.V224] 57-6046
1. Spiritual life—Catholic authors. I. Title.

VAN ZELLER, Hubert, 1905- 248
The inner search. New York, Sheed and Ward [1957] 230 p. 21 cm. Secular name: Claude Van Zeller. [BX2350.V224] 57-6046
1. Spiritual life — Catholic authors. I. Title. II. Series.

VAN ZELLER, Hubert, 1905- 248
The inner search. [Secular name: Claude Van Zeller] Garden City, N.Y., Doubleday [1967, c.1957] 234p. 18cm. (Image bk., D220) First pub. in Britain in 1957 by Sheed [BX2350.V224 1957a] .95 pap.,
1. Spiritual life—Catholic authors. I. Title.

VAN ZELLER, Hubert, Father, 1905- 248
We sing while there's voice left. London and New York, Sheed and Ward [1951] 198 p. 19 cm. [BX2350.V256] 51-8035
1. Christian life — Catholic authors. I. Title.

VAN ZELLER, Hubert, Father, 1905- 248
We work while the light lasts. New York, Sheed and Ward, 1951 [c1950] 166 p. 20 cm. [BX2350.V26 1951] 51-6899
1. Christian life — Catholic authors. I. Title.

VAN ZELLER, Hubert, Dom. 248
[Secular name: Claude Van Zeller] 1905
We live with our eyes open. Garden City, N.Y., Doubleday [1963, c.1949] 152p. 18cm. (Image bk., D162) .75 pap.,
1. Christian life—Catholic authors. I. Title.

VAN ZELLER, Hubert Father, 248
1905-SecularnameClaudeVanZeller
We work while the light lasts. Garden City, N.Y., Doubleday [1962, c.1950] 160p. 18cm. (Image bk., D146) .75 pap.,
1. Christian life—Catholic authors. I. Title.

VERHEYLEZOON, Louis. 248
Devotion to the Sacred Heart: object, ends, practice, motives. With a foreword by C. C. Martindale. Westminster, Md., Newman Press [1955] 280p. 23cm. [BX2157.V43] 55-14740
1. Sacred Heart, Devotion to. I. Title.

VERWER, George 248
Literature evangelism, a manual. Chicago, Moody [c.1963] 128p. 17cm. (Colportage lib., 498) .39 pap.,
I. Title.

VINCENTIUS FERRERIUS, Saint, 1350(ca.)-1419. 248
A treatise on the spiritual life. With a commentary by Julienne Morrell. Translated by the Dominican Nuns, Corpus Christi Monastery, Memlo [sic] Park, Calif. Westminster, Md., Newman Press, 1957. 175p. 22cm. Bibliographical footnotes. [BX2349.V52 1957] 57-1878
1. Spiritual life—Catholic authors. I. Morell, Jullenne, 1594-1653. II. Title.

VINCENTIUS FERRERIUS, Saint, 1350(ca.)-1419. 248
A treatise on the spiritual life. With a commentary by Julienne Morrell. Translated by the Cominican Nuns, Corpus Christi Monastery, Memlo [sic] Park, Calif. Westminster, Md., Newman Press, 1957. 175 p. 22 cm. Bibliographical footnotes. [BX2349.V52 1957] 57-1878
1. Spiritual life — Catholic authors. I. Morell, Julienne, 1594-1653. II. Title.

VON HILDEBRAND, Dietrich, 1889- 248
The heart : an analysis of human and divine affectivity / Dietrich von Hildebrand. Chicago : Franciscan Herald Press, c1977. 182 p. ; 22 cm. Published in 1965 under title: The sacred heart. Includes bibliographical references. [BX2157.V6 1977] 76-52744 ISBN 0-8199-0665-4 : 6.95
1. Sacred Heart, Devotion to. I. Title.

VON HILDEBRAND, Dietrich, 1889- 248
The sacred heart; an analysis of human and divine affectivity. Baltimore, Helicon [1965] 182 p. 21 cm. [BX2157.V6] 65-24130
1. Sacred Heart, Devotion to. I. Title.

VON HILDEBRAND, Dietrich, 1889- 248
The sacred heart; an analysis of human and divine affectivity. Helicon [dist. New York, Taplinger, c.1965] 182p. 21cm. [BX2157.V6] 65-24130 4.50
1. Sacred Heart, Devotion to. I. Title.

VON HILDEBRAND, Dietrich, 1889- 248
Transformation in Christ; on the Christian attitude of mind. Garden City, N.Y., Doubleday [1963, c.1960] 394p. 18cm. (Image Bk. D152) 1.35 pap.,
1. Christian life—Catholic authors. I. Title.

WAKEFIELD, Gordon Stevens. 248
The life of the spirit in the world of today, [by] Gordon S. Wakefield. [New York] Macmillan [1969] xi, 176 p. 18 cm. Bibliographical footnotes. [BV4501.2.W28] 69-10929
1. Spirituality. I. Title.

WALKER, Grace (Mathews) 248
Heaven happens here: life can be happy-heaven can be assured; abook for today (nonsectarian) based on a Christian philosophy of life. New York, Vantage Press [1955] 225p. 23cm. Prose and poems. [BV4501.W24] 54-12627
1. Christian life. I. Title.

WALKER, William Bruce. 248
Victory over suffering. Butler, Ind., Higley Press [1958] 156 p. 20 cm. [BV4909.W2] 58-33247
1. Suffering. I. Title.

WALL, Martha. 248
In crossfire of hate. Chicago, Moody Press [1970] 288 p. facsim. 22 cm. [BR1608.C66W3] 72-104827 4.95
1. Franco, Marco. 2. Persecution—Colombia. I. Title.

WALSH, James, 1920-ed. 248
Spirituality through the centuries; ascetics and mystics of the Western Church. New York, Kenedy [1964] ix, 342p. 23cm. Bibl. [BV5075.W34] 64-21181 5.50
1. Mysticism—Hist. I. Title.

WAMBLE, Irving W 248
Who is my neighbor? New York, Vantage Press [1952] 124 p. 23 cm. [BR115.S6W286] 52-6959
1. Sociology, Christian. I. Title.

WANSBROUGH, Elizabeth. 248
The Rosary: the joyful mysteries. Pictures by Cecilia Pollen. [New York] Sheed and Ward [c1951] 1 v. illus. 21 cm. [BX2163.W27] 51-14578
1. Rosary I. Title.

WATERS, Harold 248
Christ over the seven seas. [1st Amer. ed.] Wilkes-Barre. Pa., Dimension [1967] 248p. 20cm. [BV4515.2.W3 1967] 67-16817 5.95
1. Christian life—Stories. 2. Sea stories. I. Title.

WATERS, Harold. 248
Christ over the seven seas. [1st American ed.] Wilkes-Barre, Pa., Dimension Books [1967] 248 p. 20 cm. [BV4515.2W3 1967] 67-16817
1. Christian life — Stories. 2. Sea stories. I. Title.

WATSON, Harold. 248
The key to inner power; essays on religion and life. [2d ed., rev. and enl.] New York, Exposition Press [1955] 53p. 21cm. 'Some of these essays were published in 1952 under the title Let us reason together' [BV4501.W3848 1955] 55-10308
1. Christian life. I. Title.

WATTS, Marie S. 248
You are the splendor; the way to spiritual illumination. New York, Exposition [c.1963] 222p. 21cm. 5.00
I. Title.

THE way of a pilgrim, and The pilgrim continues his way. 248
Translated from the Russian, by R. M. French. New York, Harper [1954] x, 242p. maps. 20cm. [BV4839.R8O8] 54-13330
1. Devotional literature. I. French, Reginald Michael, 1884- II. The pilgrim continues his way. III. Title: r.

WE are now Catholics 248
[by] Rudolf Goethe [and others]. Edited by Karl Hardt. Translated from the German by Norman C. Reeves. With an introductory essay by Sylvester P. Theisen. Westminster, Md., Newman Press, 1959. lxvii. 223p. 23cm. 59-10404 3.95
1. Converts, Catholic. I. Goethe, Rudolf, 1880- II. Hardt, Karl, ed.

WEATHERHEAD, Leslie Dixon, 1893- 248
Prescription for anxiety. New York, Abington Press [c1956] 157p. 21cm. [BV4909.W4 1956a] 57-5284
1. Anxiety. 2. Consolation. 3. Psychology, Pastoral. I. Title.

WEATHERHEAD, Leslie Dixon, 1893- 248
Prescription for anxiety. New York, Abingdon Press [c1956] 157 p. 21 cm. [BV4909.W4 1956a] 57-5284
1. Anxiety. 2. Consolation. 3. Psychology, Pastoral. I. Title.

WEATHERHEAD, Leslie Dixon, 1893- 248
Prescription for anxiety. Nashville, Abingdon [1968,c.1956] 157p. 20cm. (Apex bks.) [BV4909.W4 1956a] 57-5284 1.25 pap.,
1. Anxiety. 2. Consolation. 3. Psychology, Pastoral. I. Title.

WEAVER, Bertrand 248
His Cross in your life. New York, St. Paul Publications [1961, c.1960] 156p. 61-8201 3.25
1. Christian life—Catholic authors. I. Title.

WEBB, Lance. 248
On the edge of the absurd. New York, Abingdon Press [1965] 158 p. 21 cm. Bibliographical references included in "Notes" (p. 155-158) [BV4501.2.W39] 65-14721
1. Christian life — Methodist authors. I. Title.

WEBB, Lance 248
On the edge of the absurd. Nashville, Abingdon [c.1965] 158p. 21cm. Bibl. [BV4501.2.W39] 65-14721 2.75
1. Christian life—Methodist authors. I. Title.

WEBBE, Gale D. 248
The night and nothing. New York, Seabury [c.]1964. 125p. 22cm. 64-14082 3.00
1. Asceticism. I. Title.

WEBSTER, Donald A 248
You can be happy; the search for the satisfying life. Mountain View, Calif, Pacific Press Pub. Association [1955] 144p. 21cm. [BV4501.W438] 55-11538
1. Christian life. I. Title.

WEIL, Simon, 1909-1943. 248
Waiting for God; translated by Emma Craufurd. With an introd. by Leslie A. Fiedler. New York, Putnam [1951] 227 p. 22 cm. [BV4817.W413] 51-7174
1. God — Worship and love. I. Title.

WEIL, Simone, 1909-1943. 248
Waiting for God; [letters and essays] Translated by Emma Craufurd. With an introd. by Leslie A. Fiedler. New York, Capricorn Books [1959, c1951] 227 p. 19 cm. (Capricorn books, CAP17) [BV4817.W413 1959] 59-14857
1. God — Worship and love. I. Title.

WEIL, Simone, 1909-1943. 248
Waiting for God; translated by Emma Craufurd. With an introd. by Leslie A. Fiedler. New York, Harper [1973, c.1951] ix, 227 p. 20 cm. (Colophon bks., CN295) [BV4817.W413] ISBN 0-06-090295-7 pap., 2.95
1. God—Worship and love. I. Title.

WEISS, Albert Maria, 1844-1925. 248
The Christian life. Translated by Sister M. Fulgence. St. Louis, Mo., B. Herder Book Co. [1956] 166p. 21cm. (Cross and crown series of spirituality, no. 7) 'A translation of part iv, volume iii, of [the author's] Apologie des Christentums.58 [BX2350.W353] 56-7718
1. Christian life— authors. I. Title.

WEISS, Albert Maria, 1844-1925. 248
The Christian life. Translated by Sister M. Fulgence. St. Louis, Mo., B. Herder Book Co. [1956] 166 p. 21 cm. (Cross and crown series of spirituality, no. 7) "A translation of part IV, volume III, of [The author's] Apologie des Christentums." [BX2350.W353] 56-7718
1. Christian life — Catholic authors. I. Title.

WEISS, George Christian, 1910- 248
The perfect will of God; a helpful handbook for saints who are seeking that "perfect will of God." Lincoln, Neb., Back to the Bible Publishers [1950] 126 p. 17 cm. (Sunrise books) [BV4501.W446] 50-3601
1. Christian life. 2. God — Will. I. Title.

WERNER, Hazen Graff, Bp., 1895- 248
Live with your emotions. New York, Abingdon-Cokesbury Press [1951] 186 p. 20 cm. [BF531.W45] 51-13502
1. Emotions. I. Title.

WERNING, Waldo J 248
The stewardship call; an approach to personal and group stewardship based on the concept of Christian vocation [by] Aldo J. Werning. Saint Louis, Concordia Pub. House [1965] 186 p. 21 cm. Bibliography: p. 185-186. [BV772.W44] 65-6734
1. Stewardship, Christian. I. Title.

WERNING, Waldo J. 248
The stewardship call; an approach to personal and group stewardship based on the concept of Christian vocation. St. Louis, Concordia [c.1965] 186p. 21cm. Bibl. [BV772.W44] 65-6734 2.25 pap.,
1. Stewardship, Christian. I. Title.

WHEELER, Joseph Clyde. 248
Winning what you want. St. Louis, Bethany Press [1960] 156 p. 21 cm. [BV4908.5.W5] 60-6229
1. Peace of mind. I. Title.

WHEELER, Joseph Clyde 248
Winning what you want. St. Louis, Bethany Press [c.1960] 156 p. 21 cm. 60-6229 2.95, bds.
1. Peace of mind. I. Title.

WHITE, Anne S 248
God can transform the world. Boston, Christopher Pub. House [1957] 107p. 21cm. [BV4501.W54] 57-20950
1. Christian life. I. Title.

WHITE, Anne S. 248
God can transform the world. Boston, Christopher Pub. House [1957] 107 p. 21 cm. [BV4501.W54] 57-20950
1. Christian life. I. Title.

WHITE, Ernest, 1887- 248
Christian life and the unconscious. New York, Harper [c1955] 190p. 20cm. [BT780.W45 1955a] 55-11487
1. Conversion—Psychology. 2. Sanctification. I. Title.

WHITE, Helen Chappell. 248
Watch for the morning. New York, Rinehart, [1958] 192 p. 20 cm. [BV4905.W54] 58-6509
1. Consolation. I. Title.

WHITE, John, 1924(Mar.5)- 248
The fight : a practical handbook for Christian living / John White. Downers Grove, Ill. : InterVarsity Press, c1976. 230 p. ; 21 cm. [BV4501.2.W4495] 76-12297 ISBN 0-87784-777-0 pbk. : 3.95
1. Christian life—1960- I. Title.

WHITE, Mary Sue. 248
I know why we give thanks. Pictures by Katherine Evans. Nashville, Broadman Press, c1956. unpaged. illus. 22cm. [BV4647.G8W5] 57-3370
1. Gratitude—Juvenile literature. I. Title.

WHITE, Mary Sue. 248
I know why we give thanks. Pictures by Katherine Evans. Nashville, Broadman Press, c1956. unpaged, illus. 22 cm. [BV4647.G8W5] 57-3370
1. Gratitude — Juvenile literature. I. Title.

WHITESELL, Faris Daniel, 1895- 248
How to slove your problems. Grand Rapids, Zondervan Pub. House [1953] 153p. 20cm. [BV4501.W562] 53-33408
1. Christian life. I. Title.

WICKLOW, William Cecil James Philip John Paul Howard, 8th earl of, ed. 248
Rome is home: the experience of converts. With a pref. by Edward Charles Rich. Fresno, Calif., Academy Library Guild [1959] 155p. 19cm. 59-12596 2.95
1. Converts, Catholic. I. Title.

*WIERWILLE, Victor Paul 248
Studies in abundant living; v.1. New Knoxville, Ohio, The Way, Inc., c.1965. xi, 131p. 19cm. Cover title. 2.00 pap.,
I. Title.

WILKIN, Eloise, illus. 248
Prayers for children. Pictures by Eloise Wilkin. New York, Simon and Schuster [1952] unpaged. illus. 21 cm. (The Little golden library, 205) [BV265.P76] 52-4401
1. Children — Prayer-books and devotions — English. I. Title.

WILKIN, Esther 248
God's child. Pictures by Lillian Obligado. New York Guild [dist. Golden, c.1963] 29p. col. illus. 20cm. (Catholic child's read-with-me bk.) 1.00 bds.,
I. Title.

WILKINSON, Marjorie. 248
Walking in the light. Nashville, Abingdon Press [1955, c1954] 60p. 20cm. First published in London in 1954 under title: The sun in our house. [BV4501.W598 1955] 55-6769
1. Christian life. I. Title.

WILLIAMS, George Huntston, 1914- 248
Wilderness and paradise in Christian thought; the Biblical experience of the desert in the history of Christianity & the paradise theme in the theological idea of the university. New York, Harper & Row [c.1962] 245p. 22cm. Bibl. 62-7307 4.50 bds.,
1. Wilderness (Theology) 2. Church and college. I. Title.

WILLIAMS, George Huntston, 1914- 248
Wilderness and pardise in Christian thought; the biblical experience of the desert in the history of Christianity & the paradise theme in the theological idea of the university. [1st ed.] New York, Harper [1962] 245 p. 22 cm. "The substance of this book was originally delivered

at Bethel College, North Newton, Kansas, in 1958." [BV5068.W5W5] 62-7307
1. Wilderness (Theology) 2. Church and college. I. Title.

WILLIAMS, Harry Abbott 248
The true wilderness. Philadelphia, Lippincott [c.1965] 168p. 19cm. [BX5133.W5485T7] 65-24166 2.95 bds.,
1. Church of England—Sermons. 2. Sermons, English. I. Title.

WILLIAMS, Harry Abbott. 248
The true wilderness, by H. A. Williams. Philadelphia, Lippincott [1965] 168 p. 19 cm. [BX5133.W5485T7] 65-24166
1. Church of England—Sermons. 2. Sermons, English. I. Title.

WILLIAMS, Jerome Oscar, 1885- 248
Let me illustrate; spiritual truth in personal experiences. Nashville, Broadman Press [1953] 135p. 20cm. [BV4225.W54] 53-11555
1. Homiletical illustrations. I. Title.

WILLIAMS, Roger, 1604?-1683. 248
Experiments of spiritual life and health; edited with a historical introd. by Winthrop S. Hudson. Philadelphia, Westminster Press [1951] 103 p. 20 cm. With reproduction of original t.p., London, 1652. [BV4500.W6] 51-7794
1. Christian life. I. Title.

WILLIAMSON, Audrey J 248
Your teen ager and you, guidance for the Christian home when young people are twelve to eighteen. Kansas City, Mo., Beacon Hill Press [1952] 96p. illus. 19cm. (Christian home series) [BV4531.W514] 52-11196
1. Youth— Religions life. I. Title.

WILSON, Ernest Charles, 1896- 248
The emerging self, by Ernest C. Wilson. Unity Village, Mo., Unity Books [1970] 191 p. 20 cm. [BX9890.U5W547] 75-120119
1. Unity School of Christianity—Doctrinal and controversial works. I. Title.

WILSON, Kenneth Lee, 1916- 248
Have faith without fear [by] Kenneth L. Wilson. [1st ed.] New York, Harper & Row [1970] 104 p. 22 cm. [BV4501.2.W56 1970] 77-124696 3.95
1. Christian life—Baptist authors. I. Title.

WINGERT, Norman Ambrose, 248
1898- ed.
Twice born, a book of conversion stories. Grand Rapids, Zondervan Pub. House [1955] 182p. 21cm. [BV4930.W63] 55-14901
1. Converts. I. Title.

WINSTON, Alexander Porter, 248
1909-
I leave you my heart. [1st ed.] Portland, Me., Juniper Press [1951] 222 p. 23 cm. [BV4501.W6517] 51-39631
1. Christian life. I. Title.

WOLD, Erling. 248
What do I have to do - break my neck? [By] Erling and Marge Wold. Minneapolis, Minn., Augsburg Pub. House [1973, c1974] 112 p. 20 cm. [BR1725.W59A37] 73-88604 ISBN 0-8066-1407-2 2.95
1. Wold, Erling. 2. Wold, Marge. I. Wold, Marge, joint author. II. Title.

WOOD, Katharine Marie, 1910- 248
Little prayers for little people. [New York? 1954] unpaged. illus. 17cm. [BX2150.W6] 54-6168
1. Children—Prayer-books and devotions—English. 2. Catholic Church—Prayer-books and devotions—English. I. Title.

WOODALL, Elizabeth Grey, 248
1908-
My yoke is easy and There is life everlasting. [1st ed.] New York, Pageant Press [1956] 43, 63p. 21cm. [BV4935.W6A3] 56-12358
1. Converts. 2. Devotional literature. I. Title. II. Title: There is life everlasting.

WOODALL, Elizabeth Grey, 248
1908-
My yoke is easy and There is life everlasting. [1st ed.] New York, Pageant Press [1956] 43, 63 p. 21 cm. [BV4935.W6A3] 56-12358
1. Converts. 2. Devotional literature. I. Title. II. Title: There is life everlasting.

WOODS, Ralph Louis, 1904- ed. 248
The consolations of Catholicism. New York, Appleton-Century-Crofts [1954] 342p. 21cm. [BX885.W6] 54-9584
1. Catholic literature (Selections: Extracts, etc.) 2. Spiritual life—Catholic authors. I. Title.

WRIGHT, Michael, writer on 248
church discussion groups.
Call to action / [by] Michael Wright. London : Mowbrays, 1976 [i.e. 1977] 141 p. ; 18 cm. (Popular Christian paperbacks) Errata slip inserted. [BV4501.2.W74] 77-364629 ISBN 0-264-66378-0 : £0.75
1. Christian life—1960- 2. Church group work. 3. Church and social problems. I. Title.

WU, Ching-hsiung, 1899- 248
Beyond East and West. New York, Sheed and Ward, 1951. xi, 364 p. ports. 22 cm. Autobiography. [BX4668.W8] 51-10658
1. Converts, Catholic. I. Title.

WU, Ching-hsiung, 1899- 248
The interior Carmel; the threefold way of love, by John C. H. Wu. New York, Sheed & Ward, 1953. 257p. 21cm. [BV4639.W8] 53-5580
1. Love (Theology) 2. Converts, Catholic. I. Title.

WYCOTT, Sara Jean (Clark) 248
1924-1960
Everywhere God; a spiritual autobiography Comp. by her mother, Odessa Grist Clark. New York, Greenwich [1962, c.1961] 53p. 21cm. 61-17890 2.50
I. Title.

WYON, Olive, 1890- 248
On the way; reflections on the Christian life. Philadelphia, Westminster Press [1958] 125 p. 20 cm. [BV4501.W9] 58-6891
1. Christian life. I. Title.

WYRTZEN, Jack, 1913- 248
Leaping flame; youth witnessing for Christ. Introd. by Charles J. Woodbridge. [Westwood, N. J.54 Revell [1954] 56p. 21cm. [BV4520.W9] 54-3174
1. Witness bearing (Christianty) I. Title.

YATES, Miles Lowell, 1890- 248
1956.
God in us; the theory and practice of Christian devotion. Edited by W. Norman Pittenger and William H. Ralston, Jr. Greenwich, Conn., Seabury Press, 1959. 206 p. 22 cm. [BV5031.2.Y3] 59-6930
1. Asceticism. 2. Devotion. 3. Spiritual life. I. Title.

YOUNGS, Robert W. 248
What it means to be a Christian / Robert W. Youngs. New York : Hawthorn Books, c1977. xxvi, 192 p. ; 22 cm. [BV4501.2.Y68 1977] 76-24225 ISBN 0-8015-8520-1 : 3.50
1. Christian life—Presbyterian authors. I. Title.

HARMAN, Dan. 248'.02'07
Get the m[a deleted e inserted above letter] ssage? Anderson, Ind., Warner Press [1971] 106 p. 19 cm. [BV4517.H35 1971] 79-150373 ISBN 0-87162-103-7
1. Christian life—Anecdotes, facetiae, satire, etc. I. Title: Get the message?

MASTON, Thomas Bufford, 248.07
1897-
The Christian in the modern world. Nashville, Broadman Press [1952] 144 p. 20 cm. [BV4511.M3] 52-12450
1. Christian life—Study and teaching. I. Title.

BOSLEY, Harold Augustus, 248.08
1907-
The mind of Christ. Nashville, Abingdon [c.1966] 143p. 20cm. [BT306.4.B6] 66-10920 2.75
1. Jesus Christ.—Biog.—Meditations. I. Title.

EDMAN, Victor Raymond, 248.08
1900-
Not somehow, but triumphantly= Lessons shared with young hearts at Wheaton College these many years and learned by them so they might become more than conquerors through the Savior, by V. Raymond Edman. Grand Rapids, Zondervan Pub. House [1965] 214 p. illus. 23 cm. [BV4832.2.E315] 65-24408
1. Devotional exercises. I. Title.

EDMAN, Victor Raymond, 248.08
1900-
Not somehow, but triumphantly! Lessons shared with young hearts at Wheaton College these many years and learned by them so they might become more than conquerors through the Savior. Grand Rapids, Mich., Zondervan [c.1965] 214p. illus. 23cm. [BV4832.2.E315] 65-24408 3.95
1. Devotional exercises. I. Title.

GUIDEPOSTS. 248.08
Seven steps to a vital faith. With special introductions by Norman Vincent Peale. Carmel, N.Y., Guideposts Associates [1965] xiii, 336 p. 22 cm. [BV4517.G8] 65-6843
1. Christian life — Stories. 2. Christian biography. I. Title.

HOLT, John Agee 248.08
Dialogue at Calvary; or The seven words to the cross. Grand Rapids, Mich., Baker Bk. [c.] 1965. 79p. 20cm. [BT456.H59] 65-27515 1.95 bds.,
1. Jesus Christ—Seven last words. I. Title. II. Title: The seven words to the cross.

MERTON, Thomas, 1915- 248'.08
1968.
The power and meaning of love / Thomas Merton. London : Sheldon Press, 1976. [7], 151 p. ; 21 cm. This edition is a selection of essays from the author's work Disputed questions. Contents.Contents.—The power and meaning of love.—A Renaissance hermit.—Philosophy of solitude.—Light in darkness.—The primitive Carmelite ideal.—Christianity and totalitarianism. [BX2350.2.M4495 1976] 76-381863 ISBN 0-85969-063-6. ISBN 0-85969-067-9 pbk.
1. Spiritual life—Catholic authors—Addresses, essays, lectures. I. Title.

PAULSON, Eric Edwin 248.08
Thunder in the wilderness; evangelical essays in an age of doubt. Minneapolis, Augsburg [1965] 283p. 22cm. [BX8011.P3] 65-28345 3.50
1. Theology—Collected works—20th cent. 2. Lutheran Church—Collected works. I. Title.

PEARCE, J Winston. 248.08
Seven first words of Jesus [by] J. Winston Pearce. Nashville, Broadman Press [c1966] 125 p. 21 cm. Bibliographical references included in "Notes" (p. 123-125) [BT306.6.P4] 66-10668
1. Jesus Christ—Words. 2. Baptists—Sermons. 3. Sermons, English. I. Title.

PEARCE, J. Winston 248.08
Seven first words of Jesus. Nashville, Broadman [c.1966] 125p. 21cm. [BT306.3.P4] 66-10668 2.75 bds.,
1. Jesus Christ—Words. 2. Baptists—Sermons. 3. Sermons, English. I. Title.

HATHAWAY, Lulu 248.081
They lived their love [by] Lulu Hathaway, Margaret Heppe. Illus. by Joseph W. Papin. New York, Friendship [1965] 127p. illus., ports. 19cm. [BV2087.H38] 65-11436 1.75
1. Missionary stories. I. Heppe, Margaret, joint author II. Title.

JOHNSTON, Minton C. 248.081
Washing elephants, and other paths to God. Nashville, Abingdon [c.1965] 127p. 19cm. [BX6333.J66W3] 65-14821 2.25 bds.,
1. Sermons, English—Canada. 2. Baptists—Sermons. I. Title.

JOHNSTON, Minton C. 248.081
Washing elephants, and other paths to God [by] Minton C. Johnston. New York, Abingdon Press [1965] 127 p. 19 cm. [BX6333.J66W3] 65-14821
1. Sermons, English — Canada. 2. Baptists — Sermons. I. Title.

MARY FRANCIS, Mother, 248.081
1921-
Spaces for silence, and other essays. Chicago, Franciscan Herald [c.1964] xi, 131p. 22cm. [BX2835.M3] 64-24285 4.50
1. Monastic and religious life. 2. Contemplation. I. Title.

PADDOCK, Charles Lee, 248.081
1891-
God's minutes Nashville, Tenn., Southern Pub. [1965] 384p. illus. (pt. col.) ports. 26cm. [BV4832.2.P3] 63-19709 14.75; 15.75 deluxe ed.,
1. Devotional literature. I. Title.

ADAIR, James R. ed. 248.082
God's power to triumph. Englewood Cliffs, N. J., Prentice [1965] ix, 198p. 22cm. [BV4513.A2] 65-13577 3.50
1. Christian life—Stories. I. Title.

ADAIR, James R 1923- ed. 248.082
God's power to triumph. Edited by James R.Adair. Englewood Cliffs, N. J., Prentice-Hall [1965] ix, 198 p. 22 cm. [BV4513.A2] 65-13577
1. Christian life—Stories. I. Title.

ADAIR, James R., 1923- 248.082
ed.
God's power to triumph. Edited by James R. Adair. Englewood Cliffs, N.J., Prentice-Hall [1965] ix, 198 p. 22 cm. [BV4513.A2] 65-13577
1. Christian life—Stories. I. Title.

BARROIS, Georges 248.082
Augustin, 1898- ed.
Pathways of the inner life; an anthology of Christian spirituality. Indianapolis, Bobbs-Merrill [1956] 263p. 24cm. [BR1700.B3] 56-13272
1. Christian biography. I. Title.

HALVERSON, Richard C., 248.082
ed.
The quiet men; the secret to personal success and effectiveness by men who practice it: Mark O. Hatfield [others] Los Angeles, 747 Seward St., Cowman [1963] 133p. 20cm. Includes biog. sketches of the authors. 63-21907 2.95
1. Christian biography. 2. U. S.—Biog. I. Title.

MCCAULEY, Leon, ed. 248.082
A treasury of faith; a personal guide to spiritual peace, edited by Leon and Elfrieda McCauley. Introd. by Edward L.R. Elson. [New York, Dell Pub. Co., 1957] 191p. 17cm. (A Dell first edition, B106) [BV4495.M23] 57-5433
1. Christian life. I. McCauley, Elfrieda, joint ed. II. Title.

HAMM, Jack. 248.084
Cartoons that live. Wheaton, Ill., Van Kampen Press [1954] 79p. illus. 22cm. [BV4515.H313] 54-10271
1. Christian life—Pictures, illustrations, etc. I. Title.

GANNON, Thomas M. 248'.09
The desert and the city; an interpretation of the history of Christian spirituality, by Thomas M. Gannon and George W. Traub. [New York] Macmillan [1969] xiii, 338 p. 22 cm. Bibliographical references included in "Notes": p. [293]-327. [BV4490.G26] 69-10502
1. Spirituality—History. I. Traub, George W., joint author. II. Title.

HYMA, Albert, 1893-. 248.09
The Christian renaissance; a history of the "Devotio moderna." 2d ed. Hamden, Conn., Archon Books, 1965. xviii, 618 p. facsim. 22 cm. With 5 additional chapters contining new material. Bibliography: p. 477-494. [BR270.H92] 65-17070
1. Devotio moderna. I. Title.

HYMA, Albert, 1893- 248.09
The Christian renaissance; a history of the 'Devotio moderna.' 2d ed. Hamden, Conn., Archon [dist. Shoe String, c.]1965 xviii, 618p. facsim. 22cm. With 5 additional chapters containing new material. Bibl. [BR270.H92] 65-17070 15.00
1. Devotio moderna. I. Title.

IMITATING Christ, 248'.09
by Edouard Cothenet [and others] Translated by Simone Inkel and Lucy Tinsley. With a pref. by John L. Boyle. St. Meinrad, Ind., Abbey Press, 1974. xiii, 122 p. 21 cm. (Religious experience series, v. 5) "Translation of the article 'Imitation du Christ' and of the second part of the article 'Imitation du Christ (livre)' which first appeared in the Dictionnaire de spiritualite, Paris, Beauchesne, 1971, vol. 7, deuxieme partie, cols. 1536-1601 and 2355-2368 respectively." Bibliography: p. 118-122. [BT304.2.I4613] 73-94173 ISBN 0-87029-029-0 3.95 (pbk.)
1. Jesus Christ—Example. 2. Spiritual life—History of doctrines. I. Cothenet, Edouard.

SHEPPARD, Lancelot Capel, 248'.09
1906-
Spiritual writers in modern times, by Lancelot Sheppard. [1st ed.] New York, Hawthorn Books [1967] 125, [3] p. 21 cm. (The Twentieth century encyclopedia of Catholicism, v. 42. Section 4: The means of redemption) Bibliography: p. [127]-[128] [BV4490.S48] 65-13397
1. Spiritual life—History of doctrines. I. Title. II. Series: The Twentieth century encyclopedia of Catholicism, v. 42

SHEPPARD, Lancelot Capel, 248'.09
1906-
Spiritual writers in modern times, by Lancelot Sheppard. [1st ed.] New York, Hawthorn Books [1967] 125, [3] p. 21 cm. (The Twentieth century encyclopedia of Catholicism, v. 42. Section 4: The means of redemption) Bibliography: p. [127]-[128] [BV4490.S48] 65-13397
1. Spiritual life—History of doctrines. I. Title. II. Series: The Twentieth century encyclopedia of Catholicism, v. 42.

BURGHARDT, Walter J 248.0922 (B)
Saints and sanctity [by] Walter J. Burghardt. Englewood Cliffs, N.J., Prentice-Hall [1965] xiv, 239 p. illus. 22 cm. Bibliographical footnotes. [BX4655.2.B8] 65-8828
1. Saints. 2. Exempla. I. Title.

BURGHARDT, Walter J. 248.0922
Saints and sanctity. Englewood Cliffs, N. J., Prentice [c.1965] xiv, 239p. illus. 22cm. Bibl. [BX4655.2.B8] 65-8828 5.50
1. Saints. 2. Exempla. I. Title.

HARCOURT, Melville 248.0922
Portraits of destiny. Illus. by Giles Harcourt. New York, Sheed [1966] 239p. ports. 22cm. [BR1700.2.H3] 66-22014 5.50
1. Dolci, Danilo. 2. Luthuli, Albert John, 1898- 3. Munk, Kaj Harold-Leininger, 1898-1944. 4. Szabo, Violette (Bushnell) 1921-1945. I. Title.

MILLER, Keith. 248'.092'2 B
The edge of adventure; an experiment in faith [by] Keith Miller [and] Bruce Larson. Waco, Tex., Word Books [1974] 226 p. 21 cm. Includes bibliographical references. [BV4501.2.M479] 74-79955 3.95
1. Miller, Keith. 2. Larson, Bruce. 3. Christian life—1960- I. Larson, Bruce, joint author. II. Title.

MILLER, Keith. 248'.092'2 B
Living the adventure : faith and "hidden" difficulties / Keith Miller & Bruce Larson. Waco, Tex. : Word Books, c1975. 251 p. ; 20 cm. Continues The edge of adventure. Includes bibliographical references. [BV4501.2.M4795] 75-27378 3.95
1. Christian life—1960- I. Larson, Bruce, joint author. II. Title.

ANTONELLIS, Costanzo J 248.0924
A saint of ardent desires; meditations on the virtues of St. Therese of Lisieux, by Costanzo J. Antonellis. [Boston] St. Paul Editions [1965] 212 p. illus. 18 cm. [BX4700.T5A78] 65-17556
1. Therese, Saint, 1873-1897. I. Title.

ANTONELLIS, Costanzo J. 248.0924
A saint of ardent desires; meditations on the virtues of St. Therese of Lisieux. [Boston] St. Paul Eds. [dist. Daughters of St. Paul, c.1965] 212p. illus. 18cm. [BX4700.T5A78] 65-17556 3.00; 2.00
1. Therese, Saint, 1873-1897. I. Title.

BASSET, Bernard. 248.0924
Born for friendship; the spirit of Sir Thomas More. New York, Sheed and Ward [1965] xv. 220 p. 22 cm. Bibliography: p. [215]-216. [DA334] 65-20862
1. More, Sir Thomas, Saint, 1478-1555. I. Title.

BASSET, Bernard 248.0924
Born for friendship; the spirit of Sir Thomas More. New York, Sheed [c.1965] xv, 220p. 22cm. Bibl. [DA334] 65-20862 4.50
1. More, Sir Thomas, Saint, 1478-1535. I. Title.

BUCKINGHAM, Jamie. 248'.092'4 B
Risky living : keys to inner healing / Jamie Buckingham. Plainfield, N.J. : Logos International, c1976. ix, 192 p. ; 22 cm. [BV4501.2.B82] 76-12033 ISBN 0-88270-175-4 : 5.95. ISBN 0-88270-177-0 pbk. :
1. Buckingham, Jamie. 2. Christian life—1960- 3. Christian biography—United States. I. Title.

COLLINS, Gary R. 248'.092'4 B
The Christian psychology of Paul Tournier [by] Gary R. Collins. Grand Rapids, Mich., Baker Book House [1973] 222 p. port. 23 cm. Bibliography: p. 211-213. [BF109.T63C64] 72-93076 4.95
1. Tournier, Paul. 2. Psychology, Religious. I. Title.

HUNTER, Frances 248'.0924 B
Gardner, 1916-
My love affair with Charles. Glendale, Calif., G/L Regal Books [1971] 197 p. 21 cm. Letters between the author and her husband, Charles Hunter. [BR1725.H83A4 1971] 72-150717 ISBN 0-8307-0099-4 4.95
I. Hunter, Charles, 1920- II. Title.

KIEMEL, Ann. 248'.092'4
I'm out to change my world. [Nashville] Impact Books [1974] 119 p. ports. 22 cm. [LA2317.K46A34] 74-81137 ISBN 0-914850-07-5 2.95
1. Kiemel, Ann. I. Title.

KIEMEL, Ann. 248'.092'4
I'm out to change my world / Ann Kiemel. New York : Pocket Books, 1977,c1974. 158p. ; 18 cm. (A Kangaroo Book) [LA2317.K46A34] pbk. : 1.50
1. Kiemel, Ann. I. Title.
L.C. card no. for 1974 Image Books ed.:74-81137.

KIEMEL, Ann. 248'.092'4
I'm out to change my world / Ann Kiemel. New York : Pocket Books, 1977,c1974. 158p. ; 18 cm. (A Kangaroo Book) [LA2317.K46A34] pbk. : 1.50
1. Kiemel, Ann. I. Title.
L.C. card no. for 1974 Image Books ed.:74-81137.

MEAD, Ruth. 248'.092'4 B
No one wins like a loser / Ruth Mead. Harrisburg, Pa. : Christian Publications, c1976. 163 p. ; 20 cm. Includes bibliographical references. [BV4501.2.M437] 76-6811 pbk. : 2.50
1. Mead, Ruth. 2. Christian life—1960- I. Title.

PEASTON, Monroe. 248'.092'4 B
Personal living; an introduction to Paul Tournier. [1st ed.] New York, Harper & Row [1972] xvii, 107 p. 22 cm. Bibliography: p. [101]-104. [BF149.P35 1972] 70-184418 4.95
1. Tournier, Paul. 2. Psychology—Addresses, essays, lectures. I. Title.

REYNOLDS, Ernest Edwin, 248.0924
1894-
Thomas More and Erasmus. New York, Fordham [1966, c.1965] x, 260p. illus., ports. 23cm. Bibl. [DA334.M8R43] 65-26739 5.00
1. More, Thomas, Saint, Sir 2. Erasmus, Desiderius, d. 1536. I. Title.

RHEE, Young Schick. 248'.0924
I cast out fear [by] Young Schick Rhee, as told to Evelyn Hannon. New York, Grosset & Dunlap [1970] 155 p. 22 cm. "A Rutledge book." [BR1725.R47A3] 74-120605 5.95
I. Hannon, Evelyn. II. Title.

RINKER, Rosalind. 248'.092'4 B
Within the circle. Grand Rapids, Zondervan Pub. House [1973] 120 p. illus. 21 cm. Bibliography: p. [119]-120. [BV3427.R526A33] 72-83867 1.95
1. Rinker, Rosalind. 2. Christian life—1960- I. Title.

ULANOV, Barry. 248.0924
The making of a modern saint; a biographical study of Therese of Lisieux. [1st ed.] Garden City, N. Y., Doubleday, 1966. ix, 372 p. port. 22 cm. [BX4700.T5U5] 65-19923
1. Therese, Saint, 1873-1897. I. Title.

WHITNEY, Eleanor 248'.0924 B
Searle.
Invitation to joy; a personal story. [1st ed.] New York, Harper & Row [1971] ix, 195 p. ports. 22 cm. [CT275.W5543A3 1971] 70-148435 5.95
I. Title.

WIGGLESWORTH, Michael, 248.0924
1631-1705
The diary of Michael Wigglesworth, 1653-1657; the conscience of a Puritan. Ed. by Edmund S. Morrgan. New York, Harper [1965, c.1946] xv, 125p. 21cm. (Harper torchbks., TB1228G. Acad. lib.) Orig. pub. in 1951 as part of Transactions, 1942-1946, v.35 of Pubns. of the Colonial Soc. of Mass. Bibl. [BX7260.W48A3] 65-25696 1.25 pap.,
I. Morgan, Edmund Sears, ed. II. Title.

WIGGLESWORTH, Michael, 248.0924
1631-1705
The diary of Michael Wigglesworth, 1653-1657; the conscience of a Puritan. Ed. by Edmund S. Morgan [Gloucester, Mass., P. Smith, 1966,c.1946] xv, 125p. 21cm. (Harper torchbk., Acad. lib. bk., TB1228G rebound) Orig. pub. in 1951 as pt. of Transactions, 1942-1946, v.35 of Pubns. of the Colonial Soc. of Massachusetts.bBibl. [BX7260.W48.A3] 3.25
I. Morgan, Edmund Sears, ed. II. Title.

WIGGLESWORTH, Michael, 248'.0924
1631-1705.
The diary of Michael Wigglesworth, 1653-1657; the conscience of a Puritan. Edited by Edmund S. Morgan. Gloucester, Mass., Peter Smith, 1970 [c1946] xv, 125 p. 21 cm. "Originally published in 1951 as part of Transactions, 1942-1946, volume XXXV of Publications of the Colonial Society of Massachusetts." Includes bibliographical references. [BX7260.W48A3 1970] 73-17093
I. Title.

WOLF, William J. 248'.0924
Lincoln's religion [by] William J. Wolf. Philadelphia, Pilgrim Press [1970] 219 p. 18 cm. First ed. published in 1959 under title: The almost chosen people. Includes bibliographical references. [E457.2.W853 1970] 70-123035 1.95
1. Lincoln, Abraham, Pres. U.S., 1809-1865—Religion. I. Title.

GILL, Theodore 248'.1'0924 B
Alexander, 1920-
Memo for a movie: a short life of Dietrich Bonhoeffer [by] Theodore A. Gill. New York, Macmillan [1971] vi, 268 p. 21 cm. Includes bibliographical references. [BX4827.B57G5] 71-80301
1. Bonhoeffer, Dietrich, 1906-1945. I. Title.

THURSTON, Herbert, *248 149.3
1856-1939.
The physical phenomena of mysticism; edited by J. H. Crehan. Chicago, H. Regnery Co., 1952. 419 p. 23 cm. Full name: Herbert Henry Charles Thurston. [BV5090.T45] 52-4542
1. Mysticism. I. Title.

JORSTAD, Erling, 1930- 248'.173
Bold in the spirit; Lutheran charismatic renewal in America today. Minneapolis, Augsburg Pub. House [1974] 128 p. 20 cm. Bibliography: p. 127-128. [BX8065.2.J67] 74-77681 ISBN 0-8066-1432-3 2.95 (pbk.)
1. Lutheran Church—Doctrinal and controversial works. 2. Pentecostalism. I. Title.

LEKEUX, Martial, 1881- 248.182
ed. and tr.
Short out to divine love. Texts collected, translated, and arranged in order by Martial Lekeux. Chicago, Franciscan Herld Press [1962] 320p. 21cm. [BX2350.2.A1L13] 61-11203
1. Spiritual life—Catholic authors. I. Title.

*AIKEN, John W. 248.2
Explorations in awareness. Socorro, N. M., The Church of the Awakening [dist. CSA Pr., Lakemont, Ga., 30552, 1966] 83p. 21cm. 2.00 pap.,
I. Title.

ALBERIONE, Giacomo 248.2
Giuseppe, 1884-
Pray always, by James Alberione. Translation by the Daughters of St. Paul. [Boston] St. Paul Editions [1966] 265 p. 19 cm. [BV210.2.A413] 65-29136
1. Prayer. I. Title.

ARNAIZ BARON, Rafael, 1911- 248.2
1938
To know how to wait. Tr. by Mairin Mitchell. Westminster, Md., Newman [1964] xviii, 381p. illus., port. 14cm. 64-55964 3.50
1. Spiritual life—Catholic authors. 2. Meditation. I. Title.

ATTACK from the spirit 248'.2
world: a compilation. Wheaton, Ill., Tyndale House Publishers [1973] 223 p. 18 cm. [BF1555.A87] 73-81003 ISBN 0-8423-0090-2 1.25 (pbk.)
1. Demoniac possession—Addresses, essays, lectures.

BACH, Marcus, 1906- 248.2
The inner ecstasy. New York, World Pub. Co. [1969] 199 p. 22 cm. [BL54.B3 1969] 70-86448 4.95
1. Glossolalia. I. Title.

*BAILEY, William Edwin 248.2
Silent witness. New York, Vantage [1966, i.e. 1967] 159p. 21cm. 3.50 bds.,
1. Christian life. I. Title.

BAIR, Bill. 248'.2 B
Love is an open door, by Bill Bair with Glenn D. Kittler. New York, Chosen Books [1974] 222 p. 21 cm. [BR1725.B3314A33] 73-17023 ISBN 0-912376-07-4 4.95
1. Bair, Bill. 2. Bair Foundation. 3. Church work with juvenile delinquents. 4. Children—Institutional care—New Wilmington, Pa. I. Kittler, Glenn D. II. Title.

BEGONE, Satan! 248'.2
Huntington, Ind., Our Sunday Visitor, inc. [1974] 96 p. 18 cm. Contents.Contents.—Pertinent definitions from the Maryknoll Catholic dictionary.—Gillese, J. P. The Devil and Anna Ecklund (p. 7-64).—Woods, R. J. The possession problem.—NC News Service. The exorcism rite and the Roman ritual. [BF1555.B35] 74-76903 ISBN 0-87973-760-3 0.95 (pbk.)
1. Demoniac possession.

*BENNETT, Bishop George W. 248.2
The meaning of eternal life. New York, Vantage [1966] 102p. 21cm. 2.95
I. Title.

BOONE, Charles Eugene. 248'.2
A miracle a day keeps the Devil away / Pat Boone. Old Tappan, N.J. : Revell, [1974] 156 p. 21 cm. [BT97.2.B63] 74-20772 ISBN 0-8007-0693-5 : 4.95
1. Boone, Charles Eugene. 2. Miracles. I. Title.

BOONE, Charles Eugene. 248'.2
A miracle a day keeps the Devil away / Pat Boone. Boston : G. K. Hall, 1976, c1974. xxvii, 301 p. ; 24 cm. "Published in large print." [BT97.2.B63 1976] 76-5898 ISBN 0-8161-6364-2 lib.bdg. : 10.95
1. Boone, Charles Eugene. 2. Miracles. 3. Sight-saving books. I. Title.

BOUQUET, Alan Coates, 1884- 248.2
Religious experience: its nature, types and validity, by A. C. Bouquet. 2nd ed., completely revised. Cambridge, Heffer, 1968. viii, 140 p. 19 cm. Bibliographical footnotes. [BL53.B64 1968] 75-385986 12/6
1. Experience (Religion) 2. Psychology, Religious. I. Title.

BOUQUET, Alan Coates, 248'.2
1884-
Religious experience : its nature, types, and validity / by A. C. Bouquet. 2d ed., completely rev. Westport, Conn. : Greenwood Press, 1976, c1968. vii, 140 p. ; 23 cm. Reprint of the ed. published by W. Heffer, Cambridge. Includes bibliographical references. [BL53.B64 1976] 75-40997 ISBN 0-8371-8714-1 lib.bdg. : 10.25
1. Experience (Religion) 2. Psychology, Religious. I. Title.

*BOUSMAN, Emma. 248.2
Christiana follows on (witness #2) [1st ed.] New York, Vantage Press [1972] 100 p. 22 cm. [BV5023] ISBN 0-533-00237-0 3.95
1. Visions. I. Title.

BULL, Geoffrey T. 1921- 248.2
The sky is red. Chicago, Moody [1966, c.1965] 254p. 22cm. Bibl. [BV3427.B79A33] 66-4124 3.95
1. Persecution—China (People's Republic of China, 1949-) 2. Missions—China (People's Republic of China, 1949-) I. Title.

CHAMBERS, Mary Jane. 248'.2 B
Here am I! Send me. Atlanta, Forum House [1973] 169 p. 23 cm. Autobiographical. [BX9225.C48A34] 72-97824 ISBN 0-913618-08-X 4.95
1. Chambers, Mary Jane. I. Title.

CHRISTENSON, Laurence. 248.2
Speaking in tongues and its significance for the church. [Minneapolis, Bethany Fellowship, 1968] 141 p. 21 cm. [BL54.C48] 68-3106
1. Glossolalia. I. Title.

CLEMO, Jack R., 1916- 248'.2
The invading gospel [by] Jack Clemo. Old Tappan, N.J., F. H. Revell Co. [1972 or 3, c1953] 128 p. 20 cm. Includes bibliographical references. [BR124.C6 1972] 73-161337 ISBN 0-8007-0573-4 3.50
1. Christianity—Essence, genius, nature. I. Title.

COGNET, Louis, 1917- 248.2
Post- Reformation spirituality. Translated from the French by P. Hepburne Scott. [1st American ed.] New York, Hawthorn Books [1959] 143p. 22cm. (The Twentieth century encyclopedia of Catholicism, v. 41. Section 4: The means of redemption) Translation of De la devotion moderne a la spritualite francaise. Includes bibliography. [BV4490.C613] 59-14522
1. Spiritual life—Hist. 2. Spiritual life—Catholic authors. I. Title.

COLLEGE Theology Society. 248.2
New dimensions in religious experience; [proceedings] George Devine, editor. Staten Island, N.Y., Alba House [1971] xii, 317 p. 22 cm. "Based on the society's last annual convention in Boston, March 29-31, 1970." Includes bibliographical references. [BL53.C645] 76-158566 ISBN 0-8189-0206-X 3.95
1. Experience (Religion) I. Devine, George, 1941- ed. II. Title.

CONN, Charles Paul. 248'.2 B
The new Johnny Cash. Old Tappan, N.J., F. H. Revell Co. [1973] 94 p. illus. 20 cm. [BV4935.C28C66] 73-2381 ISBN 0-8007-0607-2 2.95
1. Cash, Johnny. 2. Conversion. I. Title.

CUNNINGHAM, Eleanor W. 248'.2 B
He touched her, by Eleanor W. Cunningham & Doris M. McDowell. Anderson, Ind., Warner Press [1973] 107 p. 19 cm. [BX8699.N38W472] 73-8854 ISBN 0-87162-159-2
1. Wetzell, Anne Marie. 2. Faith-cure. I. McDowell, Doris M., joint author. II. Title.

CUNNINGHAM, Eleanor W. 248'.2 B
He touched her, by Eleanor W. Cunningham & Doris M. McDowell. Anderson, Ind., Warner Press [1973] 107 p. 19 cm. [BX8699.N38W472] 73-8854 ISBN 0-87162-159-2 2.50 (pbk.)
1. Wetzell, Anne Marie. 2. Faith-cure. I. McDowell, Doris M., joint author. II. Title.

DOYLE, Charles Hugo 248.2
Bitter waters; helps in the pursuit of perfection. New York, Kenedy [c.1961] 175p. 61-15822 3.95
1. Perfection (Catholic) I. Title.

DUPRE, Louis K., 1925- 248.2
The other dimension; a search for the meaning of religious attitudes [by] Louis Dupre. [1st ed.] Garden City, N.Y., Doubleday, 1972. 565 p. 22 cm. Includes bibliographical references. [BL48.D84] 78-144261 10.00
1. Religion. 2. Experience (Religion) I. Title.

EDWARDS, George, 1950- 248'.2 B
Crawling out; a young man's search for life. Grand Rapids, Mich., Zondervan Pub. House [1973] 165 p. 18 cm. [BV4935.E38A33] 73-8358 0.95 (pbk.)
1. Edwards, George, 1950- I. Title.

ELVY, Cora 248.2
Listen to the need, everybody! New York,

Pageant Press [c.1960] 41p. 21cm. 60-2225 2.50
I. Title.

EUSTACE, Cecil John, 1903- 248.2
An infinity of questions; a study of the religion of art, and of the art of religion in the lives of five women [by] Cecil Johnson Eustace. With an introd. by Michael de la Bedoyere. Freeport, N.Y., Books for Libraries Press [1969] 170 p. ports. 23 cm. (Essay index reprint series) Reprint of the 1946 ed. Contents.Contents.—The bent world.—The poetic instinct: Helen Foley.—The genius: Katherine Mansfield.—The artist in agony: France Pastorelli.—The mystic: Elizabeth Leseur.—The lover: St. Therese of Lisieux.—Epilogue. Bibliography: p. 169-170. [BV5095.A1E8 1969] 70-84356
1. Foley, Helen, 1896-1937. 2. Mansfield, Katherine, 1888-1923. 3. Pastorelli, France, Mme. 4. Leseur, Elisabeth (Arrighi) 1866-1914. 5. Therese, Saint, 1873-1897. 6. Mysticism. I. Title.

EVDOKIMOFF, Paul 248.2
The struggle with God, by Paul Evdokimov. Tr. by Sister Gertrude. Glen Rock, N.J., Paulist [1966] vi, 218p. 21cm. (Exploration bks.) Tr. of Les ages de la vie spirituel. Bibl. [BX382.E813] 66-24895 2.95 pap.,
1. Spiritual life—Orthodox Eastern authors. I. Title.

FLY, C. L., 1905- 248'.2 B
No hope but God; featuring the Christian checklist, by Claude Fly. New York, Hawthorn Books [1973] xiii, 220 p. port. 22 cm. "A Fred Bauer book." [BR1725.F52A33] 72-7768 4.95
1. Fly, C. L., 1905- 2. Christian life—Biblical teaching. I. Title.

FLY, C. L., 1905- 248'.2 B
No hope but God; featuring the Christian checklist [by] Claude L. Fly. [New York] Berkley Pub. Co. [1974, c1973] ix, 222 p. 18 cm. (A Berkley medallion book) [BR1725.F52A33] ISBN 0-425-02566-7 1.25 (pbk.)
1. Fly, C. L., 1905- 2. Christian life—Biblical teaching. I. Title.
L.C. card number for original ed.: 72-7768.

FORD, Gwen M. 248.2
Fireside stories, by Gwen M. Ford. Designed and illustrated by Peter Erhard. Nashville, Southern Pub. Association [1968] 79 p. illus. 21 cm. Short accounts of Christian experiences and the changes they wrought in the lives of many people in many times and places. [BV4515.2.F6] AC 68
1. Christian life. I. Erhard, Peter, illus. II. Title.

FORD, Josephine Massyngberde. 248.2
Baptism of the Spirit; three essays on the Pentecostal experience [by] J. Massingberd Ford. Techny, Ill., Divine Word Publications [1971] xv, 133 p. 18 cm. Contents.Contents.—Charismatic renewal.—Pentecostal blueprint.—Speaking in tongues. Includes bibliographical references. [BX8764.Z6F67] 76-164738 2.95
1. Pentecostalism—Addresses, essays, lectures. I. Title.

FORD, Josephine Massyngberde. 248.2
The pentecostal experience, by J. Massingberd Ford. Paramus, N.J., Paulist Press [1970] 60 p. 17 cm. [BX8763.F66] 72-116869 0.75
1. Pentecostalism. I. Title.

GAMMON, Roland. 248.2
All believers are brothers. Written and edited by Roland Gammon. [1st ed.] Garden City, N.Y., Doubleday, 1969. xii, 344 p. 22 cm. Testimonies of 57 international figures derived from their writings and from personal interviews. [BJ1548.G3] 68-12770 5.95
1. Conduct of life. 2. Trust in God. 3. Faith. I. Title.

GAYDOS, Michael. 248'.2 B
Eyes to behold him [by] Michael Gaydos with Russell Bixler. [1st ed.] Carol Stream, Ill., Creation House [1973] 139 p. 21 cm. [BX4705.G2693A33] 73-77531 4.95
1. Gaydos, Michael. I. Bixler, Russell, joint author. II. Title.

GELPI, Donald L., 1934- 248.2
Pentecostal piety, by Donald L. Gelpi. New York, Paulist Press [1972] v, 97 p. 19 cm. (Deus books) [BT732.5.G43] 73-190087 1.25 (pbk.)
1. Faith-cure. 2. Pentecostalism. 3. Conversion. I. Title.

GIBBS, Willa, 1917- 248.2
The shadow of His wings; a search into the riches of the Christian life. [1st ed.] Garden City, N.Y., Doubleday, 1964. 227 p. 22 cm. [BX5995.G5A3] 64-16214
1. Converts, Anglican. I. Title.

*GORDON, Prentiss M. 248.2
The high cost of living, [by] Prentiss M. Gordon. New York, Vantage Press, [1974]. 106 p. 21 cm. [BV4520] ISBN 0-533-00912-X. 4.50
1. Spiritual life. 2. Religious experience. I. Title.

GREGERSON, Jon 248.2
The transfigured cosmos; four essays in Eastern Orthodox Christianity. New York. Ungar [c.1960] 111p. 21cm. (bibl. notes: p. 99-107, footnotes) illus. 59-9153 3.50
1. Mysticism—Orthodox Eastern Church. 2. Hesychasm. I. Title.

GUTZKE, Manford George. 248'.2 B
Help thou my unbelief, by Manford Gutzke. Nashville, T. Nelson [1974] 124 p. 21 cm. [BS480.G83] 74-631 4.95
1. Gutzke, Manford George. 2. Bible—Evidences, authority, etc. I. Title.

HALL, Robert Benjamin. 248'.2
Anyone can prophesy / Robert Benjamin Hall. New York : Seabury Press, 1977. p. cm. "A Crossroad book." [BR115.P8H36] 77-8267 ISBN 0-8164-2158-7 pbk. : 3.95
1. Prophecy (Christianity) I. Title.

HARRELL, Irene Burk, comp. 248.2
God ventures; true accounts of God in the lives of men. Waco, Tex., Word Books, [1970] 131 p. 23 cm. Contents.Contents.—Cannibal talk, by J. L. Sherrill.—Something made me go, by M. Aussant.—Gang war, by D. Wilkerson.—Race to save a traitor, by E. Lundby as told to H. Cronsioe.—Facing death on the Atlantic, by D. L. Moody.—Am I my brother's keeper? By C. Coffey.—The ice-pan adventure, by W. Grenfell.—Out of the dungeon, by C. Marshall.—Four-footed angel, by O. Broadway as told to E. L. Vogt.—My grave was number 12, by J. Lee as told to E. Erny.—Blizzard, by O. A. Hunter.—A gentleman in prison, by T. Ishii.—Christmas Eve miracle, by A. Lake.—Birth on death row, by A. Sanford.—Return from tomorrow, by G. C. Ritchie, Jr.—Fire! By C. Marshall.—We thought we heard the angels sing, by J. C. Whittaker. [BR1700.2.H32 1970] 76-119888 3.95
1. Christian biography. I. Title.

HEINERMAN, Joseph. 248'.2
Temple manifestations / Joseph Heinerman. Manti, Utah : Mountain Valley Publishers, 1974. 185 p. ; 21 cm. Includes bibliographical references. [BX8643.T4H44] 74-193174 2.95
1. Temples, Mormon. I. Title.

HENDERSON, Glenna. 248'.2 B
My name is Legion. Minneapolis, Bethany Fellowship [1972] 128 p. 22 cm. Autobiographical. [BX8080.H454A35] 73-152527 ISBN 0-87123-373-8 3.95
1. Henderson, Glenna. 2. Demoniac possession. I. Title.

HENDERSON, John, 1915- 248.2
Now—would you believe? Commentary by Carlos R. Lantis. New York, Friendship Press [1967] 159 p. illus. 21 cm. [BV4515.2.H4] 67-11854
1. Christian life—Stories. 2. Christianity and other religions. I. Lantis, Carlos R. II. Title.

*HEYER, Robert, comp. 248.2
Pentecostal Catholics. New York, Paulist Press [1975 c1974] 75 p. ill. 18 cm. [BT767.3] 75-10114 ISBN 0-8091-1879-3 1.45 (pbk.)
1. Pentecostalism. I. Title.

*HOBBS, Lottie Beth 248.2
Mary and Martha who shared our daily cares. Forth Worth, Tex., Harvest Pubns. [1966] 136p. 21cm. 2.00 bds.,
I. Title.
Publisher's address: P.O. Box 3304, Fort Worth, Tex. 76105.

HODSON, Geoffrey. 248'.2
The call to the heights : guidance on the pathway to self-illumination / by Geoffrey Hodson. Wheaton, Ill. : Theosophical Pub. House, 1976. p. cm. (A Quest book) Includes index. [BP565.H635C3] 75-30656 ISBN 0-8356-0477-2
1. Theosophy. 2. Spiritual life. I. Title.

HODSON, Geoffrey. 248'.2
The call to the heights : guidance on the pathway to self-illumination / by Geoffrey Hodson. Wheaton, Ill. : Theosophical Pub. House, 1975, c1976. 213 p. ; 21 cm. (A Quest book) Includes bibliographical references and index. [BP565.H635C3] 75-30656 ISBN 0-8356-0477-2 pbk. : 3.50
1. Theosophy. 2. Spiritual life. I. Title.

HORTON, Wade H. ed. 248.2
The glossolalia phenomenon. Gen ed.: Wade H. Horton. Contributing authors: Charles W. Conn [others] [1st ed.] Cleveland, Tenn., Pathway Pr. [1966] 304p. 24cm. Bibl. [BL54.H66] 66-25794 4.95
1. Glossolalia. I. Conn, Charles W. II. Title.

HOWARD, Thomas. 248.2
Christ the tiger; a postscript to dogma. [1st ed.] Philadelphia, Lippincott [1967] 160 p. 21 cm. Autobiographical. [BR1725.H69A3] 67-24008
I. Title.

HUNTER, Charles, 1920- 248'.2
Don't limit God! : The story of Gene Lilly / by Charles [and] Frances Hunter. Houston, Tex. : Hunter Ministries Pub. Co., c1976. 101 p. ; 21 cm. [RC660.H88] 77-352045 1.95
1. Lilly, Gene, 1939- 2. Diabetes—Biography. 3. Multiple sclerosis—Biography. I. Hunter, Frances Gardner, 1916- joint author. II. Title.

INGE, William Ralph 248.2
The awakening of the soul; an introduction to Christian mysticism. Edited by A. F. Judd. [New York, Morehouse-Barlow] [1959] 61p. 19cm. 59-4793 1.00 pap.,
1. Mysticism. I. Title.

JETER, Hugh. 248'.2
By His stripes / Hugh Jeter. Springfield, Mo. : Gospel Pub. House, c1977. 208 p. ; 21 cm. Includes index. Bibliography: p. 199-202. [BT732.5.J48] 76-20893 ISBN 0-88243-521-3 pbk. : 3.95
1. Faith-cure. I. Title.

JOHN G. Finch Symposium on Psychology and Religion, 1st, Fuller Theological Seminary, 1971. 248'.2
Religious experience: its nature and function in the human psyche, by Walter Houston Clark [and others] With a foreword by Lee Edward Travis. Springfield, Ill., Thomas [1973] xi, 151 p. 24 cm. Includes bibliographies. [BL53.J5 1971] 72-79185 ISBN 0-398-02550-9 7.95
1. Experience (Religion)—Addresses, essays, lectures. I. Clark, Walter Houston, 1902- II. Title.

JOHNSON, Raynor Carey 248.2
Watcher on the hills. London, Hodder &Stoughton [1959] 188p. 23cm. Bibl. [BL625.J6] 59-65444 4.50
I. Title.
A testimony to the validity of mystical experience. Now available from Verry, Mystic, Conn.

JONES, Rufus Matthew, 1863-1948. 248.2
Spiritual reformers in the 16th and 17 centuries. Boston, Beacon Press [1959, c1914] 362p. 21cm. (Beacon paperback no. 81) Includes bibliography. [BV5075.J6 1959] 59-6392
1. Mysticism. 2. Reformers. I. Title.

KELSEY, Morton T. 248'.2
The Christian & the supernatural / Morton T. Kelsey. Minneapolis, Minn. : Augsburg Pub. House, c1976. 168 p. ; 20 cm. Bibliography: p. 159-168. [BR115.P85K44] 76-3865 ISBN 0-8066-1525-7 pbk. : 3.95
1. Christianity and psychical research. I. Title.

KELSEY, Morton T. 248'.2
God, dreams, and revelation; a Christian interpretation of dreams [by] Morton T. Kelsey. [Rev. paperback ed.] Minneapolis, Augsburg Pub. House [1973, c1974] x, 246 p. 20 cm. First ed. published in 1968 under title: Dreams: the dark speech of the spirit. Bibliography: p. [239]-246. [BF1078.K38 1974] 73-88606 ISBN 0-8066-1409-9 3.50
1. Dreams. I. Title.

KIRBY, Clyde 248.2
Then came Jesus. [1st ed.] Grand Rapids, Mich., Zondervan [1967] 157p. 23cm. [BV4515.2.K5] 67-17238 3.95 bds.,
1. Christian life—Stories. I. Title.

KIRBY, Clyde. 248.2
Then came Jesus. [1st ed.] Grand Rapids, Mich., Zondervan Pub. House [1967] 157 p. 23 cm. [BV4515.2.K5] 67-17238
1. Christian life — Stories. I. Title.

KOCH, Kurt E. 248'.2
Demonology, past and present [by] Kurt E. Koch. [Translated from the German] Grand Rapids, Kregel Publications [1973] 161 p. 18 cm. [BF1531.K6] 72-93353 ISBN 0-8254-3013-5 1.25 (pbk.)
1. Demonology. 2. Occult sciences. 3. Psychical research. I. Title.

KREYE, Eric. 248.2
Under the blood banner; the story of a Hitler youth, by Eric Kreye as told to Norman R. Youngberg. Illustrated by John Steel. Mountain View, Calif., Pacific Press Pub. Association [1968] 120 p. illus., ports. 22 cm. (Panda books, P-112) (A German lad lives through the Second World War, torn by allegiances to his Hitler youth group and love for a father whose loyalties are to the American way of life. After the war the boy emigrates to the United States and grows up as a loyal citizen and devout Seventh Day Adventist.) [BX6189.K7] AC 68
1. Converts, Seventh-Day Adventist. I. Youngberg, Norma R. II. Steel, John, illus. III. Title.

KUHLMAN, Kathryn, comp. 248'.2
Nothing is impossible with God. Englewood Cliffs, N.J., Prentice-Hall [1974] ix, 305 p. illus. 22 cm. [BT732.5.K83] 73-18030 ISBN 0-13-625293-1 6.95
1. Faith-cure—Personal narratives. I. Title.

KUHLMAN, Kathryn, comp. 248'.2
Nothing is impossible with God / [compiled by] Kathryn Kuhlman. Boston : G. K. Hall, 1975. 558 p. ; 24 cm. "Published in large print." [BT732.5.K83 1975] 75-5514 ISBN 0-8161-6278-6 lib.bdg. : 13.95
1. Faith-cure—Personal narratives. 2. Sight-saving books. I. Title.

LEE, Ernest George, 1896- 248.2
The minute particular; one man's story of God [by] E. G. Lee. Boston, Beacon [1966] 191p. 21cm. [BX9869.L4A3] 67-14107 4.95 bds.,
I. Title. II. Title: One man's story of God.

LIGHTNER, Robert Paul. 248.2
Speaking in tongues and divine healing, by Robert P. Lightner. Des Plaines, Ill. Regular Baptist Press [1965] 64 p. 19 cm. Bibliographical footnotes. [BL54.L5] 65-5805
1. Glossoialia. 2. Faith-cure. I. Title.

LIGHTNER, Robert Paul 248.2
Speaking in tongues and divine healing. Des Plaines, Ill., Regular Baptist Pr., 1800 Oakton Blvd. [c.1965] 64p. 19cm. Bibl. [BL54.L5] 65-5805 .75 pap.,
1. Glossolalia. 2. Faith-cure. I. Title.

MACDERMOT, Violet. 248'.2
The cult of the seer in the ancient Middle East; a contribution to current research on hallucinations drawn from Coptic and other texts. Berkeley, University of California Press, 1971. xii, 829 p. 26 cm. Bibliography: p. 790-800. [BV5023.M3] 79-152047 ISBN 0-520-02030-8 24.00
1. Asceticism—Early church, ca. 30-600. 2. Visions. 3. Hallucinations and illusions. 4. Coptic language—Phraseology. I. Title.

MALL, E. Jane, 1920- 248.2
My flickering torch [by] E. Jane Mall. Saint Louis, Concordia Pub. House [1968] 176 p. illus. 21 cm. Autobiographical. Sequel to P.S., I love you. [BV4908.M3] 68-12984
1. Consolation. I. Title.

MARCHETTI, Albinus 248.2
Spirituality and the states of life. Tr. by Sebastian V. Ramge. Milwaukee, 1233 S. 45 St., Spiritual Life Pr., 1963. 174p. 19cm. (Way, v.1) Bibl. 63-21920 1.50
1. Spiritual life—Catholic authors. I. Title.

MERSWIN, Rulman 248.2
Mystical writings. Edited and interpreted by Thomas S. Kepler. Philadelphia, Westminster Press [c.1960] 143p. 21cm. Contains a translation of the author's Vier anfangende Jahre (The four beginning years) and Das Buch von den neun Felsen (The book of the nine rocks) Bibliography: p.35-36. 60-5053 2.95
1. Mysticism—Middle Ages. I. Merswin, Rulman, 1307-1382. Vier anfangende Jahre. II. Merswin, Rulman, 1307-1382. Das Buch von den neun Felsen. III. Kepler, Thomas Samuel, ed. and tr. IV. Title.

MERSWIN, Rulman, 1307-1382. 248.2
Mystical writings. Edited and interpreted by Thomas S. Kepler. Philadelphia, Westminster Press [1960] 143p. 21cm. Contains a translation of the author's Vier anfangende Jahre (The four beginning years) and Das Buch von den neun Felsen (The book of the nine rocks) Bibliography: p.35-36. [BV5080.M46] 60-5053
1. Mysticism—Middle Ages. I. Merswin, Rulman, 1307-1382. Vier anfangende Jahre. II. Merswin, Rulman, 1307-1382. Das Buch von den neun Felsen. III. Kepler, Thomas Samuel, 1897- ed. and tr. IV. Title.

MEYER, Charles Robert, 1920- 248.2
The touch of God; a theological analysis of religious experience [by] Charles R. Meyer. Staten Island, N.Y., Alba House [1972] vi, 156 p. 22 cm. Bibliography: p. [149]-152. [BR110.M48] 75-38978 ISBN 0-8189-0237-X 4.50
1. Experience (Religion) I. Title.

MORGAN, Geraldine, 1927- 248'.2 B
Shadows in the sunshine. Philadelphia, Dorrance [1973] 92 p. 22 cm.

[BX7020.Z8M58] 73-77629 ISBN 0-8059-1858-2 4.00
1. Morgan, Geraldine, 1927- 2. Church of God—Sermons. 3. Sermons, American. I. Title.

OGILVIE, Lloyd John. 248'.2
You've got charisma! / Lloyd John Ogilvie. Nashville : Abingdon Press, [1975] 175 p. ; 21 cm. [BT767.3.O28] 75-14414 ISBN 0-687-47269-5 : 6.95
1. Presbyterian Church—Sermons. 2. Gifts, Spiritual—Sermons. 3. Sermons, American. I. Title.

ORSINI, Joseph E. 248.2
Hear my confession, by Joseph E. Orsini. Plainfield, N.J., Logos International [1971] 90 p. 18 cm. [BX4705.O715A3] 73-173430 ISBN 0-912106-25-5 1.00
1. Pentecostalism. I. Title.

OTTERLAND, Anders, 1920- 248'.2
Upwinds : a short report on spiritual upwinds in our time / by Anders Otterland and Lennart Sunnergren. Nashville : Nelson, [1975] p. cm. Translation of Uppvindar. [BX8763.O8713] 75-14367 ISBN 0-8407-5599-6 : 3.50
1. Pentecostalism. I. Sunnergren, Lennart, 1930- joint author. II. Title.

*PERRY, Thomas Charles. d. 1959. 248.2
Practicing Jesus' way of life. New York, Exposition [1967] 178p. 21cm. (EP45656) 4.50
1. Spiritual life. I. Title.

POPEJOY, Bill. 248'.2
The case for divine healing / Bill Popejoy. Springfield, Mo. : Gospel Pub. House, c1976. 63 p. ; 18 cm. (Radiant books) [BT732.5.P63] 75-43155 pbk. : 0.95
1. Faith-cure. I. Title.

PRICE, Eugenia. 248'.2 B
The burden is light! The autobiography of a transformed pagan who took God at His word. Boston, G. K. Hall, 1973 [c1955] 326 p. 25 cm. Large print ed. [BV4935.P75A32 1973] 73-9986 ISBN 0-8161-6137-2 9.95 (lib. bdg.)
1. Price, Eugenia. 2. Converts. I. Title.

ROBERTS, Oral 248.2
God is a good God; believe it and come alive. Indianapolis, Bobbs-Merrill [c.1960] 188p. (col front.) 23cm. 60-7419 2.95 bds.,
1. Peace of mind. I. Title.

ROBINSON, Mary Ann, 1935- 248'.2
The sparrows are looking good. Philadelphia, Dorrance [1973] 47 p. 22 cm. [BX6495.R657A3] 73-75631 ISBN 0-8059-1842-6 2.95
1. Robinson, Mary Ann, 1935- I. Title.

ROGERS, Dale Evans. 248.2
The woman at the well. Old Tappan, N.J., Revell [1970] 191 p. ports. 21 cm. [BR1725.R63A33] 78-112456 4.95
I. Title.

ROLLE, Richard, of Hampole, 1290?-1349. 248.2
The Contra amatores mundi of Richard Rolle of Hampole. Edited, with introd. and translation, by Paul F. Theiner. Berkeley, University of California Press, 1968. viii, 196 p. 24 cm. (University of California publications. English studies, 33) "This edition follows the text as given in MS. 18932 of the John Rylands Library in Manchester (M)."—p. 61. Based on the editor's thesis, Harvard University, 1962. "Textual notes": p. 113-144. Bibliography. p. 63-64. [BV5039.L3R57 1968] 68-64641
1. Mysticism—Middle Ages, 600-1500. 2. Asceticism—Middle Ages, 600-1500. I. Theiner, Paul F., ed. II. Title. III. Series: California. University. University of California publications. English studies, 33

*ROTHACKER, Viola. 248.2
I have seen the Lord. New York, Vantage [1967] 122p. 21cm. 2.95 bds.,
I. Title.

*ROTHACKER, Viola. 248.2
Walking with the master. New York, Vantage Press, [1974] 135 p. 21 cm. [BV4520] ISBN 0-533-00948-0. 3.95.
1. Religious experience. 2. Spiritual life. I. Title.

SELTZER, Louis Benson, 1897- 248.2
Six and God [by] Louis B. Seltzer. Cleveland, World Pub. Co. [1966] xi, 96 p. 21 cm. [BR1700.2.S4] 66-24997
1. Christian biography. I. Title.

SELTZER, Louis Benson, 1897- 248.2
Six and God [by] Louis B. Seltzer. Cleveland, World [1966] xi, 96p. 21cm. [BR1700.2.S4] 66-24997 3.95
1. Christian biography. I. Title.

SEWELL, Lisa. 248'.2
I called Jesus and He came leaping over mountains and skipping over hills. Philadelphia, Dorrance [1974] 153 p. 22 cm. [BT580.A1S48] 73-86945 ISBN 0-8059-1930-9 5.95
1. Visions. I. Title.

SHOEMAKER, Samuel Moor, 1893-1963. 248.2
Under new management, by Sam Shoemaker. Grand Rapids, Zondervan Pub. House [1966] 148 p. 21 cm. [BV4501.2S445] 66-28236
1. Christian life—Anglican authors. I. Title.

SMITH, Hershel. 248'.2 B
The devil and Mr. Smith [by] Hershel Smith, with Dave Hunt. Old Tappan, N.J., F. H. Revell Co. [1974] 192 p. 21 cm. Autobiographical. [BV4935.S63A33] 74-3043 ISBN 0-8007-0662-5 2.95
1. Smith, Hershel. 2. Satanism. 3. Conversion. I. Hunt, Dave, joint author. II. Title.

*SMITH, Roxie 248.2
Into each life. New York, Vantage [1967] 150p. 21cm. 3.50 bds.,
I. Title.

SMITH, Wesley E. 248'.2 B
Gateway to power, by Wesley E. Smith. [Monroeville, Pa.] Whitaker Books [1973] 144 p. 18 cm. [BR1725.S5517A33] 73-81104 ISBN 0-88368-043-2 1.25 (pbk.)
1. Smith, Wesley E. I. Title.
Publisher's address: 607 Laurel Dr. Monroeville, Pa. 15146.

SOERGEL, Mary. 248'.2
Sing a gentle breeze : a story of a disintegrating family seeking wholeness / Mary Soergel. Wheaton, Ill. : Tyndale House Publishers, 1977. 266 p. ; 21 cm. [BR1725.S65A37] 76-47301 ISBN 0-8423-5889-7 : 4.95
1. Soergel, Mary. 2. Christian biography—Wisconsin. I. Title.

STAGG, Frank, 1911- 248.2
Glossolalia; tongue speaking in Biblical, historical, and psychological perspective [by] Frank Stagg, E. Glenn Hison. Wayne E. Oates. Nashville, Abingdon [1967] 110p. 19cm. Bibl. [BL54.S65] 67-22167 1.45 pap.,
1. Glossolalia. I. Hinson, E. Glenn, joint author. II. Oates, Wayne Edward, joint author. III. Title.

STEINER, Johannes, 1902- 248'.2 B
The visions of Therese Neumann / by Johannes Steiner. New York : Alba House, c1976. xii, 244 p. : ill. ; 22 cm. Translation of Visionen der Therese Neumann. [BX4705.N47S7513] 75-34182 ISBN 0-8189-0318-X : 5.95
1. Neumann, Therese, 1898-1962. 2. Visions. I. Title.

STOLPE, Sven, 1905- 248.2
Dag Hammarskjold, a spiritual portrait. English tr. by Naomi Walford. New York, Scribners [1967, c.1966] 127p. 21cm. (Scribner lib., SL138) Tr. of Dag Hammarskjold's andliga vag. [D839.7.H3S753] 67-12027 1.25 pap.,
1. Hammarskjold, Dag, 1905-1961. I. Title.

STOLPE, Sven, 1905- 248.2
Dag Hammarskjold, a spiritual portrait. English translation by Naomi Walford. New York, Scribner [1966] 127 p. port. 22 cm. Translation of Dag Hammarskjold's andliga vag. [D839.7.H3S753] 66-12027
1. Hammarskjold, Dag, 1905-1961. I. Title.

STOLPE, Sven, 1905- 248.2
Dag Hammarskjold, a spiritual portrait. English tr. by Naomi Walford. New York, Scribners [c.1966] 127p. port. 22cm. [D839.7.H3S753] 66-12027 3.95
1. Hammarskjold, Dag, 1905-1961. I. Title.

SULLIVAN, J. C., 1907- 248'.2
They couldn't kill Sullivan: ... formerly "From crime to Christ." A true story, by J. C. Sullivan. Fort Worth, Nu-Way Foundation, Publications Dept., [1972] 127 p. illus. 18 cm. [BV4935.S83A3] 71-188610
1. Conversion. I. Title.

TAYLOR, Jack R. 248'.2
Victory over the devil; an adventure into the world of spiritual warfare [by] Jack R. Taylor. Nashville, Tenn., Broadman Press [1973] 134 p. 20 cm. [BT981.T39] 72-96149 ISBN 0-8054-5131-5 pap 2.25
1. Devil. 2. Demonology. 3. Angels. 4. Christian life—Baptist authors. I. Title.

THORNTON, Martin 248.2
Margery Kempe: an example in the English pastoral tradition. [Greenwich, Conn., The Seabury Press, c.] 1960 [i.e.1961] 120p. 61-978 3.75
1. Kempe, Margery (Burnham) b. ca.1373 I. Title.

THURIAN, Max 248.2
Modern man and spiritual life. New York, Association [1963] 80p. 19cm. (World Christian bks., 2d ser., no. 46) 64-157 1.25 pap.,
1. Spiritual life. I. Title.

TIM X. 248'.2
The Enemy; Satan's struggle for two boy's souls, by Tim and Betsy X as told to Jim Grant. Wheaton, Ill., Tyndale House Publishers [1973] 107 p. 22 cm. [BT975.T55] 73-81004 ISBN 0-8423-0691-9 2.95
1. Demonology—Case studies. 2. Trammel, Bob. 3. Trammel, Jack. I. Betsy X, joint author. II. Grant, Jim. III. Title.

TINSLEY, Ernest John. 248.2
The imitation of God in Christ; an essay on the Biblical basis of Christian spirituality. Philadelphia, Westminster Press [1960] 190 p. 23 cm. (The Library of history and doctrine) Includes bibliography. [BV4501.2.T55] 60-11146
1. Christian life—Biblical teaching. I. Title.

TINSLEY, Ernest John 248.2
The imitation of God in Christ; an essay on the Biblical basis of Christian spirituality. Philadelphia, Westminster Press [1960] 190p. (Library of history and doctrine) Bibl. 60-11146 4.00
1. Christian life—Biblical teaching. I. Title.

TOLSTOI, Lev Nikolaevich, graf, 1828-1910. 248.2
The wisdom of Tolstoy. New York, Philosophical Library; [distributed by Book Sales, inc., 1968] 128 p. 19 cm. Translation of V chem moia viera (romanized form) An abridgement of the translation by Huntington Smith first published in 1885 under title: My religion. [BR125.T7132] 68-56193 3.00
1. Christianity—19th century. I. Smith, Huntington, 1857-1926, tr. II. Title.

TOMCZAK, Larry, 1949- 248'.2 B
Clap your hands! Plainfield, N.J., Logos International [1973] 143 p. photos. 21 cm. [BX4705.T68144A33] 73-88241 ISBN 0-88270-072-3 2.50 (pbk.)
1. Tomczak, Larry, 1949- I. Title.

TORRES, Victor. 248'.2 B
Son of evil street, by Victor Torres, with Don Wilkerson. Minneapolis, Bethany Followship [1973] 160 p. 21 cm. [BV4935.T65A37] 73-10828 ISBN 0-87123-516-1 1.95
1. Torres, Victor. 2. Narcotic addicts—Personal narratives. 3. Conversion. I. Title.

TORRES, Victor. 248'.2 B
Son of evil street / Victor Torres with Don Wilkerson. 2d ed. Minneapolis : Bethany Fellowship, 1977. 166 p. ; 18 cm. (Dimension books) [BV4935.T65A37 1977] 77-150672 ISBN 0-87123-516-1 pbk. : 1.95
1. Torres, Victor. 2. Narcotic addicts—New York (State)—Brooklyn—Biography. 3. Converts—New York (State)—Brooklyn—Biography. 4. Brooklyn—Biography. I. Wilkerson, Don, joint author. II. Title.

*TORREY, R. A. 248.2
Divine healing [by] R. A. Torrey. Grand Rapids, Baker Book House [1974] 64 p. 18 cm. (Baker book house direction books) Reprint of the 1924 ed. [BT732.4] ISBN 0-8010-8828-3 0.95 (pbk.)
1. Faith—Cure. 2. Miracles—New Testament. I. Title.

DANIKEN, Erich von, 1935-. 248.2
Miracles of the gods : a new look at the supernatural Erich von Daniken ; translated by Michael Heron. New York : Dell ,1976 c1975. xi, 291 p. : ill. ; 18 cm. Bibliography: pp. 277-291. [BF1103.D3313] pbk. : 1.95
1. Visions. 2. Miracles. 3. Bible—Miscellanea. I. Title.
L.C. card no. for 1975 Souvenir Press edition: 75-332075.

DANIKEN, Erich von, 1935- 248'.2
Miracles of the gods : a new look at the supernatural / Erich von Daniken ; translated from the German by Michael Heron. 1st U.S. ed. New York : Delacorte Press, c1975. xiii, 291 p., [12] leaves of plates : ill. ; 22 cm. Translation of Erscheinungen. Bibliography: p. [277]-291. [BF1103.D3313 1975b] 75-29246 ISBN 0-440-05595-4 : 8.95
1. Bible—Miscellanea. 2. Visions. 3. Miracles. I. Title.

WAHL, Jan. 248.2 B
Juan Diego and the lady. La dama y Juan Diego. Spanish translation by Dolores Janes Garcia. Illustrated by Leonard Everett Fisher. New York, Putnam [1974] 48 p. col. illus. 24 cm. A bilingual edition of the story of the miraculous appearance of Our Lady of Guadalupe to a humble Mexican Indian in 1531. [BX4705.D513W33] 72-97317 ISBN 0-399-20356-7 4.97
1. Diego, Juan, fl. 1531—Juvenile literature. 2. Guadalupe, Nuestra Senora de—Juvenile literature. I. Fisher, Leonard Everett, illus. II. Title. III. Title: La dama y Juan Diego.

WARBURTON, John, 1776-1857 248.2
Mercies of a covenant God; being an account of some of the Lord's dealings in providence and grace with John Warburton, minister of the gospel, Trowbridge. Together with an account of the author's last days. Swengel, Pa., Reiner Pubns. 1964. xvi, 285p. illus., facsim., ports. 20cm. [BX6419.69.W3A3] 65-1231 3.95; 2.75 pap.,
I. Title.

WARD, Mildred M. 248'.2 B
The way back; a story of God's redeeming love, by Mildred M. Ward. Anderson, Ind., Warner Press [1973] 128 p. 21 cm. [BR1725.H214W37] 73-12394 ISBN 0-87162-160-6 2.95 (pbk.)
1. Hall, June. 2. Houston Christian Mission. I. Title.

WEAD, Doug. 248'.2
Hear His voice / R. Douglas Wead. Carol Stream, Ill. : Creation House, c1976. 172 p. ; 19 cm. (New leaf library) Bibliography: p. 171-172. [BT767.3.W42 1976] 76-16291 ISBN 0-88419-001-3 pbk. : 1.95
1. Gifts, Spiritual. I. Title.

WEATHERFORD, Willis Duke, 1875- 248.2
Studies in Christian experience. Nashville, Methodist Evangelistic Materials [c1962] 120 p. 20 cm. [BR110.W4] 62-14882
1. Experience (Religion) I. Title.

WEST, Marion B. 248'.2 B
Out of my bondage / Marion B. West. Nashville, Tenn. : Broadman Press, 1977, c1976. 128 p. ; 20 cm. [HQ759.W45A36] 76-5297 ISBN 0-8054-5144-7 : 2.50
1. West, Marion B. 2. Mothers—Biography. 3. Housewives—Biography. 4. Family. I. Title.

WILD, Robert, 1936- 248'.2
Enthusiasm in the Spirit / Robert Wild. Notre Dame, Ind. : Ave Maria Press, c1975. 176 p. ; 21 cm. Includes bibliographical references. [BX2350.57.W54] 75-14742 ISBN 0-87793-101-1 : 4.95 ISBN 0-87793-102-X pbk. : 2.45
1. Pentecostalism. I. Title.

WILSON, Yvonne M. 248'.2 B
Sifted gold / Yvonne M. Wilson. St. Louis : Concordia Pub. House, [1974] 126 p. ; 20 cm. [RC416.W54] 74-4743 ISBN 0-570-03235-0 : 4.95
1. Polyradiculitis—Personal narratives. I. Title.

KELSEY, Morton T. 248'.2'01
Encounter with God; a theology of Christian experience, by Morton Kelsey. Minneapolis, Bethany Fellowship [1972] 281 p. 23 cm. Bibliography: p. 262-276. [BR110.K4] 73-155993 ISBN 0-87123-123-9 5.95
1. Experience (Religion) 2. Theology, Doctrinal—History. I. Title.

ENGQUIST, Richard. comp. 248.2'0922
Living the great adventure; true stories of crisis and discovery from the pages of Faith at work, selected & ed., by Richard Engquist. Waco, Tex., Word Bks. [1968, c.1967] 206p. 21cm. [BV4515.2.E45] 67-29861 3.50
1. Christian life—Stories. I. Faith at work. II. Title.

THE Power of one 248'.2'0922 B
: men and women of faith who make a difference / edited by James L. Merrell. St. Louis : Bethany Press, c1976. 124 p. ; 22 cm. [BR1700.2.P68] 76-16064 ISBN 0-8272-2925-9 pbk. : 3.95
1. Christian biography. I. Merrell, James L.

RODENMAYER, Robert N. 248.2'0922
How many miles to Babylon? [By] Robert N. Rodenmayer. New York, Seabury Press [1967] 144 p. 22 cm. [BJ1581.2.R63] 67-20936
1. Conduct of life. I. Title.

ANDERSON, Ted, 1952- 248'.2'0924 B
The God explosion in my life / by Ted Anderson, with David Prudhomme. Wheaton, Ill. : Tyndale House Publishers, 1975. 234 p. ; 18 cm. [BV4935.A58A33] 74-21973 ISBN 0-8423-1040-1 pbk. : 1.95
1. Anderson, Ted, 1952- 2. Conversion. I. Prudhomme, David, 1917-1974, joint author. II. Title.

*BLOSE, Elcy Marie, 248.2'0924
1917-
Hello, God; the life story of Elcy Marie Blose. New York, Exposition [1968] 125p. 21cm. (EP46760) 4.50
I. Title.

BRYANT, Lee. 248.2'0924 B
Come, fill the cup. Waco, Tex., Word Books [1970] 207 p. 23 cm. [BV4935.B77A3 1970] 70-128444 4.95
I. Title.

BULLOCK, Randy. 248'.2'0924 B
It's good to know / by Randy Bullock, with Dave Balsiger. Milford, Mi. : Mott Media, [1975] 233 p. [4] leaves of plates : ports. ; 20 cm. Autobiographical. [BV4935.B84A34] 74-27321 ISBN 0-915134-00-4 : 5.95 ISBN 0-915134-01-2 pbk. : 2.95
1. Bullock, Randy. 2. Conversion. I. Balsiger, Dave. II. Title.

COLSON, Charles W. 248'.2'0924 B
Born again / Charles W. Colson. Boston : G. K. Hall, 1976. p. cm. Large print ed. [BV4935.C63A33 1976b] 76-41314 ISBN 0-8161-6428-2 : 18.95
1. Colson, Charles W. 2. Converts—United States—Biography. 3. Watergate Affair, 1972- 4. Sight-saving books. I. Title.

COLSON, Charles W. 248'.2'0924 B
Born again / Charles W. Colson. Old Tappan, N.J. : Chosen Books :distributed by F. H. Revell Co., c1976. 351 p., [8] leaves of plates : ill. ; 24 cm. Includes index. [BV4935.C63A33] 75-40462 ISBN 0-912376-13-9 : 8.95
1. Colson, Charles W. 2. Converts—United States—Biography. 3. Watergate Affair, 1972- I. Title.

COPPIN, Ezra. 248'.2'0924 B
Turn loose / by Ezra Coppin. San Diego, CA : Faith Outreach International, c1976. 137 p. : ill. ; 21 cm. On cover: The Jerry Barnard story, as told to Ezra Coppin. [BR1725.B344C66] 76-53625
1. Barnard, Jerry. 2. Christian biography—California. I. Title.

DANKER, William J. 248'.2'0924 B
More than healing, the story of Kiyoko Matsuda [by] William J. Danker and Kiyoko Matsuda. St. Louis, Concordia Pub. House [1973] 135 p. illus. 21 cm. [BR1317.M37D36] 73-78105 ISBN 0-570-03161-3 2.25
1. Matsuda, Kiyoko. I. Matsuda, Kiyoko, joint author. II. Title.

EPSTEIN, Kathie. 248'.2'0924 B
The quiet riot / Kathie Epstein. Old Tappan, N.J. : F. H. Revell Co., c1976. p. cm. [BR1725.E66A36] 76-2719 ISBN 0-8007-0789-3
1. Epstein, Kathie. I. Title.

FESCH, Jacques. 248'.2'0924
Light upon the scaffold : prison letters of Jacques Fesch, executed October 1, 1957, age twenty-seven / edited by Augustin-Michel Lemonnier ; translated by Matthew J. O'Connell ; with a foreword by Michel Quoist. St. Meinrad, IN. : Abbey Press, 1975. ix, 153 p. ; 18 cm. (A Priority edition) Translation of Lumiere sur l'echafaud. [HV9667.F4813] 75-208 ISBN 0-87029-046-0 pbk. : 2.95
1. Prisoners—France. 2. Prisons—Religious life. I. Title.

GRAEF. HILDA C. 248.2'0924
God and myself; the spirituality of John Henry Newman [by] Hilda Graef. [1st Amer. ed.] New York, Hawthorn [1968] 206p. 23cm. Bibl. [BX4705.N5G74 1968] 67-2465 5.95
1. Newman, John Henry, Cardinal, 1801-1890. I. Title.

HALL, Ennen Reaves. 248.2'0924 B
Break the glass wall. Waco, Tex., Word Books [1971] 129 p. 23 cm. [BR1725.H19A3] 75-144369 3.95
I. Title.

HARTLEY, Al. 248'.2'0924 B
Come meet my friend / Al Hartley. Old Tappan, N.J. : F. H. Revell, c1977. 61 p. ; 18 cm. (New life ventures) [BV4935.H355A33] 77-5921 ISBN 0-8007-9001-4 pbk : 0.95
1. Hartley, Al. 2. Converts—United States—Biography. 3. Cartoonists—United States—Biography. I. Title.

HEGGER, Herman J 248'.2'0924
1916-
I saw the light. Translated by H. deJongste. Edited by Eugene W. Allen. Philadelphia, Presbyterian and Reformed Pub. Co., 1961. 171p. 21cm. Autobiographical. [BV4935.H4A3] 61-11013
1. Converts. I. Title.

HELMAN, Patricia 248'.2'0924 B
Kennedy.
In league with the stones : one woman's journey of faith / by Patricia Kennedy Helman. Elgin, Ill. : Brethren Press, c1976. 143 p. ; 18 cm. [BX7843.H44A34] 76-13639 ISBN 0-87178-416-5 pbk. : 2.95
1. Helman, Patricia Kennedy. I. Title.

HERRMANN, Nina, 248'.2'0924 B
1943-
Go out in joy! / Nina Herrmann. Atlanta : John Knox Press, c1977. 221 p. ; 22 cm. [BV4335.H38] 76-44972 ISBN 0-8042-2073-5 : 7.95
1. Herrmann, Nina, 1943- 2. Chaplains, Hospital—Illinois—Chicago—Biography. 3. Chicago—Biography. 4. Sick children. I. Title.

JORDAN, Mickey. 248'.2'0924 B
Someday I'll be somebody. Foreword by Rosalind Rinker. Atlanta, Forum House [1974] 200 p. 23 cm. Autobiographical. [BR1725.J67A34] 72-97822 ISBN 0-913618-09-8 5.95
1. Jordan, Mickey. I. Title.

LIFE, Nancy. 248'.2'0924 B
Move over, Mountain : the agonizing confessions of a middle-class housewife in search of peace of mind / Nancy Life. Minneapolis : Bethany Fellowship, [1975] 139 p. ; 21 cm. [BV4935.L47A33] 74-31682 ISBN 0-87123-375-4 pbk. : 2.45
1. Life, Nancy. 2. Conversion. I. Title.

LONG, Mason, 1842- 248'.2'0924
1903.
The life of Mason Long, the converted gambler. Being a record of his experience as a white slave; a soldier in the Union Army; a professional gambler; a patron of the turf; a variety theater and minstrel manager; and, finally, a convert to the Murphy cause and to the Gospel of Christ. 4th ed. Fort Wayne, Ind., 1883. 280p. illus., ports. 18cm. [BV4935.L6A3 1883] 59-58984
I. Title.

MCLEOD, Ceil. 248'.2'0924 B
Another day, another miracle / Ceil McLeod. Wheaton, Ill. : Tyndale House Publishers, c1975. 115 p. ; 22 cm. Includes bibliographical references. [BR1725.M3154A32] 74-21964 2.95 (pbk.)
1. McLeod, Ceil. I. Title.

MCLEOD, Ceil. 248'.2'0924 B
Another day, another miracle / Ceil McLeod. Wheaton, Ill. : Tyndale House Publishers, c1975. 115 p. ; 22 cm. Includes bibliographical references. [BR1725.M3154A32] 74-21964 2.95 (pbk.)
1. McLeod, Ceil. I. Title.

MJORUD, Herbert. 248'.2'0924 B
Your authority to believe / by Herbert Mjorud. Carol Stream, Ill. : Creation House, c1975. 156 p. ; 21 cm. [BX8080.M47A33] 75-22574 ISBN 0-88419-117-6 pbk. : 2.95
1. Mjorud, Herbert. I. Title.

MORRIS, Otho Anderson, 248.20924
1891-
Shining my light, by Otho A. Morris. San Antonio, Naylor [1966] ix, 29p. ports. 22cm. [BR1725.M53A3] 66-26722 2.95
I. Title.

MURDOCK, Alma. 248'.2'0924
Crowned. San Antonio, Tex., Naylor Co. [1962] 51p. illus. 23cm. [BV4935.M8M8] 62-13062
1. Murdock, Stephen. I. Title.

NAUER, Barbara. 248'.2'0924 B
Rise up and remember / Barbara Nauer. 1st ed. Garden City, N.Y. : Doubleday, 1977. viii, 110 p. ; 21 cm. [BX4705.N284A37] 76-54011 ISBN 0-385-12955-6 pbk. : 2.95
1. Nauer, Barbara. 2. Catholics in the United States—Biography. 3. Pentecostalism—Catholic Church. I. Title.

PALE Moon, 248'.2'0924 B
Princess.
Pale Moon : the story of an Indian princess / by Princess Pale Moon. Wheaton, Ill. : Tyndale House Publishers, 1975. 110 p., [8] leaves of plates : ill. ; 22 cm. [E99.C5P25] 75-7227 ISBN 0-8423-4878-6 : 4.95
1. Pale Moon, Princess.

PROCTOR, William. 248'.2'0924 B
On the trail of God / by William Proctor. 1st ed. Garden City, N.Y. : Doubleday, 1977. xiii, 151 p. ; 22 cm. [BV4930.P73] 76-42385 ISBN 0-385-11680-2 : 6.95
1. Converts—United States—Biography. I. Title.

READ, Maureen Hay, 248'.2'0924 B
1937-
Like a watered garden / Maureen Hay Read ; introduction by Sherwood E. Wirt. Scottdale, Pa. : Herald Press, 1977. 156 p. : ill. ; 21 cm. [BR1725.R37A34] 77-5858 ISBN 0-8361-1818-9 : 5.95
1. Read, Maureen Hay, 1937- 2. Christian biography—United States. I. Title.

SIPE, Onjya, 1951- 248'.2'0924 B
Devil's dropout : Manson follower turns to Christ / by Onjya Sipe, with Robert L. McGrath. Milford, Mich. : Mott Media, c1976. 204 p. ; 21 cm. [BV4935.S56A33] 76-17648 ISBN 0-915134-16-0 : 5.95. ISBN 0-915134-17-9 pbk. : 2.95
1. Sipe, Onjya, 1951- 2. Conversion. I. McGrath, Robert L., joint author. II. Title.

SMITH, Fredrick W. 248'.2'0924 B
Journal of a fast / Fredrick W. Smith. New York : Schocken Books, 1976, c1972. 216 p. ; 21 cm. Includes bibliographical references. [BV5055.S6 1976] 75-36493 ISBN 0-8052-3609-0 : 7.95
1. Smith, Fredrick W. 2. Fasting. I. Title.

SPENCER, David V., 248'.2'0924 B
1923-
Dropping up / David V. Spencer. Carmel Valley : California/Pendleton Press, c1975. 306 p. ; 22 cm. [CT275.S6234A33] 75-37755 ISBN 0-916448-01-0
1. Spencer, David V., 1923- I. Title.

TAYLOR, Jack R. 248.2'0924 B
The key to triumphant living; an adventure in personal discovery [by] Jack R. Taylor. Nashville, Tenn., Broadman Press [1971] 160 p. illus. 21 cm. Bibliography: p. 159-160. [BV4501.2.T28] 76-166582 ISBN 0-8054-5514-0 3.95
1. Christian life—Baptist authors. I. Title.

URQUHART, Colin. 248'.2'0924 B
When the Spirit comes / Colin Urquhart. 1st U.S. ed. Minneapolis : Bethany Fellowship, 1975, c1974. 127 p. ; 18 cm. (Dimension books) [BX5195.L44S348 1975] 75-21165 ISBN 0-87123-645-1 pbk. : 1.50
1. St. Hugh's Church, Lewsey, Eng. 2. Urquhart, Colin. 3. Pentecostalism. I. Title.

VANAUKEN, Sheldon. 248'.2'0924 B
A severe mercy / by Sheldon Vanauken. 1st U.S. ed. San Francisco : Harper & Row, c1977. p. cm. Includes index. [BX5995.V33A35 1977] 77-6161 ISBN 0-06-068821-1 : 6.95
1. Vanauken, Sheldon. 2. Lewis, Clive Staples, 1898-1963—Correspondence. 3. Anglicans—United States—Biography. 4. Anglicans—England—Biography. I. Title.

VAN WADE, David 248'.2'0924 B
Second chance : a broken marriage restored / by David and Sarah Van Wade. Plainfield, N.J. : Logos International, c1975. 248 p. ; 21 cm. [BR1725.V27A35] 75-20899 ISBN 0-88270-137-1 : 5.95.
1. Van Wade, David. 2. Van Wade, Sarah. I. Van Wade, Sarah, joint author. II. Title.

WILLIAMS, Pat, 248'.2'0924 B
1940-
The gingerbread man: Pat Williams—then and now, by Pat Williams and Jerry B. Jenkins. [1st ed.] Philadelphia, A. J. Holman Co. [1974] 119 p. illus. 21 cm. [BV4935.W54A33] 74-11309 ISBN 0-87981-038-6 5.95
1. Williams, Pat, 1940- 2. Conversion. I. Jenkins, Jerry B., joint author. II. Title.

WOMACH, Merrill. 248'.2'0924 B
Tested by fire / Merrill and Virginia Womach, with Mel and Lyla White. Old Tappan, N.J. : Revell, c1976. 128 p. : ill. ; 21 cm. [BR1725.W595W65] 75-42789 ISBN 0-8007-0782-6 : 4.95
1. Womach, Merrill. 2. Womach, Virginia. I. Womach, Virginia, joint author. II. White, Mel, joint author. III. White, Lyla, joint author. IV. Title.

ARKUS, Karen A. 248'.22
A trip into the mystic mind / by Karen A. Arkus. Anaheim, Ca. : Arkus House Publications, 1977. 163 p. ; 21 cm. Includes bibliographical references. [BL625.A74] 76-27490 ISBN 0-917596-01-3 pbk. : 3.95
1. Mysticism. I. Title.

BRINTON, Howard Haines, 248.2'2
1884-
Ethical mysticism in the Society of Friends [by] Howard H. Brinton. [Wallingford, Pa., Pendle Hill Publications, 1967] 36 p. 19 cm. (Pendle Hill pamphlet 156) [BX7748.M9B7] 67-31429
1. Mysticism—Friends, Society of. I. Title.

BURROWS, Ruth. 248'.22
Guidelines for mystical prayer / [by] Ruth Burrows. London : Sheed and Ward, 1976. x, 149 p. ; 20 cm. [BV5082.2.B87] 77-354225 ISBN 0-7220-7663-0 : £2.50
1. Mysticism. I. Title.

*BUTLER, Dom Cuthbert 248.22
Western mysticism the teaching of Augustine, Gregory and Bernard on contemplation and the contemplative life. 2d ed., with afterthoughts New York, Harper, 1966 xii, 242p. 21cm. (Torchbk., TB 312 K. Cathedral Lib.) 1.75 pap.,
I. Title.

BUTLER, Edward Cuthbert, 248.2'2
1858-1934.
Western mysticism; the teaching of Augustine, Gregory, and Bernard on contemplation and the contemplative life. 3d ed. with Afterthoughts, and a new foreword by David Knowles. New York, Barnes & Noble [1968, c1967] lxxii, 242 p. 22 cm. Bibliographical footnotes. [BV5075.B8 1968] 68-6959
1. Augustinus, Aurelius, Saint, Bp. of Hippo. 2. Bernard de Clairvaux, Saint, 1091?-1153. 3. Gregorius I, the Great, Saint, Pope, 540 (ca.)-604. 4. Mysticism. 5. Contemplation. I. Title.

BUTLER, Edward Cuthbert, 248'.22
1858-1934.
Western mysticism : the teaching of SS. Augustine, Gregory, and Bernard on contemplation and the contemplative life / Cuthbert Butler. New York : Gordon Press, [1975] p. cm. Reprint of the 1922 ed. published by Constable, London. [BV5075.B8 1975] 75-20378 ISBN 0-87968-244-2 lib.bdg. : 34.95
1. Augustinus, Aurelius, Saint, Bp. of Hippo. 2. Bernard de Clairvaux, Saint, 1091?-1153. 3. Gregorius, the Great, Saint, Pope, 540 (ca.)-604. 4. Mysticism. 5. Contemplation. I. Title.

CAUSSADE, Jean Pierre de, 248'.22
d.1751.
Abandonment to divine providence / by Jean-Pierre de Caussade ; newly translated, with an introd. by John Beevers. 1st ed. Garden City, N.Y. : Image Books, 1975. 119 p. ; 18 cm. (An Image book original) Translation of L'abandon a la providence divine. [BV5080.C3 1975] 74-2827 ISBN 0-385-02544-0 pbk.: 1.45
1. Mysticism—Catholic Church. 2. Spiritual life—Catholic authors. I. Title.

CLARK, James Midgley, 248.2'2
1888-1961.
The great German mystics, Eckhart, Tauler and Suso. New York, Russell & Russell [1970] 121 p. 22 cm. Reprint of the 1949 ed. Bibliography: p. 110-117. [BV5077.G3C58 1970] 73-81493
1. Eckhart, Meister, d. 1327. 2. Tauler, Johannes, 1300 (ca.)-1361. 3. Suso, Heinrich, 1300?-1366. 4. Mysticism—Germany. I. Title.

COLLEDGE, Eric, ed. 248.22
The mediaeval mystics of England. [Elmer O'Brien general ed.] New York, Scribners [c.1961] 309p. Bibl. 61-6030 4.95 bds.,
1. Mysticism—Gt. Brit. 2. Mysticism—Middle Ages. I. Title.

COMENIUS, Johann Amos, 248.2'2
1592-1670.
The labyrinth of the world and the paradise of the heart [by] John Amos Komensky. New York, Arno Press, 1971. 347 p. 23 cm. (The Eastern Europe collection) Translation of Labyrint sveta a raj srdce. Reprint of the 1901 ed. [BV4509.C8C613 1971] 73-135812 ISBN 0-405-02754-0
1. Christian life. I. Title.

ELISABETH DE LA TRINITE, 248.22
Sister, [secular name Elisabeth Catez] 1880-1906
Spiritual writings: letters, retreats, and unpublished notes. Ed. by M. M. Philipon. New York, Kenedy [c.1962] 180p. illus. 22cm. 62-21053 3.95 bds.,
1. Mysticism—Catholic Church. I. Title.

ELIZABETH DE LA TRINITE, 248.22
Sister, 1880-1906
Spiritual writings: letters, retreats, and unpublished notes. Edited by M. M. Philipon. New York, P. J. Kenedy [c1962] 180 p. illus. 22 cm. Secular name: Elisabeth Catez. 62-21053
1. Mysticism — Catholic Church. I. Title.

GREGORIUS, Saint, Bp. of 248.22
Nyssa, fl. 379-394.
From glory to glory; texts from Gregory of Nyssa's mystical writings, selected and with an introd. by Jean Danielou. Translated and edited by Herbert Musurillo, New York, Scribner [1961] xiv, 298p. illus. 22cm. Includes bibliographical references. [BV5080.G73] 61-13370
1. Mysticism—Early church. I. Danielou, Jean, ed. II. Musurillo, Herbert Anthony, ed. and tr. III. Title.

HAPPOLD, Frederick 248.22
Crossfield, 1893-
Mysticism; a study and an anthology. Baltimore, Penguin [c.1963] 364p. 19cm. (Pelican bks., A568) 63-3395 1.45 pap.,
1. Mysticism. I. Title.

HARKNESS, Georgia Elma, 1891- 248'.22
Mysticism: its meaning and message [by] Georgia Harkness. Nashville, Abingdon Press [1973] 192 p. 23 cm. Includes bibliographical references. [BV5082.2.H37] 72-10070 ISBN 0-687-27667-5 5.50
1. Mysticism. I. Title.

HERMAN, Emily, 1876-1923. 248.2'2
The meaning and value of mysticism. 3d ed. Freeport, N.Y., Books for Libraries Press [1971] xvi, 397 p. 23 cm. Reprint of the 1923 ed. Bibliography: p. 379-389. [BV5082.H395 1971] 72-164607 ISBN 0-8369-5891-8
1. Mysticism. I. Title.

HICKS, Esther L. 248.2'2
A lantern for mine anointed Jesus [by Esther L. Hicks. Roosevelt? Utah, 1971] 12 p. 23 cm. Cover title. [BV5091.V6H5] 71-26462
1. Visions. I. Title.

HODGES, Herman. 248.2'2
How I reached the celestial heaven. [1st ed.] Taylors, S. C., Faith Print. Co. [1967] 160p. illus., port. 21cm. [BV5095.H57A3] 66-22428 2.95 pap.,
1. Mysticism—20th cent. I. Title.
Available from the author at 1115 N. Main St., Danville, Va. 24541.

HUGO of Saint-Victor, 1096or7-1141. 248.22
Hugh of Saint-Victor; selected spirtual writings. Translated by a religious of C. S. M. V. With an introd. by Aelred Squire. New York, Harper & Row [1962] 196 p. illus. 21 cm. (Classics of the contemplative life) [BV5080.H77] 62-21139
1. Spiritual life—Middle Ages. I. Title.
Contents omitted.

HUGO OF SAINT VICTOR, 1096or7-1141 248.22
Hugh of Saint-Victor; selected spiritual writings. Tr. [from Latin] by a religious of C. S. M. V. Introd. by Aelred Squire. New York, Harper [1963, c.1962] 196p. illus. 21cm. (Classics of the contemplative life) Bibl. 62-21139 5.00
1. Spiritual life—Middle Ages. I. Title.
Contents omitted.

INGE, William Ralph, 1860-1954. 248'.22
Mysticism in religion / by W. R. Inge. Westport, Conn. : Greenwood Press, 1976, c1948. 168 p. ; 24 cm. Reprint of the ed. published by University of Chicago Press, Chicago. Includes index. Bibliography: p. 166. [BL625.I5 1976] 76-15407 ISBN 0-8371-8953-5 lib. bdg. : 12.25
1. Mysticism. I. Title.

JOHNSON, Raynor Carey 248.22
Watcher on the hills; a study of some mystical experiences of ordinary people. New York, Harper [1960, c.1959] 188p. illus. 22cm. 60-11779 3.50 half cloth
1. Mysticism. I. Title.

JOHNSTON, William, 1925- 248.2'2
The mysticism of the Cloud of unknowing; a modern interpretation. With a foreword by Thomas Merton. New York, Desclee Co. [1967] xvi, 285 p. 22 cm. Bibliography: p. [257]-280. [BV5080.C6J6] 67-17678 5.50
1. Cloud of unknowing. 2. Mysticism—Middle Ages, 600-1500. I. Title.

JOHNSTON, William, 1925- 248'.22
The mysticism of the Cloud of unknowing : a modern interpretation / by William Johnston ; with a foreword by Thomas Merton. 2d ed. St. Meinrad, Ind. : Abbey Press, 1975. xviii, 285 p. ; 21 cm. (Religious experience series ; v. 8) Includes index. Bibliography: p. [275]-280. [BV5080.C6J6 1975] 74-30738 ISBN 0-87029-042-8 pbk. : 5.75
1. Cloud of unknowing. 2. Mysticism—Middle Ages, 600-1500. I. Title.

JONES, Rufus Matthew, 1863-1948. 248.2'2
The flowering of mysticism; the Friends of God in the fourteenth century. New York, Hafner Pub. Co., 1971 [c1939] 270 p. 22 cm. "Facsimile of 1939 edition." Includes bibliographical references. [BV5070.F73J6 1939a] 78-152261
1. Friends of God ("Gottesfreunde") I. Title.

JONES, Rufus Matthew, 1863-1948. 248.2'2
Studies in mystical religion. New York, Russell & Russell [1970] xxxviii, 518 p. 23 cm. Reprint of the 1909 ed. [BV5075.J62 1970] 79-102509
1. Mysticism—History. I. Title.

JULIAN and her Norwich: 248'.22 B
commemorative essays and handbook to the exhibition "Revelations of Divine Love"; editor Frank Dale Sayer. Norwich, Julian of Norwich 1973 Celebration Committee, 1973. [3], 59 p. fold. leaf, map. 26 cm. Includes a catalog of the exhibition held in Norwich Cathedral (St. Luke's Chapel), 4th May 1973. Bibliography: p. 53-57. [BV5095.J84J8] 73-178413 ISBN 0-9502886-0-8 £1.00
1. Juliana, anchoret, 1343-1443. 2. Hermits—England—Norwich. I. Sayer, Frank Dale, ed. II. Julian of Norwich 1973 Celebration Committee. III. Norwich Cathedral. St. Luke's Chapel.

KNOWLES, David, 1896- 248.22
The nature of mysticism, by M. D. Knowles. [1st ed.] New York, Hawthorn Books [1966] 140 p. 21 cm. (Twentieth century encyclopedia of Catholicism, v. 38. Section IV: The Means of redemption) Bibliography: p. 136-140. [BV5082.2.K6] 66-15244
1. Mysticism—Catholic Church. I. Title.

L'HEUREUX, Aloysius Gonzaga, Mother. 248.2'2
The mystical vocabulary of Venerable Mere Maria de l'Incarnation. New York, AMS Press [1969, c1956] xi, 193 p. 22 cm. (Catholic University of America. Studies in Romance languages and literatures, v. 53) First published under title: The mystical vocabulary of Venerable Mere Marie de l'Incarnation and its problems. Originally presented as the author's thesis, Catholic University of America. Bibliography: p. 184-190. [BV5080.M29L4 1969] 72-94190
1. Marie de l'Incarnation, Mother, 1599-1672. La relation de 1654. 2. Mysticism—Terminology. I. Title. II. Series.

MALONEY, George A., 1924- 248'.22
The breath of the mystic / by George A. Maloney. Denville, N.J. : Dimension Books, c1974. 204 p. ; 21 cm. Includes bibliographical references. [BV5082.2.M34] 75-316128 6.95
1. Mysticism. 2. Prayer. I. Title.

MECHTHILD, of Magdeburg(ca 1212-ca. 1282. 248.2'2
The revelations of Mechthild of Magdeburg (1210-1297); or, The flowing light of the Godhead. Translated from the manuscript in the library of the Monastery of Einsiedeln by Lucy Menzies. London, New York, Longmans, Green [1953] xxxvii, 263p. 22cm. Bibliography: p. xxxv-xxxvii. [BV5080.M] A54
1. Mysticism—Middle Ages. I. Title. II. Title: The flowing light of the Godhead.

MEYER, Ann Porter. 248'.22
Being a Christ! : The basic course of the teaching of the inner Christ / by Ann Porter Meyer and Peter Victor Meyer. San Diego, Calif. : Dawning Publications, 1975- v. in ; 28 cm. [BF1031.M54] 74-32528
1. Psychical research. 2. Spiritual life. I. Meyer, Peter Victor, joint author. II. Title.

MOLINARI, Paolo, 1912- 248'.22
Julian of Norwich: the teaching of a 14th century English mystic [by] Paul Molinari. [Folcroft, Pa.] Folcroft Library Editions, 1974. p. cm. Reprint of the 1958 ed. published by Longsmans, Green, London. Bibliography: p. [BV4831.J813M64 1974] 74-13160 25.00
1. Juliana, Anchoret, 1343-1443 Revelations of divine love.

MOLINARI, Paolo, 1912- 248'.22
Julian of Norwich : the teaching of a 14th century English mystic / Paul Molinari. Norwood, Pa. : Norwood Editions, 1976 [c1958] p. cm. Reprint of the ed. published by Longmans, Green, London. Includes index. Bibliography: p. [BV4831.J83M64 1976] 76-13020 ISBN 0-8482-1753-5 lib. bdg. : 25.00
1. Juliana, anchoret, 1343-1443 Revelations of divine love. 2. Devotional literature—History and criticism.

NICOLAS, Cusanus [Name originally: Nicolas Krebs (Khrypffs, Chrypffs) of Cues of Cusa.] Cardinal [Name originally: Nicolaus Krebs (Khrypffs, Chrypffs) of Cues or Cusa.] 248.22
The vision of God; with an introd. by Evelyn Underhill. [Translated from the Latin by Emma Gurney Salter] New York, Unger Pub. Co. [1960] xxx, 130p. 18cm. (Atlantic Paperbacks 503) 60-9104 1.25 pap.,
1. Mysticism—Middle Ages. I. Title.

PECK, George Terhune, 1916- 248'.22
The triple way : purgation, illumination, union / George Peck. Wallingford, Pa. : Pendle Hill Publications, 1977. 32 p. ; 20 cm. (Pendle Hill pamphlet ; 213 ISSN 0031-4250s) Bibliography: p. 30-32. [BX7748.M9P42] 77-79824 ISBN 0-87574-213-0 : 0.95
1. Mysticism—Friends, Society of. I. Title.

RAHNER, Karl, 1904- 248.22
Visions and prophecies [Tr. (from German) by Charles Henkey, richard Strachan. New York] Herder & Herder [1964, c.1963] 108p. 22cm. (Quaestiones disputatae, 10) Bibl. 63-18006 2.25 pap.,
1. Visions. 2. Private revelations. I. Title.

*RICCARDO, Martin. 248.22
Mystical consciousness : exploring an extraordinary state of awareness / by Martin Riccardo. Burbank, Ill. : MVR Books, c1977. 144p. ; 22 cm. Includes bibliographical references. [BL625] pbk. : 3.50
1. Mysticism. I. Title.
Publisher's address: 7809 So. LaPorte Ave., Burbank Illinois 60459.

SAINT GREGORIUS, Bp. of Nyssa, fl.379-394 248.22
From glory to glory; texts from Gregory of Nyssa's mystical writings, selected, introd. by Jean Danielou. Tr., ed. by Herbert Musurillo. New York. Scribners [c.1961] xiv, 298p. illus. Bibl. 61-13370 4.95
1. Mysticism—Early church. I. Danielou, Jean, ed. II. Musurillo, Herbert Anthony, ed. and tr. III. Title.

SANCHEZ-VENTURA y Pascual, Francisco. 248.2'2
The apparitions of Garabandal [by] F. Sanchez-Ventura y Pascual. Translated from the Spanish by A. de Bertodano. Detroit, San Miguel Pub. Co. [1966] 205 p. illus., maps, ports. 22 cm. Translation of Las apariciones no son un mito. [BT660.S343S2] 68-2667
1. San Sebastian de Garabandal. I. Title.

SANCHEZ-VENTURA Y PASCUAL, Francisco. 248.2'2
The apparitions of Garabandal [by] F. Sanchez-Ventura y Pascual. Translated from the Spanish by A. de Bertodano. Detroit, San Miguel Pub. Co. [1966] 205 p. illus., maps, ports. 22 cm. Translation of Las apariciones no son un mito. [BT660.S343S2] 68-2667
1. San Sebastian de Garabandal. I. Title.

*SKINNER, Betty Lee 248.22
Daws, the story of Dawson Trotman founder of the navigators. Grand Rapids, Zondervan [1974] 389 p. illus. 23 cm. [BP605] 73-22700 6.95
1. Trotman, Dawson I. Title.

SONTAG, Frederick. 248'.22
Love beyond pain : mysticism within Christianity / by Frederick Sontag. New York : Paulist Press, c1977. v, 137 p. ; 21 cm. Includes bibliographical references. [BV5082.2.S64] 76-44928 ISBN 0-8091-1998-6 pbk. : 4.50
1. Mysticism. 2. Spiritual life. I. Title.

STARCKE, Walter. 248.2'2
This double thread. [1st ed.] New York, Harper & Row [1967] xiv, 146 p. 22 cm. [BV5082.2.S7] 67-14937
1. Mysticism. I. Title.

SUSO, Heinrich, 1300?-1336. 248.2'2
The exemplar; life and writings of Blessed Henry Suso, O.P. Complete ed. based on mss., with a critical introd. and explanatory notes by Nicholas Heller. Translated from the German by Ann Edward. Dubuque, Iowa, Priory Press [1962] 2 v. illus. 22 cm. Issued in a case. Translation of Des Mystikers Heinrich Seuse, O.P.R., deutsche Schriften. Bibliographical footnotes. [BV5080.S913 1962] 62-14456
1. Mysticism—Middle Ages. I. Heller, Nikolaus, ed. II. Title.

TEILHARD de Chardin, Pierre. 248.2'2
Hymn of the universe. [Translated by Gerald Vann] New York, Harper & Row [1969, c1965] 157 p. 21 cm. (Harper colophon books, CN 173) [B2430.T373] 78-8361 1.95
1. Mysticism—Catholic Church. 2. Cosmology. 3. Creation.

UNDERHILL, Evelyn 248.22
Practical mysticism. New York, Dutton 1960 (Dutton Everyman paperback) 1.25 pap.,
1. Mysticism. I. Title.

UNDERHILL, Evelyn, 1875-1941. 248'.22
The essentials of mysticism, and other essays / by Evelyn Underhill. New York : AMS Press, [1976] p. cm. Reprint of the 1920 ed. published by J. M. Dent, London and Dutton, New York. [BV5082.U5 1976] 75-41277 ISBN 0-404-14620-1 : 15.00
1. Mysticism—Addresses, essays, lectures. I. Title.

UNDERHILL, Evelyn, 1875-1941. 248.22
The Mount of Purification, with Meditations and prayers, 1949, and Collected papers, 1946. [New York] Longmans [c.1960] 333p. (Inner life series) 61-101 3.00 bds.,
1. Mysticism. I. Title.

UNDERHILL, Evelyn, 1875-1941. 248'.22
The mystic way : a psychological study in Christian origins / by Evelyn Underhill. Folcroft, Pa. : Folcroft Library Editions, 1975. p. cm. Reprint of the 1913 ed. published by J. M. Dent, London ; Dutton, New York. Includes index. Bibliography: p. [BV5081.U5 1975] 75-34166 ISBN 0-8414-8854-1 lib. bdg. : 35.00
1. Mysticism. I. Title.

UNDERHILL, Evelyn, 1875-1941. 248.22
Mysticism; a study in the nature and development of man's spiritual consciousness. New York, Dutton, 1961. 519p. (Everyman paperback D73) 1.95 pap.,
1. Mysticism. I. Title.

VANN, Vicki. 248'.22
The growth of the soul : from impiety to ecstasy / by Vicki Vann. Marina del Rey, Calif. : DeVorss, c1977. 100 p. ; 22 cm. [BL625.V36] 77-78828 ISBN 0-87516-235-5 pbk. : 3.25
1. Mysticism. 2. Ecstasy. 3. Identification (Religion) I. Title.

VINING, Elizabeth (Gray) 1902- 248.2'2
William Penn: mystic, as reflected in his writings. [Wallingford, Pa., Pendle Hill Publications, 1969] 31 p. 19 cm. (Pendle Hill pamphlet 167) [F152.2.V79] 74-95891 0.55
1. Penn, William, 1644-1718. I. Title.

WATKIN, Edward Ingram, 1888- 248.2'2
Poets and mystics, by E. I. Watkin. Freeport, N. Y., Books for Libraries Press [1968] ix, 318 p. 23 cm. (Essay index reprint series) Reprint of the 1953 ed. Includes bibliographical references. [BV5077.G7W35 1968] 68-55862
1. Mysticism—Catholic Church. I. Title.

WAUTIER d'Aygalliers, Alfred. 248.2'2
Ruysbroeck the Admirable, by A. Wautier d'Aygalliers. Port Washington, N.Y., Kennikat Press [1969] xliii, 326 p. 22 cm. First published in 1923, as thesis, University of Paris. Bibliographical footnotes. [BV5095.J3W32 1969] 68-26207
1. Jan van Ruysbroeck, 1293-1381. 2. Philosophy, Medieval.

LEUBA, James Henry, 1868-1946. 248'.22'019
The psychology of religious mysticism. Revised ed. London, Boston, Routledge and K. Paul, 1972. xii, 336 p. 22 cm. (International library of psychology, philosophy and scientific method) Reprint of revised ed., London, K. Paul, 1929. Includes bibliographical references. [BV5083.L4 1972] 73-159944 ISBN 0-7100-7317-8 4.00
1. Mysticism—Psychology. 2. Psychology, Religious. I. Title. II. Series.

FREMANTLE, Anne (Jackson) 1909- 248.22082
The Protestant mystics. Introd. by W. H. Auden. Boston, Little [c.1964] xi, 396p. 22cm. Bibl. 64-10472 6.75
1. Mysticism—Collections. 2. Protestantism—Collections. I. Title.

FREMANTLE, Anne (Jackson) 1909- ed. 248.22082
The Protestant mystics. Introd. by W. H. Auden [New York] New Amer. Lib. [1965, c.1964] 317p. 18cm. (Mentor bk. MQ628) Bibl. [BV5072.F7] .95 pap.,
1. Mysticism—Collections. 2. Protestantism—Collections. I. Title.

FAIRWEATHER, William. 248.2'2'09
Among the mystics. Freeport, N.Y., Books for Libraries Press [1968] xvi, 145 p. 22 cm. (Essay index reprint series) Reprint of the 1936 ed. Bibliographical footnotes. [BV5075.F3 1968] 68-20298
1. Mysticism—History. I. Title.

GRAEF, Hilda C. 248.2209
The story of mysticism [by] Hilda Graef. [1st ed.] Garden City, N. Y., Doubleday, 1965. 286 p. 22 cm. Bibliography: p. [283]-286. [BV5075.G7] 65-19934
1. Mysticism—History. I. Title.

UNDERHILL, Evelyn 248.2209
The mystics of the church. New York, Schocken [1964] 259p. 21cm. Bibl. 64-22607 5.00; 1.95 pap.,
1. Mysticism—Hist. I. Title.

BOLSHAKOFF, Serge. 248'.22'0922 B
Russian mystics / by Sergius Bolshakoff ; introd. by Thomas Merton. Kalamazoo, Mich. : Cistercian Publications, 1977, c1976. xxx, 303 p. ; 23 cm. (Cistercian studies series ; no. 26) Italian translation has title: I mistici russi. Bibliography: p. 285-303. [BV5077.R8B6413]

76-15485 ISBN 0-87907-826-X : 13.95 ISBN 0-87907-926-6 pbk. : 5.50
1. Mysticism—Russia—History. 2. Mysticism—Orthodox Eastern Church, Russian—History. 3. Monasticism and religious orders—Russia—History. I. Title. II. Series.

COLEMAN, Thomas William, 1884- 248.2'2'0922
English mystics of the fourteenth century, by T. W. Coleman. Westport, Conn., Greenwood Press [1971] 176 p. 23 cm. Reprint of the 1938 ed. Contents.Contents.—Christian mysticism.—The times of the English mystics.—The Ancren riwle.—Richard Rolle.—The Cloud of unknowing.—Walter Hilton.—The Lady Julian.—Margery Kemp. Includes bibliographical references. [BV5077.G7C6 1971] 74-109723 ISBN 0-8371-4213-X
1. Mysticism—Gt. Brit. I. Title.

INGE, William Ralph, 1860-1954. 248.2'2'0922
Studies of English mystics. Freeport, N.Y., Books for Libraries Press [1969] vi, 239 p. 23 cm. (Essay index reprint series.) (St. Margaret's lectures, 1905) Reprint of the 1906 ed. Contents.Contents.—On the psychology of mysticism.—The Ancren riwle and Julian of Norwich.—Walter Hylton.—William Law.—The mysticism of Wordsworth.—The mysticism of Robert Browning. [BV5077.G7I6 1969] 69-17578
1. Mysticism—Gt. Brit. 2. Mysticism in literature. I. Title. II. Series.

ARMSTRONG, Christopher J. R., 1935- 248'.22'0924 B
Evelyn Underhill, 1875-1941 : an introduction to her life and writings / by Christopher J. R. Armstrong. Grand Rapids : Eerdmans, 1976, c1975. xxiii, 303 p. ; 22 cm. Includes index. Bibliography: p. 293-303. [BV5095.U5A75 1976] 75-33401 ISBN 0-8028-3474-4 : 7.95
1. Underhill, Evelyn, 1875-1941.

BAILEY, Raymond. 248'.22'0924
Thomas Merton on mysticism / Raymond Bailey. Garden City, N.Y. : Doubleday, 1975. 239 p. ; 22 cm. Originally presented as the author's thesis, Southern Baptist Theological Seminary, Louisville. Includes bibliographical references. [BX4705.M542B28 1975] 75-22742 ISBN 0-385-07173-6 : 7.95
1. Merton, Thomas, 1915-1968. 2. Mysticism—History. I. Title.

FADIMAN, Edwin. 248'.22'0924
The feast day, by Edwin Fadiman, Jr. Illustrated by Charles Mikolaycak. [1st ed.] Boston, Little, Brown, [1973] 93 p. illus. 25 cm. Bibliography: p. 93. Describes the events of the Feast Day on which twelve-year-old Joan of Arc receives the vision which influences the course of her life. [DC103.5.F3] 92 74-182256 ISBN 0-316-27300-7 5.95
1. Jeanne d'Arc, Saint, 1412-1431—Juvenile literature. I. Mikolaycak, Charles, illus. II. Title.

GAUDREAU, Marie M. 248'.22'0924
Mysticism and image in St. John of the Cross / Marie M. Gaudreau. Bern : Herbert Lang, 1976. 256 p. ; 23 cm. (European university papers : Series 23, Theology ; v. 66) Bibliography: p. 231-256. [BV5075.G36] 77-467124 ISBN 3-261-01932-8 : 35.00F
1. Juan de la Cruz, Saint, 1542-1591. 2. Mysticism—History. 3. Image of God—History of doctrines. I. Title. II. Series: Europaische Hochschulschriften : Reihe 23, Theologie ; Bd. 66.

JUAN de la Cruz, Saint, 1542-1591. 248'.22'0924
The poems of St. John of the Cross. Original Spanish texts and English versions newly revised and rewritten by John Frederick Nims. With an essay, A lo divino, by Robert Graves. [Rev. ed.] New York, Grove Press [1968] 151 p. 21 cm. [PQ6400.J8A17 1968] 67-27891
I. Title.

JUAN de la Cruz, Saint, 1542-1591. 248'.22'0924
Poesias completas y otras paginas / San Juan de la Cruz ; edicion, estudio y notas por Juan Manuel Blecua. 8. ed., il. Zaragoza ; New York : Ebro, c1974. 128 p. : ill. ; 18 cm. (Serie Verso ; 17) (Biblioteca clasica Ebro ; 68) Bibliography: p. [27]-28. [PQ6400.J8A17 1974] 76-460516 ISBN 8-470-64043-7
I. Blecua, Jose Manuel.

KELLEY, Carl Franklin, 1914- 248'.22'0924
Meister Eckhart on divine knowledge / C. F. Kelley. New Haven : Yale University Press, 1977. xv, 285 p. ; 25 cm. Bibliography: p. [315]-329. [BV5095.E3K44] 77-3959 ISBN 0-300-02098-8 : 17.50
1. Eckhart, Meister, d. 1327. I. Title.

KELLEY, Carl Franklin, 1914- 248'.22'0924
Meister Eckhart on divine knowledge / C. F. Kelley. New Haven : Yale University Press, 1977. xv, 285 p. ; 25 cm. Bibliography: p. [315]-329. [BV5095.E3K44] 77-3959 ISBN 0-300-02098-8 : 17.50
1. Eckhart, Meister, d. 1327. I. Title.

MARY Paul, Sister, S.L.G. 248'.22'0924
All shall be well : Julian of Norwich and the compassion of God / [by] Sister Mary Paul. Oxford : S.L.G. Press, 1976. [2], 41 p. ; 21 cm. (Fairacres publication ; 53 ISSN 0307-1405s) Includes bibliographical references. [BV5095.J84M37] 76-363857 ISBN 0-7283-0055-9 : £0.50
1. Juliana, anchoret, 1343-1443. I. Title.

MOMMAERS, Paul, 1935- 248'.22'0924
The land within : the process of possessing and being possessed by God according to the mystic Jan van Ruysbroeck / by Paul Mommaers ; translated by David N. Smith. Chicago : Franciscan Herald Press, c1975. vii, 143 p. ; 21 cm. p. cm. Translation of Waar naartoe is nu de gloed van de liefde? Includes bibliographical references. [BV5095.J3M6513] 75-19472 ISBN 0-8199-0583-6 : 6.95
1. Jan van Ruysbroeck, 1293-1381. 2. Mysticism—Middle Ages, 600-1500. I. Title.

NEWHOUSE, Flower Arlene Sechler, 1909- 248'.22'0924 B
Insights into reality : revelations through the extrasensory perception of Flower A. Newhouse / edited by Stephen and Phyllis Isaac. 1st ed. Escondido, Calif. : Christward Ministry, c1975. 191 p. ; 23 cm. [BP605.C5N424] 75-36869
1. Newhouse, Flower Arlene Sechler, 1909- 2. Christward Ministry. I. Isaac, Stephen, 1925- II. Isaac, Phyllis.

HODGSON, Geraldine Emma, 1865-1937. 248'.22'0942
English mystics. [Folcroft, Pa.] Folcroft Library Editions, 1973. p. Reprint of the 1922 ed. published by A. R. Mowbray, London; Morehouse Pub. Co., Milwaukee, Wis. Bibliography: p. [BV5077.G7H6 1973] 73-13663 20.00
1. Mysticism—Great Britain. I. Title.

HODGSON, Geraldine Emma, 1865-1937. 248'.22'0942
English mystics. [Folcroft, Pa.] Folcroft Library Editions, 1973. xi, 387 p. 24 cm. Reprint of the 1922 ed. published by A. R. Mowbray, London; Morehouse Pub. Co., Milwaukee, Wis. Bibliography: p. 380-382. [BV5077.G7H6 1973] 73-13663 ISBN 0-8414-4756-X (lib. bdg.)
1. Mysticism—Great Britain. I. Title.

*KNOWLES, David 248.220942
The English mystical tradition. New York, Harper [1965, c.1961] viii, 197p. 21cm. (Harper torchbks., TB302) 1.35 pap.,
I. Title.

KNOWLES, David, 1896- 248.220942
The English mystical tradition. [1st ed.] New York, Harper [1961] 197p. 22cm. Includes bibliography. [BV5077.G7K58] 61-7343
1. Mysticism—Gt. Brit. I. Title.

KNOWLES, David [Michael Clive Knowles] 1896- 248.220942
The English mystical tradition. New York, Harper [c.1961] 197p. Bibl. 61-7343 3.75 bds.,
1. Mysticism—Gt. Brit. I. Title.

WALSH, James, 1920- ed. 248.220942
Pre-Reformation English spirituality New York, Fordham [1966] xiii, 287p. 23cm. Bibl. [BV5077.G7W3] 65-12885 5.75
1. Mysticism—Gt. Brit. 2. Religious literature, English—Hist. &crit. I. Title.

THE Wisdom of the Spanish mystics / selected by Stephen Clissold. New York : New Directions Pub. Co., c1977. 88 p. ; 21 cm. Bibliography: p. 86-88. [BV5072.W5] 77-7650 ISBN 0-8112-0663-7 : 7.50 ISBN 0-8112-0664-5 pbk. : 2.95 248'.22'0946
1. Mysticism—Spain—Collected works. 2. Mysticism—Catholic Church—Collected works. I. Clissold, Stephen.

FEDOTOV, Georgii Petrovich, 1886-1951, ed. 248.2'2'0947
A treasury of Russian spirituality. Compiled and edited by G. P. Fedotov. Gloucester, Mass., P. Smith, 1969. xviii, 12-501 p. illus., ports. 21 cm. Reprint of the 1950 ed. Bibliography: p. 500-501. [BV5077.R8F4 1969] 76-11004 6.50
1. Mysticism—Russia. 2. Mysticism—Orthodox Eastern Church. I. Title.

ADAIR, James R 1923- comp. 248.2'4
Tom Skinner, top man of the Lords, and other stories. Edited by James R. Adair. Grand Rapids, Baker Book House [1967] 84 p. ports. 20 cm. (The Valor series, no. 17) Stories in this book are from the Sunday school papers Power life and Young teen power. [BV4930.A32] 67-26585
1. Converts. I. Title.

ADAIR, James R., 1923- comp. 248.2'4
Tom Skinner, top man of the Lords, and other stories. Edited by James R. Adair. Grand Rapids, Baker Book House [1967] 84 p. ports. 20 cm. (The Valor series, no. 17) Stories in this book are from the Sunday school papers Power life and Young teen power. [BV4930.A32] 67-26585
1. Converts. I. Title.

BAILEY, Faith Coxe. 248.24
These, too, were unshackeed; 15 dramatic stories from the Pacific Garden Mission. Adapted from the Unshackled radio scripts. With an introd. by V. Raymond Edman. Grand Rapids, Zondervan Pub. House [1962] 127p. 22cm. [BV2656.C4B3] 62-52260
1. Converits. 2. Pacific Garden Mission, Chicago. I. Unshackled (Radio program) II. Title.

BALDWIN, Lindley J. 248.2'4
The ebony saint: Samuel Morris's miraculous journey of faith, by Lindley J. Baldwin. Evesham, (Worcs), James, 1967. 125 p. front (port), illus. 18 1/2 cm. 9/6 SBN 85305-001-5 (B67-26224) [BV4935.M63B3 1967] 68-116300
1. Morros, Samuel, 1873-1893. I. Title.

BALILEY, Faith Coxe 248.24
These, too, were unshackled; 15 dramatic stories from the Pacific Garden Mission. Adapted from the Unshackled radio scripts. Introd. by V. Raymond Edman. Grand Rapids, Mich., Zondervan [c.1962] 127p. 22cm. 62-52260 1.95
1. Converts. 2. Pacific Garden Mission, Chicago. I. Unshackled (Radio program) II. Title.

BALZER, Robert Lawrence. 248.24
Beyond conflict. Indianapolis, Bobbs-Merrill [1963] 352 p. illus. 22 cm. Autobiographical. [BL1478.95.B3A3] 63-11631
1. Buddhist converts from Christianity. I. Title.

BARCLAY, William lecturer in the University of Glasgow 248.24
Turning to God: a study of conversion in the book of Acts and today. Philadelphia, Westminster Press [1964] 103 p. 20 cm. Published in London in 1963 as Peake memorial lectures, no. 8. [BV4916.B3] 64-14087
1. Conversion. I. Title.

BARCLAY, William, lecturer in the University of Glasgow. 248.24
Turning to God: a study of conversion in the book of Acts and today. Philadelphia, Westminster [c.1964] 103p. 20cm. Pub. in London in 1963 as Peake memorial lectures, no. 8. 64-14087 2.50
1. Conversion. I. Title.

BEHANNA, Gertrude Florence (Ingram) 248.2'4
The late Liz; the autobiography of an ex-pagan, by Elizabeth Burns. With an introd. by the author, Gertrude Behanna. [Rev. ed.] New York, Meredith Press [1968] x, 342 p. 21 cm. [BV4935.B4A3 1968] 68-3342
1. Converts. I. Title.

*BEST, W. E. 248.24
Regeneration and conversion [By] W. E. Best. Grand Rapids, Baker Book House, [1975] 126 p. 20 cm. [BV4916] ISBN 0-8010-0643-0 2.95 (pbk.)
1. Regeneration (Theology). 2. Conversion. I. Title.

BRANDON, Owen 248.24
The battle for the soul; aspects of religious conversion. Philadelphia, Westminster Press [1959i.e. 1960] vii, 96 p. 19 cm. Includes bibliography, p. 95-96. 60-7327 1.25 pap.,
1. Conversion—Psychology. 2. Evangelistic work I. Title.

CRUZ, Nicky. 248.2'4
Run, baby, run [by] Nicky Cruz with Jamie Buckingham. Plainfield, N.J., Logos International [1968] xv, 240 p. 21 cm. Autobiography of Nicky Cruz. [BV4935.C73A3] 68-23446 4.95
I. Buckingham, Jamie, joint author. II. Title.

DEHGANI-TAFTI, Hassan B 248.24
Design of my world. New York, Association Press, 1959. 80 p. 19 cm. (World Christian books, no. 28, 2d ser.) 59-14239
1. Converts, Anglican. 2. Converts from Mohammedanism. I. Title.

DODSON, Kenneth. 248'.24 B
From make-believe to reality: the Bill Roberts story. Old Tappan, N.J., F. H. Revell Co. [1973] 154 p. 21 cm. [BV4935.R57D62] 73-8802 ISBN 0-8007-0614-5 4.95
1. Roberts, Bill. 2. Conversion. I. Title.

EDWARDS, Josephine Cunnington. 248.2'4
"And I John saw." Nashville, Southern Pub. Association [1969] 96 p. 22 cm. [BX6193.L4E3] 79-76850
1. Lee, Johnnie. I. Title.

ENLOW, David R ed. 248.24
Men made new, by David R. Enlow. Grand Rapids, Zondervan Pub. House [1964] 150 p. ports. 21 cm. [BV4515.2E5] 64-23629
1. Christian life — Stories. 2. Christian Business Men's Committee International. I. Title.

ENLOW, David R., ed. 248.24
Men made new. Grand Rapids, Mich., Zondervan [c.1964] 150p. ports. 21cm. 64-23629 2.95 bds.,
1. Christian life—Stories. 2. Christian Business Men's Committee International. I. Title.

GELPI, Donald L., 1934- 248'.24
Charism and sacrament : a theology of Christian conversion / by Donald L. Gelpi. New York : Paulist Press, c1976. x, 258 p. ; 21 cm. Includes bibliographical references. [BT780.G44 1976] 75-44873 ISBN 0-8091-1935-8 : 5.95
1. Conversion. 2. Gifts, Spiritual. 3. Sacraments—Catholic Church. I. Title.

GORDON, Albert Isaac, 1903-1968. 248.2'4
The nature of conversion; a study of forty-five men and women who changed their religion, by Albert I. Gordon. Boston, Beacon Press [1967] xii, 333 p. 21 cm. Bibliographical references included in "Notes" (p. 327-329.) [BL53.G66 1967] 67-24894
1. Conversion—Psychology. I. Title.

GUTHRIE, William, 1620-1665. 248.24
The Christian's saving interest. Rev. and annotated, with a biographical sketch of the author by James A. Stewart. Grand Rapids, Kregel Publications, 1958. 191p. 23cm. Published in 1770 under title: The Christian's great interest. [BV4914.G8 1958] 58-13702
1. Conversion—Early works to 1800. I. Title.

HASKIN, Dorothy (Clark) 1905- 248.2'4
Tell every man; conversion stories from around the world, by Dorothy C. Haskin. Grand Rapids, Baker Book House [1968] 157 p. illus., ports. 23 cm. [BV4930.H28] 68-19208
1. Converts. I. Title.

HAUGHTON, Rosemary. 248.2'4
The transformation of man; a study of conversion and community. Springfield, Ill., Templegate, 1967. 280 p. 23 cm. [BT780.H3 1967] 67-22746
1. Conversion. I. Title.

HEFLEY, James C 248.24
Living miracles; conversion stories of famous Christians. Grand Rapids, Zondervan Pub. House [1964] 149 p. ports. 21 cm. [BX6493.H4] 64-15551
1. Converts, Baptist. I. Title. II. Title: Conversion stories of famous Christians.

HEFLEY, James C. 248.24
Living miracles; conversion stories of famous Christians. Grand Rapids, Mich., Zondervan [c.1964] 149p. ports. 21cm. 64-15551 2.50 bds.,
1. Converts, Baptist. I. Title. II. Title: Conversion stories of famous Christians.

*INGALLS, Ray Arnold 248.24
The dark cloud in between; the story of a boy, a sailor, a tragedy, a drunkard, a man thru Christ! New York, Carlton [c.1964] 56p. 21cm. 2.00
I. Title.

LEESTMA, Harold F. 248'.24
God at my elbow; the meaning of conversion [by] Harold F. Leestma. Waco, Tex., Word Books [1973, c1972] 84 p. 23 cm. [BV4916.L43] 72-84165 2.95
1. Bible—Biography. 2. Conversion. I. Title.

LUCK, Burnice 248.24
God made me new. Nashville, Broadman Press [c.1961] 70p. 61-5394 1.00 pap.,
1. Converts. I. Title.

MANDERSON, Rita, 1916- 248.2'4
The awakening. [Baltimore, Printed by Reese

Press, 1968] 213 p. ports. 22 cm. [BV4935.M28A3] 68-6922
I. Title.

MAVIS, W. Curry. 248.2'4
Personal renewal through Christian conversion, by W. Curry Mavis. Kansas City, Mo., Beacon Hill Press of Kansas City [1969] 165 p. 20 cm. Bibliography: p. 162-165. [BV4916.M3] 74-19311
1. Conversion. I. Title.

MITCHELL, Curtis. 248.24
Those who came forward; men and women who responded to the ministry of Billy Graham. Pref. by Billy Graham. Philadelphia, Chilton Books [1966] x, 281 p. 20 cm. [BV3785.G69M5] 66-20113
1. Graham, William Franklin, 1918- 2. Converts. I. Title.

MITCHELL, Curtis. 248.24
Those who came forward; an account of those whose lives were changed by the ministry of Billy Graham. Kingswood (Sy.) World's Work, 1966. 235 p. front. 20 1/2 cm. (B66-10751) [BV3785.G69M5 1966a] 66-78621
1. Graham, William Franklin, 1918- 2. Converts. I. Title.

MITCHELL, Curtis 248.24
Those who came forward; men and women who responded to the ministry of Billy Graham. Pref. by Billy Graham. Philadelphia, Chilton [c.1966] x, 281p. illus. 21cm. [BV3785.G69M5] 66-20113 3.95
1. Graham. William Franklin, 1918- 2. Converts. I. Title.

NORMAN, Joyce. 248'.24 B
Personal assignment; a newspaperwoman's search for the good news. Old Tappan, N.J., F. H. Revell [1973] 127 p. 22 cm. [BV4935.N59A3] 73-16193 ISBN 0-8007-0639-0 3.95
1. Norman, Joyce. 2. Conversion. I. Title.

OSBORN, Merton b., comp. 248.2'4
Quest for reality Chicago, Moody [1967] [BV4930.D8] 67-14386 2.95
1. eality. 2. Converts. I. Title.
Contents omitted

OSBORN, Merton B. comp. 248.2'4
Quest for reality, comp. by Merton B. Osborn. Chicago, Moody [1968,c.1967] 126p. 18cm. [BV4930.O8] 67-14386 .60 pap.,
1. Converts. I. Title.

OSBORN, Merton B., comp. 248.2'4
Quest for reality, compiled by Merton B. Osborn. Chicago, Moody Press [1967] 128 p. 22 cm. [BV4930.O8] 67-14386
1. Converts. I. Title.
CONTENTS OMITTED.

RECTOR, Hartman. 248.2'4
No more strangers [edited by] Hartman and Connie Rector. Salt Lake City, Utah, Bookcraft, 1971-73. 2 v. 24 cm. [BX8693.R4] 72-175136
1. Converts, Mormon. I. Rector, Connie, joint author. II. Title.

ROELOFS, Donet Meynell. 248.24
A testament of turning. New York, Morehouse-Barlow Co. [1960] 221p. 21cm. [BV4935.R58A3] 60-11202
1. Converts, Anglican. I. Title.

ROUNTREE, Horace G. 248.24
Thy will be done in all things; the story of a journey into faith. New York, Exposition [c.1963] 45p. 21cm. 2.50
I. Title.

ROUTLEY, Erik. 248.24
Conversion. Philadelphia, Muhlenberg Press [1960] 52p. 20cm. (Fortress books) [BT780.R66] 60-3755
1. Conversion. I. Title.

RUUD, Brian, 1946- 248'.24
The trip beyond, by Brian Ruud with Walter Wagner. Englewood Cliffs, N.J., Prentice-Hall [1972] 211 p. 21 cm. Autobiography. [BV4935.R76A3] 72-3720 ISBN 0-13-930958-6
1. Conversion. I. Wagner, Walter, 1927- II. Title.

SARGENT, Daniel, 1890- 248.2'4
Four independents. Freeport, N.Y., Books for Libraries Press [1968, c1935] 243 p. 23 cm. (Essay index reprint series) Contents.Contents.—Charles Peguy.—Paul Claudel.—Gerard Manley Hopkins.—Orestes Augustus Brownson. [BX4668.A1S26 1968] 68-55856
1. Converts, Catholic. I. Title.

SPENCE, Johnny, 1912- 248.24 (B)
Golf pro for God, by Johnny Spence, with Oscar Fraley. Foreword by Billy Graham. New York, Centaur House; distributed by Hawthorn Books [1965] 217 p. illus., ports. 22 cm. [GV964.S65A3] 65-22906
I. Fraley, Oscar, 1914- II. Title.

SPENCE, Johnny, 1912- 248.24
Golf pro for God, Johnny Spence, with Oscar Fraley. Foreword by Billy Graham. New York, Centaur House; dist. by Hawthorn [c.1965] 217p. illus., ports. 22cm. [GV964.S65A3] 65-22906 4.95
I. Fraley, Oscar, 1914- II. Title.

TEMPLE, Robert M. 248'.24
Seven words of Christian change / by Robert M. Temple, Jr. Nashville : Tidings, [1974] 95 p. ; 19 cm. [BV4916.T45] 74-14369 pbk. : 1.50
1. Conversion. 2. Christian life—Methodist authors. I. Title.

TERRY, Addie Annabell. 248.24
Tested and tried life; the true story of the Christian victory. [1st ed.] New York, Greenwich Book Publishers [1962, c1961] 78 p. 22 cm. [BV4935.T4A3 1962] 61-17932
I. Title.

WYRTZEN, Jack, 1913- comp. 248'.24
Jesus talked with me; true stories of men and women whose lives were transformed by Jesus Christ. Wheaton, Ill., Tyndale House Publishers [1973] 87 p. 18 cm. [BV4930.W95] 72-97647 ISBN 0-8423-1878-X 1.25 (pbk.)
1. Converts. I. Title.

GILLENSON, Lewis. W. 248.2'4'0922
Billy Graham, and seven who were saved [by] Lewis W. Gillenson. New York, Trident, 1967. 210p. 22cm. [BV4930.Sg5] 67-13570 4.95
1. Graham, William Franklin, 1918. 2. Converts. I. Title.
Contents omitted.

GILLENSON, Lewis W. 248.2'4'0922
Billy Graham, and seven who were saved. New York, Pocket Bks. [1968,c.1967] 212p. 18cm. (75294) [BV4930.G5] 67-13570 .75 pap.,
1. Graham, William Franklin. 1918- 2. Converts. I. Title.

GILLENSON, Lewis W. 248.2'4'0922
Billy Graham, and seven who were saved [by] Lewis W. Chllenson. New York, Trident Press, 1967. 210 p. 22 cm. [BV4930.G5] 67-13570
1. Graham, William Franklin, 1918- . 2. Converts. I. Title.
Contents omitted.

ANTHONY, Susan Brownell, 1916- 248.2'4'0924 B
The ghost in my life [by] Susan B. Anthony. Special before and after chapters by Catherine Marshall. New York, Chosen Books [1971] 221 p. 22 cm. [BV4935.A65A3] 70-159836 ISBN 0-912376-00-7 5.95
1. Converts. I. Title.

FROSSARD, Andre. 248.2'4'0924
I have met Him: God exists. Translated by Marjorie Villiers. [New York] Herder and Herder [1971, c1970] 124 p. 21 cm. Translation of Dieu existe, je l'ai recontre. [BV4935.F76A313 1971] 72-147031 4.95
1. Conversion. I. Title.

BURTON, Katherine (Kurz) 1890- 248.2'42
In no strange land; some American Catholic converts. Freeport, N.Y., Books for Libraries Press [1970, c1942] xix, 254 p. 23 cm. (Essay index reprint series) Bibliography: p. 253-254. [BX4668.A1B87 1970] 72-99619
1. Converts, Catholic. 2. Catholic Church in the United States—Biography. I. Title.

CHESTERTON, G. K. 1874-1936 248.242
The Catholic Church and conversion. New York, Macmillan, 1961 [c.1926, 1954] 115p. (Macmillan paperbacks, 79) .95 pap.,
I. Title.

LAMPING, Severin, Father, 1901- ed. 248'.242 B
Through hundred gates, by noted converts from twenty-two lands. Translation, arrangement, and foreword by Severin and Stephen Lamping. Freeport, N.Y., Books for Libraries Press [1973] p. (Essay index reprint series) Reprint of the 1939 ed. published by Bruce Pub. Co., Milwaukee, issued in series: Religion and culture series. Includes bibliographical references. [BX4668.A1L35 1973] 73-4526 ISBN 0-518-10087-1
1. Converts, Catholic. I. Lamping, Stephen, Father, 1901- joint ed. II. Title.

LUNN, Arnold Henry Moore, Sir, 1888- 248.2'42
Roman converts, by Arnold Lunn. Freeport, N.Y., Books for Libraries Press [1966] xv, 275 p. 24 cm. (Essay index reprint series) Reprint of the 1924 ed. Contents.Contents.—The problem stated.—John Henry Newman.—Henry Edward Manning.—George Tyrrell.—Ronald Knox.—G. K. Chesterton.—Bibliography (p. 267-75) [BX4668.A1L8 1966] 67-22102
1. Converts, Catholic. I. Title.

MARTINDALE, Cyril Charlie, 1879- 248.242
Jock, Jack, and the corporal. London, Campion Press; New York, Taplinger Pub. Co. [1961, c1960] 194p. 19cm. (A Campion book) [BX4668.A4M3] 60-13081
1. Converts, Catholics. I. Title.

MULLEN, James H 1924- 248.242
Against the goad. Milwaukee, Bruce Pub. Co. [1961] 201p. 21cm. [BX4668.M75] 61-13461
1. Converts, Catholic. I. Title.

O'BRIEN, John Anthony, 1893- ed. 248.242
Roads to Rome; the intimate personal stories of converts to the Catholic faith. New York, All Saints Press [dist. Pocket Bks.] [1960, c.1954] 258p. (AS 1) Bibl.: p.255-258 .60 pap.,
1. Converts, Catholic. I. Title.

SUCCOP, Margaret Phillips, 1914- 248.242
No going back; odyssey of a conversion, by Margaret Phillips. Foreword by Merle Armitage. [Fresno, Calif.] Academy Guild Press [1964] vii, 100 p. 21 cm. Autobiographical. [BX4668.S8] 64-17159
1. Converts, Catholic. I. Title.

SUCCOP, Margaret Phillips, 1914- 248.242
No going back; odyssey of a conversion, by Margaret Philips. Foreword by Merle Armitage. Fresno, Calif., Academy Guild [c.1964] vii, 100p. 21cm. 64-17159 3.50
1. Converts, Catholic. I. Title.

ANGELL, Charles. 248'.242'0924 B
Prophet of reunion : the life of Paul of Graymoor / Charles Angell, Charles LaFontaine ; with an introd. by James Stuart Wetmore. New York : Seabury Press, [1975] xi, 224 p. : ill. ; 22 cm. "A Crossroad book." [BX4705.P3842A8] 74-32239 ISBN 0-8164-0281-7 : 6.95
1. Paul James Francis, Father, 1863-1940. I. LaFontaine, Charles, joint author. II. Title.

SHOEMAKER, Samuel Moor, 1893-1963 248.243
Extraordinary living for ordinary men; excerpts from the writings of Sam Shoemaker by his daughter, Helen Shoemaker Rea and the staff of Faith at work. New York, Pyramid [1967, c.1965] 142p. 18cm. (X1673) [BV4501.2.S44] .60 pap.,
1. Christian life—Anglican authors. I. Rea, Helen (Shoemaker) comp. II. Title.

DELAPORTE, Ernest P., 1924- 248'.244
I was a Catholic priest [by] Ernest P. Delaporte. Mountain View, Calif., Pacific Press Pub. Association [1973] 127 p. 22 cm. (A Destiny book, D-140) [BX6189.D44A3] 73-80857 1.95 (pbk.)
1. Delaporte, Ernest P., 1924- 2. Converts, Seventh-Day Adventist. I. Title.

DAVIS, Charles, 1923- 248.2'44'0924
A question of conscience. [1st ed.] New York, Harper & Row [1967] viii, 278 p. 22 cm. Bibliographical footnotes. [BX1777.D3] 67-21556
1. Catholic Church—Doctrinal and controversial works. I. Title.

ABOUADAOU, Said, 1890-1964. 248.2'46 B
I was an Algerian preacher. Autobiography and parables translated and edited with a prologue, an epilogue, and a survey article by W. N. Heggoy. [1st ed.] New York, Vantage Press [1971] xiii, 92 p. illus., maps, port. 21 cm. [BV2626.4.A25A3] 76-27987 3.50
1. Converts from Islam. I. Heggoy, W. N., 1912- ed. II. Title.

ATKINS, Susan, 1948- 248'.246
Child of Satan, child of God / Susan Atkins, with Bob Slosser. Plainfield, N.J. : Logos International, c1977. vii, 290 p., [3] leaves of plates : ill. ; 22 cm. [BV4935.A86A33] 77-81947 ISBN 0-88270-229-7 : 7.95
1. Atkins, Susan, 1948- 2. Converts—California—Biography. 3. California—Biography. I. Slosser, Bob, joint author. II. Title.

BLUNT, Hugh Francis, 1877- 248.2'46
Great penitents. Freeport, N. Y., Books for Libraries Press [1967] 245 p. 22 cm. (Essay index reprint series) Reprint of the 1921 ed. [Converts, Catholic.] [BX4668.A1B5 1967] 67-30198
I. Title.
:Contents omitted

BLUNT, Hugh Francis, 1877- 248.2'46
Great penitents. Freeport, N.Y., Books for Libraries Press [1967] 245 p. 22 cm. (Essay index reprint series) Reprint of the 1921 ed. Contents.Contents.—The fool of God.—The Jesuates.—The gambler; St. Camillus de Lellis.—Abbot de Rance.—Silvio Pellico.—Paul Feval.—Father Hermann; musician and monk.—J. B. Carpeaux.—Francois Coppee.—J. K. Huysmans.—Paul Verlaine.—A litany of penitents. [BX4668.A1B5 1967] 67-30198
1. Converts, Catholic. I. Title.

BRAEMER, Alice. 248'.246 B
Cultism to charisma : my seven years with Jeane Dixon / Alice Braemer, with Dolores Hayford ; and with a foreword by Ruth D. Nickel. 1st ed. Hicksville, N.Y. : Exposition Press, c1977. 45 p. ; 22 cm. [BV4935.B65A33] 77-150260 ISBN 0-682-48755-4 : 4.00
1. Braemer, Alice. 2. Dixon, Jeane. 3. Converts—California—Biography. I. Hayford, Dolores. II. Title.

CERULLO, Morris. 248'.246
The back side of Satan. [1st ed.] Carol Stream, Ill., Creation House [1973] xii, 224 p. illus. 22 cm. Bibliography: p. 221-224. [BF1548.C47] 72-94922 4.95
1. Devil. 2. Satanism. 3. Witchcraft—United States. I. Title.

COSS, Richard David, 1944- 248'.246 B
Wanted / Richard David Coss, with Jo An Summers; introduction by Chaplain Ray. San Diego : Beta Books, c1977. p. cm. A convicted criminal relates how he found God and how his conversion affected his life. [BV4935.C634A38] 92 77-23275 ISBN 0-89293-016-0 : 2.95
1. Coss, Richard David, 1944- 2. Converts—United States—Biography. I. Summers, Jo An, joint author. II. Title.

EINSPRUCH, Henry, 1892- comp. 248.2'46
Would I? Would you? Baltimore, Lewis and Harriet Lederer Foundation [1970] 91 p. illus., ports. 22 cm. Contents.—On the bowery of New York, by W. Price.—The truth about the rabbi, by N. Brodt.—A trail blazer of Afghanistan, by L. W. Rice.—On the wings of song, by S. Gross.—The love that did not fail, by E. S. Millar.—Bernard Jean Bettelheim, M.D., by M. G. Einspruch.—Isaiah 53.—Yesha'yah nun-gimel.—Yeshaye nun-gimel.—A Jewish crusader in Brazil, by J. S. Conning.—A Tiberias rabbi, by W. M. Christie.—Bishop of Jerusalem, by A. Zolontz.—Rabbi Isaac Lichtenstein, by J. Kamer.—"I am not alone," by J. Cournos.—A lamed-vovnik, by H. Einspruch.—A Jewish bishop in China, by H. A. Levin.—Sir Leon Levison, the lion hearted, by N. Levison.—Would I? Would you? [BV2623.A1E52] 76-134718
1. Coverts from Judaism. I. Title.

EVANS, Mike, 1947- 248'.246
Young Lions of Judah [by] Mike Evans with Bob Summers. Plainfield, N.J., Logos International [1974] xii, 116 p. 18 cm. [BV2623.A1E9] 73-84781 1.25 (pbk.)
1. Converts from Judaism. I. Summers, Bob, 1942- joint author. II. Title.

FISK University, Nashville. Social Science Institute. 248.2'46
God struck me dead; religious conversion experiences and autobiographies of ex-slaves. Clifton H. Johnson, editor. Foreword by Paul Radin. Philadelphia, Pilgrim Press [1969] xix, 171 p. 22 cm. [BV4930.F5 1969] 78-77839 3.45
1. Negroes—Religion. 2. Conversion. I. Johnson, Clifton H., ed. II. Title.

FRUCHTENBAUM, Arnold G. 248'.246
Hebrew Christianity : its theology, history, and philosophy / by Arnold G. Fruchtenbaum. Washington : Canon Press, [1974]. 139 p. ; 22 cm. Includes bibliographical references. [BR158.F78] 74-186458 ISBN 0-913686-11-5 : 2.50
1. Jewish Christians. I. Title.

GOBLE, Phillip E., 1943- 248'.246
Everything you need to grow a Messianic synagogue / Philip E. Goble. South Pasadena, Calif. : William Carey Library, [1974 i.e.1975] xv, 158 p. : ill. ; 22 cm. [BR158.G6] 74-28017 ISBN 0-87808-421-5 : 2.45
1. Jewish Christians. 2. Missions to Jews. I. Title.

HOBE, Laura. 248'.246 B
Try God / by Laura Hobe ; foreword by David Wilkerson. 1st ed. Garden City, N.Y. : Doubleday, 1977. 191 p. ; 22 cm. [BV4930.H6] 76-50771 ISBN 0-385-12443-0 : 6.50

1. Walter Hoving Home. 2. Converts—United States—Biography. 3. Church work with delinquent girls—New York (State)—Garrison. I. Title.

INGLE, Clifford. 248.2'46
Children and conversion. Edited by Clifford Ingle. Nashville, Tenn., Broadman Press [1970] 160 p. 22 cm. [BV4925.I5] 79-113212 4.50
1. Children—Conversion to Christianity—Addresses, essays, lectures. 2. Children—Religious life—Addresses, essays, lectures. I. Title.

JOHNSON, Aaaron. 248'.246
The end of youngblood Johnson [by] Aaaron (Youngblood) Johnson as told to Jamie Buckingham. New York, Family Library [1974 c1973] 205 p. 18 cm. [BV4935.J64A3] ISBN 0-515-03650-1 1.25 (pbk.)
1. Buckingham, Jamie. 2. Conversion. I. Title.
L.C. card no. for original edition: 72-10240.

JOHNSON, Aaron. 248'.246
The end of Youngblood Johnson, by Aaron (Youngblood) Johnson, as told to Jamie Buckingham. [New York] Chosen Books; distributed by F. H. Revell Co., Old Tappan, N.J. [1973] 190 p. 22 cm. [BV4935.J64A3] 72-10240 ISBN 0-912376-04-X 4.95
1. Conversion. I. Buckingham, Jamie. II. Title.

KREYE, Eric. 248.2'46
Under the blood banner; the story of a Hitler youth, by Eric Kreye as told to Norma R. Youngberg. Illustrated by John Steel. Mountain View, Calif., Pacific Press Pub. Association [1968] 120 p. illus., ports. 22 cm. (Panda book, P-112) [BX6189.K7] 68-21461
1. Converts, Seventh-Day Adventist. I. Youngberg, Norma R. II. Title.

LEE, Robert Greene, 1886- 248.2'46
If I were a Jew, by Robert G. Lee. Chicago, Moody Press [1970] 62 p. 14 cm. (Moody acorn) [BV4922.L4] 78-104831 0.15
1. Jews—Conversion to Christianity. I. Title.

LEVITT, Zola. 248'.246 B
Christ in the country club / Zola Levitt and Daniel M. McGann. Scottdale, Pa. : Herald Press, c1976. 120 p. ; 18 cm. [BV2623.L45A32] 76-5299 ISBN 0-8361-1315-2 pbk. : 1.75
1. Levitt, Zola. 2. McGann, D. 3. Converts—United States—Biography. I. McGann, D., joint author. II. Title.

LIBERMAN, Paul. 248'.246
The fig tree blossoms : Messianic Judaism emerges / by Paul Liberman. Harrison, Ark. : Fountain Press, 1977, c1976. 122 p. ; 21 cm. Bibliography: p. 121-122. [BR158.L5 1977] 77-152203 ISBN 0-89350-000-3 : 2.95
1. Jewish Christians. 2. Converts from Judaism. I. Title.

LISLE, Dorothy Schwimmer 248.246
To the Jew first. Grand Rapids, Mich., Eerdmans [c.1960] 94p. 60-53091 2.50
1. Jews—Conversion to Christianity. I. Title.

MAHARAJ, Rabindranath R. 248'.246 B
Death of a guru / Rabindranath R. Maharaj, with Dave Hunt. 1st ed. Philadelphia : A. J. Holman Co., c1977. 224 p. ; 22 cm. [BV4935.M25A32] 77-5701 ISBN 0-87981-083-1 : 3.95
1. Maharaj, Rabindranath R. 2. Converts from Hinduism—Biography. I. Hunt, Dave, joint author. II. Title.

MESSER, Judy. 248'.246
To know Him is to love Him / Judy Messer. San Diego, CA : Beta Books, c1976. 175 p. ; 21 cm. [BV4916.M4] 76-7327 ISBN 0-89293-030-6 pbk. : 2.95
1. Messer, Judy. 2. Messer, Jon. 3. Conversion. I. Title.

MILLER, Hack. 248.2'46
The new Billy Casper; more important things in life than golf. Salt Lake City, Deseret Book Co., 1968. 144 p. illus., ports. 24 cm. [GV964.C3A3] 68-59516 3.95
1. Casper, Billy, 1931- 2. Converts, Mormon. I. Title.

MILLER, Keith. 248'.246
The becomers. Waco, Tex., Word Books [1973] 185 p. illus. 23 cm. Bibliography: p. 183-185. [BV4501.2.M478] 72-96363 5.95
1. Christian life—1960- I. Title.

MORGAN, Dewi, ed. 248.246
They became Christians. London, Mowbray; New York, Morehouse, 1966 vii, 157 p., 19 cm. [BV4930.M58 1966] 66-71954 2.65
1. Converts. I. Title.

MORGAN, Dewi, ed. 248.246
They became Christians. London, Mowbray; New York, Morehouse-Barlow, 1966. vii, 157 p. 18 1/2 cm. 10/6. (B 66-5884) [BV4930.M58 1966] 66-71954
1. Converts. I. Title.

MURPHY, Bob. 248'.246 B
Christianity rubs holes in my religion / by Bob Murphy. Houston : Hunter Ministries Pub. Co., c1976. 113 p. ; 20 cm. [BV4935.M84A33] 76-150938 1.95
1. Murphy, Bob. 2. Converts—United States—Biography. 3. Christian life—1960- I. Title.

NEFF, LaVonne. 248'.246 B
A heart of flesh. Mountain View, Calif., Pacific Press Pub. Association [1973] 94 p. 22 cm. (A Destiny book D-139) [BX6193.N43A3] 73-78988
1. Neff, LaVonne. I. Title.

THE New Jews 248'.246
[by] James C. Hefley. Wheaton, Ill., Tyndale House Publishers [1974] 158 p. 18 cm. Consists of 10 interviews. [BV2623.A1N48 1974] 73-92957 ISBN 0-8423-4680-5 1.45 (pbk.)
1. Converts from Judaism. I. Hefley, James C.

OESTERREICHER, John M., 1904- 248.2'46
Five in search of wisdom [by] John M. Oesterreicher. Notre Dame, University of Notre Dame Press [1967] xiii, 290 p. 21 cm. "An abridged edition of Walls are crumbling: seven Jewish philosophers discover Christ." Includes bibliographical references. [BV2623.A1O32] 67-22151
1. Converts from Judaism. I. Title.

PEDERSON, Duane. 248'.246
Day of miracles : stories of miracle-working power in the world today / Duane Pederson and Helen Kooiman. New York : Hawthorn Books, [1974] c1975. viii, 88 p. ; 21 cm. [BV4916.P42 1975] 74-2574 ISBN 0-8015-1958-6 : 2.95
1. Conversion. I. Kooiman, Helen W., joint author. II. Title.

PUTMAN, Jimmy, 1946- 248'.246 B
A new life to live : Jimmy Putman's story / [edited] by William Bradford Huie. Nashville : T. Nelson, c1977. 157 p., [4] leaves of plates : ill. ; 21 cm. [BV4935.P87A36] 77-24956 ISBN 0-8407-5124-9 : 5.95
1. Putman, Jimmy, 1946- 2. Converts—Alabama—Biography. 3. Church work with juvenile delinquents—Alabama—Oneonta. I. Huie, William Bradford, 1910- II. Title.

ROSEN, Moishe. 248'.246
Jews for Jesus [by] Moishe Rosen with William Proctor. Old Tappan, N.J., Revell [1974] 126 p. 21 cm. [BV2623.R58A34] 73-22169 ISBN 0-8007-0638-2 3.95
1. Rosen, Moishe. 2. Missions to Jews. 3. Converts from Judaism. I. Proctor, William, joint author. II. Title.

ROSEN, Moishe. 248'.246
Share the new life with a Jew / by Moishe Rosen and Ceil Rosen. Chicago : Moody Press, c1976. 80 p. ; 19 cm. [BV2620.R67] 76-7627 ISBN 0-8024-7898-0 pbk.: 1.25
1. Missions to Jews. I. Rosen, Ceil, joint author. II. Title.

THOMAS, Cal. 248'.246 B
A freedom dream / Cal Thomas. Waco, Tex. : Word Books, c1977. 144 p. : ill. ; 23 cm. [BX6495.H34T48] 76-48492 ISBN 0-87680-506-3 : 5.95
1. Hayes, Raymond Lee. 2. Thomas, Cal. 3. Converts—Texas—Biography. 4. Prisoners—Texas—Biography. 5. Baptists—Texas—Biography. 6. Texas—Biography. I. Title.

VOGEL, Traugott, 1930- 248'.246 B
Under the SS shadow / Traugott Vogel with Shirley Stephens. Nashville : Broadman Press, 1977c1976 192 p. : ill. ; 21 cm. [BX6495.V6A37] 76-27478 ISBN 0-8054-7216-9 : 6.95
1. Vogel, Traugott, 1930- 2. Baptists—Clergy—Biography. 3. Clergy—United States—Biography. 4. Converts—Germany—Biography. I. Stephens, Shirley, joint author. II. Title.

WURMBRAND, Richard. 248.2'46
Christ on the Jewish road. Glendale, Calif., Diane Books [1973, c.1970] 192 p. 18 cm. [BV2620.W78] ISBN 0-340-10504-6 1.95 (pbk.)
1. Missions to Jews. I. Title.
L.C. card no. for the London edition: 70-596138. Publisher's address: Box 488, Glendale, CA 91209.

ESSES, Michael. 248'.246'0924 B
Michael, Michael, why do you hate me? Plainfield, N.J., Logos International [1973] v, 167 p. 21 cm. [BV2623.E84A35] 73-85241 ISBN 0-88270-046-4 4.95
1. Esses, Michael. 2. Converts from Judaism. I. Title.

FABREGUES, Jean de. 248.2460924
Edith Stein. [Translated from the French by Donald M. Antoine] Staten Island, N.Y., Alba House [1965] 138 p. 20 cm. Translation of La conversion d'Edith Stein. [BX4705.S814F313] 65-25849
1. Stein, Edith, 1891-1942. 2. Converts, Catholic. I. Title.

FABREGUES, Jean de 248.2460924
Edith Stein. [Tr. from French by Donald M. Antoine] Staten Island, N.Y., Alba [c.1965] 138p. 20cm. [BX4705.S814F313] 65-25849 2.95
1. Stein, Edith, 1891-1942. 2. Converts, Catholic. I. Title.

FAGAL, William A 248.2'46'0924
Three hours to live, by William A. Fagal. Mountain View, Calif., Pacific Press Pub. Association [c1967] 63 p. 18 cm. [BV4935.T35F3] 67-29979
1. Tannyhill, Samuel Woodrow, 1929-1956. I. Title.

GOLDEN, Jerry. 248'.246'0924 B
Too tough for God / by Jerry Golden. Waco, Tex. : Word Books, c1977. 128 p. : ill. ; 21 cm. [BV4935.G6A37] 77-75460 ISBN 0-8499-0007-7 : 5.95
1. Golden, Jerry. 2. Converts—Louisiana—Biography. 3. Prisoners—Louisiana—Biography. 4. Clergy—Louisiana—Biography. I. Title.

GRAHAM, Jerry. 248'.246'0924 B
Where flies don't land : the story of a junkie, jailhouses, and Jesus / by Jerry Graham & M. L. Johnson. Plainfield, N.J. : Logos International, c1977. 141 p. ; 21 cm. [BV4935.G68A38] 76-57902 ISBN 0-88270-222-X : 2.95
1. Graham, Jerry. 2. Converts—California—Sacramento—Biography. 3. Sacramento, Calif.—Biography. 4. Church work with prisoners—California. I. Johnson, Mary L., joint author. II. Title.

GRAHAM, Jerry. 248'.246'0924 B
Where flies don't land : the story of a junkie, jailhouses, and Jesus / by Jerry Graham & M. L. Johnson. Plainfield, N.J. : Logos International, c1977. 141 p. ; 21 cm. [BV4935.G68A38] 76-57902 ISBN 0-88270-222-X : 2.95
1. Graham, Jerry. 2. Converts—California—Sacramento—Biography. 3. Sacramento, Calif.—Biography. 4. Church work with prisoners—California. I. Johnson, Mary L., joint author. II. Title.

HOW did a fat, balding, middle-aged Jew like you become a Jesus freak? 248'.246'0922 B
[By] Zola Levitt and D. McGann. Wheaton, Ill., Tyndale House Publishers [1974] 100 p. 18 cm. [BV2623.M32L48 1974] 74-80796 ISBN 0-8423-1512-8 1.45
1. McGann, D. 2. Levitt, Zola. 3. Converts from Judaism. I. McGann, D. II. Title.

HOWARD, Dorothy, 1912- 248'.246'0924 B
No longer alone / Dorothy Howard. Elgin, Ill. : D. C. Cook Pub. Co., c1976. 170 p. ; 18 cm. [BR1725.H687A34] 74-32603 ISBN 0-912692-60-X pbk. : 1.50
1. Howard, Dorothy, 1912- 2. Christian life—1960- I. Title.

HUNT, Dave. 248'.246'0924 B
God of the untouchables / Dave Hunt. Old Tappan, N.J. : Revell, c1976. p. cm. [BV3269.G86H86] 76-21858 ISBN 0-8007-0813-X : 5.95
1. Gupta, Paul. 2. Converts from Hinduism. 3. Missions—India. I. Title.

JOHNSON, Robert A. 248'.246'0924 B
Disciple in prison / Robert A. Johnson. Nashville : Tidings, [1975] ix, 63 p. ; 18 cm. [BV4935.J66A33] 74-17712
1. Johnson, Robert A. 2. Conversion. I. Title.

KEIDEL, Levi O. 248'.246'0924 B
Black Samson : an African's astounding pilgrimage to personhood / by Levi Keidel. Carol Stream, Ill. : Creation House, c1975. 144 p. ; 21 cm. Includes bibliographical references. [BV4935.M36K44 1975] 75-22577 ISBN 0-88419-116-8 : 3.50
1. Maweja Apollo. 2. Conversion. I. Title.

LEVITT, Zola. 248'.246'0924 B
Corned beef, knishes and Christ : the story of a 20th-century Levite / Zola Levitt. Wheaton, Ill. : Tyndale House Publishers, 1975. 145 p. ; 18 cm. Autobiographical. [BV2623.L45A33] 74-19647 ISBN 0-8423-0440-1 pbk. : 1.45
1. Levitt, Zola. I. Title.

LEVITT, Zola. 248'.246'0924 B
If you're there, show me / by Zola Levitt. Chicago : Moody Press, c1976. 63 p. ; 13 cm. [BV2623.L45A34] 76-15969 ISBN 0-8024-4002-9 pbk. : 0.75
1. Levitt, Zola. 2. Converts from Judaism. I. Title.

MCLEAN, Gordon R. 248'.246'0924 B
Devil at the wheel / Gordon McLean with Ken Pestana. Minneapolis : Bethany Fellowship, [1975] 142 p. : ill. ; 18 cm. (Dimension books) [BV4935.P44M3] 74-28547 ISBN 0-87123-101-8 pbk. : 1.50
1. Pestana, Ken. 2. Conversion. I. Pestana, Ken, joint author. II. Title.

ROSS, William Gordon, 1900- 248.2'46'0924 B
Why to ... Okinawa? By W. Gordon Ross. North Quincy, Mass., Christopher Pub. House [1971] 137 p. illus. 21 cm. [BR1317.K55R68] 72-171074 4.95
1. Kina, Shosei. 2. Ryukyu Islands—History. I. Title.

ROTH, Don A., 1927- 248'.246'0924 B
Mundahoi, Borneo witch doctor / by Don A. Roth. Nashville : Southern Pub. Association, c1975. 126 p. : ports. ; 21 cm. (A Crown book) [BV3342.M86R67] 75-11398 ISBN 0-8127-0098-8 pbk. : 2.95
1. Mundahoi. 2. Seventh-Day Adventists—Missions. 3. Missions—Sabah.

ROTH, Sid. 248'.246'0924 B
Something for nothing / by Sid Roth as told to Irene Burk Harrell. Plainfield, N.J. : Logos International, c1976. vii, 133 p. ; 22 cm. [BV2623.R63A35] 75-31396 ISBN 0-88270-145-2 : 5.95. ISBN 0-88270-146-0 pbk. :
1. Roth, Sid. 2. Converts from Judaism. I. Harrell, Irene Burk. II. Title.

SCHLAMM, Vera, 1923- 248'.246'0924 B
Pursued, by Vera Schlamm as told to Bob Friedman. Glendale, Calif., G/L Regal Books [1972] 212 p. 18 cm. [D810.J4S317] 72-77800 ISBN 0-8307-0153-2 1.25
1. Schlamm, Vera, 1923- 2. World War, 1939-1945—Personal narratives, Jewish. 3. Converts from Judaism. I. Friedman, Bob. II. Title.

TAHARA, Yoneko. 248'.246'0924 B
Yoneko, daughter of happiness / by Yoneko Tahara ; as told to Bernard Palmer. Chicago : Moody Press, c1976. 173 p. ; 22 cm. [BV4935.T28A38] 76-19009 ISBN 0-8024-9811-6 : 5.95
1. Tahara, Yoneko. 2. Conversion. I. Palmer, Bernard Alvin, 1914- II. Title.

HEFLEY, James C. 248'.246'094 B
The liberated Palestinian : the Anis Shorrosh story / James and Marti Hefley. Wheaton, Ill. : Victor Books, c1975. 172 p. : ill. ; 21 cm. [BV3785.S46H43] 75-36003 ISBN 0-88207-652-3 pbk. : 2.95
1. Shorrosh, Anis. I. Hefley, Marti, joint author. II. Title.

COOK, Sydney. 248'.25
The black and white book : good news for improving our every day world / by Sidney Cook and Garth Lean. Canfield, Ohio : Alba House Communications, 1975, c1972. p. cm. [HM101.C69 1975] 75-16411 0.59
1. Social change. 2. Nonviolence. I. Lean, Garth, joint author. II. Title.

DRIBERG, Tom. 248.25
The mystery of Moral Re-armament; a study of Frank Buchman and his movement. [1st American ed.] New York, Knopf, 1964 [c1964] 317 p. 22 cm. Bibliographical footnotes. [BJ10.M6D7] 64-19084
1. Buchman, Frank Nathan Daniel, 1878-1961. 2. Moral rearmament. I. Title.

HOWARD, Peter. 248.25
Frank Buchman's secret. [1st American ed.] Garden City, N.Y., Doubleday [1962, c1961] 142 p. illus. 22 cm. [BJ10.M6H567 1962] 62-15095
1. Buchman, Frank Nathan Daniel, 1878-1961. 2. Moral rearmament. I. Title.

KEYSOR, Charles W. 248'.25
Come clean! / Charles W. Keysor. Wheaton, Ill. : Victor Books, c1976. 157 p. ; 18 cm. (An Imput book) Bibliography: p. 156-157. [BJ1471.5.K49] 76-3923 ISBN 0-88207-732-5 : 1.75
1. Bible. O.T. Psalms LI—Criticism, interpretation, etc. 2. Guilt. 3. Forgiveness of sin. I. Title.

ROOTS, John McCook, ed. 248.25
Modernizing America; action papers of national purpose. Foreword by Stan Musial. Los Angeles, Pace Publications [1965] 142 p. illus., ports. 21 cm. "Addresses delivered at the Demonstration for modernizing America,

at Mackinac Island, Mich. [in 1965]" [BJ10.M6R65] 65-29225
1. Moral rearmament — Congresses. I. Title.

*WEDGE, Florence 248.2'5
What is fortitude Pulaski, Wis., Franciscan Pubs. [1967] 63p. 18cm. .25 pap.,
I. Title.

HOWARD, Peter. 248.2508
Design for dedication; selections from a series of addresses. Foreword by Richard Cardinal Cushing. Chicago, Regnery [1965, c1964] xiii, 176 p. 22 cm. [BJ10.M6H564 1965] 66-3157
1. Moral rearmament—Addresses, essays, lectures. I. Title.

HOWARD, Peter 248.25081
Design for dedication; selections from a series of addresses. Foreword by Richard Cardinal Cushing. Chicago, Regnery [c.1964] 192p. 17cm. 64-23017 .75 pap.,
1. Moral rearmament—Addresses, essays, lectures. I. Title.

SLATTERY, Sarah 248.2'5'0924 B
Lawrence, 1879-
I choose. Winchester, Mass., University Press, 1969. 161 p. illus., ports. 23 cm. Autobiography. [CT275.S5228A3] 72-93891 4.95
I. Title.

SPOERRI, Theophil, 248'.25'0924 B
1890-1975.
Dynamic out of silence : Frank Buchman's relevance today / [by] Theophil Spoerri ; [translated from the German by John Morrison and Peter Thwaites]. London : Grosvenor Books, 1976. 219 p. ; 18 cm. Translation of Dynamik aus der Stille. Bibliography: p. 219. [BJ10.M6B83613] 77-366327 ISBN 0-901269-19-0 : £1.30
1. Buchman, Frank Nathan Daniel, 1878-1961. 2. Oxford group. 3. Moral Rearmament—Biography. I. Title.

ART of Christian 248.27
relationship (The); student's resource book [Minneapolis] Augsburg [1967] 119p. illus. (pt. col.) 22cm. (Amer. Lutheran Church: Core curriculum--adult educ.) 1.50 pap.,

DUBAY, Thomas. 248'.27
A call to virginity? / Thomas Dubay. Huntington, IN : Our Sunday Visitor, inc., c1977. 63 p. ; 18 cm. [BV4647.C5D77] 76-47982 ISBN 0-87973-745-X pbk. : 1.95
1. Virginity. I. Title.

DUBAY, Thomas. 248'.27
A call to virginity? / Thomas Dubay. Huntington, IN : Our Sunday Visitor, inc., c1977. 63 p. ; 18 cm. [BV4647.C5D77] 76-47982 ISBN 0-87973-745-X pbk. : 1.95
1. Virginity. I. Title.

EVAGRIUS Ponticus, 345?- 248'.27
399?
The praktikos. Chapters on prayer. Translated, with an introd. and notes, by John Eudes Bamberger. Spencer, Mass., Cistercian Publications, 1970 [c1972] xciv, 96 p. 23 cm. (Cistercian studies series, no. 4) The 2d work is a translation of Peri proseuches, which is also attributed to Saint Nilus. Bibliography: p. 81-82. [BV5039.G7E973] 76-152483 ISBN 0-87907-804-9 10.95
1. Asceticism—Early church. 2. Prayer—Early works to 1800. I. Bamberger, John Eudes, ed. II. Nilus Ancyranus, Saint, d. ca. 430. Peri proseuches. III. Evagrius Ponticus, 345?-399? Peri proseuches. English. 1970. IV. Title. V. Title: Chapters on prayer. VI. Series.

GOBRY, Ivan 248.2'7
hrough the needle's eye. Tr. by Edmond Bonin. Westminster, Md., Newman 1967. x. 175p. 22cm. Tr. of La pauvrete du laic. [BV4647.P6G63] 66-30459 5.50 bds.,
1. Poverty (Virtur) I. Title.

GOBRY, Ivan. 248.27
Through the needle's eye. Translated by Edmund Bonin. Westminster, Md., Newman Press, 1967. x, 175 p. 22 cm. Translation of La pauvrete du laic. [BV4647.P6G63] 66-30459
1. Poverty (Virtue) I. Title.

RAGUIN, Yves, 1912- 248'.27
Celibacy for our times / by Yves Raguin ; translated by Mary Humbert Kennedy. St. Meinrad, Ind. : Abbey Press, 1974. vi, 120 p. ; 21 cm. (Religious experience series ; v. 7) Translation of Celibat pour notre temps. [BV4390.R2813] 74-84161 ISBN 0-87029-039-8 pbk. : 2.95
1. Celibacy. I. Title.

SOCIETY of Biblical 248'.27
Literature.
A symposium on eschatology, by members of the Society of Biblical Literature and Exegesis. New Haven, Pub. for the Society by the Yale University Press, 1923. 204 p. 25 cm. [BS680.E8S6] 43-33390
1. Eschatology — Biblical teaching. 2. Eschatology, Jewish. I. Title.
Contents omitted

THOMAS, George Ernest, 248.27
1907-
Disciplines of the spiritual life. [Nashville] Abingdon [c.1963] 96p. 19cm. (Faith for life ser.) 63-23648 1.25 pap.,
1. Spiritual life. I. Title.

WADE, Joseph D. 248.2'7
Chastity, sexuality & personal hangups; a guide to celibacy for religious and laity [by] Joseph D. Wade. Staten Island, N.Y., Alba House [1971] x, 174 p. 22 cm. Includes bibliographical references. [BV4390.W3] 75-148680 ISBN 0-8189-0199-3 4.95
1. Celibacy. I. Title.

*WEDGE, Florence 248.27
How to love your enemies. Pulaski, Wis., Franciscan Pubs. [c.1966] 54p. 19cm. .25 pap.,
I. Title.

*WEDGE, Florence. 248.2'7
Judgments: right or rash? Pulaski, Wis., Franciscan Pubs. [1968] 60p. 19cm. .25 pap.,
1. Judgments (Moral) I. Title.

WENNINK, H 248.2'7
The Bible on asceticism, by H. Wennik. Translated by F. Vander Heijden. De Pere, Wis., St. Norbert Abbey Press, 1966. 115, [2] p. 17 cm. Translation of De Bijbel over ascese. Bibliography: p. [117] [BS680.A8W43] 66-16988
1. Asceticism — Biblical teaching. I. Title.

ZIESLER, J. A. 248'.27
Christian asceticism [by] J. A. Ziesler. Grand Rapids, Eerdmans [1974, c1973] 118 p. 18 cm. Includes bibliographies. [BS680.A8Z53 1974] 74-2094 ISBN 0-8028-1568-5 2.25 (pbk.).
1. Asceticism—Biblical teaching. I. Title.

COLLIANDER, Tito [Fritiof 248.272
Tito Colliander] 1904-
The way of the ascetics. Tr. [from Swedish] by Katharine Ferre. Ed. with an introd. by R. M. French. New York, Harper [1961, c.1960] 123p.Bibl. 14cm. 61-7335 2.50
1. Asceticism. I. Title.

CORSTANJE, Auspicius van 248.272
The convenant with God's poor; an essay on the Biblical interpretation of the Testament of St. Francis of Assisi. Initial English tr. by Gabriel Reidy. Tev., augm. ed. by Stephen Anaclete Yonick. Chicago, Franciscan Herald [1966] xx, 172p. 21cm. Bibl. [BX3603.C613] 66-26284 3.95
1. Francesco d'Assisi, Saint, 1182-1226. Testamentum. 2. Monasticism and religious orders—Common life. 3. Franciscans. I. Title.

GREGORIUS, Saint, Bp. 248.2'72
of Nyssa, fl.379-394.
Ascetical works. Translated by Virginia Woods Callaban. Washington, Catholic University of America Press [1967] xxiii, 295 p. 22 cm. (The Fathers of the Church; a new translation. v. 58) Contents.Contents.—On virginity.—On what it means to call oneself a Christian.—On perfection.—On the Christian mode of life.—The life of Saint Macrina.—On the soul and the resurrection. Bibliography: p. xxii-xxiii. [BR60.F3G673] 66-30561
1. Asceticism—Early church, ca. 30-600. I. Title.

KESTENS, Adolph, 1863- 248.272
1925.
Spiritual guidance; fundamentals of ascetical theology based on the Franciscan ideal. Adapted from the Latin by Elmer Stoffel. Paterson, N. J., St. Anthony Guild Press [1962- . v. 23 cm. Translation of Compendium theologiae ascerticae. [BV5031.2.K413] 59-15864
1. Asceticism — Catholic Church. I. Stoffel, Elmer. II. Title.

KESTENS, Adolph, 1863- 248.272
1925
Spiritual guidance; fundamentals of ascetical theology based on the Franciscan ideal [v.1] Adapted from Latin by Elmer Stoffel. Paterson, N.J., St. Anthony Guild [c.1962] xvi, 637p. 23cm. Bibl. 59-15864 6.50
1. Asceticism—Catholic Church. I. Stoffel, Elmer. II. Title.

TERMOTE, Henri 248.272
Ascese et vie modern. [Toulouse] Privat [dist. Philadelphia, Chilton, 1964, c.1961] 122p. 19cm. (Questions posees aux catholiques) 64-9078 1.50 pap.,
1. Asceticism. I. Title.

BEALL, James Lee. 248'.273
The adventure of fasting; a practical guide. Old Tappan, N.J., F. H. Revell [1974] 128 p. 21 cm. Bibliography: p. 128. [BV5055.B4] 74-10741 ISBN 0-8007-0683-8 1.95 (pbk.)
1. Fasting. I. Title.

ROGERS, E. N. 248'.273
Fasting : the phenomenon of self-denial / by E. N. Rogers. 1st ed. Nashville : T. Nelson, c1975. p. cm. Includes index. [BV5055.R63] 74-143 ISBN 0-8407-6462-6 : 6.95
1. Fasting. I. Title.

ROGERS, Eric N. 248'.273
Fasting : the phenomenon of self-denial / Eric N. Rogers. 1st ed. Nashville : T. Nelson, c1976. 160 p. ; 21 cm. Includes index. [BV5055.R63] 76-143 ISBN 0-8407-6462-6 : 6.95
1. Fasting. I. Title.

BAKER, H. A. 248'.29
Visions beyond the veil, by H. A. Baker. [Monroeville, Pa.] Whitaker Books [1973] 144 p. 18 cm. [BT123.B24] 73-81105 ISBN 0-88368-019-X 0.95 (pbk.)
1. Baptism in the Holy Spirit. 2. Church work with children—Yunnan, China (Province) 3. Visions. I. Title.

BASHAM, Don, 1926- comp. 248'.29
The miracle of tongues. Old Tappan, N.J., F. H. Revell Co. [1974, c1973] 127 p. 21 cm. [BL54.B37 1974] 73-21974 ISBN 0-8007-0632-3 1.95 (pbk.)
1. Glossolalia—Case studies. I. Title.

BENNETT, Dennis J. 248'.29
Nine o'clock in the morning [by] Dennis J. Bennett. Plainfield, N.J., Logos International [1970] xii, 209 p. 21 cm. [BX5995.B394A3 1970] 72-85205 ISBN 0-912106-04-2 3.95
1. Baptism in the Holy Spirit. I. Title.

BRANCH, Robert. 248'.29
So your wife came home speaking in tongues? So did mine! Old Tappan, N.J., Revell [1973] 126 p. 21 cm. Bibliography: p. 125-126. [BL54.B67] 73-7521 4.50
1. Branch, Robert. 2. Glossolalia—Case studies. I. Title.
Pbk. 1.95; ISBN 0-8007-0611-0.

BYRNE, James E. 248'.29
Living in the spirit : a handbook on Catholic charismatic Christianity / by James E. Byrne. New York : Paulist Press, c1975. viii, 184 p. ; 21 cm. Bibliography: p. 177-178. [BX2350.57.B9] 75-28628 ISBN 0-8091-1902-1 pbk. : 2.95
1. Pentecostalism. I. Title.

CONGER, Wilda Lowell 248.29
Forever is now, by Wilda Lowell Conger, Elizabeth Cushman. Boston, Christopher [c.1964] 205p. 21cm. 64-15611 3.75 bds.,
1. Future life. 2. Spiritualism. I. Conger, Lowell, 1921-1936. II. Cushman, Elizabeth, joint author. III. Title.

GELPI, Donald L., 1934- 248.2'9
Pentecostalism, a theological viewpoint, by Donald L. Gelpi. New York, Paulist Press [1971] v, 234 p. 19 cm. [BX8763.G45] 73-158489 1.95
1. Pentecostalism. I. Title.

GOODMAN, Felicitas D. 248'.29
Speaking in tongues; a cross-cultural study of glossolalia [by] Felicitas D. Goodman. Chicago, University of Chicago Press [1972] xxii, 175 p. 22 cm. Bibliography: p. 162-170. [BL54.G64] 70-182871 ISBN 0-226-30324-1
1. Glossolalia. I. Title.

HAGIN, Kenneth E., 1917- 248'.29
I believe in visions [by] Kenneth E. Hagin. Old Tappan, N.J., F. H. Revell Co. [1972] 126 p. 21 cm. [BT580.A1H3] 72-10332 ISBN 0-8007-0577-7 1.95
1. Jesus Christ—Apparitions and miracles (Modern) 2. Visions. I. Title.

HARRIS, Ralph W. 248'.29
Spoken by the spirit; documented accounts of "other tongues" from Arabic to Zulu [by] Ralph W. Harris. Springfield, Mo., Gospel Pub. House [1973] 128 p. 18 cm. (Radiant books) [BL54.H28] 73-87106 1.25 (pbk.)
1. Glossolalia—Case studies. I. Title.

HELL, Vera 248.29
The great pilgrimage of the Middle Ages: the road to St. James of Compostela [by] Vera and Hellmut Hell; tr. [from German] by Alisa Jaffa. Introd. by Sir Thomas Kendrick. New York, Potter [1966] 275p. col. front., illus. (6 col. plates) maps. 33cm. Bibl. [DC20.H413] 66-22138 17.50
1. Pilgrims and pilgrimages—Santiago de Commpostela. 2. France—Descr. & trav.—Views. 3. Spain—Descr. & trav.—Views. I. Hell, Hellmut, joint author. II. Title.

HOEKEMA, Anthony A. 248.29
What about tongue-speaking? Grand Rapids, Mich., Eerdmans [c.1966] 161p. 21cm. This bk. grew out of a ser. of lects. given in Oct., 1964 at the Conservative Baptist Seminary in Denver. Bibl. [BL54.H6] 65-28568 3.50
1. Glossolalia. I. Title.

HOEKEMA, Anthony A 1913- 248.29
What about tongue-speaking? By Anthony A. Hoekema. Grand Rapids, Eerdmans [1966] 161 p. 21 cm. "This book grew out of a series of lectures given in October, 1964 at the Conservative Baptist Seminary in Denver." Bibliography: p. 151-155. [BL54.H6] 65-28568
1. Glossolalia. I. Title.

HUMPHREYS, Fisher. 248'.29
Speaking in tongues [by] Fisher Humphreys and Malcolm Tolbert. [Zachary, La., Printed by Christian Litho, 1973] viii, 94 p. 21 cm. [BL54.H84] 73-86749 2.00
1. Glossolalia. I. Tolbert, Malcolm, joint author. II. Title.

KELSEY, Morton T. 248.29
Tongue speaking; an experiment in spirtual experience [by] Morton T. Kelsey. Foreword by Upton Sinclair. [1st ed.] Garden City, N. Y., Doubleday [1968,c.1964] xii, 252p. 21cm. (Waymark bks., W16) Bibl. [BL54.K4] 64-16212 1.95 pap.,
1. Glossolalia. I. Title.

KELSEY, Morton T. 248.29
Tongue speaking; an experiment in spiritual experience [by] Morton T. Kelsey. Foreword by Upton Sinclair. [1st ed.] Garden City, N.Y., Doubleday, 1964. xii, 252 p. 22 cm. Bibliography: p.[246]-252. [BL54.K4] 64-16212
1. Glossolalia. I. Title.

KENDALL, Alan, 1939- 248.2'9
Medieval pilgrims. New York, Putnam [1970] 128 p. illus., map, ports. 23 cm. (The Putnam documentary history series) Includes bibliographical references. [BX2323.K44 1970b] 77-116148 4.95
1. Christian pilgrims and pilgrimages. I. Title.

KOCH, Kurt E. 248.2'9
The strife of tongues [by] Kurt Koch. Grand Rapids, Mich., Kregel Publications [1971?] 48 p. 17 cm. Translation of Die neue Zungenbewegung. [BL54.K613] 74-160689 ISBN 0-8254-3001-1 0.50
1. Glossolalia. I. Title.

LOWE, Harry William 248.29
Speaking in tongues; a brief history of the phenomenon known as glossolalia, or speaking in tongues. Mountain View, Calif., Pacific Pr. Pub. [c.1965] 57p. 18cm. Bibl. [BL54.L65] 65-23382 .30 pap.,
1. Glossolalia. I. Title.

*MILLIKIN, Jimmy A. 248.2'9
Testing tongues by the Word. Nashville, Broadman Pr. [1973] 48 p. 19 cm. Includes bibliographical notes. [BL54] ISBN 0-8054-1918-7 1.50 (pbk)
1. Glossolalia. I. Title.

MILLS, Watson E. 248'.29
Speaking in tongues; let's talk about it. Edited by Watson E. Mills. Waco, Tex., Word Books [1973] 162 p. 23 cm. [BL54.M52] 73-84578 4.95
1. Glossolalia—Addresses, essays, lectures.

MILLS, Watson E. 248.2'9
Understanding speaking in tongues, by Watson E. Mills. Grand Rapids, W. B. Eerdmans Pub. Co. [1972] 88 p. 22 cm. Bibliography: p. 77-83. [BL54.M53] 75-162032 1.95
1. Glossolalia. I. Title.

*NOORBERGEN, Rene. 248.2'9
Glossolalia; sweet sounds of ecstasy. Mountain View, Calif., Pacific Pr. Pub. Assn. [1973] 2 v. 18 cm. Includes bibliographical references. [BL55] 0.50 ea. (pbk.)
1. Glossolalia. I. Title.

PEREGRINATIO Aetheriae. 248.2'9
English.
Egeria: diary of a pilgrimage. Translated and annotated by George E. Gingras. New York, Newman Press, 1970. v, 287 p. 23 cm. (Ancient Christian writers; the works of the Fathers in translation, no. 38) Includes bibliographical references. [BR60.A35 no. 38] 70-119159 8.95
1. Church history—Primitive and early church—Sources. 2. Palestine—Description and travel. 3. Christian pilgrims and pilgrimages—Palestine. 4. Liturgies, Early Christian. I. Gingras, George E., tr. II. Title. III. Series.

PYLE, Hugh F. 248'.29
Truth about tongues / Hugh F. Pyle. Denver : Accent Books, c1976. 128 p. ; 18 cm. Bibliography: p. 127-128. [BL54.P94] 76-8730 ISBN 0-916406-19-9 : pbk. : 1.75
1. Glossolalia—Controversial literature. I. Title.

ROBINSON, Wayne, 1937- 248'.29
I once spoke in tongues, by Wayne A. Robinson. Atlanta, Forum House [1973] 144 p. 23 cm. Includes bibliographical references. [BL54.R6] 73-75315 ISBN 0-913618-10-1 3.95
1. Glossolalia. I. Title.

SAMARIN, William J. 248'.29
Tongues of men and angels; the religious language of Pentecostalism, by William J. Samarin. New York, Macmillan [1972] xv, 277 p. music. 22 cm. Bibliography: p. [257]-268. [BL54.S24] 70-162335
1. Glossolalia. I. Title.

STARKIE, Walter 248.29
Fitzwilliam, 1894-
The road to Santiago: pilgrims of St. James [by] Walter Starkie. Berkeley, University of California Press, 1965. x, 339 p. illus., fold. map, music 23 cm. Partly autobiographical. Bibliographical footnotes. [BX2321.S3S68] 65-5668
1. James, Saint, apostle. 2. Santiago de Compostela. 3. Pilgrims and pilgrimages—Spain. 4. Spain—Descr. & trav. I. Title.

STARKIE, Walter 248.29
Fitzwilliam, 1894-
The road to Santiago: pilgrims of St. James. Berkeley, Univ. of Calif. Pr. [c.]1965. x, 339p. illus., fold map, music. 22cm. Bibl. [BX2321.S3S68] 65-5668 5.00
1. Santiago de Compostela. 2. James, Saint, apostle. 3. Pilgrims and pilgrimages—Spain. 4. Spain—Descr. & trav. I. Title.

SULLIVAN, Kay. 248.29
Journey of love; a pilgrimage to Pope John's birthplace. Photos. by Daniel M. Madden. Book design by Edward R. Wade. With a foreword by Richard Cardinal Cushing. New York, Appleton-Century [1966] 121 p. illus., map, ports. 27 cm. [BX1378.2.S8 1966] 66-22238
1. Joannes XXIII, Pope, 1881-1963. 2. Sotto il Monte, Italy. I. Title.

TONGUES. 248.2'9
Edited by Luther B. Dyer. [1st ed.] Jefferson City, Mo., Le Roi Publishers [1971] 151 p. 21 cm. Includes bibliographical references. [BL54.T64] 73-290958
1. Glossolalia. I. Dyer, Luther B., ed.

UNGER, Merrill Frederick, 248.2'9
1909-
New Testament teaching on tongues [by] Merrill F. Unger. Grand Rapids, Kregel Publications [1971] 175 p. 18 cm. Bibliography: p. 169-175. [BL54.U53] 70-165057 ISBN 0-8254-3900-0 1.75
1. Glossolalia. I. Title.

THE Way of a pilgrim and 248'.29
The pilgrim continues his way / translated from the Russian by R. M. French. New York : Seabury Press, [1974?] x, 242 p., [2] leaves of plates : maps ; 21 cm. The 1st work is a translation of Otkrovennye rasskazy strannika dukhovnomu svoemu ottsu. "A Crossroad book." [BX597.Z9O732 1974] 74-195268 ISBN 0-8164-0259-0 : 6.00 ISBN 0-8164-2069-6 pbk. : 2.95
1. Christian pilgrims and pilgrimages. I. French, Reginald Michael, 1884- tr. II. The pilgrim continues his way. 1974.

WEATHERSPOOL, William W. 248.2'9
This big world, by W. W. Weatherspool. [1st ed.] New York, Greenwich Book Publishers [1967] xiv, 120 p. 22 cm. [DS49.7.W35] 66-23418
1. Pilgrims and pilgrimages—Levant. I. Title.

ALBERIONE, Giacomo 248.3
Giuseppe, 1884-
Pray always, by James Alberione. Tr. by the Daughters of St. Paul. Boston St. Paul Eds. [1966] 265p. 19cm. [BV210.2.A413] 65-29136 3.00; 2.00 pap.,
1. Prayer. I. Title.

AMES, David C. 248'.3
Jesus Christ is alive and well and living in His church [by] David C. Ames. Wheaton, Ill., Tyndale House Publishers [1973] 79 p. 18 cm. [BV4832.2.A47] 72-97648 ISBN 0-8423-1861-5 1.25 (pbk.)
1. Meditations. I. Title.

ASHTON, Wendell J. 248'.3
To thine own self ...; short discussions on more abundant living, by Wendell J. Ashton. Salt Lake City, Bookcraft Inc. [1972] xii, 244 p. 24 cm. Includes bibliographical references. [BV4832.2.A74] 72-77551
1. Meditations. I. Title.

AULEN, Gustaf Emanuel 248.3
Hildebrand, Bp., 1879-
Dag Hammarskjold's white book; an analysis of Markings, by Gustaf Aulen. Philadelphia, Fortress Press [1969] viii, 154 p. 22 cm. Bibliographical footnotes. [D839.7.H3A8] 75-84608 4.75
1. Hammarskjold, Dag, 1905-1961. Vagmarken. I. Title.

BAELZ, Peter R. 248.3
Prayer and providence; a background study [by] Peter R. Baelz. New York, Seabury Press [1968] 141 p. 23 cm. Bibliographical footnotes. [BV210.2.B27 1968b] 68-6128 3.25
1. Prayer. 2. Providence and government of God. I. Title.

BAKER, Mary Ellen Penny. 248'.3
Meditation: a step beyond with Edgar Cayce, by M. E. Penny Baker. Foreword by Hugh Lynn Cayce. [1st ed.] Garden City, N.Y., Doubleday, 1973. 166 p. 22 cm. Bibliography: p. [165]-166. [BL627.B34] 72-96227 ISBN 0-385-00984-4 5.95
1. Cayce, Edgar, 1877-1945. 2. Meditation. I. Title.

BAKER, Mary Ellen Penny. 248'.3
Meditation: a step beyond with Edgar Cayce, by M. E. Penny Baker. New York, Pinnacle Books [1975, c1973] 166 p. 18 cm. Bibliography: p. [165]-166. [BL627.B34] ISBN 0-523-00547-4 1.25 (pbk.)
1. Cayce, Edgar, 1877-1945 2. Meditation. I. Title.
L.C. card number for original ed.: 72-96227.

BALTHASAR, Hans Urs von, 248.3
1905-
Prayer. Tr. by A. V. Littledale. New York, Sheed & Ward [c.1961] 246p. 61-13038 5.00
1. Contemplation. I. Title.

BALTHASAR, Hans Urs von, 248.3
1905-
Prayer. Translated by A. V. Littledale. New York, Sheed & Ward [1961] 246p. 23cm. Translation of Das betrachtende Gebet. [BV5091.C7B33] 61-13038
1. Contemplation. I. Title.

BARKER, William Pierson. 248'.3
To pray is to live / William P. Barker. Old Tappan, N.J. : F. H. Revel Co., c1977. 122 p. ; 21 cm. [BV210.2.B298] 76-54315 ISBN 0-531-01214-X lib.bdg. : 4.95
1. Prayer. I. Title.

BARKER, William Pierson. 248'.3
To pray is to live / William P. Barker. Old Tappan, N.J. : F. H. Revel Co., c1977. 122 p. ; 21 cm. [BV210.2.B298] 76-54315 ISBN 0-531-01214-X lib.bdg. : 4.95
1. Prayer. I. Title.

BARREAU, Jean Claude. 248'.3
Drugs and the life of prayer / Jean-Claude Barreau ; translated by Jeremy Moiser. Grand Rapids, Mich. : W. B. Eerdmans Pub. Co., 1975. 95 p. ; 18 cm. Translation of La priere et la drogue. Includes indexes. [BV210.2.B29913] 74-28249 ISBN 0-8028-1599-5 pbk. : 1.65
1. Prayer. 2. Hallucinogenic drugs and religious experience. I. Title.

BERRIGAN, Daniel. 248'.3
Jesus Christ. Illustrated by Gregory Harris [and] Deborah Harris. [1st ed.] Garden City, N.Y., Doubleday, 1973. 1 v. (unpaged) illus. 28 cm. [BX2182.2.B43] 72-89671 4.95
1. Meditations. I. Harris, Gregory, illus. II. Harris, Deborah, illus. III. Title.

BICKERSTAFF, George. 248'.3
The gift of prayer / written by George Bickerstaff ; illustrated by Keith Christensen. Salt Lake City : Bookcraft, [1975] [24] p. : col. ill. ; 30 cm. A little girl learns the meaning of prayer. [BV212.B5] 74-33178 ISBN 0-88494-276-7
1. Prayer—Juvenile literature. I. Christensen, Keith. II. Title.

BIMLER, Richard. 248'.3
Pray, praise, and hooray. St. Louis, Concordia Pub. House [1972] 113 p. illus. 21 cm. [BV245.B55] 77-175306 ISBN 0-570-03130-3
1. Prayers. I. Title.

BLOOM, Anthony, 1914- 248'.3
Courage to pray / Anthony Bloom and Georges LeFebvre ; translated by Dinah Livingstone. New York : Paulist Press, [1974] c1973 122 p. ; 22 cm. Translation of pts. 2-3 of La priere, by A. de Robert, G. Lefebvre, and A. Bloom. Bibliography: p. [63] [BV210.2.R58213] 74-190392 ISBN 0-8091-0190-4 : 3.95
1. Prayer. I. Lefebvre, Georges, 1908- II. Title.

BOASE, Leonard. 248'.3
The prayer of faith / Leonard Boase. Huntington, Ind. : Our Sunday Visitor, c1976. 126 p. ; 21 cm. Bibliography: p. 125-126. [BV210.2.B6 1976] 76-5152 ISBN 0-87973-683-6 pbk. : 2.95
1. Prayer. I. Title.

BOROS, Ladislaus, 1927- 248'.3
Christian prayer / Ladislaus Boros ; translated by David Smith. New York : Seabury Press, c1976. p. cm. Translation of Uber das christliche Beten. "A Crossroad book." [BV210.2.B6513 1976] 76-7353 ISBN 0-8164-1199-9 : 6.95
1. Prayer. I. Title.

BOYD, Malcolm, 1923- 248.3
Human like me, Jesus. [by] Malcolm Boyd. With a new introduction to the paperback edition. Revised and abridged. New York, Pyramid Family Library [1973, c1971] 141 p. 18 cm. [BV245.B634 1973] 71-159125 ISBN 0-515-03107-0. 1.25 (pbk.)
1. Prayers. I. Title.

BOYLAN, Eugene 248.3
Difficulties in mental prayer. Westminster, Md., Newman [1966, c.1965] xiv, 127p. 19cm. [BV4813.B65] 66-1533 .95 pap.,
1. Meditation. I. Title.

*BRINGMAN, Dale S. 248.3
Prayer and the devotional life, by Dale S. Bringman, Frank W. Klos. Philadelphia, Lutheran Church [c.1964] 121p. illus. 20cm. (LCA sch. of rel. ser.) 1.25; 1.25 teacher's guide, pap.,
I. Title.

BRO, Bernard. 248.3
Learning to pray. Translated by John Morris. Staten Island, N.Y., Alba House [1966] 176 p. 22 cm. [BV210.2.B713] 66-17217
1. Prayer. I. Title.

BRO, Bernard 248.3
Learning to pray. Tr. [from French] by John Morris. Staten Island, N. Y., Alba [c.1966] 176p. 22cm. [BV210.2.B713] 66-17217 3.95
1. Prayer. I. Title.

*BROOKE, Avery. 248.3
Doorway to meditation. Text by Avery Brooke. Drawings by Robert Pinart. Noroton, Conn., Vineyard Books [1973] 110 p. illus., 23 cm. [BV4813] 3.95 (pbk.)
1. Meditations. I. Title.
Publisher's address: 129 Nearwater Lane, Noroton, Conn., 06820.

BURKE, Carl F. 248.3
Don't turn me off, Lord, and other jail house meditations [by] Carl F. Burke. New York, Association Press [1971] 128 p. 19 cm. [BV4832.2.B86] 72-167885 ISBN 0-8096-1832-X 3.50
1. Meditations. I. Title.

BUTTRICK, George Arthur, 248.3
1892-
The power of prayer today. New York, World Pub. Co. [1970] 61 p. 21 cm. (World inspirational books) Includes bibliographical references. [BV210.2.B87] 71-131562
1. Prayer. I. Title.

CARR, Jo. 248'.3
Bless this mess, & other prayers [by] Jo Carr and Imogene Sorley. Nashville, Abingdon Press [1969] 112 p. 21 cm. [BV245.C32] 69-12018 ISBN 0-687-03617-8 2.50
1. Prayers. I. Sorley, Imogene, joint author. II. Title.

CARROLL, James. 248.3
Prayer from where we are; suggestions about the possibility and practice of prayer today. Dayton, Ohio, G. A. Pflaum [1970] 120 p. illus. 17 cm. (Christian experience series. Witness book 13) Bibliography: p. 119-120. [BV210.2.C34] 71-133402 0.85
1. Prayer. I. Title.

CARTER, Edward, 1929- 248'.3
Prayer is love. St. Meinrad, Ind., Abbey Press, 1974. vii, 99 p. 21 cm. (A Priority edition) Includes bibliographical references. [BV210.2.C36] 74-78722 ISBN 0-87029-030-4 4.95
1. Prayer. I. Title.

*CARTY, James W., Jr. 248.3
Communicating with God. Nashville, Upper Room [c.1964] 64p. 19cm. .35 pap.,
I. Title.

CASSELS, Louis. 248'.3
Haircuts and holiness; discussion starters for religious encounter groups. Nashville, Abingdon Press [1972] 128 p. 20 cm. [BV4832.2.C29] 76-172817 ISBN 0-687-16475-3 1.75
1. Meditations. 2. Discussion in religious education. I. Title.

CATOIR, John T. 248'.3
We dare to believe; an exploration of faith in the modern world, by John T. Catoir. Chicago, Franciscan Herald Press [1972] 149 p. 21 cm. [BX2182.2.C36] 77-169055 ISBN 0-8199-0431-7 5.95
1. Meditations. I. Title.

CHANTAL, Jeanne Francoise 248.3
(Fremiot) de Rabutin, Baronne de, Saint, 1572-1641
St. Chantal on prayer; a translation of her writings on praver [by] A. Durand. [Boston] St. Paul Eds. [1968] 63p. 19cm. With one exception, all the extracts are to be found in vol. III of the official ed. of . . . [the author's] complete works: [Sainte Jeanne-Francoise Fremyot de Chantal, sa vie et ses oeuvres. Paris, 1876] [BV209.C48] 67-31593 1.00 pap.,
1. Prayer—Early works to 1800. 2. Meditation. I. Durand, A. comp. II. Title.

CHEESMAN, Lulu Jordan. 248'.3
From the snare of the fowler, by Lulu Jordan Cheesman with Ernest B. Rockstad. Andover, Kan., Faith and Life Publications [1972] vi, 81 p. 21 cm. [BV4935.C42] 73-187513 1.25
I. Rockstad, Ernest B., joint author. II. Title.

CHESTER, Ann E., 1901- 248'.3
Prayer, now : a response to the needs for prayer renewal / Ann E. Chester. Albany, N.Y. : Clarity Pub., [1975] 62 p. ; 28 cm. Includes bibliographical references. [BV210.2.C49] 75-3907 ISBN 0-915488-01-9 : 2.00
1. Prayer. 2. House of Prayer Movement. I. Title.

CHINMOY. 248.3
Songs of the soul. [New York] Herder and Herder [1971] 93 p. 22 cm. [BL624.C474] 79-165496 3.95
1. Meditations. I. Title.

CHRISTENSON, Evelyn. 248'.3
What happens when women pray / Evelyn Christenson, with Viola Blake. Wheaton, Ill. : Victor Books, c1975. 144 p. ; 18 cm. (An input book) [BV210.2.C53] 75-171 ISBN 0-88207-715-5 pbk. : 1.75
1. Prayer. I. Blake, Viola, 1921- joint author. II. Title.

CHRISTIANS at prayer / 248'.3
edited by John Gallen. Notre Dame, Ind. : University of Notre Dame Press, c1977. xii, 160 p. ; 24 cm. (Liturgical studies) Includes bibliographical references and index. [BV213.C46] 76-22407 ISBN 0-268-00718-7 : 9.95.
1. Prayer—Addresses, essays, lectures. I. Gallen, John. II. Series: Notre Dame, Ind. University. Liturgical studies.

CIAMPI, Luke M. 248'.3
Rebuild my church! Meditations for Franciscan laymen, by Luke M. Ciampi. Chicago, Franciscan Herald Press [1972] 49 p. illus. 26 cm. [BX2188.F7C54] 72-5770 ISBN 0-8199-0444-9 0.95 (pbk.)
1. Meditations. 2. Retreats for members of religious orders. I. Title.

COBURN, John B. 248'.3
A life to live—a way to pray [by] John B. Coburn. New York, Seabury Press [1973] x, 143 p. 21 cm. (An Original Seabury paperback, SP 80) Includes bibliographical references. [BV210.2.C57] 72-96340 ISBN 0-8164-2079-3 2.95
1. Prayer. 2. Prayers. I. Title.

COMMUNION with God. 248.3
Mountain View, Calif., Pacific Pr. Pub. [c.1964] 107p. 22cm. Devotional guide for the school of prayer, comprised of materials drawn from the Bible and the writings of Ellen G. White, and issued under auspices of the Ministerial Assn. of the Seventh-Day Adventists. 64-8715 1.25 pap.,
1. Prayer—Study and teaching. I. White, Ellen Gould (Harmon) 1827-1915. II. Seventh-Day Adventists. Ministerial Association.

CORBISHLEY, Thomas. 248'.3
The prayer of Jesus / Thomas Corbishley. London : Mowbrays, 1976. 143 p. ; 18 cm. [BT590.S65C67] 77-353560 ISBN 0-264-66068-4 : £0.75
1. Jesus Christ—Spiritual life. 2. Jesus Christ—Prayers. I. Title.

CORBISHLEY, Thomas. 248'.3
The prayer of Jesus / Thomas Corbishley. 1st ed. in the United States of America. Garden City, N.Y. : Doubleday, 1977, c1976. 119 p. ; 22 cm. [BV229.C67 1977] 76-23755 ISBN 0-385-12545-3 : 5.95
1. Jesus Christ—Prayers. 2. Jesus Christ—Spiritual life. 3. Prayer. I. Title.

COWMAN, Lettie (Burd) 248'.3
1870-1960.
God—after all, by Mrs. Charles E. Cowman. Grand Rapids, Mich., Zondervan Pub. House [1971, c1955] 139 p. 18 cm. (Zondervan books) Originally published under title: Handfuls of purpose. [BV4832.C638 1971] 76-156249 0.95
1. Devotional literature. I. Title.

CROM, Scott. 248'.3
Quaker worship and techniques of meditation / Scott Crom. [Wallingford, Pa. : Pendle Hill Publications], 1974. 30 p. ; 20 cm. (Pendle Hill pamphlet ; 195 ISSN 0031-4250s) [BX7737.C76] 74-82795 ISBN 0-87574-195-9 : 0.70
1. Friends, Society of. 2. Meditation. I. Title.

CURTIS, Lindsay R. 248'.3
Tips for 2-1/2s [by] Lindsay R. Curtis Salt Lake City, Bookcraft, 1972. viii, 103 p. illus. 24 cm. [BV4832.2.C87] 72-77553
1. Meditations. I. Title.

DANIEL, Lois, comp. 248'.3
Secrets to share; experiences of courage and faith in the lives of famouns men and women. Illustrated by James Hamil. [Kansas City, Mo., Hallmark, c1971] 61 p. illus. 20 cm. (Hallmark editions) [BV4832.2.D34] 70-112060 ISBN 0-87529-069-8 2.50
1. Meditations. I. Title.

DAVIS, Henry Grady 248.3
Why we worship. Philadelphia, Muhlenberg Press [c.1961] 54p. (Fortress bk.) 61-13582 1.00 bds.,
1. Worship. I. Title.

DEMARAY, Donald E 248.3
Alive to God through prayer; a manual on the practices of prayer, by Donald E. Demaray. Grand Rapids, Baker Book House, 1965. 156 p. 20 cm. Includes bibliographies. [BV210.2.D43] 64-8346
1. Prayer. I. Title.

DEMARAY, Donald E. 248.3
Alive to God through prayer; a manual on the practices of prayer. Grand Rapids, Mich., Baker Book [c.]1965. 156p. 20cm. Bibl. [BV210.2.D43] 64-8346 1.95 pap.,
1. Prayer. I. Title.

DEPUY, Norman R. 248'.3
The Bible alive [by] Norman R. DePuy. Valley Forge [Pa.] Judson Press [1972] 95 p. 22 cm. [BV4832.2.D46] 73-181560 ISBN 0-8170-0556-0 1.95
1. Meditations. I. Title.

DOTY, William Lodewick, 1919- 248'.3
Prayer in the spirit, by William L. Doty. Staten Island, N.Y., Alba House [1973] 154 p. 22 cm. [BV210.2.D65] 73-9580 ISBN 0-8189-0278-7 4.95
1. Prayer. 2. Pentecostalism. I. Title.

DUQUOC, Christian. 248'.3
The prayer life. Edited by Christian Duquoc and Claude Geffre. [New York] Herder and Herder [1972] 126 p. 23 cm. (Concilium: religion in the seventies. Spirituality, v. 79) On cover: The New concilium: religion in the seventies. Includes bibliographical references. [BV210.2.D85] 72-3944 ISBN 0-07-073609-X Pap. 2.95
1. Prayer. I. Geffre, Claude, joint author. II. Title. III. Series: Concilium: theology in the age of renewal, v. 79.

EASTMAN, Dick. 248.3
No easy road; inspirational thoughts on prayer. Grand Rapids, Mich., Baker Book House [1973, c.1971] 126 p. 18 cm. (Direction Books) Bibliography: p. 126. [BV210.2E28] 70-155861 ISBN 0-8010-3259-8 0.95 (pbk.)
1. Prayer. I. Title.

EATON, Kenneth Oxner. 248.3
Men who talked with God. New York, Abingdon Press [1964] 95 p. 20 cm. [BV210.2.E3] 64-10105
1. Prayer. 2. Prophets. I. Title.

EATON, Kenneth Oxner 248.3
Men who talked with God. Nashville, Abingdon [c.1964] 95p. 20cm. 64-10105 2.25 bds.,
1. Prayer. 2. Prophets. I. Title.

ECCLESTONE, Alan. 248'.3
Yes to God / Alan Ecclestone. St. Meinrad, Ind. : Abbey Press, 1975. 133 p. ; 21 cm. (A Priority edition) [BV210.2.E33 1975] 75-19923 ISBN 0-87029-050-9 pbk. : 3.95
1. Prayer. 2. Spirituality. I. Title.

EDNA MARY, Sister 248.3
This world and prayer. London, S.P.C.K. [New York, Morehouse, c.]1965. x, 85p. 19cm. (Here & now ser. Seraph bk.) Bibl. [BV213.E3] 65-6441 1.50 pap.,
1. Prayer. I. Title.

ELLUL, Jacques. 248.3
Prayer and modern man. Translated by C. Edward Hopkin. New York, Seabury Press [1970] xi, 178 p. 22 cm. [BV210.2.E43] 79-103845 4.95
1. Prayer. I. Title.

EMERY, Pierre Yves. 248'.3
Prayer at the heart of life / Pierre-Yves Emery ; translated by William J. Nottingham. Maryknoll, N.Y. : Orbis Books, c1975. xxi, 168 p. ; 20 cm. Translation of La priere au coeur de la vie. Includes bibliographical references. [BV210.2.E4713] 74-17870 ISBN 0-88344-393-7 : 4.95
1. Prayer. I. Title.

EVELY, Louis, 1910- 248.3
In His presence. Translated by J. F. Stevenson. Garden City, N.Y., Doubleday [1974, c1970] 115 p. 18 cm. (Image books) Translation of Dieu et le prochain. [BX2183.E86] ISBN 0-385-06002-5 1.45 (pbk.)
1. Meditations. I. Title.
L.C. card number for original ed.: 76-509645

EVELY, Louis, 1910- 248.3
Teach us how to pray. Translated by Edmond Bonin. Westminster, Md., Newman Press [1967] 90 p. 22 cm. Translation of the author's Apprenez-nous a prier, and Sur la priere. [BV210.2.E9] 67-26074
1. Prayer. I. Title.

EVELY, Louis, 1910- 248.3
We dare to say Our Father [Tr. from French. New York] Herder & Herder [c.1965] 128p. 22cm. [BX2350.2.E913] 64-21428 3.50
1. Christian life—Catholic authors. 2. Lord's prayer. I. Title.

FERREE, Sulon G., ed. 248'.3
Prayer in my life; witnesses by persons in various vocations. Edited by Sulon G. Ferree. Nashville, The Upper Room [1967] 80 p. ports. 16 cm. Messages delivered at The Upper Room, Nashville, Tenn., during the 1967 Easter weekend as a part of the International prayer fellowship. [BV205.P7] 67-30661
1. Prayer. I. Title.

*FERRIER, Christine M. 248.3
Guide to prayer. Chicago, Moody [1966, i.e. 1967] 127p. 18cm. (Lion ser.) Adapted from How to pray, by R. A. Torrey. .49 pap.,
1. Prayer. I. Torrev, R. A. How to pray. II. Title. III. Title: How to pray.

FIFE, Eric S. 248'.3
Prayer : common sense and the Bible / by Eric Fife. Grand Rapids : Zondervan Pub. House, c1976. 91 p. ; 18 cm. [BV210.2.F5] 76-43017 3.95 pbk. : 1.25
1. Prayer. I. Title.

FINNEY, Charles Grandison, 1792-1875 248.3
Prevailing prayer; sermons on prayer. Grand Rapids, Mich., Kregel [c.1965] 64p. 20cm. Sermons selected from the author's Sermons on the way of salvation. [BV210.F5] 65-25846 1.95; 1.00 pap.,
1. Prayer—Sermons. 2. Sermons, American. 3. Congregational churches—Sermons. I. Title.

FINNEY, Charles Grandison, 1792-1875. 248.3
Prevailing prayer; sermons on prayer. Grand Rapids, Kregel Publications [1965] 64 p. 20 cm. Sermons selected from the author's Sermons on the way of salvation. [BV210.F5 1965] 65-25846
1. Prayer — Sermons. 2. Sermons, American. 3. Congregational churches — Sermons. I. Title.

FLETCHER, Annis 248.3
A teacher's conversations with God. New York, Vantage Press [c.1959] 208p. 22cm. 3.50 bds.,
I. Title.

FOSDICK, Harry Emerson, 1878-1969. 248'.3
The meaning of prayer / Harry Emerson Fosdick ; with introduction by John R. Mott. Folcroft, Pa : Folcroft Library Editions, 1976. xii, 196 p. ; 24 cm. Reprint of the 1946 ed. published by Association Press, New York. Bibliography: p. 195-196. [BV210.F57 1976] 76-50560 ISBN 0-8414-4159-6 lib. bdg. : 15.00
1. Prayer. 2. Devotional exercises. I. Title.

FREER, Harold Wiley 248.3
Growing in the life of prayer. Nashville, Abingdon [c.1962] 176p. 21cm. Bibl. 62-9384 3.00
1. Prayer. I. Title.

FRENCH, Reginald Michael, 1884- tr. 248.3
The way of a pilgrim; and, The pilgrim continues his way. Translated from the Russian by R. M. French. New York, Seabury Press [1965] x, 242 p. maps, 21 cm. (A Seabury paperback, SP18) [BX597.Z9O732 1965] 65-4899
1. Pilgrims and Pilgramages. I. The pilgrim continues his way. II. Title.

FRIDY, Wallace. 248.3
Wings of the spirit; devotions for personal and group use. New York, Abingdon Press [1963] 144 p. 18 cm. [BV4832.2.F72] 63-16375
1. Devotional exercises. 2. Worship programs. I. Title.

FRIDY, Wallace 248.3
Wings of the spirit; devotions for personal and group use. Nashville, Abingdon [c.1963] 144p. 18cm. 63-16375 2.00
1. Devotional exercises. 2. Worship programs. I. Title.

FURLONG, Monica. 248'.3
Contemplating now. Philadelphia, Westminster Press [1972, c1971] 124 p. 19 cm. [BV5091.C7F87 1972] 72-2912 ISBN 0-664-24960-4
1. Contemplation. I. Title.

GAITHER, Gloria. 248.3
Make warm noises. Photos by Bill Grine. Nashville, Tenn., Impact Books [1971] 79 p. illus. 22 cm. [BV4832.2.G24] 71-176307 2.95
1. Meditations. I. Title.

GARRETT, Adelaide Jefferys. 248.3
Filings of light; a venture of the spirit, by Adelaide Jefferys Garrett with Elizabeth Cushman. North Quincy, Mass., Christopher Pub. House [1971] 153 p. 21 cm. [BV4832.2.G27] 79-171073 ISBN 0-8158-0266-8 3.95
1. Meditations. 2. Spirit writings. I. Cushman, Elizabeth, joint author. II. Title.

GESCH, Roy G. 248.3
Lord of the young crowd [by] Roy G. Gesch. St. Louis, Concordia Pub. House [1971] 95 p. 18 cm. [BV4850.G43] 72-162531 ISBN 0-570-03126-5
1. Youth—Prayer-books and devotions—English. I. Title.

GIBBARD, Mark. 248.3
Why pray? Valley Forge, Judson Press [1971, c1970] 125 p. 19 cm. Bibliography: p. 121. [BV210.2.G5 1971] 72-132999 ISBN 0-8170-0517-X 1.95
1. Prayer. I. Title.

GILMORE, J. Herbert. 248.3
Devotions for the home [by] J. Herbert Gilmore, Jr. Nashville, Broadman Press [1971] ix, 128 p. 21 cm. (A Broadman inner circle book) [BV4832.2.G53] 70-128854 ISBN 0-8054-8308-X
1. Meditations. I. Title.

GOLDMAN, June Parker. 248'.3
Search every corner. Nashville, Abingdon Press [1972] 96 p. 20 cm. [BV4832.2.G618] 74-186823 ISBN 0-687-37125-2 2.95
1. Meditations. I. Title.

GOLDSMITH, Joel S., 1892- 248'.3
The altitude of prayer / Joel S. Goldsmith ; edited by Lorraine Sinkler. 1st ed. New York : Harper & Row, [1975] vii, 147 p. ; 20 cm. Includes bibliographical references. [BV210.2.G64 1975] 74-25685 ISBN 0-06-063171-6 : 5.95
1. Prayer. I. Title.

GREEN, Thomas Henry, 1932- 248'.3
Opening to God : a guide to prayer / Thomas H. Green. Notre Dame, Ind. : Ave Maria Press, c1977. 110 p. ; 21 cm. Includes bibliographical references. [BV210.2.G73] 77-83197 ISBN 0-87793-135-6 : 4.95 ISBN 0-87793-136-4 pbk. : 2.45
1. Prayer. I. Title.

GREEN, Thomas Henry, 1932- 248'.3
Opening to God : a guide to prayer / Thomas H. Green. Notre Dame, Ind. : Ave Maria Press, c1977. 110 p. ; 21 cm. Includes bibliographical references. [BV210.2.G73] 77-83197 ISBN 0-87793-135-6 : 4.95 ISBN 0-87793-136-4 pbk. : 2.45
1. Prayer. I. Title.

GROU, Jean Nicolas, 1731-1803. 248'.3
How to pray; nine chapters on prayer from The school of Jesus Christ. Translated by Joseph Dalby. [Nashville] Upper Room [1973] 96 p. 19 cm. Translated from L'ecole de Jesus Christ. [BV210.G752 1973] 72-97118 1.00
1. Prayer. I. Title.

GUILLERAND, Augustin, 1877-1945. 248.3
The prayer of the presence of God. Translated from the French by a monk of Parkminster. [1st English ed.] Wilkes-Barre, Pa., Dimension Books [1966] 191 p. 21 cm. Translation of Face a Dieu. Bibliographical footnotes. [BV4813.G813] 66-22876
1. Prayer. 2. Meditation. I. Title.

GYLDENVAND, Lily M 1917- 248.3
What am I praying? Enriching the use of the Lord's prayer [by] Lily M. Gyldenvand. Minneapolis, Augsburg Pub. House [1964] 88 p. 20 cm. [BV230.G9] 64-21509
1. Lord's prayer. I. Title.

GYLDENVAND, Lily M., 1917- 248.3
What am I praying? Enriching the use of the Lord's prayer. Minneapolis, Augsburg [c.1964] 88p. 20cm. 64-21509 1.75 pap.,
1. Lord's prayer. I. Title.

HALLOCK, Edgar Francis, 1888- 248.3
Always in prayer [by] E. F. Hallock. Nashville, Broadman Press [1966] 128 p. 20 cm. [BV210.2.H35] 66-12572
1. Prayer. 2. Christian life—Baptist authors. I. Title.

HALLOCK, Edgar Francis, 1888- 248.3
Always in prayer. Nashville, Broadman [c.1966] 128p. 20cm. [BV210.2.H35] 66-12572 1.50
1. Prayer. 2. Christian life—Baptist authors. I. Title.

HAMILTON, Herbert Alfred 248.3
Conversation with God; learning to pray. Nashville, Abingdon Press [1961] 93p. 61-8408 1.75
1. Prayers. 2. Meditations. I. Title.

HAMMAN, Adalbert, 1910- 248.3
Prayer; the New Testament [by] A. Hamman. [Chicago] Franciscan Herald Press [1971] x, 238 p. 22 cm. Includes bibliographical references. [BV228.H2413] 74-85507 ISBN 0-8199-0424-4
1. Prayer—Biblical teaching. I. Title.

HAMPTON, Mack W. 248'.3
Once there were three / Mack W. Hampton. Chicago : Moody Press, c1977. 87 p. : ill. ; 22 cm. [BV4907.H33] 77-4417 ISBN 0-8024-6063-1 pbk. : 1.95
1. Hampton, Mack W. 2. Consolation. 3. Bereavement. I. Title.

HANNE, John Anthony. 248'.3
Prayer—or pretense? Grand Rapids, Zondervan Pub. House [1974] 96 p. 18 cm. [BV210.2.H354] 73-13066 0.95 (pbk.)
1. Prayer. I. Title.

HANSON, Muriel. 248.3
Honey and salt [second portion] [1st ed.] Minneapolis, His International Service [1971] 64 p. 22 cm. [BV4832.2.H28 1971] 78-185512 ISBN 0-911802-26-6 1.25
1. Meditations. I. Title.

HAPPOLD, Frederick Crossfield, 1893- 248'.3
The journey inwards : a simple introduction to the practice of contemplative meditation by normal people / F. C. Happold. Atlanta : John Knox Press, 1975, c1968. 142 p. ; 21 cm. Reprint of the ed. published by Darton, Longman & Todd, London. Bibliography: p. [137]-142. [BL627.H28 1975] 75-13460 ISBN 0-8042-2379-3
1. Meditation. 2. Contemplation. I. Title.

HARING, Bernhard, 1912- 248'.3
Prayer : the integration of faith and life / Bernard Haring. Notre Dame, Ind. : Fides Publishers, c1975. xi, 145 p. ; 23 cm. [BV210.2.H363] 75-330725 ISBN 0-8190-0609-2 : 5.95
1. Prayer. 2. Prayers. I. Title.

HAYFORD, Jack W. 248'.3
Prayer is invading the impossible / Jack W. Hayford. Plainfield, N.J. : Logos International, c1977. 150 p. ; 21 cm. [BV210.2.H39] 77-71684 ISBN 0-88270-218-1 : 2.95
1. Prayer. I. Title.

*HERHOLD, Robert M. 248.3
Freewheeling; ----meditations [by] Robert M. Herhold. Design by Jan Herhold [and] introduction [by] Joseph Sittler. Palo Alto, Calif. New Being, [1974]. 124 p. illus 21 cm. [BV284] 3.95 (pbk.)
1. Prayers. I. Title.

HIFLER, Joyce. 248.3
Think on these things. [1st ed.] Garden City, N.Y., Doubleday, 1966. 116 p. 22 cm. [PS3558.135T4] 66-20953
I. Title.

HIFLER, Joyce 248.3
Think on these things [1st ed] Garden City, Doubleday, 1966. 116 p. 22 cm [ps3558.135t4] 66-20953 3.95
1. Title. I. Title.

HIGGINS, John J. 248'.3
Thomas Merton on prayer [by] John J. Higgins. Garden City, N.Y., Doubleday, 1973 [c1971] 192 p. 22 cm. Originally published in 1971 under title: Merton's theology of prayer. Bibliography: p. [166]-192. [BV207.H53 1973] 73-151459 5.95

1. Merton, Thomas, 1915-1968. 2. Prayer—History. I. Title.

HIGGINS, John J. 248'.3
Thomas Merton on prayer [by] John J. Higgins. Garden City, N.Y., Image Books, 1975 [c1971] p. cm. Reprint of the ed. published by Cistercian Publications, Spencer, Mass. as v. 18 of the Cistercian studies series, under title: Merton's theology of prayer. Bibliography: p. [BV207.H53 1975] 74-8585 ISBN 0-385-02813-X 1.75 (pbk.)
1. Merton, Thomas, 1915-1968. 2. Prayer—History. I. Title. II. Series: Cistercian studies series, no. 18.

HOCKEN, Peter. 248'.3
Prayer, a gift of life / Peter Hocken. New York : Paulist Press, [1975 c1974] 126 p. ; 22 cm. [BV210.2.H6 1974] 75-328472 ISBN 0-8091-0199-8 : 3.95
1. Prayer. I. Title.

HOLLINGS, Michael. 248'.3
Day by day; an encouragement to pray. New York, Morehouse-Barlow Co. [1973, c1972] 125 p. 18 cm. Includes bibliographical references. [BV210.2.H63 1973] 73-84095 ISBN 0-8192-1161-3 1.95 (pbk.)
1. Prayer. I. Title.

*HOLLINGS, Michael. 248.3
The One who listens; a book of prayer [by] Michael Hollings and Etta Gullick. New York, Morehouse-Barlow [1971, c.1972] ix, 194 p. 18 cm. [BV4832] ISBN 0-8192-4037-0 pap., 2.75
1. Prayer—Collections. I. Gullick, Etta, joint author. II. Title.

HOW do I pray? / 248'.3
Edited by Robert Heyer. New York : Paulist Press, c1977. 101 p. : ill. ; 18 cm. "Articles in this book originally appeared in New Catholic world." "A New Catholic world book." [BV213.H67] 77-80808 ISBN 0-8091-2041-0 : 1.75
1. Prayer—Addresses, essays, lectures. I. Heyer, Robert J. II. New Catholic world.

HOWE, Leroy T., 1936- 248'.3
Prayer in a secular world [by] Leroy T. Howe. Philadelphia, United Church Press [1973] 159 p. 23 cm. "A Pilgrim Press book." [BV210.2.H67] 73-321 ISBN 0-8298-0248-7 5.25
1. Prayer. I. Title.

HUBBARD, David Allan. 248'.3
The problem with prayer is ... [By] David A. Hubbard. Wheaton, Ill., Tyndale House Publishers [1972] 91 p. 18 cm. [BV210.2.H77] 72-75964 ISBN 0-8423-4880-8 (pbk) 0.95 (pbk)
1. Prayer. I. Title.

HUEGEL, Frederick Julius, 1889- 248'.3
The ministry of intercession / by F. J. Huegel. 2d ed. Minneapolis : Bethany Fellowship, 1976, c1971. 74 p. ; 18 cm. (Dimension books) [BV213.H77 1976] 76-15861 ISBN 0-87123-365-7 pbk. : 1.25
1. Jesus Christ—Intercession. 2. Prayer. I. Title.

HUEGEL, Frederick Julius, 1889- 248.3
Prayer's deeper secrets. Grand Rapids, Zondervan Pub. House [1959] 96p. 20cm. [BV210.2.H8] 59-38174
1. Prayer. I. Title.

HUELSMAN, Richard J. 248'.3
Pray : [an introduction to the spiritual life for busy people] : moderator's manual / Richard J. Huelsman. New York : Paulist Press, c1976. 163 p. : ill. ; 28 cm. [BV214.H8] 76-24449 pbk. : 7.95
1. Prayer—Study and teaching. 2. Spiritual life—Catholic authors—Study and teaching. I. Title.

HULME, William Edward, 1920- 248'.3
When two become one; reflections for the newly married, by William E. Hulme. Minneapolis, Minn., Augsburg Pub. House [1972] 96 p. 21 cm. [BV4596.M3H85] 76-176481 ISBN 0-8066-1212-6 2.50
1. Married people—Prayer-books and devotions—English. I. Title.

HULTSTRAND, Donald M., 1927- 248'.3
The praying church : with study guide / Donald M. Hultstrand. New York : Seabury Press, 1977. p. cm. [BV210.2.H83] 77-8337 ISBN 0-8164-2159-5 pbk. : 3.95
1. Prayer. I. Title.

HUNTER, Frances Gardner, 1916- 248.3
Hot line to heaven, by Frances E. Gardner. Anderson, Ind., Warner Press [1970] 111 p. 19 cm. [BV210.2.H85] 72-21749
1. Prayer. I. Title.

INGERSOLL, Wendell, 1879- 248'.3
In step with the infinite for health and happiness. Philadelphia, Dorrance [1972] 72 p. 22 cm. [BV4832.2.I53] 71-187341 ISBN 0-8059-1675-X 3.00
1. Meditations. I. Title.

IRION, Mary Jean. 248'.3
Yes, world: a mosaic of meditation. New York, R. W. Baron Pub. Co., 1970. xiii, 145 p. 22 cm. [BV4832.2.I74] 76-108973 4.95
1. Meditations. I. Title.

*ISACKSEN, Frederick R., Rev., 1903- 248.3
Healing leaves, by Rev. Dr. Frederick R. Isacksen. [First ed.] New York, Vantage [1972] 120 p. 21 cm. [BV4832] 3.95
1. Meditations. I. Title.

JACOBSEN, David C. 248'.3
Clarity in prayer : telling the small t truth / David C. Jacobsen. Corte Madera, CA : Omega Books, 1976. 94, [9] p. : ill. ; 22 cm. Bibliography: p. [101]-[102] [BV210.2.J32] 76-24101 ISBN 0-89353-015-8 pbk. : 4.00
1. Prayer. I. Title.

JOHNSON, Merle Allison. 248'.3
Religious roulette & other dangerous games Christians play. Nashville, Abingdon Press [1975] 143 p. 19 cm. [BV210.2.J63] 74-17453 ISBN 0-687-36109-5 2.95 (pbk.)
1. Prayer. 2. Faith-cure. I. Title.

JONES, George Curtis, 1911- 248'.3
The good life / G. Curtis Jones. Philadelphia : United Church Press, c1976. 180 p. ; 22 cm. "A Pilgrim Press book." A collection of articles which appeared as the author's newspaper column in the Macon telegraph and news, 1970-1974. [BV4832.2.J644] 75-33410 ISBN 0-8298-0302-5 : 6.00
1. Meditations. I. Title.

JONES, Ray O. 248'.3
Top sacred: spiritual ideas in down-to-earth language [by] Ray O. Jones. Nashville, Broadman Press [1972] 128 p. 21 cm. Bibliography: p. 128. [BV4832.2.J648] 72-79170 ISBN 0-8054-5525-6 3.95
1. Meditations. I. Title.

JONES, Rufus Matthew, 1863-1948. 248'.3
The double search : studies in atonement and prayer / by Rufus M. Jones. Richmond, Ind. : Friends United Press, [1975] p. cm. Reprint of the 1906 ed. published by J. C. Winston, Philadelphia. [BT265.J6 1975] 75-14316 ISBN 0-913408-18-2
1. Atonement. 2. Prayer. I. Title.

JONES, Rufus Matthew, 1863-1948. 248'.3
The double search : studies in atonement and prayer / by Rufus M. Jones. Richmond, Ind. : Friends United Press, [1975] p. cm. Reprint of the 1906 ed. published by J. C. Winston, Philadelphia. [BT265.J6 1975] 75-14316 ISBN 0-913408-18-2 pbk. : 1.95
1. Atonement. 2. Prayer. I. Title.

KELLY, Faye L. 248.3
Prayer in sixteenth-century England, by Faye L. Kelly. Gainesville, Univ. of Fla. Pr., 1966. 68p. 23cm. (Univ. of Fla. monographs. Humanities, no. 22) Title. (Series: Florida. University, Gainesville, University of Florida monographs. Humanities, no. 22) Bibl. [BR756.K4] 66-64090 2.00 pap.,
1. Gt. Brit.—Religious life and customs. 2. Prayer—Hist. I. Title. II. Series.

KELSEY, Morton T. 248'.3
The other side of silence : a guide to Christian meditation / Morton T. Kelsey. New York : Paulist Press, c1976. viii, 314 p. : ill. ; 23 cm. Includes bibliographical references. [BV4813.K44] 76-9365 ISBN 0-8091-0208-0 : 8.50 ISBN 0-8091-1956-0 pbk. : 5.95
1. Meditation. I. Title.

KILLINGER, John. 248'.3
Bread for the wilderness, wine for the journey : the miracle of prayer and meditation / John Killinger. Waco, Tex. : Word Books, c1976. 133 p. ; 23 cm. [BV210.2.K48] 75-38049 ISBN 0-87680-443-1 : 5.95
1. Prayer. I. Title.

KIMMEL, Jo, 1931- 248'.3
Steps to prayer power. Nashville [Tenn.] Abingdon Press [1972] 112 p. 19 cm. Bibliography: p. 110-112. [BV210.2.K5] 72-702 ISBN 0-687-39341-8
1. Prayer. I. Title.

KRUTZA, Vilma. 248.3
His/hers devotionals [by] Vilma and William J. Krutza. Grand Rapids, Mich., Baker Book House [1971] 96 p. 21 cm. [BV4596.M3K78] 71-168382 ISBN 0-8010-5309-9
1. Married people—Prayer-books and devotions—English. I. Krutza, William J., joint author. II. Title.

LANDSTROM, Elsie H. 248.3
Friends, let us pray [by] Elsie H. Landstrom. [Wallingford, Pa., Pendle Hill Publications, 1970] 32 p. 20 cm. (Pendle Hill pamphlet, 174) Includes bibliographical references. [BV213.L35] 79-146679 0.70
1. Prayer. I. Title.

LAVENDER, John Allan 248.3
Why prayers are unanswered. Vally Forge [Pa.] Judson [1967] 77p. 21cm. [BV220.L38] 67-14361 2.95
1. Prayer. I. Title.

LAVENDER, John Allan. 248.3
Why prayers are unanswered. Valley Forge [Pa.] Judson Press [1967] 77 p. 21 cm. [BV220.L38] 67-14361
1. Prayer. I. Title.

LAW, William, 1686-1761. 248.3
The spirit of prayer; and, The spirit of love. The full text, edited by Sidney Spencer. Cambridge, James Clarke, 1969. 301 p. 23 cm. The spirit of prayer originally published, London, 1749-50; The spirit of love originally published, London, 1752-54. Bibliography: p. [297]-298. [BV209.L3 1969] 75-882813 ISBN 0-227-67720-X £1.75
1. Prayer. 2. Theology. 3. Mysticism. I. Law, William, 1686-1761. The spirit of love. 1969. II. Title. III. Title: The spirit of love.

**LEARNING to pray* 248.3
[teacher's guide: grades 7-9] Minneapolis, Augsburg [1967] 80p. 21cm. Prepd. for the Bd. of Parish Educ., and the Bd. of Pubn. of the Amer. Lutheran Church from the 1967 Vacation Church Sch., Ser., based on material prepd. by Clara M. Kemler, Cecelia Huglen. .95 pap.,
1. Prayer—Lutheran Church.

*LEFEBURE, Georges 248.3
Simplicity the heart of prayer translated by Dinah Livingstone. Foreword by Simon Tugwell New York, Paulist Press, [1975] 73 p. 21 cm. [BV210] ISBN 0-8091-1881-5 2.45 (pbk.)
1. Prayer. I. Title.

LEFEBVRE, Georges, 1908- 248'.3
Simplicity, the heart of prayer / Georges Lefebvre ; translated by Dinah Livingstone ; foreword by Simon Tugwell. New York : Paulist Press, [1975] 73 p. ; 21 cm. Translation of Simplicite de la priere. [BV210.2.L3813] 75-314214 ISBN 0-8091-1881-5 : 2.45
1. Prayer. I. Title.

LE GRICE, Edwin 248.3
Pattern for prayer [a work book for children] Illus. by David Pepin. New York, Morehouse [c.1963] 40p. illus. 25cm. 63-19477 .75 pap.,
1. Prayer—Juvenile literature. I. Title.

LEKEUX, Martial, 1884- 248.3
The art of prayer. Translated by Paul Joseph Oligny. Chicago, Franciscan Herald Press [1959] 306p. 20cm. [BV210.2.L413] 59-14706
1. Prayer. I. Title.

LE SAUX, Henri, 1910- 248'.3
Prayer [by] Abhishiktananda. Philadelphia, Westminster Press [1973, c1967] 81 p. 19 cm. Includes bibliographical references. [BL560.L47 1973] 73-600 ISBN 0-664-24973-6 1.95 (pbk.)
1. Prayer—Comparative studies. I. Title.

LESHAN, Lawrence L., 1920- 248'.3
How to meditate; a guide to self-discovery, by Lawrence LeShan. Boston, G. K. Hall, 1974. p. cm. Large print ed. [BL627.L47 1974b] 74-18107 ISBN 0-8161-6256-5 9.95 (lib. bdg.)
1. Meditation. 2. Sight-saving books. I. Title.

LESHAN, Lawrence L., 1920- 248'.3
How to meditate: a guide to self-discovery [by] Lawrence LeShan. Afterword by Edgar N. Jackson. [1st ed.] Boston, Little, Brown [1974] 210 p. 21 cm. Includes bibliographical references. [BL627.L47] 74-6210 ISBN 0-316-52155-8 5.95
1. Meditation. I. Title.

LESHAN, Lawrence L., 1920- 248'.3
How to meditate; a guide to self-discovery, by Lawrence Le Shan, with an afterword by Edgar N. Jackson. New York, Bantam Books, 1975, c1974. 161 p. 18 cm. Includes bibliographical references. [BL627.L47] 1.95 (pbk.)
1. Meditation. I. Title.
L.C. card no. for original edition: 74-6210.

LESTER, Muriel, 1883- 248.3
Praying: how, when, where, why. [Westwood, N. J.] F. H. Revell Co. [1960] 64p. 17cm. [BV215.L445] 60-13096
1. Prayer. I. Title.

LEWIS, Clive Staples, 1898-1963. 248.3
Letters to Malcolm; chiefly on prayer. [1st American ed.] New York, Harcourt, Brace & World [1964] 124 p. 22 cm. [BV210.2.L44] 64-11536
1. Prayer. 2. Christian life — Anglican authors. I. Title.

LEWIS, Clive Staples, 1898-1963. 248'.3
Letters to Malcolm: chiefly on prayer [by] C. S. Lewis. New York, Harcourt [1973? c.1964] 124 p. 21 cm. (Harvest Book, HB250) [BV210.2.L44] 64-11536 ISBN 0-15-650880-X pap., 1.85
1. Prayer. 2. Christian life—Anglican authors. I. Title.

LINDSELL, Harold, 1913 248.3
When you pray. Grand Rapids, Baker Book House [1975 c1969] 182 p. 20 cm. [BV210.2.L5] 78-79466 ISBN 0-8010-5554-7 2.95 (pbk.)
1. Prayer. I. Title.

LINDSELL, Harold, 1913- 248.3
When you pray. Wheaton, Ill., Tyndale House [1969] 182 p. 22 cm. Includes bibliographical references. [BV210.2.L5] 78-79466
1. Prayer. I. Title.

LOTZ, Johannes Baptist, 1903- 248.3
Interior prayer: the exercise of personality [by] Johannes B. Lotz. Translated by Dominic B. Gerlach. [New York] Herder and Herder [1968] 255 p. illus. 22 cm. Translation of Einubung ins Meditieren am Neuen Testament. [BV4813.L613] 68-22451 5.95
1. Meditation. I. Title.

LOUF, Andre. 248'.3
Lord, teach us to pray. Translated by a Sister of the Anglican community of St. Clare, Oxford. Chicago, Franciscan Herald Press [1974] p. cm. Translation of Heer, leer ons bidden. [BV210.2.L6313] 74-7309 ISBN 0-8199-0532-1
1. Prayer. I. Title.

LUTHER'S small catechism in 248.3
prayer form. Minneapolis, Augsburg [c.1963] 29p. 14cm. Based on The small catechism, by Dr. Martin Luther, pub. in 1960. price unreported pap.,

MACDONALD, Hope. 248'.3
Discovering how to pray / Hope MacDonald. Grand Rapids : Zondervan Pub. House, c1976. 120 p. ; 18 cm. [BV210.2.M28] 75-37741 pbk. : 1.75
1. Prayer. I. Title.

MCELROY, Paul Simpson, 1902- 248'.3
The meditations of my heart; a collection of short meditations and prayers for comfort and inspiration, by Paul S. McElroy. Mount Vernon, N.Y., Peter Pauper Press [1972] 62 p. 17 cm. (Gifts of gold) [BV4832.2.M179] 72-183772 1.95
1. Meditations. I. Title.

MCSORLEY, Joseph, Rev., 1874- 248.3
A primer of prayer. New York, Deus Books, Paulist Press [1961, c.1934, 1961] 120p. Bibl. 61-8815 .75 pap.,
1. Prayer. 2. Meditation. I. Title.

MCWILLIAMS, Bernard F. 248.3
Our family prayer book, edited by Bernard F. McWilliams. Charlotte, N.C., Catholic Bible House [1967] xvi, 406 p. col. illus. 18 cm. [BX2130.M3] 78-3925
1. Catholic Church—Prayer-books and devotions. 2. Family—Prayer-books and devotions. I. Title.

MADELEINE, Sister. 248'.3
Nun-sense [by] Sr. Madeleine. [Rev. ed.] Englewood Cliffs, N.J., Englewood Cliffs College Press [1972] xi, 173 p. illus. 23 cm. Includes bibliographical references. [BX2182.2.M26 1972] 76-186932 2.50
1. Meditations. I. Title.

MARSHALL, Catherine Wood, 1914- 248'.3
Adventures in prayer / Catherine Marshall ; ill. by Ned Glattauer. Boston : G. K. Hall, 1975. p. cm. Large print ed. [BV210.2.M35 1975b] 75-17978 ISBN 0-8161-6317-0 lib.bdg. : 9.95
1. Prayer. 2. Prayers. 3. Sight-saving books. I. Title.

MARVIN, John, comp. 248'.3
A walk with God. Collected by Michael James. [Hollywood, Calif.] Stanyan Books

[1972] 59 p. illus. 20 cm. (Stanyan books, 38) [BV4832.2.M33] 71-182684 ISBN 0-394-48058-9 3.00
1. Meditations. I. Title.

MASTERS, Roy. 248'.3
How to control your emotions / by Roy Masters. Los Angeles : Foundation Books, [1975], c1974. p. cm. [BL627.M35 1975] 75-15708
1. Meditation. 2. Conduct of life. I. Title.

MEAD, J. Earl. 248'.3
With God in the heights [by] J. Earl Mead. Nashville, Tenn., Broadman Press [1972] 78 p. 19 cm. [BV4832.2.M383] 72-78540 ISBN 0-8054-5526-4
1. Meditations. I. Title.

MILLER, Lee, 1940- 248'.3
Inside the husk. [1st ed.] Atlanta, Ga., Droke House/Hallux [1972] 87 p. 22 cm. Selections from his radio programs. [BV4832.2.M49] 70-187034 ISBN 0-8375-6765-3 3.95
1. Meditations. I. Inside the husk.

MISKOTTE, Kornelis Heiko, 1894- 248.3
The roads of prayer [by] Kornelis H. Miskotte. Translated by John W. Doberstein. New York, Sheed and Ward [1968] 175 p. 21 cm. Translation of De weg van het gebed. [BV210.2.M5513] 68-26032 4.50
1. Prayer. I. Title.

MITCHELL, Curtis C., 1927- 248'.3
Praying Jesus' way : a new approach to personal prayer / Curtis C. Mitchell. Old Tappan, N.J. : Revell, c1977. 156 p. ; 21 cm. [BV229.M57] 76-49879 ISBN 0-8007-0843-1 : 5.95
1. Jesus Christ—Prayers. 2. Prayer. I. Title.

MORE, Thomas, Sir, Saint, 1478-1535. 248.3
Thomas More's prayer book; a facsimile reproduction of the annotated pages. Transcription and translation with an introd. by Louis L. Martz and Richard S. Sylvester. New Haven, Published for the Elizabethan Club [by] Yale University Press, 1969. xlv, 206 p. illus., facsims. 23 cm. (The Elizabethan Club series, 4) Consists of pages from A Book of hours, reproduced in full color, on which More wrote his prayer "A Godly meditacion," and pages from a Psalter, reproduced in black and white, containing MS. annotations and pen marks. Both texts, in Latin, were annotated while More was a prisoner in the Tower of London. "A companion volume to the Yale edition of the Complete works of Sir Thomas More." [BV284.G6M6 1969] 69-15454 12.50
1. Catholic Church. Liturgy and ritual. Hours. 2. Catholic Church. Liturgy and ritual. Psalter (Sarum use.) I. Martz, Louis Lohr, ed. II. Sylvester, Richard Standish, ed. III. Title. IV. Series.

MORTON, Clement Manly. 248.3
Adventures, in prayer [by] C. Manly Morton. Westwood, N. J., F. H. Revell Co. [1966] 115 p. 21 cm. [BV210.2.M6] 66-12438
1. Prayer. I. Title.

MORTON, Clement Manly 248.3
Adventures in Prayer. Westwood, N.J., Revell [c.1966] 115p. 21cm. [BV210.2.M6] 66-12438 2.95 bds.,
1. Prayer. I. Title.

MOSCHNER, Franz Maria, 1896- 248.3
Christian prayer. Translated by Elisabeth Plettenberg. St. Louis, Herder [1962] 297p. 21cm. (Cross and crown series of spirituality, no. 23) [BV210.M783] 62-15402
1. Prayer. I. Title.

MUEHL, William. 248'.3
All the damned angels. Philadelphia, Pilgrim Press Book [1972] 126 p. 22 cm. [BV4832.2.M82] 77-185414 ISBN 0-8298-0230-4 4.95
1. Meditations. I. Title.

MURPHEY, Cecil B. 248'.3
Prayer : pitfalls & possibilities / Cecil B. Murphey. New York : Hawthorn Books, [1975] vi, 153 p. ; 21 cm. Bibliography: p. 153. [BV210.2.M8] 74-22916 ISBN 0-8015-6016-0 : 3.50
1. Prayer.

MURPHY, Carol R. 248'.3
O inward traveller / Carol R. Murphy. Wallingford, Pa. : Pendle Hill Publications, 1977. 31 p. ; 20 cm. (Pendle Hill pamphlet ; 216 ISSN 0031-4250s) Bibliography: p. 30-31. [BL627.M88] 77-91637 ISBN 0-87574-216-5 : 0.95
1. Murphy, Carol R. 2. Meditation. I. Title.

NELSON, Rosanne E. 248'.3
Dear Jesus ... I'm so human [by] Rosanne E. Nelson. [1st ed.] Garden City, N.Y., Doubleday, 1973. xiv, 104 p. 22 cm. [BV4501.2.N44] 73-79699 ISBN 0-385-05924-8 3.95
1. Christian life—1960- I. Title.

NEWHOUSE, Flower Arlene Sechler, 1909- 248'.3
Gateways into light; processes of Western meditation, by Flower A. Newhouse. [1st ed.] Escondido, Calif., Christward Ministry [1974] 160 p. 23 cm. [BL627.N48] 74-75517 4.75 (pbk.)
1. Meditation. I. Title.

NORVELL. 248'.3
The miracle power of transcendental meditation. West Nyack, N.Y., Parker Pub. Co. [1972] 200 p. 24 cm. [BL627.N67] 72-2892 ISBN 0-13-585711-2 6.95
1. Meditation. 2. Success. I. Title.

NOVAK, Michael. 248'.3
A book of elements; reflections on middle-class days. Drawings by Karen Laub-Novak. New York, Herder and Herder [1972] x, 145 p. illus. 22 cm. [BX2182.2.N68] 72-3883 ISBN 0-07-073751-7
1. Meditations. I. Laub-Novak, Karen. II. Title.

O'CONNOR, Elizabeth. 248'.3
Search for silence. Waco, Tex., Word Books [1972] 186 p. 23 cm. Bibliography: p. 183-186. [BV5091.C7O27] 74-188067 4.95
1. Contemplation. 2. Devotional exercises. I. Title.

O'FLAHERTY, Vincent M. 248.3
Let's take a trip; a guide to contemplation [by] O'Flaherty. Staten Island, N.Y., Alba House [1971] 177 p. 22 cm. Includes bibliographical references. [BV5091.C7O33] 79-148681 ISBN 0-8189-0200-0 4.95
1. Contemplation. I. Title.

OLIVER, Fay Conlee. 248'.3
Christian growth through meditation / Fay Conlee Oliver. Valley Forge, Pa. : Judson Press, [1976] p. cm. Bibliography: p. [BV4813.044] 76-23252 ISBN 0-8170-0716-4 pbk. : 3.50
1. Meditation. 2. Christian life—1960- I. Title.

OLSEN, Kermit Robert, 1914- 248.3
The magnitude of prayer. [Westwood, N.J.] Revell [c.1962] 94p. 62-10737 2.00 bds.,
1. Prayer. I. Title.

O'MALLEY, William J. 248'.3
A book about praying / by William J. O'Malley. New York : Paulist Press, c1976. v, 127 p. : ill. ; 19 cm. [BV210.2.O45] 76-20954 ISBN 0-8091-1979-X pbk. : 1.95
1. Prayer. I. Title.

ORSO, Kathryn Wickey. 248'.3
It's great to pray. New York, Morehouse-Barlow Co. [1974] 96 p. illus. 22 cm. [BV210.2.O77] 74-80379 ISBN 0-8192-1177-X 4.95
1. Prayer. 2. Christian life—Lutheran authors. I. Title.

OSBORNE, Cecil G. 248'.3
Prayer and you / Cecil G. Osborne. Waco, Tex. : Word Books, [1974] 106 p. ; 22 cm. Includes bibliographical references. [BV210.2.O8] 74-78043 3.95
1. Prayer. I. Title.

*PAULUS VI, Pope, 1897- 248.3
16 Papal documents on the Rosary: Pope Paul vi, Pope John xxiii, Pope Leo xiii. [Boston] St. Paul Eds. [1966, i.e.1967] 96p. 18cm. .50 pap.,
1. Prayer. 2. Rosary. I. Title.
Available from Daughters of St. Paul, Boston.

PENNING de Vries, Piet. 248'.3
Prayer and life / Piet Penning de Vries ; translated by W. Dudok van Heel ; foreword by Theodore Zwartkruis. 1st ed. Hicksville, N.Y. : Exposition Press, [1974] x, 221 p. ; 21 cm. (An Exposition-testament book) Translation of Gebed en leven. [BV210.2.P4313] 73-91091 ISBN 0-682-47985-3 : 8.50
1. Bible. N.T. Gospels—Commentaries. 2. Prayer. I. Title.

PENNINGTON, M. Basil. 248'.3
Daily we touch Him : practical religious experiences / M. Basil Pennington. 1st ed. Garden City, N.Y. : Doubleday, 1977. 115 p. ; 22 cm. [BV210.2.P44] 76-20836 ISBN 0-385-12478-3 : 5.95
1. Prayer. 2. Spiritual life—Catholic authors. I. Title.

PETERSEN, Mark E. 248'.3
For righteousness' sake [by] Mark E. Petersen. Salt Lake City, Bookcraft, 1972. x, 308 p. 24 cm. [BV4832.2.P48] 72-75291
1. Meditations. I. Title.

PHILLIPS, Dewi Zephaniah 248.3
The concept of prayer. New York, Schocken [c.1966] vii, 167p. 23cm. Bibl. [BV210.2.P5] 66-14086 4.95
1. Prayer. I. Title.

PIPKIN, H Wayne. 248'.3
Christian meditation, its art and practice / H. Wayne Pipkin. New York : Hawthorn Books, c1977. xiii, 176 p. ; 22 cm. Includes index. Bibliography: p. 146-160. [BV4813.P53 1977] 76-19763 ISBN 0-8015-1279-4 : 6.95
1. Meditation. I. Title.

PITTENGER, William Norman, 1905- 248'.3
Praying today: practical thoughts on prayer, by Norman Pittenger. Grand Rapids, Eerdmans [1974] 107 p. 18 cm. [BV210.2.P53] 73-20146 ISBN 0-8028-1566-9
1. Prayer. I. Title.

PONDER, Catherine. 248.3
Open your mind to prosperity. Unity Village, Mo., Unity Books [1971] 185 p. 20 cm. [BJ1611.P773] 79-155720 ISBN 0-87159-092-1
1. Success. I. Title.

PONDER, Catherine. 248.3
Pray and grow rich. West Nyack, N.Y., Parker Pub. Co. [1968] xxii, 228 p. 24 cm. Bibliographical footnotes. [BJ1611.P775] 68-29606 6.95
1. Success. 2. Prayer. I. Title.

POTTEBAUM, Gerard A. 248'.3
Hello/goodbye. Compiled by Gerard A. Pottebaum. Photos. by Jack Hamilton. Winona, Minn., St. Mary's College Press [1972] 70 p. illus. 15 cm. [BV4832.2.P63] 72-77720 2.00
1. Meditations. I. Title.

POTTEBAUM, Gerard A. 248'.3
Love is ... Written by Gerard A. Pottebaum. Photos. by Jack Hamilton. Winona, Minn., St. Mary's College Press [1972] 69 p. illus. 16 cm. [BV4639.P64] 72-77721 2.00
1. Love (Theology)—Meditations. I. Title.

POTTEBAUM, Gerard A. 248.3
1,029 private prayers for worldly Christians [by] Gerard A. Pottebaum and Joyce Winkel. Dayton, Ohio, Pflaum Press [1968] 58 p. illus. 26 cm. (A Tree house production) [BV260.P65] 68-55960
1. Prayers. I. Winkel, Joyce, joint author. II. Title.

POWERS, Isaias, 1928- 248'.3
Stereoscopic prayer : putting together scripture and self / by Isaias Powers ; photography by Philip Dattilo. New York : Alba House, [1975] viii, 176 p. : ill. ; 18 cm. [BV210.2.P63] 74-22409 ISBN 0-8189-0298-1 pbk. : 2.50
1. Prayer. I. Title.

PRATER, Arnold. 248'.3
You can pray as you ought! / By Arnold Prater. Nashville : T. Nelson, c1977. 128 p. : ill. ; 21 cm. [BV210.2.P75 1977] 77-8883 ISBN 0-8407-5631-3 pbk. : 2.95
1. Prayer. I. Title.

PRAYER and community. 248.3
Edited by Herman Schmidt. [New York] Herder and Herder [1970] 153 p. 23 cm. (Concilium: theology in the age of renewal, v. 52. Liturgy) Includes bibliographical references. [BV213.P7] 70-98257 2.95
1. Prayer—Addresses, essays, lectures. I. Schmidt, Herman, ed. II. Series: Concilium (New York) v. 52

PRAYER in my life; 248'.3
witnesses by persons in various vocations. Edited by Sulon G. Ferree. Nashville, The Upper Room [1967] 80 p. ports. 16 cm. Messages delivered at The Upper Room, Nashville, Tenn., during the 1967 Easter weekend as a part of the international prayer fellowship. [BV205.P7] 67-30661
1. Prayer. I. Ferree, Sulon G., ed.

PRICE, E. W. 248'.3
Acts in prayer / E. W. Price, Jr. Nashville : Broadman Press, [1974] 31 p. ; 14 cm. [BV213.P74] 74-15278 ISBN 0-8054-9209-7 pbk. : 0.50
1. Prayer. I. Title.

PRIME, Derek 248.3
A Christian's guide to prayer [Westwood, N. J.] Revell [1964, c.1963] 63p. 18cm. 64-583 .75 pap.,
1. Prayer. I. Title.

PROGOFF, Ira. 248.3
The well and the cathedral; a cycle of process meditation. [New York] Dialogue House Library [1971] 63 p. 21 cm. [BV4832.2.P75] 79-169085 1.95
1. Meditations. I. Title.

PROGOFF, Ira. 248'.3
The well and the cathedral : a cycle of process meditation / Ira Progoff. New York : Dialogue House Library, [1976] c1971. p. cm. [BV4832.2.P75 1976] 76-20823 1.95
1. Meditations. I. Title.

QUOIST, Michel. 248.3
Prayers. Translated by Agnes M. Forsyth and Anne Marie de Commaille. New York, Sheed and Ward [1963] x, 179 p. 21 cm. [BX2183.Q613] 63-17141
1. Devotional literature. 2. Medititations. I. Title.

QUOIST, Michel. 248.3
Prayers. Translated by Agnes M. Forsyth and Anne Marie de Commaille. [New York] Avon [1975 c1963] x, 179 p. 21 cm. (An Equinox Book) [BX2183.Q613] 63-17141 ISBN 0-380-00406-2 2.95 (pbk.)
1. Devotional literature. 2. Meditations. I. Title.

RADCLIFFE, Lynn James. 248.3
With Christ in the Garden. New York, Abingdon Press [1959] 80p. 20cm. [BV210.R32] 59-5247
1. Prayer. I. Title.

RAGUIN, Yves, 1912- 248'.3
How to pray today. Translated by John Beevers. St. Meinrad, Ind., Abbey Press, 1974. 60 p. 21 cm. (Religious experience series, v. 4) Translation of Prier a l'heure qu'il est. [BV210.2.R2513] 73-85334 ISBN 0-87029-028-2 1.50 (pbk.)
1. Prayer. I. Title.

RAGUIN, Yves, 1912- 248'.3
Paths to contemplation / by Yves Raguin ; translated by Paul Barrett. St. Meinrad, Ind. : Abbey Press, 1974. ix, 154 p. ; 21 cm. (Religious experience series ; v. 6) Translation of Chemins de la contemplation. [BV5091.C7R313] 74-84160 ISBN 0-87029-032-0 pbk. : 3.95
1. Contemplation. I. Title.

*RAHNER, Karl. 248.3
On prayer. Glen Rock, Paulist [1968, c.1958] 109p. 18cm. (Deus bks.) .95 pap.,
1. Prayer. I. Title.

*REES, Jean A. 248.3
Challenge to pray. Foreword by Ruth Graham. Grand Rapids, Mich., Zondervan [1967.c.1966] 96p. 21cm. Pub. in England in 1966 by Oliphants. 1.50 pap.,
1. Prayer. I. Title.

REIDHEAD, Paris. 248'.3
Beyond petition; six steps to successful praying. Minneapolis, Dimension Books [1974] 84 p. 18 cm. [BV210.2.R35] 74-3684 ISBN 0-87123-037-2 0.95
1. Prayer. I. Title.

REINBERGER, Francis E. 248.3
How to pray, by Francis E. Reinberger. [Rev. ed.] Philadelphia, Fortress Press [1967] 138 p. illus. 22 cm. Bibliographical footnotes. [BV210.2.R37 1967] 67-10247
1. Prayer. I. Title.

RHYMES, Douglas A. 248'.3
Through prayer to reality [by] Douglas A. Rhymes. [Nashville] Upper Room [1974] 88 p. 22 cm. Continues the author's Prayer in the secular city. Includes bibliographical references. [BV210.2.R483] 74-81813 1.25
1. Prayer. I. Title.

RICHARDS, Jean H j248.3
Why do people pray? By Jean H. Richards. Illustrated by June Goldsborough. Chicago, Rand McNally [1965] 1 v. (unpaged) col. illus. 24 cm. [BV212.R5] 65-23976
1. Prayer — Juvenile literature. I. Goldsborough, June, illus. II. Title.

RICHARDS, Jean H. 248.3
Why do people pray? Illustrated by June Goldsborough. Chicago, Rand McNally [c.1965] 1 v. (unpaged) col. illus. 24cm. [BV212.R5] 65-23976 2.00 bds.,
1. Prayer—Juvenile literature. I. Goldsborough, June, illus. II. Title.

RIESS, Walter. 248'.3
Christ's love will make you live. St. Louis, Concordia Pub. House [1973] 96 p. illus. 20 cm. [BV4832.2.R53 1973] 72-97345 ISBN 0-570-03156-7 1.50 (pbk.)
1. Meditations. I. Title.

RINKER, Rosalind. 248.3
Communicating love through prayer. Grand Rapids, Zondervan Pub. House [1966] 125 p. 21 cm. [BV210.2.R49] 66-18940
1. Prayer. I. Title.

RINKER, Rosalind 248.3
Communicating love through prayer. Grand

Rapids, Mich., Zondervan [c.1966] 125p. 21cm. [BV210.2.R49] 66-18940 2.50 bds.,
1. Prayer. I. Title.

RINKER, Rosalind. 248.3
Prayer; conversing with God. Grand Rapids, Zondervan Pub. House [1959] 116 p. illus. 20 cm. Includes bibliography. [BV210.2.R5] 59-4291
1. Prayer.

ROBERTS, William. 248'.3
Teach us to pray. Liguori, Mo., Liguori Publications [1972] 71 p. 18 cm. (A Liguorian combination book) With, as issued, Herlong, T. L. Maturity revisited. Liguori, Mo. [1972] [BV213.R553] 72-81175 1.50 (pbk.)
1. Prayer. I. Title.

ROGERS, Dale Evans. 248'.3
Finding the way; selections from the writings of Dale Evans Rogers. Old Tappan, N.J., F. H. Revell Co. [1973] 60 p. 17 cm. Published in 1969 under title: God has the answers. [BV4832.2 1973] 73-3356 ISBN 0-8007-0604-8 2.50 (pbk.)
1. Meditations. I. Title.

ROGERS, Harold, 1907- 248'.3
Learning to listen, Lord. Waco, Tex., Word Books [1974] 104 p. 21 cm. [BV210.2.R63] 73-91689 1.95 (pbk.)
1. Prayer. 2. Prayers. I. Title.

SADHU, Mouni. 248.3
Meditation: an outline for practical study. London, Allen & Unwin, 1967. 3-364p. diagrs. 23cm. Bibl. [BL627.S3] 67-101766 8.00 bds.,
1. Meditation. 2. Yoga. I. Title.
American distributor: Hillary House, New York.

SANDERS, John Oswald, 248'.3
1902-
Prayer power unlimited / by J. Oswald Sanders. Chicago : Moody Press, c1977. p. cm. Includes bibliographical references and index. [BV210.2.S26] 77-23472 ISBN 0-8024-6808-X : 5.95
1. Prayer. I. Title.

SAVON, Herve 248.3
The church and Christian prayer, v.3. Notre Dame, Ind., Fides [1966, c.1965] 168p. 21cm. (Saint Severin ser. for adult Christians, v.3; Fides paperback textbks., PBT-19) Orig. pub. in France in 1963. [BV210.2.S313] 66-3237 1.75 pap.,
1. Prayer. I. Title.

SHEDD, Charlie W. 248'.3
Getting through to the wonderful you : a Christian alternative to transcendental meditation / Charlie W. Shedd. Old Tappan, N.J. : Revell, c1976. 128 p. ; 21 cm. Includes index. [BV210.2.S48] 75-43875 ISBN 0-8007-0780-X : 4.95
1. Prayer. 2. Meditation. 3. Devotional exercises. I. Title.

SHIRKEY, Albert P 248.3
Meditations on the Lord's prayer, by Albert P. Shirkey. Nashville, The Upper room [1964] 56 p. 20 cm. [BV230.S42] 64-8891
1. Lord's prayer. I. Title.

SHIRKEY, Albert P. 248.3
Meditations on the Lord's prayer, Nashville, The Upper Room [c.1964] 56p. 20cm. [BV230.S42] 64-8891 1.00
1. Lord's prayer. I. Title.

SHOEMAKER, Helen Smith. 248'.3
Prayer and evangelism. Waco, Tex., Word Books [1974] 119 p. 23 cm. [BV210.2.S518] 73-91552 3.95, 2.25 (pbk.)
1. Prayer. 2. Evangelistic work. I. Title.

SIMCOX, Carroll Eugene, 248'.3
1912-
Notes to the overworld [by] Carroll E. Simcox. New York, Seabury Press [1972] 127 p. 22 cm. Bibliography: p. 127. [BV4832.2.S526] 72-81029 ISBN 0-8164-0242-6 4.50
1. Meditations. I. Title.

SLADE, Herbert Edwin 248'.3
William.
Exploration into contemplative prayer / Herbert Slade. New York : Paulist Press, c1975. 221 p. : ill. ; 22 cm. [BV5091.C7S55 1975b] 75-329417 ISBN 0-8091-1904-8 pbk. : 3.95
1. Contemplation. 2. Prayer. I. Title.

SLAVES of the Immaculate 248.3
Heart of Mary.
Hail Mary, full of grace. Still River [Mass] 1958. 116 p. illus. 22 cm. [BX2163.S6] 58-14484
1. Rosary. I. Title.

SMITH, Don Ian, 1918- 248'.3
Wild rivers and mountain trails. Illustrated by Roy Wallace. Nashville, Abingdon Press [1972] 126 p. illus. 20 cm. [BV4832.2.S547] 72-1566 ISBN 0-687-45536-7 3.00
1. Meditations. I. Title.

SOLLE, Dorothee. 248'.3
Suffering / by Dorothee Soelle ; translated by Everett R. Kalin. Philadelphia : Fortress Press, c1975. 178 p. ; 24 cm. Translation of Leiden. Includes bibliographical references. [BT732.7.S6513] 75-13036 ISBN 0-8006-0419-9 : 8.95
1. Suffering. I. Title.

SPONG, John Shelby. 248'.3
Honest prayer. New York, Seabury Press [1972, c1973] 126 p. 22 cm. Bibliography: p. [125]-126. [BV210.2.S66] 72-90474 ISBN 0-8164-0245-0 4.50
1. Prayer. 2. Christian life—Anglican authors. I. Title.

SQUIRE, Aelred. 248'.3
Asking the fathers : the art of meditation and prayer / Aelred Squire. 2d American ed. Wilton, Conn. : Morehouse-Barlow Co., 1976, c1973. iii, 248 p. ; 22 cm. Includes bibliographical references and index. [BX2350.2.S65 1976] 77-354628 ISBN 0-8192-1221-0 : 5.95
1. Spiritual life—Catholic authors. 2. Prayer. I. Title.

STANLEY, David Michael, 248'.3
1914-
Boasting in the Lord; the phenomenon of prayer in Saint Paul, by David M. Stanley. New York, Paulist Press [1973] vi, 192 p. 21 cm. Includes bibliographical references. [BV228.S76] 73-84361 ISBN 0-8091-1793-2 2.95 (pbk.).
1. Bible. N.T. Epistles of Paul—Criticism, interpretation, etc. 2. Prayer—Biblical teaching. I. Title.

STEDMAN, Ray C. 248'.3
Jesus teaches on prayer / Ray C. Stedman. Waco, Tex. : Word Books, c1975. 184 p. ; 21 cm. (Discovery books) [BV210.2.S69] 75-14710 4.95
1. Jesus Christ—Prayers. 2. Prayer. I. Title.

STEERE, Douglas Van, 1901- 248.3
Dimensions of prayer. [1st ed.] New York, Harper & Row [1963] ix, 130 p. 20 cm. Bibliographical footnotes. [BV210.2.S7 1963] 63-6334
1. Prayer. I. Title.

STEPHENSON, Virginia. 248'.3
Agreement : an attitude of prayer / by Virginia Stephenson. 1st ed. Redlands, CA : Allen-Greendale Publishers, c1977. 92 p. ; 15 cm. [BV213.S72] 77-81161
1. Prayer. I. Title.

STRAUSS, Lehman. 248'.3
Sense and nonsense about prayer / by Lehman Strauss. Chicago : Moody Press, [1974] 123 p. ; 22 cm. [BV210.2.S77] 74-15324 ISBN 0-8024-7700-3 : 3.95
1. Prayer. I. Title.

STREET, Noel. 248'.3
How to meditate perfectly: develop spiritually, unfold psychically [by] Noel Street [and] Judy Dupree. Lakemont, Ga., Tarnhelm Press [1973] 93 p. 21 cm. [BL627.S77] 73-75097 ISBN 0-87707-118-7 1.95
1. Meditation. I. Dupree, Judy, joint author. II. Title.

*SUBRAMUNIYA, Master. 248'.3
The fine art of meditation, by Master Subramuniya. San Francisco Comstock House [1973] [40] p., illus., 14 cm. [BL627] 1.00 (pbk.)
1. Meditations. I. Title.

SUBRAMUNIYA, Master. 248'.3
Beginning to meditate. [2d ed.] Kapaa, Hawaii, Wailua University of Contemplative Arts [1972] 18 p. illus. 14 cm. (Aloha series) [BL627.S9 1972] 73-174898 1.00
1. Meditation. I. Title. II. Series.

TAYLOR, Florence Marian 248'.3
(Tompkins) 1892-
From everlasting to everlasting; promises and prayers selected from the Bible [by] Florence M. Taylor. New York, Seabury Press [1973] ix, 178 p. 22 cm. [BV4832.2.T39] 72-96339 ISBN 0-8164-0249-3 4.95
1. Meditations. I. Title.

TAYLOR, Jack R. 248'.3
Prayer : life's limitless reach / Jack R. Taylor. Nashville : Broadman Press, c1977. 168 p. : ill. ; 22 cm. Bibliography: p. 167-168. [BV210.2.T39] 77-73984 ISBN 0-8054-5258-3 : 5.95
1. Prayer. I. Title.

*TEEPLE, Douglas M. 248.3
The artist within; moments in meditation. New York, Exposition [c.1965] 61p. 21cm. 3.00
I. Title.

THOMAS, George Ernest, 248'.3
1907-
The power of prayer in business and the professions / G. Ernest Thomas. Nashville : Tidings, [1975] viii, 67 p. ; 19 cm. [BV210.2.T45] 74-27907
1. Prayer. 2. Businessmen—Religious life. I. Title.

THOMAS, James Moulton, 248'.3
1903-
Prayer power / by J. Moulton Thomas. Waco, Tex. : Word Books, c1976. 146 p. ; 22 cm. Includes bibliographical references. [BV210.2.T46] 75-36195 ISBN 0-87680-876-3 pbk. : pbk. : 3.50
1. Prayer. I. Title.

THOMAS, Nancy White. 248.3
On bended knee. Illustrated by Charlene Miller. Richmond, John Knox Press [1966] 61 p. illus. 21 cm. [BV210.2.T47] 65-14513
1. Prayer. I. Title.

THOMAS, Nancy White 248.3
On bended knee. Illus. by Charlene Miller. Richmond, Va., Knox [c.1966] 61p. illus. 21cm. [BV210.2.T47] 65-14513 2.00 bds.,
1. Prayer. I. Title.

THOMPSON, Betty, comp. 248'.3
The healing fountain; writings selected from contemporary Christians. Photos. by John P. Taylor. [1st ed. New York, Education and Cultivation Division, Board of Global Ministries, United Methodist Church, 1973] 206 p. illus. 21 cm. Bibliography: p. 201-204. [BR53.T49] 73-76166 1.45
1. Christian literature. I. Title.

TOWNSEND, Anne J. 248'.3
Prayer without pretending / Anne J. Townsend. Chicago : Moody Press, 1976, c1973. 96 p. ; 18 cm. [BV213.T63 1976] 76-1961 ISBN 0-8024-6807-1 pbk. : 0.95
1. Prayer—Addresses, essays, lectures. I. Title.

TROEGER, Thomas H., 1945- 248'.3
Meditation : escape to reality / Thomas H. Troeger. Philadelphia : Westminster Press, c1977. 120 p. ; 21 cm. [BV4813.T76] 76-45794 ISBN 0-664-24132-8 pbk. : 4.95
1. Meditation. I. Title.

TROEGER, Thomas H., 1945- 248'.3
Rage! Reflect. Rejoice! : Praying with the psalmists / Thomas H. Troeger. 1st ed. Philadelphia : Westminster Press, c1977. p. cm. [BV210.2.T76] 77-22755 ISBN 0-664-24293-6 pbk. : 3.95
1. Bible. O.T. Psalms—Criticism, interpretation, etc. 2. Prayer. I. Title.

TRUPO, Anthony, 1908- 248.3
The miracle power of transcendental meditation [by] Norvell. New York, Barnes & Noble Books, [1974, c1972] 200 p. 21 cm. (A Barnes & Noble occult book) [BL627.T78] ISBN 0-06-464009-4 2.15 (pbk.)
1. Meditation. 2. Success. I. Title.
L.C. card no. for original ed.: 72-2892

TURRO, James. 248'.3
Reflections ... path to prayer. [Paramus, N.J., Pastoral Educational Services, 1972] 96 p. illus. 29 cm. [BX2182.2.T87] 72-75632
1. Meditations. I. Title.

VASWIG, William L. 248'.3
I prayed, He answered / William L. Vaswig ; foreword by Agnes Sanford. Minneapolis : Augsburg Pub. House, c1977. 128 p. ; 20 cm. [BR1725.V34A34] 77-72457 ISBN 0-8066-1589-3 : 3.50
1. Vaswig, William L. 2. Vaswig, Philip. 3. Sanford, Agnes Mary White. 4. Faith-cure. 5. Prayer. I. Title.

WALTERS, Annette, Sister, 248'.3
1910-
Prayer-who needs it? Camden [N.J.] T. Nelson [1970] vii, 92 p. 21 cm. (A Youth forum book, YF 12) Includes bibliographical references. Discusses how, why, when and where one prays. [BV210.2.W27] 73-127078 1.95
1. Prayer. 2. Youth—Religious life. I. Title. II. Series: Youth forum series, YF 12

WARD, William Arthur, 1921- 248.3
comp.
Prayer is— Compiled and edited by William Arthur Ward. [1st ed.] Anderson, S.C., Droke House: distributed by Grosset & Dunlap, New York [1969] 120 p. port. 23 cm. [BV205.W3] 72-79400
1. Prayer. 2. Prayers. I. Title.

THE way of a pilgrim, 248.3
and the pilgrim continues his way. Translated from the Russian, by R. M. French. New York, Ballantine Books [1974] ix, 180 p. maps. 18 cm. [BX597.Z90732 1974] ISBN 0-345-24254-8 1.50 (pbk.)
1. Pilgrims and pilgrimages. I. French, Reginald Michael, 1884-, tr. II. Title: The pilgrim continues his way.
L.C. card no. for original ed.: 65-4899.

WAY of a pilgrim (The); 248.3
and, The pilgrim continues his way. Tr. from Russian by R. M. French. New York, Seabury [1965] x. 242p. maps. 21cm. (SP18) Orig. pub. in two separate eds. [BX597.Z90732] 65-4899 1.95 pap.,
1. Pilgrims and pilgrimages. I. French. Reginald Michael, 1884- tr. II. Title: Athe pilgrim continues his way.

WELDON, Wilson O. 248.3
A plain man faces trouble [by] Wilson O. Weldon. [Nashville] The Upper Room [1971] 95 p. 20 cm. [BV4832.2.W437] 70-170107
1. Meditations. I. Title.

WENHE, Mary B. 248'.3
How to pray for healing / Mary B. Wenhe. Old Tappan, N.J. : Revell, [1975] 96 p. ; 18 cm. [BV228.W46] 74-34299 ISBN 0-8007-0741-9 : 1.50
1. Bible—Prayers. 2. Prayer—Biblical teaching. I. Title.

WESTER, Jesse M. 248.3
Are you listening, by Jesse M. Wester. [Wilkinsburg, Pa., Mercury Press, 1971] vii, 100 p. 19 cm. [BV4832.2.W47] 78-173347
1. Meditations. I. Title.

WHELAN, Joseph P. 248'.3
Benjamin; essays in prayer [by] Joseph P. Whelan. New York, Newman Press [1972] 122 p. illus. 24 cm. Includes bibliographical references. [BV210.2.W45] 72-184543 4.95
1. Prayer. 2. Contemplation. 3. Christian life—Catholic authors. I. Title.

WHISTON, Charles Francis, 248'.3
1900-
Pray: a study of distinctively Christian praying. Grand Rapids, Eerdmans [1972] 154 p. 22 cm. [BV210.2.W475] 70-162036 2.95
1. Prayer. I. Title.

WHITE, Ellen Gould (Harmon) 248.3
1827-1915.
Communion with God. 107 p. 22 cm. "A devotional guide for the school of prayer, comprosed of materials drawn from the Bible and the writings of Ellen G. White, and issued under auspices of the Ministerial Association [of the Seventh-day Adventists]" [BV214.C6] 64-8716
1. Prayer — Study and teaching. I. Seventh-Day Adventists. Ministerial Association. II. Title. III. Title: How cities grew;

WHITE, John Warren, 1939- 248'.3
comp.
What is meditation? Edited by John White. [1st ed.] Garden City, N.Y., Anchor Press, 1974. xxii, 254 p. 18 cm. Includes bibliographies. [BL627.W47] 73-81126 ISBN 0-385-07638-X 1.95 (pbk.)
1. Meditation—Addresses, essays, lectures. I. Title.

WHITMAN, Allen, 1925- 248.3
Pray for your life. Design by Donald Wallerstedt. Minneapolis, Augsburg Pub. House [1971] 91 p. 21 cm. Bibliography: p. 87-91. [BV210.2.W48] 78-159010 ISBN 0-8066-1133-2 3.50
1. Prayer. I. Title.

WHITMAN, Virginia. 248'.3
Mustard; the excitement of prayer answered. Wheaton, Ill., Tyndale House [1973] 160 p. 18 cm. [BV220.W48] 73-81012 ISBN 0-8423-4640-6 1.25
1. Prayer. I. Title.

WILKINSON, Marjorie. 248'.3
A faith for all seasons [by] Marjorie Wilkinson. [Nashville, Tenn.] The Upper Room [1972] 106 p. 21 cm. Bibliography: p. 106. [BV4832.2.W549] 72-81796 1.25
1. Meditations. I. Title.

WILLIAMS, Harry Abbott. 248'.3
The simplicity of prayer / H. A. Williams. 1st American ed. Philadelphia : Fortress Press, 1977. p. cm. [BV210.2.W49 1977] 77-78649 ISBN 0-8006-1315-5 : 2.50
1. Prayer. I. Title.

WILLIS, Edward David. 248'.3
Daring prayer / David Willis. Atlanta : John Knox Press, c1977. 157 p. ; 21 cm. Bibliography: p. [152]-157. [BV210.2.W495] 76-44975 ISBN 0-8042-2249-5 : 6.95
1. Prayer. I. Title.

*WILSON, William Croft, 248'3
1931-1963
Pastoral prayers. With a foreword by

Raymond E. Gibson. New York, Exposition Press [1973] 55 p. 21 cm. [BV4832.2] ISBN 0-682-47689-7. 3.00
1. Prayer. I. Title.

WINWARD, Stephen F. 248.3
Teach yourself to pray. New York, Harper & Row [1962, c.1961] 191p. 20cm. 62-11137 2.75 bds.,
1. Prayer. 2. Prayers. I. Title.

WORTMAN, Arthur, comp. 248.3
Springs of devotion; inspiring writings about the meaning and joy of prayer. Illustrated by William Gilmore. [Kansas City, Mo.] Hallmark Editions [1969] 61 p. 20 cm. [BV205.W66] 70-79741 ISBN 8-7529-0094- 2.50
1. Prayer. 2. Prayers. I. Title.

WORTMAN, Arthur, comp. 248'.3
Springs of devotion : writings about the joy and power of prayer / selected by Arthur Wortman ; calligraphy by Rick Cusick. Kansas City, Mo. : Hallmark, c1975. 44 p., [1] leaf of plates : ill. ; 11 x 16 cm. (Hallmark editions) [BV205.W66 1975] 74-83759 ISBN 0-87529-408-1 : 3.00
1. Prayer. 2. Prayers. I. Title.

WUELLNER, Flora Slosson. 248.3
To pray and to grow. Nashville, Abingdon Press [1970] 159 p. 20 cm. Bibliography: p. 157-159. [BV210.2.W82] 70-124757 4.25
1. Prayer. I. Title.

YOUNG, Fred L. 248.3
The Saints at prayer, by Fred L. Young. [Independence, Mo., Herald Pub. House, 1967] 176 p. 18 cm. Bibliographical footnotes. [BV214.Y6] 67-24546
1. Prayer — Study and teaching. I. Title.

YOUNG, Fred L. 248.3
The Saints at prayer, by Fred L. Young. [Independence, Mo., Herald Pub. House, 1967] 176 p. 18 cm. Bibliographical footnotes. [BV214.Y6] 67-24546
1. Prayer—Study and teaching. I. Title.

YUNGBLUT, John R. 248'.3
Rediscovering prayer [by] John R. Yungblut. New York, Seabury Press [1972] xii, 180 p. 22 cm. Includes bibliographical references. [BV210.2.Y85] 72-76349 ISBN 0-8164-0238-8 5.95
1. Prayer. I. Title.

MAX, Peter, 1937- 248'.3'0222
Meditations, selected & illustrated by Peter Max. New York, McGraw-Hill Book Co. [1972] 1 v. (unpaged) illus. 18 cm. [BV4832.2.M35] 72-5874 ISBN 0-07-040990-0 3.95
1. Meditations—Pictorial works. I. Title.

RHEA, Carolyn. 248'.3'07
Come pray with me : the power of praying together / by Carolyn Rhea. Grand Rapids : Zondervan Pub. House, c1977. 129 p. ; 21 cm. [BV214.R43] 77-4951 ISBN 0-310-35601-6 pbk. : 2.95
1. Prayer—Study and teaching. I. Title.

ACKER, Julius William 248.32
Teach us to pray. Saint Louis, Concordia [c.1961] 135p. (Concord bks.) Bibl. 60-11414 1.00 pap.,
1. Prayer. I. Title.

ACKER, Julius William. 248.32
Teach us to pray. Saint Louis, Concordia Pub. House [1961] 135p. 20cm. (Concord books) Includes bibliography. [BV2102.A3] 60-11414
1. Prayer. I. Title.

BOASE, Leonard 248.32
The prayer of faith. St. Louis, B. Herder [1963, c.1962] 147p. 22cm. 63-1370 3.25
1. Prayer. I. Title.

BOUNDS, Edward McKendnee, 248.32
1835-1913.
A treasury of prayer, from the writings of E. M. Bounds. Compiled by Leonard Ravenhill. With foreword by David Otis Fuller. Minneapolis, Bethany Fellowship [1961] 192p. sPrayer. [BV210.B635] 69-27219
I. Title.

BUTLER, Basil Christopher 248.32
Prayer in practice. Pref. by Gilbert Hess. Baltimore, Helicon [1962, c.1961] 118p. (Benedictine studies, 3) 61-16856 2.95
1. Prayer. I. Title.

CANT, Reginald 248.32
Heart in pilgrimage; a study in Christian prayer. New York, Harper [c.1961] 147p. Bibl. 61-5257 2.50
1. Prayer. I. Title.

CARRUTH, Thomas A. 248.32
Total prayer for living. Grand Rapids, Mich., Zondervan [c.1962] 116p. 21cm. Bibl. 1.95 bds.,
I. Title.

CARRUTH, Thomas A. 248.32
Total prayer for total living. Grand Rapids, Zondervan Pub. House [c1962] 116 p. 22 cm. [BV210.2.C35] 63-1759
1. Prayer. I. Title.

COLIN, Louis, 1884- 248.32
The meaning of prayer. Tr. by Francis X. Moan. Westminster, Md., Newman [c.]1962. 302p. 23cm. 62-15997 4.25
1. Prayer. 2. Catholic Church. Liturgy and ritual. I. Title.

DANIELOU, Madeleine 248.32
(Clamorgan)
How to pray. Tr. from French by Miriam Hederman. Westminster, Md., Newman [c.1963] 129p. 19cm. 63-12250 2.50
1. Prayers. 2. Church year—Meditations. I. Title.

DANIELOU, Madeline 248.32
(Clamorgan)
How to pray. Translated from the French by Miriam Hederman. Westminster, Md., Newman Press [1963] 129 p. 19 cm. Translation of Vous prierez ainsi. [BV245.D273] 63-12250
1. Prayers. 2. Church year — Meditations. I. Title.

DAWSON, John B. 248.32
People of prayer. Nashville, Upper Room [c.1963] 64p. 19cm. .35 pap.,
I. Title.

FOSDICK, Harry Emerson, 248.32
1878-
The meaning of prayer. [New York] Association [c.1949, 1962] 186p. 18cm. (Giant reflection bk. 703) 62-5499 1.50 pap.,
1. Prayer. 2. Devotional exercises. I. Title.

GERTRUDE, Sister O. M. S. 248.32
H
Christian prayer. New York, Association Press [c1959] 79 p. 19 cm. (World Christian books, 2d ser., no. 27) [BV210.2.G4] 59-14238
1. Prayer. I. Title.

GRAEF, Richard, 1899- 248.32
The power of prayer. Tr. from German by John J. Coyne. Westminster, Md., Newman [c.]1961. 139p. 61-65791 2.95
1. Prayer. I. Title.

HALL, Asa Zadel 248.32
Prayers in the space age. Grand Rapids, Mich., Zondervan [c.1963] 64p. 21cm. 1.00 pap.,
I. Title.

HAND, Thomas A 248.32
St. Augustine on prayer. Westminster, Md., Newman Press [1963] x. 133 p. 23 cm. Bibliography: p. 131. [BR65.A9H3] 63-24343
1. Augustinus, Aurelius, Saint, Bp. of Hippo. 2. Prayer—Hist. I. Title.

HAND, Thomas A. 248.32
St. Augustine on prayer. Westminster, Md., Newman [c.1963] x, 133p. 23cm. Bibl. 63-24343 3.25
1. Augustinus, Aurelius, Saint, Bp. of Hippo. 2. Prayer—Hist. I. Title.

HETTINGER, E D 248.32
Miracles through prayer. Plymouth, Pa., Helmbold Press, 1960. 166p. 20cm. Prose and poems. [BV220.H45] 60-37314
1. Prayer. 2. Miracles. I. Title.

JOHNSON, Ben C. 248.32
An adventure in prayer: a guide for groups and individuals. Nashville, Upper Room [c.1962] c64p. 17cm. Bibl. .35 pap.,
I. Title.

LOAVASIK, Lawrence George, 248.32
1913-
Prayer in Catholic life. New York, Macmillan, 1961. 197p. 22cm. [BV210.2.L65] 61-10341
1. Prayer. I. Title.

LOVASIK, Lawrence George, 248.32
1913-
Prayer in Catholic life. New York, Macmillan [c.]1961. 197p. 61-10341 3.95
1. Prayer. I. Title.

MASSEY, James Earl. 248.32
'When thou prayest'; an interpretation of Christian prayer according to the teachings of Jesus. Anderson, Ind., Warner Press [1960] 64p. 19cm. [BV215.M37] 60-11403
1. Prayer I. Title.

MURPHY, Joseph, 1898- 248.32
Techniques in prayer therapy. San Gabriel, Calif., Willing Pub. Co. [1960] 213p. 20cm. [BF639.M838] 60-37398
1. New thought. 2. Faith-cure. I. Title.

OECHSLIN, Raphael Louis, 248.32
1907-
Louis of Granada. St. Louis, B. Herder [1963, c.1962] 142p. 23cm. Bibl. 63-3129 4.20
1. Luis, de Granada, 1504-1588. 2. Prayer. I. Title.

PERRIN, Joseph Marie, 248.32
1905-
Living with God. St. Louis, B. Herder Book Co. [1961] 165p. 20cm. [BV210.2.P453] 61-2915
1. Prayer I. Title.

PRAYER--ITS deeper 248.32
dimensions; a Christian Life symposium. Grand Rapids, Mich., Zondervan [1963] 88p. 21cm. 1.95 bds.,

SANDERS, J. Oswald 248.32
Effective prayer. Chicago, Moody [1963, c.1961] 59p. 18cm. (China Inland mission bk.; compact bks., 28) .29 pap.,
I. Title.

SANGSTER, William Edwin, 248.32
1900-
Teach me to pray. Nashville, The Upper room [1959] 64p. 19cm. 'Previously published in [three booklets] ... under the titles: Teach us to pray, How to form a prayer cell [and] How to live in Christ.' [BV215.S25] 59-15667
1. Prayer. I. Sangster, William Edwin, 1900- Teach us to pray. II. Sangster, William Edwin, 1900- How to form a prayer cell. III. Sangster, aSangster, William Edwin, 1900- How to live in Christ. IV. Title.

SHEEHY, John F. 248.32
When you pray. Notre Dame, Ind., Fides Publishers Association [1961] 167 p. 21 cm. Includes bibliography. [BV210.2.S5] 61-10365
1. Prayer. I. Title.

SHEEHY, John F. 248.32
When you pray. Notre Dame, Ind., Fides [c.1961] 167p. Bibl. 61-10365 2.95 bds.,
1. Prayer. I. Title.

STEERE, Douglas Van, 1901- 248.32
Dimensions of prayer. New York, Harper [c.1962, 1963] 126p. 19cm. Bibl. 62-11822 2.50
1. Prayer. I. Title.

STEERE, Douglas Van, 1901- 248.32
Dimensions of prayer. [New York], 475 Riverside Dr., Women's Division of Christian Service Bd. of Missions, Methodist Church, [c.1962] 126p. 19cm. Bibl. 62-11822 1.00 pap.,
1. Prayer. I. Title.

TOLSON, Chester L 248.32
Peace and power through prayer [by] Chester L. Tolson and Clarence W. Lieb. With an introd. by Norman Vincent Peale. Englewood Cliffs, N.J., Prentice-Hall [1962?] 103 p. 21 cm. [BV210.2.T6] 62-17783
1. Prayer. 2. Prayers. I. Lieb, Clarence William, 1885- joint author. II. Title.

TOLSSON, Chester L. 248.32
Peace and power through prayer [by] Chester L. Tolson, Clarence W. Lieb, M.D. Introd. by Norman Vincent Peale. Englewood Cliffs, N. J., Prentice [1962] 163p. 21cm. 62-17783 3.50
1. Prayer. 2. Prayers. I. Lieb, Clarence William, 1885- joint author. II. Title.

VAN Zeller, Hubert, 1905- 248.32
Prayer in other words; a presentation for beginners. Springfield, Ill., Templegate [1963] 94 p. 20 cm. [In other words series] [BV210.2.V32] 63-25224
1. Prayer. I. Title

VAN DOOREN, L. A. T. 248.32
Prayer, the Christian's vital breath. Grand Rapids, Mich., Zondervan [1963] 88p. 21cm. 63-25418 1.00 pap.,
1. Prayer. I. Title.

VAN ZELLER, Hubert 248.32
[Secular name: Claude Van Zeller] 1905-
Prayer in other words; a presentation for beginners. Springfield, Ill., Templegate [c.1963] 94p. 20cm. (In other words ser.) 63-25224 2.95
1. Prayer. I. Title.

WEBB, Lance. 248.32
The art of personal prayer. New York, Abingdon press [1962] 100 p. 20 cm. [BV215.W4] 62-16255
1. Prayer. I. Title.

WEBB, Lance 248.32
The art of personal prayer. Nashville, Abingdon [c.1962] 160p. 20cm. Bibl. 62-16255 2.50
1. Prayer. I. Title.

WYON, Olive 248.32
Prayer. Philadelphia, Muhlenberg Press [c.1960] 68p. (bibl. footnotes) 20cm. (Fortress books) 60-3754 1.00 bds.,
1. Prayer. I. Title.

WYON, Olive 248.32
The school of prayers. New York, Macmillan [1963] 192p. 18cm. (mp 132) Bibl. .95 pap.,
1. Prayer. I. Title.

WYON, Olive, 1890- 248.32
Prayer. Philadelphia, Muhlenberg Press [1960] Includes bibliography. [BV215.W9] 60-3754
1. Prayer. I. Title.

BRICKEY, Janice 248.36
The triumphant way; rosary meditations. Foreword by Patrick J. Peyton. Pictures by Fra Angelico. St. Louis, Herder [c.1962] 95p. 18cm. 61-18371 .95 pap.,
1. Rosary—Meditations. I. Title.

FERRARO, John. 248.36
Ten series of meditations on the mysteries of the Rosary. [Boston, St. Paul Editions, 1964] 229 p. illus. 19 cm. Cover title: Mysteries of the Rosary. [BX2163.F45] 64-21600
1. Rosary—Meditations. I. Title. II. Title: Mysteries of the Rosary.

FERRARO, John 248.36
Ten series of meditations on the mysteries of the Rosary. [dist. Boston, Daughters of St. Paul [c.1964] 229p. illus. 19cm. Cover title: Mysteries of the Rosary. 64-21600 2.25; 1.25 pap.,
1. Rosary—Meditations. I. Title. II. Title: Mysteries of the Rosary.

GEARON, Patrick J. 248.36
The Rosary for boys and girls. Chicago, 6415 Woodlawn Ave., Carmelite Third Order Press, 1961 201p. 2.00
I. Title.

GEARON, Patrick J., 1890- 248.36
The Rosary for children. Chicago, Carmelite Third Order Pr. [c.1961] 150p. 2.00 bds.,
I. Title.

GENOVESE, Mary Rosalia, 248.36
Sister.
The Rosary and the living word. Baltimore, Helicon [1965] 222 p. (chiefly illus.) 16 cm. "Pictures illustrating the mysteries of the Rosary." Includes bibliographical references. [BX2163.G4] 64-22969
1. Rosaries—Meditations. I. Title.

GENOVESE, Mary Rosalia, 248.36
Sister
The Rosary and the living word. Helicon [dist. New York, Taplinger. c.1965] 222p. (chiefly illus.) 16cm. Pictures illus. the mysteries of the Rosary. Bibl. [BX2163.G4] 64-22969 4.95
1. Rosaries—Meditations. I. Title.

HAMMES, John A. 248.36
To help you say the Rosary better; practical Rosary meditations from scripture, the liturgy and the writings of the saints. Paterson, N.J. St. Anthony Guild Pr. [c.1962] 143p. 2.00; 1.50 pap.,
I. Title.

JOYFUL mysteries of the 248.36
Rosary: pictures to punch out and assemble [New York, Golden Press] c.1960. unpaged col. illus. 36cm. (A Guild punchout for Catholic boys and girls 30201) .50 pap.,

ROSS, Kenneth Needham, 248.36
1908-
The Christian mysteries. Derby [Eng.] P. Smith [dist. New York, Morehouse, 1965] 164p. 17cm. [BT303.R67] 64-1804 2.75 bds.,
1. Mysteries of the Rosary. I. Title.

THORNTON, Francis 248.36
Beauchesne, 1898-
This is the Rosary. With an introd. by Pope John xxiii. Original drawings by Alex Ross. [1st ed.] New York, Hawthorn Books [1961] 190 p. illus. 26 cm. [BX2310.R7T5] 61-13234
1. Rosary. I. Title.

THORNTON, Francis 248.36
Beauchesne. 1898-
This is the Rosary. Introd. by Pope John XXIII. Drawings by Alex Ross. New York, Hawthorn [c.1961] 190p. 26cm. Bibl. 61-13234 4.95 bds.,
1. Rosary. I. Title.

BARCLAY, William, 248.37
lecturer in the University of Glasgow.
A book of everyday prayers. New York, Harper [1960, c.1959] 128p. 20cm. 60-5326 2.50
1. Prayers. I. Title.

BARTLETT, Robert Merrill, 248.37
1898-
With one voice; prayers from around the world. New York, Crowell [1961] 181 p. 21 cm. [BL560.B3] 61-14530

1. Prayers. I. Title.

BROOKE, Avery. 248.37
Youth talks with God; a book of everyday prayers. New York, Scribner [1959] 55p. 18cm. [BV283.Y6B7] 59-11606
1. Youth—Prayer-books and devotions—English. I. Title.

CULLY, Kendig Brubaker, 248.37
ed.
Prayers for church workers. Philadelphia, Westminster Press [c.1961] 109p. 61-5076 2.00
1. Prayers. I. Title.

CUSHING, Richard James, 248.37
Cardinal, 1895-
Thoughts and reflections for Lent. [Boston] St. Paul Editions [1963] 155 p. illus. 20 cm. [BX2170.L4C8] 63-13909
1. Lent — Prayer-books and devotions — English. I. Title.

CUSHING, Richard James 248.37
Cardinal, 1895-
Thoughts and reflections for Lent. [Boston] St. Paul Eds. [dist. Daughters of St. Paul, c.1963] 155p. illus. 20cm. 63-13909 2.00; 1.00 pap.,
1. Lent—Prayer-books and devotions—English. I. Title.

DOBERSTEIN, John W. ed. 248.37
A Lutheran prayer book. Philadelphia, Muhlenberg Press [c.1960] xi, 146 p., 19 cm. illus. (6 p. bibl.) 60-6186 2.50
1. Lutheran Church—Prayer-books and devotions—English. I. Title.

GREENE, Barbara, comp. 248.37
God of a hundred names; prayers of many peoples and creeds collected and arranged by Barbara Greene and Victor Gollancz. [1st ed. in the U. S. A.] Garden City, N. Y., Doubleday, 1963 [c1962] 297 p. 22 cm. [BV245.G66 1963] 63-12347
1. Prayers. I. Gollancz, Victor, 1893-1967, joint comp. II. Title.

HAMMAN, Gauthier Adalbert 248.37
ed.
Early Christian prayers, Tr. [from French] by Walter Mitchell. Chicago, Regnery. [c.1961] xiii, 320p. Bibl. 61-65675 7.50
1. Prayers. 2. Christian literature, Early (Selections: Extracts, etc.) I. Title.

HEAD, David. 248.37
Shout for joy; a book of prayers faintly echoing the voices of seraphim and cherubim and thrones, dominions, virtues and powers, principalities, angels and archangels, the saints in light, and the great High Priest that is passed into the heavens. New York, Macmillan, 1962 [c1961] 156 p. 28 cm. [[BV260]] A62
1. Prayers. I. Title.

HEAD, David 248.37
Shout for joy; a book of prayers faintly echoing the seraphim and cherubim and thrones, dominions, virtues and powers, principalities, angels and archangels, the saints in light, and the great High Priest that is passed into the heavens. New York, Macmillan, 1962[c.1961] 156p. 18cm. A62 1.95 bds.,
1. Prayers. I. Title.

HILBURN, May Stafford 248.37
One hundred short prayers. New York, 34 W. 33 St., Macoy Pub. & Masonic Supply Co. [1963] unpaged. 16cm. 63-15810 1.50 bds.,
1. Prayers. I. Title.

HOFFMAN, Hazel 248.37
The greatest of these is love; God's holy words mingled with roses, by Hazel Hoffman; Verses and affectionate sentiments, by Audrey McDaniel. Norwalk, Conn., Knight St. C. R. Gibson Co., [c.1962] 40p. 22cm. illus. (pt. col.) 2.50; 3.50 deluxe ed.
1. Prayers—Private—Collections. I. McDaniel, Audrey, Verses and affectionate sentiments. II. Title.

KAUFFMAN, Donald T ed. 248.37
A treasury of great prayers. Donald T. Kauffman, editor. Westwood, N.J., Revell [1964] 62 p. 17 cm. (A Revell inspirational classic) [BV245.K3] 64-20191
1. Prayers. I. Title.

KAUFFMAN, Donald T. 248.37
A treasury of great prayers. Westwood, N.J., Revell [c.1964] 62p. 17cm. (Revell inspirational classic) 64-20191 1.00 bds.,
1. Prayers. I. Title.

KIELY, Martha Meister 248.37
Devotions for women at home. New York, Abingdon Press [c.1959] 127p. 18 cm. 59-5122 1.75 bds.,
1. Women—Prayer-books and devotions—English. I. Title.

LAUBACH, Frank Charles, 248.37
1884-
Frank Laubach's prayer diary. [Westwood, N.J.] Revell [1964] iv. 63 p. 20 cm. "Diary ... kept during the first six months of 1937." [BV4811.L37] 64-12201
1. Devotional calendars. I. Title. II. Title: Prayer diary.

LAUBACH, Frank Charles, 248.37
1884-
Frank Laubach's prayer diary. [Westwood, N.J.] Revell [c.1964] iv, 63p. 20cm. 64-12201 1.50 bds.,
1. Devotional calendars. I. Title. II. Title: Prayer diary.

LEWIS, Frederick White, 248.37
1873-
Prayers that are different, Grand Rapids, Eerdmans [1964] 166 p. 22 cm. [BV245.L47] 64-16583
1. Prayers. 2. Pastoral prayers. I. Title.

LEWIS, Frederick White, 248.37
1873-
Prayers that are different. Grand Rapids, Mich., Eerdmans [c.1964] 166p. 22cm. 64-16583 2.95
1. Prayers. 2. Pastoral prayers. I. Title.

LITTLE book of prayers. 248.37
Illus. by Jeff Hill. Mount Vernon, N.Y., Peter Pauper Press [1961, c.1960] 60p. col. illus. 1.00 bds.,
1. Prayer, Private—Collections. I. Peter Pauper Press, Mt. Vernon, N.Y.

MACLEOD, Earle Henry. 248.37
Prayers for everyone, to meet every need. Grand Rapids, Zondervan Pub. House [1962] 84p. 18cm. [BV260.M25] 62-16806
1. Prayers. I. Title.

MARKOWITZ, Sidney L., 248.37
1905- comp.
Prayer for a day; prayers for all occasions and for people of all denominations. Based upon the Psalms, the Prophets, and ancient supplications. New York, Citadel [c.1964] xiii, 81p. 21cm. (C174) 64-21893 1.00 pap.,
1. Prayers. I. Title.

MY God and my all. 248.37
Chicago, Franciscan Herald Press [c1960] 288p. illus. 13cm. [BX2130.M9] 60-53102
1. Catholic Church—Prayer- books and devotions—English.

MYERS, Ernest W 1906- 248.37
Prayers for laymen by a layman. [1st ed.] New York, Greenwich Book Publishers [1959] 85p. 21cm. [BV260.M9] 59-8652
1. Prayers. I. Title.

PAINE, Howard, comp. 248.37
Book of prayers for church and home [comp. by] Howard Paine, Bard Thompson. Philadelphia, Christian Educ. Pr. [dist. United Church, c.1962] 195p. 21cm. Bibl. 62-15845 3.00
1. Prayers. I. Thompson, Bard, 1925- joint comp. II. Title.

PETER Pauper Press, Mount 248.37
Vernon, N. Y.
Little book of prayers. Illustrated by Jeff Hill. Mount Vernon [1960] 60p. illus. 19cm. [BV260.P45] 60-36295
1. Prayers. I. Title.

PIUS FRANZISKUS, Father. 248.37
Mother love; a manual for Christian mothers with instructions for the Archconfraternity of Christian Mothers. English revision of 1960 by Bertin Roll. New York, F. Pustet Co. [1960] 691p. illus. 15cm. [BX2353.P513 1960] 60-794
1. Mothers—Prayer-books and devotions—English. 2. Catholic Church—Prayer-books and devotions—English. I. Cathokic Church. Liturgy and ritual. English. II. Archconfraternity of Christian Mothers. III. Title.

PIUS XII, Pope, 1876-1958. 248.37
Complete prayers. Translated from the original texts by Alastair Guinan. New York, Desclee Co. [1959] 175p. illus. 22cm. [BV245.P5] 59-12713
1. Prayers. I. Title.

*PRATT, W. Stanley 248.37
Just a moment--for life. New York, Carlton [c.1964] 396p. 21cm. 3.50
I. Title.

SANDLIN, John Lewis. 248.37
Graces and prayers. [Westwood, N. J.] Revell [1959] 125 p. 17 cm. [BV260.S28] 59-14957
1. Prayers. 2. Grace at meals. I. Title.

SELNER, John Charles, 248.37
1904- ed.
Breviary and missal prayers. Edited and compiled from approved sources by John C. Selner. New York, Benziger Bros. [1959] 199p. illus. 16cm. Most of the prayers in Latin and English. [BX2063.S4] 59-13121
1. Clergy—Prayer-books and devotions-English. 2. Catholic Church-Prayer-books and devotions— English. I. Title.

STRATON, Hillyer 248.37
Hawthorne, 1905-
Prayers in public. Valley Forge [Pa.] Judson Press [1963] 128 p. 16 cm. [BV245.S78] 63-17863
1. Prayers. I. Title.

STRATON, Hillyer 248.37
Hawthorne, 1905-
Prayers in public. Valley Forge [Pa.] Judson [c.1963] 128p. 16cm. 63-17863 2.75
1. Prayers. I. Title.

THOMPSON, Blanche 248.37
Jennings, 1887-
All day with God. Milwaukee, Bruce [c.1962] 186p. illus. 15cm. 62-4262 3.00; 3.75, deluxe ed., bxd.
1. Catholic Church—Prayer-books and devotions—English. I. Title.

ULRICH, Louis Edward, 248.37
1918-
That I may live in His kingdom; devotions based on the new translation of Luther's Small catechism. Minneapolis, Augsburg Pub. House [1963] 232 p. 22 cm. [BV198.U4] 63-16605
1. Lutheran Church — Prayer-books and devotions — English. I. Luther, Martin, Catechismus, Kleiner. II. Title.

ULRICH, Louis Edward, 248.37
Jr., 1918-
That I may live in His kingdom; devotions based on the new translation of Luther's Small catechism. Minneapolis, Augsburg [c.1963] 232p. 22cm. 63-16605 3.50 bds.,
1. Lutheran Church—Prayer-books and devotions—English. I. Luther, Martin, Catechismus, Kleiner. II. Title.

VAN ZELLER, Hubert, 1905- 248.37
A book of private prayer. Springfield, Ill., Templegate [1960] 242 p. 18 cm. Secular name: Claude Van Zeller. [BX2110.V3] 60-4419
1. Catholic Church — Prayer-books and devotions — English. I. Title. II. Series.

VAN ZELLER, Hubert 248.37
[Secular name: Claude Van Zeller] 1905-
A book of private prayer. Springfield, Ill., Templegate [1964] 189p. 17cm. 3.50
1. Catholic Church—Prayer-books and devotions—English. I. Title.

ANDREAE, Fritz. 248.372
Children's prayer book [by Fritz Andreae and Josef Quadflieg] Baltimore, Helicon Press [c1962] 95 p. illus. 16 cm. [BV4870.A373] 63-539
1. Children — Prayer-books and devotions — 1961- I. Quadflieg, Josef, 1924- joint author. II. Title.

ANDREAE, Fritz 248.372
Children's prayer book [by Fritz Andreae, Josef Quadflieg] Helicon [dist. New York, Taplinger, c.1962] 95p. col. illus. 16cm. Bibl. 63-539 1.75 bds.,
1. Children—Prayer-books and devotions—1961- I. Quadflieg, Josef, 1924- joint author. II. Title.

CAMPBELL, Margaret, ed. 248.372
A Catholic child's book of prayers, selected by Margaret Campbell. Pictures by Rachel Taft Dixon. New York, Guild Pr.; dist. Golden Pr. [c.1961] 28p. col. illus. (Read-with-me bk.) 61-19722 1.00 bds.,
1. Children—Prayer-books and devotions—English. 2. Catholic Church—Prayer-books and devotions—English. I. Title.

HERZEL, Catherine B. 248.372
A heritage of prayer for boys and girls, by Catherine Herzel. Philadelphia, Fortress Press [1965] 110 p. illus. 16 cm. "Sources of prayers": p. 100. [BV265.H4] 65-10707
1. Children — Prayer-books and devotions — 1961- I. Title.

HERZEL, Catherine B. 248.372
A heritage of prayer for boys and girls. Philadelphia, Fortress [c.1965] 110p. illus. 16cm. Bibl. [BV265.H4] 65-10707 1.25
1. Children—Prayer-books and devotions—1961- I. Title.

HOLDEN, Elizabeth W comp. 248.372
Hear me, Father; a collection of children's prayers. [n. p.] 1961. 121p. 22cm. [BV265] 61-65651
1. Children—Prayer-books and devotions—English. I. Title.

ALL our days; 248.373
a book of daily devotions for youth. Philadelphia, Christian Educ. [c.1962] 383p. illus. 17cm. 62-12680 2.50
1. Youth—Prayer-books and devotions—English.

ALL our days; 248.373
a book of daily devotions for youth. Philadelphia. Christian Education Press [1962] 383p. illus. 17cm. [BV4850.A4] 62-12680
1. Youth—Prayer-books and devotions—English.

BEIMFOHR, Herman N 248.373
Prayers for young people, for personal or group worship. [Westwood, N. J.] Revell [1960] 128p. 27cm. [BV283.Y6B4] 60-8454
1. Youth—Prayer-books and devotions—English. I. Title.

BOLLINGER, Hiel De Vere, 248.373
1898- comp.
The student at prayer. Nashville, Upper room [1960] 96p. 16cm. [BV283.C7B6] 60-14671
1. Students—Prayer-books and devotions—English. I. Title.

CAVERT, Walter Dudley, 248.373
1891-
Prayers for Scouts. New York, Abingdon Press [1964] 110 p. 13 cm. [BV4541.2.C3] 64-21130
1. Boy Scouts — Prayer-books and devotions — English. I. Title.

CAVERT, Walter Dudley, 248.373
1891-
Prayers for Scouts. Nashville, Abingdon [c.1964] 110p. 13cm. 64-21130 .50 pap.,
1. Boy Scouts—Prayer-books and devotions—English. I. Title.

CAVERT, Walter Dudley, 248.373
1891-
Prayers for youth. New York, Abingdon Press [1962] 72p. 12cm. [BV283.Y6C3] 62-11519
1. Youth—Prayer-books and devotions—English. I. Title.

COOK, Walter L. 248.373
Daily life prayers for youth. New York, Association [c.1963] 95p. 15cm. 63-10379 1.95 bds.,
1. Youth—Prayer-books and devotions—English. I. Title.

COOK, Walter L. 248.373
Everyday devotions for youth. Nashville, Abingdon [c.1961] 110p. 16cm. 61-11783 1.75 bds.,
1. Youth—Prayer-books and devotions—English. I. Title.

COUCH, Helen F. 248.373
Devotions for junior highs [by] Helen F. Couch and Sam S. Barefield. New York, Abingdon Press [1960] 111 p. 18 cm. Bibliography: p. 111. [BV4870.C65] 60-12071
1. Children—Prayer-books and devotions. I. Barefield, Sam S., joint author. II. Title.

CUDDESDON College, 248.373
Cuddesdon, Eng.
The Cuddesdon College office book. New York, Oxford [1961] xvi, 243p. 16cm. 62-151 2.40
1. Universities and colleges—Prayers. 2. Church of England—Prayer-books and devotions—English. I. Title.

HAYWARD, Percy R. 248.373
Young people's prayers: religion at work in life. Illus. by Chester Bratten. New York, Association [1962, c.1945] 122p. (Keen-age reflection bk.) .50 pap.,
I. Title.

KELLY, William L 248.373
Youth before God; prayers and thoughts. Westminster, Md., Newman Press [1958] 416p. illus. 15cm. 'Adapted ... from the German verson 'Jugend vor Gott,' by Alfonso Pereira, S. J. and from the French version 'Rabboni,' by Fernand Leiotte, S. J.' [BX2150.K4] 58-11943
1. Youth—Prayer-books and devotions—English. 2. Catholic Church—Prayer-books and devotions—English. I. Title.

MCCREARY, William Burgess 248.373
When youth prays; one hundred daily devotionals for young people in the areas of faith, witness, citizenship, outreach, and fellowship. Anderson, Ind., Warner Press [dist. Gospel Trumpet Press] [1960] 112p. 19cm. 60-7925 1.25 pap.,
1. Youth—Prayer-books and devotions—English. I. Title.

ORLEANS, Ilo. 248.373
Within Thy hand; my poem book of prayers. Illustrated by Siegmund Forst. New York, Union of American Hebrew Congregations [1961] 70p. illus. 24cm. [PS3529.R475W5] 61-15353
I. Title.

ORLEANS, Ilo Louis 248.373
Within Thy hand; my poem book of prayers. Illus. by Siegmund Forst. NewYork, Union of Amer. Hebrew Congregations [c.1961] 70p. illus. (pt. col.) 61-15353 2.95
I. Title.

WITT, Elmer N. 248.373
Time to pray; daily prayers for youth. Drawings by Jim Cummins. Saint Louis, Concordia Pub. House [c.1960] 116p. illus. 20cm. 60-3998 1.00 pap.,
1. Youth—Prayer-books and devotions—English. I. Title.

BENSON, Margaret H ed. 248.374
The second Apron-pocket book of meditation and prayer, compiled and written by Margaret H. Benson and Helen G. Smith. Greenwich, Conn., Seabury Press, 1963. 93 p. 17 cm. [BV4844.B4] 63-11057
1. Women — Prayer-books and devotions — English. I. Smith, Helen (Glass) 1906- joint ed. II. Title. III. Title: Apron-pocket book of meditation and prayer.

BENSON, Margaret H., ed. 248.374
The second Apron-pocket book of meditation and prayer, comp., written by Margaret H. Benson, Helen G. Smith. Greenwich, Conn., Seabury [c.]1963. 93p. 17cm. 63-11057 1.50, pap., plastic bdg.
1. Women—Prayer-books and devotions—English. I. Smith, Helen (Glass) 1906- joint ed. II. Title. III. Title: Apron-pocket book of meditation and prayer.

CARLSON, Betty. 248.374
Life is for living; inspirational devotions for women. Grand Rapids, Zondervan Pub. House [1962] 136p. 21cm. [BV4844.C3] 62-3052
1. Women—Prayer-books and devotions—English. I. Title.

COOK, Walter L. 248.374
Prayers for men. Nashville, Abingdon [c.1962] 72p. 12cm. 62-14666 1.25
1. Men—Prayer-books and devotions—English. I. Title.

FERRIS, Theodore Parker, 1908- 248.374
Book of prayer for everyman. Greenwich, Conn., Seabury [c.]1962. 150p. 18cm. 62-17081 2.75 bds.,
1. Prayers. I. Title.

FRIDY, Wallace 248.374
Adult devotions for public and private use. Nashville, Abingdon Press [c.1961] 144p. 16cm. 61-6475 1.75 bds.,
1. Devotional exercises. I. Title.

GEISSLER, Eugene S. 248.374
Family man. Notre Dame, Ind., Fides Publishers [c.1960] xii, 157p. illus. 21cm. 60-8446 3.50 bds.,
1. Fathers. I. Title.

GELIN, Albert. 248.374
The Psalms are our prayers. Translated by Michael J. Bell. Collegeville, Minn., Liturgical Press [1964] 61 p. 20 cm. Translation of La priere des peaumes. [BS1433.G413] 64-56825
1. Bible. O.T. Psalms—Criticism, interpretation, etc. I. Title.

HARDON, John A ed. 248.374
For Jesuits. Chicago, Loyola University Press [1963] 463 p. 15 cm. [BX2 50.F7H34] 63-5708
1. Jesuits — Prayer-books and devotions — English. I. Title.

HARDON, John A., ed. 248.374
For Jesuits. Chicago, Loyola Univ. Pr. [c.1963] 463p. 15cm. 63-5708 4.00 pap.,
1. Jesuits—Prayer-books and devotions—English. I. Title.

HEAD, David 248.374
Stammerer's tongue; a book of prayers for the infant Christian. New York, Macmillan, 1960[ ] x, 106p. 20cm. 60-14295 2.50
I. Title.

KELLY, William L 248.374
Men before God; prayers and thoughts [by] William L. Kelly. Westminister, Md., Newman Press [1962] 335 p. illus. 15 cm. "Adapted ... from the German version, Manner sprechen mit Gott, by Rev. Franz Josef Wothe." [BX2110.K3463] 63-12252
1. Catholic Church — Prayer-books and devotions — English. I. Wothe, Franz Josef. Manner sprechen mit Gott. II. Title.

KELLY, William L. 248.374
Women before God; prayers and thoughts. Westminster, Md., Newman [1962] 351p. illus. 'Adapted . . . from the German version 'Frauen vor Gott,' by Eleonore Beck and Gabriele Miller,' 62-7482 2.95
1. Women—Prayer-books and devotions—English. 2. Catholic Church—Prayer-books and devotions—English. I. Title.

LOWDER, Paul D., comp. 248.374
Let us pray; a minister's prayer book. Nashville, Upper room [c.1963] 95p. 16cm. 63-13588 .75 bds.,
1. Clergy—Prayer-books and devotions—English. I. Title.

PRICE, Eugenia 248.374
A woman's choice; living through your problems, from confusion to peace. Grand Rapids, Mich., Zondervan [c.1962] 182p. 21cm. Bibl. 62-14439 1.50 pap.,
1. Woman—Religious life. I. Title.

REID, John Calvin, 1901- 248.374
Prayer pilgrimage through the Psalms. New York, Abingdon Press [1962] 128p. 21cm. [BS1433.R4] 62-7441
1. Bible. D. T. Psalms—Meditations. I. Title.

SERGIO, Lisa, 1905- ed. 248.374
Prayers of women. [1st ed.] New York, Harper & Row [1965] [BV283.W6S4] 65-10705
I. Title.

SMALLWOOD, Kathleen Ann, 1909- 248.374
Spilled milk; litanies for living [by] Kay Smallzried. New York, Oxford University Press, 1964. 85 p. 21 cm. [BV245.S6] 64-18339
1. Prayers. 2. Christian life. I. Title. II. Title: Litanies for living.

SMALLZRIED, Kathleen Ann, 1909- 248.374
Spilled milk: litanies for living. New York, Oxford [c.]1964. 85p. 21cm. 64-18339 2.95
1. Prayers. 2. Christian life. I. Title. II. Title: Litanies for living.

SUTER, John Wallace, 1890- ed. 248.374
Prayers for a new world. New York, Scribners [c.1964] xxxvi, 244p. 21cm. Bibl. [BV245.S85] 64-22754 4.95
1. Prayers. I. Title.

WILLIAMS, Ronald Colvin 248.374
Prayers for every occasion. New York, Exposition [c.1962] 87p. 21cm. (Exposition-testament bk.) 3.00
I. Title.

LOVASIK, Lawrence George, 1913- 248.376
Jesus, joy of the suffering. [Boston? St. Paul Editions [1964] 229 p. 19 cm. [BX2170.S5L68] 64-17752
1. Suffering. 2. Catholic Church — Prayer-books and devotions — English. I. Title.

LOVASIK, Lawrence George, 1913- 248.376
Jesus, joy of the suffering [Boston] St. Paul Eds. [dist. Daughters of St. Paul, c.1964] 229p. 19cm. 64-17752 2.50; 1.50 pap.,
1. Suffering. 2. Catholic Church—Prayer-books and devotions—English. I. Title.

MCEVOY, Hubert, comp. 248.376
In time of sickness; prayers and readings. Springfield, Ill., Templegate [1963] 251p. 17cm. 3.50
I. Title.

ABATA, Russell M. 248'.4
Helps for the scrupulous / Russell M. Abata. Liguori, Mo. : Liguori Publications, 1976. 127 p. ; 18 cm. [BX1759.5.S4A2] 76-21430 ISBN 0-89243-061-3 pbk. : 1.75
1. Scruples. I. Title.

ADAMS, Harry Baker, 1924- 248'.4
Priorities and people / by Harry Baker Adams. Saint Louis : Bethany Press, c1975. p. cm. Includes bibliographical references. [BV4501.2.A28] 75-31692 ISBN 0-8272-2924-0 pbk. : 3.25
1. Christian life—1960- 2. Decision-making (Ethics) I. Title.

ADAMS, Joey, 1911- 248'.4
The God bit. New York, Mason & Lipscomb [1974] xix, 252 p. 25 cm. [BV4596.E67A3] 74-5430 ISBN 0-88405-086-6 7.95
1. Entertainers—Religious life. I. Title.

ADOLPH, Paul Ernest, 1901- 248.4
Triumphant living. Chicago, Moody Press [1959] 127p. 22cm. [BT765.A28] 59-978
1. Sanctification. 2. Bible—Biog. I. Title.

AHLEM, Lloyd H. 248'.4
Do I have to be me? The psychology of human need [by] Lloyd H. Ahlem. Glendale, Calif., G/L Regal Books [1973] 202 p. illus. 20 cm. Includes bibliographical references. [BV4501.2.A35] 73-79843 ISBN 0-8307-0248-2 2.45
1. Christian life—1960- 2. Love. I. Title.

ALDRICH, Doris (Coffin) 248'.4
The mother/daughter mixing bowl, by Doris Coffin Aldrich and Jane Aldrich Franks. Illustrated by Beva Launstein. Portland, Or., Multnomah Press [1971] 191 p. illus. 23 cm. [BV4501.2.A37] 71-184331 3.95
1. Christian life—1960- I. Franks, Jane Aldrich. II. Title.

†ALMAND, Joan. 248'.4
Establishing values / Joan Almand, Joy Wooderson. Cleveland, Tenn. : Pathway Press, c1976. 144 p. : ill. ; 18 cm. (Making life count new life series) Bibliography: p. 143-144. [BV4501.2.A44] 76-17147 ISBN 0-87148-283-5 pbk. : 1.19
1. Christian life—1960- I. Wooderson, Joy, joint author. II. Title.

ANSON, Elva. 248'.4
How to keep the family that prays together from falling apart / by Elva Anson. Chicago : Moody Press, [1975] p. cm. Bibliography: p. [BV4526.2.A57] 75-25628 ISBN 0-8024-3794-X pbk. : 2.50
1. Family—Religious life. I. Title.

*APOSTOLON, Billy 248.4
Christians in the world. Grand Rapids, Mich., Baker Bk. [c.]1965. 93p. 21cm. (Apostolon's pulpit masters' sermons) 1.00 pap.,
I. Title.

ARDEN HOUSE CONFERENCE ON FAMILY LIVING, 1962. 248'.4
The Arden House Conference on Family Living. Harriman, N.Y. [1962] 108 p. illus., ports. 28 cm. Sponsored by Modess Family Life Institute. [HQ7.A7] 67-6703
1. Family — Congresses. I. Modess Family Life Institute. II. Title.

ARNOLD, Eberhard, 1883-1935. 248'.4
Lebensbeweise lebendiger Gemeinden; die liebe zu Christus und die liebe zu den Brudern. Rifton, N.Y., Plough Pub. House [1973] 29 p. 14 cm. [BV4639.A73 1973] 73-21274 ISBN 0-87486-117-9
1. Love (Theology) 2. Christian life. I. Title.

ARNOLD, Eberhard, 1883-1935. 248'.4
Living churches: the essence of their life; love to Christ and love to the brothers. [Translated from the German and edited by the Society of Brothers at Farmington, Pennsylvania] Rifton, N.Y., Plough Pub. House [1973] 30 p. 14 cm. Translation of Lebensbeweise lebendiger Gemeinden. [BV4639.A7313 1973] 73-21273 ISBN 0-87486-116-0 0.50 (pbk.)
1. Love (Theology) 2. Christian life. I. Title.

ARNOLD, Heini, 1913- 248'.4
Freedom from sinful thoughts: Christ alone breaks the curse. Rifton, N.Y., Plough Pub. House [1974, c1973] xv, 118 p. 15 cm. [BV4832.2.A73] 73-20199 ISBN 0-87486-115-2 1.50 (pbk.)
1. Christian life—1960- I. Title.

ARNOLD, Heini, 1913- 248'.4
The living Word in men's hearts : meetings held by our Elder Heini Arnold in connection with the Lord's Supper at our Darvell Community in England, September, 1974. Rifton, N.Y. : Plough Pub. House, [1975] c1974. p. cm. [BV4501.2.A73 1975] 75-1301 ISBN 0-87486-147-0 : 4.50
1. Arnold, Eberhard, 1883-1935. Innenland. 2. Christian life—1960- 3. Lord's Supper. I. Bruderhof Communities. II. Title.

ASHBROOK, James B., 1925- 248'.4
The old me and a new i; an exploration of personal identity, by James B. Ashbrook. Valley Forge [PA.] Judson Press [1974] 128 p. illus. 22 cm. Includes bibliographical references. [BV4509.5.A83] 73-16785 ISBN 0-8170-0630-3 2.50 (pbk.).
1. Identification (Religion) I. Title.

AUGSBURGER, Myron S 248.4
Called to maturity; God's provision for spiritual growth. Scottdale, Pa., Herald Press [1960] 132p. 20cm. [BV4501.2.A9] 60-242
1. Christian life. I. Title.

AUGSBURGER, Myron S. 248.4
Called to maturity; God's provision for spiritual growth. Scottdale, Pa., Herald Press [c.1960] xi, 132p. 20cm. 60-242 2.50
1. Christian life. I. Title.

*AUSTIN, Bill R. 248.4
What would Jesus do? Nashville, Broadman Pr. [1973] 95 p. 19 cm. "Life questions answered from The living Bible." [BJ1581] ISBN 0-8054-5132-3
1. Conduct of life. 2. Christian life—1960- I. Title.

AVEBURY, John Lubbock, Baron, 1834-1913. 248'.4
The use of life. Freeport, N.Y., Books for Libraries Press [1972] vii, 316 p. 22 cm. (Essay index reprint series) Reprint of the 1894 ed. published by Macmillan, New York. Contents.Contents.—The great question.—Tact.—On money matters.—Recreation.—Health.—National education.—Self-education.—On libraries.—On reading.—Patriotism.—Citizenship.—Social life.—Industry.—Faith.—Hope.—Charity.—Character.—On peace and happiness.—Religion. Includes bibliographical references. [BJ1571.A83 1972] 72-4585 ISBN 0-8369-2961-6
1. Conduct of life. I. Title.

*BAILEY, Roscoe J. 248'4
The Man Upstairs. Parsons, West Va., McClain Printing Co., 1973. 158 p. 23 cm. [BV4501] 72-97161 ISBN 0-87012-142-1 5.95
1. Christain life. I. Title.

BAILEY, Wilfred M. 248'.4
Awakened worship; involving laymen in creative worship [by] Wilfred M. Bailey. Nashville, Abingdon Press [1972] 157 p. 20 cm. Bibliography: p. 157. [BV15.B34] 73-185543 ISBN 0-687-02338-6 2.95
1. Public worship. I. Title.

BAIRD, Jesse Hays, 1889- 248.4
They who are called Christians. Philadelphia, Westminster Press [1965] 156 p. 21 cm. [BV4501.2.B37] 65-10953
1. Christian life—Presbyterian authors. I. Title.

BAIRD, Jesse Hays, 1889- 248.4
They who are called Christians. Philadelphia. Westminster [c.1965] 156p. 21cm. [BV4501.2.B37] 65-10953 3.50
1. Christian life—Presbyterian authors. I. Title.

BAKER, Gordon Pratt 248.4
A practical theology for Christian evangelism. Henry M. Bullock, gen. ed. Nashville, Graded Pr. [dist. Abingdon. 1966, c.1965] 94p. 19cm. Bibl. [BV4501.2.B38] 66-2892 1.25 pap.,
1. Christian life—Methodist authors. I. Title.

BAKER, James Thomas. 248'.4
Faith for a dark Saturday [by] James T. Baker. Valley Forge [Pa.] Judson Press [1973] 125 p. 22 cm. Includes bibliographical references. [BS550.2.B33] 73-2612 ISBN 0-8170-0588-9 2.50
1. Bible stories, English. 2. Christian life—1960- I. Title.

BARNETTE, Henlee H 248.4
Christian calling and vocation, by Henlee H. Barnette. Grand Rapids, Baker Book House, 1965. 83 p. 22 cm. Bibliographical footnotes. Bibliography: p. 81-83. [BV4740.B3] 65-20754
1. Vocation. I. Title.

BARNETTE, Henlee H. 248.4
Christian calling and vocation. Grand Rapids, Mich., Baker Bk. [c.]1965. 83p. 22cm. Bibl. [BV4740.B3] 65-20754 1.50 pap.,
1. Vocation. I. Title.

BARNEY, Kenneth D. 248'.4
If you love me ... / Kenneth D. Barney. Springfield, Mo. : Gospel Pub. House, c1977. 126 p. ; 18 cm. (Radiant books) "Adapted from Practical Christian living by Wildon Colbaugh." [BV4501.2.B383] 75-22611 ISBN 0-88243-889-1 : 1.25
1. Christian life—1960- 2. Christian life—Biblical teaching. I. Colbaugh, Wildon. Practical Christian living. II. Title.

BATEY, Richard A., 1933- 248'.4
Thank God, I'm OK : the Gospel according to T.A. / Richard A. Batey. Nashville : Abingdon, c1976. 112 p. : ill. ; 19 cm. Includes bibliographical references and index. [BV4501.2.B3842] 76-14358 ISBN 0-687-41389-3 pbk. : 2.95
1. Christian life—1960- 2. Transactional analysis. I. Title.

BATTEN, J. Rowena 248.4
Women alive; twenty-five talks on women of the Bible. Grand Rapids, Mich., Zondervan [1965, c.1964] 184p. 23cm. [BS575.B38] 65-3172 3.95 bds.,
1. Women in the Bible. I. Title.

BAUGHMAN, John Lee. 248'.4
Beyond positive thinking; the greatest secret ever told. [1st ed.] New York, Harper & Row [1974] xii, 113 p. 20 cm. [BV4501.2.B3844 1974] 74-4621 ISBN 0-06-060660-6 5.95
1. Christian life—1960- I. Title.

BAUMAN, Edward W 248.4
Beyond belief. Philadelphia, Westminster Press [1964] 127 p. 21 cm. [BR121.2.B3] 64-14088
1. Christianity — 20th cent. I. Title.

BEALL, James Lee. 248'.4
Strong in the spirit / James Lee Beall ; Wanda Wilson, editor. Old Tappan, N.J. : F. H. Revell Co., [1975] 160 p. 21 cm.

[BV4501.2.B387] 74-32467 ISBN 0-8007-0729-X pbk. : 2.95
1. Christian life—1960- I. Title.

BEERS, Victor Gilbert, 1928- 248'.4
The discovery Bible handbook; finding God's answers to life's questions [by] V. Gilbert Beers. Wheaton, Ill., Victor Books [1974] 159 p. 18 cm. (An Input book) [BV4510.2.B36] 74-76764 1.75 (pbk.).
1. Christian life—Miscellanea. I. Title.

BELL, Ralph S. 248'.4
Soul free / Ralph S. Bell. Denver, Colo. : Accent Books, c1975. 96 p. : ill. ; 18 cm. [BV4501.2.B392] 75-17369 1.45
1. Christian life—1960- 2. Church and social problems. I. Title.

BENSON, Dennis C. 248'.4
Electric love [by] Dennis C. Benson. Richmond, John Knox Press [1973] 118 p. 21 cm. [BV4501.2.B394] 73-5343 ISBN 0-8042-2050-6 3.95
1. Christian life—1960- 2. Interpersonal relations. I. Title.

BENSON, George, 1924- 248'.4
Then joy breaks through. New York, Seabury Press [1972] 139 p. 22 cm. [BJ1471.5.B45] 72-81023 ISBN 0-8164-0243-4 4.95
1. Guilt. 2. Conversion. I. Title.

BERKELEY JOURNAL OF SOCIOLOGY. 248'.4
Berkeley, Calif. v. in 25-28 cm. annual (irregular) Began publication with issue for spring 1955. Cf. New serial titles. 1950-60. Title varies: Berkeley publications in society and institutions. Vols. for issued by the graduate students of the University of California, Dept. of Sociology (called Dept. of Sociology and Social Institutions) by the Graduate Sociology Club, Univeristy of California. [HM1.B4] 65-9165
1. Sociology — Period. I. California. University. Dept. of Sociology. II. California. University. Sociology Club. III. Title. IV. Title: Berkeley publications in society and institutions.

*BERRY, S. Stanford 248.4
The living way; a guide to conscious oneness with the divine spirit of life. New York, Vantage [c.1963] 126p. 21cm. 3.00 bds.,
I. Title.

BERVEN, Ken. 248'.4
Blest be the tie that frees. Minneapolis, Augsburg Pub. House [1973] 104 p. 20 cm. [BX8080.B455A32] 73-83784 ISBN 0-8066-1337-8 1.95 (pbk.)
1. Berven, Ken. 2. Christian life—1960- I. Title.

BIBLE. English. Selections. 1973. 248'.4
Answers, compiled by David Shibley. Wheaton, Ill., Tyndale House [1973] 80 p. 20 cm. [BS391.2.S54 1973] 72-97652 ISBN 0-8423-0080-5 1.00 (pbk.)
1. Questions and answers—Christian life. I. Shibley, David, comp. II. Title.

BICKET, Zenas J. 248'.4
Walking in the spirit : studies in the fruit of the spirit / Zenas J. Bicket. Springfield, Mo. : Gospel Pub. House, c1977. 94 p. ; 18 cm. (Radiant books) Includes bibliographical references. [BV4501.2.B46] 76-51000 ISBN 0-88243-611-2 : 1.25
1. Christian life—1960- 2. Virtues. 3. Spirituality. I. Title.

BISAGNO, John R. 248'.4
Love is something you do / John R. Bisagno. New York : Harper & Row, [1975] viii, 102 p. ; 18 cm. (Harper jubilee books ; 12) [BV835.B55 1975] 75-9314 ISBN 0-06-060792-0 pbk. : 1.75
1. Marriage. I. Title.

BLACK, Don J., 1937- 248'.4
Warm tones and tiny miracles [by] Don J. Black. [Provo, Utah] Brigham Young University Publications [1972] vii, 136 p. illus. 23 cm. [BX8695.B54A3] 78-186682 ISBN 0-8425-1409-0
I. Title.

BLACKER, Diane. 248'.4
Totally new / Diane Blacker. Old Tappan, N.J. : Revell, c1976. 64 p. : ill. ; 20 cm. Includes bibliographical references. [BV4501.2.B54] 76-10249 ISBN 0-8007-0787-7 : 2.95
1. Christian life—1960- I. Title.

BLAIKLOCK, David A. 248'.4
Living is now [by] D. A. Blaiklock. Grand Rapids, Mich., Baker Book House [1972, c1971] 127 p. 18 cm. [BV4501.2.B5526 1972] 72-85669 ISBN 0-8010-0580-9 1.50
1. Christian life—1960- I. Title.

BLAIKLOCK, E. M. 248'.4
Why didn't they tell me? By E. M. Blaiklock [and] D. A. Blaiklock. Grand Rapids, Zondervan Pub. House [1972] 173 p. 18 cm. (Zondervan books) [BV4501.2.B555] 72-83883 1.25 (pbk.)
1. Christian life—1960- I. Blaiklock, David A., joint author. II. Title.

BLOCKER, Hyacinth 248.4
Don't fall out the window. Cincinnati, St. Francis Bkshop. [1962] 214p. 23cm. 62-17240 3.95
1. Spiritual life—Catholic authors. I. Title.

BOGGS, Evelyn (Bockley) 1914- 248.4
I believe; a book of personal reflections. Foreword by Norman Vincent Peale. [1st ed.] New York, Exposition Press [1959] 101p. 21cm. [BV4501.2.B6] 59-65451
1. Christian life. I. Title.

BOGGS, Evelyn (Buckley) 248.4
I believe; a book of personal reflections. Foreword by Norman Vincent Peale. New York, Exposition Press [c.1959] 101p. 21cm. 59-65451 3.00
1. Christian life. I. Title.

BOLITHO, Axchie A. 248.4
Consider what God is doing. Anderson, Ind., Warner Press [1963] 112 p. 19 cm. [BV4515.2.B6] 63-7919
1. Christian life — Stories. 2. Affliction. I. Title.

BOLITHO, Axchie A. 248.4
Consider what God is doing. Anderson, Ind., Warner [c.1963] 112p. 19cm. 63-7919 1.50 pap.,
1. Christian life—Stories. 2. Affliction. I. Title.

*BOLLINGER, J. W. 248.4
Lightning flash! A practical guide to a God-centered and God-directed life. New York, Exposition [c.1966] 80p. 21cm. 3.00
I. Title.

BONAVENTURA, Saint, Cardinal, 1221-1274. 248.4
The way of perfection, based on the Rule for novices of St. Bonaventure. [Translated by] Anselm Romb. Edited by Method C. Billy and Salvator Pantano. Chicago, Franciscan Herald Press [c1958] 96p. 19cm. (FHP text series) [B2350.5] 58-13683
1. Perfection (Catholic) I. Romb, Anselm M., tr. II. Title.

BONNER, Gerald. 248.4
The warfare of Christ. London, Faith Press; New York, Morehouse-Barlow [1962] 122 p. 19 cm. (Studies in Christian faith and practice, 5) [BR195.C5] A 63
1. Christian life — Early church. I. Title.

BONNER, Gerald 248.4
The warfare of Christ. London, Faith Pr.; New York, Morehouse [1963, c.1962] 122p. 19cm. (Studies in Christian faith and practice, 5) A63 1.50 pap.,
1. Christian life—Early church. I. Title.

BONTRAGER, John Kenneth. 248'.4
Free the child in you; take an adventure into joyful living through transactional analysis [by] John K. Bontrager. Philadelphia, United Church Press [1974] 192 p. illus. 22 cm. "A Pilgrim Press book." Bibliography: p. 189. [BV4501.2.B62] 73-22120 ISBN 0-8298-0272-X 5.95
1. Christian life—1960- 2. Transactional analysis. I. Title.

BOSTWICK, Catherine Finney. 248'.4
What is the new life? / by C. F. Bostwick. Vineland, N.J. : New Life Books, c1975. vii, 658 p. ; 24 cm. Includes index. [BV4510.A1B6] 75-7968 9.95
1. Christian life—Biblical teaching. I. Title.

BOWERS, George K/ 248.4
God--here and now! Anderson, Ind., Warner Press [1961] 144p. 22cm. [BV4501.2.B67] 61-7026
1. Christian life. I. Title.

*BOYCE, H. Spurgeon 248.4
Thoughts to ponder. New York, Carlton [1967] 119p. 21cm. (Lyceum bk.) 3.00
1. Christian life. I. Title.

BOYD, Malcolm 248.4
If I go down to hell; man's search for meaning in contemporary life. New York, Morehouse [c.1962] 215p. 62-12134 3.75
1. Christianity—20th cent. I. Title.

BREESE, Dave W. 248.4
Discover your destiny. Waco, Tex., Word Bks. [1966, c.1965] 98p. 23cm. [BV4501.2.B69] 66-1323 3.00
1. Christian life. I. Title.

BREWIS, J S 248.4
We have a gospel. With a foreword by the Bishop of London. London, New York, Longmans, Green [1959] 120p. 18cm. [BV4501.2.B7] 58-59471
1. Christian life. I. Title.

BRISCOE, D Stuart. 248.4
The fullness of Christ, by Stuart Briscoe. Introd. by W. Ian Thomas. Grand Rapids, Zondervan Pub. House [1965] 151 p. 22 cm. [BV4501.2.B73] 64-7846
1. Christian life. I. Title.

BRISCOE, D. Stuart 248.4
The fullness of Christ. Introd. by W. Ian Thomas. Grand Rapids, Mich., Zondervan [c.1965] 151p. 22cm. [BV4501.2B73] 64-7846 2.50 bds.,
1. Christian life. I. Title.

BRISCOE, D. Stuart. 248'.4
Getting into God : practical guidelines to the Christian life / D. Stuart Briscoe. Grand Rapids : Zondervan Pub. House, c1975. 156 p. ; 18 cm. [BS600.2.B73] 75-11016 pbk. : 1.50
1. Bible—Study. 2. Prayer. 3. Witness bearing (Christianity) I. Title.

BROKHOFF, John R 248.4
This is life. [Westwood, N. J.] F. H. Revell Co. [1959] 126p. 21cm. [BV4501.2.B76] 59-8722
1. Christian life. I. Title.

BROOKS, Julian. 248.4
Sixty days in oriental waters, and other stories. New York, New City Press [1969] 212 p. 19 cm. Contents.Contents.—Women are sometimes just more domestic than men.—Timothy Trinitrotoluene.—University under siege.—If you want me to, I can wash out your shirts.—Six heads instead of one.—A plot of ground cradling a memory?—Sixty days in oriental waters.—Julie's beauty treatment.—The imperturbable Mr. Briggs.—To be a mother means ... —The files of a policewoman.—With souls bared.—A Florentine teen.—I walk with Vincent.—The cruel dilemma. [BJ1597.B75] 70-77440 3.25
1. Conduct of life. I. Title.

BRYANT, Anita. 248'.4
Bless this house. Old Tappan, N.J., Revell [1972] 156 p. illus. 21 cm. [BV4526.2.B7] 72-8409 ISBN 0-8007-0547-5 4.95
1. Family—Religious life. I. Title.

BRYANT, Anita. 248'.4
Bless this house. New York, Bantam Books [1976 c1972] 157 p. 18 cm. [BV4526.2B7] 1.50 (pbk.)
1. Family—Religious life. I. Title.
L.C. card no. of 1972 Revell edition: 72-8409.

BRYANT, Anita. 248'.4
Light my candle [by] Anita Bryant and Bob Green. Old Tappan, N.J., Revell [1974] 159 p. illus. 21 cm. [BV4501.2.B79] 74-19091 ISBN 0-8007-0690-0 5.95
1. Christian life—1960- I. Green, Bob. II. Title.

BRYANT, Anita. 248'.4
Light my candle / Anita Bryant and Bob Green. Boston : G. K. Hall, 1975, c1974. p. cm. "Published in large print." [BV4501.2.B79 1975] 75-17902 ISBN 0-8161-6315-4 lib.bdg. : 9.95
1. Christian life—1960- 2. Sight-saving books. I. Green, Bob, joint author. II. Title.

BRYANT, Anita. 248'.4
Running the good race / Anita Bryant & Bob Green. Old Tappan, N.J. : F. H. Revell Co., c1976. 157 p., [4] leaves of plates : ill. ; 21 cm. [BV4501.2.B8] 76-46766 ISBN 0-8007-0809-1 : 5.95
1. Bryant, Anita. 2. Green, Bob. 3. Christian life—1960- 4. Physical fitness—Moral and religious aspects. I. Green, Bob, joint author. II. Title.

BRYSKETT, Lodowick, ca.1545-ca.1612. 248.4
A discourse of civill life. Edited by Thomas E. Wright. Northridge, Calif., San Fernando Valley State College, 1970. xxiv, 215 p. 23 cm. (San Fernando Valley State College Renaissance editions, no. 4) "Made up primarily of Bryskett's translation [and adaptation] of Giambattista Giraldi's Tre dialoghi della vita civile, the second, non-narrative part of De gli hecatommithi, 1565." Errata slip inserted. "A select bibliography of Lodowick Bryskett": p. 214-215. [BJ1600.B78 1970] 72-633841
1. Conduct of life—Early works to 1900. I. Giraldi Cintio, Giovanni Battista, 1504-1573. Hecatommithi. II. Title. III. Series: The Renaissance editions, no. 4.

BUMP, Glen Hale. 248'.4
How to succeed in business without being a pagan. Wheaton, Ill., Victor Books [1974] 132 p. 18 cm. (An Input book) [HF5386.B884] 74-77451 ISBN 0-88207-712-0 1.50 (pbk.).
1. Success. I. Title.

BURBRIDGE, Branse. 248'.4
The sex thing: you, love, and God. Wheaton, Ill., H. Shaw Publishers [1973, c1972] 124 p. illus. 18 cm. [BT708.B87 1973] 72-94100 ISBN 0-87788-763-2 1.25 (pbk.)
1. Sex (Theology) I. Title.

BURCHETT, Randall E 248.4
Chart and compass for Christian laymen; a study of great Scriptural truths selected from the Old and New Testaments. [1st ed.] Grand Rapids, Eerdmans [1960] 159p. 23cm. [BV4501.2.B85] 60-10089
1. Christian life. I. Title.

BURKHART, Roy Abram, 1895- 248.4
The person you can be. [1st ed.] New York, Harper & Row [1962] 260 p. 22 cm. [BV4501.2.B87] 62-7447
1. Chirstian life. 2. Success. I. Title.

BURKHART, Roy Abram, 1895- 248.4
The person you can be. New York, Harper [c.1962] 260p. 22cm. 62-7447 4.50 bds.,
1. Christian life. 2. Success. I. Title.

BUSTANOBY, Andre. 248'.4
You can change your personality : make it a spiritual asset / by Andre Bustanoby. Grand Rapids : Zondervan Pub. House, c1976. 162 p. ; 21 cm. Includes bibliographical references. [BV4501.2.B94] 75-45491 5.95
1. Christian life—1960- 2. Personality. 3. Conversion. I. Title.

BUTTERWORTH, Eric. 248'.4
In the flow of life / Eric Butterworth. 1st ed. New York : Harper & Row, [1975] xi, 109 p. ; 21 cm. Includes bibliographical references. [BJ1581.2.B84 1975] 75-9316 ISBN 0-06-061269-X : 5.95
1. Conduct of life. I. Title.

BUTTERWORTH, Eric. 248'.4
Life is for loving. [1st ed.] New York, Harper & Row [1973] x, 100 p. 21 cm. Includes bibliographical references. [BV4639.B88 1973] 73-6326 ISBN 0-06-061268-1 4.95
1. Love (Theology) I. Title.

CAGIATI, Annie. 248'.4
Peace-where is it? / by Annie Cagiati ; illustrated by C. Piccinni. Boston : St. Paul Editions, [1974] ca. 100 p. : chiefly ill. ; 18 cm. [BT736.4.C3] 73-91996
1. Peace (Theology)—Caricatures and cartoons. I. Piccinni, C., ill. II. Title.

CALDWELL, Louis O. 248'.4
A birthday remembrance / Louis O. Caldwell ; drawings by Leonardo M. Ferguson. Nashville : Abingdon, 1977. 63 p. : ill. ; 20 cm. [BV4501.2.C24] 77-7043 ISBN 0-687-03555-4 : 4.95
1. Christian life—1960- 2. Birthdays. I. Title.

CALDWELL, Marge. 248'.4
Speak out with Marge ... and you'll be gladder that you're alive / Marge Caldwell with Amelia Bishop. Nashville : Broadman Press, c1976. 137 p. ; 20 cm. [BJ1581.2.C23] 75-18090 pbk. : 2.95
1. Conduct of life. I. Bishop, Amelia, joint author. II. Title.

CALIAN, Carnegie Samuel. 248.4
Grace, guts & goods; how to stay Christian in an affluent society. New York, T. Nelson [1971] 161 p. 22 cm. Bibliography: p. [156]-158. [BR121.2.C23] 75-147912 ISBN 0-8407-5029-3 4.95
1. Christianity—20th century. 2. Wealth, Ethics of. I. Title.

CALKIN, Ruth Harms. 248'.4
Two shall be one / Ruth Harms Calkin. Elgin, Ill. : D. C. Cook Pub. Co., c1977. 128 p. : ill. ; 22 cm. [BV835.C33] 76-23349 ISBN 0-89191-057-3 : 6.95
1. Marriage. I. Title.

CALLAHAN, Sidney Cornelia. 248'.4
The Magnificat : the prayer of Mary / Sidney Callahan ; photos. by Ray Ellis. New York : Seabury Press, c1975. 103 p. : ill. ; 23 cm. "A Crossroad book." [BV199.C32M358] 75-15050 ISBN 0-8164-2594-9 : 4.95
1. Magnificat. I. Title.

CAPPS, Walter H. 248'.4
Time invades the cathedral; tension in the school of hope, by Walter H. Capps. Philadelphia, Fortress Press [1972] xxiv, 152 p. 20 cm. Bibliography: p. 147-149. [BV4638.C28] 77-171496 ISBN 0-8006-0106-8 3.75
1. Hope. I. Title.

CARDENAL, Ernesto. 248.4
To live is to love. Translated by Kurt Reinhardt. New York, Herder and Herder

[1972] 152 p. 21 cm. Translation of Vida en el amor. [BX2186.C26813] 70-178873 ISBN 0-665-00002-2 4.95
1. Meditations. I. Title.

CARDENAL, Ernesto. 248.4
To live is to love. Translated by Kurt Reinhardt. New York, Image books, 1974 [c1972] 156 p., 18 cm. [Bx2186.C26813] ISBN 0-385-03055-X 1.45 (pbk.)
1. Meditations. I. Title.
L.C. card no. for the hardbound ed.: 70-178873

CARLOY, Richard A. 248'.4
Get it together with God / Richard A. Carloy. 1st ed. Dearborn, Mich. : Carloy Studio, [1975] 104 p. ; 23 cm. [BV4832.2.C268] 75-7144
1. Meditations. 2. Christian life—1960-

CARLSON, Dwight L. 248'.4
Living God's will / Dwight L. Carlson. Old Tappan, N.J. : F. H. Revell, c1976. 157 p. ; 21 cm. [BV4501.2.C315] 75-38860 ISBN 0-8007-0771-0 pbk. : 2.95
1. Christian life—1960- 2. God—Will. I. Title.

CAROTHERS, Merlin R. 248'.4
Answers to praise [by] Merlin R. Carothers. Plainfield, N.J., Logos International, 1972. 169 p. 21 cm. Letters. [BV4501.2.C317] 72-86262 ISBN 0-912106-67-0 1.95 (pbk.)
1. Christian life—1960- I. Title.

CAROTHERS, Merlin R. 248'.4
Power in praise, by Merlin R. Carothers. Edited by Jorunn Oftedal Ricketts. Plainfield, N.J., Logos International [1972] vi, 115 p. 21 cm. [BV4501.2.C32] 70-182035 ISBN 0-912106-25-5 1.95
1. Christian life—1960- I. Title.

CAROTHERS, Merlin R. 248'.4
Praise works! [By] Merlin Carothers. Plainfield, N.J., Logos International [1973] 161 p. 21 cm. [BV4501.2.C324] 73-84414 ISBN 0-88270-060-X 1.95 (pbk.).
1. Christian life—1960- 2. Pastoral counseling. I. Title.

CARTER, Del. 248'.4
Who in hell needs a shepherd? : a book for atheists and agnostics—young and old / Del Carter ; artwork by Leland Griffin. Valley Forge, PA : Judson Press, [1975] 94 p. : ill. ; 22 cm. Includes bibliographical references. [BV4501.2.C33] 74-17843 ISBN 0-8170-0648-6 : 3.50
1. Christian life—1960- I. Title.

CAUBLE, Sterling L. 248'.4
Faith wins! By Sterling L. Cauble. Foreword by Sidney Correll. [1st ed.] Sunman, Ind., Dynamic Publishers [1973] 109 p. 23 cm. [BV4637.C36] 73-89275 3.95
1. Faith. 2. Christian life—1960- I. Title.

CHAMBERS, Mary Jane. 248'.4
Get me a tambourine / Mary Jane Chambers ; with comments on the church by her teen-aged son, Craig F. Chambers. New York : Hawthorn Books, c1975. 164 p. ; 21 cm. [BV4501.2.C46 1975] 75-216 ISBN 0-8015-2948-4 pbk. : 3.95
1. Chambers, Mary Jane. 2. Chambers, Craig F. 3. Christian life—1960- I. Chambers, Craig F. II. Title.

CHAPMAN, George A. 248'.4
Research yourself. Authors: George A. Chapman [and] Don J. Campbell. [Salt Lake City, Academe Rationale, 1971- 1 v. (loose-leaf) 30 cm. [BJ1581.2.C274] 72-175912
1. Conduct of life. I. Campbell, Don J., joint author. II. Title.

*CHAPPELL, Clovis G. 248.4
Home folks; [by] Clovis G. Chappell. Grand Rapids, Baker Book House [1974, c1954] 144 p. 20 cm. (Clovis G. Chappell library) [BV4526.2] 2.50 (pbk.)
1. Family—Religious life. I. Title.

*CHARLTON, David W. 248.4
Survival is not enough; messages for our times. New York, Exposition [c.1966] 87p. 21cm. 3.00
I. Title.

CHRISTENSON, Laurence. 248'.4
The Christian couple / Larry & Nordis Christenson. Minneapolis : Bethany Fellowship, c1977. 183 p. ; 21 cm. Includes bibliographical references. [BV835.C47] 77-24085 ISBN 0-87123-053-4 : 5.95
1. Marriage. I. Christenson, Nordis, joint author. II. Title.

CHRISTENSON, Laurence. 248'.4
The Christian family / Larry Christenson. Minneapolis : Bethany Fellowship, 1974, c1970. 216 p. ; 22 cm. [BV4526.2.C44 1974] 75-324692 4.95
1. Family—Religious life. I. Title.

CHRISTENSON, Laurence. 248'.4
The renewed mind [by] Larry Christenson. Minneapolis, Bethany Fellowship [1974] 143 p. 21 cm. [BV4501.2.C5] 74-12770 2.45 (pbk.)
1. Christian life—1960- I. Title.

CHRISTIAN family /
edited by Robert Heyer. New York : Paulist Press, c1975. 102 p. : ill. ; 19 cm. "The articles in this book originally appeared in New Catholic world." [BX2351.C524] 76-24448 ISBN 0-8091-1983-8 pbk. : 1.45
1. Family—Addresses, essays, lectures. I. Heyer, Robert. II. New Catholic world.

CHRISTIAN life. 248'.4
The gift of his heart, and other short stores from Christian life [magazine. Westwood, N.J.] F. H. Revell Co. [1963] 159 p. 21 cm. [BV4515.2.C55] 63-19741
1. Christian life — Stories. I. Title.

CLARK, Miles Morton, 1920- 248.4
Every day I have a journey [by] Miles Clark. [1st ed.] New York, Harper & Row [1967] xi, 148 p. 22 cm. [BJ1581.2.C5] 67-21544
1. Conduct of life. I. Title.

CLASPER, Paul D. 248'.4
The yogi, the commissar, and the third-world church [by] Paul Clasper. Valley Forge, Judson Press [1972] 95 p. 22 cm. Includes bibliographical references. [BV4501.2.C554] 78-183648 ISBN 0-8170-0560-9 1.95
1. Christian life—1960- 2. Church and the world. I. Title.

CLEMMONS, William. 248'.4
Discovering the depths / William Clemmons. Nashville : Broadman Press, c1976. 140 p. ; 20 cm. [BV4501.2.C563] 75-22507 ISBN 0-8054-5562-0 pbk. : 2.95
1. Christian life—1960- I. Title.

CLINARD, Turner Norman. 248'.4
Becoming a Christian : response to God's grace / Turner N. Clinard. Nashville : Tidings, c1976. x, 147 p. ; 19 cm. Includes bibliographical references. [BV4501.2.C58] 75-32300
1. Christian life—1960- I. Title.

COLAW, Emerson S. 248.4
The way of the Master. Nashville, Abingdon [1965] 128p. 20cm. Bibl. [BT306.3.C6] 65-11075 2.50
1. Jesus Christ—Biog.—Sermons. 2. Sermons, American. 3. Methodist Church—Sermons. I. Title.

COLEMAN, Charles G. 248'.4
Divine guidance, that voice behind you / by Charles G. Coleman. 1st ed. Neptune, N.J. : Loizeaux Brothers, 1977. 127 p. ; 21 cm. [BV4501.2.C635] 77-6796 ISBN 0-87213-087-8 pbk. : 2.50
1. Christian life—1960- 2. God—Will. I. Title.

COLEMAN, William L. 248'.4
Lord, sometimes I need help! / William L. Coleman. New York : Hawthorn Books, c1976. 119 p. ; 22 cm. [BV4501.2.C64 1976] 75-20903 ISBN 0-8015-4676-1 : 5.95
1. Christian life—1960- I. Title.

COLEMAN, William V. 248'.4
Finding a way to follow : values for today's Christian / William V. Coleman. Wilton, Conn. : Morehouse-Barlow Co., c1977. 120 p. ; 20 cm. [BV4501.2.C642] 77-70808 ISBN 0-8192-1227-X pbk. : 3.50
1. Christian life—1960- I. Title.
Publisher's address : 78 Danbury Rd., Wilton, Conn. 06897

COLLINS, Gary R. 248'.4
Coping with Christmas / by Gary R. Collins ; photos by Stephen T. Hoke. Minneapolis : Bethany Fellowship, c1975. 64 p. : ill. ; 19 cm. Includes bibliographical references. [BV45.C59] 75-31710 ISBN 0-87123-082-8 pbk. : 2.95
1. Christmas. 2. Christmas—Psychological aspects. I. Title.

COLLINS, Marjorie A. 248'.4
Dedication, what it's all about / Marjorie A. Collins. Minneapolis : Bethany Fellowship, c1976. 154 p. ; 20 cm. [BV4501.2.C644] 76-18069 ISBN 0-87123-103-4 pbk. : 2.95
1. Christian life—1960- I. Title.

COMENIUS, Johann Amos, 248'.4
1592-1670.
The labyrinth of the world and the paradise of the heart ... Newly translated by Matthew Spinka. Ann Arbor [Dept. of Slavic Languages and Literatures, University of Michigan] 1972. xiv, 148, [55] p. 23 cm. (Michigan Slavic translation, no. 1) "Published in commemoration of the three hundred anniversary of J. A. Comenius' death by the Czechoslovak Society of Arts and Sciences in America, and the Department of Slavic Languages and Literatures of the University of Michigan." Translation of Labyrint sveta a raj srdce. Includes facsimile of the final version of The labyrinth (Amsterdam, 1663): [55] p. (at end) [BV4509.C8C613 1972] 72-619508
1. Christian life. I. Title. II. Series.

THE Concrete Christian 248.4
life. Edited by Christian Duquoc. [New York] Herder and Herder [1971] 154 p. 23 cm. (Concilium: theology in the age of renewal. Spirituality, v. 69) On cover: The New concilium: religion in the seventies. Includes bibliographical references. [BV4501.2.C647] 78-168653 2.95
1. Spirituality—Addresses, essays, lectures. I. Duquoc, Christian, ed. II. Series: Concilium (New York) v. 69.

CONWELL, Russell Herman, 248'.4
1843-1925.
Acres of diamonds [by] Russell Conwell. Essay on self-reliance [by] Ralph Waldo Emerson. As a man thinketh [by] James Allen. New Canaan, Conn., Keats Pub. [1973] 131 p. 18 cm. (A Pivot family reader) (Inspiration three, v. 1) [BX6333.C6A3 1973] 74-156290 1.25 (pbk.)
1. Success. 2. Self-reliance. 3. New Thought. I. Emerson, Ralph Waldo, 1803-1882. Self-reliance. 1973. II. Allen, James, 1864-1912. As a man thinketh. 1973. III. Title. IV. Series.

COOK, Shirley. 248'.4
Diary of a fat housewife / Shirley Cook. Denver : Accent Books, c1977. 128 p. : ill. ; 21 cm. [RM222.2.C598] 77-71003 ISBN 0-916406-65-2 pbk. : 2.95
1. Reducing. 2. Christian life—1960- 3. Self-control. I. Title.

COOK, Shirley. 248'.4
Diary of a fat housewife / Shirley Cook. Denver : Accent Books, c1977. 128 p. : ill. ; 21 cm. [RM222.2.C598] 77-71003 ISBN 0-916406-65-2 pbk. : 2.95
1. Reducing. 2. Christian life—1960- 3. Self-control. I. Title.

*COOPER, Darien B. 248'4
You can be the wife of a happy husband; by discovering the key to marital success. [by] Darien B. Cooper. [New York] Berkley Pub. Co. [1975] 168 p. 18 cm. [BV835] 1.50 (pbk.)
1. Marriage. I. Title.

COSTA, Manuel Joseph. 248'.4
Life and love, by Manuel Joseph Costa & Matthew Eussen. Dayton, Ohio, G. A. Pflaum, 1970. 128 p. illus. 18 cm. (Christian identity series) (Witness book, CI 8) Bibliography: p. 123-124. [BV4501.2.C68] 79-114725 0.95 (pbk)
1. Christian life—1960- I. Eussen, Matthew, joint author. II. Title.

CRAFTS, Wilbur Fisk, 1850- 248'.4
1922.
Successful men of to-day, and what they say of success. New York, Arno Press, 1973 [c1883] 263 p. illus. 23 cm. (Big business: economic power in a free society) Reprint of the ed. published by Funk & Wagnalls, New York. [HF5386.C892 1973] 73-2500 ISBN 0-405-05081-X 13.00
1. Success. I. Title. II. Series.

CRAWFORD, John Richard 248.4
A Christian and his money [by] John R. Crawford. Nashville, Abingdon Press [1967] 176 p. 21 cm. [HG179.C7] 67-22158
1. Finance, Personal. 2. Christian life. I. Title.

CRAWFORD, John Richard 248.4
A Christian and his money [by] John R. Crawford. Nashville, Abingdon [1967] 176p. 21cm. [HG179.C7] 67-22158 3.75 bds.,
1. Finance, Personal. 2. Christian life. I. Title.

CRIM, Mort. 248.4
Like it is! Anderson, Ind., Warner Press [1970] 124 p. 21 cm. Includes bibliographical references. [BR121.2.C7] 77-87325
1. Christianity—20th century. I. Title.

CROOK, Roger H. 248'.4
How to be nervous and enjoy it / Roger H. Crook. Nashville : Broadman Press, c1975. 136 p. ; 20 cm. Includes bibliographical references. [BJ1581.2.C77] 74-32000 ISBN 0-8054-5232-X : 4.50
1. Conduct of life. 2. Christian life—1960- I. Title.

*CROOK, Roger H. 248.4
Serving God with mammon; the economic ministry of the family. Richmond, Va., CLC Pr. [dist. Knox, 1966, c.1965] 64p. 21cm. (Covenant life curriculum; home and family nuture, 43-9633) 1.00 pap.,
I. Title.

CRUZ, Nicky. 248'.4
The corruptors. Old Tappan, N.J., F. H. Revell Co. [1974] 159 p. 21 cm. [BV4501.2.C78] 74-12104 ISBN 0-8007-0684-6 4.95
1. Christian life—1960- 2. Civilization, Modern—1950- I. Title.

CURETON, Marion H. 248'.4
Negative earthlings exposed / by Marion H. Cureton. Philadelphia : Dorrance, [1975] 66 p. ; 22 cm. [BJ1595.C77] 74-24501 ISBN 0-8059-2114-1 : 3.95
1. Conduct of life. I. Title.

CURTIS, Lindsay R. 248.4
Talks that teach. Illus. by Dean Hurst. Salt Lake City, Bookcraft [1963] 168p. illus. 22cm. 63-5866 price unreported
1. Christian life—Stories. I. Title.

CURTIS, Lindsay R. 248'.4
To strenghten family ties / Lindsay R. Curtis. Salt Lake City : Bookcraft, 1974. 97 p. ; 24 cm. [BX8643.F3C84] 74-84478 ISBN 0-88494-268-6
1. Family—Religious life. I. Title.

DAHL, Gordon. 248'.4
Work, play, and worship in a leisure-oriented society. Minneapolis, Augsburg Pub. House [1972] 125 p. 20 cm. Bibliography: p. 123-125. [BJ1498.D33] 72-78566 ISBN 0-8066-1233-9 2.95
1. Leisure. 2. Christian life—1960- I. Title.

DAME, Clarence P 248.4
Fathers of the Bible, by Clarence P. Dame. Grand Rapids, Baker Book House, 1964. 112 p. 21 cm. ([Minister's handbook series]) [BS579.F3D3] 64-16941
1. Fathers in the Bible. 2. Bible — Biog. — Sermons. 3. Sermons, American. 4. Reformed Church — Sermons. I. Title.

DAME, Clarence P. 248.4
Fathers of the Bible. Grand Rapids, Mich., Baker Bk. [c.]1964. 112p. 21cm. (Minister's handbk. ser.) 64-16941 1.95
1. Fathers in the Bible. 2. Bible.—Biog—Sermons. 3. Sermons, American. 4. ReformedChurch—Sermons. I. Title.

DAVIS, Creath. 248'.4
How to win in a crisis / by Creath Davis ; foreword by Gloria and Bill Gaither. Grand Rapids, Mich. : Zondervan, c1976. p. cm. Includes bibliographical references. [BV4012.D346] 76-4220 6.95
1. Pastoral psychology. 2. Interpersonal relations. I. Title.

DAWSON, Grace Strickler, 248'.4
1891-
Artistry in living : what is a creative life? / By Grace S. Dawson. Corte Madera, Calif. : Omega Books, c1976. 90 p. ; 22 cm. [BV4501.2.D393] 76-18617 ISBN 0-89353-007-7 pbk. : 2.50
1. Christian life—1960- I. Title.

DAY, John A 248.4
Science, change and the Christian [by] John A. Day. New York, Published for the Cooperative Publication Association by Abingdon Press [1965] 96 p. 20 cm. (Faith for life series) Bibliography: p. 95-96. [BL240.2.D3] 65-4238
1. Religion and science — 1946- I. Cooperative Publication Association. II. Title.

DAY, John A. 248.4
Science, change and the Christian [Nashville] Pub. for the Cooperative Pubn. Assn. [by] Abingdon [c.1965] 96p. 20cm. (Faith for life ser.) Bibl. [BL240.2.D3] 65-4238 1.25 pap.,
1. Religion and science—1946- I. Cooperative Publication Association. II. Title.

DAY, Peter 248.4
Saints on Main Street: the gospel for the ordinary Christian. Greenwich, Conn., Seabury [1962, c.1960] 136p. 20cm. 1.25 pap.,
1. Laity. I. Title.

DAY, Peter 248.4
Saints on Main Street: the gospel for the ordinary Christian. Greenwich, Conn., Seabury Press [c.]1960. vii, 136p. 20cm. 60-5360 2.50 half cloth,
1. Laity. I. Title.

DAYTON, Edward R. 248'.4
Tools for time management : Christian perspectives on managing priorities / Edward R. Dayton. Grand Rapids : Zondervan Pub. House, [1974] 192 p. : ill. ; 21 cm. "Resources": p. 142-154. [BV4509.5.D35] 74-196951 4.95
1. Time allocation. 2. Christian life—1960- I. Title.

DE HAAN, Richard W. 248.4
Happiness is not an accident [by] Richard W. De Haan. Grand Rapids, Mich., Zondervan Pub. House [1971] 176 p. 22 cm. [BJ1481.D424] 72-146574 3.95
1. Happiness. 2. Christian life—1960- I. Title.

DELP, Paul S. 248'.4
The gentle way / by Paul S. Delp. New York : Philosophical Library, c1977. xviii, 171 p. ; 22 cm. [BV4501.2.D438] 76-51006 ISBN 0-8022-2198-X : 8.50
1. Christian life—1960- 2. Peace (Theology) I. Title.

DELP, Paul S. 248'.4
The gentle way / by Paul S. Delp. New York : Philosophical Library, c1977. xviii, 171 p. ; 22 cm. [BV4501.2.D438] 76-51006 ISBN 0-8022-2198-X : 8.50
1. Christian life—1960- 2. Peace (Theology) I. Title.

DENNIS, Lane T. 248'.4
A reason for hope / Lane T. Dennis. Old Tappan, N.J. : F. H. Revell Co., c1976. 189 p. ; 21 cm. Includes bibliographical references. [BV4501.2.D443] 75-37715 ISBN 0-8007-0772-9 : 5.95
1. Christian life—1960- 2. Christianity and culture. 3. Country life—Michigan. I. Title.

DENNISON, Alfred Dudley, 1914- 248'.4
Give it to me straight, doctor [by] A. Dudley Dennison. Grand Rapids, Mich., Zondervan Pub. House [1972] 155 p. 22 cm. Includes bibliographies. [BV4501.2.D444] 70-189579 3.95
1. Christian life—1960- I. Title.

DENNISON, Alfred Dudley, 1914- 248'.4
Prescription for life / by A. Dudley Dennison. Grand Rapids : Zondervan Pub. House, [1975] 150 p. ; 18 cm. [BV4501.2.D4446] 74-11866 pbk. : 1.75
1. Jesus Christ—Resurrection. 2. Christian life—1960- 3. Redemption. 4. Virgin birth. I. Title.

DENNISTON, Robin. 248.4
Partly living; some understanding of experience. New York, Stein and Day [1967] 126 p. 22 cm. [BV4501.2.D45 1967b] 67-25152
1. Christian life. I. Title.

DERHAM, Arthur Morgan 248.4
The mature Christian. Foreword by Paul S. Rees. [Westwood. N. J.] Revell [1962, c.1961] 128p. 19cm. 62-4542 2.50
1. Christian life. I. Title.

DE SANTO, Charles. 248'.4
Love and sex are not enough / Charles P. De Santo ; introd. by John M. Drescher ; foreword by Anthony Campolo. Scottdale, Pa. : Herald Press, c1977. 157 p. : ill. ; 20 cm. Includes bibliographical references and indexes. [BV835.D47] 76-45731 ISBN 0-8361-1809-X pbk. : 3.95
1. Marriage. 2. Courtship. I. Title.

DEWEY, Joanna, 1936- 248'.4
Disciples of the Way : Mark on discipleship / Joanna Dewey. Cincinatti : Women's Division, Board of Global Ministries, United Methodist Church, c1976. vi, 149 p. ; 19 cm. Bibliography: p. 145-147. [BS2545.C48D48] 76-13289 1.65
1. Bible. N.T. Mark—Criticism, interpretation, etc. 2. Christian life—Biblical teaching. I. Title.

DEWEY, Joanna, 1936- 248'.4
Disciples of the Way : Mark on discipleship / Joanna Dewey. Cincinatti : Women's Division, Board of Global Ministries, United Methodist Church, c1976. vi, 149 p. ; 19 cm. Bibliography: p. 145-147. [BS2545.C48D48] 76-13289 1.65
1. Bible. N.T. Mark—Criticism, interpretation, etc. 2. Christian life—Biblical teaching. I. Title.

DEWIRE, Harry A. 248.4
Communication as commitment [by] Harry DeWire. Philadelphia, Fortress Press [1971, c1972] x, 115 p. 19 cm. Includes bibliographical references. [BV4319.D45] 70-171497 ISBN 0-8006-0104-1 2.95
1. Communication (Theology) I. Title.

DICKINSON, Charles L. 248'.4
Free men for better job performance; how a property concept can improve working conditions, output, and satisfactions to owners, and employees, by C. L. Dickinson. Menlo Park, Calif., Institute for Humane Studies [1966] 20 p. 22 cm. (Projections of liberty, no. 1) Bibliography: p. 20. [HD38.D5] 66-30818
1. Incentives in industry. 2. Employee ownership. I. Title. II. Series.

DOWLING, Gerard Patrick, 1932- 248'.4
When you're feeling that way / [by] Gerard Dowling. Melbourne : Hill of Content, 1976. xiv, 127 p. ; 22 cm. [BJ1581.2.D65] 77-357997 ISBN 0-85572-070-0
1. Conduct of life. 2. Christian life—Catholic authors. I. Title.

*DRUMMOND, Henry 248.4
The greatest thing in the world [Westwood, N.J.] Revell [1966] 63p. 17cm. 3.95
1. Christian life. I. Title.

DRYBURGH, Bob. 248'.4
How you can be sure you are a Christian / by Bob Dryburgh. New Canaan, Conn. : Keats Pub., 1975. 142 p. ; 18 cm. (A Pivot family reader) (A Pivot book) [BV4501.2.D72] 75-7806 pbk. : 1.75
1. Christian life—1960- I. Title.

EBERHART, Elvin T., 1925- 248'.4
Burnt offerings : parables for 20th-century Christians / Elvin T. Eberhart. Nashville : Abingdon, c1977. 96 p. ; 20 cm. [BV4515.2.E23] 77-23158 ISBN 0-687-04375-1 pbk. : 3.95
1. Parables. I. Title.

EIMS, Leroy. 248'.4
What every Christian should know about growing : basic steps to discipleship / LeRoy Eims. Wheaton, Ill. : Victor Books, c1976. 168 p. ; 21 cm. (An Input book) [BV4501.2.E34] 75-44842 ISBN 0-88207-727-9 pbk. : 1.95
1. Christian life—1960- I. Title.

ELLER, Vernard. 248'.4
The simple life; the Christian stance toward possessions, as taught by Jesus, interpreted by Kierkegaard. Grand Rapids, Mich., W. B. Eerdmans Pub. Co. [1973] 122 p. 21 cm. Includes bibliographical references. [BJ1496.E36] 73-6589 ISBN 0-8028-1537-5 2.25
1. Jesus Christ—Teachings. 2. Kierkegaard, Soren Aabye, 1813-1855. 3. Simplicity. I. Title.

ELLIOT, Elisabeth. 248.4
The liberty of obedience; some thoughts on Christian conduct and service. Waco, Tex., Word Books [1968] 63 p. 20 cm. [BV4501.2.E37] 68-31110 2.95
1. Christian life. I. Title.

ELLIOT, Elisabeth. 248'.4
A slow and certain light; some thoughts on the guidance of God. Waco, Tex., Word Books [1973] 122 p. 22 cm. Includes bibliographical references. [BV4501.2.E374] 73-76252 3.95
1. Christian life—1960- 2. Providence and government of God. I. Title.

ELLIOT, Elisabeth. 248'.4
A slow and certain light; some thoughts on the guidance of God. Waco, Tex., Word Books [1973] 122 p. 22 cm. Includes bibliographical references. [BV4501.2.E374] 73-76252 3.95
1. Christian life—1960- 2. Providence and government of God. I. Title.

ELLIOTT, Norman K 248.4
Great is your reward; living the Beatitudes [by] Norman K. Elliott. Westwood, N.J., F. H. Revell Co. [1966] 115 p. 21 cm. [BT382.E5] 66-17046
1. Beatitudes — Stories. I. Title.

ELLIOTT, Norman K. 248.4
Great is your reward; living the Beatitudes. Westwood, N.J., Revell [c.1966] 115p. 21cm. [BT382.E5] 66-17046 2.95
1. Beatitudes—Stories. I. Title.

ELLIS, Joe S. 248'.4
Let yourself g-r-o-w! By Joe S. Ellis. Cincinnati, Standard Pub. [1973] 160 p. 22 cm. Includes bibliographical references. [BV4501.2.E377] 73-77205 1.95 (pbk.)
1. Christian life—1960- I. Title.

ELLUI, Jacques. 248.4
The presence of the Kingdom. Introd. by William Stringfellow. [Translated by Olive Wyon] New York, Seabury Press [1967, c1948] 153 p. 21 cm. (A Seabury paperback, SP41) Translation of Presence au monde moderne. [BV4501.E588 1967] 67-21833
1. Christian life. 2. Church and social problems. I. Title. II. Series.

ELLUL, Jacques. 248.4
The presence of the Kingdom. Introd. by William Stringfellow. [Translated by Olive Wyon] New York, Seabury Press [1967, c1948] 153 p. 21 cm. (A Seabury paperback, SP41) Translation of Presence au monde moderne. [BV4501.E588 1967] 67-21833
1. Christian life. 2. Church and social problems. I. Title.

ENSIGN, Grayson. 248'.4
Letters to young Christians. Cincinnati, Standard Pub. [1974] 94 p. illus. 18 cm. (Fountain books) [BV4501.2.E59] 73-87495 1.25 (pbk.)
1. Christian life—1960- I. Title.

ERASMUS, Desiderius, d.1536 248.4
The comparation of vyrgin and a martyr (1523) Translated by Thomas Paynell. A facsim. reproduction of the Berthelet ed. of 1537 with an introd. by William James Hirten. Gainesville, Fla., Scholars' Facsimiles & Reprints, 1970. xlviii, 78 p. 23 cm. "Reproduced from a copy in the Lambeth Palace Library, London, England." Translation of Virginis et martyris comparatio. Includes bibliographical references. [BV4647.C5E713 1970] 70-101148 ISBN 0-8201-1072-8 6.00
1. Virginity. 2. Martyrdom (Christianity) I. Paynell, Thomas, fl. 1528-1567, tr. II. Berthelet, Thomas, d. ca. 1556. III. Hirten, William James. IV. Title.

ERASMUS, Desiderius, d.1536. 248.4
The enchiridion. Translated and edited by Raymond Himelick. Bloomington, Indiana University Press [1963] 222 p. 20 cm. (Midland books, MB -- 52) Translation of Enchiridion militis Christiani. Bibliographical references included in "Notes" (p. 201-222) [BV4509.L2E833] 63-16615
1. Christian life — Middle Ages. I. Himelick, Raymond, ed. and tr. II. Title.

ERASMUS, Desiderius, d.1536. 248.4
The enchiridion. Tr. [from Latin] ed. by Raymond Himelick. Bloomington, Ind. Univ. Pr. [c.1963] 222p. 20cm. (Midland bks., MB-52) Bibl. 63-16615 6.00; 2.45 pap.,
1. Christian life—Middle Ages. I. Himelick, Raymond, ed. and tr. II. Title.

ERASMUS, Desiderius, d. 1536 248.4
The enchiridion of Erasmus. Tr., ed by Raymond Himelick. [Gloucester, Mass., P. Smith, 1966, c.1963] 222p. 21cm. (Midland bks, MB-52-rebound) Bibl. [BV4509.L2E833] 4.50
1. Christian life—Middle ages. I. Himelick, Raymond, ed. and tr. II. Title.

ERNSBERGER, David J. 248.4
Education for renewal, by David J. Ernsberger. Philadelphia, Westminster Press [1965] 174 p. 21 cm. Bibliographical references included in "Notes" (p. [170]-174) [BV1488.E8] 65-10578
1. Religious education of adults. I. Title.

EVANS, William Henry, 1888- 248'.4
The queen of the home. Foreword by Leon Macon 1st ed. New York, Exposition Press [1956] 59p. illus. 21cm. [BV4526.E83] 56-10296
1. Family—Religious life. I. Title.

FAIRFIELD, James G. T., 1926- 248'.4
All that we are we give / James G. T. Fairfield. Scottdale, Pa. : Herald Press, 1977. p. cm. Bibliography: p. [BV4501.2.F28] 77-14510 ISBN 0-8361-1839-1 : 3.95
1. Christian life—1960- 2. Stewardship, Christian. I. Title.

FAIRFIELD, James G. T., 1926- 248'.4
All that we are we give / James G. T. Fairfield. Scottdale, Pa. : Herald Press, 1977. p. cm. Bibliography: p. [BV4501.2.F28] 77-14510 ISBN 0-8361-1839-1 : 3.95
1. Christian life—1960- 2. Stewardship, Christian. I. Title.

FAMILY life : 248'.4
God's view of relationships / by Ray C. Stedman ... [et al.]. Waco, Tex. : Word Books, c1976. 245 p. ; 22 cm. (Discovery books) [BV4526.2.F33] 75-36183 ISBN 0-87680-452-0 : 6.95
1. Family—Religious life. I. Stedman, Ray C.

FENTON, Horace L. 248.4
The trouble with barnacles, by Horace L. Fenton, Jr. Grand Rapids, Zondervan Pub. House [1973] 144 p. 18 cm. [BV4832.2.F46] 73-2661 0.95 (pbk.)
1. Meditations. I. Title.

FERGUSON, Ben. 248'.4
God, I've got a problem / Ben Ferguson. Santa Ana, Calif. : Vision House Publishers, [1974] 137 p. ; 18 cm. [BV4501.2.F45] 74-80778 ISBN 0-88449-007-6 : 1.45
1. Christian life—1960- I. Title.

FIELD, David, 1936- 248'.4
Free to do right. Downers Grove, Ill., InterVarsity Press [1973] 111 p. 18 cm. Includes bibliographical references. [BJ1411.F53 1973] 73-81577 ISBN 0-87784-549-2 1.25
1. Right and wrong. I. Title.

FISCHER, Helmut, 1929- 248'.4
Thematischer Dialog-Gottesdienst / Helmut Fischer. Hamburg : Furche-Verlag, 1975. 119 p. ; 20 cm. Includes bibliographical references. [BV15.F57] 76-456278 ISBN 3-7730-0254-8 : DM19.80
1. Public worship. 2. Dialogue sermons. I. Title.

FLINT, Cort R. 248'.4
The purpose of love, by Cort R. Flint. [1st ed. Anderson, S.C.] Droke House/Hallux [1973] 155 p. port. 24 cm. [BD436.F5] 73-79403 ISBN 0-8375-6741-6
1. Love. I. Title.

FLINT, Cort R. 248'.4
The purpose of love, by Cort R. Flint. [1st ed. Anderson, S.C.] Droke House/Hallux [1973] 155 p. port. 24 cm. [BD436.F5] 73-79403 ISBN 0-8375-6741-6 4.95
1. Love. I. Title.

FLORIO, Anthony. 248'.4
Two to get ready. Old Tappan, N.J., F. H. Revell Co. [1974] 155 p. 21 cm. [BV835.F55] 74-10549 ISBN 0-8007-0676-5 4.95
1. Marriage. I. Title.

FOLLETTE, John Wright. 248'.4
This wonderful venture called Christian living / [John Wright Follette.] Ashville, N.C. : distributed by Follette Books, [1974] 83 p. : port. ; 20 cm. [BV4501.2.F585] 74-77321
1. Christian life—1960- I. Title.

FORD, George L. 248.4
The miracle of America. Grand Rapids, Mich., Zondervan [c.1963] 63p. 21cm. Bibl. 1.00 pap.,
I. Title.

FOSDICK, Harry Emerson, 1878-1969. 248.4
Dear Mr. Brown; letters to a person perplexed about religion. [1st ed.] New York, Harper [1961] 190 p. 22 cm. [BR121.2.F65] 61-9645
1. Christianity—20th century. I. Title.

*FOSTER, K. Neil. 248.4
A revolution of love, by K. Neil Foster, forward by Sherwood Wirt. Minneapolis, Bethany Fellowship [1973] 92 p. 18 cm. (Dimension Books) [BV4501.2] ISBN 0-87123-486-6 0.95 (pbk.)
1. Christian life. 2. Conduct of life. I. Title.

FOSTER, Neill. 248'.4
The happen stance / by Neill Foster. Nashville : T. Nelson, c1977. p. cm. [BV4501.2.F65] 77-13263 pbk. : 1.94
1. Christian life—1960- I. Title.

FOSTER, Neill. 248'.4
The happen stance / by Neill Foster. Nashville : T. Nelson, c1977. p. cm. [BV4501.2.F65] 77-13263 pbk. : 1.94
1. Christian life—1960- I. Title.

FOX, Matthew, 1940- 248'.4
On becoming a musical, mystical bear; spirituality American style [1st ed.] New York, Harper & Row [1972] xvi, 156 p. 22 cm. Includes bibliographical references. [BV210.2.F69 1972] 72-78053 ISBN 0-06-062912-6 5.95
1. Prayer. 2. Spirituality. I. Title.

FOX, Matthew, 1940- 248'.4
On becoming a musical, mystical bear : spirituality American style / Matthew Fox. New York : Paulist Press/Deus Book, c1976. xxxiv, 156 p. ; 18 cm. Includes bibliographical references. [BV210.2.F69 1976] 75-34842 ISBN 0-8091-1913-7 : 2.25
1. Prayer. 2. Spirituality. I. Title.

FRANKE, Carl W. 248'.4
Christian, be a real person! [By] Carl W. Franke. Nashville, T. Nelson [1974] xiv, 176 p. 21 cm. Includes bibliographical references. [BV4501.2.F715] 74-3438 ISBN 0-8407-5565-1
1. Christian life—1960- I. Title.

FROST, Gerhard E 248.4
These things I remember, Illustrated by Jordan Lang. Minneapolis, Augsburg Pub. House [1963] 127 p. illus. 21 cm. [BV4515.2F7] 63-15116
1. Christian life — Stories. 2. Farm life — Minnesota. I. Title.

FROST, Gerhard E. 248.4
These things I remember. Illus. by Jordan Lang. Minneapolis, Augsburg [c.1963] 127p. illus. 21cm. 63-15116 2.95
1. Christian life—Stories. 2. Farm life—Minnesota. I. Title.

FROST, Robert C., 1926- 248.4
Overflowing life [by] Robert C. Frost. Plainfield, N.J., Logos International [1971] 140 p. 21 cm. [BV4501.2.F78] 72-146696 1.75
1. Christian life—1960- 2. Holy Spirit. I. Title.

FROTHINGHAM, Paul Revere, 1864-1926. 248.4
A confusion of tongues. Freeport, N.Y., Books for Libraries Press [1968] xii, 255 p. 22 cm. (Essay index reprint series) Reprint of the 1917 ed. Contents.Contents.—A confusion of tongues.—The conduct of life.—A motto.—The little book.—Making the best of things.—How to choose.—The "if" and "though" of faith.—Extra pennies.—The departure into Egypt.—Unshaken things. [BJ1581.F85 1968] 68-22913
1. Conduct of life. I. Title.

FRY, Thomas A 248.4
Doing what comes supernaturally [by] Thomas A. Fry, Jr. Westwood, N.J., F. H. Revell Co. [1966] 126 p. 21 cm. [BV4501.2.F79] 66-12435
1. Christian life — Presbyterian authors. I. Title.

FRY, Thomas A., Jr. 248.4
Doing what comes supernaturally. Westwood, N.J., Revell [c.1966] 126p. 21cm. [BV4501.2.F79] 66-12435 2.95 bds.,
1. Christian life—Presbyterian authors. I. Title.

*GABOURY, Placide Bernard, 1928- 248.4
Faith and creativity [by] Placide Gaboury. [First ed.] New York, Vantage [1972] 155 p. 21 cm. Includes bibliographical references [BV4501] ISBN 0-533-00273-7 4.95
1. Christian life. I. Title.

GALLOWAY, Dale E. 248'.4
We're making our home a happy place / Dale E. Galloway. Wheaton, Ill. : Tyndale House Publishers, c1976. 116 p. ; 22 cm. Includes bibliographical references. [BV4526.2.G33] 76-8679 ISBN 0-8423-7860-X : 2.95
1. Family—Religious life. I. Title.

GALLOWAY, Dale E. 248'.4
You can win with love / by Dale E. Galloway. Irvine, Calif. : Harvest House Publishers, c1976. 173 p. ; 21 cm. Includes bibliographical references. [BV4639.G34] 76-15129 ISBN 0-89081-024-9 : 2.95
1. Love (Theology) 2. Christian life—1960- I. Title.

*GANGEL, Kenneth O., comp. 248.4
Between christian parent and child [by] Kenneth O. Gangel and Elizabeth Gangel Grand Rapids, Baker Book House, [1974] 89 p. 18 cm. [BV4526] ISBN 0-8010-3680-1 1.45 (pbk.)
1. Family—Religious life. I. Gangel, Elizabeth, joint comp. II. Title.

GANGEL, Kenneth O. 248'.4
The family first [by] Kenneth O. Gangel. Minneapolis, His International Service [1972] 139 p. 19 cm. Bibliography: p. 137-139. [BV4526.2.G35] 72-75944 ISBN 0-911802-28-2
1. Family—Religious life. I. Title.

*GEE, Donald. 248.4
This is the way. Springfield, Mo., Gospel Publishing House, [1975 c1936] 64 p. 18 cm. (Radiant books) Original title: "Studies in guidance" [BV4501] ISBN 0-88243-630-9 0.95 (pbk.)
1. Immanence of God. 2. Spiritual life. I. Title.

GERKEN, John 248.4
Toward a theology of the layman. [New York] Herder & Herder [c.1963] 152p. 21cm. 63-9556 3.95
1. Laity—Catholic Church. I. Title.

GERKEN, John D 248.4
Toward a theology of the layman. [New York] Herder and Herder [1963] 152 p. 21 cm. [BX1920.G4] 63-9556
1. Laity—Catholic Church. I. Title.

†GETZ, Gene A. 248'.4
Building up one another / Gene A. Getz. Wheaton, Ill. : Victor Books, c1976. 120 p. ; 21 cm. [BV4501.2.G45 1976] 76-19918 ISBN 0-88207-744-9 pbk. : 2.25
1. Christian life—1960- 2. Interpersonal relations. I. Title.

GILLQUIST, Peter E. 248'.4
Handbook for spiritual survival. Grand Rapids, Mich., Zondervan [1973, c.1971] 138 p. Originally published in 1971 under title: Farewell to the fake I.D. [BV4501.2] 72-168649 pap., 0.95
1. Christian life—1960- I. Title.

GILLQUIST, Peter E. 248'.4
Handbook for spiritual survival [by] Peter E. Gillquist. Grand Rapids, Mich., Zondervan Pub. House [1973, c1971] 138 p. 18 cm. Published in 1971 under title: Farewell to the fake I.D. [BV4501.2.G5113 1973] 73-160803 0.95 (pbk.)
1. Christian life—1960- I. Title.

GLADDEN, Washington, 1836-1918. 248.4
Being a Christian: what it means and how to begin. Freeport, N.Y., Books for Libraries Press [1972] 76 p. 22 cm. Reprint of the 1876 ed. [BV4501.G575 1972] 72-4168 ISBN 0-8369-6880-8
1. Christian life. I. Title.

GLEASON, Robert W. 248.4
Christand the Christian. New York. Image Bks. [c.1959] 1967 154p. 18cm. (D227) Bibl. [BX 2350.2.G6] .95 pap.,
1. Christian life—Catholic authors. 2. Jesus Christ—Person and offices. I. Title.
Available from Doubleday.

GLUBB, John Bagot, Sir, 1897- 248'.4
The way of love : lessons from a long life / John Bagot Glubb. Troy, Ala. : Troy State University Press, 1976, c1974. vii, 190 ; 21 cm. Bibliography: p. 187-190. [BV4501.2.G58 1976] 75-44945 ISBN 0-916624-00-5 : 7.95
1. Christian life—1960- 2. Love. 3. God. I. Title.

GOFF, Charles Ray 248.4
Chapel in the sky. Nashville, Abingdon Press [c.1960] 127p. 20cm. 60-5472 2.00
1. Christian life. I. Title.

GOLDSMITH, Joel S., 1892- 248.4
Our spiritual resources. New York, Harper & Row [c.1962] 190p. 20cm. 62-7965 3.50 bds.,
1. New Thought. I. Title.

GOLDSMITH, Joel S., 1892-1964. 248'.4
Living between two worlds. Edited by Lorraine Sinkler. Boston, G. K. Hall, 1974. 227 p. 25 cm. Large print ed. [BL624.G64 1974b] 74-18246 ISBN 0-8161-6255-7
1. Spiritual life. 2. Sight-saving books. I. Title.

GOLDSMITH, Joel S., 1892-1964. 248'.4
Living between two worlds. Edited by Lorraine Sinkler. [1st ed.] New York, Harper & Row [1974] xii, 128 p. 20 cm. [BL624.G64 1974] 73-18679 ISBN 0-06-063191-0 4.95
1. Spiritual life. I. Title.

GOLZ, L. 248.4
Walking as He walked. Chicago, Moody [c.1963] 63p. 18cm. (Compact bks., 26) .29 pap.,
I. Title.

GONZALEZ Ruiz, Jose Maria, 1916- 248'.4
The new creation : Marxist and Christian? / By Jose Maria Gonzalez-Ruiz ; translated by Matthew J. O'Connell. Maryknoll, N.Y. : Orbis Books, c1976. ix, 150 p. ; 22 cm. Translation of Marxismo y cristianismo frente al hombre nuevo. Includes bibliographical references. [BV4506.G6613] 76-10226 ISBN 0-88344-327-9 : 6.95
1. Christian life—1960- 2. Communism and Christianity. 3. Christian ethics. I. Title.

GORDON, Ernest. 248'.4
Guidebook for the new Christian [by] Ernest Gordon and Peter Funk. [1st ed.] New York, Harper & Row [1972] 145 p. 22 cm. Bibliography: p. [135]-139. [BV4501.2.G63 1972] 72-78074 ISBN 0-06-063352-2 4.95
1. Christian life—1960- I. Funk, Peter V. K. II. Title.

GRANT, Dave. 248'.4
Compass for conscience / Dave Grant. Old Tappan, N.J. : F. H. Revell Co., [1975] 94 p. ; 21 cm. [BV4501.2.G726] 74-30090 ISBN 0-8007-0696-X pbk. : 2.50
1. Christian life—1960- 2. Christian ethics. I. Title.

GREELEY, Andrew M., 1928- 248'.4
May the wind be at your back : the prayer of St. Patrick / Andrew M. Greeley ; with photos. by the author. New York : Seabury Press, c1975. 126 p. : ill. ; 23 cm. "A Crossroad book." [BV284.F47G73] 75-13523 ISBN 0-8164-2595-7 : 4.95
1. Fet fiadha—Meditations. I. Title.

GREEN, Bryan S W 248.4
Christians alive. New York, Scribner [1959] 125p. 21cm. London ed. (Epworth) has title: Saints alive [BV4501.2.G74 1959] 59-11664
1. Christian life. I. Title.

GREGORY, Harry William, 1935- 248'.4
And the answer is yes! [By] H. William Gregory. Philadelphia, United Church Press [1973] 123 p. 22 cm. "A Pilgrim Press book." Includes bibliographical references. [BV4501.2.G747] 73-14904 ISBN 0-8298-0263-0 4.95
1. Christian life—1960- I. Title.

GRIFFIN, Kathryn. 248'.4
Blessings for blah days / Kathryn Griffin. Nashville : Broadman Press, 1977c1976 127 p. ; 20 cm. [BV4501.2.G754] 76-21476 ISBN 0-8054-5618-X pbk. : 2.50
1. Griffin, Kathryn. 2. Christian life—1960- I. Title.

GRIFFIN, Kathryn. 248'.4
Blessings for blah days / Kathryn Griffin. Nashville : Broadman Press, 1977c1976 127 p. ; 20 cm. [BV4501.2.G754] 76-21476 ISBN 0-8054-5618-X pbk. : 2.50
1. Griffin, Kathryn. 2. Christian life—1960- I. Title.

GRIFFITHS, Michael C. 248.4
Consistent Christianity. Chicago, 1519 North Astor Inter-varsity Press, [1960] 126p. 18cm. (Pocket book series) 60-2532 1.25 pap.,
1. Christian life. I. Title.

GRIFFITHS, Michael C. 248.4
Take my life [by] Michael Griffiths. [1st ed.] Chicago, Inter-varsity Press [1967] 189 p. 18 cm. [BV4501.2.G77] 66-30646
1. Christian life. I. Title.

GRIMES, Howard 248.4
Realms of our calling. New York, Friendship [1965] 64p. 19cm. Bibl. [BV4740.G7] 65-11424 .75 pap.,
1. Vocation. I. Title.

GUDER, Eileen L. 248'.4
Deliver us from fear / Eileen Guder. Waco, Tex. : Word Books, c1976. 117 p. ; 23 cm. [BV4501.2.G825] 75-36189 ISBN 0-87680-415-6 : 5.95
1. Christian life—1960- 2. Fear. I. Title.

GUDER, Eileen L. 248.4
God, but I'm bored! By Eileen Guder. [1st ed.] Garden City, N.Y., Doubleday, 1971. 140 p. 22 cm. [BV4501.2.G83] 77-157596 3.95
1. Christian life—1960- I. Title.

GUDER, Eileen L. 248.4
God, but I'm bored! [by] Eileen Guder. [New York, Dell, 1974, c1971] 156 p. 18 cm. [BV4501.2.G83] 1.25 (pbk.)
1. Christian life—1960- I. Title.
L.C. card number for original ed.: 77-157596.

GUDER, Eileen L. 248.4
The naked I; seeking God and finding identity [by] Eileen Guder. Waco, Tex., Word Books [1971] 141 p. 23 cm. [BV4509.5.G8] 73-144363 4.95
1. Identification (Religion) I. Title.

GUIDEPOSTS. 248.4
The Guideposts trilogy: Your faith can grow, introduced by Samuel M. Schoemaker; Prayer: man's way to God, introduced by Catherine Marshall [and] Finding the power that heals, introduced by Norman Vincent Peale. Carmel, N.Y., Guideposts Associates [1962] 306 p. 22 cm. [BV4515.2.G8] 63-3083
1. Christian life — Stories. I. Title. II. Title: Your faith can grow. III. Title: Prayer: man's way to God. IV. Title: Finding the power that heals.

GUILLERAND, Augustin, 1877-1945. 248.4
Where silence is praise, from the writings of Augustin Guillerand. Tr. by a monk of Parkminster. [dist. New York, Longmans, 1961, c.1960] 138p. 61-1409 2.75 bds.,
1. Spiritual life—Catholic authors. I. Title.

GUILLERAND, Augustin, 1877-1945 248.4
Where silence is praise, from the writings of Augustin Guillerand. Tr. [from French] by a monk of Parkminster. London, Darton, Longman & Todd [dist. Wilkes-Barre, Pa., Dimension Bks., 1964, c.1960] 138p. 18cm. 61-1409 2.95
1. Spiritual life—Catholic authors. I. Title.

GUINNESS, Howard. 248'.4
Sacrifice / Howard Guinness. 6th ed. Downers Grove, Ill. : Intervarsity Press, c1975. 84 p. ; 18 cm. Includes bibliographical references. [BV4501.G82 1975] 76-351355 ISBN 0-87784-307-4 pbk. : 1.95
1. Christian life. I. Title.

GUTZKE, Manford George. 248'.4
Souls in prison / Manford George Gutzke. Nashville : T. Nelson, [1975] 157 p. ; 21 cm. [BV4501.2.G87] 74-32468 ISBN 0-8407-5587-2 pbk. : 3.50
1. Christian life—1960- I. Title.

HAFFERT, John Mathias. 248.4
Sex and the mysteries, by John M. Haffert. Washington, N.J., Ave Maria Institute [1970] v, 280 p. illus. 22 cm. Includes bibliographical references. [BJ1533.C4H3] 70-14015
1. Chastity. 2. Rosary—Meditations. I. Title.

HAGGAI, John Edmund. 248'.4
The Christian's Dr. Jekyll and Mr. Hyde [by] John Haggai. Nashville, T. Nelson [1974] 32 p. 22 cm. [BV4501.2.H2624] 74-1222 ISBN 0-8407-5574-0 1.00 (pbk.).
1. Christian life—1960- I. Title.

HAGGAI, Tom. 248'.4
"Chrissie, I never had it so bad ... " Nashville, T. Nelson [1973] 160 p. 22 cm. [BJ1661.H117 1973] 72-13901 ISBN 0-8407-5044-7 4.95
1. Youth—Conduct of life. I. Title.

HALL, Sammy. 248'.4
Hooked on a good thing [by] Sammy Hall with Charles Paul Conn. Old Tappan, N.J., Revell [1972] 128 p. 21 cm. [BV4935.H24A3] 72-3826 ISBN 0-8007-0548-3
1. Conversion. I. Conn, Charles Paul, joint author. II. Title.

HALL, Thor, 1927- 248'.4
Whatever happened to the gospel? Nashville, Tidings [1973] 111 p. 19 cm. Includes bibliographical references. [BR121.2.H318] 73-87326 1.50
1. Christianity—20th century. 2. Christian life—1960- I. Title.

HAMILTON, Elizabeth, 1758-1816. 248'.4
Letters addressed to the daughter of a nobleman, on the formation of the religious and the moral principle. With an introd. for the Garland ed. by Gina Luria. New York, Garland Pub., 1974. 2v. 18 cm. (The Feminist controversy in England, 1788-1810) Reprint of the 2d ed., 1806, published by Cadell and Davies, London. Bibliography: v. 1, p. 12 (1st group) [BV4501.H267 1974] 73-22252 ISBN 0-8240-0865-0 44.00 (2 vols.)
1. Christian life. 2. Christian ethics. I. Title. II. Series.

HAMMER, Paul L. 248'.4
The gift of Shalom : Bible studies in human life and the church / by Paul L. Hammer. Philadelphia : Published for Joint Educational Development [by] United Church Press, c1976. 141 p. : ill. ; 21 cm. (A Shalom resource) Bibliography: p. 141. [BV4501.2.H296] 75-41456 ISBN 0-8298-0309-2 pbk. : 3.25
1. Christian life—Biblical teaching. 2. Shalom (The word) 3. Peace (Theology)—Biblical teaching. I. Title.

*HAMMERTON, H. J. 248.4
What manner of spirit? Foreword by the Archbishop of Canterbury. London, Faith Pr. [dist.] New York, Morehouse [1964, c.1963] 112p. 18cm. 1.50 pap.,
I. Title.

HAMMILL, Richard. 248.4
In full assurance. Nashville, Southern Pub. Association [1959] 222p. illus. 20cm. [BV4501.2.H3] 60-464
1. Christian life. I. Title.

HANCOCK, Maxine. 248'.4
Living on less and liking it more / by Maxine Hancock. Chicago : Moody Press, c1976. 158 p. ; 22 cm. Includes bibliographical references. [BV4501.2.H32] 76-40220 ISBN 0-8024-4912-3 : 4.95
1. Christian life—1960- 2. Cost and standard of living. I. Title.

HANCOCK, Maxine. 248'.4
Love, honor, and be free / by Maxine Hancock. Chicago : Moody Press, [1975] 191 p. ; 22 cm. [BV4527.H36] 75-316072 ISBN 0-8024-5021-0 : 5.95
1. Women—Religious life. 2. Woman—Biblical teaching. 3. Women. I. Title.

HARLEY, Willard F. 248'.4
Get growing, Christian! / Willard F. Harley, Jr. Elgin, Ill. : D. C. Cook Pub. Co., [1975] 95 p. ; 18 cm. [BV4501.2.H343] 74-22948 ISBN 0-912692-51-0 pbk. : 1.50
1. Christian life—1960- I. Title.

HARMAN, Dan. 248.4
A funny thing happened on the way to heaven. Illustrated by Jack Kershner. Anderson, Ind., Warner Press [1969] 112 p. illus. 19 cm. Bibliographical references included in "Notes" (p. 111-112) [BV4501.2.H345] 78-76744
1. Christian life. I. Title.

HARRELL, Irene Burk. 248'.4
Multiplied by love / Irene Burk Harrell. Nashville : Abingdon, [1976] p. cm. [BV4501.2.H358] 76-15370 ISBN 0-687-27303-X : 4.95
1. Christian life—1960- I. Title.

HARRELL, Irene Burk. 248'.4
The windows of heaven / Irene Harrell. Waco, Tex. : Word Books, c1975. 113 p. ; 21 cm. [BV4832.2.H3243] 75-19902 ISBN 0-87680-994-8 pbk. : 3.25

1. Devotional exercises. I. Title.

HARRIS, Charles D. 248'.4
Heaven? Yes! Hell? No! / By Charles D. Harris. [Waco? Tex.] : Harris, [1975] ix, 148 p. ; 24 cm. Bibliography: p. 147-148. [BV4012.H32] 75-15071
1. Pastoral psychology. 2. Christian life—1960- I. Title.

†HARTMAN, Doug. 248'.4
Guidebook to discipleship / Doug Hartman and Doug Sutherland. Irvine, Calif. : Harvest House Publishers, c1976. 173 p. : diagrs. ; 21 cm. [BV4501.2.H364] 76-20398 pbk. : 2.95
1. Christian life—1960- I. Sutherland, Doug, joint author. II. Title.

HASKIN, Dorothy (Clark) 248.4
The secret meeting, and other stories. Grand Rapids, Baker Book House [c.]1959. 76p. 20cm. (Valor series, 1) 60-511 1.50 bds.,
1. Christian life—Stories. I. Title.

HASKIN, Dorothy (Clark) 248.4
1905-
The secret meeting, and other stories. Grand Rapids, Baker Book House, 1959. 76p. 20cm. (Valor series, 1) [BV4515.H374] 60-511
1. Christian life —Stories. I. Title.

HAUGHTON, Rosemary. 248'.4
In search of tomorrow; a future to live in. St. Meinrad, Ind., Abbey Press, 1972. 106 p. illus. 18 cm. (A Priority edition) Includes bibliographical references. [CB430.H39] 72-89193 1.75 (pbk)
1. Civilization, Modern—1950- 2. Christian life—1960- I. Title.

HAUGHTON, Rosemary. 248'.4
The theology of experience. Paramus, N.J., Newman Press [1972] 168 p. 23 cm. [BR110.H33 1972] 77-188424 ISBN 0-232-51175-6 5.95
1. Experience (Religion) I. Title.

HAVERGAL, Frances Ridley, 248.4
1836-1879.
Kept for the Master's use. Westwood, N. J., Revell [1964] 64 p. 17 cm. (A Revell inspirational classic) [PR4759.H8K4 1964] 64-23347
I. Title.

HAVERGAL, Frances Ridley, 248.4
1836-1879
Kept for the Master's use. Westwood, N. J., Revell [c.1964] 64p. 17cm. (Revell inspirational classic) 64-23347 1.00 bds.,
I. Title.

HEARD, Teddy Moody. 248'.4
How to overcome stress and tension in your life / Teddy Moody Heard and Wyatt H. Heard. Old Tappan, N.J. : Revell, c1976. p. cm. [BV4501.2.H369] 76-5850 ISBN 0-8007-0791-5 : 4.95
1. Christian life—1960- 2. Stress (Physiology) I. Heard, Wyatt H., joint author. II. Title.

HEARN, Janice W. 248'.4
Peace with the restless me / Janice W. Hearn. Waco, Tex. : Word Books, c1976. 129 p. ; 21 cm. [BV4501.2.H3693] 75-36187 ISBN 0-87680-455-5 : 4.95
1. Christian life—1960- I. Title.

HEMPEL, Arthur J. 248'.4
Claim your inheritance / by Arthur J. Hempel. Boulder Creek, Calif. : Circle Press, 1975. x, 139 p. ; 21 cm. [BV4501.2.H3696] 75-40519 ISBN 0-89248-000-9
1. Christian life—1960- I. Title.

HENDRICKS, Howard G. 248'.4
Elijah; confrontation, conflict, and crisis, by Howard G. Hendricks. Chicago, Moody Press [1972] 64 p. 20 cm. [BS580.E4H45] 71-175500 ISBN 0-8024-2335-3 1.00
1. Elijah, the prophet. I. Title.

HENDRICKS, Howard G. 248'.4
Say it with love [by] Howard G. Hendricks with Ted Miller. Wheaton, Ill., Victor Books [1972] 143 p. 21 cm. (An Input book) [BV4319.H46] 72-77011 ISBN 0-88207-050-9 1.45
1. Communication (Theology) 2. Christian life—1960- I. Title.

HERTZ, Karl H. 248.4
Everyman a priest. Philadelphia, Muhlenberg Press [1961, c.1960] 56p. (Fortress book) 61-6754 1.00 bds.,
1. Priesthood, Universal. I. Title.

HESSERT, Paul. 248.4
Christian life. Philadelphia, Westminster Press [1967] 192 p. 21 cm. (New directions in theology today, v. 5) Bibliographical references included in "Notes" (p. [175]-185. [BT28.N47 vol. 5] 67-12283
1. Christian life—History. I. Title. II. Series.

HEUVEL, Albert H. van den 248.4
These rebellious powers [New York] Friendship [1965] 183p. 19cm. [BV4501.2.H39] 65-11428 1.75 pap.,
1. Christian life. 2. Power (Theology) I. Title.

*HEYMEN, Ralph. 248.4
The Christian home. Grand Rapids, Baker Book House, [1975] 79 p. 18 cm. (Contemporary discussion series) [BV4525] ISBN 0-8010-4109-0 1.25 (pbk.)
1. Pastoral counseling. 2. Marriage counseling. I. Title.

HEYNEN, Ralph. 248.4
The art of Christian living; Christian faith and mental health. [1st ed.] Grand Rapids, Baker Book House, 1963. 171 p. 23 cm. [BV4501.2.H4] 63-15079
1. Christian life. I. Title.

HEYNEN, Ralph 248.4
The art of Christian living; Christian faith and mental health. Grand Rapids, Mich., Baker Bk. [c.]1963. 171p. 23cm. 63-15079 2.95
1. Christian life. I. Title.

HEYNEN, Ralph 248.4
Building your spiritual strength. Grand Rapids, Mich., Baker Bk. [1965] 111p. 21cm. [BV4905.2.H47] 65-18262 2.95
1. Suffering. 2. Consolation. I. Title.

*HEYNEN, Ralph 248.4
Creative question on Christian living; a guidebook for group discussion. Grand Rapids. Mich., Baker Bk. [1967] 111p. 20cm. 1.50 pap.,
I. Title.

HEYNEN, Ralph. 248'.4
Where are you growing? Exploring the Christian life. Grand Rapids, Mich., Baker Book House [1972] 105 p. 18 cm. (Contemporary discussion series) [BV4501.2.H42] 72-90331 ISBN 0-8010-4067-1 1.25 (pbk.)
1. Christian life—1960- I. Title.

HILL, Harold, 1905- 248'.4
How to be a winner / Harold Hill, with Irene Burk Harrell. Plainfield, N.J. : Logos International, c1976. xix, 196 p. ; 22 cm. [BR1725.H47A32] 76-31676 ISBN 0-88270-178-9 : 5.95. ISBN 0-88270-179-7 pbk. :
1. Hill, Harold, 1905- 2. Christian life—1960- 3. Christian biography—United States. I. Harrell, Irene Burk, joint author. II. Title.

HILL, Russell Chilton. 248.4
Freedom's code. United Nations 25th anniversary ed., 1945-1970. [San Antonio, Freedom Press of Texas, 1971] vii, 63 p. 27 cm. [BJ1581.2.H54] 76-31823
1. Conduct of life. I. Title.

HILLIS, Don W. 248'.4
"What if ..." / by Don W. Hillis ; cartoons by John V. Lawing, Jr. Wheaton, Ill. : Victor Books, [1975] 96 p. : ill. ; 18 cm. [BV4832.2.H54] 74-21908 ISBN 0-88207-601-9 : 1.50
1. Bible—Caricatures and cartoons. 2. Meditations. I. Title.

HILLS, L. Rust. 248'.4
How to do things right: the revelations of a fussy man, by L. Rust Hills. [1st ed.] Garden City, N.Y., Doubleday, 1972. xvi, 145 p. 22 cm. [BJ1581.2.H55] 77-186655 4.95
1. Conduct of life. I. Title.

HODGES, Zane Clark. 248'.4
The hungry inherit; refreshing insights on salvation, discipleship, and rewards. Chicago, Moody Press [1972] 128 p. 22 cm. [BT751.2.H57] 72-175491 ISBN 0-8024-3800-8 3.95
1. Salvation. 2. Christian life—1960- I. Title.

HOEKEMA, Anthony A., 1913- 248'.4
The Christian looks at himself / by Anthony A. Hoekema. Grand Rapids : Eerdmans, [1975] 152 p. ; 18 cm. Includes indexes. Includes index. Bibliography: p. 143-144. [BT701.2.H62] 75-1285 ISBN 0-8028-1595-2 pbk. : 1.95
1. Man (Theology) 2. Christian life—Reformed authors. 3. Christianity—Psychology. I. Title.

HOFMANN, Hans F., 1923- 248.4
Breakthrough to life, by Hans Hofmann. Boston, Beacon Press [1969] vii, 215 p. 21 cm. [BJ1581.2.H6] 69-14601 5.95
1. Conduct of life. I. Title.

HOGUE, Richard. 248'.4
Sex, Satan, and Jesus. Nashville, Tenn., Broadman Press [1973] 160 p. illus. 20 cm. [BV4501.2.H536] 73-86668 ISBN 0-8054-5319-9
1. Christian life—1960- 2. Sexual ethics. I. Title.

HOLLOWAY, James Y., 1927- 248'.4
comp.
Callings! Edited by James Y. Holloway and Will D. Campbell. New York, Paulist Press [1974] vi, 280 p. 18 cm. (Deus books) "Most chapters in this book were originally published in the 1972 fall-winter issue of Katallagete, journal of the Committee of Southern Churchmen." [BV4740.H57] 73-90070 ISBN 0-8091-1806-8 1.95 (pbk.)
1. Vocation. I. Campbell, Will D., joint comp. II. Katallagete. III. Title.
Contents omitted.

HOLMES, Marjorie, 1910- 248'.4
How can I find you, God? / Marjorie Holmes ; illustrated by Betty Fraser. Boston : G. K. Hall, 1975. p. cm. Large print ed. [BV4501.2.H568 1975] 75-22253 ISBN 0-8161-6323-5 : 10.95
1. Christian life—1960- I. Title.

HOLTERMANN, Carla. 248'.4
Journey to fulfillment : a guide for the Christian life / Carla Holtermann. Minneapolis : Augsburg Pub. House, [1975] 88 p. ; 20 cm. [BV4501.2.H575] 74-14179 ISBN 0-8066-1462-5 pbk. : 2.50
1. Christian life—1960- I. Title.

HOOKER, Thomas, 1586-1647. 248'.4
The Christians two chiefe lessons, viz. selfe-deniall and selfe-tryall / Thomas Hooker. New York : Arno Press, 1972. 303 p. ; 23 cm. (Research library of colonial Americana) "Reprinted from the best available copy. Pagination was irregular (skipped from page 99 to 200) in all available copies; text appears to be complete." Reprint of the 1640 ed. printed for P. Stephens, London. [BV4500.H627 1972] 74-141112 ISBN 0-405-03325-7
1. Christian life. 2. Self-denial. I. Title. II. Series.

HOWARD, J. Grant. 248'.4
Knowing God's will—and doing it / by J. Grant Howard, Jr. Grand Rapids : Zondervan Pub. House, c1976. 126 p. ; 18 cm. [BV4501.2.H627] 75-42141 4.95
1. God—Will. 2. Christian life—1960- I. Title.

HOWARD, Thomas. 248'.4
Splendor in the ordinary / Thomas Howard. Wheaton, Ill. : Tyndale House Publishers, c1976, 1977 printing. 128 p. ; 21 cm. [BV4526.2.H67] 76-47297 ISBN 0-8423-6425-0 : 2.95
1. Family—Religious life. I. Title.

HOWARD, Wilbur F 248.4
Victorious living. Nashville, Convention Press [c1961] 131p. 20cm. Includes bibliography. [BV4501.2.H64] 62-8392
1. Christian life. I. Title.

HOWE, Reuel L., 1905- 248.4
Survival plus, by Reuel L. Howe. New York, Seabury Press [1971] xiii, 177 p. 21 cm. [BJ1581.2.H65] 76-148143 4.95
1. Conduct of life. I. Title.

HOWE, Reuel L., 1905- 248'.4
Survival plus, by Reuel L. Howe. New rev. ed. New York, Seabury Press [1974] 177 p. 21 cm. "A Crossroad book." [BJ1581.2.H65 1974] 73-21664 ISBN 0-8164-2088-2 2.95
1. Conduct of life. I. Title.

HOYER, Theodore, 1883- 248.4
The Christian view of life. Saint Louis, Concordia Pub. House [1965] 112 p. 15 cm. [BV4832.2.H67] 65-25663
1. Devotional exercises. 2. Christian life. I. Title.

HOYER, Theodore, 1883- 248.4
The Christian view of life. St. Louis, Concordia [c.1965] 112p. 15cm. [BV4832.2.H67] 65-25663 1.50
1. Devotional exercises. 2. Christian life. I. Title.

HUBBARD, David Allan. 248'.4
How to face your fears. [1st ed.] Philadelphia, A. J. Holman Co. [1972] 140 p. 22 cm. [BV4501.2.H7] 72-5670 ISBN 0-87981-013-0 3.95
1. Fear. 2. Christian life—Baptist authors. I. Title.

HUEGEL, Frederick Julius, 248.4
1889-
Reigning with Christ. Grand Rapids, Zondervan Pub. House [1963] 88 p. 21 cm. [BV4501.2.H77] 63-1273
1. Christian life. I. Title.

HUEGEL, Frederick Julius, 248.4
1889-
Reigning with Christ. Grand Rapids, Mich., Zondervan [c.1963] 88p. 21cm. 63-1273 1.95 bds.,
1. Christian life. I. Title.

HUEGEL, Frederick Julius, 248.4
1889-
Reigning with Christ, by F. J. Huegel. Minneapolis, Bethany Fellowship Inc [1973, c1963] 88 p. 18 cm. (Dimension books) [BV4501.2H77] ISBN 0-87123-480-7 0.95 (pbk.)
1. Christian life. I. Title.

HUFFMAN, John. 248'.4
Becoming a whole family / John A. Huffman, Jr. Waco, Tex. : Word Books, c1975. 156 p. ; 23 cm. [BV4526.2.H84] 75-10093 5.95
1. Family—Religious life. I. Title.

HUGHSON, Shirley Carter, 248.4
1867-1949.
To tell the godly man; selections from the writings of Shirley Carter Hughson. Arr. and edited by William Joseph Barnds. [1st ed.] West Park, N. Y., Holy Cross Press [1958] 181p. 21cm. [BV4501.2.H8] 58-14162
1. Spiritual life. I. Title.

HUNT, June. 248'.4
Above all else. Old Tappan, N.J., F. H. Revell Co. [1975] 128 p. 20 cm. [BV4501.2.H826] 74-13243 ISBN 0-8007-0689-7 3.95
1. Hunt, June. 2. Christian life—1960- I. Title.

*HUNTER, Frances. 248.4
Come alive. First ed. Van Nuys, Calif., Bible Voice Books, [1975] 146 p. 20 cm. [BV4501.2] 2.95 (pbk.)
1. Jesus Christ—Teachings. 2. Conduct of life. 3. Christian Life. I. Title.
Pub. address: P.O. Box 7491 Van Nuys, Calif 91409.

HUNTER, John Edward, 1909- 248.4

Knowing God's secrets; the secret of the effective Christian life, by John Hunter. Introd. by W. Ian Thomas. Grand Rapids, Zondervan Pub. House [1965] 151 p. 21 cm. [BV4501.2.H84] 65-19497
1. Christian life. I. Title.

HUNTER, John Edward, 1909- 248.4
Knowing God's secrets; the secret of the effective Christian life. Introd. by W. Ian Thomas. Grand Rapids, Mich., Zondervan [c.1965] 151p. 21cm. [BV4501.2.H84] 65-19497 1.50 pap.,
1. Christian life. I. Title.

HUNTER, John Edward, 1909- 248.4
Living the Christ-filled life; seving God wholeheartedly, by John E. Hunter. Grand Rapids, Zondervan Pub. House, [1969] 130 p. 22 cm. [BV4501.2.H853] 69-11635 2.95
1. Spiritual life—Addresses, essays, lectures. I. Title.

*HURLEY, Karen. 248'.4
Why Sunday mass; new views for those who go & those who don't. Edited by Karen Hurley. Cincinnati, Ohio, St Anthony Messenger Press, [1973] 123 p. illus. 18 cm. [BV4523] ISBN 0-912228-08-3 1.35 (pbk.)
1. Christian life—1960- I. Title.

HYGONET, Bernard. 248.4
Deliver us from evil. Translated from the French by Sister M. Bernarda. Chicago, Franciscan Herald Press [c1958] 125p. 18cm. [BX2373.S5H9] 58-13684
1. Suffering. I. Title.

IREDALE, Edith (Brubaker) 248.4
A promise fulfilled. Book design by Paul Dailey. Elgin, Ill., Brethren Press [1962] 208p. 21cm. 'Record of one year [1900] in the life of the family of Elder E. S. Brubaker, a Brethren farmer-preacher.'--Dust jacket. [BX7817.I6I7] 62-16018
1. Church of the Brethren—Indiana. I. Title.

JACOBS, James Vernon, 248'.4
1898-
Spiritual growth / by J. Vernon Jacobs. Cincinnati, Ohio : New Life Books, c1975. 160 p. ; 22 cm. [BV4501.2.J313] 75-18218 ISBN 0-87239-044-6
1. Christian life—1960- 2. Virtues. I. Title.

JACOBSEN, Marion Leach, 248'.4
1908-
Saints and snobs; what the church needs now is love, sweet love. Wheaton, Ill., Tyndale House Publishers [1972] 207 p. 22 cm. Includes bibliographical references. [BV4501.2.J314] 72-78876 ISBN 0-8423-5820-X 3.95
1. Christian life—1960- 2. Fellowship. I. Title.

JENTGES, Damian. 248.4
Search for sanctity. Fresno, Calif., Academy Guild Press [c.1959] 203p. illus. (ports.) 22cm. 59-10452 3.95
1. Spiritual direction. I. Title.

JOHNSON, Merle Allison. 248'.4
The kingdom seekers. Nashville, Abingdon

Press [1973] 144 p. 20 cm. [BV4501.2.J56] 72-14253 ISBN 0-687-20911-0 3.75
1. Christian life—1960- 2. Jesus people. I. Title.

JOHNSON, Raynor Carey. 248.4
The spiritual path, by Raynor C. Johnson. [1st ed.] New York, Harper & Row [1971] viii, 216 p. 22 cm. Bibliography: p. 213-216. [BL624.J64 1971] 70-160634 6.95
1. Spiritual life. I. Title.

JOHNSTON, Dorothy Grunbock. 248.4
Hey, Mom! Wheaton, Ill., Scripture Press Publications [1965] 96 p. illus. 23 cm. [BV4829.J6] 65-22376
1. Mothers — Religious life. 2. Children — Management. I. Title.

JOHNSTON, Dorothy Grunbock 248.4
Hey, Mom! Wheaton, Ill., Scripture Pr. 1825 College Ave. [c.1965] 96p. illus. 23cm. [BV4829.J6] 65-22376 1.25 pap.,
1. Mothers—Religious life. 2. Children—Management. I. Title.

JOHNSTON, Russ. 248'.4
God can make it happen / Russ Johnston with Maureen Rank ; [foreword by Lorne C. Sanny] . Wheaton, Ill. : Victor Books, c1976. 130 p. ; 21 cm. (An Input book) [BV4501.2.J583] 76-9215 ISBN 0-88207-741-4 pbk. : 1.95
1. Christian life—1960- I. Rank, Maureen, joint author. II. Title.

JONES, Eli Stanley, 1884- 248.4
Victory through surrender [by] E. Stanley Jones. Nashville, Abingdon Press [1966] 128 p. 20 cm. [BV4501.2.J6] 66-21189
1. Christian life. 2. Self-realization. I. Title.

JONES, George Curtis, 1911- 248.4
What are you doing? St. Louis, Bethany Press [1956] 100p. 21cm. [BV4501.2.J65] 56-6555
1. Christian life. I. Title.

JORDAN, Gerald Ray 248.4
Religion that is eternal. New York, Macmillan, [c.]1960. viii, 134p. 21cm. 60-8121 3.00
1. Christian life. I. Title.

JORDAN, Gerald Ray, 1896- 248.4
Religion that is eternal. New York, Macmillan, 1960. 134p. 21cm. [BV4501.2.J67] 60-8121
1. Christian life. I. Title.

†JOSEPHSON, Elmer A. 248'.4
God's key to health and happiness / Elmer A. Josephson. Old Tappan, N.J. : Revell, c1976. 224 p. ; 21 cm. [RA776.5.J57 1976] 76-151461 ISBN 0-8007-0841-5 pbk. : 3.95
1. Bible—Medicine, hygiene, etc. 2. Health. 3. Diet. I. Title.

JUNKER, Bill. 248'.4
Freedom bound / Bill Junker. Nashville : Broadman Press, c1975. 128 p. ; 18 cm. Includes bibliographical references. [BT810.2.J86] 75-2930 ISBN 0-8054-5553-1 pbk. : 1.95
1. Freedom (Theology) I. Title.

JURGENSEN, Barbara. 248'.4
God probably doesn't know I exist. Grand Rapids, Mich., Zondervan Pub. House [1973] 84 p. illus. 18 cm. [BV4501.2.J86] 72-95519 0.95 (pbk.)
1. Christian life—1960- I. Title.

JURGENSEN, Barbara. 248'.4
Quit bugging me. Illustrated by Jan and Barbara Jurgensen. Grand Rapids, Zondervan Pub. House [1972, c1968] 1 v. (unpaged) illus. 18 cm. (Zondervan books) [BV4517.J86] 68-54206 0.95
1. Christian life—Anecdotes, facetiae, satire, etc. I. Title.

JURGENSEN, Barbara. 248.4
You're out of date, God? Illustrated by Robin Jensen. Grand Rapids, Zondervan Pub. House [1971] 79 p. illus. 18 cm. [BV4517.J87] 71-156245 0.95
1. Christian life—Anecdotes, facetiae, satire, etc. I. Title.

KALOR, Earl N., 1912- 248'.4
Why people? By Erl N. Kalor. San Antonio, Naylor Co. [1972] viii, 68 p. 22 cm. [BJ1581.2.K3] 72-7236 ISBN 0-8111-0468-0 4.95
1. Conduct of life. I. Title.

KATES, Frederick Ward, 248.4
1910-
A moment between two eternities. [1st ed.] New York, Harper & Row [1965] xi, 189 p. 21 cm. (Harper chapel books, CB10) [BV4501.2.K3] 65-4276
1. Christian life. I. Title.

KATES, Frederick Ward, 248.4
1910-
A moment between two eternities. New York, Harper [c.1965] xi, 189p. 21cm. (Chapel bks. CB10) [BV4501.K3] 65-4276 1.95 pap.,
1. Christian life. I. Title.

KEATHLEY, M. F., 1905- 248.4
The road to happiness and success, by M. F. Keathley, Sr. San Antonio, Tex., Naylor Co. [1971] xiii, 119 p. illus. 22 cm. Autobiographical. [BX6495.K34A3] 79-168743 ISBN 0-8111-0420-6 4.95
I. Title.

KEEGAN, Gilbert Kearnie 248.4
Your next big step. Nashville, Broadman Press [c.1960] 64p. 16cm. 60-9533 1.25 bds.,
1. Christian life. I. Title.

KEEGAN, Gilbert Kearnie, 248.4
1907-
Your next big step. Nashville, Broadman Press [1960] 64p. 16cm. [BV4501.2.K4] 60-9533
1. Christian life. I. Title.

KEIPER, Ralph L. 248'.4
The power of Biblical thinking / Ralph L. Keiper. Old Tappan, N.J. : F. H. Revell Co., c1977. 159 p. ; 21 cm. [BV4501.2.K417] 77-2956 ISBN 0-8007-0862-8 : 5.95
1. Bible—Biography. 2. Christian life—1960- I. Title.

KEIPER, Ralph L. 248'.4
The power of Biblical thinking / Ralph L. Keiper. Old Tappan, N.J. : F. H. Revell Co., c1977. 159 p. ; 21 cm. [BV4501.2.K417] 77-2956 ISBN 0-8007-0862-8 : 5.95
1. Bible—Biography. 2. Christian life—1960- I. Title.

KEMP, Charles F., 1912- 248'.4
Thinking and acting Biblically / Charles F. Kemp. Nashville : Abingdon, c1976. 111 p. ; 20 cm. [BV4509.5.K37] 75-43850 ISBN 0-687-41739-2 pbk. : 3.50
1. Bible—Devotional literature. 2. Christian life—Biblical teaching. I. Title.

KENNEDY, Eugene C. 248.4
A time for love [by] Eugene C. Kennedy. [1st ed.] Garden City, N.Y., Doubleday, 1970. 168 p. 22 cm. [BF575.L8K43] 75-121952 4.95
1. Love. I. Title.

KENNEDY, James Hardee. 248.4
The commission of Moses and the Christian calling. Grand Rapids, Eerdmans [1964] 74 p. 21 cm. "Five lectures delivered to the Annual Pastors Conference at the New Orleans Baptist Theological Seminary in June of 1962." Bibliographical footnotes. [BS580.M6K4] 64-16585
1. Moses. I. Title.

KENNEDY, James Hardee 248.4
The commission of Moses and the Christian calling. Grand Rapids, Mich., Eerdmans [c.1964] 74p. 21cm. Five lectures delivered to the Annual Pastors Conference at the New Orleans Baptist Theological Seminary in June of 1962. Bibl. 64-16585 2.00 bds.,
1. Moses. I. Title.

KEPPLER, Paul Wilhelm von, 248'.4
Bp., 1852-1926.
More joy / by Paul Wilhelm von Keppler ; adapted into English by Joseph McSorley. New ed. / edited by Marion A. Habig. Chicago : Franciscan Herald Press, [1975] p. cm. Translation of Mehr Freude. At head of title: What the world needs now. Includes bibliographical references. [BX2350.K45 1975] 74-30048 ISBN 0-8199-0556-9
1. Christian life. 2. Joy and sorrow. I. Title. II. Title: What the world needs now.

KERR, Clarence Ware, 1893- 248'.4
Love, familystyle : "how to have a happy home" / by Clarence W. Kerr ; adapted by Nathanael Olson. Westchester, Ill. : Good News, [1974] 79 p. : ill. ; 18 cm. (One evening book) [BV835.K47] 74-18850 pbk. : 1.25
1. Marriage. 2. Family—Religious life. I. Title.

KESLER, Jay. 248'.4
The strong weak people : for those to whom perfection comes slowly / Jay Kessler. Wheaton, Ill. : Victor Books, c1976. 119 p. ; 21 cm. (An Input book) [BV4501.2.K445] 76-20918 ISBN 0-88207-739-2 pbk. : 2.25
1. Christian life—1960- I. Title.

KETTNER, Elmer A 248.4
A closer walk with God. Saint Louis, Concordia Pub. House [1959] 95p. 20cm. Includes bibliography. [BV4511.K4] 59-1017
1. Christian life—Study and teaching. I. Title.

KEYS to creative faith / 248'.4
edited by Walden Howard. Waco, Tex. : Word Books, c1976. 162 p. ; 21 cm. "Portions of this book originally appeared in Faith/at/work magazine." [BV4501.2.K484] 76-43136 ISBN 0-87680-815-1 : 3.95
1. Christian life—1960- I. Howard, Walden. II. Faith at work.

KIERKEGAARD, Soren Aabye, 248.4
1813-1855.
Works of love. Translated from the Danish by David F. Swenson and Lillian Marvin Swenson. With an introd. by Douglas V. Steere. Port Washington, Kennikat Press [1972, c1946] xiv, 317 p. 23 cm. Translation of Kjerlighedens gjerninger. Includes bibliographical references. [BV4505.K42 1972] 70-153224 ISBN 0-8046-1534-9
1. Spiritual life. I. Title.

*KIMBALL, Joe. 248'.4
Observations. New Haven, Canterbury Press [1974] 402 p. 22 cm. [BJ1581.2] 3.50 (pbk.)
1. Conduct of life. I. Title.
Publisher's address: P.O. Box 2065 New Haven, Conn. 06521

KIMMEL, Jo, 1931- 248'.4
Stop playing pious games. Nashville, Abingdon Press [1974] 126 p. 20 cm. Bibliography: p. [125]-126. [BV4501.2.K493] 73-13625 ISBN 0-687-39595-X 3.95
1. Christian life—1960- I. Title.

KINGHORN, Kenneth C. 248'.4
Dynamic discipleship [by] Kenneth C. Kinghorn. Old Tappan, N.J., F. H. Revell Co. [1973] 157 p. 21 cm. [BV4501.2.K494] 73-601 ISBN 0-8007-0591-2 4.95
1. Christian life—1960- I. Title.

KIRBAN, Salem. 248'.4
How to live above & beyond your circumstances / by Salem Kirban. Huntingdon Valley, Pa. : Kirban, c1974. 218 p. : ill. ; 18 cm. [BV4501.2.K498] 74-19641 ISBN 0-912582-20-0 : 3.95
1. Bible—Biography. 2. Christian life—1960- I. Title.

KIRK, Albert Emmanuel, 248.4
1880-
A consciousness of God; a study of the essence of genuine religion. Foreword by Gordon B. Thompson. [1st ed.] New York, Exposition Press [1962] 159p. 21cm. (An Exposition Testument book) [BV4501.2.K5] 62-21056
1. Spiritual life—Methodist authors. I. Title.

KIRK, Albert Emmanuel, 248.4
1880-
A consciousness of God; a study of the essence of genuine religion. Foreword by Gordon B. Thompson. New York, Exposition [c.1962] 159p. 21cm. (Exposition-Testament bk.) 62-21056 3.50
1. Spiritual life—Methodist authors. I. Title.

KIRKLAND, Bryant M. 248.4
Growing in Christian faith. Nashville, Tidings [c1963] 71 p. 19 cm. [BV4501.2.K52] 63-22407
1. Spiritual life. I. Title.

KLIEWER, Evelyn. 248'.4
Freedom from fat / Evelyn Kliewer ; ill. by Al Hartley. Old Tappan, N.J. : Revell, c1977. 160 p. : ill. ; 18 cm. (Spire books) Bibliography: p. 160. [RM222.2.K5727] 77-8492 ISBN 0-8007-8308-5 pbk. : 1.95
1. Reducing—Moral and religious aspects. 2. Reducing—Biography. 3. Reducing diets. 4. Kliewer, Evelyn. I. Title.

KLINKERMAN, Oscar J. 248'.4
Welcome to a new life : an introduction to the Christian faith / Oscar J. Klinkerman. St. Louis : Concordia Pub. House, c1976. 63 p. ; 19 cm. [BV4501.2.K54] 75-31786 ISBN 0-570-03720-4 : 1.00
1. Christian life—1960- I. Title.

KNIGHT, George Wendell, 248'.4
1940- comp.
The Christian home in the 70's [by] George W. Knight. Nashville, Broadman Press [1974] 125 p. 20 cm. Articles previously published in Home life. [BV4526.2.K58] 73-89525 ISBN 0-8054-8232-6 1.50
1. Family—Religious life. I. Home life (Nashville) II. Title.

*KNIGHT, Goldie. 248.4
God's great plan. New York, Carlton [1968] 73p. 21cm. (Hearthstone bk.) 2.50
I. Title.

KOOIMAN, Helen W. 248'.4
Forgiveness in action [by] Helen W. Kooiman. New York, Hawthrone Books [1974] xi, 144 p. 22 cm. Includes bibliographical references. [BJ1476.K66 1974] 73-18897 5.95
1. Forgiveness. I. Title.

KOOPMAN, Leroy. 248'.4
Beauty care for the eyes / by Leroy Koopman. Grand Rapids : Zondervan Pub. House, c1975. p. cm. [BV4501.2.K63] 75-21124 pbk. : 1.50
1. Spiritual life. I. Title.

KOOPMAN, Leroy. 248'.4
Beauty care for the hands / LeRoy Koopman. Grand Rapids : Zondervan Pub. House, c1977. 93 p. ; 18 cm. Includes index. [BV4501.2.K64] 77-3709 ISBN 0-310-26832-X pbk. : 1.50
1. Spiritual life. I. Title.

KOPPE, William A. 248'.4
How persons grow in Christian community, by William A. Koppe. Terence Y. Mullins, editor. [Philadelphia] Fortress Press [1973] 206 p. illus. 23 cm. (Yearbooks in Christian education, v. 4) Includes bibliographical references. [BV4571.2.K66] 73-171125 5.95
1. Children—Religious life—Case studies. 2. Youth—Religious life—Case studies. 3. Learning, Psychology of—Case studies. I. Title. II. Series.

*KRUTZA, William J. comp. 248.4
Facing your nation; discussions on Christian responsibility in national life. Editing and commentary by William J. Krutza and Philip P. DiCicco. Grand Rapids, Baker Book House, [1975] 160 p. 18 cm. (Contemporary discussion series) [BV4501.2] ISBN 0-8010-5372-2 1.95 (pbk.)
1. Christian life. 2. Conduct of life. I. DiCicco, Philip P. joint comp. II. Title.

KURZWEG, B F 248.4
The world that is [by] B. F. Kurzweg. Saint Louis, Concordia Pub. House [1965] 95 p. 18 cm. (The Christian encounters) Bibliography: p. 95. [BV4501.2.K8] 65-16964
1. Christian life — Lutheran authors. I. Title. II. Series.

KURZWEG, B. F. 248.4
The world that is. St. Louis, Concordia [c.1965] 95p. 18cm. (Christian encounters) Bibl. [BV4501.2.K8] 65-16964 1.00 pap.,
1. Christian life—Lutheran authors. I. Title. II. Series.

*LACOSTE, Edward, 1923- 248.4
Black nations in action, by Rev. Edward LaCoste. [First ed.] New York, Vantage [1972] 81 p. 21 cm. [BV4501] ISBN 0-533-00138-2 3.75
1. Christian life. I. Title.

LACY, Mary Lou 248.4
And God wants people. Richmond, Va., Knox [c.1962] 80p. 62-11717 2.00 bds.,
1. Love (Theology) 2. Friendship. I. Title.

LACY, Mary Lou. 248.4
Springboard to discovery. Richmond, John Knox Press [1965] 92 p. 21 cm. [BV772.L3] 65-10277
1. Stewardship, Christian. I. Title.

LACY, Mary Lou 248.4
Springboard to discovery. Richmond, Va., Knox [c.1965] 92p. 21cm. [BV772.L3] 65-10277 2.00 bds.,
1. Stewardship, Christian. I. Title.

LAHAYE, Tim F. 248'.4
Ten steps to victory over depression : from "How to win over depression / Tim LaHaye. Grand Rapids, Mich. : Zondervan Pub. House, c1974. 41 p. ; 18 cm. [BV4509.5.L33] 75-315623 0.75
1. Christian life—1960- 2. Depression, Mental. I. Title.

LAIR, Jess. 248'.4
"I ain't much, baby—but I'm all I've got." Garden City, N.Y., Doubleday, 1972. 215 p. 21 cm. Bibliography: p. [214]-215. [BJ1581.2.L23] 78-180086 2.95
1. Conduct of life. I. Title.

LAIR, Jess. 248.4
"I ain't much, baby-but I'm all I've got." Greenwich, Conn., Fawcett, [1974 c1969] [254 p.] 18 cm. (Fawcett crest book) Bibliography. p. 252-253. [BJ1581.2L23] 1.75 (pbk.)
1. Conduct of life. I. Title.

LANCASTER, Kenneth R. 1903- 248.4
Guidelines for survival, by Kenneth R. Lancaster. Minneapolis, Denison [1966] 144p. 23cm. [BV4501.2.L318] 66-28318 3.00
1. Christian life. I. Title.

LANDORF, Joyce. 248'.4
"Joyce I feel like I know you" : based on letters and conversations about life's pressure points / Joyce Landorf. Wheaton, Ill. : Victor Books, 1976. 143 p. ; 18 cm. [BV4501.2.L3182] 77-358469 ISBN 0-88207-742-2 : 1.75
1. Christian life—1960- 2. Conduct of life. I. Title.

LANDORF, Joyce. 248'.4
The richest lady in town. Grand Rapids, Mich., Zondervan Pub. House [1973] 152 p. 22 cm. [BV4501.2.L3183] 73-500 3.95
1. Landorf, Joyce. 2. Christian life—1960- I. Title.

LANDORF, Joyce. 248'.4
Tough & tender : what every women wants in

a man / Joyce Landorf. Old Tappan, N.J. : Revell, [1975] 157 p. ; 21 cm. Includes bibliographies. [BV835.L35] 75-17679 ISBN 0-8007-0753-2 : 5.95
1. Marriage. I. Title.

*LANGLEY, John Milton. 248.4
Man: master or slave? New York, Vantage [1968] 135p. 21cm. 3.75
I. Title.

LARSEN, Earnest. 248'.4
Treat me easy / Earnest Larsen. Liguori, Mo. : Liguori Publications, 1975. 122 p. : ill. ; 18 cm. [BF575.L8L28] 75-11322 pbk. : 1.50
1. Love. 2. Interpersonal relations. 3. Psychology, Religious. I. Title.

LARSEN, Lewis H. 248.4
The universal law of man, by Lewis H. Larsen. Salt Lake City, [1969] 68 p. port. 19 cm. [BJ1595.L34] 71-7148 3.75
1. Conduct of life. I. Title.

LARSON, Bruce. 248.4
Dare to live now= Grand Rapids, Zondervan Pub. House [1965] 126 p. 21 cm. [BV4501.1.L32] 65-28347
1. Christian life — Presbyterian authors. I. Title.

LARSON, Bruce 248.4
Dare to live now! Grand Rapids Mich., Zondervan [c.1965] 126p. 21cm. [BV4501.2.L32] 2.50 sChristian life--Presbyterian authors.
I. Title.

*LARSON, Muriel. 248.4
Living miracles. Anderson, Ind., Warner Pr [1973] 90 p. 18 cm. (A Portal Book) [BV4510.] ISBN 0-87162-151-7 pap. 0.95
1. Christian life. 2. Meditations. I. Title.

LAURENCE, Theodor. 248'4
The miracle power of believing / Theodor Laurence. West Nyack, N.Y. : Parker Pub. Co., c1976. 204 p. ; 24 cm. [BJ1611.2.L4] 75-35831 ISBN 0-13-585810-0 : 8.95 pbk. : 2.95
1. Apostles' Creed—Miscellanea. 2. Success. 3. Creeds—Miscellanea. I. Title.
Distributed by Prentice-Hall.

LAURENT, Bob. 248'.4
What a way to go. Elgin, Ill., D. C. Cook Pub. Co. [1973] 127 p. 18 cm. [BV4832.2.L34] 73-78714 ISBN 0-912692-20-0 1.25 (pbk.)
1. Laurent, Bob. 2. Christian life—1960- I. Title.

LAURENT, Bob. 248'.4
A world of differents / Bob Laurent. Old Tappan, N.J. : F. H. Revell Co., [1975] 127 p. ; 21 cm. [BV3790.L253] 75-20290 ISBN 0-8007-0755-9 pbk. : 2.95
1. Evangelistic work. I. Title.

LAURIE, Greg. 248'.4
A handbook on Christian dating / by Greg Laurie. Costa Mesa, Calif. : Maranatha Evangelical Assoc., c1976. p. cm. [HQ801.L33] 76-17661 pbk. : 1.25
1. Dating (Social customs) 2. Courtship. 3. Christian life—1960- I. Title.

LAWRENCE, Gene H. 248'.4
The laws of right relationship : with self, man, and God / Gene H. Lawrence. 1st ed. Hicksville, N.Y. : Exposition Press, [1974] viii, 206 p. ; 22 cm. Includes index. [BJ1581.2.L28] 74-80684 ISBN 0-682-48040-1 : 6.00
1. Conduct of life. I. Title.

LECLERCQ, Jacques 248.4
Back to Jesus. Translated from the French by Louis P. Roche. New York, P. J. Kenedy [c.1959] 213p. 21cm. 59-12898 3.95
1. Christian life—Catholic authors. 2. Christian ethics—Catholic authors. I. Title.

LECLERCQ. JACQUES, 1891- 248.4
Back to Jesus. Translated from the French by Louis P. Roche. New York, P. J. Kenedy [1959] 213p. 21cm. [BX2350.L452 1959] 59-12898
1. Christian life— Catholic authors. 2. Christian ethics—Catholic authors. I. Title.

LEDERACH, Paul M. 248'.4
The spiritual family and the biological family, by Paul M. Lederach. Scottdale, Pa., Herald Press, 1973. 31 p. port. 18 cm. (Focal pamphlet no. 24) [BV4526.2.L38] 73-4175 ISBN 0-8361-1717-4
1. Family—Religious life. I. Title.

LEE, Joseph, 1908- 248'.4
How to live a Christian; prove all things by the Word. Philadelphia, Dorrance [1974] 139 p. 22 cm. [BV4501.2.L425] 73-94390 5.95
1. Christian life—1960- I. Title.

LEENHOUTS, Keith J. 248'.4
A father, a son, and a three-mile run / Keith J. Leenhouts. Grand Rapids : Zondervan Pub. House, [1975] 140 p. : ill. ; 23 cm. [BR1725.L37L43] 74-25337 4.95
1. Leenhouts, Bill. 2. Father and child. I. Title.

LEENHOUTS, Keith J. 248'.4
A father, a son, and a three-mile run / Keith J. Leenhouts. Grand Rapids : Zondervan Pub. House, 1977, c1975. 144 p. ; 18 p. [BR1725.L37L43 1977] 77-151379 pbk. : 1.95
1. Leenhouts, Bill. 2. Leenhouts, Keith J. 3. Father and child. I. Title.

LEHMAN, Dale. 248.4
Living the Christian life. Anderson, Inc., Warner Press [1963] 96 p. 19 cm. [BV4501.2.L43] 63-17430
1. Christian life. I. Title.

LEHMAN, Dale 248.4
Living the Christian life. Anderson, Ind., Warner [c.1963] 96p. 19cm. 63-17430 1.25 pap.,
1. Christian life. I. Title.

LESLIE, Charles W 248.4
God is a spirit, by Charles W. Leslie. Boston, Christopher Pub. House [1965] 94 p. 21 cm. [BT77.L347] 65-21527
1. Theology, Doctrinal — Popular works. I. Title.

LESLIE, Charles W. 248.4
God is a spirit. Boston, Christopher [c.1965] 94p. 21cm. [BT77.L347] 65-21527 2.95
1. Theology, Doctrinal—Popular works. I. Title.

LETOURNEAU, Richard. 248'.4
Keeping your cool in a world of tension / Richard LeTourneau. Grand Rapids : Zondervan Pub. House, [1975] 141 p. : ill. ; 22 cm. [BV4501.2.L46] 74-11867 4.95
1. Christian life—1960- I. Title.

LIEGE, Pierre Andre, 1921- 248.4
Consider Christian maturity. Tr. [from French] introd. by Thomas C. Donlan. Chicago, Priory Pr. [1966, c.1965] 125p. 19cm. [BX2350.2.L4613] 65-28348 2.95
1. Christian life—Catholic authors. I. Title.

LINDSELL, Harold, 1913- 248'.4
The world, the flesh, and the Devil / Harold Lindsell. Washington : Canon Press, c1973. xiv, 227 p. ; 22 cm. [BV4501.2.L54] 75-324197 ISBN 0-913686-04-2
1. Christian life—1960- I. Title.

LITTLE foxes that hurt. 248'.4
Denver : B/P Accent Micro-books, [1973] 64 p. : ill. ; 16 cm. [BV4510.2.L57] 74-190390
1. Christian life—1960- 2. Worry. 3. Envy. 4. Anger.

LIVE in the spirit; 248'.4
a compendium of themes on the spiritual life as presented at the Council on Spiritual Life. Editorial committee: Harris Jansen, chairman, Elva Hoover [and] Gary Leggett. Springfield, Mo., Gospel Pub. House [1972] 359 p. 22 cm. Sponsored by the Assemblies of God, General Council. [BV4501.2.L59] 73-154808
1. Spiritual life—Addresses, essays, lectures. I. Jansen, Harris, ed. II. Council on Spiritual Life, Minneapolis, 1972. III. Assemblies of God, General Council.

LIVING and growing together : today's Christian family / Gary Collins, editor. Waco, Tex. : Word Books, c1976. 174 p. ; 22 cm. Papers prepared for the Continental Congress on the Family held in St. Louis, Oct. 1975. Includes bibliographical references. [BV4526.2.L58] 76-19525 ISBN 0-87680-844-5 : 4.25 248'.4
1. Family—Congresses. I. Collins, Gary R. II. Continental Congress on the Family, St. Louis, 1975.

LOCKERBIE, Jeanette W. 248'.4
The image of joy [by] Jeanette Lockerbie. Old Tappan, N.J., F. H. Revell Co. [1974] 125 p. 21 cm. [BV4832.2.L54] 73-17197 ISBN 0-8007-0640-4 3.95
1. Meditations. 2. Christian life—1960- I. Title.

LOVETTE, Roger, 1935- 248'.4
A faith of our own / by Roger Lovette. Philadelphia : United Church Press, [1976] 143 p. ; 21 cm. "A Pilgrim Press book." Includes bibliographical references. [BV4501.2.L68] 75-27086 ISBN 0-8298-0299-1
1. Christian life—1960- I. Title.

LYNCH, Etta. 248'.4
Help is only a prayer away. Old Tappan, N.J., F. H. Revell Co. [1972] 158 p. 21 cm. [BV220.L94] 72-172682 ISBN 0-8007-0496-7 3.95
1. Prayer. I. Title.

LYNCH, Frederick Henry, 1867-1934. 248'.4
The Christian in war time, by Frederick Lynch, with four additional chapters by Charles E. Jefferson [and others] With a new introd. for the Garland ed. by William F. McKee. New York, Garland Pub., 1972 [c1917] 14, 90 p. 22 cm. (The Garland library of war and peace) [D639.R4L8 1972] 71-147674 ISBN 0-8240-0431-0
1. European War, 1914-1918—Religious aspects. I. Title. II. Series.

MACARTHUR, John, 1936- 248'.4
The church, the body of Christ [by] John MacArthur, Jr. Grand Rapids, Zondervan Pub. House [1973] 199 p. illus. 18 cm. [BV600.2.M26] 73-2655 1.25 (pbk.)
1. Church. 2. Christian life—1960- I. Title.

MACARTHUR, John, 1936- 248'.4
Keys to spiritual growth / John F. MacArthur, Jr. Old Tappan, N.J. : Revell, c1976. 127 p. ; 21 cm. [BV4501.2.M16] 75-40301 ISBN 0-8007-0777-X : 4.95
1. Christian life—1960- I. Title.

MCCARTHY, Estelle, 1931- 248'.4
The power picture, by Estelle and Charles McCarthy. New York, Friendship Press [1973] 175 p. 18 cm. Includes bibliographical references. [BT745.M23] 72-14310 ISBN 0-377-03031-7 1.95 (pbk.)
1. Power (Theology) I. McCarthy, Charles, 1926- joint author. II. Title.

MCCARTHY, Joseph, 1934- 248.4
The many ways of life. Foreword by Richard Cardinal Cushing [Boston] St. Paul Eds. [dist. Daughters of St. Paul, c.1963] 243p. 22cm. 63-17307 3.00; 2.00 pap.,
1. Christian life—Catholic authors. I. Title.

MCCAW, Mabel (Niedermeyer) 248.4
This is God's world. Illustrated by Gedge Harmon. St. Louis, Bethany Press [c.1949, 1959] 94p. illus. 22cm. 60-6826 1.75 bds.,
1. Stewardship, Christian—Juvenile literature. I. Title.

MCDONALD, Cleveland 248'.4
Creating a successful Christian marriage / Cleveland McDonald. Grand Rapids : Baker Book House, [1975] 392 p. : 24 cm. Includes index. Bibliography: p. 367-380. [BV835.M2] 74-20202 ISBN 0-8010-5957-7 : 8.95
1. Marriage. I. Title.

MACE, David. 248'.4
Men, women and God : families today and tomorrow / by David and Vera Mace. Atlanta : John Knox Press, c1976. viii, 112 p. ; 22 cm. [BV4526.2.M24] 76-7225 pbk. : 5.95
1. Family—Religious life. 2. Family life education. I. Mace, Vera, joint author. II. Title.

MCGINNIS, Marilyn 248'.4
Single; the woman's view. Old Tappan, N.J., Revell [1974] 159 p. illus. 21 cm. [BJ1610.M29] 74-9837 ISBN 0-8007-0678-1 4.95
1. Single women—Conduct of life. 2. Single women—Religious life. I. Title.

MCGLOIN, Joseph T 248.4
Call me Joe! Illustrated by Don Baumgart. [1st ed.] New York(Pageant Press [1959, c1958] 189p. illus. 21cm. Inspirational essays. [BX2350.2.M25] 58-59515
1. Christian life—Catholic authors. I. Title.

MCKEE, Bill. 248'.4
Order your crowns now / by Bill McKee. [Nashville] : Impact Books, c1976. 189 p. ; 22 cm. [BV4501.2.M242] 76-21003 ISBN 0-914850-34-2 : 4.95
1. Christian life—1960- I. Title.

MCKELVEY, John W. 248.4
The now and the not yet, by John W. McKelvey. Nashville, Tidings [1968?] 96 p. 19 cm. [BV4501.2.M243] 71-114549
1. Christian life. I. Title.

MCLELLAND, Joseph C. 248.4
Living for Christ. Richmond, Va., Knox [c.1963] 109p. 21cm. Bibl. 63-9028 1.50 pap.,
1. Christian life. I. Title.

MACLENNAN, David Alexander 248.4
Be a wonder to yourself. [Westwood, N.J.] F. H. Revell Co. [c.1960] 158p. 21cm. (bibl. footnotes) 60-5502 2.75 bds.,
1. Christian life. I. Title.

MACLENNAN, David Alexander, 1903- 248.4
Be a wonder to yourself. [Westwood, N. J.] F. H. Revell Co. [1960] 158p. 21cm. Includes bibliography. [BV4501.2.M27] 60-5502
1. Christian life. I. Title.

MCNICKLE, Floyd M. 248.4
The presence of absoluteness; God is with you always [by] Floyd McNickle. [Tempe, Ariz.] Kerr Publications [1969] 250 p. 23 cm. [BV4501.2.M29] 68-59535 6.50
1. Christian life. I. Title.

MCPHERSON, Nenien C 248.4
The power of a purpose. [Westwood, N. J.] Revell [1959] 156p. 21cm. Includes bibliography. [BV4501.2.M3] 59-5499
1. Christian life. I. Title.

MACQUARRIE, John. 248'.4
Paths in spirituality. [1st U.S. ed.] New York, Harper & Row [1972] 134 p. 22 cm. Includes bibliographical references. [BV4501.2.M32 1972] 70-183765 ISBN 0-06-065366-3 4.95
1. Spiritual life. I. Title.

*MCQUILKIN, Robert C., D.D. 248.4
The life of victory, and the baptism of the spirit. Chicago, Moody [1965, c.1953] 127p. 17cm. (Colportage lib., 237) .39 pap.,
I. Title.

MAEDER, Gary. 248'.4
The Christian life : issues and answers / Gary Maeder, with Don Williams. Rev. ed. Glendale, Calif. : G/L Regal Books, 1976. 202 p. : ill. ; 21 cm. First ed. (c1973) published under title: God's will for your life. [BV4501.2.M323 1976] 76-29258 ISBN 0-8307-0470-1 : 3.50
1. Christian life—1960- I. Williams, Don, joint author. II. Title.

MAGSAM, Charles M. 248.4
The theology and practice of love. Helicon [dist. New York, Taplinger, c.1965] 295p. 21cm. Bibl. [BV4639.M265] 65-15041 5.95
1. Love (Theology) 2. Christian life—Catholic authors. I. Title.

MAHONEY, James. 248'.4
Journey into fullness. Nashville, Broadman Press [1974] 144 p. 20 cm. Includes bibliographical references. [BV4501.2.M325] 73-91615 ISBN 0-8054-5221-4 2.95 (pbk.)
1. Christian life—1960- I. Title.

MAHONEY, James. 248'.4
Journey into usefulness / James Mahoney. Nashville : Broadman Press, c1976. 162 p. : ill. ; 21 cm. Includes bibliographical references. [BV4501.2.M326] 76-9696 ISBN 0-8054-5569-8 : 4.95
1. Christian life—1960- I. Title.

*MAKELIM, Hal R. 248.4
To stand alone. New York, Exposition [1967] 95p. 21cm. 4.00
I. Title.

MALL, E. Jane, 1920- 248.4
Love in action [by] E. Jane Mall. St. Louis, Concordia Pub. House [1971] 72 p. illus. 18 cm. [BV4501.2.M33 1971] 79-162530 ISBN 0-570-03127-3
1. Christian life—1960- I. Title.

MALLORY, James D. 248'.4
The kink and I; a psychiatrist's guide to untwisted living [by] James D. Mallory, Jr., with Stanley C. Baldwin. [Wheaton, Ill.] Victor Books [1973] 224 p. 18 cm. (An Input book) [BV4501.2.M334] 73-78688 ISBN 0-88207-237-4 1.45 (pbk.)
1. Christian life—1960- I. Baldwin, Stanley C. II. Title.

MANN, Stella Terrill. 248'.4
Love is the healer. [1st ed.] New York, Harper & Row [1974] viii, 149 p. 21 cm. [BV4639.M268 1974] 72-11359 ISBN 0-06-065415-5 5.95
1. Love (Theology) I. Title.

MANTLE, John Gregory, 1852- 248'.4
Beyond humiliation : the way of the cross / by J. Gregory Mantle. Minneapolis : Dimension Books, 1975. 248 p. ; 18 cm. Published in 1922 under title: The way of the cross. [BV4501.M346 1975] 75-6163 ISBN 0-87123-040-2 pbk. : 1.95
1. Christian life. I. Title.

*MARLER, Don C. 248.4
Imprisoned in the brotherhood. [First ed.] New York, Exposition Press [1973] 62 p. 21 cm. Bibliography: p. 62. [BV4501.2] ISBN 0-682-47877-6 3.50
1. Christian life—1960- I. Title.

MARNEY, Carlyle 248.4
Beggars in velvet. Nashville, Abingdon Press [c.1960] 127p. 20cm. 60-5233 2.00 bds.,
1. Christian life. I. Title.

MARNEY, Carlyle, 1916- 248.4
Beggars in velvet. New York, Abingdon Press [1960] 127p. 20cm. [BV4501.2.M36] 60-5233
1. Christian life. I. Title.

MARNEY, Carlyle, 1916- 248.4
The recovery of the person; a Christian

humanism. [Nashville, Abingdon [c.1963] 176p. 23cm. Bibl. 63-17826 3.50
1. Identification (Religion) 2. Humanism, Religious. I. Title.

MARSH, Frederick Edward, 1858-1919. 248.4
Fully furnished; or, The Christian worker's equipment. A series of thirty-four concise studies embracing the whole scope of service for the master. [1st American ed.] Grand Rapids, Kregel Publications [1969] viii, 390 p. 23 cm. [BV4501.2.M363 1969] 68-58843 4.95
1. Christian life. I. Title.

MARTIN, Clarence S. 248'.4
Credo hoc; a book of reflections, philosophy, and faith in the twentieth century, by Clarence Samuel Martin. [Jamestown, N.D., Available from Prairie Pub., c1973] 103 p. illus. 22 cm. In English. Bibliography: p. 54. [BJ1581.2.M38] 74-160833 5.00
1. Conduct of life. 2. Meditations. I. Title.

*MASHECK, Charles L. 248.4
Design for personal living. Ed. by Wilbur G. Volker. Illus. by William C. Kautz. Philadelphia, Lutheran Church Pr. [1967] 128p. illus. (pt. col.) 21cm. (LCA Sunday church sch. ser.) .90 pap.,
1. Youth-Religious life. 2. Religious education—Young adults. I. Volker, Wilbur G., ed. II. Title.

MASON, Philip. 248'.4
The dove in harness / Philip Mason. 1st U.S. ed. New York : Harper & Row, c1976. 189 p. ; 22 cm. Based on a series of lectures given at Oxford in 1975 and sponsored by the Scott Holland Trustees. Bibliography: p. [186]-189. [BV4501.2.M3653 1976] 76-5143 ISBN 0-06-065468-6 : 8.95
1. Christian life—1960- —Addresses, essays, lectures. I. Title.

MASSEY, Craig. 248'.4
Adjust or self-destruct : a study of the believer's two natures / by Craig Massey. Chicago : Moody Press, c1977. p. cm. [BT702.M38] 77-4088 ISBN 0-8024-0137-6 : 4.95 ISBN 0-8024-0136-8 pbk. : 1.50
1. Man (Christian theology) 2. Christian life—1960- I. Title.

MASSEY, James Earl. 248'.4
The hidden disciplines. Anderson, Ind., Warner Press [1972] 111 p. 19 cm. Includes bibliographical references. [BV4501.2.M3657] 72-1776 ISBN 0-87162-137-1
1. Christian life—1960- I. Title.

MASSEY, James Earl. 248.4
The soul under siege (a fresh look at Christian experience) Anderson, Ind., Warner Press [1970] 110 p. 19 cm. [BV4501.2.M366] 70-115776
1. Christian life—1960- I. Title.

MASTON, Thomas Bufford, 1897- 248.4
The conscience of a Christian [by] T. B. Maston. Illustrated by Douglas Dillard. Waco, Tex., Word Books [1971] 156 p. illus. 23 cm. [BV4501.2.M3668] 77-160293 3.95
1. Christian life—1960- 2. Social ethics. I. Title.

*MATHEWS, Eleanor Muth 248.4
The trouble is . . . Walter A. Kortrey, ed. Art by Andrew A. Snyder [Philadelphia, Lutheran Church Pr., c.1966] 48p. illus. 23cm. (LCA Church camp ser.) .65; 1.00, pap., teacher's ed., pap.,
I. Title.

MAURIAC, Francois, 1885- 248.4
Anguish and joy of the Christian life [Tr. from French by Harold Evans] Wilkes-Barre, Pa., P.O. Box 21 Dimension Bks. [c.1964] 110p. 21cm. (Carmel series on Christian life,v.2) 64-15281 2.95 bds.,
1. Christian life—Catholic authors. I. Title. II. Series.

MAVIS, W. Curry 248.4
The psychology of Christian experience. Grand Rapids, Mich., Zondervan [c.1963] 155p. 23cm. Bibl. 63-9312 3.00
1. Christian life. I. Title.

MAXWELL, Lawrence 248.4
What stopped the music, and other stories. Illus. by James Converse. Mountain View, Calif., Pacific Pr. [1966] 96p. illus. 19cm. [BV4515.2.M37] 66-19714 .30 pap.,
1. Christian life—Stories. I. Title.

MAYS, Carl. 248'.4
You can do it! / Carl Mays. Nashville : Broadman Press, c1977. 127 p. ; 20 cm. [BV4501.2.M435] 76-59509 ISBN 0-8054-5251-6 pbk. : 2.50
1. Christian life—1960- 2. Success. I. Title.

MAYS, Carl. 248'.4
You can do it! / Carl Mays. Nashville : Broadman Press, c1977. 127 p. ; 20 cm. [BV4501.2.M435] 76-59509 ISBN 0-8054-5251-6 pbk. : 2.50
1. Christian life—1960- 2. Success. I. Title.

MEAGHER, John C. 248'.4
The gathering of the ungifted. Toward a dialogue on Christian identity. [by] John C. Meagher. New York, Paulist Press, [1975, c1972] 176 p. 18 cm. [BV4509.5.M4] 72-3827 ISBN 0-8091-1874-2 1.95 (pbk.)
1. Identification (Religion) I. Title.

MERTON, Thomas, 1915- 248.4
Conjectures of a guilty bystander. [1st ed.] Garden City, N.Y., Doubleday, 1966. vii, 328 p. 22 cm. [BX4705.M542A26] 66-24311
I. Title.

MERTON, Thomas, 1915- 248.4
Conjectures of a guilty bystander. Garden City, N.Y., Doubleday [1968,c.1966] 360p. 18cm. (Image bks., D234) [BX4705.M54.A26] 66-24311 1.25 pap.,
I. Title.

MERTON, Thomas, 1915-1968. 248.4
Conjectures of a guilty bystander. [1st ed.] Garden City, N.Y., Doubleday, 1966. vii, 328 p. 22 cm. [BX4705.M542A26] 66-24311
I. Title.

METTS, Wally. 248'.4
The brighter side / Wally Metts. Chicago : Moody Press, c1977. 96 p. ; 22 cm. [BV4905.2.M37] 77-1532 ISBN 0-8024-0928-8 pbk. : 2.25
1. Consolation. 2. Christian life—1960- I. Title.

MEYER, Frederick Brotherton 248.4
Calvary to Pentecost. Grand Rapids, Baker Book House, 1959. 90p. 21cm. 59-15532 1.75 bds.,
1. Christian life. I. Title.

MIDDLEMANN, Udo. 248'.4
Proexistence; the place of man in the circle of reality. Downers Grove, Ill., InterVarsity Press [1974] 126 p. 21 cm. Includes bibliographical references. [BD450.M495] 73-89298 ISBN 0-87784-710-X 1.95 (pbk.)
1. Man. 2. Reality. I. Title.

MIDDLETON, Robert Lee, 1894- 248.4
Patterns for life's pilgrims, by R. L. Middleton. Nashville, Broadman Press [1967] 125 p. 21 cm. Bibliographical footnotes. [BV4501.2.M47] 68-12562
1. Christian life—Baptist authors. I. Title.

MIDWEST Sociological Society. 248'.4
The Sociological quarterly. [Carbondale, Ill.] Southern Illinois University Press. v. 24 cm. Began publication with Jan. 1960 issue, superseding the Midwest sociologist. Cf. New serial titles, 1950-60. Official journal of the Midwest Sociological Society. [HM1.S69] 64-5249
1. Sociology—Period. I. Title.

MILD, Warren 248.4
Fractured questions. Valley Forge, Pa., Judson [c.1966] 125p. 22cm. [BJ1661.M54] 66-12539 1.95 pap.,
1. Youth—Conduct of life. I. Title.

MILES, Judith M., 1937- 248'.4
Mind games and hobby horses / Judith M. Miles. Minneapolis : Bethany Fellowship, c1976. 188 p. ; 20 cm. [BV4501.2.M472] 76-7042 ISBN 0-87123-379-7 pbk. : 2.95
1. Christian life—1960- 2. Games. 3. Hobbies. I. Title.

MILLER, Alexander, 1908- 248.4
Christian faith and my job. An up-to-date Reflection book ed. of the Haddam House book. New York, Association Press [1959] 128p. 16cm. (A Reflection book) Includes bibliography. [BV4740.M5 1959] 59-6838
1. Vocation. I. Title.

MILLER, June. 248'.4
The God of the impossible / June Miller. Grand Rapids, Mich. : Zondervan Pub. House, [1975] 160 p. ; 22 cm. [BV4501.2.M474] 74-31551 5.95
1. Mary, Virgin. 2. Miller, June. 3. Christian life—1960- I. Title.

MILLER, June. 248'.4
Why sink when you can swim? Grand Rapids, Zondervan Pub. House [1973] 147 p. 22 cm. [BV4501.2.M475] 73-13057 3.95
1. Christian life—1960- I. Title.

MILLER, Keith. 248.4
A second touch. Waco, Tex., Word Books [1967] 156 p. 21 cm. Sequel to The taste of new wine. Bibliographical footnotes. [BV4501.2.M48] 67-31340
1. Christian life. I. Title.

MILLER, Keith. 248.4
A second touch. Waco, Tex., Word Books [1967] 156 p. 21 cm. Sequel to The taste of new wine. Bibliographical footnotes. [BV4501.2.M48] 67-31340
1. Christian life. I. Title.

MILLER, Randolph Crump, 1910- 248.4
Living with anxiety. Philadelphia [United Church Press, 1971] 190 p. 22 cm. "A Pilgrim Press book." Includes bibliographical references. [BV4501.2.M49] 75-168525 ISBN 0-8298-0206-1 5.95
1. Christian life—1960- 2. Anxiety. I. Title.

MILLER, Randolph Crump, 1910- 248.4
Youth considers parents as people. New York, Nelson [1965] 93 p. illus. 21 cm. (Youth forum series) [HQ796.M49] 65-22013
1. Parent and child. 2. Adolescence. I. Title. II. Series.

MILLER, Randolph Crump, 1910- 248.4
Youth considers parents as people. New York, Nelson [c.1965] 93p. illus. 21cm. (Youth forum ser.) [HQ796.M49] 65-22013 1.50 pap.,
1. Parent and child. 2. Adolescence. I. Title. II. Series.

MILLER, William A., 1931- 248'.4
Big kids' Mother Goose : a Christian counselor finds new insights in old stories / William A. Miller ; ill. by Judy Swanson. Minneapolis : Augsburg Pub. House, c1976. 109 p. : ill. ; 22 cm. Contents.Contents.—Observations on truth and reality.—The little girl with the curl.—There's no joy in one-sideness.—Why are some people never satisfied?—The saga of a pussy cat.—The search for happiness.—Humpty Dumpty on integration vs. disintegration.—A marvelous example.—Pride and humility.—"I'll get even with you!—Keeping the tarnish off the golden years. [BV4501.2.M525] 75-22722 ISBN 0-8066-1500-1 : 3.25
1. Mother Goose. 2. Christian life—1960- I. Swanson, Judy. II. Mother Goose. III. Title.

MILLION, Elmer G. 248.4
Your faith and your life work. New York, Friendship Press [c.1960] 80p. 19cm. Bibl.: p.78-79 illus. 60-7452 1.00 pap.,
1. Vocation. I. Title.

MITCHELL, Curtis C., 1927- 248'.4
Let's live! Christ in everyday life [by] Curtis C. Mitchell. Old Tappan, N.J., Revell [1975] 160 p. 21 cm. [BV4501.2.M54] 74-16153 ISBN 0-8007-0716-8 4.95
1. Christian life—1960- I. Title.

MONTAGUE, George T. 248'.4
Building Christ's body : the dynamics of Christian living according to St. Paul / by George T. Montague. Chicago : Franciscan Herald Press, [1975] p. cm. (Herald scriptural library) Bibliography: p. [BS2655.C4M66] 75-14100 ISBN 0-8199-0573-9 : 4.95
1. Paul, Saint, apostle. 2. Christian life—Biblical teaching. I. Title.

*MOORE, Addison S. 248'.4
Children of God. [First ed.] New York, Vantage Press [1973] 116 p. 21 cm. [BV4501.2] ISBN 0-533-00588-4 4.50
1. Christain life—1960- I. Title.

MOORE, Hassel Guy, 1909- 248.4
The Christian life. Nashville, Convention Press [c1961] 145p. 19cm. Includes bibliography. [BV4501.2.M58] 61-11985
1. Christian life. I. Title.

MOORE, Thomas Verner [Name in religion: Pablo Maria, Father] 248.4
The life of man with God. Garden City, N. Y., Doubleday [1962, c.1956] 400p. (Image bk., D127) Bibl. 1.35 pap.,
1. Spiritual life—Catholic authors. I. Title.

MORGAN, George Campbell, D. D., 1863-1945. 248.4
Life problems. [New ed. rev.] Westwood, N.J., Revell [1962] 93p. (Campbell Morgan pocket lib.) 62-1891 .95 pap.,
1. Christian life. I. Title.

MORGAN, George Campbell, 1863-1945 248.4
The simple things of the Christian life. [New ed., rev.] Westwood, N.J., Revell [1962] 89p. (Campbell Morgan pocket lib.) 62-1890 .95 pap.,
1. Christian life. I. Title.

*MORGAN, Richard. 248'.4
God's Biblical sacrificial blueprints and specifications for reconciling the world unto himself. Nashville, Parthenon Pr. [1972] 248 p. 24 cm. [BV4501] 76-186552 8.00
1. Christian life. I. Title.

MORICH, Randy. 248'.4
God—fellowship or frustration / by Randy Morich. Costa Mesa, Calif. : Marantha Evangelical Association of Calvary Chapel. c1976. 47 p. ; 18 cm. [BV4501.2.M585] 76-15368 pbk. : 1.25
1. Christian life—1960- 2. God. I. Title.

MOUROUX, Jean 248.4
From baptism to the act of faith. Tr. [from French] by Sister M. Elizabeth, Sister M. Johnice. Introd. by Bernard J. Cooke. Boston, Allyn [c.]1964. viii, 56p. illus. 21cm. 64-2691 3.00
1. Baptism—Catholic Church. 2. Religious education of children. I. Title.

MOW, Anna B. 248'.4
Sensitivity to what? / Anna Mow. Grand Rapids : Zondervan Pub. House, [1975] 97, [9] p. ; 22 cm. Bibliography: p. [101-106] [BV4501.2.M624] 74-25336 4.95
1. Christian life—1960- 2. Group relations training. I. Title.

MOW, Anna B. 248'.4
Your experience and the Bible [by] Anna B. Mow. [1st ed.] New York, Harper & Row [1973] xii, 116 p. 21 cm. Bibliography: p. [112]-116. [BV4501.2.M63] 73-6321 ISBN 0-06-066033-3 4.95
1. Christian life. I. Title.

MUMFORD, Bob. 248'.4
The King and you. Old Tappan, N.J., Revell [1974] 252 p. illus. 21 cm. [BT94.M8] 74-10065 ISBN 0-8007-0672-2 3.50 (pbk.)
1. Kingdom of God. 2. Christian life—1960- I. Title.

MUMFORD, Bob. 248.4
Take another look at guidance; a study of divine guidance. Edited by Jorunn Oftedal Ricketts. Plainfield, N.J., Logos International [1971] xi, 156 p. 21 cm. [BT96.2.M84] 77-166498 ISBN 0-912106-17-4 4.95
1. Providence and government of God. 2. Christian life—1960- I. Title.

MURPHEY, Cecil B. 248'.4
Somebody knows I'm alive / by Cecil B. Murphey. Atlanta : John Knox Press, c1977. vi, 168 p. ; 21 cm. [BX9225.M8A37] 76-44967 ISBN 0-8042-2206-1 : 4.95
1. Murphey, Cecil B. 2. Presbyterian Church—Clergy—Biography. 3. Clergy—Georgia—Biography. I. Title.

MURPHY, Joseph, 1898- 248'.4
Great Bible truths for human problems / by Joseph Murphy. Marina del Rey, Calif. : DeVorss, 1976. 288 p. ; 20 cm. [BJ1611.2.M795] 76-19844 ISBN 0-87516-214-2 pbk. : 5.00
1. Success. I. Title.

MURRAY, Andrew, 1828-1917. 248'.4
The Master's indwelling / Andrew Murray. Minneapolis : Bethany Fellowship, c1977. 192 p. ; 18 cm. (Dimension books) [BV4501.2.M87 1977] 76-23363 ISBN 0-87123-355-X pbk. : 1.95
1. Christian life. I. Title.

MURRAY, Andrew, 1828-1917. 248'.4
Not my will : the blessedness of a life devoted to the Will of God / Andrew Murray. Grand Rapids : Zondervan Pub. House, c1977. 102 p. ; 18 cm. Translation of Niet mijn wil. [BV4501.M797613] 77-23137 ISBN 0-310-29722-2 pbk. : 1.50
1. Christian life. 2. God—Will. I. Title.

MY faith / 248'.4
Pat Boone ... [et al.] ; compiled by Roger Elwood ; designed by Wulf Stapelfeldt. Norwalk, Conn. : C. R. Gibson Co., [1975] 85 p. ; 21 cm. [BV4510.A1M88] 74-80403 ISBN 0-8378-1764-1 : 3.95
1. Christian life—Collected works. I. Boone, Charles Eugene. II. Elwood, Roger.

MYERS, T. Cecil 248.4
Faith for a time of storm. Nashville, Abingdon [c.1963] 155p. 21cm. Bibl. 63-15710 3.00
1. Devotional literature. I. Title.

NARRAMORE, Bruce. 248'.4
Guilt and freedom / Bruce Narramore and Bill Counts. Santa Ana, Calif. : Vision House Publishers, [1974] 159 p. : ill. ; 21 cm. Includes bibliographical references. [BF575.G8N37] 73-92358 ISBN 0-88449-002-5. ISBN 0-88449-003-3 pbk. : 2.25
1. Guilt. 2. Psychology, Religious. I. Counts, Bill, joint author. II. Title.

NARRAMORE, Clyde Maurice, 1916- 248'.4
How to handle pressure / Clyde M. Narramore, Ruth E. Narramore. Wheaton, Ill.

: Tyndale House, 1975. x, 150 p. ; 22 cm. [BV4501.2.N34] 75-7226 ISBN 0-8423-1513-6 : 5.95
1. Christian life—1960- I. Narramore, Ruth E., joint author. II. Title.

*NELSON, Marion H., M.D. 248.4
How to know God's will. Chicago, Moody [c.1963] 121p. 20cm. 2.50
I. Title.

*NEPTUNE, A. Ray, 1907- 248.4
On a mountain trail [by] A. Ray Neptune [First ed.] New York, Vantage [1972] viii, 250 p. 21 cm. [BV4501] ISBN 0-533-00387-3 4.95
1. Christian life. 2. Christian biography. I. Title.

NEWBERRY, Gene W. 248'.4
Soundings [by] Gene W. Newberry. Anderson, Ind., Warner Press [1972] 111 p. 19 cm. [BV4501.2.N5] 72-76777 ISBN 0-87162-136-3
1. Christian life—1960- I. Title.

NEWHOUSE, Flower Arlene 248'.4
(Sechler) 1909-
Songs of deliverance, by Flower A. Newhouse. [1st ed.] Escondido, Calif., Christward Ministry [1972] 263 p. 23 cm. [BP605.C5N457] 72-94582
1. Christward Ministry. I. Title.

NIMICK, John A. 248.4
Be still and know, by John A. Nimick. New York, Philosophical Lib. [c.1966] 47p. 22cm. [BF641.N5] 67-11989 3.00
1. New Thought. I. Title.

NOONAN, Richard H., 1916- 248'.4
52 weeks to a great new life [by] Richard H. Noonan. West Nyack, N.Y., Parker Pub. Co. [1973] 274 p. 24 cm. [BJ1470.N66] 73-12033 ISBN 0-13-314872-6 6.95
1. Self-realization. I. Title.

NORDEN, Rudolph F 248.4
Key to the full life. Saint Louis, Concordia Pub. House [c1963] 96 p. 20 cm. [BV4501.2.N6] 62-214302
1. Christian life. I. Title.

NORDEN, Rudolph F. 248.4
Key to the full life. Saint Louis, Concordia [c.1963] 96p. 20cm., 62-21430 1.00 pap.,
1. Christian life. I. Title.

NORDEN, Rudolph F 248.4
The new leisure [by] Rudolph F. Norden. Saint Louis, Concordia Pub. House [1965] 105 p. 18 cm. (The Christian encounters) Bibliography: p. 105. [BJ1498.N6] 65-16961
1. Leisure. 2. Christian life. I. Title. II. Series.

NORDEN, Rudolph F. 248.4
The new leisure. St. Louis, Concordia [c.1965] 105p. 18cm. (Christian encounters) Bibl. [BJ1498.N6] 65-16961 1.00 pap.,
1. Leisure. 2. Christian life. I. Title. II. Series.

NOUWEN, Henri J. M. 248'.4
Reaching out : the three movements of the spiritual life / Henri J. M. Nouwen. 1st ed. Garden City, N.Y. : Doubleday, 1975. 120 p. ; 22 cm. Includes bibliographical references. [BV4501.2.N68] 74-9460 ISBN 0-385-03212-9 : 5.95
1. Spiritual life. I. Title.

OATES, Wayne Edward, 1917- 248'.4
Life's detours [by] Wayne E. Oates. [Nashville] The Upper Room [1974] 86 p. 21 cm. [BJ1533.P4O2] 74-75221
1. Perseverance (Ethics) I. Title.

O'CONNOR, Elizabeth. 248.4
Eighth day of creation; gifts and creativity. Waco, Tex., Word Books [1971] 115 p. 23 cm. Bibliography: p. 113-115. [BT767.3.O25] 70-175725 3.50
1. Gifts, Spiritual. I. Title.

OLDHAM, Dale. 248.4
Give me tomorrow. Anderson, Ind., Warner Press [c1964] v, 95 p. 21 cm. [BV4501.2.O45] 64-10911
1. Christian life. I. Title.

OLDHAM, Dale 248.4
Give me tomorrow. Anderson, Ind., Warner [c.1964] v, 95p. 21cm. 64-10911 1.50 pap.,
1. Christian life. I. Title.

OLDHAM, Dale. 248.4
Just across the street; how to be a growing Christian. Anderson, Ind., Warner Press [1968] viii, 160 p. 22 cm. [BV4501.2.O46] 68-24449
1. Christian life. I. Title.

OLIVER, Lucille. 248'.4
The crystal mountain. Independence, Mo., Herald Pub. House [1974] 144 p. 18 cm. Includes bibliographical references. [BV4501.2.O47] 73-93136 ISBN 0-8309-0119-1 4.95
1. Christian life—1960- I. Title.

OLSSON, Karl A. 248'.4
Come to the party; an invitation to a freer life style [by] Karl A. Olsson. Waco, Tex., Word Books [1972] 178 p. 23 cm. Includes bibliographical references. [BV4501.2.O48] 72-84167 4.95
1. Christian life—1960- I. Title.

OLTHUIS, James H. 248'.4
I pledge you my troth : a Christian view of marriage, family, friendship / James H. Olthuis. 1st U.S. ed. New York : Harper & Row, [1975] 148 p. ; 21 cm. Includes bibliographical references. [BV835.O47 1975] 74-25695 ISBN 0-06-066394-4 : 7.95
1. Marriage. 2. Family. 3. Friendship. I. Title.

ORSO, Kathryn Wickey. 248'.4
Parenthood : a commitment in faith / Kathryn Wickey Orso. New York : Morehouse-Barlow Co., c1975. iv, 60 p. ; 22 cm. [BV4529.O67] 75-5219 ISBN 0-8192-1198-2 pbk. : 2.95
1. Family—Religious life. 2. Parent and child. 3. Moral education. I. Title.

ORTIZ, Juan Carlos, 1934- 248'.4
Cry of the human heart / Juan Carlos Ortiz. Carol Stream, Ill. : Creation House, c1977. 143 p. ; 22 cm. [BV4501.2.O7245] 76-24099 ISBN 0-88419-010-2 : 5.95
1. Christian life—1960- I. Title.

OSMUNSON, Robert Lee. 248.4
Crash landing. Illustrated by H. Larkin. Mountain View, Calif., Pacific Press Pub. Association [1963] ix, 131 p. illus. 23 cm. [BV4571.2.O8] 63-21056
1. Christian life — Stories. I. Title.

OSMUNSON, Robert Lee 248.4
Crash landing. Illus. by H. Larkin. Mountain View, Calif., Pac. Pr. Pub. [c.1963] ix, 131p. illus. 23cm. 63-21056 3.75
1. Christian life—Stories. I. Title.

OTIS, George. 248'.4
God, money, and you. Old Tappan, N.J., F. H. Revell Co. 1972] 126 p. 21 cm. [BV4501.2.O78] 71-186537 ISBN 0-8007-0523-8
1. Christian life—1960- 2. Wealth, Ethics of. I. Title.

OTIS, George. 248.4
High adventure. Old Tappan, N.J., F. H. Revell Co. [1971] 192 p. 21 cm. [BR1725.O8A3] 70-169699 ISBN 0-8007-0483-5 4.95
I. Title.

OTIS, George. 248'.4
The solution to crisis-America. Rev. and enl. ed. With a foreword by Pat Boone. Old Tappan, N.J., F. H. Revell Co. [1972] 120 p. illus. 18 cm. (Spire books) The original edition of The solution crisis-America published about 1970 was written by Pat Boone, George Otis, and Harald Bredesen. [BR526.O85 1972] 72-182932 ISBN 0-8007-8081-7 0.95
1. United States—Religion. 2. United States—Moral conditions. 3. United States—Civilization. I. Boone, Charles Eugene. The solution to crisis-America. II. Title.

*OVERHOLSER, Grace 248.4
McSpadden
God's family in god's world. Illus. by Betty Fraser. Richmond, Va., CLC Pr. [dist. Knox, 1966,c.1965] 64p. illus. (pt. col.) 21cm. (Covenant life curriculum, clem; the christian life, year 1,43-9433) 1.25 pap.,
I. Title.

OZMENT, Robert Varnell, 248.4
1927-
. . . but God can. [Westwood, N.J.] Revell [c.1962] 126p. 62-8593 2.50 bds.,
1. Christian life. I. Title.

PADOVANO, Anthony T. 248'.4
Presence and structure : a reflection on celebration, worship, and faith / by Anthony T. Padovano. New York : Paulist Press, c1976. 79 p. ; 19 cm. [BV176.P29] 75-32107 ISBN 0-8091-1912-9 : 1.95
1. Liturgics. I. Title.

PALAU, Luis. 248'.4
Walk on water, Pete! / By Luis Palau. Glendale, Calif. : G/L Regal Books, [1974] 87 p. ; 18 cm. [BV4501.2.P27] 74-79563 ISBN 0-8307-0286-5 pbk. 1.25
1. Peter, Saint, apostle. 2. Christian life—1960- I. Title.

PALMER, Everett W Bp. 248.4
You can have a new life! Nashville, Abingdon Press [1959] 127p. 20cm. [BV4501.2.P3] 59-12783
1. Christian life. I. Title.

PALMS, Roger C. 248'.4
God holds your tomorrows / Roger C. Palms. Minneapolis : Augsburg Pub. House, c1976. 104 p. ; 20 cm. [BV4501.2.P32] 76-3855 ISBN 0-8066-1527-3 pbk. : 2.95
1. God—Will. 2. Christian life—1960- I. Title.

*PATTERSON, Betsy. 248'.4
The valley of vision. Anderson, Ind., Warner Pr. [1973] 128 p. 18 cm. (A Portal Book) [BV5401] 1.25 (pbk.)
1. Christian life. I. Title.

PEALE, Norman Vincent, 248.4
1898-
Ethusiasm makes the difference. Englewood Cliffs, N.J., Prentice-Hall [1967] x, 244 p. 22 cm. 1968 ed. published under title: The new executive edition of Enthusiasm makes the difference. [BF637.S8P38] 67-26078
1. Success. 2. Enthusiasm. I. Title.

PEALE, Norman Vincent, 248.4
1898-
The new art of living. New York, Hawthorn Books [1971] ix, 185 p. 22 cm. Previous editions published under title: The art of living. [BV4501.P42 1971] 78-170195 4.95
1. Christian life—1960- I. Title.

PEALE, Norman Vincent, 248.4
1898-
The new art of living. Greenwich, Conn., Fawcett [1973, c.1971] 160 p. 18 cm. (Crest Book, M1798) Previous editions published under title: The art of living. [BV4501.P42 1971] pap., 0.95
1. Christian life—1960- I. Title.

PEDERSON, Cliff. 248'.4
Christians alive; handbook for spiritual growth. Edited by Cliff Pederson. Minneapolis, Minn., Augsburg Pub. House [1973] 112 p. illus. 21 cm. Includes bibliographical references. [BV4501.2.P364] 73-78259 1.95 (pbk.)
1. Christian life—1960- I. Title.

PEDERSON, Duane. 248'.4
On Lonely Street with God. New York, Hawthorn Books [1973] vi, 184 p. 21 cm. Includes bibliographical references. [BV4911.P35] 73-10675 2.95
1. Loneliness. 2. Christian life—1960- I. Title.

PEERMAN, Nancy. 248.4
Seasons of the soul; the adventure of being human—and Christian. Waco, Tex., Word Books [1970] 154 p. 23 cm. [BV4832.2.P44 1970] 73-111960 3.95
1. Meditations. I. Title.

PENNINGTON, Chester A 248.4
Even so, believe [by] Chester A. Pennington. Nashville, Abingdon Press [1966] 127 p. 20 cm. [BV4501.2.P37] 66-10850
1. Christian life—Methodist authors. I. Title.

PENNINGTON, Chester A. 248.4
Even so, believe. Nashville, Abingdon [c.1966] 127p. 20cm. [BV4501.2.P37] 66-10850 2.50 bds.,
1. Christian life—Methodist authors. I. Title.

PENTZ, Croft M., comp. 248.4
1001 sentence sermons, for every need--for church bulletin boards, bulletins, newspapers, etc. Grand Rapids, Mich., Zondervan [c.1962] 61p. 21cm. 1.00 pap.,
I. Title.

PETER, Laurence J. 248'.4
The Peter prescription; how to be creative, confident & competent, by Laurence J. Peter. New York, Morrow, 1972. 224 p. illus. 22 cm. [BJ1581.2.P46] 70-182953 5.95
1. Conduct of life. I. Title.

PETERSON, Wilferd Arlan, 248'.4
1900-
The art of living treasure chest / Wilferd A. Peterson. New York : Simon and Schuster, c1977. 159 p. ; 24 cm. [BJ1581.2.P5] 77-8879 ISBN 0-671-22847-1 pbk. : 2.95
1. Conduct of life. I. Title.

PHILLIPS, Allen A 248.4
Nuggets for happiness. [1st ed.] Cleveland, Tenn., Pathway Press [1959] 116p. 22cm. [BV4501.2.P5] 58-13775
1. Christian life. I. Title.

PHILLIPS, Mike, 1946- 248'.4
A Christian family in action / Mike Phillips. Minneapolis : Bethany Fellowship, c1977. 188 p. ; 21 cm. Includes bibliographical references. [BV4526.2.P47] 77-1887 ISBN 0-87123-085-2 pbk. : 2.95
1. Family—Religious life. I. Title.

PHILPOTT, Kent. 248'.4
If the devil wrote a bible / by Kent Philpott. Plainfield, N.J. : Logos International, [1975] c1974. 118 p. ; 18 cm. [BT981.P49] 74-82954 ISBN 0-88270-105-3 pbk. : 1.25
1. Devil. 2. Christian life—1960- I. Title.

*PINK, Arthur W. 248.4
Spiritual union and communion / Arthur W. Pink. Grand Rapids : Baker Book House, 1976 c1971. 165 p. ; 22 cm. Includes index [BV4501.2P554] ISBN 0-8010-6893-2 pbk. : 2.95
1. Spiritual life. 2. Trinity. I. Title.
L.C. card no. for original edition: 72-160817.

*PINK, Arthur Walkington 248.4
1886-1952
Practical Christianity [by] Arthur W. Pink. Grand Rapids, Guardian Press, [1974] 224 p. 22 cm. [BL2775] ISBN 0-89086-000-9 3.95 (pbk.)
1. Christianity. I. Title.
Distributed by Baker Books.

PINK, Arthur Walkington, 248.4
1886-1952.
Spiritual union and communion. Grand Rapids, Baker Book House [1971] 160 p. 23 cm. [BV4501.2.P554] 72-160817 ISBN 0-8010-6893-2 4.95
1. Spiritual life. 2. Trinity. I. Title.

POLSTON, Don H. 248'.4
Living without losing : a practical guide to successful living / Don H. Polston. Irvine, Calif. : Harvest House Publishers, c1975. 175 p. ; 22 cm. [BV4832.2.P594] 75-27142 ISBN 0-89081-015-X pbk. : 2.95
1. Meditations. 2. Christian life—1960- I. Title.

PONDER, Catherine Thrower 248.4
How to live a prosperous life. Lee's Summit, Mo., Unity School of Christianity [1962] 158p. 17cm. (Unity bk.) 2.00
I. Title.

POONEN, Zac. 248'.4
Where do I go from here, God? Wheaton, Ill., Tyndale House [1972, c1971] 86 p. 18 cm. Published in 1971 under title: Finding God's will. [BV4501.2.P5559] 70-188536 ISBN 0-8423-8200-3 0.95
1. Christian life—1960- I. Title.

POTTHOFF, Harvey H 248.4
A theology for Christian witnessing [by] Harvey H. Potthoff. Nashville, Tidings [1964] 63 p. 19 cm. [BV4520.P6] 64-25872
1. Witness bearing (Christianity) I. Title.

POURE, Ken. 248'.4
It's all in the family / Ken Poure ; foreword by Tim LaHaye ; prepared from Ken Poure family forum tapes by Violet T. Pearson. Denver : Accent Books, c1975. 128 p. : ill. ; 18 cm. [BV4526.2.P57] 75-17367 1.95
1. Family—Religious life. 2. Christian life—1960- I. Pearson, Violet T. II. Title.

POURE, Ken. 248'.4
Praise is a three-letter word / Ken Poure and Bob Phillips. Glendale, Calif. : G/L Regal Books, [1975] 87 p. ; 18 cm. [BV4501.2.P559] 74-16962 ISBN 0-8307-0303-9 pbk. : 1.45
1. Christian life—1960- 2. Praise of God. I. Phillips, Bob, joint author. II. Title.

POWELL, Cyril H 248.4
The lonely heart; the answer to the problem of loneliness through life. [1st ed.] Evesham, Worcs., A. James [1960] 174p. 21cm. [BV4911.P6 1960] 61-33014
1. Loneliness. I. Title.

POWELL, Cyril H. 248.4
The lonely heart; the answer to the problem of loneliness through life. Nashville, Abingdon Press [1961, c.1960] 174p. Bibl. 61-2019 2.50
1. Loneliness. I. Title.

POWELL, Cyril H 248.4
The Stranger Within: the discovery of the inner self. Manhasset, N.Y., Channel Press [1963] 160 p. 20 cm. [BV4501.2.P56] 63-17531
1. Christian life. I. Title.

POWELL, Cyril H. 248.4
The Stranger Within: the discovery of the inner self. Manhasset, N.Y., Channel [c.1963] 160p. 20cm. 63-17531 3.00 bds.,
1. Christian life. I. Title.

POWELL, Gordon George 248.4
Happiness is a habit. New York, Hawthorn Books [1960] 157p. 21cm. 60-5894 2.95 half cloth,
1. Christian life. I. Title.

*PRATT, Marsha Whitney 248.4
Sculptured in faith. New York, Exposition [c.1965] 95p. 21cm. (EP43111) 3.50
I. Title.

*PRICE, E. David 248.4
I am a Christ; the spiritual key. New York, Carlton [1967] 66p. 21cm. 2.50
1. Christian life. I. Title. II. Title: The spiritual key.

PRICE, Eugenia. 248.4
Make love your aim. Grand Rapids, Zondervan Pub. House [1967] 191 p. 23 cm. [BV4639.P67] 67-22686
1. Love (Theology) I. Title.

PRICE, Eugenia. 248.4
Make love your aim. Grand Rapids, Zondervan Pub. House [1967] 191 p. 23 cm. [BV4639.P67] 67-22686
1. Love (Theology) I. Title.

PRICE, Nelson L. 248'.4
How to find out who you are / Nelson L. Price. Nashville : Broadman Press, c1977. 128 p. ; 21 cm. Includes bibliographical references. [BV4509.5.P74] 76-49358 ISBN 0-8054-5249-4 : 3.50
1. Identification (Religious) 2. Self-perception. I. Title.

PRINCE, Derek. 248'.4
Shaping history through prayer & fasting; how Christians can change world events through the simple, yet powerful tools of prayer and fasting. Old Tappan, N.J., F. H. Revell Co. [1973] 160 p. facsim. 21 cm. [BV210.2.P72] 73-8973 ISBN 0-8007-0616-1 4.95
1. Prayer. 2. Fasting. I. Title.

QUINLAN, Edith. 248'.4
In gods we trust / Edith Quinlan. Denver : Accent Books, c1976. 127 p. ; 18 cm. [BL4851.Q56] 76-9574 ISBN 0-916406-29-6 pbk. : 1.45
1. Idols and images—Worship. I. Title.

†RAY, David A. 248'.4
The Christian power plan / David Ray. Waco, Tex. : Word Books, [c1976] 138 p. ; 22 cm. Includes bibliographical references. [BV4501.2.R35] 76-48537 ISBN 0-87680-476-8 : 5.95
1. Christian life—1960- I. Title.

RAY, David A. 248'.4
Discoveries for peaceful living [by] David A. Ray. Old Tappan, N.J., Revell [1972] 159 p. 21 cm. [BV4501.2.R355] 70-184572 ISBN 0-8007-0513-0 4.95
1. Christian life—1960- I. Title.

REAGAN, Wes. 248'.4
Return to identity / by Wes Reagan. Cincinnati : New Life Books, 1977. 96 p. ; 18 cm. [BV4509.5.R4] 76-18382 ISBN 0-87239-062-4 pbk. : 1.50
1. Identification (Religion) I. Title.
Distributed by Standard Pub.

REDHEAD, John A 248.4
Guidance from men of God [by] John A. Redhead. New York, Abingdon Press [1965] 144 p. 21 cm. [BS571.R38] 65-20365
1. Bible — Biog. I. Title.

REDHEAD, John A. 248.4
Guidance from men of God. Nashville, Abingdon [c.1965] 144p. 21cm. [BS571.R38] 65-20365 2.50
1. Bible—Biog. I. Title.

*REED, Bruce 248.4
Christian counselling. Grand Rapids, Mich., Eerdmans [1966, c.1965] 50p. 22cm. .75 pap.,
I. Title.

REID, Clyde H. 248'.4
Celebrate the temporary, by Clyde Reid. Illus. by Patricia Collins. New York, Harper & Row [1974, c1972] [89 p.] illus. 21 cm. [BJ1581.2.R44 1974] 73-160643 ISBN 0-06-066816-4 1.95 (pbk.)
1. Conduct of life. I. Title.

REIDHEAD, Paris. 248'.4
Beyond believing / Paris Reidhead. Minneapolis : Bethany Fellowship, c1976. 90 p. ; 18 cm. (Dimension books) [BV4501.2.R43] 76-29517 ISBN 0-87123-041-0 pbk. : 1.50
1. Christian life—1960- I. Title.

REISS, Marguerite. 248'.4
Holy nudges / Marguerite Reiss. Plainfield, N.J. : Logos International, c1976. xiii, 141 p. ; 20 cm. [BV4501.2.R45] 76-23362 ISBN 0-88270-185-1 : 5.95 ISBN 0-88270-186-X pbk. : 3.50
1. Reiss, Marguerite. 2. Christian life—1960- I. Title.

RELIGION and life; 248.4
the foundations of personal religion. Freeport, N. Y., Bks. for Libs. Pr. [1968] vii, 114p. 22cm. (Essay index reprint sers.) Reprint of 1923 ed. [BV4495.R4 1968] 68-22940 5.50
1. Christian life.
Contents Omitted.

RELIGION and life; the 248.4
foundations of personal religion. Freeport, N.Y., Books for Libraries Press [1968] vii, 114 p. 22 cm. (Essay index reprint series) Reprint of 1923 ed. Contents.Contents.—Faith and reason, by W. R. Inge.—The Father, by D. Cairns.—Man's need, by W. F. Halliday.—Christ, by N. S. Talbot.—The practice of prayer, by W. Brown.—Christianity as fellowship, by W. H. Frere. [BV4495.R4 1968] 68-22940
1. Christian life.

REUTER, Alan. 248'.4
Who says I'm O.K.? A Christian use of transactional analysis. St. Louis, Concordia Pub. House [1974] 125 p. illus. 21 cm. Includes bibliographical references. [BV4501.2.R47] 74-13756 ISBN 0-570-03187-7 2.95 (pbk.).
1. Christian life—1960- 2. Transactional analysis. I. Title.

RICE, Hillery C 248.4
Seeking to know the will of God. Anderson, Ind., Warner Press [1959] 128p. 20cm. [BV4501.2.R5] 59-6605
1. God—Will. 2. Christian life. I. Title.

RICHARDS, Larry. 248'.4
Becoming one in the spirit. Wheaton, Ill., Victor Books [1973] 128 p. 18 cm. (An Input book) [BX8.2.R5] 73-76812 ISBN 0-88207-235-8 1.25 (pbk.)
1. Christian union. I. Title.

RICHARDS, Larry. 248'.4
Born to grow : for new and used Christians / Larry Richards. Wheaton, Ill. : Victor Books, [1974] 143 p. : 18 cm. (An Input book) [BV4501.2.R512] 73-92609 ISBN 0-88207-708-2 : 1.75
1. Christian life—1960- I. Title.

RICHARDSON, Oman P. 248'.4
The lost lamb, by Oman P. Richardson. Boston, Branden Press [1972] 141 p. 23 cm. [BV4501.2.R513] 77-185386 ISBN 0-8283-1348-2 5.95
1. Christian life—1960- I. Title.

RIDENOUR, Fritz. 248'.4
How to be a Christian in an unchristian world. Illustrator: Joyce Thimsen. Editorial research: Georgiana Walker. Glendale, Calif., G/L Regal Books [1972, c1971] 188 p. illus. 18 cm. Includes bibliographical references. [BV4501.2.R517] 72-169603 ISBN 0-8307-0126-5 0.95
1. Christian life—1960- I. Title.

RINKER, Rosalind. 248.4
On being a Christian. Grand Rapids, Zondervan Pub. House [1963] 160 p. 21 cm. [BV4501.2.R56] 63-19172
1. Christian life. I. Title.

RINKER, Rosalind 248.4
On being a Christian. Grand Rapids, Mich., Zondervan [c.1963] 160p. 21cm. 63-19172 2.50
1. Christian life. I. Title.

RINKER, Rosalind. 248.4
The open heart. [Extensively rev. and rewritten] Grand Rapids, Mich., Zondervan Pub. House [1969] 146 p. 22 cm. 1963 ed. has title: On being a Christian. [BV4501.2.R56 1969] 76-81065 2.95
1. Christian life. I. Title.

*RIPLEY, May H. S., ed. 248.4
Cosmos at the door by Mary, Elizabeth, Annett, Helen, Elinor. Denver, Big Mountain Pr. [dist. Swallow, c.1964] 89p. illus. 22cm. Contents.pt.1. Miscellaneous essays (metaphysical and secular)--pt.2. The ten commandments (metaphysical) 2.50
I. Title.

ROACH, Fred. 248'.4
Let's talk : ideas to trigger family conversation / Fred Roach. Old Tappan, N.J. : F. H. Revell Co., c1977. p. cm. Includes index. [BV4832.2.R55] 77-13347 ISBN 0-8007-0908-X : 6.95
1. Meditations. 2. Christian life—1960- I. Title.

ROBERTS, John Robison. 248.4
The healing power of love. Philadelphia, Dorrance [1971] 127 p. 22 cm. [BV4639.R59] 76-158629 ISBN 0-8059-1574-5 4.95
1. Love (Theology) 2. Mind and body. 3. Mental healing. I. Title.

ROBERTS, Oral. 248'.4
How to live above your problems / by Oral Roberts. 1st published ed. [Tulsa, Okla. : Pinoak Publications], 1974. 132 p. : port. ; 21 cm. [BV4501.2.R613] 75-308773
1. Christian life—1960- I. Title.

ROBINSON, Haddon W. 248'.4
Eight vital relationships for the growing Christian / by Haddon Robinson and Mike Cocoris ; written and produced by EvanTell, inc .... Grand Rapids : Zondervan Pub. House, c1977. p. cm. [BV4501.2.R616] 77-23139
1. Christian life—1960- 2. Theology, Doctrinal—Popular works. I. Cocoris, Mike, joint author. II. EvanTell, inc. III. Title.

†ROBLEY, Wendell. 248'.4
Spank me if you love me / by Wendell (Rob) & Grace Robley. Harrison, Ark. : New Leaf Press, [1976] 135 p. ; 22 cm. [BV4501.2.R619] 76-1067 ISBN 0-89221-019-2 pbk. : 2.95
1. Christian life—1960- I. Robley, Grace, joint author. II. Title.

ROGERS, Dale Evans. 248.4
No two ways about it! [Westwood, N. J.] Revell [1963] 64 p. 20 cm. [BV4501.2.R64] 63-17111
1. Christian life. I. Title.

ROGERS, Dale Evans. 248'.4
Where He leads. Old Tappan, N.J., F. H. Revell Co. [1974] 126 p. 21 cm. [BR1725.R63A327] 74-1225 ISBN 0-8007-0648-X 3.95
1. Rogers, Dale Evans. I. Title.

ROGERS, Dale Evans. 248'.4
Where He leads / Dale Evans Rogers. Boston : G. K. Hall, 1975, c1974. p. cm. Large print ed. [BR1725.R63A327 1975] 75-20039 ISBN 0-8161-6321-9 lib.bdg. : 8.95
1. Rogers, Dale Evans. 2. Sight-saving books. I. Title.

ROORBACH, Harriet A. 248.4 (j)
I learn about sharing, by Harriet A. Roorbach. Nashville, Abingdon Press [1968] 31 p. illus. (part col.) 21 cm. [BV772.R64] 68-10706
1. Sharing. 2. Christian giving—Juvenile literature. I. Kurek, Sarah, illus. II. Title.

*ROTH, Paul M. 248.'4
New joy in living / Paul M. Roth. Scottdale, Pa. : Herald Press, c1976. 64p. ; 18 cm. [BV4501] 0-8361 ISBN pbk. : 0.95
1. Christian life. I. Title.

ROY, Joseph, 1935- 248'.4
Scripturegraphics; living messages for modern man. Written and illustrated by Joseph Roy. St. Meinard, Ind., Abbey Press, 1974. ix, 157 p. (chiefly illus.) 14 x 21 cm. (A Priority edition) [BV4832.2.R69] 73-94168 ISBN 0-87029-022-3 5.95 (pbk.)
1. Meditations. I. Title.

RUTLEDGE, Harold Lee. 248'.4
To be mature, by H. L. Rutledge. New Orleans, Insight Press [1974] 153 p. 20 cm. [BV4501.2.R86] 74-76988 ISBN 0-914520-03-2 2.50 (pbk.)
1. Christian life—1960- I. Title.

SACRED tradition and 248'.4
present need / edited by Jacob Needleman and Dennis Lewis. New York : Viking Press, 1975. xi, 146 p. ; 22 cm. (An Esalen book) First presented as a series of lectures sponsored by Esalen Institute in San Francisco during the summer of 1973. [BL624.S2 1975] 75-14498 ISBN 0-670-61441-6 : 10.00
1. Spiritual life—Addresses, essays, lectures. I. Needleman, Jacob. II. Lewis, Dennis. III. Esalen Institute.

SALING, Younger. 248'.4
The God I serve. Philadelphia, Dorrance [1972] 55 p. 21 cm. [BV4501.2.S165] 71-180123 ISBN 0-8059-1641-5 2.95
1. Christian life—1960- I. Title.

SAMPSON, Tom. 248'.4
Cultivating the presence : a spiritual guide for a journey toward the presence of God / Tom Sampson. New York : Crowell, c1977. xv, 212 p. ; 21 cm. Includes index. Bibliography: p. 198-203. [BV4501.2.S17] 76-27316 ISBN 0 ISBN 0-690-01205-5 : 8.95 ISBN 0-690-01206-3 pbk. : 3.25
1. Spiritual life. 2. Devotional literature. I. Title.

SANDERS, J Oswald. 248.4
On to maturity. Chicago, Moddy Press [1962] 222p. 22cm. 'A China Inland Mission book.' [BV4501.2.S18] 62-52863
1. Christian life. I. Title.

SANDERS, John Oswald, 1902- 248.4
On to maturity. Chicago, Moody Press [1962] 222 p. 22 cm. "A China Inland Mission book." [BV4501.2.S18] 62-52863
1. Christian life. I. Title.

SANDERS, John Oswald, 248'.4
1902-
The pursuit of the holy; conquest and fulfillment of attainable levels in Christian living, by J. Oswald Sanders. Grand Rapids, Mich., Zondervan Pub. House [1972] 180 p. 18 cm. (Zondervan books) Previously published under title: Christ indwelling and enthroned. [BV4510.2.S25 1972] 73-171199 1.25
1. Christian life. I. Title.

SCHAEFFER, Edith. 248'.4
A way of seeing / Edith Schaeffer. Old Tappan, N.J. : Revell, c1977. 255 p. ; 24 cm. [BV4501.2.S283] 77-4945 ISBN 0-8007-0871-7 : 7.95
1. Christian life—1960- —Addresses, essays, lectures. I. Title.

SCHAEFFER, Francis August. 248'.4
True spirituality [by] Francis A. Schaeffer. Wheaton, Ill., Tyndale House Publishers [1971] 180 p. 22 cm. [BV4501.2.S285] 73-183269 ISBN 0-8423-7350-0 3.50
1. Spirituality. I. Title.

SCHMITT, Friedrich, 1910- 248.4
Getting along with difficult people. Translated by Erich R. W. Schultz. Philadelphia, Fortress Press [1970] xiii, 113 p. 19 cm. Translation of ABC des Helfens. Includes bibliographical references. [BV4639.S3453] 79-114244 2.50
1. Charity. I. Title.

SCHROCK, Simon. 248'.4
Get on with living / Simon Schrock. Old Tappan, N.J. : F. H. Revell Co., c1976. 96 p. ; 18 cm. [BV4501.2.S298] 76-8507 ISBN 0-8007-0800-8 pbk. : 2.95
1. Christian life—1960- I. Title.

SCHULLER, Robert Harold. 248'.4
Reach out for new life / Robert H. Schuller. New York : Hawthorn Books, c1977. 216 p. ; 22 cm. [BV4501.2.S32 1977] 76-41973 ISBN 0-8015-6247-3 : 7.95
1. Christian life—Reformed authors. 2. Success. I. Title.

SCHWARZ, Jack. 248'.4
The path of action / Jack Schwarz. 1st ed. New York : Dutton, c1977. xxii, 132 p. ; 21 cm. [BL627.S44 1977] 77-2247 pbk. : 3.50
1. Meditation. 2. Spiritual life. I. Title.

SCHWEITZER, Albert, 1875- 248.4
The light within us. New York, Philosophical Library [1959] 58p. 20cm. [B3329.S53V63] 59-1813
I. Title.

SCHWEITZER, Albert, 1875- 248.4
1965.
The light within us. Westport, Conn., Greenwood Press [1971, c1959] 58 p. 23 cm. Translation of Vom Licht in uns. Bibliography: p. 58. [B3329.S53V63 1971] 75-139151 ISBN 0-8371-5767-6
I. Title.

SCOTT-MONCRIEFF, George 248.4
[Irving]
This day. With a foreword by James Walsh. Baltimore, Helicon Press [1959, i.e.,1960] 93p. 20cm. 59-14480 2.50
1. Christian life—Catholic authors. I. Title.

SCOTT MONCRIEFF, George, 248.4
1910-
This day. With a foreword by James Walsh. Baltimore, Helicon Press [c1959] 93p. 20cm. [BX2350.2.S35] 59-14480
1. Christian life—Catholic authors. I. Title.

*SCRAGG, Walter R. L. 248'4
The media, the message, and man; communicating God's love. Nashville, Southern Pub. Assoc. [1972] 153 p. 21 cm. [BV4501] 72-96066 ISBN 0-8127-0069-4 pap. 1.95
1. Christian life. I. Title.

SEAMANDS, David A. 248'.4
Problem solving in the Christian family / by David A. Seamands. Carol Stream, Ill. : Creation House, c1975. 104 p. ; 21 cm. [BV835.S38] 75-3610 ISBN 0-88419-109-5 pbk. : 2.95
1. Marriage. 2. Family—Religious life. I. Title.

SEGLER, Franklin M 248.4
The Christian layman. Nashville, Broadman Press [1964] 128 p. 21 cm. Includes bibliographies. [BV4501.2.S4] 64-10815
1. Christian life—Baptist authors. 2. Laity. I. Title.

SEGLER, Franklin M. 248.4
The Christian layman. Nashville, Broadman [c.1964] 128p. 21cm. Bibl. 64-10815 2.50
1. Christian life—Baptist authors. 2. Laity. I. Title.

SEIFERT, Harvey. 248'.4
Liberation of life : growth exercises in meditation and action / Harvey & Lois Seifert. Nashville : The Upper Room, c1976. 112 p. ; 22 cm. [BV4501.2.S42] 76-46880
1. Spiritual life. I. Seifert, Lois, joint author. II. Title.

A Selection of emblems, 248'.4
from Herman Hugo: Pia desideria; Francis Quarles: Emblemes; Edmund Arwaker: Pia desideria. Introd. by William A. McQueen. Los Angeles, William Andrews Clark

Memorial Library, University of California, 1972. x, 83 p. illus. 22 cm. (The Augustan Reprint Society. Publication no. 155-156) Reprint of 3 works each published separately in 1624, 1635, and 1686 respectively. Includes bibliographical references. [BV4515.S44 1972] 73-620544
1. Christian life. 2. Emblems. I. Hugo, Herman, 1588-1629. Pia desideria. Selections. 1972. II. Quarles, Francis, 1592-1644. Emblemes. Selections. 1972. III. Arwaker, Edmund, d. 1730. Pia desideria. Selections. 1972. IV. Title. V. Series.

SHANNON, Robert, 1930- 248.4
Belonging; a key to closer fellowship with the God of the universe and those who belong to Him in the deepest sense. Cincinnati, Ohio, Standard Pub. [1971, c1968] 96 p. 18 cm. (Fountain books) [BV1561.S48] 78-164741
1. Religious education—Text-books for adults. I. Title.

SHARP, Galen. 248'.4
The present kingdom of God. Old Tappan, N.J., Revell [1974] 160 p. 21 cm. [BV4501.2.S435] 74-6084 ISBN 0-8007-0660-9 2.95 (pbk.)
1. Christian life—1960- I. Title.

SHAW, Jean. 248'.4
Sometimes the stones are very lively : the visible church develops Christian grace / Jean Andreae Shaw. Grand Rapids : Zondervan Pub. House, c1976. 121 p. : ill. ; 18 cm. [BV4515.2.S5] 75-46613 pbk. : 1.50
1. Christian life—Stories. I. Title.

SHELLEY, Bruce Leon, 1927- 248.4
A call to Christian character; toward a recovery of Biblical piety [by] Earl S. Kalland [and others] Edited by Bruce L. Shelley. Grand Rapids, Zondervan [1970] 186 p. 22 cm. Includes bibliographical references. [BV4647.P5S46] 74-106441 4.95
1. Piety—Addresses, essays, lectures. I. Kalland, Earl S., 1910- II. Title.

SHERATON, William M. 248'.4
It's faster to heaven in a 747, by William M. Sheraton. New York, Sheed and Ward [1973] vii, 167 p. 21 cm. [TL540.S458A33] 73-5258 ISBN 0-8362-0526-X 5.95
1. Sheraton, William M. I. Title.

SIKKING, Sue. 248.4
God always says yes. [1st ed.] Garden City, N.Y., Doubleday, 1968. 143 p. 22 cm. [BV4501.2.S457] 68-18079 3.95
1. Christian life. I. Title.

SILL, Sterling W. 248.4
The three infinities: to know, to do, to be [by] Sterling W. Sill. Salt Lake City, Bookcraft, 1969. xii, 355 p. port. 24 cm. [BJ1611.S535] 70-102004 3.95
1. Success—Addresses, essays, lectures. I. Title.

SIMMONS, Robert A. 248'.4
Leadership for the new frontier / by Robert A. Simmons. North Quincy, Mass. : Christopher Pub. House, c1977. 164 p. : ill. ; 22 cm. Includes index. [BJ1581.2.S52] 76-51021 ISBN 0-8158-0348-6 : 6.50
1. Conduct of life. I. Title.

SIMON, Raphael [secular name: Kenneth Simon] 248.4
Hammer and fire; toward divine happiness and mental health. New York, P. J. Kenedy [c.1959] 257p. 22cm. Includes bibliography. 59-12900 3.95
1. Spiritual life—Catholic authors. I. Title.

SIMON, Raphael, Secular name: Kenneth Simon 1909- 248.4
Hammer and fire; toward divine happiness and mental health. New York, P.J. Kenedy [1959] 257 p. 22 cm. Includes bibliography. [BX2350.2.S5] 59-12900
1. Spiritual life — Catholic authors. I. Title.

SIMONS, George F. 248'.4
Journal for life : discovering faith and values through journal keeping / George F. Simons. Chicago : Life in Christ, c1975- v. ; 23 cm. Contents.Contents.—pt. 1. Foundations. [BV4509.5.S55] 75-17161 ISBN 0-914070-07-X
1. Spiritual life. 2. Diaries—Authorship. I. Title.

SIMONSON, Ted, ed. 248.4
The goal and the glory; America's athletes speak their faith. [Westwood, N.J.] Revell [c.1962] 128p. 21cm. 62-10732 2.95; 1.00 pap.,
1. Athletes, American, 2. Devotional literature. I. Title.

SINKLER, Lorraine. 248'.4
The alchemy of awareness / Lorraine Sinkler. 1st ed. New York : Harper & Row, c1977. ix, 149 p. ; 21 cm. [BL624.S58 1977] 76-62957 ISBN 0-06-067387-7 : 5.95
1. Spiritual life. I. Title.

SMITH, Bob, 1914- 248'.4
Dying to live : an introduction to counseling that counts / Bob Smith. Waco, Tex. : Word Books, c1976. 181 p. : ill. ; 22 cm. (Discovery books) Includes index. [BR110.S63] 75-32647 5.95
1. Christianity—Psychology. 2. Counseling. I. Title.

SMITH, Charles Merrill. 248'.4
The case of a middle class Christian. Waco, Tex., Word Books [1973] 149 p. 23 cm. [BV4501.2.S527] 73-84579 4.95
1. Christian life—1960- 2. Christianity—20th century. 3. Smith, Charles Merrill. I. Title.

SMITH, Chuck, 1927- 248'.4
Family relationships / Chuck Smith. Costa Mesa, Calif. : Maranatha Evangelical Association of Calvary Chapel, c1976. p. cm. [BV4526.2.S53] 76-44496 ISBN 0-89337-005-3 pbk. : 1.25
1. Family—Religious life. I. Title.

SMITH, Earl C. 248.4
To live by His Word; the Christian way of life: living by grace. New York, Exposition Press [c.1960] 98p. 21cm. (An Exposition-Testament book) 60-2331 2.50
1. Christian life. I. Title.

SMITH, Earl C 1894- 248.4
To live by His Word; the Christian way of life: living by grace. [1st ed.] New York, Exposition Press [1960] 98 p. 21 cm. (An Exposition-Testament book) [[BV4501.2]] 60-2331
1. Christian life. I. Title.

SMITH, Hannah Whitall, 1832-1911. 248'.4
The Christian's secret of a happy life. Boston, G. K. Hall, 1973 [c1952] 346 p. 25 cm. Large print ed. [BV4501.2.S533 1973] 73-9926 ISBN 0-8161-6133-X 9.95 (lib. bdg.)
1. Christian life. 2. Faith. I. Title.

SMITH, Hannah (Whitall) 1832-1911. 248.4
Everyday religion. [Rev. ed.] Chicago, Moody Press [1893, c1966] 249 p. 18 cm. (Moody giants, no. 45) [BV4501.S65 1966] 66-5146
1. Christian life. I. Title.

SMITH, Hannah (Whitall) 1832-1911 248.4
Everyday religion. [Rev. ed.] Chicago, Moody [c.1966] 249p. 18cm. (Moody giants, no. 45) orig. pub. in 1893 by Revell. [BV4501.S65] 66-5146 .89 pap.,
1. Christian life. I. Title.

SMITH, John 248.4
You can get the things you want; a guidebook for personal success in life. New York, Greenwich Book Publishers [c.1959] 45p. 21cm. 59-15924 2.00
1. Christian life. I. Title.

SMITH, Joyce Marie. 248'.4
Coping with life and its problems / Joyce Marie Smith. Wheaton, Ill. : Tyndale House Publishers, c1976. 64 p. ; 20 cm. (New life Bible studies) Includes bibliographies. [BV4501.2.S5343] 76-47298 pbk. : 1.25
1. Christian life—1960- I. Title. II. Series.

SMITH, Malcolm, 1938- 248'.4
The Kingdom here and now / Malcolm Smith. Old Tappan, N.J. : F. H. Revell Co., c1976. p. cm. [BV4501.2.S5344] 76-23105 ISBN 0-8007-0821-0 pbk. : 3.95
1. Christian life—1960- I. Title.

*SMITH, Martha Lang. 248.4
The key. New York, Exposition [1967] 96p. 21cm. (EP45741) 4.50
I. Title.

SNIDER, John D 248.4
The vision splendid. Washington, Review and Herald Pub. Association [1959] 125 p. 22 cm. [BV4501.2.S6] 59-4814
1. Christian life. I. Title.

STANFORD, Miles J. 248'.4
Abide above : a guide to spiritual growth / Miles J. Stanford. Grand Rapids : Zondervan Pub. House, c1977. 94, [27] p. ; 18 cm. (His The "green letters" growth series ; 5) [BV4501.2.S716] 76-51791 pbk. : 1.50
1. Christian life—1960- I. Title. II. Series.

STANFORD, Miles J. 248'.4
The green letters / Miles J. Stanford. Grand Rapids : Zondervan Pub. House, c1975. 98 p. ; 18 cm. [BV4501.2.S717] 75-21123 pbk. : 1.50
1. Christian life—1960- I. Title.

STANFORD, Miles J. 248'.4
The ground of growth : the Christian's relationship to the cross and the risen Christ / Miles J. Stanford. Grand Rapids : Zondervan Pub. House, c1976. p. cm. (His The "green letters" series) [BV4501.2.S7173] 76-26154 pbk. : 1.50
1. Christian life—1960- 2. Redemption. I. Title. II. Series.

STANFORD, Miles J. 248'.4
The principle of position / Miles J. Stanford. Grand Rapids : Zondervan Pub. House, 1976. 91 p. ; 19 cm. [BV4501.2.S718] 75-46512 pbk. : 1.50
1. Christian life—1960- I. Title.

STANFORD, Miles J. 248'.4
The reckoning that counts : the realization of spiritual growth / Miles J. Stanford. Grand Rapids, Mich. : Zondervan Pub. House, 1977 89 p. ; 18 cm. (His The "green letters" series ; no. 4) [BV4501.2.S719] 76-39688 pbk. : 1.50
1. Christian life—1960- I. Title. II. Series.

STARCKE, Walter. 248'.4
The gospel of relativity. [1st ed.] New York, Harper & Row [1973] 110 p. illus. 24 cm. [BV4501.2.S72 1973] 73-6319 ISBN 0-06-067525-X 3.95
1. Christian life—1960- I. Title.

STATON, Knofel. 248'.4
The Gospel according to Paul. Cincinnati, Standard Pub. [1973] 96 p. 18 cm. (Fountain books) [BV4501.2.S735] 73-80994 1.25 (pbk.)
1. Christian life—1960- I. Title.

STATON, Knofel. 248'.4
How to know the will of God / by Knofel Staton. Cincinnati : New Life Books, c1976. 112 p. ; 18 cm. [BV4501.2.S7353] 74-31673 ISBN 0-87239-057-8 pbk. : 1.50
1. God—Will. 2. Theodicy. I. Title.
Teacher's edition available for 1.75

STEDMAN, Ray C. 248'.4
Authentic Christianity / Ray C. Stedman. Waco, Tex. : Word Books, [1975] 184 p. ; 21 cm. (Discovery books) [BV4501.2.S738] 75-11602 4.95
1. Christian life—1960- I. Title.

STEDMAN, Ray C. 248'.4
Spiritual warfare / by Ray C. Stedman. Waco, Tex. : Word Books, [197-] 145 p. ; 21 cm. (Discovery books) [BV4501.2.S739] 75-17420 4.95
1. Christian life—1960- 2. Devil. I. Title.

STEERE, Douglas Van, 1901- 248.4
On beginning from within [and] On listening to another. [1st ed.] New York, Harper & Row [1964] 255 p. 21 cm. [BV4501.S7937 1964] 64-10913
1. Friends, Society of. 2. Spiritual life. 3. Devotion. I. Title. II. Title: On listening to another.

STEERE, Douglas Van, 1901- 248.4
On beginning from within [and] On listening to another. New York, Harper [c.1943-1964] 255p. 21cm. 64-10913 4.00
1. Friends, Society of. 2. Spiritual life. 3. Devotion. I. Title. II. Title: On listening to another.

STEIN, Edward V. 248.4
Beyond guilt [by] Edward V. Stein. Philadelphia, Fortress Press [1972] vi, 58 p. 19 cm. (Pocket counsel books) Includes bibliographical references. [BJ1471.5.S73] 79-171511 ISBN 0-8006-1107-1 1.50
1. Guilt. I. Title.

STEPHENS, Overton. 248'.4
Today is all you have [by] Overton Stephens. Edited by Richard Engquist. Foreword by Bruce Larson. Grand Rapids, Mich., Zondervan Pub. House [1972, c1971] 160 p. 21 cm. [BV4596.P5S73 1972] 70-171198 3.95
1. Christian life—1960- 2. Physicians—Religious life. I. Title.

STERNER, R. Eugene. 248.4
Where are you going, Jesus? [By] R. Eugene Sterner. Anderson, Ind., Warner Press [1971] 128 p. 19 cm. Includes bibliographical references. [BV4501.2.S757] 73-165004
1. Christian life—Church of God authors. I. Title.

STEVENSON, Dwight Eshelman, 1906- 248'.4
Monday's God / by Dwight E. Stevenson. Saint Louis : Bethany Press, c1976. 121 p. ; 22 cm. Includes bibliographical references. [BV4501.2.S759] 76-9806 ISBN pbk. : 3.95
1. Christian life—1960- 2. Christianity—20th century. 3. Church and the world. I. Title.

STONE, Sam E. 248'.4
Grounded faith for growing Christians / by Sam E. Stone. Cincinnati : New Life Books, 1975. 96 p. ; 18 cm. [BV4501.2.S78] 74-79116 ISBN 0-87239-006-3 pbk. : 1.50
1. Christian life—1960- I. Title.

STOTT, John R. W. 248'.4
Your mind matters; the place of the mind in the Christian life [by] John R. W. Stott. Downers Grove, Ill., InterVarsity Press [1973, c1972] 64 p. 18 cm. Includes bibliographical references. [BV4501.2.S79 1973] 72-94672 ISBN 0-87784-441-0 0.95 (pbk.)
1. Christian life—1960- 2. Faith and reason. I. Title.

STRAUSS, Dorothy H 248.4
Prepare yourself to serve, God's call to a life of discipline and service. Chicago, Moody Press [1960] 127 p. 20 cm. [BV4501.2.S8] 60-52357
1. Christian life — Study and teaching. I. Title.

STRAUSS, Dorothy M 248.4
Prepare yourself to serve,God's call to a life of discipline and service. Chicago, Moody Press [1960] 127 p. 20 cm. [BV4501.2.S8] 60-52357
1. Christian life — Study and teaching. I. Title.

STUHLMUELLER, Carroll. 248'.4
Thirsting for the Lord : essays in Biblical spirituality / Carroll Stuhlmueller ; edited by M. Romanus Penrose ; illustrated by Lillian Brule ; introd. by Alcuin Coyle. New York : Alba House, c1977. x, 322 p. : ill. ; 22 cm. Includes indexes. [BS680.S7S78] 76-51736 ISBN 0-8189-0341-4 : 7.95
1. Spiritual life—Biblical teaching. 2. Spiritual life—Catholic authors. 3. Liturgics—Catholic Church. I. Title.

SUELTZ, Arthur Fay. 248'.4
When the wood is green. [1st ed.] New York, Harper & Row [1973] ix, 92 p. 21 cm. Includes bibliographical references. [BV4501.2.S83 1973] 73-6346 ISBN 0-06-067759-7 4.95
1. Christian life—1960- I. Title.

SULLIVAN, James L. 248.4
Memos for Christian living [by] James L. Sullivan. Compiled by Gomer R. Lesch. Nashville, Broadman Press [1966] 125 p. 21 cm. Selections from the author's column Facts and trends, which has appeared regularly since 1957 in the News letter published by the Sunday School Board of the Southern Baptist Convention. [BV4501.2.S84] 66-11217
1. Christian life — Baptist authors. 2. Religious education. 3. Christian leadership. I. Title.

SULLIVAN, James L. 248.4
Memos for Christian living. Comp. by Gomer R. Lesch. Nashville, Broadman [c.1966] 125p. 21cm. Selections from the author's column Facts and trends, which has appeared regularly since 1957 in the News letter pub. by the Sunday Sch. Bd. of the Southern Baptist Convention [BV4501.2.S84] 66-11217 1.50 bds.,
1. Christian life—Baptist authors. 2. Religious education. 3. Christian leadership. I. Title.

SUMMERS, Jo An, comp. 248'.4
Living promises, compiled and edited by Jo An Summers. Plainfield, N.J., Logos International [1974] 116 p. 18 cm. [BV4510.A1S78] 73-93791 ISBN 0-88270-086-3 1.25 (pbk.)
1. Christian life—Biblical teaching. I. Bible. English. Authorized. Selections. 1974. II. Title.

SWEETING, George, 1924- 248'.4
How to begin the Christian life : first steps for new believers / by George Sweeting. Rev. ed. Chicago : Moody Press, c1976. 159 p. ; 18 cm. Originally published in 1970 under title: Living stones. [BV4501.2.S88 1976] 75-31694 ISBN 0-911010-55-6 : 1.25
1. Christian life—1960- I. Title.

TALBOT, Gordon. 248'.4
The breakdown of authority / Gordon Talbot. Old Tappan, N.J. : Revell, c1976. 127 p. ; 21 cm. [HM271.T24] 75-33052 ISBN 0-8007-0781-8 : 4.95
1. Authority. 2. Social conflict. 3. Christian ethics. I. Title.

TALBOT, Gordon. 248'.4
Overcoming materialism / Gordon G. Talbot. Scottdale, Pa. : Herald Press, c1977. 88 p. ; 20 cm. [BV4501.2.T25] 76-47341 ISBN 0-8361-1810-3 pbk. : 1.95
1. Christian life—1960- 2. Simplicity. 3. Stewardship, Christian. I. Title.

TAM, Stanley, 1915- 248.4
God owns my business, by Stanley Tam as told to Ken Anderson. Waco, Tex., Word Books [1969] 155 p. illus., ports. 23 cm. [BJ1611.T28] 69-18864 3.95

1. Success. I. Anderson, Kenneth, 1917- II. Title.

TATHAM, C. Ernest 248.4
Forever secure: now and hereafter. Chicago, Moody [1963] 63p. 18cm. (Compact bk. no. 25) .29 pap.,
I. Title.

TAVARD, Georges Henri, 1922- 248.4
The church, the layman, and the modern world. New York, Macmillan, 1959. 84 p. 21 cm. [BX1920.T3] 59-5988
1. Laity. 2. Christian life — Catholic authors. I. Title.

TAYLOR, Bob R., 1935- 248'.4
Being joyous [by] Bob R. Taylor. Nashville, Broadman Press [1973] 95 p. illus. 20 cm. [BJ1481.T38] 72-96151 ISBN 0-8054-6911-7 1.75
1. Joy. I. Title.

†TAYLOR, Florence Marian Tompkins, 1892- 248'.4
As for me and my family / Florence M. Taylor. Waco, Tex. : Word Books, c1976. 147 p. ; 23 cm. Bibliography: p. 145-147. [BV4526.2.T35] 76-48532 ISBN 0-87680-512-8 : 5.95
1. Family—Religious life. I. Title.

TAYLOR, Jack R. 248'.4
One home under God [by] Jack R. Taylor. Nashville, Broadman Press [1974] 157 p. 21 cm. [BV4526.2.T36] 73-91609 ISBN 0-8054-5222-2 4.95; 1.00 (study guide)
1. Family—Religious life. I. Title.

*TAYLOR, Richard S. 248.4
A return to Christian culture or, why avoid "the cult of the slob," [by] Richard S. Taylor. Minneapolis, Bethany Fellowship, [1975] 95 p. 18 cm. (Dimension Books) Bibliography: p. 95 [BJ1278] 74-28509 ISBN 0-87123-488-2 1.25 (pbk.)
1. Christian ethics. 2. Social ethics. I. Title.

TAYLOR, Richard Shelley, 1912- 248.4
The disciplined life. Kansas City, Mo., Beacon Hill [c.1962] 102p. 20cm. 62-7123 1.75
1. Christian life. I. Title.

TENNIES, Arthur C., 1931- 248'.4
A church for sinners, seekers, and sundry non-saints [by] Arthur C. Tennies. Nashville, Abingdon Press [1974] 144 p. 20 cm. [BV4501.2.T423] 73-20029 ISBN 0-687-08050-9 4.50
1. Christian life—1960- 2. Church. I. Title.

TESTERMAN, Jean. 248'.4
Eagle's wings. Anderson, Ind., Warner Press [1973] 107 p. 19 cm. Includes bibliographical references. [BR1725.T38A33] 73-8533 ISBN 0-87162-156-8 2.50 (pbk.)
1. Testerman, Jean. 2. Christian life—1960- I. Title.

THOMAS, Joan. 248'.4
Tempted by love / by Joan Thomas. Grand Rapids : W. B. Eerdmans Pub. Co., c1976. p. cm. [BV835.T47] 76-18898 ISBN 0-8028-1653-3 pbk. : 1.65
1. Marriage. 2. Temptation. 3. Adultery. I. Title.

THOMAS, Roger W. 248'.4
Standing on the promises : keys to Christian victory / by Roger W. Thomas. Cincinnati : New Life Books, 1975. 96 p. : ill. ; 18 cm. [BV4501.2.T465] 74-79115 ISBN 0-87239-005-5 pbk. : 1.50
1. Christian life—1960- I. Title.

THOMAS, W Ian 248.4
The mystery of godliness. Grand Rapids, Zondervan Pub. House [1964] 154 p. 21 cm. [BV4501.2.T47] 64-11948
1. Christian life. I. Title.

THOMAS, W. Ian 248.4
The mystery of godliness. Grand Rapids, Mich., Zondervan [c.1964] 154p. 21cm. 64-11948 2.95
1. Christian life. I. Title.

THOMAS, W. Ian. 248'.4
The mystery of godliness, by W. Ian Thomas. Grand Rapids, Zondervan Pub. House [1969, c1964] 155 p. illus. 21 cm. [BV4501.2.T47 1969] 75-81038 2.95
1. Christian life. I. Title.

*THOMAS, William Henry Griffith 248.4
Grace and power, some aspects of the spiritual life. Chicago, Moody [1964] 128p. 18cm. (Colportage lib., 502) .39 pap.,
I. Title.

THOMPSON, Luther Joe. 248.4
Through discipline to joy. Nashville, Broadman Press [1966] 128 p. 21 cm. Bibliographical references included in "Notes" (p. 123-128) [BV4501.2.T494] 66-15150
1. Christian life. I. Title.

THOMPSON, Luther Joe 248.4
Through discipline to joy. Nashville, Broadman [c.1966] 128p. 21cm. Bibl. [BV4501.2.T494] 66-15150 2.75 bds.,
1. Christian life. I. Title.

THRASH, Arline Cate. 248'.4
Little things that keep families together / Arline Cate Thrash. Nashville : Broadman Press, 1977c1976 150 p. ; 19 cm. [BV4526.2.T48] 76-24116 ISBN 0-8054-5617-1 pbk. : 2.50
1. Family—Religious life. I. Title.

**TIME to run,* 248'.4
adapted from the original Allan Sloane screenplay. Minneapolis, Bethany Fellowship [1973] 134 p. 18 cm. (Dimension books) [BV4501.] ISBN 0-87123-538-2 1.50 (pbk.)
1. Christian life—1960-

TITUS, Pauline Woodruff 248.4
Never be lonely; a practical discussion of what you can do about the problem of loneliness. Englewood Cliffs, N. J., Prentice-Hall [c.1960] 184p. 21cm. 59-7003 3.50 bds.,
1. Loneliness. I. Title.

TITUS, Pauline Woodruff, 1898- 248.4
Never be lonely; a practical discussion of what you can do about the problem of loneliness. Englewood Cliffs, N.J., Prentice-Hall [1960] 184 p. 21 cm. [BV4911.T5] 59-7003
1. Loneliness I. Title.

TODAY. 248.4
New York, Paulist Press [1969] [16] p. col. illus. 15 x 18 cm. (Rejoice books) Translation of Aujourd'hui. A little girl promises Jesus to spend her day being good and helpful to her family and friends. [BJ1631.A7813] 74-86973 0.35
1. Children—Conduct of life.

TORREY, Reuben Archer, 1856-1928. 248.4
How to succeed in the Christian life. [Westwood, N.J.] Revell [1962? c1906] 121 p. 20 cm. [BV4501.T75 1962] 62-6328
1. Christian life. I. Title.

TORREY, Reuben Archer, 1856-1928 248.4
How to succeed in the Christian life. [Westwood, N.J.] Revell [1962, c.1906] 121p. 20cm. 62-6328 2.50 bds.,
1. Christian life. I. Title.

TOURNIER, Paul. 248.4
The adventure of living. Translated by Edwin Hudson. [1st ed.] New York, Harper & Row [1965] 250 p. 22 cm. Bibliographical footnotes. [BJ1470.T613] 65-20459
1. Self-realization. I. Title.

TOURNIER, Paul, ed. 248.4
Fatigue in modern society. Tr. [from French] by James H. Farley. Richmond Va., Knox [c.1965] 79p. 19cm. (Chime paperbacks) Essays selected from Surmenage et repos, pub. 1963. [BF481.T613] 65-19582 1.00 pap.,
I. Title.

TOURNIER, Paul, M.D. 248.4
The adventure of living, Tr. [from French] by Edwin Hudson. New York. Harper [c.1965] 250p. 22cm. Bibl. [BJ1470.T613] 65-20459 3.75 bds.,
1. Self-realization. I. Title.

TOWNSEND, Anne B. 248.4
Chapel talks for school and camp. Greenwich, Conn., Seabury [c.]1961. 128p. 61-11315 3.25 bds.,
1. Youth—Religious life. 2. Sermons, American. I. Title.

TREASURE, Geoff. 248'.4
Living right side up / Geoff Treasure ; [ill., Jake Sutton]. American ed. Wheaton, Ill. : Victor Books, c1977. 158 p. : ill. ; 18 cm. (An Input book) Originally published under title: Living out a revolution. [BT380.2.T75 1977] 76-48574 ISBN 0-88207-746-5 pbk. : 1.95
1. Sermon on the mount. 2. Christian life—1960- I. Title.

TRITON, A. N. 248'.4
Living & loving [by] A. N. Triton. Downers Grove, Ill., Inter-Varsity Press [1973, c1972] 95 p. 18 cm. [BT708.T74 1973] 73-75894 ISBN 0-87784-548-4 1.25 (pbk.)
1. Sex (Theology) I. Title.

*TRUEBLOOD, Elton 248.4
The common ventures of life; marriage, birth, work, death. New York, Harper [1965, c.1949] 124p. 21cm. (Harper chapelbks., CB3) .95 pap.,
I. Title.

*TUCKER, Cyril T. 248.4
Resources for living. New York, Vantage [1966, c.1965] 59p. 21cm. 2.50 bds.,
I. Title.

TUCKETT, Guin Ream. 248'.4
Get out there and reap! / By Guin Ream Tuckett ; [ill. by Bruce Tilsley]. St. Louis, Mo. : Bethany Press, c1976. p. cm. [BV4517.T8] 76-26702 ISBN 0-8272-1229-1 pbk. : 3.50
1. Christian life—Anecdotes, facetiae, satire, etc. I. Title.

TURNER, Dean. 248.4
Lonely God, lonely man; a study in the relation of loneliness to personal development, with a re-evaluation of Christian tradition. New York, Philosophical Library [c1960] 191 p. 23 cm. [BV4911.T8] 60-13663
1. Loneliness. I. Title.

TURNER, Dean 248.4
Lonely God, lonely man; a study in the relation of loneliness to personal development, with a re-evaluation of Christian tradition. New York, Philosophical Library [c.1960] 191p. 60-13663 3.75
1. Loneliness. I. Title.

VAN BAALEN, Jan Karel, 1890- 248.4
If thou shalt confess. Grand Rapids, Mich., Eerdmans [c.1962] 65p. 18cm. 62-13402 1.50
1. Christian life. I. Title.

VAN BUREN, James G. 248'.4
The search : the living God seeks man / by James G. Van Buren. Cincinnati, : New Life Books, 1974. 94 p. : ill. ; 18 cm. [BV4501.2.V325] 74-79114 ISBN 0-87239-004-7 pbk. : 1.50
1. Christian life—1960- I. Title.

VANDERMEY, Mary A., 1901- 248'.4
The teacher's report card, and other inspiring stories / Mary A. Vandermey. Milford, Mich, : Mott Media, c1977. 146 p. ; 19 cm. [BV4515.2.V36] 77-2790 ISBN 0-915134-42-X pbk. : 2.25
1. Christian life—Fiction. I. Title.

VAN DYKE, Vonda Kay. 248.4
That girl in your mirror. Westwood, N.J., F. H. Revell Co. [1966] 123 p. 21 cm. [BJ1651.V3] 66-12437
1. Girls — Conduct of life. I. Title.

VAN DYKE, Vonda Kay 248.4
That girl in your mirror. Westwood, N. J., Revell [c.1966] 123p. 21cm. [BJ1651.V3] 66-12437 2.95; 1.00 pap.,
1. Girls—Conduct of life. I. Title.

VAN ZELLER, Dom Herbert 248.4
We sing while there's voice left. Garden City, New York, Doubleday [1964] 155p. 18cm. (Image bk., D180) .75 pap.,
I. Title.

†VAUGHT, Laud Oswald, 1925- 248'.4
Focus on the Christian family / Laud Oswald Vaught. Cleveland, Tenn. : Pathway Press, c1976. 143 p. ; 18 cm. Bibliography: p. 141-143. [BV4526.2.V37] 75-37357 ISBN 0-87148-332-7 pbk. : 2.50
1. Family—Religious life. I. Title.

VENTURES in family living. 248'.4
Edited by Roy B. Zuck and Gene A. Getz. Chicago, Moody Press [1971] 144 p. 22 cm. "Originally appeared as part II of Adult education in the church." Includes bibliographies. [BV4526.2.V45] 76-155686 1.95
1. Family—Religious life—Addresses, essays, lectures. I. Zuck, Roy B., ed. II. Getz, Gene A., ed.

VERWER, George. 248'.4
Come! Live! Die! The real revolution. Wheaton, Ill., Tyndale House Publishers [1972] 96 p. 18 cm. [BV4501.2.V42] 72-81792 ISBN 0-8423-0420-7 0.95
1. Christian life—1960- I. Title.

VINCENT, John J. 248'.4
The Jesus thing; an experiment in discipleship [by] John J. Vincent. Nashville, Abingdon Press [1973] 123 p. illus. 23 cm. Includes bibliographical references. [BV4501.2.V47] 73-322 ISBN 0-687-20221-3 pap. 2.95
1. Christian life—1960- 2. Church renewal. I. Title.

VRUWINK, John H. 248.4
The lively tradition. Indianapolis, Bobbs [c.1962] 199p. 22cm. 62-10013 3.50 bds.,
1. Joy and sorrow. 2. Christian life. I. Title.

WALKER, Alan. 248.4
A new mind for a new age. New York, Abingdon Press [1959] 143 p. 20 cm. [BV4501.2.W3] 59-7250
1. Christian life. I. Title.

WALKER, Alan, 1911- 248'.4
Jesus the Liberator. Nashville, Abingdon Press [1973] 128 p. 21 cm. [BV4832.2.W33] 73-6804 ISBN 0-687-20199-3 3.95
1. Meditations. I. Title.

WALSH, John Patrick, Sir, 1911- 248.4
Living with uncertainty, by John Walsh. Dunedin, J. McIndoe, 1968. 71 p. 22 cm. "References": p. 71. [BJ1581.2.W33] 71-442512 1.20
1. Conduct of life. I. Title.

WARD, C. M. 248'.4
The playboy comes homes / C. M. Ward. Springfield, Mo. : Gospel Pub. House, c1976. 107 p. ; 18 cm. (Radiant books) [BT378.P8W27] 75-32603 ISBN 0-88243-572-8 pbk. : 1.25
1. Prodigal son (Parable) I. Title.

*WARD, Doris H. 248.4
Goodness is not enough. New York, Vantage [c.1964] 157p. 21cm. 3.50 bds.,
I. Title.

WARMATH, William Walter. 248.4
Our God is able. Nashville, Tenn., Broadman Press [1967] 127 p. 20 cm. Bibliographical references included in "Notes" (p. 127) [BV4501.2.W35] 67-12176
1. Christian life. I. Title.

WARMATH, William Walter. 248.4
Our God is able. Nashville, Tenn., Broadman Press [1967] 127 p. 20 cm. Bibliographical references included in "Notes" (p. 127) [BV4501.2.W35] 67-12176
1. Christian life. I. Title.

WEAVER, Bertrand 248.4
Joy. New York, Sheed [c.1964] x, 182p. 21cm. 64-19912 3.95 bds.,
1. Christian life—Catholic authors. 2. Joy and sorrow. I. Title.

WEAVER, Bertrand 248.4
Joy. Garden City, N.Y., Doubleday [1966, c.1964] 157p. 18cm. (Image bk., D211) .75 pap.,
1. Christian life—Catholic authors. 2. Joy and sorrow. I. Title.

WEBB, Lance. 248.4
Discovering love. New York, Abingdon Press [1959] 176 p. 21 cm. [BV4639.W35] 59-5123
1. Love (Theology) I. Title.

WEBB, Lance. 248.4
Point of glad return. New York, Abingdon Press [1960] 224 p. 23 cm. Includes bibliography. [BV4501.2.W4] 60-5236
1. Christian life. I. Title.

WEBB, Lance 248.4
Point of glad return. New York, Abingdon Press [c.1960] 224p. 23cm. (Bibl. footnotes) 60-5236 3.50
1. Christian life. I. Title.

WEBER, George W., 1946- 248'.4
Blessings unlimited [by] George W. Weber. Old Tappan, N.J., F. H. Revell Co. [1974] 157 p. 21 cm. [BV4501.2.W415] 74-1311 ISBN 0-8007-0666-8 2.95 (pbk.)
1. Christian life—1960- 2. Success. I. Title.

*WEDGE, Florence. 248.4
Watch it! Patience. Pulaski, Wis., Franciscan Pubs. [1968] 55p. 17cm. .25 pap.,
I. Title.

WELCH, Mary Artie Barrington. 248'.4
The golden key / by Mary Welch ; foreword by Eugenia Price. Grand Rapids : Zondervan Pub. House, c1977. p. cm. [BV4501.W447 1977] 76-55727 pbk. : 1.50
1. Christian life—1960- I. Title.

WELCH, Mary Artie Barrington. 248'.4
More than sparrows : how God supplies our human needs / by Mary Welch ; foreword by Eugenia Price. Grand Rapids : Zondervan Pub. House, 1976. 123 p. ; 18 cm. [BT135.W38 1976] 75-45487 pbk. : 1.75
1. Providence and government of God. 2. Christian life—1960- I. Title.

WELCH, Reuben. 248'.4
We really do need each other. Nashville, Impact Books [1973?] 111 p. 23 cm. [BT140.W44] 73-84462 3.50
1. God—Love. 2. Fellowship. I. Title.

WENGER, A Grace. 248.4
Stewards of the gospel; a resource book for the study of Christian stewardship, by A. Grace Wenger. Illustrated by Jan Gleysteen. Scottdale, Pa., Herald Press [1964] 126 p. illus. 20 cm. 29 p. 22 cm. Bibliography: p. 126.

Leader's guide. Scottdale, Pa., Herald Press. [1964] [BV772.W43] 64-20135
1. Stewardship, Christian. I. Title.

WENGER, A. Grace 248.4
Stewards of the gospel; a resource book for the study of Christian stewardship. Illus. by Jan Gleysteen. Scottdale, Pa., Herald Pr. [c.1964] 126p. illus. 20cm. Bibl. 64-20135 1.00 pap.,
1. Stewardship, Christian. I. Title.

WHEATLEY, Melvin E. 248.4
The power of worship, by Melvin E. Wheatley, Jr. New York, World Pub. Co. [1970] 61 p. 22 cm. (World inspirational books) [BV10.2.W447] 75-131563 2.95
1. Worship. I. Title.

WHEELEY, B. Otto. 248'.4
God can work through you / B. Otto Wheeley. Valley Forge, Pa. : Judson Press, c1977. 61 p. ; 22 cm. Includes bibliographical references. [BV4501.2.W439] 77-1130 ISBN 0-8170-0739-3 pbk. : 2.50
1. Christian life—1960- 2. Witness bearing (Christianity) I. Title.

WHERRIT, Elevnora. 248'.4
Beyond disbelief. Philadelphia, Dorrance [1971] 94 p. 22 cm. [BV4501.2.W444] 77-163918 4.00
1. Jesus Christ—Person and offices. 2. Spiritual life. I. Title.

WHITAKER, Robert C. 248'.4
Hang in there : counsel for charismatics / by Robert C. Whitaker. Plainfield, N.J. : Logos International, c1974. 49, [5] p. ; 18 cm. Bibliography: p. [51]-[54] [BX8763.W44] 77-179364 ISBN 0-88270-106-1 : 0.75
1. Pentecostalism. I. Title.

*WHITE, Eleana G. de. 248.4
Mensajes para los jovenes. Mountain View, Publicaciones, Pacific Pr. Pub. [1967] 472p. port. 18cm. Comp. for el Dept. de los Misioneros Voluntarios de la Asociacion General de los Adventistos del Septimo Dia) 3.75
I. Title.

WHITE, John, 248'.4
1924(Mar.5)-
The cost of commitment / John White. Downers Grove, Ill. : InterVarsity Press, c1976. 89 p. ; 18 cm. [BV4510.2.W47] 75-21457 ISBN 0-87784-486-0 pbk. : 1.95
1. Christian life—1960- 2. Suffering. I. Title.

WHITEHEAD, Carleton. 248'.4
Creative meditation / by Carleton Whitehead. New York : Dodd, Mead, [1975] 154 p. ; 21 cm. [BL624.W47] 75-4882 ISBN 0-396-07139-2 : 6.95
1. Spiritual life. 2. Success. I. Title.

WHITESIDE, Elena S. 248'.4
The Way: living in love [by] Elena S. Whiteside. [1st ed.] New Knoxville, Ohio, American Christian Press [1972] 282 p. illus. 22 cm. [BV4486.W39W44] 72-89132 ISBN 0-910068-06-2 3.95
1. The Way Biblical Research Center. I. Title.

WHITMAN, Virginia. 248'.4 B
The power of positive sharing. Wheaton, Ill., Tyndale House Publishers [1974] 137 p. 18 cm. [BR1725.W44A36 1974] 74-79609 ISBN 0-8423-4876-X 1.45 (pbk.).
1. Whitman, Virginia. 2. Natural history—Ozark Mountains. I. Title.

WIERSBE, Warren W. 248'.4
Be real [by] Warren W. Wiersbe. Wheaton, Ill., Victor Books [1972] 190 p., 18 cm. (An Input book) [BV4501.2.W517] 72-77014 ISBN 0-88207-046-0 1.25
1. Christian life—1960- I. Title.

WIERWILLE, Victor Paul. 248'.4
Studies in abundant living. New Knoxville, Ohio, American Christian Press [1971- v. 20 cm. Contents.—v. 1. The Bible tells me so. [BV4510.A1W5] 70-176281 ISBN 0-910068-02-X
1. Christian life—Biblical teaching. I. Title.

*WILCOX, Ethel Jones 248.4
Power for Christian living. Glendale, Calif., [Gospel Light Pubns., c.1966] 208p. 18cm. (regal bks., GL 95-3) Bibl. .95 pap.,
I. Title.

*WILKERSON, Don. 248.4
A coffee house manual, by Don & Ann Wilkerson. Minneapolis, Bethany Fellowship [1972] 96 p. illus. 19 cm. [BV4501] [[TX901]] pap. 2.25
1. Christian life. 2. Coffee Houses. I. Title.

WILLIAMS, Carol M. 248'.4
Make God your friend / Carol Williams ; introd. by Rosalind Rinker. Grand Rapids : Zondervan Pub. House, [1975] 89 p. ; 18 cm. [BV4817.W52] 74-25343 pbk. : 1.25
1. God—Worship and love. I. Title.

WILLIAMS, Harold Page, 248'.4
1934-
Do yourself a favor: love your wife [by] H. Page Williams. Plainfield, N.J., Logos International [1973] xiii, 131 p. 21 cm. [BV835.W54] 73-85896 ISBN 0-88270-071-5 4.95
1. Marriage. I. Title.
Pbk., 2.50, ISBN 0-88270-055-3.

WILLIAMS, Harvell P 1922- 248.4
Your passport to illumination, by Harvell P. Williams. Los Angeles, DeVorss [1965] 260 p. 24 cm. [BV4501.2.W54] 66-3418
1. Christian life. I. Title.

WILLIAMS, Ira E., 1926- 248'.4
God in unexpected places [by] Ira E. Williams, Jr. Nashville, Abingdon Press [1974] 127 p. 21 cm. [BV4501.2.W542] 73-15522 ISBN 0-687-15122-8 3.95
1. Christian life—1960- I. Title.

WILLIAMSON, Clark M. 248'.4
God is never absent / by Clark M. Williamson. St. Louis : Bethany Press, c1977. 141 p. ; 22 cm. Includes bibliographical references. [BV4637.W53] 77-1119 ISBN 0-8272-1230-5 pbk. : 4.95
1. Faith. 2. Christian life—1960- I. Title.

WILLINGHAM, Ronald L. 248'.4
Life is what you make it; a guide for self-discovery and goal-setting [by] Ronald L. Willingham. Introd. by Maxwell Maltz. Waco, Tex., Word Books [1973] 157 p. 23 cm. Includes bibliographical references. [BF637.S8W522] 73-77950 4.95
1. Success. 2. Psychology, Religious. I. Title.

WILLS, Ann McCelvey. 248'.4
Dear Superniki Purple. Wheaton, Ill., Tyndale House Publishers [1971] 158 p. illus. 18 cm. [BV4501.2.W545] 79-123284 ISBN 0-8423-0640-4
1. Christian life. I. Title.

WILSON, Carl, 1924- 248'.4
With Christ in the school of disciple building : a study of Christ's method of building disciples / Carl Wilson. Grand Rapids : Zondervan Pub. House, c1976. 336 p. : ill. ; 22 cm. Includes indexes. Bibliography: p. 315-317. [BV4501.2.W55] 76-13214 5.95
1. Christian life—1960- 2. Evangelistic work. I. Title.

WILSON, Caroline Fry, 248'.4
1787-1846.
Christ our example / Caroline Fry. Swengel, Pa. : Reiner, 1976. 127 p. ; 22 cm. [BV4501.W615 1976] 77-366689
1. Christian life. I. Title.

*"WITH God all things are 248'.4
possible!" New York, Bantam Books [1974, c1972] 280 p. 18 cm. [BJ1581] 1.45 (pbk.)
1. Conduct of life. I. Life Study Fellowship.

WOLCOTT, Leonard T 248'.4
Twelve modern disciples; faithful witnesses in our times of change. Nashville, The Upper room [1963] 88 p. 18 cm. [BV4515.2.W58] 63-22087
1. Christian life — Stories. I. Title.

WOLD, Marge. 248'.4
Who's running your life? / Marge & Erling Wold. Minneapolis : Augsburg Pub. House, c1976. 127 p. ; 20 cm. [BV4501.2.W58] 76-375492 ISBN 0-8066-1540-0 pbk. : 3.50
1. Christian life—1960- I. Wold, Erling, joint author. II. Title.

WOODS, C. Stacey, 1909- 248'.4
Some ways of God / C. Stacey Woods. Downers Grove, Ill. : InterVarsity Press, c1975. 131 p. ; 21 cm. [BV4501.2.W63] 74-31843 ISBN 0-87784-715-0 pbk. : 2.95
1. Christian life—1960- I. Title.

WOODWARD, Thomas B. 1937- 248'.4
Turning things upside down. a theological workbook [by] Thomas B. Woodward. New York, Seabury Press [1975]. 79 p. 28 cm. "A Crossroad book." Includes bibliographical references [BV4501.2.W64] 74-31439 ISBN 0-8164-0279-5 4.50 (pbk.)
1. Christian life—1960- 2. Church. I. Title.

WOODYARD, David O. 248'.4
Strangers and exiles: living by promises, by David O. Woodyard. Philadelphia, Westminster Press [1974] 157 p. 19 cm. Includes bibliographical references. [BV4501.2.W65] 73-19591 ISBN 0-664-24980-9 3.25
1. Christian life—1960- I. Title.

WRIGHT, H. Norman. 248'.4
The Christian use of emotional power [by] H. Norman Wright. Old Tappan, N.J., F. H. Revell Co. [1974] 159 p. illus. 21 cm. Bibliography: p. 157-159. [BF561.W74] 74-10755 ISBN 0-8007-0679-X 4.95
1. Emotions. 2. Christian life—1960- I. Title.

WRIGHT, H. Norman. 248'.4
Improving your self-image / by Norman Wright. Irvine, Calif. : Harvest House Publishers, c1977. 62 p. ; 18 cm. (The Answer series) Includes bibliographical references. [BJ1533.S3W74] 76-51532 ISBN 0-89081-032-X : 0.95
1. Self-respect. I. Title. II. Series.

WRIGHT, H. Norman, comp. 248'.4
The living marriage : lessons in love from The living Bible / H. Norman Wright, compiler. Old Tappan, N.J. : F. H. Revell Co., [1975] 128 p. : ill. ; 26 cm. Includes bibliographical references. [BV835.W74] 74-31460 ISBN 0-8007-0722-2 : 5.95
1. Marriage. 2. Marriage—Biblical teaching. I. Taylor, Kenneth Nathaniel. The living Bible, paraphrased. Selections. II. Title.

WRIGLEY, Louise Scott. 248'.4
Look up, heart. Independence, Mo., Herald House [1962] 55 p. illus. 16 cm. [BV4515.2.W7] 62-21992
1. Christian life — Stories. I. Title.

WROBLEWSKI, Sergius 248.4
Christian perfection for the layman. Chicago, Franciscan Herald [c.1963] 263p. 21cm. 63-12858 3.95 bds.,
1. Christian life—Catholic authors I. Title.

WUELLNER, Flora Slosson. 248'.4
Release for trapped Christians. Nashville, Abingdon Press [1974] 94 p. 20 cm. [BV210.2.W815] 73-20034 3.75
1. Prayer. 2. Spiritual life. I. Title.

WYON, Olive, 1890- 248.4
Teaching toward Christian perfection, introducing three spiritual classics. [New York, Woman's Div. of Christian Service, Bd. of Missions, Methodist Church [c.1963] 200p. illus. 19cm. Bibl. 63-8291 1.00 pap.,
1. Spiritual life—Collections. I. Title.
Contents omitted.

WYON, Olive, 1890- 248.4
Teachings toward Christian perfection, introducing three spiritual classics. [New York, Woman's Division of Christian Service, Board of Missions, Methodist Church, 1963] 200 p. illus. 19 cm. [BV4515.W9] 63-8291
1. Spiritual life — Collections. I. Title.

YANCEY, Philip. 248'.4
After the wedding / Philip Yancey. Waco, Tex. : Word Books, c1976. 160 p. ; 23 cm. Includes bibliographical references. [BV835.Y36] 76-19537 ISBN 0-87680-456-3 : 5.95
1. Marriage—Case studies. I. Title.

YOHN, Rick. 248'.4
Beyond spiritual gifts / Rick Yohn. Wheaton, Ill. : Tyndale House Publishers, c1976. 175 p. ; 22 cm. [BV4501.2.Y63] 76-5210 ISBN 0-8423-0112-7 : 5.95. pbk. : 3.95
1. Christian life—1960- I. Title.

ZAMBONI, Camillo 248.4
Jesus speaks to you. [Boston] St. Paul Eds. [dist. Daughters of St. Paul, c.1961] 166p. 61-14570 1.75; 1.00 pap.,
1. Young women—Religious life. 2. Christian life—Catholic authors. I. Title.

ZUNKEL, Charles, 1905- 248'.4
Turn again to life [by] Charles and Cleda Zunkel. Elgin, Ill., Brethren Press [1974] 144 p. 22 cm. [BV4501.2.Z86] 74-11107 ISBN 0-87178-881-0 4.95
1. Christian life—Case studies. I. Zunkel, Cleda, 1903- joint author. II. Title.

FARRER, Carl. 248.4'02'07
Every head bowed, by Carl Farrer and Fred Bock. Introd. by Art Linkletter. Illustrated by Corny Cole. Waco, Tex., Word Books [1968] [66] p. (chiefly illus.) 15 cm. [NC1429.F292A44] 68-56987
1. Christian life—Caricatures and cartoons. I. Bock, Fred, joint author. II. Cole, Corny, illus. III. Title.

ROBERTS, Benjamin Titus, 248.403
1823-1893.
Living truths. Edited by E. D. Riggs. Winona Lake, Ind., Light and Life Press [1960] unpaged. illus. 23cm. Published in 1912 under title: Pungent truths. [BV4488.R6 1960] 60-33249
1. Christian life—Dictionaries. I. Title.

BAILEY, Harold S. 248.4'07
Intermediates in the learning fellowship [by] Harold S. Bailey. [Teacher's ed. Nashville, Tenn., Convention Press, 1967] x, 70 p. illus. 19 cm. [BV4511.B25] 67-10003
1. Christian life—Study and teaching. I. Title.

KENT, W. Herbert, 248'.4'07
ed.
Come to the feast of the Lord; "Bible Living" studies for men. W. Herbert Kent, editor. Minneapolis, Augsburg Pub. House [1965] 48 p. illus. 22 cm. Includes music. "Auspices of the Brotherhood of The American Lutheran Church." [BV4511.K37] 65-12138
1. Christian life — Biblical teaching. 2. Religious education — Textbooks for adults — Lutheran. I. The American Lutheran Church (1961-) Brotherhood. II. Title.

MATTHEWS, Victor M. 248'.4'07
Growth in grace; a manual for students with study questions [by] Victor M. Matthews. Grand Rapids, Zondervan Pub. House [1971, c1970] 142 p. illus., 21 cm. (A Zondervan book) [BV4511.M34] 71-171193 1.95 (pbk)
1. Christian life—1960- —Study and teaching. 2. Christianity—Essence, genius, nature—Study and teaching. I. Title.

WILLIAMS, Herman. 248.4'07
Attitude education : a research curriculum developed by the Union College Character Research Project / Herman Williams and Ella L. Greene. Schenectady, N.Y. : Character Research Press, c1975. 86 p. ; 28 cm. [BV4511.W54] 75-16677 ISBN 0-915744-02-3
1. Christian life—Study and teaching. I. Greene, Ella L., joint author. II. Union College, Schenectady. Character Research Project. III. Title.

REDHEAD, John A 248.4076
Putting your faith to work. New York, Abingdon Press [1959] 128p. 20cm. [BR96.R4] 59-12784
1. Questions and answers—Theology. I. Title.

LLOYD-JONES, David 248.408
Martyn.
Faith on trial [by] D. Martyn Lloyd-Jones. [1st ed.] Grand Rapids, Eerdmans [1965] 125 p. 23 cm. [BS145073d.L6] 65-29741
1. Bible. O. T. Psalms LXXIII — Sermons. 2. Sermons, English. I. Title.

LLOYD-JONES, David Martyn 248.408
Faith on trial. Grand Rapids, Mich., Eerdmans [c.1965] 125p. 23cm. [BS145073d.L6] 65-29741 2.95 bds.,
1. Bible. O. T. Psalms LXXIII—Sermons. 2. Sermons, English. I. Title.

REDPATH, Alan. 248.408
Blessings out of buffetings; studies in II Corinthians. Westwood, N.J., F.H. Revell Co. [1965] 240 p. 21 cm. [BX6333.R37B5] 65-29772
1. Bible. N.T. 2. Corinthians — Sermons. 3. Baptists — Sermons. 4. Sermons, English. I. Title.

SAVARY, Louis M., comp. 248'.4'08
Finding each other. Compiled by Louis M. Savary and Thomas J. O'Connor. New York, Newman Press, 1971. 176 p. illus. 21 cm. [BV4495.S29] 226 77-133468 2.95
1. Christian life—Collections. 2. Conduct of life—Collections. I. O'Connor, Thomas J., joint comp. II. Title.

MATHEWS, Wendell, ed. 248.4082
Images of faith; illustrations of the Christian faith by contemporary Christian thinkers. Comp., ed. by Wendell Mathews, Robert P. Wetzler. St. Louis, Concordia [c.1963] xviii, 272p. 22cm. Bibl. 63-21163 4.95
1. Christian life. I. Wetzler, Robert P., 1932- joint ed. II. Title.

REEDER, Lucille Lois. 248.40924
What faith can do. San Antonio, Naylor Co. [1966] 83 p. 22 cm. Autobiolgraphical. [BX6495.R43A3] 66-23434
I. Title.

REEDER, Lucille Lois 248.40924
What faith can do. San Antonio, Tex., Naylor [c.1966] 83p. 22cm. Autobiographical. [BX6495.R43A3] 66-23430 3.95
I. Title.

WOLHORN, Herman. 248'.4'0924
Emmet Fox's golden keys to successful living & reminiscences / Herman Wolhorn. 1st ed. New York : Harper & Row, c1977. viii, 229 p. ; 21 cm. [BF648.F6W64 1977] 76-62930 ISBN 0-06-069670-2 : 6.95
1. Fox, Emmet. 2. New Thought. 3. Clergy—United States—Biography. I. Title.

ACCOLA, Louis W. 248.42
Personal faith for human crisis [by] Louis W. Accola. Minneapolis, Augsburg Pub. House [1970] 141 p. 20 cm. Bibliography: p. 127-129. [BV4501.2.A24] 74-121968 2.75
1. Christian life—Lutheran authors. I. Title.

ADAMS, Henry L. 248.42
The eternal law. New York, Vantage [1963, c.1962] 85p. 21cm. 2.50
I. Title.

ALLAN, Ann 248.42
Streamlined thoughts. Decorations by B. S. Biro [New York, Wm.] Collins [1966, c.1965] 63p. illus. 16cm. (Collins greetings bks.) [BV4513.A4] 66-5760 1.00
1. Christian life—Quotations, maxims, etc. I. Title.

AMEN, Carol, 1933- 248'.42
Love is the motive / Carol Amen. Nashville : Southern Pub. Association, c1977. 64 p. ; 18 cm. [BJ1581.2.A46] 77-12655 ISBN 0-8127-0153-4 pbk. : 0.75
1. Conduct of life. 2. Interpersonal relations. I. Title.

ARMSTRONG, H. Parr 248.42
Living in the currents of God. St. Louis, Bethany [c.1962] 112p. 21cm. 62-20505 2.50 bds.,
1. Christian life. I. Title.

ARMSTRONG, H Parr. 248.42
Living in the currents of God. St. Louis, Bethany Press [1962] 112p. 21cm. [BV4501.2.A67] 62-20505
1. Christian life. I. Title.

ARNOLD, Arthur Olof, 1912- 248.42
You and yours. Rock Island, Ill., Augustana [c.1962] 85p. 62-12911 1.45 pap.,
1. Christian life. I. Title.

ARNOLD, Arthur Olof, 1912- 248.42
You and yours. Rock Island, Ill, Augustana Press [1962] 85p. 20cm. [BV4501.2.A7] 62-12911
1. Christian life. I. Title.

AUGSBURGER, David. 248.4'2
Man uptight! Chicago, Moody Pr. [1973, c.1970] 125 p. 18 cm. (Moody pocket books) First published under title: Man, am I uptight! [BV4501.2] 72-104819 ISBN 0-8024-5172-1 pap., 0.75
1. Christian life—Mennonite authors. I. Title.

BARCLAY, W. C. 248.42
Reaching for rapport: fulfillment through at-one-ment with God. Golden anniversary ed. Denver, Big Mountain [dist. Swallow, c.1962] 181p. 23cm. 3.75
I. Title.

BARCLAY, William lecturer in the University of Glasgow 248.42
Two minutes a day; daily Bible studies. Philadelphia, Westminster Press, 1964. 1 v. (unpaged) 20 cm. "Thirty-nine four-page folders corresponding to the weeks in a nine-month school year." [BS483.5.B3] 64-19148
1. Bible — Meditations. 2. Devotional calendars — Presbyterian Church. I. Title. II. Title: Daily Bible studies.

BARCLAY, William 248.42
Two minutes a day, daily Bible studies. Philadelphia Westminster [c.1964] 1v. (unpaged) 20cm. Thirty-nine four-page folders corresponding to the weeks in a nine-month school year. 64-19148 .75, pap., unbound
1. Bible—Meditations. 2. Devotional calendars—Presbyterian Church. I. Title. II. Title: Daily Bible studies.

BARNHOUSE, Donald Grey, 1895- 248.42
God's methods for holy living: practical lessons in experimental holiness. Grand Rapids, Mich., Eerdmans [1951, c.1961] 181p. 3.00
1. Christian life. I. Title.

BARRETT, Ethel. 248.4'2
The secret sign. Glendale, Calif., G/L Regal Books [1970] 133 p. illus. 20 cm. (A Regal venture book) Includes bibliographical references. [BJ1581.2.B348] 78-117523 0.69
1. Conduct of life. I. Title.

BELGUM, Harold J. 248.42
Family vacation idea book. Illus. by Arthur Kirchhoff. St. Louis, Concordia [c.1966] 62p. illus. 28cm. [BV4599.B4] 66-21173 1.00 pap.,
1. Vacations—Moral and religious aspects. 2. Nature—Religious interpretations. I. Title.

BELL, L. Nelson, 1894- 248.42
Convictions to live by [by] L. Nelson Bell. Grand Rapids, W. B. Eerdmans Pub. Co. [1966] 185 p. 22 cm. [BV4501.2.B39] 65-25185
1. Christian life. I. Title.

BELL, L. Nelson, 1894- 248.42
Convictions to live by. Grand Rapids, Mich., Eerdmans [c.1966] 185p. 22cm. [BV4501.2.B39] 65-25185 3.50
1. Christian life. I. Title.

BENSON, Dennis C. 248'.42
My brother Dennis / Dennis Benson. Waco, Tex. : Word Books, c1975. 187 p. ; 23 cm. [BJ1581.2.B45] 75-10092 5.95
1. Conduct of life. I. Title.

BINGHAM, Geoffrey C 248.42
Cross without velvet; studies in discipleship. Chicago, Moody Press [1960] 96p. 20cm. [BV4501.2.B5] 60-3650
1. Christian life. I. Title.

BISHOP, Edna Earl 248.42
Our gospel of love. New York, Greenwich [1962, c.1961] 96p. 22cm. 61-14161 2.75
1. Christian life. I. Title.

BLAMIRES, Harry. 248.42
The offering of man. Introd. by Bernard C. Newman. New York, Morehouse-Barlow Co., 1960. 146 p. 19 cm. [BT220.B5] 60-9769
1. Christian life. 2. Incarnation. I. Title.

BOSLEY, Harold Augustus, 1907- 248.42
Doing what is Christian. New York, Abingdon Press [1960] 128p. 20cm. [BV4501.2.B65] 60-50515
1. Christian life. 2. Church and social problems. I. Title.

BOSLEY, Harold Augustus, 1907- 248.42
Doing what is Christian. Nashville, Graded Press [1960] 128p. 20cm. (Basic Christian books) [BV4501.2.B65 1960] 61-1314
1. Christian life. 2. Church and social problems. I. Title.

BOSLEY. HAROLD AUGUSTUS 248.42
Doing what is Christian. Nashville, Abingdon Press [c.1960] 128p. 20cm. 60-50515 1.00
1. Christian life. 2. Church and social problems. I. Title.

BOVET, Theodore, 1900- 248.42
Have time and be free; toward the organization of one's life. Translated by A. J. Ungersma. Richmond, John Knox Press [1964] 61 p. 19 cm. (Chime paperbacks) [BJ1581.2.B643] 64-12502
1. Conduct of life. 2. Time. I. Title.

BOVET, Theodore, 1900- 248.42
Have time and be free; toward the organization of one's life. Tr. [from German] by A. J. Ungersma. Richmond, Va., Knox [c.1964] 61p. 19cm. (Chime paperbacks) 64-12502 1.00 pap.,
1. Conduct of life. 2. Time. I. Title.

BOWERS, George K 248.42
God's Word--and man's! A positive approach to the relationship of God's truth to man's wisdom in a time of stress. Anderson, Ind., Warner Press [1962] 192p. 21cm. Includes bibliography. [BV4501.2.B68] 62-17791
1. Christian life—Biblical teaching. I. Title.

BOWERS, George K. 248.42
God's Word--and man's! A positive approach to the relationship of God's truth to man's wisdom in a time of stress. Anderson, Ind., Warner [dist. Gospel Trumpet, c.1962] 192p. 21cm. Bibl. 62-17781 3.50
1. Christian life—Biblical teaching. I. Title.

BRETSCHER, Paul G. 248.42
The world upside down or right side up? [St. Louis] Concordia [1965, c.1964] xiv, 130p. 20cm. [BT382.B7] 64-7927 2.50 bds.,
1. Beatitudes. I. Title.

BROWN, Alberta Z. 248.4'2
For students and others fed up [by] Alberta Z. Brown. St. Louis, Bethany Press [1970] 107 p. 21 cm. [BJ1581.2.B7] 79-105054 3.95
1. Conduct of life. I. Title.

BROWN, Robert Raymond, Bp., 1910- 248.42
Alive again. New York, Morehouse-Barlow [1964] 151 p. 21 cm. [BT378.P8B74] 64-15260
1. Prodigal son (Parable) 2. Christian life — Anglican authors. I. Title.

BROWN, Robert Raymond, Bp., 1910- 248.42
Alive again. New York, Morehouse [c.1964] 151p. 21cm. 64-15260 3.95
1. Prodigal son (Parable) 2. Christian life—Anglican authors. I. Title.

BUNYAN, Hohn 248.42
Christian behaviour; or how to walk so as to please God. Swengel, Pa., Bible Truth, 1962. 111p. 20cm. 1.50 pap.,
I. Title.

BUSCAGLIA, Leo F. 248'.42
Love, by Leo F. Buscaglia. [Thorofare, N.J., C. B. Slack, 1972] 147 p. port. 21 cm. Includes bibliographical references. [BD436.B87] 72-92810
1. Love.

CARLSON, Betty 248.42
Who's beat? Rock Island, Ill., Augustana Press [c.1961] 101p. 61-10544 1.75 pap.,
1. Christian life. I. Title.

CARLSON, Dwight L. 248'.42
Run and not be weary: the Christian answer to fatigue [by] Dwight L. Carlson. Old Tappan, N.J., F. H. Revell Co. [1974] 220 p. 21 cm. Bibliography: p. 219-220. [RC351.C27] 74-848 ISBN 0-8007-0650-1 5.95
1. Fatigue, Mental. 2. Christian life—1960- I. Title.

CHALMERS, Randolph Carleton 248.42
A faith for you. Richmond, Va., John Knox [1962, c.1960] 118p. 'First pub. in 1960, under the title A gospel to proclaim.' Bibl. 62-8223 1.50 pap.,
1. Theology, Doctrinal—Popular works. I. Title.

CHANGEY, Eugene 248.42
The thinker and the hare. New York, Carlton [c.1963] 76p. 21cm. (Reflection Bk.) 2.50
I. Title.

CHEVILLE, Roy Arthur, 1897- 248.42
Spirituality in the space age. Prepared for the Dept. of Religious Education, Reorganized Church of Jesus Christ of latter Day Saints. [Independence, Mo., Herald Pub. house] 1962. 264p. 20cm. [BL254.C47] 62-12899
1. Religion and astronautics. 2. Reorganized Church of Jesus Christ of Latter-Day Saints—Sermons. I. Title.

CHEVILLE, Roy Arthur, 1897- 248.42
Spirituality in the space age. Prepared for the Dept. of Religious Education, Reorganized Church of Jesus Christ of Latter Day Saints. [Independence, Mo., Herald, c.]1962. 264p. 20cm. 62-12899 2.75
1. Religion and astronautics. 2. Reorganized Church of Jesus Christ of Latter-Day Saints—Sermons. I. Title.

CHRISTINE [PSEUD.] 248.42
Why I believe in God, immortality and the Christ, and other essays. New York, Exposition [c.1963] 94 p. 21 cm. 2.75
I. Title.

CHRISTLIKE Christian (The) by an unknown Christian. Grand Rapids, Mich., Zondervan [1962] 144p. 21cm. 1.95 bds., 248.42

CLARKE, Kathleen M. 248.42
Letters to my Heavenly Father. Introd. by Eugenia Price. Grand Rapids, Zondervan Pub. House [c.1960] 115p. 20cm. 60-1704 2.00
1. Christian life. I. Title.

CLARKE, Kathleen M 1905- 248.42
Letters to my Hevenly Father. Introd. by Eugenia Price. Grand Rapids, Zondervan Pub. House [1960] 115p. 20cm. [BV4501.2.C55] 60-1704
1. Christian life. I. Title.

CONN, Charles W. 248.42
The rudder and the rock. Cleveland, Tenn., Pathway Press [c.1960] 151p. 22cm. 60-6543 2.50
1. Christian life. I. Title.

CONVERSATIONS at Little Gidding. 248.4'2
'On the retirement of Charles V.' 'On the austere life': dialogues by members of the Ferrar family [transcribed by Nicholas Ferrar] introduction and notes, by A. M. William. London, Cambridge U.P., 1970. lxxxvi, 322 p. 5 plates, 2 illus., 3 facsims., port. 23 cm. Bibliography: p. 316-317. [BV4500.F47C6 1970] 78-85741 5/-/- ($15.00)
1. Christian life—Stories. 2. Little Gidding. I. Ferrar, Nicholas, 1592-1637. II. William, A. M., ed. III. Title: On the retirement of Charles V. IV. Title: On the austere life.

COOK, David c., 3d 248.42
Walk the high places [Elgin, Ill., Author, c.1964] 96p. 15cm. 1.50 bds.,
1. Meditations. I. Title.

COTHRAN, J. Guy, Rev. 248.42
The victorious Christian life, sermon messages. New York, Exposition [c.1963] 201p. 21cm. 3.50
I. Title.

CRANFORD, Clarence William 248.42
His life our pattern. Nashville, Broadman Press [c.1960] x, 130p. 21cm. 60-9528 2.75 bds.,
1. Christian life. I. Title.

DAILY, Starr, pseud. 248.42
You can find God. [Westwood, N. J.] Revell [c.1963] 127p. 21cm. 63-7599 2.50 bds.,
1. Christian life. I. Title.

DAILY, Starr, pseud. 248.42
You can find God. [Westwood, N.J.] Revell [1963] 127 p. 21 cm. 63-7599
1. Christian life. I. Title.

*DAVIDS, David E. 248.42
Christian Stewardship. New York, Carlton [c.1965] 67p. 21cm. (Reflection bk.) 2.00
I. Title.

DAWSON, Grace (Strickler) 1891- 248.42
For a deeper life. New York, Abingdon Press [1963] 112 p. 20 cm. Includes bibliography. [BV4509.5D3] 63-8667
1. Spiritual life — Methodist authors. 2. Prayer. I. Title.

DAWSON, Grace (Strickler) 1891- 248.42
For a deeper life. Nashville, Abingdon [c.1963] 112p. 20cm. Bibl. 63-8667 2.00
1. Spiritual life—Methodist authors. 2. Prayer. I. Title.

DEAL, William S. 248.42
Problems of the spirit-filled life. Kansas City, Mo., Beacon Hill Pr. [1961] 158p. Bibl. 61-5092 2.00
1. Spiritual life. I. Title.

DECKER, James A. 248.42
Magnificent decision. Lee's Summit, Mo., Unity Sch. of Christianity, 1963. 173p. 17cm. 2.00
I. Title.

DE KOCK, Gertrude 248.42
Live and prove! [San Antonio, Tex., Naylor, 1963] 180p. 21cm. gratis pap.,
I. Title.

DELP, Paul S 248.42
The Journey of the human spirit; the story of man's quest for fulfillment. Foreword by Glenn Randall Phillips. [1st ed.] New York, Exposition Press [1962] 104 p. 21 cm. (An Exposition-Testament book) [BV4501.2.D44] 62-21055
1. Spiritual life. I. Title.

DELP, Paul S. 248.42
The journey of the human spirit; the story of man's quest for fulfillment. Foreword by Glenn Randall Phillips. New York, Exposition [c.1962] 104p. 21cm. (ExpositioniTestament bk.) 62-21055 3.00
1. Spiritiual life. I. Title.

DEMOSS, Arthur. 248.4'2
How to change your world in 12 weeks [by] Arthur DeMoss & David R. Enlow. Old Tappan, N.J., F. H. Revell Co. [1969] 128 p. 21 cm. [BJ1611.2.D42] 69-12293 3.50
1. Success. I. Enlow, David R., joint author. II. Title.

DENNISON, Alfred Dudley, 1914- 248.4'2
Shock it to me, doctor! [by] A. Dudley Dennison. Introd. by Billy Graham. Grand Rapids, Zondervan Pub. House [1970] 152 p. 22 cm. At head of title: A look at the hang-ups of the "now" generation. [BV4501.2.D445] 75-122968 3.95
1. Christian life—1960- I. Title.

DOWNEY, Murray W 248.42
Sermons on Christian commitment; or, What is a Christian? Grand Rapids, Baker Book House, 1963. 100 p. 20 cm. (Minister's handbook series) [BV3797.D63] 63-21466
1. Christianity — Essence, genius, nature. 2. Evangelistic sermons. 3. Sermons, English — Canada. I. Title. II. Title: What is a Christian?

DOWNEY, Murray W. 248.42
Sermons on Christian commitment; or, What is a Christian? Grand Rapids, Baker Bk. [c.] 1963. 100p. 20cm. (Minister's handbk. ser.) 63-21466 1.95
1. Christianity—Essence, genius, nature. 2. Evangelistic sermons. 3. Sermons, English—Canada. I. Title. II. Title: What is a Christian?

DROWN, Harold J. 248'.42
You the graduate [by] Harold J. Drown. Nashville, Abingdon Press [1974] 64 p. 20 cm. [BJ1611.D75] 73-18380 ISBN 0-687-46856-6 2.95
1. Success. 2. Conduct of life. I. Title.

DRUMMOND, Henry, 1851-1897. 248.4'2
The greatest thing in the world; Henry Drummond's inspirational classic in a modern, readable edition, with other selected essays. Edited by William R. Webb. Illustrated by James Hamil. [Kansas City, Mo.] Hallmark Editions [1967] 58 p. illus. 20 cm. [BV4639.D7 1967] 67-17904
1. Love (Theology) I. Webb, William R., ed. II. Title.

DRUMMOND, Henry, 1851-1897 248.4'2
The greatest thing in the world Henry Drummond's inspirational classic in a modern, readable edition, with other selected essays. Ed. by William R. Webb. Illus. by James

Hamil. [Kansas City, Mo.] Hallmark Eds. [1967] 58p. illus. 20cm. [BV4639.D7 1967] 67-17904 2.50 bds.,
1. Love (Theology) I. Webb, William R., ed. II. Title.

EDMAN, V. Raymond 248.42
But God! Grand Rapids, Mich., Zondervan [c.1962] 152p. 21cm. 2.50
I. Title.

EDMAN, Victor Raymond, 1900- 248.42
But God= Little lessons of large importance learned from the Holy Scriptures, with poems by Annie Johnson Flint. Grand Rapids, Zondervan Pub. House [c9162] 152 p. illus. 21 cm. [BS483.5E3] 63-2133
1. Bible—Devotional literature. I. Flint, Annie Johnson. II. Title.

ELLISON, John Malcus, 1889- 248.42
They sang through the crisis; dealing with life's most critical issues. Chicago, Judson [c.1961] 159p. Bibl. 61-14615 3.00
1. Christian life. I. Title.

ELY, Virginia, 1899- 248.42
Stewardship: witnessing for Christ. [Westwood, N.J.] Revell [c.1962] 96p. 20cm. 62-10736 1.95
1. Stewardship, Christian. I. Title.

ENLOW, David R ed. 248.42
Men twice born; remarkable true stories of lives transformed. Grand Rapids, Zondervan Pub. House [1963] 147 p. ports. 21 cm. [BV4515.E55] 63-21648
1. Christian life — Stories. 2. Christian Business Men's Committee International. I. Title.

ENLOW, David R. ed. 248.42
Men twice born; remarkable true stories of lives transformed. Grand Rapids, Mich., Zondervan [c.1963] 147p. ports. 21cm. 63-21648 2.95
1. Christian life—Stories. 2. Christian Business Men's Committee International. I. Title.

ERASMUS, Desiderius, d. 1536. 248.42
Handbook of the militant Christian. Tr., introd. by John P. Dolan. Notre Dame, Ind., Fides [c.1962] 159p. 21cm. Bibl. 62-13638 3.95
1. Christian life. I. Dolan, John Patrick, ed. and tr. II. Title.

ERB, Paul, 1894- 248.42
Don't park here, discussions on dynamic Christian living. Scottdale, Pa., Herald Pr. [c.1962] 182p. 20cm. 62-13714 3.00
1. Christian life. I. Title.

FARRER, Austin Marsden 248.42
A faith of our own. With a pref. by C. S. Lewis. Cleveland, World Pub. Co. [1961, c.1960] 219p. 61-5802 3.75
1. Faith. 2. Christian life. I. Title.

*FILLMORE, Lowell 248.42
The prayer way to health, wealth and happiness. Lee's Summit, Mo., Unity Sch. of Christianity [1964] 252p. 24cm. 2.95 bds.,
I. Title.

FITCH, William 248.42
Enter into life. Grand Rapids, Mich., Eerdmans [c.1961] 110p. 62-403 1.25 pap.,
1. Christian life. I. Title.

FLETCHER, Grace (Nies) 248.42
I was born tomorrow. New York, Dutton [c.1961] 253 p. 62-7058 3.95
1. Christian life. I. Title.

FLYNN, Leslie B 248.42
Did I say thanks? Nashville, Broadman Press [1963] 118 p. 21 cm. [BV4647.G8F5] 63-8407
1. Gratitude. I. Title.

FLYNN, Leslie B. 248.42
Did I say thanks? Nashville, Broadman [c.1963] 118p. 21cm. 63-8407 2.50
1. Gratitude. I. Title.

FLYNN, Leslie B. 248.42
Thanksgiving messages; eight thought-provoking messages on gratitude in Christian living [by] Leslie B. Flynn. Grand Rapids, Baker Book House [1974, c1963] 118 p. 20 cm. Original title: Did I say thanks? [BV4647.G8F5] ISBN 0-8010-3466-3. 1.95 (pbk.)
1. Graditude I. Title.
L.C. card number for original ed.: 63-8407.

FORAN, Donald J. 248.4'2
Living with ambiguity; discerning God in a complex society [by] Donald J. Foran. Staten Island, Alba House [1971] xxii, 137 p. 22 cm. Includes bibliographical references. [BX2350.2.F58] 72-140282 ISBN 0-8189-0196-9 3.95
1. Christian life—Catholic authors. I. Title.

FORD, Wesley P 248.42
Gift of hope. St. Louis, Bethany Press [1963] 95 p. 21 cm. [BV4501.2.F59] 63-8822
1. Christian life. I. Title.

FORD, Wesley P. 248.42
Gift of hope. St. Louis, Bethany [c.1963] 95p. 21cm. 63-8822 1.75 bds.,
1. Christian life. I. Title.

FRAME, John Davidson, M. D. 248.42
Personality; development in the Christian life. Chicago, Moody Pr. [c.1961] 191p. 61-66181 3.25
1. Christian life. 2. Personality. I. Title.

FRAME, John Davidson. 248.4'2
Psychology and personality development; case studies in emotional problems and their implications for the Christian life [by] John D. Frame. [Rev.] Chicago, Moody Press [1967] 191 p. 22 cm. First published in 1961 under title: Personality development in the Christian life. [BV4501.2.F7 1967] 67-7390
1. Christian life. 2. Personality. I. Title.

FRANKE, Carl W. 248.4'2
Defrost your frozen assets, by Carl W. Franke. Waco, Tex., Word Books [1969] 147 p. 23 cm. Bibliographical footnotes. [BV4501.2.F717] 76-91942 3.95
1. Christian life. I. Title.

FRANKLIN, Denson N. 248.42
Which way forward? Faith at the crossroads. [Westwood, N.J.] Revell [c.1962] 124p. 62-10733 2.50
1. Christian life. I. Title.

FRASER, James Wallace 248.42
Power of a righteous life. New York, Carlton [c.] 1962. 61p. (Reflection [ser.]) 62-854 2.00
1. Christian life. I. Title.

FRENCH, Marion Flood. 248.42
To come and go on. New York, Abingdon Press [1964] 96 p. 13 cm. [BV4832.2.F66] 64-12957
1. Devotional literature. I. Title.

FRENCH, Marion Flood 248.42
To come and go on. Nashville, Abingdon [c.1964] 96p. 18cm. 64-12957 2.00 bds.,
1. Devotional literature. I. Title.

GAMMON, Roland, ed. 248.42
Faith is a star, written and edited by Roland Gammon. [1st ed.] New York, Dutton, 1963. vii, 243 p. 22 cm. Testimonies derived from personal interviews and from interviews conducted on the radio program Master control. [BV4515.G3] 62-14730
1. Christian life — Stories. I. Title.

GAMMON, Roland Irvine, ed. 248.42
Faith is a star, written, ed. by Roland Gammon. New York, Dutton [c.]1963. viii, 243p. 22cm. 63-14730 3.95
1. Christian life—Stories. I. Title.

GARA, Matthew. 248.42
On the road to happiness; 94 pointers along the way for teens. Illustrated by Edward McDonnell. Valatie, N.Y., Holy Cross Press, 1965. 119 p. illus. 23 cm. [BX2355.G3] 65-21806
1. Youth — Religious life. 2. Meditations. I. Title.

GARA, Matthew 248.42
On the road to happiness; 94 pointers along the way for teens. Illus. by Edward McDonnell. Valatie, N. Y., Holy Cross Pr. [c.] 1965. 119p. illus. 23cm. [BX2355.G3] 65-21806 3.00
1. Youth—Religious life. 2. Meditations. I. Title.

GEANEY, Dennis J 248.42
You shall be witnesses. Notre Dame, Ind., Fides Publishers [1963] 151 p. 21 cm. [BX2350.2.G44] 63-12045
1. Christian life — Catholic authors. I. Title.

GEANEY, Dennis J. 248.42
You shall be witnesses. Notre Dame, Ind., Fides [c.1963] 151p. 21cm. 63-12045 3.50
1. Christian life—Catholic authors. I. Title.

GILL, Donald H. 248.4'2
Live, Christian, live! By Donald H. Gill. Glendale, Calif., G/L Regal Books [1970] 163 p. 18 cm. [BV4501.2.G49] 71-117524 0.95
1. Christian life—1960- I. Title.

GILLQUIST, Peter E. 248.4'2
Love is now [by] Peter E. Gillquist. Foreword by Sherwood E. Wirt. Grand Rapids, Zondervan Pub. House [1970] 176 p. 21 cm. Includes bibliographical references. [BV4501.2.G5115] 76-95050 3.95
1. Christian life—1960- I. Title.

*GOLZ, Lud 248.42
Hindrances and helps to Christian living. Chicago, Moody [c.1964] 64p. 18cm. (Compact bks., 46) .29
I. Title.

GOODRICH, Robert E., Jr. 248.42
On the other side of sorrow. Nashville, Abingdon [c.1955-1962] 31p. 18cm. 1.00 bds.,
I. Title.

*GRAYSON, H. D. 248.42
The truth about life. New York, Vantage [c.1964] 214p. 21cm. 3.95 bds.,
I. Title.

GREENE, Reynolds W., Jr. 248.42
Between an atom and a star. Grand Rapids, Mich., Eerdmans [c.1963] 89p. 20cm. 2.50 bds.,
I. Title.

GUILD, Daniel R 248.42
We can have peace; victorious living in tumultuous times. Mountain View, Calif., Pacific Press Pub. Association [1960] 170p. 23cm. [BV4908.5.G84] 60-16413
1. Peace (Theology) I. Title.

HALVERSON, Richard C 248.42
Walk with God ... between Sundays, by Richard C. Halverson. Grand Rapids, Zondervan Pub. House [1965] 160 p. 21 cm. [BV4501.2.H267] 65-19508
1. Christian life—Presbyterian authors. I. Title. II. Title: Between Sundays.

HALVERSON, Richard C. 248.42
Walk with God between Sundays. Grand Rapids, Mich., Zondervan [c.1965] 160p. 21cm. Cover title: Between Sundays. [BV4501.2.H267] 65-19508 2.95 bds.,
1. Christian life—Presbyterian authors. I. Title. II. Title: Between Sundays.

HARRISON, Marie Lemoine 248.42
You are a spirit being. New York, Carlton [c.1963] 111p. 21cm. 2.50
I. Title.

HATFIELD, Mark O., 1922- 248.4'2
Conflict and conscience [by] Mark O. Hatfield. Waco, Tex., Word Books [1971] 172 p. 23 cm. Includes bibliographical references. [E840.8.H3A28] 73-165544 4.95
I. Title.

HEIGES, Donald R. 248.42
Study guide [for] The Christian's calling. Philadelphia, Muhlenberg [c.1962] 50p. 18cm. .75 pap.,
I. Title.

HEYNEN, Ralph. 248.42
The secret of Christian family living. Grand Rapids, Baker Book House, 1965. 162 p. 23 cm. [HQ10.H49] 65-16377
1. Family life education. 2. Family — Religious life. I. Title.

HEYNEN, Ralph 248.42
The secret of Christian family living. Grand Rapids, Mich., Baker Bk. [c.]1965. 162p. 23cm. [HQ10.H49] 65-16377 2.95
1. Family life education. 2. Family—Religious life. I. Title.

HIGGINBOTTOM, David B. 248.42
The great commandment and the royal law, the keys to inner contentment and universal peace. New York, Vantage [c.1963] 110p. 21cm. 2.75
I. Title.

HIGHCLIFFE, William. 248.4'2
Guide lines for young men and women. St. Albans (Herts.), Hazelwood-Lattimore Ltd., 1970. vii, 70 p. 19 cm. Bibliography: p. 69-70. [BJ1581.2] 73-451629
1. Conduct of life. I. Title.

*HILLIS, Don W. 248.42
Get with it, man; for teens with get-up-and-go. Chicago, Moody [1967] 64p. 18cm. (Teen bk.: Compact bks., no. 58) .29 pap.,
I. Title.

HOOD, E. A. 248.42
God's people are different; a study of the meaning of Christian living. New York, Exposition [c.1963] 155p. 21cm. 3.00
I. Title.

HOPE, Mary 248.42
If you ask me . . . practical answers to life's problems. Grand Rapids, Mich., Zondervan [c.1963] 152p. 21cm. 2.50 bds.,
I. Title.

*HOSTETTER, Charles, B. 248.42
Life at its best. Chicago, Moody [c.1966] 128p. 17cm. (Colportage lib., 523) .39 pap.,
I. Title.

HOUGHTON, Frank, Rt. Rev. 248.42
Faith's unclaimed inheritance. [2nd ed.] Chicago, Inter-Varsity Pr. [1961] 107p. (Christian bks. for the modern world) Originally pub. under the title: If we believe. 1.25 pap.,
I. Title.

HOUSE, E C 248.42
Why and the answer. Why Free Circulating Library ed. Parkville, Mo., Why Free Circulating Library, c1962- v. 23cm. [BV4501.2.H6] 61-18611
1. Christian life. I. Title.

HUBER, Mathias John, 1901- 248.4'2
Do you worry about the future? Edited by M. J. Huber. Liguori, Mo., Liguorian Pamphlets and Books [1970] 94 p. 18 cm. [BX2182.2.H8] 77-146937 1.00
1. Meditations. I. Title.

HUDSON, Robert Lofton. 248.4'2
Helping each other be human [by] R. Lofton Hudson. Waco, Tex., Word Books [1970] 189 p. 23 cm. Includes bibliographical references. [BV4501.2.H763 1970] 79-85831 4.95
1. Christian life—Baptist authors. I. Title.

HUDSON, Robert Lofton. 248.4'2
Persons in crisis [by] R. Lofton Hudson. Nashville, Broadman Press [1969] 127 p. 20 cm. Includes bibliographical references. [BJ1581.2.H73] 69-14367
1. Conduct of life. I. Title.

HUFFMAN, John. 248.4'2
Pot and those other things. Foreword by Norman Vincent Peale. [1st ed.] Carol Stream, Ill., Creation House [1970] 143 p. 23 cm. [BV4501.2.H78] 73-131446
1. Christian life—Presbyterian authors. I. Title.

HULME, William Edward, 1920- 248.42
Living with myself. Englewood Cliffs, N.J., Prentice-Hall [1964] xiv, 158 p. 21 cm. Bibliographical footnotes. [BJ1581.2.H75] 64-10164
1. Conduct of life. 2. Christian life—Lutheran authors. I. Title.

HULME, William Edward, 1920- 248.42
Living with myself. Englewood Cliffs, N.J., Prentice [c.1964] xiv, 158p. 21cm. Bibl. 64-10164 2.95
1. Conduct of life. 2. Christian life—Lutheran authors. I. Title.

HUNTER, John Edward, 1909- 248.42
Let us go on to maturity, by John E. Hunter. [1st ed.] Grand Rapids, Zondervan [1967] 136p. 21cm. [BV4501.2.H847] 67-17226 2.95
1. Spiritual life. I. Title.

ISAACS, Evelyn 248.42
Inchristed men; spiritual nuggets and poems. New York, Exposition [c.1965] 80p. 21cm. 3.00
I. Title.

IVERSEN, John Orville. 248.4'2
In search of a plot [by] J. O. Iversen. Washington, Review and Herald Pub. Association [1970] 128 p. 22 cm. [BV4501.2.I78] 70-106499
1. Christian life—Seventh-Day Adventist authors. I. Title.

JAUNCEY, James H. 248.42
Above ourselves; the art of true happiness. Grand Rapids, Mich., Zondervan [c.1964] 150p. 21cm. 64-25223 2.95 bds.,
1. Happiness. I. Title.

JAUNCEY, James H. 248.4'2
Guidance by God [by] James H. Jauncey. Grand Rapids, Mich., Zondervan Pub. House [1969] 160 p. 22 cm. [BV4501.2.J34] 69-11644
1. Christian life. 2. God—Will. I. Title.

JOHNSON, Alexander Bryan, 1786-1867. 248.4'2
Religion in its relation to the present life, in a series of lectures, delivered before the Young Men's Association of Utica, and published at their request. New York, Greenwood Press [1968] 180 p. 23 cm. First published in 1840. [BJ1571.J6 1968] 68-19283
1. Conduct of life—Addresses, essays, lectures. I. Young Men's Association of the City of Utica. II. Title.

JOHNSON, Frances Simington 248.42
The horizon of light. New York, Vantage [1962, c.1961] 109p. 2.95 bds.,
I. Title.

JOHNSON, Harold L. 248.42
The Christian as a businessman. New York, Association Press [1964] 192 p. illus. 29 cm. (The Haddam House series on the Christian in his vocation) A Haddam House book. "Publisher's stock number: 1539." Includes bibliographical references. [BV4596.B8J6] 64-11419
1. Businessmen — Religious life. I. Title.

*JOHNSON, Marvin E. 248.42
Desire under the sun: U.S.A. New York, Carlton [c.1964] 117p. 21cm. 2.75
I. Title.

*JOHNSON, Mel. 248.4'2
Straight from the shoulder; answers to questions teens ask. Chicago, Moody [1967] 63p. 19cm. .95 pap.,
I. Title.

JOHNSTON, Minton C. 248.42
24 hours to live. Nashville, Abingdon [c.1963] 112p. 20cm. 63-14594 2.25 bds.,
1. Sermons, English—Canada. 2. Baptist Church—Sermons. I. Title.

JOHNSTON, Minton C. 248.42
24 hours to live New York, Abingdon Press [1963] 112 p. 20 cm. Messages broadcast on the Canadian Broadcasting Corporation network. [BX6333.J66T9] 63-14594
1. Sermons, English — Canada. 2. Baptist Church — Sermons. I. Title.

JURGENSEN, Barbara. 248.4'2
The Lord is my shepherd, but ... Confessions of the natural man. Illus. by Robin Jensen. Grand Rapids, Zondervan [1969] 92 p. illus. 21 cm. [BV4510.2.J8] 69-11656
1. Christian life. I. Title.

KEITH, Noel Leonard 248.42
The human rift; bridges to peace and understanding. St. Louis, Bethany [1963] 128p. 21cm. 63-17874 2.50
1. Christian life. I. Title.

KENNEDY, Eugene C. 248'.42
The pain of being human, by Eugene Kennedy. Photos. by Todd Brennan. Chicago, Thomas More Press [1972] 254 p. illus. 24 cm. [BF637.C5K46] 73-159651 8.95
1. Conduct of life. I. Title.

KENNEDY, Eugene C. 248'.42
The pain of being human. Garden City, N.Y., Doubleday, 1974 [c1972] 277 p. 18 cm. (Image books, D329) [BF637.C5K46] ISBN 0-385-06888-3 1.75 (pbk.)
1. Conduct of life. I. Title.
L.C. card no. for the hardbound edition: 73-159651.

KENNEDY, Gerald Hamilton, Bp., 1907- 248.42
Priests, prophets, pioneers. Nashville, The Upper room [1960] 64p. 19cm. 'Previously published in [the author's] The Christian and his America.' [BV4501.K42436] 60-15970
1. Christian life. I. Title.

KERSHNER, Howard Eldred, 1891- 248.42
Diamonds, persimmons, and stars. New York, Bkmailer. [1964] 163p. 22cm. 64-18966 3.00
1. Sermons, American. I. Title.

KETCHAM, Robert Thomas, 1889- 248.42
God's provision for normal Christian living. Chicago, Moody Press [1960] 154p. 22cm. [BV4501.2.K45] 60-5153
1. Christian life. I. Title.

KETCHAM, Robert Thomas, D. D. 1889- 248.42
God's provision for normal Christian living. Chicago, Moody [1965, c.1960] 189p. 19cm. (Moody pocket bk., .87) .59 pap.,
1. Christian life. I. Title.

*KINSELLA, A. W. 248.'4"2
Your place in God's plan. Pulaski, Wis., Franciscan Pubs. [1967] 63p. 19cm. (Vocational bklets.) .25 pap.,
I. Title.

*KIRSCH, Paul J. 248.42
For good or evil. Ed. by Philip R. Hoh. Illus. by Elsa Bailey. Philadelphia, Lutheran Church Pr. [c.1965] 112p. illus. 21cm. (LCA Sunday church sch. ser.) pap., .90; teacher's guide, pap., 1.00
I. Title.

KOHN, Harold E 248.42
Reflections on the nature of the world and man, life's values and its destiny. Illustrated by the author. Grand Rapids Eerdmans [1963] 190 p. illus. 24 cm. [BD581.K55] 62-18953
1. Philosophy of nature. 2. Religion and science—1946- I. Title.

KOHN, Harold E. 248.42
Reflections on the nature of the world and man, life's values and its destiny. Illus. by the author. Grand Rapids, Mich., Eerdmans [c.1963] 190p. illus. 24cm. 62-18953 3.95 bds.,
1. Philosophy of nature. 2. Religion and science—1946- I. Title.

KOHN, Harold E 248.42
A touch of greatness, by Harold E. Kohn. Illustrated by the author. Grand Rapids, Eerdmans [1965] 205 p. illus., facsisms., ports. 23 cm. [BV4832.K64] 66-2223
1. Devotional literature. I. Title.

KOHN, Harold E. 248.42
A touch of greatness. Illus. by the author. Grand Rapids, Mich., Eerdmans [1966, c.1965] 205p. illus., facsims., ports. 23cm. [BV4832.K64] 66-2223 3.95 bds.,
1. Devotional literature. I. Title.

KOLBE, Henry E 248.42
One world under God. New York, Abingdon Press [1963] 128 p. 20 cm. [BV4647.B7K6] 63-2046
1. Brotherliness. I. Title.

KOLBE, Henry E 248.42
One world under God. Nashville, Graded Press [1963] 128 p. 20 cm. (Basic Christian books) [BV4647.B7K6] 63-5865
1. Brotherliness. I. Title.

KOLBE, Henry E. 248.42
One world under God. Nashville, Abingdon [c.1963] 128p. 20cm. 63-2046 1.00
1. Brotherliness. I. Title.

KOSTEN, Andrew 248.42
Christian courage for everyday living. Grand Rapids, Mich., Eerdmans [c.1961] 128p. 60-15302 3.00 bds.,
1. Courage I. Title.

KUHNE, Gary W. 248'.42
The dynamics of discipleship training : being and producing spiritual leaders / Gary W. Kuhne. Grand Rapids, Mich. : Zondervan Pub. House, c1977. p. cm. Companion volume to the author's The dynamics of personal follow-up. [BV4501.2.K77] 77-12651 ISBN 0-310-26961-X pbk. : 3.95
1. Christian life—1960- I. Title.

LAHAYE, Tim F. 248.4'2
Transformed temperaments [by] Tim LaHaye. Wheaton, Ill., Tyndale House Publishers [1971] 150 p. 22 cm. [BV4501.2.L3153] 77-152120 ISBN 0-8423-7305-5 2.95
1. Christian life—Baptist authors. I. Title.

LANG, David. 248'.42
Meeting God; cues for enriching your relationship with the God of the universe. Cincinnati, Standard Pub. [1972] 94 p. 18 cm. (Fountain books) [BV4501.2.L3184] 71-164742
1. Christian life—1960- I. Title.

LATHAM, Lenn Lerner 248.42
Let God in; the secret of joyous, effective living. Englewood Cliffs, N.J., Prentice-Hall [c.1961] 176p. 61-7765 3.50 bds.,
1. Christian life. I. Title.

LAUBACH, Frank Charles, 1884- 248.4'2
Living words, from the writings of Frank C. Laubach, Comp. by F. Elmo Robinson. Grand Rapids, Zondervan [1967] xii, 103p. 21cm. [BV4501.2.L355] 67-17233 2.95 bds.,
1. Christian life. I. Robinson, Fred Elmo, 1876- ed. II. Title.

LAUBACH, Frank Charles, 1884- 248.4'2
Living words, from the writings of Frank C. Laubach. Compiled by F. Elmo Robinson. Grand Rapids, Zondervan Pub. House [1967] xii, 103 p. 21 cm. [BV4501.2.L355] 67-17233
1. Christian life. I. Robinson, Fred Elmo, 1876- ed. II. Title.

LAW, William, 1686-1761. 248.42
A serious call to a devout and holy life; adapted to the state and condition of all orders of Christians. Introd. by G. W. Bromiley. Grand Rapids, Eerdmans [1966] xx, 313 p. 22 cm. "Reprinted from the edition published in 1898." Bibliographical footnotes. [BV4500.L3 1966] 66-4301
1. Christian life. I. Title.

LAW, William, 1686-1761 248.42
A serious call to a devout and holy life; adapted to the stateand condition of all orders of Christians. Introd. by G. W. Bromiley. Grand Rapids, Mich., Eerdmans [c.1966] xx, 313p. 22cm. Reprinted from the ed. pub. in 1898 by Macmillan. Bibl. [BV4500.L3] 66-4301 1.95 pap.,
1. Christian life. I. Title.

LEIBRECHT, Walter 248.42
Being a Christian in today's world. Philadelphia, Muhlenberg [c.1962] 48p. 20cm. (Fortress bk.) 62-20751 1.00 bds.,
1. Christian life. I. Title.

LIEGE, P. A. 1921- 248.42
What is Christian life? Reviewing lay spirituality. Tr. from French by A. Manson. Glen Rock, N.J., Paulist [c.1964] 143p. 18cm. (Vol. of the 20th century encv. of Catholicism; Century/Deus bks.) Bibl. .95 pap.,
1. Christian life—Catholic authors. 2. Holiness. I. Title.

LIEGE, Pierre Andre, 1921- 248.42
What is Christian life? Translated from the French by A. Manson. [1st American ed.] New York, Hawthorn Books [1961] 143 p. 21 cm. (The Twentieth century encyclopedia of Catholicism, v. 56. Section 5: The life of faith) Translation of Vivre en chretien. Includes bibliography. [BX2350.2.L473] 61-17757
1. Christian life — Catholic authors. 2. Holiness. I. Title.

LIEGE, Pierre Andre, 1921- 248.42
What is Christian life? Translated from the French by A. Manson. [1st American ed.] New York, Hawthorn Books [1961] 143 p. 21 cm. (The Twentieth century encyclopedia of Catholicism, v. 56. Section 5: The life of faith) Translation of Vivre en chretien. Includes bibliography. [BX2350.2.L473] 61-17757
1. Christian life—Catholic authors. 2. Holiness. I. Title.

LINDGREN, Donald Norman 248.42
Designs for Christian living. Minneapolis, Minn., 428 Wash. Ave., N., Bolger Pubns. [c.1962] 136p. 136p. 22cm. 62-14934 2.25 pap.,
1. Christian life. 2. Meditations. I. Title.

LOISGLOVER. 248.42
The first study book of Loisglover. Boston, Christopher Pub. House [c.1960] 73p. illus. 21cm. 60-15972 2.00
I. Title.

LOISGLOVER, 1895- 248.42
The first study book of Loisglover. Boston, Christopher Pub. House [1960] 73p. illus. 21cm. [BX9998.L6] 60-15972
I. Title.

LOWE, Arnold Hilmar, 1888- 248.42
Guidelines to courageous living. Minneapolis, Denison [c.1963] 178p. 22cm. 63-14388 3.00
1. Courage. 2. Christian life—Presbyterian authors. I. Title.

MABRY, Mildred. 248.42
That God is love. St. Louis, Bethany Press [c.1960] 93p. 20cm. 60-15571 1.25 pap.,
1. Christian life—Stories. I. Title.

MCCALL, Donald D. 248.4'2
Twice upon a time, by Donald D. McCall. Chicago, Moody Press [1971] 140 p. illus. 22 cm. [BV4501.2.M18] 75-143475 3.95
1. Aesopus. Fabulae. 2. Christian life—Presbyterian authors. I. Title.

MCCARTHY-SCHULZ 248.42
Handbook of the revolution; phase 1: back to discipline. New York, Pageant [c.1962] 109p. 21cm. 2.50
I. Title.

MCCLAIN, Roy O. 248.42
If with all your heart. Westwood, N. J., Revell co. [c.1961] 190p. 61-17106 3. 00bds.,
1. Christian life. I. Title.

MCCOY, Maurice E. 248.42
Rainwater, sunshine, and babies. New York, Carlton [c.]1962. 262p. (Reflection bk.) 62-945 4.00
1. Christian life. I. Title.

MCCRACKEN, Robert James 248.42
Putting faith to work. New York, Harper [c.1960] 179p. 22cm. Bibl.: p.175-179. 60-15271 3.00 half cloth,
1. Christian life. 2. Christianity—20th cent. I. Title.

MAINPRIZE, Don 248.42
Christian heroes of today. Grand Rapids, Mich., Baker Bk. [1967, c.1964] 81p. illus. 20cm. (Valor ser.) 1.00 pap.,
1. Christian life—Stories. I. Title.

*MAINPRIZE, Don 248.42
How to enjoy the Christian life. Grand Rapids, Mich., Zondervan [c.1966] 116p. 21cm. .79 pap.,
I. Title.

*MARSHALL, Catherine (Wood), 1914- 248.42
Beyond our selves. New York, Avon [1968, c.1961] 269p. 18cm. (N195) .95 pap.,
1. Christian life. 2. Christianity—20th cent. I. Title.

MARSHALL, Catherine (Wood) 1914- 248.42
Beyond our selves. [Reissue] New York, McGraw [1966] 266p. 22cm. [BV4501.2.M364] 61-17599 2.95
1. Christian life. 2. Faith. I. Title.

MARSHALL, Catherine (Wood) 1914- 248.42
Beyond our selves. [1st ed.] New York, McGraw-Hill [1961] 266 p. 22 cm. [BV4501.2.M364] 61-17599
1. Christian life. 2. Faith. I. Title.

MATHER, Cotton, 1663-1728 248.4'2
Bonifacius: an essay upon the good. Ed. introd. by David Levin. Cambridge, Belknap Pr. of Harvard. 1966. xxxii. 181p. facsim. 22cm. (John Harvard Lib.) Follows the orig. text of 1710, which included the Appendix on Indian Christianity and the Advertisement for Biblia Americana. Bibl. [BV4500.M35 1966] 66-14448 3.95
1. Christian life. I. Levin, David, 1924- ed. II. Title. III. Series.

MATHER, Cotton, 1663- 1728. 248.4'2
Bonifacius: an essay ... to do good. (1710) A facsimile reproduction with an introd. by Josephine K. Piercy. Gainesville, Fla., Scholars' Facsimiles & Reprints, 1967. xii, 206 p. 23 cm. "Reproduced from a copy in ... Harvard University Library." [BV4500.M35 1710a] 67-18712
1. Christian life. I. Title.

MATHER, Cotton, 1663- 1728. 248.4'2
Bonifacius: an essay ... to do good. (1710) A facsimile reproduction with an introd. by Josephine K. Piercy. Gainesville, Fla., Scholars' Facsimiles & Reprints, 1967. xii, 206 p. 23 cm. "Reproduced from a copy in ... Harvard University Library." [BV4500.M35] 67-18712
1. Christian life. I. Title.

MATHEWS, George M 248.42
Bountiful living. Washington, Review and Herald Pub. Association [1960] 192p. 22cm. Includes bibliography. [BV4501.2.M37] 60-9414
1. Christian life. I. Title.

MATHEWS, William Barnes. 248.42
The quest for life. Boston, Christopher Pub. House [1962] 290p. 21cm. [BV4501.2.M38] 62-9715
1. Christian life. I. Title.

MAXWELL, Arthur Stanley, 1896- 248.42
Courage for the crisis: strength for today, hope for tomorrow; how to find peace of mind and fortitude of spirit for the dangerous days ahead. Mountain View, Calif., Pacific Press Pub. Association [1962] 258p. illus. 18cm. [BV4908.5.M35] 62-7223
1. Peace of mind. I. Title.

MAYS, Benjamin Elijah, 1895- 248.4'2
Disturbed about man [by] Benjamin E. Mays. Richmond, John Knox Press [1969] 143 p. 21 cm. [BV4501.2.M43] 69-12370 3.95
1. Christian life—Addresses, essays, lectures. I. Title.

MEAD, Warren B 248.42
Life in the balance. New York, Carlton [c.1966] 130 p, 21 cm (reflection bk.) 3.00
I. Title.

MEREDITH, Ronald R 248.42
Hurryin' big for little reasons [by] Ronald R. Meredith. Illustrated by Kenneth K. Thompson. New York, Abingdon Press [1964] 111 p. illus. 20 cm. [CT275.M473A3] 64-21134
I. Title.

MEREDITH, Ronald R. 248.42
Hurryin' big for little reasons. Illus. by Kenneth K. Thompson. Nashville, Abingdon [c.1964] 111p. illus. 20cm. 64-21134 2.50
I. Title.

MILLER, T. Franklin 248.42
The growing Christian, a guide book on personal religious living. Anderson,Ind., Warner Press [dist. Gospel Trumpet Press] [c.1960] 94p. 21cm. 60-8649 1.25 pap.,
1. Christian life. I. Title.

MONSON, Leland H 248.42
Character and leadership, by Leland H. Monson and Clinton W. Barton. Salt Lake City, Deseret Book Co., 1964. xi, 202 p. 24 cm. Includes bibliographical references. [BJ1521.M75] 64-66454

1. Character. 2. Virtue. I. Barton, Clinton W., joint author. II. Title.

MONTGOMERY, G H 248.42
Why people like you; a Christian approach to human relations. New York, Taplinger Pub. Co. [1963] 277 p. 22 cm. [BV4501.2.M56] 63-14053
1. Christian life. I. Title.

MONTGOMERY, G. H. 248.42
Why people like you; a Christian approach to human relations. New York, Taplinger [c.1963] 277p. 22cm. 63-14053 4.50
1. Christian life. I. Title.

MOW, Anna B 248.42
Say; Yes; to life- Grand Rapids, Zondervan Pub. House [1961] 152p. 21cm. [BV4501.2.M6] 61-4300
1. Christian life. I. Title.

NAUDACK, Alice 248.42
My walk with God. New York, Carlton [c.1963] 85p. 21cm. (Reflection bk.) 2.00
I. Title.

NEAL, Emily Gardiner. 248.42
In the midst of life. New York, Morehouse-Barlow, 1963. [BX5974.N4A3] 63-12481
1. 205 p. 21 cm. I. Title.

NEAL, Emily Gardiner 248.42
In the midst of life. New York, Morehouse [c.] 1963. 205p. 21cm. 63-12481 4.50
I. Title.

*NEIDERER, Rodney P. 248.42
For when tomorrow comes; on man's quest for his immortal soul. New York, Exposition [c.1964] 63p. 21cm. (EP 42087) 2.50
I. Title.

NEILL, Stephen Charles, 248.42
Bp.
Christian holiness. New York, Harper [c.1960] 134p. Bibl. footnotes. 60-15273 3.00
1. Holiness. I. Title.

*NELSON, Boyd 248.42
What makes Christian service? New York, Friendship [1967, c.1965] 63p. 16cm. (Questions for Christians, no. 10) Bibl. .65 pap.,
I. Title.

NEWBERRY, Gene W. 248.4'2
Responding to God's call ... to live in Christ, by Gene W. Newberry. Illus. by Charles Schulz. Anderson, Ind., Warner Press [1969] iii, 128 p. illus. 19 cm. [BV4501.2.N48] 74-98337
1. Christian life. I. Title.

O'BRIEN, John Anthony, 248.42
1893-
Eternal answers for an anxious age Englewood Cliffs, N. J., Prentice-Hall [1962] 263p. 22cm. [BV4501.2.O27] 62-18835
1. Christian life. I. Title.

O'BRIEN, John Anthony, 248.42
1893-
Eternal answers for an anxious age. Englewood Cliffs, N. J., Prentice [c.1962] 263p. 22cm. 62-18835 4.95
1. Christian life. I. Title.

O'DWYER, James F. 248.4'2
Dreams of destiny, by James F. O'Dwyer. Stockton, Calif., Willow House [1970] xi, 102 p. illus. 26 cm. [BX2350.2.O32] 70-103978 5.95
1. Christian life—Catholic authors. I. Title.

OLIVER, Lucille. 248.4'2
Celebrate your existence. Prelim. design by Clarice Ward. [Independence, Mo., Herald Pub. House, 1971] 107 p. col. illus. 18 cm. Bibliography: p. 107. [BJ1581.2.O45] 79-147022 ISBN 0-8309-0042-X 3.25
1. Conduct of life. I. Title.

*PADDOCK, C.L. 248.42
Little builders. Nashville, Southern Pub. [1967] 96p. illus. 21cm. 1.00 pap.,
1. Christian life—Stories—Juvenile literature. I. Title.

PAISLEY, Sela I. 248.42
Your path to fulfillment. New York, Vantage [c.1961] 228p. 3.75
I. Title.

PARMON, Kon 248.42
This we shall do, how God's fundamental truths assure survival in today's world. New York, Exposition [c.1962] 69p. 21cm. 2.75
I. Title.

PEACE, Richard. 248.4'2
Learning to love ourselves. [1st ed.] Grand Rapids, Zondervan Pub. House [1968] 61 p. 21 cm. (His Learning to love, book 2) Includes bibliographies. [BV4511.P4] 68-12955
1. Christian life—Study and teaching. I. Title.

PEACE, Richard. 248.4'2
Learning to love people. [1st ed.] Grand Rapids, Zondervan Pub. House [1968] 73 p. 21 cm. (His Learning to love, book 3) Includes bibliographies. [BV4511.P42] 68-4255
1. Christian life—Study and teaching. I. Title.

*PEDEN, Pearle 248.42
Whispering halls. Illus. by Stanley J. Fleming. Nashville, Southern Pub. [1966, c.1959] 203p. illus. 21cm. .95 pap.,
1. Christian life—Stories—Juvenile literature. I. Title.

PENTECOST, J. Dwight 248.4'2
Pattern for maturity; conduct and conflict in the Christian life [by] J. Dwight Pentecost. Chicago, Moody [1966] 288p. 22cm. [BV4501.2.P39] 66-16226 3.95
1. Christian life. I. Title.

PETERSON, Lancie Elmer, 248.42
1899-
The Beatitudes; a Latter-Day Saint interpretation [by] L. Elmer Peterson. Salt Lake City, Deseret Book Co, 1964. xiv, 152 p. 20 cm. [BT382.P46] 64-66457
1. Beatitudes. I. Title.

PETTY, Carl Wallace, 1884- 248.42
1932
The evening altar. Nashville, Abingdon [1961, c.1940] 187 p. (Apex bks., F7) .69, pap.
1. Christian life. I. Title.

PHILLIPS, McCandlish, 248'.42
1927-
The Bible, the supernatural, and the Jews. New York, World Pub. Co. [1970] xiii, 366 p. 22 cm. [BF1434.U6P48] 77-92532 7.95
1. Supernatural. 2. Occult sciences—United States. 3. Judaism. 4. United States—Moral conditions. I. Title.

PHILLIPS, McCandlish, 248.4'2
1927-
The spirit world. Wheaton, Ill., Victor Books [1972] 192 p. 18 cm. (An Input book) "An abridgement of The Bible, the supernatural, and the Jews." [BF1434.U6P482] 72-77015 ISBN 0-88207-048-7 1.45
1. Supernatural. 2. Occult sciences—United States. 3. Judaism. 4. United States—Moral conditions. I. Title.

POWELL, Gordon George, 248.42
1911-
Release from guilt and fear. New York, Hawthorn Books [c.1961] 160p. 'Originally published in Great Britain as Freedom from fear.' 61-6707 2.95 bds.,
1. Guilt. 2. Salvation—Popular works. 3. Pastoral counseling. I. Title.

PRATER, Arnold 248.42
Parables from life. Grand Rapids, Mich., Zondervan [c.1963] 84p. 21cm. 1.95 bds.,
I. Title.

PRATT, Lillian Louise 248.42
There is a way. New York, Carlton [c.1963] 117p. 21cm. (Reflection bk.) 2.75
I. Title.

RAY, David A. 248.4'2
Where are you, God? [By] David A. Ray. Old Tappan, N.J., F. H. Revell Co. [1970] 160 p. 21 cm. [BV4501.2.R36] 71-112457 3.95
1. Christian life. I. Title.

REDHEAD, John A 248.42
Living all your life. New York, Abingdon Press [1961] 142p. 20cm. [BV4501.2.R4] 61-10815
1. Christian life. I. Title.

REDMONT, Louis 248.42
All about nothing the truth shall make you free. Stick with it. Illus. by Richard B. Igou. New York, Vantage [c.1963] 60p. 21cm. 2.50
I. Title.

REED, Marshall Russell, B 248.42
p., 1891-
Achieving Christian perfection. Nashville, Methodist Evangelistic Materials [c1962] 63 p. 29 cm. [BT766.R4] 62-20645
1. Perfection. I. Title.

RICE, Hillery C. 248.42
God's happy people. Anderson, Ind., Warner [c.1965] 80p. 21cm. [BT382.R5] 65-19203 1.25 pap.,
1. Beatitudes. I. Title.

RICE, Hillery C 248.42
Gold's happy people, by Hillery C. Rice. Anderson, Ind., Warner Press [1965] 80 p. 21 cm. [BT382.R5] 65-19203
1. Beatitudes. I. Title.

*RICHMOND, Albert E. 248.4'2
To think right is to be right how to front. 21cm. 3.50 bds.,
I. Title.

RINKER, Rosalind 248.42
You can witness with confidence. Grand Rapids, Mich., Zondervan [c.1962] 105p. 21cm. 1.95 bds.,
I. Title.

RYRIE, Charles Caldwell, 248.4'2
1925-
Balancing the Christian life. Chicago, Moody Press [1969] 191 p. 22 cm. [BV4501.2.R9] 77-12177 3.95
1. Christian life. I. Title.

SALA, Harold J. 248.4'2
Guidelines for living [by] Harold J. Sala. Grand Rapids, Baker Book House [1967] 115 p. 23 cm. [BV4501.2.S16] 67-18194
1. Christian life. I. Title.

SAMUEL, William. 248.4'2
The awareness of self discovery; how to live the real identity. [1st ed.] Mountain Brook, Ala., Mountain Brook Publications Co. [1970] 199 p. 22 cm. [BJ1581.2.S2] 79-138356 6.95
1. Conduct of life. I. Title.

SCANZONI, Letha 248.42
Why am I here? Where am I going? Youth looks at life. Westwood, N.J., F. H. Revell Co. [1966] 127p. 21cm. [BJ1661.S3] 66-17051 2.95 bds.,
1. Youth—Conduct of life. I. Title.

SCHATZMAN, Albert G 248.4'2
The age of the spirit, by Albert G. Schatzman. [Nashville, Parthenon Press, 1966] 153 p. 23 cm. [BV4501.2.S29] 67-1652
1. Christian life. I. Title.

SCHULLER, Robert 248.42
God's way to the good life. Grand Rapids, Mich., Eerdmans [c.1963] 105p. 22cm. 63-17790 2.50
1. Christian life—Reformed authors. I. Title.

SCOUGAL, Henry, 1650-1678 248.42
The life of God in the soul of man. Chicago, Intervarsity Pr. [1961] 80p. .60 pap.,
1. Christian life. I. Title.

SEGLER, Franklin M. 248.4'2
Your emotions and your faith [by] Franklin M. Segler. Nashville, Tenn., Broadman Press [1970] 125 p. 20 cm. (A Broadman inner circle book) Includes bibliographical references. [BV4637.S37] 70-95410
1. Faith. 2. Emotions. I. Title.

SHEETZ, Paul H. 248.4'2
Your fig leaf is slipping [by] Paul H. Sheetz. [1st ed.] Carol Stream, Ill., Creation House [1971] 200 p. 23 cm. Bibliography: p. 199-200. [BV4501.2.S436] 70-151979 4.95
1. Christian life—1960- I. Title.

SILVER, Benno 248.42
Toward peace. New York, Vantage [c. 1962] 94p. 21cm. 2.50
I. Title.

SMALL, Dwight Hervey 248.42
The high cost of holy living [Westwood, N. J.] Revell [1964] 189p. 21cm. 64-12203 3.50
1. Christian life. I. Title.

SMITH, Alson Jesse. 248.42
Primer for the perplexed; a working faith for an age of anxiety. New York, John Day Co. [1962] 188 p. 22 cm. [BV4501.2.S5] 62-15135
1. Christian life. I. Title.

SMITH, Alson Jesse 248.42
Primer for the perplexed; a working faith for an age of anxiety. New York, John Day [c.1962] 188p. 22cm. 62-15135 4.00
1. Christian life. I. Title.

SMOCK, Martha. 248.4'2
Halfway up the mountain. Unity Village, Mo., Unity Books [1971] 238 p. 20 cm. [BX9890.U5S58] 70-155718 ISBN 0-87159-125-1
1. Unity School of Christianity. 2. Conduct of life. I. Title.

SNOOK, John B. 248.42
Doing right and wrong [by] John B. Snook. New York, Association Press [1966] 128 p. 16 cm. (A Keen-age reflection book) [BJ1581.2.S6] 66-21546
1. Conduct of life. I. Title.

SONGHURST, George, Father 248.42
The arithmetic of life. [dist. New York, Taplinger Pub. Co., 1960] 15p. 19cm. (More books) .30 pap.,
I. Title.

SPIKE, Robert Warren. 248.42
To be a man. New York, Association Press, [1961] 123 p. 20 cm. [BV4501.2.S7] 61-14182
1. Christian life. I. Title.

SPIKE, Robert Warren 248.42
To be a man. New York, Association [c.1961] 123p. 61-14182 2.75 bds.,
1. Christian life. I. Title.

*SVANCARA-HLOSKOVA, 248.42
Katarina
The philosophy of positive life. New York, Carlton [c.1963] 291p. 21cm. (Reflection bk.) 3.95
I. Title.

SWEETING, George, 1924- 248.4'2
Living stones; guidelines for new Christians. Grand Rapids, Baker Book House [1970] 93 p. col. illus. 21 cm. [BV4501.2.S88] 70-109214
1. Christian life—1960- I. Title.

SWOR, Chester E. 248.42
If we dared! Nashville, Broadman Press [c.1961] 142p. illus. 61-12417 2.50 bds.,
1. Christian life. I. Title.

**TABLE talks;* 248.42
gifts of God for every family. Minneapolis, Augsburg, c.1965. 32p. col. illus. 28x42cm. Based on material furnished by Harold J. Belgum; illus. by John Mosand. 3.25, pap., wire bdg.,

TAEGEL, William S., 1940- 248'.42
People lovers [by] William S. Taegel. Waco, Tex., Word Books [1972] 144 p. 23 cm. Bibliography: p. 141-144. [BV4501.2.T22] 72-76442 3.95
1. Christian life—1960- I. Title.

*TAYLOR, Benjamin F. 248.4'2
Freedoms and mental fitness. New York, Vantage [1967] 80p. 21cm. 2.50 bds.,
I. Title.

THOMAS, George Ernest, 248.42
1907- ed.
A pocket book of discipleship, compiled by G. Ernest Thomas. Nashville, Upper Room [1960] 96 p. 12 cm. [BV4501.2.T46] 60-16860
1. Christian life — Methodist authors. I. Title. II. Title: Discipleship.

THOMAS, W Ian. 248.42
The saving life of Christ. Grand Rapids, Zondervan Pub. House [1961] 152 p. 22 cm. [BV4501.2.T48] 61-19963
1. Christian life. I. Title.

THOMAS, W. Ian 248.42
The saving life of Christ. Grand Rapids, Zondervan [c.1961] 152p. 61-19963 2.50 bds.,
1. Christian life. I. Title.

THOMPSON, Luther Joe. 248.42
Monday morning religion. Nashville, Broadman Press [1961] 96 p. 20 cm. Includes bibliography. [BV4501.2.T49] 61-16912
1. Christian life. I. Title.

THOMPSON, Luther Joe 248.42
Monday morning religion. Nashville, Broadman [c.1961] 96p. Bibl. 61-16912 1.95 bds.,
1. Christian life. I. Title.

THOMPSON, Olive R 248.42
The Devil and I. New York, Philosophical Library [1960] 69 p. illus. 23 cm. [BV4501.2.T5] 60-16246
1. Christian life. I. Title.

THOMPSON, Olive R. 248.42
The Devil and I. New York, Philosophical Library [c.1960] 69p. illus. 23cm. 60-16246 3.75
1. Christian life. I. Title.

THOMPSON, Olive Ross. 248.42
The Devil and I. New York, Philosophical Library [1960] 69 p. illus. 23 cm. [BV4501.2.T5] 60-16246
1. Christian life. I. Title.

*THORNTON, David. 248.'42
Faith recycling; a process for understanding your personal beliefs. Valley Forge,[Pa.] Judson Press [1975c1974] 44p. ill. 28 cm. [BV4501.2] 1.50(pbk.)
1. Christian life-1960- I. Title.

TIPPETT, Harry Moyle, 248.42
1891-
Key in your hand. Illus. by Manning de V. Lee. Washington, D.C., Review & Herald [c.1964] 128p. col. illus. 18cm. 64-14880 1.75 bds.,
1. Christian life. I. Title.

TORMEY, John C. 248.4'2
Rocks are for lizards; Live: Don't lurk: [By] John C. Tormey. Liguori, Mo., Liguorian

Books [1970] 147 p. illus., port. 11 x 18 cm. [BX2350.2.T66] 73-136564 1.75
1. Christian life—Catholic authors. I. Title.

TOWNS, Broma C. 248.42
I found the light. New York, Carleton [c.] 1962. 121p. 21cm. (Reflection Bk.) 2.75
I. Title.

TROBISCH, Walter. 248.4'2
I married you. [1st ed.] New York, Harper & Row [1971] 135 p. illus. 22 cm. [BV835.T76] 78-148437 4.95
1. Marriage. I. Title.

ULRICH, Betty Garton. 248'.42
Every day with God; devotions for families with children. Designed and illustrated by Don Wallerstedt. Minneapolis, Augsburg Pub. House [1972] 127 p. illus. 23 cm. [BV255.U47] 72-78549 ISBN 0-8066-1217-7 3.95
1. Family—Prayer-books and devotions—English. I. Title.

UNDERWAGER, Ralph C. 248'.42
I hurt inside; a Christian psychologist helps you understand and overcome feelings of fear, frustration, and failure [by] Ralph C. Underwager. Minneapolis, Augsburg Pub. House [1973] 102 p. 20 cm. (A Study of generations paperback) [BF637.C5U5] 72-90265 ISBN 0-8066-1312-2 1.95
1. Conduct of life. I. Title.

VAN BAALEN, Jan Karel 248.42
When hearts grow faint; instructions on how to live a life of joy. Grand Rapids, Mich., Eerdmans [c.1960] 119p. 21cm. 60-12642 2.00 bds.,
1. Consolation. I. Title.

VAN BAALEN, Jan Karel, 248.42
1890-
When hearts grow faint; instructions on how to live a life of joy. Grand Rapids, Eerdmans [1960] 119 p. 21 cm. [BV4905.2.V3] 60-12642
1. Consolation. I. Title.

*VOLLMER, Thomas D. 248.42
Christ and the forked tongue of man. New York, Vantage [c.1966] 299p. 21cm. 5.00 bds.,
I. Title.

WARD, Ronald Arthur. 248.42
Mind and heart; studies in Christian truth and experience, by Ronald A. Ward. Grand Rapids, Baker Book House [1966, c1965] 144 p. 23 cm. [BV4501.2.W34] 66-4483
1. Christian life. I. Title.

WARD, Ronald Arthur 248.42
Mind and heart; studies in Christian truth and experience. Grand Rapids, Mich., Baker Bk. [1966, c.1965] 144p. 23cm. [BV4501.2.W34] 66-4483 3.95
1. Christian life. I. Title.

WASHINGTON, Booker 248.4'2
Taliaferro, 1859?-1915.
Sowing and reaping. Freeport, N.Y., Books for Libraries Press, 1971. 29 p. 23 cm. (The Black heritage library collection) Reprint of the 1900 ed. [E185.97.W287 1971] 70-161275 ISBN 0-8369-8834-5
1. Conduct of life. 2. Negroes—Education. I. Title. II. Series.

WATT, Reed Loving 248.42
Memento; who am I, that you are? New York, Carlton [c.1962] 53p. 21cm. (Reflection bk.) 2.00
I. Title.

WEATHERHEAD, Leslie Dixon, 248.42
1893
Salute to a sufferer; an attempt to offer the plain man a Christian philosophy of suffering. New York, Abingdon [1963, c.1962] 95p. 20cm. 63-8669 2.00 bds.,
1. Suffering. I. Title.

WEITZ, Martin Mishli, 248.42
1907- ed.
Decalogues for our day; an anthology of ten commandments for modern living. New York, Bloch Pub. Co. [1962] 146 p. illus. 21 cm. [BJ1581.2.W4] 62-21170
1. Conduct of life. I. Title.

WEITZ, Martin Mishli, 248.42
1907- ed.
Decalogues for our day; an anthology of ten commandments for modern living. New York, Bloch [c.1962] 146p. illus. 21cm. 62-21170 3.50
1. Conduct of life. I. Title.

WENTZ, Frederick K. 248.4'2
My job and my faith; twelve Christians report on their work worlds. Frederick K. Wentz, editor. Nashville, Abingdon Press [1967] 192 p. 21 cm. [BV4740.W4] 67-22169
1. Vocation. I. Title.

WERNER, Hazen G. 248.42
Your family and God. Nashville, Upper Room [c.1962] 55p. 19cm. Bibl. .35 pap.,
1. Christian life. I. Title.

WERNER, Hazen Graff, Bp., 248.42
1895-
No saints suddenly. New York, Abingdon Press [1963] 160 p. 21 cm. [BV4501.2.W43] 63-11383
1. Christian life—Methodist authors. I. Title.

*WESTERVELT, Virginia 248.42
Youth's real-life problems. Illus. by Peter Petraglia. Philadelphia, Lutheran Church Pr. [c.1966] 64p. illus. (pt. col.) 23cm. .50 pap.,
I. Title.

WHITE, Reginald E O 248.42
The upward calling; meditations on the Christian life. [1st ed.] Grand Rapids, Eerdmans [1961] 202 p. 22 cm. [BV4501.2.W46] 61-17391
1. Christian life. I. Title.

WHITE, Reginald E. O. 248.42
The upward calling; meditations on the Christian life. Grand Rapids, Mich. Eerdmans [c.1961] 202p. 61-17391 3.50
1. Christian life. I. Title.

*WILKERSON, David 248.42
I'm not mad at God. Minneapolis, Minn., Bethany [1967] 89p. 17cm. 1.95 bds.,
I. Title.

WILKERSON, David R 248.4'2
I'm not mad at God. Minneapolis, Bethany Fellowship [1967] 89 p. 17 cm. [BV4501.2.W52] 67-7458
1. Christian life. I. Title.

WILKERSON, David R. 248.4'2
I'm not mad at God. Minneapolis, Bethany Fellowship [1967] 89 p. 17 cm. [BV4501.2.W52] 67-7458
1. Christian life. I. Title.

WILKERSON, David R. 248.4'2
Man, have I got problems [by] David Wilkerson. Old Tappan, N.J., F. H. Revell Co. [1969] 128 p. 21 cm. [BV4501.2.W523] 69-20148 2.95
1. Christian life. I. Title.

WILKERSON, David R. 248.4'2
Man, have I got problems [by] David Wilkerson. New York, Family Lib. [1973, c.1969] 93 p. 18 cm. (Pyramid Book, N3056) [BV4501.2.W523] ISBN 0-515-03056-2 pap., 0.95
1. Christian life. I. Title.
Distributed by Pyraimid Pubns.

WILSON, James I. 248.4'2
The principles of war, by James I. Wilson. [2d ed. rev.] Annapolis, Christian Books in Annapolis [1967] 68 p. 18 cm. Bibliographical footnotes. [BV4509.5.W5 1967] 76-3745 1.00
1. Christian life. I. Title.

WILSON, James Orville. 248.42
Who has your allegiance? Nashville, Southern Pub. Association [1965] 181 p. 20 cm. [BV4515.2W5] 65-2630
1. Christian life — Stories. 2. Patriotism — Juvenile literature. I. Title.

WILSON, James Orville 248.42
Who has your allegiance? Nashville, Southern Pub. [c.1965] 181p. 2 cm. [BV4515.2.W5] 65-2630 2.95
1. Christian life—Stories. 2. Patriotism—Juvenile literature. I. Title.

WOODYARD, David O. 248.4'2
To be human now, by David O. Woodyard. Philadelphia, Westminster Press [1969] 142 p. 19 cm. Bibliographical references included in "Notes" (p. [139]-142) [BT1102.W66] 70-78483 2.65
1. Apologetics—20th century. I. Title.

WRIGLEY, Louise Scott 248.42
Look up, heart. Independence, Mo., Herald [c.1962] 55p. illus. 16cm. 62-21992 1.25 bds.,
1. Christian life—Stories. I. Title.

WRIGLEY, Louise Scott 248.42
Your right to radiance. Independence, Mo., Herald House [c.1961] 76p. col. illus. 16cm. 61-12487 1.25 bds.,
1. Women—Religious life. I. Title.

PEACE, Richard. 248.4'2'076
Learning to love God. [1st ed.] Grand Rapids, Zondervan Pub. House [1968] 63 p. forms, maps. 21 cm. (His Learning to love, book 1) Includes bibliographies. [BV4511.P39] 68-6049
1. Christian life—Study and teaching. I. Title.

DYE, Harold Eldon, 248.42081
1907-
A story to remember. Nashville, Broadman Press [c1962] 126 p. 16 cm. Anecdotes. [BV4515.2.D9] 63-7335
1. Christian life—Stories. I. Title.

DYE, Harold Eldon, 248.42081
1907-
A story to remember. Nashville, Broadman [c.1962] 126p. 16cm. 63-7335 2.00 bds.,
1. Christian life—Stories. I. Title.

IKELER, Bernard C. 248.42081
Mission as decision [by] Bernard C. Ikeler, Stanley J. Rowland, Jr. New York, Friendship [1965] 47p. 19cm. [BV4515.2.I35] 65-11423 .75 pap.,
1. Christian life—Stories. I. Rowland, Stanley J., joint author. II. Title.

UNDERHILL, Evelyn, 248.42081
1875-1941.
The Evelyn Underhill reader, compiled by Thomas S. Kepler. New York, Abingdon Press [1962] 238 p. 24 cm. [BV4501.U455] 62-7438
1. Spiritual life. 2. Mysticism. I. Title.

UNDERHILL, Evelyn, 248.42081
1875-1941.
The Evelyn Underhill reader, compiled by Thomas S. Kepler. New York, Abingdon Press [1962] 238 p. 24 cm. [BV4501.U455] 62-7438
1. Spiritual life. 2. Mysticism. I. Title.

WYRICK, Neil. 248.42081
Boundaries unlimited, by Neil Wyrick, Jr. Richmond, John Knox Press [1965] 96 p. 19 cm. (Chime paperbacks) [BV4832.2.W9] 65-10699
1. Devotional literature. I. Title.

WYRICK, Neil, Jr. 248.42081
Boundaries unlimited. Richmond, Va., Knox [c.1965] 96p. 19cm. (Chime paperbacks) [BV4832.2.W9] 65-10699 1.00 pap.,
1. Devotional literature. I. Title.

STEVENSON, Herbert F., 248.42082
ed.
The ministry of Keswick; a selection from the Bible readings delivered at the Keswick Convention; 1st. ser. Grand Rapids., Mich., Zondervan [c.1963] v. 22cm. 64-426 5.95
1. Spiritual life—Addresses, essays, lectures. I. Title.
Contents omitted.

HAMM, Jack 248.42084
He will answer; a book of cartoons. Garden City, N.Y., Doubleday [c.]1961. 96 p. (chiefly illus.) 61-7651 1.00 pap.,
1. Christian life—Pictures, illustrations, etc. I. Title.

TREADWAY, Charles F. 248.4'2'0922
Fifty character stories [by] Charles and Ruby Treadway. Nashville, Tenn., Broadman Press [1969] x, 174 p. 21 cm. Bibliography: p. 173-174. Profiles of fifty famous people point out examples of Christian life and thought. [BR1704.T7] 920 74-87729 3.95
1. Christian biography—Juvenile literature. I. Treadway, Ruby Peeples, joint author. II. Title.

ZEOLI, Billy. 248'.42'0922 B
Supergoal, with Billy Zeoli. Old Tappan, N.J., Revell [1972] 127 p. illus. 21 cm. Contents.Contents.—Zeoli, B. Christianity and athletics.—Landry, T. Leadership.—Dale, C. Winning.—Staubach, R. Success.—Houston, J. Living for Christ.—Vogel, B. Faith.—Barney, L. Courage.—Evans, N. Determination.—Harraway, C. Love.—Zeoli, B. God's game plan. [BV4501.2.Z46] 72-8552 ISBN 0-8007-0584-X Pap. 1.95
1. Christian life—1960- 2. Religion and sports. I. Title.

LIBERMANN, Francois Marie 248.422
Paul [Name orig.: Jacob Libermann] 1802-1852
The spiritual letters of the Venerable Francis Libermann. Ed. tr. by Walter van de Putte, James Collery, Pittsburgh, Duquesne Univ. Pr. [c.]1963. 310p. illus. 22cm. (Duquesne studies. Spiritan ser., v. 6) Contents.v. 2, Letters to people in the world. 62-12768 4.95
1. Spiritual life—Catholic authors. I. Title.

SHOEMAKER, Samuel Moor, 248.423
1893-1963.
Extraordinary living for ordinary men; excerpts selected from the writings of Sam Shoemaker by his daughter, Helen Shoemaker Rea, and the staff of Faith at work. Grand Rapids, Zondervan Pub. House [1965] 160 p. 22 cm. [BV4501.2.S44] 65-19501
1. Christian life—Anglican authors. I. Rea, Helen (Shoemaker) comp. II. Title.

REST, Karl H 248.458
Our good enemies; a book of story sermons [by] Karl H. A. Rest. Philadelphia, United Church Press [1964] 112 p. 21 cm. [BV4315.R39] 64-19951
1. Children's sermons. I. Title.

REST, Karl H. A. 248.458
Our good enemies; a book of story sermons. Philadelphia, United Church [c.1964] 112p. 21cm. 64-19951 2.50
1. Childre's sermons. I. Title.

LEE, G. Avery. 248'.4'61
I want that mountain! [By] G. Avery Lee. Nashville, T. Nelson [1974] p. cm. Includes bibliographical references. [BX6333.L395I22] 74-13017 3.50 (pbk.).
1. Mountains in the Bible. 2. Baptists—Sermons. 3. Sermons, American. I. Title.

DURBIN, B. Paul 248.47
Everlasting goodwill and glory; outlines for Christian living. New York, Greenwich Bk. Pub. [c.1963] 63-14394 130p. 22cm. 2.75
1. Christian life—Methodist authors. I. Title.

PIERSON, Robert H. 248.473
The final countdown [by] R. H. Pierson, G. S. Stevenson. [Mountain View, Calif., Pacific Pr. 1966] 92p. 19cm. Cover title. [BV4501.2.P544] 66-23433 .30 pap.,
1. Christian life—Seventh-Day Adventist authors. I. Stevenson, G. S., joint author. II. Title.

ALLEN, James, 1864-1912. 248.48
Morning and evening thoughts. New York, R. F. Fenno [n. d.] 71 p. 17 cm. [BV4832.A44] 52-22321
1. Devotional exercises. I. Title.

BARKER, Harold P 248.48
The three weathervanes; and other illustrations of truth. New York, Loizeaux Bros [19--] 77p. 19cm. (Treasury of truth, no.117) [BV4832.B24] 56-26550
1. Devotional literature. I. Title.

BARKER, Harold P 248.48
The three weathervanes; and other illustrations of truth. New York, Loizeaux Bros. [19--] 77p. 19cm. (Treasury of truth, no. 117) [BV4832.B24] 56-26550
1. Devotional literature. I. Title.

BOREN, James Basil. 248.48
I saw God. Lawton, Okla., Clover Pub. Co., 1963. 102 p. 23 cm. Bibliographical footnotes. [BV4832.2.B65] 64-831
1. Devotional literature. I. Title.

CLAY, Donice L 248.48
To God be the glory; a book of devotions and meditations. [1st ed.] New York, Greenwich Book Publishers [c1962] 95 p. 22 cm. [BV4832.2.C54] 62-19874
1. Meditations. I. Title.

IRONSIDE, Henry Allan, 248.48
1876-1951.
The continual burnt offering; daily meditations on the Word of God. [1st ed.] New York City, Loizeaux Bros. [1953] unpaged. 15cm. A companion vol. to the author's The daily sacrifice. [BV4832.I67] 54-32596
1. Devotional calendars. I. Title.

*JESS, John D. 248.48
Coping with anxiety. Grand Rapids, Mich., Baker Book House [1973] 92 p. 18 cm. (Dimension Books) "Collection of radio messages [broadcast] on Chapel of the Air." [BV4832] ISBN 0-8010-5053-7 0.95 (pbk.)
1. Chapel of the Air (Radio program) 2. Anxiety—Addresses, essays, lectures. 3. Christian life—Addresses, essays, lectures. I. Title.

LONG, Kermit L 248.48
Hungers of the human heart. New York, Abingdon Press [1964] 96 p. 20 cm. Bibliographical footnotes. [BX8333.L65H8] 64-10440
1. Methodist Church — Sermons. 2. Sermons, American. I. Title.

LONG, Kermit L. 248.48
Hungers of the human heart. [Nashville] Abingdon [c.1964] 96p. 20cm. Bibl. 64-10440 2.00
1. Methodist Church—Sermons. 2. Sermons, American. I. Title.

MORGAN, Elise (Nevins) 248.48
1876-
The illimitable one. 3d ed. Wellesley Hills, Mass., Elisian Guild [196-, c1034] vii, 134 p. 14 cm. (Her The Meditation series) [BV4832.M565] 61-17645
1. Devotiional literature. I. Title.

MORGAN, Elise (Nevins) 248.48
1876-
Now -- This day. 5th ed. enl. Wellesley Hills, Mass., Elisian Guild [c1963] 94 p. 14 cm. (The Meditation series) [BV4832.M566 1963] 62-16342
1. Devotional literature. I. Title.

MORGAN, Elise (Nevins) 248.48
1876-
Your own path. Enl. ed. Wellesley Hills, Mass., Elisian Guild [c1961] 96p. 14cm. [BV4832.M57 1961] 61-16647
I. Title.

*PARROTT, Leslie 248.48
The power of your attitudes. Kansas City, Mo., Beacon Hill Pr. [1967] 96p. 19cm. 1.25 pap.,
1. Christian life. I. Title.

PRATER, Arnold. 248'.48
How to beat the blahs / by Arnold Prater. [Irvine, Calif. : Harvest House Publishers], c1977]. 112 p. ; 18 cm. [BV4501.2.P66] 77-24827 ISBN 0-89081-038-9 pbk. : 1.75
1. Christian life—1960- I. Title.

RINGNESS, Thomas A 248.48
Emotional reactions to learning situations as related to the learning efficiency of mentally retarded children; final report. Robert Fischer [and others] project assistants. [Madison? Wis.] 1959. 126 l. diagrs., tables. 30cm. 'The research ... was done pursuant to contract SAE6434 between the U. S. Department of Health, Education, and Welfare and the University of Wisconsin.' Bibliography: leaves 113-115. [LB1073.R5] 59-62106

SCHUTZ, Roger. 248.4'8
Unanimity in pluralism. Translated by David Flood, Brother Pascal of Taize [and] Brother Thomas of Taize. Chicago, Ill., Franciscan Herald Press [1967] x, 76 p. 29 cm. [BV4833.S413] 67-22201
1. Meditations. I. Title.

WUELLNER, Flora, Slosson. 248'.48
On the road to spiritual wholeness / Flora Slosson Wuellner. Nashville : Abingdon, c1978. p. cm. [BV4501.2.W83] 77-12232 pbk. : 3.95
1. Spiritual life. I. Title.

MURPHY, Francis 248.4'8'13
Xavier, 1914-
Moral teaching in the primitive church, by Francis X. Murphy. Glen Rock, N.J., Paulist [1968] vi, 118p. 21cm. [BR195.C5M87] 68-16664 3.95; 2.50 pap.,
1. Christian life—Early church. 2. Christian literature (Selections: Extracts, etc.) I. Title.

MAKARII, Monk, 1788- 248'.48'19
1860.
Russian letters of direction, 1834-1860 / Macarius, starets of Optino; selection, translations and foreword by Iulia de Beausobre [Crestwood, N.Y.] : St. Vladimir's Seminary Press, 1975. 115 p. ; 19 cm. Translation of the author's letters selected from the 1880 ed. published by Lavrov, Moscow, under title: Sobranie pisem blazhennyia pamiati optinskago startsa. Reprint of the 1944 ed. published by Dacre Press, Westminster. [BX382.M34213 1975] 75-1064 ISBN 0-913836-23-0 : 3.25
1. Christian life—Orthodox Eastern authors. I. Title.

AHERN, John . 248.482
8 happy people Milwaukee, Bruce Pub. Co. [1964] 71 p. 21 cm. [BX4652.A5] 64-17326
1. Beatitutdes. 2. Catholic Church—Biog. 3. Devotional literature. I. Title.

AHERN, John J. 248.482
8 happy people. Milwaukee, Bruce [c.1964] 71p. 21cm. 64-17326 1.25 pap.,
1. Beatitudes. 2. Catholic Church—Biog. 3. Devotional literature. I. Title.

ALLEMAND, Edward. 248.4/8/2
About hoping. Dayton, Ohio, Pflaum [1967] 125p. illus. 17cm. (Christian experience ser., no. 5) Witness bks., 8. Bibl. [BV4638.A55] 67-30461 .75 pap.,
1. Hope. I. Title.

ANDRE, Marie Joseph. 248.4'8'2
Equilibrium; fidelity to nature and grace, by M. J. Andre. With a pref. by Yves Congar. [Translated by David Martin] St. Louis, B. Herder Book Co. [1968] xiv, 157 p. 21 cm. (Cross and crown series of spirituality, no. 35) [BX2350.5.A6513] 68-22585
1. Spiritual life—Catholic authors. I. Title. II. Series.

ARIAS, Juan. 248'.48'2
Give Christ back to us! / by Juan Arias ; translated by Paul Barrett. St. Meinrad, Ind. : Abbey Press, 1975. x, 156 p. ; 21 cm. (A Priority edition) Translation of Cristo da riscoprire. [BX2350.2.A6413] 75-19920 ISBN 0-915862-01-8 pbk. : 3.95
1. Christian life—Catholic authors. 2. Christianity—20th century. I. Title.

ARIAS, Juan. 248'.48'2
The God I don't believe in. Translated by Paul Barrett. St. Meinrad, Ind., Abbey Press, 1973. 200 p. 21 cm. (A Priority edition) Translation of Il Dio in cui non credo. [BX2186.A7413] 73-76766 5.95
1. Devotional literature, Spanish. 2. God. I. Title.

BACH, Lester. 248'.48'2
Take time for sunsets / Lester Bach. Chicago : Franciscan Herald Press, [1975] 233 p. ; 21 cm. [BX2350.2.B27] 75-1496 ISBN 0-8199-0565-8
1. Francesco d'Assisi, Saint, 1182-1226. 2. Christian life—Catholic authors. I. Title.

BAKEWELL, Francis F 248.482
Human living in Christ. Milwaukee, Bruce Pub. Co. [1962] 156 p. 18 cm. [BX2350.2.B3] 62-18185
1. Spiritual life—Catholic authors. I. Title.

BAKEWELL, Francis F 248.482
Human living in Christ. Milwaukee, Bruce [c.1962] 156p. 18cm. 62-18185 2.75
I. Title.

BALTHASAR, Hans Urs 248.4'8'2
von, 1905-
The moment of Christian witness. Translated [BX2350.2.B3183] 68-56712 3.95
1. Christian life—Catholic authors. I. Title.

BALTHASAR, Hans Urs 248.4'8'2
von, 1905-
Who is a Christian? Translated by John Cumming. Westminster, Md., Newman Press [1967, 1968] 126 p. 21 cm. Translation of Wer ist ein Christ? Bibliographical references included in "Notes" (p. 125-126) [BX2350.2.B3213 1968] 68-4287
1. Christian life—Catholic authors. 2. Church and the world. I. Title.

BALTHASAR, Hans Urs 248.4'8'2
von, 1905-
Who is a Christian? Translated by John Cumming. Westminster, Md., Newman Press [1967, c1968] 126 p. 21 cm. Translation of Wer ist ein Christ? Bibliographical references included in "Notes" (p. 125-126) [BX2350.2.B3213 1968] 68-4287
1. Christian life—Catholic authors. 2. Church and the world. I. Title.

*BASSEL, Bernard. 248.482
We neurotics, a handbook for the half-mad. New York, Doubleday [1968,c.1962] 116 p. 18cm. (Image D248) .95 pap.,
1. Christian life—Catholic authors. I. Title.

BASSERT, Bernard. 248.482
The noonday devil; spiritual support in middle age. [1st American ed.) Fresno, Calif., Academy Guild Press [1964] xi. 178 p. 23 cm. Bibliographical references included in "Notes." (p. 172-178) [BX2350.2.B36] 64-25723
1. Christian life — Catholic authors. I. Title.

BASSET, Bernard 248.482
Best of both worlds, a guide to holiness in the suburbs. Fresno, Calif., Acad. Guild Pr. [1964, c.1963] viii, 150p. 23cm. 64-13523 3.75
1. Christian life—Catholic authors. I. Title.

BASSET, Bernard. 248.4'8'2
How to be really with it; guide to the good life. [1st ed.] Garden City, N.Y., Doubleday, 1970. 186 p. 22 cm. [BX2350.2.B335] 70-89099 4.95
1. Christian life—Catholic authors. I. Title.

BASSET, Bernard 248.482
We neurotics, a handbook for the half-mad. Fresno, Calif., Acad. Guild [1963, c.1962] 135p. 22cm. 63-12102 3.75
1. Christian life—Catholic authors. I. Title.

BAUR, Benedikt 248.482
In silence with God. Translated from the 4th German ed. by Elisabethe Corathiel-Noonan. Chicago, H. Regnery Co. [c.1960] x, 235p. 21cm. 60-9323 3.75
1. Spiritual life—Catholic authors. I. Title.

BAUR, Benedikt, 1877- 248.482
In silence with God. Translated from the 4th German ed. by Elisabethe Corathiel-Noonan. Chicago, H. Regnery Co. [1960] 235p. 21cm. [BX2350.B323 1960] 60-9323
1. Spiritual life—Catholic authors. I. Title.

BESSIERE, Gerard. 248'.48'2
Jesus ahead / Gerard Bessiere ; translated from the French by Barbara Lucas. St. Meinrad, In. : Abbey Press, 1975. 129 p. ; 21 cm. (A Priority edition) Translation of Jesus est devant. [BX2183.B47413] 75-19919 ISBN 0-87029-054-1 : 2.95
1. Meditations. 2. Christian life—Catholic authors. I. Title.

BOUYER, Louis, 1913- 248.482
Introduction to spirituality. Tr. [from French] by Mary Perkins Ryan. New York, Desclee 1961. 321p. Bibl. 61-15722 5.75
1. Spiritual life—Catholic authors. I. Title.

BRADY, Veronica. 248'.48'2
The future people: Christianity, modern culture and the future [by] Veronica Brady. Melbourne, Spectrum, 1971. 161 p. 22 cm. Includes bibliographical references. [BR115.C8B7] 73-156455 ISBN 0-909837-10-4 3.00
1. Christianity and culture. 2. Christianity—20th century. I. Title.

BRO, Bernard. 248.4'8'2
Happy those who believe. [Translated by John M. Morriss] Staten Island, N.Y., Alba House [1970] ix, 140 p. illus. 20 cm. Translation of Heureux de croire. [BX2350.2.B7313] 72-110593 3.95
1. Christian life—Catholic authors. I. Title.

BUTLER, Richard, 1918- 248.482
Themes of concern. [1st ed.] Garden City, N.Y., Doubleday, 1966. 212 p. 22 cm. Bibliographical footnotes. [BX2350.2.B8] 66-12190
1. Christian life—Catholic authors. I. Title.

CAROL, Angela 248.482
Ways of sanctity. Pulaski, Wis., Franciscan Pubs. [c.1963] 64p. 19cm. .25 pap.,
I. Title.

CARR, John, 1878- 248.482
Helps to happiness. Westminster, Md., Newman [1963] 221p. 18cm. 64-936 3.75
1. Happiness. I. Title.

CARRETTO, Carlo. 248'.48'2
In search of the beyond / Carlo Carretto ; translated by Sarah Fawcett. Maryknoll, N.Y. : Orbis Books, 1976, c1975. 175 p. ; 19 cm. Translation of Al di la delle cose. [BX2350.2.C33713] 75-35477 ISBN 0-88344-208-6 : 5.95
1. Christian life—Catholic authors. 2. Poverty (Virtue) I. Title.

CARROLL, James. 248'.48'2
Contemplation; liberating the ghost of the Church: churching the ghost of liberation. New York, Paulist Press [1972] 94 p. illus. 18 cm. (Paulist Press Deus book) [BV5091.C7C37] 77-190088 1.25
1. Contemplation. 2. Christian life—Catholic authors. 3. Christianity—20th century.

CARSWELL, Pamela, 1918- 248.482
Offbeat spirituality. Foreword by F. J. Sheed. New York, Sheed & Ward [1961, c.1960] 241p. 61-8501 3.95 bds.,
1. Spiritual life—Catholic authors. I. Title.

CARSWELL, Pamela Mary, 248.482
1918-
Offbeat spirituality. London and New York, Sheed and Ward [1960] 243p. 21cm. [BX2350.2.C34 1960] 61-65716
1. Spiritual life—Catholic authors. I. Title.

CARTER, Edward, 1929- 248'.48'2
Response in Christ; a study of the Christian life. Dayton, Ohio, Pflaum Press, 1969. xiv, 274 p. 22 cm. Bibliography: p. 263-267. [BX2350.2.C36] 69-20170 6.95
1. Spiritual life—Catholic authors. I. Title.

CASTER, Marcel van. 248.4'8'2
Values catechetics, by Marcel van Caster. Paramus, N.J., Newman Press [1970] 217 p. 22 cm. "Originally published as part II of the third edition of Dieu nous parle II." [BX2350.2.C3733] 75-116867 6.95
1. Christian life—Catholic authors. I. Title.

*CASTLE, David. 248.4'8'2
Toward caring; people building in the family. Richmond, Ind., Friends United Press [1973] vii, 60 p. illus. 21 cm. (Toward caring; a study series designed to improve dialogue amongst persons and to increase Christian care and concern) "The series is directed to family and/or intergenerational Christian education." Cover title. Bibliography: p. 59-60. ISBN 0-913408-10-7 1.50 (pbk.)
1. Christian life—Quaker authors. 2. Conduct of life. I. Title.
Publisher's address: 101 Quaker Hill Drive, Richmond, Ind. 47374.

CERESI, Vincenzo. 248.482
Quest for holiness. [Translated by Sister Gertrude] Staten Island, N.Y. Alba House [1963] 288 p. 21 cm. Includes bibliography. [BX2350.5.C413] 62-21595
1. Spirtual life — Catholic authors. I. Title.

CERESI, Vincenzo 248.482
Quest for holiness. [Tr. by Sister Gertrude] Staten Island, N.Y. Alba [c.1963] 288p. 21cm. Bibl. 63-21595 3.95
1. Spiritual life—Catholic authors. I. Title.

CHEVIGNARD, Bernard Marie 248.482
Gospel spirituality. Tr. [from French] by Angele Demand. New York, Sheed [c.1965] viii, 183p. 21cm. [BX2350.2.C513] 65-20854 3.95
1. Christian life—Catholic authors. I. Title.

CHEVIGNARD, Bernard 248.482
Marie.
Gospel spirituality, by B.-M. Chevignard. Translated by Angele Demand. New York, Sheed and Ward [1965] viii, 183 p. 21 cm. Translation of La doctrine spirituelle de l'evangile. [BX2350.2.C513] 65-20854
1. Christian life — Catholic authors. I. Title.

COLIN, Louis, 1884- 248.482
The interior life. Translated from the French by Sister Maria Constance. Westminister, Md., Newman Press, 1962. 305 p. 21 cm. [BX2350.5.C583] 61-8966
1. Spiritual life — Catholic authors. I. Title.

COLIN, Louis, 1884- 248.482
The interior life. Tr. from French by Sister Maria Constance. Westminster, Md., Newman [c.]1962. 305p. 21cm. Bibl. 61-8966 4.95
1. Spiritual life—Catholic authors. I. Title.

†CONCETTA, Sister, 248'.48'2
D.S.P., 1916-
In the light of the Bible / Sister Concetta. Boston : St. Paul Editions, c1976- v. : ill. ; 18 cm. [BX2350.2.C6134] 76-16120 1.25 (v. 1) varies
1. Christian life—Catholic authors. I. Title.

COOKE, Bernard J. 248.4'8'2
New dimensions in Catholic life, by Bernard J. Cooke. Wilkes-Barre, Pa., Dimension Books [1968] 126 p. 22 cm. [BX2350.2.C62] 68-31390 3.95
1. Christian life—Catholic authors. 2. Catholic Church—Doctrinal and controversial works—Catholic authors. I. Title.

CROSS and crown (St. 248.482
Louis)
Seeking the kingdom; a guide to Christian living. Ed. by Reginald Masterson. St. Louis, B. Herder [c.1961] 306p. 61-8041 5.25
1. Spiritual life—Catholic authors. I. Masterson, Reginald, ed. II. Title.

CURRAN, Charles E. 248.4'8'2
Christian morality today; the renewal of moral theology [by] Charles E. Curran. Notre Dame, Ind., Fides Publishers [1966] xx, 138 p. 20 cm. Includes bibliographical references. [BJ1249.C8] 66-20176
1. Christian ethics—Catholic authors. I. Title.

CUSHING, Richard James, 248.482
Cardinal
The age of lay sanctity. [Boston, Daughters of St. Paul, 1960] 16p. 19cm. .15 pap.,
I. Title.

CUSHING, Richard James, 248.482
Cardinal
Pastoral letter: the Christian and the community. Boston, Daughters of St. Paul, 1960. 31p. 22cm. .15 pap.,
I. Title.

CUSHING, Richard James, 248.482
Cardinal 1895-
The purpose of living. [Boston, Daughters of St. Paul, 1960] 12p. 19cm. .15 pap.,
I. Title.

CUSHING, Richard James, 248.482
Cardinal
The role of the Christian intellectual. Boston, Daughters of St. Paul [1960] 13p. 19cm. .15 pap.,
I. Title.

CUSHING, Richard James, 248.482
Cardinal, 1895-
Friends of God, friends of mine, by Richard Cardinal Cushing. [Boston] St. Paul Editions, [c1964] 248 p. 22 cm. [BX4652.C85] 64-66443
1. Catholic Church — Biog. I. Title.

CUSKELLY, Eugene James. 248.4'82
A heart to know thee; a practical summa of the spiritual life, by E. J. Cuskelly. New York, Paulist Press [1967] xvii, 317 p. 19 cm. (Deus books) Includes bibliographical references. [BX2350.5] 67-7269
1. Spiritual life—Catholic authors. I. Title.

CUSKELLY, Eugene James. 248.4'8'2
No cowards in the kingdom, [by] E. J. Cuskelly. Dayton, Ohio, Pflaum Press, 1969. 174 p. 22 cm. Bibliographical footnotes. [BX2350.2.C87] 75-83450 4.95
1. Christian life—Catholic authors. I. Title.

CUSKELLY, Eugene James. 248'.48'2
No cowards in the kingdom [by] E. J. Cuskelly. [Melbourne] Spectrum [1969] 150 p. 19 cm. Includes bibliographical references. [BX2350.2.C87 1969b] 73-164679
1. Christian life—Catholic authors. I. Title.

DANIELOU, Jean 248.482
The Christian today. Translated [from the French by Kathryn Sullivan. NewYork, Desclee, 1960[ ] 149p. 22cm. (Bibl. footnotes) 60-10016 2.75
1. Spiritual life—Catholic authors. I. Title.

D'ARCY, Martin Cyril, 1888- 248.4'8'2
Of God and man; thoughts on faith and morals, by Martin C. D'Arcy. [1st American paperback ed.] Notre Dame [Ind.] University of Notre Dame Press [1967, c1964] ix, 173 p. 19 cm. [BX2350.2] 67-6849
1. Christian life—Catholic authors. I. Title.

DAUGHTERS of St. Paul. 248'.48'2
Heaven / by the Daughters of St. Paul. Boston : St. Paul Editions, 1977. 156 p. : ill. ; 22 cm. [BT846.2.D38 1977] 77-4669 3.50 pbk. : 2.50
1. Heaven. 2. Christian life—Catholic authors. I. Title.

DAUGHTERS of St. Paul. 248'.48'2
Heaven / by the Daughters of St. Paul. Boston : St. Paul Editions, 1977. 156 p. : ill. ; 22 cm. [BT846.2.D38 1977] 77-4669 3.50 pbk. : 2.50
1. Heaven. 2. Christian life—Catholic authors. I. Title.

DAUJAT, Jean 248.482
The faith applied. Tr. [from French] by Norah Burke. Chicago, Scepter [1964, c.1963] 161p. 21cm. 64-6857 3.50
1. Christian life—Catholic authors. I. Title.

DE CASTILLE, Vernon. 248'.48'2
How to gain tranquillity & the pleasures of internal contentment & emotional balance without the taking of pills : statistics / Vernon De Castille. [1st ed.] [Albuquerque, N.M.] : American Classical College Press, [1977] 24 leaves ; 28 cm. Cover title. [BX2350.2.D38] 77-24402 ISBN 0-89266-048-1 : 37.50
1. Christian life—Catholic authors. I. Title: How to gain tranquillity & the pleasures of internal contentment & emotional balance ...

DEVINE, George, 1941- 248'.48'2
Transformation in Christ. Staten Island, N.Y., Alba House [1972] xii, 163 p. 23 cm. Includes bibliographical references. [BX1751.2.D395] 70-39884 ISBN 0-8189-0240-X 3.95
1. Theology, Catholic. 2. Christian life—Catholic authors. I. Title.

DOHERTY, Catherine de Hueck, 1900- 248'.48'2
The gospel without compromise / Catherine de Hueck Doherty. Notre Dame, Ind. : Ave Maria Press, c1976. 150 p. ; 22 cm. [BX2350.2.D62] 75-28619 ISBN 0-87793-105-4 : 4.95 ISBN 0-87793-104-6 pbk. : 2.45
1. Christian life—Catholic authors. I. Title.

DOMINIAN, Jacob. 248'.48'2
Affirming the human personality : psychological essays in Christian living / Jack Dominian. Huntington, Ind. : Our Sunday Visitor, inc., 1977,c1975 ix, 175 p. ; 21 cm. Includes index. [BX2350.2.D635 1975] 77-82226 ISBN 0-87973-677-1 pbk. : 3.95
1. Christian life—Catholic authors—Addresses, essays, lectures. 2. Christianity—Psychology—Addresses, essays, lectures. I. Title.

DOMINIAN, Jacob. 248'.48'2
Affirming the human personality : psychological essays in Christian living / Jack Dominian. Huntington, Ind. : Our Sunday Visitor, inc., 1977,c1975 ix, 175 p. ; 21 cm. Includes index. [BX2350.2.D635 1975] 77-82226 ISBN 0-87973-677-1 pbk. : 3.95
1. Christian life—Catholic authors—Addresses, essays, lectures. 2. Christianity—Psychology—Addresses, essays, lectures. I. Title.

DOTY, William Lodewick, 1919- 248.4'8'2
Holiness for all; Vatican II spirituality, by William L. Doty. St. Louis, B. Herder Book Co., 1969. 142 p. 18 cm. [BX2350.2.D648 1969] 71-97236 1.45
1. Vatican Council. 2d, 1962-1965. 2. Spiritual life—Catholic authors. I. Title.

DOTY, William Lodewick, 1919- 248.482
Pathways to personal peace [by] William L. Doty. St. Louis, B. Herder Book Co. [1965] ix, 188 p. 21 cm. (Cross and crown series of spirituality, no. 30) [BX2350.2.D65] 65-24040
1. Christian life — Catholic authors. 2. Peace of mind. I. Title. II. Series.

DOTY, William Lodewick, 1919- 248.482
Pathways to personal peace. St. Louis, B. Herder [c.1965] ix, 188p. 21cm. (Cross and crown ser. of spirituality, no.30) [BX2350.2.D65] 65-24040 4.25 bds.,
1. Christian life—Catholic authors. 2. Peace of mind. I. Title. II. Series.

DOTY, William Lodewick, 1919- 248.482
Virtues for our time [by] William L. Doty. St. Louis, Herder [1964] 187 p. 22 cm. [BX2350.2.D66] 64-18770
1. Christian life — Catholic authors. I. Title.

DOTY, William Lodewick. 1919- 248.482
Virtues for our time. St. Louis, B. Herder [c.1964] 187p. 22cm. 64-18770 3.75
1. Christian life—Catholic authors. I. Title.

DURRWELL, F X 248.482
In the redeeming Christ; toward a theology of spirituality, Translated by Rosemary Sheed. New York, Sheed and Ward [1963] 292 p. 22 cm. [BX2350.5.D813] 63-8545
1. Spiritual life—Catholic authors. I. Title.

DURRWELL, F. X. 248.482
In the redeeming Christ; toward a theology of spirituality. Tr. [from French] by Rosemary Sheed. New York, Sheed [c.1963] 292p. 22cm. 63-8545 5.00
1. Spiritual life—Catholic authors. I. Title.

EBERSCHWEILER, William 248.482
Stand strong in the Lord; spiritual conferences on the interior life. Tr. by Mary Aloysi Kiener. Foreword by Martin B. Hellriegel. Staten Island, N.Y., Alba House [dist. St. Paul Pubns., 1962] 348p. 21cm. 62-17038 4.00
1. Spiritual life—Catholic authors. I. Title.

ELBEE, Jean d'. 248'.48'2
I believe in love : retreat conferences on the interior life / Jean du Coeur de Jesus d'Elbee ; translated from the French by Marilyn Teichert, with Madeleine Stebbins. Chicago : Franciscan Herald Press, [1974] p. cm. Translation of Croire a l'amour. [BX2350.2.E413] 74-20671 ISBN 0-8199-0555-0
1. Spiritual life—Catholic authors. I. Title.

ESCRIVA, Jose Maria. 248.4'8'2
Woman today; an interview with Msgr. Josemaria Escriva. Chicago, Scepter, [1969] 67 p. illus., ports. 16 cm. (Scepter booklet, 15) A translation of an interview which appeared in Telva, Jan. 1968. [BX2250.E8] 77-79794 0.50
1. Conduct of life. 2. Marriage—Catholic Church. I. Title.

ESSER, Kajetan, 1913- 248.482
Love's reply, by Cajetan Esser and Engelbert Grau. Translated by Ignatius Brady. Chicago, Franciscan Herald Press [1963] 258 p. 21 cm. [BX3603.E783] 62-21883
1. Asceticism — Catholic Church. 2. Franciscans. I. Grau, Engelbert, joint author. II. Title.

ESSER, Kajetan, 1913- 248.482
Love's reply, by Cajetan Esser, Engelbert Grau. Tr. [from German] by Ignatius Brady. Chicago, Franciscan Herald [c.1963] 258p. 21cm. 62-21883 4.95
1. Asceticism—Catholic Church. 2. Franciscans. I. Grau, Engelbert, joint author. II. Title.

EVELY, Louis, 1910- 248'.48'2
In the Christian spirit. Translated by Brian and Marie-Claude Thompson. Garden City, N.Y., Image Books, 1975 [c1969] p. cm. Translation of Une spiritualite laics. Reprint of the ed. published by Herder and Herder, New York. [BX2350.2.E8613 1975] 74-8532 ISBN 0-385-06266-4 1.45 (pbk.)
1. Christian life—Catholic authors. I. Title.

EVELY, Louis, 1910- 248.4'8'2
A religion for our time. Translated by Brian and Marie-Claude Thompson. [New York] Herder and Herder [1968] 112 p. 21 cm. Translation of Une religion pour notre temps. [BR121.2.E9313] 68-9266
1. Christianity—20th century. I. Title.

EVELY, Louis, 1910- 248.4'8'2
A religion for our time. Tr. by Brian and Marie-Claude Thompson. Garden City, N.Y. Doubleday [1974, c1968] 106 p. 18 cm. (Image books) [BR121.2E9313] ISBN 0-385-03021-5 1.45 (pbk.)
1. Christianity—20th century. I. Title.
L.C. card number for original ed.: 68-9266.

EVELY, Louis, 1910- 248.482
That man is you. Translated by Edmond Bonin. Westminster, Md., Newman Press, 1964. xv, 297 p. 23 cm. [BX2183.E913] 63-23494
1. Meditations. I. Title.

EVELY, Louis, 1910- 248.4'8'2
We are all brothers. Tr. by Sister Mary Agnes. [New York] Herder & Herder [1967] 108p. 21cm. Tr. of Fraternite et evangile. [BX2350.2.E8513] 67-13297 3.50
1. Spiritual life—Catholic authors. I. Title.

EVELY, Louis, 1910- 248'.48'2
We are all brothers. Translated by Sister Mary Agnes. Garden City, N.Y., Image Books, 1975 [c1967] 119 p. 18 cm. (Image, D 347) Translation of Fraternite et evangile. Reprint of the ed. published by Herder and Herder, New York. [BX2350.2.E8513 1975] 74-8533 ISBN 0-385-04830-0 1.45 (pbk.)
1. Spiritual life—Catholic authors. I. Title.

FENELON, Francois de Salignac de La Mothe- Abp., 1651-1715. 248'.48'2
Let go; living by the cross and by faith, by Fenelon. [Monroeville, Pa.] Banner Pub. [1973] 87 p. 18 cm. [BX2183.F4L65 1973] 73-81101 ISBN 0-88368-010-6 0.95 (pbk.)
1. Christian life—Catholic authors. I. Title.

FITZPATRICK, James Joseph, 1925- 248.482
A new Pentecost, by James Fitzpatrick. St. Louis, B. Herder Book Co. [1966] xii, 208 p. 21 cm. [BX2350.2.F5] 66-17939
1. Christian life — Catholic authors. 2. Catholic Church — Addresses, essays, lectures. I. Title.

FITZPATRICK, James Joseph, 1925- 248.482
A new Pentecost. St. Louis, B. Herder [c.1966] xii, 208p. 21cm. [BX2350.2.F5] 66-17939 4.50
1. Christian life—Catholic authors. 2. Catholic Church—Addresses, essays, lectures. I. Title.

*FOLLOWING SAINT FRANCIS; NO. 5-- 248.482
Stewardship. Pulaski, Wis., Franciscan Pubs. [c.1966] 48p. 19cm. .25 pap.,
I. Title.

*FORD, John H. 248.482
Husband and father. Abbey Pr. [dist. New York, Guild Pr., 850 Third Ave., c.1965] 112p. 17cm. (Marriage paperback lib., 20011) .50 pap.,
1. Christian life—Catholic authors. I. Title.

FRANCOIS DE SAINTE MARIE, Father 248.482
The simple steps to God. [Translator: Harold Evans] Wilkes-Barre, Pa., Dimension Books [1963] 153 p. 21 cm. (The Carmel series on Christian life, v. 1) Translation of Presence a Dieu et a sol-meme. Bibliographical footnotes. [BX2350.F733] 63-20361
1. Spiritual life — Catholic authors. 2. God — Worship and love. I. Title. II. Series.

FRANCOIS DE SAINT MARIE, Father [secular name: Francois Liffort de Buffevent] 248.482
The simple steps to God. [Tr. from French by Harold Evans] Wilkes-Barre, Pa., P O. Box 21 Dimension Bks., [c.1963] 153p. 21cm. (Carmel ser. on Christian life, v.1) Bibl. 63-20361 3.50 bds.,
1. Spiritual life—Catholic authors. 2. God—Worship and love. I. Title. II. Series.

FUCHS, Josef, 1912- 248'.48'2
Human values and Christian morality. [Translated from the German by M. H. Heelan and others. Dublin] Gill and Macmillan [1971, c1970] viii, 203 p. 21 cm. Contents.Contents.—Moral theology according to Vatican II.—The Christian morality of Vatican II.—The law of Christ.—Basic freedom and morality.—Human, humanist, and Christian morality.—Moral theology and dogmatic theology.—On the theology of human progress. Includes bibliographical references. [BX1758.2.F76 1971] 72-184336 ISBN 0-7171-0269-6 £1.80
1. Christian ethics—Catholic authors. I. Title.

FUSCO, Joseph P. 248.4'8'2
Challenge to love, by Joseph P. Fusco. Philadelphia, Coleman [1969] viii, 210 p. 23 cm. Bibliography: p. 205. [BX2350.2.F8] 77-97713 5.95
1. Christian life—Catholic authors. I. Title.

GALLAGHER, Joseph. 248.4'8'2
The Christian under pressure. Notre Dame, Ind., Ave Maria Press, [1970] 160 p. 21 cm. [BX2350.2.G32] 76-105099 4.50
1. Christian life—Catholic authors. I. Title.

GARA, Matthew 248.4'8'2
Hey- lets talk it over! considerations for Catholic teens. Illus. by Dorothy Koch. North Easton, Mass., Holy Cross Pr. [1967] 111p. illus. 27cm. [BX2373.S8G32] 67-25213 3.00
1. Students—Religious life. 2. Christian life—Catholic authors. I. Title.

GEANEY, Dennis J. 248.482
The search for dialogue; parents, teachers and teenagers [by] Dennis J. Geaney. Notre Dame, Ind., Fides Publishers [1966] 157 p. 18 cm. (A Fides dome book, D-48) [BJ1661.G35] 66-20180
1. Youth—Conduct of life. 2. Christian ethics—Catholic authors. I. Title.

*GEBHARDT. G. 248.482
Handbook for Catholic parents. Tr. from German by Stephen Deacon. Staten Island, N. Y., Alba [1966] 126p. 18cm. 1.00 pap.,
I. Title.

GIBBARD, Mark. 248'.48'2
Apprentices in love. New York, Morehouse-Barlow Co. [1974] 129 p. 21 cm. Bibliography: p. 129. [BX2350.2.G49] 73-89355 ISBN 0-8192-1166-4 4.25
1. Christian life—Catholic authors. I. Title.

GLEASON, Robert W., comp. 248.4'8'2
Contemporary spirituality; current problems in religious life. Edited by Robert W. Gleason. New York, Macmillan [1968] viii, 343 p. 21 cm. Bibliographical references included in "Notes" (p. 317-343) [BX2350.2.G62] 68-15937
1. Spiritual life—Catholic authors. I. Title.

GOSLING, Justin Cyril Bertrand. 248.482
Marriage and the love of God [by] J. Gosling. New York, Sheed and Ward [1965] v, 162 p. 21 cm. [BX2350.8.G6] 65-19198
1. Marriage. 2. Married people — Religious life. I. Title.

GOSLING, Justin Cyril Bertrand 248.482
Marriage and the love of God. New York, Sheed [c.1965] v, 162p. 21cm. [BX2350.8.G6] 65-19198 3.50 bds.,
1. Marriage. 2. Married people—Religious life. I. Title.

GRANDMAISON, Leonce de, 1868-1927. 248.482
Send forth thy spirit. Selection of texts and introd. by M. Danielou. Translated by M. Angeline Bouchard. Notre Dame, Ind., Fides Publishers [c1962] 111 p. 21 cm. Translation of La vie interleure de l' apotre. [BX2350.5.G713] 62-20574
1. Spiritual life — Catholic authors. I. Title.

GREELEY, Andrew M., 1928- 248.4'8'2
Life for a wanderer [by] Andrew M. Greeley. [1st ed.] Garden City, N.Y., Doubleday, 1969. 168 p. 22 cm. [BX2350.2.G73] 70-78701 4.95
1. Spiritual life—Catholic authors. I. Title.

GREELEY, Andrew M., 1928- 248.4'8'2
The touch of the spirit [by] Andrew Greeley. New York, Herder and Herder [1971] 137 p. 22 cm. [BX2350.2.G74] 78-150311 4.50
1. Christian life—Catholic authors. 2. Holy Spirit. I. Title.

GRYGLAK, Michael A. 248.4'8'2
Flower hill; human failures and spiritual triumphs. Conferences to nuns, by Michael A. Gryglak. Translated by Edward P. Gicewicz and Ladislaus J. Kaminski. New York, Ozas Pub. Co. [1969] 159 p. 24 cm. [BX2350.2.G7813] 72-83582
1. Christian life—Catholic authors. I. Title.

GUARDINI, Romano, 1885- 248.482
The life of faith. [Translation by John Chapin] Westminster, Md., Newman Press [1961] 131p. 20cm. [BT771.2.G813] 61-3534
1. Faith. 2. Christian life—Catholic authors. I. Title.

GUARDINI, Romano, 1885- 248.482
The life of faith. [Tr. by John Chapin] Glen Rock, N.J., Paulist Pr. [1963, c.1961] 127p. 19cm. (Deus bks.) 63-20218 .75 pap.,
1. Faith. 2. Christian life—Catholic authors. I. Title.

GUELLUY, Robert. 248.4'8'2
Tune in to God. Translated from the third French ed. by Michael C. O'Brien. Pref. by C. M. Himmer. New York, Desclee Co., [1967] 267 p. 22 cm. $4.50 Translation of A L ecoute de Dieu. [BX2350.2.G833] 68-13687
1. Christian life—Catholic authors. I. Title.

GUELLUY, Robert. 248.4'8'2
Tune in to God. Translated from the third French ed. by Michael C. O'Brien. Pref. by C. M. Himmer. New York, Desclee Co. [1967] 267 p. 22 cm. Translation of A l'ecoute de Dieu. [BX2350.2.G833] 68-13687 4.50
1. Christian life—Catholic authors. I. Title.

HABIG, Marion Alphonse, 248.482
1901-
Franciscan pictorial book. With drawings by Phero Thomas, Frank Kelly Freas, and Jose Cisneros. Chicago, Franciscan Herald Press [1963-66] 2 v. illus. 23 cm. Vol. 2 has title: Franciscan pictorial book two, by Marion A. Habig and Albert J. Nimeth. [BX2182.2.H3] 63-12852
1. Catholic Church—Prayer-books and devotions—English. I. Nimeth, Albert J., joint author. II. Title.

HABIG, Marion Alphonse 248.482
[secular name: Jchn Alphonse Habig] 1901-
Franciscan pictorial; book two, by Marion A. Habig, Albert J. Nimeth. Drawings by Phero Thomas, Frank Kelly Freas, Jose Cisneros. Chicago, Franciscan Herald [1966] 104p. illus. 23cm. [BX2182.2.H3] 63-12852 2.25 pap.,
1. Catholic Church—Prayer-books andd devotions—English. I. Title.

HABIG, Marion Alphonse 248.482
[Secular name: John Alphonse Habig] 1901-
Franciscan pictorial book. Drawings by Phero Thomas, Frank Kelly Freas, Jose Cisneros. Chicago, Franciscan [c.1963] 112p. illus. 23cm. 63-12852 .95 pap.,
1. Catholic Church—Prayer-books and devotions—English. I. Title.

HAES, Paul de 248.482
On earth as it is in Heaven. Tr. [from Flemish] by Martin W. Schoenberg. Notre Dame, Ind., Fides, 1966. xiii, 287p. 21cm. [BX2350.2.H3313] 65-23116 5.95
1. Christian life—Catholic authors. I. Title.

HANLEY, Philip L. 248.482
The life of the Mystical body: the church, grace, and the sacraments. Westminster, Md., Newman Press [c.]1961. 378p. Bibl. 60-14827 4.95
1. Jesus Christ—Mystical body. I. Title.

†HARDON, John A. 248'.48'2
Holiness in the church / by John A. Hardon. Boston : St. Paul Editions, c1976. 179 p. : ill. ; 18 cm. [BX2350.2.H354] 76-15371 3.50 pbk. : 2.50
1. Spiritual life—Catholic authors—Addresses, essays, lectures. 2. Holiness—Addresses, essays, lectures. 3. Monastic and religious life—Addresses, essays, lectures. I. Title.

HARING, Bernhard, 1912- 248.4'8'2
Christian maturity [by] Bernard Haring. Tr. by Arlene Swidler. [New York] Herder & Herder [1967] 188p. 22cm. Tr. of Die gegenwartige Heilsstunde. second half. Bibl. [BX2350.2.H3214] 67-14145 4.95
1. Christian life—Catholic authors. I. Title.

HARING, Bernhard, 1912- 248.4'8'2
Christian maturity [by] Bernard Haring. Translated by Arlene Swidler. [New York] Herder and Herder [1967] 188 p. 22 cm. Translation of Die gegenwartige Heilastunde, second half. Bibliographical footnotes. [BX2350.2.H3214] 67-14145
1. Christian life — Catholic authors. I. Title.

HARING, Bernhard, 248.4'8'2
1912-
Christian renewal in a changing world, by Bernard Haring. Translated by M. Lucidia Haring. [Rev. and updated ed.] Garden City, N.Y., Image Books [1968] 433 p. 19 cm. Translation of Christ in einer neuen Welt. [BX2350.2.H313 1968] 68-7135 1.45
1. Christian life—Catholic authors. I. Title.

HARING, Bernhard, 1912- 248.482
This time of salvation. Translated by Arlene Swidler. [New York] Herder and Herder [1966] 252 p. 22 cm. Translation of Die gegenwartige Heilsstunde, first half. Bibliographical footnotes. [BX2350.2.H3213] 66-16947
1. Christian life—Catholic authors. I. Title.

HARING, Bernhard, 1912- 248.482
Toward a Christian moral theology [by] Bernard Haring. [Notre Dame, Ind.] University of Notre Dame Press, 1966. viii, 230 p. 22 cm. (The Cardinal O'Hara series. Studies and research in Christian theology at Notre Dame, v. 2) [BX1758.2.H32] 66-15502
1. Christian ethics—Catholic authors. I. Title. II. Title: A Christian moral theology. III. Series: The Cardinal O'Hara series

HAYES, Edward J. 248'.48'2
Catholicism & life / Edward J. Hayes, Paul J. Hayes. Huntington, Ind. : Our Sunday Visitor, 1976. 264 p. : ill. ; 21 cm. & teacher's manual. Includes index. Bibliography: p. 258-261. [BX930.H38] 76-6212 ISBN 0-87973-869-3 pbk. : 4.95
1. Christian education—Text-books for young people—Catholic. 2. Commandments, Ten—Study and teaching. 3. Sacraments—Catholic Church—Study and teaching. I. Hayes, Paul James, 1922- joint author. II. Title.

HAYES, Edward J. 248'.48'2
Catholicism & society / Edward J Hayes Paul J Hayes & James J Drummey Huntington, Ind. : Our Sunday Visitor, c1975. 223 p. : ill. ; 21 cm. & teacher's manual. Includes index. Bibliography: p. [217]-221. [BX1758.2.H38] 75-21600 ISBN 0-87973-859-6 pbk. : 4.95
1. Christian ethics—Catholic authors. 2. Family. 3. Church and social problems—Catholic Church. I. Hayes, Paul James, 1922- joint author. II. Drummey, James J., joint author. III. Title.

HEAGLE, John. 248'.48'2
Our journey toward God / by John Heagle. Chicago : Thomas More Press, c1977. 179 p. ; 22 cm. Includes bibliographical references. [BX2350.2.H366] 77-152311 ISBN 0-88347-071-3 : 8.95
1. Christian life—Catholic authors. 2. Spirituality. 3. Paschal mystery. I. Title.

HERMAN, Nicolas, 1611- 248.482
1691.
The practice of the presence of God, by Brother Lawrence. [Conversations and letters] With illus. by Jeff Hill. Mount Vernon, N. Y., Peter Pauper Press [c1963] 62 p. col. illus. 19 cm. "The conversations were said to have been written by M. Beaufort." Name in religion: Laurent de la Resurrection, Brother. [BX2349.H42 1963] 63-25473
1. Christian life — Catholic authors. I. Beaufort, Joseph de. II. Title.

HERMAN, Nicolas, 1611- 248'.48'2
1691.
The practice of the presence of God / by Brother Lawrence of the Resurrection [i.e. N. Herman] ; newly translated with an introd. by John J. Delaney. Garden City, N.Y. : Image Books, 1977. 112 p. ; 18 cm. Translation of La pratique de la presence de Dieu. [BX2349.H42 1977] 77-70896 ISBN 0-385-12861-4 pbk. : 2.25
1. Christian life—Catholic authors. I. Delaney, John J. II. Title.

HERMAN, Nicolas, 1611- 248.4'8'2
1691.
The spiritual maxims of Brother Lawrence. Westwood, N.J., Revell [1967] 60 p. 17 cm. (A Revell inspirational classic) Contents.Contents.—Spiritual maxims.—The character of Brother Lawrence; being the teaching of his life, by the chronicler of the conversations.—Gathered thoughts, compiled from the Life of Brother Lawrence. [BX2349.H44] 67-11074
1. Christian life—Catholic authors. I. Title.

HERMAN, Nicolas [Name in 248.482
religion: Laurent de la Resurrection, Brother] 1611-1691
The practice of the presence of God, by Brother Lawrence. Illus. by Jeff Hill. Mount Vernon, N. Y., Peter Pauper [c.1963] 62p. illus. (pt. col.) 19cm. 1.00 bds.,
1. Spiritual life—Catholic authors. I. Title.

HERTSENS, Marcel. 248.482
Lord, your servant listens. Translated by Sister M. Innocentia. Pref. by L. J. Cardinal Suenens. Westminister, Md., Newman Press, 1964. xiv, 194 p. 21 cm. [BX2183.H443] 64-15403
1. Meditations. I. Title.

HERTSENS, Marcel 248.482
Lord, your servant listens. Tr. [from French] by Sister M. Innocentia. Pref. by L. J. Cardinal Suenens. Westminster, Md., Newman [c.]1964. xiv, 194p. 21cm. 64-15403 3.95
1. Meditations. I. Title.

HIGGINS, Nicholas. 248.482
As pilgrims and strangers. New York, P. J. Kenedy [1961] 213p. 21cm. [BX2350.2.H5] 60-14109
1. Spiritual life—Catholic authors. I. Title.

HINNEBUSCH, Paul. 248'.48'2
Community in the Lord / Paul Hinnebusch. Notre Dame, Ind. : Ava Maria Press, c1975. 240 p. ; 21 cm. [BX2350.2.H517] 75-14741 ISBN 0-87793-098-8 : 5.95 ISBN 0-87793-099-6 pbk. : 3.50
1. Christian life—Catholic authors. 2. Christian communities. I. Title.

HINNEBUSCH, Paul. 248'.48'2
Friendship in the Lord. Notre Dame, Ind., Ave Maria Press [1974] 144 p. 21 cm. [BJ1533.F8H5] 73-90411 ISBN 0-87793-064-3 2.25 (pbk.)
1. Friendship. 2. Christian life—Catholic authors. I. Title.

HINNEBUSCH, Paul. 248.482
Salvation history and the religious life. New York, Sheed and Ward [1966] viii, 248 p. 22 cm. Bibliographical footnotes. [BX2350.2.H52] 66-22016
1. Christian life — Catholic authors. I. Title.

HOFFMAN, Dominic M. 248'.48'2
Maturing the spirit; a continuation of spiritual growth for contemporary men and women [by] Dominic M. Hoffman. [Boston] St. Paul Editions [1973] 357 p. 22 cm. [BX2350.2.H584] 73-77628 5.00
1. Spiritual life—Catholic authors. I. Title.

HOFFMAN, Dominic M., 248.4'8'2
1913-
Beginnings in spiritual life [by] Dominic M. Hoffman. [1st ed.] Garden City, N.Y., Doubleday, 1967. 333 p. 22 cm. [BX2350.2.H58] 67-10356
1. Spiritual life—Catholic authors. I. Title.

HOFFMAN, Dominic M., 248.482
1913-
The life within; the prayer of union, by Dominic M. Hoffman. New York, Sheed [1966] xi, 242p. 22cm. [BX2350.5.H6] 66-12276 4.50
1. Spiritual life—Catholic authors. I. Title.

HORATCZUK, Michael. 248.482
God is for everybody. Translated by Bruce Cook. Notre Dame, Ind., Fides Publishers [1964] 115 p. 21 cm. Translation of Lahme gehen zu Gott. [BX2350.2.H613] 64-23517
1. Christian life — Catholic authors. I. Title.

HORATCZUK, Michael 248.482
God is for everybody. Tr. [from German] by Bruce Cook. Notre Dame, Ind., Fides [c.1964] 115p. 21cm. 64-23517 2.95
1. Christian life—Catholic authors. I. Title.

INFORMATION (New York) 248.482
Personal problems; a selection of articles from Information magazine, edited by Kevin A. Lynch. New York, Deus Books, Paulist Press [1961] 128p. 19cm. [HN37.C3I48] 61-8817
1. Church and social problems—Catholic Church. I. Lynch, Kevin A., ed. II. Title.

IRALA, Narciso. 248'.48'2
Achieving peace of heart. Translated by Lewis Delmage. Rev. and enl. St. Meinrad, Ind., Abbey Press, 1973 [c1969] 254 p. illus. 18 cm. (A Priority edition) Translation of Control cerebral y emocional. Includes bibliographical references. [BF637.P3I713 1973] 73-157907 1.95 (pbk.)
1. Peace of mind. I. Title.

JEAN de Saint-Samson, 248'.48'2
Brother, 1571-1636.
Prayer, aspiration, and contemplation : [selections] from the writings of John of St. Samson, O. Carm., mystic and charismatic / translated and edited by Venard Poslusney. Staten Island, N.Y. : Alba House, [1975] vi, 212 p. : port. ; 21 cm. Bibliography: p. [211]-212. [BX2349.J4513] 74-30340 ISBN 0-8189-0300-7 pbk. : 3.95
1. Jean de Saint-Samson, Brother, 1571-1636. 2. Spiritual life—Catholic authors—Collected works. 3. Prayer—Collected works. 4. Contemplation—Collected works. I. Poslusney, Venard, ed. II. Title.

JUNGMANN, Josef Andreas, 248.482
1889-
The good news yesterday and today. Tr. [from German] abridged, ed. by William A. Huesman from Fr. Jungmann's The good news and our proclamation of the faith. Essays in appraisal of its contribution. General ed.: Johannes Hofinger. New York, Sadlier [1963, c.1962] xii, 228p. 21cm. Bibl. 63-25477 4.75; 1.95 pap.,
1. Kerygma. 2. Religious education. 3. Christian life—Catholic authors. I. Title.

*KELLER, James 248.482
Three minutes a day; v.7 [by] James Keller, Richard Armstrong. The Christophers [dist. New York, Guild Pr., 850 Third Ave., c.1964] xv, 365p. 17cm. (Christopher bks., 40011) .50 pap.,
1. Christian life—Catholic authors. I. Title.

KELLER, James Gregory, 248.482
1900-
Change the world from your parish. New York, Guild Pr., dist. Golden Pr. [c.1961] 468p. (Christopher handbk., 31163) 61-2815 .75 pap.,
1. Christian life-Catholic authors. I. Title.

KELLER, James Gregory, 248.482
1900-
Change the wrold from your parish. [St. Pall] Guild Press distributed by Golden Press, New York [1961] 468p. 17cm. (A Christopher handbook) [BX2350.2.K43] 61-2815
1. Christian life—Catholic authors. I. Title.

KELLY, Bernard J. 248.482
Joy in the spiritual life. Westminster, Md., Newman [1962] 167p. 62-2670 2.95
1. Spiritual life—Catholic authors. 2. Joy and sorrow. I. Title.

KELLY, George Anthony, 248.4'8'2
1916-
The Christian role in today's society [by] George A. Kelly. New York, Random House [1967] vii, 210 p. 22 cm. [BJ1249.K4] 66-21468
1. Christian ethics—Catholic authors. 2. Social ethics. I. Title.

KENNEDY, Eugene C. 248.4'8'2
In the spirit, in the flesh [by] Eugene C. Kennedy. Garden City, N.Y., Doubleday, 1971. 168 p. 22 cm. [BX2350.2.K46] 72-157604 4.95
1. Christian life—Catholic authors. I. Title.

KENNY, John J. 248'.48'2
Now that you are a Catholic, by John J. Kenny. New York, Paulist Press [1973] 98 p. illus. 18 cm. (Deus books) [BX2350.2.K464] 73-80417 ISBN 0-8091-1743-6 1.25
1. Christian life—Catholic authors. I. Title.

KIESLING, Cristopher. 248.4'8'2
Any news of God? [Dayton, Ohio] Pflaum [1971] iii, 107 p. illus. 17 cm. (Christian experience series: witness book, 16) Includes bibliographies. [BX2350.2.K48] 74-153801 0.95
1. Christian life—Catholic authors. I. Title.

KILLGALLON, James, 1914- 248.482
Beyond the commandments [by] James Killgallon, Gerard Weber [New York] Herder & Herder [c.1964] 224p. 21cm. 64-13687 3.95
1. Christian life—Catholic authors. I. Weber, Gerard p., 1918- joint author. II. Title.

KILLGALLON, James J 1914- 248.482
Beyond the commandments [by] James Killgallon [and] Gerald Weber. [New York] Herder and Herder [1964] 224 p. 21 cm. [BX2350.2.K5] 64-13687
1. Christian life — Catholic authors. I. Weber, Gerard P., 1918- joint author. II. Title.

KILLGALLON, James J 248.4'8'2
1914-
Beyond the commandments [by] James Killgallon [and] Gerard Weber. [Rev. ed. New York] Herder and Herder [1968] 219 p. 21 cm. $2.45 [BX2350.2.K5] 68-6030
1. Christian life—Catholic authors. I. Weber, Gerard p., 1918- joint author. II. Title.

KILLGALLON, James J., 248.482
1914-
Beyond the commandments [by] James Killgallon, Gerard Weber. [Rev. ed.] New York Herder & Herder [1968] 219p. 21cm. [BX2350.2.K5] 64-13687 2.45 pap.,
1. Christian life—Catholic authors. I. Weber, Gerard P., 1918- joint author. II. Title.

KOSICKI, George W., 248.4'8'2
1928-
Like a cedar of Lebanon; a biochemist looks at images of life and light [by] George W. Kosicki. New York, Sheed [1967 c.1966] 126p. 21cm. [BX2350.2.K6] 67-13757 3.50
1. Christian life—Catholic authors. I. Title.

KUCHAREK, Casimir. 248'.48'2
To settle your conscience [by] Cass Kucharek. Huntington, IN, Our Sunday Visitor, inc. [1974] 262 p. 23 cm. [BX1758.2.K8] 73-91902 ISBN 0-87973-877-4 3.95 (pbk.).
1. Commandments, Ten. 2. Christian ethics—Catholic authors. I. Title.

LANGE, Joseph. 248'.48'2
Called to service / by Joseph Lange and Anthony J. Cushing. Pecos, N.M. : Dove Publications, c1976. vi, 168 p. ; 22 cm. (The Living Christian community series ; v. 4) Includes bibliographies. [BX2350.2.L24 1976] 75-41813 ISBN 0-8091-1921-8 pbk. : 3.95
1. Christian life—Catholic authors. 2. Christian communities. I. Cushing, Anthony J., joint author. II. Title.

LANGE, Joseph. 248'.48'2
Freedom and healing / by Joseph Lange and Anthony J. Cushing. Pecos, N.M. : Dove Publications, c1976. v, 101 p. ; 22 cm. (The Living Christian community series ; v. 3) Includes bibliographies. [BX2350.2.L257] 75-40648 ISBN 0-8091-1920-X pbk. : 3.95
1. Christian life—Catholic authors. I. Cushing, Anthony J., joint author. II. Title.

LANGE, Joseph. 248'.48'2
Friendship with Jesus / by Joseph Lange and Anthony J. Cushing. Pecos, N.M. : Dove Publications, c1974. viii, 208 p. ; 22 cm. (The

Living Christian community series ; v. 1) Includes bibliographies. [BX2350.2.L26] 75-328402 3.95
1. Christian life—Catholic authors. I. Cushing, Anthony J., joint author. II. Title.

LANGE, Joseph. 248'.48'2
Worshipping community / by Joseph Lange and Anthony J. Cushing. Pecos, N.M. : Dove Publications, c1975. vii, 142 p. ; 22 cm. (Living Christian community series ; v. 2) Bibliography: p. 141-142. [BX2350.2.L28] 75-34841 ISBN 0-8091-1919-6 : 3.95
1. Christian life—Catholic authors. 2. Church. 3. Lord's Supper—Catholic Church. I. Cushing, Anthony J., joint author. II. Title.

LARSEN, Earnest. 248'.48'2
The gift of power. New York, Paulist Press [1974] 124 p. 18 cm. (Paulist Press/Deus books) [BX2350.2.L36] 74-76715 ISBN 0-8091-1833-5 1.45 (pbk.).
1. Christian life—Catholic authors. I. Title.

LARSEN, Earnest. 248'.48'2
Something wonderful is happening / by Earnest Larsen. N[ew] Y[ork] : Paulist Press, c1977. 80 p. ; 18 cm. (Emmaus books) [BX2350.2.L37] 76-24443 ISBN 0-8091-1987-0 pbk. : 1.45
1. Christian life—Catholic authors. I. Title.

LE Sage, Wilfred, 1907- 248.4'8'2
Vision of renewal; an aggiornamento. [Boston] St. Paul Editions [1967] 468 p. 19 cm. [BX2350.2.L44] 67-17697
1. Christian life — Catholic authors. I. Title.

LECLERCG, Jacques, 1891- 248.482
Christians in the world. Tr. [from French] by Kathleen Pond. New York, Sheed & Ward [c.1961] 174p. 61-8502 3.50 bds.,
1. Christian life—Catholic authors. I. Title.

LECLERCQ, Jacques, 1891- 248.482
Christians in the world. Translated by Kathleen Pond. New York, Sheed & Ward [1961] 174p. 21cm. Translation of Vivre chretiennement notre temps. [BX2350.2.L433] 61-8502
1. Christian life—Catholic authors. I. Title.

LECLERCQ, Jacques, 1891- 248.482
The interior life. Tr. [from French] by Fergus Murphy. New York, P. J. Kenedy [c.1961] 191p. 61-9449 3.95
1. Spiritual life—Catholic authors. I. Title.

LEKEUX, Martial, 1884- 248.482
ed. and tr.
Short cut to divine love. Texts collected, tr. and arr. in order by Martial Lekeux. Chicago, Franciscan Herald [c.1962] 320p. 21cm. 61-11203 4.95
1. Spiritual life—Catholic authors. I. Title.

LEPP, Ignace, 1909- 248.4'8'2
1966.
The challenges of life. [Translated by Dorothy White] Staten Island, N.Y., Alba House [1969] xiv, 210 p. 22 cm. (Mental health series, 12) Translation of Wagnisse des Daseins. [BJ1583.L5513] 75-90776 4.95
1. Conduct of life. I. Title.

LE SAGE, Wilfred, 1907- 248.4'8'2
Vision of renewal; an aggiornamento. [Boston] St. Paul Eds. [1967] 468p. 19cm. [BX2350.2.L44] 67-17697 4.00
1. Christian life—Catholic authors. I. Title.

LIGUORI, Alfonso Maria 248.482
de', Saint.
The way of St. Alphonsus Liguori. Ed. with an introd. by Barry Ulanov. New York, P. J. Kenedy [c.1961] 367p. 60-14645 4.95
1. Spiritual life—Catholic authors. I. Title.

LIGUORI, Alfonso Maria 248.482
de', Saint, 1696-1787.
The way of St. Alphonsus Liguori. Edited with an introd. by Barry Ulanov. New York, P. J. Kenedy [1961] 367p. 17cm. [BX2349.L5] 60-14645
1. Spiritual life—Catholic authors. I. Ulanov, Barry, ed. II. Title.

LORD, Daniel Aloysuis, 248.4'8'2
1888-1955.
Letters to my Lord. Edited by Thomas Gavin. [New York] Herder and Herder [1969] 121 p. 21 cm. [BX2350.2.L64 1969] 76-87759 4.50
1. Spiritual life—Catholic authors. I. Title.

†LUBICH, Chiara, 1920- 248'.48'2
Jesus in the midst : four talks / by Chiara Lubich ; [translated from the original Italian ed. Dove due o piu by the editorial staff of New City Press]. New York : New City Press, [c1976] 86 p. ; 19 cm. Includes bibliographical references. [BX2350.2.L7713] 76-18455 ISBN 0-911782-26-5 pbk. : 1.35
1. Christian life—Catholic authors. I. Title.

LUFF, S. G. A. 248.482
The breezes of the Spirit. Westminster, Md., Newman [c.1964] 112p. 22cm. 64-6058 2.95
1. Christian life—Catholic authors. I. Title.

LUFF, Stanley George 248.482
Anthony.
The breezes of the Spirit [by] S. G. A. Luff. Westminster, Md., Newman Press [1964] 112 p. 22 cm. [BX2350.2.L8] 64-6058
1. Christian life — Catholic authors. I. Title.

LUPO, Joseph F., 1919- 248'.48'2
The Trinitarian way / by Joseph F. Lupo ; drawings by Christian Blom. [Garrison, Md. : Order of the Most Holy Trinity], c1977. 32 p. : ill. ; 18 cm. Cover title: The little white book. [BX2350.2.L84] 77-150863 2.00
1. Christian life—Catholic authors. 2. Trinitarians. I. Title. II. Title: The little white book.

MCCAULEY, Michael F. 248'.48'2
On the run : spirituality for the seventies / edited by Michael F. McCauley. Chicago : Thomas More Press, [1974] 237 p. ; 22 cm. [BX2350.2.M23] 74-188853 ISBN 0-88347-042-X : 7.95
1. Spiritual life—Catholic authors. I. Title.

MCGLOIN, Joseph T. 248.482
Burn a little! or, What's love all about? Illus. by Don Baumgart. Milwaukee, Bruce [c.1961] 144p. illus. (His Love--and live, bk. 3) 61-17982 1.50 pap.,
1. Spiritual life—Catholic authors. I. Title.

MCGLOIN, Joseph T. 248.482
Learn a little! or, What's life all about? Illus. by Don Baumgart. Milwaukee, Bruce [c.1961] 97p. (His Love--and live, bk. 1) 61-17980 1.25 pap.,
1. Youth—Religious life. 2. Christian life—Catholic authors. I. Title.

MCGLOIN, Joseph T 248.482
Learn a little! or, What's life all about? Illustrated by Don Baumgart. Milwaukee, Bruce Pub. Co. [1961] 97p. illus. 21cm. (His Love--and live, book 1) [BX2355.M2] 61-17980
1. Youth—Religious life. 2. Christian life—Catholic authors. I. Title.

MCGLOIN, Joseph T. 248'.48'2
The solid gold crucifix [by] Joseph T. McGloin. Illustrated by Don Baumgart. Liguori, Mo., Liguori Publications [1972] iv, 124 p. illus. 18 cm. [BX2350.2.M252] 72-79091 1.50
1. Christian life—Catholic authors. I. Title.

MCGLOIN, Joseph T. 248.4'8'2
That's the old spirit! [By] Joseph T. McGloin. Illustrated by Don Baumgart. Liguori, Mo., Liguorian Books [1970] 207 p. illus. 18 cm. First ed. published in 1959 under title: Call me Joe! [BX2350.2.M25 1970] 73-134472 1.25
1. Christian life—Catholic authors. I. Title.

*MCGLOIN, Joseph T. 248.482
Working to beat hell. Drawings by Don Baumgart. Pulaski, Wis., Franciscan Pubs. [1966, c.1965] 78p. illus. 19cm. .25 pap.,
I. Title.

*MCGOWAN, Kilian 248.482
Your way to God. Westminster, Md., Newman, 1965. 202p. 18cm. 1.50 pap.,
I. Title.

MCHUGH, Patrick J. 248.4'8'2
Living the Christian life, by P. J. McHugh. Milwaukee, Bruce Pub. Co. [1967] vi, 250 p. 21 cm. [BX2350.2.M255] 67-24539
1. Christian life—Catholic authors. I. Title.

MCKEOWN, Francis J. 248.482
Maybe it is your attitude; a handbook for parents, teachers, and others, to be used as a basis for a correct, wholesome, complete, intelligent Christian attitude. New York, Vantage [c.1963] 117p. 21cm. 64-155 2.75 bds.,
1. Christian life—Catholic authors. I. Title.

MCMAHON, Edwin M., 248.4'8'2
1930-
Becoming a person in the whole Christ, by Edwin M. McMahon and Peter A. Campbell. New York, Sheed and Ward [1967] xiv, 306 p. 22 cm. [BX2350.5.M2] 67-13768
1. Spiritual life—Catholic authors. 2. Monastic and religious life—Psychology. I. Campbell, Peter A., 1935- joint author. II. Title.

MCNAMARA, William. 248.482
The art of being human. Milwaukee, Bruce Pub. Co. [1962] 164p. 22cm. [BX2350.2.M27] 62-20958
1. Spiritual life—Catholic authors. I. Title.

MCNAMARA, William. 248'.48'2
Mystical passion : spirituality for a bored society / by William McNamara. New York : Paulist Press, c1977. xi, 124 p. ; 23 cm. Includes bibliographical references. [BX2350.2.M276] 77-37378 pbk. : 4.95
1. Spiritual life—Catholic authors. 2. Emotions. I. Title.

MAGINNIS, Andrew. 248'.48'2
A priest to a nun; [correspondence between] Andrew Maginnis and Sister Catherine Mary. New York, Sheed and Ward [1972] 227 p. 21 cm. [BX2350.2.M313] 72-3850 ISBN 0-8362-0491-3 6.95
1. Christian life—Catholic authors. I. Catherine Mary, Sister, 1928-1966. II. Title.

MAGSAM, Charles M. 248'.48'2
The experience of God : outlines for a contemporary spirituality / Charles M. Magsam. Maryknoll, N.Y. : Orbis Books, [1975] vi, 238 p. ; 22 cm. Includes bibliographical references. [BX2350.2.M3133] 73-89314 ISBN 0-88344-123-3 : 7.95. ISBN 0-88344-124-1 pbk. : 4.95
1. Christian life—Catholic authors. I. Title.

MAGUIRE, Daniel C. 248'.48'2
Moral absolutes and the magisterium [by] Daniel Maguire. Washington [Corpus Publications, c1970] 59 p. 19 cm. (Corpus papers) Includes bibliographical references. [BX1758.2.M32] 70-135463 1.25
1. Catholic Church—Teaching office. 2. Christian ethics—Catholic authors. I. Title.

MARDUEL, Henri 248.482
The Christian pursuit. Foreword by Francis J. Ripley [Tr. from French by Daphne Knott-Bower, Angela de Hartog] New York, Kenedy [1965, c.1964] xv, 229p. 22cm. Bibl. [BX2350.2.M3413] 65-1133 4.50
1. Christian life—Catholic authors. I. Title.

MARMION, Columba, Abbot, 248.482
1858-1923
Growth of Christ; being the second part of Christ, the life of the soul. Tr. from French by a Nun of Tyburn Convent. St. Louis, B. Herder [1964] 160p. 19cm. Bibl. 64-1275 1.95 pap.,
1. Meditations. I. Title. II. Title: Christ, the life of the soul.

MARTELET, Gustave 248.482
The church's holiness and religious life. Tr. [from French] by Raymond L. Sullivant. St. Marys, Kan., 66536, Review for Religious. St. Mary's College [c.]1966. 124p. 20cm. Bibl. [BX2350.5.M293] 66-3721 2.50
1. Spiritual life—Catholic authors. 2. Manastic and religious life. 3. Church—Holiness. I. Title.

MEAGHER, Robert E. 248.4'8'2
Beckonings; moments of faith [by] Robert E. Meagher. Art interpretations by Molly Geissler Barrett. Philadelphia, Fortress Press [1969] vii, 88 p. illus. 20 cm. [BX2350.2.M39] 70-84541 2.95
1. Spiritual life—Catholic authors. I. Title.

MENARD, Eusebe M. 248'.48'2
At all times, in every age / E. M. Menard. Chicago : Franciscan Herald Press, [1977] p. cm. Translation of A toute heure. [BX1912.M4613] 77-23466 ISBN 0-8199-0663-8 : 5.95
1. Catholic Church—Clergy. 2. Christian life—Catholic authors. 3. Christianity—20th century. I. Title.

MERRY DEL VAL, Cardinal, 248.482
1865-1930
The spiritual diary of Raphael Cardinal Merry del Val, comp., ed. by Francis J. Weber. New York, Exposition [c.1964] 47p. port. 22cm. (Exposition-testament bk.) 64-56135 2.75
1. Spiritual life—Catholic authors. I. Weber, Francis J., ed. II. Title.

MERTON, Thomas, 1915- 248.482
Life and holiness. [New York] Herder and Herder [1963] 162 p. 21 cm. Name in religion: Father Louis. [BX2350.5.M37] 63-10691
1. Spiritual life — Catholic authors. I. Title.

MERTON, Thomas 1915- 248.482
Life and holiness. [New York] Herder & Herder [c.1963] 162p. 21cm. 63-10691 3.50
1. Spiritual life—Catholic authors. I. Title.

MERTON, Thomas 1915- 248.482
Life and holiness. Garden City, N.Y., Doubleday [1964, c.1963] 119p. 18cm. (Image bk. D183) .75 pap.,
1. Spiritual life—Catholic authors. I. Title.

MORE, Thomas, Saint,Sir 248.482
1478-1535
A dialogue of comfort against tribulation. Ed. for modern readers. Critical introd., notes by Leland Miles. Bloomington, Ind. Univ. Pr. [1966, c.1965] cxi, 301p. illus., ports. 21cm. Bibl. [BV4904.M62 1965] 66-26834 8.75
1. Consolation. I. Miles, Leland, ed. II. Title.

MORE, Sir Thomas, Saint 248.482
1478-1535.
A dialogue of comfort against tribulation. Ed. for modern readers. Critical introd., notes by Leland Miles. [Magnolia, Mass.] [Peter Smith] [1973, c1965] xi, 301 p. illus., 21 cm. (Indiana University paperback rebound) Includes Bibliographies. [BV4904.M62] 65-19701 ISBN 0-8446-4449-8 5.00
1. Consolation. I. Miles, Leland, ed. II. Title.

MORICE, Henri, 1873- 248.482
The apostolate of moral beauty. Translated by Sister Mary Lelia. St. Louis, Herder [1961] 142p. 21cm. [BX2350.2.M663] 61-17456
1. Spiritual life—Catholic authors. I. Title.

MORK, Wulstan. 248.482
A synthesis of the spiritual life. Milwaukee, Bruce Pub Co. [1962] 283p. 18cm. Includes bibliography. [BX2350.2.M68] 62-11166
1. Spiritual life—Catholic authors. I. Title.

MOTTE, Jean Francois, 248.482
1913-
The Catholic in the modern world. Translated by Paul J. Oligny. Chicago, Franciscan Herald Press [1963] 88 p. 22 cm. Translation of Presence a notre temps. [BX2350.2.M713] 63-12857
1. Christian life — Catholic authors. I. Title.

MOTTE, Jean Francois, 248.482
1913-
The Catholic in the modern world. Tr. [from French] by Paul J. Oligny. Chicago, Franciscan Herald [c.1963] 88p. 22cm. 63-12857 2.50
1. Christian life—Catholic authors. I. Title.

MULLIGAN, James J. 248'.48'2
The Christian experience [by] James J. Mulligan. New York, Alba House [1973] xii, 162 p. 22 cm. Includes bibliographical references. [BX2350.2.M84] 73-4005 ISBN 0-8189-0270-1 3.95
1. Spiritual life—Catholic authors. 2. Sacraments—Catholic Church. I. Title.

NIMETH, Albert J. 248.482
Instant inspiration, add only good will. Chicago, Franciscan Herald [c.1965] 278p. illus. 22cm. [BX2350.2.N5] 65-16672 3.95
1. Christian life—Catholic authors. I. Title.

NIMETH, Albert J 248.4'8'2
Sudden thoughts [by] Albert J. Nimeth. Chicago, Franciscan Herald Press [1967] ix, 260 p. illus., port. 21 cm. Bibliographical footnotes. [BX2350.2.N53] 67-31354
1. Christian life—Catholic authors. I. Title.

NIMETH, Albert J. 248.4'8'2
Sudden thoughts [by] Albert J. Nimeth. Chicago, Franciscan Herald Press [1967] ix, 260 p. illus., port. 21 cm. Bibliographical footnotes. [BX2350.2.N53] 67-31354
1. Christian life—Catholic authors. I. Title.

NOVAK, Michael. 248.4'8'2
All the Catholic people: where did all the spirit go? [New York] Herder and Herder [1971] 201 p. 21 cm. Includes bibliographical references. [BX2350.2.N68] 76-165498 5.95
1. Christian life—Catholic authors. 2. Catholics. I. Title.

O'CONNELL, David. 248'.48'2
The teachings of Saint Louis; a critical text. Chapel Hill, University of North Carolina Press [1972] 66 p. 24 cm. (Studies in the Romance languages and literatures, no. 116.) Bibliography: p. [65]-66. [DC91.A2O36] 72-611314
1. Louis IX, Saint, King of France, 1214-1270. Enseignements de Saint Louis. I. Title. II. Series: North Carolina. University. Studies in the Romance languages and literatures, no. 116.

O'FLAHERTY, Vincent M. 248.4'8'2
How to make up your mind [by] Vincent M. O'Flaherty. Staten Island, N.Y., Alba House [1969] 141 p. 22 cm. Bibliography: p. 139-141. [BJ1468.5.O35] 69-15855 3.95
1. Decision-making (Ethics) 2. Decision-making. I. Title.

O'MEARA, Thomas F., 248.4'8'2
1935-
Holiness and radicalism in religious life [by] Thomas F. O'Meara. [New York] Herder and Herder [1970] xi, 157 p. 22 cm. Bibliography: p. 155-157. [BX2435.O43] 72-110794 4.95
1. Monastic and religious life. I. Title.

*O'NEILL, David P. 248'.48'2
Christian behavior: does it matter what you do, or only what you are? Dayton, Ohio, Pflaum/Standard [1973] 95 p. illus. 16 cm. (Witness Book, 19. Christian experience series) ISBN 0-8278-2126-3 0.95 (pbk)
1. Christian life—Catholic authors. I. Title.

O'NEILL, David P. 248.4'8'2
The way of trusting; a basic option for living, by David P. O'Neill. Dayton, Ohio, G. A. Pflaum [1969] 117 p. plates. 17 cm. (Christian experience series, 8) (Witness books, 12.) [BJ1595.O5] 76-97047 0.85
1. Conduct of life. 2. Trust in God. I. Title.

ORAISON, Marc. 248.482
Love, sin, and suffering. Translated by William Barrow. New York, Macmillan [1964] 90 p. 22 cm. [BX2350.2.O713] 64-10500
1. Christian life — Catholic authors. I. Title.

ORAISON, Marc 248.482
Love, sin, and suffering. Tr. by William Barrow. New York, Macmillan [c.1964] 90p. 22cm. 64-10500 2.95
1. Christian life—Catholic authors. I. Title.

ORAISON, Marc. 248.4'82
The wound of mortality; a meditation on the human condition. Translated by Bernard Murchland. [1st ed. in the U.S.] Garden City, N.Y., Doubleday, 1971. 119 p. 22 cm. Translation of La transhumance. [BX2350.2.O7313] 70-157614 4.95
1. Christian life—Catholic authors. I. Title.

O'TOOLE, Edward J. 248.4'8'2
The better part [by] Edward J. O'Toole. Staten Island, N.Y., Alba House [1970] xii, 91 p. 22 cm. [BX2350.2.O8] 76-99139 3.95
1. Christian life—Catholic authors. I. Title.

PARENTE, Pascal P 1890- 248.482
Spiritual direction. Rev. ed. New York, St. Paul Publications [1961] 158p. 21cm. Includes bibliography. [BX2350.7.P3 1961] 61-13713
1. Spiritual direction. I. Title.

PATHWAYS to personal 248.482
peace [by] William L. Doty. St. Louis, B. Herder Book Co. [1965] ix, 188 p. 21 cm. (Cross and crown series of spirituality, no. 30) [BX2350.2.D65] 65-24040
1. Christian life — Catholic authors. 2. Peace of mind. I. Series.

PFEIFER, Carl J. 248'.48'2
The living faith in a world of change [by] Carl J. Pfeifer. Notre Dame, Ind., Ave Maria Press [1973] 126 p. 21 cm. Selected articles from the author's column in the syndicated NC News Service Know your faith series. [BV4501.2.P437] 73-83349 ISBN 0-87793-058-9 1.65 (pbk.)
1. Christian life—1960- 2. Christian life—Catholic authors. I. Title.

PHILIPS, Gerard, 1899- 248.482
Achieving Christian maturity. Pred. by L. J. Suenens. [Tr. by Eileen Kane] Chicago, Franciscan Herald [1966] 302p. 22cm. Tr. of Pour une Christianisme adulte. Bibl. [BX2348.P513] 66-28484 4.95 bds.,
1. Catholic action. 2. Christian life—Catholic authors. I. Title.

PHIPPS, John-Francis. 248.4'8'2
Look forward in joy. [Derby, Eng.] P. Smith, 1964. xviii, 123 p. 19 cm. Includes bibliographical references. [BX2350.2.P493] 70-254094 7/6
1. Christian life—Catholic authors. I. Title.

PICHON, Almire, 1843- 248.482
1919.
Seeds of the Kingdom; notes from conferences, spiritual directions, meditations. Edited and translated by Lyle Terhune. Westminster, Md., Newman Press, 1961. 271p. 23cm. [BX2350.7.P53] 60-10734
1. Spiritual direction. 2. Meditations. I. Title.

PICHON, Almire, [Auguste 248.482
Theophile Almire Pichon] 1843-1919.
Seeds of the Kingdom; notes from conferences, spiritual directions, meditations. Ed. and tr. [from French] by Lyle Terhune, Westminster, Md., Newman Press [c.] 1961. 271p. 60-10734 3.95
1. Spiritual direction. 2. Meditations. I. Title.

PINSK, Johannes, 1891- 248.482
Towards the centre of Christian living, a liturgical approach. [Translated by H. E. Winstone. New York] Herder and Herder [1961] 261p. 19cm. Translation of Schritte zur Mitte. [BX2350.2.P543 1961a] 61-11488
1. Christian life—Catholic authors. 2. Catholic Church. Liturgy and ritual. I. Title.

POLE, Karl Frederick 248.482
Michael
Health and happiness. New York. Taplinger Pub. Co. [1960] 63p. 19cm. (ACampion book) ibl. footnotes. 60-50011 1.25 pap.,
1. Happiness. 2. Christian life—Catholic authors. I. Title.

QUOIST, Michel. 248.482
The meaning of success. Translated by Donald P. Gray. Notre Dame, Ind., Fides Publishers [1963] 252 p. 21 cm. Translation of Reussir. [BX2350.2.Q613] 63-20804
1. Christian life—Catholic authors. I. Title.

RADEMACHER, Arnold, 1873- 248.482
1939
Religion and life. Westminster, Md., Newman Pr., 1962[c.1961] 200p. Bibl. 62-2118 3.95
1. Spiritual life—Catholic authors. I. Title.

RAHNER, Karl, 1904- 248.4'8'2
Belief today. With a pref. by Hans Kung. New York, Sheed and Ward [1967] 128 p. 22 cm. (Theological meditations. [v. 3]) Contents.--Everyday things.--Faith today.--Intellectual integrity and Christian faith. [BX891.R253] 67-21908
1. Christian life—Catholic authors. 2. Faith. 3. Faith and reason. I. Kung, Hans, 1928- ed. II. Title.

RAHNER, Karl, 1904- 248.4'8'2
Belief today. With a pref. by Hans Kung. New York, Sheed and Ward [1967] 128 p. 22 cm. (Theological meditations [v. 3]) Contents.Contents.—Everyday things.—Faith today.—ntellectual integrity and Christian faith. [BX891.R253 1967] 67-21908
1. Christian life—Catholic authors. 2. Faith. 3. Faith and reason. I. Kung, Hans, 1928- ed. II. Title.

RAHNER, Karl, 1904- 248.482
Meditations on hope and love / [by] Karl Rahner ; [translated from the German by V. Green]. London : Burns and Oates, 1976. 85 p. ; 22 cm. Selections from the author's Was sollen wir jetzt tun? and Gott ist Mensch geworden. [BX2182.2.R28213 1976] 77-358300 ISBN 0-86012-027-9 : £1.95
1. Meditations. I. Title.

RAYMOND, Father, 1903- 248.482
Now! Milwaukee, Bruce Pub. Co. [1961] 184p. 24cm. [BX2182.2.R35] 61-9580
1. Devotional literature. I. Title.

RAYMOND, Father [Joseph 248.482
David Flanagan] 1903-
Now! Milwaukee, Bruce [c(1961] 184p. 61-9580 4.25
1. Devotional literature. I. Title.

REDDY, Michael. 248.4'8'2
Stop the church ..., I want to get off! Liguori, Mo., Liguori Publications [1971] 127 p. 18 cm. [BX2350.2.R396] 70-160693 1.25
1. Christian life—Catholic authors. I. Title.

†REYNOLDS, Bede, 1892- 248'.48'2
Draw your strength from the Lord : counsel for menders / Bede Reynolds. Canfield, Ohio : Alba Books, c1976. 154 p. ; 19 cm. Cover title. [BX2350.2.R47] 76-7102 ISBN 0-8189-1133-6 pbk. : 1.75
1. Christian life—Catholic authors. I. Title.

REYNOLDS, Bede, 1892- 248'.48'2
Let's mend the mess! / Bede Reynolds. Canfield, Ohio : Alba Books, c1975. xiii, 221 p. ; 18 cm. [BX2350.2.R48] 75-44674 ISBN 0-8189-1130-1 : 1.65
1. Catholic Church—Doctrinal and controversial works—Catholic authors. 2. Christian life—Catholic authors. I. Title.

ROLLET, Henri 248.482
L'engagement du laic [Toulouse] Privat [dist. Philadelphia, Chilton, c.1964] 125, [3]p. 19cm. (Questions posees aux catholiques) Bibl. 64-9091 1.50 pap.,
1. Catholic action. I. Title.

ROUSTANG, Francois. 248.482
Growth in the spirit. Translated by Kathleen Pond. New York, Sheed and Ward [1966] vi, 250 p. 22 cm. Translation of Une initiation a la vie spirituelle. [BX2350.5.R5713] 65-12204
1. Spiritual life — Catholic authors. I. Title.

ROUSTANG, Francois 248.482
Growth in the spirit. Tr. by Kathleen Pond. New York, Sheed [1966] vi, 250p. 22cm. Tr. of Une initiation a la vie spirituelle. [BX2350.5.R5713] 65-12204 5.00
1. Spiritual life—Catholic authors. I. Title.

SAMSON, Henri. 248.482
Spiritual insights of a practicing psychiatrist. [Translated from the French by Paul Garvin] Staten Island, N. Y., Alba House [1966] 200 p. 22 cm. Translation of Propos spirituels d'un psychiatre. [BX2350.5.S273] 66-17218
1. Spiritual life—Catholic Church. 2. Jesus Christ—Ascension. I. Title.

SAMSON, Henri 248.482
Spiritual insights of a practicing psychiatrist. [Tr. from French by Paul Garvin] Staten Island, N. Y., Alba [c.1966] 200p. 22cm. [BX2350.5.S273] 66-17218 4.95
1. Spiritual life—Catholic Church. 2. Jesus Christ—Ascension. I. Title.

SANTANER, Marie Abdon. 248.4'8'2
God in search of man. Translated by Ruth C. Douglas. Westminster, Md., Newman Press [1968] v, 218 p. 22 cm. Translation of Dieu cherche l'homme. [BX2350.5.S313] 68-21458
1. Spiritual life—Catholic authors. I. Title.

SHAMON, Albert J. 248.482
The only life. Milwaukee, Bruce Pub. Co. [1961] 133 p. 22 cm. Includes bibliography. [BX2350.2.S43] 61-7712
1. Spiritual life — Catholic authors. I. Title.

SHAMON, Albert J., Rev. 248.482
The only life. Milwaukee, Bruce Pub. Co. [c.1961] 133p. Bibl. 61-7712 3.25
1. Spiritual life—Catholic authors. I. Title.

SHEEN, Fulton John 248.482
Go to heaven. New York, McGraw-Hill [c.1949-1960] viii, 233p. 21cm. 60-15762 4.50 bds.,
1. Christian life—Catholic authors. I. Title.

SHEEN, Fulton John, Bp., 248.482
1895-
Walk with God, by Fulton J. Sheen. [New York, Maco Magazine Corp., 1965] 96 p. illus. 24 cm. [BX2350.2.S46] 65-29709
1. Christian life—Catholic authors. I. Title.

SHEEN, Fulton John, 248.4'8'2
Bp., 1895-
Fulton J. Sheen's guide to contentment. [New York, Maco Pub. Co., 1967] 127 p. illus. 24 cm. [BX2350.2.S44] 67-2039
1. Christian life—Catholic authors. I. Title: Guide to contentment.

SHEEN, Fulton John, 248.4'82
Bp., 1895-
Fulton J. Sheen's guide to contentment. New York, Simon and Schuster [1967] 186 p. 22 cm. [BX2350.2.S44 1967b] 67-25389
1. Christian life—Catholic authors. 2. Conduct of life. I. Title: Guide to contentment.

SHEEN, Fulton John Bp., 248.482
1895-
Go to heaven. [New York, Dell, 1961, c.1958, 1960] 254p. (Chapel bk. F172) .50 pap.,
I. Title.

SHEEN, Fulton John, 248'.48'2
Bp., 1895-
Lift up your heart / by Fulton J. Sheen. Garden City, N.Y. : Image Books, [1975] c1950. 280 p. ; 18 cm. [BX2350.S49 1975] 75-303187 ISBN 0-385-09001-3 pbk. : pbk. : 1.75
1. Christian life—Catholic authors. I. Title.

SHEEN, Fulton John, 248'.48'2
Bp., 1895-
Lift up your heart / by Fulton J. Sheen. Boston : G. K. Hall, [1975] c1950. p. cm. Large print ed. [BX2350.S49 1975b] 75-17977 ISBN 0-8161-6322-7 lib.bdg. : 11.95
1. Christian life—Catholic authors. 2. Sight-saving books. I. Title.

SHEEN, Fulton John, Bp., 248.482
1895-
Way to happy living. Greenwich, Conn., Fawcett [1963, c.1955] 127p. 18cm. (Crest bk., d607) .50 pap.,
1. Christian life—Catholic authors. I. Title.

SHEEN, fulton John, Bp., 248.482
1895-
Go to heaven. [1st ed.] New York, McGraw-Hill [1960] 233 p. 21 cm. Christian life -- Catholic authors. [BX2350.2.S45 1960] 60-15762
I. Title.

SLOYAN, Gerard Stephen, 248.4'8'2
Stephen, ill 1919-
How do I know I'm doing right? Toward the formation of a Christian conscience [by] Gerard S. Sloyan. Dayton, Ohio, Pflaum [1967, c.1966] 126p. illus. 17cm. (Christian experience bks., no. 4) Witness bks., 6. Bibl. [BX1758.2.S55 1967] 67-19685 .75 pap.,
1. Christian ethics—Catholic authors. 2. Conscience. I. Title.

SMITH, Gerard. 248'.48'2
A trio of talks. [Milwaukee] Marquette University Press, 1971. 32 p. 23 cm. Contents.Contents.—Ad majorem Dei gloriam.—Humility.—Eternal joy. [BT180.G6S64] 79-140072 ISBN 0-87462-440-1
1. Glory of God. 2. Humility. 3. Joy. I. Title.

SOBOSAN, Jeffrey G., 248'.48'2
1946-
The tapestry of faith / by Jeffrey G. Sobosan. New York : Alba House, c1976. xiv, 108 p. ; 21 cm. Includes bibliographical references. [BX2350.2.S575] 76-41282 ISBN 0-8189-0334-1 pbk. :3.95 3.95
1. Christian life—Catholic authors. I. Title.

SOUTHWELL, Robert, 248'.48'2
Saint, 1561?-1595.
Two letters and Short rules of a good life. Edited by Nancy Pollard Brown. Charlottesville, Published for Folger Shakespeare Library [by] University Press of Virginia [1973] lxv, 122 p. facsim. 25 cm. (Folger documents of Tudor and Stuart civilization) Based on an early 17th century MS. acquired by the Folger Shakespeare Library, Washington, in 1964 (MS V.a. 421) Contents.Contents.—Epistle unto his father.—Short rules of a good life.—Letter to Sir Robert Cecil. Includes bibliographical references. [BX2181.S67 1973] 72-87806 ISBN 0-8139-0416-1 9.50
1. Spiritual life—Catholic authors. I. Brown, Nancy Pollard, ed. II. Title. III. Title: Epistle unto his father. IV. Title: Short rules of a good life. V. Title: Letter to Sir Robert Cecil. VI. Series.

SPICQ, Ceslaus, 1901- 248.482
The Trinity and our moral life according to St. Paul. Translated by Sister Marie Aquinas. Westminster, Md., Newman Press, 1963. xvii, 133 p. 22 cm. Bibliographical references included in "Notes" (p. 129-133) [BX2350.2.S613] 63-12232
1. Christian life — Catholic authors. 2. Christian ethics — Catholic authors. 3. Trinity I. Title.

SPICQ, Ceslaus, 1901- 248.482
The Trinity and our moral life according to St. Paul. Tr. by Sister Marie Aquinas. Westminster, Md., Newman [c.]1963. xvii, 133p. 22cm. Bibl. 63-12232 2.75
1. Christian life—Catholic authors. 2. Christian ethics—Catholic authors. 3. Trinity. I. Title.

STILLMOCK, Martin. 248.4'8'2
Teens talk of many things [by] Martin A. Stillmock. Staten Island, N.Y., Alba House [1972] x, 177 p. port. 19 cm. A Catholic priest answers letters from teen-agers about dating, sex, interracial marriage, confession, and other topics. [BJ1661.S85] 79-39708 ISBN 0-8189-0247-7 1.65
1. Youth—Conduct of life. 2. Youth—Religious life. I. Title.

SUENENS, Leon Joseph, 248.482
Cardinal, 1904-
Christian life day by day [Tr. from French by S. F. L. Tye] Westminster, Md., Newman, 1964[c.1961, 1963] 160p. 19cm. 64-15401 3.50
1. Christian life—Catholic authors. I. Title.

SULLIVAN, John J 248.482
God and the interior life; some reflections for religious on doctrine and devotion. [Boston] St. Paul Editions [1962] 283 p. 19 cm. [BX2350.2.S8] 62-22006
1. Spiritual life — Catholic authors. I. Title.

SULLIVAN, John J. 248.482
God and the interior life; some reflections for religious on doctrine and devotion. [Boston] St. Paul [dist. Daughters of St. Paul, c.1962] 283p. 19cm. 62-22006 3.00; 2.00 pap.,
1. Spiritual life—Catholic authors. I. Title.

SULLIVAN, Walter J 248.482
Live in hope. Glen Rock, N.J., Paulist Press [1964] 128 p. 19 cm. [Deus books] [BX2350.2.S83] 64-20245
1. Christian life — Catholic authors. I. Title.

SULLIVAN, Walter J. 248.482
Live in hope. Glen Rock, N. J., Paulist [c.1964] 128p. 19cm. (Deus bks.) 64-20245 .95 pap.,
1. Christian life—Catholic authors. I. Title.

TAVARD, Georges Henri, 248'.48'2
1922-
The inner life : foundations of Christian mysticism / by George H. Tavard. New York : Paulist Press, c1976. v, 104 p. ; 19 cm. Bibliography: p. 101-104. [BX2350.2.T38] 75-32858 ISBN 0-8091-1927-7 pbk. : 1.65
1. Spiritual life—Catholic authors. I. Title.

TERESA, Saint, 1515-1582. 248.482
Interior castle. Translated and edited by E. Allison Peers, from the critical ed. of P. Silverio de Santa Teresa. Garden City, N.Y., Doubleday [1961] 235 p. 19 cm. (Image books, D120) Translation of Les moradas. [BX2179.T4M63] 61-4019
1. Spiritual life — Catholic authors. I. Peers, Edgar Allison, ed. and tr. II. Title.

TERESA, Saint, 1515-1582 248.482
Interior castle. Tr., ed. by E. Allison Peers, from the critical ed. of P. Silverio de Santa Teresa. Garden City, N. Y., Doubleday [1961] 235p. (Image bks., D120) 61-4019 .75 pap.,
1. Spiritual life—Catholic authors. I. Peers, Edgar Allison, ed. and tr. II. Title.

THEAS, Pierre Marie. 248'.48'2
Lourdes, land of Mary. Translated from the

French by Earl of Wicklow. Dublin, Clonmore and Reynolds [1964] viii, 198 p. 23 cm. Translation of Lourdes, terre de Marie. [BT653.T4813] 74-172609
1. Lourdes. I. Title.

THORMAN, Donald J. 248.4'8'2
The Christian vision [by] Donald J. Thorman. [1st ed.] Garden City, N.Y., Doubleday, 1967. 215 p. 22 cm. [BX2350.2.T5] 66-12194
1. Christian life—Catholic authors. I. Title.

TOOHEY, William. 248.4'8'2
Free at last; the Christian odyssey. Notre Dame, Ind., Ave Maria Press [1970] 142 p. 18 cm. [BX2350.2.T64] 79-103644 1.35
1. Christian life—Catholic authors. I. Title.

TOOHEY, William. 248'.48'2
Fully alive / William Toohey. St. Meinrad, Ind. : Abbey Press, 1976. 116 p. ; 21 cm. (A Priority edition) [BX2350.2.T642] 76-151245 ISBN 0-87029-036-3 pbk. : 2.95
1. Christian life—Catholic authors. I. Title.

TOOHEY, William. 248'.48'2
A passion for the possible. Notre Dame, Ind., Ave Maria Press [1972] 112 p. illus. 21 cm. [BX2350.2.T644] 72-190695 ISBN 0-87793-044-9 1.35
1. Christian life—Catholic authors. I. Title.

TRESE, Leo John, 1902- 248.482
Everyman's road to heaven. Notre Dame, Ind., Fides Publishers Association [1961] 131 p. 19 cm. [BX2350.2.T7] 61-10366
1. Spiritual life — Catholic authors. I. Title.

TRESE, Leo John, 1902- 248.482
Everyman's road to heaven. Notre Dame, Ind., Fides [c.1961] 131p. 61-10366 2.95 bds.,
1. Spiritual life—Catholic authors. I. Title.

TRESE, Leo John, 1902- 248.482
Human but holy [by] Leo J. Trese. Notre Dame, Ind., Fides [1965] 132 p. 21 cm. [BX2350.2.T714] 65-13798
1. Christian life — Catholic authors. I. Title.

TRESE, Leo John, 1902- 248.482
Human but holy. Notre Dame, Ind., Fides [c.1965] 132p. 21cm. [BX2350.2.T714] 65-13798 3.25
1. Christian life—Catholic authors. I. Title.

TRESE, Leo John, 1902- 248.4'8'2
One step enough [by] Leo J. Trese. Notre Dame, Ind., Fides Publishers [1967, c1966] 191 p. 21 cm. [BX2350.2.T716] 66-28039
1. Christian life—Catholic authors. I. Title.

TRESE, Leo John, 1902- 248.482
You are called to greatness Notre Dame, Ind., Fides [c.1964] 153p. 21 cm. 64-16496 3.25
1. Spiritual life—Catholic authors. I. Title.

TRESE, Leo John, 1902- 248.482
You are called to greatness. Notre Dame, Ind., Fides [1966, c.1964] 158p. 18cm. (Dome bk., D52) .95 pap.,
1. Spiritual life—Catholic authors. I. Title.

URTEAGA LOIDI, Jesus, 1921- 248.482
Man, the saint [Tr. from Spanish] Chicago, Scepter [c.1963] xxi, 218p. 18cm. (Prow 2) Bibl. 63-23838 .95 pap.,
1. Christian life—Catholic authors. I. Title.

VANIER, Jean, 1928- 248'.48'2
Be not afraid / by Jean Vanier. New York : Paulist Press, c1975. xii, 145 p. ; 21 cm. [BX2350.2.V25 1975] 75-321768 ISBN 0-8091-1885-8 pbk. : 2.95
1. Christian life—Catholic authors. I. Title.

VANIER, Jean, 1928- 248'.48'2
Followers of Jesus / Jean Vanier. New York : Paulist Press, c1976. xi, 84 p. ; 21 cm. "A record of four talks given ... to major superiors of religious orders in Toronto." [BX2350.2.V26 1976] 76-362990 ISBN 0-8091-1941-2 pbk. : 3.50
1. Christian life—Catholic authors—Addresses, essays, lectures. I. Title.

VON HILDEBRAND, Dietrich, 1889- 248'.48'2
Transformation in Christ. [New ed.] Chicago, Franciscan Herald Press [1973, c1948] ix, 406 p. 23 cm. Translation of Die Umgestaltung in Christus. [BX2350.V5913 1973] 73-158305 ISBN 0-8199-0450-3 6.95
1. Spiritual life—Catholic authors. I. Title.

WALSH, Mary Rosamond. 248.482
Pray with me. Introd. by Richard Cardinal Cushing. New York, St. Paul Publications [c1961] 170 p. 21 cm. [BX2110.W27] 61-15621
1. Catholic Church — Prayer-books and devotions — English. I. Title.

*WALTER, Ralph N. 248.482
Life's questions as asked and answered in the Bible. New York, Vantage [1966] 212p. 21cm. 3.50 bds.,
1. Christian life—Catholic authors. I. Title.

WAYWOOD, Robert J. 248'.48'2
Hanging in there with Christ, by Robert J. Waywood. Chicago, Franciscan Herald Press [1974] vii, 130 p. 22 cm. "Originally appeared as articles in the Cord." [BX2350.2.W38] 74-1367 ISBN 0-8199-0498-8 4.50
1. Spiritual life—Catholic authors. I. Title.

*WEDGE, Florence 248.4'8'2
The single woman. Pulaski, Wis., Franciscan Pubs. [1967] 64p. 19cm. .25 pap.,
1. Spiritual life—Catholic authors. 2. Woman—Religious life—Catholic authors. I. Title.

*WEDGE, Florence 248.4'8'2
You and your thoughts. Pulaski, Wis., Franciscan Pubs. [1967] 62p. 19cm. 25 pap.,
1. Spiritual life—Catholic authors. I. Title.

WHEALON, John F. 248'.48'2
Living the Catholic faith today / by John F. Whealon. Boston : St. Paul Editions, [1975] 130 p. : ill. ; 19 cm. [BX2350.2.W48 1975] 75-6801
1. Christian life—Catholic authors. I. Title.

WINTER, David Brian. 248'.48'2
Closer than a brother; Brother Lawrence for the 70's [by David Winter. 1st ed.] Wheaton, Ill., H. Shaw, 1971. 160 p. illus. 18 cm. An adaptation of N. Herman's La pratique de la presence de Dieu. [BX2349.H422W56] 71-181991 ISBN 0-87788-129-4 1.45
1. Christian life—Catholic authors. I. Herman, Nicholas, 1611-1691. La pratique de la presence de Dieu. II. Title.

WROBLEWSKI, Sergius. 248.4'8'2
Christ-centered spirituality. Staten Island, N.Y., Alba House [1967] 211 p. 22 cm. Includes bibliographies. [BX2350.2.W69] 66-21813
1. Spiritual life—Catholic authors. I. Title.

ZIMMER, Luke B. 248'.48'2
The apostolate of Christian renewal [by] Luke Zimmer. Staten Island, N.Y., Alba House [1973, c1972] 109 p. illus. 21 cm. [BX2350.2.Z558] 73-161583 ISBN 0-8189-0269-8 1.50 (pbk.)
1. Catholic Church—Prayer-books and devotions—English. 2. Christian life—Catholic authors. I. Title.

ZIMMER, Luke B. 248'.48'2
Apostolic renewal [by] Luke Zimmer. Staten Island, N.Y., Alba House [1973] 198 p. illus. 22 cm. [BX2350.2.Z56] 73-5886 ISBN 0-8189-0275-2 1.50
1. Catholic Church—Doctrinal and controversial works—Catholic authors. 2. Catholic Church—Prayer-books and devotions—English. 3. Christian life—Catholic authors. I. Title.

TRESE, Leo John, 1902- 248.4'8'208
Book for boys and girls [by] Leo J. Trese. Notre Dame, Ind., Fides Publications [1967] 124 p. 18 cm. (A Fides dome book, D-54) "Sequel to [the author's] Book for boys." "A collection of articles that appeared in both the Catholic boy and the Catholic miss from 1961 to 1965." [BX2360.T72] 67-24804
1. Boys—Religious life. 2. Girls—Religious life. I. Title.

MARTIN, Maria Gratia. 248.4'8'20924
The spirituality of Teilhard de Chardin. Westminster, Md., Newman Press [1968] xii, 122 p. 21 cm. Bibliography: p. 119-122. [B2430.T374M27] 68-16674
1. Teilhard de Chardin, Pierre. I. Title.

NOUWEN, Henri J. M. 248'.48'20924 B
The Genesee diary : report from a Trappist monastery / Henri J. M. Nouwen. 1st ed. Garden City, N.Y. : Doubleday, 1976. xiv, 195 p. ; 22 cm. Includes bibliographical references. [BX4705.N87A33] 75-38169 ISBN 0-385-11368-4 : 6.95
1. Nouwen, Henri J. M. 2. Spiritual life—Catholic authors. I. Title.

WROBLEWSKI, Sergius. 248.48'2'0924
Bonaventurian theology of prayer. Poetry by M. Angela Sassak. Pulaski, Wis., Franciscan Publishers [1967] 143 p. 19 cm. Bibliography: p. 142-143. [BX4700.B68W7] 68-1030
1. Bonaventura, Saint, Cardinal, 1221-1274. 2. Franciscans—Spiritual life. I. Title.

ROBINSON, John Michael. 248.4'8'20967
The family apostolate and Africa, by John M. Robinson. Dublin, Helicon, 1964. xvi, 278 p. map. 22 cm. Bibliography: p. [258]-261. [BX2351.R6] 75-7591
1. Family—Religious life. 2. Family—Africa. I. Title.

BOWIE, Walter Russell, 1882- 248.4'8'3
Where you find God. [1st ed.] New York, Harper & Row [1968] 116 p. 22 cm. Bibliographical footnotes. [BT102.B62] 68-11727
1. God—Knowableness. 2. Christian life—Anglican authors. I. Title.

COBURN, John B. 248'.48'3
The hope of glory : exploring the mystery of Christ in you / John B. Coburn. New York : Seabury Press, c1976. p. cm. "A Crossroad book." [BX5937.C63H66] 75-37751 ISBN 0-8164-1208-1 : 7.95. ISBN 0-8164-2117-X pbk. : 3.95
1. Protestant Episcopal Church in the U.S.A.—Sermons. 2. Sermons, American. I. Title.

COBURN, John B. 248.4'8'3
Twentieth-century spiritual letters; an introduction to contemporary prayer, by John B. Coburn. Philadelphia, Westminster Press [1967] 170 p. 21 cm. [BV4501.2.C62] 67-21793
1. Spiritual life—Anglican authors. I. Title.

COGGAN, Frederick Donald, Abp. of York, 1909- 248.483
Christian priorities. New York, Harper & Row [1963] 172 p. illus. 23 cm. Sermons. [BX5133.C68C5] 63-12163
1. Christian life — American authors. 2. Sermons, English. 3. Church of England — Sermons. I. Title.

COGGAN, Frederick Donald, Abp. of York, 1909- 248.483
Christian priorities. New York, Harper [c.1963] 172p. illus. 23cm. 63-12163 3.50 bds.,
1. Christian life—Anglican authors. 2. Sermons, English. 3. Church of England—Sermons. I. Title.

GREEN, Edward Michael Bankes. 248'.48'3
New life, new lifestyle; a first book for new believers [by] Michael Green. Downers Grove, Ill., Inter-Varsity Press [1973] 159 p. 18 cm. [BV4501.2.G743] 73-89299 ISBN 0-87784-664-2 1.50 (pbk.)
1. Christian life—Anglican authors. I. Title.

HALL, Robert Benjamin. 248'.48'3
There's more; infinite blessings for the spirit-filled life. Plainfield, N.J., Logos International [1972] 153 p. 21 cm. [BT767.3.H33] 74-166501 ISBN 0-912106-23-9 1.50
1. Gifts, Spiritual. 2. Christian life—Anglican authors. I. Title.

HANKEY, Cyril Patrick 248.483
Sign posts on the Christian way; a guide to the devotional life. New York, Scribners [c.1962] 152 p. Bibl. 62-9640 2.95
1. Spiritual life—Anglican authors. I. Title.

HILLER, George Irvine, 1892- 248.4'8'3
The pendulum swings; churchmanship editorials. [Miami, Fla., Trinity Episcopal Cathedral, 1971] 77 p. port. 23 cm. [BV4501.2.H47] 73-178252
1. Christian life—Anglican authors. I. Title.

JEWELL, Earle B., 1896- 248.4'8'3
You can if you want to! By Earle B. Jewell. [Kansas City, Mo., Midwest Pub. Co., 1968] xiii, 141 p. port. 23 cm. [BJ1611.2.J4] 68-3819
1. Success. 2. Christian life—Anglican authors. I. Title.

KEELING, Michael. 248.4'8'3
What is right? Valley Forge [Pa.] Judson Press [1970] 124 p. illus. 19 cm. Includes bibliographical references. [BJ1251.K34 1970] 72-121055 1.95
1. Christian ethics—Anglican authors. I. Title.

LICHLITER, James Marcellus, 1911- 248.4'8'3
Inside the outside [by] James M. Lichliter. Philadelphia, Pilgrim Press [1968] xi, 147 p. 22 cm. Bibliographical references included in "Notes" (p. 145-147) [BV4501.2.L48] 68-57479 4.95
1. Christian life. I. Title.

MARTINEAU, Robert Arnold Schurhoff. 248'.48'3
Moments that matter / [by] Robert Martineau. London : S.P.C.K., 1976. 67 p. ; 19 cm. [BV4501.2.M36437] 77-353992 ISBN 0-281-02920-2 : £0.95
1. Christian life—Anglican authors. I. Title.

MURPHY, Chuck, 1922- 248'.48'3
There's no business like God's business. Nashville, Abingdon Press [1974] ix, 128 p. 19 cm. [BT77.M92] 73-20312 ISBN 0-687-41632-9 2.95 (pbk.)
1. Theology, Doctrinal—Popular works. 2. Christian life—Anglican authors. I. Title.

NASH, E. J. H. 248.483
How to succeed in the Christian life. Chicago 10, 1519 North Astor Inter-Varsity Press, [1960] 16p. 13cm. .20 pap.,
I. Title.

PEERMAN, Nancy. 248.4'8'3
The real and only life. Introd. by Keith Miller. Waco, Tex., Word Books [1968] 102 p. 21 cm. [BV4501.2.P365] 68-19482
1. Christian life—Anglican authors. I. Title.

PIKE, James Albert, Bp., 1913- 248.4'8'3
Facing the next day [by] James A. Pike. Rev. ed. New York, Macmillan [1968] xii, 175 p. 18 cm. First published in 1957 under title: The next day. [BV4501.2.P55 1968] 68-28294 1.45
1. Christian life—Anglican authors. I. Title.

PITTENGER, William Norman, 1905- 248'.48'3
Life in Christ, by Norman Pittenger. Grand Rapids, Eerdmans [1972] 128 p. 22 cm. [BV4501.2.P5547] 72-75571 ISBN 0-8028-1454-9 (pbk) 1.95 (pbk)
1. Christian life—Anglican authors. I. Title.

PITTENGER, William Norman, 1905- 248'.48'3
Trying to be a Christian, by W. Norman Pittenger. Philadelphia, Pilgrim Press [1972] 125 p. 22 cm. [BV4501.2.P555] 72-1567 ISBN 0-8298-0237-1
1. Christian life—Anglican authors. I. Title.

REID, Gavin. 248'.48'3
A new happiness : Christ's pattern for living in today's world / Gavin Reid. Nashville : Abingdon Press, [1976] c1974. p. cm. [BT382.R395 1976] 75-26504 ISBN 0-687-27785-X pbk. : 2.25
1. Beatitudes. 2. Christian life—Anglican authors. I. Title.

ROBINSON, John Arthur Thomas, Bp., 1919- 248'.48'3
The difference in being a Christian today, by John A. T. Robinson. Philadelphia, Westminster Press [1972] 92 p. 19 cm. Bibliography: p. [85]-87. [BV4501.2.R617] 75-188532 ISBN 0-664-24954-X 1.50
1. Christian life—Anglican authors. I. Title.

RODENMAYER, Robert N 248.483
According to Thy promises [1st ed.] New York, Harper & Row [1964] 159 p. 20 cm. Bibliography: p. 155-159. [BV4501.2.R62] 64-14381
1. Christian life—Anglican authors. 2. Church of England. Book of common prayer. General confession. I. Title.

RODENMAYER, Robert N. 248.483
According to Thy promises. New York, Harper [c.1964] 159p. 20cm. Bibl. 64-14381 2.75
1. Christian life—Anglican authors. 2. Church of England. Book of common prayer. General confession. I. Title.

RYLE, John Charles, Bp. of Liverpool 248.483
Practical religion; being plain papers on the daily duties, experience, dangers, and privileges of professing Christians. Edited, and with a foreword, by J. I. Packer. New York, Crowell [1960] 324p. 22cm. 'A companion to two other volumes . . . entitled Knots untied and Old paths.' 60-9163 4.50
1. Christian life—Anglican authors. I. Title.

SHERWOOD, Bill. 248'.48'3
Let's begin again / by Father Sherwood as told to Jamie Buckingham. Plainfield, N. J. : Logos International, c1975. xiv, 126 p. ; 21 cm. [BX5995.S3454A34] 74-33671 ISBN 0-88270-117-7 : 5.95 ISBN 0-88270-118-5 pbk. : 3.50
1. Sherwood, Bill. 2. Sherwood, Erma. I. Buckingham, Jamie. II. Title.

STERLING, Chandler W., Bp., 1911- 248'.48'3
The doors to perception, by Chandler W. Sterling. Philadelphia, United Church Press [1974] 127 p. 22 cm. "A Pilgrim Press book." Bibliography: p. 119-125. [BV4501.2.S755] 74-8032 ISBN 0-8298-0282-7 5.25
1. Spiritual life—Anglican authors. I. Title.

STRINGFELLOW, William 248.483
Instead of death / William Stringfellow New and expanded ed. New York : Seabury Press, 1976 112 p. ; 21 cm. [BX5875.S8] 76-2480 ISBN 0-8164-2120-X 3.95
1. Christian education—Text-books for young people—Anglican. 2. Christian life—Anglican authors. I. Title.

TAYLOR, Jeremy, Bp. of Down and Connor, 1613-1667. 248'.48'3
The rule and exercises of holy dying / Jeremy Taylor ; new introd. by Robert Kastenbaum. New York : Arno Press, 1977. [10], xvi, 288 p. ; 23 cm. (The Literature of death and dying) Reprint of the 1819 ed. printed for Longman, Hurst, Rees, Orme & Brown, London. Bibliography: p. [9-10]. [BV4500.T3 1977] 76-19590 ISBN 0-405-09585-6 : 19.00
1. Christian life—Anglican authors. 2. Sick—Prayer-books and devotions—English. I. Title. II. Series.

THORNTON, Martin 248.483
The purple headed mountain. [New York, Morehouse-Barlow, c.1962] 90p. 62-946 1.00 pap.,
1. Spiritual life—Anglican authors. I. Title.

VERDERY, John D. 248.483
It's better to believe. Evans; dist. Philadelphia, Lippincott [c.1964] 224p. 22cm. 64-20780 4.50
1. Christian life—Anglican authors. 2. Faith. I. Title.

VOGEL, Arthur Anton. 248'.48'3
Body theology; God's presence in man's world [by] Arthur A. Vogel. [1st ed.] New York, Harper & Row [1973] x, 148 p. 22 cm. Includes bibliographical references. [BR110.V6 1973] 72-11365 ISBN 0-06-068881-5 5.95
1. Experience (Religion) I. Title.

VOGEL, Arthur Anton. 248'.48'3
The power of His resurrection : the mystical life of Christians / Arthur A. Vogel. New York : Seabury Press, c1976. v, 106 p. ; 22 cm. "A Crossroad book." Includes bibliographical references. [BV4501.2.V57] 75-37762 ISBN 0-8164-0298-1 : 6.95
1. Spiritual life—Anglican authors. 2. Mysticism. I. Title.

WARD, Keith, 1938- 248'.48'3
The Christian way / [by] Keith Ward. London : S.P.C.K., 1976. 95 p. ; 19 cm. [BV4501.2.W337] 76-370410 ISBN 0-281-02893-1 : £1.25
1. Christian life—Anglican authors. I. Title.

WHITE, Anne S. 248'.48'3
Trial by fire / by Anne S. White. Winter Park, Fla. : Victorious Ministry Through Christ, [1975] 114 p. : diagrs. ; 21 cm. [BV4501.2.W449] 75-625 1.95
1. Christian life—Anglican authors. I. Title.

BURTNESS, James H. 248.4'8'4
Whatever you do; an essay on the Christian life, by James H. Burtness. Minneapolis, Augsburg Pub. House [1967] 124 p. 20 cm. (A Tower book) Bibliographical references included in "Footnotes" (p. 120-124) [BV4501.2.B89] 67-25372
1. Christian life—Lutheran authors. 2. Christian ethics—Lutheran authors. I. Title.

MOORE, David 248.484
Spirtual prescriptions for health, happiness and abundance. New York, Speller [c.1966] p. 92 18 cm pap. 1.00
I. Title.

BURTNESS, James H 248.4'8'41
Whatever you do; an essay on the Christian life, by James H. Burtness. Minneapolis, Augsburg Pub. House [1967] 124 p. 20 cm. (A Tower book) Bibliographical references included in "Footnotes" (p. 120-124) [BV4501.2.B89] 67-25372
1. Christian life—Lutheran authors. 2. Christian ethics—Lutheran authors. I. Title.

DAEHLIN, Reidar A. 248'.48'41
The family of the forgiven [by] Reidar A. Daehlin. St. Louis, Concordia Pub. House [1973] 80 p. illus. 16 cm. [BV4501.2.D27 1973] 72-96740 ISBN 0-570-03143-5 1.50 (pbk.)
1. Christian life—Lutheran authors. I. Title.

DEFFNER, Donald L. 248'.48'41
The best of your life is the rest of your life / Donald L. Deffner. Nashville : Abingdon, c1977. 95 p. ; 19 cm. [BV4501.2.D42] 76-26123 ISBN 0-687-02955-4 : 2.95
1. Christian life—Lutheran authors. I. Title.

DEFFNER, Donald L. 248'.48'41
You say you're depressed? : how God helps you overcome anxieties / Donald L. Deffner. Nashville : Abingdon Press, c1976. 112 p. ; 19 cm. [BV4501.2.D43] 75-3056 ISBN 0-687-47095-1 pbk. : 3.25
1. Christian life—Lutheran authors. 2. Depression, Mental. I. Title.

GOCKEL, Herman William, 1906- 248'.48'41
You can live above your circumstances [by] Herman W. Gockel. St. Louis, Concordia Pub. House [1973] 80 p. 18 cm. [BV4510.2.G62] 72-96741 ISBN 0-570-03154-0 1.25 (pbk.)
1. Christian life—Lutheran authors. I. Title.

GORNITZKA, A. Reuben. 248.4841
Who cares? [By] A. Reuben Gornitzka. Westwood, N.J., Revell [1966] 160 p. 21 cm. [BV4501.2.G64] 66-15082
1. Christian life — Lutheran authors. 2. Charity. I. Title.

GORNITZKA, A. Reuben 248.4841
Who cares? Westwood, N.J., Revell [c.1966] 160p. 21cm. [BV4501.2.G64] 66-15082 3.50
1. Christian life—Lutheran authors. 2. Charity. I. Title.

HALVORSON, Arndt L., 1915- 248'.48'41
All things new; meditations on the Christian life [by] Arndt L. Halvorson. Minneapolis, Augsburg Pub. House [1974] 103 p. 20 cm. [BV4501.2.H269] 74-77671 ISBN 0-8066-1418-8 2.95 (pbk.)
1. Christian life—Lutheran authors. I. Title.

HALVORSON, Arndt L 1915- 248.4841
One life to live; the image of a Christian. Minneapolis, Augsburg Pub. House [1963] 98 p. 20 cm. [BV4501.2.H27] 62-20842
1. Christian life—Lutheran authors. I. Title.

HALVORSON, Arndt L., 1915- 248.4841
One life to live; the image of a Christian. Minneapolis, Augsburg [c.1963] 93p. 20cm. 62-20842 1.75 pap.,
1. Christian life—Lutheran authors. I. Title.

HEIMARCK, Theodore 248.4841
Preaching for tethered man. Minneapolis, Augsburg [c.1962] 221p. 21cm. 62-16940 3.75
1. Lutheran Church—Sermons. 2. Sermons, American. I. Title.

HERTZ, Karl H. 248.4841
Christian behavior, by Karl H. Hertz. Edited by Phillip R. Hoh. Illustrated by John Gretzer. Philadelphia, Lutheran Church Press [c1964] 121 p. illus. 21 cm. (LCA Sunday church school series, term 3, adults) [BV4501.2.H38] 65-2235
1. Christian life — Lutheran authors. 2. Christian ethics — Lutheran authors. I. Title. II. Series.

HOLTMERMANN, Carla 248.4'8'41
Released and radiant. Westwood, N.J., Revell [1967] 60p. 17cm. [BV4501.2.H58] 67-14776 1.50 bds.,
1. Spiritual life—Lutheran authors. I. Title.

HOPE, Ludvig, 1871-1954. 248.4841
Spirit and power. Translated by Iver Olson. Minneapolis, Hauge Lutheran Innermission Federation, 1959. 197p. 24cm. [BV4501.H53448] 60-25225
1. Spiritual life. 2. Holy spirit. I. Title.

HORN, Henry E. 248.4'8'41
The Christian in modern style [by] Henry E. Horn. Philadelphia, Fortress Press [1968] viii, 184 p. 18 cm. (A Fortress paperback original) Bibliographical references included in "Notes" (p. 170-184) [BV4647.P5H63] 68-29462 2.50
1. Piety. 2. Christian life—Lutheran authors. I. Title.

HOYER, Robert. 248'.48'41
Seventy times seven / Robert Hoyer. Nashville : Abingdon, c1976. 112 p. ; 19 cm. [BV4501.2.H645] 75-30668 ISBN 0-687-38199-1 pbk. : 3.25
1. Christian life—Lutheran authors. I. Title.

KRETZMANN, Otto Paul, 1901- 248.4841
The road back to God [by] O. P. Kretzmann. [Rev. ed.] Saint Louis, Concordia Pub. House [1965, c1935] xvi, 125 p. 20 cm. [BV4310.K7] 65-9030
1. Youth — Religious life. 2. Sermons, American. 3. Lutheran Church — Sermons. I. Title.

KRETZMANN, Otto Paul, 1901- 248.4841
The road back to God [Rev. ed.] Saint Louis, Concordia [1965, c.1935] xvi, 125p. 20cm. [BV4310.K7] 65-9030 2.50
1. Youth—Religious life. 2. Sermons, American. 3. Lutheran Church—Sermons. I. Title.

LEONI, Louise. 248'.48'41
The best of New creations / by Louise Leoni. [Ely? Minn. : s.n.], c1977. 76 p. : ill. ; 22 cm. "An accumulation of some of the better New creations columns printed weekly in the Ely echo over the past 3 years." [BV4501.2.L45] 77-151486
1. Christian life—Lutheran authors. I. Title.

MARTY, Martin E. 1928- 248.4841
The hidden discipline. Saint Louis, Concordia [c.1962] 108p. 22cm. 62-21428 2.50
1. Commandments, Ten. 2. Apostles' Creed. 3. Lord's prayer. 4. Sacraments—Lutheran Church. I. Title.

MARTY, Martin E., 1928- 248'.48'41
You are promise [by] Martin E. Marty. [1st ed. Niles, Ill.] Argus Communications, 1973. 160 p. illus. 23 cm. Bibliography: p. 158-160. [BV4501.2.M3644] 73-78535 ISBN 0-913592-20-X 5.95
1. Christian life—Lutheran authors. I. Title.

MARTY, Martin E., 1928- 248'.48'41
You are promise / Martin E. Marty ; [ill. by Collin Fry]. Niles, Ill. : Argus Communications, 1974. viii, 162 p. : ill. ; 19 cm. Bibliography: p. 160-162. [BV4501.2.M3644 1974] 75-327712 ISBN 0-913592-38-2 : 1.95
1. Christian life—Lutheran authors. I. Title.

RIESS, Oswald. 248.4841
Born to live. Saint Louis, Concordia Pub. House [1963] 101 p. 20 cm. [BV4501.2.R53] 62-21431
1. Christian life — Lutheran authors. I. Title.

RIESS, Oswald. 248.4841
Born to live. St. Louis, Concordia [c.1963] 101p. 20cm. 62-21431 2.00
1. Christian life—Lutheran authors. I. Title.

ROGNESS, Alvin N., 1906- 248'.48'41
The Jesus life; a guide for young Christians [by] Alvin N. Rogness. Minneapolis, Augsburg Pub. House [1973] 112 p. 20 cm. [BV4501.2.R65] 72-90260 ISBN 0-8066-1307-6 1.95
1. Christian life—Lutheran authors. I. Title.

RUDISILL, Dorus Paul, 1902- 248.4'8'41
Love activates and acts. [1st ed.] New York, Poseidon Books [1971] vii, 120 p. 21 cm. Includes bibliographical references. [BJ1251.R8] 76-154295 ISBN 0-8181-9997-0 3.95
1. Christian ethics—Lutheran authors. I. Title.

SARDESON, Charles Thomas. 248.4841
A faith for complicated lives. Philadelphia, Fortress Press [1963] 106 p. 18 cm. [BV4501.2.S24] 63-14402
1. Christian life—Lutheran authors. I. Title.

SARDESON, Charles Thomas 248.4841
A faith for complicated lives. Philadelphia, Fortress [c.1963] 106p. 18cm. Bibl. 63-14402 1.25 pap.,
1. Christian life—Lutheran authors. I. Title.

SCHLINK, Basilea. 248.4841
And none would believe it; an answer to the new morality, by M. Basilea Schlink. Translated by M. D. Rogers and Larry Christenson. [1st ed.] Grand Rapids, Zondervan Pub. House [1967] 115 p. 21 cm. Bibliographical footnotes. [BJ1253.S343] 67-11614
1. Christian ethics—Lutheran authors. I. Title.

SCHMIDT, Ernst G., 1931- 248'.48'41
Make it happen! / Ernst G. Schmidt ; introd. by Robert H. Schuller. Nashville : Abingdon, c1976. 111 p. ; 23 cm. [BV4501.2.S296] 75-44473 ISBN 0-687-22960-X : 5.95
1. Christian life—Lutheran authors. I. Title.

SCHRAMM, John, 1931- 248'.48'41
Things that make for peace : a personal search for a new way of life / John & Mary Schramm. Minneapolis : Augsburg Pub. House, c1976. 112 p. ; 20 cm. "Study guide" by S. A. Noel published as suppl. ([8] p.) and inserted at end. Bibliography: p. 105-111. [BV4501.2.S297] 76-3861 ISBN 0-8066-1537-0 pbk. : 3.25
1. Christian life—Lutheran authors. 2. Peace (Theology) I. Schramm, Mary, joint author. II. Title.

SENFT, Kenneth C. 248.4841
God lives in word and world [by] Kenneth C. Senft. Berkeley, Calif., Mustard Hill Bks. [1966] vii, 107p. 21cm. [BV4501.2.S43] 66-17664 2.00 pap.,
1. Christian life—Lutheran authors. I. Title.

STRENG, William D. 248'.48'41
Be alive! By William D. Streng. Minneapolis, Minn., Augsburg Pub. House [1972] 94 p. 20 cm. [BV4501.2.S814] 72-78559 ISBN 0-8066-9303-7 2.50
1. Christian life—Lutheran authors. I. Title.

TENGBOM, Mildred. 248'.48'41
Is your God big enough? Minneapolis, Augsburg Pub. House [1973] 127 p. 20 cm. [BV4501.2.T4] 72-90261 ISBN 0-8066-1308-4 2.95
1. Christian life—Lutheran authors—Case studies. I. Title.

DITZEN, Lowell Russell 248.4842
Jesus and our human needs. New York, Crowell [1963, c.1962] 266p. 21cm. 62-12801 4.95
1. Christian life—Reformed authors. I. Title.

PFENDSACK, Werner. 248.4842
How to be a Christian, Translated by Ernest G. Gehman. Richmond, John Knox Press [1966] 78 p. illus. 24 cm. "Translated with adaptions from Kennst du den Weg?" [BV4501.2.P4413] 66-11952
1. Christian life—Reformed authors. I. Title.

PFENDSACK, Werner 248.4842
How to be a Christian. Tr. [from German] by Ernest G. Gehman. Richmond, Va., Knox [c.1966] 78p. illus., 24cm. [BV4501.2.P4413] 66-11952 1.50 pap.,
1. Christian life—Reformed authors. I. Title.

ALLEN, Cady Hews, 1886- 248.4'8'5
The guidance of God, by Cady H. Allen. Philadelphia, Westminster Press [1968] 121 p. 21 cm. Bibliographical references included in "Notes" (p. [119]-121) [BV4501.2.A39] 68-11371
1. God—Will. 2. Christian life—Presbyterian authors. I. Title.

ALLEN, Diogenes. 248'.48'5
Between two worlds : a guide for those who are beginning to be religious / Diogenes Allen. Atlanta : John Knox Press, c1977. 155 p. ; 21 cm. [BV4501.2.A43] 76-12395 ISBN 0-8042-1168-X : 7.95
1. Christian life—Presbyterian authors. I. Title.

BAILLIE, John, 1886-1960 248.485
Christian devotion, addresses. New York, Scribners [c.1962] 119p. 20cm. Bibl. 62-17723 2.50
1. Sermons, English. 2. Christian life—Presbyterian authors. I. Title.

BAILLIE, John, 1886-1960. 248.485
Christian devotion, addresses. New York, Scribner [1962] 119p. 20cm. Includes bibliographies. [BV4501.2.B3] 62-17723
1. Sermons, English. 2. Christian life—Presbyterian authors. I. Title.

*BEACH, Waldo 248.485
The Christian life. Richmond, Va., CLC Pr. [dist. John Knox, 1967] 319p. 20cm. (Covenant life curriculum 111) 2.95 pap.,
I. Title.

CANNON, Bryan Jay. 248'.48'5
Celebrate yourself : the secret to a life of hope and joy / by Bryan Jay Cannon. Waco, Tex. : Word Books, c1977. 138 p. ; 22 cm. Includes bibliographical references. [BV4501.2.C257] 76-48542 ISBN 0-87680-802-X pbk. : 3.95
1. Cannon, Bryan Jay. 2. Christian life—Presbyterian authors. I. Title.

ELLIOTT, William Marion, 1903- 248.485
The cure for anxiety [by] William M. Elliott, Jr. Richmond, John Knox Press [1964] 92 p. 19 cm. (Chime paperbacks) "The substance of these nine chapters appeared in ... For the living of these days." [BV4501.2.E36] 64-18326
1. Christian life. I. Title.

ELLIOTT, William Marion, Jr., 1903- 248.485
The cure for anxiety. Richmond, Va., Knox [c.1964] 92p. 19cm. (Chime paperbacks) The substance of these nine chapters appeared in For the living of these days. 64-18326 1.00 pap.,
1. Christian life. I. Title.

ELLIOTT, William Marion, 1903- 248.485
Power to master life; the message of Philippians for today. New York, Abingdon Press [1964] 143 p. 21 cm. Bibliographical footnotes. [BS2705.4.E55] 64-12956
1. Bible. N.T. Philippians — Sermons. 2. Presbyterian Church — Sermons. 3. Sermons, American. I. Title.

ELLIOTT, William Marion, 1903- 248.485
Power to master life; the message of Philippians for today. Nashville, Abingdon [c.1964] 143p. 21cm. Bibl. 64-12956 2.50
1. Bible. N.T. Philippians—Sermons. 2. Presbyterian Church—Sermons. 3. Sermons, American. I. Title.

FARLEY, Edward, 1929- 248.485
Requiem for a lost piety; the contemporary search for the Christian life. Philadelphia, Westminster Press [1966] 189 p. 21 cm. Bibliographical references in "Notes" (p. [135]-139) [BV4501.2.F3] 66-17605

1. Christian life — Presbyterian authors. I. Title.

FARLEY, Edward, 1929- 248.485
Requiem for a lost piety; the contemporary search for the Christitn life. Philadelphia, Westminster [c.1966] 139p. 21cm. [BV4501.2F3] 66-17605 2.25 pap.,
1. Christian life—Presbyterian authors. I. Title.

JONES, Gary M. 1925- 248.485
A time for boldness [by] Gary M. Jones. Nashville, Broadman Press [1966] 106 p. 21 cm. Bibliography: p. 107-108. [BV4501.2.J63] 66-16375
1. Christian life—Presbyterian authors. I. Title.

JONES, Gary M., 1925- 248.485
A time for boldness. Nashville, Broadman [c.1966] 108p. 21cm. Bibl. [BV4501.2.J63] 66-16375 2.50 bds.,
1. Christian life—Presbyterian authors. I. Title.

MORRISON, Max Merritt 248.485
Never lose heart. Garden City, N. Y., Doubleday [1967, c.1964] 143p. 21cm. (Waymark bks., W7) [BV4501.2.M59] 1.45 pap.,
1. Christian life—Presbyterian authors. I. Title.

MORRISON, Max Merritt. 248.485
Never lose heart. [1st ed.] Garden City, N. Y., Doubleday, 1964. 143 p. 22 cm. [BV4501.2.M59] 64-19291
1. Christian life—Presbyterian authors. I. Title.

PALMER, Robert E 248.485
Putting your faith to work; a series of sermons based on the book of James. Boston, Christopher Pub. House [1964] 108 p. 21 cm. [BS2785.4.P3] 64-15615
1. Bible. N. T. James — Sermons. 2. Sermons, American. 3. Presbyterian Church — Sermons. I. Title.

PALMER, Robert E. 248.485
Putting your faith to work; a series of sermons based on the book of James. Boston, Christopher [c.1964] 108p. 21cm. 64-15615 2.75
1. Bible. N.T. James—Sermons. 2. Sermons, American. 3. Presbyterian Church—Sermons. I. Title.

PICKELL, Charles N 1927- 248.485
Works count too Faith in action in the life of the Christian, by Charles N. Pickell. Grand Rapids, Zondervan Pub. House [1966] 120 p. 21 cm. [BV4501:2P54] 65-25962
1. Christian life—Presbyterian authors. I. Title.

PICKELL, Charles N., 248.485
1927-
Works count too! Faith in action in the life of the Christian. Grand Rapids. Mich., Zondervan [c.1966] 120p. 21cm. [BV4501.2.P54] 65-25962 2.95 bds.,
1. Christian life—Presbyterian authors. I. Title.

SPRING, Gardiner, 1785- 248.4'8'5
1873.
The distinguishing traits of Christian character; [essays] Philadelphia, Presbyterian & Reformed Pub. Co., 1967. 80 p. 22 cm. "Adapted from the fifth edition, published in 1829 under the title, Essays on the distinguishing traits of Christian character." [BV4501.S785 1967] 66-30202
1. Christian life. I. Title.

*TURNBULL, Ralph G. 248.485
The Christian faces his world. Grand Rapids, Mich., Baker Bk. [c.1964] 99p. 22cm. 1.00 pap.,
I. Title.

WATSON, Thomas, d.1686 248.485
The divine comforts. Swengel, Pa., Reiner Pubns., 1964. 94p. 20cm. First pub. in 1663 as A divine cordial. 64-3129 1.25 pap.,
1. Christian life—Presbyterian authors. I. Title.

ADAMS, Lane. 248'.48'51
How come it's taking me so long to get better? / Lane Adams. Wheaton, Ill. : Tyndale House, 1975. 159 p. ; 22 cm. [BV4501.2.A29] 75-15026 ISBN 0-8423-1511-X : 5.95
1. Christian life—Presbyterian authors. I. Title.

ANGELL, James W. 248'.48'51
When God made you, He knew what He was doing [by] James W. Angell. Old Tappan, N.J., Revell [1972] 192 p. 21 cm. Includes bibliographical references. [BV4501.2.A53] 70-172687 ISBN 0-8007-0486-X 4.95
1. Christian life—Presbyterian authors. 2. Self-respect. I. Title.

BARNHOUSE, Donald 248'.48'51
Grey, 1895-1960.
How to live a holy life / Donald Grey Barnhouse. Old Tappan, N.J. : F. H. Revell Co., c1975. 85 p. ; 20 cm. First published under title: God's methods for holy living. [BV4501.B265 1975] 75-10900 ISBN 0-8007-0768-0 pbk. : 1.95
1. Christian life—Presbyterian authors. I. Title.

BARNHOUSE, Donald 248'.48'51
Grey, 1895-1960.
Secrets for successful living / Donald Grey Barnhouse. Old Tappan, N.J. : Revell, c1975. 108 p. ; 20 cm. "First published under the title: God's methods for holy living (chapters 1-4)" [BV4501.B265 1975b] 75-10899 ISBN 0-8007-0767-2 pbk. : 1.95
1. Christian life—Presbyterian authors. I. Title.

BRADLEY, Preston, 248.4'8'51
1888-
Between you and me; patterns for creative living by a famous and well-loved minister. [Chicago] Aspley House [1967] 144 p. 22 cm. [BV4501.2.B685] 67-9652
1. Christian life. I. Title.

BROWN, Stephen W. 248'.48'51
So now you are a Christian ... [by] Stephen W. Brown. Old Tappan, N.J., F. H. Revell Co. [1972] 127 p. 21 cm. [BV4501.2.B768] 70-186534 ISBN 0-8007-0520-3 4.50
1. Christian life—Presbyterian authors. I. Title.

BRUERE, John, 1903- 248.4/8/51
1967
Religion that works; [essays] Cleveland, World [1967] xiv, 190p. 22cm. [BV4501.2B78] 67-18030 4.95
1. Christian life—Presbyterian authors. I. Title.

CANNON, Bryan Jay. 248.4'8'51
I give up, God. Old Tappan, N.J., Revell [1970] 192 p. 21 cm. [BV4501.2.C26] 71-96247 4.50
1. Christian life—Presbyterian authors. I. Title.

CASEBOOK for Christian 248'.48'51
living : value formation for families and congregations / Robert A. and Alice F. Evans and Louis and Carolyn Weeks. Atlanta : John Knox Press, c1977. p. cm. Includes bibliographical references. [BV4501.2.C337] 77-79587 ISBN 0-8042-2032-8 pbk. : 4.95
1. Christian life—Presbyterian authors. I. Evans, Robert A., 1937-

GALLOWAY, John T. 248'.48'51
The gospel according to superman, by John T. Galloway, Jr. [1st ed.] Philadelphia, A. J. Holman Co. [1973] 141 p. illus. 22 cm. [BV4501.2.G3] 73-1929 ISBN 0-87981-021-1 2.95
1. Superman (Comic strip) 2. Christian life—Presbyterian authors. 3. God. I. Title.

KENNEDY, Dennis James, 248'.48'51
1930-
The God of great surprises [by] D. James Kennedy. Wheaton, Ill., Tyndale House Publishers [1973] 102 p. 22 cm. [BV4501.2.K43 1973] 72-96220 ISBN 0-8423-1060-6 1.95
1. Christian life—Presbyterian authors. I. Title.

KENNEDY, Dennis James, 248'.48'51
1930-
The God of great surprises [by] D. James Kennedy. Wheaton, Ill., Tyndale House Publishers [1973] 102 p. 22 cm. [BV4501.2.K43 1973] 72-96220 ISBN 0-8423-1060-6 1.95
1. Christian life—Presbyterian authors. I. Title.

LARSON, Bruce. 248'.48'51
Ask me to dance. Waco, Tex., Words Books [1972] 126 p. 23 cm. Bibliography: p. 119-123. [BV4501.2.L319] 72-84396 3.95
1. Christian life—Presbyterian authors. I. Title.

LARSON, Bruce. 248.4'8'51
Living on the growing edge; a resource book for restless and adventurous groups and individuals. Grand Rapids, Zondervan Pub. House [1968] 115 p. 21 cm. [BV4501.2.L325] 68-22838 2.95
1. Christian life—Presbyterian authors. I. Title.

LARSON, Bruce. 248'.48'51
The one and only you. Waco, Tex., Word Books [1974] 141 p. 23 cm. Includes bibliographical references. [BV4501.2.L328] 73-91549 4.95
1. Christian life—Presbyterian authors. I. Title.

LARSON, Bruce. 248'.48'51
The relational revolution : an invitation to discover an exciting future for our life together / Bruce Larson. Waco, Tex. : Word Books, c1976. 143 p. ; 23 cm. [BV4501.2.L329] 76-19524 ISBN 0-87680-374-5 : 5.95
1. Christian life—Presbyterian authors. 2. Theology—20th century. I. Title.

MARSHALL, Catherine 248'.48'51
Wood, 1914-
Something more [by] Catherine Marshall. New York, McGraw-Hill [1974] xv, 316 p. 22 cm. Includes bibliographical references. [BV4501.2.M3643] 74-4235 ISBN 0-07-040607-3 6.95
1. Marshall, Catherine Wood, 1914- 2. Christian life—1960- I. Title.

MURPHEY, Cecil B. 248'.48'51
How to live a Christian life / Cecil B. Murphey. 1st ed. Chappaqua, N.Y. : Christian Herald Books, c1977. 128 p. ; 21 cm. [BV4501.2.M78] 77-79660 ISBN 0-915684-21-7 : 4.95 ISBN 0 ISBN 0-915684-21-7 pbk. : 2.95
1. Christian life—Presbyterian authors. I. Title.

OGILVIE, Lloyd John. 248.4'8'51
A life full of surprises. Nashville, Abingdon Press [1969] 144 p. 21 cm. [BV4501.2.O33] 79-84712 3.00
1. Christian life—Presbyterian authors. 2. Conversion. I. Title.

SMITH, Dana Prom. 248'.48'51
The debonaire disciple. Philadelphia, Fortress Press [1973] viii, 120 p. 18 cm. [BV4501.2.S532] 73-79326 ISBN 0-8006-1036-9 2.95 (pbk.)
1. Christian life—Presbyterian authors. I. Title.

STOFFEL, Ernest Lee. 248'.48'51
Believing the impossible before breakfast / Ernest Lee Stoffel. Atlanta : John Knox Press, c1977. 123 p. ; 21 cm. Includes bibliographical references. [BV4501.2.S77] 76-44977 ISBN 0-8042-2246-0 : 6.95
1. Christian life—Presbyterian authors. I. Title.

TOZER, James R. 248'.48'51
How not to be uptight in an uptight world : the message of Jesus, James, and Peter for today / James R. Tozer. Old Tappan, N.J. : F. H. Revell Co., [1975] 128 p. ; 21 cm. [BV4501.2.T68] 75-19320 ISBN 0-8007-0759-1 : 4.95
1. Christian life—Presbyterian authors. I. Title.

VIGEVENO, H. S. 248.4'8'51
Letters to saints and other sinners [by] H. S. Vigeveno. [1st ed.] Philadelphia, A. J. Holman Co. [1972] 128 p. 21 cm. [BV4905.2.V54] 70-39415 ISBN 0-87981-006-8
1. Consolation. 2. Pastoral counseling. I. Title.

LARSON, Bruce. 248.4'8'5131
Setting men free. [1st ed.] Grand Rapids, Zondervan Pub. House [1967] 120 p. 21 cm. [BV4501.2.L33] 67-17230
1. Christian life—Presbyterian authors. I. Title.

ST. Clair, Robert 248.485131
James.
The adventure of being you. Westwood, N. J., F. H. Revell Co. [1966] 186 p. 21 cm. Bibliographical references included in "Notes" (p. 183-186) [BV4501.2.S15] 66-21897
1. Christian life—Presbyterian authors. I. Title.

LINDQUIST, Raymond 248.4'8'5134
Irving.
Notes for living. [1st ed.] Philadelphia, Lippincott, 1968. 223 p. 21 cm. [BV4501.2.L52] 68-17499
1. Christian life—Presbyterian authors. I. Title.

BALL, Robert R. 248'.48'52
The "I feel" formula / Robert R. Ball. Waco, Tex. : Word Books, c1977. 120 p. ; 23 cm. Includes bibliographical references. [BV4501.2.B382] 77-152880 ISBN 0-8499-0001-8 : 5.95
1. Christian life—Presbyterian authors. 2. Psychology, Religious. I. Title.

MURPHEY, Cecil B. 248'.48'52
Put on a happy faith! / Cecil B. Murphey. 1st ed. Chappaqua, N.Y. : Christian Herald Books, c1976. 115 p. ; 21 cm. [BV4501.2.M8] 76-16600 ISBN 0-915684-08-X : 5.95
1. Christian life—Presbyterian authors. I. Title.

STEVENSON, J. W. 248.4852
God in my unbelief. New York, Harper [1963, c.1960] 159p. 22cm. 63-1496 2.75 bds.,
1. Christian life—Presbyterian authors. I. Title.

HOEK, Ann. 248.4'8'57
Committed to whom? Grand Rapids, Zondervan Pub. House [1970] 64 p. 21 cm. (A Zondervan paperback) "A group study guide including suggestions for leaders." [BV4511.H6] 70-120033 0.95
1. Christian life—Reformed authors—Study and teaching. I. Title.

*BARBER, Cyril J. 248.4858
God has the answer - - -to your problems, [by] Cyril J. Barber. Grand Rapids, Baker Book House [1974] 145 p. illus. 18 cm. [BV4509] ISBN 0-8010-0615-5 1.25 (pbk.)
1. Christian life. 2. Youth—Religious life. I. Title.

GILMORE, G. Don. 248'.48'58
Extra spiritual power; second sight and the Christian [by] Don Gilmore. Waco, Tex., Word Books [1972] 146 p. 21 cm. [BV4509.5.G48] 76-188062 3.95
1. Christian life—Congregational authors. 2. Second sight. I. Title. II. Title: ESP.

GRIFFITH, Arthur 248.4858
Leonard, 1920-
What is a Christian? Sermons on the Christian life. New York, Abingdon Press [1962] 223p. 23cm. [BV4501.2.G757] 62-51870
1. Christian life—Congregational authors. I. Title.

*HUNTING, Gardner. 248.4858
Working with God. New York, Cornerstone library [1974] 128 p. 21 cm. (The key to life bookshelf) [BV4509] 1.95 (pbk.)
1. Christian life. 2. God—Worship and love. I. Title.

JACOBS, Joan. 248'.48'58
Feelings! : Where they come from and how to handle them / Joan Jacobs. Wheaton, Ill. : Tyndale House, 1976. 143 p. ; 22 cm. [BV4501.2.J3135] 76-27573 ISBN 0-8423-0856-3 pbk. : 3.95
1. Christian life—Congregational authors. 2. Emotions. I. Title.

KOPF, Carl Heath, 248.4'8'58
1902-1958.
Windows on life. Freeport, N.Y., Books for Libraries Press [1969, c1968] x, 255 p. 23 cm. (Essay index reprint series) Reprint of the 1941 ed. [BX7233.K6W5 1969] 70-76908
1. Congregational churches—Addresses, essays, lectures. I. Title.

*MECKEL, Aaron N. 248.4858
Living can be exciting. Grand Rapids, Mich. Zondervan [1964, c.1956] 148p. 21cm. 2.95 bds.,
I. Title.

ORTLUND, Raymond C. 248'.48'58
Lord, make my life a miracle! By Raymond C. Ortlund. Glendale, Calif., G/L Regal Books [1974] 154 p. 18 cm. Includes bibliographical references. [BV4501.2.O73] 73-89714 ISBN 0-8307-0284-9 1.25 (pbk.)
1. Christian life—Congregational authors. I. Title.

STRONG, Kendrick. 248.4'8'58
The divine staircase; a guide to Christian maturity based on Isaiah's experience in the temple. [Nashville] Upper Room [1969] x, 70 p. 19 cm. [BV4501.2.S82] 71-103713
1. Isaiah, the prophet. 2. Christian life—Congregational authors. 3. Worship. I. Title.

WHISTON, Lionel A. 248.4'8'58
Are you fun to live with? By Lionel A. Whiston. Waco, Tex., Word Books [1968] 143 p. 21 cm. [BV4501.2.W448] 68-31118 3.95
1. Christian life. I. Title.

CLEVELAND, Philip 248.485832
Jerome, 1903-
Have a wonderful time! Westwood, N.J., Revell [1966] 158p. 21cm. [BV4501.2.C57] 66-21905 3.95
1. Christian life—Congregational authors. I. Title.

FREER, Harold Wiley 248.4'8'5834
God meets us where we are; an interpretation of Brother Lawrence. Nashville, Abingdon [1967] 207p. 23cm. 'Brother Lawrence: his conversations and letters on the practice of the presence of God.' (p. (179) 207) Bibl. [BV4501.2.F76] 67-14981 4.00
1. Christian life—Congregational authors. 2. Herman, Nicolas. 1611-1691. La practiaue de la presence de dieu. I. Herman, Nicolas. 1611-1691. Brother Lawrence: his conversations and letters on the practice of the presence of God. II. Title.

FREER, Harold Wiley. 248.4'8'5834
God meets us where we are; an interpretation of Brother Lawrence. Nashville, Abingdon Press [1967] 207 p. 23 cm. "Brother Lawrence: his conversations and letters on the practice of the presence of God." (p. [179]-207) Includes bibliographical footnotes. [BV4501.2.F76] 67-14981
1. Herman, Nicolas, 1611-1691. La practique de in presence de dieu. 2. Christian life — Congregational authors. I. Herman, Nicolas, 1611-1691. Brother Lawrence; his conversations and letters on the practice of the presence of God. II. Title.

KOSTYU, Frank A. 248'.48'5834
Healing life's sore spots / Frank A. Kostyu. New York : Hawthorn Books, c1976. ix, 156 p. ; 22 cm. [BV4501.2.K66 1976] 75-5040 ISBN 0-8015-3356-2 : 6.95
1. Christian life—United Church of Christ authors. I. Title.

KOSTYU, Frank A. 248'.48'5834
The time of your life is now / Frank A. Kostyu. New York : Seabury Press, c1977. p.

cm. [BV4501.2.K67] 76-41978 ISBN 0-8164-0375-9 : 6.95
1. Christian life—United Church of Christ authors. I. Title.

LLOYD-JONES, David 248.485842
Martyn.
Spiritual depression; its causes and cure [by] D. Martyn Lloyd-Jones. Grand Rapids, Eerdmans [1965] 300 p. 23 cm. Sermons. [BX7233.L57S6] 65-18094
1. Sermons, English. 2. Congregational churches — Sermons. I. Title.

LLOYD-JONES, David 248.485842
Martyn
Spiritual depression: its causes and cure. Grand Rapids. Mich., Eerdmans [c.1965] 300p. 23cm. Sermons. [BX7233.L57S6] 65-18094 3.95
1. Sermons, English. 2. Congregational churches—Sermons. I. Title.

ADAMS, Theodore Floyd, 248.486
1898-
Tell me how. [1st ed.] New York, Harper & Row [c1964] ix, 138 p. 22 cm. [BV4501.2.A3] 64-10615
1. Christian life — Baptist authors. I. Title.

ADAMS, Theodore Floyd, 248.486
1898-
Tell me how. New York, Harper [c.1964] ix, 138p. 22cm. 64-10615 3.00
1. Christian life—Baptist authors. I. Title.

ANGELL, Charles Roy. 248.486
Shields of brass [by] C. Roy Angell. Nashville, Broadman Press [1965] 128 p. 21 cm. [BV4501.2.A5] 65-19548
1. Christian life — Baptist authors. I. Title.

ANGELL, Charles Roy 248.486
Shields of brass. Nashville, Broadman [c.1965] 128p. 21cm. [BV4501.2A5] 65-19548 2.75 bds.,
1. Christian life—Baptist authors. I. Title.

ARMES, Sybil (Leonard) 248.486
Devotions from a grateful heart. [Westwood, N.J.] F. H. Revell Co. [1964] 127 p. 21 cm. [BV4501.2.A66] 64-12199
1. Christian life — Baptist authors. I. Title.

ARMES, Sybil (Leonard) 248.486
Devotions from a grateful heart [Westwood, N.J.] Revell [c.1964] 127p. 21cm. 64-12199 2.50 bds.,
1. Christian life—Baptist authors. I. Title.

BISAGNO, John R. 248.4'8'6
The power of positive living [by] John R. Bisagno. Nashville, Broadman Press [1969] 60 p. 19 cm. [BV4510.B565] 70-93913
1. Christian life—Baptist authors. I. Title.

BURNS, Freeman M., 248.4'8'6
1926-
A renewal of hope; a practical and spiritual challenge for the renewal of the minds of God's people in God's churches, by Freeman M. Burns. Boulder, Colo., Hope Pub. House [1971] 95 p. 22 cm. [BV4501.2.B88] 70-184521 3.95
1. Christian life—Baptist authors. I. Title.

BURTON, Joe Wright, 1907- 248.486
Family life; a Bible view. Nashville, Tenn., Convention Press [c1963] xv, 137 p. 20 cm. "Church study course [of the Sunday School Board of the Southern Baptist Convention]" [BV4526.2.B8] 63-21974
1. Family. 2. Christian life — Baptist authors. I. Southern Baptist Convention. Sunday School Board. II. Title.

CAMPBELL, Colin David. 248.4'86
Commitment and indifference [by] Colin D. Campbell. Valley Forge [Pa.] Judson Press [1971, c1969] 23 p. illus. 15 x 17 cm. (Life issue booklets) Includes bibliographical references. [BV4510.2.C34 1971] 71-161401 ISBN 0-8170-0523-4 0.75
1. Christian life—Baptist authors. I. Title. II. Series.

COBB, John Ross. 248.486
The spirit of a sound mind, by John R. Cobb. Grand Rapids, Zondervan Pub. House [1966] 128 p. 21 cm. Bibliographical footnotes. [BV4501.2.C6] 65-25954
1. Christian life — Baptist authors. I. Title.

COBB, John Ross 248.486
The spirit of a sound mind. Grand Rapids. Mich., Zondervan [c.1966] 128p. 21cm. Bibl. [BV4501.2.C6] 65-25954 2.95 bds.,
1. Christian life—Baptist authors. I. Title.

EDGE, Findley Bartow, 248.486
1916-
A quest for vitality in religion; a theological approach to religious education. Nashville, Broadman [c.1963] 251p. 22cm. Bibl. 63-8406 3.95

1. Christian life—Baptist authors. 2. Church membership. 3. Christianity—20th cent. I. Title.

EVANS, William Henry, 248.486
1888-
How to value life, by William H. Evans. [1st ed.] New York, American Press [c1963] 80 p. 21 cm. [BV4501.2.E9] 63-19992
1. Christian life — Baptist authors. I. Title.

FITZGERALD, Lawrence P 248.486
Adventures in Christian living. Valley Forge [Pa.] Judson Press [1964] 79 p. 20 cm. [BV4501.2.F53] 64-13127
1. Christian life — Baptist authors. I. Title.

FITZGERALD, Lawrence P. 248.486
Adventures in Christian living. Valley Forge, Pa., Judson [c.1964] 79p. 20cm. 64-13127 1.00 pap.,
1. Christian life—Baptist authors. I. Title.

FLYNN, Leslie B 248.486
The power of Christlike living. Grand Rapids, Mich., Zondervan Pub. House [c1962] 127 p. 21 cm. [BV4501.2.F58] 63-350
1. Christian life — Baptist authors. 2. Jesus Christ — Character. I. Title.

FLYNN, Leslie B. 248.486
The power of Christlike living. Grand Rapids, Mich., Zondervan [c.1962] 127p. 21cm. 62-350 2.50
1. Christian life—Baptist authors. 2. Jesus Christ—Character. I. Title.

FORD, William Herschel, 248.486
1900-
Simple sermons on the Christian life. Grand Rapids, Mich., Zondervan [c.1962] 116p. 21cm. 62-51868 1.95
1. Christian life—Baptist authors. 2. Sermons, English. 3. Baptists—Sermons. I. Title.

*GREENWAY, Betty 248.4'8'6
Reeves.
Where lifefinds expression. New York, Vantage [1967] 82p. 21cm. 2.75 bds.,
I. Title.

HARNISH, J Lester. 248.486
The harvest of the spirit [by] J. Lester Harnish. Valley Forge, Judson Press [1965] 126 p. 20 cm. [BV4501.2.H35] 65-13402
1. Christian life. I. Title.

HARNISH, J. Lester 248.486
The harvest of the spirit. Valley Forge, Pa., Judson Pr. [c.1965] 126p. 20cm. [BV4501.2.H35] 65-13402 1.75 pap.,
1. Christian life. I. Title.

HASTINGS, Robert J 248.486
The Christian man's world; a study of the total stewardship of life for Baptist men [by] Robert J. Hastings. Memphis, Brotherhood Commission, SBC, 1964. 94 p. illus. 22 cm. Bibliography: p. 93-94. [BV772.H32] 64-54538
1. Stewardship, Christian. I. Title.

HASTINGS, Robert J 248.486
How to live with yourself [by] Robert J. Hastings, Jr. Nashville, Broadman Press [1966] 94 p. 21 cm. [BJ1581.2.H34] 66-19910
1. Conduct of life. 2. Christian life — Baptist authors. I. Title.

HASTINGS, Robert J. Jr. 248.486
How to live with yourself. Nashville, Broadman [c.1966] 94p. 21cm. [BJ1581.2.H34] 66-19910 2.00 bds.,
1. Conduct of life. 2. Christian life—Baptist authors. I. Title.

HAVNER, Vance, 1901- 248.486
Why not just be Christians? Westwood, N. J., F. H. Revell Co. [1964] 128 p. 20 cm. [BX6333.H345W5] 64-20183
1. Sermons, American. 2. Christian life. 3. Baptists — Sermons. I. Title.

HAVNER. VANCE. 1901- 248.486
Why not just be Christians? Westwood. N.J., Revell [c.1964] 128p. 20cm. 64-20183 2.50 bds.,
1. Sermons, American. 2. Christian life. 3. Baptists—Sermons. I. Title.

HUDSON, Robert Lofton. 248.4'8'6
Grace is not a blue eyed blond [by] R. Lofton Hudson. Waco, Tex., Word Books [1968] 158 p. 20 cm. Bibliographical footnotes. [BV4501.2.H76] 68-21506
1. Christian life—Baptist authors. I. Title.

*HUMPHREYS, Robert Edward 248.486
Christians can conquer; challenging messages for challenging times. New York, Exposition [c.1964] 112p. 22cm. 3.00
I. Title.

LAHAYE, Tim F 248.4'8'6
Spirit-controlled temperament, by Tim LaHaye. [2d ed.] Wheaton, Ill., Tyndale House [1967, c1966] 141 p. illus. 23 cm. Spiritual life -- Baptist authors. [BV4501.2.L315] 67-28429
1. Pastoral counseling. 2. Temperament. I. Title.

LAHAYE, Tim F. 248.4'8'6
Spirit-controlled temperament, by Tim La-Haye. [2d ed.] Wheaton. Ill., Tyndale House [1967,c.1966] 141p. illus. 23cm. [BV4501.2.L315 1967] 67-28429 1.95 pap.,
1. Spiritual life—Baptist authors. 2. Pastoral counseling. 3. Temperament. I. Title.

LEAVELL, Roland Quinche, 248.486
1891-
The sheer joy of living. Grand Rapids, Eerdmans [1961] 96p. 22cm. [BV4501.2.L4] 61-18340
1. Christian life. I. Title.

LEAVELL, Roland Quinche, 248.486
1891-
The sheer joy of living. Grand Rapids, Mich., Eerdmans [c.1961] 93p. 61-18340 2.50
1. Christian life. I. Title.

LEWIS, Bill H. 248.486
How can these things be? Grand Rapids, Mich., Zondervan [c.1961] 87p. 1.95 bds.,
I. Title.

MCBAIN, Loren D. 248'.48'6
Born again & living up to it : guide to church membership / by Loren D. McBain and L. Doward McBain. Valley Forge, Pa. : Judson Press, c1976. 31 p. ; 22 cm. [BV4501.2.M17] 75-33238 ISBN 0-8170-0657-5 pbk. : 0.75
1. Christian life—Baptist authors. 2. Baptists—Doctrinal and controversial works. I. McBain, L. Doward, joint author. II. Title.

MCCLELLAN, Albert. 248.4'8'6
Openness and freedom. Nashville, Broadman Press [1970] 127 p. 20 cm. (A Broadman inner circle book) Includes bibliographical references. [BV4501.2.M213] 74-95414
1. Christian life—Baptist authors. 2. Freedom (Theology) I. Title.

MARKHAM, Meeler. 248.4'8'6
This confident faith. Nashville, Broadman Press [1968] 128 p. 20 cm. Bibliographical references included in "Notes" (p. 127-128) [BV4501.2.M353] 68-20680
1. Christian life—Baptist authors. 2. Communication (Theology) I. Title.

MASON, David E. 248.4'8'6
The compulsive Christian; to be or not to be, by David E. Mason. Foreword by Frank C. Laubach. Grand Rapids, Mich., Zondervan Pub. House [1969] 208 p. 23 cm. [BV4501.2.M365] 69-11638 4.95
1. Christian life—Baptist authors. I. Title.

MASTON, Thomas Bufford, 248.486
1897-
God's will and your life. Nashville, Tenn., Broadman [c.1964] 92p. 20cm. 64-10816 1.95 bds.,
1. Christian life—Baptist authors. I. Title.

PARSONS, E. Spencer 248.486
The Christian yes or no. Valley Forge [Pa.] Judson [1964, c.1963] 96p. 20cm. 64-10851 1.50 pap.,
1. Witness bearing (Christianity) 2. Christian life—Baptist authors. I. Title.

PEARCE, J. Winston 248.486
We covenant together. Nashville, Broadman [1964] 128p. 20cm. Bibl. 64-18271 1.50
1. Covenants (Church polity) 2. Baptists—Government. I. Title.

RADMACHER, Earl D. 248'.48'6
You & your thoughts : the power of right thinking / Earl D. Radmacher. Wheaton, Ill. : Tyndale House Publishers, 1977. 142 p. : ill. ; 18 cm. [BV4501.2.R28] 77-77358 ISBN 0-8423-8570-3 pbk. : 1.95
1. Christian life—Baptist authors. I. Title.

SANDERSON, Leonard, 248.4'8'6
1914-
Strength for living. Nashville, Broadman Press [1969] 128 p. 19 cm. [BV4501.2.S25] 75-95417
1. Christian life—Baptist authors. I. Title.

SOUTHARD, Samuel. 248.4'8'6
The imperfect disciple. Nashville, Broadman Press, [1968] 127 p. 20 cm. Bibliography: p. 127. [BV4501.2.S66] 68-20686
1. Christian life—Baptist authors. I. Title.

STEEN, John Warren 248.486
Conquering inner space. Nashville, Broadman [1964] 128p. 20cm. 64-24024 1.50
1. Christian life—Baptist authors. 2. Christianity—20th cent. I. Title.

THORN, William E 248.486
A bit of honey; after-dinner addresses of inspiration, wit, and humor. Grand Rapids, Zondervan Pub. House [1964] 120 p. 21 cm. Bibliography: p. 119-120. [BV4225.2.T47] 64.15549
1. Homiletical illustrations. 2. After-dinner speeches. I. Title.

THORN, William E. 248.486
A bit of honey; after-dinner addresses of inspiration, wit, and humor. GrandRapids, Mich., Zondervan [c.1964] 120p. 21cm. Bibl. 64-15549 2.50 bds.,
1. Homiletical illustrations. 2. After-dinner speeches. I. Title.

TRENTHAM, Charles Arthur, 248.486
1919-
Getting on top of your troubles. Nashville, Broadman [c.1966] 133p. 21cm. [BV4501.2.T7] 66-15151 2.95 bds.,
1. Christian life—Baptist authors. I. Title.

VALENTINE, Foy. 248.486
Believe and behave. Nashville, Broadman Press [1964] 128 p. 20 cm. Bibliographical references included in "Notes" (p. 126-128) [BV4501.2.V27] 64-15098
1. Christian life — Baptist authors. I. Title.

VALENTINE, Foy 248.486
Believe and behave. Nashville, Broadman [c.1964] 128p. 20cm. Bibl. 64-15098 1.50 bds.,
1. Christian life—Baptist authors. I. Title.

WEST, Bill G. 248.4'8'6
Free to be me, by Bill G. West. Waco, Tex., Word Books [1971] 149 p. 23 cm. Bibliography: p. 145-147. [BV4501.2.W434] 78-160296 3.95
1. Christian life—Baptist authors. I. Title.

WHITE, Reginald E. O. 248.486
52 seed thoughts for Christian living. Grand Rapids, Mich., Eerdmans [c.1963] 146p. 22cm. 63-11496 3.00
1. Christian life—Baptist authors. I. Title.

WHITE, Reginald E O 248.486
52 seed thoughts for Christian living Grand Rapids, Eerdmans [1963] 146 p. 22 cm. [BV4501.2.W45] 63-11496
1. Christian life — Baptist authors. I. Title.

WIERSBE, Warren W. 248.4'86
Creative Christian living [by] Warren W. Wiersbe. Westwood, N.J., F. H. Revell Co. [1967] 127 p. 21 cm. [BV4501.2.W518] 67-22576
1. Spiritual life—Baptist authors. I. Title.

WILSON, Kenneth Lee, 248'.48'6
1916-
All things considered ... ; trials, tribulations, temptations, and triumphs of being Christian in modern-day America / Kenneth L. Wilson. 1st ed. Chappaqua, N.Y. : Christian Herald Books, c1977. 127 p. ; 21 cm. [BV4501.2.W557] 76-50457 ISBN 0-915684-14-4 : 4.95
1. Christian life—Baptist authors. I. Title.

WITTY, Robert Gee. 248.4'8'6
Help yourself to happiness [by] Robert G. Witty. Nashville, Broadman Press [1968] 63 p. 19 cm. [BJ1481.W76] 68-9030
1. Happiness. I. Title.

WOOD, Bertha Vivian 248.486
Blueprints for building a better way of life [Little Rock, Ark.] Pioneer Pr., 1964. 86p. 22cm. Bibl. 64-19013 3.00, lim. ed.
1. Christian life—Baptist authors. I. Title.

SLAUGHTER, Earl. 248.48608
Religion with a smile. San Antonio, Naylor Co. [1965] xi, 154 p. 20 cm. [BV4513.S57] 65-24493
1. Christian life — Quotations, maxims, etc. 2. Homiletical illustrations. I. Title.

SLAUGHTER, Earl 248.48608
Religion with a smile. San Antonio, Tex., Naylor [c.1965] xi, 154p. 20cm. [BV4513.S57] 65-24493 3.95
1. Christian life—Quotations, maxims, etc. 2. Homiletical illustrations. I. Title.

WHITE, K. Owen 248.4'8'608
Messages on stewardship, by K. Owen White [others] Grand Rapids, Mich., Baker Bk. [1967, c.1963] 141p. 20cm. (Preaching helps ser.) 1.50 pap.,
I. Title.

ASHBROOK, James B., 248'.48'61
1925-
Humanitas; human becoming & being human [by] James B. Ashbrook. Nashville, Abingdon Press [1973] 256 p. illus. 24 cm. Bibliography: p. 240-250. [BD450.A77] 73-8840 ISBN 0-687-18030-9 7.95
1. Man. 2. Christian life. I. Title.

BAILEY, John William, 248'.48'61
1873-1969.
Life has meaning; thinking and prayers of

John William Bailey. Edited by Louise Herron Bailey. Valley Forge [Pa.] Judson Press [1974] 80 p. 22 cm. [BV4501.2.B28 1974] 73-13291 ISBN 0-8170-0624-9 1.95 (pbk.)
1. Christian life—Baptist authors. I. Bailey, Louise Herron, ed. II. Title.

BAN, Arline J. 248'.48'61
The new disciple / Arline J. Ban and Joseph D. Ban. Valley Forge, Pa. : Judson Press, c1976. 93 p. : ill. ; 22 cm. A discussion of what it means to be a disciple of Christ in today's world aimed at young people who are thinking about joining an American Baptist church. [BX6219.B35] 75-35898 ISBN 0-8170-0658-3 pbk. : 1.50
1. Baptists—Membership—Juvenile literature. 2. Christian life—Baptist authors—Juvenile literature. 3. Baptists—Doctrinal and controversial works—Juvenile literature. I. Ban, Joseph D., joint author. II. Title.

BUBECK, Mark I. 248'.48'61
The adversary : the Christian versus demon activity / Mark I. Bubeck. Chicago : Moody Press, [1975] 160 p. ; 22 cm. Bibliography: p. 159-160. [BT981.B75] 74-15343 ISBN 0-8024-0143-0 pbk. : 2.25
1. Devil. 2. Demonology. 3. Christian life—Baptist authors. I. Title.

COLEMAN, L. H. 248'.48'61
Facing life's experiences / by L. H. Coleman. Orlando, Fla. : Christ for the World Publishers, c1976. vi, 63 p. : port. ; 21 cm. [BV4501.2.C637] 75-40897
1. Christian life—Baptist authors. 2. Consolation. I. Title.

COOK, William H., 1931- 248'.48'61
Success, motivation, and the Scriptures / William H. Cook ; [foreword by Bill Bright ; introd. by Jack R. Taylor]. Nashville : Broadman Press, c1974. 170 p. ; 21 cm. Includes bibliographical references. [BV4501.2.C674] 74-82582 ISBN 0-8054-5226-5 pbk. : 3.95
1. Christian life—Baptist authors. 2. Success. I. Title.

CRISWELL, Wallie A. 248'.48'61
What to do until Jesus comes back / W. A. Criswell. Nashville : Broadman Press, c1975. 152 p. ; 20 cm. [BV4501.2.C75] 75-8327 ISBN 0-8054-5555-8 : 4.95
1. Christian life—Baptist authors. 2. Second Advent. I. Title.

DAVIS, Creath. 248'.48'61
Sent to be vulnerable; a contemporary description of the Christian life-style with suggestions for small groups. Grand Rapids, Zondervan Pub. House [1973] 180 p. 21 cm. Includes bibliographical references. [BV4501.2.D38] 72-95533 3.95
1. Christian life—Baptist authors. 2. Church group work. I. Title.

DOBBINS, Gaines Stanley, 1886- 248'.48'61
Zest for living / Gaines Dobbins. Waco, Tex. : Word Books, c1977. 123 p. ; 23 cm. [BV4501.2.D59] 76-48526 ISBN 0-87680-511-X : 5.95
1. Dobbins, Gaines Stanley, 1886- 2. Christian life—Baptist authors. I. Title.

DUNCAN, James E. 248'.48'61
Relax and let God / James E. Duncan, Jr. Nashville : Broadman Press, c1975. 128 p. ; 21 cm. [BV4501.2.D757] 75-8324 ISBN 0-8054-8240-7 pbk. : 1.95
1. Christian life—Baptist authors. I. Title.

FANNING, Buckner. 248.4'8'61
Christ in your shoes. Nashville, Broadman Press [1970] 142 p. 21 cm. [BV4501.2.F29] 74-117305 3.50
1. Christian life—Baptist authors. I. Title.

FANNING, Buckner. 248'.48'61
Throw away the garbage / Buckner Fanning. Waco, Tex. : Word Books, c1976. 114 p. ; 22 cm. [BV4501.2.F292] 76-2868 ISBN 0-87680-469-5 : 4.95
1. Christian life—Baptist authors. I. Title.

FLINT, Cort R. 248.4'8'61
To thine own self be true, by Cort R. Flint. [1st ed.] Anderson, S.C., Droke House [1969, c1968] 157 p. 24 cm. [BV4509.5.F55] 68-28780 3.95
1. Identification (Religion) 2. Self-realization. I. Title.

HARRAH, Allegra. 248'.48'61
Prayer weapons / Allegra Harrah. Old Tappan, N.J. : F. H. Revell Co., c1975. p. cm. [BV210.2.H365] 75-29426 ISBN 0-8007-0773-7 : 4.95
1. Prayer. 2. Christian life—Baptist authors. I. Title.

HENLEY, Wallace. 248'.48'61
Enter at your own risk. Old Tappan, N.J., F. H. Revell Co. [1974] 159 p. 20 cm. [BV4501.2.H373] 74-11028 ISBN 0-8007-0686-2 4.95
1. Christian life—Baptist authors. I. Title.

HINSON, E. Glenn. 248'.48'61
A serious call to a contemplative life-style [by] E. Glenn Hinson. Philadelphia, Westminster Press [1974] 125 p. 21 cm. Bibliography: p. [117]-121. [BV4501.2.H52] 74-9658 ISBN 0-664-24992-2 2.85 (pbk.).
1. Spiritual life—Baptist authors. 2. Contemplation. I. Title.

HUNTER, John Edward, 1909- 248'.48'61
Finding God's best [by] John Hunter. Nashville, Broadman Press [1974] 123 p. 20 cm. [BV4501.2.H83] 73-89524 ISBN 0-8054-8233-4 3.95
1. Christian life—Baptist authors. I. Title.

JUNKER, Bill. 248'.48'61
Knowing where you stand with God / Bill Junker. Nashville : Broadman Press, c1976. 96 p. ; 19 cm. Includes bibliographical references. [BV4501.2.J85] 76-8560 ISBN 0-8054-5241-9 pbk. : 2.25
1. Christian life—Baptist authors. I. Title.

LUTZER, Erwin W. 248'.48'61
How in this world can I be holy? / Erwin W. Lutzer. Chicago : Moody Press, c1974. 192 p. ; 19 cm. Includes bibliographical references. [BV4501.2.L87] 74-15337 ISBN 0-8024-3594-7 : 1.25
1. Christian life—Baptist authors. I. Title.

MCMILLAN, Robert M. 248'.48'61
I'm human—thank God! [By] Robert M. McMillan. Boston, G. K. Hall, 1974 [c1973] 212 p. 25 cm. Large print ed. [BV4501.2.M275 1974] 74-4342 ISBN 0-8161-6214-X 9.95 (lib. bdg.)
1. Christian life—Baptist authors. 2. Sight-saving books. I. Title.

MCMILLAN, Robert M. 248'.48'61
I'm human—Thank God! [By] Robert M. McMillan. Nashville, T. Nelson [1973] 159 p. 22 cm. [BV4501.2.M275] 73-8813 4.95
1. Christian life—Baptist authors. I. Title.

MASTON, Thomas Bufford, 1897- 248'.48'61
Real life in Christ [by] T. B. Maston. Nashville, Broadman Press [1974] 122 p. 18 cm. On cover: Bible guidance for walking the Christian way. Bibliography: p. 121-122. [BV4501.2.M3675] 73-87066 ISBN 0-8054-1923-3 1.95 (pbk.)
1. Christian life—Baptist authors. I. Title. II. Title: Bible guidance for walking the Christian way.

MASTON, Thomas Bufford, 1897- 248'.48'61
Why live the Christian life? [By] T. B. Maston. Nashville, T. Nelson [1974] p. cm. Bibliography: p. [BV4501.2.M3677] 74-14797 ISBN 0-8407-5584-8 3.50 (pbk.)
1. Christian life—Baptist authors. I. Title.

MILLER, Calvin. 248'.48'61
That elusive thing called joy / Calvin Miller. Grand Rapids : Zondervan Pub. House, [1975] 143 p. : ill. ; 23 cm. [BV4501.2.M473] 74-11865 4.95
1. Christian life—Baptist authors. 2. Joy. I. Title.

MORGAN, Darold H. 248.4861
Patterns for the pilgrimage; Biblical patterns for effective living [by] Darold H. Morgan. Mashville, Abingdon Press [1966] 142 p. 20 cm. Bibliographical references included in "Notes" (p. 141-142) [BV4501.2.M584] 66-14993
1. Christian life — Baptist authors. I. Title.

MORGAN, Darold H. 248.4861
Patterns for the pilgrimage; Biblical patterns for effective living. Nashville, Abingdon [c.1966] 142p. 20cm. Bibl. [BV4501.2.M584] 66-14993 2.75 bds.,
1. Christian life—Baptist authors. I. Title.

NEAL, Bruce W. 248'.48'61
Bite a blue apple [by] Bruce W. Neal. Nashville, Abingdon Press [1972] 127 p. 21 cm. Includes bibliographical references. [BV4501.2.N38] 77-185552 ISBN 0-687-03580-5
1. Christian life—Baptist authors. I. Title.

OLFORD, Stephen F. 248'.48'61
The grace of giving; thoughts on financial stewardship [by] Stephen Olford. Grand Rapids, Mich., Zondervan Pub. House [1972] 134, [2] p. 18 cm. (Zondervan books) Bibliography: p. [135]-[136] [BV772.O58] 72-83872 pap. 0.95
1. Stewardship, Christian—Sermons. 2. Baptists—Sermons. 3. Sermons, American. I. Title.

OSBORNE, Cecil G. 248'.48'61
You're in charge [by] Cecil G. Osborne. Waco, Tex., Word Books [1973] 154 p. 23 cm. Includes bibliographical references. [BV4501.2.O74] 72-84168 4.95
1. Christian life—Baptist authors. 2. Psychology, Religious. I. Title.

RICE, John R., 1895- 248'.48'61
Come out—or stay in? By John R. Rice. Nashville, T. Nelson [1974] p. cm. [BV4916.R45] 74-12251 ISBN 0-8407-5079-X 3.95
1. Conversion. 2. Christian life—Baptist authors. I. Title.

RICE, John R., 1895- 248'.48'61
How to make a grand success of the Christian life / John R. Rice. Nashville : T. Nelson, [1975] 234 p. ; 21 cm. [BV4501.2.R5114] 75-6968 ISBN 0-8407-5596-1 pbk. : 3.50
1. Christian life—Baptist authors. I. Title.

RIFFEL, Herman H. 248'.48'61
A living, loving way; Christian maturity and the Spirit's power [by] Herman H. Riffel. [Minneapolis] Bethany Fellowship [1973] 167 p. 21 cm. Includes bibliographical references. [BV4501.2.R54] 73-20720 ISBN 0-87123-059-3 2.45 (pbk.).
1. Christian life—Baptist authors. 2. Gifts, Spiritual. I. Title.

ROBERTS, Cecil A. 248.4861
A life worth living, by C. A. Roberts. Waco, Tex., Word Books [1966] 132 p. 21 cm. Bibliographical footnotes. [BV4501.2.R59] 66-29543
1. Christian life — Baptist authors. 2. Commandments. Ten. I. Title.

ROBERTS, Cecil A. 248.4861
This way to the cross [by] C. A. Roberts. Nashville, Broadman Press [1966] viii, 83 p. 21 cm. [BV4501.2.R6] 66-15147
1. Christian life — Baptist authors. I. Title.

ROBERTS, Cecil A. 248.4861
This way to the cross. Nashville, Broadman [c.1966] viii, 83p. 21cm. [BV4501.2.R6] 66-15147 1.95 bds.,
1. Christian life—Baptist authors. I. Title.

ROBERTSON, Pat. 248'.48'61
My prayer for you / Pat Robertson. Old Tappan, N.J. : F. H. Revell, c1977. 127 p. : ill. ; 21 cm. [BV4501.2.R6155] 77-8607 ISBN 0-8007-0869-5 : 5.95
1. Christian life—1960- I. Title.

ROBINSON, Ras B. 248'.48'61
Before the sun goes down : the spiritual journey of a layman / Ras B. Robinson, Jr. Nashville : Broadman Press, c1976. 137, [3] p. ; 20 cm. Bibliography: p. [139]-[140] [BV4501.2.R6175] 76-4243 ISBN 0-8054-8510-4 : 2.50
1. Robinson, Ras B. 2. Baptists—Biography. 3. Christian life—Baptist authors. I. Title.

SMITH, Ralph M. G. 248.4861
Living the spirit-filled life, by Ralph M. Smith. Introd. by Wallace E. Johnson. Grand Rapids, Zondervan [c.1967] 159p. 21cm. [BV4501.2.S6] 67-11610 2.95
1. Spiritual life—Baptist authors. I. Title.

SMITH, Ralph M G 248.4861
Living the spirit-filled life, by Ralph M. Smith. Introd. by Wallace E. Johnson. Grand Rapids, Zondervan Pub. House [c1967] 159 p. 21 cm. [BV4501.2.S6] 67-11610
1. Spiritual life — Baptist authors. I. Title.

SPARKMAN, Temp. 248'.48'61
Being a disciple. Nashville, Broadman Press [1972] 94 p. illus. 19 cm. Includes bibliographical references. [BV4501.2.S68] 72-189507 ISBN 0-8054-6910-9
1. Christian life—Baptist authors. I. Title.

TAYLOR, Jack R. 248'.48'61
After the spirit comes / Jack R. Taylor. Nashville : Broadman Press, c1974. 130 p. ; 20 cm. [BV4501.2.T275] 73-93908 ISBN 0-8054-5224-9 : 3.95
1. Christian life—Baptist authors. I. Title.

TAYLOR, Jack R. 248'.48'61
Much more! A view of the believer's resources in Christ [by] Jack R. Taylor. Nashville, Broadman Press [1972] 160 p. 21 cm. [BV4501.2.T283] 72-79179 ISBN 0-8054-5523-X 4.95
1. Christian life—Baptist authors. I. Title.

THOMASON, William O. 248'.48'61
The life givers [by] W. O. Thomason. Nashville, Broadman Press [1972] 124 p. 21 cm. [BV4501.2.T484] 72-90033 ISBN 0-8054-5530-2 3.50
1. Christian life—Baptist authors. 2. Empathy. I. Title.

TUCKER, Michael R. 248'.48'61
Live confidently : how to know God's will / Michael R. Tucker. Wheaton, Ill. : Tyndale House Publishers, 1976. 138 p. ; 21 cm. Includes bibliographical references. [BV4501.2.T8] 75-37235 ISBN 0-8423-2216-7 pbk. : 2.95
1. Christian life—Baptist authors. 2. God—Will. I. Title.

WILLIAMS, Robert A. 248'.48'61
A place to belong [by] Robert A. Williams. Foreword by Cecil G. Osborne. Grand Rapids, Zondervan Pub. House [1972] 175 p. 22 cm. Includes bibliographical references. [BV4501.2.W543] 72-183049 3.95
1. Christian life—1960- I. Title.

WOOD, Fred M. 248'.48'61
Dynamic living for difficult days [by] Fred M. Wood. Nashville, Broadman Press [1973] vi, 154 p. 19 cm. [BV4501.2.W614] 73-87448 ISBN 0-8054-1924-1
1. Christian life—Baptist authors. I. Title.

ASQUITH, Glenn H. 248'.48'6131
Living in the presence of God [by] Glenn H. Asquith. Valley Forge [Pa.] Judson Press [1972] 96 p. 22 cm. [BV4501.2.A777] 71-183649 ISBN 0-8170-0559-5 1.95
1. Christian life—Baptist authors. I. Title.

COOPER, Owen. 248'.48'6132
The future is before us. Nashville, Broadman Press [1973] 120 p. 21 cm. [BX6207.S68C66] 72-96155 ISBN 0-8054-5533-7 3.95
1. Southern Baptist Convention. 2. Christian life—Baptist authors. I. Title.

HAVLIK, John F. 248'.48'6132
Old wine in new bottles [by] John F. Havlik. Nashville, Broadman Press [1972] 93 p. 20 cm. [BV4501.2.H368] 72-90036 ISBN 0-8054-5314-8 1.95
1. Christian life—Baptist authors. I. Title.

HOLLOWAY, Leonard L. 248'.48'6132
Encounter with God [by] Leonard L. Holloway. Old Tappan, N.J., Revell [1972] 126 p. 21 cm. [BV4501.2.H565] 70-172684 ISBN 0-8007-0493-2 3.95
1. Spiritual life—Baptist authors. 2. God—Knowableness. I. Title.

ISHEE, John A. 248'.48'6132
From here to maturity / John A. Ishee. Nashville, Tenn. : Broadman Press, c1975. viii, 128 p. ; 18 cm. Bibliography: p. 128. [BV4501.2.I72] 75-2976 ISBN 0-8054-5233-8 pbk. : 1.95
1. Christian life—Baptist authors. I. Title.

PRICE, Nelson L. 248'.48'6132
Shadows we run from / Nelson L. Price. Nashville : Broadman Press, [1975] 122 p. ; 20 cm. [BV4501.2.P74] 74-78966 ISBN 0-8054-8237-7 pbk. : 1.95
1. Christian life—Baptist authors. I. Title.

SWADLEY, Elizabeth. 248.4'8'6132
Acknowledging my stewardship. [Teacher's ed.] Nashville, Convention Press [1967] x, 86 p. 20 cm. "Church study course [of the Sunday School Board of the Southern Baptist Convention] This book is number 2084 in category 20, section for intermediates." Bibliographical footnotes. [BV772.S88] 68-12129
1. Stewardship, Christian. 2. Christian giving. I. Southern Baptist Convention. Sunday School Board. II. Title.

GROFF, Warren F. 248'.48'65
Story time : God's story and ours / Warren F. Groff. Elgin, Ill. : Brethren Press, [1974] 141 p. ; 18 cm. Includes bibliographical references. [BR118.G68] 74-23540 ISBN 0-87178-815-2
1. Theology. 2. Christian life—Church of the Brethren authors. I. Title.

ZIEGLER, Edward Krusen, 1903- 248'.48'65
Simple living / Edward K. Ziegler. Elgin, Ill. : Brethren Press, 1974. 127 p. ; 18 cm. Bibliography: p. 124-127. [BJ1496.Z53] 74-8716 ISBN 0-87178-791-1 : 1.25
1. Simplicity. I. Title.

JONES, George Curtis, 1911- 248.4866
A man and his religion, by G. Curtis Jones. St. Louis, Bethany Press [1967] 175 p. 23 cm. Bibliographical references included in "Notes" (p. 169-175) [BV4501.2.J62] 67-27120
1. Christian life—Disciples of Christ authors. I. Title.

PAULSELL, William O. 248'.48'66
Taste and see : a personal guide to the spiritual life / William O. Paulsell. Nashville : Upper Room, c1976. 88 p. ; 20 cm. [BV4501.2.P356] 76-5634

1. Spiritual life—Christian Church (Disciples of Christ) authors. I. Title.

SEE, Frank Edmund. 248.4'8'66
Feeling kind of temporary. Westwood, N.J., F. H. Revell Co. [1968] 159 p. 21 cm. Bibliographical references included in "Notes" (p. 153-159) [BV4501.2.S38] 68-17093
1. Christian life—Disciples of Christ authors. I. Title.

WHEELER, Joseph Clyde. 248'.48'66
This way, please! [By] J. Clyde Wheeler. St. Louis, Bethany Press [1972] 128 p. 22 cm. [BV4501.2.W438] 71-184898 ISBN 0-8272-3620-4
1. Christian life—Disciples of Christ authors. I. Title.

DIEHM, Floyd L., 1925- 248'.48'663
How to be fully alive / Floyd L. Diehm. Nashville : Abingdon Press, c1976. 159 p. 19 cm. Bibliography: p. 157-159. [BV4501.2.D5] 75-26655 ISBN 0-687-17739-1 pbk. : 3.95
1. Christian life—Christian Church (Disciples of Christ) authors. I. Title.

JONES, Curtis. 248'.48'663
How come we're alive? / Curtis Jones. Waco, Tex. : Word Books, c1976. 124 p. ; 21 cm. [BV4501.2.J586] 75-36192 3.25
1. Christian life—Christian Church (Disciples of Christ) authors. 2. Death. I. Title.

MCCORD, David M. 248'.48'663
The faith; a fresh consideration of some basic Christian beliefs with an emphasis on their implications for life today, by David M. McCord. Cincinnati, Standard Pub. [1972] 96 p. 18 cm. (Fountain books) [BV4501.2.M215] 73-180748
1. Christian life—Church of Christ authors. 2. Theology, Doctrinal—Popular works. I. Title.

TAYLOR, Robert R. 248'.48'663
Christ in the home [by] Robert R. Taylor, Jr. Grand Rapids, Baker Book House [1973] 282 p. 22 cm. [BV4526.2.T38] 73-86807 ISBN 0-8010-8811-9 3.95 (pbk.).
1. Family—Religious life. I. Title.

BEACH, Walter Raymond. 248.4867
Dimensions in salvation. Washington, Review and Herald Pub. Association [1963] 329 p. col. illus. 18 cm. Bibliography: p. 319-320 [BX6154.B1] 63-17765
1. Seventh Day Adventists — Doctrinal and controversial works. 2. Christian life. I. Title.

BIETZ, Arthur Leo 248.4867
The wise have it. Mountain View, Calif., Pacific Pr. [c.1962] 107p. 23cm. 62-19058 3.50
1. Christian life—Seventh-Day Adventist authors. I. Title.

CARCICH, Theodore. 248.4867
Principles to ponder. Washington, Review and Herald Pub. Association [1963] 159 p. 20 cm. [BV4501.2C28] 63-13389
1. Christian life—Seventh-Day Adventist authors. I. Title.

CARCICH, Theodore 248.4867
Principles to ponder. Washington, D.C., Review & Herald [c.1963] 159p. 20cm. 63-13389 3.00
1. Christian life—Seventh-Day Adventist authors. I. Title.

DELAFIELD, D A 1913- 248.4867
I promise God; story talks about the Junior Missionary Volunteer pledge and law. Washington, Review and Herald Pub. Association [1963] 192 p. illus. 22 cm. [BV4515.2.D45] 63-17764
1. Christian life — Stories. 2. Seventh-day Adventists. General Conference. Young People's Missionary Volunteer Dept. I. Title.

DELAFIELD, D. A., 1913- 248.4867
I promise God; story talks about the Junior Missionary Volunteer pledge and law. Washington, D.C., Review & Herald [c.1963] 192p. illus. 22cm. 63-17764 3.75
1. Christian life—Stories. 2. Seventh-day Adventists. General Conference. Young People's Missionary Volunteer Dept. I. Title.

IVERSEN, John Orville 248.4867
Point of no return. Washington, D.C., Review & Herald [c.1964] 152p. 22cm. 64-24773 3.00
1. Christian life—Seventh-Day Adventist authors. I. Title.

KNOCHE, Keith. 248'.48'67
Knoche's law: "If something can go wrong, it will. But there's a lesson in it somewhere." Cover and other illus. by the author. Mountain View, Calif., Pacific Press Pub. Association [1973] 128 p. illus. 18 cm. (Agape 105) [BV4501.2.K56] 73-85432 1.65 (pbk.)
1. Christian life—Seventh-Day Adventist authors. I. Title.

OCHS, William Benjamin 248.4867
'Lord, is it I?' Washington, D.C., Review & Herald Pub. Assn. [1963, c.1962] 185p. 22cm. 61-11979 3.00
1. Christian life—Seventh Day Adventist authors. I. Title.

REYNOLDS, Louis Bernard, 1917- 248'.48'67
Bible answers for today's questions, by Louis B. Reynolds and Robert H. Pierson. Nashville, Southern Pub. Association [1973] 271 p. illus. 26 cm. [BV4501.2.R48] 73-78918
1. Bible—Miscellanea. 2. Christian life—Seventh-Day Adventist authors. I. Pierson, Robert H., joint author. II. Title.

WHITE, Ellen Gould (Harmon) 1827-1915. 248.4867
Life at its best. Mountain View, Calif., Pacific Press Pub. Association [c1964] 314 p. illus. (part col.) 18 cm. "Major selections from the ... [author's] The Ministry of healing, which first appeared in 1905." [BT732.W5] 64-8510
1. Medicine and religion. 2. Seventh-Davy Adventists. I. Title.

WHITE, Ellen Gould (Harmon) 1827-1915. 248.4867
Life at its best. Mountain View, Calif., Pacific Press Pub. Assn. [c.1964] 314p. illus. (pt. col.) 18cm. Major selections from the author's The ministry of healing, which first appeared in 1905. [BT732.W5] 64-8510 1.00
1. Medicine and religion. 2. Seventh-Day Adventists. I. Title.

COON, Glenn A. 248'.48'673
The God I love / Glenn A. Coon. Washington : Review and Herald Pub. Association, c1975. 191 p. ; 21 cm. [BV4501.2.C677] 75-8039
1. Christian life—Seventh-Day Adventist authors. I. Title.

COOPER, Douglas. 248'.48'673
Living God's love / Douglas Cooper. Mountain View, Calif. : Pacific Press Pub. Association, c1975. 160 p. ; 18 cm. (A Redwood paperback) [BV4639.C63] 74-27171 pbk. : 1.95
1. Love (Theology) I. Title.

DAVIS, Thomas A. 248'.48'673
How to be a victorious Christian / Thomas A. Davis. Washington : Review and Herald Pub. Association, [1975] 168 p. : ill. ; 22 cm. [BV4501.2.D39] 74-29822 3.50
1. Christian life—Seventh-Day Adventist authors. I. Title.

HILDE, Reuben. 248'.48'673
Your remarkable mind / by Reuben Hilde. Mountain View, Calif. : Pacific Press Pub. Association, 1976,c1977 144 p. ; 22 cm. (Dimension ; 123) Bibliography: p. 144. [BV4501.2.H45] 76-7851 pbk : 3.95
1. Christian life—Seventh-Day Adventist authors. 2. Intellect. I. Title.

HUTTENLOCKER, Keith. 248'.48'673
Love makes the word go round. Anderson, Ind., Warner Press [1974] 128 p. 19 cm. Includes bibliographical references. [BV4639.H89] 73-21613 ISBN 0-87162-170-3 2.50 (pbk.)
1. Love (Theology) 2. Christian life—Church of God authors. I. Title.

INTO the arena : 248'.48'673
insight essays on the Christian life / Chuck Scriven, compiler. Washington : Review and Herald Pub. Association, [1975] 157 p. ; 21 cm. Conten..Contents.—The book explained: Scriven, C. What to expect, what not to expect. Rice, R. Doctrine: do we have too much or too little?—Problems of belief: Vick, E. W. H. With all my mind. Scriven, C. Knowing that God is our maker. Rice, R. The problem of evil. Vick, E. W. H. Doubt.—On being human: Brown, D. On making yourself and making your world. Butler, J. Belief number 10: the state of the dead. Scriven, C. Our inner private world.—The significance of the cross: Larson, D. Why our hope is sure. Butler, J. The symbol of two gardens.—The experience of salvation: Scriven, C. Getting the spirit. Butler, J. Baptism, Ralph Nader, and the church. Maxwell, M. What is righteousness by faith? Battistone, J. J. Prayer in a secular age. Larson, D. Celebrating the Sabbath. Oosterwal, G. The people of God. Christian ethics: Rice, R. The unexpectedness of love. Scriven, C. Chastity and faithfulness. Butler, J. Camels and gnats. Oosterwal, G. The world my destination. Battistone, J. J. Doctor, lawyer, merchant, chief. Butler, J. Dreams, visions, and the establishment.—Ultimate fulfillment: Butler, J. Pity the planet, all joy gone. Branson, R. Can God be a stone? Includes bibliographical references. [BV4501.2.I55] 74-81647
1. Christian life—Seventh-Day Adventist authors. I. Scriven, Chuck.

OCHS, William Benjamin 248.48673
Look now toward heaven. Washington, D.C., Review Herald [1965] 160p. 22cm. [BV4501.2.O29] 64-24770 price unreported
1. Christian life—Seventh-Day Adventist authors. I. Title.

PIERSON, Robert H. 248.4'8'673
Faith on tiptoe; glimpses into the simple dynamics of practical Christian living [by] Robert H. Pierson. Nashville, Southern Pub. Association [1967] 206 p. 22 cm. [BV4501.2.P543] 67-28459
1. Christian life—Seventh-Day Adventist authors. I. Title.

†SCARBOROUGH, Peggy. 248'.48'673
Hallelujah anyway, Tim! : Based on Second Timothy / Peggy Scarborough. Cleveland, Tenn. : Pathway Press, c1976. 144 p. ; 18 cm. Bibliography: p. 143-144. [BV4501.2.S28] 75-37359 ISBN 0-87148-405-6 pbk. : 2.50
1. Bible. N.T. 2 Timothy—Meditations. 2. Christian life—Church of God authors. I. Title.

SCRAGG, Walter. 248'.48'673
Directions : a look at the paths of life / Walter R. L. Scragg. Nashville : Southern Pub. Association, c1977. 125 p. ; 20 cm. [BV4501.2.S33] 77-78101 ISBN 0-81270136-4 pbk. : 3.95
1. Christian life—Seventh-Day Adventist authors. I. Title.

SHULER, John Lewis, 1887- 248'.48'673
Help in time of need [by] J. L. Shuler. Washington, Review and Herald Pub. Association [1974] 64 p. 19 cm. [BV4501.2.S453] 74-78020 0.50 (pbk.)
1. Christian life—Seventh-Day Adventist authors. I. Title.

TAGGART, George H 248.4'8'673
Happiness is [by] George H. Taggart. Washington, Review and Herald Pub. Association [1967] 96 p. 19 cm. [BV4501.2.T23] 67-19712
1. Happiness. 2. Christian life—Seventh-Day Adventist authors. I. Title.

TAGGART, George H. 248.4'8'673
Happiness is [by] George H. Taggart. Washington, Review and Herald Pub. Association [1967] 96 p. 19 cm. [BV4501.2.T23] 67-19712
1. Happiness. 2. Christian life—Seventh-Day Adventist authors. I. Title.

TORKELSON, Ted. 248.4'8'673
Doctor upstairs. Mountain View, Calif., Pacific Press Pub. Association [1970] 64 p. 18 cm. [BV4501.2.T64] 70-103126
1. Christian life—Seventh-Day Adventist authors. 2. U.S.—Moral conditions. I. Title.

TORKELSON, Ted. 248'.48'673
One heart, one vote / T. R. Torkelson. Mountain View, Calif. : Pacific Press Pub. Association, c1975. 64 p. ; 19 cm. [BV4501.2.T65] 75-25224
1. Christian life—Seventh-Day Adventist authors. I. Title.

VANDEMAN, George E. 248.4'8'673
Happiness wall to wall, by George E. Vandeman. Mountain View, Calif., Pacific Press Pub. Association [1968] 92 p. 19 cm. [BV4529.V3] 68-56328
1. Christian life—Seventh-Day Adventist authors. 2. Family—Religious life. I. Title.

VANDEMAN, George E. 248'.48'673
Sail your own seas / George E. Vandeman. Mountain View, Calif. : Pacific Press Pub. Association, c1975. 96 p. ; 19 cm. [BV4501.2.V33] 75-324691 pbk. : 0.60
1. Christian life—Seventh-Day Adventist authors. I. Title.

WHITE, Ellen Gould (Harmon) 1827-1915. 248.4'8'673
Help in daily living. Cover and illus. by James Converse. Mountain View, Calif., Pacific Press Pub. Association [c1964] 51 p. cl. illus. 19 cm. [BV4501.W55 1964] 64-24958
1. Christian life—Seventh-Day Adventist authors. I. Title.

ALLEN, Charles Livingstone, 1913- 248.4'8'7
Life more abundant [by] Charles L. Allen. Old Tappan, N.J., F. H. Revell Co. [1968] 160 p. 21 cm. [BV4501.2.A398] 68-28432 3.50
1. Christian life—Methodist authors. I. Title.

ALLEN, Charles Livingstone. 1913- 248.487
Prayer changes things. Westwood, N. J., Revell [1964] 128p. 21cm. 64-20184 2.50
1. Christian life—Methodist authors. I. Title.

ARMSTRONG, James, 1924- 248.4'8'7
The journey that men make. Nashville, Abingdon Press [1969] 159 p. 20 cm. Includes bibliographical references. [BV4501.2.A68] 69-12016 3.50
1. Christian life—Methodist authors. I. Title.

*BAKER, Richard C. 248.487
Configurations of Christian living; a day with Christ. New York, Carlton [c.1966] 74p. 21cm. (Reflection bk.) 2.75
I. Title.

BERG, Darrel E 248.487
A piece of blue sky; the dynamics of faith, by Darrel E. Berg. Introd. by Gerald Kennedy. Grand Rapids, Zondervan Pub. House [1965] 148 p. 23 cm. [BV4501.2.B4] 65-20286
1. Christian life — Methodist authors. 2. Sermons, American. 3. Abraham, the patriarch. I. Title.

BERG, Darrell E. 248.487
A piece of blue sky; the dynamics of faith. Introd. by Gerald Kennedy. Grand Rapids, Mich., Zondervan [c.1965] 148p. 23cm. [BV4501.2.B4] 65-20286 2.95 bds.,
1. Abraham, the patriarch. 2. Christian life—Methodist authors. 3. Sermons, American. I. Title.

BISHOP, John, 1908- 248'.48'7
Courage to live / John Bishop. Valley Forge, PA : Judson Press, c1976. 127 p. ; 22 cm. Includes bibliographical references. [BV4501.2.B53] 76-999 ISBN 0-8170-0697-4 pbk. : 3.95
1. Christian life—Methodist authors. I. Title.

CONNERS, Kenneth Wray. 248.4'8'7
Stranger in the pew. Valley Forge [Pa.] Judson Press [1970] 128 p. 23 cm. Bibliography: p. 127-128. [BV4501.2.C67] 72-100966 3.95
1. Christian life—Methodist authors. 2. Church group work. I. Title.

DUNNAM, Maxie D. 248'.48'7
Barefoot days of the soul / Maxie Dunnam. Waco, Tex. : Word Books, c1975. 133 p. ; 23 cm. [BV4501.2.D767] 75-19910 4.95
1. Christian life—Methodist authors. I. Title.

DUNNAM, Maxie D. 248'.48'7
Barefoot days of the soul / Maxie Dunnam. Waco, Tex. : Word Books, c1975. 133 p. ; 23 cm. [BV4501.2.D767] 75-19910 4.95
1. Christian life—Methodist authors. I. Title.

DUNNAM, Maxie D. 248.4'8'7
Be your wholf self [by] Maxie D. Dunnam. Old Tappan, N.J., Revell [1970] 192 p. 22 cm. [BV4501.2.D768] 75-96248 4.50
1. Christian life—Methodist authors. I. Title.

ENSLEY, Francis Gerald, Bp. 248.487
Persons can change. New York, Abingdon Press [1964, c1963] 127 p. 20 cm. Bibliographical footnotes. [BV4501.2.E6] 64-4507
1. Christian life — Methodist authors. I. Title.

FOOTE, Robert M. 248.4'8.'7
Finding the real you; a psychiatrist's thoughts on man and God [by] Robert M. Foote. Westwood, N.J., Revell [1967] 159p. 21cm. [BV4501.2.F588] 67-14774 3.95
1. Christian life—Methodist authors. 2. Personality. I. Title.

GARRISON, Webb B. 248.4'8'7
Ten paths to peace and power [by] Webb Garrison. Nashville, Abingdon Press [1967] 174 p. 21 cm. [BV4501.2.G37] 67-11011
1. Christian life—Methodist authors. I. Title.

GILMORE, G Don. 248.487
The freedom to fail [by] G. Don Gilmore. Westwood, N.J., Revell [1966] 124 p. 21 cm. [BV4501.2.G53] 66-21899
1. Christian life — Methodist authors. 2. Freedom (Theology) I. Title.

GILMORE, G. Don 248.487
The freedom to fail [by] G. Don Gilmore. Westwood, N. J., Revell [1966] 124p. 21cm. [BV4501.2.G53] 66-21899 2.95 bds.,
1. Christian life—Methodist authors. 2. Freedom (Theology) I. Title.

GILMORE, G. Don. 248.4'8'7
Letters from a previously unpublished angel [by] G. Don Gilmore. Westwood, N.J., Revell [1968] 126 p. 21 cm. [BV4501.2.G55] 68-11365
1. Christian life—Methodist authors. I. Title.

GRAY, W. Arthur. 248.487
Life's eventful voyage by W. Arthur Gray. Boston, Christopher Pub. House [1964] 181 p. 21 cm. [BV4501.2.G73] 64-22911
1. Christian life—Methodist authors. I. Title.

HAGER, Wesley H 248.487
Mastering life with the Master. Grand Rapids, W. B. Eerdmans Pub, Co. [1964] 105 p. 22 cm. [BV4501.2.H26] 63-23104
1. Christian life — Methodist authors. I. Title.

HAGER, Wesley H. 248.487
Mastering life with the Master. Grand Rapids, Mich., Eerdmans [c.1964] 105p. 22cm. 63-23104 2.50
1. Christian life—Methodist authors. I. Title.

HARKNESS, Georgia Elma, 1891- 248.4'87
Disciplines of the Christian life [by] Georgia Harkness. Richmond, John Knox Press [1967] 111 p. 21 cm. Bibliographical footnotes. [BV4501.2.H34] 67-10344
1. Christian life—Methodist authors. I. Title.

JOHNSON, Barry Lee, 1943- 248'.48'7
Sometimes there's a hole in the ceiling / Barry L. Johnson. Nashville : Abingdon Press, [1975] 125 p. ; 20 cm. Includes bibliographical references. [BV4501.2.J53] 74-30431 ISBN 0-687-39084-2 pbk. : 3.50
1. Christian life—Methodist authors. I. Title.

JOHNSON, Ben Campbell. 248'.48'7
Experiencing commitment / Ben Johnson. New York : Hawthorn Books, c1975. 146 p. ; 21 cm. Bibliography: p. 145-146. [BV4501.2.J538 1975] 74-22915 ISBN 0-8015-2446-6 : 3.50
1. Christian life—Methodist authors. I. Title.

JONES, George William, 1931- 248.4'8'7
The innovator and other modern parables [by] G. William Jones. Prints by Robert O. Hodgell. Nashville, Abingdon Press [1969] 112 p. illus. 22 cm. [BV4515.2.J6] 69-13139
1. Christian life—Stories. I. Title.

MCELVANEY, William K., 1928- 248.4'8'7
The saving possibility; a contemporary refocusing of the Christian message [by] William K. McElvaney. Nashville, Abingdon Press [1971] 175 p. 19 cm. Includes bibliographical references. [BV4501.2.M234] 79-160796 ISBN 0-687-36870-7
1. Christian life—Methodist authors. I. Title.

MORRIS, Danny E 248.4'8'7
A life that really matters. The autobiography of a corporate spiritual experience as told by Danny E. Morris. [6th ed.] Atlanta, Spiritual Life Publishers [1967, 1965] xiv, 111 p. 20 cm. Bibliography: p. 104. [BV4501.2.M586] 65-26772
1. Christian life—Methodist authors. I. Title.

OZMENT, Robert Varnell, 1927- 248.487
Happy is the man. [Westwood, N.J.] Revell [c1963] 128 p. 21 cm. [BV4501.2.O92] 63-17110
1. Christian life — Methodist authors. I. Title.

OZMENT, Robert Varnell, 1927- 248.487
Happy is the man [Westwood, N.J.] Revell [c.1963] 128p. 21cm. 63-17110 2.50 bds.,
1. Christian life—Methodist authors. I. Title.

OZMENT, Robert Varnell, 1927- 248.4'8'7
Love is the answer [by] Robert V. Ozment. Westwood, N.J., Revell [1967] 158 p. 21 cm. [BV4501.2.O93] 67-22572
1. Christian life—Methodist authors. I. Title.

PALMER, Everett W Bp. 248.487
There is an answer. New York, Abingdon Press [1962] 158p. 21cm. [BV4501.2.P28] 62-14668
1. Christian life—Methodist authors. I. Title.

PLUMB, Oscar C. 248'.48'7
A search for Christian identity; a reasoning approach to believing and feeling as a Christian [by] Oscar C. Plumb. [1st ed.] New York, Exposition Press [1972] 204 p. illus. 21 cm. (An Exposition-testament book) Bibliography: p. 201-204. [BV4501.2.P5554] 72-192033 ISBN 0-682-47475-4 5.00
1. Christian life—Methodist authors. I. Title.

RAINES, Robert Arnold. 248'.48'7
Success is a moving target / Robert A. Raines. Waco, Tex. : Word Books, c1975. 152 p. : ill. ; 23 cm. Includes bibliographical references. [BJ1611.R14] 75-10091 ISBN 0-87680-395-8 : 5.95
1. Success. 2. Christian life—Methodist authors. I. Title.

RITCHIE, David Ronald. 248'.48'7
From ditches to discipleship [by] D. Ronald Ritchie. Nashville, Abingdon Press [1974] 79 p. 20 cm. [BV4501.2.R57] 74-8414 ISBN 0-687-13636-9 3.95
1. Christian life—Methodist authors. I. Title.

SCHATZMAN, Albert G. 248.4'8'7
The life Jesus brought. [Nashville, Parthenon Press, 1968] 173 p. 23 cm. [BV4501.2.S292] 68-4528
1. Christian life—Methodist authors. I. Title.

SMITH, Charles Merrill. 248.4'8'7
How to talk to God when you aren't feeling religious. Waco, Tex., Word Books [1971] 223 p. 23 cm. [BV4501.2.S53] 74-175726 4.95
1. Christian life—Methodist authors. I. Title.

TUTTLE, Robert G., 1907- 248.4'8'7
Thoughts for doubting Christians, by Robert G. Tuttle. Nashville, Upper room [1969] 77 p. 17 cm. [BV4501.2.T86] 78-77689
1. Christian life—Methodist authors. I. Title.

TWENTIETH century 248.487
Aldersgate, by ten Methodist bishops. Nashville, Methodist Evangelistic Materials [c1962] 64 p. 19 cm. "A collection of ... message by Methodist bishops on Wesley's Aldersgate experiences." [BX8495.W5T75] 62-20647
1. Wesley, John, 1708-1791. 2. Christian life — Methodist authors.

WARD, William Arthur, 1921- 248.4'8'7
Thoughts of a Christian optimist; the words of William Arthur Ward. [1st ed.] Anderson, S.C., Droke House; distributed by Grosset and Dunlap, New York [1968] 89 p. illus. 23 cm. [BJ1548.W37] 68-13823
1. Conduct of life—Quotations, maxims, etc. I. Title.

WATSON, George Douglas, 1845-1924. 248'.48'7
Tribulation worketh : a collection of chapters from G. D. Watson's books in which he explains God's loving and purposeful chastening in the lives of His choicest saints. Stoke-on-Trent : M.O.V.E. Press, 1976. 78 p. ; 19 cm. [BV4501.W38473 1976] 77-353993 ISBN 0-9504136-4-X : £0.50
1. Christian life—Methodist authors—Addresses, essays, lectures. I. Title.

WELDON, Wilson O. 248'.48'7
Mark the road; signposts for the Christian pilgrim [by] Wilson O. Weldon. [Nashville] The Upper Room [1973] 104 p. 22 cm. Includes bibliographical references. [BV4501.2.W418] 73-87636 1.50
1. Christian life—Methodist authors. I. Title.

WERNER, Hazen Graff, Bp., 1895- 248.487
The Bible and the family [by] Hazen G. Werner Nashville, Abingdon Press [1966] 111 p. 20 cm. [BS680.F3W4] 66-22915
1. Family—Biblical teaching. I. Title.

MCELVANEY, William K., 1928- 248'.48'71
Celebrations on coming alive; reflections in mini-forms through behavioral theology [by] William K. McElvaney. Nashville, Abingdon Press [1973] 126 p. 20 cm. [BV4501.2.M233] 72-10669 ISBN 0-687-04826-5 3.95
1. Christian life—Methodist authors. I. Title.

RAINES, Robert Arnold. 248'.48'71
To kiss the joy [by] Robert A. Raines. Waco, Tex., Word Books [1973] 151 p. illus. 23 cm. Includes bibliographical references. [BV4832.2.R233] 73-84577 4.95
1. Christian life—Methodist authors. I. Title.

BEACH, Walter Raymond. 248.4873
Focusing on fundamentals. Nashville, Southern Pub. Association [1966] 128 p. 28 cm. [BV4501.2.B386] 66-3672
1. Christian life — Seventh-Day Adventist authors. I. Title.

BEACH, Walter Raymond 248.4873
Focusing on fundamentals. Nashville, Southern Pub. [c.1966] 128p. 28cm. [BV4501.2.B386] 66-3672 2.50
1. Christian life—Seventh-Day Adventist authors. I. Title.

ARMSTRONG, James, 1924- 248.4'8'76
Mission: Middle America. Nashville, Abingdon Press [1971] 127 p. 21 cm. Includes bibliographical references. [BR121.2.A68] 79-172807 ISBN 0-687-27076-6 3.50
1. Christianity—20th century. 2. Church and social problems. I. Title.

BOWSER, Sam E. 248'.48'76
Roses of the ledge way, by Sam E. Bowser. Philadelphia, Dorrance [1972] xi, 106 p. 22 cm. [BX8495.B675A3] 72-75578 ISBN 0-8059-1695-4 4.95
1. Bowser, Sam E. 2. Christian life—Methodist authors. I. Title.

BRANNON, T. Leo. 248'.48'76
Doing the faith, by T. Leo Brannon. Designed and illustrated by Harold Bales. Nashville, Tidings [1973] 58 p. illus. 19 cm. [BV4501.2.B687] 72-95654 0.75 (pbk.)
1. Christian life—Methodist authors. I. Title.

CUSTER, Chester E. 248'.48'76
Called to care, by Chester E. Custer. Nashville, Tenn., Tidings [1974] 92 p. 19 cm. Includes bibliographical references. [BV4501.2.C875] 74-78610 1.50 (pbk.).
1. Christian life—Methodist authors. 2. Church work. I. Title.

DUMOND. CHARLES E. 248.4'8'76
Depth discipleship. by Charles E. DuMond. Introd. by Anna B. Mow. Grand Rapids. Zondervan [1967] 126p. 22cm. [BV4501.2.D75] 67-11620 2.95 bds.,
1. Spiritual life—Methodist authors. I. Title.

DUNNAM, Maxie D. 248'.48'76
Dancing at my funeral [by] Maxie Dunnam. Illus. by Jerry Dunnam. Foreword by Bruce Larson. Atlanta, Forum House [1973] xi, 112 p. illus. 23 cm. [BV4501.2.D769] 72-86155 4.95
1. Christian life—Methodist authors. I. Title.

HAGER, Wesley H 248.4876
Conquering, by Wesley H. Hager. Grand Rapids, Eerdmans [1965] 110 p. 22 cm. [BV4501.2.H25] 65-18101
1. Christian life — Methodist authors. 2. Consolation. I. Title.

HAGER, Wesley H. 248.4876
Conquering, Grand Rapids, Mich., Eerdmans [c.1965] 110p. 22cm. [BV4501.2.H25] 65-18101 2.95
1. Christian life—Methodist authors. 2. Consolation. I. Title.

HALE, Joe, 1935- 248'.48'76
God's moment. Nashville, Tidings [1972] 84 p. 19 cm. [BV4501.2.H2633] 72-86492 1.25 (pbk.)
1. Christian life—Methodist authors. I. Title.

HARRISON, Tank. 248'.48'76
You can't con God. Nashville, Abingdon Press [1972] 64 p. 19 cm. (An Abingdon original paperback) [BV4832.2.H325] 70-173953 ISBN 0-687-46842-6
1. Christian life—Methodist authors. I. Title.

JOHNSON, Ben Campbell. 248'.48'76 B
You are somebody [by] Ben Johnson. Atlanta, Forum House [1973] 145 p. illus. 23 cm. Bibliography: p. 144-145. [BV4501.2.J54] 73-81259 ISBN 0-913618-14-4 4.95
1. Johnson, Ben Campbell. 2. Christian life—Methodist authors. I. Title.

JONES, Eli Stanley, 1884-1973. 248'.48'76
The divine yes [by] E. Stanley Jones with the help of his daughter Eunice Jones Mathews. Nashville, Abingdon Press [1975] 160 p. 23 cm. [BV4501.2.J59 1975] 74-17119 ISBN 0-687-10988-4 5.95
1. Christian life—Methodist authors. 2. Suffering. I. Mathews, Eunice Jones. II. Title.

MYERS, T. Cecil. 248'.48'76
Living on tiptoe; the healing power of love, by T. Cecil Myers. Waco, Tex., Word Books [1972] 106 p. 21 cm. Bibliography: p. 103-106. [BV4501.2.M9] 72-84166 2.95
1. Christian life—Methodist authors. I. Title.

MYERS, T. Cecil. 248'.48'76
You can be more than you are / T. Cecil Myers. Waco, Tex. : Word Books, c1976. 122 p. ; 22 cm. [BV4501.2.M92] 76-2859 ISBN 0-87680-406-7 : 4.95
1. Christian life—Methodist authors. I. Title.

*NELSON, Wilbur E. 248'.48'76
If I were an atheist, and other stimulating devotions. Grand Rapids, Mich., Baker Book House [1973] 127 p. 18 cm. (Direction Books) [BV4501] ISBN 0-8010-6679-4 0.95 (pbk)
1. Christian life—Methodist authors—Addresses, essays, lectures. I. Title.

PENNINGTON, Chester A. 248'.48'76
Half-truths or whole Gospel? [By] Chester A. Pennington. Nashville, Abingdon Press [1972] 127 p. 19 cm. [BV4501.2.P372] 74-185546 ISBN 0-687-16513-X 2.25
1. Christian life—Methodist authors. 2. Mission of the church. I. Title.

POTTHOFF, Harvey H. 248'.48'76
A whole person in a whole world, by Harvey Potthoff. Nashville, Tidings [1972] 112 p. 19 cm. [BV4501.2.P558] 72-86491 1.25 (pbk.)
1. Christian life—Methodist authors. I. Title.

PRATER, Arnold. 248.4'8'76
Release from phoniness. Waco, Tex., Word Books [1968] 123 p. 22 cm. [BV4501.2.P67] 68-31115 3.95
1. Christian life—Methodist authors. I. Title.

PUTNAM, Roy C., 1928- 248'.48'76
Life is a celebration! / By Roy C. Putnam. [Nashville] : Impact Books, c1976. 175 p. ; 22 cm. [BV4501.2.P82] 76-21004 ISBN 0-914850-46-6 : 4.95
1. Christian life—Methodist authors. I. Title.

STEERE, Daniel C. 248'.48'76
I am, I can [by] Daniel C. Steere. Old Tappan, N.J., Revell [1973] 127 p. 21 cm. [BV4501.2.S753] 73-6921 ISBN 0-8007-0618-8 3.95 (pbk.)
1. Christian life—Methodist authors. 2. Success. I. Title.

WARD, Alice Armstrong. 248'.48'76
Servant of the light [by] Alice Armstrong Ward, with A. Dudley Ward. Nashville, Tidings [1972] 103 p. 19 cm. [BX8495.W246A3] 72-86490
1. Christian life—Methodist authors. I. Title.

WEBB, Lance. 248'.48'76
Disciplines for life in the Age of Aquarius. Waco, Tex., Word Books [1972] 177 p. 23 cm. Includes bibliographical references. [BV4832.2.W432] 71-183342 4.95
1. Christian life—Methodist authors. I. Title.

*WIERSBE, Warren W. 248'.48'76
Songs in the night; devotional messages from the worldwide radio program. Grand Rapids, Mich., Baker Book House [1973] 144 p. illus. (inside covers) 22 cm. [BV4501] ISBN 0-8010-9535-2 1.95 (pbk.)
1. Songs in the Night (Radio program) 2. Christian life—Methodist authors—Addresses, essays, lectures. I. Moody Memorial Church, Chicago. Radio Program. II. Title.

WILDMON, Donald E. 248'.48'76
Stand up to life / Donald E. Wildmon. Nashville : Abingdon Press, [1975] 111 p. ; 20 cm. [BV4501.2.W5197] 74-30209 ISBN 0-687-39290-X : 3.95.
1. Christian life—Methodist authors. I. Title.

STEERE, Daniel C. 248'.48'7633
Power for living : discover your God-given inner strengths / Daniel C. Steere. Old Tappan, N.J. : F. H. Revell Co., c1977. 158 p. ; 21 cm. [BV4501.2.S7533] 77-22384 ISBN 0-8007-0890-3 : 6.95
1. Christian life—1960- I. Title.

ASHFORD, Ray. 248'.48'792
Take it easy / Ray Ashford. Philadelphia : Fortress Press, c1976. vii, 104 p. ; 20 cm. Includes bibliographical references. [BV4501.2.A774] 75-36443 ISBN 0-8006-1219-1 pbk. : 3.25
1. Christian life—United Church of Canada authors. I. Title.

EATON, Kenneth Oxner 248.4'8'8'58
Why He came, by Kenneth O. Eaton. Nashville, Abingdon [1967] 126p. 20cm. Bibl. [BV4501.2.E27] 67-22159 2.75
1. Christian life—Congregatinal authors. I. Title.

*WEBB, Glenn M. 248.4'89
The unwritten book, a spiritual exposure. New York, Exposition [1968] 87p. 21cm. (E46819) 4.00
1. Christian life—Institute of Religious Science. I. Title.

CHEVILLE, Roy Arthur, 1897- 248.4893
Spiritual health; an exploration of the gospel of Jesus Christ as guide to wholesome living here and now, by Roy A. Cheville. [Independence, Mo., Herald Pub. House, 1966] 412 p. 21 cm. [BX8656.C48] 66-25062
1. Christian life—Mormon authors. I. Title.

CLARK, Carol. 248'.48'93
A singular life; perspectives for the single woman. Salt Lake City, Deseret Book Co., 1974. 60 p. 24 cm. [HQ800.C58] 74-81406 ISBN 0-87747-531-8 3.50
1. Single women. 2. Mormons and Mormonism. 3. Women—Religious life. I. Title.

COVEY, Stephen R. 248.4'8'93
How to succeed with people [by] Stephen R. Covey. Salt Lake City, Deseret Book Co., 1971. 141 p. 24 cm. [BJ1581.2.C67] 78-156812 ISBN 0-87747-439-7 3.95
1. Conduct of life. I. Title.

DE JONG, Gerrit, 1892- 248'.48'93
Eternal progress : the practicality and relevance of the Gospel today / Gerrit de Jong, Jr. ; with a foreword by Hugh B. Brown. Salt Lake City : Bookcraft, 1975. 172 p. ; 24 cm. Includes index. [BX8656.D4] 75-24576 ISBN 0-88494-283-X : 4.95
1. Church of Jesus Christ of Latter-Day Saints—Doctrinal and controversial works. 2. Christian life—Mormon authors. I. Title.

DE JONG, Gerrit, 1892- 248'.48'93
Eternal progress : the practicality and relevance of the Gospel today / Gerrit de Jong, Jr. ; with a foreword by Hugh B. Brown.

Salt Lake City : Bookcraft, 1975. 172 p. ; 24 cm. Includes index. [BX8656.D4] 75-24576 ISBN 0-88494-283-X : 4.95
1. Church of Jesus Christ of Latter-Day Saints—Doctrinal and controversial works. 2. Christian life—Mormon authors. I. Title.

DUNN, Paul H. 248'.48'93
Discovering the quality of success [by] Paul H. Dunn. Compiled by Gary Gough and Jeril Winget. Salt Lake City, Deseret Book Co., 1973. 140 p. 24 cm. [BF637.S8D74] 73-77365 ISBN 0-87747-493-1 3.95
1. Success. I. Title.

DUNN, Paul H. 248'.48'93
Discovering the quality of success [by] Paul H. Dunn. Compiled by Gary Gough and Jeril Winget. Salt Lake City, Deseret Book Co., 1973. 140 p. 24 cm. [BF637.S8D74] 73-77365 ISBN 0-87747-493-1 3.95
1. Success. I. Title.

DUNN, Paul H. 248.4'8'93
Meaningful living [by] Paul H. Dunn. Illus. by Richard L. Gunn. Salt Lake City, Bookcraft, 1968. 175 p. illus. 24 cm. [BJ1611.2.D8] 68-28761 3.00
1. Success. I. Title.

DUNN, Paul H. 248'.48'93
Relationships; self, family, God [by] Paul H. Dunn and Richard M. Eyre. Salt Lake City, Bookcraft [1974] 198 p. illus. 24 cm. [BX8656.D86] 74-75536 ISBN 0-88494-213-9
1. Christian life—Mormon authors. 2. Conduct of life. I. Eyre, Richard M., joint author. II. Title.

DUNN, Paul H. 248'.48'93
Relationships; self, family, God [by] Paul H. Dunn and Richard M. Eyre. Salt Lake City, Bookcraft [1974] 198 p. illus. 24 cm. [BX8656.D86] 74-75536 ISBN 0-88494-213-9 3.95
1. Christian life—Mormon authors. 2. Conduct of life. I. Eyre, Richard M., joint author. II. Title.

EBERHARD, Ernest, 248'.48'93
1909-
Is it love? / by Ernest Eberhard. Salt Lake City : Deseret Book Co., 1977. p. cm. Discusses love, dating, courtship, and marriage from a Mormon point of view. [BX8641.E24] 77-7527 ISBN 0-87747-632-2 : 6.95
1. Marriage—Mormonism—Juvenile literature. 2. Dating (Social customs)—Juvenile literature. 3. Courtship—Juvenile literature. I. Title.

EDWARDS, Francis Henry, 248.4893
1897-
The divine purpose in us. Independence, Mo., Herald Pub. House [c1963] 261 p. 21 cm. "First appeared as a set of quarterlies ... published in 1937 and 1938." Includes bibliographical references. [BX8656.E4] 63-23052
1. Christian life—Mormon authors. I. Title.

EDWARDS, Francis Henry, 248.4893
1897-
The divine purpose in us. Independence, Mo., Herald [c.1963] 261p. 21cm. First appeared as a set of quarterlies pub. in 1937 and 1938. Bibl. 63-23052 3.00
1. Christian life—Mormon authors. I. Title.

EVANS, Richard Louis, 248.4893
1906-
Faith in the future. [1st ed.] New York, Harper & Row [1963] 224 p. 22 cm. Tenth vol. of selections from the author's "spoken word" which accompanies the CBS Sunday broadcast of sacred music by the Tabernacle Choir in Salt Lake City. [BX8639.E8F3] 63-21589
1. Mormons and Mormonism — Addresses, essays, lectures. I. Title.

EVANS, Richard Louis, 248.4893
1906-
Faith in the future. New York, Harper [c.1963 524p. 22cm. Tenth vol. of selections from the author's 'spoken word' which accompanies the CBS Sunday broadcast of sacred music by the Tabernacle Choir in Salt Lake City. 63-21589 3.00
1. Mormons and Mormonism—Addresses, essays, lectures. I. Title.

HANKS, Marion D. 248'.48'93
The gift of self [by] Marion D. Hanks. Salt Lake City, Bookcraft [1974] x, 308 p. port. 24 cm. [BX8656.H36] 74-75166 ISBN 0-88494-211-2
1. Christian life—Mormon authors. I. Title.

LEA, Leonard J. 248.4893
Views from the mountain. Independence, Mo., Herald House [c.]1961. 220p. 61-9682 2.75
1. Mormons and Mormonism—Addresses, essays, lectures. I. Title.

LONGDEN, LaRue C. 248.4'8'93
It's smart to be a Latter-Day Saint, by LaRue C. Longden. Salt Lake City, Deseret Book Co., 1967. 116 p. 20 cm. [BV4531.2.L57] 67-31577
1. Christian life—Mormon authors. 2. Youth—Religious life. I. Title.

MCKAY, David Oman 248.4893
Secrets of a happy life. Compiled by Llewelyn R. McKay. Englewood Cliffs, N.J. Prentice-Hall [c.1960] xii, 175p. 21cm. 60-13049 3.50
1. Christian life—Mormon authors. I. Title.

MCKAY, David Oman, 1873- 248.4893
Treasures of life. Comp. by Clare Middlemiss from editorials pub. in The Instructor. Salt Lake City, Deseret [1963, c.1962] 562p. illus. 24cm. 63-1195 4.95
1. Christian life—Mormon authors. I. Title.

MCKAY, David Oman, 1876- 248.4893
Secrets of a happy life. Compiled by Llewelyn R. McKay. Englewood Cliffs, N. J., Prentice-Hall [1960] 175p. 21cm. [BV4501.2.M24] 60-13049
1. Christian life— Mormon authors. I. Title.

MARKHAM, Ira J 248.4893
Share a miracle. Salt Lake City, Deseret Book Co., 1962. 151p. 24cm. [BV4501.2M35] 62-38088
1. Christian life—Mormon authors. I. Title.

MAXWELL, Neal A. 248.4'8'93
... a more excellent way; essays on leadership for Latter-Day Saints [by] Neal A. Maxwell. Salt Lake City, Deseret Book Co., 1967. viii, 142 p. 24 cm. Bibliographical footnotes. [BV652.1.M38] 67-31579
1. Christian leadership. I. Title.

MAXWELL, Neal A. 248'.48'93
"Behold, I say unto you, I cannot say the smallest part which I feel." [By] Neal A. Maxwell. Salt Lake City, Deseret Book Co., 1973. 83 p. illus. 24 cm. On spine: The smallest part. [BX8656.M36] 73-87240 3.95
1. Christian life—Mormon authors. I. Title. II. Title: The smallest part.

OTTENSEN, Carol Clark. 248'.48'93
A singular life; perspectives for the single woman [by] Carol Clark. Salt Lake City, Deseret Book Co., 1974. 60 p. 24 cm. [HQ800.O82] 74-81406 ISBN 0-87747-531-8 3.50
1. Single women. 2. Mormons and Mormonism. 3. Women—Religious life. I. Title.

PAXMAN, Monroe J. 248'.48'93
Family faith and fun; helps for home evenings [by] Monroe & Shirley Paxman. Illus. by Leah Tippetts. Salt Lake City, Bookcraft, 1972. 177 p. illus. 24 cm. [BV4526.2.P39] 72-85665
1. Family—Religious life. 2. Family recreation. I. Paxman, Shirley Brockbank, joint author. II. Title.

PETERSEN, Mark E. 248.4'8'93
Live it up! [By] Mark E. Petersen. Salt Lake City, Deseret Book Co., 1971. 115 p. 24 cm. [BJ1661.P44] 70-175717 ISBN 0-87747-450-8 3.50
1. Youth—Conduct of life. I. Title.

PETERSEN, Mark E. 248.4'8'93
The way to peace [by] Mark E. Petersen. Salt Lake City, Bookcraft, 1969. x, 306 p. 24 cm. [BJ1251.P43] 74-82111
1. Christian ethics—Mormon authors. I. Title.

RUOFF, Norman D., 248.4'8'93
comp.
Testimonies of the Restoration, compiled by Norman D. Ruoff. [Independence, Mo., Herald Pub. House, 1971] 203 p. 21 cm. Selections originally published in the Restoration witness. [BX8656.R86] 75-162860 ISBN 0-8309-0050-0 4.00
1. Christian life—Mormon authors—Addresses, essays, lectures. I. Restoration witness. II. Title.

SHUTE, R Wayne, comp. 248.4'8'93
His servants speak; excerpts from devotional addresses given at Brigham Young University by general authorities of the Church of Jesus Christ of Latter-Day Saints. Selected and arr. by R. Wayne Shute. Salt Lake City, Bookcraft [1967] 143 p. 24 cm. "Excerpts from talks given ... from 1960 to 1965." [BX8656.S46] 68-3097
1. Christian life—Mormon authors. I. Church of Jesus Christ of Latter-Day Saints. II. Brigham Young University, Provo, Utah. III. Title.

SHUTE, R. Wayne, comp. 248.4'8'93
His servants speak; excerpts from devotional addresses given at Brigham Young University by general authorities of the Church of Jesus Christ of Latter-Day Saints. Selected and arr. by R. Wayne Shute. Salt Lake City, Bookcraft [1967] 143 p. 24 cm. "Excerpts from talks given ... from 1960 to 1965." [BX8656.S46] 68-3097
1. Christian life—Mormon authors. I. Church of Jesus Christ of Latter-Day Saints. II. Brigham Young University, Provo, Utah. III. Title.

SILL, Sterling W. 248.4'8'93
Making the most of yourself [by] Sterling W. Sill. Salt Lake City, Bookcraft, 1971. xi, 324 p. 24 cm. [BJ1611.2.S514] 71-177292
1. Success. I. Title.

SILL, Sterling W 248.4'8'93
The miracle of personality, by Sterling W. Sill. Salt Lake City, Bookcraft [1966] 340 p. port. 24 cm. [BX8656.S52] 67-2605
1. Christian life—Mormon authors. I. Title.

SILL, Sterling W. 248.4'8'93
The quest for excellence, by Sterling W. Sill. Salt Lake City, Bookcraft [1967] ix, 334p. port. 24cm. [BX8656.S52] 67-30254 3.75
1. Christian life—Mormon authors. I. Title.

SILL, Sterling W 248.4893
What doth it profit? By Sterling W. Sill. Salt Lake City, Bookcraft [1965] 340 p. 24 cm. [BX8656.S5] 66-6861
1. Christian life—Mormon authors. I. Title.

YOUNG, Seymour Dilworth, 248.4893
1897-
More precious than rubies; a Mormon boy and his priesthood. Salt Lake City, Bookcraft [c1959] 110 p. illus. 24 cm. [BX8643.Y6Y6] 60-29866
1. Mormons and Mormonism — Doctrinal and controversial works. 2. Youth — Religious life. I. Title.

SEARLE, Paul, comp. 248.4'8'9308
A scrapbook of inspiration, compiled by Paul and Karen Searle. Salt Lake City, Deseret Book Co., 1967. xvi, 239 p. 24 cm. "Acknowledgements" (bibliographical): p. ix-xii. [BJ1548.S4] 67-31578
1. Conduct of life—Quotations, maxims, etc. I. Searle, Karen, joint comp. II. Title.

AFFLECK, Afton Grant. 248'.48'933
Love is the gift / Afton Grant Affleck. Salt Lake City : Bookcraft, c1977. x, 149 p. ; 24 cm. [BT738.4.A35] 77-75305 ISBN 0-88494-316-X pbk. : 3.95
1. Service (Theology)—Case studies. 2. Christian life—Mormon authors—Case studies. I. Title.

ANDERSON, Leland E. 248'.48'933
Stories of power and purpose / Leland E. Anderson. Salt Lake City : Bookcraft, 1974. vi, 88 p. ; 24 cm. [BX8656.A52] 74-15807 ISBN 0-88494-269-4 : 2.95
1. Christian life—Stories. 2. Christian life—Mormon authors. I. Title.

BLACK, Don J., 1937- 248'.48'933
Seven keys to happiness [by] Don J. Black. [Provo, Utah] Brigham Young University Publications [1972] xiv, 96 p. illus. 23 cm. [BX8656.B6] 74-186681 ISBN 0-8425-1451-1
1. Christian life—Mormon authors. I. Title.

CHEVILLE, Roy Arthur, 248'.48'933
1897-
Expectations for endowed living; a consideration of the hopes of our people, by Roy A. Cheville. [Independence, Mo., Published for] the Reorganized Church of Jesus Christ of Latter Day Saints [by Herald Pub. House, 1972] 122 p. 18 cm. "Presentations made in Wichita, Kansas, as memorial to Ellis Bedwell, 1970." [BX8656.C47] 79-172649 ISBN 0-8309-0056-X 3.95
1. Christian life—Mormon authors. I. Title.

CHEVILLE, Roy Arthur, 248'.48'933
1897-
Spiritual resources are available today : an exploration in the ministering of the Holy Spirit / by Roy A. Cheville, Independence, Mo. : Herald Pub. House, [1975- v. ; 21 cm. [BX8656.C49] 74-21216 ISBN 0-8309-0138-8
1. Christian life—Mormon authors. I. Title.

DUNN, Paul H. 248'.48'933
Anxiously engaged / Paul H. Dunn. Salt Lake City : Deseret Book Co., 1974. 142 p. ; 24 cm. Includes index. [BX8656.D84] 74-28591 ISBN 0-87747-546-6 : 4.95
1. Christian life—Mormon authors. I. Title.

DUNN, Paul H. 248'.48'933
Anxiously engaged / Paul H. Dunn. Salt Lake City : Deseret Book Co., 1974. 142 p. ; 24 cm. Includes index. [BX8656.D84] 74-28591 ISBN 0-87747-546-6 : 4.95
1. Christian life—Mormon authors. I. Title.

DUNN, Paul H. 248'.48'933
Goals / Paul H. Dunn, Richard M. Eyre. Salt Lake City : Bookcraft, 1977, c1976. 28, 28 p. ; 24 cm. Opposite pages numbered in duplicate. [BX8656.D85 1977] 76-42001 ISBN 0-88494-310-0 pbk. : 3.50
1. Christian life—Mormon authors. 2. Goal (Psychology) I. Eyre, Richard M., joint author. II. Title.

DUNN, Paul H. 248'.48'933
Goals / Paul H. Dunn, Richard M. Eyre. Salt Lake City : Bookcraft, 1977, c1976. 28, 28 p. ; 24 cm. Opposite pages numbered in duplicate. [BX8656.D85 1977] 76-42001 ISBN 0-88494-310-0 pbk. : 3.50
1. Christian life—Mormon authors. 2. Goal (Psychology) I. Eyre, Richard M., joint author. II. Title.

GOATES, Lesley. 248'.48'933
Sincerely yours / Les Goates ; with a foreword by Mark E. Petersen. Salt Lake City : Bookcraft, 1975. viii, 56 p. ; 24 cm. [BX8656.G6] 75-31077 ISBN 0-88494-287-2 : 2.95
1. Christian life—Mormon authors. I. Title.

KIMBALL, Spencer W., 248'.48'933
1895-
Faith precedes the miracle; based on discourses of Spencer W. Kimball. Salt Lake City, Deseret Book Co., 1972. xx, 364 p. 24 cm. [BX8656.K54] 72-91930 ISBN 0-87747-490-7 4.95
1. Church of Jesus Christ of Latter-Day Saints—Doctrinal and controversial works. 2. Christian life—Mormon authors. I. Title.

MCKAY, David Oman, 248.4'8'933
1873-1970.
Man may know for himself; teachings of President David O. McKay. Compiled by Clare Middlemiss. Salt Lake City, Deseret Book Co., 1967. xiv, 476 p. port. 24 cm. [BX8609.M255] 67-30448
1. Christian life—Mormon authors. I. Title.

MAXWELL, Neal A. 248'.48'933
That my family should partake / Neal A. Maxwell. Salt Lake City : Deseret Book Co., 1974. 126 p. ; 24 cm. Includes index. [BX8643.F3M37] 74-84539 ISBN 0-87747-538-5 pbk. : 4.95
1. Family—Religious life. I. Title.

MAXWELL, Neal A. 248'.48'933
A time to choose [by] Neal A. Maxwell. Salt Lake City, Deseret Book Co., 1972. vii, 93 p. 24 cm. [BX8656.M38] 72-82071 ISBN 0-87747-482-6 3.95
1. Christian life—Mormon authors. I. Title.

MONSON, Thomas S., 248'.48'933
1927-
Pathways to perfection; discourses of Thomas S. Monson. [1st ed.] Salt Lake City, Deseret Book Co., 1973. xii, 302 p. illus. 24 cm. [BX8656.M66] 73-88634 ISBN 0-87747-511-3 4.95
1. Christian life—Mormon authors. I. Title.

PINEGAR, Ed J. 248'.48'933
You, your family and the scriptures / Ed J. Pinegar. Salt Lake City : Deseret Book Co., 1975. xiii, 195 p. ; 24 cm. Includes index. [BX8656.P56] 75-1621 5.95
1. Church of Jesus Christ of Latter-Day Saints—Doctrinal and controversial works. 2. Christian life—Mormon authors. I. Title.

ROMNEY, Marion G., 248.4'8'933
1897-
Look to God and live; discourses of Marion G. Romney. Compiled by George J. Romney. Salt Lake City, Utah, Deseret Book Co., 1971. xv, 291 p. port. 24 cm. [BX8639.R64L66] 70-176091 ISBN 0-87747-451-6 4.95
1. Mormons and mormonism—Addresses, essays, lectures. I. Title.

SILL, Sterling W. 248'.48'933
The laws of success / Sterling W. Sill. Salt Lake City : Deseret Book Co., 1975. 219 p. : port. ; 24 cm. Includes index. [BX8639.S5L38] 75-18818 ISBN 0-87747-556-3
1. Church of Jesus Christ of Latter-Day Saints—Sermons. 2. Sermons, American. I. Title.

SILL, Sterling W. 248'.48'933
That ye might have life / Sterling W. Sill. Salt Lake City, : Deseret Book Co., [1974] 296 p. : port. ; 24 cm. Includes index. [BX8656.S535] 74-18667 ISBN 0-87747-539-3 pbk. : 4.95
1. Christian life—Mormon authors. I. Title.

SILL, Sterling W. 248'.48'933
Thy kingdom come / Sterling W. Sill. Salt Lake City : Deseret Book Co., 1975. xiv, 239 p. : port. ; 24 cm. Includes index. [BX8656.S536] 75-37275 ISBN 0-87747-602-0
1. Christian life—Mormon authors. I. Title.

SILL, Sterling W 248'.48'933
The upward reach. Salt Lake City, Bookcraft [1962] 407 p. illus. 24 cm. [BX8639.S5U6] 62-53317

1. Mormons and Mormonism—Addresses, essays, lectures. I. Title.

SILL, Sterling W. 248'.48'933
The wealth of wisdom / Sterling W. Sill. Salt Lake City : Deseret Book Co., 1977. 220 p. ; 24 cm. Includes index. [BX8656.S54] 77-70195 ISBN 0-87747-648-9 : 5.95
1. Christian life—Mormon authors. 2. Meditations. I. Title.

SIMPSON, Robert L. 248'.48'933
Proven paths / Robert L. Simpson. Salt Lake City : Deseret Book Co., 1974. viii, 223 p. : port. ; 24 cm. Includes index. [BX8656.S55] 74-84540 ISBN 0-87747-537-7 pbk. : 4.95
1. Christian life—Mormon authors. I. Title.

PAULSEN, Dorothy E. 248'.48'95
How to know and be your self forever [by] Dorothy E. Paulsen. Philadelphia, Dorrance [1974] 93 p. 22 cm. [BV4501.2.P357] 73-89026 ISBN 0-8059-1959-7 4.95
1. Christian life—Christian Science authors. I. Title.

BRINTON, Howard 248'.48'96
Haines, 1884-
Quaker journals; varieties of religious experience among Friends [by] Howard H. Brinton. Wallingford, Pa., Pendle Hill Publications [1972] xiv, 130 p. 23 cm. Bibliography: p. 122-129. [BX7738.B74] 78-188399 ISBN 0-87574-952-6 4.75
1. Spiritual life—Society of Friends authors. I. Title.

CATTELL, Everett Lewis. 248.4896
The spirit of holiness. Grand Rapids, Eerdmans [1963] 103 p. 22 cm. [BV4501.2.C35] 62-21366
1. Christian life — Friend authors. I. Title.

CATTELL, Everett Lewis 248.4896
The spirit of holiness. Grand Rapids, Mich., Eerdmans [c.1963] 103p. 22cm. 62-21366 3.00 bds.,
1. Christian life—Friend authors. I. Title.

FRIENDS, Society of. 248.4'8'96
New England Yearly Meeting.
The Quaker queries; New England queries in past and present forms. With an introd. by Elmer Howard Brown. [Boston] Penmaen Press, 1969. vi, 12 p. 26 cm. "An edition of 100 books ... Number 67." The latest revision, which was completed in 1965, is presented with some selected queries formulated originally in 1742. [BX7607.N4A5 1969] 72-11535
1. Friends, Society of—Discipline. I. Brown, Elmer Howard, ed. II. Title.

KELLY, Thomas Raymond, 248'.48'96
1893-1941.
The eternal promise / Thomas Kelly. Richmond, Ind. : Friends United Press, 1977, c1966. 124 p. ; 17 cm. Sequel to A Testament of devotion. [BV4832.K4297 1977] 77-71637 ISBN 0-913408-30-1 pbk. : 2.50
1. Devotional literature. 2. Christian life—Friend authors. I. Title.

KELLY, Thomas Raymond, 248'.48'96
1893-1941.
The eternal promise / Thomas Kelly. Richmond, Ind. : Friends United Press, 1977, c1966. 124 p. ; 17 cm. Sequel to A Testament of devotion. [BV4832.K4297 1977] 77-71637 ISBN 0-913408-30-1 pbk. : 2.50
1. Devotional literature. 2. Christian life—Friend authors. I. Title.

PECK, George Terhune, 248'.48'96
1916-
Simplicity; a rich Quaker's view, by George Peck. [Wallingford, Pa., Pendle Hill, 1973] 32 p. 20 cm. (Pendle Hill pamphlet, 189) [BJ1496.P4] 72-97851 ISBN 0-87574-189-4 0.70
1. Simplicity.

STEERE, Douglas Van, 248'.48'96
1901-
On speaking out of the silence; vocal ministry in the unprogrammed meeting for worship, by Douglas V. Steere. [Wallingford, Pa., Pendle Hill Publications, 1972] 20 p. 20 cm. (Pendle Hill pamphlet, 182) [BX7745.S75] 72-182983 0.70
1. Pastoral theology—Friends, Society of. 2. Public worship. I. Title.

TRUEBLOOD, David 248.4'8'96
Elton, 1900-
The new man for our time [by] Elton Trueblood. [1st ed.] New York, Harper & Row [1970] 126 p. 22 cm. [BV4501.2.T76] 77-85059 2.95
1. Christian life—Friend authors. I. Title.

BRINTON, Margaret 248.4896082
Cooper, comp.
Candles in the dark; an anthology of stories to be used in education for peace. Prepared by Margaret Cooper Brinton, Mary Esther McWhirter [and] Janet E. Schroeder. [Philadelphia. 1964] 253 p. 21 cm. "Sponsored by the Religious Education Committee, Philadelphia Yearly Meeting of the Religious Society of Friends." [BV4225.2.B7] 64-21906
1. Homiletical illustrations. 2. Christian life — Stories. 3. Friends, Society of Philadelphia Yearly Meeting. Religious Education Committee. I. Title.

AUGSBURGER, A. Don. 248.4897
Creating Christian personality, by A. Don Augsburger. Scottdale, Pa., Herald Press [1966] 128, [7] p. 21 cm. (Conrad Grebel lectures 1965) Bibliographical references included in "Footnotes" (p. 128-[135]) [BV1475.9.A8] 66-23905
1. Religious education of adolescents. I. Title. II. Series.

AUGSBURGER, David W. 248.4'8'97
Be all you can be [by] David Augsburger. [1st ed.] Carol Stream, Ill., Creation House [1970] 138 p. 23 cm. Includes bibliographical references. [BV4501.2.A88] 76-131444 3.95
1. Christian life—Mennonite authors. I. Title.

AUGSBURGER, David W. 248'.48'97
Caring enough to confront; the love-fight, by David Augsburger. Glendale, Calif., G/L Regal Books [1973] 176 p. illus. 18 cm. Includes bibliographical references. [BV4501.2.A883 1973] 73-83400 ISBN 0-8307-0256-3 1.25
1. Christian life—Mennonite authors. 2. Conflict (Psychology) I. Title.

AUGSBURGER, Myron S. 248'.48'97
Walking in the Resurrection / Myron S. Augsburger ; introd. by Keith Miller. Scottdale, Pa. : Herald Press, 1976. 159 p. ; 20 cm. Includes bibliographical references. [BV4501.2.A93] 76-15566 ISBN 0-8361-1333-0 : 5.95
1. Christian life—Mennonite authors. I. Title.

BRENNEMAN, Helen Good. 248.4'8'97
The house by the side of the road. Scottdale, Pa., Herald Press [1971] 200 p. illus., ports. 21 cm. [BV4501.2.B695] 75-153969 ISBN 0-8361-1648-8 4.95
1. Christian life—Mennonite authors. I. Title.

MILLER, Ella May. 248'.48'97
The peacemakers : how to find peace and share it / Ella May Miller. Old Tappen, N.J. : F. H. Revell, c1977. 179 p. ; 21 cm. [BT736.4.M5] 77-1625 ISBN 0-8007-0865-2 : 6.95
1. Peace (Theology) 2. Christian life—Mennonite authors. I. Title.

ANDERSON, Phoebe M 248'.48'973
3's in the Christian community; a course for the church school nursery. Photos. by Sheldon Brody. Illustrated by Lawrence Scott. Boston, United Church Press [c1960] 320 p. illus. (part col.) 26 cm. Includes music. Bibliography: p. 294-295. [BV1475.7.A5] 60-5690
1. Religious education of pre-school children. I. Title.

ARNOLD, Eberhard, 248'.48'973
1883-1935.
Sendbrief from the Alm Bruderhof to the Rhon Bruderhof / by Eberhard Arnold ; edited and translated from the German by the Hutterian Society of Brothers. Rifton, N.Y. : Plough Pub. House, 1974. 55 p. ; 14 cm. [BV4501.A7613 1974] 74-23145 ISBN 0-87486-148-9
1. Bruderhof Communities. 2. Christian life. I. Arnold, Heini, 1913- II. Title.

ARNOLD, Eberhard, 248'.48'973
1883-1935.
Sendbrief vom Almbruderhof zum Rhonbruderhof, 1934 / von Eberhard Arnold. Rifton, N.Y. : Plough Pub. House, 1974. p. cm. [BV4501.A76] 75-1046 ISBN 0-87486-252-3
1. Bruderhof Communities. 2. Christian life. I. Title.

DREW, Louise C 248'.48'973
Nursery manual; a manual for administrators in the church school nursery department, by Louise C. Drew. Photos. by Sheldon Brody. Illustrated by Walter Lorraine. Boston, United Church Press [c1960] 63 p. illus. 26 cm. "One of a series of administrative manuals for use with the United Church Curriculum." Bibliography: p. 61-62. [BV1475.7.D7] 6010301
1. Religious education of pre-school children. I. Title.

DREW, Louise C 248'.48'973
Nursery manual; a manual for administrators in the church school nursery department, by Louise C. Drew. Photos. by Sheldon Brody. Illustrated by Walter Lorraine. Boston, United Church Press [c1960] 63 p. illus. 26 cm. "One of a series of administrative manuals for use with the United Church Curriculum." Bibliography: p. 61-62. [BV1475.7.D7] 6010301
1. Religious education of pre-school children. I. Title.

ERB, Alta Mae, 1891- 248'.48'973
Christian nurture of children. [2d ed.] Scottdale, Pa. Herald Press [1955] 180 p. 21 cm. [BV1475.E8 1955] 55-7811
1. Religious education of children. I. Title.

SCHMID, Jeannine. 248'.48'973
Religion, Montessori, and the home; an approach to the religious education of the young child. [2d ed.] New York, Benziger [1970] xxiv, 213 p. illus. 21 cm. Bibliography: p. 207-209. [BV1475.2.S35 1970] 68-56936
1. Christian education of children. 2. Montessori method of education. I. Title.

ARNOLD, Milo L. 248'.48'99
Life is so great, I really don't want to get off / Milo Arnold. Grand Rapids, Mich. : Zondervan Pub. House, [1975] 200 p. ; 21 cm. [BV4501.2.A74] 74-25344 5.95
1. Christian life—Nazarene authors. I. Title.

BENSON, Bob. 248'.48'99
Come share the being. [1st ed. Nashville] Impact Books [1974] 112 p. 23 cm. [BV4501.2.B393] 74-83412 ISBN 0-914850-94-6 3.95
1. Christian life—Nazarene authors. I. Title.

BENSON, Bob. 248'.48'99
Something's going on here / Bob Benson. 1st ed. Nashville : Impact Books, c1977. 170 p. ; 23 cm. [BV4501.2.B3937] 76-29334 ISBN 0-914850-77-6 : 4.95
1. Christian life—Nazarene authors. I. Title.

BUTTERWORTH, Eric. 248.4'8'99
Unity of all life. [1st ed.] New York, Harper & Row [1969] 209 p. 22 cm. Bibliographical references included in "Notes" (p. 205-209) [BX9890.U5B82] 75-85053 5.95
1. Unity School of Christianity. 2. Spiritual life. I. Title.

CARROLL, Ramon 248.4'8'99
Leonard.
Stewardship: total-life commitment. [1st ed.] Cleveland, Tenn., Pathway Press [1967] 144 p. 22 cm. [BV772.C37] 67-26668
1. Stewardship, Christian. 2. Christian life. I. Title.

CURTIS, Donald. 248'.48'99
Live it up! / by Donald Curtis. Lekemont, Ga. : CSA Press, c1976. 112 p. : port. ; 22 cm. [BF639.C8844] 76-47419 ISBN 0-87707-187-X pbk. : 2.00
1. New Thought. I. Title.

CURTIS, Donald 248.4899
Your thoughts can change your life. Englewood Cliffs, N. J., Prentice-Hall [c.1961] 218p. illus. 61-13994 4.95 bds.,
1. New Thought. I. Title.

FISCHER, William L. 248'.48'99
The master craft of living, by William L. Fischer. Unity Village, Mo., Unity Books [1974] 176 p. 20 cm. [BX9890.U5F594] 73-94281
1. Unity School of Christianity. I. Title.

FISCHER, William L. 248'.48'99
The master craft of living, by William L. Fischer. Unity Village, Mo., Unity Books [1974] 176 p. 20 cm. [BX9890.U5F594] 73-94281
1. Unity School of Christianity. I. Title.

GILLCHREST, Muriel Noyes 248.4899
The power of universal mind. Parker [dist. Englewood Cliffs, N.J., Prentice. 1966, c.1965] xiv, 242p. 24cm. Bibl. [BF639.G45] 65-28635 4.95 bds.,
1. New Thought. I. Title. II. Title: Universal mind.

GOLDSMITH, Joel S 1892- 248.4899
Conscious union with God. New York, Julian Press, 1962. 253 p. 21 cm. [BF639.G5577 1962] 62-19298
1. New Thought. I. Title.

GOLDSMITH, Joel S., 248.4899
1892-1964.
Man was not born to cry. Edited by Lorraine Sinkler. New York, Julian Press, 1964. x, 210 p. 22 cm. [BF639.G567] 64-15748
1. New Thought. I. Title.

KIEMEL, Ann. 248'.48'99
"It's incredible!" / Ann Kiemel. Wheaton, Ill. : Tyndale House Publishers, 1977. 126 p. : ill. ; 22 cm. [BV4501.2.K487] 77-152125 ISBN 0-8423-1820-8 : 4.95
1. Christian life—Nazarene authors. I. Title.

MCCLELLAN, Foster C. 248'.48'99
Thoughts for a friend / by Foster C. McClellan. Unity Village, Mo. : Unity Books, [1975] 169 p. : ill. ; 20 cm. Includes index. [BX9890.U5M22] 75-24049
1. Unity School of Christianity. I. Title.

MCCLELLAN, Foster C. 248'.48'99
Thoughts for a friend / by Foster C. McClellan. Unity Village, Mo. : Unity Books, [1975] 169 p. : ill. ; 20 cm. Includes index. [BX9890.U5M22] 75-24049 3.95
1. Unity School of Christianity. I. Title.

MACDOUGALL, Mary 248.4'8'99
Katherine.
Making love happen. [1st ed.] Garden City, N.Y., Doubleday, 1970. 236 p. 22 cm. [BF575.L8M25] 76-116232 4.95
1. Love. I. Title.

PAULSON, J. Sig. 248'.48'99
How to love your neighbor [by] J. Sig Paulson. [1st ed.] Garden City, N.Y., Doubleday, 1974. 184 p. 22 cm. [BV4639.P316] 76-89098 ISBN 0-385-04263-9 4.95
1. Love (Theology) 2. Christian life—Unity School of Christianity authors. I. Title.

PAULSON, J. Sig. 248.4'8'99
Living with purpose [by] J. Sig Paulson. [1st ed.] Garden City, N.Y., Doubleday, 1968. 146 (i.e. 143) p. 22 cm. [BV4501.2.P36] 67-19098
1. Christian life—Unity School of Christianity authors. I. Title.

PAULSON, J. Sig. 248.4'8'99
Your power to be [by] J. Sig Paulson. [1st ed.] Garden City, N.Y., Doubleday, 1969. 166 p. 22 cm. [BV4501.2.P362] 69-10976 4.95
1. Christian life—Unity School of Christianity authors. I. Title.

PONDER, Catherine 248.4899
The prospering power of love. Lee's Summit, Mo., Unity Bks., 1966. 126p. 19cm. [BJ1611.2.P63] 66-25849 1.00 pap.,
1. Success. 2. Love. I. Title.

RIGGS, Ralph M 1895- 248.4'8'99
Living in Christ; our identification with Him, by Ralph M. Riggs. Springfield, Mo., Gospel Pub. House [1967] 96 p. 19 cm. [BV4509.5.R5] 67-25874
1. Spiritual life. 2. Identification (Religion) I. Title.

RIGGS, Ralph M., 1895- 248.4'8'99
Living in Christ; our identification with Him, by Ralph M. Riggs. Springfield, Mo., Gospel Pub. House [1967] 96 p. 19 cm. [BV4509.5.R5] 67-25874
1. Spiritual life. 2. Identification (Religion) I. Title.

SCHMELIG, Randolph. 248'.48'99
Patterns for self-unfoldment / by Randolph and Leddy Schmelig. Unity Village, Mo. : Unity Books, [1975] 304 p. : ill. ; 20 cm. [BX9890.U5S34] 74-29429
1. Unity School of Christianity. I. Schmelig, Leddy, joint author. II. Title.

SKARIN, Annalee. 248.4899
Secrets of eternity. Los Angeles, DeVorss [1960] 287 p. 23 cm. [BF639.S618] 60-3545
1. New Thought. I. Title.

SMOCK, Martha. 248.4899
Meet it with faith. Lee's Summit, Mo., Unity School of Christianity, 1966. 189 p. illus. 20 cm. [BV4501.2.S58] 66-93073
1. Christian life — Unity School of Christianity authors. I. Title.

SMOCK, Martha. 248'.48'99
Turning points / by Martha Smock. Unity Village, Mo. : Unity Books, c1976. 206 p. ; 20 cm. [BX9890.U5S6] 75-41954
1. Unity School of Christianity. I. Title.

SUCCESSFUL Christian 248'.48'99
living / compiled by Douglas Wead. Harrison, Ark. : New Leaf Press, c1977. 132 p. : ports. ; 23 cm. [BV4501.2.S825] 77-75327 ISBN 0-89221-037-0 : 5.95
1. Christian life—Assemblies of God authors. I. Wead, Doug.

WILKINSON, Winifred 248.4'8'99
Focus on living. Lee's Summit. Mo., United Bks. [1967] 189p. 20cm. [BV4501.2.W53] 67-14510 2.95
1. Christian life—Unity School of Christianity authors. I. Title.

WISSMANN, Erna E. 248.4'8'99
Wealth of the mind, by Erna E. Wissmann. New York, Philosophical Library [1971] viii, 61 p. 22 cm. [BJ1581.2.W58] 70-137788 ISBN 0-8022-2047-9 4.50
1. Conduct of life. I. Title.

WOMACK, David A. 248'.48'99
Alive in Christ / David Womack ; adapted from How to live the Christian life by R. L. Brandt. Springfield, Mo. : Gospel Pub. House,

c1975. 128 p. ; 18 cm. (Radiant books) [BV4501.2.W595] 75-22609 pbk. : 1.25
1. Christian life—Assemblies of God authors. I. Brandt, R. L. How to live the Christian life. II. Title.

FAGERLIN, Elsie 248.4941
As one who serves. Gustav K. Wiencke, ed. Illus. by Kathrina Hart. Philadelphia, Lutheran [1964] c.1956. 64 p. illus. (pt. col.) 21 cm. (LCA Sunday church sch. ser. Pupil's summer bk. 9883 E64) .35, pap.
I. Title.

POLEN, O. W. 248'.4'99
Editorially speaking : a selection of twelve choice editorials on subjects of special interest / O. W. Polen. Cleveland, Tenn. : Pathway Press, [1975] 80 p. : ill. ; 21 cm. Contents.Contents.—Living in the Spirit.—Is your attitude right?—Conclusions—too quick.—If I'm sick, have I sinned?—Real sincerity will come through.—A happy marriage.—Modesty.—The fruit of the Spirit.—Not by bread alone.—The strength of the Church.—As a parent, have you ever asked what goes wrong?—It could happen anytime! [BV4501.2.P5556] 75-13730 ISBN 0-87148-300-9 pbk. : 1.00
1. Christian life—Church of God authors. I. Title.

ANDERSON, Kenneth, 1917- 248'.5
A coward's guide to witnessing [by] Ken Anderson. [1st ed.] Carol Stream, Ill., Creation House [1972] 157 p. illus. 22 cm. [BV4520.A54] 75-189627 3.95
1. Witness-bearing (Christianity) I. Title.

AUGSBURGER, David W. 248.5
Witness is withness. Chicago, Moody Press [1971] 127 p. 17 cm. [BV4520.A9] 72-143469
1. Witness bearing (Christianity) I. Title.

AUTREY, C E 248.5
The theology of evangelism [by] C. E. Autrey. Nashville, Broadman Press [c1966] 119 p. 21 cm. Bibliographical references included in "Notes" (p. 115-119) [BV3790.A82] 66-10707
1. Evangelistic work. I. Title.

AUTREY, C. E. 248.5
The theology of evangelism. Nashville, Broadman [c.1966] 119p. 21cm. Bibl. [BV3790.A82] 66-10707 2.75
1. Evangelistic work. I. Title.

BARRINGTON, Porter. 248'.5
Witnessing with power and joy. [Nashville, Tenn.] T. Nelson [1972] 118 p. 21 cm. Includes bibliographical references. [BV4520.B355] 79-39590 ISBN 0-8407-5040-4
1. Witness bearing (Christianity) I. Title.

BELLET, Maurice 248.5
Facing the unbeliever. Tr. by Eva Fleischner. [New York] Herder & Herder [1967] 223p. 21cm. Tr. of Ceux qui perdent la foi. [BV4520.B3613] 67-27540 3.95
1. Witness bearing (Christianity) I. Title.

BELLET, Maurice. 248.5
Facing the unbeliever. Translated by Eva Fleischner. [New York] Herder and Herder [1967] 223 p. 21 cm. Translation of Ceux qui perdent la fol. [BV4520.B3613] 67-27540
1. Witness bearing (Christianity) I. Title.

BENDER, Urie A 248.5
The witness: message, method, motivation, by Urie A. Bender. Scottsdale, Pa., Herald Press [1965] 159 p. 21 cm. [BV4520.B38] 65-18233
1. Witness bearing (Christianity) I. Title.

BENDER, Urie A. 248.5
The witness: message, method, motivation. Scottdale, Pa., Herald Pr. [c.1965] 159p. 21cm. [BV4520.B38] 65-18233 3.00
1. Witness bearing (Christianity) I. Title.

BLESSITT, Arthur. 248'.5
Tell the world; a Jesus people manual. Old Tappan, N.J., Revell [1972] 64 p. 18 cm. [BV4520.B52] 78-177397 ISBN 0-8007-0487-8 0.95
1. Witness bearing (Christianity) I. Title.

BOLIN, Gene. 248.5
Christian witness on campus. Introd. by Kenneth Chafin. Nashville, Broadman Press [1968] 95 p. 20 cm. Includes bibliographies. [BV639.C6B6] 68-20666
1. Witness bearing (Christianity) 2. Church work with students. 3. Evangelistic work. 4. College students—Religious life. I. Title.

BOND, Kingsley G. 248.5
A call to witness, by Kingsley G. Bond. Nashville, Methodist Evangelistic Materials [1965] 64 p. 19 cm. [BV4520.B57] 65-22516
1. Witness bearing (Christianity) I. Title.

BROCKWAY, Esther. 248'.5
Toward better witnessing / by Esther Brockway. Independence, Mo. : Herald Pub. House, c1976. 210 p. ; 21 cm. [BX8674.4.B76] 74-82511 ISBN 0-8309-0123-X
1. Reorganized Church of Jesus Christ of Latter Day Saints—Doctrinal and controversial works. 2. Witness bearing (Christianity) I. Title.

BRYANT, Anita. 248'.5
Fishers of men [by] Anita Bryant and Bob Green. Old Tappan, N.J., F. H. Revell Co. [1973] 156 p. illus. 21 cm. [BV4520.B696] 73-16091 ISBN 0-8007-0612-9 4.95
1. Witness bearing (Christianity) I. Green, Bob, joint author. II. Title.

BRYANT, Anita. 248'.5
Fishers of men [by] Anita Bryant and Bob Green. Boston, G. K. Hall [1974, c1973] p. cm. Large print ed. [BV4520.B696 1974] 74-16001 ISBN 0-8161-6237-9 8.95 (lib. bdg.)
1. Witness bearing (Christianity) 2. Sight-saving books. I. Green, Bob, joint author. II. Title.

CAMMACK, James C 1918- 248.5
Yours to share [by] James C. Cammack. [Teacher's ed.] Nashville, Convention Press [1966] vii, 72 p. illus. 19 cm. [BX6225.C3] 66-10255
1. Religious education—Text-books for adolescents—Baptist. I. Title.

CHAFIN, Kenneth. 248'.5
The reluctant witness / Kenneth L. Chafin. Nashville : Broadman Press, [1975] c1974. 143 p. ; 21 cm. [BV4520.C5 1975] 74-84548 ISBN 0-8054-5550-7 : 4.50
1. Witness bearing (Christianity) I. Title.

EIMS, Leroy. 248'.5
Winning ways; the adventure of sharing Christ. Wheaton, Ill., Victor Books [1974] 160 p. 18 cm. (An Input book) [BV4520.E35] 74-77319 ISBN 0-88207-707-4 1.75 (pbk.)
1. Witness bearing (Christianity) I. Title.

FEATHER, R. Othal. 248'.5
Outreach evangelism through the Sunday School [by] R. Othal Feather. Nashville, Convention Press [1972] xi, 145 p. illus. 20 cm. Bibliography: p. 141. [BV4520.F4] 70-186822
1. Witness bearing (Christianity) 2. Evangelistic work. 3. Visitations in Christian education. I. Title.

FLYNN, Leslie B. 248.5
Your influence is showing! [By] Leslie B. Flynn. Nashville, Broadman Press [1967] 127 p. 21 cm. Includes bibliographies. [BV4520.F55] 67-22027
1. Witness bearing (Christianity) 2. Christian life—Baptist authors. I. Title.

FRAZIER, Claude Albee, 248'.5
1920-
Notable personalities and their faith. Compiled by Claude A. Frazier. [Independence, Mo.] Independence Press [1972] 136 p. ports. 21 cm. [BV4520.F7] 72-89607 ISBN 0-8309-0083-7 3.50
1. Witness bearing (Christianity) I. Title.

GRAYUM, H. Frank, comp. 248.5
Witnessing in today's world. H. Frank Grayum, editor. Nashville, Convention Press [1970] 57 p. 21 cm. "Text for course number 3101 of subject area Christian growth and service in the New church study course." [BV4520.G7] 75-121569
1. Witness bearing (Christianity)—Study and teaching. I. Title.

HANSON, Oscar Conrad, 1908- 248.5
Good news for every person; Bible studies on personal witnessing. Prepd. under the auspices of the Comm. on Evangelism of the Amer. Lutheran Church. Minneapolis, Augsburg [c.1965, 1966] 56p. 22cm. Good news' reprint [BV3770.H3] 66-19205 1.00 pap.,
1. Evangelistic work. I. The American Lutheran Church (1961-) Commission on Evangelism. II. Title.

HITT, Russell T., comp. 248.5
Share your faith; perspectives on witnessing. Edited by Russell T. Hitt, with William J. Petersen. Grand Rapids, Zondervan Pub. House [1970] 62 p. 21 cm. (A Zondervan paperback) Contents.Contents.—The secret of effective witnessing, by R. L. Keiper.—Witnessing is not brainwashing, by J. White.—They come for coffee, by H. Kooiman.—How to be a neighborhood witness, by L. Eims.—Bashful Betty, Tacky Tom, and mistaken motives, by S. C. Baldwin.—Winning your relatives to Christ, by D. G. Barnhouse. [BV4520.H57] 76-106447 0.95
1. Witness bearing (Christianity)—Addresses, essays, lectures. I. Title.

HITT, Russell T., comp. 248'.5
Share your faith; perspectives on witnessing. Edited by Russell T. Hitt, with William J. Petersen. Grand Rapids, Zondervan Pub. House [1973, c1970] 62 p. 18 cm. Contents.Contents.—Keiper, R. L. The secret of effective witnessing.—White, J. Witnessing is not brainwashing.—Kooiman, H. They come for coffee.—Eims, L. How to be a neighborhood witness.—Baldwin, S. C. Bashful Betty, Tacky Tom, and mistaken motives.—Barnhouse, D. G. Winning your relatives to Christ. [BV4520.H57 1973] 73-160645 0.95 (pbk)
1. Witness bearing (Christianity) I. Petersen, William J., joint comp. II. Title.

HOGUE, Richard. 248'.5
The Jesus touch. Nashville, Broadman Press [1972] 108 p. illus. 19 cm. [BV4520.H63] 72-79168 ISBN 0-8054-5524-8 1.75
1. Witness bearing (Christianity) I. Title.

ISHEE, John A. 248.5
Is Christ for John Smith? Edited by John A. Ishee. Nashville, Broadman Press [1968] 127 p. 20 cm. [BV4520.I8] 68-20677
1. Witness bearing (Christianity) I. Title.

JONES, Richard M 248.5
The Man for all men [by] Richard M. Jones. Valley Forge [Pa.] Judson Press [1965] 96 p. 20 cm. Bibliographical footnotes. [BV3790.J66] 6528276
1. Evangelistic work. I. Title.

JONES, Richard M. 248.5
The Man for all men. Valley Forge [Pa.] Judson [c.1965] 96p. 20cm. Bibl. [BV3790.J66] 65-28276 1.75 pap.,
1. Evangelistic work. I. Title.

KIEMEL, Ann. 248'.5
I love the work impossible / Ann Kiemel. Wheaton, Ill. : Tyndale House Publishers, 1976. 155 p. : ill. ; 22 cm. [BV4501.2.K486] 75-42908 ISBN 0-8423-1575-6 : 5.95
1. Christian life—1960- 2. Witness bearing (Christianity) 3. Kiemel, Ann. I. Title.

KRUSE, Robert J., 1932- 248.5
To the ends of the earth; Christ here and now, by Robert J. Kruse. New York, Sheed and Ward [1969] xiv, 174 p. 21 cm. Includes bibliographical references. [BV4520.K76] 73-82596 4.50
1. Witness bearing (Christianity) I. Title.

LEVITT, Zola. 248'.5
Jesus—the Jew's Jew. Carol Stream, Ill., Creation House [1973] 106 p. 18 cm. (New leaf library) [BV2620.L45] 73-86271 ISBN 0-88419-064-1 1.45 (pbk.)
1. Missions to Jews. I. Title.

LITTLE, Paul E 248.5
Hou to give away your faith, by Paul E. Little. [Chicago] Inter-Varsity Press [1966] 131 p. illus. 22 cm. Bibliographical footnotes. [BV4520.L5] 66-20710
1. Witness bearing (Christianity) 2. Christian life. I. Title.

LITTLE, Paul E. 248.5
How to give away your faith, by Paul E. Little. [Chicago] Inter-Varsity [1966] 131p. illus. 22cm. Bibl. [BV4520.L5] 66-20710 3.50
1. Witness bearing (Christianity) 2. Christian life. I. Title.

MORRISS, L. L. 248'.5
The sound of boldness / L. L. Morriss. Nashville : Broadman Press, c1977. 117 p. ; 20 cm. [BV4520.M63] 77-75559 ISBN 0-8054-6215-5 : 5.95
1. Witness bearing (Christianity) 2. Evangelistic work. I. Title.

NEW wine, new skins : 248'.5
twenty-five people tell how they encountered the transforming power of the Spirit in the charismatic renewal / compiled by Ralph Martin. New York : Paulist Press, c1976. viii, 174 p. ; 19 cm. [BX2350.57.N48] 76-2855 ISBN 0-8091-1942-0 pbk. : 2.25
1. Pentecostalism—Personal narratives. I. Martin, Ralph, 1942-
Contents omitted

NILES, Daniel Thambyrajah 248.5
This Jesus . . . Whereof we are witnesses. Philadelphia, Westminister [1966, c.1965] 78p. 19cm. First pub. in Great Britain under title: Whereof we are witnesses. [BV4520.N5] 66-10503 1.25 [corrected entry] pap.,
1. Witness bearing (Christianity) I. Title. II. Title: Whereof we are witnesses.

NILES, Daniel Thambyrajah 248.5
Youth asks, what's life for; that they may see, by D. T. Niles. London, Camden, N.J. [etc.] Nelson [1968] 94 p. 20 1/2 cm. (Youth forum series) [BV4520.N52] 68-22130
1. Witness bearing (Christianity) I. Title. II. Series.

NOFFSINGER, Jack Ricks. 248.5
Heralds of Christ. Nashville, Convention Press [1966] viii, 119 p. 20 cm. "Church study course of the Sunday School Board of the Southern Baptist Convention] This book is number 0772 in category 7, section for young people." Includes bibliographies. [BV4520.N6] 66-10254
1. Witness bearing (Christianity) 2. Religious education — Textbooks for young people — Baptist. I. Southern Baptist Convention. Sunday School Board. II. Title.

PACKER, James Innell. 248.5
Evangelism and the sovereignty of God [by] J. I. Packer. Chicago, Inter-varsity Press [1967, c1961] 126 p. 18 cm. [BV3793.P3] 67-28875
1. Evangelistic work. 2. Providence and government of God. I. Title.

PEACE, Richard. 248'.5
Witness; a manual for use by small groups of Christians who are serious in their desire to learn how to share their faith. Foreword by Bruce Larson. Grand Rapids, Zondervan Pub. House [1971] 249 p. 21 cm. (A Zondervan horizon book) Includes bibliographical references. [BV4520.P4] 71-156253
1. Witness bearing (Christianity) I. Title.

PLEKKER, Robert J. 248'.5
Redeemed? Say so! / Robert J. Plekker. 1st ed. New York : Harper & Row, c1976. p. cm. [BV4520.P52] 76-10004 ISBN 0-06-066652-8 pbk. : 3.95
1. Witness bearing (Christianity) I. Title.

PONDER, James A. comp. 248.5
Evangelism men; motivating laymen to witness, compiled by James A. Ponder. Nashville, Broadman Press, [1975 c1974] 109 p. ports. 19 cm. [BV4520.P55] 74-20110 ISBN 0-8054-2224-2 1.95 (pbk.)
1. Witness bearing (Christianity) I. Title.

PRICHARD, Ernie. 248'.5
Salesmanship for Christ [by] Ernie "Tex" Prichard. Nashville, Broadman Press [1972] 155 p. 21 cm. [BV4520.P74] 71-178064 ISBN 0-8054-5515-9 4.50
1. Witness-bearing (Christianity) I. Title.

PRINCE, John. 248'.5
Early harvest : leading a child to Christ / [by] John Prince. London : Falcon Books, 1976. [1], 48 p. ; 20 cm. Distributed in Australia by EMU Book Agencies, Granville. Bibliography: p. 47-48. [BV4925.P74] 77-362809 ISBN 0-85491-147-2 : £0.60
1. Children—Conversion to Christianity. I. Title.

RIDENOUR, Fritz. 248.5
Tell it like it is. Illustrated by Joyce Thimsen. Research: Georgiana Walker. Glendale, Calif., G/L Regal Books [1968] 232 p. illus. 18 cm. "The gospel of John in Living New Testament paraphrase combined with personal views and experiences of present day people." Bibliographical footnotes. [BV4520.R52] 68-29315
1. Witness bearing (Christianity) I. Title.

RINKER, Rosalind. 248'.5
Sharing God's love / by Rosalind Rinker and Harry C. Griffith. Grand Rapids : Zondervan Pub. House, c1976. p. cm. [BV4520.R53] 75-37757
1. Witness bearing (Christianity) I. Griffith, Harry C., joint author. II. Title.

RUOFF, Norman D. 248'.5
1974 yearbook of testimony : testimonies from the general officers and staff of the leading departments and commissions of the world church with supporting testimonies of state and regional officers / compiled by Norman D. Rvoff Independence, Mo. : Herald Pub. House, [1974] 189 p. ; 21 cm. [BX8674.R86] 74-84192 ISBN 0-8309-0122-1 : 5.50
1. Reorganized Church of Jesus Christ of Latter-Day Saints—Doctrinal and controversial works. 2. Christian life—Mormon authors. I. Title.

RYAN, Roberta. 248.5
Keep telling the story. [Teacher's ed.] Nashville, Convention Press [1963] 102 p. illus. 19 cm. "Helps for the teacher": 16 p. bound in. [BX6225.R9] 63-8379
1. Religious education—Text-books for children—Baptists. 2. Baptists—Missions—Juvenile literature. I. Title.

*SAMUEL, Leith. 248.5
Witnessing for Christ. Grand Rapids, Zondervan Pub. House [1974, c1962] 93 p. 18 cm. Originally published under the title Personal witness. [BV4520] 74-4955 1.25 (pbk.)
1. Witness bearing (Christianity.). I. Title.

SHERROD, Paul. 248'.5
Successful soul winning; proven ideas to challenge every Christian to be a personal worker. Lubbock, Tex., P. Sherrod [1974] xi, 169 p. illus. 23 cm. Bibliography: p. 169. [BV3790.S52] 73-93945

1. Evangelistic work. I. Title.

SOUTHERN Baptist 248.5
Convention. Sunday School Board.
Little lessons for little people. Greenville, S.C. 1864- v. 12 cm. [BX6225.S6] 62-56433
1. Religious education — Text-books for children — Baptist. I. Title.

STRACHAN, Robert Kenneth, 248.5
1910-1965.
The inescapable calling; the missionary task of the church of Christ in the light of contemporary challenge and opportunity. Grand Rapids, Mich., Eerdmans [1968] 127 p. 20 cm. (A Christian world mission book) Bibliography: p. 121-122. [BV4520.S684] 68-18841
1. Witness bearing (Christianity) I. Title.

TAM, Stanley, 1915- 248'.5
Every Christian a soul winner / by Stanley Tam, as told to Ken Anderson. Nashville : T. Nelson, [1975] 168 p., [2] leaves of plates : ill. ; 22 cm. [BV3790.T25] 75-17771 ISBN 0-8407-5093-5 : 5.95
1. Evangelistic work. 2. Witness bearing (Christianity) I. Anderson, Kenneth, 1917- II. Title.

TRITES, Allison A., 1936- 248'.5
The New Testament concept of witness / Allison A. Trites. Cambridge [Eng.] ; New York : Cambridge University Press, 1977. x, 294 p. ; 22 cm. (Monograph series - Society for New Testament studies ; 31) Includes indexes. Bibliography: p. 240-254. [BS2545.W54T74] 76-11067 ISBN 0-521-21015-1 : 23.00
1. Witness bearing (Christianity)—Biblical teaching. 2. Witnesses—Biblical teaching. I. Title. II. Series: Studiorum Novi Testamenti Societas. Monograph series ; 31.

ULBRICH, Armand Henry, 248'.5
1915-
Presenting the Gospel : how to do so with confidence and joy / by Armand Ulbrich. [St. Louis : Board for Evangelism, Lutheran Church-Missouri Synod, 1977] iii, 192 p. : ill. ; 23 cm. Cover title. [BV4520.U38] 77-150370
1. Witness bearing (Christianity) 2. Evangelistic work. I. Title.

WATTS, Ewart G., 1915- 248.5
Discipleship for the 70's, by Ewart G. Watts. Nashville, Tidings [1971] 64 p. 19 cm. Includes bibliographical references. [BV4501.2.W38] 72-153116
1. Christian life—Methodist authors. I. Title.

WORRELL, George E. 248'.5
How to take the worry out of witnessing / George E. Worrell. Nashville : Broadman Press, c1976. 92 p. : ill. ; 20 cm. Includes bibliographical references. Discusses ways in which young Christians can spiritually prepare themselves for sharing their faith daily. [BV4520.W65] 76-381685 ISBN 0-8054-5568-X pbk. : 1.75
1. Witness bearing (Christianity)—Juvenile literature. 2. Youth—Religious life—Juvenile literature. I. Title.

YORK, William E. 248'.5
One to one; 15-minute Bible studies to share with a friend [by] William E. York, Jr. Downers Grove, Ill., Inter-Varsity Press [1972] 64 p. 18 cm. [BV4520.Y67] 72-78406 ISBN 0-87784-438-0 0.95
1. Witness bearing (Christianity) I. Title.

WINTER, Rebecca J. 248'.5'0922 B
The night cometh : two wealthy evangelicals face the nation / Rebecca J. Winter. South Pasadena, Calif. : William Carey Library, c1977. xii, 84 p. ; 22 cm. Includes index. Bibliography: p. 78-80. [BR1643.A1W56] 77-87594 ISBN 0-87808-429-0 pbk. : 2.95
1. Tappan, Arthur, 1786-1865. 2. Tappan, Lewis, 1788-1873. 3. Evangelicalism—United States—Biography. 4. Philanthropists—United States—Biography. I. Title.

FRANCK, Ira Stoner, 248.50924
1896-
My search for an anchor, by Ira S. Franck. Philadelphia, Dorrance [1966] 129 p. illus., ports. 21 cm. Autobiographical. [BX5995.F67A3] 66-18610
I. Title.

FRANCK, Ira Stoner, 248.50924
1896-
My search for an anchor. Philadelphia, Dorrance [c.1966] 129p. illus., ports. 21cm. Autobiographical. [BX5995.F67A3] 66-18610 3.00
I. Title.

LINSLEY, Kenneth W. 248'.5'0924 B
Advocate for God : a lawyer's experience in personal evangelism / Kenneth Williams Linsley. Valley Forge, Pa. : Judson Press, c1977. 80 p. ; 22 cm. Includes bibliographical references. [BV4520.L47] 76-48749 ISBN 0-8170-0723-7 pbk. : 2.50
1. Linsley, Kenneth Williams. 2. Witness bearing (Christianity) 3. Baptists—United States—Biography. I. Title.

MY search for an 248.50924
anchor, by Ira S. Franck. Philadelphia, Dorrance [1966] 129 p. illus., ports. 21 cm. Autobiographical. [BX5995.F67A3] 66-18610

BAILLIE, John, 1886-1960. 248.51
A reasoned faith; collected addresses. New York, Scribner [1963] 180 p. 22 cm. [BV4501.2.B33] 63-10501
1. Christian life—Presbyterian authors. 2. Sermons, English. I. Title.

BARFOOT, Earl F. 248'.6
What does the Lord want / Earl F. Barfoot, editor. Nashville, : Tidings, [1974] 55 p. ; 19 cm. [BV772.B27] 74-80892 pbk. : 1.25.
1. Stewardship, Christian—Addresses, essays, lectures. 2. Laity—Addresses, essays, lectures. I. Title.

CLARK, Henry, 1930- 248'.6
Escape from the money trap [by] Henry B. Clark. Valley Forge [Pa.] Judson Press [1973] 124 p. 22 cm. Includes bibliographical references. [BR115.E3C56] 73-2610 ISBN 0-8170-0585-4 2.35
1. Christianity and economics. 2. Stewardship, Christian. I. Title.

DIETZE, Charles E., 1919- 248'.6
God's trustees, to whom much is given / Charles E. Dietze. Saint Louis, Mo. : Bethany Press, c1976. 92 p. ; 22 cm. Includes bibliographical references. [BV772.D46] 75-43848 ISBN 0-8272-1216-X pbk. : 3.95
1. Stewardship, Christian. I. Title.

DOLLAR, Truman. 248'.6
How to carry out God's stewardship plan. Nashville, T. Nelson [1974] 191 p. 21 cm. Bibliography: p. 189-191. [BV772.D73] 74-840 6.95
1. Stewardship, Christian. I. Title.

†DOXEY, Roy Watkins, 1908- 248'.6
Tithing : the Lord's law / Roy W. Doxey. Salt Lake City : Deseret Book Co., 1976. viii, 102 p. ; 24 cm. Includes index. Bibliography: p. [96]-97. [BX8643.T5D69] 76-41587 ISBN 0-87747-615-2 : 4.95
1. Tithes—Mormonism. I. Title.

EGGERICHS, Fred W., 1912- 248'.6
A bag without holes : how to prepare for your family, your finances, your future / by Fred W. Eggerichs, with Bernard Palmer. Minneapolis : Bethany Fellowship, [1975] 95 p. ; 21 cm. [BV772.E4] 74-23435 ISBN 0-87123-532-3 ; 2.25
1. Stewardship, Christian. I. Title.

ESPIE, John C. 248'.6
Opportunities in stewardship for concerned Christians in a local church / John C. Espie, Thomas C. Rieke. Nashville : Discipleship Resources, c1975. 148 p. : ill. ; 28 cm. Includes index. Bibliography: p. 145. [BV772.E83] 75-10371
1. Stewardship, Christian. I. Rieke, Thomas C., joint author. II. Title.

FISHER, Wallace E. 248'.6
A new climate for stewardship / Wallace E. Fisher. Nashville : Abingdon Press, c1976. 127 p. ; 19 cm. [BV772.F5] 76-109 ISBN 0-687-27723-X : 3.95
1. Stewardship, Christian. I. Title.

JESUS, dollars and sense 248'.6
: a practical and effective stewardship guide for clergy and lay leaders / edited by Oscar C. Carr, Jr. ; foreword by Furman C. Stough. New York : Seabury Press, c1976. p. cm. "A Crossroad book." [BV772.J45] 76-14362 ISBN 0-8164-2132-3 pbk. : 3.95
1. Protestant Episcopal Church in the U.S.A.—Sermons. 2. Stewardship, Christian—Addresses, essays, lectures. 3. Stewardship, Christian—Sermons. 4. Sermons, American.

KAUFFMAN, Milo, 1898- 248'.6
Stewards of God. Scottdale, Pa., Herald Press, 1975. 264 p. 22 cm. Includes bibliographical references. [BV772.K33] 74-13130 ISBN 0-8361-1747-6 4.95
1. Stewardship, Christian—Biblical teaching. I. Title.

KAUFFMAN, Milo, 1898- 248'.6
Stewards of God. Scottdale, Pa., Herald Press, 1975. 264 p. 22 cm. Includes bibliographical references. [BV772.K33] 74-13130 ISBN 0-8361-1747-6 5.95
1. Stewardship, Christian—Biblical teaching. I. Title.

LINDSAY, Gordon. 248'.6
How to be enriched by giving. Carol Stream, Ill., Creation House [1974] 64 p. 18 cm. "Originally published as 20 things most people don't know about Bible giving." [BV772.L54 1974] 73-82856 ISBN 0-88419-047-1 0.95 (pbk)
1. Christian giving. I. Title.

MCBAIN, John M. 248'.6
It is required of stewards [by] John M. McBain. Nashville, Tenn., Broadman Press [1972] 128 p. 20 cm. [BV772.M27] 72-79172 ISBN 0-8054-8505-8
1. Stewardship, Christian. I. Title.

MCGEACHY, Pat, 1929- 248'.6
Traveling light / Pat McGeachy. Nashville : Abingdon Press, [1975] 112 p. ; 19 cm. Includes bibliographical references. [BV772.M3514] 75-17572 ISBN 0-687-42530-1 pbk. : 3.25
1. Stewardship, Christian. I. Title.

MACNAUGHTON, John H. 248'.6
Stewardship-myth and methods : a program guide for ministers and lay leaders / John H. MacNaughton. New York : Seabury Press, [1975] xv, 137 p. ; 21 cm. "A Crossroad book." [BV772.M355] 75-5878 ISBN 0-8164-2112-9 pbk. : 3.95
1. Stewardship, Christian. 2. Church finance. I. Title.

NATIONAL Catholic 248'.6
Stewardship Council.
Stewardship of money : a manual for parishes. Washington : National Catholic Stewardship Council, 1975. 64 p. : ill. ; 28 cm. Bibliography: p. 62-64. [BV772.N325 1975] 75-34042
1. Stewardship, Christian—Handbooks, manuals, etc. I. Title.

O'CONNELL, Hugh J., 1910- 248.6
Stewardship; call to a new way of life [by] Hugh J. O'Connell. Liguori, Mo., Liguorian Books [1969] 192 p. 18 cm. (Catholic living series, v. 10) [BV772.O3] 75-97517 1.00
1. Stewardship, Christian—Study and teaching. I. Title.

SELLS, James William. 248'.6
A partner with the living Lord / James William Sells. Nashville : Upper Room, c1975. 112 p. ; 22 cm. [BV772.S44] 75-21628 1.95
1. Stewardship, Christian. 2. Christian life—Methodist authors. I. Title.

SHEDD, Charlie W. 248'.6
The exciting church where they give their money away / Charlie W. Shedd. Waco, Tex. : Word Books, c1975. 88 p. : ill. ; 21 cm. [BV772.S518] 75-19904 3.95
1. Stewardship, Christian. 2. Christian giving. I. Title.

SMITH, Paul G. 248'.6
Managing God's goods, by Paul G. Smith. Nashville, Southern Pub. Association [1973] 126 p. illus. 21 cm. [BV772.S614] 73-84597 ISBN 0-8127-0036-8 1.95 (pbk.)
1. Stewardship, Christian. I. Title.

SORENSON, Charles M. 248'.6
Stewardship upside down : a new and exciting design for nurturing commitment to the Christian cause / Charles M. Sorenson. New York : Hawthorn Books, [1975] 76 p. ; 21 cm. Bibliography: p. 74-76. [BV772.S63 1975] 74-22914 ISBN 0-8015-7144-8 pbk. : 2.95
1. Stewardship, Christian. 2. Christian life—1960- 3. Church renewal. I. Title.

WILLIAMSON, E. Stanley, 248'.6
comp.
Faithful to the Lord. Compiled by E. Stanley Williamson. Nashville, Broadman Press [1973] 122 p. 21 cm. [BV772.W49] 72-97607 ISBN 0-8054-2219-6 3.95
1. Baptists—Sermons. 2. Stewardship, Christian—Sermons. 3. Sermons, American. I. Title.

ALBERIONE, Giacomo 248.8
Giuseppe, 1884-
Christ, model and reward of religious, by James Alberione. Transaltion by a Daughter of St. Paul. [Boston] St. Paul Editions [1963] 205 p. /19 cm. [BX2385.A59] 63-17306
1. Monastic and religious life. I. Title.

ALBERIONE, Giacomo 248.8
Giuseppe, 1884-
Christ, model and reward of religious, by James Alberione. Tr. by a Daughter of St. Paul. St. Paul Eds. [dist. Boston, Daughters of St. Paul, c.1963] 205p. 19cm. 63-17306 3.00; 2.00 pap.,
1. Monastic and religious life. I. Title.

ALBERIONE, Giacomo 248.8
Giuseppe, 1884
Growing in perfect union [Boston] St. Paul Eds. [dist. Daughters of St. Paul, c.1964] 132p. 19cm. [BX2385.A593] 63-14468 2.50; 1.50 pap.,
1. Monastic and religious life. I. Title.

ALBERIONE, Giacomo 248.8
Giuseppe, 1884-
Growing in perfect union, by James Alberione. [Boston] St. Paul Editions [c1964] 132 p. 19 cm. [BX2385.A593] 63-14468
1. Monastic and religious life. I. Title.

ALDERFER, Helen, ed. 248.8
A farthing in her hand; stewardship for women. Scottdale, Pa., Gerald Press [1964] vi, 222 p. 18 cm. Includes bibliographies. [BV772.A46] 64-23376
1. Stewardship, Christian. 2. Woman—Religious life. I. Title.

ALDERFER, Helen, ed. 248.8
A farthing in her hand; stewardship for women. Scottdale, Pa., Herald Pr. [c.1964] vi, 222p. 18cm. Bibl. [BV772.A46] 64-23376 3.50
1. Stewardship, Christian. 2. Woman—Religious life. I. Title.

BEDSOLE, Adolph 248.8
Parson to parson. Grand Rapids, Mich., Baker Bk. [1965, c.1964] 149p. 20cm. [BV4011.B39] 64-8344 2.95 bds.,
1. Pastoral theology—Baptists. I. Title.

BERGHERM, William H 248.8
No greater glory. Illustrated by Howard Larkin. Mountain View, Calif., Pacific Press Pub. Association [1959] 104p. illus. 20cm. [BV4588.B45] 59-13495
1. Soldiers—Religious life. 2. Seventh-Day Adventists. I. Title.

BERTSCHE, Leopold 248.8
Directorium sponsae: Westminster, Md., Newman Pr., c.1962, 1965 viii, 308p. 16cm. Subtitle varies. Contents.v.4, pt.1. First Sunday of Advent to vigil of Pentecost [BX4210.B383] 58-13643 3.50
1. Monastic and religious life of women—Addresses, essays, lectures. 2. Rosary—Meditations. I. Title. II. Title: Short meditations for each day of the year., v.4, pt. 1. Tr. by Maria H. Arndt.

BOWMAN, Mary D. 248.8
Mom, you gotta be kiddin' [by] Mary D. Bowman. With illus. by Don Sampson. Old Tappan, N.J., F. H. Revell [1968] 62 p. col. illus. 16 x 21 cm. [BV4847.B62] 68-28435 2.95
1. Mothers—Religious life. I. Title.

BRIGGS, Argye M 248.8
Christ and the modern woman. Grand Rapids, Eerdmans [1958] 153p. 22cm. [BV4527.B7] 58-59783
1. Woman—Religious life. I. Title.

BROWNING, Columban 248.8
Woman's highest fulfillment. Milwaukee, Bruce [c.1965] v, 98p. 17cm. [BX4210.B7] 65-12047 2.95
1. Monastic and religious life of women. I. Title.

BROWNING, Columbian. 248.8
Woman's highest fulfillment. Milwaukee Bruce Pub. Co. (c1965) v, 98 p. 17 cm. [BX4210.B7] 65-12047
1. Monastic and religious life of women. I. Title.

*CLARKSON, E. Margaret. 248.8
God's hedge; help for those who must suffer. Chicago, Moody [1968] 62p. illus. 22 cm. .95 pap.,
1. Suffering—Spiritual consolation. I. Title.

COMBS, Louis K. 248.8
So ... you're in the service, by Louis K. Combs, Jr. Glendale, Calif., G/L Regal [1968] 164p. illus. 18cm. [BV4588.C59] 68-25808 .95 pap.,
1. Soldiers—Religious life. I. Title.

DANAGHER, Edward F 248.8
Son, give me your heart. Milwaukee, Bruce Pub. Co. [1964] viii, 149 p. 17 cm. [BX2182.2.D3] 63-23266
1. Seminarians — Meditations. I. Title.

DANAGHER, Edward F. 248.8
Son, give me your heart. Milwaukee, Bruce [c.1964] viii, 149p. 17cm. 63-23266 3.00
1. Seminarians—Meditations. I. Title.

DILLENSCHNEIDER, Clement. 248.8
Christ the one priest, and we His priests. Translated by Sister M. Renelle. St. Louis, B. Herder Book Co. [1964-65] 2 v. 24 cm. Contents.-- v. 1. Dogmatic foundations of our priestly spirituality. -- v. 2. Our priestly spirituality. Bibliographical footnotes. [BX1912.5D513] 64-8811
1. Jesus Christ — Priesthood. 2. Clergy — Religious life. 3. Priests. I. Title.

DILLENSCHNEIDER, Clement 248.8
Christ the one priest, and we His priests; v.1. Tr. [from French] by Sister M. Renelle. St. Louis, B. Herder [c.1964] 306p. 24cm. Bibl.

Contents.v.1. Dogmatic foundations of our priestly spirituality. [BX1912.5.D513] 64-8811 5.75
1. Clergy—Religious life. 2. Jesus Christ—Priesthood. 3. Priests. I. Title.

EDWIN, B 248.8
Examens for retreat time [by] B. Edwin. Milwaukee, Bruce Pub. Co., [1964] 56 p. 18 cm. [BX2377.E3] 64-24338
1. Conscience, Examination of. 2. Retreats. I. Title.

EDWIN, B. 248.8
Examens for retreat time. Milwaukee, Bruce [c.1964] 56p. 18cm. 64-24338 .50 pap.,
1. Conscience, Examination of. 2. Retreats. I. Title.

EVANS, Laura Margaret 248.8
Hand in hand; mother, child, and God. [Westwood, N.J.] F. H. Revell Co. [c. 1960] 122p. 21cm. 60-5501 2.50 half cloth,
1. Children—Religious life. 2. Religious education—Home training. I. Title.

FITZGERALD, Lawrence P. 248.8
One hundred talks to teen-agers. Grand Rapids, Mich., Baker Bk. House, 1961. 106p. 61-17545 1.95
1. Youth—Religious life. I. Title.

GOLISCH, John 248.8
It's time to talk to God, by John and Joan Golisch. Minneapolis, Augsburg [c.1965] 1v. (unpaged) col. illus. 22x28cm. [BV212.G6] 65-12139 2.50
1. Prayer—Juvenile literature. I. Golisch, Joan, joint author. II. Title.

HARTON, Sibyl, 1898- 248.8
On growing old; a book of preparation for age. New York, Morehouse-Gorham Co. [1958, c1957] 126p. 19cm. [BV4580.H25 1958] 58-4995
1. Aged—Religious life. I. Title.

HASKIN, Dorothy (Clark) 248.8
1905-
Beverly's quest; a modern girl's search for truth and happiness. Grand Rapids, Zondervan Pub. House [1959] 85p. 20cm. [BV4551.2.H35] 59-16825
1. Girls—Religious life. I. Title.

*HAYES, Wanda 248.8
My thank you book [Cincinnati, Ohio, Standard Pub. Co., c.1964] unpaged. col. illus. 31cm. (3048) cover title 1.50 bds.,
I. Title.

HERTZ, Solange Strong 248.8
Women, words, and wisdom. Westminster, Md., Newman Press, [c.]1959. viii, 184p. 23cm. 59-14801 3.50
1. Christian life—Catholic authors. I. Title.

HERTZ, Solange Strong, 248.8
1920-
Women, words, and wisdom. Westminster, Md., Newman Press, 1959. 184p. 23cm. Essays. [BX2350.2.H42] 59-14801
1. Christian life—Catholic authors. I. Title.

HEYER, Robert, comp. 248.8
Discovery in song. Edited by Robert Heyer. Designed by Emil Antonucci. Photographed by Ken Wittenberg. Coordinated by Richard Payne. Written by Thomas O'Brien [and others] New Glen Rock, N.J., Paulist Press [1968] 138 p. illus. 23 cm. The themes and words of some popular songs in the folk idiom are examined for their relevance to the contemporary social and individual problems of alienation, lack of communication, and the callousness of modern life. [BV4531.2.H48] AC 68
1. Youth—Religious life. I. O'Brien, Thomas E. II. Title.

HUEGEL, Frederick Julius, 248'.8
1889-
Bone of his bone; a classic on the indwelling Christ [by] F. J. Huegel. Grand Rapids, Zondervan Pub. House [1972] 101 p. 18 cm. Originally published in 1933. [BT265.H714 1972] 72-187963 0.95
1. Atonement. 2. Christian life. I. Title.

HULME, William Edward, 248.8
1920-
God, sex, & youth. Englewood Cliffs, N. J., Prentice-Hall [1959] 179p. 21cm. [BV4780.S4H8] 59-7807
1. Sex. I. Title.

I Want to be good. 248.8
Pictures by Grace Dalles Clarke. New York, Guild Press; distributed by Golden Press [1960] c.1959. unpaged. illus. (col.) 17cm. (A First book for little Catholics; A Catechetical Guild book.) 60-278 .25 bds.,
1. Children—Religious life. I. Clarke, Grace Dalles, illus.

IVERSEN, John Orville. 248.8
More teen talks, by J. O. Iversen. Guest writers: A teen talks back [by] Bonnie Iversen; Knocking out the "T" [by] Jerre Kent Iversen. Washington, Review and Herald Pub. Association [1968] 96 p. 20 cm. A series of talks for teenagers relates Christianity to everyday life. [BV4531.2.I93] AC 68
1. Youth—Religious life. I. Title.

JARRETT, Bede, 1881-1934 248.8
For priests. Foreword by Robert W. Gleason. Chicago, Priory Pr. 2005 S Ashland Ave. [1965] 123p. 20cm. Articles which orig. appeared in the Homiletic and pastoral review. [BX1912.5.J3] 65-19358 3.50
1. Spiritual life—Catholic authors. 2. Catholic Church—Clergy—Religious life. I. Title.

*JONES, Irene 248.8
Needed: a righteous generation. Independence, Mo., Herald House [c.1964]. 64p. 22cm. .60 pap.,
I. Title.

JONES, Mary Alice, 248.8 (j)
1898-
Me, myself and God. Illustrated by Dorothy Grider. Chicago, Rand McNally, 1966, c1965. 1 v. (unpaged) col. illus. 26 cm. [BV4571.2.J63] 66-16897
1. Children—Religious life. 2. God—Juvenile literature. I. Grider, Dorothy, illus. II. Title.

JONES, Mary Alice, 1898- 248.8
Me, myself and God. Illustrated by Dorothy Grider. Chicago, Rand McNally, 1966, c1965. [32] p. col. illus. 26 cm. A small boy learns about the relationship between God and himself—that he is part of God's plan, and God loves him. [BV4571.2.J63] AC 67
1. God. I. Grider, Dorothy, illus. II. Title.

KENNEDY, Gerald Hamilton, 248.8
Bp., 1907-
For preachers and other sinners. [1st ed.] New York, Harper & Row [1964] x, 110 p. 22 cm. [BV4221.K4] 64-14379
1. Preaching — Addresses, essays, lectures. 2. Christianity — 20th cent. — Addresses, essays, lectures. I. Title.

KENNEDY, Gerald Hamilton, 248.8
Bp., 1907-
For preachers and other sinners. New York, Harper [c.1964] x, 110p. 22cm. 64-14379 3.00
1. Preaching—Addresses, essays, lectures. 2. Christianity—20th cent.—Addresses, essays, lectures. I. Title.

LECLERCQ, Dom Jean, 1911- 248.8
Alone with God. [Tr. by Elizabeth McCabe from French] New York, Farrar, Straus and Cudahy [c.1961] xxvii, 209p. Bibl. 61-11318 3.95
1. Giustiniani, Paolo, 1476-1528. I. Title.

LECLERCQ. JEAN, 1911- 248.8
Alone with God. [Translated by Elizabeth McCabe from the French] New York, Farrar, Straus and Cudahy [1961] xxvii, 209p. 21cm. [BX2845.L413] 61-11318
1. Giustiniani, Polo, 1476-1528. 2. Hermits. I. Title. II. Title: he sources : p. 201-206.

LOTZ, Johannes Baptist, 248.8
1903-
The problem of loneliness [by] J. B. Lotz. Staten Island, N.Y., Alba [1967] ix, 149p. 20cm. Tr. of Von der Einsamkeit des Menschen. Bibl. [BV4911.L613] 67-9410 3.95
1. Loneliness. I. Title.

LOTZ, Johannes Baptist, 248.8
1903-
The problem of loneliness [by] J. B. Lotz. Staten Island, N.Y., Alba House [1967] ix, 149 p. 20 cm. Translation of Von der Einsamkeit des Menschen. Bibliographical footnotes. [BV4911.L613 1967b] 67-9410
1. Loneliness. I. Title.

MCGOLDRICK, Desmond F. 248.8
Independence through submission; notes for religious sisters on the idea and implications of their religious consecration. Pittsburgh, Duquesne Univ. Pr. [c.]1964. xv, 182p. 20cm. (Duquesne sister formation ser., 3) 64-15935 3.75
1. Monastic and religious life of women. I. Title. II. Series.

MARIE EMMANUEL, Sister 248.8
1904-
Let in the sun; monthly meditations for Sisters in the active apostolate. Westminster, Md., Newman [c.]1965. xii, 153p. 22cm. [BX4214.M3] 65-18662 3.95
1. Meditations. 2. Monasticism and religious orders for women. I. Title.

MICKLEM, Caryl. 248'.8
As good as your word : a third book of contemporary prayers / by Caryl Micklem and Roger Tomes ; edited by Caryl Micklem. Grand Rapids : Eerdmans, c1975. p. cm. Includes index. [BV245.M489] 76-9048 ISBN 0-8028-1644-4
1. Prayers. I. Tomes, Roger, joint author. II. Title.

MY hospital record, 248.8
by Rev. Walter I. Greenawalt, John H. Nicholson. Henry Stewart [dist. New York, Politzer Times Tower Bldg., c.1962] unpaged. illus. (pt. col.) 1.00 bds.,
I. Greenawalt, Walter I. II. Nicholson, John H., joint author.

NELSON, Marion H 248.8
Why Christians crack up; the causes of and remedies for nervous trouble in Christians. Chicago, Moody Press [1960] 125p. 22cm. [BT732.N43] 61-3
1. Medicine and religion. 2. Mental illness. 3. Demoniac possession. I. Title.

PRICE, Eugenia 248.8
The wider place . . . where God offers freedom from anything that limits our growth. Grand Rapids, Mich., Zondervan [c.1966] 250p. 23cm. [BV4501.2.P7] 66-24574 3.95
1. Christian life. I. Title.

PRICE, Eugenia. 248.8
The wider place ... where God offers freedom from anything that limits our growth. Grand Rapids, Mich., Zondervan Pub. House [1966] 250 p. 23 cm. [BV4501.2.P7] 66-24574
1. Christian life. I. Title.

PRICE, Eugenia. 248.8
The wider place...where God offers freedom from anything that limits our growth. Grand Rapids, Zondervan [1975, c1966] 205 p. 18 cm. [BV4501.2.P7] 66-24574 1.95 (pbk.)
1. Christian life. I. Title.

PRICE, Eugenia. 248.8
Woman to woman. Grand Rapids, Zondervan Pub. House [1959] 241 p. 21 cm. [BV4527.P73] 59-4290
1. Women—Religious life. I. Title.

RAYMOND, Father, 1903- 248.8
This is your tomorrow ... and today. Milwaukee, Bruce Pub. Co. [1959] 207p. illus. 24cm. [BV4909.R3] 59-9719
1. Suffering. I. Title.

RINKER, Rosalind. 248'.8
How to have family prayers / Rosalind Rinker. Grand Rapids : Zondervan Pub. House, c1977. 170 p. : ill. ; 21 cm. Bibliography: p. 167-170. [BV4526.2.R56] 76-56797 ISBN 0-310-32160-3 : 5.95 ISBN 0-310-32161-1 pbk. : 2.95
1. Family—Religious life. 2. Family—Prayer-books and devotions—English. I. Title.

ROSENGRANT, John, comp. 248.8
Assignment: overseas. Ed. by Stanley J. Rowland, Jr. [Rev. ed.] New York, Crowell [c.1966] viii, 129p. maps. 22cm. Lects. from the insts. on overseas churchmanship. [BV4520.R65] 66-11949 4.95
1. Christians. 2. Americans in foreign countries. I. Title.

SANFORD, Edgar Lewis, 1864- 248.8
God's healing power. Englewood Cliffs, N. J., Prentice-Hall [1959] 224 p. 24 cm. [BT732.4.S23] 59-14640
1. Faith-cure. I. Title.

*SAVARD, Rev. Wilfred 248.8
The A.B.C. institute of the holy faith. New York, Vantage [c.1965] 73p. 21cm. 2.50 bds.,
I. Title.

SMITH, Tom A. 248.8
Be! A guide for personal growth, by Tom. A. Smith, Don Knipschield. Anderson, Ind., Warner [dist. Gospel Trumpet, c.1962] 64p. 62-11102 1.00 pap.,
1. Youth—Religious life. I. Knipschield, Don, joint author. II. Title.

SPENCE, Inez. 248.8
When the heart is lonely. Grand Rapids, Baker Book House [1970] 111 p. 21 cm. [BV4911.S65] 78-115640 2.95
1. Loneliness. 2. Consolation. I. Title.

STAUDACHER, Rosemarian V 248.8
In American vineyards; religious orders in the United States, by Rosemarian V. Staudacher. Illustrated by Herb Mott. New York, Vision Books [1966] 175 p. illus. 22 cm. [BX2505.S7] 66-14039
1. Monasticism and religious orders—U.S.—Juvenile literature. I. Title.

STAUDACHER, Rosemarian V. 248.8
In American vineyards; religious orders in the United States. Illus. by Herb Mott. New York, Farrar [c.1966] 175p. illus. 22cm. (Vision bks.) [BX2505.S7] 66-14039 2.25
1. Monasticism and religious orders—U.S.—Juvenile literature. I. Title.

*SWEENEY, Joseph W. 248.8
The vinedressers. New York, Exposition [1965, c.1964] 130p. 21cm. (EP42143) p3.50
I. Title.

TRESE, Leo John, 1902- 248.8
Sanctified in truth. New York, Sheed & Ward [c.1961] 183p. 61-11791 3.50
1. Clergy—Religious life. 2. Catholic Church—Clergy. I. Title.

TURNBULL, Ralph G. 248.8
A minister's obstacles. Westwood, N.J., Revell [1965, c.1964] 192p. 21cm. [BV4010.T75] 64-20189 2.95 bds.,
1. Pastoral theology. I. Title.

UNGER, Dominic J 248.8
The mystery of love for the single. Chicago, Franciscan Herald Press [1958] 192 p. 21 cm. [BX2350.9.U5] 58-10453
1. Single people — Religious life. I. Title.

UNSTEAD, R. J. 248.8
Monasteries. Illus. by J. C. B. Knight [Chester Springs, Pa.] Dufour [1965, c.1961] 48p. illus., facsim., plans. 23cm. [BX2592.U5] 65-19681 2.95 bds.,
1. Monastic and religious life—Hist. 2. Monasteries—Gt. Brit. I. Title.

WARNER, Gary. 248.8
Out to win! Christian athletes speak the language of victory. Edited by Gary Warner. Chicago Moody Press [1967] 128 p. 22 cm. [BV4501.2.W37] 67-26297
1. Christian life. I. Title.

WARNER, Gary. 248.8
Out to win! Christian athletes speak the language of victory. Edited by Gary Warner. Chicago, Moody Press [1967] 128 p. 22 cm. [BV4501.2.W37] 67-26297
1. Christian life. I. Title.

WILLIAMSON, Audrey J. 248.8
Far above rubies; meditations for the minister's wife. Kansas City, Mo., Beacon Hill Press [1961] 128 p. 20 cm. [BV4395.W54] 61-5282
1. Clergymen's wives — Religious life. I. Title.

WILLIAMSON, Audrey J. 248.8
Far above rubies; meditations for the minister's wife. Kansas City, Mo., Beacon Hill Pr. [c.1961] 128p. 61-5282 2.00
1. Clergymen's wives—Religious life. I. Title.

WILLIAMSON, William B., ed. 248.8
Personal devotions for pastors. Philadelphia, Westminister Pr. [c.1961] 202p. Bibl., 61-13305 3.50
1. Clergy—Religious life. I. Title.

WIRT, Sherwood Eliot 248.8
Not me, God. New York, Harper [c.1966] 94p. 22cm. [BV4596.B8W5] 66-20789 2.95 bds.,
1. Businessmen—Religious life. I. Title.

BRUSSELMANS, Christiane. 248'.82
A parents' guide : religion for little children : including an appendix of the 77 most asked questions and their answers / Christiane Brusselmans, with Edward Wakin. Updated and expanded. Huntington, IN : Our Sunday Visitor, 1977. 200 p. : ill. ; 21 cm. Spine title: Religion for little children. Bibliography: p. 193-200. [BV1475.2.B78 1977] 77-370434 ISBN 0-87973-825-1 : 3.50
1. Christian education of children. 2. Children—Religious life. I. Wakin, Edward, joint author. II. Title. III. Title: Religion for little children.

BUCKLEY, Francis J. 248'.82
Children and God: communion, confession, confirmation [by] Francis J. Buckley. New York [Corpus Publications, c1970] 59, [1] p. 19 cm. (Corpus papers) Bibliography: p. [60] [BV4571.2.B8] 71-135458 1.25
1. Children—Religious life. I. Title.

CARLSON, Mary Callery. 248'.82
Some people ... / by Mary Callery Carlson ; illustrated by Jack Proctor. Wheaton, Ill. : Tyndale House Publishers, c1976. [48] p. : col. ill. ; 24 cm. Offers guidance to parents in developing such Biblical character traits as honesty, gentleness, and responsibility in their children. [BJ1631.C347] 76-8669 ISBN 0-8423-6060-3 : 3.95
1. Children—Conduct of life—Juvenile literature. I. Proctor, Jack, 1930- II. Title.

CARR, Jo. 248'.82
Touch the wind ; creative worship with children / Jo Carr ; [ill. by Charla Honea]. Nashville : The Upper Room, [1975] x, 70 p. : ill. ; 20 cm. Bibliography: p. 69-70. [BV4571.2.C37] 74-33831 1.50
1. Worship (Religious education) 2. Children—Religious life. I. Title.

*COLINA, Tessa 248.82
God, we thank You: a surprise book with a

readaloud story. Illus. by Carole Wilde [New York] 342 Madison Ave., David C. Cook Pub. Co., c.1964. 12p. col. illus. 28cm. 1.39 bds.,
1. Children—Religious life. I. Title.

CORRIGAN, John E. 248.8'2
Growing up Christian; penance and the moral development of children, by John E. Corrigan. Dayton, Ohio, G. A. Pflaum [1969] 126 p. illus. 17 cm. (Parent education series, no. 3) (Witness book, 10.) Bibliography: p. 125-126. [BJ1249.C63] 69-20472 0.75
1. Christian ethics—Catholic authors. 2. Penance. 3. Children—Religious life. I. Title.

FOREHAND, Mary Anne. 248'.82
Love lives here : a think and do book about love / Mary Anne Forehand; illustrated by Karen Tureck. New York : Friendship Press, [1975] 48 p. : ill. ; 26 cm. Stories and activities for teaching the concept of love. [BF575.L8F58] 75-9850 ISBN 0-377-00028-0 pbk. : 1.95
1. Love—Juvenile literature. I. Tureck, Karen. II. Title.

GOODRICH, Donna Clark. 248'.82
Dare to be different. Cincinnati, Standard Pub. [1972] 96 p. illus. 18 cm. (Fountain books) Sixty brief discussions to meet the needs of pre-teens on such topics as understanding parents, judging others, and making decisions. [BV4870.G69] 72-82085
1. Children—Prayer-books and devotions—English. I. Title.

GREENE, Carol. 248'.82
God's my friend. Art by Jack Glover. St. Louis, Concordia Pub. House [1973] 64 p. col. illus. 22 x 27 cm. Introduces Christian principles through stories, poems, songs, activities, and prayers. [BV4870.G75] 73-78025 ISBN 0-570-06992-0 3.95 (pbk.)
1. Children—Prayer-books and devotions—English—1961- I. Glover, Jack, 1922- illus. II. Title.

HOWE, Reuel L. 1905- 248.82
Youth considers personal moods, by Reuel L. Howe. Camden, N.J., Nelson [1966] 95p. 21cm. (Youth forum ser.) [BV4531.2.H6] 66-22000 1.50 pap.,
1. Youth—Religious life. I. Title. II. Series.

JANEWAY, James, 1636?-1674. 248'.82
A token for children / James Janeway ; with a preface for the Garland ed. by Robert Miller. The Holy Bible in verse / Benjamin Harris. The history of the Holy Jesus. The school of good manners / Eleazar Moody. The prodigal daughter / with a preface for the Garland ed. by Elizabeth Williams. New York : Garland Pub., 1977. p. cm. (Classics of children's literature, 1621-1932) Reprint of 5 works published 1676-1771. Includes bibliographies. [BR1714.J3 1977] 75-32134 ISBN 0-8240-2251-3 lib.bdg. : 27.00
1. Jesus Christ—Poetry. 2. Children—Biography. 3. Children—Religious life. 4. Children—Conduct of life. 5. Theology, Puritan. I. Title. II. Series.

JANEWAY, James, 1636?-1674. 248'.82
A token for children / James Janeway ; with a preface for the Garland ed. by Robert Miller. The Holy Bible in verse / Benjamin Harris. The history of the Holy Jesus. The school of good manners / Eleazar Moody. The prodigal daughter / with a preface for the Garland ed. by Elizabeth Williams. New York : Garland Pub., 1977. p. cm. (Classics of children's literature, 1621-1932) Reprint of 5 works published 1676-1771. Includes bibliographies. [BR1714.J3 1977] 75-32134 ISBN 0-8240-2251-3 lib.bdg. : 27.00
1. Jesus Christ—Poetry. 2. Children—Biography. 3. Children—Religious life. 4. Children—Conduct of life. 5. Theology, Puritan. I. Title. II. Series.

JOHNSTON, Dorothy Grunbock. 248.82
Bob and Betty wonder; stirring devotional readings for boys and girls 9 to 11 years old. Wheaton, Ill., Scripture Press Publications [1964] 156 p. illus. 23 cm. [BV4571.2.J6] 64-16021
1. Children — Religious life. I. Title.

JOHNSTON, Dorothy Grunbock 248.82
Bob and Betty wonder; stirring devotional readings for boys and girls9 to 11 years old. Wheaton, Ill., Scripture [c.1964] 156p. illus. 23cm. 64-16021 2.95 bds.,
1. Children—Religious life. I. Title.

JONES, Chris. 248'.82
Lord, I want to tell you something. Designed and illustrated by David Koechel. Minneapolis, Augsburg Pub. House [1973] 96 p. illus. 20 cm. A collection of prayers about everyday events. [BV4855.J66] 73-78266 ISBN 0-8066-1330-0 1.95 (pbk.)
1. Boys—Prayer-books and devotions—English. I. Koechel, David, illus. II. Title.

KLINK, Johanna Louise. 248'.82
Your child and religion [by] Johanna L. Klink. [Translated by R. A. Wilson] Richmond, Va., John Knox Press [1972] 247 p. 22 cm. Translation of Kind en geloof, published as deel 1 of De theologie van de kinderen. Bibliography: p. [244]-247. [BV4579.D8K5723] 72-1764 ISBN 0-8042-2239-8 5.95
1. Children—Religious life. I. Title.

*KORFKER, Dena. 248.8'2
Good morning, Lord: devotions for children. Grand Rapids, Mich., Baker Book House [1973] 95 p. 19 cm. (Good morning, Lord series) [BV4870] ISBN 0-8010-5328-5 1.95 (pbk.)
1. Children—Prayer-books and devotions. 2. Children—Religious life. I. Title.

LEE, Florence B. Baptist leader. 248.82
When children worship [by] Florence B. Lee [and others] Valley Forge [Pa.] Judson Press [1963] 63 p. illus. 19 cm. "All the chapters of this book, with the exception of 'Wonder, work, and worship' have been previously published in the magazine Baptist leader." [BV4501.2.W44] 63-19116
1. Children — Religious life. I. Title.

MARSHALL, Catherine (Wood) 1914- 248.8'2
God loves you our family's favorite stories and prayers, by Catherine and Peter Marshall. Drawings by James Spanfeller. 2d ed. New York, McGraw-Hill [1967] 59 p. illus. (part col.) 20 cm. [BV4571.2.M3] 67-29913
1. Children—Religious life. I. Marshall, Peter, 1902-1949, joint author. II. Title.

MARSHALL, Catherine (Wood) 1914- 248.8'2
God loves you; our family's favorite stories and prayers, by Catherine and Peter Marshall. Drawings by James Spanfeller. 2d ed. New York, McGraw-Hill [1967] 59 p. illus. (part col.) 20 cm. [BV4571.2.M3 1967] 67-29913
1. Children—Religious life. I. Marshall, Peter, 1902-1949, joint author. II. Title.

MARYANNA, Sister. 248.82
With joy and gladness. [1st ed.] Garden City, N. Y., Doubleday, 1964. 190 p. 22 cm. [BX2350.2.M35] 64-11393
1. Christian life—Catholic authors. 2. Happiness. I. Title.

MOORE, Harvey Daniel, 1942- 248'.82
The irritated oyster & other object lessons for children / Harvey D. & Patsie A. Moore. Nashville : Abingdon Press, c1976. 79 p. ; 20 cm. Brief stories illustrated Christian values and principles. [BV4315.M6237] 75-30886 ISBN 0-687-19690-6 : 3.95
1. Children's sermons. I. Moore, Patsie A., joint author. II. Title.

MOORE, Jack, 1942- 248'.82
What is God's area code? : A Kelly-Duke book / by Jack Moore ; with an afterword for parents and teachers by Andrew M. Greeley. New York : Sheed and Ward, [1974] 95 p. : all ill. ; 21 cm. (Cartoons for new children) (Alligator books) [BT113.M66] 74-1545 ISBN 0-8362-0601-0. ISBN 0-8362-0582-0 pbk. : 2.25
1. God—Caricatures and cartoons. I. Title.

PRAYERS for children and young people : an anthology / edited by Nancy Martin. Philadelphia : Westminster Press, 1976, c1975. p. cm. Includes indexes. A collection of prayers for many different occasions. [BV4870.P66 1976] 75-42383 ISBN 0-664-20746-4 : 5.95 248'.82
1. Children—Prayer-books and devotions—English. 2. Youth—Prayer-books and devotions. 3. Prayers. I. Martin, Nancy.

RANWEZ, Pierre. 248.8'2
The dawn of the Christian life; the religious education of the young. Translated by Edmond Bonin. New York [Paulist Press, 1970] 128 p. illus. 18 cm. (Paulist Press Deus books) Translation of L'aube de la vie chretienne. Includes bibliographical references. [BV1475.2.R3413] 72-128143 1.75
1. Christian education of children. I. Title.

ST. Boniface, Sister, C.S.J. 248.8'2
In the beginning: a handbook for parents; Christian initiation of pre-school children [by] Sister M. St. Boniface. New York, Paulist Press [1969] vii, 150 p. illus. 19 cm. (Deus books) Bibliography: p. 149-150. [BV1475.8.S2] 68-54405 1.25
1. Christian education of preschool children. I. Title.

*SUNDQUIST, Ralph R., Jr. 248.82
Whom God chooses: the child in the church. Philadelphia, Geneva Pr. [dist.] Westminster [c.1964] 95p. 22cm. Bibl. 1.25 pap.,
I. Title.

SWEENEY, Joseph W 248.82
Angels' wings; short stories for young folks. [1st ed.] New York, Exposition Press [1962] 169 p. 21 cm. (A Exposition-Testament book) [BX2371.S9] 62-786
1. Children — Religious life. 2. Christian life — Catholic authors. I. Title.

TAYLOR, Kenneth Nathaniel. 248'.82
Living thoughts for the children's hour; devotional talks and stories for little boys and girls, by Kenneth N. Taylor. Illustrated by Robert G. Doares. Chicago, Moody Press [1972] 126 p. illus. 24 cm. Previously published under title: I see what God wants me to know. Each chapter includes a doctrinal explanation and related story, study questions, prayer, and Biblical references on some aspect of Christian life. [BV4571.2.T39 1972] 72-77943 ISBN 0-8024-4876-3 2.95
1. Children—Religious life. I. Doares, Robert G., illus. II. Title.

TRESE, Leo John, 1902- 248.82
Book for boys. With a foreword by Frank Gartland. Notre Dame. Ind., Fides Publishers Association [1961] 131 p. 21 cm. [BX2360.T7] 61-17235
1. Boys — Religious life. I. Title.

TRESE, Leo John, 1902- 248.82
Book for boys. Foreword by Frank Gartland. Notre Dame, Ind., Fides [c.1961] 131p. 61-17235 2.95 bds.,
1. Boys—Religious life. I. Title.

WALTER, Dorothy Blake 248.82
Worship time; a book of stories, finger plays, and poems for children. [Mountain View, Calif., Pacific Pr. Pub. Assn. 1962, c.1961] 165p. illus. 61-10875 3.50
1. Worship programs. 2. Children—Religious life. I. Title.

WHEN children worship 248.82
[by] Florence B. Lee [others] Valley Forge [Pa.] Judson [c.1963] 63p. illus. 19cm. All the chapters of this bk., with the exception of 'Wonder, work, and worship' have been previously pub. in the magazine Baptist leader. 63-19116 1.00 pap.,
1. Children—Religious life. I. Lee, Florence B. II. Baptist leader.

WOODALL, William Love, 1908- 248.82
Three-minute devotions for boys and girls. New York, Association Press [1962] 126 p. 20 cm. [BV4870.W63] 62-9388
1. Children — Prayer-books and devotions — English. I. Title.

WOODALL, William Love, 1908- 248.82
Three-minute devotions for boys and girls. New York, Association [c.1962] 126p. 62-9388 2.50 bds.,
1. Children—Prayer-books and devotions—English. I. Title.

ZILINSKI, Joseph 248.8'2
In their own way how young people can be living witnesses to Christ. Illus. by Dorothy Koch. North Easton, Mass., Holy Cross Pr. [1967] 60p. illus. 21cm. [BX2371.25] 67-25216 2.00
1. Children—Religious life. I. Title.

VAN DYKE, Dick. 248'.8'2'0207
Faith, hope and hilarity by Dick Van Dyke. Edited by Ray Parker. Drawings by Phil Interlandi. [New York] Warner Paperback Library [1974, c1970] 122 p. 18 cm. [PN6328.C5V3] 70-126387 0.95 (pbk.)
1. Children—Anecdotes and sayings. 2. Children—Religious life—Anecdotes, facetiae, satire, etc. I. Parker, Ray, ed. II. Title.

ADAIR, James R 1923- ed. 248.83
Teen with a future, by James R. Adair. Grand Rapids, Baker Book House, 1965. 83 p. illus., ports. 21 cm. (The Valor series, no. 12) [BV4531.2.A3] 65-25476
1. Youth — Religious life. I. Title.

AINGER, Geoffrey. 248.8'3
Time to act. Melbourne, Methodist Federal Board of Education and Presbyterian Board of Christian Education, 1968. 36 p. 22 cm. A resource book written for the National Christian Youth Convention, Sydney, January 1969. [BV4531.2.A36] 73-411900 0.40
1. Youth—Religious life. I. Methodist Federal Board of Education. II. Presbyterian Board of Christian Education. III. National Christian Youth Convention, Sydney, 1969.

AITKEN, James J 248.83
In step with Christ; trials and triumphs of Europe's Adventist young people. Illus. by James Converse. Mountain View, Calif., Pacific Press Pub. Association [1963] 84 p. illus. 21 cm. [BV4515.2.A4] 63-10646
1. Christian life—Stories. I. Title.

AITKEN, James J. 248.83
In step with Christ; trails and triumphs of Europe's Adventist young people. Illus. by James Converse. Mountain View, Calif., Pac. Pr. Pub. [c.1963] 84p. illus. 21cm. 63-10646 3.00 bds.,
1. Christian life—Stories. I. Title.

ALLEN, Charles Livingstone, 1913- 248'.83
When you graduate [by] Charles L. Allen [and] Mouzon Biggs. Old Tappan, N.J., F. H. Revell Co. [1972] 63 p. 19 cm. Advice to young people on the application of Christian principles in daily living. [BJ1661.A39] 75-189284 ISBN 0-8007-0527-0
1. Youth—Conduct of life. I. Biggs, Mouzon, joint author. II. Title.

ANDERSON, Margaret J 248.83
It's your business, teen-ager! A challenge to the teenagers. Chicago, Moody Press [1960] 96p. 20cm. [BV4531.2.A5] 60-50744
1. Youth—Religious life. I. Title.

ANSWERS for young Latter-day Saints / [compiled from the New era]. Salt Lake City : Deseret Book Co., 1977. 113 p. ; 24 cm. Includes index. A collection of answers to doctrinal and social questions raised by young adult members of the Church of Jesus Christ of Latter-day Saints. [BX8643.Y6A57] 77-3284 ISBN 0-87747-645-4 : 4.95 248'.83
1. Church of Jesus Christ of Latter-day Saints—Doctrinal and controversial works—Juvenile literature—Addresses, essays, lectures. 2. Youth—Religious life—Addresses, essays, lectures. I. Church of Jesus Christ of Latter-day Saints. II. New era (Salt Lake City)

BAILEY, James Martin, 1929- 248.8'3
From wrecks to reconciliation, by J. Martin Bailey. Illustrated by Jim Crane. New York, Friendship Press [1969] 192 p. illus. 18 cm. Includes bibliographical references. [BV1561.B24] 68-57230
1. Religious education—Textbooks for young people. I. Title.

BALY, Denis. 248.83
Academic illusion. Foreword by Stephen F. Bayne, Jr. Greenwich, Conn., Seabury Press, 1961. 179p. 22cm. [BV1610.B25] 61-5575
1. Universities and colleges—Religion. I. Title.

BALY, Denis 248.83
Academic illusion. Foreword by Stephen F. Bayne, Jr. Greenwich, Conn., Seabury Press [c.] 1960. 179p. Bibl. footnotes. 61-5575 2.25
1. Universities and colleges—Religion. I. Title.

BARKMAN, Paul Friesen. 248.8'3
Christian collegians and foreign missions [by] Paul F. Barkman, Edward R. Dayton [and] Edward L. Gruman. [Monrovia, Calif., Missions Advanced Research & Communications Center] 1969. xv, 424 p. illus., forms, map. 24 cm. [BV2390.B37] 79-84049
1. Missions—Congresses. 2. College students—Religious life. I. Dayton, Edward R., joint author. II. Gruman, Edward L., joint author. III. Title.

BECK, Hubert F. 248'.83
Why can't the church be like this? [By] Hubert Beck. St. Louis, Concordia Pub. House [1973] 104 p. illus. 20 cm. "A Perspective II book." [BV4531.2.B4] 73-9111 ISBN 0-570-03171-0 1.95 (pbk.)
1. International Student Congress on Evangelism. 2. Youth—Religious life. 3. Christianity—20th century. 4. Jesus people. I. Title.

BENNETT, Marian. 248'83
Help me, Jesus, compiled by Marian Bennett. Cincinnati, Ohio, Standard Pub. [1972] 96 p. illus. 18 cm. (Fountain books) Forty-six two page devotions concerned with teen problems such as drugs, parental pressure, and being happy. [BV4850.B45] 72-82084 Pap. 0.98
1. Youth—Prayer-books and devotions—English. I. Title.

BOWMAN, Norman. 248.8'3
College is a question mark. Nashville, Convention Press [1968] 47 p. illus. 20 cm. [LB3609.B69] 68-20667
1. College environment. 2. College students—Conduct of life. 3. College students—Religious life. I. Title.

BRISTER, C. W. 248.8'3
It's tough growing up [by] C. W. Brister.

Nashville, Broadman Press [1971] 128 p. 20 cm. Includes bibliographical references. [BJ1661.B74] 79-136134 ISBN 0-8054-5311-3 2.95
1. Youth—Conduct of life. I. Title.

*BRYANT, Hilda 248.83
Dear Pastor. Grand Rapids, Mich., Baker Bk. [c.] 1964. 106p. illus. 22cm. 1.00 pap.,
1. Christian life—Protestant authors. I. Title.

CALDWELL, Louis O. 248.8'3
After the tassel is moved; guidelines for high school graduates [by] Louis O. Caldwell. Grand Rapids, Baker Book House [1968] 80 p. 20 cm. [LB1695.C3] 68-19206
1. High school graduates—United States. 2. College, Choice of. 3. Conduct of life. I. Title.

CALDWELL LOUIS O. 248.83
His eye on youth. Illus. by Larry Shook. Grand Rapids, Baker Bk. [c.]1963. 127p. illus. 22cm. 1.00 pap.,
I. Title.

CAREY, Floyd D 248.83
Teen-agers' trail guide. Cleveland, Tenn., Pathway Press [1960] 76p. 21cm. [BJ1661.C2] 60-51492
1. Youth—Conduct of life. 2. Youth—Religious life. I. Title.

CASSELS, Louis. 248'.83
Forbid them not. Illustrated by Garry R. Hood. [Independence, Mo.] Independence Press [1973] 94 p. illus. 20 cm. [BV4531.2.C34] 73-75885 ISBN 0-8309-0097-7 2.95
1. Youth—Religious life. I. Title.

CASTAGNOLA, Lawrence A. 248.8'3
Confessions of a catechist, by Lawrence Castagnola. Staten Island, N.Y., Alba House [1970] viii, 123 p. 19 cm. [BV1485.C3] 71-117201 ISBN 0-8189-0181-0 1.95
1. Christian education of young people—Personal narratives. I. Title.

CAVERT, Walter Dudley, 248.8'3
1891-
In the days of thy youth; devotional readings for young people. Nashville, Abingdon Press [1971] 128 p. 16 cm. [BV4850.C38] 74-158674 ISBN 0-687-19355-9 2.95
1. Youth—Prayer-books and devotions—English. I. Title.

COLE, Charles Evans, 248'.83
1935-
Alternate lifestyles. Edited by Charles E. Cole. New York, Seabury Press [1974] 95 p. 28 cm. (Youth ministry notebook, 8) "A Crossroad book." Includes bibliographical references. [BV4447.C55] 73-17892 ISBN 0-8164-5707-7 4.95
1. Church work with youth. 2. Youth—Religious life. I. Title.

COOK, Walter L. 248.83
What can I believe? talks to youth on the Christian faith. Nashville Abingdon [c.1965] 112p. 20cm. [BT77.C747] 65-20360 2.00
1. Theology, Doctrinal—Popular works. I. Title.

COOPER, John Charles. 248.8'3
The new mentality. Philadelphia, Westminster Press [1969] 159 p. 21 cm. Bibliographical references included in "Notes" (p. [149]-159) [BV4531.2.C6] 69-16304 2.65
1. Youth—Religious life. 2. Symbolism. 3. U.S.—Social conditions—1960- I. Title.

CORBETT, Janice M. 248'.83
It's happening with youth [by] Janice M. Corbett & Curtis E. Johnson. [1st ed.] New York, Harper & Row [1972] 176 p. 22 cm. [BV4447.C59 1972] 79-183632 ISBN 0-06-061581-8 4.95
1. Church work with youth—United States—Case studies. I. Johnson, Curtis E., joint author. II. Title.

CRUZ, Nicky. 248.8'3
The lonely now, by Nicky Cruz, as told to Jamie Buckingham. Illus. by Jim Howard. Photos. by Keith Wegeman and Stitt-Coombs-Evans Inc. Plainfield, N.J., Logos International [1971] viii, 143 p. illus. 22 cm. [BV4921.2.C78] 72-95766 ISBN 0-912106-15-8 3.95
1. Youth—Conduct of life. 2. Conversion. I. Buckingham, Jamie. II. Title.

DARE to live: 248'.83
Taize 1974; preparing for the world-wide Council of Youth. Foreword by Samuel Wylie. New York, Seabury Press [1974] vi, 161, [2] p. 21 cm. "A Crossroad book." Translation of Audacieuse aventure. Bibliography: p. [163] [BV4532.A913] 73-17912 2.95 (pbk.)
1. Communaute de Taize. 2. Youth—Religious life. I. Communaute de Taize.

DAUGHTERS of St. Paul. 248.8'3
Your right to be informed. [Boston] St. Paul Editions [1969] 430 p. illus. 24 cm. [BX2355.D38] 68-59042
1. Youth—Religious life. 2. Christian life—Catholic authors. I. Title.

DEFFNER, Donald L. 248'.83
Bold ones on campus; a call for Christian commitment [by] Donald L. Deffner. St. Louis, Concordia Pub. House [1973] 184 p. 18 cm. [BV4531.2.D4] 73-78104 ISBN 0-570-03162-1 1.75 (pbk.)
1. College students—Prayer-books and devotions—English. I. Title.

DEFFNER, Donald L 248.83
Christ on campus; meditations for college life, by Donald L. Deffner. Saint Louis, Concordia Pub. House [1965] xii, 156 p. 20 cm. [BV4531.2.D42 1965] 65-24176
1. Students — Religious life. I. Title.

DEFFNER, Donald L. 248.83
Christ on campus; meditations for college life. St. Louis, Concordia [c.1965] xii, 156p. 20cm. [BV4531.2.D42] 65-24176 2.75
1. Students—Religious life. I. Title.

DESRIS, John Francis, 248.83
1915-
Let's take the hard road; a book on strength for young men by John Cross [pseud. 3d ed. Kenosha, Wis., Cross Publications, c1960 -- v. illus. 23 cm. Contents.-- v. 1. Morals and conduct. [GV461.D413] 60-12806
1. Gymnastics. 2. Conduct of life. I. Title.

DEWEY, Robert D. 248'.83
Commitment; a parent-teacher manual [by] Robert D. Dewey [and] Charles Murphy. [Rev. ed. New York] Herder and Herder [1968] 76 p. illus. 22 cm. (Christian commitment series) Bibliography: p. 72-76. [BV4531.2.D48 1968] 68-29893 1.75
1. Youth—Religious life. 2. Religious education—Text-books—United Church of Christ. I. Murphy, Charles, joint author. II. Title.

DUNN, Paul H. 248'.83
I challenge you ... by Paul H. Dunn in collaboration with Richard M. Eyre. Salt Lake City, Bookcraft [1972] 92 p. 24 cm. "I promise you ... by Paul H. Dunn in collaboration with Richard M. Eyre": p. 92-5 (text reversed and inverted with main text) [BV4531.2.D86] 72-90323
1. Youth—Religious life. I. Dunn, Paul H. I promise you. 1972. II. Title. III. Title: I promise you.

DUNN, Paul H. 248'.83
I challenge you ... by Paul H. Dunn in collaboration with Richard M. Eyre. Salt Lake City, Bookcraft [1972] 92 p. 24 cm. "I promise you ... by Paul H. Dunn in collaboration with Richard M. Eyre": p. 92-5 (text reversed and inverted with main text) [BV4531.2.D86] 72-90323
1. Youth—Religious life. I. Dunn, Paul H. I promise you. 1972. II. Title. III. Title: I promise you.

DURRANT, George D. 248'.83
Someone special : starring youth / George D. Durrant. Salt Lake City : Bookcraft, 1976. viii, 119 p. : ill. ; 24 cm. [BX8695.D8A35] 76-45722 ISBN 0-88494-311-9 pbk. : 3.50
1. Durrant, George D. 2. Mormons and Mormonism—Biography. 3. Youth—Conduct of life. 4. Youth—Religious life. I. Title.

DYAL, William M. 248.8/3
It's worth your life; a Christian challenge to youth today, by William M. Dyal, Jr. New York, Association [1967] 156p. 22cm. Bibl. [BV4531.2.D9] 67-14582 3.95; 1.95 pap.,
1. Christian life—Baptist authors. I. Title.

DYAL, William M. 248.8'3
It's worth your life; a Christian challenge to youth today, by William M. Dyal, Jr. New York, Association Press [1967] 156 p. 22 cm. Bibliography: p. 153-156. [BV4531.2.D9] 67-14582
1. Christian life—Baptist authors. I. Title.

EAKIN, Bill. 248.8'3
You know I can't hear you when you act that way [by] Bill Eakin and Jack Hamilton. Elgin, Ill., D. C. Cook Pub. Co. [1969] 95 p. 18 cm. [BJ1661.E24] 74-87319 0.95
1. Youth—Conduct of life. I. Hamilton, Jack. II. Title.

ELICKER, Charles W., 248'.83
1951-
Journeys without maps ... : stories of how youth are finding their ways in the church / by Chas. W. Elicker, with Sara Ashby Sawtell, Robert W. Carlson ; foreword by Robert L. Burt. Philadelphia : Published for Joint Educational Development by United Church Press, c1976. 156 p. ; 22 cm. (A Shalom resource) [BV4427.E44] 76-7545 ISBN 0-8298-0312-2 pbk. : 4.50
1. Youth in church work—United Church of Christ. 2. Youth—Religious life. 3. Church management. I. Sawtell, Sara Ashby, 1951- joint author. II. Carlson, Robert W., 1952- joint author. III. Joint Educational Development. IV. Title.

ENGELKEMIER, Joe. 248.8'3
"Really living." Washington, Review and Herald Pub. Association [1967] 157 p. 22 cm. [BV4850.E5] 67-19723
1. Christian life—Seventh-Day Adventist authors. 2. Youth—Religious life. I. Title.

FACIUS, Johannes. 248'.83
The little white book [by] Johannes Facius, Johny Noer [and] Ove Stage. [1st American ed.] Wheaton, Ill., H. Shaw [1972, c1971] 79 p. illus. 14 cm. Translation of Den lille hvide. [BJ1668.D3F313] 72-94101 ISBN 0-87788-509-5 0.75
1. Youth—Conduct of life. I. Noer, Johny, joint author. II. Stage, Ove, joint author. III. Title.

FAIR, Frank T. 248'.83
"An Orita for Black youth" / by Frank T. Fair. Valley Forge, Pa. : Judson Press, [1977] p. cm. [BR563.N4F26] 77-2607 ISBN 0-8170-0734-2 : 1.95
1. Afro-American youth—Religious life. 2. Afro-American youth—Conduct of life. I. Title.

FAIR, Frank T. 248'.83
"An Orita for Black youth" / by Frank T. Fair. Valley Forge, Pa. : Judson Press, [1977] p. cm. [BR563.N4F26] 77-2607 ISBN 0-8170-0734-2 : 1.95
1. Afro-American youth—Religious life. 2. Afro-American youth—Conduct of life. I. Title.

FAIRCHILD, Roy W. 248.8'3
The waiting game, by Roy W. Fairchild. [Camden, N.J.] T. Nelson [1971] xi, 102 p. 21 cm. (A Youth forum book, YF15) Suggestions for planning for the future and finding meaning in life in a world of changing values. [BF724.F325] 70-147916 ISBN 0-8407-5315-2 1.95
1. Adolescent psychology. I. Title. II. Series: Youth forum series, YF15.

FAITH in action. 248'.83
Cleveland, Tenn. : Pathway Press, c1975. 144 p. : ill. ; 18 cm. (Making life count new life series) Bibliography: p. 143-144. [BV4531.2.F28] 75-3504 ISBN 0-87148-331-9
1. Youth—Religious life. I. Pathway Press.

FARRELL, Melvin 248.83
First steps to the priesthood, an explanation of the Christian life for minor seminarians. Milwaukee, Bruce Pub. Co. [c.1960] 206 p. 60-15478 3.95
1. Seminarians—Religious life. I. Title.

FAULSTICH, John. 248.8'3
For man's sake; a resource book on theology for youth. Philadelphia, United Church Press [1971] 64 p. illus. 21 cm. [BV1561.F35] 74-152646
1. Religious education—Text-books for young people. I. Title.

FEATHERSTONE, Vaughn J. 248'.83
A generation of excellence : a guide for parents and youth leaders / Vaughn J. Featherstone. Salt Lake City : Bookcraft, 1975. x, 190 p. : port. ; 24 cm. Includes index. [BX8643.Y6F4] 75-34833 ISBN 0-88494-292-9
1. Church work with youth—Mormonism. 2. Youth—Religious life. I. Title.

FERGUSON, Rowena. 248.83
My life; what will I make of it? Chicago, Rand McNally [1966] 159 p. 21 cm. [BV4531.2.F4] 66-18098
1. Youth—Religious life. I. Title.

FIRNHABER, R. Paul, comp. 248.8'3
I'll let you taste my wine if I can taste yours. St. Louis, Concordia Pub. House [1969] 88 p. illus. 21 cm. (The Perspective series, 7) [BV4447.F57] 77-77627 1.25
1. Youth—Religious life. 2. Church and the world. I. Title.

FIRNHABER, R. Paul. 248.8'3
Say yes! By R. Paul Firnhaber. St. Louis, Concordia Pub. House [1968] 1 v. (unpaged) illus. (part col.) 21 cm. (The Perspective series, 6) [BV4531.2.F48] 68-25511
1. Youth—Religious life. I. Title.

FISCHER, Norma Bristol. 248'.83
Eye witness / written and illustrated by Norma Bristol Fischer. Eyewitness Greensburg, Pa. : Manna Christian Outreach, [1975] [31] p. : ill. ; 21 cm. Six young people describe their religious experiences and encounters in the Christian faith. [BV4515.2.F5] 74-24722 ISBN 0-8007-0747-8
1. Christian life—Stories. I. Title.

FISHER, Lee. 248'.83
A time to seek. Nashville, Abingdon Press [1972] 127 p. 19 cm. [BV4531.2.F49] 75-185549 ISBN 0-687-42135-7 1.95
1. Youth—Religious life. I. Title.

FLOOD, Peter 248.83
Early manhood; commonsense talks with boys in their 'teens. [dist.] New York, Taplinger Pub. Co. [1960] 38p. 18cm. (More books) .75 pap.,
I. Title.

GARA, Matthew 248.83
Don't be an oyster! And other consideration for Catholic teen-agers. Illus. by Edward McDonnell. Valatie, N. Y., Holy Cross Pr. [1966] 160p. illus. 23cm. [BX2373.S8G3] 66-7530 3.00
1. Christian life—Catholic authors. 2. Students—Religious life. I. Title.

GIBSON, Henry Louis, 248'.83
1906-
Stars through the apple tree; excerpts from open letters to an upper-classman, by H. Lou Gibson. North Quincy, Mass., Christopher Pub. House [1972] 188 p. 21 cm. [BV639.C6G5] 72-78903 4.95
1. College students—Religious life. I. Title.

GRAHAM, William Franklin, 248'.83
1918-
The Jesus generation, by Billy Graham. True spirituality, by Francis A. Schaeffer. Brethren, hang loose, by Robert C. Girard. A christianity today trilogy. New York, Produced for Christianity today [by] Iverson-Norman Associates, 1972. iii, 188, 180, 220 p. 22 cm. (Books for believers, v. 1) Includes bibliographical references. [BV4531.2.G74] 72-89780
1. Youth—Religious life. 2. Jesus People—United States. 3. Apologetics—20th century. 4. Church renewal. I. Schaeffer, Francis August. True spirituality. 1972. II. Girard, Robert C. Brethren, hang loose. 1972 III. Christianity today. IV. Title. V. Title: True spirituality. VI. Title: Brethren, hang loose. VII. Series.

GRANT, Dave. 248'.83
Heavy questions. Glendale, Calif., Regal Books [1972] 167 p. 18 cm. [BV4531.2.G76] 78-185800 ISBN 0-8307-0112-5 1.25
1. Youth—Religious life. 2. Christian life—Miscellanea. I. Title.

GREELEY, Andrew M 1928- 248.83
And young men shall see visions. Letters from Andrew M. Greeley. New York, Sheed and Ward [1964] xii, 177 p. 22 cm. [BX2350.2.G7] 64-14233
1. Christian life—Catholic authors. 2. Christianity—20th cent. I. Title.

GREELEY, Andrew M., 1928- 248.83
And young men shall see visions. Letters from Andrew M. Greeley. Garden City, N.Y., Doubleday [1968,c.1964] 160p. 18cm. (Image bks., D232) [BX2350.2.G7] .85 pap.,
1. Christian life—Catholic authors. 2. Christianity—20th cent. I. Title.

GREELEY, Andrew M., 1928- 248.83
And young men shall see visions. Letters from Andrew M. Greeley. New York, Sheed [c.1964] xii, 177p. 22cm. 64-14233 3.95
1. Christian life—Catholic authors. 2. Christianity—20th cent. I. Title.

GREELEY, Andrew M 1928- 248.83
Letters to Nancy, from Andrew M. Greeley. New York, Sheed and Ward [1964] x, 182 p. 22 cm. Bibliographical footnotes. [BX2365.G7] 64-19901
1. Woman—Religious life. I. Title.

GREELEY, Andrew M., 1928- 248.83
Letters to Nancy, from Andrew M. Greeley. Garden City, N.Y., Doubleday [1967, c.1964] x, 182p. 18cm. (Image bk., D226) Bibl. [BX2365.G7] .85 pap.,
1. Woman—Religious life. I. Title.

GREELEY, Andrew M., 1928- 248.83
Letters to Nancy, from Andrew M. Greeley. New York, Sheed [c.1964] x, 182p. 22cm. Bibl. 64-19901 3.95
1. Woman—Religious life. I. Title.

GREELEY, Andrew M., 1928- 248.8'3
Letters to Nancy, from Andrew M. Greeley. [New and rev.] Garden City, N.Y., Image Books [1967] 160 p. 19 cm. (Image D226) [BX2365.G7 1967] 67-3684
1. Woman—Religious life. I. Title.

HALLIDAY, Jerry. 248'.83
Spaced out and gathered in; a sort of an autobiography of a Jesus freak. Old Tappan, N.J., F. H. Revell Co. [1972] 126 p. 18 cm.

[BV4935.H26A3] 78-186536 ISBN 0-8007-0511-4 0.95 (pbk)
I. Title.

HANKS, Marion D., comp. 248.8'3
How glorious is youth. Compiled and edited by Marion D. Hanks, Doyle L. Green [and] Elaine Cannon. Salt Lake City, Deseret Book Co., 1968. xi, 233 p. 24 cm. Articles previously published in the Improvement era. [BX8643.Y6H3] 68-58286 3.50
1. Mormons and Mormonism—Doctrinal and controversial works. 2. Youth—Religious life. I. Green, Doyle L., joint comp. II. Cannon, Elaine, joint comp. III. Improvement era. IV. Title.

HEISER, Roy F. 248.8'3
Teens alive! Getting the best out of the teen years, by Roy F. Heiser and William J. Krutza. Grand Rapids, Baker Book House [1969] 114 p. 18 cm. [BJ1661.H45] 70-97510 1.50
1. Youth—Conduct of life. I. Krutza, William J., joint author. II. Title.

HERRING, Clyde Lee. 248'.83
If God talked out loud ... / Clyde Lee Herring. Nashville : Broadman Press, c1977. 138 p. : ill. ; 20 cm. A youth's conversations with God help to illuminate various aspects of Christian belief. [BV4531.2.H46] 76-27479 ISBN 0-8054-5325-3 pbk. : 2.25
1. Youth—Religious life. 2. Prayer—Juvenile literature. I. Title.

HEYER, Robert. comp 248.8'3
Discovery in word; readings, ed. by Robert Heyer. Viewpoints, questions written by J. Brown. Design by Emil Antonucci. Coordinated by Richard J. Payne. New York, Paulist [c.1968] 155p. illus. 23cm. (Discovery ser.) [BV4531.2.H49] 68-31256 1.95 pap.,
1. Youth—Religious life. I. Brown, James, 1949- II. Title. III. Series: The Discovery series (New York).

HEYER, Robert J., comp. 248.8'3
Discovery in song. Edited by Robert Heyer. Designed by Emil Antonucci. Photographed by Ken Wittenberg. Coordinated by Richard Payne. Written by Thomas O'Brien [and others] New Glen Rock, N.J., Paulist Press [1968] 138 p. illus. 23 cm. (Discovery series) [BV4531.2.H48] 68-28303 1.95
1. Youth—Religious life. I. O'Brien, Thomas E. II. Title.

*HILLIS, Don W. 248.83
When God calls the signals: the will of God and how to find it. Foreword by Jack Wyrtzen. Chicago, Moody [c.1965] 63p. (Compack bk. no. 54) .29, pap.,
I. Title.

*HILLIS, Don W. 248.83
Wired for sound. Chicago, Moody [c.1964] 63p. 18cm. (MP29) .29 pap.,
I. Title.

HINCKLEY, Gordon Bitner, 1910- 248'.83
From my generation to yours...with love! [By] Gordon B. Hinckley. Salt Lake City, Deseret Book Co., 1973. 85 p. port. 24 cm. [BV4531.2.H54] 73-88637 ISBN 0-87747-512-1 2.95
1. Youth—Religious life. I. Title.

HOLLAWAY, Steve. 248'.83
Working things out / Steve Hollaway and Bill Junker. Nashville : Broadman Press, [1974] 128 p. ; 19 cm. [BV639.C6H63] 74-76913 ISBN 0-8054-5219-2
1. College students—Religious life. I. Junker, Bill, joint author. II. Title.

*HOSTETLER, Paul 248.83
You're in the teen-age generation! chats with teen-agers. Grand Rapids, Mich., Baker Bk. [c.1966] 64p. 22cm. 1.00 pap.,
I. Title.

HUFF, Russell J., 1936- 248.8'3
The virtues; a discussion course for young people. Photo essays by Russell J. Huff. Parables [and] inquiries by Thomas F. McNally. [Edited by Russell J. Huff] Notre Dame, Ind., Fides Publishers [1968] 94 p. illus. (part col.) 27 cm. "First appeared as a series in Catholic boy and Catholic miss, 1966-67." [BX2355.H8] 68-15361 1.25
1. Youth—Conduct of life. 2. Virtues. I. McNally, Thomas Francis, 1887- II. Title.

HULME, William Edward, 1920- 248.8'3
When I don't like myself. New York, Popular Library [1976 c1971] 126 p. 18 cm. [BV4531.2.H83] 1.25 (pbk.)
1. Youth—Religious life. I. Title.
L.C. card no. for original edition: 79-169034.

HULME, William Edward, 1920- 248.8'3
When I don't like myself. By William E. Hulme. New York, T. Nelson [1971] v, 83 p. 21 cm. (Youth forum series YF18) Includes bibliographical references. [BV4531.2.H83] 79-169034 ISBN 0-8407-5318-7 1.95
1. Youth—Religious life. I. Title. II. Series.

HUTCHINGS, Eric 248.83
Training for triumph in victorious living. Foreword by Tom Allan. Grand Rapids, Zondervan Pub. House [1961, c.1959] 127p. 61-1588 1.95 bds.,
1. Youth—Religious life. I. Title.

IVERSEN, John O. 248.83
Teen talks. Washington, D.C., 6856 Eastern Ave., N.W. Review and Herald Pub. Assn., [1962] 92p. 20cm. 61-11980 2.00
1. Youth—Religious life. I. Title.

IVERSEN, John Orville. 248.8'3
More teen talks, by J. O. Iversen. Guest writers: A teen talks back [by] Bonnie Iversen; Knocking out the "T" [by] Jerre Kent Iversen. Washington, Review and Herald Pub. Association [1968] 96 p. 20 cm. [BV4531.2.I93] 68-18743
1. Youth—Religious life. I. Title.

*JACOB, Micheal. 248.8'3
Pop goes Jesus; an investigation of pop religion in Britain and America [1st Amer. ed.] New York, Morehouse-Barlow [1973, c.1972] 92 p. 19 cm. [BV4531.2] ISBN 0-8192-1140-0 1.95 (pbk.)
1. Youth—Religious life. 2. Jesus people—United States. 3. Jesus people—Gt. Brit. I. Title.

JACOBS, James Vernon, 1898- 248.83
Starlight talks to youth. Grand Rapids, Mich., Baker Bk. House, 1961. 168p. 61-17548 2.50
1. Youth—Religious life. 2. Astronomy. I. Title.

THE Jesus people speak out! 248'.83
Compiled by Ruben Ortega. Elgin, Ill., D. C. Cook Pub. Co. [1972] 128 p. 18 cm. Interviews conducted by the staff of Collegiate Encounter With Christ. [BV4531.2.J47] 71-187727 0.95
1. Jesus People—Addresses, essays, lectures. I. Ortega, Ruben, ed. II. Collegiate Encounter With Christ.

JOHNSON, Emmett V 248.8'3
Christian living, by Emmett V. Johnson. Chicago, Harvest Publications [c1967] 85 p. illus. 26 cm. ("Tell me, please" series, book 3) [BV4571.2.J58] 67-29104
1. Christian life. I. Title.

JOINER, Verna Jones 248.83
When love grows up [by] Verna J. Joiner. Anderson, Ind., Warner [1966] v, 96p. 21cm. [BV4531.2.J6] 66-23605 1.50 pap.,
1. Youth—Religious life. I. Title.

KAPFER, Richard G. 248'.83
Your first in college / Richard G. Kapfer. St. Louis : Concordia Pub. House, c1974. 79 p. ; 18 cm. (Crossroads) Includes bibliographical references. [LC148.K36] 73-11879 ISBN 0-570-06767-7
1. College attendance. 2. College students. I. Title.

KAVANAUGH, James J. 248.83
There's two of you; tempest in a teen-pot. Westminster, Md., Newman [c.]1964. xiv, 164p. 23cm. [BX2355.K3] 64-66035 3.75
1. Youth—Religious life. 2. Youth—Conduct of life. 3. Adolescence. I. Title.

KAY, Hether, comp. 248.83
A new look at faith and loyalties. [dist. New Rochelle, N. Y., SportShelf, 1961] 48p. (New look series) Bibl. 61-1634 1.50 pap.,
1. Young women—Religious life. I. Title.

KELLY, George Anthony, 1916- 248.83
The Catholic youth's guide to life and love. New York, Random House [1960] 209 p. 21 cm. Includes bibliography. [BX2355.K4] 60-7680
1. Youth—Religious life. 2. Christian life—Catholic authors. I. Title.

KESLER, Jay. 248'.83
I never promised you a Disneyland / by Jay Kesler, with Tim Stafford. Waco, Tex. : Word Books, c1975. 120 p., [5] leaves of plates : ill. ; 23 cm. [BV4531.2.K47] 75-10094 4.95
1. Youth—Religious life. I. Stafford, Tim. II. Title.

KESLER, Jay. 248'.83
I never promised you a Disneyland / by Jay Kesler, with Tim Stafford. Waco, Tex. : Word Books, c1975. 120 p., [5] leaves of plates : ill. ; 23 cm. [BV4531.2.K47] 75-10094 4.95
1. Youth—Religious life. I. Stafford, Tim. II. Title.

KRAMER, William Albert, 1900- 248'.83
Living for Christ; a guide for the newly confirmed, by William A. Kramer. St. Louis, Concordia Pub. House [1973] 94 p. 14 cm. [BX8074.C7K7 1973] 72-96585 1.25 (pbk.)
1. Confirmation. 2. Youth—Religious life. I. Title.

KRUTZA, William J. 248'.83
Graduate's guide to success / William J. Krutza. Grand Rapids : Baker Book House, c1976. 93 p. : ill. ; 20 cm. [BV4531.2.K78] 76-375893 ISBN 0-8010-5374-9 pbk. : 2.95
1. Youth—Religious life. I. Title.

LARSEN, Earnest. 248.8'3
Don't just stand there. [Liguori, Mo., Liguorian Books] 1969. 1 v. (unpaged) illus. 18 cm. [BV4531.2.L35] 74-84648 1.75
1. Youth—Religious life. I. Title.

LARSON, Bob. 248'.83
Hippies, Hindus and rock & roll. McCook, Neb., c1969. 90 p. port. 19 cm. [BV4596.H5L37] 73-172219 1.50
1. Hippies—Religious life. 2. Hinduism. I. Title.

LEE, Harold B., 1899- 248'.83
Decisions for successful living, by Harold B. Lee. Salt Lake City, Deseret Book Co., 1973. x, 265 p. port. 24 cm. Editions of 1945 and 1970 published under title: Youth and the church. [BX8643.Y6L4 1973] 73-168234 ISBN 0-87747-348-X 4.95
1. Youth—Religious life. 2. Mormons and Mormonism. I. Title.

LEE, Harold B., 1899- 248.8'3
Youth & the church, by Harold B. Lee. [Salt Lake City] Deseret Book Co., 1970. x, 261 p. col. port. 24 cm. Edition of 1973 published under title: Decisions for successful living. [BX8643.Y6L4 1970] 79-130323 ISBN 0-87747-348-X
1. Youth—Religious life. 2. Mormons and Mormonism. I. Title.

LINK, Mark J. 248.8'3
Life in the modern world: home, parish, neighborhood, school [by] Mark J. Link. Chicago, Loyola University Press [1970] xi, 276 p. illus. 23 cm. [BJ1661.L5] 78-108376
1. Youth—Conduct of life. I. Title.

LORIMIER, Jacques de. 248'.83
Identity and faith in young adults, by Jacques de Lorimier, Roger Graveline, and Aubert April. Translated by Matthew J. O'Connell. New York, Paulist Press [1973] viii, 275 p. 23 cm. Translation of Identite et foi. Bibliography: p. 271-275. [BV4531.2.L5813] 73-80533 ISBN 0-8091-1766-5 4.95
1. Youth—Religious life. 2. Christian education of young people. I. Graveline, Roger, joint author. II. April, Aubert, joint author. III. Title.

LOWERY, Daniel L. 248.8'3
Teenage problems, by Daniel L. Lowery. Glen Rock, N.J., Paulist Press [1968] viii, 152 p. 19 cm. (Deus books) Letters and answers originally published in the author's column, Teenage problems in the Catholic herald citizen over a period of two and one half years. [BX2355.L7] 68-57879 1.00
1. Christian life—Catholic authors. 2. Youth—Religious life. I. Title.

LUCEY, Dan, comp. 248'.83
The living loving generation / Dan and Rose Lucey. Huntington, Ind. : Our Sunday Visitor, [1975] 94 p. : ill. ; 21 cm. [BJ1661.L8 1975] 75-313209 ISBN 0-87973-783-2 pbk. : 1.50
1. Youth—Conduct of life. I. Lucey, Rose, joint comp. II. Title.

LUCEY, Dan, comp. 248.8'3
The living-loving generation. Edited by Dan and Rose Lucey. Milwaukee, Bruce Pub. Co. [1969] ix, 72 p. 21 cm. Contents.Contents.—Being is becoming, by A. L. Brassier.—Fish or cut bait, by T. Cole.—Sorry about your God, by J. L. Anderson.—Sex is for real! by J. and L. Bird.—Marriage—love-in for real, by G. and G. Raffo.—Talk to me, dad, by P. and P. Crowley.—Reach out my people, by W. and G. McNelly. [BJ1661.L8] 69-17322
1. Youth—Conduct of life. I. Lucey, Rose, joint comp. II. Title.

LUND, Gerald N. 248'.83
This is your world; four stories for modern youth, by Gerald N. Lund. Illus. by Grant L. Lund. Salt Lake City, Bookcraft [1973] viii, 91 p. illus. 24 cm. Contents.Contents.—Even as your father.—A prayer of faith.—If you love Jesus.—Foolish traditions. [BV4531.2.L84] 73-77237
1. Youth—Religious life. I. Title.

*MCGLOIN, Joseph T. 248.83
Breaking through the maturity barrier. Drawings by Don Baumgart. Pulaski, Wis. Franciscan Pubs. [c.1965] 80p. illus. 19cm. .35 pap.,
I. Title.

*MCINTYRE, Robert W. 248.83
Program pathways for young adults. Grand Rapids, Mich., Baker Bk. [c.1964] 127p. 21cm. 1.50 pap.,
I. Title.

MCKAY, David Oman, 1873-1970. 248'.83
"My young friends ..." President McKay speaks to youth. Compiled by Llewelyn R. McKay. Salt Lake City, Utah, Bookcraft [1973] 84 p. port. 24 cm. [BV4531.2.M26 1973] 73-88616
1. Youth—Religious life. I. Title.

MCKAY, David Oman, 1873-1970. 248'.83
"My young friends ..." President McKay speaks to youth. Compiled by Llewelyn R. McKay. Salt Lake City, Utah, Bookcraft [1973] 84 p. port. 24 cm. [BV4531.2.M26 1973] 73-88616
1. Youth—Religious life. I. Title.

MCKEE, Bill. 248.8'3
Happy hang up! Wheaton, Ill., Tyndale House Publishers [1969] 62 p. illus. 21 cm. [BV4531.2.M27] 79-79469
1. Youth—Religious life. I. Title.

MCLEAN, Gordon R. 248.8'3
How to raise your parents [by] Gordon R. McLean. Wheaton, Ill., Tyndale House Publishers [1970] xvii, 104 p. illus. 22 cm. A youth director counsels on the traditional areas of parent-teen conflict—dating, cars, grades—as well as on the more current issues—protests, civil disobedience, and the new morality. [BJ1661.M32 1970] 73-123288 2.95
1. Youth—Conduct of life. I. Title.

MCLEAN, Gordon R. 248'.83
Where the love is [by] Gordon R. McLean. Waco, Tex., Word Books [1973] 123 p. 23 cm. [BV4531.2.M33] 72-96352 3.95
1. Youth—Religious life. 2. Christian life—1960- I. Title.

MCLEAN, Gordon R. 248'.83
Where the love is [by] Gordon R. McLean. Waco, Tex., Word Books [1973] 123 p. 23 cm. [BV4531.2.M33] 72-96352 3.95
1. Youth—Religious life. 2. Christian life—1960- I. Title.

MCPHEE, Norma. 248'.83
Discussion programs for junior highs / Norma McPhee. Grand Rapids : Zondervan Pub. House, [1974] 128 p. ; 21 cm. [BV4531.2.M34] 73-13072 1.95
1. Youth—Religious life. 2. Youth—Conduct of life. 3. Worship programs. I. Title.

*MARTIN, Paul. 248.8'3
Good morning, Lord; more devotions for teens [by] Paul Martin. Grand Rapids, Mich., Baker Book House [1973] 64 p. 19 cm. (Good morning, Lord series) "The devotions in this book are selections from Get up and go, published in 1965 by Beacon Pr." [BV4850] ISBN 0-8010-5915-1 1.95
1. Youth—Prayer-books and devotions. 2. Youth—Religious life. I. Title.

MASTON, Thomas Bufford, 1897- 248'.83
Right or wrong? A guide for teeners and their leaders for living by Christian standards [by] T. B. Maston [and] William M. Pinson, Jr. Rev. ed. Nashville, Broadman Press [1971] 128 p. 21 cm. A guide for making decisions about such issues as drugs, dishonesty, sex, and parents. [BV4531.2.M37 1971] 75-143282 ISBN 0-8054-6101-9 3.50
1. Youth—Religious life. 2. Christian ethics. I. Pinson, William M., joint author. II. Title.

MAXWELL, Lawrence. 248'.83
The happy path / Lawrence Maxwell. Washington : Published for the Youth Dept. of the General Conference of Seventh-day Adventists [by] Review and Herald Pub. Association, c1975. 128 p. : ill. ; 19 cm. Sixteen anecdotes illustrating practical applications of scripture. [BV4531.2.M38] 74-27636
1. Youth—Religious life. I. Title.

MAXWELL, Mervyn. 248'.83
Look at it this way. Questions and answers selected from Mervyn Maxwell's column in Signs of the times magazine. Mountain View, Calif., Pacific Press Pub. Association [1972] 64 p. 19 cm. [BV4531.2.M39] 77-187400
1. Youth—Religious life. 2. Youth—Conduct of life. I. Signs of the times. II. Title.

MERIKAY. 248'.83
Huck Finn goes to church; profiles of life for young adults. Mountain View, Calif., Pacific Press Pub. Association [1972] 63 p. 19 cm. Includes brief anecdotes and articles discussing the role of religion in the lives of young people. [BV4531.2.M47] 72-83473
1. Youth—Religious life. I. Title.

MILLION, Elmer G. 248.83
You are the church. Pub. for The Cooperative Pubn. Assn. Philadelphia, Judson Pr. [c.1961] 96p. (Faith for life ser.) 1.00 pap.,
I. Title.

MITCHELL, Joan, 1940- 248'.83
Faith : a persistent hunger / Joan Mitchell. Minneapolis : Winston Press, c1977. 96 p. : ill. ; 22 cm. The author describes searching for and living with faith in today's world. [BV4531.2.M55] 77-72201 ISBN 0-03-021261-8 pbk. : 2.50
1. Youth—Religious life. 2. Faith. I. Title.

MOODY, Jess C. 248.8'3
The Jesus freaks [edited by] Jess Moody. Waco, Tex., Word Books [1971] 127 p. 23 cm. [BV4596.H5M66] 71-160297 3.95
1. Hippies—Religious life. I. Title.

MOORE, Ralph. 248.8'3
Breakout. Illustrated by John Gretzer. New York, Friendship Press [1968] 159 p. illus. 18 cm. Includes bibliographies. [BV4531.2.M6] 68-14058
1. Youth—Religious life. I. Title.

MOW, Anna B 248.83
Going steady with God; your life with God every day of the year. A practical guidebook for young people, by Anna B. Mow. Grand Rapids, Zondervan Pub. House [1965] 224 p. 21 cm. Includes bibliographies. [BV4811.M6] 64-8849
1. Devotional calendars. I. Title.

MOW, Anna B. 248.83
Going steady with God; your life with God every day of the year. Practical guidebk. for young people. Grand Rapids, Mich., Zondervan [c.1965] 224p. 21cm. Bibl. [BV4811.M6] 64-8849 2.95 bds.,
1. Devotional calendars. I. Title.

MYRA, Harold Lawrence, 1939- 248'.83
The new you; questions about this fresh newborn way of life now that you believe [by] Harold Myra. Grand Rapids, Zondervan Pub. House [1973, c1972] 115 p. illus. 18 cm. [BV4531.2.M97] 72-95527 0.95 (pbk.)
1. Youth—Religious life. 2. Questions and answers—Christian life. I. Title.

NEVER trust a God over 30; 248.8'3
new styles in campus ministry. Edited by Albert H. Friedlander. Introd. by Paul Goodman. [1st ed. New York, McGraw-Hill [1967] xii, 212 p. 22 cm. [BV639.C6N4] 67-24436
1. College students—Religious life. 2. Church work with students. I. Friedlander, Albert H., ed.

NEW York (State) University. Division of Research in Higher Education. 248'.83
College and university enrollment, New York State. [Albany] v. tables. 30 cm. Vols. for issued in the Education inventory series. Title varies: Fall enrollment in institutions of higher education in New York State. Prepared - 1960 by the Bureau of Statistical Services; 1961- by the division with the Bureau of Statistical Services. [LC148.N4] A61
1. College attendance — New York (State) I. New York (State) University. Bureau of Statistical Services. II. Title. III. Series: New York (State) University. Research Offices. Education inventory series

NOFFSINGER, Jack Ricks 248.83
It's your turn now! Nashville, Broadman [1964] 64p. 16cm. 65-7005 1.25
1. Youth—Conduct of life. I. Title.

O'DOHERTY, Eamonn Feichin. 248'.83
The religious formation of the adolescent [by] E. F. O'Doherty. Staten Island, N.Y., Alba House [1973] v, 109 p. 22 cm. [HQ796.O33] 73-12969 ISBN 0-8189-0280-9 2.95
1. Adolescence. 2. Youth—Religious life. I. Title.

OLSON, David F., 1938- 248'.83
The inner revolution; a theology for people who don't understand theology [by] David F. Olson. Valley Forge [Pa.] Judson Press [1973] 120 p. illus. 21 cm. [BV4539.S9O413] 73-3088 ISBN 0-8170-0604-4 2.50 (pbk.)
1. Youth—Religious life. I. Title.

O'MALLEY, William J. 248'.83
Meeting the living God [by] William J. O'Malley. New York, Paulist Press [1973] ix, 197 p. illus. 28 cm. [BV4531.2.O45] 73-85135 ISBN 0-8091-9525-9 2.95
1. Youth—Religious life. 2. Religious education—Text-books for young people—Catholic. I. Title.

OWEN, Bob. 248'.83
Jesus is alive and well (what Jesus People really believe). Pasadena, Calif., Compass Press [1972] 127 p. illus. 18 cm. [BT77.O86] 72-182095 1.25
1. Theology, Doctrinal—Popular works. 2. Jesus people. I. Title.

PALMS, Roger C. 248.8'3
The Jesus kids [by] Roger C. Palms. Valley Forge [Pa.] Judson Press [1971] 96 p. 22 cm. [BV4531.2.P3] 72-166486 ISBN 0-8170-0546-3 1.95
1. Jesus people. I. Title.

PARKS, Thomas David, 1917- 248.8'3
Letters to Jody [by] Thomas D. Parks. Wheaton, Ill., Tyndale House Publishers [1971] 91 p. 18 cm. [BV639.C6P37] 74-156897 ISBN 0-8423-2166-7
1. College students—Religious life. I. Title.

PEABODY, Larry D. 248.83
Fourteen for teens. Grand Rapids, Mich., Baker Bk. [c.]1965. 77p. 20cm. (Valor ser., 14) [BV4531.2.P4] 65-29510 1.95
1. Christian life—Stories. 2. Youth—Religious life. I. Title.

PEDERSON, Duane. 248.8'3
Jesus people, by Duane Pederson, with Bob Owen. Glendale, Calif. G/L Regal Books [1971] 128 p. illus. 18 cm. [BV4531.2.P43] 70-177979 ISBN 0-8307-0140-0 1.25
1. Jesus People—United States. I. Title.

PEDERSON, Duane. 248'.83
Jesus people, by Duane Pederson, with Bob Owen. Pasadena, Calif., Compass Press [1971] 127 p. illus. 18 cm. "A Jesus people book." [BV4531.2.P43 1971b] 78-189030
1. Jesus people—United States. I. Title.

PENNOCK, Dee. 248'.83
Who is God? Who am I? Who are you? Illus. by Sally Pierone. South Canaan, Pa., Early Church Publications [1973] 160 p. illus. 21 cm. [BV4531.2.P46] 73-86196 2.50
1. Youth—Religious life. I. Title.

PETERSEN, Mark E. 248.8'3
Drugs, drinks & morals [by] Mark E. Petersen. [Salt Lake City] Deseret Book Co., 1969. 79 p. map, port. 19 cm. [BJ1251.P425] 79-109605
1. Christian ethics—Mormon authors. I. Title.

PETERSEN, Mark E. 248'.83
Virtue makes sense! [By] Mark E. Petersen and Emma Marr Petersen. Salt Lake City, Utah, Deseret Book Co., 1973. 105 p. 24 cm. [BV4531.2.P48] 73-81621 ISBN 0-87747-500-8 2.95
1. Youth—Religious life. I. Petersen, Emma Marr, joint author. II. Title.

PETERSON, Eugene H., 1932- 248'.83
Growing up in Christ : a guide for families with adolescents / by Eugene H. Peterson. Atlanta : John Knox Press, c1976. 93 p. ; 21 cm. Includes bibliographical references. [BV4531.2.P485] 76-12396 ISBN 0-8042-2026-3 pbk. : 3.95
1. Youth—Religious life. 2. Parent and child. I. Title.

†PITMAN, Thomas B. 248'.83
Reaching for the sky : a challenge to young adulthood / Thomas B. Pitman III. Cleveland, Tenn. : Pathway Press, c1976. 144 p. ; 18 cm. Bibliography: p. 143-144. [BV4529.2.P57] 75-37358 ISBN 0-87148-731-4 pbk. : 2.50
1. Young adults—Religious life. I. Title.

PLOWMAN, Edward E. 248.8'3
The underground church; accounts of Christian revolutionaries in action, by Edward E. Plowman. Elgin, Ill., D. C. Cook Pub. Co. [1971] 128 p. 18 cm. [BV601.9.P57] 75-147214 0.95
1. Non-institutional churches. 2. Youth—Religious life. I. Title.

PRATNEY, Winkie, 1944- 248'.83
A handbook for followers of Jesus / by Winkie Pratney. Minneapolis : Bethany Fellowship, c1976. p. cm. Includes indexes. Bibliography: p. [BV4531.2.P7] 76-44385 ISBN 0-87123-378-9 pbk. : 3.50
1. Youth—Religious life. I. Title.

PROCTOR, William. 248'.83
Survival on the campus; a handbook for Christian students. Old Tappan, N.J., F. H. Revell Co. [1972] 157 p. 21 cm. [BV639.C6P76] 79-172681 ISBN 0-8007-0497-5 3.95
1. College students—Religious life. I. Title.

*PROTESTANT Episcopal Church in the U. S. A. National Council. Dept. of Christian Education. 248.83
Mission: the Christian's calling; leader's guide for Called to be, Bigger than all of us, These rebellious powers. For use with young people. Prepared by the Dept. of Christian Educ. of the Protestant Episcopal Church at the direction of General Convention. New York, Seabury [c.1965] 63p. 21cm. .95 pap.,
I. Title.

REAGAN, Wes. 248'.83
What are we waiting for? : Jesus is here / by Wes Reagan. Cincinnati : New Life Books, 1976. 96 p. : ill. ; 18 cm. Discusses various aspects of Biblical teaching and how they apply to everyday life. [BV4531.2.R35] 75-44589 ISBN 0-87239-061-6
1. Youth—Religious lie. I. Title.

REED, Harold W 248.83
Committed to Christ; messages to college youth. Grand Rapids, Baker Book House, 1960. 112p. 20cm. [BV4310.R37] 60-2244
1. Students—Religious life. 2. Church of the Nazarene—Sermons. 3. Sermons, American. I. Title.

THE Religious life of the adolescent / edited by Robert Heyer. 248'.83
New York : Paulist Press, c1974 [i.e.1975] v, 73 p. : ill. ; 19 cm. "A New Catholic world book." A collection of articles originally published in the Sept./Oct. 1974 issue of the New Catholic world. [BV4531.2.R38] 75-10113 ISBN 0-8091-1878-5 pbk. : 1.45
1. Youth—Religious life. I. Heyer, Robert J. II. New Catholic world.

RICHARDS, Larry. 248.8'3
Are you for real? Chicago, Moody Press [1968] 160 p. illus. 19 cm. Bibliographical references included in "Footnotes" (p. 160) [BV4531.2.R45] 68-18886
1. Youth—Religious life. I. Title.

RICHARDS, Larry. 248.8'3
How do I fit in? Chicago, Moody Press [1970] 155 p. illus. 20 cm. Cover title: Youth asks: How do I fit in? Includes bibliographical references. Explores the methods one can use to establish more meaningful relationships with people and God. [BV4531.2.R452] 79-123162 1.95
1. Youth—Religious life. I. Title. II. Title: Youth asks: How do I fit in?

RICHARDS, Larry. 248.8'3
What's in it for me? Chicago, Moody Press [1970] 143 p. illus. 19 cm. Cover title: Youth asks: What's in it for me? Includes bibliographical references. [BV4531.2.R454] 70-104829 1.95
1. Youth—Religious life. I. Title. II. Title: Youth asks: What's in it for me?

RIDENOUR, Fritz. 248.8'3
I'm a good man, but ... Edited by Fritz Ridenour. Featuring Peanuts cartoons by Charles Schulz. Glendale, Calif., G/L Regal Books [1969] 165 p. illus. 18 cm. [BV4531.2.R46 1969] 75-96702
1. Youth—Religious life. 2. Christian ethics. I. Schulz, Charles M. II. Title.

RIESS, Walter. 248.8'3
Before they start to leave; for parents of teen-agers: some quiet directions. St. Louis, Concordia Pub. House [1967] 95 p. 19 cm. [BV639.Y7R5] 67-22998
1. Youth—Religious life. I. Title.

RIESS, Walter. 248.83
Teen-ager, your church is for you. St. Louis, Concordia Pub. House [1961] 100p. illus. 19cm. [BV4531.2.R48] 60-53153
1. Youth—Religious life. I. Title.

RIESS, Walter. 248.83
Teen-ager, Christ's love will make you live. St. Louis, Concordia Pub. House [1962] 102p. illus. 19cm. [BV4531.2.R47] 62-19958
1. Youth—Religious life. I. Title.

ROBINSON, Ruth (Grace) 248.8'3
Seventeen come Sunday; a birthday letter, by Ruth Robinson. Philadelphia, Westminster Press, [c1966] 78 p. illus. 20 cm. [BV4531.2.R57] 67-12089
1. Youth—Religious life. I. Title.

ROGERS, Dale Evans. 248'.83
Cool it or lose it! Dale Evans Rogers raps with youth. Old Tappan, N.J., F. H. Revell Co. [1972] 96 p. 20 cm. Discusses the importance of religion in daily life and how it can help young people deal with problems. [BV4531.2.R585] 72-5348 ISBN 0-8007-0551-3 2.95
1. Youth—Religious life. I. Title.

ROGNESS, Alvin N 1906- 248.83
Youth asks, why bother about God? By Alvin N. Rogness. New York, T. Nelson [1965] 95. [1] p. 22 cm. (Youth forum series) Bibliography: p. [96] [BV4531.2.R6] 65-15405
1. Youth—Religious life. I. Title. II. Title: Why bother about God?

ROGNESS, Alvin N., 1906- 248.83
Youth asks, why bother about God? New York, Nelson [c.1965] 95, [1]p. 22cm. (Youth forum ser.) Bibl. [BV4531.2.R6] 65-15405 1.50 pap.,
1. Youth—Religious life. I. Title. II. Title: Why bother about God?

*RUSSELL, Wylie H. 248.8'3
Life values for young America. Berkeley, Calif., McCutcheon [1967] 58p. port. 23cm. 3.15 pap.,
I. Title.

RYDGREN, John, 1932- 248.8'3
Tomorrow is a handful of together yesterdays. Minneapolis, Augsburg Pub. House [1971] 96 p. illus., ports. 17 cm. [BV4531.2.R93] 75-159004 ISBN 0-8066-9442-4 1.95
1. Youth—Religious life. I. Title.

SAHLIN, Monte. 248'.83
Student power in Christian action; the ACT movement. Design by Dale Rusch. Mountain View, Calif., Pacific Press Pub. Association [1972] 127 p. illus. 20 cm. [BV639.C6S2] 77-187399
1. Adventist Collegiate Taskforce. 2. College students—Religious life. 3. Witness bearing (Christianity) I. Title.

SEABOUGH, Ed. 248'.83
So you're going to college. Nashville, Broadman Press [1974] 64 p. 16 cm. [BV639.C6S4] 73-91607 ISBN 0-8054-5321-0 1.95 (pbk.)
1. College students—Religious life. I. Title.

SEARCH for the sacred: 248'.83
the new spiritual quest. Edited by Myron B. Bloy, Jr. New York, Seabury Press [1972] viii, 180 p. illus. 21 cm. (Church and campus books) (An Original Seabury paperback, SP 75) Papers delivered at a consultation sponsored by the Church Society for College Work. Includes bibliographical references. [BV4531.2.S4] 72-76554 ISBN 0-8164-2074-2 3.75
1. Youth—Religious life. I. Bloy, Myron B., ed. II. Church Society for College Work.

**SERVANT of peace.* 248.8'3
New York, Harcourt [1967] (Roots of faith, bk. 3) JHS 2.40 pap.,

SIEKMANN, Theodore C. 248.83
Boys. New York, [55 Park P1., J. F. Wagner c.1961] 190p. 61-3106 3.95
1. YOuth—Religious life. I. Title.

SIEKMANN, Thodore C 248.83
Boys. New York, J. F. Wagner [1961] 190 p. 21 cm. [BX2360.S52] 61-3106
1. Youth — Religious life. I. Title.

SLOAN, Steve. 248.8'3
Calling life's signals; the Steve Sloan story, by Steve Sloan with James C. Hefley. Introd. by Paul W. (Bear) Bryant. Grand Rapids, Zondervan [1967] 143p. illus., ports. 22cm. [GV939.S6A3] 67-30567 2.95; .95 pap.,
1. Hefley, James C. I. Title.

SPARKMAN, Temp. 248.8'3
Leadership roles for youth. [Nashville, Convention Press, 1970] 96 p. illus. 20 cm. Cover title. "Text for course number 6201 of the New church study course." [BV652.1.S65] 70-134537
1. Christian leadership. 2. Youth—Religious life. I. Title.

STARCKE, Walter. 248.8'3
The ultimate revolution. [1st ed.] New York, Harper & Row [1969] 155 p. 22 cm. [BV4501.2.S73] 73-85058 4.95
1. Spiritual life. 2. Youth—Conduct of life. I. Title.

STEINKE, Peter L. 248'.83
Whose who: explorations in Christian identity [by] Peter L. Steinke. St. Louis, Concordia Pub. House [1972] 96 p. illus. 21 cm. (Perspective, 11) [BV4531.2.S78] 72-84206 ISBN 0-570-06471-6
1. Youth—Religious life. I. Title.

STEWART, Charles William. 248.8'3
Adolescent religion; a developmental study of the religion of youth. Nashville, Abingdon Press [1967] 318 p. 24 cm. Bibliography: p. 305-309. [BV4531.2.S8] 67-11712
1. Youth—Religious life. 2. Adolescence. I. Title.

THE Street people; 248.8'3
selections from "Right on," Berkeley's Christian underground student newspaper. Valley Forge [Pa.] Judson Press [1971] 62 p. illus. 28 cm. [BV4531.2.S84] 71-147962 ISBN 0-8170-0512-9 1.50
1. Youth—Religious life. I. Right on.

STREIKER, Lowell D. 248.8'3
The Jesus trip; advent of the Jesus freaks [by] Lowell D. Streiker. Nashville, Abingdon Press [1971] 128 p. illus. 23 cm. Includes bibliographical references. [BV4531.2.S85] 75-176324 ISBN 0-687-20223-X
1. Jesus People—United States. I. Title.

STROMMEN, Merton P. 248'.83
Bridging the gap; youth and adults in the church [by] Merton P. Strommen. Minneapolis, Augsburg Pub. House [1973] 104 p. 20 cm. (A Study of generations paperback) Bibliography: p. 103-104. [BV4447.S726] 72-90266 ISBN 0-8066-1313-0 1.95
1. Church work with youth. 2. Youth—Religious life. 3. Conflict of generations. I. Title.

SUGARMAN, Daniel A. 248'.83
The Seventeen guide to you and other people [by] Daniel A. Sugarman and Rolaine Hochstein. New York, Macmillan [1972] 196 p. 22 cm. [BJ1661.S94] 77-187076 5.95
1. Youth—Conduct of life. I. Hochstein, Rolaine A., joint author. II. Seventeen. III. Title.

SUGARMAN, Daniel A. 248'.83
The Seventeen guide to you and other people [by] Daniel H. Sugarman New York, Pocket Books [1974, c1972] 159 p. 18 cm. (A Washington Square book) [BJ1661.S94] ISBN 0-671-48147-9. 1.25 (pbk.)
1. Youth—Conduct of life. I. Hochstein, Rolaine A., joint author. II. Seventeen. III. Title.
L.C. card number for original ed.: 77-187076.

SWAFFORD, Mrs. Z. W. 248.83
Happy teens. Little Rock, Ark. 716 Main St. Baptist Pubns. Comm., [1962] 54p. illus. 22cm. .50 pap.,
I. Title.

SWOR, Chester E. 248.8'3
Youth at bat [by] Chester E. Swor and Jerry Merriman. Westwood, N.J., F. H. Revell Co. [1968] 127 p. 21 cm. Bibliography: p. 125-127. [BV4531.2.S9] 68-17095
1. Youth—Religious life. I. Merriman, Jerry, joint author. II. Title.

TILMANN, Klemens, 1904- 248.83
Between God and ourselves; aids to spiritual progress. Tr. [from German] by Edward Gallagher. New York, Kenedy [c.1965] 154p. 22cm. [BX2350.5.T553] 64-24621 3.95
1. Spiritual life—Catholic authors. I. Title.

TILMANN, Klemens, 1904- 248.83
Between God and ourselves; aids to spiritual progress. Translated by Edward Gallagher. New York, Kennedy c1965] 154 p. 22 cm. Translation of Das Geistliche Gesprach. [BX2350.5.T553] 64-24621
1. Spiritual life — Catholic authors. I. Title.

*TODD, Floyd. 248.8'3
Good morning, Lord; devotions for campers [by]Floyd & Pauline Todd. Grand Rapids, Mich., Baker Book House [1973] 60 p. 19 cm. (Good morning, Lord series) ISBN 0-8010-8792-9 1.95 (pbk.)
1. Campers—Prayer-books and devotions. 2. Youth—Religious life. I. Todd, Pauline, joint author. II. Title.

20TH-CENTURY teenagers 248.83
by "A friend of youth". Foreword by John P. Carroll. [Boston] St. Paul Eds. [dist. Daughters of St. Paul, c.1961] 155 p. illus., 61-14935 2.00, 1.00, pap.
1. Youth—Conduct of life. 2. Christian ethics—Catholic authors. I. "A friend of youth"

20TH-CENTURY teenagers by 248.83
"A friend of youth." Foreword by John P. Carroll. [Boston] St. Paul Editions [1961] 155 p. illus. 21 cm. [BJ1661.T9] 61-14935
1. Youth — Conduct of life. 2. Christian ethics — Catholic authors. I. "A friend of youth."

VAN DYKE, Vonda Kay. 248.8'3
Reach up. Old Tappan, N.J., F. H. Revell Co. [1971] 124 p. 21 cm. [BJ1581.2.V35] 79-149366 ISBN 0-8007-0451-7 3.95
1. Conduct of life. I. Title.

WALKER, Elmer Jerry, 1918- 248.83
Seeking a faith of your own. New York, Abingdon Press [1961] 109 p. 20 cm. [BV4310.W27] 61-5560
1. Youth — Religious life. I. Title.

WALKER, Elmer Jerry, 1918- 248.83
Seeking a faith of your own. Nashville, Abingdon Press [c.1961] 109p. 61-5560 2.00 bds.,
1. Youth—Religious life. I. Title.

WALKER, John Herbert. 248'.83
God's living room, by John Herbert Walker, Jr., with Lucille Walker and Irene Burk Harrell. Plainfield, N.J., Logos International [1972?] 141 p. 18 cm. [BV4447.W33] 79-128796 ISBN 0-912106-12-3 0.95 (pbk.)
1. Church work with youth—Greenwich Village, New York (City) I. Walker, Lucille, joint author. II. Harrell, Irene Burk, joint author. III. Title.

WARD, Hiley H. 248'.83
The far-out saints of the Jesus communes; a firsthand report and interpretation of the Jesus people movement, by Hiley H. Ward. New York, Association Press [1972] 192 p. 21 cm. Bibliography: p. [187]-190. [BV4531.2.W35] 73-189010 ISBN 0-8096-1842-7 5.95
1. Youth—Religious life. I. Title.

WARD, Ted Warren, 1930- 248'.83
Memo for the underground, by Ted Ward. [1st ed.] Carol Stream, Ill., Creation House [1971] 128 p. 23 cm. [BV4531.2.W37] 72-182853 3.95
1. Youth—Religious life. I. Title.

WARNKE, David. 248.8'3
Making it big with God. North Easton, Mass., Holy Cross Press [1969] 120 p. illus. 22 cm. [BJ1661.W33] 78-89846 3.50
1. Youth—Conduct of life. I. Title.

WEAVER, Rich. 248.8'3
Let this church die. Plainfield, N.J., Logos International [1971] xiii, 159 p. illus. 21 cm. [BR121.2.W36] 70-168749 ISBN 0-912106-20-4 3.95
1. Christianity—20th century. 2. Youth—Religious life. I. Title.

WESTERHOFF, John H. 248'.83
Learning to be free, by John H. Westerhoff, III and Joseph C. Williamson. Philadelphia, United Church Press [1972] 72 p. illus. 26 cm. Includes bibliographical references. Suggests ways in which young people can work together in groups to increase, preserve, and exercise their individual and social freedoms. [BV4531.2.W45] 72-6156
1. Youth—Religious life. 2. Freedom (Theology)—Juvenile literature. I. Williamson, Joseph C., 1932- joint author. II. Title.

WESTON, Sidney Adams, 248.83
1877-
Jesus' teachings for young people [by] Sidney A. Weston [rev. ed.] Boston, Whittemore [c.1962] 93p. 19cm. .75 pap.,
1. Youth—Religious life. I. Title.

WHALEN, William Joseph. 248.83
Catholics on campus; a guide for Catholic students in secular colleges and universities. Milwaukee, Bruce Pub. Co. [1961] 125 p. 20 cm. [BX922.W5] 61-9581
1. Students — U.S. 2. Catholics in the U.S. 3. Newman clubs. I. Title.

WIERSBE, Warren W 248.83
Be a real teenager! [By] Warren W. Wiersbe. Westwood, N.J., F.H. Revell Co. [1965] 127 p. 18 cm. [BV4531.2.W5] 65-14796
1. Youth — Religious life. 2. Youth — Conduct of life. I. Title.

WIERSBE, Warren W. 248.83
Be a real teenager! Westwood, N.J., Revell [c.1965] 127p. 18cm. [BV4531.2.W5] 65-14796 .89 pap.,
1. Youth—Religious life. 2. Youth—Conduct of life. I. Title.

WILDER, John Bunyan, 1914- 248.83
Stories to live by; true tales for young adults. Grant Rapids, Zondervan Pub. House [1964] 87 p. illus. 22 cm. [BJ661.W48] 64-15555
1. Youth — Conduct of life. I. Title.

WILDER, John Bunyan, 1914- 248.83
Stories to live by; true tales for young adults. Grand Rapids, Mich., Zondervan [c.1964] 87p. illus. 22cm. [BJ1661.W48] 64-15555 2.50 bds.,
1. Youth—Conduct of life. I. Title.

WILKERSON, David R. 248'.83
Get your hands off my throat, by David Wilkerson. Grand Rapids, Zondervan Pub. House [1971] 124 p. 22 cm. [BJ1661.W49] 76-156257 3.95
1. Youth—Conduct of life. I. Title.

WILLIAMS, Don. 248'.83
Call to the streets. Minneapolis, Augsburg Pub. House [1972] 95 p. illus. 22 cm. [BV4447.W54] 72-78552 ISBN 0-8066-1220-7 2.50
1. Church work with youth—Hollywood, Calif. 2. Jesus people. I. Title.

WILSON, R. Marshall. 248.8'3
God's guerrillas; the true story of Youth With a Mission, by R. Marshall Wilson. Illus. by Jim Howard. Plainfield, N.J., Logos International [1971] 166 p. illus. 22 cm. [BV1430.Y64W54] 71-123999 ISBN 0-912106-10-7 2.50
1. Youth with a Mission, inc. 2. Evangelistic work. 3. Youth—Religious life. I. Title.

WYCOFF, Mary Elizabeth. 248.83
Encounter with early teens. Illustrated by John Mecray. Philadelphia, Westminster Press [1965] 92 p. illus. 23 cm. [BV639.Y7W9] 65-11611
1. Youth—Religious life. I. Title.

ZINK, Jorg. 248.8'3
Tomorrow is today: a book for young people. [Tr. by L. A. Kenworthy-Brown.] Oxford, Religious Educ. Pr., 1967. 117p. illus., ports. 29cm. Tr. of Diene zeit und alle zeit. [BV4533.Z513] 67-28788 6.00
1. Youth—Religious life. I. Title.
Order from Pergamon, New York

ZUCK, Roy B. 248.8'3'0212
Christian youth, an in-depth study; profiles of 3,000 teenagers and their morals, values, doubts, religious practices, social characteristics, evaluations of themselves, their families, their churches, by Roy B. Zuck and Gene A. Getz. Chicago, Moody Press [1968] 192 p. illus. 26 cm. Bibliography: p. 188-189. [BV4531.2.Z8] 68-29503 5.95
1. Youth—Religious life—Statistics. 2. Youth—Conduct of life—Statistics. I. Getz, Gene A., joint author. II. Title.

MARIE ANGELA, Sister 248.830922
Teens triumphant [Boston] St. Paul Eds. [dist. Daughters of St. Paul, 1966, c.1965] 338p. illus. 21cm. Bibl. [BX2355.M28] 65-27249 3.50; 2.50 pap.,
1. Youth—Religious life. I. Title.

DOLLEN, Charles. 248.8'32
Ready or not! A book for young men. [Boston] St. Paul Editions [1969] 241 p. illus. 22 cm. [BJ1671.D57] 67-29164 3.00
1. Young men—Conduct of life. I. Title.

GETZ, Gene A. 248'.832
The measure of a man, by Gene A. Getz. Glendale, Calif., G/L Regal Books [1974] 219 p. 18 cm. [BV4843.G47] 74-175983 1.25
1. Men—Religious life. I. Title.

GETZ, Gene A. 248'.832
The measure of a man, by Gene A. Getz. Glendale, Calif., G/L Regal Books [1974] 219 p. 18 cm. [BV4843.G47] 74-175983 1.25 (pbk.)
1. Men—Religious life. I. Title.

SEAGREN, Daniel. 248.8'32
Letters to Chip from an older brother. Introd. by Paul S. Rees. Grand Rapids, Zondervan Pub. House [1969] 87 p. 22 cm. [BJ1671.S4] 69-11655 3.50
1. Young men—Conduct of life. I. Title.

BENNETT, Rita. 248'.833
I'm glad you asked that; timely questions women ask about the Christian life. Illustrated by Jean Beers. Edmonds, Wash., Aglow/Logos Publications [1974] xiv, 207 p. illus. 21 cm. Includes bibliographical references. [BV4527.B43] 74-81754 ISBN 0-88270-090-1 5.95
1. Woman—Religious life. I. Title.
Pbk. 2.95, ISBN 0-88270-084-7.

CALDWELL, Marge. 248.8'33
The radiant you. Nashville, Broadman Press [1968] 64 p. 20 cm. [BV4551.2.C3] 68-23559
1. Young women—Religious life. I. Title.

FANCHER, Wilda. 248'.833
The Christian woman in the Christian home. Nashville, Broadman Press [1972] 128 p. 21 cm. (A Broadman inner circle book) [BV4527.F36] 72-178059 ISBN 0-8054-8310-1
1. Woman—Religious life. I. Title.

GUDER, Eileen L. 248'.833
God wants you to smile [by] Eileen Guder. [1st ed.] New York, Doubleday, 1974. xi, 151 p. 22 cm. [BV4527.G79] 73-11706 ISBN 0-385-03521-7 4.95
1. Woman—Religious life. 2. Depression, Mental. I. Title.

GUDER, Eileen L. 248.833
We're never alone, Introd. by Raymond I. Lindquist. Grand Rapids, Mich., Zondervan [1966, c.1965] 148p. 21cm. (No. 29) [BV4527.G8] 65-19506 .89 pap.,
1. Woman—Religious life. I. Title.

GYLDENVAND, Lily M., 248.8'33
1917-
Call her blessed ... every woman who discovers the gifts of God, by Lily M. Gyldenvand. Minneapolis, Augsburg Pub. House [1967] vi, 168 p. 17 cm. [BV4844.G9] 67-11720
1. Women—Prayer-books and devotions. I. Title.

JENNINGS, Vivien, 1934- 248'.833
The valiant woman; at the heart of reconciliation. Photography by Joseph De Caro. Photo. editor: Julie Marie. New York, Alba House [1974] xi, 112 p. illus. 22 cm. [BX2353.J46] 74-6037 ISBN 0-8189-0291-4
1. Woman—Religious life. 2. Reconciliation. I. Title.

JOHNSON, Lois Walfrid. 248'.833
You're my best friend, Lord / Lois Walfrid Johnson ; art by Judy Swanson. Minneapolis : Augsburg Pub. House, c1976. 111 p. : ill. ; 20 cm. Answers questions about life and personal character asked by young girls. [BV4860.J64] 76-3866 ISBN 0-8066-1541-9 pbk. : 2.25
1. Girls—Prayer-books and devotions—English. I. Swanson, Judy. II. Title.

LARSEN, Earnest. 248'.833
"How do I change my man?" (For women only). Liguori, Mo., Liguori Publications [1974] 144 p. illus. 18 cm. [BJ1610.L3] 74-80939 1.95 (pbk.)
1. Conduct of life. 2. Woman—Religious life. I. Title.

*MILLER, Ella May 248.833
I am a woman. Chicago, Moody [1967] 123p. 17cm. (Colportage lib., 527) .39 pap.,
1. Woman—Religious life. I. Title.

NELSON, Martha. 248'.833
A woman's search for serenity. Nashville, Broadman Press [1972] 140 p. 21 cm. [BV4527.N383] 78-178063 ISBN 0-8054-5214-1 3.95
1. Woman—Religious life. I. Title.

NORDLAND, Frances. 248'.833
Dear Frances ... I have a problem. Can you help me? Chicago, Moody Press [1974] 142 p. 22 cm. Includes bibliographical references. [BV4527.N67] 74-2926 ISBN 0-8024-1765-5 2.25 (pbk.).
1. Woman—Religious life. I. Title.

ROGERS, Dale Evans. 248.833
Time out, ladies! Westwood, N. J., Revell [1966] 118 p. 21 cm. [BV4527.R6] 66-17044
1. Women—Religious life. I. Title.

ROHRBACK, Peter Thomas. 248.833
A girl and her teens; a positive program for teen-age girls. Milwaukee, Bruce Pub. Co. [1965] 123 p. 21 cm. [HQ798.R6] 65-20548
1. Girls. 2. Adolescence. I. Title.

SCHOENFELD, Elizabeth. 248.8'33
Thoughts for an LDS mother; to help me become a better wife, to help me become a better mother, to help me become a better person. Salt Lake City, Bookcraft [1967] 91 p. 21 cm. [BV4844.S35] 67-30256
1. Women—Prayer-books and devotions. 2. Quotations, English. I. Title.

STEDMAN, Elaine. 248'.833
A woman's worth / Elaine Stedman. Waco, Tex. : Word Books, [1975] 168 p. ; 23 cm. [BT704.S73] 74-27477 4.95
1. Women (Theology) I. Title.

STEVEN, Norma. 248'.833
Please, can I come home? No, you can't come home! Old Tappan, N.J., F. H. Revell Co. [1973] 126 p. illus. 19 cm. Exchange of letters between the author and her daughter Wendy. [BJ1681.S73] 73-6794 ISBN 0-8007-0619-6 1.95 (pbk.)
1. Steven, Norma. 2. Steven, Wendy. 3. Young women—Conduct of life. I. Steven, Wendy. II. Title.

STRONG, June. 248'.833 B
Journal of a happy woman. Nashville, Southern Pub. Association [1973] 160 p. 23 cm. Includes bibliographical references. [BX6193.S77A3] 73-80238 ISBN 0-8127-0072-4 4.95
1. Strong, June. I. Title.

SWIDLER, Arlene. 248'.833
Woman in a man's church; from role to person. New York, Paulist Press [1972] 111 p.

18 cm. (Deus books) Bibliography: p. 107-111. [BV4415.S94] 72-197794 ISBN 0-8091-1740-1 1.25
1. Women in church work—Catholic Church. I. Title.

WHITCOMB, Helen. 248'.833
Charm; a portfolio of activities [by] Whitcomb and Lang. [New York, Gregg Division, McGraw-Hill Book Co., 1964. 287 p. illus. 20 x 24 cm. Cover title. [BJ1681.W59] 64-25156
1. Young women — Conduct of life. 2. Success. I. Lang, Rosalind, joint author. II. Title. III. Title: A portfolio of activities.

WOLD, Margaret. 248'.833
The shalom woman / Margaret Wold. Minneapolis : Augsburg Pub. House, [1975] 128 p. ; 20 cm. Study guide inserted. Bibliography: p. 125-127. [BV4527.W58] 75-2828 ISBN 0-8066-1475-7 : 2.95
1. Women—Religious life. 2. Women. I. Title.

*WRIGLEY, Louise Scott. 248'.833
Radiance. Independence, Mo., Herald Pub. House [1973] 63 p. 18 cm. Comprises volumes previously published under titles: Your right to radiance, and Look up, heart. [BV4527]
1. Woman—Religious life. I. Title.
Available in two paperback editions, each 0.95 (pbk.) One from Independence Pr., a divn. of Herald Pr., and the other from Family Library, an imprint of Pyramid Publications, New York. L.C. card no. for the hardbound volumes: 61-12487 & 62-21992.

CROWLEY, Mary C. 248'.833'0924 B
Think mink! / Mary C. Crowley. Old Tappan, N.J. : F. H. Revell Co., c1976. 128 p. : ill. ; 21 cm. Autobiographical. [BX6495.C747A36] 76-21307 ISBN 0-8007-0810-5 : 4.95
1. Crowley, Mary C. 2. Christian life—1960- 3. Success. I. Title.

BANDAS, Rudolph George, 248.84
1896-
The Catholic layman and holiness, by Rudolph G. Bandas. Pref. by Charles P. Greco. Boston, Christoppher Pub. House [1965] 335. p. 21 cm. [BX2350.5.B3] 65-25595
1. Spiritual life — Catholic authors. I. Title.

BANDAS, Rudolph George, 248.84
1896-
The Catholic layman and holiness. Pref. by Charles P Greco. Boston, Christopher Pub. [c.1965] 335p. 21cm. [BX2350.5.B3] 65-25595 4.95
1. Spiritual life—Catholic authors. I. Title.

BARBEAU, Clayton C 248.84
The head of the family. Chicago, H. Regnery Co., 1961. 144p. 21cm. [BX2352.B3] 61-17739
1. Fathers. I. Title.

BENTON, Josephine Moffett. 248.84
The pace of a hen. Philadelphia, Christian Education Press [1961] 100 p. 21 cm. [BV4527.B45] 61-11487
1. Women—Religious life. 2. Family—Religious life. I. Title.

BRYANT, Anita. 248'.84
Raising God's children / Anita Bryant and Bob Green. Old Tappan, N.J. : Revell, c1977. p. cm. [BV4526.2.B73] 77-13762 ISBN 0-8007-0878-4 : 6.95
1. Bryant, Anita. 2. Green, Bob. 3. Family—Religious life. 4. Children—Management. I. Green, Bob, joint author. II. Title.

BURKE, Thomas William. 248.84
The gold ring; God's pattern for perfect marriage. Foreword by Maurice O'Leary. American foreword by Thomas J. O'Donnell. New York, D. McKay C. [1963] 176 p. 20 cm. [HQ734.B919] 63-12426
1. Marriage 2. Christian life — Catholic authors. I. Title.

BURKE, Thomas William 248.84
The gold ring; God's pattern for perfect marriage. Foreword by Maurice O'Leary, Amer. foreword by Thomas J. O'Donnell. New York, McKay [c.1961, 1963] 176p. 20cm. 63-12426 3.95
1. Marriage. 2. Christian life—Catholic authors. I. Title.

CALDWELL, Louis O. 248.8'4
The adventure of becoming one [by] Louis O. Caldwell. Grand Rapids, Baker Book House [1969] 80 p. 20 cm. Includes bibliographical references. [BV835.C3] 69-16930
1. Marriage. I. Title.

CARLSON, Betty 248.84
Life is for living; inspirational devotions for women. Grand Rapids, Mich., Zondervan [c.1962] 136p. 2.50 bds.,
I. Title.

CARLSON, Betty 248.84
Life is for living: inspirational devotions for women. Grand Rapids, Mich., Zondervan [c.1962] 122p. 21cm. 1.00 pap.,
I. Title.

CARLSON, Betty 248.84
Right side up, and other inspirational essays to show that happiness lies in your point of view. Grand Rapids, Mich., Zondervan [c.1963] 120p. 21cm. 63-15731 2.50 bds.,
1. Happiness. I. Title.

CARLSON, Betty. 248.84
Right side up, and other inspirational essays to show that happiness lies in your point of view. Grand Rapids, Zondervan Pub. House [1963] 120 p. 21 cm. [BJ1481.C33] 63-15731
1. Happiness. I. Title.

COOPER, John Charles. 248'.84
Religion after forty. Philadelphia, United Church Press [1973] 124 p. 22 cm. "A Pilgrim Press book." Includes bibliographical references. [BV4579.5.C66] 73-12150 ISBN 0-8298-0260-6 4.95
1. Middle age—Religious life. I. Title.

CRANE, Wendell K. 248.84
Life is a Journey. New York, Vantage [c.1962] 101p. 21cm. 2.75 bds.
I. Title.

CROOK, Roger H. 248.8'4
The Christian family in conflict; a reassuring look at the Christian family in todays troubled times [by] Roger H. Crook. Nashville, Tenn., Broadman Press [1970] 127 p. 20 cm. [BV4526.2.C7] 78-95415
1. Family—Religious life. I. Title.

DANTUMA, Angelyn Grace 248.84
The Christian woman. Grand Rapids, Mich., Eerdmans [1962, c.1961] 144p. 61-17395 3.50 bds.,
1. Woman—Religious life. I. Title.

DEAL, William S. 248.8'4
Counseling Christian parents, by William S. Deal. Grand Rapids, Zondervan Pub. House [1970] 128 p. 21 cm. (A Zondervan book) Bibliography: p. 126-128. [HQ10.D35] 77-120035 1.95
1. Family life education. 2. Family—Religious life. I. Title.

DEFFNER, Donald L. 248'.84
The possible years; thoughts after thirty on Christian adulthood, by Donald L. Deffner. St. Louis, Concordia Pub. House [1973] 95 p. illus. 20 cm. [BV4400.D43] 72-96975 1.95 (pbk.)
1. Church work. 2. Middle age. I. Title.

DOYLE, Charles Hugo. 248.84
Christian perfection for the married. Highland Falls, N.Y., Nugent Press [1964] vi, 275 p. 21 cm. [BX2350.D58] 65-1495
1. Married people — Religious life. I. Title.

DRESCHER, John M. 248.8'4
Now is the time to love, by John M. Drescher. Scottdale, Pa., Herald Press [1970] 112 p. 23 cm. Bibliography: p. [111]-112. [BV4526.2.D73] 73-123411 3.95
1. Family—Religious life. I. Title.

EVANS, Louis Hadley, 1897- 248.84
Your marriage--duel or duet? [Westwood, N.J.] Revell [c.1962] 128p. 62-8411 2.50 bds.,
1. Marriage. I. Title.

EVELY, Louis. 248.8'4
Lovers in marriage [by] Louis Evely translated by John Drury. Garden City, N.Y., Image Books 1975 [c1968] 120 p., 18 cm. Translation of: 'Amour et mariage.' [BX2250.E913] ISBN 0-385-03011-8 1.45 (pbk.)
1. Marriage—Catholic Church. I. Title.
L.C. card no. for original ed.: 68-29886.

EVELY, Louis, 1910- 248.8'4
Lovers in marriage. Translated by John Drury. [New York] Herder and Herder [1968] 144 p. 21 cm. Translation of Amour et mariage. [BX2250.E913] 68-29886 3.95
1. Marriage—Catholic Church. I. Title.

GEISSLER, Eugene S. 248.84
The meaning of parenthood. Discussion questions by Gerard Pottebaum. Notre Dame, Ind., Fides [c.1962] 159p. (Fides dome bk., D-16) At head of title: Sex, love, and life, 2. 62-1683 .95 pap.,
1. Parent and child. 2. Family—Religious life. I. Title.

GRANBERG, Lars I., 1919- 248.8'4
Marriage is for adults only [by] Lars I. Granberg. Grand Rapids, Zondervan Pub. House [1971] 96 p. 21 cm. [BT706.G7] 79-106445
1. Marriage. I. Title.

GUERNSEY, Dennis. 248'.84
Thoroughly married / Dennis Guernsey. Waco, Tex. : Word Books, c1975. 145 p. ; 23 cm. Bibliography: p. 145. [BV835.G83] 75-19903 4.95
1. Marriage. 2. Sex in marriage. I. Title.

HERTZ, Solange Strong, 248.84
1920-
Feast for a week; a retreat for housewifes [by] Slange Hertz. Westminster, Md., Newman Press, 1964. xi, 119 p. 22 cm. [BX2376.W6H4] 64-66281
1. 3. Mary, Virgin — Words. 2. Women — Religious life. 3. Retreats. I. Title.

HERTZ, Solange Strong, 248.84
1920-
Feast for a week; a retreat for housewives. Westminster, Md., Newman [c.]1964. xi, 119p. 22cm. [BX2376.W6H4] 64-66281 3.75
1. Women—Religious life. 2. Retreats. 3. Mary, Virgin—Words. I. Title.

HERTZ, Solange Strong, 248.84
1920-
Searcher of majesty. Westminster, Md., Newman Press, 1963. 283 p. 23 cm. [BX2353.H45] 63-12245
1. Woman — Religious life. 2. Spiritual life — Catholic authors. I. Title.

HERTZ, Solange Strong, 248.84
1920-
Searcher of majesty. Westminister, Md., Newman [c.]1963. 283p. 23cm. 63-12245 4.75
1. Woman—Religious life. 2. Spiritual life—Catholic authors. I. Title.

HOEK, Ann 248.84
Heart-to-heart talks with mothers. Grand Rapids, Mich., Zondervan [c.1962] 61p. 21cm. 1.00 pap.,
I. Title.

HONEYWELL, Betty 248.84
Living portraits. Programs based on character studies of Bible women. Chicago, Moody [c.1965] 127p. 22cm. 1.95 pap., spiral bdg.,
I. Title.

HUESMAN, Rose M. 248.84
Saints in aprons. Milwaukee, Bruce [c.1962] 186p. 22cm. 62-10343 3.50
1. Woman—Religious life. I. Title.

JEPSON, Sarah Anne. 248'.84
Devotions for the single set, by Sarah Jepson. [1st ed.] Carol Stream, Ill., Creation House [1972] 114 p. 22 cm. [BV4596.S5J467] 70-182855
1. Single people—Prayer-books and devotions—English. I. Title.

JEPSON, Sarah Anne. 248.8'4
For the love of singles [by] Sarah Jepson. [1st ed.] Carol Stream, Ill., Creation House [1970] 96 p. 22 cm. [BV4596.S5J47] 72-131443 2.95
1. Single people—Religious life. I. Title.

JOHNSON, John Boman. 248.84
The sin of being fifty, by John B. Johnson. Grand Rapids. Baker Book House, 1964. 77 p. illus. 29 cm. [HQ1061.J55] 64-22584
1. Middle age. 2. Aged — Religious life. I. Title.

JOHNSON, John Boman 248.84
The sin of being fifty. Grand Rapids, Mich., Baker Bk. [c.]1964. 77p. illus. 20cm. 64-22584 1.00 pap.,
1. Middle age. 2. Aged—Religious life. I. Title.

*KNUTSON, Melford S. 248.84
I write to your fathers [Hayfield, Minn., P.O. Box 11. Hayfield Pub. Co., 1964, c.1962] 103p. illus. 19cm. 1.35 pap.,
I. Title.

KOOIMAN, Helen W. 248.8'4
Small talk [by] Helen Kooiman. Wheaton, Ill., Tyndale House Publishers [1969, c1968] 60 p. illus. (part col.) 20 cm. (Heritage edition) [BV4832.2.K67] 68-56400
1. Meditations. I. Title.

LAHAYE, Tim F. 248.8'4
How to be happy though married, by Tim LaHaye. Wheaton, Ill., Tyndale House Publishers [1970, c1968] 160 p. illus. 21 cm. Includes bibliographical references. [BV835.L26] 68-31703 ISBN 0-8423-1501-2
1. Marriage. I. Title.

LANDORF, Joyce. 248.8'4
His stubborn love. Grand Rapids, Mich., Zondervan Pub. House [1971] 144 p. 22 cm. [BV835.L34] 70-133355 3.95
1. Marriage. I. Title.

LESTER, Gordon. 248'.84
Living and loving : a guide to a happy marriage / Gordon Lester. Liguori, Mo. : Liguori Publications, c1976. 128 p. (p. 127-128 advertisements) ; 18 cm. [HQ734.L398] 76-42938 ISBN 0-89243-063-X : 1.75
1. Marriage. 2. Sex. 3. Love. I. Title.

LOCKERBIE, Jeanette W. 248'.84
Fifty plus : how recycling your potential now can mean a joyous and fulfilled tomorrow / Jeanette Lockerbie. Old Tappan, N.J. : Revell, c1976. 127 p. ; 21 cm. [BV4579.5.L6] 76-6939 ISBN 0-8007-0793-1 : 4.95
1. Middle age—Religious life. 2. Retirement. I. Title.

MARRIAGE is for living. 248.8'4
With a prologue by Sam Shoemaker. Grand Rapids, Zondervan [1968] 157 p. 21 cm. "A Faith at work book." [HQ734.M389] 68-10521
1. Christian life—Stories. 2. Marriage. I. Faith at work.

MAY, Edward C. 248.8'4
Christian family living [by] Edward C. May. Edited by Oscar E. Feucht. Saint Louis, Concordia Pub. House [1970] 122 p. 21 cm. (The Discipleship series) Includes bibliographies. [BV4526.2.M34] 76-122751
1. Family—Religious life. I. Title.

MAYO, Allen. 248'.84
Contract at Mount Horeb / Allen Mayo. [San Antonio] : Tex-Mex Books, c1977. 171 p. ; 22 cm. [HN90.M6M39] 75-13402 10.95
1. United States—Moral conditions. I. Title.

MYERS, T. Cecil. 248.8'4
Happiness is still home made, by T. Cecil Myers. Waco, Tex., Word Book [1969] 127 p. 23 cm. Bibliographical footnotes. [BV4526.2.M9] 73-85827 3.95
1. Family—Religious life. 2. Marriage. I. Title.

PEPPLER, Alice Stolper. 248'.84
Divorced and Christian. St. Louis, Concordia Pub. House [1974] 93 p. 21 cm. [BT707.P46] 74-4505 ISBN 0-570-03189-3 2.95 (pbk.)
1. Divorce. I. Title.

ROUNER, Arthur Acy. 248'.84
Marryin' Sam speaks out [by] Arthur A. Rouner, Jr. Grand Rapids, Baker Book House [1973] 137 p. 18 cm. (Direction books) [BV835.R68] 73-160525 ISBN 0-8010-7611-0 0.95 (pbk)
1. Marriage. I. Title.

SPARKS, Lamar. 248.84
Living water; truth-centered guidance. Boston, Christopher Pub. House [1964] 185 p. 22 cm. Bibliographical footnotes. [BV4832.2.S68] 64-22910
1. Devotional literature. I. Title.

SPARKS, Lamar 248.84
Living water; truth-centered guidance. Boston, Christopher [c.1964] 185p. 22cm. Bibl. 64-22910 3.95 bds.,
1. Devotional literature. I. Title.

STEINKE, Peter L. 248.8'4
Is there life after thirty? [By] Peter L. Steinke. Minneapolis, Augsburg Pub. House [1971] 91 p. 17 cm. [BV4501.2.S754] 77-135229 ISBN 0-8066-9441-6 1.95
1. Christian life—1960- I. Title.

STEVEN, Norma. 248'.84
What kids katch from parents / by Norma Steven. Irvine, Calif. : Harvest House Publishers, c1976. 127 p ; 18 cm. [HQ769.S818] 76-5563 ISBN 0-89081-022-2 : 1.60
1. Children—Management. I. Title.

TOELKE, Otto W 248.84
In the presence of God; [devotions for the newly married] St. Louis, Concordia Pub. House [1962] 72 p. 19 cm. [BV255.T6] 61-18225
1. Family — Prayer-books and devotions — English. I. Title.

TOELKE, Otto W. 248.84
In the presence of God; [devotions for the newly married] St. Louis, Concordia [c.1962] 72p. 61-18225 1.50
1. Family—Prayer-books and devotions—English. I. Title.

URTEAGA, Jesus. 1921- 248.84
God and children [Tr. from Spanish by Leo Hickey] Chicago, Scepter [c.1964] 248p. 19cm. 64-20886 3.25 bds.,
1. Family—Religious life. 2. Parent and child. I. Title.

WALLACE, Helen Kingsbury 248.84
Stewardship for today's woman. [Westwood, N. J.] Revell [c. 1960] 94p. Bibl.: p.93-94 20cm. 60-13093 1.75
1. Stewardship, Christian. 2. Woman—Religious life. I. Title.

*WEYERGANS, Franz 248.84
An adventure in love. St. Meinrad, Indiana, Abbey Pr. [Dist. New York, Guild, 1966] 134p. 17cm. (20019) .75 pap.,
I. Title.

WILLIAMS, Patti. 248'.84
Husbands / by Patti Williams. Plainfield, N.J. : Logos International, c1976. ix, 94 p. ; 22 cm. [BV835.W55] 75-7477 ISBN 0-88270-147-9 : 4.95. ISBN 0-88270-148-7 pbk. :
1. Marriage. I. Title.

ANDREWS, Gini. 248'.842
Sons of freedom / Gini Andrews. Grand Rapids, Mich. : Zondervan Pub. House, [1975] 191 p. ; 21 cm. [BV4596.S5A48] 74-25329 4.95
1. Bachelors—Religious life. I. Title.

EXEL, Godfrey W. 248'842
Live happily with the woman you love / by Godfrey W. Exel. Chicago : Moody Press, c1977. p. cm. [BV835.E94] 77-10744 ISBN 0-8024-4900-X pbk. : 2.95
1. Marriage. 2. Husbands. I. Title.

EXEL, Godfrey W. 248'842
Live happily with the woman you love / by Godfrey W. Exel. Chicago : Moody Press, c1977. p. cm. [BV835.E94] 77-10744 ISBN 0-8024-4900-X pbk. : 2.95
1. Marriage. 2. Husbands. I. Title.

HERRING, Reuben 248.8'42
Men are like that. Nashville, Broadman [1967] 143p. 21cm. Bibl. [BV4843.H4] 67-17428 3.25 bds.,
1. Men—Religious life. I. Title.

MOLL, Willi. 248.842
Father and fatherhood. Translated by Elisabeth Reinecke and Paul C. Bailey. Notre Dame, Ind., Fides Publishers [1966] 157 p. 20 cm. Bibliography: p. 152-153. [BX2352.M613] 66-20177
1. Fathers. I. Title.

NELSON, Rosanne E. 248'.842
Memo from Gabriel / Rosanne E. Nelson. 1st ed. Garden City, N.Y. : Doubleday, 1976. xii, 108 p. ; 22 cm. Includes bibliographical references. [BV4527.N387] 75-44524 ISBN 0-385-11494-X : 5.95
1. Wives—Religious life. I. Title.

NIDA, Clarence. 248'.842
Before you marry ... for men only / by Clarence Nida. Chicago : Moody Bible Institute, c1977. p. cm. [BV835.N53] 77-24175 ISBN 0-8024-0481-2 pbk. : 2.50
1. Marriage. I. Title.

PINEGAR, Ed J. 248'.842
Fatherhood / Ed J. Pinegar. Salt Lake City : Deseret Book Co., 1976. 79 p. ; 24 cm. Includes index. [BX8643.F3P56] 76-7297 ISBN 0-87747-593-8 : 4.95
1. Fathers. 2. Fathers—Religious life. I. Title.

†RENICH, Fred. 248'.842
The Christian husband : how to become the husband God wants you to be / Fred Renich. Montrose, Pa. : Living Life Publications, c1976. 249 p. ; 22 cm. [HQ756.R44] 76-47727 ISBN 0-918018-01-3 : 6.95
1. Husbands. I. Title.
Publisher's address:Drawer B,Montrose Pa.18801

ACHTEMEIER, Elizabeth Rice, 1926- 248.843
The feminine crises in Christian faith [by] Elizabeth Achtemeier. New York, Abingdon Press [1965] 100 p. 21 cm. "Suggested helps for Bible study": p. 153-154. [BV639.W7A3] 65-20366
1. Women in Christianity. 2. Woman — Religious life. I. Title.

ACHTEMEIER, Elizabeth Rice, 1926- 248.843
The feminine crisis in Christian faith. Nashville, Abingdon Press [c.1965] 160p. 21cm. Bibl. [BV639.W7A3] 65-20366 2.75 bds.,
1. Women in Christianity. 2. Woman—Religious life. I. Title.

ANDERSON, Evelyn McCullough. 248.8'43
Its a woman's privilege. Grand Rapids, Mich., Baker Book House [1970] 188 p. 21 cm. [BV4527.A5] 71-115641 3.95
1. Woman—Religious life. I. Title.

ANDERSON, Evelyn McCullough. 248.8'43
New windows for women. Grand Rapids : Baker Book House, 1976c1970. 188p. ; 20 cm. Formerly published under the title, "it's a woman's privilege." [BV4527.A5] ISBN 0-8010-0101-3 pbk. : 2.95.
1. Women-Religious life. I. Title.
L. C. card no. for original ed.71-115641.

ANDREWS, Gini. 248'.843
Your half of the apple; God & the single girl. Foreword by Francis Schaeffer. Grand Rapids, Zondervan Pub. House [1972] 159 p. 22 cm. [BV4596.S5A5] 72-189574 3.95
1. Single women—Religious life. I. Title.

ARMSTRONG, Frieda. 248'.843
To be free. Illustrated by Sandy Bauer. Philadelphia, Fortress Press [1974] viii, 88 p. illus. 21 cm. (Open book 9) Includes bibliographical references. [BJ1610.A75] 73-88340 ISBN 0-8006-0126-2 2.95
1. Woman. I. Title.

BAKER, Elizabeth, 1944- 248'.843
The happy housewife / Elizabeth Baker. Wheaton, Ill. : Victor Books, [1975] 144 p. ; 18 cm. [BV4527.B3] 74-16978 ISBN 0-88207-720-1 : 1.75
1. Wives—Religious life. I. Title.

BEARDSLEY, Lou. 248'.843
The fulfilled woman / Lou Beardsley and Toni Spry. Irvine, Calif. : Harvest House Publishers, [1975] xiii, 172 p. ; 21 cm. [BV835.B38] 74-29206 ISBN 0-89081-007-9 : 2.95
1. Marriage. 2. Family. 3. Married women—Conduct of life. I. Spry, Toni, joint author. II. Title.

BEARDSLEY, Lou. 248'.843
The fulfilled woman [by] Lou Beardsly and Toni Spry. New York, Bantam Books [1976 c1975] 177 p. 18 cm. [BV835.B38] 1.50 (pbk.)
1. Marriage. 2. Family. 3. Married women—Conduct of life. I. Spry, Toni, joint author. II. Title.
L.C. card no. of 1975 Harvest House edition: 74-29206.

BIRKEY, Verna. 248'.843
You are very special / Verna Birkey. Old Tappan, N.J. : F. H. Revell Co., c1977. p. cm. [BV4527.B57] 77-23805 ISBN 0-8007-0875-X : 5.95
1. Bible—Meditations. 2. Women—Religious life. 3. Self-respect. I. Title.

BREMYER, Jayne Dickey. 248'.843
Dear God : am I important? / Jayne Bremyer. Rev. ed. Waco, Tex. : Word Books, c1976. 165 p. ; 22 cm. [BX2353.B73 1976] 76-374890 ISBN 0-87680-856-9 : 3.95
1. Women—Religious life. I. Title.

BRIGHT, Vonette Z. 248'.843
For such a time as this / Vonette Z. Bright. Old Tappan, N.J. : F.H. Revell, c1976. p. cm. [BV4527.B72] 76-25176 ISBN 0-8007-0831-8 : 4.95
1. Bright, Vonette Z. 2. Women—Religious life. 3. Christian life—1960- I. Title.

BROOKS, Pat. 248'.843
Daughters of the King / by Pat Brooks. Carol Stream, Ill. : Creation House, c1975. 144 p. ; 22 cm. Bibliography: p. 143-144. [BV4527.B75 1975] 75-22573 ISBN 0-88419-114-1 : 2.95
1. Women—Religious life. 2. Women. I. Title.

BROOME, Connie. 248'.843
Vessels unto honor / by Connie Broome. Cleveland, Tenn. : Pathway Press, 1977,c1976 128 p. ; 21 cm. [BV4527.B76] 76-22242 ISBN 0-87148-879-5 : write for information
1. Women—Religious life. 2. Women—Conduct of life. I. Title.

*CHAPPELL, Clovis G. 248.843
Feminine faces. Grand Rapids, Baker Book House [1974, c1970] 219 p. 20 cm. (Clovis G. Chappell library) [BV4527] ISBN 0-8010-2355-6. 2.95 (pbk.)
1. Woman—Religious life. I. Title.

CLARK, Vynomma. 248.8'43
So you're a woman. Abilene, Tex., Biblical Research Press [1971] vi, 51 p. 23 cm. [BV4527.C56] 70-180790 2.95
1. Woman—Religious life. I. Title.

D'ANGELO, Louise 248'.843
Too busy for God? : Think again! : A spiritual guide for working women and housewives / Louise D'Angelo. Huntington, Ind. : Our Sunday Visitor, inc., c1975. 119 p. ; 18 cm. [BX2353.D3] 75-329620 ISBN 0-87973-784-0 pbk. : 1.75
1. Women—Religious life. I. Title.

DAVIDSON, Clarissa Start. 248.8'43
On becoming a widow. New York, Family Library [1973] 124 p. 18 cm. First published in 1968 under title: When you're a widow [BV4908.D3] ISBN 0-515-03089-9 0.95 (pbk.)
1. Consolation. I. Title.
L.C. card no. for the 1968 ed.: 68-20182.

DAVIDSON, Clarissa Start. 248.8'43
When you're a widow, [by] Clarissa Start. St. Louis, Concordia Pub. House [1968] 138 p. illus. 21 cm. [BV4908.D3] 68-20182
1. Consolation. I. Title.

*DEVOS, Karen Helder. 248.8'43
A woman's worth & work : a Christian perspective. Grand Rapids : Baker Book House, 1976. 101p. ; 21 cm. [BV 4527] ISBN 0-8010-2853-1 pbk. : 2.95.
1. Women-Religious life. I. Title.

DILLOW, Linda. 248'.843
Creative counterpart / Linda Dillow. Nashville : T. Nelson, c1977. 170 p. ; 21 cm. Includes bibliographical references. [BV4527.D54] 76-30387 ISBN 0-8407-5617-8 pbk. 2.95
1. Wives—Religious life. 2. Wives—Conduct of life. I. Title.

ELLIOT, Elisabeth. 248'.843
Let me be a woman : notes on womanhood for Valerie / Elisabeth Elliot. Wheaton, Ill. : Tyndale House Publishers, c1976. 190 p. ; 22 cm. Includes bibliographical references. [BV835.E43] 76-1324 ISBN 0-8423-2160-8 : 5.95
1. Marriage—Addresses, essays, lectures. 2. Women—Religious life—Addresses, essays, lectures. I. Title.

EVANS, Colleen Townsend. 248'.843
A new joy. Boston, G. K. Hall, 1974 [c1973] 190 p. 24 cm. Large print ed. [BT382.E55 1974] 74-4419 ISBN 0-8161-6215-8 7.95
1. Beatitudes. 2. Woman—Religious life. 3. Sight-saving books. I. Title.

EVANS, Colleen Townsend. 248'.843
A new joy. Old Tappan, N.J., Revell [1973] 124 p. 21 cm. [BT382.E55] 73-3107 ISBN 0-8007-0590-4 3.95
1. Beatitudes. 2. Woman—Religious life. I. Title.

EVANS, Colleen Townsend 248.843
A new joy New York Pillar Books [1975 c1973] 128 p. 18 cm. [BT382E55] ISBN 0-89129-015-X 1.50 (pbk.)
1. Beatitudes. 2. Woman—Religious life. I. Title.
L.C. card no. for original edition: 73-3107.

FREMANTLE, Anne Jackson, 1909- 248'.843
Woman's way to God / Anne Fremantle. New York : St. Martin's Press, c1977. xvi, 255 p. ; 22 cm. [BL624.F74] 76-10553 ISBN 0-312-88690-X : 8.95
1. Women—Religious life. 2. Religions—Biography. 3. Women—Biography. I. Title.

FREMANTLE, Anne Jackson, 1909- 248'.843
Woman's way to God / Anne Fremantle. New York : St. Martin's Press, c1977. xvi, 255 p. ; 22 cm. [BL624.F74] 76-10553 ISBN 0-312-88690-X : 8.95
1. Women—Religious life. 2. Religions—Biography. 3. Women—Biography. I. Title.

GAGE, Joy P. 248'.843
But you don't know Harry [by] Joy P. Gage. Wheaton, Ill., Tyndale House Publishers [1972] 64 p. illus. 14 cm. (A Tyndale treasure) [BV4527.G34] 72-84418 ISBN 0-8423-0195-X .50
1. Woman—Religious life. I. Title.

*GLYNN, Jeanne Davis 248.843
Diary of a new mother. St. Meinrad, Ind., Abbey Pr. [1966] 132p. 17cm. (20020) .75 pap.,
I. Title.
Available from Guild in New York.

HAUGHTON, Rosemary. 248'.843
Feminine spirituality : reflections on the mysteries of the rosary / by Rosemary Haughton. New York : Paulist Press, c1976. ix, 93 p. ; 18 cm. [BX2353.H34] 76-24438 ISBN 0-8091-1982-X pbk. : 1.95
1. Women—Religious life. 2. Mysteries of the Rosary—Meditations. I. Title.

HERR, Ethel L. 248'.843
Chosen women of the Bible / Ethel L. Herr. Chicago : Moody Press, c1976. 96 p. ; 22 cm. Includes bibliographies. [BS575.H47] 75-36503 ISBN 0-8024-1297-1 pbk. : 1.50
1. Women in the Bible—Study and teaching. I. Title.

HERTZ, Jacky. 248'.843
The Christian mother : a Mary-Martha balance / Jacky Hertz. New York : Hawthorn Books, c1976. xii, 162 p. ; 22 cm. [BV4529.H47 1976] 76-15427 ISBN 0-8015-1280-8 : 6.95
1. Mothers—Religious life. I. Title.

LAHAYE, Beverly. 248'.843
The Spirit-controlled woman / Beverly LaHaye. Irvine, Calif. : Harvest House, c1976. 174 p. ; 21 cm. [BJ1610.L2] 76-5562 ISBN 0-89081-020-6 pbk. : 2.95
1. Women—Conduct of life. 2. Women—Religious life. I. Title.

*LANDORF, Joyce. 248'843
Every woman can be more beautiful. New York, Pillar Books [1975] 143 p. 18 cm. Original title: The Fragrance of Beauty. [BV4527.L33] 73-76813 ISBN 0-89129-029-X 1.25 (pbk.)
1. Woman—Religious life. 2. Beauty, Personal. I. Title.

LANDORF, Joyce. 248'.843
The fragrance of beauty. Wheaton, Ill., Victor Books [1973] 143 p. 18 cm. [BV4527.L33] 73-76813 0.95 (pbk.)
1. Woman—Religious life. 2. Beauty, Personal. I. Title.

MACINTOSH, Mike, 1944- 248'.843
Attributes of the Christian woman / Mike MacIntosh. Costa Mesa, Calif. : Maranatha Evangelical Association, c1977. p. cm. [BV4527.M2] 77-10431 ISBN 0-89337-003-7 pbk. : 1.50
1. Women—Religious life. I. Title.

NICHOLS, Jeannette, 1911- 248.8'43
Her works praise her; a study course for women. [Independence, Mo., Herald Pub. House, 1967] 133 p. 18 cm. Bibliography: p. 131-133. [BV4527.N5] 67-29797
1. Woman—Religious life. I. Title.

NICHOLS, Jeannette, 1911- 248.8'43
Her works praise her; a study course for women. [Independence, Mo., Herald Pub. House, 1967] 133 p. 18 cm. Bibliography: p. 131-133. [BV4527.N5] 67-29797
1. Woman—Religious life. I. Title.

NYBERG, Kathleen Neill. 248.8'43
The new Eve. Nashville, Abingdon Press [1967] 476 p. 21 cm. Bibliographical references included in "Notes" (p. 173-176) [BV4527.N8] 67-22762
1. Woman — Religious life. I. Title.

NYBERG, Kathleen Neill. 248.8'43
The new Eve. Nashville, Abingdon Press [1967] 176 p. 21 cm. Bibliographical references included in "Notes" (p. 173-176) [BV4527.N8] 67-22762
1. Women—Religious life. I. Title.

ORTLUND, Anne. 248'.843
Disciplines of the beautiful woman / Anne Ortlund. Waco, Tex. : Word Books, c1977. 132 p. ; 23 cm. Includes bibliographical references. [BJ1610.O77] 77-76347 ISBN 0-8499-0000-X : 4.95
1. Women—Conduct of life. I. Title.

PATTERSON, Dot. 248'.843
The sensuous woman reborn / Dot Patterson. Dallas : Crescendo Publications, c1976. 175 p. ; 18 cm. [HQ1206.P37] 76-151830 ISBN 0-89038-035-X pbk. : 1.95
1. Femininity. 2. Women—Religious life. I. Title.

PAYNE, Dorothy. 248.8'43
Women without men; creative living for singles, divorcees and widows. Philadelphia, Pilgrim Press [1969] x, 150 p. 22 cm. Includes bibliographical references. Bibliography: p. 141-150. [BJ1610.P28] 71-94758 4.95
1. Single women—Conduct of life. I. Title.

PENN-LEWIS, Jessie, 1861-1927. 248'.843
The magna charta of woman / by Jessie Penn-Lewis. Minneapolis : Bethany Fellowship, c1975. 103 p. ; 18 cm. (Dimension books) Originally published in 1919 under title: The magna charta of woman according to the scriptures. [BS680.W7P46 1975] 75-28655 ISBN 0-87123-377-0 : 1.50
1. Woman (Theology)—Biblical teaching. 2. Women—Religious life. I. Title.

†SIT, Amy Wang. 248'.843
The rib / by Amy Sit. Harrison, Ark. : New Leaf Press, 1976,c1977 140 p. ; 21 cm. Bibliography: p. 139-140. [BV4527.S47] 76-22278 ISBN 0-89221-026-5 pbk. : 2.95
1. Wives—Religious life. 2. Woman (Theology)—Biblical teaching. I. Title.

SKOGLUND, Elizabeth. 248'.843
Woman beyond roleplay / Elizabeth Skoglund. Elgin, Ill. : D. C. Cook Pub. Co., c1975. 112 p. ; 18 cm. [BV4527.S55] 75-893 ISBN 0-912692-62-6 : 1.25
1. Women—Religious life. I. Title.

SKOGLUND, Elizabeth. 248'.843
Woman beyond roleplay / Elizabeth Skoglund. Elgin, Ill. : D. C. Cook Pub. Co., c1975. 112 p. ; 18 cm. [BV4527.S55] 75-893 ISBN 0-912692-62-6 pbk. : 1.25
1. Women—Religious life. I. Title.

SPAFFORD, Belle S. 248'.843
A woman's reach [by] Belle S. Spafford. Salt Lake City, Deseret Book Co., 1974. 165 p. port. 24 cm. [BV4527.S65] 74-75032 ISBN 0-87747-518-0 4.95
1. Woman—Religious life. 2. Women in church work. I. Title.

STRUCHEN, Jeanette. 248.8'43
What do I do now, Lord? Old Tappan, N.J., Revell [1971] 120 p. 21 cm. [BV4527.S75] 76-149368 ISBN 0-8007-0445-2 3.50
1. Woman—Religious life. 2. Wives—Conduct of life. I. Title.

WIEBE, Katie Funk. 248'.843
Alone : a widow's search for joy / Katie F. Wiebe. Wheaton, Ill. : Tyndale House Publishers, 1976. 303 p. ; 21 cm. Bibliography: p. 303. [BX8143.W43A33] 76-27572 ISBN 0-8423-0062-7 : 4.95
1. Wiebe, Katie Funk. 2. Mennonites—Kansas—Hillsboro—Biography. 3. Hillsboro, Kan.—Biography. I. Title.

WOODROW, Ralph. 248'.843
Women's adornment : what does the Bible really say? / Ralph Woodrow. Riverside, Ca. : Woodrow, c1976. 61 p. : ill. ; 22 cm. Includes bibliographical references. [BS680.C65W66] 76-17711 ISBN 0-916938-01-8 pbk. : 2.00
1. Biblical costume. 2. Women in the Bible. I. Title.

WRIGLEY, Louise Scott. 248.843
A woman searches. [Independence, Mo., Herald Pub. House, 1966] 120 p. illus. 16 cm. [BV4527.W69] 66-15424
1. Woman — Religious life. I. Title.

WRIGLEY, Louise Scott 248.843
A woman searches [Independence, Mo., Herald [c.1966] 120p. col. illus. 16cm. [BV4527.W69] 66-15424 1.95 bds.,
1. Woman—Religious life. I. Title.

WRIGLEY, Louise Scott. 248.843
A woman searches. New York, Family Library [1973, c.1966] 94 p. illus. 18 cm. [BV4527.W69] ISBN 0-515-03037-6 pap., 0.95
1. Woman—Religious life. I. Title.

ZASTROW, Nancy B. 248.843
The radiant life; reflections on a woman's life in Christ [by] Nancy B. Zastrow. St. Louis, Concordia Pub. House [1966] viii, 126 p. 19 cm. Bibliography: p. 124-126. [BV4527.Z3] 66-27385
1. Women—Religious life. I. Title.

MALL, E. Jane, 248'.843'0924 B
1920-
How am I doing, God? By E. Jane Mall. St. Louis, Concordia Pub. House [1973] 160 p. 18 cm. Autobiographical. [BX8080.M22A33 1973] 72-97343 ISBN 0-570-03150-8 pap. 1.75
1. Mall, E. Jane, 1920- I. Title.

WE became wives 248'.843'0922 B
of happy husbands : true stories of personal transformation / compiled by Darien B. Cooper, with her own comments and questions for contemplation, in collaboration with Anne Kristin Carroll. Wheaton, Ill. : Victor Books, c1976. 165 p. ; 21 cm. Bibliography: p. 165. [BJ1610.W5] 76-4314 ISBN 0-88207-731-7 pbk. : 2.50
1. Wives—Conduct of life. 2. Women—United States—Biography. I. Cooper, Darien B. II. Carroll, Anne Kristin.

DEEKEN, Alfons. 248'.85
Growing old, and how to cope with it. New York, Paulist Press [1972] vi, 103 p. 19 cm. (Paulist Press/Deus book) [HQ1061.D38] 73-183419 1.25
1. Aging. 2. Aged—Religious life. I. Title.

GILHUIS, C. 248'.85
Conversations on growing older / by C. Gilhuis ; translated by Cor W. Barendrecht. Grand Rapids : Eerdmans, c1977. p. cm. Translation of Hoe dichter ik nader. [BV4580.G5413] 77-1504 ISBN pbk. : 3.95
1. Aged—Religious life. 2. Death. 3. Future life. I. Title.

GILHUIS, C. 248'.85
Conversations on growing older / by C. Gilhuis ; translated by Cor W. Barendrecht. Grand Rapids : Eerdmans, c1977. p. cm. Translation of Hoe dichter ik nader. [BV4580.G5413] 77-1504 ISBN pbk. : 3.95
1. Aged—Religious life. 2. Death. 3. Future life. I. Title.

KENNEY, Leon Fallis. 248'.85
Memories and meditations / by Leon Fallis Kenney ; decorations by Peggie Bach. Philadelphia : Westminster Press, c1977. 154 p. : ill. ; 21 cm. [BV4580.K46] 76-46643 ISBN 0-664-21290-5 : 5.95
1. Aged—Prayer-books and devotions—English. I. Title.

KENNEY, Leon Fallis. 248'.85
Memories and meditations / by Leon Fallis Kenney ; decorations by Peggie Bach. Philadelphia : Westminster Press, c1977. 154 p. : ill. ; 21 cm. [BV4580.K46] 76-46643 ISBN 0-664-21290-5 : 5.95
1. Aged—Prayer-books and devotions—English. I. Title.

LA FARGE, John, 1880- 248.85
Reflections on growing old. [1st ed.] Garden City, N.Y., Doubleday [1963] 137 p. 22 cm. Includes bibliography. [BX2372.L32] 63-18205
1. Aged—Religious life. I. Title.

MOW, Anna B. 248.8'5
So who's afraid of birthdays; for those over sixty and those who expect to be, by Anna B. Mow. [1st ed.] Philadelphia, Lippincott [1969] 128 p. 21 cm. Bibliography: p. 127-128. [BV4580.M64] 77-75176 3.95
1. Aged—Religious life. I. Title.

PYLANT, Agnes (Durant) 248.8'5
Threescore and ten ... wow! [By] Agnes D. Pylant. Nashville, Broadman Press [1971] 45 p. illus. 21 cm. Includes bibliographical references. [BV4435.P93] 70-151621 ISBN 0-8054-5213-3
1. Church work with the aged. I. Title.

RELIGION and aging; 248.8'5
the behavioral and social sciences look at religion and aging. [Los Angeles] University of Southern California [1967] vi, 84 p. illus. 23 cm. Conference held in 1965 and sponsored by the Rossmoor-Cortese Institute for the Study of Retirement and Aging, University of Southern California. Includes bibliographies. [BV4580.R45] 68-69
1. Aged—Religious life. I. Rossmoor-Cortese Institute for the Study of Retirement and Aging.

ROSSMOOR-CORTESE 248.8'5
Institute for the Study of Retirement and Aging.
Religion and aging; the behavioral and social sciences look at religion and aging. [Los Angeles] University of Southern California [1967] vl. 84 p. illus. 23 cm. Conference held in 1965 and sponsored by the Rossmoor-Cortese Institute for the Study of Retirement and Aging, University of Southern California. Includes bibliographies. [BV4580.R45] 95-69
1. Aged—Religious life. I. Title.

SOUTHERN Conference on 248*.85
Gerontology, 8th, University of Florida, 1958.
Organized religion and the older person. Edited by Delton L. Scudder. Gainesville, Published for the University of Florida Institute of Gerontology by the University of Florida Press, 1958. x, 113 p. 23 cm. (Institute of Gerontology series, v. 8) Bibliography: p. 111-113. [BV4580.S68 1958] 72-189957 2.50
1. Aged—Religious life—Addresses, essays, lectures. 2. Church work with the aged—Addresses, essays, lectures. I. Scudder, Delton Lewis, 1906- ed. II. Title. III. Series: Florida. University, Gainesville. Institute of Gerontology. Institute of Gerontology series, v. 8.

VANDENBURGH, Mildred. 248'.85
Fill your days with life / by Mildred Vandenburgh. Glendale, Calif. : G/L Regal Books, [1975] 186 p. : ill. ; 20 cm. Bibliography: p. 179-186. [BJ1691.V3] 74-16964 ISBN 0-8307-0323-3 pbk. : 1.95
1. Aged—Conduct of life. 2. Aged—Religious life. I. Title.

WHITMAN, Virginia 248.8'5
Around the corner from sixty. Chicago, Moody [1967] 142p. 22cm. [BV4580.W48] 67-14383 2.95
1. Aged—Religious life. 2. Aged—Conduct of life. I. Title.

ANDRUS, Paul F., 1931- 248'.86
Why me? Why mine? : Clear thinking about suffering / Paul F. Andrus. Nashville : Abingdon Press, [1975] 112 p. ; 19 cm. Includes bibliographical references. [BT732.7.A52] 75-12668 ISBN 0-687-45485-9 pbk. : 2.95
1. Suffering. I. Title.

BAILEY, Ralph. 248'.86
For everything a season / Ralph Bailey. New York : Hawthorn Books, c1975. xv, 100 p. ; 22 cm. [BV4907.B28 1975] 75-2564 ISBN 0-8015-2764-3 : 5.95
1. Consolation. I. Title.

BAXTER, Batsell Barrett, 248'.86
1916-
When life tumbles in : conquering life's problems / Batsell Barrett Baxter. Grand Rapids : Baker Book House, c1974. 136 p. ; 23 cm. [BV4905.2.B33] 75-306318 ISBN 0-8010-0633-3 : 3.95.
1. Consolation. 2. Churches of Christ—Sermons. 3. Sermons, American. I. Title.

BENSON, Carmen. 248'.86 B
What about us who are not healed? / [Carmen Benson]. Plainfield, N.J. : Logos International, [1975] 162 p. ; 21 cm. [BT732.5.B43] 75-2800 ISBN 0-88270-112-6 : 5.95 5.95 ISBN 0-88270-113-4 pbk. : 3.50
1. Benson, Carmen. 2. Faith-cure—Personal narratives. I. Title.

BITTNER, Vernon J. 248'.86
Make your illness count / Vernon J. Bittner. Minneapolis : Augsburg Pub. House, c1976. 126 p. ; 20 cm. [BV4910.B5] 76-3862 ISBN 0-8066-1532-X pbk. : 3.50
1. Sick—Religious life. I. Title.

BOWMAN, Leonard. 248'.86
The importance of being sick : a Christian reflection / by Leonard Bowman. [Wilmington, N.C.] : Consortium, c1976. 218 p. ; 23 cm. [BV4910.B68] 76-19774 ISBN 0-8434-0604-6 : 12.00
1. Sick—Religious life. I. Title.

BULLE, Florence. 248'.86
Lord of the valleys. Plainfield, N.J., Logos International, 1972. xvi, 206 p. 21 cm. Includes bibliographical references. [RZ401.B86] 72-85630 ISBN 0-912106-01-8 2.50
1. Mental healing. 2. Bronchiectasis—Personal narratives. I. Title.

CANTOR, Alfred Joseph, 248'.86
1913-
Immortality, pathways to peace of mind, by Alfred J. Cantor. [Flushing, N.Y.] Hippocrates Press [c1958] xix, 71 p. 23 cm. [BT732.C3] 66-91204
1. Medicine and religion. 2. Peace of mind. I. Title.

CLAYPOOL, John. 248'.86
Tracks of a fellow struggler; how to handle grief. Waco, Tex., Word Books [1974] 104 p. 21 cm. [BV4907.C55] 73-91553 3.95
1. Consolation. 2. Baptists—Sermons. 3. Sermons, American. I. Title.

DISHMAN, Pat. 248.86
10 who overcame Nashville, Broadman Press [1966] 128 p. 20 cm. [BV4910.D5] 66-15144
1. Handicapped — Religious life. I. Title.

DISHMAN, Pat 248.86
10 who overcame. Nashville, Broadman [c.1966] 128p. 20cm. [BV4910.D5] 66-15144 1.50
1. Handicapped—Religious life. I. Title.

EVANS, Barbara, 1943- 248'.86
Joy! by Barbara Evans. Correspondence with Pat Boone. [1st ed.] Carol Stream, Ill., Creation House [1973] 144 p. 22 cm. [BR1725.E89A42] 72-94923 ISBN 0-88419-060-9 3.95
1. Evans, Barbara, 1943- 2. Boone, Charles Eugene. 3. Homosexuality. I. Boone, Charles Eugene. II. Title.

FINEGAN, Jack, 1908- 248.86
At wit's end. Richmond, John Knox Press [1963] 125 p. 21 cm. [BV4908.5.F5] 63-13831
1. Peace of mind. I. Title.

FINEGAN, Jack, 1908- 248.86
At wit's end. Richmond, Va., Knox [c.1963] 125p. 21cm. 63-13831 2.75
1. Peace of mind. I. Title.

FORD, Josephine 248'.86
Massyngberde.
The hospital prayer book / J. Massyngberde Ford. New York : Paulist Press, [1975] vi, 106 p. ; 18 cm. [BV4910.F65] 74-30984 ISBN 0-8091-1838-6 pbk. : 1.65
1. Sick—Prayer-books and devotions—English. I. Title.

GREER, Virginia. 248'.86
The glory woods : a hymn of healing / Virginia Greer. 1st ed. Chappaqua, N.Y. : Christian Herald House, c1976. xiv, 138 p. ; 21 cm. [RC263.G73] 75-45858 ISBN 0-915684-04-7 : 5.95
1. Greer, Virginia. 2. Cancer—Personal narratives. I. Title.

HARTON, Sibyl, 1898- 248.86
Doors of eternity [1st Amer. ed.] New York, Morehouse [1965] 158p. 21cm. [BT825.H3] 65-5199 3.75
1. Death. I. Title.

HIGGINBOTHAM, Mary. 248'.86 B
With each passing moment / Mary Higginbotham. Tampa, Fla. : Grace Pub. Co., 1974. 78 p. ; 18 cm. [RC263.H53] 74-82816 1.25
1. Cancer—Personal narratives. 2. Faith. I. Title.

HULME, William Edward, 248'.86
1920-
Creative loneliness : a Christian counselor helps you live with yourself and others / William E. Hulme. Minneapolis : Augsburg Pub. House, c1977. 109 p. ; 20 cm. Includes bibliographical references. [BF575.L7H84] 76-27083 ISBN 0-8066-1556-7 pbk. : 3.25
1. Loneliness. I. Title.

JACKSON, Edgar Newman. 248.8'6
When someone dies [by] Edgar N. Jackson. Philadelphia, Fortress Press [1971] 58 p. 20 cm. (Pocket council books, 1-1103) [BV4905.2.J3] 76-154488 ISBN 0-8006-1103-9 1.50
1. Consolation. 2. Death. I. Title.

JOHNSON, Margaret 248'.86 B
Woods.
We lived with dying / Margaret Woods Johnson. Waco, Tex. : Word Books, [1975] 128 p. ; 21 cm. [RC263.J63] 74-82656 4.95
1. Woods, Wayne. 2. Cancer—Personal narratives. I. Title.

JOHNSON, Margaret 248'.86 B
Woods.
We lived with dying / Margaret Woods Johnson. Waco, Tex. : Word Books, [1975] 128 p. ; 21 cm. [RC263.J63] 74-82656 4.95
1. Woods, Wayne. 2. Cancer—Personal narratives. I. Title.

KURZ, Albert L. 248'.86
Let Christ take you beyond discouragement / Albert L. Kurz ; foreword by Warren Wiersbe. Denver : Accent Books, c1975. 128 p. ; 18 cm. On spine: Beyond discouragement. [BV4905.2.K84] 75-17365 1.75
1. Consolation. I. Title. II. Title: Beyond discouragement.

LANDORF, Joyce. 248'.86
Mourning song. Old Tappan, N.J., F. H. Revell Co. [1974] 184 p. 21 cm. [BT825.L35] 74-9938 ISBN 0-8007-0680-3 5.95
1. Death. I. Title.

LEAH. 248'.86
Leah. Old Tappan, N.J., F. H. Revell Co. [1973] 90 p. illus. 18 cm. Autobiographical. [HV5805.L4A3] 73-4042 ISBN 0-8007-0595-5 3.95
1. Drug abuse—Personal narratives. 2. Prostitutes—Correspondence, reminiscences, etc.

LESTER, Andrew D. 248'.86
It hurts so bad, Lord! / Andrew D. Lester. Nashville : Broadman Press, c1976. 128 p. ; 21 cm. Includes bibliographical references. [BV4905.2.L37] 75-42860 ISBN 0-8054-5238-9 : 3.95
1. Consolation. I. Title.

LEVESQUE, G Victor. 248'.86
Miracle cures for the millions, by G. Victor Levesque. Los Angeles, Sherbourne Press [1967] 154 p. 21 cm. (For the millions series, FM-9) [BT732.5.L4] 67-17560
1. Miracles. 2. Faith-cure. I. Title.

LINDELL, Paul J., 1915- 248'.86
1974.
The mystery of pain. Minneapolis, Augsburg Pub. House [1974] 80 p. 18 cm. [BJ1409.L5] 74-77676 ISBN 0-8066-1424-2 1.75 (pbk.)
1. Pain. I. Title.

LINN, Matthew. 248'.86
Healing of memories / by Matthew Linn and Dennis Linn. New York : Paulist Press, [1974] ix, 101 p. : ill. ; 19 cm. (Deus book) Includes bibliographical references. [BT732.5.L53] 74-17697 ISBN 0-8091-1854-8 pbk. : 1.45
1. Faith-cure. 2. Mental healing. I. Linn, Dennis, joint author. II. Title.

MACLENNAN, David 248'.86
Alexander, 1903-
A pocket book of healing. Nashville, The Upper room [1962] 96p. 12cm. [BT732.4.M28] 61-16508
1. Faith—Cure. I. Title.

*MOREY, Robert A. 248.86
The Bible and drug abuse [by] Robert A. Morey. Grand Rapids, Mich., Baker Book House [1973] x, 110 p, 18 cm. Bibliography: p. 107-110. [HN32] ISBN 0-8010-5944-5 1.45 (pbk.)
1. Drug abuse. 2. Church and social problems. I. Title.

NELSON, Marion H. 248.8'6
Why Christians crack up, by Marion H. Nelson. Rev. ed. Chicago, Moody [1967] 192p. 22cm. [BT732.N43 1967] 67-14384 3.95
1. Medicine and religion. 2. Mental illness. 3. Demoniac possession. I. Title.

NORDTVEDT, Matilda. 248'.86
Defeating despair & depression / Matilda Nordtvedt. Chicago : Moody Press, [1975] 125 p. ; 22 cm. [BR1725.N54A33] 75-311320 ISBN 0-8024-2082-6 pbk. : 1.95
1. Nordtvedt, Matilda. 2. Depression, Mental—Personal narratives. 3. Christian life—1960- I. Title.

OLSEN, Peder. 248'.86
Healing through prayer. Translated by John Jensen. Minneapolis, Augsburg Pub. House [1962] 158p. 20cm. [BT732.4.O413] 62-9096

1. Faith-cure. 2. Prayer. I. Title.

PARKER, Paul E. 248'.86
What's a nice person like you doing sick? / Paul E. Parker, with David Enlow. Carol Stream, Ill. : Creation House, [1974] 80 p. : ill. ; 20 cm. (New leaf library) [RC49.P35] 74-82838 ISBN 0-88419-082-X pbk. : 1.45
1. Sick—Psychology. 2. Medicine and religion. I. Enlow, David R., joint author. II. Title.

PEERMAN, Frank. 248'.86 B
See you in the morning / Frank Peerman. Nashville : Broadman Press, c1976. 94 p. ; 20 cm. [BJ1487.P4] 76-5296 ISBN 0-8054-5237-0 : 3.50
1. Peerman, Frank. 2. Grief. 3. Baptists—Biography. I. Title.

PITTS, John. 248'.86
Faith healing; fact or fiction? [Westwood, N. J.] Revell [1961] 159p. 22cm. Includes bibliography. [BT732.4.P5] 61-13618
1. Faith-cure. I. Title.

ROBERTSON, John M. 248'.86
Here I am, God, where are you? : Prayers & promises for hospital patients / John M. Robertson. Wheaton, Ill, : Tyndale House Publishers, c1976. [63] p. : ill. ; 18 cm. [BV270.R63] 75-21652 ISBN 0-8423-1416-4 pbk. : 1.45
1. Sick—Prayer-books and devotions—English. I. Title.

SALISBURY, Hugh M. 248'.86
Through sorrow into joy / by Hugh M. Salisbury. Minneapolis : Bethany Fellowship, c1977. p. cm. [BV4905.2.S22] 77-13329 ISBN 0-87123-559-5 pbk. : 2.95
1. Consolation. I. Title.

SCHERESKY, Jeanne. 248'.86 B
Diagnosis, cancer : where do we go from here? / Jeanne Scheresky. Old Tappan, N.J. : Revell, c1977. 63 p. ; 18 cm. (New life ventures) [RC280.K5S33] 77-24532 ISBN 0-8007-9003-0 pbk. : .95
1. Scheresky, Ted. 2. Kidneys—Cancer—Biography. 3. Christian biography—North Dakota. I. Title.

SEEL, David John, 1925- 248.8'6
Does my father know I'm hurt? Illustrated by Peggy Bradford Long. Wheaton, Ill., Tyndale House Publishers [1971] 96 p. illus. 18 cm. [R630.S4A3] 70-155975 ISBN 0-8423-0670-6(pbk)
1. Physicians—Correspondence, reminiscences, etc. 2. Cancer—Korea. 3. Missions, Medical—Korea. I. Title.

SIMMONS, Henry C. 248'.86
Valuing suffering as a Christian : some psychological perspectives / Henry C. Simmons. Chicago : Franciscan Herald Press, [1976] p. cm. (Synthesis series) [BT732.7.S57] 76-43247 ISBN 0-8199-0708-1 pbk. : 0.65
1. Fromm, Erich, 1900- 2. Suffering. I. Title.

SMITH, Arthur Allen, 1924- 248'.86
Rachel / Arthur A. Smith. [New York] : Morehouse-Barlow Co., 1975 c1974 55 p. ; 18 cm. [BV4907.S65] 74-80386 ISBN 0-8192-1175-3 pbk. : 1.95
1. Children—Death and future state. 2. Bereavement. 3. Consolation. I. Title.

SMITH, Helen (Reagan) 248.8'6
Jesus stood by us. Nashville, Tenn., Broadman Press [1970] 143 p. 21 cm. Bibliography: p. 143. [BV4905.2.S6] 70-113218 3.75
1. Suffering. 2. Consolation. I. Title.

SMITH, JoAnn Kelley. 248'.86 B
Free fall / by JoAnn Kelley Smith ; foreword by Elisabeth Kubler-Ross. Valley Forge, Pa. : Judson Press, [1975] 138 p. : ill. ; 23 cm. Includes bibliographical references. [RC280.B8S55] 75-6690 ISBN 0-8170-0684-2 : 5.95
1. Smith, JoAnn Kelley. 2. Breast—Cancer—Personal narratives. I. Title.

SMODIC, William J 248.8'6
The law and after-hours use of school facilities [by] William J. Smodic. Pittsburg, M/ms Press [1965] 172 p. 24 cm. [840] 65-23464
1. Educational law and legislation — U.S. — States. 2. Community centers. I. Title.

STEVENS, John, 1919- 248'.86
Suicide : an illicit lover / John Stevens. Denver : Heritage House Publications, c1976. 150 p. ; 18 cm. [HV6545.S794] 76-7690 2.95
1. Suicide. I. Title.

†SUSTAR, Bob R., 1938-1975. 248'.86
Yet will I serve Him / Bob R. Sustar, as told to Hoyt E. Stone. Cleveland, Tenn. : Pathway Press, c1976. 105 p. : port. ; 18 cm. Autobiography. [RC280.L9S85 1976] 76-1683 ISBN 0-87148-931-7 pbk. : 1.95
1. Sustar, Bob R., 1938-1975. 2. Lymphoma—Biography. I. Stone, Hoyt E., joint author. II. Title.

SWOR, Chester E. 248.86
Neither down nor out. Nashville, Broadman Press [1966] 160 p. illus. 21 cm. Bibliographical footnotes. [BV4910.S9] 67-12175
1. Handicapped—Religious life. 2. Consolation. I. Title.

TAPSCOTT, Betty. 248'.86
Inner healing through healing of memories : God's gift—peace of mind / by Betty Tapscott. [Houston, Tex.] : Tapscott, 1976, c1975. 96 p. ; 21 cm. [BT732.5.T36 1976] 76-3087 2.25
1. Faith-cure. 2. Mental healing. I. Title.

TUCK, William P. 248'.86
Facing grief and death / William P. Tuch. Nashville : Broadman Press, c1975. 153 p. ; 20 cm. Bibliography: p. 153. [BT825.T8] 75-2977 ISBN 0-8054-2409-1 : 3.95
1. Death. 2. Grief. 3. Consolation. I. Title.

TULLOCH, G Janet. 248.86
Happy issue; my handicap and the church. In collaboration with Cynthia C. Wedel. Greenwich, Conn., Seabury Press, 1962. 144 p. 20 cm. [RC388.T8] 62-9617
1. Cerebral palsy — Personal narratives. 2. Church work with the handicapped. I. Title.

TULLOCH, G. Janet 248.86
Happy issue; my handicap and the church. In collaboration with Cynthia C. Wedel. Greenwich, Conn., Seabury [c.]1962. 144p. 62-9617 3.00
1. Cerebral palsy—Personal narratives. 2. Church work with the handicapped. I. Title.

VETTER, Robert J. 248'.86
Beyond the exit door / Robert J. Vetter. Elgin, Ill. : D. C. Cook Pub. Co., [1974] 109 p. ; 18 cm. [BV4905.2.V47] 74-75539 ISBN 0-912692-36-7 pbk. : 1.25
1. Vetter, Robert J. 2. Consolation. I. Title.

VOGEL, Linda Jane. 248'.86
Helping a child understand death / by Linda Jane Vogel. Philadelphia : Fortress Press, [1975] x, 86 p. ; 20 cm. Bibliography: p. 84-86. [BF723.D3V63] 74-26325 ISBN 0-8006-1203-5 pbk. : 2.50
1. Death—Psychology. 2. Child study. I. Title.

*WEDGE, Florence 248.86
The widow. Pulaski, Wis., Franciscan Pubs. [1967] 64p. 19cm. (Help yourself ser.) .25 pap.,
1. Widows—Spiritual consolation. I. Title.

WILLIAMS, Philip W. 248'.86
When a loved one dies / Philip W. Williams ; ill. by Audrey Teeple. Minneapolis : Augsburg Pub. House, c1976. 95 p. : ill. ; 20 cm. [BV4905.2.W53] 75-22713 ISBN 0-8066-1520-6 : 2.50
1. Bereavement. 2. Consolation. I. Title.

WOLD, Erling. 248'.86 B
Thanks for the mountain / Erling and Marge Wold. Minneapolis : Augsburg Pub. House, [1975] 111 p. ; 20 cm. [BR1725.W59A35] 74-14178 ISBN 0-8066-1461-7 pbk. 2.95
1. Wold, Erling. 2. Wold, Marge. I. Wold, Marge, joint author. II. Title.

YANCEY, Philip. 248'.86
Where is God when it hurts? / By Philip Yancey. Grand Rapids, Mich. : Zondervan Pub. House, c1977. p. cm. Includes bibliographical references. [BT732.7.Y36] 77-12776 ISBN 0-310-35410-2 5.95 ISBN 0-310-35411-0 pbk. : 2.95
1. Suffering. I. Title.

BISHOP, Joseph P. 248'.86'0924 B
The eye of the storm / Joseph P. Bishop. Old Tappan, N.J. : Chosen Books : distributed by Revell, c1976. 126 p. ; 21 cm. [BV49052.B48] 76-20567 ISBN 0-912376-16-3 : 4.95
1. Bishop, Joseph P. 2. Consolation. I. Title.

CARLSON, Carole C. 248'.86'0924 B
Straw houses in the wind / C. C. Carlson. Santa Ana, Calif. : Vision House Publishers, [1974] x, 141 p. ; 21 cm. [BV4501.2.C314] 74-82550 ISBN 0-88449-009-2. ISBN 0-88449-010-6 pbk. : 2.25
1. Carlson, Carole C. 2. Christian life—1960- I. Title.

PLETT, Jake, 1936- 248'.86'0924 B
Valley of shadows / by Jake Plett. Beaverlodge, Alta. : Horizon House, c1976. 168 p. ; 18 cm. (Horizon books) [BR1725.P555A33] 77-366234 ISBN 0-88965-004-7 : 1.75
1. Plett, Jake, 1936- 2. Plett, MaryAnn, 1942-1971. 3. Christian life—1960- 4. Murder—Alberta—Edmonton. 5. Christian biography—Alberta—Edmonton. 6. Edmonton, Alta.—Biography. I. Title.

RIPPETOE, Odessa B., 1913- 248.8'6'0924 B
While heaven waited, by Odessa B. Rippetoe. Philadelphia, Dorrance [1970] 233 p. ports. 22 cm. [RC263.R5] 77-83701 ISBN 0-8059-1378-5 5.95
1. Rippetoe, Karen. 2. Cancer—Personal narratives. I. Title.

SIMPSON, Margaret Massie, 1913- 248'.86'0924 B
Coping with cancer / Margaret Simpson, with Francis A. Martin. Nashville : Broadman Press, 1977c1976 154 p. ; 19 cm. [RC280.B8S52] 76-21475 ISBN 0-8054-5245-1 pbk. : 2.50
1. Simpson, Margaret Massie, 1913- 2. Breast—Cancer—Biography. I. Martin, Francis A., joint author. II. Title.

WOODSON, Meg. 248'.86'0924 B
If I die at thirty / Meg Woodson. Grand Rapids, Mich. : Zondervan Pub. House, c1975. 166 p. ; 22 cm. [RJ456.C9W66] 75-6182 4.95
1. Woodson, Peggie. 2. Cystic fibrosis—Personal narratives. 3. Children—Religious life—Personal narratives. 4. Children—Death and future state. I. Title.

†ZUCK, Roy B. 248'.86'0926
"Barb, please wake up!" : How God helped a couple through their daughter's accident and long recovery from a nearly fatal auto accident / Roy B. Zuck. Wheaton, Ill. : Victor Books, c1976. 127 p. ; 18 cm. [RD594.Z8] 77-371325 ISBN 0-88207-653-1 pbk. : 1.75
1. Zuck, Barb. 2. Brain—Wounds and injuries—Biography. 3. Crash injuries—Biography. I. Title.

HALVERSON, Richard C. 248.87
Man to man; [a devotional book for men] Los Angeles 38, 747 Seward St., Cowman Publications [1961] 259p. Bibl. 61-977 3.95 bds.,
1. Men—Prayer-books and devotions—Englishh I. Title.

ALBERIONE, Giacomo Giuseppe, 1884- 248.874
Woman, her influence and zeal as an aid to the priesthood, by James Alberione. Tr. by the Daughters of St. Paul [Boston] St. Paul Eds. [dist. Daughters of St. Paul, 1964] 316p. 22cm. [BX2353.A553] 64-24361 3.50; 2.50 pap.,
1. Woman—Religious life. I. Title.

BOYLAN, Eugene 248.88
The priest's way to God. Westminster, Md., Newman [c.]1962. 226p. 19cm. 62-17187 3.95
1. Clergy—Religious life. I. Title.

DUNN, Branson E. 248'.88
Prayers for country living / by Branson E. Dunn. Valley Forge, Pa. : Judson Press, c1976. 62 p. : ill. ; 18 cm. [BV4596.F3D86] 75-38192 ISBN 0-8170-0703-2 : 1.95
1. Farmers—Prayer-books and devotions—English. I. Title.

ENLOW, David R. 248.88
Men aflame; the story of Christian Business Men's Committee International. Grand Rapids, Mich., Zondervan [c.1962] 120p. 22cm. 62-52227 2.50
1. Christian Business Men's Committee International. 2. Businessmen—Religious life. I. Title.

HEFLEY, James C. 248.8'8
Adventurers with God; scientists who are Christians, by James C. Hefley. [1st ed.] Grand Rapids, Zondervan Pub. House [1967] 124 p. ports. 21 cm. [Q141.H4] 67-11619
1. Scientists, American. 2. Religion and science—1946- I. Title.

HEFLEY, James C. 248.88
Play ball! Grand Rapids, Mich., Zondervan [1965, c.1964] 127p. ports. 22cm. [BV4596.A8H4] 64-22831 2.95 bds.,
1. Athletes—Religious life. 2. Christian life—Stories. I. Title.

HEFLEY, James C 248.88
Sport alive! By James C. Hefley. Grand Rapids, Zondervan Pub. House [1966] 120 p. ports. 21 cm. [BV4596.A8H42] 66-15478
1. Athletes — Religious life. I. Title.

HEFLEY, James C. 248.88
Sport alive! Grand Rapids. Mich., Zondervan3*c.1966] 120p. ports. 21cm. [BV4596.A8H42] 66-15478 2.50 bds.,
1. Athletes—Religious life. I. Title.

JOHNSON, James Leonard, 1927- 248'.88
The nine to five complex, by James L. Johnson. Grand Rapids, Zondervan Pub. House [1972] 178 p. 23 cm. [BR115.E3J63] 72-83881 4.95
1. Christianity and economics. 2. Business ethics. I. Title.

KING, LeRoy, ed. 248.88
Courage to conquer; America's athletes speak their faith. Westwood, N.J., Revell [c.1966] 127p. 21cm. [BV4596.A8K5] 66-21798 2.95; 1.00 bds., pap.,
1. Athletes—Religious life. I. Title.

LECLERCQ, Jacques, 1891- 248.8'8
The apostolic spirituality of the nursing sister. [Tr. by Norah Smaridge. Staten Island, N.Y., Alba, 1967] 138p. 20cm. Tr. of La soeur hospitaliere, [BX4240.L4] 67-15200 2.95
1. Nurses and nursing. 2. Hospitalers—Religious life. I. Title.

PIKE, Kenneth Lee, 1912- 248.8'8
Stir, change, create; [poems and essays in contemporary mood for concerned students] by Kenneth L. Pike. Grand Rapids, Eerdmans [1967] 164 p. illus. 21 cm. [PS3566.I45S7] 67-30962
I. Title.

PIKE, Kenneth Lee, 1912- 248.8'8
Stir, change, create; [poems and essays in contemporary mood for concerned students] by Kenneth L. Pike. Grand Rapids, Eerdmans [1967] 164 p. illus. 21 cm. [PS3566.I45S7] 67-30962
I. Title.

PROCTOR, William. 248'.88
Help wanted: faith required. Old Tappan, N.J., F. H. Revell Co. [1974] 158 p. 21 cm. [BV4593.P76] 73-19534 ISBN 0-8007-0642-0 3.50 (pbk.)
1. Labor and laboring classes—Religious life. 2. Business ethics. I. Title.

A Special kind of man. 248'.88
[Edited by Gary Warner. 1st ed.] Carol Stream, Ill., Creation House [1973] 236 p. 18 cm. (New leaf library) Articles by members of the Fellowship of Christian Athletes which originally appeared in the Christian athlete. [BV4501.2.S69] 73-77529 1.95 (pbk.)
1. Christian life—1960- 2. Athletes. I. Warner, Gary, ed. II. The Christian athlete.

WADE, Marion E 248.88
The Lord is my counsel; a businessman's personal experiences with the Bible, by Marion E. Wade with Glenn D. Kittler. Englewood Cliffs, N.J., Prentice-Hall [1966] ix, 178 p. 21 cm. [BV4596.B8W3] 66-19885
1. Businessmen—Religious life. I. Kittler, Glenn D. II. Title.

WADE, Marion E. 248.88
The Lord is my counsel; a businessman's personal experiences with the Bible, by Marion E. Wade with Glenn D. Kittler. Englewood Cliffs, N.J., Prentice [c.1966] ix, 178p. 21cm. [BV4596.B8W3] 66-19885 3.95 bds.,
1. Businessmen—Religious life. I. Kittler, Glenn D. II. Title.

WHITE, Jerry E., 1937- 248'.88
Your job—survival or satisfaction? / By Jerry E. White and Mary A. White ; foreword by Lorne Sanny. Grand Rapids : Zondervan Pub. House, c1977. p. cm. [BT738.5.W5] 76-45191 4.95
1. Work (Theology) 2. Job satisfaction. 3. Vocation. I. White, Mary Ann, 1935- joint author. II. Title.

ALBERIONE, Giacomo Giuseppe, 1884- 248.8'9
Personality and configuration with Christ [by] James Alberione, [Boston, Mass.] St. Paul Eds. [c1967] 185p. 21cm. [BX2350.5.A575] 67-20459 3.00; 2.00 pap.,
1. Spiritual life—Catholic authors. 2. Personality. I. Title.

BOSTON Psychotheological Symposium, 2d, Aquinas Junior College, 1976. 248'.89
Loneliness : issues of emotional living in an age of stress for clergy and religious : the Second Boston Psychotheological Symposium / Anna Polcino ... [et al.] ; edited by James P. Madden ; with a foreword by Thomas A. Kane. 1st ed. Whitinsville, Mass. : Affirmation Books, c1977. 102 p. ; 21 cm. Includes bibliographical references. [BV4398.5.B67 1976] 77-368127 4.95 pbk. : 2.95
1. Counseling for clergy—Congresses. 2. Monastic and religious life—Psychology—Congresses. 3. Psychology, Religious—Congresses. 4. Loneliness—Congresses. I. Polcino, Anna. II. Madden, James P. III. Title.

BOSTON Psychotheological Symposium, 1st, Aquinas Junior College, 1975 248'.89
Coping : issues of emotional living in an age of stress for clergy and religious : the first Boston Psycho-Theological Symposium / by Bernard J. Bush ... [et al.] ; with a foreword by Anna Polcino. 1st ed. Whitinsville, Mass. :

Affirmation Books, c1976. 83 p. ; 21 cm. Includes bibliographical references. [BX2440.B67 1975] 76-36276 2.95
1. Catholic Church—Clergy—Psychology—Congresses. 2. Monastic and religious life—Psychology—Congresses. 3. Psychology, Religious—Congresses. I. Bush, Bernard J. II. Title.

FARRELL, Melvin L 248.89
First steps to the priesthood, an explanation of the Christian life for minor seminarians [by] Melvin Farrell. Milwaukee, Bruce Pub. Co. [1960] viii, 206 p. 23 cm. [BX903.F3] 60-15478
1. Seminarians — Religious life. I. Title.

GAMBARI, Elio. 248.8'9
The religious adult in Christ; religious formation before perpetual profession, juniorate years of studies scholasticate. [Jamaica Plain, Boston] St. Paul Editions [1971] 301 p. 22 cm. Translation of Religiosi adulti in Cristo. Includes bibliographical references. [BX903.G313] 71-160577 5.00
1. Juniorate. I. Title.

MINOR Seminary 248.8'9
Conference. 12th, Catholic University of America, 1961.
Minor Seminary Conference on outcomes; the proceedings of the twelfth Minor Seminary Conference, conducted at the Catholic University of America, May 12, 13, and 14, 1961. Edited by Cornelius M. Cuyler. Washington, Catholic University of America Press, 1961. v. 90p. 22cm. [BX903.M425 1961] 61-66767
1. Seminarians. 2. Prediction of scholastic success. I. Cuyler, Cornelius M., ed. II. Title.

KINNANE, John F., 248.8'9'019
1921-
Career development for priests and religious; a framework for research and demonstration [by] John F. Kinnane. Washington, Center for Applied Research in the Apostolate, 1970. vii, 134 p. illus., 5 forms. 23 cm. On cover: CARA information service. Bibliography: p. 109-112. [BX2380.K55] 78-14927
1. Vocation (in religious orders, congregations, etc.) 2. Monastic and religious life—Psychology. I. Center for Applied Research in the Apostolate, Washington, D.C. II. Title.

BLACKMORE, James H. 248.8'92
A preacher's temptations, by James H. Blackmore, with foreword by James S. Stewart, and drawings by Allene Rose Boone. Raleigh [N.C.] Edwards & Broughton Co., 1966. 120 p. illus. 23 cm. Bibliographical references included in "Footnotes": p. 115-120. [BV4011.6.B55] 66-30712
1. Clergy—Religious life. I. Title.

D'ARCY, Paul F 1921- 248.892
The genius of the apostolate; personal growth in the candidate, the seminarian, and the priest, by Paul F. D'Arcy and Eugene C. Kennedy. Foreword by Bishop O'Donnell. New York, Sheed and Ward [1965] xiii, 273 p. 22 cm. Bibliography: p. 264-268. [BX900.D3] 65-24690
1. Theological seminaries, Catholic. 2. Catholic Church — Clergy — Appointment, call and election. 3. Seminarians. I. Kennedy, Eugene C., joint author. II. Title.

D'ARCY, Paul F., 1921- 248.892
The genius of the apostolate; personal growth in the candidate, the seminarian, and the priest, by Paul F. D'Arcy, Eugene C. Kennedy. Foreword by Bishop O'Donnell. New York, Sheed [c.1965] xiii, 273p. 22cm. Bibl. [BX900.D3] 65-24690 5.50
1. Theological seminaries, Catholic. 2. Catholic Church—Clergy—Apointment, call and election. 3. Seminarians. I. Kennedy, Eugene C., joint author. II. Title.

*DILLENSCHNEIDER, Clement 248.892
Christ the one priest, and we His Priests; v.2. Tr. [from French] by Sister M. Renelle. St. Louis, B. Herder [c.1965] 276p. 24cm. Bibl. Contents.v.2. Our priestly spirituality. [BX1912.5.D513] 64-8811 5.75
1. Clergy—Religious life. 2. Jesus Christ—Priesthood. 3. Priests. I. Title.

HOFINGER, Johannes. 248'.892
You are my witnesses : spirituality for religion teachers / Johannes Hofinger. Huntington, Ind. : Our Sunday Visitor, c1977. 112 p. ; 21 cm. [BV1530.H63] 77-79675 ISBN 0-87973-742-5 pbk. : 2.95
1. Educators, Christian—Religious life. I. Title.

MARTIN, Bernard, 1905- 248.892
If God does not die. Tr. [from French] by James H. Farley. Richmond, Va., Knox [c.1966] 79p. 21cm. [BX9439.M34A32] 66-14857 1.50 pap.,
I. Title.

RAHNER, Karl, 1904- 248.8'92
Servants of the Lord. [Translated by Richard Strachan. New York] Herder and Herder [1968] 220 p. 21 cm. "Except for the first essay, all of them have been collected and published together in German in Knechte Christi." Bibliography" p. [217]-220. [BV4011.6.R3313] 68-18067 4.95
1. Clergy—Religious life. I. Title.

ROMB, Anselm William, 248.892
1929-
As one who serves, by Anselm W. Romb. Milwaukee, Bruce Pub. Co. [1966] viii. 134 p. 21 cm. [BX903.R6] 66-24256
1. Seminarians — Religious life. I. Title.

ROMB, Anselm William, 248.892
1929-
As one who serves, by Anselm W. Romb. Milwaukee, Bruce [1966] xiii, 134p. 22cm. [BX903.R6] 66-24256 3.50
1. Seminarians—Religious life. I. Title.

TUGGY, Joy Turner 248.892
The missionary wife and her work. Chicago, Moody [c.1966] 191p. 22cm. Bibl. [BV2611.T8] 66-5659 3.50
1. Missionaries' wives. I. Title.

ALBERIONE, Giacomo 248.8'94
Giuseppe, 1884-
Living our commitment; cardinal and moral virtues for religious, by James Alberione. [Boston] St. Paul Editions [1969, c1968] 168 p. 20 cm. [BX2385.A595] 74-4416 2.50
1. Monastic and religious life. 2. Cardinal virtues. I. Title.

ALBERIONE, Giacomo 248'.894
Giuseppe, 1884-1971.
Call to total consecration / James Alberione. Boston : St. Paul Editions, 1974. 94 p. ; 19 cm. [BX2435.A397 1974] 74-79804 2.50
1. Monastic and religious life. I. Title.

ALBERIONE, Giacomo 248'.894
Giuseppe, 1884-1971.
Insights into religious life / by James Alberione. Boston : St. Paul Editions, c1977. 152 p. : ill. ; 19 cm. [BX2435.A398] 77-4862 3.00 pbk. : 2.50
1. Monastic and religious life. I. Title.

BEHA, Helen Marie. 248.8'94
The dynamics of community [by] Marie Beha. New York, Corpus Books [1970] 172 p. 21 cm. Includes bibliographical references. [BX2435.B395 1970] 72-135450 6.95
1. Monastic and religious life. I. Title.

BEHA, Helen Marie. 248.8'94
Living community. Milwaukee, Bruce Pub. Co. [1967] vii, 199 p. 21 cm. [BX2435.B4] 67-19439
1. Monastic and religious life. I. Title.

BERKERY, Patrick J. 248.8'94
Restructuring religious life; a plan for renewal [by] Patrick J. Berkery. Staten Island, N.Y., Alba House [1968] 192 p. 22 cm. (Vocational perspectives series, 4) Bibliographical footnotes. [BX2432.B4] 67-30924
1. Monasticism and religious orders. 2. Monastic and religious life. 3. Church renewal—Catholic Church. I. Title.

CATHOLIC Church. Pope. 248.8'94
The states of perfection. Selected and arr. by the Benedictine Monks of Solesmes. Translated by Mother E. O'Gorman. [Boston] St. Paul Editions [1967] 736 p. 19 cm. (Papal teachings) Bibliographical footnotes. [BX2435.C3313] 65-27248
1. Monastic and religious life—Papal documents. I. Solesmes, France. Saint-Pierre (Benedictine abbey) II. Title.

CATHOLIC Church. Pope, 248'.894
1963- (Paulus VI)
Apostolic exhortation of the Supreme Pontiff Paul VI to the members of every religious family in the Catholic world on the renewal of the religious life according to the prescriptions of the Second Ecumenical Vatican Council. [Devon, Pa., W. T. Cooke Publishing, 1971] 126 p. 20 cm. On spine: The Gospel witness. Latin and English on opposite pages. [BX2435.A333] 72-176610
1. Monastic and religious life. I. [Evangelica testificatio. English & Latin] II. Title. III. Title: The Gospel witness. IV. Title: Pauli VI Summi Pontificis adhortatio apostolica ad uniuscuiusque religiosae familiae in Catholico orbe sodales.

CEGIELKA, Francis A. 248.8'94
All things new; radical reform and the religious life, by Francis A. Cegielka. New York, Sheed and Ward [1969] 214 p. 22 cm. [BX2385.C4] 69-19251 4.95
1. Monastic and religious life. I. Title.

DAUGHTERS of St. Paul. 248.8'94
Choose your tomorrow. [Boston] St. Paul Editions [1968] 235 p. illus. 19 cm. [BX2380.D38] 68-9496 2.00
1. Vocation (in religious orders, congregations, etc.) I. Title.

DAUGHTERS of St. Paul. 248.8'94
Religious life in the light of Vatican II. Compiled by the Daughters of St. Paul [Boston] St. Paul Editions [1967] 479 p. 21 cm. [BX2385.D3] 67-24029
1. Vatican Council. 2d, 1962-1965. 2. Monastic and religious life. I. Title.

DOYLE, Stephen C. 248'.894
Covenant renewal in religious life : Biblical reflections / by Stephen C. Doyle. Chicago : Franciscan Herald Press, [1975] p. cm. Includes index. Bibliography: p. [BX2435.D68] 75-19394 ISBN 0-8199-0585-2 : 7.50
1. Monastic and religious life. 2. Spiritual life—Biblical teaching. I. Title.

DYER, Ralph J. 248.8'94
The new religious; an authentic image [by] Ralph J. Dyer. Milwaukee, Bruce Pub. Co. [1967] xiii, 171 p. 22 cm. Bibliography: p. 159-171. [BX2435.D9] 67-25938
1. Monastic and religious life. I. Title.

EDNA Mary, Sister. 248.8'94
The religious life. Harmondsworth, Penguin, 1968. 250 p. 19 cm. (Pelican book, A 961) Bibliographical references included in "Notes" (p. 209-[245]) [BV4518.E3 1968b] 73-526924 6/-
1. Monastic and religious life. I. Title.

ESSER, Kajetan, 1913- 248.8'94
Life and rule; a commentary on the Rule of the Third Order Regular of St. Francis, by Cajetan Esser. Translated by M. Honora Hau and edited by Marion A. Habig. Chicago, Franciscan Herald Press [1967] xix, 124 p. 17 cm. "Rule of the Third Order Regular of the Seraphic Father St. Francis": p. xiii-xix. [BX3654.E813] 67-21135
1. Third Order Regular of St. Francis. I. Catholic Church. Congregatio de Religiosis. Regula Tertii Ordinis Regularis Seraphici Patris S. Franisci. English. 1967. II. Title.

FACETS of the future : 248'.894
religious life USA / Ruth McGoldrick and Cassian J. Yuhaus, editors. Huntington, Ind. : Our Sunday Visitor, c1976. 238 p. ; 21 cm. Includes papers from a joint program: the CARA Symposium on the Future of Religious Life and the Sister Formation Conference futureshop on formation. Includes bibliographies. [BX2435.F3] 76-12194 ISBN 0-87973-759-X pbk. : 4.95
1. Monastic and religious life—Congresses. I. McGoldrick, Ruth. II. Yuhaus, Cassian J. III. Sister Formation Conferences. IV. Center for Applied Research in the Apostolate, Washington, D.C. V. Cara Symposium on the Future of Religious Life, Bethesda, Md., 1975.

FARICY, Robert L., 1926- 248'.894
Spirituality for religious life / by Robert Faricy. New York : Paulist Press, c1976. v, 112 p. ; 18 cm. Includes bibliographical references. [BX2435.F33] 75-44594 ISBN 0-8091-1932-3 pbk. : 1.65
1. Monastic and religious life. I. Title.

FISCHER, George L. 248.8'94
Generation of opportunity [by] George Fischer. [Glen Rock, N.J., Paulist Press, 1968] 96 p. illus. (part col.), ports. 29 cm. [BX2380.F53] 68-24480
1. Vocation, Ecclesiastical. I. Title.

GAMBARI, Elio. 248'.894
Consecration and service. Translated and abridged by Mary Magdalen Bellasis. [Boston] St. Paul Editions [1973- v. 22 cm. Translation of Manuale della vita religiosa alla luce del Vaticano II. Contents.Contents.—v. 1. The global mystery of religious life. [BX2435.G33513] 73-76311 5.00 (v. 1)
1. Vatican Council. 2d, 1962-1965. 2. Monastic and religious life. 3. Christian life—Catholic authors. I. Title. II. Title: The global mystery of religious life.

GAMBARI, Elio. 248.8'94
For me to live is the church; the ecclesiology of religious life. [Boston] St. Paul Editions [1970] 358 p. 22 cm. Translation of Per me vivere e la Chiesa. Bibliographical footnotes. [BX2435.G33613] 74-114082
1. Monastic and religious life. I. Title.

GAMBARI, Elio. 248.8'94
Journey toward renewal; meditations on the renewal of the religious life. Translated by the Daughters of St. Paul. [Boston] St. Paul Editions [1968] 161 p. 22 cm. Translation of L'itinerario del rinnovamento. [BX2435.G3313] 68-24463 4.00
1. Monastic and religious life. I. Title.

GAMBARI, Elio. 248'.894
Unfolding the mystery of religious life. Translated and abridged by Mary Magdalen Bellasis and others. [Boston] St. Paul Editions [1974] 280 p. 22 cm. (Consecration and service, v. 2) Translation of Svolgimento e pratica della vita religiosa, which was originally published as v. 2 of the author's Manuale della vita religiosa alla luce del Vaticano II. Includes bibliographical references. [BX2435.G33513 1974] 73-86210 5.00
1. Vatican Council. 2d, 1962-1965. 2. Monastic and religious life. I. Title.

GAMBARI, Elio. 248.8'94
The updating of religious formation; text and commentary on Instruction on the renewal of religious formation. [Boston] St. Paul Editions [1969] 148 p. 22 cm. [BX2435.G3513] 75-98171 2.50
1. Monastic and religious life. I. Catholic Church. Congregatio pro Religiosis et Institutis Saecularibus. Instructio de accommodata renovatione institutionis ad vitam religiosam ducendam. II. Title.

GELPI, Donald L., 1934- 248.8'94
Discerning the spirit; foundations and futures of religious life, by Donald L. Gelpi. New York, Sheed and Ward [1970] xvi, 329 p. 22 cm. Includes bibliographies. [BX2435.G38] 79-103364 6.50
1. Monastic and religious life. I. Title.

GELPI, Donald L 1934- 248.894
Functional asceticism; a guideline for American religious [by] Donald L. Gelpi. New York, Sheed and Ward [1956] 191 p. 21 cm. [BX2435.G4] 66-22012
1. Monastic and religious life. I. Title.

GLEASON, Robert W. 248.8'94
The restless religious, by Robert W. Gleason. Dayton, Ohio, Pflaum Press, 1968. ix, 251 p. 22 cm. [BX2385.G55] 68-55962 5.95
1. Monastic and religious life. I. Title.

HARDON, John A. 248'.894
Religious life today / by John A. Hardon. Boston : St. Paul Editions, c1977. 173 p. : ill. ; 19 cm. [BX2435.H28] 77-5401 3.00 pbk. : 2.00
1. Monastic and religious life. I. Title.

HARING, Bernhard, 1912- 248.8'94
Acting on the Word [by] Bernard Haring. New York, Farrar, Straus, and Giroux [1968] x, 274 p. 22 cm. [BX2432.H3] 68-24595
1. Monastic and religious life. 2. Monasticism and religious orders. I. Title.

HARING, Bernhard, 1912- 248.8'94
Acting on the Word [by] Bernard Haring. New York, Farrar, Straus, and Giroux [1968] x, 274 p. 22 cm. [BX2432.H3 1968] 68-24595
1. Monastic and religious life. 2. Monasticism and religious orders. I. Title.

HINNEBUSCH, Paul 248.894
Religious life: a living liturgy. New York, Sheed [1965] viii, 280p. 22cm. Bibl. [BX2435.H5] 65-20858 5.00
1. Monastic and religious life. 2. Catholic Church. Liturgy and ritual. I. Title.

HINNEBUSCH, Paul. 248.8'94
The signs of the times and the religious life. New York, Sheed and Ward [1967] xvii, 302 p. 22 cm. Bibliographical footnotes. [BX2435.H52] 67-21912
1. Monastic and religious life. I. Title.

HOGAN, William F. 1920- 248.894
No race apart; religious life in the mystical body [by] William F. Hogan. Valatie, N.Y., Holy Cross Pr. [1966] 74p. 22cm. Bibl. [BX2385.H6] 66-22960 1.50
1. Monastic and religious life. I. Title.

HOGAN, William F., 1920- 248.8'94
One and the same spirit; a book for domestic and manual workers in religious life, by William F. Hogan. Dayton, Ohio, Pflaum, 1967. xi, 164p. 21cm. [BX2385.H62] 67-29766 4.50
1. Spiritual life—Catholic authors. 2. Monastic and religious life. I. Title.

HOGAN, William Francis, 248.8'94
1930-
Reflections for renewal [by] William F. Hogan. No[rth] Easton, Mass., Holy Cross Press [1968] 102 p. 22 cm. [BX2385.H64] 68-21674 3.50
1. Monastic and religious life. I. Title.

INSTITUTE on Religious 248.8'94
Life in the Modern World, St. Louis University, 1966.
Vows but no walls; an analysis of religious life. Edited by Eugene E. Grollmes. St. Louis, B. Herder Book Co. [1967] xiv, 230 p. 21 cm. Contents.Contents.—Foreword, by J. C. Ritter.—Hazards of religious life; a psychiatrist's view, by B. H. Hall.—Religious poverty, by Sister M. C. B. Muckenhirn.—

Religious chastity, by B. Cooke.—Religious obedience, by Sister M. A. I. Gannon.—The value of religious community, by Sister M. A. Neal.—The place of the person within the community, by T. P. Maher.—The mission of the religious in the twentieth century, by Sister M. L. Tobin.—Bibliography (p. 216-225) [BX2385.I55 1966] 67-22562
1. Monastic and religious life—Addresses, essays, lectures. I. Grollmes, Eugene E., ed. II. Title.

*KINSELLA, A. W. 248.894
About vocations. Pulaski Wis., Franciscan Pubs. [1966] 64p. 19cm. .25 pap.,
1. Monastic and religious life. I. Title.

*KINSELLA, A. W. 248.894
You- career for Christ. Pulaski, Wis., Franciscan Pubs. [c.1966] 56p. 19cm. .25 pap.,
I. Title.

LEROY, Jules 248.894
Monks and Monasteries of Near East tk [from French] by Peter collin. London, Harrap [dist. Mystic, Conn., Verry, 1965, c.1958,1963] 208 p. illus. ports. map. 22 cm [bl631.l413] 64-39581 6.00
1. Monasteries—Near East. 2. Monasticism and religious orders—Near East. I. Title.

MATURA, Thaddee. 248'.894
The crisis of religious life. Translated by Paul Schwartz and Paul Lachance. Chicago, Franciscan Herald Press [1973] x, 122 p. 22 cm. Translation of La vie religieuse au tournant. Includes bibliographical references. [BX2435.M39413] 73-4718 ISBN 0-8199-0453-8 4.95
1. Monastic and religious life. I. Title.

MEISSNER, William W 248.894
Group dynamics in the religious life, [by] W. W. Meissner. [Notre Dame, Ind.] University of Notre Dame Press, 1965. xii, 188 p. 22 cm. Bibliographical footnotes. [BX2440.M4] 65-21070
1. Monastic and religious life — Psychology. 2. Social groups. I. Title.

MEISSNER, William W. 248.894
Group dynamics in the religious life. [Notre Dame, Ind.] Univ. of Notre Dame Pr. [c.] 1965. xii, 188p. 22cm. Bibl. [BX2440.M4] 65-21070 4.95
1. Monastic and religious life—Psychology. 2. Social groups. I. Title.

MERTON, Thomas, 1915- 248.8'94
1968.
Contemplation in a world of action. Introd. by Jean Leclercq. Garden City, N.Y., Doubleday, 1973 [c.1971] 396 p. 18 cm. (Image bk., D321) [BX2435.M46 1971] 74-21673 ISBN 0-385-02550-5 pap., 1.95
1. Monastic and religious life. I. Title.

MOORHOUSE, Geoffrey, 248.8'94
1931-
Against all reason. New York, Stein and Day [1969] xi, 436 p. illus., ports. 25 cm. Bibliography: p. 243-252. [BV4518.M6 1969b] 69-17937 10.00
1. Monastic and religious life. I. Title.

MORAN, Gabriel. 248.8'94
Experiences in community; should religious life survive? [By] Gabriel Moran and Maria Harris. [New York] Herder and Herder [1968] 203 p. 21 cm. Bibliographical footnotes. [BX2435.M6] 68-55088 4.95
1. Monastic and religious life. I. Harris, Maria, joint author. II. Title.

MORAN, Gabriel. 248.8'94
The new community; religious life in an era of change. [New York] Herder and Herder [1970] viii, 134 p. 21 cm. Includes bibliographical references. [BX2435.M63] 77-114151 4.50
1. Monastic and religious life. I. Title.

MURPHY, Margaret 248'.894
Gertrude, Sister.
St. Basil and monasticism. New York, AMS Press [1971] xix, 112 p. 23 cm. (Catholic University of America. Patristic studies, v. 25) Thesis—Catholic University of America. Reprint of the 1930 ed. Bibliography: p. ix-xi. [BR1720.B3M8 1971] 70-144661 ISBN 0-404-04543-X
1. Basilius, Saint, the Great, Abp. of Caesarea, 330 (ca)-379. 2. Monasticism and religious orders—Early church, ca. 30-600. I. Title. II. Series.

NEWMAN, John Henry, 248.8'94
Cardinal, 1801-1890.
Newman the Oratorian; his unpublished Oratory papers. Edited with an introductory study on the continuity between his Anglican and his Catholic ministry by Placid Murray. Dublin, Gill and Macmillan [1969] xxv, 500 p. 23 cm. The editor's thesis—Pontificio Ateneo S. Anselmo, Rome. Bibliography: p. [xvii]-xxv. [BX2350.N38 1969] 71-10247
1. Spiritual life—Catholic authors. I. Murray, Placid, ed. II. Title.

O'DOHERTY, Eamon 248'.894
Feichin.
Vocation, formation, consecration & vows; theological and psychological considerations [by] E. F. O'Doherty. Staten Island, N.Y., Alba House [1971] xi, 266 p. 22 cm. (Vocational perspectives series, 8) [BX2435.O3] 76-110594 ISBN 0-8189-0205-1 6.95
1. Monastic and religious life. I. Title.

O'DOHERTY, Eamonn 248'.894
Feichin.
The psychology of vocation / E. F. O'Doherty. Dublin : Dept. of Psychology, University College, 1971. 60 p. ; 22 cm. (Thornfield series ; no. 1) [BX2380.O34] 75-309961 £0.30
1. Vocation, Ecclesiastical. I. Title.

O'REILLY, John Thomas. 248.8'94
Voices of change; religious life as was and could be [by] John O'Reilly. St. Louis, B. Herder Book Co. [1970] xix, 112 p. 21 cm. [BX2435.O73] 71-119797 2.50
1. Monastic and religious life. I. Title.

ORSY, Ladislas M., 248.8'94
1921-
Open to the Spirit; religious life after Vatican II, by Ladislas M. Orsy. Washington, Corpus Books [1968] 286 p. 22 cm. [BX2435.O35] 68-10453
1. Monastic and religious life. I. Title.

PEIFER, Claude J. 248.894
Monastic spirituality, by Claude J. Peifer. New York, Sheed [1966] xvii, 555 p. 24 cm. Bibl. [BX2435.P4] 66-12267 12.00
1. Monastic and religious life. I. Title.

PREDOVICH, Nicholas A. 248.8'94
The challenge of radical renewal [by] Nicholas A. Predovich. Pref. by Joseph M. Breitenbeck. Staten Island, N.Y., Alba House [1968] 159 p. illus. 22 cm. (Vocational perspectives series, 5) Bibliographical footnotes. [BX2385.P66] 68-31514 4.95
1. Monastic and religious life. I. Title.

RAHNER, Karl, 1904- 248'.894
The religious life today / [by] Karl Rahner ; [translated from the German by V. Green]. London : Burns and Oates, 1976. [5], 88 p. ; 22 cm. Translation of selections from Wagnis des Christen. Sequel to the author's Christians at the crossroads. Includes bibliographical references. [BX2435.R3313 1976] 76-380848 ISBN 0-86012-028-7 : £1.50
1. Monastic and religious life. I. Title.

RELIGIOUS orders in the 248.894
modern world; a symp. [by] Gerard Huyghe [others. Tr.from French by Walter Mitchell] Westminster, Md., New-man [1966, c.1965] viii, 172 p. 23 cm. Bibl. [BX2432.R3713] 66-10793 4.50
1. Monasticism and religious orders. I. Huyghe, Gerard, Bp., 1909-

ROMB, Anselm William, 248.8'94
1929-
Signs of contradiction; religious life in a time of change, by Anselm W. Romb. St. Louis, B. Herder Book Co. [1967] 215 p. 21 cm. [BX2435.R57] 66-30524
1. Monastic and religious life. I. Title.

SIKORA, Joseph John. 248.8'94
Calling; a reappraisal of religious life [by] Joseph J. Sikora. [New York] Herder and Herder [1968] 206 p. 21 cm. [BX2380.S5] 68-16995
1. Vocation (in religious orders, congregations, etc.) I. Title.

SISTERS' Conference on 248.894
Spirituality, University of Portland. 6th 1965.
Religious and the Vatican Council; lectures, edited by Joseph E. Haley. Portland, Or., University of Portland Press [1966] vi, 122 p. 22 cm. Bibliography: p. 115-116. [BX2435.S55 1965aa] 65-7107
1. Vatican Council. 2d, 1962-1965. 2. Monastic and religious life. I. Haley, Joseph Edmund ed. II. Portland, Or. University. III. Title.

TILLARD, J. M. R. 248.8/94
The mystery of religious life [by] J. M. R. Tillard. Edited by R. F. Smith. St. Louis, Herder Bk. [1967] 136p. 21cm. Essays orig. appeared in Review for religious. Bibl. [BX2435.T5] 67-30747 4.95
1. Monastic and religious life. I. Title.

VAN KAAM, Adrian L., 248.8'94
1920-
Personality fulfillment in the religious life, by Adrian Van Kaam. [1st American ed.] Wilkes-Barre, Pa., Dimension Books [1967- v. 21 cm. Sequel to the author's Personality fulfillment in the spiritual life. [BX2385.V3] 67-16816
1. Monastic and religious life. I. Title.

VATICAN Council. 2d,1962- 248.894
1965.
The decree on the renewal of religious life of Vatican Council II promulgated by Pope Paul VI, October 28, 1965. Translated by Austin Flannery. Commentary by Gregory Baum. [Study-club ed.] Glen Rock, N.J., Paulist Press, 1966. 92 p. 18 cm. (Vatican II documents) At head of title: Decretum de accomodata renovatione vitae religiosae. [BX 830 1962.A45D433] 66-19150
1. Monastic and religious life. 2. Vatican Council. 2d, 1962-1965. Decretum de accomodata renovatione vitae religiosae. I. Catholic Church. Pope, 1963- (Paulus VI) II. Baum, Gregory, 1923- III. Title.

VATICAN Council. 2d, 1962- 248.894
1965
The decree on the renewal of religious life of Vatican Council II promulgated by Pope Paul VI, October 28, 1965. Tr. by Austin Flannery. Commentary by Gregory Baum. Study-club ed. Glen Rock, N.J., Paulist. 1966 92p. 18cm. (Vatican II does.) At head of title: Decretum de accomodata renovatione vitae religiosae. [BX8301962.A45D433] 66-19150 .75 pap.,
1. Monastic and religious life. 2. Vatican Council. 2d. 1962-1965. Decretum de accomodata renovatione vitae religiosae. I. Catholic Church. Pope, 1963-(Paulus VI) II. Baum, Gregory, 1923- III. Title.

VATICAN Council. 2d, 248.8'94
1962-1965.
The religious life defined; an official commentary on the deliberations of the Second Vatican Council. Edited by Ralph M. Wiltgen. Techny, Ill., Divine Word Publications [1970] 135 p. 18 cm. "This book is for the most part a translation of an official commentary on the chapter about religious in the dogmatic constitution on the Church." "Companion volume to the Abbott-Gallagher translation of The documents of Vatican II." Includes bibliographical references. [BX2435.V36] 79-134495 1.95
1. Monastic and religious life. I. Wiltgen, Ralph M., 1921- ed. II. Vatican Council. 2d, 1962-1965. The documents of Vatican II. III. Title.

VOILLAUME, Rene. 248'.894
Spirituality from the desert : retreat at Beni-Abbes / Rene Voillaume ; translated by Alan Neame. Huntington, Ind. : Our Sunday Visitor, 1975. xi, 145 p. ; 21 cm. Translation of Retraite a Beni-Abbes. [BX2435.V62713 1975b] 75-37438 ISBN 0-87973-798-0 pbk. : 2.95
1. Monastic and religious life. I. Title.

WEBER, Carlo A., 1927- 248.8'94
The time of the fugitive; from ritual to self-discovery [by] Carlo Weber. [1st ed.] Garden City, N.Y., Doubleday, 1971. ix, 203 p. 22 cm. Based on an article which appeared in Commonweal, April 18, 1969. Includes bibliographical references. [BX2440.W36] 71-139071 5.95
1. Monastic and religious life—Psychology. 2. Christianity—20th century. 3. Ex-clergy. I. Title.

WESTHUES, Kenneth. 248.8'94
The religious community and the secular state. [1st ed.] Philadelphia, Lippincott [1968] 126 p. 21 cm. Bibliography: p. 123-[127] [BX2432.W4] 68-29728 3.95
1. Monasticism and religious orders. I. Title.

*VANN, Gerald 248.8940922
To heaven with Diana! A study of Jordan of Saxony and Diana d'Andalo, with a translation of the letters of Jordan. Chicago, Regnery [1965, c.1960] 160p. 18cm. (Logos bk., L707) 1.25 pap.,
I. Title.

GASQUET, Francis 248.8'94'094
Aidan, Cardinal, 1846-1929.
Monastic life in the Middle Ages, with a note on Great Britain and the Holy See, 1792-1806. Freeport, N.Y., Books for Libraries Press [1970] vii, 342 p. 23 cm. Reprint of the 1922 ed. Contents.Contents.—Abbot Wallingford.—The making of St. Alban's Shrine.—An abbot's household account book.—How your fathers were taught in Catholic days.—Books and bookmaking in early chronicles and accounts.—A pilgrimage to the Holy Land, A.D. 1506.—A day with the abbot of St. Augustine's, Canterbury, in the sixteenth century.—Roger Bacon and the Latin Vulgate.—Adrian IV and Ireland.—Polydore Vergil's "History."—A sketch of monastic constitutional history.—The English Premonstratensians.—Great Britain and the Holy See, 1792-1806. Includes bibliographical references. [BX2470.G3 1970] 76-137377 ISBN 0-8369-5578-1
1. Catholic Church—Relations (diplomatic) with Great Britain. 2. Monasticism and religious orders—Middle Ages, 600-1500. 3. Great Britain—Foreign relations—Catholic Church. I. Title.

INTER-AMERICAN 248'.894'098
Conference on Religious, 1st, Mexico City, 1971.
Priests and religious for Latin America; proceedings and conclusions. Washington, U.S. Catholic Conference, Division for Latin America [1971] viii, 120 p. 22 cm. "The Confederation of Latin American Religious prepared and presented the papers." Includes bibliographical references. [BX2529.5.I58 1971] 77-186994 1.50
1. Monasticism and religious orders—Latin America—Congresses. I. Confederacion Latinoamericana de Religiosos. II. Title.

THE Brother in the 248.8'942
church. Compiled and edited by William Modlin. With a foreword by Laurence Cardinal Shehan. Westminster, Md., Newman Press, 1967. xi, 212 p. 23 cm. Includes bibliographies. [BX2835.B7] 66-30458
1. Brothers (in religious orders, congregations, etc.) I. Modlin, William, comp.

CIAMPI, Luke M. 248'.8942
Watering the seed : for formation and growth in Franciscanism / by Luke M. Ciampi. Chicago : Franciscan Herald Press, [1976] p. cm. [BX3603.C53] 76-22471 ISBN 0-8199-0618-2 pbk. : 3.50
1. Franciscans—Spiritual life. I. Title.

CLAY, Rotha Mary. 248.8'942
The hermits and anchorites of England. London, Methuen [1964] Detroit, Singing Tree Press, 1968. xx, 272 p. illus. 22 cm. Bibliographical footnotes. [BX2847.G7C6 1968] 68-21759
1. Hermits—England. I. Title.

[GUILLERAND, Agustin] 248'.8942
1877-1945.
They speak by silences / by a Carthusian; translated from the French by a monk of Parkminster; foreword by Gordon Wheeler. Huntington, Ind. : Our Sunday Visitor, 1975. xiii, 79 p. ; 18 cm. Translation of extracts from Silence cartusien and Voix cartusienne. [BX3303.G8413 1975b] 75-37437 ISBN 0-87973-678-X pbk. : 1.50
1. Carthusians. 2. Spiritual life—Catholic authors. I. A Carthusian. II. Guillerand, Agustin, 1877-1945. Voix cartusienne. English. Selections. 1975. III. Title.

HEIJKE, John 248.8'942
An the renewal of religious community life: Taize. Fittsburgh, ecumenical light on Duquesne Univ. Pr. [1967] ix, 203p. 22cm. (Duquesne studies. Theol. ser., 7) Bibl. [BV4408.H4] 67-15785 4.50
1. Communaute de Taize. I. Title. II. Series.

HINNEBUSCH, William A 248.8'942
Dominican spirituality; principles and practice, by William A. Hinnebusch. Illus. by Sister Mary of the Compassion. [Washington, Thomist Press, 1967, c1965] ix, 148 p. illus. 21 cm. "Originated in a series of conferences to the Dominican Sisters of the Congregation of the Most Holy Cross, Amityville, New York, ... during the Lent of 1962." Bibliography: p. 145-148. [BX3503.H55] 64-66421
1. Dominicans—Spiritual life. I. Title.

JESUIT spirit in a time 248.8'942
of change, edited by Raymond A. Schroth [and others] Westminister, Md., Newman Press [1968] vi, 250 p. 22 cm. "Essays, nearly all of which have appeared in Woodstock letters." Bibliographical footnotes. [BX3703.J4] 68-16673
1. Jesuits—Spiritual life. I. Schroth, Raymond A., comp. II. Woodstock letters.

LAZARO de Aspurz, 248'.8942
Father.
The Franciscan calling, by Lazaro Iriarte de Aspurz. Translated by Carole Marie Kelly. Chicago, Franciscan Harold Press, c1974. x, 242 p. 21 cm. Translation of Vocacion franciscana. Bibliography: p. 237-242. [BX3603.L3813] 74-10847 ISBN 0-8199-0538-0
1. Franciscans—Spiritual life. I. Title.

LESAGE, Germain. 248.8'942
Personalism and vocation. Staten Island, N.Y., Alba House [1966] 252 p. 22 cm. Bibliography: p. [251]-252. [BX2380.L56] 66-19718
1. Vocation (in religious orders, congregation, etc.) I. Title.

LOMBARDI, Riccardo. 248.8'942
Vatican II ... and now; a retreat to the fathers of the Council, November 8-11, 1965. Washington, Movement for a Better World [1967] 144 p. 19 cm. Ten meditations translated from the Italian. [BX1912.5.L6] 73-6008
1. Vatican Council. 2d, 1962-1965. 2. Clergy—Religious life. I. Title.

MCNASPY, Clement J. 248.8'942
Change not changes; new directions in religious life and priesthood, by Clement J. McNaspy. New York [Paulist Press, 1968] viii, 164 p. 18 cm. (Deus books) Bibliography: p. 158-164. [BX3703.M3] 68-21455
1. Jesuits—Spiritual life. I. Title.

**PRAYER of love and* 248.8'942
silence (The), by a Carthusian. Tr. from French by a Monk of Parkminster. Wilkes-Barre, Pa., Dimension [1968,c.1962] 18cm. 1.25 pap.,

RYELANDT, Idesbald. 248.8'942
Union with Christ; Benedictine and liturgical spirituality. [Translated from the French by Matthew Dillon] Wilkes-Barre, Pa., Dimension Books [1966] 175 p. 21 cm. [BX3003.R9313 1966a] 65-25564
1. Catholic Church. Liturgy and ritual. 2. Benedictines. 3. Spiritual life—Catholic authors. I. Title.

VANDENBROUCKE, 248'.8942
Francois.
Why monks? Translated by Leon Brockman. Washington, Cistercian Publications, 1972. xvi, 185 p. 23 cm. (Cistercian studies series, no. 17) Translation of Moines: pourquoi? Includes bibliographical references. [BX2432.V313] 75-182090 ISBN 0-87907-817-0 10.95
1. Monasticism and religious orders. 2. Monastic and religious life. I. Title. II. Series.

VICAIRE, Marie Humbert, 248.8942
1906-
The apostolic life [by] M. H. Vicaire. Pref. by John D. Fitzgerald. Chicago, Priory Press [1966] 121 p. 20 cm. Translation of L'imitation des apotres. [BX2470.V513] 66-17483
1. Monasticism and religious orders — Middle Ages. I. Title.

VICAIRE, Marie Humbert, 248.8942
1906-
The apostolic life. Pref. by John D. Fitzgerald. [Tr. from French by William E. De Naple] Chicago, Priory Pr. [c.1966] 121p. 20cm. [BX2470.V513] 66-17483 2.95
1. Monasticism and religious orders—Middle Ages. I. Title.

CALVIN, Ross, 1889- 248.89420924
Barnabas in Pittsburgh; from common clay to legend. New York, Carlton Press [1966] 170 p. 21 cm. (A Reflection book) [BX5995.H29C3] 66-5476
1. Hance, Gouverneur Provost. 2. St. Barnabas Brotherhood. I. Title.

CALVIN, Ross, 1889- 248.89420924
Barnabas in Pittsburgh, from common clay to legend. New York, Carlton [c.1966] 170 p. 21 cm (reflection bk.) [[bx5995.h29c3]] 66.5476 3.50
1. Hance, Gouverneur ProvostSt. barnabas Brotherhood. I. Title.

MERTON, 248.8'942'09769495
Thomas, 1915-.
Gethsemani; a life of praise. Text by Thomas Merton. [n.p., 1966] 1 v. (unpaged) illus. 29 cm. [BX2525.N35G3] 67-7534
1. Gethsemani (Trappist Abbey) Nelson Co., Ky. 2. Monasticism and religious life. I. Title.

ASSESSMENT of 248.8'9422
candidates for the religious life; basic psychological issues and procedures [by] Walter J. Coville [and others] Foreword by William C. Bier. Washington, Center for Applied Research in the Apostolate [1968] xxiii, 215 p. 22 cm. (CARA information service publication) Contains four papers originally presented at a workshop sponsored by the American Catholic Psychological Association held in New York City in 1966. Includes bibliographies. [BX2380.A75] 68-5252
1. Vocation (in religious orders, congregations, etc.) I. Coville, Walter J. II. American Catholic Psychological Association.

DERATANY, Edward. 248'.89422
When God calls you / Edward Deratany. Nashville : T. Nelson, [1976] 206 p. ; 21 cm. Includes bibliographical references. [BV4740.D45] 76-6539 ISBN 0-8407-5601-1 pbk. : 3.95
1. Vocation. I. Title.

WEISGERBER, Charles 248.8'9425
A., 1912-
Psychological assessment of candidates for a religious order [by] Charles A. Weisgerber. Chicago, Loyola University Press [1969] viii, 191 p. 23 cm. Includes bibliographies. [BX2440.W4] 77-91649
1. Monastic and religious life—Psychology. I. Title.

KNOWLES, David, 1896- 248.89428
From Pachomius to Ignatius: a study in the constitutional history of the religious orders. Oxford, Clarendon Pr., 1966. [7] 98p. 19cm. (Sarum lects., 1964-5) Bibl. [BX2461.2.K57] 66-73649 2.40
1. Monasticism and religious orders—Hist. 2. Monasticism and religious orders—Hist. 3. Monasticism and religious orders—Rules. I. Title. II. Series.
Available from Oxford in New York.

ALBERIONE, Giacomo 248.8943
Giuseppe, 1884-
The superior follows the master, by James Alberione. Translated by a Daughter of St. Paul. [Boston] St. Paul Editions [1965] 213 p. 19 cm. [BX4212.A413] 65-24080
1. Superiors, Religious. I. Title.

ALBERIONE, Giacomo 248.8943
Giuseppe, 1884-
The superior follows the master, by James Alberione. Tr. by a Daughter of St. Paul. [Boston] St. Paul Eds. [dist. Daughters of St. Paul, c.1965] 213p. 19cm. [BX4212.A413] 65-24080 3.00; 2.00 pap.,
1. Superiors, Religious. I. Title.

BALLA, Ignazia. 248'.8943
Our continuing yes, by M. I. B. (Mother Ignatius Balla) Translated by the Daughters of St. Paul. [Boston] St. Paul Editions [1972] 176 p. 20 cm. [BX2435.B313] 72-79298 3.00
1. Monastic and religious life. I. Title.

BOUGIER, Marie 248.8943
Witness and consecration [by] Sister Jeanne d'Arc. [Tr. by Martin Murphy] Chicago, Priory Pr. [1966] 312p. 23cm. Translation of Les religieuses dans l'eglise et dans le monde actuel. Bibl. [BX4210.B6813] 66-22551 5.95 bds.,
1. Monastic and religious life of women. I. Title.

CEGIELKA, Francis A 248'.8943
Spiritual theology for novices. Lodi, N. J., Immaculate Conception College [1961] 132p. 21cm. [BX4210.C37] 61-17401
1. Spiritual life—Catholic authors. 2. Monastic and religious life of women. I. Title.

CONSORTIUM Perfectae 248'.8943
Caritatis.
The religious woman, minister of faith : a compilation of addresses given at first international assembly, Consortium Perfectae Caritatis, February 23-March 4, 1974, Rome, Italy. Boston : St. Paul Editions, [1974] 372 p. ; 18 cm. [BX4210.C58 1974] 74-16745 pbk. : 2.50
1. Monastic and religious life of women—Congresses. I. Title.

CONSORTIUM Perfectae 248'.8943
Caritatis.
The woman religious—the heart of the Church : a compilation of addresses given at Consortium Perfectae Caritatis, April 4-6, 1975, Chicago, Illinois. Boston : St. Paul Editions, [1975] p. cm. (Magister paperback series) [BX4210.C58 1975] 75-25533
1. Monastic and religious life of women—Congresses. I. Title.

EVOY, John J. 248.8'943
The real woman in the religious life, by John J. Evoy and Van F. Christoph. New York, Sheed [1967] x, 240, [1] p. 22cm. Bibl. [BX4210.E9] 67-13773 5.00
1. Monastic and religious life of women. I. Christoph, Van Francis, joint author. II. Title.

GAMBARI, Elio. 248'.8943
The religious-apostolic formation of Sisters. Foreword by Arcadio Cardianl Larraona. New York, Fordham University Press [1964] xii, 188 p. 24 cm. Includes bibliographical references. [BX4210.5.G3] 63-23173
1. Monasticism and religious orders for women — Education. I. Title.

GARRONE, Gabriel Marie, 248.8'943
1901-
The nun: sacrament of God's saving presence. Staten Island, N.Y., Alba House [1967] 190 p. 22 cm. (Vocational perspectives series, 3) Translation of La religieuse, signe de Dieu dans le monde. [BX4214.G313] 67-21423
1. Monastic and religious life of women. 2. Retreats for members of religious orders. I. Title.

HUYGHE, Gerard, Bp., 248.8943
1909-.
Tensions and change; the problems of religious orders today. Translated by Sister Marie Florette. Westminister, Md., Newman Press, 1965. xvi, 270 p. 23 cm. Translation of Eqilibre et adaptation. [BX4205.H813] 65-25983
1. Monastic and religious life of women. I. Title.

HUYGHE, Gerard, Bp., 248.8943
1909-
Tensions and change; the problems of religious orders today. Tr. [from French] by Sister Marie Florette. Westminster, Md., Newman [c.]1965. xvi, 270p. 23cm. [BX4205.H813] 65-25983 4.95
1. Monastic and religious life of women. I. Title.

INSTITUTE on Problems 248.8943
That Unite Us, Mundelein College, 1965.
Proceedings. Dubuque, Iowa, Sisters of Charity, BVM [1966] xv, 302p. 23cm. Sponsored by the Sisters of Charity of the Blessed Virgin Mary. [BX4210.I55 1965] 66-27537 3.00
1. Monastic and religious life of women—Congresses. I. Sisters of Charity of the Blessed Virgin Mary, Dubuque, Iowa. II. Mundelein College for Women, Chicago. III. Title.

JEAN Marie, Sister, 248.8943
O.S.B.
Years of sunshine, days of rain. Westminster, Md., Newman Press, 1966. 145 p. 22 cm. [BX4210.J4] 66-28813
1. Monastic and religious life of women. 2. Meditations. I. Title.

JEAN MAIE, Sister, O. 248.8943
S. B
Years of sunshine, days of rain. Westminster, Md., Newman, 1966. 145p. 22cm. [BX4210.J4] 66-28813 .50
1. Monastic and religious life of women. 2. Meditations. I. Title.

MCALLISTER, Robert J., 248.8'943
1919-
Conflict in community, by Robert J. McAllister. Collegeville, Minn., St. John's University Press [1969] xv, 110 p. 24 cm. [BX4205.M25] 77-83089 4.50
1. Monastic and religious life of women—Psychology. I. Title.

MCCONNELL, Margaret. 248.8'943
Open then the door. [1st American ed.] New York, Transatlantic Arts [1968, c1967] vii, 183 p. 21 cm. [BX4705.M179A3 1968] 68-3401
1. Monastic and religious life of women. I. Title.

MCGOLDRICK, Desmond F. 248.8943
Fostering development; a critique, in tabloid, on the exercise of religious authority. Pittsburgh, Duquesne Univ. Pr. [c.]1965. 242p. 20cm. (Duquesne Sister formation ser., 4) [BX4212.M2] 65-22934 4.95
1. Monasticism and religious orders for women—Government. 2. Superiors, Religious. I. Title. II. Series.

MARY LAURENCE, Sister. 248.8943
Love is my calling. Staten Island, N.Y., Alba [c.1965] 149p. 21cm. Bibl. [BX4210.M323] 65-17974 3.50
1. Monastic and religious life of women. I. Title.

MEYERS, Bertrande. 248'.8943
Gleanings : Sister Bertrande Meyers, Daughter of Charity : an anthology of published articles and addresses / edited by Beatrice Brown. 1st ed. Hicksville, N.Y. : Exposition Press, c1976. xi, 132 p. ; 22 cm. (An Exposition-testament book) Bibliography: p. 130-132. [BX4210.M45 1976] 76-150154 ISBN 0-682-48522-5 : 5.50
1. Catholic Church—Education—Addresses, essays, lectures. 2. Monastic and religious life of women—Addresses, essays, lectures. I. Title.
Contents omitted

MUCKENHIRN, Charles 248.8943
Borromeo, sister ed.
The changing Sister. Contributors: Marie Augusta Neal [others] Foreword by George N. Shuster. Notre Dame, Ind., Fides, 1965. viii, 326p. 21cm. Bibl. [BX4205.M8] 65-22150 5.95; 2.95 pap.,
1. Monastic and religious life of women. I. Neal, Marie Augusta. II. Title.

MUCKENHIRN, Charles 248.8'943
Borromeo, Sister, comp.
The new nuns, edited by Sister M. Charles Borromeo. [New York] New American Library [1967] vi, 216 p. 21 cm. [BX4205.M82] 67-21801
1. Monasticism and religious orders for women. 2. Monastic and religious life of women. I. Title.

MUCKENHIRN, Charles 248.8'943
Borromeo, Sister, comp.
The new nuns, edited by Sister M. Charles Borromeo. [New York] New American Library [1967] vi, 216 p. 21 cm. [BX4205.M82] 67-21801
1. Monasticism and religious orders for women. 2. Monastic and religious life of women. I. Title.

O'KEEFE, Maureen. 248.8943
Christian love in religious life. Chicago, H. Regnery [1965] 206 p. 21 cm. [BX4210.O66] 65-26907
1. Monastic and religious life of women. 2. Charity. I. Title.

O'KEEFE, Maureen 248.8943
Christian love in religious life. Chicago, Regnery [c.1965] 206p. 21cm. [BX4210.O66] 65-26907 4.50
1. Monastic and religious life of women. 2. Charity. I. Title.

O KEEFE, Maureen Sister 248'.8943
The conyent in the modern world. Chicago, Regnery [1967, c.1963] ix, 143p. 18cm. (Logos, 71L-729) [BX4210.O67] 271 1.45 pap.,
1. Monastic and religious life of women. I. Title.

PEYRIGUERE, Albert. 248.8'943
Voice from the desert. Translated by Agnes M. Forsyth and Anne Marie de Commaille. New York, Sheed and Ward [1967] 158 p. 21 cm. "Translated from Laissez-vous salsir par le Christ." [BX2350.2.P4813] 67-13775
1. Spiritual life—Catholic authors. I. Title.

RENARD, Alexandre 248.8'943
Charles, 1906-
The new spirit in the convent, by Alexander [sic] Cardinal Renard. [Translated from the French by Sister M. Benoit. 1st American ed.] Wilkes-Barre, Pa., Dimension Books [1968] 122 p. 18 cm. Translation of Les religieuses dans le renouveau de l'Eglise. [BX4205.R413 1968] 68-13731
1. Monasticism and religious orders for women. I. Title.

ROMB, Anselm William, 248.8'943
1929-
Across the churchyard; priests and sisters in the contemporary church, by Anselm W. Romb. St. Louis, B. Herder Book Co. [1968] 105 p. 21 cm. Bibliographical footnotes. [BX4210.R63] 68-26109
1. Monastic and religious life of women. 2. Spiritual direction. I. Title.

SISTERS' Conference on 248.8943
Spirituality, University of Portland.
The Sister in America today; [selected papers from the meetings, 1960-63] Editor: Joseph E. Haley. Contributors: Sister Mary Emil [and others] Notre Dame, Ind., Fides Publishers [1965] viii, 199 p. 21 cm. Organized by the Dept. of Religion, University of Portland. Includes bibliographies. [BX4210.S525] 65-13799
1. Monastic and religious life of women — Congresses. I. Haley, Joseph Edmund. ed. II. Portland, Or. University, Dept. of Religion. III. Title.

SISTERS' Conference on 248.8943
Spirituality, University of Portland.
The Sister in America today; [selected papers from the meetings, 1960-63] Ed.: Joseph E. Haley. Contrib. Sister Mary Emil [others] Notre Dame, Ind., Fides [c.1965] viii, 199p. 21cm. Org. by the Dept. of Religion, Univ. of Portland. Bibl. [BX4210.S525] 65-13799 4.95; 2.95 pap.,
1. Monastic and religious life of women—Congresses. I. Haley, Joseph Edmund, ed. II. Portland, Or. University. Dept. of Religion. III. Title.

SISTERS' Conference on 248'.8943
Spirituality, University of Portland, 1964.
Mental health and religious; lectures. Edited by Joseph E. Haley. Portland, Or., University of Portland Press [1965] vi, 136 p. 22 cm. Organized by the Dept. of Religion, University of Portland. [BX4210.S526 1964aa] 248 65-5153
1. Monastic and religious life of women — Congresses. I. Haley, Joseph Edmund, ed. II. Portland, Or. University. Dept. of Religion. III. Title.

SMITH, Hilary. 248.8'943
Realism in renewal; a guide to survival for sisters and others. Techny, Ill., Divine Word Publications [1969] 177 p. 21 cm. Bibliographical footnotes. [BX4205.S56] 69-20418 4.50
1. Monastic and religious life of women. I. Title.

TATE, Judith 248.8943
Sisters for the world. [New York] Herder &

Herder [1966] 141p. 21cm. Bibl. [BX4210.T3] 66-26678 3.50
1. Monastic and religious life of women. I. Title.

VALENTINE, Mary Hester. 248.8'943
The post-conciliar nun. [1st ed.] New York, Hawthorn Books [1968] 157 p. 22 cm. (Catholic perspectives) Bibliographical references included in "Notes" (p. 153-157) [BX4205.V3] 68-19113
1. Monastic and religious life of women. I. Title.

PSYCHOLOGICAL 248.8'943'019
dimensions of the religious life [by] Charles A. Curran, John I. Nurnberger [and] Sister Annette. [Notre Dame, Ind.] University of Notre Dame Press, 1966. 172 p. 21 cm. (Religious life in the modern world v. 6) "Articles ... published previously in the Proceedings of the Sisters' Institute of Spirituality 1959 and 1960 and the Proceedings of the Institute for Local Superiors 1962." Contents.Contents.—Counseling and guidance, by C. A. Curran.—Personality disorders and procedures, by J. I. Nurnberger.—Psychological aspects of modern-day religious life, by Sister Annette. Includes bibliographical references. [BX4205.P75] 66-21170 1.95
1. Monastic and religious life of women—Psychology. I. Curran, Charles Arthur. Counseling and guidance. II. Nurnberger, John I. Personality disorders and procedures. III. Walters, Annette, Sister, 1910- Psychological aspects of modern-day religious life. IV. Title. V. Series.

SISTERS' Conference on 248.894308
Spirituality, University of Portland.
New directions in religious life. Selected lectures from the Sisters' Conference on Spirituality, University of Portland. Edited by Joseph E. Haley. Portland, Or., University of Portland Press [1965] v, 134 p. 22 cm. [BX4210.S523] 65-29551
1. Monastic and religious life of women — Congresses. 2. Christian life — Congresses. I. Haley, Joseph Edmund, ed. II. Title.

AGNES Martha, 248.8'943'0924
Sister, S.C.H.
Nothing on earth. Milwaukee, Bruce [1967] ix, 148 p. 21 cm. [BX4210.A4] 67-21494
1. Nuns—Correspondence, reminiscences, etc. I. Title.

CODE, Joseph 248.8'943'0922
Bernard, 1899-
Great American foundresses, by Joseph B. Code. Freeport, N.Y., Books for Libraries Press [1968] xviii, 512 p. ports. 22 cm. (Essay index reprint series) "First published 1929." Contents.Contents.—Mother D'Youville, of the Grey Nuns of Montreal.—Mother Clare Joseph Dickinson, of the Carmelites of Maryland.—Mother Elizabeth Ann Seton, of the Sisters of Charity of St. Vincent de Paul.—Mother Mary Rhodes, of the Sisters of Loretto at the Foot of the Cross.—Mother Catherine Spalding, of the Sisters of Charity of Nazareth.—Mother Teresa Lalor, of the Nuns of the Visitation of Georgetown.—Mother Philippine Duchesne, of the Religious of the Sacred Heart.—Mother Angela Sansbury, of the Dominicans of Kentucky.—Mother Mary Francis Clarke, of the Sisters of Charity of the Blessed Virgin Mary.—Mother Theodore Guerin, of the Sisters of Providence of St. Mary-of-the-Woods.—Mother Gamelin, of the Sisters of Charity of Providence.—Mother Mary Xavier Warde, of the Sisters of Mercy.—Mother Mary Rose Durocher, of the Sisters of the Holy Names of Jesus and Mary.—Mother Cornelia Connelly, of the Religious of the Holy Child Jesus.—Mother Mary Amadeus of the Heart of Jesus, of the Ursulines of Montana and Alaska.—Mother Alphonsa Lathrop, of the Dominican Sisters, Servants of Relief for Incurable Cancer. [BX4225.C6 1968] 68-20291
1. Nuns. 2. Women—United States—Biography. I. Title.

HARRIS, Sara. 248.8'943'0973
The sisters; the changing world of the American nun. Indianapolis, Bobbs-Merrill [1971, c1970] 333 p. 22 cm. [BX4220.U6H35] 71-81289 7.50
1. Monastic and religious life of women—U.S. I. Title.

DUBAY, Thomas. 248.8'9432
Ecclesial women; towards a theology of the religious state. Staten Island, N.Y., Alba House [1970] ix, 119 p. 22 cm. (Vocational perspectives series, 7) Includes bibliographical references. [BX4210.D8] 77-110589 3.95
1. Monastic and religious life of women. I. Title.

HENDERSON, Nancy. 248.8'943'2
Out of the curtained world; the story of an American nun who left the convent. [1st ed.] Garden City, N.Y., Doubleday, 1972. 276 p. 22 cm. [BX4668.3.H45A35] 74-171297 6.95
1. Ex-nuns—Personal narratives. I. Title.

HENDERSON, Nancy. 248.8'943'2
Out of the curtained world. New York Pyramid Books [1974, c1972] 285 p. 18 cm. [BX4668.3.H45A35] ISBN 0-515-03383-9 1.50 (pbk.)
1. Ex-nuns—Personal narratives. I. Title.
L.C. card no. for original edition: 74-1711297.

MARY Maureen, Sister, 248.8'9432
S. M. S. M.
Your calling as a nun; a sense of mission. [1st ed.] New York, R. Rosen Press [1967] 142 p. illus. 22 cm. (Careers in depth) Bibliography: p. 115-120. Bibliographical footnotes. [BX4210.M328] 66-10997
1. Monastic and religious life of women. 2. Vocation. I. Title.

ANCREN riwle. 248.8'9438
The nun's rule, being the Ancren riwle modernised by James Morton, with introd. by Abbot Gasquet. New York, Cooper Square Publishers, 1966. xxvii, 339 p. front. 17 cm. (The Medieval library) [PR1808.M6 1966] 66-23314
1. Monasticism and religious orders for women. 2. Monasticism and religious orders—Rules. I. Morton, James, 1783-1865. II. Gasquet, Francis Aidan, Cardinal, 1846-1929. III. Title.

GROSS, Mynette, sister 248.89438
1911-
The contemporary sister in the apostolate of home visitation. Washington, D.C., Catholic Univ. [c.1966] vi, 121p. 22cm. Bibl. [BX4205.G7] 66-17753 2.95 pap.,
1. Visitations (church work) 2. Monasticism and religious orders for women. I. Title.

HANSEL, Robert R. 248.9'
Free to be Christian in high school. New York, Seabury [1967] 78p. illus. 21cm. Prepd. under the auspices of the Dept. of Christian Educ. of the Episcopal Church (Senior high sch. unit. Study units on contemp. concerns) .95 pap.,
I. Title.

JONES, Franklin, comp. 248'.9'19
The spiritual instructions of Saint Seraphim of Sarov. Edited and with an introd. by Franklin Jones (Bubba Free John). Los Angeles, Dawn Horse Press [1973] xi, 83 p. 21 cm. [BX597.S37J57] 73-89308 ISBN 0-913922-05-6 1.95 (pbk.)
1. Serafim, Saint, 1759-1833. I. Motovilov, Nikolai Aleksandrovich. II. Dobbie-Bateman, A. F. The life and spiritual instructions of St. Seraphim of Sarov. 1973. III. Serafim, Saint, 1759-1833. A conversation of St. Seraphim of Sarov with Nicholas Motovilov concerning the aim of a Christian life. 1973. IV. Title.
Contents omitted.

JONES, Franklin, comp. 248'.9'19
The spiritual instructions of Saint Seraphim of Sarov. Edited and with an introd. by Franklin Jones (Bubba Free John). Los Angeles, Dawn Horse Press [1973] xi, 83 p. 21 cm. Contents.Contents.—The life and spiritual instructions of St. Seraphim of Sarov, by A. F. Dobbie-Bateman.—A conversation of St. Seraphim of Sarov with Nicholas Motovilov concerning the aim of a Christian life.—The spiritual technique of St. Seraphim and the Adept-Saints of the Eastern Christian Church. [BX597.S37J57] 73-89308 ISBN 0-913922-05-6 1.95
1. Serafim, Saint, 1759-1833. I. Motovilov, Nikolai Aleksandrovich. II. Dobbie-Bateman, A. F. The life and spiritual instructions of St. Seraphim of Sarov. 1973. III. Serafim, Saint, 1759-1833. A conversation of St. Seraphim of Sarov with Nicholas Motovilov concerning the aim of a Christian life. 1973. IV. Title.

MCNAMARA, William. 248'.9'2
The human adventure; contemplation for everyman. [1st ed.] Garden City, N.Y., Doubleday, 1974. 190 p. 22 cm. Bibliography: p. [189]-190. [BX2350.2.M274] 73-10862 ISBN 0-385-08993-7 5.95
1. Christian life—Catholic authors. 2. Experience (Religion) 3. Mysticism. I. Title.

MCNAMARA, William 248.92
The human adventure : contemplation for everyman. Garden City, N. Y. : Doubleday [1976c1974] 195p. ; 18 cm. (Image books) Bibliography: p. 194-195. [BX2350.2.M274] ISBN 0-385-11370-6 pbk. : 1.75
1. Christian life-Catholic authors. 2. Experience(religion). 3. Mysticism. I. Title.
L. C. card no. for original edition: 73-10862.

MANTON, Joseph E., 1904- 248.9'2
Happiness over the hill; reflections for everyday Christian living, by Joseph E. Manton. Huntington, Ind., Our Sunday Visitor [1970] 190 p. 21 cm. [BX2350.2.M325] 76-138603 1.95
1. Christian life—Catholic authors. I. Title.

MARTIN, Ralph, 1942- 248'.9'2
Hungry for God; practical help in personal prayer. [1st ed.] Garden City, N.Y., Doubleday 1974. 168 p. 21 cm. Includes bibliographical references. [BX2350.57.M37] 74-4830 ISBN 0-385-09535-X 5.95
1. Pentecostalism. 2. Spiritual life—Catholic authors. 3. Prayer. I. Title.

O'MEARA, Thomas F., 248'.9'2
1935-
Loose in the world, by Thomas Franklin O'Meara. New York, Paulist Press [1974] 120 p. 19 cm. (Deus books) Includes bibliographical references. [BR121.2.O48] 73-94214 ISBN 0-8091-1819-X 1.45 (pbk.)
1. Christianity—20th century. I. Title.

O'REILLY, James D. 248'.9'2
Lay and religious states of life : their distinction and complementarity / [James O'Reilly] Chicago : Franciscan Herald Press, 1977, c1976 54 p. ; 18 cm. (Synthesis series) [BX2435.O72] 76-43048 ISBN 0-8199-0715-4 pbk. : 0.65
1. Monastic and religious life. 2. Christian life—Catholic authors. I. Title.

RATZINGER, Joseph. 248.9'2
Being Christian. Translated by David Walls. [Chicago] Franciscan Herald Press [1970] x, 85 p. 20 cm. The first three items in this work were originally published under title: Vom Sinn des Christseins. [BX2350.2.R37] 70-123594 ISBN 0-8199-0409-0 3.95
1. Christian life—Catholic authors. I. Title.

HEYER, Robert J., 248.9'2'08
comp.
The aware person in today's church [by] Robert J. Heyer [and] Daniel J. Gatti. New York, Holt, Rinehart and Winston [1969] 268 p. illus. 23 cm. [BV4501.2.H395] 74-20207 ISBN 0-03-081488-X
1. Christian life—1960- 2. Church renewal. I. Gatti, Daniel J., joint comp. II. Title.

NEWTON, John, 1725- [248]922.342
1807.
Voice of the heart: Cardiphonia. With a biographical sketch of the author by William Culbertson. Chicago, Moody Press, 1950. 432 p. 23 cm. (The Wycliffe series of Christian classics) Previous editions published under title: Cardiphonia. Bibliography: p. 22. [BX5199.N55A35] 51-1389
I. Title. II. Series.

BOYD, Malcolm, 1923- 248'.9'3
The runner. Waco, Tex., Word Books [1974] 203 p. 23 cm. [BT202.B677] 73-91012 5.95
1. Jesus Christ—Person and offices. 2. Christian life—Anglican authors. I. Title.

JONES, Alan W., 1940- 248'.9'3
Journey into Christ / Alan Jones. New York : Seabury Press, 1977. p. cm. "A crossroad book." Bibliography: p. [BV4501.2.J585] 76-30656 ISBN 0-8164-0338-4 : 8.95
1. Spiritual life—Anglican authors. I. Title.

JONES, Alan W., 1940- 248'.9'3
Journey into Christ / Alan Jones. New York : Seabury Press, 1977. p. cm. "A crossroad book." Bibliography: p. [BV4501.2.J585] 76-30656 ISBN 0-8164-0338-4 : 8.95
1. Spiritual life—Anglican authors. I. Title.

LAW, William, 1686-1761. 248'.9'3
Wholly for God : selections from the writings of William Law / edited by Andrew Murray. Minneapolis : Bethany Fellowship, 1976. xxxii, 328 p. ; 18 cm. (Dimension books) Reprint of the 1894 ed. published by J. Nisbet, London. Includes bibliographical references. [BV4500.L34 1976] 76-6622 ISBN 0-87123-602-8 pbk. : 2.75
1. Spiritual life—Anglican authors—Addresses, essays, lectures. I. Title.

MCGEE, James Sears, 248'.9'3
1942-
The godly man in Stuart England : Anglicans, Puritans, and the two Tables, 1620-1670 / J. Sears McGee. New Haven : Yale University Press, 1976. xviii, 299 p. ; 22 cm. (Yale historical publications : Miscellany ; 110) Includes index. Bibliography: p. 275-291. [BX5075.M3] 75-43325 ISBN 0-300-01637-9 : 17.50
1. Anglicans. 2. Puritans—England. 3. Great Britain—Religion—17th century. 4. Great Britain—History—Civil War, 1642-1649. I. Title. II. Series.

WILLIAMS, Harry Abbott. 248'.9'3
Tensions : necessary conflicts in life and love / [by] H. A. Williams. London : Mitchell Beazley, 1976. 120 p. ; 22 cm. [BV4501.2.W537 1976] 76-376546 ISBN 0-85533-079-1 : £2.00
1. Christian life—Anglican authors. I. Title.

LLOYD, Sarah, pseud. 248.9'4'1
Claimed by God, a course for seventh and eighth grades, by Sarah Lloyd [pseud.] & Jane Evans [pseud.] Boston, United Church Press [1963] 128 p. illus. 26 cm. "JH I-1." [BX9884.A3L55] 63-7420
1. Religious education — Text-books for children — United Church of Christ. I. Evans, Jane, pseud. joint author. II. Title.

SCHULTZ, Richard J. 248.9'4'1
The Christian's mission [by] Richard J. Schultz. Edited by Oscar E. Feucht. Saint Louis, Concordia Pub. House [1970] 96 p. 21 cm. (The Discipleship series) Includes bibliographies. [BV601.8.S36 1970] 70-119917
1. Mission of the church. I. Title.

UNITED Dhurch of 248.9'4'1
Christ.
Year book. 1962- [New York] v. 24 cm. Formed by the merger of the Year book of the Congregational Christian churches and the Year book of the Evangelical and Reformed Church. Each vol. contains statistics for the previous year. Vols. for 1962- include statistics for Congregational Christian churches which had not yet voted and for those which had voted to remain outside the United Church of Christ. [BX9884.A1U55] 65-29474
1. United Church of Christ — Yearbooks. I. Title.

WETZEL, Willard W 248.9'4'1
The Christian view of man. Boston, United Church Press [c1963] 234 p. illus. 21 cm. [BX9884.A3W4] 63-19207
1. Religious education — Text-books for adults — United Church of Christ. I. Title.

CALIAN, Carnegie Samuel. 248'.9'5
The gospel according to the Wall Street journal / Carnegie Samuel Calian. Atlanta : John Knox Press, [1975] 114 p. ; 21 cm. Includes bibliographical references. [PN4899.N42W24] 74-19971 ISBN 0-8042-0826-3 pbk : 3.95
1. Wall Street journal. 2. Christianity and economics. 3. Christian life—1960- I. Title.

GOD'S hand in my life 248'.9'673
/ compiled by Lawrence T. Geraty. Nashville : Southern Pub. Association, [1977] p. cm. [BX6191.G63] 77-12585 ISBN 0-8127-0151-8 pbk. : 4.95
1. Seventh-Day Adventists—Biography. 2. Christian life—Seventh-Day Adventist authors. I. Geraty, Lawrence T.

WESLEY, John, 1703-1791. 248'.97
Fire of love : the spirituality of John Wesley / [compiled by] Gordon Wakefield. London : Darton, Longman and Todd, 1976. 80 p. ; 19 cm. Includes bibliographies. [BV4510.A1W45 1976] 77-350375 ISBN 0-232-51357-0 : £0.95
1. Christian life—Methodist authors—Collected works. I. Title.

CANNON, D. James. 248.9'93
Mormon essays [by] D. James Cannon. Salt Lake City, Deseret Book Co., 1970. 221 p. 18 cm. At head of title: "... experiment upon my words ..." [BX8656.C3] 72-148055 ISBN 0-87747-412-5 3.95
1. Christian life—Mormon authors. I. Title.

ROBINSON, Christine 248.9'93
Hinckley.
Inspirational truths from the doctrine and covenants [by] Christine H. Robinson. Salt Lake City, Deseret Book Co., 1970. xv, 239 p. 24 cm. Includes bibliographical references. [BX8656.R6] 70-149511 ISBN 0-87747-389-7 3.95
1. Christian life—Mormon authors. I. Title.

LONSDALE, Kathleen 248'.9'96
Yardley, Dame, 1903-1971.
The Christian life lived experimentally : an anthology of the writings of Kathleen Lonsdale / selected by James Hough. London : Friends Home Service Committee, 1976. 59 p. ; 19 cm. Bibliography: p. 58-59. [BX7795.L65A25 1976] 76-376812 ISBN 0-85245-121-0 : £0.90
I. Title.

MARK Age, 1922- 248.9'99
How to do all things; your use of divine power. [1st ed.] Miami, Fla., Published for the Hierarchal Board by Mark-Age [1970] 144 p. 24 cm. [BJ1581.2.M34] 72-121118 5.00
1. Conduct of life. I. Title.

249 Worship In Family Life

AASENG, Rolf E. 249
Come, Lord Jesus; devotions for families with children, by Rolf E. Aaseng. Designed and illustrated by Don Wallerstedt. Minneapolis, Augsburg Pub. House [1974] 144 p. illus. 22 cm. [BV255.A17] 74-77675 ISBN 0-8066-1423-4 3.50 (pbk.)

1. Family—Prayer-books and devotions—English. I. Title.

ANDERSON, Doris (Jones) 249
How to raise a Christian family; a mother shows that living together can be fun. Grand Rapids, Mich., Zondervan Pub. House [c.1960] 117p. 20cm. 60-2522 2.00 bds.,
1. Family—Religious life. I. Title.

ANDERSON, Doris (Jones) 1918- 249
How to raise a Christian family: a mother shows that living together can be fun. Grand Rapids, Zondervan Pub. House, 1960 117p. 20cm. [BV4526.A65] 60-2522
1. Family—Religious life. I. Title.

ANDERSON, Margaret J 249
Happy m0ments with God; devotions especially written for families with young children. Grand Rapids, Mich., Zondervan [c.1962] 186p. illus. 24cm. 62-4925 2.95
1. Family—Prayer-books and devotions—English. I. Title.

ANDERSON, Margaret J 249
Happy moments with God; devotions especially written for families with young children. Grand Rapids, Zondervan Pub. House [1962] 186p. illus. 21cm. [BV255.A56] 62-4925
1. Youth— Prayer-books and devotions—English. I. Title.

ANDERSON, Margaret J. 249
Happy moments with God; devotions especially written for families with young children. Minneapolis, Minn., Bethany Fellowship [1973, c.1962] 186 p. illus. 22 cm. [BV255.A56] ISBN 0-87123-212-X 2.25 (pbk.)
1. Family—Prayer-books and devotions—English. I. Title.
L.C. card no. for hardbound edition: 62-4925.

ANDERSON, Margaret J. 249
Let's talk about God : devotions for families with young children / Margaret J. Anderson. Minneapolis : Bethany Fellowship, c1975. 191 p. : ill. ; 22 cm. One hundred devotionals for small children, each of which includes an anecdote, something to think about, a Bible verse, and a prayer. [BV4870.A35] 75-6055 ISBN 0-87123-3401 pbk. : 2.95
1. Children—Prayer-books and devotions—English—1961- I. Title.

ARENA, auditorium, stadium 249
guide. New York, National Sports Publication. v. illus. 19 cm. [GV182.A74] 54-27224
1. Public buildings—Direct.

BANIGAN, Sharon (Church) 249
1912- comp.
Hear our grace, selected and illustrated by Sharon Banigan. Garden City, N. Y., Garden City Books [1955] 60p. illus. 29 x 14cm. 'Catholic edition. --Dust jacket. [BV265.B3 1955a] 55-4368
1. Children— Prayer-books and devotions—English. 2. Grace at meals. I. Title.

BARRETT, Thomas van Braam. 249
The Christian family. New York, Morehouse-Gorham, 1958. 118p. 19cm. [BV4526.B35] 58-11486
1. Family—Religious life. I. Title.

BEDSOLE, Adolph. 249
Sermon outlines on the family and the home. Grand Rapids, Baker Book House, 1959. 105p. 20cm. (Minister's handbook series) [BV4526.B43] 59-8336
1. Family—Religious life—Sermons—Outlines. I. Title.

BELGUM, Harold J. 249
Great days for the family; how to make birthdays, big days, church days, nation days, nature days interesting and exciting [by] Harold J. Belgum. Illus. by John Ferguson. Saint Louis, Concordia Pub. House [1969] 124 p. illus. 24 cm. [GV182.8.B44] 70-89879 3.95
1. Family recreation. I. Title.

BLUMHORST, Roy. 249
Design for family living: devotions for families with teen-agers. Saint Louis, Concordia Pub. House [1963] 112 p. 20 cm. (The Family worship series) [BV255.B5] 63-19964
1. Family — Prayer-books and devotions — English I. Title.

BLUMHORST, Roy 249
Design for family living; devotions for families with teen-agers. St. Louis, Concordia [c.1963] 112p. 20cm. (Family worship ser.) 63-19964 1.00 pap.,
1. Family—Prayer-books and devotions—English. I. Title.

BOCK, Lois. 249
Happiness is a family time together / Lois Bock and Miji Working. Old Tappan, N.J. : Revell, [1975] 160 p. : ill. ; 28 cm. [BV4526.2.B58] 75-22059 ISBN 0-8007-0761-3 pbk. : 4.95
1. Family—Religious life. I. Working, Miji, joint author. II. Title.

BOCK, Lois. 249
Happiness is a family walk with God / Lois Bock & Miji Working ; ill. by Patty Eckman. Old Tappan, N.J. : Revell, c1977. 160 p. : ill. ; 28 cm. [BV4526.2.B583] 76-55000 ISBN 0-8007-0850-4 pbk. : 4.95
1. Family—Religious life. I. Working, Miji, joint author. II. Title.

BOUYER, Marie Dominique. 249
Table prayer [by] M. D. Bouyer. Translated and adapted by Anselm Jaskolka. [New York] Herder and Herder [1967] 128 p. 22 cm. Translation of Prieres pour le repas. [BV283.G7B613] 67-27733
1. Grace at meals. I. Title.

BOUYER, Marie Dominique. 249
Table prayer [by] M. D. Bouyer. Translated and adapted by Anselm Jaskolka. [New York] Herder and Herder [1967] 128 p. 22 cm. Translation of Prieres pour le repas. [BV283.G7B613] 67-27733
1. Grace at meals. I. Title.

BRADFORD, Reed H. 249
And they shall teach their children. Salt Lake City, Deseret [c.]1964. 218p. illus. 24cm. Formerly pub. in the Intsructor magazine. 64-3336 3.50
1. Family—Religious life. 2. Christian life—Mormon authors. I. Title.

BRADLEY, Ruth Olive, 1901- 249
Great themes from the Book of Mormon for family activities, by Ruth O. Bradley. [Independence, Mo., Herald Pub. House, 1974] 200 p. col. illus. 21 cm. Prepared under the direction of the Dept. of Christian Education, Reorganized Church of Jesus Christ of Latter-Day Saints. Bibliography: p. 200. [BV4526.2.B679] 73-19257 ISBN 0-8309-0115-9 7.95
1. Family—Religious life. I. Reorganized Church of Jesus Christ of Latter-Day Saints. Dept. of Christian Education. II. Book of Mormon. III. Title.

BRANDT, Henry R. 249
Building a Christian home, by Henry R. Brandt and Homer E. Dowdy. Wheaton, Ill., Scripture Press [c.1960] 158p. illus., diagrs. Bibl.: p.151-152 60-53592 3.00
1. Family—Religious life. I. Dowdy, Homer E., joint author. II. Title.

BREIG, Joseph Anthony, 1905- 249
The family and the Cross; the Stations of the Cross and their relation to family life. Illustrated by Margaret Goldsmith. Chicago, H. Regnery Co., 1959. 83p. illus. 20cm. [BX2040.B7] 59-7861
1. Stations of the Cross. 2. Family— Religious life. I. Title.

BROWN, Leslie Wilfrid, Bp. 249
The Christian family [by] Leslie and Winifred Brown. New York, Association Press [c.1959] 80p. 19cm. (World Christian books, 2d ser., no. 29) 60-6572 1.00 pap.,
1. Family—Religious life. I. Brown. Winifred (Megaw) joint author. II. Title.

BROWN, Leslie Wilfrid, Bp., 249
1912-
The Christian family [by] Leslie and Winifred Brown. New York, Association Press [1959] 80p. 19cm. (World Christian books, 2d ser., no. 29) [BV4526.B68] 60-6572
1. Family—Religious life. I. Brown, Winifred (Megaw) 1914- joint author. II. Title.

BUNCH, Josephine. 249
Prayers for the family, by Josephine and Christopher Bunch. [Westwood, N. J.] Revell [1961] 62p. 17cm. 'Published in Great Britain under the title: Prayers at home.' [BV255.B84 1961] 61-5928
1. Family—Prayer-books and devotions—English. I. Bunch. Christopher, joint author. II. Title.

BUNCH, Josephine 249
Prayers for the family, by Josephine and Christopher Bunch. [Westwood, N. J.] Revell [c.1961] 62p. 'Published in Great Britain under the title: Prayers at home' 61-5928 1.50 bds.,
1. Family—Prayer-books and devotions—English. I. Bunch, Christopher, joint author. II. Title.

CARLTON, Anna Lee. 249
Guidelines for family worship. Anderson, Ind., Warner Press [1964] 103 p. 21 cm. [BV426.2.C3] 64-22160
1. Family — Religious life. I. Title.

CARLTON, Anna Lee 249
Guidelines for family worship. Anderson, Ind., Warner [c.1964] 103p. 21cm. 64-22160 1.50 pap.,
1. Family—Religious life. I. Title.

CATHOLIC University of 249
America. Workshop on the Catholic Elementary School Program for Christian Family Living, 1954.
The Catholic elementary school program for Christian family living; the proceedings of the Workshop on the Catholic Elementary School Program for Christian Family Living conducted at the Catholic University of America, June 11 to June 22, 1954. Edited by Sister Mary Ramon Langdon. Washington, Catholic University of America Press, 1955. vii, 209p. illus. 22cm. Bibliography: p.197-207. [BX2351.C3 1954] 55-2616
1. Family—Religious life. I. Langdon, Mary Rames, Sister, ed. II. Title.

CHANNELS, Vera. 249
The layman builds a Christian home. St. Louis, Bethany Press [1959] 95p. 21cm. [BV4526.C43] 59-14680
1. Family—Religious life. I. Title.

CHEVILLE, Roy Arthur, 1897- 249
Ten considerations for family living. Independence, Mo., Herald House [1958] 150p. 20cm. [BX8672.C47] 58-11854
1. Christian life—Study and teaching. 2. Christian life—Mormon authors. I. Title.

CLOUGH, William A. 1899- 249
Father, we thank Thee. graces and prayers for the home. Nashville, iAbingdon [1967] 112p. 16cm. [BV255.C67] 49 8430 .95 pap.,
1. Family—Prayer-books and devotions — English. I. Title.

COAKLEY, Mary Lewis, 1907- 249
Our child--God's child. Milwaukee, Bruce Pub. Co. [1953] 233p. 21cm. [BX2351.C53] 53-3959
1. Family—Religious life. I. Title.

COFFMAN, Harry E. 249
Bible family life seminar : strengthening—the church, the home : how to implement Bible life principles into daily victories in the home and church / by Harry E. Coffman. Portland, Or. : Coffman, c1977. 31 leaves in various foliations ; 30 cm. [BV4510.2.C6] 78-100219
1. Christian life—1960- 2. Family—Religious life. I. Title. II. Title: Strengthening—the church, the home.

COOK, Walter L. 249
Mealtime graces for the family [by] Walter L. Cook. Nashville, Abingdon Press [1966] 72 p. 12 cm. [BV283.G7C6] 66-28023
1. Grace at meals. I. Title.

CROOK, Roger H. 249
The changing American family; a study of family problems from a Christian perspective. St. Louis, Bethany Press [c.1960] 160p. Bibl.: p.157-160. 21cm. 60-14649 2.95
1. Family—Religious life. I. Title.

CROUCH, W Perry. 249
Guidance for Christian home life. Nashville, Convention Press [1955] 129p. 20cm. [BV4526.C7] 55-14888
1. Family—Religious life. I. Title.

EDENS, David, 1926- 249
Making the most of family worship [by] David and Virginia Edens. Nashville, Broadman Press [1968] 128 p. 20 cm. Includes bibliographical references. [BV200.E3] 68-15851
1. Family—Religious life. 2. Family—Prayer-books and devotions—English. I. Edens, Virginia, joint author. II. Title.

FAIRCHILD, Roy W. 249
Families in the church; a Protestant survey, by Roy W. Fairchild, John Charles Wynn. New York. Association Press [c.1961] xii, 302p. Bibl. 61-7109 5.75 bds.,
1. Family—Religious life. I. Wynn, John Charles, joint author. II. Title.

FEE, Zephyrus Roy, 1890- 249
Home sweet home, here and hereafter. Dallas, Wilkinson Pub. Co. [1952] 113 p. illus. 18 cm. [BV4526.F4] 52-10261
1. Family—Religious life. I. Title.

FLOWER, Alice Reynolds. 249
The home, a divine sanctuary. Springfield, Mo., Gospel Pub. House [1955] 185p. 20cm. Includes bibliography. [BV4526.F56] 56-16596
1. Family—Religious life. I. Title.

GANGSEI, Virginia 249
Home is where God is; a devotional book for family reading. Illus. by Ollie Jacobson. Minneapolis, Augsburg [c.1961] 165p. illus. 61-13885 1.00
1. Family—Prayer-books and devotions—English. I. Title.

GEBHARD, Anna Laura (Munro) 249
1914-
Guideposts to creative family worship [by] Anna Laura and Edward W. Gebhard. Nashville, Abingdon-Cokesbury Press [1953] 173p. 21cm. [BV4526.G4] 53-6350
1. Family—Religious life. 2. Family—Prayer-books and devotions—English. I. Gebhard, Edward W., joint author. II. Title.

GEISSLER, Eugene S 249
Father of the family. Chicago, Fides Publishers Association [1957] 157p. illus. 21cm. [BX2352.G4] 57-7961
1. Fathers. I. Title.

GETZ, Gene A. 249
The Christian home in a changing world, by Gene A. Getz. Chicago, Moody Press [1972] 107 p. 22 cm. "Portions of this book are reprinted from the author's The Christian home, a Moody manna booklet." Bibliography: p. 106-107. [BV4526.2.G47] 72-77950 ISBN 0-8024-1352-8 1.95
1. Family—Religious life. I. Title.

HAAKONSON, Reidar Pareli, 249
1903-
Family altar readings. Chicago, Moody Press [c1956] 367p. 22cm. [BV4832.H23] 57-1289
1. Devotional calendars—Lutheran Church. I. Title.

HAGER, Wesley H. 249
Whom God hath joined together; a devotional guide for husband and wife. Nashville, Upper Room [c.1962] 96p. 16cm. 62-16903 .75 bds.,
1. Family—Prayer-books and devotions. I. Title.

HART, W Neill. 249
Home and church working together. New York, Abingdon- Cokesbury Press [1951] 157 p. 19 cm. [BV4526.H34] 52-555
1. Family—Religious life. 2. Religious education—Home training. I. Title.

HEIN, Lucille E. 249
One small circle. a book of family devotions. Nashville, Abingdon [c.1962] 128p. 20cm. 62-16254 2.50
1. Family—Prayer-books and devotions—English. I. Title.

HERZEL, Catherine. 249
The family worships together. Philadelphia, Muhlenberg Press [1957] 108p. 18cm. [BV255.H48] 57-9594
1. Family— Prayer-books and devotions—English. I. Title.

HERZEL, Catherine B 249
The family worships together. Philadelphia, Muhlenberg Press [1957] 108p. 18cm. [BV255.H48] 57-9594
1. Family— Prayer-books and devotions—English. I. Title.

HERZEL, Catherine B. 249
The family worships together. Philadelphia, Muhlenberg Press [1957] 108 p. 18 cm. [BV255.H48] 57-9594
1. Family — Prayer-books and devotions — English. I. Title.

THE home and its inner 249
spiritual life; a treatise on the mental hygiene of the home, by a Carthusian of Miraflores. Westminster, Md., Newman Press, 1952. 256 p. 22 cm. [BX2351.H6] 52-1589
1. Family—Religious. I. A Carthusian of Miraflores.

HOOLE, Daryl (Van Dam) 249
The art of teaching children. Illus. [by] Dick and Mary Scopes. Salt Lake City, Deseret [c.] 1964. xix, 230p. illus. 24cm. 64-4289 3.95
1. Mormons and Mormonism—Education. 2. Religious education of children. I. Bentley, Ellen F., arr. Hang up the baby's stocking. II. Title.

HOPE, Wingfield. 249
Other people. New York, Sheed & Ward [1957] 181p. 21cm. [BX2351.H65] 57-6048
1. Family—Religious life. I. Title.

HOWARD, Barbara, 1930- 249
Be swift to love / by Barbara Howard. Independence, Mo. : Herald Pub. House, [1974] 186 p. : ill. ; 21 cm. Bibliography: p. 185-186. [BX8675.H68] 74-82423 ISBN 0-8309-0128-0 : 7.00
1. Reorganized Church of Jesus Christ of Latter-Day Saints—Prayer-books and devotions—English. 2. Family—Prayer-books and devotions—English. I. Title.

HUDSON, Robert Lofton. 249
Home is the place [by] R. Lofton Hudson. Nashville, Broadman Press [1967] 128 p. 20 cm. Bibliography: p. 127-128. [BV4526.2.H8] 67-121728
1. Family—Religious life. I. Title.

HUDSON, Robert Lofton. 249
Home is the place [by] R. Lofton Hudson. Nashville, Broadman Press [1967] 128 p. 20 cm. Bibliography: p. 127-128. [BV4526.2.H8] 67-12172
1. Family—Religious life. I. Title.

INGZEL, Marjorie, comp. 249
Table graces for the family. New York, Nelson [c.1964] 64p. 16cm. 64-13997 1.00
1. Grace at meals. I. Title.

JAHSMANN, Allan Hart. 249
Little visits with God; devotions for families with small children, by Allan Hart Jahsmann and Martin P. Simon. Illus. by Frances Hook. St. Louis, Concordia Pub. House [1957] 286p. illus. 24cm. [BV255.J25] 55-12480
1. Family— Prayer-books and devotions—English. I. Simon, Martin Paul William, 1903- joint author. II. Title.

JAHSMANN, Allan Hart. 249
More little visits with God; devotions for families with young children, by Allan Hart Jahsmann and Martin P. Simon. Illus. by Frances Hook. Saint Louis, Concordia Pub. House [1961] 319p. illus. 24cm. [BV255.J26] 61-11549
1. Family—Prayer-books and devotions—English. I. Simon, Martin Paul William, 1903- joint II. Title.

JOHNSON, Early Ashby, 1917- 249
Communion with young saints. With illus. by Doyle Robinson. Richmond, John Knox Press [1959] 111p. illus. 21cm. The author's conversations with his sons, David and Paul. [BV4526.J58] 59-8231
1. Johnson, David. 2. Johnson, Paul, 1945 or 6- 3. Family—Religious life. I. Title.

JOINER, Verna Jones. 249
This home we build. Anderson, Ind., Warner Press [1959] 80p. 19cm. [BV4526.2J6] 59-8789
1. Family— Religious life. I. Title.

KERR, Clarence Ware, 1893- 249
God's pattern for the home. Los Angeles, Cowman Publications [1953] 147p. 20cm. [BV4526.K4] 54-16103
1. Family—Religious life. I. Title.

LARSEN, Earnest. 249
Liturgy begins at home [by] Earnest Larsen and Patricia Galvin. Liguori, Mo., Liguori Publications [1973] 143 p. illus. 18 cm. [BX1970.L28] 73-91410 1.75 (pbk.)
1. Liturgics—Catholic Church. 2. Family—Religious life. I. Galvin, Patricia, joint author. II. Title.

MCBRIDE, Charles R 249
The Christian home in a rural setting. [1st ed.] Philadelphia, Judson Press [1953] 111p. 21cm. [BV4526.M25] 53-8556
1. Family—Religious life. 2. Rural churches—U.S. I. Title.

MCBRIDE, Clarence Ralph. 249
The Christian home in a rural setting. [1st ed.] Philadelphia, Judson Press [1953] 111p. 21cm. [BV4526.M25] 53-8556
1. Family—Religious life. 2. Rural churches—U. S. I. Title.

MCCAULEY, Elfrieda, ed. 249
A book of family worship. Edited by Elfrieda and Leon McCauley, with the counsel of an interdenominational committee: Water Russell Bowie [and others] Foreword by Walter Russell Bowie. New York, Scribner [1959] 176p. 22cm. Includes bibliography. [BV255.M27] 59-5917
1. Family—Prayer-books and devotions—English. I. McCauley, Leon, joint ed. II. Title.

MCLOUGHLIN, Helen 249
My nameday--come for dessert. Collegeville, Minn., Liturgical Pr. [1963, c.1962] 320p. illus., 21cm. 63-3393 2.75
1. Patron saints. 2. Desserts. 3. Saints—Prayerbooks and devotions—English. I. Title.

MCNAIRY, Philip F Bp. 249
Family story. Greenwich, Conn., Seabury Press, 1960. 138p. 21cm. In part a series of radio addresses given in Buffalo, New York.' [BV4526.M32] 60-14118
1. Family—Religious life. I. Title.

MARSHALL, Catherine (Wood) 249
1914-
God loves you; our family's favorite stories and prayers, by Catherine and Peter Marshall. Drawings by James Spanfeller. 2d ed. New York, McGraw-Hill [1967] 59 p. illus. (part col.) 20 cm. Prayers, poetry and brief stories illustrate God's love and Christian principles. [BV4571.2.M3 1967] AC 68
1. Family—Religious life. I. Marshall, Peter, 1902-1949, joint author. II. Spanfeller, James J., illus. III. Title.

MARTIN, Dorothy McKay, 1921- 249
Creative family worship / Dorothy Martin. Chicago : Moody Press, c1976. 126 p. ; 18 cm. [BV4526.2.M29] 76-8822 ISBN 0-8024-1641-1 pbk. : 1.25
1. Family—Religious life. I. Title.

MAY, Edward C. 249
Family worship idea book. St. Louis, Concordia [c.1965] 64p. illus. 28cm. Bibl. [BV255.M38] 65-27694 1.00 pap.,
1. Family—Prayer-books and devotions—English. I. Title.

MAYNARD, Donald More. 249
Your home can be Christian; illustrated by Janet Smalley. New York, Abingdon-Cokesbury Press [1952] 160 p. illus. 20 cm. [BV4526.M38] 52-8841
1. Family. Religious life. I. Title.

*MILLIKAN, Marilyn 249
Devotions with Julie and Jack. Kansas City, Mo., Beacon Hill [c.1964] 201p. illus. 24cm. 2.95
I. Title.

MOW, Anna B. 249
Your teen-ager and you [by] Anna B. Mow. Grand Rapids, Zondervan [1967] 95, [1] p. 21cm. Bibl. [BV4526.2.M6] 67-14103 2.95 pap.,
1. Parent and child. 2. Family—Religious life. I. Title.

MUELLER, Charles S 249
God's wonderful world of words; devotions for families with children ages 9-13. Saint Louis, Concordia Pub. House [1963] 102 p. 20 cm. (The Family worship series) [BV255.M9] 63-19963
1. Family — Prayer-books and devotions — English. I. Title.

MUELLER, Charles S. 249
God's wonderful world of words; devotions for families with children ages 9-13. St. Louis, Concordia [c.1963] 102p. 20cm. (Family worship ser.) 63-19963 1.00 pap.,
1. Family—Prayer-books and devotions—English. I. Title.

MUELLER, Therese. 249
Guide for the Christian homemaker. Illus. by Gertrud Mueller Nelson. St. Meinrad, Ind., Abbey Press Publications [1965] 94 p. illus. 17 cm. (Marriage paperback library, 20010) [BX2351.M82] 66-6311
1. Family — Religious life. I. Title.

MURPHREE, Clyde E. 249
Resource use and income implications of outdoor recreation; [the impact of a demand for indigenous resources generated by nonresidents on the economy of a rural county in north Florida, by] Clyde E. Murphree. Gainesville, Agricultural Experiment Stations, University of Florida, 1965. 55 p. illus., maps. 23 cm. ([University of Florida. Agricultural Experiment Station, Gainesville] Bulletin 690) Bibliography: p. 52. [GV182.2.M8] 65-64838
1. Outdoor recreation — Economic aspects — Florida. I. Title. II. Series: Florida. Agricultural Experiment Station. Gainesville. Bulletin 690

*NEWLAND, Mary (Reed) 249
Religion in the home, a parents' guide. Grs. 1-3. New York, Sadlier [1968] .80 pap., ea.,
I. Title.

NORFLEET, Mary Crockett. 249
With happy voices; stories for prayertime in families with young children. Illus. by Katherine La Bruce Rowe. Richmond, John Knox Press [1959] 191p. illus. 24cm. [BV4571.2.N6] 59-5097
1. Children—Religious life. I. Title.

O'BRIEN, Joachim. 249
Parish family life and social action : a handbook for parish pastoral councillors / Joachim O'Brien. Chicago : Franciscan Herald Press, c1977. 32 p. : ill. ; 18 x 25 cm. [BX2351.O23] 77-3573 ISBN 0-8199-0673-5 pbk. : 1.50
1. Catholic Church—Charities. 2. Family—Religious life. 3. Social service. I. Title.

PISTOLE, Hollis. 249
The church in thy house; how home and church can work together [by] Hollis and Elizabeth Pistole. Anderson, Ind., Warner Press [1959] 94p. 21cm. [BV4526.P53] 59-1358
1. Family— Religious life. I. Pistole, Elizabeth, joint author. II. Title.

PLUS, Raoul, 1882- 249
Christ in the home; a translation from the French. New York, F. Pustet Co., 1951. 343 p. 21 cm. [BX2351.P613] 52-19918
1. Family — Religious life. 2. Christian life — Catholic authors. I. Title.

PORTER, Blaine R., comp. 249
The Latter-Day Saint family; a book of selected readings [by] Blaine R. Porter. Salt Lake City, Deseret Book Co., 1966. xii, 438 p. 24 cm. Published in 1963 under title: Selected readings in the Latter-Day Saint family. Bibliographical footnotes. [BV4526.2.P6 1966] 66-29996
1. Family—Religious life. I. Title.

PORTER, Blaine R comp. 249
Selected readings in the Latter-Day Saint family. Dubuque, Iowa, W. C. Brown Book Co. [1963] 498 p. 23 cm. [BV4526.2.P6] 63-4147
1. Family—Religious life. I. Title.

PREUS, Johan Carl Keyser, 249
1881-
God's promises and our prayers. With contributions by Conrad M. Thompson [and] Oscar Engebretson. Minneapolis, Augsburg Pub. House [1961] 158p. 21cm. [BV255.P84] 61-6999
1. Family—Prayer-books and devotions—English. 2. Lutheran Church-Prayer-books and devotions—English. I. Title.

RANDOLPH, Abigail Graves, 249
comp.
The family at prayer; a guide for family worship. An interpretation of family worship, with prayers for family use by Hazen G. Werner. Nashville, Upper Room [1958] 128p. 25cm. [BV255.R2] 58-12816
1. Family—Prayer-books and devotions—English. I. Title.

REST, Karl, ed. 249
Prayer book for the family circle and for personal devotions. Philadelphia, Christian Education Press [c1950] vii. 184 p. 20 cm. [BV255.R47] 51-9875
1. Family — Prayer books and devotions — English. I. Title.

ROBINSON, Ella May (White) 249
1882-
Happy home stories. Mountain View, Calif., Pacific Press Pub. Association [1955] 137p. illus. 23cm. [BV4515.R594] 55-9129
1. Christian life—Stories. I. Title.

ROLFSRUD, Erling Nicolai, 249
1912-
Happy Acres. Illustrated by Dorothy Divers. Minneapolis, Augsburg Pub. House [1956] 167p. illus. 21cm. [BV4526.R63] 56-11793
1. Family—Religious life. I. Title.

*ROPER, Gayle G. 249
Wife, mate, mother, me! [By] Gayle G. Roper. Grand Rapids, Baker Book House [1975] 98p. 23 cm. [BV4526.2] ISBN 0-8010-7633-1 4.95.
1. Woman-Religious life 2. Conduct of life. I. Title.

SANDLIN, John Lewis 249
A book of table graces. [Westwood, N.J.] Revell [c.1963] 64p. 17cm. 63-7597 1.00 bds.,
1. Grace at meals. I. Title.

SIMON, Martin Paul William, 249
1903-
Glad moments with God, by Martin P. Simon. Grand Rapids, Zondervan Pub. House [1964] 1 v. (unpaged) illus. 21 cm. [BV255.S56] 64-15560
1. Family — Prayer-books and devotions — English. I. Title.

SIMON, Martin Paul William, 249
1903-
Glad moments with God. Grand Rapids, Mich., Zondervan [c.1964] lv. (unpaged) illus. 21cm. [BV255.S56] 64-15560 3.95 bds.,
1. Family—Prayer-books and devotions—English. I. Title.

SNYDER, Ross. 249
Inscape. Design and illus. by Giorgetta Bell. Nashville, Abingdon Press [1968] 94 p. illus. 20 cm. Verse and prose. [BV4526.2.S55] 68-19320
1. Family—Religious life. I. Title.

TAYLOR, Florence Marian 249
Tompkins, 1892-
Your children's faith, a guide for parents, by Florence M. Taylor. [1st ed.] Garden City, N. Y., Doubleday, 1964. xiii, 174 p. 22 cm. Bibliography: p. [166]-174. [BV1590.T33] 64-19273
1. Bible—Study. 2. Family—Religious life. 3. Religious education—Home training. I. Title.

THOMAS, John Lawrence. 249
The family clinic; a book of questions and answers. Westminster, Md., Newman Press, 1958. 336 p. 23 cm. [BX2351.T5] 58-13641
1. Questions and answers — Theology. 2. Family — Religious life. 3. Church and social problems — Catholic Church. I. Title.

THOMPSON, William Taliaferro, 249
1886-
An adventure in love; Christian family living. Richmond, John Knox Press [1956] 155p. 22cm. [BV4526.T46] 56-6717
1. Family—Religious life. 2. Marriage. I. Title.

THOMPSON, William Taliaferro, 249
1886-
An adventure in love; Christian family living. Richmond, John Knox Press [1956] 155 p. 22 cm. [BV4526.T46] 56-6717
1. Family—Religious life. 2. Marriage. I. Title.

THOUGHTS of God for boys and 249
girls. As we think with God; selections. Ed. by Phyllis N. Maramarco, Edith Frances Welker. Illus. by Arnold Dobrin. Nashville, Abingdon [c.1948-1962] 111p. illus. 22cm. 62-11153 2.25
1. Children—Prayer-books and devotions—English. I. Maramarco, Phyllis Newcomb, ed. II. Welker Edith Frances, ed.

TRAPP, Maria Augusta. 249
Yesterday, today, and forever. [1st ed.] Philadelphia, Lippincott [1952] 220 p. 21 cm. [BX2351.T7] 52-12170
1. Family—Religious life. 2. Christian life—Catholic authors. I. Title.

TRAPP, Maria Augusta 249
Yesterday, today, and forever. Garden City, N.Y., Doubleday [1966, c.1952] 200p. 18cm. (Echo bk. E34) [BX2351.T7] .85 pap.,
1. Family—Religious life. 2. Christian life—Catholic authors. I. Title.

VANDER VELDE, Frances. 249
Christian home and family living. Grand Rapids, Zondervan Pub. House [1959] 119 p. 20 cm. [BV4626.V28] 59-4363
1. Family — Religious life. I. Title.

VOGEL, Lois. 249
God and your family; devotions for families with young children. Saint Louis, Concordia Pub. House [1963] 102 p. 20 cm. (The Family worship series) [BV255.V58] 63-19961
1. Family—Prayer-books and devotions—English. I. Title.

VOGEL, Lois 249
God and your family devotions for families with young children. St. Louis, Concordia [c.1963] 102p. 20cm. (Family worship ser.) 63-19961 1.00 pap.,
1. Family—Prayer-books and devotions—English. I. Title.

WALLIS, Charles Langworthy, 249
1921-
365 table graces for the Christian home [by] Charles L. Wallis. [1st ed.] New York, Harper [1967] 117p. 17cm. [BV283.G7W3] 67-14939 2.50
1. Grace at meals. I. Title.

WATSON, Ethel May 249
Where is thy flock? Mountain View, Calif., Pacific Press Pub. Assn. [c.1961] 130 p. 61-10876 3.00
1. Family—Religious life. I. Title.

WATSON, Ethel May. 249
Where is thy flock? Mountain View, Calif., Pacific Press Pub. Association [1961] 130 p. 21 cm. [BV4526.W34] 61-10876
1. Family — Religious life. I. Title.

WEBB, Barbara Owen. 249
Devotions for families: fruit of the spirit. Illustrated by Marlise A. Reidenbach. Valley Forge [Pa.] Judson Press [1974, c1973] 48 p. illus. 28 cm. [BV255.W37 1974] 74-7516 ISBN 0-8170-0640-0 1.50 (pbk.).
1. Family—Prayer-books and devotions—English. I. Title.

WEISER, Francis Xavier, 1901- 249
The year of the Lord in the Christian home, by Francis X. Weiser. Collegeville, Minn., Liturgical Press [1964] 126, [2] p. 19 cm. (Popular liturgical library) "Recommended reading": p. [127] [BX2351.W4] 64-56307
1. Family — Religious life. I. Title.

WIDMER, Frederick W 249
How home and church can work together. Illustrated by Ruth Ensign. Richmond, Published for the Cooperative Publication Association, by John Knox Press [1960] 94 p. illus. 21 cm. (The Cooperative series) Includes bibliography. [BV4526.W472] 60-9209
1. Family — Religious life. I. Title.

WIDMER, Frederick W. 249
How home and church can work together. Illustrated by Ruth Ensign. Richmond, Virginia, Published for the Cooperative Publication Association, by John Knox Press [c.1960] 94p. Includes bibliography. illus. 21cm. (The Cooperative series) 60-9209 1.50 pap.,
1. Family—Religious life. I. Title.

WIDMER, Frederick W 249
Living together in Christian homes; a leader's guide for leadership course 420b, the Christian home. Richmond, John Knox Press [1956] 52 p. 21 cm. [BV4526.W473] 56-9251
1. Family — Religious life. I. Title.

WILKINSON, Frances. 249
Growing up in Christ; family life and family religion. Foreword by Stephen F. Bayne, Jr. Greenwich, Conn., Seabury Press [1960] 149 p. 21 cm. Includes bibliography. [BV4526.W52] 60-50881
1. Family — Religious life. I. Title.

WILLIAMS, Norman V 249
How to have a family altar. Chicago, Moody Press [c1951] 127 p. 18 cm. (Colportage library, 212) [BV4526.W53] 52-20936
1. Family—Religious life. I. Title.

WYNN, John Charles, ed. 249
Sermons on marriage and family life; teachings from Protestant pulpits concerning the Christian home. New York, Abingdon Press [1956] 173 p. 21 cm. [BV837.W9] 56-7767
1. Marriage — Sermons. 2. Family-Religious life. I. Title.

WYNN, John Charles, ed. 249
Sermons on marriage and family life; teachings from Protestant pulpits concerning the Christian home. Nashville, Abingdon [1963, c.1956] 173p. 21cm. (Apex bk., M8) .95 pap.,
1. Marriage—Sermons. 2. Family—Religious life. I. Title.

ZINK, Heidi, comp. 249
This child of God shall meet no harm; prayers for parents and children. [Compiled by Heidi Zink and Joerg Zink] Translated by Erich Hopka. Saint Louis, Concordia Pub. House [1964] 96 p. illus. (part col.) 14 cm. Translation of Dies Kind soll unverletzet sein. [BV255.Z513] 64-21138
1. Family — Prayer-books and devotions — English. 2. Lutheran Church — Prayer-books and devotions — English. I. Zink, Joerg, joint comp. II. Title.

ZINK, Heidi, comp. 249
This child of God shall meet no harm; prayers for parents and children [Comp. by Heidi Zink, Joerg Zink] Tr. [from German] by Erich Hopka. St. Louis, Concordia [c.1962, 1964] 96p. illus. (pt. col.) 14cm. 64-21138 1.00 bds.,
1. Family—Prayer-books and devotions—English. 2. Lutheran Church—Prayer-books and devotions—English. I. Zink, Joerg, joint comp. II. Title.

*PERKINS, Richard F. 249.07
The image of a Christian family. CLC Pr. [dist.] Richmond, Va. [Knox, c.1964] 108p. 21cm. (Covenant life curriculum) 1.25 pp.,
I. Title.

PHILLIPS, Dewi Zephaniah. 249.3
The concept of prayer, by D. Z. Phillips. New York, Schocken Books [1966] vii, 167 p. 23 cm. Bibliography: p. 161-164. [BV210.2.P5] 66-14086
1. Prayer. I. Title.

*DOBBINS, Richard O. 249.7
Train up a child . . . guidelines for parents. Grand Rapids, Mich., Baker Book House [1973] 87 p. 18 cm. [BV4571] ISBN 0-8010-2824-8 0.95 (pbk.)
1. Children—Religious life. 2. Religious education of children. I. Title.

*TEMPLE, Joe 249.7
Know your child Grand Rapids, Baker Book House [1974] x., 149 p. 20 cm. [BV4571] ISBN 0-8010-8820-8 2.95 (pbk.)
1. Children—Religious life. I. Title.

250 LOCAL CHURCH & RELIGIOUS ORDERS

ADAMS, Arthur Merrihew, 250
Pastoral administration. Philadelphia, Westminster Press [1964] 174 p. 21 cm. Bibliography: p. [166]-170. [BV652.A35] 64-18686
1. Church work. I. Title.

ADAMS, Arthur Merrihew 250
Pastoral administration. Philadelphia. Westminster [c.1964] 174p. 21cm. Bibl. 64-18686 4.50
1. Church work. I. Title.

ANDERSON, Park Harris, 1880- 250
Christ's preachers, according to the New Testament. [2d ed.] Boston, Christopher Pub. House [1951] 200 p. 21 cm. [BV660.A5 1951] 51-1984
1. Clergy—Office. 2. Sermons—Outlines. I. Title.

BARR, Browne. 250
The ministering congregation, by Browne Barr and Mary Eakin. Philadelphia, United Church Press [1972] 127 p. 22 cm. "A Pilgrim Press book." Includes bibliographical references. [BV4011.B367] 72-5587 ISBN 0-8298-0243-6 4.95
1. Pastoral theology. 2. Church work. I. Eakin, Mary (Mulford) 1914- joint author. II. Title.

BARRETT, George West. 250
Demands on ministry today; the issue of integrity [by] George W. Barrett. New York, Seabury Press [1969] viii, 165 p. 21 cm. (An Original Seabury paperback, SP58) [BV660.2.B33] 69-19145 3.50 (pbk)
1. Clergy. I. Title.

BAXTER, Richard, 1615-1691 250
The reformed pastor. Ed. by Hugh Martin. Richmond, Va., Knox [1963] 125p. 19cm. Orig. pub. under title: Gildas Salvianus; or The reformed pastor. 63-16412 1.50 pap.,
1. Pastoral theology—Early works to 1900. I. Title.

BENSON, Dennis C. 250
Dennis C. Benson's Recycle catalogue. Nashville : Abingdon Press, [1975]. 208 p. : ill. ; 31 cm. Includes index. [BV3.B4 1975] 75-313743 ISBN 0-687-35854-X pbk. : 6.95
1. Theology, Practical—Miscellanea. I. Title. II. Title: Recycle catalogue.

BENSON, Dennis C. 250
Recycle catalogue II : fabulous flea market / Dennis C. Benson. Nashville : Abingdon, c1977. 159 p. : ill. ; 31 cm. Includes indexes. [BV3.B42] 77-23978 ISBN 0-687-35855-8 pbk. : 6.95
1. Theology, Practical—Miscellanea. I. Title.

BERG, Orley. 250
The work of the pastor. Nashville, Southern Pub. Association [1966] 180 p. 22 cm. [BV4011.B45] 66-4718
1. Pastroal theology — Seventh-Day Adventist. I. Title.

BERG, Orley 250
The work of the pastor. Nashville, Southern Pub. [c.1966] 189p. 22cm. [BV4011.B45] 66-4718 4.95
1. Pastoral theology—Seventh-Day Adventist. I. Title.

BINGHAM, Robert E. 250
Serving with the saints; down-to-earth help for church staff members in their many roles [by] Robert E. Bingham and Ernest Loessner. Nashville, Broadman Press [1970] 127 p. 21 cm. Includes bibliographical references. [BV705.B5] 73-93914 3.50
1. Church officers. 2. Interpersonal relations. I. Loessner, Ernest J., joint author. II. Title.

BLIEWEIS, Theodor 250
The diary of a parish priest. Tr. by Barbara Waldstein. Westminster, Md., Newman [1965] 126p. 18cm. [BX1913.B543] 65-3424 1.50 pap.,
1. Catholic Church—Clergy—Correspondence, reminiscences, etc. 2. Pastoral theology—Catholic Church. I. Title.

BOCKELMAN, Wilfred. 250
Toward better church committees. Minneapolis, Augsburg Pub. House [1962] 80p. 20cm. [BV705.B6] 62-9098
1. Church officers. I. Title.

CALKINS, Gladys Gilkey. 250
Follow those women ; church women in the ecumenical movement, a history of the development of united work among women of the Protestant churches in the United States. [New York, Published for United Church Women, National Council of the Churches of Christ in U.S.A. by the Office of Publication and Distribution, c1961] 108 p. 21 cm. "Presented by the officers and staff of United Church Women as the report of the triennium, 1958-1961." [BV4415.C25] 61-17252
1. Women in church work—U.S. 2. National Council of the Churches of Christ in the United States of America. Dept. of United Church Women. I. National Council of the Churches of Christ in the United States of America. Dept. of United Church Women. II. Title.

CARR, James McLeod 250
Our church meeting human needs. Progressive Farmer [dist. New York, Putnam, 1963, c.1962] 152p. illus. 23cm. 62-21440 2.00; 1.00 pap.,
1. Church work. I. Title.

CASEY, Thomas Francis, 1923- 250
Pastoral manual for new priests. Foreword by Richard Cardinal Cushing. Milwaukee, Bruce Pub. Co. [1962] 164p. 23cm. [BX1913.C3] 62-12431
I. Pastoral theology—Catholic Church. I. Title.

CHAPMAN, John Wilbur, 1859- 250
The minister's handicap, by J. Wilbur Chapman ... xii, 13-155p. 20cm. New York, N. Y. American tract society) [BV4010.C5] 18-18979
1. Theology, Pastoral. I. American tract society. II. Title. III. Series.

CICOGNANI, Amleto Giovanni, Abp., 1883- comp. 250
The priest in the Epistles of St. Paul. 3d ed. Paterson. N.J., St. Anthony Guild Press [1955] 209 p. illus. 17 cm. d. [BX1912.C5 1955] 56-17892
1. Catholic Church—Clergy. I. Title.

CLARK, Howard Gordon. 250
A handbook for vestrymen; a lay vocation in the service of the church. New York, Morehouse-Barlow Co. [1962] 72p. 19cm. Includes bibliography. [BX5967.5.C5] 62-19255
1. Church officers. 2. Protestant Episcopal Church in the U.S.A.— Government. I. Title.

COLTON, Clarence Eugene, 1914- 250
The minister's mission, a survey of ministerial responsibilities and relationships. Dallas, Story Book Press ['1951] 343 p. 20 cm. [BV4010.C57] 52-556
1. Theology. Pastoral. I. Title.

COLTON, Clarence Eugene, 1914- 250
The minister's mission; a survey of ministerial responsibilities and relationships. [Rev. ed.] Grand Rapids, Zondervan Pub. House [1961, c.1951] 223p. Bibl. 61-4320 3.50
1. Pastoral theology. I. Title.

DAWSON, David Miles, 1885- 250
More power to the preacher; a pastoral theology. Grand Rapids, Zondervan Pub. House [1956] 153p. 20cm. [BV4010.D29] 56-41990
1. Theology, Pastoral. I. Title.

DE HUECK, Catherine, 1900- 250
Dear Seminarian. Milwaukee, Bruce [1950] 87 p. 19 cm. [BX903.D4] 51-2185
1. Seminarians—Religious life. I. Title.

DITTES, James E 250
The church in the way, by James E. Dittes. New York, Scribner,[1967] xix, 358 p. 24 cm. [BV4011.D54] 67-24041
1. Pastoral theology. I. Title.

DITTES, James E. 250
The church in the way, by James E. Dittes. New York, Scribner [1967] xix, 358 p. 24 cm. [BV4011.D54] 67-24041
1. Pastoral theology. I. Title.

DOING, Robert B. 250
Answering Christ's call. Foreword by Henry I. Louttit. New York, Seabury Pr. [1965, c.1959] 192p. 19cm. First pub. under title Witness by word and life. 1.95 pap.,
I. Title.

DONALDSON, Margaret F 250
How to put church members to work. [Westwood, N.J.] Revell [1963] 63 p. forms. 21 cm. (Revell's better church series) [BV652.D582] 63-17114
1. Church work. 2. Church officers. I. Title.

DONALDSON, Margaret F. 250
How to put church members to work. [Westwood, N. J.] Revell [c.1963] 63p. forms. 21cm. (Revell's better church ser.) 63-17114 1.00 pap.,
1. Church work. 2. Church officers. I. Title.

DURKIN, Mary G., 1934- 250
The suburban woman : her changing role in the Church / Mary G. Durkin. New York : Seabury Press, c1975. p. cm. "A Crossroad book." Bibliography: p. [BV4415.D83] 75-29147 ISBN 0-8164-1200-6 : 6.95
1. Women in church work. 2. Women. 3. Suburban life. I. Title.

ESPINOSA POLIT, Aurelio. 250
Our happy lot; out vocation in the light of the Gospels and Epistles. Translated by William J. Young. St. Louis, Herder, 1951. xi, 245 p. 21 cm. [BX1912.E7] 51-992
1. Clergy—Appointment, call, and election. 2. Vocation (in religious orders, congregations. etc.) 3. Clergy—Religious life. I. Title.

FACKRE, Gabriel J 250
The pastor and the world; the public sector witness of the parish minister [by] Gabriel J. Fackre. Philadelphia, United Church Press [1964] 126 p. 24 cm. Bibliographical references included in "Notes" (p. 119-126) [BV4011.F27] 64-25364
1. Pastoral theology — United Church of Christ. I. Title.

FACKRE, Gabriel J. 250
The pastor and the world; the public sector witness of the parish minister. Philadelphia. United Church Pr. [c.1964] 126p. 24cm. Bibl. 64-25364 1.75 pap.,
1. Pastoral theology—United Church of Christ. I. Title.

FALLAW, Wesner. 250
The case method in pastoral and lay education. Philadelphia, Westminster Press [1963] 207 p. 21 cm. [BV4020.F3] 63-7343
1. Pastoral theology — Study and teaching. I. Title.

FALLAW, Wesner 250
The case method in pastoral and lay education. Philadelphia, Westminister [c.1963] 207p. 21cm. 63-7343 4.00
1. Pastoral theology—Study and teaching. I. Title.

FENN, Don Frank, 1890- 250
Parish administration. 2d ed. New York, Morehouse-Gorham Co., 1951. 334 p. 23 cm. [BX5965.F4 1951] 51-8948
1. Theology, Pastoral—Anglican communion. 2. Church work. 3. Sunday-schools. I. Title.

FLORISTAN, Casiano, 1926- 250
The parish, eucharistic community. Translated by John F. Byrne, with a foreword by Louis J. Putz. Notre Dame, Ind., Fides Publishers [1964] 240 p. 21 cm. Bibliography: p. 208-240. [BV700.F513] 64-23519
1. Parishes. 2. Pastoral theology — Catholic Church. I. Title.

FLORISTAN, Casiano, 1926- 250
The parish. eucharistic community. Tr. [from Spanish] by John F Byrne. Foreword by Louis J. Putz. Notre Dame, Ind., Fides [c.1964] 240p. 21cm. Bibl. 64-23519 4.95
1. Parishes. 2. Pastoral theology—Catholic Church. I. Title.

FORRESTER, William Roxburgh, 1892- 250
Christian vocation; studies in faith and work, being the Cunningham lectures, 1950, in New College, Edinburgh. New York, Scribner, 1953. 223p. 21cm. [BV4740.F6 1953] 53-9436
1. Vocation. I. Title.

GIFFORD, Frank Dean, 1891- 250
This ministry and service; a textbook of pastoral care and parish administration. New York, Morehouse-Gorham [1956] 192p. 21cm. [BV4010.G47] 56-86456
1. Theology, Pastoral. I. Title.

GOULOOZE, William, 1903- 250
The Christian worker's handbook. Grand Rapids, Baker Book House, 1953. 218p. 17cm. [BV4016.G6] 53-28239
1. Theology, Pastoral—Handbooks, manuals, etc. I. Title.

GOULOOZE, William, 1903- 250
Pastoral psychology; applied psychology in pastoral theology in America. Grand Rapids, Baker Book House, 1950. 266 p. 24 cm. Bibliography: p. [211]-236. [BV4012.G58] 50-4210
1. Psychology, Pastoral. I. Title.

GREELEY, Andrew M., 1928- 250
The crucible of change; the social dynamics of pastoral practice [by] Andrew M. Greeley. New York, Sheed and Ward [1968] 188 p. 21 cm. [BV4011.G69] 68-26039 4.50
1. Pastoral theology—Catholic Church. I. Title.

GREEVES, Frederic, 1903- 250
Theology and the cure of souls; an introduction to pastoral theology. Manhasset, N.Y., Channel Press [1962] 180 p. 21 cm. (The Cato lecture of 1960) [[BV4011.G7]] 62-18047
1. Pastoral theology — Methodist Church. I. Title.

GREEVES, Frederic, 1903- 250
Theology and the cure of souls; an introduction to pastoral theology. Manhasset, N.Y., Channel [c.1962] 180p. 21cm. (Cato lect. of 1960) 62-18047 3.75
1. Pastoral theology—Methodist Church. I. Title.

GREGORIUS I, the Great, Saint, Pope, 540 (ca.)-604. 250
Pastoral care; translated and annotated by Henry Davis. Westminster, Md., Newman Press, 1950. 281 p. 23 cm. (Ancient Christian writers; the works of the Fathers in translation, no. 11) Bibliographical references included in "Notes" (p. [239]-270) [BR60.A35 no. 11] 50-10904
1. Theology, Pastoral—Catholic Church. I. Davis, Henry, 1866- ed. and tr. II. Title. III. Series.

GUFFIN, Gilbert Lee. 250
Called of God: the work of the ministry. Introd. by Andrew W. Blackwood. Westwood, N. J., Revell ['1951] 128 p. 20 cm. [BV660.G8] 51-14839
1. Clergy. I. Title.

GUFFIN, Gilbert Lee. 250
Pastor and church; a manual for pastoral leadership. Foreword by Davis C. Woolley. Nashville, Broadman Press [1955] 154p. 21cm. [BV4010.G85] 55-14075
1. Theology, Pastoral. I. Title.

GUFFIN, Gilbert Lee 250
Pastor and church; a manual for pastoral leadership.4th ed. Birmingham, Ala., Banner Pr. [1963, c.1955] xii, 160p. 22cm. Bibl. 63-21959 2.65 pap.,
1. Pastoral theology. I. Title.

HALVERSON, Richard C. 250
How I changed my thinking about the church [by] Richard C. Halverson. Grand Rapids, Zondervan Pub. House [1972] 120 p. 21 cm. [BV600.2.H26] 72-85567 3.95
1. Church. 2. Christian life—Presbyterian authors. I. Title.

HARMON, Nolan Bailey, 1892- 250
Ministerial ethics and etiquette. Rev. ed. New York, Abingdon-Cokesbury Press [1950] 215 p. 21 cm. [BV4012.H3 1950] 50-8100
1. Theology, Pastoral. I. Title.

HEENAN, John Carmel, 1905- 250
The people's priest. London and New York, Sheed and Ward [1951] 243 p. 21 cm. [BX1912.H36 1951] 51-8077
1. Theology, Pastoral—Catholic Church. I. Title.

HEENAN, John Carmel, 250
Cardinal, 1905-
The people's priest. New York, Sheed and Ward, 1952 [c1951] 243 p. 21 cm. [BX1913.H36] 52-1489
1. Pastoral theology—Catholic Church. I. Title.

HEENAN, John Carmel, 250
Cardinal, 1905-
The people's priest. London and New York, Sheed and Ward [1951] 243 p. 21 cm. [BX1913.H36] 51-8077
1. Pastoral theology—Catholic Church. I. Title.

HERRMANN, John Ewald, 1902- 250
The chief steward; a manual on pastoral leadership. St. Louis, Concordia Pub. House [1951] 113 p. illus. 24 cm. [BV652.H4] 51-8114
1. Church work. 2. Stewardship, Christian. I. Title.

HILTNER, Seward, 1909- 250
Preface to pastoral theology. New York, Abingdon Press [1958] 240p. 24cm. (The Ayer lectures, 1954) Includes bibliography. [BV4011.H5] 58-5398
1. Pastoral theology. 2. Spencer, Ichabod, 1798-1854. A pastor's sketches. I. Title.

HOLLAND, Cornelius Joseph, 250
1873-
The shepherd and his flock; on the duties and responsibilities of Catholic pastors. New York, D. McKay Co. [1953] 220p. 21cm. [BX1912.H63] 53-7931
1. Theology, Pastoral—Catholic Church. I. Title.

HOLMES, Urban Tigner, 1930- 250
The future shape of ministry, a theological projection [by] Urban T. Holmes III. New York, Seabury Press [1971] vi, 310 p. 21 cm. Includes bibliographical references. [BV4011.H58] 72-150697 4.50
1. Pastoral theology. I. Title.

HOPKIN, Charles Edward, 1900- 250
The watchman. New York, Crowell [1960] 117p. 21cm. [BV4011.H6] 60-8253
1. Pastoral theology. 2. Apologetics—20th cent. I. Title.

HOUTART, Francois, 1925- 250
Sociology and pastoral care. Translated from the French by Malachy Carroll. Chicago, Franciscan Herald Press [1965] vi, 77 p. 21 cm. [BX1913.H613] 65-25839
1. Pastoral theology — Catholic Church. 2. Religion and sociology. I. Title.

HOUTART, Francois, 1925- 250
Sociology and pastoral care. Tr. from French by Malachy Carroll. Chicago, Franciscan Herald [c.1965] vi, 77p. 21cm. [BX1913.H613] 65-25839 price unreported pap.,
1. Pastoral theology—Catholic Church. 2. Religion and sociology. I. Title.

HUTCHINSON, John Alexander, 250
1912-
Language and faith; studies in sign, symbol, and meaning. Philadelphia, Westminster Press [1963] 316 p. 21 cm. [BV4319.H8] 63-10334
1. Communication (Theology) 2. Religion and language. I. Title.

HUTCHISON, John Alexander, 250
1912-.
Language and faith; studies in sign, symbol, and meaning. Philadelphia, Westminister Press [1963] 316 p. 21 cm. [BV4319.H8] 63-10334
1. Communication (Theology) 2. Religion and language. I. Title.

JACKSON, Benjamin Franklin, 250
1907-
Communication for churchmen series. B. F. Jackson, Jr., editor. Nashville, Abingdon Press [1968- v. illus. 25 cm. [BV4319.J3] 68-28826 5.95
1. Communication(Theology) 2. Communication—Audio-visual aids. 3. Religious education. I. Title.

JOHNSON, Paul Emanuel, 1898- 250
Psychology of pastoral care. Nashville, Abingdon-Cokesbury [1953] 362p. 24cm. [BV4012.J64] 53-8134
1. Psychology, Pastoral. 2. Theology, Pastoral. I. Title.

JOHNSON, Paul Emanuel, 1898- 250
Psychology of pastoral care. Nashville, Abingdon [1964, c.1953] 362p. 23cm. (Apex bks., R2) 1.95 pap.,
1. Psychology, Pastoral. 2. Theology, Pastoral. I. Title.

JUNGMANN, Josef Andreas, 250
1889-
Announcing the word of God, by Josef A. Jungmann. Translated by Ronald Walls. [New York, Herder and Herder, 1967, c1968] 176 p. 22 cm. Translation of Glaubensverkundigung im Lichte der Frohbotschaft. Bibliographical footnotes. [BX1912.J8413] 68-17328
1. Pastoral theology—Catholic Church. 2. Kerygma. I. Title.

JUNGMANN, Josef Andreas, 250
1889-
Announcing the word of God, by Josef A. Jungmann. [New York, Herder and Herder, 1967, c1968] 176 p. 22 cm. Translation of Glaubensverkundigung im Lichte der Frohbotschaft. Bibliographical footnotes. [BX1912.J8413] 68-17328
1. Pastoral Theology—Catholic Church. 2. Kerygma. I. Title.

KEECH, William J 250
The life I owe; Christian stewardship as a way of life. Valley Forge, Judson Press [1963] 108 p. 21 cm. Includes bibliographies. [BV772.K4] 63-13989
1. Stewardship, Christian. I. Title.

KEECH, William J. 250
The life I owe; Christian stewardship as a way of life. Valley Forge, Judson [c.1963] 108p. 21cm. Bibl. 63-13989 1.50 pap.,
1. Stewardship, Christian. I. Title.

KEECH, William J 250
Our church plans for missionary and stewardship education. Valley Forge [Pa.] Judson Press [1963] 104 p. illus. 19 cm. [BV602.K4] 62-17000
1. Stewardship, Christian — Study and teaching. 2. Missions — Study and teaching. I. Title.

KEECH, William J. 250
Our church plans for missionary and stewardship education. Valley Forge [Pa.] Judson [c.1963] 104p. illus. 19cm. 62-17000 1.25 pap.,
1. Stewardship, Christian—Study and teaching. 2. Missions—Study and teaching. I. Title.

†KEELER, Ronald F. 250
To the work! : What you can do after the sermon / Ronald F. Keeler. Cincinnati : Standard Pub., c1976. 87 p. ; 22 cm. [BV4400.K38] 76-26296 ISBN 0-87239-135-3 pbk. : 2.95
1. Church work. 2. Christian life—1960- I. Title.

KENNEDY, Gerald Hamilton, 250
Bp., 1907-
The seven worlds of the minister [by] Gerald Kennedy. [1st ed.] New York, Harper & Row [1968] xiii, 173 p. 21 cm. [BV4011.K44] 68-17580
1. Pastoral theology. I. Title.

KENT, Homer Austin, 1898- 250
The pastor and his work, by Homer A. Kent, Sr. Chicago, Moody Press [1963] 301 p. illus. 24 cm. Includes bibliographical references. [BV4011.K45] 63-14563
1. Pastoral theology. I. Title.

KENT, Homer Austin, 1926- 250
The pastor and his work. Chicago, Moody [c.1963] 301p. illus. 24cm. Bibl. 63-14563 4.50
1. Pastoral theology. I. Title.

KITAGAWA, Daisuke. 250
The pastor and the race issue. New York, Seabury Press [1965] 139, [2] p. 21 cm. Bibliography: p. [141] [BT734.2.K49] 65-14645
1. Church and race problems. I. Title.

KITAGAWA, Daisuke 250
The pastor and the race issue. New York, Seabury [c.1965] 139[2]p. 21cm. Bibl. [BT734.2.K49] 65-14645 3.50
1. Church and race problems. I. Title.

KUNTZ, Kenneth A 250
Wooden chalices, new ideas for stewardship. St. Louis, Bethany Press [1963] 192 p. 23 cm. [BV772.K8] 62-22316
1. Stewardship, Christian. I. Title.

KUNTZ, Kenneth A. 250
Wooden chalices, new ideas for stewardship. St. Louis, Bethany [c.1963] 192p. 23cm. Bibl. 62-22316 3.50
1. Stewardship, Christian. I. Title.

LAWRENCE, William Appleton, 250
Bp., 1889-
Parsons. vestries, and parishes: a manual. Greenwich, Conn., Seabury Pr. [c.]1961 304p. Bibl. 61-12427 6.00
1. Pastoral theology—Anglican Communion—Hand-books. manuals, etc. I. Title.

LAWRENCE, William Appleton, 250
Bp., 1889-
Parsons, vestries, and parishes: a manual. New York, Seabury [1964, c.1961] 304p. 21cm. (SP12) Bibl. 1.95 pap.,
1. Pastoral theology—Anglican Communion—Hand-books, manuals, etc. I. Title.

LAWRENCE, William Appleton, 250
Bp., 1889-
Parsons, vestries, and parishes: a manual. Greenwich, Conn., Seabury Press, 1961. 304p. 22cm. Includes bibliography. [BX5965.L3] 61-12427
1. Pastoral theology —Anglican Communion—Handbooks, manuals, etc. I. Title.

LEACH, William Herman, 1888- 250
Handbook of church management. Englewood Cliffs, N. J., Prentice-Hall, 1958. 504 p. illus. 22 cm. [BV4011.L4] 58-12327
1. Pastoral theology. 2. Church work. I. Title: Church management.

LESCH, Gomer R. 250
Creative Christian communication. Nashville, Broadman [c.1965] 128p. 20cm. Bibl. [BV4319.L4] 65-23047 1.50 bds.,
1. Communication (Theology) I. Title.

MCKAY, Arthur R. 250
Servants and stewards; the teaching and practice of stewardship. Geneva Pr. dist. Philadelphia, Westminster, c.1963 76p. 20cm. hristian. 63-12597 1.25
I. Title.

MCLANE, Edwin D. 250
The 7:05 and the church alive; dynamic and successful programs in today's churches. Englewood Cliffs, N.J., Prentice [c.1963] xiv, 207p. 22cm. Bibl. 63-19619 4.95
1. Pastoral theology. I. Title.

MCLAUGHLIN, Raymond W. 250
Communication for the church [by] Raymond W. McLaughlin. Grand Rapids, Zondervan Pub. House [1968] 228 p. 23 cm. Bibliography: p. 213-223. [BV4319.M2] 68-12953
1. Communication (Theology) I. Title.

MCMULLEN, John S. 250
Stewardship unlimited, a cooperative text, pub. for the Cooperative Pubn. Assn. Richmond, Va., John Knox [1962, c.1961] 94p. 20cm. (Faith for life ser.) 62-19445 1.00, 1.25 pap., after Jan. 1,
1. Stewardship, Christian. I. Title.

MCNEIL, Jesse Jai. 250
Men in the local church. New and rev. ed. Nashville, Townsend Press [1960] 128p. illus. 20cm. [BV4440.M3 1960] 60-37400
1. Men in church work. 2. Laity. I. Title.

MARSHALL, David F., comp. 250
Creative ministries. Philadelphia, Pilgrim Press [1968] 124 p. illus. 21 cm. [BV4400.M38] 68-8396 2.95
1. Church work. I. Title.

MELTON, William Walter, 1879- 250
The making of a preacher. Introd. by W. R. White. Grand Rapids, Zondervan Pub. House [1953] 150p. 21cm. [BV4010.M393] 53-36893
1. Theology, Pastoral. I. Title.

MERKENS, Guido A 250
Living Lutheran leadership [by Guido Merkens. 1st ed. Austin, Tex., C. E. Saegert Pub. Co., c1964] 1 v. (various pagings) illus., forms. 28 cm. Includes bibliography. [BV652.M47] 64-66451
1. Church work — Handbooks, manuals, etc. I. Title.

MERKENS, Guido A 250
Organized for action; how to build a successful parish and its program. St. Louis, Concordia Pub. House [1959] St. Louis, Concordia Pub. House [1961] 125p. illus. 24cm. 68p. 23cm. [BM652.M48] 61-15971
1. Church work. 2. Laity. I. Title. II. Title: — Training lay leadership;

MICHONNEAU, G 250
Revolution in a city parish. With a foreword by Archbishop Cushing. Westminster, Md., Newman Press, 1950. xxi, 189 p. 23 cm. [BX2347.M5] 50-9047
1. Theology, Pastoral — Catholic Church. 2. Church work. 3. Catholic Churh in France. I. Title.

MICHONNEAU, Georges, 1899- 250
Revolution in a city parish. With a foreword by Archbishop Cushing. Westminster, Md., Newman Press, 1950. xxi, 189p. 23cm. [BX2347.M5] 50-9047
1. Theology, Pastoral—Catholic Church. 2. Church work. 3. Catholic Church in France. I. Title.

MIDWESTERN Institute of 250
Pastoral Theology. 1st, Sacred Heart Seminary, 1961.
Sharing the Christian message. [Proceedings of the] first annual institute, August 27-30, 1961. Detroit, 1962. 120 p. illus. 22 cm. Sponsored by St. John's Provincial Seminary and Sacred Heart Seminary. Includes bibliographical references. [BX1913.A1M5] 63-3808
1. Pastoral theology — Catholic Church — Congresses. 2. Religious education — Congresses. I. St. John's Provincial Seminary. Plymouth, Mich. II. Detroit. Sacred Heart Seminary. III. Title.

MONDALE, Robert Lester, 1904- 250
Preachers in purgatory, with reference to accounts of more than a hundred ministers reporting on crisis situations, by Lester Mondale. Boston, Beacon Press [1966] xii, 243 p. 22 cm. Bibliographical references included in "Notes" (p. 240-243) [BV4011.M6] 66-15071
1. Pastoral theology. I. Title.

MONDALE, Robert Lester, 1904- 250
Preachers in purgatory, with reference to accounts of more than a hundred ministers reporting on crisis situations. Boston, Beacon [c.1966] xii, 243p. 22cm. Bibl. [BV4011.M6] 66-15071 4.95 bds.,
1. Pastoral theology. I. Title.

MUELLER, Charles S 250
The strategy of evangelism; a primer for congregational evangelism committees [by] Charles S. Mueller. Saint Louis, Concordia Pub. House [1965] 96 p. 20 cm. Evangelistic work. Bibliography: p. 96. [BV3790.M836] 65-23702
I. Title.

MUELLER, Charles S. 250
The strategy of evangelism; a primer for congregational evangelismcommittees. St. Louis, Concordia [c.1965] 96p. 20cm. Bibl. [BV3790.M836] 65-23702 1.25 pap.,
1. Evangelistic work. I. Title.

MULLEN, Thomas James, 1934- 250
The renewal of the ministry. With an introd. by D. Elton Trueblood. New York, Abingdon Press [1963] 143 p. 21 cm. [BV4011.M8] 63-14596
1. Pastoral theology. I. Title.

MULLEN, Thomas James, 1934- 250
The renewal of the ministry. Introd. by D. Elton Trueblood. Nashville, Abingdon [c.1963] 143p. 21cm. 63-14596 3.00
1. Pastoral theology. I. Title.

NAVAGH, James J 250
The apostolic parish. New York, P. J. Kenedy [c1950] xiii, 166 p. 20 cm. [BX1912.N3] 51-3471
1. Theology, Pastoral — Catholic Church. I. Title.

NEILL, Stephen Charles, Bp. 250
Fulfill thy ministry. [1st ed.] New York, Harper [1952] 152 p. 20 cm. [BV4010.N4] 51-11944
1. Theology, Pastoral. I. Title.

THE New shape of pastoral 250
theology; essays in honor of Seward Hiltner. Edited by William B. Oglesby, Jr. Nashville, Abingdon Press [1969] 383 p. port. 24 cm.

Includes bibliographical references. [BV4017.N37] 72-84721 ISBN 6-87278-791-7.95
1. Pastoral theology—Addresses, essays, lectures. I. Hiltner, Seward, 1909- II. Oglesby, William B., ed.

NOUWEN, Henri J. M. 250
Creative ministry [by] Henri J. M. Nouwen. [1st ed.] Garden City, N.Y., Doubleday, 1971. xxi, 119 p. 22 cm. [BV4011.N68] 73-139050 4.95
1. Pastoral theology. I. Title.

OATES, Wayne E 1917- 250
The Christian pastor. Philadelphia, Westminster Press [1951] 171 p. 21 cm. [BV4010.O2] 51-9873
1. Theology. Pastoral. 2. Psychology, Pastoral. I. Title.

OATES, Wayne Edward, 1917- 250
The Christian pastor. Philadelphia, Westminster Press [1951] 171p. 21cm. [BV4010.O2] 51-9873
1. Theology, Pastoral. 2. Psychology, Pastoral. I. Title.

OMAN, John Wood, 1860-1939 250
Concerning the ministry. Richmond, Va., John Knox [1963] 248p. 22cm. 63-8126 2.50 pap.,
1. Preaching. I. Title.

OSTER, Henri. 250
The paschal mystery in parish life. Translated by Michael O'Brien. [New York] Herder and Herder [1967] 144 p. 22 cm. Translation of Le mystere pascal dans la pastorale. Bibliographical footnotes. [BX1913.O813] 66-13070
1. Pastoral theology—Catholic Church. 2. Paschal mystery. I. Title.

PELLEGRINO, Michele. 250
The true priest; the priesthood as preached and practised by St. Augustine. Translated by Arthur Gibson. [New York] Philosophical Library [1968] 184 p. 23 cm. Translation of Verus sacerdos. Articles published between 1962 and 1965 in the Seminarium. Bibliographical footnotes. [BR1720.A9P363] 68-7498 6.00
1. Augustinus, Aurelius, Saint, Bp. of Hippo. 2. Pastoral theology—History of doctrines. I. Title.

PFLIEGLER, Michael, 1891- 250
Pastoral theology. Translated by John Drury. Westminster, Md., Newman Press 1966. x, 311 p. 23 cm. [BX1913.P413] 65-25981
1. Pastoral theology—Catholic Church. I. Title.

PLEUTHNER, Willard Augustus 250
Building up your congregation; help from tested business methods. [Rev. ed.] Chicago, Wilcox & Follett [1951] 135 p. illus. 25 cm. [BV652.P6 1951] 51-6120
1. Church work I. Title.

PLEUTHNER, Willard Augustus. 250
Building up your congregation; help from tested business methods. [Rev. ed.] Chicago, Wilcox & Follett [1951] 135p. illus. 25cm. [BV652.P6 1951] 51-6120
1. Church work. I. Title.

PLEUTHNER, Willard Augustus 250
Building up your congregation; help from tested business methods. Chicago, Wilcox & Follett [1950] viii, 135 p. illus. 2 cm. Bibliography: p. 130-132. [BV652.P6] 50-9873
1. Church work. I. Title.

PLEUTHNER, Willard Augustus 250
More power for your church; proven plans and projects, by Willard Augustus Pleuthner, with the assistance of several hundred clergy and church workers of different denominations and faiths. [Limited 1st ed.] New York, Farrar, Straus and Young [1952] 408 p. illus. 22 cm. [BV652.P62] 52-14064
1. Church work. I. Title.

PLEUTHNER. WILLARD AUGUSTUS. 250
More power for your church Building up your congregation. With the assistance of several hundred clergy and church workers of different denominations and faiths. New York, Farrar, Straus and Cudahy [1959] 287p. illus. 21cm. Condensed versions of the author's More power for your church and Building up your congregation, with additional chapters. [BV652.P63] 59-6589
1. Church work. I. Title. II. Title: Building up your congregation.

RAHNER, Karl, 1904- 250
The Christian commitment; essays in pastoral theology. Translated by Cecily Hastings. New York, Sheed and Ward [1963] vi, 218 p. 22 cm. One of 3 vols., each with distinctive title, which together represent the English translation of the author's Sendung und Gnade, published in London under title: Mission and grace. Bibliographical references included in "Notes" (p. 200-204, 217-218) [BX1913.R313] 63-17146
1. Pastoral theology—Catholic Church—Addresses, essays, lectures. I. Title.

RAHNER, Karl, 1904- 250
Christian in the market place. Translated by Cecily Hastings. New York, Sheed & Ward [1966] 184 p. 21 cm. One of 3 vols., each with distinctive title, which together represent the English translation of the author's Sendung und Gnade, published in London under title: Mission and grace. Includes bibliographical references. [BX1913.R29] 66-22022
1. Pastoral theology—Catholic Church. I. Title.

RAHNER, Karl, 1904- 250
Theology of pastoral action. [Translated by W. J. O'Hara and adapted for an English-speaking audience by Daniel Morrissey. New York] Herder and Herder [1968] 144 p. 22 cm. (Studies in pastoral theology, v. 1) Translation of Grundlegung der Pastoraltheologie als praktische Theologie. Bibliography: p. 135-139. [BV600.2.R3413] 67-18253 4.50
1. Church. 2. Pastoral theology—Catholic Church. I. Title.

RAINES, Robert Arnold. 250
Reshaping the Christian life. [1st ed.] New York, Harper & Row [1964] x, 174 p. 22 cm. Bibliography: p. 167-168. Bibliographical references included in "Notes" (p. 169-172) [BV4501.2.R3] 63-15954
1. Christian life—Methodist authors. 2. Church group work. I. Title.

RAINES, Robert Arnold 250
Reshaping the Christian life. New York, Harper [c.1964] x, 174p. 22cm. Bibl. 63-15954 3.00
1. Christian life—Methodist authors. 2. Church group work. I. Title.

REES, Tom. 250
Break-through. Waco, Tex., Word Books [1970] 196 p. illus. 23 cm. [BV652.2.R37] 75-107949 4.95
1. Church group work. I. Title.

REORGANIZED Church of Jesus Christ of Latter Day Saints. 250
The priesthood manual. Prepared under the direction of the director of priesthood education. Rev. Independence, Mo., Herald House, 1957. 164p. 19cm. [BX8675.A45 1957] 57-1208
1. Pastoral theology—Mormon Church. I. Title.

REORGANIZED Church of Jesus Christ of Latter--Day Saints. 250
The priesthood manual. Prepared under the direction of the director of priesthood education. Rev. Independence, Mo., Herald House, 1957. 164p. 19cm. [BX8675.A45 1957] 57-1208
1. Pastoral theology—Mormon Church. I. Title.

REORGANIZED Church of Jesus Christ of Latter Day Saints. 250
The priesthood manual; prepared under the direction of Floyd M. McDowell. Independence, Mo., Herald House, 1950 [c1949] 165 p. diagrs. 19 cm. "New edition" -- Dust jacket. [BX8671.A544 1950] 51-1175
1. Theology. Pastoral — Mormon Church. I. McDowell, Floyd Marion. II. Title.

REORGANIZED Church of Jesus Christ of Latter-Day Saints. 250
The priesthood manual. Prepared under the direction of the Office of Priesthood and Leadership Education. [New ed.] Independence, Mo., Herald House, 1964. 214 p. 18 cm. (Pastors' reference library) Bibliography: p. 209-210. [BX8675.A45] 64-25012
1. Pastoral theology — Mormon Church. I. Title.

REORGANIZED Church of Jesus Christ of Latter-Day Saints 250
The priesthood manual. Prep. under the direction of the Office of Priesthood and Leadership Educ. [New ed.] Independence, Mo., Herald [c.]1964. 214p. 18cm. (Pastors' ref. lib.) Bibl. 64-25012 2.50
1. Pastoral theology—Mormon Church. I. Title.

REORGANIZED Church of Jesus Christ of Latter-Day Saints. 250
The Priesthood manual, prepared by Alfred H. Yale. [Completely rev. ed.] [Independence, Mo., Herald Press, 1972] 317 p. 18 cm. (Pastor's reference library) Bibliography: p. 316-317. [BX8675.A45 1972] 72-177206 ISBN 0-8309-0065-9
1. Pastoral theology—Mormonism. I. Yale, Alfred H. II. Title.

REYNOLDS, Ralph Vincent. 250
Making full proof of our ministry; a handbook of elementary pastoral studies based on the Scriptures. [Winnipeg, Columbia Press, 1953] 145p. 20cm. [BV4010.R4] 53-30886
1. Theology, Pastoral. I. Title.

RHODES, John D 250
Success secrets for pastors, by John Rhodes. Mountain View, Calif., Pacific Press Pub. Association [1965] viii, 166 p. illus., facsims., forms. 26 cm. Bibliography: p. 160-162. [BV4011.R5] 64-8744
1. Pastoral theology — Seventh-Day Adventists. I. Title.

RHODES, John D. 250
Success secrets for pastors. Mountain View, Calif., Pacific Pr. [c.1965] viii, 166p. illus. facisms., forms. 26cm. Bibl. [BV4011.R5] 64-8744 5.50
1. Pastoral theology—Seventh-Day Adventists. I. Title.

*RICE, John R. 250
Why our churches do not win souls. Murfreesboro, Tenn., Sword of the Lord, Box 1099 [c.1966] 178p. 21cm. 2.50
I. Title.

RILEY, William Bell, 1861-1947. 250
Pastoral problems. [Westwood, N. J.] F. H. Revell Co. [1959] 192p. 21cm. (Revell's preaching and pastoral aid series) [BV4010.R5 1959] 59-5503
1. Pastoral theology. I. Title.

RITSCHIL DIETRICH. 250
Christ our life; the protestant church at worship and work. Translated by J. Colin Campbell. Ednburgh, Olifver and Boyd, 1960. 114p. 23cm. Translation of Vom Leben in der Kirche. [BV652.R563] 60-52329
1. Church work. I. Title.

RODENMAYER, Robert N 250
We have this ministry. [1st ed.] New York, Harper [1959] 126p. 20cm. (The Kellogg lectures at the Episcopal Theological School, Cambridge, Massachusetts, 1958) Bibliographical references included in 'Notes' (p. 125-126) [BV4011.R6] 59-5548
1. Pastoral theology. I. Title. II. Series: The Kellogg lectures. 1958

ROTH, Arnold C 250
Learing to work together, by Arnold Roth. Scottdale, Pa., Herald Press [1967] 96 p. 19 cm. (Christian service training series) [BV652.R67] 67-28310
1. Church work. I. Title.

ROTH, Arnold C. 250
Learning to work together, by Arnold Roth. Scottdale, Pa., Herald Pr. [1967] 96p. 19cm. (Christian serv. training ser.) [BV652.R67] 67-28310 1.25 pap.,
1. Church work. I. Title.

SANGSTER, William Edwin, 1900- 250
The approach to preaching. Philadelphia, Westminster Press [1952] 112p. 20cm. [BV4010.S16] 52-7115
1. Theology, Pastoral. I. Title.

SANGSTER, William Edwin Robert, 1900- 250
The approach to preaching [by] W. E. Sangster Grand Rapids Baker Book House [1974, c1952] 112 p. 20 cm. [BV4010.S16] ISBN 0-8010-8023-1 1.95 (pbk.)
1. Theology, Pastoral. I. Title.
L.C. card no. for original edition: 52-7115.

SEGLER, Franklin M. 250
The Broadman minister's manual [by] Franklin M. Segler. Nashville, Broadman Press [1968] iv, 154 p. 17 cm. [BV4016.S37] 68-26920
1. Pastoral theology—Handbooks, manuals, etc. I. Title. II. Title: Minister's manual.

SELLMAIR, Josef, 1896- 250
The priest in the world. [Translation by Brian Battershaw] Westminster, Md. [1954?] 238p. 23cm. [BX1912.S483] 55-7042
1. Catholic Church—Clergy. 2. Clergy—Office. 3. Theology, Pastoral—Catholic Church. I. Title.

SHANNON, Harper. 250
Trumpets in the morning. Nashville, Tenn., Broadman Press [1969] 156 p. 21 cm. (Broadman books) [BV4011.S46] 76-93912 3.50
1. Pastoral theology. I. Title.

SHOEMAKER, Samuel Moor, 1893- 250
The church alive. [1st ed.] New York, Dutton, 1950. 160 p. 20 cm. [BV4010.S535] 50-7524
1. Theology, Pastoral. 2. Church work. I. Title.

SHRADER, Wesley. 250
Dear Charles; letters to a young minister. New York, Macmillan, 1954. 109p. 21cm. [BV4015.S35] 54-12798
1. Theology, Pastoral. I. Title.

SMITH, Karl Franklin. 250
The Scriptural view of the Christian pastorate. [Columbus? Ohio, 1951] 154 p. 19 cm. [BV4012.S56 1951] 51-39053
1. Theology, Pastoral. I. Title.

SMITH, Roy Lemon, 1887- 250
Winning ways for working churches [by] Roy L. Smith. New York. Cincinnati [etc.] The Abingdon press [c1932] 240 p. 19 1/2 cm. [BV4400.S617] 32-11669
1. Church work. 2. Pastoral theology. I. Title.

SOUTHCOTT, Ernest William. 250
The parish comes alive. Foreword by Horace W. B. Donegan, Bishop of New York. New York, Morehouse-Gorham Co. [1957, c1956] 143p. 21cm. (The Annual Bishop of New York books, 1957) [BX5132.S6 1957] 57-5287
1. Theology, Pastoral—Church of England. I. Title.

SOUTHCOTT, Ernest William. 250
The parish comes alive. Foreword by Horace W. B. Donegan, Bishop of New York. New York, Morehouse-Gorham Co. [1957, c1956] 143 p. 21 cm. (The Annual Bishop of New York books, 1957) [BX5132.S6 1957] 57-5287
1. Theology, Pastoral — Church of England. I. Title.

STARKEY, Lycurgus Monroe. 250
The Holy Spirit at work in the church [by] Lycurgus M. Starkey, Jr. New York, Abingdon Press [1965] 160 p. 21 cm. Bibliographical footnotes. [BT121.2.S8] 65-20370
1. Holy Spirit. I. Title.

STARKEY, Lycurgus Monroe, Jr. 250
The Holy Spirit at work in the church. Nashville, Abingdon [c.1965] 160p. 21cm. Bibl. [BT121.2.S8] 65-20370 3.00
1. Holy Spirit. I. Title.

STERNER, R. Eugene 250
You have a ministry; Christian laymen are called to serve. Anderson, Ind., Warner [c.1963] 110p. 21cm. 63-15212 1.50 pap.,
1. Laity. I. Title.

STORER, James Wilson. 250
The preacher, his belief and behavior. Nashville, Broadman Press [1953] 104p. 20cm. [BV4010.S757] 53-9034
1. Theology. Pastoral. I. Title.

STRAUSS, Dorothy M 250
Christian worker's handbook. Boston, W. A. Wilde Co. [1957] 125 p. 20 cm. Includes bibliography. [BV652.S82] 57-13175
1. Church work. I. Title.

THORNTON, Martin. 250
Feed my lambs; essays in pastoral reconstruction. [American ed.] Greenwich, Conn., Seabury Press 1961. 142 p. 23 cm. Includes bibliography. [BV4011.T45] 61-979
1. Pastoral theology—Anglican Communion. I. Title.

THORNTON, Martin 250
Feed my lambs; essays in pastoral reconstruction. Greenwich, Conn., Seabury Press, 1961[ ] 142p. Bibl. 61-979 3.95
1. Pastoral theology—Anglican Communion. I. Title.

TORBET, Robert George, 1912- 250
The baptist ministery: then and now. Foreword by Lynn Leavenworth. Philadelphia, Judson Press [1953] 134p. 20cm. [BX6345.T6] 53-6776
1. Baptists—Clergy. I. Title.

TOWNS, Elmer L. 250
America's fastest growing churches; why 10 Sunday Schools are growing fast, by Elmer L. Towns. Nashville, Impact Books [1972] 218 p. illus. 23 cm. [BV652.25.T68] 72-76395 4.95
1. Church growth—Case studies. I. Title.

TOWNS, Elmer L. 250
Great soul-winning churches, by Elmer L. Towns. Murfreesboro, Tenn., Sword of the Lord Publishers [1973] 245 p. illus. 21 cm. A collection of articles which originally appeared in the Sword of the Lord, 1972-1973. [BV652.25.T69] 73-87082 4.50
1. Church growth—Case studies. 2. Evangelistic work—Case studies. I. Title.

WEBER, Hans-Ruedi 250
Salty christians. New York, Seabury [c.1963] 64p. 21cm. Prepared under the auspices of The Dept. of Christian Educ., Protestant Episcopal Church. .75 pap.,
I. Title.

WEDEL, Theodore Otto, 1892- 250
The gospel in a strange, new world. Philadelphia, Westminster Press [1963] 141 p.

21 cm. (Westminster studies in Christian communication) Includes bibliography. [BV4319.W4] 63-8161
1. Communication (Theology) I. Title.

WEDEL, Theodore Otto, 1892- 250
The gospel in a strange, new world. Philadelphia, Westminster [c.1963] 141p. 21cm. (Westminster studies in Christian communication) Bibl. 63-8161 3.75
1. Communication (Theology) I. Title.

WEITZEL, Eugene J., ed. 250
Pastoral ministry in a time of change. Eugene J. Weitzel, participating editor. Milwaukee, Bruce Pub. Co. [1966] xiv, 494 p. 23 cm. Bibliography: p. 447-478. [BX1913.W4] 66-29713
1. Pastoral theology—Catholic Church—Addresses, essays, lectures. I. Title.

WELLMAN, Sterrie Austin, 1879- 250
Your stewardship and mine, its blessings and responsibilities. Washington, Review and Herald Pub. Association [1950] 192 p. 20 cm. [BV770.W45] 50-1765
1. Stewardship, Christian. I. Title.

WORLEY, Robert C. 250
A gathering of strangers : understanding the life of your church / Robert C. Worley. Philadelphia : Westminster Press, c1976. p. cm. Includes bibliographical references. [BV600.2.W66] 76-21091 ISBN 0-664-24124-7 : 4.95
1. Church. 2. Theology, Practical. I. Title.

MIDWESTERN Institute of Pastoral Theology. 4th Sacred Heart Seminary,1964. 250.07152
The priest: the teacher of morality. [Proceedings of the] fourth annual institute, August 24-27, 1964. Detroit, 1964 [i.e. 1965] 157 p. 22 cm. Sponsored by the faculties of St. John's Provincial Seminary and Sacred Heart Seminary. [BX1913.A1M5] 65-29265
1. Pastoral theology — Catholic Church — Congresses. 2. Christian ethics — Study and teaching — Congresses. I. St. John's Provincial Seminary, Plymouth, Mich. II. Detroit. Sacred Heart Seminary. III. Title.

BERTRAM, Robert W. 250.08
The lively function of the Gospel; essays in honor of Richard R. Caemmerer on completion of 25 years as professor of practical theology at Concordia Seminary, Saint Louis. Robert W. Bertram, editor. Saint Louis, Concordia Pub. House [1966] ix. 196 24 cm. Bibliographical footnotes. [BR50.B44] 66-19143
1. Theology — Addresses, essays, lectures. I. Caemmerer, Richard Rudolf, 1904- II. Title.
CONTENTS OMITTED

BERTRAM, Robert W. ed. 250.08
The lively function of the Gospel; essays in honor of Richard R. Caemmerer on completion of 25 years as professor of practical theology at Concordia Seminary, Saint Louis. St. Louis, Concordia [c.1966] ix, 196p. front. 24cm. Bibl. [BR50.B44] 66-19143 5.00
1. Theology—Addresses, essays, lectures. I. Caemmerer,Richard Rudolf, 1904- II. Title.

DUFFIE, David. 250'.1'9
Psychology and the Christian religion. Nashville, Southern Pub. [1967,c.1968] 160p. 22cm. Bibl. [BV4012.D84] 67-31387 4.50
1. Pastoral psychology. I. Title.

DUFFIE, David. 250'.1'9
Psychology and the Christian religion. Nashville, Southern Pub. Association [1967, c1968] 160 p. 22 cm. Bibliography: p. 155-157. [BV4012.D84] 67-31387
1. Pastoral psychology. I. Title.

ULEYN, Arnold. 250'.1'9
Is it I, Lord? Pastoral psychology and the recognition of guilt. Translated by Mary Ilford. [1st ed.] New York, Holt, Rinehart and Winston [1969] xiv, 240 p. 22 cm. Translation of Actualite de la fonction prophetique. Includes bibliographical references. [BV4011.U413] 69-10763 5.95
1. Pastoral theology. I. Title.

DAVIDSON, Charles Theodore, 1905- 250.2
Minister's manual; some helps for the busy minister: funerals, dedications [and] weddings. Cleveland, Tenn., White Wing Pub. House & Press [1952] 91 p. illus. 16 cm. [BV4016.D35] 52-64999
1. Theology, Pastoral—Handbooks, manuals, etc. I. Title.

DAVIDSON, Charles Theodore, Bp., 1905- 250.2
Minister's manual; some helps for the busy minister: funerals, dedications [and] Weddings. Cleveland, Tenn., White Wing Pub. House & Press [1952] 91p. illus. 16cm. [BV4016)06.D35] 52-64999
1. Theology Pastoral-Handbooks, manuals, etc. I. Title.

KOON, Warren L ed. 250.2
Ministers' manual and discipline. [1st ed.] New York, Vantage Press [1957] 86p. 21cm. Includes bibliography. [BV4016.K6] 56-12307
1. Pastoral theology—Handbooks, manuals, etc. I. Title.

MCNEIL, Jesse Jai. 250.2
Minister's service book for pulpit and parish. Grand Rapids, Eerdmans [1961] 212p. 18cm. [BV4016.M26] 61-10860
1. Pastoral theology—Handbooks, manuals, etc. I. Title.

TRAYLOR, Melvin Alvah. 250'.2'07
The nomenclatural standing of clericus polydenominata [by] Melvin A. Traylor. Gurnee, Ill., Vanishing Press, 1967. 11 p. 14 cm. (Vanishing Press natural history references, no. 2) (A Vanishing Press monograph.) [PN6231.C5T7] 75-10256
1. Pastoral theology—Anecdotes, facetiae, satire, etc. I. Title.

DAVISON, Frank Elon, 1887- 250.76
Let's talk it over; questions on church work and church problems asked by ministers and lay people, answered with brevity, candor, humor, and understanding. St. Louis, Bethany Press [1953] 159p. 21cm. [BR96.D35] 53-32883
1. Questions and answers—Theology. 2. Church work. I. Title.

CLEVELAND, Philip Jerome, 1903- 250.8
It's bright in my valley. [Westwood, N. J.] Revell [1962] 192p. 21cm. [BV4015.C54] 62-10734
1. Pastoral theology—Anecdotes, facetiae, satire, etc. I. Title.

BARR, Browne. 250.81
Parish back talk. New York, Abingdon Press [1964] 127 p. 20 cm. (Lyman Beecher lectures, 1963) Bibliographical footnotes. [BV4011.B37] 64-16145
1. Pastoral theology — Addresses, essays, lectures. I. Title. II. Series: Lyman Beecher lectures on preaching. Yale University, 1963

BARR, Browne 250.81
Parish back talk. Nashville, Abingdon [c.1964] 127p. 20cm. (Lyman Beecher lects., 1963) Bibl. 64-16145 2.50
1. Pastoral theology—Addresses, essays, lectures. I. Title. II. Series: Lyman Beecher lectures on preaching, Yale University, 1963

LARGE, John Ellis 250.81
The small needle of Dr. Large. Englewood Cliffs, N. J., Prentice [c.1962] 177p. 22cm. 62-10175 3.50
1. Pastoral theology—Anecdotes, facetiae, satire, etc. I. Title.

ANDERSON, Kenneth, 1917- 250.88
It only happens to preachers. Grand Rapids, Zondervan Pub. House [1956] 185p. 20cm. [BV4015.A5] 56-41991
1. Theology. Pastoral—Anecdotes, fecetiae, satire, etc. I. Title.

CLEVELAND, Philip Jerome 250.88
Three churches and a Model T. [Westwood, N.J.] Revell [c.1960] 189p. 22cm. 60-5504 3.50 bds.,
1. Pastoral theology—Anecdotes, facetiae, satire, etc. I. Title.

CLEVELAND, Philip Jerome, 1903- 250.88
Three churches and a Model T. [Westwood, N. J.] Revell [1960] 189p. 22cm. [BV4015.C55] 60-5504
1. Pastoral theology—Anecdotes, facetiae, satire, etc. I. Title.

CLOWNEY, Edmund P. 250.88
Eutychus and his pin, edited with an apology. Grand Rapids, Mich., Eerdmans [c.1960] 102p. illus. 60-53092 2.50 bds.,
I. Title.

CLOWNEY, Edmund P 250.88
Eutychus and his pin, edited with an apology. Grand Rapids, Erdmans [1960] 102p. illus. 23cm. A selection of the author's articles which originally 'appeared in Christianity today's letter section, 'Eutychus and his skin.' ' [BV4015.C57] 60-53092
I. Title.

OWENS, Loulie (Latimer) 250.88
Minnie Belle. Illustrated by Murray McKeehan. Nashville, Broadman Press [1956] 109p. illus. 22cm. [PS3529.W4419M5] 56-8671
1. Theology, Pastoral—Anecdotes, facetiae, satire, etc. I. Title.

*MCNEILL, John T. 250.9
A history of the cure of souls. New York, Harper [1965, c.1951] 371p. 21cm. (Harper Torchbk.; Cloister lib., TB126) 2.25 pap.,
I. Title.

NOYCE, Gaylord B. 250'.9'04
The church is not expendable, by Gaylord B. Noyce. Philadelphia, Westminster Press [1969] 128 p. 21 cm. Bibliography: p. [126]-128. [BV601.8.N6] 69-10900 ISBN 6-642-08495-3.95
1. Mission of the church. 2. Church renewal. I. Title.

MULLIN, Joseph 250.96
The Catholic Church in modern Africa; a pastoral theology. London, G. Chapman [New York, Herder & Herder, 1966, c. 1965] ix, 256p. 23cm. Bibl. [BX1913.M8] 66-3287 4.95 bds.,
1. Pastoral theology—Catholic Church. 2. Missions—Africa. 3. Catholic Church in Africa. I. Title.

251 Preaching (Homiletics)

ABBEY, Merrill R. 251
Living doctrine in a vital pulpit [by] Merrill R. Abbey. New York, Abingdon Press [1964] 208 p. 21 cm. Bibliographical footnotes. [BV4211.2.A18] 64-21129
1. Preaching. I. Title.

ABBEY, Merrill R. 251
Living doctrine in a vital pulpit. Nashville. Abingdon [c.1964] 208p. 21cm. Bibl. 64-21129 3.50
1. Preaching. I. Title.

ABBEY, Merrill R. 251
Preaching to the contemporary mind. New York, Abingdon Press [1963] 192 p. 23 cm. [BV4211.2.A2] 63-7763
I. Title. II. Title: Preaching.

ABBEY, Merrill R. 251
Preaching to the contemporary mind. Nashville, Abingdon [c.1963] 192p. 23cm. 63-7763 4.00
1. Preaching. I. Title.

ABBEY, Merrill R. 251
The word interprets us [by] Merrill Abbey. New York, Abingdon Press [1967] 208 p. 21 cm. Bibliographical footnotes. [BV4211.2.A23] 67-11008
1. Bible—Homiletical use. 2. Preaching. I. Title.

*ADAMS, Jay E. 251
The homiletical innovations of Andrew W. Blackwood / Jay E. Adams. Grand Rapids : Baker Book House, 1976c1975. 166p. ; 22 cm. (Studies in preaching ; 3) Bibliography: pp. [159]-166. [BV4226] ISBN 0-8010-0105-6 pbk. : 3.50
1. Blackwood, Andrew W. D. 1966. 2. Homiletical illustrations. 3. Preaching. I. Title.

*ADAMS, Jay E. 251
Sense appeal in the sermons of Charles Haddon Spurgeon / Jay E. Adams. Grand Rapids : Baker Book House, 1976 c1975. [viii], 62 p. ; 22 cm. (Studies in preaching ; 1) Bibliography: pp. 60-62. [BV4222] ISBN 0-8010-0102-1 pbk. : 1.95
1. Spurgeon, Charles Haddon—Sermons. 2. Preaching. I. Title.

ALLMEN, Jean Jacques von. 251
Preaching and congregation. Tr. [from French] by B. L. Nicholas. Richmond, Va. Knox [1962] 67p. 22cm. (Ecumenical studies in worship, no. 10) 62-16769 1.50 pap.,
1. Preaching. I. Title.

APPELMAN, Hyman, 1902- 251
Pointed sermon outlines and illustrations. Grand Rapids, Zondervan Pub. House [1953] 118p. 21cm. [BV4223.A63] 53-1944
1. Sermons—Outlines. 2. Homiletical illustrations. I. Title. II. Title: Sermon outlines and illustrations.

APPELMAN, Hyman Jedidiah, 1902- 251
Pointed sermon outlines and illustrations. Grand Rapids, Zondervan Pub. House [1953] 118 p. 21 cm. [BV4223.A63] 53-1244
1. Sermons — Outlines. 2. Homiletical illustrations. I. Title. II. Title: Sermon outlines and illustrations.

ARMSTRONG, James, 1924- 251
Telling truth : the foolishness of preaching in a real world / James Armstrong. Waco, Tex. : Word Books, c1977. 114 p. ; 23 cm. [BV4222.A75] 76-53986 ISBN 0-87680-501-2 : 5.95
1. Preaching—Addresses, essays, lectures. I. Title.

AUGUSTINUS, Aurelius, Saint, Bp. of Hippo. 251
On Christian doctrine. Translated with an introd., by D. W. Robertson, Jr. New York, Liberal Arts Press [1958] xxii, 169p. 21cm. (The Library of liberal arts, no. 80) Bibliography: p. xxi-xxii. [BR65.A655E5] [BR65.A655E5] 281.4 58-9956 58-9956
1. Bible—Hermeneutics. 2. Preaching. I. Robertson, Durant Waite, tr. II. Title.

BAAB, Otto Justice. 251
Prophetic preaching: a new approach. Nashville, Abingdon Press [1958] 159p. 21cm. [BV4211.2.B22] 58-6590
1. Preaching. I. Title.

BABIN, David E. 251
Week in, week out : a new look at liturgical preaching / David E. Babin. New York : Seabury Press, c1976. x, 130 p. ; 22 cm. "A Crossroad book." Includes bibliographical references. [BV4211.2.B224] 75-37814 ISBN 0-8164-0287-6 : 5.95
1. Preaching. I. Title.

BACH, T J. 251
Pearls from many seas; colorful quotations for message and meditation. Wheaton, Ill., Van Kampen Press [1951] 104 p. 20 cm. [BV4225.B2] 51-4459
1. Homiletical illustrations. I. Title.

BAILLARGEON, Anatole O. 251
New media: new forms; contemporary forms of preaching. Anatole Baillargeon, editor. Chicago, Franciscan Herald Press [1968] vii, 230 p. 21 cm. Companion volume to the author's Handbook for special preaching. Includes bibliographies. [BV4211.2.B32] 67-28207
1. Preaching. I. Title.

BARTH, Karl, 1886- 251
The preaching of the gospel. Translated by B. E. Hooke. Philadelphia, Westminister Press [1963] 94 p. 20 cm. "The French text ... published on the occasion of the author's seventy-fifth birthday, was prepared by the Rev. A. Roulin from notes taken by students." [BV4211.2.B253] 63-7926
1. Preaching. I. Title.

BARTH, Karl, 1886- 251
The preaching of the gospel. Tr. [from French] by B. E. Hooke. Philadelphia, Westminster [c.1963] 94p. 20cm. 63-7926 2.50
1. Preaching. I. Title.

BARTLETT, Gene E 251
The audacity of preaching. [1st ed.] New York, Harper [1962] 159p. 22cm. (The Lyman Beecher lectures, Yale Divinity School, 1961) Includes bibliography. [BV4211.2.B26] 62-11123
1. Preaching. I. Title.

BASS, George M. 251
The renewal of liturgical preaching, by George M. Bass. Minneapolis, Augsburg [1967] xi, 155p. 22cm. Bibl. [BV4221.B3] 67-25364 4.50
1. Preaching. 2. Church year. I. Title.

BASS, George M 251
The renewal of liturgical preaching, by George M. Bass. Minneapolis, Augsburg Pub. House,[1967] xi, 155 p. 22 cm. Bibliograph p. 153-155. [BV4221.B3] 67-25364
1. Preaching. 2. Church year. I. Title.

BAUMANN, J. Daniel. 251
An introduction to contemporary preaching [by] J. Daniel Baumann. Grand Rapids, Baker Book House [1972] 302 p. 24 cm. Includes bibliographical references. [BV4211.2.B29] 72-76649 ISBN 0-8010-0572-8 6.95
1. Preaching. I. Title.

BAYBROOK, Gar 251
Will you be the speaker? Mountain View, Calif., Pacific Press Pub. Association [c.1961] 162p. illus. 61-6480 3.50
1. Preaching. 2. Seventh-Day Adventists. I. Title.

*BLACKWOOD, Andrew W. 251
Leading in public prayer [by] Andrew W. Blackwood. Grand Rapids: Baker Book, 1975 c1957. 207 p.; 20 cm. Bibliography, p. 197-202. [BV4211 2B55] ISBN 0-8010-0642-2 2.95 (pbk.)
I. Preaching. I. Title.

*BLACKWOOD, Andrew W. 251
Preaching from the Bible [by] Andrew W. Blackwood. Grand Rapids, Baker Book House [1974, c1969] 224 p. 20 cm. (Notable books on preaching.) Bibliography: 227-239. [BV4223] ISBN 0-8010-0619-8 2.95 (pbk.)
1. Preaching. I. Title.

BLACKWOOD, Andrew Watterson, 1882- 251
Biographical preaching for today; the pulpit

use of Bible cases. Nashville, Abingdon Press [1954] 224 p. 21cm. [BV4211.B515] 54-8237
1. Preaching. I. Title.

BLACKWOOD, Andrew Watterson, 1882- 251
Doctrinal preaching for today; case studies of Bible teachings. New York, Abingdon Press [1956] 224p. 21cm. [BV4211.2.B55] 56-8739
1. Preaching. I. Title.

BLACKWOOD, Andrew Watterson, 1882- 251
Doctrinal preaching for today: case studies of Bible teachings. Grand Rapids: Baker Book House, [1975 c1956] 224 p.; 20 cm. (Andrew W. Blackwood library) Bibliography: p. 209-215. [BV4211.2.B55] 56-8739 ISBN 0-8010-0638-4 2.95 (pbk.)
1. Preaching. I. Title.

BLACKWOOD, Andrew Watterson, 1882- 251
Planning a year's pulpit work. Nashville, Abingdon [1963, c.1942] 240p. 21cm. (N1) Bibl. 1.25 pap.,
1. Preaching. I. Title.

BLACKWOOD, Andrew Watterson, 1882- 251
Preaching from the Bible. Nashville, Abingdon [1961, c.1941] 247p. (Apex bk. H1) 1.25 pap.,
1. Preaching. I. Title.

BLOCKER, Simon, 1881- 251
The secret of pulpit power through thematic Christian preaching. Grand Rapids, W. B. Eerdmans Pub. Co., 1951. 209 p. 23 cm. [BV4211.B533] 51-8686
1. Preaching. I. Title.

BOWIE, Walter Russell, 1882- 251
Preachingz. Nashville, Abingdon Press [1954] 224p. 21cm. [BV4211.B538] 54-5508
1. Preaching. I. Title.

BRACK, Harold Arthur, 1923- 251
Public speaking and discussion for religious leaders [by] Harold A. Brack [and] Kenneth G. Hance. Englewood Cliffs, N. J., Prentice-Hall, 1961. 259p. illus. 22cm. [BV4211.2.B67] 61-14151
1. Preaching. 2. Discussion. I. Hance, Kenneth Gordon, 1903- joint author. II. Title.

BRACK, Harold Arthur, 1923- 251
Public speaking and discussion for religious leaders [by] Harold A. Brack, Kenneth G. Hance. Englewood Cliffs, N. J., Prentice-Hall [c.]1961. 259p. illus. 61-14151 6.35
1. Preaching. 2. Discussion. I. Hance, Kenneth Gordon, 1903- joint author. II. Title.

BRADFORD, Charles E. 251
Preaching to the times : the preaching ministry in the Seventh-day Adventist Church / Charles E. Bradford. Washington : Review and Herald Pub. Association, [1975] 144 p. ; 21 cm. (Discovery paperbacks) Bibliography: p. 143-144. [BV4211.2.B672] 75-318950 3.25
1. Seventh-Day Adventists—Doctrinal and controversial works. 2. Preaching. I. Title.

BROCKS, Phillips, Bp., 1835-1893 251
On preaching. Introd. by Theodore Parker Ferris. New York, Seabury Press [1964] vi, 281 p. 21 cm. (A Seabury paperback, SP14) First published in 1877 under title: Lectures on preaching. [BV4211.B7] 64-23901
1. Preaching. I. Title.

BROOKS, Phillips, Bp., 1835-1893. 251
The excellence of our calling; an abridgment of Phillips Brooks' Lectures on preaching, by Thomas F. Chilcote, Jr. [1st ed.] New York, Dutton, 1954. 192p. 22cm. [BV4211.B7 1954] 54-10919
1. Preaching. I. Chilcote, Thomas F. II. Title.

BROOKS. PHILLIPS, Bp., 1835-1893. 251
On preaching. Introd. by Theodore Parker Ferris. New York, Seabury [c.1964] vi, 281p. 21cm. (SP14) First pub. in 1877 under title: Lectures on preaching. 64-23901 1.95 pap.,
1. Preaching. I. Title.

BROWN, Henry Clifton. 251
A Christian layman's guide to public speaking [by] H. C. Brown, Jr. Nashville, Broadman Press [1966] 76 p. 20 cm. [BV4235.L3B7] 67-12167
1. Preaching, Lay. I. Title.

BROWN, Henry Clifton, ed. 251
Messages for men; for laymen and ministers. Grand Rapids, Zondervan Pub. House [1960] 150p. 21cm. [BV4205.B7] 61-712
1. Preaching. 2. Laity. I. Title.

BROWN, Henry Clifton. 251
A quest for reformation in preaching, by H. C. Brown, Jr. Waco, Tex., Word Bks. [1968] 251p. forms. 23cm. Annotated texts of 10 sermons by Karl Barth, others. Bibl. footnotes. [BV4211.2.B68] 67-26938 5.95
1. Preaching. I. Title.

BROWN, Henry Clifton. 251
Steps to the sermon; a plan for sermon preparation, by H. C. Brown, Jr., H. Gordon Clinard and Jesse J. Northcutt. Nashville, Broadman Press [1963] ix, 202 p. 22 cm. Bibliography: p. 197-202. [BV4211.1.B69] 63-19068
1. Preaching. I. Title.

BROWN, Henry Clifton 251
Steps to the sermon; a plan for sermon preparation, by H. C. Brown, Jr., H. Gordon Cinard, Jesse J. Northcutt. Nashville, Broadman [c.1963] ix, 202p. 22cm. Bibl. 63-19068 4.50
1. Preaching. I. Title.

BROWNE, Benjamin P 251
Let there be light; the art of sermon illustration. [Westwood, N. J.] Revell [1956] 157p. 21cm. [BV4211.2.B7] 56-7443
1. Preaching. 2. Homiletical illustrations. I. Title.

BROWNE, Robert Eric Charles. 251
The ministry of the word / Robert E. C. Browne. 1st American ed. Philadelphia : Fortress Press, 1976, c1975. 128 p. ; 22 cm. Includes bibliographical references and index. [BV4211.2.B73 1976] 76-1310 ISBN 0-8006-1229-9 pbk. : 3.50
1. Preaching. I. Title.

BROWNLOW, Leroy, 1914- 251
Sermons you can preach. Fort Worth, Tex., Brownlow Publications [1958] 143p. illus. 21cm. [BV4223.B73] 58-19106
1. Sermons—Outlines. I. Title.

BRYANT, Al, 1926- ed. 251
1,000 new illustrations. Grand Rapids, Zondervan Pub. House [1957] 254p. 22cm. [BV4225.B73] 57-37887
1. Homiletical illustrations. I. Title.

BRYANT, Al, 1926- ed. 251
Sermon outlines for worship and devotional services. Grand Rapids, Zondervan Pub. House [1954] 122p. 20cm. [BV4223.B76] 55-249
1. Sermons—Outlines. I. Title.

BUECHNER, Frederick, 1926- 251
Telling the truth : the Gospel as tragedy, comedy, and fairy tale / Frederick Buechner. San Francisco : Harper & Row, [1977] p. cm. [BV4211.2.B78] 77-10586 ISBN 0-06-061156-1 : 5.95
1. Preaching. 2. Communication (Theology) I. Title.

CAEMMERER, Richard Rudolph, 1904- 251
Preaching for the church. Saint Louis, Concordia Pub. House [1959] 353p. 24cm. Includes bibliography. [BV4211.2.C2] 58-13260
1. Preaching. I. Title.

CALDWELL, Frank H 251
Preaching angles. Nashville, Abingdon Press [1954] 126p. 20cm. [BV4211.C265] 54-5228
1. Preaching. I. Title.

CATHOLIC Church. Liturgy and ritual. Missal. English. 251
Jesus, Mary, and Joseph, daily missal; the official prayers of the Catholic Church arr. for participation in the Mass. Under the editorial supervision of Bede Babo [and others] New York, Benziger Bros. [c1962] 1408 p. illus. 17 cm. (A Catholic family library edition) [BX2015.A4B23] 63-1778
I. Catholic Church. Liturgy and ritual. English. II. Babo, Bede, 1900- ed. III. Title.

*CHAPPELL, Clovis G. 251
The village tragedy and other sermons / Clovis G. Chappell. Grand Rapids : Baker Book House, 1976. ix, 182 p. ; 20 cm. (Clovis G. Chappell library.) [BV4211.2] ISBN 0-8010-2386-6 pbk. : 2.95
1. Preaching. I. Title.

CHAPPELL, Clovis Gillham, 1882- 251
Anointed to preach. Nashville, Abingdon-Cokesbury Press [1951] 124 p. 20 cm. [BV4211.C43] 51-9215
1. Preaching. I. Title.

CHELEY, John Austin. 251
Stories for talks with boys and girls; a revision of his father's classic Stories for talks to boys. New York, Association Press [1958] 380p. 20cm. [BV1160.C54] 58-6472
1. Church work with children. 2. Homiletical illustrations. I. Cheley, Frank Hobart, 1889-1941. Stories for talks to boys. II. Title.

CLARKE, James W 251
Dynamic preaching. [Westwood, N. J.] F. H. Revell Co. [1960] 128p. 21cm. Includes bibliography. [BV4211.2.C5] 60-8457
1. Preaching. I. Title.

CLELAND, James T. 251
Preaching to be understood. Nashville, Abingdon [1965] 126p. 20cm. (Warrack lects. on preaching, 1964) Bibl. [BV4222.C55] 65-13145 2.75
1. Preaching—Addresses, essays, lectures. I. Title. II. Series.

CLELAND, James T 251
The true and lively Word. New York, Scribner, 1954. 120p. 20cm. [BV4211.C52] 54-6304
1. Preaching. I. Title.

CLOWNEY, Edmund P 251
Preaching and Biblical theology. Grand Rapids, Eerdmans [1961] 124p. 21cm. Includes bibliography. [BV4211.2.C53] 60-53094
1. Preaching. 2. Bible—Homiletical use. I. Title.

COFFIN, Henry Sloane, 1877- 251
Communion through preaching; the monstrance of the Gospel. New York, Scribner, 1952. 124 p. 20 cm. (The George Craig Stewart lectures on preaching) [BV4211.C54] 52-14246
1. Preaching. 2. Lord's Supper. I. Title.

COLQUHOUN, Frank. 251
Christ's ambassadors; the priority of preaching. Philadelphia, Westminster Press [c1965] 93 p. 19 cm. (Christian foundations) Bibliographical footnotes. [BV1211.2.C58] 67-10471
1. Preaching. I. Title.

*COMPTON, W. H. 251
Salvation sermon outlines, comp. by W. H. Compton. Grand Rapids, Baker Book House [1973, c.1961] 62 p. 22 cm. (Dollar sermon library) [BV4223] ISBN 0-8010-2349-1 1.00 (pbk.)
1. Sermons—Outlines. 2. Preaching. I. Title.

CONNELL, Francis Jeremiah, 1888- 251
Sunday sermon outlines. Foreword by Patrick A. O'Boyle. New York, F. Pustet Co., 1955. 324p. 24cm. [BX1756.A1C6] 55-43368
1. Sermons—Outlines. I. Title.

CONWAY, Marion H., comp. 251
Sermon suggestions; or, Pulpit points. Grand Rapids, Mich., Baker Bk. 1965]c.1957] 91p. 21cm. ((1.00 sermon lib.) [BV4223.C59] 1.00 pap.,
1. Sermons—Outlines. I. Title.

COOKE, John Blair Deaver, 1901- 251
The Carpenter's method of preaching. Philadelphia, Seaboard Press [1953] 96p. illus. 20cm. [BV4211.C63] 53-32884
1. Preaching. I. Title.

COWAN, Arthur Aitken. 251
The primacy of preaching today. New York, Scribner [1955] 128p. 19cm. (The Warrack lectures for 1954) [BV4211.2.C6] 56-13730
1. Preaching. I. Title.

COX, James William, 1923- 251
A guide to biblical preaching / James W. Cox. Nashville : Abingdon, [1976] p. cm. Includes bibliographical references and index. [BV4211.2.C64] 76-13491 ISBN 0-687-16229-7 : 6.50
1. Bible—Homiletical use. 2. Preaching. I. Title.

CRADDOCK, Fred B. 251
As one without authority; essays on inductive preaching [by] Fred B. Craddock. Enid, Okla., Phillips University Press [1971] ix, 159 p. 21 cm. Includes bibliographical references. [BV4211.2.C7] 75-152003
1. Preaching. I. Title.

CRAIG, Archibald C 251
Preaching in a scientific age. New York, Scribner 1954 119p. 20cm. (The Warrack lectures for 1953) [BV4211.C67 1954a] 54-3863
1. Preaching. I. Title.

CRUM, Milton. 251
Manual on preaching / Milton Crum, Jr. Valley Forge, Pa. : Judson Press, [1977] p. cm. Includes bibliographical references and index. [BV4211.2.C78] 77-79775 ISBN 0-8170-0744-X : 8.95
1. Preaching. I. Title.

CRUM, Milton. 251
Manual on preaching / Milton Crum, Jr. Valley Forge, Pa. : Judson Press, [1977] p. cm. Includes bibliographical references and index. [BV4211.2.C78] 77-79775 ISBN 0-8170-0744-X : 8.95
1. Preaching. I. Title.

DAILY bread. 251
405 worship illustrations; selections from Daily bread. Independence, Mo., Herald House [1956] 327p. 27cm. [BV4225.D3] 56-8471
1. Homiletical illustrations. I. Title.

DEMARAY, Donald E. 251
An introduction to homiletics [by] Donald E. Demaray. Grand Rapids, Mich., Baker Book House [1974] 156 p. 23 cm. Bibliography: p. 149-152. [BV4211.2.D38] 74-176239 4.95
1. Preaching. I. Title.

DIRKS, Marvin J. 251
Laymen look at preaching; lay expectation factors in relation to the preaching of Helmut Thielicke, by Marvin J. Dirks. North Quincy, Mass., Christopher Pub. House [1972] 326 p. port. 21 cm. Bibliography: p. 317-326. [BV4211.2.D5] 79-189364 6.50
1. Thielicke, Helmut, 1908- 2. Preaching. I. Title.

DOUGLASS, Truman B 251
Preaching and the new reformation. [1st ed.] New York, Harper [1956] 142p. 22cm. (The Lyman Beecher lectures) [BV4211.2.D6] 56-7032
1. Preaching. I. Title.

DRINKWATER, Francis Harold, 1886- 251
Third book of catechism stories; a teachers' aid-book in four parts. Westminster, Md., Newman Press [1956] 243p. 20cm. [BV4225.D74] 56-11429
1. Homiletical illustrations. I. Title.

DRURY, Ronan, ed. 251
Preaching. New York, Sheed [1963, c.1962] 149p. 22cm. 63-8543 3.50
1. Preaching—Addresses, essays, lectures. I. Title.

DUFFEY, William Richard, 1892- 251
Preaching well; the rhetoric and delivery of sacred discourse. Milwaukee, Bruce [1950] xvii, 284 p. 23 cm. [BV4211.D8] 50-13438
1. Preaching. I. Title.

ELLISON, John Malcus, 1889- 251
They who preach. Nashville, Broadman Press [1956] 180 p. 21 cm. [BV4211.2.E4] 56-13821
1. Preaching. I. Title.

ELLISON, John Malcus, 1892- 251
They who preach. Nashville, Broadman Press [1956] 180p. 21cm. [BV4211.2.E4] 56-13821
1. Preaching. I. Title.

ENGSTROM, Theodore Wilhelm, 1916- ed. 251
188 heart-reaching sermon outlines. Grand Rapids, Zondervan [1950] 112 p. 20 cm. [BV4223.E64] 50-11976
1. Sermons—Outlines. I. Title.

ERDAHL, Lowell O. 251
Better preaching / by Lowell Erdahl. St. Louis : Concordia Pub. House, c1977. p. cm. (The Preacher's workshop series ; 9) [BV4211.2.E69] 77-21826 ISBN 0-570-07408-8 pbk. : 1.95
1. Preaching. I. Title. II. Series.

ERDAHL, Lowell O. 251
Better preaching / by Lowell Erdahl. St. Louis : Concordia Pub. House, c1977. p. cm. (The Preacher's workshop series ; 9) [BV4211.2.E69] 77-21826 ISBN 0-570-07408-8 pbk. : 1.95
1. Preaching. I. Title. II. Series.

ERDAHL, Lowell O. 251
Preaching for the people / Lowell O. Erdahl. Nashville : Abingdon, c1976. 127 p. ; 20 cm. Includes bibliographical references. [BV4211.2.E7] 75-43934 ISBN 0-687-33865-4 : 5.95
1. Preaching. I. Title.

EVANS, John R 25,no.1
An economic bypass study of the St. George, Utah area, by John R. Evans, Katherine L. Lueck [and] Gordon S. Thompson. [Salt Lake City] Bureau of Economic and Business Research, College of Business, University of Utah, 1965. vii, 78 p. maps. 28 cm. (University of Utah. Bureau of Economic and Business Research. Studies in business and economics, v. 25, no. 1) [HC107.U8U7 vol.] 67-63831
1. Express highways—Economic aspects—St. George, Utah. 2. Highway bypasses. I. Lueck, Katherine L., joint author. II. Thompson, Gordon Stuart, 1930- joint author. III. Title. IV. Series: Utah. University. Bureau of Economic and Business Research. Studies in business and economics, v. 25, no. 1

FANT, Clyde E. 251
Preaching for today / Clyde E. Fant. 1st ed. New York : Harper & Row, [1975] xvi, 196 p. ; 21 cm. Includes bibliographical references. [BV4211.2.F36 1975] 74-4640 ISBN 0-06-062331-4 : 8.95
1. Preaching. I. Title.

FARMER, Herbert Henry, 1892- 251
The servant of the Word. Philadelphia, Fortress [1964, c.1942] ix, 115p. 18cm. (Preacher's paperback lib., v.1) 64-20405 2.45 pap.,
1. Preaching. I. Title.

FERRIS, Theodore Parker, 1908- 251
Go tell the people. New York, Scribner, 1951. 116 p. 20 cm. (George Craig Stewart lectures on preaching) [BV4211.F45] 51-3166
1. Preaching. I. Title. II. Series.

FISH, Roy J. 251
Giving a good invitation / Roy J. Fish. Nashville, Tenn. : Broadman Press, c1974. 55 p. ; 19 cm. Includes bibliographical references. [BV3793.F48] 74-18043 ISBN 0-8054-2107-6 pbk. : 1.50
1. Evangelistic invitations. I. Title.

*FORSYTH, P. T. 251
Positive preaching and the modern mind. Grand Rapids, Mich., Eerdmans [1964] 258p. 20cm. 1.95 pap.,
I. Title.

FOSTER, Elon, ed. 251
6,000 windows for sermons. Grand Rapids, Baker Book House, 1953. 791p. 25cm. 'A companion volume to 6,000 sermon illustrations.' [BV4225.F735] 57-3801
1. Homiletical illustrations. 2. Quotations. I. Title.

FRANCOIS DE SALES, Saint, Bp. of Geneva, 1567-1622. 251
On the preacher and preaching. Translated, with an introd. and notes, by John K. Ryan. [Chicago] H. Regnery Co., 1964. 110 p. 22 cm. Translation of a letter to Andre Fremyot, archbishop of Bourges, dated Oct. 5, 1604. Bibliographical references included in "Notes" [p. [75]-103) Bibliography: p. 107-108. [BV4210.F713] 64-14601
1. Preaching — Early works to 1800. I. Ryan, John Kenneth, 1887- ed. and tr. II. Title.

FRANCOIS DE SALES, Saint, Bp. of Geneva, 1567-1622 251
On the preacher and preaching. Tr., introd., notes, by John K. Ryan [Chicago] Regnery [c.1964] 110p. 22cm. Tr. of a letter to Andre Fremyot, archbishop of Bourges, dated Oct. 5, 1604. Bibl. 64-14601 2.95
1. Preaching—Early works to 1800. I. Ryan, John Kenneth, 1887- ed. and tr. II. Title.

GARRISON, Webb B. 251
Creative imagination in preaching. Nashville, Abingdon Press [c.1960] 175p. 21cm. (bibl. notes: p.163-166) 60-9197 3.00
1. Preaching. 2. Creation (Literary, artistic, etc.) I. Title.

GARRISON, Webb B 251
The preacher and his audience. [Westwood, N.J.] Revell [1954] 285p. illus. 22cm. Includes bibliography. [BV4211.G33] 54-8003
1. Preaching. I. Title.

GATTI, Arno, 1925- 251
Study of the growth parameters involved in synthesizing boron carbide filaments, by A. Gatti [and others] Springfield, Va., For sale by the Clearinghouse for Federal Scientific and Technical Information [1965] vii, 57 p. illus. 27 cm. (NASA contractor report. NASA CR-251) "Prepared under contract no. NASw -- 937 by General Electric Company, Philadelphia, Pa., for National Aeronautics and Space Administration." Bibliography: p. 32. 65-62066
1. Boron carbine. 2. Composite materials. I. General Electric Company. II. U.S. National Aeronautics and Space Administration. III. Title. IV. Series: U.S. National Aeronautics and Space Administration. NASA contractor report. CR-251

GERICKE, Paul. 251
The preaching of Robert G. Lee; adorning the doctrine of God. Orlando, Fla., Christ for the World Publishers [1967] 180 p. 22 cm. Bibliography: p. 176-180. [BX6495.L39G4] 66-30553
1. Lee, Robert Greene, 1886- 2. Preaching—History—20th century. I. Title.

GIBSON, George Miles, 1896- 251
Planned preaching. Philadelphia, Westminster Press [1954] 140p. 21cm. [BV4211.G5] 54-5653
1. Preaching. I. Title.

GILMORE, Alec. 251
Tomorrow's pulpit. Valley Forge, Pa., Judson Press [1975] 95 p. 22 cm. Originally presented as the Edwin Griffith Memorial lectures, Cardiff Baptist College, June 12-13, 1973. Bibliography: p. 89-92. [BV4211.2.G5] 74-13494 ISBN 0-8170-0641-9 3.50 (pbk.)
1. Preaching. I. Title.

GOULOOZE, William, 1903-1955. 251
1500 themes for series preaching. Grand Rapids, Baker Book House, 1956. 156p. 20cm. [BV4223.G6] 56-7576
1. Sermons—Texts for sermons. I. Title.

GRASSO, Domenico, 1917- 251
Proclaiming God's message: a study in the theology of preaching. [Notre Dame, Ind.] University of Notre Dame Press, 1965. xxxiii, 272 p. 24 cm. (Notre Dame [Ind.] University. Liturgical studies, v. 8) Bibliography: p. 255-266. [BV4211.2.G7] 65-14739
1. Preaching. 2. Kerygma. I. Title. II. Series.

GRASSO, Domenico, 1917- 251
Proclaiming God's message: a study in the theology of preaching. [Notre Dame, Ind.] Univ. of Notre Dame Pr. [c.]1965. xxxiii, 272p. 24cm. (Notre Dame Univ. Liturgical studies, v. 8) Bibl. [BV4211.2.G7] 65-14739 bds., 6.00; text ed., 4.00
1. Kerygma. 2. Preaching. I. Title. II. Series.

GRITTI, Jules 251
Precher aux hommes de notre temps [Toulouse] Privat [dist. Philadelphia, Chilton, 1964] 159p. 19cm. (Question posees aux catholiques) Bibl. 64-9075 1.00 pap.,
1. Preaching. I. Title.

*HAGEMAN, Howard G. 251
Proclamation: aids for interpreting the Church year; Easter, [by] Howard G. Hageman and J. C. Beker. Philadelphia, Fortress Press [1974] v, 57 p. 22 cm. (Series c) [BV421.P73] 73-88346 ISBN 0-8006-4055-1 1.95 (pbk.)
1. Church year sermons. 2. Sermons, American. 3. Bible—Liturgical lessons, English. I. Beker, J. C., joint author II. Title.

HALL, Thor, 1927- 251
The future shape of preaching. Philadelphia, Fortress Press [1971] xx, 140 p. 22 cm. Includes bibliographical references. [BV4211.2.H25] 77-157537 ISBN 0-8006-0019-3 3.50
1. Preaching. I. Title.

HALLOCK, Gerard Benjamin Fleet, 1856- ed. 251
New sermon illustrations for all occasions. Westwood, N. J., F. H. Revell Co. [1953] 445p. 21cm. [BV4225.H32] 53-10527
1. Homiletical illustrations. I. Title.

HARRIS, James, 1709-1780. 251
An essay on the action proper for the pulpit. New York, Garland Pub., 1971. 86 p. 21 cm. Bound with the author's Upon the rise and progress of criticism. New York, 1971. Facsim. of the 1753 ed. [B809.3.H37 1752a] [BV4210] [BV4210] 224 016.329 78-112117
1. Preaching. I. Title.

HASELDEN, Kyle. 251
The urgency of preaching. [1st ed.] New York, Harper & Row [1963] 121 p. 20 cm. [BV2311.2.H3] 63-10751
1. Preaching. I. Title.

HASELDEN, Kyle 251
The urgency of preaching. New York, Harper [c.1963] 121p. 20cm. 63-10751 2.75 bds.,
1. Preaching. I. Title.

HENRY, Matthew, 1662-1714. 251
Sermon outlines, a choice collection of thirty-five model sermons; selected and edited by Sheldon B. Quincer. [1st ed.] Grand Rapids, W. B. Eerdmans Pub. Co., 1955. 148p. 23cm. (The World's great sermons in outline) [BV4223.H36] 55-1079
1. Sermons—Outlines. I. Title. II. Series.

HITZ, Paul. 251
To preach the gospel. Translated by Rosemary Sheed. New York, Sheed and Ward [1963] 209 p. 21 cm. Translation of L'annonce missionaire de l'evangile. [BV4211.2.H513] 63-11552
1. Preaching. 2. Kerygma. I. Title.

HITZ, Paul 251
To preach the gospel Tr. by Rosemary Sheed. New York, Sheed [c.1963] 209p. 21cm. 63-11552 3.95
1. Preaching. 2. Kerygma. I. Title.

HOEFLER, Richard Carl. 251
Oral writing; the art of effective manuscript preaching. Introd. by E. Eppling Reinartz. [Columbia, S.C.? 1964] 118 p. 21 cm. Bibliographical references included in "Notes" (p. 117-118) [BV4211.2.H6] 65-461
1. Preaching. I. Title.

HOLDCRAFT, Paul Ellsworth, 1891- 251
440 more snappy sermon starters New York, Abingdon Press [1954] 127p. 20cm. [BV4223.H6] 54-4102
1. Sermons—Outlines. I. Title.

HOLDCRAFT, Paul Ellsworth, 1891- 251
Texts and themes for the Christian year. New Ywrk, Abingdon Press [1957] 96p. 23cm. [BV4223.H62] 57-2266
1. Church year sermons—Outlines. 2. Sermons—Texts for sermons. 3. Church year. I. Title.

HOLMES, George. 251
Toward an effective pulpit ministry. Springfield, Mo., Gospel Pub. House [1971] 176 p. 20 cm. [BV4211.2.H63] 72-152056
1. Preaching. I. Title.

HORNE, Chevis F. 251
Crisis in the pulpit : the pulpit faces future shock / Chevis F. Horne. Grand Rapids : Baker Book House, [1975] 144 p. ; 23 cm. Includes bibliographical references. [BV4211.2.H66] 74-20203 ISBN 0-8010-4108-2 : 4.95
1. Preaching. I. Title.

HOWE, Reuel L. 251
Partners in preaching; clergy and laity in dialogue [by] Reuel L. Howe. New York, Seabury [1967] 127p. 22cm. In an earlier form these chapters were the Princeton Seminary Alumni lects., delivered in Sept. 1965. [BV4221.H6] 67-20937 3.50
1. Preaching. 2. Communication (Theology) I. Title.

HUMBERT DE ROMANS, 1194?-1277. 251
Treatise on preaching. Translated by the Dominican students, Province of St. Joseph; edited by Walter M. Conlon. Westminster, Md., Newman Press, 1951. xiii, 160 p. 21 cm. Translation of Liber de eruditione praedicationis. [BV4209.H83] 51-10275
1. Preaching. I. Title.

JACKSON, Edgar Newman. 251
A psychology for preaching Pref. by Harry Emerson Fosdick. Great Neck, N. Y., Channel Press [1961] 191p. 21cm. [BV4211.2.J3] 61-7573
1. Preaching. I. Title.

JACKSON, Edgar Newman 251
A psychology for preaching. Pref. by Harry Emerson Fosdick. Great Neck, N. Y., Channel Press [c.1961] 191p. Bibl. 61-7573 3.50 bds.,
1. Preaching. I. Title.

JACOBS, James Vernon, 1898- ed. 251
450 true stories from church history; a unique collection of facts, highlights, striking incidents, and illustrative anecdotes from the lives of famous church leaders. [1st ed.] Grand Rapids, Eerdmans, 1955. 147p. 24cm. [BV4225.J26] 55-691
1. Homiletical illustrations. I. Title.

JACOBS, James Vernon, 1898- 251
Illustrations from great literature. Butler, Ind., Higley Press [1952] 224p. 20cm. [BV4225.J28] 53-16275
1. Homiletical illustrations. I. Title.

JASPER, K G 251
Living helps for preacher and people. New York, Comet Press Books, 1958. 79p. 21cm. (A Relections book) [BV4223.J3] 58-4083
1. Sermons—Outlines. 2. Homilectieal illustrations. I. Title.

JOHNSON, Howard Albert, 1915- ed. 251
Preaching the Christian year [by] Hughell E. W. Fosbroke [and others] Edited for the Dean and Chapter of the Cathedral Church of St. John the Divine. With a foreword by James A. Pike. New York, Scribner [1957] 243p. 22cm. Includes bibliography. [BV4211.2.J57] 57-12061
1. Preaching. 2. Church year. I. Fosbroke, Hughell E. W. II. Title.

JOHNSON, Howard Albert, 1915- ed. 251
Preaching the Christian year [by] Hughell E.W. Fosbroke [and others] Edited for the Dean and Chapter of the Cathedral Church of St. John the Divine. With a foreword by James A. Pike. New York, Scribner [1957] 243p. 22cm. Includes bibliography. [BV4211.2.J57] 57-12061
1. Preaching. 2. Church year. I. Fosbroke, Hughell E.W. II. Title.

JONES, Bob 251
How to improve your preaching. New enl. ed. Grand Rapids, Kregel Publication [c.1945, 1960] 151p. 20cm. (bibl.: p.148-151) 59-14905 2.50
1. Preaching. I. Title.

JONES, Bob, 1911- 251
How to improve your preaching. New enl. ed. Grand Rapids, Kregel Publications [1960] 151p. 20cm. Includes bibliography. [BV4211.J6 1960] 59-14905
1. Preaching. I. Title.

JONES, Ilion Tingal, 1889- 251
Principles and practice of preaching. New York, Abingdon Press [1956] 272p. 23cm. [BV4211.2.J6] 56-7761
1. Preaching. I. Title.

JONES, Ilion Tingnal, 1889- 251
Principles and practice of preaching. New York, Abingdon Press [1956] 272p. 23cm. [BV4211.2.J6] 56-7761
1. Preaching. I. Title.

JORDAN, Gerald Ray, 1896- 251
Preaching during a revolution: patterns of procedure. Anderson, Ind., Warner Press [1962] 192p. 22cm. [BV4211.2.J62] 62-11773
1. Preaching. I. Title.

JORDAN, Gerald Ray, 1896- 251
You can preach! Building and delivering the sermon. New York, Revell [1951] 256 p. 22 cm. [BV4211.J63] 51-11399
1. Preaching. I. Title.

JORDAN, Gerald Ray, 1896- 251
You can preach! Building and delivering the sermon. [Westwood, N. J.] Revell [c1958] 256p. 21cm. (Revell's preaching and pastoral aid series) [BV4211.2.J63 1958] 59-5501
1. Preaching. I. Title.

KAHMANN, J 251
The Bible on the preaching of the World, by J. Kahmann. Translated by T. J. Holmes. De Pere, Wis., St. Norbert Abbey Press, 1965. 117 p. 17 cm. [BV4207.K313] 65-29090
1. Preaching — Biblical teaching. 2. Kerygma. I. Title.

KEIGHTON, Robert Elwood, 1896- 251
The man who would preach. New York, Abingdon Press [1956] 128p. 20cm. [BV4211.2.K38] 56-7762
1. Preaching. I. Title.

KEMP, Charles F 1912 ed. 251
Life-situation preaching. St. Louis, Bethany Press [1956] 224p. 23cm. [BV4241.K42] 56-10170
1. Sermons, English. I. Title.

KEMP, Charles F. 1912- ed. 251
Pastoral preaching. St. Louis, Bethany Press [1963] 252 p. 22 cm. [BV4211.2.K39] 63-13913
1. Preaching. 2. Sermons, American. I. Title.

KEMP, Charles F., 1912- ed. 251
Pastoral preaching. St. Louis, Bethany [c.1963] 252p. 22cm. 63-13913 4.00
1. Preaching. 2. Sermons, American. I. Title.

KEMP, Charles F. 1912- ed. 251
The preaching pastor, by Charles F. Kemp. St. Louis, Bethany Press [1966] 251 p. 21 cm. Bibliographical footnotes. [BV4211.2.K393] 66-22922
1. Preaching. 2. Sermons, American — Collections. I. Title.

KENNEDY, Gerald Hamilton, Bp., 1907- 251
God's good news. [1st ed.] New York, Harper [1955] 182p. 22cm. [BV4211.2.K4] 54-116629
1. Preaching. I. Title.

KENNEDY, Gerald Hamilton, Bp., 1907- 251
Who speaks for God? Nashville, Abingdon Press [1954] 139 p. 23 cm. [BV4211.K417] 54-9196
1. Preaching. I. Title.

KILLINGER, John. 251
The centrality of preaching in the total task of the ministry. Waco, Tex., Word Books [1969] 123 p. 23 cm. [BV4211.2.K5] 69-12817 3.95
1. Preaching. 2. Clergy—Office. I. Title.

KNIGHT, Walter Brown, comp. 251
Master book of new illustrations. Grand Rapids, W. B. Eerdmans Pub. Co., 1956. 760p. 24cm. [BV4225.K58] 56-13890
1. Homiletical illustrations. I. Title.

KNOX, John, 1900- 251
The integrity of preaching. New York, Abingdon Press [1957] 96p. 20cm. (Lectures on the James A. Gray Fund of the Divinity School of Duke University, Durham, North Carolina) [BV4211.2.K56] 57-5279
1. Preaching. I. Title.

KNOX, John, 1900- 251
The intergrity of preaching. New York, Abingdon Press [1957] 96p. 20cm. (Lectures on the James A. Gray Fund of the Divinity School of Duke University, Durham, North Carolina) [BV4211.2.K56] 57-5279
1. Preaching. I. Title.

KOLLER, Charles W., 1886- 251
Expository preaching without notes. Grand Rapids, Mich., Baker Bk. [c.]1962. 132p. 20cm. (Evangelical pulpit lib.) 62-21703 2.50
1. Preaching. I. Title.

KOLLER, Charles W 1896- 251
Expository preaching without notes. Grand Rapids, Baker Book House, 1962. 132 p. 29 cm. [Evangelical pulpit library) [BV4211.2.K6] 62-21703
1. Preaching. I. Title.

KRAUS, Hans Joachim. 251
The threat and the power. Translated by Keith Crim. Richmond, Va., John Knox Press [1971] 107 p. 21 cm. Translation of Predigt aus Vollmacht. Bibliography: p. [105]-107. [BV4214.K713] 73-93827 3.95
1. Preaching. I. Title.

KURFEES, Marshall Clement, 1856-1931. 251
Outlines of sermons and inspirational talks. Lufkin, Tex., 1953. 62p. 24 cm. [BV4223.K82] 53-19469
1. Sermons—Outlines. I. Title.

LANGHORNE, John, 1735-1779. 251
Letters on the eloquence of the pulpit. New York, Garland Pub., 1970. 75, [1] p. 22 cm. Facsim. of a Yale University Library copy with imprint: London, Printed for T. Becket and P. A. de Hondt, 1765. "Books written by Mr. Langhorne": p. [76] Bound with Webb, Daniel. Literary amusements, in verse and prose. New York, 1970; Whally, Peter. An essay on the manner of writing history. New York, 1970; and Manwaring, Edward. Harmony and numbers in Latin and English. New York, 1970. [BV4210.L34 1765a] 70-112174
1. Preaching. I. Title.

LEE, Robert Greene, 1886- 251
Modern illustrations for public speakers; likings and leavings. Grand Rapids, Zondervan Pub. House [1955] 121p. 21cm. [BV4225.L375] 55-42018
1. Homilectical illustrations. I. Title.

LEHMAN, H. T. 251
Heralds of the Gospel. Philadelphia, Muhlenberg Press [1953] 76p. 20cm. [BV4211.L43] 53-9215
1. Preaching. I. Title.

LEHMANN, Helmut T 251
Heralds of the Gospel. Philadelphia, Muhlenberg Press [1953] 76 p. 20 cm. [BV4211.2.L44] 53-9215
1. Preaching. I. Title.

*LENSKI, R. C. H. 251
Preaching on John; sermon outlines, sermons, homiletical hints. Grand Rapids, Baker Book House [1973] 194 p. 20 cm. First published in 1933 under title: Saint John. [BV4223] 2.95 (pbk.)
1. Sermons—Outlines. I. Title.

LENSKI, Richard Charles Henry, 1864-1936. 251
The sermon; its homiletical construction. Introd. by Ralph G. Turnbull. Grand Rapids, Baker Book House [1968] 314 p. 20 cm. (Notable books on preaching) First published in 1927. [BV4211.L425 1968] 68-3995
1. Preaching. I. Title.

LEWIS, Ralph Loren, 1919- 251
Speech for persuasive preaching [by] Ralph L. Lewis. Wilmore, Ky. [1968] x, 276 p. 23 cm. Bibliography: p. 266-270. [BV4211.2.L48] 68-3037
1. Preaching. I. Title.

LISKE, Thomas V. 251
Effective preaching. New York, Macmillan, 1951. 293 p. 21 cm. [BV4211.L5] 51-14326
1. Preaching. I. Title.

LISKE, Thomas V 251
Effective preaching. 2d ed. New York, Macmillan, 1960. 349p. 21cm. Includes bibliography. [BV4211.2.L54 1960] 60-15046
1. Preaching. I. Title.

*LOCKYER, Herbert. 251
The art and craft of preaching. Grand Rapids, Baker Book House [1975] 118 p. 19 cm. [BV4211.2] ISBN 0-8010-5556-3 2.95 (pbk.)
1. Preaching. I. Title.

LOGSDON, S Franklin. 251
Original sermon outlines, plus hints and helps on how to make sermon outlines. Grand Rapids, Zondervan Pub. House [1954] 128p. 20cm. [BV4223.L6] 54-34229
1. Sermons— Outlines. 2. Preaching. I. Title.

LOUTTIT, Henry Irving, Bp., 1903- 251
Commanded to preach, by Henry I. Louttit. New York, Seabury Press [1965] 111 p. 19cm. (George Craig Stewart Memorial lectures) Bibliography: p. 109-111. [BV4222.L6] 64-19632
1. Preaching — Addresses, essays, lectures. I. Title. II. Series: George Craig Stewart lectures on preaching

LOUTTIT, Henry Irving, Bp., 1903- 251
Commanded to preach. New York, Seabury [c.1965] 111p. 19cm. (George Craig Stewart memorial lects.) Bibl. Title. (Series: George Craig Stewart lectures on preaching) [BV4222.L6] 64-19632 1.95 pap.,
1. Preaching—Addresses, essays, lectures. I. Title. II. Series.

LUCCOCK, Halford Edward, 1885- 251
Communicating the Gospel. [1st ed.] New York, Harper [c1954] 183p. 22cm. (The Lyman Beecher lectures on preaching, Yale University. 1958) [BV4211.L78] 53-10974
1. Preaching. I. Title.

LUCCOCK, Halford Edward, 1885- 251
Unfinished business; short diversions on religious themes. [1st ed.] New York, Harper [1956] 191p. 22cm. [bV4225.L8] 55-11480
1. Homiletical illustrations. I. Title.

LUTHI, Walter 251
Preaching. Confession. The Lord's Supper. [By] Walter Luthi [and] Eduard Thurneysen. Translated [from the German] by Francis J. Brooke, III. Richmond, Va., John Knox Press [c.1960] 121p. 21cm. 60-9291 2.50
1. Preaching. 2. Confession. 3. Lord's Supper. I. Thurneysen, Eduard Evangelical confession. II. Title.

LUTHI, Walter, 1901- 251
Preaching. Confession. The Lord's Supper. [By] Walter Luthi [and] Eduard. Thurneysen. Translated by Francis J. Brooke, III. Richmond. John Knox Press [1960] 121p. 21cm. [BV4211.2.L813] 60-9291
1. Preaching. 2. Confession. 3. Lord's Supper. I. Thurneysen, Eduard, 1888- Evangelical confession. II. Title.

*LYNN, Thomas. 251
150 biographical illustrations, by Thomas Lynn with Jimmy Law. Grand Rapids, Baker Book House, [1975 c1973] 96 p. 20 cm. [BV4223] 1.95 (pbk.)
1. Sermons—Outlines. 2. Homiletical illustrations. I. Law, Jimmy. joint author II. Title.

*MACARTNEY, Clarence Edward. 251
Preaching without notes / by Clarence Edward Macartney. Grand Rapids : Baker Book House, 1976c1946. 186p. ; 20 cm. (Notable books on preaching) [BV4211.2] ISBN 0-8010-5992-5 pbk. : 2.95
1. Preaching. I. Title.

MCCLUNG, Fred W 1909- 251
God's picture gallery. Fayetteville, Ark. [1953] 172p. illus. 22cm. [BV4223.M2] 53-26459
1. Sermons—Outlines. I. Title.

MCCRACKEN, Robert James. 251
The making of the sermon. [1st ed.] New York, Harper [c1956] 104p. 20cm. [BV4211.M22] 55-11481
1. Preaching. I. Title.

MCGINTY, Claudius Lamar, 1885- 251
Sermon outlines. [Westwood, N. J.] Revell [1957- v. 19cm. [BV4223.M17] 57-6853
1. Sermons—Outlines. I. Title.

MCLAREN, Alexander, 1826-1910. 251
Sermon seeds; [outlines from the writings of Alexander Maclaren, and others. Grand Rapids, Baker Book House, 1956. 95 p. 21 cm. (Minister's handbook series, v. 10) [BV4223.S45] 56-10682
1. Sermons — Outlines. I. Title.

MCLAREN, Alexander, 1826-1910. 251
Sermon outlines; a choice collection of thirty-five mode sermons, selected and edited by Sheldon B. Quincer. Grand Rapids, Eerdmans, 1954. 151p. 23cm. (The World's great sermons in outline) [BV4223.M2] 54-6232
1. Sermons—Outlines. I. Title.

MCLAUGHLIN, Raymond W. 251
Drastic discipleship, and other expository sermons, by Raymond W. McLaughlin and others. Grand Rapids, Baker Book House, 1963. 116 p. 20 cm. (Evangelical pulpit library) [BV4241.D7] 63-21470
1. Sermons, English. I. Title.

MACLENNAN, David Alexander, 1903- 251
Entrusted with the gospel. Philadelphia, Westminster Press [1956] 128p. 20cm. (Warrack lectures on preaching) [BV4211.2.M17] 56-8426
1. Preaching. I. Title.

MACLENNAN, David Alexander, 1903- 251
Pastoral preaching. Philadelphia, Westminister Press. [c1955] 157p. 21cm. [BV4211.M263] 55-5176
1. Preaching. I. Title.

MACLENNAN, David Alexander, 1903- 251
Resources for sermon preparation. Philadelphia, Westminster Press [1957] 239p. 21cm. [BV4223.M22] 57-9604
1. Sermons—Outlines. I. Title.

MACLEOD, Donald, 1914- ed. 251
Here is my method; the art of sermon construction. Westwood, N. J., F. H. Revell Co. [1952] 191 p. 21 cm. [BV4211.M265] 52-14107
1. Preaching. I. Title.

MCNAMARA, Robert Francis, 1910- 251
Catholic Sunday preaching : the American guidelines, 1791-1975 / by Robert F. McNamara. 1st ed. Washington : Word of God Institute, 1975. 62 p. ; 22 cm. (Special studies series - Word of God Institute) Includes bibliographical references. [BV4208.U6M34] 75-36695 1.95
1. Catholic Church in the United States—Clergy. 2. Preaching—History—United States. I. Title. II. Series: Word of God Institute. Special studies series — Word of God Institute.

MCNEIL, Jesse Jai. 251
The preacher-prophet in mass society. Grand Rapids, Eerdmans [1961] 116p. 21cm. Includes bibliography. [BV4211.2.M176] 61-18335
1. Prenching. 2. Pastoral theology. I. Title.

MACNUTT, Sylvester F 251
Ganging sermon effectiveness. Dubuque, Iowa, Priory Press [c1960] 139p. illus. 21cm. [BV4211.2.M18] 61-9450
1. Preaching. I. Title.

MACPHERSON, Ian, 1912- 251
The art of illustrating sermons. Nashville, Abingdon [c.1964] 219p. 23cm. Bibl. 64-15759 3.50
1. Preaching. 2. Homiletical illustrations. I. Title.

MACPHERSON, Ian, 1912- 251
The art of illustrating sermons. Grand Rapids : Baker Book House, 1976c1966. 219p. ; 20 cm. (Minister's paperback library) Includes bibliographical references and index. [BV4211.2M19] ISBN 0-8010-5987-9 pbk. : 3.95
1. Preaching. 2. Homiletical illustrations. I. Title.
L. C. card no. for original ed. 64-15759.

MACPHERSON, Ian, 1912- 251
The burden of the Lord. New York, Abingdon Press [1955] 157p. 21cm. [BV4211.2.M2 1955a] 56-5126
1. Preaching. I. Title.

MALCOMSON, William L. 251
The preaching event [by] William L. Malcomson. Philadelphia, Westminister Press [1968] 144 p. 20 cm. [BV4211.2.M25] 68-23449 3.95
1. Preaching. I. Title.

MANNEBACH, Wayne C. 251
Speaking from the pulpit [by] Wayne C. Mannebach [and] Joseph M. Mazza. Valley Forge [Pa.] Judson Press [1969] 128 p. 23 cm. Includes bibliographical references. [BV4211.2.M26] 74-81445 ISBN 0-8170-0437-8 4.95
1. Preaching. I. Mazza, Joseph M., joint author. II. Title.

MARCEL, Pierre Charles Raymond 251
The relevance of preaching. Tr. from French by Rob Roy McGregor. Grand Rapids, Mich., Baker Bk. [c.]1963. 110p. 23cm. 63-15823 2.95
1. Preaching. I. Title.

MARSH, Frederick Edward, 1858- 251
Pearls, points and parables. Grand Rapids, Baker Book House, 1954. xxviii, 269p. 20cm. [BV4225.M3 1954] 54-11073
1. Homiletical illustrations. I. Title.

MASSEY, James Earl. 251
The responsible pulpit. Anderson, Ind., Warner Press [1974] 115 p. 22 cm. Includes bibliographical references. [BV4211.2.M28] 74-939 ISBN 0-87162-169-X 5.95
1. Preaching. 2. Clergy—Religious life. I. Title.

MASSEY, James Earl. 251
The responsible pulpit. Anderson, Ind., Warner Press [1974] p. cm. Includes bibliographical references. [BV4211.2.M28] 74-939 ISBN 0-87162-169-X 5.95
1. Preaching. 2. Clergy—Religious life. I. Title.

MASSEY, James Earl. 251
The sermon in perspective : a study of communication and charisma / James Earl Massey. Grand Rapids : Baker Book House, c1976. 116 p. ; 23 cm. Delivered in part as the Mary Claire Gautschi Lectures at Fuller Theological Seminary, Pasadena, Calif., in 1975, as the 1975 Fall Lectures at Ashland Theological Seminary, Ashland, Ohio, and at Gulf-Coast Bible College, Houston, Tex. in Feb. 1976 during the Fourteenth Annual Ministers' Refresher Institute. Includes bibliographical references and index. [BV4222.M28] 76-150073 ISBN 0-8010-6003-6 : 4.95
1. Preaching—Addresses, essays, lectures. I. Title.

MAST, Russell L. 251
Preach the word [by] Russell L. Mast. Newton, Kan., Faith and Life Press [1968] 90 p. 20 cm. Includes bibliographical references. [BV4222.M3] 68-28782
1. Preaching—Addresses, essays, lectures. I. Title.

MEDLER, William H. 251
God's lamb; a series of Lenten sermons on Isaiah 53, the "gospel in the Old Testament," including sermons for Maundy Thursday, Good Friday, and Easter. [1st ed.] New York, Greenwich Book Publishers [1964] 88 p. 22 cm. [BV4277.M4] 64-11223
1. Lenten sermons. 2. Lutheran Church — Sermons. 3. Sermons, American. I. Title.

MICHAUX, Lightfoot. 251
Sparks from the anvil of Elder Michaux, compiled and edited by Pauline Lark. Washington, Happy News Pub. Co., 1950. ix, 139 p. port. 24 cm. [BV4225.M5] 50-2492
1. Homiletical illustrations. I. Title.

MICHONNEAU, Georges, 1899- 251
From pulpit to people; thoughts on dynamic preaching, by Georges Michonneau and Francois Varillon. Translated by Edmond Bonin. Westminister, Md., Newman Press, 1965. vii, 224 p. 22 cm. Tranlsation of Propos sur ia predication. Bibliographical footnotes. [BV4211.2.M4413] 65-25982
1. Preaching. I. Varillon, Francois, 1905- joint author. II. Title.

MICHONNEAU, Georges, 1899- 251
From pulpit to people; thoughts on dynamic preaching, by Georges Michonneau, Francois Varillon. Tr. [from French] by Edmond Bonin. Westminster, Md, Newman [c.]1965. vii, 224p. 22cm. Bibl. [BV4211.2.M4413] 65-25982 3.95
1. Preaching. I. Varillon, Francois, 1905- joint author. II. Title.

MIDDLETON, Robert G. 251
Tensions in modern faith [by] Robert G. Middleton. Valley Forge [Pa.] Judson Press [1965] 158 p. 21 cm. [BV4211.2.M46] 65-22001
1. Preaching — Addresses, essays, lectures. 2. Christianity — 20th cent. — Addresses, essays, lectures. I. Title.

MIDDLETON, Robert G. 251
Tensions in modern faith. Valley Forge [Pa.] Judson [c.1965] 158p. 21cm. [BV4211.2.M46] 65-22001 3.95
1. Preaching—Addresses, essays, lectures. 2. Christianity—20th cent.—Addresses, essays, lectures. I. Title.

MILLER, Donald G 251
Fire in thy mouth. Nashville, Abingdon Press [c1954] 160p. 21cm. [BV4211.M48] 54-5229
1. Preaching. I. Title.

MILLER, Donald G. 251
Fire in thy mouth / Donald G. Miller. Grand Rapids : Baker Book House, 1976c1954. 160p. ; 20 cm. (Notable books on preaching) Includes bibliographical references and index. [BV4211.M48] ISBN 0-8010-5986-0 pbk. : 2.95.
1. Preaching. I. Title.
L. C. card no. for original ed.54-5229.

MILLER, Donald G 251
The way to Biblical preaching. New York, Abingdon Press [1957] 160p. 21cm. [BV4211.2.M5] 57-11012
1. Preaching. I. Title.

MILLER, Milburn H 251
Ideas for sermons and talks. Anderson, Ind., Warner Press [1957] 149p. 19cm. [BV4223.M48] 57-3912
1. Sermons—Outlines. I. Title.

MILLER, Milburn H 251
Ideas for sermons and talks. Anderson, Ind., Warner Press [1957] 149p. 19cm. [BV4223.M48] 57-3912
1. Sermons— Outlines. I. Title.

MITCHELL, Henry H. 251
The recovery of preaching / by Henry H. Mitchell. New York : Harper & Row, [1977] p. cm. Includes bibliographical references. [BV4222.M5] 76-62959 ISBN 0-06-065763-4 : pbk. : 3.95
1. Preaching—Addresses, essays, lectures. I. Title.

MOORE, Hight C 1871- 251
Nuggets from golden texts. Nashville, Broadman Press [1953] 112p. 20cm. [BV4223.M56] 53-12023
1. Sermons—Outlines. I. Title.

MOOREHEAD, Lee C 251
Freedom of the pulpit. New York, Abingdon Press [1961] 94p. 20cm. Includes bibliography. [BV4211.2.M65] 61-5558
1. Preaching. I. Title.

MORRIS, Colin M. 251
The Word and the words / Colin Morris. Nashville : Abingdon Press, 1975. 174 p. ; 22 cm. Includes bibliographical references. [BV4211.2.M67 1975] 75-15955 ISBN 0-687-46045-X pbk. : 3.95
1. Preaching. I. Title.

MORRIS, Frederick M 251
Preach the Word of God. Foreword by Alden Drew Kelley. New York, Morehouse- Gorham Co., 1954. 157p. 21cm. [BV4211.M645] 54-3982
1. Preaching. I. Title.

MUNSON, Edwin C 251
The mysterious presence, communion sermons. Philadelphia, Fortress Press [1963] 112 p. 21 cm. [BV4257.5.M8] 62-20739
1. Communion sermons. 2. Lutheran Church — Sermons. 3. Sermons, American. I. Title.

NASBY, Asher Gordon, 1909- ed. 251
Treasury of the Christian world; an anthology of illustrations, ideas, and expositions drawn from eighty years of sermon publication in the Christian world pulpit and from columns of the Christian world. Foreword by George M. Docherty. [1st ed.] New York, Harper [1953] 397p. 25cm. [BV4225.N3] 53-5443
1. Homiletical illustrations. I. Title.

NASBY, Gordon Asher, 1909- ed. 251
1041 sermon illustrations, ideas, and expositions / compiled and edited by A. Gordon Nasby Grand Rapids : Baker Book House, 1976,c1953. 397p. ; 20 cm. (Treasury of the Christian World) Includes index. [BV4225.N3] ISBN 0-8010-6682-4 pbk. : 4.95
1. Homiletical illustrations. I. Title.
L.C. card no. for 1953 Harper and Row ed.:53-5443

NES, William Hamilton, 1895- 251
The excellency of the word, by William H. Nes, together with A survey of homiletics education, by Noah E. Fehl. New York, Morehouse- Gorham Co. [1956] 158p. 19cm. (The George Craig Stewart memorial lectures in preaching. 1954) [BV4211.2.N4] 56-5286
1. Preaching. I. Title.

NESPER, Paul William, 1891- 251
Biblical texts. [2d ed.] Columbus, Ohio, Wartburg Press [1952] 442p. 20cm. First published in 1923 under title: Biblical texts for special occassions. [BV4223.N35 1952] 54-28198
1. Sermons—Texts for sermons. 2. Lectionaries —Hist. & crit. I. Title.

NICOLL, William Robertson, Sir 1851-1923, ed. 251
The sermon outline Bible. Grand Rapids, Baker Book House, 1958- v. 23cm. 'Previously printed ... under the title, The sermon Bible.' [BS491.N53] 57-14758
1. Bible—Sermons—Outlines. I. Title.

NICOLL, William Robertson, Sir 1851-1923, ed. 251
300 sermon outlines on the New Testament. Grand Rapids, Baker Book House, 1956. 279p. 21cm. [BV4223.N53 1956] 56-7588
1. Sermons—Outlines. I. Title.

NILES, Daniel T 251
Preaching the gospel of the resurrection. Philadelphia, Westminster Press [1954] 93p. 20cm. (The Bevan memorial lectures) [BV4211.N55 1954] 54-6325
1. Preaching. I. Title.

NILES, Daniel Thambyrajah. 251
The preacher's task and the stone of stumbling. [1st ed.] New York, Harper [1958] 125p. 20cm. (The Lyman Beecher lectures, 1957) [BV4211.2.N5] 57-12986
1. Preaching. I. Title.

NILES, Daniel Thambyrajah. 251
Preaching the gospel of the resurrection. Philadelphia, Westminster Press [1954] 93p. 20cm. (The Bevan memorial lectures) [BV4211.2.N52 1954] 54-6325
1. Preaching. I. Title.

101 select sermon outlines by 251
Vaughan, Exell, Spurgeon, Robinson, and others. Grand Rapids, Baker Book House, 1953. 95p. 21cm. (Minister's handbook series) [BV4223.O5] 54-16109
1. Sermans—Outlines.

1,001 sermon illustrations 251
and quotations [from] Geikie, Cowper, and others. Grand Rapids, Baker Book House, 1952. 116p. 21cm. (Minister's handbook series) [BV4225.O53] 52-14831
1. Hornilectical illustrations. I. Geikie, John Cunningham, 1824-1906.

OTT, Heinrich. 251
Theology and preaching; a programme of work in dogmatics, arranged with reference to Questions I-II of the Heidelberg catechism. Translated by Harold Knight. Philadelphia, Westminster Press [1965] 158 p. 23 cm. Translation of Dogmatik und Verkundigung. [BV4214.O813] 65-12513
1. Preaching. 2. Kerygma. 3. Sin. I. Heidelberg catechism. II. Title.

OXNAM, Garfield Bromley, Bp., 1891-1963. 251
Preaching in a revolutionary age. Freeport, N.Y., Books for Libraries Press [1971, c1944] 207 p. 23 cm. (Lyman Beecher lectures on preaching, 1943-44) (Essay index reprint series) Includes bibliographical references. [BV4211.O9 1971] 75-142687 ISBN 0-8369-2421-5
1. Preaching. 2. Clergy. 3. Church and social problems. I. Title. II. Series: Lyman Beecher lectures, 1944.

PACK, Frank, 1916- 251
Preaching to modern man [by] Frank Pack and Prentice Meador, Jr. Abilene, Tex., Biblical Research Press [1969] vii, 173 p. 23 cm. Bibliography: p. 172-173. [BV4222.P28] 73-75928 3.95
1. Preaching—Addresses, essays, lectures. I. Meador, Prentice, 1938- joint author. II. Title.

PARKER, Joseph, 1830-1902. 251
Sermon outlines; a choice collection of thirty-five model sermons. Selected and edited by Sheldon B. Quincer. Grand Rapids, Eerdmans [1958] 150p. 23cm. (The World's great sermons in outline, v. 4) [BV4223.P34] 58-7570
1. Sermons—Outlines. I. Title.

PEARSON, Roy Messer, 1914- 251
The ministry of preaching. [1st ed.] New York, Harper [1959] 127p. 20cm. Includes bibliography. [BV4211.2.P4] 59-7158
1. Preaching. I. Title.

PEARSON, Roy Messer, 1914- 251
The preacher: his purpose and practice. Philadelphia,Westminister Press, [1962] 224 p. 21 cm. [BV660.2.P4] 62-15163
1. Preaching. I. Title.

PEARSON, Roy Messer, 1914- 251
The preacher: his purpose and practice. Philadelphia, Westminster [c1962] 224p. 21cm. 62-15163 4.50
1. Preaching. I. Title.

PENNINGTON, Chester A. 251
God has a communication problem / Chester Pennington. New York : Hawthorn Books, c1976. viii, 136 p. ; 22 cm. Bibliography: p. 134-136. [BV4211.2.P42 1976] 75-28692 ISBN 0-8015-3044-X : 6.95
1. Preaching. I. Title.

PERRY, Lloyd Merle. 251
Biblical preaching for today's world, by Lloyd M. Perry. Chicago, Moody Press [1973] 208 p. 22 cm. Based on the Lyman Stewart memorial lectures for 1971-72, delivered at Talbot Theological Seminary, La Mirada, Calif. Bibliography: p. 201-205. [BV4211.2.P433] 73-7471 ISBN 0-8024-0707-2 4.95
1. Preaching. I. Title.

PERRY, Lloyd Merle. 251
Biblical sermon guide; a step-by-step procedure for the preparation and presentation, by Lloyd M. Perry. Grand Rapids, Baker Book House [1970] 131 p. illus. 23 cm. Bibliography: p. 125-128. [BV4211.2.P435] 75-115642 4.95
1. Preaching. 2. Sermons—Outlines. I. Title.

PERRY, Lloyd Merle. 251
A manual for Biblical preaching. Grand Rapids, Mich., Baker Book House, 1965. 215 p. 29 cm. Bibliography: p. 207-215. [CBV1211.2.P44] 65-9730
1. Preaching, I. Title. II. Title: Biblical preaching.

PERRY, Lloyd Merle 251
A manual for Biblical preaching. Grand Rapids, Mich., Baker [c.]1965. 215p. 29cm. Bibl. [BV4211.2.P44] 65-9730 4.95
1. Preaching. I. Title. II. Title: Biblical preaching.

PICKELL, Charles N 1927- 251
Preaching to meet men's needs; the meaning of the Acts as a guide for preaching today. [1st ed.] New York, Exposition Press [1958] 82p. 21cm. Includes bibliography. [BV4211.2.P5] 58-3691
1. Preaching. 2. Bible. N. T. Acts—Criticism, interpretation,etc. I. Title.

PIKE, James Albert, Bp., 1913-1969. 251
A new look in preaching. New York, Scribner [1961] 107 p. 19 cm. (The George Craig Stewart memorial lectures) [BV4211.P53] 61-13607
1. Preaching. I. Title.

PIPES, William Harrison, 1912- 251
Say amen, brother! Old-time Negro preaching: a study in American frustration. New York, William-Frederick Press, 1951. 1, 210 p. 24 cm. Bibliography: p. 201-205. [BR563.N4P53] 51-11631
1. Negroes — Religion. 2. Preaching — Hist. — U.S. I. Title. II. Title: Old-time Negro preaching.

PITTENGER, William Norman, 1905- 251
Proclaiming Christ today. Greenwich, Conn., Seabury Press, 1962. 148p. 20cm. Includes bibliography. [BV4211.2.P56] 62-9616
1. Preaching. I. Title.

POOVEY, William Arthur, 1913- 251
And Pilate asked ... Sermons for Lent [by] W. A. Poovey. Minneapolis, Augsburg Pub. House [c1965] 92 p. 20 cm. [BV4277.P6] 252
1. Lenten sermons. 2. Sermons, American. 3. Lutheran Church—Sermons. I. Title.

PROCHNOW, Herbert Victor, 1897- ed. 251
The speaker's treasury for Sunday school teachers. Boston, W. A. Wilde Co. [1955] 175p. 21cm. [BV4225.P7] 55-10546
1. Homiletical illustrations. I. Title.

PROCLAMATION: aids for 251
interpreting the lessons of the church year. Philadelphia, Fortress Press [197 v. 22 cm. Contents.Contents.— —Series C. [1] Watermulder, D. B. and Krodel, G. Advent-Christmas. [2] Achtemeier, P. J. and Achtemeier, E. R. Epiphany. [3] Stuempfle, H. G. and Kearney, P. J. Lent. [4] Stevick, D. B. and Johnson, B. Holy week. [BV4241.P73] 73-79329 1.95 (pbk.)
1. Bible—Liturgical lessons, English. 2. Church year sermons. 3. Sermons, American.

PULPIT themes; 251
one hundred outlines of sermons, by Matthew Henry, Christmas Evans, Andrew Fuller, and others. Grand Rapids, Baker Book House, 1954. 227p. 20cm. [Co-operative reprint library] 'A reprint of Pulpit themes and Preacher's assistant, part II.' [BV4223.P84] 54-11088
1. Sermons—Outlines. I. Henry, Matthew, 1662-1714.

PUNT, Neal. 251
Baker's textual and topical filing system. Grand Rapids, Baker Book House [c1960] 1v. (unpaged) 29cm. An aid to Christian clergymen and religious workers for the organization of study material: 'Textual index' of Biblical books, chapters, and verses; 'Topical index'; and 'Reference space' section of blank spaces numbered 1 to 2000. [BV4379.P8] 60-53376
1. Files and filing (Documents) 2. Pastoral theology. I. Title.

RAD, Gerhard von, 1901-1971. 251
Biblical interpretations in preaching / Gerhard von Rad ; translated by John E. Steely. Nashville : Abingdon, c1977. 125 p. ; 21 cm. Translation of Predigt-Meditationen. [BX8066.R22P7413] 76-43248 ISBN 0-687-03444-2 : 5.95
1. Lutheran Church—Sermons. 2. Bible—Homiletical use. 3. Sermons, German. I. Title.

RANDOLPH, David James, 1934- 251
The renewal of preaching. Philadelphia, Fortress Press [1969] xi, 137 p. 23 cm. Bibliographical footnotes. [BV4211.2.R3] 69-14623 3.95
1. Bible—Hermeneutics. 2. Bible—Homiletical use. 3. Preaching. I. Title.

READ, David Haxton Carswell. 251
The communication of the gospel. London, SCM press [label: Chicago, A. R. Alienson, 1952] 96p. 19cm. (The Warrack lectures for 1951) [BV4211.R33] 53-37774
1. Preaching. I. Title.

READ, David Haxton Carswell. 251
Sent from God; the enduring power and mystery of preaching [by] David H. C. Read. Nashville, Abingdon Press [1974] 112 p. 20 cm. [BV4211.2.R36] 73-18241 3.95
1. Preaching. I. Title.

REES, Paul Stromberg. 251
The Epistles to the Philippians, Colossians, and Philemon. Grand Rapids, Baker Book House, 1964. 143 p. 21 cm. (Proclaiming the New Testament, 9) Bibliography: p. 141-143. [BS2705.5.R4] 64-14823
1. Bible. N.T. Philipians — Homiletical use. I. Title.

REES, Paul Stromberg 251
The Epistles to the Philippians, Colossians, and Philemon. Grand Rapids, Mich., Baker Bk. House [c.]1964. 143p. 21cm. (Proclaiming the New Testament, 9) Bibl. 64-14823 2.95 bds.,
1. Bible. N. T. Philippians—Homiletical use. I. Title.

THE Renewal of preaching: 251
theory and practice, edited by Karl Rahner. New York, Paulist Press [1968] ix, 195 p. 24 cm. (Concilium: theology in the age of renewal: Pastoral theology, v. 33) Includes articles translated from several languages by various persons. Bibliographical footnotes. [BV4211.2.R43] 68-22795
1. Preaching. I. Rahner, Karl, 1904- ed. II. Series: Concilium (New York) v. 33

REU, Johann Michael, 1869-1943. 251
Homiletics; a manual of the theory and practice of preaching. Translated into English by Albert Steinhaeuser. Grand Rapids, Baker Book House [1967, c1924] 639 p. 23 cm. (Limited editions library) [BV4211.R4 1967] 67-4175
1. Preaching. I. Title.

RICE, Charles Lynvel, 1936- 251
Interpretation and imagination; the preacher and contemporary literature [by] Charles L. Rice. Philadelphia, Fortress Press [1970] xiv, 158 p. 18 cm. (The Preacher's paperback library) Includes bibliographical references. [BV4211.2.R48] 78-116463 3.50 (pbk)
1. Preaching. 2. Religion and literature. 3. Sermons, American. I. Title.

RICHARDS, Harold Marshall Sylvester, 1894- 251
Feed my sheep. Washington, Review and Herald Pub. Association [c1958] 446p. 22cm. [BV4211.2.R5] 59-20241
1. Preaching. I. Title.

RITSCHL, Dietrich 251
A theology of proclamation. Richmond, Va. John Knox Press [c.1960] 190p. 60-15296 3.50
1. Preaching. I. Title.

ROBERTSON, Archibald Thomas, 1863-1934. 251
The glory of the ministry; Paul's exultation in preaching. Introd. by Ralph G. Turnbull. Grand Rapids, Baker Book House [1967] 243 p. 20 cm. First published 1911. Bibliographical footnotes. [BV4010.R63 1967] 67-18193
1. Preaching. 2. Pastoral theology. I. Title.

ROBINSON, James Herman. 251
Adventurous preaching. [1st ed.] Great Neck, N. Y., Channel Press [1956] 186p. 21cm. (The Lyman Beecher lectures at Yale, 1955 [BV4211.2.R6] 56-13819
1. Preaching. 2. Theology. Postoral. I. Title.

ROCK, Augustine. 251
Unless they be sent; a theological study of the nature and purpose of preaching. Dubuque, W. C. Brown Co. [1953] 208p. 21cm. (Dominican Fathers, Province of St. Albert the Great. The Aquinas library. Doctrinal studies, 4) [BV4211.R65] 53-1632
1. Preaching. I. Title.

ROHRBACH, Peter Thomas. 251
The art of dynamic preaching; a practical

guide to better preaching. [1st ed.] Garden City, N.Y., Doubleday, 1965. 190 p. 22 cm. [BV4211.2.R65] 65-23781
1. Preaching. I. Title.

ROHRBACH, Peter Thomas 251
The art of dynamic preaching; a practical guide to better preaching. Garden City, N. Y., Doubleday [c.]1965. 190p. 22cm. [BV4211.2.R65] 65-23781 4.50
1. Preaching. I. Title.

SANFORD, Jack D 251
Make your preaching relevant. Nashville, Broadman Press [1963] 93 p. 20 cm.SPreaching. [BV4211.2.S28] 63-11167
I. Title.

SANFORD, Jack D. 251
Make your preaching relevant. Nashville, Broadman [c.1963] 93p. 20cm. 63-11167 1.50 pap.,
1. Preaching. I. Title.

SANGSTER, P E 251
Speech in the pulpit. New York, Philosophical Library [1958] 84 p. illus. 20cm. [PN4173.S3] 58-59644
1. Preaching. 2. Oratory. I. Title.

*SANGSTER, W. E. 1900-1960 251
Power in preaching W. E. Sangster. Grand Rapids. : Baker Book House, 1976 c1958. 110 p. ; 20 cm. (Notable books on preaching) Includes index. [BV4211.2] ISBN 0-8010-8075-4 pbk. : 1.95
1. Preaching. I. Title.
L.C. card no. for 1958 Epworth Press ed.: 58-10462.

SANGSTER, William Edwin, 251
1900-
The craft of sermon construction. [A source book for ministers] Philadelphia, Westminster Press [1951] 208 p. 21 cm. (The Westminster source books) [BV4211.S24] 51-7833
1. Preaching. I. Title. II. Title: Sermon construction.

SANGSTER, William Edwin, 251
1900-
The craft of sermon illustration. Philadelphia, Westminster Press [1950] 125 p. 21 cm. (The Westminster source books) On cover: A source book for ministers. [BV4226.S3] 50-9924
1. Homiletical illustrations. 2. Preaching. I. Title.

SANGSTER, William Edwin, 251
1900-
Power in preaching. New York, Abingdon Press [1958] 110p. 20cm. (The Fondren lectures, 39) [BV4211.2.S3] 58-10462
1. Preaching. I. Title.

SANGSTER, William Edwin 251
Robert.
The craft of sermon illustration [by] W. E. Sangster. Introd. by Ralph G. Turnbull Grand Rapids, Mich., Baker Book House [1973, c.1950] 125 p. 20 cm. (Notable books on preaching) [BV4226.S3] 1.95 (pbk.)
1. Homiletical illustrations. 2. Preaching. I. Title.
L.C. card no. for hardbound ed.: 50-9924.

SAYRES, Alfred Nevin. 251
That one good sermon. Philadelphia, United Church Press [1963] 95 p. 20 cm. [BV4211.2.S34] 63-21519
1. Preaching. I. Title.

SAYRES, Alfred Nevin 251
That one good sermon. Philadelphia, United Church Pr. [c.1963] 95p. 20cm. 63-21519 2.50 bds.,
1. Preaching. I. Title.

*SCHERER, Paul 251
For we have this treasure. New York, Harper [1965, c.1944] 212p. 21cm. (Lyman Beecher lects., Yale Univ.; Harper chapelbks, CB4) Bibl. 1.95 pap.,
I. Title.

*SCHERER, Paul. 251
For we have this treasure : the Yale lectures on preaching, 1943. Grand Rapids : Baker Book House, 1976c1944. 212p. ; 20 cm. (Notable books on preaching) Includes bibliographical references. [BV4211] ISBN 0-8010-8073-8 pbk. : 2.95.
1. Preaching. 2. Communication (Theology) I. Title.

SCHERER, Paul, 1892- 251
The word God sent / Paul Scherer. Grand Rapids, Mich. : Baker Book House, 1977,c1965. 272p. ; 20 cm. Includes index. [BV4211.2S36] ISBN 0-8010-8102-5 pbk. : 3.95
1. Preaching. 2. Sermons, American. 3. Lutheran Church-Sermons. I. Title.

L.C. card no. for 1965 Harper & Row ed.: 65-20457.

SCHERER, Paul, 1892- 251
The work God sent. New York. Harper [c.1965] xiii, 272p. 22cm. Bibl. [BV4211.2.S36] 65-20457 4.95
1. Preaching. 2. Sermons, American. 3. Lutheran Church—Sermons. I. Title.

SCHMAUS, Michael, 1897- 251
Preaching as a saving encounter. [Translated by J. Holland Smith] Staten Island, N.Y., Alba House [1966] 151 p. 20 cm. Translation of: Wahrheit als Heilsbegegnung. Bibliographical references included in "Annotations" (p. [137]-151) [BV4214.S5213] 66-21814
1. Preaching. I. Title.

SCHNEIDER, Stanley D. 251
As one who speaks for God; the why and how of preaching. Minneapolis, Augsburg [c.1965] vi, 114p. 22cm. Bibl. [BV4211.2.S38] 65-22842 3.50
1. Preaching. I. Title.

SCHROEDER, Frederick W 251
Preaching the Word with authority. Philadelphia, Westminister Press [1954] 128p. 20cm. [BV4211.S28] 54-8838
1. Preaching. I. Title.

SCHROEDER, George W 251
You can speak for God; 130 devotional talk outlines for laymen. Nashville, Broadman Press [1958] 132p. 22cm. [BV4223.S35] 58-5415
1. Sermons—Outlines. I. Title.

SEAVER, Paul S. 251
The Puritan lectureships; the politics of religious dissent, 1560-1662 [by] Paul S. Seaver. Stanford, Stanford University Press, 1970. ix, 402 p. 24 cm. Bibliography: p. [311]-373. [BX9334.2.S4] 71-93497 12.50
1. Puritans—Gt. Brit. 2. Preaching—History—Gt. Brit. 3. Church and state in Great Britain. I. Title.

SELLE, Frank Frederick, 1877- 251
comp.
Quotations and illustrations for sermons, compiled by F. F. Selle and Ewald Plass. Saint Louis, Concordia Pub. House [c1951] 196 p. 23 cm. First published as v. 7 of the Concordia pulpit, under title: Sermon illustrations. [BV4225.S413 1951] 52-18345
1. Homiletical illustrations. I. Title.

SEMMELROTH, Otto. 251
The preaching word; on the theology of proclamation. [Translated by John Jay Hughes. New York] Herder and Herder [1965] 256 p. 22 cm. Translation of Wirkendes Wort. Bibliographical references included in "Footnotes" (p. 247-252) [BV4211.2.S413] 64-19737
1. Kerygma. 2. Preaching. I. Title.

SEMMELROTH, Otto 251
The preaching word; on the theology of proclamation. [Tr. from German by John Jay Hughes. New York] Herder & Herder [c.1965] 256p. 22cm. Tr. of Wirkendes Wort. Bibl. [BV4211.2.S413] 64-19737 4.95
1. Kerygma. 2. Preaching. I. Title.

SERMON outlines, 251
by Charles Simon and others. Grand Rapids, Baker Book House, 1954. 2v. in 1. 24cm. 'Formerly publishec as Theological sketchbook; or, Skeletons of sermons.' [BV4223.S43] 54-3031
1. Sermons—Outlines. I. Simeon, Charles, 1759-1836.

SERMON seeds; 251
[outlines from the writings of Alexander Maclaren, and others. Grand Rapids, Baker Book House, 1956. 95p. 21cm. (Minister's handbook series, v. 10) [BV4223.S45] 56-10682
1. Sermons—Outlines. I. McLaren, Alexander, 1826-1910.

SEVENTH-DAY Adventists. 251
General Conference. Dept. of Education.
Treasury of devotional aids for home and school. Washington, Review and Herald Pub. Association [1951] 352 p. 24 cm. [BV4225.S45] 51-38573
1. Homiletical illustrations. 2. Children's sermons. I. Title.

SHINN, George Wolfe, 1839- 251
1910, comp.
Helps to a better Christian life; new readings for Lent. New York, T. Whittaker [1900] 239 p. 19 cm. [BV4277.S46] 0-2329
1. Lenten sermons. 2. Sermons, English. I. Title.

SITTLER, Joseph. 251
The anguish of preaching. Philadelphia, Fortress Press [1966] vii, 70 p. 22 cm. [BV4222.S53] 66-25261
1. Preaching—Addresses, essays, lectures. I. Title.

SITTLER, Joseph. 251
The ecology of faith. Philadelphia, Muhlenberg Press [1961] 104 p. 21 cm. [BV4211.2.S5] 61-10278
1. Preaching. I. Title.

SITTLER, Joseph 251
The ecology of faith. Philadelphia, Muhlenberg [c.1961] 104p. 61-10278 2.25
1. Preaching. I. Title.

SKINNER, Craig. 251
The teaching ministry of the pulpit; its history, theology, psychology, and practice for today. Grand Rapids, Mich., Baker Book House [1973] 255 p. illus. 23 cm. Bibliography: p. 237-246. [BV4211.2.S533] 72-93334 ISBN 0-8010-7981-0 5.95
1. Preaching. I. Title.

SLEETH, Ronald Eugene. 251
Persuasive preaching. [1st ed.] New York, Harper [1956] 96 p. 20 cm. [BV4211.2.S55] 55-8527
1. Preaching. I. Title.

SLEETH, Ronald Eugene 251
Proclaiming the Word. Nashville, Abingdon [c.1964] 142p. 20cm. Bibl. 64-10605 2.75 bds.,
1. Preaching. I. Title.

SMITH, Charles William 251
Frederick
Biblical authority for modern preaching. Philadelphia, Westminster Press [c.1960] 176 p. 21 cm. Bibl. and bibl. notes: p. 170-176 60-7190 3.50
1. Preaching. I. Title.

SMITH, Charles William 251
Frederick, 1905-
Biblical authority for modern preaching. Philadelphia, Westminster Press [1960] 176 p. 21 cm. Includes bibliography. [BV4211.2.S6] 60-7190
1. Preaching. I. Title.

SOLLITT, Kenneth Walter. 251
Preaching from pictures. A handbook for worship leaders explaining and illustrating with twelve complete services of worship the preaching power of pictures. [New rev. ed.] Boston, W. A. Wilde [1953,c1938] 150p. illus. 21cm. [BV4227] 53-9054
1. Art and religion. 2. Sermons, American. 3. Preaching. 4. Public worship. I. Title.

SOPER, Donald Oliver, 1903- 251
The advocacy of the Gospel. New York, Abingdon Press [1961] 119 p. 18 cm. [BV4211,2.S65] 61-66124
1. Preaching. I. Title.

SOPER, Donald Oliver, 1903- 251
The advocacy of the Gospel. Nashville, Abingdon [c.1961] 119p. 61-66124 2.50 bds.,
1. Preaching. I. Title.

SPURGEON, Charles Haddon, 251
1834-1892.
Choice sermon notes. Grand Rapids, Zondervan Pub. House [1952] 215 p. illus. 20 cm. [BV4223.S58] 52-3466
1. Sermons — Outlines. I. Title.

SPURGEON, Charles Haddon, 251
1834-1892.
Encounter with Spurgeon [by] Helmut Thielicke. Translated by John W. Doberstein. Grand Rapids: Baker Book House, [1975 c1963] [ix,] 283 p.; 20 cm. Translation of Vom geistlichen Reden: Begegnung mit Spurgeon. [BV4211.S6943] 63-12536 ISBN 0-8010-8825-9 3.95 (pbk.)
1. Preaching. I. Thielicke, Helmut, 1908- II. Title.

SPURGEON, Charles Haddon, 251
1834-1892.
My sermon notes; a selection from outlines of discourses delivered at the Metropolitan Tabernacle, with anecdotes and illus. [Westwood, N.J.] Revell [1956?] 1067p. 21cm. [BV4223] 56-9829
1. Sermons—Outlines. I. Title.

SPURGEON, Charles Haddon, 251
1834-1892.
My sermon notes; a selection from outlines of discourses delivered at the Metropolitan Tabernacle, with anecdotes and illus. [Westwood, N.J., Revell [1956.] 1067 p. 21 cm. [[BV4223]] 56-9829
1. Sermons-Outlines. I. Title.

STALKER, James, 1848-1927. 251
The preacher and his models. Introd. by Ralph G. Turnbull. Grand Rapids, Baker Book House [1967] 284 p. 20 cm. (Notable books on preaching) (The Yale lectures on preaching, 1891.) Bibliographical footnotes. [BV4211.S7 1967] 67-18196
1. Preaching. I. Title. II. Series: Lyman Beecher lectures, 1891.

STAMM, Frederick Keller, 251
1883-
So you want to preach. New York, Abingdon Press [1958] 109 p. 20 cm. [BV4011.S8] 58-8124
1. Pastoral theology. 2. Preaching. I. Title.

STANFIELD, Vernon L. 251
Effective evangelistic preaching. Grand Rapids, Mich., Baker Bk. [c.]1965. 78p. 23cm. [BV4211.2.S72] 65-29537 2.00
1. Preaching. 2. Evangelistic sermons. I. Title.

STAUFFER, Joshua, 1891- 251
"Give ye them to eat"; or, Sermon outlines. Berne, Ind., Light and Hope Publications [c1951] 192 p. 20 cm. [BV4223.S76] 52-20938
1. Sermons — Outlines. I. Title.

STEERE, Douglas Van, 1901- 251
Bethlehem revisited, by Douglas V. Steere. [Wallingford, Pa., Pendle Hill Publications 1965] 18 p. 20 cm. (Pendle Hill pamphlet 144) [BV4257.S7] 65-26995
1. Christmas sermons. I. Title.

*STENDAHL, Krister 251
Proclamation: aids for interpreting the lessons of the Church Year. Philadelphia, Fortress Press, [1974] 58 p. 22 cm. (Series A) [BV421] 74-76926 ISBN 0-8006-4064-0 1.95 (pbk.)
1. Bible—Liturgical lessons. I. Title.

STEVENSON, Dwight Eshelman, 251
1906-
Reaching people from the pulpit; a guide to effective sermon delivery, by Dwight E. Stevenson and Charles F. Diehl. [1st ed.] New York, Harper [1958] 172 p. illus. 22 cm. Includes bibliography. [BV4211.2.S75] 58-7104
1. Preaching. 2. Elocution. I. Diehl, Charles F., joint author. II. Title.

STEWART, James Stuart, 1896- 251
A faith to proclaim [by] James S. Stewart. Grand Rapids, Mich., Baker Book House [1972, c.1953] 160 p. 19 cm. (James S. Stewart library) [BR121.S86] 53-2290 ISBN 0-8010-7977-2 pap., 1.95
1. Christianity—20th century. 2. Preaching. I. Title.

STEWART, James Stuart, 1896- 251
A faith to procliam. New York, Scribner, 1953. 160p. 20cm. (The Lyman Beecher lectures at Yale University) [BR121.S86 1953a] 53-2290
1. Christianity—20th cent. 2. Preaching. I. Title.

STOTT, John R. W 251
The preacher's portrait; some New Testament word studies. Grand Rapids, Eerdmans [1961] 124 p. 21 cm. Includes bibliography. [BV4211.S8] 61-17392
1. Preaching — Biblical teaching. I. Title.

STOTT, John R. W. 251
The preacher's portrait; some New Testament word studies. Grand Rapids, Eerdmans [c.1961] 124p. Bibl. 61-17392 3.00
1. Preaching—Biblical teaching. I. Title.

STOWE, Everett M 251
Communicating reality through symbols [by] Everett M. Stowe. Philadelphia, Westminster Press [1966] 158 p. 21 cm. (Westminster studies in Christian communication) Bibliographical references included in "Notes" (p. 151-158) [BV4319.S7] 66-18509
1. Communication (Theology) 2. Symbolism in communication. I. Title. II. Series.

STOWE, Everett M. 251
Communicating reality through symbols [by] Everett M. Stowe. Philadelphia, Westminster [1966] 158p. 21cm. (Westminster studies in Christian communication) Bibl. [BV4319.S7] 66-18509 4.95
1. Communication (Theology) 2. Symbolism in communication. I. Title. II. Series.

SWEAZEY, George Edgar, 1905- 251
Preaching the good news / George E. Sweazey. Englewood Cliffs, N.J. : Prentice-Hall, [1976] viii, 339 p. ; 24 cm. Includes index. Bibliography: p. 319-326. [BV4211.2.S93] 75-4997 ISBN 0-13-694802-2 : 10.95
1. Preaching. I. Title.

TAYLOR, Richard Shelley, 251
1912-
Preaching holiness today, by Richard S. Taylor. Kansas City, Mo., Beacon Hill Press [1968] 216 p. 21 cm. Bibliography: p. 206-210. [BV4221.T3] 68-3324
1. Preaching. 2. Holiness. I. Title.

TEIKMANIS, Arthur L., 1914- 251
Preaching and pastoral care. Englewood Cliffs, N.J., Prentice [c.1964] 144p. 21cm. (Successful pastoral counseling ser.) 64-23551 2.95
1. Preaching. I. Title. II. Series.

THARP, Zeno Chandler, 1896- 251
Favorite stories and illustrations. [1st ed.] Cleveland, Tenn., Church of God Pub. House, 1956. 144p. 21cm. [BV4225.T44] 56-8668
1. Homiletical illustrations. I. Title.

THARP, Zeno Chandler, 1896- 251
Favorite stories and illustrations. [1st ed.] Cleveland, Tenn., Church of God Pub. House, 1956. 144 p. 21 cm. [BV4225.T44] 56-8668
1. Homiletical illustrations. I. Title.

THIELICKE, Helmut, 1908- 251
The trouble with the church; a call for renewal. Translated and edited by John W. Doberstein. [1st ed.] New York, Harper & Row [1965] xvi, 136 p. 21 cm. Translation of Leiden an der Kirche; ein personliches Wort. [BV4214.T473] 65-20458
1. Preaching. 2. Kerygma. I. Title.

THOMPSON, William D. 251
Dialogue preaching; the shared sermon [by] William D. Thompson [and] Gordon C. Bennett. Valley Forge [Pa.] Judson Press [1969] 158 p. 23 cm. "An anthology of dialogue sermons": p. 73-158. Bibliographical footnotes. [BV4307.D5T5] 69-16387 4.95
1. Dialogue sermons. 2. Sermons, American. I. Bennett, Gordon C., joint author. II. Title.

THOMPSON, William D. 251
A listener's guide to preaching. Nashville, Abingdon [c.1966] 110p. illus. 18cm. [BV4211.2.T5] 66-14996 1.25 pap.,
1. Preaching. I. Title.

TODD, Galbraith Hall. 251
O angel of the garden. Grand Rapids, Baker BookHouse, 1961. 96 p. 21 cm. [BV4259.T6] 61-17551
1. Easter — Sermons. 2. Presbyterian Church — Sermons. 3. Sermons, American. I. Title.

TRUSS, Cyprian. 251
Say it with stories; a compilation of true stories, anecdotes, and examples for the use of preachers, teachers, public speakers, and lecturere. New York, J. F. Wagner [c1955] 189p. 21cm. [BV4225.T7] 56-965
1. Homiletical illustrations. I. Title.

VALENTINE, Ferdinand. 251
The art of preaching; a practical guide. Westminster, Md., Newman Press, 1952. 224p. 22cm. [BV4211.V2 1952] 52-9506
1. Preaching. I. Title.

VOLBEDA, Samuel 251
The pastoral genius of preaching. Compiled and edited by Robert Evenhuis. Grand Rapids, Mich., Zondervan Pub. House [c.1960] 85p. 21cm. 60-3430 2.00 bds.,
1. Preaching. I. Title.

VOLBEDA, Samuel, 1881-1953. 251
The pastoral genius of preaching. Compiled and edited by Robert Evenhuis. Grand Rapids, Zondervan Pub. House [1960] 85 p. 21 cm. [BV4211.2.V6] 60-3430
1. Preaching. I. Title.

WAGNER, Don M 251
The expository method of G. Campbell Morgan. [Westwood, N.J.] Revell [1957] 128p. 20cm. Includes bibliography. [BS501.M6W3] 57-5709
1. Morgan, George Campbell, 1863-1945. 2. Bible—Hermeneutics. I. Title.

WAGNER, Don M 251
The expository method of G. Campbell Morgan. [Westwood, N.J.] Revell [1957] 128 p. 20 cm. Includes bibliography. [BS501.M6W3] 57-5409
1. Morgan, George Campbell, 1863-1945. 2. Bible — Hermeneutics. I. Title.

WALKER, Granville T 251
Preaching in the thought of Alexander Campbell. St. Louis, Bethany Press [1954] 271p. 23cm. [Bethany history series] 'The original work ... was submitted as a doctoral dissertation to the Yale faculty in 1948.' [BX7343.C2W3] 54-14505
1. Campbell, Alexander, 1788-1866. 2. Preaching—Hist.—U. S. I. Title.

WALLIS, Charles Langworthy, 251
1921- ed.
Lenten-Easter sourcebook. New York, Abingdon Press [1961] 224 p. 23 cm. [BV85.W32] 61-5200
1. Lent. 2. Easter. I. Title.

WALLIS, Charles Langworthy, 251
1921- ed.
Lenten-Easter sourcebook. Nashville, Abingdon Press [c.1961] 224p. 61-5200 2.95
1. Lent. 2. Easter. I. Title.

WALLIS, Charles Langworthy, 251
1921- ed.
A treasury of sermon illustrations. Nes York, Abindyon-Cokesbury Press [1950] 319 p. 24 cm. [BV4225.W25] 50-10619
1. Homiletical illustrations. I. Title.

WALLIS, Charles Langworthy, 251
1921- ed.
A treasury of sermon illustrations. Nashville, Abingdon [1968, c.1950] 319p. 24cm. (Apex bks.) [BV4225.W25] 50-10619 1.95 pap.,
1. Homiletical illustrations. I. Title.

WEATHERSPOON, Jesse Burton, 251
1886-
Sent forth to preach; studies in apositolic preaching. [1st ed.] New York, Harper [1954] 182p. 21cm. Bibliography: p. 181-182. [BV4211.W38] 54-5855
1. Preaching. I. Title.

WEDEL, Alton F. 251
The mighty word / by Alton Wedel. St. Louis : Concordia Pub. House, c1977. p. cm. (The Preacher's workshop series ; book 1) Includes bibliographical references. [BV4211.2.W38] 77-21778 ISBN 0-570-07400-2 pbk. : 1.95
1. Preaching. I. Title. II. Series.

WEDEL, Theodore Otto, 1892- 251
The pulpit rediscovers theology. Greenwich, Conn., Seabury Press, 1956. 181p. 22cm. [BV4211.2.W4] 56-7969
1. Preaching. I. Title.

WEDEL, Theodore Otto, 1892- 251
The pulpit rediscovers theology. Greenwich, Conn., Seabury Press, 1956. 181 p. 22 cm. [BV4211.2.W4] 56-7969
1. Preaching. I. Title.

WEISHEIT, Eldon. 251
A sermon is more than words / by Eldon Weisheit. St. Louis : Concordia Pub. House, c1977. p. cm. (The Preacher's workshop series ; book 8) [BV4227.W43] 77-21557 ISBN 0-570-07407-X pbk. : 1.95
1. Preaching—Audio-visual aids. I. Title. II. Series.

WELSH, Clement, 1913- 251
Preaching in a new key: Studies in the psychology of thinking and listening. Philadelphia, United Church Press [1974] 128 p. 22 cm. "A Pilgrim Press book." Includes bibliographical references. [BV4211.2.W42] 74-5268 ISBN 0-8298-0273-8 5.95
1. Preaching. 2. Perception. 3. Cognition. I. Title.

WEST, Emerson Roy. 251
How to speak in church / Emerson Roy West. Salt Lake City : Deseret Book Co., 1976. viii, 168 p. : ill. ; 24 cm. Includes index. Bibliography: p. 162-163. [BX8638.W47] 76-3818 5.95
1. Church of Jesus Christ of Latter-Day Saints. 2. Public speaking. 3. Preaching. I. Title.

WEST, Emerson Roy 251
When you speak in church: purpose, preparation, presentation. Salt Lake City, Deseret, 1966 [c.1965] 196p. illus. 24cm. Bibl. [BV4211.2.W43] 65-28866 price unreported
1. Preaching. I. Title.

WHITE, Douglas Malcolm, 1909- 251
The excellence of exposition / by Douglas M. White ; foreword by Stephen F. Olford. Neptune, N.J. : Loizeaux Bros., c1977. 191 p. ; 21 cm. Includes indexes. Bibliography: p. 179-184. [BV4211.2.W433] 77-6807 ISBN 0-87213-938-7 : 4.25
1. Preaching. I. Title.

WHITE, Douglas Malcolm, 1909- 251
"He ezpounded"; a guide to ezpository preaching. Chicago, Moody Press [1952] 159 p. 20 cm. [BV4211.W43] 52-1588
1. Preaching. I. Title.

WHITE, Reginald E. O. 251
A guide to preaching; a practical primer of homiletics [by] R. E. O. White. [1st American ed.] Grand Rapids, W. B. Eerdmans Pub. Co. [1973] vii, 244 p. 21 cm. Bibliography: p. 241-244. [BV4211.2.W435 1973] 73-76535 ISBN 0-8028-1540-5 3.95
1. Preaching. I. Title.

WHITEFIELD, George, 1714- 251
1770.
Sermon outlines; a choice collection of thirty-five model sermons. Selected and edited by Sheldon B. Quincer. Grand Rapids, Erdmans, 1956. 150p. 23cm. (The World's great sermons in outline) [BV4223.W444] 56-13871
1. Sermons—Outlines. I. Title.

WHITESELL, Faris Daniel, 251
1895-
Power in expository preaching. [Westwood, N.J.] Revell [1963] 174 p. 21 cm. [BV4211.2.W44] 63-10393
1. Preaching. I. Title.

WHITESELL, Faris Daniel, 251
1895-
Power in expository preaching. [Westwood, N.J.] Revell [c.1963] 174p. 21cm. 63-10393 4.00 bds.,
1. Preaching. I. Title.

WHITESELL, Faris Daniel, 251
1895-
Preaching on Bible characters. [1st ed.] Grand Rapids, Barker Book House, 1955. 150p. 20cm. Includes bibliography. [BV4211.2.W45] 55-6506
1. Preaching. 2. Preaching—Hist. 3. Bible—Biog.—Bibl. I. Title.

WHITESELL, Faris Daniel, 251
1895-
Variety in your preaching [by] Faris D. Whitesell [and] Lloyd M. Perry. [Westwood, N. J.], F. H. Revell Co. [1954] 219p. 22cm. [BV4211.W46] 54-5437
1. Preaching. I. Perry, Lloyd M., joint author. II. Title.

WOOD, Arthur Skevington. 251
The art of preaching; message, method, and motive in preaching. [American ed.] Grand Rapids, Zondervan Pub. House [1964, c1963] 126 p. 22 cm. Published in London in 1963 under title: Heralds of the gospel. [BV4211.2.W6 1964] 64-11954
1. Preaching. I. Title.

WOOD, Arthur Skevington 251
The art of preaching; message, method, and motive in preaching. Grand Rapids, Mich., Zondervan [1964, c.1963] 126p. 22cm. Pub. in London in 1963 under title: Herald of the gospel. 64-11954 2.50
1. Preaching. I. Title.

YOHN, David Waite. 251
The contemporary preacher and his task. Grand Rapids, Mich., W. B. Eerdmans [1969] 159 p. 21 cm. Bibliography: p. 154-159. [BV4211.2.Y6] 67-28379 2.95
1. Preaching. 2. Clergy—Office. I. Title.

ZIEGLER, Edward Krusen, 1903- 251
Rural preaching. [Westwood, N. J.] F. H. Revell Co. [1954] 158p. 21cm. [BV4211.2.Z5] 54-8002
1. Preaching. 2. Rural churches. I. Title.

DARGAN, Edwin Charles, 251'.009
1852-1930.
A history of preaching. New York, B. Franklin [1968] 2 v. 24 cm. (Burt Franklin: research and source works series, no. 177) (Art history and reference series, no. 19.) Reprint of the 1905-1912 ed. Contents.Contents.—v. 1. From the apostolic fathers to the great reformers, A.D. 70-1572.—v. 2. From the close of the Reformation period to the end of the nineteenth century, 1572-1900. Includes bibliographies. [BV4207] 68-4837
1. Preaching—History. I. Title.

ECHLIN, Edward P. 251'.009
The priest as preacher, past and future, by Edward P. Echlin. Notre Dame, Ind., Fides Publishers [1973] 91 p. 18 cm. (Theology today, no. 33) Bibliography: p. 88-90. [BV4207.E25] 73-176542 ISBN 0-85342-322-9 0.95 (pbk.)
1. Catholic Church—Clergy. 2. Preaching—History. I. Title.

JONES, Edgar De Witt, 251'.009
1876-1956.
The royalty of the pulpit; a survey and appreciation of the Lyman Beecher lectures on preaching founded at Yale Divinity School 1871 and given annually (with four exceptions) since 1872. Freeport, N.Y., Books for Libraries Press [1970, c1951] xxx, 447 p. 23 cm. (Essay index reprint series) Bibliography: p. 432-439. [BV4207.J65 1970] 79-134105 ISBN 0-8369-1979-3
1. Preaching—History. 2. Lyman Beecher lectures. I. Title.

KIESSLING, Elmer 251'.009'02
Carl, 1895-
The early sermons of Luther and their relation to the pre-reformation sermon. Grand Rapids, Zondervan Pub. House, 1935. [New York, AMS Press, 1971] 157 p. 18 cm. Thesis (Ph.D.)—University of Chicago, 1935. Bibliography: p. 151-157. [BR332.S75K5 1971] 75-171064 ISBN 0-404-03669-4 5.00
1. Luther, Martin, 1483-1546. 2. Preaching—History—Germany. 3. Preaching—History—Middle Ages, 600-1500. I. Title.

BRASTOW, Lewis 251'.00922
Orsmond, 1834-1912.
Representative modern preachers. Freeport, N.Y., Books for Libraries Press [1968] xv, 423 p. 23 cm. (Essay index reprint series) Reprint of the 1904 ed. Contents.Contents.—Friedrich Daniel Ernst Schleiermacher.—Fredrick William Robertson.—Henry Ward Beecher.—Horace Bushnell.—Phillips Brooks.—John Henry Newman.—James Bowling Mozley.—Thomas Guthrie.—Charles Haddon Spurgeon. [BV4207.B7 1968] 68-57306
1. Preaching—History. I. Title.

DEMARAY, Donald E. 251'.009'22 B
Pulpit giants; what made them great, by Donald E. Demaray. Chicago, Moody Press [1973] 174 p. ports. 22 cm. [BV4207.D38] 72-95026 ISBN 0-8024-6950-7 3.95
1. Preaching—History. 2. Christian biography. I. Title.
Contents Omitted.

GOTAAS, Mary C., 1907- 251'.00922
Bossuet and Vieira; [a study in national, epochal, and individual style, by Mary C. Gotaas] New York, AMS Press [1970, c1953] xix, 136 p. 23 cm. (Catholic University of America. Studies in Romance languages and literatures, v. 46) Part of the author's thesis, Catholic University of America, 1953. Bibliography: p. [131]-136. [BV4207.G68 1970] 75-128929 ISBN 0-404-50346-2
1. Bossuet, Jacques Benigne, Bp. of Meaux, 1627-1704. 2. Vieira, Antonio, 1608-1697. 3. Preaching—History—France. 4. Preaching—History—Portugal. I. Title. II. Series.

MACARTNEY, Clarence 251'.00922
Edward Noble, 1879-1957.
Six kings of the American pulpit. Freeport, N.Y., Books for Libraries Press [1971, c1942] 210 p. 23 cm. (The Smyth lectures, 1939) (Essay index reprint series) [BV4208.U6M3 1971] 75-152192 ISBN 0-8369-2323-5
1. Preaching—History—U.S. I. Title. II. Series: Thomas Smyth lectures, Columbia Theological Seminary, Decatur, Ga., 1939.

CROCKER, Lionel 251'.00924
George, 1897- comp.
Harry Emerson Fosdick's art of preaching; an anthology. Compiled and edited by Lionel Crocker. Springfield, Ill., Thomas [1971] xii, 283 p. 24 cm. Contents.Contents.—Essays on preaching, by H. E. Fosdick: Learning to preach. What is the matter with preaching? How I prepare my sermons. Animated conversation. Personal counseling and preaching. The Christian ministry. To those interested in the profession of the ministry.—A young preacher listens to Fosdick, by S. H. Miller.—How Dr. Fosdick uses the Bible in preaching, by E. May.—Harry Emerson Fosdick and Reinhold Niebuhr: a contrast in the methods of the teaching preacher, by E. Harris.—Harry Emerson Fosdick: realist and idealist, by E. D. Jones.—Harry Emerson Fosdick: titan of the pulpit, by E. D. Jones.—Harry Emerson Fosdick: a study in sources of effectiveness, by R. C. McCall.—Harry Emerson Fosdick: the growth of a great preacher, by R. D. Clark.—Selected bibliography: (p. 181-185)—Harry Emerson Fosdick and the techniques of organization, by E. H. Linn.—Structural analysis of the sermons of Dr. Harry Emerson Fosdick, by G. S. Macvaugh.—Harry Emerson Fosdick: the methods of a master, by C. F. Kemp.—The rhetorical theory of Harry Emerson Fosdick, by L. Crocker.—Henry Ward Beecher and Harry Emerson Fosdick, by L. Crocker.—Phillips Brooks and Harry Emerson Fosdick, by L. Crocker.—A rhetorical analysis of Harry Emerson Fosdick's sermon, "The power to see it through," by L. Crocker.—Studies in the preaching of Harry Emerson Fosdick (bibliographical: p. 274-275) [BV4207.C75] 74-130922
1. Fosdick, Harry Emerson, 1878-1969. 2. Preaching—History—20th century. I. Fosdick, Harry Emerson, 1878-1969. II. Title.

*DAY, Richard 251.'0092'4
Ellsworth
The shadow of the broad brim : the life story of Charles Hadden Spurgeon, heir of the Puritans. Grand Rapids : Baker Book House, 1976c1934. 236p. : ill., ports. ; 20 cm. [BX6495.S7.] [B] ISBN 0-8010-2855-8 pbk. : 3.95.
1. Spurgeon, Charles Haddon, 1834-1892. 2. Preaching. I. Title.

WORLEY, Robert C 251'.00924
Preaching and teaching in the earliest church, by Robert C. Worley. Philadelphia, Westminster Press [1967] 199 p. 21 cm. Based on the author's doctoral study. Bibliographical references included in "Notes" (p. [153]-194) [BX4827.D6W6] 67-20613
1. Dodd, Charles Harold, 1884- 2. Preaching—Hist.—Early church. 3. Religious education—Hist.—Early church. 4. Kerygma. I. Title.

WORLEY, Robert C. 251'.00924
Preaching and teaching in the earliest church, by Robert C. Worley. Philadelphia, Westminster Press [1967] 199 p. 21 cm. Based on the author's doctoral study. Bibliographical

references included in "Notes" (p. [153]-194) [BX4827.D6W6] 67-20613
1. Dodd, Charles Harold, 1884- 2. Preaching—History—Early church. 3. Religious education—History—Early church. 4. Kerygma. I. Title.

DOWNEY, James. 251'.00942
The eighteenth century pulpit. A study of the sermons of Butler, Berkeley, Secker, Sterne, Whitefield and Wesley. Oxford, Clarendon Press, 1969. ix, 254 p. ports. 22 cm. Bibliography: p. [234]-247. [BV4208.G7D6] 75-438031 unpriced
1. Preaching—History—England. I. Title.

GATCH, Milton McC. 251'.00942
Preaching and theology in Anglo-Saxon England : Aelfric and Wulfstan / Milton McC. Gatch. Toronto ; Buffalo : University of Toronto Press, c1977. p. cm. "Aelfric's excerpts from Julian of Toledo, Prognosticon futuri saeculi": p. Includes indexes. Bibliography: p. [BV4208.G7G37] 77-3277 ISBN 0-8020-5347-5 : 15.00
1. Aelfric, Abbot of Eynsham. 2. Wulfstan II, Abp. of York, d. 1023. 3. Preaching—History—England. 4. Eschatology—History of doctrines—Middle Ages, 600-1500. I. Julianus, Saint, Bp. of Toledo, d. 690. Prognosticon futuri seculi. Selections. 1977.

GATCH, Milton McC. 251'.00942
Preaching and theology in Anglo-Saxon England : Aelfric and Wulfstan / Milton McC. Gatch. Toronto ; Buffalo : University of Toronto Press, c1977. p. cm. "Aelfric's excerpts from Julian of Toledo, Prognosticon futuri saeculi": p. Includes indexes. Bibliography: p. [BV4208.G7G37] 77-3277 ISBN 0-8020-5347-5 : 15.00
1. Aelfric, Abbot of Eynsham. 2. Wulfstan II, Abp. of York, d. 1023. 3. Preaching—History—England. 4. Eschatology—History of doctrines—Middle Ages, 600-1500. I. Julianus, Saint, Bp. of Toledo, d. 690. Prognosticon futuri seculi. Selections. 1977.

OWST, Gerald Robert, 1894- 251.00942
Preaching in medieval England; an introduction to sermon manuscripts of the period c. 1350-1450, by G. R. Owst. New York, Russell & Russell, 1965. xviii, 381 p. illus., facsim. 23 cm. (Cambridge studies in medieval life and thought) "First published in 1926." Based on thesis, University of London. Bibliographical footnotes. [BV4208.G7O8] 65-18825
1. Preaching — Hist. — England. I. Title. II. Series.

OWST, Gerald Robert, 1894- 251.00942
Preaching in medieval England; an introduction to sermon manuscripts of the period c. 1350-1450. New York, Russell & Russell, 1965. xviii, 381p. illus., facsim. 23cm. (Cambridge studies in medieval life and thought) Bibl. [BV4208.G708] 65-18825 8.50
1. Preaching—Hist.—England. I. Title. II. Series.

WILSON, John Frederick. 251'.00942
Pulpit in Parliament; Puritanism during the English civil wars, 1640-1648, by John F. Wilson. Princeton, N.J., Princeton University Press, 1969. x, 289 p. 23 cm. Bibliographical footnotes. [BX9333.W5] 69-18074 ISBN 0-691-07157-8 10.00
1. Puritans—England. 2. Preaching—History—England. I. Title.

MITCHELL, Henry H. 251'.00973
Black preaching [by] Henry H. Mitchell. [1st ed.] Philadelphia, Lippincott [1970] 248 p. 21 cm. (C. Eric Lincoln series on Black religion) Includes bibliographical references. [BV4208.U6M57 1970] 72-124546 5.50
1. Preaching—History—United States. 2. Negroes—Religion. I. Title.

PIPES, William Harrison, 1912- 251'.00973
Say amen, brother! Old-time Negro preaching: a study in American frustration, by William H. Pipes. Westport, Conn., Negro Universities Press [1970, c1951] i, 210 p. 24 cm. Bibliography: p. 201-205. [BR563.N4P53 1970] 73-111585 ISBN 0-8371-4611-9
1. Negroes—Religion. 2. Preaching—History—U.S. I. Title.

ROSENBERG, Bruce A. 251'.00973
The art of the American folk preacher [by] Bruce A. Rosenberg. New York, Oxford University Press, 1970. x, 265 p. 24 cm. Includes bibliographical references. [BV4208.U6R67] 77-111649 8.50
1. Preaching—History—U.S. I. Title.

STEVENSON, Dwight Eshelman, 1906- 251'.00973
Disciple preaching in the first generation; an ecological study, by Dwight E. Stevenson. Nashville, Disciples of Christ Historical Society, 1969. 109 p. 23 cm. (The Forrest F. Reed lectures for 1969) Includes bibliographical references. [BV4208.U6S73] 70-22610
1. Disciples of Christ. 2. Preaching—History—U.S. I. Title. II. Series: The Reed lectures for 1969

LEVY, Babette May, 1907- 251'.00974
Preaching in the first half century of New England history. New York, Russell & Russell [1967, c.1945] xii, 215p. 24cm. (Studies in church hist., v.6) Reprint of thesis. Columbia Univ. Bibl. [BV4208.U6L4 1967] 66-27116 8.50
1. Preaching—Hist.—New England. 2. Theology, Doctrinal—Hist.—New England. 3. New England—Church history. 4. Puritans. I. American Society of Church History. II. Title. III. Series.

LEVY, Babette May, 1907- 251'.00974
Preaching in the first half century of New England history. New York, Russell & Russell [1967], c1945] vii, 215 p. 24 cm. (Studies in church history, v. 6) Reprint of thesis, Columbia University. Bibliography: p. 177-207. [BV4208.U6L4] 66-27116
1. Preaching — Hist. — New England. 2. Theology, Doctrinal — Hist. — New England 3. New England — Church history. 4. Puritans. I. American Society of Church History. II. Title. III. Series.

ASQUITH, Glenn H. 251'.01
Preaching according to plan [by] Glenn H. Asquith. Valley Forge, Pa., Judson Press [1968] 79 p. 20 cm. [BV4211.2.A8] 68-13606
1. Preaching. I. Title.

BRAGA, James. 251'.01
How to prepare Bible messages; a manual on homiletics for Bible students. Portland, Or., Multnomah Press [1971, c1969] xv, 216 p. 22 cm. Bibliography: p. 207-208. [BV4211.2.B674] 75-88213 4.95
1. Preaching. I. Title.

BROWN, Henry Clifton. 251'.01
Sermon analysis for pulpit power [by] H. C. Brown, Jr. Nashville, Broadman Press [1971] 61 p. 19 cm. [BV4211.2.B686] 72-145979 ISBN 0-8054-2105-X
1. Preaching. I. Title.

LINN, Edmund Holt. 251.01
Preaching as counseling; the unique method of Harry Emerson Fosdick. Valley Forge [Pa.] Judson Press [1966] 159 p. 23 cm. Bibliographical references included in "Notes" (p. 157-159) [BV4211.2.L52] 66-28296
1. Fosdick, Harry Emerson, 1878- 2. Preaching. I. Title.

*LOCKYER, Herbert. 1886- 251.01
Triple truths of Scripture; unique expositions of Scriptural Trilogies. Grand Rapids, Mich., Baker Book House [1973] 3 v., 21 cm. (The Lockyer Bible preacher's library). [BV4379] ISBN 0-8010-5529-6 1.95 ea. (pbk.)
1. Sermons. I. Title.

*LOCKYER, Herbert. 1886- 251.01
Twin truths of Scripture: a unique study of the pairing of Biblical themes. Grand Rapids, Mich, Baker Book House [1973] 2 v., 21 cm. (The Lockyer Bible preacher's library) [BV4379] ISBN 0-8010-5529-6 1.95 ea. (pbk.)
1. Sermons. I. Title.

*MEYER, F. B. 251.01
Expository preaching: plans and methods. Grand Rapids, Baker Book House [1974] 127 p. 20 cm. [BV4211] ISBN 0-8010-5945-3 1.25 (pbk.)
1. Preaching. I. Title.

*MORGAN, Campbell G. 251.01
Preaching [by] G. Campbell Morgan. Grand Rapids, Baker Book House [1974] 90 p. 18 cm. (G. Campbell Morgan library) [BV4226] ISBN 0-8010-5953-4 1.95 (pbk.)
1. Preaching. I. Title.

PEARCE, J. Winston. 251'.01
Planning your preaching [by] J. Winston Pearce. Nashville, Broadman Press [1967] vii, 197 p. 22 cm. Bibliography: p. 189-194. [BV4211.2.P38] 67-19398
1. Preaching. I. Title.

*STEWART, James Stuart, 1896- 251.01
Heralds of God [by] James S. Stewart. Grand Rapids, Mich., Baker Book House [1972, c.1946] 221 p. 20 cm. (James S. Stewart library) [BV4211] ISBN 0-8010-7976-4 pap., 1.95
1. Preaching. I. Title.

TURNBULL, Ralph G. 251.01
The preacher's heritage, task, and resources, by Ralph G. Turnbull. Grand Rapids, Baker Bk. [1968] 178p. 20cm. Bibl. [BV4211.2.T87] 68-19215 2.95 pap.,
1. Preaching. I. Title.

*APOSTOLON, Billy. 251'.02
Choice sermon outlines. Grand Rapids, Mich., Baker Book House [1973, c.1972] 55 p. 22 cm. (Dollar sermon library) ISBN 0-8010-0046-7 1.00 (pbk.)
1. Sermons—Outlines. I. Title.

*APOSTOLON, Billy, comp. 251.02
Heart-touching sermon outlines. Grand Rapids, Mich., Baker Book House, [1974] 61 p. 22 cm. [BV4223] ISBN 0-8010-0078-5 1.00 (pbk.)
1. Sermons—Outlines. I. Title.

*APPELMAN, Hyman. 251.02
Appelman's sermon outlines & illustrations. Grand Rapids, Baker Book House [1974 c1944] 121 p. 20 cm. Title on spine: Sermon outlines & illustrations. [BX1756.Q5] ISBN 0-8010-0072-6 1.95 (pbk.)
1. Sermons—Outlines. I. Title. II. Title: Sermon outlines & illustrations.

AUSTIN, William R. 251.02
The Zondervan pastor's annual, 1966. Grand Rapids, Mich., Zondervan [c.1965] 383p. 21cm. [BX6333.A1A8] 65-19507 3.95
1. Sermons—Outlines. 2. Baptists—Sermons—Outlines. I. Title.

AUSTIN, William R. 251.02
The Zondervan pastor's manual for 1967. Grand Rapids, Mich., Zondervan [1966] 383p. 21cm. [BX6333.A1A8] 65-19507 3.95 bds.,
1. Sermons—Outlines. 2. Baptists—Sermons—Outlines. I. Title. II. Title: Pastor's manual.

*BOLICK, James H. 251'.02
Sermon outlines for saints and sinners. Grand Rapids, Mich., Baker Book House [1973] 64 p. 22 cm. (Dollar sermon library) ISBN 0-8010-0596-5 1.00 (pbk.)
1. Sermons—Outlines. I. Title.

BONELL, Harold C. 251'.02
Sparks of the kindling [by] Harold C. Bonell. Valley Forge [Pa.] Judson Press [1968] 128 p. 23 cm. [BV4223.B6] 68-22754 3.95
1. Sermons—Outlines. 2. Meditations. I. Title.

BROOKS, George, Rev., of Johnstone. 251'.02
201 sermon outlines. Grand Rapids, Baker Book House [1966] 110 p. 20 cm. (Minister's handbook series) Selections from the author's Five hundred plans of sermons, 1863. [BV4223.B68] 67-2597
1. Sermons — Outlines. I. Title. II. Title: Sermon outlines.

BROOKS, George, Rev. of Johnstone 251'.02
201 sermon outlines. Grand Rapids. Baker Bk. [1966] 110p. 20cm. (Minister's handbk. ser.) Seleceions from the author's Five hundred plans of sermons, 1863. [BV4223.B68] 67-2597 1.98
1. Sermons—Outlines. I. Titles Sermon outlines. II. Title.

BURNS, Jabez, 1805-1876. 251'.02
200 Scriptural sermon outlines. [1st American ed. Grand Rapids, Kregel Publications [1969] 424 p. 21 cm. (His Sermon outline series) First published in 1875 under title: Two hundred sketches and outlines of sermons. [BV4223.B86 1969] 75-92502 4.95
1. Sermons—Outlines. I. Title.

*COMPTON, W. H. 251.02
Funeral sermon outlines. Grand Rapids, Mich., Baker Bk. [c.]1965. 91p. 22cm. ((1.00 sermon lib.) 1.00 pap.,
I. Title.

*COMPTON, W. H. 251'.02
Vital sermon outlines. Grand Rapids, Baker Book House [1972] 66 p. 22 cm. (Dollar sermon library) [BV4223] ISBN 0-8010-2340-8 pap., 1.00
1. Sermons—Outlines. I. Title.

COOPER, Harold E., 1928- 251'.02
Doctrines from the beloved disciple; outlines from the Gospel according to John, by Harold E. Cooper. [Little Rock, Ark., Baptist Publications Committee, 1972] 137 p. 19 cm. [BS2615.4.C66] 72-88392 pap. 1.00
1. Bible. N.T. John—Sermons—Outlines. I. Title.

CRABTREE, T. T. 251.02
The Zondervan pastor's annual, 1968. Grand Rapids, Zondervan [1967] v. 21cm. [BX6333.A1A8] 65-19507 3.95
1. Sermons—Outlines. 2. Baptists—Sermons Outlines. I. Title.

ELLIS, J., comp. 251.02
The seed basket; 300 sermon outlines and suggestions, compiled by J. Ellis. Grand Rapids, Baker Book House [1966] 90 p. 22 cm. [BV4223.E62] 66-31709
1. Sermons—Outlines. I. Title.

ERDMAN, F. E. 251.02
Sketches of funeral sermons, by F. E. Erdman, J. M. Rinker, others. Grand Rapids, Mich., Baker Bk., 1965. 105p. 20cm. (Minister's handbk. ser.) [BV4275.E7] 66-904 1.95 bds.,
1. Funeral sermons—Outlines. I. Title.

*FREY, Lash 251.02
Crusade for souls, and other sermon outlines, by Lash Frey, William Willis. Grand Rapids, Mich., Baker Bk. [c.]1965. 91p. 23cm. ((1.00 sermon lib.) 1.00 pap.,
1. Sermons—Text for sermons. I. Willis, William, joint author. II. Title.

GIERTZ, Bo Harald, Bp., 1905- 251'.02
Preaching from the whole Bible; background studies in the preaching texts for the church year, by Bo Giertz. Translated by Clifford Ansgar Nelson. Minneapolis, Augsburg Pub. House [1967] 141 p. 22 cm. Translation of Vad sager Guds ord. [BV4223.G513] 67-25363
1. Bible—Homiletical use. 2. Church year sermons—Outlines. I. Title.

*HALLOCK, E. F. 251.02
Bible-centered Sermon Starters, by E. F. Hallock. Grand Rapids, Mich., Baker Book House, [1974] 63 p. 22 cm. [BV4223] ISBN 0-8010-4112-0 1.00 (pbk.)
1. Sermons—Outlines. I. Title.

*HAYDEN, Eric. 251.02
Complete Sermon outlines. Grand Rapids, Mich., Baker Book House, [1974]. 62 p. 22 cm. [BV4223] ISBN 0-8010-4113-9. 1.00 (pbk.)
1. Sermons—Outlines. I. Title.

HENRY, James A. 251'.02
Prescriptions from the beloved physician. Fifty outlines from Luke; fifty outlines from Acts, by James A. Henry. [Little Rock, Ark., Baptist Publications Committee, 1972] 108 p. 19 cm. [BS2589.H45] 72-88383 pap. 1.00
1. Bible. N.T. Luke and Acts—Sermons—Outlines. I. Title.

*HORNBERGER, J. C. 251.02
Sketches of revival sermons, original and selected. Grand Rapids, Mich., Baker Bk. [1967 69p. 22cm. ((1.00 sermon lib.) 1.00 pap.,
1. Sermons—Outlines. I. Title.

*HORRELL, B. C. 251.02
Fifty sermon outlines on conversion. Grand Rapids, Mich., Baker Bk. [c.1966] 70p. 22cm. 1.00 pap.,
I. Title.

*HORRELL, B. C. 251.02
Fifty sermon outlines on forgiveness. Grand Rapids, Mich., Baker Bk. [1966] 70p. 22cm. ((1.00 sermon lib.) 1.00 pap.,
I. Title.

*HORRELL, Benjamin. 251'.02
150 topical sermon outlines on Christ. Grand Rapids, Mich., Baker Book House [1973] 54 p. 22 cm. (Dollar sermon library) ISBN 0-8010-4065-5 1.00 (pbk.)
1. Sermons—Outlines. I. Title.

*HORRELL, Benjamin C. 251.02
150 topical sermon outlines on Romans, [by] Benjamin C. Horrell. Grand Rapids, Baker Book House [1974] 58 p. 22 cm. (Dollar sermon library) [BV4223] ISBN 0-8010-4101-5 1.00 (pbk.)
1. Sermons—Outlines. I. Title.

*INGLIS, Charles. 251'.02
Dynamic sermon outlines. Grand Rapids, Mich., Baker Book House [1973] 61 p. 22 cm. (Dollar sermon Library) [BV4223] ISBN 0-8010-5028-6 1.00 (pbk.)
1. Sermons—Outlines. I. Title.

*JOHNSON, Carl G. 251.'02
Preaching truths for perilous times / Carl G. Johnson. Grand Rapids : Baker Book House, 1976. 93p. ; 20 cm. [BV4223] ISBN 0-8010-5062-6 pbk. : 1.95
1. Sermons-Outlines. 2. Preaching. I. Title.

*JOHNSON, Carl G. 251.02
Scriptural sermon outlines. Grand Rapids, Mich., Baker Bk. [c.]1965. 112p. 22cm. (1.00 sermon lib.) 1.00 pap.
1. Sermons—Texts for sermons. I. Title.

LUECKE, Richard Henry, 1923- 251'.02
Violent sleep; notes toward the development of sermons for the modern city. Philadelphia, Fortress Press [1968, c1969] xv, 139 p. 18 cm.

(The Preacher's paperback library, v. 9) [BV4277.L8 1969] 69-14510 1.95
1. Lenten sermons—Outlines. I. Title.

*MC KENZIE, E. C. comp. 251.02
2700 quotes for sermons and addresses comp. by E. C. McKenzie. Grand Rapids, Baker Book House [1974] 140 p. 22 cm. [BV4223] ISBN 0-8010-5948-8 1.95 (pbk.)
1. Sermons, American. 2. Quotations. I. Title.

*MACLAREN, Alexander 251.02
Sermon outlines on the Psalms, by Alexander Maclaren [others] Grand Rapids. Mich., Baker Bk. [1966] 142p. 20cm. (Preaching helps ser.) Reprinted from the orig. ed. pub. by Hodder & Stoughton, London, in 1900. 1.50 pap.,
1. Sermons—Outlines. I. Title.

*MACPHERSON, Ian. 251.02
Bible sermon outlines / Ian Macpherson. Grand Rapids : Baker Book House, 1976c1966. 191p. ; 20 cm. Includes index. [BV4223] ISBN 0-8010-5993-3 pbk. : 2.95
1. Sermon-Outlines. I. Title.

*MACPHERSON, Ian. 251.02
Live sermon outlines. Grand Rapids, Baker Book House [1974] 64 p. 22 cm. (Dollar sermon library) [BV4223] ISBN 0-8010-5956-9 1.00 (pbk.)
1. Sermons—Outlines. I. Title.

MACPHERSON, Ian, 1912- 251.02
Bible sermon outlines. Nashville, Abingdon [c.1966] 191p. 23cm. Bibl. [BV4223.M23] 66-12926 3.95
1. Sermons—Outlines. 2. Bible—Sermons—Outlines. I. Title.

MACPHERSON, Ian, 1912- 251'.02
Kindlings; outlines and sermon starters. Old Tappan, N.J., Revell [1969] 159 p. 21 cm. [BV4223.M235] 72-77481 3.95
1. Sermons—Outlines. I. Title.

*MEES, Otto. 251.02
Outlines for funeral sermons; and other helps. Grand Rapids, Baker Book House [1974] 320 p. 20 cm. (Minister's handbook series) [BV4223] ISBN 0-8010-5946-1 2.95 (pbk.)
1. Sermons—outlines. I. Title.

MINISTERS' research 251'.02
service. William F. Kerr, general editor. Wheaton, Ill., Tyndale House Publishers [1970] 854 p. 26 cm. Includes bibliographies. [BV4223.M53] 76-103985
1. Sermons—Outlines. 2. Pastoral theology. I. Kerr, William F., ed.

*MOODY, D. L. 251.02
Notes from my Bible; from Genesis to Revelation, By D. L. Moody. Grand Rapids, Baker Book House, [1975] 236 p. 20 cm. [BV4223] ISBN 0-8010-5982-8 4.95
1. Bible—Study. 2. Homiletical illustrations. 3. Sermons—Outlines. I. Title.

*PENTZ, Croft M. 251.02
52 simple sermon outlines. Grand Rapids, Baker Bk. [1968] 82p. 22cm. (Dollar sermon lib.) 1.00 pap.,
1. Sermons—Outlines. I. Title.

*PENTZ, Croft M. 251.02
Expository outlines on the gospel of John, [by] Croft M. Pentz. Grand Rapids, Baker Book House [1974] 53 p. 22 cm. (Dollar sermon library) [BV4223] ISBN 0-8010-6960-2 1.00 (pbk.)
1. Sermons—Outlines. I. Title.

*PENTZ, Croft M. 251.02
48 simple sermon outlines. Grand Rapids, Mich., Baker Bk [c.]1965. 82p. 22cm. 1.00 pap.,
I. Title.

*PENTZ, Croft M. 251.02
Sermon outlines from the psalms, [by] Croft M. Pentz. Grand Rapids, Mich., Baker Book House, [1974] 63 p. 22 cm. [BV4223] ISBN 0-8010-6974-2 1.00 (pbk.)
1. Sermons—Outlines. I. Title.

PIERSON, Robert H 251.02
What shall I speak about? 250 suggestions and helps in preparing talks and sermons for many occasions, by Robert H. Pierson. Nashville, Southern Pub. Association [1966] 255 p. 22 cm. [BV4223.P53] 66-3991
1. Sermons—Outlines. I. Title.

PIERSON, Robert H. 251.02
What shall I speak about? 250 suggestions and helps in preparing talks and sermons for many occasions. Nashville, Southern Pub. [c.1966] 255p. 22cm. [BV4223.P53] 66-3991 4.95
1. Sermons—Outlines. I. Title.

QUINN, Alexander James, 251'.02
1932-
Thoughts for sowing; reflections on the liturgical readings for Sundays and holidays [by] A. James Quinn and James A. Griffin. Staten Island, N.Y., Alba House [1970] xii, 108 p. 21 cm. [BX1756.Q5T45] 72-140432 2.50
1. Catholic Church—Sermons. 2. Church year sermons. 3. Sermons, American. I. Griffin, James A., joint author. II. Title.

SELF, William L. 251'.02
The Saturday night special : [sermons] / William L. Self. Waco, Tex. : Word Books, c1977. 135 p. ; 23 cm. [BV4223.S42] 77-75469 ISBN 0-8499-0013-1 : 5.95
1. Sermons—Outlines. I. Title.

SHERRICK, Marvin Manam, 251'.02
1868-
Topical sermon notes, by Marvin M. Sherrick. Grand Rapids, Baker Bk. [1967] 76p. 22cm. [BV4233] 67-6258 1.00 pap.,
1. Sermons—Outlines. I. Title.

*SPURGEON, Charles 251'.02
Haddon, 1834-1892.
Stimulating sermon outlines, by Charles H. Spurgeon and others. Grand Rapids, Mich., Baker Book House [1973, c.1972] 61 p. 22 cm. (Dollar sermon library) ISBN 0-8010-7962-4 1.00 (pbk.)
1. Sermons—Outlines. I. Title.

*TAYLOR, Richard S. 251'.02
Timely sermon outlines; compiled by Richard S. Taylor. Grand Rapids, Mich., Baker Book House [1973] 64 p. 22 cm. (Dollar sermon library) ISBN 0-8010-8789-9 1.00 (pbk.)
1. Sermons—Outlines. I. Title.

*TORREY, Reuben Archer, 251'.02
1856-1928
Suggestive sermon outlines, ed. by R. A. Torrey. Grand Rapids, Baker Bk. [1968] 77p. 22cm. ($1.00 sermon lib.) 1.00 pap.,
1. Sermons—Outlines. I. Title.

*TURNBULL, Ralph G. 251.02
Growing as Christians. Grand Rapids, Mich., Baker Bk. [c.]1965. 86p. 22cm. (Bible companion ser. for lesson and sermon prep.) 1.00 pap.,
I. Title.

*TURNBULL, Ralph G. 251.02
Old Testament biographies. Grand Rapids, Mich., Baker Bk. [c.1965] 86p. 22cm. (Bible companion ser. for lesson and sermon preparation) 1.00 pap.,
I. Title.

TURNBULL, Ralph G. 251.02
Spokesmen for God (Isaiah, Jeremiah) by Ralph G. Turnbull. Grand Rapids, Baker Bk. [1966] 88p. 22cm. (Bible companion ser. for lesson and sermon preparation) [BV4223.T87] 66-9309 1.00 pap.,
1. Sermons—Outlines. I. Title.

TURNBULL, Ralph G. 251.02
Spokesmen for God (Isaiah, Jeremiah) by Ralph G. Turnbull. Grand Rapids, Baker Book House [1966] 88 p. 22 cm. (His Bible companion series for lesson and sermon preparation) [BV4223.T87] 66-9309
1. Sermons—Outlines. I. Title.

WEBER, Gerald P., 1918- 251.02
Witness to the world; homilies on the Sunday Gospels [by] Gerard Weber, James Killgallon. Staten Island, N.Y., Alba [c.1965] 145p. 22cm. [BX1756.A2W4] 65-28504 1.75 pap.,
1. Church year sermons. 2. Catholic Church—Sermons. 3. Sermons, American. I. Killgallon, James, 1914- joint author. II. Title.

WEBER, Gerard P., 1918- 251.02
Love one another; sermon outlines for Sundays and holydays, by Gerard Weber, James Killgallon. Foreword by Albert Meyer. Staten Island, N.Y., Alba [c.1965] 175p. 22cm. [BV4223.W43] 65-17978 3.95
1. Sermons—Outlines. 2. Love (Theology)—Sermons. I. Killgallon, James, 1914- joint author. II. Title.

WEBER, Gerard P 1918- 251.02
Love one another; sermon outlines for Sundays and holydays. by Gerard Weber and James Killgallon. Foreword by Albert Meyer. Staten Island, N.Y., Alba House [1965] 175 p. 22 cm. [BV4223.W43] 65-17978
1. Sermons — Outlines. 2. Love (Theology) — Sermons. I. Killgallon, James, 1914- joint author. II. Title.

WEBER, Gerard P., 1918- 251.02
Praise the Lord; homilies on the Sunday Gospels [by] Gerard Weber and James Killgallon. Staten Island, N.Y., Alba House [1966] 167 p. 22 cm. [BX1756.A1W43] 66-27534
1. Church year sermons—Outlines. I. Killgallon, James J., 1914- joint author. II. Title.

WEBER, Gerard P., 1918- 251'.02
To be church; source material for homilies on the Sunday Scripture readings, 1967-68 [by] Gerard Weber & James Killgallon. Staten Island, N.Y., Alba House [1967] 184 p. 22 cm. Bibliography: p. 185. [BX1756.A1W44] 67-24922
1. Church year sermons—Outlines. I. Killgallon, James J., 1914- joint author. II. Title.

WEBER, Gerard P 1918- 251.02
Witness to the world; homilies on the Sunday Gospels [by] Gerard Weber & James Killgallon. Staten Island, N.Y., Alba House [1965] 145 p. 22 cm. [BX1756.A2W4] 65-28504
1. Church year sermons. 2. Catholic Church — Sermons. 3. Sermons, American. I. Killgallon, James, 1914- joint author. II. Title.

*WHITE, Douglas M. 251'.02
Pulpit capsules; twenty-six expositions in embryo. Grand Rapids, Baker Bk. [1967] 98p. 22cm. ($1.00 sermon lib.) 1.00 pap.,
1. Homiletical illustrations. I. Title.

*WHITE, R. E. O. 251.02
Invitation to adventure; contemporary sermon suggestions, [by] R. E. O. White. Grand Rapids, Baker Book House, [1975 c1974] vi, 226 p. 23 cm. [BV4223] ISBN 0-8010-9565-4 5.95
1. Bible—Sermons—N.T. I. Title.

WHITE, Reginald E. O. 251.02
Sermon suggestions in outline. Grand Rapids, Mich., Eerdmans [1966, c.1965] 75p. 22cm. Contents.Ser. 1 January-June [BV4223.W437] 65-25194 145 pap.,
1. Sermons—Outines. I. Title.

WILLIAMS, Ernest Swing, 251'.02
1885-
My sermon notes; the Gospels and Acts, by E. S. Williams. Springfield, Mo., Gospel Pub. House [1967] 224 p. (p. 213-224, blank for "Notes") 23 cm. [BV4223.W447] 67-27320
1. Sermons—Outlines. I. Title.

THE Zondervan pastor's 251'.02
annual for 1969. Grand Rapids. Zondervan. v. 21cm. [BX6333.A1A8] 65-19507 3.95 bds.,
1. Sermons—Outlines. 2. Baptists—Sermons—Outlines.

APOSTOLON, Billy 251.027
Searchlights from the Scriptures. Grand Rapids, Mich., Baker Bk. [c.1963] 103p. 22cm. (Apostolon's great sermon outlines) 1.00 pap.,
I. Title.

APPELMAN, Hyman 251.027
Sermons on the Holy Spirit. Grand Rapids, Mich., Baker [c.]1962. 77p. 22cm. 1.00 pap.,
I. Title.

*BOLICK, James H. 251.027
Sermon outlines for revival preaching. Grand Rapids, Mich., Baker Bk. [c.1964] 105p. 22cm. (1.00 sermon lib.) 1.00 pap.,
I. Title.

BROWN, Jeff D. 251.027
Sermon outlines on the Old Testament. Grand Rapids, Mich., Baker [c.]1962. 111p. 22cm. 1.00 pap.,
1. Sermons—Outlines. I. Title.

BROWN, Jeff D. 251.027
Sermon outlines on Timothy to Revelation. Grand Rapids, Mich., Baker Bk. [c.1962] 95p. 22cm. 1.00 pap.,
I. Title.

BRYANT, Al [Thomas Alton 251.027
Bryant] ed.
Sermon outlines for messages to children. Grand Rapids, Mich., Zondervan Pub. House [c.1960] 64p. 22cm. (Zondervan loose-leaf sermon outline library, no. 19) 60-2021 1.00 pap.,
1. Children's sermons—Outlines. I. Title.

BURNS, Jabez, 1805-1876. 251.027
500 sketches and skeletons of sermons; includes nearly one hundred on types and metaphors Grand Rapids, Kregel publications, 1963. viii, 638 p. 24 cm. "Five volumes complete in one." [BV4223.B82] 63-11463
1. Sermons — Outlines I. Title.

BUTLER, Burris 251.027
Doctrinal sermon outlines. Cincinnati, Standard [c.1962] 64p. 22cm. (Sermon outline ser.) 1.00 pap.,
I. Title.

BUTLER, Burris 251.027
Evangelistic sermon outlines. Cincinnati, Standard [c.1962] 64p. 22cm. (Sermon outline ser.) 1.00 pap.,
I. Title.

CAIN, Benjamin H. 251.027
The town and country pulpit; sermon blueprints for forty special days. Anderson, Ind., Warner Press [dist. by Gospel Trumpet Press] [c.1960] 112p. illus. 19cm. 60-6470 1.25 pap.,
1. Occasional sermons—Outlines. I. Title.

CHANDLER, Ward B 251.027
Chandler's choice series sermon outlines. Grand Rapids, Baker Book House, 1958. 161p. 20cm. [BV4223.C48] 58-83834
1. Sermons—Outlines. I. Title. II. Title: Choice series sermon outlines.

CLEMENS, E. Bryan. 251.027
Sermon outlines you can preach. Natick, Mass., W.A. Wilde [1963] 79p. 22cm. 63-22171 1.25 pap.,
1. Sermons—Outlines. I. Title.

COMPTON, W. H. 251.027
Fifty select sermon outlines. Grand Rapids, Mich., Baker Bk. [c.]1963. 79p. 22cm. 1.00 pap.,
I. Title.

COMPTON, W. H., comp. 251.027
Sermon outlines from God's word. [Westwood, N.J.] Revell [c.1961] 64p. (Revell's sermon outline ser.) 61-9246 1.00 pap.,
I. Title.

COX, Frank 251.027
Select sermon materials. Grand Rapids, Mich., Baker Bk. [c.]1963. 93p. 22cm. (Sermon lib.) 1.00 pap.,
I. Title.

DE JONG, Jerome 251.027
Sermon outlines on a spiritual pilgrimage [Based on Israel's journey from Egypt to Canaan] Grand Rapids, Mich., Baker Bk. [c.] 1962. 90p. 22cm. 1.00 pap.,
I. Title.

FALLIS, William J., comp. 251.027
Broadman sermon outlines. Nashville, Broadman Press [c.1960] 64p. 21cm. 60-9531 1.00 pap.,
1. Sermons—Outlines. I. Title.

GREENWAY, Alfred L 251.027
Sermon plans and story illustrations. Grand Rapids, Baker Book House, 1959. 96p. 21cm. (Minister's handbook series) [BV4223.G65] 60-1141
1. Sermons—Outlines. I. Title.

[HARRIS, W] Prebyterian 251.027
minister.
Miracles and parables of the Old Testament; homiletic outlines. by a London minister. Grand Rapids, Baker Book House, 1959. 427p. 23cm. First published in 1878 under title: Outlines of sermons on the miracles and parables of the Old Testament. [BV4223.H32 1959] 59-8345
1. Sermons—Outlines. 2. Miracles. 3. Parables. I. A London minister. II. Title.

HENRY, Matthew, 1662-1714 251.027
Bible themes from Matthew Henry. Passages selected from Matthew Henry's Commentary, arr., ed. under doctrinal subjects by Selwyn Gummer, with a sermon outline on each subject [Enl. ed. Westwood, N.J.] Revell [1965] 384p. 23cm. [BS490.H4] 65-3027 5.95
1. Bible—Sermons—Outlines. I. Gummer, Selwyn, ed. II. Title.

HERRERA, Oria, Angel, 251.027
Bp., 1886- ed.
The preacher's encyclopedia [v.3] Comp., ed. under the supervision of His Eminence Angel Cardinal Herrera, Bp. of Malaga. Eng. version tr. [from Spanish] ed. by David Greenstock. Westminster, Md. Newman [c.1955, 1965] xvi, 704p. 26cm. Contents.v.3. Twelfth to last Sundays after Pentecost [BX1756.A1H43] 65-2580 15.00
1. Church year sermons—Outlines. 2. Catholic Church—Sermons—Outlines. 3. Sermons—Outlines. I. Greenstock, David L., ed. and tr. II. Title.

HERRERA ORIA, Angel, 251.027
Bp., 1886- ed.
The preacher's encyclopedia; v.1. Comp., ed. under the supervision of Angel Herrera. Eng. version tr., ed. by David Greenstock. Forewords by Archbishop Cardinale, Archbishop O'Hara. Westminster. Md. Newman Pr. [1965, c.1964] xxiv, 734p. 26cm. Contents.v.1. Lent and Eastertide [BX1756.A1H43] 65-2580 15.00
1. Church year sermons—Outlines. 2. Catholic Church—Sermons—Outlines. 3. Sermons—Outlines. I. Greenstock, David L., ed. and tr. II. Title.

HERRERA ORIA, Angel, 251.027
Bp., 1886- ed.
The preacher's encyclopedia [v.4] comp., ed. under the supervision of His Eminence Angel

Cardinal Herrera, Bp. of Malaga. Eng. version tr. [from Spanish] ed. by David Greenstock. Westminster, Md., Newman [c.1955, 1965] xix, 737p. 26cm. Contents.v. 4. Advent to Quinqwagesima [BX1756.A1H43] 65-2580 15.00
1. uinquagesima p15.00 2. Church year sermons—Outlines. 3. Catholic Church—Sermons—Outlines. 4. Sermons—Outlines. I. Greenstock, David L., ed. and tr. II. Title.

HERRERA ORIA, Angel, 251.027
Bp., 1886- ed.
The preacher's encyclopedia [v.2.] Comp. ed. under the supervision of Angel Herrera. Eng. version tr., (from Spanish) ed. by David Greenstock. Forewords by Archbishop Cardinale and the late Archbishop O'Hara. Westminister, Md., Newman [c.1955, 1965] xvi, 668p. 26cm. Contents.v.2. Sunday after Ascension to eleventh Sunday after Pentecost. [BX1756.A1H43] 65-2580 15.00
1. Church year sermons—Outlines. 2. Catholic Church—Sermons—Outlines. 3. Sermons—Outlines. I. Greenstock, David L. ed., and tr. II. Title.

KERR, David W 251.027
Sermon outlines on great Bible texts. [Westwood, N. J.] Revell [1959] 64p. 21cm. (Revell's sermon outline series) [BV4223.K4] 59-8729
1. Sermons—Outlines. I. Title.

MCDERMOTT, Andrew W., 251.027
comp.
Evangelistic sermon outlines. [Westwood, N. J.] Revell [1959] 64p. 21cm. (Revell's sermon outline series) [BV3797.M24] 59-8730
1. Evangelistic sermons— Outlines. I. Title.

MCDERMOTT, Andrew W., 251.027
comp.
Sermon outlines from great preachers. [Westwood, N. J.] Revell [1959] 64p. 21cm. (Revell's sermon outline series) [BV4223.M16] 59-8731
1. Sermons—Outlines. I. Title.

MCGINTY, Claudius Lamar 251.027
Sermon outlines for holy living. [Westwood, N. J.] Revell [c.1960] 64p. 21cm. (Revell's sermon outline series) 60-8462 1.00 pap.,
1. Sermons—Outlines. I. Title.

MCGINTY, Claudius Lamar, 251.027
1885-
Sermon outlines for holy living. [Westwood, N. Y.] Revell [1960] 64p. 21cm. (Revell's sermon outline series) [BV4223.M18] 60-8462
1. Sermons—Outlines. I. Title.

MCGINTY, Claudius Lamar, 251.027
1885-
Sermon outlines from the four Gospels. [Westwood, N.J.] Revell [c.1961] 64p. (Revell's sermon outline series) 61-9244 1.00 pap.,
1. Bible. N.T. Gospels—Sermons—Outlines. I. Title.

MACPHERSON, Ian, 1912- 251.027
Sermon outlines from sermon masters. New York, Abingdon Press [1960-62] 2v. 20cm. Contents.[1] New Testament.--[2] Old Testament. [BV4223.M24] 60-5474
1. Sermons— Outlines. I. Title.

MACPHERSON, Ian [John 251.027
Cook Macpherson] 1912-
Sermon outlines from sermon masters--Old Testament. Nashville, Abingdon [c.1962] 240p. 20cm. 60-5474 3.00
1. Sermons—Outlines. I. Title.

MACPHERSON, Ian [real 251.027
name: John Cook Macpherson]
Sermon outlines from sermon masters. Nashville, Abingdon Press [c.1960] 224p. 20cm. 60-5474 2.50 bds.,
1. Sermons—Outlines. I. Title.

MARK, Harry Clayton, 251.027
1906-
Patterns for preaching; the art of sermon making. Grand Rapids, Zondervan Pub. House [1959] 183p. 23cm. [BV4223.M28] 59-39706
1. Sermons—Outlines. 2. Preaching. I. Title.

MINISTERS manual (The): 251.027
a study and pulpit guide for the calendar year 1961. 36th annual issue, compiled and edited by Rev. M. K. W. Heicher. New York, Harper [c.1960] xii, 388p. 21cm. Title varies: 1926-46, Doran's ministers manual (cover title, 1947: The Doran's ministers manual) 25-21658 3.50 half cloth,
1. Sermons—Outlines. 2. Homiletical illustrations. I. Heicher, M. K. W., ed.

MOORE, Walter Lane, 1905- 251.027
Outlines for preaching [by] Walter L. Moore. Nashville, Broadman Press [1965] 80 p. 21 cm. [BV4223.M58] 65-15602
1. Sermons — Outlines. I. Title.

MOORE, Walter Lane, 1905- 251.027
Outlines for preaching. Nashville, Broadman [c.1965] 80p. 21cm. [BV4223.M58] 65-15602 1.50 pap.,
1. Sermons—Outlines. I. Title.

PENTZ, Croft M. 251.027
175 simple sermon outlines. Grand Rapids, Mich., Baker Bk. [c.]1963. 87p. 22cm. (Sermon lib.) 1.00 pap.,
I. Title.

REU, Johann Michael, 251.027
1869-1943.
Thomasius Old Testament selections, with interpretation and homiletical adaptation by M. Reu. Translated from the German by Max L. Steuer. Columbus, Ohio, Wartburg Press, 1959. 704p. 23cm. Translation of Die alttestamentlichen Perikopen nach der Auswahl von Professor Dr. Thomasius. [BX8066.R428T53] 59-9290
1. Church year sermons—Outlines. I. Thomasius, Gottfried, 1802-1875. II. Title.

STRONG, Charles O., comp. 251.027
Selected sermon outlines. Grand Rapids, Mich., Zondervan [c.1963] 119p. 21cm. 2.50 bds.,
I. Title.

TONNE, Arthur, Rt. Rev. 251.027
Msgr.
Stories for sermons; 513 stories on God, with complete index and cross index; v.14 [Emporia, Kans., Didde, c.1963 161p. 23cm. 2.50 pap.,
I. Title.

TONNE, Arthur, Rt. Rev. 251.027
Msgr.
Stories for sermons. v.13, Fortitude to God, Existence of, inclusive (with complete index and cross-index) Emporia, Kans., Didde [1962] 130p. 23cm. 2.50 pap.,
I. Title.

*TURNBULL, Ralph G. 251.027
Letters to Christian leaders. Grand Rapids, Mich., Baker Bk. [c.1964] 96p. 22cm. 1.00 pap.,
I. Title.
Contents omitted.

TURNBULL, Ralph G. 251.027
Mark--gospel of action. Grand Rapids, Mich., Baker Bk. [c.]1962. 86p. 22cm. (Bible companion ser. for lesson and sermon preparation) 1.00 pap.,
I. Title.

TURNBULL, Ralph G. 251.027
Personalities around Jesus. Grand Rapids, Mich., Baker Bk. [c.]1963. 99p. 22cm. (Bible companion ser. for lesson and sermon preparation) 1.00 pap.,
I. Title.

TURNBULL, Ralph G 251.027
Sermon substance. Grand Rapids, Baker Book House, 1958. 224 p. 23 cm. [BV4223.T85] 58-59824
1. Sermons — Outlines. I. Title.

VAN WYK, William P. 251.027
My sermon notes for special days. Grand Rapids, Mich., Baker Bk. [c.]1962. 79p. 22cm. 1.00 pap.,
I. Title.

WEBER, Gerard P 1918- 251.027
The God who loves us, a program of instructions originally prepared for use in the Archdiocese of Chicago, by Gerard P. Weber [and] James Killgallon. Collegeville, Minn., Liturgical Press [c1962] 121 p. 23 cm. Bibliography: p. 6-7. [BX1756.A1W4] 63-3109
1. Church year sermons. 2. Sermons — Outlines. I. Killgallon, James, 1914- joint author. II. Title.

WHITESELL, Faris Daniel, 251.027
1895-
Expository sermon outlines: Old and New Testament. [Westwood, N.J.] Revell [1959] 64 p. 21 cm. (Revell's sermon outline series) [BV4223.W446] 59-8728
1. Sermons — Outlines. I. Title.

WILLIAMS, Jerome Oscar, 251.027
1885-
Sermons in outline. Nashville, Broadman Press [1960, c.1943] 210p. (Broadman Starbooks) 1.50 pap.,
1. Sermons—Outlines. I. Title.

BAIRD, John Edward. 251'.03
Preparing for platform and pulpit [by] John E. Baird. Nashville, Abingdon Press [1968] 222 p. 23 cm. Bibliography: p. 215-220. [BV4211.2.B24] 68-11468
1. Preaching. I. Title.

REID, Clyde H. 251'.03
The empty pulpit; a study in preaching as communication [by] Clyde Reid. [1st ed.] New York, Harper & Row [1967] 122 p. 22 cm. Bibliographical footnotes. [BV4211.2.R4] 67-21552
1. Preaching. 2. Communication (Theology) I. Title.

MINISTERS manual (The); 251.058
a study and pulpit guide. 1968- New York, Harper. v. 21cm. annual. Title varies. Ed.: 1968- Vols. 1-5 were pub. by Doubleday, Doran [etc.] [BV4223.M5] 25-21658 3.95 bds.,
1. Sermons—Outlines. 2. Homiletical illustrations. I. Heicher, M.K.W. ed.

MINISTERS manual (The) 251.058
(Doran's Comp., ed. by M. K. W. Heicher. 42nd annual issue. New York, Harper [c.1966] xii, 372p. 21cm. Title varies. annual. 25-21658 3.95 bds.,
1. Sermons—Outlines. 2. Homiletical illustrations. I. Heicher, M. K. W., ed. II. Title: Doran's minister's manual.

MINISTERS manual (The) 251.058
(Doran's) Comp., ed. by M.K.W. Heicher. 41st annual issue. New York, Harper [c.1965] xviii, 357p. 22cm. Title varies. annual. 25-21658 3.95 bds.,
1. Sermons—Outlines. 2. Homelectical illustrations. I. Heicher, M.K.W., ed. II. Title: Doran's minister's manual.

LEE, Robert Greene, 1886- 251.061
The wonderful Saviour. Grand Rapids, Mich., Zondervan [1966, c.1965] 139p. 22cm. [BX6333.L3953W6] 65-19498 2.50 bds.,
1. Baptists—Sermons. 2. Sermons, American. I. Title.

*RILEY, Miles O'Brian. 251.077
To whom it may concern, introd by Merla Zellerbach. 1st ed. [Los Altos,Calif., Practical Press, 1975] x,110p. 21cm. [BV4235] 75-13134 5.00(pbk.)
1. Sermons,American .sPreaching. I. Title.
Pub. address: P.o.Box 960,94022.

APOSTOLON, Billy, ed. 251.08
Fifty-two evangelistic illustrations. Grand Rapids, Baker Book House, 1965. 122 p. 20 cm. (Preaching helps series) [BV4225.2.A6] 65-29503
1. Homiletical illustrations. I. Title. II. Series.

APOSTOLON, Billy, ed. 251.08
Fifty-two evangelistic illustrations. Grand Rapids, Mich., Baker Bk. [c.]1965. 122p. 20cm. (Preaching helps ser.) [BV.4225.2.A6] 65-29503 1.50 pap.,
1. Homiletical illustrations. I. Title. II. Series.

*APOSTOLON, Billy. 251.08
52 simple invitation illustrations. Grand Rapids, Baker Book House [1974] 122 p. 20 cm. (Minister's handbook series) [BV4225.2] ISBN 0-8010-0068-8 1.95 (pbk.)
1. Homeiletical illustrations. I. Title.

*APOSTOLON, Billy. 251.08
52 special-day invitation illustrations. Grand Rapids, Baker Book House, [1975] 107 p. 20 cm. [BV4225.2] ISBN 0-8010-0082-3 1.95 (pbk.)
1. Occasional, sermons. 2. Hamiletical illustrations. I. Title.

BAILLARGEON, Anatole O ed. 251.08
Handbook for special preaching, edited by Anatole O. Baillargeon. [New York] Herder and Herder [1965] 192 p. 22 cm. Includes bibliographies. [BV4211.2.B23] 65-21942
1. Preaching I. Title.

BAILLARGEON, Anatole O. 251.08
ed.
Handbook for special preaching [New York] Herder & Herder [c.1965] 192p. 22cm. Bibl. [BV4211.2.B23] 65-21942 4.50
1. Preaching. I. Title.

BARNHOUSE, Donald Grey, 251'.08
1895-1960.
Let me illustrate; stories, anecdotes, illustrations. Westwood, N.J., F. H. Revell Co. [1967] 379 p. 21 cm. [BV4225.2.B35] 67-11064
1. Homiletical illustrations. I. Title.

BROWNE, Benjamin P. 251'.08
Illustrations for preaching / Benjamin P. Browne. Nashville : Broadman Press, c1977. 191 p. ; 21 cm. [BV4225.2.B74] 76-39713 ISBN 0-8054-2228-5 : 6.95
1. Homiletical illustrations. I. Title.

*CARTER, James E. 251'.08
People parables. Grand Rapids, Mich., Baker Book House [1973] 115 p. 20 cm. (Preaching helps series) [BV4225.2] ISBN 0-8010-2348-3 1.95 (pbk.)
1. Homelitical illustrations. I. Title.

CATHOLIC University of 251.08
America. Work-shop on the Renewal in Scriptural and Liturgical Preaching, 1965.
The Sunday homily; scriptural and liturgical renewal. Ed. by John Burke. [Washington, D. C., Thomist Pr., c.1966] iv, 141p. 22cm. Papers delivered at the 1965 Workshop on the Renewal in Scriptural and Liturgical Preaching conducted at the Catholic Univ. of America. bBibl. [BV4211.2.C3 1965] 66-26068 2.75 pap.,
1. Preaching—Congresses. I. Burke, John, 1928- ed. II. Title.

CATHOLIC University of 251.08
America. Workshop on the Renewal in Scriptural and Liturgical Preaching, 1965.
The Sunday homily; scriptural and liturgical renewal. Edited by John Burke. [Washington, D.C., Thomist Press, 1966] iv, 141 p. 22 cm. Papers delivered at the 1965 Workshop on the Renewal in Scriptural and Liturgical Preaching conducted at the Catholic University of America. Includes bibliographies. [BV4211.2.C3] 66-26068
1. Preaching — Congresses. I. Burke, John, 1928- ed. II. Title.

CURTIS, Lindsay R 251'.08
2 1/2 minute talk treasury. Salt Lake City, Bookcraft [1962] 158 p. illus. 22 cm. [BV4225.2.C8] 62-53411
1. Homilletical illustrations. I. Title.

CURTIS, Lindsay R 251.08
Thoughts for 2 1/2 minute talks, by Lindsay R. Curtis. Salt Lake City, Bookcraft [c1965] 208 p. illus. 24 cm. [BV4225.2C79] 66-6860
1. Homilletical illustrations. I. Title.

DIO, "dictionary of 251'.08
illustrations and outlines." Jefferson City, Mo., Le Roi Publishers [1972- v. 22 cm. Vol. 1 compiled by A. H. Stainback. [BV4225.D2] 72-86593
1. Homiletical illustrations. 2. Sermons—Outlines. I. Stainback, Arthur House, comp.

*DODD, Monroe E. 251'.08
Stewardship helps for fifty-two Sundays. Grand Rapids, Mich., Baker Bk. [1968] 125p. 20cm. (Preaching helps ser.) Orig. pub. under title Concerning the collcction. 1.50 pap.,
1. Homelitical illustrations. I. Title.

EAVEY, Charles Benton, 251.08
1889-
300 thought stimulators for sermons and addresses, byC. B Eavey [BV4225.2.E22] 66-18313
1. Homiletical illustrations. I. Title.

EAVEY, Charles Benton, 251.08
1889-
300 thought stimulators for sermons and addresses. Grand Rapids, Mich., Baker Bk. [c.] 1966. 151p. 20cm. [BV4225.2.E22] 66-18313 1.95 bds.,
1. Homiletical illustrations. I. Title.

EDWARDS, Otis Carl, 1928- 251'.08
The living and active word : one way to preach from the Bible today / by O. C. Edwards, Jr. New York : Seabury Press, [1975] 178 p. ; 22 cm. "A Crossroad book." Bibliography: p. [173]-178. [BS534.5.E38] 74-30038 ISBN 0-8164-0265-5 : 6.95
1. Protestant Episcopal Church in the U.S.A.—Sermons. 2. Bible—Homiletical use. 3. Preaching. 4. Sermons, American. I. Title.

FOSTER, Elon, comp. 251'.08
6,000 classic sermon illustrations; a companion volume to 6,000 sermon illustrations. Grand Rapids, Baker Book House [1974] 791 p. 25 cm. Previously published as v. 2 of New cyclopaedia of prose illustrations; later published under special title: 6,000 windows for sermons. [BV4225.F722 1974] 74-167260 ISBN 0-8010-3463-9 8.95
1. Homiletical illustrations. I. Title.

*FOSTER, Elon. 251'.08
6000 sermon illustrations; an omnibus of classic sermon illustrations Grand Rapids, Baker Book House [1972] 704 p. 25 cm. "Previously published as New Encyclopaedia of prose illustrations." [BV4225.2] ISBN 0-8010-3455-8 7.95
1. Homeiletical illustrations. I. Title.

HARROP, G. Gerald, 1917- 251'.08
Elijah speaks today : the long road into Naboth's vineyard / G. Gerald Harrop. Nashville : Abingdon Press, [1975] 175 p. ; 19 cm. Includes bibliographical references and index. [BS580.E4H33] 75-12755 ISBN 0-687-11654-6 pbk. : 4.95
1. Elijah, the prophet. 2. Naboth (Biblical character) 3. Bible. O.T. Prophets—Homiletical use. I. Title.

HASTINGS, Robert J. 251'.08
Hastings' illustrations [by] Robert J. Hastings. Nashville, Broadman Press [1971] 136 p. 21

cm. Anecdotes. [BV4225.2.H37] 74-145982 ISBN 0-8054-3611-1
1. Homiletical illustrations. I. Title.

HAVNER, Vance, 1901- 251.08
Pepper 'n salt. Westwood, N. J., F. H. Revell Co. [1966] 125 p. 20 cm. Short stories, sayings, etc. culled from the author's preaching and writing. [BX6495.H288A25] 66-12432
1. Baptists — Clergy — Correspondence, reminiscences, etc. 2. Evangelists — Correspondence, reminiscences, etc. I. Title.

HAVNER, Vance, 1901- 251.08
Pepper n' salt. Westwood, N.J., Revell [c.1966] 125p. 20cm. [BX6495.H288A25] 66-12432 2.95 bds.,
1. Baptists—Clergy—Correspondence, reminiscences, etc. 2. Evangelists—Correspondence, reminiscences, etc. I. Title.

JOHNSON, Carl G. 251'.08
My favorite illustration, by Carl G. Johnson. Grand Rapids, Baker Book House [1972] 137 p. 20 cm. (Preaching helps series) [BV4225.2.J6] 72-85718 ISBN 0-8010-5016-2 1.95 (pbk.)
1. Homiletical illustrations. I. Title. II. Series.

KAUFFMAN, Donald T., comp. 251'.08
For instance ... Current insights, anecdotes, quotations, questions for teachers, ministers, speakers, and discussion leaders [collected by] Donald T. Kauffman. [1st ed.] Garden City, N.Y., Doubleday, 1970. 263 p. 22 cm. Includes bibliographical references. [BV4225.2.K3] 77-123699 5.95
1. Homiletical illustrations. I. Title.

KNIGHT, Walter Brown, comp. 251'.08
Knight's Illustrations for today [by] Walter B. Knight. Chicago, Moody Press [1970] 359 p. 24 cm. [BV4225.2.K59 1970] 70-123157 5.95
1. Homiletical illustrations. I. Title: Illustrations for today.

LEHMAN, Louis Paul. 251'.08
Put a door on it! : The "how" and "why" of sermon illustration / by Louis Paul Lehman. 1st ed. Grand Rapids : Kregel Publications, 1975. 102 p. ; 21 cm. [BV4226.L43] 75-12109 ISBN 0-8254-3110-7 : 3.50
1. Homiletical illustrations. 2. Preaching. I. Title.

LIBER exemplorum ad usum praedicantium: saeculo XIII compositus a quodam fratre minore Anglico de privincia Hiberniae; secundum codicem Dunelmensem editus per A. G. Little. Farnborough (Hants.), Gregg Pr., 1966. iii-xxx, 177p. 20cm. Facsimile reprint of 1st ed., Aberdeen, Aberdeen U. P., 1908. Bibl. [BV4224.L5 1966] 67-87699 12.50 251'(08
1. Exempla. I. Little, Andrew George, 1863-1945, ed.
Distributed by Gregg Pr., Ridgewood, N.J.

MCDONALD, Erwin Lawrence. 251'.08
Stories for speakers and writers; a compendium of wit, humor, and inspiration from everyday life, by Erwin L. McDonald. Gran Rapids, Baker Book House [1970] 101 p. 20 cm. (Speakers' and toastmasters' library) [BV4225.2.M22] 72-126559 ISBN 0-8010-5853-8 1.95
1. Homiletical illustrations. I. Title.

MOTTE, Gonzague. 251'.08
Homilies for the liturgical year. Translated by John Drury. Chicago, Franciscan Herald Press [1973- v. 21 cm. Translation of Homelies pour une annee. Contents.Contents.— —v. C. Covering the Sundays and feast days of liturgical year C. [BX1756.M686H613] 73-17144 ISBN 0-8199-0461-9 6.95
1. Catholic Church—Sermons. 2. Church year sermons. 3. Sermons, French—Translations into English. 4. Sermons, American—Translations from French. I. Title.

NELSON, Wilbur E. 251'.08
Anecdotes and illustrations, by Wilbur E. Nelson. Grand Rapids, Baker Book House [1971] 101 p. 20 cm. (Preaching helps series) [BV4225.2.N45] 79-157315 ISBN 0-8010-6677-8 1.95
1. Homiletical illustrations. I. Title. II. Series.

PERSON, Amy L. 251.08
Illustrations from literature, by Amy L. Person. Grand Rapids, Baker Book House [1966] 95 p. 20 cm. (Preaching helps series) [BV4225.2.P4] 66-31742
1. Homiletical illustrations. I. Title. II. Series.

PIERSON, Robert H 251.08
501 Adventist illustrations and stories, by Robert H. Pierson. Nashville, Southern Pub. Association [c1965] 308 p. 22 cm. [BV4225.2P5] 66-3986
1. Homiletic illustrations. I. Title.

ROBERTSON, James Douglas, ed. 251'.08
Handbook of preaching resources from literature; comp. & edited by James Douglas Robertson. Grand Rapids, Mich., Baker Book House [1973 c.1972] xiv, 268 p. 20 cm. (Sourcebooks for ministers) [BV4225.2.R58] 62-8566 ISBN 0-8010-7608-0 2.95 (pbk)
1. Homiletical illustrations. 2. English literature—Selections, extracts, etc. 3. Quotations. I. Title. II. Title: Preaching resources from literature.

STRAIT, C. Neil, comp. 251'.08
The speaker's book of inspiration; a treasury of contemporary religious & inspirational thought. Compiled by C. Neil Strait. [1st ed.] Atlanta, Ga., Droke House/Hallux [1972] 197 p. 24 cm. Includes bibliographical references. [BV4225.2.S87] 76-160893 ISBN 0-8375-6759-9 5.95
1. Homiletical illustrations. I. Title.

SUMNER, Robert Leslie, 1922- 251'.08
Sumner's incidents and illustrations, by Robert L. Sumner. Brownsburg, Ind., Biblical Evangelism Press [1969] 480 p. 29 cm. [BV4225.2.S94] 78-12634 7.95
1. Hamiletical illustrations. I. Title.

TREASURY of quotations on religious subjects from the great writers and preachers of all ages / [compiled] by F. B. Proctor. Grand Rapids : Kregel Publications, c1977. xvi, 816 p. ; 27 cm. Includes indexes. [BV4225.2.T73] 76-15741 ISBN 0-8254-3500-5 : 14.95 251'.08
1. Homiletical illustrations. 2. Religion—Quotations, maxims, etc. I. Proctor, F. B.

WELTER, Jean Thiebaut, 1877- 251'.08
L'exemplum dans la litterature religieuse et didactique du Moyen age, par J.-Th. Welter. Paris, Occitania, 1927. [New York, AMS Press, 1973] 564 p. 23 cm. Original ed. issued in series: Bibliotheque d'histoire ecclesiastique de France. Originally presented as the author's thesis, Paris. Bibliography: p. [503]-518. [BV4224.W44 1973] 70-178558 ISBN 0-404-56688-X
1. Exempla. 2. Homiletical illustrations. 3. Christian literature—History and criticism. 4. Literature, Medieval—History and criticism. I. Title. II. Series: Bibliotheque de la Societe d'histoire ecclesiastique de la France.

*WHITMAN, Virginia. 251.08
Devotional talks from familiar things. Chicago, Moody [1967] 64p. 22cm. 1.00 pap.,
1. Homiletic illustrations. I. Title.

WHITMAN, Virginia. 251.08
Illustrations from nature; for preachers and speakers. Grand Rapids, Baker Book House, 1965. 132 p. 20 cm. (Preaching helps series) [BV4225.2.W48] 65-9699
1. Homiletical illustrations. 2. Sermons — Texts for sermons. I. Title. II. Series.

WHITMAN, Virginia 251.08
Illustrations from nature; for preachers and speakers. Grand Rapids, Mich., Baker Bk. [c.] 1965. 132p. 20cm. (Preaching helps ser.) [BV4225.2.W48] 65-9699 1.50 pap.,
1. Homiletical illustrations. 2. Sermons—texts for sermons. I. Title. II. Series.

*WILLER, Earl C. 251.08
A treasury of inspirational illustrations, [by] Earl C. Willer Grand Rapids, Baker Book House, [1975] 115 p. 20 cm. [BV4226] ISBN 0-8010-9557-3 2.95 (pbk.)
1. Homiletical illustrations. I. Title.

WINDOWS, ladders, and bridges : an anthology of illustrations for public speakers and ministers / [compiled] by A. Dudley Dennison, Jr. Grand Rapids : Zondervan Pub. House, c1976. 214 p. ; 23 cm. [BV4225.2.W55] 75-38642 7.95 251'.08
1. Homiletical illustrations. I. Dennison, Alfred Dudley, 1914-

ZOBELL, Albert L comp. 251.08
Notes to quote. Compiled by Albert L. Zobell, Jr. Salt Lake City, Bookcraft [c1965] 132 p. 16 cm. [BV4225.2.Z58] 66-8261
1. Homiletical illustrations. I. Title.

ZOBELL, Albert L comp. 251.08
Only on the threshold, compiled by Albert L. Zobell, Jr. Salt Lake City, Deseret Book Co., 1966. 100 p. 17 cm. [BV4225.2.Z6] 66-20708
1. Homiletical illustrations. I. Title.

ZOBELL, Albert L. comp. 251.08
Only on the threshold, comp. by Albert L. Zobell, Jr. Salt Lake City, Deseret, 1966. 100p. 17cm. [BV4225.2.Z6] 66-20708 1.25
1. Homiletical illustrations. I. Title.

HEFLEY, James C. 251'.08'03
A dictionary of illustrations; over 900 illustrations for teachers, speakers, and ministers [by] James C. Hefley. Grand Rapids, Mich., Zondervan Pub. House [1971] 313 p. 24 cm. [BV4225.2.H4] 75-133359 6.95
1. Homiletical illustrations. I. Title.

ANDERSON, Roy Allan. 251.081
Preachers of righteousness. Nashville, Tenn., Southern Pub. Association [1963] 212 p. illus. 22 cm. [BV4211.2.A44] 63-12808
1. Preaching — Addresses, essays, lectures. I. Title.

ANDERSON, Roy Allan 251.081
Preachers of righteousness. Nashville, Tenn., Southern Pub. Assn. [c.1963] 212p. illus. 22cm. Bibl. 63-12808 3.75
1. Preaching—Addresses, essays, lectures. I. Title.

RODDY, Clarence Stonelynn, ed. 251.082
We prepare and preach; the practice of sermon construction and delivery. Chicago, Moody Press [1959] 190p. 22cm. [BV4211.2.R63] 59-1089
1. Preaching. I. Title.

ALLEE, George Franklin, 1897- ed. 251.0822
Evangelistic illustrations, for pulpit and platform. Chicago, Moody Press [1961] 400p. 24cm. [BV4225.2.A4] 62-231
1. Homiletical illustrations. I. Title.

BACH, T. J. 251.0822
Pearls from many seas; 710 pointed quotations and illustrations. Grand Rapids, Mich., Baker Bk. [1963, c.1951] 104p. 20cm. 1.00 pap.,
1. Homiletical illustrations. I. Title.

BRYANT, Al 251.0822
Evangelistic illustrations. Grand Rapids, Mich., Zondervan [c.1961] 120p. 1.95 bds.,
1. Homilectics—Illustrations. I. Title.

DRINKWATER, Francis Harold, 1886- 251.0822
Fourth book of catechism stories; a teachers' aidbook. [Dist. New York, St. Martin's, 1962, c.]1961. 220p. 19cm. A62 2.95
1. Homiletical illustrations. I. Title. II. Title: Catechism stories.

EAVEY, Charles Benton, 1889- 251.0822
Speaker's handbook for occasional talks. Grand Rapids, Baker Book House, 1963. 158 p. 20 cm. [BV4225.2.E2] 63-12752
1. Homilectical illustrations. I. Title.

EAVEY, Charles Benton, 1889- 251.0822
Speaker's handbook for occasional talks. Grand Rapids, Mich., Baker Bk. [c.]1963. 158p. 20cm. 63-12752 2.50
1. Homiletical illustrations. I. Title.

HASTINGS, Robert J. 251.0822
A word fitly spoken. Nashville, Broadman Pr. [c.1962] 122p. illus. 62-9197 2.50
1. Homiletical illustrations. 2. Quotations. 3. Anecdotes. I. Title.

KNIGHT, Alice Marie (Neighbour) 1901- 251.0822
Mrs. Knight's book of illustrations for children and young people, by Alice Marie Knight. Grand Rapids, W. B. Eerdmans Pub. Co. [1964] xix, 403 p. 23 cm. [BV4225.2K58] 63-17787
1. Homiletical illustrations. I. Title.

KNIGHT, Alice Marie (Neighbour) 1901- 251.0822
Mrs. Knight's book of illustrations for children and young people. Grand Rapids, Mich., Eerdmans [c.1964] xix, 403p. 23cm. 63-17787 5.95
1. Homiletical illustrations. I. Title.

KNIGHT, Walter Brown, comp. 251.0822
Treasury of illustrations. Grand Rapids, Eerdmans [1963] 451 p. 24 cm. [BV4225.2K6] 62-21375
1. Homiletical illustrations. I. Title.

KNIGHT, Walter Brown, comp. 251.0822
Treasury of illustrations. Grand Rapids, Mich., Eerdmans [c.1963] 451p. 24cm. 62-21375 5.95
1. Homiletical illustrations. I. Title.

KOSTEN, Andrew, ed. 251.0822
A minister's scrapbook of sermon illustrations and quotations. Grand Rapids, Baker House, 1961. 119p. 22cm. [BV4225.2.K65] 61-10542
1. Homiletical illustrations. I. Title.

LEE, Robert G. 251.0822
Quotable illustrations. Grand Rapids, Mich., Zondervan [c.1962] 152p. 21cm. 2.50
I. Title.

LEE, Robert Green, 1886- 251.0822
Robert G. Lee's sourcebook of 500 illustrations. For public speakers, ministers, Sunday school teachers. Grand Rapids, Mich., Zondervan [c.1964] 218p. 24cm. [BV4225.2.L43] 64-22907 3.95 bds.,
1. Homiletical illustrations. I. Title. II. Title: Sourcebook of 500 illustrations.

LEE, Robert Greene, 1886- 251.0822
Choice pickings; illustrations for pulpit and platform. Grand Rapids, Mich., Zondervan Pub. House [1960, c.1961] 119p. 61-710 1.95 bds.,
1. Homiletical illustrations. I. Title.

LEE, Robert Greene, 1886- 251.0822
Quotable illustrations. Grand Rapids, Zondervan Pub. House [c1962] 152 p. 21 cm. [BV4225.2.L42] 63-1904
1. Homilectical illustrations. I. Title.

LEE, Robert Greene, 1886- 251.0822
Robert G. Lee's sourcebook of 500 illustrations. For public speakers, ministers, Sunday school teachers. Grand Rapids, Zondervan [1964] 218 p. 24 cm. [BV4225.2.L43] 64-22907
1. Homiletical illustrations. I. Title. II. Title: Sourcebook of 500 illustrations.

LUDWIG, Charles, 1918- 251.0822
On target: illustrations for Christian messages. Anderson, Ind., Warner Press [1963] 110 p. 21 cm. [BV4225.2.L8] 63-10212
1. Homiletical illustrations. I. Full name: Charles Shelton Ludwig. II. Title.

LUDWIG, Charles Shelton, 1918- 251.0822
On target: illustrations for Christian messages. Anderson, Ind., Warner [c.1963] 110p. 21cm. 63-10212 1.50 pap.,
1. Homiletical illustrations. I. Title.

MCDONALD, Erwin Lawrence 251.0822
75 stories and illustrations from everyday life. Grand Rapids, Mich., Baker [c.]1964. 105p. 20cm. 64-16943 1.95 bds.,
1. Homiletical illustrations. I. Title.

MACLENNAN, David Alexander, 1903- 251.0822
Preaching week by week: ideas, insights, illustrations. [Westwood, N.J.] Revell [c.1963] 158p. 21cm. 63-10392 3.00
1. Homiletical illustrations. I. Title.

MILLER, Milburn H. 251.0822
Notes and quotes for church speakers. Anderson, Ind., Warner Press [dist. by Gospel Trumpet Press, c.1960] 192p. 21cm. 60-6938 3.00
1. Homiletical illustrations. I. Title.

POWELL, Ivor 251.0822
Bible windows. With a foreword by W. L. Jarvis. Grand Rapids, Mich., Zondervan Pub. House [1960] 180p. 22cm. 60-4640 2.50
1. Homiletical illustrations. I. Title.

RICHARDS, Le Grand, Bp., 1886- 251.0822
Just to illustrate. Salt Lake City, Bookcraft [1961] 324p. illus. -3cm. [BV4225.2.R5] 61-47642
1. Homlletical illustrations. I. Title.

ROBERTSON, James Douglas, ed. 251.0822
Handbook of preaching resources from English literature. New York, Macmillan, 1962. 268p. 22cm. [BV4225.2.R58] 62-8566
1 Homiletical illustrations. 2. English literature (Selections: Extracts, etc.) 3. Quotations. I. Title. II. Title: Preaching resources from English literature.

ROSELL, Garth, comp. 251.0822
Shoe-leather faith, compiled by Garth & Merv Rosell. Saint Paul, Printed by the Bruce Pub. Co. [1960] unpaged. 24cm. [BV4225.2.R6] 60-615
1. Homiletical illustrations. I. Rosell, Mervin E., joint comp. II. Title.

SELECTED poetry for sermons and addresses. Grand Rapids, Baker Book House, 1960. 112p. 20cm. (Minister's handbook series) [BV4225.2.S4] 60-16793 251.0822
1. Homiletical illustrations.

TICKEMYER, Garland E 251.0822
Story illustrations for church and home; 114 appropriate stories and word pictures, including a section of illustrations for special days. Independence, Mo., Herald House, 1961. 176 p. 20 cm. [BV4225.2.T5] 61-17948
1. Homiletical illustrations. I. Title.

TICKEMYER, Garland E. 251.0822
Story illustrations for church and home; 114

appropriate stories and word pictures, including a section of illustrations for special days. Independence, Mo., Herald House [c.] 1961. 176p. 61-17948 2.00
1. Homiletical illustrations. I. Title.

WALLIS, Charles 251.0822
Langworthy, 1921- ed.
1010 sermon illustrations from the Bible. [1st ed.] New York, Harper & Row [1963] 242 p. 22 cm. [BV4225.2.W3] 63-7610
1. Homiletical illustrations. 2. Bible — Indexes, Topical. I. Title.

WALLIS, Charles 251.0822
Langworthy, 1921- ed.
1010 sermon illustrations from the Bible. Edited by Charles L. Wallis. Grand Rapids: Baker Book House, [1975 c1963] xiii, 242 p.; 20 cm. (Charles L. Wallis library of pulpit helps) [BV4225.2.W3] 63-7610 ISBN 0-8010-9552-2 2.95 (pbk.)
1. Homiletical illustrations. 2. Bible—Indexes, Topical. I. Title.

WILDER, John Bunyan, 251.0822
1914-
Stories for pulpit and platform. Grand Rapids, Zondervan Pub. House [1963] 117 p. 21 cm. [BV4225.2.W5] 63-3081
1. Homiletical illustrations. I. Title.

WILDER, John Bunyan, 251.0822
1914-
Stories for pulpit and platform. Grand Rapids, Mich., Zondervan [c.1963] 117p. 21cm. 63-3081 1.95 bds.,
1. Homiletical illustrations. I. Title.

BRILIOTH, Yngve Torgny, 251.09
Abp. 1891-1959.
A brief history of preaching. Translated by Karl E. Mattson. Philadelphia, Fortress Press [1965] x. 229 p. 18 cm. (The Preacher's paperback library) "Translated from Predikans historia." Bibliography: p. 217-223. [BV4207.B7313] 65-13256
1. Preaching — Hist. I. Title.

BRILIOTH, Yngve Torgny, 251.09
Abp., 1891-1959
A brief history of preaching. Tr. by Karl E. Mattson. Philadelphia, Fortress [c.1965] x, 229p. 18cm. (Preacher's paperback lib.) Bibl. [BV4207.B7313] 65-13256 2.95 pap.,
1. Preaching—Hist. I. Title.

CALKINS, Harold L 251.09
Master preachers: their study and devotional habits. Washington, Review and Heaald Pub. Association [c1960] 128p. 21cm. Includes bibliography. [BV4208.G7C3] 60-15509
1. Preaching— Hist.—Gt. Brit. 2. Preaching—Hist.—U. S. I. Title.

DARGAN, Edwin Charles, 251.09
1852-1930.
A history of preaching. Introd. by J. B. Weatherspoon. Grand Rapids, Baker Book House, 1954. 2v. in 1. 23cm. Includes bibliographical references. [BV4207.D3 1954] 54-2653
1. Preaching-Hist. I. Title.

DARGAN, Edwin Charles, 251.09
1852-1930
A history of preaching. Introd. by J. B. Weatherspoon. Great Rapids, Baker Bk. [1968] 2v. 22cm. (Twin Brooks ser.) Contents.v. 1. From the apostolic fathers to the great reformers, A.D. 70-1572.--v. 2. From the close of the Reformation period to the end of the nineteenth century, 1572-1900. Bibl. [BV4207.D3] 54-2653 3.95 pap., ea.,
1. Preaching—Hist. I. Title.

JONES, Edgar De Witt, 251.09
1876-
The royalty of the pulpit; a survey and appreciation of the Lyman Beecher lectures on preaching founded at Yale Divinity School 1871 and given annually (with four exceptions) since 1872. [1st ed.] New York, Harper [1951] xxx, 447 p. 22 cm. Bibliography: p. 432-439. [BV4207.J65] 51-9797
1. Preaching—Hist. 2. Lyman Beecher lectures on preaching, Yale University. I. Title.

MCGRAW, James 251.09
Great evangelical preachers of yesterday. Nashville, Abingdon [c.1961] 159p. Bibl. 61-11785 2.75 bds.,
1. Preaching—Hist. I. Title.

PETRY, Ray C., 1903- 251.09
Preaching in the great tradition, neglected chapters in the history of preaching. Philadelphia, Westminster Press [1950] 122 p. 20 cm. (The Samuel A. Crozer lectures for 1949) [BV4207.P4] 50-7643
1. Preaching — Hist. I. Title. II. Series.

JONES, Edgar De Witt, 251'.0922 B
1876-1956.
American preachers of to-day; intimate appraisals of thirty-two leaders. Freeport, N.Y., Books for Libraries Press [1971, 1933] 317 p. 23 cm. (Essay index reprint series) [BV4208.U6J65] 76-156667 ISBN 0-8369-2279-4
1. Preaching—History—U.S. I. Title.

NEWTON, Joseph Fort, 251'.0922 B
1876-1950.
Some living masters of the pulpit; studies in religious personality. Freeport, N.Y., Books for Libraries Press [1971, c1923] 261 p. 23 cm. (Essay index reprint series) Contents.Contents.—George A. Gordon.—John A. Hutton.—Dean Inge, of St. Paul's.—Charles E. Jefferson.—W. E. Orchard.—Charles D. Williams.—A. Maude Royden.—Samuel McChord Crothers.—T. Reaveley Glover.—S. Parkes Cadman.—Reginald J. Campbell.—William E. Quayle.—George W. Truett.—Edward L. Powell.—Frank W. Gunsaulus: In memoriam. [BR1700.N4 1971] 71-152203 ISBN 0-8369-2287-5
1. Christian biography. 2. Preaching. I. Title.

BLENCH, J. W. 251.0942
Preaching in England in the late fifteenth and sixteenth centuries; a study of English sermons 1450-c. 1600, by J. W. Blench. New York, Barnes & Noble, 1964. xv, 378 p. front. 23 cm. Bibliography: p. [350]-368. [BV4208.B7B55] 64-4249
1. Preaching — Hist. — England. 2. Sermons, English — 16th cent. — Hist. & crit. I. Title.

BLENCH, J. W. 251.0942
Preaching in England in the late fifteenth and sixteenth centuries: a study of English sermons 1450-c. 1600, by J. W. Blench. New York, Barnes & Noble [c.]1964. xv, 378p. front. 23cm. Bibl. 64-4249 10.00
1. Preaching—Hist.—England. 2. Sermons, English—16th cent.—Hist. & crit. I. Title.

DAVIES, Horton 251.0942
Varieties of English preaching, 1900-1960. London, SCM Pr.; Englewood Cliffs, N. J., Prentice [c.1963] 276p. illus. 23cm. Bibl 63-11791 6.60
1. Preaching—Hist.—England. I. Title.

DAVIES, Horton. 251.0942
Varieties of English preaching,1900-1960 London, SCM Press; Englewood Cliffs, N.J., Prentice-Hall [1963] 276 p. illus. 23 cm. Includes bibliography. [BV4208.G7D3] 63-11791
1. Preaching — Hist. — England. I. Title.

MITCHELL, William 251.0942
Fraser, 1900-
English pulpit oratory, from Andrewes to Tillotson: a study of its literary aspects. New York, Russell, 1962. xii, 516p. Bibl. 61-17196 10.00
1. Preaching—Hist.—England. 2. Church of England—Clergy. 3. Clergy—England. I. Title.

OTT, Heinrich 251165-12513
Theology and preaching; a programme of work in dogmatics, arranged with reference to questions I-II of the Heidelberg catechism. Tr. [from German] by Harold Knight. Philadelphia, Westminister [c.1965] 158p. 23cm. [BV4214.O813] 4.50
1. Kerygma. 2. Preaching. 3. Sin. I. Heidelberg catechism. II. Title.

GOLLADAY, Robert Emory, 251.6
1867-
Lenten sermon outlines, by R. E. Golladay and others. [Special ed.] Minneapolis, Augsburg Pub. House [1954] 510p. 22cm. 'Abridged edition of Lenten outlines and sermons.' [BV4277.G62] 54-682
1. Lenten sermons-Outlines. I. Title.

SCHNEIDER, Stanley D 251.6
Facing the cross; sermon sketches for Lent, by Stanley D. Schneider and others. Columbus, Ohio, Wartburg Press [1955] 279p. 20cm. [BV4277.S37] 55-768
1. Lenten sermons—Outlines. I. Title.

REYNOLDS, Quentin James, 251.74
1902-1965.
The F.B.I. New York, Random House [1954] 180 p. illus. 22 cm. (Landmark books, 46) [HV8141.R4] 364.12* 54-6267
1. United States. Federal Bureau of Investigation—Juvenile literature.

BLACKWOOD, Andrew 251.8
Watterson, 1882-
Expository preaching for today; case studies of Bible passages. Nashville, Abingdon-Cokesbury Press [1953] 224p. 21cm. Includes bibliography. [BV4211.B518] 53-5392
1. Preaching. I. Title.

BLACKWOOD, Andrew 251.8
Watterson, 1882-
Expository preaching for today: case studies of Bible passages. Grand Rapids: Baker Book House, [1975 c1943] 224 p. 20 cm. (Andrew W. Blackwood library) Bibliography: p. 209-214. [BV4211.B518] 53-5392 ISBN 0-8010-0639-2 2.95 (pbk.)
1. Preaching. I. Title.

LITTORIN, Frank T 1900- 251.8
How to preach the Word with variety. Grand Rapids, Baker Book House, 1953. 157p. 21cm. [BV4211.L55] 53-3411
1. Preaching. I. Title.

UNGER, Merrill Fredierick, 251.8
1909-
Principles of expository preaching. Grand Rapids, Zondervan Pub. House [1955] 267p. 22cm. Includes bibliographies. [BV4211.2.U5] 55-42014
1. Preaching. I. Title.

252 Texts Of Sermons

AMICK, Fred A 252
Hearing for eternity. Rosemead, Calif., Old Paths Book Club, 1954- v. illus. 21cm. [BV4301.A6] 54-40237
1. Sermons, American. 2. Sermons, American. I. Title.

ANDERSON, Norman G 252
Power for tomorrow. Minneapolis, T. S. Denison [1961] 223p. 22cm. [BV4301.A65] 61-16790
1. Sermons, American. I. Title.

ANGELL, Charles Roy. 252
Rejoicing on great days [by] C. Roy Angell. Nashville, Broadman Press [1968] 126 p. 21 cm. Bibliographical footnotes. [BV4254.2.A54] 68-20665
1. Occasional sermons. 2. Baptists—Sermons. 3. Sermons, American. I. Title.

*APOSTOLON, Billy 252
Hands full of honey. Grand Rapids, Mich., Baker Bk. [c.1964] 83p. 22cm. 1.00 pap.,
I. Title.

APOSTOLON, Billy 252
The riches of God's grace. Grand Rapids, Mich., Baker Bk. [c.]1963. 85p. 22cm. (Pulpit masters' sermons) 1.00 pap.,
I. Title.

*APPELMAN, Hyman 252
Revival sermons. Grand Rapids, Mich., Baker Bk. [c.1966] 85p. 22cm. ((1.00 sermon lib.) 1.00 pap.,
I. Title.

*APPELMAN, Hyman. 252
Sermons on evangelism. Grand Rapids, Baker Book House [1974] 98 p. 20 cm. (Minister's handbook series) [BV3797] ISBN 0-8010-0068-8 1.95 (pbk.)
1. Evangelistic sermons. 2. Sermons, American. I. Title.

BARTH, Karl, 1886- 252
Deliverance to the captives. [Sermons translated by Marguerite Wieser. 1st ed.] New York, Harper [1961] 160p. 22cm. [BV4316.P7B33] 61-7333
1. Prisons—Sermons. I. Title.

BEAN, George M 1918- 252
No other gods; sermons preached to the Class of 1956 by their chaplain. New York, Morehouse-Gorham Co., 1956. 117p. 16cm. [BV4316.S7B43] 56-10120
1. Sermons. American. 2. U. S. Military Academy, West Point. I. Title.

BEECHER, Lyman, 1775-1863. 252
Lyman Beecher and the reform of society: four sermons, 1804-1828. New York, Arno Press, 1972. 107 p. 23 cm. (Religion in America, series II) Contents.Contents.—The practicality of suppressing vice by means of societies instituted for that purpose.—A reformation of morals practicable and indispensable.—The remedy for duelling.—Six sermons on the nature, occasions, signs, evils, and remedy of intemperance. [BV4253.B4] 71-38437 ISBN 0-405-04058-X
1. Sermons, American. I. Title.

BENNETT, Elbert Lansing, 252
1899-
Fifty object talks for your junior congregation. Westwood, N. J., Revell [1952] 159 p. 20 cm. [BV4315.B36] 52-9312
1. Children's sermons. 2. Object-teaching. I. Title.

BISAGNO, John R. 252
The power of positive preaching to the saved [by] John R. Bisagno. Nashville, Broadman Press [1971] 126 p. 20 cm. [BV3797.B52] 79-145978 ISBN 0-8054-2215-3 2.95
1. Evangelistic sermons. 2. Baptists—Sermons. 3. Sermons, American. I. Title.

BLACK, V. P., 1918- 252
We persuade men, by V. P. Black. Abilene, Tex., Biblical Research Press [1969] iv, 226 p. 23 cm. (The 20th century sermons series, v. 2) [BV4253.B47] 72-87861
1. Sermons, American. I. Title.

BLACKWOOD, Andrew Watterson, 252
1915-
From the rock to the gates of hell, by Andrew W. Blackwood, Jr. Grand Rapids, Baker Book House [1968] 127 p. 23 cm. [BV603.B48] 68-19203
1. Church—Sermons. 2. Sermons, American. I. Title.

BLAIR, Charles E. 252
The silent thousands suddenly speak! [By] Charles E. Blair. Foreword by J. Sidlow Baxter. Grand Rapids, Zondervan Pub. House [1968] 149 p. 23 cm. [BV4253.B5] 68-22833
1. Sermons, American. I. Title.

BOSWORTH, Fred Francis, 1877- 252
Christ, the healer [by] F. F. Bosworth. Old Tappan, N.J., F. H. Revell Co. [1974, c1973] 241 p. 20 cm. Reprint of the 8th ed., with a new introd. [BT732.5.B67 1974] 73-17492 ISBN 0-8007-0647-1 2.95 (pbk.)
1. Faith-cure. I. Title.

BOWERS, George K 252
Firecracker Christians; a book of children's sermons. Philadelphia, Muhlenberg Press [1958] 112p. 19cm. [BV4315.B62] 58-8945
1. Children's sermons. I. Title.

BOYCE, Edward H. 252
With Christ in the mount; mountain experiences in the life of Christ. [Sermons] New York, Exposition Press [1951] 128 p. 23 cm. [BV4253.B64] 51-5040
1. Sermons. American. I. Title.

BRISCOE, D. Stuart. 252
What works when life doesn't / Stuart Briscoe. Wheaton, Ill. : Victor Books, c1976. 143 p. ; 21 cm. [BS1430.4.B677] 75-26443 ISBN 0-88207-725-2 pbk. : 1.95
1. Bible. O.T. Psalms—Sermons. 2. Sermons, American. I. Title.

BROWNE, Benjamin P 252
52 story sermons. Illus. by Oliver F. Grimley 1st ed. Philadelphia, Judson Press [1958] 179p. illus. 22cm. [BV4315.B73] 58-9988
1. Children's sermons. I. Title.

BROWNSON, William. 252
Do you believe? : Contemporary insight on the question of faith / William Brownson. Grand Rapids, Mich. : Zondervan Pub. House, c1975. 217 p. ; 18 cm. [BS2615.4.B76] 74-25324 1.95
1. Bible. N.T. John—Sermons. 2. Sermons, American. I. Title.

BRUNNER, Heinrich Emil, 1889- 252
The great invitation, and other sermons. Translated by Harold nninght. Philadelphia, Westminster Press [1955] 188p. 22cm. Translation of Fraumunster-Predigten. [BX9435.B675 1955] 55-8594
1. Reformed Church—Sermons. 2. Sermons, German —Translations into English. 3. Sermons, English—Translations from German. I. Title.

*CHAPPELL, Clovis G. 252
The sermon on the Mount by Clovis G. Chappell Grand Rapids, Baker Book [1975] 227 p. 20 cm. (Clovis G. Chappell Library) [BV4253] ISBN 0-8010-2363-7 2.95 (pbk.)
1. Sermons. I. Title.

*CHAPPELL, Clovis G. 252
Sermons from the miracles [by] Clovis G. Chappell Grand Rapids Baker Book [1975 c1965] 224 p. 20 cm. (Clovis G. Chappell Library) [BV4253] ISBN 0-8010-2362-9 2.95 (pbk.)
1. Sermons. I. Title.

CHILDREN'S sermons, outlines, 252
and illustrations [by] James Stalker, John R. MacDuff, Richard Newton, and others. Grand Rapids, Baker Book House, 1956. 96p. 21cm. (Minister's handbook series) [BV4315.C57] 56-6827
1. Children's sermons. 2. Homiletical illustrations. I. Stalker, James, 1848-1927.

COFFEY, John W. 252
Grace in the wilderness, by John W. Coffey, Jr. [Nashville, T. Nelson, 1974] p. cm. "Nelson giant print inspirational." [BV4253.C63] 74-18292 ISBN 0-8407-5579-1 3.50 (pbk.)
1. Sermons, American. 2. Sight-saving books. I. Title.

COX, Frank Lucius, 1895- 252
Moses' last birthday, and other sermons.

Nashville, Gospel Advocate Co., 1956. 136p. 22cm. [BV4223.C65] 57-31388
1. Sermons—Outlines. I. Title.

CRAVNER, William Charles 252
The daystar at midnight. New York, Vantage [c.1962] 91p. front. port. 21cm. 2.75 bds.,
I. Title.

CROWLEY, Dale. 252
Fifty radio sermons; evangelist Dale Crowley's golden anniversary book. Washington, National Bible Knowledge Association [1972] xii, 221 p. 22 cm. [BV4253.C77] 72-89559 5.00
1. Sermons, American. I. Title.

CULBERTSON, William. 252
The faith once delivered; keynote messages from Moody Founder's Week. Chicago, Moody Press [1972] 192 p. 22 cm. Addresses delivered annually, 1953-1971. [BV4253.C84] 76-181585 ISBN 0-8024-2520-8 4.95
1. Sermons, American. I. Moody Bible Institute of Chicago. II. Title.

CULBERTSON, William. 252
The faith once delivered; keynote messages from Moody Founder's Week. Chicago, Moody Press [1972] 192 p. 22 cm. Addresses delivered annually, 1953-1971. [BV4253.C84] 72-181584 ISBN 0-8024-2520-8 4.95
1. Sermons, American. I. Moody Bible Institute of Chicago. II. Title.

DAANE, James. 252
The freedom of God; a study of election and pulpit. Grand Rapids, Eerdmans [1973] 208 p. 23 cm. Includes bibliographical references. [BT810.2.D32] 72-77189 ISBN 0-8028-3421-3 5.95
1. Election (Theology) 2. Preaching. I. Title.

DE HAAN, Martin Ralph, 1891- 252
Signs of the times, and other prophetic messages. Grand Rapids, Zondervan Pub. House [1951] 182 p. 20 cm. [BV4301.D382] 51-11552
1. Sermons, American. I. Title.

DE HAAN, Martin Ralph, 1891- 252
The tabernacle, the house of blood. Grand Rapids, Zondervan Pub. House [1955] 185p. illus. 20cm. [BV4301.D385] 55-14895
1. Sermons, American. I. Title.

DOUGLAS, Lloyd Cassel, 1877- 252
1951.
The living faith [by] Lloyd C. Douglas, from his selected sermons. Boston, Houghton Mifflin, 1955. 344 p. 22 cm. [BV4253.D68] 55-6127
1. Sermons, American. I. Title.

EAVEY, Charles Benton, 1889- 252
Ninety-five brief talks for various occasions. Grand Rapids, Baker Book House, 1956. 103p. 21cm. [BV425.2.E3] 56-12748
1. Occasional sermons. I. Title.

EAVEY, Charles Benton, 1889- 252
Ninty-five brief talks for various occasions. Grand Rapids, Baker Bk. [1967, c.1956] 103p. 20cm. (Preaching helps ser.) [BV4254.2.E3] 56-12748 1.50 pap.,
1. Occasional sermons. I. Title.

THE 11 o'clock news & other 252
experimental sermons / edited by John Killinger. Nashville : Abingdon Press, [1975] 156 p. : ill. ; 23 cm. [BV4241.E55] 75-16357 ISBN 0-687-11639-2 : 6.95
1. Sermons, American. I. Killinger, John.

FERGUSON, Charles Wright, 252
1901-
Great themes of the Christian faith, as presented by G. Campbell Morgan [and others] Arr. by Charles W. Ferguson. Freeport, N.Y., Books for Libraries Press [1969, c1930] viii, 204 p. 23 cm. (Essay index reprint series) [BV4241.F4 1969] 68-58788
1. Sermons, American. I. Morgan, George Campbell, 1863-1945. II. Title.

FERRE, Gustave A comp. 252
The Upper Room Chapel talks. Nashville, The Upper room [1957] 128p. 19cm. [BV4241.F44] 57-13007
1. Sermons, English. I. The Upper room. II. Title.

FERRE, Nels Fredrick 252
Solomon, 1908-
The extreme center [by] Nels F. S. Ferre. Waco, Tex., Word Books [1973] 184 p. 23 cm. Includes bibliographical references. [BV4253.F428] 73-84581 5.95
1. Sermons, American. I. Title.

FERRE, Nels Fredrick Solomon, 252
1908-
God's new age, a book of sermons. New York, Harper [c.1956-1962] 160p. 62-7285 3.00 bds.,
1. Sermons, American. I. Title.

FICHTNER, Joseph. 252
Proclaim His word; homiletic themes for Sundays and holydays. New York, Alba House [1973- v. 21 cm. Contents.Contents.—v. 1. Cycle C. [BX1756.F46P76] 73-5726 ISBN 0-8189-0273-6 3.95
1. Catholic Church—Sermons. 2. Church year sermons. 3. Sermons, American. I. Title.

FINE, William M., ed. 252
That day with God. Edited by William M. Fine. Foreword by Richard Cardinal Cushing. [1st ed.] New York, McGraw-Hill [1965] xiv, 213 p. 24 cm. Principally excerpts from sermons. [E842.9.F5] 64-66265
1. Kennedy, John Fitzgerald, Pres. U.S., 1917-1963—Funeral and memorial services. 2. Sermons, English. I. Title.

FINNEY, Charles Grandison, 252
1792-1875.
True saints; revival messages. Grand Rapids, Kregel Publications [1967] 119 p. 20 cm. (Revival sermon series) "Sermons selected from [the author's] Lectures to professing Christians." [BV3797.F543] 66-24880
1. Evangelistic sermons. 2. Sermons, American. 3. Congregational churches—Sermons. I. Title.

FINNEY, Charles Grandison, 252
1792-1875.
True submission; revival messages [by] Charles G. Finney. Grand Rapids, Kregel Publications [1967] 128 p. 20 cm. (The Charles G. Finney memorial library. Revival sermon series) Sermons selected from the author's Lectures to professing Christians and The way of salvation. [BV3797.F544] 66-24881
1. Evangelistic sermons. 2. Sermons, American. I. Title.

FISCHBACH, Julius, 1894- 252
Children's sermons in stories. Nashville, Abingdon Press [1955] 127p. 20cm. [BV4315.F47] 55-6762
1. Children's sermons. 2. Baptists—Sermons. 3. Sermons, American. I. Title.

FORD, William Herschel, 1900- 252
Simple sermons for a world in crisis / by W. Herschel Ford. Grand Rapids : Zondervan Pub. House, c1977. 107 p. ; 21 cm. [BX6333.F568S473] 76-51354 ISBN 0-310-24461-7 pbk. : 1.95
1. Baptists—Sermons. 2. Sermons, American. I. Title.

FORD, William Herschel, 1900- 252
Simple sermons for a world in crisis / by W. Herschel Ford. Grand Rapids : Zondervan Pub. House, c1977. 107 p. ; 21 cm. [BX6333.F568S473] 76-51354 ISBN 0-310-24461-7 pbk. : 1.95
1. Baptists—Sermons. 2. Sermons, American. I. Title.

FORD, William Herschel, 1900- 252
Simple sermons on Old Testament texts / by W. Herschel Ford. Grand Rapids : Zondervan Pub. House, c1975. 102 p. ; 21 cm. [BS1151.5.F67] 74-25331 pbk. : 1.95
1. Bible. O.T.—Sermons. 2. Baptists—Sermons. 3. Sermons, American. I. Title. II. Title: Old Testament texts.

FOUSHEE, Clyde C 1900- 252
Animated object talks. [Westwood, N. J.] Revell [1956] 159p. 20cm. [BV4315.F617] 56-7440
1. Object teaching. 2. Children's sermons. I. Title.

FOUSHEE, Clyde C, 1900- 252
52 workable youth object lessons. Grand Rapids, Zondervan Pub. House [1951] 120 p. 20 cm. [BV4315.F62] 52-18160
1. Object-teaching. 2. Children's sermons. I. Title.

FROST, S. S. Jr. ed. 252
The world's great sermons, edited by S. E. Frost, jr. Garden City, N. Y., Garden City Books, 1960 [c.1943] xiii, 395p. 22cm. Each sermon preceded by a biographical sketch of the author. 2.95 bds.,
1. Sermons. I. Title.

GLENNIE, Alexander. 252
Sermons preached on plantations. Freeport, N.Y., Books for Libraries Press, 1971. viii, 161 p. 23 cm. (Black heritage library collection) Reprint of the 1844 ed. published under title: Sermons preached on plantations to congregations of Negroes. [BV4316.S6G45 1971] 75-161260 ISBN 0-8369-8819-1
1. Sermons, American. I. Title. II. Series.

GOSSELINK, Marion Gerard. 252
Inspiring talks to juniors (the days of youth) Boston, Wilde [c1956] 144p. 20cm. [BV4315.G62] 56-11660
1. Children's sermons. I. Title.

GOSSELINK, Marion Gerard. 252
Junior story talks, from Rally Day to Children's Day. Boston, W. A. Wilde Co. [1953] 128p. 20cm. [BV4315.G63] 53-9052
1. Children's sermons. I. Title.

GUNTHER, Peter F comp. 252
Great sermons by great preachers. Chicago, Moody Press [1960] 159p. 19cm. (Moody pocket books, 56) [BV4241.G84] 60-50743
1. Sermons, English. I. Title.

HAMILTON, James Wallace, 252
1900-
Ride the wild horses! The Christian use of our untamed impulses. Westwood, N. J., Revell [1952] 160 p. 22 cm. [BV4253.H33] 52-8205
1. Sermons, American. I. Title.

HAMILTON, James Wallace, 252
1900-1968.
Still the trumpet sounds. Old Tappan, N.Y., Revell [1970] 191 p. 21 cm. [BV4253.H335] 77-112461 4.50
1. Sermons, American. I. Title.

HAMILTON, James Wallace, 252
1900-1968.
What about tomorrow? Old Tappan, N.J., Revell [1972] 187 p. port. 21 cm. [BV4253.H342] 74-177396 ISBN 0-8007-0491-6 4.95
1. Sermons, American. I. Title.

HAMILTON, James Wallace, 252
1900-1968.
Where now is thy God? [By] J. Wallace Hamilton. Old Tappan, N.J., F. H. Revell Co. [1969] 128 p. 21 cm. [BV4253.H343] 69-12837 3.50
1. Sermons, American. I. Title.

HENRY, Carl Ferdinand Howard, 252
1913-
New strides of faith, by Carl F. H. Henry. Chicago, Moody Press [1972] 140 p. 22 cm. (Moody evangelical focus) Bibliography: p. 139-140. [BV4253.H46] 72-77956 ISBN 0-8024-5917-X 2.25
1. Sermons, American. I. Title.

HIBBS, Ben, 1901- comp. 252
White House sermons. Edited by Ben Hibbs. Introduction by Richard Nixon. [1st ed.] New York, Harper & Row [1972] xii, 216 p. 22 cm. [BV4241.H5] 70-184407 ISBN 0-06-063897-4 5.95
1. Sermons, American. I. Title.

HODGES, Graham R 252
50 children's sermons. New York, Abingdon Press [1957] 95p. 20cm. [BV4315.H53] 57-12390
1. Childern's sermons. I. Title.

HOLDCRAFT, Paul Ellsworth, 252
1891- comp.
101 snappy sermonettes for the children's church New York, Abingdon-Cokesbury Press [1951] 126 p. 20 cm. [BV4315.H56] 51-7709
1. Children's sermons. I. Title.

HUMBARD, Rex, 1919- 252
The third dimension. Old Tappan, N.J., F. H. Revell [1972] 154 p. 21 cm. [BV3797.H745] 72-4223 ISBN 0-8007-0549-1
1. Evangelistic sermons. 2. Sermons, American. I. Title.

*HUTCHINSON, Charles 252
Portrait of the cross. New York, Vantage [c.1964] 60p. 21cm. 2.00
I. Title.

HUTTENLOCKER, Keith. 252
Alive; steps to personal renewal. Anderson, Ind., Warner Press [1970] 111 p. port. 19 cm. [BV4253.H84] 75-102374
1. Sermons, American. I. Title.

IF I could preach just once 252
[by] Bertrand Russell [and others] Freeport, N.Y., Books for Libraries Press [1971, c1929] 255 p. 23 cm. (Essay index reprint series) Contents.—The power of the word, by J. Drinkwater.—The pagan in the heart, by L. Lewisohn.—The unknown future, by P. Gibbs.—Lucifer; or, The root of evil, by G. K. Chesterton.—There came one running, by H. N. MacCracken.—How to become a Christian, by H. Cecil.—For all bishops and other clergy, by S. Kaye-Smith.—The importance of style, by H. S. Canby.—Behind the veil of death, by A. C. Doyle.—The three voices of nature, by J. A. Thomson.—Morals and health, by T. Horder.—On the evils due to fear, by B. Russell.—The road to redemption, by J. Collins. [BV4241.I5 1971] 73-167364 ISBN 0-8369-2457-6
1. Sermons, English. I. Russell, Bertrand Russell, Hon., 3d Earl, 1872-1970.

IRONSIDE, Henry Allan, 1876- 252
1951.
Miscellaneous papers. New York, Loizeaux Bros. [1945] 2v. 20cm. [BR85.I7] 54-37436
1. Theology—Addresses, essays, lectures. I. Title.

JAY, William, 1769-1853. 252
Sixty-two sermons. Grand Rapids, Baker Book House, 1955. 454p. 21cm. [Co-operative reprint library] First published in 1879 under title: Sunday evening sermons and Thursday evening lectures. [BX5201] 55-8791
1. Sermons, English. I. Title.

*JONES,J.D. 252
The gospel of grace / by J.D.Jones Grand Rapids : Baker Book house, 1976. vii, 282, [1] p. ; 20 cm. (Minister's paperback library) [BV 253] ISBN 0-8010-5067-7 pbk. : 3.95
1. Sermons. I. Title.

*JONES, Sam. 252
Sam Jones. Introduction by Bishop Ivan Lee Holt. Grand Rapids, Mich., Baker Book House [1973, c1950] 256 p. 19 cm. (Great pulpit masters series) [BV3797] ISBN 0-8010-5054-5. 2.95 (pbk.)
1. Evangelistic sermons. 2. Sermons, American. I. Title.

KELSEY, Alice (Geer) 252
Story sermons for juniors. Nashville, Abingdon-Cokesbury Press [c1954] 127p. 20cm. [BV4571.K39] 53-11340
I. Title.

KILLINGER, John, comp. 252
Experimental preaching. Edited by John Killinger. Nashville, Abingdon Press [1973] 175 p. 21 cm. [BV4241.K48] 72-8419 ISBN 0-687-12423-9 3.95
1. Sermons, American. 2. Preaching. I. Title.
Contents omitted.

KILLINGER, John. 252
The thickness of glory. New York, Abingdon Press [1965] 158 p. 20 cm. [BV4253.K5 1965] 65-10811
1. Sermons, American. I. Title.

KILLINGER, John 252
The thickness of glory. Nashville, Abingdon [c.1964, 1965] 158p. 20cm. [BV4253.K5] 65-10811 2.75 bds.,
1. Sermons, American. I. Title.

KRONER, Richard, 1884- 252
The new dimension of the soul; chapel addresses. Foreword by Henry Pitney Van Dusen. Edited by John E. Skinner. Philadelphia, Fortress Press [1964, c1963] xi, 147 p. 18 cm. [BV4316.T5K7] 63-19549
1. Sermons, American. 2. Theological seminaries — Sermons. I. Title.

KRONER, Richard, 1884- 252
The new dimension of the soul; chapel addresses. Foreword by Henry Pitney Van Dusen. Ed. by Joh Philadelphia, Fortress [1964, c.1963] xi, 147p. 18cm. 63-19549 1.75 pap.,
1. Sermons, American. 2. Theological seminaries—Sermons. I. Title.

LEESTMA, Harold F. 252
Listen to the wind : how to live your faith / Harold F. Leestma. Waco, Tex. : Word Books, [1974] 100 p. ; 21 cm. Consists of previously delivered messages. [BV4253.L33] 74-82659 pbk. : 2.95
1. Sermons, American. I. Title.

LITTELL, Franklin Hamlin, ed. 252
Sermons to intellectuals from three continents [by] William Sloane Coffin, Jr. [others] New York, Macmillan [1963] 160p. 22cm. 63-10003 3.95
1. Sermons. I. Title.

LLOYD-JONES, David Martyn 252
Romans : an exposition of chapter 8:5-17, the sons of God / D. M. Lloyd-Jones. Grand Rapids : Zondervan, 1975, c1974. xi, 438 p. ; 23 cm. "Sermons ... preached in Westminster Chapel between March 1960 and April 1961." Includes text of Romans VIII, 5-17. Includes bibliographical references. [BS2665.4.L585 1975] 75-321704 8.95
1. Bible. N.T. Romans VIII, 5-17—Sermons. 2. Sermons, English. I. Bible. N.T. Romans VIII, 5-17. English. 1975. II. Title.

LOUGHHEAD, LaRue A. 252
Eyewitnesses at the cross [by] LaRue A. Loughhead. Valley Forge [Pa.] Judson Press [1974] 125 p. 23 cm. Includes bibliographical references. [BV4277.L68] 73-16692 ISBN 0-8170-0626-5 4.95
1. Lenten sermons. 2. Dialogue sermons. 3. Sermons, American. I. Title.

MCCRACKEN, Robert James. 252
Questions people ask. New York, Harper [1951] 188 p. 21 cm. [BV4253.M27] 51-8607

1. Sermons, American. I. Title.

MCGEE, J Vernon. 252
The fruit of the sycamore tree, and other sermons. Wheaton, Ill., Van Kampen Press [1952] 81 p. 20 cm. [BV4253.M37] 52-1202
1. Sermons, American. I. Title.

MCGEE, John Vernon, 1904- 252
The fruit of the sycamore tree, and other sermons. Wheaton, Ill., Van Kampen Press [1952] 81p. 20cm. [BV4253.M37] 52-1202
1. Sermons, American. I. Title.

MACLENNAN, David Alexander, 1903- 252
Preaching values in Today's English version [by] David A. MacLennan. Nashville, Abingdon Press [1971, c1972] 192 p. 23 cm. "Based on texts selected from Good news for modern man, the New Testament in Today's English version." [BS2361.M335 1972] 74-172811 ISBN 0-687-33880-8 4.75
1. Bible. N.T.—Homiletical use. I. Title.

MACLURE, Millar. 252
The Paul's Cross sermons, 1534-1642. [Toronto] University of Toronto Press [1958] 261p. illus. 24cm. (University of Toronto. Dept. of English. Studies and texts, no. 6) Includes bibliography. [BV4208.E5M2] 58-2173
1. Preaching—Hist.—England. 2. London. St. Paul's Cathedral. I. Title.

MARSH, Frederick Edward, 1858-1919. 252
Night scenes of the Bible, by F. E. Marsh. Grand Rapids, Baker Book House [1967, c1904] 131 p. 20 cm. [BV4253.M4] 67-18185
1. Sermons, English. I. Title.

MARSH, Frederick Edward, 1858-1919. 252
Night scenes of the Bible, by F. E. Marsh. Grand Rapids, Baker Book House [1967, c1904] 131 p. 20 cm. [BV4253.M4 1967] 67-18185
1. Sermons, English. I. Title.

MARTIN, William Benjamin James. 252
Sermons for special days / W. B. J. Martin. Nashville : Abingdon Press, [1975] 157 p. ; 19 cm. [BV4254.2.M37] 74-34062 ISBN 0-687-37989-X pbk. : 3.95
1. Occasional sermons. 2. Sermons, American. I. Title.

MOODY, Dwight Lyman, 1837-1899. 252
The best of D. L. Moody; sixteen sermons by the great evangelist. Edited by Wilbur M. Smith. Chicago, Moody Press [1971] 223 p. 22 cm. [BV3797.M7B47] 75-143467 4.95
1. Evangelistic sermons. 2. Sermons, American. I. Smith, Wilbur Moorehead, 1894- ed. II. Title.

MOODY, Dwight Lyman, 1837-1899 252
Moody's latest sermons. Authorized ed. Grand Rapids, Mich., Baker Bk. [1965] 126p. facsim. 20cm. [BV3797.M7L3] 65-20555 1.95 bds.,
1. Sermons, American. 2. Evangelistic sermons. I. Title.

MOORE, Harvey Daniel, 1942- 252
Little threads, and other object lessons for children. Nashville, Abingdon Press [1974] 80 p. 19 cm. [BV4315.M624] 73-21959 ISBN 0-687-22169-2 3.50
1. Children's sermons. I. Title.

MURRY, John Middleton, 1889-1957. 252
Not as the scribes; lay sermons. Edited with an introd. by Alec R. Vidler. [New York, Horizon Press] [1960] 255p. Bibl. footnotes. 60-14654 3.75
1. Sermons, English. I. Title.

NIEBUHR, Reinhold, 1892-1971. 252
Justice and mercy. Edited by Ursula M. Niebuhr. [1st ed.] New York, Harper & Row [1974] x, 139 p. 21 cm. Includes bibliographical references. [BV4253.N5 1974] 73-18704 ISBN 0-06-066171-2 5.95
1. Sermons, American. 2. Prayers. I. Title.

OUTSTANDING Black sermons / 252
J. Alfred Smith, Sr., editor. Valley Forge, Pa. : Judson Press, [1976] 96 p. ; 22 cm. Contents.Contents.—Belk, L. S. The eyes of the Lord.—Blanford, C. The church and its mission.—Booth, L. V. The master dreamer.—Clark, E. M. How a people make history.—Gregory, H. C. The shepherd.—Jones, O. C. The preacher's dilemma.—Matthews, J. V. When, from our exile ....—Moyd, O. P. Membership or movement?—Shaw, W. J. A day of trouble.—Smith, J. A. The future of the Black church.—Stewart, J. H. The cost of citizenship.—Thomas, R. C. The gateway to life.—Wright, H. S. Rules for the road. Includes bibliographical references. [BV4241.5.O9] 76-2084 ISBN 0-8170-0664-8 pbk. : 2.95
1. Sermons, American—Negro authors. I. Smith, James Alfred.
Contents omitted.

PATTEN, Bebe. 252
Give me back my soul. [1st ed.] Oakland, Calif., Patten Foundation, 1972. 190 p. 22 cm. Sermons preached in Christian Cathedral, Oakland, Calif., 1962-72, and first published in the Trumpet call. [BV4253.P27] 73-158771 4.95
1. Sermons, American. I. Title.

PENTECOST, J. Dwight. 252
Man's problems—God's answers, by J. Dwight Pentecost. Chicago, Moody Press [1971] 192 p. 22 cm. [BV4253.P38] 72-155685 3.95
1. Sermons, American. I. Title.

PETRUS CHRYSOLOGUS, Saint, Bp. of Ravenna. 252
Saint Peter Chrysologus: selected sermons, and Saint Valerian: homilies. Translated by George E. Ganss. Washington, Catholic University of America Press [1965, c1953] viii, 454 p. 22 cm. (The Fathers of the Church, a new translation. v. 17) Bibliography: p. 24. Bibliographical footnotes. [BR60.F3P473] 65-27500
1. Sermons, Latin—Translations into English. 2. Sermons, English—Translations from Latin. I. Valerianus Saint, Bp. of Cintez. II. Title. III. Series.

PHILPOT, William M., comp. 252
Best Black sermons. Editor: William M. Philpot. Valley Forge [Pa.] Judson Press [1972] 96 p. 22 cm. Contents.Contents.—Introduction, by G. C. Taylor.—Three dimensions of a complete life, by M. L. King, Jr.—Handicapped lives, by W. H. Borders, Sr.—The God who takes off chariot wheels, by D. E. King.—What man lives by, B. E. Mays.—The hot winds of change, by S. B. McKinney.—Going from disgrace to dignity, by O. Moss, Jr.—A strange song in a strange land, by D. T. Shannon.—Time is winding Up! By K. M. Smith.—What is your name? By H. H. Watts.—The relevancy of the Black church to the new generation, by H. L. Williams.—Black theology, by G. S. Wilmore, Jr.—Suggested tools for the preacher, by W. B. Hoard (p. 95-96) [BV4241.5.P48] 72-75358 ISBN 0-8170-0533-1 1.95
1. Sermons, American—Negro authors. I. Title.

*PIERSON, Arthur T. 252
Outline studies of great themes of the Bible. Grand Rapids, Mich., Baker Book House [1973] 64 p. 21 cm. (Dollar sermon library) [BV4223] ISBN 0-8010-6950-5 1.00 (pbk.)
1. Bible—Sermons. 2. Sermons—Outlines. I. Title.

PIPPIN, Frank Johnson, 1906- 252
The roads we travel. St. Louis, Bethany Press [1966] 128 p. 21 cm. Includes bibliographical references. [BV4241.P52] 66-14599
1. Sermons, American. I. Title.

PIPPIN, Frank Johnson, 1906- 252
The roads we travel. St. Louis, Bethany Pr. [c.1966] 128p. 21cm. Bibl. [BV4241.P52] 66-145996 3.50 bds.,
1. Sermons, American. I. Title.

PREACHING on national holidays / edited by Alton M. Motter. 252
Philadelphia : Fortress Press, c1976. viii, 120 p. ; 22 cm. Includes bibliographical references. [BV4254.2.P73] 75-36445 ISBN 0-8006-1222-1 pbk. : 2.95
1. Occasional sermons. 2. Sermons, American. I. Motter, Alton M.

PULLEY, Frank Easton, 1906- 252
Soldiers of the cross; sermons preached to the Class of 1950 by their chaplain. New York, Morehouse-Gorham Co., 1950. 108 p. 16 cm. Bibliography: p. 107-108. [BV4316.S7P796] 50-8439
1. U.S. Military Academy, West Point. 2. Sermons, American. I. Title.

PULLEY, Frank Easton, 1906- 252
Thine is the kingdom; sermons preached to the Class of 1954 by their chaplain. New York, Morehouse-Gorham Co., 1954. 120p. 16cm. [BV4316.S7P797] 54-2882
1. Sermon, American. 2. U. S. Military Academy, West Point. I. Title.

PURVIS, Cleo. 252
Christ and the common man. Louisville, Ky., Herald Press [1956] 114p. illus. 20cm. [BV4253.P8] 56-42691
1. Sermons, American. I. Title.

RATIFF, Dale Hedrick, 1928- 252
The challenge of Christ; a book of sermons. [1st ed.] New York, Exposition Press [1955] 77p. 21cm. [BV4253.R37] 55-9410
1. Sermons, American. I. Title.

REST, Karl. 252
When stones hurt your feet, and other sermons. Philadelphia, Muhlenberg Press [1954] 104p. 20cm. [BV4315.R42] 54-7587
1. Children's sermons. I. Title.

REST, Karl H A 252
Story talks for children; the village parson in the junior church (junior sermons for boys and girls) By Karl Rest. Columbus, Ohio, Wartburg Press [1942] 135 p. 19 cm. [BV4315.R4] 42-7057
1. Children's sermons. I. Title.

SCHAEFFER, Francis August. 252
No little people; sixteen sermons for the twentieth century [by] Francis A. Schaeffer. Downers Grove, Ill., InterVarsity Press [1974] 271 p. 21 cm. [BV4253.S34] 74-78675 ISBN 0-87784-765-7 3.50
1. Sermons, American. I. Title.

SCHOFIELD, Joseph Anderson, 1807- 252
53 object Sunday talks to children. Boston, W. A. Wilde Co. [1951] 190 p. 20 cm. [BV4315.S3178] 51-13871
1. Children's sermons. I. Title.

SCHOFIELD, Joseph Anderson, 1897- 252
Dynamic Sunday talks to children. Boston, W. A. Wilde Co. [1955] 184p. 20cm. [BV4315.S3175] 55-9730
1. Children's sermons. I. Title.

SCHWEIZER, Eduard, 1913- 252
God's inescapable nearness. Translated and edited by James W. Cox. Waco, Tex., Word Books [1971] 124 p. 23 cm. Includes bibliographical references. [BV4254.G3S34] 77-134938 3.95
1. Sermons, German—Translation into English. 2. Sermons, English—Translations from German. I. Title.

SESSLER, Jacob John, 1899- 252
Junior character sermons. New York, Revell [1950] 140 p. 20 cm. [BV4315.S465] 50-4726
1. Children's sermons. 2. Virtue. I. Title.

SEWELL, George A. 252
A motif for living and other sermons. New York, Vantage [c.1963] 66p. 21cm. 2.00
I. Title.

SHORT, John, 1896- 252
Triumphant believing. New York, Scribner, 1952. 177 p. 21 cm. [BX9882.S5] 52-8721
1. United Church of Canada—Sermons. 2. Sermons, English—Canada. I. Title.

SIMMONS, William James. 252
One great fellowship. [1st ed.] Nashville, Marshall & Bruce [1967] xi, 158 p. 20 cm. Sermons originally delivered over Station WSM-TV, Nashville, Tenn., on the Community worship program. Bibliographical footnotes. [BV4301.S5] 67-31551
1. Sermons, American. I. Title.

SIMMONS, William James. 252
One great fellowship. [1st ed.] Nashville, Marshall & Bruce [1967] xi, 158 p. 20 cm. Sermons originally delivered over Station WSM-TV, Nashville, Tenn., on the Community worship program. Bibliographical footnotes. [BV4301.S5] 67-31551
1. Sermons, American. I. Title.

SKINNER, Clarence Russell, 1881-1949, ed. 252
A free pulpit in action. Edited by Clarence R. Skinner. Freeport, N.Y., Books for Libraries Press [1971] vi, 328 p. 23 cm. (Essay index reprint series) Reprint of the 1931 ed. Sermons delivered at the Boston Community Church. [BV4241.S545 1971] 71-156718 ISBN 0-8369-2333-2
1. Sermons, American. I. Boston. Community Church. II. Title.

SMITH, Andre. 252
How beautiful : a series of short sermons / Andre Smith. Aberdeen : University Press, 1971. 84 p. ; 19 cm. [BV4253.S725] 75-314125 £0.35
1. Sermons, English—Scotland. I. Title.

SMITH, Daniel, 1907- 252
Worship and remembrance / by Daniel Smith. Neptune, N.J. : Loizeaux Brothers, [1975] p. cm. [BX8800.S55] 75-23215 ISBN 0-87213-790-2
1. Plymouth Brethren—Sermons. 2. Sermons, American. I. Title.

*SMITH, Mabel G. 252
Honey out of the rock. New York, Vantage [1967] 318p. 21cm. 4.95 bds.,
I. Title.

*SPEARS, Gene, Jr. 252
Seventy feet nearer the stars: sermons to help build your church. New York, Vantage [c.1964] 112p. 21cm. 2.50 bds.,
I. Title.

*SPURGEON, C. H. 252
Christ's glorious achievements by C. H. Spurgeon Grand Rapids Baker Book. [1975] 128 p. 20 cm. [BV42.53] ISBN 0-8010-8042-8 1.95 (pbk.)
1. Sermons, American. I. Title.

*SPURGEON, C. H. 252
Twelve sermons on conversion, [by] C. H. Spurgeon. Grand Rapids, Baker Book House, [1974] 147 p. 20 cm. [BV4222] ISBN 0-8010-8027-4. 1.95 (pbk.)
1. Sermons—Addresses, essays, lectures, etc. I. Title.

*SPURGEON, C. H. 252
Twelve sermons on repentance, [by] C. H. Spurgeon. Grand Rapids, Baker Book House, [1974] 131 p. 20 cm. [BV4222] ISBN 0-8010-8028-2 1.95 (pbk.)
1. Sermons—Addresses, essays, lectures, etc. I. Title.

*SPURGEON, C. H. 252
Twelve sermons on various subjects [by] C. H. Spurgeon. Grand Rapids, Baker Book House, [1974] 125 p. 20 cm. [BV4222] ISBN 0-8010-8029-0 1.95 (pbk.)
1. Sermons—Addresses, essays, lectures, etc. I. Title.

STEVENSON, Dwight Eshelman, 1906- 252
Faith takes a name. [1st ed.] New York, Harper [c1954] 189p. 22cm. [BV4253.S77] 53-10979
1. Sermons, American. 2. Christiana—Name. I. Title.

STEVENSON, Herbert F ed. 252
Keswick's triumphant voice; forty-eight outstanding addresses delivered at the Keswick Convention, 1882-1962. Grand Rapids, Zondervan Pub. House [1963] 408 p. col. illus. 23 cm. [BV4487.K5S8] 63-6331
1. Evangelistic sermons. 2. Keswick movement. I. Keswick Convention. II. Title.

STEVENSON, Herbert F., ed. 252
Keswick's triumphant voice; forty-eight outstanding addresses delivered at the Keswick Convention, 1882-1962. Grand Rapids, Mich., Zondervan [c.1963] 408p. col. illus. 23cm. 63-6331 5.95
1. Evangelistic sermons. 2. Keswick movement. I. Keswick Convention. II. Title.

STUEMPFLE, Herman G., comp. 252
Preaching in the witnessing community. Edited by Herman G. Stuempfle, Jr. [Philadelphia, Fortress Press, 1973] xiv, 104 p. 19 cm. Contents.Contents.—Stuempfle, H. G., Jr. Introduction: preaching in the witnessing community.—Doan, G. E. An impotent God?—Achtemeier, P. J. The hidden God.—Sloyan, G. S. The church's missionary call.—Hageman, H. G. Jesus freaks and Christian fools.—Muehl, W. The cult of the publican.—Neuhaus, R. J. Change for the Kingdom's sake.—Napier, D. Of dogs and angels and violins.—Rice, C. An uncommonly common grace.—Wentz, F. K. You are the light of the world.—Vivian, C. T. Peter: the profound Nigger.—Hale, R. J. The Christian and the poor.—Santmire, H. P. The three wise men.—Sittler, J. Evangelism and the care of the earth. Includes bibliographical references. [BV3797.A1S8] 72-91524 ISBN 0-8006-0135-1 2.95
1. Evangelistic sermons. 2. Sermons, American. I. Title.
Contents omitted.

SUNDAY, William Ashley, 1862-1935. 252
The best of Billy Sunday; 17 burning sermons from the most spectacular evangelist the world has ever known. Compiled and edited by John R. Rice. Murfreesboro, Tenn., Sword of the Lord Publishers [1965] 350 p. ports. 21 cm. [BV3797.S8B4] 65-5232
1. Evangelistic sermons. 2. Sermons, American. I. Title.

SUTHERLAND, Robert T 252
We learn to worship God; illustrated by Edwin Pike. Chicago, Moody Prees [1954] 127p. illus. 20cm. [BV4571.S88] 55-24351
1. Children—Religious life. I. Title.

SWEETING, George, 1924- 252
The city; a matter of conscience, and other messages. Chicago, Moody Press [1972] 128 p. 22 cm. [BV4253.S83] 72-77947 ISBN 0-8024-1565-2 2.95
1. Sermons, American. I. Title.

SWEETING, George, 1924- 252
Special sermons for special days : eighteen

condensed sermons for the twentieth century / by George Sweeting. Chicago : Moody Press, c1977. 157 p. ; 22 cm. [BV4254.2.S93] 77-1218 ISBN 0-8024-8206-6 : 2.95
1. Occasional sermons. 2. Sermons, American. I. Title.

*TASSELL, Paul. 252
Outline studies of Jeremiah. Grand Rapids, Mich., Baker Bk. [1968] 60p. 22cm. ($100 sermon lib.) 1.00 pap.,
1. Jeremiah—Sermons. I. Title.

THIS great company : 252
sermons by outstanding preachers of the Christian tradition / selected and edited by David Poling ; foreword by Keith Miller. New Canaan, Conn. : Keats Pub., c1976. xiv, 200 p., [1] leaf of plates : ill. ; 23 cm. Bibliography: p. 200. [BV4241.T47] 74-75977 ISBN 0-87983-123-5 : 4.95
1. Sermons, English. I. Poling, David, 1928-

TILLICH, Paul, 1886- 252
The eternal now. New York, Scribners [1965, c.1956-1963] 185p. 21cm. (SL114) [BV4253.T575] 1.25 pap.,
1. Sermons, American. I. Title.

TILLICH, Paul Johannes Oskar, 252
1886-
The eternal now. New York, Scribners [c.1963] 185p. 21cm. 63-17938 2.95
1. Sermons, American. I. Title.

TO God be the glory; 252
sermons in honor of George Arthur Buttrick. Edited by Theodore A. Gill. Nashville, Abingdon Press [1973] 159 p. 24 cm. Contents.Contents.—Stewart, J. S. To God be the glory!—Robinson, J. A. T. Evil and the God of love.—Read, D. H. C. News from another network.—Ferris, T. P. On leaving home.—Little, G. One thing I do.—Marney, C. Our present higher good.—Steere, D. V. The ultimate underpinning.—Bennett, J. C. The radicalism of Jesus.—Lehmann, P. Which way is left?—Terrien, S. A time to speak.—Williams, G. H. Creatures of a Creator, members of a body, subjects of a kingdom.—Abbey, M. R. Christ's liberating mandate.—Harrelson, W. Resisting and welcoming the new.—Winn, A. C. The plaines and simplest thing in the world.—Buechner, F. Air for two voices.—Buttrick, D. G. The commandment will not change.—Campbell, E. T. Every battle isn't Armageddon.—Farley, E. Boundedness: the provincialist capture of the church of our Lord and Savior Jesus Christ. [BV4241.T63] 73-8690 ISBN 0-687-42233-7 5.50
1. Buttrick, George Arthur, 1892- 2. Sermons, American. I. Buttrick, George Arthur, 1892- II. Gill, Theodore Alexander, 1920- ed.
Contents omitted.

TORREY, Reuben Archer, 1856- 252
1928
The treasury of R. A. Torrey. Introd. by George T. B. Davis. Grand Rapids, Baker Bk. [1967, c.1954] 254p. 20cm. [BV3797.T59] 1.95 pap.,
1. Evangelistic sermons. I. Title.

TRUEBLOOD, David Elton, 1900- 252
The yoke of Christ, and other sermons. [1st ed.] New York, Harper [1958] 192 p. 22 cm. [BV4253.T7] 58-10364
1. Sermons, American. I. Title.

*TRUETT, George Washington, 252
1867-1944.
"Follow thou Me." Grand Rapids, Mich., Baker Book House [1973, c.1959] 241 p. 20 cm. (Minister's paperback library) First published in 1932. [BV4253] ISBN 0-8010-8791-0 pap., 2.95
1. Sermons, American. I. Title.

TUCKER, Julius Lafayette, 252
1895-
God in the shadows, by J. L. Tucker. Nashville, Southern Pub. Association [1972] 63 p. 19 cm. (Better living series) [BV4253.T77] 72-88859 ISBN 0-8127-0067-8
1. Sermons, American. I. Title.

VALLOWE, Ed. F. 252
Revival or ruin. Grand Rapids, Mich., Baker Bk. [c.1963] 91p. 22cm. 1.00 pap.,
I. Title.

VERSTEEG, Robert John 252
The secret life of the Good Samaritan, and other stories. [Nashville, Abingdon, c.1963] 96p. 20cm. 63-7482 2.00 bds.,
1. Sermon stories. I. Title.

VERSTEEG, Robert John. 252
The secret life of the Good Samaritan, and other stories. [New York, Abingdon Press, 1963] 96 p. 20 cm. [BV4307.S7V4] 63-7482
1. Sermon stories. I. Title.

VIRGINIA Council of Churches. 252
Watchers of the springs; a collection of rural life sermons and addresses. Richmond [1950] ix, 132 p. 23 cm. [BV4241.V5] 51-18848
1. Sermons, American. 2. Rural churches. I. Title. II. Title: Rural life sermons.

WALKER, Alan. 252
God is where you are. Grand Rapids, Eerdmans [1962] 128 p. 20 cm. (Preaching for today) [BV4253.W32] 62-5296
1. Sermons, Australian. I. Title.

WALKER, Alan 252
God is where you are. Grand Rapids, Mich., Eerdmans [c.1962] 128p. 20cm. (Preaching for today) 62-5296 2.00 bds.,
1. Sermons, Australian. I. Title.

WALKER, William Bruce 252
What think ye of Christ, and other evangelistic sermons. Grands Rapids, Mich., Baker Bk. [c.] 1962. 69p. 22cm. 1.00 pap.,
I. Title.

WALLIS, Charles Langworthy, 252
1921- ed.
A treasury of story-sermons for children. [1st ed.] New York, Harper [1957] 266p. 22cm. [BV4315.W27] 57-7343
1. Children's sermons. I. Title.

WALLIS, Charles Langworthy, 252
1921- ed.
A treasury of story-sermons for children. [1st ed.] New York, Harper [1957] 266 p. 22 cm. [BV4315.W27] 57-7343
1. Children's sermons. I. Title.

WALLIS, Charles Langworthy, 252
1921-
A treasury of story sermons for children edited by Charles L. Wallis. Grand Rapids: ,Baker Book, [1975] c1957. xx., 266 p.; 20 cm. [BV4315.W27] 57-7343 ISBN 0-8010-9556-5 3.50 (pbk.)
1. Children's sermons. I. Title.

WARNER, Amos Griswold, 1861- 252
1900.
Lay sermons. With a biographical sketch by George Elliott Howard. Baltimore, Johns Hopkins Press, 1904. [New York, Johnson Reprint Corp., 1973] p. Original ed. issued as Notes supplementary to the Johns Hopkins studies in historical and political science. Bibliography: p. [BV4310.W36 1973] 73-3355 pap. 4.00
1. Universities and colleges—Sermons. 2. Sermons, American. I. Title. II. Series: Johns Hopkins University. Studies in historical and political science. Notes supplementary.

WATT, John A. 252
The old, old story from the Old Testament; a series of addresses by John Watt. New York, Loizeaux Bros. [1954?] 192 p. 19 cm. [BS1151.5.W37] 75-304078
1. Bible. O.T.—Sermons. 2. Sermons, American. I. Title.

WEIST, Carl Sireno, 1886- 252
Fire on a drumhead; a year of sermons for girls and boys. [1st ed.] New York, Harper [1955] 157p. 20cm. [BV4315.W386] 55-6790
1. Children's sermons. I. Title.

WELCH, Reuben. 252
When you run out of fantastic ... persevere / Reuben Welch. [Nashville] : Impact Books, c1976. 147 p. ; 22 cm. [BS2775.4.W44] 76-20999 ISBN 0-914850-42-3 : 4.95
1. Bible. N.T. Hebrews—Sermons. 2. Sermons, American. I. Title.

*WESBERRY, James P. 252
When hell trembles and other sermons for revival [by] James P. Wesberry Grand Rapids, Baker Book House [1974] 118 p. 20 cm. [BV3797] ISBN 0-8010-9558-1 3.95
1. Sermons, American. I. Title.

WHITE, John Wesley. 252
Mission control. Grand Rapids, Mich., Zondervan Pub. House [1971] 184 p. 22 cm. [BV3797.W425] 76-146567 3.95
1. Evangelistic sermons. 2. Sermons, English—Canada. I. Title.

WHITESELL, Faris Daniel, 252
1895- comp.
Great expository sermons, compiled by Faris D. Whitesell. Westwood, N.J., F. H. Revell Co.[1964] 190 p. 21 cm. [BV4241.W5] 64-20188
1. Sermons. I. Title.

WHITESELL, Faris Daniel, 252
1895- comp.
Great expository sermons. Westwood, N. J., Revell [c.1964] 190p. 21cm. 64-20188 3.50 bds.,
1. Sermons. I. Title.

WOMACK, Don L., comp. 252
Let the fire fall! Compiled by Don L. Womack. Nashville, Broadman Press [1968] 143 p. 22 cm. [BV3797.A1W6] 68-28361
1. Evangelistic sermons. 2. Sermons, American. I. Title.

YOUNGDAHL, Reuben K 1911- 252
The unconquerable partnership. Rock Island, Ill., Augustana Press [1960] 258 p. 21 cm. [BX8066.Y68U5] 041 60-16828
1. Lutheran Church — Sermons. 2. Sermons, American. I. Title.

BURNS, Jabez, 1805-1876. 252.002
300 sermon sketches on Old and New Testament texts Grand Rapids, Kregel Publications, 1961. 394 p. 24 cm. "Originally published in a volume entitled The pulpit encyclopedia." [BV4223.B85] 61-14902
1. Sermons — Outlines. I. Title.

HALLOCK, Gerard Benjamin 252.002
Fleet, 1856-
Five hundred sermon themes. Westwood, N. J., Revell [1952] 448 p. 21 cm. [BV4223.H18] 52-11091
1. Sermons—Outlines. I. Title.

FANT, Clyde E., comp. 252'.008
20 centuries of great preaching; an encyclopedia of preaching [by Clyde E Fant, Jr. and William M. Pinson Jr. Donald E. Hammer, research associate. Waco, Tex., Word Books [1971] 13 v. illus. 24 cm. Includes bibliographies. [BV4241.F34] 78-156697
1. Sermons. 2. Preaching—History. I. Pinson, William M., joint comp. II. Title.

MACPHERSON, Ian, 1912- 252'.008
comp.
More sermons I should like to have preached, edited by Ian Macpherson. Westwood, N.J., F. H. Revell Co. [1967] 178 p. 20 cm. Contents.Contents.—What is vital in life, by G. T. Bellhouse.—The perfect worker, by G. N. M. Collins.—The sin of prayerlessness, by G. B. Duncan.—The wind of the spirit, by R. A. Finlayson.—The unshaken kingdom, by D. MacLeod.—The psalm of the two ways, by G. C. Morgan.—The proof of greatness, by K. E. Roach.—How to be saved, by W. E. Sangster.—Sin and forgiveness, by A. Ross.—The power of His Resurrection, by J. S. Stewart.—His greatest hour, by D. P. Thomson.—I have kept the faith, by J. K. Thomson.—Blast-off, by J. H. Withers.—Our unrestricted God, by A. S. Wood.—Treasure in earthen vessels, by G. Kennedy.—On being finely aware and richly responsible, by R. J. McCracken.—Let's celebrate! By D. A. MacLennan.—On explaining everything, by D. H. C. Read.—Shepherd, guide, and host, by W. G. Scroggie.—The water of the well at Bethlehem, by G. S. Wakefield. [BV4241.M329 1967] 67-9264
1. Sermons, English. I. Title.

MONTEFIORE, Hugh, comp. 252'.008
For God's sake; sermons from Great St. Mary's. [1st American ed.] Philadelphia, Fortress Press [1969, c1968] 287 p. 18 cm. First published in 1968 under title: Sermons from Great St. Mary's. [BV4241.M57 1969] 71-84544
1. Sermons, English. I. Cambridge, Eng. St. Mary the Great (Church) II. Title.

SMUCKER, Donovan 252.'.008
Ebersole, 1915- comp.
Rockefeller chapel sermons of recent years, compiled by Donovan E. Smucker. Chicago, University of Chicago Press [1967] xx, 226 p. 23 cm. [BV4241.S57] 66-30215
1. Sermons, American. I. Chicago. University. Rockefeller Memorial Chapel. II. Title.

*SPURGEON, Charles 252'.008
Haddon, 1834-1892.
Charles H. Spurgeon. Introd. by Andrew W. Blackwood. Grand Rapids, Baker Book House [1972, c.1949] 256 p. 19 cm. (Great pulpit masters) [BV4241] pap., 2.95
1. Sermons, English—Collections. I. Title.

TREASURY of the world's 252'.008
great sermons / compiled by Warren W. Wiersbe. Grand Rapids : Kregel Publications, c1977. x, 662 p. ; 26 cm. Based on The world's great sermons, compiled by G. Kleiser, and Modern sermons by world scholars, edited by R. Scott and W. C. Stiles. Includes indexes. [BV4241.T73] 77-72366 ISBN 0-8254-4011-4 : 12.95
1. Sermons. I. Wiersbe, Warren W. II. Kleiser, Grenville, 1868-1953, comp. The world's great sermons. III. Scott, Robert, 1860- ed. Modern sermons by world scholars.

TURNBULL, Ralph G. ed. 252.008
If I had only one sermon to preach, ed. by Ralph G. Turnbull. Grand Rapids, Baker Bk. [1966] 151p. 21cm. [BV4241.T83] 66-18304 2.95
1. Sermons, English. I. Title.

ASSOCIATION Press, New 252.0082
York.
Words to change lives; a kaleidoscopic view of contemporary religious expression. New York [c1957] 128p. 16cm. (An Association Press reflection book) [BV4241.A76] 57-5494
1. Sermons, American (Selections: Extracts, etc.) I. Title.

BEST sermons 252.0082
x- 1966-1968 New York Trident Pr. v. 22-25cm. irregular. Ed.: 1944- G. P. Butler Vols. for 1959-68 called "Protestant edition" [BV4241.B38] 7.95
1. Sermons. I. Butler, George Paul, 1900- ed.

BEST sermons; 252.0082
v.9. 1964. Protestant ed. Princeton, N.J., Van Nostrand [c.1964] 321p. 24cm. irregular. Ed.: 1964--G. P. Butler. 44-51581 5.95 bds.,
1. Sermons. I. Butler, George Paul, 1900- ed.

BEST sermons; 252.0082
v.8. 1962. Protestant Ed. Ed. by G. Paul Butler. Foreword by Bishop Gerald Kennedy. Princeton, N.J., Van Nostrand [c.1962] 328p. 24cm. 44-51581 5.95
1. Sermons. I. Butler, George Paul, 1900- ed.

DASKAM, Max F ed. 252.0082
Sermons from an ecumenical pulpit. Boston, Starr King Press [1956] 254p. 22cm. [BV4241.D28] 56-10078
1. Sermons, American. I. Title.

ENGSTROM, Theodore 252.0082
Wilhelm, 1916- ed.
Great sermons from master preachers of all ages. First series. Grand Rapids, Zondervan Pub. House [1951] 180 p. illus. 20 cm. [BV4241.E673] 51-11553
1. Sermons. I. Title.

MACPHERSON, Ian, 1912- 252.0082
ed.
Sermons I should like to have preached [Westwood, N.J.] Revell [1965, c.1964] 131p. 20cm. [BV4241.M33] 65-3846 2.95 bds.,
1. Sermons, English. I. Title.

MEAD, Frank Spencer, 252.0082
1898- ed.
The pulpit in the South; sermons of today. New York, Revell [1950] 220 p. 21 cm. [BV4241.M4] 50-11379
1. Sermons, American. I. Title.

MOTTER, Alton M ed. 252.0082
Great preaching today; a collection of 25 sermons delivered at the Chicago Sunday Evening Club. [1st ed.] New York, Harper [c1955] 255p. 22cm. [BV4241.M72] 54-12330
1. Sermons, English. I. Title.

MOTTER, Alton M ed. 252.0082
Sunday evening sermons; fifteen selected addresses delivered before the noted Chicago Sunday Evening Club. Introd. by Harry Emerson Fosdick. [1st ed.] New York, Harper [1952] 191 p. 20 cm. [BV4241.M73] 52-11443
1. Sermons, American. I. Title.

PULPIT digest. 252.0082
The best from Pulpit digest. Great Neck, N.Y., Pulpit Digest Pub. Co. [1951] 319 p. 21 cm. [BV4241.P763] 51-2778
1. Sermons, American. I. Title.

SADLER, William Alan, 252.0082
ed.
Master sermons through the ages. [1st ed.] New York, Harper & Row [1963] 228 p. 22 cm. [BV4241.S2] 63-7608
1. Sermons. I. Title.

SADLER, William Alan, 252.0082
ed.
Master sermons through the ages. New York, Harper [c.1963] 228p. 22cm. 63-7608 3.95
1. Sermons. I. Title.

WALLIS, Charles 252.0082
Langworthy, 1921- ed.
Notable sermons from Protestant pulpits. New York, Abingdon Press [1958] 206 p. 23 cm. [BV4241.W3] 58-9526
1. Sermons, American. I. Title.

AELFRIC, Abbot of 252'.00924
Eynsham.
Homilies of AElfric: a supplementary collection, being twenty-one full homilies of his middle and later career for the most part no previously edited with some shorter pieces mainly passages added to the second and third series; edited from all the known manuscripts with introduction, notes, Latin sources and a glossary by John C. Pope. London, New York [etc.] Oxford U. P. for the Early English Text Society, 1967- v. fronts., plates (facsims.). 22 1/2 cm. Includes bibliographical references. [PR1119.A2 no. 259, etc.] (v.1 67-90497
1. Sermons, Anglo- Saxon. I. (Early English Text Society. [Publications. Original series] no.

259) v. 1: II. Pope, John Collins, 1904- ed. III. Title.

FERRY, John G comp. 252'.00971
Outstanding sermons from Canadian pulpits, edited by John G. Ferry. Vancouver, Evergreen Press, c1966. x, 149 p. ports. 23 cm. unpriced (C 67-4250) [BV4241.F46] 68-75081
1. Sermons, English—Canada. I. Title.

FERRY, John G., comp. 252'.00971
Outstanding sermons from Canadian pulpits, edited by John G. Ferry. Vancouver, Evergreen Press, c1966. x, 149 p. ports. 23 cm. [BV4241.F46] 68-75081
1. Sermons, English—Canada. I. Title.

BRITE Divinity School. 252'.00973
The word we preach; sermons in honor of Dean Elmer D. Henson, by faculty and trustees of Brite Divinity School, Texas Christian University. Edited by Hunter Beckelhymer. [Fort Worth, Texas Christian University Press, c1970] xi, 149 p. port. 24 cm. Contents.Contents.—A tribute, by J. M. Moody.—Our Father, who art in heaven, by W. O. Harrison.—This Jesus whom you crucified, by H. Beckelhymer.—The meaning of Easter, by M. J. Suggs.—The family of God, by J. W. Stewart.—What matters is faith, by W. D. Hall.—The full blessing of Christ's gospel, by A. T. DeGroot.—The citadel of hope, by G. Routt.—Under new management, by N. J. Robison.—The marks of a Christian, by W. R. Baird.—Making your life count, by R. A. Olsen.—Between God and Caesar, by H. L. Lunger.—The problem of grief, by C. H. Sanders.—Go placidly amid the noise and haste, by G. T. Walker.—Christianity—A spectator sport? By G. A. Shelton.—On the way, by R. A. Hoehn.—A people for the future, by G. L. Smith.—A ministry without hocus-pocus, by W. R. Naff.—The ministry of compassion, by C. F. Kemp.—Violent physicians, by M. D. Bryant.—Treasure in earthen vessels, by W. E. Tucker. Includes bibliographical references. [BV4241.B627] 79-143563
1. Sermons, American. I. Henson, Elmer D., 1901- II. Beckelhymer, Hunter, ed. III. Title.

*MOODY, Dwight Lyman, 252'.00973
1837-1899.
Dwight L. Moody. Introduction by Charles R. Erdman. Grand Rapids, Mich., Baker Book House [1972, c.1949] 256 p. 19 cm. (Great pulpit masters) [BV3797] ISBN 0-8010-5911-9 pap., 2.95
1. Evangelistic sermons—Collections. I. Title.

PREACHING the gospel 252'.00973
/ Henry J. Young, editor ; with contributions by William Holmes Borders ... [et al.]. Philadelphia : Fortress Press, c1976. vi, 89 p. ; 22 cm. [BV4241.5.P73] 75-36449 ISBN 0-8006-1223-X pbk. : 2.95
1. Sermons, American—Afro-American authors. I. Young, Henry J. II. Borders, William Holmes, 1905-

STEDMAN, Ray C. 252'.00973
Growth of the body : [Acts 13-20] / Ray C. Stedman. Santa Ana, Calif. : Vision House Publishers, c1976. 202 p. ; 21 cm. [BS2625.4.S74] 76-47845 ISBN 0-88449-059-9 : 2.95
1. Bible. N.T. Acts XIII-XX—Sermons. 2. Sermons, American. I. Title.

SUNDAY, William 252'.00973
Ashley, 1862-1935.
Billy Sunday speaks. Introd. by Oral Roberts. Edited by Karen Gullen. New York, Chelsea House Publishers, 1970. 217 p. illus., ports. 25 cm. [BV3797.S8B48] 76-127017 6.95
1. Evangelistic sermons. 2. Sermons, American. I. Title.

WIRT, Sherwood Eliot, 252'.00973
comp.
Great preaching; evangelical messages by contemporary Christians. Edited by Sherwood Eliot Wirt and Viola Blake. Waco, Tex., Word Books [1970] 173 p. 23 cm. Contents.Contents.—When Christ becomes real, by M. S. Augsburger.—From Galilee to Manhattan, by D. H. C. Read.—God's universe, by G. B. Wilson.—"I am ...," by T. Rees.—The rending of the veil, by M. L. Loane.—The Holy Spirit in action, by O. C. J. Hoffmann.—Made, marred, mended, by B. Graham.—The third he, by H. J. Ockenga.—Repent, by J. E. Haggai.—This business of being converted, by R. G. Turnbull.—You can be sure, by D. J. Kennedy.—Touched by Jesus, by O. Roberts.—The burning heart, by H. O. Jones.—The Christian extra, by P. S. Rees.—Living in high gear, by P. M. Nagano.—Redeeming the time, by S. F. Olford.—Christian responsibility to a changing world, by R. B. Munger.—The source of our life, by E. L. R. Elson.—The wasteland and the springs, by G. Kennedy.—A living hope, by L. Ford.—The crown of life, by W. Fitch.—Coming! By W. A. Criswell. [BV4241.W57] 76-134253 4.50
1. Sermons, American. I. Blake, Viola, 1921- joint comp. II. Title.

WOMEN and the world, 252'.00973
sermons / edited by Helen Gray Crotwell. Philadelphia : Fortress Press, c1977. p. cm. [BV4241.W65] 77-78627 ISBN 0-8006-1318-X pbk. : 4.25
1. Sermons, American—Women authors. I. Crotwell, Helen Gray, 1925-

CONIARIS, Anthony M. 252'.01'9
Gems from the Sunday gospels in the Orthodox Church : talks based on the yearly cycle of Sunday Gospel lessons / by Anthony M. Coniaris. Minneapolis : Light and Life Pub. Co., [1975- v. ; 21 cm. Contents.Contents.—v. 1. January through June. [BX330.C62] 74-81199 ISBN pbk. : 3.95
1. Orthodox Eastern Church—Sermons. 2. Sermons, English. I. Title.

MAKRAKES, Apostolos, 252.019
1831-1905.
A revelation of treasure hid, together with three important lectures ... and apostolical canons respecting baptism; translated out of the original Greek by D. Cummings. Chicago, Orthodox Christian Educational Society, 1952. 80p. illus. 23cm. [BX616.M3] 53-8789
1. Orthodox Eastern Church, Greek—Addresses, essays, lectures. I. Title.

ALBION, Gordon, 1906- 252.02
Christians awake. London, New York, Longmans, Green [1957] 294p. 19cm. [BX1756.A52C4] 57-4937
1. Catholic Church—Sermons. 2. Sermons, English. I. Title.

AUGUSTINUS, Aurelius, 252.02
Saint, Bp. of Hippo.
Selected sermons. Translated and edited by Quincy Howe, Jr. [1st ed.] New York, Holt, Rinehart and Winston [1966] xix, 234 p. 22 cm. [BR65.A52E6] 6610265
I. Howe, Quincy, 1934 — ed. and tr. II. Title.

AUGUSTINUS, Aurelius, 252.02
Saint, Bp. of Hippo.
Selected sermons. Tr., ed. by Quincy Howe, Jr. New York, Holt [c.1966] xix, 234p. 22cm. [BR65.A52E6] 66-10265 6.00
I. Howe, Quincy, 1934- ed. and tr. II. Title.

BECK, Frederick O. 252'.02
The faith for all seasons; the main tenets of the Church explained in the light of Vatican II, arranged according to the liturgical year, by Frederick O. Beck. St. Charles, Ill., St. Charles' House, 1971. 223 p. 22 cm. [BX1756.B3497F3] 71-149652 5.25
1. Catholic Church—Sermons. 2. Church year sermons. 3. Sermons, American. I. Title.

BENSON, Robert Hugh, 1871- 252.02
1914.
The friendship of Christ; [sermons] Westminster, Md., Newman Press, 1955. 167p. 20cm. [BX1756.B4F7 1955] 55-8666
1. Catholic Church—Sermons. 2. Sermons, English. I. Title.

BONAVENTURA, Saint, 252'.02
Cardinal, 1221-1274.
Rooted in faith: homilies to a contemporary world. Translation and introductory essay by Marigwen Schumacher. Foreword by Peter Damian Fehlner. Chicago, Franciscan Herald Press [1974] xxxii, 133 p. illus. 21 cm. [BX1756.B58S413] 73-19533 ISBN 0-8199-0465-1 5.95
1. Catholic Church—Sermons. 2. Sermons, Latin—Translations into English. 3. Sermons, English—Translations from Latin. I. Title. Contents omitted.

BRENNAN, Gerald Thomas, 252.02
1898-
Angel food for Jack and Jill; little talks to little folks. Milwaukee, Bruce [1950] viii, 113 p. 20 cm. (His The Angel food series) [BX1756.Z9B67] 50-12691
1. Children's sermons. 2. Catholic Church—Sermons. 3. Sermons, American. I. Title.

BRENNAN, Gerald Thomas, 252.02
1898-
Angel food time; little talks to little folks. Milwaukee, Bruce Pub. Co. [1953] 126p. illus. 20cm. (His The angel food series) [BX1756.Z9B72] 53-3704
1. Children's sermons. 2. Catholic Church—Sermons. 3. Sermons, American. I. Title.

BUDDY, Charles Francis, 252.02
Bp.
The thoughts of His heart, and selected writings. [Paterson? N. J.] 1954. 363p. illus. 21cm. [BX1756.B824T5] 54-30269
1. Occasional sermons. 2. Catholic Church—Sermons. 3. Sermons, American. I. Title.

BURGHARDT, Walter J 252.02
All lost in wonder; sermons on theology and life. Westminster, Md., Newman Press, 1960. 220p. 23cm. [BX1756.B828A4] 60-10724
1. Catholic Church—Sermons. 2. Sermons, American. I. Title.

CARBONI, Romolo, Abp. 252.02
An apostolic delegate speaks: addresses of Romolo Carbom, apostolic delegate to Australia, New Zealand, and Oceania, 1953-1959. Paterson, N. J., St. Anthony Guild Pr. [c.1961] 537p. 60-16431 6.00
1. Catholic Church—Addresses, essays, lectures. I. Title.

CROCK, Clement Henry, 252.02
1890-
Encyclopedia of preaching. New York, J. F. Wagner [1956,(1955] 1 v. 24 cm. Each pt. published also separately. [BX1756.C7E5] 57-2369
1. Catholic Church—Sermons. 2. Sermons, American. I. Title.
Contents omitted.

DEVINE, George, 1941- 252'.02
If I were to preach. New York, Alba House [1974- v. 21 cm. Contents.Contents.—A. Liturgical homiletic aids for cycle A. Includes bibliographical references. [BX1756.D47I3] 74-9914 ISBN 0-8189-0297-3
1. Catholic Church—Sermons. 2. Church year sermons. 3. Sermons, American. I. Title.

DEVINE, George, 1941- 252'.02 s
Liturgical homiletic aids for cycle A. New York, Alba House [1974] xvi, 192 p. 21 cm. (His If I were to preach, A) Includes bibliographical references. [BX1756.D47I3 vol. 1] 251'.08 74-9915 ISBN 0-8189-0293-0
1. Catholic Church—Sermons. 2. Church year sermons. 3. Sermons, American. I. Title.

DEVINE, George, 1941- 252'.02 s
Liturgical-homiletic aids for cycle B / by George Devine. New York : Alba House, [1975] 196 p. ; 21 cm. (His If I were to preach ; v. 2) [BX1756.D47I3 vol. 2] 251'.08 75-15822 ISBN 0-8189-0320-1 : 4.95
1. Catholic Church—Sermons. 2. Church year sermons. 3. Sermons, American. I. Title.

DEVINE, George, 1941- 252'.02 s
Liturgical-homiletic aids for cycle C / George Devine. New York : Alba House, c1976. p. cm. (His If I were to preach ; v. 3) Includes bibliographical references. [BX1756.D47I3 vol. 3] 251'.08 75-45320 ISBN 0-8189-0324-4 pbk. : 4.95
1. Catholic Church—Sermons. 2. Church year sermons. 3. Sermons, American. I. Title.

DRINKWATER, Francis 252.02
Harold, 1886-
Sermon notes on the Sunday propers. Westminster, Md., Newman Press, 1950. 119 p. 19 cm. [BX1756.A 1D7] 51-29674
1. Catholic Church—Sermons—Outlines. 2. Propers (Liturgy) I. Title.

*ELLIS, J. comp. 252.02
Sermons in a nutshell; outlines for sermons and addresses, comp., arranged by J. Ellis. Grand Rapids, Mich., Baker Bk. [1968] 66p. 22cm. ($1.00 sermon lib.) 1.00 pap.,
1. Sermons—Outlines. I. Title.

ESCRIVA de Balaguer, 252'.02
Jose Maria, 1902-
Christ is passing by : homilies / Josemaria Escriva de Balaguer. Chicago : Scepter Press, [1974] 276 p., [18] leaves of plates : ill. ; 22 cm. Translation of Es Cristo que pasa. Includes bibliographical references and indexes. [BX1756.E77E813] 74-78783
1. Catholic Church—Sermons. 2. Sermons, English—Translations from Spanish. 3. Sermons, Spanish—Translations into English. I. Title.

GIBBONS, James, 252'.02
Cardinal, 1834-1921.
A retrospect of fifty years. New York, Arno Press, 1972 [c1916] 2 v. in 1. 22 cm. (Religion in America, series II) [BX890.G47 1972] 79-38447 ISBN 0-405-04066-0
I. Title.

GROUES, Henri, 1910- 252.02
Man is your brother; television talks and sermons by the Abbe Pierre [pseud.] Translated by Ronald Matthews. Westminster, Md., Newman Press, 1958. 135p. 19cm. 'Originally published in 1956 under the title, Vers Phomme.' [BX1756.G77V43] 58-4403
1. Catholic Church—Sermons. 2. Sermons, French—Translations into English. 3. Sermons, English—Translations from French. I. Title.

HOSTY, Thomas J. 252.02
Good morning, boys and girls! Milwaukee, Bruce Pub. Co. [1952] 146 p. 21 cm. [BX1756.Z9H58] 52-4505
1. Children's sermons. 2. Catholic Church—Sermons. 3. Sermons, American. I. Title.

KNOX, Ronald Arbuthnott 252.02
Pastoral sermons. Edited, with an introd., by Philip Caraman. New York, Sheed & Ward [1960] xvi, 532p. 23cm. (bibl. foonotes) 60-16137 8.50
1. Catholic Church—Sermons. 2. Sermons, English. I. Title.

KNOX, Ronald Arbuthnott, 252.02
1888-
The Gospel in slow motion. New York, Sheed & Ward, 1950. x, 182 p. 21 cm. [BX1756.K68G6] 50-10287
1. Catholic Church—Sermons. 2. Sermons, English. I. Title.

KNOX, Ronald Arbuthnott, 252.02
1888-
Stimuli. London and New York, Sheed and Ward [1951] ix, 148 p. 21 cm. [BX1756.K68S8 1951] 51-5460
1. Catholic Church—Sermons. 2. Sermons, English. I. Title.

KNOX, Ronald Arbuthnott, 252.02
1888-1957.
Occasional sermons. Edited, with an introd., by Philip Caraman. New York, Sheed & Ward [1960] xv, 426 p. 22 cm. Bibliographical references included in footnotes. [BX1756.K68O3 1960 a] 60-14646
1. Catholic Church—Sermons. 2. Sermons, English. I. Title.

KNOX, Ronald Arbuthnott, 252.02
1888-1957.
Stimuli. New York, Sheed and Ward, 1951. 214 p. 20 cm. [BX1756.K68S8 1951a] 51-7176
1. Catholic Church—Sermons. 2. Sermons, English. I. Title.

KNOX, Ronald Arbuthnott, 252.02
1888-1957
University sermons, together with sermons preached on variousoccasions. Ed., introd. by Philip Caraman. New York, Sheed [1964, c.1963] xiii, 522p. 22cm. 64-10797 9.50
1. Catholic Church—Sermons. 2. Sermons, English. I. Caraman, Philip, 1911- ed. II. Title.

LELEN, Joseph Mary, Rev., 252.02
1873-
The gospel of a country pastor; sketches and sermons, by the Rev. J. M. Lelen. St. Louis, B. Herder [1962] xvi 179p. 20cm. 22-12182 2.95
I. Title.

MCNALLY, James J 252.02
Until the day dawns. New York, J. F. Wagner [1956] 244p. 21cm. Sermons. [BX1756.M258U5] 56-3021
1. Church year sermons. 2. Catholic Church—Sermons. 3. Sermons, American. I. Title.

MANTON, Joseph E 1904- 252.02
Pennies from a poor box. Foreword by Richard Cardinal Cushing. [Boston] St. Paul Editions [1962] 566p. 22 cm. [BX1756.M2924P4] 62-14507
1. Catholic Church—Sermons. 2. Sermons, American. I. Title.

MILLER, Charles Edward, 252.02
1929-
Announcing the good news; homilies on the "A" cycle of readings for Sundays and holy days [by] Charles E. Miller, Oscar J. Miller, and Michael M. Roebert. Staten Island, N.Y., Alba House [1971] xii, 196 p. 21 cm. [BX1756.A2M55] 74-169144 ISBN 0-8189-0215-9 3.95
1. Catholic Church—Sermons. 2. Sermons, American. I. Miller, Oscar J., 1913- II. Roebert, Michael M. III. Title.

MILLER, Charles Edward, 252'.02
1929-
Breaking the bread; homilies on the "B" cycle of readings for Sundays and holy days [by] Charles E. Miller, Oscar J. Miller [and] Michael M. Roebert. Staten Island, N.Y., Alba House [1972] xi, 214 p. 21 cm. [BX1756.A2M56] 72-6155 ISBN 0-8189-0254-X 3.95
1. Catholic Church—Sermons. 2. Sermons, American. I. Miller, Oscar J., 1913- II. Roebert, Michael M. III. Title.

MILLER, Charles Edward, 252'.02
1929-
Living in Christ; sacramental and occasional homilies [by] Charles E. Miller. New York, Alba House [1974] 121 p. 21 cm. Includes bibliographical references. [BV4254.2.M53] 73-22092 2.95 (pbk.)
1. Catholic Church—Sermons. 2. Occasional sermons. 3. Sermons, American. I. Title.

MOHR, Heinrich, 1874- 252.02
God and the soul; sermons for the Sundays of the year. Translated by F. J. Klemmer. St.

Louis, Herder, 1950. viii, 315 p. 21 cm. Catholic Church -- Sermons. Translation of Die Seele im Herrgottswinkel. [BX1756.M59S44] 50-3069
1. Church year sermons. 2. Sermons. German — Translations into English. 3. Sermons, English — Translations from German. I. Title.

NEWMAN, John Henry, Cardinal, 1801-1890. 252.02
The parting of friends; a sermon preached on the anniversary of the consecration of a chapel. Westminster, Md., Newman [1962, c.1961] 23p. 62-1136 1.50 bds.,
1. Farewell sermons. I. Title.

NEWMAN, John Henry, Cardinal, 1801-1890. 252.02
Faith and prejudice, and other unpublished sermons. Edited by the Birmingham Oratory. New York, Sheed & Ward [1956] 128p. 21cm. [BX1756.N5F3] 56-9529
1. Catholic Church—Sermons. 2. Sermons, English. I. Title.

NEWMAN, John Henry, Cardinal, 1801-1890. 252.02
Sermons preached on various occasions. Westminster, Md., Christian Classics, inc., 1968. xi, 337p. 21cm. (Works of Cardinal Newman) [BX890.N458 1968] 68-24032 8.00
1. Catholic Church—Sermons. 2. Sermons, English. I. Title.
Publisher's address: 205 Willis St., Westminster, Md. 21157

NEWMAN, John Henry, Cardinal, 1801-1890. 252.02
Discourses addressed to mixed congregations. Westminister, Md., Christian Classics, 1966. viii, 376 p. 21 cm. (His Works) Reprints of the edition published in 1902. [BX1756.N5D5] 66-20431
1. Catholic Church — Sermons. 2. Sermons, English. I. Title.

NEWMAN, John Henry, Cardinal, 1801-1890 252.02
Discourses addressed to mixed congregations. Westminister, Md., 21157 Christian Classics, [205 Willis St.] 1966. viii, 376p. 21cm. (His Works) Reprints of the ed. pub. in 1902 [BX1756.N5D5] 66-20431 8.00
1. Catholic Church—Sermons. 2. Sermons, English. I. Title.

O'SULLIVAN, Kevin. 252'.02
The Sunday readings, "cycle C" (3); an explanation and application of the Sunday readings. Chicago, Franciscan Herald Press [1973] vii, 437 p. 24 cm. "Text of the Old and New Testaments ... from the Revised Standard version Bible, Catholic edition." [BS391.2.O8] 74-141766 ISBN 0-87236-312-0 7.50
1. Catholic Church—Sermons. 2. Bible—Liturgical lessons, English. 3. Church year sermons. 4. Sermons, American. I. Catholic Church. Liturgy and ritual. Lectionary (1969). English. Selections. 1973. II. Title.

RAHNER, Karl, 1904- 252.02
Biblical homilies. [Translated by Desmond Forristal and Richard Strachan. New York] Herder and Herder [1966] 191 p. 21 cm. Delivered in the university church, Innsbruck, 1953-1958. [BX1756.R25B53] 66-24386
1. Catholic Church—Sermons. 2. Sermons, German—Translations into English. 3. Sermons, English—Translations from German. I. Title.

RAHNER, Karl, 1904- 252.02
Biblical homilies. [Translated by Desmond Forristal and Richard Strachan. New York] Herder and Herder [1966] 191 p. 21 cm. Delivered in the university church, Innsbruck, 1953-1958. [BX1756.R25B53] 66-24386
1. Catholic Church—Sermons. 2. Sermons, German—Translations into English. 3. Sermons, English—Translations from German. I. Title.

SATOLLI, Francesco, Cardinal, 1839-1910. 252'.02
Loyalty to church and state. New York, Arno Press, 1972 [c1895] 249 p. port. 22 cm. (Religion in America, series II) [BX890.S3 1972] 71-38461 ISBN 0-405-04082-2
I. Title.

SAVAGE, Thomas G. 252'.02
And now a word from our Creator [by] Thomas G. Savage. Chicago, Loyola University Press [1972] xix, 280 p. illus. 24 cm. [BX1756.Z8S28] 72-1370 ISBN 0-8294-0213-6 5.95
1. Catholic Church—Sermons. 2. Universities and colleges—Sermons. 3. Sermons, American. I. Title.

SHEEN, Fulton John, Bp., 1895- 252.02
Footprints in a darkened forest [by] Fulton J. Sheen. [1st ed.] New York, Meredith Press [1967] 272 p. 24 cm. [BX1756.S45F6] 67-16514
1. Catholic Church—Sermons. 2. Sermons, American. I. Title.

SLOYAN, Gerard Stephen, 1919- 252.02
Nothing of yesterday preaches; homilies for contemporaries [by] Gerard S. Sloyan. [New York] Herder & Herder [1966] 256p. 22cm. [BX1756.S58N6] 66-26677 4.95
1. Catholic Church—Sermons. 2. Sermons, American. 3. Church year sermons. I. Title.

TAULER, Johannes, 1300(ca.)-1361. 252.02
Spiritual conferences. Translated and edited by Eric Colledge and Sister M. Jane. St. Louis, Herder [1961] 283 p. 21 cm. (Cross and crown series of spirituality, no. 20) "Translation of selected sermons compiled from Die Predigten Taulers, published ... 1910, in the series: Deutsche Texte des Mittelaiters, vol. xi." [BV5080.T257] 61-15363
1. Sermons, German — Middle High German — Translations into English. 2. Sermons, English — Translations from German — Middle High German. I. Title.

TAULER, Johannes, 1300 (ca.)-1361 252.02
Spiritual conferences. Tr. [from German] and ed. by Eric Colledge, Sister M. Jane. St. Louis, Herder [c.1961] 283p. (Cross and crown ser. of spirituality, no. 20) 61-15363 4.25
1. Sermons. German—Middle High German—Translations into English. 2. Sermons, English—Translations from German—Middle High German. I. Title.

*TONNE, Arthur J. 252.02
Object talks [Emporia, Kan., Didde Print., c.1964] 50p. illus. 21cm. .75 pap.,
I. Title.

VANN, Gerald, 1906- 252.02
The high green hill. [Essays and addresses] New York, Sheed and Ward, 1951. viii, 136 p. 20 cm. [BX890.V265] 51-10194
1. Catholic Church — Addresses, essays, lectures. I. Title.

VIANNEY, Jean Baptiste Marie, Saint 252.02
The sermons of the Cure of Ars. Translated [from the French] by Una Morrissy, with a special foreword to the English translation by Lancelot Sheppard. Chicago, H. Regnery Co., [c.]1960. xxii, 195p. 22cm. 60-7921 4.00
1. Catholic Church—Sermons. 2. Sermons, French—Translations into English. 3. Sermons, English—Translations from French. I. Title.

WIMBLEDON, R. 252.02
Wimbledon's sermon: Redde rationem villicationis tue; a Middle English sermon of the fourteenth century. Edited by Ione Kemp Knight. Pittsburgh, Duquesne University Press [1967] vii, 147 p. 27 cm. (Duquesne studies. Philological series, 9) "The text is ... based on Corpus Christi MS. 357." First published under title: A sermon no lesse fruteful than famous. Bibliographical footnotes. [BX890.W48 1967] 66-29692
1. Sermons, English—Middle English, 1100-1500. I. Knight, Ione Kemp, ed. II. Title. III. Title: Redde rationem villicationis tue. IV. Series.

WRIGHT, John Joseph, Bp., 1909- 252.02
The Christian and the law, selected Red Mass sermons. Notre Dame, Ind., Fides Publishers [1962] 98 p. 21 cm. [BX1756.W7C5] 62-20572
1. Red Mass sermons. 2. Catholic Church — Sermons. 3. Sermons, American. I. Title.

WYSZYNSKI, Stefan, Cardinal, 1901- 252.02
The deeds of faith, by Cardinal Wyszynski. Selected and translated by Alexander T. Jordan [1st ed.] New York, Harper & Row [1966] 187 p. illus., port. 25 cm. London ed. (Chapman) has title: A strong man armed. [BX1756.W9D43 1966] 66-20794
1. Catholic Church — Sermons. 2. Sermons, Polish — Translations into English. 3. Sermons, English — Translations from Polish. I. Title.

WYSZYNSKI, Stefan, Cardinal, 1901- 252.02
The deeds of faith, by Cardinal Wyszynski. Selected, tr. by Alexander T. Jordan. [1st ed.] New York, Harper [1966] 187p. illus., port. 25cm. London ed. (Chapman) has title: A strong man armed. [BX1756.W9D43 1966] 66-20794 5.95
1. Catholic Church—Sermons. 2. Sermons, Polish—Translations into English. 3. Sermons, English—Translations from Polish. I. Title.

MORRIS, Richard, 1833-1894, ed. 252'.0242
Old English homilies and homiletic treatises (Sawles warde, and Pe wohunge of Ure Lauerd: Ureisuns of Ure Louerd and of Ure Lefdi, &c.) of the twelfth and thirteenth centuries. Edited from mss. in the British Museum, Lambeth, and Bodleian Libraries, with introd., translation, and notes, by Richard Morris. New York, Greenwood Press [1969] lxiii, 330 p. 23 cm. (Early English Text Society. [Publications] O. S. 29 & 34) Reprint of the 1868 ed. [PR1119.A2 no. 29, 34 1969] 69-19533
1. Sermons, English—Middle English, 1100-1500. I. Title. II. Series: Early English Text Society. Publications. Original series, no. 29, 34

SMALL, John, 1828-1886, ed. 252'.02'42
English metrical homilies: from manuscripts of the fourteenth century, with an introd. and notes. [Folcroft, Pa.] Folcroft Library Editions, 1973. p. Reprint of the 1862 ed. published by W. Paterson, Edinburgh. [PR1120.S6 1973b] 73-16187 7.25
1. English poetry—Middle English (1100-1500) 2. Sermons, English—Middle English (1100-1500) I. Title.

SMALL, John, 1828-1886, ed. 252'.02'42
English metrical homilies from manuscripts of the fourteenth century, with an introd. and notes by John Small. Edinburgh, W. Paterson, 1862. [New York, AMS Press, 1973] xxii, 188 p. 23 cm. [PR1120.S6 1973] 79-178504
1. English poetry—Middle English, 1100-1500. 2. Sermons, English—Middle English, 1100-1500. I. Title.

JACOBUS de Vitriaco, Cardinal, d.1240. 252.02'44
The exempla or illustrative stories from the sermones vulgares of Jacques de Vitry. Edited, with introd., analysis, and notes, by Thomas Frederick Crane. New York, B. Franklin [1971] cxvi, 303 p. 22 cm. (Burt Franklin research and source works series, 742) Reprint of the 1890 ed. Text in Latin. [BV4224.J3 1971] 74-128839 ISBN 0-8337-0715-9
1. Exempla. I. Crane, Thomas Frederick, 1844-1927, ed.

DAVES, Michael 252.027
Sermon outlines on Romans. [Westwood, N.J.] Revell [c.1962] 64p. 21cm. (Revell's sermon outline ser.) 62-10741 1.00 pap.,
1. Bible. N. T. Romans—Sermons. 2. Sermons—Outlines. I. Title.

WHITESELL, Faris Daniel, 1895- 252.027
Sermon outlines on favorite Bible chapters. [Westwood, N.J.] Revell [c.1962] 64p. 21cm. (Revell's sermon outline ser.) 62-10740 1.00 pap.,
1. Sermons—Outlines. I. Title.

WHITESELL, Faris Daniel, 1895- 252.027
Sermon outlines on women of the Bible. [Westwood, N.J.] Revell [c.1962] 64p. 21cm (Revell's sermon outline ser.) 62-10739 1.00 pap.,
1. Women in the Bible. 2. Sermons—Outlines. I. Title.

WHITESELL, Jack R. 252.027
Sermon outlines for soul winning. [Westwood, N.J.] Revell [c.1962] 64p. 21cm. (Revell's sermon outline ser) 62-10742 1.00 pap.,
1. Evangelistic sermons—Outlines. I. Title.

ANDREWES, Lancelot, Bp. of Winchester, 1555-1626. 252.03
Sermons; selected and edited with an introduction by G. M. Story. Oxford, Clarendon P., 1967. iii, 295 p. front. (port.) 19 1/2 cm. 52/6 [BX5133.A6S4 1967] 67-88073
1. Church of England — Sermons. 2. Sermons, English. I. Story, George Morley, 1927- ed. II. Title.

ANDREWES, Lancelot, Bp. of Winchester, 1555-1626 252.03
Sermons; selected, ed., introd. by G. M. Story. Oxford, Clarendon Pr., 1967. lii, 295p. front. (port.). 20cm. [BX5133.A6S4 1967] 67-88073 6.75
1. Church of England— Sermons. 2. Sermons, English. I. Story, George Morley, 1927- ed. II. Title.
Available from publisher's New York office.

BRENT, Charles Henry, Bp., 1862-1929. 252.03
No other wealth: the prayers of a modern-day saint, edited by Frederick Ward Kates. With a biographical memoir by Malcolm Endicott Peabody. Nashville. The Upper Room [1965] 143 p. 18 cm. [BV245.B66] 65-18870
1. Prayers. I. Kates, Frederick Ward, 1910-ed. II. Title.

BRENT, Charles Henry, Bp., 1862-1929. 252.03
No other wealth; the prayers of a modern-day saint, ed. by Frederick Ward Kates. Biographical memoir by Malcolm Endicott Peabody. Nashville, Upper Room [c.1965] 143p. 18cm. [BV245.B66] 65-18870 1.00 bds.,
1. Prayers. I. Kates, Frederick Ward, 1910-ed. II. Title.

BROWN, Robert R 252.03
Friendly enemies, putting your troubles to work. [Westwood, N. J.] Revell [1955] 159p. 22cm. [BX5937.B86F7] 55-6626
1 Protestant Episcopal Church in the U. S. A.—Sermons. 2. Sermons, American. I. Title.

BROWN, Robert Raymond, Bp., 1910- 252.03
Friendly enemies, putting your troubles to work. [Westwood, N. J.] Revell [1955] 159p. 22cm. [BX5937.B86F7] 55-6626
1. Protestant Episcopal Church in the U. S. A.—Sermons. 2. Sermons. American. I. Title.

BUTLER, Joseph, Bp. of Durham, 1692-1752. 252.03
Five sermons preached at the Rolls Chapel; and, A dissertation upon the nature of virtue. With an introd. by Stuart M. Brown, Jr. New York, Liberal Arts Press, 1950. x, 90 p. 21 cm. (The Little library of liberal arts. no. 21) Sermons I, II, III, XI, and XII of [the author's] The fifteen sermons preached at the Rolls Chapel [and] ... 'Dissertation II, appended to the first edition of [his] The analogy of religion." Bibliography: p. vi. [BX5133.B87F55] 50-4922
1. Church of England—Sermons. 2. Sermons, English. I. Title. II. Series.

CALEY, James Cowin, comp. 252.03
The Apostles doctrine and fellowship a symposium on the Christian year, scraments and services, some aspects of the outreach of the church. Written by one hundred and twenty-five bishops of the Anglican (Episcopal) Church throughout the world. [San Francisco?] c1958. 426p. illus. 24cm. [BX5008.A1C3] 59-22681
1. Church uear sermons. 2. Anglican Communion—Sermons. 3. Sermons, English. I. Title.

CARRITHERS, Gale H., 1932- 252'.03
Donne at sermons; a Christian existential world [by] Gale H. Carrithers, Jr. [1st ed.] Albany, State University of New York Press, 1972. x, 319 p. 24 cm. Includes the complete texts of four sermons by Donne: The sermon of valediction. The third sermon on John 1.8. The sermon on Psalm 63.7. The two-part sermon on fishers of men. Includes bibliographical references. [PR2248.C35] 74-171183 ISBN 0-87395-122-0 10.00
1. Donne, John, 1572-1631. 2. Church of England—Sermons. 3. Preaching—History—England. 4. Sermons, English. I. Donne, John, 1572-1631. Selected works. 1972. II. Title.

CHAMBERLIN, John S. 252'.03
Increase and multiply : arts-of-discourse procedure in the preaching of Donne / by John S. Chamberlin. Chapel Hill : University of North Carolina Press, c1976. p. cm. Based on the author's thesis, University of Toronto, 1970. Includes bibliographical references. [PR2248.C48] 76-6998 ISBN 0-8078-1266-8 : 12.95
1. Donne, John, 1572-1631—Prose. 2. Preaching—History. I. Title.

CHARLES-EDWARDS, Mervyn, 1902- 252.03
Saints alive! With a foreword by the Bishop of London. London, Mowbray; New York, Morehouse-Gorham Co. [1953] 132p. 19cm. [BS2440.C37] 54-3940
1. Church of England—Sermons. 2. Aposties. I. Title.

CHURCH of England. Homilies. 252.03
Certaine sermons or Homilies, appointed to be read in churches, in the time of Queen Elizabeth I, 1547-1571. 2 vols. in 1. Gainesville, Fla., Scholars' Facsimiles & Reprints, 1968. xii, 323 p. 23 cm. "A facsimile reproduction of the edition of 1623 with an introduction by Mary Ellen Rickey and Thomas B. Stroup." [BX5133.A1A3 1623a] 68-17016 ISBN 0-8201-1008-6
1. Church of England—Sermons. 2. Sermons, English. I. Title.

CRAVNER, William Charles 252.03
The dreamer in Galilee. New York, Vantage Press, [c.1960] 109p. port., 21cm. 2.95 bds.,
I. Title.

CRAVNER, William Charles 252.03
The faith magnificent. New York, Vantage Press [c.1961] 93p. front. port. 2.95 bds.,
1. Sermons, Episcopalian. I. Title.

DE BLANK, Joost, Abp. 252.03
A working faith; sermons for the man in the street. Grand Rapids, Mich., Eerdmans [c.1960] 108p. 20cm. (Preaching for today) 60-12925 2.00
1. Church of the Province of South Africa—Sermons. 2. Sermons, English—Africa, South. I. Title.

DONNE, John, 1573-1631. 252.03
Sermons. Edited with introductions and critical apparatus by George R. Potter and Evelyn M. Simpson. Berkeley, University of California Press, 1953- v. facsims. 25cm. 'On the bibliography of the sermons': v.1, p. 1-32. [BX5133.D6S4] 53-7179
1. Church of England—Sermons. 2. Sermons, English. I. Title.

DONNE, John, 1573-1631 252.03
Sermons, v.10. Ed., introds., critical apparatus by George R. Potter, Evelyn M. Simpson. Berkeley, Univ. of Calif. Pr. [c.]1962. 479p. 25cm. Bibl. 53-7179 10.00
1. Church of England—Sermons. 2. Sermons, English. I. Title.

DONNE, John, 1573-1631. 252.03
The showing forth of Christ; sermons. Selected and edited with an introd. by Edmund Fuller. [1st ed.] New York, Harper & Row [1964] xviii, 230 p. 22 cm. [BX5133.D6S5 1964] 64-23294
1. Church of England—Sermons. English. I. Fuller, Edmund, 1914- ed. II. Title.

EARP, Ernest C 252.03
The unfailing God; sermons and meditations. [1st ed.] New York, Exposition Press [1956] 115p. illus. 21cm. [BX5937.E2U5] 56-11587
1. Protestant Episcopal Church in the U. S. A.—Sermons. 2. Sermons, American. I. Title.

EPISCOPAL series of the 252.03
Protestant hour (The) (Radio program) The word on the air. Ed. by Girault M. Jones. Foreword by Henry I. Louttit. New York, Seabury [c.]1964. 157p. 21cm. Twenty-six sermons preached on TheEpiscopal hour during the past decade. 64-14889 1.95 pap.,
1. Sermons, American. 2. Protestant Episcopal Church in the U.S.A.—Sermons. I. Jones, Girault M., Bp., ed.

THE EPISCOPAL SERIES OF 252.03
THE PROTESTANT HOUR (RADIO PROGRAM)
The word on the air. Edited by Girault M. Jones. Foreword by Henry I. Loutit. New York, Seabury Press, 1964. 157 p. 21 cm. "Twenty -- six sermons preached on The Episcopal hour during the past decade." [BX5937.A1E6] 64-14889
1. Sermons. American. 2. Protestant Episcopal Church in the U.S.A. — Sermons. I. Jones, Girault M., Bp., ed. II. Title.

FARRER, Austin Marsden. 252'.03
The end of man. Grand Rapids, W. B. Eerdmans [1974, c1973] xii, 176 p. 21 cm. Sermons. [BX5133.F33E52 1974] 74-3061 ISBN 0-8028-1579-0
1. Church of England—Sermons. 2. Sermons, English. I. Title.

FARRER, Austin Marsden. 252'.03
The end of man. Grand Rapids, W. B. Eerdmans [1974, c1973] p. cm. Sermons. [BX5133.F33E52 1974] 74-3061 ISBN 0-8028-1579-0 3.45 (pbk.).
1. Church of England—Sermons. 2. Sermons, English. I. Title.

FERRIS, Theodore Parker, 252.03
1908-
The image of God. New York, Oxford, 1965. vi, 184p. 20cm. [BX5937.F414] 65-15612 4.25
1. Protestant Episcopal Church in the U. S. A.—Sermons. 2. Sermons, American. I. Title.

FERRIS, Theodore Parker, 252.03
1908-
The new life. Greenwich, Conn., Seabury Press, [c.]1961. 130p. 61-5574 2.50 half cloth.,
1. Lenten sermons. 2. Protestant Episcopal Church in the U. S. A.—Sermons. 3. Sermons, American. I. Title.

FERRIS, Theodore Parker, 252.03
1908-
This is the day. Chicago, Wilcox and Follett Co. [1951] 191 p. 22 cm. [BX5937.F42T5] 51-14838
1. Protestant Episcopal Church in the U. S. A.—Sermons. 2. Sermons, American. I. Title.

FORD, Douglas William 252.03
Cleverley
An expository preacher's notebook. New York, Harper [1961, c.1960] 220p. 22cm. 61-7334 3.50 half cloth,
1. Church of England—Sermons. 2. Sermons, English. I. Title.

GIFFORD, Frank Dean, 1891- 252.03
ed.
The Anglican pulpit to-day; representative sermons by leading preachers of the Anglican communion. New York, Morehouse-Gorham, 1953. 235p. 22cm. [BX5008.A1G5] 53-12886
1. Anglican Communion—Sermons. 2. Sermons, English. I. Title.

GIFFORD, Frank Dean, 1891- 252.03
Signposts on the King's Highway; a book of sermons especially suitable for lay readers. New York, Morehouse-Gorham Co., 1952. 188 p. 21 cm. [BX5937.G5S5] 52-7949
1. Protestant Episcopal Church in the U. S. A.—Sermons. 2. Sermons, American. I. Title.

GRAY, James, 1923- 252'.03
Johnson's sermons: a study. Oxford, Clarendon Press, 1972. xv, 263 p., iv leaves. ports. 23 cm. Bibliography: p. [245]-255. [PR3534.G7] 73-158318 ISBN 0-19-812033-8
1. Johnson, Samuel, 1709-1784. 2. Sermons, English—18th century—History and criticism. I. Title.
Distributed by Oxford University Press N.Y. 13.75.

HEUSS, John, 1908- 252.03
Do you want inward power? Foreword by Horace W. B. Donegan. Greenwich, Conn., Seabury Press [1953] 172p. 21cm. [BX5937.H46D6] 53-13367
1. Protestant Episcopal Church in the U. S. A.—Sermons. 2. Sermons, American. I. Title.

INGE, William Ralph, 1860- 252.03
1954.
The things that remain. Introd. by W. R. Matthews. [1st American ed.] New York, Harper [1958] 140p. 22cm. London ed. (Mowbray) has title: Goodness and truth. [BX5133.I5T53] 58-10372
1. Church of England—Sermons. 2. Sermons, English. I. Title.

LATIMER, Hugh, Bp. of 252.03
Worcester, 1485?-1555.
Selected sermons of Hugh Latimer. Edited by Allan G. Chester. Charlottesville, Published for the Folger Shakespeare Library [Washington, by] University of Virginia Press [1968] xxxiv, 209 p. 23 cm. (Folger documents of Tudor and Stuart civilization) Contents.Contents.—A chronological table.—Introduction.—Convocation sermon. —Sermon on the plowers.—First sermon before Edward VI.—Second sermon before Edward VI.—Sixth sermon before Edward VI.—Seventh sermon before Edward VI.—Last sermon before Edward VI.—First sermon on the Lord's Prayer.—Sermon for Christmas Day.—Sermon for St. Stephen's Day. [BX5133.L3S4] 68-14091
1. Church of England—Sermons. 2. Sermons, English. I. Chester, Allan Griffith, 1900- ed. II. Title. III. Series.

LATIMER, Hugh, Bp. of 252'.03
Worcester, 1485?-1555.
Sermons. New York, AMS Press [1971] xvii, 379 p. 19 cm. Reprint of the 1906 ed., which was issued as no. 40 of Everyman's library: theology and philosophy. [BX5133.L3 1971] 76-172301 ISBN 0-404-03886-7 15.00
1. Church of England—Sermons. 2. Sermons, English.

MELISH, William Howard, 252.03
1910-
Strength for struggle; Christian social witness in the crucible of our times. New York, Bromwell Press, 1953. 248p. illus. 21cm. [BX5937.M45S8] 53-11777
1. Protestant Episcopal Church in the U. S. A.—Sermons. 2. Sermons, American. 3. Church and social problems. 4. Brooklyn. Church of the Holy Trinity (Protestant Episcopal) I. Title.

MERCER, Robert Hampton. 252.03
The soul's anchorage. Boston, Christopher Publ. House [1964] 209 p. 21 cm. [BX5937.M523S6] 64-15616
1. Sermons, American. 2. Protestant Episcopal Church in the U.S.A. — Sermons. I. Title.

MERCER, Robert Hampton 252.03
The soul's anchorage. Boston, Christopher [c.1964] 209p. 21cm. 64-15616 2.75
1. Sermons, American. 2. Protestant Episcopal Church in the U.S.A.—Sermons. I. Title.

MORRIS, Frederick M. 252.03
God in action, by Frederick M. Morris. Grand Rapids, W. B. Eerdmans Pub. Co. [1968] 77 p. 21 cm. [BX5937.M65G59] 68-12789
1. Protestant Episcopal Church in the U.S.A.—Sermons. 2. Sermons, American. I. Title.

MORRIS, Frederick M 252.03
God's way and ours. [1st ed.] New York, Exposition Press [1952] 124 p. 21 cm. [BX5937.M65G6] 52-12344
1. Protestant Episcopal Church in the U.S.A. — Sermons. 2. Sermons, American. I. Title.

NEWMAN, John Henry, 252.03
Cardinal, 1801-1890
Cardinal Newman's best plain sermons, ed. by Vincent Ferrer Blehl. Foreword by Muriel Spark [New York] Herder & Herder [c.196454 xix, 171p. 21cm. 64-19732 3.95
1. Church of England—Sermons. 2. Sermons, English. I. Blehl, Vincent Ferrer, ed. II. Title.

NEWMAN, John Henry, 252.03
Cardinal, 1801-1890
Newman at St. Mary's; a selection of the Parochial and plain sermons. Ed., introd. by Lawrence F. Barmann. Westminster, Md., Newman [c.]1962. 211p. 23cm. 62-21487 4.50
1. Chuch of England—Sermons. 2. Sermons—English. I. Title.

NEWMAN, John Henry, 252.03
Cardinal, 1801-1890.
The preaching of John Henry Newman. Edited and with an introd. by W. D. White. Philadelphia, Fortress Press [1969] x, 227 p. 18 cm. (The Preacher's paperback library, 10) Bibliographical footnotes. [BX5133.N4P7 1969] 77-84540 2.45
1. Church of England—Sermons. 2. Sermons, English. I. White, W. D., ed. II. Title.

NEWMAN, John Henry, 252.03
Cardinal, 1801-1890.
Cardinal Newman's best plain sermons, edited by Vincent Ferrer Blehl. Foreword by Muriel Spark. [New York] Herder and Herder [1964] xix, 171 p. 21 cm. [BX5133.N4C3] 64-19732
1. Church of England — Sermons. 2. Sermons, English. I. Blehl, Vincent Ferrer, ed. II. Title.

NEWMAN, John Henry, 252.03
Cardinal, 1801-1890
Fifteen sermons preached before the University of Oxford between A. D. 1826 and 1843. Westminster, Md., 21157, Christian Classics, [205 Willis St.] 1966. xxiii, 351p. 21cm. (His Works) On spine: Oxford University sermons. First pub. in 1918. [BX5133.N4F5 1966] 66-20432 8.00
1. Church of England—Sermons. 2. Sermons, English. I. Title. II. Title: Oxford University sermons.

NEWMAN, John Henry, 252.03
Cardinal, 1801-1890.
Parochial and plain sermons; v.1-3 Westminster, Md., Christian Classics, inc., 1966. 3v. 21cm. [BX5133.N4P32] 67-10298 8.00 ea.,
1. Church of England—Sermons. 2. Sermons, English. I. Title.

PACKARD, A. Appleton 252.03
An open door; sermons by A. Appleton Packard. Boston, Christopher Pub. House [1966] 328p. 20cm. Bibl. [BX5937.P26O6] 66-19216 4.00; 2.50 pap.,
1. Protestant Episcopal Church in the U.S.A.—Sermons. 2. Sermons, American. I. Title.

PAUL, James Albert 252.03
Faith is the victory; a selection of sermons. Edited by Horace W. B. Donegan. New York, Morehouse-Barlow Co., [c.] 1959. 143 p. 16 cm. 59-14477 2.50, pap.
1. Protestant Episcopal Church in the U.S.A.—Sermons. 2. Sermons—English. I. Title.

PAUL, James Albert, 1905- 252.03
1957.
Faith is the victory; a selection of sermons. Edited by Horace W.B. Donegan. New York, Morehouse-Barlow Co., 1959. 143p. 16cm. [BX5937.P36F3] 59-14477
1. Protestant Episcopal Church in the U.S.A.—Sermons. 2. Sermons, American. I. Title.

PHILLIPS, John Bertram, 252.03
1906-
Plain Christianity, and other broadcast talks. New York, Macmillan, 1954. 87 p. 21 cm. [BX5133.P52P5] 54-8822
1. Church of England—Sermons. 2. Sermons, English. I. Title.

ROBERTSON, Frederick 252.03
William, 1816-1853.
The preaching of F. W. Robertson. Edited by Gilbert E. Doan, Jr. Philadelphia, Fortress Press [1964] vii, 209 p. 18 cm. (The Preacher's paperback library) "Bibliographical notes": p. 207. [BS5133.R6P7] 64-20116
1. Church of England — Sermons. 2. Sermons, English. I. Doan, Gilbert E., ed. II. Title.

ROBERTSON, Frederick, 252.03
William, 1816-1853
The preaching of F. W. Robertson. Ed. by Gilbert E. Doan, Jr. Philadelphia, Fortress [c.1964] vii, 209p. 18cm. (Preacher's paperback lib.) Bibl. 64-20116 2.45 pap.,
1. Church of England—Sermons. 2. Sermons, English. I. Doan, Gilbert E., ed. II. Title.

SHOEMAKER, Samuel Moor, 252.03
1893-1963
And thy neighbor: Sam Shoemaker; talk[s] about creative living. Arr. by Cecile Cox Offill. Foreword by Cuthbert Bardsley. Waco, Tex., Word Bks. [1967] 200p. 21cm. [BX5937.S45A5] 67-26935 3.50 bds.,
1. Protestant Episocpal Church in the U.S.A.—Sermons. 2. Sermons, American. I. Offill, Cecile Cox. II. Title.

STEWART, Alexander Doig. 252.03
The shock of revelation [by] Alexander Stewart. New York, Seabury Press [1967] vii, 152 p. 22 cm. Based on a series of television appearances.—Cf. dust jacket. Bibliographical references included in "Notes" (p. 149-152) [BX5937.S842S5] 67-11469
1. Protestant Episcopal Church in the U.S.A.—Sermons. 2. Sermons, American. I. Title.

STEWART, William Ward. 252.03
Thoughts for victorious living. Austin, Tex., Von Boeckmann-Jones Co., 1968. 227 p. 23 cm. [BX5937.S78T5] 68-331
1. Protestant Episcopal Church in the U. S. A.—Sermons. 2. Sermons, American. I. Title.

STEWART, William Ward. 252.03
Thoughts for victorious living. Austin, Tex., Von Boeckmann-Jones Co., 1968. 227 p. 23 cm. [BX5937.S78T5] 68-3316
1. Protestant Episcopal Church in the U.S.A.—Sermons. 2. Sermons, American. I. Title.

WATSON, Orville Ernest, 252.03
1857-1951.
Selected sermons; edited by Lacy Lockert. Nashville, Printed for Kenyon College by the Parthenon Press [1955] 297p. illus. 22cm. [BX5937.W388S4] 55-28231
1. Protestant Episcopal Church in the U. S. A.—Sermons 2. Sermons, American. I. Title.

WEDEL, Theodore Otto, 252.03
1892- ed.
Go preach/ Thirty sermons for the laity, edited by Theodore O. Wedel and George W. R. MacCray. Foreword by Henry Know Sherrill. Greenwich, Conn., Seabury Press, 1954. 242p. 22cm. [BX5937.A1W4] 54-9213
1. Protestant Episcopal Church in the U. S. A.—Sermons. 2. Sermons, American. I. MacCray, George W. R., joint ed. II. Title.

FARRER, Austin 252'.03'08
Marsden.
The brink of mystery / Austin Farrer ; edited by Charles C. Conti ; foreword by J. L. Houlden. London : SPCK, 1976. x, 171 p. ; 23 cm. [BX5133.F33B74] 76-373635 ISBN 0-281-02896-6 : £3.95
1. Church of England—Sermons. 2. Sermons, English. I. Conti, Charles C. II. Title.

NEWMAN, John Henry, 252.03'08
Cardinal, 1801-1890.
Sermons bearing on subjects of the day. Westminster, Md., Christian Classics, 1968. xxi, 424 p. 21 cm. Bibliographical footnotes. [BX5133.N4S4 1968] 68-24084
1. Church of England—Sermons. 2. Sermons, English. I. Title.

READ, David Haxton 252.03'131
Carswell
The pattern of Christ, by David H. C. Read. New York, Scribners [1967] 94p. 19cm. [BT382.R37] 67-13654 2.95
1. Beatitudes—Sermons. 2. Presbyterian Church—Sermons. 3. Sermons, American. I. Title.

WILLIAMS, Granville 252'.03'3
Mercer, 1889-
Joy in the Lord [by] Granville M. Williams. Wakefield, Mass., Parameter Press [1972] 123 p. 24 cm. "Retreat addresses given at various times to the Sisters of the Society of St. Margaret." [BX5937.W475J69] 71-189764 ISBN 0-88203-001-9 2.00
1. Protestant Episcopal Church in the U.S.A.—Sermons. 2. Sermons, American. I. Title.

DONNE, John, 1572-1631. 252.03'42
Donne's Prebend sermons. Edited, with an introd. and commentary, by Janel M. Mueller. Cambridge, Mass., Harvard University Press, 1971. xi, 361 p. 25 cm. First published in LXXX sermons preached by that learned and reverend divine, John Donne, Dr in Divinitie, London, 1640. Includes bibliographical references. [BX5133.D61M8] 77-143229 ISBN 0-674-21485-4 10.00
1. Church of England—Sermons. 2. Sermons, English. 3. Preaching—History—England. I. Mueller, Janel M., 1938- ed. II. Title: Prebend sermons.

BROOKS, Phillips, Bp., 1835-1893. 252.03'73
Selected sermons, edited and with an introd. by William Scarlett. Freeport, N.Y., Books for Libraries Press [1971, c1949] 377 p. port. 23 cm. (Essay index reprint series) [BX5937.B83S39 1971] 79-142610 ISBN 0-8369-2146-1
1. Protestant Episcopal Church in the U.S.A.—Sermons. 2. Sermons, American.

DOUGLASS, William, of Philadelphia. 252.03'73
Sermons preached. Freeport, N.Y., Books for Libraries Press, 1971. 251 p. 23 cm. (The Black heritage library collection) Reprint of the 1854 ed. published under title: Sermons preached in the African Episcopal Church of St. Thomas', Philadelphia. Includes bibliographical references. [BX5937.D75S4 1971] 79-157366 ISBN 0-8369-8804-3
1. Episcopalians, Negro—Sermons. 2. Sermons, American. I. Title. II. Series.

BLACKWOOD, Andrew Watterson, 1882- comp. 252.04
The Protestant pulpit, an anthology of master sermons from the Reformation to our own day. Nashville, Abingdon [1966, c.1947] 318p. 23cm. (Apex bk., W2) [BV4241.B5] 47-12188 1.95 pap.,
1. Sermons. I. Title.

TILLICH, Paul, 1886-1965. 252.04
The new being. New York, Scribner, 1955. 179 p. 21 cm. Companion vol. to the author's The shaking of the foundations. [BV4253.T58] 55-7198
1. Sermons, American. I. Title.

ANDERSON, Norman G. 252.04'1
The priceless ingredient [by] Norman G. Anderson. Old Tappan, N.J., F. H. Revell Co. [1971] 124 p. 21 cm. Short sermons based on the author's television program, Power for tomorrow. [BX8066.A53P75] 79-139609 ISBN 0-8007-0427-4 3.50
1. Lutheran Church—Sermons. 2. Sermons, American. I. Power for tomorrow. II. Title.

AUGSBURG sermons; 252'.04'1
sermons on Gospel texts from the new lectionary and calendar. Minneapolis, Minn., Augsburg Pub. House [1973-75; v. 1, 1974, v. 3, 1973] 3 v. 23 cm. [BX8066.A1A9] 73-78262 ISBN 0-8066-1489-7 (v. 2) 7.95 (v. 1)
1. Lutheran Church—Sermons. 2. Church year sermons. 3. Sermons, American. I. Augsburg Publishing House.

AUGSBURG sermons: 252'.04'1
sermons on Gospel texts from the new lectionary and calendar: series C. Minneapolis, Minn., Augsburg Pub. House [1973] 287 p. 23 cm. [BX8066.A1A9] 73-78262 ISBN 0-8066-9485-8 7.95
1. Lutheran Church—Sermons. 2. Church year sermons. 3. Sermons, American. I. Augsburg Publishing House.

BARD, Andreas, 1873- 252.041
A vitamin called faith. New York, Greenberg; trade distributor: Arco Pub. Co. [1958] 147p. 21cm. (A Benadum book) [BR85.B414] 58-11481
1. Christianity— Addresses, essays, lectures. I. Title.

BECK, Victor Emanuel, 1894- ed. 252.041
The gospel we preach; sermons on a series of gospels for the church year. Editorial committee: Victor Emanuel Beck, Clifford Ansgar Nelson [and] Ernest Edwin Ryden. Rock Island, Ill., Augustana Press [1956] 367p. 21cm. [BX8066.A1B4] 56-11985
1. Church year sermons. 2. Lutheran Church—Sermons. 3. Sermons, American. I. Title.

BECK, Victor Emanuel, 1894- ed. 252.041
The gospel we preach; sermons on a series of gospels for the church year. Second series, by sixty-five Lutheran pastors. Editorial committee: Victor Emanuel Beck, G. Erik Hagg [and] Clifford Ansgar Nelson. Rock Island, Ill., Augustana Press [1958] xv, 347p. 21cm. 'Sermons on a series of gospels of the church year, usually known as the 'Second series." --Dust jacket. [BX8066.A1B42] 59-1478
1. Church year sermons. 2. Lutheran church—Sermons. 3. Sermons, American. I. Title.

BEHNKEN, John William, 1884- 252.041
Mercies manifold: radio messages broadcast during the summer of 1949. St. Louis, Concordia Pub. House, 1950 [i. e. 1951] ix, 147 p. 22 cm. [BX8066.B33M4] 51-1465
1. Lutheran Church—Sermons. 2. Sermons. American. I. Lutheran hour (Radio program) II. Title.

BLUMHARDT, Christoph, 1842-1919. 252.041
Christoph Blumhardt and his message [by] R. Lejeune. [Translated by Hela Ehrlich and Nicoline Maas] Rifton, N. Y., Plough Pub. House [1963] 238 p. 23 cm. Full name: Christoph Friedrich Blumhardt. [BX8011.B523] 63-15816
1. Lutheran Church — Sermons. 2. Sermons, German — Translations into English. 3. Sermons, English — Translations from German. I. Lejeune, Robert, ed. II. Title.

BLUMHARDT, Christoph Friedrich, 1842-1919. 252.041
Christoph Blumhardt and his message [by] R. Lejeune. [Tr. from German by Hela Ehrlich, Nicoline Mass] Rifton, N. Y., Plough [c.1963] 238p. 23cm. 63-15816 3.75
1. Lutheran Church—Sermons. 2. Sermons, German—Translations into English. 3. Sermons, English—Translations from German. I. Lejeune, Robert, ed. II. Title.

BRAATEN, Carl E., 1929- 252'.04'1
The whole counsel of God, by Carl E. Braaten. Philadelphia, Fortress Press [1974] x, 166 p. 23 cm. Sermons. [BX8066.B65W47] 73-88345 ISBN 0-8006-1064-4 5.95
1. Lutheran Church—Sermons. 2. Sermons, American. I. Title.

BULTMANN, Rudolf [Karl] 252.041
This world and the beyond, Marburg sermons. [Translation from the German by Harold Knight] New York, Scribner [c.1960] 248p. 21cm. (Bibl. footnotes) 60-14019 3.50
1. Lutheran Church—Sermons. 2. Sermons, German—Translations into English. 3. Sermons, English—Translations from German. I. Title.

BULTMANN, Rudolf Karl, 1884- 252.041
This world and the beyond, Marburg sermons. [Translation by Harold Knight] New York, Scribner [1960] 248p. 21cm. Translation of Marburger Predigten. [BX8066.B8T53] 60-14019
1. Lutheran Church—Sermons. 2. Sermons, German —Translations into English. 3. Sermons, English—Translations from German. I. Title.

CLAUSEN, Robert Howard, comp. 252'.04'1
The cross and the cries of human need; messages for Lent and every season. The meaning of the cross for human problems portrayed in six selections from the plays of Arthur Miller, John Osborne, Edward Albee, Frank D. Gilroy, Eugene Ionesco. Minneapolis, Augsburg Pub. House [1973] 127 p. 20 cm. [BX8066.C5C76] 72-90255 ISBN 0-8066-1301-7 2.95
1. Lutheran Church—Sermons. 2. Sermons, American. 3. Christianity and literature. I. Title.
Contents Omitted.

FISHER, Wallace E. 252.041
Preaching and parish renewal [by] Wallace E. Fisher. Nashville, Abingdon [1966] 208p. 21cm. Bibl. [BX8066.F52P7] 66-22916 4.00
1. Lutheran Church—Sermons. 2. Sermons, American. I. Title.

FORCE, Maynard Alfred, 1904- 252.041
Our refuge and strength; sermons and meditations. Rock Island, Ill., Augustana Book Concern [1954] 140p. 21cm. [BX8066.F6O54] 54-34230
1. Lutheran Church—Sermons. 2. Sermons, American. I. Title.

GRAF, Arthur E. 252.041
Bought with a price; lenten and stewardship sermons, as well as sermons for various occasions. Springfield, Ill., 3524 Sherman Faith Pubns., [c.1961] 140p. illus. 61-14616 3.00
1. Lutheran Church—Sermons, 2. Lenten sermons. 3. Sermons, American. I. Title.

GRAF, Arthur E. 252.04'1
Sermons for special occasions; funerals, weddings, and various other occasions, by Arthur E. Graf. Giddings, Tex., Faith Publications [1972] 151 p. 20 cm. [BV4254.2.G69] 70-183106
1. Lutheran Church—Sermons. 2. Occasional sermons. 3. Sermons, American. I. Title.

GRAF, Arthur E. 252.04'1
Walking and talking with God; two sermon series, by Arthur E. Graf. Jefferson City, Mo., Faith Publications [1969] 174 p. 20 cm. [BX8066.G7W3] 73-81749
1. Lutheran Church—Sermons. 2. Sermons, American. I. Title.

GULLIXSON, Thaddeus Frank, 1882- 252.04'1
Down into the arena, and other sermons, by T. F. Gullixson. Minneapolis, Augsburg Pub. House [1968] v, 175 p. 21 cm. [BX8066.G8D6] 68-25800 3.95
1. Lutheran Church—Sermons. 2. Sermons, American. I. Title.

HAGG, G Erik. 252.041
Sermons for special days. Rock Island, Ill., Augustana Press [1962] 160p. 20cm. [BX8066.H37S4] 62-12912
1. Sermons, American. 2. Lutheran Church—Sermons. I. Title.

HANSON, Oscar Conrad, 1908- 252.041
Out of old ruts. Minneapolis, Augsburg Pub. House [c.1961] 104p. 61-6994 1.75 pap.,
1. Lutheran Church—Sermons. 2. Sermons, American. I. Title.

HARRISVILLE, Roy A. 252.04'1
Pick up your trumpet [by] Roy A. Harrisville. Minneapolis, Augsburg Pub. House [1970] 135 p. 20 cm. [BX8066.H46P5] 70-101110 2.50
1. Lutheran Church—Sermons. 2. Sermons, American. I. Title.

HERSHEY, Robert D 252.041
Think about these things; sermons. Philadelphia, Muhlenberg Press [1958] 198p. 20cm. [BX8066.H57T5] 58-11738
1. Lutheran Church—Sermons. 2. Sermons, American. I. Title.

HOFFMANN, Oswald C. J. 252.04'1
God is no island [by] Oswald C. J. Hoffmann. Saint Louis, Concordia Pub. House [1969] 111 p. 20 cm. [BX8066.H583G6] 71-80998 2.75
1. Lutheran Church—Sermons. 2. Sermons, American. I. Title.

JENSEN, Kai, 1899- 252.041
The answer of faith; translated by John M. Jensen. Mineapolis, Augsburg Pub. House [1961] 115p. 21cm. 'A translation of selections from two books ...: Hjertets uro og troens svar, published in 1952, and Den evige lengsel, published in 1954.' [BX8066.J45A5] 61-6995
1. Lutheran Church—Sermons. 2. Sermons, Danish—Translations into English. 3. Sermons, English—Translations from Danish. I. Title.

KILDAHL, John Nathan, 1857- 252.041
Concerning sin and grace; sermons for the church year based on Gospel texts. Translated by Bernhard H. J. Habel. Minneapolis, Augsburg Pub. House [1954] 428p. 22cm. Translation of Synd og naade. [BX8066.K48S92] 54-11372
1. Lutheran Church— Sermons. 2. Sermons, Norwegian—Translations into English. 3. Sermons, English—Translations from Norwegian. I. Title.

KOBERLE, Adolf, 1898- 252.04'1
The invitation of God. Translated by Roy Barlag. Saint Louis, Concordia Pub. House [1968] 238 p. 22 cm. Sermons preached 1950-1957 at the university church in Tubingen, Germany. Translation of Die Einladung Gottes. [BX8066.K583E53] 68-12893
1. Lutheran Church—Sermons. 2. Sermons, English—Translations from German. 3. Sermons, German—Translations into English. I. Title.

LEE, Knute, 1916- 252.041
Plain talk in an Artic chapel. Minneapolis, Augsburg Pub. House [1954] 182p. illus. 20cm. [BX8066.L395P6] 54-11482
1. Lutheran Church—Sermons. 2. Sermons, American. I. Title.

LOEW, Ralph W 252.041
The hinges of destiny. Philadelphia, Muhlenberg Press [1955] 173p. 20cm. [BX8066.L594H5] 55-7762
1. Lutheran Church—Sermons. 2. Sermons, American. I. Title.

LUTHER, Martin, 1483-1546 252.041
Alone with God; devotions from Martin Luther. ed. from his sermons by Theodore J. Kleinhans. Saint Louis, Concordia [1962] 104p. 19cm. 62-14143 2.50
1. Devotional calendars—Lutheran Church. I. Kleinhans, Theodore, Jr., ed. and tr. II. Title.

MAIER, Walter Arthur, 1893-1950. 252.041
Go quickly and tell: radio messages for the second part of the fifteenth Lutheran hour. Saint Louis, Concordia Pub House [c1950] xii, 444 p. 20 cm. [BX8066.M25G6] 51-28420
1. Lutheran Church—Sermons 2. Sermons, American. I. Lutheran hour (Radio program) II. Title.

MAIER, Walter Arthur, 1893-1950. 252.041
One thousand radio voices for Christ; radio messages for the first part of the fifteenth Lutheran hour. Saint Louis, Concordia Pub. House [c1950] x, 454 p. 20 cm. [BX8066.M2505] 50-8806
1. Lutheran Church—Sermons 2. Sermons, American. I. Lutheran hour (Radio program) II. Title.

MEZERS VALDIS 252.041
The great light; sermons and meditations. Boston, Christopher Pub. House [1957] 139p. 21cm. [BX8066.M46G7] 57-13133
1. Lutheran Church—Sermons. 2. Sermons, American. I. Title.

MEZEZERS, Valdis. 252.041
God and man; sermons and meditations. Jacket illus. by Leonids Linants. [1st ed.] New York, Vantage Press [1956] 132p. 21cm. [BX8066] 56-5820
1. Lutheran Church—Sermons. 2. Sermons, American. I. Title.

MEZEZERS, Valdis. 252.041
The great light; sermons and meditations. Boston, Christopher Pub. House [1957] 139p. 21cm. [BX8066.M46G7] 57-13133
1. Lutheran Church—Sermons. 2. Sermons, American. I. Title.

MOLTMANN, Jurgen. 252'.04'1
The gospel of liberation. Translated by H. Wayne Pipkin. Waco, Tex., Word Books [1973] 136 p. 23 cm. [BX8066.M6G67] 73-77952 5.95
1. Lutheran Church—Sermons. 2. Sermons, German—Translations into English. 3. Sermons, English—Translations from German. I. Title.

MUNSON, Edwin C. 252.041
The mysterious presence, communion sermons. Philadelphia, Fortress [c.1963] 112p. 21cm. 62-20739 2.95
1. Communion sermons. 2. Lutheran Church—Sermons. 3. Sermons, American. I. Title.

NEIPP, Paul C 252.041
Soul-searching sermons. Ridgecrest, Calif. [1957] 117p. 23cm. [BX8066.N49Sb] 57-47480
1. Lutheran Church—Sermons. 2. Sermons, American. I. Title.

NORDEN, Rudolph F. 252.041
The voice of the prophets; sixteen timely pulpit meditations based on texts from the sixteen Old Testament prophets. St. Louis, Concordia [c.1963] xi, 161p. 23cm. 63-20177 2.75
1. Sermons, American. 2. Lutheran Church—Sermons. I. Title.

OBERMEIER, Arnold, 1915- 252.041
What shall I say? Devotional addresses for special occasions. Saint Louis, Concordia Pub. House [1954] 95p. 21cm. [BV4254.2.O2] 54-3555
1. Occasional sermons. 2. Lutheran Church—Sermons. 3. Sermons, American. I. Title.

OLDSEN, Armin Charles, 1910- 252.041
A message from God; a collection of sermons most frequently requested during the nineteenth year of the Lutheran hour. Saint Louis, Concordia Pub. House [1953] 147p. 22cm. [BX8066.O5M4] 54-7389
1. Lutheran Church—Sermons. 2. Sermons, American. I. Lutheran hour (Radio program) II. Title.

POLACK, William Gustave, 1890-1950. 252.041
Beside still waters. Saint Louis, Concordia Pub. House [c1950] xi, 73 p. port. 20 cm. [BX8066.P65B4] 50-8979
1. Luthern Church — Sermons. 2. Sermons, America. I. Title.

RIESS, Oswald. 252.041
For such a time as this; inspirational messages for 20th century Christians. Saint Louis, Concordia Pub. House [1959] 140p. 22cm. Includes bibliography. [BX8066.R47F6] 58-13258
1. Lutheran Church—Sermons. 2. Sermons, American. I. Title.

RILLING, John William, 1906- 252.041
Have a good day, and other sermons. Philadelphia, Muhlenberg Press [1958] 177p. 20cm. [BX8066.R48H3] 58-13830
1. Lutheran Church—Sermons. 2. Sermons, American. I. Title.

ROGNESS, Alvin N 1906- 252.041
Who shall be God? A selection of sermons. Minneapolis, Augsburg Pub. House [1954] 183p. 21cm. [BX8066.R63W45] 54-10809
1. Lutheran Church—Sermons. 2. Sermons, American. I. Title.

SEGERHAMMAR, Carl William. 252.041
God lifts my sights; National radio pulpit sermons. Rock Island, Ill., Augustana Press [1957] 88p. 21cm. [BX8066.S39G6] 57-9553

1. Lutheran Church— Sermons. 2. Sermons, American. I. Title.

STEIMLE, Edmund A 252.041
Are you looking for God and other sermons. Philadelphia, Muhlenberg Press [1957] 154p. 20cm. [BX8066.S716A7] 57-5757
1. Lutheran Church—Sermons. 2. Sermons, American. I. Title.

STEIMLE, Edmund A 252.041
Are you looking for God? and other sermons. Philadelphia, Muhlenberg Press [1957] 154 p. 20 cm. [BX8066.S716A7] 57-5757
1. Lutheran Church — Sermons. 2. Sermons, American. I. Title.

STEIMLE, Edmund A. 252.04'1
Disturbed by joy; sermons, by Edmund A. Steimle. Philadelphia, Fortress Press [1967] ix, 182 p. 18 cm. [BX8066.S716D5] 67-13059
1. Lutheran Church—Sermons. 2. Sermons, American. I. Title.

STEIMLE, Edmund A. 252'.04'1
From death to birth: sermons, by Edmund A. Steimle. Philadelphia, Fortress Press [1973] ix, 128, [3] p. 22 cm. Bibliography; p. [131] [BX8066.S716F7] 73-79327 ISBN 0-8006-1037-7 3.25
1. Lutheran Church—Sermons. 2. Sermons, American. I. Title.

STEIMLE, Edmund A., ed. 252.041
Renewal in the pulpit; sermons, by younger preachers. Edited and with an introd. by Edmund A. Steimle. Philadelphia, Fortress Press [1966] xvii, 190 p. 17 cm. (The Preacher's paperback library, v. 7) [BX8066.A1S73] 66-19980
1. Lutheran Church—Sermons—Collections. 2. Sermons, American—Collections. I. Title.

THIELICKE, Helmut, 1908- 252.041
Christ and the meaning of life; a book of sermons and meditations. Edited and translated by John W. Doberstein. [1st ed.] New York, Harper [1962] 186 p. 21 cm. [BX8066.T46C5] 62-7304
1. Lutheran Church — Sermons. 2. Sermons, German — Translations into English. 3. Sermons, English — Translations from German. I. Title.

THIELICKE, Helmut, 1908- 252.041
Christ and the meaning of life: a book of sermons and meditations. Edited and translated by John W. Doberstein. Grand Rapids: Baker Book House, [1975 c1962] 186 p.; 20 cm. [BX8066.T46C5] 62-7304 ISBN 0-8010-8824-0 2.95 (pbk.)
1. Lutheran Church—Sermons. 2. Sermons, German—Translations into English. 3. Sermons, English—Translations from German. I. Title.

THIELICKE, Helmut, 252'.04'1
1908-
How to believe again. Translated by H. George Anderson. Philadelphia, Fortress Press [1972] 220 p. 22 cm. Translation of Und wenn Gott ware. [BX8066.T46U5313] 72-75656 ISBN 0-8006-0123-8 3.95
1. Lutheran Church—Sermons. 2. Sermons, German. I. Title.

THIELICKE, Helmut, 1908- 252.041
.
Man in God's world. Translated and edited by John W. Doberstein. [1st American ed.] New York, Harper & Row [1963] 223 p. 22 cm. "This book is a revision and translation of chapters 18 to 32 of Der Glaube der Christenheit ... Chapter 12 is from Fragen des Christentums an die moderne Welt." Includes bibliography. [BX8066.T46M3 1963] 63-14971
1. Lutheran Church — Sermons. 2. Sermons, German — Translations into English. 3. Sermons, English — Translations from German. I. Title.

THIELICKE, Helmut, 1908- 252.041
Man in God's world. Tr. [from German] ed. by John W. Doberstein. New York, Harper [c.1963] 223p. 22cm. Bibl. 63-14971 3.95
1. Lutheran Church—Sermons. 2. Sermons, German—Translations into English. 3. Sermons, English—Translations from German. I. Title.

THIELICKE, Helmut, 1908- 252.041
The silence of God. Introd. and translation by G. W. Bromiley. Grand Rapids, Mich., Eerdmans [1962] 92 p. 21 cm. [BX8066.T46S5] 62-11248
1. Lutheran Church — Sermons. 2. Sermons, German — Translations into English. 3. Sermons, English — Translations from German. I. Title.

THIELICKE, Helmut, 1908- 252.041
The silence of God. Introd., tr. [from German] by G. W. Bromiley. Grand Rapids, Mich., Eerdmans [c.1962] 92p. 21cm. 62-11248 2.50
1. Lutheran Church—Sermons. 2. Sermons, German—Translations into English. 3. Sermons, English—Translations from German. I. Title.

TILLICH, Paul [Johannes 252.041
Oskar]
The new being. New York, Scribner [c.1955] 179p. 21cm. Companion vol. to the author's The shaking of the foundations. (Scribner library SL20) 1.25 pap.,
1. Sermons, American. I. Title.

TILLICH, Paul [Johannes 252.041
Oskar]
The shaking of the foundations. New York, Scribner [c.1948] 186p. 21cm. (Scribner Library, SL 30) 1.25 pap.,
1. Sermons, American. I. Title.

*WURMBRAND, Richard. 252.04'1
The Wurmbrand letters. Glendale, Calif., Diane Books [1973? c.1972] 157 p. 18 cm. [BR1608] 1.95 (pbk.)
1. Persecution—Rumania. 2. Prisoners—Rumania—Personal narratives. I. Title.
Publisher's address: Box 488, Glendale, CA 91209.

YOUNGDAHL, Reuben K 1911- 252.041
A house for tomorrow, and other sermons. Rock Island, Ill., Augustana Book Concern [1952] 138 p. 20 cm. [BX8066.Y68H67] 52-14453
1. Lutheran Church — Sermons. 2. Sermons, American. I. Title.

YOUNGDAHL, Reuben K 1911- 252.041
Looking God's way, by Reuben K. Youngdahl. Minneapolis, Augsburg Pub. House [1966] 170 p. 21 cm. [BX8066.Y68L6] 66-13054
1. Lutheran Church — Sermons. 2. Sermons, American. I. Title.

YOUNGDAHL, Reuben K., 252.041
1911-
Looking God's way. Minneapolis, Augsburg [c.1966] 170p. 21cm. [BX8066.Y68L6] 66-13054 3.95
1. Lutheran Church—Sermons. 2. Sermons, American. I. Title.

YOUNGDAHL, Reuben K 1911- 252.041
The pathway to peace. Minneapolis, T. S. Denison [1957] 221p. 22cm. [BX8066.Y68P3] 57-12698
1. Lutheran Church—Sermons. 2. Sermons, American. I. Title.

YOUNGDAHL, Reuben K 1911- 252.041
The pathway to peace. Minneapolis, T. S. Denison, [1957] 221 p. 22 cm. [BX8066.Y68P3] 57-12698
1. Lutheran Church — Sermons. 2. Sermons, American. I. Title.

YOUNGDAHL, Reuben K 1911- 252.041
The secret of greatness. [Westwood, N. J.] Revell [1955] 188p. 22cm. [BX8066.Y68S4] 55-8763
1. Lutheran Church—Sermons. 2. Sermons, American. I. Title.

YOUNGDAHL, Reuben K 1911- 252.041
Trumpets in the morning. Rock Island, Ill., Augustana Press [1962] 167 p. 21 cm. [BX8066.Y68T7] 62-21692
1. Lutheran Church — Sermons. 2. Sermons, American. I. Title.

YOUNGDAHL, Reuben K., 252.041
1911-
Trumpets in the morning. Rock Island, Ill., Augustana [c.1962] 167p. 21cm. 62-216926 3.00
1. Lutheran Church—Sermons. 2. Sermons, American. I. Title.

YOUNGDAHL, Reuben K 1911- 252.041
Turbulent world, tranquil God. [Westwood, N.J., Revell [1958] 157 p. 22 cm. [BX8066.Y68T8] 58-11021
1. Lutheran Church — Sermons. 2. Sermons, American. I. Title.

YOUNGDAHL, Reuben K., 252.041
1911-
The unconquerable partnership. Rock Island, Ill., Augustana Press [c.1960] 258p. 60-16828 3.00
1. Lutheran Church—Sermons. 2. Sermons, American. I. Title.

SCHWEITZER, Albert, 252.04'143
1875-1965.
Reverence for life. Translated by Reginald H. Fuller. [1st ed.] New York, Harper & Row [1969] 153 p. 22 cm. Translation of Strassburger Predigten. [BV4244.S3613] 71-85052 4.95
1. Sermons, German. I. Title.

BARTH, Karl, 1886- 252.04'2
Call for God. [Tr. by A. T. Mackay. 1st U. S. ed.] New York, Harper [1967] 125p. 22cm. Tr. of Rufe mich an. Collection of 12 sermons delivered to convicts in a prison at base. [BX9435.B2613] 67-21543 3.95
1. Reformed Church—Sermons. 2. Sermons, English—Translations from German. 3. Sermons, German — Translations into English. 4. Prisons — Sermons. I. Title.

BARTH, Karl, 1886- 252.04'2
Call for God. [Translated by A. T. Mackay. 1st U.S. ed.] New York. Harper & Row [1967] 125 p. 22 cm. Translation of Rufe mich an. Collection of 12 sermons delivered to convicts in a prison at Basel. [BX9435.B2613] 67-21543
1. Reformed Church — Sermons. 2. Sermons, English — Translations from German. 3. Sermons. German — Translations into English. 4. Prisons — Sermons. I. Title.

BARTH, Karl, 1886- 252.04'2
Call for God: new sermons from Basel Prison; translated [from the German] by A. T. Mackay. London, S. C. M. Press, 1967. 125 p. 19 1/2 cm. 12/6 (B67-14128) Originally published as 'Rufe mich an.' Zurich, Evangelischer Veriag, 1965. [BX9426.B3R813] 67-100978
1. Reformed Church — Sermons. 2. Sermons, German — Translations into English. 3. Sermons, English — Translations from German. I. Title.

THE deity of Christ, and 252.042
other sermons; translated from the French and Latin by Leroy Nixon. Grand Rapids, Eerdmans, 1950. 302 p. 23 cm. [BX 420. A32 Nd] 50-8898
1. Reformed Church—Sermons. 2. Sermons, English—Translations from French. 3. Sermons, English—Translations from Latin. 4. Sermons, French—Translations into English. Sermons, Latin—Translations into English. 5. Jesus Christ—Divialty—Sermons.

ZINZENDORF, Nicolaus 252'.04'6
Ludwig, Graf von, 1700-1760.
Nine public lectures on important subjects in religion, preached in Fetter Lane Chapel in London in the year 1746. Translated & edited by George W. Forell. Iowa City, University of Iowa Press, 1973. xxxii, 138 p. 24 cm. Bibliography: p. [105]-138. [BX8577.Z5N56] 72-93784 ISBN 0-87745-036-6
1. Moravian Church—Sermons. 2. Sermons, English. I. Title.

REES, Paul Stromberg. 252.047
Christian: commit yourself! [Westwood, N. J.] Revell [1957] 158p. 21cm [BX7549.Z6R35] 57-5405
1. Evangelical Mission Covenant Church of America—Sermons. 2. Sermons, American. I. Title.

REES, Paul Stromberg. 252.047
The face of our Lord. Grand Rapids, Eerdmans, 1951. 119 p. 20 cm. [BX7549.Z6R39] 51-9752
1. Evangelical Mission Covenant Church of America — Sermons. 2. Sermons, American. I. Title.

BLACKWOOD, Andrew 252.05
Watterson, 1915-
The Holy Spirit in your life. Grand Rapids, Baker Book House, 1957. 169p. 21cm. [BX9178.B662H6] 57-14662
1. Presbyterian Church—Sermons. 2. Sermons, American. I. Title.

BURNETT, Andrew Ian. 252.05
Lord of all life. New York, Rinehart [1952] 205p. 22cm. [BX9178.B78L6] 52-11251
1. Presbyterian Church— Sermons. 2. Sermons, English—Canada. I. Title.

CONNING, Gordon. 252.05
The new shape of life. Wilmington, Del., Mercantile Press [1968] 157 p. illus. 24 cm. [BV4501.C71338] 68-59443
1. Presbyterian Church—Sermons. 2. Christian life—Presbyterian authors. 3. Sermons, American. I. Title.

ELLIOTT, William Marion, 252.05
1903-
Lift high that banner! Richmond, John Knox Press, 1950. 153 p. 21 cm. "References and acknowledgments": p. [145]-153. [BX9178.E48L5] 50-5990
1. Presbyterian Church—Sermons. 2. Sermons, American. I. Title.

ELSON, Edward Lee Roy, 252.05
1906-
The inevitable encounter. Grand Rapids, Mich., Eerdmans [c.1962] 68p. 21cm. (Preaching for today) 62-21372 2.25
1. Presbyterian Church—Sermons. 2. Sermons, American. I. Title.

EVANS, Louis Hadley, 1897- 252.05
This is America's hour. [Westwood, N.J.] Revell [1957] 128p. 21cm. [BX9178.E84T5] 57-11323
1. Presbyterian Church—Sermons. 2. Sermons, American. 3. Lincoln, Abraham, Pres.U.S., 1809-1865. I. Title.

FERRIS, Frank Halliday. 252.05
Standing up to life. [1st ed.] Indianapolis, Bobbs-Merrill [1953] 190p. illus. 20cm. [BX9178.F43S8] 53-5231
1. Presbyterian Church—Sermons. 2. Sermons, American. I. Title.

LOVE, Larry. 252.05
Called to be servants. Grand Rapids, Zondervan Pub. House [1957] 119p. 20cm. [BX9178.L72C32] 58-15405
1. Presbyterin Church—Sermons. 2. Sermons, American. I. Title.

LOWE, Arnold Hilmar, 1888- 252.05
Beliefs have consequences. New York, Crowell [1959] 178p. 21cm. [BX9178.L73B4] 59-14573
1. Presbyterian Church—Sermons. 2. Sermons, American. I. Title.

LOWE, Arnold Hilmar, 1888- 252.05
Start where you are. [1st ed.] New York, Harper [1950] vii, 179 p. 20 cm. [BX9178.L73S7] 50-10793
1. Presbyterian Church—Sermons. 2. Sermons, American. I. Title.

MACARTNEY, Clarence Edward 252.05
Noble, 1879-1957.
Along life's highway. Compiled and edited by Harry E. Farra. Grand Rapids, Mich., Baker Book House [1969] 103 p. 21 cm. ([The New minister's handbook series]) [BX9178.M172A63] 75-97726 2.95
1. Presbyterian Church—Sermons. 2. Sermons, American. I. Title.

*MCGEE, C. Lincoln 252.05
God in action. New York, Carlton [c.1964] 70p. 21cm. 2.50
I. Title.

MARSHALL, Peter, 1902- 252.05
1949.
John Doe, disciple; sermons for the young in spirit. Edited and with introd. by Catherine Marshall. Pref. by Peter John Marshall. New York, McGraw-Hill [1963] 222 p. 22 cm. [BX9178.M363J6 1963] 63-20813
1. Presbyterian Church—Sermons. 2. Sermons, American. I. Title.

MARSHALL, Peter, 1902- 252.05
1949.
Keepers of the springs, and other messages from Mr. Jones, meet the Master. [Westwood, N. J.] Revell [1962] 60p. 17cm. [BX9178.M363M52] 61-13622
1. Presbyterian Church—Sermons. 2. Sermons, American. I. Title.

MUNGER, Robert Boyd. 252.05
What Jesus says; the master teacher and life's problems. [Westwood, N. J.] F. H. Revell Co. [1955] 185p. 22cm. [BX9178.M664W5] 55-8764
1. Presbyterian Church —Sermons. 2. Sermons, American. I. Title.

PHILIPS, T Roland., 252.05
God hath spoken. Grand Rapids, Eerdmans [1959] 181p. illus. 23cm. [BX9178.P54G6] 59-12935
1. Sermons, American. 2. Presbyterian Church—Sermons. I. Title.

READ, David Haxton 252'.05
Carswell.
An expanding faith, by David H. C. Read. Grand Rapids, Eerdmans [1973] 116 p. 18 cm. (An Eerdmans evangelical paperback) [BX9178.R367E96] 73-7620 ISBN 0-8028-1539-1 1.95 (pbk.)
1. Presbyterian Church—Sermons. 2. Sermons, American. I. Title.

READ, David Haxton 252.05
Carswell
I am persuaded. New York, Scribners [1962, c.1961] 182p. 62-9641 3.00
1. Presbyterian Church—Sermons. 2. Sermons, American. I. Title.

READ, David Haxton 252.05
Carswell.
Religion without wrappings, by David H. C. Read. Grand Rapids, Mich., Eerdmans [1970] 216 p. 21 cm. [BX9178.R367R4] 79-127626 4.95
1. Presbyterian Church—Sermons. 2. Sermons, American. I. Title.

READ, David Haxton 252.05
Carswell.
Sons of Anak; the gospel and the modern giants, sermons. New York, Scribner [1964] 208 p. 21 cm. [BX9178.R367S6] 64-12835
1. Sermons, American. 2. Presbyterian Church—Sermons. I. Title. II. Title: The gospel and the modern giants.

REDHEAD, John A. 252.05
Getting to know God, and other sermons. Nashville, Abingdon [1964, c.1954] 126p. 18cm. (Apex bks., Q6) .95 pap.,
1. Presbyterian Church—Sermons. 2. Sermons, American. I. Title.

REDHEAD, John A 252.05
Getting to know God, and other sermons. Nashville, Abingdon Press [c1954] 126p. 20cm. [BX9178.R368G4] 54-5230
1. Presbyterian Church—Sermons. 2. Sermons, American. I. Title.

ROBSHAW, Charles P 252.05
The wisdom that does not change. New York, Abingdon Press [1962] 125p. 20cm. [BX9178.R63W5] 62-8106
1. Presbyterian Church—Sermons. 2. Sermons, American. I. Title.

SMART, James D 252.05
The recovery of humanity. Philadelphia, Westminster Press [1953] 157p. 21cm. [BX9178.S526R4] 53-8528
1. Presbyterian Church—Sermons. 2. Sermons, American. I. Title.

*STEWART, James Stuart, 252'.05
1896-
The gates of new life [by] James S. Stewart. Grand Rapids, Mich., Baker Book House [1972] x, 251 p. 20 cm. (James S. Stewart library) First published in Edinburgh as part of the Scholar as preacher series. [BV4241] ISBN 0-8010-7974-8 pap., 2.95
1. Sermons, English. I. Title.

SUTPHIN, Wyn Blair. 252.05
No greater love. Richmond, John Knox Press [1965] 71 p. 21 cm. Includes bibliographical references. [BT456.S8] 65-25514
1. Jesus Christ — Seven last words. 2. Prestbyterian Church — Sermons. 3. Sermons, American. I. Title.

SUTPHIN, Wyn Blair 252.05
No greater love. Richmond, Va., John Knox [c.1965] 71p. 21cm. Bibl. [BT456.S8] 65-25514 2.00 bds.,
1. Jesus Christ—Seven last words. 2. Presbyterian Church—Sermons. 3. Sermons, American. I. Title.

THOMAS, D Reginald. 252.05
Love so amazing. [Westwood, N.J.] Revell [1961] 127 p. 21 cm. [BX9178.T37L6] 61-5926
1. Presbyterian Church — Sermons. 2. Sermons, American. I. Title.

THOMAS, D. Reginald 252.05
Love so amazing. [Westwood, N. J.] Revell [c.1961] 127p. 61-5926 2.50 bds.,
1. Presbyterian Church—Sermons. 2. Sermons, American. I. Title.

WARFIELD, Benjamin 252'.05
Breckinridge, 1851-1921.
Faith and life / Benjamin B. Warfield. Edinburgh ; Carlisle, Pa. : Banner of Truth Trust, 1974. viii, 458 p. ; 19 cm. First published 1916. [BX9178.W33F3 1974] 75-320416 ISBN 0-85151-188-0 : £0.90
1. Presbyterian Church—Sermons. 2. Sermons, American. I. Title.

WASSON, Samuel Carson, 252.05
1908-
Eleven o'clock Sunday morning; book of sermons. [Rye? N.Y., 1960] 245 p. illus. 20 cm. Includes bibliography. [BX9178.W347E4] 61-21272
1. Presbyterian Church — Sermons. 2. Sermons, American. I. Title.

ANDERSON, Harrison Ray. 252.051
God's way; messages for our time. [Westwood, N. J., Revell [1955] 160p. 21cm. [BX9178.A497G6] 55-6627
1. Presbyterian Church—Sermons. 2. Sermons. American I. Title.

BONNELL, John Sutherland, 252.051
1893-
What are you living for? [Sermons] New York, Abingdon-Cokesbury Press [1950] 188 p. 20 cm. [BX9178.B66653W5] 50-5254
1. Presbyterian Church—Sermons. 2. Sermons, American. I. Title.

BUECHNER, Frederick, 252.051
1926-
The magnificent defeat. New York, Seabury Press [1966] 144 p. 22 cm. [BX9178.B75M3] 66-12638
1. Sermons, American. 2. Presbyterian Church — Sermons. I. Title.

BUECHNER, Frederick, 252.051
1926-
The magnificent defeat. New York, Seabury [c.1966] 144p. 22cm. [BX9178.B75M3] 66-12638 3.50
1. Sermons, American. 2. Presbyterian Church—Sermons. I. Title.

CUSTIS, W. Keith. 252'.05'1
Into a new age and other sermons / W. Keith Custis. [Upper Marlboro? Md.] : Custis, c1975. 200 p. ; 24 cm. Includes bibliographical references. [BX9178.C85I57] 75-29693
1. Presbyterian Church—Sermons. 2. Sermons, American. I. Title.

EVANS, Louis Hadley, 252.051
1897-
Youth seeks a master. Westwood, N.J., F. H. Revell Co. [c1964] 126 p. 20 cm. [BV4310.E75 1964] 64-16868
1. Youth — Religious life. 2. Presbyterian Church — Sermons. 3. Sermons, American. I. Title.

EVANS, Louis Hadley, 252.051
1897-
Youth seeks a master. Westwood, N.J., Revell [c.1964] 126p. 20cm. 64-16868 2.75 bds.,
1. Youth—Religious life. 2. Presbyterian Church—Sermons. 3. Sermons, American. I. Title.

FRY, John R. 252'.051
Fire and blackstone [by] John R. Fry. [1st ed.] Philadelphia, Lippincott [1969] vi, 248 p. 22 cm. [BX9178.F79F5] 73-91672 5.95
1. Presbyterian Chruch—Sermons. 2. Sermons, American. I. Title.

GORDON, Ernest. 252.051
A living faith for today. New York, Coward-McCann [1956] 255p. 22cm. [BX9178.G55L5] 56-10622
1. Presbyterian Church—Sermons. 2. Sermons, American. I. Title.

HALVERSON, Richard C 252.051
Christian maturity. Los Angeles, Cowman Publications [1956] 137p. 21cm. [BX9178.H32C5] 57-32400
1. Presbyterian Church—Sermons. 2. Sermons, American. I. Title.

HELTZEL, Massey Mott. 252.051
The invincible Christ. Nashville, Abingdon Press [1957] 142p. 20cm. [BX9178.H39 I 5] 57-5278
1. Presbyterian Church—Sermons. 2. Sermons, American. I. Title.

HUDNUT, Robert K. 252'.05'1
An active man and the Christ, by Robert K. Hudnut. Philadelphia, Fortress Press [1972] xiv, 114 p. 18 cm. Includes bibliographical references. [BX9178.H7A25] 72-75650 ISBN 0-8006-0119-X 2.50
1. Presbyterian Church—Sermons. 2. Sermons, American. I. Title.

HUTTON, John Alexander, 252.051
1868-1947.
The best of John A. Hutton, edited with an introd. by Edgar De Witt Jones. [1st ed.] New York, Harper [1950] xiv, 176 p. 21 cm. [BX9178.H75B4] 50-5295
1. Presbyterian Church—Sermons. 2. Sermons. American. I. Title.

IMES, William Lloyd, 252.051
1889-
The black pastures, an American pilgrimage in two centuries; essays and sermons. [1st ed.] Nashville, Hemphill Press, 1957. 146p. illus. 24cm. [BX9178.I5B5] 57-11472
1. Presbyterian Church—Sermons. 2. Sermons, American. 3. U. S.—Race question. I. Title.

JONES, Ilion Tingnal, 252.05'1
1889-
God's everlasting "yes", and other sermons [by] Ilion T. Jones. Waco, Tex., Word Books [1969] 138 p. 23 cm. [BX9178.J59G6] 69-12816 3.95
1. Presbyterian Church—Sermons. 2. Sermons, American. I. Title.

KEARNS, Ralph D 252.051
Handling life; sermons of inspiration and coruage for living. [1st ed.] New York, Exposition Press [1957] 77p. 21cm. [BX9178.K25H3] 57-7658
1. Presbyterian Church—Sermons. 2. Sermons, American. I. Title.

KERR, Clarence Ware, 252.051
1893-
Questions that must be answered. Los Angeles, Cowman Publications [1956] 190p. 20cm. [BR96.K4] 56-2694
1. Questions and answers—Theology. 2. Presbyterian Church— Sermons. 3. Sermons, American. I. Title.

KERR, Hugh Thomson, 1871- 252.051
1950.
Design for Christian living sermons edited by Donald Craig Kerr Philadelphia, Westminster Press [1953] 157p. 21cm. [BX9178.K4D4] 52-11757
1. Presbyterian Church—Sermons. 2. Sermons, American. I. Title.

LOVE, Larry. 252.051
Called to be saints. Grand Rapids, Zondervan Pub. House [1955] 137p. 20cm. [BX9178.L72C3] 55-24614
1. Presbyterian Church—Sermons. 2. Sermons. 3. Sermons, American. I. Title.

LOWE, Arnold Hilmar, 252.051
1888-
When God moves in. [1st ed.] New York, Harper, [1952] 191 p. 21 cm. [BX9178.L73W45] 52-8482
1. Presbyterian Church—Sermons. 2. Sermons, American. I. Title.

MACARTNEY, Clarence 252.051
Edward Noble, 1879-
The faith once delivered. New York, Abingdon-Cokesbury Press [1952] 175 p. 20 cm. [BX9178.M172F32] 52-5384
1. Presbyterian Church—Sermons. 2. Sermons, American. I. Title.

MACARTNEY, Clarence 252.051
Edward Noble, 1879-
Great nights of the Bible. Nashville, Abingdon [1964, c.1943] 224p. 18cm. (Apex bk. Q4-125) 1.25 pap.,
1. Presbyterian church—Sermons. 2. Sermons, American. I. Title.

MACARTNEY, Clarence 252.051
Edward Noble, 1879-
The greatest words in the Bible and in Human speech, by Clarence Edward Macartney. Nashville, Abingdon [1963, c.1938] 193p. 18cm. (Apex Bks., M5) .95 pap.,
1. Presbyterian church—Sermons. 2. Sermons, American. I. Title.

MACARTNEY, Clarence 252.051
Edward Noble, 1879-
Mountains and mountain men of the Bible. New York, Abingdon-Cokesbury Press [1950] 188 p. 20 cm. [BX9178.M174M6] 50-7310
1. Mountains—Palestine. 2. Bible—Biog. 3. Presbyterian Church—Sermons. 4. Sermons, American. I. Title.

MACARTNEY, Clarence 252.051
Edward Noble, 1879-
Strange texts, but grand truths. Nashville, Abingdon-Cokesbury Press [1953] 192p. 20cm. [BX9178.M174S8] 52-13756
1. Presbyterian Church—Sermons. 2. Sermons, American. I. Title.

MACARTNEY, Clarence 252.051
Edward Noble, 1879-
Trials of great men of the Bible, by Clarence Edward Macartney. New York, Nashville, Abingdon [1967, c.1946] 189p. 18cm. (Apex bks., AA5-125) [BX9178.M172T7] 46-3923 1.25 pap.,
1. Presbyterian church—Sermons. 2. Sermons, American. I. Title.

MACARTNEY, Clarence 252.051
Edward Noble, 1879-
You can conquer. Nashville, Abingdon Press [1954] 158p. 20cm. [BX9178.M172Y6] 54-5507
1. Presbyterian Church—Sermons. 2. Sermons, American. I. Title.

MACARTNEY, Clarence 252.051
Edward Noble, 1879-1957.
Salute thy soul. New York, Abingdon Press [1957] 144p. 20cm. [BX9178.M172S3] 57-9787
1. Presbyterian Church—Sermons. 2. Sermons, American. I. Title.

MCCOMB, John Hess, 1898- 252.051
Sermons on Bible themes. Wheaton, Ill., Van Kampen Press [1955] 99p. 20cm. [BX9178.M192S4] 55-33683
1. Presbyterian Church—Sermons. 2. Sermons, American. I. Title.

MCCONKEY, F Paul. 252.051
The ebony jewel box, and other sermons. Grand Rapids, W.B. Eerdmans Pub. Co., 1956. 150p. 23cm. [BX9178.M197E2] 56-14353
1. Presbyterian Church—Sermons. 2. Sermons, American. I. Title.

MACLENNAN, David 252.05'1
Alexander, 1903-
Sermons from Thanksgiving to Easter [by] David A. MacLennan. Valley Forge [Pa.] Judson Press [1968] 156 p. 23 cm. [BX9178.M1786S4] 68-13607 3.95
1. Presbyterian Church—Sermons. 2. Sermons, American. I. Title.

MARSHALL, Peter, 1902- 252.051
1949
Mr. Jones, meet the Master; sermons and prayers. [New York] Dell [1961, c.1949, 1950] 253p. (F127) Bibl. .50 pap.,
1. Presbyterian Church—Sermons. 2. Sermons, American. 3. Prayers. I. Title.

MARSHALL, Peter, 1902- 252.051
1949.
Mr. Jones, meet the Master; sermons and prayers. [Rev.] New York, Revell [1950] 192 p. port. 22 cm. [BX9178.M363M5 1950] 50-13247
1. Presbyterian Church—Sermons. 2. Sermons, American. 3. Prayers. I. Title.

MARSHALL, Peter, 1902- 252'.05'1
1949.
Mr. Jones, meet the Master; sermons and prayers of Peter Marshall. Boston, G. K. Hall, 1973 [c1950] 330 p. 25 cm. Large print ed. Includes bibliographical references. [BX9178.M363M5 1973] 73-9911 ISBN 0-8161-6132-1 9.95 (lib. bdg.)
1. Presbyterian Church—Sermons. 2. Sermons, American. 3. Prayers. I. Title.

MARTIN, William T 1921- 252.051
1956.
The power of an upward look, and other sermons. Tallahassee, Peninsular Pub. Co. [1957] 176p. illus. 24cm. [BX9178. 3653P6] 57-29433
1. Presbyterian Church—Sermons. 2. Sermons, American. I. Title.

OGILVIE, Lloyd John. 252'.05'1
Drumbeat of love : the unlimited power of the Spirit as revealed in the Book of Acts / Lloyd John Ogilvie. Waco, Tex. : Word Books, c1976. 291 p. ; 23 cm. Includes bibliographical references. [BS2625.4.O36] 76-19535 ISBN 0-87680-483-0 : 7.95
1. Presbyterian Church—Sermons. 2. Bible. N.T. Acts—Sermons. 3. Sermons, American. I. Title.

ROBERTS, David Everett, 252.051
1911-1955.
The grandeur and misery of man; [sermons] New York, Oxford University Press, 1955. 186p. 20cm. [BX9178.R56G7] 55-10931
1. Presbyterian Church—Sermons. 2. Sermons, American. I. Title.

ROSE, Stephen C. 252'.05'1
Sermons not preached in the White House, by Stephen C. Rose. Introductory essay by Reinhold Niebuhr. New York, R. W. Baron Pub. Co., 1970. 155 p. 21 cm. "A Cambria Press book." [BX9178.R67S47] 70-108974 4.95
1. Presbyterian Church—Sermons. 2. Sermons, American. I. Title.

SAY, David Lester. 252'.05'1
Brothers of the Bible. Parsons, W. Va., McClain Print. Co., 1973. 77 p. 22 cm. [BS579.B7S29] 72-89116
1. Brothers in the Bible. I. Title.

SCHOFIELD, Joseph 252.051
Anderson, 1897-
53 nature Sunday talks to children. Boston, W. A. Wilde Co. [1952] 189 p. 20 cm. [BV4315.S3177] 52-4527
1. Children's sermons. I. Title.

SCHOFIELD, Joseph 252.051
Anderson, 1897-
A year of children's sermons. Rev. ed. Boston, Wilde [1950] 219 p. 20 cm. [BV4315.S32 1950] 50-12735
1. Children's sermons. I. Title.

SPEAKMAN, Frederick B. 252.051
Love is something you do. [Westwood, N.J.] Revell [1959] 154 p. 22 cm. [BX9178.S68L6] 59-8724
1. Presbyterian Church — Sermons. 2. Sermons, American. I. Title.

SPEAKMAN, Frederick B 252.051
The salty tang; messages for today. [Westwood, N. J.] F. H. Revell Co. [1954] 160p. 21cm. [BX9178.S68S3] 54-5435
1. Presbyterian Church— sermons. 2. Sermons, American. I. Title.

STEWART, James Stuart, 252'.05'1
1896-
King for ever / James S. Stewart. Nashville, Tenn. : Abingdon Press, [1975] 160 p. ; 23 cm. [BX9178.S7917K5] 75-313215 ISBN 0-687-20883-1 : 5.95
1. Presbyterian Church—Sermons. 2. Sermons, English—Scotland. I. Title.

STOFFEL, Ernest Lee. 252.051
The strong comfort of God. Richmond, John Knox Press [1958] 159 p. 21 cm. [BX9178.S7932S7] 58-7774
1. Presbyterian Church — Sermons. 2. Sermons, American. I. Title.

*TALMAGE, T. DeWitt. 252'.051
T. DeWitt Talmage. Introduction by Daniel A. Poling. Grand Rapids, Mich., Baker Book House [1973, c1950] 254 p. 19 cm. (Great

pulpit masters series) [BX9178] ISBN 0-8010-8812-7. 2.95 (pbk.)
1. Presbyterian Church—Sermons. 2. Sermons, American. I. Title.

TALMAGE, Thomas De Witt, 1832-1902. 252.051
500 selected sermons Grand Rapids, Baker Book House, 1956- v. illus. 22cm. 'A reprint of the printing originally made by the Christian herald in 1900.' [BX9178] 56-10681
1. Presbyterian Church—Sermons. 2. Sermons, American. I. Title.

TALMAGE, Thomas De Witt, 1832-1902. 252.051
500 selected sermons. Grand Rapids, Baker Book House, 1956- v. illus. 22 cm. "A reprint of the printing originally made by the Christian herald in 1900." [[BN9178]] 56-10681
1. Presbyterian Church — Sermons. 2. Sermons, American. I. Title.

TEMPLETON, Charles Bradley, 1915- 252.051
Life looks up. [1st ed.] New York, Harper [c1955] 192p. 22cm. [BX9178.T345L5] 54-12812
1. Presbyterian Church—Sermons. 2. Sermons, American. I. Title.

TEMPLETON, Charles Bradley, 1915- 252.051
Life looks up. [1st ed.] New York, Harper [c1955] 192 p. 22 cm. [BX9178.T345L5] 54-12812
1. Presbyterian Church — Sermons. 2. Sermons, American. I. Title.

WALKER, Harold Blake. 252.051
Upper room on Main Street. [1st ed.] New York, Harper [1954] 191p. 22cm. [BX9178.W29U6] 53-10981
1. Presbyterian Church—Sermons. 2. Sermons, American. I. Title.

READ, David Haxton Carswell. 252.05'131
The pattern of Christ, by David H. C. Read. New York, Scribner [1967] 94 p. 19 cm. [BT382.R37] 67-13634
1. Beatitudes — Sermons. 2. Presbyterian Church — Sermons. 3. Sermons, American. I. Title.

READ, David Haxton Carswell. 252.05'131
The presence of Christ; sermons [by] David H. C. Read. [Denville, N.J.] Pannonia Press, 1968. 91 p. 21 cm. [BX9178.R367P7] 68-31878
1. Presbyterian Church—Sermons. 2. Sermons, American. I. Title.

READ, David Haxton Carswell. 252.05'131
Virginia Woolf meets Charlie Brown, by David H. C. Read. Grand Rapids, Eerdmans [1968] 225 p. 23 cm. A collection of sermons. [BX9178.R367V5] 68-28854 4.95
1. Presbyterian Church—Sermons. 2. Sermons, American. I. Title.

THOMAS, D. Reginald. 252.05131
To know God's way [by] D. Reginald Thomas. Westwood, N.J., Revell [1966] 154 p. 21 cm. [BX9178.T37T6] 66-21895
1. Presbyterian Church—Sermons. 2. Sermons, American. 3. Christian life—Presbyterian authors. I. Title.

ARMSTRONG, James Francis, 1750-1816. 252'.05'2
Light to my path : sermons / by James F. Armstrong ; edited by Marian B. McLeod. Trenton : First Presbyterian Church, c1976. 68 p. : ill. ; 22 cm. [BX9178.A67L53] 77-366763
1. Presbyterian Church—Sermons. 2. Sermons, American. I. Title.

BAILLE, Donald Macpherson, 1887-1954. 252.052
To whom shall we go? [By] D. M. Baille. Together with a biographical introd. by John Dow. Grand Rapids, Baker Book House [1974, c1955] 199 p. 18 cm. [BX9178.B325T6] ISBN 0-8010-0613-9 2.95 (pbk.)
1. Church of Scotland—Sermons. 2. Sermons, English—Scotland. I. Title.
L.C. card no. for original ed.: 56-15908.

BAILLIE, Donald Macpherson, 1887-1954. 252.052
Out of Nazareth; a selection of sermons and lectures. Edited by John Baillie. New York, Scribner [1959, c1958] 211p. 22cm. [BX9178.B325O8] 59-7204
1. Church of Scotland—Sermons. 2. Sermons, English—Scotland. 3. Theology—Addresses, essays, lectures. I. Title.

BAILLIE, Donald Macpherson, 1887-1954. 252.052
To whom shall we go? Together with a biographical introd. by John Dow. New York, Scribner [c1955] 199p. illus. 22cm. [BX9178.B325T6 1955a] 56-7128
1. Church of Scotland—Sermons. 2. Sermons, English—Scotland. I. Title.

BONAR, Horatius, 1808-1889. 252.052
Fifty-two sermons. Grand Rapids, Baker Book House, 1954. 464p. 21cm. [Co-operative reprint library] 'Originally published under the title, Family sermons.' [BX9178] 54-2688
1. Free Church of Scotland—Sermons. 2. Sermons, English—Scotland. I. Title.

BOSTON, Thomas, 1677-1732. 252.052
The crook in the lot; or, The sovereignty and wisdom of God in the afflictions of men displayed. With a brief memoir, and a portrait of the author. Swengel, Pa., Bible Truth Depot, 1961. 143p. illus. 20cm. [BX9178.B6668S6 1961] 61-65720
1. Church of Scotland—Sermons. 2. Affliction. 3. Providence and government of God—Sermons. I. Title.

COWAN, Arthur Aitken. 252.052
Bright is the shaken torch. New York, Scribner, 1950. xi, 148 p. 22 cm. (The Scholar as preacher) [BX9178.C68B7] 50-14247
1. Church of Scotland—Sermons. 2. Sermons, English—Scotland. I. Title. II. Series.

MCCARTNEY, Albert Joseph. 252.052
The empire of silence and selected sermons. Boston, Christopher Pub. House [1957] 191p. 21cm. [BX9178.M1746E5 252.085] 57-9839
1. Presbyterian Church—Sermons. 2. Sermons, American. I. Title.

MACDONALD, Murdo Ewen, 1914- 252.052
The vitality of faith. New York, Abingdon Press [1955] 158p. 21cm. [BX9178.M2233V5 1955a] 56-8741
1. Church of Scotland—Sermons. 2. Sermons, English—Scotland. I. Title.

MACLEAN, Alistair, 1885-1936. 252.052
High country; studies of the inner life with some interpretative aids from modern literature. With a foreword by Henry Sloane Coffin. New York Scribner, 1952. 255 p. 20 cm. [BX9178.M262H5] 52-13544
1. Presbyterian Church—Sermons. 2. Sermons, English—Scotland. I. Title.

MORRISON, George Herbert 252.052
Greatest sermons. With an introd. by George M. Docherty. New York, Harper [1960, c.1959] 256p. 22cm. 60-7960 3.50 half cloth,
1. United Free Church of Scotland—Sermons. 2. Sermons, English—Scotland. I. Title.

STEWART, James Stuart, 1896- 252'.05'2
River of life, by James S. Stewart. Nashville, Abingdon Press [1972] 160 p. 23 cm. [BX9178.S7917R58] 72-2031 ISBN 0-687-36480-9 3.50
1. Presbyterian Church—Sermons. 2. Sermons, English—Scotland. I. Title.

STEWART, James Stuart, 1896- 252.05'2
The wind of the spirit [by] James S. Stewart. Nashville, Abingdon Press [1969, c1968] 191 p. 23 cm. [BX9178.S7917W5 1969] 69-18447 3.95
1. Presbyterian Church—Sermons. 2. Sermons, English—Scotland. I. Title.

WHYTE, Alexander, 1837-1921 252.052
The treasury of Alexander Whyte; ed. by Ralph G. Turnbull. Foreword by Clarence E. Macartney. Grand Rapids, Mich., Baker Bk. [1968, c. 1953] 256p. 19cm. (Treasury ser.) [BX9178.W55T7] 1.95 pap.,
1. Presbyterian Church—Sermons. 2. Sermons. 3. Sermons, English—Scotland. I. Title.

DUNCAN, John, 1796-1870. 252.05'2'41
Pulpit and communion table; edited by David Brown. [New ed.] Inverness, Free Presbyterian Publications, 1969. [8], 243 p. 23 cm. [BX9178.D754P8] 72-497581 ISBN 0-902506-01-3 12/6
1. Free Church of Scotland—Sermons. 2. Sermons, English—Scotland. 3. Lord's Supper—Meditations. I. Brown, David, 1803-1897, ed. II. Title.

TORRANCE, Thomas Forsyth, 1913- 252.05241
When Christ comes and comes again. Grand Rapids, Eerdmans [1957] 192 p. 19 cm. [BX9178.T6W5] 58-14280
1. Church of Scotland — Sermons. 2. Sermons, English — Scotland. I. Title.

TORRENCE, Thomas Forsyth, 1913- 252'.05'2411
The centrality of Christ : devotions and addresses [at] the General Assembly of the Church of Scotland, May 1976 / [by] Thomas F. Torrence. Edinburgh : St. Andrew Press, 1976. v, 30 p. : 1 ill. ; 21 cm. [BT202.T67] 77-351033 ISBN 0-7152-0341-X : £0.50
1. Jesus Christ—Person and offices—Addresses, essays, lectures. 2. Devotional exercises. I. Church of Scotland. General Assembly. II. Title.

READ, David Haxton Carswell. 252'.05'242
Curious Christians [by] David H. C. Read. Nashville, Abingdon Press [1973] 144 p. 19 cm. [BX9178.R367C87 1973] 72-5201 ISBN 0-687-10101-8 pap. 1.95
1. Presbyterian Church—Sermons. 2. Sermons, American. I. Title.

ELDERSVELD, Peter H 252.057
Of law and love; the Ten commandments and the cross of Christ.[1st ed.] Grand Rapids, Eerdmans, 1954. 85p. 23cm. [BV4655.E62] 54-4995
1. Commandments, Ten—Sermons. 2. Christian Reformed Church—Sermons. 3. Sermons, American. I. Title.

ELDERSVELD, Peter H. 252.057
The Word of the Cross. Grand Rapids, Eerdmans [c.1959] 97p. 21cm. 59-16501 2.00
1. Christian Reformed Church—Sermons. 2. Sermons, American. I. Title.

EPPINGA, Jacob D 252.057
A pastor speaks to the soul of the city. [1st ed.] Grand Rapids, W. B. Eerdmans Pub. Co., 1954. 93 p. 23 cm. [BR517.E7] 54-14203
1. Cities and towns—U. S.—Religious life. I. Title.

GOULOOZE, William, 1903- 252.057
Consider Christ Jesus. Grand Rapids, Mich., Baker Bk., 1964[c.1947] 121p. 22cm. 1.00 pap.,
1. Reformed Church—Sermons. 2. Sermons, American. I. Temple time (Radio program) II. Title.

MILLER, Charles Ervine, 1867-1939. 252.05'7
Sermons and addresses. Edited by Herman Albert Klahr. Fostoria, Ohio, Gray Print. Co., 1967. xi, 328 p. port. 24 cm. [BX9426.M5S4] 67-28570
1. Reformed Church—Sermons. 2. Sermons, American. I. Klahr, Herman Albert, ed. II. Title.

ELDERSVELD, Peter H. 252.05731
Nothing but the Gospel; radio messages presented by Peter H. Eldersveld. Collected by the Radio Committee of the Christian Reformed Church. Grand Rapids, W. B. Eerdmans Pub. Co. [1966] xix, 162 p. port. 23 cm. [BX6827.E4N6] 66-30327
1. Christian Reformed Church—Sermons. 2. Sermons, American. I. Christian Reformed Church. Radio committee. II. Title.

GIROD, Gordon H 252.05732
God is not dead, by Gordon H. Girod. Grand Rapids, Baker Book House [1966] 125 p. 20 cm. [BX9527.G5G6] 66-19327
1. Evangelistic sermons. 2. Reformed Church in American-Sermons. 3. Sermons, American. I. Title.

GIROD, Gordon H. 252.05732
God is not dead. Grand Rapids, Mich., Baker Bk. [c.1966] 125p. 20cm. [BX9527.G5G6] 66-19327 2.95
1. Evangelistic sermons. 2. Reformed Church in America—Sermons. 3. Sermons, American. I. Title.

GOSSELINK, Marion Gerard. 252.05'732
The things eternal; sermons of a Dutch dominie. Grand Rapids, Baker Book House, 1967. 85 p. 22 cm. [BX9527.G57T49] 67-28326
1. Reformed Church in America—Sermons. 2. Sermons, American. I. Title.

BARR, Browne. 252.058
East Bay and Eden; sermons on the drama of redemption to a contemporary congregation. New York, Abingdon Press [1963] 159 p. 21 cm. [BX7233.B298E2] 63-17824
1. Congregational churches — Sermons. 2. Sermons, American. I. Title.

BARR, Browne 252.058
East Bay and Eden; sermons on the drama of redemption to a contemporary congregation. Nashville, Abingdon [c.1963] 159p. 21cm. 63-17824 3.00
1. Congregational churches—Sermons. 2. Sermons, American. I. Title.

CLAXTON, John W. 252.058
Facets of our faith; with an introd. by Judge Archie McComb. Green Bay, Wis., Reliance Pub. Co., 1951. 116 p. 20 cm. [BX7233.C664F3] 52-18162
1. Congregational churches—Sermons. 2. Sermons, American. I. Title.

DAVIES, John Trevor, 1907- 252.058
Lord of all. New York, Abingdon-Cokesbury Press [1953, '1951] 175 p. 20 cm. [BX7233.D252L6] 52-11310
1. Congregational churches—Sermons. 2. Sermons, English. I. Title.

FINNEY, Charles Grandison, 1792-1875. 252.05'8
Victory over the world; revival messages [by] Charles G. Finney. Grand Rapids, Kregel Publications [c1966] 123 p. 20 cm. (The Charles G. Finney memorial library. Revival sermon series) Sermons selected from the author's Lectures to professing Christians and Sermons on Gospel themes. [BV3797.F547] 66-24870
1. Evangelistic sermons. 2. Sermons, American. 3. Congregational churches — Sermons. I. Title.

HERRON, George Davis, 1862-1925. 252.05'8
Social meanings of religious experiences. With a new introd. by Timothy L. Smith. New York, Johnson Reprint Corp., 1969 [c1896] xxvi, 237 p. 18 cm. (Series in American studies) Bibliography: p. xxv-xxvi. [BT738.H46 1969] 74-79658
1. Social gospel—Sermons. 2. Congregational churches—Sermons. 3. Sermons, American. I. Title. II. Series.

INGLIS, Ervine P 252.058
What Christianity has to say. Webster Groves, Mo., Woman's Association of the First Congregational Church (United Church of Christ) [1962] 55p. illus. 23cm. [BX7233.I5W5] 62-20099
1. Sermons, English. 2. Congregational churches—Sermons. I. Title.

JACOBS, Charles Fredrick, 1908- 252.058
The dignity of the undefeated & other sermons suggested by modern fiction and biography. Boston, Christopher Pub. House [1958] 174p. 21cm. [BX7233.J2D5] 58-14172
1. Congregational churches—Sermons. 2. Sermons, American. I. Title.

JACOBS, Charles Fredrick, 1908- 252.058
New world calling, & other sermons suggested by Modern novels. [Waterloo? Iowa, 1951] xvii, 126 p. 21 cm. [BX7233.J2N4] 51-5043
1. Congregational Churches—Sermons. 2. Sermons, American. I. Title.

JEFFERSON, Charles Edward, 1860-1937 252.058
The best of Charles E. Jefferson. Selected, introd. by Frederick Kellar Stamm. New York, Crowell [1961, c.1960] 268p. 60-9216 3.95
1. Congregational churches—Sermons. 2. Sermons, American. I. Title.

JOWETT, John Henry, 1864-1923. 252.058
The school of Calvary; or, Sharing His suffering. Grand Rapids, Baker Book House, 1956. 125p. 18cm. 'Reprint of the original edition ... London ... 1911.' [BX7233] 55-10431
1. Suffering. 2. Congregational churches—Sermons. 3. Sermons, English. I. Title. II. Title: Sharing His suffering.

LOWE, Arnold Hilmar, 1888- 252.058
The worth of a man. [1st ed.] New York, Harper [1956] 184p. 22cm. [BR123.L69] 56-10211
1. Christianity—Addresses, essays, lectures. I. Title.

*MACDONALD, Angus 252.058
Called to be free. With introd. by Russell J. Clinchy [Chicago, 60610, Chas. Hallberg & Co. Pubs., 110 W. Grand Ave., c.1965] 126p. 19cm. 2.95 bds.,
I. Title.

MACDONALD, George, 1824-1905. 252'.05'8
Creation in Christ / George Macdonald ; edited by Rolland Hein from the three v. of Unspoken sermons. Wheaton, Ill. : H. Shaw Publishers, 1976. 342 p. ; 21 cm. (Wheaton literary series) A condensation of the author's Epea aptera. Unspoken sermons, 1st-3d ser., originally published, 1867-1889. [BV4253.M322 1976] 76-11282 ISBN 0-87788-860-4 : 4.95
1. Sermons, English. I. Title.

MARCH, Daniel, 1816- 252'.05'8
1909.
Night scenes in the Bible. Grand Rapids, Kregel Publications [1972] vii, 336 p. 21 cm. Reprint of the 1868 ed. [BX7233.M2667N5 1972] 77-189204 ISBN 0-8254-3211-1 5.95
1. Congregational churches—Sermons. 2. Sermons, American. I. Title.

MATHER, Cotton, 1663- 252'.05'8
1728.
Days of humiliation, times of affliction and disaster; nine sermons for restoring favor with an angry God, 1696-1727. Facsim. reproductions, with an introd. by George Harrison Orians. Gainesville, Fla., Scholars' Facsimiles & Reprints, 1970. xxiv, 381 p. 23 cm. Contents.Contents.—Things for a distress'd people to think upon.—Humiliations follow'd with deliverances.—Advice from Taberah.—Advice from the watch tower.—The Saviour with His rainbow.—A voice from heaven.—The voice of God in a tempest.—The terror of the lord.—Boanerges. [BX7233.M32D36 1970] 68-24211 15.00
1. Congregational churches—Sermons. 2. Sermons, American. I. Title.

MECKEL, Aaron Nathaniel, 252.058
1904-
Faith alive! The secret of joyful living. Grand Rapids. Mich., Ondervan [c.1965] 149p. 22cm. [BX7233.M447F3] 65-19509 2.95 bds.,
1. Congregational Churches—Sermons. 2. Sermons, American. I. Title.

MECKEL, Aaron Nathaniel, 252.058
1904-
Living can be exciting. Foreword by Halford E. Luccock. [1st ed.] New York, Dutton, 1956. 250 p. 21 cm. [BX7233.M447L5] 56-8282
1. Congregational churches—Sermons. 2. Sermons, American. I. Title.

MEEK, Frederick M 252.058
The life to live; [sermons] New York, Oxford University Press, 1955. 151p. 21cm. [BX7233.M45L5] 55-8120
1. Beatitudes—Sermons. 2. Congregational churches—Sermons. 3. Sermons, American. I. Title.

MEEK, Frederick M 252.058
Monday to Friday is not enough. New York, Oxford University Press, 1951. 240 p. 21 cm. [BX7233.M45M6] 51-13310
1. Congregational Churches — Sermons. 2. Sermons, American. I. Title.

MORGAN, George Campbell, 252.058
1863-1945.
The Westminster pulpit; the preaching of G. Campbell Morgan. [Westwood, N. J.] F. H. Revell Co. [1954- v. 22cm. [BX7233.M63W4] 54-5438
1. Congregational churches—Sermons. 2. Sermons, English. I. Title.

ROUTLEY, Erik. 252'.05'8
Saul among the prophets. [Abridged ed. Nashville, Tenn.] The Upper Room [1972] vi, 91 p. 20 cm. Includes bibliographical references. [BS573.R682] 79-188604 1.25
1. Patriarchs (Bible)—Sermons. 2. Congregational churches—Sermons. 3. Sermons, English. I. Title.

SECCOMBE, Joseph, 1706- 252.05'8
1760.
A discourse utter'd in part at Ammauskeeg-Falls in the fishing season, 1739. With an introd. by C. K. Shipton and illustrated with wood engravings by Michael McCurdy. Barre, Mass., Barre Publishers, 1971. 43 p. illus. 28 cm. On spine: A discourse at Ammauskeeg-Falls. "The illustrations ... are printed from the original wood block." Issued in a case. First published in 1743 under title: Business and diversion inoffensive to God, and necessary for the comfort of human society; a discourse ... 1739. [BX7233.S44B8 1971] 77-148059
1. Amusements—Moral and religious aspects. 2. Congregational churches—Sermons. 3. Sermons, American. I. Title.

SWANSON, Harvey. 252'.05'8
It is time to rebuild: our faith, our character, our America. With a foreword by Hardin B. Jones. Los Angeles, Crescent Publications [1974] vi, 159 p. 18 cm. [BX7233.S884I85] 74-80006 ISBN 0-914184-11-3 2.75 (pbk.)
1. Congregational churches—Sermons. 2. Sermons, American. I. Title.

TAYLOR, Edward, 1642- 252.058
1729.
Christographia. Edited by Norman S. Grabo. New Haven, Yale University Press, 1962. xviii, 507 p. facsim. 25 cm. The author's sermons delivered between 1701 and 1703, each with a corresponding poetic mediation. Bibliographical footnotes. [BX7117.T3] 62-10317
1. Congregational churches — Sermons. 2. Sermons, American. I. Grabo, Norman S., ed. II. Title.

TAYLOR, Edward, 1642-1729 252.058
Christographia. Ed. by Norman S. Grabo. New Haven, Conn., Yale [c.]1962. xlviii, 507p. facsim. 25cm. Bibl. 62-10317 15.00
1. Congregational churches—Sermons. 2. Sermons, American. I. Grabo, Norman S., ed. II. Title.

*TORREY, Reuben Archer, 252'058
1856-1928
R. A. Torrey. Introd. by William Culbertson. Grand Rapids, Mich. Baker Book House [1972, c.1950] 256 p. 20 cm. (Great Pulpit Masters) [BV7233] ISBN 0-8010-8788-0 pap., 2.95
1. Congregational Church—Sermons. I. Title.

VERNON, Ambrose White, 252.058
1870-1951.
The nobler risk, and other sermons. Selected and edited by Roy B Chamberlain. Hanover, N.H. Dartmouth Publications, 1955. 148p. illus. 24cm. [BX7233.V4N6] 56-19048
1. Congregational churches—Sermons. 2. Sermons, American. I. Title.

FINNEY, Charles 252.05832
Grandison, 1792-1875
So great salvation; evangelistic messages. Grand Rapids, Mich. Kregel [1966, c.1965] 128p. 20cm. (His Charles G. Finney memorial lib. Evangelistic sermon ser.) Sermons selected from the author's Sermons on the way of salvation [BV3797.F54] 65-25844 2.50
1. Evangelistic sermons. 2. Sermons, American. 3. Congregational churches—Sermons. I. Title.

FINNEY, Charles 252.05832
Grandison, 1792-1875.
True and false repentance; evangelistic messages. Grand Rapids, Kregel Publications [1966] 122 p. 20 cm. (The Charles G. Finney memorial library. Evangelistic sermon series) Sermons selected from the author's Lectures to professing Christians and his Gospel themes. [BV3797.F542 1966] 66-10576
1. Evangelistic sermons. 2. Sermons, American. 3. Congregational churches — Sermons. I. Title.

FINNEY, Charles 252.05832
Grandison, 1792-1875
True and false repentance; evangelistic messages. Grand Rapids, Mich., Kregel [c.1966] 122p. 20cm. (Charles G. Finney memorial lib. Evangelistic sermon ser.) Sermons selected from the author's Lectures to professing Christians and his Gospel themes. [BV3797.F542] 66-10576 2.50
1. Evangelistic sermons. 2. Sermons, American. 3. Congregational churches—Sermons. I. Title.

*SCOFIELD, C.I. 252.05832
In many pulpits. Grand Rapids, Mich., Baker Bk. 1966 [c.1922] 317p. 22cm. 3.95
I. Title.

BRUEGGEMANN, Walter. 252'.05'834
Living toward a vision : Biblical reflections on shalom / by Walter Grueggemann. Philadelphia : United Church Press, c1976. p. cm. (A Shalom resource) Includes bibliographical references. [BX9886.Z6B78] 76-22172 ISBN 0-8298-0322-X pbk. : 4.95
1. United Church of Christ—Sermons. 2. Sermons, American. I. Title.

SALVATION in New 252'.05'874
England : selections from the sermons of the first preachers / edited by Phyllis M. Jones and Nicholas R. Jones. Austin : University of Texas Press, c1977. xiii, 198 p. : ill. ; 24 cm. Bibliography: p. [163]-165. [BX7233.A1S34] 76-46554 ISBN 0-292-77532-6 : 12.95
1. Congregational churches—Sermons. 2. Sermons, American. 3. Preaching—History—New England. I. Jones, Phyllis M., 1945- II. Jones, Nicholas R., 1946-

*ANGELL, C. Roy. 252.06
Iron shoes [By] Charles Roy Angell. Nashville, Broadman Press, [1975 c1953] 117 p. 24 cm. [BX6333.A5I7] ISBN 0-8054-5136-6 2.95 (pbk.)
1. Babtists—Sermons. 2. Sermons, American. I. Title.

ANGELL, Charles Roy. 252.06
Baskets of silver. Nashville, Broadman Press [1955] 138p. 21cm. [BX6333.A5B3] 55-14611
1. Baptists—Sermons. 2. Sermons, American. I. Title.

ANGELL, Charles Roy 252.06
God's gold mines. Nashville, Broadman [c.1962] 118p. 21cm. 62-9194 2.50 bds.,
1. Baptists—Sermons. 2. Sermons, American. I. Title.

ANGELL, Charles Roy. 252.06
God's gold mines. Nashville, Broadman Press [1962] 118p. 21cm. [BX6333.A5G6] 62-9194
1. Baptists— Sermons. 2. Sermons, American. I. Title.

ANGELL, Charles Roy. 252.06
Iron shoes. Nashville, Broadman Press [1953] 117p. 21cm. [BX6333.A5 I7] 54-500
1. Baptists—Sermons. 2. Sermons. American. I. Title.

ANGELL, Charles Roy. 252.06
The price tags of life. Nashville, Broadman Press [1959] 125p. 21cm. [CM333.A5P7] 59-9692
1. Baptists—Sermons. 2. Sermons, American. I. Title.

BAXTER, James Sidlow. 252.06
Studies in problem texts; being a short series of elucidatory and applicatory expositions of certain Scripture passages which have occasioned perplexity. Grand Rapids, Zondervan Pub. House [1960] 192p. 22cm. [BX6333.B39S7] 60-50194
1. Baptists—Sermons. 2. Sermons, English. I. Title. II. Title: Problem texts.

BELL, Robert Emmet, 1872- 252.06
The fourth man in the fire, and other sermons. [1st ed.] New York, American Press [1961] 79p. 21cm. [BX6333.B44F6] 61-11490
1. Baptists—Sermons. 2. Sermons, American. I. Title.

BENNETT, William L 252.06
The trumpet of the Lord; messages of no uncertain sound. Grand Rapids, Zondervan Pub. House [1959] 118p. 21cm. [BX6333.B455T7] 59-2744
1. Baptists—Sermons. 2. Sermons, American. I. Title.

BROADUS, John Albert, 252.06
1827-1895.
Favorite sermons of John A. Broadus. Edited with an introd. by Vernon Latrelle Stanfield. [1st ed.] New York, Harper [1959] 147p. 22cm. [BX6333.B67F3] 59-7148
1. Baptists—Sermons. 2. Sermons, American. I. Title.

BRONG, Rosco, D. D. 252.06
Love builds up: a simple score of short sermons addressed to saints and sinners. Lexington, Ky., 657 St. Anthony Dr., Amen Bk. Loft, c.1963. 80p. 23cm. 3.00; 1.00 pap.,
I. Title.

BRONG, Rosco, 1908- 252.06
For His name's sake; a simple score of short sermons fitting first truths to last days. [1st ed.] New York, Greenwich Book Publishers [c1963] 82 p. 21 cm. [BX6333.B685F6] 63-22175
1. Sermons, American. 2. Baptists — Sermons. I. Title.

BROWN, Henry Clifton, ed. 252.06
Chapel messages, compiled and edited by H. C. Brown and Charles P. Johnson. Grand Rapids, Baker Book House [1966] 143 p. 21 cm. Thirteen addresses given at Southwestern Baptist Theological Seminary chapel services. [BX6333.A1B69] 66-18315
1. Baptists — Sermons. 2. Sermons, American. I. Johnson, Charles P., joint ed. II. Fort Worth, Tex. Southwestern Baptist Theological Seminary. III. Title.

BROWN, Henry Clifton, ed. 252.06
Chapel messages, comp. ed. by H. C. Brown, Charles P. Johnson. Grand Rapids, Mich., Baker Bk. [c.1966] 143p. 21cm. 13 addresses given at Southwestern Baptist Theological Seminary chapel services. [BX6333.A1B69] 66-18315 2.50
1. Baptists—Sermons. 2. Sermons, American. I. Johnson, Charles P., joint ed. II. Fort Worth, Tex. Southwestern Baptist Theological Seminary. III. Title.

BROWN, Henry Clifton, ed. 252.06
Southwestern sermons. Nashville, Broadman Press [1960] 212p. 22cm. Thirty-two sermons by members of the faculty of Southwestern Baptist Theological Seminary. [BX6333.A1B72] 60-5629
1. Baptists—Sermons. 2. Sermons, American. I. Fort Worth, Tex. Southwestern Baptist Theological Seminary. II. Title.

BUNYAN, John, 1628-1688. 252.06
The heavenly footman; or, A description of the man that gets to heaven; together with the way he runs in, the marks he goes by, also, some directions how to run so as to obtain. Swengel, Pa., Reiner Publications, 1967. xv, 48 p. port. 19 cm. "The text of the present edition is from that of George Offor's edition of 1860." [BR75.B78 1967] 68-399
I. Offor, George, 1787-1864, ed. II. Title.

CAMPBELL, Robert Clifford, 252.06
1888-
How firm a foundation; a book of sermons. introd. by Robert G. Lee. [Westwood, N. J.,)0] 0Revell [1954] 159p. 20cm. [BX6333.C354H6] 54-9682
1. Baptists—Sermons. 2. Sermons, American. I. Title.

CHAPPELLE, E. E. 252.06
The voice of God. New York, Carlton [c.1963] 119p. 21cm. 2.50
I. Title.

COLTON, Clarence Eugene, 252.06
1914-
Questions Christians ask [by] C. E. Colton. Nashville, Broadman Press [1969] 128 p. 20 cm. (A Broadman inner circle book) [BX6333.C58Q4] 69-17898
1. Baptists—Sermons. 2. Sermons, American. I. Title.

CRISWELL, Wallie A 252.06
These issues we must face. Grand Rapids, Zondervan Pub. House [1953] 137 p. 20 cm. [BX6333.C77T5] 53-13124
1. Baptists—Sermons. 2. Sermons, American. I. Title.

DEHONEY, Wayne 252.06
Challenges to the cross. Nashville, Broadman [c.1962] 116p. Bibl. 62-9196 2.50 bds.,
1. Baptists—Sermons. 2. Sermons, American. I. Title.

DIXON, Amzi Clarence, D. 252.06
D., 1854-1925.
The glories of the Cross. Grand Rapids, Mich., Eerdmans [c.1962] 253p. 20cm. 62-3917 3.00 bds.,
1. Evangelistic sermons. 2. Baptists—Sermons. 3. Sermons, English. I. Title.

EDDLEMAN, H Leo. 252.06
To make men free. Nashville, Broadman Press [1954] 128p. 21cm. [BX6333.E3T6] 54-12917
1. Baptists—Sermons. 2. Sermons, American. I. Title.

EWTON, Maynard Franklin, 252.06
1903-
The joys of Jesus. [Enid, Okla.] 1952. 282 p. 20 cm. [BX6333.E85J6] 52-20940
1. Baptists—Sermons. 2. Sermons, American. I. Title.

FAGERBURG, Frank Bentamin, 252.06
1898-
Here for a purpose. Valley Forge, Pa., Judson [c.1963] 95p. 20cm. 63-19833 1.75 pap.,
1. Sermons, American. 2. Baptist Church—Sermons. I. Title.

FISCHBACH, Julius, 1894- 252.06
The children's moment; a year of story sermons for boys and . girls. Illus. by the author. Valley Forge, Judson Press [1966] 128 p. illus. 21 cm. [BV4315.F46] 66-20531
1. Children's sermons. 2. Baptists — Sermons. I. Title.

FISCHBACH, Julius 1894- 252.06
The children's moment; a year of story sermons for boys and girls. Illus. by the author. Valley Forge, Pa., Judson Pr. [c.1966] 128p. illus. 21cm. [BV4315.F46] 66-20531 2.95
1. Children's sermons. 2. Baptists—Sermons. I. Title.

FORD, William Herschel, 252.06
1900-
Simple sermons about Jesus Christ. Grand Rapids, Mich., Zondervan [c.1961] 104p. 61-16233 1.95 bds.,
1. Baptists—Sermons. 2. Sermons, American. I. Title.

FORD, William Herschel, 252.06
1900-
Simple sermons for Sunday evening, by W. Herschel Ford. Grand Rapids, Zondervan Pub. House [1967] 126 p. 21 cm. [BX6333.F568S4815] 67-22685
1. Baptists—Sermons. 2. Sermons, American. I. Title.

FORD, William Herschel, 252.06
1900-
Simple sermons for Sunday morning, by W. Herschel Ford. Grand Rapids, Zondervan [1966] 127p. 21cm. [BX6333.F568S482] 66-27003 2.50 bds.,
1. Baptists—Sermons. 2. Sermons, American. I. Title.

FORD, William Herschel, 252.06
1900-
Simple sermons for times like these, by W. Herschel Ford. Grand Rapids, Zondervan Pub. House [1965] 135 p. 21 cm. [BX6333.F568C4845] 65-19499
1. Baptists—Sermons. 2. Sermons, American. I. Title.

FORD, William Herschel, 1900- 252.06
Simple sermons for times like these. Grand Rapids, Mich., Zondervan [c.1965] 135p. 21cm. [BX6333.F568C4845] 65-19499 2.50 bds.,
1. Baptists—Sermons. 2. Sermons, American. I. Title.

FORD, William Herschel, 1900- 252.06
Simple sermons for today's world. Introd. by W. Ramsey Pollard. Grand Rapids, Zondervan Pub. House [c.1960] 120p. 20cm. (Simple sermons ser.) 60-51161 1.95 bds.,
1. Baptists—Sermons. 2. Sermons, American. I. Title.

FORD, William Herschel, 1900- 252.06
Simple sermons on salvation and service. Introd. by James Le Roy Steele. Grand Rapids, Zondervan Pub. House [c1955] 136p. 20cm. [BX6333.F568S49] 55-227
1. Baptists— Sermons. 2. Sermons, American. I. Title.

FORD, William Herschel, 1900- 252.06
Simple sermons on the old-time religion, by W. Herschel Ford. Introd. by W. A. Criswell. Grand Rapids, Zondervan Pub. House [1968] 120 p. 21 cm. [BX6333.F568S52] 68-19842
1. Baptists—Sermons. 2. Sermons, American. I. Title.

FORD, William Herschel, 1900- 252.06
Simple talks for Christian workers. Grand Rapids, Mich., Zondervan [c.1961] 120p. 61-19960 1.95 bds.,
1. Baptists—Sermons. 2. Sermons, American. I. Title.

FREEMAN, Thomas Franklin. 252.06
The choice of the pew, a volume of sermons. [1st ed.] New York, American Press [c1963] 148 p. 22 cm. [BX6333.F77C5] 63-14590
1. Baptists — Sermons. 2. Sermons, American. I. Title.

GARNER, Lloyd W., Rev. 252.06
Could it be you? 'T.V.' sermons. New York, Exposition Press [c.1961] 107p. 2.50
1. Baptist Church—Sermons. I. Title.

GLADSTONE, John N. 252.06
The valley of the verdict [by] John N. Gladstone. Nashville, Abingdon Press [1968] 144 p. 20 cm. [BX6333.G55V3] 68-25360 3.00
1. Baptists—Sermons. 2. Sermons, English—Canada. I. Title.

GRAHAM, William Franklin, 1918- 252.06
The challenge; sermons from Madison Square Garden [by] Billy Graham. [1st ed.] Garden City, N.Y., Doubleday, 1969. x, 173 p. 22 cm. [BV3797.G679] 78-100047 4.50
1. Evangelistic sermons. 2. Baptists—Sermons. 3. Sermons, American. I. Title.

GUNN, John R 252.06
Bulwark never failing. Rindge, N. H., R. R. Smith, 1955. 157p. 23cm. [BX6333.G8B8] 55-9045
1. Baptists— Sermons. 2. Sermons, American. I. Title.

HENDERSON, Joseph Luke, 1890- 252.06
The trial of Christ. [Crestview? Fla., 1954] 167p. illus. 20cm. [BX6333.H38T7] 55-24540
1. Baptists—Sermons. 2. Sermons, American. I. Title.

HILBUN, Bruce S 1893- 252.06
That ye may know; sermons for Christian living. [1st ed.] New York, Exposition Press [1955] 103p. 21cm. [BX6333.H49T5] 55-12283
1. Baptists—Sermons. 2. Sermons, American. I. Title.

HOBBS, Herschel H. 252.06
Cowards or conquerors. [1st ed.] Philadelphia, Judson Press [1951] 240 p. 20 cm. Bibliographical references included in "Acknowledgments" (p. 239-240) [BX6333.H59C6] 51-10399
1. Baptists—Sermons. 2. Sermons, American. I. Title.

HOOD, David 252.06
My Father's world; messages on themes from God's great out-of-doors. Grand Rapids, Mich., Zondervan Pub. House [c.1960] 124p. illus. 20cm. 60-51234 1.95 bds.,
1. Baptists—Sermons. 2. Sermons, American. I. Title.

HUDSON, Robert Lofton. 252.06
For our age of anxiety. Nashville, Broadman Press [1956] 160p. 21cm. [BX6333.H8F6] 56-10285
1. Baptists— Sermons. 2. Sermons, American. I. Title.

HUNTLEY, Thomas Elliott. 252.06
As I saw it, not comm Unism but commOnism a prophetic appraisal of the status quo, a message for our times and for all times, for America and for all nations. New York, Comet Press Books [1955, c1954] 146p. 23cm. 'The Central Baptist Church on Wheels': p. 119-146. [BX6452.H8] 55-874
1. Communism and religion. 2. U. S.—Race question. 3. St. Louis. Central Baptist Church. 4. Baptists— Sermons. 5. Sermons, American. I. Title.

HURT, John Jeter. 252.06
Sermons: short, medium, long. Atlanta [1959] 284p. 23cm. [BX6333.H83S4] 59-15663
1. Baptists— Sermons. 2. Sermons, American. I. Title.

HUSS, John Ervin, 1910- 252.06
I felt God's presence in the nation's Capital. Grand Rapids, Mich., Zondervan Pub. House [c.1960] 133p. illus. 61-199 2.50 bds.,
1. Baptists—Sermons. 2. Sermons, American. 3. Washington, D. C.—Descr.—1951- I. Title.

HUSS, John Ervin, 1910- 252.06
I met God there; messages from nature. Introd. by G. A. Leichliter. Grand Rapids, Zondervan Pub. House [1956] 88p. 21cm. [BX6333.H85I2] 56-25034
1. Baptists— Sermons. 2. Sermons, American. I. Title. II. Title: Nature messages.

JONES, John Ithel. 252.06
Facing the new world, and other sermons, by J. Ithel Jones. Waco, Tex., Word Books [1968] 128 p. 22 cm. [BX6333.J73F3] 68-21744
1. Baptists—Sermons. 2. Sermons, English. I. Title.

KEPNER, Frank M. 252.06
Answering God's call; informal sermons dealing with life's eternal verities. With a foreword by John Bunyan Smith. Philadelphia, Judson Press [1952] 110 p. 21 cm. [BX6333.K43A5] 52-11353
1. Baptists—Sermons. 2. Sermons, American. I. Title.

KETCHAM, Robert Thomas, 1889- 252.06
Sermons, by Robert T. Ketcham. Des Plaines, Ill., Regular Baptist Press [1966] 2 v. 20 cm. Contents.CONTENTS. -- v. 1. The death hymn of Christ, and other sermons. -- v. 2. Why was Christ a carpenter, and other sermons. [BX6333.K45S4] 66-15924
1. Baptists — Sermons. 2. Sermons, American. I. Title.

KETCHAM, Robert Thomas, 1889- 252.06
Sermons [2v.] Des Plaines, Ill., Regular Baptist Pr. 188 Oakton Blvd. [c.1966] 2v. (176; 176p.) 20cm. Contents.v.1. The death hymn of Christ, and other sermons.--v.2. Why was Christ a carpenter, and other sermons. [BX6333.K45S4] 66-15924 2.95 ea., sBaptists--Sermons.
1. Sermons, American. 2. Sermons, American. I. Title.

KING, Geoffrey R 252.06
Truth for our time. Grand Rapids, Eerdmans [c1957] 140p. 20cm. (Preaching for today) [BX6333.K55T7] 57-14468
1. Baptists—Sermons. 2. Sermons, English. I. Title.

KING, Martin Luther 252.06
Strength to love. New York, Pocket Bks. [1964, c.1963] 179p. 18cm. (50001) .50 pap.,
1. Baptists, Negro—Sermons. 2. Sermons, American. I. Title.

KING, Martin Luther. 252.06
Strength to love. [1st ed.] New York, Harper & Row [1963] 146 p. 22 cm. [BX6452.K5] 63-12051
1. Baptists, Negro—Sermons. 2. Sermons, American. I. Title.

LAMBDIN, Jerry Elmer, 1889- comp. 252.06
Be strong in the Lord; twelve sermons on the 1955 Training Union theme. Nashville, Broadman Press [1954] 132p. 20cm. [BX6333.A1L18] 54-12918
1. Baptists— Sermons. 2. Sermons, American. 3. Baptist Training Union. I. Title.

LAMBDIN, Jerry Elmer, 1889- ed. 252.06
Keeping the faith. Nashville, Broadman Press [1953] 135p. 20cm. [BX6333.L3K4] 53-13403
1. Baptists—Sermons. 2. Sermons, American. I. Title.

LAMBDIN, Jerry Elmer, 1889- ed. 252.06
Learn from me. Nashville, Broadman Press [1952] 125p. 20cm. 'Sermons on the twelve monthly themes of the Training Union.' [BX6333.A1L2] 52-14654
1. Baptists— Sermons. 2. Sermons, American. 3. Baptist Training Union. I. Title.

LEE, Robert Greene 252.06
The must of the second birth, and other sermons. [Westwood, N.J.] Revell [1960, c.1959] 127p. 21cm. 60-5499 2.50 bds.,
1. Baptists—Sermons. 2. Sermons, American. I. Title.

LEE, Robert Greene, 1886- 252.06
Bought by the blood. Grand Rapids, Zondervan Pub. House [1957] 184p. 21cm. [BX6333.L3953B6] 58-20565
1. Baptists—Sermons—Sermons. 2. Sermons, American. I. Title.

LEE, Robert Greene, 1886- 252.06
A charge to keep, and other messages. Grand Rapids, Zondervan Pub. House [1959] 120p. 20cm. [BX6333.L3953C5] 60-17172
1. Baptists—Addresses, essays, lectures. I. Title.

LEE, Robert Greene, D. D., 1886- 252.06
Christ above all, and other messages. Grand Rapids, Mich., Zondervan [c.1963] 154p. 22cm. 63-21172 2.50 bds.,
1. Baptists—Sermons. 2. Sermons, American. I. Title.

LEE, Robert Greene, 1886- 252.06
Christ above all, and other messages. Grand Rapids, Zondervan Pub. House [c1963] 154 p. 22 cm. [BX6333.L3953C5] 63-21172
1. Baptists — Sermons. 2. Sermons, American. I. Title.

LEE, Robert Greene, 1886- 252.06
From death to life through Christ, by Robert G. Lee. Grand Rapids, Mich., Zondervan [1966] 120p. 21cm. [BX6333.L3953F7] 66-18944 2.95 bds.,
1. Baptists—Sermons. 2. Sermons, American. I. Title.

LEE, Robert Greene, 1886- 252.06
God's answer to man's question, and other messages. Grand Rapids, Mich., Zondervan [c.1962] 149p. 21cm. 62-4809 2.50 bds.,
1. Baptists—Sermons. 2. Sermons, American. I. Title.

LEE, Robert Greene, 1886- 252.06
Salvation in Christ, and other messages. Grand Rapids, Zondervan [c.1961] 152p. 61-16238 2.50 bds.,
1. Baptists—Sermons. 2. Sermons, American. I. Title.

LORD, Fred Townley, 1893- 252.06
The treasure of the Gospel. Nashville, Broadman Press [1952] 109 p. 20 cm. [BV3797.L65] 52-14148
1. Evangelistic sermons. 2. Baptists—Sermons. 3. Sermons, English I. Title.

MCLAREN, Alexander, 1826-1910. 252'.06
The best of Alexander MacLaren. Edited, with an introd. by Gaius Glenn Atkins. Freeport, N.Y., Books for Libraries Press [1971, c1949] xix, 167 p. 23 cm. (Biography index reprint series) [BX6333.M365B4 1971] 74-179733 ISBN 0-8369-8101-4
1. Baptists—Sermons. 2. Sermons, English. I. Title.

MARNEY, Carlyle, 1916- 252.06
These things remain. Nashville, Abingdon-Cokesbury Press [1953] 174p. 20cm. [BX6333.M3668T5] 53-5398
1. Baptists—Sermons. 2. Sermons, American. I. Title.

MARTINEZ, Angel, 1921or2- 252.06
The destiny of the species, and other messages. Grand Rapids, Zondervan Pub. House [1959] 119p. 20cm. [BX6333.M3682D4] 59-43147
1. Baptists—Sermons. 2. Sermons, American. I. Title.

MARTINEZ, Angel, 1921or2- 252.06
Revival at midnight, and other messages. Foreword by Robert G. Lee. Grand Rapids, Zondervan Pub. House [c1956] 119p. 20cm. [BV3797.M316] 57-23352
1. Evangelistc sermons. 2. Baptists—Sermons. 3. Sermons, American. I. Title.

MELTON, William Walter, 1879- 252.06
The Christian heritage; sermons upon the meanings of our common faith. [1st ed.] New York, American Press [1959] 70p. 21cm. [BX6333.M39C5] 59-9403
1. Baptists— Sermons. 2. Sermons, American. I. Title.

*MEYER, F. B. 252'.06
F. B. Meyer. Introduction by Robert G. Lee. Grand Rapids, Mich., Baker Book House [1973, c1950] 256 p. 19 cm. (Great pulpit masters series) [BX6333] ISBN 0-8010-5943-7. 2.95 (pbk.)
1. Baptists—Sermons. 2. Sermons, English. I. Title.

MILLER, Calvin. 252'.06
Burning bushes & moon walks. Waco, Tex., Word Books [1972] 108 p. 21 cm. Includes bibliographical references. [BX6333.M53B87] 77-188065 ISBN 0-87680-275-7 Pap. $1.95
1. Baptists—Sermons. 2. Sermons, American. I. Title.

MILLER, Calvin. 252.06
Sixteen days on the church calendar. Grand Rapids, Baker Book House [1968] 130 p. 21 cm. ([The New minister's handbook series]) [BV4254.2.M5] 68-31475 2.95
1. Occasional sermons. 2. Baptists—Sermons. 3. Sermons, American. I. Title.

MOODY, Jess C. 252'.06
A drink at Joel's Place, by Jess Moody. Waco, Tex., Word Books [1967] 125 p. 21 cm. [BX6333.M55D7] 67-24570
1. Baptists—Sermons. 2. Sermons, American. I. Title.

MORGANS, G. J. 252.06
The danger, duty, and delight of life, by G. J. Morgans. Uniontown, Pa., Great Bethel Baptist Church [1971] 61 p. 20 cm. [BX6333.M64D35] 79-176376
1. Baptists—Sermons. 2. Sermons, American. I. Title.

MURRAY, Ralph L. 252.06
Christ and the city [by] Ralph L. Murray. Nashville, Tenn., Broadman Press [1970] 126 p. 20 cm. (A Broadman inner circle book) Includes bibliographical references. [BX6333.M83C5] 70-95413
1. Baptists—Sermons. 2. Sermons, American. I. Title.

OATES, Wayne Edward, 1917- 252.06
The revelation of God in human suffering. Philadelphia, Westminster Press [1959] 143p. 20cm. [BV4909.O2] 59-8226
1. Baptists—Sermons. 2. Sermons, American. I. Title.

OLFORD, Stephen F 252.06
Christianity and you. [1st ed.] Grand Rapids, Eerdmans [1958] 123p. 21cm. (Preaching for today) [BX6333.O4C47] 58-9547
1. Baptists—Sermons. 2. Sermons, English. I. Title.

PALMER, Gordon, 1888- 252.06
By freedom's holy light; a selection of patriotic messages. With a foreword by John W. Bradbury. New York, Devin-Adair Co., 1964. vii, 162 p. 21 cm. [BX6333.P3B9] 64-8224
1. Baptists — Sermons. 2. Sermons, American. 3. Christianity and politics. I. Title.

PEARCE, J Winston. 252.06
I believe. Nashville, Broadman Press [1954] 120p. 21cm. [BX6333.P4I2] 54-9444
1. Baptists— Sermons. 2. Sermons, American. I. Title.

PEARCE, J Winston. 252.06
The window sill of heaven. Nashville, Broadman Press [1958] 166p. 21cm. [BX6333.P4W5] 58-5412
1. Baptists- -Sermons. 2. Sermons, American. I. Title.

PHILLIPS, Harold Cooke, 1892- 252.06
The timeless gospel. New York, Abingdon Press [1956] 171p. 21cm. [BX6333.P54T5] 56-7765
1. Baptists—Sermons. 2. Sermons, American. 3. Christianity—Essence, genlus, nature. I. Title.

POTEAT, Edwin McNeill, 1892- 252.06
The dimension of depth. [1st ed.] New York, Harper [1957] 114p. 20cm. [BX6333.P785D5] 56-7031
1. Baptists—Sermons. 2. Sermons, American. I. Title.

POWELL, Adam Clayton, 1908-1972. 252.06
Keep the faith, baby! New York, Trident Press, 1967. 293 p. 22 cm. [BX6452.P59] 67-16402
1. Baptists, Afro-Americans—Sermons. 2. Sermons, American. I. Title.

POWELL, Ivor 252.06
Bible highways. Foreword by Thomas B. McDormand. Grand Rapids, Mich., Zondervan Pub. House [1959] 171p. 19cm. 60-2523 2.50 bds.,

1. Baptists—Sermons. 2. Sermons, English—Canada. 3. Homiletical illustrations. I. Title.

PRUDEN, Edward Hughes. 252.06
Interpreters needed; the eternal gospel and our contemporary society. Philadelphia, Judson Press [1951] 128 p. 21 cm. [BX6333.P78915] 51-11475
1. Baptists—Sermons. 2. Sermons, American. I. Title.

RANSOME, William Lee, 1879- 252.06
An old story for this new day, and other sermons and addresses. Richmond, Central Pub. Co., 1954. 207p. 20cm. [BX6452.R35] 54-37090
1. Baptists—Sermons. 2. Sermons, American. I. Title.

REDPATH, Alan. 252.06
The Bible speaks to our times. Westwood, N.J., Revell [1968] 124 p. 21 cm. [BV4253.R38] 68-11370
1. Sermons, American. 2. Sermons, English. I. Title.

REDPATH, Alan. 252.06
Learning to live. Grand Rapids, Eerdmans [1961] 132p. 20cm. (Preaching for today) [BX6333.R37L4] 61-10856
1. Baptists—Sermons. 2. Sermons, American. I. Title.

SANDERS, Robert Neal, 1931- comp. 252.06
Light for life's dark riddle; timely sermons from today's pulpits. R. N. Sanders, editor. Waco, Tex., Word Books [1968] 139 p. 21 cm. [BX6333.A1S3] 68-24011
1. Baptists—Sermons. 2. Sermons, American. I. Title.

SHAMBLIN, J. Kenneth. 252.06
Life comes as choice [by] J. Kenneth Shamblin. Nashville, Abingdon Press [1967] 175 p. 21 cm. [BX8333.S45L5] 67-11018
1. Methodist Church—Sermons. 2. Sermons, American. I. Title.

*SPURGEON, Charles Haddon, 1834-1892 252.06
Lectures to my students [by] C. H. Spurgeon. Grand Rapids, Mich., Zondervan [1972] 443 p. 23 cm. This is a new ed. containing Selected Lectures from Series 1, 2 and 3, 1954. [BX63333.] 6.95
1. Sermons—English—Baptist—Collections. I. Title.

SPURGEON, Charles Haddon, 1834-1892. 252.06
The new Park Street pulpit; containing sermons preached and rev.; v.1. Grand Rapids, Mich., Zondervan [1963] v. 23cm. Contents.v.1 [1855] Facsimile of the orig. [pub.] in 1856-61 by Passmore & Alabaster, London. 64-79 4.95
1. Baptists—Sermons. 2. Sermons, English. I. Title.

SPURGEON, Charles Haddon, 1834-1892 252.06
The new Park Street pulpit; containing sermons preached and rev. by the Rev. C. H. Spurgeon, minister of the Chapel; vs. 3 & 4. Grand Rapids, Mich., Zondervan [1964] 2v. (459; 479p.) 23cm. Contents.v.3, 1857.--v.4, 1858. Facsimile of the orig. pub. in 1858 and 1859 by Passmore & Alabaster, London. 64-79 4.95 ea.,
1. Baptists—Sermons. 2. Sermons—English. I. Title.

SPURGEON, Charles Haddon, 1834-1892. 252.06
The treasury of Charles H. Spurgeon. Introd. by Wilbur M. Smith. [Westwood, N.J.] F.H. Revell Co. [1955] 256p. 21cm. [BX6217.S67] 55-9251
1. Theology—Collected works—19th cent. 2. Baptists—Collected works. I. Title.

SPURGEON, Charles Haddon, 1834-1892 252.06
The treasury of Charles H. Spurgeon. Introd. by Wilbur M. Smith. Grand Rapids, Mich., Baker Bk. [1967,c.1955] 256p. 20cm. (Treasury ser.) [BX6217.S67] 1.95 pap.,
1. Theology—Collected works—19th cent. 2. Baptists—Collected works. I. Title.

STANFIELD, Vernon L 252.06
Effective evangelistic messages, by V. L. Stanfield. Grand Rapids, Baker Book House [1967] 67 p. 23 cm. [BV3797.S682] 67-26586
1. Evangelistic sermons. 2. Sermons, American. 3. Baptists—Sermons. I. Title.

STANFIELD, Vernon L. 252.06
Effective evangelistic messages, by V. L. Stanfield. Grand Rapids, Baker Book House [1967] 67 p. 23 cm. [BV3797.S682] 67-26586
1. Evangelistic sermons. 2. Sermons, American. 3. Baptists—Sermons. I. Title.

THE Struggle for meaning / William Powell Tuck, editor. Valley Forge, Pa. : Judson Press, c1977. 144 p. ; 22 cm. Includes bibliographical references. [BX6333.A1S77] 76-48747 ISBN 0-8170-0724-5 pbk. : 4.95 252'.06
1. Baptists—Sermons. 2. Sermons, American. I. Tuck, William P.

THURMAN, Howard, 1899- 252.06
The growing edge. [1st ed. New York] Harper [1956] 181p. 22cm. [BX6333.T5G7] 56-12058
1. Baptists—Sermons. 2. Sermons, American. I. Title.

THURMAN, Howard, 1899- 252.06
The growing edge. [1st ed. New York] Harper [1956] 181 p. 22 cm. [BX6333.T5G7] 56-12058
1. Baptists—Sermons. 2. Sermons, America. I. Title.

TRUETT, George Washington, 1867-1944. 252.06
After His likeness; compiled and edited by Powhatan W. James. [1st ed.] Grand Rapids, Eerdmans, 1954. 176p. 21cm. (Truett memorial series, v. 8) Sermons. [BX6333.T8A35] 54-4832
1. Baptists—Sermons. 2. Sermons,American. I. Title.

TRUETT, George Washington, 1867-1944 252.06
Follow thou Me.' Nashville, Broadman Press [1960] 241p. (Broadman Starbooks) 1.50 pap.,
1. Evangelistic sermons. 2. Baptists—Sermons. 3. Sermons, American. I. Title.

TRUETT, George Washington, 1867-1944. 252.06
A guest for souls; [sermons and addresses] Compiled and edited by J. B. Cranfill. Grand Rapids, Eerdmans [1961, c1917] 379 p. 20 cm. [BX6333.T8Q5] 61-2917
1. Baptists — Sermons. 2. Sermons, American. I. Title.

TRUETT, George Washington, 1867-1944. 252.06
The inspiration of ideals; compiled and edited by Powhatan W. James. Grand Rapids, Eerdmans, 1950. 195 p. 20 cm. (Truett memorial series, v. 5) [BV4254.2.T7] 51-1114
1. Occasional sermons. 2. Baptists — Sermons. 3. Sermons, American. I. Title.

TRUETT, George Washington, 1867-1944. 252'.06
The inspiration of ideals, by George W. Truett. Compiled & edited by Powhatan W. James. Grand Rapids, Mich., Baker Book House [1973, c.1950] 195 p. 20 cm. (George W. Truett library) At head of title: Vol. V in the Truett Memorial series. [BV4254.2T7] ISBN 0-8010-8800-3 2.95 (pbk.)
1. Occasional sermons. 2. Baptists—Sermons. 3. Sermons, American. I. Title.
L.C. card no. for the 1950 edition: 51-1114.

TRUETT, George Washington, 1867-1944. 252'.06
On eagle wings, by George W. Truett. Comp. & edited by Powhatan W. James. Grand Rapids, Mich., Baker Book House [1973, c.1953] 186 p. 20 cm. (George W. Truett library) At head of title: Vol. VII in the Truett memorial series. [BX6333.T805] ISBN 0-8010-8803-8 2.95 (pbk.)
1. Baptists—Sermons. 2. Sermons, American. I. James, Powhatan W., ed. II. Title. III. Series: Truett memorial series, v. 7
L.C. card no. for the 1953 edition: 53-8069.

TRUETT, George Washington, 1867-1944. 252.06
A quest for souls; [sermons and addresses] Comp. and ed. by J. B. Cranfill. Grand Rapids, Mass., Eerdmans [1961, c.1917] 379p. 61-2917 2.45 pap.,
1. Baptists—Sermons. 2. Sermons, American. I. Title.

WARBURTON, John, 1776-1857. 252'.06
The Gospel of a Covenant God : 10 sermons / by John Warburton ; with foreword by K. W. H. Howard. Sheffield : Zoar Publications, 1976. [7], 151 p., leaf of plate, [2] p. of plates : col. ill., col. port. ; 19 cm. [BX6333.W267G67 1976] 76-375009 ISBN 0-904435-08-3 : £3.75
1. Baptists—Sermons. 2. Sermons, English. I. Title.

WARMATH, William Walter. 252.06
When He calls me. Nashville, Broadman Press [1969] 127 p. 20 cm. [BX6333.W27W48] 69-10725
1. Baptists—Sermons. 2. Sermons, American. I. Title.

WEBB, Perry F. 252.06
He made the stars also, by Perry F. Webb. San Antonio, Naylor Co. [1968] vii, 99 p. 20 cm. [BX6333.W333H4] 68-54389 3.95

1. Baptists—Sermons. 2. Sermons, American. I. Title.

WELLDORN, Charles. 252.06
This is God's hour. Nashville, Broadman Press [1952] 101p. 20cm. [BX6333.W36T45] 52-14442
1. Baptists— Sermons. 2. Sermons, American. I. Title.

WHITE, Reginald E O 252.06
A relevant salvation. Grand Rapids, Eerdmans [1963] 132 p. 21 cm. (Preaching for today) Includes bibliographical references) [BX6333.W435R4] 63-23792
1. Baptists — Sermons. 2. Sermons, English. I. Title.

WIGHTON, R W 1901- 252.06
A pendant of pearls. [1st ed.] New York, Pageant Press [1961] 110 p. 21 cm. [BX6333.W48P4] 61-19010
1. Baptists — Sermons. 2. Sermons, American. I. Title.

WIGHTON, R. W., 1901- 252.06
A pendant of pearls. New York, Pageant Pr. [c.1961] 110p. 61-19010 2.50
1. Baptist—Sermons. 2. Sermons, American. I. Title.

WOOTTON, William Robert. 252.06
Steam cycles for nuclear power plant. New York, Simmons-Boardman [1958] Boston, Christopher Pub. House, [1961] 66 p. diagrs. 22 cm. 142 p. 21 cm. (Nuclear engineering monographs, 6) [(TK1078.W)] [BX6333.W69W5] A 59 61-13066
1. Atomic power-plants. 2. Steam engineering. 3. Baptists — Sermons. 4. Sermons, American I. Worboys, James Samuel Alphaeus. II. Title. III. Title: The winning move. IV. Series.

WORBOYS, James Samuel Alphaeus 252.06
The winning move. Boston, Christopher Pub. House [c.1961] 142p. 61-13066 3.00
1. Baptists—Sermons. 2. Sermons, American. I. Title.

YATES, Kyle Monroe, 1895- 252.06
Preaching from great Bible chapters [by] Kyle M. Yates. [2d ed.] Waco, Tex., Word Books [1968, c1957] xii, 209 p. 22 cm. Bibliographical footnotes. [BX6333.Y3P7 1968] 68-7270 4.95
1. Baptists—Sermons. 2. Sermons, American. I. Title.

CRISWELL, Wallie A. 252.06'08
Fifty years of preaching at the Palace, by W. A. Criswell [and George W. Truett] Grand Rapids, Mich., Zondervan Pub. House [1969] 142 p. illus., ports. 22 cm. [BX6333.C77F48] 68-59097 2.95
1. Baptists—Sermons. 2. Sermons, American. I. Truett, George Washington, 1867-1944. II. Title.

ALLEN, R. Earl. 252.061
Bible paradoxes. [Westwood, N.J.] Revell [1963] 128 p. 21 cm. [BX6333.A3B5] 63-17107
1. Sermons. America. 2. Southern Baptist Convention — Sermons. I. Title.

ALLEN, R. Earl 252.061
Bible paradoxes. [Westwood, N. J.] Revell [c.1963] 128p 21cm. 63-17107 2.50 bds.,
1. Sermons, American. 2. Southern Baptist Convention—Sermons. I. Title.

BAKER, Bo. 252'.06'1
Made for the mountains / Bo Baker. Waco, Tex. : Word Books, c1977. 85 p. ; 22 cm. [BX6333.B348M33] 76-48503 ISBN 0-87680-504-7 : 3.95
1. Baptists—Sermons. 2. Sermons, American. I. Title.

BISAGNO, John R. 252'.06'1
The word of the Lord [by] John R. Bisagno. Nashville, Broadman Press [1973] 149 p. 21 cm. [BX6333.B46] 72-96153 ISBN 0-8054-2221-8 4.95
1. Baptists—Sermons. 2. Sermons, American. I. Title.

BROUGHER, James Whitcomb, 1870- 252.061
Life and laughter, popular lectures. [1st ed.] Philadelphia, Judson Press [1950] 229 p. 20 cm. [BX6333.B73L5] 50-13364
1. Baptists—Addresses, essays, lectures. I. Title.

BROWN, Henry Clifton, ed. 252.061
More Southern Baptist preaching. Compiled and edited by H. C. Brown, Jr. Nashville, Broadman Press [1964] viii, 165 p. 22 cm. [BX6333.A1B73] 64-14074
1. Baptists — Sermons. 2. Sermons, American. 3. Preaching. I. Title. II. Title: Southern Baptist preaching.

BROWN, Henry Clifton, Jr., ed. 252.061
More Southern Baptist preaching. Comp., ed. by H. C. Brown, Jr. Nashville, Broadman [c.1964] viii, 165p. 22cm. 64-14074 2.95 bds.,
1. Baptists—Sermons. 2. Sermons, American. 3. Preaching. I. Title. II. Title: Southern Baptist preaching.

BROWN, Henry Clifton, ed. 252.061
Southern Baptist preaching. Nashville, Broadman Press [1959] 227p. 22cm. [BX6333.A1B7] 59-9695
1. Baptists—Sermons. 2. Sermons, American. 3. Preaching. I. Title.

BRYANT, Carvin C. 252'.06'1
The love slave / Carvin C. Bryant. [Cincinnati : Clarion Pub. Co., c1977] 103 p. ; 21 cm. [BX6333.B79L68] 76-51604 ISBN 0-89422-001-2 : 5.95
1. Baptists—Sermons. 2. Sermons, American. I. Title.

CAMPBELL, Robert Clifford, 1888- 252.061
Answered by the Master. Nashville, Broadman Press ['1951] 138 p. 20 cm. [BX6333.C354A5] 51-14367
1. Baptists—Sermons. 2. Sermons, American. I. Title.

CARLETON, J Paul, 1907- 252.061
Are you as big as you think you are? Shawnee, Printed by Oklahoma Baptist University Press [1952] 151 p. 20 cm. Sermons. [BX6333.C358A7] 52-1709
1. Raptists—Sermons. 2. Sermons, American. I. Title.

CAYLOR, John, 1894- 252.061
The great 'I am's' of Jesus. Grand Rapids, Zondervan Pub. House [1957] 86p. 20cm. [BX6333.C38G7] 57-36859
1. Baptists—Sermons. 2. Sermons, American. I. Title. II. Title: 'I am's' of Jesus.

COLEMAN, L. H. 252'.06'1
Christ's call to commitment / by L. H. Coleman. Orlando, Fla. : Christ for the World Publishers, c1976. 117 p. ; 22 cm. [BX6333.C575C48] 76-39751
1. Baptists—Sermons. 2. Sermons, American. I. Title.

CRISWELL, Wallie A. 252.06'1
The scarlet thread through the Bible [by] W. A. Criswell. Nashville, Broadman Press [1971, c1970] 80 p. 20 cm. [BX6333.C77S3] 70-132923
1. Baptists—Sermons. 2. Sermons, American. I. Title.

DEHONEY, Wayne. 252'.06'1
Preaching to change lives / Wayne Dehoney. Nashville : Broadman Press, [1974] 124 p. ; 19 cm. [BX6333.D43P74] 74-80339 ISBN 0-8054-2223-4 pbk. : 2.50
1. Baptists—Sermons. 2. Sermons, American. I. Title.

DRAPER, James T. 252'.06'1
Say neighbor—your house is on fire! / By James T. Draper, Jr. ; with foreword by Cliff Barrows. Dallas : Crescendo Book Publications, [1975] 190 p. ; 21 cm. [BX6333.D68S29] 75-6207 ISBN 0-89038-021-X
1. Baptists—Sermons. 2. Sermons, American. I. Title.

ELLISON, John Malcus, 1889- 252.061
The art of friendship, by John Malcus Ellison ... Richmond, Va., 1943. 6 p.l., 15-103 p. 19 cm. [BX6333.E4A7] 43-12480
1. Baptists — Sermons. 2. Sermons, American. I. Title.

EXPERIENCING, living, sharing Christ : sermons on the Evangelistic Life Style / edited by J. Richard Hawley. Valley Forge, Pa. : Judson Press, c1976. 91 p. : ports. ; 22 cm. Includes bibliographical references. [BX6333.A1E87] 75-33905 ISBN 0-13-778704-9 : 12.95 ISBN 0-8170-0704-0 pbk. : 252'.06'1
1. Baptists—Sermons. 2. Sermons, American. I. Hawley, J. Richard.

FORD, William Herschel, 1900- 252.06'1
Simple sermons for a sinful age [by] W. Herschel Ford. Grand Rapids, Zondervan Pub. House [1970] 128 p. 22 cm. [BX6333.F568S47] 77-106431 2.95
1. Baptists—Sermons. 2. Sermons, American. I. Title.

FORD, William Herschel, 1900- 252.061
Simple sermons for saints and sinners. Grand Rapids, Zondervan Pub. House [1954] 152p. 20cm. [BX6333.F568S48] 54-1163

1. Baptists—Sermons. 2. Sermons, American. I. Title.

FORD, William Herschel, 1900- 252.06'1
Simple sermons for twentieth century Christians. by W. Herschel Ford. [1st ed.] Grand Rapids. Zondervan [1967] 116p. 21cm. [BX6333.F568S487] 67-17229 2.50 bds.,
1. Baptists—Sermons. 2. Sermons, American. I. Title.

FORD, William Herschel, 1900- 252.06'1
Simple sermons for twentieth century Christians, by W. Herschel Ford. [1st ed.] Grand Rapids, Zondervan Pub. House [1967] 116 p. 21 cm. [BX6333.F568S487] 67-17229
1. Baptists—Sermons. 2. Sermons, American. I. Title.

FORD, William Herschel, 1900- 252.06'1
Simple sermons on evangelistic themes, by W. Herschel Ford. Grand Rapids, Mich., Zondervan Pub. House [1970] 128 p. 22 cm. [BV3797.F57] 73-146569 2.95
1. Evangelistic sermons. 2. Baptists—Sermons. 3. Sermons, American.

FORD, William Herschel, 1900- 252'.06'1
Simple sermons on New Testament texts / by W. Herschel Ford. Grand Rapids : Zondervan Pub. House, c1974. 109 p. ; 21 cm. [BX6333.F568S4895] 73-22697 1.95
1. Baptists—Sermons. 2. Sermons, American. I. Title. II. Title: New Testament texts.

FORD, William Herschel, 1900- 252.061
Simple sermons on simple themes. Introd. by L. R. Scarborough. Grand Rapids, Zondervan Pub. House [1957] 118p. 20cm. First published in 1941 under title: God bless, America, and other sermons. [BX6333.F568G6 1957] 57-4753
1. Baptists—Sermons. 2. Sermons, American. I. Title.

FOSDICK, Harry Emerson, 1878- 252.061
The secret of victorious living. New York, Harper [c.1934-1966] 208p. 21cm. (Chapelbks., 19 H) [BX6333.F57S4] 34-39191 1.45 pap.,
1. Sermons, American. I. Title.

FOSDICK, Harry Emerson, 1878-1969. 252.06'1
A great time to be alive; sermons on Christianity in wartime. Freeport, N.Y., Books for Libraries Press [1972, c1944] vi, 235 p. 23 cm. (Essay index reprint series) [BX6333.F57G7 1972] 78-167341 ISBN 0-8369-2688-9
1. Sermons, American. 2. World War, 1939-1945—Addresses, sermons, etc. I. Title.

FOSDICK, Harry Emerson, 1878-1969. 252.061
What is vital in religion; sermons on contemporary Christian problems. [1st ed.] New York, Harper [1955] 238 p. 22 cm. [BX6333.F57W5] 55-8522
1. Sermons, American. I. Title.

HARMS, Abraham John. 252.061
The quest for Christ; a series of messages on finding Christ. Chicago, Good News Publishers [1950] 168 p. 20 cm. [BX6333.H328Q4] 50-4667
1. Baptists—Sermons. 2. Sermons, American. I. Title.

HAVNER, Vance, 1901- 252.06'1
In times like these. Old Tappan, N.J., Revell [1969] 128 p. 20 cm. [BX6333.H345I5] 71-85308 3.50
1. Baptists—Sermons. 2. Sermons, American. I. Title.

HAWK, Charles Nathaniel. 252'.06'1
The search for truth [by] C. Nathaniel Hawk. Philadelphia, Dorrance [1974] 181 p. 22 cm. [BX6333.H348S4] 73-88168 ISBN 0-8059-1931-7 6.95
1. Baptists—Sermons. 2. Sermons, American. I. Title.

HOWINGTON, Nolan P. 252'.06'1
Growing disciples through preaching / Nolan P. Howington, Alton H. McEachern, William M. Pinson, Jr. Nashville : Broadman Press, c1976. 136 p. ; 20 cm. Includes bibliographical references. [BX6333.H74G76] 75-41741 ISBN 0-8054-2227-7 pbk. : 2.95
1. Baptists—Sermons. 2. Sermons, American. I. McEachern, Alton H., joint author. II. Pinson, William M., joint author. III. Title.

HUBBARD, David Allan. 252'.06'1
Colossians speaks to the sickness of our times / David Allan Hubbard. Waco, Tex. : Word Books, c1976. 96 p. ; 21 cm. "Originally radio talks given on the international broadcast: The Joyful sound." [BS2715.4.H82] 76-19527 ISBN 0-87680-843-7 : 2.25
1. Bible. N.T. Colossians—Sermons. 2. Baptists—Sermons. 3. Sermons, American. I. Joyful sound. II. Title.

HUBBARD, David Allan. 252'.06'1
Happiness : you can find the secret / David A. Hubbard. Wheaton, Ill. : Tyndale House Publishers, c1976. 96 p. ; 18 cm. Most of the content of this book was presented as radio addresses by the author on the program, The joyful sound. [BT382.H8] 76-5214 ISBN 0-8423-1297-8 pbk. : 1.45
1. Beatitudes—Sermons. 2. Baptists—Sermons. 3. Sermons, American. I. Title.

HUBBARD, David Allan. 252'.06'1
An honest search for a righteous life / David A. Hubbard. Wheaton, Ill. : Tyndale House Publishers, 1975. 128 p. ; 18 cm. Originally presented as a series of messages on the network radio program "The joyful sound" by the author. [BX6333.H78H66] 75-596 ISBN 0-8423-1508-X pbk. : 1.45
1. Baptists—Sermons. 2. Sermons, American. I. Title.

HUBBARD, David Allan. 252.06'1
What's God been doing all this time? Glendale, Calif., G/L Regal Books [1970] 116 p. 18 cm. [BX6333.A1H8] 70-122885 0.95
1. Baptists—Sermons. 2. Sermons, American. I. Title.

HUBBARD, David Allan. 252.06'1
What's new? Thoughts on the new things happening to God's people. Waco, Tex., Word Books [1970] 80 p. 22 cm. [BX6333.H78W45 1970] 71-132858 2.95
1. Baptists—Sermons. 2. Sermons, American. I. Title.

JACKSON, Richard Allen, 1938- 252'.06'1
Freedom is never free : [sermons] / Richard A. Jackson. Nashville : Broadman Press, c1976. 135 p. ; 20 cm. [BX6333.J3F73] 75-42861 ISBN 0-8054-1936-5 : 4.95
1. Baptists—Sermons. 2. Sermons, American. I. Title.

KOLLER, Charles W 1896- 252.061
Sermons preached without notes. Grand Rapids, Baker Book House, 1964. 145 p. 20 cm. [[Evangelical pulpit library]] [BX6333.K63S4] 64-15866
1. Baptists — Sermons. 2. Sermons, American. I. Title.

KOLLER, Charles W., 1896- 252.061
Sermons preached without notes. Grand Rapids, Mich., Baker Bk. House, [c.]1964. 145p. 20cm. (Evangelical pulpit lib.) 64-15866 2.50 bds.,
1. Baptists—Sermons. 2. Sermons, American. I. Title.

LEE, G Avery. 252.061
Life's everyday questions. Nashville, Broadman Press [1953] 123p. 20cm. [BX6333.L395L5] 53-12016
1. Baptists—Sermons. 2. Sermons, American. I. Title.

LEE, Robert Greene, 1886- 252'.06'1
Grapes from Gospel vines / R. G. Lee. Nashville : Broadman Press, c1976. 149 p. ; 20 cm. [BX6333.L3953G67] 75-39448 ISBN 0-8054-5142-0 : 4.95
1. Baptists—Sermons. 2. Sermons, American. I. Title.

LEE, Robert Greene, 1886- 252'.06'1
Latest of Lee [by] Robert G. Lee. Jefferson City, Mo., Le Roi Publishers [1973] 123 p. 22 cm. Sermons. [BX6333.L3953L37] 72-94717 4.95
1. Sermons, American. 2. Baptists—Sermons. I. Title.

LEE, Robert Greene, 1886- 252.061
Seven swords, and other messages. Grand Rapids, Zondervan Pub. House [c1958] 120p. 20cm. [BX6333.L3953S4] 59-29221
1. Baptists—Sermons. 2. Sermons, American. I. Title.

LEE, Robert Greene, 1886- 252.061
Yielded bodies. Grand Rapids, Zondervan Pub. House [1954] 180p. 20cm. [BX6333.L3953Y5] 54-3806
1. Man (Theology)—Sermons. 2. Baptists—Sermons. 3. Sermons, American. I. Title.

LELAND, John, 1754-1841. 252.06'1
The writings of John Leland. Edited by L. F. Greene. New York, Arno Press, 1969. 744 p. port. 24 cm. (Religion in America) Reprint of the 1845 ed. [BX6495.L43A2 1969] 73-83420
I. Greene, L. F., ed.

LINGER, O. Afton. 252'.06'1
Pilot aboard; sermonettes, by O. Afton Linger. Lake Mills, Iowa, Graphic Pub. Co., 1971. vi, 229 p. 23 cm. [BX6333.L48P5] 79-169846
1. Baptists—Sermons. 2. Sermons, American. I. Title.

LORD, Fred Townley, 1893- 252.061
The faith that sings. [Essays] Nashville, Broadman Press [1951] 119 p. 20 cm. [BX6333.L57F3] 51-11400
1. Sermons, English (Selections: Extracts, etc.) I. Title.

*MALONE, Tom 252.061
With Jesus after sinners. 12 Bible messages as blessed of God in conferences on revival and soul winning. Introd. by John R. Rice. Murfreesboro, Tenn., Sword of the Lord Pubs. [c.1966] 200p. ports. 21cm. 2.75
I. Title.

MINTON, Frank D. 252'.06'1
Baseball's sermon on the mound / Frank D. Minton. Nashville : Broadman Press, c1976. 96 p. : port. ; 20 cm. [BX6333.M54B37] 75-36887 ISBN 0-8054-5566-3 : 3.25
1. Baptists—Sermons. 2. Sermons, American. I. Title.

MORRIS, Bernard Newth, 1919- 252'.06'1
Harmony of sermons. Philadelphia, Dorrance [1973] 91 p. 22 cm. [BX6333.M647H37] 72-96800 ISBN 0-8059-1826-4 3.95
1. Baptists—Sermons. 2. Sermons, American. I. Title.
Contents omitted.

PARKER, Henry Allen. 252'.06'1
Living at peace in a turbulent world. Nashville, Broadman Press [1973] 127 p. 21 cm. Includes bibliographical references. [BX6333.P33L48] 72-97603 ISBN 0-8054-8507-4 1.50 (pbk.)
1. Baptists—Sermons. 2. Sermons, American. I. Title.

PATTERSON, W. Morgan, ed. 252.061
Professor in the pulpit; sermons preached in Alumni Memorial Chapel by the faculty of the Southern Baptist Theological Seminary, comp., ed. by W. Morgan Patterson, Raymond Bryan Brown. Nashville, Tenn., Broadman Press [c.1963] vi, 150 p. 21 cm. Bibl. 63-19073 2.25, pap.
1. Sermons, American. 2. Southern Baptist Convention—Sermons. I. Brown, Raymond Bryan, joint ed. II. Louisville, Ky. Southern Baptist Theological Seminary. III. Title.

PATTERSON, W. Morgan, ed. 252.061
Professor in the pulpit; sermons preached in Alumni Memorial Chapel by the faculty of the Southern Baptist Theological Seminary. compiled and edited by W. Morgan Patterson and Raymond Bryan Brown. Nashville, Tenn., Broadman Press [1963] vi, 150 p. 21 cm. Includes bibliographies. [BX6333.P35P7] 63-19073
1. Sermons, American. 2. Southern Baptist Convention—Sermons. I. Brown, Raymond Bryan, joint ed. II. Louisville, Ky. Southern Baptist Theological Seminary. III. Title.

PAULLIN, Norman, 1906-1968. 252.06'1
In step with Jesus; sermons. Valley Forge, Judson Press [1970] 79 p. 20 cm. [BX6333.P394I5] 70-131421 1.95
1. Baptists—Sermons. 2. Sermons, American. I. Title.

RICE, John R., 1895- 252'.06'1
Preaching that built a great church / John R. Rice. Murfreesboro, Tenn. : Sword of the Lord, c1974. 585 p. ; 20 cm. Sermons originally published in Sword of the Lord. [BX6333.R48P73] 75-312705 3.95
1. Baptists—Sermons. 2. Sermons, American. I. Title.

SCOTT, Manuel Lee. 252'.06'1
The Gospel for the ghetto; sermons from a Black pulpit [by] Manuel L. Scott. Nashville, Broadman Press [1973] 125 p. 21 cm. [BX6333.S39G67] 72-97605 ISBN 0-8054-5532-9 3.95
1. Baptists—Sermons. 2. Sermons, American. I. Title.

SHERMAN, Cecil E. 252'.06'1
Modern myths [by] Cecil E. Sherman. Nashville, Broadman Press [1973] 122 p. 20 cm. [BX6333.S48M62] 72-94401 ISBN 0-8054-5216-8 1.50 (pbk.)
1. Sermons, American. 2. Baptists—Sermons. I. Title.

SMITH, Ralph M. G. 252'.06'1
Let me explain; direct answers to disturbing doubts, by Ralph M. Smith. With foreword by W. A. Criswell. [Dallas, Crescendo Book Publications, c1970] 198 p. 23 cm. [BX6333.S55L4] 71-122687
1. Baptists—Sermons. 2. Sermons, American. I. Title.

THURMAN, Howard, 1899- 252'.06'1
The growing edge. Richmond, Ind., Friends United Press [1974, i.e.1975 c1956] p. cm. Reprint of the ed. published by Harper, New York. [BX6333.T5G7 1974] 74-14866 ISBN 0-913408-14-X 2.95 (pbk.)
1. Baptists—Sermons. 2. Sermons, American. I. Title.

TRENT, John Scott. 252.061
Revival crusade sermons. Grand Rapids, Baker Book House, 1966. 97 p. 20 cm. [BV3797.T74] 66-15953
1. Evangelistic sermons. 2. Sermons, American. 3. Baptists — Sermons. I. Title.

TRENT, John Scott 252.061
Revival crusade sermons. Grand Rapids, Mich., Baker Bk. [c.]1966. 97p. 20cm. [BV3797.T74] 66-15953 2.00 bds.,
1. Evangelistic sermons. 2. Sermons, American. 3. Baptists—Sermons. I. Title.

TRUETT, George Washington, 1867-1944. 252.06'1
After his likeness, by George W. Truett. Comp. & edited by Powhatan W. James. Grand Rapids, Mich., Baker Book House [1973, c.1954] 182 p. 20 cm. (George W. Truett library) At head of title: Volume VII in the Truett Memorial series. [BX6333.T8A35] ISBN 0-8010-8804-6 2.95 (pbk.)
1. Baptists—Sermons. 2. Sermons, American. I. Title.
L.C. card no. for hardbound edition: 54-12947.

TRUETT, George Washington, 1867-1944. 252.061
On eagle wings; compiled and edited by Powhatan W. James. Grand Rapids, W. B. Eerdmans Pub. Co., 1953. 186p. 20cm. (The Truett memorial series, v. 7) [BX6333.T8O5] 53-8069
1. Baptists—Sermons. 2. Sermons, American. I. Title.

*TRUETT, George Washington, 1867-1944. 252.06'1
The prophet's mantle, by George W. Truett. Edited by Powhatan W. James. Grand Rapids, Mich., Baker Book House [1973, c.1948] 206 p. 20 cm. (George W. Truett library) At head of title: Volume III in the Truett Memorial series. [BX6333] ISBN 0-8010-8798-8 2.95 (pbk.)
1. Baptists—Sermons. 2. Bible. O.T.—Sermons. I. Title.

TRUETT, George Washington, 1867-1944. 252'.061
The salt of the earth, by George W. Truett. Edited by Powhatan W. James. Grand Rapids, Baker Book House [1973, c.1949] 191 p. 20 cm. (George W. Truett library) At head of title: Volume IV in the Truett Memorial series) [BX6333.T8W45] ISBN 0-8010-8799-6 2.95 (pbk.)
1. Baptists—Sermons. 2. Sermons, American. I. Title.
L.C. card no. for the hardbound edition: 49-8976.

TRUETT, George Washington, 1867-1944. 252.061
Who is Jesus? Compiled and edited by Powhatan W. James. Grand Rapids, W. B. Eerdmans Pub. Co., 1952. 171 p. 21 cm. (Truett memorial series, v. 6) [BX6333.T8W45] 52-2204
1. Baptists — Sermons. 2. Sermons, American. I. Title.

TRUETT, George Washington, 1867-1944. 252.06'1
Who is Jesus? By George W. Truett. Comp. & edited by Powhatan W. James. Grand Rapids, Mich., Baker Book House [1973, c.1952] 171 p. 20 cm. (George W. Truett library) At head of title: Vol. VI in the Truett memorial series. [BX6333.T8W45] ISBN 0-8010-8801-1 2.95 (pbk.)
1. Baptists—Sermons. 2. Sermons, American. I. James, Powhatan W., ed. II. Title. III. Series: Truett memorial series, v. 6
L.C. card no. for the 1952 edition: 52-2204.

VALENTINE, Foy, comp. 252.061
Christian faith in action; fourteen sermons on current moral issues, by J. B. Weatherspoon [and others] Nashville, Broadman Press [1956] 136p. 21cm. [BX6333.A1V3] 56-8672
1. Baptists—Sermons. 2. Sermons, American. I. Weatherspoon, Jesse Burton, 1886- II. Title.

VALENTINE, Foy, comp. 252.061
Christian faith in action; fourteen sermons on current moral issues, by J. B. Weatherspoon [and others] Nashville, Broadman Press [1956] 136 p. 21 cm. [BX6333.A1V3] 56-8672
1. Baptists — Sermons. 2. Sermons, American. I. Weatherspoon, Jesse Burton, 1886- II. Title.

WEBB, Perry F 252.061
Doves in the dust. Nashville, Broadman Press [1953] 115p. 22cm. [BX6333.W333D6] 53-9550
1. Baptists— Sermons. 2. Sermons, American. I. Title.

WESBERRY, James 252'.06'1
Pickett.
Evangelistic sermons [by] James P. Wesberry. Nashville, Tenn., Broadman Press [1973] 124 p. 20 cm. [BV3797.W422] 73-80775 ISBN 0-8054-2220-X
1. Evangelistic sermons. 2. Baptists—Sermons. 3. Sermons, American.

WILLIAMSON, E. Stanley. 252'.06'1
The people builder / E. Stanley Williamson. Nashville : Broadman Press, [1975] 152 p. ; 20 cm. [BX6333.W54P46] 75-8328 ISBN 0-8054-5138-2 : 4.95
1. Baptists—Sermons. 2. Sermons, American. I. Title.
Contents omitted

*YOUNGBLOOD, Ronald. 252.06'1
Special day sermons. Grand Rapids, Mich., Baker Book House [1973] 120 p. 19 cm. (Preaching Helps Series) [BX6333] ISBN 0-8010-9901-3 pap., 1.95
1. Baptists—Sermons. 2. Sermons, American. I. Title.

THE Laymen's hour 252.06131
(Radio program)
Four-minute talks for laymen [by] Gene E. Bartlett [and others] Valley Forge [Pa.] Judson Press [1966] 128 p. 22 cm. "52 talks which were broadcast on The Laymen's hour." Bibliographical footnotes. [BX6333.A1L26] 66-12538
1. Sermons, American. 2. Baptists — Sermons. I. Bartlett, Gene E. II. Title.

LAYMEN'S hour (The) 252.06131
(Radio program) Four-minute talks for laymen [by] Gene E. Bartlett [others] Valley Forge[Pa.] Judson Pr. [1966] 128p. 22cm. 52 talks which were broadcast on the layman's hour. Bibl. [BX6333.A1L26] 66-12538 1.95 pap.,
1. Sermons, American. 2. Baptists—Sermons. I. Bartlett, Gene E.

MARNEY, Carlyle, 252'.06'131
1916-
The Carpenter's Son. Nashville, Abingdon Press [1967] 95 p. 20 cm. [BX6333.M3668C3] 67-11017
1. Baptists—Sermons. 2. Sermons, American. I. Title.

ALLEN, R. Earl. 252.06'132
Silent Saturday, by R. Earl Allen. Grand Rapids, Baker Book House [1968] 98 p. 21 cm. [BX6333.A3S5] 68-54237 2.95
1. Baptists—Sermons. 2. Sermons, American. I. Title.

BISAGNO, John R. 252'.06'132
The power of positive preaching to the lost [by] John R. Bisagno. Nashville, Broadman Press [1972] 128 p. 20 cm. [BV3797.B519] 71-178056 ISBN 0-8054-2217-X 3.50
1. Evangelistic sermons. 2. Baptists—Sermons. 3. Sermons, American. I. Title.

CRISWELL, Wallie A. 252.06132
The Holy Spirit in today's world, by W. A. Criswell. [1st ed.] Grand Rapids, Zondervan [1966] 193p. 21cm. [BT122.C85] 66-29826 2.95
1. Holy Spirit—Sermons. 2. Sermons, American. 3. Baptists—Sermons. I. Title.

CRISWELL, Wallie A 252.06132
The Holy Spirit in today's world, by W. A. Criswell. [1st ed.] Grand Rapids, Zondervan Pub. House [1966] 193 p. 21 cm. [BT122.C85] 66-29826
1. Holy Spirit—Sermons. 2. Sermons, American. 3. Baptists—Sermons. I. Title.

CRISWELL, Wallie A. 252.06'132
In defense of the faith, by W. A. Criswell. [1st ed.] Grand Rapids, Zondervan [1967] 88p. 21cm. [BX6333.C77I5] 67-28311 2.50 bds.,
1. Baptists—Sermons. 2. Sermons, American. I. Title.

CRISWELL, Wallie A 252.06'132
In defense of the faith, by W. A. Criswell. [1st ed.,] Grand Rapids, Zondervan Pub. House [1967] 88 p. 21 cm. [BX6333.C77I5] 67-28311
1. Baptists—Sermons. 2. Sermons, American. I. Title.

*GORDON, Adoniram 252.06'132
Jordan.
A. J. Gordon. Introduction by Nathan R. Wood. Grand Rapids, Mich., Baker Book House [1973, c1951] 256 p. 19 cm. (Great pulpit masters series) [BX6333] ISBN 0-8010-3675-5. 2.95 (pbk.)
1. Baptists—Sermons. 2. Sermons, American. I. Title.

JORDAN, Clarence. 252'.06'132
The substance of faith, and other cotton patch sermons. Edited by Dallas Lee. New York, Association Press [1972] 160 p. 23 cm. (A Koinonia publication) [BX6333.J76S9] 74-189013 ISBN 0-8096-1843-5 4.95
1. Baptists—Sermons. 2. Sermons, American. I. Title.

LAFAVRE, Robert E. 252'.06'132
The Gospel according to ... By Robert E. LaFavre. [Jefferson City, Mo., LeRoi Publishers, 1972] 91 p. 22 cm. [BX6333.L25G67] 72-92935
1. Baptists—Sermons. 2. Sermons, American. I. Title.

*MACON, Leon 252.06132
You choose a cross. Grand Rapids, Baker Bk. [1966] 107p. 22cm. 1.00 pap.,
I. Title.

MARTIN, Gerald E., 252.06'132
1921- comp.
Great Southern Baptist doctrinal preaching. Edited by Gerald Martin. Foreword by J. D. Grey. Grand Rapids, Zondervan [1969] 121 p. 21 cm. "A companion volume to Great Southern Baptist evangelistic preaching." Contents.Contents.—Foreword, by J. D. Grey.—Our source of authority: the Bible, by C. Pinnock.—Our Father's Book, by K. O. White.—The promised Messiah, by E. S. James.—The Deity of Jesus, by R. G. Lee.—The old rugged cross, by J. Glisson.—The bodily resurrection of Jesus, by J. N. Palmer.—The Lordship of Christ, by H. Hobbs.—The Priesthood of Christ, by R. Pollard.—The doctrine of the Devil, by G. Martin.—The doctrine of the future life, by J. C. Evans. [BX6333.A1M37] 74-81043
1. Baptists—Sermons. 2. Sermons, American. I. Title.

MARTIN, Gerald E., 252.06'132
1921- comp.
Great Southern Baptist evangelistic preaching. Edited by Gerald Martin. Foreword by Robert G. Lee. Grand Rapids, Zondervan [1969] 104 p. 22 cm. Contents.Contents.—Foreword, by R. G. Lee.—The marvel of saving grace, by J. D. Grey.—The new birth, by F. S. Hardee.—The guttermost to the uttermost, by H. R. Bumpas.—Obedience- -the real evidence, by S. Price.—The saving of the saved, by J. Weber.—The preservation of the saints, by A. B. Van Arsdale.—The lost are to be evangelized, by P. B. Leath.—The persons involved in evangelism, by W. M. Jones.—The power for evangelism, by E. L. Williams.—The command to be filled with the Holy Spirit, by W. A. Criswell. [BX6333.A1M39] 70-81042 3.50
1. Baptists—Sermons. 2. Sermons, American. I. Title.

SCARBOROUGH, Lee 252.06'132
Rutland, 1870-1945.
The tears of Jesus; sermons to aid soul-winners. Grand Rapids, Baker Book House [1967] viii, 125 p. 20 cm. (Minister's paperback library) Reprint of the 1922 ed. [BV3797.S33 1967] 67-18195
1. Evangelistic sermons. 2. Sermons, American. 3. Baptists—Sermons. I. Title.

SCARBOROUGH, Lee 252.06'132
Rutland, 1870-1945.
The tears of Jesus; sermons to aid soul-winners. Grand Rapids, Baker Book House [1967] viii, 125 p. 20 cm. (Minister's paperback library) Reprint of the 1922 ed. [BV3797.S33 1967] 67-18195
1. Evangelistic sermons. 2. Sermons, American. 3. Baptists—Sermons. I. Title.

VALENTINE, Foy. 252.06132
The cross in the marketplace. Waco, Tex., Word Books [1966] 122 p. 21 cm. [BX6333.V28C7] 66-29544
1. Baptists—Sermons. 2. Sermons, American. I. Title.

HERE they stand : 252'.06'147
biblical sermons from Eastern Europe / compiled and edited by Lewis A. Drummond. London : Marshall, Morgan and Scott, 1976. v, 186 p. : maps ; 22 cm. [BX6333.A1H47] 77-373921 ISBN 0-551-05539-1 : £2.95
1. Sermons. 2. Baptists—Sermons. I. Drummond, Lewis A.

ALLEN, J. P., 1912- 252'.06'173
A shouting in the desert : Jesus' kind of kingdom / J. P. Allen. Nashville : Broadman Press, c1976. viii, 125 p. ; 20 cm. [BX6333.A28S55] 76-2239 ISBN 0-8054-8128-1 : 2.50
1. Baptists—Sermons. 2. Sermons, American. I. Title.

BRAWLEY, Edward M., 252.06'173
comp.
The Negro Baptist pulpit; a collection of sermons and papers by Colored Baptist ministers. Edited by Edward M. Brawley. Freeport, N.Y., Books for Libraries Press, 1971 [c1890] 300 p. 23 cm. (The Black heritage library collection) [BX6452.B7 1971] 74-154072 ISBN 0-8369-8783-7
1. Baptists—Sermons. 2. Sermons, American. 3. Baptists, Negro. I. Title. II. Series.

CONLEY, Thomas H. 252'.06173
Two in the pulpit; sermons in dialogue [by] Thomas H. Conley. Waco, Tex., Word Books [1973] 116 p. 21 cm. Includes bibliographical references. [BV4307.D5C65] 72-96360 2.95
1. Dialogue sermons. 2. Baptists—Sermons. 3. Sermons, American. I. Title.

BANKS, Gabriel Conklyn 252.063
Echoes from alter, sermons. New York, Expostion [c.1966] 21 cm 177 p. 4.00
I. Title.

BANOWSKY, William 252.06'3
Slater.
The now generation, and other sermons [by] William S. Banowsky. Austin, Tex., Sweet Pub. Co. [1969] 128 p. 20 cm. [BX7077.Z6B34] 77-101147
1. Churches of Christ—Sermons. 2. Sermons, American. I. Title.

WALKER, Granville T. 252'.06'3
Go placidly amid the noise and haste : meditations on the "Desiderata" / by Granville T. Walker. St. Louis : Bethany Press, c1975. 102 p. ; 22 cm. Includes bibliographical references. [BX7327.W28G6 1975] 75-37546 ISBN 0-8272-1217-8 pbk. : 3.95
1. Christian Church (Disciples of Christ)—Sermons. 2. Sermons, American. I. Title.

ANDERSON, Leroy Dean, 252.066
1876-
What we believe. [Fort Worth? Tex., 1957] 151p. illus. 21cm. [BX7327.A54W5] 58-19691
1. Disciples of Christ—Sermons. 2. Sermons, American. 3. Disciples of Christ—Doctrinal and controversial works. I. Title.

ASH, Anthony Lee. 252'.06'6
The word of faith. Abilene, Tex., Biblical Research Press [1973] v, 218 p. 23 cm. (The 20th century sermon series, v. 8) [BX7327.A75W6] 73-89757 4.95
1. Disciples of Christ—Sermons. 2. Sermons, American. I. Title.

BECKELHYMER, Hunter. 252.066
Questions God asks. New York, Abingdon Press [1961] 142p. 20cm. [BX7327.B4Q4] 61-5192
1. Disciples of Christ—Sermons. 2. Sermons, American. I. Title.

BECKELHYMER, Hunter, 252.06'6
comp.
The vital pulpit of the Christian church; a series of sermons by representative men among the Disciples of Christ. With introd. and a brief biographical sketch of each contributor. St. Louis Bethany Press [1969] 287 p. ports. 24 cm. [BX7327.A1B37] 69-17883
1. Disciples of Christ—Sermons. 2. Sermons, American. I. Title.

BOOK, Morris Butler, 252.066
1907-
Gospel trail blazers; 10 positive sermons. [Orlando? Fla., 1954] 124p. 21cm. [BX7327.B68G6] 55-16555
1. Disciples of Christ—Sermons. 2. Sermons, American. I. Title.

GREAT preachers of 252.066
today. Edited by J.D. Thomas. [1st ed.] Abilene, Tex., Biblical Research Press, 1960- v. port. 23cm. [BX7077.Z6A35] 61-26629
1. Churches of Christ—Sermons. 2. Sermons, American. I. Thomas, James David, 1910- ed.

HOVEN, Ard, 1906- 252.066
Christ is all! Cincinnati, Standard Press [1954] 128p. 19cm. [BX7327.H65C5] 54-4739
1. Disciples of Christ —Sermons. 2. Sermons, American. I. Title.

JONES, Edgar De Witt, 252.066
1876-
Sermons I love to preach. [1st ed.] New York, Harper [1953] 191p. 22cm. [BX7327.J8S4] 53-5441
1. Disciples of Christ—Sermons. 2. Sermons, American. I. Title.

JONES, George Curtis, 252.066
1911-
On being your best. New York, Macmillan, 1950. xvi, 129p. 20cm. A selection of weekly radio addresses given by the author over station WLEE, Richmond, Va., under the title: Tomorrow is Sunday. [BX7327.J83O5] 50-5993
1. Disciples of Christ— Addresses, essays, lectures. I. Title.

JONES, George Curtis, 252.066
1911-
Which way is progress? St. Louis, Bethany Press [1953] 160p. 21cm. [BX7327.J83W5] 54-21456
1. Disciples of Christ—Sermons. 2. Sermons, American. I. Title.

KELCY, Raymond C, 1916- 252.066
Why I believe in God, and other sermons. [Tulsa? Okla., 1951] 156 p. 21 cm. [BX7094.C95K4] 51-5039
1. Churches of Christ—Sermons. 2. Sermons. American. I. Title.

LADD, James Earl, 1901- 252.066
1951.
"As much as in me is ..." and other sermons. Portland, Or., Printed by Beattie [1951] 225 p. illus. 24 cm. [BX7327.L3A8] 51-38725
1. Disciples of Christ—Sermons. 2. Sermons, American. I. Title.

LEMMON, Clarence Eugene, 252.066
1888- ed.
Preaching on New Testament themes; sermons by active pastors of present-day Christian Churches (Disciples of Christ) St. Louis, Bethany Press, 1964. 144 p. 23 cm. [BX7327.A1L4 1964] 64-13406
1. Disciples of Christ — Sermons. 2. Sermons, American. 3. Disciples of Christ — Biog. I. Title.

LEMMON, Clarence Eugene, 252.066
1888- ed.
Preaching on New Testament themes; sermons by active pastors of present-day Christian Churches (Disciples of Christ) St. Louis, Bethany [c.]1964. 144p. 23cm. 64-13406 2.50
1. Disciples of Christ—Sermons. 2. Sermons, American. 3. Disciples of Christ—Biog. I. Title.

LEMMON, Clarence Eugene, 252.066
1888- ed.
Preaching on Old Testament themes; sermons by active pastors of present-day Christian Churches (Disciples of Christ) St. Louis, Bethany Press, 1963. 128 p. 23 cm. "Sponsored by the Committee on the Ministry of the Home Missions and Planning Council of the Christian Churches (Disciples of Christ)" [BX7328.A1L4] 63-8823
1. Disciples of Christ — Sermons. 2. Sermons, American. 3. Disciples of Christ — Biog. I. Title.

LEMMON, Clarence Eugene 252.066
1888- ed.
Preaching on Old Testament themes; sermons by active pastors of present-day Christian Churches. (Disciples of Christ) St. Louis, Bethany [c.]1963. 128p. 23cm. Sponsored by the Comm. on the Ministry of the Home Missions and Planning Council of the Christian Churches (Disciples of Christ) 63-8823 2.50
1. Disciples of Christ—Sermons. 2. Sermons, American. 3. Disciples of Christ—Biog. I. Title.

LUNGER, Harold L 252.066
Finding holy goround. St. Louis, Bethany Press [1957] 192p. 21cm. [BX7327.L8F5] 57-7265
1. Discipies of Christ—Sermons. 2. Sermons, American. I. Title.

LUNGER, Harold L 252.066
Finding holy ground. St. Louis, Bethany Press [1957] 192p. 21cm. [BX7327.L8F5] 57-7265
1. Disciples of Christ—Sermons. 2. Sermons, American. I. Title.

LUNGER, Harold L 252.066
A pocket full of seeds, and other sermons. St. Louis, Bethany Press [1954] 160p. 21cm. [BX7327.L8P6] 54-21716
1. Disciples of Christ—Sermons. 2. Sermons, American. I. Title.

MOORE, William Thomas, 252.066
1832-1926, ed.
Biographies and sermons of pioneer preachers, arr. and edited by B. C. Goodpasture and W. T. Moore. Nashville, B. C. Goodpasture, 1954. vi, 2, 589p. ports. 23cm. Published in 1868 under the editorship of W T. Moore, with title: The living pulpit of the Christian Church. [BX7327.A1M78 1954] 55-20571
1. Disciples of Christ—Sermons. 2. Disciples of Christ—Biog. 3. Sermons, American. I. Goodpasture, Benjamin Cordell, 1895- ed. II. Title.

NICHOL, Charles Ready, 252.066
1876-
Sermons. Clifton, Tex., Nichol Pub. Co., 1956- v. illus. 21cm. [BX7094.C95N49] 57-37689

1. Churches of Christ—Sermons. 2. Sermons, American. I. Title.

PICKUP, Harry Wilson, 252.066
1900-
Sermons by Pickup ... delivered in the church building at Clearwater, Florida, on February 25 through March 6, 1952. Clearwater, Fla., Philips Publications [1953] 214p. illus. 22cm. [BX7094.C95P5] 53-26248
1. Churches of Christ— Sermons. 2. Sermons, American. I. Title.

SHAW, Roud. 252.066
Pentecost and God's hurry. Boston, Christopher Pub. House [1956] 276p. 21cm. [BX7327.S45P4] 56-44895
1. Disciples of Christ—Sermons. 2. Sermons, American. I. Title.

SHAW, Roud. 252.066
Pentecost and God's hurry. Boston, Christopher Pub. House [1956] 176 p. 21 cm. [BX7327.S45P4] 56-44895
1. Disciples of Christ — Sermons. 2. Sermons, American. I. Title.

THOMAS, James David, 252'.06'6
1910- comp.
Spiritual power. Edited by J. D. Thomas. Abilene, Tex., Biblical Research Press [1972] viii, 338 p. 23 cm. At head of title: Great single sermons. [BX7327.A1T43] 74-170920
1. Disciples of Christ—Sermons. 2. Sermons, American. I. Title. II. Title: Great single sermons.

THOMPSON, Rhodes, ed. 252.066
Voices from Cane Ridge. St. Louis, Bethany Press [1954] 259p. illus. 23cm. 'Including the story of the historic meetinghouse: facsimile reproduction of The biography of Barton Warren Stone, its minister; and voices from the First National Laymen's Retreat (1949) and subsequent annual Cane Ridge meetings (1950-53)' [BX7309.S8T5] 54-31944
1. Disciples of Christ—Addresses, essays, lectures. 2. Stone, Barton Warren, 1772-1844 3. Christian union. I. Title.

WELSH, Wiley A 252.066
Villains on white horses; sermons on passages from Paul, by W. A. Welsh. Saint Louis, Bethany Press [1964] 155 p. 23 cm. [BX7327.W38V5] 64-25219
1. Sermons, American. 2. Disciples of Christ — Sermons. I. Title.

WELSH, Wiley A. 252.066
Villains on white horses; sermons on pasages from Paul. St. Louis, Bethany [c.1964] 155p. 23cm. 64-25219 2.95
1. Sermons, American. 2. Disciples of Christ—Sermons. I. Title.

WHEELER, J Clyde. 252.066
Claim these victories. St. Louis, Bethany Press [1956] 144p. 21cm. [BX7327.W47C35] 56-8099
1. Disciples of Christ—Sermons. 2. Sermons, American. 3. Psychology, Pastoral. I. Title.

WHEELER, J. Clyde. 252.066
Claim these victories. St. Louis, Bethany Press [1956] 144 p. 21 cm. [BX7327.W47C35] 56-8099
1. Disciples of Christ — Sermons. 2. Sermons, American. 3. Psychology, Pastoral. I. Title.

WHEELER, Joseph Clyde. 252.066
Claim these victories. St. Louis, Bethany Press [1956] 144 p. 21 cm. [BX7327.W47C35] 56-8099
1. Disciples of Christ — Sermons. 2. Sermons, American. 3. Pastoral psychology. I. Title.

MERRITT, George W. 252'.06'63
Truth for today : [five-minute radio sermons] / by George W. Merritt ; illustrated by Merlyn Jones. Nashville : Gospel Advocate Co., c1976. x, 187 p. : ill. ; 20 cm. [BX7327.M584T78] 76-18471 ISBN 0-89225-203-0
1. Christian Church (Disciples of Christ)—Sermons. 2. Sermons, American. I. Title.

NICHOLS, Gus, 1892- 252.0663
Sermons of Gus Nichols. Edited by J. D. Thomas. [1st ed.] Abilene, Tex., Biblical Research Press [1966] viii, 275 p. port. 23 cm. (Great preachers of today, 9) [BX7077.Z6A35 vol. 9] 66-9306
1. Churches of Christ—Sermons. 2. Sermons, American. I. Title. II. Series.

BELLAH, Charles Greeley, 252.067
1873-
The King's highway. Washington, Review and Herald Pub. Association [1953] 279p. 21cm. [BX6123.B43] 53-36892
1. Seventh-Day Adventists—Sermons. 2. Sermons, American. I. Title.

DOUGLASS, Herbert E., 252'.06'7
comp.
If I had one sermon to preach. Edited by Herbert E. Douglass. Washington, Review and Herald Pub. Association [1972] 190 p. ports. 21 cm. (Review and Herald sermon library series) (Discovery paperbacks) Contents.Contents.—Alexander, W. Mingled motives.—Bradford, C. E. Rich man, poor man, Christian.—Brooks, C. D. A hope called blessed.—Bush, F. F. The church called Christian.—Dower, N. R. That I may win Christ.—Fearing, A. The song of Moses and the lamb.—Hackett, W. J. How man finds freedom.—Hegstad, R. R. An offbeat subject.—Lesher, W. R. Two ways with people.—Loveless, W. A. Burn your labeling machine.—Osborn, J. W. The magnificent decision.—Pease, N. F. The answered question.—Pierson, R. H. Hope and help for you!—Spangler, J. R. Is the Cross out of date?—Venden, L. Two lost boys.—Vitrano, S. P. Keeping the great commandment.—Wood, K. H. The leukemia of noncommitment. Includes bibliographical references. [BX6123.D68] 72-78420
1. Seventh-Day Adventists—Sermons. 2. Sermons, American. I. Title.

HARE, Eric B. 252.067
Fullness of joy. Washington, Review and Herold Pub. Association [1952] 254 p. 21 cm. [BV4310.H28] 52-64332
1. Youth—Religious life. 2. Seventh-day Adventists—Sermons. 3. Sermons, American. I. Title.

RICHARDS, Harold Marshall 252.067
Sylvester, 1894-
Day after tomorrow, and other sermons Washington, Review and Herald Pub. Association [1956] 188p. 21cm. [BX6123.R48] 56-35989
1. Seventh-Day Adventists—Sermons. 2. Sermon, American. I. Title.

RICHARDS, Harold Marshall 252.067
Sylvester, 1894-
Day after tomorrow, and other sermons. Washington, Review and Herald Pub. Association [1956] 188p. 21cm. [BX6123.R48] 56-35989
1. Seventh-Day Adventists— Sermons. 2. Sermons, American. I. Title.

RICHARDS, Harold Marshall 252.067
Sylvester, 1894-
Radio sermons. Washington, Review and Herald Pub. Assoication [1952] 253 p. 22 cm. [BX6123.R52] 52-32721
1. Seventh-Day Adventists — Sermons. 2. Sermons, American. I. Title.

CARCICH, Theodore. 252'.06'73
So what's there to live for? Nashville, Southern Pub. Association [1972] 63 p. 19 cm. [BX6123.C37] 72-88858 ISBN 0-8127-0064-3 Pap. 0.50
1. Seventh-Day Adventists—Sermons. 2. Sermons, American. I. Title.

REYNOLDS, Louis 252'.06'73
Bernard, 1917-
Great texts from Romans, by Louis B. Reynolds. Nashville, Tenn., Southern Pub. Association [1972] 94 p. 18 cm. [BS2665.4.R48] 72-75378
1. Seventh-Day Adventists—Sermons. 2. Bible. N.T. Romans—Sermons. 3. Sermons, American. I. Title.

WILLIAMS, Carl 252'.06'73
Carnelius, 1903-
Chicken coops or sky scrapers [by] Carl C. Williams. Anderson, Ind., Warner Press [1973] 112 p. 19 cm. [BV3797.W46] 73-3312 ISBN 0-87162-153-3 pap. 2.50
1. Church of God (Anderson, Ind.)—Sermons. 2. Evangelistic sermons. 3. Sermons, American. I. Title.

ABBEY, Merrill R. 252.07
Encounter with Christ; a preaching venture in the Gospel of John. Nashville, Abingdon [c.1961] 176p. 61-11782 3.00
1. Methodist Church—Sermons. 2. Sermons, American. I. Title.

ABBEY, Merrill R 252.07
Encounter with Christ; a preaching venture in the Gospel of John. New York, Abingdon Press [1961] 176p. 21cm. [BX8333.A25E5] 61-11782
1. Methodist Church—Sermons. 2. Sermons, American. I. Title.

ARMSTRONG, James, 1924- 252.07
The urgent now; sermons on contemporary issues. Nashville, Abingdon Press [1970] 160 p. 21 cm. Includes bibliographical references. [BX8333.A67U7 1970] 75-109671 3.75
1. Methodist Church—Sermons. 2. Sermons, American. I. Title.

BOSLEY, Harold Augustus, 252.07
1907-
The church militant. [1st ed.] New York, Harper [1952] 159 p. 20 cm. (The Carnahan Jectures [1951]) [BX8333.B565C5] 51-11886
1. Methodist Church—Sermons. 2. Sermons, American. I. Title. II. Series.

BOSLEY, Harold Augustus, 252'.07
1907-
Men who build churches; interpretations of the life of Paul [by] Harold A. Bosley. Nashville, Abingdon Press [1972] 158 p. 19 cm. [BS2506.B65] 72-701 ISBN 0-687-24801-9
1. Paul, Saint, apostle—Sermons. 2. Methodist Church—Sermons. 3. Sermons, American. I. Title.

BOSLEY, Harold Augustus, 252.07
1907-
Preaching on controversial issues; a free pulpit in a free society. [1st ed.] New York, Harper [1953] 221p. 22cm. [BX8333.B565P7] 53-5001
1. Methodist Church— Sermons. 2. Sermons, American. 3. Preaching. I. Title.

BRAUN, Andrew Christian. 252.07
The conquest of life; messages for the young and young in heart. [Westwood, N. J.] F. H. Revell Co. [1957] 128p. 21cm. [BX8333.B68C6] 57-6854
1. Methodist Church—Sermons. 2. Sermons, American. I. Title.

BUTTERWORTH, Frank E 252.07
So now He speaks again. New York, Abingdon Press [1963] 125 p. 20 cm. [BX8333.B86S] 63-7477
1. Methodist Church—Sermons. 2. Sermons, American. I. Title.

BUTTERWORTH, Frank E. 252.07
So now He speaks again. Nashville, Abingdon [c.1963] 125p. 20cm. 63-7477 2.50 bds.,
1. Methodist Church—Sermons. 2. Sermons, American. I. Title.

CHAPPELL, Clovis Gilham, 252.07
1882-
Values that last. Nashville, Abingdon [1964, c.1939] 216p. 18cm. (Apex bk., Q1-125) 1.25 pap.,
1. Methodist church—Sermons. 2. Sermons, American. I. Title.

CHAPPELL, Clovis Gillham 252.07
The cross before Calvary. Nashville, Abingdon Press [c.1960] 62p. 20cm. 60-12070 1.50
1. Methodist Church—Sermons. 2. Sermons, American. I. Title.

CHAPPELL, Clovis Gillham, 252.07
1882-
The cross before Calvary. New York, Abingdon Press [1960] 62p. 20cm. [BX8333.C5C7] 60-12070
1. Methodist Church—Sermons. 2. Sermons, American. I. Title.

CHAPPELL, Clovis Gillham, 252.07
1882-
If I were young. Nashville, Abingdon [1963, c.1945] 217p. 18cm. (Apex Bks. MI) .95 pap.,
1. Methodist church—Sermons. 2. Sermons, American. I. Title.

CHAPPELL, Clovis Gillham, 252.07
1882-
Questions Jesus asked. Grand Rapids, Baker Book House [1974, c1948] 181 p. 19 cm. "A Clovis G. Chappell Library Book" [BX8333.C5Q4] ISBN 0-8010-2352-1 2.95 (pbk.)
1. Methodist Church—Sermons. 2. Sermons, American. I. Title.
L.C. card number for original edition: 48-10044.

CHAPPELL, Wallace D 252.07
His continued witness. New York, Abingdon Press [1964] 140 p. 20 cm. [BX8333.C522H5] 64-16146
1. Sermons, American. 2. Methodist Church — Sermons. I. Title.

CHAPPELL, Wallace D. 252.07
His continued witness. Nashville, Abingdon [c.1964] 140p. 20cm. 64-16146 2.50 bds.,
1. Sermons, American. 2. Methodist Church—Sermons. I. Title.

CHAPPELL, Wallace D 252.07
Receiving God's fullness. New York, Abingdon Press [1960] 126p. 20cm. [BX8333.C522R4] 60-9196
1. Sermons, American. 2. Methodist Church—Sermons. I. Title.

CHAPPELL, Wallace D 252.07
When morning comes; [sermons, by] Wallace D. Chappell. Nashville, Abingdon Press [1966] 112 p. 20 cm. [BX8333.C522W48] 66-19806
1. Methodist Church — Sermons. 2. Sermons, American. 3. Evangelistic sermons. I. Title.

CHAPPELL, Wallace D. 252.07
When morning comes; [sermons.] Nashville, Abingdon [c.1966] 112p. 20cm. [BX8333.C522W48] 66-19806 2.50 bds.,
1. Methodist Church—Sermons. 2. Sermons, American. 3. Evangelistic sermons. I. Title.

CHAPPELL, Wallace D. 252.07
Who Jesus says you are. Nashville, Abingdon [c.1962] 96p. 62-7225 2.00 bds.,
1. Sermons, American. 2. Methodist Church—Sermons. I. Title.

CROWE, Charles M. 252.07
Sermons for special days. New York, Abingdon-Cokesbury Press [1951] 171 p. 20 cm. [BV4254.2.C7] 51-10932
1. Occasional sermons. 2. Methodist Church—Sermons. 3. Sermons, American. I. Title.

CROWE, Charles M. 252.07
Sermons for special days. Nashville, Abingdon Press [1961, c.1951] 171p. (Apex bk., F3) .95 pap.,
1. Occasional sermons. 2. Methodist Church—Sermons 3. Sermons, American. I. Title.

CROWE, Charles M. 252.07
Stewardship sermons. Nashville, Abingdon Press [c.1960] 141p. 21cm. 60-12072 2.50
1. Stewardship, Christian—Sermons. 2. Methodist Church—Sermons. 3. Sermons, American. I. Title.

DUNNINGTON, Lewis Le Roy, 252.07
1890-
Keys to richer living. New York, Macmillan, 1952. 136 p. 21 cm. [BX8333.D83K4] 52-9146
1. Methodist Church—Sermons. 2. Sermons, American. I. Title.

FERGUSON, John Lambuth, 252.07
1892-1950.
Our God is able, and other sermons. Nashville, Men's Club, Belmont Methodist Church [1951] 174 p. illus. 21 cm. [BX8333.F4O8] 52-18574
1. Methodist Church—Sermons. 2. Sermons, American. I. Title.

FRANKLIN, Denson N. 252.07
We dream, we climb [by] Denson N. Franklin. Nashville, Abingdon Press [1969] 144 p. 20 cm. [BV4515.2.F68] 69-18440 3.50
1. Christian life—Stories. 2. Sermon stories. 3. Sermons, American. I. Title.

GOFF, Charles Ray. 252.07
A better hope, and other sermons. New York, Revell [1951] 192 p. 21 cm. [BX8333.G55B4] 51-5322
1. Methodist Church—Sermons. 2. Sermons, American. I. Title.

GOFF, Charles Ray 252.07
Shelters and sanctuaries. Nashville, Abingdon [c.1961] 128p. 61-10812 2.25 bds.,
1. Methodist Church—Sermons. 2. Sermons, American. I. Title.

GOODRICH, Robert Edward 252.07
Reach for the sky; life at its highest. [Westwood, N. J.] Revell [c.1960] 126p. 21cm. 60-8456 2.50 bds.,
1. Methodist Church—Sermons. 2. Sermons, American. I. Title.

GOODRICH, Robert Edward, 252.07
1909-
Reach for the sky; life at its highest. Nashville, Abingdon [1967, c.1960] 126p. 18cm. (Apex bks., AA 3-100) [BX8333.G63R4] 1.00 pap.,
1. Methodist Church— Sermons. 2. Sermons, American. I. Title.

GUY, Norman M. 252.07
Windows of faith. [Madison? N. J., 1951] 192 p. 20 cm. [BT771.G85] 51-38572
1. Faith—Sermons. 2. Methodist Church—Sermons. 3. Sermons, American. I. Title.

HARRELL, Costen Jordan, 252.07
1885-
Christian affirmations. New York, Abingdon Press [1961] 126p. 20cm. [BX333H235C45] 61-11036
1. Sermons, American. 2. Methodist Church—Sermons. I. Title.

HEINSOHN, Edmund. 252.07
The new world; edited and designed by Mary L. Kennedy. [Austin, University Methodist Church, 1952] 98 p. 27 cm. [BX8333.H38N4] 52-34954
1. Methodist Church—Sermons. 2. Sermons, American. I. Title.

KENNEDY, Gerald Hamilton, 252.07
Bp., 1907-
Fresh every morning, by Gerald Kennedy. [1st ed.] New York, Harper & Row [1966] 194 p. 21 cm. [BX8333.K42F7] 66-15042
1. Methodist Church — Sermons. 2. Sermons, American. I. Title.

KENNEDY, Gerald Hamilton, Bp., 1907- 252.07
Fresh every morning. New York, Harper [c.1966] 194p. 21cm. [BX8333.K42F7] 66-15042 3.95 bds.,
1. Methodist Church—Sermons. 2. Sermons, American. I. Title.

KIRKPATRICK, Dow. 252.07
Six days and Sunday; a pew-pulpit dialogue. Nashville, Abingdon [1968] 158p. 19cm. [BX8333.K55S5] 68-17439 1.95 pap.,
1. Methodist Church—Sermons. 2. Sermons, American I. Title.

LEHMBERG, Ben F 252.07
What's right with the world? Colorado Springs, First Methodist Church [c1957] 140p. 21cm. [BX8333.L43W5] 58-21606
1. Methodist Church—Sermons. 2. Sermons, American. I. Title.

LUCCOCK, Halford Edward, 1885- 252.07
Marching off the map, and other sermons. New York, Harper [1952] 192 p. 22 cm. [BX8333.L8M3] 52-5463
1. Methodist Church—Sermons. 2. Sermons, American. I. Title.

LUCCOCK, Robert Edward, 1915- 252.07
If God be for us; sermons on the gifts of the Gospel. [1st ed.] New York, Harper [1954] 189p. 22cm. [BX8333.L825 I35] 54-8967
1. Methodist Church—Sermons. 2. Sermons, American. I. Title.

METHODIST Church (United States) Dept. of Evangelists. 252.07
This faith we share; ten sermons written by staff members of the Department of Evangelists, Ed Beck, director. Nashville [1965] 100 p. ports. 19 cm. Bibliographical footnotes. [BV3797.A1M4] 65-17349
1. Evangelistic sermons. 2. Methodist Church — Sermons. 3. Sermons, American. I. Title.

MOORE, Arthur James, Bp., 1888- 252.07
Fight on! Fear not! [Sermons] Nashville, Abingdon [c.1962] 144p. 21cm. 62-19133 2.50
1. Sermons, American. 2. Methodist Church—Sermons. I. Title.

OVERTON, James H comp. 252.07
Sermons from the Upper room chapel. Nashville, The Upper room [1962] 149 p. 19 cm. [BX8333.A1O9] 62-21269
1. Methodist Church — Sermons. 2. Sermons, American. I. Title.

OVERTON, James H., comp. 252.07
Sermons from the Upper room chapel. Nashville, Upper Room [c.1962] 149p. 19cm. 62-21269 .75 pap.,
1. Methodist Church—Sermons. 2. Sermons, American. I. Title.

PEELOR, Harry N. 252.07
Angel with a slingshot. Nashville, Abingdon [1962, c.1961] 127p. 23cm. 62-16811 2.50
1. Sermons, American. 2. Methodist Church—Sermons. I. Title.

PHILPOT, Ford 252.07
So you want a mountain. Grand Rapids, Mich., Baker Bk., 1964. 113p. 20cm. 64-23175 2.50
1. Evangelistic sermons. 2. Methodist Church—Sermons. 3. Sermons, American. I. Title.

PRATER, Arnold. 252.07
A model-T king? Boston, Christopher Pub. House [1957] 167p. 21cm. Sermons. [BX8333.P7M6] 57-28026
1. Methodist Church—Sermons. 2. Sermons, American. I. Title.

QUILLIAN, Paul. 252.07
Not a sparrow falls, and other sermons. Nashville, Abingdon-Cokesbury Press [1952] 156 p. 20 cm. [BX8333.Q5N6] 52-11318
1. Methodist Church — Sermons. 2. Sermons, American. I. Title.

SANGSTER, William Edwin, 1900-1960 252.07
Can I know God? and other sermons [by] W. E. Sangster. Grand Rapids, Baker Books, [1975 c1960] 176 p. 20 cm. [BX8333.S25W42] 61-5198 ISBN 0-8010-8058-4 2.95 (pbk.)
1. Methodist Church—Sermons. 2. Sermons, English. I. Title.

SANGSTER, William Edwin, 1900-1960. 252.07
Can I know God? and other sermons. New York, Abingdon Press [1961- c1960- v. 21cm. First published in London in 1960 under title: Westminster sermons. [BX8333.S25W42] 61-5198
1. Methodist Church—Sermons. 2. Sermons, English. I. Title.

*SANGSTER, William Edwin, 1900-1960. 252.07
He is able [by] W. E. Sangster. Grand Rapids, Baker Book House [1975 c1965] 199 p. 20 cm. (W. E. Sangster Library) [BX8333] ISBN 0-8010-8056-8 2.95 (pbk.)
1. Methodist Church—Sermons. I. Title.

SHULER, Robert Pierce, 1880- 252.07
Some [logs I have known. and other gospel sermons, by Robert P. (Bob) Shuler. With one sermon by J. W. W. Shuler, father, one sermon each by sons, R. P. Shuler, Jr., Jack, and Phil. Wheaton, Ill., Sword of the Lord Publishers [1953] 142p. illus., ports. 21cm. At head of title: Three generations of Shulers preach. [BX8333.S52S6] 53-2270
1. Methodist Church—Sermons. 2. Sermons, American. I. Title.

SOCKMAN, Ralph Washington, 1889- 252.07
Now to live! Nashville, Abingdon [1962, c.1946] 214p. 18cm. 95. pap.,
1. Methodist church—Sermons. 2. Sermons, American. I. Title.

STOWE, William McFerrin, 1913- 252.07
Characteristics of Jesus. New York, Abingdon Press [1962] 128 p. 20 cm. [BX8333.S758C5] 62-10416
1. Jesus Christ — Character. 2. Methodist Church — Sermons. 3. Sermons, American. I. Title.

STOWE, William McFerrin, 1913- 252.07
Characteristics of Jesus. Nashville, Abingdon [c.1962] 128p. 20cm. 62-10416 2.50
1. Jesus Christ—Character. 2. Methodist Church—Sermons. 3. Sermons, American. I. Title.

STOWE, William McFerrin, 1913- 252.07
It all began with God [by] W. McFerrin Stowe. New York, Abingdon Press [1965] 112 p. 20 cm. [BX8333.S758I 8] 65-11078
1. Methodist Church — Sermons. 2. Sermons, American. I. Title.

STOWE, William McFerrin, 1913- 252.07
It all began with God. Nashville, Abingdon [c.1965] 112p. 20cm. [BX8333.S75818] 65-11078 2.50 bds.,
1. Methodist Church—Sermons. 2. Sermons, American. I. Title.

STOWE, William McFerrin, 1913- 252.07
Power of Paul. New York, Abingdon Press [1963] 128 p. 20 cm. [BS2506.S78] 63-11382
1. Paul, Saint, Apostle. 2. Methodist Church — Sermons. 3. Sermons, American. I. Title.

STOWE, William McFerrin, 1913- 252.07
Power of Paul. New York, Abingdon [c.1963] 128p. 20cm. 63-11382 2.50
1. Paul, Saint, Apostle. 2. Methodist Church—Sermons. 3. Sermons, American. I. Title.

STRAYER, James H 252.07
The living landscape; reflections on living today. With foreword by Donald Harvey Tippett. [1st ed.] New York, Exposition Press [1953] 96p. 21cm. [BR123.S82] 53-9796
1. Christianity—Addresses, essays, lectures. I. Title.

THOMAS, George Ernest, 1907- 252.07
Through Christ Our Lord; sermons on the mission of Christ. Nashville, Tidings [1959] 79 p. illus. 19 cm. (Christian materials) [BX8333.T47T5] 59-15727
1. Methodist Church — Sermons. 2. Sermons, American. I. Title.

THOMPSON, Gordon, 1918- 252.07
His words on happiness. [Atlanta, Parke Pub. Co., 1953] 58p. 19cm. [BX8333.T477H5] 54-22111
1. Methodist Church—Sermons. 2. Sermons, American. I. Title.

TITTLE, Ernest Fremont, 1885-1949. 252.07
A mighty fortress. With a foreword, Portrait of a preacher, by Paul Hutchinson. [1st ed.] New York, Harper [1950] xxxv, 179 p. port. 22 cm. [BX8333.T5M5] 50-8672
1. Methodist Church — Sermons. 2. Sermons, American. I. Title.

WALKER, Alan, 1911- 252'.07
God, the disturber. Waco, Tex., Word Books [1973] 136 p. 23 cm. [BX8333.W224G6] 73-76967 3.95
1. Methodist Church—Sermons. 2. Sermons, English—Australia. I. Title.

WEATHERHEAD, Leslie Dixon, 1893- 252.07
Key next door; [sermons] New York, Abingdon Press [1961, c1960] 255 p. 21 cm. [BX8333.W416K4 1961] 61-6395
1. Methodist Church—Sermons. 2. Sermons, English. I. Title.

WEATHERHEAD, Leslie Dixon, 1893- 252.07
That immortal sea. Nashville, Abingdon Press [1954, c1953] 217p. 21cm. [BX8333.W416T5 1954] 54-5944
1. Methodist Church—Sermons. 2. Sermons, English. I. Title.

WEBB, Lance. 252'.07
God's surprises / Lance Webb. Nashville : Abingdon, c1976. 175 p. ; 20 cm. Includes bibliographical references. [BX8333.W4164G6] 75-44495 ISBN 0-687-15447-2 : 6.95
1. Methodist Church—Sermons. 2. Sermons, American. I. Title.

WHEATLEY, Melvin E 252.07
Going His i[Westwood, N. J.] F. H. Revell Co. [1957] 155p. 22cm. [BX8333.W42G6] 57-6974
1. Methodist Church—Sermons. 2. Sermons, American. I. Title.

WHEATLEY, Melvin E. 252.07
Going His way. [Westwood, N.J.,] F.H. Revell Co. [1957] 155 p. 22 cm. [BX8333.W42G6] 57-6974
1. Methodist Church — Sermons. 2. Sermons, American. I. Title.

WHITING, Thomas A. 252'.07
Don't be afraid of the dark [by] Thomas A. Whiting. St. Louis, Bethany Press [1970] 176 p. 23 cm. Includes bibliographical references. [BX8333.W425D6] 74-112439 4.95
1. Methodist Church—Sermons. 2. Sermons, American. I. Title.

WYNN, Daniel Webster, 1919- 252.07
Timeless issues [by] Daniel W. Wynn. New York, Philosophical Library [1967] x, 144 p. 22 cm. [BX8472.W9] 66-20219
1. Methodist Church—Sermons. 2. Sermons, American. I. Title.

MORRIS, Colin M. 252'.07'1
Mankind my church [by] Colin Morris. Nashville, Abingdon Press [1972, c1971] 160 p. 22 cm. Includes bibliographical references. [BX8333.M584M35 1972] 78-185547 ISBN 0-687-23137-X 2.45
1. Methodist Church—Sermons. 2. Sermons, English. I. Title.

*LEE, Luther, 1800-1889. 252.07173
Five sermons and a tract, edited with and introduction by Donald W. Dayton. Chicago, Holrad House, 1975. 135 p. 23 cm. [BV4211] 3.00 (pbk.)
1. Sermons, American. 2. Wesleyan Methodist Church of America. I. Title.
Publisher's address: 5104 N. Christiana Ave. 60625.

CARCICH, Theodore. 252'.07'3
Carcich at 7:30 : sermons preached at camp meetings / by Theodore Carcich. Nashville : Southern Pub. Association, [1975] 95 p. ; 21 cm. [BX6123.C36] 74-30869 ISBN 0-8127-0091-0
1. Seventh-Day Adventists—Sermons. 2. Sermons, American. I. Title.

ADAMS, James Clyde. 252.07'6
The Bishop of Heard County preaches [by] J. C. Adams. With an introd. by Arthur J. Moore. Nashville, Printed for the author by the Methodist Pub. House [1962] 160 p. illus., ports. 21 cm. [BX8333.A3B5] 70-271754
1. Methodist Church—Sermons. 2. Sermons, American. I. Title.

*BOSLEY, Harold A. 252.076
Sermons on the Psalms. Nashville, Abingdon [1966, c.1956] 208p. 21cm. (Apex bks., Y2-195) 1.95 pap.,
I. Title.

CHAPPELL, Clovis Gillham, 1882- 252.07'6
Surprises in the Bible [by] Clovis G. Chappell. Nashville, Abingdon Press [1967] 126 p. 20 cm. [BX8333.C5S8] 67-15635
1. Methodist Church — Sermons. 2. Sermons, American I. Title.

CHAPPELL, Clovis Gillham, 1882- 252.07'6
Surprises in the Bible [by] Clovis G. Chappell. Nashville, Abingdon [1967] 126p. 20cm. [BX8333.C5S8] 67-15635 2.50 bds.,
1. Methodist Church—Sermons. 2. Sermons, American. I. Title.

CHAPPELL, Wallace D. 252'.07'6
All for Jesus! / Wallace D. Chappell. Nashville : Broadman Press, [1975] 95 p. ; 20 cm. [BX8333.C522A44] 74-27926 ISBN 0-8054-5231-1 : 3.50
1. Methodist Church—Sermons. 2. Sermons, American. I. Title.

GOODRICH, Robert Eugene, 1909- 252.07'6
Dear God, where are you? [By] Robert E. Goodrich, Jr. Waco, Tex., Word Books [1969] 138 p. 23 cm. Bibliographical footnotes. [BX8333.G65D4] 79-91940 3.95
1. Methodist Church—Sermons. 2. Sermons, American. I. Title.

HAMBY, Warren C., 1924- 252.07'6
Winds of change; finding God's direction in turbulent times [by] Warren C. Hamby. Old Tappan, N.J., Revell [1971] 159 p. 21 cm. [BS1525.4.H34] 78-149371 ISBN 0-8007-0449-5 3.95
1. Bible. O.T. Jeremiah—Sermons. 2. Methodist Church—Sermons. 3. Sermons, American. I. Title.

LACY, Donald Charles, 1933- 252'.07'6
Gems from James / by Donald Charles Lacy. Philadelphia : Dorrance, [1974] 61 p. ; 22 cm. [BS2785.4.L32] 74-78302 ISBN 0-8059-2024-2 : 4.95
1. Methodist Church—Sermons. 2. Bible. N.T. James—Sermons. 3. Sermons, American. I. Title.

MANN, Leonard W. 252'.07'6
The best of the good news / edited by Leonard W. Mann. Nashville : Tidings, [1974] v, 98 p. ; 19 cm. [BX8333.A1M3] 74-80894 pbk. : 1.50
1. Methodist Church—Sermons. 2. Sermons, American. I. Title.

MOORE, Arthur James, Bp., 1888- 252.076
The mighty Saviour. [Sermons] New York, Abingdon-Cokesbury Press [1952] 154 p. 20 cm. [BX8333.M5647M5] 52-8840
1. Methodist Church — Sermons. 2. Sermons, American. I. Title.

MYERS, T. Cecil 252.07'6
When crisis comes [by] T. Cecil Myers. Nashville, Abingdon [1967] 176p. 20cm. [BX8333.M95W5] 67-14984 3.00
1. Methodist Church—Sermons. 2. Sermons, American. I. Title.

PALMER, Everett W., Bp. 252.07'6
The glorious imperative [by] Everett W. Palmer. Nashville, Abingdon [1967] 160p. 21cm. [BX8333.P28G55] 67-14985 3.00
1. Methodist Church—Sermons. 2. Sermons, American. 3. Pastoral theology. I. Title.

PALMER, Everett W., Bp. 252.07'6
The glorious imperative [by] Everett W. Palmer. Nashville, Abingdon Press [1967] 160 p. 21 cm. [BX8333.P28G55] 67-14985
1. Methodist Church — Sermons. 2. Sermons, American. 3. Pastoral theology. I. Title.

RICE, John Andrew, 1862-1930. 252.076
Emotions Jesus stirred; sermons. Tulsa, Okla., Printed by Standard Print. Co., 1950. 66 p. port. 22 cm. [BX8333.R48E5] 51-22598
1. Methodist Church — Sermons. 2. Sermons, American. I. Title.

SLEETH, Ronald Eugene. 252.07'6
Splinters in the quick [by] Ronald E. Sleeth. Waco, Tex., Word Books [1971] 144 p. 23 cm. Sermons. Includes bibliographical references. [BX8333.S5726S65] 78-144359 3.95
1. Sermons, American. 2. Methodist Church—Sermons. I. Title.

SMITH, Chester Allen, 1884- 252.076
Be of good cheer; a layman's sermons. Foreword by Bishop James H. Straughn. [1st ed.] Peekskill, N. Y., Friendly Town Association, 1956. 116p. 22cm. [BX8333.S5728B4] 56-8522
1. Methodist Church—Sermons. 2. Sermons, American. I. Title.

SMITH, Chester Allen, 1884- 252.076
Be of good cheer: a layman's sermons. Foreword by Bishop James H. Straughn. [1st ed.] Peekskill, N.Y., Friendly Town Association, 1956. 116 p. 22 cm. [BX8333.S5728B4] 56-8522
1. Methodist Church — Sermons. 2. Sermons, American. I. Title.

*THORNE, Milton 252.076
Everbody is a somebody. New York, Carlton [1966] 63p. 21cm. (Reflection bk.) 2.00
I. Title.

WATTS, Ewart G., 1915- 252'.07'6
Bench marks of faith, by Ewart G. Watts. Study aids by John P. Gilbert. Nashville, Tidings [1974] 104 p. 19 cm. Includes bibliographical references. [BT77.W37] 73-90773 1.25 (pbk.).
1. Theology, Doctrinal—Popular works. 2. Christian life—Methodist authors. I. Gilbert, John Peyton, 1936- II. Title.

JOHNSON, Merle 252'.07'674
Allison.
Ancient fires for modern man, by Merle Allison Johnson "Pastor X." Nashville, Tidings [1973] 87 p. 19 cm. [BX8333.J58A6] 72-95672 1.25 (pbk.)
1. Methodist Church—Sermons. 2. Sermons, American. I. Title.

COOPER, William A. 252.078
The awakening; sermons and sermonettes on special occasions. New York, Expostion [c.1963] 120p. 21cm. 3.00
I. Title.

PAYNE, Daniel 252.07'83
Alexander, Bp., 1811-1893.
Sermons and addresses, 1853-1891. Edited, with an introd. by Charles Killian. New York, Arno Press, 1972. 1 v. (various pagings) ports. 24 cm. (Religion in America, series II) [BX8449.P3A5 1972] 70-38458 ISBN 0-405-04079-2
1. Methodist Church—Sermons. 2. Sermons, American. I. Title.

ARCHIBALD, Frank E. 252'.07'92
An essential greatness, by Frank E. Archibald. Windsor, N.S., Lancelot Press [1968] 164 p. 21 cm. [BX9882.A8 1968] 72-180379 2.50
1. United Church of Canada—Sermons. 2. Apostles' Creed. 3. Sermons, English—Canada. I. Title.

GRIFFITH, Arthur 252'.07'92
Leonard, 1920-
Ephesians : a positive affirmation : the Ephesian letter today / Leonard Griffith. Waco, Tex. : Word Books, [1975] 173 p. ; 23 cm. Includes bibliographical references. [BS2695.4.G74] 75-3638 5.95
1. United Church of Canada—Sermons. 2. Bible. N.T. Ephesians—Sermons. 3. Sermons, English—Canada. I. Title.

BARTH, Joseph, 1906- 252.08
The art of staying sane. Foreword by Pierre Van Paassen. Freeport, N.Y., Books for Libraries Press [1970, c1948] viii, 192 p. 23 cm. (Essay index reprint series) Contents.—The art of staying sane.—How to lose your soul.—The God I believe in.—The fact of brotherhood.—The art of not dealing with evil.—The worst enemy of the better.—The dangers of being intelligent.—Why is mysticism?—Women in the new world to come.—Mr. Capital and Mrs. Labor.—That man, John L. Lewis.—America's most intolerant man.—Can democracy survive?—The end of the world.—The liberal looks at the cross.—When the atom bomb falls. [BX9843.B288A7 1970] 70-117757
1. Unitarian churches—Addresses, essays, lectures. I. Title.

BUEHRER, Edwin T 252.08
The changing climate of religion; humanist sermon-essays, by Edwin T. Buehrer. [1st ed.] New York, Pageant Press [1965] 227 p. 21 cm. [BX9843.B98C5] 65-19370
1. Unitarian Churches — Sermons. 2. Sermons, America. I. Title.

BUEHRER, Edwin T. 252.08
The changing climate of religion; humanist sermonessays. New York, Pageant [c.1965] 227p. 21cm. [BX9843.B98C5] 65-19370 4.50
1. Unitarian Churches—Sermons. 2. Sermons, American. I. Title.

CAMERON, Kenneth Walter, 252.08
1908-
Index-concordance to Emerson's sermons; with homiletical papers. Hartford [Conn.] Transcendental Books [1963] 2 v. (709 l.) ports. 29 cm. Includes bibliographical references. [BX9843.E487S47] 63-4377
1. Emerson, Ralph Waldo, 1803-1882—Dictionaries, indexes, etc. 2. Sermons, American—Indexes. I. Title.

DAVIES, Arthur Powell. 252.08
The temptation to be good; a book of unconventional sermons. New York, Farrar, Straus and Young [1952] 210 p. 22 cm. [BX9843.D29T4] 52-12565
1. Unitarian churches—Sermons. 2. Sermons, American. I. Title.

EMERSON, Ralph Waldo, 252.08
1803-1882.
Young Emerson speaks; unpublished discourses on many subjects. Edited by Arthur Cushman McGiffert, Jr. Port Washington, N.Y., Kennikat Press [1968, c1938] xxxix, 275 p. 23 cm. (Essay and general literature index reprint series) [BX9843.E487Y6 1968] 68-8237
1. Unitarian churches—Sermons. 2. Sermons, American. I. McGiffert, Arthur Cushman, 1892- ed. II. Title.

MATSON, Howard, 1907- 252.08
The fourth wise man; a quest for reasonable certainties. [Laguna Beach, Calif.] Carlborg Blades [1954] 139p. illus. 25cm. [B29.M37] 54-13393
1. Philosophy—Addresses, essays, lectures. I. Title.

MAYHEW, Jonathan, 1720- 252.08
1766.
Sermons: Seven sermons. A discourse, concerning the unlimited submission and non-resistance to the higher powers. The snare broken. New York, Arno Press, 1969. 162, 48, vii, 44 p. 23 cm. (Religion in America) Reprint of the author's works previously published separately between 1749 and 1766. [BX9843.M35S43 1969] 76-83429
1. Charles I, King of Great Britain. 2. Unitarian churches—Sermons. 3. Sermons, American. 4. Government, Resistance to. I. Mayhew, Jonathan, 1720-1766. Seven sermons. 1969. II. Mayhew, Jonathan, 1720-1766. A discourse, concerning the unlimited submission and non-resistance to the higher powers. 1969. III. Mayhew, Jonathan, 1720-1766. The snare broken. 1969. IV. Title: The snare broken.

PARK, Charles Edwards, 252.08
1873-
Creative faith. [Sermons] Foreword by Palfrey Perkins. Boston, Beacon Press [1951] 250 p. illus. 22 cm. [BX9843.P293C7] 52-6265
1. Unitarian churches — Sermons. 2. Sermons, American. I. Title.

SEAWARD, Carl Albert. 252.08
Light on dark horizons; optimism of liberal Christianity. Boston, Beacon Press [1953] 152p. 22cm. [BX9843.S42L5] 53-7596
1. Unitarian churches—Sermons. 2. Sermons, American. 3. Liberalism (Religion) I. Title.

MACKINNON, John G. 252.08'33
The MacKinnon years [by John G. MacKinnon] Indianapolis, Ind., All Souls Unitarian Church [1968] xii, 144 p. port. 24 cm. [BX9843.M23M3] 68-58353 4.95
1. Unitarian churches—Sermons. 2. Sermons, American. I. Title.

FINNEY, Charles 252.085
Grandison, 1792-1875.
God's love for a sinning world; evangelistic messages. Grand Rapids, Kregel Publications [1966] 122 p. 20 cm. (The Charles G. Finney memorial library. Evangelistic sermon series) Sermons selected from the author's Sermons on Gospel themes. [BV3797.F527 1966] 66-19200
1. Evangelistic sermons. 2. Sermons, American. 3. Congregational churches — Sermons. I. Title.

FINNEY, Charles 252.085
Grandison, 1792-1875
God's love for a sinning world; evangelistic messages. Grand Rapids, Mich., Kregel [c.1966] 122p. 20cm. (Charles G. Finney memorial lib. Evangelistic sermon ser.) Sermons selected from the author's Sermons on Gospel themes. [BV3797.F527] 66-19200 2.50
1. Evangelistic sermons. 2. Sermons, American. 3. Congregational churches—Sermons. I. Title.

MCCARTNEY, Albert Joseph. 252.085
The empire of silence and selected sermons. Boston, Christopher Pub. House [1957] 191p. 21cm. [BX9178.M1746E5] 57-9839
1. Presbyterian Church—Sermons. 2. Sermons, American. I. Title.

AWARD winning 252'.08'6
sermons. Nashville : Broadman Press, c1977- v. ; 21 cm. [BX6333.A1A9] 77-71576 ISBN 0-8054-2229-3 bds. : 4.95
1. Baptists—Sermons. 2. Sermons, American.

WHITE, Reginald E. O. 252.086
A relevant salvation. Grand Rapids, Mich., Eerdmans [c.1963] 132p. 21cm. (Preaching for today) Bibl. 63-23792 2.25
1. Baptists—Sermons. 2. Sermons, English. I. Title.

ALLEN, R. Earl. 252'.086'1
Bible comparatives [by] R. Earl Allen. Foreword by Kenneth Chafin. Waco, Tex., Word Books [1973] 128 p. 23 cm. [BX6333.A3B48] 73-76253 3.95
1. Baptists—Sermons. 2. Sermons, American. I. Title.

LEAVELL, Landrum P. 252'.08'61
The harvest of the spirit / Landrum P. Leavell. Nashville : Broadman Press, c1976. 93 p. ; 20 cm. [BS2685.4.L43] 76-4373 ISBN 0-8054-1937-3 pbk. : 2.25
1. Bible. N.T. Galatians V, 22—Sermons. 2. Baptists—Sermons. 3. Sermons, American. I. Title.

BLAKEMORE, William 252.0866
Barnett, 1912-
Encountering God, by Wm. Barnett Blakemore. St. Louis, Bethany Press [1965] 207 p. 23 cm. [BX7327.B5E5] 64-24117
1. Disciples of Christ — Sermons 2. Sermons, American. I. Title.

BLAKEMORE, William 252.0866
Barnett, 1912-
Encountering God. St. Louis, Bethany [c.1965] 207p. 23cm. [BX7327.B5E5] 64-24117 3.50
1. Disciples of Christ—Sermons. 2. Sermons, American. I. Title.

CLYMER, Wayne Kenton, 252.08'7'6
1917-
Affirmation, by Wayne K. Clymer. Nashville, Tidings [1971] 90 p. 19 cm. "A series of sermons delivered on The Protestant hour, produced by The Protestant Radio and Television Center, inc., Atlanta, Georgia." [BX8382.2.Z6C57] 79-161576
1. Methodist Church—Sermons. 2. Sermons, American. I. Title.

BUEHRER, Edwin T. 252.08'773'11
The art of being [by] Edwin T. Buehrer. [1st ed.] Chicago, Ill., Third Unitarian Church of Chicago [1971] 129 p. 23 cm. [BJ1581.2.B77] 75-162600 4.50
1. Conduct of life. 2. Religion. 3. Liberalism (Religion) I. Title.

SMITH, Joseph Fielding, 252.0893
1876-
Take heed to yourselves, by Joseph Fielding Smith. Salt Lake City, Deseret, 1966. viii, 453p. port. 24cm. [BX8639.S57T3] 66-25511 4.95
1. Mormons and Mormonism—Sermons. 2. Sermons, American. I. Title.

WIRTHLIN, Joseph 252.0893
Leopold, 1893-
A heritage of faith, by Joseph L. Wirthlin. Richard Bitner Wirthlin, compiler. Salt Lake City, Utah, Deseret Book Co., 1964. x, 262 p. port. 24 cm. [BX8639.W5H4] 64-66456
1. Mormons and Mormonism — Sermons. 2. Sermons, American. I. Wirthlin, Richard Bitner, comp. II. Title.

CHAPIN, Edwin Hubbell, 252'.09'1
1814-1880.
Humanity in the city. New York, Arno Press, 1974 [c1854] 252 p. port. 23 cm. (Metropolitan America) Reprint of the ed. published by De Witt & Davenport, New York. [BX9943.C5H85 1974] 73-11901 ISBN 0-405-05389-4 12.00
1. Universalist Church—Sermons. 2. Sermons, American. I. Title. II. Series.

NEWTON, Joseph Fort, 252.091
1876-1950.
Everyday religion. New York, Abingdon-Cokesbury Press [1950] 240 p. 16 cm. [BX9943.N4E9] 50-7150
I. Title.

BENNION, Adam Samuel, 252.093
1886-
The candle of the Lord. Salt Lake City, Deseret Book Co., 1958. 339p. 24cm. [BX8609.B4] 58-27485
1. Mormons and Mormonism—Addresses, essays, lectures. I. Title.

CASE, Oscar, 1872- 252.093
My book of acts; missionary experiences and short sermons . . . [Independence? Mo.] c1956. 198p. illus. 20cm. [BX8678.C3A3] 56-32561
1. Reorganized Church of Jesus Christ of Latter-Day Saints—Sermons. I. Title.

COWLEY, Matthew, 1897- 252.093
1953.
Matthew Cowley speaks; discourses of Elder Matthew Cowley of the Quorum of the Twelve of the Church of Jesus Christ of Latter-Day Saints. Salt Lake City, Deseret Book Co., 1954. 456p. illus. 24cm. [BX8639.C6M3] 54-2010
1. Mormons and Mormonism—Addresses, essays, lectures. I. Title.

CRITCHLOW, William J., 252.09'3
1892-1968.
Gospel insights, from the sermons and stories of William J. Critchlow, Jr. Compiled by Eleanor Knowles. Salt Lake City, Deseret Book Co., 1969. viii, 149 p. 24 cm. [BX8639.C7G6] 78-82120 3.95
1. Mormons and Mormonism—Sermons. 2. Sermons, American. I. Knowles, Eleanor, ed. II. Title.

ETTINGER, Cecil Ray, 252.093
1922-
Thy kingdom come, a study in Christian ethics [by] Cecil R. Ettinger. Independence, Mo., Herald Pub. House [1965] 96 p. 18 cm. Includes bibliographies. [BX8676.E8] 65-18921
1. Reorganized Church of Jesus Christ of Latter-Day Saints — Sermons. 2. Sermons, American. I. Title.

ETTINGER, Cecil Ray, 252.093
1922-
Thy kingdom come, a study in Christian ethics. Independence, Mo., Herald House [c.1965] 96p. 18cm. Bibl. [BX8676.E8] 65-18921 1.75 bds.,
1. Reorganized Church of Jesus Christ of Latter-Day Saints—Sermons. 2. Sermons, American. I. Title.

EVANS, Richard Louis, 252.093
1906-
The everlasting things, [1st ed.] New York, Harper [1957] 255p. 22cm. Seventh vol. of selections from the author's 'spoken word' which accompanies the CBS Sunday morning broadcast of sacred music by the Tabernacle choir in Salt Lake City. [BX8639.E8E9] 57-10532
1. Mormons and Mormonism—Addresses, essays, lectures. I. Title.

EVANS, Richard Louis, 252.093
1906-
From the crossroads . . . [1st ed.] New York, Harper [1955] 256p. 22cm. A 6th vol. of selections from the author's talks which accompany the CBS Sunday morning broadcast of sacred music by the Tabernacle choir and organ in Salt Lake City. [BX8639.E8F7] 55-9688
1. Mormons and Mormonism—Addresses, essays, lectures. I. Title.

EVANS, Richard Louis, 252.093
1906-
Tonic for our times. [1st ed.] New York, Harper [1952] 256 p. 22 cm. [BJ1581.E8] 52-12774
1. Conduct of life. I. Title.

FRY, Evan Anselm, 1902- 252.093
1959
The restoration faith. Independence, Mo., Herald House [c.1962] 377p. 21cm. 62-12901 3.75
1. Reorganized Church of Jesus Christ of Latter Day Saints—Sermons. 2. Sermons, American. I. Title.

HACKWORTH, Dorothy South, 252.093
comp.
The Master's touch. Salt Lake City, Bookcraft [1962, c1961] 290p. 24cm. [BX8676.H3 1962] 62-53005
1. Mormons and Mormonism—Addresses, essays, lectures. 2. Witness bearing (Christianity) I. Title.

MCKAY, David Oman, 1873- 252.093
Gospel ideals; selections from the discourses of David O. McKay. [Salt Lake City] 1953. 598 p. illus. 24 cm. "An Improvement era publication." [BX8635.M325] 54-17880
1. Mormons and Mormonism—Doctrinal and controversial works. I. Title.

MCKAY, David Oman, 1873- 252.093
1970.
Gospel ideals; selections from the discourses of David O. McKay. Salt Lake City 1953. 598 p. illus. 24 cm. "An improvement era publication." [BX8635.M325] 54-17880
1. Mormons and Mormonism—Doctrinal and controversial works. I. Title.

MCKINLAY, Lynn A 252.093
Life eternal; a series of lectures, delivered to the Young People's Temple Group of the South Davis Stake. Life eternal [n.p., c1950] 189p. illus. 24cm. [BX8635.M327] 54-31232
1. Mormons and Mormonism—Doctrinal and controversial works. I. Title.

OAKMAN, Arthur A 252.093
He who is. Independence, Mo., Herald Pub. House [c1963] 136 p. 20 cm. [BX8676.O3] 63-22369
1. Reorganized Church of Jesus Christ of Latter-Day Saints — Sermons. 2. Sermons, American. I. Title.

OAKMAN, Arthur A. 252.093
He who is. Independence, Mo., Herald Pub. [c.1963] 136p. 20cm. 63-22369 2.00
1. Reorganized Church of Jesus Christ of Latter-Day Saints—Sermons. 2. Sermons, American. I. Title.

REORGANIZED Church of 252.093
Jesus Christ of Latter-Day Saints.
The kingdom of heaven is like . . . A symposium of nineteen sermons. Independence, Mo., Herald Pub. House [1954] 231p. 21cm. [BX8671.A46] 55-16794

1. Reorganized Church of Jesus Christ of Latter-Day Saints—Sermons. 2. Sermons, American. I. Title.

SILL, Sterling W. 252.09'3
The power of believing [by] Sterling W. Sill. Salt Lake City, Bookcraft, 1968. x, 330 p. illus. 24 cm. [BX8639.S5P6] 68-59023 3.75
1. Mormons and Mormonism—Sermons. 2. Sermons, American. I. Title.

SILL, Sterling W. 252'.09'3
Principles, promises, and powers [by] Sterling W. Sill. Salt Lake City, Utah, Deseret Book Co., 1973. xiii, 308 p. 24 cm. [BX8639.S5P7] 73-87714 ISBN 0-87747-506-7 3.95
1. Church of Jesus Christ of Latter-Day Saints—Sermons. 2. Sermons, American. I. Title.

SPERRY, Sidney Branton, 1895- 252.093
Knowledge is power. Salt Lake City, Bookcraft [1958] 269 p. 24 cm. [BX8609.S67] 58-43141
1. Mormons and Mormonism — Addresses, essays, lectures. I. Title.

SPERRY, Sidney Branton, 1895- 252.093
Themes of the restored gospel; a series of gospel discourses as contained in the sermons and articles of Sidney B. Sperry. Salt Lake City, Bookcraft Pub. Co., 1950. 165 p. 20 cm. [BX8639.S8T45] 52-64564
1. Mormons and Mormonism — Sermons. 2. Sermons, American. I. Title.

YARN, David H 252.093
Faith in a day of unbelief. Salt Lake City, Deseret Book Co. [1960] 189 p. 20 cm. "Prepared originally as radio addresses which were delivered weekly on the Sunday evening hour of the Church of Jesus Christ of Latter-Day Saints on radio station KSL in Salt Lake City from February 10, 1952 through June 29, 1952." [BX8639.Y3F3] 60-3651
1. Mormons and Mormonism — Addresses, essays, lectures. I. Title.

YARN, David H. 252.093
Faith in a day of unbelief. Salt Lake City, Utah, Deseret Book Co. [c.1960] 189p. 60-3651 1.95
1. Mormons and Mormonism—Addresses, essays, lectures. I. Title.

FRY, Evan, 1902-1959. 252'.09'33
Evan Fry : illustrations from radio sermons / edited and compiled by Norman D. Ruoff. [Independence, Mo.] : Herald House, c1975. 160 p. ; 21 cm. Compiled from the author's radio sermons delivered under the title: Hear ye Him. [BX8676.F67 1975] 74-84763 ISBN 0-8309-0131-0 : 6.50
1. Reorganized Church of Jesus Christ of Latter-Day Saints—Sermons. 2. Sermons, American. I. Title: Illustrations from radio sermons.

KINARD, J. Spencer, 1940- 252'.09'33
The worth of a smile : spoken words for daily living / by J. Spencer Kinard. Englewood Cliffs, N.J. : Prentice-Hall, c1976. 217 p. ; 21 cm. Essays delivered by the author on the Mormon Tabernacle Choir's weekly program, Music and the spoken word. Includes bibliographical references and index. [BX8639.K56W67] 75-42298 ISBN 0-13-969139-1 : 5.95
1. Church of Jesus Christ of Latter-Day Saints—Sermons. 2. Sermons, American. I. Title.

LANDON, Donald D. 252.0933
To be the salt of the earth: messages on the nature of Christ, the church. and discipleship [Independence, Mo.] Dept. of Religious Education, Reorganized Churchof Jesus Christ of Latter Day Saints [dist. Herald House, c.1965] 214p. 21cm. [BX8676.L3] 65-26305 2.25; 1.50 pap.,
1. Reorganized Church of Jesus Christ of Latter Day Saints—Sermons. 2. Sermons, American. I. Reorganized Church of Jesus Christ of Latter Day Saints. Dept. of Religious Education. II. Title.

REORGANIZED Church of Jesus Christ of Latter-Day Saints. Council of Twelve Apostles. 252'.093'3
Twelve sermons. Independence, Mo., Herald Pub. House, 1972] 151 p. 18 cm. [BX8676.A2] 76-182436 ISBN 0-8309-0069-1 3.00
1. Reorganized Church of Latter-Day Saints—Sermons. 2. Sermons, American. I. Title.

RUSSELL, William D., 1938- comp. 252.09'3'3
The word became flesh; sermons on New Testament texts, edited by William D. Russell. [Independence, Mo.] Herald Pub. House [1967] 284 p. 21 cm. Bibliographical footnotes. [BX8676.R8] 67-26969
1. Reorganized Church of Jesus Christ of Latter-Day Saints—Sermons. 2. Sermons, American. I. Title.

ROBERTS, Arthur O. 252.096
Move over, Elijah; sermons in poetry and prose, by Arthur O. Roberts. Newberg, Or., Barclay Press [1967] vii, 161 p. 23 cm. [BX7733.R6] 67-24903
1. Friends, Society of—Sermons. 2. Sermons, American. I. Title.

WAINWRIGHT House, Rye, N.Y. 252.096
Search for meaning, [by] Eugene Exman. Thomas E. Powers [and] Douglas V. Steere. Rye, N.Y. [1961] viii, 88 p. illus., port. 19 cm. "Lectures . . . delivered at Wainwright House in the spring of 1900 in memory of Louise Mendenhall, Wainwright House librarian." Bibliographical footnotes. [BX7733.A1W3] 61-19962
1. Friends, Society of — Addresses, essays, lectures. 2. Mendenhall, Louise. 3. Hilgel, Friedrich, Frelherr von, 1852-1925. I. Exman, Eugene. II. Title.

ERB, Paul, 1894- ed. 252.097
From the Mennonite pulpit: twenty-six sermons from Mennonite ministers. Scottdale, Pa., Herald Press [1965] 200 p. 20 cm. [BX8127.A1E7] 65-18234
1. Mennonite Church — Sermons. 2. Sermons, American. I. Title.

ERB, Paul, 1984- ed. 252.097
From the Mennonite pulpit: twenty-six sermons from Mennonite ministers. Scottdale, Pa., Herald Pr. [c.1965] 200p. 20cm. [BX8127.A1E7] 65-18234 3.75
1. Mennonite Church—Sermons. 2. Sermons, American. I. Title.

KAUFMAN, Edmund George. 252.097
Living creatively [by] Edmund G. Kaufman. Newton, Kan., Faith and Life Press [1966] 169 p. 20 cm. Bibliographical footnotes. [BX8127.K3L5] 66-20385
1. Sermons, English. 2. Mennonites — Sermons. I. Title.

KAUFMAN, Edmund George 252.097
Living creatively. Newton, Kan., Faith & Life [c.1966] 169p. 20cm. Bibl. [BX8127.K3L5] 66-20385 2.95
1. Sermons, English. 2. Mennonites—Sermons. I. Title.

SILL, Sterling W 252.097
The glory of the sun. Salt Lake City, Bookcraft [1961] 387 p. 24 cm. Fifty-two messages from the radio program: "Sunday evening from Temple Square." [BX8639.S5G5] 61-7643
1. Mormons and Mormonism — Addresses, essays, lectures. I. Title.

TSCHETTER, P P 1886- 252.097
What manner of child? And other sermons. [1st ed.] New York, Greenwich Book Publishers [c1956] 96p. 22cm. [BS571.T8] 56-13256
1. Bible—Biog. 2. Mennonites—Sermons. 3. Sermons, American. I. Title.

TSCHETTER, P P 1886- 252.097
What manner of child? And other sermons. [1st ed.] New York, Greenwich Book Publishers [c1956] 93 p. 22 cm. [BS571.T8] 56-13256
1. Bible — Biog. 2. Mennonites — Sermons. 3. Sermons, American. I. Title.

BRESEE, Phineas Franklin, 1838-1915. 252.099
The certainties of faith; ten sermons by the founder of the Church of the Nazarene. With an introd. and notes on the author's life by Timothy L. Smith. [Kansas City, Mo.] Nazarene Pub. House [1958] 95p. 20cm. [BX8699.N3B7] 58-32639
1. Church of the Nazarene—Sermons. 2. Sermons, American. I. Title.

CROSS, James A 1911- 252.099
The glorious gospel. Cleveland, Tenn., Church of God Pub. House, 1956. 135p. 21cm. [BX7094.C73C7] 56-36201
1. Church of God (General Assembly)—Sermons. 2. Sermons, American. I. Title.

DE LONG, Ressell Victor, 1901- 252.099
Facts we hate to face, and other radio sermons. Kansas City, Mo., Beacon Hill Press [1952] 108 p. 20 cm. [BX8699N3D42] 52-10225
1. Church of the Nazarene—Sermons. 2. Sermons, American. I. Title.

DE LONG, Russell Victor, 1901- 252.099
Beyond tragedy--what? And other sermons. Kansas City, Mo., Beacon Hill Press [1956] 96p. 20cm. [BX8699.N3D38] 57-20738
1. Church of the Nazarene —Sermons. 2. Sermons, American. I. Title.

DE LONG, Russell Victor, 1901- 252.099
Clouds and rainbows, and other radio sermons. Kansas City, No., Beacon Hill Press [1950] 112 p. 20 cm. [BX8699.N3D4] 50-37009
1. Church of the Nazarene—Sermons. 2. Sermons, American. I. Title.

DE LONG, Russell Victor, 1901- 252.099
Mastering our midnights, and other sermons. Kansas City, Mo., Beacon Hill Press [c1953] 103p. 20cm. [BX8699.N3D44] 54-7768
1. Church of the Nazarene—Sermons. 2. Sermons, American. I. Title.

HECKART, Robert H 252.099
Behold sPilgrim Holiness Church--Sermons. [BX8795.P456H4] 60-17848
1. Sermons, American. I. Title.

HORTON, Wade H. 252'.09'9
Evangel sermons / Wade H. Horton. Cleveland, Tenn. : Pathway Press, c1977. 127 p. ; 21 cm. Sermons printed in the Church of God evangel, 1974-1976. [BX7034.Z6H673] 76-57860 ISBN 0-87148-287-8 : 2.50
1. Church of God (Cleveland, Tenn.)—Sermons. 2. Sermons, American. I. Title.

HUGHES, Ray H 252.099
Religion on fire. [1st ed.] Cleveland, Tenn., Pathway Press [1956] 159p. 21cm. [BX7094.C73H8] 56-8017
1. Church of God (General Assembly)—Sermons. 2. Sermons, American. I. Title.

KRING, James Arthur, 1873- 252.099
Vital gospel truths; sixteen sermons presenting the teaching of Scripture relative to sin and Christ's remedy for the universal malady. Kansas City, Mo., Beacon Hill Press [1955] 123p. 20cm. [BX8699] 55-14590
1. Church of the Nazarene— Sermons. 2. Sermons, American. I. Title.

LEMONS, Frank W., 1901- 252.09'9
Perennial Pentecost [by] Frank W. Lemons. [1st ed.] Cleveland, Tenn., Pathway Press [1971] 126 p. 16 cm. [BX7020.Z6L45] 74-167943
1. Church of God—Sermons. 2. Sermons, American. I. Title.

MCCUMBER, W. E. 252.099
A good word, and other sermons. Kansas City, Mo., Beacon Hill Press [1959] 77p. 20cm. [BX8699.N36M3] 59-8364
1. Church of the Nazarene—Sermons. I. Title.

MALLOUGH, Don. 252.09'9
Crowded detours. Grand Rapids, Mich., Baker Book House [1970] 111 p. 21 cm. [BX6198.A7M3] 72-115636 2.95
1. Assemblies of God, General Council—Sermons. 2. Sermons, American. I. Title.

MALLOUGH, Don 252.099
If I were God. Grand Rapids, Baker Bk. [c.1966] 109p. 21cm. [BV4253.M377] 67-2290 1.95
1. Sermons, American. I. Title.

MUELLER, Reuben H. 252.099
His church [by] Reuben H. Mueller. Nashville, Abingdon Press [1966] 143 p. 20 cm. [BV603.M74] 66-28025
1. Evangelical United Brethren Church—Sermons. 2. Church—Sermons. 3. Sermons, American. I. Title.

OLDHAM, W Dale, 1903- 252.099
The enduring Word; a book of doctrinal sermons. Anderson, Ind., Gospel Trumpet Co., 1952. 127 p. 19 cm. [BX7094.C676O43] 52-36169
1. Church of God (Anderson Ind.)—Sermons. 2. Sermons, American. I. Title.

OLDHAM, W Dale, 1903- 252.099
Messages of Christian brotherhood. Anderson, Ind., Warner Press [1951] 128 p. 20 cm. [BX7094.C676O44] 51-9966
1. Church of God (Anderson, Ind.)—Sermons. 2. Sermons, American. I. Title.

PRICE, Ross E., ed. 252.099
Faith in these times; sermons by Pasadena College ministers, commemorating fifty years of service by Pasadena College in the city of Pasadena, California, 1910 to 1960. Ed. by Ross E. Price, Oscar F. Reed. Kansas City, Mo., Beacon Hill Pr. [c.1961] 117p. 61-12007 1.50
1. Church of the Nazarene—Sermons. 2. Sermons, American. 3. Pasadena College, Pasadena, Calif. I. Reed, Oscar F., joint ed. II. Title.

PRICE, Ross E ed. 252.099
Faith in these times; sermons by Pasadena College ministers, commemorating fifty years of service by Pasadena College in the city of Pasadena, California, 1910 to 1960. Edited by Ross E. Price [and] Oscar F. Reed. Kansas City, Mo., Beacon Hill Press [1961] 117p. 20cm. [BX8699.N36A3] 61-12007
1. Church of the Nazarene—Sermons. 2. Sermons, American. 3. Pasadena College, Pasadena, Calif. I. Reed, Oscar F., joint ed. II. Title.

SMITH, Bernie, 1920- 252.099
The thirteenth apostle. Kansas City, Mo., Beacon Hill Press [1955] 95p. 20cm. [BX8699] 55-14596
1. Church of the Nazarene—Sermons. 2. Sermons, American. I. Title.

THARP, Zeno Chandler, 1896- 252.099
Inspirational short sermons. [1st ed.] Cleveland, Tenn. Church of God Pub. House, 1956. 150p. 21cm. [BX7094.C73T5] 56-7648
1. Church of God (General Assembly)—Sermons. 2. Sermons, American. I. Title.

THARP, Zeno Chandler, 1896- 252.099
Inspirational short sermons. [1st ed.] Cleveland, Tenn., Church of God Pub. House, 1956. 150 p. 21 cm. [BX7094.C73T5] 56-7648
1. Church of God (General Assembly) — Sermons. 2. Sermons, American. I. Title.

THOMAS, James Melton, 1917- 252.099
Great three-sixteens of the New Testament. Kansas City, Mo., Beacon Hill Press [1955] 80p. 20cm. [BX8699] 55-14597
1. Church of the Nazarene—Sermons. 2. Sermons, American. I. Title.

WARD, C M 252.099
What happens to sinners? [By] C. M. Ward. Westwood, N. J., Fleming H. Revell Co. [1967] 127 p. 21 cm. [BX6198.A7W33] 67-22575
1. Assemblies of God, General Council—Sermons. I. Title.

WARD, C. M. 252.099
What happens to sinners? [By] C. M. Ward. Westwood, N.J., Fleming H. Revell Co. [1967] 127 p. 21 cm. [BX6198.A7W33] 67-22575
1. Assemblies of God, General Council—Sermons. I. Title.

WHITESIDE, Robertson Lafayette, 1869- 252.099
Doctrinal discourses. Denton, Tex., I. Whiteside, 1955. 386p. 20cm. [BX7094.C95W45] 252.066 55-59114
1. Churches of Christ—Sermons. 2. Sermons, American. I. Title.

WILEY, Henry Orton, 1877- 252.099
God has the answer. Kansas City, Mo., Beacon Hill Press [1956] 124p. 20cm. [BX8699.N3W5] 56-2147
1. Church of the Nazarene—Sermons. 2. Sermons, American. I. Title.

WILEY, Henry Orton, 1877- 252.099
God has the answer. Kansas City, Mo., Beacon Hill Press [1956] 124 p. 20 cm. [BX8699.N3W5] 56-2147
1. Church of the Nazarene — Sermons. 2. Sermons, American. I. Title.

WILLIAMS, Smallwood Edmond, 1907- 252.09'9
Significant sermons. Washington, Bible Way Church [1970] 164 p. 20 cm. [BX6510.B676W54] 77-117015 3.50
1. Bible Way Churches of Our Lord Jesus Christ World Wide—Sermons. 2. Sermons, American. I. Title.

ALLEN, R Earl. 252.1
Memorial messages. Nashville, Broadman Press [1964] 96 p. 20 cm. Bibliography: p. 95-96. [BV4275.A48] 64-12408
1. Funeral sermons. 2. Sermons, American. 3. Baptists — Sermons. I. Title.

ALLEN, R. Earl 252.1
Memorial messages. Nashville, Broadman [c.1964] 96p. 20cm. Bibl. 64-12408 1.95 bds.,
1. Funeral sermons. 2. Sermons, American. 3. Baptists—Sermons. I. Title.

BACON, Leonard, 1802-1881. 252'.1
A discourse preached in the Center Church, in New Haven, August 27, 1828. Freeport, N.Y., Books for Libraries Press, 1971. 36 p. 23 cm. (The Black heritage library collection) "Preached ... at the funeral of Jehudi Ashmun ... with the address at the grave; by R. R. Gurley." Reprint of the 1828 ed. [E448.A825 1971] 78-168507 ISBN 0-8369-8861-2
1. Ashmun, Jehudi, 1794-1828. 2. Liberia. I. Gurley, Ralph Randolph, 1797-1872. II. Title. III. Series.

BAIRD, William Robb, 1887- 252.1
Funeral mediations [by] William R. Baird, Sr., and John E. Baird. Nashville, Abingdon Press [1966] 128 p. 20 cm. [BV4275.B26] 66-14990
1. Funeral sermons. 2. Sermons, American. I. Baird, John Edward, joint author. II. Title.

BAIRD, William Robb, 1887- 252.1
Funeral meditations [by] William R. Baird, Sr., John E. Baird. Nashville, Abingdon [c.1966] 128p. 20cm. [BV4275.B26] 66-14990 2.50 bds.,
1. Funeral sermons. 2. Sermons, American. I. Baird, John Edward, joint author. II. Title.

CHILES, John Russell, 1879- 252.1
A treasury of funeral messages: beauty for ashes [Reissue] Grand Rapids, Baker Bk. [1966, c.1946] 161p. 23cm. First pub. in 1946 under title: Beauty for ashes. [BV4275.C47] 60-3072 1.50 pap.,
1. Funeral sermons. 2. Baptists—Sermons. 3. Sermons, American. I. Title.

CHILES, JOHN RUSSELL, 1879- 252.1
A treasury of funeral messages: beauty for ashes. Grand Rapids Baker Book House, 1960 [c1946] 161p. 23cm. Published in 1946 under title: Beauty for ashes. [BV4275.C47 1960] 60-3072
1. Funeral sermons. 2. Baptists—Sermons. 3. Sermons, American. I. Title.

FORD, W. Herschel, D. D. 252.1
Simple sermons for funeral services. Grand Rapids, Mich., Zondervan [c.1962] 54p. 21cm. 1.50 bds.,
I. Title.

FORD, William Herschel, 1900- 252.1
Simple sermons for funeral services. Grand Rapids, Zondervan Pub. House [c1962] 54 p. 21 cm. [BV4275.F6] 63-1752
1. Funeral sermons. 2. Baptists—Sermons. 3. Sermons, American. I. Title.

HARTENBERGER, John Henry, 1871-1937. 252'.1
Asleep in Jesus; funeral sermons, by J. H. Hartenberger. Revised in part and prepared for publication by his son, Henry W. Hartenberger. With a pref. by Walter A. Maier. Grand Rapids, Baker Book House [1967, c1937] 120 p. 20 cm. (Preaching helps series) [BV4275.H28 1967] 67-18177
1. Lutheran Church—Sermons. 2. Funeral sermons. 3. Sermons, American. I. Hartenberger, Henry William, 1900- ed. II. Title. III. Series.

LAMONT, Corliss, 1902- 252'.1
A Humanist funeral service / by Corliss Lamont. New ed. rev. Buffalo : Prometheus Books, c1977. 48 p. ; 20 cm. [BV199.F8L3 1977] 77-76001 ISBN 0-87975-093-6. ISBN 0-87975-090-1 pbk.
1. Funeral service. I. Title.

ONE thousand thoughts for funeral occasions. 252'.1
Introd. by Russell H. Conwell. New York, Harper. Detroit, Gale Research Co., 1973 [c1912] p. Published by Hodder & Stoughton in 1912 under title: One thousand thoughts for memorial addresses. [BV4275.O5 1973] 73-2884
1. Funeral sermons. 2. Sermons, American. 3. Homiletical illustrations.

PIUS XII, Pope, 1876-1958 252.1
The dignity and happiness of marriage; selected addresses of Pope Pius XII to married couples. Translated by John Joyce. Foreword by the Marchioness of Lothian. London, Campion Press [dist. New York, Taplinger Pub. Co., 1960] 106p. 19cm. (Campion bk.) 60-2277 1.25 pap.,
1. Marriage—Catholic Church. I. Title.

ROGUET, A. M., 1906- 252'.1
Homilies for the celebration of marriage / by A. M. Roguet ; translated by Jerome J. DuCharme. Chicago : Franciscan Herald Press, [1977] p. cm. Translation of Homelies pour le mariage. Includes readings pertaining to marriage from the 1969 Lectionary. [BV4278.R6313] 76-53538 ISBN 0-8199-0656-5 pbk. : 3.50
1. Catholic Church—Sermons. 2. Wedding sermons. 3. Sermons, English—Translations from French. 4. Sermons, French—Translations into English. I. Catholic Church. Liturgy and ritual. Lectionary (1969, English, U.S.). Marriage. 1977. II. Title.

ROGUET, A. M., 1906- 252'.1
Homilies for the celebration of marriage / by A. M. Roguet ; translated by Jerome J. DuCharme. Chicago : Franciscan Herald Press, [1977] p. cm. Translation of Homelies pour le mariage. Includes readings pertaining to marriage from the 1969 Lectionary. [BV4278.R6313] 76-53538 ISBN 0-8199-0656-5 pbk. : 3.50
1. Catholic Church—Sermons. 2. Wedding sermons. 3. Sermons, English—Translations from French. 4. Sermons, French—Translations into English. I. Catholic Church. Liturgy and ritual. Lectionary (1969, English, U.S.). Marriage. 1977. II. Title.

VINCENT, Arthur M ed. 252.1
Join your right hands; addresses and worship aids for church weddings. Arthur M. Vincent, editor. St. Louis, Concordia Pub. House [1965] 143 p. 20 cm. Bibliographical reference included in "Notes" (p. 23) [BV4278.V55] 65-27799
1. Wedding sermons. 2. Marriage service. I. Title.

VINCENT, Arthur M., ed. 252.1
Join your right hands; addresses and worship aids for church weddings. St. Louis, Concordia [c.1965] 143p. 20cm. Bibl. [BV4278.V55] 65-27799 3.00
1. Wedding sermons. 2. Marriage service. I. Title.

WALLIS, Charles Langworthy, 1921- ed. 252.1
The funeral encyclopedia, a source book. Edited by Charles L. Wallis. Grand Rapids, Mich., Baker Book House [1973, c1953] xiv, 327 p. 20 cm. (Source books for ministers) [BV4275.W2] ISBN 0-8010-9539-5 3.95 (pbk.)
1. Funeral sermons. 2. Funeral service. I. Title. L.C. card no. for the hardbound edition: 52-11447.

*APOSTOLON, Billy 252.3
The preaching of the cross. Grand Rapids, Mich. Baker Bk. [c.]1963. 82p. 22cm. (Apostolon's pulpit master's sermons) 1.00 pap.,
I. Title.

LEA, Henry Charles, 1825-1909. 252..3
The history of sacerdotal celibacy in the Christian church. New York, Russell & Russell, 1957. xvii, 611p. 22cm. First published in 1867 under title An historical sketch of sacerdotal celitacy in the Christian church. [BV4390.L4] 57-8673
1. Celitary. 2. Catholic Church—Clergy. I. Title.

LEA, Henry Charles, 1825-1909. 252.3
The history of sacerdotal celibacy in the Christian church. New York, Russell & Russell, 1957. xvii, 611p. 22cm. First published in 1867 under title: An historical sketch of sacerdotal celibacy in the Christian church. [BV4390.L4 1957] 57-8673
1. Celibacy. 2. Catholic Church—Clergy. I. Title.

SPURGEON, Charles Haddon, 1834-1892 252.3
Sermons on the second coming of Christ. Selected, ed. by Chas. T. Cook. Grand Rapids, Mich., Zondervan [c.1962] 256p. 23cm. (Lib. of Spurgeon's sermons v.18) A62 2.95
1. Second Advent—Sermons. I. Title.

ADLER, Elisabeth, ed. 252.4
Here for a reason; Christian voices in a Communist state. [Tr. by Leslie Seiffert] New York, Macmillan [1964] 136p. 21cm. 64-17716 2.95
1. Sermons, German—Translations into English. 2. Sermons, English—Translations from German. 3. Germany (Democratic Republic, 1949-)—Religion. I. Title. II. Title: Christian voices in a Communist state.

*DEVIN, John N., D.D. 252.4
The wine gave out. New York, Carlton [c.1964] 107p. 21cm. (Reflection bk.) 2.75
I. Title.

DRASTIC discipleship, 252.4
and other expository sermons, by Raymond W. McLaughlin, others. Grand Rapids, Mich., Baker Bk. [c.]1963. 116p. 20cm. (Evangelical pulpit lib.) 63-21470 2.95 bds.,
1. Sermons, English. I. McLaughlin, Raymond W.

HOVEY, Byron P. 252.4
Living in the eye of a hurricane: sermons for every day. New York, Exposition [c.1962] 56p. 21cm. 2.75
I. Title.

MALLOUGH, Don 252.4
Stop the merry-go-round. Grand Rapids, Mich., Baker Bk. House [c.]1964. 97p. 21cm. 64-15865 1.95 bds.,
1. Evangelistic sermons. 2. Sermons, American. I. Title.

RUOPP, Harold W., 1899-1961 252.4
One life isn't enough; the life and thought of Harold W. Ruopp, collected, by Julia Phillips Ruopp. St. Paul, Minn., Macalester Park Pub. Co., 1571 Grand Ave. [1965] 160p. 22cm. Bibl. [BX8333.R805] 65-3844 3.50
1. Methodist Church—Sermons. 2. Sermons, American. I. Ruopp, Julia Phillips, ed. II. Title.

STRATON, Hillyer Hawthorne, 1905- 252.4
Solving life's problems, methods of the Master. St. Louis, Bethany Press [1954] 160p. 20cm. [BX6333.S729S6] 54-21457
1. Baptists—Sermons. 2. Sermons, American. I. Title.

WHITE, Kenneth Owen, 1902- 252.4
Nehemiah speaks again. Nashville, Broadman Press [1964] 122 p. 21 cm. [BS1365.4.W5] 64-14047
1. Bible. O.T. Nehemiah — Sermons. 2. Baptists — Sermons. 3. Sermons, American. I. Title.

WHITE, Kenneth Owen, 1902- 252.4
Nehemiah speaks again. Nashville, Broadman [c.1964] 122p. 21cm. 64-14047 2.50 bds.,
1. Bible. O.T. Nehemiah—Sermons. 2. Baptists—Sermons. 3. Sermons, American. I. Title.

WILLIAMS, Joseph W 1883- 252.4
Songs in the night. [1st ed.] New York, Pageant Press [1952] 245 p. 21 cm. [BV4253.W44] 52-4914
1. Sermons, American. I. Title.

APPLEBAUM, Morton M ed. 252.5
Sermonettes for young people. Compiled and edited by Morton M. Applebaum and Samuel M. Silver. New York, Bloch Pub. Co. [1964] vi, 218 p. 22 cm. [BM743.A6] 64-19140
1. Children's sermons, Jewish. I. Silver, Samuel M., joint ed. II. Title.

APPLEBAUM, Morton M., ed. 252.5
Sermonettes for young people. Comp., ed. by Morton M. Applebaum, Samuel M. Silver. New York, Bloch [c.1964] vi, 218p. 22cm. 64-19140 4.50
1. Children's sermons, Jewish. I. Silver, SamuelM., joint ed. II. Title.

BEAN, George M 1918- 252.5
The armor of God; sermons preached to the Class of 1957. New York, Morehouse-Gorham, 1957. 125p. 16cm. [BV4316.S7B39] 57-10616
1. Sermons, American. 2. U. S. Military Academy, West Point. I. Title.

BEAN, George M 1918- 252.5
Be not conformed to this world; sermons preached to the Class of 1955 by their chaplain. New York, Morehouse-Gorham Co., 1955. 117p. 16cm. [BV4316.S7B4] 55-37389
1. Sermons, American. 2. U. S. Military Academy, West Point. I. Title.

BEAN, George M 1918- 252.5
The power of His might; sermons preached to the Class of 1958 by their chaplain. [West Point? N. Y.] 1958. 93p. 16cm. [BV4316.S7B44] 58-2435
1. Sermons, American. 2. U. S. Military Academy, West Point. I. Title.

*BOYER, Frank J. 252.5
Sermon outlines for special occasions. Grand Rapids, Mich., Baker Bk. [1967] 114p. 21cm. (Preaching helps ser.) 1.50 pap.,
1. Sermons, American. 2. Presbyterian Church—Sermons. I. Title.

COATES, Thomas, 1910- 252.5
The chapel hour. Saint Louis, Concordia Pub. House [1955] 184p. 23cm. [BV4310.C57] 55-7714
1. Universities and colleges—Sermons. 2. Lutheran Church—Sermons. 3. Sermons, American. I. Title.

FROST, Gerhard E 252.5
Chapel time, by Gerhard E. Frost & Gerhard L. Belgum. Minneapolis, Augsburg Pub. House [1956] 149p. 21cm. [BV4310.F7] 56-9460
1. Universities and colleges—Sermons. 2. Lutheran Church—Sermons. 3. Sermons, American. I. Belgum, Gerhard L., joint author. II. Title.

HEDLEY, George Percy, 1899- 252.5
Religion on the campus; some sermons in the chapel of Mills College. New York, Macmillan, 1955. 194p. 21cm. [BV4310.H433] 55-3565
1. Universities and colleges—Sermons. 2. Sermons, American. I. Title.

HERGET, John Francis, 1873- 252.5
Never failing wells. [2d ed.] Cincinnati [1952] 114 p. 20 cm. [BV4255.H32 1952] 52-22787
1. Baccalaureate addresses—William Jewell College. I. Title.

JONES, Bob, 1883- 252.5
Things I have learned; chapel talks at Bob Jones College. New York, Loizeaux Bros. [1952] 224p. 20cm. [BV4310.J59] 54-40323
1. Universities and colleges—Sermons. 2. Sermons, American. I. Title.

JOSEPH, Frances (Henry) 252.5
Addresses to children by Mrs. Morris Joseph and by Bethel Halford. London, Society for the Distribution of Jewish Literature; New York, Bloch Pub. Co., 1920. 127p. 19cm. On cover: Addresses to Jewish children. [BM743.J65] 57-54703
1. Children's sermons—Jewish authors. I. Halford, Bethel. II. Title.

NORRIS, Louis William. 252.5
The good new days. New York, Bookman Associates [1956] 132p. 23cm. [BV4310.N74] 56-58669
1. Universities and colleges—Sermons. 2. Sermons, American. I. Title.

PRINCE, Samuel Henry. 252.5
The legacy of adoration; homiliae Columbiae. With a foreword by Grayson Kirk. [1st ed.] New York, Exposition Press [1955] 73p. 21cm. (Exposition-university book) [BV4310.P68] 54-12992
1. Universities and colleges—Sermons. I. Title.

PULLEY, Frank Easton, 1906- 252.5
Blessed are the peacemakers; sermons preached to the Class of 1953 by their chaplain. New York, Morehouse-Gorham Co., 1953. 128p. 16cm. [BV4316.S7P78] 53-2293
1. Sermons, American. 2. U. S. Military Academy, West Point. I. Title.

PULLEY, Frank Easton, 1906- 252.5
Christ, thy Captain; sermons preached to the Class of 1952 by their chaplain. New York, Morehouse-Gorham Co., 1952. 135 p. 16 cm. [BV4316.S7P792] 52-4012
1. U.S. Military Academy, West Point. 2. Sermons, American. I. Title.

PULLEY, Frank Easton, 1906- 252.5
Help from the hills; sermons preached to the Class of 1951 by their chaplain. New York, Morehouse-Gorham Co., 1951. 127 p. 16 cm. [BV4316.S7P793] 51-4938
1. U.S. Military Academy, West Point. 2. Sermons, American. I. Title.

REID, Albert Clayton, 1894- 252.5
100 chapel talks. combined ed., containing the talks originally published in Invitation to Worship and Resources for Worship Nashville, Abingdon Press [c1955] 304p. 18cm. [BV4310.R43] 55-5043
1. Universities and colleges—Sermons. 2. Sermons, American. 3. Devotional literature. I. Title.

SPERRY, Willard Learoyd, 1882- 252.5
Sermons preached at Harvard. [1st ed.] New York, Harper [1953] 188p. 22cm. [BV4310.S56] 53-8374
1. Universities and colleges—Sermons. 2. Sermons, American. I. Title.

WYNN, Daniel Webster, 1919- 252.5
The chaplain speaks. Boston, Bruce Humphries [c1956] 50p. 21cm. [BR123.W95] 56-5896
1. Christianity— Addresses, essays, lectures. I. Title.

WYNN, Daniel Webster, 1919- 252.5
The chaplain speaks. Boston, Bruce Humphries [c1956] 50 p. 21 cm. [BR123.W95] 56-5896
1. Christianity — Addresses, essays, lectures. I. Title.

KANE, H. Victor. 252'.52
Tell it to the children [by] H. Victor Kane. Valley Forge, Judson Press [1970] 124 p. 21 cm. "Suggestions for 52 story sermons." [BV4315.K27] 73-116723 ISBN 8-17-004823-
1. Children's sermons. I. Title.

BAUER, E. Charles. 252'.53
Little lessons to live by [by] E. Charles Bauer. St. Louis, Concordia Pub. House [1972] 114 p. illus. 21 cm. Fifty-six short sermons based on selected Bible passages from the Old and New Testaments. [BV4315.B29] 79-175143 ISBN 0-570-03131-1
1. Children's sermons. I. Title.

BAUER, E. Charles. 252'.53
More little lessons to live by [by] E. Charles Bauer. St. Louis, Concordia Pub. House [1972] 115 p. illus. 21 cm. [BV4315.B293] 79-185531 ISBN 0-570-03135-4
1. Children's sermons. I. Title.

BENNETT, Robinson Potter Dunn, 1869- 252'.53
What I tell my junior congregation; a series of object sermons preached to the junior congregation of Summit Presbyterian church, Germantown, Pa., by the pastor, Robinson P. D. Bennett ... with an introduction by Alexander Henry ... Philadelphia, Westminster press, 1912. 173 p. 18 1/2 cm. [BV4315.B4] 12-10828

1. Children's sermons. 2. Presbyterian Church — Sermons. 3. Sermons, American. I. Title.

BOWMAN, George W 252.53
Sermons for the junior congregation. Grand Rapids, Baker Book House, 1962. 118p. 20cm. (Minister's handbook series) [BV4315.B67] 62-12668
1. Children's sermons. 2. Baptists—Sermons. I. Title.

CASTLE, Leon W. 252'.53
A year of children's sermons / Leon W. Castle. Nashville : Broadman Press, c1976. 121 p. ; 19 cm. [BV4315.C32] 76-6717 ISBN 0-8054-4918-3 pbk. : 2.95
1. Children's sermons. I. Title.

*CROSS, Luther S. 252.53
Story sermons for children. Grand Rapids, Mich., Baker Bk. [1966] 102p. illus. 20cm. 1.50 pap.,
1. Sermons for children—Lutheran Church. I. Title.

DAVES, Michael 252.53
Devotional talks for children. Grand Rapids, Mich., Baker Bk. House [c.]1961. 92p. (Minister's handbk. ser.) 61-10003 1.95 bds.,
1. Children's sermons. 2. Methodist Church—Sermons. 3. Sermons, American. I. Title.

FISCHBACH, Julius, 1894- 252.53
Story sermons for boys and girls. Nashville, Abingdon [1963, c.1947] 192p. 20cm. (Apex bk., M2) .95 pap.,
1. Children's sermons. I. Title.

FRANCIS, Dorothy Brenner. 252'.53
Piggy-bank minds and 49 other object lessons for children / Dorothy Brenner Francis. Nashville : Abingdon, c1977. 127 p. ; 19 cm. [BV4315.F64] 76-49639 ISBN 0-687-31420-8 pbk. : 3.95
1. Children's sermons. I. Title.

FRANCIS, Dorothy Brenner. 252'.53
Piggy-bank minds and 49 other object lessons for children / Dorothy Brenner Francis. Nashville : Abingdon, c1977. 127 p. ; 19 cm. [BV4315.F64] 76-49639 ISBN 0-687-31420-8 pbk. : 3.95
1. Children's sermons. I. Title.

FRANZEN, Lavern G. 252'.53
Good news from Luke : visual messages for children / Lavern G. Franzen. Minneapolis : Augsburg Pub. House, c1976. 128 p. ; 20 cm. [BV4315.F658] 76-3869 ISBN 0-8066-1528-1 pbk. : 2.95
1. Bible. N.T. Luke—Sermons. 2. Children's sermons. 3. Sermons, American. I. Title.

FRANZEN, Lavern G. 252'.53
Smile! God loves you; 59 gospel talks for children to see and hear, by Lavern G. Franzen. Minneapolis, Augsburg Pub. House [1973] 128 p. 20 cm. Includes bibliographical references. [BV4315.F66] 72-90257 ISBN 0-8066-1304-1 2.95
1. Children's sermons. I. Title.

FRANZEN, Lavern G. 252'.53
Smile! Jesus is Lord : 50 messages for children to see and hear / Lavern G. Franzen. Minneapolis : Augsburg Pub. House, [1974] c1975. 112 p. ; 20 cm. [BV4315.F665] 74-14175 ISBN 0-8066-1458-7 pbk. : 2.95
1. Children's sermons. I. Title.

*GOSSELINK, Marion G. 252.53
Children's talks for Sundays and holidays. 80p. 22cm. ((1.00 sermon lib.) 1.00 pap.,
I. Title. II. Title: Grand Rapids, Mich.,

GOSSELINK, Marion Gerard, 252.53
D. D.
52 three minute talks to children. Boston, W. A. Wilde [c.1961] 160p. 61-17636 2.95 bds.,
1. Children's sermons. I. Title.

GOSSELINK, Marion Gerard 252.53
Up to date Bible talks for children. Natick, Mass., W. A. Wilde [c.1963] 32p. 22cm. 63-22170 price unreported
1. Children's sermons. I. Title.

HENDERSON, Martha Gray, 252'.53
1945-
Being a kid ain't easy / Martha Gray Henderson. Nashville : Abingdon, c1977. 111 p. ; 20 cm. Stories dealing with the real problems of children emphasizing that God can help with solutions. [BV4315.H39] 77-2135 ISBN 0-687-02814-0 pbk. : 3.95
1. Children's sermons. I. Title.

HODGES, Graham R. 252'.53
42 sermons for children; inspirational talks for church, Sunday school, camp, home, and wherever children gather [by] Graham Hodges. Nashville, Abingdon Press [1968] 111 p. 20 cm. [BV4315.H517] 68-11464
1. Children's sermons. I. Title.

HODGES, Graham R 252.53
Object lessons for children's sermons. New York, Abingdon Press [1963] 110 p. 20 cm. [BV4315.H52] 63-7481
1. Children's sermons. 2. Object-teaching. I. Title.

HODGES, Graham R. 252.53
Object lessons for children's sermons. Nashville, Abingdon [c.1961-1963] 110p. 20cm. 63-7481 2.50
1. Children's sermons. 2. Object-teaching. I. Title.

HODGES, Graham R 252.53
Sermons in stories for children. New York, Abingdon Press [1959] 96p. 20cm. [BV4315.H54] 59-10360
1. Children's sermons. I. Title.

HODGES, Graham R. 252.53
Thoughts are things, and 51 other children's sermons. Nashville, Abingdon [c.1960, 1961] 112p. 61-13194 2.25 bds.,
1. Children's sermons. I. Title.

ISAAC, Reid 252'.53
What's God doing today? Talks with parents and children. New York, Seabury [1967] 128p. 22cm. [BV4315.I8] 67-13315 3.95
1. Children's sermons. I. Title.

JENKINS, Holt M. 252'.53
A haunted house and other sermons for the family service, by Holt M. Jenkins. New York, Morehouse-Barlow Co. [1967] 128 p. 21 cm. [BV4315.J47] 67-12970
1. Protestant Episcopal Church in the U.S.A.—Sermons. 2. Children's sermons. 3. Sermons, American. I. Title.

JOHNSON, Samuel Lawrence. 252'.53
Captain Ducky & other children's sermons / S. Lawrence Johnson. Nashville : Abingdon, c1976. 125 p. ; 19 cm. Thirty-eight stories with a moral, including such titles as "Growing Up," "Too Much Is Too Much," and "Do You Chicken?" [BV4315.J627] 76-4913 ISBN 0-687-04630-0 : 3.95
I. Title.

JOHNSON, Samuel Lawrence. 252'.53
Cats and dogs together, and other children's sermons / S. Lawrence Johnson. Nashville : Abingdon, [1975] 78 p. ; 20 cm. A collection of brief sermons illustrating various Christian principles. [BV4315.J63] 74-23105 ISBN 0-687-04768-4 : 3.95.
1. Children's sermons. I. Title.

JOHNSON, Samuel Lawrence. 252'.53
The pig's brother, and other children's sermons [by] S. Lawrence Johnson. Nashville, Abingdon Press [1970] 128 p. 20 cm. [BV4315.J64] 79-97577 ISBN 0-687-31423-2 3.00
1. Children's sermons. 2. Congregational churches—Sermons. 3. Sermons, American. I. Title.

JOHNSON, Samuel Lawrence. 252'.53
The squirrel's bank account, and other children's sermons [by] S. Lawrence Johnson. Nashville, Abingdon Press [1972] 127 p. 20 cm. A collection of brief sermons based on natural history, historical events, and everyday occurrences. [BV4315.J65] 79-186827 ISBN 0-687-39268-3 3.00
1. Children's sermons. 2. Congregational churches—Sermons. 3. Sermons, American. I. Title.

LANKLER, Ralph Conover. 252'.53
Inspiring stories for children / Ralph Conover Lankler ; introd. by Norman Vincent Peale. New York : Hawthorn Books, c1974. xii, 115 p. ; 21 cm. Fifty-five brief essays stressing moral behavior and spiritual idealism. [BV4315.L26 1974] 73-10645 2.95 ($3.25 Can)
1. Children's sermons. I. Title.

LEHMAN, Louis Paul 252.53
Five-minute talks for Sunday school leaders. Grand Rapids, Mich., Zondervan Pub. House [c.1960] 64p. (The Sunday school 'know-how' series) 60-51856 1.00 pap.,
1. Children's sermons. I. Title.

MIELKE, Arthur W. 252.53
Sermons on questions children ask, each paired with one for adults on the same theme. New York, Crowell [c.1960] x, 245p. 21cm. 60-9217 3.75
1. Children's questions and answers. 2. Questions and answers—Theology. 3. Children's sermons. 4. Sermons, American. I. Title.

MIELKE, Arthur W. 252.53
Sermons on questions children ask, each paired with one for adults on the same theme. Expanded ed. New York, Crowell [1963] 287 p. 21 cm. [BR96.M5 1963] 63-15100
1. Children's questions and answers. 2. Questions and answers—Theology. 3. Children's sermons. 4. Sermons, American. I. Title.

MIELKE, Arthur W 252.53
Sermons on questions children ask, each paired with one for adults on the same theme. New York, Crowell [1960] 245p. 21cm. [BR96.M5] 60-9217
1. Children's questions and answers. 2. Questions and answers—Theology. 3. Children's sermons. 4. Sermons, American. I. Title.

MYERS, Alexander John 252.53
William, 1877-
Children's adventures with nature and people; a collection of stories for children about animals, plants, biblical and other events to be narratived by ministers, teachers, and parents. [1st ed.] New York, Exposition Press [1959] 108p. 21cm. [BV4571.2.M9] 59-3770
1. Children's stories. I. Title.

PARSONS, William Edward, 252'.53
1936-
Silly putty, and other children's sermons [by] William E. Parsons, Jr. Nashville, Abingdon Press [1973] 112 p. 20 cm. Includes forty-five story sermons, each introduced by a Bible verse, stressing a particular aspect of Christian teaching. [BV4315.P33] 73-3451 ISBN 0-687-38463-X 3.00
1. Children's sermons. I. Title.

SARGENT, John Henry, 1891- 252.53
52 parables; short talks to young folks. Natick, Mass., W. A. Wilde [c.1961] 112p. 61-17634 2.45 bds.,
1. Children's sermons. I. Title.

SASSER, Harper J. 252.53
Children's sermonettes: adapted from The Upper Room. Nashville, Upper Room [c.1962] 56p. 15cm. .35 pap.,
I. Title.

*SCHOFIELD, Joseph 252'.53
Anderson, 1897-
All occasion talks for children [by] Joseph A. Schofield, Jr. Grand Rapids, Baker Book House [1973, c.1947] 158 p. 20 cm. (Paperback program series) [BV4315] ISBN 0-8010-7978-0 pap., 1.50
1. Children's sermons. I. Title.

*THOMPSON, Orin D. 252.53
Even if I'm bad? sermons for children. Illus. by William R. Johnson. Minneapolis, Augsburg [c.1966] 80p. illus. 22cm. 1.75 pap.,
I. Title.

*TRULL, Joe E. 252.53
40 object sermons for children, [by] Joe E. Trull. Grand Rapids, Baker Book House, [1975] 93 p. 20 cm. [BV4315] [BV4227] ISBN 0-8010-8831-3 1.95 (pbk.)
1. Children's sermons. I. Title.

UHL, Harold J. 252'.53
The Gospel for children : object messages from the Gospel of Mark / Harold J. Uhl. Minneapolis, Minn. : Augsburg Pub. House, c1975. 127 p. ; 20 cm. [BV4315.U36] 75-14695 ISBN 0-8066-1493-5 pbk. : 2.95
1. Bible stories, English—N.T. Mark. 2. Children's sermons. I. Title.

WEISHEIT, Eldon. 252'.53
The Gospel for kids, series A / Eldon Weisheit. St. Louis : Concordia Pub. House, c1977. 128 p. ; 20 cm. [BV4315.W373] 77-9601 ISBN 0-570-03265-2 : 4.95
1. Children's sermons. I. Title.

WEISHEIT, Eldon. 252'.53
Sixty-one worship talks for children, with suggested objects for illustration. St. Louis, Concordia Pub. House [1968] 134 p. 20 cm. [BV4315.W36] 68-20728
1. Children's sermons. I. Title.

WEISHEIT, Eldon. 252'.53
To the kid in the pew : 60 chapel talks / Eldon Weisheit. St. Louis : Concordia Pub. House, c1974. 128 p. ; 20 cm. [BV4315.W375] 74-4548 ISBN 0-570-03238-5 : 4.25
1. Children's sermons. I. Title.

WELCH, Emily H. 252.53
Talks for teenagers. Minneapolis, Burgess Pub. Co. [1959] 80 p. 22 cm. [BV4315.W389] 59-10745
1. Children's sermons. I. Title.

*WELLS, Harold Philmore 252.53
Sermons in magic. Chicago, Moody Press, [1975 c1968] 119 p. ill. 19 cm. Formerly entitled: "Sermons in magic for youngsters" Vols. 1-4. Includes bibliographical references. [BV4315] 74-15333 ISBN 0-8024-7823-9 1.95 (pbk.)
1. Magic—Juvenile literature. 2. Children's sermons. I. Title.

BINNS, Walter Pope 252.55
Behold the Man! Nashville, Broadman Press [c.1960] 128p. 21cm. 60-14144 2.50 bds.,
1. Baccalaureate addresses—William Jewell College. I. Title.

BUTTRICK, George Arthur, 252.55
1892-
Sermons preached in a university church. New York, Abingdon Press [1959] 222p. 22cm. Includes bibliography. [BV4310.B85] 59-8194
1. Universities and colleges—Sermons. 2. Sermons, American. I. Title.

CARLSON, Edgar Magnus, 252.55
1908-
The classic Christian faith; chapel meditations based on Luther's Small catechism. Rock Island, Ill., Augustana Press [1959] 171p. 20cm. [BV4310.C34] 59-9093
1. Catechetical sermons. 2. Universities and colleges—Sermons. 3. Lutheran Church—Sermons. 4. Sermons, American. I. Title.

CUSHING, Richard James, 252.55
Cardinal
Hands that care, sermon delivered on the occasion of the capping ceremony, School of Nursing, Boston College, Sunday, January 31, 1960. Boston, Daughters of St. Paul, 1960. 16p. front. (port.) 16cm. .15 pap.,
I. Title.

DAVIES, William David, 252'.55
1911-
The new creation; university sermons [by] W. D. Davies. Philadelphia, Fortress Press [1971] iv, 107 p. 18 cm. [BV4310.D28] 78-133034 2.50
1. Universities and colleges—Sermons. 2. Sermons, American. I. Title.

*EAVEY, C. B. 252.55
Chapel talks. Grand Rapids, Mich., Baker Bk., 1965 [c.1959] 116p. 20cm. (Preaching helps ser.) 1.50
I. Title.

FIFE, Robert O. 252'.55
Under the chapel spire; dynamic talks to students [by] Robert O. Fife. Grand Rapids, Mich., Baker Book House [1972] 127 p. 20 cm. [BV4310.F4] 70-188232 ISBN 0-8010-3453-1 1.95
1. Universities and colleges—Sermons. 2. Sermons, American. I. Title.

KRUENER, Harry H 252.55
Specifically to youth; a book of sermons. [1st ed.] New York, Harper [1959] 146p. 22cm. [BV4310.K76] 59-7152
1. Universities and colleges—Sermons. 2. Sermons, American. I. Title.

MADSEN, Thorvald Berner. 252.55
'What is your life?' and other chapel challenges. Minneapolis, Free Church Publications [1960] 88p. 18cm. [BV4310.M32] 61-21729
1. Universities and colleges—Sermons. 2. Students— Religious life. I. Title.

MARSCHALK, Nicolaus. 252'.55
Nicolai Marscalci Thurii oratio habita Albiori Academia in Alemania... Nicolaus Marschalk's commencement address delivered at the University of Wittenberg, January 18, 1503. Translated into English with introd. and notes by Edgar C. Reinke and Gottfried G. Krodel. [St. Louis, Printed by Concordia Pub. House, c1967] x, 66, [1] p. facsims., port. 26 cm. On spine: Oratio, 1503. Facsimile of the original Latin text (p. [59]-[67]) made from a microfilm of the University of Halle copy. Bibliographical footnotes. [PA8547.M538T5] 67-31102
I. Reinke, Edgar Carl, 1906- ed. II. Krodel, Gottfried G., ed. III. Title.

MARSCHALK, Nicolaus. 252'.55
Nicolai Marscalci Thurii oratio habita Albiori Academia in Alemania ... Nicolaus Marschalk's commencement address delivered at the University of Wittenberg, January 18, 1503. Translated into English with introd. and notes by Edgar C. Reinke and Gottfried G. Krodel. [St. Louis, Printed by Concordia Pub. House, c1967] x, 66, [1] p. facsims., port. 26 cm. On spine: Oratio, 1503. Facsimile of the original Latin text (p. [59]-[67]) made from a microfilm of the University of Halle copy. Bibliographical footnotes. [PA8547.M538T5 1967] 67-31102
I. Reinke, Edgar Carl, 1906- ed. II. Krodel, Gottfried G., ed. III. Title: Commencement address.

SITTLER, Joseph 252.55
The care of the earth, and other university sermons. Philadelphia, Fortress [c.1964] ix, 149p. 18cm. Bibl. 64-20114 2.45 pap.,
1. Universities and colleges—Sermons. 2. Sermons, American. I. Title.

SITTLER, Joseph. 252.55
The care of the earth, and other university sermons. Philadelphia, Fortress Press [1964] ix, 149 p. 18 cm. (The Preacher's paperback library, v. 2) Bibliographical footnotes. [BV4310.S47] 64-20114
1. Universities and colleges — Sermons. 2. Sermons, American. I. Title.

*SPURGEON, Charles H. 252.'55
1834-1892.
12 sermons to young people / Charles H. Spurgeon. Grand Rapids : Baker Book House, 1976. 143p. ; 20 cm. (His Library) Formerly printed under the title "Twelve sermons to young men" [BV 4310] ISBN 0-8010-8065-7 pbk. : 1.95.
1. Sermons, English. 2. Young adults. I. Title.

WRIGHT, Ronald Selby, 252'.55
1908-
Take up God's armour: talks to schools and colleges. London, Oxford U.P., 1967. xii, 212 p. 19 cm. Includes bibliographical references [BX9178.W73T3] 67-101002
1. Church of Scotland—Sermons. 2. Sermons, English. I. Title.

BEAN, George M 252.550974731
1918-
Be filled with gladness; sermons preached to the Class of 1959 by their chaplain. [West Point? N. Y.] 1959. 110p. 16cm. [BV4316.S7B395] 59-43545
1. Sermons, American. 2. U. S. Military Academy, West Point. I. Title.

SERMONS from hell : 252'.56
help for the distressed / edited by Ward A. Knights, Jr. St. Louis : Bethany Press, [1975] 191 p. ; 22 cm. Includes bibliographical references. [BV4908.5.S44] 75-4830 ISBN 0-8272-3414-7 pbk. : 5.95
1. Consolation. 2. Sermons, American. I. Knights, Ward A., 1927-

SPURGEON, Charles Haddon, 252.58
1834-1892
Farm sermons. Grand Rapids, Mich., Baker Bk. 1965. 328p. illus. 19cm. Reprinted from the orig. ed. of 1882 [BV4316.F3S6] 65-18268 1.95 pap.,
1. Baptists—Sermons. 2. Sermons, English. 3. Farmers—Religious life. I. Title.

*ALLEN, R. Earl 252.6
Days to remember; sermons for special days [by] R. Earl Allen Grand Rapids, Baker Book House, [1975] 136 p. 20 cm. [BV4254.2] ISBN 0-8010-0077-7 2.95 (pbk.)
1. Occasional sermons. 2. Sermons, American. I. Title.

APOSTOLON, Billy 252.6
These days we remember. Grand Rapids, Mich., Baker Bk. [c.]1962. 103p. 22cm. 1.00 pap.,
1. Sermons—Outlines. I. Title.

AUGSBURG sermons : 252'.6
sermons on Epistle texts from the new lectionary and calendar. Minneapolis : Augsburg Pub. House, 1976 v. ; 23 cm. [BX8066.A1A89] 76-3868 ISBN 0-8066-1523-0 (v. 3) : 8.50
1. Lutheran Church—Sermons. 2. Church year sermons. 3. Sermons, American. I. Augsburg Publishing House.

AUGUSTINUS, Aurelius, 252.6
Saint, Bp. of Hippo.
Sermons on the liturgical seasons. Translated by Mary Sarah Muldowney. New York, Fathers of the Church, inc., 1959. xxii, 451p. 22cm. (Writings of Saint Augustine, v. 17) The Fathers of the church, a new translation, v. 38. Translation of Sermones de tempore. Bibliography: p. xxii, Bibliographical footnotes. [BR60.F3A8 vol.38] 59-4211
1. Church year sermons. 2. Sermons, Latin—Translations into English. 3. Sermons, English—Translations from Latin. I. Title.

BAKER, Joseph Baer, 1877- 252.6
Sermons on our mothers. Grand Rapids, Mich., Baker Bk., 1963. 125p. 20cm. First pub. in 1926 under title: Sermons on our mothers and those other heroic, self-sacrificing souls. 63-12753 1.95 bds.,
1. Mother's Day sermons. 2. Lutheran Church—Sermons. 3. Sermons, English. I. Title.

BARRON, Vance, 1916- 252'.6
Sermons for the celebration of the Christian year / Vance Barron. Nashville : Abingdon, c1977. 95 p. ; 19 cm. [BX9178.B375S47] 76-51402 ISBN 0-687-37775-7 pbk. : 3.95
1. Presbyterian Church—Sermons. 2. Church year sermons. 3. Sermons, American. I. Title.

BAUMGAERTNER, John H 252.6
Declaration of dependence; sermons for national holidays by, John H. Baumgaertner. Saint Louis, Concordia Pub. House [1965] 135 p. 23 cm. [BV4254.2B3] 65-18456
1. Occasional sermons. 2. Sermons. American. 3. Lutheran Church — Sermons. I. Title.

BAUMGAERTNER, John H. 252.6
Declaration of dependence; sermons for national holidays. St. Louis, Concordia [c.1965] 135p. 23cm. [BV4254.2.B3] 65-18456 2.00 pap.,
1. Occasional sermons. 2. Sermons. American. 3. Lutheran Church—Sermons. I. Title.

BUESSING, Venantius, 252.6
Father.
Dearly beloved; plain and simple talks for the Sundays and holydays of the year. Foreword by Clement Neubauer. New York, J. F. Wagner ['1951] 208 p. 24 cm. [BX1756.B825D4] 52-28102
1. Church year sermons. 2. Catholic Church—Sermons. 3. Sermons, American. I. Title.

BY the obedience of one; 252.6
pre-Lenten and Lenten sermons by pastors of the Evangelical Lutheran Church. Minneapolis, Augsburg Pub. House [1950] 340 p. front. 21 cm. [BV4277.B8] 50-863
1. Lenten sermons. 2. Lutheran Church—Sermons. 3. Sermons, American.

CALDWELL, Martin, ed. 252.6
Lift up your hearts; an anthology of Lenten essays. New York, Morehouse-Gorham [c1956] 144p. 22cm. [BV85.C34] 56-5284
1. Lent—Prayer-books and devotions—English. I. Title.

CALDWELL, Martin, ed. 252.6
Lift up your hearts; an anthology of Lenten essays. New York, Morehouse-Gorham [c1956] 144p. 22cm. [BV85.C34] 56-5284
1. Lent—Prayer-books and devotions—English. I. Title.

*CHAPPELL, Clovis G. 252.6
Chappell's special day sermons / Clovis G. Chappell. Grand Rapids : Baker Book House, 1976c1964. 204p. ; 20 cm. [BV4254] ISBN 0-8010-2383-1 : 2.95
1. Sermons. I. Title.

*CLAUSEN, Bernard C. 252.6
Pen-pictures in the upper room; fourteen communion sermons. Grand Rapdis, Mich., Baker Bk. [1967] 187p. 20cm. (Preaching helps ser.) 1.50 pap.,
1. Communion sermons. I. Title.

CROSSING the Kidron; 252.6
a series of sermons for Lent and Easter, by pastors of the Lutheran Church --Missouri Synod. Saint Louis, Concordia Pub. House [1954] 108p. 19cm. [BV4277.C7] 54-1925
1. Lenten sermons. 2. Easter-Sermons. 3. Lutheran Church— Sermons. 4. Sermons, American.

DAVES, Michael. 252.6
Come with faith. New York, Abingdon Press [1965] 159 p. 20 cm. Bibliographical references included in "Notes" (p. 156-159) [BV4257.5.D3] 65-20361
1. Communion sermons. 2. Methodist Church — Sermons. 3. Sermons, American. I. Title.

DAVES, Michael 252.6
Come with faith. Nashville, Abingdon [c.1964, 1965] 159p. 20cm. Bibl. [BV4257.5.D34] 65-20361 2.75
1. Communion sermons. 2. Methodist Church—Sermons. 3. Sermons, American. I. Title.

DONAGHY, William Andrew, 252.6
1909-
That we may have hope; reflections on the Epistles for the Sunday Masses and some of the feasts. New York, America Press [1954] 205 p. 21 cm. [BX1756.D633T5] 54-10159
1. Church year sermons. 2. Catholic Church—Sermons. 3. Sermons. American. I. Title.

DONDERS, Adolf. 252.6
The message of Christ; sermon sketches. Translated by Rudolph Kraus. St. Louis, Herder, 1950. xi, 477 p. 25 cm. [BX1756.A1D62] 50-27841
1. Church year sermons—Outlines. 2. Catholic Church—Sermons. 3. Sermons, German. I. Title.

ENGELBERT, E. F. 252.6
A still small voice. Grand Rapids, Mich., Eerdmans [1965, c.1964] 216p. 21cm. [BX8066.E57S7] 64-8906 3.50 bds.,
1. Sermons, American. 2. Lutheran Church—Sermons. I. Title.

EVELY, Louis, 1910- 252'.6
The word of God; homolies. Translated by Sister Mary Agnes. [New York] Herder and Herder [1967] 295 p. 22 cm. [BX1756.E85W6] 67-27736
1. Catholic Church—Sermons. 2. Church year sermons. I. Title.

FORD, William Herschel, 252.6
1900-
Simple sermons for special days and occasions. Introd. by Forrest C. Feezor. Grand Rapids, Zondervan Pub. House [c1956] 136p. 20cm. [BV4254.2.F6] 57-23347
1. Occasional sermons. 2. Baptists—Sermons. 3. Sermons, American. I. Title.

FORD, William Herschel, 252'.6
1900-
Simple sermons for the midweek service, by W. Herschel Ford. Grand Rapids, Mich., Zondervan Pub. House [1970] 104 p. 21 cm. [BX6333.F568S483] 73-120042 2.95
1. Baptists—Sermons. 2. Sermons, American. I. Title.

FORELL, George Wolfgang ed. 252.6
The Christian year; sermons of the Fathers, compiled and edited by George W. Forell. New York, Nelson [1964-65] 2 v. 22 cm. Vol. 2 has imprint: London, New York, Nelson. "Sources and acknowledgments": v. 1, p. 347-349; v. 2, p. 373-375. Contents.--v. 1. From Advent to Pentecost. v. 2. From Trinity Sunday to Advent. [BV30.F57] 64-25283
1. Church year sermons—Collections. I. Title.

FORELL, George Wolfgang, 252.6
ed.
The Christian year; sermons of the Fathers; v.1. New York, Nelson [c.1964] 349p. 22cm. Contents.v.1. From Advent to Pentecost. Bibl. 64-25283 6.50
1. Church year sermons—Collections. I. Title.

FORELL, George Wolfgang, 252.6
ed.
The Christian year; sermons of the Fathers, v.2. New York, Nelson [c.1965] 375p. 22cm. Bibl. Contents.v.2. From Trinity Sunday to Advent. [BV30.F78] 64-25283 6.50
1. Church year sermons—Collections. I. Title.

FRANZMANN, Martin H. 252.6
Ha! Ha! among the trumpets. St. Louis, Concordia [c.1966] 109p. 20cm. [BX8066.F67H3] 66-15516 2.95 bds.,
1. Lutheran Church—Sermons. 2. Sermons, American. I. Title.

FRANZMANN, Martin H 252.6
Ha! Ha! among the trumpets, by Martin H. Branzmann. Saint Louis, Concordia Pub. House [1966] 109 p. 20 cm. [BX8066.F67H3] 66-15516
1. Lutheran Church — Sermons. 2. Sermons, American. I. Title.

FRANZMANN, Martin H 252.6
Ha! Ha! among the trumpets, by Martin H. Franzmann. Saint Louis, Concordia Pub. House [1966] [BX8066.F67H3] 66-15516
1. Sermons, American. I. Title.

†GEALY, Fred Daniel. 252'.6
Let us break bread together : thoughts on the meaning of Christ / Fred Daniel Gealy. Los Angeles : Acton House, c1976. 143 p. ; 21 cm. "Except for a change in the subtitle and the updating of the introduction, the sermons are printed as they first appeared" in the 1960 ed. Includes index. [BX8333.G37L4 1976] 76-151764 ISBN 0-89202-008-3 : 4.95
1. Methodist Church—Sermons. 2. Church year sermons. 3. Sermons, American. I. Title.

GEISEMAN, Otto Albert, 252.6
1893-
Old truths for a new day; a selection of sermons ... based on texts taken from the Epistles. Saint Louis, Concordia Pub. House, 1949-50. 2 v. 21 cm. [BX8066.G38O5] 50-363
1. Church year sermons. 2. Lutheran Church—Sermons. 3. Sermons. American. I. Title.

GORNITZKA, A Reuben. 252.6
Seriously, now; thought-starters for Lent. Minneapolis Augsburg Pub. House [c1956] 81p. 20cm. [BV4277.G65] 56-724
1. Lenten sermons. 2. Lutheran Church—Sermons. 3. Serm American. I. Title.

GRAF, Arthur E. 252'.6
Joybells of life; Advent to Easter sermons, includes a Lenten series on favorite hymns, by Arthur E. Graf. Giddings, Tex., Faith Publications [1973] 216 p. 20 cm. [BX8066.G7J69] 73-84707
1. Lutheran Church—Sermons. 2. Sermons, American. 3. Hymns, English—History and criticism. I. Title.

GRANT, Frederick Clifton, 252.6
1891-
The passion of the King; a book for Holy Week and Easter. New York, Macmillan, 1955. 107p. illus. 21cm. [BV4298.G68] 55-14124
1. Holy Week sermons. 2. Protestant Episcopal Church in the U.S.A.—Sermons. 3. Sermons, American. I. Title.

GRANT, James Ralph, 1908- 252.6
The Word of the Lord for special days. Grand Rapids, Mich., Baker Bk., 1964. 174p. 20cm. 64-20451 2.95
1. Occasional sermons. 2. Sermons, American. 3. Baptists—Sermons. I. Title.

GRIFFITH, Arnnhur Leonard, 252.6
1920-
God's time and ours [by] Leonard Griffith. Nashville, Abingdon [1965, c.1964] 212p. 23cm. [BX7233.G763G6] 65-10809 3.00
1. Church year sermons. 2. Sermons, English. 3. Congregational churches—Sermons. I. Title.

GUERRICUS, Abbot of Igny, 252'.6
d.ca.1157.
Liturgical sermons [by] Guerric of Igny. Introd. and translation by monks of Mount Saint Bernard Abbey. Spencer, Mass., Cistercian Publications, 1970- v. 23 cm. (Cistercian Fathers series, no. 8) Includes bibliographical references. [BX1756.G86L57] 75-148203
1. Catholic Church—Sermons. 2. Church year sermons. 3. Sermons, Latin—Translations into English. 4. Sermons, English—Translations from Latin. I. Title.

GWYNNE, John Harold, 1899- 252.6
Nearer the cross. [1st ed.] New York, Vantage Press [1955] 150p. 23cm. [BV4277.G9] 54-12635
1. Lenten sermons. 2. Presbyterian Church—Sermons. 3. Sermons, American. I. Title.

HAGG, G Erik. 252.6
Passion perspectives; sermons for Lent. Rock Island, Ill., Augustana Press [1958] 79p. 21cm. [BV4277.H28] 57-14188
1. Lenten sermons. 2. Lutheran Church—Sermons. 3. Sermons, American. I. Title.

HAMBY, Warren C., 1924- 252'.6
Eight keys to happiness; a new look at the Beatitudes [by] Warren C. Hamby. Old Tappan, N.J., F. H. Revell Co. [1969] 127 p. 20 cm. [BV652.7.H3] 69-20146 3.50
1. Beatitudes. I. Title.

HAMELL, Patrick J., ed. 252.6
Sunday and feast homilies, by 62 Irish priests. Ed. by Patrick J. Hamell. Dublin, Browne & Nolan [dist. Mystic, Conn., Verry,1965] 128p. 23cm. [BX1756.A2] 65-7960 3.50 bds.,
1. Sermons, English—Ireland. 2. Catholic Church—Sermons. 3. Church year—Sermons. I. Title.

HARRISVILLE, Roy A 252.6
God incognito; a series of Lenten sermons on the passion according to St. John. Minneapolis, Augusburg Pub. House [c1956] 79p. 20cm. [BV4277.H317] 56-7248
1. Lenten sermons. 2. Lutheran Church—Sermons. 3. Sermons, American. I. Title.

HEINTZEN, Erich H 252.6
Were you there? Sermons for Lent and Easter. Saint Louis, Concordia Pub. House [1957, c1958] 77p. 19cm. [BV4277.H38] 57-11908
1. Lenten sermons. 2. Easter—Sermons. 3. Lutheran Church—Sermons. 4. Sermons, American. I. Title.

HERSHEY, Robert D. 252.6
The secret of God. Philadelphia, Muhlenberg Press [1951] x, 162 p. 20 cm. [BV4277.H4] 51-9542
1. Lenten sermons. 2. Lutheran Church—Sermons. 3. Sermons, American. I. Title.

HOBBS, Herschel H 252.6
Welcome speeches, and emergency addresses for all occasions. Grand Rapids, Zondervan Pub. House [1960] 64p. 20cm. [BV4254.2.H6] 60-51664
1. Occasional sermons. I. Title.

HOLT, John Agee. 252.6
Sermons for special Sundays. Nashville, Broadman Press [1963] 116 p. 21 cm. [BV4254.3.H6] 63-8408
1. Festival-day sermons. 2. Sermons, American. 3. Baptists — Sermons. I. Title.

HOLT, John Agee 252.6
Sermons for special Sundays. Nashville, Broadman [c.1963] 116p. 21cm. Bibl. 63-8408 2.50 bds.,
1. Festival-day sermons. 2. Sermons, American. 3. Baptists—Sermons. I. Title.

*HOVEY, Bryon P. 252.6
Holy day sermons. New York, Exposition [c.1964] 106p. 21cm. 3.00
I. Title.

HOWELL, Clifford, 1902- 252.6
Preparing for Easter. Collegeville, Minn., Liturgical Press [1955] 127p. 18cm. (Popular liturgical library) [BX2045.H6H6] 55-4766

1. Catholic Church. Liturgy and ritual. Rite of Holy Saturday. 2. Lenten sermons. I. Title.

HOYER, George W. 252.6
In time...for eternity, a series of sermons on the Eisenach Epistle lessons in the Revised standard version. By George W. Hoyer [and] Justus P. Kretzmann. St. Louis, Concordia Pub. House [1963] 353 p. 24 cm. [BX8066.H65I4] 62-19957
1. Church year sermons. 2. Lutheran Church—Sermons. 3. Sermons, American. I. Kretzmann, Justus P. II. Title. III. Title: Eisenach Epistle lessons.

HOYER, George W. 252.6
In time . . . for eternity, a series of sermons on the Eisenach Epistle lessons in the Rev. standard version. By George W. Hoyer, Justus P. Kretzmann. St. Louis, Concordia [c.1963] 353p. 24cm. 62-19957 5.95
1. Church year sermons. 2. Lutheran Church—Sermons. 3. Sermons, American. I. Kretzmann, Justus P. II. Title. III. Title: Eisenach Epistle lessons.

HUXHOLD, Harry N. 252.6
The promise and the presence [by] Harry N. Huxhold. Saint Louis, Concordia Pub. House [1965] viii, 252 p. 22 cm. [BS1151.5.H8] 65-13136
1. Bible. O. T. — Sermons. 2. Sermons, American. 3. Lutheran Church — Sermons. I. Title.

HUXHOLD, Harry N. 252.6
The promise and the presence. St. Louis, Concordia [c.1965] viii, 252p. 22cm. [BS1151.5.H8] 65-13136 4.50
1. Bible. O. T.—Sermons. 2. Sermons, American. 3. Lutheran Church—Sermons. I. Title.

*JARRETT, Bede 252.6
No abiding city: Lenten conferences. Springfield, Ill., Templegate [1964] 86p. 15cm. (Temple bk.; Paraclete bks.) 1.25 pap.,
I. Title.

JOHNSON, Merle Allison. 252'.6
Sermons for Christian seasons / Merle Allison Johnson. Nashville : Abingdon, c1976. 111 p. ; 19 cm. [BX8333.J58S47] 75-44210 ISBN 0-687-37809-5 pbk. : 3.50
1. Methodist Church—Sermons. 2. Church year sermons. 3. Sermons, American. I. Title.

JONES, George Curtis, 1911- 252.6
March of the year; especial sermons for special days. St. Louis, Bethany Press [1959] 192p. 21cm. [BV4254.2.J6] 59-13167
1. Occasional sermons. 2. Disciples of Christ—Sermons. 3. Sermons, American. I. Title.

KEAN, Charles Duell, 1910- 252.6
When you preach; [a sermon series for the Christian year] Greenwich, Conn., Seabury Press, 1959. 3 v. 21cm. [BX5937.K38W5] 59-10757
1. Church year sermons. 2. Protestant Episcopal Church in the U. S. A.—Sermons. 3. Sermons, American. I. Title.

KEMP, Thomas L. 252'.6
Homilies on the Sunday gospels : in three cycles, with holy days of obligation / Thomas L. Kemp. Huntington, IN : Our Sunday Visitor, c1976. 361 p. ; 24 cm. [BX1756.K42H65] 76-675 ISBN 0-87973-883-9 : 15.95
1. Catholic Church—Sermons. 2. Church year sermons. 3. Sermons, American. I. Title.

KETTNER, Elmer A 252.6
Life victorious; a series of Lenten sermons by Elmer A. Kettner and Paul G. Hansen. Saint Louis, Concordia Pub. House [c1956] 112p. 19cm. [BV4277.K4] 56-8949
1. Lenten sermons. 2. Lutheran Church—Sermons. 3. Sermons, American. I. Hansen, Paul G. II. Title.

KRETZMANN, Reinhard, 1901- 252.6
Voices of the Passion; meditations for the Lenten and Easter season, by O. P. Kretzmann and A. C. Oldsen. Minneapolis, Augsburg Pub. House [c1954] 127p. 21cm. [BV4277] 55-669
1. Lenten sermons. 2. Jesus Christ—Seven last words. 3. Lutheran Church—Sermons. 4. Sermons, American. I. Oldsen, Armin Charles, 1910- joint author. II. Title.

LAWRENCE, Emeric Anthony, 252.6
1908-
Homilies for the year and prayers for the faithful. Collegeville, Minn., Liturgical [1965] xv, 327p. 22cm. [BX1756.L32H6] 65-6844 price unreported
1. Church year sermons. 2. Catholic Church—Sermons. 3. Pastoral prayers. I. Title.

LENTEN counsellors; 252.6
a catena of Lent sermons for devotional reading. London, A. R. Mowbray; New York, Morehouse-Gorham [1951] 116 p. 19 cm. [BV4277.L4] 52-6304
1. Lenten sermons. 2. Church of England—Sermons. 3. Protestant Episcopal Church in the U. S. A.—Sermons. 4. Sermons, English.

LINDEMANN, Herbert. 252.6
Dead or alive, a series of sermons for Lent and Easter Saint Louis, Concordia Pub. House [1955] 120p. 19cm. [BV4277.L5] 55-9894
1. Lenten sermons. 2. Easter—Sermons. 3. Lutheran Church—Sermons. 4. Sermons, American. I. Title.

LINDEMANN, Herbert Fred, 252.6
1909-
Dead or alive; a series of sermons for Lent and Easter. Saint Louis, Concordia Pub. House [1955] 120 p. 19 cm. [BV4277.L5] 55-9894
1. Lenten sermons. 2. Easter — Sermons. 3. Lutheran Church — Sermons. 4. Sermons, American. I. Title.

LITTLETON, William H 252.6
Good morning forever [by] William H. Littleton. Westwood, N.J., Revell [1966] 158 p. 21 cm. Bibilography: p. 157-158. [BX5937.L5G6] 66-12433
1. Church year sermons. 2. Sermons, American. 3. Protestant Episcopal Church in the U.S.A. — Sermons. I. Title.

LITTLETON, William H. 252.6
Good morning forever. Westwood, N.J., Revell [c.1966] 158p. 21cm. Bibl. [BX5937.L5G6] 66-12433 3.50 bds.,
1. Church year sermons. 2. Sermons, American. 3. Protestant Episcopal Church in the U.S.A.—Sermons. I. Title.

LOCKYER, Herbert. 252'.6
All the holy days and holidays; or, Sermons on all national and religious memorial days. Grand Rapids, Mich., Zondervan Pub. House [1968] 283 p. 25 cm. Bibliography: p. 283. [BV4254.3.L6] 68-27463 4.95
1. Festival-day sermons. 2. Occasional sermons. 3. Sermons, American. I. Title.

LUCCOCK, Robert Edward 252.6
The power of His name; a book of sermons. New York, Harper [c.1960] 159p. 22cm. 60-8138 3.00 half cloth,
1. Sermons, American. I. Title.

LUCCOCK, Robert Edward, 252.6
1915-
The power of His name; a book of sermons. [1st ed.] New York, Harper [1960] 159p. 22cm. [BV4253.L824] 60-8138
1. Sermons, American. I. Title.

MCBRIDGE, Alfred 252.6
Homilies for the new liturgy. Milwaukee, Bruce [c.1965] xii, 177p. 21cm. [BX1756.M19] 65-15302 3.95
1. Church year sermons. 2. Sermons, American. 3. Catholic Church—Sermons. I. Title.

MACLENNAN, David Alexander, 252.6
1903-
Joyous adventure; sermons for the Christian year. [1st ed.] New York, Harper [1952] 192 p. 22 cm. [BV4253.M374] 52-8483
1. Church year sermons. 2. Sermons, American. I. Title.

MACLENNAN, David Alexander, 252.6
1903-
Sermons of faith and hope [by] David A. MacLennan. Valley Forge [Pa.] Judson Press [1971] 144 p. 23 cm. Includes bibliographical references. [BX9178.M265S4] 73-144083 ISBN 0-8170-0509-9 4.95
1. Presbyterian Church—Sermons. 2. Sermons, American. I. Title.

MCNALLY, James J 252.6
Rock of truth. [Sermons] New York, J. F. Wagner [c1952] 245p. 21cm. [BX1756.M258R6] 53-2103
1. Church year sermons. 2. Catholic Church—Sermons. 3. Sermons, American. I. Title.

MASLOWSKI, Stanley J. 252'.6
What's the good word? Contemporary homilies, by Stanley Maslowski. Milwaukee, Bruce Pub. Co. [1967] viii, 134 p. 22 cm. Bibliographical footnotes. [BX1756.M295W4] 67-29591
1. Catholic Church—Sermons. 2. Church year sermons. 3. Sermons, American. I. Title.

MEISENHEIMER, Thomas. 252'.6
Formed by the word; homilies for Sundays and feastdays. Milwaukee, Bruce Pub. Co. [1968] xii, 181 p. 23 cm. [BX1756.M38F6] 68-20897
1. Church year sermons. I. Title.

MILLER, Randolph Crump, 252.6
1910-
A symphony of the Christian year. Greenwich, Conn., Seabury Press, 1954. 230p. 22cm. [BX5937.M53S9] 54-9090
1. Church year sermons. 2. Protestant Episcopal Church in the U. S. A.—Sermons. 3. Sermons, American. I. Title.

MOORE, Harmon D ed. 252.6
And our defense is sure; sermons and addresses from the Pentagon Protestant pulpit. Edited by Harmon D. Moore, Ernest A. Ham [and] Clarence E. Hobgood. New York, Abingdon Press [1964] 191 p. 23 cm. "The Pentagon Protestant pulpit is the outgrowth of occasional weekday noon-hour services conducted by chaplains in the concourse of the Pentagon ... The pulpit now operates under a committee of chaplains of the Army, Navy, and Air Force." [BV4241.M58] 64-14618
1. Sermons, American. I. Title. II. Title: Pentagon Protestant pulpit.

MOORE, Harmon D., ed. 252.6
And our defense is sure; sermons and addresses from the Pentagon Protestant pulpit. Ed. by Harmon D. Moore, Ernest A. Ham, Clarence E Hobgood. Nashville, Abingdon [c.1964] 191p. 23cm. 64-14618 2.50
1. Sermons, American. I. Title. II. Title: Pentagon Protestant pulpit.

MOTTER, Alton M. ed. 252.6
Preaching the Nativity; nineteen great sermons for Advent, Christmas, and Epiphany. Philadelphia, Muhlenberg [c.1961] 136p. 61-13580 1.95 pap.,
1. Advent sermons. 2. Christmas sermons. 3. Epiphany sermons. I. Title.

MUNSON, Edwin C 252.6
Ancient truths for today's needs; sermons on the Old Testament lessons. Rock Island, Ill., Augustana Press [1962] 392p. 20cm. [BX8066.M74A5] 62-11206
1. Church year sermons. 2. Lutheran Church—Sermons. 3. Sermons, American. I. Title.

MUNSON, Edwin C 252.6
Through the year with Christ; sermons on the church year. Gospels of the first series. Rock Island, Ill., Augustana Press [1957] 383p. 21cm. [BX8066.M74T44] 57-36651
1. Church year sermons. 2. Lutheran Church—Sermons. 3. Sermons, American. I. Title.

MUNSON, Edwin C 252.6
Through the year with Christ; sermons on the church year. Gospels of the third series. Rock Island, Ill., Augustana Press [1959] 389p. 21cm. [BX8066.M74T46] 59-11996
1. Church year sermons. 2. Lutheran Church—Sermons. 3. Sermons, American. I. Title.

MUNSON, Edwin C 252.6
Through the year with Christ; sermons on the church year. Gospels of the second series. Rock Island, Ill., Augustana Press [1955] 312p. 20cm. [BX8066.M74T45] 56-18624
1. Church year sermons. 2. Lutheran Church—Sermons. 3. Sermons, American. I. Title.

NEAL, Bruce W 252.6
The table is for eating [by] Bruce W. Neal. Nashville, Abingdon Press [1966] 112 p. 20 cm. [BV4257.5.N4] 66-19807
1. Communion sermons. 2. Sermons, American. 3. Baptists — Sermons. I. Title.

NEAL, Bruce W. 252.6
The table is for eating [by] Bruce W. Neal. Nashville, Abingdon [1966] 112p. 20cm. [BV4257.5.N4] 66-19807 2.50
1. Communion sermons. 2. Sermons, American. 3. Baptists—Sermons. I. Title.

OCKENGA, Harold John, 1905- 252.6
Protestant preaching in Lent. Grand Rapids, Eerdmans, 1957. 285p. 23cm. [BV4277.O25] 57-6672
1. Lenten sermons. 2. Congregational churches—Sermons 3. Sermons. American. I. Title.

O'NEALL, Kelly. 252.6
Paths the Master trod, Lenten mediations. St. Louis, Bethany Press [1951] 127 p. 21 cm. [BV4277.O6] 51-1390
1. Lenten sermons. 2. Disciples of Chirst—Sermons. 3. Sermons, American. I. Title.

REID, John Calvin, 1901- 252.6
We knew Jesus; a series of Lenten messages. Grand Rapids, W. B. Eerdmans Pub. Co., 1954. 148p. 23cm. [BV4277.R4] 54-6231
1. Bible. N. T.—Biog. 2. Lenten sermons. 3. Presbyterian Church—Sermons. 4. Sermons, American. I. Title.

ROMOSER, Harold Wolfangle, 252.6
1907-
Christ's "No!" A series of Lenten sermons. Sant Louis, Concordia Pub. House, 1950 [c1949] 77 p. 20 cm. [BV4277.R6] 50-2948
1. Lenten sermons. 2. Lutheran Church — Sermons. 3. Sermons. American. I. Title.

SANGSTER, William Edwin 252.6
Robert, 1900-1960.
Special-day sermons. Nashville, Abingdon [1962 c.1960] 160p. 21cm. First pub. in England as his Westminster sermons. v.2: At fast and festival. 62-9995 2.50 bds.,
1. Methodist Church—Sermons. 2. Sermons, English. I. Title.

SLOYAN, Gerard Stephan, 252.6
1919-
To hear the word of God; homilies at Mass [by] Gerard S. Sloyan. [New York] Herder and Herder [1965] 304 p. 22 cm. [BX1756.S58T6] 65-25913
1. Church year sermons. 2. Catholic Church — Sermons. 3. Sermons, American. I. Title.

SLOYAN, Gerard Stephen, 252.6
19189
To hear the word of god; homilies at Mass [New York] Herder & Herder [c.1965] 304p. 22cm. [BX1756.S58T6] 65-25913 4.95
1. Church year sermons. 2. Catholic Church—Sermons. 3. Sermons, American. I. Title.

TAULER, Johannes 252.6
1300(ca.)-1361.
Signposts to perfection; a selection from the sermons of Johann Tauler. Selected, edited, and translated by Elizabeth Strakosch. St. Louis, Herder [1958] 140 p. 19 cm. [BV5080.T25 1958] 59-900
1. Sermons, German — Middle High German — Translations into English. 2. Sermons, English — Translations from German — Middle High German. I. Title.

THOMPSON, Gjermund S 252.6
The cross is urgent. [Minneapolis] Augsburg Pub. House [1952] 117 p. 21 cm. [BV4277.T5] 52-6312
1. Lenten sermons. 2. Lutheran Church — Sermons. 3. Sermons, American. I. Title.

TODD, Galbraith Hall. 252.6
The gamblers at Golgotha. [1st ed.] Grand Rapids, Baker Book House, 1957. 151 p. 20 cm. [BV4277.T6] 57-14757
1. Lenten sermons. 2. Presbyterian Church — Sermons. 3. Sermons, American. I. Title.

20 occasional sermons, 252.6
by pastors of the Evangelical Lutheran Church Minneapolis, Augsburg Pub. House [1953] 234p. 21cm. [BV4254.2.T9] 53-12930
1. Occasional sermons. 2. Lutheran Church—Sermons. 3. Sermons, American. I. Evangelical Lutheran Church.

UNDERWOOD, W. I. 252.6
Heavenly fragrance. New York, Exposition [c.1966] 120p. 22cm. 3.50
I. Title.

UNGER, Merrill Frederick, 252.6
1909-
Principles of expository preaching, by Merrill F. Unger. Grand Rapids, Mich., Zondervan Pub. House [1973, c1953] 267 p. 21 cm. Includes bibliographies. [BV4211.2.U5] 55-42014 4.95 (pbk.)
1. Preaching. I. Title.

WAGNER, H Hughes, 1903- 252.6
The word in season. New York, Abingdon-Cokesbury Press [1951] 176 p. 20 cm. [BX8333.W18W6] 51-1879
1. Church year sermons. 2. Sermons, American. I. Methodist Church — Sermons. II. Title.

BECK, Victor Emanuel, 252.6082
ed.
The gospel we preach; sermons on a series of gospels for the church year. First series, by sixty-eight Lutheran pastors. Editorial committee: Victor Emanuel Beck, G. Erik Hagg [and] Clifford Ansgar Nelson. Rock Island, Ill., Augustana Press [c.1960] xv, 374p. 21cm. 60-9575 3.75
1. Church year sermons. 2. Lutheran Church—Sermons. 3. Sermons, American. I. Title.

BECK, Victor Emanuel, 252.6082
1894- ed.
The gospel we preach; sermons on a series of gospels for the church year. First series, by Sixty-eight Lutheran pastors. Editorial committee: Victor Emanuel Beck, G. Erik Hagg [and] Clifford Ansgar Nelson. Rock Island, Ill., Augustana Press [1960] 374p. 21cm. [BX8066.A1B39] 60-9575
1. Church year sermons. 2. Lutheran Church—Sermons. 3. Sermons, American. I. Title.

HAMELL, Patrick J., ed. 252.6082
Sermons for Sundays & feasts, by 68 Irish priests and prelates. Dublin, Browne & Nolan [dist. Mystic, Conn., Lawrence Verry, 1964] xii, 522p. 22cm. Bibl. 64-9585 6.00
1. Sermons, English—Ireland. 2. Catholic Church—Sermons. I. Title.

CAEMMERER, Richard Rudolph, 1904- comp. 252'.61
Come, Immanuel; preaching from Advent to Epiphany. Richard R. Caemmerer, Sr., editor. Saint Louis, Concordia Pub. House [1968] 168 p. 21 cm. Bibliography: p. 23-24. [BV4254.5.A1C3] 68-20199
1. Lutheran Church—Sermons. 2. Advent sermons. 3. Sermons, American. I. Title.

FLYNN, Leslie B. 252.61
Christmas messages, by Leslie B. Flynn. Grand rapids, Baker Bk. [1967, c. 1964] 113p. 20cm. ([Minister's handbk. ser.]) [BV4257.F55] 64-23173 1.50 pap.,
1. Christmas sermons. 2. Sermons, American. 3. Baptists—Sermons. I. Title.

GUERRICUS, Abbot of Igny, d.ca.1157. 252.61
The Christmas sermons of Bl. Guerric of Igny. An essay by Thomas Merton. Sermons translated by Sister Rose of Lima. [Trappist Ky., 1959] 62p. 24cm. [BV4257.G813] 60-23697
1. Christmas sermons. 2. Catholic Church—Sermons. 3. Sermons, Latin—Translations into English. 4. Sermons, English— Translations from Latin. I. Merton, Thomas, 1915- II. Title.

*HALL, Thor. 252.61
Advent Christmas [by] Thor Hall and James L. Price. Philadelphia, Fortress Press, [1975] vi, 58 p. 22 cm. (Proclamation; aids for interpreting the lessons of the church year.) (Series B.) Includes bibliographical references. [BV4257] [BV45] 74-24899 ISBN 0-8006-4071-3 1.95 (pbk.)
1. Bible—Liturgical lessons. 2. Christmas Sermons. 3. Advent Sermons. I. Price, James L. joint author. II. Title.

HE has come! : 252'.61
Messages proclaiming the birth of Christ / compiled and edited by W. Glyn Evans. Nashville : Broadman Press, c1975. 140 p. ; 19 cm. [BV4257.H39] 75-18089 ISBN 0-8054-1934-9 pbk. : 2.95
1. Christmas sermons. 2. Baptists—Sermons. 3. Sermons, American. I. Evans, William Glyn. Contents omitted.

LoNNING, Per. 252'.61
The fourth candle; messages for Advent, Christmas, and Epiphany. Translated by O. G. Malmin. Minneapolis, Augsburg Pub. House [1970] 110 p. 20 cm. Translation of Det fjerde lys. [BV4254.5.L613] 76-121963 2.50
1. Advent sermons. 2. Christmas sermons. I. Title.

MCCOLLISTER, John, comp. 252'.61
A child is born: messages for Advent, Christmas, Epiphany. Minneapolis, Augsburg Pub. House [1972] 95 p. 20 cm. [BV40.M25] 72-78562 ISBN 0-8066-1228-2 2.50
1. Advent sermons. 2. Christmas sermons. 3. Sermons, American. I. Title.

PAULUS VI, Pope 1897 252.61
Homilies on Christmas and Epiphany, by Giovanni Bastista Cardinal Montini [Tr. from Italian by Michael Campo] Helion [dist. New York, Taplinger, c.1964] 137p. 21cm. [BV4257.P313] 64-20230 3.50
1. Christmas sermons. 2. Epiphany—Sermons. 3. Catholic Church—Sermons. I. Title.

PAULUS VI Pope, 1897- 252.61
Homilies on Christmas and Epiphany, by Giovanni Batista Cardinal Montini. [Translated by Michael Campo] Baltimore, Helicon [1964] 137 p. 21 cm. "From the original Italian Discorsi per il Natale e l'Epifania (1955-1961) edited by Ufficio studi archivescovili de Milano." [BV4257.P313] 64-20230
1. Christmas sermons. 2. Epiphany—Sermons. 3. Catholic Church—Sermons. I. Title.

SCHMIDT, John, 1905- 252.61
They welcomed the child; sermons for Advent and Christmas. Minneapolis, Augsburg Pub. House [1965] 127 p. 20 cm. [BV4254.5.S3] 65-22833
1. Advent sermons. 2. Christmas sermons. 3. Lutheran Church—Sermons. 4. Sermons, American. I. Title.

SCHMIDT. JOHN, 1905- 252.61
They welcomed the child; sermons for Advent and Christmas. Minneapolis, Augsburg [c.1965] 127p. 20cm. [BV4254.5.S3] 65-22833 1.95 pap.,
1. Advent sermons. 2. Christmas sermons. 3. Lutheran Church—Sermons. 4. Sermons, American. I. Title.

SCHREIBER, Vernon R. 252'.61
My redeemer lives : messages from the Book of Job for Lent and Easter / Vernon R. Schreiber. Minneapolis, : Augsburg Pub. House, [1974] 79 p. ; 20 cm. [BS1415.4.S37] 74-14170 ISBN 0-8066-1453-6 pbk. : 2.50
1. Lutheran Church—Sermons. 2. Bible. O.T. Job—Sermons. 3. Sermons, American. I. Title.

SILL, Sterling W. 252'.61
Christmas sermons [by] Sterling W. Sill. Salt Lake City, Deseret Book Co., 1973. 164 p. port. 24 cm. [BV4257.S5] 73-86165 ISBN 0-87747-503-2 3.50
1. Church of Jesus Christ of Latter-Day Saints—Sermons. 2. Christmas sermons. 3. Sermons, American.

WOLBER, David A. 252'.61
Getting ready for Christmas, by David A. Wolber. Minneapolis, Augsburg Pub. House [1969] 62 p. 20 cm. [BV4254.5.W6] 71-84808 1.95
1. Advent sermons. I. Title.

SMITH, Wilbur Moorehead, 1894- ed. 252.61082
Great sermons on the birth of Christ, by celebrated preachers. With biographical sketches and bibliographies. Natick, Mass., W. A. Wilde Co., [c1963] 236 p. 21 cm. Includes bibliographies. [BV4257.S55] 63-22166
1. Christmas sermons. 2. Sermons. I. Title.

SMITH, Wilbur Moorehead, 1894- ed. 252.61082
Great sermons on the birth of Christ, by celebrated preachers. Biographical sketches, bibliographies. Natick, Mass., W. A. Wilde [c.1963] 236p. 21cm. Bibl. 63-22166 4.50
1. Christmas sermons. 2. Sermons. I. Title.

ANDERSON, Dennis A. 252'.62
Jesus our brother in suffering : messages for Lent and Easter / Dennis A. Anderson. Minneapolis : Augsburg Pub. House, c1977. 96 p. ; 20 cm. Bibliography: p. 91-96. [BV4277.A48] 76-27076 ISBN 0-8066-1562-1 pbk. : 2.95
1. Lenten sermons. 2. Sermons, American. I. Title.

ANDERSON, Robert L 1926- 252.62
Crossroads of Lent; sermons for the Lenten season, by Robert L. Anderson. Minneapolis, Augsburg Pub. House [c1966] 103 p. 20 cm. Includes bibliographies. [BV4277.A5] 66-13048
1. Lenten sermons. 2. Sermons. American. 3. Lutheran Church — Sermons. I. Title.

BASS, George M. 252'.62
The garden and the graveyard; sermons on Genesis for Lent and Easter, by George M. Bass. Minneapolis, Augsburg Pub. House [1970, c1971] 96 p. 20 cm. [BS1235.4.B38 1971] 71-135214 ISBN 0-8066-1101-4 2.50
1. Lutheran Church—Sermons. 2. Bible. O.T. Genesis—Sermons. 3. Lenten sermons. 4. Sermons, American. I. Title.

BASS, George M. 252'.62
The pilgrims & the Passion; messages for Lent and Easter [by] George M. Bass. Minneapolis, Augsburg Pub. House [1972, c1973] 88 p. 20 cm. [BV4277.B32] 72-90256 ISBN 0-8066-1303-3 2.50
1. Lutheran Church—Sermons. 2. Lenten sermons. 3. Sermons, American.

BAUMGAERTNER, John H. 252'.62
Friends in the underground church; sermons for Lent and Easter, by John H. Baumgaertner. Minneapolis, Minn., Augsburg Pub. House [1970, c1971] 121 p. 20 cm. [BV4277.B345] 78-135213
1. Lutheran Church—Sermons. 2. Bible. N.T. Romans XVI—Biography—Sermons. 3. Lenten sermons. 4. Sermons, American. I. Title.

BAUMGAERTNER, John H 252.62
On a hill far away; two complete Lenten sermon series [by] J. H. Baumqaertner and Elmer A. Kettner. St. Louis, Concordia Pub. House [1962] 120p. 21cm. [BV4277.B35 1962] 61-18223
1. Leateu sermons. 2. Lutheran Church—Sermons. 3. Sermons, American. I. Kettner, Elmer A. II. Title.

*BEDSOLE, Adolph 252.62
My God, my God, why ...? Messages on the Seven Last Words. Grand Rapids, Mich., Baker Bk. [c.] 1965. 67p. 21cm. 1.00 pap.,
I. Title.

BELGUM, David Rudolph, 1922- 252.62
The Cross & the Creed; the seven last words in light of the third article of the Creed, by David Belgum. Minneapolis, Augsburg Pub. House [c1966] 94 p. 20 cm. [BV4277.B44] 66-13047
1. Jesus Christ — Seven last words — Sermons. 2. Apostles' Creed — Sermons. 3. Lenten sermons. 4. Sermons, American. 5. Lutheran Church — Sermons. I. Title.

BELGUM, David Rudolph, 1922- 252.62
The Cross & the Creed; the seven last words in light of the third article of the Creed. Minneapolis, Augsburg [c.1966] 94p. 20cm. [BV4277.B44] 66-13047 1.95 pap.,
1. Jesus Christ—Seven last words—Sermons. 2. Apostles' Creed—Sermons. 3. Lenten sermons. 4. Sermons, American. 5. Lutheran Church—Sermons. I. Title.

BUEGE, William A. 252.62
The cross of Christ, and a meditation on the seven last words from the cross. St. Louis, Concordia Pub. House [1962, c1963] 122 p. 20 cm. [BV4298.B8] 62-14144
1. Jesus Christ — Passion — Sermons. 2. Sermons, English. 3. Lutheran Church — Sermons. I. Title.

BUEGE, William A. 252.62
The cross of Christ, and a meditation on the seven last words from the cross. St. Louis, Concordia [1962, c.1963] 122p. 20cm. 62-14144 1.50 pap.,
1. Jesus Christ—Passion—Sermons. 2. Sermons, English. 3. Lutheran Church—Sermons. I. Title.

CAEMMERER, Richard Rudolph, 1904- 252'.62
Jesus, why? Sermons for Lent and Easter [by] Richard R. Caemmerer, Sr. Saint Louis, Concordia Pub. House [1969, c1970] 93 p. 19 cm. Bibliographical references included in "Notes" (p. 28) [BV4277.C33] 73-98543 1.95
1. Lentan sermons. 2. Lutheran Church—Sermons. 3. Sermons, American. I. Title.

CHAPPELL, Wallace D. 252'.62
Eight days that rocked the world [by] Wallace D. Chappell. Waco, Tex., Word Books [1969] 90 p. 20 cm. [BV4298.C48] 78-96289 2.95
1. Holy-Week sermons. 2. Methodist Church—Sermons. 3. Sermons, American. I. Title.

CRISWELL, Wallie A. 252'.62
Christ the Savior of the world / by W. A. Criswell ; with foreword by James T. Draper, Jr. Dallas : Crescendo Book Publications, [1975] 95 p. ; 20 cm. [BV4298.C74] 75-1711 ISBN 0-89038-020-1
1. Holy Week sermons. 2. Baptists—Sermons. 3. Sermons, American. I. Title.

EIFERT, William H 252.62
The Lamb and the blessed; a series of sermons for Lent and Easter, by William H. Eifert and Daniel A. Brockhoff. Saint Louis, Concordia Pub. House [1964] 86 p. 19 cm. Cover title: The Lamb and the blessed; sermons for Lent and Easter based on the Beatitudes. [BT431.E5] 63-22340
1. Jesus Christ — Passion — Sermons. 2. Beatitudes — Sermons. 3. Sermons, American. 4. Lutheran Church — Sermons. I. Brockhoff, Daniel A., joint author. II. Title.

EIFERT, William H. 252.62
The Lamb and the blessed; a series of sermons for Lent and Easter, by William H. Eifert, Daniel A. Brockhoff. St. Louis, Concordia [c.1964] 86p. 19cm. Cover title: The Lamb and the blessed; sermons for Lent and Easter based on the Beautitudes. 63-22340 1.50 pap.,
1. Jesus Christ—Passion—Sermons. 2. Beatitudes—Sermons. 3. Sermons, American. 4. Lutheran Church—Sermons. I. Brockhoff, Daniel A., joint author. II. Title.

ERDAHL, Lowell O. 252'.62
Unwitting witnesses : messages for Lent and Easter / Lowell O. Erdahl. Minneapolis : Augsburg Pub. House, [1974] c1975. 96 p. ; 20 cm. [BV4277.E72] 74-14171 ISBN 0-8066-1455-2 pbk. : 2.95
1. Lutheran Church—Sermons. 2. Lenten sermons. 3. Sermons, American. I. Title.

FETTY, Maurice A., 1936- 252'.62
Putting your life on the line / Maurice A. Fetty. Nashville : Abingdon, c1977. 95 p. ; 19 cm. [BV4277.F47] 76-43351 ISBN 0-687-34945-1 pbk. : 2.95
1. Lenten sermons. 2. Congregational churches—Sermons. 3. Sermons, American. I. Title.

FRYHLING, Paul P 252.62
Prelude to the Cross, and other sermons, by Paul P. Fryhling. Grand Rapids, Baker Book House, 1965. 149 p. 20 cm. [BT431.F7] 64-8347
1. Jesus Christ — Passion — Sermons. 2. Sermons, American. 3. Evangelistic sermons. I. Title.

HAYDEN, Eric W. 252'.62
Miracle of time; provocative reflections on the Christ, the cross, and the resurrection, by Eric W. Hayden. Grand Rapids, Mich., Zondervan Pub. House [1969] 123 p. 21 cm. [BV4277.H34] 70-95043 2.95
1. Lenten sermons. 2. Baptists—Sermons. 3. Sermons, English. I. Title.

HEINECKEN, Martin J. 252.62
The meaning of the cross. [Philadelphia] Muhlenberg [c.1962] 122p. (Muhlenberg Pr. bk. for Lent) 62-8201 1.50 pap.,
1. Lenten sermons. 2. Lutheran Church—Sermons. 3. Sermons, American. I. Title.

*HORDERN, William. 252.62
Lent, [by] William Hordern and John Otwell. Philadelphia, Fortress Press, [1975] vii, 49 p. 22 cm. (Proclamation; aids for interpreting the lessons of the church year) (Series B) [BV4277] [BV85] 74-24901 ISBN 0-8006-4073-X 1.95 (pbk.)
1. Bible—Liturgical lessons. 2. Lent. I. Otwell, John. joint author. II. Title.

HOVERSTEN, Chester E. 252.62
The prince and the prophet: [sermons for Lent] Minneapolis, Augsburg Pub. House [1963] 122 p. 20 cm. [BV4277.H6] 62-21816
1. Lenten sermons. 2. Lutheran Church — Sermons. 3. Sermons, American. I. Title.

HOVERSTEN, Chester E. 252.62
The prince and the prophet; [sermons for Lent] Minneapolis, Augsburg [c.1963] 122p. 20cm. 62-21816 1.75 pap.,
1. Lenten sermons. 2. Lutheran Church—Sermons. 3. Sermons, American. I. Title.

JACKSON, Gordon Duffield 252.62
Judgement and acquittal; Lenten addresses. Dist. Greenwich, Conn., Seabury [c.]1962. 87p. 19cm. 1.50 pap.,
1. Lenten sermons. 2. Sermons, English. I. Title.

*JONES, John Daniel, 1865-1942. 252'.62
The Lord of life and death [by] J. D. Jones. Grand Rapids, Mich., Baker Book House [1972] 224 p. 20 cm. (Minister's paperback lib.) [BV4277] ISBN 0-8010-5018-9 pap., 2.95
1. Lenten sermons. 2. Holy-Week sermons. I. Title.

KRETZMANN, Otto Paul, 1901- 252.62
The sign of the cross, a series of Lenten sermons. Saint Louis, Concordia Pub. House [1959] 86p. 19cm. [BV4277.K7] 59-6231
1. Lenten sermons. 2. Lutheran Church—Sermons. 3. Sermons, American. I. Title.

KUNTZ, Arnold G 252.62
On trial; sermons for Lent and Easter, by Arnold G. Kuntz. Saint Louis, Concordia Pub. House [c1965] 102 p. 19 cm. [BV4277.K82] 64-24266
1. Lenten sermons. 2. Easter — Sermons. I. Title.

KUNTZ, Arnold G. 252.62
On trial; sermons for Lent and Easter. Kuntz. St. Louis, Concordia [c.1965] 102p. 19cm. (12-2241) [BV4277.K82] 64-24266 1.50 pap.,
1. Lenten sermons. 2. Easter—Sermons. I. Title.

KURTH, Erwin, 1898- 252.62
The passion pilgrimage. Saint Louis, Concordia Pub. House [1961] 123p. 20cm. [BV4277.K85 1960] 60-15578
1. Lenten sermons. 2. Lutheran Church—Sermons. 3. Sermons, American. I. Title.

KURTH, Erwin [William Emil] 1898- 252.62
The passion pilgrimage. Saint Louis, Mo., Concordia Pub. House [c.1961] 123p. 60-15578 1.50 pap.,
1. Lenten sermons. 2. Lutheran Church—Sermons. 3. Sermons, American. I. Title.

KVAMME, Rodney A. 252.62
Profiles of the Christ; meditations for the Lenten season, by Rodney A. Kvamme. Minneapolis, Augsburg Pub. House [1966, c1967] 95 p. 20 cm. [BV4277.K87] 67-11714
1. Lutheran Church—Sermons. 2. Lenten sermons. 3. Sermons, American. I. Title.

LEE, Harris W. 252'.62
Time for questions : messages for Lent and Easter / Harris W. Lee. Minneapolis : Augsburg Pub. House, c1976. 95 p. ; 20 cm. [BV4277.L35] 75-22716 ISBN 0-8066-1518-4 pbk. : 2.95
1. Lutheran Church—Sermons. 2. Lenten sermons. 3. Sermons, American. I. Title.

LINDEMANN, Herbert Fred, 1909- 252'.62
The Cross in agony and ecstasy; Lenten sermons [by] Herbert F. Lindemann and George F. Lobien. St. Louis, Concordia Pub. House [1973] 136 p. 19 cm. [BV4277.L48 1973] 72-89625 ISBN 0-570-06383-3 2.75

1. Lutheran Church—Sermons. 2. Lenten sermons. 3. Sermons, American. I. Lobien, George F., joint author. II. Title.

MCCARTHY, John M. 252'.62
Weekday homilies for Lent [by] John M. McCarthy. Milwaukee, Bruce Pub. Co. [1968] 46 p. 20 cm. [BV4277.M26] 68-16812
1. Catholic Church—Sermons. 2. Lenten sermons. 3. Sermons, American. I. Title.

MANEY, Carlyle 1916- 252.62
The suffering servant; a Holy Week exposition of Isaiah 52:13-53:12. Nashville, Abingdon [c.1965] 93p. 20cm. [BV4298.M35] 65-15234 2.00
1. Holy Week sermons. 2. Bible. O. T. Isaiah Lii, 13-Liii, 12—Sermons. 3. Sermons, American. 4. Baptists—Sermons. I. Title.

MANZ, James G. 252'.62
The call of Lent; sermons for the season [by] James G. Manz. Minneapolis, Augsburg Pub. House [1968, c1969] 92 p. 20 cm. [BV4277.M28] 69-14179 2.25
1. Lutheran Church—Sermons. 2. Lenten sermons. 3. Sermons, American. I. Title.

NEIPP, Paul C 252.62
The challenge of Lent. Nashville, Parthenon Press [1960] 134p. 20cm. [BV4277.N38] 60-50742
1. Lenten sermons. 2. Lutheran Church—Sermons. 3. Sermons, American. I. Title.

NOREN, Paul H. A. 252.62
Profiles of the Passion; Lenten sermons. Rock Island, Ill., Augustana Press [c.1961] 76p. Bibl. footnotes 61-7246 1.50 pap.,
1. Lenten sermons. 2. Lutheran Church—Sermons. 3. Sermons, American. I. Title.

NOREN, Paul H A 252.62
Profiles of the Passion; Lenten sermons. Rock Island, Ill., Augustana Press [1961] 76p. 20cm. [BV4277.N65] 61-7246
1. Lenten sermons. 2. Lutheran Church—Sermons. 3. Sermons, American. I. Title.

POOVEY, William Arthur, 252.62
1913-
And pilate asked ... Sermons for Lent. Minneapolis, Augsburg [c.1965] 92p. 20cm. [BV4277.P6] 65-12132 1.75 pap.,
1. Lenten sermons. 2. Sermons, American. 3. Lutheran Church—Sermons. I. Title.

QUINN, Alexander James, 252'.62
1932-
Ashes from the cathedral; liturgical reflections for the lenten weekdays, edited by A. James Quinn and James A. Griffin. New York, Alba House [1974] 90 p. 21 cm. [BV4277.Q56] 73-22299 ISBN 0-8189-0287-6 2.95
1. Catholic Church—Sermons. 2. Lenten sermons. 3. Sermons, American. I. Griffin, James A., joint author. II. Title.

ROGNESS, Alvin N., 1906- 252'.62
The wonder of being loved; messages for Lent and every season [by] Alvin N. Rogness. Minneapolis, Augsburg Pub. House [1971, c1972] 72 p. 20 cm. [BV4277.R57 1972] 72-176472 ISBN 0-8066-1203-7 2.25
1. Lutheran Church—Sermons. 2. Lenten sermons. 3. Sermons, American. I. Title.

SHEETS, Herchel H. 252'.62
The look that redeemed, by Herchel H. Sheets. Nashville, Tidings [1972] 63 p. 20 cm. Includes bibliographical references. [BV4277.S43] 73-188379 0.65
1. Methodist Church—Sermons. 2. Lenten sermons. 3. Sermons, American. I. Title.

SIEGEL, William J 252.62
Men who faced the Cross; sermons for Lent. Rock Island, Ill.,Augustana Press [1959] 85 p. 21 cm. [BV4277.S5] 59-5757
1. Lenten sermons. 2. Luteran Church — Sermons. 3. Sermons, American. I. Title.

SMITH, James Roy. 252'.62
His finest week. [Nashville] The Upper room [1971] 63 p. 21 cm. [BT414.S56] 77-175803
1. Holy Week—Meditations. I. Title.

STRENG, William D 252.62
What language shall I borrow! Thirty Lenten meditations. Minneapolis, Augsburg Pub. House [1961] 191 p. 21 cm. [BV4277.S79] 61-7000
1. Lenten sermons. 2. Lutheran Church — Sermons. 3. Sermons, American. I. Title.

STRENG, William D. 252.62
What language shall I borrow? Thirty Lenten meditations. Minneapolis, Minn., Augsburg Pub. House [c.1961] 191p. 61-7000 3.00
1. Lenten sermons: 2. Lutheran Church—Sermons. 3. Sermons, American. I. Title.

TAYLOR, Gardner C. 252'.62
How shall they preach / by Gardner C. Taylor. Elgin, IL : Progressive Baptist Pub. House, c1977. 148 p. ; 22 cm. Includes bibliographical references. [BV4211.2.T38] 77-76732 ISBN 0-89191-097-2 : 7.50
1. Preaching—Addresses, essays, lectures. 2. Lenten sermons. I. Title.

THESE forty days, 252.62
Lenten counsels by twenty-one Anglicans. New York, Morehouse-Barlow [c.1962] 145p. 62-12135 2.50 bds.,
1. Lenten sermons. 2. Anglican Communion—Sermons. 3. Sermons, English.

TONNE, Arthur J., Rt. 252.62
Rev. Msgr.
Lent and the laws of the church; seven sermons plus--one for Good Friday, one for Easter. [Emporia, Kan., Didde Printing Co., 1962, c.1961] 64p., 1.50, pap., plastic binding
I. Title.

VIETS, Wallace T 252.62
My God, why? and other questions from the Passion [by] Wallace T. Viets. Nashville, Abingdon Press [1966] 112 p. 20 cm. Bibliographical references included in "Notes" (p. 111-112) [BV4277.V5] 66-10848
1. Lenten sermons. 2. Sermons, American. 3. Methodist Church — Sermons. I. Title.

VIETS, Wallace T. 252.62
My God, why? and other questions from the Passion. Nashville, Abingdon [c.1966] 112p. 20cm. Bibl. [BV4277.V5] 66-10848 2.25 bds.,
1. Lenten sermons. 2. Sermons, American. 3. Methodist Church—Sermons. I. Title.

VIETS, Wallace T 252.62
Seven days that changed the world; Lenten sermons based upon the events of the last week in the life of Jesus. New York, Abingdon Press [1962] 92 p. 18 cm. [BV4298.V5] 62-8109
1. Holy Week sermons. 2. Methodist Church — Sermons. 3. Sermons, American. I. Title.

VIETS, Wallace T. 252.62
Seven days that changed the world; Lenten sermons based upon the events of the last week in the life of Jesus. Nashville, Abingdon [c.1962] 92p. 62-8109 2.00 bds.,
1. Holy Week sermons. 2. Methodist Church—Sermons. 3. Sermons, American. I. Title.

WEBB, Wheaton Phillips, 252'.62
1911-
The dramatic silences of his last week. Nashville, Abingdon Press [1971, c1972] 64 p. 20 cm. Includes bibliographical references. [BV4277.W39 1972] 74-173949 ISBN 0-687-11231-1 2.50
1. Methodist Church—Sermons. 2. Lenten sermons. 3. Sermons, American. I. Title.

WEDEL, Alton F. 252.62
A cross to glory [by] Alton F. Wedel. [St. Louis] Concordia [1966] 104p. 20cm. [BV4277.W4] 66-25446 1.95 pap.,
1. Lenten sermons. 2. Lutheran Church—Sermons. 3. Sermons, American. I. Title.

WERBERIG, Robert J. 252'.62
Journey to joy [by] Robert J. Werberig. St. Louis, Concordia Pub. House [1971] 62 p. 19 cm. [BV4277.W45 1971] 72-153648 ISBN 0-570-06382-5
1. Lenten sermons. 2. Sermons, American. I. Title.

LEHMBERG, Ben F. 252'.62'08
Food for fasting, by Ben F. Lehmberg. Nashville, Tidings [1969] 80 p. 19 cm. [BX8333.L43F6] 68-59144
1. Methodist Church—Sermons. 2. Sermons, American. I. Title.

MOTTER, Alton M., ed. 252.62082
Preaching the Passion; twenty-four outstanding sermons for the Lenten season. Philadelphia, Fortress [1964, c.1963] vi, 193p. 19cm. 64-10648 1.95 pap.,
1. Lenten sermons. 2. Sermons, English. I. Title.

AUGUSTINUS. AURELIUS, 252.63
Saint, Bp. of Hippo.
Selected Easter sermons of Saint Augustine: with introd., text of thirty sermons, notes, and commentary by Philip T. Weller. St. Louis, Herder [1959] 329p. 21cm. Includes bibliography. [BV4259.A783] 59-9774
1. Easter Sermons. 2. Sermons, Latin—Translations into English. 3. Sermons. English—Translations from Latin. I. Weller, Philip T., hist. ed. and tr. II. Title.

CALVARY 's cross, 252'.63
by Dwight L. Moody . . . and others. Grand Rapids, Baker Bk. [1966] 97p. 20cm. (Minister's handbk. ser.) [BV4241.C3] 67-2873 1.95 bds.,
1. Sermons. I. Moody, Dwight Lyman, 1837-1899.
Contents omitted.

GADDY, C. Welton. 252'.63
Easter proclamation: remembrance, and renewal [by] C. Welton Gaddy. Nashville, Broadman Press [1974] 95 p. 19 cm. Includes bibliographical references. [BT481.G32] 73-87065 ISBN 0-8054-1921-7 1.95 (pbk.)
1. Jesus Christ—Resurrection—Sermons. 2. Jesus Christ—Passion—Sermons. 3. Baptists—Sermons. 4. Sermons, American. I. Title.

GORDON, John M. 252.63
Resurrection messages, by John M. Gordon. Grand Rapids, Baker Book House, 1964. 141 p. 22 cm. [RV4259.G6] 64-8348
1. Easter — Sermons. 2. Sermons, American. 3. Presbyterian Church — Sermons. I. Title.

GORDON, John M. 252.63
Resurrection messages. Grand Rapids, Mich. Baker Bk. [c.]1964. 141p. 22cm. [BV4259.G6] 64-8348 2.50 bds.,
1. Easter—Sermons. 2. Sermons, American. 3. Presbyterian Church—Sermons. I. Title.

MARNEY, Carlyle, 1916- 252'.63
The crucible of redemption. Nashville, Abingdon Press [1968] 63 p. 20 cm. [BV4298.M34] 68-11712
1. Holy-Week sermons. 2. Sermons, American. 3. Baptists—Sermons. I. Title.

MOODY, Dwight Lyman, 1837- 252'.63
1899.
Calvary's cross, by Dwight L. Moody ... and others. Grand Rapids, Baker Book House [1966] 97 p. 20 cm. (Minister's handbook series) [BV4241.C3] 67-2873
1. Sermons. I. Title.

*RICE, Charles. 252.63
Easter, [by] Charles Rice and J. Louis Martyn. Philadelphia, Fortress Press, [1975] vi, 58 p. 22 cm. (Proclamation; aids for interpreting the lessons of the church year.) (Series B) Includes bibliographical references. [BV4259] [BV55] 74-24958 1.95 (pbk.)
1. Bible—Liturgical lessons. 2. Easter. I. Martyn, J. Louis. joint author. II. Title.

TODD, Galbraith Hall 252.63
O angel of the garden. Grand Rapids, Mich., Baker Bk. House, 1961. 96p. 61-17551 1.50
1. Easter—Sermons. 2. Presbyterian Church—Sermons. 3. Sermons, American. I. Title.

MCGAUGHEY, C. E., 1905- 252.6'63
The hope of the world, by C. E. McGaughey. Abilene, Tex., Biblical Research Press [1971] v, 198 p. 23 cm. (The 20th century sermons series, v. 6) On spine: 20th century sermons. [BX7077.Z6M24] 74-180791 4.50
1. Churches of Christ—Sermons. 2. Sermons, American. I. Title.

MOTTER, Alton M., ed. 252.67
Preaching on Pentecost and Christian unity; thirty outstanding sermons dealing with theme of Pentecost and the ecumenical movement. Philadelphia, Fortress [1966, c.1965] viii, 248p. 19cm. Bibl. [BV4300.5.M6] 66-10157 2.48 pap.,
1. Pentecost—Sermons. 2. Christian union—Sermons. 3. Sermons, English. I. Title.

TODD, Galbraith Hall. 252.67
Sermons for special days and occasions. Grand Rapids, Baker Book House, 1962. 157 p. 21 cm. (Evangelical pulpit library) [BV4254.3.T6] 62-21706
1. Festival-day sermons. I. Title.

PLUMSTEAD, A. W. comp. 252'.68
The wall and the garden; selected Massachusetts election sermons, 1670-1755, ed. by A. W. Plumstead. Minneapolis. Univ. of Minn. Pr. [1968] viii, 390p. facsims. 24cm. Bibl. [F67.P65 1968] 68-19742 8.50
1. Election sermons—Massachusetts. I. Title.

PLUMSTEAD, A. W., comp. 252'.68
The wall and the garden; selected Massachusetts election sermons, 1670-1775, edited by A. W. Plumstead. Minneapolis, University of Minnesota Press [1968] viii, 390 p. facsims. 24 cm. Bibliographical footnotes. [F67.P65 1968] 68-19742
1. Election sermons—Massachusetts. I. Title.

ALBRECHT, Joseph H. 252.7
The Gospel in our day; collected sermons. New York, Vantage [1962, c.1961] 96p. 2.50 bds.,
I. Title.

*MCCANDLESS, Oleta R. 252.7
Installation services for arious occasions / by Oleta R. McCandless. Grand Rapids : Baker Book House, 1976c1966. 103p. ; 20 cm. Formerly published under the title, "Twenty-four installation services. [BV199.I5] ISBN 0-8010-5985-2 pbk. : 1.95.
1. Installation service (Church officers) 2. Dedication services. 3. &devotional exercises. I. Title.

MCGINTY, Claudius Lamar, 252.7
1885-
A book of dedications. Nashville, Broadman Press [1955] 112p. 21cm. [BV199.D4M3] 55-13936
1. Dedication services. I. Title.

BELTER, Robert Rudolph, 252.9
1899-
To die is gain; funeral sermons for special and general use. Burlington, Iowa, Lutheran Literary Board [1951] 88 p. 20 cm. [BV4275.B45] 52-18168
1. Funeral sermons. 2. Lutheran Church—Sermons. 3. Sermons, American. I. Title.

BOLDING, Amy. 252'.9
Installation services for all groups. Nashville, Tenn., Broadman Press [1969] 126 p. 21 cm. [BV199.I5B6] 71-84501 2.95
1. Installation service (Church officers) I. Title.

BONNER, William Jones. 252.9
When sorrow comes; funeral sermon suggestions. Anderson, Ind., Warner Press [1958] 80p. 19cm. [BV4275.B6] 58-9454
1. Funeral sermons—Outlines. I. Title.

FUNERAL orations 252.9
by Saint Gregory Nazianzen and Saint Ambrose;translated by Leo P. McCauley [and others] With an introd. on the early Christian funeral oration by Martin R. P. McGuire. New York, Fathers of the Church, inc., 1953. xxiii, 344p. 22cm. (The Fathers of the church, a new translation, v. 22) Bibliography: p. xxii-xxiii. [BR60.F3F8] 54-962
1. Funeral sermons. I. Grogorius Nazianzenus, Saint, Patriarch of Constantinople. II. Ambrosius, Saint, Bp. of Milan. III. McGuire, Martin Rawson Patrick, 1897- IV. Series.

FUNERAL orations by Saint 252'.9
Gregory Nazianzen and Saint Ambrose; translated by Leo P. McCauley [and others] With an introd. on the early Christian funeral oration by Martin R. P. McGuire. Washington, Catholic University of America Press [1968, c1953] xxiii, 351 p. (p. 345-351 advertisements) 22 cm. (The Fathers of the church, a new translation, v. 22) Bibliography: p. xxii-xxiii. [BR60.F3F8 1968] 67-28586 7.90
1. Funeral sermons. I. Gregorius Nazianzenus, Saint, Patriarch of Constantinople. II. Ambrosius, Saint, Bp. of Milan. III. Title. IV. Series.

FUNERAL sermons and 252.9
outlines, by F. B. Meyer, Charles H. Spurgeon, Albert Barnes, and others. Grand Rapids, Baker Book House, 1951. 107 p. 21 cm. Prose and poetry. [BV4275.F83] 52-6829
1. Funeral sermons. I. Meyer, Frederick Brotherton, 1847-1929.

20 funeral sermons, 252.9
by pastors of the Evangelical Lutheran Church Minneapolis, Augsburg Pub. House [1952] 202p. 21cm. [BV4275.T9] 52-14491
1. Funeral sermons. 2. Lutheran Church—Sermons. 3. Sermons, American. 4. Evangelical Lutheran Church.

VAN WYK, William Peter, 252.9
1874-1943.
Notes for addresses at funeral occasions. Grand Rapids, Baker Book House, 1955 [c1945] 140p. 20cm. First published in 1945 under title: My notes for addresses at funeral occasions. [BV4275.V3 1955] 55-6616
1. Funeral sermons. 2. Sermons—Outlines. I. Title.

WALLIS, Charles Langworthy, 252.9
1921- ed.
The funeral encyclopedia, a source book. New York, Harper [1953] 327p. 24cm. [BV4275.W2] 52-11447
1. Funeral sermons. 2. Funeral service. I. Title.

253 Secular Clergymen & Duties

ABBEY, Merrill R. 253
Communication in pulpit and parish, by Merrill R. Abbey. Philadelphia, Westminster Press [1973] 237 p. 22 cm. Includes bibliographical references. [BV4319.A23] 72-14329 ISBN 0-664-20967-X 7.50
1. Communication (Theology) 2. Preaching. I. Title.

*ADAMS, Jay E. 253
Shepherding God's flock / Jay E. Adams. Grand Rapids : Baker Book House, 1976c1975. v,199p. : ill., chart ; 22 cm. Contents.Contents: v.3.Pastoral leadership Includes bibliographical references. [BV 420] ISBN 0-8010-0091-2 pbk. : 3.75.
1. Pastoral theology. 2. Group ministry. 3. Clergy. I. Title.

ALEXANDER, Walter Richardson, 253
1889-
Two o clock in the morning, and other true

stories of practical Christianity. Grand Rapids, Eerdmans, 1956. 86p. 23cm. [BX6495.A4A3] 56-12803
1. Baptists—Clergy—Correspondence, reminiscences, etc. I. Title.

ALEXANDER, Walter Richardson, 1889- 253
Two o'clock in the morning, and other true stories of practical Christianity. Grand Rapids, Eerdmans, 1956. 86p. 23cm. [BX6495.A4A3] 56-12803
1. Baptists— Clergy—Correspondence, reminiscences, etc. I. Title.

ANDERSON, Roy Allan. 253
The shepherd-evangelist; his life, ministry, and reward. Washington, Review and Herald Pub. Association [1950] 672 p. illus. 21 cm. Bibliographical footnotes. [BV3790.A5] 50-14166
1. Evangelistic work. I. Title.

ARNOLD, Charles Harvey. 253
Near the edge of battle; a short history of the Divinity School and the Chicago school of theology, 1866-1966. [Chicago, Divinity School Association, University of Chicago, c1966] viii, 131 p. 21 cm. Bibliography: p. 119-131. [BV4070.C525A8] 207'.744'5 68-407
1. Chicago. University. Divinity School—History. I. Title.

BARTLETT, Laile E. 253
The vanishing parson [by] Laile E. Bartlett. Boston, Beacon Press [1971] x, 241 p. 22 cm. [BV660.2.B35 1971] 79-136221 ISBN 0-8070-1142-8 7.50
1. Clergy. 2. Christianity—20th century. I. Title.

BASTIAN, Ralph J. 253
Priesthood and ministry, by Ralph J. Bastian. Glen Rock, N.J., Paulist Press [1969] ix, 99 p. 21 cm. (Guide to the Fathers of the church, 5) Bibliography: p. 95. [BR63.B3] 69-18372 2.95
1. Priests. 2. Christian literature, Early. I. Title.

BAXTER, Richard, 1615-1691. 253
The reformed pastor / Richard Baxter ; edited by William Brown. Edinburgh ; Carlisle, Pa. : The Banner of Truth Trust, 1974. 256 p. ; 19 cm. (Puritan paperbacks) Originally published under title: Gildas Salvianus. Includes bibliographical references. [BV4009.B3 1974] 74-189719 ISBN 0-85151-191-0 : £0.65
1. Pastoral theology—Early works to 1900. I. Title.

BELL, Arthur Donald. 253
How to get along with people in the church. Grand Rapids, Zondervan Pub. House [1960] 109p. 21cm. Includes bibliography. [BV652.1.B4] 60-3667
1. Leadership. 2. hurch work. 3. Pastoral psychology. I. Title.

*BICKET, Zenas J. 253
The effective pastor. Comp. and edited by Zenas J. Bicket under the direction of the Assemblies of God Committee on Mission. Springfield, Mo., Gospel Publishing House [1973] 184 p. illus. 21 cm. Bibliography: p. 179-180. [BV600.2] 3.95
1. Clergy—Office. I. Assemblies of God Committee on Mission. II. Title.

BLACKWOOD, Andrew Watterson 253
The growing minister, his opportunities and obstacles. Nashville, Abingdon Press [c.1960] 192p. 23cm. (bibl.:184-187, footnotes) 60-9194 3.00
1. Pastoral theology. I. Title.

BLACKWOOD, Andrew Watterson, 1882- 253
The growing minister, his opportunities and obstacles. New York, Abingdon Press [1960] 192p. 23cm. Includes bibliography. [BV4011.B55] 60-9194
1. Pastoral theology. I. Title.

BLACKWOOD, Carolyn Philips. 253
The pastor's wife. Introd. by Andrew W. Blackwood. Philadelphia, Westminster Press [1951] 187 p. 21 cm. Includes bibliographies. [BV4395.B65] 51-9792
1. Clergymen's wives. I. Title.

BOHREN, Rudolf 253
Preaching and community. Tr. [from German] by David E. Green. Richmond, Va., Knox [1966, c.1965] 238p. 21cm. Bibl. [HV4214.B613] 65-12284 4.95 bds.,
1. Preaching. I. Title.

BREITIGAM, R R. 253
The challenge of child evangelism. Nashville, Southern Pub. Association [1950] 250 p. front. 21 cm. Bibliography: p. 238-242. [BV1475.B7] 51-22595
1. Religious education of children. 2. Evangelistic work. I. Title.

BROWN, Jeff D 253
A handbook for the preacher at work. Grand Rapids, Baker Book House, 1958. 90p. 21cm. [Minister's handbook series] [BV4011.B7] 59-20730
1. Pastoral theology. I. Title. II. Title: The Preacher at work.

BROWN, Raymond Edward. 253
Priest and bishop; Biblical reflections, by Raymond E. Brown. Paramus, Paulist Press [1970] v, 86 p. 21 cm. Includes bibliographical references. [BX1912.B77] 78-139594 1.50
1. Priesthood—Biblical teaching. 2. Bishops—Biblical teaching. I. Title.

BROWN, Stephen W. 253
Where the action is [by] Stephen W. Brown. Old Tappan, N.J., F. H. Revell Co. [1971] 128 p. 21 cm. [BT1102.B72] 79-137446 ISBN 0-8007-0430-4 3.95
1. Apologetics—20th century. 2. Clergy—Office. I. Title.

BROWNING, Don S. 253
The moral context of pastoral care / Don S. Browning. Philadelphia : Westminster Press, c1976. p. cm. Includes bibliographical references. [BV4011.5.B76] 76-5858 ISBN 0-664-20742-1
1. Pastoral theology—Addresses, essays, lectures. 2. Pastoral counseling—Addresses, essays, lectures. I. Title.

BUTMAN, Harry R. 253
Serve with gladness, by Harry R. Butman. [Wauwatosa, Wis.] Swannet Press [1971] xii, 234 p. 22 cm. [BX7260.B93A3] 79-130402
1. Clergy—Office. I. Title.

BYERS, Laurence P. 253
Christians in crossfire; the face of my parish, by Laurence P. Byers. Philadelphia, Westminster Press [1967] 151 p. 21 cm. Bibliography: p. 149-151. [BV4011.B9] 67-18726
1. Pastoral theology. I. Title.

CALIAN, Carnegie Samuel. 253
Today's pastor in tomorrow's world / Carnegie Samuel Calian. New York : Hawthorn Books, c1977. xii, 153 p. ; 22 cm. Includes index. Bibliography: p. 145-148. [BV4011.C24 1977] 76-15419 ISBN 0-8015-7761-6 : 6.95
1. Pastoral theology. I. Title.

CAPLAN, Ruth B. 253
Helping the helpers to help; mental health consultation to aid clergymen in pastoral work, by Ruth B. Caplan in collaboration with Gerald Caplan [and others] New York, Seabury Press [1972] x, 241 p. 22 cm. Includes bibliographical references. [BV4012.C315] 72-81024 ISBN 0-8164-0239-6 6.95
1. Pastoral psychology. I. Title.

CARLSON, Oscar W. 253
The Church's singular task. Philadelphia, Muhlenberg Press [1950] 90 p. 21 cm. (The Knubel-Miller Foundation lectures [5th ser.]) [BV3790.C28] 51-313
1. Evangelistic work. I. Title. II. Series: United Lutheran Church in America. Knubel-Miller Foundation. Lectures, 5th ser.

CARRE, Ambrosius Maria. 1908- 253
The everlasting priest. [Tr. from French by Ronald Matthews and A. V. Littledale] New York, P. J. Kenedy [1961, c.1960] 132p. 19cm. Bibl. 61-6855 3.50
1. Catholic Church—Clergy. I. Title.

CASE studies in the campus ministry; an occasional paper. [Editor: Clement W. Welsh. Cambridge, Mass.] Church Society for College Work [1968] 62 p. 28 cm. Cover title. "This collection of essays ... [presented] to Jones B. Shannon." [BV1610.C34] 75-303368 253
1. Shannon, Jones B. 2. Church work with students—Addresses, essays, lectures. 3. Chaplains, University and college—Addresses, essays, lectures. I. Shannon, Jones B. II. Welsh, Clement, 1913- ed. III. Church Society for College Work.

CHARUE, Antoine Marie, Bp. 253
The diocesan clergy; history and spirituality. Tr. by Michael J. Wrenn. New York, Desclee, 1963. 327p. illus. 22cm. Bibl. 63-20669 4.75
1. Catholic Church—Clergy. 2. Clergy—Hist. I. Title.

CHURCH of the Nazarene. 253
Commission of the Mid-Century Crusade for Souls.
He that winneth souls; illustrations of personal evangelism in the mid-century crusade for souls. Edited by Alpin P. Bowes. Kansas City, Mo., Nazarene Pub. House [1950] 125 p. 19 cm. [BV3790.C5634] 50-31887
1. Evangelistic work. I. Bowes, Alpin P. ed. II. Title.

CLARK, Faye (Aldridge) 253
I married a preacher. New York, Vantage Press [1953] 51p. 23cm. [BV4395.C45] 53-6466
1. Clergymen's wives. I. Title.

CLIFFORD, Paul Rowntree. 253
The pastoral calling. Great Neck, N. Y., Channel Press [1961] 144p. 21cm. Includes bibliography. [BV4011.C55 1961] 61-7570
1. Pastoral theology. I. Title.

CLINEBELL, Howard John, 1922- 253
The mental health ministry of the local church [by] Howard J. Clinebell, Jr. Nashville, Abingdon Press [1972] 300 p. 23 cm. 1965 ed. published under title: Mental health through Christian community. Bibliography: p. 285-289. [BV4012.C56 1972] 73-185551 ISBN 0-687-24829-9 2.95
1. Pastoral psychology. 2. Mental hygiene. I. Title.

COBURN, John B. 253
Minister: man-in-the-middle. New York, Macmillan [1963] 205 p. 22 cm. (Career book series) [BV660.2.C58] 63-8662
1. Clergy — Office. I. Title.

COBURN, John B. 253
Minister: man-in-the-middle. New York, Macmillan [c.1963] 205p. 22cm. (Career bk. ser.) 63-8662 3.95
1. Clergy—Office. I. Title.

COLLINS, Gary R. 253
Man in transition; the psychology of human development [by] Gary R. Collins. [1st ed.] Carol Stream, Ill., Creation House [1971] 203 p. 22 cm. (Psychology for church leaders series) Bibliography: p. 189-198. [BV4012.C59] 79-163763 4.95
1. Pastoral psychology. 2. Christian leadership. I. Title.

THE Continuing quest; 253
opportunities, resources, and programs in post-seminary education. James B. Hofrenning, editor. Minneapolis, Augsburg Pub. House [1970] 154 p. 23 cm. Includes bibliographical references. [BV4165.C65] 78-121969 4.95
1. Clergy—Post-ordination training—Addresses, essays, lectures. I. Hofrenning, James B., ed.

DAEHLIN, Reidar A 253
Pastor to pastor; conversations with parish ministers, by Reidar R. Daehlin. Minneapolis, Augsburg Pub. House [1966] 124 p. 19 cm. [BV4011.D3] 66-13056
1. Pastoral theology — Lutheran Church. I. Title.

DAEHLIN, Reidar A. 253
Pastor to pastor; conversations with parish ministers. Minneapolis, Augsburg [c.1966] 124p. 19cm. [BV4011.D3] 66-13056 2.50 pap.,
1. Pastoral theology—Lutheran Church. I. Title.

DAVIS, Martin Winfrid. 253
The sister as campus minister; a survey-study of the religious sister's role and status in the campus ministry. Washington, Center for Applied Research in the Apostolate, 1970. xvi, 124 p. illus. 22 cm. [BV4376.D38] 76-23062
1. Nuns in campus ministry—Statistics. I. Title.

A dictionary of pastoral psychology. New York, Philosophical Library [c1955] xi, 336p. 22cm. [BV4012.F44] [BV4012.F44] 258 54-13510 54-13510 253
1. Psychology, Pastoral—Dictionaries. 2. Psychology—Dictionaries. I. Ferm, Vergilius Ture Anselm, 1896-

DIEHL, William E. 253
Christianity and real life / William E. Diehl. Philadelphia : Fortress Press, c1976. viii, 120 p. ; 20 cm. Includes bibliographical references. [BV677.D53] 76-7860 ISBN 0-8006-1231-0 pbk. : 3.50
1. Lay ministry. I. Title.

DILLENSCHNEDIDR, Clement 253
The Holy Spirit and the priest, toward an interiorization of our priesthood. Tr. [from French] by Sister M. Renelle. St. Louis, B. Herder [c.1965] xv, 151p. 24cm. Bibl. [BT121.2.D513] 65-19770 4.00
1. Holy Spirit. 2. Priests. I. Title.

DILLENSCHNEIDER, Clement. 253
The Holy Spirit and the priest, toward an interiorization of our priesthood. Translated by Sister. M. Renelle. St. Louis, Herder [1965] xv, 151 p. 24 cm. Bibliographical footnotes. [BT121.2.D513] 65-19770
1. Holy Spirit. 2. Priests. I. Title.

DITTES, James E. 253
Minister on the spot [by] James E. Dittes. Philadelphia, Pilgrim Press [1970] 138 p. 21 cm. [BV660.2.D54] 79-114051
1. Clergy—Office. I. Title.

DITTES, James E 253
Vocational guidance of theological students: a manual for the use of the Theological school inventory [by] James E. Dittes. [Dayton, Ohio, Ministry Studies Board, 1964] 1 v. (various pagings) illus. 28 cm. "The Theological school inventory was developed in research conducted by Educational Testing Service, directed by Frederick R. Kling, supported by Lilly Endowment, inc." [BV4011.4.D5] 68-2363
1. Theological school inventory. I. Title.

DOBERSTEIN, John W. ed. 253
Minister's prayer book; an order of prayers and readings. Philadelphia, Muhlenberg Press [1959] xxiv, 492p. 19cm. (21p. bibl. notes) 59-10533 3.75 6.00 lea. cl.
1. Lutheran Church—Prayer-books and devotions—English. 2. Clergy—Religious life. I. Title.

DONNELLY, Dody. 253
Team : theory and practice of team ministry / by Dody Donnelly. New York : Paulist Press, c1977. 161 p. : ill. ; 21 cm. Bibliography: p. 160-161. [BV675.D66] 77-74584 ISBN 0-8091-2013-5 pbk. : 4.95
1. Group ministry. I. Title.

DONNELLY, Dody. 253
Team : theory and practice of team ministry / by Dody Donnelly. New York : Paulist Press, c1977. 161 p. : ill. ; 21 cm. Bibliography: p. 160-161. [BV675.D66] 77-74584 ISBN 0-8091-2013-5 pbk. : 4.95
1. Group ministry. I. Title.

DRESSELHAUS, Richard L. 253
The deacon and his ministry / Richard L. Dresselhaus. Springfield, Mo. : Gospel Pub. House, c1977. 96 p. (p. 85-96 blank) ; 18 cm. [BX6198.A7D68] 77-73518 ISBN 0-88243-493-4 pbk. : 2.25
1. Assemblies of God, General Council—Government. 2. Deacons.

DRESSELHAUS, Richard L. 253
The deacon and his ministry / Richard L. Dresselhaus. Springfield, Mo. : Gospel Pub. House, c1977. 96 p. (p. 85-96 blank) ; 18 cm. [BX6198.A7D68] 77-73518 ISBN 0-88243-493-4 pbk. : 2.25
1. Assemblies of God, General Council—Government. 2. Deacons.

DUGGAR, John W. 253
Ministerial ethics. biblically presented. Little Rock, Ark., 716 Main St. Baptist Pubns. Comm., [1962] 104p. 21cm. Bibl. 1.00 pap.,
I. Title.

DUQUESNE, Jacques, 1930- 253
A church without priests? Translated from the French by Bernard Murchland. [New York] Macmillan [1969] 192 p. 22 cm. Translation of Demain, une Eglise sans pretres? Bibliographical footnotes. [BX1912.D8913] 69-19578
1. Catholic Church—Clergy. I. Title.

DYNAMIC interpersonalism for ministry; essays in honor of Paul E. Johnson. Edited by Orlo Strunk, Jr. Nashville, Abingdon Press [1973] 320 p. 23 cm. Includes bibliographical references. [BV4012.D96] 73-7813 11.95 253
1. Johnson, Paul Emanuel, 1898- 2. Pastoral psychology—Addresses, essays, lectures. 3. Pastoral theology—Addresses, essays, lectures. I. Johnson, Paul Emanuel, 1898- II. Strunk, Orlo, ed.
Contents omitted. Contents omitted.

EARL Blue Associates. 253
The Earl Blue report on clergy disaffection. Prepared by the Earl Blue staff. Written by Michael Donahoe and Earl Blue. [San Francisco, 1970] 76 p. illus. 23 cm. Cover title. [BV672.5.E27] 74-11506
1. Ex-clergy. 2. Ex-priests, Catholic. I. Donahoe, Michael. II. Blue, Earl. III. Title.

*ECHLIN, Edward. 253
The priest as preacher, past and future, by Edward P. Echlin, S. J. General editor: Edward Yarnhold, S. J. Notre Dame, Ind., Fides Publishers [1973] 91 p. 18 cm. (Theology today series, no. 33) [BV660.2] ISBN 0-8190-0579-7. 0.95 (pbk.)
1. Clergy—Office. I. Yarnhold, Edward ed. II. Title.

ECHLIN, Edward P. 253
The deacon in the Church; past time and future [by] Edward P. Echlin. Staten Island, N.Y., Alba House [1971] xiii, 139 p. 22 cm. Bibliography: p. 137-139. [BV680.E25] 75-158571 ISBN 0-8189-0213-2 3.95
1. Deacons—History. I. Title.

EIMS, Leroy. 253
Be the leader you were meant to be : what the

Bible says about leadership / LeRoy Eims ; [foreword by Theodore H. Epp]. Wheaton, Ill. : Victor Books, c1975. 132 p. ; 21 cm. (An Input book) [BS680.L4E37] 75-5392 ISBN 0-88207-723-6 : pbk. : 1.95
1. Christian leadership—Biblical teaching. I. Title.

EVOLVING religious careers. 253
Edited by Willis E. Bartlett. Foreword by Theodore M. Hesburgh. Washington, Center for Applied Research in the Apostolate [1970] xii, 207 p. illus. 23 cm. (CARA information service) "Based on the conference on Vocational development of religious careers, cosponsored by the Center for the Study of Man in Contemporary Society and the Department of Graduate Studies in Education, University of Notre Dame." Includes bibliographies. [BX2380.E9] 70-24375
1. Vocation, Ecclesiastical—Addresses, essays, lectures. I. Bartlett, Willis E., ed. II. Notre Dame, Ind. University. Center for the Study of Man in Contemporary Society. III. Notre Dame, Ind. University. Graduate School. Dept. of Education. IV. Center for Applied Research in the Apostolate, Washington, D.C.

FACKRE, Gabriel J. 253
The purpose and work of the ministry; a mission pastor's point of view. Philadelphia, Christian Education Press [c.1959] xi, 141p. 21cm. (bibl. footnotes) 59-14166 2.50
1. Pastoral theology. I. Title.

FLYNN, Leslie B. 253
How to save time in the ministry. Nashville, Broadman [c.1966] 95p. 20cm. Bibl. [BV652.F55] 65-23049 1.50 pap.,
1. Church management. I. Title.

FORSYTH, Nathaniel Frederick, ed. 253
The minister and Christian nurture. New York, Abingdon Press [1957] 250p. 23cm. [BV4360.F57] 57-6755
1. Pastoral theology. 2. Religious education. I. Title.

FOUR faces of Christian ministry; essays in honor of A. Dale Fiers. 253
Essyas, by Granville T. Walker [and others] With a biographical essay by Robert I. Friedly. St. Louis, Bethany Press [1973] 64 p. port. 21 cm. [BR50.F63] 73-9560 ISBN 0-8272-1005-1 1.95
1. Theology—Addresses, essays, lectures. 2. Fiers, Alan Dale. I. Fiers, Alan Dale. II. Walker, Granville T.
Contents omitted.

GARRIGOU-LAGRANGE, Reginald, Father, 1877- 253
The priest in union with Christ. Translated by G. W. Shelton. Westminster, Md., Newman Press, 1952. 220 p. 22 cm. [BX1912.G34] 52-10969
1. Clergy—Religious life. I. Title.

GATEWOOD, Otis. 253
You can do personal work. [3d ed., rev.] Lubbock, Tex. [1951] xii, 209 p. 21 cm. Bibliography: p. 209. [BV3790.G35 1951] 51-26515
1. Evangelistic work. I. Title.

GEBHARD, Anna Laura Munro, 1914- 253
Parsonage doorway; illustrated by Janet Smalley. New York, Abingdon-Cokesbury [1950] 144 p. illus. 20 cm. [BV4395.G4] 50-10109
I. Title.

GERDES, Egon W. 253
Informed ministry : theological reflections on the practice of ministry in methodism / Egon W. Gerdes. Zurich : Publishing House of the United Methodist Church, 1976. 94 p. ; 21 cm. (Studies in Methodism and related movements : Series A, Monographs ; v. 1) [BV4011.G45] 76-370415 ISBN 3-85706-186-3 : 19.00F
1. Pastoral theology—Methodist Church. I. Title. II. Series.

GLASSE, James D. 253
Profession: minister [by] James D. Glasse. Nashville, Abingdon Press [1968] 174 p. 21 cm. Bibliographical references included in "Notes" (p. 159-169) [BV660.2.G55] 68-17447
1. Clergy—Office. 2. Clergy—United States. I. Title.

GLASSE, James D. 253
Putting it together in the parish [by] James D. Glasse. Nashville, Abingdon Press [1972] 159 p. illus. 23 cm. (Currie lectures, 1970) [BV4011.G55] 71-185548 ISBN 0-687-34932-X 3.95
1. Pastoral theology. I. Title. II. Series.

GLEN, John Stanley, 1907- 253
The recovery of the teaching ministry. Philadelphia, Westminster [1967, c.1966] 125p. 20cm. Bibl. [BV4360.G55] 60-10955 1.85 pap.,
1. Clergy. 2. Religious education. I. Title.

GOODYKOONTZ, Harry G. 253
The minister in the Reformed tradition. Richmond, John Knox Press [1963] 176 p. 21 cm. Bibliographical references included in "Notes and acknowledgments" (p. 157-169) Bibliography: p. 170-174. [BV660.2.G6] 63-15199
1. Clergy—Office. I. Title.

*GORMAN, F. E. 253
Rocking the pulpit the pastor as biblical shepherd. New York, Exposition [1967] 80p. 21cm. [EP45683] 3.50
1. Pastoral theology—Baptist Church I. Title.

GREEN, Bryan S. W. 253
The practice of evangelism; with a foreword by Henry Knox Sherrill. New York, Scribner, 1951. 258 p. 21 cm. [BV3790.G77 1951a] 51-14552
1. Evangelistic work. I. Title.

GRESHAM, Perry Epler. 253
Disciplines of the high calling. St. Louis, Bethany Press [1954] 176p. 21cm. [BV4010.G78] 54-31949
1. Theology, Pastoral. I. Title.

GRIFFITH, Earle Gordon. 253
The pastor as God's minister / Earle G. Griffith ; foreword by Charles H. Stevens. Schaumburg, Ill. : Regular Baptist Press, [1977] p. cm. [BV4011.G74] 76-50694 ISBN 0-87227-054-8 : 7.95
1. Pastoral theology. I. Title.

A Guide for good priesthood ministry, edited by Norman D. Ruoff. 253
[Independence, Mo., Herald Pub. House, 1971] 408 p. illus. 21 cm. Includes bibliographical references. [BV4011.G83] 75-150660 ISBN 0-8309-0044-6
1. Pastoral theology—Mormonism. I. Ruoff, Norman D., ed.

GUPTILL, Nathanael M. 253
How to be a pastor in a mad, mod world, by Nathanael M. Guptill. St. Louis, Bethany Press [1970] 75 p. 20 cm. [BV660.2.G83] 76-105056
1. Clergy—Office. I. Title.

HALL, David D. 253
The faithful shepherd; a history of the New England ministry in the seventeenth century, by David D. Hall. Chapel Hill, Published for the Institute of Early American History and Culture, Williamsburg, Va., by the University of North Carolina Press [1972] xvi, 301 p. 24 cm. Includes bibliographical references. [BR520.H3] 72-81326 ISBN 0-8078-1193-9 11.95
1. Pastoral theology—History of doctrines. 2. Clergy—New England. 3. New England—Church history. I. Title.

HALL, David D. 253
The faithful shepherd; a history of the New England ministry in the seventeenth century, by David D. Hall. New York, Norton [1974, c1972] xvi, 301 p. 20 cm. (The Norton library, N719) Reprint of the ed. published by the University of North Carolina Press, Chapel Hill, for the Institute of Early American History and Culture, Williamsburg, Va. Bibliography: p. [279]-290. [BR520.H3 1974] 74-818 ISBN 0-393-00719-7 3.45 (pbk.)
1. Pastoral theology—History of doctrines. 2. Clergy—New England. 3. New England—Church history. I. Institute of Early American History and Culture, Williamsburg, Va. II. Title.

HALL, Douglas T., 1940- 253
Organizational climates and careers; the work lives of priests [by] Douglas T. Hall [and] Benjamin Schneider. New York, Seminar Press, 1973. xix, 291 p. illus. 24 cm. (Quantitative studies in social relations) Based on a survey conducted by the authors for the Archdiocese of Hartford, Conn. Bibliography: p. 281-288. [BX1912.H32] 78-187261 ISBN 0-12-842550-4 11.95
1. Catholic Church in the United States—Clergy. 2. Occupations. I. Schneider, Benjamin, joint author. II. Hartford (Archdiocese) III. Title.

HALL, Douglas T., 1940- 253
A study of work experiences and career growth of Roman Catholic doicesan [sic] priests, by Douglas T. Hall and Benjamin Schneider. [New Haven, Conn.] Dept. of Administrative Sciences, Yale University, 1969. 164 l. illus., forms. 29 cm. Bibliography: leaves 132-133. [BX1912.H33] 72-11298
1. Catholic Church in the United States—Clergy. I. Schneider, Benjamin, 1938- joint author. II. Title.

HAMILTON, Charles V. 253
The Black preacher in America [by] Charles V. Hamilton. New York, Morrow, 1972. 246 p. 21 cm. Includes bibliographical references. [BR563.N4H34] 78-170231 ISBN 0-688-00006-1
1. Negro clergy—United States. I. Title.

HART, Arthur Tindal 253
The country priest in English history. London, Phoenix House [1959, i.e.,1960 dist., Hollywood-by-the-Sea, Fla., Transatlantic Arts] 176p. Bibl.: p.163-167. illus., ports. 23cm. 60-2015 6.25
1. Rural clergy—Gt. Brit. 2. Clergy—Gt. Brit. I. Title.

HAYNES, Carlyle Boynton, 1882-1958. 253
Carlyle B. Haynes speaks to young ministers. Nashville, Tenn., Southern Pub. Association [1968] vi, 63 p. 23 cm. [BV4011.H35] 68-25168
1. Clergy. 2. Pastoral theology. I. Title.

HAYWARD, Helen (Harry). 253
The other foot. New York, Vantage Press [1951] 122 p. 23 cm. Autobiographical. [BR1725.H28A3] 51-8782
I. Title.

HEICHER, Merlo Karl Wordsworth, 1882- 253
The Heicher filing system for ministers, missionaries, church school teachers, and other church workers. Grand Rapids, Baker Book House, 1957 c86p. 22cm. [BV4379.H4] 57-10681
1. Files and filing (Documents) 2. Pastoral theology. I. Title.

HENRY, Carl Ferdinand Howard, 1913- 253
Evangelical responsibility in contemporary theology. Grand Rapids, Eerdmans [1957] 89 p. 19 cm. (Pathway books; a series of contemporary evangelical studies) [B479.H44] 57-13036
1. Theology—20th cent. 2. Evangelicalism. I. Title.

HICKS, H. Beecher. 253
Images of the Black preacher : the man nobody knows / by H. Beecher Hicks, Jr. Valley Forge, Pa. : Judson Press, [1977] p. cm. Bibliography: p. [BR563.N4H5] 77-79777 ISBN 0-8170-0759-8 : 5.95
1. Afro-American clergy. I. Title.

[HILKERT, Robert C]. 253
Everybody calls me Father, by Father X. New York, Sheed and Ward, 1951. 180 p. 20 cm. [BX1912.H5] 51-9545
1. Catholic Church—Clergy. I. Title.

HILTNER, Seward, 1909- 253
Ferment in the ministry. Nashville, Abingdon Press [1969] 222 p. 23 cm. [BV4011.H48] 69-18441 4.95
1. Pastoral theology. I. Title.

HINCHEY, Roy W. 253
Plain talk about the pastorate / Roy W. Hinchey. Nashville : : Broadman Press, c1975. 64 p. ; 19 cm. Includes bibliographical references. [BV4011.H53] 76-352205 ISBN 0-8054-2410-5 pbk. : 1.50
1. Pastoral theology—Baptists. I. Title.

HOFMANN, Hans F. 1923- ed. 253
Making the ministry relevant. New York Scribner [1960] xvii, 169 p. 21 cm. Bibliographical footnotes. [BV4165.H6] 60-14020
1. Clergy — Post-ordination training. 2. Pastoral psychology. I. Title.

HOFMANN, Hans Fritz, 1923- ed. 253
Making the ministry relevant. New York, Scribners [c.1960] xvii, 169p. Bibl. 60-14020 3.50
1. Clergy—Post-ordination training. 2. Pastoral psychology. I. Title.

HOLMES, Urban Tigner, 1930- 253
Ministry and imagination / Urban T. Holmes III. New York : Seabury Press, c1976. 279 p. ; 24 cm. "A Crossroad book." Includes bibliographical references. [BV4011.H583] 76-1851 ISBN 0-8164-0292-2 : 10.95
1. Pastoral theology. 2. Experience (Religion) I. Title.

HOLST, Lawrence E. 253
Toward a creative chaplaincy. Edited by Lawrence E. Holst and Harold P. Kurtz. With a foreword by Carroll A. Wise. Springfield, Ill., C. C. Thomas [1973] xix, 160 p. 24 cm. Includes bibliographical references. [BV4335.H63] 72-88446 ISBN 0-398-02673-4 6.95
1. Chaplains, Hospital. 2. Pastoral medicine. I. Kurtz, Harold P., joint author. II. Title.

HOVEY, Byron P., 1894- 253
The minister's work, an outline of his duties and obligations. New York, Exposition Press [c.1961] 44p. 61-3520 2.50
1. Clergy—Office. I. Title.

HOWE, Reuel L. 253
The miracle of dialogue. New York, Seabury [1964, c.1963] 154p. 20cm. (SP 9) 1.65 pap.,
1. Discussion. 2. Pastoral counseling. I. Title.

HUDNUT, Robert K. 253
Surprised by God; what it means to be a minister in middle-class America today, by Robert K. Hudnut. New York, Association Press [1967] 127 p. 20 cm. [BV4011.H75] 67-21144
1. Pastoral theology. I. Title.

HUDNUT, Robert K. 253
Surprised by God; what it means to be a minister in middle-class America today, by Robert K. Hudnut. New York, Association Press [1967] 127 p. 20 cm. [BV4011.H75] 67-21144
1. Pastoral theology. I. Title.

HULME, William Edward, 1920- 253
Two ways of caring; a Biblical design for balanced ministry [by] William E. Hulme. Minneapolis, Augsburg Pub. House [1973] 107 p. 20 cm. [BV3.H84] 73-78270 ISBN 0-8066-1334-3 2.95 (pbk.)
1. Theology, Practical. 2. Pastoral theology. 3. Church and social problems. I. Title.

HURLEY, Denis E. 253
Vatican II on priests and seminaries [by] Denis E. Hurley and Joseph Cunnane. [1st ed.] Dublin, Chicago, Scepter Books [1967] 254 p. 22 cm. Documents in Latin and English. Contents.Contents.—The ministry and life of priests, by J. Cunnane.—Documents (p. [62]-167)—The training of priests, by D. E. Hurley.—Documents (p. [214]-251) Includes bibliographical references. [BX1912.H85] 70-262493
1. Catholic Church—Clergy. 2. Catholic Church—Clergy, Training of. I. Vatican Council. 2d, 1962-1965. II. Cunnane, Joseph. The ministry and life of priests. 1967. III. Title.

HUSS, John Ervin, 1910- 253
Ideas for a successful pastorate. Grand Rapids, Zondervan Pub. House [1953] 144p. 20cm. [BV4010.H87] 53-29145
1. Theology, Pastoral. I. Title.

HUTTENLOCKER, Keith. 253
"Be-attitudes" for the church. Anderson, Ind., Warner Press [1971] 112 p. 19 cm. Includes bibliographical references. [BV3.H88] 70-165003 ISBN 0-87162-125-8
1. Theology, Practical. 2. Christian life—1960- I. Title.

THE Identity of the priest. 253
Edited by Karl Rahner. New York, Paulist Press [1969] ix, 197 p. 24 cm. (Concilium: theology in the age of renewal. Pastoral theology, v. 43) Includes bibliographical references. [BX1913.I3] 70-81227 4.50
1. Catholic church—Clergy. I. Rahner, Karl, 1904- ed. II. Series: Concilium (New York) v. 43

IF I had my ministry to live over, I would .... / compiled by Rick Ingle. 253
Nashville : Broadman Press, c1977. 131 p. ; 20 cm. [BV660.2.I53] 77-78154 ISBN 0-8054-2704-X pbk. : 2.50
1. Southern Baptist Convention—Clergy—Anecdotes, facetiae, satire, etc. 2. Clergy—Office—Anecdotes, facetiae, satire, etc. 3. Pastoral theology—Anecdotes, facetiae, satire, etc. 4. Clergy United States—Anecdotes, facetiae, satire, etc. I. Ingle, Rick.

JACOBSEN, David C. 253
The positive use of the minister's role, by David C. Jacobsen. Philadelphia, Westminster [1967] 111, [1] p. 21cm. Bibl. [BV4011.J3] 67-15870 3.25
1. Pastoral theology. 2. Clergy. I. Title.

JOHNSON, Joseph Andrew, 1914- 253
The soul of the Black preacher, by Joseph A. Johnson, Jr. Philadelphia, Pilgrim Press [1971] 173 p. 22 cm. Contents.Contents.—The soul of the Black preacher.—Conflict, challenge, defeat, victory.—The triumphant adequacy of Jesus.—Wholeness through Jesus Christ.—Man's helplessness and the power of Christ.—The principle of identical harvest.—Jesus, the leader.—Jesus, the disturber.—Jesus, the emancipator.—Jesus, the liberator.—Jesus, the word of life.—The Christian's call, commitment, and commission.—"All is of grace and grace is for all."—"Even we have believed in Jesus Christ."—The imperative of beyondness.—The Christian faith and the Black experience. Includes bibliographical references. [BR563.N4J58] 70-162411 ISBN 0-8298-0193-6 4.95

1. Negroes—Religion. 2. Negro clergy. I. Title.

JOHNSON, Merle Allison.
How to murder a minister [by] Pastor X. Old Tappan, N.J., F. H. Revell [1970] 156 p. 21 cm. [BV660.2.J57] 75-112458 3.95
1. Clergy—Office. I. X, Pastor. II. Title.

JOHNSON, Orien. 253
Recovery of ministry: a guide for the laity. Valley Forge [Pa.] Judson Press [1972] 62 p. 23 cm. Includes bibliographical references. [BV4011.J64] 72-433 ISBN 0-8170-0566-8 1.50
1. Pastoral theology. 2. Christian life—1960- I. Title.

JONES, Ilion Tingnal, 1889- 253
The pastor: the man and his ministry. Philadelphia, Westminster Pr. [c.1961] 158p. 61-12105 3.50
1. Clergy—Office. I. Title.

JONES, Ilion Tingnal, 1889- 253
The pastor: the man and his ministry. Philadelphia Westminster Press [1961] 158p. 21cm. [BV660.2.J6] 61-12105
1. Clergy—Office. I. Title.

JORDAN, Bert. 253
On roads to the healing Christ / by Bert Jordan. Evesham : James, 1976. 122 p. ; 10 cm. [BT732.5.J68] 77-350372 ISBN 0-85305-187-9 : £2.00
1. Faith-cure. I. Title.

JURGENSEN, Barbara. 253
Don't bug me, preacher! Illustrated by Jan, Marie, and Barbara Jurgensen. Grand Rapids, Zondervan Pub. House [1972] [75] p. illus. 18 cm. [BV663.J87] 73-159631 0.95
1. Clergy. I. Title.

KEAN, Charles Duell, 1910- 253
Christian faith and pastoral care. Greenwich, Conn., Seabury Press [c.]1961. 139p. Bibl. 61-5573 3.75
1. Pastoral theology. I. Title.

KELLEY, Ann Elizabeth. 253
Women in campus ministry; a report from consultations with Catholic women campus ministers. [Cambridge, Mass.] National Center for Campus Ministry, 1973. xiii, 37 p. 22 cm. (National Center for Campus Ministry. Research paper no. 1) A report of the meetings held in Boston, Sept. 8-9; San Francisco, Sept. 15-16; New Orleans, Sept. 29-30; and Chicago, Oct. 6-7, 1972. [BV4376.K44] 73-158792
1. Women in campus ministry—Congresses. I. Title. II. Title: Catholic women campus ministers. III. Series.

KEMP, Charles F. 253
The pastor and community resources. St. Louis, Bethany Press [c.1960] 96p. 'Published for the Department of Social Welfare, National Council of the Churches of Christ in the U.S.A.' 18cm. 59-10370 1.50, pap., spiral binding
1. Pastoral theology 2. Church and social problems. I. Title.

KEMP, Charles F 1912- 253
The pastor and community resources. St. Louis, Bethany Press [1960] 96p. 18cm. 'Published for the Department of Social Welfare, National Council of the Churches of Christ in the U. S. A.' [BV4325.K4] 59-10370
1. Pastoral theology. 2. Church and social problems. I. Title.

KEMP, Charles F 1912- 253
Preparing for the ministry. St. Louis, Mo., Bethany Press [1959] 128p. 20cm. [BV4011.4.K4] 59-10369
1. Clergy—Appointment, call, and election. I. Title.

KENNEDY, Eugene C. 253
Comfort my people; the pastoral presence of the church, by Eugene C. Kennedy. New York, Sheed and Ward [1968] xiii, 208 p. 21 cm. Includes bibliographies. [BX1913.K4] 68-26037 4.95
1. Catholic Church—Clergy. 2. Pastoral theology—Catholic Church. I. Title.

KENNEDY, Gerald Hamilton, 253
Bp., 1907-
With singleness of heart. [1st ed.] New York, Harper [1951] 157 p. 20 cm. (The Slover lectures, Southwestern University, 1950) [BV4010.K42] 51-10340
1. Theology, Pastoral. I. Title.

KENNEDY, James William, 1905- 253
Minister's shop-talk, by James W. Kennedy. [1st ed.] New York, Harper & Row [1965] 211 p. 22 cm. Bibliographical references included in "Notes" (p. [199]-206) [BV4011.K43] 65-20454
1. Pastoral theology. I. Title.

KENNEDY, James William, 1905- 253
Minister's shop-talk. New York, Harper [c.1965] 211p. 22cm. Bibl. [BV4011.K43] 65-20454 3.95 bds.,
1. Pastoral theology. I. Title.

KLEIN, Walter Conrad, Bp., 253
1904-
A priest forever. New York, Morehouse [1965, c.1964] viii, 132p. 21cm. Bibl. [BX5965.K55] 65-14454 4.50
1. Priests. 2. Pastoral theology—Anglican Communion. I. Title.

KNOX, Ronald Arbuthnott, 253
1888-1957.
The priestly life; a retreat. New York, Sheed & Ward [1958] 176p. 21cm. [BX1912.K6] 58-5889
1. Clergy—Religious life. I. Title.

KOLLER, Charles W., 1896- 253
Pointers for pastors / Charles W. Koller. Dallas : Crescendo Book Publications, [1974] 144 p. ; 20 cm. [BV4011.K63] 74-76738 ISBN 0-89038-016-3 : 2.95 2.95
1. Pastoral theology. I. Title.

LEAS, Speed, 1937- 253
Church fights; managing conflict in the local church, by Speed Leas and Paul Kittlaus. Philadelphia, Westminster Press [1973] 186 p. 19 cm. Bibliography: p. [185]-186. [BV652.L39] 73-6790 ISBN 0-664-24974-4 3.50
1. Church management. 2. Conflict (Psychology) I. Kittlaus, Paul, 1934- joint author. II. Title.

LEE, Mark W. 253
The minister and his ministry. Grand Rapids, Mich., Zondervan Pub. House [c.1960] 280p. Includes bibliography. illus. 23cm. 60-1374 3.95
1. Pastoral theology. I. Title.

LEE, Mark W 1923- 253
The minister and his ministry. Grand Rapids, Zondervan Pub. House [1960] 280p. illus. 23cm. Includes bibliography. [BV4011.L43] 60-1374
1. Pastoral theology. I. Title.

LINGER, O. Afton. 253
Church management guidelines [by] O. Afton Linger. Hendersonville, N.C., Fruitland Baptist Bible Institute [1972] v, 95, [7] p. illus. 29 cm. Bibliography: p. [100] [BV4011.L53] 72-87864
1. Pastoral theology. I. Title.

LITTLE, Lawrence Calvin, 253
1897-
Toward understanding the church and the clergy; contributions of selected doctoral dissertations. Pittsburgh, Dept. of Religious Education, University of Pittsburgh, 1963. ix, 218 p. 29 cm. Bibliography: p. 214-218. [BV4011.L55] 63-23863
1. Pastoral theology — Research. 2. Dissertations, Academic — U.S. — Abstracts. I. Title.

LONG, Louise, 1908- 253
Door of hope. Nashville, Abingdon Press [1972] 189 p. 22 cm. [BV4012.2.L65] 70-185545 ISBN 0-687-11179-X 2.95
1. Pastoral counseling. 2. Pastoral psychology. I. Title.

LOWDER, Paul D. 253
Feed whose sheep? [by] Paul D. Lowder. Waco, Tex., Word Books [1973] 127 p. 23 cm. Includes bibliographical references. [BV4011.L6o] 72-96358 3.95
1. Lowder, Paul D. 2. Pastoral theology—Methodist Church. I. Title.

LYONS, Bob E. 253
Kingdom of priests / Bob E. Lyons. Cleveland, Tenn. : Pathway Press, c1977. 160 p. ; 21 cm. "A publication of the Department of General Education." Bibliography: p. 160. [BT767.5.L96] 77-92990 ISBN 0-87148-478-1
1. Priesthood, Universal. 2. Laity—Church of God (Cleveland, Tenn.) I. Title.

MCCABE, Joseph E., 1912- 253
How to find time for better preaching and better pastoring, by Joseph E. McCabe. Philadelphia, Westminster Press [1973] 112 p. 20 cm. [BV4011.M23] 73-10264 ISBN 0-664-20983-1 4.50
1. Pastoral theology. 2. Preaching. I. Title.

MCCABE, Joseph E 1912- 253
The power of God in a parish program. Philadelphia, Westminster Press [1959] 164p. 21cm. [BV4015.M27] 59-6481
1. Theology, Pastoral. I. Title.

MCGOEY, John H 253
Fathering-forth. Milwaukee, Bruce Pub. Co. [1958] 188p. 22cm. [BX1912.M16] 58-9760
1. Catholic Church— Clergy. I. Title.

MAGNER, James Aloysius, 1901- 253
The Catholic priest in the modern world. Milwaukee, Bruce Pub. Co. [1957] 291p. 23cm. [BX1912.M22] 57-6319
1. Pastoral theology—Catholic Church. I. Title.

MARTIN, William Benjamin 253
James.
The diary of Peter Parson pseud. New York, Abingdon Press [1958, c1957] 174p. 21cm. First published in London in 1957 under title: Five minutes to twelve. [BR123.M37 1958] 58-7435
1. Christianity—Addresses, essays, lectures. I. Title.

MATTHEWS, Charles Evert, 253
1887-
Every Christian's job. Nashville, Broadman Press [1951] 132 p. 20 cm. [BV3790.M45] 51-6134
1. Evangelistic work. I. Title.

MATTHEWS, DeWitt. 253
Capers of the clergy : the human side of the ministry / DeWitt Matthews. Grand Rapids : Baker Book House, c1976. 140 p. ; 22 cm. [BV4011.M39] 76-378854 ISBN 0-8010-5990-9 : 4.95
1. Pastoral theology. I. Title.

MATTHEWS, Stanley G. 253
The night pastors, by Stanley G. Matthews. [1st ed.] New York, Hawthorn Books [1967] 224 p. ports. 22 cm. [BV2653.M3] 67-15555
1. City missions. 2. City clergy. I. Title.

METHODIST Church (United 253
States) Council of Bishops.
Who is the parish minister? Edited by T. Otto Nall. New York, Abingdon Press [1965] 128 p. 19 cm. [BV4011.M46] 65-26732
1. Pastoral theology — Methodist Church. I. Nall, Torney Otto, 1900- ed. II. Title.

METHODIST Church (United 253
States) Council of Bishops
Who is the parish minister? Ed. by T. Otto Nall. Nashville, Abingdon [c.1965] 128p. 19cm. [BV4011.M46] 65-26732 1.25 pap.,
1. Pastoral theology—Methodist Church. I. Nall, Torney Otto, 1900- ed. II. Title.

MEYER, Charles Robert, 1920- 253
Man of God; a study of the priesthood [by] Charles R. Meyer. [1st ed.] Garden City, N.Y., Doubleday, 1974. 168 p. 22 cm. Bibliography: p. [160]-168. [BX1912.M517] 73-10813 ISBN 0-385-01024-9 5.95
1. Priests. 2. Priesthood—History of doctrines. I. Title.

MEYER, Jack. 253
The preacher and his work; college lectures to student preachers. Athens, Ala., C. E. I. Store, c1955. 176p. 23cm. [BV4010.M46] 56-2139
1. Theology, Pastoral. I. Title.

MICHONNEAU, Georges, 1899- 253
My father's business; a priest in France. [English translation by Edmund Gilpin. New York] Herder and Herder [1959] 154p. 19cm. 'Based on the original version of Le cure.' [BX1913.M543 1959a] 59-10890
1. Pastoral theology—Catholic Church. 2. Catholic Church—Clergy. I. Title.

MICKEY, Paul A., 1937- 253
Conflict and resolution [by] Paul A. Mickey and Robert L. Wilson. Nashville, Abingdon Press [1973] 160 p. 20 cm. [BV4013.M5] 73-4974 ISBN 0-687-09400-3 4.50
1. Pastoral theology—Case studies. I. Wilson, Robert Leroy, 1925- joint author. II. Title.

MIDDLETON, Robert G. 253
Privilege and burden [by] Robert G. Middleton. Valley Forge [Pa.] Judson Press [1969] 157 p. 21 cm. Bibliographical footnotes. [BV660.2.M48] 72-86872 4.95
1. Clergy—Office. 2. Church. I. Title.

MIGUENS, Manuel. 253
Church ministries in New Testament times / Manuel Miguens. Arlington, Va. : Christian Culture Press, c1976. xvii, 221 p. ; 23 cm. Includes bibliographical references and indexes. [BV648.M5] 76-152025 12.95
1. Church polity—Early church, ca. 30-600. 2. Pastoral theology—Biblical teaching. 3. Pastoral theology—History of doctrines. I. Title.

MILLER, Paul M 253
Servant of God's servants; the work of a Christian minister, by Paul M. Miller. Scottdale, Pa., Herald Press [1964] 236 p. 20 cm. (The Conrad Grebel lectures, 1963) Bibliography: p. 233-236. [BV4011.M5] 63-15499
1. Pastoral theology — Mennonites. I. Title. II. Series.

MILLER, Paul M. 253
Servant of God's servants; the work of a Christian minister. Scottdale, Pa., Herald Pr. [c.1964] 236p. 20cm. (Conrad Grebel lectures, 1963) Bibl. 63-15499 4.50
1. Pastoral theology—Mennonites. I. Title. II. Series.

MILLET, Robert L. 253
Magnifying priesthood power / Robert L. Millet. Bountiful, Utah : Horizon Publishers, c1974. 169 p. ; 24 cm. Includes indexes. Bibliography: p. 138-141. [BX8659.M54] 75-312753 ISBN 0-88290-037-4 : 5.95
1. Church of Jesus Christ of Latter-Day Saints—Doctrinal and controversial works. 2. Melchizedek Priesthood (Mormonism) I. Title.

MITCHELL, Kenneth R 253
Psychological and theological relationships in the multiple staff ministry, by Kenneth R. Mitchell. Philadelphia, Westminster Press [1966] 273 p. 22 cm. Bibliography: p. [265]-269. [BV675.M5] 66-13597
1. Group ministry. 2. Pastoral theology — Presbyterian Church. I. Title.

MITCHELL, Kenneth R. 253
Psychological and theological relationships in the multiple staff ministry. Philadelphia, Westminster [c.1966] 273p. 22cm. Bibl. [BV675.M5] 66-13597 6.50
1. Group ministry. 2. Pastoral theology—Presbyterian Church. I. Title.

MOODY, Jess C 253
You can't lose for winning; a candid look at minister, layman, and church in a changing world, by Jess C. Moody. Introd. by Billy Graham. Grand Rapids, Zondervan Pub. House [1965] 152 p. 22 cm. [BX6345.M6] 65-19496
1. Baptists — Clergy — Correspondence, reminiscences, etc. 2. Pastoral theology. 3. Evangelistic work. I. Title.

MOODY, Jess C. 253
You can't lose for winning; a candid look at minister, layman, and churchin a changing world. Introd. by Billy Graham. Grand Rapids, Mich., Zondervan [c.1965] 152p. 22cm. [BX6345.M6] 65-19496 2.95 bds.,
1. Baptists—Clergy—Correspondence, reminiscences, etc. 2. Pastoral theology. 3. Evangelistic work. I. Title.

MOORE, Edward Roberts, 1894- 253
Roman collar, New York, Macmillan, 1950. xiii, 251 p. 21 cm. [BX1912.M74] 50-11067
1. Catholic Church — Clergy. I. Title.

MORGAN, George Campbell, 253
1863-1945.
The ministry of the Word. Grand Rapids, Baker Book House [1970] 252 p. 20 cm. (Notable books on preaching) Reprint of the 1919 ed. with a new introd. by Ralph G. Turnbull. [BV4010.M6 1970] 73-129056 ISBN 8-01-058589- 2.95
1. Pastoral theology. I. Title.

MOSSHAMER, Ottilie. 253
The priest and womanhood. Translated by Robert J. Voigt. Westminster, Md., Newman Press, 1964. xi, 388 p. 22 cm. "Sources": p. 369-379. [BX2347.8.W6M613] 63-12242
1. Church work with women — Catholic Church. I. Title.

MOSSHAMER, Ottilie 253
The priest and womanhood. Tr. [from German] by Robert J. Voigt. Westminster, Md., Newman [c.]1964. xi, 388p. 23cm. 63-12242 5.75
1. Church work with women—Catholic Church. I. Title.

MOXCEY, Mary Eliza, 1875- 253
Some qualities associated with success in the Christian ministry, by Mary E. Moxcey. New York, Teachers College, Columbia University, 1922. [New York, AMS Press, 1973] 101 p. illus. 22 cm. Reprint of the 1922 ed., issued in series: Teachers College, Columbia University. Contributions to education, no. 122. Originally presented as the author's thesis, Columbia. [BV660.M7 1972] 76-177095 ISBN 0-404-55122-X 10.00
1. Clergy. 2. Theology—Study and teaching. I. Title. II. Series: Columbia University. Teachers College. Contributions to education, no. 122.

MUELLER, Charles S. 253
What's this I hear about our church? : An action guide for congregation leaders / Charles S. Mueller. Minneapolis : Augsburg Pub. House, [1974] 104 p. : ill. ; 20 cm. (A Study of generations paperback) [BV3.M83] 74-77683 ISBN 0-8066-1434-X pbk. : 2.50 2.50
1. Theology, Practical. I. Title.

NATIONAL Campus Ministry 253
convocation. Theme: personal wholeness and professional identity in the campus ministry. [Athens, University of Georgia, 1966?] 75 p.

28 cm. Proceedings of a conference held at the University of Georgia Center for Continuing Education, June 20-24, 1966 and sponsored by the National Campus Ministry Association and the University of Georgia. [BV660.2.N3] 68-65136
1. Chaplains, University and college—Congresses. I. National Campus Ministry Association. II. Georgia. University. III. Title: Personal wholeness and professional identity in the campus ministry.

NATIONAL Opinion Research Center. 253
American priests; a report. Prepared for the United States Catholic Conference. [Chicago] 1971. xix, 486 p. illus. 27 cm. Bibliography: p. 485-486. [BX1912.N28] 78-29420
1. Catholic Church—Clergy—Statistics. 2. Clergy—U.S.—Statistics. I. United States Catholic Conference. II. Title.

NAVY Supervisory Chaplains Conference, Washington, D.C., 1966. 253
Navy Supervisory Chaplains Conference; [proceedings] Washington, 1966. 245 p. port. 26 cm. Cover title. [BV4017.N34 1966] 76-10894
1. Pastoral theology—Addresses, essays, lectures. 2. Chaplains, Military—U.S.—Addresses, essays, lectures. I. Title.

NEW York Academy of Medicine. 253
Ministry and medicine in human relations. Iago Galdston, editor. Freeport, N.Y., Books for Libraries Press [1971, c1955] xviii, 165 p. 23 cm. (Essay index reprint series) Papers presented at conferences held by the academy, May 11, 1950 and April 18-19, 1952. Includes bibliographical references. [BF47.N48 1971] 77-142682 ISBN 0-8369-2120-8
1. Psychology. 2. Ethics. 3. Pastoral psychology. I. Galdston, Iago, 1895- ed. II. Title.

NEWBIGIN, James Edward Lesslie, Bp. 253
"The Good Shepherd" : meditations on Christian ministry in today's world / Lesslie Newbigin ; foreword by the Archbishop of Canterbury. Grand Rapids : Eerdmans, 1977. 158 p. ; 21 cm. "A revised edition; originally published by the Christian Literature Society, Madras." [BV4017.N38 1977] 77-740 ISBN 0-8028-1686-X pbk. : 2.95
1. Pastoral theology—Addresses, essays, lectures. I. Title.

NIKLAS, Gerald R. 253
Ministry to the hospitalized / by Gerald R. Niklas and Charlotte Stefanics. New York : Paulist Press, c1975. v, 135 p. ; 21 cm. Includes bibliographies. [BX2347.8.S5N5] 75-22986 ISBN 0-8091-1899-8 : 3.95
1. Pastoral medicine—Catholic Church. 2. Church work with the sick. I. Stefanics, Charlotte, joint author. II. Title.

NILES, Daniel T 253
That they may have life. [1st ed.] New York, Published in association with the Student Volunteer Movement for Christian Missions by Harper [1951] 121 p. 20 cm. [BV3790.N5] 51-10822
1. Evangelistic work. I. Title.

NILES, Daniel Thambyrajah. 253
The preacher's calling to be servant. New York, Harper [1959] 143p. 20cm. [BV660.2.N5 1959a] 59-10349
1. Clergy—Appointment, call, and election. 2. Clergy—Office. I. Title.

NILES, Daniel Thambyrajah. 253
That they may have life. [1st ed.] New York, Published in association with the Student Volunteer Movement for Christian Missions by Harper [1951] 121p. 20cm. [BV3790.N5] 51-10822
1. Evangelistic work. I. Title.

NOUWEN, Henri J. M. 253
The wounded healer; ministry in contemporary society [by] Henri J. M. Nouwen. Illus. by Roel de Jong. [1st ed.] Garden City, N.Y., Doubleday, 1972. xiv, 104 p. illus. 22 cm. [BV4011.N683] 72-186312 ISBN 0-385-02856-3 5.95
1. Pastoral theology. I. Title.

NUGENT, Francis Edward, comp. 253
The priest in our day. Westminster, Md., Newman Press, 1954. 194p. 21cm. [BX1912.N78] 54-5898
1. Catholic Church—Clergy. 2. Clergy—Religious life. I. Title.

OATES, Wayne Edward, 1917- 253
The Christian pastor. Rev. and enl. ed. Philadelphia, Westminster Press [1964] xii, 258 p. 21 cm. Bibliography: p. 247-253. [BV4011.O2] 63-18553
1. Pastoral theology. 2. Pastoral psychology. I. Title.

OATES, Wayne Edward, 1917- 253
The Christian pastor. Rev. and enl. ed. Philadelphia, Westminster [c.1961, 1964] xii, 258p. 21cm. Bibl. 63-18553 5.00
1. Pastoral theology. 2. Pastoral psychology. I. Title.

OATES, Wayne Edward, 1917- 253
New dimensions in pastoral care, by Wayne E. Oates. Philadelphia, Fortress Press [1970] 86 p. 19 cm. Based on lectures originally presented by the author as the Zimmerman lectures at the Lutheran Theological Seminary, Gettysburg, Pa., May 1-2, 1968. Bibliography: p. 84-86. [BV4012.O225] 73-122832 1.95
1. Pastoral psychology. 2. Clergy—Psychology. I. Title.

OFFICE and ministry in the Church. 253
Edited by Bas van Iersel and Roland Murphy. [New York] Herder and Herder [1972] 150 p. 23 cm. (Concilium religion in the seventies, v. 80) On cover: The new concilium: religion in the seventies. Includes bibliographical references. [BV660.2.O34] 72-3946 ISBN 0-07-073610-3 2.95
1. Clergy—Office. 2. Pastoral theology. I. Iersel, Bastiaan Martinus Franciscus van, ed. II. Murphy, Roland Edmund, 1917- ed. III. Series: Concilium: theology in the age of renewal, v. 80.

*OLSON, Richard Allan, comp. 253
The pastor's role in educational ministry., edited with introductions by Richard Allan Olson. Philadelphia Fortress Press [1974] 285 p. 23 cm. (Yearbooks in Christian education, vol., 5) [BV1473] 8.95 (pbk.)
1. Religious education. 2. Clergy. I. Title.

O'NEILL, David P. 253
The priest in crisis; a study in role change [by] David P. O'Neill. Dayton, Ohio, Pflaum Press, 1968. xiv, 233 p. 22 cm. Bibliography: p. 225-227. Bibliographical footnotes. [BX1913.O48] 68-21240
1. Catholic Church—Clergy. I. Title.

O'NEILL, Joseph H. 253
A pastor's point of view. Milwaukee, Bruce [c.1963] x, 267p. 22cm. Bibl. 63-17494 5.00
1. Pastoral theology—Catholic Church. I. Title.

OSBORN, Ronald E. 253
In Christ's place; Christian ministry in today's world [by] Ronald E. Osborn. St. Louis, Bethany Pr. [1967] 288p. 23cm. Bibl. [BV660.2.O8] 67-27121 6.45
I. Title.

OSBORN, Ronald E 253
In Christ's place; Christian ministry in today's world [by] Ronald E. Osborn. St. Louis, Bethany Press [1967] 288 p. 23 cm. Includes bibliographical references. [BV660.2.O8] 67-27121
1. Clergy — Office. I. Title.

THE Pastor at work. 253
Authors: Richard R. Caemmerer [and others] Saint Louis, Concordia Pub. House [1960] 414p. 24cm. Includes bibliography. [BV4011.P34] 59-11470
1. Pastoral theology— Lutheran Church. I. Caemmerer, Richard Rudolph, 1904-

PASTOR at work (The). 253
Authors: Richard R. Caemmerer [and others] Saint Louis, Concordia Pub. House [c.1960] viii, 414p. 24cm. (bibls.) 59-11470 6.50
1. Pastoral theology—Lutheran Church. I. Caemmerer, Richard Rudolph.

PASTORAL pointers / 253
[O. W. Polen, editor in chief]. Cleveland, Tenn. : Pathway Press, 1976c1975 92 p. : ill. ; 20 cm. [BV4017.P28] 75-18284 ISBN 0-87148-686-5 pbk. : 1.95
1. Pastoral theology—Church of God—Addresses, essays, lectures. I. Polen, O. W.

PASTOR'S manual of the A.M.E. Church / 253
G. Lovelace Champion, editor. [Nashville] : H. Belin, c1976. 2 v. : ill. ; 23 cm. Contents.Contents.—v. 1. Toward deaconate orders.—v. 2. Toward elders orders. Includes bibliographies. [BX8447.P34] 76-360432
1. African Methodist Episcopal Church—Doctrinal and controversial works. 2. Pastoral theology—African Methodist Episcopal Church—Handbooks, manuals, etc. I. Champion, G. Lovelace.

PATTISON, E. Mansell, 1933- 253
Pastor and parish : a systems approach / E. Mansell Pattison. Philadelphia : Fortress Press, c1977. viii, 88 p. ; 22 cm. (Creative pastoral care and counseling series) Bibliography: p. 88. [BV4011.P35] 76-62619 ISBN 0-8006-0559-4 pbk. : 2.95
1. Pastoral theology. 2. System theory. 3. Pastoral psychology. I. Title.

PAULUS VI Pope, 1897- 253
The priest, by Giovanni Battista Cardinal Montini. [Tr. by Serge Hughes] Helicon [dist. New York, Taplinger, 1966, c.1965] 209p. 21cm. Bibl. [BX1912.P3413] 65-24126 4.95 bds.,
1. Clergy—Office. 2. Catholic Church—Clergy. I. Title.

PERRY, Lloyd Merle. 253
A manual of pastoral problems and procedures, by Lloyd Merle Perry and Edward John Lias. Grand Rapids, Mich., Baker BookHouse, 1964[c1962] 171 p. 29 cm. Includes bibliographies. [BV4016.P44] 65-4895
1. Pastoral theology—Handbooks, manuals, etc. I. Lias, Edward John joint author. II. Title.

PETTEY, Richard J. 253
In His footsteps : the priest and the Catholic charismatic renewal / by Richard J. Pettey. New York : Paulist Press, c1977. 106 p. ; 19 cm. (A Deus book) Bibliography: p. 93-106. [BX2350.57.P48] 76-45274 ISBN 0-8091-2007-0 pbk. : 2.45
1. Pentecostalism—Catholic Church. 2. Pastoral theology—Catholic Church. I. Title.

PINSON, William M. 253
The local church in ministry [by] William M. Pinson, Jr. Nashville, Broadman Press [1973] 145 p. 22 cm. Bibliography: p. 132-138. [BV4011.P5] 73-75629 ISBN 0-8054-6304-6
1. Pastoral theology. I. Title.

THE Plurality of ministries. 253
Edited by Hans Kung and Walter Kasper. [New York] Herder and Herder [1972] 152 p. 23 cm. (Concilium: religion in the seventies. Ecumenism, v. 74) On cover: The New concilium: religion in the seventies. Includes bibliographical references. [BV4011.P58] 76-185750 2.95 (pbk)
1. Pastoral theology—Addresses, essays, lectures. I. Kung, Hans, ed. II. Kasper, Walter, ed. III. Series: Concilium: theology in the age of renewal, v. 74.

POHLSCHNEIDER, Johannes, Bp., 1899- 253
Adsum a bishop speaks to his priests. Tr. [from German], adapted by Henry J. Grimmelsman. St. Louis, B. Herder [c.1962] 172p. 22cm. 62-15405 3.25
1. Priests. 2. Pastoral theology—Catholic church. I. Title.

PRATER, Arnold. 253
Seven keys to a more fruitful ministry. Foreword by Eugene M. Frank. Grand Rapids, Zondervan Pub. House [1960] 120p. 21cm. [BV4011.6.P7] 60-4356
1. Pastoral theology. I. Title.

PRESTWOOD, Charles. 253
The new breed of clergy. Grand Rapids, Eerdmans [1972] 108 p. 21 cm. Includes bibliographical references. [BV660.2.P67] 78-184696 ISBN 0-8028-1448-4 1.95
1. Clergy—Office. I. Title.

PRUYSER, Paul W. 253
The minister as diagnostician : personal problems in pastoral perspective / Paul W. Pruyser. Philadelphia : Westminster Press, c1976. p. cm. Includes bibliographical references and index. [BV4011.P7] 76-8922 ISBN 0-664-24123-9 pbk. : 4.95
1. Pastoral theology. 2. Pastoral psychology. 3. Clergy—Office. I. Title.

RAMSEY, Arthur Michael, Abp. of Canterbury, 1904- 253
The Christian priest today [by] Michael Ramsey. New York, Morehouse-Barlow [1972] 100 p. 19 cm. [BV660.2.R34] 72-192670 ISBN 0-8192-1133-8
1. Clergy—Office. I. Title.

REBELS in the church. 253
Ben Campbell Johnson, editor. Waco, Tex., Word Books [1971, c1970] 131 p. 23 cm. [BV660.2.R36 1971] 70-134939 3.95
1. Clergy—Office. 2. Church renewal. I. Johnson, Ben Campbell, ed.

REESE, J Irving. 253
A service manual for ministers, by J. Irving Reese. Des Plaines, Ill., Regular Baptist Press [1966] vii, 184 p. (p. 184 blank for "Notes") 15 cm. [BV4016.R4] 66-23726
1. Clergy — Handbooks, manuals, etc. I. Title.

REESE, J. Irving. 253
A service manual for ministers. Des Plaines, Ill., Regular Baptist Pr. [c.1966] vii, 184p. 15cm. [BV4016.R4] 66-23726 2.75 pap.,
1. Clergy—Handbooks, manuals, etc. I. Title.

RENGSTORF, Karl Heinrich, 1903- 253
Apostolate and ministry; the New Testament doctrine of the office of the ministry. Translator: Paul D. Pahl. Saint Louis, Concordia Pub. House [1969] 124 p. 22 cm. Translation of Apostolat und Predigtamt. Bibliographical references included in "Notes" (p. [115]-124) [BV660.2.R413] 69-12767 4.95
1. Clergy—Biblical teaching. I. Title.

SCHUETTE, Walter Erwin. 253
The minister's personal guide. [1st ed.] New York, Harper [1953] 183p. 22cm. [BV4012.S29] 53-5448
1. Theology, Pastoral. I. Title.

SCHUETZE, Armin W. 253
The shepherd under Christ : a textbook for pastoral theology / Armin W. Schuetze, Irwin J. Habeck. Milwaukee : Northwestern Pub. House, 1974. xvi, 389 p. : forms ; 24 cm. Includes bibliographical references. [BV4011.S357] 74-81794 10.00
1. Pastoral theology. I. Habeck, Irwin J., joint author. II. Title.

SECULAR priest in the new church, 253
edited by Gerard S. Sloyan. [New York] Herder and Herder [1967] 252 p. 22 cm. Contents.Contents.—Theology of the priesthood, by J. Powell.—Spirituality for the secular priesthood, by G. S. Sloyan.—Vatican II and the secular priest, by J. A. O'Donohoe.—Future laws for the secular priest, by P. M. Shannon.—The priest as liturgist, by J. T. Nolan.—The priest and his bishop, by J. K. Mussio.—The office of pastor, by J. G. Chatham.—The parish assistant, by A. M. Greeley.—The social mission of the secular priest, by J. V. Coffield.—The priest and the intellectual life, by J. T. Ellis.—The human side, by H. Fehren.—Ministry in the church of the future, by R. Ruether.—Notes on contributors. Bibliographical footnotes. [BX1913.S4] 67-25885
1. Catholic Church—Clergy. 2. Pastoral theology—Catholic Church. I. Sloyan, Gerard Stephen, 1919- ed.

SEGLER, Franklin M 253
A theology of church and ministry. Nashville, Broadman Press [1960] 272p. 22cm. Includes bibliography. [BV4011.S4] 60-14146
1. Clergy—Office. 2. Pastoral theology. I. Title.

SEVENTH-DAY Adventists. General Conference. Home Missionary Dept. 253
Lift Him up; a training course in Christ-centered lay evangelism. Washington, Review and Herald Pub. Association [1951] 253 p. illus. 18 cm. [BV3790.S46] 51-34674
1. Evangelistic work. I. Title.

SHEDD, Charlie W 253
The pastoral ministry of church officers, by Charlie W. Shedd. Richmond, John Knox Press [1965] 71 p. 21 cm. [BV705.S5] 65-11504
1. Church officers. 2. Church work. I. Title.

SHEDD, Charlie W. 253
The pastoral ministry of church officers. Richmond, Va., Knox [c.1965] 71p. 21cm. [BV705.S5] 65-11504 1.25 pap.,
1. Church officers. 2. Church work. I. Title.

SHIPLEY, David O., 1925- 253
Neither Black nor white; the whole church for a broken world [by] David O. Shipley. Waco, Tex., Word Books [1971] 164 p. 23 cm. Includes bibliographies. [BT734.2.S47] 73-134937 4.95
1. Church and race problems. I. Title.

SHIPMAN, Raymond M 253
We ordinary preachers, by one of them. [1st ed.] New York, Vantage Press [1957] 255p. 21cm. [BV4011.S48] 57-7816
1. Pastoral theology. I. Title.

SHOEMAKER, Samuel Moor, 1893- 253
Beginning your ministry. [1st ed.] New York, Harper & Row [1963] 127 p. 22 cm. [BV660.2.S5] 63-14974
1. Clergy—Office. I. Title.

SHOEMAKER, Samuel Moor, 1893- 253
Beginning your ministry. New York, Harper [c.1963] 127p. 22cm. 63-14974 3.00
1. Clergy—Office. I. Title.

SIMONET, Andre. 253
The priest and his bishop. [Translation by Angeline Bouchard] Foreword by Philip Delhaye. St. Louis, B. Herder Book Co., 1969. xxi, 129 p. 18 cm. "An Intex selection." Translation of Saisi par la charite de Dieu. [BX1912.S513] 70-107385 1.45
1. Catholic Church—Clergy. I. Title.

SMART, James D 253
The rebirth of ministry; a study of the biblical character of the church's ministry. Philadelphia, Westminster Press [1960] 192 p. 21 cm. Includes bibliography. [BV660.2.S6] 60-6189
1. Clergy — Office. I. Title.

SMART, James D. 253
The rebirth of ministry; a study of the biblical character of the church's ministry. Philadelphia, Westminster Press [c.1960] 192p. (2p. bibl.) 21cm. 60-6189 3.50
1. Clergy—Office. I. Title.

SMITH, Wilbur Moorehead, 1894- 253
The minister in his study, by Wilbur M. Smith. Chicago, Moody Press [1973] 128 p. 22 cm. Includes bibliographical references. [Z7751.S66] 73-7329 ISBN 0-8024-5295-7 3.95
1. Theology—Bibliography. 2. Bibliography—Best books—Theology. I. Title.

SMITH, William Martin, 1916- 253
Servants without hire; emerging concepts of the Christian ministry in the Campbell-Stone movement. Nashville, Tenn., Disciples of Christ Historical Society, 1968. 95 p. 23 cm. (The Reed lectures for 1967) Includes bibliographical references. [BX7326.S63] 75-19314
1. Disciples of Christ—Clergy—Addresses, essays, lectures. 2. Pastoral theology—Disciples of Christ—Addresses, essays, lectures. I. Title. II. Series.

SOUTHARD, Samuel. 253
Pastoral authority in personal relationships. Nashville, Abingdon Press [1969] 144 p. 20 cm. [BV660.2.S63] 69-12021 3.00
1. Clergy—Office. 2. Pastoral theology. 3. Pastoral psychology. I. Title.

SPENCE, Hartzell, 1908- 253
The clergy and what they do. New York, F. Watts [1961] 195 p. 22 cm. [BV660.2S7] 61-10081
1. Clergy — Office. I. Title.

SPENCE, Hartzell, 1908- 253
The clergy and what they do. New York, F. Watts [1961] 195 p. 22 cm. [BV660.2.S7] 61-10081
1. Clergy—Office. I. Title.

SPRUCE, Fletcher Clarke. 253
Of grasshoppers and giants : a formula for achieving ministers / by Fletcher Spruce. Kansas City, Mo. : Beacon Hill Press of Kansas City, c1975. 160 p. ; 20 cm. Includes bibliographical references. [BV4011.S68] 76-356021 ISBN 0-8341-0357-5
1. Pastoral theology—Church of the Nazarene. I. Title.

SPURGEON, Charles Haddon, 1834-1892. 253
An all round ministry; addresses to ministers and students [by] C. H. Spurgeon. [London, Carlisle, Pa.] Banner of Truth Trust [1972] xxii, 399 p. 19 cm. Includes bibliographical references. [BV4011.6.S68 1972] 73-178080 £0.55
1. Clergy—Religious life. 2. Clergy—Office. I. Title.

STEELE, James E. 253
I have a ghetto in my heart; a portrait of the Chicago challenge—youth action reaching the lost of a large city, by James E. Steele with Neigel and Peggy Scarborough. [Cleveland, Tenn., Pathway Press, 1973] 121 p. 18 cm. [BV4447.S687] 73-82727 ISBN 0-87148-428-5 1.50 (pbk.)
1. Church work with youth—Chicago. I. Scarborough, Neigel. II. Scarborough, Peggy. III. Title.

STEVENS, George Dewey 253
A pastor's diary; 'all in a day's work' for a Baptist minister. New York, Exposition Press [c.1960] 187p. 3.00
I. Title.

STEVENSON, Dwight Eshelman, 1906- 253
The false prophet [by] Dwight E. Stevenson. New York, Abingdon Press [1965] 142 p. 21 cm. Bibliographical footnotes. [BV4211.2.S74] 65-13058
1. Preaching. I. Title.

STEVENSON, Dwight Eshelman, 1906- 253
The false prophet. Nashville, Abingdon [c.1965] 142p. 21cm. Bibl. [BV4211.2.S74] 65-13058 2.75
1. Preaching. I. Title.

STIRES, Ernest Van R. 253
Not as a man pleaser; John Doe & the church, by Ernest Van R. Stires. Darien, Ga., Printed for the author at the Ashantilly Press, 1965. 50 p. 25 cm. [BX5175.S7] 331.1'1 68-2180
1. Pastoral theology—Anglican communion. I. Title. II. Title: John Doe & the church.

STOTT, John R. W. 253
One people [by] John R. W. Stott. Downers Grove, Ill., Inter-Varsity Press [1971] 93, [1] p. 20 cm. "Revision and expansion of the Pastoral theology lectures delivered in Durham University in February 1968." Bibliography: p. 93-[94] [BV4011.S87] 72-127931 ISBN 0-87784-694-4
1. Pastoral theology. I. Title.

STOVALL, Charles E 253
Training for greater service; a study of various phases of church work for Christian men who desire to render a greater service to the Lord and His cause. Lebanon, Tenn., Noble Searcher, 1956. 158 p. 20 cm. [BV652.S8] 56-31569
1. Church work. I. Title.

STRAIN, Dudley. 253
The measure of a minister. St. Louis, Bethany Press [1964] 127 p. 23 cm. Bibliographical footnotes. [BV660.2.S8] 64-13405
1. Clergy — Office. I. Title.

SUGDEN, Howard F. 253
When pastors wonder how [by] Howard F. Sugden & Warren W. Wiersbe. Chicago, Moody Press [1973] 160 p. 22 cm. [BV4011.S93] 73-179180 ISBN 0-8024-9431-5 3.95
1. Pastoral theology. I. Wiersbe, Warren W., joint author. II. Title.

SWEENEY, Joseph W 253
The knight of the sanctuary; the priest in our times. Foreword by Bryan Joseph McEntegart. [1st ed.] New York, Exposition Press [c1959] 226 p. 21 cm. (An Exposition-testament book) [BX1912.5.S9] 60-240
1. Clergy — Religious life. I. Title.

SWEENEY, Joseph W. 253
The knight of the sanctuary; the priest in our times. Foreword by Bryan Joseph McEntegart. New York, Exposition Press [c.1959] 226p. 21cm. (An Exposition-testament book) 60-240 3.50
1. Clergy—Religious life. I. Title.

TATLOCK, Richard. 253
Proving preaching, and teaching, an inquiry into the nature and technique of apologetics and communication in the context of the Christian religion. London, Faith Press New York Morehouse-Barlow Co. [1963] 131 p. 19 cm. (Studies in Christian faith and practice, 8) Includes bibliographical references. [BV4319.T34] 63-25475
1. Apologetics—20th cent.—Addresses, essays, lectures. 2. Communication (Theology) I. Title.

TATLOCK, Richard 253
Proving, preaching, and teaching, an inquiry into the nature and technique of apologetics and communication in the context of the Christian religion. London, Faith Pr.; New York, Morehouse [c.1963] 131p. 19cm. (Studies in Christian faith and practice, 8) Bibl. 63-25475 1.50 pap.,
1. Apologetics—20th cent.—Addresses, essays, lectures. 2. Communication (Theology) I. Title.

*TAYLOR, William M. 1829-1895 253
The ministry of the word, [by] William M. Taylor. Grand Rapids, Baker Book House, [1975] vi, 318 p. 20 cm. (Notable books on preaching) Includes bibliographical references and index. [BV662] ISBN 0-8010-8830-5 3.95 (pbk.)
1. Church work. 2. Communication (Theology) 3. Pastoral Theology. I. Title.

TERRY, Mary. 253
Winsome witnessing; how to tell your neighbors about Christ. With an introd. by M. E. Dodd. Chicago, Moody Press [1951?] 127 p. 18 cm. (Colportage library, 210) [BV4520.T4] 52-20937
1. Witness bearing (Christianity) I. Title.

THIESSEN, John Caldwell. 253
Pastoring the smaller church. Grand Rapids, Zondervan Pub. House [1962] 168 p. 23 cm. [BV4011.T43] 62-51429
1. Pastoral theology. I. Title.

THIESSEN, John Caldwell 253
Pastoring the smaller church. Grand Rapids, Mich., Zondervan [c.1962] 168p. 23cm. 62-51429 2.95
1. Pastoral theology. I. Title.

THILS, Gustave, 1909-. 253
The diocesan priest; the nature and spirituality of the diocesan clergy. Translated by Albert J. La Mothe, Jr. Notre Dame, Ind., Fides Publishers [1964] 368 p. 23 cm. Translation of Nature et spiritualite de clerge diocesain. Bibliographical footnotes. [BX1912.T4853] 64-16500
1. Clergy — Religious life. I. Title.

THILS, Gustave, 1909- 253
The diocesan priest; the nature and spirituality of the diocesan clergy. Tr. [from French] by Albert J. La Mothe, Jr. Notre Dame, Ind., Fides [c.1964] 368p. 23cm. Bibl. 64-16500 5.50 bds.,
1. Clergy—Religious life. I. Title.

TOWNS, Elmer L. 253
Successful ministry to the retarded, by Elmer L. Towns and Roberta L. Groff. Chicago, Moody Press [1972] 144 p. 21 cm. Bibliography: p. 135-144. [BV4461.T68] 70-181589 ISBN 0-8024-8425-5 2.25
1. Church work with mentally handicapped children. I. Groff, Roberta L., joint author. II. Title.

TRESE, Leo John, 1902- 253
Vessel of clay. New York, Sheed & Ward, 1950. viii, 115p. 20cm. [BX1912.T7] 50-6709
1. Clergy— Religious life. I. Title.

TURNBULL, Ralph G 253
A minister's obstacles. [Westwood, N. J.] F. H. Revell Co. [1959] 159 p. 21 cm. (Revell's preaching and pastoral aid series) [BV4010.T75] 59-5504
1. Pastoral theology. I. Title.

UNITED Church of Christ. Task Force on Ministries to Military Personnel. 253
Ministries to military personnel; report of a United Church task force to the Ninth General Synod, St. Louis, Missouri, June 22-26, 1973. Philadelphia, Published by United Church Press, for the United Church Board for Homeland Ministries, and the Council for Church and Ministry, United Church of Christ [1973] 126 p. 21 cm. [UH23.U54 1973] 73-178292 1.95 (pbk.)
1. Chaplains, Military—United Church of Christ—Congresses. 2. Chaplains, Military—United States—Congresses. I. United Church of Christ. General Synod, 9th, St. Louis, 1973. II. United Church Board for Homeland Ministries. III. United Church of Christ. Council for Church and Ministry. IV. Title.

V8COURTOIS, Gaston 253
The young priest [Tr. from French by Michael C. O'Brien, New York] Herder ; Herder [c.1965] 110p. 21cm. [BX1912.5.C623] 65-13488 2.75
1. Clergy—Religious life. 2. Meditations. I. Title.

WAGNER, Charles U. 253
The pastor, his life and work / Charles U. Wagner. Schaumburg, Ill. : Regular Baptist Press, c1976. xiii, 274 p. ; 24 cm. Includes bibliographical references and index. [BV4011.W27] 76-22402 ISBN 0-87227-001-7 : 7.95
1. Pastoral theology. I. Title.

WALTERS, Orville Selkirk, 1903- 253
You can win others; how to adventure in sharing the good news. Winons Lake, Ind., Light and Life Press, 1951. 82 p. illus. 17 cm. [BV3790.W32] 52-16767
1. Evangelistic work. I. Title.

WATSON, Louis E. 253
Oceans of love [by] Louis E. Watson. Philadelphia, Dorrance [1973] 97 p. 22 cm. [BX6495.W35A3] 72-91280 ISBN 0-8059-1778-0 4.00
1. Watson, Louis E. I. Title.

WEATHERLY, Owen Milton. 253
Help your minister to do his best [by] Owen M. Weatherly. Illus. by Russell Keeter. Valley Forge [Pa.] Judson Press [1965] 156 p. illus. 21 cm. [BV4015.W4] 65-22000
1. Pastoral theology. I. Title.

WEATHERLY, Owen Milton 253
Help your minister to do his best. Illus. by Russell Keeter. Valley Forge [Pa.] Judson [c.1965] 156p. illus. 21cm. [BV4015.W4] 65-22000 3.95
1. Pastoral theology. I. Title.

WEED, Michael R., comp. 253
The minister and his work [compiled by] Michael R. Weed. Austin, Tex., Sweet Pub. Co. [1970] 192 p. 21 cm. "The essays contained in this volume formerly appeared in a column in the Christian chronicle entitled 'For the minister.'" Includes bibliographies. [BV4011.W36] 72-134689 ISBN 0-8344-0063-4
1. Pastoral theology. 2. Clergy—Office. I. Christian chronicle. II. Title.

WERNING, Waldo J 253
Winning them back; new life for inactive church members. Minneapolis, Augsburg Pub. House [1963] 79 p. 20 cm. [BV4011.W4] 63-16606
1. Church membership. I. Title.

WERNING, Waldo J. 253
Winning them back; new life for inactive church members. Minneapolis, Augsburg [c.1963] 79p. 20cm. 63-16606 1.75 pap.,
1. Church membership. I. Title.

WHITE, Reginald E. O. 253
A guide to pastoral care : a practical primer of pastoral theology / [by] R. E. O. White. London : Pickering and Inglis, 1976. ix, 325 p. ; 21 cm. Bibliography: p. 321-324. [BV4011.W45] 77-363285 ISBN 0-7208-0377-2 : £7.50
1. Pastoral theology. I. Title.

WHITLEY, Henry Charles 253
Laughter in heaven. Westwood, N.J., Revell [1964, c.1962] 189p. port. 22cm. 64-9896 3.50 bds.,
I. Title.

WILKINS, Chester, 1918- 253
A handbook for personal soul-winning. Berne, Ind., Light & Hope Publications [1950] 301 p. 20 cm. Bibliography: p. [299-301. [BV3790.W49] 50-29204
1. Evangelistic work. I. Title.

WITTKOFSKI, Joseph N:cholas, 1912- 253
The pastoral use of hypnotic technique, by Joseph Wittkofski. With a foreword by T. J. Freeborn, Jr., and an introd. by Austin Pardue. Springfield, Ill., Thomas [1971] xvi, 111 p. 22 cm. Bibliography: p. 107. [BV4012.W55 1971] 74-21535
1. Pastoral psychology. 2. Hypnotism—Therapeutic use. I. Title.

WITTY, Robert Gee. 253
Church visitation: theory and practice [by] Robert G. Witty. Nashville, Broadman Press [1967] 74p. 20 cm. [BV4320.W5] 68-12318
1. Visitations (Church work) I. Title.

WITTY, Robert Gee. 253
Church visitation: theory and practice [by] Robert G. Witty. Nashville, Broadman Press [1967] 74 p. 20 cm. [BV4320.W5] 68-12318
1. Visitations (Church work) I. Title.

YOUTH ministry : 253
a book of readings / edited by Michael Warren. New York : Paulist Press, c1977. 212 p. ; 19 cm. (A Deus book) Includes bibliographical references. [BX2347.8.Y7Y68] 77-70639 ISBN 0-8091-2018-6 pbk. : 2.95
1. Church work with youth—Catholic Church—Addresses, essays, lectures. I. Warren, Michael.

ULEYN, Arnold. 253'.01'9
The recognition of guilt; a study in pastoral psychology. Translated by Mary Ilford. [Dublin] Gill and Macmillan [1969] xiv, 240 p. 22 cm. Translation of Actualite de la fonction prophetique. Includes bibliographical references. [BV4012.U413] 71-254089 ISBN 0-7171-0266-1 36/-
1. Pastoral psychology. I. Title.

PERRY, Lloyd Merle. 253.02
A manual of pastoral problems and procedures, by Lloyd Merle Perry and Edward John Lias. Grand Rapids, Baker Book House, 1962. 171p. 29cm. Includes bibliography. [BV4016.P44] 62-4310
1. Pastoral theology—Handbooks, manuals, etc. I. Lias, Edward John, joint author. II. Title. III. Title: Pastoral problems and procedures.

BASSET, Bernard 253.0207
Priest in the presbytery; a psycho-ecclesiastical extravaganza. Illus. by Penelope Harter. [New York] Herder & Herder [1966, c.1964] 104p. illus. 21cm. [BV4015.B27] 65-29206 3.50
1. Pastoral theology—Anecdotes, facetiae, satire, etc. I. Title.

CARTWRIGHT, Charles. 253'.02'07
Choice chuckles. Grand Rapids, Kregel Publications [1968] [64] p. (chiefly illus.) 19 cm. (His Church chuckles cartoon series) [NC1429.C4A44] 68-31127 1.00
1. Clergy—Caricatures and cartoons. I. Title.

FREEMAN, Gary. 253'.02'07
A funny thing happened on the way to heaven. Illustrated by Jim Crane. [1st ed.] New York, Harper & Row [1969] 126 p. illus. 22 cm. [PN6231.C5F7] 69-17012 3.95
1. Pastoral theology—Anecdotes, facetiae, satire, etc. I. Title.

MILHAM, Richard. 253'.02'07
Brother Fred Chicken, superpastor. Nashville, Broadman Press [1968] 96 p. illus. 20 cm. [BV4015.M5] 68-20682
1. Pastoral theology—Anecdotes, facetiae, satire, etc. I. Title.

TORMEY, John C. 253'.02'07
What's cooking in the priesthood? / John C. Tormey. Canfield, Ohio : Alba Books, [1975] 128 p. : ill. ; 18 cm. [BX1912.T6] 74-28963 pbk. : 1.25
1. Catholic Church—Clergy—Caricatures and cartoons. 2. Pastoral theology—Catholic Church. I. Title.

FLOYD, William A., 1928- 253'.023
Your future as a minister [by] William A. Floyd. [1st ed.] New York, R. Rosen Press [1969] 158 p. illus., ports. 23 cm. ([Careers in depth, 92]) Cover title: A definitive study of your future as a minister. Bibliography: p. 152-158. Describes the educational requirements for and the advantages and disadvantages of a career as a minister. [BV660.2.F55] 72-77299 ISBN 0-8239-0062-2 3.78
1. Clergy—Office. I. Title. II. Title: A definitive study of your future as a minister.

SCOTT, Manuel Lee. 253.06'1
From a Black brother. Nashville, Broadman Press [1971] 128 p. 21 cm. [BX6333.S39F7] 76-145988 2.95
1. Baptists—Sermons. 2. Sermons, American. I. Title.

*MECKLENBURG, George, D. D. 253.081
Never a dull moment; reflections on sixty years in the Protestant ministry. New York, Exposition [c.1964] 128p. 22cm. (EP42114) 3.00
I. Title.

CATHOLIC Church. Pope. 253.082
The Catholic priesthood, according to the teaching of the Church; bk. 2 [Ed. by] Pierre Veuillot. Pref. by His Excellency Monsignor Montini. Westminster, Md., Newman [1965, c.1964] xxxix, 302p. 22cm. Bibl. [BX1912.A323] 58-1447 7.50
1. Priesthood—Papal documents. 2. Pastoral theology—Catholic Church—Addresses, essays, lectures. I. Veuillot, Pierre, ed. II. Title. Contents omitted.

JOHNSON, Emeroy, ed. 253.082
Why I became a pastor; twenty true stories by Lutheran pastors. Edited by Emeroy Johnson and Thomas W. Wersell. Rock Island, Ill., Augustana Press [1958] 131p. 20cm. [BX8049.J6] 58-9643
1. Augustana Evangelical Lutheran Church—Clergy. I. Wersell, Thomas W., joint ed. II. Title.

MCCULLOH, Gerald O., ed. 253.082
Heralds of Christ. Gerald O. McCulloh, W. Thomas Smith, eds. Prep., ed. by Dept. of Ministerial Educ., Div. of Higher Educ., Bd. of Educ., The Methodist Church. Nashville, Abingdon [c.1963] 128p. 19cm. 64-554 .50 pap.,
1. Clergy—Office—Collections. 2. Clergy—Hist. I. Smith, Warren Thomas, 1923- joint ed. II. Title.

BOUSMAN, Gary. 253.088
The human side of the ministry. Fargo, N. D., Fireside Press [1959] 106p. illus. 22cm. [BV4015.B53] 60-18501
1. Pastoral theology—Ancedotes, facetiae, satire, etc. I. Title.

BRODE, Anthony. 253.088
Wayward vicarage. Illustrated by Fritz Kredel. Philadelphia, Lippincott, 1959. 190 p. illus. 21 cm. Autobiographical. "Published in England under the title, Picture a country vicarage." [BV4015.B6 1959] 59-7110
1. Pastoral theology—Anecdotes, facetiae, satire, etc. I. Title.

PORTER, Alyene 253.088
Papa was a preacher. Illus. by Janet Smalley. Nashville, Abingdon Pr., [1960, c.1944] 167p. (Apex Bks. E5) 1.00 pap.,
1. Theology, Pastoral—Anecdotes, facetiae, satire, etc. I. Title.

SEGERHAMMAR, Robert E 253.088
Just call me Pastor; a Peter Pulpitpounder book. Illustrated by Donald J. Wallerstedt. Rock Island, Ill., Augustana Press [1959] 91p. illus. 20cm. [BV4015.S32] 59-9092
1. Pastoral theology—Anecdotes, facetiae, satire, etc. I. Title.

SEGERHAMMAR, Robert E 253.088
Peter Pulpitpounder, B. D. Rock Island, Ill., Augustana Press [1957] 54p. illus. 20cm. [BV4015.S33] 57-7761
1. Pastoral theology—Anecdotes, facetiae, satire, etc. I. Title.

COOKE, Bernard J. 253'.09
Ministry to word and sacraments : history and theology / Bernard Cooke. Philadelphia : Fortress Press, c1976. ix, 677 p. ; 27 cm. Includes bibliographies and indexes. [BV4006.C66] 75-36459 ISBN 0-8006-0440-7 : 25.00
1. Pastoral theology—History of doctrines. I. Title.

CARTER, Lawrence. 253'.0924
Can't you here me calling! New York, Seabury Press [1969] xii, 146 p. 22 cm. [BV600.2.C34] 68-24006 4.95
1. Church renewal—Case studies. 2. City churches. I. Title.

CUNNINGHAM, James F 253.0924
American pastor in Rome [by] James F. Cunningham. [1st ed.] Garden City, N.Y., Doubleday, 1966. 285 p. illus., ports. 22 cm. Autobiographical. 66-20921
1. Catholic Church — Clergy — Correspondence, reminiscences, etc. I. Title.

CUNNINGHAM, James F. 253.0924
American pastor in Rome [by] James F. Cunningham.[1st ed.] Garden City, N.Y., Doubleday, 1966. 285p. illus., ports. 22cm. Autobiographical. [BX4705.C792A3] 66-20921 4.95
1. Catholic Church—Clergy—Correspondence, reminiscences, etc. I. Title.

DAVIES, Samuel, 1723-1761. 253'.0924
The Reverend Samuel Davies abroad; the diary of a journey to England and Scotland, 1753-55. Edited, with an introd., by George William Pilcher. Urbana, University of Illinois Press, 1967. xv, 176 p. 24 cm. Bibliographical footnotes. [BX9225.D33A3] 67-12991
1. Great Britain—Description and travel—1701-1800. I. Pilcher, George William, ed. II. Title.

DISPENZA, Joseph 253.0924
Forgotten patriot; a story of Father Pierre Gibault, by Brother Joseph Dispenza. Decorations by Carolyn Lee Jagodits. Notre Dame, Ind., Dujarie [1966] 95p. illus. 24cm. [BX4705.G49D5] 66-22270 2.25
1. Gibault, Pierre. 1737-1804. I. Title.

HEWITT, Arthur Wentworth, 1883- 253.0924
The old brick manse. [1st ed.]) New York, Harper & Row [c1966] vi, 246 p. 22 cm. Autobiography. [BX8495.H52A3] 66-10674
I. Title.

HEWITT, Arthur Wentworth, 1883- 253.0924
The old brick manse. New York, Harper [c.1966] vi, 246p. 22cm. Autobiography. [BX8495.H52A3] 66-10674 4.95
I. Title.

POWELL, W. H. R. 253'.0924 B
Illustrations from a supervised life, by W. H. R. Powell. [Philadelphia, Printed by Continental Press, 1968] 263 p. illus. 22 cm. Autobiographical. [BX6455.P65A3] 68-7980 4.50
I. Title.

RAPKING, Aaron Henry, 1886- 253'.0924
Stick to it farmer boy; an autobiography, by Aaron H. Rapking. Nashville, Parthenon Press, 1967. 188 p. 19 cm. [BX8495.R28A3] 67-8781
I. Title.

RUSSELL, Stephen. 253'.0924
A man in the middle; the journal of a young priest in conflict with himself. Dayton, Ohio, Pflaum Press, 1969. viii, 130 p. 22 cm. [BX1912.R83] 69-20167 3.95
1. Catholic Church—Clergy—Correspondence, reminiscences, etc. I. Title.

HART, Arthur Tindal 253.0942
Country counting house; the story of two eighteenthcentury clerical account books. London, Phoenix House [dist. Hollywood-by-the-Sea, Fla., Transatlantic, c.1962] xxix, 142p. illus. 23cm. Bibl. 63-1753 6.25
1. Payne, Squier, 1676?-1751. 2. Mease, Henry, 1680 or 81-1746. 3. Clergy—England. 4. Church finance—England—Hist.—Sources. I. Title.

HEENEY, William Brian Danford, 1933- 253'.0942
A different kind of gentleman : parish clergy as professional men in early and mid-Victorian England / by Brian Heeney. Hamden, Conn. : Published for the Conference on British Studies and Wittenberg University by Archon Books, 1976. p. cm. (Studies in British history and culture ; v. 5) Includes index. Bibliography: p. [BR759.H4] 76-17329 ISBN 0-208-01460-8 : 12.50
1. Clergy—England. I. Title. II. Series.

MCCLATCHEY, Diana 253.094257
Oxfordshire clergy, 1777-1869; a study of the established church and of therole of its clergy in local society. Oxford, Clarendon Press, 1960. [dist., New York, Oxford University Press] vi, 252p. fold. maps, tables. 22cm. Bibl.: p.[232]-241. 60-50762 7.20
1. Clergy—England—Oxfordshire. I. Title.

CHILD, Frank Samuel, 1854-1922. 253'.0974
The colonial parson of New England; a picture. Ann Arbor, Mich., Gryphon Books, 1971. 226 p. 22 cm. "Facsimile reprint of the 1896 edition." [BR520.C49 1869a] 76-145527
1. Clergy—New England. 2. New England—Church history. I. Title.

CHILD, Frank Samuel, 1854-1922. 253'.0974
The colonial parson of New England; a picture. New York, Baker & Taylor Co. Detroit, Gale Research Co., 1974. 226 p. 18 cm. Reprint of the 1896 ed. [BR520.C49 1974] 73-19532 10.00
1. Clergy—New England. 2. New England—Church history. I. Title.

YOUNGS, John William Theodore, 1941- 253'.0974
God's messengers, : religious leadership in colonial New England, 1700-1750 / by J. William T. Youngs, Jr. Baltimore : Johns Hopkins University Press, c1976. xi, 176 p. ; 24 cm. "Frank S. and Elizabeth D. Brewer prize essay of the American Society of Church History." Includes index. Bibliography: p. 167-169. [BX7136.Y68] 76-8544 ISBN 0-8018-1799-4 : 10.00
1. Congregational churches in New England—Clergy. 2. Clergy—New England. 3. New England—History—Colonial period, ca. 1600-1775. I. Title.

GUFFIN, Gilbert Lee. 253.1
Called of God; the work of the ministry [by] Gilbert L. Guffin. Introd. by Andrew W. Blackwood. [Rev. ed.] Boston, Christopher Pub. House [1965] 140 p. 21 cm. [BV660.2.G8] 65-26314
1. Clergy. I. Title.

GUFFIN, Gilbert Lee 253.1
Called of God; the work of the ministry. Introd. by Andrew W. Blackwood. [Rev. ed.] Boston, Christopher Pub. [c.1951, 1965] 140p. 21cm. [BV660.2.G8] 65-26314 2.95
1. Clergy. I. Title.

*ARNOLD, Milo L. 253.2
The adventure of the Christian ministry. Kansas City, Mo., Beacon Hill Pr. [1967] 138p. 21cm. 2.25
I. Title.

ASHBROOK, James B., 1925- 253'.2
In human presence - hope [by] James B. Ashbrook. Valley Forge [Pa.] Judson Press [1971] 220 p. illus. 23 cm. Includes bibliographical references. [BJ1581.2.A78] 77-147847 ISBN 0-8170-0491-2 6.95
1. Conduct of life. 2. Pastoral theology. I. Title.

AUDET, Jean Paul. 253'.2
Structures of Christian priesthood; a study of home, marriage, and celibacy in the pastoral service of the church. Translated by Rosemary Sheed. [1st American ed.] New York, Macmillan [1968] xiii, 112 p. 22 cm. Translation of Mariage et celibat dans le service pastoral de l'Eglise. Bibliographical footnotes. [BV4390.A913 1968] 67-31350
1. Catholic Church—Clergy. 2. Celibacy. I. Title.

BAARS, Conrad W. 253'.2
How to treat and prevent the crisis in the priesthood [by] Conrad W. Baars. [Chicago, Franciscan Herald Press, c1972] 39 p. 18 cm. (Synthesis series) [BX1912.B13] 73-157886 0.50
1. Catholic Church—Clergy—Psychology. I. Title.

BAARS, Conrad W. 253'.2
A priest for all seasons; masculine and celibate [by] Conrad W. Baars. Chicago, Franciscan Herald Press [1972] 50 p. 18 cm. (Synthesis series) Includes bibliographical references. [BX1912.B15] 72-77446 0.50
1. Catholic Church—Clergy. I. Title.

BASSETT, William W. 253'.2
Celibacy in the church. Edited by William Bassett and Peter Huizing. [New York] Herder and Herder [1972] 156 p. 23 cm. (Concilium: religion in the seventies, v. 78. Canon law) Includes bibliographical references. [BV4390.B34] 72-3943 ISBN 0-07-073608-1 2.95
1. Celibacy. I. Huizing, Petrus, 1911- joint author. II. Title. III. Series: Concilium: theology in the age of renewal, v. 78.

BEATTIE, Carol. 253.2
For goodness' sake. New York, Prentice-Hall [1952] 242 p. 21 cm. Autobiographical. [BR1725.B387A3] 52-8805
I. Title.

BEDSOLE, Adolph. 253.2
The pastor in profile. Grand Rapids, Baker Book House, 1960 [c1958] 163p. 21cm. [BV4011.B4] 58-10857
1. Pastoral theology. I. Title.

BERTRAMS, Wilhelm 253.2
The celibacy of the priest; meaning and basis. Tr. by P. Byrne. Westminster,Md., Newman [c.1963] 127p. 19cm. Bibl. 63-25080 2.50
1. Celibacy. I. Title.

BERTRAMS, Wilhelm. 253.2
The celibacy of the priest; meaning and basis. Translated by P. Byrne. Westminster, Md., Newman Press [1963] 127 p. 10 cm. Bibliographical references included in "Notes" (p. 108-127) [BV4390.B413] 63-25080
1. Celibacy. I. Title.

BLENKINSOPP, Joseph, 1927- 253'.2
Celibacy, ministry, church; an enquiry into the possibility of reform in the present self-understanding of the Roman Catholic Church and its practice of ministry. [New York] Herder and Herder [1968] 252 p. 22 cm. Bibliographical footnotes. [BV4390.B54] 68-55081 5.95
1. Catholic Church—Clergy. 2. Celibacy. 3. Clergy—Biblical teaching. I. Title.

CASE histories of tentmakers / edited by James L. Lowery, Jr. Wilton, Conn. : Morehouse-Barlow Co., c1976. xvii, 83 p. ; 22 cm. Includes bibliographical references. [BV676.5.C37] 76-374762 ISBN 0-8192-1216-4 pbk. : 3.50 253'.2
1. Protestant Episcopal Church in the U.S.A.—Clergy. 2. Clergy, Part-time—Case studies. I. Lowery, James L.

CASE, Mabel (Hamm) 1883-1952. 253.2
The singing years. New York, Vantage Press [1953] 105p. 23cm. Autobiography. [BV4395.C3] 52-11907
1. Clergymen's wives. I. Title.

CATHOLIC Church. Pope, 1958- 253.2
(Joannes XXIII) Sacerdotii nostri primordia (1 Aug. 1959) English.
From the beginning of our priesthood. 'Sacerdotii nostri primordia.' As provided by N. C. W. C. [Boston] St.Paul Editions [dist. Daughters of St. Paul] [1959] 32p. 19cm. 60-197 .25 pap.,
1. Vianney, Jean Baptiste Marie, Saint, 1786-1859. 2. Clergy—Religious life. I. Title.

CLARK, Wayne C 253.2
The minister looks at himself ... Philadelphia, Judson Press [1957] 135p. 21cm. [BV4010.C55] 57-7628
1. Pastoral theology. I. Title.

CLEARY, William H. 253'.2
Hyphenated priests: the ministry of the future. Edited by William H. Cleary. Washington, Corpus Books [1969] xii, 167 p. 21 cm. [BX1912.C54] 79-76570
1. Catholic Church—Clergy—Addresses, essays, lectures. I. Title.

CREATING an intentional ministry / edited by John E. Biersdorf. Nashville : Abingdon, c1976. 237 p. ; 22 cm. Includes bibliographical references and index. [BV4011.C68] 75-40463 ISBN 0-687-09810-6 pbk. : 5.75 253'.2
1. Pastoral theology—Addresses, essays, lectures. I. Biersdorf, John E., 1930-

CURRAN, Charles E. 253'.2
The crisis in priestly ministry [by] Charles E. Curran. Notre Dame, Ind., Fides Publishers [1972] vii, 146 p. 18 cm. (A Fides dome book, D-82) Includes bibliographical references. [BX1913.C86] 72-80236 ISBN 0-8190-0577-0 1.50
1. Pastoral theology—Catholic Church. I. Title.

DENTON, Wallace 253.2
The role of the minister's wife. Philadelphia, Westminster [c.1962] 175p. illus. 21cm. Bibl. 62-7474 3.50
1. Clergymen's wives. I. Title.

DE SATGE, John. 253'.2
Letters to an ordinand : a study in vocation / [by] John de Satge. London : S.P.C.K. : Advisory Council for the Church's Ministry, 1976. x, 45 p. ; 19 cm. [BX5175.D44] 77-350373 ISBN 0-281-02948-2 : £0.95
1. Pastoral theology—Anglican Communion. 2. Vocation, Ecclesiastical. I. Title.

THE Dimensions of the priesthood: theological, Christological, liturgical, ecclesial, apostolic, Marian. Compiled by the Daughters of St. Paul. [Boston] St. Paul Editions [1973] 322 p. 22 cm. "A compilation of 325 selected passages from the documents of Vatican II; from postconciliar documents; from the writings 253'.2

and addresses of Popes Pius XII, John XXIII, Paul VI, and the 1971 World Synod of Bishops." [BX1913.D53] 73-76310 5.00
1. Catholic Church—Clergy—Collections. 2. Pastoral theology—Catholic Church—Collections. I. Daughters of St. Paul.

DOTY, Harry L., 1911- 253'.2
Letters to Ron / by Harry L. Doty. Independence, Mo. : Herald Pub. House, c1976. 98 p. ; 21 cm. [BV4011.D67] 74-28091 ISBN 0-8309-0142-6 : 5.00
1. Doty, Harry L., 1911- 2. Pastoral theology. I. Title.

DOUGLAS, William G. T. 253.2
Ministers' wives [by] William Douglas. [1st ed.] New York, Harper & Row [1965] xv, 265 p. 22 cm. Bibliography: p. 253-260. [BV4395.D6] 65-20449
1. Clergymen's wives. I. Title.

FENHAGEN, James C. 253'.2
Mutual ministry : new vitality in the local church / James C. Fenhagen. New York : Seabury Press, 1977. p. cm. "A Crossroad book." [BV4011.F45] 76-49997 ISBN 0-8164-0332-5 : 6.95
1. Pastoral theology. 2. Church. I. Title.

FLYNN, Leslie B. 253.2
How to save time in the ministry [by] Leslie B. Flynn. Grand Rapids Baker Book House [1975 c1966] 95 p. 20 cm. (Source books for ministers) [BV652.F55] 65-23049 ISBN 0-8010-3470-1 2.95 (pbk.)
1. Church management. I. Title.

FRAY, Harold R. 253'.2
The pain and joy of ministry [by] Harold R. Fray, Jr. Philadelphia, Pilgrim Press [1972] 127 p. 22 cm. Includes bibliographical references. [BV4011.F7] 72-182234 ISBN 0-8298-0221-5 4.95
1. Pastoral theology. 2. Christianity—20th century. I. Title.

FRAZIER, Claude Albee, 1920- 253'.2
Should preachers play God? Compiled by Claude A. Frazier. [Independence, Mo.] Independence Press [1973] 224 p. 21 cm. [BV660.2.F7] 72-91073 ISBN 0-8309-0084-5 4.95
1. Clergy—Office. I. Title.

FRIST, Elizabeth (Ferran) 253.2
No wings in the manse; life and laughter under the preacher's roof. Text illustrated by Jane Frist. [Westwood, N. J.] Revell [c1956] 159p. illus. 22cm. Autobiographical. [BV4395.F7] 56-5236
1. Clergymen's wives. I. Title.

GARRIGOU-LAGRANGE, Reginald, Father, 1877- 253.2
The priesthood and perfection. Translated by E. Hayden. Westminster, Md., Newman Press, 1955. 208p. 22cm. [BX2350.5.G355] 55-7046
1. Perfection—Catholic authors. 2. Clergy—Religions life. I. Title.

GOERGEN, Donald. 253'.2
The sexual celibate / Donald Goergen. New York : Seabury Press, [1975] c1974. vi, 266 p. ; 22 cm. "A Crossroad book." Includes index. Bibliography: p. 249-262. [BV4390.G59 1975] 74-30103 ISBN 0-8164-0268-X : 8.95
1. Celibacy. I. Title.

GORRES, Ida Friederike (Coudenhove) 1901- 253.2
Is celibacy outdated? Tr. [from German] by Barbara Waldstein-Wartenberg in collaboration with the author. Westminster, Md., Newman [c.1965] 95p. 18cm. [BV4390.G613] 65-29811 .95 pap.,
1. Celibacy. I. Title.

GRABNER-HAIDER, Anton. 253'.2
Letters to a young priest from a laicized priest / Anton Grabner-Haider. St. Meinrad, IN : Abbey Press, 1975. 63 p. ; 21 cm. (A Priority edition) Translation of An einen jungen Priester. [BX1912.G6813] 75-19922 ISBN 0-87029-052-5 : 1.50
1. Catholic Church—Clergy. I. Title.

GREELEY, Andrew M., 1928- 253'.2
Priests in the United States; reflections on a survey [by] Andrew M. Greeley. [1st ed.] Garden City, N.Y., Doubleday, 1972. 213 p. 22 cm. Includes bibliographical references. [BX1912.G744] 75-175378 5.95
1. Catholic Church—Clergy. 2. Clergy—U.S. I. Title.

GREY, J. D., 1906- 253'.2
Epitaphs for eager preachers [by] J. D. Grey. Nashville, Broadman Press [1972] 126 p. 21 cm. [BV4011.G73] 72-79167 ISBN 0-8054-7904-X
1. Pastoral theology. I. Title.

GUERRETTE, Richard H. 253'.2
A new identity for the priest; toward an ecumenical ministry, by Richard H. Guerrette. Paramus, N.J., Paulist Press [1973] v, 100 p. 21 cm. Includes bibliographical references. [BX1912.G83] 72-95651 ISBN 0-8091-1764-9 2.95
1. Catholic Church—Clergy. 2. Pastoral theology—Catholic Church. I. Title.

HALL, Ennen Reaves. 253.2
One saint and seven sinners. New York, Crowell [1959] 243 p. 21 cm. [BV4396.H3] 58-14308
1. Clergymen's families. I. Title.

HARKX, Peter. 253'.2
The Fathers on celibacy. [Translated by Religious Book Consultants] De Pere, Wis., St. Norbert Abbey Press, 1968. 91 p. 17 cm. On spine: 1. Includes bibliographical references. [BV4390.H35] 69-20287 ISBN 0-8316-1050-6
1. Celibacy—History. I. Title.

HEBERT, Albert J., 1913- 253'.2
Priestly celibacy—recurrent battle and lasting values, by Albert J. Hebert. Houston, Tex., Lumen Christi Press [1971] 198 p. 23 cm. Includes bibliographical references. [BV4390.H38] 72-29763 6.00
1. Catholic Church—Clergy. 2. Celibacy. I. Title.

HEDLEY, George Percy, 1899- 253.2
The minister behind the scenes. New York, Macmillan, 1956. xii, 147p. 21cm. (The James A. Gray lectures at Duke University, 1955) [GV4010.H413] 56-7305
1. Theology, Pastoral. I. Title. II. Series.

HERMAND, Pierre 253.2
The priest: celibate or married. Helicon, [dist. New York, Taplinger] 1966[c.1965] 144p. 20cm. Bibl. [BV4390.H413] 65-28350 3.75 bds.,
1. Celibacy. I. Title.

HEWITT, Emily C. 253'.2
Women priests: yes or no? [By] Emily C. Hewitt [and] Suzanne R. Hiatt. New York, Seabury Press [1973] 128 p. 21 cm. Bibliography: p. 126-128. [BV676.H48] 72-81027 ISBN 0-8164-2076-9 2.95
1. Ordination of women—Protestant Episcopal Church. I. Hiatt, Suzanne R., joint author. II. Title.

HEYER, Robert J. 253'.2
Women and orders, edited by Robert J. Heyer. New York, Paulist Press [1974] xi, 104 p. 19 cm. (Deus books) Includes bibliographical references. [BV676.H5] 74-80262 ISBN 0-8091-1841-6 1.65 (pbk.).
1. Ordination of women. I. Title.

HICKMAN, Martha. 253'.2
How to marry a minister. [1st ed.] Philadelphia, Lippincott [1968] 191 p. 21 cm. [BV4395.H5] 68-29730 3.95
1. Clergymen's wives. I. Title.

HUGHES, John Jay. 253.2
Man for others; reflections on Christian priesthood. Huntington, Ind., Our Sunday Visitor [1971] 111 p. 21 cm. [BV660.2.H78 1971] 71-154291 1.95
1. Clergy—Office. 2. Vocation. I. Title.

HULME, William Edward, 1920- 253.2
Your pastor's problems; a guide for ministers and laymen. Minneapolis, Minn., Augsburg [1967,c.1966] 165p. 22cm. Bibl. [BV660.2.H8] 66-12249 1.95 pap.,
1. Clergy—Psychology. I. Title.

HULME, William Edward, 1920- 253.2
Your pastor's problems; a guide for ministers and laymen, by William E. Hulme. [1st ed.] Garden City, N. Y., Doubleday, 1966. 165 p. 22 cm. Bibliographical references included in "Notes" (p. [163]-165) [BV660.2.H8] 66-12249
1. Clergy—Psychology. I. Title.

JENNINGS, Ray. 253'.2
Rev. Ms. Evelyn Morgan Jones, I love you : letters to a woman in ministry, addressed to a representative of the emerging breed of women in ministry by a middle-aged male minister / Ray Jennings. Valley Forge, Pa. : Judson Press, [1975] 64 p. ; 22 cm. Includes bibliographical references. [BV676.J46] 75-9959 ISBN 0-8170-0672-9 pbk. : 2.95
1. Women ministers. I. Title.

JOHNSON, H. Eugene. 253'.2
Duly and scripturally qualified : a study of the ministry of the Christian Church movement / by H. Eugene Johnson. Cincinnati : New Life Books, [1975] 176 p. ; 22 cm. Includes bibliographical references. [BX7326.J63] 75-12445 ISBN 0-87239-054-3 pbk. : 3.95
1. Pastoral theology—Christian Church (Disciples of Christ) 2. Pastoral theology—Churches of Christ. I. Title.

JUD, Gerald John. 253'.2
Ex-pastors; why men leave the parish ministry [by] Gerald J. Jud, Edgar W. Mills, Jr. [and] Genevieve Walters Burch. Philadelphia, Pilgrim Press [1970] xiii, 191 p. 23 cm. Bibliography: p. 187-191. [BV672.5.J8] 75-106558 3.45
1. Ex-clergy. I. Mills, Edgar W., 1928- joint author. II. Burch, Genevieve Walters, joint author.

JURY, Paul, 1878-1953 253.2
Journal of a psychoanalyst-priest. Tr. [from French] by Albert R. Teichner. New York, Lyle Stuart [1965, c.1935, 1956] 158p. 21cm. [BX1765.2.J853] 64-13874 4.00 bds.,
I. Title.

KASSIEPE, Max, 1867-1948. 253.2
Priestly beatitudes, retreat sermons; translated by A. Simon. St. Louis, Herder, 1952. 393 p. 22 cm. [BX1912.K233] 52-10358
1. Clergy—Religious life. 2. Catholic Church—Sermons. 3. Sermons, German—Translations into English. 4. Sermons, English—Translations from German. I. Title.

KLOPPENBURG, Boaventura, 1919- 253'.2
The priest: living instrument and minister of Christ, the eternal priest, by Bonaventure Kloppenburg. Translated by Matthew J. O'Connell. Chicago, Franciscan Herald Press [1974] xiv, 233 p. 21 cm. Translation of O ser do padre. [BX1912.K54913] 73-23059 ISBN 0-8199-0495-3 5.95
1. Catholic Church—Clergy. 2. Pastoral theology—Catholic Church. I. Title.

LAVENDER, Lucille. 253'.2
They cry, too! : What you always wanted to know about your minister but didn't know whom to ask / Lucille Lavender. New York : Hawthorn Books, c1976. 152 p. ; 22 cm. Includes bibliographical references. [BV660.2.L34 1976] 75-20905 ISBN 0-8015-7594-X : 6.95
1. Clergy. I. Title.

LEA, Henry Charles, 1825-1909. 253.2
History of sacerdotal celibacy in the Christian Church. [New Hyde Park, N.Y.] University Books [1966] xvii, 611 p. 24 cm. First published in 1867 under title: An historical sketch of sacerdotal celibacy in the Christian church. [BV4390.L4] 66-19723
1. Celibacy. 2. Catholic Church — Clergy. I. Title.

LEA, Henry Charles, 1825-1909 253.2
History of sacerdotal celibacy in the Christian Church [4th ed., rev.] [New Hyde Park, N.Y.] University Bks. [c.1966] xvii, 611p. 24cm. First pub. in 1867 under title: An historical sketch of sacerdotal celibacy in the Christian church. [BV4390.L4 1966] 66-19723 10.00 bds.,
1. Celibacy. 2. Catholic Church—Clergy. I. Title.

LECUYER, Joseph. 253.2
What is a priest? Translated from the French by Lancelot C. Sheppard. [1st American ed.] New York, Hawthorn Books [1959] 125p. 22cm. (The Twentieth century encyclopedia of Catholicism, v. 53. Section 5: The life of faith) Translation of Pretres du Christ. [BX2240.L383] 59-6730
1. Ordination— Catholic Church. 2. Clergy—Office. I. Title.

LEIFFER, Murray Howard, 1902- 253'.2
Changing expectations and ethics in the professional ministry; a research report on the attitudes of ministers in five Protestant denominations [by] Murray H. Leiffer. Evanston, Ill., Garrett Theological Seminary; [distributed by Bureau of Social and Religious Research, 1969] 189 p. forms. 23 cm. Project of the Bureau of Social and Religious Research, Garrett Theological Seminary. [BR517.L4] 75-17257 2.00
1. Clergy—U.S.—Statistics. 2. Protestant churches—U.S. I. Garrett Theological Seminary. Bureau of Social and Religious Research. II. Title.

LOBSENZ, NORMAN M 1919- 253.2
The minister's complete guide to successful retirement. Great Neck, N. Y., Channel Press [1955] 192p. illus. 21cm. [BV4382.L6] 56-56
1. Clergy— Retirement. I. Title.

LOBSENZ, Norman. 253.2
The minister's complete guide to successful retirement. Great Neck, N. Y., Channel Press [1955] 192p. illus. 21cm. [BV4382.L6] 56-56
1. Clergy—Retirement. I. Title.

LOVASIK, Lawrence George, 1913- ed. 253.2
Priestly holiness, according to the spirit of Jesus Christ,St. Paul, and Pope Pius XII. [Boston] St. Paul Editions [dist. Daughters of St. Paul, c.1961] 183p. 61-10930 3.00;2.00 pap.,
1. Clergy—Religious life. I. Title.

LOWERY, James L. 253'.2
Peers, tents, and owls; some solutions to problems of the clergy today, by James L. Lowery, Jr. New York, Morehouse-Barlow Co. [1973] 155 p. 21 cm. Includes bibliographical references. [BV660.2.L68] 73-84090 ISBN 0-8192-1155-9 3.95 (pbk.)
1. Clergy—Office. I. Title.

MCCABE, Herb, 1936- 253'.2 B
Love letters of Herb and Sandy McCabe. St. Louis, Concordia Pub. House [1973] 188 p. 18 cm. [CT275.M29A45 1973] 73-78879 ISBN 0-570-03169-9 0.95 (pbk)
1. McCabe, Herb, 1936- 2. McCabe, Sandy. I. McCabe, Sandy, joint author. II. Title.

MCGOLDRICK, Desmond F. 253'.2
Living the celibate life; an essay in the higher psychology of faith, by Desmond F. McGoldrick. [1st ed.] New York, Vantage Press [1969, c1970] 145 p. 21 cm. Includes bibliographical references. [BV4390.M24] 75-9143 3.95
1. Celibacy. I. Title.

MEER, Haye van der. 253'.2
Women priests in the Catholic Church? A theological-historical investigation. Translated and with a foreword and afterword by Arlene and Leonard Swidler. Foreword by Cynthia C. Wedel. Philadelphia, Temple University Press [1973] xxix, 199 p. 23 cm. Translation of Priestertum der Frau? Originally presented as the author's thesis, Innsbruck, 1962. Bibliography: p. 169-191. [BV676.M4413] 73-79480 ISBN 0-87722-059-X 10.00
1. Women as ministers. I. Title.

MILLER, Althea S. 253'.2
Under the parsonage roof, by Althea S. Miller. Chicago, Moody Press [1969] 96 p. illus. 20 cm. [BV4395.M5] 78-80946 2.50
1. Clergymen's wives. I. Title.

MOFFATT, Gene E 253'.2
The anatomy of the ministry [by] Gene E. Moffatt. Atlanta, Pendulum Books [c1966] 287 p. 20 cm. [BV660.2.M57] 66-23720
1. Clergy. I. Title.

MOFFATT, Gene E. 253'2
The anatomy of the ministry [by] Gene E. Moffatt. Atlanta, Pendulum Bks. [c.1966] 287p. 20cm. [BV660.2.M57] 66-23720 2.95 pap.,
1. Clergy. I. Title.
Publisher s address. 123 Simpson St., N. W., Atlanta, Ga. 30313.

MOORE, Jenny, 1923- 253'.2
The people on Second Street. With an introd. by Malcolm Boyd. New York, Morrow, 1968. 218 p. 22 cm. [BV4395.M6 1968] 68-21541
1. Clergymen's wives. 2. City churches. I. Title.

NEUMEYER, Murray W., 1937- 253'.2
Your own steps along the way / Murray W. Neumeyer. New York : United Church Press, c1977. p. cm. [BV660.2.N44] 77-21993 ISBN 0-8298-0334-3 : 5.95
1. Clergy—Office. 2. Theology, Practical. I. Title.

NORDLAND, Frances. 253'.2
The unprivate life of a pastor's wife. Chicago, Moody Press [1972] 176 p. 22 cm. Includes bibliographical references. [BV4395.N67] 72-77945 ISBN 0-8024-9041-7 3.95
1. Clergymen's wives. I. Title.

NYBERG, Kathleen Neill. 253.2
The care and feeding of ministers. New York, Abingdon Press [1961] 141p. 19cm. [BV4395.N9] 61-7629
1. Clergyman's wives. 2. Theology, Pastoral. I. Title.

OATES, Wayne Edward, 1917- 253'.2
Before you marry them : a premarital guidebook for pastors / Wayne E. Oates and Wade Rowatt. Nashville : Broadman Press, c1975. 137 p. ; 20 cm. Original ed. published in 1958 under title: Premarital pastoral care and counseling. Bibliography: p. 121-129. [HQ10.O18 1975] 74-80340 ISBN 0-8054-2408-3 : 4.50
1. Marriage counseling. 2. Pastoral counseling. I. Rowatt, Wade, joint author. II. Title.

O'BRIEN, John Anthony, 1893- 253'.2
Why priests leave; the intimate stories of twelve who did, edited by John A. O'Brien.

[1st ed.] New York, Hawthorn Books [1969] 200 p. 24 cm. [BX4669.O26] 70-79078 5.95
1. Ex-priests, Catholic—Personal narratives. I. Title.

ODEN, Marilyn Brown. 253.2
The minister's wife: person or position? Nashville, Abingdon Press [1966] 111 p. 20 cm. Bibliography: p. 109-111. [BV4395.O3] 66-14999
1. Clergymen's wives. I. Title.

ODEN, Marilyn Brown 253.2
The minister's wife: person or position? Nashville, Abingdon [c.1966] 111p. 20cm. Bibl. [BV4395.O3] 66-14999 2.50 bds.,
1. Clergymen's wives. I. Title.

OLDHAM, Pauline E. 253.2
The parsonage family and you. Anderson, Ind., Warner [dist. Gospel Trumpet, c.1962] 80p. 21cm. 62-16349 2.50
1. Clergymen's families. I. Title.

O'NEALL, Freda Schwartz. 253.2
The better half of the ministry. Boston, Christopher Pub. House [c1963] 83 p. 21 cm. [BV4395.O6] 63-20779
1. Clergymen's wives. I. Title.

O'NEALL, Freda Schwartz 253.2
The better half of the ministry. Boston, Christopher Pub. [c.1963] 83p. 21cm. 63-20779 2.75
1. Clergymen's wives. I. Title.

O'NEILL, David P. 253.2
Priestly celibacy and maturity. New York, Sheed [1965] 182p. 22cm. Bibl. [BV4390.O5] 65-24691 3.95
1. Celibacy. I. Title.

THE Ordination of 253'.2
women—pro and con / edited by Michael P. Hamilton and Nancy S. Montgomery. New York : Morehouse-Barlow Co., [1975] xi, 212 p. ; 22 cm. Includes bibliographical references. [BV676.O73] 76-350554 ISBN 0-8192-1203-2 pbk. : 4.95
1. Ordination of women—Addresses, essays, lectures. I. Hamilton, Michael Pollock, 1927- II. Montgomery, Nancy S.

PARROTT, Lora Lee 253.2
(Montgomery) 1923-
How to be a preacher's wife and like it. Introd. by Mrs. Billy Graham. Grand Rapids, Zondervan Pub. House [1956] 120p. 21cm. [BV4395.P36] 56-1479
1. Clergymen's wives. I. Title.

PENTECOST, Dorothy 253.2
Harrison.
The pastor's wife and the church. Chicago, Moody Press [1964] 316 p. 21 cm. [BV4395.P4] 63-23169
1. Clergymen's wives. I. Title.

PFFIEGLER, Michael, 1891- 253.2
Priestly existence. Translated from the German by Francis P. Dinneen. Westminster, Md., Newman Press, 1957. 425p. 22cm. [BX1912.P463] 56-11422
1. Clergy—Religious life. 2. Catholic Church—Clergy. I. Title.

PROCTOR, Priscilla, 1945- 253'.2
Women in the pulpit : is God an equal opportunity employer? / Priscilla and William Proctor. 1st ed. Garden City, N.Y. : Doubleday, 1976. 176 p. ; 22 cm. [BV676.P77] 75-14838 ISBN 0-385-00916-X : 6.95
1. Women clergy. I. Proctor, William, joint author. II. Title.

QUINLEY, Harold E. 253'.2
The prophetic clergy: social activism among Protestant ministers [by] Harold E. Quinley. New York, Wiley [1974] ix, 369 p. illus. 24 cm. "A Wiley-Interscience publication." Includes bibliographical references. [BR517.Q56] 74-5175 ISBN 0-471-70265-X
1. Protestant churches—United States—Clergy. 2. Church and social problems—United States. I. Title.

RENDTORFF, Heinrich, 1888- 253.2
The pastor's personal life. Translated from the German by Walter G. Tillmanns. Minneapolis, Augsburg Pub. House [1959] 68p. 20cm. Translation of Das personlliche Leben des evangelischen Botschafters. [BV4011.6.R413] 59-11763
1. Clergy—Religious life. I. Title.

RIPLEY, Francis J. 253.2
A priest for ever. Westminster, Md., Newman Press [c.1960] 233p. 21cm. 61-8960 3.95
1. Clergy—Religious life. I. Title.

RIPLEY, Francis J. 253.2
Priest of Christ. With a foreword by Cardinal Godfrey, Archbishop of Westminster. Westminster, Md., Newman Press [1959, i.e., 1960] viii, 198p. 23cm. (bibl.: p.196) 60-16075 3.95
1. Clergy—Religious life. I. Title.

RIPLEY, Francis Joseph, 253.2
1912-
A priest for ever. Westminster, Md., Newman Press [c1960] 233p. 22cm. [BX1912.5.R48] 61-8960
1. Clergy—Religious life. I. Title.

RIPLEY, Francis Joseph, 253.2
1912-
A priest for ever. Westminster, Md., Newman Press [c1960] 233 p. 22 cm. [BX1912.5.R48] 61-8960
1. Clergy — Religious life. I. Title.

RIPLEY, Francis Joseph, 253.2
1912-
Priest of Christ. With a foreword by Cardinal Godfrey, Archbishop of Westminster. Westminster, Md., Newman Press [c1959] 198 p. 23 cm. Includes bibliography. [BX1912.5.R5] 60-16075
1. Clergy — Religious life. I. Title.

ROY, Lucien, 1913- comp. 253'.2
Step beyond impasse; chronicle of the Dutch Church, Amsterdam, October 27, 1968 - March 2, 1969, edited by Lucien Roy [and] Forrest Ingram. [Translators: Harry Fleddermann and others] New York, Newman Press, 1969. 247 p. 20 cm. [BV4390.R68] 76-92627 3.95
1. Celibacy. 2. Catholic Church in the Netherlands. I. Ingram, Forrest L., joint comp. II. Title.

RUTLER, George William. 253'.2
Priest and priestess. Ambler, Pa., Trinity Press [1973] xi, 99 p. 22 cm. Includes bibliographical references. [BV676.R87] 73-75334 ISBN 0-912046-09-0
1. Ordination of women—Church of England. I. Title.

ST. CLAIR, Robert James. 253.2
Neurotics in the church. [Westwood, N.J.] Revell [1963] 251 p. 21 cm. [BV4011.S3] 63-13360
1. Pastoral psychology. 2. Pastoral theology—Anecdotes, facetiae, satire, etc. I. Title.

ST. CLAIR, Robert James 253.2
Neurotics in the church. [Westwood, N.J.] Revell [c.1963] 251p. 21cm. Bibl. 63-13360 4.50 bds.,
1. Pastoral psychology. 2. Pastoral theology—Anecdotes, facetiae, satire, etc. I. Title.

SCHILLEBEECKX, Edward 253'.2
Cornelis Florentius Alfons, 1914-
Celibacy, by E. Schillebeeckx. Translated by C. A. L. Jarrott. New York, Sheed and Ward [1968] 142 p. 21 cm. Translation of Het ambts-celibaat in de branding. Bibliographical footnotes. [BV4390.S313] 68-13845 3.95
1. Catholic Church—Clergy. 2. Celibacy. I. Title.

SHEEN, Fulton John, Bp., 253'.2
1895-
Those mysterious priests [by] Fulton J. Sheen. [1st ed.] Garden City, N.Y., Doubleday, 1974. 333 p. 22 cm. Includes bibliographical references. [BX1912.S493] 74-1508 ISBN 0-385-08102-2 7.95
1. Priests. I. Title.

SHRADER, Wesley. 253'.2
Anguished men of God. [1st ed.] New York, Harper & Row [1970] xii, 145 p. 22 cm. [BV660.2.S53 1970] 75-109060 4.95
1. Clergy. 2. Christianity—20th century. I. Title.

SMITH, Donald P., 1922- 253'.2
Clergy in the cross fire: coping with role conflicts in the ministry, by Donald P. Smith. Philadelphia, Westminster Press [1973] 232 p. 24 cm. Bibliography: p. [223]-232. [BV660.2.S623] 72-8009 ISBN 0-664-20964-5 7.50
1. Clergy—Office. I. Title.

SMITH, William Martin, 253.2
1916-
For the support of the ministry; a history of ministerial support, relief, and pensions among Disciples of Christ. Indianapolis, Pension Fund of Disciples of Christ [c1956] 240p. 22cm. Includes bibliography. [BX7326.S6] 56-13387
1. Disciples of Christ—Clergy—Salaries, pensions, etc. 2. Disciples of Christ. Pension Fund of Disciples of Christ. I. Title.

SOUTHARD, Samuel. 253'.2
Comprehensive pastoral care / by Samuel Southard. Valley Forge, Pa. : Judson Press, [1975] p. cm. Includes bibliographical references. [BV4011.S59] 74-22518 ISBN 0-8170-0655-9 pbk. : 3.50 with cassette : 9.95
1. Pastoral theology. 2. Laity. 3. Church management. 4. Christian leadership. I. Title.

SPARKS, James Allen, 1933- 253'.2
Potshots at the preacher / James Allen Sparks. Nashville : Abingdon, c1977. 128 p. ; 19 cm. Bibliography: p. 126-128. [BV4011.S6] 76-30753 ISBN 0-687-33240-0 pbk. : 4.95
1. Pastoral theology. 2. Clergy—Psychology. 3. Church controversies. I. Title.

SPICQ, Ceslaus, 1901- 253.2
The mystery of godliness; translated by Jex Martin. Chicago, Fides Publishers Association [1954] 183p. 21cm. Translation of Spiritualite sacerdotale d'apre's Saint Paul. [BX1912.S682] 54-10355
1. Clergy—Religious life. I. Title.

STARK, Phyllis. 253.2
I chose a parson; illustrated by Vito Giallo. New York, Oxford University Press, 1956. 240p. illus. 21cm. [BV4395.S74] 56-9430
1. Clergymen's wives. I. Title.

STARK, Phyllis. 253.2
I chose a parson; illustrated by Vito Giallo. New York, Oxford University Press, 1956. 240 p. illus. 21 cm. [BV4395.S74] 56-9430
1. Clergymen's wives. I. Title.

STEWART, Charles William. 253'.2
Person and profession; career development in the ministry. Nashville, Abingdon Press [1974] 172 p. 21 cm. Includes bibliographical references. [BV660.2.S75] 74-11334 ISBN 0-687-30779-1
1. Clergy—Office. I. Title.

SYMPOSIUM on Clerical 253'.2
Celibacy, University of Notre Dame, 1967.
Celibacy: the necessary option. Edited by George H. Frein. [New York] Herder and Herder [1968] 176 p. 22 cm. Papers which were presented at the symposium held Sept. 6-8, 1967 at the University of Notre Dame and sponsored by the National Association for Pastoral Renewal. Bibliographical footnotes. [BV4390.S9 1967] 68-20404
1. Catholic Church—Clergy. 2. Celibacy. I. Frein, George H., ed. II. National Association for Pastoral Renewal. III. Title.

TARTRE, Raymond A. 253.2
The postconciliar priest; comments on some aspects of theDecree on the ministry and life of priests [by] Raymond A. Tartre. New York, Kenedy [1966] viii, 172p. 22cm. Includes tr. of the Decree taken from The documents of Vatican II. Bibl. [BX830 1962.A45D467] 66-25142 3.95
1. Vatican Council. 2d, 1962-1965. Decretum de presbyterorum ministerio et vita. I. Vatican Council. 2d, 1962-1965. Decree on the ministry and life of priests. II. Title. III. Title: Decree on the ministry and life of priests.

TAYLOR, Alice, 1909- 253'.2
How to be a minister's wife and love it; life in a goldfish bowl. Foreword by Helen Smith Shoemaker. Grand Rapids, Zondervan Pub. House [1968] 118 p. 21 cm. [BV4395.T3] 68-12956
1. Clergymen's wives. I. Title.

TRUMAN, Ruth, 1931- 253'.2
Underground manual for ministers' wives. Nashville, Abingdon Press [1974] 173 p. 21 cm. [BV4395.T7] 73-23060 ISBN 0-687-42796-7 4.95
1. Clergymen's wives. I. Title.

VERDESI, Elizabeth Howell, 253'.2
1922-
In but still out : women in the church / Elizabeth Howell Verdesi. Philadelphia : Westminster Press, c1976. 218 p. : ill. ; 19 cm. Based on the author's thesis, Columbia University and Union Theological Seminary, New York, 1975. Bibliography: p. [209]-218. [BV4415.V45 1976] 75-34365 ISBN 0-664-24788-1 pbk. : 3.95
1. Women in church work—Presbyterian Church. I. Title.

VON HILDEBRAND, Dietrich, 253'.2
1889-
Celibacy and the crisis of faith. [Translated into English by John Crosby. Chicago] Franciscan Herald Press [1971] lv, 116 p. 22 cm. Translation of Zolibat und Glaubenskrise. Includes bibliographical references. [BV4390.V613] 72-155851 ISBN 0-8199-0428-7 4.95
1. Catholic Church—Clergy. 2. Celibacy. I. Title.

WALKER, Daniel D 253.2
The human problems of the minister. New York, Harper [1960] 203 p. 22 cm. Includes bibliography. [BV4011.W3] 60-8134
I. Title.

WALKER, Daniel D. 253.2
The human problems of the minister. New York, Harper [c.1960] xiv, 203p. 22cm. (bibl. notes: p.197-198) 60-8134 3.95 half cloth,
1. Pastoral theology. I. Title.

WAYWARD shepherds: 253'.2
prejudice and the Protestant clergy [by] Rodney Stark [and others. 1st ed.] New York, Harper & Row [1971] x, 138 p. 24 cm. (Patterns of American prejudice series, v. 6) Includes bibliographical references. [BX5965.W38] 76-144187 ISBN 0-06-013973-0 6.95
1. Protestant churches—Clergy. 2. Antisemitism—United States. I. Stark, Rodney. II. Title. III. Series.

WENGER, Elwyn D 253.2
The pastor as husband, father, clergyman, by E. D. Wenger. Long Prairie, Minn., Green Lake Books [1965] 93 p. 20 cm. [BV4396.W45] 66-456
1. Clergy — Office. 2. Clergymen's families. I. Title.

WENGER, Elwyn D. 253.2
The pastor as husband, father, clergyman. Long Prairie, Minn., 56347. Green Lake Bks. Box 389 [c.1965] 93p. 20cm. [BV4396.W45] 66-456 2.00 pap.,
1. Clergy—Office. 2. Clergymen's families. I. Title.

WHITLOCK, Glenn E. 253'.2
From call to service; the making of a minister, by Glenn E. Whitlock. Philadelphia, Westminster Press [1968] 122 p. 21 cm. Bibliography: p. [119]-122. [BV664.W48] 68-11214
1. Clergy—Appointment, call, and election. I. Title.

WILLARD, Frances 253'.2
Elizabeth, 1839-1898.
Woman in the pulpit / by Frances E. Willard. Washington : Zenger Pub. Co., 1975, c1889. p. cm. Reprint of the ed. published by the Woman's Temperance Publication Association, Chicago. [BV676.W5 1975] 75-34240 ISBN 0-89201-014-2 : 11.95
1. Women clergy. I. Title.

WILLIAMS, Cicely. 253.2
Bishop's wife, but still myself. [1st American ed.] Garden City, N.Y., Doubleday, 1961. 259 p. 22 cm. Autobiographical. [BV4395.W48 1961a] 61-9569
1. Clergymen's wives. I. Title.

WILLIAMS, Cicely 253.2
Bishop's wife, but still myself. Garden City, N. Y., Doubleday [c.]1961. 259p. 61-9569 3.95
1. Clergymen's wives. I. Title.

WOOD, Miriam. 253'.2
Two hands, no wings. Washington, Review and Herald Pub. Association [1968] 192 p. illus. 22 cm. [BX6193.W64A3] 68-26904
1. Clergymen's wives. I. Title.

WUERL, Donald W. 253'.2
The priesthood : the Catholic concept today / by Donald W. Wuerl. Chicago : Franciscan Herald Press, c1976. 192 p. ; 21 cm. Bibliography: p. 167-192. [BX1912.W83] 75-33171 ISBN 0-8199-0591-7 : 6.95
1. Catholic Church—Clergy. 2. Priesthood—History of doctrines. I. Title.

KENNEDY, Eugene C. 253'.2'019
The Loyola psychological study of the ministry and life of the American priest [by] Eugene C. Kennedy and Victor J. Heckler. [Washington, National Conference of Catholic Bishops] 1971. vi, 342 p. forms. 29 cm. Bibliography: p. 335-342. [BX1912.K35] 76-28180
1. Catholic Church—Clergy—Psychology. I. Heckler, Victor J., 1942- joint author. II. Title.

BODDIE, Charles 253'.2'0922 B
Emerson.
God's "bad boys." Valley Forge [Pa.] Judson Press [1972] 125 p. ports. 23 cm. [BR563.N4B64] 72-75360 ISBN 0-8170-0534-X 4.95
1. Negro clergy—United States—Biography. I. Title.

THE Hills beyond 253'.2'0922 B
the hills; "400 years in the ministry" [by] Paul F. Swarthout [and others] Lakemont, N.Y., North Country Books [1971] 327 p. illus. 24 cm. Autobiographical accounts by eight Christian ministers. [BR1700.2.H53] 79-32293 6.75
1. Clergy—Correspondence, reminiscences, etc. I. Swarthout, Paul Franklin.

NELSON, Martha. 253'.2'0922
On being a deacon's wife. Nashville, Broadman Press [1973] 96 p. 21 cm. Includes bibliographical references. [BV4527.N382] 72-96150 ISBN 0-8054-3505-0 2.95
1. Wives—Religious life. 2. Deacons. I. Title.

CROPLEY, Ruve. 253'.2'0924 B
Forty "odd" years in a manse. [Granville, Australia, Printed by Ambassador Press, 1962]

100 p. illus. 23 cm. [BX9225.C763A3] 73-172017
1. Cropley, Ruve. I. Title.

DAVIS, Almond H. 253'.2'0924 B
The female preacher; or, Memoir of Salome Lincoln, by Almond H. Davis. New York, Arno Press, 1972 [c1843] viii, 162 p. 20 cm. (American women: images and realities) [BR1725.M68D38 1972] 72-2599 ISBN 0-405-04489-5 7.00
1. Mowry, Salome Lincoln, 1807-1841. I. Title. II. Series.

LONGO, Joan. 253'.2'0924 B
I married a priest. New York, Grosset & Dunlap [1969] 242 p. 22 cm. [BX4705.L717L6] 70-75324 5.95
1. Longo, Gabriel Anthony, 1926- 2. Ex-priests, Catholic—Personal narratives. I. Title.

VARKER, Philip J 253.20924 (B)
The Lord will provide, by Philip J. Varker. Illustrated by Robert L. Varker. [New Brunswick? N.J., 1965] 170 p. 23 cm. Autobiographical [BX8495.V34A3] 65-27994
I. Title.

VARKER, Philip J. 253.20924
The Lord will provide. Illus. by Robert L. Varker [Highland Park, N.J., Author, 228 Donlsn, c.1965] 170p. 23cm. Autobiographical. [BX8495.V34A3] 65-27994 1.95 pap.,
I. Title.

MCMURRY, Mildred (Dodson) 253.2'924
Letters from Mother [ed. by] Billie McMurry Emmons. Nashville, Broadman [1967] 128p. 21cm. [CT275.M44415A4] 67-17427 2.95 bds.,
I. Emmons, Billie McMurray, ed. II. Title.

*ADAMS, Jay E. 253.5
The Christian counselor's casebook, by Jay E. Adams. Grand Rapids, Baker Book House, [1974]. ix, 213 p. 22 cm. A workbook designed for individual or class use in conjunction with competent to counsel and the Christian counselor's manual. [BV4012.2] 74-81707 ISBN 0-8010-0075-0. 3.50 (pbk.).
1. Pastoral counselling. I. Title.

*ADAMS, Jay E. 253.5
The use of the Scriptures in counseling, [by] Jay E. Adams. Grand Rapids, Baker Book House, [1975] vii, 105 p. 18 cm. (Direction books) Includes bibliographical references. [BV4012.2] ISBN 0-8010-0099-8 1.50 (pbk.)
1. Pastoral counseling. I. Title.

*ADAMS, Jay E. 253.5
Your place in the counseling revolution, [by] Jay E. Adams. Grand Rapids, Baker Book House, [1975] vii, 62 p. 18 cm. (Direction books) [BV4012.2] ISBN 0-8010-0100-5 0.95 (pbk.)
1. Pastoral counseling. I. Title.

ALCOHOLICS are God's 253.5
children, too; a guide to understanding for the clergyman. Co-authors: O. T. Binkley [and others. Raleigh, 195-] 50p. 20cm. [HV5175.N6] [HV5175.N6] 258 57-63175 57-63175
1. Alcoholism and religion. I. North Carolina. Alcoholic Rehabilitation Program. II. Binkley, Olin Trivette, 1908-

ALDRICH, Clarence Knight, 1914- 253.5
A pastoral counseling casebook, by C. Knight Aldrich and Carl Nighswonger. Philadelphia, Westminster Press [1968] 224 p. illus. 21 cm. Bibliography: p. 215-220. [BV4012.2.A4] 68-24677 5.95
1. Pastoral counseling. I. Nighswonger, Carl, joint author. II. Title.

ASHBROOK, James B., 1925- 253.5
Responding to human pain / by James B. Ashbrook. Valley Forge, Pa. : Judson Press, [1975] p. cm. [BJ1409.A83] 75-12190 ISBN 0-8170-0677-X : 10.00
1. Includes bibliographical references. 2. Pain. 3. Suffering. I. Title.

BACHMANN, C. Charles 253.5
Ministering to the grief sufferer. Philadelphia, Fortress [1967, c.1964] 144p. 21cm. (Successful pastoral counseling ser.) Bibl. 1.50 pap.,
1. Joy and sorrow. 2. Pastoral psychology. 3. Funeral service. I. Title. II. Title: The grief sufferer.

BACHMANN, C. Charles 253.5
Ministering to the grief sufferer. Englewood Cliffs, N. J., Prentice [c.1964] 144p. 21cm. (Successful pastoral counseling ser.) Bibl. 64-14539 2.95 bds.,
1. Joy and sorrow. 2. Pastoral psychology. 3. Funeral service. I. Title. II. Title: The grief sufferer III. Series.

BAILEY, Robert W. 253'.5
The minister and grief / Robert W. Bailey. New York : Hawthorn Books, c1976. viii, 114 p. ; 22 cm. Includes bibliographical references. [BT825.B26 1976] 75-39351 ISBN 0-8015-5074-2 : 5.95
1. Death. 2. Funeral service. 3. Grief. I. Title.

BARLOW, T. Ed, 1931- 253.5
Small group ministry in the contemporary church, by T. Ed Barlow. [Independence, Mo., Herald Pub. House, 1972] 190 p. 20 cm. Bibliography: p. 187-190. [BV652.2.B37] 72-90357 ISBN 0-8309-0080-2
1. Church group work. I. Title.

BECKER, Russell J. 253.5
Family pastoral care. Philadelphia, Fortress [1968,c.1965] 144p. illus. 21cm. (Successful pastoral counseling ser.) Bibl. [BV4438.B4] 1.50 pap.,
1. Church work with families. 2. Pastoral counseling. I. Title. II. Series.

BECKER, Russell J 253.5
Family pastoral care [by] Russell J. Becker. Englewood Cliffs, N.J., Prentice-Hall [1965] 144 p. illus. 21 cm. (Successful pastoral counseling series) Bibliography: p. 137-142. [BV4438.B4] 65-22197
1. Church work with families. 2. Pastoral counseling. I. Title. II. Series.

BECKER, Russell J. 253.5
Family pastoral care. Englewood Cliffs, N. J., Prentice [c.1965] 144p. illus. 21cm. (Successful pastoral counseling ser.) Bibl. [BV4438.B4] 65-22197 2.95 bds.,
1. Church work with families. 2. Pastoral counseling. I. Title. II. Series.

BELL, Walter Presley. 253.5
The case for pastoral clinical training. Boston, Christopher Pub. House [1967] 147 p. 21 cm. Bibliography: p. 143-146. [BV4012.B382] 66-28033
1. Council for the Clinical Training of Theological Students. 2. Pastoral psychology. I. Title.

BIBLICAL and psychological 253.5
perspectives for Christian counselors. Robert K. Bower, editor. [Contributions by] Kenneth B. Mulholland [and others. South Pasadena, Calif.] Publishers Services [1974] x, 310 p. illus. 23 cm. "Each presentation is based on a doctoral dissertation conducted by the respective author while in residence at the Fuller Theological Seminary." Includes bibliographical references. [BV4012.B45] 74-12239 ISBN 0-87808-951-9 5.45 (pbk. text ed.)
1. Pastoral psychology. 2. Pastoral counseling. I. Bower, Robert K., ed. II. Mulholland, Kenneth B.

BLEES, Robert A. 253.5
Counseling with teen-agers [by] Rob ert A. Blees and staff of First Community Church, Columbus, Ohio. Englewood Cliffs, N. J., Prentice-Hall [1965] 144 p. 21 cm. (Successful pastoral counseling series) [BV4447.B63] 65-21973
1. Church work with youth. 2. Pastoral counseling. I. Columbus, Ohio. First Community Church. II. Title. III. Series.

BLEES, Robert A. 253.5
Counseling with teen-agers [by] Robert A. Blees and staff of First Community Church, Columbus, Ohio. Englewood Cliffs, N.J., Prentice-Hall [1965] 144 p. 21 cm. (Successful pastoral counseling series) [BV4447.B63] 65-21973
1. Church work with youth. 2. Pastoral counseling. I. Columbus, Ohio. First Community Church. II. Title. III. Series.

BLEIDORN, Eugene F. 253.5
Help me, Father; a technique of spiritual direction. Milwaukee, Bruce Pub. Co. [c.1960] 134p. Bibl. 60-15476 3.00
1. Spiritual direction. I. Title.

BONNELL, John Sutherland, 1893- 253.5
No escape form life. [1st ed.] New York, Harper [1958] 215p. 22cm. [BV4012.2.B6] [BV4012.2.B6] 258 57-12933 57-12933
1. Pastoral counselling. I. Title.

BOVET, Theodore, 1900- 253.5
The road to salvation; a handbook on the Christian care of persons, by Theodor Bovet. Translated by F. A. Baker. [1st ed. in the U. S. A.] Garden City, N. Y., Doubleday, 1964. xiv, 249 p. 22 cm. Translation of Lebendige Seelsorge. Bibliography: p. 235-242. [BV4011.B613 1964a] 64-20575
1. Pastoral theology. I. Title.

BRAND, Ralph A., 1924- 253.5
Simplified techniques of counseling; an aid to improving the counseling efficiency of pastors, teachers, and Christian workers, by Ralph A. Brand. Little Rock, Ark., Baptist Publications Committee [1972] 132 p. 21 cm. Bibliography: p. 130-132. [BF637.C6B68] 72-83959
1. Counseling. 2. Pastoral counseling. I. Title.

BRANDT, Henry R. 253.5
Christians have troubles, too; a psychologist finds the answers in the Bible [by] Henry R. Brandt & Homer E. Dowdy. Old Tappan, N.J., Revell [1968] 127 p. 22 cm. [BV4012.2.B7] 68-28436 3.50
1. Pastoral counseling. I. Dowdy, Homer E., joint author. II. Title.

BRILLENBURG WURTH, Gerrit. 253.5
Christian counseling in the light of modern psychology. [Translation by H. de Jongste] Philadelphia, Presbyterian and Reformed Pub. Co., 1962. 307p. 22cm. [BV4012.B853] 61-16942
1. Pastoral psychology. 2. Pastoral theology. I. Title.

BRISTER, C W 253.5
Pastoral care in the church [by] C. W. Brister. [1st ed.] New York, Harper & Row [1964] xxiv, 262 p. 22 cm. Includes bibliographical references. [BV4011.B7] 64-19497
1. Pastoral theology — Baptists. I. Title.

BRISTER, C. W. 253.5
Pastoral care in the church. New York, Harper [c.1964] xxiv, 262p. 22cm. Bibl. 64-19497 5.00
1. Pastoral theology—Baptists. I. Title.

BROWN, J. Paul. 253.5
Counseling with senior citizens [by] J. Paul Brown, Philadelphia, Fortress [1968,c.1964] 144p. 21cm. (Successful pastoral counseling ser.) Bibl. [BV4435.B7] 1.50 pap.,
1. Church work with the aged. 2. Pastoral counseling. I. Title.

BROWN, J Paul 253.5
Counseling with senior citizens [by] J. Paul Brown. Englewood Cliffs, N. J., Prentice-Hall [1964] 144 p. 21 cm. (Successful pastoral counseling series) Bibliography: p. 127-138. [BV4435.B7] 64-15217
1. Church work with the aged. 2. Pastoral counseling. I. Title. II. Series.

BROWN, J. Paul 253.5
Counseling with senior citizens. Englewood Cliffs, N. J., Prentice [c.1964] 144p. 21cm. (Successful pastoral counseling ser.) Bibl. 64-15217 2.95 bds.,
1. Church work with the aged. 2. Pastoral counseling. I. Title. II. Series.

BROWN, Stanley C. 253.5
Folly or power? : Encounter groups in the church / Stanley C. Brown and Robert H. Deits. New York : Hawthorn Books, [1975] 160 p. ; 22 cm. Bibliography: p. 155-160. [BV652.2.B7 1975] 74-22919 ISBN 0-8015-2732-5 : 5.95
1. Church group work. 2. Group relations training. I. Deits, Robert H., joint author. II. Title.

BROWN, Stanley C. 253.5
God's plan for marriage / by Stanley C. Brown. Philadelphia : Westminster Press, c1977. p. cm. [BV835.B74] 77-6674 ISBN 0-664-24758-X pbk. : 4.95
1. Marriage. I. Title.

BRUDER, Ernest E. 253.5
Ministering to deeply troubled people. Philadelphia, Fortress [1967, c.1964] 144p. 21cm. (Successful pastoral counseling ser.) Bibl. 1.50 pap.,
1. Church work with the mentally ill. 2. Pastoral psychology. I. Title. II. Series.

BRUDER, Ernest E 253.5
Ministering to deeply troubled people. Englewood Cliffs, N.J., Prentice-Hall [c1963] 144 p. 21 cm. (Successful pastoral counseling series) Bibliography: p. 135-142. [BV4012.B88] 63-18120
1. Church work with the mentally ill. 2. Pastoral psychology. I. Title. II. Series.

BRUDER, Ernest E. 253.5
Ministering to deeply troubled people. Englewood Cliffs, N.J., Prentice [c.1963] 144p. 21cm. (Successful pastoral counseling ser.) Bibl. 63-18120 2.95
1. Church work with the mentally ill. 2. Pastoral psychology. I. Title. II. Series.

BUTTRY, Lucas Wayne. 253.5
The calling program of the local church. Butler, Ind., Higley Press [c1956] 96p. 20cm. [BV652.B85] 57-21733
1. Church work. I. Title.

CARE for the dying : 253.5
resources of theology / edited with an introd. by Richard N. Soulen. Atlanta : John Knox Press, [1975] x, 141 p. ; 22 cm. Includes bibliographical references. [BV4012.2.C28] 74-19968 ISBN 0-8042-1098-5 pbk. : 4.95
1. Pastoral counseling—Addresses, essays, lectures. 2. Death—Addresses, essays, lectures. I. Soulen, Richard N., 1933-

CARRINGTON, William Langley. 253.5
Psychology, religion, and human need; a guide for ministers, doctors, teachers, and social workers. Great Neck, N. Y., Channel Press [1957] 315p. illus. 21cm. [BV4012.C32] 258 57-12036
1. Pastoral psychology. I. Title.

CAVANAGH, John R 1904- 253.5
Fundamental pastoral counseling; technic and psychology. Milwaukee, Bruce Pub. Co. [1962] 326p. 24cm. Includes bibliography. [BV4012.2.C3] 62-10437
1. Pastoral counseling. I. Title.

CHRISTENSEN, James L 253.5
The pastor's counseling handbook. [Westwood, N.J.] Revell [1963] 181 p. 22 cm. [BV4012.2.C5] 63-10394
1. Pastoral counseling. I. Title.

CHRISTENSEN, James L. 253.5
The pastor's counseling handbook. [Westwood, N. J.] Revell [c.1963] 181p. 22cm. 63-10394 3.95 bds.,
1. Pastoral counseling. I. Title.

CLINEBELL, Charlotte H. 253.5
Counseling for liberation / Charlotte Holt Clinebell. Philadelphia : Fortress Press, c1976. viii, 88 p. ; 22 cm. (Creative pastoral care and counseling series) Bibliography: p. 84-88. [BV4012.2.C52] 75-36447 ISBN 0-8006-0555-1 pbk. : 2.95
1. Pastoral counseling. 2. Pastoral psychology. I. Title.

CLINEBELL, Howard John, 1922- 253.5
Basic types of pastoral counseling [by] Howard Clinebell, Jr. Nashville, Abingdon [1966] 318p. 24cm.) Bibl. [BV4012.2.C53] 66-21187 6.00
1. Pastoral counseling. I. Title.

CLINEBELL, Howard, John, 1922- 253.5
Mental health through Christian community; the local church's ministry of growth and healing [by] Howard J. Clinebell, Jr. New York, Abingdon Press [1965] 300 p. 24 cm. "Reading by chapters": p. 285-289. Bibliographical footnotes. [BV4012.C56] 65-15230
1. Pastoral psychology. 2. Mental hygiene. I. Title.

CLINEBELL, Howard John, 1922- 253.5
Mental health through Christian community; the local church's ministry of growth and healing. Nashville, Abingdon [c.1965] 300p. 24cm. Bibl. [BV4012.C56] 65-15230 4.75
1. Pastoral psychology. 2. Mental hygiene. I. Title.

COBB, John B. 253.5
Theology and pastoral care / John B. Cobb, Jr. Philadelphia : Fortress Press, c1977. xii, 79 p. ; 22 cm. (Creative pastoral care and counseling series) Bibliography: p. 77-79. [BV4012.2.C55] 76-7862 ISBN 0-8006-0557-8 pbk. : 2.95
1. Pastoral counseling. 2. Pastoral theology. I. Title.

COLLINS, Gary R. 253.5
Man in motion; the psychology of human motivation [by] Gary R. Collins. [1st ed.] Carol Stream, Ill., Creation House [1973] 167 p. illus. 22 cm. (Psychology for church leaders series) Bibliography: p. 155-161. [BR110.C624] 72-94832 2.95
1. Christianity—Psychology. 2. Motivation (Psychology) I. Title.

COLSTON, Lowell G. 253.5
Judgment in pastoral counseling [by] Lowell G. Colston. Nashville, Abingdon Press [1969] 207 p. 23 cm. Bibliographical footnotes. [BV4012.2.C57] 77-84717 4.50
1. Pastoral counseling. 2. Judgment. I. Title.

CONLEY, Thomas H. 253.5
Pastoral care for personal growth / by Tom Conley. Valley Forge, Pa. : Judson Press, [1977] p. cm. Includes bibliographical references. [BV4012.C64] 77-79776 ISBN 0-8170-0754-7 pbk. : 3.50
1. Pastoral psychology. 2. Church group work. I. Title.

CRABB, Lawrence J. 253.5
Basic principles of Biblical counseling / Lawrence J. Crabb, Jr. Grand Rapids : Zondervan Pub. House, c1975. 111 p. ; 23 cm. [BR110.C75] 75-6186 4.95
1. Christianity—Psychology. 2. Counseling. 3. Man (Theology) I. Title.

CRABB, Lawrence J. 253.5
Effective biblical counseling / Lawrence J.

Crabb, Jr. Grand Rapids : Zondervan Pub. House, c1977. 191 p. : ill. ; 23 cm. [BR110.C76] 77-2146 6.95
1. Christianity—Psychology. 2. Counseling. I. Title.

CRANE, William E. 253.5
Where God comes in; the divine "plus" in counseling [by] William E. Crane. Waco, Tex., Word Books [1970] 147 p. 23 cm. Bibliography: p. 145-147. [BV4012.2.C7 1970] 79-111959 3.95
1. Pastoral counseling. I. Title.

CRYER, Newman S., ed. 253.5
Casebook in pastoral counseling, ed. by Newman S. Cryer, Jr., John Monroe Vayhinger. Nashville, Abingdon [c.1952-1962] 320p. 62-8105 4.95
1. Pastoral counseling. I. Vayhinger, John Monroe, joint ed. II. Title.

CURRAN, Charles Arthur. 253.5
Counseling in Catholic life and education. Pref. by Eugene Cardinal Tisserant, foreword by Michael J. Ready. New York, Macmillan [1952] 462 p. 22 cm. [BF637.C6C8] 258 52-8584
1. Counseling. 2. Theology, Pastoral—Catholic Church. I. Title.

CURRAN, Charles Arthur. 253.5
Religious values in counseling and psychotherapy, by Charles A. Curran. New York, Sheed and Ward [1969] viii, 398 p. illus. 22 cm. Includes bibliographical references. [BV4012.2.C85] 69-16992 7.50
1. Pastoral counseling. I. Title.

DEATH and ministry : 253.5
pastoral care of the dying and the bereaved / J. Donald Bane ... [et al.] editors. New York : Seabury Press, [1975] p. cm. "A Crossroad book." [BV4330.D4] 75-14134 ISBN 0-8164-0260-4 : 13.95
1. Death—Addresses, essays, lectures. 2. Bereavement—Addresses, essays, lectures. 3. Pastoral medicine—Addresses, essays, lectures. I. Bane, J. Donald.

DENTON, Wallace 253.5
The minister's wife as a counselor. Philadelphia, Westminster [1966, c.1965] 172p. 21cm. Bibl. [BV4012.2.D45] 66-10704 3.95
1. Pastoral counseling. 2. Clergymen's wives. I. Title.

DICKS, Russell Leslie 253.5
Toward health and wholeness. New York, Macmillan, [c.]1960. x, 158p. 22cm. 60-11812 3.50
1. Mental healing. I. Title.

DICKS, Russell Leslie, 253.5
1906-
Principles and practices of pastoral care. Englewood Cliffs, N.J., Prentice-Hall [1963] 143 p. 21 cm. [Successful pastoral counseling series] [BV4012.2D55] 63-8623
1. Pastoral counseling. I. Title.

DOTY, William Lodewick, 253.5
1919-
Encountering Christian crises [by] William L. Doty. Liguori, Mo., Liguori Publications [1973] 224 p. 18 cm. [BV4012.2.D67] 73-88240 2.00
1. Pastroral counseling—Case studies. I. Title.

DOTY, William Lodewick, 253.5
1919-
Encountering Christian crises [by] William L. Doty. Liguori, Mo., Liguori Publications [1973] 224 p. 18 cm. [BV4012.2.D67] 73-88240 2.00 (pbk.)
1. Pastroral counseling—Case studies. I. Title.

DRAKEFORD, John W. 253.5
Counseling for church leaders. Nashville, Broadman [c.1961] 150p. Bibl. 61-12412 2.95
1. Pastoral counseling. I. Title.

DRAKEFORD, John W. 253.5
Integrity therapy [by] John W. Drakeford. Nashville, Broadman Press [1967] 153 p. illus. 21 cm. "Notes" (bibliographical): p. 149-153. [RC480.5.D7] 67-19396
1. Psychotherapy. 2. Guilt. I. Title.

DRAPER, Edgar, 1926- 253.5
Psychiatry and pastoral care. Philadelphia, Fortress [1967, c.1965] 138p. 21cm. (Successful pastoral counseling ser.) Bibl. [BV4012.D7] 65-23861 1.50 pap.,
1. Pastoral psychology. 2. Pastoral counseling. I. Title. II. Series.

DRAPER, Edgar, 1926- 253.5
Psychiatry and pastoral care. Englewood Cliffs, N.J., Prentice [1966] 138p. 21cm. (Successful pastoral counseling ser.) Bibl. [BV4012.D7] 65-23861 2.95 pap.,
1. Pastoral psychology. 2. Pastoral counseling. I. Title. II. Series.

DUCKER, E. N. 253.5
A Christian therapy for a neurotic world. Foreword by Frank Lake. London, Allen & Unwin [Mystic, Conn., Verry, 1964, c.1961] 225p. illus. 23cm. Bibl. 62-32733 4.50
1. Pastoral psychology. I. Title.

DUCKER, E. N. 253.5
A Christian therapy for a neurotic world. Foreword by Frank Lake. Introd. to the Amer. ed. by Charles Di Salvo. New York, Taplinger [1963, c.1961] 225p. 22cm. Bibl. 62-8355 4.95
1. Pastoral counseling. 2. Psychiatry and religion. I. Title.

DUCKER, E. N. 253.5
Psychotherapy: a Christian approach. Foreword by E. Graham Howe. London, Allen & Unwin [dist. New York, Hillary, 1965, c.1964] 126p. 23cm. [BV4012.2.D83] 64-6109 4.00 bds.,
1. Pastoral counseling. 2. Psychiatry and religion. I. Title.

EDMONSON, George. 253.5
Me, you, and God; group experiments for Christians. Waco, Tex., Word Books [1973] 158 p. 23 cm. [BV652.2.E35] 73-76254 4.95
1. Church group work. I. Title.

FABER, Heije, 1907- 253.5
The art of pastoral conversation [by] Heije Faber and Ebel van der Schoot. [Translation by Abingdon Press] New York, Abingdon Press [1965] Arnhem, Van Loghum Slaterus, 1961. 223 p. 21 cm. 126 p. 21 cm. (The Church in a changing society, 1) Translation of Het pastorale gesprek. Bibliographical footnotes. [BV4012.2.F313] [BV4012.F3] 65-21977 63-44900
1. Pastoral counseling. 2. Pastoral psychology — Study and teaching. 3. Clergy — U.S. I. Schoot, Ebel van der, joint author. II. Faber, Heije, 1907- III. Title. IV. Title: Pastoral care and clinical training in America; V. Series.

FABER, Heije, 1907- 253.5
The art of pastoral conversation [by] Heije Faber, Ebel van der Schoot. Nashville, Abingdon [c.1965] 223p. 21cm. Bibl. [BV4012.2.F313] 65-21977 3.75
1. Pastoral counseling. I. Schoot, Ebel van der, joint author. II. Title.

FAGAL, William A 253.5
Pastor, this is my problem. Mountain View, Calif., Pacific Press Pub. Association [1963] 144 p. 23 cm. [BV4612.F3] 63-10645
1. Questions and answers — Christian life. 2. Casuistry. I. Title.

FAGAL, William A. 253.5
Pastor. this is my problem. Mountain View, Calif., Pac. Pr. Pub. [c.1963] 144p. 23cm. 63-10645 3.75 bds.,
1. Questions and answers—Christian life. 2. Casuistry. I. Title.

FAITH is the answer; 253.5
a pastor and a psychiatrist discuss your problems [by] Norman Vincent Peale [and] Smiley Blanton. [Enl. and rev. ed.] Carmel, N. Y., Guideposts Associates [1955] 280 p. 22 cm. In the 1940 ed. Blanton's name appeared first on the title page. [BV4012.B53 1955] [BV4012.B53 1955] 258 55-4168 55-4168
1. Psychology, Pastoral. I. Blanton, Smiley, 1882- II. Peale, Norman Vincent, 1898-

FAITH is the answer; 253.5
a pastor and a psychiatrist discuss your problems [by] Norman Vincent Peale [and] Smiley Blanton. [Enl. and rev. ed.] Englewood Cliffs, N. J., Prentice-Hall [1955] 280 p. 21 cm. In the 1940 ed. Blanton's name appeared first on the title page. [BV4012.B53 1955a] [BV4012.B53 1955a] 258 56-5645 56-5645
1. Psychology, Pastoral. I. Blanton, Smiley, 1882- II. Peale, Norman Vincent, 1898-

FEUCHT, Oscar E 253.5
Ministry to families; a handbook for Christian congregations. St. Louis, Concordia Pub. House [1963] 94 p. illus. 20 cm. [BV4438.F4] 63-2691
1. Church work with families. 2. Family—Religious life. I. Title.

FRELLICK, Francis I. 253.5
Helping youth in conflict. Philadelphia, Fortress [1968,c.1965] 144p. 21cm. (Successful pastoral counseling ser.) Bibl. [BV4464.5.F7] 1.50 pap.,
1. Church work with juvenile delinquents. I. Title. II. Series.

FRELLICK, Francis I. 253.5
Helping youth in conflict. Englewood Cliffs, N. J., Prentice [1966] 144p. 21cm. (Successful pastoral counseling ser.) Bibl. [BV4464.5.F7] 65-11884 2.95 pap.,
1. Church work with juvenile delinquents. I. Title. II. Series.

GODIN, Andre. 253.5
The pastor as counselor. Translated by Bernard Phillips. [1st ed.] New York, Holt, Rinehart and Winston [1965] vi, 182 p. 22 cm. Translation of La relation humaine dans le dialogue pastoral. "Notes and bibliography": p. [145]-182. [BV4012.2.G613] 65-15056
1. Pastoral counseling. I. Title.

GODIN, Andre. 253.5
The priest as counselor. Tr. by Bernard Phillips. Techny, Ill., Divine Word [1968, c.1965. 182p. 22cm. Tr. of La relation humaine dans le dialogue pastoral. Orig: pub. by Holt undertitle "The pastor as counselor. Notes & Bibl. [BV4012.2.G613] 1.85 pap.,
1. Pastoral counseling. I. Title.

GOLDBRUNNER, Josef. 253.5
Holiness is wholeness, and other essays. Notre Dame, Ind., University of Notre Dame Press, 1964. 101 p. 18 cm. (Notre Dame pocket library, PL-5) Translation of Helligkeit und Gesundheit. [BX2350.G643] 64-23667
1. Christian life — Catholic authors. 2. Pastoral psychology. I. Title.

GOLDBRUNNER, Josef 253.5
Holiness is wholeness, and other essays [Tr. from German. Notre Dame, Ind.] Univ. of Notre Dame Pr. [c.]1964. 101p. 18cm. (Notre Dame pocket lib., PL-5) [BX2350.G643] 64-23667 .95 pap.,
1. Christian life—Catholic authors. 2. Pastoral psychology. I. Title.

GOLDBRUNNER, Josef 253.5
Realization; anthropology of pastoral care. Tr. by Paul C. Bailey, Elisabeth Reinecke. [Notre Dame, Ind.] Univ. of Notre Dame Pr., 1966. ix, 221p. 24cm. (Liturgical studies, v.9) Bibl. [BV4012.G5513] 66-14629 6.00 bds.,
1. Pastoral psychology. I. Title. II. Series: Nortre Dame, Ind., University, Liturgical studies, v. 9

GORDON, Ernest. 253.5
Meet me at the door. [1st ed.] New York, Harper & Row [1969] 154 p. 22 cm. [BV1610.G6] 71-85044 4.95
1. Church work with students. 2. Chaplains, University and college. I. Title.

HAGMAIER, George. 253.5
Counselling the Catholic; modern techniques and emtional conflicts [by] George Hagmaier and Robert W. Gleason. New York, Sheed & Ward [1959] 301p. 22cm. [BV4012.2.H3] 59-12094
1. Pastoral counseling. I. Gleason, Robert W., joint author. II. Title.

HAMILTON, James D., 1926- 253.5
The ministry of pastoral counseling [by] James D. Hamilton. Grand Rapids, Baker Book House [1972] 126 p. 19 cm. (Source books for ministers) Includes bibliographical references. [BV4012.2.H33 1972] 73-152922 ISBN 0-8010-4069-8 1.95 (pbk.)
1. Pastoral counseling. I. Title.

HARRIS, Thomas Allen, 1919- 253.5
Counseling the serviceman and his family [by] Thomas A. Harris. Englewood Cliffs, N.J., Prentice-Hall [1964] 144 p. 21 cm. (Successful pastoral counseling series) Bibliography: p. 137-138. [BV4457.H3] 64-20749
1. Church work with military personnel. 2. Pastoral counseling. I. Title. II. Series.

HARRIS, Thomas Allen, 1919- 253.5
Counseling the serviceman and his family [by] Thomas A. Harris. Englewood Cliffs, N.J., Prentice [1964] 144p. 21cm. (Sucessful pastoral counseling ser.) Bibl. [BV4457.H3] 64-20749 1.50 pap.,
1. Church work with military personnel. 2. Pastoral counseling. I. Title. II. Series.

HATFIELD, Louis Duane. 253.5
As the twig is bent; therapeutic values in the use of drama and the dramatic in the church. [1st ed.] New York, Vantage Press [1965] 166 p. 22 cm. Includes bibliographical references. [BV1534.4.H3] 65-4363
1. Religious drama — Hist. & crit. 2. Psychodrama. I. Title.

HATFIELD, Louis Duane 253.5
As the twig is bent; therapeutic values in the use of drama and the dramatic in the church. New York, Vantage [c.1965] 166p. Bibl. [BV1534.4.H3] 65-4363 2.95
1. Religious drama—Hist. & crit. 2. Psychodrama. I. Title.

HAUCK, Paul A. 253.5
Reason in pastoral counseling, by Paul A. Hauck. Philadelphia, Westminster Press [1972] 236 p. 22 cm. Bibliography: p. [231]-233. [BV4012.2.H37] 72-76436 ISBN 0-664-20945-9 5.95
1. Pastoral counseling. 2. Pastoral psychology. I. Title.

HILTNER, Seward, 1909- 253.5
The Christian shepherd; some aspects of pastoral care. New York, Abingdon Press [1959] 190p. 21cm. [BV4012.2.H48] 59-7246
1. Pastoral counseling. I. Title.

HILTNER, Seward, 1909- 253.5
The context of pastoral counseling [by] Seward Hiltner and Lowell G. Colston. New York, Abingdon Press [1961] 272p. 24cm. Includes bibliography. [BV4012.2.H49] 61-13193
1. Pastoral counseling. I. Colston, Lowell G., joint author. II. Title.

HOFMANN, Hans, 1923- ed. 253.5
The ministry and mental health. New York, Association Press [1960] 251p. 26cm. Includes bibliographies. [BV4012.3.H6] 60-13142
1. Church work with the mentally ill. 2. Pastoral psychology. I. Title.

HOFMANN, Hans, 1923- 253.5
Religion and mental health; a casebook with commentary, and An essay on pertinent literature. [1st ed.] New York, Harper [1961] 333p. 22cm. Includes bibliography. [BV4012.H63] 61-5262
1. Pastroal psychology. 2. Psychotherapy—Cases, clinical reports, statistics. I. Title.

HOFMANN, Hans F. 1923- ed. 253.5
The ministry and mental health. New York Association Press [1960] 251 p. 26 cm. Includes bibliographies. [BV4012.3.H6] 60-13142
1. Church work with the mentally ill. 2. Pastoral psychology. I. Title.

HOFMANN, Hans F., 1923- 253.5
Religion and mental health a casebook with commentary, and An essay on pertinent literature. [1st ed.] New York Harper [1961] 333 p. 22 cm. Includes bibliography. [BV4012.H63] 61-5262
1. Pastoral psychology. 2. Psychotherapy — Cases, clinical reports, statistics. I. Title.

HOFMANN, Hans [Fritz] 1923- 253.5
ed.
The ministry and mental health. New York, Association Press [c.1960] 251p. 26cm. Bibl. 60-13142 5.00 bds.,
1. Church work with the mentally ill. 2. Pastoral psychology. I. Title.

HOFMANN, Hans Fritz, 1923- 253.5
Religion and mental health; a casebook with commentary, and An essay on pertinent literature. New York, Harper [c.1961] 333p. Bibl. 61-5262 5.00
1. Pastoral psychology. 2. Psychotherapy—Cases, clinical reports, statistics. I. Title.

HOSTIE, Raymond, 1920- 253.5
Pastoral counseling, Tr. by Gilbert Barth. New York, Sheed [1966] xii, 243p. 22cm. First pub. in 1963 under title: L'entretien pastoral. Bibl. [BV4012.2H5713] 66-12275 5.00
1. Pastoral counseling. I. Title.

HOWE, Reuel L. 1905- 253.5
The miracle of dialogue. Greenwich, Conn., Seabury Press, 1963. 154 p. 22 cm. [BV4012.2.H6] 62-17080
1. Discussion. 2. Pastoral counseling. I. Title.

HOWE, Reuel L., 1905- 253.5
The miracle of dialogue. Greenwich, Conn., Seabury Press, 1963. 154 p. 22 cm. [BV4012.2.H6] 62-17080
1. Discussion. 2. Pastoral counseling. I. Title.

HUDSON, Robert Lofton. 253.5
Sir, I have a problem. New York, Crowell [1959] 148p. 21cm. [BV4012.2.H77] 59-7757
1. Pastoral counseling. 2. Questions and answers—Theology. I. Title.

HULME, William Edward. 253.5
How to start counseling; building the counseling program in the local church. New York, Abingdon Press [1955] 157p. 21cm. Includes bibliography. [BV4012.H83] 55-5735
1. Counseling. 2. Psychology, Pastoral. I. Title.

HULME, William Edward, 253.5
1920-
Counseling and theology. Philadelphia, Fortress [1967, c.1956] 249p. 18cm. [BV4012.2.H8] 1.95 pap.,
1. Pastoral counseling. I. Title.

HULME, William Edward, 253.5
1920-
Counseling and theology. Philadelphia, Muhlenberg Press [1956] 249p. 22cm. [BV4012.H827] 258 56-5643
1. Psychology, Pastoral. 2. Counseling. I. Title.

HULME, William Edward, 253.5
1920-
Pastoral care come of age [by] William E. Hulme. Nashville, Abingdon Press [1970] 175 p. 23 cm. Includes bibliographical references. [BV4012.2.H827] 79-109680 4.50

1. Pastoral counseling. 2. Pastoral theology. I. Title.

HULME, William Edward, 1920- 253.5
The pastoral care of families, its theology and practice. Nashville, Abingdon [c.1962] 208p. Bibl. 61-11784 3.50
1. Pastoral counseling. 2. Pastoral theology. I. Title.

IRWIN, Paul B. 253.5
The care and counseling of youth in the Church / Paul B. Irwin. Philadelphia : Fortress Press, c1975. xv, 80 p. ; 22 cm. (Creative pastoral care and counseling series) Bibliography: p. 77-80. [BV4447.I7] 74-26334 ISBN 0-8006-0552-7 pbk. : 2.95
1. Church work with youth. I. Title.

JACKSON, Edgar Newman. 253.5
Group counseling; dynamic possibilities of small groups [by] Edgar N. Jackson. Philadelphia, Pilgrim Press [1969] ix, 129 p. 21 cm. Bibliography: p. 128-129. [BV652.2.J3] 73-91167 2.95
1. Church group work. I. Title.

JACKSON, Edgar Newman. 253.5
Parish counseling / by Edgar N. Jackson. New York : J. Aronson, c1975. xviii, 221 p. ; 24 cm. Includes index. Bibliography p. [212]-[216] [BV4012.2.J3] 75-29698 ISBN 0-87668-222-0 : 10.00
1. Pastoral counseling. I. Title.

JACKSON, Edgar Newman. 253.5
The pastor and his people; a psychology for parish work. Introd. by James A. Knight. Manhasset, N.Y., Channel Press [c1963] 224 p. 21 cm. [BV4012.J25] 62-18046
1. Pastorial psychology. I. Title.

JOHNSON, Paul Emanuel, 1898- 253.5
Person and counselor [by] Paul E. Johnson. Nashville, Abingdon Press [1967] 208 p. 21 cm. Bibliographical footnotes. [BV4012.2.J6] 67-11710
1. Pastoral counseling. I. Title.

KEMP, Charles F. 253.5
Counseling with college students. Philadelphia, Fortress [1967, c.1964] 143p. 20cm. (Successful pastoral counseling ser.) [BV1610.K4] 1.50 pap.,
1. Church work with students. 2. Pastoral counseling. I. Title.

KEMP, Charles F. 1912- 253.5
Counseling with college students [by] Charles F. Kemp. Englewood Cliffs, N. J., Prentice-Hall [1964] 143 p. 21 cm. (Successful pastoral counseling series) Bibliographical references included in "Notes" (p. 131-134) Bibliography: p. 135-138. [BV1610.K4] 64-23561
1. Church work with students. 2. Pastoral counseling. I. Title. II. Series. III. Series

KEMP, Charles F., 1912- 253.5
Counseling with college students. Englewood Cliffs, N. J., Prentice [c.1964] 143p. 21cm. (Successful pastoral counseling ser.) Bibl. 64-23561 2.95 bds.,
1. Church work with students. 2. Pastoral counseling. I. Title. II. Series.

KEMP, Charles F 1912- 253.5
The pastor and vocational counseling. St. Louis, Bethany Press [1961] 190p. 21cm. Includes bibliography. [BV4012.2.K44] 61-8602
1. Pastoral counseling. 2. Vocational guidance. I. Title.

KLINK, Thomas W. 253.5
Depth perspectives in pastoral work [by] Thomas W. Klink. Englewood Cliffs. N. J., Prentice Hall [1965] 144 p. 21 cm. (Successful pastoral counseling series) Bibliographical footnotes. [BV4012.2K5] 65-22190
1. Pastoral counseling. I. Title. II. Series.

KLINK, Thomas W. 253.5
Depth perspectives in pastoral work. Englewood Cliffs, N.J., Prentice [c.1965] 144p. 21cm. (Successful counseling ser.) Bibl. [BV4012.2.K5] 65-22190 2.95 bds.,
1. Pastoral counseling. I. Title. II. Series.

KNIGHTS, Ward A., 1927- 253.5
My church was a mental hospital, by Ward A. Knights, Jr. Philadelphia, United Church Press [1974] 125 p. 22 cm. "A Pilgrim Press book." [BV4012.3.K58] 74-12018 ISBN 0-8298-0287-8 5.50
1. Church work with the mentally ill. 2. Pastoral psychology. I. Title.

KNOWLES, Joseph W. 253.5
Group counseling. Philadelphia, Fortress [1967, c.1964] 144p. 20cm. (Successful pastoral counseling ser.) [BV4012.2.K6] 1.50 pap.,
1. Church group work. 2. Group counseling. 3. Pastoral counseling. I. Title.

KNOWLES, Joseph W 253.5
Group counseling. Englewood Cliffs, N. J., Prentice-Hall [1964] 144 p. 21 cm. (Successful pastoral counseling series) [BV4012.2K6] 64-12849
1. Church group work. 2. Group counseling. 3. Pastoral counseling. I. Title. II. Series.

KNOWLES, Joseph W. 253.5
Group counseling. Englewood Cliffs, N.J., Prentice [c.1964] 144p. 21cm. (Successful pastoral counseling ser.) Bibl. 64-12849 2.95
1. Church group work. 2. Group counseling. 3. Pastoral counseling. I. Title. II. Series.

KNUBEL, Frederick R 253.5
Pastoral counseling. Philadelphia, Muhlenberg Press [1952] 102p. 21cm. (The Knubel-Miller Foundation lectures) [BV4012.K58] 53-8945
1. Theology, Pastoral. 2. Psychology, Pastoral. I. Title.

KOCH, Kurt E 253.5
Christian counseling and occultism; the Christian counseling of persons who are psychically vexed or ailing because of involvement in occultism. A practical theological and systematic investigation in consultation with medical and pyschological bordering sciences, by Kurt E. Koch. Translated from the German by Andrew Petter. Grand Rapids, Kregel Publications, 1965. 299 p. 24 cm. Translation of Seeisorge und Okkultismus. Bibliography: p. 293-299. [BF1033.K573 1965] 65-23118
1. Occult sciences. 2. Pastoral psychology. I. Title.

KOCH, Kurt E. 253.5
Christian counseling and occultism; the Christian counseling of persons who are psychically vexed or ailing because of involvement in occultism. A practical theological and systematic investigation in consultation with medical and psychological bordering sciences. Tr. from German by Andrew Petter. Grand Rapids, Mich., Kregel [c.]1965. 299p. 24cm. Bibl. [BF1033.K573] 65-23118 4.95
1. Occult sciences. 2. Pastoral psychology. I. Title.

KOCH, Kurt E. 253.5
Christian counselling and occultism; the counselling of the psychically disturbed and those oppressed through involvement in occultism. A practical, theological and systematic investigation in the light of present day psychological and medical knowledge, by Kurt E. Koch. [21st ed.] Grand Rapids, Kregel Publications, 1972. 338 p. 23 cm. Translation of the 15th ed. of Seelsorge und Okkultismus. Includes bibliographical references. [BR115.P85K613 1972] 73-151940
1. Christianity and psychical research. 2. Christianity and occult sciences. 3. Pastoral psychology. I. Title.

LAPLACE, Jean, S. J. 253.5
The direction of conscience. Translated by John C. Guinness. [New York] Herder and Herder [1967] 192 p. 21 cm. [BV4012.2.L2413] 67-13295
1. Pastoral counseling. 2. Spiritual direction. I. Title.

LAUTERBACH, William Albert, 1903- *253.5
Ministering to the sick. Saint Louis, Concordia Pub. House [1955] 191p. 18cm. [BV4335.L3] 258 55-7576
1. Church work with the sick. I. Title.

LAYCOCK, Samuel Ralph, 1891- 253.5
Pastoral counseling for mental health. [Nashville] Abingdon [c.1958, 1961] 96p. 61-17154 1.00 pap.,
1. Pastoral counseling. I. Title.

LEACH, Max, 1909- 253.5
Christianity and mental health. Dubuque, Iowa. W. C. Brown [1957] 135p. 23cm. [BV4012.L39] 258 57-2298
1. Pastoral psychology. 2. Mental hygiene. I. Title.

MCCANN, Richard Vincent 253.5
The churches and mental health. A report to the staff director, Jack R. Ewalt, New York, Basic [c.]1962. x, 278p. 24cm. (Joint Comm. on Mental Illness and Health. Monograph ser., no. 8) Bibl. 62-11204 6.00
1. Pastoral psychology. I. Title. II. Series.

MCINTOSH, Ian F. 253.5
Pastoral care and pastoral theology, by Ian F. McIntosh. Philadelphia, Westminster Press [1972] 160 p. 21 cm. Includes bibliographical references. [BV4011.M26] 71-169599 ISBN 0-664-20924-6 5.50
1. Pastoral theology. 2. Pastoral counseling. I. Title.

MCLEMORE, Clinton W., 1946- 253.5
Clergyman's psychological handbook; clinical information for pastoral counseling, by Clinton W. McLemore. Grand Rapids, Eerdmans [1974] 146 p. 22 cm. Includes bibliographies. [BV4012.2.M24] 74-2011 ISBN 0-8028-1576-6 2.45 (pbk.).
1. Pastoral counseling. I. Title.

MARTIN, John R., 1928- 253.5
Divorce and remarriage; a perspective for counseling [by] John R. Martin. Scottdale, Pa., Herald Press, 1974. 136 p. port. 23 cm. Originally presented as the author's thesis (Th.M.), Eastern Baptist Theological Seminary, 1972. Bibliography: p. 132-133. [BV835.M25 1974] 73-18038 ISBN 0-8361-1729-8 4.95
1. Marriage. 2. Divorce. 3. Remarriage. 4. Pastoral counseling. I. Title.

MAVES, Paul B ed. 253.5
The church and mental health. New York, Scribner, 1953. 303p. 24cm. Includes bibliography. [BV4012.M36] [BV4012.M36] 258 53-12856 53-12856
1. Psychology, Pastoral. 2. Mental hygiene. I. Title.

MEET Joe Ross. 253.5
New York, Abingdon Press [1957] 159p. 21cm. [BV4012.2.D5] [BV4012.2.D5] 258 57-11008 57-11008
1. Pastoral counseling. I. Dicks, Russell Leslie, 1906-

MICHALSON, Carl. 253.5
Faith for personal crises. New York, Scribner [1958] 184p. 21cm. [BR110.M5] 258 58-5720
1. Christianity— Psychology. I. Title.

MICHALSON, Carl 253.5
Faith for personal crises. Nashville, Abingdon [1967, c.1958] 184p. 21cm. [BR110.M5] 1.45 pap.,
1. Christianity—Psychology. I. Title.

MIDWESTERN Institute of Pastoral Theology. 2d, Sacred Heart Seminary, 1962. 253.5
Pastoral counseling. [Proceedings of the] second annual institute, August 27-30, 1962. Detroit, 1962. 136 p. 22 cm. Sponsored by St. John's Provincial Seminary and Sacred Heart Seminary. Includes bibliographies. [BX1913.A1M5] 62-22108
1. Pastoral theology — Catholic Church — Congresses. 2. Pastoral psychology — Congresses. I. St. John's Provincial Seminary, Plymouth, Mich. II. Detroit. Sacred Heart Seminary. III. Title.

MIDWESTERN Institute of Pastoral Theology. Conference. 2d, Detroit, 1962. 253.5
Pastoral counseling; proceedings. Detroit, Midwestern Institute of Pastoral Theology, Sacred Heart Seminary, 1962. 136 p. 22 cm. Includes bibliographies. [BX1913.A1M5] 62-22108
1. Pastoral theology — Catholic Church — Congresses. 2. Pastoral psychology. I. Title.

MIKESELL, William Henry, 1887- 253.5
Counseling for ministers. Boston, Christopher Pub. House [1961] 190p. 21cm. [BV4012.2.M5] 61-15194
1. Pastoral counseling. I. Title.

THE missionary spirit in parish life. 253.5
Westminster, Md., Newman Press, 1952. 194p. 22cm. [BX2347.M48] 258 52-7997
1. Theology, Pastoral—Catholic Church. 2. Evangelistic work. I. Michonneau, Georges, 1899-

MITCHELL, Kenneth R. 253.5
Hospital chaplain, by Kenneth R. Mitchell. Philadelphia, Westminster Press [1972] 128 p. 21 cm. [BV4335.M58] 72-76438 ISBN 0-664-20946-7
1. Chaplains, Hospital. I. Title.

MORRIS, James Kenneth, 1896- 253.5
Marriage counseling; a manual for ministers [by] J. Kenneth Morris. Englewood Cliffs, N. J., Prentice-Hall [1965] xvii. 329 p. illus. 21 cm. Includes bibliographies. [HQ10.M675] 65-17575
1. Marriage counseling. I. Title.

MORRIS, James Kenneth, 1896- 253.5
Marriage counseling; a manual for ministers. Englewood Cliffs, N.J., Prentice [c.1965] xvii, 329p. illus. 22cm. Bibl. [HQ10.M675] 65-17575 7.95 bds.,
1. Marriage counseling. I. Title.

MORRIS, Paul D. 253.5
Love therapy [by] Paul D. Morris. Wheaton, Ill., Tyndale House Publishers [1974] 167 p. 22 cm. Bibliography: p. 165-167. [BV4501.2.M588] 74-80151 ISBN 0-8423-3860-8 4.95
1. Christian life—1960- 2. Love. 3. Psychotherapy. I. Title.

MOSER, Leslie E 253.5
Counseling: a modern emphasis in religion. Englewood Cliffs, N. J., Prentice-Hall, 1962. 354p. 22cm. Includes bibliography. [BV4012.2.M6] 62-8569
1. Pastoral counselling. 2. Counseling. I. Title.

NARRAMORE, Clyde Maurice, 1916- 253.5
Counseling with youth at church, school, and camp. Grand Rapids, Mich., Zondervan [c.1966] 113p. 21cm. [BV4447.N33] 66-23186 2.95
1. Church work with youth. 2. Pastoral counseling. I. Title.

NARRAMORE, Clyde Maurice, 1916- 253.5
Counseling with youth at church, school, and camp, by Clyde M. Narramore. Grand Rapids, Zondervan Pub. Co. [1966] 113 p. 21 cm. [BV4447.N33] 66-23186
1. Church work with youth. 2. Pastoral counseling. I. Title.

NARRAMORE, Clyde Maurice, 1916- 253.5
The psychology of counseling; professional techniques for pastors, teachers, youth leaders, and all who are engaged in the incomparable art of counseling. Grand Rapids, Zondervan Pub. House [1960] 303 p. 23 cm. Includes bibliography. [BV4012.2.N3] 60-10242
1. Pastoral counseling. 2. Psychology—Dictionaries. I. Title.

NATALE, Samuel. 253.5
Pastoral counselling : reflections and concerns / by Samuel M. Natale, in collaboration with Richard J. Wolff. New York : Paulist Press, c1977. v, 117 p. ; 21 cm. (An Exploration book) Includes bibliographical references. [BV4012.2.N34] 76-57341 ISBN 0-8091-2008-9 pbk. : 3.95
1. Pastoral counseling. I. Wolff, Richard, 1927- joint author. II. Title.

NOUWEN, Henri J. M. 253.5
Intimacy; pastoral psychological essays [by] Henri J. M. Nouwen. Notre Dame, Ind., Fides Publishers [1969] ix, 164 p. 21 cm. Bibliographical footnotes. [BV4012.N63] 79-79241 2.50
1. Pastoral psychology—Addresses, essays, lectures. 2. Pastoral theology—Catholic Church—Addresses, essays, lectures. 3. Intimacy (Psychology)—Addresses, essays, lectures. I. Title.

OATES, Wayne Edward, 1917- ed. 253.5
An introduction to pastoral counseling. Nashville, Broadman Press [1959] 331p. 22cm. [BV4012.2.O22] 59-9688
1. Pastoral counselling. I. Title.

OATES, Wayne Edward, 1917- 253.5
Pastoral care and counseling in grief and separation / Wayne E. Oates. Philadelphia : Fortress Press, c1976. ix, 86 p. ; 22 cm. (Creative pastoral care and counseling series) Bibliography: p. 84-86. [BV4011.O25] 75-13048 ISBN 0-8006-0554-3 pbk. : 2.95
1. Pastoral theology. 2. Pastoral counseling. 3. Bereavement. I. Title.

OATES, Wayne Edward, 1917- 253.5
Pastoral counseling, by Wayne E. Oates. Philadelphia, Westminster Press [1974] 240 p. 22 cm. [BV4012.2.O23] 73-19719 ISBN 0-664-20992-0 7.50
1. Pastoral counseling. I. Title.

OATES, Wayne Edward, 1917- 253.5
Pastoral counseling in social problems: extremism, race, sex, divorce, by Wayne E. Oates. Philadelphia, Westminster [1966] 128p. 21cm. Bibl. [BV4012.O23] 66-15962 1.75
1. Pastoral counseling. 2. Church and social problems. I. Title.

OATES, Wayne Edward, 1917- 253.5
Pastoral counseling in social problems: extremism, race, sex, divorce, by Warren E. Oates. Grand Rapids, Mich., Baker Book House [1974, c1966] 128 p. 20 cm. (Source books for ministers) [BV4012.O23] 66-15962 ISBN 0-8010-6656-5. 2.45 (pbk.)
1. Pastoral counseling. 2. Church and social problems. I. Title.

OATES, Wayne Edward, 1917- 253.5
Protestant pastoral counseling. Philadelphia, Westminster [c.1962] 256p. 21cm. 62-9228 4.50
1. Pastoral counseling. I. Title.

OATES, Wayne Edward, 1917- 253.5
Religious factors in mental illness. New York, Association Press [1955] 239p. 20cm. [BV4012.O24] [BV4012.O24] 258 55-7416 55-7416
1. Psychology, Pastoral. 2. Psychology, Religious. 3. Mental illness. I. Title.

OATES, Wayne Edward, 1917- 253.5
When religion gets sick, by Wayne E. Oates. Philadelphia, Westminster Press [1970] 199 p. 19 cm. [BL53.O334] 76-114727 2.95
1. Psychology, Religious. I. Title.

OATES, Wayne Edward, 1917- 253.5
Where to go for help. Philadelphia, Westminster Press [1957] 118p. 21cm. [HQ10.O2] [HQ10.O2] 258 57-5623 57-5623
1. Counselling. I. Title.

O'BRIEN, Michael J. 253.5
An introduction to pastoral counseling [by] Michael J. O'Brien. Staten Island, N.Y., Alba House [1968] 272 p. 22 cm. (Mental health series, 10) Includes bibliographical references. [BV4012.2.O27] 68-31511 4.95
1. Pastoral counseling. I. Title. II. Title: Pastoral counseling.

ODEN, Thomas C 253.5
Kerygma and counseling; toward a covenant ontology for secular psychotherapy, by Thomas C. Oden. Philadelphia, Westminster Press [1966] 186 p. 21 cm. Bibliographical references included in "Notes" (p. [171]-186) [BV4012.O27] 66-11516
1. Rogers, Carl Ransom, 1902- 2. Barth, Karl, 1886- 3. Pastoral psychology. 4. Psychotherapy. I. Title.

ODEN, Thomas C. 253.5
Kerygma and counseling; toward a covenant ontology for secular psychotherapy. Philadelphia, Westminster [c.1966] 186p. 21cm. Bibl. [BV4012.O27] 66-11516 5.00
1. Rogers, Carl Ransom, 1902- 2. Barth, Karl, 1886- 3. Pastoral psychology. 4. Psychotherapy. I. Title.

O'DOHERTY, Eamonn Feichin, ed. 253.5
The priest and mental health, edited by E. F. O'Doherty [and] S. Desmond McGrath. Staten Island, N.Y., Alba House [1963] xi, 251 p. 22 cm. Papers presented at the first Stillorgan conference held in 1960. Includes bibliographies. [BV4012.O3] 63-14316
1. Pastoral psychology. I. McGrath, Sean Desmond, joint ed. II. Title.

O'DOHERTY, Eamonn Feichin, ed. 253.5
The priest and mental health, ed. by E. F. O'Doherty, S. Desmond McGrath. Staten Island, N.Y., St. Paul Pubns. [dist.] Alba House [c.1963] xi, 251p. 22cm. Bibl. 63-14316 4.95
1. Pastoral psychology. I. McGrath, Sean Desmond, joint ed. II. Title.

OGLESBY, William B. 253.5
Referral in pastoral counseling [by] William B. Oglesby, Jr. Englewood Cliffs, N.J., Prentice-Hall [1968] 139 p. 21 cm. (Successful pastoral counseling series) [BV4012.2.O35] 68-11945
1. Pastoral counseling. I. Title. II. Series.

OLSEN, Peder 253.5
Pastoral care and psychotherapy; a study in cooperation between physician and pastor. Tr. [From Norwegian] by Herman E. Jorgensen. Minneapolis. Augsburg Pub. House [c.1961] 144p. Bibl. 61-6997 3.50
1. Pastoral psychology. 2. Psychotherapy. I. Title.

OUTLER, Albert Cook, 1908- 253.5
Psychotherapy and the Christian message. [1st ed.] New York, Harper [1954] 286p. 22cm. [BV4012.O72] [BV4012.O72] 258 53-10975 53-10975
1. Psychology, Pastoral. 2. Psychotherapy. I. Title.

PASTORAL care in crucial 253.5
human situations. [Edited by] Wayne E. Oates and Andrew D. Lester. Valley Forge [Pa.] Judson Press [1969] 206 p. 23 cm. Includes bibliographical references. [BV4012.P3] 70-81444 6.50
1. Pastoral psychology. 2. Pastoral counseling. I. Oates, Wayne Edward, 1917- ed. II. Lester, Andrew D., ed.

PASTORAL care in health 253.5
facilities : a book of readings / edited by Ward A. Knights, Jr. St. Louis : Catholic Hospital Association, c1977. viii, 114 p. ; 23 cm. Includes bibliographical references. [BV4335.P37] 76-26994 ISBN 0-87125-035-7 pbk. : 6.50
1. Pastoral medicine—Addresses, essays, lectures. I. Knights, Ward A., 1927-

PASTORAL care in the 253'.5
liberal churches. Edited by James Luther Adams and Seward Hiltner. Nashville, Abingdon Press [1970] 256 p. 21 cm. Includes bibliographical references. [BV4012.2.P28] 70-97572 4.75
1. Pastoral counseling—Addresses, essays, lectures. 2. Liberalism (Religion)—Addresses, essays, lectures. I. Adams, James Luther, 1901- ed. II. Hiltner, Seward, 1909- ed.

PASTORAL ministry to 253.5
families. Philadelphia, Westminster Press [1957] 214p. 21cm. Includes bibliography. [BV4320.W9] 258 57-6553
1. Pastoral theology. 2. Family—Religious life. I. Wynn, John Charles.

PASTORAL psychology. 253.5
The minister's consultation clinic; pastoral psychology in action, a selection of questions submitted by ministers to the magazine Pastoral psychology, and answered by a board of psychiatrists, psychologists, social scientists, and clergymen. Edited by Simon Doniger. Great Neck, N. Y., Channel Press [1955] 316p. illus. 21cm. [BV4012.P34] [BV4012.P34] 258 55-4568 55-4568
1. Psychology, Pastoral. I. Doniger, Simon, ed. II. Title.

PASTORAL psychology in 253.5
practice; contributions to a psychology for priests and educators. Translated from the German by Joachim Werner Conway. New York, P. J. Kenedy [1955] 249p. 23cm. [BX1912] [BX1912] 258 55-8364 55-8364
1. Psychology, Pastoral. 2. Theology, Pastoral—Catholic Church. I. Demal, Willibald, 1908-

PEALE, Norman Vincent, 1898- 253.5
The art of real happiness, by Norman Vincent Peale and Smiley Blanton. 2d ed. Englewood Cliffs, N. J., Prentice-Hall [1956] 280p. 21cm. [BV4012.P35 1956] [BV4012.P35 1956] 258 56-9773 56-9773
1. Psychology, Pastoral. I. Blanton, Smiley, 1882- joint author. II. Title.

PROFESSIONAL growth for 253.5
clergymen, through supervised training in marriage counseling and family problems. Edited by Robert C. Leslie & Emily Hartshorne Mudd. Nashville, Abingdon Press [1970] 192 p. 21 cm. "Written by participants in a pilot project called Advanced training for seminary teachers of pastoral care." Sponsored by National Institute of Mental Health and the Marriage Council of Philadelphia. Includes bibliographical references. [BV4165.P74] 72-124755 4.75
1. Clergy—Post-ordination training. 2. Pastoral counseling. I. Leslie, Robert Campbell, 1917- ed. II. Mudd, Emily (Hartshorne) ed. III. U.S. National Institute of Mental Health. IV. Marriage Council of Philadelphia.

PSYCHIATRY and religious 253.5
experience, by Louis Linn and Leo W. Schwarz. New York, Random House [1958] 307p. 22cm. [BV4012.L54] 258 58-9873
1. Pastoral psychology. 2. Psychology, Religious. I. Linn, Louis. II. Schwarz, Leo Walder, 1906- joint author.

PSYCHIATRY, the clergy, and 253.5
pastoral counseling; the St. John's story. Editors: Dana L. Farnsworth [and] Francis J. Braceland. Collegeville, Minn., Institute for Mental Health, St. John's University Press [1969] xviii, 356 p. 24 cm. Adapted from lectures given at the annual seminars of the psychiatric-pastoral workshops conducted by the Institute for Mental Health at St. John's University since 1954. Includes bibliographical references. [BV4012.2.P75] 73-83088 6.50
1. Pastoral counseling. 2. Psychiatry and religion. I. Farnsworth, Dana L., ed. II. Braceland, Francis James, 1900- ed. III. St. John's University, Collegeville, Minn. Institute for Mental Health.

RASSIEUR, Charles L., 1938- 253.5
The problem clergymen don't talk about / by Charles L. Rassieur. Philadelphia : Westminster Press, c1976. 157 p. ; 19 cm. Includes bibliographical references. [BV4012.2.R33] 75-40306 ISBN 0-664-24790-3 pbk. : 3.95
1. Pastoral counseling. 2. Clergy—Sexual behavior. I. Title.

REEVES, Robert B., comp. 253.5
Pastoral care of the dying and the bereaved: selected readings. Edited by Robert B. Reeves, Jr., Robert E. Neale & Austin H. Kutscher for the Foundation of Thanatology. New York, Health Sciences Pub. Corp., 1973. vii, 160 p. illus. 28 cm. (Journal reprint series) Includes bibliographical references. [BT825.R4] 72-75177 ISBN 0-88238-503-8 3.95
1. Death—Collected works. 2. Grief—Collected works. I. Neale, Robert E., joint comp. II. Kutscher, Austin H., joint comp. III. Foundation of Thanatology. IV. Title.

THE Role of the minister in 253.5
caring for the dying patient and the bereaved / edited by Brian O'Connor, Daniel J. Cherico, Austin H. Kutscher, et al. ; with the editorial assistance of Lillian G. Kutscher. New York : MSS Information Corp., [1975] p. cm. (Continuing series on thanatology) [BT732.7.R64] 75-5716 ISBN 0-8422-7279-8 : 13.50
1. Pastoral medicine. 2. Church work with the bereaved. I. O'Connor, Brian. II. Cherico, Daniel J. III. Kutshcer, Austin H.

RUNESTAM, Arvid, 1887- 253.5
Psychoanalysis and Christianity. Translated by Oscar Winfield. Rock Island, Ill., Augustana Press [1958] 194p. 21cm. [BV4012.R84] 258 58-6526
1. Pastoral psychology. 2. Psychoanalysis. I. Title.

SAINT Elizabeths Hospital, Washington, D. C. Chaplain Services Branch. 253.5
A survey of ten years of clinical pastoral training at Saint Elizabeths Hospital, by Ernest E. Bruder and Marian L. Barb. [Washington] 1956. iv, 98p. tables. 28cm. [BV4012.3.S3] 258 56-62388
1. Pastoral psychology—Study and teaching. I. Bruder, Ernest E. II. Barb, Marian L. III. Title.

SEIFERT, Harvey. 253.5
Personal growth and social change; a guide for ministers and laymen as change agents, by Harvey Seifert and Howard J. Clinebell, Jr. Philadelphia, Westminster Press [1969] 240 p. 22 cm. Bibliographical references included in "Notes" (p. [220]-236) [BV4012.2.S4] 73-80977 6.95
1. Pastoral counseling. 2. Church and social problems. I. Clinebell, Howard John, 1915- joint author. II. Title.

SHARPE, William Donald, 1927- 253.5
Medicine and the ministry; a medical basis for pastoral care [by] William D. Sharpe. Pref. by Lauriston. L. Scaife. [1st ed.] New York, Appleton-Century [1966] xix, 356p. 24cm. Bibl. [BV4012.S47] 66-19997 6.95
1. Pastoral psychology. 2. Pastoral medicine. I. Title.

SHRADER, Wesley. 253.5
Of men and angels. New York, Rinehart [1957] 184p. 21cm. [BV4012.2.S5] [BV4012.2.S5] 258 57-6574 57-6574
1. Pastroral counselling. I. Title.

SOLOMON, Charles R. 253.5
Counseling with the mind of Christ : the dynamics of spirituotherapy / Charles R. Solomon. Old Tappan, N.J. : F. H. Revell Co., c1977. 159 p. : ill. ; 21 cm. Bibliography: p. 157-159. [BV4012.2.S64] 77-12227 ISBN 0-8007-0889-X pbk. : 3.95
1. Pastoral counseling. 2. Counseling. I. Title.

SOUTHARD, Samuel. 253.5
Counseling for church vocations. Nashville, Broadman Press [1957] 126p. 20cm. [BV660.S65] 57-8660
1. Clergy—Office. I. Title.

SOUTHARD, Samuel. *253.5
Counseling for church vocations. Nashville, Broadman Press [1957] 126 p. 20 cm. [BV660.S65] 57-8660
1. Clergy — Office. I. Title.

STEIN, Calvert, 1903- 253.5
Practical pastoral counseling. Springfield, Ill., Thomas [1970] xiii, 283 p. illus. 24 cm. Includes bibliographies. [BV4012.2.S7] 76-97536
1. Pastoral counseling. I. Title.

STEWARD, Charles William. 253.5
The minister as marriage counselor. Rev. Nashville, Abingdon Press [1970] 224 p. 24 cm. Bibliography: p. 212-216. [HQ728.S85 1970] 71-18087 4.75
1. Marriage counseling. 2. Pastoral counseling. I. Title.

STONE, Howard W. 253.5
Crisis counseling / Howard W. Stone. Philadelphia : Fortress Press, c1976. xiv, 81 p. ; 22 cm. (Creative pastoral care and counseling series) Bibliography: p. 79-81. [BV4012.2.S75] 75-13047 ISBN 0-8006-0553-5 pbk. : 2.95
1. Pastoral counseling. 2. Counseling. I. Title.

STROUP, Herbert W. 253.5
Sexuality and the counseling pastor [by] Herbert W. Stroup, Jr. & Norma Schweitzer Wood. Philadelphia, Fortress Press [1974] xi, 122 p. 23 cm. Bibliography: p. [119]-122. [BV4012.2.S8] 73-88344 ISBN 0-8006-0264-1 5.25
1. Pastoral counseling—Case studies. 2. Sex (Theology) I. Wood, Norma Schweitzer, joint author. II. Title.

STULTZ, Owen Glennard. 253.5
Pastoral care of the pastoral family / by Owen Glennard Stultz. [s.l. : s.n.], 1976 (Roanoke, Va. : Toler) vii, 131 p. ; 23 cm. Thesis—Bethany Theological Seminary, Oak Brook, Ill. Bibliography: p. 127-131. [BV4396.S87] 76-150614
1. Clergymen's families. I. Title.

SWITZER, David K., 1925- 253.5
The minister as crisis counselor [by] David K. Switzer. Nashville, Abingdon Press [1974] 288 p. illus. 23 cm. Includes bibliographical references. [BV4012.2.S9] 73-13722 ISBN 0-687-26953-9 6.95
1. Pastoral counseling. I. Title.

TERKELSEN, Helen E. 253.5
Counseling the unwed mother [by] Helen E. Terkelsen. Philadelphia, Fortress [1967, c. 1964] 144p. 21cm. (Successful pastoral counseling ser.) [HV700.5.T4] 1.50 pap.,
1. Unmarried mothers. 2. Pastoral counseling. I. Title. II. Series.

TERKELSEN, Helen E 253.5
Counseling the unwed mother [by] Helen E. Terkelson. Englewood Cliffs, N.J., Prentice-Hall [1964] 144 p. 21 cm. (Successful pastoral counseling series) Bibliography: p. 131-135. [HV700.5.T4] 64-20746
1. Unmarried mothers. 2. Pastoral counseling. I. Title. II. Series.

THILO, Hans Joachim, 1914- 253.5
Unfragmented man; a study in pastoral psychology. Translated from the German by Arthur J. Seegers. Minneapolis, Augsburg Pub. House [1964] 208 p. 22 cm. "Notes and references": p. 201-208. [BV4012.T483] 64-13433
1. Pastoral psychology. 2. Psychology, Religious. I. Title.

THILO, Hans Joachim, 1914- 253.5
Unfragmented man; a study in pastoral psychology. Tr. from German by Arthur J. Seegers. Minneapolis, Augsburg [c.1964] 208p. 22cm. Bibl. 64-13433 5.00
1. Pastoral psychology. 2. Psychology, Religious. I. Title.

THORNTON, Edward E. 253.5
Professional education for ministry; a history of clinical pastoral education [by] Edward E. Thornton. Nashville, Abingdon Press [1970] 301 p. illus., ports. 24 cm. Bibliography: p. 265-293. [BV4012.T53] 79-97569 7.50
1. Pastoral psychology—Study and teaching—History. I. Title.

THORNTON, Edward E. 253.5
Theology and pastoral counseling. Philadelphia, Fortress [1967, c.1964] 144p. 21cm. (Successful pastoral counseling ser.) Bibl. [BV4012.2.T5] 1.50 pap.,
1. Pastoral counseling. I. Title. II. Series.

THORNTON, Edward E. 253.5
Theology and pastoral counseling. Englewood Cliffs, N.J., Prentice [c.1964] 144p. 21cm. (Successful counseling ser.) 64-12847 2.95 bds.,
1. Pastoral counseling. I. Title. II. Series.

THURNEYSEN, Eduard, 1888- 253.5
A theology of pastoral care. Basic tr. by Jack A. Worthington, Thomas Wieser asst. by a panel of advisers. Richmond, John Knox [c.1962] 343p. 62-8614 5.50
1. Pastoral theology. I. Title.

TSCHUDY, James Jay. 253.5
The art of counseling. Salt Lake City, Deseret Book Co., 1963. 242 p. illus. 24 cm. [BV4012.2.T8] 63-3392
1. Pastoral counseling. I. Title.

TSCHUDY, James Jay 253.5
The art of counseling. Salt Lake City, Deseret [c.]1963. 242p. illus. 24cm. 63-3392 3.50
1. Pastoral counseling. I. Title.

TURNER, F. Bernadette. 253.5
God-centered therapy; how to live abundantly, a scriptural approach to problem living [by] F. Bernadette Turner. New York, R. Speller [1968] xvii, 277 p. 23 cm. [BV4012.2.T9] 68-21749
1. Pastoral counseling. 2. Christian life. I. Title.

UMPHREY, Marjorie. 253.5
Why don't I feel ok? / By Marjorie Umphrey & Richard Laird. Irvine, Calif. : Harvest House Publishers, c1977. 160 p. ; 21 cm. Bibliography: p. 160. [BR110.U45] 77-24826 ISBN 0-89081-049-9 : pbk. : 2.95
1. Psychology, Religious. 2. Transactional

analysis. I. Laird, Richard, joint author. II. Title.

VANDERPOOL, James A. 253.5
Person to person : a handbook for pastoral counseling / by James A. Vanderpool. 1st ed. Garden City, N.Y. : Doubleday, 1977. 156 p. ; 22 cm. Bibliography: p. [151]-156. [BV4012.2.V28] 76-20837 ISBN 0-385-12518-6 : 6.95
1. Pastoral counseling—Handbooks, manuals, etc. I. Title.

VAN DEUSEN, Dayton G. 253.5
Redemptive counseling; relating psychotherapy to the personal meanings in redemption. Richmond, John Knox Press [1960] 191 p. 21 cm. Includes bibliography. [BV4012.2.V3] 60-14142
1. Pastoral counseling. I. Title.

VAN DEUSEN, Dayton G. 253.5
Redemptive counseling; relating psychotherapy to the personal meanings in redemption. Richmond, Va., John Knox Press [c.1960] 191p. 21cm. Bibl.: p.179-182 60-14142 3.50
1. Pastoral conseling. I. Title.

VAUGHAN, Richard Patrick. 253.5
An introduction to religious counseling: a Christian humanistic approach [by] Richard P. Vaughan. Englewood Cliffs, N.J., Prentice-Hall [1969] x, 164 p. 22 cm. Includes bibliographical references. [BV4012.2.V38] 74-86957 ISBN 1-349-52839- 5.95
1. Pastoral counseling. I. Title.

WEBER, Carlo A., 1927- 253.5
Pastoral psychology; new trends in theory and practice [by] Carlo A. Weber. New York, Sheed and Ward [1970] 160 p. 21 cm. Includes bibliographical references. [BV4012.W37] 73-101548 ISBN 0-8362-1420-X 6.00
1. Pastoral psychology.

WEITZEL, Eugene J. 253.5
Contemporary pastoral counseling. Eugene J. Weitzel, participating editor. New York, Bruce Pub. Co. [1969] xiii, 299 p. 24 cm. Includes bibliographical references. [BV4012.2.W4] 75-75032
1. Pastoral counseling. I. Title.

WESTBERG, Granger E 253.5
Community psychiatry and the clergyman, by Granger E. Westberg and Edgar Draper. Springfield, Ill., C. C. Thomas [1966] xxi, 110 p. 24 cm. [BV4012.W428] 66-14277
1. Social psychiatry. 2. Pastoral counseling. 3. Psychiatry and religion. I. Draper, Edgar, 1926- joint author. II. Title.

WESTBERG, Granger E. 253.5
Community psychiatry and the clergyman, by Granger E. Westberg, Edgar Draper. Springfield, Ill., Thomas [c.1966] xxi, 110p. 24cm. [BV4012.W428] 66-14277 5.75
1. Social psychiatry. 2. Pastoral counseling. 3. Psychiatry and religion. I. Draper, Edgar, 1926- joint author. II. Title.

WESTBERG, Granger E. 253.5
Minister and doctor meet. [1st ed.] New York, Harper [1961] 179 p. 22 cm. [BV4012.W43] 61-7352
1. Pastoral psychology. 2. Medicine and religion. I. Title.

WESTBERG, Granger E. 253.5
Minister and doctor meet. New York, Harper [c.1961] 179p. 61-7352 3.50 bds.,
1. Pastoral psychology. 2. Medicine and religion. I. Title.

WHITLOCK, Glenn E. 253.5
Preventive psychology and the church, by Glenn E. Whitlock. Philadelphia, Westminster Press [1973] 74 p. 22 cm. Bibliography: p. [171]-174. [BV4012.2.W44] 72-8359 ISBN 0-664-20959-9 5.95
1. Pastoral counseling. 2. Pastoral psychology. 3. Mental hygiene. I. Title.

WILKE, Richard B., 1930- 253.5
The pastor and marriage group counseling, [by] Richard B. Wilke. Nashville, Abingdon Press [1974] 173 p. 21 cm. Bibliography: p. 171-173. [HQ10.W487] 73-18351 ISBN 0-687-30129-7 5.75
1. Marriage counseling. 2. Group counseling. 3. Pastoral counseling. I. Title.

WILKERSON, David R. 253'.5
The untapped generation, by David & Don Wilkerson. Grand Rapids, Zondervan Pub. House [1971] 256 p. illus. 22 cm. [RC554.W54] 75-146572 4.95
1. Personality, Disorders of. 2. Youth. 3. Counseling. 4. Psychology, Religious. I. Wilkerson, Don, joint author. II. Title.

WILLIAMS, Daniel Day, 1910- 253.5
The minister and the care of souls. [1st ed.] New York, Harper [1961] 157 p. 22 cm. Incudes bibliography. [BV4012.2.W48] 61-12836
1. Pastoral counseling. I. Title.

WILLIAMS, Daniel Day, 1910- 253.5
The minister and the care of souls. New York, Harper [c.1961] 157p. Bibl. 61-12936 3.50 bds.,
1. Pastoral counseling. I. Title.

WISE, Carroll Alonzo, 1903- 253.5
Pastoral counseling, its theory and practice. [1st ed.] New York, Harper [1951] xi, 231p. 22cm. 'Notes and references': p. 223-227. [BV4012.2.W5] 258 51-9232
1. Pastoral counseling. I. Title.

WISE, Carroll Alonzo, 1903- 253.5
Psychiatry and the Bible. [1st ed.] New York, Harper [1956] 169p. 22cm. [BV4012.W53] 258 56-7025
1. Psychology, Pastoral. 2. Bible—Psychology. 3. Medicine and religion. I. Title.

WISE, Carroll Alonzo, 1903- 253.5
Psychiatry and the Bible. New York, Harper [1966, c.1956] 169p. 21cm. (Harper Chapel bk., CB23H) [BV4012.W53] 56-7025 1.45 pap.,
1. Psychology, Pastoral. 2. Bible—Psychology. 3. Medicine and religion. I. Title.

WITTKOFSKI, Joseph Nicholas, 1912- 253.5
The pastoral use of hypnotic technique. With a foreword by T. J. Freeborn, Jr., and an introd. by Austin Pardue. New York, Macmillan, 1961. 111 p. 22 cm. Includes bibliography. [BV4012.W55] 61-14715
1. Pastoral psychology. 2. Hypnotism — Therapeutic use. I. Title.

WITTKOFSKI, Joseph Nicholas, 1912- 253.5
The pastoral use of hypnotic technique. Foreword by T. J. Freeborn, Jr., introd. by Austin Pardue. New York, Macmillan [c.] 1961. 111p. Bibl. 61-14715 2.50
1. Pastoral psychology. 2. Hypnotism—Therapeutic use. I. Title.

WORKSHOP in Pastoral Counseling, University of Florida, 1959. 253.5
Proceedings. Edited by J. Milan Kolarik. [Gainesville, Fla., 1959] 85 p. 23 cm. Includes bibliographies. [BV4012.2.W6 1959] A60
1. Pastoral counseling. I. Kolarik J. Millan, ed. II. Title.

YOUNG, Richard K 253.5
The pastor's hospital ministry. Nashville, Broadman Press [1954] 139p. 21cm. [BV4335.Y6] 54-4469
1. Church work with the stick. I. Title.

YOUNG, Richard K 253.5
Spiritual therapy; how the physician, psychiatrist and minister collaborate in healing [by] Richard K Young and Albert L. Meiburg. New York, Harper [1960] 184 p. 22 cm. Includes bibliography. [BV4012.2.Y6] 60-7958
1. Pastoral counseling. 2. Medicine, Psychosomatic — Cases, clinical reports, statistics. I. Meiburg, Albert L. joint author. II. Title.

YOUNG, Richard K. 253.5
Spiritual therapy; how the physician, psychiatrist and minister collaborate in healing [by] Richard K. Young and Albert L. Meiburg. New York, Harper [c.1960] 184p. Includes bibliography.22cm. 60-7958 3.50
1. Pastoral counseling. 2. Medicine, Psychosomatic—Cases, clinical reports, statistics. I. Meiburg, Albert L., joint author. II. Title.

MATTHEWS, Victor M. 253.5'01'86
Confessions to a counselor; responses to the plea, "Confidentially, I need help." Grand Rapids, Zondervan Pub. House [1969] 96 p. 21 cm. (A Zondervan paperback) [BV4012.2.M3] 69-11633 0.95
1. Pastoral counseling—Case studies. I. Title.

HEALER, Carl T., 1925- 253.5'01'9
Freud and Saint Paul (an exploratory study of two great men who have had a profound influence upon Western civilization) by Carl T. Healer. Philadelphia, Dorrance [1972] 55 p. 22 cm. Bibliography: p. 53-55. [BF173.F85H35] 70-187015 ISBN 0-8059-1672-5 3.00
1. Freud, Sigmund, 1856-1939. 2. Paul, Saint, Apostle.

HILLMAN, James. 253.5'019
Insearch; psychology and religion. New York, Scribner [1968, c1967] 126 p. 22 cm. [BV4012.H5 1968] 67-24042
1. Pastoral psychology. 2. Soul. I. Title.

SOFIELD, Loughlan. 253.5'025'73
A directory of counseling centers for priests and religious in the United States 1973, by Loughlan Sofield [and] Angelo D'Agostino. Washington, Center for Applied Research in the Apostolate, 1973. v, 48 p. 22 cm. (CARA information service) [BV4398.5.S63] 73-163830
1. Counseling for clergy—Directories. 2. Community mental health services—United States—Directories. I. D'Agostino, Angelo A., 1926- joint author. II. Title.

CATHOLIC University of America. Workshop on Spiritual Formation and Guidance-Counseling in the CCD Program, 1961. 253.5082
Spiritual formation and guidance-counseling in the CCD program; the proceedings of the Workshop on Spiritual Formation and Guidance-Counseling in the CCD Program, conducted at the Catholic Univ. of America, June 16 to June 27, 1961. Ed. by Joseph B. Collins. Washington, D.C., Catholic Univ. [c.] 1962. ix, 248 p. 22 cm. Bibl. 62-4669 2.50, pap.
1. Spiritual direction. 2. Pastoral counseling. 3. Catholic Church—Education. 4. Confraternity of Christian Doctrine. I. Collins, Joseph Burns, 1897- ed. II. Title.

HEALING: 253.5082
human and divine; man's search for health and wholeness through science, faith, and prayer. New York, Association Press [1957] 254p. 20cm. (Pastoral psychology series) [BV4012.D617] [BV4012.D617] 258 57-6889 57-6889
1. Pastoral psychology—Addresses, essays, lectures. I. Doniger, Simon, ed.

INSTITUTE of Pastoral Psychology, Fordham University. 1st, 1955. 253.5082
Personality and sexual problems in pastoral psychology. Edited by William C. Bier. New York, Fordham University Press [1964] xiii, 256 p. 24 cm. (The Pastoral psychology series, no. 1) Contains "papers...derived from the 1955 and 1957 institutes" sponsored by the Dept. of Psychology, Fordham University. Includes bibliographies. [BV4012.I 48] 62-16224
1. Pastoral psychology — Addresses, essays, lectures. I. Blier, William Christian, 1911- ed. II. Institute of Pastoral Psychology, Fordham University. 2d, 1957. III. Fordham University, New York. Dept. of Psychology. IV. Title. V. Series.

INSTITUTE of Pastoral Psychology, Fordham University. 1st, 1955. 253.5082
Personality and sexual problems in pastoral psychology. Ed. by William C. Bier. New York, Fordham Univ. Pr. [c.1964] xiii, 256p. 24cm. (Pastoral psych. ser., no. 1) Contains papers derived from the 1955 and 1957 institutes sponsored by the Dept. of Psychology, Fordham Univ. Bibl. 62-16224 5.00
1. Pastoral psychology—Addresses, essays, lectures. I. Bier, William Christian, 1911- ed. II. Institute of Pastoral Psychology, Fordham University. 2d, 1957. III. Fordham University, New York. Dept. of Psychology. IV. Title. V. Series.

CLEBSCH, William A. 253.509
Pastoral care in historical perspective, an essay with exhibits, by William A. Clebsch, Charles R. Jaekle. New York, Harper [1967, c.1964] x, 344p. 21cm. (Torch bks., 148) Twenty-one exhibits of the history of the pastoral art: p.87-335. Bibl. [BV4005.C64] 2.75 pap.,
1. Pastoral theology—Hist. 2. Pastoral theology—Collections. I. Jaekle, Charles R., joint author. II. Title.

CLEBSCH, William A 253.509
Pastoral care in historical perspective, an essay with exhibits, by William A. Clebsch and Charles R. Jackle. Englewood Cliffs, N.J., Prentice-Hall [1964] x, 344 p. 22 cm. "Twenty-one exhibits of the history of the pastoral art": p. 87-335. Bibliographical footnotes. [BV4005.C64] 64-10746
1. Pastoral theology — Hist. 2. Pastoral theology — Collections. I. Jackle, Charles R., joint author. II. Title.

CLEBSCH, William A. 253.509
Pastoral care in historical perspective, an essay with exhibits, by William A. Clebsch, Charles R. Jaekle. Englewood Cliffs, N.J., Prentice [c.1964] x, 344p. 22cm. Bibl. 64-10746 7.95
1. Pastoral theology—Hist. 2. Pastoral theology—Collections. I. Jaekle, Charles R., joint author. II. Title.

ISHEE, John A. 253.5'0926
When trouble comes, compiled by John Ishee. Nashville, Tenn., Broadman Press [1970] 128 p. 20 cm. (A Broadman inner circle book) Includes bibliographical references. [BV4012.2.I8] 75-113211
1. Pastoral counseling—Case studies. I. Title.

MICHONNEAU, G *253.5 258
The missionary spirit in parish life. Westminster, Md., Newman Press, 1952. 194 p. 22 cm. [BX2347.M48] 52-7997
1. Theology, Pastoral — Catholic Church. 2. Evangelistic work. I. Title.

WHAT, then, is man? *253.5 258
A symposium of theology, psychology, and psychiatry. St. Louis, Concordia Pub. House [1958] ix, 356 p. 22 cm. ([Concordia Theological Seminary, St. Louis. School for Graduate Studies] Graduate study no. 3) Bibliography: p. 341-344. [BF51.W43 1958] 58-9438
1. Man (Theology) 2. Psychology. 3. Psychiatry. I. Series.

WISE, Carroll Alonzo, 1903- *253.5 258
Psychiatry and the Bible. [1st ed.] New York, Harper [1956] 169 p. 22 cm. [BV4012.W53] 56-7025
1. Psychology, Pastoral. 2. Bible — Psychology. 3. Medicine and religion. I. Title.

WYNN, John Charles. *253.5 258
Pastoral ministry to families. Philadelphia, Westminster Press [1957] 214 p. 21 cm. Includes bibliography. [BV4320.W9] 57-6553
1. Pastoral theology. 2. Family — Religious life. I. Title.

AUGSBURGER, Myron S 253.7
Invitation to discipleship: the message of evangelism, by Myron S. Augsburger. Scottdale, Pa., Herald Press [1964] 114 p. 21 cm. Bibliography: p. 110-114. [BV3790.A78] 64-18731
1. Evangelistic work. I. Title.

AUGSBURGER, Myron S. 253.7
Invitation to discipleship: the message of evangelism. Scottdale, Pa., Herald Pr. [c.1964] 114p. 21cm. Bibl. 64-18731 2.50
1. Evangelistic work. I. Title.

AUTREY, C E 253.7
Basic evangelism. Grand Rapids, Zondervan Pub. House [1959] 183p. 23cm. Includes bibliography. [BV3790.A8] 59-4475
1. Evangelistic work. I. Title.

AUTREY, C. E. 253.7
You can win souls. Nashville, Broadman Press [c.1961] 160p. Bibl.: p.156-160. 61-5392 2.75 bds.,
1. Evangelistic work. I. Title.

AUTREY, C E 253.7
You can win souls. Nashville, Broadman Press [1961] 160p. 22cm. Includes bibliography. [BV3790.A83] 61-5392
1. Evangelistic work. I. Title.

BAKER, Gordon Pratt, ed. 253.7
Evangelism and contemporary issues. Nashville, Tidings [1964] 158p. 21cm. Bibl. 64-21896 1.50
1. Evangelistic work. I. Title.

BAKER, Gordon Pratt, ed. 253.7
A year of evangelism in the local church. Gordon Pratt Baker [and] Edward Ferguson, Jr., editors. Nashville, Tidings [1960] 224p. illus. 21cm. [BV3790.B27] 60-8790
1. Evangelistic work. I. Ferguson, Edward, joint ed. II. Title.

BISAGNO, John R. 253.7
How to build an evangelistic church [by] John R. Bisagno. Nashville, Broadman Press [1971] 160 p. 21 cm. [BV3790.B485] 78-178055 ISBN 0-8054-2524-1 3.95
1. Evangelistic work. I. Title.

BROCK, Raymond T 253.7
Into the highways and hedges; ways of perpetuating evangelism in and through the Sunday school. Springfield, Mo., Gospel Pub. House [c1961] 117p. 20cm. Includes bibliography. [BV3793.B68] 61-18608
1. Evangelistic work. 2. Sunday-schools. I. Title.

CLAMPIT, Vernon L. 253.7
Behind the church curtain; adventures in faith. New York, Exposition [c.1962] 143p. front. 3.00
1. Evangelistic work. I. Title.

COLEMAN, Robert Emerson, 1928- 253.7
Evangelism in perspective / by Robert E. Coleman. Harrisburg, Pa. : Christian Publications, c1975. 109 p. : port. ; 20 cm. (L. W. Pippert memorial lectures ; 1974) Includes bibliographical references. [BV3795.C79] 76-354631
1. Evangelistic work—Addresses, essays, lectures. I. Title. II. Series.

CONANT, Judson E. 253.7
Soul-winning evangelism; the good news in action. Grand Rapids, Mich., Zondervan [1963] 168p. 22cm. 63-17754 2.95 bds.,
1. Evangelistic work. I. Title.

COUNCIL on Evangelism, St. Louis, 1968. 253.7
Our mission in today's world; official papers and reports. Editorial Committee: Richard Champion, chairman; Edward S. Caldwell; Gary Leggett. Springfield, Mo., Gospel Pub. House [1968] 217 p. 29 cm. Sponsored by the Assemblies of God, General Council. [BV3755.C63 1968] 73-2853
1. Evangelistic work—Congresses. 2. Pentecostal churches—Doctrinal and controversial works. I. Champion, Richard, 1931- ed. II. Caldwell, Edward S., ed. III. Leggett, Gary, ed. IV. Assemblies of God, General Council. V. Title.

DE JONG, Peter Ymen, 1915- 253.7
A theology of evangelistic concern. Nashville, Tidings [1963] 72 p. 19 cm. Bibliographical references included in "Notes" (p. 65-67) and "References" (p. 68-71) [BV3793.D43] 63-22406
1. Evangelistic work. I. Title.

DEUTSCHER Evangelischer Missionstag, Hermannsburg, Ger., 1974. 253.7
Evangelisation in der Erwartung des Reiches Gottes : Hauptreferat u. Bibelarbeiten d. Dt. Evang. Missionstages 1974 / Siegfried Liebschner, Anselm Schulz, Herwig Wagner. Hamburg : Verlag der Evang. Missionshilfe, 1975. 68 p. ; 21 cm. (Studienheft der Deutschen Evangelischen Missionshilfe ; 4) Includes index. [BV3755.D48 1974] 76-458572
1. Evangelistic work—Congresses. I. Liebschner, Siegfried. II. Schulz, Anselm. III. Wagner, Herwig. IV. Title. V. Series: Deutsche Evangelische Missions-Hilfe. Studienheft der Deutschen Evangelischen Missionshilfe ; 4.

DEWIRE, Harry A. 253.7
The Christian as communicator. Philadelphia, Westminster Press [c.1961] 198p. 21cm. (Westminster studies in Christian communication) Bibl.: p.191-194. 60-14681 4.50
1. Witness bearing (Christianity) I. Title.

DOUGLAS, Mack R 253.7
How to build an evangelistic church. Grand Rapids, Zondervan Pub. House [1963] 88 p. 21 cm. [BV3790.D66] 63-15728
1. Evangelistic work. I. Title.

DOUGLAS, Mack R. 253.7
How to build an evangelistic church. Grand Rapids, Mich., Zondervan [c.1963] 88p. 21cm. Bibl. 63-15728 1.50 pap.,
1. Evangelistic work. I. Title.

ELLER, Eugene R. 253.7
Every boy needs a man [by] E. R. Eller. Illus. by Johnny J. Davis. Pickens, S.C., Pickens sentinel [1969] 167 p. port. 22 cm. [BX6495.E4A3] 71-5529
1. Baptists—Clergy—Correspondence, reminiscences, etc. 2. Church work with youth. I. Title.

ELLIS, Howard W 253.7
Evangelism for teen-agers for a new day [by] Howard W. Ellis. [Rev. ed.] Nashville. Abingdon Press [1966] 109 p. 19 cm. Bibliographical references included in "Notes" (p. 103-109) [BV3795.E4] 66-20457
1. Evangelistic work — Study and teaching. I. Title.

ELLIS, Howard W. 253.7
Evangelism for teenagers for a new day [by] Howard W. Ellis. [Rev. ed.] Nashville, Abingdon [1966] 109p. 19cm. Bibl. [BV3795.E4 1966] 66-20457 1.50 pap.,
1. Evangelistic work—Study and teaching. I. Title.

FINNEY, Charles Grandison. 1792-1875. 253.7
Lectures on revivals of religion. Edited by William G. McLoughlin. Cambridge, Mass., Belknap Press of Harvard University Press [c.] 1960. lix. 470p. 25cm. (The John Harvard library) (Bibl. footnotes) 60-11558 5.95
1. Revivals. 2. Evangelistic work. 3. Sermons, American. I. Title.

FINNEY, Charles Grandison, 1792-1875 253.7
Revivals of religion. Chicago, Moody [1963, c.1962] 352p. 18cm. (MP129) Condensation of the author's Lectures on revivals of religion, first publ. in 1835. 63-1685 .89 pap.,
1. Revivals. 2. Evangelistic work. 3. Sermons, American. I. Title.

FORD, Leighton 253.7
The Christian persuader. New York, Harper [1966] 159p. 22cm. [BV3790.F63] 66-22043 3.95 bds.,
1. Evangelistic work. I. Title.

FORD, Leighton 253.7
The Christian persuader New York Harper and Row [1976 c1966] 159 p.; 20 cm. [BV3790] ISBN 0-06-062679-8 pbk.: 3.95
1. Evangelistic work. I. Title.
L.C. card no. for original edition: 66-22043.

GERBER, Vergil. 253.7
A manual for evangelism/church growth. South Pasadena, Calif., William Carey Library [1973] 91 p. illus. 22 cm. Includes bibliographical references. [BV3790.G45] 72-97998 ISBN 0-87808-123-2
1. Evangelistic work. I. Title.

GERBER, Vergil. 253.7
A manual for evangelism/church growth. South Pasadena, Calif., William Carey Library [1973] 91 p. illus. 22 cm. Includes bibliographical references. [BV3790.G45] 72-97998 ISBN 0-87808-123-2 1.25 (pbk.)
1. Evangelistic work. I. Title.

GOLAY, Eugene E. 253.7
Organizing the local church for effective lay visitation evangelism. Nashville, 1908 Grand Ave. Tidings, [c.1961] 84p. illus. Bibl. 61-9628 .50 pap.,
1. Evangelistic work. 2. Visitations (Church work) I. Title.

GOLDBERG, Louis, 1923- 253.7
Our Jewish friends / by Louis Goldberg. Chicago : Moody Press, c1977. 188 p. ; 22 cm. Bibliography: p. 188. [BM580.G58] 76-56773 ISBN 0-8024-6217-0 pbk. : 3.95
1. Judaism. 2. Missions to Jews. I. Title.

GRAF, Arthur E. 253.7
The church in the community; an effective evangelism program for the Christian congregation. Grand Rapids, Mich. Eerdmans [c.1965] 207p. forms. 23cm. Bibl. [BV4011.G67] 64-22019 3.95
1. Pastoral theology—Lutheran Church. I. Title.

HARRINGTON, Bob, 1927- 253.7
Motivating men for the Master. Nashville, Broadman Press [1971] 176 p. illus. 21 cm. [BV3797.H348] 71-155682 4.95
1. Evangelistic work—U.S. 2. Converts. I. Title.

HASKIN, Dorothy C. 253.7
Soul-winning, the Christian's business. Grand Rapids, Mich., Baker Book House [c.]1959. 53p. 22cm. .75 pap.,
I. Title.

HOLLOWAY, Fred Garrigus, B, p., 1898- 253.7
New Testament foundations for Christian evangelism [by] Fred G. Holloway. Nashville, Tidings [1965] 64 p. 19 cm. [BV3793.H63] 65-28308
1. Evangelistic work. 2. Bible. N.T. — Criticism, interpretation, etc. I. Title.

KETTNER, Elmer A. 253.7
Adventures in evangelism. St. Louis, Concordia Pub. House [c1964] 133 p. 19 cm. [BV3790.K49] 63-23488
1. Evangelistic work — Handbooks, manuals, etc. I. Title.

KETTNER, Elmer A. 253.7
Adventures in evangelism. St. Louis, Concordia [c.1964] 133p. 19cm. 63-23488 1.50 pap.,
1. Evangelistic work—Handbooks, manuals, etc. I. Title.

*KINGSLEY, Charles W. 253.7
Go! revolutionary New Testament Christianity, by Charles W. Kingsley, George Delamarter. Grand Rapids, Mich., Zondervan [c.1965] 95p. 23cm. 1.50 pap.,
I. Title.

KUHNE, Gary W. 253.7
The dynamics of personal follow-up / Gary W. Kuhne. Grand Rapids, Mich. : Zondervan, c1975. p. cm. Includes bibliographical references. [BV3790] pbk. : 2.95
1. Evangelistic work. 2. Christian life—1960- I. Title.

LEAVELL, Roland Quinche, 1891-1963 253.7
The Christian's business: being a witness. Nashville, Broadman [1964] 128p. 20cm. 64-18272 1.50
1. Evangelistic work. I. Title.

MCCOY, Charles S 253.7
The gospel on campus; rediscovering evangelism in the academic community [by] Charles S. McCoy [and] Neely D. McCarter. Richmond, John Knox Press [1959] 123p. 21cm. Includes bibliography. [BV4531.2.M2] 59-6077
1. Students—Religious life. 2. Universities and colleges—Religion. 3. Evangelistic work. I. McCarter, Neely D., joint author. II. Title.

MALLOUGH, Don. 253.7
Grassroots evangelism. Grand Rapids, Baker Book House [1971] 143 p. 18 cm. [BV3796.M33] 72-172299 ISBN 0-8010-5880-5 1.25
1. Evangelistic work—Study and teaching. I. Title.

MALONE, Tom. 253.7
Essentials of evangelism. Foreword by Bob Jones, Jr. Grand Rapids, Kregel Publications [c1958] 152p. 21cm. (The Bob Jones University lectures on evangelism for 1958) [BV3790.M35] 58-59550
1. Evangelistic work. I. Title.

METCALF, Harold E 253.7
The magic of telephone evangelism, by Harold E. Metcalf. Atlanta, Southern Union Conference [of Seventh-Day Adventists, 1967] 448 p. illus. 21 cm. [BV656.4.M4] 68-801
1. Telephone in church work. I. Title. II. Title: Telephone evangelism.

METCALF, Harold E. 253.7
The magic of telephone evangelism, by Harold E. Metcalf. Atlanta, Southern Union Conference [of Seventh-Day Adventists, 1967] 448 p. illus. 21 cm. [BV656.4.M4] 68-801
1. Telephone in church work. I. Title. II. Title: Telephone evangelism.

MEYER, Bernard F. 1891- 253.7
The whole world is my neighbor, by Bernard F. Meyer, with an introd. by Richard Cardinal Cushing. Notre Dame, Ind., Fides Publishers [1964] xiii, 324 p. 21 cm. First published in 1962 under title: Your life to share. [BX2348.M43] 64-22893
1. Catholic action. 2. Catholic Church — Missions. I. Title.

MEYER, Bernard F., 1891- 253.7
The whole world is my neighbor. Introd. by Richard Cardinal Cushing. Notre Dame, Ind., Fides [c.1964] xiii, 324p. 21cm. [BX2348.M43] 64-22893 4.95
1. Catholic action. 2. Catholic Church—Missions. I. Title.

MITCHELL, John D ed. 253.7
The parish priest's guide to inquiry classes. Foreword by Richard Cardinal Cushing. New York, Paulist Press [1960] 256p. illus. 21cm. Includes bibliography. [BX2347.4.M55] 60-11595
1. Evangelistic work. 2. Church membership—Study and teaching. 3. Catholic Church—Doctrinal and controversial works, Popular. I. Title.

MUMMA, Howard E. 253.7
Take it to the people; new ways in soul winning—unconventional Evangelism [by] Howard. E. Mumma. New York, World Pub. Co. [1969] 124 p. 22 cm. Bibliographical footnotes. [BV3793.M8] 68-26844 3.95
1. Evangelistic work. I. Title.

NATIONAL Council of the Churches of Christ in the United States of America. 253.7
The local church manual for the National Christian Teaching Mission. New York, c1956. 72p. 23cm. [BV3793.N36] 62-2623
1. Evangelistic work. I. National Christian Teaching Mission. II. Title.

NIDA, Eugene Albert 253.7
Message and mission; the communication of the Christian faith. New York, Harper [c.1960] xvii, 253p. illus. 22cm: Bibl.: p.239-248. 60-11785 5.00
1. Evangelism. 2. Missions. 3. Intercultural communication. I. Title.

NIDA, Eugene Albert, 1914- 253.7
Message and mission; the communication of the Christian faith. [1st ed.] New York, Harper [1960] 253p. illus. 22cm. Includes bibliography. [BV3793.N5] 60-11785
1. Evangelism. 2. Missions. 3. Intercultural communication. I. Title.

PERRY, John D. 253.7
The coffee house ministry, by John D. Perry, Jr. Foreword by Malcolm Boyd. Richmond, John Knox Press [1966] 127 p. illus., ports. 21 cm. Includes bibliographies. [BV4377.P4] 66-17597
1. Coffee house ministry. I. Title.

PHILIBERT, Michel Andre Jean 253.7
Christ's preaching, and ours. [Tr. from French by David Lewis. American ed.] Richmond, Va., Knox [1964, c.1963] 55p. 22cm. (World Council of Churches. Commission on World Mission and Evangelism. Study pamph., no. 1) Bibl. 64-12262 1.00 pap.,
1. Preaching. I. Title.

POWELL, Ivor. 253.7
Don't lose that fish- Grand Rapids. Zondervan Pub. House [1960] 3151p. 21cm. [BV3790.P67] 60-50190
1. Evangelistic work. I. Title.

PRIOR, Kenneth Francis William. 253.7
The Gospel in a pagan society : a book for modern evangelists / Kenneth F. W. Prior. Downers Grove, Ill. : InterVarsity Press, 1975. 126 p. ; 18 cm. Includes bibliographical references. [BV3793.P7 1975] 75-7248 ISBN 0-87784-484-4 pbk. : 2.25
1. Paul, Saint, apostle. 2. Bible. N.T. Acts XVII, 16-34—Criticism, interpretation, etc. 3. Evangelistic work. I. Title.

QUERE, Ralph W. 253.7
Evangelical witness : the message, medium, mission, and method of evangelism / Ralph W. Quere. Minneapolis : Augsburg Pub. House, [1975] 160 p. ; 20 cm. Includes bibliographical references. [BV3790.Q47] 75-2839 ISBN 0-8066-1485-4 pbk. : 3.75
1. Evangelistic work. I. Title.

RAINES, Robert Arnold 253.7
New life in the church. New York, Harper [c.1961] 155 p. Bibl. notes: p. 147-149. 61-5267 3.00, half cloth
1. Laity. 2. Church work. I. Title.

RINKER, Rosalind. 253.7
You can witness with confidence. Grand Rapids, Zondervan Pub. House [1962] 105 p. 21 cm. [BV4520.R54] 63-1197
1. Witness bearing (Christianity) I. Title.

ROWELL, J. B. 253.7
How to lead Roman Catholics to Christ; methods of approach, factual, spiritual, practical, by J. B. Rowell. Grand Rapids, Kregel Publications [1966] 80 p. 19 cm. Bibliography: p. 80. [BV3790.R68] 66-19199
1. Evangelistic work. I. Title.

SOUTHARD, Samuel. 253.7
Pastoral evangelism. Nashville, Broadman Press [1962] 196 p. 22 cm. Includes bibliographies. [BV3790.S74] 62-15327
1. Evangelistic work. I. Title.

SOUTHARD, Samuel 253.7
Pastoral evangelism. Nashville, Broadman [c.1962] 198p. 22cm. Bibl. 62-15327 3.75
1. Evangelistic work. I. Title.

SOUTHERN Baptist Convention. Home Mission Board. Division of Evangelism. 253.7
Handbook on evangelism; a program of evangelism for Southern Baptists. Produced by the Division of Evangelism, Home Mission Board of the Southern Baptist Convention. Edited by Newman R. McLarry. Nashville, Convention Press [c1965] 127 p. 20 cm. Includes bibliographical references. [BV3790.S745] 65-10341
1. Evangelistic work. I. McLarry, Newman R., ed. II. Title.

STILSON, Max 253.7
How to deal with Roman Catholics. Grand Rapids, Mich., Zondervan [c.1963] 66p. 21cm. 1.00 pap.,
I. Title.

SUMNER, Robert Leslie, 1922- 253.7
Evangelism: the church on fire. Chicago, Regular Baptist Press [1960] 220 p. 21 cm. [BV3797.S76] 61-23521
1. Evangelistic work I. Title.

TOWNSEND, Arthur H 253.7
How to consider the church evangelist. Tahlequah, Okla., Pan Press [1960] 53 p. 22 cm. [BV3793.T65] 60-10183
1. Evangelistic work. I. Title.

*VERWER, George 253.7
Literature evangelism, a manual. Chicago, Moody [c.1963] 128p. 17cm. (Colorportage lib., 498) .39 pap.,
I. Title.

WATMOUGH, George. 253.7
Hitchhiking on purpose. Neptune, N.J., Loizeaux Bros. [1965] 64 p. 19 cm. [BR1725.W343A3] 65-27057
I. Title.

WATMOUGH, George 253.7
Hitchhiking on purpose. Neptune, N.J., Loizeaux Bros. 1238 Corlies Ave. [c.1965] 64p. 19cm. [BR1725.W343A3] 65-27057 1.00 pap.,
I. Title.

WENGER, A. Grace 253.7
God builds the church through congregational witness; a resource book for the study of Christian Witnessing. Scottdale, Pa., Herald [1963, c.1962] 128p. 20cm. 62-17325 1.00 pap.,
1. Witness bearing (Christianity) I. Title.

WHITE, Robert Andrew, 1937- 253.7
How to win a soul, by Robert A. White. Nashville, Tenn., Southern Pub. Association

[1971] 95 p. 19 cm. [BV3790.W474] 76-165794
1. Evangelistic work. 2. Witness bearing (Christianity) I. Title.

WOOD, Arthur Skevington. 253.7
Evangelism; its theology and practice, by A. Skevington Wood. Grand Rapids, Zondervan Pub. House [1966] 119 p. 21 cm. [BV3790.W58] 65-25960
1. Evangelistic work. I. Title.

WOOD, Arthur Skevington 253.7
Evangelism; its theology and practice. Grand Rapids, Mich., Zondervan [c.1966] 119p. 21cm. [BV3790.W58] 65-25960 2.95 bds.,
1. Evangelistic work. I. Title.

HALL, Gordon Langley. 253.709
The sawdust trail; the story of American evangelism. Philadelphia, Macrae Smith Co. [1964] 249 p. ports. 22 cm. Bibliography: p. [241]-249. [BV3773.H3] 64-14870
1. Evangelistic work—Hist. I. Title.

HALL, Gordon Langley 253.709
The sawdust trail; the story of American evangelism. Philadelphia, Macrae [c.1964] 249p. ports. 22cm. Bibl. 64-14870 4.50 bds.,
1. E. Evangelistic work—Hist. I. Title.

BACON, Ernest 253.7'0924 (B)
Wallace.
Spurgeon, heir of the Puritans [by] Ernest W. Bacon. [1st U. S. A. ed.] Grand Rapids, Mich., W. B. Eerdmans Pub. Co. [1968, 1967] 184 p. port. 23 cm. Bibliography: p. 178-179. [BX6495.S7B3] 67-30115
1. Spurgeon, Charles Haddon, 1834-1892. I. Title.

BACON, Ernest Wallace. 253.7'0924
Spurgeon, heir of the Puritans [by] Ernest W. Bacon. [1st U.S.A. ed.] Grand Rapids, Mich., Eerdmans [1968, c1967] 184p. port. 23cm. Bibl. [BX6495.S7B3] (B) 67-30115 3.95
1. Spurgeon, Charles Haddon, 1834-1892. I. Title.

BROWN, Leo Kingsbury. 253.7'0924
The private devotional lives of Finney, Moody, and Spurgeon. [San Rafael? Calif., c1963] 91 p. illus., ports. 23 cm. Bibliography: p. 78. [BV3780.B7] 64-28496
1. Finney, Charles Grandison, 1792-1875. 2. Moody, Dwight Lyman, 1837-1890. 3. Spurgeon, Charles Haddon, 1834-1892. I. Title.

FULLERTON, William 253.70924 B
Young, 1857-1932.
Charles Haddon Spurgeon; a biography. Chicago, Moody Press [1966] 283 p. 23 cm. (The Tyndale series of great biographies) "First published, 1920." [BX6495.S7F8 1966] 66-8933
1. Spurgeon, Charles Haddon, 1834-1892. I. Title. II. Series.

GAGE, Freddie, 1933- 253.70924
Pulpit in the shadows, by Freddie Gage with Stan Redding. Englewood Cliffs, N. J., Prentice-Hall [1966] viii, 182 p. 22 cm. [BV4935.G27A3] 66-22079
1. Converts. I. Redding, Stanley N. II. Title.

*KUHLMAN, Kathryn. 253.7'0924
Never to late. Minneapolis, Bethany Fellowship [1975] 79p. ill 18 cm. (Dimension books) [BV3777] 75-32235 ISBN 0-87123-397-5 0.95 (pbk.)
1. Evangelists. 2. evangelistic work. I. Title.

*GENTRY, Gardiner. 253.'7'3
Bus them in / by Gardiner Gentry. Grand Rapids : Baker Book House, 1976c1973. [ix], 151p. : ill. ports. ; 22 cm. [BV1523.A7] ISBN 0-8010-3705-0 pbk. : 2.95
1. Motor bus driving-Moral and religious aspects. 2. Evangelistic work-United States. I. Title.

*GOODMAN, Carlton T. 253.'7'3
How to be a successful bus pastor or bus captain / Carlton T. Goodman. Grand Rapids : Baker Book House, 1976c1974. 183p. ; 22 cm. First published 1974 by Church Growth Publications. [BV1523.A7] ISBN 0-8010-3661-5 pbk. : 2.95
1. Motor bus driving-Moral and religious aspects. 2. Evangelistic work-United States. I. Title.

CHAPLAIN Ray, 1913- 253.7'5
God's prison gang / Chaplain Ray with Walter Wagner. Old Tappan, N.J. : F. H. Revell Co., c1977. 159 p. ; 21 cm. [BV4340.C46] 76-49571 ISBN 0-8007-0840-7 : 5.95
1. Church work with prisoners—United States. 2. Prisoners—United States. 3. Conversion. I. Wagner, Walter, 1927- joint author. II. Title.

KANDLE, George C. 253.7'5
Ministering to prisoners and their families [by] George C. Kandle and Henry H. Cassler. Englewood Cliffs, N.J., Prentice-Hall [1968] 140 p. illus. 21 cm. (Successful pastoral counseling series) Bibliography: p. 133-136. [BV4465.K3] 68-11944
1. Prisons—Missions and charities. 2. Pastoral counseling. I. Cassler, Henry H., joint author. II. Title. III. Series.

SMITH, Leon, 1918- 253.7'6
Family ministry : an educational resource for the local church / Leon Smith. Nashville : Discipleship Resources, c1975. 159 p. : ill. ; 22 cm. Includes bibliographical references. [BV4438.S55] 74-33832
1. Church work with families. 2. Family—Religious life. I. Title.

ELLENS, J. Harold, 1932- 253.7'8
Models of religious broadcasting, by J. Harold Ellens. [Grand Rapids] Eerdmans [1974] 168 p. 21 cm. Bibliography: p. 153-163. [BV656.E43] 74-8382 ISBN 0-8028-3437-X 3.45 (pbk.)
1. Radio in religion. 2. Television in religion. I. Title.

FREED, Paul E. 253.7'8
Towers to eternity, by Paul E. Freed. Waco, Tex., Word Books [1968] 154 p. 22 cm. [BV2082.R3F7] 68-54118 3.95
1. Trans World Radio. 2. Radio in missionary work. I. Title.

*JESS, John D. 253.78
Escape from emptiness, [by] John D. Jess. Grand Rapids, Baker Book House, [1975 c1968] 87 p. 18 cm. (Direction books) [BV4301] ISBN 0-8010-5071-5 1.25 (pbk.)
1. Radio in religion. I. Title.

254 Parish Government & Administration

AMERICAN Baptist Convention. 254
Ministers and Missionaries Benefit Board.
Report. [Rochester? N. Y.] v. 23cm. Issued 19 by the board under the convention's earlier name: Northern Baptist Convention. [BX6345.5.A653] 35-24714
1. American Baptist Convention—Clergy—Salaries, pensions, etc. I. Title.

ANDERSON, James D. 254
To come alive! New proposal for revitalizing the local church [by] James D. Anderson. [1st ed.] New York, Harper & Row [1973] viii, 141 p. 22 cm. "A Project Test Pattern book in parish development." Includes bibliographical references. [BV600.2.A5 1973] 72-11351 ISBN 0-06-060234-1 4.95
1. Church renewal. 2. Sociology, Christian. I. Title.

ANDERSON, Marin, 1882- 254
Multiple ministries; staffing the local church. Minneapolis, Augsburg Pub. House [1965] 104 p. 22 cm. [BV652.A7] 6522837
1. Church management. 2. Church officers. 3. Pastoral theology — Lutheran Church. 4. City churches. I. Title.

ANDERSON, Martin, 1882- 254
Mutiple ministries; staffing the local church. Minneapolis, Augsburg [c.1965] 104p. 22cm. [BV652.A7] 65-22837 2.50 pap.,
1. Church management. 2. Church officers. 3. Pastoral theology—Lutheran Church. 4. City churches. I. Title.

ANDERSON, Philip A 254
Church meetings that matter [by] Philip A. Anderson. Philadelphia, United Church Press [1965] 111 p. 21 cm. Includes bibliographical references. [BV652.15.A5] 65-13499
1. Church meetings. I. Title.

ANDERSON, Philip A. 254
Church meetings that matter. Philadelphia, United Church [c.1965] 111p. 21cm. Bibl. [BV652.15.A5] 65-13499 1.60 pap.,
1. Church meetings. I. Title.

BALK, Alfred. 254
The religion business. Richmond, John Knox Press [1968] 96 p. 22 cm. "Appendix: Some representative policy statements on churches and taxes (excerpts)": (p. [55]-96) Bibliographical footnotes. [BV777.B34] 68-25011 3.00
1. Church property—United States. 2. Taxation, Exemption from—United States. 3. United States—Religion—1945- I. Title.

BARTOW, Donald W. 254
Creative churchmanship [by] Donald W. Bartow. New York, World Pub. Co. [1969] 200 p. 21 cm. [BV600.B375 1969] 70-90922 4.95
1. Church renewal. 2. Church management. I. Title.

BELEW, M. Wendell. 254
Churches and how they grow [by] M. Wendell Belew. Nashville, Broadman Press [1971] 144 p. 21 cm. [BV652.25.B43] 79-157402 ISBN 0-8054-2522-5 3.95
1. Church growth. I. Title.

BOCKELMAN, Wilfred 254
Toward better church committees. Minneapolis, Augsburg [c.1962] 80p. 62-9098 1.50 pap.,
1. Church officers. I. Title.

BRAMER, John C. 254
Efficient church business management. Philadelphia, Westminster Press [c.1960] 150p. 21cm. Bibl.: p.147-150. tables. 60-7471 3.50
1. Church work. I. Title.

BRODERICK, Robert C., 1913- 254
The parish council handbook; a handbook to bring the power of renewal to your parish, by Robert C. Broderick. Chicago, Franciscan Herald Press [1968] vii, 76 p. 21 cm. [BV652.9.B7] 68-21817
1. Parish councils. I. Title.

BRODERICK, Robert C., 1913- 254
Your parish—where the action is; parish leadership in the modern church, by Robert C. Broderick. Chicago, Franciscan Herald Press [1974] v, 50 p. illus. 21 cm. [BV652.1.B76] 74-572 ISBN 0-8199-0493-7 2.50 (pbk.).
1. Christian leadership. 2. Parishes. I. Title.

CARR, James McLeod. 254
Working together in the larger parish. Atlanta [Board of Church Extension, Presbyterian Church in the United States, 1960] 105p. illus. 23cm. Includes bibliography. [BV638.4.C3] 60-8633
1. Larger parishes. I. Title.

CHAMPLIN, Joseph M. 254
The living parish : a believing, caring, praying people / Joseph M. Champlin. Notre Dame, Ind. : Ave Maria Press, c1977. 156 p. : ill. ; 22 cm. [BV700.C47] 76-51887 ISBN 0-87793-129-1 pbk. : 2.95
1. Parishes. I. Title.

CHRISTENSEN, James L. 254
How to increase church attendance. [Westwood, N. J.] F. H. Revell Co. [c.1961] 126p. Bibl. 61-9240 2.00 bds.,
1. Church attendance. I. Title.

DITZEN, Lowell Russell 254
Handbook for the church secretary. Englewood Cliffs, N.J., Prentice [1964, c.1963] xi, 229p. forms, tables. 24cm. 63-19429 5.95 bds,
1. Church secretaries. I. Title.

DITZEN, Lowell Russell 254
Handbook of church administration. New York, Macmillan [c.]1962. 390p. illus. 22cm. 62-11914 7.00
1. Church work. I. Title.

DOBBINS, Gaines Stanley 254
A ministering church. Nashville, Broadman Press [c.1960] viii, 231p. 22cm. Bibl. 60-9530 .220-227. 3.95
1. Church work. 2. Pastoral theology. I. Title.

DONALDSON, Margaret F 254
Giving and growing: finance and public relations in the local church. [Westwood, N. J.] F. H. Revell Co. [1956] 154 p. 21 cm. [BV652.D58] 56-10892
1. Church work. 2. Church finance. 3. Advertising—Churches. I. Title.

DUBLIN. St. Patrick's 254
Cathedral.
The "Dignitas decani" of St. Patrick's Cathedral, Dublin. Edited by Newport B. White. With introd. by Aubrey Gwynn. Dublin, Stationery Office, 1957. xxvii, 205 p. 25 cm. At head of title: Coimisiun Laimhscribhinni na hEireann. Irish Manuscripts Commission. Text chiefly in Latin. [BX4632.D75S242 1957] 74-187142
1. Dublin. St. Patrick's Cathedral—History—Sources. I. White, Newport Benjamin, ed. II. Ireland (Eire). Irish Manuscripts Commission. III. Title.

DUNNAM, Maxie D. 254
The manipulator and the church [by] Maxie D. Dunnam, Gary J. Herbertson [and] Everett L. Shostrom. Nashville, Abingdon Press [1968] 176 p. illus. 21 cm. Includes bibliographical references. [BV652.2.D8] 68-27627 3.50
1. Self-realization. 2. Church renewal. 3. Church group work. I. Herbertson, Gary J., joint author. II. Shostrom, Everett L., 1921- joint author. III. Title.

ELY, Virginia, 1899- 254
The church secretary. Chicago, Moody Press [1956] 190 p. 22 cm. [BV705.E47] 56-2878
1. Church secretaries. I. Title.

ENGSTROM, Theodore Wilhelm, 254
1916-
The making of a Christian leader / by Ted W. Engstrom ; foreword by W. Stanley Mooneyham. Grand Rapids : Zondervan Pub. House, c1976. 214 p. ; 23 cm. Includes indexes. Bibliography: p. [209] [BV652.1.E53] 76-13220 6.95
1. Christian leadership. I. Title.

FELDMAN, Julian, 1920- 254
Church purchasing procedures [by] Julian Feldman and contributing author G. Henry Richert. Englewood Cliffs, N.J., Prentice [1964] 192p. forms. 22cm. (Church bus. mgmt. ser.) [BV652.75.F4] 64-7827 3.95
1. Church purchasing. I. Title. II. Series.

FORD, George Lonnie, 1914- 254
Manual on management for Christian workers. Grand Rapids, Mich., Zondervan [c.1964] 152 p. 21 cm. 64-15550 2.95, bds.
1. Church work. I. Title.

FORD, George Lonnie, 1914- 254
Manual on management for Christian workers. Grand Rapids, Zondervan Pub. House [1964] 152 p. 21 cm. [BV4400.F66] 64-15550
1. Church work. I. Title.

GENERAL Council of the 254
Congregational and Christian Churches of the United States.
Pension boards, Congregational Christian Churches; the Annuity Fund for Congregational Ministers, Retirement Fund for Lay Workers, Ministerial Relief Division of the Board of Home Missions. [Reports] New York. v, illus. 18 cm. annual. Title varies: Reports of the Congregational pension boards; the Annuity Fund for Congregational Ministers. Retirement Fund for Lay Workers, Ministerial Relief Division of the Board of Home Missions. [BX7245.5.G4] 52-17246
1. Congregational Churches—Clergy—Salaries, pensions, etc. I. Title.

GILCHRIST, Jack. 254
The vacant pulpit. Valley Forge [Pa.] Judson Press [1969] 159 p. 20 cm. [BV664.G5] 77-81443 2.95
1. Clergy—Appointment, call and election. I. Title.

GRANT, Perley Cummings 254
The prophet of Calvary church. New York, Vantage [c.1962] 142p. 21cm. 3.00 bds.,
I. Title.

GREEN, Hollis L. 254
Why churches die; a guide to basic evangelism and church growth, by Hollis L. Green. Minneapolis, Bethany Fellowship [1972] 219 p. 21 cm. [BV652.25.G7] 73-152940 ISBN 0-87123-642-7 1.95
1. Church growth. 2. Evangelistic work. I. Title.

GRENELL, Zelotes, 1841-1918. 254
The work of the clerk [by] Zelotes Grenell and Agnes Grenell Goss. [Rev.] Valley Forge [Pa.] Judson Press [1967] 63 p. forms. 18 cm. Previous ed. published in 1909 under title: The church clerk. [BV705.G7 1967] 67-25895
1. Church officers. I. Goss, Agnes Grenell, joint author. II. Title.

HAHN, Celia A. 254
The minister is leaving: a Project Test Pattern book in parish development [by] Celia A. Hahn. New York, Seabury Press [1974] 120 p. 21 cm. "A crossroad book." [BV664.H34] 74-9943 ISBN 0-8164-2099-8 3.50 (pbk.).
1. Clergy—Appointment, call, and election—Case studies. I. Project Test Pattern. II. Title.

HAHN, Celia A. 254
Patterns for parish development, edited by Celia A. Hahn. Foreword by Martin E. Marty. New York, Seabury Press [1974] xviii, 169 p. 21 cm. "A Crossroad book." Includes bibliographical references. [BV700.H3] 74-11189 ISBN 0-8164-2098-X 3.95
1. Parishes. I. Title.

HALL, Asa Zadel, M. D. 254
What goes on your bulletin board Chicago, Moody [1961, c.1960] 80p. illus. 1.00 pap.,
I. Title.

HARRAL, Stewart, 1906-1964. 254
Handbook of effective church letters. New York, Abingdon Press [1965] 208 p. 21 cm. [BV652.H35] 65-15233
1. Church correspondence. I. Title.

HARRAL, Stewart, 1906-1964 254
Handbook of effective church letters. Nashville, Abingdon [c.1965] 208p. 21cm. [BV652.H35] 65-15233 3.50
1. Church correspondence. I. Title.

HARTRIDGE, Reginald Alfred 254
Rupert.
A history of vicarages in the Middle Ages, by R. A. R. Hartridge. New York, Barnes & Noble [1968] x, 273 p. 23 cm. On spine: Vicarages in the Middle Ages. Reprint of the

1930 ed. Bibliography: p. [230]-242. [BV775.H3 1968] 68-23763
1. Church property. I. Title. II. Title: Vicarages in the Middle Ages.

HATCH, C W, 1903- 254
Stewardship enriches life. Anderson, Ind., Warner Press [1951] 107 p. 20 cm. [BV772.H34] 51-13778
1. Stewardship, Christian. I. Title.

HATCH, Clarence W 1903-1960. 254
Stewardship enriches life. Anderson, Ind., Warner Press [1951] 107 p. 20 cm. [BV772.H34] 51-13778
1. Stewardship, Christian. I. Title.

HENDRIX, Olan, 1927- 254
Management for the Christian worker / by Olan Hendrix. Libertyville, Ill. : Quill Publications, c1976. p. cm. Bibliography: p. [BV652.H39] 76-3510 ISBN 0-916608-01-8 : 6.95
1. Religious and ecclesiastical institutions—Management. 2. Church management. 3. Management. I. Title.

HILL, Leonard, 1929- 254
Your work on the pulpit committee. Nashville, Broadman Press [1970] 66 p. illus. 17 cm. [BV664.H5] 70-93916
1. Clergy—Appointment, call, and election. I. Title.

HILLOCK, Wilfred M. 254
Involved : an introduction to church participation and management / Wilfred M. Hillock ; [edited by Gerald Wheeler]. Nashville : Southern Pub. Association, c1977. 155 p. ; 22 cm. Bibliography: p. 147-155. [BV652.H5] 77-78102 ISBN 0-8127-0140-2 pbk. : 7.95
1. Church management. I. Title.

THE House church evolving / 254
edited by Arthur L. Foster. Chicago : Exploration Press, c1976. 126 p. ; 23 cm. (Studies in ministry and parish life) Includes bibliographical references. [BV601.85.H68] 76-4198 ISBN 0-913552-04-6 : 8.00 ISBN 0-913552-05-4 pbk. : 3.50
1. House churches—Addresses, essays, lectures. I. Foster, Arthur Lorne, 1922- II. Series.

HOWSE, William Lewis, 1905- 254
The church staff and its work. Nashville, Broadman Press [1959] 174p. 21cm. [BV652.H6] 59-5857
1. Church work. 2. Church officers. I. Title.

HUBBARD, La Fayette Ronald, 1911- 254
The organization executive course : an encyclopedia of scientology policy / by L. Ron Hubbard. Los Angeles : American Saint Hill Organization, 1974. 8 v. : ill. ; 32 cm. Vols. numbered 0-7. Includes index. [BP605.S2H826] 74-195055 ISBN 0-88404-033-X
1. Scientology. I. Title.

HUBER, Evelyn. 254
Enlist, train, support church leaders / Evelyn M. Huber. Valley Forge, Pa. : Judson Press, [1975] 32 p. ; 22 cm. Includes bibliographical references. [BV652.1.H8] 74-22521 ISBN 0-8170-0667-2 : 1.50.
1. Christian leadership. I. Title.

HUDNUT, Robert K. 254
Arousing the sleeping giant; how to organize your church for action [by] Robert K. Hudnut. [1st ed.] New York, Harper & Row [1973] p. Includes bibliographical references. [BV652.H75] 73-6334 ISBN 0-06-064064-2 5.95
1. Church management. I. Title.

INFORMAL groups in the church 254
: papers of the second Cerdic colloquium, Strasbourg, May 13-15, 1971 / edited by Rene Metz and Jean Schlick ; translated by Matthew J. O'Connell. Pittsburgh : Pickwick Press, 1975. p. cm. (Pittsburgh theological monograph series ; 7) Translation of Les Groupes informels dans l'Eglise. Includes bibliographical references. [BV652.2.G6813] 75-25591 ISBN 0-915138-08-5
1. Church group work—Congresses. 2. Sociology, Christian—Congresses. I. Metz, Rene. II. Schlick, Jean. III. Title. IV. Series.

JACOBS, James Vernon, 1898- 254
500 plans and ideas for church officers Cincinnati, Standard Pub. Foundation [1957] 110p. illus. 20cm. [DV652.J3] 57-32414
1. Church work. 2. Church officers. I. Title.

JENSEN, Mary, 1939- 254
Audiovisual idea book for churches [by] Mary and Andrew Jensen. Minneapolis, Augsburg Pub. House [1974] 160 p. 22 cm. Bibliography: p. 159-160. [BV1535.J46] 73-88612 ISBN 0-8066-1415-3 3.95 (pbk.).
1. Church work—Audio-visual aids. I. Jensen, Andrew, 1938- joint author. II. Title.

JOHNSON, Alvin D. 254
The work of the usher [by] Alvin D. Johnson. Valley Forge [Pa.] Judson Press [1966] 64 p. illus. 17 cm. [BV705.J6] 66-22519
1. Church ushers. I. Title.

JOHNSON, Douglas W., 1934- 254
Managing change in the church [by] Douglas W. Johnson. New York, Friendship Press [1974] 96 p. 22 cm. Includes bibliographical references. [BV600.2.J56] 74-12458 ISBN 0-377-00017-5 3.50 (pbk.).
1. Church renewal. I. Title.

JONES, Ezra Earl. 254
Strategies for new churches / Ezra Earl Jones. 1st ed. New York : Harper & Row, c1976. xiv, 178 p. : ill. ; 21 cm. Bibliography: p. 177-178. [BV652.24.J66 1976] 75-36731 ISBN 0-06-064183-5 : 7.95
1. Church development, New. I. Title.

JONES, George Curtis, 1911- 254
The church parking lot [by] G. Curtis Jones. Philadelphia, Fortress [1967] xi, 97p. plans. 18cm. Bibl. [HE370.J68] 67-16467 1.75 pap.,
1. Churches—Parking facilities. I. Title.

JONES, George Curtis, 1911- 254
Handbook of church correspondence. New York, Macmillan [1962] 216p. illus. 22cm. [BV652.9.J6] 62-15689
1. Church correspondence. I. Title.

JUDY, Marvin T. 254
The cooperative parish in nonmetropolitan areas [by] Marvin T. Judy. Nashville, Abingdon Press [1967] 208 p. illus. 21 cm. Based on the author's The larger parish and group ministry and his Parish development aids. Bibliography: p. 197-204. [BV638.4.J79] 67-22761
1. Larger parishes. I. Title.

JUDY, Marvin T 254
The larger parish and group ministry. New York, Abingdon Press [1959] 175p. illus. 21cm. 'Enlarged from [the author's] Serve to survive.' Includes bibliography. [BV638.4.J8 1959] 59-5409
1. Larger parishes. 2. Sociology, Rural. I. Title.

JUDY, Marvin T. 254
The multiple staff ministry [by] Marvin T. Judy. With the cooperation of Murlene O. Judy. Nashville, Abingdon Press [1969] 287 p. illus. 25 cm. Bibliography: p. 274-282. [BV650.2.J8] 69-18442 6.95
1. Church polity. 2. Church officers. 3. City clergy. I. Title.

JUDY, Marvin T. 254
The parish development process [by] Marvin T. Judy. Nashville, Abingdon Press [1973] 207 p. illus. 23 cm. "An enlargement and revision of The cooperative parish in nonmetropolitan areas." Bibliography: p. 201-204. [BV638.4.J792] 72-8819 ISBN 0-687-30086-X 5.75
1. Larger parishes. I. Title.

KILINSKI, Kenneth K. 254
Organization and leadership in the local church [by] Kenneth K. Kilinski and Jerry C. Wofford. Grand Rapids, Zondervan Pub. House [1973] 253 p. illus. 23 cm. Bibliography: p. 247-250. [BV652.K49] 72-95532 5.95
1. Church management. 2. Christian leadership. 3. Spiritual life. I. Wofford, Jerry C., joint author. II. Title.

KNIGHT, Walker L., 1924- 254
Seven beginnings : the human touch in starting new churches / written by Walker Knight ; photographed by Ken Touchton ; editor/designer, Elaine Selcraig Furlow, editorial assistant, Patti Benton ; photographic lab technician, Paul Obregon ; artist, Debbie Petticord. Atlanta : Home Mission Board, Southern Baptist Convention, 1976. p. cm. (Crossing barriers in national missions) [BV652.24.K58] 75-44496 5.95
1. Church development, New—Case studies. I. Touchton, Ken. II. Title.

LAMBERT, Norman M. 254
Managing church groups / by Norman M. Lambert. Dayton, Ohio : Pflaum Pub., c1975. x, 85 p. : ill. ; 28 cm. Bibliography: p. 85. [BV652.L33] 75-14637 ISBN 0-8278-0005-3 pbk. : 3.95
1. Church management. I. Title.

LARSON, Martin Alfred, 1897- 254
The churches: their riches, revenues, and immunities; an analysis of tax-exempt property, by Martin A. Larson and C. Stanley Lowell. Washington, R. B. Luce [1969] 301 p. 22 cm. Includes bibliographies. [BV777.L33] 73-85878
1. Church property—Taxation—U.S. 2. Church and state in the United States. I. Lowell, C. Stanley, joint author. II. Title.

LARSON, Philip M. 254
Vital church management / Philip M. Larson, Jr. Atlanta : John Knox Press, c1977. p. cm. [BV652.L35] 76-12394 ISBN 0-8042-1883-8 pbk. : 4.95
1. Church management. I. Title.

LESSEL, William M 254
Duplicating and publicity manual for Christian workers. Chicago, Moody Press [1957] 94p. illus. 28cm. [BV653.L18] 57-37886
1. Office equipment and supplies. 2. Church work. I. Title.

LINAMEN, Harold F 254
Business handbook for churches. Anderson, Ind., Warner Press [1957] 168p. illus. 21cm. [BV652.L5] 57-30919
1. Church work. I. Title.

LINAMEN, Harold F 254
Business handbook for churches, by Harold F. Linamen. Rev. ed. Anderson, Ind., Warner Press [c1964] 176 p. forms. 21 cm. [BV652.L5] 65-12586
1. Church management. I. Title.

LINAMEN, Harold F. 254
The church says . . . welcome! Anderson, Ind., Warner Press [dist. Gospel Trumpet Press, c.1960] 63p. illus. 28cm. 60-7926 2.00, pap., plastic binding.
1. Church work. I. Title.

LINAMEN, Harold F 254
Letter writing for the church. Anderson, Ind., Warner Press [1958] 100p. 28cm. [BV652.L52] 58-6420
1. Church correspondence. I. Title.

LINDGREN, Alvin J 254
Foundations for purposeful church administration [by] Alvin J. Lindgren. New York, Abingdon Press [1966] 302 p. illus. 24 cm. Includes bibliographical references. [BV652.L55] 65-16459
1. Church management. I. Title.

LINDGREN, Alvin J. 254
Foundations for purposeful church administration. Nashville, Abingdon [c.1965] 302p. illus. 24cm. Bibl. [BV652.L55] 65-16459 5.50
1. Church management. I. Title.

LINDGREN, Alvin J. 254
Management for your church / Alvin J. Lindgren, Norman Shawchuck. Nashville : Abingdon, c1977. 160 p. : ill. ; 23 cm. Includes index. Bibliography: p. 153-156. [BV652.L57] 77-425 ISBN 0-687-23062-4 : 7.95
1. Church management. I. Shawchuck, Norman, 1935- joint author. II. Title.

LIVESAY, George Benton. 254
Leadership training in the local church (including the Christian day school) / by George Banton Livesay. [San Diego? Calif. : s.n.], c1976. vii, 117 p. : ill. ; 20 cm. Bibliography: p. 113-114. [BV652.1.L58] 76-47753
1. Christian leadership. 2. Christian education. I. Title: Leadership training in the local church ...

LUFFBERRY, Henry Benner. 254
A new manual for vestrymen [by] Henry B. Luffberry. Philadelphia, Fortress Press [1972] 87 p. 20 cm. [BV705.L8 1972] 72-75651 ISBN 0-8006-0122-X 2.50
1. Church officers. I. Title. II. Title. Manual for vestrymen.

LUNT, William Edward, 1882- 254
ed. and tr.
Papal revenues in the middle ages, by William E. Lunt. New York, Octagon, 1965. 2 v. 24 cm. (Records of civilization: sources and studies, ed. under the auspices of the Dept. of history, Columbia university ... no. xix) A collection of the original records of the papal camera, in translation, with historical introduction. cf. Pref. "Bibliography of works cited": vol. II, p. [539]-565. [BX1950.L8] 34-15984
1. Catholic church—France. 2. Catholic church—History—Sources. I. Catholic church. Camera apostolica. II. Title.

LUNT, William Edward, 1882-1956. 254
Financial relations of the papacy with England. Cambridge, Mass., Mediaeval Academy of America, 1939-62. 2 v. 26 cm. (Mediaeval academy of America. Publication no. 33, 74. Studies in Anglo-papal relations during the middle ages, 1-2) Series: Mediaeval Academy of America. Studies in Anglo-papal relations during the Contents.Contents. -- [1] To 1327. -- [2] 1327-1534. Bibliography: v. 1, p. 687-721. Bibliographical footnotes. [BR747.A1M4 vol. 1-2] 39-29743
1. Taxation, Papal. 2. Taxation — Gt. Brit. — Hist. 3. Catholic Church — Relations — Gt. Brit. 4. Gt. Brit. — Relations (general) with Catholic Church. 5. Annates. I. Title. II. Series.

LYONS, Bernard. 254
Parish councils; renewing the Christian community. Foreword by John J. Wright. Techny, Ill., Divine Word [1967] xvii, 149p. 22cm. Bibl. [BV652.9.L9] 67-29363 2.25 pap.,
1. Parish councils. I. Title.

LYONS, Bernard. 254
Programs for parish councils; an action manual. Introd. by Mr. and Mrs. Patrick F. Crowley. Techny, Ill., Divine Word Publications [1969] xix, 124 p. illus. 22 cm. Includes bibliographies. [BV652.9.L92] 69-20417 1.50
1. Parish councils. I. Title.

MCCARTT, Clara Anniss 254
How to organize your church office. [Westwood, N.J.] Revell [1962] 63p. 22cm. (Revell's better church res.) 62-17111 1.00 pap.,
1. Office practice in churches. I. Title.

MCCUDDEN, John. 254
The parish in crisis, edited by John McCudden. Techny, Ill., Divine World Publications [1967] xiv, 193 p. 21 cm. Bibliographical footnotes. [BX1913.M3] 67-19034
1. Parishes. 2. Pastoral theology—Catholic Church. I. Title.

MCDONOUGH, Reginald M. 254
Working with volunteer leaders in the church / Reginald M. McDonough. Nashville : Broadman Press, c1976. 146 p. : ill. ; 19 cm. Bibliography: p. 145-146. [BV652.1.M3] 76-372425 ISBN 0-8054-3214-0 pbk. : 2.95
1. Christian leadership. 2. Church work. I. Title.

MCGAVRAN, Donald Anderson, 1897- 254
How to grow a church, by Donald A. McGavran with Win C. Arn. Glendale, Calif., Regal Books [1973] 180 p. illus. 19 cm. Bibliography: p. 179. [BV652.25.M28] 73-80207 ISBN 0-8307-0238-5 2.95
1. Church growth. I. Arn, Winfield. II. Title.

MCGAVRAN, Donald Anderson, 1897- 254
How to grow a church, by Donald A. McGavran with Win C. Arn. Glendale, Calif., Regal Books [1973] 180 p. illus. 19 cm. Bibliography: p. 179. [BV652.25.M28] 73-80207 ISBN 0-8307-0238-5 2.95
1. Church growth. I. Arn, Winfield. II. Title.

*MACNAIR, Donald J. 254
The birth, care, and feeding of a local church. / Donald J. MacNair. Grand Rapids : Baker Book House, 1976 c1971. xii, 211 p. : plan ; 22 cm. (A Canon Press book). Includes index. [BV652] ISBN 0-8010-5996-8 pbk. : 3.95
1. Church management. I. Title.

MACNAIR, Donald J., 1922- 254
The birth, care, and feeding of a local church / Donald J. MacNair. Washington : Canon Press, c1973. x, 212 p. ; 24 cm. Includes index. [BV3.M3] 75-312222 ISBN 0-913686-08-5
1. Theology, Practical. I. Title.

MADSEN, Paul O. 254
The small church—valid, vital, victorious / by Paul O. Madsen. Valley Forge, Pa. : Judson Press, [1975] 126 p. ; 22 cm. [BV637.8.M32] 74-22519 ISBN 0-8170-0669-9 pbk. : 3.95
1. Small churches. I. Title.

MANUAL for church officers 254
and boards [workbk.] St. Louis, Concordia [c.1961] 90p. 28cm. 1.00 pap.,
1. Church—Administration.

*MARTIN, George 254
Parish renewable : a charismatic approach / George Martin. Ann Arbor, Mich. : Word of Life, c1976. 135 p. ; 21 cm. [BV700] ISBN 0-89283-030-1 pbk. : 1.95
1. Church renewal. 2. Parishes. I. Title.
Publisher's address: P.O. Box 331, Ann Arbor, Mich.

MICKEY, Paul A., 1937- 254
What new creation? / Paul A. Mickey & Robert L. Wilson. Nashville : Abingdon, c1977. 192 p. ; 21 cm. Includes bibliographical references. [BV652.M5] 76-49559 ISBN 0-687-44850-6 pbk. : 5.95
1. Church management. I. Wilson, Robert Leroy, 1925- joint author. II. Title.

MOORE, Paul, 1942- 254
The art of Christian promotion / Paul Moore,

with William Proctor. Old Tappan, N.J. : Revell, [1975] 127 p. ; 21 cm. [BV3790.M7] 75-2450 ISBN 0-8007-0734-6 : 4.95
1. Evangelistic work. 2. Communication (Theology) 3. Mass media in religion. I. Proctor, William, joint author. II. Title.

MOORHOUS, Carl W. 254
Growing new churches : step-by step procedures in new church planting / Carl W. Moorhous ; foreword by Paul Benjamin. Gary, Ind. : Moorhous, 1975. xv, 96 p. : ill. ; 22 cm. Bibliography: p. 95. [BV652.25.M66] 75-13333
1. Church growth—Handbooks, manuals, etc. I. Title.

MURPHY, Bonneau Pernell, 1909- 254
The building and care of Methodist Church property. New York, Division of Home Missions and Church Extension, Board of Missions and Church Extension, Methodist Church [1951] 54 p. 23 cm. [BV604.M8] 52-28964
1. Church property — Maintenance and repair. 2. Churches, Methodist. I. Title.

MURPHY, Bonneau Pernell, 1909- 254
The building and care of Methodist Church property. [Rev. and enl.] New York, Division of National Missions, Board of Missions, Methodist Church [1961] 131p. illus. 23cm. Includes bibliography. [BV604.M8 1961] 61-2649
1. Church property—Maintenance and repair. 2. Churches. Methodist. I. Title.

MYERS, Katie Lea. 254
The church secretary: her calling and her work. New York, Seabury Press [1965] 128 p. 20 cm. Bibliography: p. 125-128. [BV705.M9] 65-21313
1. Church secretaries.

NEITHOLD, Eugene C., 1939- 254
Church business policies outlined / Eugene C. Neithold. Newark, Del. : Church Books, c1976. p. cm. Includes index. [BV773.N44] 76-4051 ISBN 0-916778-01-0 : 3.50
1. Church finance. 2. Church management. I. Title.

NYGAARD, Norman Eugene, 1897- 254
A practical church administration handbook. Grand Rapids, Mich., Baker Bk. [c.]1962. 103p. illus. 23cm. 62-19236 1.95 bds.,
1. Church work. I. Title.

OLSEN, Charles M. 254
The base church; creating community through multiple forms [by] Charles M. Olsen. Atlanta, Forum House [1973] xvi, 167 p. illus. 24 cm. Includes bibliographical references. [BV600.2.O38] 73-81260 ISBN 0-913618-13-6 4.95
1. Church renewal. 2. Church group work. I. Title.

PAGE, Harry Robert. 254
Church budget development. Englewood Cliffs, N.J., Prentice-Hall [1964] 192 p. illus. 21 cm. (Church business management series) Bibliography: p. 179-180. [BV773.P3] 63-18113
1. Church finance — Accounting. I. Title. II. Series.

PAGE, Harry Robert 254
Church budget development. Englewood Cliffs, N.J., Prentice [c.1964] 192p. illus. 21cm. (Church bus. mgmt. ser.) Bibl. 63-18113 3.95 bds.,
1. Church finance—Accounting. I. Title. II. Series.

PALMER, Bernard Alvin, 1914- 254
Pattern for a total church : Sherman Williams and his staff share ways any church can grow / Bernard Palmer. Wheaton, Ill. : Victor Books, c1975. 135 p. : ill. ; 21 cm. Includes index. [BX9999.C3P34] 75-8026 ISBN 0-88207-717-1 : 2.50
1. Redwood Chapel Community Church, Castro Valley, Calif. I. Williams, Sherman. II. Title.

PARROTT, Leslie, 1922- 254
The usher's manual; a spiritual and practical guidebook. Grand Rapids, Zondervan Pub. House [1970] 64 p. illus. 21 cm. [BV705.P33] 72-95041
1. Church ushers. I. Title.

PFNUR, Vinzenz. 254
Kirche und Amt : neuere Literatur zur okumenischen Diskussion um die Amtsfrage / zusammengestellt von Vinzenz Pfnur ; mit einem Geleitwort von Albert Brandenburg. Munster, Westfalen : Aschendorff, c1975. 32 p. ; 25 cm. (Catholica : Beiheft ; 1) Cover title. [Z7820.P43] [BV4011] 016.2621 75-518521 ISBN 3-402-07243-2
1. Pastoral theology—Bibliography. 2. Christian union—Bibliography. 3. Pastoral theology and Christian union—Bibliography. I. Title. II. Series.

PLANNING for planning; 254
perspectives on diocesan research and planning. Edited by George M. Pope, III and Bernard Quinn. Washington, Center for Applied Research in the Apostolate [1972] v, 58 p. 28 cm. (CARA information service R-0-10) "Papers of a conference held at Duquesne University, May 16-17, 1972." "TCRRC project no. 157, August 1972." Bibliography: p. 57-58. [BV652.P57] 72-197467 1.25
1. Church management. I. Pope, George M., ed. II. Quinn, Bernard, 1928- ed. III. Center for Applied Research in the Apostolate, Washington, D.C.

POSTCONCILIAR parish (The) 254
ed. by James O'Gara. New York, Kenedy [1967] xiii, 197p. 22cm. Bibl. [BX1913.P63] 67-18428 4.95
1. Pastoral theology—Catholic Church. 2. Parishes—U. S. I. O'Gara, James, ed.

PRESCRIPTIONS for parishes, 254
by Jean M. Haldane [and others] New York, Seabury Press [1973] 123 p. 21 cm. (An Original Seabury paperback, 81) [BV700.P74] 73-76062 ISBN 0-8164-2080-7 2.95
1. Parishes. 2. Church renewal. I. Haldane, Jean M.

RADEMACHER, William J., 1928- 254
Working with parish councils? / W. J. Rademacher. Canfield, Ohio : Alba Books, [1977?] 186 p. ; 18 cm. Bibliography: p. 185-186. [BV652.9.R3] 77-71024 ISBN 0-8189-1149-2 pbk. : 1.75
1. Parish councils. I. Title.

REID, Clyde H. 254
Groups alive—church alive; the effective use of small groups in the local church, by Clyde Reid. [1st ed.] New York, Harper & Row [1969] 126 p. illus. 22 cm. Includes bibliographical references. [BV652.2.R4] 69-17008 3.95
1. Church group work. I. Title.

REIN, Remus C 1905- 254
The congregation at work. Saint Louis, Concordia Pub. House [1962] 247p. illus. 24cm. Includes bibliography. [BV652.R38 1962] 61-18221
1. Church work. I. Title.

REITZ, Rudiger. 254
The church in experiment; studies in new congregational structures and functional mission. Nashville, Abingdon Press [1969] 205 p. 23 cm. Bibliography: p. 193-198. [BV600.2.R4] 73-84716 4.75
1. Church renewal—Case studies. I. Title.

ROBINSON, Godfrey Clive. 254
Church worker's handbook [by] Godfrey C. Robinson [and] Stephen F. Winward. Valley Forge [Pa.] Judson Press [1973, c1972] 96 p. 18 cm. A revision of the work first published in 1957 under title: The King's business. [BV4400.R63 1973] 73-4983 ISBN 0-8170-0606-0 1.50 (pbk.)
1. Church work—Handbooks, manuals, etc. I. Winward, Stephen F., joint author. II. Title.

RUDGE, Peter Frederick. 254
Management in the church / Peter F. Rudge. London ; New York : McGraw-Hill, c1976. p. cm. Includes index. Bibliography: p. [BV652.R79] 76-16121 ISBN 0-07-084478-X : £5.25
1. Church management. I. Title.

RUSBULDT, Richard E. 254
Local church planning manual : contains all needed instructions and worksheets / Richard E. Rusbuldt, Richard K. Gladden, Norman M. Green, Jr. Valley Forge, PA : Judson Press, c1977. 248 p. : ill. ; 28 cm. Bibliography: p. 99. [BV652.R87] 77-7109 ISBN 0-8170-0753-9 pbk. : 13.50
1. Church management—Handbooks, manuals, etc. I. Gladden, Richard K., joint author. II. Green, Norman M., joint author. III. Title.

SCHALLER, Lyle E. 254
Creative church administration / Lyle E. Schaller and Charles A. Tidwell. Nashville : Abingdon, [1975] 208 p. ; 22 cm. Bibliography: p. 204-208. [BV652.S28] 75-15953 ISBN 0-687-09816-5 pbk. : 4.95
1. Church management. I. Tidwell, Charles A., joint author. II. Title.

SCHALLER, Lyle E. 254
The decision-makers; how to improve the quality of decision-making in the churches [by] Lyle E. Schaller. Nashville, Abingdon Press [1974] 223 p. 23 cm. Includes bibliographical references. [BV652.S29] 73-16411 ISBN 0-687-10402-5 5.95
1. Church management. 2. Decision-making. I. Title.

SCHALLER, Lyle E. 254
Hey, that's our church! [By] Lyle E. Schaller. Nashville, Abingdon Press [1975] 192 p. illus. 22 cm. Includes bibliographical references. [BV652.S293] 74-17094 ISBN 0-687-16955-0 4.50
1. Church management. I. Title.

SCHALLER, Lyle E. 254
The local church looks to the future [by] Lyle E. Schaller. Nashville, Abingdon Press [1968] 240 p. 20 cm. Bibliography: p. 239-240. [BV652.S3] 68-17449
1. Church management. 2. Pastoral theology. I. Title.

SCHALLER, Lyle E. 254
Parish planning [by] Lyle E. Schaller. Nashville, Abingdon Press [1971] 240 p. 22 cm. Includes bibliographical references. [BV652.S33] 70-148076 ISBN 0-687-30102-5
1. Church management. I. Title.

SCHALLER, Lyle E. 254
The pastor and the people; building a new partnership for effective ministry [by] Lyle E. Schaller. Nashville, Abingdon Press [1973] 176 p. 20 cm. Includes bibliographical references. [BV4011.S33] 72-8567 ISBN 0-687-30136-X pap. 2.45
1. Pastoral theology. 2. Theology, Practical. I. Title.

SCHALLER, Lyle E. 254
Survival tactics in the parish / Lyle E. Schaller. Nashville : Abingdon, c1977. 208 p. ; 21 cm. [BV4011.S34] 76-54751 ISBN 0-687-40757-5 pbk. : 4.95
1. Pastoral theology. 2. Parishes. I. Title.

SCHWARTZ, Seymour S., 1915- 254
Rigidized inflatable solar energy concentrators, by S. Schwartz and J. Bagby. Springfield, Va., For sale by the Clearinghouse for Federal Scientific and Technical Information [1965] xi, 82 p. illus. 27 cm. (NASA contractor report, NASA CR-254) "Prepared under contract no. NAS 1-3244 by Hughes Aircraft Company, Culver City, Calif., for National Aeronautics and Space Administration." [TL521.3.C6A3 no.] 65-62375
1. Space vehicles—Solar engines—Collected works. I. Bagby, John Pendleton, 1924- joint author. II. Hughes Aircraft Company. III. U. S. National Aeronautics and Space Administration. IV. Title. V. Series. VI. Series: U. S. National Aeronautics and Space Administration. NASA contractor report CR-254

SEBOLDT, Roland H A ed. 254
God and our parish; worship resources for the parish. Saint Louis, Concordia Pub. House [1963] 295 p. 21 cm. [BV198.S35] 63-14986
1. Worship programs. I. Title.

SEBOLDT, Ronald H. A., ed. 254
God and our parish; worship resources for the parish. St. Louis, Concordia [c.1963] 295p. 21cm. 63-14986 5.00
1. Worship programs. I. Title.

SENFT, Kenneth C. 254
New life in the parish, by Kenneth C. Senft. Minneapolis, Augsburg Pub. House [1970] 90 p. 20 cm. Includes bibliographical references. [BV600.2.S45] 78-101107 2.50
1. Church renewal. I. Title.

SOUTHERN Baptist Convention. Baptist Brotherhood Commission. 254
Church program guidebook. 1964/65- [Nashville, Tenn., Convention Press] v. 28 cm. annual. Supersedes the Curriculum guide issued by the Sunday School Board of the Southern Baptist Convention. Produced jointly by the commission (called Brotherhood Commission) various departments of the convention's Sunday School Board, and the convention's Woman's Missionary Union. [BV652.A1S6] 64-16878
1. Church work—Handbooks, manuals, etc. 2. Religious education—Curricula. I. Title.

STOTTS, Herbert Edward, 1916- *254
The church inventory handbook. Denver, Wesley Press [1952] 235 p. illus. 24 cm. [BV652.S77] 52-27459
1. Social surveys. 2. Church work. I. Title.

SWEET, Herman J 1899- 254
The multiple staff in the local church. Philadelphia, Westminster Press [1963] 122 p. 21 cm. [BV705.S9] 63-11562
1. Church officers. I. Title.

SWEET, Herman J., 1899- 254
The multiple staff in the local church. Philadelphia, Westminster [c.1963] 122p. 21cm. 63-11562 2.75
1. Church officers. I. Title.

TAYLOR, Robert C 254
How to maintain your church buildings and grounds. [Westwood, N.J.] Revell [1962] 64 p. 21 cm. (Revell's better church series) [BV652.7.T3] 62-8416
1. Church property — Maintenance and repair. I. Title.

TAYLOR, Robert C. 254
How to maintain your church buildings and grounds. [Westwood, N.J.] Revell [c.1962] 64p. (Revell's better church ser.) 62-8416 1.00 pap.,
1. Church property—Maintenance and repair. I. Title.

TIDWELL, Charles A. 254
Working together through the church council [by] Charles A. Tidwell. Nashville, Convention Press [1968] xii, 114 p. 19 cm. "Church study course [of the Sunday School Board of the Southern Baptist Convention] This book is number 1606 in category 16, section for adults and young people." [BV652.9.T5] 68-10608
1. Parish councils. I. Southern Baptist Convention. Sunday School Board. II. Title.

TOWNS, Elmer L. 254
Getting a church started in the face of insurmountable odds with limited resources in unlikely circumstances : how to establish a church based on a study of 10 new small prospering congregations / by Elmer L. Towns. [Nashville] : Impact Books, [1975] 175 p. : ill. ; 23 cm. Includes bibliographical references. [BV652.25.T687] 74-28990 ISBN 0-914850-23-7 : 4.95
1. Church growth—Case studies. 2. Evangelistic work—Case studies. I. Title.

UNITY on the ground; 254
edited by Colin Buchanan. London, S.P.C.K., 1972. vi, 72 p. map. 22 cm. [BR759.U54] 72-195688 ISBN 0-281-02672-6
1. Christian union—England. I. Buchanan, Colin Ogilvie, ed.
Available from Allenson, pap. 3.65

WALKER, Alan 254
As close as the telephone; the dramatic story of the Australian Life Line Movement. Nashville, Abingdon [1967] 159p. 19cm. [BV656.4.W3] 67-22168 2.25 pap.,
1. Life Line Movement. 2. Telephone in church work. I. Title.

WEDEL, Leonard E. 254
Building & maintaining a church staff [by] Leonard E. Wedel. Nashville, Broadman Press [1967, c1966] 158 p. 22 cm. [BV652.W4] 67-12177
1. Church management. 2. Personnel management. I. Title.

WERNING, Waldo J. 254
Where does the money go? The Christian philosophy of money and a practical approach for Christian family budgeting, by Waldo J. Werning. [St. Louis, Church-Craft Pictures, inc., 1964] 85 p. 23 cm. Bbiliography: p. 85. [BV773.W445] 67-6140
1. Stewardship, Christian. 2. Christian giving. I. Title.

WHEELEY, B. Otto. 254
Church planning and management : a guide for pastors and laymen / by B. Otto Wheeley ; with Thomas H. Cable. Philadelphia : Dorrance, [1975] 218 p., [3] leaves of plates : ill. ; 22 cm. [BV652.W48] 74-84485 ISBN 0-8059-2074-9 : 8.95
1. Church management. I. Cable, Thomas H. II. Title.

WIEST, Elam G 254
How to organize your church staff. [Westwood, N.J., Revell [1962] 64 p. illus. 21 cm. (Revell's better church series) [BV652.W54] 62-8415
1. Church work. I. Title.

WIEST, Elam G. 254
How to organize your church staff. [Westwood, N.J.] Revell [c.1962] 64p.illus. (Revell's better church ser.) 62-8415 1.00 pap.,
1. Church work. I. Title.

WOOD, Herbert George, 1879- 254
Belief and unbelief since 1850. Belief and unbelief since eighteen fifty Cambridge [Eng.] University Press, 1955. 142p. 19cm. Includes bibliography. [BR759.W65] 55-14513
1. Gt. Brit.—Religion. 2. Religious thought—Gt. Brit. 3. Theology, Doctrinal—Hist.—Gt. Brit. I. Title.

DOWDY, Augustus W. 254'.0028
Phone power / Augustus W. Dowdy, Jr. Valley Forge, PA. : Judson Press, [1975] 96 p. ; 18 cm. Includes index. Bibliography: p. 92-94. [BV656.4D68] 74-22368 ISBN 0-8170-0652-4 : 2.95
1. Telephone in church work. I. Title.

BORDELON, Marvin. 254'.02
The parish in a time of change, edited by Marvin Bordelon. Notre Dame, Ind., Fides

Publishers [1967] x, 227 p. 23 cm. Includes bibliographical references. [BX1912.B67] 66-30590
1. Pastoral theology—Catholic Church—Addresses, essays, lectures. I. Title.

BRODERICK, Robert C., 1913- 254'.02
Your parish comes alive, by Robert C. Broderick. [Chicago] Franciscan Herald Press [1970] ix, 72 p. 21 cm. [BV652.9.B73] 76-130463 ISBN 8-19-904139- 1.95
1. Parish councils. I. Title.

DIGNAN, Patrick Joseph, 1905- 254'.02
A history of the legal incorporation of Catholic Church property in the United States (1784-1932), by Patrick J. Dignan. Washington, Catholic University of America, 1933. [New York, AMS Press, 1974] viii, 289 p. 23 cm. Reprint of the author's thesis, Catholic University of America, 1933, which was issued as v. 14 of the Catholic University of America. Studies in American church history. Bibliography: p. 270-285. [BX1407.P8D5 1974] 73-3569 ISBN 0-404-57764-4 12.00
1. Catholic Church in the United States. 2. Church property—United States. 3. Corporations, Religious—United States. 4. Church and state in the United States. 5. Ecclesiastical law—United States. I. Title. II. Series: Catholic University of America. Studies in American church history, v. 14.

BOWEN, V. S. 254'.03
A vestryman's guide, by V. S. Bowen. New York, Seabury Press [1972] 64 p. illus. 21 cm. [BX5967.5.B68] 72-82210 ISBN 0-8164-2078-5 1.25
1. Protestant Episcopal Church in the U.S.A.—Government. 2. Church officers. I. Title.

BOWEN, V. S. 254'.03'73
A vestryman's guide / by Van S. Bowen. Rev. ed. New York : Seabury Press, 1976. 70 p. ; 21 cm. "Sponsored by the Episcopal Church Foundation." "A Crossroad book." includes index. Bibliography: p. 67. [BX5967.5.B68 1976] 76-44386 ISBN 0-8164-2136-6 : 2.50
1. Protestant Episcopal Church in the U.S.A.—Government. 2. Church officers. I. Title.

TRURO Parish, Va. Vestry. 254'.03'755291
Minutes of the Vestry, Truro Parish Virginia, 1732-1785. Lorton, Va. : Pohick Church, 1974. vi, 153 p. : ill. ; 24 cm. Includes index. [BX5980.L75T787 1974] 74-81678 12.00
1. Truro Parish, Va.—History—Sources. I. Title.

HARKINS, George F. 254.041
Handbook for committees of congregations of the Lutheran Church in America, by George F. Harkins. Philadelphia, Bd. of Pubn. of the Lutheran Church in Amer. [c.1967] vii, 81p. 23cm. Based on the approved constitution for congregations, prepd. by the Lutheran Chruch in Amer. Bibl. [BX8048.2.H3] 67-14315 .50 pap.,
1. Lutheran Church in America—Government. 2. Church committees—Lutheran Church. I. Lutheran Church in America. II. Title.

HARKINS, George F 254.041
Handbook for committees of congregations of the Lutheran Church in America, by George F. Harkins. Philadelphia, Board of Publication of the Lutheran Church in America [c1967] vii, 81 p. 23 cm. "Based on the approved constitution for congregations, prepared by the Lutheran Church in America." Includes bibiolographies. [BX8048.2.H3] 67-14315
1. Lutheran Church in America — Government. 2. Church committees — Lutheran Church. I. Lutheran Church in America. II. Title.

REINBOTH, Oscar H. 254'.04'1
Calls and vacancies. Oscar H. Reinboth: editor. Saint Louis, Concordia Pub. House [1967] 70 p. 21 cm. (Concordia paperback) Contents.Contents.—When a pastor receives a call, by V. G. Albers.—Filling the vacancy, by L. H. Goetz.—The congregation's ministry during a vacancy, by O. H. Reinboth. [BX8071.R4] 67-27154
1. Lutheran Church—Clergy—Appointment, call, and election. I. Title.

MASSEY, Floyd. 254'.06'1
Church administration in Black perspective / Floyd Massey, Jr. and Samuel Berry McKinney. Valley Forge, Pa. : Judson Press, c1976. 172 p. ; 22 cm. Includes index. Bibliography: p. 139-144. [BX6448.M37] 76-9874 ISBN 0-8170-0710-5 pbk. : 5.95
1. Afro-American Baptists. 2. Afro-American churches. 3. Church management. I. McKinney, Samuel Berry, joint author. II. Title.

COBB, Jesse E., 1890-1971. 254'.06'173
Cobb's Baptist church manual. [Rev. ed.] Little Rock, Ark., Baptist Publications Committee of the Baptist Missionary Association of America [1972] 212 p. 16 cm. Published in 1941 under title: A new manual for Baptist churches. [BX6349.58.C6 1972] 72-88391 2.95
1. American Baptist Association—Government. I. Title. II. Title: Baptist church manual.
pap. 1.00.

KUNTZ, Kenneth A. 254'.06'6
The congregation as church [by] Kenneth A. Kuntz. St. Louis, Bethany Press [1971] 176 p. 20 cm. Bibliography: p. [171]-176. [BV601.8.K85] 70-168892 ISBN 0-8272-0434-5
1. Mission of the church. 2. Church renewal—Disciples of Christ. I. Title.

DUNN, Paul H. 254'.09'3
The ten most wanted men, by Paul H. Dunn. Salt Lake City, Bookcraft [1967] 405p. illus. 24cm. [BV652.1.D8] 67-17928 price unreported
1. Christian leadership. I. Title.

BUTT, Edmund Dargan, 1898- 254.2
Preach there also; a study of the town and country work of the Episcopal Church. With a foreword by Alden Drew Kelley. Evanston, Ill., Seabury- Western Theological Seminary, 1954. 140p. 24cm. [BV638.B867] 261 54-2361
1. Rural churches. 2. Protestant Episcopal Church in the U. S. A. I. Title.

CANTELON, John E 254.2
A Protestant approach to the campus ministry. Philadelphia, Westminster Press [1964] 127 p. 19 cm. Bibliographical references included in "Notes" (p. 121-127) [BV1610.C3] 64-12142
1. Universities and colleges—Religion. I. Title.

CANTELON, John E. 254.2
A Protestant approach to the campus ministry. Philadelphia, Westminster [c.1964] New York, Paulist Pr. [c.1959, 1963] 127p. n3 192p. 18cm. (Deus bk.) 254.2 254.2 64-12142 .95 pap.,
1. Suburban churches. I. Greeley, Andrew M., 1928- II. Title. III. Title: The church and the n3 IV. Title: The church and the suburbs.

CARR, James McLeod. 254.2
Bright future a new day for the town and country church. Illustrated by Ruth S. Ensign. Richmond, Published for Board of Church Extension, Presbyterian Church in the United States, by John Knox Press [1956] 162p. illus. 21cm. [BV638.C3] [BV638.C3] 261 56-10740 56-10740
1. Rural churches—Southern States. 2. Presbyterian Church in the U.S.—Missions. I. Title.

THE church, the university, and social policy: 254.2
the Danforth study of campus ministries. [1st ed.] Middletown, Conn., Wesleyan University Press [1969] 2 v. forms. 24 cm. Contents.Contents.—v. 1. Report of the director, by K. Underwood.—v. 2. Working and technical papers, edited and with introductions by K. Underwood. Bibliography: p. v. 1, p. [603]-618. [BV1610.C52] 69-17794 15.00
1. Church work with students. 2. Chaplains, University and college. 3. Sociology, Christian. 4. Protestant churches—United States—Clergy. I. Underwood, Kenneth Wilson. II. Title: The Danforth study of campus ministries.

GREELEY, Andrew M 1928- 254.2
The church and the suburbs. New York, Sheed & Ward [1959] 206p. 21cm. Essays. [BX1407.S8G7] 59-12089
1. Suburban churches. I. Title.

*GREENWAY, Roger S comp. 254.'2
Guidlines for urban church planting / Roger S. Greenway, editor. Grand Rapids : Baker Book House, c1976. 128 p. ; 21 cm. [BV637] ISBN 0-8010-3707-7 pbk. : 1.95
1. City churches. 2. Church work with apartment dwellers. I. Title.

HOYES, Herbert 254.2
Spiritual suburbia: the church in a new and growing community. New York, Vantage Press [c.1959] 63p. 21cm. 2.00 bds.,
I. Title.

KLOETZLI, Walter. 254.2
Urban church planning; the church discovers its community [by] Walter Kloetzli and Arthur Hillman. Philadelphia, Muhlenberg Press [1958] 186p. illus. 20cm. Includes bibliography. [BV637.K55] 261 58-11737
1. City churches. 2. Social surveys. I. Hillman, Arthur, 1909- joint author. II. Title.

LEIFFER, Murray Howard, 1902- 254.2
The effective city church. Rev. ed. Nashville, Abingdon Press [1955] 232 p. illus. 24 cm. [BV637.L414 1955] [BV637.L414 1955] 260 55-11070 55-11070
1. City churches. I. Title.

MCCONNELL, Charles Melvin. 254.2
High hours of Methodism in town-country communities. [1st ed.] New York, Editorial Dept., Joint Section of Education and Cultivation, Board of Missions of the Methodist Church, 1956. 109p. illus. 20cm. [BV638.M15] 261 56-10362
1. Rural churches—U. S. 2. Methodist Church—Missions. I. Title.

METHODISM looks at the city; 254.2
addresses, section reports, and supplemental data. Edited by Robert A. McKibben. [New York, 1954] 236p. illus., group ports., map. 23cm. Includes bibliographies. [BV637.C6 1954] [BV637.C6 1954] 261 54-4061 54-4061
1. City churches. I. McKibben, Robert A, 1895- ed.

PROTESTANT parish; 254.2
a case study of rural and urban parish patterns, by Earl D. C. Brewer [and others] Atlanta, Communicative Arts Press [1967] viii, 129 p. 22 cm. Project sponsored by the National Division of the Board of Missions of the Methodist Church. Bibliography: p. 124-129. [BV637.P7] 67-28402
1. Rural churches. 2. City churches. I. Brewer, Earl D. C. II. Methodist Church (United States). Board of Missions. National Division.

RICH, Mark. 254.2
The rural church movement. Columbia, Mo., Juniper Knoll Press, 1957. ii, 251p. 28cm. Includes bibliographies. [BV638.R44] A58 261
1. Rural churches—U. S. 2. Interdenominational cooperation. I. Title.

RURAL churches in transition. 254.2
Nashville, Broadman Press [1959] 145p. 21cm. [BV638.C546] 261 59-5853
1. Rural churches. I. Clark, Carl Anderson, 1905-

SCHALLER, Lyle E 254.2
Planning for Protestantism in urban America [by] Lyle E. Schaller. New York, Abingdon Press [1965] 223 p. 22 cm. Bibliography: p. 215-217. [BV637.S36] 65-10812
1. City churches. I. Title.

SCHALLER, Lyle E. 254.2
Planning for Protestantism in urban America. Nashville, Tenn., Abingdon [c.1965] 223p. 22cm. Bibl. [BV637.S36] 65-10812 4.50
1. City churches. I. Title.

SCHNUCKER, Calvin. 254.2
How to plan the rural church program. Philadelphia, Westminster Press [1954] 158 p. 21 cm. [BV638.S35] 261 54-5281
1. Rural churches. 2. Church work. I. Title.

SHIPPEY, Frederick Alexander, 1908- *254.2
Church work in the city. New York, Abingdon-Cokesbury Press [1952] 255 p. illus. 24 cm. [BV637.S5] 52-8838
1. City churches. 2. Church work. I. Title.

SMITH, Rockwell Carter, 1908- 254.2
The church in our town; a study of the relationship between the church and the rural community. Rev. and enl. ed. New York, Abingdon Press [1955] 220p. illus. 23cm. [BV638.S6 1955] [BV638.S6 1955] 261 55-8612 55-8612
1. Rural churches. 2. Sociology, Rural. I. Title.

SMITH, Rockwell Carter, 1908- 254.2
Rural church administration. Nashville, Abingdon-Cokesbury Press [1953] 176p. 20cm. [BV638.S62] [BV638.S62] 261 53-5402 53-5402
1. Rural churches. I. Title.

WARD, Leo Richard, 1893- 254.2
The living parish. Notre Dame, Ind., Fides Publishers Association [1959] 191 p. 21 cm. [BX1913.W35] 59-14097
1. Parishes — U.S. 2. Pastoral theology — Catholic Church. I. Title.

FOSTER, Virgil E. 254.20973
By deed and design. New York, Friendship [c.1961] 120p. illus. 61-6633 2.95
1. Church work. 2. City churches. 3. Suburban churches. I. Title.

JANSSEN, Lawrence H. 254.22
These cities glorious. New York, Friendship Pr. [c.1963] 175p. 19cm. Bibl. 63-8677 1.75 pap.,
1. City churches. I. Title.

JONES, Ezra Earl. 254.2'2
What's ahead for old first church [by] Ezra Earl Jones & Robert L. Wilson. [1st ed.] New York, Harper & Row [1974] xi, 132 p. 21 cm. [BV637.J6 1974] 74-4616 ISBN 0-06-064200-9 5.95
1. City churches—United States. I. Wilson, Robert Leroy, 1925- joint author. II. Title.

KLOETZLI, Walter. 254.22
The church and the urban challenge. Philadelphia, Muhlenberg Press [1961] 83p. 21cm. Includes bibliography. [BV637.K53] 61-14757
1. City churches. 2. Church and social problems— U. S. I. Title.

KLOETZLI, Walter. 254.22
The city church--death or renewal; a study of eight urban Lutheran churches. With foreword by Lauris B. Whitman, afterword By Charles Y. Glock. Philadelphia, Muhlenberg Press [1961] xi, 224p. diagrs. 24cm. 'Part of ... the Effective city church study, sponsored by the National Council of the Churches of Christ in the U. S. A.' Includes bibliography. [BV637.K54] 61-6751
1. City churches. 2. Social surveys—U. S. I. Title.

LEE, Robert, ed. 254.22
The church and the exploding metropolis. Richmond, Va., Knox [c.1965] 125p. 21cm. Bibl. [BV637.L33] 65-10347 1.50 pap.,
1. City churches. I. Title.

LEIFFER, Murray Howard, 1902- 254.22
The effective city church. 2d rev. ed. Nashville, Abingdon Press [c.1961] 232p. illus. Bibl. 60-15810 4.00
1. City churches. I. Title.

MOORE, Paul, 1919- 254.22
The church reclaims the city. Foreword by Marshal L. Scott. New York, Seabury Press, 1964. xiii, 241 p. 22 cm. Bibliography: p. [223]-230. [BV2653.M6] 63-16285
1. City missions. I. Title.

MOORE, Paul, Jr., 1919- 254.22
The church reclaims the city. Foreword by Marshal L. Scott. New York, Seabury [c.] 1964. xiii, 241p. 22cm. Bibl. 63-16285 4.95
1. City missions. I. Title.

MOORE, Richard E. 254.22
Urban church breakthrough [by] Richard E. Moore, Duane L. Day. [1st. ed.] New York, Harper [1966] xii, 183p. 22cm. Bibl. [BV637.M6] 66-20781 4.50 bds.,
1. City churches. I. Day, Duane L., joint author. II. Title.

MUSSELMAN, G Paul. 254.22
The church on the urban frontier. Greenwich, Conn., Seabury Press, 1960. 136p. 22cm. [BV637.M85] 60-14117
1. City churches. 2. Church work. I. Title.

NORTON, Perry L 254.22
Church and metropolis; a city planner's viewpoint of the slow-changing church in the fast-changing metropolis [by] Perry L. Norton. New York, Seabury Press [1964] 128 p. 20 cm. [BV637.N6] 64-24129
1. City churches. I. Title.

NORTON, Perry L. 254.22
Church and metropolis; a city planner's viewpoint of the slow-changing church in the fast-changing metropelis. New York, Seabury [c.1964] 128p. 20cm. 64-24129 2.95
1. City churches. I. Title.

PEACHEY, Paul, 1918- 254.22
The church in the city. Newton, Kan., Faith and Life Press [1963] 115 p. 23 cm. (Institute of Mennonite Studies series, no. 2) Bibliography: p. 104-115. [BV637.P4] 63-25145
1. City churches. I. Title. II. Series.

PEACHEY, Paul, 1918- 254.22
The church in the city. Newton, Kan., Faith & Life [c.1963] 115p. 23cm. (Inst. of Mennonite Studies ser., no. 2) Bibl. 63-25145 1.95 pap.,
1. City churches. I. Title. II. Series.

SCHUYLER, Joseph B. 254.22
Northern parish; a sociological and pastoral study. Chicago, Loyola University Press [c.] 1960 xxi, 360p. Bibliography: p.333-341. illus., col. maps, diagrs. (part col.) tables. 24cm. (Jesuit studies; contributions to the arts and sciences by members of the Society of Jesus) 60-9600 8.00
1. New York. Our Lady of Mercy (Church) 2. Social survey — New York (City) 3. Church and social problems — New York (City) 4. Catholics in New York (City). I. Title.

SCHUYLER, Joseph B 1921- 254.22
Northern parish; a sociological and pastoral study. Chicago, Loyola University Press, 1960. xxi, 360p. illus., col. maps, diagrs. (part col.) tables. 24cm. (Jesuit studies: contributions

to the arts and sciences by members of the Society of Jesus) Bibliography: p. 333-341. [BX4603.N6O72] 60-9600
1. New York. Our Lady of Mercy (Church) 2. Social survey—New York (City) 3. Church and social problems—New York (City) 4. Catholics in New York (City) I. Title.

SEGER, Imogen 254.22
Responsibility for the community; a new norm confronts tradition in Lutheran city churches. Totowa, N.J., Vreeland Ave., Paterson 2 Bedminster, [c.]1963 viii, 366p. diagrs., tables. 26cm. Bibl. 63-18090 pap., price unreported
1. City churches. 2. Lutheran Church in the U.S. 3. Sociology, Christian (Lutheran) I. Title.

WALKER, Alan. 254.22
A ringing call to mission. New York, Abingdon Press [1966] 127 p. 20 cm. [BV637.W3] 66-10852
1. City churches. I. Title.

WALKER, Alan 254.22
A ringing call to mission. Nashville, Abingdon [c.1966] 127p. 20cm. [BV637.W3] 66-10852 2.50 bds.,
1. City churches. I. Title.

WEBBER, George W 254.22
The congregation in mission; emerging structures for the church in an urban society. New York, Abingdon Press [1964] 208 p. 23 cm. Bibliography: p. 203-208. [BV637.W37] 64-16152
1. City churches. I. Title.

WEBBER, George W. 254.22
The congregation in mission; emerging structures for the church in an urban society. Nashville, Abingdon [c.1964] 208p. 23cm. Bibl. 64-16152 3.50
1. City churches. I. Title.

WINTER, Gibson. 254.22
The new creation as metropolis. New York, Macmillan [1963] 152 p. 21 cm. [BV637.W54] 63-15703
1. City churches. I. Title.

WINTER, Gibson 254.22
The new creation as metropolis. New York, Macmillan [1965, c.1963] 152p. 18cm. Bibl. [BV637.W54] .95 pap.,
1. City churches. I. Title.

YOUNGER, George D 254.22
The church and urban power structure. Philadelphia, Westminster Press [1963] 88 p. 19 cm. (Christian perspectives on social problems) [BV637.Y6] 63-9774
1. City churches. I. Title.

YOUNGER, George D. 254.22
The church and urban power structure. Philadelphia, Westminster [c.1963] 88p. 19cm. (Christian perspectives on soc. problems) 63-9774 1.25 pap.,
1. City churches. I. Title.

YOUNGER, George D 254.22
The church and urban renewal [by] George D. Younger. [1st ed.] Philadelphia, Lippincott [1965] 216 p. 22 cm. Bibliography: p. 208-212. [BV637.Y62] 65-14899
1. City churches. 2. Urban renewal. I. Title.

YOUNGER, George D. 254.22
The church and urban renewal. Philadelphia, Lippincott [c.1965] 216p. 22cm. Bibl. [BV637.Y62] 65-14899 4.50 bds.,
1. City churches. 2. Urban renewal. I. Title.

CROSS, Robert D. ed. 254.2'208
The church and the city. 1865-1910. Ed. by Robert D. Cross. Indianapolis. Bobbs [1967 xlv, 359p. 21cm. (Amer. heritage ser.) Bibl. [BV637.C7] 66-17273 7.50
1. City churches—Collections. 2. U.S.—Religion—Collections I. Title.

CROSS, Robert D ed. 254.2'208
The church and the city, 1865-1910. Edited by Robert D. Cross. Indianapolis, Bobbs-Merrill Co. [1967] xiv, 350 p. 21 cm. (The American heritage series) Bibliographical footnotes. [BV637.C7] 66-17273
1. City churches — Collections. 2. U.S. — Religion — Collections. I. Title.

HOME Missions 254.22082
Conference, Chicago, 1961
Challenge and response in the city; a theological consultation on the urban church. Ed. by Walter Kloetzli. Rock Island, Ill., Augustana Pr. [c.1962] viii, 156p. Bibl. 62-11167 2.00 pap.,
1. City churches. I. Kloetzli, Walter, ed. II. Title.

LEE, Robert, ed. 254.22082
Cities and churches; readings on the urban church. Philadelphia, Westminster [c.1962] 366p. Bibl. 62-7325 3.50 pap.,
1. City churches. I. Title.

FACKRE, Gabriel J. 254.2'3
Second fronts in metropolitan mission, by Gabriel Fackre. Grand Rapids, Eerdmans [1968] 30 p. 21 cm. (A Reformed journal monograph) "First appeared in ... The Reformed journal." [BV637.7.F3] 68-7824 0.75
1. Suburban churches. 2. Segregation in education—Lancaster, Pa. I. Title.

METZ, Donald L. 254.2'3
New congregations; security and mission in conflict, by Donald L. Metz. With a foreword by Charles Y. Glock. Philadelphia, Westminster Press [1967] 170 p. 22 cm. Bibliography: p. [161]-165. [BV637.7.M4] 67-10276
1. Suburban churches. I. Title.

WINTER, Gibson 254.23
The suburban captivity of the churches. ; an analysis of Protestant responsibility in the expanding metropolis. New York, Macmillan [c.1962] 255p. 18cm. Bibl. 1.45 pap.,
1. Surburban churches. 2. City churches. I. Title.

WINTER, Gibson. 254.23
The suburban captivity of the churches; an analysis of Protestant responsibility in the expanding metropolis. [1st ed.] Garden City, N.Y., Doubleday, 1961. 216 p. 22 cm. Includes bibliography. [BV637.7.W5] 61-7667
1. Suburban churches. 2. City churches. I. Title.

BAILEY, James Martin, 254.24
1929-
Windbreaks; six stories of the rural church in action. Illustrated by Brinton Turkle. New York, Friendship Press [1959] 111p. illus. 23cm. [BV638.8.B3] 59-6039
1. Rural churches—Stories. I. Title.

FELTON, Ralph Almon 254.24
The pulpit and the plow. New York, Friendship Press [c.1960] viii, 168p. 20cm. 60-8323 2.95; 1.75 half cloth, pap.,
1. Rural churches. I. Title.

GREENE, Shirley Edward 254.24
Ferment on the fringe; studies of rural churches in transition. Philadelphia, Christian Education Press [c.1960] 174p. 60-53027 2.00 pap.,
1. Rural churches. I. Title.

LONGENECKER, Harold. 254.2'4
Building town and country churches. [Rev. ed.] Chicago, Moody Press [1973] 122 p. 22 cm. Published in 1961 under title: The village church: its pastor and program. Includes bibliographical references. [BV638.L6 1973] 73-7333 ISBN 0-8024-0997-0 1.95 (pbk.)
1. Rural churches. 2. Rural clergy. I. Title.

LONGENECKER, Harold. 254.24
The village church; its pastor and program. Chicago, Moody Press [1961] 192p. 26cm. []wBV638.L6] 61-19635
1. Rural churches. 2. Rural clergy. I. Title.

MCBRIDE, Charles R 254.24
Protestant churchmanship for rural America. Valley Forge [Pa.] Judson Press [1962] 334p. 23cm. Includes bibliography. [BV638.M13] 61-8938
1. Rural churches—U. S. I. Title.

MCBRIDE, Clarence Ralph 254.24
Protestant churchmanship for rural America. Valley Forge [Pa.] Judson [c.1962] 334p. 23cm. Bibl. 61-8938 4.95
1. Rural churches—U.S. I. Title.

SMITH, Rockwell Carter, 254.24
1908-
People, land and churches. New York, Friendship Press [1959] 164 p. 20 cm. Includes bibliography. [BV638.S617] 59-6035
1. Rural churches. 2. U.S. — Rural conditions. I. Title.

SMITH, Rockwell Carter, 254.2'4
1908-
Rural ministry and the changing community [by] Rockwell C. Smith. Nashville, Abingdon Press [1971] 206 p. 21 cm. Includes bibliographical references. [BV638.S623] 73-158671 ISBN 0-687-36661-5 4.75
1. Rural churches. I. Title.

BOCKELMAN, Wilfred. 254.24097
On good soil. New York, Friendship Press [1959] 173p. 21cm. [BV638.B6] 59-6036
1. Rural churches. I. Title.

BRUNNER, Edmund de 254.2'4'0975
Schweinitz, 1889-
Church life in the rural South; a study of the opportunity of Protestantism based upon data from seventy counties, by Edmund deS. Brunner. New York, Negro Universities Press [1969] 117 p. illus., maps. 24 cm. At head of title: Committee on Social and Religious Surveys, Town and Country Department. Reprint of the 1923 ed. Bibliography: p. 117. [BV638.B844 1969] 70-90129
1. Rural churches—Southern States. 2. Social surveys—Southern States. I. Title.

CRISIS in communication; 254.3
a Christian examination of the mass media. Garden City, N. Y., Doubleday, 1957. 128p. 22cm. [BV653.B6] [BV653.B6] 259 57-5781 57-5781
1. Evangelistic work. 2. Communication. 3. Public relations—Churches. 4. Christianity—Influence. I. Boyd, Malcolm.

CUNNINGHAM, Milton E. 254.3
New drums over Africa [by Milton E. Cunningham, Jr.] Nashville, Convention Press [1971] 115 p. illus., map, ports. 20 cm. (Foreign mission graded series) "Text for course number 5136-17 of the New church study course." [BV2082.R3C85] 78-139665
1. Radio in missionary work. 2. Missions—Africa, East. 3. Baptists—Missions. I. Title.

FREEMAN, Wendell K, 1928- 254.3
Why not broadcast the gospel? Radio broadcasting methods, sermons, questions. [Huntington? W. Va.] 1952. 179 p. illus. 20 cm. [BV656.F7] 259 52-32351
1. Radio in religion. 2. Churches of Christ—Sermons. 3. Sermons, American. I. Title.

GRISWOLD, Clayton T comp. 254.3
Broadcasting religion, compiled by Clayton T. Griswold and Charles H. Schmitz. [Rev., enl. ed.] New York, National Council of the Churches of Christ, Broadcasting and Film Commission [c1954] 103p. illus. 23cm. Bibliography: p. 102. [BV656.G7 1954] 259 55-4080
1. Radio in religion. 2. Radio broadcasting. 3. Television broadcasting. I. Schmitz, Charles Henry, joint comp. II. Title.

GRISWOLD, Clayton T comp. *254.3
How you can broadcast religion, compiled by Clayton T. Griswold and Charles H. Schmitz; edited by Lois J. Anderson. New York, National Council of the Churches of Christ in the United States of America, Broadcasting and Film Commission [1957] 128p. illus. 23cm. [BV656.G72] 259 57-4638
1. Radio in religion. 2. Radio broadcasting. 3. Television broadcasting. I. Schmitz, Charles Henry., joint comp. II. Title.

HOW to conduct religious 254.3
radio programs. St. Louis, Bethany Press [1958] 63p. 22cm. 'Originally part of the author's thesis written in the School of Religion in Butler University ... for the bachelor of divinity degree.' Includes bibliography. [BV656.K5] 259 58-12745
1. Radio in religion. 2. Radio broadcasting. I. Kimsey, James E

IVERSEN, John Orville. 254.3
So you're going on the air, written and compiled by J. Orville Iversen. [Washington, Review and Herald Pub. Association, 1969] 320 p. illus., ports. 24 cm. Bibliography: p. 315-320. [BV656.I9] 68-57039
1. Radio in religion. I. Title.

PARKER, Everett C. 254.3
Religious television; what to do and how. New York, Harper [c.1961] 244p. 61-5265 4.00 bds.,
1. Television in religion. I. Title.

PARKER, Everett C 254.3
The television-radio audience and religion [by] Everett C. Parker, David W. Barry [and] Dallas W. Smythe. New York, Harper [1955] xxx, 464p. diagrs., tables. 25cm. (Studies in the mass media of communication) Bibliography: p. 15. Bibliographical footnotes. [BV656.3.P3] [BV656.3.P3] 259 55-8526 55-8526
1. Television in religion. 2. Radio in religion. 3. U. S.—Religion. I. Title. II. Series.

WILSON, Ron, 1932- 254.3
Multimedia handbook for the church / Ron Wilson. Elgin, Ill. : D.C. Cook Pub. Co., [1975] 142 p. : diagrs. ; 18 cm. (Christian education series) Bibliography: p. 130-140. [BV652.95.W54] 74-29049 ISBN 0-912692-55-3 pbk. : 1.95
1. Mass media in religion. I. Title.

BOYD, Malcolm, 1923- *254.3 259
Crisis in communication; a Christian examination of the mass media. Garden City, N. Y., Doubleday, 1957. 128 p. 22 cm. [BV653.B6] 57-5781
1. Evangelistic work. 2. Communication (Theology) 3. Public relations—Churches. 4. Christianity—Influence. I. Title.

AUSTIN, Charles Marshall, 254.4
1941-
Let the people know : a media handbook for churches / Charles M. Austin ; designed by Judy Swanson. Minneapolis : Augsburg Pub. House, [1975] 91 p. : ill. ; 20 cm. Bibliography: p. 91. [BV653.A93] 75-2841 ISBN 0-8066-1486-2 pbk. : 2.95
1. Church publicity. 2. Mass media in religion. I. Title.

BARROWS, William J 254.4
How to publicize church activities. [Westwood, N.J.] Revell [1962] 62 p. illus. 21 cm. (Revell's better church series) [BV653.B3] 62-17112
1. Public relations — Churches. I. Title.

BARROWS, William J. 254.4
How to publicize church activities. [Westwood, N.J.] Revell [c.1962] 62p. illus. 21cm. (Revell's better church ser.) 62-17112 1.00 pap.,
1. Public relations—Churches. I. Title.

BREWER, Jack A. 254.4
Fellowships from A to Z [by] Jack A. Brewer. Nashville, Broadman Press [1968] 48 p. 22 cm. [BV1620.B7] 68-12320
1. Church entertainments. I. Title.

BRODIE, William Austin, 254.4
1901-
Keeping your church in the news. [Westwood, N. J., F. H. Revell Co. [1959] 125p. 21cm. (Revell's preaching and pastoral aid series) [BV653.B7 1959] 59-5502
1. Advertising—Churches. I. Title.

BROWN, Richmond O 254.4
Practical church publicity. Nashville, Broadman Press [1953] 174p. illus. 21cm. [BV653.B78] 53-8493
1. Advertising—Churches. I. Title.

COMMUNICATIONS Seminar, 254.4
Manhattan College, 1959.
The church and communications arts; [proceedings. 2d ed.] Washington, D.C., 1312 Massachusetts Ave. Bur. of Info., Natl. Catholic Welfare Conference, [1962] 183p. 26cm. 62-16968 3.00 pap.,
1. Public relations—Churches. 2. Communication. I. Title.

CRAIG, Floyd A. 254.4
Christian communicator's handbook; a practical guide for church public relations [by] Floyd A. Craig. Nashville, Broadman Press [1969] 96 p. illus. 28 cm. Includes bibliographical references. [BV653.C7] 69-17893
1. Public relations—Churches. I. Title.

CROCKETT, William David, 254.4
1919-
Promotion and publicity for churches / W. David Crockett. New York : Morehouse-Barlow Co., c1974. iv, 43 p. : ill. ; 28 cm. [BV653.C76] 74-80382 ISBN 0-8192-1181-8 pbk. : 3.50
1. Church publicity. I. Title.

GARRISON, Webb B 254.4
Improve your church bulletins; helps for church bulletins, parish papers, and outdoor bulletin boards. [Westwood, N.J.] Revell [1957] 127p. 21cm. [BV653.G3] 57-9965
1. Advertising—Churches. I. Title.

GREIF, Edward L. 254.4
The silent pulpit; a guide to church public relations. New York, Holt [1964] x, 213p. 22cm. 64-11277 4.95
1. Public relations—Churches. I. Title. II. Title: A guide to church public relations.

HESS, Geraldine. 254.4
Planning the church bulletin for effective worship. Foreword by George McDonough. [1st ed.] New York, Exposition Press [1962] 141p. 22cm. (An Exposition- testament book) [BV653.3.H45] 62-560
1. Church bulletins. I. Title.

HOLDCRAFT, Paul Ellsworth, 254.4
1891- comp.
Sayings and sentences for church bulletins [by] Paul E. Holdcraft. Nashville, Abingdon Press [1967] 80 p. 23 cm. [BV653.3.H6] 67-15638
1. Church bulletins. 2. Aphoriams and apothegms. Title. I. Title.

KIRBAN, Salem. 254.4
Church promotion handbook. [Huntingdon Valley? Pa.] 1963. 172 l. illus. 30 cm. [BV653.K5] 63-18718
1. Advertising — Churches. I. Title.

KIRBAN, Salem 254.4
Church promotion handbook. [Huntingdon Valley, Pa.] 2117 Kent Rd., Kirban Associates, c.1963. 1721. illus. (pt. col.) 30cm. 63-18718 10.00
1. Advertising—Churches. I. Title.

LEIDT, William E. 254.4
Publicity goes to church. Greenwich, Conn., Seabury Press, 1959. 122 p. 20 cm. Includes bibliography. [BV653.L45] 58-9227

1. Public relations—Churches. 2. Advertising—Churches. I. Title.

LESCH, Gomer R 254.4
Church public relations at work. Nashville, Convention Press [1962] 142p. 19cm. Includes bibliography. [BV653.L47] 62-9621
1. Public relations—Churches. I. Title.

LESSEL, William M. 254.4
Church publicity; basic principles and practices for churches and church-related organizations, by William M. Lessel. Camden, T. Nelson [1970] 221 p. illus. 26 cm. [BV653.L479] 74-131118 4.95
1. Church publicity.

MARTY, Martin E 1928- 254.4
The improper opinion: mass media and the Christian faith. Philadelphia, Westminster Press [1961] 144p. 21cm. (Westminster studies in Christian communication) Includes bibliography. [BV653.M3] 61-10298
1. Evangelistic work. 2. Public relations—Churches. 3. Communication. I. Title.

MEAD, Frank Spencer, 1898- ed. 254.4
Reaching beyond your pulpit. [Westwood, N.J.] Revell [1962] 190p. 21cm. 62-10730 3.50 bds.,
1. Public relations—Clergy. I. Title.

MECCA, Raymond G. 254.4
Your church is news / Raymond G. Mecca. Valley Forge, Pa. : Judson Press, [1975] 94 p. : ill. ; 18 cm. [BV653.M4] 75-9655 ISBN 0-8170-0670-2 pbk. : 3.50
1. Church publicity. I. Title.

SOUTHERN Baptist Convention. Sunday School Board. 254.4
The church public relations committee. [Nashville, 1972] 23 p. 21 cm. (Its Program help series) Cover title. Bibliography: p. 22-23. [BV653.S74] 73-150730
1. Public relations—Churches. I. Title.

STEWART, John T 254.4
How to get your church news in print. St. Louis, Bethany Press [1960] 64 p. 22 cm. [BV653.S82] 60-10642
1. Advertising — Churches. I. Title.

STEWART, John T. 254.4
How to get your church news in print. St. Louis, Bethany Press [c.1960] 64p. 22cm. 60-10642 1.00 pap.,
1. Advertising—Churches. I. Title.

TODD, Wayne E. 254.4
Media on the move : reaching out with resources / compiled by Wayne E. Todd ; assisted by C. Keith Mee, Jacqulyn Anderson, Wanda Lineberry. Nashville : Convention Press, [1974] 123 p. : ill. ; 20 cm. "This book is the text for course 6911 of subject area 69, Program and Administrative Services, of the Church Study Course [Sunday School Board, Southern Baptist Convention]" Bibliography: p. 97-112. [BV652.95.T6] 75-301776
1. Mass media in religion. I. Southern Baptist Convention. Sunday School Board. II. Title.

CATHOLIC Press Association. Venezuela Study Committee. 254.4'0987
Mass communications and the church in Venezuela; a report prepared for His Excellency, the Apostolic Nuncio to Venezuela, Archbishop Luigi Dadaglio. [New York, 1962] 149 l. illus. 28 cm. [BV652.95.C37 1962] 74-179518
1. Mass media in religion—Venezuela. 2. Mass media—Venezuela. I. Dadaglio, Luigi, 1914- II. Title.

BOW, Russell. 254'.5
The integrity of church membership. Waco, Tex., Word Books [1968] 133 p. 21 cm. "References" p. 131-133. [BV820.B68] 67-26937
1. Church membership. 2. Church renewal. I. Title.

HODGES, Melvin L. 254'.5
A guide to church planting, by Melvin L. Hodges. Chicago, Moody Press [1973] 95 p. 22 cm. Includes bibliographical references. [BV3790.H58] 73-7334 ISBN 0-8024-3380-4 1.50 (pbk.)
1. Evangelistic work. 2. Mission of the church. I. Title.

MCGAVRAN, Donald Anderson, 1897- 254'.5
Ten steps for church growth / Donald A. McGavran and Winfield C. Arn. 1st ed. San Francisco : Harper & Row, c1977. p. cm. [BV652.25.M29 1977] 76-62950 ISBN 0-06-065351-5 : 6.95. ISBN 0-06-065352-3 pbk. : 2.95
1. Church growth. I. Arn, Winfield, joint author. II. Title.

MILLER, Herb. 254'.5
Evangelism's open secrets / Herb Miller. St. Louis : Bethany Press, c1977. 112 p. ; 23 cm. Bibliography: 111-112. [BV3790.M6] 77-23468 ISBN 0-8272-0803-0 pbk. : 4.25
1. Evangelistic work. 2. Church growth. I. Title.

PALMER, Bernard Alvin, 1914- 254'.5
How churches grow / by Bernard and Marjorie Palmer. Minneapolis : Bethany Fellowship, c1976. p. cm. [BV652.25.P34] 76-40927 ISBN 0-87123-229-4 pbk. : 3.50
1. Church growth—Case studies. 2. Evangelistic work—Case studies. I. Palmer, Marjorie, joint author. II. Title.

SMITH, Ebbie C. 254'.5
A manual for church growth surveys / Ebbie C. Smith. South Pasadena, Calif. : William Carey Library, c1975. p. cm. Bibliography: p. [BV652.25.S55] 75-25999 ISBN 0-87808-145-3 pbk. : 2.95
1. Church growth—Handbooks, manuals, etc. I. Title.

THOMAS, George Ernest, 1907- 254'.5
25 ways to assimilate new members [by G. Ernest Thomas Nashville, Tidings [1973] 38 p. illus. 19 cm. [BV820.T53] 73-77729
1. Church membership. I. Title.

WERNING, Waldo J. 254'.5
Vision and strategy for church growth / by Waldo J. Werning. Chicago : Moody Press, c1977. 125 p. ; 22 cm. Includes bibliographical references. [BV652.25.W47] 77-1539 ISBN 0-8024-9175-8 pbk. : 2.95
1. Church growth. I. Title.

WOMACK, David A. 254'.5
The pyramid principle of church growth / by David A. Womack. Minneapolis : Bethany Fellowship, c1977. 140 p. ; 21 cm. [BV652.25.W65] 76-46312 ISBN 0-87123-462-9 pbk. : 2.95
1. Church growth. I. Title.

BAUMANN, Dan. 254'.5'0722
All originality makes a dull church / Dan Baumann. Santa Ana, Calif. : Vision House Publishers, c1976. 141 p. ; 21 cm. Includes bibliographies. [BV652.25.B38] 75-42852 ISBN 0-88449-053-X : 2.50
1. Church growth—Case studies. 2. Churches—United States. I. Title.

POPE, Robert G. 254'.5'0974
The half-way covenant; church membership in Puritan New England, by Robert G. Pope. Princeton, N.J., Princeton University Press, 1969. xi, 321 p. 21 cm. Bibliography: p. 287-307. [BX9353.P6] 69-18067 10.00
1. Church membership. 2. Covenants (Church polity) 3. Puritans—New England. I. Title.

ANDERSON, Philip A. 254'.6
The house church [by] Philip and Phoebe Anderson. Nashville, Abingdon Press [1975] 176 p. illus. 22 cm. Bibliography: p. 174-176. [BV601.85.A5] 74-19144 ISBN 0-687-17437-6 4.50 (pbk.)
1. House churches. I. Anderson, Phoebe M., joint author. II. Title.

APPS, Jerold W., 1934- 254'.6
Ideas for better church meetings / Jerold W. Apps. Minneapolis : Augsburg Pub. House, [1975] 128 p. : ill. ; 20 cm. Includes bibliographical references. [BV652.15.A66] 75-2842 ISBN 0-8066-1487-0 : 2.95
1. Church meetings. I. Title.

CROWE, Jimmy P. 254.6
Church leader training handbook [by] Jimmy P. Crowe. Nashville, Convention Press [1970] 96 p. 21 cm. "This book is number 6407 in the Christian leadership series of the New church study course." Bibliography: p. 96. [BV652.1.C75] 75-118305
1. Christian leadership. I. Title.

DESPORTES, Elisa L. 254'.6
Congregations in change; a Project Test Pattern book in parish development [by] Elisa L. DesPortes. Foreword by Cynthia C. Wedel. Pref. by Loren B. Mead. New York, Seabury Press [1973] xvi, 201 p. illus. 21 cm. "A Crossroad book." [BV600.2.D49] 73-77768 ISBN 0-8164-2085-8 3.95
1. Project Test Pattern. 2. Church renewal—Case studies. I. Title.

ENGSTROM, W. A., 1925- 254'.6
Multi-media in the church: a beginner's guide for putting it all together [by] W. A. Engstrom, Richmond, Va., John Knox Press [1973] 128 p. illus. 24 cm. Bibliography: p. 118-121. [BV1535.E55] 72-11165 ISBN 0-8042-1730-0 3.50
1. Church work—Audio-visual aids. 2. Public worship. I. Title.

FORLITI, John E. 254'.6
Program planning for youth ministry / by John E. Forliti. Winona, Minn. : St. Mary's College Press, [1975] 60 p. ; 28 cm. [BX2347.8.Y7F67] 75-143 ISBN 0-88489-061-9
1. Church work with youth—Catholic Church. I. Title.

FORLITI, John E. 254'.6
Program planning for youth ministry / by John E. Forliti. Winona, Minn. : St. Mary's College Press, [1975] 60 p. ; 28 cm. [BX2347.8.Y7F67] 75-143 ISBN 0-88489-061-9 pbk. : 4.50
1. Church work with youth—Catholic Church. I. Title.

HODGES, Norman E. 254'.6
The association and church training [by] Norman E. Hodges. Nashville, Convention Press [1970] iv, 156 p. illus. 21 cm. Bibliography: p. 155-156. [BV652.1.H6] 76-101353
1. Christian leadership. I. Title.

JOHNSON, Alvin D. 254'.6
Celebrating your church anniversary [by] Alvin D. Johnson. Valley Forge [Pa.] Judson Press [1968] 95 p. illus. 22 cm. Bibliography: p. 83. [BV652.9.J58] 68-28077 2.50
1. Church anniversaries. I. Title.

KOSTYU, Frank A. 254'.6
Ways to spark your church program, by Frank A. Kostyu. Nashville, Abingdon Press [1974] 141 p. illus. 19 cm. [BV4011.K67] 73-12236 ISBN 0-687-44236-2 2.95 (pbk.)
1. Pastoral theology. I. Title.

LOUTHAN, Sheldon. 254'.6
Toward better families / by Sheldon Louthan and Grant Martin. Newberg, Or. : Barclay Press, c1976. viii, 80 p. : ill. ; 28 cm. Includes bibliographical references. [BV4438.L68] 76-22904 ISBN 0-913342-21-1 : 4.95
1. Church work with families. I. Martin, Grant, joint author. II. Title.

LUTHERAN Church in America. Task Group for Long-Range Planning. 254'.6
Significant issues for the 1970's; report. [Philadelphia, Board of Publication of the Lutheran Church in America, 1968] 122 l. 28 cm. Includes bibliographies. [BV4011.L8] 68-5334
1. Pastoral theology—Lutheran Church. 2. Sociology, Christian (Lutheran) I. Title.

LUTHERAN Church in America. Task Group for Long-range Planning. 254'.6
Significant issues for the 1970's; report. Edward W. Uthe, director. Philadelphia, Fortress Press [1968] 172 p. 21 cm. Includes bibliographies. [BV4011.L8 1968b] 68-9485
1. Pastoral theology—Lutheran Church. 2. Sociology, Christian (Lutheran) I. Uthe, Edward W. II. Title.

PEARL, Virginia L. 254'.6
A bunch of daisies : model for a family program / Virginia L. Pearl ; introd. by Alfred McBride. Kansas City, Kan. : Sheed and Ward, 1975. 192 p. : ill. ; 26 cm. Bibliography: p. 188-192. [BX2351.P38] 75-17051 ISBN 0-8362-0598-7 : 7.95 ($8.95 Can)
1. Family—Religious life. I. Title.

SHEDD, Charlie W. 254'.6
The exciting church : where people really pray / Charlie W. Shedd. Waco, Tex. : Word Books, [1974] 105 p. ; 22 cm. [BX9211.J43J447] 74-78039 3.95
1. Jekyll Presbyterian Community Church, Jekyll Island. 2. Prayer. I. Title.

SMITH, Lyndsay L. 254'.6
Creative leadership; programme ideas and leadership techniques for boys' club leaders, girls' club leaders, teachers, and all interested in giving a leadership which will be creative in the development of Australian youth, [edited by] L. L. Smith. [Rev. ed. Melbourne] Explorer Boys' Clubs Movement of the Department of Christian Education of the Churches of Christ in Victoria & Tasmania [1969] 168 p. diagrs. 21 cm. Includes bibliographies. [BV4447.S62 1969] 73-885836
1. Church work with youth. 2. Christian leadership. I. Churches of Christ in Victoria and Tasmania. Explorer Boys' Club Auxiliary. II. Title.

THOMAS, George Ernest, 1907- 254'.6
Christian growth; the cultivation of congregational life, by G. Ernest Thomas. Nashville, Tenn., Tidings [1973] 32 p. 19 cm. [BV4501.2.T45] 73-85524 0.50
1. Christian life—1960- 2. Church work. I. Title.

VANDER Kaay, Dorothy. 254'.6
Women's world handbook of ideas and procedures for ladies groups. Des Plaines, Ill., Regular Baptist Press [1974] 133 p. 19 cm. [BV2610.V36] 74-79541 1.50 (pbk.).
1. Women in missionary work. I. Title.

WEIDENBACH, Nell L. 254'.6
Just a touch of drama : programs for women / Nell L. Weidenbach. Chicago : Moody Press, [1975] 64 p. ; 22 cm. Includes bibliographies. [BV4415.W38] 74-15346 ISBN 0-8024-4496-2 pbk. : 1.25
1. Women in church work. 2. Women—Prayer-books and devotions—English. I. Title.

HARRELL, William Asa, 1903- 254'.7
Providing adequate church property and buildings [by] William A. Harrell. Nashville, Convention Press [1969] x, 69 p. 20 cm. [BV604.H3] 68-19361
1. Church facilities—Planning. I. Title.

ANDERSON, Martin, 1882- 254.8
A guide to church building and fund raising. Minneapolis, Augsburg Pub. House. [1959] 69p. illus. 29cm. [BV604.A5] 59-5611
1. Churches. 2. Church architecture. 3. Fund raising. I. Title.

APPLEGARTH, Margaret Tyson, 1886- 254.8
Twelve baskets full. [1st ed.] New York, Harper [1957] 245p. 22cm. [BV772.A65] 56-12059
1. Stewardship, Christian. I. Title.

APPLEGARTH, Margaret Tyson, 1886- 254.8
Twelve baskets full, by Margaret T. Applegarth. Grand Rapids, Mich., Baker Book House [1973, c1947] 245 p. 19 cm. [BV772.A65 1973] 2.95 (pbk.)
1. Stewardship, Christian. I. Title.
L.C. card no. for original ed.: 56-12059.

ATKINSON, Charles Harry, 1894- 254.8
How to finance your church building program. [Westwood N.J.] Revell [1963] 64 p. illus. 21 cm. (Revell's better church series) Bibliography: p. 64. [BV772.5.A8] 63-17113
1. Church finance. 2. Fund raising. I. Title.

ATKINSON, Charles Harry, 1894- 254.8
How to finance your church building program. [Westwood, N.J.] Revell [c.1963] 64p. illus. 21cm. (Revell's better church ser.) Bibl. 63-17113 1.00 pap.,
1. Church finance. 2. Fund raising. I. Title.

AZARIAH, Vedanayakam Samuel, Bp., 1874-1945. 254.8
Christian giving. New York, Association Press [1955] 96p. 20cm. (World Christian books) [BV772.A97] 55-7404
1. Christian giving. I. Title.

AZARIAH, Vedanayakam Samuel, Bp., 1874-1945. 254.8
Christian giving. New York, Association Press [1955] 96p. 20cm. (World Christian books. [2]) [BV772.A97] 55-7404
1. Christian giving. I. Title.

BALCOMB, Raymond E. 254.8
Stir what you've got! and other stewardship studies [by] Raymond E. Balcomb. Nashville, Abingdon Press [1968] 160 p. 21 cm. [BV772.B25] 68-17443
1. Stewardship, Christian. I. Title.

BRACEWELL, Joseph Searcy, 1892 254.8
Building churches through income financing. Fresno, Calif., CBF Press [1961] 108p. illus. 22cm. [BV770.B66] 61-35994
1. Church finance. 2. Churches. I. Title.

BROOKS, Lawrence E. 254.8
Better church finance. Anderson, Ind., Warner Press [dist. Gospel Trumpet Press, c.1960] 64p. illus. 28cm. 60-13190 2.00, pap., spiral binding
1. Church finance. I. Title.

BUCK, Carlton C 254.8
At the Lord's treasury; a stewardship manual. St. Louis, Bethany Press [1959] 192p. 16cm. Includes bibliography. [BV772.B77] 58-59535
1. Stewardship, Christian. I. Title.

BYFIELD, Richard. 254.8
Your money and your church, by Richard Byfield and James P. Shaw. [1st ed.] Garden City, N. Y., Doubleday, 1959. 238p. 22cm. [BV772.B9] 59-12025
1. Christian giving. 2. Church finance. I. Shaw, James, P., joint author. II. Title.

CLEARWATERS, Richard V 254.8
Stewardship sermonettes. Grand Rapids, Baker

Book House, 1955. 120p. 21cm. [BV772] 55-12086
1. Stewardship, Christian—Sermons. 2. Baptists—Sermons. 3. Sermons, American. I. Title.

CLEARWATERS, Richard V 254.8
Stewardship sermonettes. Wheaton, Ill., Van Kampen Press [1955] 120p. 20cm. [BV772.C54] 55-33689
1. Stewardship. Christian—Sermons. 2. Baptists—Sermons. 3. Sermons, American. I. Title.

CONFERENCE on Philanthropy in Action, San Francisco, 1966. 254.8
Proceedings. [New York] Commn. on Stewardship & Benevolence, Natl. Council of the Churches of Christ [1966] 96p. 21cm. [Sponsored by] the Commn. on Stewardship and Benevolence. Committee on Wills and Special Gifts. Bibl. [GV770.C58 1966] 66-8430 5.00 pap.,
1. Church finance. I. National Council of the Churches of Christ in the United States of America. Commission on Stewardship and Benevolence. Committee on Wills and Special Gifts. II. Title.

COSTELOE, Michael P. 254.8
Church wealth in Mexico: a study of the 'Juzgado de Capellanias' in the archbishopric of Mexico 1800-1856, by Michael P. Costeloe. London, Cambridge U.P., 1967 ix, 139 p. 22 1/2 cm. (Cambridge Latin American studies, no. 2) Bibliography: p. 133-136. [BX1428.2.C6] 67-18310 ISBN 0-521-04729-3
1. Catholic Church in Mexico—Finance. 2. Church and state in Mexico. I. Title. II. Title: Juzgado de Capellanias.

COWLING, Ellis, 1905- 254.8
Let's think about money. New York, Abingdon Press [1957] 95p. 19cm. [BV772.C76] 57-1588
1. Stewardship, Christian. I. Title.

DURHAM, Eng. University. Durham Colleges. Dept. of Palaeography and Diplomatic. 254.8
Durham diocesan records; list of tithe apportionments and plans for County Durham. Durham, Dept. of Palaeography and Diplomatic, University of Durham, 1971. ii, 51 l. 30 cm. [DA670.D9D86 1971] 75-301621
1. Durham, Eng. (County)—History—Sources. I. Title.

FLYNN, Leslie B. 254.8
Your God and your gold. Grand Rapids, Mich., Zondervan [c.1961] 137p. 61-66732 2.50 bds.,
1. Stewardship, Christian. I. Title.

FOX, John Frederick, 1918- 254.8
Church loans by commercial banks. [Rochester? N. Y., 1954] vi, 100 l. 28cm. 'Submitted in partial fulfilment of the requirements of the Graduate School of Banking conducted by the American Bankers Association at Rutgers University.' Bibliography: leaves 95-97. [BV770.F65] 55-16797
1. Church finance. I. Title.

GRAVES, Allen Willis, 1915- 254.8
Using and maintaining church property, by Allen W. Graves. Englewood Cliffs, N.J., Prentice-Hall [1965] 186 p. 21 cm. (Church business management series) Bibliography: p. 178-179. [BV652.7.G7] 65-24695
1. Church property—Maintenance and repair. 2. Church management. I. Title. II. Series.

GRAVES, Allen Willis, 1915- 254.8
Using and maintaining church property. Englewood Cliffs, N.J., Prentice [c.1965] 186p. 21cm. (Church bus. mgmt. ser.) Bibl. [BV652.7.G7] 65-24695 3.95 bds.,
1. Church property—Maintenance and repair. 2. Church management. I. Title. II. Series.

HARRELL, Costen Jordan, 1885- 254.8
Stewardship and the tithe. Nashville, Abingdon-Cokesbury Press [1953] 61p. 20c4. [BV772.H225] 54-3107
1. Stewardship, Christian. I. Title.

HARRISON, George W. 254.8
Church fund raising [by] George W. Harrison, Howell Farnworth and Chester A. Myrom. Englewood Cliffs, N.J., Prentice [1964] 175p. illus. 21cm. (Church bus. mgmt. ser.) Bibl. 64-19677 3.95
1. Church finance. 2. Fund raising. I. Title.

HASTINGS, Robert J. 254.8
My money and God. Nashville, Broadman Press [c.1961] 127p. Bibl. notes: p.126-127. 61-5393 2.50
1. Stewardship, Christian. I. Title.

HESS, Bartlett L., 1910- 254.8
How to have a giving church [by] Bartlett L. Hess and Margaret Johnston Hess. Nashville, Abingdon Press [1974] 127 p. 19 cm. [BV772.H45] 74-6186 ISBN 0-687-17808-8 2.95 (pbk.)
1. Christian giving. 2. Church finance. I. Hess, Margaret Johnston, joint author. II. Title.

HICKERSON, May Josephine (compere.) 254.8
These dared to share. [Teacher's ed.] Nashville, Broadman Press [1952] 102 p. illus. 20 cm. [BV772.H5] 52-38081
1. Stewardship, Christian. I. Title.

HILL, Christopher. 254.8
Economic problems of the church, from Archbishop Whitgift to the Long Parliament. Oxford, Clarendon Press, 1956. xiv, 367p. 23cm. Bibliographical footnotes. [BX5165.H55] 56-58783
1. Church of England—Finance. I. Title.

HOLCK, Manfred. 254.8
Complete handbook of church accounting / Manfred Holck, Jr., with Manfred Holck, Sr. Englewood Cliffs, N.J. : Prentice-Hall, 1977c1978 p. cm. Includes index. Bibliography: p. [BV773.H63] 77-23882 ISBN 0-13-160895-9 : 17.95
1. Church finance. 2. Church work—Forms, blanks, etc. I. Holck, Manfred, 1902- joint author. II. Title.

HOLCK, Manfred. 254.8
Money and your church : how to raise more, how to manage it better / Manfred Holck, Jr. New Canaan, Conn. : Keats Pub., 1974. 189 p. : ill. ; 22 cm. Bibliography: p. 187-189. [BV770.H617] 74-75979 ISBN 0-87983-080-8 : 7.95
1. Church finance. I. Title.

HOLT, David R. 254.8
Handbook of church finance. New York, Macmillan, [c.]1960. 201p. 22cm. Bibl.: p.173-176. 60-8543 5.00
1. Church finance. I. Title.

HOWELL, Roy Wilbur. 254.8
Saved to serve; accent on stewardship. Grand Rapids, Baker Book House, 1965. 132 p. 20 cm. Bibliography: p. 131-132. [BV772.H63] 65-28579
1. Stewardship, Christian. I. Title.

HOWELL, Roy Wilbur 254.8
Saved to serve; accent on stewardship. Grand Rapids, Mich., Baker Bk. [c.]1965. 132p. 20cm. Bibl. [BV772.H63] 65-28579 1.95 pap.,
1. Stewardship, Christian. I. Title.

JOHNSON, Frederick Ernest, 1884- 254.8
The church as employer, money raiser, and investor, by F. Ernest Johnson and J. Emory Ackerman. [1st ed.] New York, Harper [1959] 184p. 22cm. (Series on ethics and economic life) [BV770.J6] 58-11043
1. Church finance. 2. Clergy— Salaries, pensions, etc. 3. Christianity and economics. I. Ackerman, J. Emory, joint author. II. Title.

JOHNSON, Philip A 254.8
Telling the good news; a public relations handbook for churches, edited by Philip A. Johnson, Norman Temme [and] Charles C. Hushaw. Saint Louis, Concordia Pub. House [1962] 202p. illus. 21cm. [BV653.J6] 62-14145
1. Public relations—Churches. I. Title.

KING, Julius, 1893- ed. 254.8
Successful fund-raising sermons. New York, Funk & Wagnalls, 1953. 274p. 22cm. [BV772.K53] 53-6986
1. Fund raising. 2. Church finance. 3. Sermons. American. I. Title.

KNUDSEN, Raymond B. 254.8
New models for financing the local church; fresh approaches to giving in the computer age [by] Raymond B. Knudsen. New York, Association Press [1974] 157 p. illus. 22 cm. [BV770.K58] 74-11208 ISBN 0-8096-1892-3 5.95
1. Church finance. I. Title.

LANSDELL, Henry 254.8
The tithe in scripture. Grand Rapids, Mich., Baker Bk. [1966, c.1963] 156p. 22cm. Embodies the portions of the author's The sacred tenth which deals with the scriptural teaching on the tithe. First pub. in England in 1908. 1.50 pap.,
1. Tithes. I. Title.

LANSDELL, Henry, 1841-1919. 254.8
The sacred tenth; or, Studies in tithe-giving, ancient and modern. Grand Rapids, Baker Book House, 1955- v. 23cm. [Co-operative reprint library] [BV771.L32] 54-11072
1. Tithes. 2. Tithes—Gt. Brit. I. Title.

LANSDELL, Henry, 1841-1919 254.8
The tithe in Scripture. Grand Rapids, Mich., Baker Bk., 1963. 156p. 23cm. Embodies the portions of the author's The sacred tenth which deal with the Scriptural teaching on the tithe. 63-12030 2.95
1. Tithes. I. Title.

LUMLEY, Arthur W. 254.8
Raising money for church building projects. Nashville, Abingdon Press [1954] 128p. illus. 20cm. [BV772.L85] 54-8240
1. Fund raising. 2. Church finance. I. Title.

MCKEOWN, Boyd M 254.8
Stewardship in Methodism. Nashville, Methodist Pub. House [1953] 156p. 20cm. Published in 1942 under title: Achieving results in church finance. [BV770.M34 1953] 52-13757
1. Church finance. 2. Stewardship, Christian. I. Title.

MILLER, Basil William, 1897- *254.8
Treasury of stewardship illustrations; 164 sparkling illustrations of march to fame and infamy. [1st ed.] Kansas City, Mo., Beacon Hill Press [1952] 192 p. 20 cm. [BV772.M5] 52.9724
1. Stewardship, Christian. 2. Homiletical illustrations. I. Title.

MILLICAN, Charles N 254.8
Church financing by financial institutions in the United States,1946-1952. [Gainesville, Fla.] c1954. 1v. illus. 28cm. Condensed reports of chapters 2-4 of the author's dissertation. [BV770.M48] 55-32540
1. Church finance. I. Title.

OLSON, Raymond M 254.8
Stewards appointed; ten studies in Christian stewardship based on Luther's small catechism. Minneapolis, Augsburg Pub. House [1958] 141p. 20cm. Includes bibliography. [BV772.O6] 58-10319
1. Luther, Martin. Catechismus, Kleiner. 2. Stewardship, Christian. I. Title.

PAPPENHEIM, Eugene, 1913- 254.8
Stewardship without failure; the complete day-by-day how-to-do-it manual for all Christian churches. Milwaukee, Agape [1974] xii, 335 p. illus. 25 cm. [BV772.5.P36] 74-79559 ISBN 0-914618-00-8 20.00
1. Church finance. 2. Stewardship, Christian. I. Title.
Publisher's address: 10721 West Capitol Drive, Suite 203, Milwaukee, Wisconsin 53222.

PENDLETON, Othniel Alsop, 1911- 254.8
New techniques for church fund raising; a ten-step plan to increase your pledges and strengthen your church. Foreword by W. Appleton Lawrence, Bishop of the Diocese of Western Massachusetts, the Protestant Episcopal Church. New York, McGraw-Hill, 1955. 256, K 109p. illus. 24cm. [BV770.P4] 55-6166
1. Church finance. 2. Fund raising. I. Title.

PETERSON, Robert E 254.8
Handling the church's money; a handbook for church treasurers, financial secretaries, stewardship leaders, by Robert E. Peterson. St. Louis, Bethany Press [1965] 64 p. (p. [62]-64, blank for "Notes") 22 cm. [BV773.P4] 65-12291
1. Church finance—Accounting. I. Title.

PETERSON, Robert E. 254.8
Handling the church's money; a handbook for church treasurers, financial secretaries, stewardship leaders. St. Louis, Bethany [c.1965] 64p. 22cm. [BV773.P4] 65-12291 1.00 pap.,
1. Church finance—Accounting. I. Title.

PIAT, Stephane Joseph, 1899- 254.8
Riches and the spirit. Translated from the French by Paul J. Oligny. Chicago, Franciscan Herald Press [1958] 254p. 21cm. [BV772.P483] 58-12950
1. Stewardship, Christian. I. Title.

POWELL, Luther P 254.8
Money and the church. New York, Association Press [1962] 252p. 21cm. [BV770.P6] 62-11030
1. Church finance— Hist. I. Title.

POWELL, Luther P. 254.8
Money and the church. New York, Association [1963, c.1962] 252p. 18cm. (Giant reflection bk., 704) 1.50
1. Church finance—Hist. I. Title.

POWERS, Charles W. 254.8
Social responsibility & investments [by] Charles W. Powers. Nashville, Abingdon Press [1971] 224 p. 20 cm. (An Original Abingdon paperback) Includes bibliographical references. [BV774.5.P69] 72-148859 ISBN 0-687-38925-9
1. Church finance. 2. Investments. I. Title.

RAY, George McNeill. 254.8
Tall in His presence; a manual of Christian stewardship. Greenwich, Conn., Seabury Press, 1961. 127p. 20cm. [BV772.R28] 61-9108
1. Stewardship, Christian. I. Title.

REBOK, D. E. 254.8
Les richesses de Dieu entre mes mains [in French] Mountain View, Calif., Pac. Pr. Pub. [c.1963] 79p. 18cm. .50 pap.,
I. Title.

REBOK, Denton Edward, 1897- 254.8
God's gold in my hand. Mountain View, Calif., Pacific Press Pub. Association [c1959] 82p. illus. 19cm. [BV772.R34] 59-9707
1. Stewardship, Christian. 2. Tithes. I. Title.

REEVE, Jack V., ed. 254.8
A God to glorify, through Christian stewardship. St. Louis, Bethany [c.1964] 160p. 23cm. Bibl. 64-20802 2.95
1. Stewardship, Christian—Sermons. 2. Sermons, American. 3. Disciples of Christ—Sermons. I. Title.

REEVE, Jack V ed. 254.8
A God to glorify, through Christian stewardship. Edited by Jack Reeve. St. Louis, Bethany Press [1964] 160 p. 23 cm. Bibliographical footnotes. [BV772.R36] 64-20802
1. Stewardship, Christian — Sermons. 2. Sermons, American. 3. Disciples of Christ — Sermons. I. Title.

REIN, Remus C 1905- 254.8
First fruits: God's guide for giving. Saint Louis, Concordia Pub. House [1959] 111p. 22cm. [BV772] 59-16764
1. Stewardship, Christian—Study and teaching. I. Title.

SALSTRAND, George A. E. 254.8
The tithe; the minimum standard for Christian giving. Grand Rapids, Mich., Baker Bk. [1963, c.1952] 55p. 20cm. Bibl. .85 pap.,
I. Title.

SAYERS, Carl R 254.8
Tithing and the church's mission, by Carl R. Sayers and Bertram T. White. Pref. by Richard S. Emrich. New York, Morehouse-Barlow Co. [1962] 65p. illus. 19cm. [BV772.S33] 62-19256
1. Stewardship, Christian. I. White, Bertram T., joint author. II. Title.

SEAMAN, Ralph. 254.8
101 ways to raise money for your church; including The living light, a royalty-free Christmas pageant. New York, F. Fell [1952] 138p. 20cm. [BV770.S4] A53
1. Church finance. 2. Fund raising. I. Title. II. Title: The living light.

SEAMAN, Ralph. 254.8
101 ways to raise money for your church; including The living light, a royalty-free Christmas pageant. New York, F. Fell [1952] 138 p. 20 cm. [BV770.S4] A 53
1. Church finance. 2. Fund raising. I. Title. II. Title: The living light.

SHEDD, Charlie W. 254.8
How to develop a tithing church. New York, Abingdon Press [1961] 123 p. 19 cm. [BV772.S52] 61-2942
1. Stewardship, Christian. I. Title.

SHEDD, Charlie W. 254.8
How to develop a tithing church. Nashville, Abingdon Press [c.1961] 123p. 61-2942 1.25 pap.,
1. Stewardship, Christian. I. Title.

STEWART, Ivan Robert. 254.8
From house to house; a manual on personal work. Albuquerque, N. M., c1956. 204p. illus. 21cm. [BV652.3.S73] 56-42689
1. Canvassing (Church work) 2. Evangelistic work. I. Title.

STEWART, Ivan Robert. *254.8
From house to house, a manual on personal work. Albuquerque, N.M., c1956. 204 p. illus. 21 cm. [BV652.3.S73] 56-42689
1. Canvassing (Church work) 2. Evangelistic work. I. Title.

STILES, Joseph 254.8
Acquiring and developing church real estate. Englewood Cliffs, N.J., Prentice [1965] 189p. 21cm. (Church bus, mgmt. ser.) Bibl. [BV775.S68] 65-24694 3.95 bds.,
1. Church property. 2. Church management. I. Title. II. Series.

SUTTON, Jack A. 254.8
Witness beyond barriers, by Jack A. Sutton. St. Louis, Bethany Press [1968] 158 p. 23 cm. [BV772.S87] 68-26113 4.95
1. Tithes. 2. Christian giving. I. Title.

THOMPSON, David W. 254.8
How to increase memorial giving. [Westwood, N. J.] Revell [c.1963] 63p. 21cm. (Revell's better church ser.) 63-17116 1.00 pap.,
1. Church finance. 2. Fund raising. 3. Memorials. I. Title.

THOMPSON, David Wilson, 254.8
1935-
How to increase memorial giving. [Westwood, N.J.] Revell [1963] 63 p. 21 cm. [(Reyell's better church series)] [BV772.5.T5] 63-17116
1. Church finance. 2. Fund raising. 3. Memorials. I. Title.

THOMPSON, Thomas K 254.8
Handbook of stewardship procedures, by T. K. Thompson. Englewood Cliffs, N.J., Prentice-Hall [1964] x, 115 p. 21 cm. (Library of Christian stewardship, LCS-1) "An annotated bibliography": p. 59-72. [BV772.T46] 64-20977
1. Stewardship, Christian. 2. Church finance. I. Title.

THOMPSON, Thomas K. 254.8
Handbook of stewardship procedures. Englewood Cliffs, N.J., Prentice [c.1964] x, 115p. 21cm. (Lib. of Christian stewardship, LCS-1) Bibl. 64-20977 2.75; 1.50 pap.,
1. Stewardship, Christian. 2. Church finance. I. Title.

THOMPSON, Thomas K ed. 254.8
Stewardship in contemporary theology. New York, Association Press [1960] 252 p. 20 cm. Include bibliography. [BV772.T47] 60-6564
1. Stewardship. Christian. I. Title.

THOMPSON, Thomas K., ed. 254.8
Stewardship in contemporary theology. New York, Association Press [c.1960] 252p. 20cm. (bibl.) 60-6564 3.50 bds.,
1. Stewardship, Christian. I. Title.

USSERY, Annie (Wright) 254.8
Christian sharing of possessions. [Nashville] Convention Press [1961] 141 p. 10 cm. Includes bibliography. [BV772.U8] 61-11006
1. Stewardship, Christian — Biblical teaching. I. Title.

*YOUNG, Samuel. 254-8
Giving and living : foundations for Christian Stewardship / by Samuel Young. Grand Rapids : Baker Book House, 1976c1974. 94p. ; 20cm. Bibliography: p. 93-94. [BV772] ISBN 0-8010-9911-0 pbk. : 1.95
1. Stewardship, Christian. I. Title.

LUNT, William Edward, 254.8'0942
1882-1956.
Accounts rendered by papal collectors in England, 1317-1378. Transcribed with annotations and introd. by William E. Lunt. Edited, with additions and revisions by Edgar B. Graves. Philadelphia, American Philosophical Society, 1968. liv, 579 p. facsims. 31 cm. (Memoirs of the American Philosophical Society, v. 70) Includes bibliographical references. [BX1950.L78] 67-19647
1. Catholic Church—Finance. 2. Catholic Church. Camera Apostolica. 3. Catholic Church—History—Sources. 4. Taxation, Papal. I. Graves, Edgar B., ed. II. Title. III. Title: Papal collectors in England. IV. Series: American Philosophical Society, Philadelphia. Memoirs, v. 70.

255 Religious Congregations & Orders

CLARKE, Thomas E. 255
New Pentecost or new Passion? The direction of religious life today [by] Thomas E. Clarke. Paramus [N.J.] Paulist Press [1973] 181 p. 21 cm. Includes bibliographical references. [BX2435.C55] 73-84049 ISBN 0-8091-1792-4 3.95 (pbk.)
1. Monastic and religious life. I. Title.

FUTRELL, John Carroll. 255
Making an apostolic community of love; the role of the superior according to St. Ignatius of Loyola. St. Louis, Institute of Jesuit Sources, 1970. 231 p. 24 cm. "A condensation of a ... dissertation." Bibliography: p. 217-221. [BX2434.F87] 73-139365 8.50
1. Loyola, Ignacio de, Saint, 1491-1556. 2. Superiors, Religious. I. Title.

GALOT, Jean. 255
Inspiritor of the community; the new role of the religious superior. Staten Island, N.Y., Alba House [1971] vii, 110 p. 22 cm. Translation of Animatrice de communaute. [BX4209.G3313] 75-169147 ISBN 0-8189-0235-3 3.95
1. Superiors, Religious. I. Title.

HEROLD, Duchesne. 255
New life: preparation of religious for retirement. St. Louis, Catholic Hospital Association [1973] xiv, 154 p. 28 cm. Bibliography: p. 152-154. [BX2437.5.H47] 73-76987 ISBN 0-87125-007-1 5.00
1. Monastic and religious orders—Retirement. I. Title.

LECLERCQ, Jean, 1911- 255
Contemplative life. Translated by Sr. M. Elizabeth. [Spencer, Mass.] Cistercian Publications; [distributed by] Consortium Press, Washington, 1973. p. cm. (Cistercian studies series, no. 19) Translation of Vie religieuse et vie contemplative. Includes bibliographical references. [BX2435.L42513] 74-8484 ISBN 0-87907-819-7 10.95
1. Monastic and religious life. I. Title. II. Series.

LIBELLUS de diversis 255
ordinibus et professionibus qui sunt in aecclesia; edited and translated [from the Latin] with introduction and notes by G. Constable and B. Smith. Oxford, Clarendon Press, 1972. xxix, 125 p., leaf. facsim. 22 cm. (Oxford medieval texts) Attributed by some to Reimbald. Parallel Latin text and English translation, English introduction and notes. "The Latin text ... is printed here from British Museum ms. Add. 21244 ..." [BX2470.L5] 73-162115 ISBN 0-19-822218-1 £3.50
1. Monasticism and religious orders—Middle Ages, 600-1500. I. Constable, Giles, ed. II. Smith, Bernard, 1925- ed. III. Reimbaldus, d. 1149. IV. British Museum. Mss. Additional 21244. V. Title. VI. Series.

MEETING of the Monastic 255
Superiors in the Far East, Bangkok, Thailand, 1968.
A new charter for monasticism; proceedings. Edited, and with an introd., by John Moffitt. Foreword by George N. Shuster. Notre Dame, University of Notre Dame Press, 1970. xv, 335 p. 24 cm. Includes bibliographical references. [BX2410.M4 1968] 70-122049
1. Monasticism and religious orders—Congresses. I. Moffitt, John, ed. II. Title.

MOHLER, James A. 255
The heresy of monasticism; the Christian monks: types and anti-types; an historical survey [by] James A. Mohler. Staten Island, N.Y., Alba House [1971] xviii, 263 p. illus., maps. 22 cm. Bibliography: p. 241-250. [BX2461.2.M58] 76-148683 ISBN 0-8189-0183-7 5.95
1. Monastic and religious life—History of doctrines. 2. Monasticism and religious orders—History. I. Title.

REGULA Magistri. English. 255
The rule of the Master = Regula magistri / translated by Luke Eberle. Kalamazoo, Mich. : Cistercian Publications, c1977. p. cm. (Cictercian studies series ; 6) [BX2436.5.M3E5 1977] 77-3986 ISBN 0-87907-806-5 : 12.95
1. Monasticism and religious orders—Rules. I. Eberle, Luke. II. Title. III. Series.

SALMON, Pierre, 255
Aug.23,1896-
The abbot in monastic tradition; a contribution to the history of the perpetual character of the office of religious superiors in the West. Translated by Claire Lavoie. Washington, Cistercian Publications, Consortium Press, 1972. xv, 160 p. 23 cm. (Cistercian studies series, no. 14) Translation of L'abbe dans la tradition monastique. Bibliography: p. 151-153. [BX2434.2.S2413 1972] 78-158955 ISBN 0-87907-814-6 9.95
1. Superiors, Religious. 2. Monasticism and religious orders—History. I. Title. II. Series.

THEOLOGICAL Institute for 255
Local Superiors, University of Notre Dame.
Dimensions of authority in the religious life [by] Joseph H. Fichter [others] Notre Dame, Univ. of Notre Dame Pr. [c.] 1966. 179p. 21cm. (Religious life in the mod., world, v.5) Articles previously pub. in the Proceedings of the Sisters' Inst. of Spirituality, 1958-1959. Bibl. [BX4212.T47] 66-14632 1.95 pap.,
1. Monasticism and religious orders for women—Discipline. 2. Superiors, Religious. I. Fichter, Joseph Henry, 1908. II. Notre Dame, Ind. University. III. Title. IV. Series.

THEOLOGICAL INSTITUTE FOR 255
LOCAL SUPERIORS, University of Notre Dame.
Dimensions of authority in the religious life [by] Joseph H. Fichter [and others] Notre Dame, University of Notre Dame Press, 1966. 179 p. 21 cm. (Religious life in the modern world, v. 5) "Articles ... previously published in the Proceedings of the Sisters' Institute of Spirituality, 1958-1959." Includes bibliographies. Bibliographical footnotes. [BX4212.T47] 66-14632
1. Monasticism and religious orders for women — Discipline. 2. Superiors, Religious. I. Fichter, Joseph Henry, 1908- . II. Notre Dame, Ind. University. III. Title. IV. Series.

VATICAN Council. 2d, 1962- 255
1965.
Religious life—a mystery in Christ and the church : a collated study according to Vatican Council II and subsequent papal and ecclesial documents / edited by Rose Eileen Masterman. New York : Alba House, [1975] xi, 289 p. ; 21 cm. Includes indexes. [BX2435.V37 1975] 75-8729 ISBN 0-8189-0303-1 : 4.95
1. Monastic and religious life—Collected works. I. Masterman, Rose Eileen. II. Title.

DOCUMENTS on renewal for 255'.008
religious. [Boston] St. Paul Editions [1974] 394 p. 18 cm. (Magister books) Includes bibliographical references. [BX2435.D63] 74-75621 2.50 (pbk.)
1. Monastic and religious life—Collected works.

THE Monk's community 255'.009'02
: the monastery / Dawn Cline Trueman, John H. Trueman. Toronto ; New York : McGraw-Hill Ryerson, [1974] 113 p. : ill. ; 24 cm. (Ancient and medieval history series) Bibliography: p. 108-111. [BX2470.M66] 75-305647 ISBN 0-07-077648-2
1. Monasticism and religious orders—Middle Ages, 600-1500. 2. Civilization, Medieval. I. Trueman, Dawn Cline. II. Trueman, John Herbert, 1925-

RYAN, John, 1894- 255'.009415
Irish monasticism; origins and early development. New introd. and bibliography. Shannon, Irish University Press [1972] xv, 481, xiv p. 25 cm. Facsimile reproduction of the ed. published in Dublin by Talbot Press in 1931. Bibliography: p. 415-481. [BX2600.R8 1931a] 72-171613 ISBN 0-7165-0578-9
1. Monasticism and religious orders—Ireland. I. Title.
Available from Cornell Univ. Pr., 12.50, 0-8014-40613-7.

CONTEMPLATIVE 255'.01
community; an interdisciplinary symposium. Edited by M. Basil Pennington. Washington, Cistercian Publications, 1972. 366 p. 23 cm. (Cistercian studies series, no. 21) Papers presented at the third Cistercian symposium held at the Abbey of Notre Dame du Lac, Aug. 30-Sept. 6, 1971. Includes bibliographical references. [BX2810.C65] 70-184548 ISBN 0-87907-821-9
1. Contemplative orders—Addresses, essays, lectures. 2. Monastic and religious life—Addresses, essays, lectures. I. Pennington, M. Basil, ed. II. Title. III. Series.

**FOLLOWING Saint* 255.09
Francis; no. 6. Pulaski, Wis., Franciscan Pubs. [c.1966] 63p. 19cm. no. 6. The Counsels. Reprinted from the Franciscan message. .25 pap.,

THIERRY, Jean Jacques. 255'.095
Opus Dei : a close-up / Jean-Jacques Thierry ; translated by Gilda Roberts. New York : Cortland Press, c1975. 197 p. : 23 cm. Bibliography: p. [195]-197. [BX809.S49T4713] 75-325600 pbk. : 5.95
1. Societas Sacerdotalis Sanctae Crucis. I. Title.
Publisher's address: 505 Fifth Ave., N.Y., N.Y. 10017.

HEATH, Robert George, 255'.1
1923-
Crux imperatorium philosophia : imperial horizons of the Cluniac confraternitas, 964-1109 / by Robert G. Heath. Pittsburgh : Pickwick Press, 1976[i.e.1977] xx, 260 p., [2] leaves of plates : ill. ; 22 cm. (Pittsburgh theological monograph series ; no. 13) Includes index. Bibliography: p. 223-251. [BX2615.C63H42] 76-56099 ISBN 0-915138-17-4 pbk. : 8.50
1. Cluny, France (Benedictine abbey) I. Title. II. Series.

HUNT, Noreen. 255'.1
Cluny under Saint Hugh, 1049-1109. [1st American ed. Notre Dame, Ind.] University of Notre Dame Press [1968, c1967] xii, 228 p. illus. 25 cm. Bibliography: p. [214]-223. [BX2615.C63H8 1968] 68-11411 6.95
1. Cluny, France (Benedictine abbey) I. Title.

DEEGAN, Paul J., 255'.1'00977647
1937-
The monastery: life in a religious community, by Paul J. Deegan. Photos. by Bruce Larson. Mankato, Minn., Creative Educational Society [1970] 79 p. illus. 28 cm. "An Amecus Street book." [BX2525.C65D4] 70-125912 ISBN 0-87191-043-8
1. St. John's Abbey, Collegeville, Minn. I. Title.

BENEDICTUS, Saint, 255'.1'06
Abbot of Monte Cassino.
The rule of St. Benedict / translated, with introd. and notes by Anthony C. Meisel and M. L. del Mastro. 1st Garden City, N.Y. : Image Books, 1975. 117 p. ; 18 cm. (An Image book original) Translation of Regula. Bibliography: p. 116-117. [BX3004.E6 1975] 74-33611 ISBN 0-385-00948-8 pbk. : 1.45
I. Meisel, Anthony C., 1943- II. Del Mastro, M. L. III. Title.

SCHROLL, Mary Alfred, 255'.1'06
Sister, 1900-
Benedictine monasticism as reflected in the Warnefrid-Hildemar commentaries on the Rule, by M. Alfred Schroll. New York, AMS Press, 1967 [c1941] 217 p. 23 cm. (Studies in history, economics and public law, no. 478) Originally presented as the author's thesis, Columbia, 1941. Bibliography: p. 206-212. [BX3004.Z5S35 1967] 73-29916
1. Benedictus, Saint, Abbot of Monte Cassino. Regula. 2. Paulus Diaconus, 720 (ca.)-797? 3. Hildemarus, Monk of Civate, fl. 833. I. Title. II. Series: Columbia studies in the social sciences, no. 478.

WATHEN, Ambrose G., 255'.1'06
1931-
Silence; the meaning of silence in the rule of St. Benedict [by] Ambrose G. Wathen. Washington, Cistercian Publications, 1973. xviii, 240 p. illus. 23 cm. (Cistercian studies series, no. 22) Originally presented as the author's thesis, St. Paul University, Ottawa. Bibliography: p. 235-240. [BX3004.Z5W37 1973] 74-188556 ISBN 0-87907-822-7
1. Benedictus, Saint, Abbot of Monte Cassino. Regula. 2. Silence. I. Title. II. Series.

FOWLER, George 255.1'0924 B
Bingham, 1903-
Intellectual interests of Engelbert of Admont. New York, AMS Press, 1967 [c1947] 251 p. front. 23 cm. (Studies in history, economics, and public law, no. 530) Originally presented as the author's thesis, Columbia University. "A list of the works of Engelbert of Admont": p. 183-221. Bibliography: p. 223-235. [BX4705.E655F6 1967] 75-168131
1. Engelbert von Admont, 1250 (ca.)-1331. I. Title. II. Series: Columbia studies in the social sciences, 530.

HAYS, Rhys W. 255.12094292
The history of the Abbey of Aberconway, 1186-1537. Cardiff, Univ. of Wales Pr. [Mystic, Conn., Verry, 1966] xiii, 210p. maps. 22cm. Bibl. [BX2596.A2H3] 66-4815 7.00 bds.,
1. Aberconway Abbey. 2. Maenan Abbey. I. Title.

MCINECRY, Dennis 255'.125'00924 B
Q.
Thomas Merton; the man and his work [by] Dennis Q. McInerny. Kalamazoo, Mich., Cistercian Publications, 1974. p. cm. (Cistercian studies series, no. 27) [BX4705.M542M3] 74-4319 ISBN 0-87907-827-8 7.95
1. Merton, Thomas, 1915-1968. I. Title. II. Series.

NOUWEN, Henri J. 255'.125'024 B
M.
Pray to live. Thomas Merton: a contemplative critic [by] Henri J. M. Nouwen. [Translated from the Dutch by David Schlaver] Notre Dame, Ind., Fides Publishers [1972] x, 157 p. 21 cm. Translation of Bidden om het leven. Includes texts by T. Merton. Bibliography: p. 153-157. [BX4705.M542N6813] 72-10395 ISBN 0-8190-0580-0 2.95
1. Merton, Thomas, 1915-1968. I. Merton, Thomas, 1915-1968. II. Title.

FLOOD, David Ethelbert. 255'.3
The birth of a movement : a study of the First rule of Saint Francis / by David Flood and Thaddee Matura ; translated by Paul Schwartz and Paul Lachance. Chicago : Franciscan Herald Press, [1975] p. cm. Translation of La naissance d'un charisme. "The First rule of Saint Francis": p. Includes index. Bibliography: p. [BX3604.Z5F5313] 75-8783 ISBN 0-8199-0567-4 : 6.95
1. Monasticism and religious orders—Rules. 2. Franciscans. I. Matura, Thaddee. II. Francesco d'Assisi, Saint, 1182-1226. Regula non bullata. English & Latin. 1975. III. Title.

LANDINI, Lawrence C. 255'.3
The causes of the clericalization of the order of Friars Minor, 1209-1260 in the light of early Franciscan sources. Auctore Laurentio C. Landini. Chicago, Pontifica Universitas Gregoriana, Facultas Historiae Ecclesiasticae, 1968. xxvi, 149 p. 23 cm. Thesis—Pontificia Universitas Gregoriana, Chicago. Bibliography: p. xiii-xx. [BX3606.2.L35 1968] 68-56626
1. Franciscans—History. 2. Clericalism. I. Title.

LAPSANSKI, Duane V. 255'.3
The first Franciscans and the Gospel / Duane V. Lapsanski. Chicago : Franciscan Herald Press, [1975] p. cm. Translation of Das Leben

nach dem Evangelium am Anfang des Minderbruderordens. Includes index. Bibliography: p. [BX3603.L3513] 75-8685 ISBN 0-8199-0568-2 : 6.95
1. Franciscans—Spiritual life. I. Title.

MARQUARD, Philip, 1914- 255'.3
Formation of lay Franciscans. Chicago, Franciscan Herald Press [1973] v, 75 p. illus. 23 cm. Bibliography: p. 75. [BX3654.M37] 73-12908 ISBN 0-8199-0470-8 0.95 (pbk.)
1. Franciscans. Third Order. I. Title.

ZACATECAS, Mexico 255'.3'009764
(City). Apostolico Colegio de Nuestra Senora de Guadalupe.
The Zacatecan missionaries in Texas, 1716-1834: excerpts from the Libros de los decretos of the Missionary College of Zacatecas, 1707-1828, translated by Benedict Leutenegger, and A biographical dictionary, by Marion A. Habig. Austin, Texas Historical Survey Committee, 1973. 181 p. illus. 28 cm. (Office of the State Archeologist reports, no. 23) Bibliography: p. 177-181. [BV2803.T4Z32 1973] 74-154408
1. Missions—Texas—History—Sources. 2. Franciscans in Texas—History—Sources. 3. Franciscans—Missions—History—Sources. 4. Texas—History—To 1846—Sources. I. Leutenegger, Benedict, tr. II. Habig, Marion Alphonse, 1901- A biographical dictionary. 1973. III. Title. IV. Series: Texas. Office of the State Archeologist. Reports, no. 23.

ESSER, Kajetan, 1913- 255'.3'06
Rule and Testament of St. Francis : conferences to the modern followers of Francis / by Cajetan Esser. Chicago : Franciscan Herald Press, [1977] p. cm. [BX3604.Z5E835] 77-5318 ISBN 0-8199-0674-3 : 5.95
1. Francesco d'Assisi, Saint, 1182-1226. Regula non bullata. 2. Francesco d'Assisi, Saint, 1182-1226. Testamentum. I. Title.

ESSER, Kajetan, 1913- 255'.3'06
Rule and Testament of St. Francis : conferences to the modern followers of Francis / by Cajetan Esser. Chicago : Franciscan Herald Press, [1977] p. cm. [BX3604.Z5E835] 77-5318 ISBN 0-8199-0674-3 : 5.95
1. Francesco d'Assisi, Saint, 1182-1226. Regula non bullata. 2. Francesco d'Assisi, Saint, 1182-1226. Testamentum. I. Title.

JESUITS. Constitutiones. 255'.5
English.
The constitutions of the Society of Jesus [by] Saint Ignatius of Loyola. Translated, with an introd. and a commentary, by George E. Ganss. St. Louis, Institute of Jesuit Sources, 1970. xii, 420 p. illus., facsims. 24 cm. Based on the Spanish text D of 1594, Sancti Ignatii de Loyola Constitutiones Societatis Jesu, edited by Father Arturo Codina, tomus secundus, Textus Hispanus, Rome, 1936. Bibliography: p. 363-370. [BX3704.E5 1970] 72-108258 14.50
I. Loyola, Ignacio de, Saint, 1491-1556. II. Ganss, George E., 1905- tr. III. Title.

JESUITS. Decreta 255'.53
congregationum. English.
Documents of the 31st and 32nd general congregations of the Society of Jesus : an English translation of the official Latin texts of the general congregations and of the accompanying papal documents / [prepared by the Jesuit Conference ; and edited by John W. Padberg]. Saint Louis : Institute of Jesuit Sources, 1977. x, 598 p. ; 20 cm. (Jesuit primary sources in English translation ; no. 2) Translation of Decreta congregationis generalis XXXI ... annis 1965-1966 and Decreta congregationis generalis XXXII ... annis 1974-1975. Includes bibliographical references and index. [BX3704.E5 1977] 77-70881 ISBN 0-912422-25-4 : 7.00. ISBN 0-912422-26-2 pbk. : 6.00
1. Jesuits. I. Padberg, John W. II. Jesuit Conference. III. Title. IV. Series.
Publisher's address: Fusz Memorial (of St. Louis Univ.), 3700 W. Pine Blve., St. Louis, Mo 63108

PASSIONISTS. Province of 255'.62
St. Paul of the Cross. Research and Planning Project.
The Passionists / Research and Planning Project, St. Paul of the Cross Province ; [directors] Herbert E. Stotts ... [et al.]. [Union City, N.J. : Provincial Print. Office, 1974- v. ; 23 cm. Cover title. Contents.Contents.—v. 1. The religious. Includes bibliographies. [BX3880.A1P37 1974] 75-305489
1. Passionists—Collected works. I. Stotts, Herbert Edward, 1916- II. Title.

CARMEL'S call; 255*.73
a manual for tertiaries of Our Lady of Mount Carmel, by the Carmelite Fathers. [3d ed.] Chicago, Carmelite Third Order Press, 1951. 269 p. illus. 19 cm. "This edition ... combines three Third Order books: 1) the manual of Carmelite tertiaries, 2) the Little office of the B. V. M. for the tertiaries, both compiled by the Rev. Stephen J. McDonald, O.Carm. ... and 3) Carmel's call, edited by the Rev. Alexis E. McCarthy, O.Carm." "Rule of the Third Order Secular of Our Lady of Mount Carmel": p. 21-34. "The Little office of the Blessed Virgin Mary according to the Carmelite rite": p. 149-215. [BX3252.E5 1951] 70-256080
1. Carmelites. Third Order—Handbooks, manuals, etc. I. McDonald, Stephen James, Father, 1875-1963. II. Carmelites. III. Carmelites. Rule of the Third Order Secular. English. 1951. IV. Catholic Church. Liturgy and ritual. Little office of the Blessed Virgin Mary (Carmelite) English. 1951.

SOTTEK, James J. 255'.76
A star rose in the West; a short account of the Toledo foundations of the Oblates of St. Francis de Sales from 1943 to 1972, by James J. Sottek. [Toledo, Printed by Magers Print., 1972] v, 110 p. illus. 22 cm. Appendices (p. 102-110): A. Significant dates in the history of the Toledo foundations.—B. Necrology of the Oblates of St. Francis de Sales who have served in the Toledo-Detroit Province. [BX3825.Z6T67] 75-304180 2.95
1. Oblates of St. Francis de Sales. Toledo-Detroit Province. I. Title.

GABRIS, P. Paul. 255'.79'0097731
The past fifty years [by] P. Paul Gabris. [Chicago] Marian Fathers, 1964. 119 p. illus. 20 cm. [BX3782.Z6S34] 75-304525
1. Marian Fathers. St. Casimir Province. I. Title.

BLOESCH, Donald G., 1928- 255'.8
Wellsprings of renewal: promise in Christian communal life, by Donald G. Bloesch. Grand Rapids, Eerdmans [1974] 124 p. illus. 21 cm. Bibliography: p. 114-118. [BV4405.B57] 72-93618 ISBN 0-8028-1500-6
1. Monasticism and religious orders, Protestant. I. Title.

COMMUNAUTE de Taize. 255'.8
The Rule of Taize in French and in English / [Br. Roger]. New York : Seabury Press, c1968. 142 p. ; 16 cm. Translation of Le Regle de Taize. "A Crossroad book." [BV4408.A3 1968] 74-10118 ISBN 0-8164-2564-7 : 2.95
1. Monasticism and religious orders, Protestant—Rules. I. Schutz, Roger. II. Title.

ROBINSON, Nalbro' Frazier. 255'.8
Monasticism in the orthodox churches, by N. F. Robinson. London, Cope and Fenwick; Milwaukee, Wis., Young Churchman Co., 1916. [New York, AMS Press, 1971] x, 175 p. illus., plan. 19 cm. Includes bibliographical references. [BX385.A1R6 1971] 72-131506 ISBN 0-404-05375-0
1. Monasticism and religious orders, Orthodox Eastern. I. Title.

STOKL, Andreas, 1939- 255'.8
Taize : Geschichte u. Leben d. Bruder von Taize / Andreas Stokl. Hamburg : Siebenstern Taschenbuch Verlag, 1975. 242 p. : 11 ill. ; 19 cm. (Siebenstern-Taschenbuch ; 184) A revision of the author's thesis, Universitat Erlangen-Nurnberg, Erlangen, 1973, presented under the title: Die Communaute de Taize. Bibliography: p. 240-[243] [BV4408.S68 1975] 75-514126 ISBN 3-7970-0145-2 : DM7.90
1. Communaute de Taize. I. Title.

ANCREN riwle. 255'.9
The ancren riwle; a treatise on the rules and duties of monastic life. Edited and translated from a semi-Saxon ms. of the thirteenth century by James Morton. New York, AMS Press [1968] xxviii, 479 p. 24 cm. Anglo-Saxon text and English translation on opposite pages. Text is that of the Cottonian manuscript (Nero A. XIV.) in the British Museum, collated with Titus D. XVIII. and Cleopatra C. VI. Reprint of the 1853 ed., which was issued as no. 57 of the Camden Society publications. [BX4210.A58 1968] 72-158250
1. Monasticism and religious orders for women. 2. Monasticism and religious orders—Rules. I. Morton, James, 1783-1865, ed. II. Series: Camden Society, London. Publications, no. 57.

EBAUGH, Helen Rose Fuchs, 255'.9
1942-
Out of the cloister : a study of organizational dilemmas / Helen Rose Fuchs Ebaugh. Austin : University of Texas Press, c1977. xxii, 155 p. ; 24 cm. Bibliography: p. [149]-155. [BX4200.E25] 76-54503 ISBN 0-292-76007-8 : 12.95
1. Monasticism and religious orders for women. I. Title.

TATE, Judith. 255'.9
Religious women in the modern world. [New York] Herder and Herder [1970] x, 102 p. 21 cm. Includes bibliographical references. [BX4210.T29] 70-122902 4.50
1. Monastic and religious life of women. I. Title.

DOBSON, Eric John. 255'.901
Moralities on the Gospels : a new source of Ancrene wisse / by E. J. Dobson. Oxford : Clarendon Press, 1975. 182 p. ; 20 cm. English or Latin. Includes bibliographical references. [PR1810.D58] 76-376493 ISBN 0-19-812056-7 : 16.75
1. Ancrene riwle—Sources. 2. Moralia super evangelia. I. Grosseteste, Robert, Bp. of Lincoln, 1175?-1253. II. Title.
Distributed by Oxford University Press N.Y. N.Y.

DOBSON, Eric John. 255'.901
The origins of Ancrene wisse / by E. J. Dobson. Oxford [Eng.] : Clarendon Press, 1976. 441 p. ; 19 cm. Includes bibliographical references and index. [PR1810.D6] 76-367043 ISBN 0-19-811864-3 : 37.50
1. Limebrook Priory. 2. Ancren riwle. 3. Monasticism and religious orders for women—England. 4. Monasticism and religious orders—Middle Ages, 600-1500. 5. Augustinians in England. I. Title.
Distributed by Oxford University Press N.Y. N.Y.

CATHOLIC Church. 255'.97
Congregatio de Propaganda Fide.
Documents: Nerinckx—Kentucky—Loretto, 1804-1851, in archives Propaganda Fide, Rome. Co-editors: Augustin C. Wand and M. Lilliana Owens. St. Louis, Mo., Mary Loretto Press, 1972. 305 p. 23 cm. Bibliography: p. 292-305. [BX4705.N4C37 1972] 76-189662
1. Nerinckx, Charles, 1761-1824. 2. Sisters of Loretto at the Foot of the Cross. I. Wand, Augustin C., ed. II. Owens, Lilliana, 1898- ed. III. Title.

MARY Thomas, 255'.977'0924 B
Sister, P.B.V.M.
Not words but deeds; the story of Nano Nagle. Illustrated by Carolyn Lee Jagodits. Notre Dame, [Ind.] Dujarie Press [1968] 92 p. illus. 22 cm. A biography of the Irish woman who, despite the strictness of the English Penal Laws, opened schools for poor Catholic children, and founded the order of the Sisters of the Presentation. [PZ7.M3688No] 92 AC 68
1. Nagle, Nano, 1718-1784. I. Jagodits, Carolyn Lee, illus. II. Title.

TJADER, Marguerite. 255'.979 B
Mother Elisabeth; the resurgence of the Order of Saint Birgitta. New York, Herder and Herder [1972] viii, 231 p. front. 22 cm. Bibliography: p. 231. [BX4705.H564T58] 72-3010 ISBN 0-07-073812-2
1. Birgittines. 2. Hesselblad, Maria Elisabeth, 1870-1957. I. Title.

258 Social Welfare Work Of Church

ANDERSON, Stanley Edwin. 258
Every pastor a counselor. Wheaton, Ill., Van Kampen Press [1949] 111p. 20cm. Bibliography: p. 107-111. [BV4012.A6] 49-8239
1. Psychology, Pastoral. I. Title.

AUTTON, Norman 258
The pastoral care of the mentally ill, Forewords by Bishop of Lichfield, Desmond Pond. London, S. P. O. K. [dist. New York, Seabury, c.]1963. 223p. 23cm. Bibl. 63-6802 5.00
1. Church work with the mentally ill. 2. Psychiatry and religion. 3. Pastoral theology—Anglican Communion. I. Title.

BEASLEY, A Roy. 258
In prison ... and visited me, by Prison Parson A. Roy Beasley; as told to Ewart A. Autry. Grand Rapids, Mich., Eerdman, 1952. 188 p. 21 cm. [BV4465.B36] 52-10795
1. Prisons—Missions and charities. I. Autry. Ewart A. II. Title.

BELGUM, David. 258
Clinical training for pastoral care. Philadelphia, Westminster Press [1956] 136p. illus. 21cm. [BV4012.B38] 56-5102
1. Psychology, Pastoral. I. Title.

BELGUM, David Rudolph, 1922- 258
Clinical training for pastoral care. Philadelphia, West-minster Press [1956] 136p. illus. 21cm. [BV4012.B38] 56-5102
1. Psychology, Pastoral. I. Title.

BELGUM, David Rudolph, 1922- 258
Clinical training for pastoral care. Philadelphia, Westminster Press [1956] 136 p. illus. 21 cm. [BV4012.B38] 56-5102
1. Pastoral Sychology. I. Title.

BERGSTEN, Gote. 258
Pastoral psychology; a study in the care of souls. London. Allen and Unwin; New York, Macmillan [1951] 227 p. 22 cm. [BV4012.B4] 51-10759
1. Psychology. Pastoral. I. Title.

BERGSTEN, Gote 258
Pastoral psychology; a study in the care of souls. London, Allen & Unwin [dist. Mystic, Conn., Verry, 1964] 227p. 23cm. 4.50
1. Psychology, Pastoral. I. Title.

BONNELL, John Sutherland, 258
1893-
No escape from life. New York, Harper [1965, c.1958] 215p. 21cm. (Harper chapel bk. CB14J) [BV4012.2.B6] 1.60 pap.,
1. Pastoral counseling. I. Title.

BROWN, Brian A., 1942- 258
The sacramental ministry to the sick, by Brian A. Brown. [1st ed.] New York, Exposition Press [1968] 86 p. 18 cm. (An Exposition-testament book) Bibliography: p. [83]-86. [BV4335.B7] 68-4564
1. Church work with the sick. 2. Sacraments. I. Title.

BURNET, Mary. 258
Abe of literacy. [Paris] UNESCO [1965] 64 p. illus. 21 cm. [LC149.B87] 65-9846
1. Illiteracy. I. Title.

CAMPBELL, Ora Mae, 1916- 258
Them that sit in darkness. Cleveland, Tenn., White Wing Pub. House & Press [1953] 174p. 20cm. [BV4595.C3] 54-17874
1. Prisons—Religious life. I. Title.

CARRIER, Blanche, 1895- 258
Free to grow. [1st ed.] New York, Harper [1951] vii, 241 p. 22 cm. Bibliography:p. 235-238. [BL53.C28] 51-11275
1. Psychology, Religious. 2. Psychology, Pastoral. I. Title.

COMMUNITY mental health: 258
the role of church & temple. Howard J. Clinebell, Jr., editor. Nashville, Abingdon Press [1970] 288 p. 22 cm. Includes bibliographical references. [RA790.6.C6] 71-124752 4.25
1. Community mental health services—U.S. 2. Church work with the mentally ill. I. Clinebell, Howard John, 1922- ed.

DICKS, Russell Leslie, 1906- 258
How to make pastoral calls, for ministers and laymen. [2d rev. ed.] St. Louis, Bethany [c.1962] 63p. 22cm. 62-17916 1.00 pap.,
1. Visitations (Church work) I. Title.

DOLLOFF, Eugene Dinsomore. 258
The romance of doorbells; a guide to effective pastoral calling. [1st ed.] Philadelphia, Judson Press [1951] 197 p. 21 cm. Bibliography: p. 196-197. [BV4320.D6] 51-11459
1. Theology, Pastoral. I. Title.

GROUES, Henri, 1910- 258
Abbe Pierre speaks; speeches collected by L. C. Repland, translated by Cecily Hastings and George Lamb. New York, Sheed & Ward [1956] 203p. illus. 22cm. [BX890.G75] 56-11530
1. Catholic Church—Addresses, essays, lectures. I. Title.

GROUES, Henri, 1910- 258
Abbe Pierre speaks; speeches collected by L. C. Repland, translated by Cecily Hastings and George Lamb. New York, Sheed & Ward [1956] 203p. illus. 22cm. [BX890.G75] 56-11530
1. Catholic Church—Addresses, essays, lectures. I. Title.

GUERRA, Vincent. 258
The turning point. Anderson, Ind. Warner Press [1970] 144 p. 19 cm. [BV4470.G8] 76-127139
1. Church work with narcotic addicts. I. Title.

HILTNER, Seward, 1909- 258
The counselor in counseling; case notes in pastoral counseling. New York, Abingdon-Cokesbury Press [1952] 188 p. 22 cm. [BV4012.H48] 52-375
1. Psychology, Pastoral. 2. Counseling. I. Title.

HOWELL, Robert Lee. 258
Fish for my people. New York, Morehouse-Barlow Co. [1968] 93 p. 19 cm. [BV4403.H6] 68-56916
1. Fish movement (Christianity) I. Title.

KELLER, John E 1924- 258
Ministering to alcoholics, by John E. Keller. Minneapolis, Augsburg Pub. House [1966] x, 158 p. 22 cm. [BV4460.5.K4] 66-22560
1. Church work with alcoholics. I. Title.

KELLER, John E. 1924- 258
Ministering to alcoholics. Minneapolis, Augsburg [c.1966] x, 158p. 22cm. [BV4460.5.K4] 66-22560 4.75
1. Church work with alcoholics. I. Title.

KENRICK, Bruce 258
Come out the wilderness: the story of East Harlem Protestant parish. Drawings by Joseph Papin. New York, Harper [1966, c.1962] ix, 220p. illus. 21cm. (Chapel bks., CB31) 1.60 pap.,
1. Church and social problems—New York (City) 2. East Harlem Protestant Parish, New York. I. Title.

LAUBACH Literacy Fund. 258
Laubach literacy. [Syracuse, N.Y.] v. 23-28 cm. annual. Report year ends May 31. Title varies: -1962/63, Report. [LC149.L35] 68-41931
1. Illiteracy—Societies, etc. I. Title.

LYNN, Robert Charles. 258
The church faces the problem of juvenile delinquency, by Robert C. Lynn. New York, Carlton Press [1965] 61 p. 21 cm. (A Reflection book) Bibliography: p. 60-61. [BV4464.5.L9] 65-9200
1. Church work with juvenile delinquents. I. Title.

LYNN, Robert Charles 258
The church faces the problem of juvenile delinquency. New York, Carlton [c.1965] 61p. 21cm. (Reflection bk.) Bibl. [BV4464.5.L9] 65-9200 2.00
1. Church work with juvenile delinquents. I. Title.

MCKENZIE, John Grant, 1882- 258
Nervous disorders and religion; a study of souls in the making. New York, Collier [1962] 160p. 18cm. (Tate lects., 1947) (AS407V) Bibl. .95 pap.,
1. Psychology, Pastoral. 2. Psychotherapy. I. Title.

MARTIN, Bernard, 1905- 258
Healing for you. Tr. by A. A. Jones. Richmond, Va., Knox [1966, c.1963] 194p. 23cm. Bibl. [BV4335.M3713] 66-10352 4.50
1. Church work with the sick. I. Title.

MASON, David E. 258
Reaching the silent billion; the opportunity of literacy missions [by] David E. Mason. Grand Rapids, Zondervan [1967] 190p. illus. 23cm. Bibl. [BV2082.I45M3] 67-17232 4.95 bds.,
1. Illiteracy. 2. Missions—Educational work. I. Title.

MORSE-BOYCOTT Desmond Lionel, 258
1892-
A golden legend of the slums, being the true tale of life as lived there and the beautiful vision seen there and the wonderous thing that came about there. London. New York, Skeffington [1952] 200 p. illus. 24 cm. [HV4088.L8M58] 52-33536
1. St. Mary-of-the-Angels Song School, Addlestone, Eng. 2. London — Soc. condit. 3. London — Poor. I. Title.

NATIONAL Association of 258
Catholic Chaplains.
The apostolate to the sick; a guide for the Catholic chaplain in health care facilities. St. Louis, Catholic Hospital Association [1967] xii, 128 p. 21 cm. Bibliography: p. 121-124. [BX2347.8.S5N3] 67-26608
1. Church work with the sick. 2. Chaplains, Hospital—Catholic church. I. Title.

O'BRIEN, Virgil Patrick, 258
1917-
A handbook for hospital chaplains. St. Louis, B. Herder Book Co., [1959] 362p. 21cm. Includes bibliography. [BX2390.S5O3] 59-7438
1. Church work with the sick. 2. Chaplains, Hospital—Catholic Church. I. Title.

OUTLER, Albert Cook, 1908- 258
Psychotherapy and the Christian message. New York, Harper [1966, c.1954] 286p. 21cm. (Chapel bks., CB26K) [BV4012.O72] 53-10975 1.75 pap.,
1. Psychology, Pastoral. 2. Psychotherapy. I. Title.

*PAETKAU, Walter 258
Start where you are: a guide to local Christian service. Drawings by Esther Groves. Newton, Kan., Faith & Life [1966, c.1965] 73p. illus. 21cm. 1.00 pap.,
I. Title.

PEALE, Norman Vincent, 1898- 258
The art of real happiness, by Norman Vincent Peale and Smiley Blanton. [1st ed.] New York, Prentice-Hall [1950] vi, 247 p. 21 cm. [BV4012.P35] 50-5426
1. Psychology, Pastoral. I. Blanton, Smiley, 1882- joint author. II. Title.

PEALE, Norman Vincent, 1898- 258
The art of real happiness / Norman Vincent Peale and Smiley Blanton revised edition Greenwich, Coon. : Fawcett Crest [1976 c1950] 204 p. ; 18 cm. [BV4012.P35] ISBN 0-449-23039-2 pbk. : 1.75
1. Psychology, Pastoral. I. Blanton, Smiley, 1882- , joint author. II. Title.
L.C. card no. for 1950 Prentice-Hall edition: 50-5426.

PETERSEN, Sigurd D. 258
Retarded children: God's children. Philadelphia, Westminster Press [1960] 156 p. 21 cm. Includes bibliography. [BV4012.3.P45] 60-6190
1. Church work with mentally handicapped children. 2. Pastoral psychology. I. Title.

THE Poor church; 258
a symposium, edited by William J. Richardson. Maryknoll, N.Y., Maryknoll Publications, 1967. ix, 166 p. 19 cm. Selected papers from the annual meeting of the Mission Secretariat held at Washington, D.C., fall 1966. Includes bibliographies. [BV639.P6P6] 67-25221
1. Church and the poor. I. Richardson, William Jerome, 1929- ed. II. Society for the Propagation of the Faith. United States. Mission Secretariat.

ROBERTSON, Josephine. 258
How to help through understanding. New York, Abingdon Press [1961] 124p. 20cm. [BV4400.R6] 61-11786
1. Church work. I. Title.

SCHERZER, Carl J. 258
And you visited me: a guide for lay visitors to the sick, by Carl J. Scherzer. Philadelphia, Fortress [1966] xii, 84p. 18cm. [BV4335.S28] 66-24860 1.50
1. Church work with the sick. I. Title.

SCHERZER, Carl J. 258
Ministering to the physically sick. Philadelphia, Fortress [1968,c.1963] 142p. 21cm. ([Successful pastoral counseling ser.]) [BV4335.S3] 1.50 pap.,
1. Church work with the sick. I. Title.

SCHERZER, Carl J 258
Ministering to the physically sick. Englewood Cliffs, N. J., Prentice-Hall [1963] 142 p. 21 cm. [Successful pastoral counseling series] [BV4335.S3] 63-8624
1. Church work with the sick. I. Title.

SCHERZER, Carl J. 258
Ministering to the physically sick. Englewood Cliffs, N.J., Prentice [c.1963] 142p. 21cm. (Successful pastoral counseling ser.) Bibl. 63-8624 2.95 bds.,
1. Church work with the sick. I. Title.

SHULTZ, Lawrence W 258
The story of Camp Alexander Mack, 1924-1955. Milford, Ind., Camp Alexander Mack [1956] 128p. illus. 22cm. [BX7830.C3S45] 56-25230
1. Camp Alexander Mack, Milford, Ind. 2. Church of the Brethren. I. Title.

SOUTHARD, Samuel. 258
The family and mental illness. Philadelphia, Westminster Press [1957] 96p. 20cm. (The Westminster pastoral aid books) Includes bibliography. [RC455.S65] 57-5572
1. Mental illness. I. Title.

SOUTHARD, Samuel. 258
The family and mental illness. Philadelphia, Westminster Press [1957] 96 p. 20 cm. (The Westminster pastoral aid books) Includes bibliography. [RC455.S65] 57-5572
1. Mental illness. I. Title.

SPANN, John Richard, 1891- 258
ed.
Pastoral care. New York, Abingdon-Cokesbury Press [1951] 272 p. 23 cm. [BV4010.S63] 51-13150
1. Theology, Pastoral. I. Title.

STOLL, George. 258
Laymen at work; how to meet human needs in your town. Edited by Albert L. Meibury. Nashville, Abingdon Press [1956] 93p. 20cm. Includes bibliography. [BV4400.S73] 56-10150
1. Church work. I. Title.

STOLL, George. 258
Laymen at work; how to meet human needs in your town, Edited by Albert L. Meiburg. Nashvill, Abingdon Press [1956] 93 p. 20 cm. Includes bibliography. [BV4400.S73] 56-10150
1. Church work. I. Title.

TUCKER, Park. 258
Prison is my parish; the story of Park Tucker as told to George Burnham. [Westwood, N. J.] Revell [1957] 191p. illus. 22cm. [BV4340.T8] 57-9963
1. Prisons—Missions and charities. I. Burnham, George. II. Title.

TUCKER, Park. 258
Prison is my parish; the story of Park Tucker as told to George Burnham. [Westwood, N.J.] Revell [1957] 191 p. illus. 22 cm. [BV4340.T8] 57-9963
1. Prisons — Missions and charities. I. Burnham, George. II. Title.

UNITED Presbyterian Church in 258
the U.S.A. Commission on Ecumenical Mission and Relations. Office for Research.
The struggle against illiteracy. W. Stanley Eycroft [Secretary for research] and Myrtle M. Clemmer [research assistant] New York, 1964. 1 v. (various pagings) 28 cm. Cover title. Bibliography: p. 48-50. [LC149.U59] 65-4000
1. Illiteracy — Stat. I. Rycroft, William Stanley. II. Clemmer, Myrtle M. III. Title.

WEATHERHEAD, Leslie Dixon, 258
1893-
Wounded spirits. Nashville, Abingdon [1963, c.1962] 173p. 21cm. 63-10563 3.00
1. Faith-cure. 2. Pastoral medicine—Case studies. I. Title.

WEBBER, George W. 258
God's colony in man's world. New York, Abingdon Press [1960] 155 p. 21 cm. [BV2805.N5W4] 60-9203
1. City missions. I. Title.

WEBBER, George W. 258
God's colony in man's world. Nashville, Abingdon [1966, c.1960] 155p. 20cm. [BV2805.N5W4] 1.25 pap.,
1. City missions. I. Title.

WEBBER, George W. 258
God's colony in man's world. Nashville, Abingdon Press [c.1960] 155p. 21cm. (3p. bibl.) 60-9203 2.75 bds.,
1. City missions. I. Title.

WHITE, Ellen Gould (Harmon) 258
1827-1915.
Welfare ministry; instruction in Christian neighborhood service. Washington, Review and Herald Pub. Assn. [1952] 349 p. 18 cm. (Christian home library) [BV4400.W45] 52-1493
1. Social service. 2. Church work. 3. Seventh-Day Adventists—Charities. I. Title.

WILKERSON, David 258
The cross and the switchblade, by David Wilkerson. with John and Elizabeth Sherrill. New York, Pyramid [1964, c.1963] 174p. 18cm. (R-980) .50 pap.,
1. Church work with juvenile delinquents. I. Title.

WILKERSON, David 258
Twelve angels from hell [by] David Wilkerson, with Leonard Ravenhill. Westwood, N.J., Revell [c.1965] 152p. 21cm. [BV4464.5.W52] 65-14800 2.95 bds.,
1. Church work with juvenile delinquents. I. Ravenhill, Leonard. II. Title.

WILKERSON, David R 258
The cross and the switchblade, by David Wilkerson, with John & Elizabeth Sherrill. New York, B. Geis Associates; distributed by Random House [1963] 217 p. 22 cm. [BV4464.5.W5 1963] 63-9442
1. Church work with juvenile delinquents. I. Title.

WILKERSON, David R. 258
The cross and the switchblade, by David Wilkerson, with John & Elizabeth Sherrill. [New York] B. Geis Associates; distributed by Random House [1963] 217 p. 22 cm. [BV4464.5.W5 1963] 63-9442
1. Church work with juvenile delinquents. I. Title.

WILKERSON, David R 258
Twelve angels from hell [by] David Wilkerson, with Leonard Ravenhill. Westwood, N.J. F.H. Revell Co. [1965] 152 p. 21 cm. [BV4464.5.W52] 65-14800
1. Church work with juvenile delinquents. I. Ravenhill, Leonard. II. Title.

WILKERSON, David R. 258
Twelve angels from hell [by] David Wilkerson, with Leonard Ravenhill. Westwood, N. J., F. H. Revell Co. [1965] 152 p. 21 cm. [BV4464.5.W52] 65-14800
1. Church work with juvenile delinquents. I. Ravenhill, Leonard. II. Title.

WILKERSON, Don. 258
The gutter and the ghetto, by Don Wilkerson with Herm Weiskopf. Waco, Tex., Word Books [1969] 179 p. illus. 23 cm. [BV4470.W53] 70-91938 4.95
1. Church work with narcotic addicts. I. Weiskopf, Herman. II. Title.

WILLING, Ora Mae (Campbell) 258
1916-
Them that sit in darkness. Cleveland, Tenn., White Wing Pub. House & Press [1953] 174 p. 20 cm. [BV4595.W5] 54-17874
1. Prisons — Religious life. I. Title.

WISE, Carroll A 258
Pastoral counseling, its theory and practice. [1st ed.] New York, Harper [1951] xi, 231 p. 22 cm. "Notes and references": p. 223-227. [BV4012.W5] 51-9232
1. Counseling. 2. Theology, Pastoral. I. Title.

WOODRUFF, C. Roy. 258
Alcoholism and Christian experience, by C. Roy Woodruff. Foreword by Wayne E. Oates. Philadelphia, Westminster Press [1968] 156 p. 21 cm. Includes bibliographical references. [BV4460.5.W6] 68-15438
1. Church work with alcoholics. 2. Conversion—Psychology. I. Title.

WORKSHOP for Baptists on 258
Deafness and Rehabilitation, University of Tennessee, 1965.
Workshop for Baptists on Deafness and Rehabilitation; [proceedings. Washington, U.S. Dept. of Health, Education, and Welfare, Vocational Rehabilitation Administration, 1966] vii, 105 p. illus. 24 cm. Financed by Training Grant No. VRA 412-T-63 and VRA 412-T-66 from the Vocational Rehabilitation Administration to the University of Tennessee. [BV4463.W6 1965] 67-60123
1. Church work with the deaf—Congresses. 2. Deaf—Rehabilitation—Congresses. I. Tennessee. University. II. United States. Dept. of Health, Education, and Welfare. Vocational Rehabilitation Administration.

SCHWARTZ, Aloysius. 258.0924
The starved and the silent. [1st ed.] Garden City, N. Y., Doubleday [1966] 216 p. 22 cm. [BV3462.S35A3] 66-11721
1. Missions—Korea. 2. Church and the poor. I. Title.

259 Parochial Activities

ALBRITTON, Walter M. 259
Koinonia ministries guidebook, by Walter M. Albritton. Nashville, Tidings [1969] 51 p. 19 cm. Includes bibliographical references. [BV652.2.A55] 71-78557
1. Church group work. I. Title.

*AULTMAN, Donald S. 259
Guiding youth. Cleveland, Tenn., Pathway [c.] 1965. 109p. 20cm. 1.50; 1.00 pap.,
I. Title.

BACHMAN, John W. 259
The church in the world of radio-television. New York, Association Press [c.1960] 191p. 22cm. (7p. bibl. notes) 60-6554 3.50
1. Radio in religion. 2. Television in religion. I. Title.

BACHMAN, John W 259
The church in the world of radio-television. New York, Association Press [1960] 191p. 22cm. Includes bibliography. [BV656.B3] 60-6554
1. Radio in religion. 2. Television in religion. I. Title.

BARTLETT, Bob. 259
The Soul Patrol: "Here comes the God Squad." With Jorunn Oftedal. Plainfield, N.J., Logos International [1970] 170 p. 21 cm. [BV4447.B37] 71-107609 3.95
1. Teen Challenge. 2. Church work with youth—Philadelphia. I. Title.

BENTON, John, 1933- 259
Debs, dolls & dope. Old Tappan, N.J., F. H. Revell [1968] 128 p. 21 cm. [BV4464.5.B4] 68-28434 3.50
1. Church work with narcotic addicts. 2. Church work with juvenile delinquents. I. Title.

BIMLER, Richard. 259
77 ways of involving youth in the church / Rich Bimler. Saint Louis : Concordia Pub. House, c1977. 64 p. : ill. ; 21 x 28 cm.

Bibliography: p. 64. [BV4447.B54] 76-25739 ISBN 0-570-03737-9 pbk. : 3.95
1. Church work with youth—Lutheran Church. I. Title.

BLACKWOOD, Carolyn Philips. 259
How to be an effective church woman. With an introd. by Andrew W. Blackwood. Philadelphia, Westminster Press [1955] 189 p. 21 cm. [BV4415.B55] 55-7088
1. Women in church work. I. Title.

BLESSITT, Arthur. 259
Life's greatest trip. Waco, Tex., Word Books [1970] 92 p. illus., ports. 16 cm. [BV4447.B638] 78-132132 2.95
1. Church work with youth—Los Angeles. I. Title.

BOCKELMAN, Eleanor. 259
The stewardess. Columbus, Ohio, Wartburg Press [1956] 71p. 20cm. [BV772.B6] 56-57288
1. Stewardship, Christian. 2. Woman—Religious life. I. Title.

BOWMAN, Clarice Margurette, 259
1910-
Spiritual values in camping. New York, Association Press, 1954. 240p. 20cm. [BV1650.B6] 54-9339
1. Camping. 2. Church work with children. I. Title.

BOWMAN, Clarice Margurette, 259
1910-
Worship ways for camp. New York, Association Press [1955] 182p. 20cm. [BV1650.B62] 55-7408
1. Camping. 2. Worship programs. I. Title.

BOYD, Bob M. 259
Recreation for churches, compiled by Bob M. Boyd. Nashville, Convention Press [1967] x. 146 p. 19 cm. "Church study course [of the Sundy School Board of Southern Baptist Convention] This book is number 1109 in category 11, section for adults and young people." Bibliography: p. 142-146. [BV1640.B6] 67-21665
1. Recreation in church work. I. Southern Baptist Convention. Sunday School Board. II. Title.

BURKE, Edmund M 259
How to work with parish groups. Milwaukee, Bruce Publ. co. c1964] iv, 76 p. illus. 20 cm. [BV652.2.B8] 63-23136
1. Church group work. I. Title.

BURKE, Edmund M. 259
How to work with parish groups. Milwaukee, Bruce [c.1964] iv, 76p. illus. 20cm. 63-23136 1.50 pap.,
1. Church group work. I. Title.

BURTON, Janet. 259
A guidebook for developing the church youth program. Grand Rapids, Baker Book House [1968] 123 p. 21 cm. [BV4447.B85] 68-19204
1. Church work with youth. I. Title. II. Title: Developing the church youth program.

THE campus ministry 259
[by] George L. Earnshaw [and others] Valley Forge, Judson Press [1964] 329 p. illus. 23 cm. Bibliography: p. 323-329. [BV1610.E2] 64-15798
1. Church and college—Addresses, essays,lectures.

CASTEEL, John Laurence, 1903- 259
The creative role of interpersonal groups in the church today, edited by John L. Casteel. New York, Association Press [1968] 221 p. 21 cm. Bibliographical references included in "Notes" (p. 217-221) [BV652.2.C3] 68-17776
1. Church group work—Addresses, essays, lectures. I. Title.

CASTEEL, John Laurence, 1903- 259
ed.
Spiritual renewal through personal groups; edited with an introd. and an interpretation. New York, Association Press [1957] 220 p. 21 cm. [BV4501.C3454] 57-11602
1. Spiritual life. 2. Church group work. I. Title.

CATHOLIC Church. Pope. 259
The popes on youth; principles for forming and guiding youth from Popes Leo XIII to Pius XII, compiled and edited by Raymond B. Fullam. New York, D. McKay Co. [c1956] 442p. 24cm. [BX2390.Y7A4 1956a] 57-4398
1. Church work with youth. 2. Youth—Religious life. 3. Religious education of young people. I. Fullam, Raymond B., ed. II. Title.

CATHOLIC Church. Pope. 259
The popes on youth; principles for forming and guiding youth from Popes Leo XIII to Pius XII, compiled and edited by Raymond B. Fullam. Buffalo, Canisius High School, 1956. xvii, 442p. 24cm. Bibliography: p. [385]-409. [BX2390.Y7A4] 55-12380
1. Church work with youth. 2. Youth—Religious life. 3. Religious education of young people. I. Fullam, Raymond B., ed. II. Title.

CHAMBERLIN, John Gordon. 259
Churches and the campus. Philadelphia, Westminster Press [1963] 189 p. 21 cm. Bibliographical footnotes. [BV1610.C47] 63-9303
1. Universities and colleges—Religion. 2. Church work with students. I. Title.

CLARK, M. Edward 259
The church creative; a reader on the renewal of the church, ed. by M. Edward Clark, William L. Malcomson, Warren Lane Molton. Nashville, Abingdon [1967] 208p. 22cm. Bibl. [BV4400.C58] 67-22157 4.50
1. Church work. I. Malcomson, William L., joint author. II. Molton, Warren Lane, joint author. III. Title.
Contents omitted.

CLARK, M. Edward. 259
The church creative; a reader on the renewal of the church, edited by M. Edward Clark, William L. Malcomson [and] Warren Lane Molton. Nashville, Abingdon Press [1967] 208 p. 22 cm. Contents.Contents. -- Girding laity for mission, by K. W. Connors. -- Interfaith Commission on Labor Relations, by R. C. Phibbs. -- The changing face of a church, by P. C. contemporary literature, by A. L. Reed. -- Breakthrough by C. L. Graham. -- The ministry of Bethany, by J. C. Garvin. -- Newlook church in California, by J. T. Harrington. -- Fractured forms, by R. W. Shaffer. -- See ya Sunday! by M. F. Crawford. -- The night ministry, by W. R. Grace. -- Giving form to feeling: art and communication, by J. T. Leamon. -- Biblical concepts through contemporary literature, by A. L. Reed. -- Breakthrough communication, by J. T. Leamon. -- Biblical concepts through in Burlington, by W. N. Aswad. -- New ministries of the church, by R. E. Dowdy. -- Encounter: adults and the Gospel, by P. R. Long. -- Ministry in high-rise apartments, by D. C. Rich. -- Dialogue in Goshen, by R. C. Phibbs. -- Senior citizens' fellowship, by O. deW. Cummings. Bibliographical footnotes. [BV4400.C58] 67-22157
1. Church work. I. Malcomson, William L., joint author. II. Molton, Warren Lane, joint author. III. Title.

CLEMENS, Frances, ed. 259
Recreation and the local church, edited by Frances Clemens, Robert Tully [and] Edward Crill. Illustrated by Frances Clemens. Elgin, Ill., Brethren Pub. House [1956] 191p. illus. 24cm. Includes bibliographies. [BV1640.C56] 57-18412
1. Recreation. 2. Church work. I. Title.

CLEMMONS, Robert S 259
Young adults in the church. New York, Published for the Cooperative Publication Association by Abingdon Press [1959] 138p. 19cm. (The Cooperative series) Includes bibliography. [BV4446.C55] 59-3661
1. Church work with young adults. I. Title.

CLEMMONS, William. 259
Growth through groups [by] William Clemmons and Harvey Hester. Introd. by Findley B. Edge. Nashville, Broadman Press [1974] 160 p. 21 cm. Bibliography: p. 158-160. [BV652.2.C55] 74-77359 ISBN 0-8054-5546-9 4.95
1. Church group work. I. Hester, Harvey, joint author. II. Title.

CLENDINNING, B. A. 259
Family ministry in today's church, edited by B. A. Clendinning, Jr. Nashville, Convention Press [1970, c1971] iv, 139 p. 21 cm. "Text for course 6106 in the Christian leadership courses of the New church study course." Includes bibliographical references. [BV4438.C55] 72-123522
1. Church work with families. I. Title.

COMBS, Bob. 259
God's turf. Old Tappan, N.J., Revell [1969] 127 p. illus., ports. 26 cm. [BV4470.C57] 69-20144
1. Church work with narcotic addicts. I. Title.

CONVOCATION on Preaching in 259
College and University Communities, 1st, Cincinnati, 1961.
On the work of the ministry in university communities [papers] Ed.: Richard N. Bender. Nashville, Div. of Higher Educ., Bd., of Educ., Methodist Church [1963] 264p. 24cm. Bibl. 63-3369 apply
1. Universities and colleges—Religion. 2. Church work with students. I. Bender, Richard N., ed. II. Methodist Church (United States) Division of Higher Education. III. Title.

CROSSLAND, Weldon Frank, 259
1890-
Better leaders for your church. Nashville, Abingdon Press [1955] 128p. illus. 20cm. [BV652.C7] 55-9138
1. Church work. 2. Leadership. I. Title.

CUES for church camping 259
for counselors of juniors and junior highs. Philadelphia, Geneva Pr. [dist. Westminster, 1963, c.1962] 80p. illus. 22cm. Bibl. 1.00 pap.,

CULVER, Elsie Thomas 259
New church programs with the aging. New York, Association Press [c.1961] 152p. Bibl. 61-7467 3.50 bds.,
1. Church work with the aged. I. Title.

CUMMINGS, Oliver DeWolf, 259
1900--
The youth fellowship, a vital church program for youth. Philadelphia, Published for the Cooperative Publication Association by the Judson Press [1956] 192p. 20cm. (The Cooperative series leadership training texts) [BV29.C8] 56-9297
1. Young people's meetings (Church work) I. Title.

DAVIES, John Gordon, 1919- 259
The secular use of church buildings [by] J. G. Davies. New York, Seabury Press [1968] xiii, 305 p. illus. 23 cm. Bibliographical references included in "Notes" (p. [265]-293) [BV640.D3] 68-17844
1. Churches—Secular use. I. Title.

DAVIS, Robert Pickens, 1911- 259
Church camping; administrative manual for sponsoring units, planning committees, and directors. Art by Ruth Ensign. Richmond, John Knox Press [1969] 140 p. illus. 23 cm. Bibliography: p. [132]-140. [BV1650.D33] 70-85427 ISBN 8-04-211809- 3.25
1. Church camps. I. Title.

DAY, Leroy J. 259
Dynamic Christian fellowship. Philadelphia, Judson Press [c.1960] 101p. illus. 20cm. (bibls.) 1.00 pap.,
I. Title.

DEBONVILLE, Bob. 259
Every fourth Tuesday / by Bob DeBonville. Milwaukee : Agape Publishers, c1976. 173 p. ; 18 cm. [BV4340.D4] 75-9246 ISBN 0-914618-02-4 pbk. : 2.25
1. Church work with prisoners—Wisconsin—Green Bay. I. Title.

DOBBINS, Gaines Stanley, 259
1866-
Winning the children. Nashville, Broadman Press [1953] 172p. 21cm. [BV639.C4D6] 53-3801
1. Church work with children. I. Title.

DOLAN, Joseph M. 259
Give comfort to my people / by Joseph M. Dolan. New York : Paulist Press, c1977. vi, 122 p. ; 18 cm. (A Deus book) [BX2347.8.S5D64] 77-80804 ISBN 0-8091-2037-2 pbk. : 1.95
1. Church work with the sick. 2. Pastoral medicine—Catholic Church. I. Title.

DOLAN, Joseph M. 259
Give comfort to my people / by Joseph M. Dolan. New York : Paulist Press, c1977. vi, 122 p. ; 18 cm. (A Deus book) [BX2347.8.S5D64] 77-80804 ISBN 0-8091-2037-2 pbk. : 1.95
1. Church work with the sick. 2. Pastoral medicine—Catholic Church. I. Title.

DOUGLASS, Paul Franklin, 259
1904-
The group workshop way in the church. Visuals by Mary Eleanor Spear. New York, Association Press [1956] 174p. illus. 24cm. [BV652.D64] 56-10967
1. Church work. 2. Sociac group work. I. Title.

DOUTY, Mary Alice. 259
How to work with church groups. Nashville, Abingdon Press [1957] 170p. illus. 21cm. Includes bibliography. [BV1534.D67] 57-5076
1. Religious education— Teaching methods. 2. Leadership. 3. Discussion. I. Title. II. Title: Church groups.

DOWDY, Rufus Edward, 1915- 259
The church is families [by] Edward and Harriet Dowdy. Valley Forge, Pa., Pub. for Coop. Pubn. Assn. by Judson [c.1965] 158p. illus. 20cm. Bibl. [BV4438.D6] 65-13403 2.00 pap.,
1. Church work with families. I. Dowdy, Harriet, joint author. II. Cooperative Publication Association. III. Title.

EARNSHAW, George L., ed. 259
The campus ministry [by] George L. Earnshaw [others] Vallev Forge, Pa., Judson [c.1964] 329p. illus. 23cm. Bibl. [BV1610.E2] 64-15798 6.95
1. Church and college—Addresses, essays, lectures. I. Title.

EARSHAW, George L ed. 259
The campus ministry [by] George L. Earnshaw [and others] Valley Forge, Judson Press [1964] 329 p. illus. 23 cm. Bibliography: p. 323-329. [BV1610.E2] 64-15798
1. Church and college—Addresses, essays,lectures. I. Title.

EVANS, David M., 1929- 259
Shaping the church's ministry with youth. Valley Forge, Judson [c.1965] 127p. 20cm. Bibl. [BV4447.E9] 65-22676 1.75 pap.,
1. Church work with youth. I. Title.

EVERETT, Harvey A. 259
The future won't wait. Illus. by Warren Johnson. New York, Friendship Press [c.] 1961. 128p. 61-604 2.95; 1.75 bds., pap.,
1. Church work with youth. 2. Churches—Location. 3. Missions, Home. I. Title.

FACING the future : 259
church and family together / Gary Collins, editor. Waco, Tex. : Word Books, c1976. 186 p. : ill. ; 22 cm. Includes bibliographies. [BV4438.F3] 76-19522 ISBN 0-87680-844-5 : 3.95
1. Church work with families—Addresses, essays, lectures. I. Collins, Gary R.

FAHERTY, William Barbey, 259
1914-
The destiny of modern woman in the light of papal teaching. Westminster, Md., Newman Press, 1950. xvii, 206 p. 21 cm. Bibliography: p. 195-199. [BV639.W7F3] 50-10660
1. Women in Christianity. 2. Church and social problems—Catholic Church. I. Title.

FERGUSON, Dowena 259
The church's ministry with senior highs; a guide for adult workers. Nashville, Grade Pr. [dist. Abingdon, c.1963] 158p. 19cm. 1.50 pap.,
I. Title.

FERGUSON, Rowena. 259
The church's ministry with senior highs. Henry M. Bullock, general editor. Rev. Nashville, Graded Press [1968] 160 p. 19 cm. (A Guide for adult workers) Bibliography: p. 159-160. [BV4447.F47] 68-7939
1. Church work with youth. I. Bullock, Henry Morton, ed. II. Title.

FEUCHT, Oscar E. 259
Ministry to families; a handbook for Christian congregations. St. Louis, Concordia [c.1963] 94p. illus. 20cm. (Family Life Comm. of the Bd. of Parish Educ. pubn., Lutheran Church Mo. Synod) 63-2691 1.00 pap.,
1. Church work with families. 2. Family—Religious life. I. Title.

FORDHAM, Forrest B 1910- 259
Our church plans for youth, a manual on administration. Philadelphia, Judson Press [1953] 96p. illus. 20cm. [BV639.Y7F6] 53-8754
1. Church work with youth. I. Title.

FRANKLIN, Lottie M. 259
So you work with young adults. Anderson, Ind., Warner Press [dist. Gospel Trumpet Press, c.1960] 64p. 21cm. 60-11404 1.00 pap.,
1. Church work with young adults. I. Title.

GARMON, William Sewell. 259
Who are the criminals? [By] William S. Garmon. Nashville, Broadman Press [1968] 127 p. 20 cm. Bibliographical references included in "Notes" (p. 117-127) [BV4464.7.G3] 68-20674
1. Church work with criminals. I. Title.

GEYER, Nancy. 259
Team building in church groups [by] Nancy Geyer and Shirley Noll. Valley Forge [Pa.] Judson Press [1970] 32 p. illus. 22 cm. [BV652.2.G48] 76-107653 1.00
1. Church group work. I. Noll, Shirley, joint author. II. Title.

GLASS, William. 259
Free at last / Bill Glass. Waco, Tex. : Word Books, c1976. 164 p. : ill. ; 23 cm. [BV4340.G58] 76-19532 ISBN 0-87680-489-X : 5.95
1. Church work with prisoners—United States. I. Title.

GLEASON, George, 1875- 259
Horizons for older people ... New York, Macmillan, 1956. 137p. 22cm. [BV4435.G55] 56-11574
1. Church work with the aged. I. Title.

GLEASON, George, 1875- 259
Single young adults in the church. New York, Associated Press, 1952. 120p. 22cm. [BV4446.G53] 52-12724
1. Church work with young adults. I. Title.

GRAY, Robert M. 259
The church and the older person, by Robert

M. Gray, David O. Moberg. Foreword by Ernest W. Burgess. Grand Rapids, Mich., Eerdmans [c.1962] 162p. Bibl. 61-18341 3.50
1. Church work with the aged. I. Moberg, David O., joint author. II. Title.

GRAY, Robert M. 259
The church and the older person / by Robert M. Gray and David O. Moberg ; with a foreword by Ernest W. Burgess. Rev. ed. Grand Rapids : Eerdmans, c1977. 227 p. ; 22 cm. Includes index. Bibliography: p. 215-218. [BV4435.G7 1977] 76-51286 ISBN 0-8028-1091-8 pbk. : 3.95
1. Church work with the aged. 2. Aged—Religious life. I. Moberg, David O., joint author. II. Title.

GRAY, Robert M. 259
The church and the older person / by Robert M. Gray and David O. Moberg ; with a foreword by Ernest W. Burgess. Rev. ed. Grand Rapids : Eerdmans, c1977. 227 p. ; 22 cm. Includes index. Bibliography: p. 215-218. [BV4435.G7 1977] 76-51286 ISBN 0-8028-1091-8 pbk. : 3.95
1. Church work with the aged. 2. Aged—Religious life. I. Moberg, David O., joint author. II. Title.

GROUPS that work; 259
the missing ingredient. Perceptive chapters by Bruce Larson [and others] Grand Rapids, Zondervan Pub. House [1967] 142 p. 21 cm. "The chapters ... originally appeared in Faith at work magazine or the Faith at work edition of Groups that work, c1964." [BV652.2.G7] 67-25730
1. Church group work. I. Larson, Bruce. II. Faith at work.

HAMMOND, Phillip E. 259
The campus clergyman [by] Phillip E. Hammond. Foreword by Kenneth W. Underwood. New York, Basic [1966] xvi, 171p. 22cm. Bibl. [BV4375.H3] 66-28793 5.95
1. Chaplains, University and college. 2. Church work with students. I. Title.

HEUVEL, Albert H. van den, 3d. 259
The new creation and the new generation; a forum for youth workers, edited by Albert H. van den Heuvel. New York, Friendship Press [1965] 127 p. 19 cm. "Footnotes": p. 123-125. [BV4447.H4] 65-27265
1. Church work with youth — Addresses, essays, lectures. I. Title.

HEUVEL, Albert H. van den, ed. 259
The new creation and the new generation; a forum for youth workers. New York, Friendship [c.1965] 127p. 19cm. Bibl. [BV4447.H4] 65-27265 1.75 pap.,
1. Church work with youth—Addresses, essays, lectures. I. Title.

HOGLUND, Gunnar. 259
Youth groups. Chicago, Harvest Publications [c1967] 148 p. 19 cm. (A Harvest learning-for-serving book) On cover: Success handbook for youth groups. [BV29.H54] 67-27425
1. Young people's meetings (Church work) I. Title. II. Title: Success handbook for youth groups.

HUGEN, M D 259
The church's ministry to the older unmarried. Grand Rapids, Eerdmans [1959] 122p. 22cm. Includes bibliography. [BV639.S5H8] 60-724
1. Church work with single people. I. Title.

IDEAS for youth outreach. 259
Compiled by Billie Pate. [Nashville, Convention Press, 1970- v. illus. 21 cm. Cover title. Includes bibliographical references. [BV4447.I3] 72-132633
1. Church work with youth. I. Pate, Billie, ed.

JANSS, Edmund W 259
Help your boy or girl to be Christian. Boston, W. A. Wilde Co., 1956. 188p. 20cm. [BV639.C4J3] 56-11246
1. Church work with children. I. Title.

JOHNSON, L. Ted. 259
Blueprint for quality; administrative guidelines for Christ-centered camping, by L. Ted Johnson and Lee M. Kingsley. Chicago, Harvest Publications [1969] 180 p. 18 cm. [BV1650.J6] 69-16918
1. Church camps. I. Kingsley, Lee M., joint author. II. Title.

JONES, Mary Alice, 1898- 259
The Christian faith speaks to children. New York, Published for the Cooperative Publication Association by Abingdon Press [1965] 175 p. illus. 19 cm. (The Cooperative series) Bibliography: p. 172-175. [BV639.C4J6] 65-4401
1. Church work with children. I. Title.

JONES, Mary Alice, 1898- 259
The Christian faith speaks to children. Nashville, Pub. for the Cooperative Pubn. Assn. by Abingdon [c.1965] 175p. illus. 19cm. (Cooperative ser.) Bibl. [BV639.C4J6] 64-4401 1.75 pap.,
1. Church work with children. I. Title.

JUNIOR-HI; 259
a program guide for junior high fellowships and clubs plus material for the adviser. Philadelphia, Westminster Press [19 no. illus. 28cm. annual. Editor: N. F. Langford. [BV29.J83] 54-28460
1. Young People's meetings (Church work) 2. Worship programs. I. Langford, Norman F., 1914- ed.

*KIDNEY, Dorothy Boone 259
Lively youth meetings. Chicago, Moody [c.1965] 64p. illus. 28cm. (MP125. 30-4925) 1.25 pap.,
1. Church work with young people. I. Title.

KILGORE, James E 259
Pastoral care of the hospitalized child, by James E. Kilgore. [1st ed.] New York, Exposition Press [1968] 104 p. 21 cm. (An Exposition-testament book) Bibliography: p. [97]-104. [BV4460.K5] 68-13259
1. Church work with sick children. 2. Chaplains, Hospital. I. Title.

KILGORE, James E. 259
Pastoral care of the hospitalized child, by James E. Kilgore. [1st ed.] New York, Exposition Press [1968] 104 p. 21 cm. (An Exposition-testament book) Bibliography: p. [97]-104. [BV4460.K5] 68-13259
1. Chaplains, Hospital. 2. Church work with sick children. I. Title.

KIRK, Jane. 259
Group activities for church women. [1st ed.] New York, Harper [1954] 245 p. illus. 22 cm. [BV4415.K5] 54-8961
1. Women in church work. I. Title.

*KLAMMER, Enno E. 259
A manual for Boy Scout troops in churches for God and country. Grand Rapids, Mich., Baker Bk. [c.]1965. 81p. 19cm. 1.00 pap.,
I. Title.

KUHN, Margaret E 259
You can't be human alone; handbook on group procedures for the local church. [New York, Published for the Division of Christian Life and Work and the Division of Christian Education by] National Council of the Churches of Christ in the U. S. A. [c1956] iii, 55p. illus. 22cm. Bibliography: p. 37-42. [BV652.2.K8] 57-2023
1. Church group work. I. National Council of the Churches of Christ in the United States of America. II. Title.

LANGEVIN, Gene. 259
Way to go, baby! Nashville, Abingdon Press [1970] 172 p. 20 cm. Includes bibliographical references. An account of a program evolved by a minister to bring religion to street youths on their own terms. [BV4447.L35] 79-124754 ISBN 0-687-44181-1 2.95
1. Church work with youth—Quincy, Mass. 2. Worship programs. I. Title.

LARSON, Bruce. 259
Groups that work; the missing ingredient. Perceptive chapters by Bruce Larson [and others] Grand Rapids, Zondervan Pub. House [1967] 142 p. 21 cm. "The chapters...originally appeared in Faith at work magazine or the Faith at work edition of Groups that work, c1964." [BV652.2.G7] 67-25730
1. Church group work. I. Faith at work. II. Title.

LEDERACH, Paul M. 259
Mennonite youth; report of Mennonite youth research, by Paul M. Lederach. Scottdale, Pa., Herald Press [1971] 109 p. 22 cm. [BV639.Y7L4] 70-155174 ISBN 0-8361-1636-4
1. Youth—Religious life. 2. Church work with youth—Mennonites. I. Title.

LITTLE, Sara. 259
Youth, world, and church. Richmond, John Knox Press [1968] 201 p. 20 cm. Bibliographical references included in "Acknowledgments" (p. [189]-195) [BV4447.L5] 68-11684
1. Church work with youth. I. Title.

LOEW, Ralph W 259
The church and the amateur adult. Philadelphia, Muhlenberg Press [1955] 108p. 21cm. [BV639.Y7L6] 55-11780
1. Church work with youth. I. Title.

LOS Angeles City School District. 259
It's worth a visit; catalog of school journeys for elementary schools. [Los Angeles] 1956. 174p. illus. 28cm. (Los Angeles City School Districts. Division of Instructional Services. Publication no. EC-146) [LB1047.L65] 61-40649
1. School excursions—Los Angeles. I. Title.

MCADAMS, Daniel A 259
Ringing doorbells for God. Washington, Review and Herald Pub. Association [1958] 192p. illus. 18cm. [BV2369.M27] 58-22709
1. Religious literature—Publication and distribution. 2. Seventh-Day Adventists—Missions. I. Title.

MCADAMS, Daniel A 259
Successful leadership. Washington, Review and Herald Pub. Association [c1954] 320p. 18cm. [BV2369.M28] 55-18137
1. Religious literature—Publication and distribution. 2. Booksellers and bookselling—Colportage, subscription trade, etc. 3. Seventh-Day Adventists. I. Title.

MACHOLTZ, James D 259
Good times together; plans for fun and fellowship in the church. Anderson, Ind., Warner Press [1958] 80p. illus. 21cm. [BV1620.M15] 58-9453
1. Church entertainments. I. Title.

*MACKAY, Joy 259
Creative counseling for Christian camps. Wheaton, Ill., Scripture Pr. [c.1966] 127p. illus. 23cm. Bibl. 1.50 pap.,
I. Title.

MCLEAN, Gordon R. 259
We're holding your son [by] Gordon R. McLean. Old Tappan, N.J., Revell [1969] 160 p. 21 cm. Bibliography: p. 159-160. [BV4464.5.M3] 69-12297 3.95
1. Church work with juvenile delinquents. 2. Juvenile delinquency—U.S. I. Title.

MCMANIS, Lester W. 259
Handbook on Christian education in the inner city [by] Lester W. McManis. New York, Seabury [1966] 96p. illus. 28cm. Prepd. under the auspices of the Dept. of Christian Educ., Executive Council of the Protestant Episcopal Church. Bibl. [BV637.M24] 66-28452 2.95 pap.,
1. City churches. 2. Religious education. I. Protestant Episcopal Church in the U.S.A. National Council. Dept. of Christian Education. II. Title.

MCMURRY, Mildred Dodson. 259
Educating youth in missions. Nashville, Convention Press [1960] vi, 140p. 20cm. (WMU aims series) Prepared for the Woman's Missionary Union. Bibliographical references included in 'Notes' (p. 137-138) Bibliography: p. 139. [BV639.Y7M3] 60-9531
1. Church work with youth. 2. Missions—Study and teaching. I. Southern Baptist Convention. Woman's Missionary Union. II. Title.

MADSEN, Paul O. 259
Ventures in mission [by] Paul O. Madsen. New York, Friendship Press [1968] 159 p. 19 cm. [BV4400.M36] 68-14056
1. Church work. I. Title.

MANSHIP, David 259
Learning to live; a description and discussion of an inductive approach to training. [1st ed.] Oxford, New York, Pergamon [1967] x, 88p. 21cm. (Pergamon lib. for youth leaders) [BV4447.M28 1967] 67-27486 1.50 pap.,
1. Church work with youth. 2. Religious education of youth. 3. Church group work. I. Title.

MARIE Lucita, Sister. 259
Manhattan mission. [1st ed.] Garden City, N.Y., Doubleday, 1967. 192 p. 22 cm. [BV2657.M35A3] 67-10393
1. Social work with delinquents and criminals—New York (City) 2. Church work with juvenile delinquents. 3. Evangelistic work—New York (City) I. Title.

MARTIN, C. Lewis, 1915- 259
Exceptional children: a special ministry [by] C. Lewis Martin [and] John T. Travis. Valley Forge [Pa.] Judson Press [1968] 63 p. illus. 17 cm. Bibliography: p. 61-63. [BV4460.M35] 68-8289 1.25
1. Church work with exceptional children. I. Travis, John T., joint author. II. Title.

MARVIN, Ernest. 259
Odds against evens; young people and the church. With an introd. by Bruce Kenrick. Philadelphia, Westminster [c.1968] xii, 124p. 19cm. First pub. in 1967 under title: Odds against. Bibl. [BV4447.M34 1968] 68-10459 1.65 pap.,
1. Church work with youth. I. Title.

MAY, Helen, 1915- 259
Impactivity: youth program resources. Nashville, Broadman Press [1974] 120 p. 21 cm. Bibliography: p. 117-120. [BV4447.M346] 73-91611 ISBN 0-8054-3614-6 3.95
1. Church work with youth. I. Title.

MILLER, Alice Gail. 259
The God squad. Illus. by James G. Macdonell. New York, Morehouse-Barlow Co. [1969] 139 p. illus. 22 cm. [BV4377.M5] 76-97264
1. Coffee house ministry. I. Title.

MORRIS, Charles Eugene. 259
The group leader as counselor, Drawn from Counseling with young people. New York, Association Press [1963] 64 p. 17 cm. (A Working with youth book) [BF637.C6M62] 63-17420
1. Counseling. 2. Adolescence. I. Title.

MORRIS, Charles Eugene 259
The group leader as counselor. Drawn from Counseling with young people. New York, Association [c.1963] 64p. 17cm. (Working with youth bk.) 63-17420 1.50 pap.,
1. Counseling. 2. Adolescence. I. Title.

MORTON, Nelle. 259
Living together as Christians; a guide for camp leaders on creating Christian community. Illustrated by Ruth Singley Ensign. Philadelphia, Published for the Cooperative Publication Association [by] Christian Education Press [1952] 144 p. illus. 23 cm. Includes bibliography. [BV1650.M64] 52-33959
1. Camping. I. Title.

MOWRY, Charles E. 259
The church and the new generation [by] Charles E. Mowry. Nashville, Abingdon Press [1968, c1969] 175 p. 20 cm. Bibliographical references included in "Notes" (p. 173-175) [BV4446.M6] 69-12013
1. Church work with young adults. 2. Mission of the church. I. Title.

MUELLER, Elwin W., 1908- ed. 259
Missions in the American outdoors; concerns of the church in leisure-recreation. E. W. Mueller, Giles C. Ekola, eds. St. Louis, Concordia [1966] 165p. 22cm. Based on the working papers of a seminar on outdoor recreation which was sponsored by the Natl. Lutheran Council, Div. of Amer. Missions, and held in Chicago in 1964. Bibl. [BX4467.M8] 66-23038 4.95
1. Church work with tourists, travelers, etc. 2. Outdoor recreation—Moral and religious aspects. I. Ekola, Giles C., joint ed. II. National Lutheran Council. Division of American Missions. III. Title.

NATIONAL Council of the Churches of Christ in the United States of America. Bureau of Research and Survey. 259
A study of youth work in Protestant churches, by Helen F. Spaulding [director of Christian education research] and Olga Haley [research assistant] Produced for the Committee on Youth Work, National Council of Churches. Chicago, National Council of the Churches of Christ in the U. S. A. [1956?] vi, 123 l. form. tables. 28cm. Cover title. [BV4447.N35] 56-58082
1. Church work with youth. I. Spaulding, Helen F. II. Haley, Olga. III. Title. IV. Title: Youth work in Protestant Churches.

NOFFS, Ted. 259
The Wayside Chapel; a radical Christian experiment in today's world. Valley Forge, Judson Press [1970, c1969] 192 p. 19 cm. Includes bibliographical references. [BV2656.S9W37] 79-121054
1. Sydney. Wayside Chapel. 2. City missions—Sydney. I. Title.

ON becoming a group. 259
John Hendrix, editor. Nashville, Tenn., Broadman Press [1969] v, 118 p. 21 cm. (Broadman books) Contents.Contents.—Becoming: introducing group processes, by D. Wright.—Reconciling: being in the world, by T. Conley.—Remembering: the past in the present, by R. Hester.—Enabling: realizing the other's potential, by F. Pryor.—Sensing: hearing the feeling, by C. Marsh.—Sharing: the Gospel and the self, by K. Harris.—Supporting: their brother's keeper, by J. Drakeford.—Guiding: finding help for living, by S. Watson.—Deciding: decisions and life's demands, by B. Cusack.—Confronting: readiness for or resistance to change, by R. Brown.—Analyzing: campus ministry groups, by K. Harris.—Retreating: the renewal of life's resources, by R. Myers. Includes bibliographical references. [BV652.2.O5] 77-87727
1. Church group work—Addresses, essays, lectures. 2. Small groups—Addresses, essays, lectures. I. Hendrix, John, ed. II. Title: Becoming a group.

OSWALD, Evan 259
Manual for leaders of boys' clubs. Illus. by Jan

Gleysteen. Scottdale, Pa., Herald Pr. [c.1963] 162p. illus. 22cm. Bibl. 2.50, pap., spiral bdg.
I. Title.

OVERHOLT, William A. 259
Religion in American colleges and universities [by] William A. Overholt. Washington, American College Personnel Association [1970] 60 p. 28 cm. (Student personnel series, no. 14) Bibliography: p. 58-60. [BV1610.O9] 71-22569 2.50
1. Universities and colleges—U.S.—Religion. 2. College students—Religious life. I. Title. II. Series.

PACE, Dale K. 259
A Christian's guide to effective jail & prison ministries / Dale K. Pace ; foreword by Myrl E. Alexander. Old Tappan, N.J. : F. H. Revell Co., c1976 318 p. : ill. ; 24 cm. Includes index. Bibliography: p. 295-308. [BV4340.P3] 76-41797 ISBN 0-8007-0844-X : 11.95
1. Church work with prisoners. I. Title.

PALMER, Charles E 259
The church and the exceptional person. New York, Published for the Cooperative Publication Association by Abingdon Press [1961] 174p. illus. 19cm. (The Cooperative series: leadership training texts) Includes bibliography. [BV4460.P3] 61-4540
1. Church work with the handicapped. 2. Church work with exceptional children. I. Title.

PERSON, Peter P 259
The church and modern youth. Grand Rapids, Zondervan Pub. House [1963] 151 p. 23 cm. Includes bibliography. [BV4447.P38] 63-9316
1. Church work with youth. I. Title.

PERSON, Peter P. 259
The church and modern youth. Grand Rapids, Mich., Zondervan [c.1963] 151p. 23cm. Bibl. 63-9316 3.50
1. Church work with youth. I. Title.

PETHYBRIDGE, Bill 259
A manual of Christian youth work, by Bill and Ena Pethybridge. Minneapolis, Minn., Bethany Fellowship [c.1963] 119p. 21cm. 1.50 pap.,
I. Title.

PROHL, Russell C 259
Woman in the church; a restudy of woman's place in building the kingdom. Grand Rapids, Eerdmans [c1957] 86p. 23cm. Includes bibliography. [BV639.W7P7] 58-76
1. Women in Christianity. I. Title.

PYLANT, Agnes (Durant) 259
Church recreation. Nashville, Convention Press [c1959] 150p. illus. 19cm. Includes bibliography. [BV1620.P9] 60-507
1. Recreation. 2. Church entertainments. I. Title.

PYLANT, Agnes Durant. 259
Fun plans for church recreation. Illustrated by Murray McKeehan. Nashville, Broadman Press [1958] 125p. illus. 22cm. Includes bibliography. [BV1640.P9] 58-8924
1. Recreation. 2. Church entertainments. I. Title.

REESE, Lawrence M 259
Youth work in today's church. Philadelphia, Muhlenberg Press [1956] 141p. illus. 21cm. [BV4447.R4] 56-2837
1. Church work with youth. I. Title.

RICHARDS, Lawrence O. 259
Youth ministry; its renewal in the local church [by] Lawrence O. Richards. Grand Rapids, Zondervan Pub. House [1972] 364 p. illus. 25 cm. Includes bibliographical references. [BV4447.R46] 79-189581 6.95
1. Church work with youth. I. Title.

RISMILLER, Arthur P. 259
Older members in the congregation, by Arthur P. Rismiller. Minneapolis, Augsburg Pub. House [1964] 127 p. 29 cm. Bibliography: p. 123-127. [BV4435.R5] 64-21507
1. Church work with the aged. I. Title.

RISMILLER, Arthur P. 259
Older members in the congregation. Minneapolis, Augsburg [c.1964] 127p. 20cm. Bibl. 64-21507 1.95 pap.,
1. Church work with the aged. I. Title.

ROLFSRUD, Erling Nicolai, 1912- 259
One to one; communicating the gospel to the deaf and the blind. Minneapolis, Augsburg Pub. House [1961] 116p. 20cm. Includes bibliographies. [BV4463.R6] 61-13886
1. Church work with the handicapped. I. Title.

RYRIE, Charles Caldwell, 1925- 259
The place of women in the church. New York, Macmillan, 1958. 155p. 22cm. [BR163.R9] 58-8329
1. Women in Christianity. 2. Woman—History and condition of women. I. Title.

RYRIE, Charles Caldwell, 1925- 259
The place of women in the church. Chicago, Moody [1968, c.1958] 155p. 22cm. [BR195.W6R9] 2.95
1. Women in Christianity. 2. Woman—History and condition of women. I. Title.

SCHREIVOGEL, Paul A. 259
The world of art—the world of youth; a primer on the use of arts in youth ministry [by] Paul A. Schreivogel. Design and illus. [by] Robert Friederichsen. Minneapolis, Augsburg Pub. House [1968] 67 p. illus. (part col.) 31 cm. Includes bibliographies. [BV4447.S29] 68-13430
1. Church work with youth. 2. Mass media in religion. 3. Art and religion. I. Friederichsen, Robert, illus. II. Title.

SCHULLER, David 259
The church's ministry to youth in trouble. Saint Louis, Concordia Pub. House [c.1959] 35p. Includes bibliography. illus. (col.) 19cm. (Lutheran Round Table, pamphlet no. 6) 59-65452 .35 pap.,
1. Church work with youth. I. Title.

SEGER, Doris Louise 259
Ten teen programs. Chicago, Moody [c.1963] 95p. illus. 22cm. 1.35, pap., plastic bdg.
I. Title.

SEVENTH-DAY Adventists. General Conference. Publishing Dept. 259
Essentials of Christian salesmanship, a compilation of principles and procedures by Publishing Dept. leaders. Washington, Review and Herald Pub. Association [1956] 316p. 18cm. [BV2369.S4] 56-28909
1. Religious literature—Publication and distribution. 2. Booksellers and bookselling—Colportage, subscription trade, etc. I. Title.

SEVENTH DAY ADVENTISTS. GENERAL CONFERENCE. PUBLISHING DEPT. 259
Essentials of Christian salesmanship; a compilation of principles and procedures by Publishing Dept. leaders. Washington, Review and Herald Pub. Association [1956] 316 p. 18 cm. [BV2369.S4] 56-28909
1. Religious literature — Publications and distribution. 2. Booksellers and bookselling-Colportage, subscription trade, etc. I. Title.

SIMMS, Ruthanna M., 1880- 259
As long as the sun gives light; an account of Friends' work with American Indians in Oklahoma from 1917 to 1967, by Ruthanna M. Simms. [Richmond, Ind.] Associated Executive Committee of Friends on Indian Affairs; [distributed by Friends Book and Supply House] 1970. 146 p. illus., map, ports. 29 cm. "Deals primarily with work sponsored by the Associated Executive Committee of Friends on Indian Affairs." Bibliography: p. 145-146. [E98.M6S55] 76-147879
1. Friends, Society of. Associated Executive Committee on Indian Affairs. 2. Indians of North America—Missions. I. Title.

SMITH, Seymour A 259
The American college chaplaincy. New York, Association Press [1954] 180p. 20cm. [BV4447.S63] 54-13400
1. Chaplains, University and college. 2. Universities and colleges—Religion. 3. Church work with students. I. Title.

SMITH, Wesley E. 259
Mission impossible [by] Wesley E. Smith. Wheaton, Ill., Tyndale House Publishers [1969] 111 p. illus. 18 cm. [BV4447.S635] 79-75250
1. Church work with youth—Personal narratives. 2. Evangelistic work. I. Title.

STEVENS, Ewing Campbell. 259
Sunday alive; a story of youth and the Church [by] Ewing Stevens. Dunedin, McIndoe [1970] 134 p. illus., group ports. 22 cm. [BV4447.S69] 79-857407 3.30
1. Church work with youth—Dunedin, N.Z. I. Title.

STROMMEN, Merton P 259
Profiles of church youth; report on a four-year study of 3,000 Lutheran high school youth. Saint Louis, Concordia Pub. House [1963] xxiv, 356 p. illus., tables. 24 cm. Bibliography: [339]-342. [BV639.Y7S8] 63-20178
1. Youth — Religious life. 2. Church work with youth — Lutheran Church. I. Lutheran Youth Research. II. Title.

STROMMEN, Merton P. 259
Profiles of church youth; report on a four-year study of 3,000 Lutheran high-school youth. Saint Louis, Concordia [c.1963] xxiv, 356p. illus., tables. 24cm. Bibl. 63-20178 5.95
1. Youth—Religious life. 2. Church work with youth—Lutheran Church. I. Lutheran Youth Research. II. Title.

STUBBLEFIELD, Harold W 259
The church's ministry in mental retardation [by] Harold W. Stubblefield. Nashville, Broadman Press [c1965] viii, 147 p. 22 cm. Bibliography: p. 145-147. [BV4461.S8] 65-10343
1. Church work with the mentally handicapped. I. Title.

STUBBLEFIELD, Harold W. 259
The church's ministry in mental retardation. Nashville, Broadman [c.1965] viii, 147p. 22cm. Bibl. [BV4461.S8] 65-10343 4.00 bds.,
1. Church work with the mentally handicapped. I. Title.

TANI, Henry N 259
Ventures in youth work. Philadelphia, Christian Education Press [1957] 197p. 21cm. Includes bibliography. [BV4447.T3] 57-9060
1. Church work with youth. I. Title.

TANI, Henry N 259
Ventures in youth work. Philadelphia, Christian Education Press [1957] 197 p. 21 cm. Includes bibliography. [BV4447.T3] 57-9060
1. Church work with youth. I. Title.

THOMPSON, Yancy Samuel. 259
Industrial chaplaincy; the concept of industrial evangelism in the light of the general thinking of the evangelical movement. Boston, Christopher Pub. House [1956] 81p. 21cm. [BV2695.W6T5] 57-15549
1. Chaplains, industrial. 2. Welfare work in industry. I. Title.

THOMPSON, Yancy Samuel. 259
Industrial chaplaincy; the concept of industrial evangelism in the light of the general thinking of the evangelical movement. Boston, Christopher Pub. House [1956] 81 p. 21 cm. [BV2695.W6T5] 57-15549
1. Chaplains, Industrial 2. Welfare work in industry. I. Title.

TINNING, Graham, ed. 259
Year book of Christian camping. North Hollywood, Calif. v. 28 cm. Editor: G. Tinning. [BV1650.A1Y4] 59-43074
1. Church camps — Yearbooks. I. Title.

TOWNS, Elmer. 259
The single adult and the church. Glendale, Calif., G/L Regal Books [1967] 125 p. illus. 20 cm. Bibliography: p. 121-123. [BV639.S5T6] 67-9603
1. Church work with single people. I. Title.

TOWNS, Elmer L. 259
The single adult and the church. Glendale, Calif., G/L Regal Books [1967] 125 p. illus. 20 cm. Bibliography: p. 121-123. [BV639.S5T6] 67-9603
1. Church work with single people. I. Title.

*TREMMEL, William C. 259
A different drum, a manual on interreligious campus affairs. New York, Natl. Conf. of Christians & Jews [1964] 63p. 23cm. .50 pap.,
I. Title.

UEHLING, Carl T. 259
Blood, sweat & love; the Circus Kirk story, by Carl T. Uehling. Philadelphia, Fortress Press [1970] 126 p. illus., ports. 21 cm. (Open books, 3) [BV4447.U33] 79-119764 2.50
1. Church work with youth—Pennsylvania. 2. Circus—Pennsylvania. I. Title. II. Title: Circus Kirk.

VITTORIA, Theodore J ed. 259
Adolescent conflicts; [a manual for those engaged in the guidance of youth] Buffalo, Saint Paul Publications [c1951] 189 p. 19 cm. Includes bibliography. [BX2347.8.Y7V5] 60-16564
1. Church work with youth. I. Title.

WEISHEIT, Eldon. 259
Abortion? : Resources for pastoral counseling / Eldon Weisheit. St. Louis : Concordia Pub. House, c1976. 173 p. ; 21 cm. Bibliography: p. 169-172. [HQ767.3.W45] 75-43587 ISBN 0-570-03259-8 : 6.95
1. Abortion. 2. Abortion—Religious aspects. 3. Pastoral counseling. I. Title.

WHITE, Emma Jane. 259
Let's do more with persons with disabilities. Edited by Emma Jane White. Nashville, Tenn., Local Church Education, Board of Discipleship of the United Methodist Church [1973] vi, 73 p. illus. 22 cm. Bibliography: p. 71-72. [BV4460.W45] 73-169463 1.00
1. Church work with the handicapped. I. Title.

WILKERSON, David R. 259
Beyond the cross and the switchblade [by] David Wilkerson. Special introd. by John and Elizabeth Sherrill. Old Tappan, N.J., Chosen Books; distributed by F. H. Revell [1974] 191 p. 21 cm. [BV4470.W48] 74-12155 ISBN 0-912376-08-2
1. Wilkerson, David R. 2. Church work with narcotic addicts. I. Title.

WILKERSON, David R. 259
Hey, Preach—you're comin' through! [By] David Wilkerson. Westwood, N. J., Revell [1968] 160 p. 21 cm. [BV4464.5.W513] 68-17096
1. Church work with juvenile delinquents. I. Title.

WILKERSON, David R. 259
Purple violet squish [by] David Wilkerson. Grand Rapids, Zondervan Pub. House [1969] 152 p. 22 cm. [BV4470.W5] 79-81055 2.95
1. Church work with narcotic addicts. 2. Hippies. I. Title.

WILLIAMS, Gomer. 259
History of the Liverpool privateers and letters of marque, with an account of the Liverpool slave trade. New York, A. M. Kelley, 1966. xv, 718 p. illus. 23 cm. (Reprints of economic classics) Reprint of the first ed., 1897. [DA690.L8W55 1966] 66-24413
1. Liverpool—History, Naval. 2. Privateering. 3. Slave-trade—Great Britain—Liverpool. I. Title.

WOLSELEY, Roland Edgar, 1904- 259
Interpreting the church through press and radio. Philadelphia, Muhlenberg Press [1951] xv, 352 p. illus. 22 cm. "A booklist for the church journalist": p. 337-341. [BV653.W6] 51-11395
1. Public relations — Churches. I. Title.

WYKER, Mossie Allman. 259
Church women in the scheme of things. St. Louis, Bethany Press [1953] 117p. 20cm. [BV4415.W9] 53-3867
1. Women in church work. I. Title.

*YAXLEY, Grace 259
Here's how youth meetings. Chicago, Moody [c.1964] 64p. illus. 28cm. 1.25 pap.,
I. Title.

YODER, Gideon G 259
The nurture and evangelism of children. Scottdale, Pa., Herald Press [1959] 188 p. 21 cm. (The Conrad Grebel lectures, 1956) Includes bibliography. [BV639.C4Y6] 59-7877
1. Church work with children. 2. Religious education of children. I. Title.

YOUTH fellowship kit; 259
discussion topics and year-round program suggestions for young people's fellowships, societies, and clubs. Philadelphia, Westminster Press [19 v. illus. 28cm. annual. Editor: N. F. Langford. [BV29.Y6] 54-2806
1. Young people's meetings (Church work) 2. Worship programs. I. Langford, Norman F., 1914-

YOUTH fellowship kit; 259
discussion topics and year-round program suggestions for young people's fellowships,societies, and clubs, v.19. Eds.: Norman F. Langford, Donald L. Leonard, J. Wilbur Patterson. Philadelphia, Westminster Press [c.1961] 232p. illus. (part col.) 28cm. Bibl. 54-2806 3.50 pap.,
1. Young people's meetings (Church work) 2. Worship programs. I. Langford, Norman F., ed.

260 SOCIAL & ECCLESIASTICAL THEOLOGY

ADAMS, Jeremy duQuesnay. 260
The populus of Augustine and Jerome; a study in the patristic sense of community. New Haven, Yale University Press, 1971. viii, 278 p. 23 cm. Bibliography: p. 252-266. [BR166.A3] 70-140521 ISBN 0-300-01402-3 12.50
1. Augustinus, Aurelius, Saint, Bp. of Hippo—Sociology. 2. Hieronymus, Saint. 3. Sociology, Christian—Early church, ca. 30-600. 4. Populus (The Latin word) I. Title.

ADKINS, Edward T. 260
Study-action manual for "Mission: the Christmas calling", by Edward T. Adkins. New York, Friendship Press [1965] 96 p. 19 cm. "Program for adults, for use with Voices of protest and hope: The Word with power: Mission as decision; Babylon by choice; [and] Realms of our calling." [BV1561.A2] 65-11420
1. Religious education — Text-books for adults. 2. Missions — Study and teaching I. Title.

ADOLFS, Robert, 1922- 260
The grave of God; has the church a future? Tr. by N. D. Smith. [1st Amer. ed.] New York, Harper [1967] 156, [1]p. 22cm. Tr. of Het graf

van God; heeft de kerk nog toekomst? Bibl. [BR115.W6A33 1967] 67-14940 4.50
1. Church and the world. I. Title.

ANDERSON, Stanley Edwin. 260
Real churches or a fog : a defense of real, local churches, a denial of a foggy, universal church / by S. E. Anderson. Texarkana, Tex. : Bogard Press, [1975] 168 p. ; 22 cm. [BS2545.C5A5] 74-29675
1. Church—Biblical teaching. I. Title.

BAKER, Wesley C. 260
The split-level fellowship. Philadelphia, Westminster [1965] 151p. 21cm. Bibl. [BV4011.B33] 65-10080 4.50
1. Pastoral theology—Presbyterian Church. 2. Church membership. I. Title.

BANNERMAN, David Douglas. 260
The Scripture doctrine of the church historically and exegetically considered. Grand Rapids, Eerdmans, 1955. 580p. 23cm. (The Cunningham lectures, 11th ser.) 'A reproduction of the 1887 edition printed in Edinburgh.' [BV600.B342] 55-2840
1. Church—Biblical teaching. I. Title.

BANNERMAN, James, 1807-1868. 260
The Church of Christ : a treatise on the nature, powers, ordinances, discipline, and government of the Christian Church / James Bannerman. Edinburgh ; Carlisle, Pa. : Banner of Truth Trust, 1974. 2 v. : port. ; 23 cm. (Students' reformed theological library) Reprint of the 1869 ed. published by T. and T. Clark, Edinburgh. Includes bibliographical references and index. [BV600.B343 1974] 75-322515 ISBN 0-85151-186-4 : £4.00
1. Church. 2. Sacraments. 3. Church polity. I. Title.

BARBOUR, Robert Stewart. 260
What is the Church for? [By] R. S. Barbour. Aberdeen, R. S. Barbour, 1973. 76 p. 21 cm. [BV601.8.B37] 74-165753 ISBN 0-9503201-0-2 £0.50
1. Mission of the church. I. Title.

BATES, Francis Van Ness How. 260
Christianity and cosmopolitan civilization; a study of spiritual and global factors in modern society, based on an anthology of conventional verse entitled, Reason in rhyme. Boston, Christopher Pub. House [1966] xxvi, 375 p. illus. 21 cm. [BR124.B3] 65-25596
1. Christianity—20th cent.—Addresses, essays, lectures. I. Title.

BATES, Francis Van Ness How 260
Christianity and cosmopolitan civilization; a study of spiritual and global factors in modern society, based on an anthology of conventional verse entitled, Reason in rhyme. Boston, Christopher Pub. House [c.1966] xxvi, 375p. illus. 21cm. [BR124.B3] 65-25596 4.95
1. Christianity—20th cent.—Addresses, essays, lectures. I. Title.

BATES, Francis Van Ness How. 260
Christisanity and cosmopolitan civilization; a study of spiritual and global factors in modern society, based on an anthology of conventional verse entitled, Reason in rhyme. Boston, Christopher Pub. House [1966] xxvi, 375 p. illus. 21 cm. [BR124.B3] 65-25596
1. Christianity — 20th cent. — Addresses, essays, lectures. I. Title.

BEA, Augustin, Cardinal, 260
1881-1968.
The church and mankind. Chicago, Franciscan Herald Press [1967] vi, 282 p. 23 cm. Translation of La chiesa e l'umanita. Includes bibliographical references. [BX1746.B413] 67-8390
1. Vatican Council. 2d, 1962-1965. 2. Church. 3. Church and the world. I. Title.

BEKKERS, Willem Marinus, 260
Bp., 1908-1966.
God's people on the march; a modern Bishop speaks to his people [by] Mgr. Willem Bekkers; [introd., comp. by Michel van der Plas] tr. [from Dutch] by Catherine Jarrott. Techny, Ill., Divine Word [1967,c.1966] 180p. 18cm. (DWP14) Orig. published as God's volk onder weg, Amboboeken, Utrecht, 1964. The English edition first appeared in 1966 under the title God's people on the way. [BX891.B4132] 1.50 pap.,
1. Catholic Church—Addresses, essays, lectures. I. Title.

BELGUM, David Rudolph, 1922-- 260

The church and its ministry. Englewood Cliffs, N.J. Prentice-Hall, 1963. 188 p. illus. 24 cm. [BV640.B43] 63-10668
1. Church. 2. Pastoral theology. I. Title.

BELGUM, David Rudolph, 1922- 260
The church and its ministry. Englewood Cliffs, N.J., Prentice [c.] 1963 188 p. illus. 24 cm. Bibl. 63-10668 6.60
1. Church. 2. Pastoral theology. I. Title.

BERTON, Pierre, 1920- 260
The comfortable pew; a critical look at Christianity and the religious establishment in the new age. With a foreward by Ernest Harrison and a special pref. to the U.S. ed. Philadelphia, Lippincott [1965] xxx, 137 p. 21 cm. Bibliographical references included in "Notes" (p. 131-137) [BR123.B42] 65-23204
1. Christianity — 20th cent. — Addresses, essays, lectures. I. Title.

BERTON, Pierre, 1920- 260
The comfortable pew; a critical look at Christianity and the religious establishment in the new age. With a foreword by Ernest Harrison and a special pref. to the U.S. ed. Philadelphia, Lippincott [1965] xxx, 137 p. 21 cm. Bibliographical references included in "Notes" (p. 131-137) [BR123.B42 1965] 65-23204
1. Christianity—20th century—Addresses, essays, lectures. I. Title.

BLUMHORST, Roy. 260
Faithful rebels; does the old-style religion fit the new style of life? Saint Louis, Concordia Pub. House [1967] 100 p. illus. 22 cm. [BV637.B55] 67-23985
1. City churches. 2. Church work with apartment dwellers. 3. High-rise apartment buildings. I. Title.

BOCKELMAN, Wilfred. 260
You can help make it happen. Illustrated by Ray Barton. Minneapolis, Augsburg Pub. House [1971] 88 p. illus. 18 cm. Bibliography: p. 86-88. [BV4400.B63] 72-135217 ISBN 0-8066-1104-9
1. Church work. I. Title.

BONHOFFER, Dietrich, 1906- 260
1945
The communion of saints; a dogmatic inquiry into the sociology of the church. New York, Harper [1964, c.1963] 256p. 22cm. Tr. is pub. in Great Britain under the title: Sanctorum communio based on the third German edition of 1960. Bibl. 64-10749 4.00
1. Communion of saints. 2. Church. 3. Sociology, Christian. I. Title.

BOWER, William Clayton, 1878- 260
The church at work in the modern world, written in collaboration by William Clayton Bower, editor, Edward Scribner Ames [and others] Freeport, N.Y., Books for Libraries Press [1967] xi, 304 p. maps. 22 cm. (Essay index reprint series) Reprint of the 1935 ed. Includes bibliographies. [BV3.B6 1967] 67-26717
1. Theology, Practical. 2. Church work. 3. Protestant churches—United States. I. Ames, Edward Scribner, 1870-1958. II. Title.

BOYD, Malcolm, ed. 260
On the battle lines. New York, Morehouse-Barlow Co. [1964] 259 p. 22 cm. Bibliographical footnotes. [BV625.B6] 64-16830
1. Christianity — 20th cent. — Addresses, essays, lectures. 2. Church and social problems — Addresses, essays, lectures. I. Title.

BOYD, Malcolm, ed. 260
On the battle lines. New York, Morehouse [c.1964] 259p. 22cm. Bibl. 64-16830 5.95
1. Christianity—20th cent.—Addresses, essays, lectures. 2. Church and social problems—Addresses, essays, lectures. I. Title.

BOYD, Malcolm, 1923- ed. 260
On the battle lines. New York, Morehouse-Barlow Co. [1964] 259 p. 22 cm. Bibliographical footnotes. [BV625.B6] 64-16830
1. Christianity—20th cent.—Addresses, essays, lectures. 2. Church and social problems—Addresses, essays, lectures. I. Title.

BOYD, Malcolm, 1923- 260
The underground church. Ed. by Malcolm Boyd. New York, Sheed [1968] x, 246p. 21 cm. Bibl. footnotes. [BV601.9.B6] 68-17361 4.95
1. Non-institutional churches. 2. Christianity—20th cent. I. Title.

BOYD, Malcolm, 1923- 260
The underground church, edited by Malcolm Boyd. [Rev. ed. Baltimore] Penguin Books [1969] xx, 271 p. 18 cm. (A Pelican book, A1109) [BV601.9.B6 1969] 76-5321 0.95
1. Non-institutional churches. 2. Christianity—20th century. I. Title.

BRAATEN, Carl E., 1929- 260
The flaming center : a theology of the Christian mission / Carl E. Braaten. Philadelphia : Fortress Press, c1977. vi, 170 p. ; 24 cm. Includes bibliographical references. [BV601.8.B68] 76-62605 ISBN 0-8006-0490-3 : 8.50
1. Mission of the church. I. Title.

BRAY, Allen F. 260
The return to self-concern. Philadelphia, Westminister Press [1964] 142 p. 21 cm. Bibliographical references included in "Notes" (p. 135-142) [BV4006.B7] 64-10517
1. Pastoral theology — Hist. 2. Identification (Religion) 3. Individuality. I. Title.

BRAY, Allen F. 260
The return to self-concern. Philadelphia, Westminster [c.1964] 142p. 21cm. Bibl. 64-10517 3.50
1. Pastoral theology—Hist. 2. Identification (Religion) 3. Individuality. I. Title.

BRENT, Charles Henry, Bp., 260
1862-1929.
The inspiration of responsibility, and other papers. Freeport, N.Y., Books for Libraries Press [1966] 236 p. 19 cm. (Essay index reprint series) Reprint of the 1915 ed. [BR125.B7216 1966] 67-22081
1. Christianity—Addresses, essays, lectures. I. Title.

BROHOLM, Richard R 260
The man of faith in the new age [by] Richard R. Broholm. Valley Forge, Judson Press [1964] 111 p. illus. 20 cm. Bibliography: p. 111. [BR123.B72] 64-15794
1. Christianity — 20th cent. — Addresses, essays, lectures. I. Title.

BROHOLM, Richard R. 260
The man of faith in the new age. Valley Forge, Judson [c.1964] 111p. illus. 20cm. Bibl. 64-15794 1.50 pap.,
1. Christianity—20th cent.—Addresses, essays, lectures. I. Title.

BROKHOFF, John R. 260
This is the church [by] John R. Brokhoff. Frank W. Klos, ed. Helen Woods. illus. Philadelphia, Lutheran Church [1964] 137p. illus. 21cm. (LCA sch. of rel. ser.) Bibl. 64-56345 1.25; 1.25 pap., teacher's guide, pap.
1. Church. I. Title.

BROWN, Bob W. 260
The church is people / Bob W. Brown. Nashville : Broadman Press, c1976. 128 p. ; 18 cm. [BV600.2.B723] 75-22506 ISBN 0-8054-5563-9 pbk. : 1.95
1. Church. 2. Christian life—Baptist authors. I. Title.

BROWN, Dale W., 1926- 260
So send I you. Newton, Kan., Faith and Life Press [1969] 32 p. 20 cm. (The Schowalter memorial lecture series) Contents.Contents.—The nature of our mission to the world.—The nature of the unity we seek. [BR115.W6B75] 79-97735
1. Church and the world. 2. Christian union. I. Title. II. Series.

BUHLMANN, Walbert. 260
The coming of the Third Church : an analysis of the present and future of the Church / [by] Walbert Buhlmann. Slough : St. Paul Publications, 1976. xi, 419 p. : maps, plans ; 22 cm. Revised translation from the Italian ed. and the original German manuscript of Es kommt die dritte Kirche. Includes index. Bibliography: p. 408-413. [BR121.B74313] 76-363041 ISBN 0-85439-119-3 : £4.50
1. Christianity—20th century. I. Title.

BURNS, Patrick J ed. 260
Mission and witness; the life of the church. Selected and edited with commentary and pref. by Patrick J. Burns. Westminster, Md., Newman Press, 1964. xii, 382 p. 22 cm. Includes bibliographical references. [BV600.A1B8] 63-17438
1. Church — Addresses, essays, lectures. I. Title.

BURNS, Patrick J., ed. 260
Mission and witness the life of the church. Selected and edited with commentary and pref. by Patrick J. Burns. Westminster, Md., Newman [c.]1964. xiii, 382p. 22cm. Bibl. 63-17438 5.75; 2.50 pap.,
1. Church—Addresses, essays, lectures. I. Title.

BUTLER, Basil Christopher 260
The idea of the church. Helicon [dist. New York, Taplinger, 1963, c.1962] 236p. 23cm. Bibl. 62-19068 4.95
1. Church—History of doctrines. I. Title.

BYFIELD, Ted 260
Just think, Mr. Berton, a little harder. Illus. by Peter Kuch. Foreword by William Pollard [1st Amer. ed] New York, Morehouse [c.1965] 149p. 19cm. A reply to The comfortable pew, by Pierre Berton [BR123.B9] 65-9170 2.25 pap.,
1. Christianity—20th cent.—Addresses, essays, lectures. I. Berton. Pierre, 1920- The comfortable pew. II. Title.

BYFIELD, Ted. 260
Just think, Mr. Berton, a little harder. With illus. by Peter Kuch and a foreword by William Pollard. [1st American ed.] New York, Morehouse-Barlow Co. [1965] 149 p. 19 cm. A reply to The comfortable pew, by Pierre Berton. [BR123.B9] 65-9170
1. Christianity—20th cent.—Addresses, essays, lectures. I. Berton, Pierre, 1920- The comfortable pew. II. Title.

CAEMMERER, Richard Rudolph, 260
1904-
Christ builds His church. Saint Louis, Concordia Pub. House [1963] 94 p. 19 cm. (Concord books) [BV600.8C3] 63-14989
1. Church—Foundation. I. Title.

CAEMMERER, Richard Rudolph, 260
1904-
Christ builds His church. Saint Louis, Concordia [c.1963] 94p. 19cm. (Concord bks.) 63-14989 1.00 pap.,
1. Church—Foundation. I. Title.

CAN Christianity survive? 260
By the staff of Time. Edited by Joe David Brown. New York, Time-Life Books [1968] 123 p. 20 cm. [BR123.C33] 68-26081
1. Christianity—20th century—Addresses, essays, lectures. I. Brown, Joe David, ed. II. Time, inc.

CARTER, James Everard, 1906- 260
The mission of the church [by] James E. Carter. Nashville, Broadman Press [1973, c1974] 123 p. 20 cm. "Originally this material was prepared as a twelve-part Bible study for Royal service." Includes bibliographical references. [BV601.8.C37] 73-83832 ISBN 0-8054-8509-0 1.50
1. Mission of the church.

CATHOLIC Church. Pope, 1939- 260
1958 (Pius XII) Exsul familia (1 Aug. 1952) English.
The church's Magna charta for migrants. Edited by Giulivo Tessarolo, with commentaries. Introd. by Edward E. Swanstrom. Staten Island, N. Y., St. Charles Seminary [1962] 300p. 20cm. At head of title: Exsul familia. [BV2180.A353] 62-15993
1. Emigration and immigration—Religious aspects. I. Tessarolo, Giulivo, ed. II. Title.

CHURCH as the body of Christ 260
(The) [by] K. E. Skydsgaard [others. Notre Dame, Ind.] Univ. of Notre Dame Pr. [c.] 1963. xii, 145p. 22cm. (Cardinal O'Hara Ser.; studies and res. in Christian theology at Notre Dame, v.1) Three of the papers were presented at the 1962 Notre Dame Colloquium. Bibl. 63-13473 2.95
1. Jesus Christ—Mystical body. I. Skydsgaard, Krister E. II. Notre Dame Colloquium. 2d, University of Notre Dame, 1962. III. Series: The Cardinal O'Hara series, v.1

THE Church emerging : 260
a U.S. Lutheran case study / edited by John Reumann ; with contributions by James A. Bergquist ... [et al.]. Philadelphia : Fortress Press, c1977. ix, 275 p. ; 23 cm. Includes bibliographical references. [BV600.2.C447] 76-62618 ISBN 0-8006-1259-0 pbk. : 9.95
1. Lutheran Church in the United States. 2. Church. 3. Mission of the Church. 4. Sociology, Christian. I. Reumann, John Henry Paul. II. Bergquist, James A.

CHURCH in Christian faith and 260
life (The); a study course to prepare local churches for the use of the curriculum Christian faith and life, a program for church and home. 3d ed. Pub. by the Bd. of Christian Educ. of the United Presbyterian Church in the United States of America. [dist. Philadelphia, Westminster, c.1962] 63p. Bibl. .60 pap.,

CHURCH of England in 260
Australia. Missionary and Ecumenical Council.
Renewal, by the Missionary and Ecumenical Council of the Church of England and the Australian Council of Churches. [Melbourne, General Board of Religious Education of the Church of England in Australia, 1967?] 32 p. illus. 22 cm. [BV601.8.C47] 73-494428
1. Mission of the church. 2. Church renewal. I. Australian Council of Churches. II. Title.

COATES, Thomas, 1910- 260
Authority in the Church. Saint Louis, Concordia Pub. House [1964] 98 p. 21 cm. Bibliographical references included in "Notes" (p. 91-93) Bibliography: p. [95]-96. [BT91.C6] 63-23148
1. Church — Authority. I. Title.

COATES, Thomas, 1910- 260
Authority in the Church. St. Louis, Concordia [c.1964] 98p. 21cm. Bibl. 63-23148 1.50 pap.,
1. Church—Authority. I. Title.

COBB, John B. 260
Can the church think again? / John B. Cobb, Jr. [Nashville, TN] : United Methodist Board of Higher Education and Ministry, 1976. 11 p. ; 28 cm. (Occasional papers - United Methodist Board of Higher Education and Ministry ; v. 1, no. 12) Caption title. [BR148.C6] 77-356708
1. Religious thought—History—Addresses, essays, lectures. I. Title. II. Series: United Methodist Church (United States). Board of Higher Education and Ministry. Occasional papers — United Methodist Board of Higher Education and Ministry ; v. 1, no. 12.

COGGINS, Ross 260
To change the world. Nashville, Broadman [1964] viii, 117p. 20cm. Bibl. 64-24026 1.50
1. Christianity—20th cent.—Addresses, essays, lectues. I. Title.

COME, Arnold B. 260
Agents of reconciliation. Rev. and enl, ed. Philadelphia, Westminster Press [c1964] 178 p. 21 cm. [BV600.2.C6] 63-25767
1. Church 2. Clergy. I. Title.

COME, Arnold B. 260
Agents of reconciliation. Philadelphia, Westminster Press [c.1960] 176p. 21cm. 60-8634 3.95
1. Church. 2. Clergy. 3. Laity. I. Title.

COME, Arnold B. 260
Agents of reconciliation, Rev., enl. ed. Philadelphia, Westminster [c.1964] 178p. 21cm. 63-25767 1.95 pap.,
1. Church. 2. Clergy. 3. Laity. I. Title.

CONFERENCE on the Communication and Interpretation of the World Mission of the Church, New York, 1965. 260
Report. [New York, Published for Interpretation and Promotion Division of Overseas Ministries by the Dept. of Publication Services, National Council of the Churches of Christ in the U.S.A., 1966] v, 97 p. 28 cm. Cover title. "Sponsored by: the Division of Overseas Ministries (National Council of the Churches of Christ in the U.S.A.) and the Division of Inter-Church Aid, Refugee and World Service; the Division of World Mission and Evangelism; the Department of Information (World Council of Churches)" [BV4319.C6 1965] 70-24210
1. Communication (Theology)—Congresses. 2. Mission of the church—Congresses. I. National Council of the Churches of Christ in the United States of America. Division of Overseas Ministries.

*CONWAY, Martin 260
The undivided vision: students explore a worldly Christianity. Philadelphia, Fortress [1967, c.1966] 122p. 18cm. First pub. in England in 1966. 2.50 pap.,
I. Title.

COOKE, Bernard J. 260
Christian community: response to reality [by] Bernard J. Cooke. New York, Holt, Rinehart, and Winston [1970] viii, 187 p. 22 cm. [BT1102.C6 1970] 77-102022 4.95
1. Apologetics—20th century. I. Title.

COOKE, Bernard J. 260
Christian community: response to reality. Garden City, N.Y., Doubleday, 1973 200 p., 18 cm. (Image Books) [BT1102.C6 1973] ISBN 0-385-08565-6 pap. 1.45
1. Apologetics—20th century I. Title.
L.C. card no. for the orig. ed.: 77-102022

COOPER, Mattie Lula. 260
The church is a friendly place; a weekday church school course for grades 1 and 2. Teacher's book. Dayton, Ohio, Published for the Cooperative Publication Association [by] the Otterbein Press [1955] 176p. illus. 20cm. (The Co-operative series texts for weekday religious educations classes and released time religious education instruction) [BV1583.C64] 55-11377
1. Week-day church schools—Teachers' manuals. I. Title.

CORSON, Fred Pierce, 1896- 260
Your church and you. [1st ed.] Philadelphia. Winston [1951] 171 p. 22 cm. [BV600.C77] 51-12831
1. Church 2. Laity. I. Title.

CRAGG, Kenneth. 260
Christianity in world perspective. New York, Oxford University Press, 1968. 227 p. 23 cm. [BR115.C8C68] 68-23577
1. Christianity and culture. 2. Christianity and other religions. 3. Christianity—Essence, genius, nature. I. Title.

CRISIS in the church; 260
essays in honor of Truman B. Douglass. Everett C. Parker, editor. Philadelphia, Pilgrim Press [1968] 143 p. 21 cm. Contents.Contents.—Preface, by E. C. Parker.—The lover's quarrel of the church with the world, by R. L. Shinn.—The revolution that has begun in home missions, by J. L. Regier.—The local church and the Big Daddy fantasy, by G. J. Jud.—A look over Jordan, by H. Schachern.—Church education for a new age, by E. A. Powers.—Meeting the crisis in church-related higher education, by W. A. Hotchkiss.—Communications; the new ministry, by E. L. Greif.—Truman Douglass in the ecumenical movement. 1943-1968, by D. Horton.—The ecumenical vision of the church as mission, by D. G. Colwell.—The mission that is to be, by T. B. Douglass. Bibliographical references included in "Notes" (p. [139]-143) [BR50.C67] 68-57478 2.95
1. Douglass, Truman B. 2. Christianity—20th century—Addresses, essays, lectures. I. Douglass, Truman B. II. Parker, Everett C., ed.

CROWTHER, Clarence Edward. 260
Where religion gets lost in the church, by C. Edward Crowther. New York, Morehouse-Barlow [1968] 158 p. 22 cm. Bibliographical footnotes. [BR115.W6C697] 68-56915
1. Church and the world. I. Title.

CUDNEY, Gerald E. 260
Administering the ministry, by Gerald E. Cudney. Grand Rapids, Diadem Productions [1970] 96 p. illus. 22 cm. [BV652.C8] 77-129798 1.95
1. Church management. I. Title.

CUNNEEN, Sally. 260
Sex: female; religion: Catholic. [1st ed.] New York, Holt, Rinehart and Winston [1968] xv, 171 p. 22 cm. Includes bibliographical references. [BX2347.8.W6C8] 68-10075
1. Women in Christianity. I. Title.

DANKER, Frederick W 260
The kingdom in action [by] Frederick W. Danker. [St. Louis] concordia Pub. House, [1965] 112 p. 21 cm. (The Witnessing church series) "The substance of a series of lectures delivered to a group of pastors at Concordia Seminary, St. Louis, Mo., in summer 1963." Includes bibliographies. [BV600.2D3] 65-16285
1. Church — Addresses, essays, lectures. I. Title.

DANKER, Frederick W. 260
The kingdom in action. [St. Louis] Concordia [c.1965] 112p. 21cm. (Witnessing church ser.) Substance of a ser. of lects. delivered to a group of pastors at Concordia Seminary, St. Louis, Mo., in summer 1963. Bibl. [BV600.2.D3] 65-16285 1.75 pap.,
1. Church—Addresses, essays, lectures. I. Title.

DAVIS, Henry, 1866- 260
Moral and pastoral theology, a summary. New York, Sheed and Ward, 1952. 484 p. 22 cm. [BX1758.D32] 52-9315
1. Christian ethics—Catholic authors. 2. Theology, Pastoral—Catholic Church. I. Title.

DAVIS, Henry, 1866-1952. 260
Moral and pastoral theology; a summary. London, New York, Sheed and Ward [1952] 486p. 23cm. (Heythrop series, 3) [BX1758.D32 1952a] 53-1494
1. Christian ethics—Catholic authors. 2. Theology. Pastoral—Catholic Church. I. Title.

DEWOLF, Lotan Harold, 1905- 260
A hard rain and a cross; faith for a church under fire [by] L. Harold DeWolf. Nashville, Abingdon Press [1966] 224 p. 23 cm. Bibliography footnotes. [BR121.2.D44] 66-14997
1. Christianity — 20th cent. 2. Church. I. Title.

DEWOLF, Lotan Harold, 1905- 260
A hard rain and a cross; faith for a church under fire. Nashville, Abingdon [c.1966] 224p. 23cm. Bibl. [BR121.2.D44] 66-14997 4.00
1. Christianity—20th cent. 2. Church. I. Title.

DOLLOFF, Eugene Dinsmore 260
The pastor's public relations. Philadelphia, Judson Press [c.1959] 188 p. 21 cm. (2 p. bibl.) 59-15432 3.00
1. Church work. 2. Pastoral theology. I. Title.

DORNER, Isaak August, 1809-1884 260
Geschichte der protestantischen theologie, besonders in Deutschland, nach ihrer principiellen bewegung und im zusammenhang mit dem religiosen, sittlichen und intellectuellen leben betrachtet, von dr. I. A. Dorner. Munchen, J. G. Cotta, 1867; New York, Johnson Reprint, 1966. 2 p. 1., 924 p. 23 cm. 2 cm. (Geschichte der wissenschaften in Deutschland. Neuere zeit. 5. bd.) 28.00
I. Title.

DRAPER, James T. 260
The Church Christ approves [by] James T. Draper, Jr. Nashville, Broadman Press [1974] 128 p. 21 cm. Includes bibliographical references. [BV4501.2.D68] 73-89856 ISBN 0-8054-1922-5 3.95
1. Christian life—Baptist authors. 2. Mission of the church. 3. Christianity—20th century. I. Title.

DRIVER, John, 1924- 260
Community and commitment / John Driver ; introd. by Wilbert Shenk. Scottdale, Pa. : Herald Press, c1976. 92 p. ; 20 cm. (Mission forum series ; 4) [BV600.2.D68] 76-41463 ISBN 0-8361-1802-2 pbk. : 2.95
1. Church. 2. Christian life—Mennonite authors. I. Title. II. Series.

ERASMUS, Desiderius, d.1536. 260
Praise of folly; and, Letter to Martin Dorp, 1515 [by] Eramus of Rotterdam; translated by Betty Radice; with an introduction and notes by A. H. T. Levi. Harmondsworth, Penguin, 1971. 265 p. 19 cm. (Penguin classics) Translation of Moria encomium. Bibliography: p. 51. [PA8514.E5 1971] 76-28783 ISBN 0-14-044240-5 £0.40
1. Folly. I. Erasmus, Desiderius, d. 1536. Letter to Martin Dorp. 1971. II. Title.

ERNSBERGER, David J. 260
Reviving the local church [by] David J. Ernsberger. Philadelphia, Fortress Press [1969] x, 86 p. 19 cm. (Church-in-mission series, v. 1) Based on lectures at Concordia Seminary's 11th annual Institute of the Church in Mission, Aug., 1967. Includes bibliographical references. [BV601.8.E75] 69-14624 1.95
1. Mission of the church. 2. Church renewal. I. Title.

FACKRE, Gabriel J. 260
Secular impact; the promise of mission [by] Gabriel Fackre. Philadelphia, Pilgrim Press [1968] xii, 146 p. 22 cm. Bibliographical references included in "Notes" (p. 142-146) [BR115.W6F3] 68-29713 4.95
1. Church and the world. 2. Mission of the church. I. Title.

FACKRE, Gabriel J. 260
Under the steeple [by] Gabriel and Dorothy Fackre. New York, Abingdon Press [1957] 128 p. 20 cm. [BX8.F3] 57-11009
1. Ecumenical movement. 2. Evangelistic work. I. Fackre, Dorothy Ashman, joint author. II. Title.

FERGUSON, Everett, 1933- 260
The New Testament church. Abilene, Tex., Biblical Research Press [1968] 93 p. 22 cm. (The Way of life series, no. 108) Bibliography: p. 5. [BV597.F4] 68-55790 1.00
1. Church—Biblical teaching. 2. Theology, Doctrinal—History—Early church, ca. 30-600. I. Title.

FISHER, Wallace E. 260
The affable enemy, by Wallace E. Fisher. Nashville, Abingdon Press [1970] 157 p. 21 cm. Includes bibliographical references. [BR123.F557] 71-97567 3.95
1. Christianity—20th century. I. Title.

FORESI, Pasquale M., 1929- 260
Theology of social man, by Pascal M. Foresi Tr. by Julian Stead. Jamaica, N.Y., New City Pr. [1967] 190p. 20cm. Tr. of Teologia della socialita. Bibl. [BX1754.F5713] 67-15776 3.25 bds.,
1. Catholic Church—Doctrinal and controversial works, Popular. 2. Sociology, Christian (Catholic) I. Title.
Publishers address: 148-18 85th Dr., Jamaica, N.Y. 11435.

FORSTMAN, H. Jackson. 260
Christian faith and the church, by H. Jackson Forstman. St. Louis, Bethany Press [1965] 191 p. 23 cm. Bibliographical footnotes. [BV600.2.F6] 65-18204
1. Church. 2. Faith. I. Title.

FROST, Gerhard E. 260
Life in Christ. [by] Gerhard E. Frost, A. Thomas Kraabel. Minneapolis, Augsburg [c.1963] 80p. 21cm. 1.00 pap.,
I. Title.

GARDNER, Eugene Norfleet, 1804- 260
Changing patterns in Christian programs, by E. Norfleet Gardner. Boston, Christopher Pub. House [1964] 161 p. 21 cm. Includes bibliographies. [HN64.G26] 64-8589
1. Church and social problems — U.S. I. Title.

GARDNER, Eugene Norfleet, 1894- 260
Changing patterns in Christian programs. Boston, Christopher Pub. [c.1964] 161p. 21cm. Bibl. [HN64.G26] 64-8589 3.50
1. Church and social problems—U.S. I. Title.

GARDNER-SMITH, Percival, 1888- ed. 260
The roads converge; a contribution to the question of Christian reunion, by members of Jesus College, Cambridge. Introd. by C. H. Dodd. New York, St. Martin's [1964, c.]1963. x, 253p. 23cm. Bibl. 64-10301 7.00 bds.,
1. Theology—Addresses, essays, lectures. 2. Christianity—Addresses, essays, lectures. I. Cambridge. University. Jesus College. II. Title.

GATTI, Enzo. 260
Rich church—poor church? Some Biblical perspectives. Translated by Matthew J. O'Connell. Maryknoll, N.Y., Orbis Books [1974] xi, 127 p. 19 cm. Translation of Colui che sa il dolore dell'uomo. Includes bibliographical references. [BV601.8.G3313] 74-77432 ISBN 0-88344-437-2 4.95
1. Mission of the church. 2. Missions. 3. Freedom (Theology) I. Title.

GATTI, Enzo. 260
Rich church—poor church? Some Biblical perspectives. Translated by Matthew J. O'Connell. Maryknoll, N.Y., Orbis Books [1974] xi, 127 p. 19 cm. Translation of Colui che sa il dolore dell'uomo. Includes bibliographical references. [BV601.8.G3313] 74-77432 ISBN 0-88344-437-2 4.95
1. Mission of the church. 2. Missions. 3. Freedom (Theology) I. Title.

GETZ, Gene A. 260
The measure of a church / by Gene A. Getz. Glendale, Calif. : G/L Regal Books, c1975. 159 p. ; 18 cm. [BV600.2.G43] 75-17160 ISBN 0-8307-0398-5 : 1.65
1. Church. 2. Love (Theology) 3. Hope. 4. Faith. I. Title.

GETZ, Gene A. 260
The measure of a church / by Gene A. Getz. Glendale, Calif. : G/L Regal Books, c1975. 159 p. ; 18 cm. [BV600.2.G43] 75-17160 ISBN 0-8307-0398-5 pbk. : 1.65
1. Church. 2. Love (Theology) 3. Hope. 4. Faith. I. Title.

GETZ, Gene A. 260
Sharpening the focus of the church, by Gene A. Getz. Introd. by George W. Peters. Chicago, Moody Press [1974] 320 p. 24 cm. Bibliography: p. 317. [BV600.2.G44] 74-162924 ISBN 0-8024-7901-4 5.95
1. Church. 2. Theology, Practical. I. Title.

GILKEY, Langdon Brown, 1919- 260
How the church can minister to the world without losing itself. New York, Harper [c.1964] viii, 151p. 21cm. 64-14378 3.75
1. Christianity—20th cent. 2. Church. I. Title.

GILLIOM, James O. 260
Sent on a mission; a resource and discussion book for youth, by James O. Gilliom. Illustrated by Carol Bachenheimer. Boston, United Church Press [1968] 76 p. illus. 22 cm. (Confirmation education series) "Part of the United Church curriculum, prepared and published by the Division of Christian Education and the Division of Publication of the United Church Board for Homeland Ministries." [BX9884.A3G54] 68-10035
1. Mission of the church. 2. Religious education—Text-books for young people—United Church of Christ. I. United Church Board for Homeland Ministries. Division of Christian Education. II. United Church Board for Homeland Ministries. Division of Publication. III. Title.

GOD, man and church growth. 260
Edited by A. R. Tippett. Grand Rapids, Eerdmans [1973] xii, 447 p. port. 22 cm. "A festschrift in honor of Donald Anderson McGarran." Includes bibliographies. [BV652.25.G63] 72-91125 ISBN 0-8028-3424-8 7.95
1. McGarran, Donald Anderson, 1897- 2. Church growth—Addresses, essays, lectures. 3. Missions—Addresses, essays, lectures. I. McGarran, Donald Anderson, 1897- II. Tippett, Alan Richard, ed.

GOODMAN, Grace Ann. 260
Rocking the ark; nine case studies of traditional churches in process of change with a foreword by Robert A. Raines. [New York] Division of Evangelism, United Presbyterian Church in the U.S.A. [1968] 214 p. 23 cm. [BV600.2.G6] 73-1367 1.95
1. Church renewal—Case studies. I. United Presbyterian Church in the U.S.A. Division of Evangelism. II. Title.

GOTTWALD, Norman Karol, 1926- 260
The church unbound; a human church in a human world, by Norman K. Gottwald. [1st ed.] Philadelphia, Lippincott [1967] 188p. 21cm. Bibl. [BR115.W6G68] 67-14365 4.95 bds.,
1. Church and the world. 2. Christianity and culture. I. Title.

GOTTWALD, Norman Karol, 1926- 260
The church unbound; a human church in a human world, by Norman K. Gottwald. [1st ed.] Philadelphia, Lippincott [1967] 188 p. 21 cm. Includes bibliographies. [BR115.W6G68] 67-14365
1. Church and the world. 2. Christianity and culture. I. Title.

GREELEY, Andrew M., 1928- 260
A future to hope in; socio-religious speculations [by] Andrew M. Greeley. [1st ed.] Garden City, N.Y., Doubleday, 1969. 286 p. 22 cm. Bibliographical footnotes. [BR121.2.G695] 69-10968 5.95
1. Christianity—20th century. I. Title.

*GRIMES. HOWARD 260
The church and my life; a course for junior high youth in vacation church schools. youth week programs, and other settings [2v] Nashville, Pub. for the Cooperative Pubn. Assn. by Abingdon [c.1965] 2v. (128; 48p.) illus. 23cm. 1.25, 40 pap., teacher's ed., pupil's ed.,
I. Title.

GUSTAFSON, James M. 260
Treasure in earthen vessel; the church as a human community. New York, Harper [c.1961] 141p. Bibl. 61-12827 3.50 bds.,
1. Church. I. Title.

GUSTAFSON, James M 260
Treasure in earthen vessels; the church as a human community. [1st ed.] New York, Harper [1961] 141p. 22cm. [BV600.G85] 61-12827
1. Church. I. Title.

HALVERSON, Richard C. 260
Relevance; the role of Christianity in the twentieth century, by Richard C. Halverson. Waco, Tax., Word Books [1968] 102 p. 22 cm. [BR121.2.H32] 68-31111 2.95
1. Christianity—20th century. I. Title.

HALVORSON, Loren E 1927- 260
Exodus into the world [by] Loren E. Halvorson. Minneapolis, Augsburg Pub. House [1966] Viii, 115 p. 20 cm. (A Tower book) Includes bibliographical references. [BR123.H26] 66-13050
1. Christianity—20th cent.—Addresses, essays, lectures. I. Title.

HALVORSON, Loren E., 1927- 260
Exodus into the world. Minneapolis, Augsburg [c.1966] viii, 115p. 20cm. (Tower bk.) Bibl. [BR123.H26] 66-13050 1.50 pap.,
1. Christianity—20th cent.—Addresses, essays, lectures. I. Title.

HANDY, Robert T. 260
Members one of another; studies in the nature of the church as it relates to evangelism [Valley Forge, Pa.] Judson [1964, c.1959] 114p. 19cm. Bibl. 59-14337 1.50 pap.,
1. Church. 2. Evangelistic work. I. Title.

HANSON, James H 260
What is the church? Its nature and function. Minneapolis, Augsburg Pub. House [1961] 183p. 20cm. [BV600.2.H33] 61-13882
1. Church. I. Title.

HANSON, James H. 260
What is the church? its nature and function. Minneapolis, Augsburg [c.1961] 133p. 1.25 pap.,
1. Church, Christian. 2. Ministry. I. Title.

HANSSLER, Bernhard 260
The Church and God's people. Tr. by Gregory Roettger. Helicon [dist. New York, Taplinger, 1964, c.1963] 182p. 23cm. Bibl. 63-19408 4.50
1. Church. I. Title.

HARRISON, Ernest Wilfrid. 260
A church without God [by] Ernest Harrison. Philadelphia, Lippincott, 1967. 149 p. 21 cm. [BR121.2.H34] 67-20437
1. Christianity—20th century. I. Title.

HARRISON, Ernest Wilfrid. 260
Let God go free, by Ernest Harrison. New York, Seabury Press [1965] 78 p. 21 cm. [BR123.H34] 65-21847
1. Christianity — 20th cent. — Addresses, essays, lectures. I. Title.

HARRISON, Ernest Wilfrid 260
Let God go free, by Ernest Harrison. New York, Seabury [c.1965] 78p. 21cm. [BR123.H34] 65-21847 1.50 pap.,
1. Christianity—20th cent.—Addresses, essays, lectures. I. Title.

HASELDEN, Kyle. 260
Flux and fidelity. Richmond, John Knox Press [1968] 79 p. 21 cm. [BR121.2.H35] 68-13667
1. Christianity—20th century. I. Title.

HASTINGS, Adrian. 260
The faces of God : reflections on church and society / Adrian Hastings. Maryknoll, N.Y. : Orbis Books, 1976, c1975. viii, 156 p. ; 21 cm. [BX1756.H345F3 1976] 76-4575 ISBN 0-88344-128-4 pbk. : 4.95
1. Catholic Church—Doctrinal and controversial works—Catholic authors. 2. Christianity—20th century—Addresses, essays, lectures. I. Title.

HASTINGS, Adrian 260
One and apostolic. New York, Sheed [1964, c.1963] xiv, 200p. 22cm. Bibl. 64-13568 4.50
1. Church—Marks. I. Title.

HEADLEY, John M 260
Luther's view of church history. New Haven, Yale University Press, 1963. xvi, 301 p. 23 cm. (Yale publications in religion, 6) "First presented as a doctoral dissertation in the Department of History, Yale University." Bibliography: p. [272]-283. [BR333.5.C5H4] 63-7935
1. Luther, Martin, 1483-1546. 2. Church — History of doctrines. I. Title. II. Series.

HEADLEY, John M. 260
Luther's view of church history. New Haven, Conn., Yale [c.]1963. xvi, 301p. 23cm. (Yale pubns. in religion, 6) Bibl. 63-7935 6.75
1. Luther, Martin, 1483-1546. 2. Church—History of Doctrines. I. Title. II. Series.

HENNESSY, Nancy. 260
Decision; church, teacher's introduction with idea-lines [by] Nancy Hennessy and Carol White. [New York] Herder and Herder [1970] 95 p. 21 cm. [BX930.H42] 75-87756 1.95
1. Religious education—Text-books—Catholic. I. White, Carol, joint author. II. Title.

HENRY, Carl Ferdinand Howard, 260
1913-
The God who shows himself by Carl F. H. Henry. Waco, Tex., Word Books [1966] 138 p. 22 cm. [BR121.1.H396] 66-3918
1. Christianity — 20th cent. — Addresses, essays, lectures. I. Title.

HENRY, Carl Ferdinand Howard, 260
1913-
The God who shows himself. Waco, Tex., Word Bks. [c.1966] 138p. 22cm. [BR121.2.H36] 66-3918 3.50
1. Christianity—20th cent.—Addresses, essays, lectures. I. Title.

HINSON, E. Glenn. 260
The church: design for survival [by] E. Glenn Hinson. Nashville, Broadman Press [1967] 128 p. 21 cm. Bibliographical references included in "Notes" (p. 127-128) [BV600.2.H5] 67-22028
1. Church. 2. Christianity—20th century. I. Title.

HOEKENDIJK, Hans. 260
Horizons of hope. Nashville, Tidings [1970] 47 p. 19 cm. Lecture delivered at the Candler School of Theology, Emory University, Atlanta, Georgia, Jan. 1970. Includes bibliographical references. [BV3795.H59] 74-122512 1.00
1. Evangelistic work—Addresses, essays, lectures. I. Title.

HOEKENDIJK, Johannes 260
Christiaan
The church inside out. Ed. by L. A. Hoedemaker, Pieter Tijmes. Tr. [from Dutch] by Isaac C. Rottenberg. Philadelphia, Westminster [c.1964, 1966] 212p. 19cm. (Adventures in faith) Bibl. [BV600.2.H5713] 66-10600 1.95 pap.,
1. Church—Addresses, essays, lectures. 2. Christianity—20th cent.—Addresses, essays, lectures. I. Title.

HOMRIGHAUSEN, Elmer George, 260
1900-
I believe in the church. New York, Abingdon Press [1959] 108p. 20cm. [BV600.2.H6] 59-7247
1. Church. I. Title.

HOOKER, Thomas, 1586-1647. 260
A survey of the summe of church-discipline / Thomas Hooker. New York : Arno Press, 1972. 493 p. in various pagings ; 24 cm. (Research library of colonial Americana) Reprint of the 1648 ed. printed by A. M. for J. Bellamy, London. [BV649.H93 1972] 78-141113 ISBN 0-405-03326-5 : 30.00
1. Church polity. 2. Church discipline. 3. Congregational churches in New England. I. Title. II. Series.

HOUGH, Lynn Harold, 1877- 260
The living church. St. Louis, Bethany Press [1959] 125p. 21cm. [BV600.2.H65] 59-10368
1. Church. 2. Christianity—20th cent. I. Title.

HOWARD, David M. 260
The great commission for today / David M. Howard. Downers Grove, Ill. : InterVarsity Press, c1976. 112 p. ; 21 cm. Includes bibliographical references. [BV2074.H68] 76-12302 ISBN 0-87784-646-4 pbk. : 1.95
1. Great Commission (Bible) I. Title.

HOWLETT, Duncan. 260
Man against the church; the struggle to free man's religious spirit. Boston, Beacon Press [1954] 247p. 22cm. [BV640.H68] 54-8423
1. Church. 2. Liberalism (Religion) I. Title.

HUDNUT, Robert K. 260
Church growth is not the point / Robert K. Hudnut. 1st ed. New York : Harper & Row, [1975] xi, 143 p. ; 21 cm. Includes bibliographical references. [BR121.2.H77 1975] 74-25692 ISBN 0-06-064062-6 : 7.95
1. Christianity—20th century. 2. Church membership. 3. Christian life—Presbyterian authors. I. Title.

HUNT, George Laird. 260
Rediscovering the church. New York, Association Press [1956] 178p. 21cm. [BV600.H78] 56-5030
1. Chruch. I. Title.

HUS, Jan, 1369?-1415. 260
The church, by John Huss. Translated, with notes and introd. by David S. Schaff. Westport, Conn., Greenwood Press [1974, c1915] xlvi, 304 p. 22 cm. Translation of De ecclesia. Reprint of the ed. published by Scribner, New York. Includes bibliographical references. [BV600.A2H95 1974] 72-109752 ISBN 0-8371-4242-3 13.00
1. Church. I. Title.

ILLANES, Jose Luis, 1933- 260
On the theology of work; translated [from the Spanish] by Michael Adams. 2nd ed. Dublin, Chicago, Scepter Books, 1968. 3-72 p. 22 cm. Translation of La santificacion del trabajo: tema de nuestro tiempo. Bibliographical references included in "Notes" (p. 64-72) [BT738.5.I413 1968] 74-362339 8/6
1. Work (Theology) I. Title.

INGWALSON, Kenneth W. 260
Your church, their target; what's going on in the Protestant churches, a symposium by Harry R. Butman [others] Comp. by Kenneth W. Ingwalson. Arlington, Va., Better Bks. [1966] 275p. ports. 21cm. Bibl. [BR515.I46] 66-17578 4.50; 3.00 bds., pap.,
1. Protestant churches—U. S.—Addresses, essays, lectures. I. Butman, Harry R. II. Title.

INRIG, Gary. 260
Life in His body : discovering purpose, form, and freedom in His church / Gary Inrig. Wheaton, Ill. : H. Shaw Publishers, c1975. 182 p. ; 21 cm. Bibliography: p. [178]-182. [BV597.I57] 76-358946 ISBN 0-87788-500-1
1. Church—Biblical teaching. I. Title.

JENKINS, Daniel Thomas, 1914- 260
Beyond religion; the truth and error in 'religionless Christianity.' Philadelphia, Westminster [c.1962] 128p. 20cm. 62-14175 2.75
1. Church. 2. Christianity—20th cent. 3. Liberalism (Religion) I. Title. II. Title: Religionless Christianity.

JONES, Mary Alice, 1898- j260
God's church is everywhere. With illus. by Bernard Case. New York, Friendship Press [1965] 61 p. illus. (part col.) 23 cm. [BV602.5.J6] 65-11438
1. Church—Juvenile literature. I. Case, Bernard, illus. II. Title.

JONES, Mary Alice, 1898- 260
God's church is everywhere. Illus. by Bernard Case. New York, Friendship [c.1965] 61 p. illus. (pt. col.) 23cm. [BV602.5.J6] 65-11438 2.75; 1.75 bds., pap.,
1. Church—Juvenile literature. I. Case, Bernard, illus. II. Title.

JUBILEE : 260
a study resource for the bicentennial / contributors, Walter Rauschenbusch ... [et al.] ; study guide, Mark Matheny. Nashville : Upper Room, c1976. x, 101 p. ; 20 cm. Bibliography: p. 100-101. [BR50.J8] 75-39964 2.50
1. Theology—Addresses, essays, lectures. I. Rauschenbusch, Walter, 1861-1918.
Contents omitted.

JUD, Gerald John 260
Pilgrim's process; how the local church can respond to the new age [by] Gerald J. Jud. Philadelphia, United Church Pr. [1967] 127p. illus. 22cm. Bibl. [BV700.J8] 67-21651 2.95; 1.95 pap.,
1. Church. 2. Chritianity—20th cent. 3. Parishes. I. Title.

JUD, Gerald John. 260
Pilgrim's process: how the local church can respond to the new age [by] Gerald J. Jud. Philadelphia, United Church Press [1967] 127 p. illus. 22 cm. Bibliographical references included in "Notes" (p. 125-127) [BV700.J8] 67-21651
1. Church. 2. Christianity — 20th cent. 3. Parishes. I. Title.

KEUCHER, William F. 260
An exodus for the church [by] William F. Keucher. Valley Forge, Pa., Judson Press [1973] 126 p. 22 cm. Cover title: An exodus for the church; from yesterday to tomorrow. Includes bibliographical references [BR121.2K47] 72-7591 ISBN 0-8170-0508-0 2.50 (pbk.)
1. Christianity—20th century. I. Title.

KIERKEGAARD, Soren Aabye, 260
1813-1855
Kierkegaard's attack upon "Christendom," 1854-1855; tr. with an introduction, by Walter Lowrie. Princeton, N.J., Princeton Univ. Pr. [1968, c.1944] xviii, 303p. 21cm. Bibl. [BR85.K456] A45 2.95 pap.,
1. Christianity—19th cent. I. Lowrie, Walter, 1868- tr. II. Title.
Contents Omitted.

KILBOURN, William, ed. 260
The restless church; a response to The comfortable pew. Philadelphia, Lippincott [c.1966] 145p. 21cm. Bibl. [BR123.K5] 66-18678 3.50; 1.95 pap.,
1. Christianity—20th cent.—Addresses, essays, lectures. I. Berton, Pierre, 1920- The comfortable pew. II. Title.

KIRK, Albert Emmanuel, 1880- 260
It can happen in the church. Philadelphia, Dorrance [1951] 199 p. 20 cm. [BV600.K54] 51-7102
1. Church. I. Title.

KROMMINGA, John H., 1918- 260
All one body we; the doctrine of the church in ecumenical perspective, by John H. Kromminga. Grand Rapids, Eerdmans [1970] 227 p. 22 cm. Bibliography: p. 215-222. [BV598.K77] 76-120844 3.95
1. World Council of Churches. 2. Church—History of doctrines—20th century. I. Title.

KRUITHOF, Bastian. 260
Man in God's milieu. Grand Rapids, Baker Book House [1968] 144 p. 20 cm. Includes bibliographies. [BR115.C8K67] 68-19211
1. Christianity and culture. 2. Christianity—20th century. I. Title.

LATOURETTE, Kenneth Scott, 260
1884-1968, ed.
The Gospel, the church and the world. Freeport, N.Y., Books for Library Press [1970, c1946] xvi, 229 p. 23 cm. (Essay index reprint series) "Originally published as Volume III of the Interseminary series." Includes bibliographies. [BV600.L345 1970] 76-134107 ISBN 0-8369-1972-6
1. Church—Addresses, essays, lectures. 2. Christianity—Essence, genius, nature—Addresses, essays, lectures. 3. Sociology, Christian—Addresses, essays, lectures. I. Title.

LECKY, Robert S. 260
Can these bones live? The failure of church renewal [by] Robert S. Lecky and H. Elliot Wright. With a foreword by Rosemary Ruether. New York, Sheed and Ward [1969] xviii, 201 p. 22 cm. Includes bibliographical references. [BV600.2.L38] 71-82602 5.50
1. Church renewal. I. Wright, H. Elliott, 1937- joint author. II. Title.

LEE, G. Avery. 260
What's right with the church? [by] G. Avery Lee. Nashville, Broadman Press [1967] 128 p. 20 cm. Includes bibliographies. [BV600.2.L4] 67-12173
1. Church. I. Title.

LEEUWEN, Arend Theodoor van, 260
1918-
Prophecy in a technocratic era. With foreword by Harvey G. Cox. New York, Scribner [1968] 130 p. 23 cm. [BR115.W6L4] 68-12509
1. Church and the world. 2. Sociology, Christian. 3. Technocracy. I. Title.

LIGGETT, Thomas J. 260
Where tomorrow struggles to be born; the Americas in transition [by] Thomas J. Liggett. New York, Friendship Press [1970] 160 p. 18 cm. [HN39.L3L53] 70-102949
1. Church and social problems—Latin America. 2. Latin America—Social conditions—1945- I. Title.

LONG, Robert W., 1935- ed. 260
Renewing the congregation, edited by Robert

W. Long. Minneapolis, Augsburg Pub. House [1966] ix, 213 p. illus. 22 cm. Bibliography: p. 209-213. [BV625.L6] 66-22567
1. Sociology, Christian. 2. Pastoral theology. I. Title.

LUECKE, Richard, 1923- 260
New meanings for new beings. Philadelphia, Fortress Press [1964] xvii, 267 p. 22 cm. Bibliographical references included in "Notes" (p. 255-267) [BR123.L8] 64-12992
1. Christianity — 20th cent. — Addresses, essays, lectures. I. Title.

LUECKE, Richard, 1923- 260
New meanings for new beings. Philadelphia, Fortress [c.1964] xvii, 267p. 22cm. Bibl. 64-12992 3.50
1. Christianity—20th cent.—Addresses, essays, lectures. I. Title.

LYONS, Bernard. 260
Voices from the back pew; Catholics and former Catholics talk of their experiences and understandings of the Church. New York, Bruce Pub. Co. [1970] 174 p. 21 cm. [BX1746.L96] 74-123142
1. Church renewal—Catholic Church. 2. Christian life—1960- I. Title.

MCBRIEN, Richard P. 260
Church: the continuing quest, by Richard P. McBrien. Paramus, N.J., Newman Press [1970] v, 85 p. 21 cm. Includes bibliographical references. [BV598.M29] 70-118700 1.95
1. Church—History of doctrines—20th century. I. Title.

MACGREGOR, Geddes. 260
Corpus Christi; the nature of the church according to the Reformed tradition. Philadelphia, Westminster Press [c1958] 302p. 24cm. Includes bibliography. [BV600.2.M3] 59-5514
1. Church. 2. Church—History of doctrines. 3. Jesus Christ—Mystical body. 4. Reformed Church—Doctrinal and controversial works. I. Title.

MACKAY, John Alexander, 1889- 260
Ecumenics; the science of the church universal [by] John A. Mackay. Englewood Cliffs, N.J., Prentice [1965, c.1964] ix, 294p. 24cm. Bibl. [BV600.2.M33] 64-22800 5.95
1. Church. I. Title.

MACKENZIE, Ross, 1927- 260
Trying new sandals. Atlanta, John Knox Press [1974] 118 p. illus. 21 cm. Includes bibliographical references. [BV600.2.M34] 73-5348 ISBN 0-8042-1509-X 4.95
1. Church. 2. Christianity—20th century. I. Title.

MCNEIL, Jesse Jai 260
Mission in metropolis. Grand Rapids, Mich., Eerdmans [c.1965] 148p. 23cm. Bibl. [BV637.M25] 65-6164 3.50
1. City churches. I. Title.

MARTIN, Noah S. 260
Beyond renewal / Noah S. Martin ; introd. by Dale W. Brown. Scottdale, Pa. : Herald Press, c1976. 211 p. ; 18 cm. Includes bibliographical references and index. [BV600.2.M347] 75-36675 1.95
1. Church. 2. Christianity—20th century. I. Title.

MARTY, Martin E. 1928- 260
Babylon by choice; new environment for mission, New York, Friendship [1965] 63p. 19cm. [BV637.M3] 65-11422 .75 pap.,
1. City churches. I. Title.

MARTY, Martin E., 1928- 260
The search for a usable future, by Martin E. Marty. [1st ed.] New York, Harper & Row [1968, c1969] 157 p. 21 cm. Bibliographical references included in "Notes" (p. 147-151) [BR121.2.M35] 69-10473 4.95
1. Christianity—20th century. I. Title.

MEYER, Ben F., 1927- 260
The church in three tenses [by] Ben F. Meyer. [1st ed.] Garden City, N.Y., Doubleday, 1971. xii, 174 p. 22 cm. Includes bibliographical references. [BV600.2.M49] 70-131097 5.95
1. Church. I. Title.

MILLER, Samuel Howard, 1900- 260
The life of the church. [1st ed.] New York, Harper [1953] 154p. 20cm. [BV600.M52] 52-12776
1. Church. 2. Christianity—Essence, genius, nature. I. Title.

MINEAR, Paul Sevier, 1906- 260
Horizons of Christian community. St. Louis, Bethany Press [1959] 127p. 20cm. (Hoover lectues [1957]) [BV600.M53] 59-10103
1. Church. I. Title.

MOL, J. J. 260
The breaking of traditions: theological convictions in colonial America [by] J. J. Mol. Berkeley, Glendessary Press [1968] 94 p. 21 cm. Bibliography: p. 73-78. [BL60.M6] 68-25005
1. Religion and sociology. 2. Assimilation (Sociology) 3. United States—Church history—Colonial period, ca. 1600-1775. I. Title.

MOLTMANN, Jurgen. 260
The passion for life : a messianic lifestyle / by Jurgen Moltmann ; translated with an introd. by M. Douglas Meeks. Philadelphia : Fortress Press, c1977. p. cm. A freely adapted translation of Neuer Lebensstil: Schritte zur Gemeinde. [BV603.M43 1977] 77-78636 ISBN 0-8006-0508-X : 5.95
1. Church—Addresses, essays, lectures. 2. Christian life—1960- —Addresses, essays, lectures. I. Meeks, M. Douglas. II. Title.

MONTAGUE, George T. 260
The Biblical theology of the secular [by] George T. Montague. Milwaukee, Bruce Pub. Co. [1968] viii, 90 p. 23 cm. (Impact books) "Essays were originally written as lectures for the Chicago Biblical Institute in ... 1967." Bibliographical footnotes. [BR115.W6M6] 68-14112
1. Church and the world—Biblical teaching. I. Title.

MONTCHEUIL, Yves de. 260
Aspects of the church; translated by Albert J. La Mothe, Jr. Chicago, Fides Publishers Association [1955] 197p. 21cm. [BX1751.M594] 55-11503
1. Church. 2. Catholic Church. I. Title.

MONTGOMERY, John Warwick. 260
Damned through the church. Minneapolis, Bethany Fellowship [1970] 96 p. 22 cm. Four lectures delivered at the Elim Lodge Retreat of the Evangelical Lutheran Synod of Eastern Canada, Sept. 7-9, 1962. [BV603.M64] 71-13809 2.95
1. Church—Addresses, essays, lectures. I. Title.

MONTGOMERY, John Warwick. 260
Damned through the church. Minneapolis, Minn., Bethany Fellowship [1973, c.1970] 96 p. 18 cm. (Dimension Books) Four lectures delivered at the Elim Lodge Retreat of the Evangelical Lutheran Synod of Eastern Canada, Sept. 7-9, 1962. [BV603.M64] 71-13808 ISBN 0-8712-3090-9 0.95 (pbk.)
1. Church—Addresses, essays, lectures. I. Title.

MORRIS, Danny E. 260
How to tell a church (as in recognize) / Danny E. Morris. Nashville : Tidings, c1975. xiv, 139 p. ; 19 cm. [BV600.2.M66] 74-84316
1. Church. 2. Christian life—Methodist authors. I. Title.

MORTON, Thomas Ralph. 260
Community of faith; the changing pattern of the church's life. With chapters by Alexander Miller and John Oliver Nelson. New York, Association Press [1954] 153p. 20cm. 'A Haddam House book.' First published in Glasgow, 1951, under title: The household of faith. [BV600.M63 1954] 54-12573
1. Church. 2. Sociology, Christian. 3. Christianity and economics. I. Title.

MORTON, Thomas Ralph. 260
The household of faith; an essay on the changing pattern of the church's life. Glasgow, Iona Community [1951] 131p. 19cm. [BV600.M63] 52-19919
1. Church. 2. Sociology, Christian. 3. Christianity and economics. I. Title.

MULLER, Gladys (Blanchard) 260
I seen him when he does it; a handbook on Christian etiquette, by Gladys Blanchard Muller and Dorothy Blanchard Bennett. Wheaton, Ill., Van Kampen Press [1951] 70 p. illus. 20 cm. [BJ2019.M8] 51-9888
1. Church etiquette. I. Bennett, Dorothy (Blanchard) joint author. II. Title.

MYERS, Richard A 260
Cooperative church extension planning. [Chicago;]1959. 64 l. illus. 28cm. [BR555.I3M9] 59-44934
1. Churches— Location. 2. Cities and towns—Planning—Illinois. I. Title.

NATIONAL Catholic Welfare 260
Conference. Press Dept.
Council day book: Vatican II, session 3. Ed. by Floyd Anderson, director. Washington, D. C., Author, 1312 Mass. Ave. N.W., [c.1965] xv, 368p. illus., group ports. 28cm. Record of press releases at the time the Council was in session. Bibl. [BX830.1962.N3] 65-17303 5.00 pap.,
1. Vatican Council, 2d. I. Anderson, Floyd, 1906- ed. II. Title.

NATIONAL Catholic Welfare 260
Conference. Press Dept.
Council daybook: Vatican II, session 4, Sept. 14, 1965 to Dec. 8, 1965. Ed. by Floyd Anderson. Washington, D. C., Author [c.1966] xiii, 454p. illus., group ports. 28cm. A record of press releases at the time the Council was in session. Bibl. [BX830.N3] 65-17303 7.50 pap.,
1. Vatican Council, 2d. I. Anderson, Floyd, ed. II. Title.

NEBREDA, Alfonso M 260
Kerygma in crisis [By] Alfonso M. Nebreda. Chicago, Loyola University Press, 1965. xi, 140 p. 24 cm. (Loyola pastoral series) Bibliographical footnotes. [BV4317.N4] 65-14911
1. Communication (Theology) 2. Kerygma. I. Title.

NEBREDA, Alfonso M. 260
Kerygma in crists? Chicago, Loyola Univ. Pr. [c.] 1965. xi, 140p. 24cm. (Loyola pastoral ser.) Bibl. [BV4317.N4] 65-14911 3.50
1. Kerygma. 2. Communication (Theology) I. Title.

NEEDS of the church to-day 260
(The): a course of sermons preached during the Michaelmas term, 1964, in the chapel of Pusey House, Oxford. London. A. R. Mowbray; New York, Morehouse [1966] ix, 55p. 19cm. (Pusey House sermons) Bibl. [BV603.N4] 66-3417 1.50
1. Church—Sermons. 2. Sermons, English. I. Pusey House, Oxford. II. Series.

NELSON, Carl Ellis, 1916- 260
Where faith begins [by] C. Ellis Nelson. Richmond, John Knox Press [1967] 231 p. 21 cm. (The James Sprunt lectures, 1965) Bibliographical references included in "Notes and acknowledgments" (p. [212]-222) [BV1471.2.N4] 67-22004
1. Communication (Theology) 2. Religious education. I. Title. II. Series.

NELSON, John Robert, 1920- 260
Criterion for the church. Nashville, Abingdon [1963] 144p. 21cm. 63-23791 3.00
1. Christianity—20th cent. I. Title.

NEWBIGIN, James Edward 260
Leslie, Bp.
A faith for this one world? New York, Harper [c1961] 128 p. 20 cm. [BT60] 61-7346
1. Christianity — Essence, genius, nature. 2. Christianity and other religions. 3. Missions — Theory. I. Title.

NEWBIGIN, James Edward 260
Lesslie, Bp.
A faith for this one world? New York, Harper & Row [1962, c.1961] 128p. 20cm. 61-7346 2.75 bds.,
1. Christianity—Essence, genius, nature. 2. Christianity and other religions. 3. Missions—Theory. I. Title.

NYGREN, Anders, Bp., 1890- 260
ed.
This is the church; edited by Anders Nygren with Gustaf Aulen [and others] Translated by Carl C. Rasmussen. Philadelphia, Muhlenberg Press [1952] 353 p. 22 cm. "Translated from en bok om kyrkan, av svenska teologer." [BV600.A1B63] 52-10140
1. Church. I. Title.

O'DEA, Thomas F. 260
Alienation, atheism, and the religious crisis [by] Thomas F. O'Dea. New York, Sheed and Ward [1969] 189 p. 21 cm. Includes bibliographies. [BR121.2.O3] 69-19254 4.95
1. Christianity—20th century. 2. Man (Theology) I. Title.

*OSTWALT, Adeline Hill 260
The church is for all people. Illus. by William Steinel. Richmond, Va., CLC Pr. [dist. Knox, 1966, c.1965] 64p. illus. (pt. col.) 21cm. (Coyenant life curriculum., elem.; the Church year, 1, 43-9432) 1.25 pap.,
I. Title.

OURSLER, William Charles, 260
1913-
Protestant power and the coming revolution [by] Will Oursler. [1st ed.] Garden City, N.Y., Doubleday, 1971. xi, 203 p. 22 cm. [BX4805.2.O9] 78-131099 5.95
1. Protestantism—20th century. I. Title.

OURSLER, William Charles, 260
1913-
Religion: out or way out [by] Will Oursler. [Harrisburg, Pa.] Stackpole Books [1968] 147 p. 24 cm. "A Giniger book." Bibliographical footnotes. [BR121.2.O9] 68-9131 5.95
1. Christianity—20th century. I. Title.

OVERHOLSER, James A. 260
A contemporary Christian philosophy of religion. Chicago, Regnery [1965,c.1964] ix, 214p. 22cm. Bibl. [BR479.O9] 64-66120 5.95
1. Christianity—20th cent. I. Title.

PAULUS VI Pope, 1897- 260
The Church, light of all mankind [by] Pope Paul VI. Compiled by the Daughters of St. Paul. [Texts of the Pope's speeches N.C.W.C. translation. Boston] St. Paul Editions [1967] 152 p. 22 cm. [BX1746.P313] 67-29691
1. Church—Addresses, essays, lectures. I. Daughters of St. Paul. II. Title.

PERSPECTIVES on charismatic 260
renewal / editor, Edward D. O'Connor. Notre Dame, Ind. : University of Notre Dame Press, [1975] p. cm. Includes bibliographical references and index. [BX8762.P47] 75-19875 ISBN 0-268-01516-3 : 9.95 ISBN 0-268-01517-1 pbk. : 3.95
1. Holy Spirit—Addresses, essays, lectures. 2. Pentecostalism—History—Addresses, essays, lectures. 3. Pentecostalism—Bibliography. I. O'Connor, Edward Dennis.

PINSON, William M. 260
Contemporary Christian trends; perspectives on the present. Edited by William M. Pinson, Jr. & Clyde E. Fant, Jr. Waco, Tex., Word Books [1972] 217 p. 23 cm. Includes bibliographical references. [BR123.P53] 71-188069 5.95
1. Christianity—20th century—Addresses, essays, lectures. 2. Theology—20th century—Addresses, essays, lectures. I. Fant, Clyde E., joint author. II. Title.

PITTENGER, Norman. 260
Process-thought and Christian faith. [1st American ed.] New York, Macmillan [1968] xii, 99 p. illus. 21 cm. Bibliography: p. [97]-99. [BR100.P615] 68-8711
1. Christianity—Philosophy. 2. Process theology. I. Title.

PITTENGER, William Norman, 260
1905-
The Church, the ministry, and reunion Greenwich, Conn., Seabury Press, 1957. 147p. 19cm. Includes bibliography. [BV600.P52] 57-5797
1. Church. 2. Clergy—Office. 3. Christian union. I. Title.

PITTENGER, William Norman, 260
1905-
The church, the ministry, and reunion. Greenwich, Conn., Seabury Press, 1957. 147p. 19cm. Includes bibliography [BV600.P52] 57-5797
1. Church. 2. Clergy—Office. 3. Christian union. I. Title.

PONNUTHURAI, C. S., 1909- 260
Being the people of god; a symposium compiled in connection with a resolution on the same subject, at the annual session of the Diocesan Council of the Diocese of Colombo, October 1968. Edited by C. S. Ponnuthurai. [Colombo, Printed at Wesley Press, 1968?] vi, 59 p. 22 cm. [BV603.P6] 70-903624 2.00
1. Church—Addresses, essays, lectures. I. Colombo, Ceylon (Diocese). Diocesan Council. II. Title.

POWELL, Oliver 260
Household of power; the task and testing of the church in our time. Boston, United Church Pr. [c.1962] 114p. 22cm. (Pilgrim Press pubn.) 62-18361 1.45 pap.,
1. Theology, Practical. 2. Christian life. I. Title.

PRESBYTERIAN Church in the 260
U.S.A. Board of Christian Education.
The church in Christian faith and life. [A program for church and home. Philadelphia, 1950] 125 p. 19 cm. [BV602.P7] 50-3935
1. Church — Study and teaching. 2. Religious education. I. Title.

PUSEY House, Oxford. 260
The Needs of the church to-day; a course of sermons preached during the Michaelmas term, 1964, in the chapel of Pusey House, Oxford. London, A. R. Mowbray; New York, Morehouse-Barlow [1966] ix, 55 p. 19 cm. (Pusey house sermons) Bibliographical footnotes. [BV603.N4] 66-3417
1. Church — Sermons. 2. Sermons, English. I. Title. II. Series.

RAHNER, Karl, 1904- 260
The church after the council. New York, Herder and Herder [1966] 106 p. 21 cm. Translation by D. C. Herron and R. Albrecht of the author's Das Konzil: Ein neuer Beginn, Das neue Bild der Kirche, and Die Herausforderung der Theologie durch das II. Vatikanische Konzil. Contents.Contents.—The council: a new beginning.—The church: a new image.—Theology: a new challenge. [BX891.R253 1966] 66-26676
1. Vatican Council. 2d, 1962-1965—Addresses,

essays, lectures. 2. Catholic Church—Addresses, essays, lectures. I. Title.

RAHNER, Karl, 1904- 260
The dynamic element in the church. [Translated by W. J. O'Hara. New York] Herder and Herder [1964] 169 p. 22 cm. (Quaestiones disputatae, 12) Translation of Das Dynamische in der Kirche. Bibliographical footnotes. [BV600.2.R313] 64-16554
1. Church—Addresses, essays, lectures. 2. Spiritual life—Catholic authors. 3. Christian ethics—Catholic authors. I. Title.

RAHNER, Karl, 1904- 260
The dynamic element in the church [Tr. from German by W. J. O'Hara. New York] Herder & Herder [c.1964] 169p. 22cm. (Quaestiones dis-utatae, 12) Bibl. 64-16554 2.75 pap.,
1. Church—Addresses, essays, lectures. 2. Spiritual life—Catholic authors. 3. Christian ethics—Catholic authors. I. Title.

RAINES, Robert Arnold. 260
The secular congregation [by] Robert A. Raines. [1st ed.] New York, Harper & Row [1968] viii, 144 p. 21 cm. Bibliographical references included in "Notes" (p. 133-142) [BR115.W6R25] 68-17584
1. Church and the world—Case studies. I. Title.

*RAMSAY, William M. 260
The church; a believing fellowship, by William M. Ramsay, John H. Leith. Art by M. Milton Hull. Richmond, Va., CLC Pr. [dist. Knox, 1966, c.1965] 224p. col. illus. 24cm. 2.95 pap.,
I. Title.

RANDALL, Claire. 260
Study-action manual on "new forms of mission." New York, Friendship Press [1968] 94 p. music. 19 cm. This guide has been designed for use with Mandate for mission and Ventures in Mission. Includes bibliographical references. [BR115.W6R33] 68-25936
1. Church and the world. I. Madsen, Paul O. Ventures in mission. II. Smith, Eugene Lewis, 1912- Mandate for mission. III. Title. IV. Title: New forms of mission.

RATZINGER, Joseph. 260
The open circle; the meaning of Christian brotherhood. Translated by W. A. Glen-Doeple. New York, Sheed and Ward [1966] 128 p. 21 cm. "Originally published as Die christliche Bruderlichkeit. Kosel-Veriag KG. Munich (1960)." Bibliographical footnotes. [BV4647.B7R323] 66-22023
1. Brotherliness. I. Title.

READ, Ralph Harlow, 1903- ed. 260
The younger churchmen look at the church. Edited by Ralph H. Read. With an introd. by Kirby Page. Freeport, N.Y., Books for Libraries Press [1971] xvi, 345 p. 23 cm. (Essay index reprint series) Reprint of the 1935 ed. "Reference books": p. 335-336. [BV600.R4 1971] 74-156708 ISBN 0-8369-2330-8
1. Church—Addresses, essays, lectures. 2. Sociology, Christian—Addresses, essays, lectures. I. Title.

REALITIES and visions : 260
the church's mission today / edited by Furman C. Stough and Urban T. Holmes III. New York : Seabury Press, c1976. p. cm. "A Crossroad book." Bibliography: p. [BX5935.R4] 76-21086 pbk. : 4.95
1. Protestant Episcopal Church in the U.S.A.—Doctrinal and controversial works—Addresses, essays, lectures. 2. Mission of the church—Addresses, essays, lectures. I. Stough, Furman C., 1928- II. Holmes, Urban Tigner, 1930-

RECONCILIATION in today's 260
world; six study papers [by Donald G. Miller and others] introducing the theme of the uniting general council of the World Alliance of Reformed and Presbyterian Churches and the International Congregational Council, Nairobi, Kenya, August 1970. Grand Rapids, Eerdmans [1969] 122 p. 20 cm. "Prepared ... for the North American Area Theological Committee of the World Alliance of Reformed and Presbyterian Churches, Allen O. Miller, chairman and editor." [BT265.2.R4] 70-95464 1.95
1. Reconciliation—Addresses, essays, lectures. I. Miller, Allen O., ed. II. Miller, Donald G. III. Alliance of Reformed Churches throughout the World Holding the Presbyterian System. North American Area. Theological Committee.

REDEKOP, Calvin Wall, 1925- 260
The church functions with purpose; an essay on church organization, by Calvin Redekop. Scottdale, Pa., Herald Press [1967] 40 p. 20 cm. (Focal pamphlet series, no. 11) (John F. Funk lectures 5) "Footnotes": p. 38-40. [BV603.R38] 67-7077
1. Church. I. Title. II. Series.

REDEKOP, Calvin Wall, 1925- 260
The free church and seductive culture, by Calvin Redekop. Diagrams by Ivan Moon. Scottdale, Pa., Herald Press [1970] 189 p. port. 20 cm. Includes bibliographical references. [BT738.R39] 78-114844
1. Sociology, Christian. 2. Dissenters, Religious. I. Title.

RELIGIOUS progress on the 260
Pacific slope; addresses and papers at the celebration of the semi-centennial anniversary of Pacific School of Religion, Berkeley, California. Freeport, N.Y., Books for Libraries Press [1968] vi, 326 p. ports. 22 cm. Reprint of the 1917 ed. [BR550.R4 1968] 68-22941
1. Christianity—Addresses, essays, lectures. I. Berkeley, Calif. Pacific School of Religion.

RHOADES, Donald H 260
A faith for fellowship, by Donald H. Rhoades. Philadelphia, Westminster Press [1965] 139 p. 21 cm. Bibliography: p. [135]-139. [BV820.R5] 65-10348
1. Church membership. I. Title.

*RICHARDS, H. F. 260
The church for our time: the kind of church needed for today's world. New York, Vantage [c.1964] 112p. 21cm. 2.75 bds.,
I. Title.

RICHARDS, Lawrence O. 260
A new face for the church [by] Lawrence O. Richards. Grand Rapids, Mich., Zondervan Pub. House [1970] 288 p. illus. 23 cm. Bibliography: p. 283-285. [BR121.2.R48] 78-120038 5.95
1. Christianity—20th century. 2. Church—Biblical teaching. I. Title.

RIGA, Peter J. 260
The church and revolution; some reflections on the relationship of the church to the modern world, by Peter J. Riga. Milwaukee, Bruce Pub. Co. [1967] vii, 195 p. 22 cm. [BR115.W6R55] 67-28887
1. Church and the world. I. Title.

RIPLINGER, Thomas. 260
An American vision of the church : the church in American protestant theology, 1937-1967 / Thomas Riplinger. Frankfurt/M. : Peter Lang, 1976. [iv], vi, 320 p. ; 21 cm. (European university papers : Series 23, Theology ; v. 76) Bibliography: p. [302]-320. [BV598.R5] 77-361315 ISBN 3-261-02093-8 : 52.00F
1. Church—History of doctrines—20th century. 2. Theology, Protestant—North America. I. Title. II. Series: Europaische Hochschulschriften : Reihe 23, Theologie ; Bd. 76.

ROBINSON, John Arthur Thomas, 260
Bp., 1919-
The new Reformation? By John A. T. Robinson. Philadelphia, Westminster Press [1965] 142 p. 19 cm. An expanded and revised version of the author's lectures given in May 1964 as the Purdy lectures at Hartford Seminary, Connecticut, and as the Thorp lectures at Cornell University. Bibliographical footnotes. [BT55.R62] 65-17645
1. Christianity—20th century—Addresses, essays, lectures. 2. Christianity—Essence, genius, nature. I. Title.

ROYCE, Josiah, 1855-1916. 260
The problem of Christianity. With a new introd. by John E. Smith. Chicago, University of Chicago Press [1968] v, 412 p. 24 cm. Reprint of the 1913 ed. Contents.Contents.—The Christian doctrine of life.—The real world and the Christian ideas. Bibliographical footnotes. [BR121.R67 1968] 68-16716
1. Christianity—Essence, genius, nature. 2. Christianity—Philosophy. I. Title.

ROYCE, Josiah, 1855-1916. 260
The problem of Christianity; lectures delivered at the Lowell Institute in Boston, and at Manchester College, Oxford. [Hamden, Conn.] Archon Books, 1967. 2 v. in 1. 22 cm. Reprint of the 1913 ed. Contents.Contents.—v. 1. The Christian doctrine of life.—v. 2. The real world and the Christian ideas. Bibliographical footnotes. [BR121.R67 1967] 67-22305
1. Christianity—Essence, genius, nature. 2. Christianity—Philosophy. I. Title.

RUETHER, Rosemary Radford. 260
The church against itself; an inquiry into the conditions of historical existence for the eschatological community. [New York] Herder and Herder [1967] 245 p. 21 cm. Bibliography: p. [238]-245. Bibliographical footnotes. [BX1746.R8] 68-12019
1. Church—Addresses, essays, lectures. I. Title.

RUETHER, Rosemary Radford. 260
The church against itself; an inquiry into the conditions of historical existence for the eschatological community. [New York] Herder and Herder [1967] 245 p. 21 cm. Bibliography: p. [238]-245. Bibliographical footnotes. [BX1746.R8 1967b] 68-12019
1. Church—Addresses, essays, lectures. I. Title.

SAVORY, Jerold. 260
Tuned-in Christians. Valley Forge [Pa.] Judson Press [1968] 96 p. 22 cm. Bibliographical footnotes. [BR115.W6S2] 68-22751 1.95
1. Church and the world. 2. Christianity—20th century. I. Title.

SCHALL, James V. 260
Redeeming the time [by] James V. Schall. New York, Sheed and Ward [1968] ix, 244 p. 22 cm. Essays. Includes bibliographical references. [BR115.W6S26] 68-13842
1. Church and the world. I. Title.

SCHALLER, Lyle E. 260
The impact of the future [by] Lyle E. Schaller. Nashville, Abingdon Press [1969] 256 p. 21 cm. Includes bibliographies. [BV601.8.S3] 69-18455 4.75
1. Church renewal. 2. Christianity—20th century. I. Title.

SCHEPERS, Maurice 260
Bonaventure.
The church of Christ. Englewood Cliffs, N.J., Prentice-Hall [1963] 118 p. illus. 24 cm. (Foundations of Catholic theology series) Includes bibliography. [BV600.2.S3] 63-14735
1. Church. I. Title.

SCHEPERS, Maurice Bonaventure 260
The church of Christ. Englewood Cliffs, N. J., Prentice [c.1963] 118p. illus. 24cm. (Founds, of Catholic theology ser.) Bibl. 63-14735 3.95; 1.50 pap.,
1. Church. I. Title.

SCHILLEBEECKX, Edward 260
Cornelis Florentius Alfons, 1914-
God, the future of man, by E. Schillebeeckx. Translated by N. D. Smith. New York, Sheed and Ward [1968] xi, 207 p. 22 cm. Essays. Includes bibliographical references. [BT83.7.S3] 68-26036 4.95
1. Church and the world. 2. Secularization (Theology) I. Title.

SCHWEIZER, Eduard, 1913- 260
The church as the body of Christ. Richmond, John Knox Press [1964] 78 p. 19 cm. (T. V. Moore lectures, 1962) Chime paperbacks. [BV600.5.S3] 64-16282
1. Jesus Christ—Mystical body. I. Title. II. Series: T. V. Moore lectures, San Francisco Theological Seminary, San Anselmo, Calif., 1962

SCHWEIZER, Eduard, 1913 260
The church as the body of Christ. Richmond, Va., Knox [c.1964] 78p. 19cm. (T. V. Moore lectures, 1962; Chime paperbacks) 64-16282 1.00 pap.,
1. Jesus Christ—Mystical body. I. Title. II. Series: T. V. Moore lectures, San Francisco Theological Seminary, San Anselmo, Calif., 1962

SEIFERT, Harvey. 260
Power where the action is. Philadelphia, Westminster Press [1968] 157 p. 19 cm. [BJ1251.S38] 68-19898
1. Christian ethics. 2. Sociology, Christian. I. Title.

SHANDS, Alfred Rives, 1928- 260
The liturgical movement and the local church [by] Alfred R. Shands. [Rev. ed.] New York, Morehouse-Barlow [1965] 159 p. 19 cm. Bibliography: p. [147]-156. [BX5141.S45 1965] 65-6017
1. Liturgical movement—Anglican Communion. I. Title.

SHANDS, Alfred Rives, 1928- 260
The liturgical movement and the local church [Rev. ed.] New York, Morehouse [1965] 159p. 19cm. Bibl. [BX5141.S45] 65-6017 1.95 pap.,
1. Liturgical movement—Anglican Communion. I. Title.

*SHANNON, Robert C. 260
The New Testament church; study course for youth and adults. Cincinnati, Ohio, Standard [c.1964] 112p. 21cm. (Training for serv. ser.) 1.25 pap.,
I. Title.

SHARP, David G. 260
No stained-glass-window saints : the Church in the New Testament and today / [by] David G. Sharp. London : Epworth Press, 1976. 128 p. ; 19 cm. Includes bibliographies. [BS2545.C5S53] 77-359980 ISBN 0-7162-0268-9 : £1.50
1. Church—Biblical teaching. 2. Church history—Primitive and early church, ca. 30-600. 3. Christianity—20th century. I. Title.

SIMMONS, Robert A. 260
O church awake, by Robert A. Simmons. North Quincy, Mass., Christopher Pub. House [1969] 152 p. 21 cm. [BV601.8.S5] 75-78034 3.95
1. Church. 2. Mission of the church. 3. Church and social problems. I. Title.

SKYDSGAARD, Krister E. 260
The Church as the body of Christ [by] K. E. Skydsgaard [and others. Notre Dame, Ind.] University of Notre Dame Press, 1963. xii, 145 p. 22 cm. (The Cardinal O'Hara series: studies and research in Christian theology at Notre Dame, v. 1) Three of the papers were presented at the 1962 Notre Dame Colloquium. Bibliographical footnotes. [BV600.5.C5] 63-13473
1. Jesus Christ — Mystical body. I. Notre Dame Colloquium. 2d. University of Notre Dame, 1962. II. Title. III. Series. IV. Series: The Cardinal O'Hara series, v. 1

SMITH, James Roy. 260
God still speaks in the space age. Kansas City, Mo., Beacon Hill Press [1967] 172 p. 20 cm. Bibliographical references included in "Notes" (p. 171-172) [BR121.2.S6] 67-25725
1. Christianity—20th century. I. Title.

SNYDER, Howard A. 260
The problem of wine skins : church structure in a technological age / Howard A. Snyder. Downers Grove, Ill. : Inter-Varsity Press, [1975] 214 p. ; 21 cm. [BR123.S713] 74-31842 ISBN 0-87784-874-2 : 5.95 ISBN 0-87784-769-X pbk. : 3.95
1. Christianity—20th century—Addresses, essays, lectures. I. Title.

SOMMERFELD, Richard Edwin, 260
1928-
The church of the 21st century: prospects and proposals [by] Richard Sommerfeld. Saint Louis, Concordia Pub. House [1965] 103 p. 21 cm. [BV603.S6] 65-14318
1. Church—Addresses, essays, lectures. I. Title.

SOMMERFELD, Richard Edwin, 260
1928-
The church of the 21st century: prospects and proposals. St. Louis, Concordia [c.1965] 103p. 21cm. [BV603.S6] 65-14318 1.50 pap.,
1. Church—Addresses, essays, lectures. I. Title.

SPONHEIM, Paul R 260
Contemporary forms of faith, by Paul R. Sponheim. Minneapolis, Augsburg Pub. House [1967] 122 p. illus. 20 cm. (A Tower book) Includes bibliographical references. [BT60.S65] 67-25371
1. Christianity—Essence, genius, nature. 2. Religious thought—20th cent. I. Title.

SPONHEIM, Paul R. 260
Contemporary forms of faith, by Paul R. Sponheim. Minneapolis, Augsburg Pub. House [1967] 122 p. illus. 20 cm. (A Tower book) Includes bibliographical references. [BT60.S65] 67-25371
1. Christianity—Essence, genius, nature. 2. Religious thought—20th century. I. Title.

STAHLIN, Wilhelm, Bp., 1883- 260
The mystery of God. Translated from the German by R. Birch Hoyle. St. Louis, Concordia Pub. House [1964] 223 p. 21 cm. (Concordia paperback) [BV600.S725 1964] 64-19432
1. Church. 2. Clergy — Office. 3. Sacraments. 4. Lutheran Church — Doctrinal and controversial works. I. Title.

STAHLIN, Wilhelm, Bp, 1883- 260
The mystery of God. Tr. from German by R. Birch Hoyle. St. Louis, Concordia [c.1964] 223p. 21cm. 64-19432 2.50 pap.,
1. Church. 2. Clergy—Office. 3. Sacraments. 4. Lutheran Church—Doctrinal and controversial works. I. Title.

STAMM, Frederick Keller, 260
1883-
If this be religion— New York, J. Day Co. [1950] x, 116 p. 20 cm. [BR121.S8] 50-10315
1. Christianity—20th century. I. Title.

STAMMLER, Eberhard. 260
Churchless Protestants. Translated by Jack A. Worthington. Philadelphia, Westminster Press [c1964] 223 p. 21 cm. Bibliographical references included in "Notes" (p. 203-223) [BV640.S783] 64-10075
1. Christianity—20th cent. 2. Indifferentism (Religion) I. Title.

STAMMLER, Eberhard 260
Churchless Protestants. Tr. [from German] by Jack A. Worthington. Philadelphia, Westminster [c.1964] 223p. 21cm. Bibl. 64-10075 4.50
1. Christianity—20th cent. 2. Indifferentism (Religion) I. Title.

STAUDERMAN, Albert P 260
Understanding my congregation. Philadelphia, Muhlenberg Press [c1952] 139p. illus. 20cm. Includes bibliography. [BX8065.S8] 52-13636
1. Lutheran Church—Government. 2. Church work. I. Title.

STERNER, R. Eugene. 260
Being the community of Christian love [by] R. Eugene Sterner. Anderson, Ind., Warner Press [1971] 128 p. 19 cm. Includes bibliographical references. [BV600.2.S8] 72-139685 ISBN 0-87162-058-8
1. Church. I. Title.

STROBE, Donald B., 1928- 260
Faith under fire; challenges to the church in a changing world [by] Donald B. Strobe. Waco, Tex., Word Books [1969] 182 p. 22 cm. Includes bibliographical references. [BR121.2.S78] 72-91941 4.50
1. Christianity—20th century. I. Title.

STRUCTURES of the church. 260
Edited by Teodoro Jimenez Urresti. [New York] Herder and Herder [1970] 160 p. 23 cm. (Concilium: theology in the age of renewal, v. 58: Canon law) On cover: The New concilium: religion in the seventies. Includes bibliographical references. [BX1746.S76] 74-129757 2.95
1. Church—Addresses, essays, lectures. 2. Church and the world—Addresses, essays, lectures. I. Jimenez Urresti, Teodoro Ignacio, ed. II. Series: Concilium (New York) v. 58

SUHARD, Emmanuel, Cardinal 260
The church today, Growth or decline? Translated by James J. Corbett [5th ed.] Foreword by John Courtney Murray. Notre Dame, Ind., Fides Publishers [1960, c.1948] 126p. 18cm. (Fides dome bk.) Bibl. notes: p.113-126. .95 pap.,
I. Title.

SUMMERS, Stanford. 260
Secular films and the church's ministry. New York, Seabury Press [1969] 64 p. illus. 28 cm. Includes bibliographical references. [BV1643.S9] 73-19430 1.95
1. Moving-pictures in church work. I. Title.

SUSSMAN, Irving. 260
This train is bound for glory [by] Irving & Cornelia Sussman. Chicago, Franciscan Herald Press [1968, c1969] 174 p. illus. (on lining papers) 21 cm. [BR121.2.S8] 69-13723 4.95
1. Christianity—20th century. 2. Church renewal—Catholic Church. I. Sussman, Cornelia, joint author. II. Title.

TALEC, Pierre 260
Christian presence in the neighborhood. Tr. by Nels Challe. Westminster, Md., Newman [1967] 128p. 22cm. Tr. of Initiation al la mission. Bibl. [BX2347.T313] 67-23601 3.50
1. Church work—Catholic Church. 2. Evangelistic work. I. Title.

TAYLOR, Michael J., comp. 260
The sacred and the secular [compiled by] Michael J. Taylor. Englewood Cliffs, N.J., Prentice-Hall [1968] vi, 239 p. 22 cm. Bibliography: p. 237-239. Bibliographical footnotes. [BR115.W6T3] 68-21291
1. Church and the world—Addresses, essays, lectures. I. Title.

THORNTON, Martin. 260
The rock and the river; an encounter between traditional spirituality and modern thought. [1st American ed.] New York, Morehouse-Barlow Co. [1965] 158 p. 21 cm. Bibliographical footnotes. [BV4501.2.T515] 65-27001
1. Christian life — Anglican authors. 2. Christianity — 20th cent. — Addresses, essays, lectures. I. Title.

THORNTON, Martin 260
The rock and the river; an encounter between traditional spirituality and modern thought. [1st Amer. ed.] New York, Morehouse [c.1965] 158p. 21cm. Bibl. [BV4501.T515] 65-27001 3.75 bds.,
1. Christian life—Anglican authors. 2. Christianity—20th cent.—Addresses, essays, lectures. I. Title.

TRUEBLOOD, David Elton, 1900- 260
The incendiary fellowship [by] Elton Trueblood. [1st ed.] New York, Harper [1967] 121 p. 22 cm. Bibliographical footnotes. [BV640.T7] 67-11508
1. Church. 2. Christianity—20th century. I. Title.

VAJTA, Vilmos. 260
The Gospel and the ambiguity of the Church, edited by Vilmos Vajta. Philadelphia, Fortress Press [1974] viii, 243 p. 23 cm. (The Gospel encounters history series) Includes bibliographical references. [BV603.V34] 73-88358 ISBN 0-8006-0278-1 8.95
1. Church—Addresses, essays, lectures. I. Title. II. Series.

VALLQUIST, Gunnel. 260
Churches on the move. Translated by Ingalill Hellman Hjelm. Philadelphia, Fortress Press [1970] viii, 183 p. 21 cm. Translation of Kyrkor i uppbrott. [BV600.2.V313] 70-101428 3.50
1. Church renewal. 2. Christianity—Europe. I. Title.

VASSADY, Bela. 260
Christ's church: evangelical, catholic, and reformed. Grand Rapids, Eerdmans [1965] 173 p. 20 cm. [BX8.2.V35] 64-22028
1. Christian union — Addresses, essays, lectures. 2. Consultation on Church Union. I. Title.

VASSADY, Bela 260
Christ's church: evangelical, catholic, and reformed. Grand Rapids, Mich., Eerdmans [c.1965] 173p. 20cm. [BX8.2.V35] 64-22028 1.95 pap.,
1. Christian union—Addresses, essays, lectures. 2. Consultation on Church Union. I. Title.

VATICAN Council, 2d. 260
De ecclesia; the Constitution on the Church of Vatican Council II proclaimed by Pope Paul VI, November 21, 1964. Ed. by Edward H. Peters. Foreword by Basil C. Butler. Commentary by Gregory Baum [Study club ed.] Glen Rock, N. J., Paulist [c.1965] 192p. 18cm. (Deus bks.) Bibl. [BX830.A45C43] 65-17864 .95 pap.,
1. Church. I. Peters, Edward H., ed. II. Baum, Gregory, 1923- III. Title. IV. Title: The Constitution on the Church of Vatican Council II.

VATICAN Council, 2d, 1962-1965. 260
The church today; readings from Vatican II. Edited with commentary by Mary Kathleen Wright in association with the Curriculum Committee, Dept. of Education, Archdiocese of San Francisco, San Francisco, Calif. Los Angeles, Lawrence Pub. Co. [1967] ix, 107 p. illus. 22 cm. [BX830 1962.A3W7] 67-4027
I. Wright, Mary Kathleen, ed. II. Title.

VATICAN Council. 2d, 1962-1965. 260
De ecclesia; the Constitution on the Church of Vatican Council II proclaimed by Pope Paul VI, November 21, 1964. Edited by Edward H. Peters. Foreword by Basil C. Butler. With a commentary by Gregory Baum. [Study club ed.] Glen Rock, N.J., Paulist Press [1965] 192 p. 18 cm. (Deus books) Bibliographical footnotes. [BX830 1962.A45C43] 65-17864
1. Church. I. Peters, Edward H., ed. II. Baum, Gregory, 1923- III. Title. IV. Title: The Constitution on the Church of Vatican Council II.

VATICAN Council. 2d, 1962-1965. 260
Men and nations; Vatican II's pastoral constitution on the church in the modern world. Part 2: Problems of special urgency. Text and commentary edited by Peter Foote [and others. Translations: William Schafer and John McCudden] Chicago, Catholic Action Federations [1968] 95 p. illus. 28 cm. Text and commentary on facing pages. Bibliographical references included in "Footnotes" (p. 93) [BX830 1962.A45C932] 68-22200 1.95
1. Church and the world. I. Foote, Peter, ed. II. Vatican Council. 2d, 1962-1965. Constitutio pastoralis de ecclesia in mundo huius temporis. III. Title.

VATICAN COUNCIL, 2d, 1962-1965 260
Constitution on the church; De ecclesia, proclaimed November 21, 1964 [Prepd. by Claude Leetham, Campion Clifford] Notre Dame, Ind., Fides [1966] 96p. 22cm. (Fides paperback textbk., PBT-22) [BX830.1962.A45C425] 66-5203 1.00 pap.,
1. Church. I. Leetham, Claude Richard Harbord, ed. II. Clifford, Campion, ed. III. Title. IV. Title: De ecclesia.

VATICAN COUNCIL. 2D, 1962-1965. 260
Vatican II: the church constitution. Ed.: Austin Flanney. Chicago, Priory Pr. [1966] 207p. 23cm. Tr. & commentary on the constitution Constitutio de ecclesia. Appeared first in Doctrine & life. Bibl. [BX830 1962.A45 C423] 66-24108 4.95
1. Vatican Council. 2d, 1962-1965. Constitutio de ecclesia. I. Flannery, Austin, ed. II. Title.

WALSH, Eva. 260
Why go to church? By Eva and Chad Walsh. New York, Association Press [1962] 124 p. 16 cm. (A Keen-age reflection book) [BV600.2.W3] 62-9381
1. Church. I. Walsh, Chad, 1914- joint author. II. Title.

WALSH, Eva 260
Why go to church? By Eva and Chad Walsh. New York, Association [c.1962] 124p. 16cm. (Teen-age reflection bk.) 62-9381 .50 pap.,
1. Church. I. Walsh, Chad, 1914- joint author. II. Title.

WALSH, Marion Michael. 260
A new Christendom : how we will build it / by Marion Michael Walsh. Omaha : Help of Christians Publications, c1976. 124 p. ; 22 cm. Includes index. Bibliography: p. 110-113. [BX1753.W27] 75-39175 2.00
1. Sociology, Christian (Catholic) 2. Civilization, Christian. I. Title.

WALVOORD, John F 260
The church in prophecy, by John F. Walvoord. Grand Rapids, Zondervan Pub. House [1964] 183 p. 21 cm. [BV603.W3] 64-11955
1. Church — Addresses, essays, lectures. I. Title.

WALVOORD, John F. 260
The church in prophecy. Grand Rapids, Mich., Zondervan [c.1964] 183p. 21cm. 64-11955 2.95
1. Church—Addresses, essays, lectures. I. Title.

WAND, John William Charles, Bp. of London 260
The church today. [Baltimore, Md.] Penguin Bks. [c.1960] 192p. 18cm. (Pelican A471) .95 pap.,
1. Church. I. Title.

WASHINGTON, Joseph R. 260
The politics of God, by Joseph R. Washington, Jr. Boston, Beacon Press [1967] ix, 234 p. 21 cm. Bibliographical footnotes. [BR563.N4W33] 67-14108
1. Negroes—Religion. 2. Church and race problems—United States. I. Title.

WEBER, Hans Ruedi. 260
The militant ministry; People and pastors of the early church and today. Philadelphia, Fortress Press [1963] x, 108 p. 21 cm. Bibliographical references included in "Notes" (p. 96-108) [BV687.W4] 64-12990
1. Laity. 2. Christianity — 20th cent. I. Title. II. Title: People and pastors of the early church and today.

WEBER, Hans-Ruedi 260
The militant ministry; people and pastors of the early church and today. Philadelphia, Fortress [c.1963] x, 108p. 21cm. Bibl. 64-12990 2.00
1. Laity. 2. Christianity—20th cent. I. Title. II. Title: People and pastors of the early church and today.

WHITE, Mary Sue. 260
Helpers at my church. Pictures by Beatrice Derwinski. Nashville, Broadman Press, c1959. unpaged. illus. 21 cm. [BV600.W48] 59-5868
1. Church — Juvenile literature. I. Title.

WHY the Church? / 260
Edited by Walter J. Burghardt and William G. Thompson ; contributors, J. Peter Schineller ... [et al.]. New York : Paulist Press, c1977. ix, 138 p. ; 23 cm. "Originally a special issue of the journal Theological studies (December 1976)" Includes bibliographical references. [BX1746.W5] 77-74583 ISBN 0-8091-2028-3 : 4.95
1. Church—Addresses, essays, lectures. I. Burghardt, Walter J. II. Thompson, William G. III. Schineller, J. Peter. IV. Theological studies.

WIETZKE, Walter R. 260
Believers incorporated : the message of Ephesians for evangelical outreach / Walter R. Wietzke. Minneapolis : Augsburg Pub. House, c1977. 112 p. ; 20 cm. [BS2695.2.W53] 76-27073 ISBN 0-8066-1553-2 pbk. : 2.95
1. Bible. N.T. Ephesians—Criticism, interpretation, etc. 2. Church. 3. Christianity—20th century. I. Title.

WILLIAMS, Colin Wilbur, 1921- 260
The church, by Colin W. Williams. Philadelphia, Westminster Press [1968] 187 p. 20 cm. (New directions in theology today, v. 4) Bibliographical references included in "Notes" (p. [173]-182) [BT28.N47] 68-22647 2.45
1. Church. I. Title. II. Series.

WILLIAMS, John Bigelow 260
Christ or clergy.? New York, Exposition [c.1963] 215p. 21cm. 4.00
I. Title.

WILSON, William Joseph, 1936- 260
Demands for Chirstian renewal, edited by William J. Wilson. Maryknoll, N.Y., Maryknoll Publications, 1968. viii, 179 p. 21 cm. Bibliographical footnotes. [BV601.8.W5] 68-23545
1. Mission of the church. 2. Church and the world. I. Title.

WINTER, Ralph D. 260
The twenty-five unbelievable years, 1945 to 1969 [by] Ralph D. Winter. South Pasadena, William Carey Library [1970] 112 p. illus. 25 cm. A commentary in essay form covering the period following K. S. Latourette's A history of the expansion of Christianity published 1937-45. "Selected books by Latourette": p. 92. [BR121.2.W53] 73-125459 1.95
1. Christianity—20th century. 2. Missions—History. I. Latourette, Kenneth Scott, 1884-1968. A history of the expansion of Christianity. II. Title.

WOOD, Herbert George, 1879-1963. 260
Living issues in religious thought, from George Fox to Bertrand Russell. Freeport, N.Y., Books for Libraries Press [1966] 187 p. 22 cm. (Essay index reprint series) Reprint of the 1924 ed. Contents.Contents.—Religion and the unknown.—Logic and pessimism.—The moral scepticism of today.—A disciple of Spinoza.—Liberal Protestantism and modernist criticism.—The attitude of Mr. H. G. Wells towards Jesus Christ.—G. Bernard Shaw and religion.—The next revival of religion.—Quakerism.—Personal religion and social progress, a study of John Woolman. [BR85.W6 1966] 67-22128
1. Religious thought—Great Britain. I. Title.

WRIGHT, Ralph Justus 260
One man's views. New York, Carlton [c.1963] 58 p. 21 cm. (Reflection bk.) 2.00
I. Title.

CONTROVERSY in the 260'.08 s
Middle East : U.N. Resolution 242 : an elusive hope for peace? / IDOC in association with the Arab-Israeli Research and Relations Project ; [Mary Jo Cooney, guest editor ; Katherine Carr, editorial consultant for the Arab-Israeli Research and Relations Project]. New York : IDOC-North America, 1973. 60 p. : ill. ; 28 cm. (IDOC international/North American edition ; no. 55) Cover title. Includes bibliographical references. [BR115.P7I17 no. 55] [DS119.7] 320.9'56 75-308573 2.95
1. United Nations—Palestine—Addresses, essays, lectures. 2. Jewish-Arab relations—1967-1973—Addresses, essays, lectures. I. Cooney, Mary Jo, ed. II. Idoc. III. Arab-Israeli Research and Relations Project. IV. Title. V. Series.

POLING, David, 1928- 260'.09'04
The last years of the church. [1st ed.] Garden City, N.Y., Doubleday, 1969. xii, 153 p. 22 cm. [BR121.2.P585] 69-10954 4.95
1. Christianity—20th century. I. Title.

WHITE, Ray L. 260'.19
On getting things done, by Ray L. White. Salt Lake City, Bookcraft, 1968. 164 p. illus. 24 cm. [BV652.1.W48] 68-9793
1. Christian leadership. I. Title.

RINKER, Richard N. 260'.2'07
The East Burlap parables [by] Richard N. Rinker. Illustrated by Jack Brodie. Lincoln, University of Nebraska Press [1969] xiii, 169 p. illus. 22 cm. [PN6231.C35R5] 69-11775 3.95
1. Christianity—Anecdotes, facetiae, satire, etc. I. Title.

MCCABE, Joseph E., 1912- 260.23
Challenging careers in the church. New York, McGraw [c.1966] 180p. 21cm. [BV683.M23] 65-28133 4.50 bds.,
1. Church work as a profession. I. Title.

ANDERSON, Kenneth, 1917- 260'.2'7
Stains on glass windows, written by Ken Anderson. Drawings by Robin Jensen. Waco, Tex., Word Books [1969] [45] p. illus. 15 cm. [BV4.A5] 74-91939 1.95
1. Theology, Practical—Anecdotes, facetiae, satire, etc. I. Title.

MISSIONS Advanced Research and Communication Center. 260'.28'54
The church and the computer; an analysis of a survey of religious organizations on their use of electronic data processing. Monrovia, Calif. [1969?] iii, 25 p. 30 cm. [BV652.97.M57] 72-191603 1.00
1. Electronic data processing—Church work. I. Title.

STEWART, William, 1910- 260'.3
50 key words: the church. Richmond, Va., John Knox Press [1970] 84 p. 20 cm. On spine: Fifty key words: church. [BR95.S76] 79-82935 1.65
1. Theology—Dictionaries. I. Title. II. Title: The church.

CHRISTIAN Information Bureau, Elkhorn, Wis. 260.58
The Christian information directory; 1000 important names and addresses for your convenience in Christian work. [Elkhorn, Wis., 1954] 51p. 18cm. Cover title. [BV652.C48] 54-39024
1. Church work —Direct. I. Title.

DOWN, Goldie M. 260.6'7'0922
If I have twelve sons, by Goldie Down. Nashville, Southern Pub. [1968] 95p. 22cm. [BV2495.D68] 68-55391 3.75
1. Seventh-Day Adventists—Missions. 2. Converts, Seventh-Day Adventist. I. Title.

NELSON, John Oliver, 1909- 260.69
Vocation and Protestant religious occupations. New York, Vocational Guidance Manuals [1964,c.1963] 160p. 20cm. (VGM career ser., V145) Bibl. 63-19638 2.65; 1.45 pap.,
1. Church work as a profession. 2. Clergy—Appointment, call, and election. I. Title.

GRIMME, Jeannette. 260.7
What is the church? A weekday church school course for grades 3 and 4. Teacher's book. Nashville, Published for Cooperative Publication Association by Abingdon Press [1955] 160p. 20cm. (The Cooperative series: texts for weekday religious education classes and released time religious education instruction) Includes bibliography. [BV602.G7] 55-10268
1. Church—Study and teaching. 2. Week-day church schools—Teachers' manuals. I. Title.

HUDSON, Winthrop Still, 1911- comp. 260.7
Nationalism and religion in America: concepts of American identity and mission, edited by Winthrop S. Hudson. [1st ed.] New York, Harper & Row [1970] xxxiii, 211 p. 21 cm. (Harper forum books, RD 10) Includes bibliographical references. [BL65.N3H8 1970] 76-109063 3.50
1. Nationalism and religion—U.S. 2. Messianism, American. 3. Religion and state—U.S. I. Title.

MAKRAKES, Apostolos, 1831-1905. 260.7
The political philosophy of the Orthodox Church, by Apostolos Makrakis. Translated from the Greek by D. Cummings. Chicago, Orthodox Christian Educational Society, 1965. 162 p. 21 cm. [BL51.M24813] 77-16996
1. Orthodox Eastern Church—Doctrinal and controversial works. 2. Philosophy and religion. 3. Political science. I. Title.

REID, Clyde H 260.7
I belong, a course for seventh and eighth grades, by Clyde Reid. Boston, United Church Press [c1964] 124 p. illus. (part col.) fold. col. map. 26 cm. "Part of the United Church Curriculum prepared and published by the Division of Christian Education and the Division of Publication of the United Church Board for Homeland Ministries." Bibliography: p. 122-123. [BX9884.A3R4] 64-19462
1. Religious education — Test-books for adolescents — United Church of Christ. I. United Church Board for Homeland Ministries. Division of Christian Education. II. United Church Board for Homeland Ministries. Division of Publication. III. Title.

SHEPARD, Lillian (White) 1896- 260.7
Our part in the world-wide church; a unit of study for grades nine and ten in weekday religious education classes. Teacher's guide. Nashville, Published for the Cooperative Publication Association by Abingdon Press [1954] 142p. 20cm. (The Cooperative series texts for weekday religious education classes and released time religious education Instruction) [BV1583.S5] 54-7032
1. Week-day church schools—Teachers' manuals. 2. Church—Study and teaching. 3. Church and social problems—Study and teaching. 4. Christian union—Study and teaching. I. Title.

CHRISTIANITY today 260'.8
Christianity today. (Title orig.: A Christianity today reader.) Ed., introd. by Frank E. Gaebelain. New York, Pyramid [1968,c.1966] 333p. 18cm. (T-1791) [BR50.C553] .75 pap.,
1. Christianity—Collections. I. Gaebelein, Frank Ely, 1890- ed. II. Title.
Also available from Revell in a Spire Books edition at the same price.

CHRISTIANITY today. 260'.8
A Christianity today reader. Edited, and with an introd., by Frank E. Gaebelein. [1st ed.] New York, Meredith Press [1967, c1966] vi, 271 p. illus. 24 cm. [BR50.C553] 66-27904
1. Christianity—Collections. I. Gaebelein, Frank Ely, 1899- ed. II. Title.

DAHLBERG, Edwin Theodore, 1892- ed. 260.8
Herald of the Evangel 60 years of American Christianity [by] Samuel McCrae Cavert [others] Ed. by Edwin T. Dahlberg. St. Louis, Bethany [c.1965] 221p. col. port. 23cm. [BR50.D3] 65-22349 4.95
1. Bader, Jesse Moren, 1886-1963. 2. Christianity—Addresses, essays, lectures. I. Bader, Jesse Moren, 1886-1963. II. Cavert, Samuel McCrae, 1888- III. Title.

DAHLBERG, Edwin Theodore, 1892- ed. 260.8
Herald of the Evangel; 60 years of American Christianity [by] Samuel McCrae Cavert [and others] Edited by Edwin T. Dahlberg. St. Louis, Bethany Press [1965] 221 p. col. port. 23 cm. "A tribute honoring the life and work of Jesse Moreen Bader." Contents.-- Jesse Moren Bader: evangelist and ecumenical churchman, by S. M. Cavert -- Jesus Christ: Lord of all life, by E. C. Blake. -- The communication of the Gospel, by D. H. C. Read. -- Evangelism is every Christian's business by B. Graham. -- Motive and method in Christian teaching, by R. H. Mueller. -- The layman and his pastor, by C. P. Taft. -- Women in the church, by Mrs. J. D. Wyker. -- Cooperative Christianity in the local community, by E. G. Homrighausen. -- The contributions of separation to American life, by H. E. Short. -- Toward wholeness for God's household on earth, by H. S. Leiper. -- When churches grow younger, by E. T. Dahlberg. -- Heralds of the Evangel, by J. Bader. -- An epilogue: I remember, by D. Poling. [BR50.D3] 65-22349
1. Bader, Jesse More, 1886-1963. 2. Christianity — Addresses, essays, lectures. I. Bader, Jesse Moren, 1886-1963. II. Cavert, Samuel McCrea, 1886- III. Title.

DIRKSWAGER, Edward J., comp. 260'.8
Readings in the theology of the church [by] Edward J. Dirkswager, Jr. Englewood Cliffs, Prentice-Hall [1970] viii, 257 p. 22 cm. Contents.Contents.—Introduction: secular awareness and the dark night of the church, by A. Morawska.—The church and mankind, by E. Schillebeeckx.—Man and the sacraments, by B. Bro.—The ecclesial reality of the other churches, by G. Baum.—Intercommunion, by S. Butler.—Is the Catholic Church relevant today? By C. Davis and J. L. McKenzie.—Are you a Catholic? By F. Sontag.—What is the essence of apostolic succession? By H. Kung.—Bishops, presbyters, and priests in Ignatius of Antioch, by J. F. McCue.—The Petrine office, by H. Kung.—Public opinion in the church, by S. E. Kutz.—Vatican I, infallibility, and doctrinal renewal, by G. Baum.—Dogma as an ecumenical problem, by A. Dulles.—Schism of consciousness, by R. Ruether.—Church as movement, by G. Baum. Includes bibliographical references. [BX1746.D5] 73-97921
1. Church—Addresses, essays, lectures. I. Title.

ROBINSON, John Arthur Thomas, Bp., 1919- 260'.8
On being the Church in the world [by] John A. T. Robinson. Harmondsworth, Penguin, 1969. 190 p. 19 cm. (Pelican books, A1021) [BV600.2.R6 1969] 72-406173 5/-
1. Church—Addresses, essays, lectures. I. Title.

LICHTENBERGER, Arthur. 260.81
The day is at hand. New York, Seabury Press [1964] 124 p. 22 cm. "Largely based on addresses, sermons, and seasonal messages." [BV4011.L5] 64-19625
1. Pastoral theology — Angilcan Crmmunion — Addresses, essays, lectures. I. Title.

LICHTENBERGER, Arthur 260.81
The day is at hand. New York, Seabury [c.1964] 124p. 22cm. 64-19625 3.00 bds.,
1. Pastoral theology—Anglican Communion—Addresses, essays, lectures. I. Title.

RAHNER, Karl, 1904- 260.81
Theology for renewal: bishops, priests, laity. Tr. [from German] by Cecily Hastings, Richard Strachan. New York, Sheed [1965, c.1964] vii, 183p. 21cm. One of 3 vols., each with distinctive title. Bibl. [BV600.2.R333] 65-1786 4.00
1. Church—Addresses, essays, lectures. 2. Laity—Catholic Church. I. Title.

ROBINSON, John Arthur Thomas, Bp., 1919- 260.81
On being the church in the world. Philadelphia, Westminster [1962, c.1960] 158p. 23cm. Bibl. 62-14939 3.50
1. Church—Addresses, essays, lectures. I. Title.

THE Church and mankind. 260.82
Glen Rock, N.J., Paulist Press [1965] viii, 177 p. 24 cm. (Concilium theology in the age of renewal: Dogma, v. 1) Contents.Contents.—General introduction, by K. Rahner and E. Schillebeeckx.—Preface, by E. Schillebeeckx.—Articles: The church, the people of God, by Y. Congar; translated by K. Sullivan. The pastoral implications of episcopal collegiality, by J. Ratzinger; translated by T. Rattler. The church and mankind, by E. Schillebeeckx; translated by J. A. Byrne and T. L. Westow. Diversity of structures and freedom within structures of the church, by M. Novak.—Bibliographical survey: The church as the people of God, by R. Schnackenburg and J. Dupont; translated by H. A. Musurillo. Who belongs to the church? By B. Willems; translated by T. L. Westow.—DO-C: Documentation concilium: Introduction, by L. A. von Geusau and M. J. Le Guillou. Eucharistic congresses from Leo XIII to Paul VI, by R. Aubert; translated by E. O'Gorman. The dialogue between the church and contemporary cultures, by Van Kets; translated by T. L. Westow. Bibliographical footnotes. [BX1746.C5] 65-15249
1. Church. I. Schillebeeckx, Edward Cornelis Florentinius Alfans, 1914- II. Series: Concilium (New York) v. 1

CHURCH and mankind (The) 260.82
[Edward Schillebeeckx, edit. direct. English tr. by Paulist Fathers and Stichting Concilium] Glen Rock, N.J., Paulist [c.1965] viii, 177p. 24cm. (Concilium theology in the age of renewal: Dogma, v.1) Bibl. [BX1746.C5] 65-15249 4.50
1. Church. I. Schillebeeckx, Edward Cornelis Florentinius Alfans, 1914- (Series)

OXFORD Institute on Methodist Theological Studies, 1962 260.82
The doctrine of the church. Dow Kirkpatrick, ed. Prepared under the dir. of the World Methodist Council. Nashville, Abingdon [c.1964] 215p. 23cm. Bibl. 64-15757 3.00
1. Church—Addresses, essays, lectures. 2. Methodism—Addresses, essays, lectures. I. Kirkpatrick, Dow, ed. II. World Methodist Council. III. Title.

OXFORD Institute on Methodist Theological Studies. 2d, 1962. 260.82
The doctrine of the church. Dow Kirkpatrick, editor. Prepared under the direction of the World Methodist Council. New York, Abingdon Press [1964] 215 p. 23 cm. Includes bibliographies. [BV600.A1O9] 64-15757
1. Church — Addresses, essays, lectures. 2. Methodism — Addresses, essays, lectures. I. Kirkpatrick, Dow, ed. II. World Methodist Council. III. Title.

THE Pastoral mission of the church. 260.82
Glen Rock, N. J., Paulist Press [1965] vi, 186 p. 24 cm. (Concilium theology in the age of renewal: Pastoral theology, v. 3) Includes bibliographies. [BX1913.P3] 65-19634
1. Pastoral theology—Catholic Church. 2. Religion and sociology. I. Series.

PASTORAL mission of the church (The) v.3. 260.82
Glen Rock, N. J., Paulist Pr. [c.1965] vi, 186p. 24cm. (Concilium theology in the age of renewal: Pastoral theology, v.3) Bibl. [BX1913.P3] 65-19634 4.50
1. Pastoral theology—Catholic Church. 2. Religion and sociology. (Series)

SCHILLEBEECKX, Edward Cornelis Florentinius Alfans, 1914- 260.82
The Church and mankind. Glen Rock, N.J., Paulist Press [1965] viii, 177 p. 24 cm. (Concilium theology in the age of renewal: Dogma, v. 1) Contents.General introduction, by K. Rahner and E. Schillebeeckx. -- Preface, by E. Schillebeeckx. -- Articles: The church, the people of God, by Y. Congar; translated by K. Sullivan. The pastoral implications of episcopal collegiality, by J. Ratzinger; translated by T. Rattler. The church and mankind, by E. Schillebeeckx: translated by J. A. Byrne and T. L. Westow. Diversity of structures and freedom within structures of the church, by M. Novak. -- Bibliographical survey: The church as the people of God, by R. Schnackenburg and J. Dupont; translated by H. A. Musurillo. Who belongs to the church? By B. Willems; translated by T. L. Westow. -- DO-C: Documentation concilium: Introduction, by L. A. von Geusau and M. J. Le Guillou. Eucharistic congresses from Leo XIII to Paul VI, by R. Aubert; translated by E. O'Gorman. The dialogue between the church and contemporary cultures, by R. Van Kets; translated by T. L. Westow. Bibliographical footnotes. [BX1746.C5] 65-15249
1. Church. I. Title. II. Series.

SCHALLER, Lyle E 260.83
Community organization: conflict and reconciliation [by] Lyle E. Schaller. Nashville, Abingdon Press [1966] 176 p. 20 cm. Bibliographical footnotes. [HN65.S4] 66-10921
1. Church and social problems—U. S. 2. Community organization. 3. Social change. I. Title.

SCHALLER, Lyle E. 260.83
Community organization: conflict and reconciliation Nashville, Abingdon [c.1966] 176p. 20cm. (140) Bibl. [HN65.S4] 66-10921 1.95 pap.,
1. Church and social problems—U.S. 2. Community organization. 3. Social change. I. Title.

THE Urban crisis; 260.8'3
a symposium on the racial problem in the inner city. General editor: David McKenna. Grand Rapids, Zondervan Pub. House [1969] 146 p. 21 cm. Papers presented at a seminar held at Spring Arbor College in Jan. 1968. Bibliographical footnotes. [HN39.U6U72] 69-11658 3.95
1. Church and social problems—U.S.—Addresses, essays, lectures. I. McKenna, David Loren, 1929- ed. II. Spring Arbor College.

CRONIN, John Francis, 1908- 260.85
The church and the workingman, by John F. Cronin and Harry W. Flannery. 1st ed.] New York, Hawthorn Books [1965] 159, [1] p. 22 cm. (The Twentieth century encyclopedia of Catholicism, v. 104. Section 9: The church and the modern world) Bibliography: p. [160] [HD6338.C75] 65-13027
1. Church and labor. I. Flannery, Harry W., 1900- joint author. II. Title. III. Title: The Twentieth century encyclopedia of Catholicism, v. 104) IV. Series.

CRONIN, John Francis, 1908- 260.85
The church and the workingman, by John F. Cronin, Harry W. Flannery. New York, Hawthorn [c.1965] 159, [1]p. 22cm. (20th century ency. of Catholicism, v. 104. Sect. 9: The church and the mod. world) Bibl. [HD6338.C75] 65-13027 3.50 bds.,
1. Church and labor. I. Flannery, Harry W., 1900- joint author. II. Title. III. Series: The Twentieth century encyclopedia of Catholicism, v. 104

GHEDDO, Piero. 260.8'5
Why is the Third World poor? Translated by Kathryn Sullivan. [Maryknoll, N.Y., Orbis Books, 1973] xv, 143 p. 21 cm. Translation of Terzo mondo: perche povero? Includes bibliographical references. [HC59.7.G4813] 72-85793 ISBN 0-88344-757-6 3.95
1. Underdeveloped areas. I. Title.

GHEDDO, Piero. 260.8'5
Why is the Third World poor? Translated by Kathryn Sullivan. [Maryknoll, N.Y., Orbis Books, 1973] xv, 143 p. 21 cm. Translation of Terzo mondo: perche povero? Includes bibliographical references. [HC59.7.G4813] 72-85793 ISBN 0-88344-757-6 3.95
1. Underdeveloped areas. I. Title.

RICHARDSON, Peter. 260.'901
Israel in the apostolic Church. London, Cambridge U.P., 1969. xiii, 257 p. 23 cm. (Society for New Testament Studies. Monograph series, 10) Originally presented as

the author's thesis, Cambridge, 1965. Includes bibliographical references. [BM535.R48 1969] 74-79055 ISBN 0-521-07592-0 80/- ($12.50)
1. Christianity and other religions—Judaism. 2. Judaism—Relations—Christianity. 3. Church history—Primitive and early church. I. Title. II. Series: Studiorum Novi Testamenti Societas. Monograph series, 10

LUEKER, Erwin Louis, 1914- 260'.9'04
Change and the church, by Erwin L. Lueker. Saint Louis, Concordia Pub. House [1969] 134 p. 21 cm. Bibliographical references included in "Notes" (p. [126]-134) [BV600.2.L8] 70-77888 3.25
1. Church. 2. Church renewal—Lutheran Church. I. Title.

BETHGE, Eberhard, 1909- 260'.968
Bonhoeffer, exile and martyr / Eberhard Bethge ; edited and with an essay by John W. de Gruchy. New York : Seabury Press, c1975. 191 p. ; 22 cm. "A Crossroad book." Includes bibliographical references and index. [BX4827.B57B39 1975b] 75-33303 ISBN 0-8164-1211-1 : 7.95
1. Bonhoeffer, Dietrich, 1906-1945. 2. Christianity—South Africa. I. De Gruchy, John W. II. Title.

KOENIG, Richard Edwin. 260'.973
A creative minority: the church in a new age [by] Richard E. Koenig. Minneapolis, Augsburg Pub. House [1971] 123 p. 20 cm. Includes bibliographical references. [BR121.2.K63] 70-159008 ISBN 0-8066-1121-9 2.50
1. Christianity—20th century. I. Title.

261 Social Theology

ABELL, Aaron Ignatius, 1903- 1965, comp. 261
American Catholic thought on social questions. Indianapolis, Bobbs-Merrill [1968] lv, 571 p. 21 cm. (The American heritage series, 58) Bibliography: p. xliii-liv. [BX1753.A6] 66-30548
1. Sociology, Christian (Catholic) I. Title.

ALPENFELS, Ethel Josephine. [261]
Brothers all, a course for the junior high age; illus. by John Leamon. Teacher's ed. Boston, Pilgrim Press [1950] xiv, 54, v-vi, 88 p. illus. 21 cm. (Pilgrim series) The "Pupil's book" (v-vi, 88 p.) is preceded by the "Teacher's guide" (xiv, 54 p.) Bibliography: p. xiii. [BV1548.A4] 268.433 50-2139
1. Religions education—Text-books for adolescents—Congregational. 2. Church and social problems—Study and teaching. I. Title.

AMARIU, Constantin. 261
The church in the service of liberty. Translated by Paul A. Barrett. St. Louis, Herder [1963] vii. 214 p. 21 cm. [HN37.C3A553] 63-21561
1. Church and social problems — Catholic Church. 2. Liberty. I. Title.

AMARIU, Constantin 261
The church in the service of liberty. Tr. by Paul A. Barrett. St. Louis, Herder [c.1963] viii, 214p. 21cm. 63-21561 3.95
1. Church and social problems—Catholic Church. 2. Liberty. I. Title.

ANDELSON, Robert V., 1931- 261
Imputed rights; an essay in Christian social theory [by] Robert V. Andelson. Athens, University of Georgia Press [1971] xvi, 153 p. 24 cm. Includes bibliographical references. [JC571.A53] 70-135183 ISBN 0-8203-0270-8 6.00
1. Civil rights. I. Title.

ANNAN, Noel Gilroy Annan, Baron, 1916- 261
The headmaster; Roxburgh of Stowe and his influence in English education [by] Noel Annan. New York, Schocken Books [1966] xiii, 216 p. 22 cm. First published in London in 1965 under title: Roxburgh of Stowe. Roxburgh, John Fergusson, 1888-1954. Bibliographical footnotes. [LF795.B87934R63 1966] 66-16310
1. Stowe School, Buckingham, Eng. I. Title.

ARMERDING, Hudson T. 261
Christianity and the world of thought, edited by Hudson T. Armerding. Contributors: Beatrice Batson [and others] Chicago, Moody Press [1968] 350 p. 24 cm. Includes bibliographies. [BR115.C8A7] 68-18884
1. Christianity and culture. I. Batson, Beatrice. II. Title.

ARMERDING, Hudson T. 261
Christianity and the world of thought, edited by Hudson T. Armerding. Contributors: Beatrice Batson [and others] Chicago, Moody Press [1968] 350 p. 24 cm. Includes bibliographies. [BR115.C8A7] 68-18884
1. Christianity and culture. I. Batson, Beatrice. II. Title.

AUER, Alfons. 261
The Christian and the world; readings in theology [by] Alfons Auer [and others]. Foreword by John J. Wright. Compiled at the Canisianum, Innsbruck. Canisianum, Innsbruck. New York, P. J. Kenedy [1965] xx, 229 p. 22 cm. Translated from German or French. Includes bibliographical references. [BR123.C58] 65-22645
1. Christianity — 20th cent. — Addresses, essays, lectures. 2. Christian life — Catholic authors. I. Title. II. Title: The world.

BALY, Denis. 261
Besieged city; the church in the world. Greenwich, Conn., Seabury Press, 1958. 146p. 22cm. [BV600.B32] 58-9228
1. Church. I. Title.

*BAYNE, Stephen F. 261
What future for Christianity? by Stephen F. Bayne,Jr. New York, Friendship [1967] 63p. 16cm. (Questions for Christians, no. 9) Bibl. .65 pap.,
I. Title.

BAYNE, Stephen Fielding, Bp., 1908- 261
The optional God. New York, Oxford University Press [1953] 145p. 20cm. [BR481.B35] 53-9182
1. Christianity—20th cent. 2. U.S.—Religion. I. Title.

BEAVER, Gilbert A. 261
Christ and community; an exploration of co-operative fellowship (koinonia) [New York] Association Press, 1950. 367 p. 23 cm. Bibliographical references included in "Notes" (p. 339-361) [BV625.B4] 50-11031
1. Church. 2. Interdenominational cooperation. 3. Church and social problems. I. Title.

*BEGUESSE, H. Hugh. 261
Man--evolution's unfinished product. New York, Vantage [1967] 118p. 21cm. 3.00 bds.,
I. Title.

BENNETT, John Coleman, 1902- ed. 261
Christian social ethics in a changing world; an ecumenical theological inquiry. New York, Association [c.1966] 381p. 21cm. Working papers prepd. under the sponsorship of the Dept. on Church and Society, World Council of Churches, for the 1966 world conf. Bibl. [BT738.B4] 66-10118 5.50
1. Sociology, Christian—Addresses, essays, lectures. I. World Council of Churches. Division of Studies. Dept. on Church and Society. II. World Conference on Church and Society, Geneva, 1966. III. Title.

BERDIAEV, Nikolai Aleksandrovich, 1874-1948 261
The bourgeois mind and other essays, by Nicholas Berdyaev. Freeport, N.Y., Bks. for Libs. Pr. [1966] 130p. 19cm. First pub. 1934. The bourgeois mind and Man and machine are tr. from Russian by Countess Bennigsen; the other two essays are from French. The whole collection has been rev. by Donald Attwater, who also tr. the last essay. (Essay index reprint ser.) [BR115.C5B37] 67-22072 5.00
1. Civilization, Christian. 2. Civilization, Modern. 3. Middle classes. I. Title.
Contents omitted.

BERDIAEV, Nikolai Aleksandrovich, 1874-1948. 261
The bourgeois mind and other essays, by Nicholas Berdyaey. Freeport, N. Y., Books for Libraries Press [1966] 130 p. 19 cm. (Essay index reprint series) "First published 1934." "The bourgeois mind and Man and machine are translated from the Russian by Countess Bennigsen; the other two essays are from the French. The whole collection has been revised by Donald Attwater, who also translated the last essay." [BR115.C5B37] 67-22072
1. Civilization. Christian. 2. Civilization. Modern. 3. Middle classes. I. Title.

BERLIN, Isaiah, Sir ed. 261
Two concepts of liberty; an inaugural lecture delivered before the University of Oxford, on 31 October 1958. Oxford, Clarendon Press, 1958. 57p. 22cm. [JC585.B42] 59-2289
1. Liberty. I. Title.

BIANCHI, Eugene C. 261
Reconciliation; the function of the church [by] Eugene C. Bianchi. New York, Sheed and Ward [1969] xii, 211 p. 21 cm. Includes bibliographical references. [BV601.8.B52] 68-13853 5.50
1. Mission of the church. 2. Secularization (Theology) I. Title.

BIEBER, Agnes Reiniger. 261
Salt of the earth. New York, Vantage Press [1955] 135p. 23cm. [BV640.B5] 54-10234
1. Christianity— 20th cent. I. Title.

BIELER, Andre. 261
The social humanism of Calvin. Translated by Paul T. Fuhrmann. Foreword by W. A. Visser't Hooft. Richmond, John Knox Press [1964] 79 p. 21 cm. [BX9418.B513] 64-11878
1. Calvin, Jean, 1509-1564. 2. Sociology, Christian. I. Title.

BIELER, Andre 261
The social humanism of Calvin. Tr. [from French] by Paul T. Fuhrmann. Foreword by W. A. Visser't Hooft. Richmond, Va., Knox [c.1964] 79p. 21cm. 64-11878 1.50 pap.,
1. Calvin, Jean, 1509-1564. 2. Sociology, Christian. I. Title.

BILHEIMER, Robert S., 1917- 261
What must the church do? [By] Robert S. Bilheimer. Freeport, N.Y., Books for Libraries Press [1971, c1947] xi, 148 p. 23 cm. (Essay index reprint series) (The Interseminary series, v. 5) "Complete index, volumes I-V, The Interseminary series": p. 125-148. Includes bibliographical references. [BV600.B47 1971] 70-134053 ISBN 0-8369-2384-7
1. Church. I. Title. II. Series.

BLAIR, Morris Myers. 261
Christ, Christianity and communism. Cincinnati, Standard Pub. Co. [1950] 139 p. 23 cm. [BT1240.B55] 50-29214
1. Apologetics—20th cent. 2. Communism and religion. I. Title.

BLOY, Myron B., Jr. 261
The crisis of cultural change, a Christian viewpoint. New York, Seabury [1967, c.1965] 139p. 21cm. (SP33) Bibl. [BR123.B567] 1.65 pap.,
1. Christianity — 20th cent. —Addresses, essays, lectures. I. Title.

BLOY, Myron B. 261
The crisis of cultural change, a Christian viewpoint, by Myron B. Bloy, Jr. New York, Seabury Press [1965] 139 p. 22 cm. Bibliographical references included in "Notes" (p. 131-139) [BR123.B576] 64-19623
1. Christianity — 20th cent. — Addresses, essays, lectures. I. Title.

BLOY, Myron B. jr. 261
The crisis of cultural change, a Christian viewpoint, New York, Seabury [c.1965] 139p. 22cm. Bibl. [BR123.B567] 64-19623 3.95 bds.,
1. Christianity—20th cent.—Addresses, essays, lectures. I. Title.

BODO, John R 261
The Protestant clergy and public issues, 1812-1848. Princeton, PrincetonUniversity Press, 1954. xiv, 291p. 23cm. Bibliography: p.261-284. [BR525.B63] 53-6379
1. U. S.—Church history. 2. Church and state in the U. S. I. Title.

BOLLEN, John David. 261
Protestantism and social reform in New South Wales 1890-1910 [by] J. D. Bollen. Clayton, Vic., Melbourne University Press, 1972. xiii, 199 p. illus., 4 plates, ports., tables. 23 cm. Bibliography: p. 187-193. [BR1483.N5B64] 73-163210 ISBN 0-522-84023-X
1. Protestant churches—New South Wales. 2. Church and social problems—New South Wales. I. Title.
Distributed by International Scholarly Book Service, 11.70.

BOYD, Malcolm. 261
The hunger, the thirst; the questions of students and young adults. New York, Morehouse-Barlow [1964] 128 p. 19 m. [HN39.U6B65] 64-8097
1. Church and social problems — U.S. 2. Civilization, Modern — 20th cent. I. Title.

BOYD, Malcolm. 261
The hunger, the thirst; the questions of students and young adults. [New York, Dell, 1968,c.1964] 128p. 18cm. (Laurel ed., 3931) [HN39.U6B65] .50 pap.,
1. Church and social problems—U. S. 2. Civilization, Modern—20th cent. I. Title.

BOYD, Malcom 261
The hunger, the thirst; the questions of students and young adults. New York, Morehouse [c.1964] 128p. 19cm. 64-8097 1.50 pap.,
1. Church and social problems—U. S. 2. Civilization, Modern—20th cent. I. Title.

BRINSON, George W. 261
Satan's release. Boston, Christopher Pub. House [1950] 114 p. 21 cm. [BR126.B647] 50-10135
I. Title.

BROCKWAY, Allan R., 1932- 261
The secular saint [by] Allan R. Brockway. [1st ed.] Garden City, N.Y., Doubleday, 1968. 238 p. 22 cm. Bibliography: p. [233]-238. [BR121.2.B7] 68-10560
1. Christianity—20th century. 2. Secularization (Theology) I. Title.

BRODRICK, James, 1891- 261
The economic morals of the Jesuits; an answer to Dr. H. M. Robertson. New York, Arno Press, 1972. 158 p. 23 cm. (The Evolution of capitalism) Reprint of the 1934 ed. [BR115.E3R623 1972] 76-38248 ISBN 0-405-04113-6
1. Robertson, Hector Menteith. Aspects of the rise of economic individualism. 2. Jesuits. 3. Christianity and economics. I. Title. II. Series.

BROWN, Robert McAfee, 1920- 261
The significance of the church. Philadelphia, Westminster Press [1956] 96p. 20cm. (Layman's theological library) [BV600.B852] 56-6172
1. Church. I. Title.

BROWN, Robert McAffe, 1920- 261
The significance of the church. Philadelphia, Westminster Press [1956] 96p. 20cm. (Layman's theological library) [BV600.B852] 56-6172
1. Church. I. Title.

BRUNNER, Heinrich Emil, 1889- 261
The misunderstanding of the church; translated by Harold Knight. Philadelphia, Westminster Press [1953] 132p. 23cm. [BV600.B8663] 53-6558
1. Church. I. Title.

BUTTERFIELD, Herbert, 1900- 261
Christianity, diplomacy and war. New York, Abingdon-Cokesbury Press [1953] 125 p. 19 cm. (The Beckly social service lecture) [BR115.P7B79] 53-13186
1. Christianity and politics. 2. War and religion. I. Title.

CAILLIET, Emile, 1894- 261
The Christian approach to culture. Nashville, Abingdon-Cokesbury Press [1953] 288p. 24cm. [BR115.,c8C29] 52-13754
1. Culture. 2. Christianity—Philosophy. I. Title.

CARTER, Paul Allen, 1926- 261
The idea of progress in American Protestant thought, 1930-1960, by Paul A. Carter. Philadelphia, Fortress Press [1969] xi, 27 p. 20 cm. (Facet books. Historical series, 11) First published in Church history, [v.] XXXII, no. 1 (March, 1963), [p.] 75-94, under title: The idea of progress in most recent American Protestant thought, 1930-1960. Includes bibliographical references. [BR479.C33] 69-14621 0.85
1. Progress. 2. Religious thought—20th century. I. Title.

CATHOLIC Church. Pope. 261
The woman in the modern world. Selected and arr. by the monks of Solesmes. [Boston] St. Paul Editions [1959] 1v. 20cm. (Papal teachings) Translation of Le probleme feminin. [BV639.W7C33] 59-16227
1. Women in Christianity—Papal documents. I. Solesmes, France. Saint-Pierre (Benedictine abbey) II. Title.

CATHOLIC Church. Pope, 1878-1903 (Leo XIII) 261
The church speaks to the modern world; the social teachings of Leo XIII. Edited, annotated and with an introd. by Etienne Gilson. Garden City, N. Y., Image Books [1954] viii, 348p. 18cm. (A Doubleday image book, D7) Bibliography: p. 334-338. [HN37.C3A3 1954] 54-9930
1. Church and social problems—Catholic Church. I. Gilson, Etienne Henry, 1884- ed. II. Title.

CATHOLIC Church. Pope, 1922-1939 (Pius XI) 261
The church and the reconstruction of the modern world; the social encyclicals of Pope Pius XI. Edited, annotated, and with an introd. by Terence P. McLaughlin. Garden City, N. Y., Image Books [1957] 433p. 18cm. (A Doubleday image book, D54) Includes bibliography. [HN37.C3A3 1957] 57-10459
1. Church and social problems—Catholic Church. I. McLaughlin, Terence Patrick, 1903- ed. II. Title.

CENTER for the Study of Democratic Institutions. 261
Religion and American society, a statement of principles [by] William Clancy [and others] With an introd. by Henry P. Van Dusen. Santa Barbara, Calif. [1961] 79 p. 22 cm. (Its A contribution to the discussion of the free society) [BR517.C4] 63-91
1. U.S. — Religion. 2. Sociology, Christian. I. Clancy, William. II. Title.

CHERESO, James C. 261
Here & now; the sacred secular, by James C.

Chereso. Dayton, Ohio, G. A. Pflaum, 1969. 128 p. illus. 18 cm. (Witness book, C14) (Christian identity series.) Includes bibliographical references. [BT83.7.C44] 79-97045 0.95
1. Secularization (Theology) 2. Secularism. I. Title.

CHRIST and humanity. 261
Ivar Asheim, editor. Foreword by Mikko Juva. Philadelphia, Fortress Press [1970] xiii, 185 p. 21 cm. "This study volume summarizes the study undertaken by the Commission on Theology of the Lutheran World Federation." Bibliographical footnotes. [BT703.C49] 73-101426 3.50
1. Jesus Christ—Person and offices. 2. Man (Theology) 3. Social ethics. I. Asheim, Ivar, ed. II. Lutheran World Federation. Commission on Theology.

CHRISTIAN and the world 261
(The); readings in theology [by] Alfons Auer [others] Foreword by John J. Wright. Comp. at the Canisianum, Innsbruck. New York, Kenedy [c.1965] xx, 229p. 22cm. Tr. from German or French. Bibl. [BR123.C58] 65-22645 4.95
1. Christianity—20th cent.—Addresses, essays, lectures. 2. Christian life—Catholic authors. I. Auer, Alfons. II. Title: The world.

CHRISTIAN bases of world 261
order, by Henry A. Wallace [and others] Freeport, N.Y., Books for Libraries Press [1971, c1943] 255 p. 23 cm. (The Merrick lectures for 1943) (Essay index reprint series) Original ed. issued as The Merrick lectures for 1943. These lectures were a part of the Conference on Christian Bases of World Order held at Ohio Wesleyan University, March 8-12, 1943. Bibliography: p. 159-160. [HN31.C43 1971] 75-134068 ISBN 0-8369-2490-8
1. Church and social problems—Addresses, essays, lectures. 2. Christianity—20th century. I. Conference on Christian Bases of World Order, Ohio Wesleyan University, 1943. II. Wallace, Henry Agard, 1888-1965. III. Series: Ohio Wesleyan University. The Merrick-McDowell lectures, 1943.

THE Christian centuries; 261
a new history of the Catholic Church. [New York, McGraw-Hill, 1964- v. illus., maps (1 fold.) ports. 23 cm. Contents.v. 1. The first six hundred years, by J. Danielou and H. Marrou. Bibliography: v. 1, p. [463]-494. [BR145.2.C46] 64-55698
1. Church history. 2. Catholic Church — Hist.

CHRISTIAN in the world. 261
(The) General ed.: Reginald Doherty. [Authors: Francis Kelly, others] Dubuque, Iowa, Priory [c.1963] viii, 527p. maps. 24cm. (Challenge of Christ, no. 4) 63-21761 3.95
1. Religious education—Text-books for young people—Catholic. I. Doherty, Reginald, ed. II. Series.

CHRISTIAN social conscience 261
(The), v.4, by a group of laymen [Tr. from French] NotreDame, Ind., Fides [1966, c.1965] 112p. 21cm. (St. Severin ser. for adult Christians, v.4; Fides paper back textbks., PBT-20) [BT738.M613] 66-3247 1.75 pap.,
1. Sociology, Christian (Catholic)

THE Church amid revolution; 261
a selection of the essays prepared for the World Council of Churches Geneva Conference on Church and Society. Edited by Harvey G. Cox. New York, Association Press [1967] 256 p. 21 cm. [BT738.C52] 67-21140
1. Sociology, Christian—Addresses, essays, lectures. I. Cox, Harvey Gallagher, ed. II. World Conference on Church and Society, Geneva, 1966.

THE Church and human society 261
at the threshold of the third millennium / edited by Joseph Papin. Villanova, Pa. : Villanova University Press, c1974. x, 344 p. ; 23 cm. (The Villanova University symposium ; v. 6, 1973) Includes bibliographical references and indexes. [BR123.C623] 73-189873 ISBN 0-7112-3016-1 : 6.95
1. Christianity—20th century—Addresses, essays, lectures. I. Papin, Joseph, 1914- II. Title. III. Series.

CIANFARRA, Camille 261
Maximilian, 1907-
The Vatican and the Kremlin. [1st ed.] New York, Dutton [1950] 258 p. 22 cm. [HX536.C4] 50-12701
1. Communism and religion. I. Title.

CLUMP, Cyril C 261
A Catholic's guide to social and political action. [Completely rev. ed.] Oxford, Catholic Social Guild [1955] 127p. 19cm. [HN37.C3C529 1955] 57-39518
1. Church and social problems—Catholic Church. 2. Church and state—Catholic Church. 3. Christianity and politics. 4. Questions and answers—Theology. I. Title.

COGGLE, Betrand J. 261
Christian social ethics; a Methodist approach. By Bertrand J. Coggle, John P. K. Byrnes., Foreword by Edward Rogers. London, Epworth Pr. [dist. Mystic, Conn., Verry, 1964] 178p. 19cm. 56-44899 2.50 bds.,
1. Church and social problems. 2. Christian ethics. 3. Social ethics. I. Byrnes, John P. K., joint author. II. Title.

COLE, Chlries Chester. 261
The social ideas of the northern evangelists, 1826-1860. New York, Columbia University Press, 1954. 268p. 24cm. (Columbia studies in the social sciences, no. 580) Bibliography: p. [243]-262. [H31.C7 no.580] 54-6480
1. Evangelists—U. S. 2. U. S.—Church history. 3. Church and social problems—U.S. I. Title. II. Series.

CONFERENCE on Christian 261
Humanism, Asheville, N.C.
The divine synthesis; some lectures, 1961-1964. [Raleigh? N.C., c1968] iv, 352 p. illus. 21 cm. Half title: Some lectures of the Conference on Christian Humanism, 1961-1964. Includes bibliographies. [BX1404.C6] 77-2854
1. Catholic Church in the United States—Congresses. I. Title.

CONGAR, Yves Marie Joseph, 261
1904-
Christians active in the world [by] Yves Congar. Translated by P. J. Hepburne-Scott. [New York] Herder and Herder [1968] viii, 227 p. 22 cm. Translation of Sacerdoce et laicat, second half. Includes bibliographical references. [BX891.C5813 1968] 67-14142 5.95
1. Catholic Church—Collected works. 2. Theology—Collected works—20th century. I. Title.

CORBISHLEY, Thomas 261
The contemporary Christian. [1st Amer. ed.] New York, hawthorn [1967, c.1966] 191 [1]p. 21cm. (Twentieth century ency. of Catholicism, v. 134. Section 14: Outside the church Bibl. [BR123.C69 1967] 67-13949 3.95 bds.,
1. Christianity—20th cent.—Addresses, essays, lectures. I. Title. II. Series.

COX, Harvey Gallagher, ed. 261
The Church amid revolution; a selection of the essays prepared for the World Council of Churches Geneva Conference on Church and Society. Edited by Harvey G. Cox. New York, Association Press [1967] 256 p. 21 cm. [BT738.C52] 67-21140
1. Sociology Christian—Addresses, essays, lectures. I. World Conference on Church and Society, Geneva, 1966. II. Title.

COX, Harvey Gallagher. 261
On not leaving it to the snake, by Harvey G. Cox. New York, Macmillan [1967] xviii, 174 p. 22 cm. [BR123.C726] 67-26056
1. Christianity—20th century—Addresses, essays, lectures. I. Title.

CRANCH, Raymond Greenleaf. 261
Justice in social relations. Bryn Athyn, Pa., 1951. 111 p. 24 cm. [HN37.N4C7] 51-35828
1. Church and social problems—New Jerusalem Church. I. Title.

CREDO, pseud. 261
Man in danger. London, New York, S. Paul [1950] 94 p. 19 cm. [BR115.C5C7] 52-19103
1. Civilization. Christian. I. Title.

CRIPPS, Richard Stafford, 261
Sir, 1889-1952.
Towards Christian democracy. Westport, Conn., Greenwood Press [1970, c1945] 90 p. 23 cm. [BT738.C73 1970] 76-100226
1. Sociology, Christian. 2. Christianity—20th century. I. Title.

CROWE, Charles M 261
In this free land. New York, Abingdon Press [1964] 224 p. 24 cm. Bibliographical footnotes. [BR115.P7C75] 64-16147
1. Christianity and politics. 2. U.S. — Pol. & govt. I. Title.

CROWE, Charles M. 261
In this free land. Nashville, Abingdon [c.1964] 224p. 24cm. Bibl. 64-16147 4.00
1. Christianity and politics. 2. U.S.—Pol. & govt. I. Title.

CULLY, Kendig Brubaker. [261]
We can live together; a reading and study guide for older young people and adults. Boston, Pilgrim Press [1950] 96 p. 21 cm. (Pilgrim series) [BV1550.C8] 268.434 50-2138
1. Religions education —Textbooks for adults—Congregational. 2. Church and social problems—Study and teaching. I. Title.

DALY, Mary. 261
The church and the second sex. [1st ed.] New York, Harper & Row [1968] 187 p. 22 cm. Bibliographical footnotes. [BV639.W7D28] 68-11737
1. Women in Christianity. I. Title.

DANIEL, John. 261
Labor, industry, and the church; a study of the interrelationships involving the church, labor, and management. Saint Louis, Concordia Pub. House [1957] 229p. illus. 21cm. Includes bibliography. [HD6338.D26] 56-12854
1. Church and labor. 2. Industrial relations—U. S. I. Title.

DANIELOU, Jean. 261
Prayer as a political problem, edited and translated by J. R. Kirwan. New York, Sheed and Ward [1967] 123 p. 21 cm. Translation of L'oraison, probleme politique. [BR115.W6D33] 67-21913
1. Church and the world. I. Title.

DANIELOU, Jean, S. J. 261
The scandal of truth. Tr. [from French] by W. J. Kerrigan. Helicon [dist. New York, Taplinger, c.1962] 154 p. 23 cm. 62-18774 3.95, bds.
1. Christianity—20th cent. I. Title.

DANIELOU, Jean. 261
The scandal of truth. Translated by W. J. Kerrigan. Baltimore, Helicon Press [1962] 154 p. 23 cm. Translation of Scandaleuse verite. [BR121.2.D313] 62-18774
1. Christianity — 20th cent. I. Title.

DAUGHTERS of St. Paul. 261
One family under God. [Boston] St. Paul Editions [1968] 98 p. 22 cm. [BR115.W6D34] 68-9497 2.50
1. Church and the world. I. Title.

DAVIDSON, James West. 261
The logic of millennial thought : eighteenth-century New England / James West Davidson. New Haven : Yale University Press, 1977. xii, 308 p. ; 22 cm. (Yale historical publications : Miscellany ; 112) Includes index. Bibliography: p. 298-302. [BR520.D29] 75-43315 ISBN 0-300-01947-5 : 17.50
1. Bible. N.T. Revelation—Criticism, interpretation, etc.—History—18th century. 2. Millennium—History of doctrines. 3. Religious thought—New England. I. Title. II. Series.

DAVIDSON, James West. 261
The logic of millennial thought : eighteenth-century New England / James West Davidson. New Haven : Yale University Press, 1977. xii, 308 p. ; 22 cm. (Yale historical publications : Miscellany ; 112) Includes index. Bibliography: p. 298-302. [BR520.D29] 75-43315 ISBN 0-300-01947-5 : 17.50
1. Bible. N.T. Revelation—Criticism, interpretation, etc.—History—18th century. 2. Millennium—History of doctrines. 3. Religious thought—New England. I. Title. II. Series.

*DAWSON, Christopher 261
The historic reality of Christian culture; a way to the renewal of human life. New York, Harper [1965, c.1960] 131p. 21cm. (Harper torchbks.; Cathedral lib., TB305) Bibl. .95 pap.,
1. Culture. 2. Civilization, Christian. I. Title.

DAWSON, Christopher Henry, 261
1889-
The historic reality of Christian culture; a way to the renewal of human life. New York, Harper [1960] 124 p. 22 cm. (Religious perspectives, v. 1) Includes bibliography. [BR115.C8D3] 60-5291
1. Culture. 2. Civilization, Christian. I. Title. II. Series.

DAWSON, Christopher Henry, 261
1889-1970.
The formation of Christendom, by Christopher Dawson. New York, Sheed and Ward [1967] x, 309 p. 22 cm. Bibliographical footnotes. [BR115.C5D363] 66-22011
1. Civilization, Christian. 2. Civilization, Medieval. 3. Christianity and culture. I. Title.

DAWSON, Christopher Henry, 261
1889-1970.
The historic reality of Christian culture : a way to the renewal of human life / by Christopher Dawson. Westport, Conn. : Greenwood Press, 1976. p. cm. Reprint of the 1960 ed. published by Routledge and Kegan Paul, London, which was issued as v. 1 of Religious perspectives. Includes index. Bibliography: p. [BR115.C8D3 1976] 76-21783 ISBN 0-8371-9001-0 lib.bdg. : 10.75
1. Christianity and culture. 2. Civilization, Christian. I. Title. II. Series: Religious perspectives ; v. 1.

DEBLANK, Joost, Abp. 261
The return of the sacred; forword by the Archibishop of Canterbury. London, Faith Pr.; New York, Morehouse, 1968. 77p. 19cm. (Archbishop of Canterbury's Lent bk.) [BR115.W6D4] 68-85404 1.95 pap.,
1. Church and the world. I. Title. II. Series.

DELESPESSE, Max. 261
The church community; leaven & life-style. Notre Dame, Ind., Ave Maria Press [1973] 143 p. 21 cm. Translation of Cette communaute qu'on appelle Eglise. Includes bibliographical references. [BX1746.D3813 1973] 73-80089 ISBN 0-87793-057-0 1.95
1. Church. I. Title.

DICKEY, Christina Robinson, 261
1888-
An emerging civilization. Dallas, Story Book Press [1952] 214p. 20cm. [BR115.H5D5] 53-1398
1. History—Philosophy. 2. Civilization, Christian. 3. Anglo-Israelism. I. Title.

DIRKSEN, Cletus Francis, 261
1907-
Catholic social principles. St. Louis, Herder [c.1961] 247p. Bibl. 61-17788 4.00
1. Sociology, Christian (Catholic) 2. Individuality. 3. Liberty. I. Title.

DROLET, Francis K. 261
New communities for Christians [by] Francis K. Drolet. Staten Island, N.Y., Alba House [1972] xviii, 396 p. 22 cm. Bibliography: p. [377]-384. [BX2350.2.A1D76] 79-39629 ISBN 0-8189-0242-6 3.95
1. Christian life—Societies, etc. 2. Christian life—Catholic authors. I. Title.

DRUMMOND, William Francis. 261
Every man a brother, by William F. Drummond. Foreword by John F. Cronin. Washington, Corpus Bks. [1968] 160p. 22cm. Bibl. [HN37.C3D69] 68-10449 4.95
1. Church and social problems—Catholic Church. 2. Encyclicals, Papal. I. Title.
Publisher's address: 1330 Massachusetts Ave., N.W., Washington, D.C. 20005.

DULLES, Avery Robert, 1918- 261
The dimensions of the church; a postconciliar reflection, by Avery Dulles. Westminster, Md., Newman Press, 1967. ix, 118 p. 21 cm. (Woodstock papers; occasional essays for theology, no. 8) Bibliographical footnotes. [BX1746.D8] 67-20429
1. Church. I. Title. II. Series.

DULLES, John Foster, 1888- 261
1959.
The spiritual legacy of John Foster Dulles: selections from his articles and addresses. Edited with an introd. by Henry P. Van Dusen. Freeport, N.Y., Books for Libraries Press [1972, c1960] xxii, 232 p. 22 cm. (Essay index reprint series) [BR115.I7D8 1972] 72-3360 ISBN 0-8369-2899-7
1. Christianity and international affairs—Addresses, essays, lectures. 2. United States—Religion—Addresses, essays, lectures. I. Title.

DUSHAW, Amos Isaac, 1877- 261
No room for Him. Brooklyn, Tolerance Press [1950] 127 p. 18 cm. [BR1610.D8] 50-8526
1. Toleration. 2. Race problems. I. Title.

EAGLETON, Terence, 1943- 261
The New Left church [essays] Baltimore, Helicon [1966] x, 180 p. 18 cm. (A Helicon paperbook) Bibliographical footnotes. [BR115.C8E3] 66-24850
1. Christianity and culture. I. Title.

EBERHARD, Kenneth D. 261
The alienated Christian: a theology of alienation [by] Kenneth D. Eberhard. Philadelphia, Pilgrim Press Book [1971] 190 p. 22 cm. Includes bibliographical references. [BT731.E2] 78-155657 ISBN 0-8298-0194-4 6.95
1. Alienation (Theology) I. Title.

ECCLESIASTICAL History 261
Society, London.
Sanctity and secularity; the church and the world. Papers read at the eleventh summer meeting and the twelfth winter meeting of the Ecclesiastical History Society; edited by Derek Baker. Oxford [Eng.] Published for the Ecclesiastical History Society by B. Blackwell, 1973. xiii, 223 p. 23 cm. (Studies in church history (London) no. 10) Includes bibliographical references. [BR141.S84 vol. 10] 73-82131 ISBN 0-631-15120-6 £5.00
1. Church history—Congresses. 2. Church and the world—Congresses. I. Baker, Derek, ed. II. Title. III. Series.

ECCLESIASTICAL History 261
Society, London.
Sanctity and secularity: the church and the world; papers read at the eleventh summer meeting and the twelfth winter meeting of the Ecclesiastical History Society. Edited by Derek Baker. New York, Barnes & Noble [1973] xiii, 223 p. 23 cm. (Studies in church

history, 10) Includes bibliographical references. [BR140.E28 1973] 74-159033 ISBN 0-06-490296-X 17.50
1. Church history—Congresses. 2. Church and the world—Congresses. I. Baker, Derek, ed. II. Title. III. Series: Studies in church history (New York), 10.

ELLIOTT, Ralph H. 261
Reconciliation and the new age [by] Ralph H. Elliott. Valley Forge [Pa.] Judson Press [1973] 125 p. 22 cm. (Lakeview books) Includes bibliographical references. [BS680.R28E45] 72-9568 ISBN 0-8170-0586-2 2.95
1. Reconciliation—Biblical teaching. I. Title.

EPSOM College, Epsom, Eng. 261
Register, 1855-1954, edited by T. R. Thomson. Oxford, Printed at the University Press for the Old Epsomian Club, 1955. 620 p. illus. 23 cm. [LF795.E6A65] 56-23431
I. Thomson, Theodore Radford, 1897- ed. II. Title.

EVELY, Louis, 1910- 261
If the Church is to survive... Translated by J. F. Bernard. [1st ed.] Garden City, N.Y., Doubleday, 1972. 144 p. 22 cm. Translation of Si l'Eglise ne meurt... Includes bibliographical references. [BX1746.E913] 72-79374 ISBN 0-385-03846-1 4.95
1. Church. I. Title.

FANFANI, Amintore 261
Catechism of Catholic social teaching. Translated [From the Italian] by Henry J. Yannone. Westminster, Med., Newman Press [c.]1960. xxvii, 208p. 22cm. Bibl.: p.xiii-xvi 60-10719 2.95
1. Sociology, Christian (Catholic) 2. Church and state—Catholic Church. I. Title.

FERRE, Nels Fredrick Solomon, 1908- 261
Christianity and society. [1st ed.] New York, Harper [1950] viii, 280 p. 22 cm. (His Reason and the Christian faith, v. 8) Bibliographical footnotes. [BR115.S6F44] 50-6197
1. Sociology, Christian. I. Title.

FERRE, Nels Fredrick Solomon, 1908- 261
Christianity and society, by Nels F. S. Ferre. Freeport, N.Y., Books for Libraries Press [1970, c1950] viii, 280 p. 23 cm. (Essay index reprint series) "Originally published as volume III of [the author's] Reason and the Christian faith series." Includes bibliographical references. [BT738.F47 1970] 78-117791
1. Sociology, Christian. I. Title.

FERWERDA, Vernon L. 261
East and West: one world, or two? New York, Friendship [1965] 63p. 16cm. (Questions for Christians, no. 4) Bibl. [JX1395.F45] 65-11432 .65 pap.,
1. International relations. 2. World politics—1945- 3. Christianity and international affairs. I. Title. II. Series.

FISHER, Wallace E. 261
Can man hope to be human? [By] Wallace E. Fisher. Nashville, Abingdon Press [1971] 160 p. 23 cm. Includes bibliographical references. [BR115.W6F57] 75-138276 ISBN 0-687-04613-0 3.95
1. Church and the world. I. Title.

FORWARD, Carnice E. 261
If one be lifted up; the nucleus of peace. New York, Carlton [dist. Comet, c.]1962. 21p. (Reflection bk.) 1.95
I. Title.

FREED, David A 261
My case for freedom. San Antonio, Naylor Co. [1962] 112 p. 22 cm. [JC585.] 62-19537
1. Liberty. I. Title.

FREED, David A 261
My case for freedom. San Antonio, Naylor Co. [1962] 112 p. 22 cm. [JC585.F65] 62-19537
1. Liberty. I. Title.

FRY, Thomas A. 261
Change, chaos, and Christianity [by] Thomas A. Fry, Jr. Westwood, N.J., F. H. Revell Co. [1967] 124 p. 21 cm. [BR121.2.F7] 67-22568
1. Christianity—20th century. 2. Protestant churches—United States. I. Title.

GALLOWAY, Allan Douglas, 1920- 261
Faith in a changing culture; Kerr lectures. delivered at Glasgow University. 1966, by Allan D. Galloway. London, Allen & Unwin. 1967. 3-122p. 23cm. (Kerr lects., 1966) Bibl. [BR115.C8G3] 67-111154 4.50 bds.,
1. Christianity and culture—Addresses, essays, lectures. I. Title. II. Series.
Distributed by Humanities, New York.

GARAUDY, Roger. 261
A Christian-Communist dialogue [by] Roger Garaudy and Quentin Lauer. [1st ed.] Garden City, N.Y., Doubleday, 1968. 190 p. 22 cm. Bibliography: p. [189]-190. [BR128.A8G3] 68-27118 4.95
1. Communism and Christianity. I. Lauer, Quentin, joint author. II. Title.

GEORGETOWN University 261
Colloquium on the Church in the Modern World, 1966.
The church in the world, Ed. by Charles P. O'Donnell. Milwaukee, Bruce [1967] xiv, 173p. 22cm. Bibl. [BR115.W6 G4 1966] 67-28888 5.95
1. Church and the world. I. O'Donnell, Charles P., 1904- ed. II. Title.

GILMORE, Conal Gregory. 261
History of King Edward VI School, Stafford Oxford, Printed at the University Press by C. Batey, 1953. 137p. illus. 23cm. [LF795.S73G5] 56-46773
1. Stafford, Eng. King Edward VI School. I. Title.

GLEASON, Philip. 261
The conservative reformers; German-American Catholics and the social order. Notre Dame, University of Notre Dame Press [1968] x, 272 p. 24 cm. Includes bibliographical references. [HN39.U6G56] 68-17062
1. Church and social problems—Catholic Church. 2. Germans in the United States. 3. Catholic Church in the Unites States. I. Title.

GLOCK, Charles Y. 261
To comfort and to challenge; a dilemma of the contemporary church, by Charles Y. Glock, Benjamin B. Ringer, Earl R. Babbie. Berkeley, Univ. of Calif. Pr., 1967. 268p. 24cm. Based on res. done in 1952 by the Bur. of Applied Soc. Res. of Columbia Univ. for the Dept. of Christian Soc. Relationsof the Natl. Council of the protestant Episcopal Church. Bibl. [BT738.G54] 67-15560 5.75
1. Sociology, Christia. 2. u.S.—Religion. I. Ringer, Benjamin Bernard, 1920- joint author. II. Babbie, Earl R., joint author. III. Columbia University. Bureau of Applied Social Research. IV. Protestant Episcopal Church in the U. S. A. National Council. Dept. of Christian Social Relations. V. Title.

GLOCK, Charles Y. 261
To comfort and to challenge: a dilemma of the contemporary church, by Charles Y. Glock, Benjamin B. Ringer [and] Earl R. Babbie. Berkeley, University of California Press, 1967. 268 p. 24 cm. Based on research done in 1952 by the Bureau of Applied Social Research of Columbia University for the Dept. of Christian Social Relations of the National Council of the Protestant Episcopal Church. Bibliographical footnotes. [BT738.G54] 67-15560
1. Sociology, Christian. 2. U.S. — Religion. I. Ringer, Benjamin Ber4ard, 1920- joint author. II. Babbie, Earl R., Joint author. III. Columbia University. Bureau of Applied Social Research. IV. Protestant Episcopal Church in the U.S.A. National Council. Dept. of Christian Social Relations. V. Title.

GOLDWIN, Robert A 1922- ed. 261
Liberalism and conservatism four essays by Samuel H. Beer [and others] eidted by Robert A. Goldwin. [Chicago] University of Chicago, Public Affairs Conference Center [1965] 1 v. (various pagings) 30 cm. Bibliographical references included in footnotes. [JC585.G67] 66-3748
1. Liberalism — Addresses, essays, lectures 2. Conservatism — Addresses, essays, lectures. I. Beer, Samuel Hutchinson, 1911- II. Title.

GOLLWITZER, Helmut. 261
The Christian faith and the Marxist criticism of religion. [Translated by David Cairns] New York, Scribner [1970] ix, 173 p. 20 cm. Translation of Die marxistiche Religionskritik und der christliche Glaube. Includes bibliographical references. [BR128.A8G613 1970b] 69-17055 5.95
1. Communism and Christianity. I. Title.

GONZALEZ Ruiz, Jose Maria, 1916- 261
Atheistic humanism and the Biblical God. Translation by Amado Jose Sandoval. Milwaukee, Bruce [1969] xi, 180 p. 22 cm. Translation of El cristianismo no es un humanismo. Includes bibliographical references. [BR115.W6G6613] 69-18134 7.95
1. Church and the world. 2. Christianity—20th century. I. Title.

GRAHAM, W. Fred, 1930- 261
Picking up the pieces / W. Fred Graham. Grand Rapids : Eerdmans, [1975] 232 p. ; 21 cm. Bibliography: p. 230-232. [BT1102.G72] 74-26818 ISBN 0-8028-1593-6 pbk. : 3.95
1. Apologetics—20th century. 2. Religion and sociology. 3. Secularism. 4. Religion and science—1946- I. Title.

GREMILLION, Joseph B. 261
Continuing Christ in the modern world; teaching Christian social concepts in the light of Vatican Council II, by Joseph Gremillion. Dayton, Ohio, Paflaum [1967] 189p. illus, map. 17cm. Bibl. [BX1753.G7] 67-28059 1.00 pap.,
1. Sociology, Christian (Catholic)—Study and teaching. I. Title.

GREMILLION, Joseph B. 261
The other dialogue [by] Joseph Gremillion. [1st ed.] Garden City, N. Y., Doubleday, 1965. 308 p. 22 cm. [HN37.C3G68] 64-19259
1. Church and social problems—Catholic Church. I. Title.

GRIFFITHS, Michael C. 261
God's forgetful pilgrims : recalling the church to its reason for being / Michael Griffiths. Grand Rapids : Eerdmans, [1975] 176 p. ; 18 cm. Includes bibliographical references. [BV600.2.G754 1975] 75-16166 ISBN 0-8028-3463-9
1. Church. I. Title.

GRIMES, Howard 261
The church redemptive. New York, Abingdon [1967, c.1958] 191p. 20cm. [BV820.G74] 58-7431 1.45 pap.,
1. Church membership. I. Title.

GRUNDMANN, Elisabeth. 261
Bevolkerungsentwicklung und Beschaftigung in Lateinamerika : ausgewalte neuere Literatur = Desarrollo demografico y empleo en America Latina : bibliografia selecta / Bearbeitung, Elisabeth Grundmann. Hamburg : Institut fur Iberamerika-Kunde, Dokumentations-Leitstelle Lateinamerika, 1975. xiv, 226 p. ; 30 cm. (Dokumentationsdienst Lateinamerika ; Reihe A, 1) Introductory material in German and Spanish; list of bibliographical works in English, French, German, Portuguese, Russian, and Spanish. Includes index. [Z7165.L3G78] [HN110.5.A8] 016.016916'03 76-458371 DM20.00
1. Latin America—Social conditions—Bibliography. 2. Labor and laboring classes—Latin America—Bibliography. I. Title. II. Title: Desarrollo demografico y empleo en America Latina. III. Series.

HAMILTON, James Wallace, 1900- 261
The thunder of bare feet. [Westwood, N.J.] Revell [1964] 100 p. 21 cm. (Sermons on Christian social concerns) [BV4253.H34] 64-12200
1. Sermons, American. I. Title.

HAMILTON, James Wallace, 1900- 261
The thunder of bare feet. [Westwood, N.J.] Revell [c.1964] 160p. 21cm. (Sermons on Christian soc. concerns) 64-12200 2.95
1. Sermons, American. I. Title.

HANDY, Robert T. ed. 261
The Social Gospel in america, 1870-1920. New York, oxford [c.1966]. xii, 399 24 cm (lib. of Protestant thought) Contents.Gladden Ely.—Rauchenbusch Bibl. [BT738.H29] 66-14977
1. Social Gospel. sociology, Christian—Hist. series. I. Title. II. Series.

HANDY, Robert T. ed. 261
The Social Gospel in America, 1870-1920. New York, Oxford [c.1966.] xii, 399p. 24cm. (Lib. of Protestant thought) Bi2l*Contents omitted. [BT738.H29] 66-14977 7.00
1. Social Gospel. 2. Sociology, Christian—Hist. Series) I. Title.
Contents omitted.

HANDY, Robert T ed. 261
The Social Gospel in America, 1870-1920, edited by Robert T. Handy. New York, Oxford University Press, 1966. xii, 399 p. 24 cm. (A Library of Protestant thought) Contents.Contents.--Gladden.--Ely.--Rauschenbusch. Bibliography: p. 391-393. [BT38.H29] 66-14977
1. Social Gospel. 2. Sociology, Christian—Hist. I. Title. II. Series.

HANKE, Howard A 261
Christ and the church in the Old Testament; a survey of redemptive unity in the testaments. Foreword by Russell C. Murphy. Grand Rapids, Mich., Zondervan Pub. House [1957] 187p. 20cm. [BV600.H27] 57-34943
1. Church—Biblical teaching. 2. Bible. N. T.—Relation to O. T. I. Title.

HANKO, Charles William, 1920- 261
Christianity mobilizing. Newark, N. J., Washington Irving Pub. Co., 1955. 197p. 22cm. [BR121.H256] 55-10881
1. Christianity—20th cent. 2. Christian life. 3. Success. I. Title.

HARKNESS, Georgia Elma, 1891- 261
The methodist Church in social thought and action. Edited by the Board of Social and Economic Relations of the Methodist Church. New York, Abingdon Press [1964] 172 p. 23 cm. [BT738.H3] 64-16150
1. Sociology, Christian (Methodist) I. Methodist Church (United States) Board of Social and Economic Relations. II. Title.

HARKNESS, Georgia Elma, 1891- 261
The Methodist Church in social thought and action. Ed. by the Bd. of Soc. & Econ. Relations of the Methodist Church. Nashville, Abingdon [c.1964] 172p. 23cm. 64-16150 1.50 pap.,
1. Sociology, Christian (Methodist) I. Methodist Church (United States) Board of Social and Economic Relations. II. Title.

HARKNESS, Georgia Elma, 1891- 261
The ministry of reconciliation [by] Georgia Harkness. Nashville, Abingdon Press [1971] 160 p. 20 cm. [BV4509.5.H3] 79-134243 2.45
1. Reconciliation. I. Title.

HEISS, Willard. 261
A list of all the Friends Meetings that exist or ever have existed in Indiana, 1807-1955. Rev. Indianapolis, Indiana Quaker records, 1961. 85p. 21cm. [BX7648.I5H4 1961] 62-5786
1. Friends, Society of. Indiana. 2. Churches—Indiana. I. Title.

HEISS, Willard C comp. 261
Indiana Quaker records. Indianapolis, 19 v. 36 cm. Contents.v. 6. Milford Monthly Meeting, Wayne County, Indiana. [BX7648.85H38] 63-42754
1. Friends, Society of. Indiana — Hist. — Sources. I. Title.

HEISS, Willard C 261
A list of all the Friends Meetings that exist or ever have existed in Indiana. 1807-1955. Rev. Indianapolis, Indiana Quaker records, 1961. 85 p. 21 cm. Friends, Society of. Indiana. [BX7648.I5H4 1961] 62-5786
I. Title.

HENRY, Carl Ferdinand Howard, 1913- 261
Aspects of Christian social ethics [by] Carl F. H. Henry. Grand Rapids, W. B. Eerdmans Pub. Co. [1964] 190 p. 22 cm. (The Payton lectures, 1963) Bibliographical footnotes. [BT38.H4] 63-20686
1. Sociology, Christian. I. Title. II. Series.

HENRY, Carl Ferdinand Howard, 1913- 261
Aspects of Christian social ethics. Grand Rapids, Mich., Eerdmans [c.1964] 190p. 22cm. (Payton lect. 1963) Bibl. 63-20686 8.95
1. Sociology, Christian. I. Title. II. Series.

HERRON, George Davis, 1862-1925. 261
The Christian society. With a new introd. by Milton Cantor. New York, Johnson Reprint Corp., 1969. xxix, 158 p. 18 cm. (Series in American studies) Reprint of the 1894 ed. Bibliography: p. xxviii-xxix. [BT738.H45 1969] 78-79659
1. Sociology, Christian. 2. Social gospel. I. Title. II. Series.

HESSERT, Paul. 261
Introduction to Christianity. Englewood Cliffs, N. J., Prentice-Hall, 1958. 383p. 22cm. Includes bibliography. [BR121.2.H4] 59-5039
1. Christianity—Essence, genius, nature. I. Title.

HEYER, Robert J., comp. 261
Discovery in politics: humanizing the world and its structures [compiled by] Robert J. Heyer, Richard J. Payne [and] Mary E. Tierney. New York, Paulist Press [1971] 160 p. illus. 21 cm. (Discovery series) [BV1561.H46] 70-152574 2.50
1. Religious education—Text-books for young people. I. Payne, Richard J., joint comp. II. Tierney, Mary E., joint comp. III. Title.

HEYNE, William P. 261
This is our destiny. Boston, Christopher Pub. House [1952] 210 p. 21 cm. [BR126.H47] 52-946
I. Title.

HODGSON, Peter Crafts, 1934- 261
New birth of freedom : a theology of bondage and liberation / Peter C. Hodgson. Philadelphia : Fortress Press, c1976. xvi, 368 p. ; 24 cm. Includes bibliographical references and indexes. [BT810.2.H58] 75-37145 ISBN 0-8006-0437-7 : 14.95. ISBN 0-8006-1437-2 pbk. :
1. Freedom (Theology) I. Title.

HOFFNER, Joseph, Bp. 261
Fundamentals of Christian sociology. Translated by Geoffrey Stevens. Westminster, Md. Newman Press [1965] 196 p. 22 cm. Translation of Christliche Gesellschaftslehre. [BT738.H613 1965] 65-26782

1. Sociology, Christian (Catholic) I. Title.

HOFFNER, Joseph 261
Fundamentals of Christian sociology. Tr. [from German] by Geoffrey Stevens. Westminster, Md. Newman [1965] 196p. 22cm. [BT738.H613] 65-26782 4.75
1. Sociology, Christian (Catholic) I. Title.

HOPKINS, Charles Howard, 1905- 261
The rise of the social gospel in American Protestantism: 1865-1915, by Charles Howard Hopkins. New Haven, Yale [1967,c.1940] xiv. 352p. 21cm. (Half-title: Yale Studies in religious educ. xiv) Presented for the degree of Ph.D at Yale [1937] Pub. under the joint sponsorship of the Samuel B. Smeath memorial pubns. fund of the Yale divinity sch. and the Rauschenbusch memorial lectship. found. of the Colgate-Rochester divinity sch. [HN39.U6H6 1967] 41-1101 8.50; 2.45 pap.,
1. Sociology, Christian—Hist. 2. Theology, Doctrinal—Hist.—U. S. I. Title. II. Title: The social gospel in American Protestantism.

*HOPPS, Abe Albert, M.D. 261
Facts, fantasy and comparison. New York, Vantage [c.1965] 99p. 21cm. 2.75 bds.,
I. Title.

HOUTART, Francois, 1925- 261
The challenge to change; the church confronts the future. Edited by Mary Anne Chouteau. New York, Sheed and Ward [1964] xi, 212 p. 21 cm. "Edited from a series of ten lectures given in August, 1963 ... [by the author at the] Fifth Marquette University Workshop in Curriculum and Role of the Faculty in the Formation of Sisters." [BX1746.H6] 64-20406
1. Catholic Church—Addresses, essays, lectures. 2. Christianity—20th century. 3. Pastoral theology—Catholic Church. I. Title.

HOUTEPEN, Anton W. J., 1940- 261
Theology of the Saeculum : a study of the concept of Saeculum in the documents of Vatican II and of the World Council of Churches, 1961-1972 / Anton Houtepen ; [translation, M. Goosen-Mallory]. Kampen : Kok, [1976] 170 p. ; 25 cm. Translation of Theologie van het saeculum. Includes bibliographical references and index. [BR115.W6H6713] 76-368388 ISBN 9-02-421392-4 : fl 42.00
1. Vatican Council, 2d, 1962-1965. 2. World Council of Churches. 3. Church and the world—History—Addresses, essays, lectures. 4. History (Theology)—History of doctrines—Addresses, essays, lectures. I. Title.

HUDNUT, Robert K. 261
The sleeping giant; arousing church power in America [by] Robert K. Hudnut. [1st ed.] New York, Harper & Row [1971] 164 p. 22 cm. Includes bibliographical references. [BR121.2.H78 1971] 72-163161 ISBN 0-06-064063-4 5.95
1. Christianity—20th century. 2. Church and social problems. I. Title.

HUNTER, Gordon C. 261
When the walls come tumblin' down, by Gordon C. Hunter. Foreword by Bruce Larson. Waco, Tex., Word Books [1970] 139 p. 23 cm. Includes bibliographical references. [BV4509.5.H85] 79-135354 3.95
1. Reconciliation. I. Title.

INGE, William Ralph, 1860-1954. 261
Christian ethics and modern problems. Westport, Conn., Greenwood Press [1970] ix, 427 p. 23 cm. Reprint of the 1930 ed. [BJ1251.I54 1970] 72-104283 ISBN 0-8371-3960-0
1. Christian ethics. 2. Social problems. I. Title.

INSTITUTE of Spirituality. 261
The world in the church. Jordan Aumann, editor. Chicago, Priory Press [1969] 161 p. 23 cm. (Its Special lectures, v. 4, 1968) Bibliographical footnotes. [BR115.W615] 79-95907 5.95
1. Church and the world—Addresses, essays, lectures. I. Aumann, Jordan, ed. II. Title. III. Series.

JACKSON, Edgar Newman. 261
How to preach to people's needs. New York, Abingdon Press [c1956] 191p. 21cm. [BV4211.J25] 55-10269
1. Preaching. 2. Psychology, Pastoral. I. Title.

JACOBS, Donald R. 261
The Christian stance in a revolutionary age, by Donald R. Jacobs. Scottdale, Pa., Herald Press [1968] 32 p. 20 cm. (Focal pamphlet series, no. 14) Bibliography: p. 30-32. [BR125.J243] 68-7502 0.35
1. Christianity—20th century. I. Title.

JENKINS, Daniel Thomas, 1914- 261
The strangeness of the church. [1st ed.] Garden City, N. Y., Doubleday, 1955. 188p. 22cm. (Christian faith series) [BV600.J43] 55-8404
1. Church. I. Title.

JOHNSON, Merle Allison. 261
Beyond disenchantment. Old Tappan, N.J., F. H. Revell Co. [1972] 123 p. 21 cm. [BR121.5.J64] 76-172683 ISBN 0-8007-0495-9 3.50
1. Christianity—20th century. I. Title.

JONAS, Gerald, 1935- 261
On doing good. New York, Scribners [1973, c.1971] 177 p. 21 cm. (Lyceum Editions, SL416) [BX7631.2.J64] 79-143914 pap., 2.45
1. Friends, Society of—History. 2. Friends, Society of, American Friends Service Committee. I. Title.

KALT, William J. 261
The community of the free [by] William J. Kalt and Ronald J. Wilkins. Chicago, Regnery [1968] ii, 121 p. illus. 23 cm. (To live is Christ. Discussion booklet 6) Bibliographical footnotes. [BT38.K3] 68-55751
1. Sociology, Christian (Catholic)—Study and teaching. I. Wilkins, Ronald J., joint author. II. Title.

KANTZENBACH, Friedrich Wilhelm. 261
Christentum in der Gesellschaft : Grundlinien d. Kirchengeschichte / Friedrich Wilhelm Kantzenbach. Orig.-Veroffentlichung. Hamburg : Siebenstern-Taschenbuch-Verlag, 1975- v. ; 19 cm. (Siebenstern-Taschenbuch ; 185) Includes index. Contents.Contents.—Bd. 1. Alte Kirche und Mittelalter. Bibliography: v. 1, 299-309. [BR145.2.K35] 75-510392 ISBN 3-7970-0146-0 (v. 1) : DM11.90 (v. 1)
1. Church history. 2. Socilogy, Christian. I. Title.

KEAN, Charles Duell, 1910- 261
The Christian gospel and the parish church; an introduction to parish dynamics. Greenwich, Conn., Seabury Press, 1953. 142p. 22cm. [BX5930.K35] 53-12395
1. Protestant Episcopal Church in the U. S. A.—Doctrinal and controversial works. I. Title.

KELLEY, Dean M. 261
Why conservative churches are growing; a study in sociology of religion [by] Dean M. Kelley. [1st ed.] New York, Harper & Row [1972] xiii, 184 p. illus. 22 cm. Includes bibliographical references. [BT738.K38] 77-175156 6.95
1. Sociology, Christian. 2. Church growth. I. Title.

KELLY, George Anthony, 1916- 261
Who should run the Catholic Church? : Social scientists, theologians, or bishops? / George A. Kelly. Huntington, IN : Our Sunday Visitor, inc., c1976. 224 p. ; 22 cm. Includes bibliographical references and index. [BX1751.2.K37] 76-3291 ISBN 0-87973-755-7 : 8.95
1. Catholic Church—Doctrinal and controversial works—Catholic authors. 2. Sociology, Christian (Catholic) I. Title.

KENNEDY, Gerald Hamilton, Bp., 1907- 261
The Christian and his America. [1st ed.] New York, Harper [1956] 175p. 22cm. [BR516.K4] 56-12068
1. U. S.—Religion. 2. Christianity—Addresses, essays, lectures. I. Title.

KERSTEN, Lawrence K. 261
The Lutheran ethic; the impact of religion on laymen and clergy, by Lawrence K. Kersten. Detroit, Wayne State University Press, 1970. 309 p. 21 cm. Includes bibliographical references. [BX8041.K45 1970] 71-102200 ISBN 0-8143-1416-3 8.95
1. Lutherans in the United States—Statistics. 2. Sociology, Christian (Lutheran)—Statistics. I. Title.

KNUDTEN, Richard D., comp. 261
The sociology of religion, an anthology, ed. by Richard D. Knudten. New York, Appleton [1967] xiii, 560p. illus. 24cm. (Sociology ser.) Bibl. [BL60.K55] 67-14572 6.95
1. Religion and sociology. I. Title.

KNUDTEN, Richard D., comp. 261
the sociology of religion, an anthology, edited by Richard D. Knudten. New York, Appleton-Century-Crofts [1967] xiii, 500 p. illus. 24 cm. (Sociology series) Bibliographical footnotes. [BL60.K55] 67-14572
1. Religion and sociology. I. Title.

KRAMER, Leonard J ed. 261
Man amid change in world affairs. Edited with an introd. by Leonard J. Kramer. New York, Friendship Press, 1964. 175 p. 19 cm. Bibliography: p. [171]-175. [D844.K7314] 64-22938
1. World politics — 1965- 2. Christianity and international affairs. I. Title.

KRAMER, Leonard J., ed. 261
Man amid changes in world affairs. New York, Friendship [c.]1964. 175p. 19cm. Bibl. 64-22938 1.95 pap.,
1. World politics—1965- 2. Christianity and international affairs. I. Title.

KRUTZA, William J. 261
Facing the issues [by] William J. Krutza and Phillip P. DiCicco. Grand Rapids, Mich., Baker Book House [1969] 119 p. 18 cm. (Contemporary discussion series, 1) Includes bibliographical references. [BR115.W6K7] 76-10693 1.25
1. Church and the world. I. Di Cicco, Phillip P., joint author. II. Title.

KUHNELT-LEDDIHN, Erik Maria, Ritter von, 1909- 261
The timeless Christian [by] Erik von Kuehnelt-Leddihn. [Translated by Ronald Walls. Chicago] Franciscan Herald Press [1969] xxi, 220 p. illus. 22 cm. Translation of Hirn, Herz, und Ruckgrat. Bibliographical references included in "Notes" (p. 207-220) [BR124.K813] 73-106047 4.50
1. Christianity—Miscellanea. I. Title.

KUIPER, Rienk Bouke, 1886- 261
The glorious body of Christ. Grand Rapids, Mich., Eerdmans [1958?] 383p. 23cm. [BV600.K8] 58-13510
1. Church. I. Title.

LANDWEHR, Arthur J., 1934- 261
In the third place: an alternative for the Christian [by] Arthur J. Landwehr II. Nashville, Abingdon Press [1971, c1972] 128 p. illus. 19 cm. Includes bibliographical references. [BR115.W6L36 1972] 70-172810 ISBN 0-687-19427-X
1. Church and the world. I. Title.

LA ROE, Wilbur, 1888- 261
The church we love. Nashville, Abingdon-Cokesbury Press [1953] 79p. 21cm. [BV600.L34] 53-10009
1. Church. 2. Laity. I. Title.

LATOURETTE, Kenneth Scott, 1884- 261
Challenge and conformity; studies in the interaction of Christianity and the world of today. [1st ed.] New York, Harper [1955] 126p. 20cm. [BR481.L28] 55-6787
1. Christianity—20th cent. 2. Christianity—Influence. I. Title. II. Title: Interaction of Christianity and the world.

LAW, church, and society : 261
essays in honor of Stephan Kuttner / edited by Kenneth Pennington and Robert Somerville. [Philadelphia] : University of Pennsylvania Press, 1977. p. cm. (The Middle Ages) Includes index. [BR252.L38] 76-53199 ISBN 0-8122-7726-0 : 22.50
1. Kuttner, Stephen George, 1907- 2. Christianity—Middle Ages, 600-1500—Addresses, essays, lectures. 3. Canon law—Addresses, essays, lectures. I. Kuttner, Stephan Georg, 1907- II. Pennington, Kenneth, 1941- III. Somerville, Robert, 1940- IV. Series.
Contents omitted

LEE, Robert, ed. 261
Religion and social conflict, based upon lectures given at the Institute of Ethics and Society at San Francisco Theological Seminary. Edited by Robert Lee [and] Martin E. Marty. New York, Oxford University Press, 1964. vii, 193 p. 21 cm. Includes bibliographical references. [BR516.L44] 64-11231
1. Christianity and politics. 2. United States—Religion—1945- 3. Social conflict. I. Marty, Martin E., 1928- joint ed. II. San Francisco Theological Seminary, San Anselmo, Calif. Institute of Ethics and Society. III. Title.

LEUBA, James Henry, 1868-1946. 261
The reformation of the churches. Boston, Beacon Press, 1950. xiii, 219 p. 22 cm. Bibliographical footnotes. [BT78.L4] 50-6154
1. Modernism. 2. Humanism, Religions. I. Title.

LINCOLN, Anthony. 261
Some political & social ideas of English dissent, 1763-1800. New York, Octagon Books, 1971. 292 p. 21 cm. Reprint of the 1938 ed. Bibliography: p. [275]-285. [BX5203.L5 1971] 72-120642 ISBN 0-374-95012-1
1. Dissenters, Religious—England. 2. Political science—History—Gt. Brit. 3. Church and social problems—Gt. Brit. I. Title.

LINK, Mark J. 261
Man in the modern world; perspectives, problems, profiles [by] Mark J. Link. Chicago, Loyola University Press [1967] x, 256 p. illus. 24 cm. [BT738.L5] 67-3706
1. Sociology, Christian (Catholic) 2. Religious education—Text-books for young people—Catholic Church. I. Title.

LITTLE, Paul E. 261
Lost audience [a brief discussion of evangelism] Chicago 10, 1519 North Astor, Inter-Varsity Press, [1960] 24p. 13cm. .25 pap.,
I. Title.

LOEW, Jacques, 1908- 261
Mission to the poorest. With an introd. and epilogue by Maisie Ward. Foreword by Archbishop Cushing. New York, Sheed and Ward, 1950. vii, 184p. 21cm. 'A translation by Pamela Carswell of [v. 1 of] En mission proletarienne by Pere Loew.' [HN39.F8L62] 50-9864
1. Church and social problems—France. 2. Church and social problems—Catholic Church. I. Title.

LOEW, M. R. 261
Mission to the poorest. With an introd. and epilogue by Maisie Ward. Foreword by Archbishop Cushing. New York, Sheed and Ward, 1950. vii. 184 p. 21 cm. "A translation by Pamela Carswell of [v. 1 of] En mission proletarienne, by Pere Loew." [HN39.F8L62] 50-9864
1. Church and social problems—France. 2. Church and social problems—Catholic Church. Name in religion: Jacques Lowe, Father. I. Title.

LOMBARDI, Riccardo. 261
Towards a new world. Translated and condensed from the Italian. New York, Philosophical Library [1958] 276p. illus. 22cm. [BX1753.L633] 58-4833
1. Sociology, Christian (Catholic) 2. Civilization, Christian. I. Title.

LORACK, George. 261
It just doesn't make sense. [1st ed.] New York, Vantage Press [1971] 381 p. 22 cm. Conduct of life. Common sense. [BJ1581.2.L67] 76-24670 7.50
I. Title.

LUBAC, Henri de, 1896- 261
The splendour of the church; translated by Michael Mason. New York, Sheed and Ward [1956] 289p. 22cm. 'Translation of the second edition of Meditation surl eglise' [BX1751.L933] 55-9454
1. Church. 2. Catholic Church. I. Title.

LUBAC, Henri de, 1896- 261
The splendour of the church. Translated by Michael Mason. Glen Rock, N.J. Paulist Press [1963, c1956] 352 p. 18 cm. (Deus books) "A translation of the second edition of Meditation sur l'Eglise." Bibliographical references included in "Footnotes" (p. 236-352) [BX1746.L933] 63-20217
1. Catholic Church. 2. Church. I. Title.

LUBAC, Henri de, 1896- 261
The splendour of the church, Tr. by Michael Mason. Glen Rock, N.J., Paulist Pr. [1963, c.1956] 352p. 18cm. (Deus bks.) Bibl. 63-20217 1.25 pap.,
1. Church. 2. Catholic Church. I. Title.

LYNCH, William F., 1908- 261
Christ and Prometheus; a new image of the secular [by] William F. Lynch. [Notre Dame, Ind.] University of Notre Dame Press [1970] 153 p. 23 cm. Includes bibliographical references. [BT83.7.L9] 70-122046 5.95
1. Secularization (Theology) I. Title.

LYON, David, 1948- 261
Christians & sociology : the challenge of sociology, a Christian response / David Lyon. Downers Grove, Ill. : InterVarsity Press, [1976] c1975. 89, [4] p. ; 18 cm. Bibliography: p. [93] [BT738.L93 1976] 76-21458 ISBN 0-87784-578-6 pbk. : 1.95
1. Sociology, Christian. I. Title.

MCCLELLAN, Albert. 261
The new times. Nashville, Broadman Press [1968] 128 p. 20 cm. Includes bibliographical references. [BR121.2.M27] 69-13133
1. Christianity—20th century. I. Title.

MCFALL, Ernest A. 261
Approaching the Nuer of Africa through the Old Testament [by Ernest A. McFall. South Pasadena, Calif., William Carey Library, c1970] iv, 99 l. 28 cm. Bibliography: leaves 95-98. [DT132.M27] 72-136099 ISBN 0-87808-104-6
1. Jews—Social life and customs. 2. Nuer (African tribe) 3. Sociology, Biblical. I. Title.

MCKENNEY, Charles R 261
Moral problems in social work. Milwaukee, Bruce [1951] 131 p. 22 cm. (Science and culture series) [HV43.M25] 51-8471

1. Social case work. 2. Christian ethics—Catholic authors. I. Title.

MCNEILL, Robert B 261
Prophet, speak now. Richmond, John Knox Press [1961] 92p. 21cm. [BV625.M33] 61-7871
1. Church and social problems. 2. Preaching. I. Title.

MCNEILL, Robert B. 261
Prophet, Speak now. Richmond, John Knox Press [c.1961] 92p. 61-7871 2.50
1. Church and social problems. 2. Preaching. I. Title.

MAINS, David R. 261
Full circle; the creative church for today's society [by] David R. Mains. Waco, Tex., Word Books [1971] 217 p. illus. 23 cm. [BV601.8.M3] 77-181100 4.95
1. Chicago. Circle Church. 2. Mission of the church—Case studies. I. Title.

MARCINIAK, Ed. 261
Tomorrow's Christian. Dayton, Ohio, Pflaum Press, 1969. xiv, 189 p. 22 cm. Bibliographical footnotes. [BR115.W6M28] 69-20168 5.95
1. Church and the world. I. Title.

MARTY, Martin E., 1928- 261
The modern schism; three paths to the secular [by] Martin E. Marty. [1st U.S. ed.] New York, Harper & Row [1969] 191 p. 22 cm. Includes bibliographical references. [BL2747.8.M37 1969] 74-85042 5.95
1. Secularism. I. Title.

MASS means of communication. 261
[Edited by the Daughters of St. Paul. Boston] St. Paul Editions [1967] 202 p. illus., ports. 28 cm. Contents.Contents.—Foreword.—Decree on the media of social communication (p. [17]-144)—Motu proprio of Pope Paul VI, In fructibus.—Pope Pius XI on motion pictures, Vigilanti cura.—Pope Pius XII on motion pictures, radio and television, Miranda prorsus. Bibliography: p. 149. [BX830 1962.A451733] 67-25827
1. Vatican Council. 2d, 1962-1965. Decretum de instrumentis communicationis socialis. 2. Communication (Theology) I. Daughters of St. Paul. II. Vatican Council. 2d, 1962-1965. Decretum de instrumentis communicationis socialis. English. 1967.

MATSON, Theodore E 261
Edge of the edge. New York, Friendship Press [1961] 165p. 20cm. Includes bibliography. [BV600.2.M35] 61-6627
1. Church. 2. Church work. I. Title.

MAURY, Philippe 261
Politics and evangelism. [Translated from the French by Marguerite Wieser.] Garden City, N. Y., Doubleday [c.1959] 120p. 22cm. 60-5939 2.95
1. Christianity and politics. I. Title.

MAURY, Philippe. 261
Polities anc evangelism. [Translated by Marguerite Wieser. Special ed.] Garden City, N. Y., Doubleday [1959] 120p. 21cm. Translation of Evangelisation et politique. [BR115.P7M3433] 60-5939
1. Christianity and politics. I. Title.

MAY, Henry Farnham, 1915- 261
Protestant churches and industrial America. New introd. by the author. New York. Harper [1967] xviii, 297p. 21cm. (Torchbk. TB1334) Bibl. [HN39.U6M38] 2.25 pap.,
1. Church and social problems—U. S. 2. U. S.—Church history. I. Title.

MAYNOOTH Union Summer School, 1967. 261
The Christian in his world; papers. Edited by Brendan Devlin. Dublin, Gill [1968] xiv, 148 p. 21 cm. Bibliography: p. 147-148. [BR115.W6M358] 70-19310
1. Church and the world—Addresses, essays, lectures. I. Devlin, Brendan, ed. II. Title.

MELAND, Bernard Eugene, 1899- 261
The realities of faith; the revolution in cultural forms. New York, Oxford [c.] 1962. 368 p. 22 cm. Bibl. 62-9826 6.50, bds.
1. Christianity—20th cent. I. Title.

MELAND, Bernard Eugene, 1899- 261
The secularization of modern cultures. New York, Oxford 1966. xii, 163p. 21cm. (Barrows lects., 1964-65) [bR115.W6M4] 66-22266 4.75
1. Church and the world. I. Title. II. Series.

MERTON, Thomas, 1915- 261
Seeds of destruction. New York, Macmillan [1967, c.1964] 224p. 18cm. (MP08769) [BT734.2.M4] 1.45 pap.,
1. Church and race problems—U.S. 2. Christianity—20th century—Addresses, essays, lectures. 3. Catholic Church—Clergy—Correspondence, reminiscences, etc. I. Title.

MERTON, Thomas, 1915-1968. 261
Seeds of destruction. New York, Farrar, Straus and Giroux [1965, c1964] xvi, 328 p. 21 cm. Contents.Contents.—Black revolution: Letters to a white liberal. The legend of Tucker Caliban.—The diaspora: The Christian in world crisis. The Christian in the diaspora. A tribute to Gandhi.—Letters in a time of crisis. [BT734.2.M4] 64-19515
1. Catholic Church—Clergy—Correspondence, reminiscences, etc. 2. Church and race problems—United States. 3. Christianity—20th century—Addresses, essays, lectures. I. Title.

METZLER, Edgar. 261
Let's talk about extremism. Scottdale, Pa., Herald Press [1968] 25 p. 20 cm. (Focal pamphlet series, no. 12) [BF575.F16M4] 68-2824
1. Fanaticism. I. Title. II. Title: Extremism.

MILLER, Donald G 261
The nature and mission of the church. Richmond, John Knox Press [1957] 134p. 21cm. [BV600.M44] 57-9443
1. Church. I. Title.

MILLER, Haskell M 261
A Christian critique of culture [by] Haskell M. Miller. New York, Published for the Cooperative Publication Association by Abingdon Press [1965] 96 p. 19 cm. (Faith for life series) [BR115.C8M5] 65-9148
1. Christianity — 20th cent. 2. Culture. I. Title.

MILLER, Haskell M. 261
A Christian critique of culture. Pub. for the Cooperative Pubn. Assn., Nashville, Abingdon [c.1965] 96p. 19cm. (Faith for life ser.) [BR115.C8M5] 65-9148 1.25 pap.,
1. Christianity—20th cent. 2. Culture. I. Title.

MILLER, Randolph Crump, 1910- ed. 261
The church and organized movements. Freeport, N.Y., Books for Libraries Press [1971, c1946] xvi, 255 p. 23 cm. (Essay index reprint series) Contents.Contents.—Introduction, by R. C. Miller.—The general perspective: The discovery of resistance and resource, by R. C. Miller. The new comparative religion, by E. Trueblood.—Contemporary live options: the anti-opium league (secular radicalism) by G. Hedley. The Fascist masquerade, by H. Thurman. Welfare work: ally or alternative? By B. G. Gallagher. The church and organized fraternalism, by D. C. Smith. Christianity and organized education, by F. West. The cults, by P. Parker.—The church; basic response: Christianity and the non-Christian religions, by H. V. White. Resources in a genuinely Christian church, by E. L. Parsons. Includes bibliographies. [BV600.M515 1971] 76-134115 ISBN 0-8369-1998-X
1. Church. 2. Social groups. 3. Christianity and other religions. I. Title.

MINEAR, Paul Sevier, 1906- 261
Jesus and His people. New York, Association Press [1956] 96p. 21cm. (World Christian books) [BV600.M54] 56-6457
1. Church. I. Title.

MITCHELL, S. John D. 261
Perse : a history of the Perse School, 1615-1976 / [by] S. J. D. Mitchell. Cambridge : Oleander Press, 1976. viii, 263 p. : ill., coat of arms, map, plans, ports. ; 22 cm. Includes bibliographical references and index. [LF795.C185M57] 77-357892 ISBN 0-902675-71-0 : £4.95
1. Perse Grammar School, Cambridge, Eng. 2. Cambridge, Eng.—Schools—History. I. Title.

MOBERG, David O. 261
The great reversal : evangelism and social concern / David O. Moberg. Rev. ed. Philadelphia : Lippincott, c1977. 228 p. ; 21 cm. "A Holman book." Includes index. Bibliography: p. 218-221. [BV3793.M56 1977] 77-745 ISBN 0-87981-073-4 pbk. : 3.45
1. Evangelistic work. 2. Church and social problems. I. Title.

MOBERG, David O. 261
The great reversal; evangelism versus social concern [by] David O. Moberg. [1st ed.] Philadelphia, Lippincott [1972] 194 p. 21 cm. (Evangelical perspectives) "A Holman book." Includes bibliographical references. [BV3793.M56] 72-2153 ISBN 0-87981-009-2 5.95
1. Evangelistic work. 2. Church and social problems. I. Title.

MORGAN, Everett J., comp. 261
Readings in social theology, edited by Everett J. Morgan. Dayton, Ohio, Pflaum Press, 1969. xi, 332 p. 22 cm. Includes bibliographical references. [BX1395.M58] 69-20169 5.95
1. Church and social problems—Catholic Church. I. Title.

MORGAN, Everett J., ed. 261
The social conscience of a Catholic; the social doctrine of the church applied to problems in our contemporary society. Rev. ed. by Everett J. Morgan. Foreword by Louis J. Twomey. [Milwaukee, dist. Marquette Univ. Bkstore, c.1964] x, 293p. 28cm. Substance of this bk. was orig. comp. by the students: priests, sisters, seminarians, lay students, who attended the 1st Social Doctrine Inst. at Marquette, 1963. Bibl. 64-18403 3.75 pap.,
1. Church and social problems—Catholic Church. I. Marquette University, Milwaukee. Social Doctrine Institute. II. Title.

MORGAN, Thomas Brynmor, 1886- 261
Faith is a weapon. New York, Putnam [1952] 278 p. 22 cm. [BX1397.M6] 52-5279
1. Socialism and Catholic Church. 2. Communism and religion. 3. Catholic Church — Relations (diplomatic) I. Title.

MORRIS, Colin M. 261
The hammer of the Lord; signs of hope [by] Colin Morris. Nashville, Abingdon Press [1974, c1973] 160 p. 20 cm. Includes bibliographical references. [BX8333.M584H35 1974] 73-12234 ISBN 0-687-16547-4 4.75
1. Methodist Church—Sermons. 2. Sermons, English. I. Title.

MORTON, Nelle. 261
The church we cannot see. Illus. by Jim Lee. New York, Friendship Press [1953] 116p. illus. 21cm. [BV600.M62] 53-9283
1. Church. I. Title.

MUDGE, Lewis Seymour. 261
Why is the church in the world? [by] Lewis S. Mudge, Jr. [Philadelphia?] Board of Christian Education, United Presbyterian Church in the United States of America [1967] 95 p. 21 cm. [BR115.W6M8] 67-9285
1. United Presbyterian Church in the U.S.A.—Doctrinal and controversial works. 2. Church and the world. I. United Presbyterian Church in the U.S.A. Board of Christian Education. II. Title.

MUNBY, D. L. 261
The idea of a secular society, and its significance for Christians. New York, Oxford [c.]1963. 91p. 19cm. (Riddell. memorial lect. 34th ser., Univ. of Durham pubns.) 63-1609 3.00 bds.,
1. Church and state—Addresses, essays, lectures. 2. Secularism—Addresses, essays, lectures. I. Title.

MUNBY, Denys Lawrence. 261
The idea of a secular society, and its significance for Christians. London, New York, Oxford University Press, 1963. 91 p. 19 cm. (The Riddell memorial lectures, 34th ser.) Series: Durham, Eng. University. Publications) University of Durham publications. [BV631.M8 1963] 63-1609
1. Church and state — Addresses, essays, lectures. 2. Secularism — Addresses, essays, lectures. I. Title. II. Series.

MURTAGH, James G. 261
Australia; the Catholic chapter, by James G. Murtagh. Melbourne, Polding Press, 1969. xx, 261 p. 22 cm. Includes bibliographical references. [BX1685.M8 1969] 75-488629
1. Catholic Church in Australia. 2. Australia—History. I. Title.

NAPIER, Bunyan Davie. 261
On new creation [by] B. D. Napier. Baton Rouge, Louisiana State University Press [1971] x, 114 p. 23 cm. (Rockwell lectures) Includes bibliographical references. [BR121.2.N3] 70-134553 ISBN 0-8071-0524-4 4.95
1. Christianity—20th century. 2. Civilization. I. Title. II. Series.

NEF, John Ulric, 1899- 261
Religion and study of man. Houston [Tex.] Univ. of St. Thomas [c.1961] 53p. illus. 16cm. (Smith hist. lecture, 1961) 61-65160 2.00 pap.,
1. Religion and sociology. I. Title.

NEF, John Ulric, 1899- 261
Religion and the study of man. Houston [Tex.] University of Saint Thomas, 1961. 53p. illus. 16cm. (The Smith history lecture, 1961) [BL60.N4] 61-65160
1. Religion and sociology. I. Title.

NEILL, Thomas Patrick, 1915- 261
Renewing the face of the earth; essays in contemporary church-world relationships, by Thomas P. Neill. Edited by Harry J. Cargas. Milwaukee, Bruce Pub. Co. [1968] xiv, 146 p. 22 cm. [BX891.N37] 68-55282
1. Catholic Church—Addresses, essays, lectures. 2. Church and the world—Addresses, essays, lectures. I. Title.

NELSON, John Oliver, 1909- 261
Dare to reconcile; seven settings for creating community. New York, Friendship Press [1969] 127 p. 19 cm. [BV1534.5.N4] 68-59134 1.50
1. Discussion in religious education. 2. Reconciliation. 3. Church and social problems. I. Title.

NESIOTES, Nikos A., 1925- 261
Discerning the times; the church in today's world [by] Philip Maury, Nikos A. Nissiotis [and] P. A. Liege. Translated by Agnes Cunningham. Techny, Ill., Divine World Publications [1968] x, 165 p. 18 cm. (Churches in dialogue) In the original ed. Nissiotis' name appeared first on the t.p. Translation of L'Eglise dans le monde. Bibliographical footnotes. [BR115.W6N513] 68-8361 1.95
1. Church and the world. I. Maury, Philippe. II. Liege, Pierre Andre, 1921- III. Title.

NEWBIGIN, James Edward Lesslie, Bp. 261
The household of God; lectures on the nature of the church. New York, Friendship Press [c1954] 177p. 21cm. (The Kerr lectures, 1952) [BV600.N46] 54-5573
1. Church. I. Title.

NEWQUIST, Jerreld L., comp. 261
Prophets, principles and national survival Salt Lake City, Publishers Pr., 1881 WN Temple [1964] 575p. 24cm. Bibl. [BX8608.N4] 64-57193 4.95
1. Mormons and Mormonism—Collections. 2. Sociology, Christian (Mormon)—Collections. I. Title.

NIDA, Eugene Albert, 1914- 261
Religion across cultures; a study in the communication of Christian faith [by] Eugene A. Nida. [1st ed.] New York, Harper & Row [1968] vii, 111 p. 22 cm. Bibliography: p. [93]-95. [BV4319.N53] 68-11733
1. Communication (Theology) I. Title.

NIEBUHR, Helmut Richard, 1894- 261
The kingdom of God in America. Hamden, Conn., Shoe String Press, 1956 [c1935] 215p. 21cm. [BT94] 56-6352
1. Kingdom of God. 2. U. S.—Church history. I. Title.

NIEBUHR, Reinhold, 1892- 261
Christianity and power politics. [Hamden, Conn.] Archon Books, 1969 [c1940] xi, 226 p. 19 cm. [BR115.P7N55 1969] 69-12421 ISBN 0-208-00740-7
1. Christianity and politics. 2. Europe—Politics and government—1918-1945. 3. World War, 1939-1945—Religious aspects. I. Title.

NIEMOLLER, Martin, 1892- 261
The challenge to the church; the Niemoller-Blake conversations, Lent, 1965. Edited by Marlene Maertens. Philadelphia, Westminister Press [1965] 138 p. 21 cm. [BV4307.D5N5] 65-24514
1. Dialogue sermons. 2. Sermons, American. I. Blake, Eugene Carson, 1906- II. Maertens, Marlene, ed. III. Title.

NIEMOLLER, Martin, 1892- 261
The challenge to the church; the Niemoller-Blake conversations, Lent, 1965. Ed. by Marlene Maertens. Philadelphia, Westminster [c.1965] 138p. 21cm. [BV4307.D5N5] 65-24514 1.65 pap.,
1. Dialogue sermons. 2. Sermons, American. I. Blake, Eugene Carson, 1906- II. Maertens, Marlene, ed. III. Title.

NIXON, Justin Wroe, 1886- 261
Responsible Christianity; leaven of a free society. [1st ed.] New York, Harper [1950] 190 p. 21 cm. "References": p. 177-183. [BR481.N5] 50-7151
1. Christianity—20th century. 2. Religious thought—U.S. 3. Christianity—Philosophy. I. Title.

NOBLE, Charles C 261
Faith for the future. New York, Association Press, 1950. 136 p. 21 cm. Includes bibliographies. [HN31.N57] 51-1185
1. Church and social problems. I. Title.

NORMAN, Edward R. 261
Church and society in England 1770-1970 : a historical study / by e.R. Norman Oxford : Clarendon Press, 1976. 507 p. ; 24 cm. Includes index. Bibliography: p. [475]-494. [BR744.N67] 76-377182 ISBN 0-19-826435-6 : 25.50
1. Sociology, Christian—England—History. I. Title.
Distributed by Oxford University Press, NY

NYGREN, Anders, Bp., 1890- 261
Christ and His church. Translated by Alan Carlsten. Philadelphia, Westminster Press [1956] 125p. 20cm. [BV600.N92] 56-7769
1. Chruch. I. Title.

O'DEA, Thomas F., comp. 261
Readings on the sociology of religion [compiled by] Thomas F. O'Dea [and] Janet K. O'Dea. Englewood Cliffs, N.J., Prentice-Hall [1973] xi, 244 p. illus. 23 cm. (Readings in modern sociology series) Includes bibliographical references. [BL60.O27] 72-8593 ISBN 0-13-761940-5 5.95
1. Religion and sociology—Collections. I. O'Dea, Janet K., joint author. II. Title.

OLD and the new in the church 261
(The) [by] World Council of Churches Commission on Faith and Order, two interim reports. Preface by Paul S. Minear. Minneapolis, Augsburg [1962, c.1961] 91p. (Faith and order studies) 1.25 pap.,

OLDHAM, Joseph Houldsworth, 1874- 261
Life is commitment. New York, Harper [1953?] 140p. 22cm. [BR121.O47] 53-2505
1. Christianity—Essence, genius, nature. I. Title.

OLDHAM, Joseph Houldsworth, 1874- 261
Life is commitment. New York, Association Press [1959] 127p. 16cm. (An Association Press reflection book) Abridged ed. Includes bibliography. [BR121.O472 1959] 59-6839
1. Christianity—Essence, genius, nature. I. Title.

OSGNIACH, Augustine John, Father, 1891- 261
Must it be communism? A philosophical inquiry into the major issues of today. With 3 chapters comprising pt. 4, by Jerome L. Toner. New York, Wagner [1950] ix. 486 p. 22 cm. Bibliography: p. 461-477. [HN37.C3O68] 50-3424
1. Church and social problems—Catholic Church. 2. Socialism and Catholic Church. I. Toner, Jerome Leo, 1899- II. Secular name: John Osgniach. III. Title.

OWENS, Jimmy. 261
If my people ... : a handbook for national intercession / by Jimmy and Carol Owens. Waco, Tex. : Word Books, c1974 [i.e.1975] 153 p. ; 22 cm. Includes bibliographical references. [BV4501.2.O87] 75-5181 pbk : 3.25
1. Christian life—1960- 2. United States—Moral conditions. I. Owens, Carol, joint author. II. Title.

OXNAM, Garfield Bromley, Bp., 1891- 261
The Church and contemporary change. New York, Macmillan, 1950. xiii, 132 p. 21 cm. [BR481.O9] 50-10839
1. Christianity — 20th cent. I. Title.

PALMER, Parker J. 261
The church, the university, and urban society: focus on the church [by] Parker J. Palmer [and] Elden Jacobson. [New York, Dept. of Higher Education, National Council of Churches, 1971] viii, 37 p. 28 cm. "Paper number 2 in a series of seven reports produced for the project on church, university, and urban society of the Department of Higher Education, National Council of Churches." [BT738.P28] 73-29861 0.50
1. Sociology, Christian. 2. Urban churches. 3. Religious and ecclesiastical institutions. I. Jacobson, Elden, joint author. II. National Council of the Churches of Christ in the United States of America. Dept. of Higher Education. III. Title.

PICHON, Charles, 1893-1963. 261
The Vatican and its role in world affairs. Translated from the French by Jean Misrahi. Westport, Conn., Greenwood Press [1969, c1950] 382 p. illus., ports. 23 cm. Translation of Histoire du Vatican. [BX946.P514 1969] 72-97350 ISBN 8-371-28285-
1. Catholic Church—History. 2. Catholic Church—Relations. 3. Catholic Church—Relations (diplomatic) I. Title.

PIKE, James Albert, 1913- 261
The church, politics, and society; dialoguex on current problems, by James A. Pike and John W. Pyle. New York, Morehouse-Gorham Co., 1955. 159p. 21cm. 'Based on the script of eleven dialogues presented by the authors ... over the ABC radio network under the auspices of the National Council of the Churches of Christ in the U. S. A.' [HN31.P43] 55-7435
1. Church and social problems. I. Pyle, John W. II. Title.

PINSON, William M 261
How to deal with controversial issues [by] William M. Pinson, Jr. Nashville, Broadman Press [1966] 128 p. 20 cm. Bibliographical references included in "Notes" (p. 122-128) [BV4521.P5] 66-12059
1. Christian leadership. I. Title. II. Title: Controversial issues.

PINSON, William. M., Jr. 261
How to deal with controversial issues. Nashville, Broadman Pr. [c.1966] 128p. 20cm. Bibl. [BV4521.P5] 66-12059 1.50 bds.,
1. Christian leadership. I. Title. II. Title: Controversial issues.

POPE, Liston 261
Millhands & preachers, a study of Gastonia [with a new introd.] New Haven, Conn., Yale [1965, c.1942] xlx, 369p. tables, map. 21cm. (Y-144) Bibl. [HD6338.P6] 7.50; 2.45 pap.,
1. Gastonia, N.C. 2. Church and labor. 3. Gaston co., N.C. I. Yale university. John Addison Porter prize. II. Title.

POULTON, John. 261
Dear Archbishop / by John Poulton ; [with a foreword by the Archbishop of Canterbury]. London : Hodder and Stoughton, 1976. 159 p. ; 18 cm. (Hodder Christian paperbacks) [HN385.5.P62] 76-383781 £0.60
1. Great Britain—Social conditions—1945- 2. Great Britain—Moral conditions. 3. Church and social problems—Great Britain. I. Title.

PREACHING in American 261
history; selected issues in the American pulpit, 1630-1967. Prepared under the auspices of the Speech Association of America. DeWitte Holland, editor. Jess Yoder and Hubert Vance Taylor, associate editors. Nashville, Abingdon Press [1969] 436 p. 25 cm. Includes bibliographical references. [BV4208.U6P7] 69-18453 8.95
1. Preaching—History—U.S.—Addresses, essays, lectures. I. Holland, DeWitte Talmadge, 1923- ed. II. Speech Association of America.

RAHNER, Karl, 1904- 261
The pastoral approach to atheism, ed. by Karl Rahner. [Tr. by Theodore L. Westow, others] New York, Paulist [1967] viii, 181p. 24cm. (Concilium theol. in the age of renewal: Pastoral theol., v.23) [BR128.A8R3] 67-21347 4.50
1. Christianity and atheism—Addresses, essays, lectures. I. Title. II. Series: Concilium theology in the age of renewal, v.23
Contents omitted.

RAMSEY, Paul. 261
Who speaks for the church? Nashville, Abingdon Press [1967] 189 p. 22 cm. "A critique of the 1966 Geneva Conference on Church and Society." Bibliographical references included in "Notes" (p. 169-189) [BT38.W58] 67-24331
1. World Conference on Church and Society, Geneva, 1966. I. Title.

RAMSEY, Paul. 261
Who speaks for the church? Nashville, Abingdon Press [1967] 189 p. 22 cm. "A critique of the 1966 Geneva Conference on Church and Society." Bibliographical references included in "Notes" (p. 169-189) [BT738.W58 1966sr] 67-24331
1. World Conference on Church and Society, Geneva, 1966. I. Title.

RAUSCHENBUSCH, Walter, 1861-1918. 261
Christianity and the social crisis. Edited by Robert D. Cross. New York, Harper & Row [1964] xxv, 429 p. 21 cm. (American perspectives) Harper torchbooks. The University library, TB3059. Bibliographical footnotes. [BT738.R34 1964] 64-57260
1. Sociology, Christian. I. Title.

RAUSCHENBUSCH, Walter, 1861-1918. 261
The righteousness of the kingdom, edited and introduced by Max L. Stackhouse. Nashville, Abingdon Press [1968] 320 p. 24 cm. Bibliography: p. 289-312. [BT738.R345] 68-17441
1. Sociology, Christian. 2. Kingdom of God. I. Title.

RAUSCHENBUSCH, Walter, 1861-1918. 261
The social principles of Jesus / by Walter Rauschenbusch ; written under the direction of Sub-committee on College Courses, Sunday School Council of Evangelical Denominations and Committee on Voluntary Study, Council of North American Student Movements. Folcroft, Pa. : Folcroft Library Editions, 1976. 198 p. ; 26 cm. Reprint of the 1916 ed. published by Association Press, New York, which was issued as 4th year, pt. 1 of College voluntary study courses. [BS2417.S7R3 1976] 76-50566 ISBN 0-8414-7308-0 lib. bdg. : 15.00
1. Jesus Christ—Teachings. 2. Sociology, Christian. 3. Christian ethics. I. Title. II. Series: College voluntary study courses ; 4th year, pt. 1.

RAUSCHENBUSCH, Walter, 1861-1918. 261
A theology for the social gospel. Nashville, Abingdon Press [1961, c.1917] 279p. 21cm. (Apex books, E7) 61-40 1.75 pap.,
1. Sociology. Christian. 2. Theology, Doctrinal. I. Title.

READ, Leonard Edward, 1898- 261
Elements of libertarian leadership; notes on the theor, methods, and practice of freedom. Irvington-on-Hudson N. Y., Foundation for Economic Education, 1962. 183p. illus. 20cm. Includes bibliography. [JC585.R4] 62-3043
1. Liberalism. I. Title. II. Title: Libertarian leadership.

RECKITT, Maurice Benington, 1888- 261
Maurice to Temple; a century of the social movement in the Church of England. London, Faber & Faber [Mystic, Conn., Verry, 1966] 245p. 23cm. (Scott Holland Memorial lects., 1946) Series: Holland Memorial lectures. Bibl. [HN37.A6R4] 48-12000 4.50
1. Church and social problems—Church of England. I. Title. II. Series.

RELIGION & freedom of 261
thought, by Perry Miller [and others] Foreword by Henry P. Van Dusen. Freeport, N.Y., Books for Libraries Press [1971, c1954] 64 p. 24 cm. (Essay index reprint series) Addresses, given at the one-day conference on "The relation between religion and freedom of the mind" which was held by the Union Theological Seminary as a tribute to Columbia University on the occasion of its bicentennial. Contents.Contents.—The location of American religious freedom, by P. Miller.—The historical relations between religion and intellectual freedom, by R. L. Calhoun.—Religion's role in liberal education, by N. M. Pusey.—The commitment of the self and the freedom of the mind, by R. Niebuhr. [BV741.R42 1971] 78-128296 ISBN 0-8369-2199-2
1. Religious liberty. 2. Church and education. I. Miller, Perry, 1905-

REUMANN, John Henry Paul. 261
Righteousness and society, ecumenical dialog in a revolutionary age, by John Reumann and William Lazareth. Philadelphia, Fortress Press [1967] xi, 242 p. 18 cm. Bibliographical footnotes. [BT738.R5] 68-12326
1. Sociology, Christian. I. Lazareth, William Henry, 1928- II. Title.

REUMANN, John Henry Paul. 261
Righteousness and society, ecumenical dialog in a revolutionary age, by John Reumann and William Lazareth. Philadelphia, Fortress Press [1967] xi, 242 p. 18 cm. Bibliographical footnotes. [BT738.R5] 68-12326
1. Sociology, Christian. I. Lazareth, William Henry, 1928- II. Title.

RICH, Mark. 261
Rural prospect. New York, Friendship Press [1950] viii, 183 p. illus. 20 cm. Bibliography: p. [173]-176. [BV638.R45] 50-8260
1. Rural churches. 2. Interdenominational cooperation. I. Title.

RIDDLE, Oscar, 1877- 261
The unleashing of evolutionary thought. New York, Vantage Press [c1954] 414p. 23cm. [QH367.R53] 54-10246
1. Evolution. 2. Religion and science. I. Title.

RIGA, Peter. 261
A guide to Pacem in terris for students (with discussion questions) Glen Rock, N.J., Paulist Press [1964] 126 p. 18 cm. (An Original Deus book) [BX1793.A26R49] 64-24515
1. Catholic Church. Pope, 1958-1963 (Joannes XXIII) Pacem in terris (11 Apr. 1963) I. Title.

RIGA, Peter. 261
Peace on earth; a commentary on Pope John's encyclical. [New York] Herder and Herder [1964] 254 p. 21 cm. "Pacem in terris": p. [195]-249. [BX1793.A26R5] 64-13691
1. Catholic Church. Pope, 1958-1963 (Joannes XXIII) Pacem in terris (11 Apr. 1963) I. Catholic Church. Pope, 1958-1963 (Joannes XXIII) Pacem in terris (11 Apr. 1963) English. II. Title.

RIGA, Peter J. 261
The church made relevant; a commentary on the pastoral constitution of Vatican II [by] Peter J. Riga. Notre Dame, Ind., Fides Publishers [1967] 337 p. 23 cm. [BX830.1962.A45C765] 66-30587
1. Vatican Council. 2d, 1962-1965. Constitutio pastoralis de ecclesia in mundo huius temporis. 2. Church and the world. I. Title.

RIGA, Peter J 261
A guide to Pacem in terris for students (with discussion questions) Glen Rock, N. J., Paulist Press [1964] 126 p. 18 cm. (Original Deus book) [BX1793.A26R49] 64-24515
1. Catholic Church. Pope, 1958-1963 (Joannes XXIII) Pacem in terris (11 Apr. 1963) I. Title.

RIGA, Peter J 261
Peace on earth; a commentary on Pope John's encyclical. [New York] Herder and Herder [1964] 254 p. 21 cm. "Pacem in terris": p. [195]-249. [BX1793.A26R5] 64-13691
1. Catholic Church. Pope, 1958-1963 (Joannes XXIII) Pacem in terris(11 Apr. 1963) I. Catholic Church. Pope, 1958-1963 (Joannes XXIII) Pacem in terris(11 Apr. 1963) English. II. Title.

ROBERTSON, D. B., ed. 261
Voluntary associations, a study of groups in free societies; essays in honor of James Luther Adams. Ed. by D. B. Robertson. Richmond, Knox [1966] 448p. port. 24cm. [BT738.R6] 66-21648 9.75
1. Sociology, Christian—Addresses, essays, lectures. 2. Church— Addresses, essays, lectures. 3. Associations, institutions, etc. I. Adms, James Luther, 1901- II. Title.
Contents omitted.

ROBERTSON, D. B. ed. 261
Voluntary associations, a study of groups in free societies: essays in honor of James Luther Adams. Edited by D. B. Robertson. Richmond, John Knox Press [1966] 448 p. port. 24 cm. Contents.The nature of voluntary associations, by K. Hertz. -- Associational thought in early Calvinism, by F. S. Carney. -- The religious background of the idea of a loyal opposition, by G. H. Williams. -- The meaning of "church" in Anabatism and Roman Catholicism: past and present, by M. Novak. -- Hobbe's theory of associations in the seventeenth-century milieu, by D. H. Robertson. -- The voluntary principle in religion and religious freedom in America, by R. T. Handy. -- The political theory of voluntary association in early nineteenty-century German liberal thought, by G. G. Iggers. -- Rauschenbusch's view of the church as a dynamic voluntary association, by D. E. Smucker. -- A note on creative freedom and the state in the social philosophy of Nicolas Berdyaev, by D. E. Sturm -- Missionary societies and the development of other forms of associations in India, by R. W. Taylor. -- The communaute de travail: experimentation in Integral association, by V. H. Fletcher. -- "The politics of mass society": significance for the churches, by W. A. Pitcher. -- A new pattern of community, by F. H. Littell. -- The crisis of the congregation: a debate, by G. Fackre. -- The voluntary church: a moral appraisal, by J. M. Gustafason. -- SANE as a voluntary organization, by H. A. Jack. -- James Luther Adams: a biographical and intellectual sketch, by M. L. Stackhouse. -- Voluntary associations as a key to history, by J. D. Hunt. -- A bibliography of the writings of James Luther Adams, by R. B. Potter. [BT738.R6] 66-21648
1. Sociology, Christian — Addresses, essays, lectures. 2. Church — Addresses, essays, lectures. 3. Associations, institutions, etc. I. Adams, James Luther, 1901- II. Title.

ROBINSON, William, 1888- 261
The Biblical doctrine of the church. Rev. ed. St. Louis, Bethany Press [1955] 245p. 20cm. [BV600.R62 1955] 55-12948
1. Church. 2. Church—Biblical teaching. I. Title.

ROSE, Stephen C 261
Alarms and visions; churches and the American crisis, by Stephen C. Rose. [Chicago, Renewal magazine, 1967] 175 p. 21 cm. (A Renewal paperback) [BR121.2.R59] 68-2885
1. Christianity—20th cent. 2. Sociology, Christian. I. Title.

ROSE, Stephen C. 261
Alarms and visions; churches and the American crisis, by Stephen C. Rose. [Chicago, Renewal magazine, c1967] 175 p. 21 cm. (A Renewal paperback) [BR121.2.R59] 68-2885
1. Christianity—20th century. 2. Sociology, Christian. I. Title.

ROSENSTOCK-HUESSY, Eugen Friedrich Moritz 1888- 261
The Christian future; or, The modern mind outrun. Introd. by Harold Stahmer. [New ed. New York] Harper [1966, c.1946] lviii, 248p. 21cm. (Harper torchbk., Cloister lib., TB., 143) [BR479.R6] 2.25 pap.,
1. Christianity-20th cent. 2. Civilization, Modern. I. Title.

ROSS, Floyd Hiatt. 261
Addressed to Christians: isolationism vs. world community. [1st ed.] New York, Harper [1950] 154 p. 20 cm. Bibliography: p. 145-149. [BR127.R64] 50-5311
1. Christianity and other religions. I. Title.

RUPP, Ernest Gordon. 261
Principalities and powers; studies in the Christian conflict in history. New York,

Abingdon-Cokesbury Press [1952] 143 p. 20 cm. [BR115.H5R76] 52-376
1. History — Philosophy. 2. Good and evil. I. Title.

RUSSELL, Ralph, father. 261
Essays in reconstruction. Port Washington, N.Y., Kennikat Press [1968] xi, 176 p. 22 cm. (Essay and general literature index reprint series) Reprint of the 1946 ed. Contents.Contents.—Reconstruction and the natural man, by R. Russell.—The leaven, by R. Russell.—The Catholic action, by I. Trethowan.—Christian education, by C. Butler.—Catholicism and science, by F. S. Taylor.—Catholicism and English literature, by H. Steuert and S. Moore.—The reconstruction of philosophic thought, by I. Trethowan.—Catholics and economic reconstruction, by M. Fogarty.—The aims of youth in peace and war, by A. Lytton-Milbanke.—Youth and the young Christian workers, by J. Fitzsimons. Bibliographical footnotes. [D825.R88 1968] 68-15835
1. Reconstruction (1939-1951)—Religious aspects. 2. Church and social problems—Catholic Church. I. Title.

RUTENBER, Culbert Gerow, 1909- 261
The dagger and the cross; an examination of Christian pacifism. [New York] Fellowship Publications [1950] 134 p. 21 cm. [BR115.W2R8] 51-7132
1. War and religion. I. Title.

SANDERSON, Ross Warren, 1884- 261
The church serves the changing city, by Ross W. Sanderson for the Dept. of the Urban Church, with the co-operation of the Committee on Field Research, National Council of Churches. [1st ed.] New York, Harper [1955] 252p. illus. 22cm. [BV4400.S35] 55-6788
1. Social service. 2. Church work. 3. City churches. I. Title.

SAVARY, Louis M. 261
Man, his world, and his work [by] Louis M. Savary. New York, Paulist [1967] vii, 232p. 21cm. (Exploration bks.) Bibl. [BT738.5.S3] 67-15719 4.95; 2.95 pap.,
1. Work (Theology) I. Title.

SCHNEIDER, Louis, 1915- 261
Sociological approach to religion. New York, Wiley [1970] viii, 188 p. 23 cm. Includes bibliographical references. [BL60.S32] 78-94915
1. Religion and sociology. I. Title.

SCHONFIELD, Hugh Joseph, 1901- 261
The politics of God [by] Hugh J. Schonfield. Chicago, Regnery [1971, c1970] xx, 231 p. 22 cm. Includes bibliographical references. [BL65.P7S33 1971] 77-143848 5.95
1. Religion and politics. 2. Messianism. 3. Judaism—Relations—Christianity. 4. Christianity and other religions—Judaism. I. Title.

SCHROEDER, W. Widick. 261
Cognitive structures and religious research; essays in sociology and theology, by W. Widick Schroeder. East Lansing, Michigan State University Press, 1970. xiii, 211 p. 25 cm. Includes bibliographical references. [BT738.S36494] 76-136266 ISBN 0-87013-150-8 7.50
1. Sociology, Christian. I. Title.

SCHULLER, David S. 261
Emerging shapes of the church [by] David S. Schuller. [St. Louis, Concordia Pub. House, 1967] ix, 84 p. 21 cm. (The Witnessing church series) Includes bibliographical references. [BR115.W6S3] 67-12901
1. Church and the world. 2. Church renewal. I. Title.

SEEK, find, share. 261
[Edited by J. Floyd Moore. Greensboro, N.C., The Fourth World Conference of Friends, 1967] 159 p. 22 cm. "Study volume number two, preparatory to the Fourth World Conference of Friends, 1967, Guilford College, Greensboro, North Carolina." A sequel to No time but this present, by Friends World Committee for Consultation. [BX7615.S4] 67-16166
1. Friends, Society of—Addresses, essays, lectures. I. Moore, J. Floyd, ed. II. Friends World Conference. 4th, Guilford, N.C., 1967.

SEGUNDO, Juan Luis. 261
Liberation of theology / Juan Luis Segundo ; translated by John Drury. Maryknoll, N.Y. : Orbis Books, c1976. p. cm. Translation of Liberation de la teologia. Includes bibliographical references. [BT738] 76-7049 ISBN 0-88344-285-X : 10.95 ISBN 0-88344-286-8 pbk. : 6.95
1. Liberation theology. 2. Sociology, Christian. 3. Theology—20th century. I. Title.

SERMONS in American history; 261 selected issues in the American pulpit, 1630-1967. Prepared under the auspices of the Speech Communication Association. DeWitte Holland, editor. Hubert Vance Taylor and Jess Yoder, assistant editors. [Nashville, Abingdon Press, 1971] 542 p. 25 cm. [BV4241.S4186] 76-148072 ISBN 0-687-37794-3 11.95
1. Sermons, American. I. Holland, DeWitte Talmadge, 1923- ed. II. Speech Communication Association.

THE 70's: opportunities for your church. 261 Edited by James Daniel and Elaine Dickson Nashville, Convention Press [1969] 160 p. illus. 21 cm. Includes 6 resource papers from intensive studies conducted by the Southern Baptist Convention. [BX6225.S43] 69-17890
1. Religious education—Text-books for adults—Baptist. I. Daniel, James H., ed. II. Dickson, Elaine, ed. III. Southern Baptist Convention.

SHACKLOCK, Floyd. 261
This revolutionary faith. New York, Friendship Press [1955] 176p. 20cm. Includes bibliography. [BR121.S477] 55-6839
1. Christianity.—Essence, genius, nature. I. Title.

SLUSSER, Gerald H. 261
A Christian look at secular society, by Gerald H. Slusser. Philadelphia, Published for the Cooperative Publication Association by the Westminster Press [1968, c1969] 112 p. 22 cm. Bibliographical references included in "Notes" (p. [109]-112) [BR115.C8S58] 69-11338 ISBN 0-664-21282-4
1. Christianity and culture. I. Title.

SMALL churches are beautiful 261
/ edited by Jackson W. Carroll. 1st ed. New York : Harper & Row, c1977. p. cm. Includes bibliographical references. [BV637.8.S62 1977] 76-62948 ISBN 0-06-061319-X : 7.95
1. Small churches—Addresses, essays, lectures. I. Carroll, Jackson W.

SMITH, Eugene Lewis, 1912- 261
Mandate for mission [by] Eugene L. Smith. New York, Friendship [1968] 157p. 19cm. Bibl. [BR115.W6S5] 68-14055 1.75 pap.,
1. Church and the world. I. Title.

SMITH, George Leslie, 1940- 261
Religion and trade in New Netherland; Dutch origins and American development [by] George L. Smith. Ithaca, Cornell University Press [1973] xiii, 266 p. 23 cm. Bibliography: p. 249-259. [BR555.N7S62] 73-8403 ISBN 0-8014-0790-7 12.50
1. New York (State)—Religion. 2. New York (State)—Commerce. 3. Netherlands—Religion. 4. Netherlands—Commerce. 5. Christianity and economics—History. I. Title.

SMITH, Harry E. 261
Secularization and the university, by Harry E. Smith. Foreword by Harvey Cox. Richmond, Va., John Knox Press [1968] 172 p. 21 cm. Bibliographical references included in "Notes" (p. [161]-172) [BT83.7.S6] 68-25015 2.95
1. Secularization (Theology) 2. Universities and colleges—Religion. I. Title.

SMITH, William Edward, 1881- 261
The divine creation and perfection of man. Boston, Meador Pub. Co. [1951] 273 p. 21 cm. [BR126.S494] 51-14034
I. Title.

SMITH, William Edward, 1881- 261
The Holy Spirit, state, church, and school. Boston, Meador Pub. Co. [1959] 494 p. 21 cm. [BT123.S68] 58-14170
1. Holy Spirit. 2. Civilization, Christian. I. Title.

SMYTHE, Lewis Strong Casey. 261
The Christian in today's world : inner city to world community / Lewis Smythe. 1st ed. Hicksville, N.Y. : Exposition Press, [1974] 174 p. ; 21 cm. Includes bibliographical references. [BT738.S59] 75-300670 ISBN 0-682-48055-X : 6.50
1. Sociology, Christian. 2. Church and social problems. I. Title.

SOCIOLOGY, theology, and conflict. 261 Edited by D. E. H. Whiteley and R. Martin. New York, Barnes & Noble, 1969. vii, 167 p. 23 cm. Papers from a conference organized by the Modern Churchmen's Union held at Oxford, Easter 1968. Bibliographical footnotes. [BL60.S63] 78-5351 5.50
1. Religion and sociology. I. Whiteley, Denys Edward Hugh, ed. II. Martin, Roderick, ed. III. Modern Churchmen's Union.

SPIKE, Robert Warren. 261
In but not of the world; a notebook of theology and practice in the local church. New York, Published for the Interseminary Committee of the National Council of Churches [by]Association Press [1957] 110p. 20cm. [BV600.S583] 57-6883
1. Church. 2. Church work. I. Title.

SPIKE, Robert Warren. 261
In but not of the world; a notebook of theology and practice in the local church. New York, Published for the Interseminary Committee of the National Council of Churches [by] Association Press, [1957] 110 p. 20 cm. [BV600.S583] 57-6883
1. Church. 2. Church work. I. Title.

SPIKE, Robert Warren. 261
Tests of a living church, reprinting the popular In but not of the world. New York, Association Press [1961, c1957] 124 p. 15 cm. (An Association Press reflection book, 547) [BV600.S583 1961] 61-7464
1. Church 2. Church work. I. Title.

SPIKE, Robert Warren 261
Tests of a living church, reprinting the popular In but not of the world. NewYork, Association [1961, c.1957] 124p. (Association Pr. reflection bk., 547) 61-7464 .50 pap.,
1. Church. 2. Church work. I. Title.

SPIRITUALITY in the secular city. 261 New York, Paulist Press [1966] viii, 184 p. 24 cm. (Councilium theology in the age of renewal, v. 19) Bibliographical footnotes. [BR115.W6S6] 66-30386
1. Church and the world. 2. Spirituality. I. Series.

SPIRITUALITY in the secular city. 261 New York, Paulist Press [1966] viii, 184 p. 24 cm. (Concilium theology in the age of renewal, v. 19) Bibliographical footnotes. [BR115.W6S6] 66-30386
1. Church and the world. 2. Spirituality. I. Title. II. Series.

STALEY, Ronald. 261
Catholic principles of social justice: including the entire text of the encyclical: Pacem in terris. Foreword by Sister Patricia Marie. Los Angeles, Lawrence Pub. Co. [1964] xiv, 98 p. maps, ports. 22 cm. Bibliography: p. 98. [BT738.S7] 64-5986
1. Sociology, Christian (Catholic) I. Catholic Church. Pope, 1958-1963 (Joannes XXIII) Pacem in Terris (11 Apr. 1963) II. Title.

STALEY, Ronald 261
Catholic principles of social justice; including the entire text of the encyclical: Pacem in terris. Foreword by Sister Patricia Marie. Los Angeles, Lawrence [c.1964] xiv, 98p. maps, ports. 22cm. Bibl. 64-5986 1.00 pap.,
1. Sociology, Christian (Catholic) I. Catholic Church. Pope, 1958-1963 (Joannes XXIII) Pacem in terris (11 Apr. 1963) II. Title.

STERLING, Chandler W., Bp., 1911- 261
The arrogance of piety; religion in America [by] Chandler W. Sterling. New York, Morehouse-Barlow Co. [1969] 140 p. 22 cm. [BR121.2.S73] 70-97265
1. Christianity—20th century. I. Title.

STREYFFELER, Alan. 261
Prophets, priests, and politicians. Valley Forge, Judson Press [1971] 160 p. 23 cm. Bibliography: p. 153-158. [BT28.S74] 71-129487 ISBN 0-8170-0502-1 4.95
1. Theology—20th century. 2. Secularism. 3. Christianity and politics. I. Title.

TAWNEY, Richard Henry, 1880- 261
Religion and the rise of capitalism, a historical study. Gloucester, Mass., Peter Smith [1963, c.1926] 337p. 21cm. (Holland memorial lects., 1922) Bibl. 4.00
1. Religious thought—Hist. 2. Christianity and economics—Hist. 3. Gt. Brit.—Soc. condit. 4. Capitalism. I. Title.

TEMPLE, William, Abp. of Canterbury, 1881-1944. 261
Christianity and social order / William Temple ; foreword by Edward Heath ; introd. by Ronald H. Preston. London : Shepheard-Walwyn, 1976. 119 p. ; 20 cm. Reprint of the 1942 ed. published by Penguin Books, Harmondsworth; with new foreword and introd. Includes bibliographical references. [BT738.T36 1976] 76-377418 ISBN 0-281-02898-2 : £2.95. ISBN 0-281-02897-4 pbk.
1. Sociology, Christian. I. Title.

TEPPERMAN, Lorne. 261
Social mobility in Canada / Lorne Tepperman. Toronto ; New York : McGraw-Hill Ryerson, c1975. xi, 220 p. : ill. ; 23 cm. (McGraw-Hill Ryerson series in Canadian sociology) Includes index. Bibliography: p. [206]-212. [HN110.Z9S658] 76-357312 ISBN 0-07-082257-3
1. Social mobility—Canada. 2. Occupational mobility. I. Title.

THANKSGIVING Workshop on 261
Evangelicals and Social Concern, Chicago, 1973.
The Chicago declaration. Ronald J. Sider, editor. Carol Stream, Ill., Creation House [1974] 144 p. 18 cm. (New leaf library) Includes bibliographical references. [BR1640.A2T45 1973] 74-82506 ISBN 0-88419-048-X 2.45 (pbk.)
1. Evangelicalism—Congresses. 2. Church and social problems—Congresses. I. Sider, Ronald J., ed. II. Title.

TIBBETTS, Orlando L. 261
The reconciling community [by] Orlando L. Tibbetts. Valley Forge [Pa.] Judson Press [1969] 128 p. 20 cm. On cover: Task force for church renewal. Bibliographical footnotes. [BV600.2.T5] 69-16386 ISBN 8-17-004157-2.50
1. Church renewal. 2. Reconciliation. 3. Church and social problems. I. Title. II. Title: Task force for church renewal.

TILLICH, Paul, 1886- 261
The world situation. Philadelphia, Fortress [1965] xi, 51p. 19cm. (Facet bks. Soc. ethics ser., 2) This essay was first pub. as a chapter in the symposium The Christian Answer. Bibl. [BR115.I7T5] 65-12765 .85 pap.,
1. Christianity and international affairs. I. Title. II. Series.

TILSON, Charles Everett. 261
The conscience of culture. Nashville, National Methodist Student Movement [1953] 126p. 19cm. [BR115.C8T5] 54-14307
1. Culture. 2. Civilization, Christian. I. Title.

TORRANCE, Thomas Forsyth, 1913- 261
Kingdom and church; a study in the theology of the Reformation. Fair Lawn, N. J., Essential Books, 1956. 168p. 23cm. [BV600.T58] 56-58460
1. Church— History of doctrines—16th cent. I. Title.

TORRANCE, Thomas Forsyth, 1913- 261
Kingdom and church; a study in the theology of the Reformation. Fair Lawn, N.J., Essential Books, 1956. 168 p. 23 cm. [BV600.T58] 56-58460
1. Church — History of doctrines — 16th cent. I. Title.

TORRANCE, Thomas Forsyth, 1913- 261
Kingdom and church; a study in the theology of the Reformation. Edinburgh, Oliver & Boyd [dist. Mystic, Conn., Verry, 1965] viii, 168p. 23cm. Bibl. [BV600.T58] A56 3.50 bds.,
1. Church—History of doctrines—16th cent. I. Title.

TROCME, Andre, 1901- 261
The politics of repentance; translated by John Clark. New York, Fellowship Publications [1953] 111p. 20cm. (The Robert Treat Paine lectures, 1951) [BV600.T7] 53-13224
1. Church. 2. Church and state. 3. Church and social problems. I. Title.

TROELTSCH, Ernest, 1865-1923. 261
The social teaching of the Christian churches [2.v.] by Ernst Troeltsch.Translated [from the German] by Olive Wyon, with an introduction by H. Richard Niebuhr. New York, Harper [c.1960] 2v. 1019p. 21cm. (Harper Torchbooks, The Cloister library, TB-71; TB-72) Paged continuosly. Bibl. notes. pap., v.1, 2.25; v.2, 2.45
1. Sociology, Christian—Hist. 2. Church history. I. Wyon, Olive, tr. II. Title.

TROELTSCH, Ernst, 1865-1923. 261
Christian thought, its history and application. Edited with an introd. and index by Baron F. von Hugel. New York, Meridian Books, 1957. 191 p. 19 cm. (Living age books, LA12) [BR83.T74] 57-6686
1. Christianity — Addresses, essays, lectures. I. Title.

TROELTSCH, Ernst, 1865-1923 261
The social teaching of the Christian churches [2v.] Tr. [From German] by Olive Wyon. Introd. note by Charles Gore.* London, Allen & Unwin New York, Barnes & Noble [1963] 2v. (1019p.) 25cm. (Halley Stewart pubns., 1) Bibl. 63-25855 12.50 set,
1. Church and social problems—Hist. 2. Church history. I. Title. II. Series.

TRUMAN, Tom. 261
Catholic action and politics. [Rev. and enl. 2d ed.] Melbourne, Georgian House [1960] 283 p. 22 cm. Includes bibliography. [BX1685.T75] 61-65435
1. Catholic Church in Australia. 2. Church and state in Australia. 3. Catholic action — Australia. Full name: Thomas Charles Truman. I. Title.

TWO kingdoms and one world 261
/ edited by Karl H. Hertz. Minneapolis : Augsburg Pub. House, c1976. 379 p. ; 22 cm. Bibliography: p. 375-377. [BX8066.A1T85] 76-3852 ISBN 0-8066-1538-9 : 9.50
1. Theology, Lutheran—History.—Addresses, essays, lectures. 2. Christianity and politics—History—Addresses, essays, lectures. 3. Church and the world—History—Addresses, essays, lectures. 4. Social ethics—Addresses, essays, lectures. I. Hertz, Karl H.

ULLMAN, Walter, 1910- 261
The growth of papal government in the Middle Ages; a study in the ideological relation of clerical to lay power. New York, Barnes & Noble [1956] xviii, 482 p. front. 23 cm. [(BX955.U)] A59
1. Papacy — Hist. 2. Popes — Temporal power. 3. Church and state — Hist. I. Title.

USHER-WILSON, R.N. 261
The Church must modernize men [by] R. N. Usher-Wilson. Grand Rapids, Eerdmans [1967] 32 p. 21 cm. Bibliographical footnotes. [BT738.U72] 68-1864
1. Sociology, Christian—Addresses, essays, lectures. I. Title.

VALLIER, Ivan. 261
Catholicism, social control, and modernization in Latin America. Englewood Cliffs, N.J., Prentice-Hall [1970] x, 172 p. 24 cm. (Modernization of traditional societies series) Includes bibliographical references. [BX1426.2.V4] 77-99742
1. Catholic Church in Latin America. 2. Sociology, Christian (Catholic) I. Title. II. Series.

VALYI Nagy, Ervin. 261
Church as dialogue [by] Ervin Valyi Nagy [and] Heinrich Ott. Translated by Reinhard Ulrich. Philadelphia, Pilgrim Press [1969] 128 p. 22 cm. Translation of Kirche als Dialog. Bibliographical references included in "Notes" (p. 105-128) [BR115.W6V313] 69-16929 4.95
1. Church and the world. I. Ott, Heinrich. II. Title.

VATH, Mary Loyola. 261
Visualized church history. New ed., with 1959 suppl. New York, Oxford Book Co. [1959] 356 p. illus. 19 cm. Includes bibliography. [BR147.V3] 270
1. Church history. 2. Catholic Church — Hist. 3. Catholic Church in the U.S. I. Title.

VELAZCO MEDINA, Jose Luis, 261
1926-
What's mine? what's yours? New Yrok, Friendship [1966] 63p. 16cm. (Questions for Christians, no. 7) Bibl. [BV772.V35] 66-1132 .65 pap.,
1. Stewardship, Christian. I. Title. II. Series.

VISSER'T Hooft, Willem 261
Adolph, 1900-
The renewal of the church. Philadelphia, Westminster Press [1957] 128 p. 21 cm. (The Dale lectures, 1955) [BV600.V54] 57-5059
1. Church. I. Title.

VISSER 'T HOOFT, William 261
Adolph, 1900-
The renewal of the church. Philadelphia, Westminster Press [1957] 128p. 21cm. (The Dale lectures, 1955) [BV600.V54] 57-5059
1. Church. I. Title.

VRIES, Egbert de, 1901- ed. 261
Man in community; Christian concern for the human in changing society. New York, Association Press [1966] 382 p. 21 cm. Working papers prepared under the sponsorship of the Dept. on Church and Society, World Council of Churches, for the 1966 world conference. Bibliographical footnotes. [BT738.V7] 66-11797
1. Sociology, Christian—Addresses, essays, lectures. I. World Council of Churches. Division of Studies. Dept. on Church and Society. II. World Conference on Church Society, Geneva, 1966. III. Title.

VRIES, Egbert de, 1901- ed. 261
Man in community; Christian concern for the human in changing society. New York, Association [c.1966] 382p. 21cm. Working papers prepd. under the sponsorship of the Dept. on Church and Society, World Council of Churches, for the 1966 world conf. Bibl. [BT738.V7] 66-11797 5.50
1. Sociology, Christian—Addresses, essays, lectures. I. World Council of Churches. Division of Studies. Dept. on Church and Society. II. World Conference on Church Society, Geneva, 1966. III. Title.

WALMSLEY, John, 1947- 261
Neill & Summerhill: a man and his work: a pictorial study. Harmondsworth, Penguin, 1969. [96] p. (chiefly illus.). 20 cm. (Penguin education specials) (Penguin education.) [LF795.L692953W3 1969b] 79-574622 ISBN 0-14-080134-0 7/-
1. Summerhill School, Leiston, Eng. 2. Neill, Alexander Sutherland, 1883- I. Title.

WALSH, Chad, 1914- 261
Early Christians of the 21st century. Westport, Conn., Greenwood Press [1972, c1950] 188 p. 22 cm. [BR115.C5W26 1972] 78-138136 ISBN 0-8371-5709-9
1. Civilization, Christian. I. Title.

WARD, Alfred Dudley, 1914- 261
Secular man in sacred mission; the story of spiritual reality and service [by Dudley Ward. Nashville, Tidings, 1968] 114 p. 19 cm. Bibliographical footnotes. [BV601.8.W37] 68-59145
1. Mission of the church. 2. Church and the world. I. Title.

WARD, Alfred Dudley, 1914- 261
The social creed of the Methodist Church, a living document. Rev. ed. Nashville, Abingdon [c.1961, 1965] 160p. 22cm. Bibl. [HN37.M4W27] 65-15236 1.75 pap.,
1. Church and social problems—Methodist Church. 2. Church and social problems—U. s. I. Title.

WARD, Alfred Dudley, 1914- 261
The social creed of the Methodist Church, a living document [by] A. Dudley War. Rev. ed. New York, Abingdon Press [1965] 160 p. 22 cm. Bibliography: p. 155-156. [HN37.M4W27] 65-15236
1. Church and social problems — Methodist Church. 2. Church and social problems — U.S. I. Title.

WARD, William George, 1812- 261
1882.
The ideal of a Christian Church considered in comparison with existing practice, containing a defence of certain articles in the British critic in reply to remarks on them in Mr. Palmer's "Narrative" / by W. G. Ward. 2d ed. New York : AMS Press, 1977. xiv, 601 p. ; 23 cm. Reprint of the 1844 ed. published by J. Toovey, London. Includes bibliographical references. [BV600.W35 1977] 75-30040 ISBN 0-404-14044-0 : 37.50
1. Church of England—Doctrinal and controversial works. 2. Palmer, William, 1803-1885. A narrative of events ... 3. Church. I. Title: The ideal of a Christian Church considered in comparison with existing practice ...

WELCH, Claude. 261
The reality of the church. New York, Scribner [1958] 254 p. 21 cm. Includes bibliography. [BV600.W38] 58-11639
1. Church. I. Title.

WELLINGTON, Paul A., comp. 261
Challenges to kingdom building; a symposium on contemporary issues, edited and compiled by Paul A. Wellington. [Independence, Mo., Herald Pub. House, 1968] 380 p. 21 cm. A selection of articles which originally appeared in the Saints' herald. [BX8674.W4] 68-15216
1. Reorganized Church of Jesus Christ of Latter-Day Saints—Doctrinal and controversial works. I. The Saints' herald. II. Title.

WELTY, Eberhard 261
A handbook of Christian social ethics, v.1. [Translated from the German by Gregor Kirstein, rev. and adapted by John Fitzsimons. New York] Herder and Herder [1960] xvi. [395]p. 22cm. Contents.v. 1. Man in society. Bibl.: p. 359-368 59-14749 6.95
1. Sociology, Christian (Catholic) I. Title. II. Title: Christian social ethics.

WENTZ, Frederick K. 261
Set free for others [by] Frederick K. Wentz. Drawings by Edith Aberle. New York, Friendship Press [1969] 157 p. illus. 19 cm. Bibliography: p. 156-157. [BT738.W42] 68-59133 ISBN 3-7709-0115- 1.50
1. Sociology, Christian. 2. Church and the world. I. Title.

WEST, Charles C. 261
Outside the camp; the Christian and the world. [Special ed. for the Commission on World Mission of the National Student Christian Federation] Garden City, N.Y., Doubleday, 1959. 168 p. 21 cm. [BR481.W43] 59-9130
1. Christianity — 20th cent. 2. Civilization, Modern. I. Title.

WESTOW, Theodore L 261
The variety of Catholic attitudes. [New York] Herder and Herder [1963] 159 p. 21 cm. Bibliographical footnotes. [BX1793.W45] 63-18160
1. Personalism. 2. Individualism. 3. Sociology, Christian (Catholic) 4. Man (Theology) 5. Christianity — 20th cent. I. Title.

WESTOW, Theodore L. 261
The variety of Catholic attitudes. [New York] Herder & Herder [c.1963] 159p. 21cm. Bibl. 63-18160 3.50
1. Personalism. 2. Individualism. 3. Sociology, Christian (Catholic) 4. Man (Theology) 5. Christianity—20th cent. I. Title.

WHEELER, J Clyde. 261
Here lies our hope. Boston, Christopher Pub. House [1955] 118p. 21cm. [BR481.W48] 55-14094
1. Christianity—20th cent. 2. Church history—1945 I. Title.

WHEELER, Joseph Clyde. 261
Here lies our hope. Boston, Christopher Pub. House [1955] 118 p. 21 cm. [BR481.W48] 55-14094
1. Christianity — 20th cent. 2. Church history — 1945- I. Title.

WHITLEY, Oliver Read. 261
The church: mirror or window? Images of the church in American society. St. Louis, Mo., Bethany Press [1969] 189 p. 22 cm. Includes bibliographical references. [BV625.W47] 77-79585 4.95
1. Church. 2. Sociology, Christian. I. Title.

WICKER, Brian, 1929- 261
Culture and liturgy. New York, Sheed [1964, c.1963] xii, 212p. 20cm. Bibl. 64-13571 3.50
1. Sociology, Christian (Catholic) I. Title.

WILLIAMS, Melvin J 261
Catholic social thought; its approach to contemporary problems. With a foreword by Paul Hanly Furfey. New York, Ronald Press Co. [1950] xv. 567 p. 24 cm. Bibliography: p. 495-530. [HM19.W5] 50-7775
1. Sociology—Hist. 2. Sociology, Christian—Catholic authors. I. Title.

WILLIAMSON, Eugene L 261
The liberalism of Thomas Arnold, a study of his religious and political writings [by] Eugene L. Williamson, Jr. University, University of Alabama Press [1964] 261 p. 21 cm. Bibliography: p. [251]-258. [LF795.R92W53] 63-17401
1. Arnold, Thomas, 1795-1842. I. Title.

WILLIAMSON, Eugene L., Jr. 261
The liberalism of Thomas Arnold, a study of his religious and political writings. University, Univ. of Ala. Pr. [c.1964] 261p. 21cm. Bibl. 63-1740 5.95
1. Arnold, Thomas, 1795-1842. I. Title.

WIRT, Sherwood Eliot. 261
The social conscience of the evangelical. [1st ed.] New York, Harper & Row [1968] xiii, 177 p. 22 cm. Includes bibliographical references. [BT738.W53] 68-11736
1. Sociology, Christian. 2. Evangelicalism. I. Title.

WOOD, Herbert George, 1879- 261
1963.
Christianity and civilisation. New York, Octagon Books, 1973. 128 p. 19 cm. Based on 6 lectures delivered at the invitation of the Divinity Board in Cambridge in 1942. Reprint of the 1943 ed. published by the University Press, Cambridge [Eng.] which was issued as no. 16 of Current problems. Includes bibliographical references. [BR115.C5W6 1973] 73-17694 ISBN 0-374-98713-0 8.00 (lib. bdg.).
1. Civilization, Christian. I. Title. II. Series: Current problems.

WOOLLARD, A. G. B. 261
Progress: a Christian doctrine? [By] A. G. B. Woollard. Valley Forge [Pa.] Judson Press [1973, c1972] 92 p. 22 cm. Includes bibliographical references. [BR115.P77W66 1973] 72-7724 ISBN 0-8170-0576-5 1.95
1. Christianity and progress. 2. Theology—20th century. I. Title.

WOOLLARD, A. G. B. 261
Progress: a Christian doctrine? [By] A. G. B. Woollard. Valley Forge [Pa.] Judson Press [1973] p. Includes bibliographical references. [BR115.P77W66] 72-7726 ISBN 0-8170-0576-5
1. Christianity and progress. 2. Theology—20th century. I. Title.

WORLD Conference on Faith and 261
Order. Continuation Committee.
The nature of the church; papers presented to the theological commission appointed by the Continuation Committee of the World Conference on Faith and Order. Edited by R. Newton Flew. New York, Harper [c1952] 347p. 23cm. Bibliographical footnotes. [BV600.A1W62 1952a] 52-5434
1. Church. I. Flew, Robert Newton, 1886- ed. II. Title.

WORLD Council of Churches. 261
Commission on Faith and Order. Theological Commission on the Church.
The nature of the church; papers presented to the Theological Commission appointed by the Continuation Committee of the World Conference on Faith and Order. Edited by R. Newton Flew, chairman. New York, Harper [1952] 347 p. 23 cm. [BV600.A1W62 1952a] 52-5434
1. Church. I. Flew, Robert Newton, 1886- ed. II. Title.

WORLD Evaluation Conference 261
on Christian Education, Geneva, 1969.
Christian education in a secular society. Gustav K. Wiencke, editor. [Philadelphia] Fortress Press [1970] 230 p. 23 cm. (Yearbooks in Christian education, v. 2) "A study document of the Commission on Education of the Lutheran World Federation, summarizing the results of a five-year consultation and study program, 1965-69." "Annotated listing of study papers, prepared by Dr. Herbert G. Schaefer": p. [209]-230. [BV1463.W63 1969b] 73-11416
1. Religious education—Congresses. 2. Secularism—Congresses. I. Wiencke, Gustav K., ed. II. Lutheran World Federation. Commission on Education. III. Title. IV. Series.

WORLEY, Robert C. 261
Change in the Church; a source of hope, by Robert C. Worley. Philadelphia, Westminster Press [1971] 127 p. 19 cm. [BV600.2.W65] 78-126354 ISBN 0-664-24901-9 2.25
1. Church. 2. Sociology, Christian. I. Title.

WRIGHT, John Joseph, 261
Cardinal, 1909-
The Church: hope of the world [by] John Wright. Edited by Donald W. Wuerl. Kenosha, Wis., Prow Books [1972] xiv, 192 p. 23 cm. Contents.Contents.—The church of promise.—Teachers of the faith.—Faith and the theologies.—The point of contemporary catechetics.—Christ head of the church and the priest.—Priestly maturity.—The Resurrection: fact or myth?—Justice exalts.—Faith and social action.—The blessed vision of peace.—The cult of Mary in the age of the cult of the flesh.—The Roman loyalty of the English martyrs.—Toast to the Holy Father.—Pope John and his secret. Includes bibliographical references. [BX891.W74] 76-158917 5.95
1. Catholic Church—Addresses, essays, lectures. I. Title.

YOUNGER, George D 261
The Bible calls for action. Philadelphia, Judson Press [1959] 107 p. 19 cm. [TB738.Y6] 59-8732
1. Sociology, Christian — Study and teaching. I. Title.

WALGRAVE, Jan Henricus, 261.01
1911-
Person and society; a Christian view, by John H. Walgrave. Pittsburgh, Duquesne University Press [1965] 182 p. 23 mcm. (Duquesne studies. Theological series, 5) "The original edition of this book was published in Dutch as the introduction to a four volume set entitled Welfare, well-being and happiness. It was translated by Walter van de Putte." Bibliographical footnotes. [BT738.W29] 65-22936
1. Sociology, Christian (Catholic) I. Title.

WALGRAVE, Jan Henricus, 261.01
1911-
Person and society; a Christian view. Pittsburgh, Duquesne Univ. Pr. [c.1965] 182p. 23cm. (Duquesne studies. Theological ser., 5) Orig. ed. pub. in Dutch as the introd. to a four vol. set entitled Welfare, well-being and happiness, tr. by Walter van de Putte. Bibl. [BT738.W29] 65-22936 4.25
1. Sociology, Christian (Catholic) I. Title. II. Series.

HUTCHISON, John Alexander, 261.04
1912- ed.
Christian faith and social action; a symposium by John A. Hutchison [and others] New York, Scribner, 1953. 246p. 24cm. Bibliographical footnotes. [HN31.H85] 53-9669
1. Church and social problems—Addresses, essays, lectures. I. Title.
Contents omitted.

WORLD Conference on 261.0631
Church, Community, and State, Oxford, 1937
Foundations of ecumenical social thought; the Oxford Conference report, ed. by J. H. Oldham. [New] introd. by Harold L. Lunger. Philadelphia, Fortress Press [1966, c.1937] xv, 211p. 20cm. First pub. in 1937 under titles: The churches survey their task (London, G. Allen & Unwin) and The Oxford Conference official report (New York, Willett, Clark) [BV630.A1W6] 66-14244 5.00

1. Church and state—Congresses. 2. Sociology, Christian—Congresses. I. Oldham, Joseph Houldsworth, 1874- ed. II. Title.

KATHAN, Boardman. 261'.071'2
Youth—where the action is, by Boardman and Joyce Kathan. Grades 7 and 8. Philadelphia, Published for the Cooperative Publication Association by United Church Press [1970] 2 v. illus. 22 cm. (The Cooperative through-the-week series) Consists of a teacher's book with outlines and study guides and a student's book with reading material. Bibliography: v. [1] p. 184-186. [BV1561.K3] 71-122924 ISBN 0-8298-0161-8 (teacher's book)
1. Religious education—Text-books for young people. I. Kathan, Joyce, joint author. II. Cooperative Publication Association. III. Title.

BROTHERS, Joan, 1938- ed. 261'.08
Readings in the sociology of religion. [1st ed.] Oxford, New York, Pergamon Press [1967] x, 239 p. 20 cm. (The Commonwealth and international library. Readings in sociology) Includes bibliographical references. [BL60.B7 1967] 66-29582
1. Religion and sociology—Collections. I. Title.

CELL, Edward, comp. 261'08
Religion and contemporary Western culture; selected readings. Nashville. Abingdon [1967] 399p. 26cm. Bibl. [BR115.C8C4] 67-14980 7.95
1. Christianity and culture—Collections. I. Title.

DEEDY, John G ed. 261.08
Eyes on the modern world; views on Schema 13, edited by John G. Deedy, Jr. [Contributors] Richard Horchler [and others] New York, P. J. Kenedy [1965] 186 p. 22 cm. [BR123.D43] 65-22644
1. Christianity — 20th cent. — Addresses, essays, lectures. 2. Vatican Council, 2d. I. Horchler, Richard. II. Title. III. Title: Views on Schema 13.

DEEDY, John G., Jr., ed. 261.08
Eyes on the modern world; views on Schema 13, ed. by John G. Deedy, Jr. [Contribs.] Richard Horchler [others] New York, Kenedy [c.1965] 186p. 22cm. [BR123.D43] 65-22644 4.95
1. Christianity—20th cent.—Addresses, essays, lectures. 2. Vatican Council, 2d I. Horchler, Richard. II. Title. III. Title: Views on Schema 13.

FORELL, George Wolfgang, 261'.08 ed.
Christian social teachings; a reader in Christian social ethics from the Bible to the present. Compiled and edited by George W. Forell. Garden City, N.Y., Anchor Books, 1966. xx, 491 p. 19 cm. Bibliography: p. 481-491. [BR53.F6] 66-21010
1. Christian literature. 2. Sociology, Christian—Collections. I. Title.

NIEBUHR, Reinhold, 1892- 261.08
The godly and the ungodly; essays on the religious and secular dimensions of modern life. London, Faber & Faber [Mystic, Conn., Verry, 1966, c.1958] x, 150p. 23cm. [BR123.N53] 66-2142 4.50
1. Christianity—Addresses, essays, lectures. I. Title.

TURNER, Denys, 1942- 261'.08
The Church in the world: essays on the Second Vatican Council's pastoral constitution on the Church in the World Today with texts of Church teaching on social questions. Dublin, Scepter Publishers, 1968. 230 p. 22 cm. Bibliography: p. 222-225. [BX830 1962.A45C988] 77-417617 25/-
1. Church and the world. I. Vatican Council. 2d, 1962-1965. Pastoral constitution on the Church in the world today. II. Title.

WENZ, Helmut, writer 261'.08 s on theology.
Theologie des Reiches Gottes : hat Jesus sich geirrt? / Helmut Wenz. Hamburg : H. Reich, Evangelischer Verlag, 1975. 103 p. ; 21 cm. (Evangelische Zeitstimmen ; 73) Includes bibliographical references and index. [AC30.E83 Nr. 73] [BT94] 231'.7 75-505853 ISBN 3-7924-0271-8
1. Kingdom of God. I. Title. II. Series.

SAYRE, Leslie C ed. 261.084
Where there is life. [New York? 1953] unpaged (chiefly illus.) 23cm. [BV595.S3] 53-11891
1. Church—Pictorial works. I. Title.

BIKLE, George B. 261'.092'4
The new Jerusalem : aspects of utopianism in the thought of Kagawa Toyohiko / George B. Bikle, Jr. Tucson : Published for the Association for Asian Studies by the University of Arizona Press, [1976] 343 p. ; 24 cm. (Monographs of the Association for Asian Studies ; no. 30) Includes index. Bibliography: p. 327-334. [BV3457.K3B54] 75-36125 ISBN 0-8165-0550-0 : 8.95. ISBN 0-8165-0531-4 pbk. : 4.95
1. Kagawa, Toyohiko, 1888-1960. I. Association for Asian Studies. II. Title. III. Series: Association for Asian Studies. Monographs of the Association for Asian Studies ; no. 30.

LEE, Robert. 261'.0924
The promise of Bennett; Christian realism and social responsibility. [1st ed.] Philadelphia, Lippincott [1969] 111 p. 21 cm. (The Promise of theology) Bibliographical references included in "Notes" (p. 107-109) [BX9886.Z8B4] 79-88738 3.50
1. Bennett, John Coleman, 1902- I. Title.

SMITH, David H., 1939- 261'.0924
The achievement of John C. Bennett [by] David H. Smith. [New York] Herder and Herder [1970] 204 p. 22 cm. Includes bibliographical references. "The works of John C. Bennett": p. 195-202. [BX9886.Z8B43] 78-87770 6.95
1. Bennett, John Coleman, 1902- I. Title.

SOLLE, Dorothee. 261'.092'4
Political theology. Translated and with an introd. by John Shelley. Philadelphia, Fortress Press [1974] xx, 107 p. 19 cm. Includes bibliographical references. [BX4827.B78S6413] 73-88349 ISBN 0-8006-1065-2 3.50
1. Bultmann, Rudolf Karl, 1884- 2. Christianity and politics. I. Title.

CONGREGATIONAL 261'.09'33
readings from the Scriptures ..., hymns, inspirational writings / compiled by Cecil R. Ettinger. Independence, Mo. : Herald Pub. House, [1975] p. cm. Includes index. [BX8675.C66] 75-8596 ISBN 0-8309-0145-0
1. Reorganized Church of Jesus Christ of Latter-Day Saints—Prayer-books and devotions—English. 2. Responsive worship. I. Ettinger, Cecil Ray, 1922-

LITTLE, David. 261'.0942
Religion, order, and law; a study in pre-Revolutionary England. [1st ed.] New York, Harper & Row [1969] v, 269 p. 21 cm. (Harper torchbooks. The Library of religion and culture, TB1418.) Includes bibliographical references. [BR757.L66] 70-84041 2.95
1. Weber, Max, 1864-1920. Dieprotestantische Ethik und der Geist des Kapitalismus. 2. Church of England—Doctrinal and controversial works. 3. Sociology, Christian—Gt. Brit. 4. Religion and law. 5. Puritans. I. Title.

DRU, Alexander. 261.0943
The contribution of German Catholicism. [1st ed.] New York, Hawthorn Books [1963] 124, [1] p. 21 cm. (Twentieth century encyclopedia of Catholicism, vol. 101. Section 9: The church and the modern world) Bibliography: p. [125] [BX1536.D74] 63-20562
1. Catholic Church in Germany — Hist. — 19th cent. I. Title. II. Series. III. Series: Twentieth century encyclopedia of Catholicism, v. 101

DRU, Alexander 261.0943
The contribution of German Catholicism. New York, Hawthorn [c.1963] 124, [1]p. 21cm. (Twentieth cent. ency. of Catholicism, v. 101. Sect. 9: The church and the modern world) Bibl. 63-20562 3.50 bds.,
1. Catholic Church in Germany—Hist.—19th cent. I. Title. II. Series: Twentieth century encyclopedia of Catholicism, v. 101

BEACH, Waldo. 261'.0973
Christian community and American society. Philadelphia, Westminster Press [1969] 190 p. 21 cm. Includes bibliographical references. [BT738.B33] 69-14196 6.00
1. Sociology, Christian. 2. U.S.—Social history—1945- I. Title.

COLE, Charles Chester, 261.0973 Jr.
The social ideas of the northern evangelists, 1826-1860, New York, Octagon, 1966[c.1954] 268p. 24cm. (Columbia studies in the soc. scis., no. 580) Issued also as thesis, Columbia Univ., in microfilm form under title: The secular ideas of the northern evangelists, 1826-1860. Bibl. [H31.C7no.580] 66-17507 7.50
1. Evangelists—U. S. 2. U. S.—Church history. 3. Church and social problems—U. S. I. Title. II. Series.

MCNAMARA, Patrick H., 261'.0973 comp.
Religion American style. Edited by Patrick H. McNamara. New York, Harper & Row [1974] xiv, 408 p. 24 cm. Includes bibliographical references. [BR515.M2] 73-10686 ISBN 0-06-044377-4 4.95 (pbk.).
1. United States—Religion—Collected works. I. Title.

WHITE, Donald Cedric, 261'.0973 1939-
The social gospel : religion and reform in changing America / Ronald C. White, Jr. and C. Howard Hopkins ; with an essay by John C. Bennett. Philadelphia : Temple University Press, 1976. xix, 306 p. : ill. ; 22 cm. Includes bibliographical references and index. [BT738.W45] 75-34745 ISBN 0-87722-083-2 : 15.00 ISBN 0-87722-084-0 pbk. :
1. Social gospel. 2. Sociology, Christian—United States. I. Hopkins, Charles Howard, 1905- joint author. II. Title.

MOL, J. J. 261'.0994
Christianity in chains; a sociologist's interpretation of the churches' dilemma in a secular world [by] Hans Mol. [Melbourne] Nelson [1969] vii, 120 p. 22 cm. (Nelson's Australasian paperbacks) Bibliography: p. 110-115. [BT738.M55] 72-493507 2.95
1. Sociology, Christian—Australia. 2. Christianity—20th century. I. Title.

BARTLETT, David Lyon, 1941- 261.1
"Paul's vision for the teaching church" / David L. Bartlett. Valley Forge, Pa. : Judson Press, c1977. 141 p. ; 22 cm. Revision and expansion of lectures given at the Learning One '76 Conference at the American Baptist Assembly, Green Lake, Wis. Includes index. Bibliography: p. 137-138. [BS2655.C5B37] 77-1106 ISBN 0-8170-0738-5 pbk. : 4.95
1. Bible. N.T. Epistles of Paul—Theology—Addresses, essays, lectures. 2. Church—Teaching office—Biblical teaching—Addresses, essays, lectures. I. Title.

BLOESCH, Donald G., 1928- 261.1
The invaded church / Donald G. Bloesch. Waco, Tex. : Word Books, c1975. 133 p. ; 22 cm. Contents.Contents.—A church divided.—Burying the Gospel.—The church and social involvement.—The missing dimension.—How Christians can change the world. Includes bibliographical references and index. [BR115.W6B54] 74-27487 ISBN 0-87680-376-1 : 4.95
1. Church and the world. 2. Christianity—20th century. I. Title.

A Christian declaration of 261.1
human rights : theological studies of the World Alliance of Reformed Churches / edited by Allen O. Miller. Grand Rapids, MI : Eerdmans, c1977. 190 p. ; 21 cm. [BT738.15.C47] 77-2796 ISBN 0-8028-1717-3 pbk. : 4.95
1. Church and civil rights—Addresses, essays, lectures. I. Miller, Allen O. II. World Alliance of Reformed Churches (Presbyterian and Congregational).

CHURCH and Society Study 261.1 Conference, Chicago, 1961.
Christian responsibility to society, a Biblical-theological statement. Newton, Kan., Faith and Life Press [1963] 18 p. 23 cm. (Church and society series, no. 2) "Published for the Board of Christian Service of the General Conference Mennonite Church." [BT738.C5] 63-3226
1. Sociology, Christian. I. General Conference Mennonite Church. Board of Christian Service. II. Title.

CORWIN, Charles. 261.1
East to Eden? Religion and the dynamics of social change. Grand Rapids, Eerdmans [1972] 190 p. 21 cm. Includes bibliographical references. [BL60.C67] 77-184693 ISBN 0-8028-1444-1 2.95
1. Religion and sociology. 2. Asia—Religion. I. Title.

COUNCIL for Social Welfare. 261.1
Planning for social development : what needs to be done / Council for Social Welfare (a committee of the Catholic Bishops' Conference). Dublin : The Council, 1976. [3], 29 p. ; 30 cm. Includes bibliographical references. [HN382.5.C68 1976] 77-364044 ISBN 0-9503413-3-9
1. Great Britain—Social policy. 2. Social service—Great Britain. I. Title.

DOUGLASS, Harlan Paul, 261.1 1871-1953.
The Protestant church as a social institution, by H. Paul Douglass and Edmund deS. Brunner. New York, Russell & Russell [1972] xv, 368 p. illus. 24 cm. (Institute of Social and Religious Research studies) (Institute of Social and Religious Research Studies) Reprint of the 1935 ed. Bibliography: p. 356-362. [BR517.D6 1972] 72-173517
1. Protestant churches—United States. 2. Sociology, Christian. I. Brunner, Edmund de Schweinitz, 1889- joint author. II. Title. III. Series. IV. Series: Institute of Social and Religious Research. Studies.

EASTMAN, Albert Theodore, 261.1 1928-
Chosen and sent: calling the church to mission [by] A. Theodore Eastman. Grand Rapids, Mich., W. B. Eerdmans Pub. Co. [1971] 144 p. 20 cm. (A Christian world mission book) Bibliography: p. 140-141. [BV601.8.E23] 71-127624 2.95
1. Mission of the church. 2. Church and the world. I. Title.

ELLUL, Jacques. 261.1
False presence of the kingdom. Translated by C. Edward Hopkin. New York, Seabury Press [1972] viii, 211 p. 22 cm. Translation of Fausse presence au monde moderne. [BR115.W6E4313] 77-163969 ISBN 0-8164-0235-3 4.95
1. Church and the world. I. Title.

EPPSTEIN, John, 1895- 261.1
The cult of revolution in the church. New Rochelle, N.Y., Arlington House [1974] 159 p. 23 cm. Includes bibliographical references. [BT738.3.E66] 73-18470 ISBN 0-87000-241-4 6.95
1. Revolution (Theology) 2. Violence—Moral and religious aspects. 3. Social ethics. I. Title.

FLORY, Charles. 261.1
Le catholicisme social devant la crise de civilisation; recherches et perspectives. Pref 'd alain Barrere, Postface de Joseph Folliet [Lyon] Chronique sociale de France, 1960. [New York, Kraus Reprint Corp., 1966] 259 p. 23 cm. ix, 141 p. illus. (Society for Research in Child Development. Monographs, v.1, no. 3) (Series. Series: Chicago. University. Committee on Child Development. Study no.1) Chicago. University. Committee on Child Development. Study no.1. [BT738.F5] 63-40661 67-12417
1. Sociology, Christian (Catholic) 2. Semaine sociale de France. 3. Growth. 4. Hand. 5. Child study. I. Flory, Charles D 1902- II. Title. III. Title: Osseous development in the hand as an index of skeletal development. Washington Society for Research in Child Development, National Research Council, 1936. IV. Series.

GLENN, Leslie, 1900- 261.1
A scornful wonder : what's right with the Church / C. Leslie Glenn. New York : D. McKay Co., c1977. xvii, 235 p. : ill. ; 22 cm. [BV600.2.G56] 77-5712 ISBN 0-679-50740-X : 9.95
1. Church. 2. Christian life—Anglican authors. I. Title.

GLENN, Leslie, 1900- 261.1
A scornful wonder : what's right with the Church / C. Leslie Glenn. New York : D. McKay Co., c1977. xvii, 235 p. : ill. ; 22 cm. [BV600.2.G56] 77-5712 ISBN 0-679-50740-X : 9.95
1. Church. 2. Christian life—Anglican authors. I. Title.

GRANT, Robert McQueen, 261.1 1917-
Early Christianity and society : seven studies / Robert M. Grant. New York : Harper & Row, [1977] p. cm. Includes index. Bibliography: p. [BR166.G7] 77-7844 ISBN 0-06-063411-1 : 10.95
1. Sociology, Christian—Early church, ca. 30-600—Addresses, essays, lectures. I. Title.

GRANT, Robert McQueen, 261.1 1917-
Early Christianity and society : seven studies / Robert M. Grant. New York : Harper & Row, [1977] p. cm. Includes index. Bibliography: p. [BR166.G7] 77-7844 ISBN 0-06-063411-1 : 10.95
1. Sociology, Christian—Early church, ca. 30-600—Addresses, essays, lectures. I. Title.

HARDENBERG, Friedrich, 261.1 Freiherr von, 1772-1801.
Spiritual saturnalia; fragments of existence [by] Novalis. Translation and introd. by John N. Ritter. [1st ed.] New York, Exposition Press [1971] 82 p. 21 cm. (An Exposition-university book) Translation of the author's Die Christenheit oder Europa and translations of some of his notes. [BR115.C8H37] 71-146914 ISBN 0-682-47246-8 5.95
1. Christianity and culture. I. Title.

HARING, Bernhard, 1912- 261.1
The church on the move. Staten Island, N.Y., Alba House [1970] vii, 85 p. illus. (part col.) 28 cm. Translation of Zusage an die Welt. Includes bibliographical references. [BR115.W6H313] 72-129175 ISBN 0-8189-0192-6 4.95
1. Church and the world. I. Title.

IS revolution change? 261.1
Edited by Brian Griffiths. Downers Grove, Ill., Inter-Varsity Press [1972] 111 p. 18 cm. Includes bibliographical references. [BT738.3.I8] 74-186350 ISBN 0-87784-545-X
1. Revolution (Theology)—Addresses, essays, lectures. 2. Church and social problems—

Addresses, essays, lectures. I. Griffiths, Brian, ed.

JONES, George Curtis, 1911- 261.1
Candles in the city [by] G. Curtis Jones. Waco, Tex., Word Books [1973?] 92, [1] p. 22 cm. Bibliography: p. [93] [BS2825.4.J66] 72-96356 3.50
1. Disciples of Christ—Sermons. 2. The seven churches—Sermons. 3. Sermons, American. 4. City churches. I. Title.

JONES, George Curtis, 1911- 261.1
Candles in the city [by] G. Curtis Jones. Waco, Tex., Word Books [1973?] 92, [1] p. 22 cm. Bibliography: p. [93] [BS2825.4.J66] 72-96356 3.50
1. Disciples of Christ—Sermons. 2. The seven churches—Sermons. 3. Sermons, American. 4. City churches. I. Title.

KEUCHER, William F. 261.1
Main Street and the mind of God [by] William F. Keucher. Valley Forge [Pa.] Judson Press [1974] 127 p. 22 cm. Includes bibliographical references. [BR115.W6K48] 74-4425 ISBN 0-8170-0639-7 2.65 (pbk.)
1. Church and the world. 2. Mission of the church. 3. God. I. Title.

*LANCASTER, John. 261.1
The spirit-filled church. Springfield, Mo., Gospel Publishing House, [1975] 112 p. 18 cm. (Radiant books) [BV600.8] ISBN 0-88243-601-5 1.25 (pbk.)
1. Church—Study and teaching. 2. Church and the world. I. Title.

LOOMIS, Samuel Lane, 1856-1938. 261.1
Modern cities and their religious problems. New York, Arno Press, 1970 [c1887] 219 p. 23 cm. (The Rise of urban America) Includes bibliographical references. [HT151.L64 1970] 73-112558
1. Cities and towns. 2. Social problems. 3. Cities and towns—Religious life. 4. City missions. I. Title. II. Series.

LUECKE, Richard Henry, 1923- 261.1
Perchings; reflections on society and ministry. Chicago, Urban Training Center Press [1972] 151 p. 21 cm. [BV637.5.L8] 72-179632 2.95
1. City clergy—Addresses, essays, lectures. 2. Pastoral theology—Addresses, essays, lectures. I. Title.

MCCUE, George, ed. 261.1
American Institute of Architects.
The Press and the building of cities; proceedings of a working conference for 30 reporters from metropolitan newspapers. Proceedings editor, George McCue. Washington, American Institute of Architects [1962?] x, 170 p. illus. 28 cm. "[The conference was] conducted by the Graduate School of Journalism and the School of Architecture, Columbia University, and supported by the American Institute of Architects; October 1-3, 1962, Columbia University." Bibliography: p. 167-170. [NA9050.P7] 68-4045
1. City planning and the press—Congresses. I. Columbia University. Graduate School of Journalism. II. Columbia University. School of Architecture. III. Title.

MCGAVRAN, Donald Anderson, 1897- 261.1
The clash between Christianity and cultures / Donald McGavran. Washington : Canon Press, [1974] 84 p. ; 22 cm. Includes bibliographical references. [BR115.C8M22] 74-187763 ISBN 0-913686-12-3 pbk. : 1.75
1. Christianity and culture. I. Title.

*O'NEILL, David P. 261.1
Christian behavior; does it matter what you do, or only what you are? Dayton, Ohio, Pflaum [1973] 95 p. illus. 16 cm. (Christian experience series: Witness Book 19) [BR115] ISBN 0-8278-2126-3 0.95 (pbk.)
1. Sociology, Christian. 2. Christianity—20th century. I. Title.

PATERNOSTER, Michael. 261.1
Man, the world's high priest : an ecological approach / [by] Michael Paternoster. Oxford : S.L.G. Press, 1976. [1], 12 p. ; 21 cm. (Fairacres publications ; no. 58 ISSN 0307-1405s) Cover title.Includes bibliographical references. [GF80.P37] 77-362813 ISBN 0-7283-0063-X : £0.15
1. Human ecology—Moral and religious aspects. 2. Nature (Theology) I. Title.

PITTENGER, William Norman, 1905- 261.1
The Christian church as social process. [By] Norman Pittenger. Philadelphia, Westminster Press [1972, c1971] ix, 131 p. 19 cm. [BV600.2.P58 1972] 76-187972 ISBN 0-664-24953-1 Pap. $2.75
1. Church. 2. Clergy—Office. 3. Process theology. I. Title.

THE Press and the building 261.1
of cities; proceedings of a working conference for 30 reporters from metropolitan newspapers. Proceedings editor, George McCue. Washington, American Institute of Architects [1962?] x, 170 p. illus. 28 cm. "[The conference was] conducted by the Graduate School of Journalism and the School of Architecture, Columbia University, and supported by the American Institute of Architects; October 1-3, 1962, Columbia University." Bibliography: p. 167-170. [NA9050.P7] 68-4045
1. City planning and the press—Congresses. I. McCue, George, ed. II. American Institute of Architects. III. Columbia University. Graduate School of Journalism. IV. Columbia University. School of Architecture.

*SCHADE, Sigmund C. 261.1
Love is for real; practical Christian living for space-age humans. New York, Exposition Pr. [1973] 173 p. 21 cm. [BR115] ISBN 0-682-47650-1 6.50
1. Church and the world. 2. Christianity—20th century. I. Title.

SNOW, John H., 1924- 261.1
The Gospel in a broken world [by] John H. Snow. Philadelphia, United Church Press [1972] 124 p. 22 cm. "A Pilgrim Press book." [BR123.S68] 72-6476 ISBN 0-8298-0241-X
1. Christianity—20th century—Addresses, essays, lectures. 2. Theology—Addresses, essays, lectures. I. Title.

STACKHOUSE, Max L. 261.1
Ethics and the urban ethos; an essay in social theory and theological reconstruction [by] Max L. Stackhouse. Boston, Beacon Press [1972] 220 p. 21 cm. Includes bibliographical references. [BT738.S695 1972] 77-179155 ISBN 0-8070-1136-3 7.95
1. Sociology, Christian. 2. Sociology, Urban. I. Title.

VERNEY, Stephen. 261.1
People and cities [by] Stephen Verney, with contributions by Colin Buchanan [and others] Old Tappan, N.J., Revell [1971, c1969] 221 p. 21 cm. Bibliography: p. 220-221. [HT151.V43 1971] 73-146865 ISBN 0-8007-0437-1
1. Cities and towns. 2. City churches. I. Title.

WESTERHOFF, John H. 261.1
Tomorrow's church : a community of change / John J. Westerhoff. Waco, Tex. : Word Books, c1976. 130 p. ; 23 cm. [BR121.2.W38] 76-2864 ISBN 0-87680-448-2 : 5.95
1. Christianity—20th century. 2. Church and social problems. 3. Christian education. I. Title.

WILMORE, Gayraud S. 261.1
The secular relevance of the church. Philadelphia, Westminster Press [1962] 89 p. 19, cm. (Christian perspectives on social problems) [BT738.W5] 62-14177
1. Sociology, Christian. I. Title.

THE Story of research 261.1'07'2
in sociology of religion: Garrett Theological Seminary, 1929-1972, including the Bureau of Social and Religious Research, established 1941. Evanston, Ill., Garrett Theological Seminary [1972] 53 p. 23 cm. [BT738.S76] 72-186163 1.25
1. Garrett Theological Seminary. 2. Sociology, Christian—Study and teaching. I. Garrett Theological Seminary. II. Garrett Theological Seminary. Bureau of Social and Religious Research.

KITSON Clark, George 261.1'0942
Sidney Roberts, 1900-
Churchmen and the condition of England, 1832-1885; a study in the development of social ideas and practice from the Old Regime to the Modern State [by] G. Kitson Clark. [London] Methuen [1973] xxi, 353 p. 22 cm. Distributed in the U.S.A. by Harper & Row Publishers, Barnes & Noble Import Division. Includes bibliographical references. [HN389.K58 1973] 73-159878 ISBN 0-416-13240-5 15.75
1. Church and social problems—Church of England. 2. Church and state in Great Britain. I. Title.

EDEN, Lynn. 261.1'09775'82
Crisis in Watertown; the polarization of an American community. Ann Arbor, University of Michigan Press [1972] 218 p. 22 cm. [BX7255.W38F5 1972] 77-185150 ISBN 0-472-29875-5 6.95
1. First Congregational United Church of Christ, Watertown, Wis. 2. Kromholz, Alan. 3. Church and social problems—Case studies. I. Title.

MICKLEM, Caryl, ed. 261'.13
Contemporary prayers for public worship, by Anthony Coates [and others]; edited by Caryl Micklem. [1st American ed.] Grand Rapids, W. B. Eerdmans Pub. Co. [1967] 141 p. 21 cm. [BV250.C6] 67-28374
1. Pastoral prayers. I. Coates, Anthony. II. Title.

ALTHOUSE, LaVonne. 261.2
When Jew and Christian meet. With an afterword by Balfour Brickner and David R. Hunter. New York, Friendship Press [1966] 94 p. illus. 19 cm. Bibliography: p. 93-94. [BM535.A53] 66-11136
1. Judaism — Relations — Christianity and other religious — Judaism. I. Title.

ALTHOUSE, LaVonne 261.2
When Jew and Christian meet. Afterword by Balfour Brickner, David R. Hunter. New York, Friendship [c.1966] 94p. illus. 19cm. Bibl. [BM535.A53] 66-11136 1.50 pap.,
1. Judaism—Relations—Christianity. 2. Christianity and other religions—Judaism. I. Title.

AMERICAN Jewish Committee. 261.2
Institute of Human Relations.
Report. 1960- [New York] v. illus. 26 cm. annual [DS140.A8] 67-1383
1. Jews — Political and social conditions — 1948 — — Societies, etc. I. Title.

BANKI, Judith. 261.2
Vatican Council II's statement on the Jews: five years later; a survey of progress and problems in implementing the Conciliar declaration in Europe, Israel, Latin America, the United States, and Canada. [New York, American Jewish Committee, Institute of Human Relations, 1971] 31 p. 28 cm. "[Data] compiled by the Foreign Affairs and Interreligious Affairs Departments of the American Jewish Committee." Includes bibliographical references. [BX830 1962.A45E27] 73-170483 0.25
1. Vatican Council. 2d, 1962-1965. Declaratio de Ecclesiae habitudine ad religiones non-Christianas. 2. Catholic Church—Relations—Judaism. 3. Judaism—Relations—Catholic Church. I. American Jewish Committee. Foreign Affairs Dept. II. American Jewish Committee. Interreligious Affairs Dept. III. Title.

BAVINCK, Johan Herman, 1895-1965 261.2
The Church between temple and mosque; a study of the relationship between the Christian faith and other religions, by J. H. Bavinck. Grand Rapids, Eerdmans [1966] 206p. 21cm. [BR127.B35] 2.65 pap.,
1. Christianity and other religions. I. Title.

BAVINCK, Johan Herman, 1895-1965. 261.2
The Church between temple and mosque; a study of the relationship between the Christian faith and other religions, by J. H. Bavinck. Grand Rapids, W. B. Eerdmans Pub. Co. [1966] 206 p. 21 cm. Footnotes. [BR127.B35] 66-22946
1. Christianity and other religions. I. Title.

BEA, Augustin Cardinal 1881- 261.2
The Church and the Jewish people; a commentary on the Second Vatican Councils Declaration on the relation of the Church to non-Christian religions [by] Augustin Cardinal Bea. Tr. by Philip Loretz. New York, Harper [1966] 172p. 21cm. the text of the Declaration on the relation of the Church to non-Christian religions Bibl. [BX830 1962.A45D433] 66-20790 4.50
1. Vatican Council. 2d, 1962-1965. Declaratio de Ecclesiae habitudine ad religiones non-Christianas. 2. Catholic Church—Relations—Judaism. 3. Judaism—Relations—Catholic Church. I. Title.

BECKER, Carl Heinrich, 1876-1933. 261.2
Christianity and Islam. Translated by H. J. Chaytor. New York, B. Franklin Reprints [1974] viii, 113, [1] p. 18 cm. (Burt Franklin research & source works series. Philosophy & religious history monographs, 141) Reprint of the 1909 ed. published by Harper, London, New York, in series: Harper's library of living thought. Translation of Christentum und Islam. Bibliography: p. 110-[114] [BP172.B4 1974] 74-608 ISBN 0-8337-4816-5 11.50
1. Christianity and other religions—Islam. 2. Islam—Relations—Christianity. I. Title.

BELL, Richard, 1876- 261.2
The origin of Islam in its Christian environment: the Gunning lectures, Edinburgh University 1925. 1st ed., new impression. London, Cass, 1968. vii, 224p. 23cm. (Islam & the Muslim world, no. 10) Series: The Gunning lectures, 1925) Gunning lects., 1925. Bibl. footnotes. [BP172.B45 1968] 68-112517 8.75
1. Christianity and other religions—Islam. 2. Islam—Origin. 3. Islam—Relations—Christianity. I. Title. II. Series.
Order from Barnes & Noble, New York.

BISHOP, Claire Huchet. 261.2
How Catholics look at Jews; inquiries into Italian, Spanish, and French teaching materials. Pref. by Olin J. Murdick. New York, Paulist Press [1974] 164 p. illus. 23 cm. Bibliography: p. 153-158. [BM535.B5] 73-91371 ISBN 0-8091-1813-0 4.50
1. Christian education—Text-books—Catholic Church—Attitude toward Judaism. 2. Christianity and antisemitism. I. Title.

BOKSER, Ben Zion, 1907- 261.2
Judaism and the Christian predicament. With a foreword by Frederick C. Grant. [1st ed.] New York, Knopf, 1967 [c1966] viii, 384 p. 22 cm. Bibliography: p. 379-384. [BM535.B6] 66-19370
1. Judaism—Relations—Christianity. 2. Christianity and other religions—Judaism. I. Title.

BOUQUET, Alan Coates, 1884- 261.2
The Christian faith and non-Christian religions / A. C. Bouquet. Westport, Conn. : Greenwood Press, 1976, c1958. p. cm. Reprint of the ed. published by J. Nisbet, Walwyn, Eng., in series: the Library of constructive theology. [BR127.B64 1976] 76-13920 ISBN 0-8371-7974-2 lib.bdg. : 24.00
1. Christianity and other religions. 2. Religions. I. Title. II. Series: The Library of constructive theology.

BRATTON, Fred Gladstone, 1896- 261.2
The crime of Christendom; the theological sources of Christian anti-Semitism. Boston, Beacon Press [1969] xii, 241 p. 22 cm. Bibliography: p. [225]-232. [BM535.B67] 69-14596 5.95
1. Christianity and antisemitism. I. Title.

BROWN, David Allan, 1922- 261.2
A new threshold : guidelines for the churches in their relations with Muslim communities / [by] David Brown. London : British Council of Churches : Conference of Missionary Societies in Great Britain and Ireland, 1976. v, 44 p. ; 21 cm. Prepared for the BCC/CBMS Advisory Group on the Presence of Islam in Britain. Bibliography: p. 40-41. [BP172.B77 1976] 76-369201 ISBN 0-85169-050-5 : £0.50
1. Christianity and other religions—Islam. 2. Islam—Relations—Christianity. 3. Muslims in Great Britain. I. BCC/CBMS Advisory Group on the Presence of Islam in Britain. II. Title.

CADDELL, Cecilia Mary, d.1877. 261.2
History of the missions in Japan and Paraguay. New York, D. & J. Sadlier [n. d.] 1 v. illus. 20 cm. [BV3445.C3] 52-29033
1. Missions—Japan. 2. Missions—Paraguay. 3. Jesuits—Missions. I. Title.

CALLAWAY, Tucker N. 261.2
Zen way, Jesus way / Tucker N. Callaway. Rutland, Vermont : C. E. Tuttle, 1976. 263 p. ; 20 cm. Includes index. [BQ9269.4.C5C34] 76-6032 8.50
1. Callaway, Tucker N. 2. Zen Buddhism—Relations—Christianity. 3. Christianity and other religions—Zen Buddhism. I. Title.

CARPENTER, George Wayland 261.2
Encounter of the faiths. New York, Friendship [1967] 174p. 19cm. Bibl. [BR127.C27] 67-11852 1.75 pap.,
1. Christianity and other religions. I. Title.

CAVE, Sydney, 1883- 261.2
Redemption: Hindu and Christian. Freeport, N.Y., Books for Libraries Press [1969] x, 263 p. 23 cm. (Select bibliographies reprint series) Reprint of the 1919 ed. Bibliography: p. [251]-255. [BR128.H5C3 1969] 73-102230
1. Christianity and other religions—Hinduism. 2. Hinduism—Relations—Christianity. 3. Redemption—Comparative studies. I. Title.

CHESTERTON, Gilbert Keith, 1874-1936. 261.2
The everlasting man. Westport, Conn., Greenwood Press [1974, c1925] xxv, 344 p. 22 cm. Reprint of the ed. published by Dodd, Mead, New York. [BL48.C5 1974] 72-11233 ISBN 0-8371-6636-5 14.50
1. Catholic Church—Apologetic works. 2. Religion. 3. Christianity and other religions. I. Title.

CHESTERTON, Gilbert Keith, 1874-1936. 261.2
The everlasting man [by] G. K. Chesterton. Garden City, N.Y., Doubleday, [1974] 280 p. 18 cm. (Image books) [BL48.C5] ISBN 0-385-07198-1. 1.95 (pbk.)
1. Catholic Church—Apologetic works. 2. Religion. 3. Christianity and other religions. I. Title.
L.C. card no. for original ed.: 72-11233.

CONFERENCE on Judaism and the Christian Seminary Curriculum, Chicago, 1965. 261.2
Judaism and the Christian seminary curriculum. Editor: J. Bruce Long. Editorial consultants: Joseph P. Cahill [and] J. Coert Rylaarsdam. Chicago, Loyola University Press [1966] x, 166 p. 23 cm. Contents.Contents.—Contains papers from "a Catholic-Protestant Conference which was convened and sponsored by the Anti-defamation League of B'nai B'rith." "Select bibliography [by] J. Bruce Long": p. 156-66. [BM535.C62 1965aa] 66-27702
1. Christianity and other religions—Judaism—Congresses. 2. Judaism—Relations—Christianity—Congresses. 3. Theological seminaries—Curricula. I. Long, J. Bruce, ed. II. Anti-defamation League. III. Title.

DAVIES, Alan T. 261.2
Anti-Semitism and the Christian mind; the crisis of conscience after Auschwitz [by] Alan T. Davies. [New York] Herder and Herder [1969] 192 p. 22 cm. Bibliographical footnotes. [BM535.D345] 78-87754 5.95
1. Christianity and other religions—Judaism. 2. Judaism—Relations—Christianity. 3. Antisemitism. I. Title.

DEAN, Thomas, 1938- 261.2
Post-theistic thinking : the Marxist-Christian dialogue in radical perspective / Thomas Dean Philadelphia : Temple University Press, [1975] xvi, 300 p. ; 23 cm. Includes index. Bibliography: p. 283-287. [BT83.7.D4] 74-83202 ISBN 0-87722-037-9 : 12.95
1. Marx, Karl, 1818-1883. 2. Secularization (Theology) 3. Communism and Christianity. I. Title.

DE LANGE, Nicholas Robert Michael, 1944- 261.2
Origen and the Jews : studies in Jewish-Christian relations in third-century Palestine / N. R. M. de Lange. Cambridge ; New York : Cambridge University Press, 1976. p. cm. (University of Cambridge oriental publications ; 25) Based on the author's thesis, Oxford University, 1970. Bibliography: p. [BM535.D44] 75-36293 ISBN 0-521-20542-5 : 14.95
1. Origenes. 2. Bible. O.T.—Criticism, interpretation, etc., Jewish. 3. Judaism—Relations—Christianity. 4. Christianity and other religions—Judaism. I. Title. II. Series: Cambridge. University. Oriental publications ; 25.

DERRICK, Christopher, 1921- 261.2
Light of revelation and non-Christians. [Staten Island, N.Y., Alba House, 1965] 141 p. 21 cm. [BR115.C8D4] 65-23239
1. Culture. 2. Christianity and other religions. 3. Catholic Church — Missions — Addresses, essays, lectures. I. Title.

DERRICK, Christopher, 1921- ed., 261.2
Light of revelation and non-Christians [Staten Island, N.Y., Alba, c.1965] 141p. 21cm. [BR115.C8D4] 65-23239 3.95 bds.,
1. Culture. 2. Christianity and other religions. 3. Catholic Church—Missions—Addresses, essays, lectures. I. Title.

DEVARAJA, Nand Kishore, 1917- 261.2
Hinduism and Christianity [by] N. K. Devaraja. Bombay, New York, Asia Pub. House [1969] xi, 126 p. 22 cm. (Brahmananda Keshab Chandra Sen memorial lectures on comparative religion, 1965) Includes bibliographical references. [BR128.H5D46] 71-905203 18.00
1. Hinduism—Relations—Christianity. 2. Christianity and other religions—Hinduism. I. Title. II. Series.

ECKARDT, Arthur Roy, 1918- 261.2
Your people, my people: the meeting of Jews and Christians [by] A. Roy Eckardt. [New York] Quadrangle [1974] xiv, 275 p. 22 cm. Includes bibliographical references. [BM535.E264 1974] 73-90162 ISBN 0-8129-0412-5 8.95
1. Judaism—Relations—Christianity. 2. Christianity and other religions—Judaism. 3. Jewish-Arab relations. I. Title.

FILTHAUT, Theodor, ed. 261.2
Israel in Christian religious instruction [Notre Dame, Ind.] Univ. of Notre Dame Pr., 1965. v, 125p. 18cm. (Contemp. catechetics ser.) First pub. in 1963 under title: Israel in der Christlichen Unterweisung. Bibl. [BM535.F513] 65-14738 1.25
1. Catholic Church—Relations—Judaism. 2. Judaism—Relations—Catholic Church. 3. Judaism—Study and teaching. I. Title.

FLEISCHNER, Eva, 1925- 261.2
Judaism in German Christian theology since 1945 : Christianity and Israel considered in terms of mission / by Eva Fleischner. Metuchen, N.J. : Scarecrow Press, 1975. p. cm. (ATLA monograph series ; no. 8) Includes index. Bibliography: p. [BM535.F56 1975] 75-22374 ISBN 0-8108-0835-8
1. Judaism—Relations—Christianity. 2. Christianity and other religions—Judaism. 3. Missions to Jews—Germany. 4. Judaism (Christian theology) I. Title. II. Series: American Theological Library Association. ATLA monograph series ; no. 8.

FLEISCHNER, Eva, 1925- 261.2
Judaism in German Christian theology since 1945 : Christianity and Israel considered in terms of mission / by Eva Fleischner. Metuchen, N.J. : Scarecrow Press, 1975. 205 p. ; 22 cm. (ATLA monograph series ; no. 8) Includes index. Bibliography: p. 181-192. [BM535.F56 1975] 75-22374 ISBN 0-8108-0835-8 : 7.50
1. Judaism—Relations—Christianity. 2. Christianity and other religions—Judaism. 3. Missions to Jews—Germany. 4. Judaism (Christian theology) I. Title. II. Series: American Theological Library Association. ATLA monograph series ; no. 8.

GLOCK, Charles Y. 261.2
Christian beliefs and anti-Semitism [by] Charles Y. Glock and Rodney Stark. New York, Harper & Row [1969, c1966] xxi, 266, 24 p. illus., facsims. 21 cm. (Harper torchbooks, TB 1454) Bibliographical footnotes. [DS145] 74-5472 1.95
1. Christianity and antisemitism. 2. Antisemitism—U.S. I. Stark, Rodney, joint author. II. Title.

GLOCK, Charles Y. 261.2
Christian beliefs and anti-Semitism [by] Charles Y. Glock and Rodney Stark. [1st ed.] New York, Harper & Row [1966] xxi, 266, 24 p. facsims., form. 24 cm. (Patterns of American prejudice series, 1) Bibliographical footnotes. [DS145.G49] 65-21002
1. Christianity and antisemitism. 2. Antisemitism—United States. I. Stark, Rodney, joint author. II. Title.

GRAHAM, Aelred, 1907- 261.2
Conversations: Christian and Buddhist: encounters in Japan. [1st ed.] New York, Harcourt, Brace & World [1968] xvi, 206 p. 21 cm. [BR128.B8G7] 68-24390
1. Christianity and other religions—Buddhism. 2. Buddha and Buddhism—Relations—Christianity. I. Title.

GRAYZEL, Solomon, 1896- 261.2
The church and the Jews in the XIIIth century: a study of their relations during the years 1198-1254, based on the papal letters and the conciliar decrees of the period. Rev. 2d ed. New York, Hermon Pr., 1966. ix, 378p. 24cm. Revision of the author's thesis, Dropsie Coll. Bibl. [BM535.G7 1966] 66-19755 6.75
1. Jewish question. 2. Jews—Hist.—70-1789 A.D. 3. Jews—Civil rights. 4. Church history—Middle Ages. 5. Christianity and other religions—Judaism. 6. Missions to Jews. 7. Letters, Papal. I. Catholic Church. Pope. II. Catholic Church. Canons, decretals, etc. III. Title.

GRIFFITHS, Bede, 1906- 261.2
Christ in India; essays towards a Hindu-Christian dialogue. New York, Scribner [1967, c1966] 249 p. illus., ports. 22 cm. First published in 1966 under title: Christian Ashram. [BR128.H5G7] 67-15729
1. Christianity and other religions — Hinduism. 2. Hinduism — Relations — Christianity. I. Title.

GRIFFITHS, Bede, 1906- 261.2
Christ in India; essays towards a Hindu-Christian dialogue. New York, Scribners [1967,c.1966] 249p. illus., ports. 22cm. First pub. in 1966 under title: Christian Ashram. [BR128.H5G7 1967] 67-15729 4.95
1. Christianity and other religions—Hinduism., 2. Hinduism—Relations—Christianity. I. Title.

HARGROVE, Katharine T ed. 261.2
The star and the cross; essays on Jewish-Christian relations, edited by Katharine T. Hargrove. Milwaukee, Bruce Pub. Co. [1966] x, 318 p. 24 cm. Bibliographical footnotes. [BM535.H3] 66-18059
1. Christianity and other religions — Judaism. 2. Judaism — Relations — Christianity. I. Title.

HARGROVE, Katharine T., ed. 261.2
The star and the cross; essays on Jewish-Christian relations. Milwaukee, Bruce [c.1966] x, 318p. 24cm. Bibl. [BM535.H3] 66-18059 6.75
1. Christianity and other religions—Judaism. 2. Judaism—Relations—Christianity. I. Title.

HUNT, John, 1827-ca.1908. 261.2
Pantheism and Christianity. Port Washington, N.Y., Kennikat Press [1970] viii, 397 p. 23 cm. "First published in 1884." Based on the author's An essay on Pantheism. [BL220.H8 1970] 78-102573
1. Pantheism. 2. Christianity and the other religion. 3. Idealism. 4. Transcendentalism. I. Title.

JEWISH-CHRISTIAN relations / edited by Robert Heyer. New York : Paulist Press, c1974. v, 86 p. : ill. ; 19 cm. "The articles in this book originally appeared in the Jan./Feb. 1974 issue of New Catholic world." "A New Catholic world book." [BM535.J45] 75-73 ISBN 0-8091-1869-6 pbk. : 1.45 261.2
1. Judaism—Relations—Christianity—Addresses, essays, lectures. 2. Christianity and other religions—Judaism—Addresses, essays, lectures. I. Heyer, Robert. II. New Catholic world.

JONES, A. Jase. 261.2
Neighbors yet strangers [by] A. Jase Jones. Nashville, Broadman Press [1968] viii, 102 p. 20 cm. Bibliography: p. 99-100. [BV2620.J63] 68-20678
1. Missions to Jews. I. Title.

JUDAISM and Christianity. 261.2
Prolegomenon by Ellis Rivkin. New York, Ktav Pub. House, 1969. 3 v. in 1. 24 cm. Reprint of the 1937-38 ed. Contents.Contents.—v. 1. The age of transition, edited by W. O. E. Oesterley.—v. 2. The contact of Pharisaism with other cultures, edited by H. Loewe.—v. 3. Law and religion, edited by E. I. J. Rosenthal. Includes bibliographical references. [BM535.J82] 68-25717
1. Christianity and other religions—Judaism. 2. Judaism—Relations—Christianity. 3. Pharisees. I. Oesterley, William Oscar Emil, 1866-1950, ed. II. Loewe, Herbert Martin James, 1882-ed. III. Rosenthal, Erwin Isak Jakob, 1904- ed.

KIRSCH, Paul J. 261.2
We Christians and Jews / Paul J. Kirsch. Philadelphia : Fortress Press, [1975] x, 150 p. ; 20 cm. Includes index. Bibliography: p. 142-145. [BM535.K48] 74-26332 ISBN 0-8006-1094-6 pbk. : 3.95
1. Christianity and other religions—Judaism. 2. Judaism—Relations—Christianity. I. Title.

LAPIDE, Phinn E., 1922- 261.2
Three Popes and the Jews [by] Pinchas E. Lapide. [1st ed.] New York, Hawthorn Books [1967] 384 p. ports. 23 cm. Includes bibliographies. [BM535.L3 1967b] 67-11768
1. Catholic Church—Relations—Judaism. 2. Judaism—Relations—Catholic Church. I. Title.

LEE, Kun Sam. 261.2
The Christian confrontation with Shinto nationalism; a historical and critical study of the conflict of Christianity and Shinto in Japan in the period between the Meiji restoration and the end of World War II (1868-1945) Philadelphia, Presbyterian and Reformed Pub. Co., 1966. xi, 270 p. 20 cm. (International library of philosophy and theology) Includes bibliographical references. [BR128.S5L4] 66-18124
1. Christianity and other religions — Shinto. 2. Shinto — Relations — Christianity. 3. Japan — Church history — 1867-1945. 4. Nationalism and religion — Japan. I. Title. II. Series.

LEEUWEN, Arend Theodoor van, 1918- 261.2
Christianity in world history; the meeting of the faiths of East and West. Foreword by Hendrik Kraemer. Tr. [from Dutch] by H. H. Hoskins. New York, Scribners [1968, c.1964] xi, 487p. 21cm. (SL 151) Bibl. [BR115.C5.L43] 65-28805 2.95 pap.,
1. Christianity and other religions. 2. East and West. 3. Christianity and culture. I. Title.

LEEUWEN, Arend Theodoor van, 1918- 261.2
Christianity in world history; the meeting of the faiths of East and West. Foreword by Hendrik Kraemer. Tr. [from Dutch] by H. H. Hoskins. New York, Scribners [1966, c.1964] 487p. 22cm. Bibl. [BR115.C5L43] 65-28805 8.50
1. Christianity and other religions. 2. East and West. 3. Christianity and culture. I. Title.

LE SAUX, Henri, 1910-1973. 261.2
Hindu-Christian meeting point, within the cave of the heart / Abhishiktananda [i.e. H. Le Saux]. Rev. ed. Delhi : ISPCK, 1976. xiii, 128 p. ; 23 cm. Translation of La rencontre de l'hindouisme et du christianisme. First published in 1969 by Institute of Indian Culture, Bombay. Includes bibliographical references and index. [BR128.H5L4313 1976] 76-904678 Rs15.00 ($3.50 U.S.)
1. Christianity and other religions—Hinduism. 2. Hinduism—Relations—Christianity. I. Title.

LOCHMAN, Jan Milic. 261.2
Encountering Marx : bonds and barriers between Christians and Marxists / Jan Milic Lochman ; translated by Edwin H. Robertson. Philadelphia : Fortress Press, c1977. 136 p. ; 18 cm. Translation of Marx begegnen. Bibliography: p. 136. [HX536.L6613] 75-55827 ISBN 0-8006-1249-3 : 4.25
1. Communism and Christianity. I. Title.

MCGARRY, Michael B. 261.2
Christology after Auschwitz / by Michael B. McGarry. New York : Paulist Press, c1977. vii, 119 p. ; 21 cm. (An Exploration book) Bibliography: p. 108-119. [BM535.M3] 77-73977 ISBN 0-8091-2024-0 pbk. : 3.95
1. Christianity and other religions—Judaism—1945- 2. Judaism—Relations—Christianity—1945- I. Title.

MARITAIN, Jacques, 1882-1973. 261.2
A Christian looks at the Jewish question. New York, Arno Press, 1973 [c1939] v, 90 p. 21 cm. (The Jewish people: history, religion, literature) Translation of Les Juifs parmi les nations. Reprint of the ed. published by Longmans, Green, New York. Includes bibliographical references. [DS145.M2513 1973] 73-2216 ISBN 0-405-05280-4 7.00
1. Christianity and antisemitism. I. Title. II. Series.

MODERN mission dialogue; 261.2
theory and practice. Edited by Jan Kerkhofs. Pref. by Franz Hengsbach. Introd. by Frank de Graeve. New York, Newman Press [1969] xxii, 263 p. 23 cm. At head of title: Commissioned by Pro Mundi Vita, Brussels. Bibliographical footnotes. [BV2170.M67] 69-19959 6.50
1. Catholic Church—Missions. 2. Catholic Church—Relations. I. Kerkhofs, Jan, 1924- ed. II. Pro Mundi Vita (Society)

NEILL, Stephen Charles, Bp. 261.2
Christian faith and other faiths: the Christian dialogue with other religions [by] Stephen Neill. 2nd ed. London, New York, Oxford U.P., 1970. vii, 245 p. 21 cm. (Oxford paperbacks, 196) Bibliography: p. 235-239. [BR127.N37 1970] 79-549128 ISBN 0-19-283011-2 15/-
1. Christianity and other religions. 2. Religions. I. Title.

NEILL, Stephen Charles, Bp. 261.2
Salvation tomorrow / by Stephen Neill. Guildford [Eng.] : Lutterworth Press, 1976. x, 150 p. ; 22 cm. [BR127.N373] 76-383264 ISBN 0-7188-2272-2 ; £1.75
1. Christianity and other religions—Addresses, essays, lectures. 2. Missions—Addresses, essays, lectures. 3. Christianity—20th century—Addresses, essays, lectures. I. Title.

THE New China : 261.2
a Catholic response / edited by Michael Chu. New York : Paulist Press, c1977. v, 165 p. ; 21 cm. (An Exploration book) Includes bibliographical references. [DS777.55.N47] 76-56958 ISBN 0-8091-2004-6 pbk. : 4.95
1. China—Politics and government—1949- — Addresses, essays, lectures. 2. Christianity—China—Addresses, essays, lectures. I. Chu, Michael.

NEWBIGIN, James Edward Lesslie, Bp. 261.2
The finality of Christ [by] Lesslie Newbigin. Richmond, Va., John Knox Press [1969] 120 p. 20 cm. Bibliography: p. 117. [BR127.N39 1969] 72-76216 2.50
1. Christianity and other religions—Addresses, essays, lectures. 2. Christianity—Essence, nature, genius—Addresses, essays, lectures. I. Title.

NILES, Daniel Thambyrajah. 261.2
Buddhism and the claims of Christ, by D. T. Niles. Richmond, Va., John Knox Press [1967] 88 p. 21 cm. [BT60.N5] 67-27054
1. Christianity—Essence, genius, nature. 2. Christianity and other religions—Buddhism. 3. Buddha and Buddhism—Relations—Christianity. I. Title.

NILES, Daniel Thambyrajah. 261.2
Buddhism and the claims of Christ, by D. T. Niles. Richmond, Va., John Knox Press [1967] 88 p. 21 cm. [BT60.N5] 67-27054
1. Christianity—Essence, genius, nature. 2. Christianity and other religions—Buddhism. 3. Buddha and Buddhism—Relations—Christianity. I. Title.

ODEBERG, Hugo, 1898- 261.2
Pharisaism and Christianity. Translated by J. M. Moe. Saint Louis, Concordia Pub. House [c1964] 112 p. 21 cm. [BM535.O413] 63-21162
1. Christianity and other religions — Judaism. 2. Pharisees. I. Title.

OPENINGS for Marxist-Christian dialogue. 261.2
Thomas W. Ogletree, editor. Nashville, Abingdon Press [1969] 174

p. 20 cm. Contains the Alden-Tuthill lectures presented in 1968 at the Chicago Theological Seminary. Bibliographical footnotes. [BR128.A8O6] 69-12768 3.75
1. Communism and Christianity. I. Ogletree, Thomas W., ed. II. Chicago Theological Seminary.

THE ox, the ass, the oyster 261.2
/ edited by Henry and Marie Einspruch. Baltimore : Lewis and Harriet Lederer Foundation, [1975] 90 p. : ill. ; 21 cm. [BV2620.O9] 74-25243
1. Missions to Jews. 2. Christianity and other religions—Judaism. 3. Judaism—Relations—Christianity. I. Einspruch, Henry, 1892- II. Einspruch, Marie.

PINAY, Maurice. 261.2
The plot against the Church. Los Angeles, St. Anthony Press, 1967. 710 p. 23 cm. Translation of Complotto contro la Chiesa. Bibliography: p. 677-696. [BM535.P4813] 67-6032
1. Catholic Church—Relations—Judaism. 2. Judaism—Relations—Catholic Church. I. Title.

RIDENOUR, Fritz. 261.2
So, what's the difference? A Biblical comparison of orthodox Christianity with major religions and major cults. Editor: Fritz Ridenour. Writing and research consultants: Jack Durkee [and others] Illustrator: Joyce Thimsen. Glendale, Calif., Regal Books [1967] 168 p. illus. 18 cm. Includes bibliographies. [BR127.R5] 67-31426
1. Christianity and other religions. 2. Sects. I. Title.

SCHARPER, Philip, ed. 261.2
Torah and gospel; Jewish and Catholic theology in dialogue. New York, Sheed [c.1966] xiii, 305p. 22cm. Papers delivered at a symp. held Jan. 1965, at St. Vincent Archabbey, Latrobe, Pa. Bibl. [BM535.S26] 66-12273 6.00
1. Judaism—Relations—Catholic Church. 2. Catholic Church—Relations—Judaism. I. St. Vincent Archabbey, Latrobe, Pa. II. Title.

SCHLETTE, Heinz Robert. 261.2
Towards a theology of religions. [Translated by W. J. O'Hara. New York] Herder and Herder [1966] 151 p. 22 cm. (Quaestiones disputatae, 14) Translation of the author's Die Religionen als Thema der Theologie. Bibliography: p. 144-151. [BR127.S2413] 66-10760
1. Religion—Philosophy. 2. Christianity and other religions. I. Title.

SCHLETTE, Heinz Robert 261.2
Towards a theology of religions. [Tr. from German by W. J. O'Hara. New York] Herder & Herder [c.1966] 151p. 22cm. (Quaestiones disputatae, 14) Bibl. [BR127.S2413] 66-10760 2.50 pap.,
1. Religion—Philosophy. 2. Christianity and other religions. I. Title.

SCHNEIDER, Herman Peter 261.2
The dialogue of Christians and Jews [by] Peter Schneider. New York, Seabury [1967, c.1966] 196p. 21cm. (Seabury paperback, SP 42) Bibl. [BM535.S282 1967] 67-21834 1.95 pap.,
1. Christianity and other religions—Judaism. 2. Judaism—Relations—Christianity. I. Title.

SCOTT, Archibald, 1837- 261.2
1909.
Buddhism and Christianity; a parallel and a contrast. Port Washington, N.Y., Kennikat Press [1971] xiv, 391 p. 22 cm. (The Croall lecture, 1889-90) Reprint of the 1890 ed. Includes bibliographical references. [BR128.B8S35 1971] 78-118547 ISBN 0-8046-1172-6
1. Christianity and other religions—Buddhism. 2. Buddha and Buddhism—Relations—Christianity. I. Title. II. Series: The Croall lectures, 1889-90.

SEIFERTH, Wolfgang S. 261.2
Synagogue and church in the Middle Ages; two symbols in art and literature [by] Wolfgang S. Seiferth. Translated by Lee Chadeayne and Paul Gottwald. New York, Ungar [1970] ix, 213 p. illus. 23 cm. Translation of Synagoge und Kirche im Mittelalter. Bibliography: p. 183-187. [BM535.S3313] 75-107031 10.00
1. Christianity and other religions—Judaism. 2. Judaism—Relations—Christianity. 3. Christian art and symbolism. I. Title.

SMITH, Henry Preserved, 261.2
1847-1927.
The Bible and Islam; or, The influence of the Old and New Testaments on the religion of Mohammed. New York, Arno Press, 1973 [c1897] 319 p. 23 cm. (The Jewish people: history, religion, literature) Reprint of the ed. published by Scribner, New York, which was issued as the Ely lectures for 1897. Includes bibliographical references. [BP172.S6 1973] 73-2227 ISBN 0-405-05288-X 18.00
1. Islam—Relations—Christianity. 2. Christianity and other religions—Islam. I. Title. II. Series. III. Series: The Elias P. Ely lectures on the evidences of Christianity, 1897.

SNOEK, Johan M. 261.2
The grey book; a collection of protests against anti-semitism and the persecution of Jews, issued by non-Roman Catholic churches and church leaders during Hitler's rule [by] Johan M. Snoek. Introd. by Uriel Tal. New York, Humanities Press, 1970. xxvi, 315 p. 23 cm. Bibliography: p. 308-315. [BM535.S64 1970] 77-11417 10.50
1. Antisemitism. 2. Protestant churches—Europe. 3. Judaism—Relations—Christianity. 4. Christianity and other religions—Judaism. I. Title.

SOBEL, B. Zvi, 1933- 261.2
Hebrew Christianity; the thirteenth tribe [by] B. Z. Sobel. New York, Wiley [1974] xi, 413 p. 22 cm. (Contemporary religious movements) "A Wiley-Interscience publication." Bibliography: p. 321-340. [BV2620.S65] 74-3351 ISBN 0-471-81025-8
1. Missions to Jews—History. 2. Religion and sociology. I. Title.

STANG, Hakon. 261.2
Westernness and Islam / by Hakon Stang. Oslo : Chair in Conflict and Peace Research, University of Oslo, [1976] 96 p. ; 30 cm. (Papers - Chair in Conflict and Peace Research, University of Oslo ; no. 27) (Trends in Western civilization project ; no. 7) Cover title. Includes bibliographical references. [BP172.S78] 77-353911
1. Islam—Relations—Christianity. 2. Christianity and other religions—Islam. I. Title. II. Series. III. Series: Oslo. Universitet. Professoratet i konflikt- og fredsforskning. Papers — Chair in Conflict and Peace Research, University of Oslo ; no. 27.

SWEARER, Donald K., 1934- 261.2
Dialogue, the key to understanding other religions / Donald K. Swearer. Philadelphia : Westminster Press, c1977. p. cm. (Biblical perspectives on current issues) Includes bibliographical references. [BR127.S93] 77-3964 ISBN 0-664-24138-7 pbk. : 4.95
1. Christianity and other religions. 2. Christianity and other religions—Buddhism. 3. Buddhism—Relations—Christianity. I. Title. II. Series.

SYNAN, Edward A 261.2
The popes and the Jews in the Middle Ages, by Edward A. Synan. Pref. by John M. Oesterreicher. New York, Macmillan, 1965. x, 246 p. 22 cm. (Quest books) Bibliographical references included in "Notes" (p. 165-214) [BM535.S9] 65-20172
1. Christianity and other religions — Judaism. 2. Judaism — Relations — Christianity. 3. Papacy — Hist. I. Title.

SYNAN, Edward A. 261.2
The popes and the Jews in the Middle Ages. Pref. by John M. Oesterreicher. New York, Macmillan [c.]1965. x, 246p. 22cm. (Quest bks.) Bibl. [BM535.S9] 65-20172 5.95
1. Christianity and other religions—Judaism. 2. Judaism—Relations—Christianity. 3. Papacy—Hist. I. Title.

THOMAS, Owen C., 1922- 261.2
comp.
Attitudes toward other religions; some Christian interpretations, edited by Owen C. Thomas. [1st U.S. ed.] New York, Harper & Row [1969] x, 236 p. 21 cm. (Harper forum books, RD9) Contents.Contents.—Rationalism: Common notions concerning religion, by Herbert of Cherbury.— Romanticism: Religion and the religions, by F. Schleiermacher.—Relativism: The place of Christianity among the world religions, by E. Troeltsch.—Exclusivism: The revelation of God as the abolition of religion, by K. Barth.—Dialectic: Revelation and religion, by E. Brunner.—Reconception: The way of reconception, by W. E. Hocking.—Tolerance: What should be the Christian approach to the contemporary non-Christian faiths? By A. Toynbee. —Dialogue: A Christian-Buddhist conversation, by P. Tillich.—Catholicism: The freedom of religion, by H. Kung.—Presence: Christian amid African religion, by M. A. C. Warren and J. Taylor. Bibliographical footnotes. [BR127.T52 1969] 69-17004 3.50
1. Christianity and other religions—Addresses, essays, lectures. I. Title.

TROWBRIDGE, Buel. 261.2
What do you believe, Tovarish? : An imaginary dialogue between an American Protestant "believer" and a Soviet atheist / by Buel Trowbridge. Boston : Branden Press, c1975. 32 p. ; 22 cm. [BR128.A8T74] 75-22629 ISBN 0-8283-1641-4 : 1.25
1. Christianity and atheism. I. Title.

VAN TIL, Cornelius, 1895- 261.2
Christ and the Jews. [Philadelphia] Presbyterian and Reformed Pub. Co., 1968. v, 99 p. 23 cm. (International library of philosophy and theology: Biblical and theological studies) Includes bibliographical references. [BM535.V3] 68-25835
1. Philo Judaeus. 2. Buber, Martin, 1878-1965. 3. Judaism—Relations—Christianity. 4. Christianity and other religions—Judaism. I. Title. II. Series: International library of philosophy and theology: Biblical and theological studies series.

VATICAN COUNCIL. 2D. 1962- 261.2
1965
The Declaration on the relation of the Church to non-Christian religions. promulgated by Pope Paul VI, October 28, 1965. Commentary by Rene Laurentin, Joseph Neuner. Study-club ed. Glen Rock. N.J., Paulist. 1966. 104p. 18cm. (Vatican II docs.) Bibl. [BX8301962.A45D353] 66-26208 .75 pap.,
1. Vatican Council. 2d. 1962-1965. Declaratio de Ecclesiae habitudine ad religiones non-Christianas. 2. Catholic Church—Relations. I. Laurentin, Rene. II. Neuner, Josef. III. Title.

*VOEHRINGER, Erich 261.2
Christianity and other world religions, by Erich Voehringer; ed. by Jerome Nilssen. Artists: Vinayak S. Masoji, Setsuo Hosiyama, Azarish Mbatha. Philadelphia, Lutheran Church Pr. [1967] 128p. illus. 21cm. (LCA Sunday church school ser.) With teachers guide. pap., .90; teachers guide, pap., 1.00
1. Christianity. 2. Christianity and other religions I. Nilssen, Jerome, ed. II. Title.

VOS, Johannes G. 261.2
A Christian introduction to religions of the world. Grand Rapids, Mich., Baker Bk. [c.] 1965. 79p. 19cm. [BL80.2.V63] 65-5709 1.50 pap.,
1. Religions. 2. Christianity and other religions. I. Title.

WATTS, Alan Wilson, 1915- 261.2
Beyond theology; the art of Godmanship [by] Alan Watts. New York, Vintage Books [1973, c1964] xiii, 231 p. 19 cm. Includes bibliographical references. [BR127.W28 1973] 73-4542 1.95 (pbk.)
1. Christianity and other religions. I. Title.

WEHRLI, Eugene S. 261.2
The Gospel and conflicting faiths [by] Eugene S. Wehrli. Boston, United Church Press [1969] 192 p. illus. 22 cm. (The Cooperative through-the-week series) Bibliographical references included in "Notes and acknowledgments" (p. 189-192) [BR127.W4] 69-13710 2.50
1. Christianity and other religions. I. Title.

WILKEN, Robert Louis, 1936- 261.2
Judaism and the early Christian mind; a study of Cyril of Alexandria's exegesis and theology, by Robert L. Wilken. New Haven, Yale University Press, 1971. xiv, 257 p. 22 cm. (Yale publications in religion, 15) Bibliography: p. 231-247. [BM535.W49] 74-140541 ISBN 0-300-01383-3 8.75
1. Cyrillus, Saint, Patriarch of Alexandria, 370 (ca.)-444. 2. Christianity and other religions—Judaism. 3. Judaism—Relations—Christianity. I. Title. II. Series.

WU, Ching-hsiung, 1899- 261.2
Chinese humanism and Christian spirituality; essays of John C. H. Wu. Ed. by Paul K. T. Sih. Jamaica, N.Y., St. John's Univ. Pr. [c.] 1965. ix, 227p. 21cm. (Asian philosophical studies, no. 2) Bibl. [BR128.C4W8] 65-24405 5.00 pap.,
1. Christianity and other religions—Chinese. 2. Mysticism—Comparative studies. I. Title. II. Series.

HUNTER, Carman St. 261.2'02'02
John.
Study-action manual on Christ and the faiths of men. New York, Friendship Press [1967] 96 p. 19 cm. Includes bibliographical references. [BR127.H8] 67-18246
1. Christianity and other religions—Outlines, syllabi, etc. I. Title.

HUNTER, Carman St. 261.2'02'02
John.
Study-action manual on Christ and the faiths of men. New York, Friendship Press [1967] 96 p. 19 cm. Includes bibliographical references. [BR127.H8] 67-18246
1. Christianity and other religions—Outlines, syllabi, etc. I. Title. II. Title: Christ and the faiths of men.

PAUW, Berthold 261.2'0968'7
Adolf.
Christianity and Xhosa tradition : belief and ritual among Xhosa-speaking Christians / B. A. Pauw. Cape Town ; New York : Oxford University Press, 1975. xiv, 390 p., 4 leaves of plates : ill. ; 22 cm. Includes index. Bibliography: p. 366-376. [BR1450.P38] 75-325209 ISBN 0-19-570046-5 : 27.00
1. Christians in South Africa. 2. Xosa—Religion. 3. Xosa—Social life and customs. I. Title.

BOOTH, Alan. 261.3
Christians and power politics. [New York] Association Press [1961] 126p. 19cm. [BR115.I7B6 1961a] 61-14169
1. Christianity and international affairs. I. Title.

EDWARDS, Richard Henry, 261.4
1877-
Christianity and amusements, by by Richard Henry Edwards ... New York, London, Association Press, 1915. 157p. 17cm. [BV4597.E3] 15-3891
1. Amusements—Moral and religious aspects. 2. Christian life. I. Title.

BARNES, Harry Elmer, 1889- 261.5
1968.
The twilight of Christianity / by Harry Elmer Barnes. New York : Revisionist Press, 1975, c1929. p. cm. Reprint of the ed. published by the Vanguard Press, New York. Includes bibliographical references and index. [BL2775.B327 1975] 75-26524 ISBN 0-87700-037-9
1. Christianity—Controversial literature. 2. Religion and science—1926-1945. 3. Religion. I. Title.

BELGUM, David Rudolph, 261.5
1922- comp.
Religion and medicine; essays on meaning, value, and health. David Belgum, editor. 1st ed. Ames, Iowa State University Press [1967] xxiii 345 p. 24 cm. (Iowa studies in religion and medicine) Bibligraphical footnotes. [BL65.M4B4] 67-26060
1. Medicine and religion—Addresses, essays, lectures. I. Title. II. Series.

BELGUM, David Rudolph, 261.5
1922- comp.
Religion and medicine; essays on meaning, values, and health. David Belgum, editor. [1st ed.] Ames, Iowa State University Press [1967] xxiii, 345 p. 24 cm. (Iowa studies in religion and medicine) Bibliographical footnotes. [BL65.M4B4] 67-26060
1. Medicine and religion—Addresses, essays, lectures. I. Title. II. Series.

BENZ, Ernst, 1907- 261.5
Evolution and Christian hope; man's concept of the future from the early Fathers to Teilhard de Chardin. Tr. from German by Heinz G. Frank. Garden City, N.Y., Doubleday [1968,c.1966] 270p. 18cm. (Anchor bk., A607) Tr. of Schopfungsglaube und Endzeiterwartung. Bibl. [B818.B413] 66-20935 1.25 pap.,
1. Evolution—Hist. I. Title.

BENZ, Ernst, 1907- 261.5
Evolution and Christian hope; man's concept of the future from the early Fathers to Teilhard de Chardin. Tr. from German by Heinz G. Frank. [1st ed. in the U.S.A.] Garden City, N.Y., Doubleday, 1966. ix, 270p. 22cm. Tr. of Schopfungsglaube und Endzeiterwartung. Bibl. [B818.B413] 66-20935 4.95
1. Evolution—Hist. I. Title.

BOZEMAN, Theodore Dwight, 261.5
1942-
Protestants in an age of science : the Baconian ideal and ante-bellum American religious thought / by Theodore Dwight Bozeman. Chapel Hill : University of North Carolina Press, c1977. xv, 243 p. ; 24 cm. Includes index. Bibliography: p. 211-239. [BL245.B7] 76-25962 ISBN 0-8078-1299-4 : 14.95
1. Bacon, Francis, Viscount St. Albans, 1561-1626. 2. Religion and science—History of controversy—United States. 3. Protestantism. I. Title.

CHRIST & the modern mind. 261.5
Edited by Robert W. Smith. Downers Grove, Ill., InterVarsity Press [1972] viii, 312 p. illus. 22 cm. Includes bibliographical references. [BR115.C8C44] 70-186349 ISBN 0-87784-863-7
1. Christianity and culture—Addresses, essays, lectures. 2. Learning and scholarship—Addresses, essays, lectures. I. Smith, Robert Wayne, 1926- ed.

THE Church and the visual 261.5
arts. Andrew J. Buehner, editor. Saint Louis, Mo., Lutheran Academy for Scholarship [1968] 190 p. 21 cm. Papers presented at a conference in May 1968, sponsored by the Lutheran Academy for Scholarship. Includes bibliographies. [NX175.C5] 74-677
1. Art and religion. 2. The arts—Psychology. I. Buehner, Andrew J., ed. II. Lutheran Academy for Scholarship.

CONNOR, Edward. 261.5
Prophecy for today. Fresno, Calif., Academy Library Guild, 1956. 110p. 21cm. [BX961] 57-524
1. Prophecies. I. Title.

COULSON, Charles Alfred. 261.5
Faith and technology, by C. A. Coulson. Being the inaugural lecture of the Luton Industrial College, delivered 14th September, 1968. [Nashville, Upper room, 1971] 31 p. 19 cm. [BJ59.C65 1971] 70-24927
1. Technology and ethics. I. Luton Industrial College. II. Title.

DYE, David L. 261.5
Faith and the physical world: a comprehensive view, by David L. Dye. Grand Rapids, W. B. Eerdmans Pub. Co. [1966] 214 p. illus. 21 cm. Bibliography: p. 183-199. [BL240.2.D9] 66-18729
1. Religion and science—1946- I. Title.

GARRIGAN, Owen. 261.5
Man's intervention in nature. [1st ed.] New York, Hawthorn Books [1967] 190, [2] p. 22 cm. (Twentieth century encyclopedia of Catholicism, v. 133. Section 13: Catholicism and science) The Twentieth century encyclopedia of Catholicism, v. 133) Bibliography: p. [191] [HQ753.G3] 65-13028
1. Eugenics. 2. Religion and science—1946- I. Title. II. Series.

GARRIGAN, Owen. 261.5
Man's intervention in nature. [1st ed.] New York, Hawthorn Books [1967] 190, [2] p. 22 cm. (Twentieth century encyclopedia of Catholicism, v. 133. Section 13: Catholicism and science) Bibliography: p. [191] [HQ753.G3] 65-13028
1. Eugenics. 2. Religion and science—1946- I. Title. II. Series: The Twentieth century encyclopedia of Catholicism, v. 133

HARTT, Julian Norris. 261.5
Theology and the church in the university, by Julian N. Hartt. Philadelphia, Westminster Press [1969] 204 p. 20 cm. "Some of the material of this essay was first presented as Danforth lectures given at Brown University in the academic year 1964-1965." [BV1610.H33] 69-14198 3.25 (pbk)
1. Universities and colleges—Religion. 2. Universities and colleges—Chapel exercises. I. Title.

HAZO, Samuel, John, ed. 261.5
The Christian intellectual; studies in the relation of Catholicism to the human sciences. Prefatory note by John J. Wright. Pittsburgh, Duquesne University Press, 1963. xxvi, 179 p. 23 cm. Includes bibliographical references. [BX961.I5H3] 63-17590
1. Catholics — Intellectual life. I. Title.

HAZO, Samuel John, ed. 261.5
The Christian intellectual: studies in the relation of Catholicism to the human sciences. Pref. note by John J. Wright. Pittsburgh, Duquesne [c.]1963. xxvi, 179p. 23cm. Bibl. 63-17590 4.50
1. Catholics—Intellectual life. I. Title.

HOLUM, John R 261.5
Of test tubes & testaments; thoughts for youth on science and the Christian faith, by John R. Holum. Minneapolis, Augsburg Pub. House [1965] ix, 69 p. illus. 20 cm. "Reprint of articles in One magazine, February, June, and October, 1963, and February and June, 1964." Bibliographical footnotes. [BL241.H625] 65-22832
1. Religion and science — 1946- — Addresses, essays, lectures. I. Title.

HOLUM, John R. 261.5
Of test tubes & testaments; thoughts for youth on science and the Christian faith. Minneapolis, Augsburg [c.1965] ix, 69p. illus. 20cm. Reprint of articles in One magazine, Feb., June, Oct., 1963; Feb., June, 1964. Bibl. [BL241.H625] 65-228323 1.50 pap.,
1. Religion and science—1946- —Addresses, essays, lectures. I. Title.

KUHNS, William. 261.5
Environmental man. [1st ed.] New York, Harper & Row [1969] 156 p. 22 cm. Includes bibliographical references. [BR115.C8K8] 69-10472 4.95
1. Christianity and culture. 2. Man—Influence of environment. 3. Technology and civilization. I. Title.

MACKAY, Donald MacCrimmon, 261.5
1922-
The clock work image : a Christian perspective on science / Donald M. MacKay. Downers Grove, Ill. : InterVarsity Press, 1974. 112 p. ; 18 cm. Includes index. [BL240.2.M29] 74-83475 ISBN 0-87784-557-3 pbk. : 2.25
1. Religion and science—1946- I. Title.

MARSH, Frank Lewis, 1899- 261.5
Life, man, and time. Rev. ed. Escondido, Calif., Outdoor Pictures [1967] 238 p. illus. 23 cm. Bibliography: p. 226-229. [BL240.2.M39 1967] 66-21121
1. Religion and science—1946- I. Title.

MORRIS, Henry Madison, 261.5
1918-
Evolution and the modern Christian, by Henry M. Morris. Philadelphia, Presbyterian and Reformed Pub. Co. [1967] 72 p. 20 cm. Bibliography: p. 69-72. [BL263.M58] 68-2233
1. Religion and science—1945- 2. Evolution. I. Title.

MORRIS, Henry Madison, 261.5
1918-
Evolution and the modern Christian, by Henry M. Morris. Philadelphia, Presbyterian and Reformed Pub. Co. [1967] 72 p. 20 cm. Bibliography: p. 69-72. [BL263.M585] 68-2233
1. Religion and science—1946- 2. Evolution. I. Title.

REAM, Robert J. 261.5
A Christian approach to science and science teaching, by Robert J. Ream. [Nutley, N.J.] Presbyterian and Reformed Pub. Co., 1972. v, 130 p. 21 cm. Cover title: Science teaching: a Christian approach. [BL240.2.R37] 78-187332
1. Religion and science—1946- I. Title. II. Title: Science teaching: a Christian approach.

RENO, Cora A. 261.5
Evolution on trial, by Cora A. Reno. Chicago, Moody Press [1970] 192 p. illus. 22 cm. Bibliography: p. 185-189. [BS659.R4] 71-80947 3.95
1. Bible and evolution. I. Title.

*THOMAS, Owen C. 261.5
Science challenges faith. New York, Seabury [1967] 80p. illus. 21cm. (Senior-high-sch. unit. Study units on contemp. concerns.) Prepd. under the auspices of the Dept. of Christian Educ. of the Episcopal Church. .95 pap.,
I. Title.

TURNER, Frank Miller. 261.5
Between science and religion; the reaction to scientific naturalism in late Victorian England. New Haven, Yale University Press, 1974. x, 273 p. 25 cm. (Yale historical publications, miscellany, 100) Based on the author's thesis, Yale. Bibliography: p. 257-267. [BL245.T87] 73-86920 ISBN 0-300-01678-6 12.50
1. Religion and science—History of controversy—England. I. Title. II. Series: Yale historical publications. Miscellany 100.

WARD, Rita Rhodes. 261.5
In the beginning; a study of creation versus evolution for young people. Illus. by Charles Valentine. Grand Rapids, Baker Book House [1967, c1965] 110 p. (p. 110 blank for "Notes") illus. 22 cm. Includes bibliographies. [BL263.W3] 67-18200
1. Religion and science—1946- 2. Evolution—Study and teaching. 3. Creation—Study and teaching. I. Title.

WELLS, George Ross, 1884- 261.5
Sense and nonsense in religion. New York, Vantage [c.1961] 182p. 3.50 bds.,
1. Christianity—Hist. and growth. I. Title.

ADDISON, James Thayer, 261.6
1887-
War, peace, and the Christian mind; a review of recent thought. Foreword by Henry Knox Sherrill. Greenwich, Conn., Seabury Press, 1953. 112p. 20cm. [BR115.W2A4] 53-12393
1. War and religion. I. Title.

ALFORD, Neal B 261.6
The invisible road to peace. Boston, Meador Pub. Co. [1957] 96p. 21cm. [HN31.A59] 58-26538
1. Church and social problems. 2. Peace. I. Title.

BOOTH, Alan 261.6
Christians and power politics. [New York] Association [c.1961] 126p. 61-14169 3.00 bds.,
1. Christianity and international affairs. I. Title.

BOOTH, Alan R 261.6
Christians and power politics. [New York] Association Press [1961] 126 p. 19 cm. [BR115.I7B6] 61-14169
1. Christianity and international affairs. I. Title.

CAEMMERER, Richard Rudolph, 261.6
1904-
The church in the world. [Rev.] Saint Louis, Concordia [1961, c.1949] 108p. Bibl. 61-13457 1.00 pap.,
1. Church. 2. Witness bearing (Christianity) 3. Christian life. I. Title.

CHUDOBA, Bohdan. 261.6
The meaning of civilization. New York, P. J. Kenedy [1951] 314 p. 20 cm. [BR115.C5C5] 51-14962
1. Civilization, Christian. 2. Civilization—Philosophy. I. Title.

DELAVIGNETTE, Robert Louis, 261.6
1897-
Christianity and colonialism, by Robert Delavignette. Translated from the French by J. R. Foster. [1st American ed.] New York, Hawthorn Books [1964] 172 p. 21 cm. (The Twentieth century encyclopedia of Catholicism, v. 97. Section 9: The church and the modern world) Bibliography: p. [171]-172. [JV321.D413] 64-14158
1. Colonies. 2. Church and social problems — Catholic Church. I. Title. II. Series. III. Series: The Twentieth century encyclopedia of Catholicism, v. 97

DELAVIGNETTE, Robert Louis, 261.6
1897-
Christianity and colonialism. Tr. from French by J. R. Foster. New York, Hawthorn [c.1964] 172p. 21cm. (20th century encyc. of Catholicism, v.97. Sect. 9: The church & the mod. world) Bibl. 64-14158 3.50
1. Colonies. 2. Church and social problems—Catholic Church. I. Title. II. Series: The Twentieth century encyclopedia of Catholicism, v.97

DULLES, John Foster 261.6
The spiritual legacy of John Foster Dulles: selections from his articles andaddresses, edited with an introd. by Henry P. Van Dusen. Philadelphia, Westminster Press [c.1960] xxii, 232p. 21cm. 60-8635 3.95
1. Christianity and international affairs. 2. Church and state. 3. U.S.—Religion. 4. Christian life. I. Title.

FORMAN, Charles W 261.6
A faith for the nations. Philadelphia, Westminster Press [1957] 94p. 20cm. (Layman's theological library) Includes bibliography. [BR121.F6519] 57-9601
1. Christianity— Essence, genius, nature. I. Title.

GARBETT, Cyril Forster, 261.6
Abp. of York, 1875-
In an age of revolution. New York, Oxford University Press, 1952. 318 p. 23 cm. [BR115.C5G3 1952a] 52-13197
1. Civilization, Christian. 2. Civilization, Modern. 3. Gt. Brit.—Religion. 4. Christianity—20th cent. I. Title.

GARBETT, Cyril Forster, 261.6
Abp. of York, 1875-
World problems of today. New York, Morehouse-Gorham [1955] 186p. 19cm. [HN37] 55-13717
1. Church and social problems—Church of England. 2. Civilization, Christian. I. Title.

GEYER, Alan F. 261.6
Piety and politics: American Protestantism in the world arena. Richmond, John Knox Press [1963] 173 p. illus. 21 cm. A revision of the author's thesis, Boston University, with title: American Protestantism and world politics, 1898-1960. Bibliographical references included in "Notes and acknowledgments" (p. [157]-167) Bibliography: p. [168]-169. [BR115.P7G44] 63-15198
1. Christianity and politics. 2. Christianity and international affairs. I. Title.

GOLLWITZER, Helmut. 261.6
The demands of freedom; papers by a Christian in West Germany. With an introductory essay by Paul Oestreicher, [Translated from the German by Robert W. Fenn. 1st ed.] New York, Harper & Row [1965] 176 p. 22 cm. "Selected and translated from the German Forderungen der Freiheit... with additional papers." [BR115.P7G63] 65-10370
1. Christianity and politics — Addresses, essays, lectures. I. Title.

GOLLWITZER, Helmut 261.6
The demands of freedom; papers by a Christian in West Germany. Introd. essay by Paul Oestreicher [Tr. from German by Robert W. Fenn] New York, Harper [c.1965] 176p. 22cm. [BR115.P7G63] 65-10370 3.00
1. Christianity and politics—Addresses, essays, lectures. I. Title.

GUERRY, Emile Maurice, 261.6
Abp., 1891-
The popes and world government. Foreword by Paul Emile Cardinal Leger. Tr. [from French] by Gregory J. Roettger.* Helicon [dist. New York, Taplinger, c.1964] xvi, 254p. 23cm. Bibl. 63-19409 5.50
1. Church and international organization—Catholic Church. I. Title.

GUERRY, Emile Maurice, 261.6
Abp.,1891-
The popes and world government. Foreword by Paul Emile Cardinal Leger. Translated by Gregory J. Roettger. Baltimore, Helicon [c1964] xvi, 254 p. 23 cm. Translation of L'Eglise et la communaute des peuples. Bibliographical footnotes. [JX1954.G733] 63-19409
1. Church and international organization — Catholic Church. I. Title.

HERSHBERGER, Guy Franklin, 261.6
1896-
War, peace, and nonresistance. [Rev. ed.] Scottdale, Pa., Herald Press, 1953. 375p. 24cm. [BR115.P4H4 1953] 53-7586
1. Peace. 2. Mennonites—Hist. 3. Facifism. I. Title.

HIEBERT, Erwin N 1919- 261.6
The impact of atomic energy. Newton, Kan. Faith and Life Press [1961] 302p. 24cm. Includes bibliography. [BR115.A85H5] 61-1553
1. Atomic bomb—Moral and religious aspects. 2. Nuclear physics—Hist. I. Title.

HILL, Norman Llewellyn, 261.6
1895-
If the churches want world peace [by] Norman Hill and Doniver A. Lund. New York, Macmillan, 1958. 148p. 22cm. [BR115.I 7H5] 58-11542
1. Christianity and international affairs. 2. U. S.—For. rel.—20th cent. 3. Peace. I. Lund, Doniver Adolph, joint author. II. Title.

LECLERCQ, Jacques, 1891- 261.6
The Christian and world integration. Translated from the French by P. J. Hepburne-Scott. 1st ed. New York, Hawthorn Books [1963] 126, [1] p. 21 cm. (The Twentieth century encyclopedia of Catholicism, v. 95. Section 9: The Church and the modern world) Translation of Le Chretien devant ia planetarisation du monde. Bibliography: p. [127] [BR115.I7L43] 63-13109
1. Christianity and international affairs. 2. International cooperation. I. Title. II. Series: The Twentieth century encyclopedia of Catholicism, v. 95

LECLERCQ, Jacques, 1891- 261.6
The Christian and world integration. Tr. from French by P. J. Hepburne-Scott. New York, Hawthorn [c.1963] 126, [1]p. 21cm. (Twentieth cent. ency. of Catholicism, v.95. Section 9: The Church and the modern world) Bibl. 63-13109 3.50 bds.,
1. Christianity and international affairs. 2. International cooperation. I. Title. II. Series: The Twentieth century encyclopedia of Catholicism, v.95

LINTON, Clair Starrett, 261.6
1898-
The fundamentals of peace and war. New York, Vantage Press [c1953] 132p. 23cm. [HX86.L72] 53-10297
1. Socialism. 2. Individualism. 3. Peace. I. Title.

LOOS, Amandus William, 261.6
1908- ed.
Religious faith and world culture. [1st ed.] New York, Prentice-Hall [1951] viii, 294 p. 24 cm. "Symposium...planned under the guidance of the joint Education Committee of the Church Peace Union and its affiliate, the World Alliance for International Friendship through Religion." Includes bibliographies. [BR115.C5L64] 51-8314
1. Civilization, Christian. I. Title.

MACKENZIE, Kenneth M 261.6
The robe and the sword; the Methodist Church and the rise of American imperialism. Washington, Public Affairs Press [1961] 128p. 24cm. Includes bibliography. [BX8237.M24] 61-8444
1. Methodist Church in the U. S. 2. Christianity and politics. I. Title.

MALIK, Charles. 261.6
Christ and crisis. Grand Rapids, Eerdmans [1962] 101 p. 21 cm. [BR115.I7M3] 62-13403
1. Christianity and international affairs. I. Title.

MASTON, Thomas Bufford, 261.6
1897-
A world in travail; a study of the contemporary world crisis. Nashville, Broadman Press [1954] 139p. 21cm. [BR115.C5M33] 54-8246
1. Civilization, Modern. 2. Civilization, Christian. 3. Christianity—20th cent. I. Title.

MOELLERING, Ralph Luther. 261.6
Modern war and the American churches; a factual study of the Christian conscience on trial from 1939 to the cold war crisis of today. [1st ed.] New York, American Press [c1956] 141p. 21cm. Includes bibliography. [BR115.W2M56] 56-9006
1. War and religion. I. Title.

MONTCHEUIL, Yves de. 261.6
Guide for social action. Chicago, Fides Publishers Association [1954] 85p. 19cm. Translation of L'eglise et le monde actuel. [BR115.C5M582] 54-2077
1. Civilization, Christian. 2. Christianity—20th cent. 3. Church and state—Catholic Church. I. Title.

NIEBUHR, Helmut Richard, 261.6
1894-
Christ and culture. [1st ed.] New York, Harper [1951] x, 259 p. 22 cm. Bibliographical footnotes. [BR115.C8N5] 51-11010
1. Culture. 2. Christianity—20th century. I. Title.

NIEBUHR, Helmut Richard, 261.6
1894-
Christ and culture [Gloucester, Mass., P. Smith, 1965, c.1951] xii, 259p. 21cm. (Harper torchbk.; Cloister lib. bk. rebound) Bibl. [BR115.C8N5] 3.65
1. Culture. 2. Christianity—20th cent. I. Title.

ONE world or none. 261.6
[Washington] United World Federalists. v. illus. 28cm. annual. [JX1954.O56] 61-29023
1. International organization—Popular works. I. United World Federalists.

RAVEN, Charles Earle, *261.6
1885-
The theological basis of Christian pacifism. New York, Fellowship Publications [1951] 87 p. 20 cm. (The Robert Treat Paine lectures, 1950) [BR115.P4R3] 52-6753
1. Pacifism. I. Title.

REISSIG, Herman F 261.6
Man's new home; a Christian approach to changing world problems [by] Herman F. Reissig. Philadelphia, United Church Press [1964] 191 p. 21 cm. Bibliography: p. 188-191. [BR115.I7R4] 64-18118
1. Christianity and international affairs. I. Title.

REISSIG, Herman F. 261.6
Man's new home; a Christian approach to changing world problems [by] Herman F. Reissig. Philadelphia, United Church [c.1964] 191p. 21cm. Bibl. 64-18118 2.50 pap.,
1. Christianity and international affairs. I. Title.

SEIFERT, Harvey 261.6
Ethical resources for international relations. Philadelphia, Westminster [c.1964] 88p. 19cm. (Christian perspectives on soc. probs.) 64-10194 1.25 pap.,
1. Christianity and international affairs. I. Title.

SMITH, Roy Lemon, 1887- 261.6
The future is upon us. New York, Abingdon Press [1962] 252 p. 24 cm. [BR115.I7S5] 62-16812
1. Christianity and international affairs. I. Title.

SORAS, Alfred de. 261.6
International morality. Translated from the French by S. J. Tester. [1st ed.] New York, Hawthorn Books [1963] 128 p. 21 cm. (The Twentieth century encyclopedia of Catholicism, v. 106. Section 9: the church and the modern world) [BR115.I7S63] 63-17331
1. Christianity and international affairs. I. Title.

SORAS, Alfred de 261.6
International morality. Tr. from French by S. J. Tester. New York, Hawthorn [c.1963] 128p. 21cm. (Twentieth cent. encyclopedia of Catholicism, v.106. Section 9: the church and the modern world) Bibl. 63-17331 3.50
1. Christianity and international affairs. I. Title.

STRATMANN, Franziskus 261.6
Maria, 1883-
War & Christianity today. Translated by John Doebele. Westminster, Md., Newman Press [1956] 134p. illus. 22cm. [BR115.W2S642] 57-791
1. War and religion. I. Title.

STRATMANN, Franziskus *261.6
Maria, 1883-
War & Christianity today. Translated by John Doebele. Westminster, Md., Newman Press [1956] 134 p. illus. 22 cm. [BR115.W2S612] 57-791
1. War and religion. I. Title.

TSIRINTANES, Alexandros 261.6
Nikolaos, 1903-
Towards a Christian civilization; a draft issued by the Christian Union of Professional Men of Greece. Athens, Damascus Publications, 1950. 270 p. 25 cm. [BR115.C5T7] 50-24453
1. Civilization, Christian. I. Christianike Henosis Epistemonon. II. Title.

WOOD, John Simpson, 1927- 261.6
Whose world? A handbook on international relations. Illustrated by Mine Okubo. New York, Friendship Press [1960] 80 p. illus. 29 cm. Includes bibliography. [BR115.I7W6] 60-7453
1. Christianity and international affairs. I. Title.

WOOD, John Sumner 261.6
Whose world? A handbook on international relations. Illustrated by Mine Okubo. New York, Friendship Press [c.1960] 80p. illus. 29cm. (bibls.) 60-7453 1.00 pap.,
1. Christianity and international affairs. I. Title.

WOOD, John Sumner, 1902- 261.6
Whose world? A handbook on international relations, Illustrated by Mine Okubo. New York, Friendship Press [1960] 80 p. illus. 29 cm. Includes bibliography. [BR115.I7W6] 60-7453
1. Christianity and international affairs. I. Title.

YODER, John Howard. 261.6
The Christian witness to the State. Newton, Kan., Faith and Life Press [1964] 90 p. illus. 23 cm. (Institute of Mennonite studies series, no. 8) Bibliographical footnotes. [BV631.Y6] 64-4807
1. Church and state — Mennonites. 2. Sociology, Christian (Mennonite) I. Title. II. Series.

YODER, John Howard 261.6
The Christian witness to the State. Newton, Kan., Faith & Life Pr. [c.1964] 90p. illus. 23cm. (Inst. of Mennonite studies ser., no. 3) Bibl. 64-4807 1.50 pap.,
1. Church and state—Mennonites. 2. Sociology (Mennonite) I. Title. II. Series.

BAINTON, Roland Herbert, 261.63
1894-
Christian attitudes toward war and peace; a historical survey and critical re-evaluation. New York, Abingdon Press [1960] 299 p. illus. 24 cm. Includes bibliography. [BT736.2.B3] 60-12064
1. War and religion—History of doctrines. 2. Church history. I. Title.

CENTER for the Study of 261.63
Democratic Institutions
'. . . therefore choose life, that thou mayest live, thou and thy seed.' (Deut. 30:19) [By Norman Cousins, others] Santa Barbara, Calif., Author, P.O. Box 4068 [1965] 70p. 22cm. (Its Papers on peace) Pub. in connection with the Center's Convocation on ways to peace. Feb. 18-20, 1965, N.Y.C. [BX1793.A26C4] 65-1757 pap., gratis
1. Catholic Church. Pope, 1958-1963 (Joannes XXIII) Pacem in terris (11 Apr. 1963) I. Cousins, Norman. II. Title. III. Series.

EATHERLY, Claude Robert 261.63
Burning conscience; the case of the Hiroshima pilot, Claude Eatherly, told in his letters to Gunther Anders [Tr. from German] Postscript for Amer. readers by Anders. Pref. by Bertrand Russell. Foreword by Robert Jungk. New York, Monthly Review [1962, c.1961] 139p. illus. 21cm. 62-15160 4.00
1. Atomic warfare—Moral and religious aspects. I. Anders, Gunther, 1902- II. Title.

FLANNERY, Harry W., 1900- 261.63
ed.
Pattern for peace. Catholic statements on international order. Westminster, Md., Newman [c.]1962. 411p. 61-16575 5.75
1. Christianity and international affairs—Papal documents. I. Title.

GOLLANCZ, Victor, 1893- 261.63
1967.
The Devil's repertoire; or, Nuclear bombing and the life of man. Garden City, N. Y., Doubleday, 1959 [c1958] 192 p. illus. 22 cm. [BR115.A85G63 1959] 59-8403
1. Atomic bomb—Moral and religious aspects. I. Title.

KEYS, Donald, ed. 261.63
God and the H-bomb. Foreword by Steve Allen. [New York] Macfadden [1962, c.1961] 176p. 18cm. (50-128) Bibl. .50 pap.,
1. Atomic warfare—Moral and religious aspects. I. Title.

KEYS, Donald, ed. 261.63
God and the H-bomb. Foreword by Steve Allen. [New York] Bellmeadows Press; distributed by Random House [1961] 224 p. 22 cm. Includes bibliography. [BR115.A85K4] 61-15782
1. Atomic warfare—Moral and religious aspects. I. Title.

LASSERRE, Jean, of 261.63
Epernay.
War and the Gospel. Translated by Oliver Coburn. Scottdale, Pa., Herald Press [1962] 243 p. 23 cm. [BT736.2.L313] 62-52667
1. War and religion—Biblical teaching. 2. Church and state. 3. Commandments, Ten—Murder. I. Title.

METHODIST Church (United 261.63
States) Commission to Study the Christian Faith and War in the Nuclear Age.
The Christian faith and war in the nuclear age. Nashville, Abingdon [c.1963] 108p. 19cm. Bibl. 63-22301 1.00 pap.,
1. War and religion. 2. Christianity and international affairs. I. Title.

NUCLEAR weapons, 261.63
a Catholic response [by] G. E. M. Anscombe [others] Foreword by T. D. Roberts. New York, Sheed [1962, c.1961] 151p. 21cm. 62-15284 5.50
1. Atomic warfare—Moral and religious aspects. I. Anscombe, G. E. M.

RAMSEY, Paul. 261.63
War and the Christian conscience; how shall modern war be conducted justly? Durham, N. C., Published for the Lilly Endowment Research Program in Christianity and Politics by Duke University Press, 1961. 331 p. 22cm. [BR115.W2R25] 61-10666
1. War and religion. I. Title.

RAMSEY, Paul [Robert Paul 261.63
Ramsey]
War and the Christian conscience; how shall modern war be conducted justly? Durham, N.C., Published for the Lilly Endowment Research Program in Christianity and Politics by Duke Univ. Press [c.]1961. 331p. Bibl. 61-10666 6.00
1. War and religion. I. Title.

ACTON, John Emerich Edward 261.7
Dalberg Acton, Baron, 1834-1902.
Essays on church and state, by Lord Acton. Introd. by Douglas Woodruff. New York, Crowell [1968] vi, 518 p. 20 cm. (Apollo editions, A-186) Bibliographical footnotes. [BV630.A3 1968] 68-8638 2.95
1. Church and state. I. Title.

ALLEY, Robert S., 1932- 261.7
So help me God: religion and the Presidency, Wilson to Nixon, by Robert S. Alley. Richmond, John Knox Press [1972] 160 p. illus. 20 cm. [BR516.A7] 70-37418 ISBN 0-8042-1045-4
1. Presidents—United States—Religion. 2. Nationalism and religion—United States. 3. Messianism, American. I. Title.

ANDREW, Brother. 261.7
The ethics of smuggling. With a foreword by Corrie ten Boom. Wheaton, Ill., Tyndale House Publishers [1974] 139 p. 18 cm. [BV4501.2.A48] 74-80770 ISBN 0-8423-0730-3 1.45
1. Christian life—Baptist authors. 2. Smuggling—Moral and religious aspects. 3. Communism and Christianity. I. Title.

AUGUSTIN, Pius. 261.7
Religious freedom in church and state; a study in doctrinal development. Baltimore, Helicon [1966] 328 p. 21 cm. Bibliography: p. 317-321. Bibliographical footnotes. [BX1791.A9] 66-26479
1. Church and state—Catholic Church. 2. Religious liberty. I. Title.

BAIERL, Joseph John, 1884- 261.7
1955.
The Catholic Church and the modern state; a study of their mutual juridical claims. Rochester, N. Y., St. Bernard s Seminary, 1955. 243p. 23cm. [BX1790.B27] 55-43712
1. Church and state—Catholic Church. I. Title.

*BALES, James D. 261.7
Two worlds, Christianity and communism; study course for youth and adults. Cincinnati, Ohio, 45231, Standard Publishing, 8121 Hamilton Av. [c.1965] 128p. 22cm. (3313) 1.25 pap.,
I. Title.

BARON, Salo Wittmayer, 261.7
1895-
Modern nationalism and religion. Freeport, N.Y., Books for Libraries Press [1971, c1947] x, 363 p. 24 cm. (Essay index reprint series) Includes bibliographical references. [BL65.N3B3 1971] 79-134050 ISBN 0-8369-2142-9
1. Nationalism and religion. I. Title.

BARRETT, Patricia, 1914- 261.7
Religious liberty and the American Presidency; a study in church-state relations. [New York] Herder and Herder [1963] 166 p. 21 cm. Includes bibliography. [BR516.B35] 63-9558
1. Church and state in the U.S. 2. Catholic Church in the U.S. 3. Toleration. 4. Presidents—U.S.—Election—1960. I. Title.

BAUMAN, Richard. 261.7
For the reputation of truth; politics, religion, and conflict among the Pennsylvania Quakers, 1750-1800. Baltimore, Johns Hopkins Press [1971] xviii, 258 p. 24 cm. Bibliography: p. 249-254. [BX7648.P4B38 1971] 79-143626 ISBN 0-8018-1178-3 10.00
1. Friends, Society of. Pennsylvania. 2. Friends, Society of—Political activity. I. Title.

BAYNE, Charles Gerwien, 261.7
1860-1947.
Anglo-Roman relations, 1558-1565, by C. G. Bayne Oxford, Clarendon P., 1968. 335 p. 23 cm. Reprint of 1st ed., 1913. Bibliographical footnotes. [DA356.B34 1968] 75-356675 unpriced
1. Catholic Church—Relations (diplomatic) with Gt. Brit. 2. Gt. Brit.—Foreign relations—Catholic church. I. Title.

BEAVER, Robert Pierce, 261.7
1906-
Church, state, and the American Indians; two and a half centuries of partnership in missions between Protestant churches and government [by] R. Pierce Beaver. Saint Louis, Concordia Pub. House [1966] 230 p. 24 cm. Based on the I. M. Dawson lectures on church and state, Baylor University, 1962. Bibliography: p. [213]-222. [BR516.B37] 66-27692
1. Church and state in the United States. 2. Indians of North America—Missions—History. I. Title.

BELLARMINO, Roberto 261.7
Francesco Romolo, Saint, 1542-1621.
Reply to the principal points of the argument, which is falsely entitled Catholic, for the succession of Henry of Navarre to the Kingdom of France. by Francisco Romulo [pseud.] 1587. Translated and edited by George Albert Moore. [2d ed.] Chevy Chase, Md., Country Dollar Press [1950, '1949] xiv, (i. e. xvii), 85 p. port. 28 cm. (The Moore series of English translations of source books) Half title: Bellarmine's reply to Belloy. Authority of Pope in politics. "Collector's edition ... limited to fifty (50) signed and numbered copies. of which this is no. 7." [BX1529.B455B] A 51
1. Belloy, Pierre de, 1540?-1609? Apologie catholique. 2. Henri rv. King of France. 1553-1610. 3. Catholic Church in France. 4. France—Kings and rulers—Succession. 5. Church and state—Catholic Church. I. Title.

BENNETT, John Coleman, 261.7
1902-
The Christian as citizen. New York, Association Press [c1955] 93p. 20cm. (World Christian books) [BR115.P7B38] 55-9115
1. Christianity and politics. I. Title.

BENNETT, John Coleman, 261.7
1902-
When Christians make political decisions. New York, Association [c.1964] 123p. 16cm. (Reffection bk.) Bibl. 64-12561 .50 pap.,
1. Christianity and politics. I. Title.

BERRIGAN, Daniel. 261.7
The dark night of resistance. [1st ed.] Garden City, N.Y., Doubleday, 1971. vi, 181 p. 22 cm. Contains personal narrative, poetry, and prose. [BX4705.B3845A29] 74-150282 5.95
1. U.S.—Social conditions—1960- 2. Government, Resistance to. I. Title.

THE Best of Church & state, 261.7
1948-1975 / edited and with an introd. by Albert J. Menendez ; pref. by Glenn L. Archer. [Silver Spring, Md. : Americans United for Separation of Church and State], c1975. xi, 194 p. ; 21 cm. [BV631.B44] 75-29680 5.95
1. Church and state—Addresses, essays, lectures. I. Menendez, Albert J. II. Church and state.

THE Best of Church & state, 261.7
1948-1975 / edited and with an introd. by Albert J. Menendez; pref. by Glenn L. Archer [Silver Spring, Md. : Americans United for Separation of Church and State], c1975. xi, 194 p. ; 21 cm. [BV631.B44] 75-29680 5.95
1. Church and state—Addresses, essays, lectures. I. Menendez, Albert J. II. Church and state.

BETH, Loren P 261.7
The American theory of church and state. Gainesville, University of Florida Press, 1958. vii, 183p. 24cm. Bibliography: p.171-175. [BR516.B4] 58-13204
1. Church and state in the U. S. I. Title.

BIGLER, Robert M. 261.7
The politics of German Protestantism; the rise of the Protestant Church elite in Prussia, 1815-1848 [by] Robert M. Bigler. Berkeley, University of California Press [1972] xiv, 300 p. 24 cm. A revision of the author's thesis, University of California at Berkeley.

Bibliography: p. 268-290. [BX4844.B53 1972] 77-142055 ISBN 0-520-01881-8
1. Protestant churches—Prussia. 2. Clergy—Prussia. 3. Christianity and politics. I. Title.

BLAKE, Eugene Carson, 1906- 261.7
Christian faith, bulwark of freedom. Houston, Elsevier Press, 1956. 57p. 22cm. (The Rockwell lectures [1955]) [BR115.P7B635] 55-10887
1. Christianity and polities. 2. Church and education. I. Title.

BLAKE, Eugene Carson, 1906- 261.7
Christian faith, bulwark of freedom. [Reissue, New York] Amer. Elsevier [1963] 57p. 22cm. (Rockwell lectures [1955] 2.75
1. Christianity and politics. 2. Church and education. I. Title.

BOONE, Abbott 261.7
Our hypocritical new national motto: In God we trust; a study of the congressional substitution for E pluribus unum and its theological implications. New York, Expostion [c.1963] 114p. 21cm. 62-21054 3.00
1. Religion and state—U.S. 2. Religion—Controversial literature. 3. Mottoes. I. Title.

BOONE, Abbott. 261.7
Our hypocritical new national motto: In God we trust; a study of the congressional substitution for E pluribus unum and its theological implications. [1st ed.] New York, Exposition Press [1963] 114 p. 21 cm. [BL2775.2.B6] 62-21054
1. Religion and state — U.S. 2. Religion — Controversial literature. 3. Mottoes. I. Title.

BORNKAMM, Heinrich, 1909- 261.7
Luther's doctrine of the two kingdoms in the context of his theology. Tr. by Karl H. Hertz. Philadelphia, Fortress [1966] v, 41p. 19cm. (Facet bks. Soc. ethics ser., 14) Bibl. [BR333.5.P6B63] 66-24862 .85 pap.,
1. Luther, Martin, 1483-1546. 2. Church and state—Hist. I. Title. II. Series.

BRIDSTON, Keith R. 261.7
Church politics [by] Keith R. Bridston. New York, World Pub. Co. [1969] 173 p. 21 cm. Bibliographical references included in "Notes" (p. 167-173) [BR115.P7B69 1969] 70-84549 4.95
1. Christianity and politics. I. Title.

BROOKES, Edgar Harry. 261.7
The city of God and the politics of crisis. London, New York, Oxford University Press, 1960. 111p. illus. 19cm. [BR65.A65B7 1960] 61-238
1. Augustinus, Aurelius, Saint, Bp. of Hippo. De civitate Del. 2. Christianity and politics. I. Title.

BRUCKBERGER, Raymond Leopold, 1907- 261.7
God and politics [by] R. L. Bruckberger. Translated from the French by Eleanor Levieux. Chicago, J. P. O'Hara [1972, c1971] 100 p. 23 cm. "A Howard Greenfeld book." Translation of Dieu et la politique. [BR115.P7B69713] 78-190754 ISBN 0-87955-302-2 6.95
1. Christianity and politics. 2. Revolution (Theology) 3. Church and state—Catholic Church. I. Title.

BUTTS, R. Freeman, 1910- 261.7
The American tradition in religion and education. Boston, Beacon Press, 1950. xiv, 230 p. 22 cm. (Beacon Press studies in freedom and power) Bibliographical references included in "Notes" (p. 213-224) [BR516.B85] 50-7586
1. Church and state in the U. S. 2. Church and education in the U. S. I. Title.

BUTTS, Robert Freeman, 1910- 261.7
The American tradition in religion and education. Boston, Beacon Press, 1950. xiv, 230p. 22cm. (Beacon Press studies in freedom and power) Bibliographical references included in 'Notes' (p. 213-224) [BR516.B85] 50-7586
1. Church and state in the U. S. 2. Church and education in the U. S. I. Title.

CALHOON, Robert McCluer. 261.7
Religion and the American Revolution in North Carolina / by Robert M. Calhoon. Raleigh : [North Carolina State University Graphics], 1976. x, 81 p. : ill. ; 23 cm. (North Carolina bicentennial pamphlet series ; 11) Bibliography: p. 79-80. [E263.N8C25] 76-383347
1. North Carolina—History—Revolution, 1775-1783—Religious aspects. I. Title. II. Series.

CALHOUN, Malcolm P ed. 261.7
Christians are citizens; the role of the responsible Christian citizen in an era of crisis [by] Edward L. Long, Jr. [and others] Illustrated by Ruth S. Ensign. Richmond, Published for the Board of Church Extension, Presbyterian Church in the United States by John Knox Press [1957] 139p. illus. 21cm. Includes bibliography. [BR115.P7C25] 57-9522
1. Christianity and politics. I. Long, Edward Le Roy. II. Title.

CARAYON, Jean. 261.7
Essai sur les rapports du pouvoir politique et du pouvoir religieux chez Montesquieu. New York, B. Franklin [1973] p. Reprint of the 1903 ed. Bibliography: p. [JC179.M8C25 1973] 75-168919 ISBN 0-8337-4024-5
1. Montesquieu, Charles Louis de Secondat, baron de La Brede et de, 1689-1755—Political science. 2. Religion and state. I. Title.

CATHOLIC Church. Pope. 261.7
Papal pronouncements on politics, compiled and edited by Francis J. Powers. Washington, '1950. 1 v. (unpaged) 28 cm. Bibliography: 4 leaves at end. [BX1790.A2 1950] 51-616
1. Church and state—Catholic Church. 2. Christianity and politics. 3. Church and social problems—Catholic Church. I. Powers, Francis Joseph, 1913- ed. II. Title.

CATHOLIC Church. Pope. 261.7
Papal pronouncements on the political order, compiled and edited by Francis J. Powers. Westminster, Md., Newman Press, 1952 ['1950] xii, 245 p. 22 cm. "Selected excerpts from the documents, messages and allocutions of the supreme pontiffs from Leo XIII in 1878 to Pius XII in 1951." First published in 1950 under title: Papal pronouncements on politics. Bibliography: p. 221-225. [BX1790.A2 1952] 52-6807
1. Church and state—Catholic Church. 2. Christianity and politics. 3. Church and social problems—Catholic Church. I. Powers, Francis Joseph, 1913- ed. II. Title.

CATHOLIC Church. Pope. 261.7
Papal thought on the state; excerpts from encyclicals and other writings of recent popes, edited by Gerard F. Yates. New York, Appleton-Century-Crofts [1958] 139p. 18cm. (Crofts classics) [BX1790.C2694] 58-5745
1. Church and state—Catholic Church. I. Yates, Gerard F., ed. II. Title.

CATHOLIC Church. Pope, 1958-1963 (joannesXXiI) Pacem in terris (11Apr. 1963)English. 261.7
Peace on earth; an encyclical letter of His Holiness Pope John XXIII. Photos. by Magnum. [Editors: Jerry Mason and Fred R. Sammis] New York, Ridge Press/Odyssey Press [1964] 159 p. illus. 30 cm. "Footnotes": p. 158-159. [BX1793.A253 1964] 64-25011
1. Peace (Theology) 2. Christianity—20th century. 3. Christianity and politics. I. Mason, Jerry, ed. II. Sammis, Fred R., ed. III. Magnum Photos, Inc.

CATHOLIC Church. Pope, 1958-1963(Joannesxxiii)Paceminterris(11Apr.1963) English. 261.7
Pacem in terris. Peace on Earth; encyclical letter of His Holiness Pope John xxiii. [English tr. from Latin] Ed. by William J. Gibbons. With study-club outline. New York, Paulist Pr. [c.1963] 80p. 18cm. (Deus bk.) Bibl. 63-4423 .35 pap.,
1. Peace (Theology) 2. Christianity—20th cent. 3. Christianity and politics. I. Gibbons, William Joseph. 1912- ed. II. Title.

CATHOLIC Church. Pope, 1958-1963(JoannesXXIII)Paceminterris(11Apr.1963)English. 261.7
Pacem in terris. Peace on earth; encyclical letter of His Holiness Pope John XXIII. Edited by William J. Gibbons. With study-club outline. New York, Paulist Press [1963] 80 p. 18 cm. Text in English. "Selected references": p. 78-80. [BX1793.A253 1963a] 63-4423
1. Peace (Theology) 2. Christianity — 20th cent. 3. Christianity and politics. I. Gibbons, William Joseph, 1912- ed. II. Title.

CATHOLIC Church. Pope, 1958-1963(Joannesxxiii)Pacem,interris(11Apr.1963)English 261.7
Pacem in terris. Peace on earth; encyclical letter of Pope John xxiii. Ed. for class and study-group use, with topical outline, selected reading list, commentary, and questions for discussion. [New York] America Pr. [1963] 80p. 19cm. Cover title. Text in English. 63-4376 .50 pap.,
1. Peace (Theology) 2. Christianity—20th cent. 3. Christianity and politics. I. Title.

CENTER for Hermeneutical Studies in Hellenistic and Modern Culture. 261.7
Greek and Christian concepts of justice : protocol of the tenth colloquy, 24 February 1974 / the Center for Hermeneutical Studies in Hellenistic and Modern Culture ; Albrecht Dihle ; W. Wuellner, editor. Berkeley, CA : The Center, c1974. 72 p. ; 21 cm. (Protocol series of the colloquies of the Center for Hermeneutical Studies in Hellenistic and Modern Culture ; nr. 10) Includes bibliographical references. [JC578.C46 1974] 75-24153
1. Justice. 2. Justice—Biblical teaching. 3. Political science—History—Greece. I. Dihle, Albrecht. II. Wuellner, Wilhelm H., 1927- III. Title. IV. Series: Center for Hermeneutical Studies in Hellenistic and Modern Culture. Protocol series of the colloquies ; nr. 10.

CENTER for the Study of Democratic Institutions. 261.7
The churches and the public [by] Robert Lekachman [and others] Santa Barbara, Calif., 1960] 70p. 22cm. Includes bibliography. [BR115.P7C36] 60-1546
1. Christianity and politics. I. Lekachman, Robert. II. Title.

CHRISTIANITY today. 261.7
The challenge of the cults; a Christianity today symposium, by Harold Lindsell [and others] Grand Rapids, Zondervan Pub. House [1961] 80p. 21cm. 'Most of the articles ... first appeared in the Dec. 19, 1960 issue of Christianity today.' Includes bibliography. [BR516.5.C45] 61-42475
1. Sects—U. S. I. Lindsell, Harold, 1913- II. Title.

A Christian's handbook on communism [by Pedro Vazquex Lopez and others] New York, Distributed by Committee on World Literacy and Christian Literature, National Council of the Churches of Christ in the US.A. [1952] 71p. 22cm. [HX536.C38] 52-67154 261.7
1. Communism and religion. I. Vazque Lopez, Pedro. aNational Council of the Churches of Christ in the United States of America. Committee on World Literacy and Christian Literature.

CHURCH of Scotland. General Assembly. Commission on Communism. 261.7
The Church faces the challenge; report. London, New York, Longmans, Green [1955] 124 p. 19 cm. [HN37.C45A5] 56-736
1. Church and social problems—Church of Scotland. 2. Communism and religion. I. Title.

CHURCH of Scotland. General Assembly. Commission on Communism. 261.7
The Church under communism. New York, Philosophical Library [1953] 79 p. 22 cm. [BR481.C525] 53-7901
1. Church and communism. 2. Russia—Church history—1917- I. Title.

CLAHOUN, Malcolm P ed. 261.7
Christians are citizens; the role of the responsible Christian in an era of crisis [by] Edward L. Long. Jr. [and others] Illustrated by Ruth S. Ensign. Richmond, Published for the Board of Church Extension, Presbyterian Church in the United State by John Knox Press [1957] 139p. illus. 21cm. Includes bibliography. [BR115.P7C25] 57-9522
1. Christianity and politics. I. Long, Edward Le Roy. II. Title.

CLEMENT, Marcel. 261.7
Christ and revolution. Translated from the French by Alice von Hildebrand, with Marilyn Teichert. New Rochelle, N.Y., Arlington House [1974] 123 p. 21 cm. Translation of Le Christ et la revolution. Includes bibliographical references. [BT738.C5513] 74-3060 ISBN 0-87000-233-3 6.95
1. Sociology, Christian. 2. Socialism. I. Title.

COATS, William R., 1936- 261.7
God in public: political theology beyond Niebuhr [by] William R. Coats. Grand Rapids, Mich., Eerdmans [1974] 215 p. 24 cm. Bibliography: p. 201-204. [BR115.P7C58] 74-632 7.95
1. Christianity and politics. 2. United States—Economic conditions—1945- 3. Socialism, Christian. I. Title.

COBBET, Thomas, 1608-1685. 261.7
The civil magistrates power in matters of religion modestly debated, impartially stated according to the bounds and grounds of Scripture : and answer returned to those objections against the same which seem to have any weight in them, together with A brief answer to a certain slanderous pamphlet called Ill news from New-England; or A narrative of New-Englands persecution, by John Clark ... / by Thomas Cobbet. New York : Arno Press, 1975. 108, 52 p. ; 24 cm. (Research library of colonial Americana) Reprint of the 1653 ed. printed by W. Wilson for Stephens, London. [BV629.C6 1975] 74-141104 ISBN 0-405-03318-4 : 12.00
1. Church and state. 2. Church and state in New England. I. Clarke, John, 1609-1676. Ill newes from New-England. II. Cobbet, Thomas, 1608-1685. A brief answer to a certain slanderous pamphlet called Ill news from New-England. 1972. III. Title: The civil magistrates power in matters of religion modestly debated ...

COLE, Franklin P. 261.7
They preached liberty : an anthology of timely quotations from New England ministers of the American Revolution on the subject of liberty, its source, nature, obigations, types, and blessings / with an introductory essay and biographical sketches by Franklin P. Cole. Indianapolis : Liberty Press, [1976] p. cm. Includes bibliographical references and index. [E211.C66 1976] 76-26327 ISBN 0-913966-16-9 : 5.95. ISBN 0-913966-20-7 pbk. : 1.25
1. United States—Politics and government—Revolution, 1775-1783—Addresses, essays, lectures. 2. Liberty—Addresses, essays, lectures. 3. Clergy—United States—Addresses, essays, lectures. I. Title.

COMAN, Peter. 261.7
Catholics and the welfare state / Peter Goman. London ; New York : Longman, 1977. ix, 118 p. ; 23 cm. Includes index. Bibliography: p. 111-114. [BX1493.2.C65] 76-49523 ISBN 0-582-48543-6 : 11.50
1. Catholics in England. 2. Church and state—Catholic Church. 3. England—Social policy. I. Title.

CONFERENCE on the Meaning of the First Amendment, Indianapolis, 1963. 261.7
A dialogue on church and state; unabridged addresses. Indianapolis [Methodist Public Relations] 1963. 51 p. ports. (on cover) 22 cm. Cover title. "Sponsored by the Indiana area of the Methodist Church." [BR516.C69] 64-26089
1. Church and state in the U.S. 2. U.S. Constitution. 1st amendment. I. Methodits Church (United States) II. Title.

COTTON, John, 1584-1652. 261.7
The bloudy tenent, washed, and made white in the bloud of the Lambe / by John Cotton. New York : Arno Press, 1972. 144 p. ; 24 cm. (Research library of colonial Americana) Reprint of the 1647 ed. published by H. Allen, London. [BV741.W58C6 1972] 78-141105 ISBN 0-405-03319-2 : 20.00
1. Williams, Roger, 1604?-1683. The bloudy tenent of persecution, for cause of conscience. 2. Liberty of conscience. I. Title. II. Series.

COWHERD, Raymond Gibson, 1910- 261.7
The politics of English dissent; the religious aspects of liberal and humanitarian reform movements from 1815 to 1848. New York, New York University Press, 1956. 242 p. 25 cm. [HN385.C63] 56-9977
1. Gt. Brit.—Social policy. 2. Church and social problems—Gt. Brit. 3. Dissenters—Gt. Brit. I. Title.

CREEDON, Lawrence P. 261.7
United for separation; an analysis of POAU assaults on Catholicism, by Lawrence P. Creedon and William D. Falcon. Milwaukee, Bruce Pub. Co. [c.1959] 259p. 23cm. (bibl. footnotes) 59-13646 3.95
1. Protestants and Other Americans United for Separation of Church and State. 2. Church and state in the U. S. 3. Catholic Church—Doctrinal and controversial works—Catholic authors. I. Falcon, William D., joint author. II. Title.

CULVER, Robert D. 261.7
Toward a Biblical view of civil government / Robert Duncan Culver. Chicago : Moody Press, c1974. 308 p. ; 24 cm. Includes bibliographical references and indexes. [BS680.P45C84] 75-308406 ISBN 0-8024-8796-3 : 6.95
1. Bible—Political science. I. Title.

CURTISS, John Shelton, 1899-- 261.7
The Russian church and the Soviet state, 1917-1950. 1st ed. Boston, Little, Brown [1953] x, 387p. 21cm. Bibliography:p. 371-378 [BR936.C8] 53-10235
1. Church and state in Russia—1917— 2. Russia—Church history—1917- 3. Orthodox Eastern Church, Russian—Hist. I. Title.

CURTISS, John Shelton, 1899- 261.7
The Russian church and the Soviet state. 1917-1950. Gloucester, Mass., P. Smith [1966, c.1953] x, 387p. 21cm. First pub. in 1953 by Little. Bibl. [BR936.C8] 66-3186 5.50
1. Church and state in Russia—1917- 2. Russia—Church history—1917- 3. Orthodox Eastern Church, Russian—Hist. I. Title.

DAIM, Wilfried. 261.7
Christianity, Judaism, and revolution. Translated by Peter Tirner. New York, Ungar [1973] ix, 181 p. 22 cm. Translation of Christentum und Revolution. [BT738.D313] 73-163148 ISBN 0-8044-5266-0 7.50
1. Sociology, Christian. 2. Revolution (Theology) I. Title.

DAIM, Wilfried. 261.7
The Vatican and Eastern Europe. Translated

by Alexander Gode. New York, Ungar [1970] vii, 189 p. 22 cm. Translation of Der Vatikan und der Osten. Includes bibliographical references. [BX1401.A1D313] 77-98343 7.00
1. Catholic Church—Relations (diplomatic) with Communist countries. 2. Communist countries—Foreign relations—Catholic Church. I. Title.

DANTE Alighieri, 1265-1321. 261.7
Monarchy, and Three political letters. With an introd. by Donald Nicholl, and a note on the chronology of Dante's political works by Colin Hardie. With a new introd. for the Garland ed. by Walter F. Bense. New York, Garland Pub., 1972. 40, xxi, 121 p. 22 cm. (The Garland library of war and peace) Monarchy translated by D. Nicholl; Three political letters translated by C. Hardie. Reprint of the 1954 ed., issued in series: Library of ideas. Bibliography: p. 36-40. [PQ4315.62.N5 1972] 74-147412 ISBN 0-8240-0210-5 11.00
1. Church and state. 2. Italy—Politics and government—476-1268. I. Nicholl, Donald, 1923- tr. II. Hardie, Colin Graham, 1906- tr. III. Dante Alighieri, 1265-1321. Epistolae. English. 1972. IV. Title. V. Title: Three political letters. VI. Series. VII. Series: Library of ideas.

D'ARCY, Martin Cyrill, 261.7
1888-
Communism and Christianity. [Harmondsworth, Middlesex] Penguin Books [1956] 190p. 18cm. (A Penguin special, S163) [HX246.D17] 56-3900
1. Communism. 2. Communism and religion. I. Title.

DAVIES, John Gordon, 1919- 261.7
Christians, politics and violent revolution / [by] J. G. Davies. London : S.C.M. Press, 1976. vii, 216 p. ; 22 cm. Includes index. Bibliography: p. 203-211. [BT738.3.D38] 76-362839 ISBN 0-334-00287-7 : £2.50
1. Revolution (Theology) 2. Christianity and politics. 3. Violence—Moral and religious aspects. I. Title.

DAVIES, John Gordon, 1919- 261.7
Christians, politics and violent revolution / J. G. Davies. Maryknoll, N.Y. : Orbis Books, c1976. 216 p. ; 22 cm. Includes bibliographical references and index. [BR115.P7D28] 75-42517 ISBN 0-88344-061-X pbk. : 4.95
1. Christianity and politics. 2. Revolution (Theology) 3. Violence—Moral and religious aspects. I. Title.

DRINAN, Robert F. 261.7
Religion, the courts, and public policy. [1st ed.] New York, McGraw-Hill [1963] 261 p. 22 cm. Includes bibliography. [BR516.D7] 63-16195
1. Church and state in the U.S. 2. Religion in the public schools. 3. Church and education in the U.S. I. Title.

DRINAN, Robert F. 261.7
Religion, the courts, and public policy. New York, McGraw [c.1963] 261p. 22cm. Bibl. 63-16195 5.95
1. Church and state in the U. S. 2. Religion in the public schools. 3. Church and education in the U. S. I. Title.

EBERSOLE, Luke Eugene, 261.7
1918-
Church lobbying in the Nation's Capital. New York, Macmillan, 1951. x, 195 p. 21 cm. "Notes and references": p. 182-195. [BR516.E35] 51-9346
1. Church and state in the U. S. 2. Lobbying. I. Title.

ELBRECHT, Paul G 261.7
Politics and government [by] Paul G. Elbrecht. Saint Louis, Concordia Pub. House [1965] 95 p. 18 cm. (The Christian encounters) Bibliography: p. 95. [BR115.P7E53] 65-16963
1. Christianity and politics. I. Title. II. Series.

ELBRECHT, Paul G. 261.7
Politics and government. Saint Louis, Concordia [c.1965] 95p. 18cm. (Christian encounters) Bibl. [BR115.P7E53] 65-16963 1.00 pap.,
1. Christianity and politics. I. Title. II. Series.

EVANS, Hiram Wesley. 261.7
The rising storm / Hiram W. Evans. New York : Arno Press, 1977. xviii, 345 p. ; 23 cm. (Anti-movements in America) Reprint of the 1930 ed. published by Buckhead Pub. Co., Atlanta. Bibliography: p. xvii-xviii. [BX1770.E8 1977] 76-46075 ISBN 0-405-09948-7 : 20.00
1. Catholic Church in the United States. 2. Church and state in the United States. I. Title. II. Series.

EVANS, Hiram Wesley. 261.7
The rising storm / Hiram W. Evans. New York : Arno Press, 1977. xviii, 345 p. ; 23 cm. (Anti-movements in America) Reprint of the 1930 ed. published by Buckhead Pub. Co., Atlanta. Bibliography: p. xvii-xviii. [BX1770.E8 1977] 76-46075 ISBN 0-405-09948-7 : 20.00
1. Catholic Church in the United States. 2. Church and state in the United States. I. Title. II. Series.

FABER, Richard. 261.7
Die Verkundigung Vergils : Reich, Kirche, Staat : zur Kritik d. politischen Theologie / Richard Faber. Hildesheim ; New York : Olms, 1975. xiv, 443 p. ; 21 cm. (Altertumswissenschaftliche Texte und Studien ; Bd. 4) Bibliography: p. 423-437. [BR115.P7F26] 76-453715 ISBN 3-487-05755-7 : DM58.00
1. Christianity and politics—History. 2. Religion and politics—History. 3. Sociology, Christian—History. 4. Conservatism—Europe—History. I. Title.

FAITH and the world of 261.7
politics. Edited by Johannes B. Metz. New York, Paulist Press [1968] viii, 183 p. 24 cm. (Concilium: theology in the age of renewal: Fundamental theology, v. 36) Includes bibliographical references. [BR115.P7F28] 68-31786
1. Christianity and politics—Addresses, essays, lectures. I. Metz, Johannes Baptist, 1928- ed. II. Series: Concilium (New York) v. 36

FENTON, Geoffrey, Sir, 261.7
1539?-1608.
A form of Christian policy gathered out of French. Introductory note by Peter Davison. New York, Johnson Reprint Corp., 1972. 352 p. 22 cm. (Theatrum redivivum) Reprint of the 1574 ed. imprinted by H. Middleton for Rafe Newbery, London under title: A forme of Christian pollicie gathered out of French (STC 10793a) Includes bibliographical references. [JC393.B3F4 1972] 78-175656
1. Education of princes. 2. Political ethics. 3. Political science—Early works to 1700. 4. Conduct of life—Early works to 1900. I. Title.

FENTON, John H. 261.7
The Catholic vote. New Orleans, Hauser Press [c.1960] 146p. 23cm. (Galleon books) Bibl. note: p.121-123. 60-12512 4.75
1. Catholics in the U. S. 2. Christianity and politics. 3. Voting—U.S. I. Title.

FIERRO Bardaji, Alfredo, 261.7
1936-
The militant gospel : a critical introduction to political theologies / Alfredo Fierro ; translated by John Drury. Maryknoll, N.Y. : Orbis Books, c1977. xv, 459 p. ; 22 cm. Translation of El evangelio beligerante. Includes index. Bibliography: p. 427-453. [BR115.P7F4713] 77-1652 ISBN 0-88344-310-4 : 12.95 pbk. : 6.95
1. Christianity and politics. 2. Theology—20th century. 3. Communism and Christianity. I. Title.

FIGGIS, John Neville, 1866- 261.7
1919
The political aspects of St. Augustine's 'City of God', Gloucester, Mass., Peter Smith 1963[c.1921] 132p. 22cm. Bibl. 3.00
I. Title.

FOGARTY, Michael Patrick. 261.7
Christian democracy in Western Europe, 1820-1953. Notre Dame, Ind., University of Notre Dame Press [1957] xviii, 461p. illus., maps, tables. 24cm. (International studies of the Committee on International Relations, University of Notre Dame) Bibliography: p. 436-452. [HN373.F6] 57-7387
1. Christian democracy. 2. Europe Soc. condut. I. Title. II. Series: Notre Dame, Ind. University. Committee on International Relations. International studies

FORMAN, Charles W. 261.7
The nation and the kingdom; Christian mission in the new nations. New York, Friendship [c.1964] 174p. 19cm. Bibl. 64-10996 1.75 pap.,
1. Missions. 2. Nationalism and religion. 3. Indigenous church administration. I. Title.

FOSTER, Paul. 261.7
Two cities; a study of the church-state conflict. West-minister, Md., Newman Press, 1955. 110p. 18cm. [BV630.F63] 55-4602
1. Church and state—Hist. I. Title.

FOWLER, Ira E. 261.7
Is it too late? Boston, Christopher Pub. House [c.1960] 115p. 60-15782 2.75 bds.,
1. U.S.—Religion. I. Title.

FRAZIER, Claude Albee, 261.7
1920-
Politics & religion can mix! / [edited by] Claude A. Frazier. Nashville : Broadman Press, [1974] 128 p. : ports; 18 cm. [BR115.P7F74] 74-79489 ISBN 0-8054-5549-3 pbk. : 1.50
1. Christianity and politics—Addresses, essays, lectures. 2. Statesmen—United States—Religious life—Addresses, essays, lectures. I. Title.

GARDINER, Stephen, Bp. of 261.7
Winchester, 1483?-1555.
Obedience in church & state; three political tracts. Edited, with an introd., translation, and notes by Pierre Janelle. New York, Greenwood Press, 1968. lxx, 221 p. facsim. 22 cm. English and Latin. Reprint of the 1930 ed. Contents.Contents.—Gardiner's address to the legates.—The Pope's brief to Francis I.—Gardiner's tract on Fisher's execution.—The oration of true obedience.—Gardiner's answer to Bucer. Bibliographical footnotes. [BV629.G27 1968] 68-19272
1. Catholic Church—Doctrinal and controversial works. 2. Church and state. 3. Great Britain—History—Henry VIII, 1509-1547—Sources. 4. Obedience. I. Janelle, Pierre, ed. II. Title.

GILBY, Thomas, 1902- 261.7
Between community and society; a philosophy and theology of the state. London, New York, Longmans, Green [1953] 344p. 23cm. [BV630.G47] 53-1827
1. Church and state. 2. State, The. I. Title.

GILLETT, Henry Tregelles. 261.7
The spiritual basis of democracy; the living way thorugh Christianity. With a foreword by Janet Whitney. [1st American rev. ed.] New York, Exposition Press [1954] 97p. 21cm. [BR115.P7G5 1954] 54-10071
1. Christianity and politics. I. Title.

GOD and Caesar; 261.7
case studies in the relationship between Christianity and the state. Edited with an introd. by Robert D. Linder. Longview, Tex., Conference on Faith and History, 1971. vii, 140 p. 22 cm. Papers presented at a meeting sponsored by the Conference on Faith and History and the Concordia Teachers College and held Oct. 3-4, 1969. Includes bibliographical references. [BV631.G6] 78-187900 1.95
1. Church and state—Addresses, essays, lectures. I. Linder, Robert Dean, ed. II. Conference on Faith and History. III. Concordia Teachers College, River Forest, Ill.

GOERNER, Edward Alfred, 261.7
1929-
Peter and Caesar; the Catholic Church and political authority [by] E. A. Goerner, [New York] Herder and Herder [1965] Westminster, Md., Newman Press [1965] 282 p. 22cm. 95 p. 18cm. Translation of Laiengedanken zum Zolibat. Bibliographical footnotes. [BX1791.G6] [BV4390.G613] 253.2 65-21945 65-29811
1. Church and state — Catholic Church. 2. Celibacy. I. Gorres, Eda Friederike (Coudenhove) 1901- II. Title. III. Title: Is celibacy outdated?

GOERNER, Edward Alfred, 261.7
1929-
Peter and Caesar; the Catholic Church and political authority. [New York] Herder & Herder [c.1965] 282p. 22cm. Bibl. [BX1791.G6] 65-21945 5.95
1. Church and state—Catholic Church. I. Title.

GRANT, Daniel R. 261.7
The Christian and politics [by] Daniel R. Grant. Nashville, Broadman Press [1968] 127 p. 19 cm. Bibliographical footnotes. [BR115.P7G72] 68-6413
1. Christianity and politics. I. Title.

GROUNDS, Vernon C. 261.7
Revolution and the Christian faith / Vernon C. Grounds. 1st ed. Philadelphia : Lippincott, 1971. 240 p. ; 21 cm. (Evangelical perspectives) "A Holman book." Bibliography: p. [231]-240. [BT738.3.G76] 75-156368 4.95
1. Revolution (Theology) 2. Revolutions. I. Title.

HANFF, Helene 261.7
Religious freedom; the American story. Pictures by Charles Waterhouse.Consultant and co-author: Lloyd L. Smith. New York, Grosset [c.1966] 61p. illus. 24cm. (Who, when, where bk.) [BR516.H3] 66-14290 1.95
1. Religious liberty—U. S.—Juvenile literature. I. Smith, Lloyd Lowell, 1929- joint author. II. Title.

HEBBLETHWAITE, Peter. 261.7
The Christian-Marxist dialogue : beginnings, present status, and beyond / by Peter Hebblethwaite. New York : Paulist Press, c1977. v, 122 p. ; 21 cm. (An Exploration book) Includes index. [HX536.H373] 77-70644 ISBN 0-8091-2019-4 pbk. : 3.95
1. Communism and Christianity. I. Title.

HEERING, Gerrit Jan, 1879- 261.7
The fall of Christianity; a study of Christianity, the state, and war. Translated from the Dutch by J. W. Thompson, with a foreword by E. Stanley Jones. With a new introd. for the Garland ed., by Walter F. Bense. New York, Garland Pub., 1972. 47, x, 243 p. 22 cm. (The Garland library of war and peace) Reprint of the 1930 ed. Translation of De zondeval van het Christendom. Includes bibliographical references. [BT736.2.G3613 1972] 77-147670 ISBN 0-8240-0428-0 15.00
1. War and religion. 2. Civilization, Christian. 3. State, The. 4. Church and state. I. Title. II. Series.

HELMREICH, Ernst Christian, 261.7
ed.
A free church in a free state? The Catholic Church, Italy, Germany, France, 1864-1914. Edited with an introd. by Ernst C. Helmreich. Boston, Heath [1964] xvi, 111 p. 24 cm. (Problems in European civilization) Bibliography: p. 109-111. [BX1791.H4] 63-23317
1. Catholic Church in Italy. 2. Catholic Church in Germany. 3. Catholic Church in France. 4. Church and state—Catholic Church. I. Title. II. Series.

HENRY, Paul B. 261.7
Politics for evangelicals. [By]Paul Henry. Valley Forge, Pa., Judson Press [1974] 127 p. 18 cm. Includes bibliographical references. [BR115.P7H46] 74-2893 ISBN 0-8170-0636-2 1.95 (pbk.)
1. Christianity and politics. I. Title.

HERING, Jean. 261.7
A good and a bad government, according to the New Testament. [Translated by O. Stilling] Springfield, Ill., C. C. Thomas [1954] 68p. 23cm. (American lecture series, publication no. 221. American lectures in philosophy) [BS2545.C55H4] 54-6561
1. Church and state—Biblical teaching. I. Title.

HERTZ, Karl H. 261.7
Politics is a way of helping people : a Christian perspective for times of crisis / Karl H. Hertz. Minneapolis, Minn. : Augsburg Pub. House, [1974] 150 p. ; 20 cm. Bibliography: p. 149-150. [BR115.P7H47] 74-77686 ISBN 0-8066-1437-4 pbk. : 3.95
1. Christianity and politics. I. Title.

HINSHAW, Cecil E 261.7
Toward political responsibility. Wallingford, Pa., Pendle Hill [1954] 39p. 19cm. (A Pendle Hill pamphlet, sChristianity and politics. [BR115.P7H54] 54-13103
1. Evil, Non-resistance to. 2. Friends, Society of —Doctrinal and controversial works. I. Title.

HOFFMANN, Gerhard, 261.7
fl.1968- comp.
World mission and world communism. Edited by Gerhard Hoffmann and Wilhelm Wille. Translation edited by David Cairns. Richmond, John Knox Press [1971, c1970] 142 p. 21 cm. Translation of Weltmission und Weltkommunismus. Contents.Contents.—Church and revolution, by H.-D. Wendland.—The Christian world mission in confrontation with communism, by L. Rutti.—Christian presence in a revolutionary society, by J. de Santa Ana.—Communism and African socialism, by H.-G. Schatte.—The mission of the church in Asia confronting the challenge of communism.—The church's response to the Communist challenge in India, by J. W. Sadiq.—Basic ideological concepts of Chinese communism (Maoism), by G. Brakelmann. Includes bibliographical references. [BR115.W6H6313 1971] 75-117391 2.45
1. Church and the world—Addresses, essays, lectures. 2. Communism and religion—Addresses, essays, lectures. I. Wille, Wilhelm, joint comp. II. Title.

HUDSON, Winthrop Still, 261.7
1911-
The great tradition of the American churches [Gloucester, Mass., P. Smith, 1963, c.1953] 282p. 21cm. (Harper torchbk., Acad. lib., TB98 rebound) Bibl. 3.75
1. Church and state in the U.S. 2. U.S.—Church history. I. Title.

HUGHES, John, Abp., 1797- 261.7
1864.
A discussion: Is the Roman Catholic religion inimical to civil or religious liberty? Is the Presbyterian religion inimical to civil or religious liberty? By John Hughes and John Breckinridge. New York, Da Capo Press, 1970 [c1836] 546 p. 24 cm. (Civil liberties in American history) Facsim. of original t.p. has title: A discussion of the question, Is the Roman Catholic region, in any or in all its principles or doctrines, inimical to civil or religious liberty? And of the question, Is the Presbyterian religion, in any or in all its principles or doctrines, inimical to civil or religious liberty? On spine: A discussion on civil and religious liberty. [BV741.H78 1970] 76-122167

1. Catholic Church—Doctrinal and controversial works—Debates, etc. 2. Presbyterian Church—Doctrinal and controversial works—Debates, etc. 3. Religious liberty. I. Breckinridge, John, 1797-1841. II. Title. III. Title: Is the Roman Catholic religion inimical to civil or religious liberty? IV. Title: Is the Presbyterian religion inimical to civil or religious liberty? V. Title: A discussion on civil and religious liberty. VI. Series.

HUTCHISON, John Alexander, 1912- 261.7
The two cities; a study of God and human politics. [1st ed.] Garden City, N. Y., Doubleday, 1957. 190p. 22cm. (Christian faith series) [BR115.P7H84] 57-7826
1. Christianity and politics. I. Title.

HUTCHISON, John Alexander, 1912- 261.7
The two cities; a study of God and human politics, [1st ed.] Garden City, N. Y., Doubleday, 1957. 190p. 22cm. (Christian faith series) [BR115.P7H84] 57-7826
1. Christianity and politics. I. Title.

JAMES, Arthur Walter, 1912- 261.7
The Christian in politics. London, New York, Oxford University Press, 1962. 216p. 23cm. [BR115.P7J35] 62-51942
1. Christianity and politics. I. Title.

JERROLD, Douglas, 1893- 261.7
The future of freedom; notes on Christianity and politics. Freeport, N.Y., Books for Libraries Press [1968] ix, 306 p. 22 cm. (Essay index reprint series) Reprint of the 1938 ed. [BX1397.J4 1968] 68-20311
1. Christianity and politics. 2. Christianity—20th century. 3. Civilization, Christian. 4. World politics—20th century. I. Title.

JUHNKE, James C. 261.7
A people of two kingdoms : the political acculturation of the Kansas Mennonites / James C. Juhnke. Newton, Kan. : Faith and Life Press, [1975] xii, 215 p. : ill. ; 24 cm. (Mennonite historical series) Originally presented as the author's thesis, Indiana University. Includes index. Bibliography: p. [198]-209. [BX8117.K2J83 1975] 74-84697 ISBN 0-87303-662-X
1. Mennonites in Kansas. 2. Mennonites—Political activity. I. Title. II. Series.

JUHNKE, James C. 261.7
A people of two kingdoms : the political acculturation of the Kansas Mennonites / James C. Juhnke. Newton, Kan. : Faith and Life Press, [1975] xii, 215 p. : ill. ; 24 cm. (Mennonite historical series) Originally presented as the author's thesis, Indiana University. Includes index. Bibliography: p. [198]-209. [BX8117.K2J83 1975] 74-84697 ISBN 0-87303-662-X : 7.95
1. Mennonites in Kansas. 2. Mennonites—Political activity. I. Title. II. Series.

KAY, Thomas O. 261.7
The Christian answer to communism; an NAE study series. Grand Rapids, Mich., Zondervan [c.1961] 125p. Bibl. 61-16237 1.95; 1.00 bds., pap.,
1. Communism. 2. Communism and religion. I. Title.

KELLEY, Alden Drew, 1903- 261.7
Christianity and political responsibility. Philadelphia, Westminster Press [1961] 239 p. 21 cm. (Westminster studies in Christian communication) [BR115.P7K37] 61-7306
1. Christianity and politics.

KENNARD, Joseph Spencer, 1890- 261.7
Render to God; a study of the tribute passage. New York, Oxford University Press, 1950. x, 148 p. illus. 21 cm. Includes bibliographical references. [BS2545.C55K4] 50-12335
1. Church and state—Biblical teaching. I. Title.

KERWIN, Jerome Gregory 261.7
Catholic viewpoint on church and state. Garden City, N. Y., Hanover House [c.]1960. 192p. 22cm. (The Catholic viewpoint series) (Bibl. footnotes) 60-11842 3.50
1. Church and state—Catholic Church. I. Title.

KERWIN, Jerome Gregory, 1896- 261.7
Catholic viewpoint on church and state. [1st ed.] Garden City, N. Y., Hanover House, 1960. 192p. 22cm. (The Catholic viewpoint series) Includes bibliography. [BX1791.K45] 60-11842
1. Church and state—Catholic Church. I. Title.

KINNEY, Charles B 261.7
Church & state; the struggle for separation in New Hampshire, 1630-1900. New York, Teachers College, Columbia University, 1955. vii, 198p. 24cm. (Teachers College studies in education) Bibliography: p. 179-186. [BR555.N4K5] 55-6548
1. Church and state in New Hampshire. 2. New Hampshire—Church history. I. Title. II. Series.

KOENKER, Ernest Benjamin. 261.7
Secular salvations; the rites and symbols of political religions [by] Ernest B. Koenker. Philadelphia, Fortress Press [1965] xii, 220 p. 22 cm. Bibliography: p. 211-213. Bibliographical footnotes. [BL65.N3K6] 65-22554
1. Nationalism and religion. 2. Rites and ceremonies—Germany. 3. Rites and ceremonies—Communist countries. I. Title.

KOENKER, Ernest Benjamin 261.7
Secular salvations; the rites and smybols of political religions. Philadelphia, Fortress [c.1965] xii, 220p. 22cm. Bibl. [BL65.N3K6] 65-22554 3.75
1. Nationalism and religion. 2. Rites and ceremonies—Germany. 3. Rites and ceremonies—Communist countries. I. Title.

THE Left hand of God : 261.7
essays on discipleship and patriotism / edited by William H. Lazareth ; with contributions by Gerhard A. Krodel ... [et al.]. Philadelphia : Fortress Press, c1976. xvii, 172 p. ; 20 cm. (Confrontation books) Includes bibliographical references. [BX8041.L43] 75-36457 ISBN 0-8006-1452-6 : 4.75
1. Lutherans in the United States—Addresses, essays, lectures. 2. Church and state—History—Addresses, essays, lectures. 3. Christianity and politics—Addresses, essays, lectures. 4. Church and state—Lutheran Church—Addresses, essays, lectures. I. Lazareth, William Henry, 1928- II. Krodel, Gerhard, 1926-

LEHMANN, Paul Louis, 1906- 261.7
The transfiguration of politics / Paul Lehmann. 1st ed. New York : Harper & Row, [1975] xv, 366 p. ; 22 cm. Includes indexes. Bibliography: p. 351-355. [BR115.P7L327 1975] 74-4636 ISBN 0-06-065229-2 12.95
1. Christianity and politics. I. Title.

LEVITT, Albert 261.7
Vaticanism: the political principles of the Roman Catholic Church. New York, Vantage Press [c.1960] 160p. Bibliography: p. 156-160. 22cm. (Flagstones library, no. 1) 60-11350 3.00 bds.,
1. Catholic Church—Doctrinal and controversial works—Protestant authors. 2. Church and state—Catholic Church. 3. Christianity and politics. I. Title.

LEVITT, Albert, 1887- 261.7
Vaticanism: the political principles of the Roman Catholic Church. [1st ed.] New York, Vantage Press [1960] 160p. 22cm. (Flagstones library, no. 1) Bibliography: p. 156-160. [BX1770.L47] 60-11350
1. Catholic Church—Doctrinal and controversial works—Protestant authors. 2. Church and state—Catholic Church. 3. Christianity and politics. I. Title.

LINDER, Robert Dean. 261.7
Politics: a case for Christian action [by] Robert D. Linder & Richard V. Pierard. Downers Grove, Ill., Inter Varsity Press [1973] 160 p. 18 cm. Bibliography: p. [147]-155. [BR115.P7L46] 73-77850 ISBN 0-87784-356-2 1.75 (pbk.)
1. Christianity and politics. I. Pierard, Richard V., 1934- joint author. II. Title.

LINDSAY, Alexander Dunlop, Baron Lindsay of Birker, 1879-1952. 261.7
Religion, science, and society in the modern world. Freeport, N.Y., Books for Libraries Press [1972, c1943] vi, 73 p. 23 cm. (Essay index reprint series) Original ed. issued in series: The Terry lectures. [BL241.L55 1972] 70-37847 ISBN 0-8369-2604-8
1. Religion and science—1926-1945—Addresses, essays, lectures. 2. Sociology, Christian—Addresses, essays, lectures. I. Title. II. Series: The Terry lectures, Yale University.

LINDSTROM, David Edgar, 1899- 261.7
American foundations of religious liberty. Champaign, Ill., Garrard Press, 1950. xii, 107 p. 20 cm. (Rauschenbusch lectures, 1950) Bibliographical footnotes. [BR516.L6] 51-1464
1. Religious liberty—U. S. 2. Rural churches—U. S. I. Title. II. Series: Rauschenbusch lectures, Colgate Rochester Divinity School Rochester, N. Y., 1950

LOEWEN, M E 261.7
Religious liberty and the Seventh-Day Adventist, by M. E. Loewen. Nashville, Southern Pub. Association [1964] 62 p. illus. 18 cm. [BX6154.L55] 64-56249
1. Church and state — Seventh-Day Adventists. I. Title.

LOEWEN, M. E. 261.7
Religious liberty and the Seventh-Day Adventist. Nashville, Southern Pub. Assn. [c.1964] 62p. illus. 18cm. 64-56249 .35 pap.,
1. Church and state—Seventh-Day Adventists. I. Title.

LOVE, Thomas T. 261.7
John Courtney Murray: contemporary church-state theory. Garden City, N.Y., Doubleday, 1965[c.1964, 1965] 239p. 22cm. Bibl. [BX4705.M977L6] 65-12357 4.95
1. Murray, John Courtney. 2. Church and state—Catholic Church. I. Title.

LOWELL, C. Stanley. 261.7
Embattled wall; Americans United: an idea and a man, by C. Stanley Lowell. [Washington, Protestants and Other Americans United for Separation of Church and State, 1966] vi,162p. illus., ports. 24cm. Bibl. [BR516.L78] 66-24865 3.95
1. Archer, Glenn L. 2. Church and state in the U.S. 3. Protestants and Other Americans United for Separation of Church and State. I. Title.

MCKENZIE, Leon. 261.7
Designs for progress; an introduction to Catholic social doctrine. [Boston] St. Paul Eds. [1968] 126, [3] p. 22cm. Bibl. [BX1753.M234] 67-31069 2.00; 1.00 pap.,
1. Sociology, Christian (Catholic) I. Title.

MCKENZIE, Leon. 261.7
Designs for progress; an introduction to Catholic social doctrine. [Boston] St. Paul Editions [1968] 126, [3] p. 22 cm. Bibliography: p. [127]-[128] [BX1753.M234] 67-31069
1. Sociology, Christian (Catholic) I. Title.

MACKINNON, Donald MacKenzie, 1913- ed. 261.7
Christian faith and Communist faith; a series of studies by members of the Anglican Communion. London, Macmillan; New York, St. Martin's Press, 1953. xii, 260p. 24cm. Bibliography: p. 257-258. [BT1240.M38] 53-4149
1. Apologetics—20th cent. 2. Communism. 3. Communism and religion. I. Title.

MCLELLAN, David. 261.7
Marxism : an introduction / by David McLellan. London : Catholic Truth Society, [1976] 7 p. ; 19 cm. Caption title. [HX40.M235] 76-382501 ISBN 0-85183-171-0 : £0.10
1. Communism. I. Title.

MAIER, Hans, 1931- 261.7
Revolution and church; the early history of Christian democracy, 1789-1901. Translated by Emily M. Schossberger. Notre Dame, University of Notre Dame Press [1969] xiv, 326 p. 24 cm. (Studies in Christian democracy, v. 4) Translation of Revolution und Kirche. Bibliography: p. 298-314. [HN373.M213] 68-27577 10.00
1. Christian democracy. 2. Church and state—Catholic Church. I. Title. II. Series.

MAURY, Philippe. 261.7
Politics and evangelism. [Translated by Marguerite Wieser. Garden City, N. Y., Doubleday [1960, c1959] 120p. 22cm. Translation of Evangelisation et politique. [BR115.P7M3433 1960] 60-658
1. Christianity and politics. I. Title.

MEINHOLD, Peter, 1907- 261.7
Caesar's or God's? The conflict of church and state in modern society. Translated by Walter G. Tillmanns. Minneapolis, Augsburg Pub. House [1962] 170 p. 22 cm. Translation of Romer 13. [BV630.2.M413] 62-9095
1. Church and state. 2. War and religion. I. Title.

MEYER, Donald B. 261.7
The Protestant search for political realism, 1919-1941 [by] Donald B. Meyer. Westport, Conn., Greenwood Press [1973, c1960] x, 482 p. 23 cm. Bibliography: p. 463-474. [HN39.U6M45 1973] 72-12314 ISBN 0-8371-6698-5 19.25
1. Niebuhr, Reinhold, 1892-1971. 2. Church and social problems—United States. 3. Protestant churches—United States. 4. Christianity and politics. I. Title.

MEYER, Donald B. 261.7
The Protestant search for political realism, 1919-1941 Berkeley, University of California Press, 1960. x, 482 p. 24 cm. [HN39.U6M45] 60-9648
1. Church and social problems—U.S. 2. Protestant churches—U.S. 3. Niebuhr, Reinhold, 1892- 4. Christianity and politics. I. Title.

MICKLEM, Nathaniel, 1888- 261.7
The theology of politics. Freeport, N.Y., Books for Libraries Press [1973] p. Reprint of the 1941 ed. [BR115.P7M53 1973] 72-10611 ISBN 0-8369-7119-1
1. Christianity and politics. 2. Totalitarianism. I. Title.

MIGUEZ Bonino, Jose. 261.7
Christians and Marxists : the mutual challenge to revolution / by Jose Miguez Bonino. Grand Rapids, Mich. : Eerdmans, c1976. 157 p. ; 22 cm. "First delivered as the 1974 London lecture in contemporary Christianity." Includes bibliographical references and index. [HX536.M46 1976] 75-45042 ISBN 0-8028-3477-9 : 6.95
1. Communism and Christianity—Addresses, essays, lectures. I. Title.

MIGUEZ Bonino, Jose. 261.7
Christians and Marxists : the mutual challenge to revolution / by Jose Miguez Bonino. London : Hodder and Stoughton, 1976. 158 p. ; 22 cm. (Ecclesia books) "First delivered as the 1974 London lecture in contemporary Christianity." Includes bibliographical references and index. [HX536.M46 1976b] 76-369696 ISBN 0-340-19396-4 : £2.50
1. Communism and Christianity—Addresses, essays, lectures. I. Title.

MILLER, William Lee. 261.7
The Protestant and politics. Philadelphia, Westminster Press [1958] 92p. 20cm. (Layman's theological library) [BR115.P7M54] 58-8256
1. Christianity and polities. I. Title.

MINEAR, Paul Sevier, 1906- 261.7
I pledge allegiance : patriotism and the Bible / by Paul S. Minear. Philadelphia : Geneva Press, [1975] 140 p. ; 21 cm. Includes bibliographies. Examines various national issues, such as civil disobedience, amnesty, and segregation, from Biblical perspectives. [BR115.P7M543] 74-31489 ISBN 0-664-24819-5 pbk. : 2.65
1. Patriotism—Moral and religious aspects. I. Title.

MOEHLMAN, Conrad Henry, 1879- 261.7
The wall of separation between church and state; an historical study of recent criticism of the religious clause of the first amendment. Boston, Beacon Press, 1951. xvi, 239 p. 23 cm. (Beacon studies in freedom and power) Bibliography: p. 222-231. [BR516.M64] 51-3272
1. Church and state in the U.S. 2. Church and education in the U.S. I. Title.

MONSMA, Stephen V., 1936- 261.7
The unraveling of America : wherein the author analyzes the inadequacy of current political options and responds with a Christian approach to government / Stephen V. Monsma. Downers Grove, Ill. : InterVarsity Press, c1974. 228 p. ; 22 cm. Includes bibliographical references and index. [JA84.U5M68] 74-14302 4.95
1. Political science—History—United States. I. Title.

MORRISON, Stanley Andrew. 261.7
Religious liberty in the Near East. London, New York, World Dominion Press [1948] 50p. 22cm. (Post war survey series, no. 1) 'Postacript on Egypt': leaf inserted. [BR1070.M6] 48-27428
1. Religious liberty—Levant. I. Title. II. Series.

MOSSE, George Lachmann. 261.7
The holy pretence; a study in Christianity and reason of state from William Perkins to John Winthrop [by] George L. Mosse. New York, H. Fertig, 1968 [c1957] 159 p. 23 cm. Bibliographical footnotes. [BR115.P7M57 1968] 68-14552
1. Christianity and politics. 2. Political ethics. 3. Puritans. I. Title.

MOUW, Richard J. 261.7
Political evangelism [by] Richard J. Mouw. Grand Rapids, Eerdmans [1974, c1973] 111 p. 21 cm. [BR115.P7M59] 73-16213 ISBN 0-8028-1544-8 1.95 (pbk.)
1. Christianity and politics. 2. Social ethics. I. Title.

MOUW, Richard J. 261.7
Politics and the Biblical drama / by Richard J. Mouw. Grand Rapids : Eerdmans, c1976. p. cm. [BR115.P7M593] 76-25004 ISBN 0-8028-1657-6 pbk. : 3.95
1. Bible—Political science. 2. Christianity and politics. I. Title.

MUEHL, William. 261.7
Mixing religion and politics. New York, Association Press [1958] 128 p. 16 cm. (An Association Press reflection book) Excerpted from the author's Politics for Christians, published in 1956. [BR115.P7M82] 58-11530
1. Christianity and politics. I. Title.

MUEHL, William. 261.7
Politics for Christians. New York, Association

Press [1956] 181p. 20cm. (A Haddam House book) [BR115.P7M8] 56-6443
1. Christianity and politics. I. Title.

MUELLER, William A. 261.7
Church and state in Luther and Calvin. a comparative study. Garden City, N.Y., Doubleday [1965, c.1954] 187p. 18cm. (Anchor bk. A454) [BV630.M8] .95 pap.,
1. Luther, Martin, 1483-1546. 2. Calvin, Jean, 1509-1564. 3. Church and state—Hist. I. Title.

MULLER, Alois 1924- comp. 261.7
Political commitment and Christian community. Edited by Alois Muller and Norbert Greinacher. [New York] Herder and Herder [1973] 154 p. 23 cm. (Concilium: religion in the seventies, 84) Includes bibliographical references. [BR115.P7M826] 72-12422 ISBN 0-8164-2540-X 3.95 (pbk.)
1. Christianity and politics. I. Greinacher, Norbert, 1931- joint comp. II. Title. III. Series: Concilium (New York) 84.

MULLER, Herbert Joseph, 1905- 261.7
Religion and freedom in the modern world. Chicago, University of Chicago Press [1963] vii, 129 p. 22 cm. Lectures sponsored by the Frank L. Weil Institute for Studies in Religion and the Humanities. [BR115.P7M85] 63-20911
1. Christianity and politics. I. Frank L. Weil Institute for Studies in Religion and the Humanities. II. Title.

MURPHY, Francis Xavier, 1914- 261.7
Politics and the early Christian. Foreword by Hubert H. Humphrey. New York, Desclee Co. [1967] viii, 184pm 21cm. Bibl. footnoes. [BR115.P7M87] 67-30762 3.50 pap.,
1. Christianity and politics. 2. Church history—Primitive and early church. I. Title.
Distributed by Herder Bk. Ctr.

MURRAY, Albert Victor, 1890- 261.7
The state and the church in a free society. Cambridge [Eng] University Press, 1958. 190p. 23cm. (The Hibbert lectures, 1957) [BL25.H5 1957] 58-1675
1. Church and state. I. Title.

MURRAY, John Courtney. 261.7
We hold these truths; Catholic reflections on the American proposition. Garden City. N. Y., Doubleday [1964, c.1960] 317p. 18cm. (Image bk. D181) 1.25 pap.,
1. Church and state in the U. S. 2. Catholic Church in the U. S. 3. U. S.—Pol. & govt. I. Title.

MURRAY, John Courtney. 261.7
We hold these truths; Catholic reflections on the American proposition. New York, Sheed and Ward [1960] 336 p. 22 cm. [BR516.M84] 60-12876
1. Catholic Church in the United States. 2. Church and state in the United States. 3. United States—Politics and government.

MUTCHLER, David E. 261.7
The church as a political factor in Latin America; with particular reference to Colombia and Chile [by] David E. Mutchler. Foreword by Irving Louis Horowitz. New York, Praeger [1971] xxviii, 460 p. 25 cm. (Praeger special studies in international politics and public affairs) Originally issued as the author's thesis, Washington University, St. Louis. Bibliography: p. [429]-445. [BX1426.2.M88] 74-153836
1. Catholic Church in Latin America. 2. Christianity and politics. I. Title.

NATIONAL Conference on Church and State, 15th, Denver, 1963. 261.7
The current challenge to church-state separation; selected addresses. [Washington] Protestants and Other Americans United for Separation of Church and State [1963] 61 p. 22 cm. Proceedings of the 15th of a series of meetings; proceedings of the 14th are entered under: Protestants and Other Americans United for Separation of Church and State. [BR516.N27 1963] 74-151647
1. Church and state in the United States—Congresses. I. Protestants and Other Americans United for Separation of Church and State. II. Title.

NEMEC, Ludvik. 261.7
Church and state in Czechoslovakia; historically, juridiscally, and theologically documented. New York, Vantage Press [1955] 577p. 23cm. Includes bibliography. [BR1050.C9N4] 54-7406
1. Church and state in the Czechoslovak Republic. I. Title.

NEWMAN and Gladstone: 261.7
the Vatican decrees. Introd. by Alan S. Ryan. [Notre Dame, Ind.] Univ. of Notre Dame Pr. [c.]1962 xxii, 228p. (ndp 11) 62-1066 1.95 pap.,
1. Vatican Council, 1869-1870. 2. Popes—Infallibility. 3. Allegiance. I. Ryan, Alvan Sherman, 1912- II. Gladstone, William Ewart, 1809-1898. The Vatican decrees in their bearing on civil allegiance. III. New man, John Henry, Cardinal, 1801-1890. A letter addressed to His Grace the Duke of Norfolk.

NEWMAN, Jeremiah 261.7
Studies in political morality. Chicago 2, 30 N. LaSalle St. Scepter Pr., [1963] 459p. 22cm. (Corinth ser.) Bibl. 63-20072 6.25
1. Church and state—Catholic Church. 2. State, The. 3. Church and state in Ireland. I. Title. II. Title: Political morality.

NICHOLS, James Hastings, 1915- 261.7
Democracy and the churches. Philadelphia, Westminster Press [1951] 298 p. 24 cm. Bibliography: p. [280]-284. [BR115.P7N52] 51-10765
1. Christianity and politics. 2. Democracy. I. Title.

NICHOLS, James Hastings, 1915- 261.7
Democracy and the churches. New York, Greenwood Press [1969, c1951] 298 p. 23 cm. Includes bibliographical references. [BR115.P7N52 1969] 70-97387 ISBN 0-8371-2695-9
1. Christianity and democracy. 2. Democracy. I. Title.

NIEBUHR, Reinhold, 1892-1971. 261.7
Christian realism and political problems. New York, Scribner, 1953. 203 p. 21 cm. [BR115.P7N54] 53-12785
1. Christianity and politics. I. Title.

NOVAK, Michael. 261.7
A theology for radical politics. [New York] Herder and Herder [1969] 128 p. 21 cm. Includes bibliographical references. [BT738.3.N68] 69-17073 1.95
1. Revolution (Theology) 2. Students—United States—Conduct of life. I. Title.

OAKLEY, Francis. 261.7
Kingship and the gods: the Western apostasy. Houston, University of Saint Thomas, 1968. 51 p. port. 16 cm. (The Smith history lecture 1968) Bibliographical references included in "Footnotes" (p. 51) [BV631.O2] 68-7995
1. Church and state—History. I. Title. II. Series: The Smith lecture 1968

ODEGARD, Holtan Peter, 1923- 261.7
Sin and science; Reinhold Niebuhr as political theologian. Yellow Springs, Ohio. Antioh Press [1956] 245p. 22cm. Bibliography:p. [221]-234. [BX4827.N5O3] 56-8247
1. Niebuhr, Reinhold, 1892- 2. Sin. 3. Christianity and politics. I. Title.

ODEGARD, Holtan Peter, 1923- 261.7
Sin and science; Reinhold Niebuhr as political theologian, by Holtan P. Odegard. Westport, Conn., Greenwood Press [1972, c1956] 245 p. 22 cm. Bibliography: p. [221]-234. [BX4827.N5O3 1972] 72-6928 ISBN 0-8371-6505-9 11.25
1. Niebuhr, Reinhold, 1892-1971. 2. Sin. 3. Christianity and politics. I. Title.

ODEGARD, Holton P 261.7
Sin and science; Reinhold Niebuhr as political theologian. Yellow Springs, Ohio, Antioch Press [1956] 245p. 22cm. Bibliography: p. [221]-234. [BX4827.N5O3] 56-8247
1. Niebuhr, Reinhold, 1802- 2. Christianity and politics. 3. Sin I. Title.

ODEGARD, Peter H., 1901- ed. 261.7
Religion and politics. Introd. by Lewis Webster Jones. [New York] Published for the Eagleton Institute of Politics at Rutgers, the State University, by Oceana Publications [1960] xii, 219 p. illus., diagrs., tables. 23 cm. (America's politics series, no. 1) Bibliographical footnotes. [BR115.P7O3] 60-10209
1. Christianity and politics. 2. Presidents—U.S.—Election. 3. Catholic Church in the U.S. 4. Religious liberty—U.S. I. Title. II. Series.

O'NEILL, James Milton, 1881- 261.7
Catholics in controversy. New York, McMullen Books [1954] 227p. 21cm. [BR516.O5] 54-7092
1. Church and state in the U. S. 2. Catholics in the U. S. 3. Catholic Church—Apologetic works. I. Title.

PAUPERT, Jean Marie, 1927- 261.7
The politics of the Gospel. Foreword by Daniel Berrigan. [Translated from the French by Gregor Roy. 1st ed.] New York, Holt, Rinehart, and Winston [1969] xviii, 174 p. 22 cm. Translation of Pour une politique evangelique. Bibliographical footnotes. [BR115.P7P3613] 69-10227 4.95
1. Christianity and politics. I. Title.

PEACHAM, Henry, 1576?-1643? 261.7
The complete gentleman, The truth of our times, and The art of living in London. Edited by Virgil B. Heltzel. Ithaca, N. Y., Published for the Folger Shakespeare Library by Cornell University Press [1962] xx, 250p. 23cm. (Folger documents of tudor and Stuart civillization) Bibliographical footnotes. [LC4945.G7P4 1962] 62-16358
1. Education—Early works to 1800. 2. Courtesy. I. Heltzel, Virgil Barney, 1896- ed. II. Title. III. Title: The truth in our times. IV. Title: The art of living in London. V. Series.

PEARL, Reuben. 261.7
The road to peace. New York, Philosophical Library [1957] 189p. 22cm. [BR115.P4P42] 57-13953
1. Peace. I. Title.

PENNER, Archie. 261.7
The Christian, the state, and the New Testament. Scottdale, Pa., Herald Press, 1959. 128p. 20cm. Includes bibliography. [BV630.2.P44] 58-14061
1. Church and state—Biblical teaching. 2. Church and state—Hist. I. Title.

PETULLA, Joseph M. 261.7
Christian political theology; a Marxian guide [by] Joseph M. Petulla. Foreword by George A. Mueller. Maryknoll, N.Y., Orbis Books [1972] x, 256 p. 22 cm. Bibliography: p. 253-256. [BR115.P7P47] 77-190167 3.95
1. Marx, Karl, 1818-1885. 2. Christianity and politics. 3. Communism and Christianity. I. Title.

PFEFFER, Leo, 1910- 261.7
Church, State, and freedom. Boston, Beacon Press [1953] xvi, 675p. 24cm. [Beacon studies in church and state] Bibliography: p. [650]-654. [BV630.P53] 53-6617
1. Church and state. 2. Church andstate in the U. S. 3. Bible in the schools. 4. Religious liberty—U. S. I. Title.

PFEFFER, Leo, 1910- 261.7
Church, state, and freedom. Rev. ed. Boston, Beacon Press [1967] xiii, 832 p. 24 cm. Bibliography: p. 794-802. [BR516.P45 1967] 66-23582
1. Church and state in the United States. I. Title.

PIKE, James Albert, Bp. 261.7
A Roman Catholic in the White House. In collaboration with Richard Byfield. Garden City. N.Y., Doubleday [c.]1960. 143p. 22cm. (Bibl. notes p.134-136 bibl. p. 137-38) 60-10331 2.50
1. Church and state in the U.S. 2. Catholic Church in the U.S. 3. Presidents—U.S.—Election—1960. I. Title.

PIKE, James Albert, Bp., 1913- 261.7
A Roman Catholic in the White House. In collaboration with Richard Byfield. [1st ed.] Garden City, N. Y., Doubleday, 1960. 143p. 22cm. Includes bibliography. [BR516.P5] 60-10331
1. Church and state in the U. S. 2. Catholic Church in the U. S. 3. Presidents—U. S.—Election—1960. I. Title.

PIKE, James Albert, Bp., 1913-1969. 261.7
A Roman Catholic in the White House. In collaboration with Richard Byfield. Westport, Conn., Greenwood Press [1972, c1960] 143 p. 22 cm. Bibliography: p. [137]-138. [BR516.P5 1972] 72-7508 ISBN 0-8371-6514-8 8.25
1. Catholic Church in the United States. 2. Church and state in the United States. 3. Presidents—United States—Election—1960. I. Title.

PIPPERT, Wesley. 261.7
Memo for 1976; some political options. Downers Grove, Ill., InterVarsity Press [1974] 120 p. 21 cm. [BR115.P7P49] 73-89301 ISBN 0-87784-704-5 1.95 (pbk.)
1. Christianity and politics. I. Title.

PRADERA, Victor, 1872- 261.7
The new state. Translated from the Spanish by Bernard Malley, with a foreword by the Prince of Asturias. London, Sands. [New York, AMS Press, 1974] 320 p. port. 23 cm. Translation of El estado nuevo. Reprint of the 1939 ed. Includes bibliographical references. [JC271.P72 1974] 79-180421 ISBN 0-404-56196-9 16.00
1. Church and state—Catholic Church. 2. State, The. I. Title.

PROTESTANTS and Other Americans United for Separation of Church and State. 261.7
Preserving our tradition in Church and State; highlights of the 11th National Conference. Chicago, Illinois, February 5 and 6, 1962. Washington [1962] 46 p. ports. 22 cm. [BR516.P747] 66-85338
1. Church and state in the U.S.—Congresses. I. Title.

REDEKOP, John Harold. 261.7
Making political decisions; a Christian perspective, by John H. Redekop. Scottdale, Pa., Herald Press [1972] 46 p. illus. 18 cm. (Focal pamphlet series, no. 23) Includes bibliographical references. [BR115.P7R432] 72-185900 ISBN 0-8361-1678-X 0.75
1. Christianity and politics. I. Title.

REGAMEY, Raymond, 1900- 261.7
Non-violence and the Christian conscience [by] P. Regamey. With a Pref. by Thomas Merton and a foreword by Stanley Windass. [New York] Herder & Herder [1966] 272p. 22cm. Bibl. [BT736.6.R413 1966] 66-22610 5.95
1. Passive resistance to government. I. Title.

REGAN, Richard J 261.7
American pluralism and the Catholic conscience. With a foreword by John Courtney Murray. New York, Macmillan [1963] 288 p. 22 cm. [BX1793.R4] 63-13182
1. Church and state — Catholic Church. 2. Church and state in the U.S. 3. Law and ethics. 4. Christianity and politics. I. Title.

REGAN, Richard J. 261.7
American pluralism and the Catholic conscience. With a foreword by John Courtney Murray. New York, Macmillan [1963] 288 p. 22 cm. [BX1793.R4] 63-13182
1. Church and state—Catholic Church. 2. Church and state in the U.S. 3. Law and ethics. 4. Christianity and politics. I. Title.

RELIGION and political 261.7
society [by] Jurgen Moltmann [and others] Edited and translated in the Institute of Christian Thought. [1st ed.] New York, Harper & Row [1974] p. cm. (A Harper forum book) Includes bibliographical references. [BR115.P7R434 1974] 73-18424 ISBN 0-06-065564-X 3.95
1. Christianity and politics—Addresses, essays, lectures. 2. Eschatology—Addresses, essays, lectures. 3. Religion and sociology—Addresses, essays, lectures. I. Moltmann, Jurgen. II. Institute of Christian Thought.

RELIGION and the law : 261.7
a handbook of suggestions for laymen and clergymen preparing Law Day addresses. [Chicago : American Bar Association, c1975] 64 p. ; 23 cm. Cover title. Bibliography: p. 59-62. [BL65.L33R44] 76-356405 pbk. : 0.75
1. Religion and law. I. American Bar Association.

RELIGIOUS Liberty Conference, 14th, Washington, D.C., 1970. 261.7
Dissent in church and state; compilation of background study papers prepared for use by participants. John W. Baker: editor. Washington, Baptist Joint Committee on Public Affairs [1970] iii, 60 p. ports. 27 cm. Sponsored by the Baptist Joint Committee on Public Affairs, Aug. 4-6, 1970. Includes bibliographical references. [BR516.R42] 74-19303
1. Dissenters, Religious—U.S.—Addresses, essays, lectures. 2. Dissenters—Addresses, essays, lectures. I. Baker, John Wesley, 1920- ed. II. Baptist Joint Committee on Public Affairs. III. Title.

RIGA, Peter 261.7
Peace on earth; a commentary on Pope John's encyclical [New York] Herder & Herder [c.1964] 254p. 21cm. 64-13691 4.95
1. Catholic Church. Pope. 1958-1963 (Joannes XXIII) Pacem in terris (11 Apr. 1963) I. Catholic Church. Pope, 1958-1963 (Joannes XXIII) Pacem in terris (11 Apr. 1963) English. II. Title.

RUFF, G Elson, 1904- 261.7
The dilemma of church and state. Philadelphia, Muhlenberg Press, 1954. 103p. 21cm. [BV630.R85] 53-13514
1. Church and state. I. Title.

SANDERS, Thomas G. 261.7
Protestant concepts of church and state; historical backgrounds and approaches for the future. Garden City, N.Y., Doubleday [1965, c.1964] x, 388p. 18cm. (Anchor bk. A471) Bibl. [BV630.2.S3] 1.45 pap.,
1. Church and state—Hist. I. Title. II. Series.

SANDERS, Thomas Griffin, 1932- 261.7
Protestant concepts of church and state: historical backgrounds and approaches for the

future. New York, Holt [1964] x. 339p. 22cm. (Studies of church and state) Bibl. 64-11275 7.50
1. Church and state—Hist. I. Title. II. Series.

SHANNON, Thomas Anthony, 1940- 261.7
Render unto God; a theology of selective obedience, by Thomas A. Shannon. New York, Paulist Press [1974] ix, 180 p. 21 cm. Bibliography: p. 173-180. [BX1791.S5] 73-92233 ISBN 0-8091-1802-5 4.50 (pbk.)
1. Church and state—Catholic Church. I. Title.

SHEED, Francis Joseph 261.7
God and politics. New York, Sheed and Ward [c.1960] 96p. 18cm. (Canterbury books) 'From Communism and man. 60-7322 .75 pap.,
1. Christianity and politics. I. Title.

SHEED, Francis Joseph, 1897- 261.7
God and politics. New York, Sheed and Ward [1960] 96 p. 18 cm. (Canterbury books) "From Communism and man." [BR115.P7S46] 60-7322
1. Christianity and politics. I. Title.

SHEEN, Fulton John, Bp., 1895- 261.7
Crisis in history. St. Paul, Catechetical Guild Educational Society [1952] 64p. 17cm. [BR115.H5S45] 53-20862
1. History—Philosophy. 2. World politics—1945- I. Title.

SHIELS, William Eugene, 1897- 261.7
King and church; the rise and fall of the Patronato Real. Chicago, Loyola Univ. Press [c.]1961. xxiii, 399p (Jesuit studies; contributions to the arts and sciences by members of the Society of Jesus) Bibl. 61-11113 6.00
1. Patronage, Ecclesiastical—Spain—Colonies. 2. Church and state in Spain. I. Title.

SINGH, Surjit. 261.7
Communism, Christianity, democracy. Richmond, John Knox Press [1965] 127 p. 21 cm. [HX536.S484] 65-10654
1. Communism and religion. 2. Christianity and politics. 3. Democracy. I. Title.

SINGH, Surjit 261.7
Communism, Christianity, democracy. Richmond, Va., Knox [c.1965] 127p. 21cm. [HX536.S484] 65-10654 3.00; 1.95 pap.,
1. Communism and religion. 2. Christianity and politics. 3. Democracy. I. Title.

SLANT manifesto: Catholics and the left, by Adrian Cunningham [and others] With an introd. by Neil Middleton. [U.S. ed.] Springfield, Ill., Templegate [1968] xviii, 206 p. 18 cm. Bibliography: p. 53-54. [BR115.P7S54 1968] 67-31528 261.7
1. Christianity and politics. 2. Socialism and Catholic Church. I. Cunningham, Adrian. II. Title: Catholics and the left.

SMITH, William Edward, 1881- 261.7
Divine democracy. Boston, Meador Pub. Co. [1957] 504p. 21cm. [BR126.S495] 57-13672
I. Title.

SMITH, William Edward, 1881- 261.7
Divine democracy. Boston, Meador Pub. Co. [1957] 504 p. 21 cm. [BR126.S495] 57-13672
I. Title.

STEDMAN, Murray Salisbury, 1917- 261.7
Religion and politics in America [by] Murray S. Stedman, Jr. New York, Harcourt, Brace & World [1964] vii, 168 p. 21 cm. Bibliography: p. 159-161. [BR516.S8] 64-19366
1. Church and state in the U.S. I. Title.

STEDMAN, Murray Salisbury, Jr., 1917- 261.7
Religion and politics in America. New York, Harcourt [c.1964] vii, 168p. 21cm. Bibl. 64-19366 4.95; 2.95 pap.,
1. Church and state in the U. S. I. Title.

STOKES, Anson Phelps, 1874- 261.7
Church and state in the United States... Introd. by Ralph Henry Gabriel. [1st ed.] New York, Harper [1950] 8 v. illus., ports., facsims. 25 cm. "Critical and classified selected bibliography": v. 3. p. 789-836. [BR516.S85] 50-7978
1. Church and state in the U.S. I. Title.

STOKES, Anson Phelps, 1874-1958. 261.7
Church and state in the United States, by Anson Phelps Stokes and Leo Pfeffer. Rev. one-volume ed. [1st ed.] New York, Harper & Row [1964] xii, 660 p. 24 cm. Bibliography: p. 623-631. [BR516.S85 1964] 64-14382
1. Church and state in the United States. I. Pfeffer, Leo, 1910-

STRICKLAND, Reba Carolyn, 1904- 261.7
Religion and the state in Georgia in the eighteenth century. New York, AMS Press, 1967 [c1939] 211 p. 23 cm. (Studies in history, economics, and public law, no. 460) Originally presented as the author's thesis, Columbia University. Bibliography: p. 187-197. [BR555.G4S8 1967] 73-29198
1. Church and state in Georgia. 2. Georgia—Church history. I. Title. II. Series: Columbia studies in the social sciences, no. 460.

STRINGFELLOW, William. 261.7
Conscience & obedience : the politics of Romans 13 and Revelation 13 in light of the Second Coming / William Stringfellow. Waco, Tex. : Word Books, c1977. 112 p. ; 23 cm. [BS2545.C55S8] 76-19538 ISBN 0-87680-345-1 : 5.95
1. Bible. N.T. Romans XIII—Political science. 2. Bible. N.T. Revelation—Political science. 3. Christianity and politics. I. Title.

STRUBE, William P 261.7
The Star over the Kremlin. Grand Rapids, Baker Book House, 1962. 108 p. 21 cm. [HX536.S84] 62-17679
1. Communism and religion. I. Title.

STUMPF, Samuel Enoch, 1918- 261.7
A democratic manifesto; the impact of dynamic Christianity upon public life and government. Nashville, Vanderbilt University Press, 1954. 168p. 22cm. [BR115.P7S76] 54-4773
1. Democracy. 2. Christianity and politics. I. Title.

STURZO, Luigi, 1871- 261.7
Church and state. [2 vs.] Introd. by A. Robert Caponigri. [Tr. by Barbara Barclay Carter. Notre Dame, Ind.] Univ. of Notre Dame Pr. [c.]1962. 2 v. (584p.) Bibl. 62-12467 2.25 pap., ea.,
1. Church and state—Catholic Church. 2. Church and social problems—Catholic Church. I. Title.

SUAREZ, Francisco, 1548-1617. 261.7
Extracts: politics and government from Defense of the faith, Laws and God the Lawgiver. Tract on faith [and] Tract on charity; translated and edited by George Albert Moore. Chevy Chase, Md., Country Dollar Press [c1950] xiii, 138 p. port. 28 cm. (The Moore series of English translations of source books) "Collector's edition...limited to sixty copies (60), signed and numbered...No. 3. [Signed] G. A. Moore." Cover title: Political excerpts. 51-4359
1. Church and state. 2. Jurisprudence. 3. Canon law. I. Moore, George Albert, 1893- ed. and tr. II. Title. III. Title: Political excerpts.

SUGDEN, Christopher. 261.7
A different dream : non-violence as practical politics / by Christopher Sugden. Bramcote : Grove Books, 1976. 24 p. ; 22 cm. (Grove booklet on ethics ; no. 12 ISSN 0305-4241s) Includes bibliographical references. [BT736.6.S83] 77-374343 ISBN 0-901710-95-4 : £0.30
1. Nonviolence—Moral and religious aspects. I. Title.

TAYLOR, Ernest Richard. 261.7
Methodism & politics, 1791-1851 : Thirlwall and Gladstone prize essay, 1933 / by E. R. Taylor New York : Russell & Russell, 1975. x, 226 p. ; 20 cm. Reprint of the 1935 ed. published by Cambridge University Press, Cambridge, Eng. Includes index. Bibliography: p. 217-222. [BX8276.T3 1975] 73-94149 ISBN 0-8462-1781-3 : 16.00
1. Methodism—History. 2. Great Britain—Politics and government—19th century. 3. Church and state in Great Britain. I. Title.

THOMPSON, Kenneth W 1921- 261.7
Christian ethics and the dilemmas of foreign policy. Durham, N.C., Published for the Lilly Endowment Research Program in Christianity and Politics by the Duke University Press, 1959. 148 p. 22 cm. Includes bibliography. [BR115.P7T49] 59-15344
1. Christianity and politics. 2. International relations. 3. Christian ethics. I. Title.

THORNTON, John Wingate, 1818-1878, ed. 261.7
The pulpit of the American Revolution; political sermons of the period of 1776. Historical introd. and notes by John Wingate Thornton. New York, Da Capo Press, 1970. 537 p. 23 cm. (The Era of the American Revolution) Reprint of the 1860 ed. published by Gould and Lincoln, Boston. Contents.Contents.—Dr. Mayhew's sermon of Jan. 30, 1750.—Dr. Chauncy's thanksgiving sermon on the repeal of the Stamp act, 1766.—Mr. Cooke's election sermon, 1770.—Mr. Gordon's thanksgiving sermon, 1774.—Dr. Langdon's election sermon at Watertown 1775.—Mr. West's election sermon, 1776.—Mr. Payson's election sermon, 1778.—Mr. Howard's election sermon, 1780.—Dr. Stiles's election sermon, 1783. [E297.T5 1970b] 71-109611 ISBN 0-306-71907-X
1. United States—History—Revolution, 1775-1783—Addresses, sermons, etc. I. Title.

THORNTON, John Wingate, 1818-1878, ed. 261.7
The pulpit of the American Revolution; or, The political sermons of the period of 1776. With a historical introd., notes, and illus. by John Wingate Thornton. New York, B. Franklin [1970] 537 p. illus., port. 23 cm. (American classics in history and social science, 109) (Research and source works series, 440.) Reprint of the 1860 ed. Contents.Contents.—Dr. Mayhew's sermon of Jan. 30, 1750.—Dr. Chauncy's thanksgiving sermon on the repeal of the Stamp act, 1766.—Mr. Cooke's election sermon, 1770.—Mr. Gordon's thanksgiving sermon, 1774.—Dr. Langdon's election sermon at Watertown, 1775.—Mr. West's election sermon, 1776.—Mr. Payson's election sermon, 1778.—Mr. Howard's election sermon, 1780.—Dr. Stiles's election sermon, 1783. [E297.T51 1970] 77-114833
1. United States—History—Revolution, 1775-1783—Addresses, essays, lectures. I. Title.

TOLERANCE and the Catholic, a symposium; translated by George Lamb. New York, Sheed and Ward, 1955. viii, 199p. 22cm. Translation of Tolerance et communaute humaine. Bibliographical footnotes. [BR1610.T615] 55-7485 261.7
1. Toleration.

TURNER, Frederick C. 261.7
Catholicism and political development in Latin America, by Frederick C. Turner. Chapel Hill, University of North Carolina Press [1971] xv, 272 p. 24 cm. Bibliography: p. 255-259. [BX1426.2.T87] 78-123100 ISBN 0-8078-1164-5 8.75
1. Catholic Church in Latin America. 2. Latin America—Politics and government—1948- I. Title.

VALENTINE, Foy. 261.7
Citizenship for Christians. Nashville, Broadman Press [1965] 127 p. 20 cm. Bibliographical references included in "Notes" (p. 124-127) [BR115.P7V3] 65-21197
1. Christianity and politics. 2. Citizenship. I. Title.

VALENTINE, Foy. 261.7
Citizenship for Christians. Nashville, Broadman Press, [1974, c1965] 128 p. 18 cm. Includes bibliographical references. [BR115.P7V3] ISBN 0-8054-6112-4. 1.50 (pbk.)
1. Christianity and politics. 2. Citizenship. I. Title.
L.C. card no. for original ed.: 65-21197.

VEKEMANS, Roger. 261.7
Caesar and God; the priesthood and politics. Maryknoll, N.Y., Orbis Books [1972] x, 118 p. 21 cm. Translation of Iglesia y mundo politico, sacerdocio y politica. Includes bibliographical references. [BR115.P7V32813] 77-179959 3.95
1. Christianity and politics. I. Title.

VERDUIN, Leonard. 261.7
The anatomy of a hybrid : a study in church-state relationships / by Leonard Verduin. Grand Rapids, Mich. : Eerdmans, c1976. 274 p. ; 21 cm. Includes bibliographical references and index. [BV630.2.V47] 76-3654 ISBN 0-8028-1615-0 pbk. : 3.95
1. Church and state—History. 2. Religious liberty—History. I. Title.

VON DER MEHDEN, Fred R 261.7
Religion and nationalism in Southeast Asia: Burma, Indonesia, the Philippines. Madison, University of Wisconsin Press, 1963. 253 p. illus. 23 cm. [BL65.N3V6] 63-13743
1. Nationalism and religion—Asia, Southeastern. 2. Asia, Southeastern—Religion. I. Title.

VON DER MEHDEN, Fred R. 261.7
Religion and nationalism in Southeast Asia: Burma, Indonesia, the Philippines. Madison, University of Wisconsin Press, 1963. 253 p. illus. 23 cm. [BL65.N3V6] 63-13743
1. Nationalism and religion—Asia, Southeastern. 2. Asia, Southeastern—Religion. I. Title.

VREE, Dale, 1944- 261.7
On synthesizing Marxism and Christianity / Dale Vree. New York : Wiley, [1976] p. cm. "A Wiley-Interscience publication." Bibliography: p. [HX536.V74] 76-27706 ISBN 0-471-01603-9 : 9.95
1. Communism and Christianity. I. Title.

WALDROP, W. Earl 261.7
How to combat communism. St. Louis, Bethany [c.1962] 62p. 22cm. Bibl. 62-17918 1.00 pap.,
1. Communism and religion. I. Title.

WALSH, Henry Horace, 1899- 261.7
The Concordat of 1801: a study of the problem of nationalism in the relations of church and state, by Henry H. Walsh New York, AMS Press, 1967. 259 p. 23 cm. Reprint of the 1933 ed., which was issued as no. 387 of Studies in history, economics and public law. Originally presented as the author's thesis, Columbia, 1933. Bibliography: p. 247-249. [DC192.6.W3 1967] 72-188261
1. Catholic Church in France. 2. Catholic Church—Relations (diplomatic) with France. 3. Concordat of 1801 (France) 4. Church and state in France. 5. France—Foreign relations—Catholic Church. 6. France—History—Consulate and Empire, 1799-1815. 7. Nationalism and religion—France. I. Title. II. Series: Columbia studies in the social sciences, no. 387.

WEST, Charles C. 261.7
Communism and the theologians; study of an encounter. New York, Macmillan [1963, c.1958] 399p. 23cm. 63-2966 1.95 pap.,
1. Theology, Doctrinal—Hist.—20th cent. 2. Communism and religion. 3. Christianity—Philosophy. I. Title.

WEST, Charles C. 261.7
Communism and the theologians; study of an encounter. Philadelphia, Westminster Press [1958] 399 p. 24 cm. "The substance of the book was originally presented to Yale University in partial fulfilment of the requirements for the degree of doctor of philosophy [under title: Recent theological encounters with communism]" Bibliographical footnotes. [BT1240.W4] 58-9095
1. Communism and religion. 2. Apologetics—20th cent. I. Title.

WHO'S who in the P. O. A. U.? Huntington, Ind., Our Sunday Visitor Press, 1951. 128p. 20cm. [BR516.W45] 53-26243 261.7
1. Protestants and Other Americans United for Separation of Church and State. 2. Church and state in the U S. 3. Catholic Church—Doctrinal and controversial works—Catholic authors.

WICKER, Brian, 1929- 261.7
First the political kingdom; a personal appraisal of the Catholic left in Britain. [1st American ed.] Notre Dame [Ind.] University of Notre Dame Press [1968, c1967] xv, 141 p. 21 cm. Bibliography: p. 135-137. [BR115.P7W46 1968] 68-16171
1. Christianity and politics. 2. Socialism and Catholic Church. I. Title.

WILLIAMSON, Rene de Visme. 261.7
Independence and involvement; a Christian reorientation in political science. [Baton Rouge] Louisiana State University Press, 1964. xii, 269 p. 25 cm. Bibliographical references included in "Notes" (p. 257-269) [BT736.W5] 64-13637
1. Christianity and politics. I. Title.

WILLIAMSON, Rene de Visme 261.7
Independence and involvement; a Christian reorientation in political science. [Baton Rouge] La. State Univ. Pr. [c.]1964. xii, 269p. 25cm. Bibl. 64-13637 7.50
1. Christianity and politics. I. Title.

WILLIAMSON, Rene de Visme. 261.7
Politics and Protestant theology : an interpretation of Tillich, Barth, Bonhoeffer, and Brunner / Rene de Visme Williamson. Baton Rouge : Louisiana State University Press, c1976. p. cm. Includes bibliographical references. [BR115.P7W49] 76-20817 ISBN 0-8071-0193-1 : 10.95
1. Tillich, Paul, 1886-1965. 2. Barth, Karl, 1886-1968. 3. Bonhoeffer, Dietrich, 1906-1945. 4. Brunner, Heinrich Emil, 1889-1966. 5. Christianity and politics—History. I. Title.

WOOD, James Edward. 261.7
Church and state in Scripture, history, and constitutional law, by James E. Wood, Jr., E. Bruce Thompson [and] Robert T. Miller. Waco, Tex., Baylor University Press, 1958. vii, 148 p. 24 cm. (The J. M. Dawson studies in church and state) Bibliography: p. 146-147. [BV630.2.W6] 59-21543
1. Church and state. I. Title. II. Series.

WOODRUFF, Douglas, 1897- 261.7
Church and state. [1st ed.] New York, Hawthorn Books [1961] 128 p. 21 cm. (The Twentieth century encyclopedia of Catholicism, v. 89. Section 9: The church and the modern world) Includes bibliography. [BX1791.W65] 61-18916

1. Church and state — Catholic church. I. Title.

BARTH, Karl, 1886- 261.704
Community, state, and church; three essays. [Tr. from German] Introd. by Will Herberg. [Gloucester, Mass., Peter Smith, 1961, c.] 1960. 193p. (Anchor books, A221 rebound in cloth) 3.00
1. Theology—20th cent.—Addresses, essays, lectures. 2. Reformed Church—Addresses, essays, lectures. I. Title.

BARTH, Karl, 1886-1968. 261.704
Community, state, and church; three essays. With an introd. by Will Herberg. [1st ed.] Garden City, N.Y., Doubleday, 1960. 193 p. 18 cm. (Anchor books, A221) Translated from the German. Contents.Contents.—Gospel and law.—Church and state.—The Christian community and the civil community.—Bibliography (p. 191-193) [BX9410.B323] 60-13233
1. Reformed Church—Addresses, essays, lectures. 2. Theology—20th century—Addresses, essays, lectures. I. Title.

FEY, Harold Edward, 1898- 261.7'06'273
With sovereign reverence; the first twenty-five years of Americans United, by Harold E. Fey. Rockville, Md., R. Williams Press [1974] 87 p. illus. 21 cm. [BR516.F48] 73-94001 4.95
1. Protestants and Other Americans United for Separation of Church and State. 2. Church and state in the United States. I. Title.

EHLER, Sidney Z., ed. and tr. 261.7'08
Church and state through the centuries; a collection of historic documents with commentaries, translated and edited by Sidney Z. Ehler and John B. Morrall. New York, Biblo and Tannen, 1967. xii, 625 p. 24 cm. [BV630.A1E37 1967] 66-30406
1. Church and state—History—Sources. I. Morrall, John B., joint ed. and tr.

HUNT, George Laird, ed. 261.708
Calvinism and the political order; essays prepared for the Woodrow Wilson Lectureship of the National Presbyterian Center, Washington, D. C. George L. Hunt, Editor; John T. McNeill, consulting editor. Philadelphia, Westminster Press [1965] 216 p. 21 cm. [BV631.H8] 65-23269
1. Church and state—Addresses, essays, lectures. I. United Presbyterian Church in the U.S.A. Council for the National Presbyterian Church and Center. II. Title.

SMITH, Elwyn Allen, 1919- ed. 261.708
Church-state relations in ecumenical perspective, ed.by Elwyn A. Smith. [Pittsburgh] Duquesne Univ. Pr., 1966. 280p. 22cm. With one exception, these essays were delivered during the academic year 1956-66, to the grad. Seminar in Ecumenics conducted by Duquesne Univ. (Pittsburgh) & the Pittsburgn Theological Seminary (United Presbyterian) Bibl. [BV630.2S6] 66-18450 4.95
1. Church and state—Addresses, essays, lectures. I. Duquesne University, Pittsburgh. II. Pittsburgh. Theological Seminary. III. Title.

EHLER, Sidney Z ed. and tr. 261.7082
Church and state through the centuries; a collection of historic documents with commentaries, translated and edited by Sidney Z. Ehler and John B. Morrall. Westminster, Md., Newman Press [1954] 625 p. 22 cm. [BV630.A1E37] 54-12446
1. Church and state—Hist.—Sources. I. Morrall, John B., joint ed. and tr. II. Title.

EHLER, Sidney Z 261.709
Twenty centuries of church and state; a survey of their relations in past and present. Westminster, Md., Newman Press, 1957. 160 p. illus. 21 cm. (A Newman paperback) [BV630.E4] 57-8612
1. Church and state—Hist. I. Title.

CHURCH and government in the Middle Ages : essays presented to C. R. Cheney on his seventieth birthday / and edited by C. N. L. Brooke ... [et al.]. Cambridge ; New York : Cambridge University Press, c1976. p. cm. Includes index. Bibliography: p. [BR252.C54] 75-41614 ISBN 0-521-21172-7 : 26.50 261.7'09'02
1. Cheney, Christopher Robert, 1906- 2. Church history—Middle Ages, 600-1500—Addresses, essays, lectures. 3. Middle Ages—History—Addresses, essays, lectures. 4. Middle Ages—Historiography—Addresses, essays, lectures. 5. Canon law—History—Addresses, essays, lectures. I. Brooke, Christopher Nugent Lawrence. II. Cheney, Christopher Robert, 1906-
Contents omitted

TELLENBACH, Gerd, 1903- 261.7'09'021
Church, state, and Christian society at the time of the investiture contest. Translated by R. F. Bennett. New York, Harper & Row [1970, c1959] xxiii, 196 p. 21 cm. (Harper torchbooks) Translation of Libertas; Kirche und Weltordnung im Zeitalter des Investiturstreites. Includes bibliographical references. [BX1790.T43 1970] 75-19373 1.95
1. Church and state—History. 2. Investiture. 3. Liberty. I. Title.

HENLEY, Wallace. 261.7'092'4 B
The White House mystique / Wallace Henley. Old Tappan, N.J. : Revell, c1976. 126 p. ; 21 cm. [BX6495.H454A33] 75-30774 ISBN 0-8007-0774-5 : 4.95
1. Henley, Wallace. 2. Christianity and politics. I. Title.

LUTHER, Martin, 1483-1546. 261.7'092'4
Luther—selected political writings / edited and with an introd. by J. M. Porter. Philadelphia : Fortress Press, [1974] v, 153 p. ; 21 cm. Bibliography: p. 23-24. [BR333.5.P6P67] 74-76931 ISBN 0-8006-1079-2 pbk. : 3.50 3.50
1. Luther, Martin, 1483-1546—Political science. I. Porter, Jene M., ed.
Contents omitted.

MORINO, Claudio. 261.7'0924
Church and state in the teaching of St. Ambrose. Translated by M. Joseph Costelloe. Washington, Catholic University of America Press, 1969. viii, 218 p. ports. 24 cm. Translation of Chiesa e stato nella dottrina di S. Ambrogio. Includes bibliographical references. [BV630.2.M613] 67-31282 9.95
1. Ambrosius, Saint, Bp. of Milan. 2. Church and state. I. Title.

PELOTTE, Donald E. 261.7'092'4
John Courtney Murray : theologian in conflict / by Donald E. Pelotte. New York : Paulist Press, c1976. xi, 210 p. ; 24 cm. Includes index. Bibliography: p. 191-206. [BX4705.M977P44] 76-18046 ISBN 0-8091-0212-9 : 9.95
1. Murray, John Courtney. 2. Catholic Church—Biography. 3. Theologians—United States—Biography.

ROTMANN, Bernhard, ca.1495-1535? 261.7'092'4
Earthly and temporal power; translated and edited by George Albert Moore. Chevy Chase, Md., Country Dollar Press [1950] x, [xi], xi b-xi d, xiii-xx, 81 p. 28 cm. (The Moore series of English translations of source books) "Collector's edition ... limited to fifty (50) signed and numbered copies ... No. 27. [Signed]: G. A. Moore." German and English. Bibliography: p. xi d. [JC141.R63] 51-7395
1. State, The. 2. Anabaptists. I. Moore, George Albert, 1893- ed. and tr. II. Title.

SETTON, Kenneth Meyer, 1914- 261.7'0937
Christian attitude towards the emperor in the fourth century, especially as shown in addresses to the emperor, by Kenneth M. Setton. New York, AMS Press, 1967 [c1941] 239 p. 24 cm. (Studies in history, economics, and public law, no. 482) Originally presented as the author's thesis, Columbia, 1941. Includes bibliographical references. [BR170.S63 1967] 77-29917
1. Church and state in Rome. 2. Roman emperors. I. Title. II. Series: Columbia studies in the social sciences, 482.

RYLE, John Charles, Bp. of Liverpool, 1816-1900. 261.7'0941
Five Christian leaders of the eighteenth century. [London] Banner of Truth Trust, 1960;[stamped: distributed by Bible Truth Depot, Swengel, Pa.] 192p. 19cm. [BR758.R92 1960] 60-16371
1. Clergy—Gt. Brit. 2. Preaching— Hist.—Gt. Brit. I. Title.

SYKES, Norman, 1897-1961. 261.7'0941
Church and state in England in the XVIIIth century / by Norman Sykes. New York : Octagon Books, 1975. p. cm. (The Birkbeck lectures ; 1931-3) Reprint of the 1934 ed. published by the University Press, Cambridge, Eng. Includes index. Bibliography: p. [BR758.S9 1975] 75-29470 ISBN 0-374-97690-2 lib.bdg. : 15.50
1. Church of England—History. 2. Church and state in England. I. Title. II. Series.

MILLER, David W., 1940- 261.7'09415
Church, state, and nation in Ireland, 1898-1921 [by] David W. Miller. [Pittsburgh] University of Pittsburgh Press [1973] x, 579 p. map. 22 cm. Bibliography: p. [561]-567. [BX1505.M54 1973] 72-95453 ISBN 0-8229-1108-6 14.95
1. Catholic Church in Ireland. 2. Ireland—Politics and government—1901-1910. 3. Ireland—Politics and government—1910-1921. I. Title.

MILLER, David W., 1940- 261.7'09415
Church, state, and nation in Ireland, 1898-1921 [by] David W. Miller. [Dublin] Gill and Macmillan [1973] x, 579 p. 23 cm. Based on the author's thesis, University of Chicago. Bibliography: p. [561]-567. [BX1505.M54 1973b] 74-165171 ISBN 0-7171-0645-4 £8.25
1. Catholic Church in Ireland. 2. Ireland—Politics and government—1901-1910. 3. Ireland—Politics and government—1910-1921. I. Title.

WHYTE, John Henry, 1928- 261.7'09415
Church and state in modern Ireland, 1923-1970 [by] J. H. Whyte. [Dublin] Gill and Macmillan [1971] xii, 466 p. 23 cm. Bibliography: p. 433-448. [BR793.W49] 77-31562 ISBN 0-7171-0486-9 £4.25
1. Church and state in Ireland. I. Title.

CHILD, Gilbert William, 1832or3-1896. 261.7'0942
Church and state under the Tudors. New York, B. Franklin [1974] xix, 429 p. 23 cm. (Burt Franklin research & source works series. Philosophy & religious history monographs, 150) Reprint of the 1890 ed. published by Longmans, Green, London. Includes bibliographical references. [BR756.C5 1974] 73-183695 ISBN 0-8337-4041-5 19.50
1. Church and state in Great Britain. 2. Great Britain—Church history—16th century. I. Title.

FIGGIS, John Neville, 1866-1919. 261.7'0942
Churches in the modern state. 2d ed. New York, Russell & Russell [1973] xiii, 272 p. 20 cm. "The four lectures which make the main matter of this volume were delivered to the clergy in Gloucester in June, 1911." Reprint of the 1914 ed. published by Longmans, Green, London. Includes bibliographical references. [BV630.F5 1973] 72-173525 ISBN 0-8462-1700-7 14.00
1. Church of England. 2. Church and state. 3. Church and state in Great Britain. I. Title.
Contents Omitted.

HOOKER, Richard, 1553or4-1600. 261.7'0942
Ecclesiastical polity, book VIII. With an introd. by Raymond Aaron Houk. New York, Columbia University Press, 1931. [New York, AMS Press, 1973] xii, 346 p. 19 cm. Original ed. issued in series: Columbia University studies in English and comparative literature. Originally presented as Houk's thesis, Columbia, 1931. [BV649.H88 1973] 77-170046 ISBN 0-404-03329-6 10.50
1. Church and state in Great Britain. 2. Church polity. I. Houk, Raymond Aaron, 1888- II. Title. III. Series: Columbia University studies in English and comparative literature.

LYON, Thomas, 1912- 261.7'0942
The theory of religious liberty in England, 1603-39 / by T Lyon New York : Octagon Books, 1976. viii, 241 p. ; 20 cm. Reprint of the 1937 ed. published by University Press, Cambridge, Eng., which was issued as the Thirlwall prize essay, 1937. Includes index. [BR757.L96 1976] 76-6526 ISBN 0-374-95212-4 : 12.00
1. Religious liberty—England. 2. Great Britain—Politics and government—1603-1625. 3. Church and state in England. I. Title. II. Series: Thirlwall prize essay ; 1937.

SPOTTS, Frederic. 261.7'0942
The churches and politics in Germany. [1st ed.] Middletown, Conn., Wesleyan University Press [1973] xii, 419 p. illus. 24 cm. Bibliography: p. 367-399. [BR856.3.S6] 72-11050 ISBN 0-8195-4059-5 12.50
1. Church and state in Germany (Federal Republic, 1949-) I. Title.

SYKES, Norman, 1897- 261.70942
Church and state in England in the XVIIIth century. Hamden, Conn., Archon Books, 1962 [c1934] 455 p. 23 cm. (The Birkbeck lectures in ecclesiastical history, 1931-3) Includes bibliography. [BR758.S9 1962] 61-66508
1. Church and state in Great Britain. 2. Church of England — Hist. I. Title.

SYKES, Norman, 1897- 261.70942
Church and state in England in the XVIIIth century. Hamden. Conn., Archon Bks. [dist. Shoe String] 1962[c.1934] 455p. (Birkbeck lecturesin ecclesiastical hist. 1931-3) Bib. 61-66508 11.75
1. Church and state in Great Britain. 2. Church of England—Hist. I. Title.

HERMAN, Stewart Winfield, 1909- 261.7'0943
It's your souls we want, by Stewart W. Herman, Jr. New York, Harper, 1943. [New York, AMS Press, 1973] xv, 315 p. 23 cm. Includes bibliographical references. [BR856.H45 1973] 72-180406 ISBN 0-404-56130-6 17.00
1. Germany—Religion—1933-1945. 2. Church and state in Germany—1933-1945. I. Title.

INTERNATIONAL Scholars' Conference, 1st, Wayne State University, 1970. 261.7'0943
The German church struggle and the Holocaust. Edited by Franklin H. Littell [and] Hubert G. Locke. Detroit, Wayne State University Press, 1974. 328 p. 24 cm. Sponsored by the Walker and Gertrude Cisler Library of the Grosberg Religious Center. Includes bibliographical references. [BR856.I57 1970] 72-9352 ISBN 0-8143-1492-9 15.95
1. Church and state in Germany—1933-1945—Congresses. 2. Holocaust, Jewish (1939-1945)—Congresses. I. Littell, Franklin Hamlin, ed. II. Locke, Hubert G., ed. III. Walker and Gertrude Cisler Library. IV. Title.

ZABEL, James A. 261.7'0943
Nazism and the pastors : a study of the ideas of three Deutsche Christen groups / by James A. Zabel. Missoula, Mont. : Published by Scholars Press for the American Academy of Religion, c1976. xv, 243 p. ; 22 cm. (Dissertation series - American Academy of Religion ; no. 14) Bibliography: p. 235-243. [BR856.Z23] 75-30607 ISBN 0-89130-040-6 : 4.20
1. Deutsche Christen (Nationalkirchliche Einung) 2. Glaubensbewegung "Deutsche Christen". 3. Luther-Deutsche (Reformatorische Reichskirche) 4. Church and state in Germany—1933-1945. 5. National socialism. I. American Academy of Religion. II. Title. III. Series: American Academy of Religion. Dissertation series — American Academy of Religion ; no. 14.

BERNARD, Paul P. 261.7'09436
The origins of Josephinism; two studies [by] Paul P. Bernard. Colorado Springs, Research Committee, Colorado College, 1964. 52 p. 23 cm. (The Colorado College studies, no. 7) Contents.Contents.—Joseph I and the reforms of Joseph II.—On the ideological origins of Josephinism. Bibliographical footnotes. [AS36.C563 no. 7] 70-10768
1. Josephinism. I. Title. II. Series: Colorado College, Colorado Springs. Research Committee. The Colorado College studies, no. 7

GALTON, Arthur Howard, 1852-1921. 261.7'0944
Church and state in France, 1300-1907. New York, B. Franklin [1972] xxiv, 290 p. 23 cm. (Burt Franklin research and source works series. Selected studies in history, economics & social science: n.s. 4(c) Modern European studies) "Loi du 9 decembre, 1905, concernant la separation des eglises et de l'etat": p. [269]-283. Bibliography: p. [xvii]-xxi. [DC59.5.G2 1972] 70-185939 ISBN 0-8337-4124-1 15.00
1. Church and state in France. I. France. Laws, statutes, etc. Loi du 9 decembre, 1905, concernant la separation des eglises et de l'etat. 1972. II. Title.

RAUCH, Rufus William. 261.7'0944
Politics and belief in contemporary France: Emmanuel Mounier and Christian democracy, 1932-1950, by R. William Rauch, Jr. The Hague, Nijhoff, 1972. 363 p. 24 cm. Includes bibliographical references. [D2430.M694R38] 73-160173 ISBN 9-02-471281-5
1. Mounier, Emmanuel, 1905-1950. 2. Mouvement republicain populaire. 3. Esprit; revue internationale. 4. Center parties—France. I. Title.
Distributed by Humanities; 15.00.

JEMOLO, Arturo Carlo, 1891- 261.70945
Church and state in Italy, 1850-1950. Tr. [from Italian] by David Moore. Philadelphia, Dufour 1961 [c1960] 344p. 60-16882 6.50
1. Church and state in Italy. I. Title.

MID-EUROPEAN Law Project. 261.7'0947
Church and state behind the Iron Curtain: Czechoslovakia, Hungary, Poland, Romania, with an introduction on the Soviet Union. Prepared under the general editorship of Vladimir Gsovski. Westport, Conn., Greenwood Press [1973, c1955] xxxi, 311 p. 22 cm. Original ed. issued as no. 17 of Praeger publications in Russian history and world communism and in the series: Research studies of the Mid-European Law Project. Includes bibliographies. [BR738.6.M5 1973] 72-12333 ISBN 0-8371-6726-4 13.50
1. Church and state in Eastern Europe. I. Gsovski, Vladimir, 1891-1961, ed. II. Title.

RELIGION and atheism 261.7'0947
in the U.S.S.R. and Eastern Europe / edited by Bohdan R. Bociurkiw and John W. Strong, assisted by Jean K. Laux. Toronto ; Buffalo : University of Toronto Press, 1975. xviii, 412 p. ; 23 cm. (The Carleton series in Soviet and East European studies) "The idea of this volume was conceived at an international symposium ... organised at Carleton University in April 1971 by the Institute of Soviet and East European Studies." Includes bibliographical references and index. [HX536.R437 1975] 73-89059 ISBN 0-8020-2115-8 : 17.50
1. Communism and religion—Addresses, essays, lectures. 2. Church and state in Russia—Addresses, essays, lectures. 3. Church and state in Eastern Europe—Addresses, essays, lectures. I. Bociurkiw, Bohdan R. II. Strong, John W., 1930- III. Laux, Jean K. IV. Series.

RELIGION and atheism 261.7'0947
in the U.S.S.R. and Eastern Europe / edited by Bohdan R. Bociurkiw and John W. Strong, assisted by Jean K. Laux. Toronto ; Buffalo : University of Toronto Press, 1975. xviii, 412 p. ; 23 cm. (The Carleton series in Soviet and East European studies) "The idea of this volume was conceived at an international symposium ... organised at Carleton University in April 1971 by the Institute of Soviet and East European Studies." Includes bibliographical references and index. [HX536.R437 1975] 73-89059 ISBN 0-8020-2115-8 : 17.50
1. Communism and religion—Addresses, essays, lectures. 2. Church and state in Russia—Addresses, essays, lectures. 3. Church and state in Eastern Europe—Addresses, essays, lectures. I. Bociurkiw, Bohdan R. II. Strong, John W., 1930- III. Laux, Jean K. IV. Title. V. Series.

SIMON, Gerhard. 261.7'0947
Church, state, and opposition in the U.S.S.R. Translated by Kathleen Matchett in collaboration with the Centre for the Study of Religion and Communism. Berkeley, University of California Press [1974] x, 248 p. 23 cm. Translation of Die Kirchen in Russland. Bibliography: p. 242-244. [BR933.S5413] 73-87754 ISBN 0-520-02612-8 12.00
1. Church and state in Russia. I. Title.

CLAYTON, Geoffrey Hare, 261.70968
Abp., 1884-1957.
Where we stand; Archbishop Clayton's charges, 1948-57, chiefly relating to church and state in South Africa. Edited by C. T. Wood. Cape Town, New York, Oxford University Press, 1960. 55p. 22cm. [BX5700.6.C5] 60-51515
1. Church of the Province of South Africa—Pastoral letters and charges. 2. Church and state in South Africa. I. Title.

LEDIT, Joseph Henry, 261.70972
1898-
Rise of the downtrodden. Translated by Joseph Ledit & Anthony Santacruz. New York. Society of St. Paul [1959] 260p. 22cm. Translation of Le front des pauvres. [BX1428.2.L413] 60-1516
1. Catholic Church in Mexico. I. Title.

HOLLERAN, Mary 261.7'097281
Patricia, 1905-
Church and state in Guatemala. New York, Octagon Books, 1974 [c1949] 359 p. illus. 24 cm. Reprint of the ed. published by Columbia University Press, New York, in series: Studies in history, economics, and public law, no. 549. Bibliography: p. 341-345. [BX1438.H64 1974] 73-19956 ISBN 0-374-93929-2 13.00
1. Church and state in Guatemala. 2. Patronage, Ecclesiastical—Guatemala. I. Title. II. Series: Columbia studies in the social sciences, no. 549.

DEWART, Leslie. 261.7097291
Christianity and revolution; the lesson of Cuba. New York, Herder and Herder [1963] 320 p. 21 cm. [BR115.P7D46] 63-19832
1. Christianity and politics. 2. Communism — Cuba. 3. Cuba — Hist. — 1959- 4. Church and state in Cuba. I. Title.

DEWART, Leslie 261.7097291
Christianity and revolution the lesson of Cuba. [New York] Herder & Herder [c.1963] 320p. 21cm. 63-19832 5.50
1. Christianity and politics. 2. Communism—Cuba 3. Cuba—Hist.—1959- 4. Church and state in Cuba. I. Title.

BLANSHARD, Paul, 1892- 261.70973
God and man in Washngton. Boston, Beacon Press [c1960] 251p. 22cm. Includes bibliography. [BR516.B58] 60-5815
1. Church and state in the U. S. I. Title.

BLANSHARD, Paul 261.70973
[Bleecher]
God and man in Washington. Boston, Beacon Press [c.1960] 251p. 22cm. (16p. bibl. notes) 60-5815 3.50 bds.,
1. Church and state in the U. S. I. Title.

BUTTS, Robert Freeman, 261.7'0973
1910-
The American tradition in religion and education, by R. Freeman Butts. Westport, Conn., Greenwood Press [1974, c1950] xiv, 230 p. 22 cm. Reprint of the ed. published by Beacon Press, Boston, in series: Beacon Press studies in freedom and power. Includes bibliographical references. [BR516.B85 1974] 73-20903 ISBN 0-8371-5875-3 11.00
1. Church and state in the United States. 2. Church and education in the United States. I. Title.

CHERRY, C. Conrad, ed. 261.70973
Religion in the public domain; proceedings [of the] consultation at University Park, Pa., May 1-3, 1966. Edited by C. Conrad Cherry and John Y. Fenton. [University Park? Pa., 1966] iv, 211 p. 28 cm. "Sponsored by the Pennsylvania State University Department of Religious Studies and the Center for Continuing Liberal Education in cooperation with the American Jewish Committee [and others]" Bibliography: p. 165-168. Bibliographical footnotes. [BR516.C46] 67-136
1. Church and state in the United States—Congresses. 2. United States—Religion—Congresses. I. Fenton, John Y., joint ed. II. Pennsylvania. State University. Dept. of Religious Studies. III. Pennsylvania. State University. Center for Continuing Liberal Education. IV. Title.

COGLEY, John, ed. 261.70973
Religion in America; original essays on religion in a free society. New York, Meridian Books [1958] 288p. 18cm. (Meridian books, M60) [BR516.C68] 58-12381
1. U. S.—Religion. 2. Church and state and state in the U. S. I. Title.

COLWELL, Stephen, 261.7'0973
1800-1871.
The position of Christianity in the United States, in its relations with our political institutions, and specially with reference to religious instruction in the public schools. New York, Arno Press, 1972 [c1854] 175 p. 23 cm. (Religion in America, series II) [BR525.C63 1972] 78-38444 ISBN 0-405-04063-6
1. Catholic Church—Education. 2. Church and state in the United States. 3. Religious education—United States. I. Title.

COTHAM, Perry C. 261.7'0973
Politics, Americanism, and Christianity / Perry C. Cotham. Grand Rapids : Baker Book House, c1976. 335 p. ; 23 cm. "A Canon Press book." Includes index. Bibliography: p. 321-326. [BR115.P7C688] 75-39165 ISBN 0-8010-2377-7 : 8.95
1. Christianity and politics. 2. United States—Religion. I. Title.

GADDY, C. Welton. 261.7'0973
Proclaim liberty! / C. Welton Gaddy. Nashville : Broadman Press, c1975. 154 p. ; 20 cm. Includes bibliographical references. [BR115.P7G267] 75-2931 ISBN 0-8054-2225-0 : 2.95
1. Christianity and politics. 2. Allegiance—United States. 3. Sermons, American. 4. Worship programs. I. Title.

GADDY, C. Welton. 261.7'0973
Profile of a Christian citizen / C. Welton Gaddy. Nashville : Broadman Press, [1975] c1974. 125 p. ; 20 cm. Includes bibliographical references. [BR115.P7G27 1975] 74-82584 ISBN 0-8054-8420-5 : 1.95
1. Christianity and politics. 2. Citizenship. I. Title.

GREENE, Evarts 261.7'0973
Boutell, 1870-1947.
Religion and the state : the making and testing of an American tradition / by Evarts B. Greene. New York : AMS Press, 1976. 172 p. ; 22 cm. Reprint of the 1941 ed. published by New York University Press, New York, in series: Anson G. Phelps lectureship on early American history, New York University, Stokes Foundation. Includes bibliographical references and index. [BR516.G67 1976] 75-41122 ISBN 0-404-14548-5 : 14.50
1. Church and state in the United States. 2. Religious liberty—United States. I. Title. II. Series: New York University. Stokes Foundation. Anson G. Phelps lectureship on early American history.

HARPER, William A., 261.7'0973
comp.
Toward a new politics, edited by William A. Harper. New York, MSS Information Corp. [1973] p. [BR115.P7H354] 73-12924 ISBN 0-8422-5122-7 10.00
1. Christianity and politics—Addresses, essays, lectures. 2. United States—Politics and government—Addresses, essays, lectures. I. Title.
Contents omitted.

HEFLEY, James C. 261.7'0973
Washington : Christians in the corridors of power / James C. Hefley and Edward E. Plowman. Wheaton, Ill. : Tyndale House Publishers, 1975. 200 p. ; 21 cm. Includes bibliographical references. [BR115.P7H43] 75-13635 ISBN 0-8423-7815-4 pbk. : 3.95
1. Christianity and politics. 2. Statesmen—United States—Religious life. I. Plowman, Edward E., joint author. II. Title.

HEIMERT, Alan E. 261.70973
Religion and the American mind, from the Great Awakening to the Revolution [by] Alan Heimert. Cambridge, Harvard University Press, 1966. x, 668 p. 25 cm. "Biographical glossary": p. 555-563. Bibliographical references included in "Sources" & "Notes" (p. 564-629) [BR520.H4] 66-14444
1. Religious thought—United States. 2. United States—Church history. I. Title.

KRAYBILL, Donald B. 261.7'0973
Our star-spangled faith / Donald B. Kraybill ; introd. by Martin E. Marty. Scottdale, Pa. : Herald Press, c1976. 216 p. : ill. ; 18 cm. Includes bibliographical references. [BR516.K68 1976] 75-46167 ISBN 0-8361-1797-2 pbk. : 2.50
1. Church and state in the United States. 2. United States—Religion. I. Title.

LOWELL, C. Stanley. 261.7'0973
The great church-state fraud [by] C. Stanley Lowell. Washington, R. B. Luce [1973] 224 p. 23 cm. Includes bibliographical references. [BR516.L783] 72-94949 7.50
1. Church and state in the United States. I. Title.

MENENDEZ, Albert J. 261.7'0973
Religion at the polls / by Albert J. Menendez. Philadelphia : Westminster Press, c1977. 248 p. ; 21 cm. Bibliography: p. 237-248. [BL2530.U6M46] 76-30655 ISBN 0-664-24117-4 pbk. : 5.95
1. Religion and politics—United States. 2. Presidents—United States—Election—History. I. Title.

NICHOLS, Roy Franklin, 261.70973
1896-
Religion and American democracy. Baton Rouge, Louisiana State University Press, 1959. 108p. 21cm. (Rockwell lectures) Includes bibliography. [BR516.N5] 59-9085
1. U. S.—Religion. 2. Church and state in the U. S. I. Title.

PROTESTANTS and Other 261.70973
Americans United for Separation of Church and State.
Studies in church-state relations: the American way. Washington, 1963. 71 p. 23 cm. 63-37042
1. Church and state in the U.S. I. Title.

*RIGA, Peter J. 261.7'0973
Give unto Caesar what are God's: the Christian and political life, [by] Peter J. Riga. 1st. ed. [Jericho] N.Y., Exposition Press [1974, c1973] 175 p. 22 cm. [BR516.] ISBN 0-682-47843-1 6.00
1. Church and State in the United States. I. Title.

ROY, Ralph Lord. 261.70973
Communism and the churches. [1st ed.] New York, Harcourt, Brace [1960] 495p. 22cm. (Communism in American life) Includes bibliography. [BR517.R64] 60-10941
1. U. S.—Religion. 2. Communism—U. S. I. Title.

SCHAFF, Philip, 1819- 261.7'0973
1893.
Church and state in the United States; or, The American idea of religious liberty and its practical effects. New York, Arno Press, 1972 [c1888] 183 p. 24 cm. (Religion in America, series II) Original ed. issued as vol. 2, no. 4 of the Papers of the American Historical Association series. [BR516.S3 1972] 75-38462 ISBN 0-405-04083-0
1. Church and state in the United States. 2. Religious liberty—United States. I. Title. II. Series. III. Series: American Historical Association. Papers, v. 2, no. 4.

STOKES, Anson Phelps, 261.7'0973
1874-1958.
Church and state in the United States / by Anson Phelps Stokes and Leo Pfeffer. Rev. one-volume ed. Westport, Conn. : Greenwood Press, 1975, c1964. xii, 660 p. ; 23 cm. Reprint of the ed. published by Harper & Row, New York. Includes indexes. Bibliography: p. 623-631. [BR516.S85 1975] 73-15318 ISBN 0-8371-7186-5 lib.bdg. : 30.00
1. Church and state in the United States. I. Pfeffer, Leo, 1910- II. Title.

*SWEET, William 261.7'0973
Warren.
The story of religion in America. Grand Rapids, Mich., Baker Book House [1973, c1950] ix, 492 p, 22 cm. (Twin brooks series) [BL65.S8] ISBN 0-8010-8019-3 4.95 (pbk.)
1. Religion and state.—U.S. I. Title.

UNDER God, a new birth 261.7'0973
of freedom : award-winning bicentennial sermons / contributors, Giles Conwill ... [et al.]. Nashville : Upper Room, c1976. ix, 102 p. ; 20 cm. Includes bibliographical references. [BV4254.75.A1U52] 76-365611 2.50
1. American Revolution Bicentennial, 1776-1976—Sermons. 2. Sermons, American. I. Conwill, Giles.
Contents omitted.

WHITEHEAD, John W., 261.7'0973
1946-
The separation illusion : a lawyer examines the First amendment / by John W. Whitehead. Milford, MI : Mott Media, c1977. p. cm. Includes index. Bibliography: p. [BR516.W447] 77-7045 ISBN 0-915134-41-1 pbk. : 4.25
1. Church and state in the United States—History. 2. Christianity—United States. 3. United States—Moral conditions. I. Title.

HATCH, Nathan O. 261.7'0974
The sacred cause of liberty : republican thought and the millennium in Revolutionary New England / Nathan O. Hatch. New Haven : Yale University Press, 1977. p. cm. Includes index. Bibliography: p. [BR520.H34] 77-6626 ISBN 0-300-02092-9 : 12.50
1. Religious thought—New England. 2. Political science—New England. 3. Millennialism. 4. Clergy—New England. I. Title.

HANLEY, Thomas O'Brien 261.709752
Their rights and liberties; the beginnings of religious and political freedom in Maryland. Westminster, Md., Newman Press, [c.] 1959. xv, 142p. 23cm. (p. bibl.) illus. 59-14758 2.75
1. Church and state in Maryland. 2. Religious liberty—Maryland. I. Title.

BUCKLEY, Thomas E., 261.7'09755
1939-
Church and state in Revolutionary Virginia, 1776-1787 / Thomas E. Buckley. Charlottesville : University Press of Virginia, 1977. p. cm. Includes index. Bibliography: p. [BR555.V8B8] 77-4283 ISBN 0-8139-0692-X : 10.00
1. Church and state in Virginia—History. 2. Religious liberty—Virginia—History. I. Title.

MECHAM, John Lloyd, 261.7098
1893-
Church and state in Latin America; a history of politicoecclesiastical relations, by J. Lloyd Mecham. Rev. ed. Chapel Hill, University of North Carolina Press [1966] viii, 465 p. 24 cm. Bibliography: p. [429]-452. [BR600.M4 1966] 66-15511
1. Catholic Church in Latin America. 2. Church and state in Latin America.

ANTOINE, Charles, 261.7'0981
1929-
Church and power in Brazil. Translated by Peter Nelson. Maryknoll, N.Y., Orbis Books [1973] xi, 275 p. 22 cm. Translation of L'Eglise et le pouvoir au Bresil. Includes bibliographical references. [BX1466.2.A6413] 72-93341 4.95
1. Catholic Church in Brazil. 2. Church and state in Brazil. I. Title.

BRUNEAU, Thomas C. 261.7'0981
The political transformation of the Brazilian Catholic Church [by] Thomas C. Bruneau. [London, New York] Cambridge University Press [1974] xiv, 270 p. map. 23 cm. (Perspectives on development [2]) Based on the author's thesis, University of California, Berkeley. Bibliography: p. [253]-264. [BX1466.2.B78] 73-79318 ISBN 0-521-20256-6 £5.50 ($16.50 U.S.)
1. Catholic Church in Brazil. 2. Church and state in Brazil. I. Title. II. Series.

BRENNAN, Niall. 261.7'0994
The politics of Catholics [by] Niall Brennan. Melbourne, Hill Publishing, 1972. 116 p. 23 cm. [BX1685.B73] 73-163206 ISBN 0-85572-044-1 4.25
1. Catholic Church in Australia. 2. Australia—Politics and government. I. Title.

BENDER, Harold Stauffer, 261.7'2
1897-1962.
The Anabaptists and religious liberty in the sixteenth century. Philadelphia, Fortress Press [1970] viii, 27 p. (p. 25-27 advertisement) 19 cm. (Facet books. Historical series, 16) "First published in Archiv fuer Reformationsgeschichte, 44 (1953), 32-50."

Bibliography: p. 23-24. [BX4931.2.B4 1970] 73-99611 1.00
1. Anabaptists. 2. Religious liberty—History—16th century. I. Title.

BYRD, Valois. 261.72
Pioneers of religious liberty. Nashville, Convention Press [1963, c1964] 101 p. 19 cm. Bibliographical footnotes. [BV741.B9] 63-22242
1. Religious liberty. 2. Baptists—Doctrinal and controversial works. I. Title.

CARLSON, Carl Emanuel, 261.72
1906-
Religious liberty; case studies in current church-state issues [by] C. Emanuel Carlson and W. Barry Garrett. Nashville, Convention Press [1964] ix, 149 p. 20 cm. Bibliography: p. 146-149. [BR516.C3] 63-22243
1. Religious liberty—U.S. I. Garrett, Wilkins Barry, 1915- joint author. II. Title.

CARLYLE, Alexander James, 261.7'2
1861-1943.
The Christian Church and liberty. New York, B. Franklin [1968] 159 p. 19 cm. (Selected essays in history & social science, 24) (Burt Franklin Research & source works, 214.) Reprint of the 1924 ed. [BV741] 68-56734
1. Religious liberty. I. Title.

CARRILLO DE ALBORNOZ, 261.72
Angel Francisco, 1905-
The basis of religious liberty. New York, Association Press [1963] 182 p. 23 cm. Includes bibliography. [BV741.C34] 63-16047
1. Religious liberty. I. Title.

COBB, Sanford Hoadley, 261.7'2
1838-1910.
The rise of religious liberty in America. New introd. by Leo Pfeffer. New York, Da Capo Press, 1973. p. (Civil liberties in American history) Reprint of the 1902 ed. published by Macmillan, New York. Bibliography: p. [BR516.C66 1973] 70-164514 ISBN 0-306-70289-4
1. Religious liberty—United States. 2. Church and state in the United States. I. Title.

DORRIES, Hermann. 261.72
Constantine and religious liberty. Translated from the German by Roland H. Bainton. New Haven, [Conn.] Yale University Press [c.] 1960. xi, 141 p. 21 cm. (The Terry lectures) (Bibl. note 133-134 & Bibl. footnotes) 60-7823 4.00
1. Constantinus I, the Great, Emperor of Rome, d. 337. 2. Religious liberty—Rome. I. Title.

KAMEN, Henry Arthur 261.7'2
Francis.
The rise of toleration [by] Henry Kamen. New York, McGraw-Hill [1967] 256 p. illus. (part col.), ports. 20 cm. (World university library) Bibliography: p. 249-250. [BR1610.K3 1967b] 66-24158
1. Toleration. 2. Religious liberty—History. I. Title.

KRISHNASWAMI, Arcot. 261.72
Study of discrimination in the matter of religious rights and practices. New York, United Naions, 1960. x, 79p. 23cm. (United Nations. [Document] E/CN.4/sub.2/200/rev.1) 'United Nations publication. Catalogue no.: 60. XIV. 2.' Bibliographical footnotes. [JX1977.A2 E/CN.4/sub.2/200/rev.1] 61-2431
1. Religious liberty. I. Title. II. Series.

LECLER, Joseph 261.72
Toleration and the Reformation. 2v. Tr. [from French] by T. L. Westow. New York, Association Press [1960] 432, 544p. 23cm. Bibl. 60-12723 25.00, bxd.
1. Toleration. 2. Religious liberty—Europe. 3. Reformation. I. Title.

LOANE, Marcus L., Bp. 261.72
Makers of religious freedom in the seventeenth century: Henderson, Rutherford, Bunyan, Baxter. [1st ed.] Grand Rapids, Eerdmans [1961] 240 p. illus. 23 cm. Includes bibliography. [BR757.L68] 59-6951
1. Religious liberty—Gt. Brit. 2. Henderson, Alexander, 1583-1646. 3. Rutherford, Samuel, 1600?-1661. 4. Bunyan, John, 1628-1688. 5. Baxter, Richard, 1615-1691. I. Title.

MCDONAGH, Enda. 261.7'2
Freedom or tolerance? The Declaration on religious freedom of Vatican Council II, the text with commentary in the context of the church-state discussion. [New York] Magi Books [1967] 155 p. 19 cm. First published under title: The Declaration on religious freedom of Vatican Council II. Bibliographical footnotes. [BX830.1962.A45L55 1967b] 67-21467
1. Religious liberty. I. Vatican Council. 2d, 1962-1965. The Declaration on religious freedom. II. Title.

MURRAY, John Courtney. 261.72
The problem of religious freedom. Westminster, Md., Newman Press, 1965. 112 p. 22 cm. (Woodstock papers; occasional essays for theology, no. 7) "Appeared originally in Theological studies 25, 1964." Bibliographical references included in "Notes" (p. 111-112) [BV741.M86] 65-19454
1. Religious liberty. I. Title. II. Series.

MURRAY, John Courtney 261.72
The problem of religious freedom. Westminster, Md., Newman [c.]1965. 112p. 22cm. (Woodstock papers; occasional essays for theology, no. 7) Appeared orig. in Theological studies, 25, 1964. Bibl. [BV741.M86] 65-19454 1.50 pap.,
1. Religious liberty. I. Title. II. Series.

REGAN, Richard J. 261.7'2
Conflict and consensus; religious freedom and the second Vatican Council [by] Richard J. Regan. New York, Macmillan [1967] 212 p. 21 cm. Includes bibliographies. [BX830 1962.A45L58] 67-19679
1. Vatican Council. 2d, 1962-1965. Declaratio de libertate religiosa. I. Title.

RELIGIOUS freedom, 1965 261.7'2
and 1975 : a symposium on a historic document / edited by Walter J. Burghardt New York : Paulist Press, 1976, c1977. v, 74 p. ; 21 cm. (Woodstock studies ; 1) Includes bibliographical references. [BX830 1962.A45L584] 76-45938 ISBN 0-8091-1993-5 pbk. : 2.45
1. Vatican Council. 2d, 1962-1965. Declaratio de libertate religiosa—Congresses. 2. Religious liberty—Congresses. I. Burghardt, Walter J. II. Title. III. Series.

SMITH, Elwyn Allen, 1919- 261.7'2
Religious liberty in the United States; the development of church-state thought since the Revolutionary era [by] Elwyn A. Smith. Philadelphia, Fortress Press [1972] xiv, 386 p. 24 cm. Includes bibliographical references. [BR516.S57] 70-178093 ISBN 0-8006-0071-1 10.95
1. Religious liberty—United States. 2. Church and state in the United States. I. Title.

SWIDLER, Leonard J. 261.7'2
Freedom in the church [by] Leonard Swidler. Dayton, Ohio, Pflaum Press, 1969. x, 142 p. 21 cm. (Themes for today) Bibliographical footnotes. [BV741.S94] 76-93013 2.95
1. Catholic Church—Doctrinal and controversial works—Catholic authors. 2. Religious liberty. I. Title.

UNDERHILL, Edward Bean, 261.7'2
1813-1901.
Tracts on liberty of conscience and persecution, 1614-1661, with an historical introduction. New York, B. Franklin [1966] cxxviii, 401 p. 24 cm. (Burt Franklin research source works series, 189) (Philosophy monographs, 11) Reprint of the 1846 ed., published for the Hanserd Knollys Society. Bibliographical footnotes. [BR757.U5 1966] 79-6729
1. Liberty of conscience—History. 2. Religious liberty—England. I. Title.

VATICAN Council. 2d,1962- 261.7'2
1965.
Declaration on religious freedom of Vatican Council II. Promulgated by Pope Paul VI, December 7, 1965, Commentary by Thomas F, Stransky New York, Paulist Press [1967] 190 p. 19 cm. (Vatican II documents) Contents.CONTENTS. -- Commentary, by T. F. Stransky. -- Study club questions. -- Outline of the declaration. -- Declaration on religious freedom. -- Appendix I: Bishop de Smedt's report on religious liberty. -- Appendix II: The method and principles of the declaration (Relatio, issued by the Secretariat for Promoting Christian Unity). -- Appendix III: The Declaration on religious freedom, by J. C. Murray. -- Appendix IV, part one: The declaration and the World Council of Churches. -- Appendix IV, part two: Religious freedom and the World Council of Churches, by L. Vischer. -- Selected bibliography (p. 187-190) [BX830 1962.A45D415] 67-16718
1. Religious liberty. I. Stransky, Thomas F., ed. II. Title.

WOGAMAN, J. Philip 261.7'2
Protestant faith and religious liberty [by] Philip Wogaman. Nashville, Abingdon [1967] 254p. 23cm. Bibl. [BV741.W65] 67-14993 4.75
1. Religious liberty. 2. Theology, Protestant. I. Title.

WOGAMAN, J. Philip. 261.7'2
Protestant faith and religious liberty [by] Philip Wogaman. Nashville, Abingdon Press [1967] 254 p. 23 cm. Includes bibliographies. [BV741.W65] 67-14993
1. Religious liberty. 2. Theology, Protestant. I. Title.

WOOD, Herbert George, 261.7'2
1879-1963.
Religious liberty to-day. New York, Octagon Books, 1973. viii, 149 p. 19 cm. Reprint of the 1949 ed. published by University Press, Cambridge, Eng., which was issued as no. 31 of Current problems. Includes bibliographical references. [BV741.W68 1973] 73-17441 ISBN 0-374-98716-5 8.00
1. Religious liberty. I. Title. II. Series: Current problems, 31.

WOOLLEY, Davis C 1908- 261.72
Champions of religious freedom. Rev. in 1963 from the book Champions of religious liberty by Rufus W. Weaver. Nashville, Convention Press [1964] xiv, 125 p. 20 cm. "Church study course of the Sunday School Board of the Southern Baptist Convention] This book is number 0871 in category 8, section for young people." Bibliographical footnotes. [BV741.W69] 63-22241
1. Religious liberty. 2. Baptists — Doctrinal and controversial works. I. Weaver, Rufus Washington, 1870-1947. Champions of religious liberty. II. Southern Baptist Convention. Sunday School Board. III. Title.

KETCHAM, Charles B., 261.7'2'08
comp.
Faith and freedom; essays in contemporary theology. Edited by Charles B. Ketcham and James F. Day. New York, Weybright and Talley [1969] x, 292 p. 22 cm. Bibliography: p. 277-280. [BV740.K37] 74-81496
1. Freedom (Theology)—Addresses, essays, lectures. I. Day, James F., 1920- joint comp. II. Title.

POLISHOOK, Irwin H. 261.7'2'08
Roger Williams, John Cotton, and religious freedom; a controversy in new and old England [by] Irwin H. Polishook. Englewood Cliffs, N.J., Prentice-Hall [1967] vi, 122 p. 21 cm. (American historical sources series: research and interpretation) Includes bibliographical references. [F82.W792] 67-20229
1. Williams, Roger, 1604?-1683. 2. Cotton, John, 1584-1652. 3. Religious liberty. I. Title.

BAINTON, Roland 261.7'2'0922
Herbert, 1894-
The travail of religious liberty; nine biographical studies, by Roland H. Bainton. [Hamden, Conn.] Archon Books, 1971 [c1951] 272 p. illus. 23 cm. Bibliography: p. [261]-266. [BV741.B26 1971] 76-122412 ISBN 0-208-01085-8 8.50
1. Religious liberty. 2. Christian biography. I. Title.

EDWARDS, Robert 261.7'2'09415
Dudley.
Church and state in Tudor Ireland; a history of penal laws against Irish Catholics, 1534-1603. With a foreword by Mary Hayden. New York, Russell & Russell [1972] xliii, 352 p. 23 cm. Reprint of the 1935 ed. Bibliography: p. 313-332. [BR795.E4 1972] 76-180608
1. Catholic Church in Ireland. 2. Church and state in Ireland. 3. Ireland—Politics and government. 4. Penal laws (against nonconformists)—Ireland. 5. Ireland—Religion. I. Title.

WILLIAMS, Roger, 261.7'2'0942
1604?-1683.
The fourth paper presented by Major Butler, with other papers edited and published by Roger Williams in London, 1652. With an introd. and notes by Clarence Saunders Brigham. New York, B. Franklin [1968] xxiii, 49 p. 24 cm. (Burt Franklin research & source works series, 312) (American classics in history & social science, 60.) On spine: Roger Williams on Major Butler's Fourth paper on religious tolerance. "Mr. Goads letter to Maior Butler" (p. [5]-10) signed Christopher Goad. Reprint of 1903 ed. which included a facsim. (p. 1-23) of the 1652 ed. [BV741.W6 1968] 68-57125
1. Religious liberty—Gt. Brit. 2. Gt. Brit.—Politics and government—1649-1660. I. Butler, William, 17th cent. II. Goad, Christopher, fl. 1651. III. Brigham, Clarence Saunders, 1877-1963, ed. IV. Title.

EVANS, Austin 261.7'2'094332
Patterson.
An episode in the struggle for religious freedom. New York, AMS Press [1970, c1924] xi, 235 p. 19 cm. Bibliography: p. 207-230. [BR359.N8E8 1970] 74-130618 ISBN 0-404-02357-6
1. Nuremberg—Church history. 2. Reformation—Germany—Nuremberg. 3. Religious liberty—Germany. I. Title.

O'BRIEN, Charles H. 261.7'2'09436
Ideas of religious toleration at the time of Joseph II; a study of the enlightenment among Catholics in Austria [by] Charles H. O'Brien. Philadelphia, American Philosophical Society, 1969. 80 p. 30 cm. (Transactions of the American Philosophical Society. New ser., v. 59, pt. 7) Bibliography: p. 72-76. [Q11.P6 n.s., vol. 59, pt. 7] 76-93502 2.50
1. Catholic Church in Austria. 2. Religious liberty—Austria. 3. Dissenters, Religious—Austria. I. Title. II. Series: American Philosophical Society, Philadelphia. Transactions, new ser., v. 59, pt. 7

HUGHEY, John David. 261.7'2'0946
Religious freedom in Spain: its ebb and flow. Freeport, N.Y., Books for Libraries Press [1970] xi, 211 p. 23 cm. Reprint of the 1955 ed. A revision of the author's thesis, Columbia University. Bibliography: p. 201-207. [BR1023.H8 1970] 77-119935
1. Religious liberty—Spain. 2. Protestants in Spain. 3. Church and state in Spain. I. Title.

COBB, Sanford 261.7'2'0973
Hoadley, 1838-1910.
The rise of religious liberty in America; a history. New York, Cooper Square Publishers, 1968. xx, 541 p. 24 cm. Reprint of the 1902 ed. Includes bibliographical references. [BR515.C6 1968] 68-27517
1. Religious liberty—United States. 2. Church and state in the United States. I. Title.

COBB, Sanford 261.7'2'0973
Hoadley, 1838-1910.
The rise of religious liberty in America; a history. With a new introd. by Paul L. Murphy. New York, Johnson Reprint Corp., 1970. xviii, xx, 541 p. 23 cm. (Series in American studies) Reprint of the 1902 ed. Bibliography: p. xviii (1st group) [BR516.C66 1970] 76-105360
1. Religious liberty—U.S. 2. Church and state in the United States. I. Title. II. Series.

COBB, Sanford 261.7'2'0973
Hoadley, 1838-1910.
The rise of religious liberty in America; a history. New York, B. Franklin [1970] xx, 541 p. 23 cm. (American classics in history and social science 140) (Burt Franklin research and source works series 529.) Reprint of the 1902 ed. Includes bibliographical references. [BR516.C66 1970b] 70-129031
1. Religious liberty—U.S. 2. Church and state in the United States. I. Title.

RELIGIOUS liberty. 261.7'2'0973
[New York] Board of Social Ministry, Lutheran Church in America, 1968. vi, 88 p. 20 cm. On cover: Christian social responsibility. Contents.Contents.—Christian freedom and religious liberty, by G. W. Forell.—Legal aspects of religious liberty, by P. G. Kauper.—Religious liberty and current tensions: problems beyond the constitution, by D. Oberholtzer. Includes bibliographical references. [BR516.R38] 68-3836
1. Religious liberty—United States. I. Lutheran Church in America. Board of Social Ministry. II. Title: Christian social responsibility.

COCKBURN, James Hutchison, 261.73
1882-
Religious freedom in eastern Europe. Richmond, John Knox Press [1953] 140p. 21cm. [BR735.C6] 53-6969
1. Religious liberty—Europe. I. Title.

CUNINGGIM, Merrimon, 1911- 261.73
-
Freedom's holy light. [1st ed.] New York, Harper [1955] 192p. 22cm. Includes bibliography. [BR516.C9] 54-11660
1. Religious liberty—U. S. 2. Church and state in the U. S. I. Title.

DAWSON, Joseph Martin, 261.73
1879-
America's way in church, state, and society. New York, Macmillan, 1953. 189p. 21cm. Includes bibliography. [BR516.D297] 53-1549
1. Church and state in the U. S. 2. Religions liberty—U. S. I. Title.

DELPECH, Jacques, 1887- 261.73
The oppression of Protestants in Spain. Translation from the French by Tom and Dolores Johnson. Pref. by Howard Schomer; introd. by John A. Mackay. Boston, Beacon Press [1955] 114p. 22cm. [BX4851.D415] 55-7802
1. Protestants in Spain. 2. Religious liberty—Spain. I. Title.

LAGO, Mary M 261.73
They live in the city. Photos. by Edward C. Meyer. New York, Friendship Press [1954] Friendship Press, 1954. c117p. illus. 21cm. 48p. 21cm. [BV625.L3] 54-6194
1. Church and social problems—Study and teaching. I. Poff, Betty. II. Title. III. Title: — How to use They live in the city,

LOCKE, John, 1632-1704. 261.73
Concerning civil government, second essay in Locke, John, 1632-1704. A letter concerning toleration. Chicago, Encyclopaedia Britannica [1955, c1952] [AC1.G72 vol. 35] 55-10342

I. Title.

LOCKE, John, 1632-1704. 261.73
A letter concerning toleration. [Translated by William Popple] Concerning civil government, second essay. An essay concerning human understanding. By John Locke. The principles of human knowledge, by George Berkeley. An enquiry concerning human understanding, by David Hume. Chicago, Encyclopaedia Britannica [1955, c1952] x, 509p. 25cm. (Great books of the Western World, v. 35) Bibliographical footnotes. [AC1.G72 vol. 35] 55-10342
1. Toleration. I. Locke, John, 1632-1704. Concerning civil government, second essay. II. Locke, John, 1632-1704. An essay concerning human understanding. III. Berkeley, George, Bp. of Cloyne, 1685-1753. The principles of human knowledge. IV. Hume, David, 1711-1776. An enquiry concerning human understanding. V. Popple, William, d. 1708, tr. VI. Title. VII. Title: Human understanding.

O'CONNELL, David A 261.73
Christian liberty. Westminster, Md., Newman Press [c1952] 142p. 22cm. (Thomlstic studies, no. 5) Includes bibliography. [BV741.O25] 53-1550
1. Religious liberty. I. Title.

RIDDELL, Walter 261.7'3
Alexander, 1881-1963.
The rise of ecclesiastical control in Quebec. [1st AMS ed.] New York, AMS Press [1968] 197 p. 23 cm. (Columbia University studies in the social sciences, 174) Reprint of the 1916 ed. Bibliography: p. 189-195. [BR575.Q3R5 1968] 75-76703
1. Church and state in Quebec. 2. Quebec (Province)—Social conditions. I. Title. II. Series: Columbia studies in the social sciences, 174

SCHAPIRO, Jacob Salwyn, 261.7'3
1879-
Anticlericalism; conflict between church and state in France, Italy, and Spain [by] J. Salwyn Schapiro. Princeton, N.J., Van Nostrand [1967] 207 p. 19 cm. (An Anvil original, 91) Bibliography: p. 203-205. [BX1791.S33] 67-5310
1. Church and state—Catholic church. 2. Anticlericalism. I. Title.

KRISHNASWAMI, Arcot. 261.74
Study of discrimination in the matter of religious rights and practices; report. [New York] 1959. 95p. 28cm. (United Nations. [Document] E/CN.4/Sub.2/200) [JX1977.A2 E/CN.4/Sub.2/200] 60-1252
1. Religious liberty. I. Title.

CHEN, Philip Stanley, 261.75
1903-
A new look at God. South Lancaster, Mass., Chemical Elements [c.]1962. 238p. 23cm. 62-4924 3.95
1. Religion and science—1946- I. Title.

DE HAAN, Martin Ralph, 261.75
1891-
Genesis and evolution. Grand Rapids, Zondervan Pub. House [1962] 152 p. 21 cm. [BS651.D43] 62-6076
1. Bible and science. I. Title.

HODGES, Herbert Arthur, 261.75
1905-
Christianity and the modern world view [2d ed. Dist. Greenwich, Conn., Seabury] 1962. 56p. 19cm. (Seraph) 1.00 pap.,
1. Christianity—20th cent. I. Title. II. Series: Viewpoints: contemporary issuesof thought and life, no. 13

MIXTER, Russell Lowell, 261.75
1906- ed.
Evolution and Christian thought today. [Contributors] V. Elving Anderson [and others] [1st ed.] Grand Rapids, Eerdmans [1959] 224 p. illus., diagrs. 24 cm. Bibliographical footnotes. [BL263.M54] 59-15641
1. Evolution. 2. Religion and science—1900- I. Anderson, Victor Elving, 1921- II. Title.

STUERMANN, Walter Earl, 261.75
1919-
Logic and faith, a study of the relations between science and religion. Philadelphia, Westminster Press [1962] 192 p. illus. 21 cm. (Westminster studies in Christian communication) [BL240.2.S8] 62-12647
1. Religion and science—1946- I. Title.

STUERMANN, Walter Earl, 261.75
1919-
Logic and faith, a study of the relations between science and religion. Philadelphia, Westminster [c.1962] 192p. illus. 21cm. (Westminster studies in Christian communication) Bibl. 62-12647 4.50
1. Religion and science—1946- I. Title.

WELLS, Albert N. 261.75
The Christian message in a scientific age. Richmond, John Knox Press [1962] 160 p. 21 cm. Bibliographical footnotes. [BL240.2.W4] 62-19483
1. Religion and science — 1900- I. Title.

WELLS, Albert N. 261.75
The Christian message in a scientific age. Richmond, Va., Knox [c.1962] 160p. 21cm. Bibl. 62-19483 3.75
1. Religion and science—1900- I. Title.

ABBOTT, Lyman, 1835-1922. 261.8
Christianity and social problems. With a new introd. by Timothy L. Smith. New York, Johnson Reprint Corp., 1970. xxi, v, 370 p. 19 cm. (Series in American studies) Reprint of the 1896 ed. Includes bibliographical references. [BT738.A2 1970] 70-110386
1. Sociology, Christian. I. Title.

ADAMS, Theodore Floyd, 261.8
1898-
Making your marriage succeed; the Christian basis for love and marriage. [1st ed.] New York, Harper [1953] 156p. 20cm. [HQ734.A243] [HQ734.A243] 173.1 52-13215 52-13215
1. Marriage. 2. Home. I. Title.

†ALBERIONE, Giacomo 261.8
Giuseppe, 1884-1971.
Design for a just society = (originally entitled Fundamentals of Christian sociology) / by James Alberione ; updated by the Daughters of St. Paul. [Boston] : St. Paul Editions, c1976. 247 p. : ill. ; 23 cm. Includes index. Bibliography: p. 223-224. [BT738.A4 1976] 76-975 4.00 pbk. : 3.00
1. Sociology, Christian (Catholic) I. Daughters of St. Paul. II. Title.

ARNOLD, Joan, 1929- 261.8
Shalom is ... whole community / by Joan Arnold. Philadelphia : United Church Press, [1975] p. cm. (A Shalom resource) "Published for Joint Educational Development." Bibliography: p. [HM131.A75] 75-22492 ISBN 0-8298-0298-3
1. Community. I. Title.

ASSMANN, Hugo, 1933- 261.8
Theology for a nomad church / Hugo Assmann ; translated by Paul Burns ; introd. by Frederick Herzog. Maryknoll, N.Y. : Orbis Books, c1975. 146 p. ; 23 cm. Translation of Teologia desde la praxis de la liberacion. Includes bibliographical references. [BT83.57.A8713 1975b] 75-13878 ISBN 0-88344-493-3 : 7.95. ISBN 0-88344-494-1 pbk. : 4.95
1. Liberation theology. I. Title.

AUER, Alfons 261.8
Open to the world: an analysis of lay spirituality. Tr. by Dennis Doherty, Carmel Callaghan. Baltimore, Helicon [1966] 337p. 22cm. Tr. of Weltoffener Christ. Bibl. [BX2350.5.A813] 66-25741 5.95
1. Spiritual life— Catholic authors. I. Title.
Available from Taplinger in New York.

*BAJEMA, Clifford E. 261.8
Abortion and the meaning of personhood [by] Clifford E. Bajema. Grand Rapids, Baker Book House [1974] 114 p. 22 cm. [HQ767.5] ISBN 0-8010-0624-4 3.95
1. Abortion—United States. 2. Pastoral counseling. I. Title.

BAUM, Gregory, 1923- 261.8
Religion and alienation : a theological reading of sociology / Gregory Baum. New York : Paulist Press, c1975. v, 296 p. ; 23 cm. Includes bibliographies and index. [BT738.B32] 75-28652 ISBN 0-8091-0205-6 : 10.95 ISBN 0-8091-1917-X pbk. : 6.95
1. Sociology, Christian. 2. Alienation (Theology) I. Title.

BEECHER, Henry Ward, 1813- 261.8
1887.
Freedom and war. Freeport, N.Y., Books for Libraries Press, 1971. iv, 445 p. 23 cm. (The Black heritage library collection) Reprint of the 1863 ed. [E458.B4 1971] 70-157361 ISBN 0-8369-8799-3
1. United States—Politics and government—Civil War, 1861-1865. 2. Slavery in the United States—Controversial literature—1859-1863. 3. United States—History—Civil War, 1861-1865—Addresses, sermons, etc. I. Title. II. Series.

BENJAMIN, Philip S. 261.8
The Philadelphia Quakers in the industrial age, 1865-1920 / Philip S. Benjamin. Philadelphia : Temple University Press, 1976. ix, 301 p. ; 22 cm. Includes index. Bibliography: p. 267-286. [BX7649.P5B46] 76-22967 ISBN 0-87722-086-7 : 12.50
1. Friends, Society of. Philadelphia. 2. Church and social problems—Friends, Society of. I. Title.

BERGER, Peter L. 261.8
The precarious vision; a sociologist looks at social fictions and Christian faith. [1st ed.] Garden City, N.Y., Doubleday, 1961. 238 p. 22 cm. Includes bibliography. [BL60.B4] 61-12493
1. Religion and sociology. 2. Sociology, Christian. I. Title.

BERGER, Peter L. 261.8
The precarious vision : a sociologist looks at social fictions and Christian faith / Peter L. Berger. Westport, Conn. : Greenwood Press, 1976, c1961. 238 p. ; 23 cm. Reprint of the ed. published by Doubleday, Garden City, N.Y. Includes bibliographical references. [BL60.B4 1976] 76-1981 ISBN 0-8371-8657-9 lib.bdg. : 14.00
1. Religion and sociology. 2. Sociology, Christian. I. Title.

BERRIGAN, Daniel. 261.8
Consequences: truth and ... New York, Macmillan [1967] ix, 123 p. 21 cm. [BV625.B45] 67-12794
1. Christianity—20th century. 2. Church and social problems. 3. Social ethics. I. Title.

BLAKE, Eugene Carson, 1906- 261.8
The church in the next decade. New York, Macmillan [1966] viii, 152p. 21cm. [BR115.W6.B5] 66-25501 4.95
1. Church and the world. I. Title.

BLANCHARD, Jonathan, 1811- 261.8
1892.
A debate on slavery [by] Jonathan Blanchard and N. L. Rice. New York, Arno Press, 1969. 482 p. 23 cm. (The Anti-slavery crusade in America) Reprint of the 1846 ed. [E449.B638 1969c] 72-82175
1. Slavery in the United States—Controversial literature—1846. 2. Slavery—Justification. I. Rice, Nathan Lewis, 1807-1877. II. Title. III. Series.

BLANCHARD, Jonathan, 1811- 261'.8
1892.
A debate on slavery, held in the city of Cincinnati on the first, second, third, and sixth days of October 1845 upon the question: Is slave-holding in itself sinful, and the relation between master and slave, a sinful relation? Affirmative: J. Blanchard. Negative: N. L. Rice. Cincinnati, W. H. Moore, 1846. Detroit, Negro History Press [1969?] 482 p. 23 cm. [E449.B638 1969b] 70-92419
1. Slavery in the United States—Controversial literature—1846. 2. Slavery—Justification. I. Rice, Nathan Lewis, 1807-1877. II. Title.

BLANCHARD, Jonathan, 1811- 261.8
1892.
A debate on slavery, held in the city of Cincinnati, on the first, second, third, and sixth days of October, 1845, upon the question: Is slave-holding in itself sinful, and the relation between master and slave, a sinful relation? Affirmative: J. Blanchard. Negative: N. L. Rice. New York, Negro Universities Press [1969] 482 p. 23 cm. Reprint of the 1846 ed. [E449.B638 1969] 70-76853
1. Slavery in the United States—Controversial literature—1846. 2. Slavery—Justification. I. Rice, Nathan Lewis, 1807-1877. II. Title.

BLAND, Salem Goldworth, 261'.8
1859-1950.
The new Christianity; or, The religion of the new age. Introd. by Richard Allen. [Toronto, Buffalo] University of Toronto Press [1973] xxvi, 89 p. 22 cm. (The Social history of Canada) "The original edition of the work appeared in 1920." Includes bibliographical references. [BT738.B54 1973] 73-95815 ISBN 0-8020-1954-4 2.50 (pbk.)
1. Sociology, Christian. 2. Church and social problems. I. Title. II. Series.

BLOWERS, Russ. 261.8
Listen! A plea for those who are bewildered by the confusion and chaos of our age to listen to what Jesus has to say about the crucial issues of our time. Cincinnati, Standard Pub. [1972] 96 p. 18 cm. (Fountain books) [BR121.2.B53] 76-180746
1. Christianity—20th century. I. Title.

BOCK, Paul, 1922- 261.8
In search of a responsible world society; the social teachings of the World Council of Churches. Philadelphia, Westminster Press [1974] 251 p. 21 cm. Bibliography: p. [243]-244. [HN31.B68] 74-9986 ISBN 0-664-20708-1 10.00
1. World Council of Churches. 2. Church and social problems. I. Title.

BOER, Hans Alfred de. 261.8
The bridge is love; jottings from a traveller's notebook. Foreword by Martin Niemoller. [1st English ed.] Grand Rapids, Eerdmans, 1958. 255p. illus. 23cm. Translation of Unterwegs notiert: Bericht einer Weitreise. [BT734.2.B613 1958] 58-3886

1. Race problems. 2. Voyages around the world. I. Title.

BOESAK, Allan Aubrey, 1946- 261.8
Farewell to innocence : a socio-ethical study on Black theology and Black power / Allan Aubrey Boesak. Maryknoll, N.Y. : Orbis Books, 1977, c1976. xii, 185 p. ; 21 cm. Includes index. Bibliography: p. 173-182. [BT82.7.B63 1977] 77-5578 ISBN 0-88344-130-6 pbk. : 4.95
1. Black theology. 2. Black power. I. Title.

BOURNE, George, 1780-1845. 261.8
The Book and slavery irreconcilable. New York, Arno Press, 1969. 141 p. 23 cm. (The Anti-slavery crusade in America) "With animadversions upon Dr. Smith's philosophy." Reprint of the 1816 ed. [E446.B77 1969] 76-82176
1. Smith, Samuel Stanhope, 1750-1819. Lectures ... on the subjects of moral and political philosophy. 2. Slavery in the United States—Controversial literature—1816. I. Title. II. Series.

BRAND, Mary Vivian. 261.8
The Social Catholic movement in England, 1920-1955 [by] M. Vivian Brand. [New York] Pageant Press, 1963. 216 p. 21 cm. Thesis—St. Louis University. Bibliography: p. 207-216. [HN39.G7B65] 68-568
1. Church and social problems—Catholic Church. 2. Church and social problems—Great Britain. I. Title.

BRILL, Earl H 261.8
The creative edge of American Protestantism [by] Earl H. Brill. New York, Seabury Press [1966] vii. 248 p. 22 cm. Bibliography: p. 239-243. [BR526.B7] 66-10834
1. Protestant churches — U.S. 2. Church and social problems — U.S. I. Title.

BRILL, Earl H. 261.8
The creative edge of American Protestantism. New York, Seabury [c.1966] vii, 248p. 22cm. Bibl. [BR526.B7] 66-10834 5.95
1. Protestant churches—U. S. 2. Church and social problems—U. S. I. Title.

BROWN, Dale W., 1926- 261.8
The Christian revolutionary [by] Dale W. Brown. Grand Rapids, Eerdmans [1971] 147 p. 21 cm. Includes bibliographical references. [BT738.3.B76] 77-142903 2.45
1. Revolution (Theology) 2. Theology—20th century. I. Title.

BROWN, John Pairman. 261.8
The liberated zone; a guide to Christian resistance. Richmond, Va., John Knox Press [1969] 203 p. 21 cm. [BR85.B837] 69-14679 4.95
1. Christianity—20th century—Addresses, essays, lectures. I. Title.

BRUEGGEMANN, Walter. 261.8
In man we trust; the neglected side of Biblical faith. Richmond, Va., John Knox Press [1973, c1972] 144 p. 21 cm. Includes bibliographical references. [BS1455.B78 1973] 72-1761 ISBN 0-8042-0199-4 4.95
1. Jews—History—To 586 B.C. 2. Wisdom literature—Criticism, interpretation, etc. 3. Theology—20th century. I. Title.

CALVEZ, Jean Yves, 1927- 261.8
The social thought of John XXIII: Mater et magistra. Tr. [from French] by George J. M. McKenzie. Chicago, Regnery [c.1965] xi, 121p. 23cm. Sequel to The church and social justice; the social teaching of the popes from Leo XIII to Pius XII. Bibl. [HN37.C3A3] 64-66118 3.75
1. Catholic Church. Pope, 1958-1963 (Joannes XXIII) Mater et magistra (15 May 1961) I. Title.

CALVEZ, Jean Yves, 1927- 261.8
The social thought of John XXIII : Mater et magistra / by Jean-Yves Calvez ; translated by George J. M. McKenzie. Westport, Conn. : Greenwood Press, 1977. xi, 121 p. ; 23 cm. Translation of Eglise et societe economique (L'enseignement social de Jean XXIII) Sequel to The church and social justice; the social teaching of the popes from Leo XIII to Pius XII. Reprint of the 1965 ed. published by Regnery, Chicago. Includes bibliographical references and index. [HN37.C3A3 1976] 75-40992 ISBN 0-8371-8711-7 lib.bdg. : 10.75
1. Catholic Church. Pope, 1958-1963 (Joannes XXIII). Mater et magistra. I. Title.

CALVEZ, Jean Yves, 1947- 261.8
he social thought of John XXIII: Mater et magistra. Chicago, H. Regnery Co. [1965] xi, 121 p. 23 cm. Translation of Eglise et societe economique (L'enseignement social de Jean XXIII) Sequel to The Church and social justice; the social teaching of the popes from Leo XIII to Pius XII. "References": p. 100-118. [HN37.C3A3] 64-66118
1. Catholic Church. Pope, 1958-1963 (Joannes

XXIII) Mater et Magistra (15 May 1961) I. Title. II. Title: Translated by George J. M. McKenzie.

CAMARA, Helder, 1909- 261.8
The church and colonialism; the betrayal of the third world. Translated by William McSweeney. [1st American ed.] Denville, N.J., Dimension Books [1969] v, 181 p. 21 cm. Translation of Terzo mondo defraudato. [HN37.C3C2642 1969b] 70-94535 5.95
1. Church and social problems—Catholic Church—Addresses, essays, lectures. 2. Underderveloped areas—Social conditions—Addresses, essays, lectures. 3. Church and social problems—Brazil—Addresses, essays, lectures. I. Title.

CAMARA, Helder, 1909- 261.8
Revolution through peace. Translated from the Portuguese by Amparo McLean. [1st U.S. ed.] New York, Harper & Row [1971] xix, 149 p. 22 cm. (World perspectives, v. 45) Translation of Revolucao dentro da Paz. [BX1466.2.C313 1971] 71-138713 ISBN 0-06-010597-6 5.95
1. Catholic Church in Brazil—Addresses, essays, lectures. I. Title.

CAMERON, Richard Morgan, 1898- 261.8
Methodism and society in historical perspective. Ed. by the Board of Social and Economic Relations of the Methodist Church. Nashville, Abingdon Press [c.1961] 349p. (Methodism and society, v.1) Bibl. 61-8407 5.00
1. Church and social problems—Methodist Church. I. Methodist Church (United States) Board of Social and Economic Relations. II. Title. III. Series.

CAMPBELL, Ernest T. 261.8
Locked in a room with open doors [by] Ernest T. Campbell. Waco, Tex., Word Books [1974] 180 p. 23 cm. Includes bibliographical references. [BX9178.C26L6] 73-91554 5.95
1. Presbyterian Church—Sermons. 2. Sermons, American. I. Title.

CAMPBELL, Thomas Charles, 1929- 261.8
The fragmented layman; an empirical study of lay attitudes, by Thomas C. Campbell and Yoshio Fukuyama. Philadelphia, Pilgrim Press [1970] xvi, 252 p. 24 cm. (Studies in religion and society) Includes bibliographical references. [BT738.C34] 79-125960 ISBN 0-8298-0182-0 12.00
1. Sociology, Christian—U.S. 2. Laity—United Church of Christ. I. Fukuyama, Yoshio, 1921- joint author. II. Title. III. Series: Studies in religion and society series

CAMPBELL, Will D. 261.8
Up to our steeples in politics, by Will D. Campbell and James Y. Holloway. New York, Paulist Press [1970] v, 153 p. 21 cm. [BR121.2.C248] 70-127791 1.95
1. Christianity—20th century. 2. Social action. I. Holloway, James Y., 1927- joint author. II. Title.

CARLSON, Edgar Magnus, 1908- 261.8
The church and the public conscience. Philadelphia, Muhlenberg Press [c1956] 104p. 20cm. [BR115.S6C27] 55-11782
1. Sociology, Christian (Lutheran) I. Title.

CARMEN, Arlene. 261.8
Abortion counseling and social change from illegal act to medical practice; the story of the clergy consultation service on abortion [by] Arlene Carmen and Howard Moody. Valley Forge [Pa.] Judson Press [1973] 122 p. 22 cm. [HQ767.5.U5C37] 72-11221 ISBN 0-8170-0579-X pap. 2.95
1. Abortion—United States. 2. Pastoral counseling. I. Moody, Howard, joint author. II. Title.

CATHOLIC Church in the U.S. Bishops. 261.8
U.S. bishops' Pastoral letter on human life in our day, November 15, 1968. Commentary by John B. Sheerin. Glen Rock, N.J., Paulist Press [1969] 72 p. 19 cm. Cover title: Human life in our day. [BX1405.A58] 74-5046 0.50
1. Catholic Church—Pastoral letters and charges. 2. Catholic Church. Pope, 1963- (Paulus VI) Humanae vitae. 3. Church and the world. 4. Birth control—Religious aspects. I. Sheerin, John B., ed. II. Title. III. Title: Human life in our day.

CATHOLIC Church. Pope, 1963- (Paulus VI) 261.8
Encyclical letter of His Holiness Pope Paul VI on the development of peoples. Commentary by Barbara Ward. [New York, Paulist Press, 1967] 80 p. illus., ports. 12 x 18 cm. [HN37.C3A35 1967b] 67-28692
1. Church and social problems—Catholic Church—Papal documents. 2. Underdeveloped areas. I. Jackson, Barbara (Ward) Lady, 1914- II. [Populorum progressio. English.]

CATHOLIC Inter-American Cooperation Program. 261.8
CICOP working papers. Davenport, Iowa, Latin America Bureau [1967]- pts. 28 cm. Consists of papers presented at the 4th annual CICOP conference, sponsored by the Bishops' Committee for Latin America. Includes bibliographical references. [F1410.C32] 68-5425
1. Church and social problems—Latin America. 2. Latin American federation. 3. Church and international organization. 4. Pan-Americanism. I. Catholic Church. National Conference of Catholic Bishops Bishops' Committee for Latin America. II. Title.

CAUTHEN Wilfred Kenneth. 261.8
The ethics of enjoyment : the Christian's pursuit of happiness / by Kenneth Cauthen. Atlanta : John Knox Press, c1975. 124 p. ; 21 cm. Includes bibliographical references. [HN18.C32] 75-13466 ISBN 0-8042-0815-8
1. Social history—1960- 2. Social ethics. 3. Church and social problems. 4. Technology and ethics. I. Title.

CHEEVER, George Barrell, 1807-1890. 261.8
God against slavery. New York, Arno Press, 1969. 272 p. 23 cm. (The Anti-slavery crusade in America) Reprint of the 1857 ed. [E449.C49 1969c] 79-82182
1. Slavery in the United States—Controversial literature—1857. I. Title. II. Series.

CHEEVER, George Barrell, 1807-1890. 261.8
God against slavery, and the freedom and duty of the pulpit to rebuke it, as a sin against God. New York, Negro Universities Press [1969] 272 p. 24 cm. Reprint of the 1857 ed. [E449.C49 1969b] 70-97360
1. Slavery in the United States—Controversial literature—1857. I. Title.

CHEEVER, George Barrell, 1807-1890. 261.8
God against slavery: and the freedom and duty of the pulpit to rebuke it, as a sin against God. Miami, Fla., Mnemosyne Pub. Inc., 1969. viii, 272 p. 23 cm. Reprint of the 1857 ed. [E449.C49 1969] 76-78995
1. Slavery in the United States—Controversial literature—1857. I. Title.

CHILDS, Marquis William, 1903- 261.8*
Ethics in a business society, by Marquis W. Childs and Douglass Cater. [1st ed.] New York, Harper [1954] 191 p. 22 cm. Includes bibliography. [HB72.C45] 54-6442
1. Christianity and economics. 2. Church and social problems. 3. Ethics. 4. United States—Economic policy. I. Cater, Douglass, 1923- joint author. II. Title.

CHOU, Po-chin, 1891- 261.8
Commonism, a plan for implementing the Christian answer to A communism, by Pik Kum Chau. With forewords by Hollington K. Tong and John W. Bailey, and a biographical sketch of the author by Charles R. Shepherd. [1st ed.] New York, Exposition Press [1957] 256p. illus. 21cm. [HN18.C3884] 57-10656
1. Social problems. I. Title.

CHRISTENSEN, Winnie. 261.8
Caught with my hands full; opportunity in my community. Wheaton, Ill., H. Shaw [1970] 141 p. illus. 18 cm. Includes bibliographical references. [BR115.W6C494] 71-133985
1. Church and the world. I. Title.

THE Christian message for the world today; a joint statement of the world-wide mission of the Christian Church. Freeport, N.Y., Books for Libraries Press [1971] 203 p. 23 cm. (Essay index reprint series) Foreword signed: E. Stanley Jones [and others] Reprint of the 1934 ed. [BR479.C37 1971] 77-152163 ISBN 0-8369-2184-4 261.8
1. Christianity—20th century. I. Jones, Eli Stanley, 1884-

CHRISTIAN perspectives on psychology / edited by Richard Ruble. New York : MSS Information Corp., [1975] p. cm. [BF121.C49] 75-15956 ISBN 0-8422-0456-3 pbk. : 3.75 261.8
1. Psychology. 2. Psychology, Religious. I. Ruble, Richard.

CHRISTIAN stewardship and church finance. Foreword by J. D. Grey. Grand Rapids, Zondervan Pub. House [1953] 153p. 20cm. [BV770.E4] [BV770.E4] 254 53-28736 53-28736 261.8
1. Stewardship, Christian. I. Ellis, Hallett West, 1882-

CHURCH League of America. 261.8
The record of the National Council of Churches. Wheaton, Ill. [1969] 161 p. 28 cm. [BX6.N2C49] 73-289636 3.00
1. National Council of the Churches of Christ in the United States of America. I. Title.

CLOUSE, Robert G., 1931- 261.8
Protest and politics; Christianity and contemporary affairs, edited by Robert G. Clouse, Robert D. Linder [and] Richard V. Pierard. Greenwood, S.C., Attic Press, 1968. vi, 271 p. 24 cm. Includes bibliographical references. [BR115.P7C48] 68-58884 5.95
1. Christianity and politics—Addresses, essays, lectures. 2. Evangelicalism—United States. I. Linder, Robert Dean, joint author. II. Pierard, Richard V., 1934- joint author. III. Title.

COLWELL, Stephen, 1800-1871. 261.8
New themes for the Protestant clergy. New York, Arno Press, 1969. xv, 383 p. 23 cm. (Religion in America) Reprint of the 1851 ed. Includes bibliographical references. [BT38.C65] 71-83417
1. Sociology, Christian. 2. Charity. 3. Protestantism. I. Title.

COUGHLIN, Bernard J. 261.8
Church and state in social welfare. New York, Columbia [c.1964, 1965] xii, 189p. illus., maps. 24cm. Bibl. [HN39.U6C6] 65-16309 6.95
1. Church and social problems—U.S. 2. Church and state in the U.S. 3. Church charities. I. Title.

COX, Harvey 261.8
God's revolution and man's responsibility. Valley Forge, Pa., Judson [c.1965] 128p. 20cm. [BR123.C72] 65-23541 1.50 pap.,
1. Christianity—20th cent.—Addresses, essays, lectures. I. Title.

CRAIG, Archibald Gordon, 1873- 261.8
The golden age. Rindge, N. H., R. R. Smith, 1956. 140p. 23cm. [HN31.C74] 56-9204
1. Church and social problems. I. Title.

CRAIG, Clarence Tucker, 1895-1953, ed. 261.8
The challenge of our culture. Freeport, N.Y., Books for Libraries Press [1972, c1946] xi, 205 p. 23 cm. (Essay index reprint series) Original ed. issued as v. 1 of The Interseminary series. Includes bibliographies. [BR115.C8C69] 70-167331 ISBN 0-8369-2765-6
1. Culture—Addresses, essays, lectures. 2. Christianity—20th century—Addresses, essays, lectures. 3. Church and social problems—Addresses, essays, lectures. I. Title. II. Series: The Interseminary series, v. 1.

CRAIN, James Andrew, 1886- 261.8
The development of social ideas among the Disciples of Christ, by James A. Crain. St. Louis, Mo., Bethany Press [1969] 336 p. 23 cm. Includes bibliographies. [BX7321.2.C7] 71-86155
1. Disciples of Christ. 2. Church and social problems—History. I. Title.

CRONIN, John Francis, 1908- 261.8
Christianity and social progress; a commentary on Mater et magistra, by John F. Cronin. Baltimore, Helicon [1965] vi, 223 p. 21 cm. "Based on a series of articles which first appeared in Our Sunday visitor ... The text uses the translation of Father H. E. Winstone, as adapted by The Pope speaks. References to the encyclical area based on the paragraph numbers used in the Winstone version." "Reading list": p. 216-217. [HN37.C3C694] 65-15037
1. Church and social problems—Catholic Church. 2. Catholic Church. Pope, 1958-1963 (Joannes xxiii) Mater et magistra (15 May 1961) I. Title.

CRONIN, John Francis, 1908- 261.8
Christianity and social progress; a commentary on Mater et magistra. Helicon [dist. New York, Taplinger, c.1965] vi, 223p. 21cm. Based on a ser. of articles which first appeared in Our Sunday visitor. Text uses the tr. of Father H. E. Winstone, as adapted by The Pope speaks. Refs. to the encyclical are based on the paragraph numbers used in the Winstone version. Bibl. [HN37.C3C694] 65-15037 4.95 bds.,
1. Church and social problems—Catholic Church. 2. Catholic Church. Pope, 1958-1963 (Joannes XXIII) Mater et magistra (15 May 1961) I. Title.

CRONIN, John Francis, 1908- 261.8
Social principles and economic life [by] John F. Cronin. Rev. ed. Milwaukee, Bruce Pub. Co. [1966] xxxiii, 429 p. 23 cm. Includes bibliographical references. [HN37.C3C72 1966] 66-24254
1. Church and social problems—Catholic Church. I. Title.

CRONIN, John Francis, 1908- 261.8
Social principles and economic life. Rev. ed. Milwaukee, Bruce [1964] xxiii, 429p. 24cm. Bibl. [HN37.C3C72] 64-66114 6.50
1. Church and social problems—Catholic Church. I. Title.

CRONIN, John Francis, 1908- 261.8
The social teaching of Pope John XXIII Milwaukee, Bruce Pub. Co. [1963] ix, 83 p. 23 cm. [HN37.C3C74] 63-22039
1. Joannes XXIII, Pope, 1881-1963. 2. Church and social problems—Catholic Church—Papal documents. I. Title.

CRONIN, John Francis, 1908- 261.8
The social teaching of Pope John XXIII. Milwaukee, Bruce [c.1963] ix, 83p. 23cm. 63-22039 1.35 pap.,
1. Joannes XXIII. Pope 1881-1963. 2. Church and social problems—Catholic Church—Papal documents. I. Title.

DANA, Ellis Huntington. 261.8
Congregationalism as a social action pioneer. Some possible ways by which we may still improve our total strategy and effectiveness. [Madison? Wis., 1951] 97 p. illus. 23 cm. [HN37.C6D3] 54-16633
1. Church and social problems—Congregational churches. I. Title.

DAVIS, Jerome, 1891- 261.8
Religion in action. Introd. by E. Stanley Jones. New York, Philosophical Library [1956] 319p. 24cm. [HN31.D33] 56-58114
1. Church and social problems. I. Title.

DEANE, Herbert Andrew, 1921- 261.8
The political and social ideas of St. Augustine. New York, Columbia University Press, 1963. 356 p. 28 cm. [BR65.A9D4] 63-9809
1. Augustinus, Aurelius, Saint, Bp. of Hippo — Sociology. 2. Sociology, Christian. I. Title.

DEANE, Herbert Andrew, 1921- 261.8
The political and social ideas of St. Augustine. NewYork, Columbia [1966, c.1963] 356p. 21cm. (Columbia paperback, 69) [BR65.A9D4] 63-9809 2.45 pap.,
1. Augustinus. Aurelius. Saint, Bp. of Hippo—Sociology. 2. Sociology, Christian. I. Title.

DE BOER, Cecil. 261.8
Responsible society. Grand Rapids, Eerdmans [1957] 247p. 23cm. [BX9410.D4] 57-6670
1. Reformed Church—Addresses, essays, lectures. 2. Church and social problems—Reformed Church. I. Title.

DRAKE Conference, Drake University, 1944. 261.8
The church and the new world mind, by William E. Hocking [and others] Freeport, N.Y., Books for Libraries Press [1968, c1944] 256 p. 23 cm. (The Drake lectures for 1944) (Essay index reprint series.) Contents.Contents.—Faith and world order, by W. E. Hocking.—Culture and peace, by W. E. Hocking.—Statesmanship and Christianity, by W. E. Hocking.—The church, the press, and world opinion, by W. Lewis.—Toward peace in the Orient, by M. S. Bates.—A Christian view of inter-American relationships, by G. Baez-Camargo.—Peace begins at home, by C. W. Blackburn.—The racial issue and the Christian church, by G. Harkness.—How can the churches in America work for peace? By W. W. Van Kirk.—The church and the new world mind, by R. M. Jones. Bibliographical footnotes. [BR115.P7D7 1944aab] 68-57311
1. Christianity and politics. I. Hocking, William Ernest, 1873-1966. II. Title. III. Series: Drake Conference, Drake University, 1944. Drake lectures.

DRUMMOND, William Francis. 261.8
Every man a brother, by William F. Drummond. With a foreword by John F. Cronin. Washington, Corpus Books [1968] 160 p. 22 cm. Bibliography: p. 155-160. [HN37.C3D69] 68-10449
1. Church and social problems—Catholic Church. 2. Encyclicals, Papal. I. Title.

DRUMMOND, William Francis. 261.8
Social justice. Milwaukee, Bruce Pub. Co. [1956, c1955] 132p. 21cm. [HN37.C3D7] 55-12386
1. Justice. 2. Church and social problems—Catholic Church. I. Title.

DULLES, Avery Robert, 1918- 261.8
The resilient church : the necessity and limits of adaptation / Avery Dulles. 1st ed. Garden City, N.Y. : Doubleday, 1977. 229 p. ; 22 cm. Includes bibliographical references and index. [BX1746.D82] 76-29790 ISBN 0-385-11610-1 : 6.95
1. Catholic Church—Doctrinal and controversial works—Catholic authors. 2. Church. I. Title.

DULLES, Avery Robert, 1918- 261.8
The resilient church : the necessity and limits

of adaptation / Avery Dulles. 1st ed. Garden City, N.Y. : Doubleday, 1977. 229 p. ; 22 cm. Includes bibliographical references and index. [BX1746.D82] 76-29790 ISBN 0-385-11610-1 : 6.95
1. Catholic Church—Doctrinal and controversial works—Catholic authors. 2. Church. I. Title.

DURLAND, William R., 1931- 261.8
No king but Caesar? : A Catholic lawyer looks at Christian violence / William R. Durland ; introd. by Richard T. McSorley. Scottdale, Pa. : Herald Press, 1975. 182 p. : port. ; 23 cm. (The Christian peace shelf ; no. 7) Includes index. Bibliography: p. 175-177. [BT736.15.D87] 74-30093 ISBN 0-8361-1757-3 : 5.95
1. Violence—Moral and religious aspects. I. Title.

DURLAND, William R., 1931- 261.8
No king but Caesar? : A Catholic lawyer looks at Christian violence / William R. Durland ; introd. by Richard T. McSorley. Scottdale, Pa. : Herald Press, 1975. 182 p. : port. ; 23 cm. (The Christian peace shelf ; no. 7) Includes index. Bibliography: p. 175-177. [BT736.15.D87] 74-30093 ISBN 0-8361-1757-3 : 5.95
1. Violence—Moral and religious aspects. I. Title.

EAGLESON, John, comp. 261.8
The radical Bible. Adapted by John Eagleson and Philip Scharper from Bibel provokativ, edited by Hellmut Haug and Ju[e]rgen Rump. Translated by Erika J. Papp. Maryknoll, N.Y., Orbis Books, 1972. vi, 161 p. 13 cm. Scriptural quotations as they were used in the Bibel provokativ, and a completely new selection of contemporary comments. Bibliography: p. 153-157. [BR115.U6E34] 76-190164 1.95
1. Church and underdeveloped areas. I. Scharper, Philip J., joint comp. II. Haug, Hellmut, comp. Bibel provokativ. III. Bible. English. Revised standard. Selections. 1972. IV. Title.

EARLE, John R., 1935- 261.8
Spindles and spires : a re-study of religion and social change in Gastonia / by John R. Earle, Dean D. Knudsen, and Donald W. Shriver, Jr. Atlanta : John Knox Press, c1976. 382 p. ; 24 cm. Includes index. Bibliography: p. 348-353. [HN39.U6E27] 73-13461 ISBN 0-8042-0854-9 16.95 ISBN 0-8042-0853-0 pbk. : 5.95
1. Church and social problems—Gastonia, N.C. 2. Church and industry—North Carolina—Gastonia. 3. Church and labor—Gastonia, N.C. I. Knudsen, Dean D., 1932- joint author. II. Shriver, Donald W., joint author. III. Title.

EBY, Kermit. 261.8
The God in you, by Kermit Eby with the assistance of Ray Montgomery. [Chicago] University of Chicago Press [1954] 161p. 20cm. [HN37.C3E2] 54-8454
1. Church and social problems—Church of the Brethren. I. Title.

FAHEY, Sheila Macmanus. 261.8
Charismatic social action : reflection/resource manual / by Sheila Macmanus Fahey. New York : Paulist Press, c1977. xvii, 174 p. ; 21 cm. (An Exploration book) Includes bibliographies. [BR1644.F34] 77-70633 ISBN 0-8091-2014-3 pbk. : 4.95
1. Pentecostalism. 2. Church and social problems. I. Title.

FAHEY, Sheila Macmanus. 261.8
Charismatic social action : reflection/resource manual / by Sheila Macmanus Fahey. New York : Paulist Press, c1977. xvii, 174 p. ; 21 cm. (An Exploration book) Includes bibliographies. [BR1644.F34] 77-70633 ISBN 0-8091-2014-3 pbk. : 4.95
1. Pentecostalism. 2. Church and social problems. I. Title.

THE Faith that does justice 261.8
: examining the Christian sources for social change / edited by John C. Haughey. New York : Paulist Press, c1977. vi, 295 p. ; 21 cm. (Woodstock studies ; v. 2) Includes bibliographical references and index. [BR115.J8F34] 77-151395 ISBN 0-8091-2026-7 pbk. : 5.95
1. Christianity and justice—Addresses, essays, lectures. I. Haughey, John C. II. Series.
Contents omitted

THE Faith that does justice 261.8
: examining the Christian sources for social change / edited by John C. Haughey. New York : Paulist Press, c1977. vi, 295 p. ; 21 cm. (Woodstock studies ; v. 2) Includes bibliographical references and index. [BR115.J8F34] 77-151395 ISBN 0-8091-2026-7 pbk. : 5.95
1. Christianity and justice—Addresses, essays, lectures. I. Haughey, John C. II. Series.
Contents omitted

FALLAW, Wesner. 261.8
Toward spiritual security. Philadelphia, Westminster Press [1952] 192 p. 21 cm. [BV625.F3] 52-7117
1. Church and social problems. 2. Family—Religious life. 3. Psychology. Pastoral. I. Title.

FICHTER, Joseph Henry, 261.8
1908-
Social relations in the urban parish. [Chicago] University of Chicago Press [1954] 263p. 24cm. [BV637.F5] 54-11207
1. City churches. 2. Church and social problems—Catholic Church. I. Title.

FINNERTY, Adam, 1944- 261.8
No more plastic Jesus : global justice and Christian lifestyle / Adam Finnerty. Maryknoll, N.Y. : Orbis Books, 1977c1976 p. cm. Bibliography: p. Discusses the seriousness of the worldwide dilemma of hunger, depletion of natural resources, and pollution and suggests ways to "reclaim the planet", particularly ways that the church as an institution can help and also ways responsive adults in adopting a simple, truly Christian lifestyle can contribute to global change. [BJ1496.F5] 76-13174 ISBN 0-88344-340-6 : 8.95 ISBN 0-88344-341-4 pbk. : 3.95
1. Simplicity. 2. Church and social problems. 3. Civilization, Modern—1950- I. Title.

FINNERTY, Adam, 1944- 261.8
No more plastic Jesus : global justice and Christian lifestyle / Adam Finnerty. Maryknoll, N.Y. : Orbis Books, 1977c1976 p. cm. Bibliography: p. Discusses the seriousness of the worldwide dilemma of hunger, depletion of natural resources, and pollution and suggests ways to "reclaim the planet", particularly ways that the church as an institution can help and also ways responsive adults in adopting a simple, truly Christian lifestyle can contribute to global change. [BJ1496.F5] 76-13174 ISBN 0-88344-340-6 : 8.95 ISBN 0-88344-341-4 pbk. : 3.95
1. Simplicity. 2. Church and social problems. 3. Civilization, Modern—1950- I. Title.

FOGARTY, Michael Patrick. 261.8
Christian democracy in Western Europe, 1820-1953, by Michael P. Fogarty. Westport, Conn., Greenwood Press [1974] p. Reprint of the 1957 ed. published by Routledge & K. Paul, London. Bibliography: p. [HN373.F6 1974] 73-11997 ISBN 0-8371-7114-8
1. Christian democracy. 2. Europe—Social conditions. I. Title.

FOGARTY, Michael Patrick. 261.8
Christian democracy in Western Europe, 1820-1953, by Michael P. Fogarty. Westport, Conn., Greenwood Press [1974] p. Reprint of the 1957 ed. published by Routledge & K. Paul, London. Bibliography: p. [HN373.F6 1974] 73-11997 ISBN 0-8371-7114-8 20.00
1. Christian democracy. 2. Europe—Social conditions. I. Title.

FORDHAM-RURAL Life Socio- 261.8
Economic Conference Maryknoll, N. Y., 1958.
The missionary's role in socio-economic betterment. Edited by John J. Considine. [Westminster, Md.] Newman Press [c.]1960. xi, 330 p. 21 cm. Includes bibliographies. 60-12058 3.75; 1.75 pap.,
1. Church and social problems—Congresses. 2. Church and social problems—Congresses. 3. Church and social problems—Catholic Church. 4. Catholic Church—Missions—Congresses. 5. Rural churches. I. Considine, John Joseph, ed. II. Title.

FOUND faithful; 261.8
Christian stewardship in personal and church life. Nashville, Broadman Press [1953] 142p. illus. 19cm. [BV772.M55] 254 53-12600
1. Stewardship, Christian. I. Moore, Merrill Dennis, 1904-

FOWLER, Grady. 261.8
Three races under God. [1st ed.] New York, Vantage Press [1956] 172p. illus. 21cm. [BR115.R3F6] 55-11657
1. Race. I. Title.

FOX, Mary Harrita, Sister, 261.8
1900-
Peter E. Dietz, labor priest. With a foreword by Aaron I. Abell. Notre Dame, Ind., University of Notre Dame Press [1953] ix, 285p. illus., ports. 24cm. 'Prepared originally as a dissertation ... at the University of Notre Dame.' Bibliography: p. 282-285. [HD8073.D5F6] 53-7348
1. Dietz, Peter Ernest, 1878-1947. I. Title.

GARDINER, Robert Kweku 261.8
Atta.
The development of social administration [by] Robert Kweku Gardiner [and] Helen O. Judd. London, Oxford University Press, 1954. 208p. 19cm. [HN18.G29] 56-1903
1. Social policy. 2. Africa, West—Social policy. 3. Gt. Brit.—Social policy. I. Judd, Helen O., joint author. II. Title.

GARDNER, Edward Clinton, 261.8
1920-
The church as a prophetic community, by E. Clinton Gardner. Philadelphia, Westminster Press [1967] 254 p. 21 cm. Bibliographical references included in "Notes" (p. [239]-246) [BR115.W6G3] 67-10612
1. Church and the world. 2. United States—Religion. I. Title.

GAUTHIER, Paul 261.8
Christ, the church, and the poor. Tr. by Edward Fitzgerald. Westminster, Md., Newman, 1965[c.1964] 157p. 21cm. [BV639.P6G33] 65-1407 3.50
1. Church and the poor. 2. Companions of Jesus the Carpenter. I. Title.

GIORDANI, Igino, 1894- 261.8
The social message of the early church fathers / Igino Giordani ; translated by Alba I. Zizzamia. Boston : St. Paul Editions, c1977. x, 356 p. ; 19 cm. Translation of Il messaggio sociale dei primi padri della chiesa. Reprint of the 1944 ed. published by St. Anthony Guild Press, Paterson, N.J. Includes index. Bibliography: p. 335-345. [BR166.G5613 1977] 77-4935 4.50 pbk. : 3.50
1. Sociology, Christian—Early church, ca. 30-600. 2. Fathers of the church. I. Title.

GIORDANI, Igino, 1894- 261.8
The social message of the early church fathers / Igino Giordani ; translated by Alba I. Zizzamia. Boston : St. Paul Editions, c1977. x, 356 p. ; 19 cm. Translation of Il messaggio sociale dei primi padri della chiesa. Reprint of the 1944 ed. published by St. Anthony Guild Press, Paterson, N.J. Includes index. Bibliography: p. 335-345. [BR166.G5613 1977] 77-4935 4.50 pbk. : 3.50
1. Sociology, Christian—Early church, ca. 30-600. 2. Fathers of the church. I. Title.

GISH, Arthur G. 261.8
Beyond the rat race [by] Arthur G. Gish. Scottdale, Pa., Herald Press [1973] 192 p. 18 cm. Sequel to The New Left and Christian radicalism. Bibliography: p. 183-189. [BJ1496.G57] 73-9336 ISBN 0-8361-1724-7 1.45
1. Simplicity. I. Title.

GISH, Arthur G. 261.8
Beyond the rat race [by] Arthur G. Gish. Scottdale, Pa., Herald Press [1973] 192 p. 18 cm. Sequel to The New Left and Christian radicalism. Bibliography: p. 183-189. [BJ1496.G57] 73-9336 ISBN 0-8361-1724-7 1.45 (pbk.)
1. Simplicity. I. Title.

GISH, Arthur G. 261.8
The New Left and Christian radicalism, by Arthur G. Gish. Grand Rapids, Mich., Eerdmans [1970] 158 p. 20 cm. Bibliography: p. 143-151. [BT738.3.G55] 75-107618 2.45
1. Revolution (Theology) 2. Radicalism—U.S. 3. Anabaptists. I. Title.

GLEASON, Robert W., ed. 261.8
Problems and progress; a theological and psychological inquiry. Westminster, Md., Newman [c.]1962. ix, 152p. 22cm. 62-17190 3.00
1. Catholic Church—Doctrinal and controversial works—Catholic authors. 2. Church and social problems—Catholic Church. 3. Psychology, Religious. I. Title.

GOLLWITZER, Helmut. 261.8
The rich Christians and poor Lazarus. Translated by David Cairns. [New York] Macmillan [1970] xi, 108 p. 21 cm. Translation of Die reichen Christen und der arme Lazarus. Includes bibliographical references. [BR115.P7G65513] 78-107048 1.45
1. World Council of Churches, 4th Assembly, Uppsala, 1968. 2. Christianity and politics. 3. Church and social problems. I. Title.

GOOD stewards. 261.8
Nashville, Broadman Press [1953] 141p. 20cm. Includes bibliography. [BV772.D48] [BV772.D48] 254 53-12597 53-12597
1. Stewardship, Christian. I. Dillard, James Edgar, 1879-

GRAEF, Hilda C. 261.8
The Word of God in the world of today; contemporary problems in the light of Scripture. Garden City, N. Y., Hanover House [c.]1960. 138p. 22cm. 60-13734 2.95
1. Apologetics—20th cent. 2. Catholic Church—Apologetic works. I. Title.

GRAHAM, W. Fred, 1930- 261.8
The constructive revolutionary; John Calvin & his socio-economic impact, by W. Fred Graham. Richmond, John Knox Press [1971] 251 p. port. 21 cm. Bibliography: p. [243]-251. [BX9418.G7] 72-107321 ISBN 0-8042-0880-8 7.95
1. Calvin, Jean, 1509-1564—Sociology. I. Title.

GRIMKE, Angelina Emily, 261.8
1805-1879.
Appeal to the Christian women of the South. New York, Arno Press, 1969. 36 p. 22 cm. (The Anti-slavery crusade in America) Reprint of the 1836 ed. On spine: To Christian women of the South. [E449.G863 1969] 77-82195
1. Slavery in the United States—Controversial literature—1836. I. Title. II. Title: To Christian women of the South. III. Series.

GRIMM. ROBERT 261.8
Love and sexuality. Tr. [from French] foreword. by David R. Mace. New York, Association [c.1964] 127p. 20cm. 64-19746 3.50
1. Sexual ethics. 2. Sex and religion. I. Title.

HAAKE, Alfred Paul, 1885- 261.8
Faith and fact; a guide to economics through Christian understanding. [1st ed.] Harrisburg, Pa., Stackpole Co. [1953] 223p. 23cm. [BR115.E3H3] 53-7169
1. Christianity and economics. I. Title.

HAIPT, Maria Carl, Mother. 261.8
Social aspects of the Christian faith contained in Mater et magistra and Pacem in terris. Glen Rock, N.J., Paulist [c.1965] 95p. 18cm. (Deus bks.) At head of title: Study guide. Bibl. [BT738.H28] 65-14764 .75 pap.,
1. Sociology, Christian (Catholic) 2. Catholic Church. Pope, 1958-1963 (Joannes XXIII) Mater et magistra (15 May 1961) 3. Catholic Church. Pope, 1958-1963 (Joannes XXIII) Pacem in terris (11 Apr. 1963). I. Title.

HALL, Douglas John, 1928- 261.8
The reality of the Gospel and the unreality of the churches / by Douglas John Hall. Philadelphia : Westminster Press, [1975] 190 p. ; 20 cm. Includes bibliographical references. [BR115.W6H34] 75-12852 ISBN 0-664-24775-X pbk. : 3.45
1. Church and the world. 2. Christianity—20th century. I. Title.

HARDISTY, George. 261.8
Honest questions—honest answers to enrich your marriage / by George and Margaret Hardisty. Irvine, Calif. : Harvest House, c1977. 222 p. ; 21 cm. Bibliography: p. 219-220. [HQ10.H26] 77-24828 ISBN 0-89081-039-7 : pbk. : 2.95
1. Family life education. I. Hardisty, Margaret, joint author. II. Title.

HARING, Bernhard, 1912- 261.8
A theology of protest [by] Bernard Haring. New York, Farrar, Straus and Giroux [1970] xvii, 189 p. 22 cm. [BT736.6.H3 1970] 70-109556 5.95
1. Nonviolence—Moral and religious aspects. 2. Authority (Religion) I. Title.

HARTE, Thomas Joseph, 1914- 261.8
Papal social principles; a guide and digest. Milwaukee, Bruce Pub. Co. [1956] ix, 207p. 23cm. Includes bibliographical references. Bibliography: p.193-196. [HN37.C3H35] 56-11150
1. Church and social problems—Catholic Church. I. Title.

HAYNES, Leonard L 1923- 261.8
The Negro community within American Protestantism, 1619-1844. Boston, Christopher Pub. House [1953] 264p. 21cm. [BR563.N4H38] 53-4230
1. Negroes—Religion. 2. Protestant churches—U. S. I. Title.

HENGEL, Martin. 261.8
Victory over violence, Jesus and the revolutionists. Translated by David E. Green. With an introd. by Robin Scroggs. Philadelphia, Fortress Press [1973] xxvi, 67 p. 19 cm. Translation of Gewalt und Gewaltlosigkeit. Includes bibliographical references. [BT736.15.H4513] 73-79035 ISBN 0-8006-0167-X 2.50
1. Violence—Moral and religious aspects. I. Title.

HENRY, Carl Ferdinand 261.8
Howard, 1913-
A plea for evangelical demonstration, by Carl F. H. Henry. Grand Rapids, Baker Book House [1971] 124 p. 21 cm. [BR1640.H43] 78-159778 ISBN 0-8010-4019-1 3.95
1. Evangelicalism—Addresses, essays, lectures. 2. Social ethics—Addresses, essays, lectures. I. Title.

HERRON, George Davis, 1862- 261.8
1925.
Between Caesar and Jesus : a course of eight Monday-noon lectures given in Willard Hall,

Chicago, for the Christian Citizenship League, upon the subject of the relation of the Christian conscience to the existing social system, beginning October 24 and closing December 12, 1898 / by George D. Herron. Westport, Conn. : Hyperion Press, 1975, c1899. p. cm. (The Radical tradition in America) Reprint of the ed. published by T. Y. Crowell, New York. [HN31.H45 1975] 75-324 ISBN 0-88355-227-2 : 18.00
1. Churuch and social problems—Addresses, essays, lectures. 2. Sociology, Christian—Addresses, essays, lectures. I. Title.

HERSHBERGER, Guy Franklin, 1896- 261.8
The way of the cross in human relations. Scottdale, Pa., Herald Press [1958] 424p. 23cm. 'An expansion of the Conrad Grebel lectures delivered in 1954.' [HN31.H52] 58-10992
1. Church and social problems. I. Title.

HIGGINS, Herbert Ralph, 1902- 261.8
Christianity and America's social problems. New York, Comet Press Books [1952] 125p. 23cm. [HN37.A6H5] 53-20394
1. Church and social problems—Anglican communion. I. Title.

HOBBS, Herschel H 261.8
The gospel of giving. Nashville, Broadman Press [c1954] 146p. 20cm. [BV772.H52] 254 55-24353
1. Stewardship, Christian—Sermons. 2. Baptists—Sermons. 3. Sermons, American. I. Title.

HOFFMAN, John Leslie. 261.8
Catholicism and mental deficiency. Cambridge, Mass. [1967] vii, 168 l. fold. map. 29 cm. Thesis—Harvard University, 1964. Bibliography: l. 162-168. [BX2347.8.M4H6] 68-2457
1. Catholic Church and the mentally handicapped. 2. Mentally handicapped children. I. Title.

*HORN, James G. 261.8
Major social concerns. Frank W. Klos, ed. William C. Kautz, illus. Philadelphia, Lutheran Church Pr. [c.1966] 175p. illus. 21cm. (School of religion ser., LB431) 1.50; 1.25 pap., teacher's guide,
I. Title.

HOWES, Robert Gerard. 261.8
Steeples in metropolis [by] Robert G. Howes. Dayton, Ohio, Pflaum Press, 1969. xiii, 200 p. 22 cm. Bibliography: p. 195-200. [BV637.H66] 69-20171 5.50
1. City churches. 2. Cities and towns—Planning—U.S. I. Title.

HUGHLEY, Judge Neal, 1907- 261.8
Trends in Protestant social idealism [by] J. Neal Hughley. Freeport, N.Y., Books for Libraries Press [1972, c1948] xiii, 184 p. 23 cm. (Essay index reprint series) Bibliography: p. 167-179. [HN31.H783 1972] 74-167359 ISBN 0-8369-2771-0
1. Church and social problems. 2. Sociology, Christian. 3. Protestantism. 4. Protestants in the U.S. I. Title.

HUNTLEY, Thomas Elliott 261.8
When people behave like sputniks (as I saw them). New York, Vantage Press [c. 1960] 112p. 22cm. 2.50 bds.,
I. Title.

JOHNS, Hazel T., 1920- 261.8
Peaceworld / Hazel T. Johns, Michael McIntyre, Sister Luke Tobin ; cartoons by Claudius. New York : Friendship Press, 1976. p. cm. Includes bibliographical references. [BT736.4.J63] 76-12410 ISBN 0-377-00054-X pbk. : 2.50
1. Peace (Theology) 2. Violence—Moral and religious aspects. 3. Nonviolence—Moral and religious aspects. 4. Peace. I. McIntyre, Michael, 1942- joint author. II. Tobin, Luke, 1908- joint author. III. Title.

JONES, George Curtis, 1911- 261.8
Christian stewardship: what are you worth? St. Louis, Bethany Press [1954] 159p. 20cm. [BV772.J6] 254 54-2649
1. Stewardship, Christian. I. Title. II. Title: What are you worth?

KANE, John Joseph, 1909- 261.8
Marriage and the family; a Catholic approach. New York, Dryden Press [1952] 341 p. 22 cm. Includes bibliography. [HQ728.K3] 392.3 52-11466
1. Family. 2. Marriage. I. Title.

KANTONEN. TAITO ALMAR, 1900- 261.8
A theology for Christian stewardship. Philadelphia, Muhlenberg Press [1956] ix, 126p. 21cm. Bibliographical footnotes. [BV772.K26] 254 56-9341
1. Stewardship, Christian. 2. Theology, Doctrinal. I. Title.

KAUFFMAN, Milo, 1898- 261.8
The challenge of Christian stewardship. Scottdale, Pa., Herald Press [1955] xii, 180p. 21cm. (The Conrad Grebel lectures for 1953) Bibliography: p. 169-175. [BV772.K3] 254 55-9814
1. Stewardship, Christian. I. Title. II. Series.

KAVANAUGH, John, 1912- ed. 261.8
The Quaker approach to contemporary problems. Edited by John Kavanaugh. Westport, Conn., Greenwood Press [1970, c1953] xi, 243 p. 23 cm. Contents.Contents.—Introduction, by J. Whitney.—Peace and war, by H. J. Cadbury.—Relief and reconstruction, by R. C. Wilson.—Economic life, by K. E. Boulding.—Business and industry, by D. R. Yarnall.—Education, by H. H. Brinton.—Race relations, by I. D. Reid.—Civil liberties, by H. A. Freeman.—Crime and punishment, by C. Bok.—Prisons and prisoners, by H. Van Etten.—Science, by K. Lonsdale.—Health and healing, by H. E. Collier.—Present secular philosophies, by D. E. Trueblood.—Quakers and the Russians, by E. Jackson.—Epilogue, by C. E. Pickett. [HN18.K3 1970] 70-110047
1. Social problems. 2. Church and social problems—Friends, Society of. I. Title.

KEACH, Richard L. 261.8
The purple pulpit [by] Richard L. Keach. Valley Forge [Pa.] Judson Press [1971] 128 p. illus. 20 cm. [BX6480.W37C45] 70-147848 ISBN 0-8170-0530-7 2.95
1. Wayne, Pa. Central Baptist Church. 2. Church renewal. I. Title.

KERANS, Patrick. 261.8
Sinful social structures. New York, Paulist Press [1974] vi, 113 p. 18 cm. (Topics in moral argument) Includes bibliographical references. [BT738.K39] 74-76716 ISBN 0-8091-1830-0 1.45 (pbk.).
1. Sin. 2. Social ethics. I. Title.

KERSHNER, Howard Eldred, 1891- 261.8
God, gold and government; the interrelationship of Christianity, freedom, self-government and economic well-being. Englw0)ewood Cliffs, N. J., Prentice-Hall [1957] 146p. 21cm. [HN31.K44] 57-6176
1. Church and social problems. I. Title.

KERSHNER, Howard Eldred, 1891- 261.8
God, gold and government; the interrelationship of Christianity, freedom, self-government and economic well-being. Englewood Cliffs, N.J., Prentice-Hall [1957] 146p. 21cm. [HN31.K44] 57-6176
1. Church and social problems. I. Title.

KLEMME, Huber F 261.8
Your churc and your community. Philadelphia, Published for the Co-operative Publication Association [by] Christian Education Press [1957] 121p. 20cm. (The Co-operative series. Leadership training texts& [BV625.K4] 57-10956
1. Church and social problems. I. Title.

KLEMME, Huber F 261.8
Your church and your community. Philadelphia, Published for the Co-operative Publication Association [by] Christian Education Press [1957] 121p. 20cm. (The Co-operative series. Leadership training texts) [BV625.K4] 57-10956
1. Church and social problems. I. Title.

KRUMBHOLZ, Clarence E. 261.8
Christianizing community life. Arthur H. Getz, editor. Philadelphia, Muhlenberg Press ['1951] 96 p. illus. 18 cm. (Elective series for young people and adults) Includes bibliography. [BV625.K7] 52-64327
1. Church and social problams—Study and teaching. I. Title.

LA FARGE, John, 1880- *261.8
The Catholic viewpoint on race relations. [1st ed.] Garden City, N. Y., Hanover House [1956] 190p. 22cm. (The Catholic viewpoint series) [HT1521.L18] 56-10767
1. Race problems. 2. Church and social problems—Catholic Church. 3. U. S.—Race question. I. Title.

LEE, Robert. 261.8
The schizophrenic church; conflict over community organization, by Robert Lee and Russell Galloway, with assistance of William Eichorn. Philadelphia, Westminister [i.e. Westminster] Press [1969] 192 p. illus. 21 cm. "Project by the Institute of Ethics and Society, San Francisco Theological Seminary, commissioned by the Division of Lay Education and the Office of Church and Society of the Board of Christian Education, the United Presbyterian Church U.S.A." [BV601.8.L4] 69-12490 2.65
1. Mission of the church—Case studies. I. Galloway, Russell, joint author. II. San Francisco Theological Seminary, San Anselmo, Calif. Institute of Ethics and Society. III. Title.

LENSKI, Gerhard Emmanuel, 1924- 261.8
The religious factor; a sociological study of religion's impact on politics, economics, and family life. Garden City, N.Y., Doubleday, [c.] 1961 xvi, 381p. illus., 61-9197 5.95
1. Religion and sociology—Case studies. I. Title.

LENSKI, Gerhard Emmanuel, 1924- 261.8
The religious factor; a sociological study of religion's impact on politics, econimics, and family life. Rev. ed. Garden City, N.Y., Doubleday [c.1961, 1963] xvi, 414p. 18cm. (Anchor bk., A337) Bibl. 1.45 pap.,
1. Religion and sociology—Case studies. I. Title.

LENSKI, Gerhard Emmanuel, 1924- 261.8
The religious factor : a sociological study of religion's impact on politics, economics, and family life / by Gerhard Lenski. Westport, Conn. : Greenwood Press, [1977, c1961] p. cm. Reprint of the 1st ed. published by Doubleday, Garden City, N.Y. Includes bibliographical references and indexes. [BL60.L44 1977] 77-1275 ISBN 0-8371-9506-3 lib.bdg. : 21.75
1. Religion and sociology—Case studies. 2. Detroit—Religion—Case studies. I. Title.

LEPPICH, John 261.8
Cries from the half-world. Tr. [from German] by Father Patrick. Detroit. Saint Paul Publications [dist. Daughters of St. Paul] [1961, c.1960] 181p. 60-11246 3.50
1. Church and social problems—Catholic Church. I. Title.

LETTS, Harold C ed. 261.8
Christian social responsibility; a symposium in three volumes. Philadelphia, Muhlenberg Press [1957] 3v. 20cm. Contents.v. 1. Existence today.--v. 2. The Lutheran heritage.--v. 3. Life in community. Includes bibliography. [HN37.L8L4] 57-11300
1. Church and social problems—Lutheran Church. 2. Sociology, Christian (Lutheran) I. Title.

LICORISH, David Nathaniel, 1904- 261.8
Tommorrow's church in today's world; a study of the twentieth -century challenge to religion. [1st ed.] New York, Exposition Press [1956] 172p. 21cm. [HN31.L55] 55-9403
1. Church and social problems. 2. Church. I. Title.

LOCKERBIE, D. Bruce. 261.8
The cosmic center / by D. Bruce Lockerbie. Grand Rapids : Eerdmans, c1977. p. cm. [BR115.C8L6] 77-737 ISBN 0-8028-1692-4 pbk. : 4.95
1. Jesus Christ—Person and offices. 2. Christianity and culture. 3. Secularism. I. Title.

LOOS, Amandus William, 1908- ed. 261.8
Religious faith and world culture. Freeport, N.Y., Books for Libraries Press [1970, c1951] viii, 294 p. 23 cm. (Essay index reprint series) Contents.Contents.—Introduction, by A. W. Loos.—What do we mean by religion? By H. E. Fosdick.—The situation we face: a sociological analysis, by K. G. Collier.—The situation we face: a psychological analysis, by G. W. Allport.—Religion and reality, by M. Buber, translated by N. Guterman.—Individualism reconsidered, by D. Riesman.—The individual and authority, D. J. Bradley.—Technology and personality, by J. E. Burchard.—Faith and freedom, by N. F. S. Ferre.—Prophetic religion and world culture, by A. H. Silver.—The world impact of the Russian Revolution, by P. E. Mosely.—The whole world in revolt, by M. S. Bates.—The unity of interdependence: a case study in international economics, by J. P. Condliffe.—Religious faith and human brotherhood, by A. Paton.—Ideal democracy and global anarchy, by M. B. Lucas.—World organization and world culture, by E. D. Canham.—Individual ethics and world culture, by W. R. Matthews.—World faith for world peace, by A. Chakravarty.—Is there a nascent world culture? By M. C. D'Arcy.—Cathedral lamp, translated by F. Mousseau. Bibliography (p. 285-287) [BL65.C8L6 1970] 71-128270 ISBN 0-8369-1976-9
1. Religion and culture—Addresses, essays, lectures. I. Title.

LOPEZ Trujillo, Alfonso. 261.8
Liberation or revolution? : An examination of the priest's role in the socioeconomic class struggle in Latin America / Alfonso Lopez Trujillo. Huntington, Ind. : Our Sunday Visitor, c1977. 128 p. ; 21 cm. Translation of ?Liberacion o revolucion? Includes bibliographical references. [BX1426.2.L6813] 77-70281 ISBN 0-87973-684-4 pbk. : 3.95
1. Catholic Church in Latin America—Clergy. 2. Liberation theology. 3. Revolution (Theology) I. Title.

MCCLELLAND, William Grigor. 261.8
And a new earth : making tomorrow's society better than today's / by W. Grigor McClelland. London : Friends Home Service Committee, 1976. [7], 91 p. ; 19 cm. (Swarthmore lecture ; 1976) Includes bibliographical references. [HN18.M214] 76-382485 ISBN 0-85245-122-9 : £0.90
1. Social history—20th century. 2. Friends. I. Title.

MCCORMACK, Arthur 261.8
World poverty and the Christian. New York, Hawthorn [c.1963] 158p. 22cm. (Twentieth cent. ency. of Catholicism, v.132. Section 13: Catholicism and science) Bibl. 63-13108 3.50 bds.,
1. Poverty. 2. Population. 3. Food supply. 4. Church and social problems—Catholic Church. I. Title.

MACDONALD, Allan John Macdonald, 1887- 261.8
Trade politics and Christianity in Africa and the East, by A. J. Macdonald. With an introd. by Sir Harry Johnston. New York, Negro Universities Press [1969] xxi, 295 p. 23 cm. "Originally published in 1916." Includes bibliographical references. [BV2105.M3 1969] 77-89007
1. Race problems. 2. Native races. 3. Missions. I. Title. II. Title: Christianity in Africa and the East.

MCKIEVER, Charles Fitzgerald. 261.8
Slavery and the emigration of North Carolina Friends. Murfreesboro, N.C., Johnson Pub. Co. [1970] viii, 88 p. 21 cm. Bibliography: p. [81]-88. [BX7648.N8M3] 79-18192
1. Friends, Society of. North Carolina. 2. Slavery in the United States—North Carolina. I. Title.

MCRAE, Glenn, 1887- 261.8
Teaching Christian stewardship. St. Louis, Bethany Press [1954] 158p. 20cm. [BV772.M357] [BV772.M357] 254 54-37559 54-37559
1. Stewardship, Christian—Study and teaching. I. Title.

MALHERBE, Abraham J. 261.8
Social aspects of early Christianity / Abraham J. Malherbe. Baton Rouge : Louisiana State University Press, c1977. xii, 98 p. ; 23 cm. (Rockwell lectures) Delivered at Rice University, April 1975. Includes bibliographical references and index. [BR166.M34] 77-3876 ISBN 0-8071-0261-X : 7.95
1. Sociology, Christian—Early church, ca. 30-600—Addresses, essays, lectures. I. Title. II. Series.

MARGERIE, Bertrand de. 261.8
The sacraments and social progress. Translated by Malachy Carroll. Chicago, Franciscan Herald Press [1974] p. Bibliography: p. [BX2203.M3713] 74-1451 ISBN 0-8199-0499-6 5.50
1. Sacraments—Catholic Church. 2. Sociology, Christian (Catholic) I. Title.

MARXISM and radical religion; essays toward a revolutionary humanism. Edited by John C. Raines and Thomas Dean. Philadelphia, Temple University Press, 1970. xvi, 176 p. 22 cm. "This book grows out of a two-day conference ... held at Temple University in April 1969 under the sponsorship of the Department of Religion." Includes bibliographical references. [BT738.3.M35] 78-119903 261.8
1. Revolution (Theology)—Addresses, essays, lectures. 2. Communism and religion—Addresses, essays, lectures. I. Raines, John C., ed. II. Dean, Thomas, 1938- ed. III. Philadelphia. Temple University. Dept. of Religion.

'MASON, Philip. 261.8
Christianity and race. New York, St. Martin's Press, 1957. 174p. 19cm. (The Burroughs memorial lectures, 1956) [BR115.R3M27 1957] 57-816
1. Race problems. 2. Church and social problems. I. Title.

MASSE, Benjamin Louis, 1905- ed. 261.8
The church and social progress; background readings for Pope John's Mater et magistra. Milwaukee Bruce [c.1966] xi, 248p. 23cm. Bibl. [HN37.C3M469] 66-19747 5.50
1. Church and social problems—Catholic Church—Addresses. essays, lectures. 2.

Catholic Church. Pope 1958-1963 (Joannes XXVI) Mater et magistra (15 may 1961) I. Title.

MASTON, Thomas Bufford, 1897- 261.8
Christianity and world issues. New York, Macmillan, 1957. 374 p. 22 cm. [HN31.M243] 57-5221
1. Church and social problems. I. Title.

MATHEWS, Donald G. 261.8
Slavery and Methodism; a chapter in American morality, 1780-1845, by Donald G. Mathews. Princeton, N.J., Princeton University Press, 1965. xi, 329 p. 21 cm. Bibliography: p. 305-324. [E449.M428] 65-17148
1. Slavery and the church—Methodist Episcopal Church. I. Title.

MATHEWS, Shailer, 1863-1941. 261.8
Jesus on social institutions, by Shailer Mathews. Edited, and with an introd., by Kenneth Cauthen. Philadelphia, Fortress Press [1971] lxxiii, 166 p. 19 cm. (Lives of Jesus series) Reprint of the 1928 ed., with a new introd. Based on the author's Social teaching of Jesus. Includes bibliographical references. [BS2417.S7M3 1971] 72-139346 5.95
1. Jesus Christ—Teachings. 2. Sociology, Biblical. I. Title.

MAYS, Benjamin Elijah, 1895- 261.8
Seeking to be Christian in race relations. New York, Friendship Press, 1957. 84p. 20cm. [BR115.R3M3 1957] 57-6580
1. Race problems. 2. Church and social problems. I. Title.

MERTON, Thomas, 1915- 261.8
Faith and violence; Christian teaching and Christian practice. [Notre Dame, Ind.] University of Notre Dame Press, 1968. x, 291 p. 21 cm. Bibliographical footnotes. [BT736.15.M4] 68-20438 1.95
1. Violence—Moral and religious aspects. I. Title.

MIDWESTERN Institute of Pastoral Theology. 3d, Detroit, 1963. 261.8
The teenage parishioner; [proceedings] Detroit, Midwestern Institute of Pastoral Theology, Sacred Heart Seminary, 1963. 84 p. 22 cm. Sponsored by the faculties of St. John's Provincial Seminary and Sacred Heart Seminary. Includes bibliographical references. [BX2347.8.Y7M5] 63-23228
1. Church work with youth — Catholic Church — Congresses. I. St. John's Provincial Seminary, Plymouth, Mich. II. Detroit. Sacred Heart Seminary. III. Title.

MIGUEZ Bonino, Jose. 261.8
Doing theology in a revolutionary situation / Jose Miguez Bonino. Philadelphia : Fortress Press, [1975] xxviii, 179 p. ; 20 cm. (Confrontation books) Bibliography: p. 175-179. [BT83.57.M53] 74-80424 ISBN 0-8006-1451-8 pbk. : 3.95
1. Liberation theology. I. Title.

MILLER, Haskell M. 261.8
Compassion and community; an appraisal of the church's changing role in social welfare. New York, Association Press [c.1961] 288p. Bibl. 61-7465 3.50 bds.,
1. Church and social problems. 2. Church charities. 3. Public welfare—U. S. I. Title.

MILLER, Robert Mcats. 261.8
American Protestantism and social issues, 1919-1939. Chapel Hill University of North Caroline Press [1958] 385p. 24cm. Includes bibliography. [HN3689.U6M59] 58-1243
1. Church and social problems—U. S. 2. Protestant churches—U. S. 3. U. S— Church history—20th cent. I. Title.

MOOMAW, I W 261.8
Deep furrows; goals, methods, and results of those who work toward a brighter tomorrow New York, Published by Agricultural Missions for the Rural Missions Cooperating Committee of the Division of Foreign Missions [1957] 192p. illus. 23cm. [HN32.M6] 57-9966
1. Community development. 2. Missions—Agricultural work. I. Title.

MOORE, Merrill Dennis, 1904- 261.8
Found faithful; Christian stewardship in personal and church life. Nashville Convention Press [1958, c1953] 146p. illus. 20cm. [BV772.M55 1958] 254 58-10985
1. Stewardship, Christian. I. Title.

MORGAN, Dewi. 261.8
God and sons. New York, Weybright and Talley [1968, c1967] 165 p. 22 cm. Bibliographical footnotes. [BT77.M83 1968] 68-28269 6.50

1. Theology, Doctrinal—Popular works. I. Title.

MORGAN, Everett J. 261.8
Social commitment; the social doctrine of the Church as applied to the current problems of our contemporary world: religion made relevant to the secular city [by] Everett J. Morgan. Berkeley, Calif., McCutchan Pub. [1967] xii, 257p. 28cm. Companion vol. to the author's The social conscience of a Catholic. Bibl. [HN37.C3M75] 67-16655 3.75
1. Church and social problems—Catholic Church. I. Title.

MORGAN, Everett J 261.8
Social commitment; the social doctrine of the Church as applied to the current problems of our contemporary world: religion made relevant to the secular city [by] Everett J. Morgan. Berkeley, Calif., McCutchan Pub. Corp. [1967] xii, 257 p. 28 cm. A companion vol. to the author's The social conscience of a Catholic. Includes bibliographies. [HN37.C3M75] 67-16655
1. Church and social problems — Catholic Church. I. Title.

MORGAN, Everett J ed. 261.8
The social conscience of a Catholic; the social doctrine of the church applied to problems in our contemporary society, edited by Everett J. Morgan. With a foreword by Louis J. Twomey. [Milwaukee, Distributed by Marquette University Bookstore, 1964] x, 293 p. 28 cm. "The substance of this book ... was originally composed by the students: priests, sisters, seminarians, lay students, who attended the first Social Doctrine Institute of Marquette University, summer 1963." Includes bibliographies. [HN37.C3M76] 64-18403
1. Church and social problems — Catholic Church. I. Marquette University. Milwaukee. Social Doctrine Institute. II. Title.

MUELDER, Walter George, 1907- 261.8
Methodism and society in the twentieth centry. Edited by the Board of Social and Economic Relations of the Methodist Church. New York, Abingdon Press [1961] 446p. 24cm. (Methodism and society, v.2) Includes bibliography. [HN37.M4M8] 61-10814
1. Church and social problems—Methodist Church. 2. Church and social problems—U. S. I. Methodist Church (United States) Board of Social and Economic Relations. II. Title.

MUELDER, Walter George, 1907- 261.8
Methodism and society in the twentieth century. Ed. by the Board of Social and Economic Relations of the Methodist Church. Nashville, Abingdon [c.1961] 446p. (Methodism and society, v.2) Bibl. 61-10814 6.50
1. Church and social problems—Methodist Church. 2. Church and social problems—U. S. I. Methodist Church (United States) Board of Social and Economic Relations. II. Title.

MUNBY, D L 261.8
Christianity and economic problems. London, Macmillan; New York, St. Martin's Press, 1956. ix, 290p. 23cm. Bibliographical footnotes. [BR115.E3M85] 56-14325
1. Christianity and economics. I. Title.

MUNBY, D. L. 261.8
God and the rich society; a study of Christians in a world of abundance. London, New York, Oxford University Press, 1961. 209 p. 22 cm. [BR115.E3M86 1961] 61-19285
1. Christianity and economics. I. Title.

MUNBY, Denys Lawrence. *261.8
Christianity and economic problems. London, Macmillan; New York, St. Martin's Press, 1956. ix, 290 p. 28 cm. Bibliographical footnotes. [BR115.E3M85] 56-14325
1. Christianity and economics. I. Title.

MUNBY, Denys Lawrence. 261.8
God and the rich society; a study of Christians in a world of abundance. London, New York, Oxford University Press, 1961. 209 p. 22 cm. [BR115.E3M86] 61-19285
1. Christianity and economics. I. Title.

THE Mystical and political dimension of the Christian faith / edited by Claude Geffre and Gustavo Guttierez [sic]. New York : Herder and Herder, 1974. 160 p. ; 23 cm. (Concilium ; new ser., v. 6, no. 10 (96), Theology of liberation) On cover: The New concilium: religion in the seventies. Includes bibliographical references. [BT83.57.M95] 73-17896 ISBN 0-8164-2580-9 pbk. : 3.95 261.8
1. Liberation theology. I. Geffre, Claude, ed. II. Gutierrez, Gustavo, 1928- ed. III. Series: Concilium (New York) ; 96.

NEAL, Marie Augusta. 261.8
A socio-theology of letting go : the role of a First World church facing Third World peoples / by Marie Augusta Neal. New York : Paulist Press, c1977. vii, 118 p. ; 21 cm. (An Exploration book) Bibliography: p. 112-118. [BR85.N28] 76-50953 ISBN 0-8091-2012-7 pbk. : 3.95
1. Theology—Addresses, essays, lectures. 2. United States—Religion—1945- —Addresses, essays, lectures. 3. Church and social problems—Addresses, essays, lectures. I. Title.

NELSEN, Hart M. 261.8
Black church in the sixties / Hart M. Nelsen & Anne Kusener Nelsen. Lexington : University Press of Kentucky, [1975] x, 172 p. ; 22 cm. Includes bibliographical references and index. [BR563.N4N45] 74-18937 ISBN 0-8131-1324-5 : 11.50
1. Afro-American churches. 2. Afro-Americans—Religion. I. Nelsen, Anne K., joint author. II. Title.

NELSON, Claud D 261.8
Religion and society; the ecumenical impact, by Claud D. Nelson. With a pref. by Lewis Webster Jones. New York, Sheed and Ward [1966] viii, 181 p. 22 cm. Bibliography: p. [179]-181. [HN31.N44] 66-22020
1. Church and social problems. I. Title.

NELSON, Claud D. 261.8
Religion and society; the ecumenical impact, by Claud D. Nelson. With a pref. by Lewis Webster Jones. New York, Sheed and Ward [1966] viii, 181 p. 22 cm. Bibliography: p. [179]-181. [HN31.N44] 66-22020
1. Church and social problems. I. Title.

NELSON, John Oliver, 1909- ed. 261.8
Work and vocation, a Christian discussion. [1st ed.] New York. Harper [1954] 224p. 22cm. Bibliography: p. 213-224. [BV4740.N4] 54-5856
1. Vocation. I. Title.

NIEBUHR, Reinhold, 1892- 261.8
Love and justice; selections from the shorter writings of Reinhold Niebuhr. Edited by D. B. Robertson. Philadelphia, Westminster Press [1957] 309p. 24cm. [HN18.N5] 57-9745
1. Social problems. I. Title.

NIEBUHR, Reinhold, 1892- 261.8
Love and justice; selections from the shorter writings of Reinhold Niebuhr. Ed. by D. B. Robertson. [Magnolia, Mass., P. Smith. 1967.c. 1957] 309p. 20cm. (Meridian bk. rebound) [HN18.N5] 4.00
1. Social problem. I. Title.

NIEBUHR, Reinhold, 1892- 261.8
Love and Justice; selections from the shorter writings of Reinhold Niebuhr. Edited by D. B. Robertson. Philadelphia. Westminster Press [1957] 309p. 24cm. [HN18.N5] 57-9745
1. Social problems. I. Title.

OBENHAUS, Victor. 261.8
The responsible Christian. [Chicago] University of Chicago Press [1957] 218p. 24cm. Includes bibliography. [HN31.O2] 57-11211
1. Church and social problems. 2. Christianity and economics. I. Title.

O'CONNOR, Daniel A. 261.8
Catholic social doctrine. Westminster, Md., Newman Press, 1956. 204p. 23cm. [BX1753.O27] 55-10551
1. Pius XII, Pope, 1876- 2. Sociology, Christian (Catholic) I. Title.

O'CONNOR, Daniel A 261.8
Catholic social Locke [a critical introduction] London, Baltimore, Christian (Catholic) [BX1753.O27] 55-105518
1. Pius XII, Pope, 1876- I. Title.

O'CONNOR, Elizabeth. 261.8
The new community / Elizabeth O'Connor. 1st ed. New York : Harper & Row, c1976. 121 p. : ill. ; 22 cm. Includes bibliographical references. [BV4501.2.O32 1976] 76-9964 ISBN 0-06-066337-5 pbk. : 3.95
1. Washington, D.C. Church of the Saviour. 2. Christian life—1960- 3. Christian communities. 4. Church and the poor—Case studies. I. Title.

PASTORAL psychology. 261.8
Sex and religion today, edited by Simon Doniger. New York, Association Press [1953] 238p. 20cm. (Pastoral psychology series) 'Articles ... selected ... from the pages of ... Pastoral psychology.'--Dust jacket. [BL65.S4P3] 53-11816
1. Sex and religion. 2. Psychology, Pastoral. I. Doniger, Simon, ed. II. Title.

PERKINS, William Allen, 1926- 261.8
When we work together. New York, Friendship Press [1960] 64p. illus. 21cm. Includes bibliography. [HD4869.P4] 60-7451
1. Labor camps. 2. Students in church work. I. Title.

PIERARD, Richard V., 1934- 261.8
The unequal yoke; evangelical Christianity and political conservatism [by] Richard V. Pierard. [1st ed.] Philadelphia, Lippincott [1970] 191 p. 21 cm. (Evangelical perspectives) Bibliography: p. 188-191. [BR1642.U5P5] 70-127085 5.95
1. Evangelicalism—United States. 2. Conservatism—United States. I. Title.

POWELL, Oliver. 261.8
Citizens for the new world, a course for older young people and adults. Teacher's ed. Boston, Pilgrim Press [1953] 66, 92p. 21cm. (Pilgrim series) [HN31.P73 1953] 53-1077
1. Church and social problems—Study and teaching. I. Title.

PROTESTANT Episcopal Church in the U. S. A. Albany (Diocese) *261.8
Man at work in God's world; papers delivered at the church and work congress held in Albany, New York, October 19-20, 1955. Edited by G. E. DeMille. [1st ed.] New York, Longmans, Green, 1956. xviii, 205p. 22cm. [BV627.P7] 56-9214
1. Church and labor. 2. Church and social problems. I. De Mille, George Edmed, 1898- ed. II. Title.

RAUSCHENBUSCH, Walter, 1861-1918. *261.8
A Rauschenbusch reader; the kingdom of God and the social gospel. Compiled by Benson Y. Landis; with an interpretation of the life and work of Walter Rauschenbush by Harry Emerson Fosdick. [1st ed.] New York, Harper [1957] 167 p. 22 cm. [BR115.S6R39] 57-7351
1. Sociology, Christian. I. Landis, Benson Young, 1897- comp. II. Title.

READING, Benjamin F 261.8
Democracy can succeed-how? [New York] Printed by the Parthenon Press [1956] 163p. 20cm. [HN31.R42] 56-3507
1. Church and social problems. 2. Democracy. 3. U. S.—Pol. & govt. I. Title.

RECKITT, Maurice Bennington, 1888- 261.8
Militant here in earth; considerations on the prophetic function of the church in the twentieth centrry. London, New York, Longmans, Green [1958] 160p. 19cm. [BR115.S6R523] 58-14551
1. Sociology, Christian. 2. Civilization, Modern. I. Title.

RELIGION and social change; a report on a series of five seminars with ministers and social scientists. Raleigh, Agricultural Policy Institute, North Carolina State University, 1968. vi, 209 p. 28 cm. "Summaries were written by Mrs. Marion Gregory." Seminars held Oct. 9-10, 1967-April 1-2, 1968, at Quail Roost Conference Center, Rougemont, N.C., sponsored by Agricultural Policy Institute of North Carolina State University, Raleigh, and others. Includes bibliographies. [HN31.R44] 70-628044 261.8
1. Church and social problems. 2. Church and economics. I. North Carolina. State University, Raleigh. Agricultural Policy Institute.

RICHARDS, Herbert Forest. 261.8
The church for our time; the kind of church needed for today's world, by H. F. Richards. [1st ed.] New York, Vantage Press [1964] 112 p. 21 cm. [BV4017.R52] 64-6060
1. Pastoral theology — Addresses, essays, lectures. I. Title.

RICHARDSON, William J., 1921- 261.8
Social action vs. evangelism : an essay on the contemporary crisis / by William J. Richardson. South Pasadena, Calif. : W. Carey Library, [1977] p. cm. Includes bibliographical references. [BV601.8.R49] 77-22669 ISBN 0-87808-160-7 : 1.95
1. Mission of the church. 2. Evangelistic work. 3. Social action. 4. Church and social problems. I. Title.

RIGA, Peter 261.8
John XXIII and the city of man. Westminster, Md., Newman [c.]1966. xiii, 239p. 23cm. Bibl. [HN37.C3A3] 66-16569 5.50
1. Catholic Church. Pope, 1958-1963 (Joannes XXIII) Mater et magistra (15 May, 1961) I. Title.

RIGA, Peter J 261.8
John XXIII and the city of man. Westminster, Md., Newman Press, 1966. xiii, 239 p. 22 cm. Bibliographical footnotes. [HN37.C3A3 1966] 66-16569
1. Catholic Church. Pope, 1958-1963 (Joannes XXIII) Mater et magistra (15 May 1961) I. Title.

ROBERTS, Guy L 261.8
How the church can help where delinquency

begins. Richmond, John Knox Press [1958] 157p. 21cm. Includes bibliography. [BV4464.R6] 58-7770
1. Title.

ROOT, Robert. 261.8
Progress against prejudice; the church confronts the race problem. New York, Friendship Press [1957] 165p. 21cm. [BR115.R3R6] 57-6158
1. U. S.—Race question. 2. Church and social problems—U. S. I. Title.

RUETHER, Rosemary Radford. 261.8
The radical kingdom; the Western experience of Messianic hope. [1st ed.] New York, Harper & Row [1970] viii, 304 p. 22 cm. Includes bibliographical references. [BT738.3.R8 1970] 70-109080 7.50
1. Revolution (Theology) 2. Messianism. 3. Sociology, Christian. I. Title.

RUETHER, Rosemary Radford. 261.8
The radical Kingdom; the Western experience of Messianic hope. New York, Paulist Press, [1975 c1970] viii, 304 p. 21 cm. Includes bibliographical references and index. [BT738.3.R8] ISBN 0-8091-1860-2 3.95 (pbk.)
1. Revolution (Theology). 2. Sociology, Christian. 3. Messianism. I. Title.
L.C. card no. for original edition: 70-109080.

RUNES, Dagobert David, 1902- 261.8
The Jew and the cross [by] Dagobert D. Runes. New York, Philosophical Library [1965] 94 p. 22 cm. Bibliography: p. 93-94. [DS145.R85] 65-26567
1. Antisemitism—Hist. I. Title.

RUNES, Dagobert David, 1902- 261.8
The Jew and the cross [by] Dagobert D. Runes. [2d ed.] New York, Citadel Press [1966, c1965] 96 p. 21 cm. Bibliography: p. 93-94. [DS145.R85] 66-1680
1. Antisemitism—Hist. I. Title.

RUNES, Dagobert David, 1902- 261.8
The Jew and the cross. New York, Philosophical [c.1965] 94p. 22cm. Bibl. [DS145.R85] 65-26567 2.75
1. Antisemitism—Hist. I. Title.

RUNES, Dagobert David, 1902- 261.8
The Jew and the cross. New York, Citadel [1966, c.1965] 96p. 21cm. (C-216) Bibl. [DS145.R85] .95 pap.,
1. Antisemitism—Hist. I. Title.

RUSHDOONY, Rousas John. 261.8
Bread upon the waters; columns from the California farmer, by Rousas J. Rushdoony. Nutley, N.J., Craig Press, 1969. 102 p. 22 cm. [BR115.E3R87] 70-81504
1. Christianity and economics. 2. Church and social problems—United States. I. California farmer. II. Title.

RUSHDOONY, Rousas John. 261.8
Politics of guilt and pity. Nutley, N.J., Craig Press, 1970. 371 p. 20 cm. Includes bibliographical references. [BR115.P7R9] 70-133083 6.50
1. Christianity and politics. 2. Christianity and economics. 3. Social ethics. I. Title.

RUTLEDGE, Arthur B *261.8
Homes that last. Nashville, Broadman Press [1952] 134p. 19cm. [BV4526.R85] 173.1 52-14769
1. Family—Religious life. I. Title.

RYAN, Rosalie, 1915- comp. 261.8
New Testament themes for contemporary man [by] Rosalie M. Ryan. Englewood Cliffs, N.J., Prentice-Hall [1969] xi, 274 p. 22 cm. Bibliographical footnotes. [BR85.R87] 69-20491 ISBN 1-361-59710- 3.75
1. Christianity—20th century—Addresses, essays, lectures. I. Title.

SACRIFICE and song. 261.8
[Teacher's ed.] Nashville, Broadman Press [1953] 136p. 20cm. 'A publication of the Woman's Missionary Union, Birmingham, Alabama.' [BV772.F35] [BV772.F35] 254 53-9362 53-9362
1. Stewardship, Christian. I. Farmer, Foy (Johnson) 1887-

SALSTRAND, George A E 1908- 261.8
The story of stewardship in the United States of America. Grand Rapids, Baker Book House, 1956. 169p. illus. 23cm. Includes bibliography. [BV772.S3] [BV772.S3] 254 56-7586 56-7586
1. Stewardship, Christian. I. Title.

SANDERS, Robert Neal, 1931- 261.8
Radical voices in the wilderness; the social implications of the prophets [by] Robert N. Sanders. Waco, Texas, Word Books [1970] 172 p. 23 cm. Includes bibliographical references. [BS1505.4.S25] 74-135350 4.95
1. Bible. O.T. Prophets—Sermons. 2. Baptists—Sermons. 3. Sermons, American. I. Title.

SANDIFORD, Ralph, 1693-1733. 261.8
A brief examination of the practice of the times. New York, Arno Press, 1969. 74 p. 23 cm. (The Anti-slavery crusade in America) Reprint of the 1729 ed. [E446,S36 1969] 70-82221
1. Slavery in the United States—Controversial literature—1729. I. Title. II. Series.

SCHAEFFER, Francis August. 261.8
The church at the end of the 20th century, by Francis A. Schaeffer. Downers Grove, Ill., Inter-Varsity Press [1970] 153 p. 22 cm. [BR121.2.S22] 73-134795 ISBN 0-87784-889-0 3.95
1. Christianity—20th century. I. Title.

SCHAEFFER, Francis August. 261.8
Pollution and the death of man; the Christian view of ecology [by] Francis A. Schaeffer. Wheaton, Ill., Tyndale House Publishers [1970] 125 p. 22 cm. [GF80.S3] 72-123293 ISBN 0-8423-4840-9 2.95
1. Human ecology—Moral and religious aspects. 2. Nature—Religious interpretations. I. Title.

SCHERER, James A. 261.8
Global living here and now [by] James A. Scherer. New York, Friendship Press [1974] 128 p. illus. 20 cm. Includes bibliographical references. [BR121.2.S32] 74-5344 ISBN 0-377-00003-5 1.95 (pbk.)
1. Christianity—20th century. 2. Church and the world. 3. Civilization, Modern—1950- I. Title.

SEE, Ruth Douglas, 1910 261.8
What can we do? An action handbook. New York, Friendship Press [1957] 64p. 19cm. [BR115.R3S4] 57-6161
1. U. S.—Race question. 2. Church and social problems—Study and teaching. I. Title.

SEE, Ruth Douglas, 1910- 261.8
What can we do? An action handbook. New York, Friendship Press [1957] 64p. 19cm. [BR115.R3S4] 57-6161
1. U. S.—Race question. 2. Church and social problems—Study and teaching. I. Title.

SEIFERT, Harvey. *261.8
The church in community action. New York, Abingdon-Cokesbury Press [1952] 240 p. 21 cm. Includes bibliography. [BV625.S43] 52-5379
1. Church and social problems. I. Title.

SEIFERT, Harvey. 261.8
Good news for rich and poor : Christian approaches to a new economic order / by Harvey Seifert. Philadelphia : United Church Press, c1976. p. cm. (A Doing the word study/action resource) Bibliography: p. [BR115.E3S38] 76-40211 ISBN 0-8298-0324-6 pbk. : 3.95
1. Christianity and economics. I. Title.

SELLERS, James Earl. 261.8
Public ethics; American morals and manners [by] James Sellers. [1st ed.] New York, Harper & Row [1970] 349 p. 22 cm. Bibliographical references included in "Notes" (p. 313-342) [E169.12.S43 1970] 70-85049 8.95
1. U.S.—Moral conditions. 2. Church and the world. I. Title. II. Title: American morals and manners.

SHAW, Roud. 261.8
The lost Christ in a lost world. Boston, Christopher Pub. House [1969] 182 p. 23 cm. [BR121.2.S5] 69-16271 3.95
1. Christianity—20th century. 2. Social problems. I. Title.

SHEED, Francis Joseph, 1897- 261.8
Society and sanity. London, New York, Sheed and Ward [1953] 225p. 22cm. [BX1753.S49 1953] 53-3135
1. Sociology, Christian (Catholic) I. Title.

SHERMAN, Franklin. 26.18
The courage to care; a study in Christian social responsibility. Editor: Arthur H. Getz. Philadelphia, Muhlenberg Press [1959] 96 p. illus. 28 cm. [HN37.L8S45] 59-4297
1. Church and social problems — Lutheran Church. I. Title.

SKINNER, Tom, 1942- 261.8
Words of revolution; a call to involvement in the real revolution. Grand Rapids, Zondervan Pub. House [1970] 171 p. 22 cm. [BV3797.S47] 76-132973 3.95
1. Evangelistic sermons. 2. Sermons, American. 3. Revolution (Theology) I. Title.

SMITH, John Owen. 261.8
Give the whole gospel a chance / John Owen Smith. Nashville : Tidings, [1974?] x, 101 p. ; 19 cm. Includes bibliographical references. [BT738.S565] 74-27908
1. Sociology, Christian. 2. Church and social problems. I. Title.

SMITH, Roy Lemon, 1887- 261.8
Stewardship studies. Nashville, Abingdon Press [1954] 256p. 21cm. [BV772.S615] [BV772.S615] 254 54-8242 54-8242
1. Stewardship, Christian. I. Title.

SPANN, John Richard, 1891-- ed. 261.8
The church and social responsibility. Nashville, Abingdon- Cokesbury Press [1953] 272p. 23cm. [HN31.S75] 53-8136
1. Church and social problems. I. Title.

STRINGFELLOW, William. 261.8
Imposters of God: inquiries into favorite idols. Dayton, Ohio, G. A. Pflaum [1969] 127 p. plates. 17 cm. (Christian experience series, 7) (Witness books, 11.) [BL485.S8] 72-97046 0.85
1. Idols and images—Worship. I. Title.

SYMANOWSKI, Horst. 261.8
The Christian witness in an industrial society. Translated by George H. Kehm. Introd. by Robert B. Starbuck. Philadelphia, Westminster Press [1964] 160 p. 21 cm. Bibliographical references included in "Notes" (p. 156-160) [HD6338.S943] 64-12391
1. Church and labor — Addresses, essays, and lectures. 2. Church and social problems — Lutheran Church — Addresses, Essays, lectures, I. Title.

SYMANOWSKI, Horst 261.8
The Christian witness in an industrial society. Tr. [from German] by George H. Kehm. Introd. by Robert B. Starbuck. Philadelphia, Westminster [c.1964] 160p. 21cm. Bibl. 64-12391 3.75
1. Church and labor—Addresses, essays, lectures. 2. Church and social problems—Lutheran Church—Addresses, essays, lectures. I. Title.

TAYLOR, Eustace Lovatt Hebden, 1925- 261.8
Reformation or revolution; a study of modern society in the light of a reformational and scriptural pluralism, by E. L. Hebden Taylor. Nutley, N.J., Craig Press, 1970. xiv, 633 p. 23 cm. Includes bibliographical references. [BR115.E3T37] 77-115822
1. Christianity and economics. 2. Sociology, Christian. 3. Labor and laboring classes. I. Title.

TAYLOR, Robert N. 261.8
This damned campus; as seen by a college chaplain [by] Robert N. Taylor, Jr. Philadelphia, Pilgrim Press [1969] x, 130 p. illus. 21 cm. Bibliographical references included in "Notes" (p. 127-130) [BV639.C6T33] 77-76086 2.95
1. Universities and colleges—Religion. I. Title.

TECHNOLOGY and social justice; 261.8
an international symposium on the social and economic teaching of the World Council of Churches from Geneva 1966 to Uppsala 1968. Edited by Ronald H. Preston. [1st American ed.] Valley Forge, Judson Press [1971] xx, 472 p. 24 cm. "Sponsored by the International Humanum Foundation." Includes bibliographical references. [HN31.T4 1971] 78-152584 ISBN 0-8170-0536-6 10.95
1. World Council of Churches. 2. Church and social problems—Addresses, essays, lectures. I. Preston, Ronald H., 1913- ed. II. International Foundation Humanum.

TEMPLE, William, Abp. of Canterbury, 1881-1944. 261.8
Christianity and social order / William Temple ; introduction by Ronald H. Preston. New York : Seabury Press, 1977, c1976. 119 p. ; 22 cm. "A Crossroad book." Includes bibliographical references. [BT738.T36 1977] 77-23138 ISBN 0-8164-0348-1 : 6.95
1. Sociology, Christian. I. Title.

THOMAS, Madathilparampil M *261.8
Revolution and redemption, by M. M. Thomas and Paul E. Converse. New York, Friendship Press [1955] 58p. 19cm. [BV2063.T37] 55-5764
1. Church and social problems. 2. Missions. I. Converse, Paul E., joint author. II. Title.

TOTTRESS, Richard E *261.8
Heaven's entrance requirements for the races. [Rev. ed.] New York, Comet Press Books, 1957. 50p. 21cm. (A Reflection book) [BR115.R3T6 1957] 57-8115
1. U. S.—Race question. I. Title.

TOTTRESS, Richard E *261.8
Heaven's entrance requirements for the races. [Rev. ed.] New York, Comet Press Books, 1957. 50 p. 21 cm. (A Reflection book) [BR115.R3T6 1957] 57-8115
1. U.S. — Race question. I. Title.

TRIMBLE, Malcome Calvis. *261.8
Our awakening social conscience; the emerging kingdom of God. [1st ed.] New York, Vantage Press [1958] 158 p. 21 cm. [BT738.T7] 58-10676
1. Sociology, Christian. 2. Kingdom of God. I. Title.

WAKIN, Edward. 261.8
Controversial conversations with Catholics. Dayton, Ohio, Pflaum Press, 1969. xiv, 211 p. 22 cm. [BV600.2.W28] 69-20173 5.95
1. Church renewal—Catholic Church. 2. Church and the world. I. Title.

WALSH, Chad, 1914- 261.8
Campus gods on trial. New York, Macmillan, 1953. 138 p. 20 cm. [BV1610.W25] 53-1048
1. Universities and colleges—Religion. 2. Apologetics—20th cent. I. Title.

WALSH, Chad, 1914- 261.8
Campus gods on trial. Rev., enl. ed. New York, Macmillan, 1962 [c.1953, 1962] 154p. Bibl. 62-8559 3.00
1. Universities and colleges—Religion. 2. Apologetics—20th cent. I. Title.

WARNER, Wellman Joel, 1897- 261.8
The Wesleyan movement in the industrial revolution, by Wellman J. Warner. New York, Russell & Russell [1967] x, 299 p. 23 cm. First published in 1930. Bibliography: p. 283-296. [HN37.M4W3 1967] 66-24768
1. Wesley, John, 1703-1791. 2. Church and social problems—Methodist Church. 3. Church and social problems—Great Britain. 4. Great Britain—Social conditions. 5. Methodism. I. Title.

WEATHERFORD, Willis Duke, 1875- 261.8
American churches and the Negro; an historical study from early slave days to the present. Boston, Christopher Pub. House [1957] 310p. 21cm. [BR563.N4W4] 57-9842
1. U. S.—Race question. 2. Slavery and the church. I. Title.

WEATHERFORD, Willis Duke, 1875- *261.8
American churches and the Negro; an historical study from early slave days to the present. Boston, Christopher Pub. House [1957] 310 p. 21 cm. [BR563.N4W4] 57-9842
1. U.S. — Race question. 2. Slavery and the church. I. Title.

WEBB, Muriel S ed. 261.8
Wealth and want in one world; a symposium, edited by Muriel S. Webb. New York, Friendship Press [1966] 126 p. ports. 21 cm. [HN18.W38] 66-11126
1. Poverty — Addresses, essays, lectures. 2. Social history — 1945- I. Title.

WELSBY, Paul A., comp. 261.8
Sermons and society: an Anglican anthology; edited by Paul A. Welsby. Harmondsworth, Penguin, 1970. 364 p. 19 cm. (Pelican books, A1173) Bibliography: p. 360-[362] [BX5133.A1W4] 79-22020 ISBN 0-14-021173-X 10/-
1. Church of England—Sermons. 2. Sermons, English. 3. Great Britain—Social conditions—Collections. I. Title.

WHEELER, Richard Shaw, 1935- 261.8
Pagans in the pulpit [by] Richard S. Wheeler. New Rochelle, N.Y., Arlington House Publishers [1974] 137 p. 25 cm. [BR115.P7W44] 74-10903 ISBN 0-87000-264-3 7.95
1. Christianity and politics. 2. Church and social problems. 3. Liberalism (Religion) I. Title.

WICKHAM, Edward Ralph, Bp., 1911- 261.8
Encounter with modern society. New York, Seabury [1965, c.1964] 125p. 20cm. Bibl. [BR123.W49] 65-937 1.50 pap.,
1. Christianity—20th cent.—Addresses, essays, lectures. 2. Missions—Theory. I. Title.

WILLIAMS, Colin Wilbur, 1921- 261.8
Faith in a secular age, by Colin Williams. New York, Harper [1966] 128p. 21cm. (Harper chapel bks., CB28) Bibl. [BR115.W6W5 1966] 66-8597 1.25 pap.,
1. Church and the world. I. Title.

WILLIAMS, William Thomas. 261.8
Civilization of right relationships; a study of life and its urge for fellowship. [1st ed.] New York, Exposition Press [1953] 229p. 21cm. [BR115.P7W48] 53-8520

1. Christian life. 2. Church and social problems. 3. Democracy. I. Title.

WILLIE, Charles Vert, 1927- 261.8
Church action in the world; studies in sociology and religion, by Charles V. Willie. New York, Morehouse-Barlow Co., 1969. xv, 160 p. 23 cm. [BV601.8.W48] 68-56919
1. Mission of the church. 2. Sociology, Christian. I. Title.

YINGER, John Milton 261.8
Religion in the struggle for power; a study in the Sociology of religion. New York, Russell & Russell, 1961 [c.1946] 275p. (Duke Univ. Pr. soc. ser., 3) Bibl. 61-13820 6.50
1. Religion and sociology. 2. Church and social Problems. I. Title.

CHRISTIANITY and crisis. 261.804
What the Christian hopes for in society. Selections from Christianity and crisis, with a foreword by Reinhold Niebuhr. Edited by Wayne H. Cowan. New York, Association Press [1957] 125p. 16cm. (An Association Press reflection book) [BR123.C62] 57-11610
1. Christianity— Addresses, essays, lectures. 2. Church and social problems— Addresses, essays, lectures. I. Cowan, Wayne H., ed. II. Title.

CHRISTIANITY and crisis. 261.804
What the Christian hopes for in society. Selections from Christianity and crisis, with a foreword by Reinhold Niebuhr. Edited by Wayne H. Cowan. New York, Association Press [1957] 125 p. 16 cm. (An Association Press reflection book) [BR123.C62] 57-11610
1. Christianity—Addresses, essays, lectures. 2. Church and social problems—Addresses, essays, lectures. I. Cowan, Wayne H., ed. II. Title.

FENTON, Thomas P. 261.8'07
Education for justice : a resource manual / edited by Thomas P. Fenton. Maryknoll, N.Y. : Orbis Books, 1975. xvi, 464 p. : ill. ; 28 cm. Includes bibliographies. [JX1293.U6F4] 74-83519 ISBN 0-88344-154-3 pbk. : 3.95
1. International relations—Study and teaching. 2. Justice. I. Title.

MCCOLLOUGH, Charles R., 261.8'07
1934-
Morality of power : a notebook on Christian education for social change / by Charles R. McCollough. Philadelphia : United Church Press, c1977. 142 p. : ill. ; 28 cm. (A Doing the word resource published for Christian education) Bibliography: p. 141-142. [BV1565.S6M3] 76-56243 ISBN 0-8298-0329-7 pbk. : 5.95
1. Christian education—Text-books for adults. 2. Church and social problems—Study and teaching. I. Title.

BOASE, Paul H., comp. 261.8'08
The rhetoric of Christian socialism [by] Paul H. Boase. New York, Random House [1969] ix, 173 p. 21 cm. (A Random house study in speech, SSP9) (Issues and spokesmen series.) Contents.Contents.—Infidel attack on property, by J. Cook.—Labor's view of the situation, by R. H. Newton.—The church and the gospel of push, by W. D. P. Bliss.—Christianity versus socialism, by L. Abbott.—The coming brotherhood, by F. Willard.—The problem of the city, by J. Strong.—The opportunity of the church, by G. D. Herron.—The new apostolate, by W. Rauschenbusch.—The new evangel, by W. Gladden.—My account with the unknown soldier, by H. E. Fosdick.—The Koinonia story, by C. Jordan.—A knock at midnight, by M. L. King. Includes bibliographical references. [BT738.B57] 69-14470 1.95
1. Social gospel—Addresses, essays, lectures. I. Title.

THE Church today; 261.8'08
commentaries on the Pastoral constitution on the Church in the modern world. [Translated by John Drury, Denis Barrett, and Michael L. Mazzarese.] Edited by Group 2000. Westminster, Md., Newman Press [1967, c1968] vi, 319 p. 21 cm. Bibliographical footnotes. [BX830 1962.A45C975] 68-20847
1. Vatican Council. 2d, 1962-1965. Constitutio pastoralis de ecclesia in mundo huius temporis. 2. Church and the world. I. Group 2000.

GROUP 2000. 261.8'08
The Church today; commentaries on the Pastoral constitution on the Church in the modern world. [translated by John Drury, Denis Barrett, and Michael L. Mazzarese.] Edited by Group 2000. Westminster, Md., Newman Press [1967, c1968] vi, 319 p. 21 cm. Bibliographical footnotes. [BX830 1962.A45C975] 68-20847
1. Vatican Council. 2d, 1962-1965. Constitutio pastoralis de eccesia in mundo huius temporis. 2. Church and the world. I. Title.

JOANNES XXIII, Pope 1881- 261.808
1963.
A Pope John memorial miniature, 4v. [New York, Random, c.1966] 4v. unpaged ports. 10x7cm. [BX891.J6] 66-18333 2.95, set, bxd.
1. Catholic Church—Collected works. 2. Theology—Collected works—20th cent. 3. Bibliography and miniature editions—Specimens. I. Catholic Church. Pope, 1958-1963 (Joannes XXIII) Pacem in terris (11 Apr. 1963) English. II. Title.
Contents omitted.

SYMPOSIUM on Pacem in 261.808
Terris by Pope John XXIII, University of Notre Dame, 1965.
Proceedings. Edited by Mark J. Fitzgerald. [Notre Dame, Ind., 1965] 78 p. 23 cm. Organized by the Dept. of Economics in cooperation with the college faculties of the University of Notre Dame and the Catholic Economic Association. Includes bibliographies. [BX1793.A26S9 1965] 66-293
1. Catholic Church. Pope, 1958-1963 (Joannes XXIII) Pacem in terris (11 Apr. 1963) — Congresses. 2. Christianity and international affairs — Congresses. I. Fitzgerald, Mark J., ed. II. Notre Dame, Ind. University. Dept. of Economics. III. Catholic Economic Association. IV. Title.

SYMPOSIUM on Pacem in 261.808
Terris by Pope John XXIII, University of Notre Dame, 1965
Proceedings. Ed. by Mark J. Fitzgerald. [Notre Dame, Ind.] Univ. of Notre Dame [c.1965] 78p. 23cm. Org. by the Dept. of Econ. in coop. with the coll. faculties of the Univ. of Notre Dame and the Catholic Econ. Assn. Bibl. [BX1793.A26S91965] 66-293 1.25 pap.,
1. Catholic Church. Pope, 1958-1963 (Johannes XXIII) Pacem in terris (11 Apr. 1963)—Congresses. 2. Christianity and international affairs—Congresses. I. Fitzgerald, Mark J., ed. II. Notre Dame, Ind. University. Dept. of Economics. III. Catholic Economic Association. IV. Title.

TILLICH, Paul, 1886- 261.8'08
1965.
Political expectation. [1st ed.] New York, Harper & Row [1971] xx, 187 p. 22 cm. Contents.Contents.—Introduction, by J. L. Adams.—Christianity and modern society.—Protestantism as a critical and creative principle.—Religious socialism.—Basic principles of religious socialism.—Christianity and Marxism.—The state as expectation and demand.—Shadow and substance: a theory of power.—The political meaning of Utopia. [BT738.T54 1971] 78-124700 5.95
1. Sociology, Christian—Addresses, essays, lectures. 2. Socialism, Christian—Addresses, essays, lectures. 3. Political science—Addresses, essays, lectures. I. Title.

HANOVER College, 261.8082
Hanover, Ind. Insitute, 1960.
Christian perspectives in contemporary culture ... proceedings. Edited by Frank S. Baker. New York, Twayne Publishers, 1962. 148 p. group port. 23 cm. [BR115.C5H3] 62-19357
1. Civilization, Christian — Addresses, essays, lecture. I. Baker, Frank S., ed. II. Hanover College, Hanover, Ind. III. Title.

HANOVER COLLEGE, 261.8082
Hanover, Ind. Institute, 1960
Christian perspectives in contemporary culture . . . proceedings. Ed. by Frank S. Baker. New York, Twayne [c.]1962. 148p. group port. 23cm. 62-19357 3.50
1. Civilization, Christian—Addresses, essasy, lectures. I. Baker, Frank S., ed. II. Hanover College, Hanover, Ind. III. Title.

MUELLER, Elwin W., 1908- 261.8082
ed.
The silent struggle for mid-America; the church in town and country today. E. W. Mueller, Giles C. Ekola, editors. Minneapolis, Augsburg [c.1963] xi, 167p. map. 22cm. Lects. and findings of a workshop on 'The church's concern for town and country communities in mid-America' sponsored by the office of Church in Town and Country of the Div. of Amer, Missions, Natl. Lutheran Council. Bibl. 63-16602 3.50 pap.,
1. Rural churches—U.S. 2. Sociolgy, Christian (Lutheran) I. Ekola, Giles C., joint ed. II. National Lutheran Council. Division of American Missions. Church in Town and Country. III. Title.

MUELLER, Elwin W. 1908- 261.8082
ed.
The silent struggle for mid-America; the church in town and country today. E. W. Mueller and Giles C. Ekola, editors. Minneapolis, Augsburg Pub. House [c1963] xi, 167 p. map. 22 cm. Lectures and findings of a workshop on "The church's concern for town and country communities in mid-America" sponsored by the office of Church in Town and Courtry of the Division of American Missions, National Lutheran Council. Bibliography: p. 165-167. [BV638.M77] 63-16602
1. Rural churches — U.S. 2. Sociology, Christian (Lutheran) I. Ekola, Giles C., joint ed. II. National Lutheran Council. Division of American Missions. Church in Town and Country. III. Title.

BIGO, Pierre. 261.8'09172'4
The church and Third World revolution / Pierre Bigo ; translated by Sister Jeanne Marie Lyons. Maryknoll, N.Y. : Orbis Books, c1977. iv, 316 p. ; 22 cm. Translation of L'Eglise et la revolution du Tiers Monde. Includes bibliographical references and index. [BR115.U6B513] 76-55388 ISBN 0-88344-071-7 : 8.95 ISBN 0-88344-072-5 pbk. : 4.95
1. Church and underdeveloped areas. 2. Sociology, Christian. 3. Christianity and politics. 4. Communism and Christianity. I. Title.

DUNNE, George 261.8'09172'4
Harold, 1905-
The right to development, by George H. Dunne. New York, Paulist Press [1974] 141 p. 18 cm. (Topics in moral argument) (Paulist Press/Deus books) Includes bibliographical references. [BR115.U6D86] 74-78418 ISBN 0-8091-1837-8 1.65 (pbk.).
1. Church and underdeveloped areas. I. Title.

GOULET, Denis. 261.8'09172'4
A new moral order : studies in development ethics and liberation theology / Denis Goulet ; with a foreword by Paulo Freire. Maryknoll, N.Y. : Orbis Books, 1974. xiv, 142 p. ; 21 cm. Includes bibliographical references. [BR115.U6G68] 73-89313 ISBN 0-88344-330-9 : 3.95
1. Church and underdeveloped areas. 2. Social ethics. 3. Liberation theology. I. Title.

GOULET, Denis. 261.8'09172'4
A new moral order : studies in development ethics and liberation theology / Denis Goulet ; with a foreword by Paulo Freire. Maryknoll, N.Y. : Orbis Books, 1974. xiv, 142 p. ; 21 cm. Includes bibliographical references. [BR115.U6G68] 73-89313 ISBN 0-88344-330-9 : 3.95
1. Church and underdeveloped areas. 2. Social ethics. 3. Liberation theology. I. Title.

TAYLOR, John 261.8'09172'2
Vernon, 1914-
Enough is enough : a biblical call for moderation in a consumer-oriented society / John V. Taylor. 1st U.S. ed. Minneapolis : Augsburg Pub. House, 1977, c1975. 124 p. ; 20 cm. Bibliography: p. 118-124. [HD82.T365 1977] 77-72456 ISBN 0-8066-1584-2 pbk. : 3.50
1. Economic development—Moral and religious aspects. 2. Simplicity. I. Title.

BALDWIN, John W. 261.8'0924
Masters, princes, and merchants; the social views of Peter the Chanter & his circle, by John W. Baldwin. Princeton, Princeton University Press, 1970. 2 v. illus., facsims. 25 cm. Contents.Contents.—v. 1. Text.—v. 2. Notes. Bibliographical references included in v. 2. [BX4705.P439B3] 69-18049 22.50
1. Petrus Cantor, d. 1197. 2. Paris—Intellectual life. 3. Social ethics—History. I. Title.

HOLLOWAY, James Y., 261.8'0924
1927- comp.
Introducing Jacques Ellul. Edited by James Y. Holloway. Grand Rapids, Eerdmans [1970] 183 p. port. 22 cm. "Essays ... first appeared in Katallagete: Be reconciled, Winter/Spring 1970." [BX4827.E5H64] 77-132034 2.45
1. Ellul, Jacques. I. Title.

THOMPSON, David 261.8'0924
Decamp, 1852-1908.
John Wesley as a social reformer. Freeport, N.Y., Books for Libraries Press, 1971. 111 p. port 23 cm. (The Black heritage library collection) Reprint of the 1898 ed. [BX8495.W5T5 1971] 70-164396 ISBN 0-8369-8855-8
1. Wesley, John, 1703-1791. I. Title. II. Series.

SCHLATTER, Richard 261.8'0942
Bulger, 1912-
The social ideas of religious leaders, 1660-1688, by Richard B. Schlatter. New York, Octagon Books, 1971. vii, 248 p. 24 cm. Reprint of the 1940 ed. Includes bibliographical references. [BR757.S35 1971] 70-120663
1. Gt. Brit.—Church history—17th century. 2. Church and social problems—Gt. Brit. 3. Gt. Brit.—Social conditions. I. Title.

SHORTER, Aylward. 261.8'096
African culture and the Christian church; an introduction to social and pastoral anthropology. Maryknoll, N.Y., Orbis Books, 1974 [c1973] xi, 229 p. 22 cm. Includes bibliographies. [BR1360.S5 1974] 73-79481 ISBN 0-88344-004-0 6.50
1. Christianity—Africa. 2. Ethnology—Africa. I. Title.

ANDREWS, James F., 261.8'0973
1936-
The citizen Christian, by James F. Andrews. With an introd. by Theodore M. Hesburgh. New York, Sheed and Ward [1968] 190 p. 21 cm. Includes bibliographies. [HN58.A53] 68-26035 4.50
1. United States—Social conditions. 2. Church and social problems—United States. I. Title.

EASTMAN, Dick. 261.8'0973
Up with Jesus. Grand Rapids, Mich., Baker Book House, [1973, c1971] 147 p. 18 cm. [HN31] ISBN 0-8010-3264-4 pap., 0.95
1. Church and Social problems—Protestant Church. I. Title.
Hardcover 3.95 ISBN 0-8010-3263-6

FORUM : 261.8'0973
religious faith speaks to American issues : a Bicentennial discussion stimulator / edited by William A. Norgren. New York : Friendship Press, [1975] 56 p. : ill. ; 28 cm. Bibliography: p. 55-56. [BR517.F58] 75-11874 ISBN 0-377-00044-2 pbk. : 2.95
1. United States—Religion—Addresses, essays, lectures. 2. United States—Civilization—Addresses, essays, lectures. I. Norgren, William A.
Contents omitted.

JOHNSON, Robert Leon, 261.8'0973
1930-
Counter culture and the vision of God [by] Robert L. Johnson. Foreword by Tom Driver. Minneapolis, Augsburg Pub. House [1971] 168 p. 21 cm. Includes bibliographical references. [BR121.2.J583] 78-159002 ISBN 0-8066-1125-1 4.50
1. Christianity—20th century. 2. Mysticism. 3. Youth—Conduct of life. I. Title.

MOONEY, Christopher 261.8'0973
F., 1925-
Religion and the American dream : the search for freedom under God / by Christopher F. Mooney. Philadelphia : Westminster Press, c1977. 144 p. ; 21 cm. First presented as the Bicentennial Lectures at St. Joseph's College, Philadelphia, 1975-1976. Includes bibliographical references. [BR516.M66] 76-54332 ISBN 0-664-241352 : 4.95
1. United States—Religion—Addresses, essays, lectures. 2. Church and state in the United States—Addresses, essays, lectures. 3. Justice—Addresses, essays, lectures. 4. Liberty—Addresses, essays, lectures. I. Title.

ROOHAN, James Edmund. 261.8'0973
American Catholics and the social question, 1865-1900 / James Edmund Roohan New York : Arno Press, 1976. p. cm. (The Irish-Americans) Reprint of the author's thesis, Yale, 1952. Bibliography: p. [BX1406.2.R57] 76-6364 ISBN 0-405-09356-X : 28.00
1. Catholic Church in the United States. 2. Church and social problems—Catholic Church. I. Title. II. Series.

TLAPA, Richard J. 261.8'0973
The new apostles : the mission to the inner-city / by Richard J. Tlapa. Chicago : Franciscan Herald Press, [1977] p. cm. [BV637.T55] 76-58395 ISBN 0-8199-0667-0 : 6.95
1. City churches—United States. I. Title.

WHAT the religious 261.8'0973
revolutionaries are saying. Elwyn A. Smith, editor. Philadelphia, Fortress Press [1971] v, 154 p. 20 cm. Includes bibliographical references. [BR515.W48] 72-155949 ISBN 0-8006-0133-5 3.50
1. United States—Religion—Addresses, essays, lectures. I. Smith, Elwyn Allen, 1919- ed.

BODE, Frederick A., 261.8'09756
1940-
Protestantism and the new South : Baptists and Methodists in political crisis, North Carolina, 1894-1903 / Frederick A. Bode. Charlottesville : University Press of Virginia, 1975. p. cm. Includes bibliographical references and index. [BR555.N78B62] 75-1289 ISBN 0-8139-0597-4 : 9.75
1. North Carolina—Religion. 2. Protestant churches—North Carolina. 3. North Carolina—Social conditions. I. Title.

ELLACURIA, Ignacio. 261.8'098
Freedom made flesh : the mission of Christ and His church / Ignacio Ellacuria ; translated by John Drury. Maryknoll, N.Y. : Orbis Books, c1976. ix, 246 p. ; 22 cm. [BX1426.2.E4413] 76-23172 ISBN 0-88344-140-3 : 8.95. ISBN 0-88344-141-1 pbk. : 4.95
1. Catholic Church in Latin America. 2. Mission of the church. I. Title.

BAILEY, Derrick *261.8 173.1
Sherwin, 1910-
The mystery of love and marriage; a study in the theology of sexual relation. New York, Harper [1952] 145 p. 21 cm. [HQ1051.B3 1952a] 52-10755
1. Marriage. 2. Love. I. Title.

WARD, Hiley H *261.8 254
Creative giving. New York, Macmillan, 1958. 170 p. 22 cm. [BV772.W3] 58-12072
1. Christian giving. I. Title.

ABELL, Aaron Ignatius, 261.83
1903-
American Catholicism and social action: a search for social justice, 1865-1950. [Notre Dame, Ind.] Notre Dame Univ. Pr., 1963 [c.1960] 306p. 21cm. (Ndp 34) 1.95 pap.,
1. Church and social problems—Catholic Church. I. Title.

ABELL, Aaron Ignatius, 261.83
1903-
American Catholicism and social action: a search for social justice, 1863-1950. [1st ed.] Garden City, N. Y., Hanover House, 1960. 306p. 22cm. Includes bibliography. [HN37.C3A4] 60-15164
1. Church and social problems— Catholic Church. I. Title.

ABELL, Aron Ignatius, 261.83
1903-
American Catholicism and social action: a search for social justice, 1865-1950. Garden City, N. Y., Hanover House [c]1960. 306p. Includes bibliograaphy. 22cm. 60-15164 4.95 half cloth,
1. Church and social problems—Catholic Church. I. Title.

AHMANN, Mathew II., ed. 261.8'3
The Church and the urban racial crisis, edited by Mathew Ahmann and Margaret Roach. Techny, Ill., Divine Word Publications [1967] viii, 262 p. 22 cm. "The major addresses and background papers prepared for the August, 1967, convention of the National Catholic Conference for Interracial Justice held at Rockhurst College in Kansas City, Missouri." [E185.615.C58] 67-29364
1. Negroes—Addresses, essays, lectures. 2. Church and race problems—U. S.—Addresses, essays, lectures. I. Roach, Margaret, ed. II. National Catholic Conference for Interracial Justice. III. Rockhurst College, Kansas City, Mo. IV. Title.

ALLAN, Doug, comp. 261.83
Safari. Introd. by Lowell Thomas, Jr. New York, Rolton House [1963] ix, 214 p. maps. 22 cm. [DT4.A56 1963] 63-22278
1. Africa—Descr. & trav.—Addresses, essays, lectures. 2. Adventure and adventures. I. Title.

THE American Lutheran 261.8'3
Church (1961-)
Conscience and action; social statements of The American Lutheran Church, 1961-1970. Edited by Carl F. Reuss. Minneapolis, Augsburg Pub. House [1971] 184 p. 22 cm. [HN37.L8A65] 75-135223 ISBN 0-8066-1106-5
1. Church and social problems—Lutheran Church. I. Reuss, Carl F., ed. II. Title.

ANDERSON, Floyd, 1906- 261.8'3
The birth control encyclical; a newsman's view. [St. Meinrad, Ind., Abbey Press, 1969] 158 p. 19 cm. (Marriage paperback library) "Pope Paul's encyclical": p. [55]-78. Includes bibliographical references. [HQ766.3.A5] 72-10972 1.50
1. Birth control—Religious aspects. I. Catholic Church. Pope, 1963- (Paulus VI) Humanae vitae. English. II. Title.

ARNOLD, Eberhard, 1883- 261.83
1935.
Love and marriage in the spirit; talks and writings by Eberhard Arnold. Edited and translated from the German at the Society of Brothers, Arnold. [Edited and translated from the German at the Society of Brothers, Woodcrest, Rifton, N.Y.] Rifton, N.Y. Plough Pub. House, 1965. xviii, 237 p. 19 cm. [BX8129.B65A73] 64-24321
1. Marriage — Bruderhof Communities. 2. Love (Theology) I. Title.

ARNOLD, Eberhard, 1883- 261.83
1935
Love and marriage in the spirit; talks and writings [Ed., tr. from German at the Soc. of Brothers] Rifton, N. Y., Plough [c.]1965. xviii, 237p. 19cm. [BX8129.B65A73] 64-24321 4.00
1. Marriage—Bruderhof Communities. 2. Love (Theology) I. Title.

ARTER, Rhetta Marie. 261.8'3
Assignment: race; report of inventory, United States summary, by Rhetta M. Arter. New York, Research and Action [1966] 63 p. illus. (part col.), maps. 29 cm. Report of phase 1 of the United Church Women's assignment: race project. [BT734.2.A7] 77-8326
1. Church and race problems—U.S.—Case studies. I. National Council of the Churches of Christ in the United States of America. Dept. of United Church Women. II. Title.

ASPEN Interreligious 261.8'3
Consultation, 1974.
Global justice & development : report of the Aspen Interreligious Consultation, Aspen, Colorado, June 1974 / sponsored by the Overseas Development Council with the support of the Aspen Institute for Humanistic Studies and the Johnson Foundation. Washington : The Council, c1975. 175 p. ; 26 cm. Bibliography: p. 117-123. [BR115.U6A86 1974] 5-13891 pbk. : 2.50
1. Church and underdeveloped areas—Congresses. 2. Justice—Congresses. 3. Church and social problems—Congresses. I. Overseas Development Council. II. Aspen Institute for Humanistic Studies. III. Johnson Foundation, Racine, Wis. IV. Title.

ASSOCIATION for Promoting 261.83
the Discovery of the Interior Parts of Africa.
Records of the African Association 1788-1831. Edited with an introd. by Robin Hallett for the Royal Geographical Society. London, New York, T. Nelson [1964] viii, 318 p. maps (2 fold. in pocket) 25 cm. Includes bibliographies. [DT1.R657] 67-2476
1. Africa — Disc. & explor. — British. I. Hallett, Robin, ed. II. Royal Geographical Society, London. III. Title.

BACON, Leonard, 1802- 261.8'3
1881.
Slavery discussed in occasional essays, 1833-1846. New York, Arno Press, 1969. 247 p. 22 cm. (The Anti-slavery crusade in America) Reprint of the 1846 ed. Includes bibliographical references. [E449.B12 1969b] 72-82167
1. Slavery in the United States. I. Title. II. Series.

BACON, Leonard, 1802- 261.8'3
1881.
Slavery discussed in occasional essays, from 1833 to 1846. Miami, Fla., Mnemosyne Pub. Co., 1969. 247 p. 23 cm. Reprint of the 1846 ed. [E449.B12 1969] 70-83954
1. Slavery in the United States. I. Title.

BAKER, George, self- 261.8'3
named Father Divine.
A treatise on overpopulation taken from interviews, sermons, and lectures by Father Divine. Philadelphia, New Day Pub. Co., 1967. v, 41 p. 28 cm. [BX7350.A25 1967] 73-172243
1. Christian life. 2. Population. I. Title.

BAN, Joseph D. 261.8'3
Facing today's demands [by] Joseph D. Ban. Valley Forge, Judson Press [1970] 126 p. 22 cm. [BR121.2.B285] 72-91243 2.50
1. Christianity—20th century. I. Title.

BARBOUR, Russel B 261.8'3
Black and white together; plain talk for white Christians [by] Russell B. Barbour. Philadelphia, United Church Press [1967] viii, 166 p. illus. 21 cm. Bibliography: p. 163-166. [BT734.2.B3] 67-26983
1. Church and race problems—U. S. I. Title.

BARBOUR, Russell B. 261.8'3
Black and white together; plain talk for white Christians [by] Russell B. Barbour. Philadelphia, United Church Press [1967] viii, 166 p. illus. 21 cm. Bibliography: p. 163-166. [BT734.2.B3] 67-26983
1. Church and race problems—United States. I. Title.

BARNES, Albert, 1798- 261.8'3
1870.
The church and slavery. With an appendix. Philadelphia, Parry & McMillan, 1857. Detroit, Negro History Press [1969?] 204 p. 22 cm. [E449.B26 1969] 79-92416
1. Slavery in the United States—Controversial literature—1857. 2. Slavery and the church. 3. Slavery and the church—Presbyterian Church. I. Title.

BARNES, Albert, 1798- 261.8'3
1870.
The church and slavery. New York, Negro Universities Press [1969] 204 p. 23 cm. Reprint of the 1857 ed. Includes bibliographical references. [E449.B26 1969b] 71-98714 ISBN 0-8371-2771-8
1. Slavery in the United States—Controversial literature—1857. 2. Slavery and the church. 3. Slavery and the church—Presbyterian Church. I. Title.

BARNES, Albert, 1798- 261.8'3
1870.
An inquiry into the scriptural views of slavery. New York, Negro Universities Press [1969] 384 p. 23 cm. On spine: Scriptural views of slavery. Reprint of the 1857 ed. Bibliographical footnotes. [E449.B262 1969] 68-58048
1. Slavery in the United States—Controversial literature—1846. 2. Slavery in the Bible. I. Title. II. Title: Scriptural views of slavery.

BARNES, Albert, 1798- 261.8'3
1870.
An inquiry into the scriptural views of slavery. Philadelphia, Parry & McMillan, 1855. Detroit, Negro History Press [1969] 384 p. 22 cm. Title on spine: Scriptural views of slavery. Bibliographical footnotes. [E449.B262 1969b] 75-92415
1. Slavery in the United States—Controversial literature—1846. 2. Slavery in the Bible. I. Title. II. Title: Scriptural views of slavery.

BARNES, Roswell Parkhurst, 261.83
1901-
Under orders; the churches and public affairs. Garden City, N. Y., Doubleday [c.]1961. 138p. 61-8873 2.95
1. Church and social problems. I. Title.

BARNES, Roswell Parkhurst, 261.83
1901-
Under orders; the churches and public affairs. [1st ed.] Garden City, N. Y., Doubleday. 1961. 138p. 24cm. [HN31.B173] 61-8873
1. Church and social problems. I. Title.

BARNETTE, Henlee H. 261.8'3
The church and the ecological crisis, by Henlee H. Barnette. Grand Rapids, Eerdmans [1972] 114 p. 22 cm. Bibliography: p. 112-114. [BT695.5.B37] 72-77175 ISBN 0-8028-1457-3 (pbk) 2.25 (pbk)
1. Nature (Theology) 2. Human ecology—Moral and religious aspects. I. Title.

BARNETTE, Henlee H. 261.8'3
Crucial problems in Christian perspective, by Henlee H. Barnette. Philadelphia, Westminster Press [1970] 144 p. 19 cm. Includes bibliographical references. [HN39.U6B37] 71-110113 2.45
1. Church and social problems—U.S. I. Title.

BASEN, Carol. 261.8'3
Showdown at Seattle. New York, Seabury Press [1968] 80 p. 21 cm. "Prepared under the auspices of the Executive Council of the Episcopal Church." Report, including excerpts from the proceedings, of the meetings of the women of the church during the national convention of the Protestant Episcopal Church in the U.S.A., Seattle, Sept. 1967. Bibliography: p. [79]-80. [BT734.2.B34] 74-3033 1.95
1. Church and race problems—U.S. I. Protestant Episcopal Church in the U.S.A. Executive Council. II. Title.

BECK, Hubert F. 261.8'3
The age of technology [by] Hubert F. Beck. Art work by Art Kirchhoff. St. Louis, Concordia Pub. House [1970] 133 p. illus. 18 cm. (The Christian encounters) Bibliography: p. 131-133. [BJ59.B4 1970] 79-112440
1. Technology and ethics. I. Title. II. Series.

BELGUM, David Rudolph, 261.8'3
1922-
The church and sex education, by David Belgum. Wilbur G. Volker, ed. Philadelphia, Lutheran Church Pr. [c1967] 128p. 21cm. (Consult ser., no. 3) Bibl. ref. [HQ56.B325] 68-2696 1.50
1. Sex instruction. I. Title.

BELGUM, David Rudolph, 261.8'3
1922-
The church and sex education, by David Belgum. Wilbur G. Volker, editor. Philadelphia, Lutheran Church Press [c1967] 128 p. 21 cm. (Consult series, no. 3) Includes bibliographical references. [HQ56.B325] 68-2696
1. Sex instruction. I. Title.

BELLOC, Hilaire, 1870- 261.8'3
1953.
The crisis of civilization. Westport, Conn., Greenwood Press [1973] 245 p. 22 cm. Reprint of the 1937 ed. Contents.Contents.—The foundation of Christendom.—Christendom established.—The Reformation and its immediate consequences.—The ultimate consequences of the Reformation.—Restoration. [BR115.C5B33 1973] 73-114465 ISBN 0-8371-4761-1 10.75
1. Civilization, Christian. 2. Sociology, Christian (Catholic) I. Title.

BENSON, Dennis C. 261.8'3
The now generation [by] Dennis C. Benson. Richmond, John Knox Press [1969] 143 p. 21 cm. Bibliographical references included in "Notes" (p. [137]-143) [BV639.Y7B4] 68-25012 ISBN 0-8042-1979-6 2.45
1. Youth—Religious life. 2. Youth—United States. 3. Church work with youth. I. Title.

BERRIGAN, Philip. 261.83
No more strangers. Introd. by Thomas Merton. New York, Macmillan [1965] xx, 181 p. 21 cm. [BT734.2.B4] 65-18322
1. Church and race problems. I. Title.

BERRIGAN, Philip 261.83
No more strangers. Introd. by Thomas Merton. New York, Macmillan [c.1965] xx, 181p. 21cm. [BT734.2.B4] 65-18322 4.95
1. Church and race problems. I. Title.

BERRIGAN, Philip. 261.8'3
A punishment for peace. [New York] Macmillan [1969] 178 p. 21 cm. Bibliographical references included in "Notes" (p. 175-178) [HN39.U6B4] 78-77969
1. Church and social problems—United States. 2. United States—Social conditions—1960- 3. United States—Race question. 4. United States—Foreign relations. I. Title.

BIELER, Andre. 261.8'3
The politics of hope. Pref. by Helder Camara. Translated by Dennis Pardee. [Grand Rapids] Eerdmans [1974] 152 p. 21 cm. Translation of Une politique de l'esperance. Includes bibliographical references. [BR115.W6B4513] 74-14980 ISBN 0-8028-1588-X
1. Church and the world. 2. Church renewal. 3. Civilization, Modern—1950- I. Title.

BIEZANEK, Anne C. 261.83
All things new, a declaration of faith [1st Amer. ed.] New York, Harper [1965, c.1964] 152p. ports. 22cm. [HQ766.3.B46] 65-14689 3.50
1. Birth control—Religious aspects. I. Title.

BIEZANEK, Anne C. 261.8'3
All things new; the declaration of faith of Anne C. Biezanek ... a twentieth-century Roman Catholic woman. [Derby] P. Smith, 1964. 152 p. illus., ports. 23 cm. [HQ766.3] 78-9192
1. Birth control—Religious aspects. I. Title.

BIRMINGHAM, William, ed. 261.83
What modern Catholics think about birth control a new symposium. [New York] New American Library [1964] 256 p. 18 cm. (Signet books) "T2577." Includes bibliographical references. [HQ766.3.B5] 64-56822
1. Birth control—Religious aspects. 2. Woman—History and condition of woman. I. Title.

BIRMINGHAM, William, ed. 261.83
What modern Catholics think about birth control; a new symposium [New York] New Amer. Lib. [c.1964] 256p. 18cm. (Signet bks.; T2577) Bibl. 64-56822 .75 pap.,
1. Birth control—Religious aspects. 2. Woman—History and condition of women. I. Title.

BIRNEY, James Gillespie, 261.8'3
1792-1857.
The American churches: the bulwarks of American slavery. New York, Arno Press, 1969. 44 p. 23 cm. (The Anti-slavery crusade in America) Reprint of the 1842 ed. [E449.B617 1969] 79-82174
1. Slavery and the church. I. Title. II. Series.

BLACK militancy and the 261.8'3
university; report of a conference for campus clergy, November 29-December 1, 1968 at Shaw University, Raleigh, N.C. Washington, National Newman Apostolate [1969] vi, 26 p. 28 cm. Sponsored by the National Newman Apostolate. [BT734.2.B54] 72-8330
1. Church and race problems. 2. Race (Theology) 3. Negroes. I. National Newman Apostolate. II. Shaw University, Raleigh, N.C.

BOISEN, Anton Theophilus, 261.8'3
1876-
Religion in crisis and custom; a sociological and psychological study, by Anton T. Boisen. Westport, Conn., Greenwood Press [1973, c1955] xv, 271 p. 22 cm. Includes bibliographical references. [BL53.B62 1973] 72-10977 ISBN 0-8371-6642-X 14.25
1. Psychology, Religious. 2. Religion and sociology.. 3. United States—Religion. I. Title.

BRAUN, Theodore A. 261.8'3
Witnessing in the world; a resource and discussion book for youth [by] Theodore A. Braun. Illustrated by Don Herzbach. Boston, United Church Press [1968] v, 73 p. illus. 22 cm. (Confirmation education series) "Part of the United Church curriculum, prepared and published by the Division of Christian Education and the Division of Publication of the United Church Board for Homeland Ministries." [BR115.W6B7] 68-10315
1. Church and the world. 2. Church and social problems. I. United Board for Homeland Ministries. Division of Christian Education. II. United Church Board for Homeland Ministries. Division of Publication. III. Title.

BROCKMAN, Norbert, comp. 261.8'3
Contemporary religion and social responsibility. Edited by Norbert Brockman [and] Nicholas Piediscalzi. New York, Alba House [1973] xvi, 366 p. 23 cm. Includes bibliographical references. [BL60.B68] 72-11982 ISBN 0-8189-0257-4 4.95 (pbk.)
1. Religion and sociology—Collections. 2. Social ethics—Collections. I. Piediscalzi, Nicholas, joint comp. II. Title.

BROMLEY, Dorothy (Dunbar) 261.83
Catholics and birth control; contemporary views on doctrine. Foreword by Richard Cardinal Cushing. Pref. by John L. Thomas. New York, Devin-Adair [1965] xv, 207p. 21cm. Bibl. [HQ766.3.B7] 64-23750 4.95
1. Birth control—Religious aspects. I. Title.

BROWN, Harold O. J., 261.8'3
1933-
Christianity and the class struggle [by] Harold O. J. Brown. New Rochelle, N.Y., Arlington House [1970] 221 p. 21 cm. Includes bibliographical references. [HM136.B74] 73-101958 7.00
1. Social conflict. 2. Apologetics—20th century. I. Title.

BURKE, Fred G 261.83
Political evolution in Kenya [by] Fred G. Burke. [Syracuse? N. Y., International Programs, Center for Overseas Operations and Research, 1964?] 55, vi l. 28 cm. (Program of East African Studies. Occasional paper no. 2) "Paper presented to the Seminar in Political Anthropology, spring 1964." Bibliographical references included in "Footnotes" (leaves i-vi) [DT1.S915] 67-9524
1. Kenya—Pol. & govt. I. Title. II. Series: Syracuse University. Program of Eastern African Studies. Occasional paper no. 2

CALLAHAN, Sidney 261.8'3
Cornelia.
Christian family planning and sex education [by] Sidney Callahan. Notre Dame, Ind., Ave Maria Press [1969] 72 p. illus. 19 cm. [HQ766.3.C275] 71-92272 0.75
1. Birth control—Religious aspects. 2. Sexual ethics. I. Title.

CAMPBELL, Ernest Queener. 261.83
Christians in racial crisis; a study of Little Rock's ministry, by Ernest Q. Campbell and Thomas F. Pettigrew. Including statements on desegregation and race relations by the leading religious denominations of the United States. Washington, Public Affairs Press [1959] x, 196 p. 24 cm. "Reference notes": p. 172-194. [BR560.L5C3] 59-10228
1. Clergy—Arkansas—Little Rock. 2. Segregation in education. 3. Race problems. I. Pettigrew, Thomas F., joint author. II. Title.

CAMPBELL, Will D. 261.83
Race and the renewal of the church. Philadelphia, Westminster [c.1962] 90p. 19cm. (Christian perspectives on soc. problems) 62-12146 1.25 pap.,
1. Race problems. 2. Segregation—Religious aspects. I. Title.

CAROTHERS, J. Edward 261.83
Keepers of the poor [by] J. Edward Carothers. [Cincinnati, Jt. Commn. on Educ. & Cultivation, Bd. of Missions of the Methodist Church, 1966] 161p. illus. 29cm. Bibl. [BV639.P6C3] 66-21409 1.00 pap.,
1. Church and the poor. I. Methodist Church (United States) Joint Commission on Education and Cultivation. II. Title.

CASEBOOK on church and 261.8'3
society. Edited by Keith R. Bridston [and others] Nashville, Abingdon Press [1974] 220 p. 22 cm. Bibliography: p. 220. [BV3.C37] 74-13419 ISBN 0-687-04709-9 5.95 (pbk.)
1. Theology, Practical—Case studies. 2. Church and social problems—Case studies. I. Bridston, Keith R., ed.

CATHOLIC Church. National 261.8'3
Conference of Catholic Bishops. Respect Life Committee.
Respect life! Washington : Respect Life Committee, National Conference of Catholic Bishops, 1976. 52 p. : ill. ; 28 cm. Includes bibliographical references. [HQ767.5.U5C38 1976] 76-151063
1. Abortion—Religious aspects. 2. Church work with families—United States. I. Title.

CATHOLIC Church. Pope, 261.83
1958- (Joannes XXIII) Mater et magistra (15 May 1961) English.
Mater et magistra, Christianity and social progress an encyclical letter. Edited by Donald R. Campion and Eugene K. Culhane. New York, America Press [1961] 96p. 19cm. Bibliography: p. 81-89. [HN37.C3A3 1961] 61-65157
1. Church and social problems— Catholic Church—Papal documents. I. Campion, Donald R., ed. II. Culhane, Eugene K., ed. III. Title.

CATHOLIC Church. Pope, 261.83
1958- (Joannes XXIII) Mater et magistra (15 May 1961) English.
Mater et magistra, encyclical letter on Christianity and social progress. [English translation by William J. Gibbons, assisted by a committee of Catholic scholars] Washington, National Catholic Welfare Conference [1961] 80p. 18cm. Bibliographical footnotes. [HN37.C3A3 1961c] 62-25011
1. Church and social problems —Catholic Church—Papal documents. I. Gibbons, William Joseph, 1912- ed. and tr. II. Title.

CATHOLIC Church. Pope, 261.83
1958- (Joannes XXIII) Mater et magistra (15 May 1961) English.
Mater et magistra, encyclical letter Christianity and social progress. Translated by William J. Gibbons, assisted by a committee of Catholic scholars. New York, Paulist Press [1961] 96p. 18cm. 'Teaching-aid outline, byWilliam J. Bertsch and William J. Gibbons': p. 83-90. 'Annotations and selected references': p. 91-96. [HN37.C3A3 1961b] 62-608
1. Church and social problems—Catholic Church —Papal documents. I. Gibbons, William Joseph, 1912- ed. and tr. II. Title.

CATHOLIC Church, Pope, 261.83
1958- (Joannes XXIII) Mater et magistra (15 May 1961) English.
Mater et magistra, an encyclical letter. Chicago 11, 154 E. Erie St. Discoverers Pr., [c.1962] 79p. 24cm. Bibl. 62-4896 7.50
1. Church and social problems—Catholic Church—Papal documents. I. Title.

CATHOLIC Church. Pope, 261.83
1958- (Joannes XXIII) Mater et magistra (15 May 1961) English.
On recent developments of the social question in the light of Christian teaching, Mater et magistra; encyclical letter. Vatican translation. [Boston] St. Paul Editions [dist. Daughters of St. Paul, 1961] 60p. Bibl. 61-65155 .25 pap.,
1. Church and social problems—Catholic Church—Papal documents. I. Title.

CATHOLIC Church. Pope, 261.83
1958- (Joannes XXIII) Mater et nagistra (15 May 1961) English.
Mater et magistra, an encyclical letter. Chicago, Discoverers Press [1962] 79p. 24cm. [HN37.C3A3 1962] 62-4896
I. Pius XII, Pope, 1876-1958. II. Title.

CATHOLIC Church. Pope, 261.8'3
1963- (Paulus VI)
Encyclical letter on the regulation of birth (Humanae vitae) of Pope Paul VI. Melbourne, A.C.T.S. Publications, 1968. 27 p. 18 cm. Bibliographical footnotes. [HQ766.3.C32 1968b] 70-469623 0.18
1. Catholic Church. Pope, 1963- (Paulus VI) Humanae vitae. 2. Birth control—Religious aspects. I. [Humanae vitae. English]

CATHOLIC Students' Mission 261.83
Crusade, United States of America Africa Research Committee.
College readings on Africa; a collection of discussions on the cultural, economic, political and religious aspects of present-day Africa, contributed by His Eminence Laurean Cardinal Rugambwa [and others] Edited by Robert S. Payne, chairman. [Cincinnati, CSMC Press, 1963] xii, 143 p. illus. group ports, fold. map. 22 cm. (World cultures and religion series) Bibliography: p. 123-130. [DT30.C35] 63-24261
1. Africa — Collections. I. Payne, Robert S. ed. II. Title.

CENTER for Hermeneutical 261.83
Studies in Hellenistic and Modern Culture.
A social context to the religious crisis of the third century A.D. : protocol of the fourteenth colloquy, 9 February 1975 / The Center for Hermeneutical Studies in Hellenistic and Modern Culture ; Peter R. L. Brown. Berkeley, CA : The Center, c1975. 52 p. ; 21 cm. (Protocol series of the colloquies of the Center for Hermeneutical Studies in Hellenistic and Modern Culture ; no. 14 ISSN 0098-0900s) Includes bibliographical references..[BL60.C43 1975] 75-38688IISBN 0-89242-013-8XV
1. Religion and sociology—History—Congresses. 2. Sociology, Christian—Early church, ca. 30-600—Congresses. I. Brown, Peter Robert Lamont. II. Title. III. Series: Center for Hermeneutical Studies in Hellenistic and Modern Culture. Protocol series of the colloquies ; no. 14.

CHRISTENSON, Laurence. 261.8'3
A charismatic approach to social action, by Larry Christenson. Minneapolis, Bethany Fellowship [inc., 1974] 122 p. 22 cm. Includes bibliographical references. [BX8763.C48] 74-1326 ISBN 0-87123-389-4 3.95
1. Pentecostalism. 2. Church and social problems. I. Title.

CHRISTENSON, Laurence. 261.8'3
Social action, Jesus style / Larry Christenson. 2d ed. Minneapolis : Bethany Fellowship, 1976, c1974. 112 p. ; 18 cm. (Dimension books) First ed. published in 1976 under title: A charismatic approach to social action. Includes bibliographical references. [BX8763.C48 1976] 75-44927 ISBN 0-87123-504-8 pbk. : 1.50
1. Pentecostalism. 2. Church and social problems. I. Title.

CHRISTIE, John W. 261.8'3
George Bourne and The Book and slavery irreconcilable, by John W. Christie and Dwight L. Dumond. Wilmington, Historical Society of Delaware [1969] xi, 206 p. 24 cm. (Presbyterian Historical Society. [Publications], v. 9) "A chronological list of the publications of George Bourne": p. 99-101. [E446.B77C45] 75-12112 5.00
1. Bourne, George, 1780-1845. 2. Slavery in the United States—Controversial literature—1816. I. Dumond, Dwight Lowell, 1895- joint author. II. Delaware Historical Society. III. Bourne, George, 1780-1845. The Book and slavery irreconcilable. 1969. IV. Title. V. Series.

CHRISTOFF, Nicholas B., 261.8'3
1939-
Saturday night, Sunday morning : singles and the church / Nicholas B. Christoff. New York : Harper & Row, [1977] p. cm. [BV4437.C48] 77-23976 ISBN 0-06-061380-7 pbk. : 3.95
1. Church work with single people. 2. Single people—Religious life. I. Title.

CHRISTY, David, b.1802- 261.8'3
Pulpit politics; or, Ecclesiastical legislation on slavery, in its disturbing influences on the American Union. New York, Negro Universities Press [1969] 624 p. port. 23 cm. Reprint of the 1862 ed. Bibliographical footnotes. [E449.C5573 1969] 77-77197
1. Slavery in the United States—History. 2. Slavery and the church. I. Title.

CHURCH and the urban 261.8'3
racial crisis (The). ed. by Mathew Ahmann, Margaret Roach. Techny, Ill., Divine World [1967] viii, 262p. 22cm. The major addresses and background papers prepd. for the Aug. 1967, convention of the Natl. Catholic Conf. for Interracial Justice held at Rockhurst Coll. in Kansas City, Mo. [E185.615.C58] 67-29364 2.95
1. Negroes—Addresses, essays, lectures. 2. Church and race problems—U. S.—Address essays, lectures. I. Ahmann. Mathew H. ed. II. Roach, Margaret. ed. III. National Catholic Conference for Interracial Justice. IV. Rockhurst College, Kansas City, Mo.

CHURCHILL, Rhona. 261.83
White man's God. Pref. by Joost de Blank. New York, Morrow, 1962. 205 p. illus. 22 cm. [BR1450.C5 1962a] 62-15759
1. Segregation—Religious aspects. 2. Africa, South—Race question. I. Title.

CIVARDI, Luigi 261.83
Christianity and social justice. Fresno, Calif., Academy Guild [1962, c.1961] 176p. 22cm. 61-16771 3.95; 1.95 pap.,
1. Church and social problems—Catholic Church. I. Title.

CLARK, Henry, 1930- 261.83
The Christian case against poverty. New York, Association Press [1965] 126 p. 16 cm. (A Reflection book) Includes bibliographical references. [BV639.P6C5] 65-11083
1. Church and the poor. I. Title.

CLARK, Henry, 1930- 261.83
The Christian case against poverty. New York, Association [c.1965] 126p. 16cm. (Reflection bk.) Bibl. [BV639.P6C5] 65-11083 .50 pap.,
1. Church and the poor. I. Title.

CLARK, Henry, 1930- 261.83
The church and residential desegregation; a case study of an open housing covenant campaign. New Haven, College & University Press [1965] 254 p. 21 cm. Bibliographical references included in "Notes" (P. 234-254) [E185.89.H6C55] 64-20663
1. Negroes — Housing. 2. Discrimination in housing — U.S. 3. Church and race problems — U.S. I. Title.

CLARK, Henry, 1930- 261.83
The church and residential desegregation; a case study of an open housing covenant campaign. New Haven, Conn., Coll. & Univ. Pr. [c.1965] 254p. 21cm. Bibl. [E185.89H6C55] 64-20663 5.00
1. Negroes—Housing. 2. Discrimination in housing—U.S. 3. Church and race problems—U.S. I. Title.

CLEVELAND, Earl E. 261.8'3
The middle wall [by] E. E. Cleveland. Washington, Review and Herald Pub. Association [1969] 96 p. 18 cm. [BT734.C56] 77-81305
1. Race (Theology) I. Title.

CLOUSE, Robert G., 1931- 261.8'3
The Cross & the flag. [Edited by] Clouse, Linder [and] Pierard. [1st ed.] Carol Stream, Ill., Creation House [1972] 261 p. 21 cm. Erratum sheet inserted. Includes bibliographical references. [BR1640.C55] 72-85415 2.95 (pbk)
1. Evangelicalism. 2. Christianity and politics. 3. Church and social problems. I. Linder, Robert Dean, joint author. II. Pierard, Richard V., 1934- joint author. III. Title.

COLACCI, Mario. 261.83
Christian marriage today; a comparison of Roman Catholic and Protestant views with special reference to mixed marriages. Foreword by Bernhard Christensen. [Rev. ed.] Minneapolis, Augsburg Pub. House [1965] xi, 203 p. 22 cm. Bibliography: p. 183-191. [HQ518.C6] 64-4169
1. Marriage. 2. Marriage, Mixed. I. Title.

COLACCI, Mario 261.83
Christian marriage today; a comparison of Roman Catholic and Protestant views with special reference to mixed marriages. Foreword by Bernhard Christensen [Rev. ed.] Minneapolis, Augsburg [c.1958, 1965] xi, 203p. 22cm. Bibl. [HQ518.C6] 65-4169 1.95 pap.,
1. Marriage. 2. Marriage, Mixed. I. Title.

COLES, Robert. 261.8'3
A spectacle unto the world; the Catholic Worker Movement. Photos. by Jon Erikson. New York, Viking Press [1973] xv, [49], 71 p. illus. 23 cm. [BX809.C33C64 1973] 72-11060 ISBN 0-670-66212-7 10.00
1. Catholic Worker Movement. I. Erikson, Jon, 1933- illus. II. Title.

COLLEGE Theology Society. 261.8'3
Liberation, revolution, and freedom : theological perspectives : proceedings of the College Theology Society / edited by Thomas M. McFadden. New York : Seabury Press, [1975] viii, 214 p. ; 22 cm. "A Crossroad book." "The essays included here were, with one exception, delivered at the 1974 convention of the College Theology Society Society at the University of Dayton. Includes bibliographical references. [BT83.57.C64 1975] 74-28391 ISBN 0-8164-0271-X : 7.95
1. Liberation theology—Addresses, essays, lectures. 2. Violence—Moral and religious aspects—Addresses, essays, lectures. I. McFadden, Thomas M., ed. II. Title.

COMMONS, John Rogers, 261.8'3
1862-1945.
Social reform & the church. New York, A. M. Kelley Publishers, 1967. x, 176 p. 21 cm. (Reprints of economic classics) Reprint of the 1894 ed. [HN31.C63 1967] 66-21663
1. Church and social problems. I. Title.

CONE, James H. 261.8'3
Black theology and black power [by] James H. Cone. New York, Seabury Press [1969] x, 165 p. 21 cm. (An Original Seabury paperback, SP 59) Bibliographical references included in "Notes" (p. 153-161) [BT734.2.C6] 70-76462 2.95
1. Church and race problems. 2. Negroes—Religion. I. Title. II. Title: Black power.

CONNERY, John R., 1913- 261.8'3
Abortion, the development of the Roman Catholic perspective / by John R. Connery. Chicago : Loyola University Press, [1977] p. cm. [HQ767.3.C66] 76-51217 ISBN 0-8294-0257-8 : 7.95
1. Abortion—Religious aspects—Catholic Church. I. Title.

CONSIDINE, John Joseph, 261.83
1897-
Fundamental Catholic teaching on the human race. Maryknoll, N. Y., Maryknoll Publications [c.1961] 92p. 25cm. (World horizon reports. Report no. 27) Bibl. 61-9083 1.00 pap.,
1. Race. I. Title.

CONTRACEPTION and 261.83
holiness; the Catholic predicament; introduced by Thomas D. Roberts [New York] Herder & Herder [c.1964] 346p. 22cm. Bibl. 64-8201 5.50
1. Birth control—Religious aspects. I. Roberts, Thomas D'Esterre, Abp., 1893-

CORNELL, Thomas Charles, 261.8'3
1934- comp.
A penny a copy; readings from the Catholic

worker, edited by Thomas C. Cornell and James H. Forest. New York, Macmillan [1968] xvi, 271 p. 21 cm. [HV530.C65] 68-18870
1. Catholic Church—Charities. 2. Church and social problems—Catholic Church. I. Forest, James H., joint comp. II. The Catholic worker. III. Title.

CULLY, Kendig Brubaker, comp. 261.8'3
Will the church lose the city? Edited by Kendig Brubaker Cully and F. Nile Harper. New York, World Pub. Co. [1969] 256 p. 22 cm. Contents.Contents.—Part I: Viewpoints on the city: A historical view, by R. W. Friedrichs. A sociological view, by D. W. Dodson. An economic view, by R. Kaminsky. A psychological view, by J. P. Kildahl. An aesthetic view, by R. S. Jackson. An integrative view, by M. E. Marty.—Part II: Viewpoints on the church in the city: The city and the church: historical interlockings, by R. T. Handy. The city from a Biblical standpoint, by W. Klassen. The churches and the challenges of poverty, by L. E. Schaller. The Black church in search of a new theology, by G. S. Wilmore, Jr. Religion, church, and culture, by W. Hamilton. Leadership for change in church and society, by G. W. Webber. The church in the city as a locale for humanizing life, by H. Moody.—Part III: Actualities and prospects: What are the churches actually doing in the city? I, by D. W. Barry. What are the churches actually doing in the city? II, by G. H. J. Woodard. Prospects and parables, by F. N. Harper. Focus and future, by K. B. Cully. Bibliography: p. [245]-250. [BV637.C8 1969] 73-86449 5.95
1. City churches—Addresses, essays, lectures. 2. Cities and towns—Addresses, essays, lectures. I. Harper, F. Nile, joint comp. II. Title.

THE Cutting edge; 261.8'3
critical questions for contemporary Christians. Compiled by H. C. Brown, Jr. Waco, Tex., Word Books [1969] 2 v. 23 cm. Bibliographical footnotes. [BT734.2.C85] 70-76726
1. Church and race problems—U.S.—Addresses, essays, lectures. 2. Church and social problems—Addresses, essays, lectures. 3. Social ethics—Addresses, essays, lectures. I. Brown, Henry Clifton, ed.

DAVIES, Alfred T ed. 261.83
The pulpit speaks on race. Edited by Alfred T. Davies. New York, Abingdon Press [1965] 191 p. 23 cm. [BT734.2.D3 1965] 65-11515
1. Church and race problems. 2. Sermons, American. I. Title.

DAVIES, Alfred T., ed. 261.83
The pulpit speaks on race. Ed. by Alfred T. Davies. Nashville, Tenn., Abingdon [c.1956-1965] 191p. 23cm. [BT734.2.D3] 65-11515 3.95 bds.,
1. Church and race problems. 2. Sermons, American. I. Title.

DEMANT, Vigo Auguste, 1893- 261.83
Christian sex ethics; an introduction, by V. A. Demant. [1st ed.] New York, Harper & Row [1963] 127 p. 20 cm. "Notes and references": p. 123-127. [HQ63.D4 1963a] 64-15481
1. Sex and religion. 2. Sexual ethics. I. Title.

DERR, Thomas Sieger, 1931- 261.8'3
Ecology and human need / by Thomas Sieger Derr. Philadelphia : Westminster Press, [1975] 174 p. ; 21 cm. Published in 1973 under title: Ecology and human liberation. Includes bibliographical references. [GF80.D47 1975] 74-22126 ISBN 0-664-24806-3
1. Human ecology—Moral and religious aspects. I. Title.

DERRICK, Christopher, 1921- 261.8'3
Honest love and human life: is the Pope right about contraception? [1st American ed.] New York, Coward-McCann [1969] 158 p. 21 cm. Includes bibliographical references. [HQ766.3.D47 1969] 74-91387 4.95
1. Catholic Church. Pope, 1963- (Paulus VI) Humanae vitae. I. Title.

DESAI, Ram, ed. 261.83
Christianity in Africa as seen by Africans. Edited, with an introd., by Ram Desai. Denver, A. Swallow [1962] 135 p. 23 cm. [BR1360.D42] 62-19349
1. Church and social problems — Africa. 2. Christians in Africa. I. Title.

DESAI, Ram, ed. 261.83
Christianity in Africa as seen by Africans, Ed., introd., by Ram Desai. Denver, Swallow [c.1962] 135p. 23cm. Bibl. 62-19349 3.50; 1.65 pap.,
1. Church and social problems—Africa. 2. Christians in Africa. I. Title.

DESROCHE, Henri. 261.8'3
Jacob and the angel; an essay in sociologies of religion. Translated by John K. Savacool. Amherst, University of Massachusetts Press [1973] xiv, 187 p. 24 cm. Translation of Sociologies religieuses. Includes bibliographical references. [BL60.D4813] 72-77575 12.50
1. Religion and sociology. I. Title.

DILEMMAS of tomorrow's world. 261.8'3
Edited by Franz Bockle [and] Theo Beemer. New York, Paulist Press [1969] viii, 174 p. 24 cm. (Concilium: theology in the age of renewal. Moral theology, v. 45) Bibliographical footnotes. [BJ1249.D53] 78-86974 4.50
1. Church and social problems—Catholic Church. I. Bockle, Franz, ed. II. Beemer, Th. C. J., 1927- ed. III. Series: Concilium (New York) v. 45

DISSENT in and for the church; 261.8'3
theologians and Humanae vitae, by Charles E. Curran [and] Robert E. Hunt and the subject professors, with John F. Hunt and Terrence R. Connelly. New York, Sheed & Ward [1970, c1969] xii, 237 p. 21 cm. (A Search book) This volume is substantially the first part of the testimony prepared by the professors subject to the inquiry at Catholic University, and their counsel. The second part of the written testimony by the counsel forms the nucleus of a companion volume: The responsibility of dissent: the church and academic freedom, by John F. Hunt and Terrence R. Connelly. Includes bibliographies. [BX1753.D53] 70-92530 3.95 (pbk)
1. Catholic Church—Doctrinal and controversial works—Catholic authors. 2. Catholic Church. Pope, 1963- (Paulus VI) Humanae vitae. 3. Catholic University of America. I. Curran, Charles E. II. Hunt, Robert E.

DOLLEN, Charles, ed. 261.83
Civil rights, a source book [Boston] St. Paul [1964] 123p. illus. 22cm. [JC585.D55] 64-7926 2.00; 1.00 pap.,
1. Civil rights. 2. Church and social problems—Catholic Church. I. Title.

DOXIADES, Konstantinos Apostolou, 1913- 261.83
The new world of urban man [by] Constantinos A. Doxiadis [and] Truman B. Douglass. Philadelphia, United Church Press [1965] 127 p. 21 cm. Bibliography: p. 127. [HT151.D6] 65-23113
1. Cities and towns. Church and social problems. I. Douglass, Truman B., joint author. II. Title.

DOXIADES, Konstantinos Apostolou, 1913- 261.83
The new world of urban man [by] Constantinos A. Doxiadis, Truman B. Douglass. Philadelphia, United Church Pr. [c.1965] 127p. 21cm. [HT151.D6] 65-23113 1.60 pap.,
1. Cities and towns. 2. Church and social problems. I. Dougless, Truman B., joint author. II. Title.

DUPRE, Louis K., 1925- 261.83
Contraception and Catholics: a new appraisal, by Louis Dupre. Baltimore, Helicon [1964] 94 p. 21 cm. Bibliography: p. 89-94. [HQ766.D83] 64-23614
1. Birth control—Religious aspects. I. Title.

EGNER, G. 261.83
Contraception vs. tradition; a Catholic critique [by] G. Egner. [New York] Herder & Herder [1967] x, 205p. 22cm. Bibl. [HQ766.3.E32] 67-14144 4.95
1. Birth control—Religious aspects. I. Title.

EIGHMY, John Lee. 261.8'3
Churches in cultural captivity; a history of the social attitudes of Southern Baptists. With an introd. and epilogue by Samuel S. Hill, Jr. [1st ed.] Knoxville, University of Tennessee Press [1972] xvii, 249 p. 24 cm. Bibliography: p. 211-240. [HN39.U6E38] 70-111047 ISBN 0-87049-115-6 11.50
1. Southern Baptist Convention. 2. Church and social problems—Baptists. 3. Southern States—Social conditions. I. Title.

ELIOT, Thomas Stearns 261.83
Christianity and culture: The idea of a Christian society and Notes toward the definition of culture. New York, Harcourt, Brace [1960, c.1940, 1949] 202p. 21cm. (A Harvest book, HB32) 60-1931 1.95 pap.,
1. Sociology, Christian. 2. Culture. I. Title.

ELLUL, Jacques. 261.8'3
Violence; reflections from a Christian perspective. Translated by Cecelia Gaul Kings. New York, Seabury Press [1969] 179 p. 22 cm. Bibliographical footnotes. [BT736.15.E413] 69-13540 4.95
1. Violence—Moral and religious aspects. I. Title.

ENGLAND, John, Bp., 1786-1842. 261.8'3
Letters of the late Bishop England to the Hon. John Forsyth, on the subject of domestic slavery: to which are prefixed copies, in Latin and English, of the Pope's apostolic letter, concerning the African slave trade, with some introductory remarks, etc. New York, Negro Universities Press [1969] xi, 156 p. 23 cm. Reprint of the 1844 ed. [E449.E58 1969] 74-97400
1. Slavery in the United States—Controversial literature—1844. 2. Slavery—Justification. I. Forsyth, John, 1780-1841.

EVANS, Louis Hadley, 1926- 261.8'3
Creative love / Louis H. Evans, Jr. Old Tappan, N.J. : F. H. Revell Co., c1977. 127 p. ; 21 cm. [BV652.2.E9] 77-4238 ISBN 0-8007-0860-1 : 5.95
1. Church group work. I. Title.

EVANS, Louis Hadley, 1926- 261.8'3
Creative love / Louis H. Evans, Jr. Old Tappan, N.J. : F. H. Revell Co., c1977. 127 p. ; 21 cm. [BV652.2.E9] 77-4238 ISBN 0-8007-0860-1 : 5.95
1. Church group work. I. Title.

FARAMELLI, Norman J. 261.8'3
Technethics; Christian mission in an age of technology [by] Norman J. Faramelli. New York, Friendship Press [1971] 160 p. 18 cm. Bibliography: p. 157-160. [BJ59.F37] 77-146630 ISBN 0-377-01001-4 1.75
1. Technology and ethics. I. Title.

FEE, John Gregg, 1816-1901. 261.8'3
An anti-slavery manual. New York, Arno Press, 1969. 230 p. 22 cm. (The Anti-slavery crusade in America) Reprint of the 1848 ed. [E449.F29 1969] 74-82189
1. Slavery in the United States—Controversial literature—1848. I. Title. II. Series.

FOLSOM, Paul. 261.8'3
And thou shalt die in a polluted land; an approach to Christian ecology. Liguori, Mo., Liguorian Pamphlets & Books [1971] 99, [2] p. illus. 18 cm. Bibliography: p. [101] [GF80.F6] 75-158338 1.50
1. Human ecology—Moral and religious aspects. I. Title.

FOSTER, Stephen Symonds, 1809-1881. 261.8'3
The brotherhood of thieves. New York, Arno Press, 1969. 75 p. 23 cm. (The Anti-slavery crusade in America) Reprint of the 1886 ed. [E449.F765 1969] 79-82190
1. Slavery in the United States—Controversial literature—1843. 2. Slavery and the church. I. Title. II. Series.

FRIESEN, Duane K. 261.8'3
Moral issues in the control of birth [by] Duane K. Friesen. Newton, Kan., Faith and Life Press [1974] 69 p. illus. 20 cm. Includes bibliographical references. [HQ766.35.F74] 74-76587 ISBN 0-87303-561-5
1. Birth control—Religious aspects—Protestant churches. 2. Abortion—Religious aspects. I. Title.

FRIESEN, Duane K. 261.8'3
Moral issues in the control of birth [by] Duane K. Friesen. Newton, Kan., Faith and Life Press [1974] 69 p. illus. 20 cm. Includes bibliographical references. [HQ766.35.F74] 74-76587 ISBN 0-87303-561-5 1.95 (pbk.).
1. Birth control—Religious aspects—Protestant churches. 2. Abortion—Religious aspects. I. Title.

FRY, Thomas A. 261.83
Get off the fence! Morals for moderns [Westwood, N. J.] Revell [c.1963] 127p. 21cm. 63-22556 2.50 bds.,
1. Christian ethics—Presbyterian authors. I. Title.

FRY, Thomas A 261.83
Get off the fence! Morals for moderns. [Westwood] N.J.] F. H. Revell [c1963] 127 p. 21 cm. [BJ1251.F76] 63-22556
1. Christian ethics — Presbyterian authors. I. Title.

FURFEY, Paul Hanly, 1896- 261.83
The respectable murderers; social evil and Christian conscience. [New York] Herder and Herder [1966] 192 p. 21 cm. Bibliographical references included in "Notes": p. 168-187. [HN31.F82] 66-26816
1. Church and social problems. 2. Social ethics. I. Title.

THE future of marriage as institution. 261.8'3
Edited by Franz Bockle. [New York] Herder and Herder [1970] 171 p. 23 cm. (Concilium: theology in the age of renewal, v. 55) Includes bibliographical references. [BX2250.F86] 70-113057 2.95
1. Marriage—Catholic Church. I. Bockle, Franz, ed. II. Series: Concilium (New York) v. 55.

GENNE, Elizabeth 261.83
Christians and the crisis in sex morality; the church looks at the facts about sex and marriage today, by Elizabeth and William Genne. New York, Association [c.1962] 123p. 16cm. (Association Pr. reflection bk.) 62-9379 .50 pap.,
1. Sex and religion. 2. Sexual ethics. I. Gennee, William H., joint author. II. Title.

GINGERICH, Melvin, 1902- 261.8'3
The Christian and revolution. Scottdale, Pa., Herald Press [1968] 229 p. 20 cm. (The Conrad Grebel lectures, 1967) Bibliography: p. [209]-224. [BT738.G5] 68-12028 4.50
1. Sociology, Christian—Addresses, essays, lectures. I. Title. II. Series.

GLADDEN, Washington, 1836-1918. 261.8'3
Applied Christianity : moral aspects of social questions / Washington Gladden. New York : Arno Press, 1976 [c1886] 320 p. ; 21 cm. (Social problems and social policy—the American experience) Reprint of the ed. published by Houghton, Mifflin, Boston. [HN31.G54 1976] 75-17224 ISBN 0-405-07494-8 : 18.00
1. Sociology Christian. I. Title. II. Series.

GLADDEN, Washington, 1836-1918. 261.8'3
Social salvation / Washington Gladden. Reprint ed. with a new introd. Hicksville, N.Y. : Regina Press, 1975, c1902. 5, v, 240 p. ; 23 cm. Reprint of the ed. published by Houghton Mifflin, Boston, which was issued as the 1902 Lyman Beecher lecture. Contents.Contents.—Religion and the social question.—The care of the poor.—The state and the unemployed.—Our brothers in bonds.—Social vices.—Public education.—The redemption of the city. Bibliography: p. [237]-240. [HN31.G65 1975] 74-78270 ISBN 0-88271-008-7
1. Sociology, Christian. 2. Social ethics. I. Title. II. Series: Lyman Beecher lectures ; 1902.

GOODWIN, Daniel Raynes, 1811-1890. 261.8'3
Southern slavery in its present aspects: containing a reply to a late work of the Bishop of Vermont on slavery. New York, Negro Universities Press [1969] 343 p. 23 cm. Reprint of the 1864 ed. Includes bibliographical references. [E449.H793G6 1969] 78-97452
1. Hopkins, John Henry, Bp., 1792-1868. A scriptural, ecclesiastical and historical view. 2. Slavery in the United States—Controversial literature—1864. I. Title.

THE Gospel of peace and justice : 261.8'3
Catholic social teaching since Pope John / presented by Joseph Gremillion. Maryknoll, N.Y. : Orbis Books, c1976. xiv, 623 p. ; 24 cm. Includes bibliographical references and indexes. [HN37.C3G66] 75-39892 ISBN 0-88344-165-9 : 15.95. ISBN 0-88344-166-7 pbk. : 8.95
1. Joannes XIII, Pope, 1881-1963. 2. Paulus VI, Pope, 1897- 3. Church and social problems—Catholic Church—Papal documents. 4. Social justice. I. Gremillion, Joseph B.

GRANT, Fern (Babcock) 1904- 261.83
Ministries of mercy. New York, Friendship [c.1962] 167p. 20cm. Bibl. 62-7847 2.95; 1.95 bds., pap.,
1. Church work with the handicapped. 2. Church and social problems—U. S. I. Title.

GRAYBILL, Ronald D. 261.8'3
E. G. White and church race relations [by] Ronald D. Graybill. Washington, Review and Herald Pub. Association [1970] 128 p. 22 cm. On spine: Church race relations. Bibliography: p. 124-128. [BX6193.W5G7] 76-122392
1. White, Ellen Gould (Harmon) 1827-1915. 2. Church and race relations—U.S. I. Title. II. Title: Church race relations.

GREET, Kenneth G. 261.83
The mutual society; aspects of the relationship of men and women. London, Epworth Pr. [dist. Mystic, Conn., Verry, 1964, c.1962] 170p. 19cm. (Beckly soc. service lect., 1962) Bibl. 64-5177 2.50 bds.,
1. Sex and religion. I. Title. II. Series.

GRIFFIN, Graeme Maxwell, 1932- 261.8'3
Towards a Christian approach to sex, by Graeme M. Griffin. Melbourne [Presbyterian Board of Christian Education] 1969. 54 p. 22 cm. Includes bibliographical references. [HQ32.G63] 70-526114 1.25

1. Sexual ethics. 2. Sex and religion. I. Presbyterian Church of Australia. Board of Christian Education. II. Title.

GRIFFIN, John Howard, 1920- 261.8'3
The church and the black man. Dayton, Ohio, Pflaum Press, 1969. vii, 132 p. illus., ports. and phonodisc (2 s. 7 in. 33 1/3 rpm. microgroove) in pocket. 28 cm. [BT734.2.G74] 68-55961 2.95
1. Church and race problems—U.S. I. Title.

GROUNDS, Vernon C. 261.8'3
Evangelicalism and social responsibility, by Vernon C. Grounds. Scottdale, Pa., Herald Press [1969] 39 p. 20 cm. (Focal pamphlet no. 16) "This paper was read at the Evangelicals in Social Action Peace Witness Seminar held at Eastern Mennonite College, Harrisonburg, Virginia, November 30, 1967." Bibliographical references included in "Footnotes" (p. 39) [BT738.G75] 79-4724 0.50 (pbk)
1. Sociology, Christian. 2. Evangelicalism. I. Title.

GUERRY, Emile Maurice, Abp., 1891- 261.83
The social doctrine of the Catholic Church. Tr. by Miriam Hederman. New York, Alba House [dist. St. Paul, 1962] 287p. 21cm. Bibl. 62-13995 4.95
1. Sociology, Christian (Catholic) I. Title.

GUERRY, Emile Maurice, Abp.,1891- 261.83
The social doctrine of the Catholic Church. Translated by Miriam Hederman. New York, Alba House [c1961] 287 p. 21 cm. Translation of La doctrine sociale de l'Eglise. Includes bibliography. [BT738.G813] 62-13995
1. Sociology, Christian (Catholic) I. Title.

HACKETT, Allen, 1905- 261.83
For the open door. Philadelphia, United Church Press [1964] 110 p. 19 cm. Bibliographical footnotes. [BX7255.S28P5] 64-25363
1. St. Louis. Pilgrim Congregational Church. 2. Church and race problems — St. Louis. I. Title.

HACKETT, Allen, 1905- 261.83
For the open door. Philadelphia, United Church [c.1964] 110p. 19cm. Bibl. 64-25363 1.45 pap.,
1. St. Louis. Pilgrim Congregational Church. 2. Church and race problems—St. Louis. I. Title.

HADDEN, Jeffrey K. 261.8'3
Gideon's gang: a case study of the church in social action [by] Jeffrey K. Hadden and Charles F. Longino, Jr, with the assistance of Myer S. Reed, Jr. Philadelphia, United Church Press [1974] 245 p. 22 cm. "A Pilgrim Press book." Includes bibliographical references. [BX9886.Z7D3944] 74-6156 ISBN 0-8298-0275-4 6.95
1. Congregation for Reconciliation, Dayton, Ohio. 2. Congregation for Reconciliation, Cincinnati. 3. Social action—Case studies. I. Longino, Charles F., 1938- joint author. II. Title.

HALL, Mary Penelope, 1904- 261.83
The church in social work; a study of moral welfare work undertaken by the Church of England, by M. Penelope Hall and Ismene V. Howes. London, Routledge & K. Paul; New York, Humanities Press [1965] x, 306 p. 22 cm. (International library of sociology and social reconstruction) Bibliographical references included in "Notes" (p. 273-299) [HV530.H3] 65-4701
1. Church of England—Charities—Hist. 2. Church and social problems—Church of England. I. Howes, Ismene V., joint author. II. Title. III. Series. IV. Series: International library of sociology and social reconstruction (London)

HALL, Mary Penelope, 1904- 261.83
The church in social work; a study of moral welfare work undertaken by the Church of England, by M. Penelope Hall, Ismene V. Howes. London, Routledge & K. Paul; New York, Humanities [c.1965] x, 306p. 22cm. (Intl. lib. of soc. and soc. reconstruction) Bibl. Title. (Series: International library of sociology and social reconstruction (London) [HV530.H3] 65-4701 6.50
1. Church of England—Charities—Hist. 2. Church and social problems—Church of England. I. Howes, Ismene V., joint author. II. Title. III. Series.

HALVORSON, Lawrence W ed. 261.83
The church in a diverse society. Minneapolis, Augsburg Pub. House [1964] 179 p. diagr. 22 cm. Includes bibliographical references. [BV4468.H3] 64-13434
1. Church work with minorities. 2. Sociology, Christian (Lutheran) 3. Minorities—U.S. I. Title.

HALVORSON, Lawrence W., ed. 261.83
The church in a diverse society. Minneapolis, Augsburg [c.1964] 179p. diagr. 22cm. Bibl. 64-13434 3.95 pap.,
1. Church work with minorities. 2. Sociology, Christian (Lutheran) 3. Minorities—U.S. I. Title.

HALVORSON, Loren E., 1927- 261.8'3
Peace on Earth handbook / Loren E. Halvorson. Minneapolis : Augsburg Pub. House, c1976. 128 p. : ill. ; 20 cm. [HN30.H28] 75-22718 ISBN 0-8066-1516-8 pbk. : 3.50
1. Church and social problems. 2. Social action. 3. Social action—Societies, etc.—Directories. 4. Church and underdeveloped areas. I. Title.

HAMILL, Robert H. 261.8'3
Plenty and trouble; the impact of technology on people [by] Robert H. Hamill. Nashville, Abingdon Press [1971] 192 p. 19 cm. Bibliography: p. 185-189. [CB478.H34] 73-148066 ISBN 0-687-31655-3
1. Technology and civilization. I. Title.

HARRINGTON, Janette T. 261.83
Who cares? A project-guide book on the church's mission and persons of special need [by] Janette T. Harrington. Muriel S. Webb. New York, Friendship [1962, c.1961] 160p. 21cm. Bibl. 61-16828 1.75 pap.,
1. Church work with the handicapped. I. Webb, Muriel S., joint author. II. Title.

HARRINGTON, Paul V 261.83
Woman's sublime call, by Paul V. Harrington. [Boston] St. Paul Editions [1964] 90 p. 22 cm. [BX2353.H3] 64-66106
1. Woman — Religious life. I. Title.

HARRINGTON, Paul V. 261.83
Woman's sublime call [Boston] St. Paul Eds. [dist. Daughters of St. Paul, c.1964] 90p. 22cm. [BX2353.H3] 64-66106 1.50; 1.00 pap.,
1. Woman—Religious life. I. Title.

HASELDEN, Kyle 261.83
Mandate for white Christians. Richmond, Knox [1966] 127p. 21cm. [BT734.2.H3] 66-12595 3.00
1. Church and race problems. I. Title.

HENDERSON, George, 1932- 261.8'3
A religious foundation of human relations : beyond games / by George Henderson. Norman : University of Oklahoma Press, c1977. p. cm. Includes bibliographical references and index. [HN31.H43] 76-62510 ISBN 0-8061-1398-7 : 9.95
1. Church and social problems. 2. Sociology, Christian. I. Title.

HENRY, Paul Mare. 261.83
Africa aeterna; the pictorial chronicle of a continent. Text by Paul Mare Henry. Translated by Joel Carmichael. [Lausanne, 1965] 342 p. illus. (part col., col. maps, ports. (part col.) 32 cm. [DT20.H413] 67-6986
1. "Conceived and produced by Georges and Rosamond Bernier." 2. Africa — Hist. I. Bernier, Georges. II. Bernier, Rosamond. III. Title.

HESSEL, Dieter T. 261.8'3
Reconciliation and conflict; church controversy over social involvement [by] Dieter T. Hessel. Philadelphia, Westminster Press [1969] 172 p. 21 cm. Bibliographical references included in "Notes" (p. [157]-172) [HN39.U6H4] 75-85857 2.95
1. Church and social problems—U.S. 2. Protestant churches—U.S. I. Title.

HEYER, Robert, comp. 261.8'3
Discovery in the press [compiled by] Robert Heyer [and] Tom Sheehan. Paramus, N.J., Paulist Press [1969] 132 p. illus. 21 cm. (Discovery series) [BV4531.2.H483] 71-79921 1.95
1. Social problems. 2. Youth—Religious life. I. Sheehan, Tom, joint comp. II. Title.

HILL, Clifford S 261.83
West Indian migrants and the London churches. London, New York, Oxford University Press, 1963. 89 p. tables. 19 cm. "Issued under the auspices of the Institute of Race Relations, London." [BV4404.G7115] 63-25728
1. Church and race problems — London. 2. West Indians in London. I. Title.

HILL, Clifford S. 261.83
West Indian migrants and the London churches. New York, Oxford [c.]1963. 89p. tables. 19cm. Issued under the auspices of the Inst. of Race Relations, London. 63-25728 1.95 pap.,
1. Church and race problems—London. 2. West Indians in London. I. Title.

HILTON, Bruce. 261.8'3
The Delta Ministry. [New York] Macmillan [1969] 240 p. illus., map, ports. 21 cm. [BV4470.H5] 69-17345
1. Delta Ministry. 2. Church and race problems—Mississippi.

HILTON, Bruce. 261.83
My brother is a stranger. New York, Friendship Press [1963] 128 p. illus. 21 cm. [HN39.U6H5] 63-8678
1. Church and social problems — U.S. 2. Sociology, Urban. I. Title.

HILTON, Bruce [ed.] 261.83
My brother is a stranger. New York, Friendship Pr. [c.1963] 128p. illus. 21cm. 63-8678 1.75 pap.,
1. Church and social problems—U.S. 2. Sociology, Urban. I. Title.

HODGSON, Robert David, 1923- 261.83
The changing map of Africa, by Robert D. Hodgson and Elvyn A. Stoneman. Princeton, N.J., Van Nostrand [c1963] 143 p. maps. 21 cm. (Van Nostrand searchlight book, 16) Bibliography: p. 137-138. [DT20.H58] 63-23636
1. Africa — Hist. I. Stoneman, Evlyn A., joint author. II. Title.

HOLLIS, Harry. 261.8'3
The shoot-'em-up society / Harry Hollis, Jr. Nashville : Broadman Press, [1974] 126 p. ; 18 cm. Includes bibliographical references. [BT736.15.H64] 74-78964 ISBN 0-8054-6113-2 pbk. : 1.50
1. Violence—Moral and religious aspects. I. Title.

HOLMES, Thomas Joseph. 261.8'3
Ashes for breakfast [by] Thomas J. Holmes. In collaboration with Gainer E. Bryan, Jr. Valley Forge [Pa.] Judson Press [1969] 127 p. 23 cm. [BX6480.M23H6] 74-79729 3.95
1. Macon, Ga. Tattnall Square Baptist Church. 2. Church and race problems—Macon, Ga. I. Bryan, Gainer E., joint author. II. Title.

HOLTROP, Donald. 261.8'3
Notes on Christian racism. Grand Rapids, Mich., Eerdmans [1969] 46 p. 21 cm. (A Reformed journal monograph) [BT734.2.H6] 73-95462 0.95
1. Church and race problems—U.S. I. Title.

HOOTON, Caradine R. 261.83
What shall we say about alcohol? Nashville, Abingdon Press [1960] 127 p. 20 cm. [HV5186.H6] 60-6931
1. Temperance. I. Title.

HORNE, George, 1895- 261.83
The twentieth-century cross; a book for every thinking, patriotic, Christian American in our time. [1st ed.] New York, Greenwich Book Publishers [1960- v. 21cm. [BT734.3.H6] 60-10772
1. Segregation—Religious aspects. 2. U.S.—Race question. I. Title.

HOUGH, Joseph C. 261.8'3
Black power and white Protestants; a Christian response to the new Negro pluralism [by] Joseph C. Hough, Jr. New York, Oxford University Press, 1968. ix, 228 p. 21 cm. Bibliographical footnotes. [BT734.2.H63] 68-19767
1. Church and race problems—United States. 2. Black power. I. Title.

HOWES, Robert G. 261.83
The church and the change; an initial study of the role of the Roman Catholic Church in the changing American community. [Boston] St. Paul Eds. [dist. Daughters of St. Paul, c.1961] 180p. Bibl. 61-14571 3.00; 2.00 pap.,
1. Church and social problems—Catholic Church. I. Title.

HOWES, Robert Gerard. 261.83
The church and the change; an initial study of the role of the Roman Catholic Church in the changing American community. [Boston] St. Paul Editions [1961] 180 p. 22 cm. Includes bibliographies. [HN37.C3H6] 61-14571
1. Church and social problems—Catholic Church. I. Title.

INGRAM, Tolbert Robert, 1913- ed. 261.83
Essays on segregation. Boston, St. Thomas Press, 1960. v, 106p. 19cm. [BT734.3.I5] 60-13820
1. Segregation—Religious aspects. I. Title.

INTERNATIONAL Congress of Africanists. 261.83
Proceedings. 1st- 1962- [Evanston, Ill.] Northwestern University Press. v. illus. 23 cm. Editors: 1962- L. Brown and M. Crowder. [DT1.I57] 64-16276
1. African studies — Congresses. I. Bown, Lalage J., ed. II. Crowder, Michael, 1934- ed. III. Title.

JARRETT-KERR, Martin 1912- 261.83
Christ and the new nations. New York, Morehouse, 1966. viii, 120p. 19cm. (Here & now) Seraph. Bibl. [HN32.J3] 66-5931 1.95
1. Church and social problems. 2. Missions. I. Title.

JENNINGS, Sir William Ivor, 1903- 261.83
Democracy in Africa. Cambridge [Eng.] University Press, 1963. 89 p. 22 cm. [DT30.J4] 63-23577
1. Africa — Politics — 1960- 2. Nationalism — Africa. I. Title.

JERSILD, Paul T., 1931- comp. 261.8'3
Moral issues and Christian response, edited by Paul T. Jersild [and] Dale A. Johnson. New York, Holt, Rinehart and Winston [1971] x, 467 p. illus. 24 cm. Includes bibliographical references. [HN39.U6J44] 72-125003 ISBN 0-03-083309-4
1. Church and social problems—U.S.—Addresses, essays, lectures. I. Johnson, Dale A., 1936- joint comp. II. Title.

JERSILD, Paul T., 1931- comp. 261.8'3
Moral issues and Christian response / edited by Paul T. Jersild, Dale A. Johnson. 2d ed. New York : Holt, Rinehart and Winston, c1976. vi, 410 p. : ill. ; 23 cm. Includes bibliographical references and index. [HN39.U6J44 1976] 75-38909 ISBN 0-03-089802-1 : 7.50
1. Church and social problems—United States—Addresses, essays, lectures. I. Johnson, Dale A., 1936- II. Title.

JONES, Howard O. 261.83
Shall we overcome? A challenge to Negro and white Christians [by] Howard O. Jones. Westwood, N.J., Revell [1966] 146p. 21cm. [BT734.2.J6] 66-17048 3.50 bds.,
1. Church and race problems—U.S. 2. Negroes—Religion. I. Title.

KEITH-LUCAS, Alan 261.83
The church and social welfare. Philadelphia, Westminster [c.1962] 84p. 19cm. (Christian perspectives on soc. problems) 62-15164 1.25 pap.,
1. Church charities. 2. Church and social problems. I. Title.

KELSEY, George D. 261.83
Racism and the Christian understanding of man, by George D. Kelsey. New York, Scribner [1965] 178 p. 24 cm. Bibliographical footnotes. [BT734.2.K42] 65-27241
1. Church and race problems. 2. Race discrimination. I. Title.

KELSEY, George D. 261.83
Racism and the Christian understanding of man. New York, Scribners [c.1965] 178p. 24cm. (Studies in contemp. theol., 34325) Bibl. [BT734.2.K42] 65-27241 2.95 pap.,
1. Church and race problems. 2. Race discrimination. I. Title.

KERNS, Joseph E. 261.83
The theology of marriage; the historical development of Christian attitudes toward sex and sanctity in marriage. New York, Sheed and Ward [1964] xiv, 302 p. 22 cm. Bibliography: p. 295-302. [BX2250.K42] 63-17145
1. Marriage — Catholic Church. I. Title.

KERNS, Joseph E. 261.83
The theology of marriage; the historical development of Christian attitudes toward sex and sanctity in marriage. New York, Sheed [c.1964] xiv, 302p. 22cm. Bibl. 63-17145 6.00
1. Marriage—Catholic Church. I. Title.

KING, Morton Brandon, 1913- 261.8'3
Measuring religious dimensions; studies of congregational involvement [by] Morton B. King [and] Richard A. Hunt. Dallas, Southern Methodist University [1972] 136 p. 23 cm. (Studies in social science, no. 1) Bibliography: p. 64-68. [BR555.T4K56] 72-195903
1. Sociology, Christian—Texas—Dallas Co.—Case studies. 2. Dallas Co., Tex.—Religious life and customs—Case studies. I. Hunt, Richard A., 1931- joint author. II. Title. III. Series: Studies in social science (Dallas) no. 1.

KIPPLEY, John F. 261.8'3
Covenant, Christ, and contraception [by] John F. Kippley. Staten Island, N.Y., Alba House [1970] xxviii, 160 p. 22 cm. Includes bibliographical references. [HQ766.3.K53] 79-129174 4.95
1. Birth control—Religious aspects. 2. Church. 3. Sex (Theology) I. Title.

KITAGAWA, Daisuke. 261.83
Race relations and Christian mission. New York, Friendship Press [1964] 191 p. 19 cm. [BT734.2.K5] 64-11007
1. Church and race problems. I. Title.

KITAGAWA, Daisuke 261.83
Race relations and Christian mission. New York, Friendship [c.1964] 191p. 19cm. 64-11007 1.95 pap.,
1. Church and race problems. I. Title.

KLEMME, Huber F. 261.83
Poverty and plenty in our time; a coursebook for leaders of adults [by] Huber F. Klemme. Boston, United Church Pr. [1966] 122p. illus. 21cm. Pt. of the United Church curriculum. prepd. & pub. by the Div. of Christian Educ. & the Div. of Publication of the United Church Bd. for Homeland Ministries. Bibl. [HC110.P6K55] 66-20543 1.00 pap.,
1. Poor—U. S. 2. Church and social problems. 3. Social work education. I. United Church Board for Homeland Ministries. Division of Christian Education. II. United Church Board for Homeland Ministries. Division of Publication. III. Title.

KLEMME, Huber F. 261.83
Poverty and plenty in our time; a coursebook for leaders of adults [by] Huber F. Klemme. Boston, United Church Press [1966] 122 p. illus. 21 cm. "Part of the United Church curriculum, prepared and published by the Division of Christian Education and the Division of Publication of the United Church Board for Homeland Ministries." Bibliography: p. 24-27. [HC110.P6K55] 66-20543
1. Poor—U.S. 2. Church and social problems. 3. Social work education. I. United Church Board for Homeland Ministries. Division of Christian Education. II. United Church Board for Homeland Ministries. Division of Publication. III. Title.

KNOX, John, 1900- ed. 261.8'3
Religion and the present crisis. Freeport, N.Y., Books for Libraries Press [1973, c1942] p. (Essay index reprint series) Original ed. issued in series: Chicago. University. Charles R. Walgreen foundation lectures. Contents.Contents.—Colwell, E. C. Christianity refinding itself.—Aubrey, E. E. Building a better democracy.—Knox, J. Re-examining pacifism.—Holman, C. T. Maintaining fellowship across lines of conflict.—Wieman, H. N. Achieving personal stability.—Gilkey, C. W. Anticipating the post-war mind.—McNeill, J. T. Preparing for durable peace.—Bower, W. C. Educating for a new world-order.—Pauck, W. Redeeming culture through crisis. [BR115.C5K63 1973] 72-10731 ISBN 0-8369-7225-2
1. Civilization, Christian. 2. Christianity—United States. I. Title. II. Series: Chicago. University. Charles R. Walgreen Foundation for the Study of American Institutions. Lectures.

LAFARGE, John. 261.83
The Catholic viewpoint on race relations. Introd. by John J. Delaney. Rev. ed. Garden City, N. Y., Hanover House, 1960 [c.1956, 1960] 192 p. 22 cm. (Catholic viewpoint series) (Bibl. footnotes) 60-9760 3.50
1. Race problems. 2. Church and social problems—Catholic Church. 3. U. S.—Race question. I. Title.

LACY, Creighton, ed. 261.83
Christianity amid rising men and nations [by] Barbara Ward [and others] New York, Association Press [1965] 192 p. 21 cm. Papers from an interdisciplinary symposium sponsored by the Divinity School of Duke University with the aid of the Ford Foundation. April 9-12, 1964. Bibliographical references included in "Notes" (p. 183-185) "Supplementary reading list": p. 187-192. [BV2061.L3] 65-11080
1. Missions — Congresses. I. Duke University, Durham, N.C. Divinity School. II. Title.

LACY, Creighton, ed. 261.83
Christianity amid rising men and nations [by] Barbara Ward [others] New York, Association [c.1965] 192p. 21cm. Papers from an interdisciplinary symp. sponsored by the Divinity Sch. of Duke Univ. with the aid of the Ford Found. April 9-12, 1964. Bibl. [BV2061.L3] 65-11080 2.25 pap.,
1. Missions—Congresses. I. Duke University, Durham, N.C. Divinity School. II. Title.

LANDIS, Benson Young, 1897- 261.83
Protestant experience with United States immigration, 1910-1960, a study paper. [New York? 1961] 81p. 19cm. Includes bibliography. [BV639.I4L3] 61-11038
1. U. S.—Emig. & immig. 2. Church and social problems—U. S. I. Title.

LANIER, Jesse Alvin 261.83
The impact of science and scriptures on delinquency. New York, Vantage 1962 c.1961 82p. 2.50
I. Title.

LAURENTIN, Rene. 261.8'3
Liberation, development, and salvation. Translated by Charles Underhill Quinn. Maryknoll, N.Y., Orbis Books [1972] xvii, 238 p. 24 cm. Translation of Developpement et salut. Bibliography: p. 235-238. [BT738.L3513] 72-156970 5.95
1. Sociology, Christian (Catholic) 2. Church and underdeveloped areas. I. Title.

LAY, Benjamin, 1677-1759. 261.8'3
All slave-keepers that keep the innocent in bondage. New York, Arno Press, 1969. 271 p. 23 cm. (The Anti-slavery crusade in America) Reprint of the 1737 ed. [E446.L4 1969] 72-82203
1. Slavery in the United States—Controversial literature—1737. 2. Slavery and the church—Friends, Society of. I. Title. II. Series.

LECKY, Robert S. 261.8'3
Black manifesto; religion, racism, and reparations, edited by Robert S. Lecky and H. Elliott Wright. New York, Sheed and Ward [1969] x, 182 p. 21 cm. (A Search book) Bibliography: p. [179]-182. [E185.615.L4] 78-98090 5.00
1. Negroes—Economic conditions. 2. Church and social problems—U.S. I. Wright, H. Elliott, 1937- joint author. II. Title.

LENGYEL, Emil, 1895- 261.83
Africa: past, present, and future. New York, Oxford Book Co. [1966] 152 p. illus., maps. 19 cm. (Oxford unit texts) [DT5.L37] 66-31553
1. Africa. I. Title.

LEONARD, Joseph T. 261.83
Theology and race relations. Foreword by Patrick A. O'Boyle. Milwaukee, Bruce [1964, c.1963] x, 316p. 23cm. Bibl. 63-23264 5.00
1. Church and race problems. I. Title.

LEPP, Ignace, 1909- 261.83
The Christian failure. Tr. by Elizabeth Strakosch. Westminster, Md., Newman [c.] 1962] 192p. illus. 19cm. 62-51062 3.50
1. Sociology, Christian (Catholic) 2. Catholic Church—Relations. I. Title.

LIPMAN, Eugene J., ed. 261.83
A tale of ten cities; the triple ghetto in American religious life. Ed. by Eugene J. Lipman, Albert Vorspan. New York, Union of Amer. Hebrew Cong. [c.1962] 344p. 22cm. 62-9651 4.95
1. Church and social problems—U. S. 2. Judaism and social problems. I. Vorspan, Albert, joint ed. II. Title.

LIPMAN, Eugene J ed. 261.83
A tale of ten cities; the triple ghetto in American religious life. Edited by Eugene J. Lipman and Albert Vorspan. New York, Union of American Hebrew Congregations [1962] 344p. 22cm. [HN39.U6L5] 62-9651
1. Church and social problems— U. S. 2. Judaism and social problems. I. Vorspan, Albert, joint ed. II. Title.

LOVASIK, Lawrence George, 1913- 261.83
Catholic marriage and child care. Boston, Christopher [c.1962] 361p. 62-11879 4.95
1. Marriage—Catholic Church. 2. Religious education—Home training. I. Title.

LUCAS, Lawrence, 1933- 261.8'3
Black priest/white church; Catholics and racism. [1st ed.] New York, Random House [1970] 270 p. 22 cm. [BX4705.L795A3] 72-102317 6.95
1. Church and race problems—U.S. I. Title.

LUTHERAN Church--Missouri Synod. Family Life Committee. 261.83
Sex and the church; a sociological, historical, and theological investigation of sex attitudes. Oscar E. Feucht. ed. [others] St. Louis. Concordia Pub. House [c.1961] xiv, 277p. illus. (Marriage and family research series, v.5) Bibl. 60-5351 3.50
1. Sex and religion. 2. Sexual ethics. I. Feucht, Oscar E., ed. II. Title. III. Series.

LUTZE, Karl E 261.83
To mend the broken; the Christian response to the challenge of human relations problems by Karl E. Lutze. Saint Louis, Concordia Pub. House [1966] 99 p. illus. 21 cm. [BT734.1.L8] 66-14567
1. Church and race problems — U.S. I. Title.

LUTZE, Karl E. 261.83
To mend the broken; the Christian response to the challenge of humanrelations problems. St. Louis, Concordia [c.1966] 99p. illus. 21cm. [BT734.2.L8] 66-14567 1.95 pap.,
1. Church and race problems—U.S. I. Title.

LYON, William, 1927- 261.8'3
A pew for one, please : the church and the single person / William Lyon. New York : Seabury Press, 1977. xii, 120 p. ; 22 cm. "A Crossroad book." Includes bibliographical references. [BV4437.L95] 76-41976 ISBN 0-8164-0374-0 : 6.95
1. Church work with single people. I. Title.

MCCORMACK, Arthur, ed. 261.83
Christian responsibility and world poverty; a symposium. Westminster, Md., Newman [c.1963] xiii, 314p. 23cm. Bibl. 63-25858 6.50
1. Church and social problems—Catholic Church—Congresses. 2. Poverty—Congresses. 3. Population—Congresses. I. Title.

MACE, David Robert. 261.8'3
The Christian response to the sexual revolution [by] David R. Mace. Nashville, Abingdon Press [1970] 142 p. 19 cm. Bibliography: p. 137-142. [BT708.M3] 76-124748
1. Sex (Theology) I. Title.

MCFADDEN, Charles Joseph, 1909- 261.8'3
The dignity of life : moral values in a changing society / Charles J. McFadden. Huntington, IN : Our Sunday Visitor, c1976. 296 p. ; 22 cm. Includes index. [HM216.M243] 75-42902 ISBN 0-87973-891-X : 8.50
1. Moral conditions. 2. Medical ethics. 3. Christian ethics. I. Title.

MCLAIN, C. E. 261.83
Place of race. New York, Vantage [c.1965] 56p. 21cm. Bibl. [BT734.M22] 65-4154 2.50 bds.,
1. Race. I. Title.

MACLURE, Millar, ed. 261.83
Africa: the political pattern; [essays by] Jaja Wachuku [and others] Edited by Millar MacLure [and] Douglas Anglin. [Toronto] University of Toronto Press, 1961. 63-124p. 24cm. (University of Toronto quarterly. Supplements, 6) [DT30.M25] 62-5327
1. Africa—Politics. 2. States, New. I. Anglin, Douglas, joint ed. II. Wachuku, Jaja. III. Title.

MCMANUS, Eugene P 261.83
Studies in race relations. Baltimore, Josephite Press, 1961. 163p. 23cm. Includes bibliography. [HT1521.M23] 61-18523
1. Race problems. 2. U. S.—Race question. 3. Church and social problems—Catholic Church. I. Title.

MCNEILL, Robert B. 261.83
God wills us free: the ordeal of a Southern minister, by Robert McNeill. Introd. by Ralph McGill. New York, Hill and Wang [1965] xii, 210 p. 22 cm. Bibliographical footnotes. [BX9225.M287A3] 65-15862
1. Church and race problems—Southern States. 2. Southern States—Race question. I. Title.

THE Manipulated man. 261.8'3
Edited by Franz Bockle. [New York] Herder and Herder [1971] 144 p. 23 cm. (Concilium: religion in the seventies. Moral theology, v. 65) On cover: The New concilium: religion in the seventies. Includes bibliographical references. [BT701.2.M353] 74-150302 2.95
1. Man (Theology) 2. Science and ethics. 3. Social ethics. I. Bockle, Franz, ed. II. Series: Concilium (New York) v. 65

MARSHALL, John, 1922- 261.83
Catholics, marriage, and contraception. Helicon, [dist. New York,] Taplinger, c.1965 xv, 212p. 22cm. Bibl. [HQ766.3.M35] 65-24125 4.50 bds.,
1. Birth control—Religious aspects. I. Title.

MASTON, Thomas Bufford, 1897- 261.8'3
The Christian, the church, and contemporary problems, by T. B. Maston. Waco, Tex., Word Books [1968] 248 p. 22 cm. Bibliographical references included in "Notes" (p. 229-240) [HN31.M242] 68-23116 5.95
1. Church and social problems. I. Title.

MASTON, Thomas Bufford, 1897- 261.83
Segregation and desegregation: a Christian approach. New York, Macmillan, 1959. 178p. 22cm. Includes bibliography. [BT734.3.M3] 59-8224
1. Segregation— Religious aspects. I. Title.

MAY, Henry Farnham, 1915- 261.83
Protestant churches and industrial America. New York, 175 5th Ave., Octagon Bks., 1963[c.1949] 297p. 24cm. Bibl. 63-14345 7.50
1. Church and social problems—U.S. 2. U.S.—Church history. I. Title.

MESSER, Mary Burt. 261.83
The science of society; the identity of each as Godlike, embracing all. New York, Philosophical Library [1959] 239p. 21cm. [HN37.C4M4] 59-16088
1. Christian Science. 2. Church and social problems—Christian Science. I. Title.

METHODIST Church (United States) Dept. of Research and Survey. 261.83
The church in the racially changing community [by] Robert L. Wilson [executive secretary] and James H. Davis [director] New York, Abingdon Press [1966] 159 p. 19 cm. "For further reading": p. 157-159. [E185.89.H6M45] 66-11060
1. Church and race problems — U.S. 2. Negroes — Housing. 3. Race discrimination — U.S. I. Wilson, Robert Leroy, 1925- . II. Davis, James Hill 1931- . III. Title.

METHODIST Church (United States) Dept. of Research and Survey 261.83
The church in the racially changing community [by] Robert L. Wilson [executive secretary] & James H. Davis [director] Nashville, Abingdon [c.1966] 159p. 19cm. Bibl. [E185.89.H6M45] 66-11060 1.25 pap.,
1. Church and race problems—U.S. 2. Negroes—Housing. 3. Race discrimination—U.S. I. Wilson, Robert Leroy, 1925- II. Davis, James Hill. 1931- III. Title.

MILLER, William D., 1916- 261.8'3
A harsh and dreadful love; Dorothy Day and the Catholic Worker Movement [by] William D. Miller. New York, Liveright [1973] xvi, 370 p. illus. 23 cm. Bibliography: p. [351]-357. [BX810.M5] 72-87098 ISBN 0-87140-558-X 9.95
1. Catholic Worker Movement. 2. Day, Dorothy, 1897- 3. The Catholic worker. I. Title.

MILLER, William D., 1916- 261.8'3
A harsh and dreadful love; Dorothy Day and the Catholic Worker Movement. Garden City, N.Y., Doubleday, 1974 [c1973] 356 p. 18 cm. (Image book, D331) Bibliography: p. [338]-344. [BX810.M5] ISBN 0-385-08915-5 1.95 (pbk.)
1. Day, Dorothy, 1897- 2. Catholic Worker Movement. I. Title.
L.C. card no. for the hardbound edition: 72-87098.

MOBERG, David O. 261.83
The church as a social institution; the sociology of American religion. Englewood Cliffs, N. J., Prentice-Hall, 1962. 569 p. 24 cm. (Prentice-Hall sociology series) Includes bibliography. [BV625.M6] 62-10140
1. Sociology, Christian. 2. Religion and sociology. 3. U.S.—Religion. I. Title.

MOBERG, David O 261.83
Inasmuch: Christian social responsibility in the twentieth century, by David O. Moberg. Grand Rapids, Eerdmans [1965] 216 p. 21 cm. Includes bibliographies. [HN31.M67] 65-18093
1. Church and social problems. 2. Sociology, Christian. I. Title.

MOBERG, David O. 261.83
Inasmuch; Christian social responsibility in the twentieth century. Grand Rapids, Mich., Eerdmans [c.1965] 216p. 21cm. Bibl. [HN31.M67] 65-18093 2.45 pap.,
1. Church and social problems. 2. Sociology, Christian. I. Title.

MOELLERING, Ralph Luther. 261.83
Christian conscience and Negro emancipation [by] Ralph L. Moellering. Philadelphia. Fortress Press [1965] x, 214 p. 22 cm. Bibliographical footnotes. [BT734.2.M6] 65-18282
1. Church and race problems — U.S. 2. Negroes — Civil rights. I. Title.

MOELLERING, Ralph Luther 261.83
Christian conscience and Negro emancipation. Philadelphia, Fortress [c.1965] x, 214p. 22cm. Bibl. [BT734.2.M6] 65-18282 3.75
1. Church and race problems—U.S. 2. Negroes—Civil rights. I. Title.

MOODY, Joseph Nestor, 1904- ed. 261.83
The challenge of Mater et magistra. Edited by Joseph N. Moody and Justus George Lawler. [New York] Herder and Herder [1963] 280 p. 22 cm. Includes bibliography. [HN37.C3M72] 63-11309
1. Catholic Church. Pope, 1958- (Joannes XXIII) Mater et magistra (15 May 1961) 2. Church and social problems — Catholic Church — Papal documents. I. Lawler, Justus George, joint ed. II. Title.

MOODY, Joseph Nestor, 1904- ed. 261.83
The challenge of Mater et magistra. Ed. by Joseph N. Moody, Justus George Lawler. [New York] Herder & Herder [c.1963] 280p. 22cm. Bibl. 63-11309 4.95
1. Catholic Church. Pope, 1958- (Joannes XXIII) Mater et magistra (15 May, 1961) 2.

Church and social problems—Catholic Church—Papal documents. I. Lawler, Justus George, joint ed. II. Title.

MOORE, Maurice J. 261.8'3
Death of a dogma? The American Catholic clergy's views of contraception, by Maurice J. Moore. [Chicago] Community and Family Study Center, University of Chicago [1973] xiii, 142 p. illus. 23 cm. Includes bibliographical references. [HQ766.3.M63] 73-176504
1. Birth control—Religious aspects—Catholic Church. 2. Birth control—United States. I. Title.

MORGAN, Richard. 261.83
God's message and the messengers. Philadelphia, Dorrance [1960] 377p. 24cm. [BR124.M65] 60-8556
1. Christianity —20th cent. I. Title.

MORRIS, Colin M. 261.8'3
Unyoung, uncolored, unpoor [by] Colin Morris. Nashville, Abingdon Press [1969] 158 p. 20 cm. Includes bibliographical references. [BT736.15.M6] 73-10321
1. Violence—Moral and religious aspects. I. Title.

THE Most holy 261.8'3
principle. [Murray, Utah] GEMS [1970-71] 3v. 24 cm. Contents.Contents.—v. 1. The law and the testimony, 5 Dec. 1805-3 Mar. 1887.—v. 2. The horn made war with the saints and prevailed, 3 Mar. 1887-2 Sep. 1898.—v. 3. A history problem, 23 Dec. 1805-Jun. 1970. [BX8641.M65] 72-16602
1. Mormons and Mormonism. 2. Polygamy.

MULLEN, Thomas James, 261.83
1934-
The ghetto of indifference [by] Thomas J. Mullen. Nashville, Abingdon Press [1966] 111 p. 20 cm. [HN31.M8] 66-14994
1. Church and social problems. I. Title.

MULLEN, Thomas James, 261.83
1934-
The ghetto of indifference. Nashville. Abingdon [c.1966] 111p. 20cm. [HN31.M8] 66-14994 2.25 bds.,
1. Church and social problems. I. Title.

MURPHY, Magdalen B. 261.8'3
The church and non-profit housing: a survey. Prepared by Magdalen B. Murphy. Washington, National Conference of Catholic Charities [1972] v, 80 p. 23 cm. [HD7293.M87] 72-197073 2.00
1. Housing—United States. 2. Church and social problems—Catholic Church. I. National Conference of Catholic Charities. II. Title.

NARRAMORE, Clyde Maurice, 261.8'3
1916-
How to succeed in family living, by Clyde M. Narramore. Glendale, Calif., G/L Regal Bks. [1968] 119p. 18cm. (GL95-14) [HQ734.N28] 67-31425 .95 pap.,
1. Family. I. Title. II. Title: Family living.

NATIONAL Conference on 261.83
Religion and Race, Chicago, 1963.
Race: challenge to religion, original essays and An appeal to the conscience. Edited by Mathew Ahmann. Chicago, H. Regnery Co., 1963. 178 p. 21 cm. "Convened by the Department of Racial and Cultural Relations of the National Council of Churches, the Social Action Commission of the Synagogue Council of America, and the Social Action Department of the National Catholic Welfare Conference." Includes bibliography. [BT734.2.N3] 63-13762
1. Church and race problems — U.S. I. Ahmann, Mathew, ed. II. National Council of the Churches of Christ in the United States of America. Dept. of Racial and Cultural Relations. III. Title.

NATIONAL Conference on 261.83
Religion and Race, Chicago, 1963.
Race: challenge to religion, original essays and An appeal to the conscience. Edited by Mathew Ahmann. Chicago, H. Regnery Co., 1963. 178 p. 21 cm. "Convened by the Department of Racial and Cultural Relations of the National Council of Churches, the Social Action Commission of the Synagogue Council of America, and the Social Action Department of the National Catholic Welfare Conference." Includes bibliography. [BT734.2.N3 1963c] 63-13762
1. Church and race problems—United States. I. Ahmann, Mathew H., ed. II. National Council of the Churches of Christ in the United States of America. Dept. of Racial and Cultural Relations.

NEDERHOOD, Joel H. 261.8'3
The holy triangle [by] Joel Nederhood. Grand Rapids, Baker Book House [1970?] 143 p. 18 cm. [BT706.N4] 72-132195 1.25
1. Marriage. I. Title.

NEUHAUS, Richard John. 261.8'3
Christian faith & public policy, thinking and acting in the courage of uncertainty / Richard John Neuhaus. Minneapolis : Augsburg Pub. House, c1977. 224 p. ;22 cm. Bibliography: p. 211-224. [HN31.N47] 76-27086 ISBN 0-8066-1554-0 : 4.95
1. Church and social problems. 2. Church and state. 3. Christian ethics. 4. United States—Social policy. I. Title: Christian faith & public policy ...

A New ethic for a new 261.8'3
earth. Edited by Glenn C. Stone. [New York] Published by Friendship Press for the Faith-Man-Nature Group and the Section on Stewardship and Benevolence of the National Council of Churches [1971] 176 p. 19 cm. (F/M/N papers, no. 2) Includes papers presented at the Faith-Man-Nature Group's 4th national conference, Airlie House, Nov. 28-30, 1969. Pages 173-176 blank for "Notes." Bibliography: p. 163-172. [BL435.N48] 77-152084 1.95
1. Nature—Religious interpretations. 2. Human ecology—Moral and religious aspects. I. Stone, Glenn C., ed. II. Faith-Man-Nature Group. III. Series: Faith-Man-Nature Group. F/M/N papers, no. 2

*NEW world's a' coming; 261.83
a study guide on human rights. Prepd. by a joint working party appointed by Church Women United, Natl. Council of Catholic Women, for use by ecumenical groups in local communities. Pub. for Church Women United, Natl. Council of Catholic Women. [New York Council Pr., [Glen Rock, New Jersey] Paulist [1968] 96p. 18cm. .95 pap.,

NOONAN, John Thomas, 261.83
1926-
Contraception: a history of its treatment by the Catholic theologians and canonists. New York, New Amer. Lib. [1967, c.1965] 667p. 18cm. (Mentor-Omega bk., MW720) [HQ766.3.N6] 1.50 pap.,
1. Birth control — Religious aspects. I. Title.

NOONAN, John Thomas, 1926- 261.83
Contraception; a history of its treatment by the Catholic theologians and canonists [by] John T. Noonan, Jr. Cambridge, Belknap Press of Harvard University Press, 1965. x, 561 p. illus., 25 cm. Bibliographical footnotes. [HQ766.3.N6] 65-16687
1. Birth control—Religious aspects. I. Title.

NOONAN, John Thomas, Jr., 261.83
1926-
Contraception; a history of its treatment by the Catholic theologians and canonists. Cambridge, Mass., Belknap Pr. of Harvard [c.] 1965. x, 561p. illus. 25cm. Bibl. [HQ766.3.N6] 65-16687 7.95
1. Birth control—Religious aspects. I. Title.

NORTH Conway Institute. 261.8'3
Time for a change; attitudes on alcohol and drugs [Edited by L. Dana Gatlin] Boston [1970] 32 p. 28 cm. Condensation of the speeches given at the 15th annual conference of the North Conway Institute held June, 1969, in North Conway, N.H. Bibliography: p. 32. [HV5175.N63] 72-22616
1. Alcoholism and religion. 2. Drug abuse. I. Gatlin, L. Dana, 1930- ed. II. Title.

NOYCE, Gaylord B. 261.8'3
Survival and mission for the city church / by Gaylord B. Noyce. Philadelphia : Westminster Press, [1975] 162 p. ; 22 cm. Includes bibliographical references. [BV637.N66] 74-23160 ISBN 0-664-24813-6 pbk. : 3.95
1. City churches. I. Title.

OATES, Wayne Edward, 1917- 261.83
Alcohol in and out of the church [by] Wayne E. Oates. Nashville, Broadman Press [1966] vi, 136 p. 21 cm. Bibliography: p. 133-136. [HV5175.O18] 66-15146
1. Alcoholism and religion. I. Title.

OATES, Wayne Edward, 1917- 261.83
Alcohol in and out of the church. Nashville, Broadman [c.1966] vi, 136p. 21cm. Bibl [HV5175.O18] 66-15146 3.95
1. Alcoholism and religion. I. Title.

O'GRADY, Desmond 261.83
Eat from God's hand; Paul Gauthier and the church of the poor. London, G. Chapman [New York, Herder & Herder. 1966, c.1965] 162p. 21cm. [BV639.P6O34] 66-3209 3.50
1. Gauthier, Paul. 2. Church and the poor. I. Title.

OLDHAM, Joseph 261.8'3
Houldsworth, 1874-1969.
Christianity and the race problem. New York, Negro Universities Press [1969] xx, 280 p. 23 cm. Reprint of the 1924 ed. Bibliographical footnotes. [BT734.2.04 1969] 73-75534
1. Race problems. I. Title.

OLIVER, C Herbert, 1925- 261.83
No flesh shall glory. [Nutley, N. J.] Presbyterian and Reformed Pub. Co., 1959. 96p. 21cm. [BT734.O4] 59-14513
1. Race. 2. Segregation—Religious aspects. 3. Sociology, Biblical. I. Title.

O'NEILL, Joseph Eugene, 261.83
1910- ed.
A Catholic case against segregation. Foreword by Richard Cardinal Cushing; New York, Macmillan, 1961. xiv, 155 p. 22 cm. Bibliographical footnotes. [LB3062.O5] 61-16759
1. Segregation in education. 2. Church and social problems—Catholic Church. I. Title.

OPPEN, Dietrich von. 261.8'3
The age of the person; society in the twentieth century. Translated by Frank Clarke. Foreword by James Luther Adams. Philadelphia, Fortress Press [1969] xii, 211 p. 23 cm. Translation of Das personale Zeitalter. Bibliographical footnotes. [BT738.O613] 71-84536 5.50
1. Sociology, Christian. I. Title.

O'REILLY, James D. 261.8'3
The moral problem of contraception / by James O'Reilly. Chicago : Franciscan Herald Press, c1972. p. cm. (Synthesis series ; no. 27) Bibliography: p. [HQ766.3.O54] 74-31013 ISBN 0-8199-0363-9
1. Birth control—Catholic Church. 2. Conception—Prevention. I. Title.

OSBORNE, William Audley, 261.8'3
1919-
The segregated covenant; race relations and American Catholics [by] William A. Osborne. [New York] Herder & Herder [1967] 252p. 22cm. Bibl. [BT734.2O8] 67-17623 5.95
1. Church and race problems — U. S. 2. Church and race problems — Catholic Church. I. Title.

PELT, John. 261.8'3
The soul, the pill, and the fetus. Philadelphia, Dorrance [1973] 130 p. 22 cm. Bibliography: p. 125-130. [HQ766.3.P44] 72-91938 ISBN 0-8059-1781-0 4.95
1. Birth control—Religious aspects. I. Title.

PHILLIPS, Keith W. 261.8'3
Everybody's afraid in the ghetto / by Keith W. Phillips. Glendale, Calif. : G/L Regal Books, [1975] 182 p. : ill. ; 18 cm. [BV4464.5.P47] 73-87286 ISBN 0-8307-0262-8 pbk. : 1.45
1. Church work with juvenile delinquints. 2. City missions. 3. Conversion—Case studies. I. Title.

PHIPPS, William E., 1930- 261.8'3
The sexuality of Jesus: theological and literary perspectives [by] William E. Phipps. [1st ed.] New York, Harper & Row [1973] 172 p. 21 cm. Includes bibliographical references. [BL65.S4P5] 72-78067 ISBN 0-06-066561-0 5.95
1. Jesus Christ—Biography. 2. Sex and religion—History. I. Title.

PHIPPS, William E., 1930- 261.8'3
Was Jesus married? The distortion of sexuality in the Christian tradition [by] William E. Phipps. [1st ed.] New York, Harper & Row [1970] vii, 239 p. 22 cm. [BT708.P47 1970] 74-126282 5.95
1. Jesus Christ. 2. Paul, Saint, apostle. 3. Sex (Theology)—History of doctrines. I. Title.

PIKE, Esther, ed. 261.83
Who is my neighbor? Greenwich, Conn., Seabury Press, 1960. 230 p. 22 cm. [HN31.P42] 60-5373
1. Church and social problems. I. Title.

PIKE, James Albert, Bp., 261.83
1913-
Our Christmas challenge. New York, Sterling Pub. Co. [1961] 64p. 18cm. [BR481.P48] 61-15856
1. Christianity—20th cent. 2. U. S.—Race question. 3. Church and social problems—U. S. I. Title.

PYLE, Leo, ed. 261.83
The pill and birth regulation; the Catholic debate, including statements, articles, and letters from the Pope, bishops, priests, and married and unmarried laity, edited and introduced by Leo Pyle. Baltimore, Helicon Press [1964] x, 225 p. 19 cm. (A Helicon paperbook) [HQ766.3.P9] 64-8012
1. Birth control—Religious aspects. I. Title.

PYLE, Leo, ed. 261.83
The pill and birth regulation; the Catholic debate, including statements, articles, and letters from the Pope, bishops, priests, and married and unmarried laity, edited and introduced by Leo Pyle. Baltimore, Helicon Press [1964] x, 225 p. 19 cm. (A Helicon paperbook) [HQ766.3.P9] 64-8012

1. Birth control—Religious aspects. I. Title.

QUEST for reality: 261.8'3
Christianity and the counter culture [by] Carl F. H. Henry and others. Downers Grove, Ill., InterVarsity Press [1973] 161 p. 21 cm. Papers presented at a conference sponsored by the Institute for Advanced Christian Studies, held in Chicago, Oct., 1971. Includes bibliographical references. [BR115.W6Q47] 73-75892 ISBN 0-87784-761-4 2.95
1. Sociology, Christian—Addresses, essays, lectures. 2. Civilization, Secular—Addresses, essays, lectures. I. Henry, Carl F. H. II. Institute for Advanced Christian Studies. III. Title: Counter culture.

RAHTJEN, Bruce D 261.83
Scripture and social action [by] Bruce D. Rahtjen. Nashville, Abingdon Press [1966] 144 p. 19 cm. "Selected bibliography": p. 137-141. [HN31.R3] 66-20458
1. Church and social problems. I. Title.

RAHTJEN, Bruce D. 261.83
Scripture and social action [by] Bruce D. Rahtjen. Nashville, Abingdon [1966] 144p. 19cm. Bibl. [HN31.R3] 66-20458 1.50 pap.,
1. Churches and social problems. I. Title.

RAMSEY, Paul. 261.83
Christian ethics and the sit-in. New York, Association Press [1961] 128p. 20cm. [BT734.3.R3] 61-8182
1. Segregation—Religious aspects. 2. Negroes—Segregation. I. Title.

RAMSEY, Paul [Robert Paul 261.83
Ramsey]
Christian ethics and the sit-in. New York, AssociationPress [c.1961] 128p. Bibl. 61-8182 2.50 bds.,
1. Segregation—Religious aspects. 2. Negroes—Segregation. I. Title.

REIMERS, David M. 261.83
White Protestantism and the Negro [by] David M. Reimers. New York, Oxford University Press, 1965. ix, 236 p. 21 cm. Bibliographical references included in "Notes" (p. 190-222) Bibliography: p. 223-227. [E185.61.R36] 65-22800
1. Negroes—Segregation. 2. Church and race problems—United States. 3. Protestant churches—United States. I. Title.

RENEWING the earth : 261.8'3
Catholic documents on peace, justice, and liberation / edited by David J. O'Brien and Thomas A. Shannon. Garden City, N.Y. : Image Book, 1977. p. cm. Includes bibliographical references and index. [HN37.C3R397] 76-52008 ISBN 0-385-12954-8 : 3.95
1. Church and social problems—United States—Catholic Church. 2. Church and social problems—Latin America—Catholic Church. 3. Church and social problems—Catholic Church—Papal documents. I. O'Brien, David J. II. Shannon, Thomas Anthony, 1940-

REUTER, George Sylvester, 261.83
1920-
One blood; the Christian approach to the civil rights problem, by George S. Reuter, Jr., August M. Hintz, and Helen H. Reuter. Foreword by Harry Homewood; introd. by John Roy Wolfe. [1st ed.] New York, Exposition Press [1964] 72 p. 21 cm. [E184.A1R45] 64-2385
1. Minorities — U.S. 2. Discrimination — U.S. 3. Church and race problems. 4. Equality. I. Title. II. Title: The Christian approach to the civil rights problem.

REUTER, George Sylvester, 261.83
Jr., 1920-
One blood: the Christian approach to the civil rights problem, by George S. Reuter, Jr., August M. Hintz, Helen H. Reuter. Foreword by Harry Homewood; introd. by John Roy Wolfe. New York, Exposition [c.1964] 72p. 21cm. 64-2385 3.00
1. Minorities—U.S. 2. Discrimination—U.S. 3. Church and race problems. 4. Equality. I. Title. II. Title: The Christian approach to the civil rights problem.

RHYMES, Douglas A 261.83
No new morality; Christian personal values and sexual morality [by] Douglas Rhymes. Indianapolis, Bobbs-Merrill [1964] 155 p. 22 cm. Bibliography: p. 151-155. [HQ1051.R45] 64-24646
1. Sex. I. Title.

RHYMES, Douglas A. 261.83
No new morality; Christian personal values and sexual morality. Indianapolis, Bobbs [c.1964] 155p. 22cm. Bibl. 64-24646 3.50 bds.,
1. Sex. I. Title.

RIGA, Peter J. 261.8'3
The church of the poor; a commentary on Paul VI's encyclical On the development of

peoples. Techny, Ill., Divine Word Publications [1968] ix, 155 p. 22 cm. Bibliographical references included in "Encyclical footnotes" (p. 154-155) [HN37.C3R53] 68-18374
1. Catholic Church. Pope, 1963- (Paulus VI) Populorum progressio. 2. Church and social problems—Catholic Church. 3. Underdeveloped areas. I. Title.

ROBINSON, James Herman. 261.83
Africa at the crossroads. Philadelphia, Westminster Press [1962] 83 p. 19 cm. (Christian perspectives on social problems) [DT30.R56] 62-17810
1. Africa. 2. Church and social problems — Africa. I. Title.

ROBINSON, James Herman. 261.83
Africa at the crossroads. Philadelphia, Westminster Press [1962] 83 p. 19 cm. (Christian perspectives of social problems) [DT30.R56] 62-17810
1. Africa. 2. Church and social problems—Africa. I. Title.

ROOT, Robert. 261.83
Struggle of decency; religion and race in modern America [by] Robert Root and Shirley W. Hall. New York, Friendship Press [1965] 174 p. 19 cm. [E185.61.R77] 65-11440
1. Negroes — Civil rights. 2. Church and race problems — U.S. I. Hall, Shirley W., joint author. II. Title.

ROOT, Robert 261.83
Struggle of decency: religion and race in modern America [by] Robert Root, Shirley W. Hall. New York, Friendship [c.1965] 174p. 19cm. [E185.61.R77] 65-11440 1.95 pap.,
1. Negroes—Civil rights. 2. Church and race problems—U.S. I. Hall, Shirley W., joint author. II. Title.

ROSS, Frederick Augustus, 261.8'3
1796-1883.
Slavery ordained of God. Miami, Fla., Mnemosyne Pub. Co. [1969] 186 p. 23 cm. Reprint of the 1857 ed. [E449.R82 1969b] 74-83876
1. Slavery in the United States—Controversial literature—1857. 2. Slavery—Justification. 3. Slavery and the church—Presbyterian Church. I. Title.

ROSS, Frederick Augustus, 261.8'3
1796-1883.
Slavery ordained of God. New York, Negro Universities Press [1969] 186 p. 18 cm. Reprint of the 1857 ed. [E449.R82 1969] 69-16570
1. Slavery in the United States—Controversial literature—1857. 2. Slavery—Justification. 3. Slavery and the church—Presbyterian Church. I. Title.

ROSS, Frederick Augustus, 261.8'3
1796-1883.
Slavery ordained of God. New York, Haskell House Publishers, 1970. 186 p. 23 cm. Reprint of the 1857 ed. [E449.R82 1970] 70-95445
1. Slavery in the United States—Controversial literature—1857. 2. Slavery—Justification. 3. Slavery and the church—Presbyterian Church. I. Title.

RUSSELL, Jean. 261.8'3
God's lost cause; a study of the Church and the racial problem. Valley Forge, Judson Press [1969, c1968] 143 p. 22 cm. Bibliographical footnotes. [BT734.2.R8 1969] 78-82155 ISBN 8-17-004580- 2.50
1. Church and race problems—History. I. Title.

RYAN, John Augustine, 261.8'3
1869-1945.
Questions of the day. Freeport, N.Y., Books for Libraries Press [1967] 333 p. 22 cm. (Essay index reprint series) Reprint of the 1931 ed. Bibliographical footnotes. [HN39.U6R9 1967] 67-26779
1. Catholic Church in the United States. 2. Church and social problems—Catholic Church. 3. Prohibition—United States. 4. United States—Economic conditions—1918-1945. I. Title.

SANTAMARIA, Bartholomew 261.8'3
Augustine, 1915-
Contraception; refelections on the Pope's ruling [by] B. A. Santamaria. [2d ed. Melbourne, Freedom Publ. Co., 1968] 32 p. 22 cm. [HQ766.3.S26] 74-457771 0.20
1. Birth control—Religious aspects. I. Title.

SAPPINGTON, Roger Edwin, 261.83
1929-
Brethren social policy, 1908-1958. Elgin, Ill., Brethren Press [1961] 220p. 22cm. Includes bibliography. [HN37.C18S2] 61-1081
1. Church and social problems—Church of the Brethren. I. Title.

SCHILLING, Sylvester Paul 261.83
Methodism and society in theological perspective. Edited by the Board of Social and Economic Relations of the Methodist Church. Nashville, Abingdon Press [c.1960] 318p. 24cm. (Methodism and society, v. 3) Bibl.: p.309-311. tables. 60-11221 5.00
1. Sociology, Christian (Methodist). I. Methodist Church (United States) Board of Social and Economic Relations. II. Title. III. Series.

SCHILLING, Sylvester Paul, 261.83
1904-
Methodism and society in theological perspective. Edited by the Board of Social and Economic Relations of the Methodist Church. New York, Abingdon Press [1960] 318p. tables. 24cm. (Methodism and society, v.3) Bibliography: p.300-311. [BT738.S36] 60-11221
1. Sociology, Christian (Methodist) I. Methodist Church (United States) Board of Social and Economic Relations. II. Title. III. Series.

SCHULLER, David S. 261.83
The new urban society. St. Louis, Concordia [c.1966] 101p. 18cm. (Christian encounters) Bibl. [HT151.S295] 65-25383 1.00 pap.,
1. Sociology, Urban. I. Title. II. Series.

SCHULLER, David S. 261.8'3
Power structures and and the church [by] David S. Schuller. Saint Louis, Concordia Pub. House [1969] 90 p. illus. 21 cm. Bibliographical references included in "Notes" (p. 87-90) [BR115.W6S33] 70-79996 1.75
1. Church and the world. 2. Christianity and culture. I. Title.

SCHUTZ, Roger. 261.8'3
Violent for peace. Translated by C. J. Moore. Philadelphia, Westminster Press [1971, c1970] 144 p. 19 cm. Translation of Violence des pacifiques. Includes bibliographical references. [BT736.15.S3513 1971] 76-151348 ISBN 0-664-24922-1 2.65
1. Violence—Moral and religious aspects. I. Title.

SCOTT, Orange, 1800-1847. 261.8'3
The grounds of seccession from the M. E. Church. New York, Arno Press, 1969. 229 p. 23 cm. (The Anti-slavery crusade in America) Reprint of the 1848 ed. [E449.S3 1969] 71-82219
1. Methodist Episcopal Church—Doctrinal and controversial works. 2. Slavery and the church—Methodist Episcopal Church. I. Title. II. Series.

SCUDDER, C. W., 1915- ed. 261.83
Crises in morality, edited by C. W. Scudder. Nashville, Broadman Press [1964] vii, 156 p. 22 cm. Includes bibliographies. [HN39.U6S35] 64-18189
1. Church and social problems—U.S. 2. U.S.—Moral conditions. I. Title.

SCUDDER, C W 1915- 261.83
Danger ahead: a Christian approach to some current problems. Nashville, Broadman Press [c1961] 180p. 22cm. Includes bibliography. [HN31.S38] 61-5395
1. Church and social problems. I. Title.

SEE, Ruth Douglas, 1910- 261.83
What can we do? An Action handbook. Rev. ed. New York, Friendship Press, 1965. 64 p. 19 cm. [E185.61.S4 1965] 65-12248
1. U. S.—Race question. 2. Church and race problems—Study and teaching. I. Title.

SELLERS, James Earl. 261.83
The South and Christian ethics. New York, Association Press [1962] 190 p. 20 cm. [E185.61.S48] 62-16877
1. Segregation—Religious aspects. 2. Negroes—Segregation. I. Title.

SHAW, Wayne. 261.8'3
Birth of a revolution; how the church can change the world, by Wayne Shaw and James Strauss. Cincinnati, Ohio, Standard Pub. [1974] 94 p. 18 cm. Includes bibliographies. [BR115.W6S45] 73-87494 1.25 (pbk.)
1. Church and the world. I. Strauss, James, joint author. II. Title.

SHEPHERD, George W 261.83
The politics of African nationalism; challenge to American policy. New York Praeger [1962] 244 p. illus. 21 cm. (Books that matter) Includes bibliography. [DT30.S5] 62-13737
1. Africa — Politics. 2. Pan-Africanism. I. Title.

SHERIDAN, John V. 261.8'3
The Church yesterday & today / John V. Sheridan. Huntington, IN : Our Sunday Visitor, c1975. 312 p. ; 23 cm. Includes index. [BX1751.2.S465] 74-21572 ISBN 0-87973-867-7 pbk. : 4.50
1. Catholic Church—Doctrinal and controversial works—Catholic authors. I. Title.

SHERMAN, Franklin. 261.8'3
The problem of abortion after the Supreme Court decision, by Franklin E. Sherman. [New York] Division for Mission in North America, Lutheran Church in America, 1974. ix, 37 p. 20 cm. (Studies in man, medicine, and theology) (Christian social responsibility) Bibliography: p. 25-26. [HQ767.5.U5S47] 74-171038
1. Abortion—United States. 2. Abortion—Religious aspects. I. Title. II. Series. III. Series: Studies in man, medicine, and theology.

SHERRIFF, D A 261.83
Africa, by D. A. Sherriff. 2d ed. [London] Oxford University Press, 1963. 95 p. illus., col. maps. 26 cm. (The Oxford visual geographies) [DT5.S45] 67-1276
1. Africa—Descr. & trav.—1951- I. Title.

SHIPPEY, Frederick 261.83
Alexander, 1908-
Protestantism in suburban life [by] Frederick A. Shippey. New York, Abingdon Press [1964] 221 p. 24 cm. Bibliography: p. 203-212. [BV637.7.S46] 64-20521
1. Suburban churches. I. Title.

SHRIVER, Donald W ed. 261.83
The unsilent South; prophetic preaching in racial crisis, edited by Donald W. Shriver, Jr. Richmond, John Knox Press [1965] 169 p. 21 cm. Bibliographical references included in "Notes" (p. 166-169) [BT734.2.S5] 65-20546
1. Church and race problems—Sermons. 2. Sermons, American. 3. Church and race problems—Southern States. I. Title.

SHRIVER, Donald W., ed. 261.83
The unsilent South; prophetic preaching in racial crisis. Richmond, Va., Knox [c.1965] 169p. 21cm. ibl. [BT734.2.S5] 65-20546 2.25 pap.,
1. Church and race problems—Sermons. 2. Sermons, American. 3. Church and race problems—Southern States. I. Title.

SKALA, John J 261.83
The marriage maze, by John J. Skala. [Boston] St. Paul Editions [1965] 129 p. 21 cm. [HQ734.S614] 65-24078
1. Marriage. I. Title.

SKALA, John J. 261.83
The marriage maze, by John J. Skala [Boston] St. Paul Eds. [dist. Daughters of St. Paul, c.1965] 129p. 21cm. [HQ734.S614] 65-24078 2.25; 1.25 pap.,
1. Marriage. I. Title.

SMEDT, Emile Joseph de, 261.83
Bp.
Married love; an enquiry and a dialogue with his people, a pastoral letter [Tr. from French by Jennifer Nicholson] Notre Dame, Ind., Fides [1965, c.1964] 125p. 21cm. [HQ728.S593] 64-23516 2.95; 1.50 pap.,
1. Marriage. I. Title.

SOCIAL Work Conference, 261.8'3
Valparaiso University, 1968.
Theology and social welfare, redemption and good works; papers. St. Louis, Lutheran Academy for Scholarship [1968] ii, 111 p. 29 cm. Cover title. Sponsored by the Lutheran Academy for Scholarship. Includes bibliographies. [HN37.L8S6 1968aa] 68-126161
1. Church and social problems—Lutheran Church. 2. Sociology, Christian (Lutheran) I. Lutheran Academy for Scholarship. II. Title. III. Title: Redemption and good works.

SPAIN, Rufus B. 261.8'3
At ease in Zion; social history of Southern Baptists, 1865-1900 [by] Rufus B. Spain. Nashville, Vanderbilt University Press [1967] xiii, 247 p. 24 cm. Bibliography: p. 222-228. [HN39.U6S6] 66-10367
1. Southern Baptist Convention. 2. Church and social problems—Baptists. I. Title.

SPARKS, Jack. 261.8'3
God's forever family, by Jack Sparks, with special help from a lot of other brothers and sisters in Berkeley. Grand Rapids, Zondervan Pub. House [1974] 287 p. 18 cm. [BV3775.B47S68] 73-13069 1.95
1. Evangelistic work—Berkeley, Calif. I. Title.

SPERRY, Willard Learoyd, 261.83
1882-1954, ed.
Religion and our racial tensions, one of a series of volumes on religion in the post-war world, edited by Willard L. Sperry. By Clyde Kluckhohn [and others] College Park, Md., McGrath Pub. Co. [1969, c1945] ix, 106 p. 23 cm. (Religion in the post-war world, v. 3) Contents.Contents.—The myth of race, by C. Kluckhohn.—The right to be different, by E. R. Clinchy.—Color and Christianity, by E. R. Embree.—How religion has fared in the melting pot, by M. Mead.—Agencies of inter-racial cooperation, by B. S. Abernethy. [BR525.S72 vol. 3] 74-84108
1. U.S.—Race question. 2. Race problems. I. Kluckhohn, Clyde, 1905-1960. II. Title.

SPIKE, Robert Warren. 261.83
The freedom revolution and the churches, by Robert W. Spike. New York, Association Press [1965] 128 p. 20 cm. [E185.61.S73] 64-20240
1. Church and race problems. 2. Negroes — Civil rights. I. Title.

SPIKE, Robert Warren 261.83
The freedom revolution and the churches. New York, Association [c.1965] 128p. 20cm. [E185.61.S73] 64-20240 2.95
1. Church and race problems. 2. Negroes—Civil rights. I. Title.

SPLIT-LEVEL lives 261.8'3
Divine Word [1967] ix, 169p. 22cm. Essays developed from lects., experiences, & seminars by members of traveling workshop teams sponsored by the Natl. Catholic Conf. for Interracial Justice. [BT734.2S6] 67-29362 2.50 pap.,
1. Church and race problems—Addresses, essays, lectures. I. Traxler, Mary Peter, ed. II. National Catholic Conference for Interracial Justice.
Contents omitted.

STAHMER, Harold, ed. 261.83
Religion & contemporary society. New York, Macmillan [1963] 282 p. 21 cm. [BL60.S67] 63-15052
1. Religion and sociology. 2. U.S.—Religion. I. Title.

STEPHENS, Bill, comp. 261.8'3
The issues we face ... and some biblical answers. Nashville, Tenn., Broadman Press [1974] 128 p. 20 cm. Includes bibliographical references. [HN39.U6S8] 73-85702 ISBN 0-8054-8230-X 1.50
1. Church and social problems—United States. 2. Social ethics. 3. Christian ethics. I. Title.

STOTTS, Herbert Edward, 261.83
1916-
Methodism and society: guidelines for strategy [by] Herbert E. Stotts and Paul Deats, Jr. Edited by the Board of Social and Economic Relations of the Methodist Church. New York, Abingdon Press [1962] 383 p. illus., tables. 24 cm. (Methodism and society, v. 4) Bibliography: p. 374-375. [HN37.M4S78] 62-9997
1. Church and social problems — Methodist Church I. Deats, Paul, joint author. II. Methodist Church (United States) Board of Social and Economic Relations. III. Title. IV. Series.

STOTTS, Herbert Edward, 261.83
1916-
Methodism and society: guidelines for strategy, v.4 [by] Herbert E. Stotts, Paul Deats, Jr. Ed. by the Bd. of Soc. and Econ. Relations of the Methodist Church. Nashville, Abingdon [c.1962] 383p. illus. 24cm. (Methodism and soc., v.4) Bibl. 62-9997 5.50
1. Church and social problems—Methodist Church. I. Deats, Paul, joint author. II. Methodist Church (United States) Board of Social and Economic Relations. III. Title. IV. Series.

STRINGFELLOW, William. 261.83
Dissenter in a great society; a Christian view of America in crisis, [1st ed.] New York, Holt, Rinehart and Winston [1966] x, 164 p. 22 cm. [HN57.S86] 65-22472
1. U.S. — Soc. condit. 2. U.S. — Moral conditions. I. Title.

STUDENTS, religion, and 261.8'3
the contemporary university. Charles E. Minneman, editor. [Ypsilanti] Eastern Michigan University Press, 1970. xxi, 188 p. 24 cm. Contents.Contents.—Religion, the university, and the future of the American society, by E. S. Muskie.—The futureless generation, by E. J. Shoben, Jr.—In search of soul, by D. Berrigan and J. L. Smith.—Secularity in higher education, by F. H. Littell.—Coordinating university religious affairs, by E. de F. Bennett.—The co-curriculum in religion, by G. W. Jones.—The sanctions of celebration, by R. E. Wentz.—Moral exercise in the intellectual community, by C. Wellborn.—The search for church-university relational models, by L. H. Harshbarger.—Toward an international community of man under God, by A. Schaffer.—University cities and the city of God: looking toward the year 2000, by H. G. Locke. [BV639.C6S74] 70-132320 6.95
1. College students—Religious life—Addresses, essays, lectures. 2. Universities and colleges—

Religion—Addresses, essays, lectures. I. Minneman, Charles E., ed.

SWANEY, Charles Baumer, 1888- 261.8'3
Episcopal Methodism and slavery, with sidelights on ecclesiastical politics. New York, Negro Universities Press [1969] 356 p. 23 cm. Reprint of the 1926 ed. Bibliography: p. 341-351. [E449.S96 1969] 69-16562
1. Slavery and the church—Methodist Episcopal Church. I. Title.

TASTE & see '72; 261.8'3
selections from the Liguorian (a disscussion book) Liguori, Mo., Liguori Publications [1972] 155 p. 18 cm. Contents.Contents.—Earl, R. Has the Church gone soft?—Higgins, J. J. How rich is the Catholic Church?—Weber, P. J. Is shared prayer the new devotion?—Earl, R. Why confess to a priest?—Larsen, E. Cool is dead.—Sex and the college girl.—Rick M. "Police brutality?"—Cosgrove, T. Marriage: Sacramental mystery or romantic myth?—Shanahan, L. Are marriage vows on the way out?—Hughes, J. J. Does the Church need new marriage laws?—Rue, J. J. What to look for in a marriage counselor.—Higgins, J. J. Are schools bad for kids?—Diamond, J. J. Suicide American style: the danger of birth rate decline.—Engel, R. Will your government abolish large families?—Jann, P. Questions about abortion.—Take a look at your drinking.—Miller, L. G. Busy ... but bored.—Bertha, M. K. Help is the name of the game. [HN65.T34] 72-89230 1.50
1. United States—Social conditions—1960- — Addresses, essays, lectures. 2. Church and social problems—Catholic Church—Addresses, essays, lectures. I. The Liguorian.

TAYLOR, Richard K. 261.8'3
Friends & the racial crisis [by] Richard K. Taylor. [Wallingford, Pa., Pendle Hill, 1970] 36 p. 20 cm. (Pendle Hill pamphlet 172) Includes bibliographical references. [BX7748.R3T38] 70-129552 0.55
1. Friends, Society of. 2. Church and race problems—U.S. I. Title.

THOMAS, John Lawrence. 261.83
Catholic viewpoint on marriage and the family [by] John L. Thomas. Rev. ed. Garden City, N.Y., Image Books [1965] 200 p. 19 cm. (The Catholic viewpoint series) [HQ734.T44 1965] 66-268
1. Marriage. 2. Family. I. Title. II. Title: On marriage and the family.

THOMAS, John Lawrence. 261.83
Looking toward marriage [by] John L. Thomas. With teaching aids by Jane Marie Murray. Notre Dame, Ind., Fides [1964] xii, 340 p. illus. 22 cm. Pages 334-340 blank. [HQ734.T444] 64-22892
1. Marriage. I. Title.

THOMAS, John Lawrence 261.83
Looking toward marriage. With teaching aids by Jane Marie Murray. Notre Dame, Ind., Fides [c.1964] xii, 340p. illus. 22cm. (Christian Life ser.) 64-22892 2.45 pap.,
1. Marriage. I. Title.

THOMPSON, Ernest Trice, 1894- 261.83
Plenty and want; the responsibility of the church. Nashville, Tenn., Presbyterian Church U.S. [1966] 114 p. illus. 21 cm. "Joint season of witness." Includes bibliographical references. [BV639.P6T48] 66-26242
1. Church and the poor. I. Title.

THORNING, Joseph Francis, 1896- 261.8'3
Builders of the social order, by Joseph F. Thorning. Freeport, N.Y., Books for Libraries Press [1968, c1943] xv, 183 p. 23 cm. (Essay index reprint series) [HN37.C3T45 1968] 68-57340
1. Church and social problems—Catholic Church. I. Title.

*TIMMS, Noel 261.83
The Christian family today, its major problems. Glen Rock, N. J., Paulist [c.1965] 63p. 18cm. (Insight ser.) Orig. pub. under the title: The Christian family in the mid-twentieth century. .50 pap.,
I. Title.

TO love or to perish: 261.8'3
the technological crisis and the churches. Edited by J. Edward Carothers [and others] New York, Friendship Press [1972] 152 p. 21 cm. "Report of the U.S.A. Task Force on the Future of Mankind and the Role of the Christian Churches in a World of Science-based Technology." [BJ59.T6] 72-11504 1.95
1. Technology and ethics. I. Carothers, J. Edward, ed. II. U.S.A. Task Force on the Future of Mankind and the Role of the Christian Churches in a World of Science-based Technology.

TRAVERSO, Edmund. 261.83
Immigration: a study in American values. [Teachers ed.] Boston, Heath [1964] ix, 145, 15 p. illus. 20 cm. (New dimension in American history) [JV6465.T7] 64-4320
1. U.S. — Emig. & immig. — Collections. I. Title.

TRAXLER, Mary Peter. 261.8'3
New works of new nuns, edited by Sister M. Peter Traxler. St. Louis, B. Herder Book Co. [1968] xi, 179 p. 21 cm. [BX4205.T7] 68-55600 5.95
1. Women in church work—Catholic Church. 2. Church and social problems—Catholic Church. 3. Monastic and religious life of women. I. Title.

TROELTSCH, Ernst, 1865-1923. 261.83
The social teaching of the Christian churches. Translated by Olive Wyon; with an introd. by H. Richard Neibuhr. New York, Harper [1960- v. 21 cm. (Harper torchbooks, TB71-The Cloister library) Includes bibliographical references. [HN31.T752] 60-50842
1. Church and social problems — Hist. 2. Church history. I. Title.

UNDERWOOD, Kenneth Wilson. 261.8'3
Protestant and Catholic: religious and social interaction in an industrial community. Westport, Conn., Greenwood Press [1973, c1957] xxi, 484 p. illus. 22 cm. Bibliography: p. 409-417. [BR560.H7U5 1973] 72-9051 ISBN 0-8371-6567-9 18.25
1. Catholic Church—Relations—Protestant churches. 2. Sociology, Christian—Massachusetts—Holyoke. 3. Protestant churches—Relations—Catholic Church. I. Title.

VERKUYL, Johannes. 261.8'3
Responsible revolution; means and ends for transforming society, by Johannes Verkuyl and H. G. Schulte Nordholt. Translated and edited by Lewis Smedes. Grand Rapids, Eerdmans [1974] 101 p. 21 cm. Translation of Verantwoorde revolutie. [BT738.3.V413] 73-13560 ISBN 0-8028-1546-4 1.95 (pbk.).
1. Revolution (Theology) 2. Revolution. I. Schulte Nordholt, H. G. II. Title.

VIOLENCE in Ireland : 261.8'3
a report to the churches. Belfast : Christian Journals Ltd., 1976. 128 p. ; 18 cm. "This report comes from the fifth Working Party appointed by the Irish Council of Churches/Roman Catholic Church Joint Group on Social Questions." Bibliography: p. 127. [DA950.V56] 77-356900 ISBN 0-904302-27-X : £0.90
1. Irish question. 2. Violence—Moral and religious aspects. I. Joint Group on Social Questions.

WALTON, Rus. 261.8'3
One nation under God / by Rus Walton. Washington : Third Century Publishers, [1975] 311 p. ; 21 cm. Bibliography: p. 311. [HC106.6.W24] 75-7975 3.45
1. United States—Economic conditions—1961- 2. United States—Moral conditions. 3. Church and social problems. I. Title.

WARD, Alfred Dudley, 1914- 261.83
The social creed of the Methodist Church; a living document. New York, Abingdon Press [1961] 176 p. 20 cm. Includes bibliography. [HN37.M4W27] 61-8415
1. Church and social problems — Methodist Church. 2. Church and social problems — U.S. I. Title.

WARD, Alfred Dudley, 1914- 261.83
The social creed of the Methodist Church; a living document. Nashville, Abingdon Press [c.1961] 176p. Bibl. 61-8415 1.50 pap.,
1. Church and social problems—Methodist Church. 2. Church and social problems—U.S. I. Title.

WELD, Wayne. 261.8'3
Principles of church growth / Wayne Weld & Donald A. McGavran. 2d ed. South Pasadena, Calif. : William Carey Library, [1974] 462 p. in various pagings ; 23 cm. Translation of Principios del crecimiento de la iglesia first published in 1970. Includes bibliography. [BV652.25.W4413 1974] 74-18617 ISBN 0-87808-720-6 pbk. : 4.95
1. Church growth—Study and teaching. 2. Sociology, Christian—Study and teaching. I. McGavran, Donald Anderson, 1897- joint author. II. Title.

*WERR, Donald F. 261.83
Today's world; a textual guide for the college course in Catholic and modern problems [dist. Berkeley, Calif., 94704, McCutchan] 1966. 128p. 28cm. Bibl. price unreported pap.,
I. Title.

WEST, Robert Frederick 261.83
Preaching on race. St. Louis, Bethany Press [1962] 160 p. 23 cm. [BT734.2.W45] 62-8760
1. Race problems. 2. Sermons, American. 3. Disciples of Christ — Sermons. I. Title.

WEST, Robert Frederick 261.83
Preaching on race. St. Louis, Bethany [c.1962] 160p. 23cm. 62-8760 3.50
1. Race problems. 2. Sermons, American. 3. Disciples of Christ—Sermons. I. Title.

WHEN all else fails; 261.8'3
Christian arguments on violent revolution. Edited by IDO-C. Philadelphia, Pilgrim Press [1970] vi, 230 p. 22 cm. "Based on a book published originally ... as Vangelo, violenza, rivoluzione." Contents.Contents.—The Gospels and the Church as a revolutionary force, by H. D. Wendland.—Revolution and violence, by A. Bezerra de Melo.—A theological perspective on human liberation, by R. Shaull.—Why the Gospels are revolutionary, by V. Borovoj.—Christianity and the socialist revolution, by J. M. Gonzalez-Ruiz.—The Christian faith and Marxism in revolution, by P. Blanquart.—Search for a phenomenology of revolution, by P. L. Geschiere and H. G. Schulte Nordholt.—The stages of the revolution in the Third World, by A. P. Lentin.—Latin America - land of revolution, by the IDO-C Staff, et al.—Violence or nonviolence in the transformation of society, by the IDO-C staff. Includes bibliographical references. [BT738.3.W48] 74-131205 ISBN 8-298-01871- 7.95
1. Revolution (Theology)—Addresses, essays, lectures. 2. Revolutions—Addresses, essays, lectures. I. Idoc. II. Vangelo, violenza, rivoluzione.

WILKERSON, David 261.83
The little people [by] David Wilkerson, with Phyllis Murphy. Westwood, N.J., Revell [1966] 159p. 21cm. [BV4464.5.W515] 66-21904 2.95
1. Church work with juvenile delinquents. I. Murphy, Phyllis. II. Title.

WILKERSON, David R 261.83
The little people [by] David Wilkerson, with Phyllis Murphy. Westwood, N.J. F.H. Revell Co. [1966] 159 p. 21 cm. [BV4464.5.W515] 66-21904
1. Church work with juvenile delinquents. I. Murphy, Phyllis. II. Title.

WILKERSON, David R. 261.83
The little people [by] David Wilkerson, with Phyllis Murphy. Westwood, N. J., F. H. Revell Co. [1966] 159 p. 21 cm. [BV4464.5.W515] 66-21904
1. Church work with juvenile delinquents. I. Murphy, Phyllis. II. Title.

WILMORE, Gayraud S. 261.83
The secular relevance of the church. Philadelphia, Westminster [c.1962] 89p. 19cm. (Christian perspectices on soc. problems) 62-14177 1.25 pap.,
1. Sociology, Christian. I. Title.

WITT, Raymond H 1912- 261.83
It ain't been easy, Charlie, by Raymond H. Witt. [1st ed.] New York, Pageant Press [1965] 105 p. 21 cm. [BX8076.C5S28] 65-27305
1. Chicago. St. Stephen's Lutheran Church. 2. Church and race problems — Chicago. I. Title.

WOGAMAN, J Philip. 261.83
Methodism's challenge in race relations; a study of strategy. Boston, Boston University Press, 1960. 76 p. 29 cm. "Originally developed as a dissertation ... for the degree of doctor of philosophy in the Division of Theological Studies of Boston University Graduate School, under the title A strategy for racial desegregation in the Methodist Church." Includes bibliography. [BX8388.W57 1960] 60-11712
1. Methodist Church (United States) — Government. 2. U.S. — Race Question. I. Title.

WOGAMAN, J. Philip 261.83
Methodism's challenge in race relations; a study of strategy. Foreword by Edward K. Graham. Washington, Public Affairs Press [c.1960] viii, 76p. 29cm. 'Originally developed as a dissertation . . . for the degree of doctor of philosophy in the Division of Theological Studies of Boston University Graduate School, under the title A. strategy for racial desegregation in the Methodist Church.' Bibl. p.71-76 60-2996 2.00 pap.,
1. Methodist Church (United States)—Government. 2. U.S.—Race question. I. Title.

WOGAMAN, J Philip. 261.83
Methodism's challenge in race relations; a study of strategy. Foreword by Edward K. Graham. Washington, Public Affairs Press [1960] 76 p. 29 cm. "Originally developed as a dissertation ... for the degree of doctor of philosophy in the Division of Theological Studies of Boston University Graduate School, under the title A strategy for racial desegregation in the Methodist Church." [BX8388.W57 1960a] 60-2996
1. Methodist Church (United States) — Government 2. U.S. — Race question. I. Title.

YINGER, John Milton. 261.83
Sociology looks at religion. New York, Macmillan [1963] 192 p. 18 cm. (Macmillan paperbacks, 139) [BL60.Y53] 63-15705
1. Religion and sociology. I. Title.

CONFERENCE on Inner City Research, Catholic University of America, 1965. 261.8308
The church in the changing city, ed. by Louis J. Luzbetak. Techny, Ill., Divine World [1966] vii, 197p. 22cm. Sponsored by the Ctr. for Applied Res. in the Apostolate and held on Nov. 20-21, 1965. Bibl. [BV637.C57 1965] 66-28387 2.25 pap.,
1. City churches. I. Luzbetak, Louis J., ed. II. Center for Applied Research in the Apostolate, Washington, D.C. III. Catholic University of America. IV. Title.

CONFERENCE on Inner City Research Catholic University of America, 1965. 261.8308
The church in the changing city, edited by Louis J. Luzbetak. Techny, Ill., Divine World Publications [1966] viii, 197 p. 22 cm. Sponsored by the Center for Applied Research in the Apostolate and held on Nov. 20-21, 1965. Bibliography: p. 191-197. [BV637.C57 1965] 66-28387
1. City churches. I. Luzbetak, Louis J., ed. II. Center for Applied Research in the Apostolate, Washington, D.C. III. Catholic University of America. IV. Title.

DAANE, James. 261.8308
The anatomy of anti-semitism, and other essays on religion and race. Grand Rapids, Eerdmans [1965] 84 p. 21 cm. [BT734.D3] 65-18090
1. Race — Addresses, essays, lectures. I. Title.

DAANE, James 261.8308
The anatomy of anti-semitism, and other essays on religion and race Grand Rapids, Mich., Eerdmans [c.1965] 84p. 21cm. [BT734.D3] 65-18090 1.45 pap.,
1. Race—Addresses, essays, lectures. I. Title.

SCHUSTER, Kay Lathrop, comp. 261.8'3'08
Hope for our broken world. Edited by Kay Lathrop Schuster. Introductions by Everett H. Jones, Stephen A. Leven and O. Eugene Slater. North Quincy, Mass., Christopher Pub. House [1969] 156 p. 21 cm. Bibliographical footnotes. [BV4647.B7S36] 78-78032 4.95
1. Brotherliness. 2. Prejudices and antipathies. 3. Love (Theology) I. Title.

BOYLAN, Marguerite Theresa, 1887- ed. 261.83082
The Catholic Church and social welfare; a symposium. New York, Greenwich [1962, c.1961] 217p. 21cm. 61-17766 5.00
1. Church and social problems—Catholic Church. I. Title.

FREMANTLE, Anne (Jackson) 1909- ed. 261.83082
The social teachings of the church. [New York] New American Library [1963] 320 p. 18 cm. (A Mentor-Omega book) Bibliographical footnotes. [HN37.C3F73] 63-23027
1. "MT549." 2. Church and social problems — Catholic Church — Papal documents. I. Title.

FREMANTLE, Anne (Jackson) 1909- ed. 261.83082
The social teachings of the church. [New York] New Amer. Lib. [c.1963] 320p. 18cm. (Mentor-Omega bk.; MT549) Bibl. 63-23027 .75 pap.,
1. Church and social problems—Catholic Church—Papal documents. I. Title.

NATIONAL Conference on the Churches and Social Welfare. 2d, Cleveland, 1961. 261.83082
Concern and response; report. Edited by Margaret Williamson. New York, Friendship Press [1962] 222p. 21cm. 'Held... under the auspices of the Department of Social Welfare of the National Council of the Churches of Christ in the U. S. A.' [HV530.N34 1961c] 62-5698
1. Church charities. 2. Church and social problems—U. S.— Congresses. I. Williamson, Margaret, 1889- ed. II. National Council of the Churches of Christ in the United States of America. Dept. of Social Welfare. III. Title.

MARTIN, Hugh, 1890- ed. 261.8'3'0922
Christian social reformers of the nineteenth century, by James Adderley [and others]

Freeport, N.Y., Books for Libraries Press [1970] vi, 242 p. illus., ports. 23 cm. (Essay index reprint series) Reprint of the 1927 ed. Contents.Contents.—Introduction: The Christian social movement in the nineteenth century, by W. Temple.—John Howard, by S. K. Ruck.—William Wilberforce, by R. Coupland.—Anthony Ashley Cooper, by C. Smith.—Charles Dickens, by A. J. Carlyle.—Florence Nightingale, by M. Scharlieb.—John Malcolm Ludlow, by C. E. Raven.—William Morris, by H. Martin.—George Cadbury, by H. G. Wood.—Henry Scott Holland, by J. Adderley.—James Keir Hardie, by A. F. Brockway. [HN385.M3 1970] 70-107725
1. Social reformers—Gt. Brit. 2. Sociology, Christian. I. Adderley, James Granville, 1861-1942. II. Title.

WASHBURN, Henry Bradford, 1869-1962. 261.8'3'0922
The religious motive in philanthropy: studies in biography. Freeport, N.Y., Books for Libraries Press [1970, c1931] 172 p. 23 cm. (Essay index reprint series) Contents.Contents.—Introduction.—Samuel Barnett.—Vincent de Paul.—Francis of Assisi.—Jesus of Nazareth. [BT738.4.W36 1970] 72-105047 ISBN 8-369-16344-
1. Service (Theology) 2. Christian biography. I. Title.

CHARTIER, Myron Raymond. 261.8'3'0924
The social views of Dwight L. Moody and their relation to the workingman of 1860-1900. [Hays, Fort Hays Kansas State College] 1969. x, 79 p. port. 23 cm. (Fort Hays studies. New series. History series, no. 6) Bibliography: p. 74-79. [D6.F6 no. 6] 77-627350
1. Moody, Dwight Lyman, 1837-1899. 2. Religion and labor. I. Title. II. Series.

CAIRNS, Earle Edwin 261.830942
Saints and society; the social impact of eighteenth century English revivals and its contemporary relevance. Chicago, Moody Press [c.1960] 192p. 22cm. Bibl.: p.181-187 60-16235 3.25
1. Church and social problems—Gt. Brit. 2. Revivals—Gt. Brit. I. Title.

CAIRNS, Earle Edwin, 1910- 261.8'3'0942
The Christian in society, by Earle E. Cairns. [Rev. ed.] Chicago, Moody Press [1973] 188 p. 22 cm. (Moody evangelical focus) First ed. published in 1960 under title: Saints and society. Bibliography: p. 177-184. [HN39.G7C3 1973] 72-95034 ISBN 0-8024-1353-6 2.25
1. Church and social problems—Great Britain. 2. Revivals—Great Britain. I. Title.

CAIRNS, Earle Edwin, 1910- 261.830942
Saints and society; the social impact of eighteenth century English revivals and its contemporary relevance. Chicago, Moody Press [1960] 192p. 22cm. Includes bibliography. [HN39.G7C3] 60-16235
1. Church and social problems—Gt. Brit. 2. Revivals—Gt. Brit. I. Title.

CARTER, Paul Allen, 1926- 261.8'3'0973
The decline and revival of the social Gospel; social and political liberalism in American Protestant churches, 1920-1940, by Paul A. Carter. [Hamden, Conn.] Archon Books, 1971. xxvi, 265 p. 24 cm. Based on the author's thesis, Columbia, 1954. Bibliography: p. 251-260. [HN39.U6C35 1971] 70-122413 ISBN 0-208-01083-1 10.00
1. Church and social problems—U.S. 2. Protestant churches—U.S. 3. Social gospel. I. Title.

FURNESS, Charles Y. 261.8'3'0973
The Christian and social action [by] Charles Y. Furness. Old Tappan, N.J., F. H. Revell Co. [1972] 254 p. 21 cm. Bibliography: p. 247-250. [HN39.U6F9] 72-4527 ISBN 0-8007-0564-5
1. Church and social problems—United States. 2. Social action. 3. Evangelicalism. I. Title.

MILLER, Robert Moats. 261.8'3'0973
American Protestantism and social issues, 1919-1939 / by Robert Moats Miller Westport, Conn. : Greenwood Press, 1977. p. cm. Reprint of the 1958 ed. published by University of North Carolina Press, Chapel Hill. Includes index. Bibliography: p. [HN39.U6M49 1977] 77-22031 ISBN 0-8371-9777-5 lib.bdg. : 21.75
1. Church and social problems—United States. 2. Protestant churches—United States. 3. United States—Church history—20th century. I. Title.

PANNELL, William E. 261.8'3'0973
My friend, the enemy, by William E. Pannell. Waco, Tex., Word Books [1968] 131 p. 20 cm. Includes bibliographical references. [BT734.2.P3] 68-21861
1. Church and race problems—United States. I. Title.

SCHULZE, Andrew. 261.8'3'0973
Fire from the throne; race relations in the church. Saint Louis, Concordia Pub. House [1968] 203 p. 24 cm. Bibliographical references included in "Notes" (p. 199-203) [BT734.2.S3] 68-21833
1. Church and race problems—United States. I. Title.

FARISH, Hunter Dickinson, 1897-1945. 261.8'3'0975
The circuit rider dismounts; a social history of Southern Methodism, 1865-1900. New York, Da Capo Press, 1969 [c1938] 400 p. ports. 24 cm. (The American scene: comments and commentators) (A Da Capo Press reprint series.) (A Da Capo Press reprint edition.) Thesis—Harvard University, 1936. Bibliography: p. [371]-378. [BX8237.F3 1969] 77-87534
1. Methodist Episcopal Church, South—History. 2. Southern States—Social conditions. I. Title.

PERKINS, John, 1930- 261.8'3'09762
A quiet revolution : the Christian response to human need, a strategy for today / John Perkins. Waco, Tex. : Word Books, c1976. 226 p. ; 22 cm. Includes bibliographical references. [HN39.U6P47] 76-48541 ISBN 0-87680-793-7 : 4.50
1. Voice of Calvary (Organization) 2. Church and social problems—Mississippi. 3. Church and race problems—Mississippi. 4. Social action. I. Title.

THE Edge of the ghetto; 261.8'3'0977311
a study of church involvement in community organization [by] John Fish [and others. 1st ed.] New York, Seabury Press [1968, c1966] xix, 188 p. 21 cm. "SP47." Bibliography: p. 187-188. [HN80.C5E3 1968] 68-4903
1. Church and race problems—Chicago. 2. Chicago—Race question. 3. Community organization—Case studies. I. Fish, John.

CONSULTA Latinoamericana de Iglesia y Sociedad. 2d, El Tabo, Chile, 1966. 261.8'3'098
Social justice and the Latin churches. Translated by Jorge Lara-Braud. Richmond, Va., John Knox Press [1969] 137 p. 21 cm. "[Edited] summary of the discussions and reports presented at the second Latin American Conference on Church and Society." Sponsored by Church and Society in Latin America. Translation of America hoy. [HN39.L3C613 1966c] 72-79313 ISBN 0-8042-1505-7 2.95
1. Social justice. 2. Church and social problems—Latin America. 3. Protestant churches—Latin America. I. Iglesia y Sociedad en America Latina. II. Title.

LUM, Ada. 261.8'3'1
Single & human / Ada Lum. Downers Grove, Ill. : InterVarsity Press, c1976. 81 p. ; 18 cm. Includes bibliographical references. [HQ800.L84] 75-44625 ISBN 0-87784-361-9 : 1.95
1. Single people—Conduct of life. 2. Single people—Religious life. I. Title.

BARRELL, Dilys. 261.8'32
You don't need to have an abortion / by Dilys Barrell. London : Catholic Truth Society, 1976. 12 p. ; 19 cm. "S 318" [HV700.G7B29] 77-363541 ISBN 0-85183-186-9 . £0.15
1. Pregnancy, Unwanted—Great Britain. 2. Child welfare—Great Britain. I. Title.

GRAY, Marjorie V. 261.8'32'1
Soul-winning helps : for members of the healing professions / Marjorie V. Gray. Mountain View, Calif. : Pacific Press Pub. Association, c1975. 80 p. ; 19 cm. [BV4460.G73] 75-18268
1. Gray, Marjorie V. 2. Church work with the sick. I. Title.

THE Updated chaplaincy; 261.8'32'1
workshop proceedings. Adapted from Dept. of Pastoral Care conference held in St. Louis, San Francisco, and Philadelphia. St. Louis, Mo., Catholic Hospital Association [1973] v, 81 p. 29 cm. Includes bibliographical references. [BX2347.8.S5U63] 73-76621 ISBN 0-87125-008-X 4.00
1. Church work with the sick. 2. Chaplains, Hospital—Catholic Church. I. Catholic Hospital Association. Dept. of Pastoral Care Services.

VAN DOLSON, Leo R. 261.8'32'1
Healthy, happy, holy / Leo R. Van Dolson, J. Robert Spangler. Washington : Review and Herald Pub. Association, [1975] 208 p. ; 23 cm. Bibliography: p. 206-208. [BX6154.V24] 74-21006 3.50
1. Seventh-Day Adventists—Doctrinal and controversial works. 2. Medicine and religion. 3. Evangelistic work. 4. Missions, Medical. I. Spangler, J. Robert, joint author. II. Title.

DOWLING, Michael J., 1949- 261.8'32'10973
Health care and the church / by Michael J. Dowling ; Robert E. Koenig, editor. Philadelphia : United Church Press, c1977. 115 p. ; 21 cm. (A Doing the word resource published for Christian education) Bibliography: p. 105-111. [RA395.A3D68] 77-1242 ISBN 0-8298-0333-5 pbk. : 3.95
1. Medical care—United States. 2. Medical policy—United States—Citizen participation. 3. Medicine and Christianity. I. Title. II. Series.

DOWLING, Michael J., 1949- 261.8'32'10973
Health care and the church / by Michael J. Dowling ; Robert E. Koenig, editor. Philadelphia : United Church Press, c1977. 115 p. ; 21 cm. (A Doing the word resource published for Christian education) Bibliography: p. 105-111. [RA395.A3D68] 77-1242 ISBN 0-8298-0333-5 pbk. : 3.95
1. Medical care—United States. 2. Medical policy—United States—Citizen participation. 3. Medicine and Christianity. I. Title. II. Series.

JOHN G. Finch Symposium on Psychology and Religion, 2d, Pasadena, Calif., 1973. 261.8'32'2
After therapy, what? Lay therapeutic resources in religious perspective. Finch lectures by Thomas C. Oden, with responses by Neil C. Warren [and others] Edited by Neil C. Warren. Springfield, Ill., Thomas [1974] 205 p. 24 cm. Includes bibliographical references. [RC480.5.J63 1973] 73-21983 ISBN 0-398-03105-3
1. Psychiatry and religion—Congresses. 2. Psychotherapy—Congresses. 3. Pastoral counseling—Congresses. I. Oden, Thomas C. II. Warren, Neil Clark, ed. III. Title.

SOUTHARD, Samuel. 261.8'32'2
Christians and mental health. Nashville, Broadman Press [1972] 128 p. 20 cm. (A Broadman inner circle book) [BR110.S67] 79-189506 ISBN 0-8054-8414-0
1. Christianity—Psychology. 2. Mental hygiene. I. Title.

TOLSTOI, Lev Nikolaevich, graf, 1828-1910. 261.8'32'29
Why do men stupefy themselves? : and other writings / by Leo Tolstoy; translated by Aylmer Maude; edited by Meredith Murray and the editors of 24 Magazine. Hankins, N.Y. : Strength Books : Blauvelt, N.Y. : distributed by Steinerbooks, [1975] 164 p. : ill. ; 18 cm. Translation of Dlia chego liudi odurmanivaiutsia? Contents.Contents.—Why do men stupefy themselves?—The first step.—Industry and idleness. [HV5801.T64D5213 1975] 74-16880 ISBN 0-914896-08-3 pbk. : 2.50
1. Drug abuse—Addresses, essays, lectures. 2. Alcoholism—Addresses, essays, lectures. 3. Smoking—Addresses, essays, lectures. 4. Moral conditions—Addresses, essays, lectures. I. Title.

MCCLUNG, Floyd. 261.8'32'2930924 B
Just off Chicken Street / Floyd McClung, Jr. with Charles Paul Conn. Old Tappan, N.J. : Revell, [1975] 123 p. ; 21 cm. [BV4447.M23] 74-31256 ISBN 0-8007-0699-4 pbk. 1.95
1. Church work with youth. I. Conn, Charles Paul, joint author. II. Title.

PALMQUIST, Al. 261.8'32'293
Miracle at city hall, by Al Palmquist, with Kay Nelson. Minneapolis, Bethany Fellowship [1974] 173 p. illus. 21 cm. [BV4470.P27] 74-11738 ISBN 0-87123-364-9 2.45 (pbk.)
1. Midwest Challenge (Center) 2. Church work with narcotic addicts—Minneapolis. I. Nelson, Kay, joint author. II. Title.

CLARK, Dorothy. 261.8'32'3
Look at me, please look at me [by] Dorothy Clark & Jane Dahl [and] Lois Gonzenbach. Elgin, Ill., D. C. Cook Pub. Co., [1973] 125 p. 18 cm. "A collection of true incidents evolving from the work of Dorothy Clark and Jane Dahl with the mentally handicapped..." [BV4461.C55] 73-76698 ISBN 0-912692-11-1 1.25 (pbk.)
1. Church work with the mentally handicapped. I. Dahl, Jane. II. Gonzenbach, Lois. III. Title.

YOUNT, William R. 261.8'32'42
Be opened! : An introduction to ministry with the deaf / William R. Yount. Nashville : Broadman Press, c1976. 225 p. : ill. ; 21 cm. Originally entitled Ephphatha! and written for use in the author's classroom. Bibliography: p. 223-225. [BV4463.Y68 1976] 76-2238 ISBN 0-8054-3216-7 bds. : 7.95
1. Church work with the deaf. 2. Deaf—Education. I. Title.

JENNINGS, William H. 261.8'32'5
Poor people and churchgoers [by] William H. Jennings. New York, Seabury Press [1972] 128 p. 21 cm. (An Original Seabury paperback, SP76) Bibliography: p. 125-128. [BV639.P6J45] 72-81028 ISBN 0-8164-2075-0 2.95
1. Church and the poor. I. Title.

ROBERTSON, Hector Menteith. 261.8'32'5
Aspects of the rise of economic individualism; a criticism of Max Weber and his school, by H. M. Robertson. [1st ed.] Clifton [N.J.] A. M. Kelley, 1973. xvi, 223, [18] p. 22 cm. (Reprints of economic classics) "With the addition of 'European economic developments in the 16th century', reprinted from the South African journal of economics, March 1950." Based on the author's thesis, University of Cambridge, 1928-29. Reprint of the 1933 ed. published by the University Press, Cambridge, Eng. in series: Cambridge studies in economic history. Includes bibliographical references. [BR115.E3R62 1973] 73-17059 ISBN 0-678-00867-1 11.50
1. Weber, Max, 1864-1920. Die protestantische Ethik und der Geist des Kapitalismus. 2. Christianity and economics—History. 3. Religion and sociology. 4. Capitalism. I. Weber, Max, 1864-1920. Die protestantische Ethik und der Geist des Kapitalismus. II. Robertson, Hector Menteith. European economic developments in the 16th century. 1974. III. Title.

TAYLOR, Richard K. 261.8'32'50973
Economics and the Gospel; a primer on shalom as economic justice, by Richard K. Taylor. Philadelphia, Published for Joint Educational Development [by] United Church Press [1973] 125 p. 22 cm. (A Shalom resource) Includes bibliographies. [BR115.E3T38] 73-12570
1. Christianity and economics. 2. United States—Economic conditions—1961- I. Joint Educational Development. II. Title.

PEDERSON, Duane. 261.8'33'1522
Going sideways : hope, love, life versus suicide / Duane Pederson and Helen W. Kooiman. New York : Hawthorn Books, [1974] viii, 135 p. ; 21 cm. Includes bibliographical references. [HV6545.P43] 74-335 ISBN 0-8015-3056-3 : 2.95
1. Suicide. 2. Suicide—Prevention—United States—Directories. I. Kooiman, Helen W., joint author. II. Title.

O'REILLY, Sean, 1922- 261.8'34
In the image of God; a guide to sex education for parents. Middleburg, Va., Notre Dame Institute Press [1974] iv, 53 p. 22 cm. Bibliography: p. 53. [HQ57.2.O73] 74-76101 1.85 (pbk.)
1. Sex instruction. 2. Sex and religion. I. Title.

BIANCHI, Eugene C. 261.8'34'1
From machismo to mutuality : essays on sexism and woman-man liberation / by Eugene C. Bianchi and Rosemary R. Ruether. New York : Paulist Press, c1976. v, 142 p. ; 22 cm. Includes bibliographical references. [HQ61.B53] 75-25443 ISBN 0-8091-0202-1 : 5.95
1. Sex and religion. 2. Sexual ethics. 3. Sex discrimination. I. Ruether, Rosemary Radford, joint author. II. Title.

BRIFFAULT, Robert, 1876-1948. 261.8'34'1
Sin and sex / Robert Briffault. New York : AMS Press, 1976. 253 p. ; 19 cm. Reprint of the 1931 ed. published by Macaulay Co., New York. [HQ61.B7 1976] 72-9623 ISBN 0-404-57418-1 : 12.50
1. Sex. 2. Sex and religion. 3. Ethics—History. 4. Christian ethics. I. Title.

EVENING, Margaret. 261.8'34'1
Who walk alone : a consideration of the single life / Margaret Evening. Downers Grove, Ill. : InterVarsity Press, 1974. 222 p. ; 22 cm. Bibliography: p. 221-222. [HQ800.E85 1974b] 75-24160 ISBN 0-87784-767-3 : 3.95
1. Single people. 2. Single people—Sexual behavior. I. Title.

GREEN, Ernest L. 261.8'34'1
Male and female created He them / by Ernest L. Green. Grand Rapids : Kregel Publications, c1977. 86 p. ; 19 cm. [BT708.G68] 77-79188 ISBN 0-8254-2717-7 pbk. : 1.95
1. Sex (Theology) 2. Marriage. I. Title.

GREEN, Ernest L. 261.8'34'1
Male and female created He them / by Ernest L. Green. Grand Rapids : Kregel Publications,

c1977. 86 p. ; 19 cm. [BT708.G68] 77-79188 ISBN 0-8254-2717-7 pbk. : 1.95
1. Sex (Theology) 2. Marriage. I. Title.

HAMILTON, Kenneth. 261.8'34'1
To be a man, to be a woman / Kenneth & Alice Hamilton. Nashville : Abingdon Press, 1975, c1972. 159 p. : ill. ; 22 cm. [HQ734.H2588 1975] 75-306287 ISBN 0-687-42149-7 pbk. : 2.95
1. Sex in marriage. 2. Conduct of life. I. Hamilton, Alice, joint author. II. Title.

HIS guide to sex, 261.8'34'1
singleness & marriage / C. Stephen Board & others. Downers Grove, Ill. : InterVarsity Press, [1974] 130 p. ; 18 cm. [HQ31.H57] 74-83476 pbk. : 1.95
1. Sexual ethics. 2. Marriage. I. Board, Stephen. II. His.
Contents omitted.

HOLLIS, Harry. 261.8'34'1
Thank God for sex : a Christian model for sexual understanding and behavior / Harry Hollis, Jr. Nashville : Broadman Press, [1975] 167 p. ; 21 cm. Includes bibliographical references. [BT708.H63] 75-3730 ISBN 0-8054-6114-0 : 4.95
1. Sex (Theology) I. Title.

HOWARD, Clifford, 261.8'34'1
1868-
Sex and religion : a study of their relationship and its bearing upon civilization / by Clifford Howard. New York : AMS Press, 1975. xi, 201 p. ; 19 cm. Reprint of the 1925 ed. published by Williams and Norgate, London. [HQ63.H6 1975] 72-9654 ISBN 0-404-57463-7 : 16.00
1. Sex and religion.

HUMAN sexuality : 261.8'34'1
new directions in American Catholic thought : a study / commissioned by the Catholic Theological Society of America ; Anthony Kosnik, chairperson ... [et al.]. New York : Paulist Press, c1977. xvi, 322 p. ; 24 cm. Includes index. Bibliography: p. 275-291. [HQ32.H822] 77-74586 ISBN 0-8091-0223-4 : 8.50
1. Sexual ethics. 2. Sex (Theology) I. Kosnik, Anthony. II. Catholic Theological Society of America.

IT'S O.K. to be single 261.8'34'1
: a guidebook for singles and the church / edited by Gary R. Collins. Waco, Tex. : Word Books, c1976. 165 p. ; 22 cm. Includes bibliographical references. [BV639.S5I77] 76-2857 ISBN 0-87680-858-5 : 3.95
1. Church work with single people. 2. Single people—Religious life. I. Collins, Gary R.

JOHANSEN, Ruthann 261.8'34'1
Knechel, 1942-
Coming together : male and female in a renamed garden / Ruthann Knechel Johansen. Elgin, Ill. : Brethren Press, c1977. 151 p. ; 21 cm. Bibliography: p. [147]-151. [BV639.W7J64] 77-6301 ISBN 0-87178-156-5 pbk. : 3.95
1. Women in Christianity. 2. Sex role. 3. Sex discrimination against women. 4. Sex (Theology) I. Title.

MCGOEY, John H. 261.8'34'1
Dare I love? / John H. McGoey. Huntington, Ind. : Our Sunday Visitor, 1974, c1971. ix, 131 p. : ill. ; 20 cm. [HQ31.M1844] 74-16464 ISBN 0-87973-762-X pbk. : 2.75
1. Sexual ethics. 2. Love. I. Title.

MALE and female : 261.8'34'1
Christian approaches to sexuality / edited by Ruth Tiffany Barnhouse, and Urban T. Holmes, III ; with a foreword by John Maury Allin. New York : Seabury Press, c1976. xiii, 274 p. ; 23 cm. "A Crossroad book." Bibliography: p. 271-274. [BT708.M34] 75-42380 ISBN 0-8164-2118-8 : 4.95
1. Sex (Theology)—Addresses, essays, lectures. 2. Sex—Addresses, essays, lectures. 3. Marriage—Addresses, essays, lectures. 4. Women—Addresses, essays, lectures. 5. Homosexuality—Addresses, essays, lectures. I. Barnhouse, Ruth Tiffany, 1923- II. Holmes, Urban Tigner, 1930-

MICKLEY, Richard R. 261.8'34'1
Christian sexuality : a reflection on being Christian and sexual / by Richard R. Mickley ; illustrated by Shelagh. 2d ed. rev., with study guide. Los Angeles : Universal Fellowship Press, c1976. 186 p. : ill. ; 22 cm. "A chi-rho book." Includes bibliographical references. [BT708.M5 1976] 77-670034 3.95
1. Sex (Theology) 2. Sexual ethics. I. Title.

REYNOLDS, Jim, 1942- 261.8'34'1
Secrets of Eden : God and human sexuality / Jim Reynolds. Austin, Tex. : Sweet Pub. Co., [1975] 191 p. ; 18 cm. Includes bibliographies. [HQ31.R444] 74-25859 ISBN 0-8344-0087-1 pbk. : 1.95
1. Sex. 2. Sexual ethics. 3. Marriage. I. Title.

RUETHER, Rosemary 261.8'34'1
Radford.
New woman/new earth : sexist ideologies and human liberation / Rosemary Radford Ruether. New York : Seabury Press, [1975] p. cm. "A Crossroad book." Includes index. Bibliography: p. [HQ1154.R83] 75-17649 ISBN 0-8164-1205-7 : 8.95
1. Sex discrimination against women—Addresses, essays, lectures. 2. Women in Christianity—Addresses, essays, lectures. 3. Race discrimination—Addresses, essays, lectures. 4. Sex role—Addresses, essays, lectures. I. Title.

SAPP, Stephen. 261.8'34'1
Sexuality, the Bible, and science / by Stephen Sapp. Philadelphia : Fortress Press, c1977. xi, 140 p. ; 24 cm. Bibliography: p. 136-140. [BT708.S25] 76-62617 ISBN 0-8006-0503-9 : 8.25
1. Sex (Theology) 2. Sex in the Bible. 3. Sex differences. I. Title.

SHARP, Watson. 261.8'34'1
The Catholic & the Jewish approach to sex & their relative influence upon the cultural character of our society / Watson Sharp. [1st ed.]. [Albuquerque, N.M.] : American Classical College Press, [1977] 17 leaves ; 28 cm. Cover title. [HQ63.S45] 77-24674 ISBN 0-89266-012-0 : 37.75
1. Sex and religion. I. Title: The Catholic & the Jewish approach to sex & their relative influence ...

SMEDES, Lewis B. 261.8'34'1
Sex for Christians : the limits and liberties of sexual living / by Lewis B. Smedes. Grand Rapids : Eerdmans, c1976. 250 p. ; 18 cm. [HQ32.S55] 76-791 ISBN 0-8028-1618-5 pbk. : 2.95
1. Sexual ethics. 2. Sex in marriage. 3. Christian ethics. I. Title.

STEINMETZ, Urban G. 261.8'34'1
The sexual Christian [by] Urban G. Steinmetz. St. Meinrad, Ind., Abbey Press, 1972. ix, 98 p. 21 cm. (A Priority edition) [HQ63.S73] 72-85374 1.50
1. Sexual ethics. 2. Sex and religion. I. Title.

VALENTE, Michael F. 261.8'34'1
Sex: the radical view of a Catholic theologian, by Michael F. Valente. New York, Bruce Pub. Co. [1970] 158 p. 21 cm. Includes bibliographical references. [HQ63.V32] 79-132466 2.95
1. Sex and religion. 2. Sexual ethics. 3. Sex (Theology) I. Title.

GRANT, Wilson W., 261.8'34'107
1941-
From parent to child about sex; including questions for discussion and thought, by Wilson W. Grant. Grand Rapids, Zondervan Pub. House [1973] 183 p. 21 cm. Bibliography: p. 175-177. [HQ57.G69] 72-85572 pap. 1.95
1. Sex instruction for children. I. Title.

GRANT, Wilson W., 261.8'34'107
1941-
Love and sex, what it's all about / by W. W. Grant. Grand Rapids, Mich. : Zondervan Pub. House, [1974] 172 p. : ill. ; 18 cm. Includes index. [HQ35.G73] 74-4962 pbk. : 1.50
1. Sex instruction for youth. I. Title.

BOLDREY, Richard. 261.8'34'12
Chauvinist or feminist? : Paul's view of women / Richard and Joyce Boldrey ; foreword by David M. Scholer. Grand Rapids : Baker Book House, c1976. 89 p. ; 22 cm. "A Canon Press book." Includes indexes. Bibliography: p. 73-82. [BS2655.W5B64] 75-38236 ISBN 0-8010-0657-0 : 2.95
1. Bible. N.T. Epistles of Paul—Theology. 2. Woman (Theology)—Biblical teaching. I. Boldrey, Joyce, joint author. II. Title.

BRITTAIN, Alfred. 261.8'34'12
Women of early Christianity / by Alfred Brittain and Mitchell Carroll ; with an introd. by J. Cullen Ayre, Jr. New York : Gordon Press, 1976. p. cm. (Woman in all ages and in all countries) Reprint of v. 3 of the 1907 ed. of Woman in all ages and in all countries, published by Rittenhouse Press, Philadelphia. [BR195.W6B74 1976] [BR195.W6] 76-5490 ISBN 0-87968-268-X
1. Women in Christianity—Early church, ca. 30-600. 2. Women—Biography. 3. Christian biography. I. Carroll, Mitchell, 1870-1925, joint author. II. Title. III. Series.

CHANDLER, Sandie. 261.8'34'12
Lovingly liberated : a Christian woman's response to the liberation movement / Sandie Chandler. Old Tappan, N.J. : Revell, [1975] 122 p. ; 20 cm. [HQ1426.C457] 75-20141 ISBN 0-8007-0750-8 : 3.95
1. Feminism—United States. 2. Women—Religious life. I. Title.

CHRISTIAN freedom for 261.8'34'12
women and other human beings / Harry N. Hollis, Jr. ... [et al.]. Nashville : Broadman Press, [1975] 192 p. ; 21 cm. [BV639.W7C45] 74-21566 ISBN 0-8054-5552-3 : 4.95
1. Women in Christianity—Addresses, essays, lectures. 2. Women—Addresses, essays, lectures. I. Hollis, Harry.

CLARK, Elizabeth, 261.8'34'12
1938-
Women and religion : a feminist sourcebook of Christian thought / Elizabeth Clark and Herbert Richardson. 1st ed. New York : Harper & Row, c1977. viii, 296 p. ; 21 cm. (Harper forum books ; RD 178) Includes bibliographical references. [BT704.C53 1977] 76-9975 ISBN 0-06-061398-X : 4.95
1. Woman (Theology)—Addresses, essays, lectures. 2. Women and religion—Addresses, essays, lectures. I. Richardson, Herbert Warren, joint author. II. Title.

COLLINS, Sheila D. 261.8'34'12
A different heaven and earth [by] Sheila D. Collins. Valley Forge [Pa.] Judson Press [1974] 253 p. 23 cm. Includes bibliographical references. [BV639.W7C57] 74-2890 ISBN 0-8170-0620-6
1. Women in Christianity. I. Title.

DALY, Mary. 261.8'34'12
The Church and the second sex / Mary Daly ; with a new feminist postchristian introd. by the author. New York : Harper & Row, 1975. 229 p. ; 21 cm. (Harper colophon books) Includes bibliographical references and index. [BV639.W7D28 1975] 75-301799 pbk. : 3.45
1. Women in Christianity. I. Title.

EMSWILER, Sharon 261.8'34'12
Neufer.
The ongoing journey : women and the Bible / by Sharon Neufer Emswiler. [New York] : Women's Division, Board of Global Ministries, United Methodist Church, c1977. 144 p. ; 19 cm. Bibliography: p. 139-142. [BS575.E55] 77-151179 1.50
1. Women in the Bible. 2. Woman (Theology)—Biblical teaching. I. Title.

GILMAN, Charlotte 261.8'341'2
Perkins Stetson, 1860-1935.
His religion and hers : a study of the faith of our fathers and the work of our mothers / by Charlotte Perkins Gilman. Westport, Conn. : Hyperion Press, 1976, c1923. p. cm. (Pioneers of the woman's movement) Reprint of the ed. published by Century Co., New York. [HQ1221.G53 1976] 75-29509 ISBN 0-88355-377-5
1. Women—Social and moral questions. 2. Religion. I. Title.

GILMAN, Charlotte 261.8'341'2
Perkins Stetson, 1860-1935.
His religion and hers : a study of the faith of our fathers and the work of our mothers / by Charlotte Perkins Gilman. Westport, Conn. : Hyperion Press, 1976, c1923. xi, 300 p. ; 23 cm. (Pioneers of the woman's movement) Reprint of the ed. published by Century Co., New York. [HQ1221.G53 1976] 75-29509 ISBN 0-88355-377-5 : 21.50
1. Women—Social and moral questions. 2. Religion. I. Title.

HARKNESS, Georgia 261.8'34'12
Elma, 1891-
Women in church and society; a historical and theological inquiry [by] Georgia Harkness. Nashville, Abingdon Press [1971, c1972] 240 p. 20 cm. Includes bibliographical references. [BV639.W7H28 1972] 76-172809 ISBN 0-687-45965-6 4.75
1. Women in Christianity. 2. Woman—History and condition of women. 3. Ordination of women. I. Title.

HUNT, Gladys M. 261.8'34'12
Ms. means myself, by Gladys Hunt. Grand Rapids, Mich., Zondervan Pub. House [1972] 145 p. 22 cm. [HQ1206.H85] 72-85566 3.95
1. Woman—Psychology. 2. Conduct of life. I. Title.

HUNT, Gladys M. 261.8'34'12
Ms. means myself, by Gladys Hunt. New York, Bantam Books [1974, c1973] 146 p. 18 cm. [HQ1206.H85] 1.50 (pbk.)
1. Woman—Psychology. 2. Conduct of life. I. Title.
L.C. card number for original ed.: 72-85566.

KRESS, Robert. 261.8'34'12
Whither womankind? : The humanity of women / by Robert Kress. St. Meinrad, Ind. : Abbey Press, 1975. 336 p. ; 21 cm. (A Priority edition) Includes index. Bibliography: p. [321]-327. [BT704.K73] 75-207 ISBN 0-87029-045-2 pbk. : 4.75
1. Woman (Theology)—History of doctrines. 2. Feminism. I. Title.

LUDER, Hope 261.8'34'12
Elizabeth.
Women and Quakerism / Hope Elizabeth Luder. Wallingford, Pa. : [Pendle Hill], 1974. 36 p. ; 19 cm. (Pendle Hill pamphlet ; 196) Bibliography: p. 35-36. [HQ1394.L84] 74-82914 ISBN 0-87574-196-7 : 0.70
1. Friends, Society of—History. 2. Women and religion. I. Title.

*MCGRATH, Sister 261.'8'34'12
Albertus Magnus.
Women and the Church. / by Sister Albertus Magnus McGrath, O. P. Garden City, N.Y. : Doubleday, 1976 c1972. 158 p. ; 18 cm. (Doubleday Image Books). Original title : What a modern Catholic believes about women Includes bibliographical references. [BL458] pbk. : 1.95
1. Women and religion. 2. Church work with women. I. Title.

MOLLENKOTT, Virginia 261.8'34'12
R.
Women, men, and the Bible / Virginia R. Mollenkott. Nashville : Abingdon Press, [1977] p. cm. Includes bibliographical references. [BT704.M64] 76-40446 ISBN 0-687-45970-2 pbk. : 3.95
1. Woman (Theology) 2. Woman (Theology)—Biblical teaching. I. Title.

MORAN, Miriam G., 261.8'34'12
comp.
What you should know about Women's Lib / edited by Miriam G. Moran. New Canaan, Conn. : Keats Pub., 1974. 118 p. ; 18 cm. (A Pivot book) [HQ1395.M67] 74-75980 pbk. : 1.50
1. Feminism—Addresses, essays, lectures. 2. Women in the Bible—Addresses, essays, lectures. I. Title.
Contents omitted.

PAPE, Dorothy. 261.8'34'12
In search of God's ideal woman : a personal examination of the New Testament / Dorothy R. Pape. Downers Grove, Ill. : Inter-Varsity Press, c1976. 370 p. ; 21 cm. Bibliography: p. 363-365. [BS2545.W65P36] 75-21453 ISBN 0-87784-854-8 : 4.95
1. Jesus Christ—Attitude towards women. 2. Woman (Theology)—Biblical teaching. 3. Women in Christianity. I. Title.

PETERSEN, Evelyn R., 261.8'34'12
comp.
For women only; the fine art of being a woman. Edited by Evelyn R. Petersen and J. Allan Petersen. Wheaton, Ill., Tyndale [1974] 296 p. 22 cm. [HQ1420.P48] 73-93968 ISBN 0-8423-0896-2 3.95 (pbk.).
1. Women in the United States—Addresses, essays, lectures. 2. Conduct of life—Addresses, essays, lectures. 3. Family—United States—Addresses, essays, lectures. I. Petersen, J. Allan, joint comp. II. Title.

RUETHER, Rosemary 261.8'34'12
Radford.
Religion and sexism; images of woman in the Jewish and Christian traditions. Edited by Rosemary Radford Ruether. New York, Simon and Schuster [1974] 356 p. 22 cm. Bibliography: p. [345] [BV639.W7R8] 74-2791 ISBN 0-671-21692-9 9.95
1. Women in Christianity. 2. Women in the Bible. 3. Women in the Talmud. I. Title.
Pbk. 3.95, ISBN 0-671-21693-7.

RUSSELL, Letty M. 261.8'34'12
Human liberation in a feminist perspective—a theology, by Letty M. Russell. Philadelphia, Westminster Press [1974] 213 p. 21 cm. Includes bibliographical references. [BT810.2.R87] 74-10613 ISBN 0-664-24991-4 3.95 (pbk.).
1. Freedom (Theology) 2. Salvation. 3. Woman (Theology) I. Title.

SANNELLA, Lucia. 261.8'34'12
The female Pentecost / by Lucia Sannella. 1st ed. Port Washington, N.Y. : Ashley Books, c1976. 281 p. ; 23 cm. [BS680.W7S25 1976] 75-16565 ISBN 0-87949-043-8 : 12.95
1. Bible and feminism. 2. Women in the Bible. I. Title.

SCANZONI, Letha. 261.8'34'12
All we're meant to be : a Biblical approach to women's liberation / Letha Scanzoni, Nancy Hardesty. Waco, Tex. : Word Books, [1974] 233 p. ; 23 cm. Includes bibliographical references and index. [BS680.W7S28] 74-78041 6.95
1. Woman (Theology)—Biblical teaching. 2. Women—Social conditions. I. Hardesty, Nancy, joint author. II. Title.

SEXISM and church law 261.8'34'12
: equal rights and affirmative action / edited by James A. Coriden. New York : Paulist Press, c1977. ix, 192 p. ; 21 cm. (An Exploration book) Includes bibliographical

references and index. [BV639.W7S49] 77-70638 ISBN 0-8091-2010-0 pbk. : 7.95
1. Women in Christianity—Addresses, essays, lectures. 2. Women in church work—Catholic Church—Addresses, essays, lectures. 3. Women—Legal status, laws, etc. (Canon law)—Addresses, essays, lectures. I. Coriden, James A.

SWIDLER, Arlene. 261.8'34'12
Woman in a man's church; from role to person. New York, Paulist Press [1972] 111 p. 19 cm. (Deus books) Bibliography: p. 107-111. [BV639.W7S94] 72-86596 ISBN 0-8091-1740-1 1.25
1. Women in Christianity. 2. Women in church work—Catholic Church. I. Title.

TAVARD, George Henri, 1922- 261.8'34'12
Woman in Christian tradition [by] George H. Tavard. Notre Dame [Ind.] University of Notre Dame Press [1973] xi, 257 p. 24 cm. Includes bibliographical references. [BV639.W7T38] 72-12637 ISBN 0-268-00490-0 9.95
1. Women in Christianity. I. Title.

UNSWORTH, Richard P. 261.8'34'12
Dignity & exploitation : Christian reflections on images of sex in the 1970s : a study document prepared at the request of and approved by the Advisory Council on Church and Society, the United Presbyterian Church in the U.S.A. / Richard P. Unsworth. New York : [Advisory Council on Church and Society of the United Presbyterian Church in the U.S.A. : available from Presbyterian Distribution Service, 1974] 49 p. ; 22 cm. Bibliography: p. 43-48. [BT708.U57] 74-190628 pbk. : 1.00
1. Sex (Theology) I. United Presbyterian Church in the U.S.A. Advisory Council on Church and Society. II. Title.

WOMEN in a strange 261.8'34'12
land : search for a new image / edited by Clare Benedicks Fischer, Betsy Brenneman, and Anne McGrew Bennett. Philadelphia : Fortress Press, [1975] x, 133 p. ; 22 cm. Bibliography: p. 131-133. [HQ1394.W64] 74-26326 ISBN 0-8006-1204-3 pbk. : 3.50
1. Women in Christianity—Addresses, essays, lectures. 2. Feminism—United States—Addresses, essays, lectures. I. Fischer, Clare Benedicks. II. Brennemans, Betsy. III. Bennett, Anne McGrew.
Contents omitted.

WOMEN'S liberation 261.8'34'12
and the church: the new demand for freedom in the life of the Christian Church. Edited, with introduction by Sarah Bentley Doely. Published in co-operation with IDOC-North America. New York, Association Press [1970] 158 p. 23 cm. Bibliography: p. [149]-154. [BV639.W7W64] 70-129441 ISBN 0-8096-1814-1 5.95
1. Women in christianity—Addresses, essays, lectures. I. Doely, Sarah Bentley, ed.

MILES, Herbert Jackson, 1907- 261.8'341'4
The dating game / Herbert J. Miles. Grand Rapids : Zondervan Pub. House, [1975] 168 p. ; 21 cm. Bibliography: p. 167-168. [HQ801.M56] 74-25332 pbk. : 2.95
1. Dating (Social customs) 2. Youth—Sexual behavior. 3. Weddings—United States. I. Title.

HARTLEY, Fred. 261.8'34'142
Update / by Fred Hartley. Old Tappan, N.J. : F. H. Revell Co., c1977. 155 p. ; 21 cm. [HQ801.H34] 77-1763 ISBN 0-8007-0861-X pbk. :3.95
1. Dating (Social customs) 2. Youth—Conduct of life. 3. Youth—Sexual behavior. I. Title.

WHITE, John, 1924(Mar.5)- 261.8'34'15
Eros defiled : the Christian & sexual sin / John White. Downers Grove, Ill. : Inter-Varsity Press, c1977. 169, [3] p. ; 21 cm. Includes bibliographical references. [HQ31.W5] 76-39711 ISBN 0-87784-781-9 pbk. : 3.95
1. Sexual ethics. 2. Sexual deviation. I. Title.

VIGEVENO, H. S. 261.8'34'153
I'm in love with a married man / H. S. Vigeveno. Philadelphia : A. J. Holman Co., 1976. 132 p. ; 22 cm. [HQ806.V53] 76-22495 ISBN 0-87981-067-X : 3.45
1. Adultery—Case studies. 2. Women—Religious life—Case studies. I. Title.

DRAKEFORD, John W. 261.8'34'157
A Christian view of homosexuality / John W. Drakeford. Nashville : Broadman Press, c1977. 140 p. ; 20 cm. Includes bibliographical references. [HQ76.3.U5D7] 76-41474 ISBN 0-8054-56201 pbk. : 2.95
1. Homosexuality—United States. I. Title.

DRAKEFORD, John W. 261.8'34'157
A Christian view of homosexuality / John W. Drakeford. Nashville : Broadman Press, c1977. 140 p. ; 20 cm. Includes bibliographical references. [HQ76.3.U5D7] 76-41474 ISBN 0-8054-56201 pbk. : 2.95
1. Homosexuality—United States. I. Title.

ENROTH, Ronald M. 261.8'34'157
The gay church, by Ronald M. Enroth [and] Gerald E. Jamison. Grand Rapids, Eerdmans [1974] 144 p. 22 cm. Bibliography: p. 141. [BV4470.E57] 73-16483 ISBN 0-8028-1543-X 2.95
1. Universal Fellowship of Metropolitan Community Churches. 2. Church work with homosexuals. I. Jamison, Gerald E., joint author. II. Title.

FIELD, David, 1921- 261.8'34'157
The homosexual way, a Christian option? / by David Field. Bramcote : Grove Books, 1976. 24 p. ; 22 cm. (Grove booklets on ethics ; no. 9 ISSN 0305-4241s) Includes bibliographical references. [BR115.H6F53] 77-350376 ISBN 0-901710-83-0 : £0.30
1. Homosexuality and Christianity. I. Title.

GEARHART, Sally Miller, 1931- 261.8'34'157
Loving women/loving men; gay liberation and the church. Edited/authored by Sally Gearhart and William R. Johnson. [San Francisco] Glide Publications [1974] xi, 165 p. 24 cm. Bibliography: p. 153-160. [BR115.H6G4] 74-11339 ISBN 0-912078-41-3
1. Homosexuality and Christianity. 2. Gay liberation movement. I. Johnson, William Reagan, 1946- joint author. II. Title.

GEARHART, Sally Miller, 1931- 261.8'34'157
Loving women/loving men; gay liberation and the church. Edited/authored by Sally Gearhart and William R. Johnson. [San Francisco] Glide Publications [1974] p. cm. [BR115.H6G4] 74-11339 ISBN 0-912078-41-3 6.95 (pbk.)
1. Homosexuality and Christianity. 2. Gay liberation movement. I. Johnson, William Reagan, 1946- joint author. II. Title.

MCNEILL, John J. 261.8'34'157
The church and the homosexual / by John J. McNeill. Kansas City [Kan.] : Sheed and Ward, c1976. p. cm. Includes bibliographical references. [HQ76.M156] 76-18844 ISBN 0-8362-0683-5 : 10.00
1. Homosexuality. 2. Homosexuality in the Bible. 3. Church work with homosexuals. I. Title.

PITTENGER, William Norman, 1905- 261.83'4'157
Time for consent : a Christian's approach to homosexuality / [by] Norman Pittenger. 3rd revised and enlarged ed. London : S.C.M. Press, 1976. [7], 104 p. ; 22 cm. [HQ76.P5 1976] 77-363876 ISBN 0-334-01660-6 : £1.80
1. Homosexuality. I. Title.

PRESBYTERIAN Church in the U.S. Council on Theology and Culture. 261.8'34'157
The Church and homosexuality : a preliminary study. Atlanta : Office of the Stated Clerk, Presbyterian Church in the United States, c1977. 37 p. ; 26 cm. Bibliography: p. 33-34. [BR115.H6P73 1977] 77-154207 0.50
1. Homosexuality and Christianity. I. Title.

WOODS, Richard. 261.8'34'157
Another kind of love : homosexuality and spirituality / by Richard Woods. Chicago : Thomas More Press, c1977. 163 p. ; 21 cm. Bibliography: p. 161-162. [HQ76.25.W66] 77-151667 ISBN 0-88347-075-6 pbk. : 3.95
1. Homosexuality. 2. Sex and religion. I. Title.

RATLIFF, Dale Hedrick, 1928- 261.8'34'158
Minor sexual deviance : diagnosis and pastoral treatment / Dale H. Ratliff. Dubuque, Iowa : Kendall/Hunt Pub. Co., c1976. ix, 54 p. ; 23 cm. Bibliography: p. 51-54. [HQ72.U53R37] 76-29284 ISBN 0-8403-1605-4 : 3.50
1. Sexual deviation—United States. 2. Pastoral counseling. I. Title.

GINDER, Richard. 261.8'34'17
Binding with briars : sex and sin in the Catholic Church / Richard Ginder. Englewood Cliffs, N.J. : Prentice-Hall, [1975] ix, 251 p. ; 24 cm. Includes index. Bibliography: p. 237-244. [HQ59.G56] 75-11610 ISBN 0-13-076299-7
1. Catholic Church—Doctrinal and controversial works—Catholic authors. 2. Sexual ethics. 3. Sex and religion. I. Title.

NORTHCOTE, Hugh. 261.8'34'17
Christianity and sex problems. 2d ed. rev. and enl. Philadelphia, F. A. Davis Co., 1916. [New York, AMS Press, 1974] xvi, 478 p. 23 cm. Includes bibliographical references. [HQ31.N87 1974] 72-9668 ISBN 0-404-57486-6
1. Sexual ethics. I. Title.

**THE secrets of our* 261.8'34'17
sexuality : role liberation for the Christian / edited by Gary R. Collins. Waco, Tex. : Word Books, c1976. 185p. ; 22 cm. (Continental congress on the family) [AQ61] 76-2865 ISBN 0-87680-847-X pbk. : 3.95
1. Sex and religion. I. Collins, Gary R. comp.

SOMMER, Joseph, 1915- 261.8'34'17
Catholic thought on contraception through the centuries. Liguori, Mo., Liguorian Pamphlets and Books [1970] 96 p. 18 cm. [HQ766.3.S6] 77-145913 1.00
1. Birth control—Religious aspects. I. Title.

SUENENS, Leon Joseph, Cardinal, 1904- 261.8'34'17
Christian love and human sexuality / [by] Cardinal Suenens. London : Catholic Truth Society, 1976. [2], 32 p. ; 19 cm. Cover title. Includes bibliographical references. [BV4647.C5S83] 77-359989 ISBN 0-85183-181-8 : £0.20
1. Chastity. 2. Love. 3. Sexual ethics. I. Title.

VALENTINI, Norberto. 261.8'34'17
Sex and the confessional [by] Norberto Valentini [and] Clara Di Meglio. Translated by Melton S. Davis. New York, Stein and Day [1974] 213 p. 25 cm. Translation of Il sesso in confessionale. [HQ63.V3413] 73-91861 ISBN 0-8128-1681-1 6.95
1. Sex and religion. 2. Sexual ethics. 3. Confession. I. Di Meglio, Clara, joint author. II. Title.

DRAKEFORD, John W. 261.8'34'175
Made for each other [by] John W. Drakeford. Nashville, Broadman Press [1973] 152 p. 21 cm. Includes bibliographical references. [HQ35.D67] 72-90039 ISBN 0-8054-5608-2 4.95
1. Sex instruction for youth. 2. Sexual ethics. I. Title.

CONVERSATIONS on love 261.8'34'18
and sex in marriage [by] Jim and June Cicero, Ivan and Joyce Fahs. Waco, Tex., Word Books [1972] 138 p. 22 cm. [HQ31.C755] 72-84157 3.50
1. Sexual ethics. 2. Sex in marriage. I. Cicero, Jim.

CONVERSATIONS on love 261.8'34'18
and sex in marriage [by] Jim and June Cicero, Ivan and Joyce Fahs. Waco, Tex., Word Books [1972] 138 p. 22 cm. [HQ31.C755] 72-84157 3.50
1. Sexual ethics. 2. Sex in marriage. I. Cicero, Jim.

†DEATRICK, Mary. 261.8'34'18
Sexual maturity for women / Mary Deatrick. Santa Ana, Calif. : Vision House, c1976. 162 p. : ill. ; 21 cm. Bibliography: p. [161]-162. [HQ46.D38] 76-40715 ISBN 0-88449-058-0 : 2.95
1. Sex instruction for women. I. Title.

MILES, Herbert Jackson, 1907- 261.8'34'18
Sexual happiness in marriage : a Christian interpretation of sexual adjustment in marriage / Herbert J. Miles ; ill. by R. Earl Cleveland. Rev. ed. Grand Rapids : Zondervan Pub. House, c1976. p. cm. Bibliography: p. [HQ31.M63 1976] 76-29620 pbk. : 1.75
1. Sex in marriage. I. Title.

WHEAT, Ed. 261.8'34'18
Intended for pleasure / Ed Wheat and Gaye Wheat. Old Tappan, N.J. : F. H. Revell Co., c1977. 223 p. : ill. ; 24 cm. Includes index. Bibliogrphy: p. 211-213. [HQ734.W52] 76-52997 ISBN 0-8007-0824-5 : 7.95
1. Marriage. 2. Sex instruction. 3. Sex in marriage. 4. Family—Biblical teaching. I. Wheat, Gaye, joint author. II. Title.

BAILEY, Derrick Sherwin, 1910- 261.8'34'2
The mystery of love and marriage : a study in the theology of sexual relation / Derrick Sherwin Bailey. Westport, Conn. : Greenwood Press, 1977, c1952. x, 145 p. ; 22 cm. Reprint of the ed. published by Harper, New York. Includes index. Bibliography: p. 137-139. [HQ1051.B3 1977] 77-3313 ISBN 0-8371-9577-2 lib.bdg. : 12.50
1. Marriage. 2. Marriage—Biblical teaching. 3. Love. 4. Sex (Theology) I. Title.

BEAR, Robert L. 261.8'34'2
Delivered unto Satan / by Robert L. Bear. Carlisle, Pa. : Bear, c1974. 331 p. ; 23 cm. [BX8129.R4B4] 75-303200 6.95
1. Reformed Mennonite Church—Doctrinal and controversial works. 2. Bear, Robert L. 3. Excommunication. I. Title.
Distributed by Stackpole Books

CONSTANTELOS, Demetrios J. 261.8'34'2
Marriage, sexuality & celibacy : a Greek Orthodox perspective / by Demetrios J. Constantelos. Minneapolis : Light and Life Pub. Co., [1975] 93 p. ; 21 cm. Includes bibliographical references. [BX378.M2C66] 74-27604
1. Marriage—Orthodox Eastern Church. I. Title.

COOPER, Darien B. 261.8'34'2
You can be the wife of a happy husband / Darien B. Cooper, [foreword by Tim LaHaye]. Wheaton, Ill. : Victor Books, [1974] 156 p. : ill. ; 21 cm. (An Input book) Bibliography: p. 155-156. [HQ734.C854] 74-77450 ISBN 0-88207-711-2 pbk. : 1.95
1. Marriage. 2. Wives. 3. Women—Conduct of life. I. Title.

DOHERTY, Dennis. 261.8'34'2
Divorce & remarriage : resolving a Catholic dilemma / by Dennis J. Doherty. St. Meinrad, Ind. : Abbey Press, 1974. ix, 194 p. ; 20 cm. (A Priority edition) Includes bibliographical references and index. [BX2250.D54] 74-82237 ISBN 0-87029-036-3 pbk. : 4.95
1. Marriage—Catholic Church 2. Divorce. I. Title.

DUFRESNE, Edward R. 261.8'34'2
Partnership : marriage and the committed life / Edward R. Dufresne ; photos. by John Foraste ; with a foreword by Henri J. M. Nouwen. New York : Paulist Press, [1975] xvi, 135 p. : ill. ; 21 cm. [HQ734.D88] 74-27423 ISBN 0-8091-1866-1 pbk. : 5.95
1. Marriage. 2. Conduct of life. I. Title.

ELLISEN, Stanley A. 261.8'34'2
Divorce and remarriage in the church / Stanley A. Ellisen. Grand Rapids : Zondervan, c1977. p. cm. [BT707.E47] 77-9945 ISBN 0-310-35551-6 pbk. : 2.95
1. Divorce. 2. Remarriage. I. Title.

EVANS, Colleen Townsend. 261.8'34'2
My lover, my friend / Colleen Townsend Evans and Louis H. Evans, Jr. Old Tappan, N.J. : Revell, c1976. 159 p. ; 21 cm. [HQ734.E87] 76-22480 ISBN 0-8007-0751-6 : 5.95
1. Marriage. 2. Christian life—Presbyterian authors. I. Evans, Louis Hadley, 1926- joint author. II. Title.

THE Family in today's 261.8'34'2
society. Levi Miller, editor. Scottdale, Pa., Herald Press [1972, c1971] 109 p. 20 cm. Includes bibliographies. [HQ10.F34] 79-170198 ISBN 0-8361-1659-3 1.75
1. Family life education. I. Miller, Levi, ed.

HAUGHTON, Rosemary. 261.8'34'2
The theology of marriage. Notre Dame, Ind., Fides Publishers [1971] 92 p. 18 cm. (Theology today, no. 31) Bibliography: p. 91-92. [BT706.H38] 72-185903 ISBN 0-85342-277-X
1. Marriage. I. Title.

HENDRICKS, Howard G. 261.8'342
Heaven help the home! [by] Howard G. Hendricks. [New York] Berkeley Pub. Co. [1975, c1974] 148 p. 18 cm. (A Berkley medallion book) Includes bibliographical references. [HQ734.H48] 73-78689 ISBN 0-425-02896-8 1.25 (pbk.)
1. Marriage. 2. Family—United States. I. Title.

HUBBARD, David Allan. 261.8'3'42
Is the family here to stay? Waco, Tex., Word Books [1971] 97 p. 21 cm. [BS680.M35H8] 74-170912 2.95
1. Marriage—Biblical teaching. 2. Family—Religious life. I. Title.

HUNTER, Charles, 1920- 261.8'34'2
How to make your marriage exciting, by Charles [and] Frances Hunter. Glendale, Calif., G/L Regal Books [1972] 162 p. 18 cm. [HQ734.H935] 79-180988 ISBN 0-8307-0147-8 1.45
1. Marriage. 2. Conduct of life. I. Hunter, Frances Gardner, 1916- joint author. II. Title.

HYDER, O. Quentin, 1930- 261.8'34'2
The people you live with / O. Quentin Hyder. Old Tappan, N.J. : Revell, [1975] 192 p. ; 21 cm. Bibliography: p. 191-192. [HQ734.H97] 74-32317 ISBN 0-8007-0697-8 : 4.95
1. Marriage. 2. Family. 3. Conduct of life. I. Title.

MACDONALD, Gordon. 261.8'34'2
Magnificent marriage / by Gordon MacDonald. Wheaton, Ill. : Tyndale House, c1976. xii, 183 p. ; 21 cm. Includes bibliographical references. [HQ734.M182 1976] 76-42115 ISBN 0-8423-3890-X : 3.95
1. Marriage. I. Title.

MARRIAGE & family in a world of change / edited by Angela M. Schreiber. Notre Dame, Ind. : Ave Maria Press, c1975. 184 p. : ill. ; 21 cm. "Excerpts from the Know your faith series, the Wedding supplement for 1974, and the Wedding supplement for 1975." Bibliography: p. [182]-184. [HQ734.M387] 75-14740 ISBN 0-87793-097-X : 2.25 261.8'34'2
1. Marriage—Addresses, essays, lectures. 2. Family—Addresses, essays, lectures. 3. Conduct of life—Addresses, essays, lectures. 4. Family life education. I. Schreiber, Angela M.

MUMFORD, Bob. 261.8'34'2
Living happily ever after. Old Tappan, N.J., F. H. Revell Co. [1973] 64 p. illus. 20 cm. [HQ734.M885] 73-4607 ISBN 0-8007-0596-3 2.95
1. Marriage. 2. Conduct of life. I. Title.

OPPENHEIMER, Helen, Lady, 1926- 261.8'34'2
The marriage bond / [by] Helen Oppenheimer. Leighton Buzzard : Faith Press, 1976. 110 p. ; 19 cm. Includes index. [BX5149.M2O66] 76-376820 £1.35
1. Marriage—Church of England. 2. Divorce. I. Title.

OSGOOD, Don. 261.8'34'2
The family and the corporation man / Don Osgood. 1st ed. New York : Harper & Row, [1975] viii, 148 p. : ill. ; 21 cm. [HQ535.O75 1975] 74-25696 6.95
1. Osgood, Don. 2. Family—United States. 3. Executives—United States. 4. Family—Religious life. I. Title.

PACKER, Boyd K. 261.8'34'2
Eternal love [by] Boyd K. Packer. Salt Lake City, Deseret Book Co., 1973. 22 p. 16 cm. "Adapted from an address given to students at Brigham Young University." [BX8643.M3P3] 73-88635 ISBN 0-87747-514-8 1.25
1. Marriage—Church of Jesus Christ of Latter-Day Saints. 2. Love. I. Title.

RIGA, Peter J. 261.8'34'2
Problems of marriage and sexuality today [by] Peter J. Riga. [1st ed.] New York, Exposition Press [1973] 126 p. 21 cm. [HQ35.R55] 73-155136 ISBN 0-682-47638-2 5.00
1. Sex instruction for youth. 2. Marriage counseling. I. Title.

SEX, marriage, and family : a contemporary Christian perspective / edited by Cedric W. Tilberg. [New York] : Lutheran Church in America, Division for Mission in North America, [1975] 93 p. ; 20 cm. (Christian social responsibility) Includes bibliographical references. [BV835.S45] 75-320695 pbk. : 1.50 261.8'34'2
1. Marriage. 2. Sex (Theology) 3. Family. I. Tilberg, Cedric W. II. Series.

SHANAHAN, Louise. 261.8'34'2
All about Eve ... and Adam and Jane and Johnnie. Liguori, Mo., Liguori Publications [1972] 192 p. 18 cm. [HQ10.S157] 72-91081 1.75
1. Family life education. 2. Marriage—Catholic Church. I. Title.

STATON, Knofel. 261.8'34'2
Home can be a happy place / by Knofel Staton. Cincinnati : New Life Books, 1975. 112 p. ; 18 cm. [BV835.S84] 74-84669 ISBN 0-87239-009-8 pbk. : 1.50
1. Marriage. 2. Family—Religious life. I. Title.

STRAUSS, Richard L. 261.8'34'2
Marriage is for love [by] Richard L. Strauss. Wheaton, Ill., Tyndale House Publishers [1973] 116 p. 22 cm. Includes bibliographical references. [HQ728.S863] 73-81007 ISBN 0-8423-4180-3 2.95
1. Marriage. I. Title.

TOMPKINS, Iverna. 261.8'34'2
How to be happy in no man's land : a book for singles / by Iverna Tompkins, with Irene Burk Harrell. Plainfield, N.J. : Logos International, [1975] xii, 132 p. ; 21 cm. [HQ800.T65] 74-31676 pbk. : 3.50
1. Single women. 2. Divorcees. I. Harrell, Irene Burk, joint author. II. Title.

TRIMMER, Ellen McKay. 261.8'34'2
You and yours; building interpersonal relationships. Chicago, Moody Press [1972] 224 p. 22 cm. Bibliography: p. 214-219. [HQ734.T84] 78-175498 ISBN 0-8024-9820-5 3.95
1. Family. 2. Marriage. 3. Interpersonal relations. 4. Christian life. I. Title.

WRENN, Lawrence G. 261.8'34'2
Divorce and remarriage in the Catholic Church. Edited by Lawrence G. Wrenn. New York, Newman Press [1973] viii, 152 p. 23 cm. Includes bibliographical references. [BX2250.W73] 73-75744 ISBN 0-8091-0183-1 4.95
1. Marriage—Catholic Church. 2. Divorce. I. Title.

HILLMAN, Eugene. 261.8'34'223096
Polygamy reconsidered : African plural marriage and the Christian churches / Eugene Hillman. Maryknoll, N.Y. : Orbis Books, c1975. x, 266 p. ; 22 cm. Includes index. Bibliography: p. 241-259. [BT707.5.H54] 74-19967 ISBN 0-88344-391-0 : 15.00
1. Christianity and polygamy. 2. Polygamy—Africa, Sub-Saharan. I. Title.

REIMANN, Paul E., 1904- 261.8'34'223
Plural marriage, limited, by Paul E. Reimann. [Salt Lake City, Printed by Utah Print. Co., 1974] xiv, 286 p. 24 cm. [BX8641.R47] 74-166198
1. Marriage—Church of Jesus Christ of Latter-Day Saints. 2. Polygamy. I. Title.

BOYLE, John P. 261.8'34'26
The sterlization controversy : a new crisis for the Catholic hospital? / By John P. Boyle. New York : Paulist Press, c1977. ix, 101 p. ; 21 cm. (An Exploration book) Includes bibliographical references and index. [RD585.B69] 77-7378 ISBN 0-8091-2016-X pbk. : 3.50
1. Sterlization (Birth control)—Moral and religious aspects—Catholic Church. 2. Catholic hospitals. I. Title.

QUESNELL, John G. 261.8'34'26
The family planning dilemma revisited / John G. Quesnell. Chicago : Franciscan Herald Press, [1975] p. cm. (Synthesis series) "A supplement to the author's book Marriage: a discovery together." Bibliography: p. [HQ766.3.Q43] 75-1344 ISBN 0-8199-0364-7 pbk. : 0.65
1. Birth control—Religious aspects—Catholic Church. I. Quesnell, John G. Marriage : a discovery together. II. Title.

SUBBIAH, B. V., 1917- 261.8'34'26
The tragedy of a papal decree (in a crowded world) by B. V. Subbiah. [1st ed.] New York, Vantage Press [1971] 144 p. 21 cm. [HQ766.S8777] 78-28072 3.95
1. Birth control. 2. Birth control—Religious aspects. 3. Population. I. Title.

TROBISCH, Walter. 261.8'34'26
Please help me! Please love me! Downers Grove, Ill., Inter-varsity Press [1970] 63 p. 18 cm. On cover: A Christian view of contraception. [HQ766.3.T65] 73-131592 0.95
1. Birth control—Religious aspects. I. Title. II. Title: A Christian view of contraception.

WOOLSEY, Raymond H. 261.8'342'6
Christian sex & family planning / Raymond H. Woolsey. Washington : Review and Herald Pub. Association, c1974. 64 p. ; 19 cm. [HQ744.W65] 74-16785
1. Marriage. 2. Birth control—Religious aspects. 3. Sex in the Bible. I. Title.

BRANDT, Henry R. 261.8'342'7
I want to enjoy my children : a handbook on parenthood / Henry Brandt, Phil Landrum. Grand Rapids, Mich. : Zondervan Pub. House, [1975] 184 p. ; 21 cm. [HQ772.B6815] 75-21115 pbk. : 2.95
1. Parent and child. 2. Family—Religious life. I. Landrum, Phil, joint author. II. Title.

GAULKE, Earle H. 261.8'342'7
You can have a family where everybody wins / Earl H. Gaulke. St. Louis : Concordia Pub. House, [1975] p. cm. [HQ769.G296] 75-25570 ISBN 0-570-03723-9 : 1.95
1. Children—Management. 2. Parent and child. 3. Family—Religious life. I. Title.

GAULKE, Earle H. 261.8'342'7
You can have a family where everybody wins : Christian perspectives on parent effectiveness training / Earl H. Gaulke. St. Louis : Concordia Pub. House, [1975] 93 p. : ill. ; 21 cm. [HQ769.G296] 75-23574 ISBN 0-570-03723-9 : 1.95
1. Children—Management. 2. Parent and child. 3. Family—Religious life. I. Title.

MACDONALD, Gordon. 261.8'34'27
The effective father / Gordon MacDonald. Wheaton, Ill. : Tyndale House Publishers, 1977. 256 p. ; 22 cm. [HQ756.M2] 76-58136 ISBN 0-8423-0680-3 : 3.95
1. Father and child. 2. Fathers in the Bible. 3. Fathers—Religious life. I. Title.

SMALL, Dwight Hervey. 261.8'34'27
The right to remarry / Dwight Hervey Small. Old Tappan, N.J. : F. H. Revell Co., [1975] 190 p. ; 21 cm. Bibliography: p. 189-190. [HQ824.S57] 75-17655 ISBN 0-8007-0758-3 : 5.95
1. Divorce—Biblical teaching. 2. Remarriage. I. Title.

TROBISCH, Ingrid Hult. 261.8'34'27
The joy of being a woman ... and what a man can do / Ingrid Trobisch. 1st ed. New York : Harper & Row, [1975] xvi, 136 p. : ill. ; 18 cm. (Harper jubilee books ; HJ 13) Bibliography: p. 129-131. [HQ734.T846 1975] 75-9324 ISBN 0-06-068448-8 pbk. : 1.95
1. Marriage. 2. Sex in marriage. 3. Femininity (Psychology) 4. Women—Health and hygiene. I. Title.

WELTER, Paul, 1928- 261.8'34'27
Family problems and predicaments : how to respond / by Paul Welter. Wheaton, Ill. : Tyndale House Publishers, c1977. 255 p. : ill. ; 21 cm. Includes bibliographical references and index. [HQ734.W4843] 77-72444 ISBN 0-8423-0853-9 : 4.95
1. Family. 2. Parent and child. 3. Problem family. I. Title.

WHAT they did right : reflections on parents by their children / edited by Virginia Hearn. Wheaton, Ill. : Tyndale House Publishers, c1974. 294 p. ; 21 cm. [HQ772.W42] 74-23717 ISBN 0-8423-7920-7 : 3.95 261.8'34'27
1. Parent and child—Personal narratives. 2. Children—Religious life—Personal narratives. 3. Family—Religious life—Personal narratives. I. Hearn, Virginia.

WRIGHT, H. Norman. 261.8'34'27
Communication: key to your marriage; practical, Biblical ways to improve communication and enrich your marriage [by] H. Norman Wright. Edited by Fritz Ridenour. Glendale, Calif., G/L Regal Books [1974] 194 p. illus. 20 cm. Bibliography: p. 191-194. [HQ734.W948] 73-88317 ISBN 0-8307-0255-5 1.95 (pbk.)
1. Marriage. 2. Interpersonal relations. I. Title.

HOSIER, Helen Kooiman. 261.8'34'284
The other side of divorce / Helen Kooiman Hosier. New York : Hawthorn Books, c1975. ix, 198 p. ; 21 cm. Includes bibliographical references. [HQ834.H67] 74-15642 ISBN 0-8015-5644-9 : 3.95
1. Divorce—United States. 2. Divorce—Biblical teaching. I. Title.

HUDSON, Robert Lofton. 261.8'34'284
'Til divorce do us part; a Christian looks at divorce, by R. Lofton Hudson. Nashville, T. Nelson [1973] 132 p. 22 cm. Includes bibliographical references. [HQ823.H83] 73-5667 4.95
1. Divorce—United States. I. Title.

MARTIN, Norma. 261.8'34'284
Divorce, a Christian dilemma / Norma Martin and Zola Levitt ; introduction by John R. Martin. Scottdale, Pa. : Herald Press, c1977. 158 p. ; 18 cm. [HQ824.M37] 76-45939 ISBN 0-8361-1808-1 : 1.95
1. Divorce—Biblical teaching. 2. Remarriage. I. Levitt, Zola, joint author. II. Title.

RUE, James J. 261.8'34'284
A catechism for divorced catholics / by James J. Rue and Louise Shanahan. St. Meinrad, Ind. : Abbey Press, 1976. xiii, 66 p. ; 21 cm. [HQ823.R79] 76-16170 ISBN 0-87029-063-0 : 1.95
1. Divorcees. 2. Marriage—Catholic Church. 3. Divorce (Canon law) I. Shanahan, Louise, joint author. II. Title.

RUE, James J. 261.8'34'284
The divorced Catholic, by James J. Rue and Louise Shanahan. Paramus, N.J., Paulist Press [1972] viii, 312 p. 18 cm. (Deus books) Bibliography: p. 308-312. [HQ823.R8] 70-184990 1.95
1. Divorce. 2. Marriage—Catholic Church. 3. Divorce (Canon law) I. Shanahan, Louise, joint author. II. Title.

SMOKE, Jim. 261.8'34'284
Growing through divorce / by Jim Smoke. Irvine, Calif. : Harvest House, c1976. 168 p. ; 21 cm. Bibliography: p. 167-168. [HQ814.S66] 76-21980 ISBN 0-89081-081-8 : 2.95
1. Divorce. I. Title.

ALLEN, Charles Livingstone, 1913- 261.8'34'2860924
12 ways to solve your problem. [Westwood, N. J.] Revell [1961] 64p. 17cm. [BV4908.5.A43] 61-14589
1. Peace of mind. I. Title.

DECKER, Beatrice. 261.8'34'2860924
After the flowers have gone, by Beatrice Decker as told to Gladys Kooiman. Grand Rapids, Zondervan Pub. House [1973] 184 p. 21 cm. Bibliography: p. 183-184. [BV4908.D4] 73-2668 3.95
1. Decker, Beatrice. 2. Theos Foundation. 3. Church work with the bereaved. I. Kooiman, Gladys. II. Title.

PENDLETON, Winston K 261.8'34'2860924
Aw, stop worryin', by Winston K. Pendleton. St. Louis, Bethany Press [1966] 80 p. 21 cm. [BV4908.5.P43] 66-19811
1. Peace of mind. I. Title.

STEPHENS, Simon. 261.8'34'286
Death comes home. [1st American ed.] New York, Morehouse-Barlow Co. [1973, c1972] xv, 110 p. 19 cm. Bibliography: p. 109-110. [BV4907.S7 1973] 73-84094 ISBN 0-8192-1137-0 2.50 (pbk.).
1. Bereavement. 2. Consolation. 3. Death. I. Title.

LUKA, Ronald. 261.8'34'29
When a Christian and a Jew marry, by Ronald Luka. With a Jewish perspective by Bernard M. Zlotowitz. New York, Paulist Press [1973] v, 89 p. 19 cm. (Deus books) [HQ1031.L85] 73-77393 ISBN 0-8091-1748-7 1.25 (pbk.)
1. Marriage, Mixed. 2. Marriage—Jews. I. Zlotowitz, Bernard M. II. Title.

SAYERS, Stanley E., 1933- 261.8'34'31
Bridging the generation gap and bringing it back to God / by Stanley E. Sayers. Nashville, Tenn. : Gospel Advocate Co., 1975. ix, 169 p. ; 23 cm. Bibliography: p. 166-169. [BV4531.2.S29] 75-34639 ISBN 0-89225-201-4
1. Youth—Religious life. 2. Conflict of generations. I. Title.

SLATER, Peter Gregg, 1940- 261.8'34'314
Children in the New England mind : in death and in life / by Peter Gregg Slater. Hamden, Conn. : Archon Books, 1977. p. cm. Includes index. Bibliography: p. [BV4907.S58] 77-7352 ISBN 0-208-01652-X : 14.50
1. Children—Death and future state. 2. Children (Christian theology)—History of doctrines. 3. Children—Management. 4. Puritans—New England. I. Title.

BOLTON, Stacey. 261.8'34'315
Randy, please call home / by Stacey and Lee Bolton. Wheaton, Ill. : Tyndale House, 1975. 119 p. ; 18 cn, Includes bibliographical references. [BV4447.B65] 74-19643 ISBN 0-8423-5140-X pbk. : 1.45
1. Bolton, Stacey. 2. Church work with youth. 3. Hippies—Religious life. I. Bolton, Lee, joint author. II. Title.

DRANE, James F. 261.8'34'315
A new American reformation; a study of youth culture and religion, by James Drane. New York, Philosophical Library [1973] 166 p. 23 cm. Includes bibliographical references. [HQ799.7.D7] 73-82161 ISBN 0-8022-2123-8 7.50
1. Young adults—United States. 2. Youth—Religious life. 3. Jesus People. I. Title.

FORD, Clay. 261.8'34'315
Berkeley journal; Jesus and the street people—a firsthand report. [1st ed.] New York, Harper & Row [1972] xii, 109 p. 22 cm. [BV4447.F65 1972] 77-163165 4.95
1. Church work with youth—Berkeley, Calif. I. Title.

TOWNS, Elmer L. 261.8'34'315
Successful Biblical youth work, by Elmer L. Towns. [Rev. ed.] Nashville, Impact Books [1973] 375 p. illus. 24 cm. Published in 1966 under title: Successful youth work. Bibliography: p. 371-373. [BV4447.T68 1973] 73-75988 5.95
1. Church work with youth. I. Title.

DOW, Robert Arthur. 261.8'34'34
"Ministry with single adults" / by Robert Arthur Dow. Valley Forge, Pa. : Judson Press, [1977] p. cm. [BV639.S5D69] 76-48518 ISBN 0-8170-0693-1 pbk. : 5.95
1. Church work with single people. I. Title.

DOW, Robert Arthur. 261.8'34'34
"Ministry with single adults" / by Robert Arthur Dow. Valley Forge, Pa. : Judson Press, [1977] p. cm. [BV639.S5D69] 76-48518 ISBN 0-8170-0693-1 pbk. : 5.95
1. Church work with single people. I. Title.

COOK, Thomas C. 261.8'34'35
The religious sector explores its mission in aging : a report on the survey of programs for the aging under religious auspices / by Thomas C. Cook, Jr. [Athens, Ga.] : National Interfaith Coalition on Aging, 1976. xiv, 84 p. : ill. ; 29 cm. Includes bibliographical references. [BV4435.C66] 77-368627 15.00
1. Church work with the aged. I. National Interfaith Coalition on Aging. II. Title.

COOK, Thomas C. 261.8'34'35
The religious sector explores its mission in aging : a report on the survey of programs for

the aging under religious auspices / by Thomas C. Cook, Jr. [Athens, Ga.] : National Interfaith Coalition on Aging, 1976. xiv, 164, 84 p. : ill. ; 29 cm. Includes bibliographical references. [BV4435.C66] 77-368627 15.00
1. Church work with the aged. I. National Interfaith Coalition on Aging. II. Title.

REICHERT, Sara. 261.8'34'35
In wisdom and the spirit : a religious education program for those over sixty-five / by Sara and Richard Reichert. New York : Paulist Press, c1976. 87 p. : ill. ; 23 cm. Bibliography: p. 86-87. [BV1489.R44] 76-14221 ISBN 0-8091-1969-2 pbk. : 3.95
1. Christian education of the aged. 2. Aged—Religious life. I. Reichert, Richard, joint author. II. Title.

SEMINAR on 261.8'34'35
Responsibility of Churches to the Aging, Park City, Utah, 1968.
Proceedings. [Salt Lake City, Division of Continuing Education, University of Utah, 1968?] viii, 92 p. 28 cm. "Sponsored by: University of Utah, Division of Continuing Education, Utah Council on Aging, [and] churches of Utah." [BV4435.S45 1968] 72-612543
1. Church work with the aged—Congresses. 2. Aged—Congresses. I. Utah. University. Division of Continuing Education.

UNITED Church of 261.8'34'350973
Christ. Vermont Conference. Dept. of Christian Education.
Understanding aging, prepared by the Department of Christian Education of the Vermont Conference, United Church of Christ. Edited by Pamela L. Parker. Philadelphia, Published for Joint Educational Development by United Church Press [1974] 47 p. illus. 21 cm. (A Shalom resource) Bibliography: p. 43-47. [HQ1064.U5U5 1974] 74-8795 ISBN 0-8298-0291-6 2.50 (pbk.).
1. Aged—United States—Juvenile literature. 2. Old age—Juvenile literature. I. Parker, Pamela L., 1943- ed. II. Joint Educational Development. III. Title.

BATEY, Richard A., 261.8'34'41
1933-
Jesus and the poor [by] Richard Batey. [1st ed.] New York, Harper & Row [1972] xi, 114 p. 22 cm. Includes bibliographical references. [BV639.P6B38 1972] 70-160637 4.95
1. Church and the poor—History. I. Title.

KELLY, George 261.8'34'41
Anthony, 1916-
The Catholic Church and the American poor / George A. Kelly. New York : Alba House, [1976] p. cm. Includes bibliographical references. [BV639.P6K42] 75-16293 ISBN 0-8189-0321-X : 5.95
1. Church and the poor. 2. Poor—United States. 3. Church and social problems—Catholic Church. I. Title.

CARAVAGLIOS, 261.8'34'4930973
Maria Genoino.
The American Catholic Church and the Negro problem in the XVIII-XIX centuries / Maria Genoino Caravaglios ; edited by Ernest L. Unterkoefler. Charleston, S.C. : Caravaglios, [1974] xv, 375 p. : facsims. ; 25 cm. Includes index. Bibliography: p. [353]-368. [HT917.C3C37] 74-195927
1. Slavery and the church—Catholic Church. 2. Slavery in the United States. I. Title.

HARRIS, William 261.8'34'493
Logan, Bp., 1817-1887.
The constitutional powers of the General Conference, with a special application to the subject of slaveholding. Freeport, N.Y., Books for Libraries Press, 1971. 156 p. 23 cm. (The Black heritage library collection) Reprint of the 1860 ed. Includes bibliographical references. [HT917.M4H37 1971] 74-146265 ISBN 0-8369-8740-3
1. Methodist Episcopal Church. General Conference, 1856. 2. Slavery and the church—Methodist Episcopal Church. I. Title. II. Series.

HOSMER, William. 261.8'34'493
Slavery and the church. New York, Negro Universities Press [1969] 200 p. 22 cm. [E449.H823 1969] 70-82465 ISBN 0-8371-1646-5
1. Slavery in the United States—Controversial literature—1853. 2. Slavery and the church. I. Title.

HOSMER, William. 261.83'4'493
Slavery and the church. Freeport, N.Y., Books for Libraries Press, 1970 [c1853] 200 p. 23 cm. (The Black heritage library collection) [E449.H823 1970] 78-133156 ISBN 0-8369-8711-X
1. Slavery in the United States—Controversial literature—1853. 2. Slavery and the church. I. Title. II. Series.

HOW, Samuel 261.83'4'493
Blanchard, 1790-1868.
Slaveholding not sinful. Slavery, the punishment of man's sin, its remedy, the gospel of Christ. Freeport, N.Y., Books for Libraries Press, 1971 [c1855] 136 p. 23 cm. (The Black heritage library collection) "An argument before the General Synod of the Reformed Protestant Dutch Church, October, 1855." Includes bibliographical references. [E449.H842 1971] 70-152922 ISBN 0-8369-8766-7
1. Slavery in the United States—Controversial literature—1856. 2. Slavery—Justification. I. Reformed Church in America. General Synod. II. Title. III. Series.

MATTISON, Hiram, 261.8'34'493
1811-1868.
The impending crisis of 1860; or, The present connection of the Methodist Episcopal Church with slavery. Freeport, N.Y., Books for Libraries Press, 1971. 136 p. 23 cm. (The Black heritage library collection) Reprint of the 1858 ed. Includes bibliographical references. [HT917.M4M35 1971] 75-149870 ISBN 0-8369-8750-0
1. Slavery and the church—Methodist Episcopal Church. I. Title. II. Series.

[NEWCOMB, Harvey, 261.83'4'493
1803-1863]
The "Negro pew": being an inquiry concerning the propriety of distinctions in the house of God, on account of color. Freeport, N.Y., Books for Libraries Press, 1971. 108 p. 23 cm. (The Black heritage library collection) Reprint of the 1837 ed. [E185.7.N48 1971] 76-149873 ISBN 0-8369-8753-5
1. Negroes—Religion. 2. Negroes—Segregation. I. Title. II. Series.

SCHERER, Lester 261.8'34'4930973
B., 1931-
Slavery and the churches in early America, 1619-1819 / by Lester B. Scherer Grand Rapids : Eerdmans, [1975] 163 p. ; 23 cm. Includes bibliographical references and index. [HT913.S33] 75-5817 ISBN 0-8028-1580-4 : 7.95
1. Slavery and the Church. 2. Slavery in the United States—History. I. Title.

STANGE, Douglas 261.8'34'4930973
C.
Patterns of antislavery among American Unitarians, 1831-1860 / Douglas C. Stange. Rutherford, N.J. : Fairleigh Dickinson University Press, c1977. p. cm. A revision of the author's thesis, Harvard University. Includes index. Bibliography: p. [E449.S898] 75-18245 ISBN 0-8386-1797-2 : 15.00
1. Slavery in the United States—Anti-slavery movements. 2. Slavery and the church—Unitarian churches. 3. Abolitionists—United States. I. Title.

LINKH, Richard M. 261.8'34'5
American Catholicism and European immigrants, 1900-1924 / by Richard M. Linkh. 1st ed. Staten Island, N.Y. : Center for Migration Studies, 1975. x, 200 p. ; 23 cm. Bibliography: p. 198-200. [BX1407.I45L56] 74-79914 ISBN 0-913256-17-X : 7.95
1. Catholics in the United States. 2. United States—Emigration and immigration. I. Title.

CAMPBELL, Charles 261.8'34'51
Grimshaw, 1912-1953.
Race and religion. Westport, Conn., Greenwood Press [1970] viii, 238 p. 23 cm. Reprint of the 1953 ed. Includes bibliographical references. [BL65.R3C3 1970] 71-104256 ISBN 0-8371-3262-2
1. Religion and race. I. Title.

GILMORE, J. Herbert. 261.8'34'51
When love prevails; a pastor speaks to a church in crisis [by] J. Herbert Gilmore. Grand Rapids, Eerdmans [1971] 141 p. 23 cm. "Sermons were preached in the First Baptist Church in Birmingham, Alabama." [BT734.2.G53] 70-162039 3.95
1. Sermons, American. 2. Baptists—Sermons. 3. Church and race problems—Sermons. I. Title.

REIST, Benjamin A. 261.8'34'51
Theology in red, white, and black / by Benjamin A. Reist. Philadelphia : Westminster Press, [1975] 203 p. ; 22 cm. Includes bibliographical references. [BT734.R44] 74-27936 ISBN 0-664-20723-5 : 7.50
1. Race (Theology) I. Title.

VERKUYL, Johannes. 261.8'34'51
Break down the walls; a Christian cry for racial justice. Edited and translated by Lewis B. Smedes. Grand Rapids, W. B. Eerdmans Pub. Co. [1973] 166 p. 21 cm. Translation of Breek de muren af! Om gerechtigheid in de rassenverhoudingen. [BT734.2.V4513] 72-93620 2.95 (pbk.)
1. Church and race problems. I. Title.

CAMPBELL, Will D., 261.8'34'51042
comp.
The failure and the hope; essays of Southern churchmen. Edited, with an introd., by Will D. Campbell and James Y. Holloway. Grand Rapids, Eerdmans [1972] 266 p. 21 cm. "All the essays ... appeared first ... in Katallagete—Be reconciled, the journal of the Committee of Southern Churchmen." [BT734.2.C25] 72-75575 ISBN 0-8028-1479-4 3.95
1. Church and race problems—Addresses, essays, lectures. I. Holloway, James Y., 1927- joint comp. II. Katallagete. III. Title.
Contents Omitted.

HUMAN relations 261.8'34'51042
and the South African scene in the light of scripture : official translation of the report Ras, volk en nasie en volkereverhoudinge in die lig van die Skrif : approved and accepted by the General Synod of the Dutch Reformed Church, October 1974. Cape Town : Dutch Reformed Church Publishers, 1976. 100 p. ; 22 cm. [BS680.R2R3713] 77-463450 ISBN 0-86991-158-9
1. Reformed Church in South Africa. 2. Race (Theology)—Biblical teaching. 3. Church and social problems—South Africa. 4. Church and race problems—South Africa. I. Nederduits Gereformeerde Kerk (South Africa). Algemene Sinode.

INGRAM, Tolbert 261.8'34'51042
Robert, 1913- ed.
Essays on segregation, edited by T. Robert Ingram. [Rev. ed.] Houston [Tex., St. Thomas Press, 1960 [i.e. 1963] iv, 108 p. 19 cm. [BT734.3.I 5] 66-3174
1. Segregation — Religious aspects. I. Title.

MARTIN, William 261.8'34'51042
Curtis, 1937-
Christians in conflict, by William C. Martin. [Chicago, Center for the Scientific Study of Religion, 1972] vi, 106 p. 23 cm. (Studies in religion and society) Bibliography: p. 101-106. [BT734.2.M26] 72-88018 ISBN 0-913348-01-5
1. Alinsky, Saul David, 1909- 2. Church and race problems—Rochester, N.Y. 3. Clergy—New York—Rochester. I. Title. II. Series: Studies in religion and society series.

NELSON, 261.8'34'510420973
William Stuart, 1895- ed.
The Christian way in race relations. Freeport, N.Y., Books for Libraries Press [1971, c1948] ix, 256 p. 23 cm. (Essay index reprint series) "The result of a co-operative enterprise on the part of the members of the Institute of Religion [Howard University]" Includes bibliographical references. [BT734.2.N44 1971] 79-134121 ISBN 0-8369-2004-X
1. U.S.—Race question. 2. Church and race problems—U.S. I. Institute of Religion, Howard University, Washington, D.C. II. Title.

ROBERTS, James 261.8'34'51042
Deotis.
Liberation and reconciliation: a Black theology, by J. Deotis Roberts. Philadelphia, Westminster Press [1971] 205 p. 19 cm. Includes bibliographical references. [BT734.2.R6] 73-140601 ISBN 0-664-24911-6 3.50
1. Race (Theology) 2. Negroes—Religion. I. Title. II. Title: Black theology.

SALLEY, Columbus. 261.8'34'51042
Your God is too white [by] Columbus Salley & Ronald Behm. Downers Grove, Ill., Inter-Varsity Press [1970] 114 p. 21 cm. Includes bibliographical references. [BT734.2.S25] 76-132957 ISBN 0-87784-478-X
1. Race (Theology) I. Behm, Ronald, joint author. II. Title.

SCHULZE, Andrew. 261.8'34'51042
Race against time; a history of race relations in the Lutheran Church—Missouri Synod from the perspective of the author's involvement, 1920-1970. Valparaiso, Ind., Lutheran Human Relations Association of America [1972] ix, 153 p. illus. 23 cm. [BT734.2.S33] 72-171264 2.00
1. Lutheran Church—Missouri Synod. 2. Church and race problems—United States. I. Title.

SHOCKLEY, Donald 261.8'34'51042
G., 1937-
Free, white, and Christian [by] Donald G. Shockley. Nashville, Abingdon Press [1975] 142 p. 20 cm. Includes bibliographical references. [BR517.S42] 74-19276 ISBN 0-687-13502-8 3.50 (pbk.)
1. Church and race problems—United States. 2. Protestant churches—United States. 3. United States—Race question. I. Title.

SPEAKS, Ruben Lee. 261.8'34'51042
The church and Black liberation. [Charlotte, N.C., 1973] 94 p. 22 cm. Bibliography: p. 94. [BV600.2.S65] 73-161347
1. Church. 2. Negro churches—United States. 3. Sermons, American. I. Title.

WINTER, Colin 261.8'34'5109688
O'Brien.
Namibia / by Colin O'Brien Winter. Grand Rapids, MI : Eerdmans, c1977. v, 234 p. ; 22 cm. [DT709.W56] 76-56830 pbk. : 3.95
1. Winter, Colin O'Brien. 2. Church of England—Bishops—Biography. 3. Africa, Southwest—Race relations. 4. Church and race problems—Africa, Southwest. 5. Bishops—Africa, Southwest—Biography. I. Title.

TOMASI, 261.8'34'515107471
Silvano M.
Piety and power; the role of the Italian parishes in the New York metropolitan area, 1880-1930, by Silvano M. Tomasi. 1st ed. [Staten Island, N.Y.], Center for Migration Studies, 1975. xi, 201 p. 24 cm. Bibliography: p. 187-201. [BX1407.I8T65] 74-79913 9.95.
1. Catholics, Italian. 2. Catholics in the United States. 3. Catholic Church in the United States. 4. Italian Americans—New York metropolitan area. 5. Parishes—New York metropolitan area. I. Title.

ORTEGON, 261.8'34'516872079494
Samuel M.
Mexican religious population of Los Angeles, by Samuel M. Ortegon. [San Francisco, R and E Research Associates, 1972] iv, 52 p. illus. 28 cm. On cover: The religious status of the Mexican population of Los Angeles. Thesis (M.A.)—University of Southern California, 1932. Bibliography: p. 51-52. [BR560.L67O77 1972] 79-147290 ISBN 0-88247-196-1
1. Los Angeles—Religion. 2. Mexican Americans—California—Los Angeles. I. Title. II. Title: The religious status of the Mexican population of Los Angeles.

BALTAZAR, Eulalio 261.8'34'5196
R.
The dark center; a process theology of Blackness [by] Eulalio R. Baltazar. New York, Paulist Press [1973] 181 p. 23 cm. Includes bibliographical references. [BT734.B3] 73-83811 ISBN 0-8091-1788-6 4.95
1. Race (Theology) 2. Black (in religion, folk-lore, etc.) 3. Symbolism. I. Title.

BARNHART, Phil. 261.8'34'5196073
Don't call me preacher; for laymen and other ministers. Atlanta, Forum House [1972, i.e. 1973] 118 p. 23 cm. [BX8495.B326A33] 72-87066 ISBN 0-8028-1517-0 3.95
1. East Lake Church, Atlanta. 2. Church and race problems—Atlanta. I. Title.

CLEVELAND, 261.8'34'5196073
Edward Earl.
Living soul; "we shall overcome" [by] E. E. Cleveland. Nashville, Southern Pub. Association [1974] 219 p. illus. 21 cm. [BX6123.C56] 73-91286 ISBN 0-8127-0078-3 1.95 (pbk.).
1. Seventh-Day Adventists—Sermons. 2. Sermons, American. 3. United States—Race question. I. Title.

CONE, James H. 261.8'34'5196073
God of the oppressed / James H. Cone. New York : Seabury Press, [1975] viii, 280 p. ; 22 cm. "A Crossroad book." Includes bibliographical references and index. [BT83.57.C67] 74-31474 ISBN 0-8164-0263-9 : 9.95
1. Liberation theology—Addresses, essays, lectures. 2. Negroes—Religion—Addresses, essays, lectures. 3. Theology—Addresses, essays, lectures. I. Title.

CROOK, William 261.8'34'5196073
H., 1925-
Seven who fought [by] William H. Crook [and] Ross Coggins. Waco, Tex., Word Books [1971] 143 p. 23 cm. [BT734.2.C7] 78-91712 4.95
1. Church and race problems—U.S.—Case studies. I. Coggins, Ross, joint author. II. Title.

FIFE, Robert O. 261.8'34'5196073
Teeth on edge [by] Robert O. Fife. Grand Rapids, Mich., Baker Book House [1971] 135 p. 21 cm. Includes bibliographical references. [BT734.2.F5] 76-143277 ISBN 0-8010-3450-7 1.95
1. Church and race problems—U.S. I. Title.

*FIGART, Thomas 261.8'345196073
O.
A Biblical perspective on the race problem. Grand Rapids, Mich., Baker Book House [1973] 185 p. 20 cm. Bibliography: p. 171-176. [BR563] ISBN 0-8010-3457-4 3.95 (pbk.)
1. Race—Biblical teaching. 2. Church and social problems. I. Title.

GUTTERIDGE, 261.8'345'1924043
Richard Joseph Cooke.
The German Evangelical Church and the Jews, 1879-1950 / Richard Gutteridge. New York : Barnes & Noble Books, 1976. 374 p. ;

22 cm. Includes index. Bibliography: p. [358]-370. [DS146.G4G87] 76-12068 ISBN 0-06-492620-6 : 18.50
1. Antisemitism—Germany. 2. Christianity and antisemitism. 3. Protestant churches—Germany. 4. Germany—Church history—1933-1945. I. Title.

GUTTERIDGE, 261.8'34'51924043
Richard Joseph Cooke.
Open thy mouth for the dumb! : the German Evangelical church and the Jews, 1879-1950 / Richard Gutteridge. Oxford : Blackwell, c1976. 374 p. ; 22 cm. Includes index. Bibliography: p. [358]-370. [BX8020.G88] 76-369403 ISBN 0-631-16380-8 : £10.00
1. Deutsche Evangelische Kirche. 2. Christianity and antisemitism. 3. Antisemitism—Germany. 4. Jews in Germany—History—1933-1945. I. Title.

HARRELL, David 261.8'34'5196073
Edwin.
White sects and Black men in the recent South. Foreword by Edwin S. Gaustad. Nashville, Vanderbilt University Press, 1971. xix, 161 p. 21 cm. Bibliography: p. 135-152. [BR535.H37] 72-157742 ISBN 0-8265-1171-6 6.50
1. Sects—Southern States. 2. Church and race problems—Southern States. I. Title.

HARRISON, Bob. 261.8'34'5196073
When God was Black, by Bob Harrison with Jim Montgomery. Grand Rapids, Mich., Zondervan Pub. House [1971] 160 p. 22 cm. [BV3785.H349A3] 70-156250 3.95
1. Church and race problems—United States. 2. Evangelistic work. I. Montgomery, Jim, joint author. II. Title.

HASSKARL, Gottlieb 261.8'34'5196
Christopher Henry, 1855-1929.
"The missing link;" or, The Negro's ethnological status ... Chambersburg, Pa., The Democratic news. [New York, AMS Press, 1972] 176 p. port. 19 cm. "Reprinted from the Eastern Lutheran." Reprint of the 1898 ed. [GN645.H28 1972] 77-144636 ISBN 0-404-00170-X
I. Title.

HODGSON, Peter 261.8'34'5196073
Crafts, 1934-
Children of freedom; Black liberation in Christian perspective [by] Peter C. Hodgson. Foreword by Gayraud S. Wilmore. Philadelphia, Fortress Press [1974] x, 86 p. 18 cm. Includes bibliographical references. [BT810.H63] 74-76930 ISBN 0-8006-1304-X 2.95 (pbk.)
1. Freedom (Theology) I. Title.

JACKSON, Warner. 261.8'34'5196073
Theology: White, Black, or Christian? Scottdale, Pa., Herald Press, 1974. 47 p. 18 cm. (Focal pamphlet no. 25) [BT734.J3] 74-6543 ISBN 0-8361-1743-3 0.75
1. Race (Theology) I. Title.

JACKSON, Warner. 261.8'34'5196073
Theology: White, Black, or Christian? Scottdale, Pa., Herald Press, 1974. 47 p. 18 cm. (Focal pamphlet no. 25) [BT734.J3] 74-6543 ISBN 0-8361-1743-3 0.75 (pbk.)
1. Race (Theology) I. Title.

JONES, Howard O. 261.8'34'5196073
White questions to a Black Christian / by Howard O. Jones. Grand Rapids, Mich. : Zondervan Pub. House, [1975] 215 p. ; 18 cm. Bibliography: p. 211-215. [BR563.N4J63] 74-11859 pbk. : 1.75
1. Negroes—Religion. I. Title.

LABBE, 261'.8'34'51960730763
Dolores Egger.
Jim Crow comes to church; the establishment of segregated Catholic parishes in South Louisiana. 2d ed. Lafayette, University of Southwestern Louisiana, 1971. 104 p. 23 cm. (The USL history series, no. 4) Bibliography: p. 96-100. [BX1415.L9L3] 73-620838
1. Catholic Church in Louisiana. 2. Church and race problems—Louisiana. I. Title. II. Series: Louisiana. University of Southwestern Louisiana, Lafayette. The U.S.L. history series, no. 4.

LITTELL, Franklin 261.8'34'51924
Hamlin.
The crucifixion of the Jews / Franklin H. Littell. 1st ed. New York : Harper & Row, [1975] 153 p. ; 22 cm. Includes bibliographical references. [BM535.L53 1975] 74-32288 ISBN 0-06-065251-9 : 7.95
1. Christianity and antisemitism. I. Title.

LOESCHER, Frank 261.8'34'5196073
Samuel.
The Protestant church and the Negro; a pattern of segregation, by Frank S. Loescher. With a foreword by William Scarlett. Westport, Conn., Negro Universities Press [1971, c1948] 159 p. 23 cm. Includes bibliographical references. [BR563.N4L6 1971] 76-135601 ISBN 0-8371-5193-7
1. United States—Race question. 2. Protestant churches—United States. 3. Negroes. I. Title.

PARKES, James 261.8'34'51924
William, 1896-
The conflict of the church and the synagogue : a study of the origins of antisemitism / James Parkes. New York : Hermon Press, 1974. xxiv, 430 p. ; 24 cm. Reprint of the 1934 ed. published by the Soncino Press, London. Originally presented as the author's thesis, Oxford. Includes bibliographical references. [BM535.P195 1974] 74-78327 ISBN 0-87203-043-1 : 14.95
1. Christianity and antisemitism. 2. Judaism—Relations—Christianity. 3. Christianity and other religions—Judaism. I. Title.

RUETHER, Rosemary 261.8'34'51924
Radford.
Faith and fratricide: the theological roots of anti-Semitism. New York, Seabury Press [1974] ix, 294 p. 22 cm. "A Crossroad book." [BM535.R8] 74-11341 ISBN 0-8164-1183-2 9.50
1. Christianity and antisemitism—History. I. Title.

SKINNER, Tom, 261.8'34'5196073
1942-
If Christ is the answer, what are the questions? / Tom Skinner. Grand Rapids : Zondervan Pub. House, [1974] 219 p. ; 21 cm. [BV4501.2.S475] 73-22696 pbk. : 2.95
1. Christian life—1960- 2. Church and social problems. 3. Negroes—Religion. I. Title.

SMITH, Hilrie 261.8'34'5196073075
Shelton, 1893-
In his image, but ... Racism in Southern religion, 1780-1910 [by] H. Shelton Smith. Durham, N.C., Duke University Press, 1972. x, 318 p. 25 cm. Includes bibliographical references. [BT734.2.S56] 72-81338 ISBN 0-8223-0273-X
1. Church and race problems—Southern States. I. Title.

STEWART, John J. 261.8'34'5196073
Mormonism and the Negro; an explanation and defense of the doctrine of the Church of Jesus Christ of Latter-Day Saints in regard to Negroes and others of negroid blood, by John J. Stewart. With a historical supplement, The church and the negroid people, by William E. Berrett. [3d ed. Orem, Utah, Bookmark, 1967, c1960] 55, 23 p. 19 cm. Includes bibliographical references. [BX8643.N4S8 1967] 73-172525
1. Mormons and Mormonism, Negro. I. Berrett, William Edwin. The church and the negroid people. 1967. II. Title.

BETTEN, Neil. 261.8'5
Catholic activism and the industrial worker / Neil Betten. Gainesville : University Presses of Florida, c1976. x, 191 p. ; 24 cm. "A Florida State University book." Includes bibliographical references and index. [HD6338.2.U5B47] 76-17280 ISBN 0-8130-0503-5 : 10.00
1. Church and labor—United States—History. 2. Church and social problems—Catholic Church. I. Title.

BROWNE, Henry Joseph, 261.8'5
1919-
The Catholic Church and the Knights of Labor / Henry J. Browne. New York : Arno Press, 1976, c1949. p. cm. (The Irish Americans) Reprint of the ed. published by Catholic University of America Press, Washington, which was issued as v. 38 of Studies in American church history. Originally presented as the author's thesis, Catholic University of America, 1949. Bibliography: p. [HD6338.2.U5B76 1976] 76-6326 ISBN 0-405-09323-3 : 26.00
1. Knights of Labor—History. 2. Church and labor—United States—History. 3. Church and labor—History. I. Title. II. Series. III. Series: Catholic University of America. Studies in American church history ; v. 38.

CALVEZ, Jean Yves, 1927- 261.85
The church and social justice; the social teaching of the popes from Leo XIII to Pius XII, 1878-1958, by Jean-Yves Calvez, Jacques Perrin. [Tr. by J. R. Kirwan] Chicago, Regnery Co. [1962] 466p. 23cm. 62-52204 7.50
1. Sociology, Christian (Catholic) I. Perrin, Jacques, 1901- joint author. II. Title.

CANTELON, Willard. 261.8'5
Money master of the world / Willard Cantelon. Plainfield, N.J. : Logos International, c1976. vii, 147 p. ; 21 cm. [BS647.2.C36] 75-38197 ISBN 0-88270-151-7 : 5.95 ISBN 0-88270-152-5 pbk. : 2.95
1. Bible—Prophecies. 2. Money. 3. Communism. I. Title.

CHENU, Marie Dominique, 261.85
1895-
The theology of work; an exploration. Tr. by Lilian Soiron. Chicago, Regnery [1966, c.1963] vii, 114p. 18cm. (Logos, 51L-708) Bibl. [BX1753.C4213] 66-3744 1.25 pap.,
1. Sociology, Christian (Catholic) 2. Christianity and economics. 3. Work (Theology) I. Title.

CHRISTIAN values and 261.85
economic life [by] John C. Bennett [and others] [1st ed.] New York, Harper [1954] 272 p. 22 cm. (Series on ethics and economic life) [BR115.E3C5] 54-6443
1. Christianity and economics. I. Bennett, John Coleman, 1902-

CHRISTIAN values and 261.8'5
economic life [by] John C. Bennett [and others] Freeport, N.Y., Books for Libraries Press [1970, c1954] xv, 272 p. 23 cm. (Essay index reprint series) Bibliographical footnotes. [BR115.E3C5 1970] 71-99624
1. Christianity and economics. I. Bennett, John Coleman, 1902-

THE Church and industry 261.8'5
/ edited by Temple Kingston. Windsor, Ont. : Canterbury College, University of Windsor, [1974] xi, 31 p. ; 22 cm. Includes bibliographical references. [BV628.C48] 75-319209
1. Church and industry—Addresses, essays, lectures. I. Kingston, Temple.

CONFERENCE on Business and 261.85
the Social Order, Valparaiso University, 1965.
The Christian in business; thoughts on business and the social order. Andrew J. Buehner, editor. St. Louis, Lutheran Academy for Scholarship [1966] 104 p. 21 cm. [BR115.E3C63 1965d] 66-31669
1. Christianity and economics—Congresses. 2. Business ethics—Congresses. I. Buehner, Andrew J., ed. II. Valparaiso University, Valparaiso, Ind. III. Title.

CONFERENCE on Society, 261.8'5
Development, and Peace, Beirut, 1968.
World development: challenge to the churches; the official report and the papers. Edited by Denys Munby. Washington, Corpus Books [1969] xvi, 208 p. 21 cm. "Held ... under the joint auspices of the Vatican Commission on Peace and Freedom and the World Council of Churches." Includes bibliographical references. [BR115.U6C634 1968] 72-91286 5.95
1. Church and underdeveloped areas—Congresses. I. Munby, Denys Lawrence, ed. II. Vatican Commission on Peace and Freedom. III. World Council of Churches. IV. Title.

DAVIES, Joseph Kenneth, 261.8'5
1925-
Deseret's sons of toil : a history of the worker movement of Territorial Utah / J. Kenneth Davies. Salt Lake City : Olympus Pub. Co., c1976. p. cm. Includes bibliographies and index. [HD6338.2.U52U82] 76-26459 ISBN 0-913420-64-6 : 12.50
1. Church of Jesus Christ of Latter-Day Saints. 2. Church and labor—Utah—History. 3. Trade-unions—Utah—History. I. Title.

DEMANT, Vigo Auguste, 261.85
1893-
Religion and the decline of capitalism. New York, Scribner [1952] 204 p. 23 cm. (The Holland lectures for 1949) [BR115.E3D4 1952a] 52-4544
1. Christianity and economics. I. Title.

DUNN, James M. 261.8'5
Endangered species / James M. Dunn, Ben E. Loring, Phil D. Strickland. Nashville : Broadman Press, c1976. 153 p. : ill. ; 20 cm. Bibliography: p. 151-153. [HD9000.6.D85] 76-27481 ISBN 0-8054-6117-5 pbk. : 2.50
1. Food supply. 2. Church and social problems. I. Loring, Ben E., joint author. II. Strickland, Phil, 1941- joint author. III. Title.

EDWARDS, David Lawrence. 261.85
The state of the nation : a Christian approach to Britain's economic crisis / [by] David L. Edwards. London : Church Information Office for the General Synod Board for Social Responsibility, 1976. [4], 35 p. ; 21 cm. (Anglican comment on current affairs) "An occasional paper of the General Synod Board for Social Responsibility." [HC256.6.E3] 76-363406 ISBN 0-7151-6546-1 : £0.45
1. Great Britain—Economic conditions—1945- 2. Church and social problems—Church of England. I. Title.

EISENSTADT, Shmuel Noah, 261.8'5
1923- comp.
The Protestant ethic and modernization; a comparative view, edited by S. N. Eisenstadt. New York, Basic Books [1968] viii, 407 p. 25 cm. Bibliography: p. 385-400. [BR115.E3E4] 68-16156
1. Weber, Max, 1864-1920. 2. Christian ethics. 3. Social ethics. 4. Christianity and economics. I. Title.

FAITH-MAN-NATURE Group. 261.8'5
Christians and the good earth; addresses and discussions at the third national conference of the Faith-Man-Nature Group. Alexandria, Va. [1968?] 190 p. 20 cm. (Its F/M/N papers, no. 1) [S912.F33] 75-5459 1.25
1. Conservation of natural resources—Religious aspects—Congresses. I. Title. II. Series.

FLORIDI, Ulisse Alessio, 261.8'5
1920-
The uncertain alliance: the Catholic Church and labor in Latin America [by] Alexis U. Floridi [and] Annette E. Stiefbold. Coral Gables, Fla., Center for Advanced International Studies, University of Miami [1973] vii, 108 p. 23 cm. (Monographs in international affairs) Includes bibliographical references. [HD6338.2.L3F54] 73-92382 4.95
1. Church and labor—Latin America. I. Stiefbold, Annette E., joint author. II. Title. III. Series.

FREUDENBERGER, C. Dean, 261.8'5
1930-
Christian responsibility in a hungry world / C. Dean Freudenberger, Paul M. Minus. Nashville : Abingdon, c1976. 128 p. ; 19 cm. Bibliography: p. 125-128. [HD9000.5.F74] 75-43764 ISBN 0-687-07567-X pbk. : 2.50
1. Food supply. 2. Church and social problems—United States. I. Minus, Paul M., joint author. II. Title.

FULLER, Reginald Horace. 261.8'5
Christianity and the affluent society, by Reginald H. Fuller and Brian K. Rice. Grand Rapids, W. B. Eerdmans Pub. Co. [1967, c1966] 191 p. 23 cm. [BR115.E3F8 1967] 67-19337
1. Christianity and economics. 2. Christian giving. I. Rice, Brian Keith, 1932- II. Title.

GLADDEN, Washington, 261.8'5
1836-1918.
Tools and the man : property and industry under the Christian law / by Washington Gladden. Westport, Conn. : Hyperion Press, 1975. p. cm. (The Radical tradition in America) Reprint of the 1893 ed. published by Houghton, Mifflin, Boston, in series: Lyman Beecher lectures, 1886-87. [HB171.G49 1975] 75-353 ISBN 0-88355-222-1
1. Economics. 2. Sociology, Christian. 3. Socialism, Christian. I. Title. II. Series: Lyman Beecher lectures ; 1886-87.

GLADDEN, Washington, 261.8'5
1836-1918.
Tools and the man : property and industry under the Christian law / by Washington Gladden. Westport, Conn. : Hyperion Press, 1975. p. cm. (The Radical tradition in America) Reprint of the 1893 ed. published by Houghton, Mifflin, Boston, in series: Lyman Beecher lectures, 1886-87. [HB171.G49 1975] 75-353 ISBN 0-88355-222-1 : 19.00
1. Economics. 2. Sociology, Christian. 3. Socialism, Christian. I. Title. II. Series: Lyman Beecher lectures ; 1886-87.

GREEN, Robert W., ed. 261.85
Protestantism and capitalism; the Weber thesis and its critics. Boston, Heath [1959] xii, 116 p. 24 cm. (Problems in European civilization) Second ed. published in 1973 under title: Protestantism, capitalism, and social science. "Suggestions for additional reading": p. 115-116. [BR115.E3G7] 59-8437
1. Capitalism. 2. Christianity and economics. 3. Protestantism. I. Title. II. Series.

GREEN, Robert W., ed. 261.8'5
Protestantism, capitalism, and social science; the Weber thesis controversy. Edited and with an introd. by Robert W. Green. 2d ed. Lexington, Mass., Heath [1973] xviii, 195 p. 21 cm. (Problems in European civilization) Published in 1959 under title: Protestantism and capitalism. [BR115.E3G7 1973] 72-13639 ISBN 0-669-81737-6
1. Weber, Max, 1864-1920. Die protestantische Ethik und der Geist des Kapitalismus—Addresses, essays, lectures. 2. Christianity and economics—Addresses, essays, lectures. 3. Religion and sociology—Addresses, essays, lectures. 4. Capitalism—Addresses, essays, lectures. I. Title. II. Series. Contents omitted.

HARRISON, Anthony John, 261.85
1938-
The framework of economic activity: the international economy and the rise of the state in the twentieth century [by] Anthony Harrison. London, Melbourne [etc.] Macmillan; New York, St. Martin's P., 1967. c.xiii, 189 p. 21 cm. (The Making of the twentieth century) 25/-(12/6 pbk.)

Bibliography: p. [171]-181. [HC54.H27] 67-11419
1. Economic history — 20th cent. 2. Industry and state. I. Title.

HENGEL, Martin. 261.8'5
Property and riches in the early church : aspects of a social history of early Christianity / Martin Hengel ; translated by John Bowden from the German. 1st American ed. Philadelphia : Fortress Press, 1974. viii, 96 p. ; 22 cm. Translation of Eigentum und Reichtum in der fruhen Kirche. Includes bibliographical references. [BR166.H4513 1974] 75-305658 ISBN 0-8006-1201-9 pbk. : 2.95
1. Property—Moral and religious aspects—History. 2. Wealth, Ethics of—History. 3. Sociology, Christian—Early church, ca. 30-600. I. Title.

HEYNE, Paul T. 261.85
The world of economics. St. Louis, Concordia [1966, c.1965] 117p. 18cm. (Christain encounters) Bibl. [HB171.7.H46] 65-27497 1.00 pap.,
1. Economics. I. Title. II. Series.

HOLLIS, Allen. 261.8'5
The Bible and money / Allen Hollis. New York : Hawthorn Books, c1976. 129 p. ; 21 cm. [BS680.M57H64 1976] 75-41798 ISBN 0-8015-0616-6 pbk.: 3.95
1. Money—Biblical teaching. I. Title.

HOLLIS, Christopher, 1902- 261.85
Christianity and economics. [1st ed.] New York, Hawthorn Books [1961] 112p. 21cm. (Twentieth century encyclopedia of Catholicism, v. 90. Section 9: The church and the modern world) Includes bibliography. [BR115.E3H64] 61-9456
1. Christianity and economics. I. Title.

HOLLIS, Christopher 261.85
[Maurice Christopher Hollis] 1902-
Christianity and economics. New York, Hawthorn Books [c.1961] 112p. (Twentieth century encyclopedia of Catholicism, v. 90. Section 9: The church and the modern world) Bibl. 61-9456 3.50 half cloth,
1. Christianity and economics. I. Title.

HOWARD, Irving E. 261.85
The Christian alternative to socialism [by] Irvin E. Howard. Introd. by Howard E. Kershner. Arlington, Va., Better Bks., 1966 [i.e.1967] xiii, 153p. ports. 21cm. [HX536.H78] 66-29719 2.50 pap.,
1. Socialism and religion. I. Title.

JOHNSON, Tilden W 261.85
Prosperity is Christian duty. Los Angeles, Employment Purchase Expediter [1956] 83p. illus. 22cm. [HN31.T64] 56-23223
1. Church and social problems. 2. Social policy. I. Title.

KAISER, Edwin G. 1893- 261.85
Theology of work, by Edwin G. Kaiser. Westminster. Md., Newman 1966 [i.e.,1967] xxi, 521p. 24cm. Bibl. [BT738.5.K3] 66-16568 10.50
1. Work (Theology) I. Title.

KELLER, Edward A 261.85
Christianity and American capitalism. Chicago, Published for the Council of Business and Professional Men of the Catholic Faith by the Heritage Foundation [1953] 92p. 22cm. [HN37.C3K45] 54-1296
1. Chruch and social problems—Catholic Church. 2. Church and social problems—U. S. I. Title.

KITCH, M. J., comp. 261.8'5
Capitalism and the Reformation. New York, Barnes & Noble [1968, c1967] xx, 217 p. 22 cm. (Problems and perspectives in history) Bibliography: p. 209-212. [BR115.E3K52 1968] 68-2564
1. Protestantism and capitalism. I. Title.

KOSTYU, Frank A. 261.8'5
Shadows in the valley; the story of one man's struggle for justice [by] Frank A. Kostyu. [1st ed.] Garden City, N.Y., Doubleday, 1970. 192 p. maps. 22 cm. [BV2695.M5K6] 79-84388 4.95
1. Krueger, Edgar A. 2. Church work with migrant labor—Rio Grande Valley. 3. Mexicans in the U.S. I. Title.

KUHN, Margaret E., ed. 261.85
Christians in a rapidly changing economy; a study book for reading, discussion, action by church people and groups during the 1963-64 coordinated emphasis in Christian life and work. [New York, Pub. for the Dept. of the Church and Econ. Life, Div. of Christian Life and Work, Natl. Council of the Churches of Christ in the U.S.A. by the Office of Pubn. and Dist., Natl. Council of Churches, 1963] 96p. illus. 23cm. Bibl. 63-5945 1.00
1. Christianity and economics. I. Title. II. Title: Coordinated emphasis in Christian life and work.

LAUBACH, Frank Charles, 261.85
1884-
What Jesus had to say about money, by Frank C. Laubach. Grand Rapids, Zondervan Pub. House [1966] 63 p. 21 cm. [BV772.L36] 64-8845
1. Stewardship, Christian. I. Title.

LAUBACH, Frank Charles, 261.85
1884-
What Jesus had to say about money. Grand Rapids, Mich., Zondervan [c.1966] 63p. 21cm. [BV772.L36] 64-8845 1.00 pap.,
1. Stewardship, Christian. I. Title.

LECLERCQ, Jacques, 1891- 261.85
Christianity and money. Translated from the French by Eric Earnshaw Smith. [1st American ed.] New York, Hawthorn Books [1959] 126p. 22cm. (The Twentieth century encyclopedia of Catholicism, v.59. Section 5: The life of faith) Translation of Le chretien deva at l'argent. Includes bibliography. [HN37.C3L3773] 59-6727
1. Church and social problems—Catholic Church. 2. Christianity and economics. I. Title.

LETTS, Harold C 261.85
Christian action in economic life. Arthur H. Getz, editor. Philadelphia, Muhlenberg Press [1953] 96p. illus. 18cm. [BR115.E3L4] 53-3490
1. Christianity and economics. I. Title.

LEWIS, John, 1889- ed. 261.8'5
Christianity and the social revolution. Edited by John Lewis, Karl Polanyi [and] Donald K. Kitchin. Freeport, N.Y., Books for Libraries Press [1972] 526 p. 23 cm. Reprint of the 1935 ed. Includes bibliographical references. [HX51.L53 1972] 79-37892 ISBN 0-8369-6729-1
1. Socialism, Christian—Addresses, essays, lectures. 2. Communism—Addresses, essays, lectures. 3. Communism and religion—Addresses, essays, lectures. I. Polanyi, Karl, 1886-1964, joint ed. II. Kitchin, Donald K., joint ed. III. Title.

MCLELLAND, Joseph C. 261.85
The other six days; the Christian meaning of work and property. Richmond, John Knox Pr. [1961] 121p. Bibl. 61-6687 1.50 pap.,
1. Christianity and economics. 2. Sociology, Christian. I. Title.

MASSE, Benjamin Louis, 261.85
1905-
Justice for all; an introduction to the social teaching of the Catholic Church. Milwaukee, Bruce [c.1964] ix, 196p. 22cm. Bibl. 64-22860 3.95
1. Church and social problems—Catholic Church. I. Title.

MORGAN, Bruce. 261.85
Christians, the church, and property; ethics and the economy in a supramarket world. Philadelphia, Westminster Press [1963] 304 p.21 cm. Bibliography:286-300. [HB199.M58] 62-15407
1. Christianity and economics. I. Title.

MORGAN, Bruce 261.85
Christians, the church, and property; ethics and the economy in a supermarket world. Philadelphia, Westminster [c.1963] 304p. 21cm. 62-15407 5.95
1. Christianity and economics. I. Title.

MUELDER, Walter George, 261.85
1907-
Religion and economic responsibility. New York, Scribner, 1953. xvii, 264p. 21cm. Bibliography: p. 253-260. [BR115.E3M8] 53-1193
1. Christianity and economics. I. Title.

MUNRO, Duncan. 261.8'5
Trade, justice and the wealth of nations / by Duncan Munro. Bramcote : Grove Books, 1976. 24 p. ; 22 cm. (Grove booklet on ethics ; no. 14 ISSN 0305-4241s) Includes bibliographical references. [HF1411.M854] 77-371341 ISBN 0-905422-00-7 : £0.30
1. International economic relations. 2. Commerce. 3. Justice. I. Title.

NORTH, Gary. 261.8'5
An introduction to Christian economics. [Nutley, N.J.] Craig Press, 1973. xii, 413 p. 23 cm. Includes bibliographical references. [BR115.E3N6] 73-75292 9.95
1. Christianity and economics. I. Title.

NOYES, John Humphrey, 261.85
1811-1886
History of American socialism. New introd. by Mark Holloway [Magnolia, Mass., P. Smith, 1967, c.1966] xxii, 678p. 21cm. (Dover bk. rebound) Unaltered, unabridged repubn. of the work first pub. in 1875. Bibl. [HX83. N9 1966] 4.75
1. Socialism in the U.S. 2. Communism—U.S. I. Title.

OPITZ, Edmund A. 261.8'5
Religion and capitalism: allies, not enemies [by] Edmund A. Opitz. New Rochelle, N.Y., Arlington House [1970] 318 p. 24 cm. Bibliography: p. [303]-309. [BR115.E3O6] 72-101955 ISBN 0-87000-079-9 7.00
1. Religion and economics. 2. Capitalism. I. Title.

OTSUKA, Hisao, 1907- 261.8'5
Max Weber on the spirit of capitalism / Otsuka Hisao ; translated by Kondo Masaomi. Tokyo : Institute of Developing Economies, 1976. 95 p. ; 25 cm. (I.D.E. occasional papers series ; no. 13) Includes bibliographical references. [BR115.E3W43513] 76-376652
1. Weber, Max, 1864-1920. Die protestantische Ethik und der Geist des Kapitalismus. 2. Religion and sociology—Addresses, essays, lectures. 3. Christian ethics—Addresses, essays, lectures. 4. Protestantism and capitalism—Addresses, essays, lectures. I. Title. II. Series: Ajia Keizai Kenkyujo, Tokyo. I.D.E. occasional papers series ; no. 13.

OXENFELDT, Alfred Richard, 261.85
1917-
Economic systems in action; the United States, the Soviet Union and France. 3d ed. [by] Alfred R. Oxenfeldt [and] Vsevolod Holubnychy. New York, Holt, Rinehart and Winston [1965] vii, 264 p. illus. 23 cm. [HC54.O9] 65-14872
1. U.S. — Econ. condit. 2. Russia — Econ. condit. I. Holubnychy, Vsevolod, joint author. II. Title.

PARADISE, Scott I. 261.8'5
Detroit Industrial Mission; a personal narrative [by] Scott I. Paradise. [1st ed.] New York, Harper & Row [1968] xviii, 158 p. 21 cm. [HD6338.2.U52D46] 68-17586
1. Detroit Industrial Mission. 2. Church and labor—Detroit.

PROJECT Equality Council. 261.8'5
Project Equality; affirmative action for equal employment opportunity through churches, synagogues and related institutions. [Rev. ed.] Chicago, 1967. 36 p. 23 cm. [HD4903.5.U58P75 1967] 70-269171
1. Discrimination in employment—U.S. 2. Church and labor. I. Title.

RASMUSSEN, Albert Terrill, 261.85
1910-
Christian responsibility in economic life. Philadelphia, Westminster Press [c1965] 90 p. 19 cm. (Christian perspectives on social problems) [BR115.E3R3] 65-10209
1. Christianity and economics. I. Title.

RASMUSSEN, Albert Terrill, 261.85
1910-
Christian responsibility in economic life. Philadelphia, Westminster [c.1965] 90p. 19cm. (Chrustian perspectives on soc. probs.) [BR115.E3R3] 65-10209 1.25 pap.,
1. Christianity and economics. I. Title.

RICHARDSON, John R 261.85
Christian economics; studies in the Christian message to the market place, by John R. Richardson. [Houston, Tex., St. Thomas Press, 1966] x, 169 p. 24 cm. Bibliographical footnotes. [BR115.E5R5] 66-19947
1. Christianity and economics. I. Title.

ROGERS, Edward, 1909- 261.85
God's business; a study in the relationship between economics and theology. London, Epworth Pr. [dist. Mystic, Conn., Verry, 1964] 105p. 19cm. (Beckly social serv. lect., 1957) 58-2116 2.00 bds.,
1. Christianity and economics. I. Title.

SAMUELSSON, Kurt 261.85
Religion and economic action; a critique of Max Weber. Tr. from Swedish by E. Geoffrey French. Ed., introd. by D. C. Coleman. New York, Harper [1964, c.1957, 1961] 156p. 21cm. (Harper torchbk.; Acad. Lib. TB1131) Bibl. 1.45 pap.,
1. Christianity and economics. I. Title.

SAMUELSSON, Kurt. 261.85
Religion and economic action. Translated from the Swedish by E. Geoffrey French. Edited and with an introd. by D. C. Coleman. New York, Basic Books [1961] 156 p. 23 cm. Translation of Ekonomi och religion. Includes bibliography. [BR115.E3S33 1961a] 61-6822
1. Christianity and economics. I. Title.

SCHWARTZ, Aloysius. 261.8'5
Poverty: sign of our times. Staten Island, Alba House [1970] xvi, 151 p. illus. 22 cm. (Vocational perspectives series, 6) [BV639.P6S35] 79-109384 4.95
1. Church and the poor. I. Title.

SHRIVER, Donald W. 261.8'5
Rich man poor man [by] Donald W. Shriver, Jr. Cartoons by Jim Crane. Richmond, John Knox Press [1972] 112 p. illus. 19 cm. (Christian ethics for modern man) (Chime paperbacks) Includes bibliographical references. [BR115.E3S47] 71-37003 ISBN 0-8042-9092-X 1.00
1. Christianity and economics. 2. Christian ethics. I. Title.

SIDER, Ronald J. 261.8'5
Rich Christians in an age of hunger : a Biblical study / Ronald J. Sider. Downers Grove, Ill. : Intervarsity Press, c1977. 249 p. ; 21 cm. Includes indexes. Bibliography: p. [245]-249. [BS670.S48] 76-45106 ISBN 0-87784-793-2 pbk. : 4.95
1. Bible—Economics. 2. Hunger. 3. Food supply. 4. Simplicity. I. Title.

SIMON, Paul, 1928- 261.85
A hungry world. St. Louis, Concordia Pub. House [1966] 101 p. 18 cm. (The Christian encounters) Bibliography: p. 101. [HD9000.6.S5] 65-27495
1. Food supply. 2. Food relief. I. Title. II. Series.

SIMON, Paul, 1928- 261.85
A hungry world. St. Louis, Concordia [c.1966] 101p. 18cm. (Christian encounters) Bibl. [HD9000.6.S5] 65-27495 1.00 pap.,
1. Food supply. 2. Food relief. I. Title. II. Series.

SLEEMAN, John F. 261.8'5
Economic crisis : a Christian perspective / [by] John F. Sleeman. London : S.C.M. Press, 1976. xi, 196 p. ; 22 cm. Includes index. Bibliography: p. [193] [BR115.E3S62] 76-361894 ISBN 0-334-00367-9 : £2.50
1. Christianity and economics. I. Title.

TAWNEY, Richard Henry, 261.85
1880-1962.
Religion and the rise of capitalism; a historical study. Gloucester Mass., P. Smith, 1962, [c1926] 337 p. 21 cm. (Holland memorial lectures, 1922) [BR115.E3T3] 63-1429
1. Religious thought—Hist. 2. Christianity and economics—Hist. 3. Gt. Brit.—Soc. condit. 4. Capitalism. I. Title.

TAWNEY, Richard Henry, 261.85
1880-1962
Religion and the rise of capitalism; a historical studv. London, E. Murray [Mystic, Conn., Verry, 1965] 339p. 23cm. [BR115.E3T3] 6.00 bds.,
1. Religious thought—Hist. 2. Christianity and economics—Hist. 3. Gt. Brit.—Soc. condit. 4. Capitalism. I. Title.

VILLAIN, Jean 261.85
L'Eglise et le capitalisme [Toulouse] Privat [dist. Philadelphia, Chilton, 1964, c.1960] 134p. 19cm. (Questions posees aux catholiques) Bibl. 64-9060 1.00 pap.,
1. Christianity and economics. I. Title.

WEBER, Max 261.85
The Protestant ethic and the spirit of capitalism. Translated [from the German] by Talcott Parsons. With a foreword by R. H. Tawney. New York, Scribner [c.1958] xvii, 1(a)-1(e), 292p. 21cm. (Scribner library SL21) Bibliographical references included in Notes (p. 185-284) 1.45 pap.,
1. Religion and sociology. 2. Christian ethics. 3. Capitalism. 4. Christianity and economics. 5. Protestantism I. Title.

WEBER, Max, 1864-1920. 261.85*
The Protestant ethic and the spirit of capitalism. Translated by Talcott Parsons. With a foreword by R. H. Tawney. [Student's ed.] New York, Scribner [1958] xvii, 292 p. 21 cm. Bibliographical references included in "Notes" (p. 185-284) [BR115.E3W4 1958] 58-4170
1. Religion and sociology. 2. Christian ethics. 3. Protestantism and captialism. I. Title.

WATSON, Kenneth, 261.8'5'0973
1913-
Religion in the market place; or, Religious characteristics of business and labor leaders in America. Tujunga, Calif., 196- vi, 174 [5] l. 28 cm. Bibliography: leaves [175]-[180] [HB72.W34] 72-192080
1. Religion and economics. I. Title.

THE Church and the 261.8'5'0975
rural poor / edited by James A. Cogswell. Atlanta : John Knox Press, [1975] p. cm. Includes bibliographical references. [HC107.A133P613] 74-7616 ISBN 0-8042-0797-6 : 1.95
1. Poor—Southern States—Addresses, essays, lectures. 2. Church and Social problems—Southern States—Addresses, essays, lectures. I. Cogswell, James A.

BENNETT, John Coleman, 1902- 261.8'7
United States foreign policy and Christian ethics / by John C. Bennett and Harvey Seifert. 1st ed. Philadelphia : Westminster Press, c1977. 235 p. ; 21 cm. Bibliography: p. [233]-235. [JX1255.B45] 77-5062 ISBN 0-664-24756-3 pbk. : 7.95
1. International relations—Moral and religious aspects. 2. United States—Foreign relations—1945- I. Seifert, Harvey, joint author. II. Title.

BRIGHT, Laurence, ed. 261.87
Christians and world freedom; [essays] Baltimore, Helicon [1966] 246 p. 18 cm. (A Helicon paperbook) Includes bibliographical references. [BR115.I7B7] 66-24849
1. Christianity and international affairs. 2. Liberty. I. Title.

*BROOMHALL, A. J. 261.87
Time for action; Christian responsibility to a non-Christian world. Chicago, Inter-Varsity [1966] 152p. 18cm. Bibl. 1.25 pap.,
I. Title.

DONNER, Andreas Matthias, 1918- 261.8'7
The Christian and the nations, by Andre Donner. Grand Rapids, Eerdmans [1968] 72 p. 23 cm. [BR115.I7D65] 67-19328 3.95
1. Christianity and international affairs. I. Title.

GAY, Jules, 1867- 261.8'7
Le Pape Clement VIet les affaires d'Orient (1342-1352) New York, B. Franklin [1972] 188 p. 22 cm. (Burt Franklin research & source works series. Selected studies in history, economics & social science, n.s. 15. (b) Medieval, Renaissance & Reformation studies) Reprint of the 1904 ed. These—Paris. Bibliography: p. [179]-182. [BX1279.G38 1972] 71-187037 ISBN 0-8337-1301-9 15.00
1. Catholic Church—Relations (diplomatic) I. Title.

GREAT Britain. Legation (Holy See) 261.8'7
Anglo-Vatican relations, 1914-1939: confidential annual reports of the British Ministers to the Holy See. Edited by Thomas E. Hachey. Boston, G. K. Hall, 1972. xli, 403 p. 27 cm. "Annual reports of the British Ministers to the Vatican from the F. O. General Correspondence (Political) held in the Public Record Office (FO371)" Includes bibliographical references. [BX1493.A5] 72-5361 ISBN 0-8161-0991-5 18.00
1. Catholic Church—Relations (diplomatic) with Great Britain. 2. Great Britain—Foreign relations—Catholic Church. I. Hachey, Thomas E., ed. II. Title.

KIRKEMO, Ronald B. 261.8'7
Between the eagle & the dove : the Christian & American foreign policy / Ronald Kirkemo. Downers Grove, Ill. : InterVarsity Press, c1976. 218 p. : ill. ; 21 cm. Includes bibliographies and index. [JX1417.K57] 76-12300 ISBN 0-87784-775-4 pbk. : 4.95
1. United States—Foreign relations—1945- 2. International relations—Moral and religious aspects. I. Title.

MILFORD, Theodore Richard. 261.8'7
Christian decision in the nuclear age, by T. R. Milford. Philadelphia, Fortress Press [1967] vi, 53 p. 19 cm. (Facet books. Social ethics series 15) Revised reprint of the author's The valley of decision: the Christian dilemma in the nuclear age, first published in 1964. Bibliography: p. 49. [BR115.I7M5 1967] 67-13058
1. Christianity and international affairs. 2. War and religion. I. Title.

NOLDE, Otto Frederick, 1899- 261.8'7
The churches and the nations, by O. Frederick Nolde. Foreword by W. A. Visser 't Hooft. Philadelphia, Fortress Press [1970] viii, 184 p. illus., ports. 23 cm. Includes bibliographical references. [BR115.I7N6] 73-99461 7.50
1. Christianity and international affairs. I. Title.

WEBER, Theodore R. 261.8'7
Foreign policy is your business, [by] Theodore R. Weber. Cartoons by Jim Crane. Richmond, John Knox Press [1972] 125 p. illus. 19 cm. (Christian ethics for modern man) (Chime paperbacks) Includes bibliographical references. [BR115.I7W4] 74-37769 ISBN 0-8042-9091-1 1.00
1. Christianity and international affairs. 2. United States—Foreign relations. I. Title.

WILSON, Bryan R. 261.87
Religion in secular society: A sociological comment. London, C. A. Watts, 1966. xix, 252p. 19cm. (New thinker's lib., 15) Bibl. [BR115.W6W53] 66-67339 3.75 bds.,
1. Church and the world. I. Title.
Distributed by Intl. Pubns. Serv., New York.

WILSON, Bryan R. 261.8'7
Religion in secular society [by] Bryan R. Wilson. Harmondsworth, Penguin, 1969. 286 p. 19 cm. (Pelican books) Bibliography: p. 267-277. [BR115.W6W53 1969] 70-403500 6/-
1. Church and the world. I. Title.

VATICAN Council. 2d, 1962-1965 261.8'7'0904
De ecclesia in mundo huius temporis: The pastoral constitution on the church in the modern world, promulgated by Pope Paul VI, Dec. 7, 1965. Commentary by Gregory Baum, Donald Campion. [Study-club ed.] Glen Rock [N.J.] Paulist [1968, c1967] vi, 232p. 18cm. (Vatican II documents) Cover title: Pastoral constitution on the church in the modern world of Vatican Council II. Tr. of Constitutio pastoralis de ecclesia in mundo huius temporis. Bibl. [BX830 1962.A45C935] 68-16669 1.95 pap.,
1. Church and the world. I. Baum, Gregory, 1923- II. Campion, Donald R. III. Title. IV. Title: Pastoral constitution on the church in the modern world of Vatican Council II.

APPLEWHITE, Harry. 261.8'73
Waging peace: a way out of war. Philadelphia, Published for Joint Educational Development [by] United Church Press [1974] 190 p. 22 cm. (A Shalom resource) Includes bibliographies. [JX1953.A6463] 73-20080 ISBN 0-8298-0266-5 2.95 (pbk.)
1. Peace. 2. War and religion. I. Joint Educational Development. II. Title.

ARIZONA Model United Nations General Assembly. 261.873
Papers. 2d- 1964- Tucson, Published for the Institute of Government Research by the University of Arizona Press. v. 23 cm. annual. (Arizona. University. Institute og Government Research. International relations studies) First assembly held in 1963. Sponsored by the Dept. of Government and the Institute of Government Research of the University of Arizona. Editor: 1964- C. E. Wilson. [JX68.A7] 64-64708
1. United Nationa. 2. International relations — Study and teaching. I. Wilson, Clifton E., ed. II. Arizona. University. Dept of Government. III. Arizona. University. Institute of Government Research. IV. Title. V. Series.

ARIZONA. University. Institute of Government Research. 261.873
International relations studies. no. 1- Tucson, University of Arizona Press, 1964- No. 23 cm. [JX68.A7] 65-63533
1. International relations — Collections. I. Title.

BOOTH, Alan R. 261.8'73
Not only peace; Christian realism and the conflicts of the twentieth century [by] Alan R. Booth. New York, Seabury [1967] 141p. 23cm. Bibl. [BT736.2.B63] 67-15735 3.50 bds.,
1. War and religion. 2. Peace (Theology) I. Title.

BOWMAN, Rufus David, 1899- 261.8'73
The Church of the Brethren and war, 1708-1941, by Rufus D. Bowman. With a new introd. for the Garland ed. by Donald F. Durnbaugh. New York, Garland Pub., 1971 [i.e. 1972, c1944] 21, 348 p. illus. 23 cm. (The Garland library of war and peace) Bibliography: p. [334]-348. [BX7815.B6 1972] 75-147667 ISBN 0-8240-0425-6
1. Church of the Brethren—History. 2. War and religion. I. Title. II. Series.

BROCK, Peter, 1920- 261.8'73
Pacifism in Europe to 1914. Princeton, N.J., Princeton University Press, 1972. x, 556 p. 25 cm. (His A History of pacifism, v. 1) Bibliography: p. 505-544. [JX1938.B76] 75-166362 ISBN 0-691-04608-5 17.50
1. Pacifism—History. I. Title.

BROWN, Robert McAfee, 1920- 261.8'73
Religion and violence; a primer for white Americans. Philadelphia, Westminster Press [1973] xv, 112 p. illus. 23 cm. Bibliography: p. 104-112. [BT736.15.B76] 73-14710 ISBN 0-664-24977-9 3.95
1. Violence—Moral and religious aspects. I. Title.

BROWN, Robert McAfee, 1920- 261.8'73
Religion and violence; a primer for white Americans. Stanford, Calif., Stanford Alumni Association, 1973. xv, 112 p. illus. 23 cm. (The Portable Stanford) Bibliography: p. 104-112. [BT736.15.B76 1973b] 73-85363
1. Violence—Moral and religious aspects. I. Title.

CADOUX, Cecil John, 1883-1947. 261.8'73
The early Christian attitude to war : a contribution to the history of Christian ethics / by C. John Cadoux ; with a foreword by W. E. Orchard. New York : Gordon Press, 1975. xxxii, 272 p. ; 24 cm. First published in 1919. Includes bibliographical references and index. [JX1941.C3 1975] 75-3884 ISBN 0-87968-198-5 lib.bdg. : 34.95
1. War. 2. Evil, Non-resistance to. 3. Christian ethics—Early church. I. Title.

DODGE, David Low, 1774-1852. 261.8'73
War inconsistent with the religion of Jesus Christ. With an introd. by Edwin D. Mead. Boston, Published for the International Union [by] Ginn, 1905. [New York, J. S. Ozer, 1972] xxiv, 168 p. port. 22 cm. (The Peace movement in America) Facsim. ed. [JX1949.D7 1905a] 75-137540 9.95 (Library Ed.)
1. War and religion. 2. Peace. I. Title. II. Series.

DOUGLASS, James W. 261.8'73
The non-violent cross; a theology of revolution and peace, by James W. Douglass. New York, Macmillan [1968] xv, 301 p. 21 cm. Includes bibliographical references. [BT736.4.D6 1968] 68-31276
1. Peace (Theology) I. Title.

DRESNER, Samuel H. 261.873
God, man, and atomic war, by Samuel H. Dresner. With a pref. by Lewis L. Strauss. New York, Living Books [1966] 227 p. 23 cm. [BR115.A85D7] 66-14026
1. Atomic warfare—Moral and religious aspects. I. Title.

DRINAN, Robert F. 261.8'73
Vietnam and Armageddon; peace, war and the Christian conscience, by Robert F. Drinan. New York, Sheed and Ward [1970] vi, 210 p. 21 cm. Includes bibliographical references. [BT736.2.D7] 71-101550 ISBN 0-8362-0484-0 5.95
1. War and religion. 2. Vietnamese Conflict, 1961-1975—Moral aspects. I. Title.

DYMOND, Jonathan, 1796-1828. 261.8'73
An inquiry into the accordancy of war. With a new introd. for the Garland ed. by Naomi Churgin Miller. New York, Garland Pub., 1973. 11, 158 p. 22 cm. (The Garland library of war and peace) Reprint of the 1835 ed., which was published under title: An inquiry into the accordancy of war with the principles of Christianity. [BT736.2.D9 1973] 79-147432 ISBN 0-8240-0222-9 16.00
1. War and religion. 2. Pacifism. I. Title. II. Series.

ELLER, Vernard. 261.8'73
King Jesus' manual of arms for the 'armless; war and peace from Genesis to Revelation. Nashville, Abingdon Press [1973] 205 p. 23 cm. [BS680.W2E43] 72-8638 ISBN 0-687-20885-8 4.75
1. War—Biblical teaching. 2. Peace (Theology)—Biblical teaching. I. Title.

ENZ, Jacob J. 261.8'73
The Christian and warfare; the roots of pacifism in the Old Testament, by Jacob J. Enz. Scottdale, Pa., Herald Press [1972] 95 p. 18 cm. (Christian peace shelf series, 3) "Substance of the Menno Simons Lectures as originally delivered at Bethel College, North Newton, Kansas, in 1957." Includes bibliographical references. [BS680.P4E59] 72-192756 ISBN 0-8361-1684-4
1. Peace (Theology)—Biblical teaching. I. Title.

EPP, Frank H., 1929- 261.8'73
A strategy for peace: reflections of a Christian pacifist, by Frank H. Epp. Grand Rapids, Eerdmans [1973] 128 p. 21 cm. Includes bibliographical references. [BT736.4.E66] 73-2290 ISBN 0-8028-1516-2 2.45 (pbk.)
1. Peace (Theology) I. Title. II. Title: Reflections of a Christian pacifist.
Contents omitted.

FINN, James, ed. 261.873
Peace, the churches, and the bomb. [New York] Council on Religion and International Affairs [1965] 103 p. 23 cm. Bibliographical footnotes. [JX1974.7.F5] 65-24574
1. Atomic weapons and disarmament. 2. Christianity and international affairs. I. Council on Religion and International Affairs. II. Title.

FINN, James, ed. 261.873
Peace, the churches, and the bomb [New York] Council on Religion and Intl. Affairs, 170 E. 64th St. [c.1965] 103p. 23cm. Bibl. [JX1974.7.F5] 65-24574 2.00 pap.,
1. Atomic weapons and disarmament. 2. Christianity and international affairs. I. Council on Religion and International Affairs. II. Title.

THE First American peace movement; 261.8'73
comprising War inconsistent with the religion of Jesus Christ, by David Low Dodge, with an introd. by Edwin D. Mead; The lawfulness of war for Christians, examined, by James Mott [and] A solemn review of the custom of war, by Noah Worcester. With a new introd. for the Garland ed. by Peter Brock. New York, Garland Pub., 1972. 11, xx [i.e. xxiv], 168, 33, 23 p. 22 cm. (The Garland library of war and peace) Reprint of three works originally published in 1905, 1814, and 1815, respectively. [JX1949.F57 1972] 73-147428 ISBN 0-8240-0220-2
1. Peace—Addresses, essays, lectures. 2. War—Addresses, essays, lectures. I. Dodge, David Low, 1774-1852. War inconsistent with the religion of Jesus Christ. 1972. II. Mott, James, 1788-1868. The lawfulness of war for Christians, examined. 1972. III. Worcester, Noah, 1758-1837. A solemn review of the custom of war. 1972. IV. Title. V. Series.

GARDINER, Robert W., 1932- 261.8'73
The cool arm of destruction; modern weapons and moral insensitivity, by Robert W. Gardiner. Philadelphia, Westminster Press [1974] 169 p. 22 cm. Bibliography: p. [165]-169. [BR115.A85G37] 74-4351 ISBN 0-664-20701-4
1. Atomic warfare—Moral and religious aspects. I. Title.

GRIFFITHS, Brian, comp. 261.8'73
Is revolution change? edited by Brian Griffiths. London, Inter-Varsity Press, 1972. 111 p. 18 cm. (I.V.P. Pocketbook) Contents.Contents.—The law and order issue, by B. Griffiths.—Reform or revolution? by F. Catherwood.—The way of Christ, by A. Kreider.—Revolution and revelation, by R. Padilla.—The social impact of the Gospel, by S. Escobar.—Conclusion: the Christian way. Includes bibliographical references. [BT738.G73] 72-176215 ISBN 0-85110-355-3
1. Sociology, Christian—Addresses, essays, lectures. 2. Revolutions—Addresses, essays, lectures. 3. Church and social problems—Addresses, essays, lectures. I. Title.
Available from Inter-Varsiy, Pap 1.25, ISBN 0-87784-545-X

GUINAN, Edward, comp. 261.8'73
Peace and nonviolence; basic writings. New York, Paulist Press [1973] ix, 174 p. 23 cm. On cover: Peace and nonviolence; basic writings by prophetic voices in the world religions. Includes bibliographies. [BT736.6.G84] 73-75741 ISBN 0-8091-1770-3 4.50
1. Nonviolence—Moral and religious aspects—Addresses, essays, lectures. 2. Peace (Theology)—Addresses, essays, lectures. I. Title.

HERSHBERGER, Guy Franklin, 1896- 261.8'73
War, peace, and nonresistance. [3d ed., rev.] Scottdale, Pa., Herald Press [1969] xvi, 382 p. 23 cm. Includes bibliographical references. [BT736.4.H47 1969] 72-8199 5.00
1. Peace (Theology) 2. Mennonites—History. 3. Pacifism. I. Title.

HORMANN, Karl. 261.873
Peace and modern war in the judgment of the church. Translated by Caroline Hemesath. Westminster, Md., Newman Press, 1966. vii, 162 p. 22 cm. Bibliographical references included in "Notes" (p. 103-158) [BT736.2H613] 66-16570
1. War and religion. 2. Peace (Theology) I. Title.

HORMANN, Karl 261.873
Peace and modern war in the judgment of the church. Tr. [from German] by Caroline Hemesath. Westminster, Md., Newman [c.] 1966. vii, 162p. 22cm. Bibl. [BT736.2.H613] 66-16570 3.50
1. War and religion. 2. Peace (Theology) I. Title.

INTERNATIONAL Inter-Religious Symposium on Peace, New Delhi, 1968. 261.8'73
World religions and world peace. Edited by Homer A. Jack. Pref. by Zakir Husain. Introd. by Dana McLean Greeley. Boston, Beacon Press [1968] xvi, 208 p. 21 cm. Bibliography: p. 206. [JX1963.I65 1968] 68-54849 4.95
1. Peace—Addresses, essays, lectures. 2. Religions—Addresses, essays, lectures. I. Jack, Homer Alexander, ed. II. Title.

ISBELL, Allen C 261.873
War and conscience, by Allen C. Isbell. Abilene, Tex., Biblical Research Press [1966] x, 221 p. 23 cm. Bibliography: p. 221.

Bibliographical footnotes. [BT736.2.I8] 66-1666
1. War and religion. I. Title.

JOHNSON, James Turner. 261.8'73
Ideology, reason, and the limitation of war : religious and secular concepts, 1200-1740 / James Turner Johnson. Princeton, N.J. : Princeton University Press, [1975] x, 291 p. ; 23 cm. Includes index. Bibliography: p. 275-285. [B105.W3J63] 74-25618 ISBN 0-691-07209-4 : 12.50
1. Just war doctrine—History. I. Title.

JONES, Rufus Matthew, 261.8'73
1863-1948, ed.
The church, the gospel, and war. With a new introd. for the Garland ed. by Henry Cadbury. New York, Garland Pub., 1971 [i.e. 1972, c1948] 9, xii, 169 p. 23 cm. (The Garland library of war and peace) Includes bibliographical references. [BT736.2.J65 1972] 79-147625 ISBN 0-8240-0400-0
1. War and religion—Addresses, essays, lectures. I. Title. II. Series.

JONES, Thomas Canby, 261.8'73
1921-
George Fox's attitude toward war; a documentary study, by T. Canby Jones. Annapolis, Academic Fellowship, 1972. 125, 13 p. facsim. 23 cm. Includes bibliographical references. [BT736.2.J66] 79-187544
1. Fox, George, 1624-1691. 2. War and religion—History of doctrines. I. Title.

KAUFMAN, Donald D. 261.8'73
What belongs to Caesar? A discussion on the Christian's response to payment of war taxes, by Donald D. Kaufman. Scottdale, Pa. Herald Press [1970, c1969] 128 p. 20 cm. Bibliography: p. 105-122. [HJ2305.K3] 70-109939
1. Taxation. 2. Tax evasion. I. Title.

KNOX, John Dunn. 261.8'73
Eternal war; the why of conscientious objection [by] John D. Knox. [Melbourne, John D. Knox, 199 Napier Street, 1967] 94 p. illus., diagrs., facsim. 19 cm. [BT736.2.K6] 70-362153 unpriced
1. War and religion. 2. Conscientious objectors. I. Title.

LONG, Edward Le Roy. 261.8'73
War and conscience in America. Philadelphia, Westminster Press [1968] xiv, 130 p. 19 cm. Bibliographical references included in "Notes" (p. 125-130) [BT736.2.L6] 68-22645
1. War and religion. I. Title.

LOQUE, Bertrand de. 261.8'73
Discourses of warre and single combat. Translated by John Eliot. A Renaissance library facsim. ed., with an introd. by Alice Shalvi. Jerusalem, New York, Israel Universities Press; [distributed by International Scholarly Book Services, Portland, Or., c1968] xii, 67 p. 22 cm. (Renaissance library) Original t.p. reads: Discovres of vvarre and single combat. Translated out of French by I. Eliot. London, Printed by Iohn Wolfe, and are to be solde at his shop right ouer against the great South dore of Paules, 1591. "A treatise of single combate" (p. 43-67) has special t.p. Part 1 has running title: A discourse of Christian war; pt. 2: A discourse of single combat. Translation of Deux traitez, l'un de la guerre, l'autre du duel. STC 16810. Includes bibliographical references. [BT736.2.L6413 1591a] 72-178223 ISBN 0-7065-0051-2 5.00
1. War and religion. 2. Dueling. I. Eliot, John, fl. 1593, tr. II. Title. III. Title: A treatise of single combate. IV. Title: A discourse of Christian warre. V. Title: A discourse of single combat.

MCCREADY, Adelaide M. 261.8'73
Two letters to a peacemaker, by Adelaide M. McCready. New York, Philosophical Library [1970] viii, 48 p. 22 cm. Bibliography: p. 37-39. [BL2780.M325] 73-129064 3.95
1. Christianity—Controversial literature. I. Title.

MACQUARRIE, John. 261.8'73
The concept of peace. [1st U.S. ed.] New York, Harper & Row [1973] 82 p. 21 cm. Includes bibliographical references. [BT736.4.M25 1973] 73-6325 ISBN 0-06-065365-5 4.95
1. Peace (Theology) I. Title.

MARRIN, Albert. 261.8'73
The last crusade; the Church of England in the First World War. Durham, N.C., Duke University Press, 1974. xi, 303 p. 25 cm. Bibliography: p. [283]-293. [D639.C54M37] 72-97471 ISBN 0-8223-0298-5
1. Church of England—History. 2. European War, 1914-1918—Church of England. I. Title.

MERTON, Thomas, 1915- 261.8'73
1968.
Thomas Merton on peace / [by] Thomas Merton. London : Mowbrays, 1976. 156 p. ; 22 cm. [JX1963.M549 1976] 77-358970 ISBN 0-264-66339-X : £2.25
1. Peace—Addresses, essays, lectures. 2. Nonviolence—Addresses, essays, lectures. 3. Christianity and international affairs—Addresses, essays, lectures. I. Title.

MERTON, Thomas, 1915- 261.8'73
1968.
Thomas Merton on peace. With an introd. by Gordon C. Zahn. New York, McCall Pub. Co. [1971] xli, 269 p. 22 cm. [JX1963.M549 1971] 75-122148 ISBN 0-8415-0060-6 7.95
1. Peace—Addresses, essays, lectures. 2. Nonviolence—Addresses, essays, lectures. 3. Christianity and international affairs—Addresses, essays, lectures. I. Title.

MOELLERING, Ralph 261.8'73
Luther.
Modern war and the Christian. Minneapolis, Augsburg Pub. House [1969] 94 p. 20 cm. Includes bibliographical references. [JX1963.M645] 69-14186 2.50
1. Christianity and international affairs. 2. Peace. I. Title.

MUSTE, Abraham John, 261.8'73
1885-1967.
Not by might; Christianity: the way to human decency, and Of holy disobedience. With a new introd. for the Garland ed. by Jo Ann Robinson. New York, Garland Pub., 1971 [i.e. 1972, c1947] 15, xiii, 227, 34 p. 23 cm. (The Garland library of war and peace) Reprint of 2 works first published in 1947 and 1952 respectively. [BT736.4.M88] 70-147628 ISBN 0-8240-0403-5
1. Peace (Theology) 2. Conscientious objectors. 3. Pacifism. I. Muste, Abraham John, 1885-1967. Of holy disobedience. 1971. II. Title. III. Title: Of holy disobedience. IV. Series.

NATIONAL Inter-Religious 261.87'3
Conference on Peace Washington, D.C., 1966.
Religion and peace; papers from the National Inter-Religious Conference on Peace. Edited by Homer A. Jack. Indianapolis, Bobbs-Merrill [1966] xvi, 137 p. 21 cm. [JX1963.N24 1966aa] 66-27885
1. Peace—Addresses, essays, lectures. 2. Christianity and international affairs—Addresses, essays, lectures. I. Jack, Homer Alexander, ed. II. Title.

O'BRIEN, William 261.8'73
Vincent.
Nuclear war, deterrence, and morality [by] William V. O'Brien. Westminster [Md.] Newman Press [1967] viii, 120 p. 21 cm. Bibliography: p. 111-120. [BR115.A85O2] 67-15720
1. Atomic warfare — Moral and religious aspects. 2. War and religion. I. Title.

O BRIEN, William Vincent 261.8'73
Nuclear war, deterrence, and morality [by] William V. O'Brien. Westminster [Md.] Newman [1967] viii. 120p. 21cm. Bibl. [BR115.A85O2] 67-15620 3.75
1. Atomic warfare—Moral and religious aspects. 2. War and religion. I. Title.

O'BRIEN, William Vincent, 261.873
ed.
The Yearbook of world polity. v. 1- New York, Praeger, 1957- v. 23 cm. irregular. Title varies: v. 1-2, World polity; a yearbook of studies in international law and organization. Some vols. have also a distinctive title: v. 3, The new nations in International law and diplomacy. Issued by the Institute of World Polity, Georgetown University. Editor: v. 3- W. V. O'Brien. Vols. 1-2 published by Spectrum Publishers, Utrecht. [JX68.W6] 65-13962
1. International law — Collections. 2. International organization — Collections. I. Georgetown University, Washington, D.C. Institute of World Polity. II. Title. III. Title: World polity. IV. Title: The new nations in international law and diplomacy.

ORMONDE, Paul. 261.8'73
Catholics in revolution; challenging new views on communism and war edited by Paul Ormonde. [Melbourne] Lansdowne [1968] 199 p. 22 cm. Bibliographical references included in "Reference notes" (p. 188-199). [BX1396.4.O7] 70-382136 5.95
1. Communism and religion. 2. War and religion. 3. Church and social problems—Catholic Church. I. Title.

PEACE, on not leaving it 261.8'73
to the pacifists / edited by Gerald O. Pedersen ; with contributions by William Lesher ... [et al.] ; and a foreword by Gerhard L. Belgum. Philadelphia : Fortress Press, [1975] viii, 88 p. ; 19 cm. Bibliography: p. 85-87. [JX1963.P334] 74-26328 ISBN 0-8006-1092-X pbk. : 2.95
1. Peace—Addresses, essays, lectures. I. Pedersen, Gerald O. II. Lesher, William.

PEACE! Peace! 261.8'73
Waco, Tex., Word Books [1967] 162 p. 21 cm. Chapters were first presented at conferences sponsored by the Christian Life Commission of the Southern Baptist Convention, and held in Glorieta, N.M., and Ridgecrest, N.C. Bibliographical footnotes. [BT736.4.P4] 67-23975
1. Peace (Theology)—Addresses, essays, lectures. I. Valentine, Foy, ed. II. Southern Baptist Convention. Christian Life Commission.

POTTER, Ralph B. 261.8'73
War and moral discourse [by] Ralph B. Potter. Richmond, John Knox Press [1969] 123 p. 21 cm. Includes bibliographical references. [BT736.2.P63] 69-18111 2.45 (pbk)
1. War and religion. 2. War and religion—Bibliography. I. Title.

QUIGLEY, Thomas E., 261.8'73
comp.
American Catholics and Vietnam, edited by Thomas E. Quigley. Grand Rapids, Mich., by W. B. Eerdmans [1968] 197 p. 22 cm. "Bibliographical notes": p. 9-13. [BT736.2.Q5] 68-54102 4.50
1. War and religion. 2. Vietnamese Conflict, 1961-1975—Religious aspects. 3. Catholic Church in Vietnam. I. Title.

RAVEN, Charles Earle, 261.8'73
1885-
War and the Christian, by Charles E. Raven. With a new introd. for the Garland ed. by Franklin H. Littell. New York, Garland Pub., 1972. 9, 185 p. 22 cm. (The Garland library of war and peace) Reprint of the 1938 ed. [BT736.2.R38 1972] 75-147675 ISBN 0-8240-0432-9
1. World Conference on Church, Community and State, Oxford, 1937. 2. War and religion. I. Title. II. Series.

REED, Edward, ed. 261.873
Peace on earth: Pacem in terris. Proceedings of an Intl. Convocation on the requirements of peace. Sponsored by the Center for the Study of Democratic Institutions. New York, Pocket Bks. [c.1965] 260p. 18cm. (95019) .95 pap.,
I. Title.

ROAD to peace (The); 261.873
Christian approaches to defence and disarmament [by] John C. Bennett [others] Philadelphia, Fortress [1966] 54, [1] p. 20cm. (Facet bks. Soc. ethics ser., 10) Bibl. [JX1963.R62 1966] 66-14795 .85 pap.,
1. Peace—Addresses, essays, lectures. 2. Christianity and international affairs—Addresses, essays, lectures. I. Bennett, John Coleman, 1902-(Series)
Contents omitted

ROGERS, W. Henry 261.873
There shall be no peace unless. 2nd ed. New York, Vantage [c.1955, 1966] 79p. 20cm. 2.50 bds.,
I. Title.

RUSSELL, Chester. 261.8'73
Was Jesus a pacifist? Nashville, Tenn., Broadman Press [1971] 96 p. 21 cm. Includes bibliographies. [BT736.4.R87] 72-145987 ISBN 0-8054-5511-6 2.95
1. Peace (Theology) I. Title.

SHEERIN, John B. 261.8'73
Peace, war, and the young Catholic, by John B. Sheerin. New York, Paulist Press [1972, c1973] viii, 109 p. 18 cm. (Deus books) Bibliography: p. 108-109. [BT736.2.S46] 72-91458 ISBN 0-8091-1733-9 1.25
1. War and religion. I. Title.

STOTTS, Jack L. 261.8'73
Shalom: the search for a peaceable city. Nashville, Abingdon [1973] 224 p. 21 cm. Includes bibliographical references. [BT736.4.S85] 72-6970 ISBN 0-687-38324-2 5.95
1. Peace (Theology) I. Title.

STRATMANN, Franziskus 261.8'73
Maria, 1883-
The church and war, a Catholic study, by Franziskus Stratmann. With a new introd. for the Garland ed. by Gerard A. Vanderhaar. New York, Garland Pub., 1971. 23, 219 p. 22 cm. (The Garland library of war and peace) Reprint of the 1928 ed. Includes bibliographical references. [BT736.2.S67 1971] 72-147677 ISBN 0-8240-0434-5
1. War and religion. I. Title. II. Series.

TOLSTOI, Lev 261.8'73
Nikolaevich, graf, 1828-1910.
The law of love and the law of violence [by] Leo Tolstoy. Translated by Mary Koutouzow Tolstoy. With a foreword by Baroness Budberg. [1st ed.] New York, Holt, Rinehart and Winston [1970] x, 101 p. 22 cm. Translation of La loi de l'amour et la loi de la violence. [HM278.T6313 1970] 73-105433 3.95
1. Pacifism. 2. Government, Resistance to. I. Title.

UNITED Nations. Office of 261.873
Public Information.
Never again war! A documented account of the visit to the United Nations of His Holiness Pope Paul VI, with texts of the encyclical letter of Pope John XXIII, Pacem in terris, and the United Nations Universal declaration of human rights. New York 1965. 134 p. illus., facsims. (1 col.) ports. (1 mounted col.) 28 cm. "Sales no.: 65.I.27." Bibliographical references included in "Footnotes" (p. 125-126). [BX1378.3.U48] 66-995
1. Paulus VI, Pope, 1897- 2. Peace. I. Paulus VI, Pope, 1897- II. Catholic Church. Pope, 1958-1963 (Joannes XXIII) Pacem in terris (11 Apr. 1963) III. Title.

UNITED Nations. Office of 261.873
Public Information
Never again war! A documented account of the visit to the U. N. of His Holiness Pope Paul VI, with texts of the encyclical letter of Pope John XXIII, Pacem in terris, and the U. N. Universal declaration of human rights. New York, Author [c.]1965 134p. illus., facsims. (1 col.) ports. (1 mounted col.) 28cm. (U. N. Sales no.: 65.I.27.) Bibl. [BX1378.3.U48] 66-995 5.50
1. Paulus VI, Pope, 1897- 2. Peace. I. Paulus VI, Pope, 1897- II. Catholic Church. Pope, 1958-1963 (Joannes XXIII) Pacem in terris (11 Apr. 1963) III. Title.

WALLACE, Foy Esco, 1896- 261.8'73
The Christian and the government [and other articles] by Foy E. Wallace, Jr. With review of the Lipscomb theory of civil government, by O. C. Lambert. Nashville, Tenn., F. E. Wallace, Jr. Publications [1969? c1968] 324 p. ports. 24 cm. Addendum (p. [239]-324):—Christians in uniform, by F. A. Amick.—The relation of the Christian to civil government and war, by G. E. Green. [BV630.2.W3] 72-270353
1. Church and state. 2. Christianity and politics. 3. War and religion. I. Title.

WEBER, Theodore R. 261.8'73
Modern war and the pursuit of peace, by Theodore R. Weber. [New York] Council on Religion and International Affairs [1968] 39 p. 23 cm. (Ethics and foreign policy series) Address delivered at the World Peace Center of the Catholic Adult Education Center in 1967. Bibliographical references included in "Notes" (p. 37-39) [BT736.2.W37] 68-29422
1. War and religion. 2. Politics and war. I. Title.

WELLS, John I. 261.8'73
An essay on war. Proving that the spirit of war, existing in the rational mind, is ever inimical to the spirit of the Gospel; that the wars mentioned in the history of the Jews, were for the happiness of that people, the punishment of idolatrous nations, and the instruction of mankind generally. Also, that the spirit of war is wholly excluded from the Christian Church. Hartford, Printed by Hudson and Goodwin, 1808. [New York, J. S. Ozer, 1972] 52 p. 22 cm. (The Peace movement in America) Facsim. reprint. [BT736.2.W42 1808a] 70-137560 5.95
1. War and religion. I. Title. II. Series.

WENGER, John Christian, 261.8'73
1910-
Pacifism and Biblical nonresistance, by J. C. Wenger. Scottdale, Pa., Herald Press [1968] 28 p. 20 cm. (Focal pamphlet series, no. 15) "Papers ... read at the Peace Witness Seminar, Evangelicals in Social Action, Eastern Mennonite College, Harrisonburg, Virginia, November 30, 1968." [BT736.4.W4] 68-7991
1. Pacifism. 2. Evil, Non-resistance to. I. Title.

THE Witness of U.S. 261.8'73
Lutherans on peace, war, conscience : prepared for the Division for Parish Services of the Lutheran Church in America, the Division for Life and Mission in the Congregation of the American Lutheran Church, and the Board of Parish Education of the Lutheran Church—Missouri Synod / John E. Schramm, consultant ; Hartland H. Gifford, editor .... [Minneapolis] : Augsburg Pub. House, [1975] 32 p. : ill. ; 28 cm. Cover title: Peace, war, conscience. Caption title. Bibliography: p. 32. [BT736.4.W55] 75-308067
1. Lutheran Church—Doctrinal and controversial works. 2. Peace (Theology) 3. War and religion. 4. Conscience. I. Schramm, John, 1931- II. Gifford, Hartland H. III. Lutheran Church in America. Division for Parish Services. IV. American Lutheran Church (1961-) Division for Life and Mission. V. Lutheran Church—Missouri Synod. Board of Parish Education.

YODER, John Howard. 261.8'73
The original revolution; essays on Christian pacifism, by John H. Yoder. Scottdale, Pa., Herald Press [1972, c1971] 189 p. 21 cm. (Christian peace shelf series, 3) Includes bibliographical references. [BT736.2.Y6 1972] 76-181577 ISBN 0-8361-1572-4 5.95
1. War and religion—Addresses, essays, lectures. I. Title.

ZAHN, Gordon Charles, 1918- 261.8'73
War, conscience, and dissent [by] Gordon C. Zahn. [1st ed.] New York, Hawthorn [1967] 317p. 22cm. Bibl. [BT736.2.Z37] 67-14856 5.95 bds.,
1. War and religion. 2. War and morals. 3. Conscientious objectors. I. Title.

MARRIN, Albert, comp. 261.8'73'08
War and the Christian conscience: from Augustine to Martin Luther King, Jr. Chicago, Regnery [1971] ix, 342 p. 21 cm. "Gateway edition." Bibliography: p. 335-342. [BT736.2.M375] 73-143855 3.95
1. War and religion. I. Title.

262 Ecclesiology

ARCHIEPISCOPAL and 262
patriarchal autonomy; a symposium held on July 15, 1972, at Lincoln Center Campus. Editors: Thomas E. Bird [and] Eva Piddubcheshen. New York, Fordham University, 1972. 74 p. 23 cm. Includes bibliographical references. [BX4711.62.A7] 72-11841
1. Catholic Church. Byzantine rite (Ukrainian)—Congresses. 2. Patriarchs and patriarchate (Catholic Oriental)—Congresses. I. Bird, Thomas E., 1888- ed. II. Piddubcheshen, Eva, ed. III. Fordham University, New York.

BERKOUWER, Gerrit Cornelis, 1903- 262
The church / by G. C. Berkouwer ; [translated by James E. Davison. Grand Rapids, Mich. : W. B. Eerdmans Pub. Co., c1976. 438 p. ; 22 cm. (His Studies in dogmatics) Translation of De kerk. Includes bibliographical references and indexes. [BV601.B4513] 75-45202 ISBN 0-8028-3433-7 : 10.95
1. Church—Marks. I. Title.

BREWER, Grover Cleveland, 1884-1956. 262
The model church. Nashville, Gospel Advocate Co., 1957. 166p. 20cm. [BV600.B7 1957] 57-21805
1. Church sChurches of Christ—Government. I. Title.

BROW, Robert. 262
The church: an organic picture of its life and mission. Grand Rapids, Eerdmans [1968] 122 p. 20 cm. Bibliography: p. 118-122. [BV600.2.B72] 68-28849 1.95
1. Church. I. Title.

BURTON, Malcolm K 262
Destiny for Congregationalism. Oklahoma City, Modern Publishers, 1953. 304p. 23cm. [BX7240.B85] 53-1514
1. Congregational churches—Government. 2. General Council of the Congregational and Christian Churches of the United States—Relations— Evangelical and Reformed Church. 3. Evangelical and Reformed Church— Relations—General Council of the Congregational and Christian Churches in the United States. I. Title.

CARR, Warren. 262
At the risk of idolatry. Valley Forge [Pa.] Judson Press [1972] 144 p. 23 cm. Includes bibliographical references. [BV600.2.C338] 72-75356 ISBN 0-8170-0564-1 4.95
1. Church. 2. Institutionalism (Religion) I. Title.

THE Case for freedom; 262
human rights in the church. Edited by James A. Coriden. Foreword by Ladislas M. Orsy. Washington, Corpus Books [1969] x, 175 p. 21 cm. "[Papers prepared for] a symposium held at the Catholic University of America, Washington, D.C., on October 5-6, 1968 ... [and] co-sponsored by the Canon Law Society of America and the School of Canon Law of Catholic University." [BT810.2.C37] 72-83515 5.50
1. Catholic Church—Doctrinal and controversial works—Addresses, essays, lectures. 2. Freedom (Theology)—Addresses, essays, lectures. I. Coriden, James A., ed. II. Canon Law Society of America. III. Catholic University of America. School of Canon Law.

CATHOLIC Reporter, The 262
Kansas City, Mo. The layman and the Council; conversations between John Cogley, Daniel Callahan, Donald J. Thorman, Martin H. Work. Ed. by Michael Greene. Springfield, Ill., Templegate [1965] 128p. 19cm. Appeared serially in the Catholic reporter of the Diocese of Kansas City-St. Joseph, Mo. [BX830 1962.C35] 65-3173 3.95
1. Vatican Council, 2d. I. Cogley, John. II. Greene, Michael J., ed.

DEMOCRATIZATION of the 262
church. Edited by Alois Muller. [New York] Herder and Herder [1971] 160 p. 23 cm. (Concilium: religion in the seventies, v. 63. Pastoral theology) On cover: The New concilium: religion in the seventies. Includes bibliographical references. [BV647.2.D43] 73-147026 2.95
1. Church polity—Addresses, essays, lectures. 2. Democracy—Addresses, essays, lectures. I. Muller, Alois, 1924- ed. II. Series: Concilium: theology in the age of renewal, v. 63

DIDASCALIA apostolorum. 262
English. Didascalia apostolorum; the Syriac version tr. and accompanied by the Verona Latin fragments. Introd. notes by R. Hugh Connolly. Oxford, Clarendon Press[dist. New York, Oxford, 1962] xci, 280p. 24cm. English and Latin on opposite pages. 6.75
1. Church orders, Ancient. I. Didascalia apostolorum. Latin. II. Didascalia apostolorum. Syriac version. English. III. Connolly, Richard Hugh, 1873- ed. and tr.

ERMARTH, Margaret Sittler. 262
Adam's fractured rib; observations on women in the church. Philadelphia, Fortress Press [1970] xvi, 159 p. 20 cm. Based upon the findings of the Subcommittee on the Role of Women in the Life of the Church of the Lutheran Church in America's Commission on the Comprehensive Study of the Doctrine of the Ministry. Bibliography: p. 157-159. [BV639.W7E7] 78-117976 3.25
1. Women in Christianity. 2. Ordination of women. I. Title.

ERVIN, Spencer, 1886- 262
The polity of the Church of the Province of South Africa. Ambler, Pa., Trinity Press [c1964] xii, 157 p. 22 cm. "Vol. 2 of a series on the government of the churches of the Anglican communion." Errata slip inserted. Bibliographical footnotes. [BX5700.6.Z5E7] 65-2456
1. Church of the Province of South Africa — Government. I. Title.

ERVIN, Spencer, 1886- 262
The polity of the Church of the Province of South Africa. Ambler, Pa., Trinity Pr. [c.1964] xii, 157p. 22cm. Vol. 2 of a ser. on the govt. of the churches of the Anglican communion. Bibl. [BX5700..6.Z5E7] 65-2456 price unreported
1. Church of the Province of South Africa— Government. I. Title.

FLUCKIGER, Wilford Lynn 262
Dynamic leadership. [Salt Lake City] Deseret [1963, c.]1962. 113p. 24cm. 63-952 2.00
1. Christian leadership. I. Title.

FORD, LeRoy. 262
Developing skills for church leaders. Nashville, Convention Press [1968] 61 p. illus., forms. 20 cm. [BV652.1.F6] 68-31558
1. Christian leadership—Study and teaching. I. Title.

FOSHEE, Howard B., 1925- 262
The work of church officers and committees [by] Howard B. Foshee, Reginald M. McDonough [and] James A. Sheffield. Nashville, Convention Press [1968] x, 133 p. 20 cm. "Church study course [of the Sunday School Board of the Southern Baptist Convention] This book is number 1607 in category 16, section for adults and young people." Bibliography: p. 131. [BV705.F66] 68-19362
1. Church officers. 2. Church committees—Baptist. I. McDonough, Reginald M., joint author. II. Sheffield, James A., joint author. III. Southern Baptist Convention. Sunday School Board. IV. Title.

GANGEL, Kenneth O. 262
Leadership for church education, by Kenneth O. Gangel. Chicago, Moody Press [1970] 392 p. 24 cm. Includes bibliographies. [BV1471.2.G3] 79-104826 5.95
1. Christian education. 2. Christian leadership. I. Title.

GRAVES, Harold K 1912- 262
The nature and functions of a church. Nashville, Convention Press [1963] 136 p. 20 cm. [BX6340.G7] 63-7546
1. Baptists—Government. I. Title.

GRINDSTAFF, Wilmer E 1912- 262
Our cooperative program [by] W. E. Grindstaff. Nashville, Convention Press [1965] x, 144 p. 20 cm. "Church study course [of the Sunday School Board of the Southern Baptist Convention] This book is number 1402 in category 14, section for adults and young people." [BX6346.5.G7] 65-18867
1. Baptists — Finance. I. Southern Baptist Convention. Sunday School Board. II. Title.

GUITTON, Jean 262
The Church and the laity: from Newman to Vatican II. Tr. [from French] by Malachy Gerard Carroll. Staten Island, N.Y., Alba [c.1965] 176p. 22cm. [BX1920.G813] 65-15730 3.50
1. Newman, John Henry, Cardinal. 1801-1890. 2. Laity—Catholic Church. I. Title.

GUITTON, Jean. 262
The Church and the laity: from Newman to Vatican II. Translated by Malachy Gerard Carroll. Staten Island, N.Y., Alba House [1965] 176 p. 22 cm. [BX1920.G813] 65-15730
1. Laity — Catholic Church. 2. Newman, John Henry, Cardinal, 1801-1890. I. Title.

HAGOOD, Lewis Marshall, 1853-1936. 262
The colored man in the Methodist Episcopal Church. Westport, Conn., Negro Universities Press [1970] 327 p. illus., ports. 23 cm. Reprint of the 1890 ed. [BX8435.H3 1970] 73-111577 ISBN 0-8371-4602-X
1. Methodist Episcopal Church. 2. Methodists, Negro. I. Title.

HAGOOD, Lewis Marshall, 1853-1936. 262
The colored man in the Methodist Episcopal Church. Freeport, N.Y., Books for Libraries Press, 1971 [c1890] 327 p. illus., ports. 23 cm. (The Black heritage library collection) [BX8435.H3 1971] 77-149868 ISBN 0-8369-8631-8
1. Methodist Episcopal Church. 2. Methodists, Negro. I. Title. II. Series.

HARMON, Nolan Bailey, 1892- ed. 262
The district superitendent: his office and work in the Methodist Church. Prepared by present and former district superintendents. Nashville, Methodist Pub. House [1954] 128p. 20cm. [BX8388.H27] 54-5945
1. Methodist Church (United States)—Government. I. Title.

HARMON, Nolan Bailey, 1892- 262
The organization of the Methodist Church; historic development and present working structure. 2d rev. ed. Nashville, Methodist Pub. House [1962] 287p. 24cm. [BX8388.H3 1962] 62-12436
1. Methodist Church (United States)—Government. I. Title.

HARMON, Nolan Bailey, 1892- 262
The organization of the Methodist Church; historic development and present working structure. Rev. ed. Nashville, Methodist Pub. House [1953] 288p. 24cm. [BX8388.H3 1953] 53-5396
1. Methodist Church (United States)—Government. I. Title.

HARRELL, Costen Jordan, 1885- 262
The local church in Methodism. Nashville, Methodist Pub. House [c1952] 63p. 20cm. [BX8340.H34] 55-42350
1. Methodist Church—Government. I. Title.

HARRIS, William Coe, 1899- 262
Shepherds of the flock of God; the responsibilities of the Christian elder in the church government planned by Jesus. [1st ed.] New York, Exposition Press [1967] 125 p. 21 cm. [BV650.2.H37] 67-24274
1. Church—Government. 2. Elders (Church officers) I. Title.

HATCH, Edwin, 1835-1889. 262
The organization of the early Christian churches. Eight lectures delivered before the University of Oxford, in the year, 1880. New York, B. Franklin [1972] xxviii, 216 p. 22 cm. (Burt Franklin research and source works series. Philosophy and religious history monographs, 94) Spine title: Early Christian churches. Reprint of the 1881 ed., issued in series: Bampton lectures. Includes bibliographical references. [BV648.H4 1972] 77-183696 ISBN 0-8337-4163-2 12.50
1. Church polity—Early church. 2. Church history—Primitive and early church. I. Title. II. Title: Early Christian churches. III. Series: Bampton lectures, 1880.

HEBBLETHWAITE, Peter. 262
The theology of the church. Notre Dame, Ind., Fides Publishers [1969] 93 p. 18 cm. (Theology today, no. 8) Bibliography: p. 92. [BV600.2.H39] 74-8387 0.95
1. Church. I. Title.

HIPPOLYTUS Saint fl.217-235. 262
Apostolic tradition. Tr. into English, introd., and notes by Burton Scott Easton. [Hamden, Conn.] Archon [dist. Shoe String] 1962 [c.1934] [xi], 112p. 22cm. Bibl. 62-5122 3.50
1. Church orders, Ancient. I. Easton, Burton Scott, 1877-1950, ed. and tr. II. Title.

HOH, Paul Jacob, 1893- 262
Parish practice, a manual of church administration. Rev. ed. Philadelphia, Muhlenberg Press [1956] 248p. 23cm. [BX8065.H73 1956] 56-3820
1. Lugheran Church—Government. 2. Theology, Pastoral—Lutheran Church. 3. Church work. I. Title.

HOOKER, Richard, 1553or4-1600. 262
The works of that learned and judicious divine, Mr. Richard Hooker; with an account of his life and death, by Isaac Walton. Arranged by John Keble. 7th ed. Rev. by R. W. Church and F. Paget. New York, B. Franklin [1970] 3 v. geneal. table, facsim. 24 cm. (Philosophy monograph series, 34) (Burt Franklin research and source works series, 546.) Commonly referred to as Ecclesiastical polity. Reprint of the 1888 ed. Bibliography: v. 3, p. [730]-736. [BV649.H8 1970] 76-125020
1. Church of England—Doctrinal and controversial works. 2. Ecclesiastical law. 3. Church polity. 4. Sermons, English. I. Keble, John, 1792-1866, ed. II. Church, Richard William, 1815-1890, ed.

HOWELL, Margaret 262
Regalian right in medieval England. [Dist. New York, Oxford, c.]1962. xv, 264p. illus. 23cm. (Univ. of London historical studies, 9) Bibl. 62-6241 6.75
1. Patronage, Ecclesiastical—Gt. Brit. I. Title. II. Series: London. University. Historical studies, 9

HOWSE, William Lewis, 1905- 262
A church organized and functioning [by] W.L. Howse and W.O. Thomason. Nashville, Convention Press [1963] 148 p. 20 cm. [BX6340.H6] 63-8299
1. Baptists—Government. I. Thomason, William O., joint author. II. Title.

HOYER, Harvey Conrad, 1907- 262
Ecumenopolis U.S.A.: the church in mission in community [by] H. Conrad Hoyer. Minneapolis, Augsburg Pub. House [1971] 159 p. illus. 20 cm. Bibliography: p. 157-159. [BV601.8.H69] 74-158997 ISBN 0-8066-1120-0 2.95
1. Mission of the church. 2. Sociology, Christian. I. Title.

HUMMEL, Margaret Gibson. 262
The amazing heritage. References and resources assembled by Mildred Roe. Philadelphia, Geneva Press [1970] 144 p. illus., ports. 21 cm. Bibliography: p. [142]-144. [BV4415.H77] 75-111040 2.00
1. Women in church work—United Presbyterian Church in the U.S.A. I. Title.

JOURNET, Charles. 262
The Church of the Word Incarnate; an essay in speculative theology. Translated by A.H. C. Downes. London, New York, Sheed and Ward [1955- v. 25cm. [BX1751.J685] 55-2643
1. Catholic Church. 2. Catholic Church—Government. 3. Catholic Church—Clergy. I. Title.

JUMPER, Andrew A 262
Chosen to serve: the deacon; a practical manual for the operation of the board of deacons in the Presbyterian Church in the United States. Richmond, John Knox Press [1961] 128p. 21cm. [BX8966.J78] 61-18257
1. Presbyterian Church in the United States—Government. 2. Deacons. I. Title.

JUMPER, Andrew A. 262
The noble task: the elder; a practical manual for the operation of the church session in the Presbyterian Church in the United States. Richmond, Va., John Knox [c.1961] 143p. 61-18256 1.50 pap.,
1. Presbyterian Church in the U.S.—Government. I. Title.

KRAUS, Clyde Norman. 262
The community of the spirit, by C. Norman Kraus. Grand Rapids, Eerdmans [1974] 104 p. 21 cm. Includes bibliographical references. [BV600.2.K68] 74-1479 ISBN 0-8028-1562-6 2.45 (pbk.)
1. Church. I. Title.

KUNG, Hans, 1928- 262
Structures of the church. Tr. from German by Salvator Attanasio. New York, Nelson [c.1964] xviii, 394p. 22cm. 63-19353 7.50
1. Church. 2. Councils and synods, Ecumenical. I. Title.

LOLLIS, Lorraine. 262
The shape of Adam's rib: a lively history of women's work in the Christian Church. Illus. by Thelma Pyatt. St. Louis, Mo., Bethany

Press [1970] 219 p. illus. 23 cm. Bibliography: p. 215-219. [BV4415.L6 1970] 70-117336 3.95
1. Women in church work—Disciples of Christ. 2. Women in missionary work. I. Title.

LUNT, William Edward. 1882- 262
1956. ed. and tr.
Papal revenues in the Middle Ages. NewYork, Octagon. 1965[c.1934, 1962] 2v. (341:665p.) 24cm. (Records of civilization: sources and studies, no. 19) Bibl. [BX1950.L8] 65-25616 25.00 set,
1. Catholic Church—Finance. 2. Catholic Church—Hist.—Sources. I. Catholic Church. Camera Apostolica. II. Title. III. Series.

LYNSKEY, Elizabeth M 262
The government of the Catholic Church. Introd. by John J. Meng: with a foreword by George N. Shuster. New York, P. J. Kennedy [1952] 99 p. 23 cm. [BX1801.I9] 52-11496
1. Catholic Church—Government. I. Title.

MCNUTT, William Roy, 1879- 262
Polity and practice in Baptist churches. Foreword by Douglas Clyde Macintosh. [Rev.] Chicago, Judson Press [1954 206p. 20cm. Includes bibliography. [BX6340.M25 1959] 59-7279
1. Baptists—Government. I. Title.

MATHER, Richard, 1596-1669. 262
Church covenant : two tracts. New York : Arno Press, 1972. 84, 78 p. ; 24 cm. (Research library of colonial Americana) Reprint of the 1643 ed. published by B. Allen, London, under title: Church-government and church-covenant discussed. Contents.Contents.—Mather, R. Church-government and church-covenant discussed.—Mather, R. An apologie of the churches in New England for church-covenant.—Davenport, J. An answer of the elders of the severall churches in New England. [BX7240.M32 1972] 75-141115 ISBN 0-405-03329-X
1. Church polity. I. Mather, Richard, 1596-1669. An apologie of the churches in New England for church-covenant. 1972. II. Davenport, John, 1597-1670. An answer of the elders of the severall churches in New England. 1972. III. Title. IV. Series.

MAYFIELD, Guy. 262
The Church of England: its members and its business. London, New York, Oxford University Press, 1958. 211p. 23cm. Includes bibliography. [BX5150.M37] 58-777
1. Church of England—Government. I. Title.

METHODIST Church (United 262
States) Co-ordinating Council.
The study of the general superintendency of the Methodist Church; a report to the General Conference of 1964, consisting of proposed legislation and recommendations, together with abridgements of the four basic research reports. [Nashville?] 1964. 134 p. 23 cm. [BX8340.A54] 64-1711
1. Methodist Church — Government. I. Title. II. Title: The general superintendency of the Methodist Church.

MORE, George Voiers, 1897- 262
Better church leaders. St. Louis, Bethany Press [1950] 127 p. diagr. 20 cm. Includes bibliographies. [BV705.M6] 50-11550
1. Church officers. I. Title.

MUELLER, Arnold Carl, 1891- 262
The ministry of the Lutheran teacher; a study to determine the position of the Lutheran parish school teacher within the public ministry of the church, by Arnold C. Mueller. St. Louis, Concordia Pub. House [1964] 174 p. front. 21 cm. Bibliography: p. 173-174. [BX8071.M8] 64-18882
1. Religious education as a profession. 2. Clergy — Office. 3. Lutheran Church — Clergy. I. Title.

MUELLER, Arnold Carl, 1891- 262
The ministry of the Lutheran teacher; a study to determine the position of the Lutheran parish school teacher within the public ministry of the church. St. Louis, Concordia [c.1964] 174p. front. 21cm. (12-2237) Bibl. 64-18882 3.00 pap.,
1. Religious education as a profession. 2. Clergy—Office. 3. Lutheran Church—Clergy. I. Title.

MURA, Ernest, 1900- 262
The nature of the mystical body. Translated by M. Angeline Bouchard. [St. Louis] B. Herder Book Co. [c1963] xxv, 293 p. 24 cm. "Translation of the first volume of Le corps mystique du Christ." Bibliographical footnotes. [BV600.5.M813] 63-22744
1. Jesus Christ — Mystical body. I. Title.

MURA, Ernest, 1900- 262
The nature of the mystical body. Tr. [from French] by M. Angeline Bouchard. [St. Louis] Herder [c.1963] xxv, 293p. 24cm. Bibl. 63-22744 5.75
1. Jesus Christ—Mystical body. I. Title.

NEW *visions, new roles* : 262
women in the church. Washington : Leadership Conference of Women Religious of the United States, 1975. 78 p. ; 26 cm. Bibliography: p. 77-78. [BX4210.N48] 76-355786
1. Monastic and religious life of women—Addresses, essays, lectures. 2. Women in church work—Catholic Church—Addresses, essays, lectures. 3. Feminism—Addresses, essays, lectures. I. Leadership Conference of Women Religious of the United States.

ODEN, Thomas C. 262
Beyond revolution; a response to the underground church, by Thomas C. Oden. Philadelphia, Westminster Press [1970] 142 p. 19 cm. Includes bibliographical references. [BV600.2.O3] 72-120409 ISBN 6-642-48950-2.45
1. Church renewal. 2. Non-institutional churches. I. Title.

OSBORN, Ronald E. 262
A church for these times [by] Ronald E. Osborn. New York, Abingdon Press [1965] 192 p. 20 cm. Some of the material was presented as the McFadin lectures, University Christian Church, Fort Worth, Tex., 1964. Bibliographical references included in "Notes" (p. 181-185) [BX8.2.O8] 65-14720
1. Christian union—Addresses, essays, lectures. 2. Consultation on Church Union. I. Title.

PALMER, Lee A 262
Aaronic priesthood through the centuries [by] Lee A. Palmer. Salt Lake City, Deseret Book Co., 1964. xi, 430 p. illus. 24 cm. Bibliography: p. [411]-414. [BX8657.P3] 64-66455
1. Priesthood — Hist. 2. Mormons and Mormonism — Clergy. I. Title.

PARSCH, Pius, 1884-1956 262
We are Christ's body. Tr. [from German] adapted by Clifford Howell. Notre Dame, Ind., Fides [1963, c.1962] 102p. 20cm. 63-24158 2.95
1. Jesus Christ—Mystical body—Sermons. 2. Catholic Church—Sermons. 3. Sermons, German—Translations into English. 4. Sermons, English—Translations from German. I. Title.

PIERSON, Robert H 262
So you want to be a leader! A spiritual, human relations, and promotional approach to church leadership and administration, by Robert H. Pierson. Mountain View, Calif., Pacific Press Pub. Association [1966] 452 p. 22 cm. Bibliographical footnotes. [BV652.1.P5] 66-20341
1. Christian leadership. I. Title.

PIERSON, Robert H. 262
So you want to be a leader! A spiritual, human relations, and promotional approach to church leadership and administration Mountain View, Calif., Pacific Pr. Pub. [c.1966] 152p. 22cm. Bibl [BV652.1.P5] 66-20341 2.50 pap.,
1. Christian leadership. I. Title.

POLE, Reginald, Cardinal, 262
1500-1558.
Defense of the unity of the church. Translated with introd. by Jospeh G. Dwyer. Westminster, Md., Newman Press, 1965. xii, 349 p. port. 24 cm. Bibliography: p. 345-346. [BR377.P713] 65-25980
1. Henry viii, King of England, 1491-1547. 2. Reformation—England. 3. Church—Unity. I. Dwyer, Joseph G., ed. and tr. il. II. Title.

POLE, Reginald Cardinal 1500- 262
1558
Defense of the unity of the church. Tr. [from Latin] introd. by Joseph G. Dwyer. Wesminster, Md., Newman [c.]1965. xli, 349p. port. 24cm. Bibl. [BR377.P713] 65-25980 6.50
1. Henry VIII, King of England, 1491-1547. 2. Reformation—England. 3. Church—Unity. I. Dwyer, Joseph G., ed. and tr. II. Title.

PRESBYTERIAN Church in the U. 262
S. Board of Christian Education. Division of Men's Work.
The work of the church--whose responsibility? Church officer's guide and notebook. [Rev.] Richmond, John Knox Press [1956] 88p. illus. col. maps, diagrs. (part col.) 28cm. 'Originally prepared in 1949 by Cameron D. Deans for the Division of Men's Work.' [BX8966.A44 1956] 56-9759
1. Presbyterian Church— Government. 2. Church officers. I. Title.

PRESBYTERIAN Church in the U. 262
S. General Assembly.
The book of church order of the Presbyterian Church in the United States. Rev. ed. [n. p.] Printed by the Board of Christian Education for the General Assembly of the Presbyterian Church in the United States, 1961. 174p. 21cm. [BX8966.A45 1961] 61-42474
1. Presbyterian Church in the U. S.—Government. I. Title.

ROSE, Stephen C. 262
The grass roots church; a manifesto for Protestant renewal [by] Stephen C. Rose. Introd. by Harvey Cox. [1st ed.] New York, Holt, Rinehart and Winston [1966] xviii, 174 p. 22 cm. [BV600.2.R66] 66-22067
1. Church renewal. I. Title.

SCHARP, Heinrich, 1899- 262
How the Catholic Church is governed. [Translation by Annelise Derrick. New York] Herder and Herder [1960] 167p. illus. 19cm. 'Based on the original German version of 'Wie die Kirche regiert wird." [BX1801.S313 1960a] 60-6658
1. Catholic Church—Government. I. Title.

SCHARP, Heinrich, 1899- 262
How the Catholic Church is governed. [Tr. [from German] by Annelise Derrick] New York, Paulist Pr. [1962, c.1960] 128p. (Deus bks.) .75 pap.,
1. Catholic Church—Government. I. Title.

SIGMUND, Paul E 262
Nicholas of Cusa and medieval political thought. Cambridge, Mass., Harvard University Press, 1963. viii, 335 p. port. 22 cm. (Harvard political studies) Bibliography: p. 317-330. [BX4705.N58S5] 63-20772
1. Nicolaus Cusanus, Cardinal, 1401-1464. 2. Conciliar theory. 3. Church and state—Catholic Church. I. Title. II. Series.

SIGMUND, Paul E. 262
Nicholas of Cusa and medieval political thought. Cambridge, Mass., Harvard [c.]1963. viii, 335p. port. 22cm. (Harvard pol. studies) Bibl. 63-20772 6.95
1. Nicolaus Cusanus, Cardinal, 1401-1464. 2. Conciliar theory. 3. Church and state—Catholic Church. I. Title. II. Series.

SISK, John P., 1914- 262
Person and institution [by] John P. Sisk. Notre Dame, Ind., Fides Publishers [1970] xiii, 90 p. 19 cm. (A Fides dome book, D-69) [BV640.S57] 73-79245 0.95
1. Institutionalism (Religion) I. Title.

SISSON, Charles Jasper, 1885- 262
1966.
The judicious marriage of Mr. Hooker and the birth of The laws of ecclesiastical polity. New York, Octagon Books, 1974. xvi, 203 p. 21 cm. Reprint of the 1940 ed. published at the University Press, Cambridge, Eng. [BV649.H9S5 1974] 74-9652 ISBN 0-374-97465-9 10.50
1. Hooker, Richard, 1553 or 4-1600. Ecclesiastical polity. I. Title.

TAVARD, George Henri, 1922- 262
The church tomorrow. Garden City, N.Y., Doubleday [1966, c.1965] 152p. (Image bk., D212) p.85 pap., [BX830 1962. T3]
1. Vatican Council, 2d. 2. Theology—20th cent. I. Title.

THOMPSON, Alexander Hamilton, 262
1873-
The English clergy and their organization in the later Middle Ages. Oxford, Clarendon Pr., 1947. xv, 327p. 23cm. (Ford lectures, 1933) Bibl. [BR750.T5] A48 5.60
1. Gt. Brit.—Church history—Medieval period. I. Title. II. Series.
Available from Oxford Univ. Pr., New York.

VATICAN Council. 2d, 1962- 262
1965.
Church; Vatican II's dogmatic constitution on the church; text and commentary, edited by Peter Foote [and others] New York, Holt, Rinehart and Winston [1969] 142 p. illus. 28 cm. (The Church in dialogue series) (The Holt program in religious education. Adult education group.) Translation of Constitutio dogmatica de ecclesia. Bibliographical references included in "Footnotes" (p. 134-137) [BX830 1962.A45C8733] 69-19557
1. Church. I. Foote, Peter, ed. II. Title.

VATICAN Council. 2d, 1962- 262
1965.
Dogmatic constitution on the Church: Lumen gentium, solemnly promulgated by His Holiness, Pope Paul VI on November 21, 1964. [N.C.W.C. translation. Boston] St. Paul Editions [1965?] 82 p. 18 cm. "This unofficial translation is based on the Latin text appearing in L'Osservatore romano, Nov. 25, 1964." "Supplementary notes" (bibliographical): p. 73-82. [BX830 1962.A45C823] 79-10281
1. Church. I. [Constitutio dogmatica de Ecclesia. English] II. Title.

WALLACE, Gervias Knox, 1903- 262
Wallace-Ketcherside debate, held near Paragould, Arkansas, June 30 July 4, 1952. Tape recorded; transcribed by Wm. Wayne Anderson. 1st ed. Longview, Wash., Telegram Book Co., 1952 [i.e.1953] 286p. illus. 22cm. [BX7094.C95W2] 53-25512
1. Churches of Christ—Government. I. Ketcherside, W. Carl. II. Title.

WINTER, Gibson. 262
Religious identity; a study of religious organization. New York, Macmillan [1968] ix, 143 p. 18 cm. (Studies in religion and society series) Part of the material included was previously published in v. 1. of The emergent American society, edited by W. Lloyd Warner. Bibliographical footnotes. [BR517.W55] 68-9701 1.45
1. Religious and ecclesiastical institutions—United States. 2. Institutionalism (Religion) 3. United States—Religion. I. Title. II. Series.

WOOD-LEGH, Kathleen Louise. 262
Perpetual chantries in Britain, by K. L. Wood-Legh. Cambridge [Eng.] University Press, 1965. xii, 356 p. illus. 33 cm. Bibliography: p. 331-344. [BX1956.W6] 65-28505
1. Chantries. I. Title.

WOOD-LEGH, Kathleen Louise 262
Perpetual chantries in Britain [New York] Cambridge [c.]1965. xii, 356p. illus. 33cm. Bibl. [BX1956.W6] 65-28505 13.50
1. Chantries. I. Title.

MCBRIEN, Richard P. 262.000924
The church in the thought of Bishop John Robinson [by] Richard P. McBrien. Philadelphia, Westminster [1966] xv, 160p. 23cm. Bibl. [BX5199.R722M3 1966a] 66-23087 3.95
1. Robinson, John Arthur Thomas, Bp., 1919-2. Church—History of doctrines—20th cent. I. Title.

ABBOT, Carolyn T. 262'.001
One church; a grass-roots view of the Protestant ecumenical movement, by Carolyn T. Abbot. [1st ed.] New York, Exposition Press [1967] 135 p. 21 cm. Bibliography: p. [126]-135. [BX8.2.A2] 67-24257
1. United Church of Christ—Doctrinal and controversial works. 2. Christian union. I. Title.

ADAMS, Michael, ed. 262.001
Vatican II on ecumenism. [1st ed.] Dublin, Chicago, Scepter Bks. [1966] 117p. 22cm. Bibl. [BX830 1962.A45O462] 66-9026 1.50 pap.,
1. Vatican Council, 2d, 1962-1965. De Oecumenismo. I. Title.

ALLEN, Donald R., 1930- 262'.001
Barefoot in the church [by] Donald R. Allen. Richmond, Va., John Knox Press [1972] 187 p. 21 cm. Includes bibliographical references. [BV600.2.A4] 72-1759 ISBN 0-8042-1540-5
1. Harrisonburg, Va. Trinity Presbyterian Church. 2. Church renewal—Case studies. I. Title.

ALTING VON GEUSAU, Leo 262.001
George Marie, ed.
Ecumenism and the Roman Catholic Church. Ed. by Leo Alting von Geusau. Tr. by H. J. J. Vaughan, J. S. Harding, and the Documentation Ctr. (DO-C) Westminster, Md., Newman [1966] v, 186p. 19cm. (DO-C dossiers, 2) Working papers for the Second Vatican Council. [BX8.2.A1A4] 66-31525 3.95
1. Christian union—Addresses, essays, lectures. I. Vatican Council. 2d., 1962-1965. II. Title. III. Series: Documentatie-Centrum Concilie. DO-C dossiers, 2

ANGLICAN/ROMAN Catholic 262'.001
Joint Preparatory Commission.
Anglican/Roman Catholic dialogue; the work of the Preparatory Commission, edited by Alan C. Clark and Colin Davey. London, New York, Oxford University Press, 1974. 129 p. 22 cm. Includes bibliographical references. [BX5129.A53 1974] 74-163055 ISBN 0-19-213425-6 3.25 (pbk.)
1. Church of England—Relations—Catholic Church. 2. Catholic Church—Relations—Church of England. I. Clark, Alan C., ed. II. Davey, Colin, 1934- ed. III. Title.

ARROWSMITH, John. 262'.001
Visible unity and the ten propositions / [by] John Arrowsmith, Peter Boulton, Derek Gibbs. London : Church Literature Association, 1976. [2], 7 p. ; 21 cm. (Dolphin papers ; 3) Cover title. [BX8.2.A7] 76-383987 ISBN 0-85191-080-7 : £0.18
1. Christian union—Anglican Communion. I. Boulton, Peter, joint author. II. Gibbs, Derek, joint author. III. Title.

BARR, Browne. 262'.001
The well church book / Browne Barr. New York : Seabury Press, c1976. p. cm. "A Crossroad book." [BV600.2.B36] 76-18291 ISBN 0-8164-0304-X : 7.95

1. Church renewal—Addresses, essays, lectures. 2. Church—Addresses, essays, lectures. I. Title.

BAUM, Gregory, 1923- 262'.001
comp.
Ecumenical theology today. Glen Rock, N. J., Paulist Press [1964-] v. 19 cm. (An Original Deus book) Vol. 2 has title: Ecumenical theology. "A short bibliography of ecumenical literature, [by] Paul Broadhurst": v. [1] p. 245-256. [BX9.B34] 64-24514
1. Christian union—Addresses, essays, lectures. I. Title.

BAXTER, James Sidlow. 262'.001
Rethinking our priorities; the church: its pastor and people ... By J. Sidlow Baxter. Grand Rapids, Zondervan Pub. House [1974] 255 p. 23 cm. [BR1640.B38] 73-22698 6.95
1. Evangelicalism. I. Title.

BEA, Augustin, 262'.001
Cardinal, 1881-
The way to unity after the Council. [New York] Herder and Herder [1967] 256 p. 23 cm. Bibliographical footnotes. [BX8.2.B38] 67-19546
1. Christian union-Catholic Church. 2. Vatican Council. 2d. 1962-1965. I. Title.

BEA, Augustin, Cardinal, 262.001
1881-1968.
Peace among Christians [by] Augustin Bea and Willem A. Visser 't Hooft. Translated by Judith Moses. New York, Association Press [1967] 236 p. 22 cm. Translation of Friede zwischen Christen. Bibliographical footnotes. [BX8.2.A1B373] 67-25877
1. Christian union—Addresses, essays, lectures. I. Visser 't Hooft, Willem Adolph, 1900- II. Title.

BENJAMIN, Paul. 262'.001
The growing congregation. Lincoln, Ill., Lincoln Christian College Press [1972] xvi, 94 p. 21 cm. [BV652.25.B45] 73-189037
1. Church growth. I. Title.

BLACK, Antony. 262'.001
Monarchy and community; political ideas in the later conciliar controversy 1430-1450. Cambridge [Eng.] University Press, 1970. xii, 189 p. 23 cm. (Cambridge studies in medieval life and thought, 3d ser., no. 2) Bibliography: p. 173-182. [BV720.B57] 72-108101 ISBN 0-521-07739-7 65/- ($10.50)
1. Conciliar theory. 2. Political science—History. I. Title. II. Series.

BLOESCH, Donald G., 262'.001
1928-
The reform of the church, by Donald G. Bloesch. Grand Rapids, Mich., Eerdmans [1970] 199 p. 23 cm. Includes bibliographical references. [BV600.2.B57] 77-95463 4.95
1. Church renewal. I. Title.

BROHOLM, Richard R. 262'.001
Strategic planning for church organizations [by] Richard R. Broholm. Valley Forge [Pa.] Judson Press [1969] 32 p. 22 cm. [BV652.B68] 69-16393 1.00
1. Church management. I. Title.

BROWN, Robert McAfee, 262'.001
1920-
The ecumenical revolution; an interpretation of the Catholic-Protestant dialogue. [1st ed.] Garden City, N.Y., Doubleday, 1967. xix, 388 p. 22 cm. Based on the William Belden Noble lectures for 1964-65. Bibliography: p. [366]-380. [BX6.5.B75] 67-12862
1. Catholic Church—Relations—Protestant churches. 2. Ecumenical movement—History. 3. Protestant churches—Relations—Catholic Church. I. Title. II. Series: William Belden Noble lectures, Harvard University, 1965.

BROWN, Robert McAfee, 262'.001
1920-
Frontiers for the church today. New York, Oxford University Press, 1973. xvii, 149 p. 21 cm. Bibliography: p. [136]-143. [BV600.2.B725] 73-82662 ISBN 0-19-501700-5 5.95
1. Church. 2. Christianity—20th century. I. Title.

CATHOLIC Church. 262'.001
Ecumenical Commission for England and Wales.
The Roman Catholic Church in England and the Ten Propositions of the Churches' Unity Commission : a paper / by the Ecumenical Commission of England and Wales. Abbots Langley : Catholic Information Office, 1976. [1], 8 p. ; 21 cm. Cover title. A provisional response to the report of the Churches' Unity Commission entitled: Visible unity: ten propositions. [BX1784.C35 1976] 77-359592 ISBN 0-905241-04-5 : £0.15
1. Catholic Church. Unity Commission. Visible unity. 2. Catholic Church in England. 3. Christian union—Catholic Church. I. Title: The Roman Catholic Church in England and the Ten Propositions ...

CAVERT, Samuel McCrea, 262'.001
1888-
The American churches in the ecumenical movement, 1900-1968. American churches in the ecumenical movement nineteen hundred--nineteen sixty-eight New York, Association Press [1968] 288 p. 28 cm. Includes bibliographical references. [BX6.5.C37] 68-17775
1. Ecumenical movement—History. 2. Christian union—United States. I. Title.

CHITWOOD, Billy J. 262'.001
What the church needs now; a plan for renewal [by] B. J. Chitwood. Old Tappan, N.J., F. H. Revell Co. [1973] 160 p. 21 cm. Bibliography: p. 157-160. [BV600.2.C43] 73-2732 ISBN 0-8007-0588-2 4.95
1. Church renewal. I. Title.

CLARK, Henry, 1930- 262'.001
Ministries of dialogue; the church confronts the power structure. New York, Association Press [1971] 224 p. 22 cm. "Ministries of dialogue—a listing": p. [12]-[13] Includes bibliographical references. [BR115.W6C58] 70-152894 ISBN 0-8096-1829-X 6.95
1. Church and the world. I. Title.

CLARK, Stephen B. 262'.001
Building Christian communities; strategy for renewing the church [by] Stephen B. Clark. Notre Dame, Ind., Ave Maria Press [1972] 189 p. 21 cm. Bibliography: p. 187-189. [BX1746.C53] 75-189990 ISBN 0-87793-043-0 (pbk.) 1.50
1. Church renewal—Catholic Church. I. Title.

CLARK, Stephen B. 262'.001
Unordained elders and renewal communities / by Stephen B. Clark. New York : Paulist Press, c1976. v, 105 p. ; 21 cm. Bibliography: p. 95-105. [BX1746.C5324] 75-35329 ISBN 0-8091-1916-1 pbk. : 3.50
1. Church renewal—Catholic Church. 2. Pentecostalism. 3. Asceticism—History. 4. Elders (Church officers) 5. Ordination—Catholic Church. I. Title.

COLEMAN, Richard J. 262'.001
Issues of theological warfare: evangelicals and liberals, by Richard J. Coleman. Grand Rapids, Eerdmans [1972] 206 p. 21 cm. Includes bibliographical references. [BR1615.C63] 71-180785 ISBN 0-8028-1438-7 3.45
1. Liberalism (Religion)—United States. 2. Evangelicalism—United States. I. Title.

CONGAR, Yves Marie 262'.001
Joseph, 1904-
Dialogue between Christians: Catholic contributions to ecumenism [by] Yves M. -J. Congar. Translated by Philip Loretz. Westminster, Md., Newman Press, 1966. vii, 472 p. 23 cm. Bibliographical footnotes. [BX8.2.C5813 1966a] 66-27909
1. Christian union—Addresses, essays, lectures. I. Title.

CONGAR, Yves Marie 262'.001
Joseph, 1904-
Ecumenism and the future of the Church [by] Yves Congar. Chicago, Priory Pr. [1967] 181p. 21cm. First 6 chapters are a tr. of Aspects de l'oecumenisme. The last chapter is a tr. of L'avenir de l'Eglise, orig. pub. in L'Avenir in 1963. [BX8.2.C583] 67-14012 3.95
1. Christian union—Addresses. essays, lectures. I. Title.

CONSULTATION on Church 262'.001
Union.
Consultation on Church Union, 1967 : principles of Church Union, guidelines for structure, and a study guide [Cincinnati : Forward Movement Publications, c1967] 142 p. ; 17 cm. (A Forward Movement miniature book) Bibliography: p. 140-142. [BX6.C6823] 75-303683 0.25
1. Consultation on Church Union. 2. Christian union.

CONSULTATION on Church 262'.001
Union.
A plan of union for the Church of Christ Uniting. Princeton, N.J. [1970] 104 p. 23 cm. [BX6.C6825] 70-23669 0.65
1. Church of Christ Uniting. I. Title.

CORNELL, George W. 262.001
Voyage of faith; the Catholic Church in transition New York, Odyssey [c.1966] 250p. 24cm. [BX8.2.C6] 65-27074 5.00 bds.,
1. Paulus VI, 1897- 2. Christian union—Catholic Church. I. Title.

CROW, Paul A. 262'.001
Church union at midpoint. Edited by Paul A. Crow, Jr. and William Jerry Boney. New York, Association Press [1972] 253 p. 23 cm. Bibliography: p. 243-248. [BR516.5.C76] 72-4341 ISBN 0-8096-1848-6 Pap 7.95
1. Consultation on Church Union—Addresses, essays, lectures. 2. Christian union—United States—Addresses, essays, lectures. I. Boney, William Jerry, joint author. II. Title.

CURRY, Lerond. 262'.001
Protestant-Catholic relations in America, World War I through Vatican II. [Lexington] University Press of Kentucky [1972] xi, 124 p. 23 cm. Includes bibliographical references. [BX4818.3.C87] 79-183352 ISBN 0-8131-1265-6 7.25
1. Catholic Church—Relations—Protestant churches. 2. Protestant churches—Relations—Catholic Church. 3. United States—Religion. I. Title.

CURTIS, Charles J 262'.001
Facets of ecumenicity, by C. J. Curtis. [Chicago? c1966] 76 p. illus. 22 cm. (Loyola Ecumenical Forum. Public lectures, 1966) Bibliography: p. 75-76. [BX8.2.C8] 66-29984
1. Christian union. I. Title. II. Series.

CURTIS, Charles J. 262'.001
Facets of ecumenicity, by C. J. Curtis. [Chicago? c1966] 76 p. illus. 22 cm. (Loyola Ecumenical Forum. Public lectures, 1966) Bibliography: p. 75-76. [BX8.2.C8] 66-29984
1. Christian union. I. Title. II. Series.

DAY, Peter. 262'.001
Tomorrow's church: catholic, evangelical, reformed. New York, Seabury Press [1969] 192 p. 21 cm. (A Seabury paperback, SP50) Bibliographical footnotes. [BX8.2.D33] 68-24009 2.95
1. Christian union. 2. Consultation on Church Union. I. Title.

DEHONEY, Wayne. 262'.001
Set the church afire! Nashville, Broadman Press [1971] 156 p. 21 cm. [BV600.2.D48] 72-136135 4.50
1. Church renewal—Southern Baptist Convention. I. Title.

DIRKS, Lee E. 262'.001
The ecumenical movement, by Lee E. Dirks. [1st ed. New York, Public Affairs Committee, 1969] 28 p. group ports. 19 cm. (Public affairs pamphlet no. 431) [BX8.2.D5] 79-3743 0.25
1. World Council of Churches. 2. Christian union—History. I. Title.

DO we know the others? 262.001
New York, Paulist [1966.i.e.,1967] ix, 180p. 24cm. (Concilium theol. in the age of renewal; Ecumenical. theol., v. 14) Bibl. [BX1784.D6] 66-20895 4.50
1. Catholic Church — Relations — Addresses, essays, lectures. 2. Christian union — Addresses, essays, lectures. I. Series: Councilium theology in the age of reneval, v.14

DOLAN, Rex Robert, 1921- 262'.001
The big change; the challenge to radical change in the church, by Rex R. Dolan. Philadelphia, Westminster Press [1968, c1967] 122 p. 19 cm. [BV600.2.D6 1968] 68-11031
1. Church renewal. 2. Christianity—20th century. I. Title.

ECUMENISM and religious 262.001
education [by] Le Guillou [others] Chicago, Loyola Univ. Pr. [c.]1965. viii, 276p. 24cm. (Loyola pastoral ser.: Lumen vitae studies) Consists chiefly of articles first pub. in Lumen vitae, v.19, 1964. Bibl. [BX8.2.A1E25] 65-28199 4.00
1. Christian union—Addresses, essays, lectures. 2. Religious education. I. Le Guillou, M. J. II. Lumen vitae.

EDGE, Findley Bartow, 262'.001
1916-
The greening of the church [by] Findley B. Edge. Waco, Tex., Word Books [1971] 195 p. 23 cm. Bibliography: p. 193-195. [BV600.2.E3] 70-170911 4.95
1. Church renewal. 2. Mission of the church. I. Title.

EHRLICH, Rudolf J. 262.001
Rome, opponent or partner? Philadelphia, Westminster [1966, c.1965] 295p. 23cm. Bibl. [BX4818.3.E4] 66-10260 5.00
1. Catholic Church—Relations—Protestant Churches. 2. Protestant churches—Relations—Catholic Church. I. Title.

ERASMUS, Desiderius, 262'.001
d.1536.
Erasmus and the seamless coat of Jesus. De sarcienda Ecclesiae concordia (On restoring the unity of the Church). With selections from the Letters and Ecclesiastes. Translations with introd. and notes by Raymond Himelick. Lafayette, Ind., Purdue University Studies, 1971. ix, 222 p. 24 cm. Bibliography: p. 220-222. [BR350.E7A2513] 70-151515 ISBN 0-911198-29-6 6.25
I. Himelick, Raymond, ed. II. Title.

ESTEP, William Roscoe, 262.001
1920-
Baptists and Christian unity [by] William R. Estep. Nashville, Broadman Press [1966] 200 p. 23 cm. Bibliography: p. 195-199. [BX8.2.E78] 67-12169
1. Christian union—Baptists. I. Title.

FIFE, Robert O. 262'.001
Disciples and the church universal, by Robert O. Fife, David Edwin Harrell, Jr. [and] Ronald E. Osborn. Nashville, Tenn., Disciples of Christ Historical Society, 1967. 64 p. 23 cm. (The Reed lectures for 1966) Includes bibliographical references. [BX9.F52] 78-17204
1. Christian union—Disciples of Christ—Addresses, essays, lectures. I. Harrell, David Edwin, joint author. II. Osborn, Ronald E., joint author. III. Disciples of Christ Historical Society. IV. Title. V. Series.

FIOLET, Hermanus 262'.001
Antonius Maria.
Ecumenical breakthrough; an integration of the Catholic and the Reformational faith, by Herman A. Fiolet. Pittsburg, Duquesne University Press [1969] 475 p. 22 cm. (Duquesne studies. Theological series, 9) "This book is a combination and revision of the author's original Dutch works, Onvermoed perspectief of de oecumene and Dilemma doorbroken ... supplemented by additional materials." Includes bibliographical references. [BX8.2.F5] 71-98548 9.95
1. Christian union—Catholic Church. 2. Theology, Doctrinal. 3. Church. I. Title. II. Series.

FIRST steps in Christian 262'.001
renewal, edited by Abigail Q. McCarthy. Wilkes-Barre, Pa., Dimension Books [1967] 211 p. 21 cm. "Papers ... originally presented at a workshop, 'Let's educate for ecumenism,' held at Trinity College, Washington, D.C."—p. 209. [BX8.2.A1F5] 67-27132
1. Ecumenical movement—Collections. I. McCarthy, Abigail Quigley, ed. II. Trinity College, Washington, D.C.

FLINT, Edward. 262'.001
Family of believers; Christians in dialogue. Dayton, Ohio, G. A. Pflaum, 1969. 127 p. illus. 18 cm. (Christian identity series) (Witness book CI 2.) Bibliography: p. 123-124. [BX1751.2.F55] 74-97041 0.95
1. Catholic Church—Doctrinal and controversial works—Catholic authors. 2. Christian union. I. Title.

FORD, Josephine 262'.001
Massyngberde.
Which way for Catholic pentecostals? / J. Massyngberde Ford. 1st ed. New York : Harper & Row, c1976. x, 143 p. ; 21 cm. Bibliography: p. [137]-143. [BX2350.57.F67 1976] 75-36757 ISBN 0-06-062672-0 : 6.95
1. Pentecostalism. I. Title.

FOX, Robert Joseph, 262'.001
1927-
Renewal for all God's people / Robert J. Fox. Huntington, Ind. : Our Sunday Visitor, inc., c1975. 256 p. ; 18 cm. [BX1751.2.F67] 74-33128 ISBN 0-87973-790-5 pbk. : 2.50
1. Catholic Church—Doctrinal and controversial works—Catholic authors. I. Title.

THE Future of 262'.001
ecumenism. Edited by Hans Kung. New York, Paulist Press [1969] x, 181 p. 24 cm. (Concilium: theology in the age of renewal. Ecumenical theology, v. 44) Bibliographical footnotes. [BX6.9.F84] 71-84552 4.50
1. Ecumenical movement—Addresses, essays, lectures. I. Kung, Hans, 1928- ed. II. Series: Concilium (New York) v. 44

GAINES, David P. 262.001
The World Council of Churches, a study of its background and history, by David P. Gaines. [1st ed.] Peterborough, N.H., R. R. Smith [1966] xviii, 1302 p. 25 cm. Bibliography: p. 1265-1281. [BX6.W78G3] 63-17177
1. World Council of Churches.

GENTZ, William H., 262'.001 B
1918-
The world of Philip Potter [by] William H. Gentz. New York, Friendship Press [1974] 96 p. illus. 20 cm. Includes excerpts from P. Potter's speeches. Includes bibliographical references. [BX6.8.P67G46] 74-9918 ISBN 0-377-00006-X 2.95 (pbk.)
1. Potter, Philip. I. Potter, Philip. The world of Philip Potter. 1974. II. Title.

GERARD, Francois C., 262'.001
1924-
The future of the church : the theology of renewal of Willem Adolf Visser't Hooft / Francois C. Gerard. Pittsburgh : Pickwick Press, 1974. xii, 239 p. : port. ; 22 cm. (Pittsburgh theological monograph series ; 2) Bibliography: p. 232-239. [BV600.2.G42] 74-26564 ISBN 0-915138-01-8 6.95

1. Visser't Hooft, Willem Adolph, 1900- 2. Church renewal—History of doctrines. I. Title. II. Series.

GIRARD, Robert C. 262'.001
Brethren, hang loose; or, What's happening to my church? [by] Robert C. Girard. Introd. by Lawrence O. Richards. Grand Rapids, Mich., Zondervan Pub. House [1972] 220 p. 21 cm. Includes bibliographical references. [BV600.2.G49] 77-183050 4.95
1. Church renewal. I. Title.
Pap. $1.95

GREEN, Edward Michael Bankes 262.001
Called to serve; ministry and ministers in the church, by Michael Green [pseud.] Philadelphia, Westminster [1965, c.1964] 94p. 19cm. (Christian founds.) Bibl. [BV660.2.G7] 65-16838 1.25 pap.,
1. Clergy—Office. 2. Episcopacy. I. Title.

GREENSPUN, William B., ed. 262.001
Living room dialogues, ed. by William B. Greenspun,William A. Norgren. [New York] Natl. Council of the Churches of Christ [1965] 256p. form. 19cm. [BX8.2.A1G7] 65-28465 1.00 pap.,
1. Christian union—Collections. I. Norgren, William A., joint ed. II. Title.

GREENSPUN, William B., ed. 262.001
Second living room dialogues, ed. by William B. Greenspun, and William A. Norgren. [New York] Friendship Pr., Natl. Council of the Churches of Christ in the U.S.A. and Paulist Pr., Glen Rock, N.J. Paulist [1967] v. 18cm. [BX8.2.a1G7] 1.00 pap.,
1. Christian union—Colleections. I. Norgren, William A., joint ed. II. Title.

GRIFFITH, Arthur Leonard, 1920- 262'.001
We have this ministry [by] Leonard Griffith. Waco, Tex., Word Books [1973] 122 p. 23 cm. [BV600.2.G75] 73-84580 3.95
1. Church renewal. I. Title.

GUNDERSEN, Valborg J 262'.001 (B)
Long shadow; the living story of a layman and his Lord, by Valborg J. Gundersen. Minneapolis, Beacon Publications, 1966] 126 p. port. 22 cm. [BX7547.Z8G85] 67-8634
1. Gundersen, Carl A., 1897-1964. I. Title.

HAMANN, Henry Paul. 262'.001
Unity and fellowship and ecumenicity [by] Henry Hamann. St. Louis, Concordia Pub. House [1973] 48 p. 23 cm. (Contemporary theology series) Includes bibliographical references. [BX8.2.H3] 73-80313 ISBN 0-570-06725-1 1.95
1. Christian union. 2. Fellowship. I. Title.

HANEY, David. 262'.001
The idea of the laity. Grand Rapids, Zondervan Pub. House [1973] 188 p. 21 cm. Bibliography: p. 185. [BV600.2.H315] 73-2654 1.95 (pbk.)
1. Church renewal. 2. Laity. I. Title.

HANEY, David. 262'.001
Renew my church; a group study book. Grand Rapids, Zondervan Pub. House [1972] 95 p. 21 cm. "An Evangelism Research Foundation book." Includes bibliographies. [BV600.H265] 76-187964
1. Church renewal. I. Title.

HARMON, Francis Stuart, 1895- 262'.001
The Interchurch Center : reminiscences of an incorrigible promoter / by Francis Stuart Harmon. [New York] : Harmon, c1972. 385 p. : ill. ; 28 cm. Includes index. [BX6.N2H37] 70-185585
1. New York (City). Interchurch Center. 2. National Council of the Churches of Christ in the United States of America. I. Title.

HARPER, Michael. 262'.001
Let my people grow : ministry and leadership in the church / Michael Harper. Plainfield, N.J. : Logos International, c1977. 254 p. ; 21 cm. Includes index. Bibliography: p. [247]-248. [BV600.2.H35] 77-73840 ISBN 0-88270-236-X : 3.50
1. Church renewal—Church of England. 2. Church polity. 3. Christian leadership.

HEIDEMAN, Eugene P. 262'.001
Reformed bishops and catholic elders, by Eugene Heideman. Grand Rapids, Eerdmans [1970] 267 p. 23 cm. Includes bibliographical references. [BX9.5.C5H4] 67-19335 6.95
1. Church polity and Christian union. I. Title.

HENDERSON, Ian, 1910- 262'.001
Power without glory; a study in ecumenical politics. [American ed.] Richmond, John Knox Press [1969, c1967] xiii, 184 p. 21 cm. Bibliographical footnotes. [BX8.2.H4 1969] 69-19857 4.50
1. Church of England—Relations—Church of Scotland. 2. Church of Scotland—Relations—Church of England. 3. Christian union. I. Title.

HERLONG, T. L. 262'.001
Maturity revisited, by T. L. Herlong. Liguori, Mo., Liguori Publications [1972] 40 p. 19 cm. (A Liguorian combination book) With, as issued, Roberts, William. Teach us to pray. Liguori, Mo. [1972] [BV213.R553] 72-187089 1.50
1. Church renewal—Catholic Church. I. Title.

HOLMES, William A. 262'.001
Tomorrow's church, a cosmopolitan community; a radical experiment in church renewal [by] William A. Holmes. Nashville, Abingdon Press [1968] 176 p. 21 cm. [BV600.2.H59] 68-17437
1. Church renewal—Case studies. 2. Suburban churches. I. Title.

THE Holy Spirit and power 262'.001
: the Catholic charismatic renewal / Kilian McDonnell, editor. 1st ed. Garden City, N.Y. : Doubleday, 1975. 186 p. ; 21 cm. Includes bibliographical references. [BX2350.57.H64] 74-32573 ISBN 0-385-09909-6 pbk. : 2.95
1. Pentecostalism. I. McDonnell, Kilian.

HORTON, Douglas, 1891- 262'.001
Toward an undivided church. With a foreword by Richard Cardinal Cushing. New York, Association Press [1967] 96 p. 20 cm. "Addresses to the Protestant and Orthodox observers and guests at Vatican II, 1962-1965, [by Pope John XXIII, Pope Paul VI, and Augustin Cardinal Bea]": (p. 63-96) Bibliographical footnotes. [BX8.2.H6] 67-10932
1. Vatican Council. 2d, 1962-1965. 2. Christian union—Catholic Church. I. Title.

HUBER, Roger. 262'.001
No middle ground; a celebration of the liberation from religion. Introd. by George W. Webber. Nashville, Abingdon Press [1971] 153 p. 22 cm. Includes bibliographical references. [BV600.2.H8] 78-158675 ISBN 0-687-28033-8
1. Church renewal. I. Title.

IRISH directory on ecumenism. 262'.001
Issued by the Irish hierarchy, January 1969. [Dublin] Catholic Truth Society of Ireland [1969] 12 p. 19 cm. [BX8.2.I7] 74-151166 1/-
1. Christian union—Catholic Church. I. Catholic Truth Society of Ireland.

JACKSON, Joseph Harrison, 1900- 262'.001
Nairobi—a joke, a junket, or a journey? : Reflections upon the fifth Assembly of the World Council of Churches, November 27-December 8, 1975 / by J. H. Jackson. Nashville : Townsend Press, 1976. xix, 130 p. : ill. ; 23 cm. Includes index. Bibliography: p. 125-126. [BX6.W77 1975.J3] 76-27046 5.50
1. World Council of Churches. 5th Assembly, Nairobi, 1975. I. Title.

JAEGER, Lorenz, Cardinal, 1892- 262.001
A stand on ecumenism: the Council's decree [by] Lorenz Cardinal Jaeger. Translated by Hilda Graef. New York, P. J. Kenedy [1965] xiii, 242 p. 22 cm. Translation of Konzilsdekret "Uber den Okumenismus." "Sources of the decree 'On ecumenism'": p. 223-236. 65-26330
1. Vatican Council, 2d. De oecumenismo. I. Title.

JAEGER, Lorenz, Cardinal, 1892- 262.001
A stand on ecumenism: the Council's decree. Tr. [from German] by Hilda Graef. New York, Kenedy [c.1965] xiii, 242p. 22cm. Bibl. [BX8301962.A45D4653] 65-26330 4.95
1. Vatican Council, 2d. De oecumenismo. I. Title.

JONES, Eli Stanley, 1884- 262'.001
The reconstruction of the Church—on what pattern? [by] E. Stanley Jones. Nashville, Abingdon Press [1970] 208 p. 23 cm. [BV600.2.J6] 72-124747 4.95
1. Church renewal. I. Title.

JONES, James William, 1943- 262'.001
Filled with new wine; the charismatic renewal of the church [by] James W. Jones. [1st ed.] New York, Harper & Row [1974] xiii, 141 p. 21 cm. Includes bibliographical references. [BX8763.J65] 73-6342 5.95
1. Pentecostalism. 2. Church renewal. I. Title.

KELLEY, Hugh N., 1911- 262'.001
The profile of a parish, by H. N. Kelley. New York, Morehouse-Barlow Co. [1973] xiii, 111 p. 19 cm. Pages 48 and 49 misplated. [BX5980.D394S334] 73-84096 ISBN 0-8192-1163-X 3.50 (pbk.)
1. St. Gregory's Church, Deerfield, Ill. 2. Church renewal—Case studies. I. Title.

KENT, John, 1923- 262.001
The age of disunity. London, Epworth P., 1966. xii, 209 p. tables. 22 1/2 cm. 30/- (B 66-5893) [BX5129.8.M4K4] 66-71072
1. Methodist Church — Relations — Church of England. 2. Church of England — Relations — Methodist Church. I. Title.

KNAPP, Forrest Lamar, 1899- 262.001
Church cooperation: dead-end street or highway to unity? Garden City, N.Y., Doubleday [c.]1966. xi, 249p. 22cm. Bibl. [BX8.2.K55] 66-17390 4.95
1. Christian union. 2. Interdenominational cooperation. I. Title.

KNAPP, Forrest Lamar, 1899- 262.001
Church cooperation: dead-end street or highway to unity? [By] Forrest L. Knapp. [1st ed.] Garden City, N.Y., Doubleday, 1966. xi, 249 p. 22 cm. Bibliographical references included in "Notes" (p. [243]-249) [BX8.2.K55] 66-17390
1. Christian union. 2. Interdenominational cooperation. I. Title.

KUNG, Hans, 1928- 262'.001
Truthfulness; the future of the church. New York, Sheed and Ward [1968] vi, 185 p. 22 cm. Essays, some translated from the German. Includes bibliographical references. [BV600.2.K823] 68-9369 4.50
1. Catholic Church—Doctrinal and controversial works. 2. Church renewal—Catholic church. I. Title.

LAMBERT, Bernard 262'.001
Ecumenism: theology and history: tr. [from French] by Lancelot C. Sheppard. London, Burns & Oates. New York, Herder & Herder [1967] x, 533p. 25cm. Orig. pub. as Le probleme oecumenique. Paris. Editions du Centurions. 1962. Bibl. [BX8.2.L2713 1967] 67-21091 13.50
1. Christian union. I. Title.

LAMBERT, Bernard. 262'.001
Ecumenism: theology and history; translated [from the French] by Lancelot C. Sheppard. London, Burns & Oates; New York, Herder & Herder [1967] x, 533 p. 24 1/2 cm. 90/- (B 67-19374) Bibliographical footnotes. [BX8.2.L2713] 67-21091
1. Originally published as Le probleme oecumenique. Paris, Editions du Centurions, 1962. 2. Christian union. I. Title.

LASH, Nicholas, comp. 262'.001
... until He comes; a study in the progress toward Christian unity. Dayton, Ohio, Pflaum Press, 1968 [c1967] xii, 223 p. 21 cm. Bibliographical footnotes. [BX8.2.L29] 68-21237
1. Christian union—Addresses, essays, lectures. I. Title.

LEFEVER, Harry G. 262'.001
The house church in the twentieth century; a study of Trinity Presbyterian Church, Harrisonburg, Virginia, by Harry G. Lefever. Atlanta, Board of National Ministries, Presbyterian Church in the United States [1969] iii, 94 l. 29 cm. Bibliography: leaves 93-94. [BX9211.H22L4] 76-19928
1. Harrisonburg, Va. Trinity Presbyterian Church. 2. Church renewal. 3. House churches—Virginia—Harrisonburg. I. Title.

LIGHTNER, Robert Paul. 262'.001
Church union: a layman's guide, by Robert P. Lightner. Des Plaines, Ill., Regular Baptist Press [1971] 163 p. 21 cm. Bibliography: p. 155-156. [BX8.2.L48] 72-176318
1. Ecumenical movement—Controversial literature. I. Title.

LINTHICUM, Robert C. 262'.001
Christian revolution for church renewal, by Robert C. Linthicum. Philadelphia, Westminster Press [1972] 173 p. 19 cm. Bibliography: p. [169]-173. [BV600.2.L54] 72-1410 ISBN 0-664-24959-0 3.25
1. Church renewal. I. Title.

LOETSCHER, Lefferts Augustine, 1904- 262'.001
The problem of Christian unity in early nineteenth-century America, by Lefferts A. Loetscher. Philadelphia, Fortress Press [1969] ix, 25 p. 20 cm. (Facet books. Historical series, 12) "First published in Church history, [v.] XXXII (March, 1963), [p.] 3-16." Includes bibliographical references. [BX6.5.L6] 69-14622 0.85
1. Christian union—U.S.—History. I. Title.

LOWELL, C. Stanley. 262'.001
The ecumenical mirage, by C. Stanley Lowell. Grand Rapids, Baker Book House [1967] 205 p. 23 cm. Includes bibliographical references. [BX8.2.L6] 67-18182
1. Christian union. I. Title.

LUBICH, Chiara, 1920- 262'.001
That all men be one; origins and life of the Focolare Movement. New York, New City Press [1969] 105 p. 19 cm. [BX809.F6L8] 71-77438 2.50
1. Focolare Movement. I. Title.

LUNDIN, Jack W. 262'.001
A church for an open future : Biblical roots and parish renewal / Jack W. Lundin ; with a foreword by Martin E. Marty. Philadelphia : Fortress Press, c1977. p. cm. [BV600.2.L86] 77-78634 ISBN 0-8006-1307-4 pbk. : 4.25
1. Community of Christ the Servant—Lombard, Ill. 2. Church renewal—Lutheran Church—Case studies. 3. Pastoral theology—Biblical teaching. I. Title.

LUNDIN, Jack W. 262'.001
A church for an open future : Biblical roots and parish renewal / Jack W. Lundin ; with a foreword by Martin E. Marty. Philadelphia : Fortress Press, c1977. p. cm. [BV600.2.L86] 77-78634 ISBN 0-8006-1307-4 pbk. : 4.25
1. Community of Christ the Servant—Lombard, Ill. 2. Church renewal—Lutheran Church—Case studies. 3. Pastoral theology—Biblical teaching. I. Title.

MCBRIEN, Richard P. 262'.001
The remaking of the church; an agenda for reform [by] Richard P. McBrien [1st ed.] New York, Harper & Row [1973] xv, 175 p. 21 cm. Includes bibliographical references. [BX1746.M18] 73-6333 ISBN 0-06-065327-2 6.95
1. Church renewal—Catholic Church. I. Title.

MCCARTHY, Abigail Quigley, ed. 262'.001
First steps in Christian renewal, edited by Abigail Q. McCarthy. Wilkes-Barre, Pa., Dimension Books [1967] 211 p. 21 cm. "Papers ... originally presented at a workshop, 'Let's educate for ecumenism,' held at Trinity College, Washington, D. C."--p. 209. [BX8.2.A1F5] 67-27132
1. Ecumenical movement—Collections. I. Trinity College, Washington, D. C. II. Title.

MACQUARRIE, John. 262'.001
Christian unity and Christian diversity / John Macquarrie. Philadelphia : Westminster Press, [1975] 118 p. ; 20 cm. Includes bibliographical references and index. [BX8.2.M325] 75-9674 ISBN 0-664-24782-2 pbk. : 2.85
1. Christian union. 2. Christianity and other religions. I. Title.

MCQUILKIN, J. Robertson, 1927- 262'.001
How Biblical is the church growth movement? By J. Robertson McQuilkin. Chicago, Moody Press [1973] ix, 99 p. 21 cm. [BV652.25.M32] 73-12833 ISBN 0-87808-136-4 1.95 (pbk.)
1. Church growth. I. Title.

MASSACHUSETTS Council of Churches. 262'.001
Goals and guidelines for use in strenghtening and expanding interchurch cooperation in Massachusetts as a whole, in clusters of towns and cities, in neighborhoods and towns. [Boston, c1969] 104 p. 28 cm. Cover title: Toward oneness in mission. "Report of a Committee appointed by the Massachusetts Council of Churches to make a comprehensive study of the cooperative movement of religious bodies in Massachusetts." [BR555.M4M37] 73-172060 2.00
1. Christian union—Massachusetts. I. Title. II. Title: Toward oneness in Mission.

MATHEWS, James Kenneth, 1913- 262'.001
A church truly catholic [by] James K. Mathews. Nashville, Abingdon Press [1969] 160 p. 19 cm. Bibliographical footnotes. [BR123.M39] 69-14311 2.45
1. Christianity—20th century—Addresses, essays, lectures. I. Title.

MEAD, Loren B. 262'.001
New hope for congregations; a Project Test Pattern book in parish development [by] Loren B. Mead, with research assistance of Elisa L. DesPortes. Foreword by Reuel L. Howe. New York, Seabury Press [1972] 128 p. 21 cm. (An Original Seabury paperback, SP 78) [BV600.2.M4] 72-80715 ISBN 0-8164-2077-7 2.95
1. Project Test Pattern. 2. Church renewal. I. DesPortes, Elisa L. II. Project Test Pattern. III. Title.

METHODIST Church (United States). Committee Appointed to Study the National Council of the Churches of Christ in the U.S.A. 262'.001
Report to the South Carolina Annual Conference, Southeastern Jurisdiction of the Methodist Church. [Columbia? S.C.] 1965. 95 p. 23 cm. Bibliography: p. 61-69. [BX6.N2M45] 75-19322
1. National Council of the Churches of Christ in the United States of America. I. Methodist Church (United States). Conferences. South Carolina. II. Title.

MEYENDORFF, Jean, 1926- 262'.001
Orthodoxy and catholicity [by] John Meyendorff. New York, Sheed & Ward [1966] vi, 180 p. 21 cm. Includes bibliographical references. [BX324.3.M4513] 66-22017
1. Orthodox Eastern Church—Relations—Catholic Church. 2. Catholic Church—Relations—Orthodox Eastern Church. I. Title.

MINUS, Paul M.
The Catholic rediscovery of Protestantism : a history of Roman Catholic ecumenical pioneering / by Paul M. Minus, Jr. New York : Paulist Press, c1976. vi, 261 p. ; 21 cm. (An Exploration book) Includes bibliographical references and index. [BX1784.M56] 75-44804 pbk. : 5.95
1. Catholic Church—Relations—Protestant churches. 2. Christian union—Catholic Church—History. 3. Protestant churches—Relations—Catholic Church. I. Title.

MODRAS, Ronald E. 262'.001
Paths to unity; American religion today and tomorrow, by Ronald E. Modras. New York, Sheed and Ward [1968] ix, 309 p. 21 cm. Includes bibliographies. [BX8.2.M58] 68-13855
1. Christian union—Catholic Church. I. Title.

MOLNAR, Thomas Steven. 262'.001
Dialogues and ideologues / Thomas Molnar. Chicago : Franciscan Herald Press, [1977] p. cm. Edition of 1968 published under title: Ecumenism or new reformation? Includes bibliographical references and index. [BX1746.M64 1977] 77-24084 ISBN 0-8199-0679-4 : 6.95
1. Catholic Church—History—20th century. 2. Church renewal—Catholic Church. I. Title.

MONTGOMERY, John Warwick. 262'.001
Ecumenicity, evangelicals, and Rome. Grand Rapids, Zondervan Pub. House [1969] 107 p. 21 cm. Bibliographical footnotes. [BX8.2.M59] 69-11634 3.50
1. Christian union—Addresses, essays, lectures. I. Title.

MOORE, George Voiers, 1897- 262'.001
Interchurch cooperation in Kentucky, 1865 to 1965. [Private ed.] Lexington, Printed by Keystone Printery, 1965] ii, 238 p. 22 cm. [BR555.K4M66] 76-17426
1. Kentucky—Church history. 2. Christian education—Kentucky. I. Title.

MORAN, Gabriel. 262'.001
Religious body: design for a new reformation. New York, Seabury Press [1974] 245 p. 22 cm. "A Crossroad book." Includes bibliographical references. [BV600.2.M65] 74-12103 ISBN 0-8164-1176-X 8.95
1. Church renewal. I. Title.

MORRISON, Charles Clayton, 1874- 262'001
The unfinished Reformation. Freeport, N.Y., Books for Libraries Press [1968, c1953] xvi, 236 p. 22 cm. (Essay index reprint series) "William Henry Hoover lectures in Christian unity for 1951." Contents.Contents.—The ecumenical awakening.—A critique of denominationalism.—The churchism of the denomination.—the Christian life in a united church.—Protestant unity and Roman Catholic unity compared.—The illusion of restorationism.—Surmounting three major obstacles.—Loyalty and freedom in a united church.—Epilogue. [BX8.2.M63 1968] 68-20322
1. Ecumenical movement. I. Title. II. Series: Disciples Divinity House, University of Chicago. Hoover lectures on Christian unity, 1951

MUDGE, Lewis Seymour. 262'.001
The crumbling walls, by Lewis S. Mudge. Philadelphia, Westminster Press [1970] 171 p. 19 cm. Includes bibliographical references. [BR121.2.M78] 74-101366 2.65
1. Christianity—20th century. 2. Christian union. I. Title.

MULLER, Alois, 1924- comp. 262'.001
Ongoing reform of the church. Edited by Alois Muller and Norbert Greinacher. [New York, Herder and Herder [1972] 151 p. 23 cm. (Concilium; religion in the seventies, v. 73) Contents.Contents.—Church reform and society in evolutionary perspective, by T. F. O'Dea.—Pathology of the Catholic Church, by S. Pfurtner.—Renewal of the spirit and reform of the institution, by Y. Congar.—The theological objectives of church reform, by K.-H. Ohlig.—Practical theology of church reform, by A. Muller.—Change of consciousness and church reform, by A. Exeler.—Should reform start from the top or from the ground level? by A. Hastings.—Comments on the revision of Canon law, by P. Huitzing.—Conflicts and conflict resolution in the church, by I. Hermann.—Church reform in Bohemia, by J. Nemec and B. Rouse.—The ecumenical student parish in the Free University of West Berlin, by M. Kramer and T. Gawron.—Reform of the church in the archdiocese of Chicago, by W. McCready.—Examples of attempts at reform in the church of Ceylon, by T. Balasuriya. Includes bibliographical references. [BX1746.M845] 71-185749 2.95
1. Church renewal—Catholic Church—Addresses, essays, lectures. I. Greinacher, Norbert, 1931- joint comp. II. Title. III. Series: Concilium: theology in the age of renewal, v. 73.

NEIGHBOUR, Ralph Webster, 1929- 262'.001
The seven last words of the church; or we never tried it that way before by Ralph Neighbour. Foreword by Leighton Ford. Grand Rapids, Zondervan Pub. House [1973] 182 p. 18 cm. Bibliography: p. 181-182. [BV600.2.N38] 72-95512 1.25
1. Church renewal. I. Title.

NEILL, Stephen Charles, Bp. 262'.001
The Church and Christian union [by] Stephen Neill. London, New York, Oxford Univ. Pr., 1968. ix, 423p. 23cm. (Bampton lecs., 1964) Bibl. [BR45.B3 1967] 68-87751 10.10
1. Christian union. 2. Church. I. Title. II. Series.

NELSON, John Robert, 1920- 262'.001
Church union in focus; guide for adult group study [by] J. Robert Nelson. Boston, United Church Press [1968] vii, 87 p. illus. 21 cm. "Part of the United Church curriculum, prepared and published by the Division of Christian Education and the Division of Publication of the United Church Board of Homeland Ministries." Bibliography: p. 87. [BX8.2.N44] 68-10065
1. Christian union—Study and teaching. I. United Church Board for Homeland Ministries. Division of Christian Education. II. United Church Board for Homeland Ministries. Division of Publication. III. Title.

NOLDE, Otto Frederick, 1899- ed. 262'.001
Toward world-wide Christianity. O. Frederick Nolde, editor. Port Washington N.Y., Kennikat Press [1969, c1946] xvi, 263 p. 22 cm. (Essay and general literature index reprint series.) (The interseminary series, v. 4) Contents.Contents.—Introduction by O. F. Nolde.—Christianity and the churches, by M. Spinka.—The Biblical and theological bases for the ecumenical goal, by J. A. MacKay.—The forms of ecumenical Christianity, by J. C. Bennett.—The rise of ecumenical organizations, by H. S. Leiper and A. R. Wentz.—Ecumenical fellowship during the war, by C. W. Iglehart.—Christian community and world order, by O. F. Nolde.—Ecumenicity in America, by H. P. Douglass.—Achieving the ecumenical ideal, by W. S. Rycroft.—Implementing the ecumenical ideal at the parish level, by E. M. McKee. Bibliography: p. 258-260. Bibliographical footnotes. [BV600.N55 1969] 70-86049
1. Christian union. I. Title. II. Series.

OLSON, William George. 262'.001
The charismatic church. Minneapolis, Bethany Fellowship, 1974. 152 p. 21 cm. Includes bibliographical references. [BX8763.O43] 74-10600 ISBN 0-87123-080-1 2.25 (pbk.)
1. Pentecostalism. 2. Church polity. I. Title.

OUTLER, Albert Cook, 1908- 262.001
That the world may believe; a study of Christian unity [by] Albert C. Outler. [New York] Joint Commission on Education and Cultivation, Board of Missions of the Methodist Church, 1966] xii, 195 p. 19 cm. Bibliography: p. 181-189. [BX8.2.O85] 66-13569
1. Christian union. I. Methodist Church (United States) Joint Commission on Education and Cultivation. II. Title.

OUTLER, Albert Cook, 1908- 262.001
That the world may believe; a study of Christian unity [by] Albert C. Outler. [New York, Jt. Commn. on Educ. & Cultivation, Bd. of Missions of the Methodist Church, 1966] xii, 195p. 19cm. Bibl. [BX8.2.O85] 66-13569 1.00 pap.,
1. Christian union. I. Methodist Church (United States) Joint Commission on Education and Cultivation. II. Title.

PALMER, Bernard Alvin, 1914- 262'.001
The winds of God are blowing [by] Bernard and Marjorie Palmer. Wheaton, Ill., Tyndale House Publishers [1973] 186 p. 22 cm. [BX8763.P34] 72-97654 ISBN 0-8423-8220-8 3.95
1. Pentecostalism. I. Palmer, Marjorie, joint author. II. Title.

PERKINS, Benjamin Paul, 1934- 262'.001
Black Christians' tragedies; an analysis of Black youth and their church [by] Benjamin Paul Perkins, Sr. [1st ed.] New York, Exposition Press [1972] 64 p. 22 cm. [E185.7.P4] 72-185996 ISBN 0-682-47510-6 3.00
1. Negroes—Religion. 2. Negro youth. I. Title.

PERRY, Lloyd Merle. 262'.001
Getting the church on target / by Lloyd Perry. Chicago : Moody Press, c1977. 256 p. : ill. ; 24 cm. Includes index. Bibliography: p. 247-254. [BV600.2.P46] 77-150244 ISBN 0-8024-2924-6 : 6.95
1. Church renewal. I. Title.

PEYTON, Thomas A. 262'.001
Reflections on a Christian community; a study in pastoral theology [by] Thomas A. Peyton. Notre Dame, Ind., Catholic Action Office [1970] 109 p. 19 cm. (New perspectives no. 5) [BX1746.P46] 70-123681 2.50
1. Church renewal—Catholic Church. I. Title. II. Series: New perspectives (Notre Dame, Ind.), no. 5

PORTER, Harry Boone, 1923- 262'.001
Growth and life in the local church [by] H. Boone Porter, Jr. New York, Seabury Press [1968] 124 p. 21 cm. Bibliographical references included in "Author's notes" (p. [117]-124) [BV4011.P6] 68-11592
1. Church renewal. 2. Pastoral theology. I. Title.

PORTER, Harry Boone, 1923- 262'.001
Growth and life in the local church [by] H. Boone Porter, Jr. South Pasadena, Calif., William Carey Library [1974, c1968] 124 p. 22 cm. Reprint of the ed. published by Seabury Press, New York. Chapters 1, 3-5 based on McMath lectures in the Diocese of Michigan. Includes bibliographical references. [BV4011.P6 1974] 73-19847 ISBN 0-87808-141-0
1. Church renewal. 2. Pastoral theology. I. Title.

POST-ECUMENICAL 262'.001
Christianity. Edited by Hans Kung [New York] Herder and Herder [1970] 160 p. 23 cm. (Concilium: theology in the age of renewal. Ecumenism, v. 54) Includes bibliographical references. [BX9.P6] 70-110788 2.95
1. Christian union—Addresses, essays, lectures. I. Kung, Hans, 1928- ed. II. Series: Concilium (New York) v. 54

PRESBYTERIAN Church in the U.S. 262'.001
Study draft of a plan for union of the Presbyterian Church in the United States and the United Presbyterian Church in the United States of America. Submitted to the 111th General Assembly (1971) of the Presbyterian Church in the United States and the 183d General Assembly (1971) of the United Presbyterian Church in the United States of America. [Philadelphia, 1971] 160 p. 23 cm. [BX9171.A1P73] 79-159762 0.50
1. Presbyterian Church in the U.S.—Relations—United Presbyterian Church in the U.S.A. 2. United Presbyterian Church in the U.S.A.—Relations—Presbyterian Church in the U.S. 3. Christian union—Presbyterian Church. I. United Presbyterian Church in the U.S.A. II. Title. III. Title: A plan for union.

PRESBYTERIAN Church in the U.S. Ecumenical Consultation. 262'.001
Report of the Ecumenical Consultation, Kanuga Conference Center, Hendersonville, North Carolina, October 27-31, 1975. [Atlanta] : Office of the Stated Clerk, Presbyterian Church in the United States : available from Materials Distribution Service, c1976. 55 p. ; 25 cm. [BX9171.A1P73 1976] 77-150902 0.50
1. Presbyterian Church in the U.S.—Relations—Addresses, essays, lectures. 2. Christian union—Presbyterian Church—Addresses, essays, lectures.

QUANBECK, Warren A. 262'.001
Search for understanding; Lutheran conversations with Reformed, Anglican, and Roman Catholic Churches [by] Warren A. Quanbeck. Minneapolis, Augsburg Pub. House [1972] 125 p. 20 cm. Bibliography: p. 125. [BX8063.7.A1Q3] 72-90259 ISBN 0-8066-1306-8 2.95
1. Lutheran Church—Relations. I. Title.

RICHARDS, Lawrence O. 262'.001
Three churches in renewal / Lawrence O. Richards. Grand Rapids : Zondervan Pub. House, c1975. 128 p. ; 21 cm. [BV600.2.R48] 74-25345 pbk. : 2.95
1. Our Heritage Wesleyan Church, Scottsdale, Ariz. 2. Mariners Church, Newport Beach Calif. 3. Trinity Church, Seattle. 4. Church renewal—Case studies. I. Title.

RODGER, Patrick Campbell, ed. 262'.001
Ecumenical dialogue in Europe, edited by Patrick C. Rodger. Richmond, John Knox Press [1966] 83 p. 22 cm. (Ecumenical studies in history, no. 6) Papers relating to a series of inter-church meetings held 1937-1962 in Switzerland and France. Contents.Contents.—Introduction, by R. Beaupere.—History of the inter-confessional group of Les Dombes, by M. Villain.—What ecumenicity means for us, by J. Bosc.—Commentary on the theses, by J. de Baciocchi.—The theses.—Bibliography (p. 60-61)—Conclusion: A Protestant point of view, by H. Bruston. A Catholic point of view, by G. Martelet. [BX8.2.A1R58] 66-25163
1. Christian union—Europe. I. Title. II. Series.

ROMEU, Luis V ed. 262.001
Ecumenical experiences, edited by Louis V. Romeu. Westminster, Md., Newman Press [1965] x, 203 p. group ports. 21 cm. Translation of Dialogos de la Cristiandad, edited by Lancelot C. Sheppard. [BX8.2.A1R613] 65-26784
1. Christian union — Addresses, essays, lectures. I. Sheppard, Lancelot Capel,..1906- ed. II. Title.

ROMEU, Luis V., ed. 262.001
Ecumenical experiences [Tr. from Spanish] Westminster, Md., Newman [c.1964, 1965] x, 203p. group ports. 21cm. Tr., ed. by Lancelot C. Sheppard. [BX8.2.A1R613] 65-26784 4.50
1. Christian union—Addresses, essays, lectures. I. Sheppard, Lancelot Capel, 1906- ed. II. Title.

ROSSER, Harold C., 1924- 262'.001
For lack of a meddlesome preacher [by] Harold C. Rosser. Philadelphia, Dorrance [1973] 55 p. 22 cm. [BR125.R7] 73-85343 ISBN 0-8059-1912-0 3.95
1. Christianity—20th century. I. Title.

ROUNER, Arthur Acy. 262'.001
The free church today; new life for the whole church, by Arthur A. Rouner, Jr. New York, Association Press [1968] 159 p. 21 cm. Bibliographical footnotes. [BV600.2.R67] 68-11486
1. Church. 2. Christian union. I. Title.

SCALISE, Victor F. 262'.001
Merging for mission [by] Victor F. Scalise, Jr. Valley Forge [Pa.] Judson Press [1972] 127 p. 22 cm. Includes bibliographical references. [BX9999.B76U557] 70-173771 ISBN 0-8170-0545-5 2.95
1. Brookline, Mass. United Parish. I. Title.

SCHLINK, Edmund, 1903- 262'.001
The coming Christ and the coming church. Philadelphia, Fortress Press [1968, c1967] xiii, 333 p. 23 cm. Translation of Der kommende Christus und die kirchlichen Traditionen. Bibliographical footnotes. [BX8.2.S2713 1968] 68-3670
1. Christian union—Addresses, essays, lectures. I. Title.

SCHUTZ, Roger. 262'.001
The power of the provisional. Translated by Philip Parsons and Timothy Wilson. Philadelphia, Pilgrim Press [1969] 80 p. 19 cm. Translation of Dynamique du provisoire. Bibliographical references included in "Notes" (p. 80) [BX8.2.S283] 69-15436 3.95
1. Christian union. 2. Christianity—20th century. I. Title.

SEIFERT, Harvey. 262'.001
New power for the church / by Harvey Seifert. Philadelphia : Westminster Press, c1976. 175 p. ; 19 cm. Includes bibliographical references. [BV600.2.S43] 75-40063 ISBN 0-664-24791-1 pbk. : 3.95
1. Church renewal. 2. Christianity—20th century. I. Title.

SHEERIN, John B 262.001
Christian reunion: the ecumenical movement and American Catholics, by John B. Sheerin. [1st ed.] New York, Hawthorn Books [1966] 287 p. 22 cm. (Catholic perspectives)

Bibliographical references included in "Notes" (p. 271-275) [BX8.2.S47] 66-13619
1. Christian union—Catholic Church. I. Title.

SHEERIN, John B. 262.001
Christian reunion: the ecumenical movement and American Catholics. New York, Hawthorn [c.1966] 287p. 22cm. (Catholic perspectives) bBibl. [BX8.2.S47] 66-13619 4.95
1. Christian union—Catholic Church. I. Title.

SHEERIN, John B 262'.001
A practical guide to ecumenism, by John B. Sheerin. Rev. ed. New York, Paulist Press [1967] 262 p. 18 cm. (Deus books) First ed. published in 1966 under title: Christian reunion: the ecumenical movement and American Catholics. Bibliographical footnotes. [BX8.2.S47 1967] 68-77
1. Christian union—Catholic Church. I. Title.

SHEERIN, John B. 262'.001
A practical guide to ecumenism, by John B. Sheerin. Rev. ed. New York, Paulist Press [1967] 262 p. 18 cm. (Deus books) First ed. published in 1966 under title: Christian reunion: the ecumenical movement and American Catholics. Bibliographical footnotes. [BX8.2.S47 1967] 68-77
1. Christian union—Catholic Church. I. Title.

SILLS, Horace S., ed. 262.001
Grassroots ecumenicity; case studies in local church consolidation [edited by] Horace S. Sills. Philadelphia, United Church Press [1967] vii, 140 p. 21 cm. [BX6.5.S5] 66-23993
1. Christian union—History. 2. Interdenominational cooperation. I. Title.

SIMPSON, Ervin Peter Young. 262.001
Ordination and Christian unity [by] E. P. Y. Simpson. Valley Forge [Pa.] Judson Press [1966] 184 p. 23 cm. Bibliographical references included in "Notes" (p. 173-179) [BX9.5.C5S5] 66-20532
1. Church polity and Christian union. 2. Pastoral theology and Christian union. I. Title.

SINGER, Charles Gregg, 1910- 262'.001
The unholy alliance : a study of the National Council of Churches / C. Gregg Singer. New Rochelle, N.Y. : Arlington House, [1975] p. cm. Includes index. Bibliography: p. [BX6.N2S56] 75-11598 ISBN 0-87000-327-5 : 11.95
1. National Council of the Churches of Christ in the United States of America. 2. Federal Council of the Churches of Christ in America. I. Title.

SKIBBE, Eugene M. 262'.001
Protestant agreement on the Lord's Supper [by] Eugene M. Skibbe. Minneapolis, Augsburg Pub. House [1968] 143 p. 23 cm. Bibliographical references included in "Notes" (p. 139-143) [BX9.5.S2S57] 68-13426
1. Lord's Supper and Christian union. 2. Theology, Protestant. I. Title.

SLACK, Kenneth. 262'.001
Nairobi narrative : the story of the Fifth Assembly of the World Council of Churches, 23 November-10 December, 1975 / [by] Kenneth Slack. London : S.C.M. Press, 1976. vi, 90 p. ; 20 cm. Includes index. Bibliography: p. 88. [BX6.W77 1975.S5] 76-370414 ISBN 0-334-01096-9 : £0.90
1. World Council of Churches. Assembly, 5th, Nairobi, 1975. I. World Council of Churches. II. Title.

SONTAG, Frederick. 262'.001
The crisis of faith; a Protestant witness in Rome. [1st ed.] Garden City, N.Y., Doubleday, 1969. 285 p. 22 cm. [BX1765.2.S65] 69-12194 5.95
1. Catholic Church—Doctrinal and controversial works—Protestant authors. 2. Church renewal—Catholic Church. I. Title.

STEERE, Douglas Van, 1901- 262'.001
Mutual irradiation; a Quaker view of ecumenism, by Douglas V. Steere. [Wallingford, Pa., Pendle Hill Publications, 1971] 32 p. 19 cm. (Pendle Hill pamphlet 175) Originally presented in German as the Richard Cary Lecture of 1968 at the German Yearly Meeting in Bad Pyrmont. [BX7732.S784] 73-146680
1. Christian union—Friends, Society of. 2. Christianity and other religions. I. Title.

STENBERG, Odin K. 262'.001
A church without walls / Odin K. Stenberg. Minneapolis : Bethany Fellowship, c1976. 158 p. ; 18 cm. (Dimension books) Includes bibliographical references. [BV600.2.S78] 76-7702 ISBN 0-87123-056-9 pbk. : 2.45
1. Church renewal. I. Title.

STOWE, David M. 262'.001
Ecumenicity and evangelism, by David M. Stowe. Grand Rapids, Eerdmans [1970] 94 p. 20 cm. Bibliography: p. 89-91. [BV3793.S7] 79-112948 2.45
1. Evangelistic work. 2. Christian union. I. Title.

STRIGHT, Hayden L. 262'.001
Together; the story of church cooperation in Minnesota, by Hayden L. Stright. With a foreword by Forrest L. Richeson. Minneapolis, Denison [1971] xvi, 300 p. illus. 24 cm. Bibliography: p. 289-290. [BR555.M6S76] 71-29728 6.95
1. Christian union—Minnesota. I. Title.

SWARTZ, Fred W., 1938- 262'.001
All in God's family : Brethren and the quest for Christian unity / Fred W. Swartz. Elgin, Ill. : Brethren Press, c1977. 143 p. : Ill. ; 18 cm. Bibliography: p. 128-129. [BX7823.4.S95] 77-6375 ISBN 0-87178-021-6 pbk. : 2.95
1. Christian union—Church of the Brethren. I. Title.

SWIDLER, Leonard J. 262.001
The ecumenical vanguard; the history of the Una Sancta Movement. Foreword by Hans Kung. Pittsburgh, Duquesne Univ. Pr. [c.1966] xv, 287p. 23cm. Bibl. [BR856.S95] 66-15156 7.75
1. Metzger, Max Josef, 1887-1944. 2. Christian union—Germany. 3. Christian union—Catholic Church. 4. Una Sancta Movement. I. Title.

SWIDLER, Leonard J. comp. 262'.001
Ecumenism, the spirit, and worship, ed. by Leonard Swidler. [Pittsburgh, P.] Duquesne, 1967. 258p. 22cm. Essays selected from the papers delivered at the 1964 and 1965 graduate seminars in ecumenism jointly offered by Duquesne University and the Pittsburgh Thelogical Seminary and at a symposium held in 1965 and sponsored by the editorial board of the Journal of ecumenical studies and the Dept. of Theology, Duquesne University. Bibl. [BX8.2A1S9] 67-15784 4.95
1. Christian union— Addresses, essays, lectures. I. Duquesne University, Pittsburgh. II. Pittsburgh. Theological Seminary. III. Journal of ecumenical studies. IV. Title.
Contents omitted.

THATCHER, Joan. 262'.001
The church responds. Valley Forge [Pa.] Judson Press [1970] 160 p. 22 cm. Bibliography: p. 147-154. [BV600.2.T48] 77-116724 ISBN 8-17-004661- 2.95
1. Church renewal—Case studies. 2. Christianity—20th century. I. Title.

THORMAN, Donald J. 262'.001
Power to the people of God, by Donald J. Thorman. Paramus, N.J., Paulist Press [1970] 63 p. 17 cm. [BX1746.T48] 72-111487 0.75
1. Church renewal—Catholic Church. I. Title.

TIETJEN, John H. 262.001
Which way to Lutheran unity? A history of efforts to unite the Lutherans of America [by] John H. Tietjen. St. Louis, Concordia [1966] vii, 176p. illus. 21cm. Bibl. [BX8043.5.T5] 66-25270 4.95
1. Christian union—Lutheran Church. 2. Lutheran Church in the U.S. I. Title.

TILL, Barry. 262'.001
The churches search for unity. [Harmondsworth, Eng., Baltimore] Penguin Books [1972] 555 p. 19 cm. (Pelican books, A1443) Bibliography: p. 524-[550] [BX6.5.T53] 72-170600 ISBN 0-14-021443-7 3.50 (U.S.)
1. Christian union—History. I. Title.

TORBET, Robert George, 1912- 262'.001
Ecumenism; free church dilemma [by] Robert G. Torbet. Valley Forge [Pa.] Judson Press [1968] 127 p. 21 cm. Bibliography: p. 119-121. Bibliographical footnotes. [BX4817.T6] 68-22757 3.95
1. Dissenters, Religious. 2. Christian union. I. Title.

TORRANCE, Thomas Forsyth, 1913- 262'.001
Theology in reconciliation : essays towards Evangelical and Catholic unity in East and West / Thomas F. Torrance. Grand Rapids : Eerdmans, 1975. p. cm. Includes indexes. [BX9.T67] 75-33373 ISBN 0-8028-3475-2 : 8.95
1. Christian union—Addresses, essays, lectures. 2. Theology—Addresses, essays, lectures. I. Title.

TREXLER, Edgar R., comp. 262'.001
Creative congregations; tested strategies for today's churches, edited by Edgar R. Trexler. With commentary by Lyle E. Schaller. Nashville, Abingdon Press [1972] 143 p. illus. 22 cm. Contents.Contents.—Introduction, by E. R. Trexler.—Laymen in action: Do it now! By C. T. Uehling. A force for every task, by D. C. Collins. This minister is a building inspector, by W. E. Diehl. Laymen in action: a commentary, by L. E. Schaller.—The new minorities: Women are equals, by L. Powell. The "right time" for youth, by B. Curler. Reaching for the sky to help the aging, by E. R. Trexler. Where the singles are, by N. B. Read, Jr. The new minorities: a commentary, by L. E. Schaller.—Diversity is magic: They worship in a barn, by B. Gunnerson. Excitement on Lexington Ave, by E. R. Trexler. Changing the face of a city, by J. Willis. Diversity is magic: a commentary, by L. E. Schaller.—Let's get together: Nine rural churches discover each other, by E. R. Trexler. Growing up ecumenical, by P. Hainline. Merger may not be the answer, by H. L. Berg. Interchurch cooperation: a commentary, by L. E. Schaller.—Suburban revival: Planned city, planned church, by M. Tengbom. Organized for outreach, by E. R. Trexler. When change brings trouble, by D. W. Holland. Suburban revival: a commentary, by L. E. Schaller. [BV603.T73] 72-3009 ISBN 0-687-09824-6
1. Church renewal—Addresses, essays, lectures. I. Title.

TREXLER, Edgar R., comp. 262'.001
Ways to wake up your church, edited by Edgar R. Trexler. Philadelphia, Fortress Press [1969] viii, 152 p. illus. 22 cm. Contents.Contents.—Introduction.—Parking lots are for people, by W. L. Thorkelson.—Living room listening, by J. Mathe.—Eight rural churches think big, by E. R. Trexler.—Evangelism and the passing parade, by L. E. Schaller.—Hang-loose mission to a city, by R. C. Underwood.—The church is their stage, by E. R. Trexler.—Make those committees work! By O. L. Shealy.—New hope for the Baileys, by E. R. Trexler.—We split ... to grow, by W. C. White.—Ministers in the suburbs, by C. G. Karsch.—Anniversaries can be different, by E. R. Trexler.—No buildings, few Sunday services, by E. A. Daley.—Celebrate life, by E. R. Trexler.—Confidence through controversy, by D. F. Marshall.—Tenements don't have to be slums, by E. R. Trexler.—Seven-day church, by C. G. Karsch.—A budget is people, by L. E. Schaller.—Playing it bold in Dallas, by N. Cryer.—Wednesday's church, by J. Mathe.—Easton's interfaith adventure, by E. R. Trexler.—Key to the campus, by R. C. Underwood.—Loneliness can be shared, by J. Harbison.—Making the scene at Luther Place, by W. A. Harper.—Perking up the congregational meeting, by B. Bohling.—Invading the drug scene, by E. R. Trexler. [BV600.2.T75] 78-84543 2.95
1. Church renewal—Case studies. I. Title.

VATICAN Council. 2d,1962-1965. 262.001
The decree on ecumenism of the Second Vatican Council. A new translation by the Secretariat for Promoting Christian Unity. With a commentary by Thomas F. Stransky. Study-club ed. Glen Rock, N.J., Paulist Press [1965] 86 p. 18 cm. Translation of De Oecumenismo. [BX830 1962.A45D42] 65-8641
1. Catholic Church — Relations. 2. Christian union — Catholic Church. I. Stransky, Thomas F. II. Title.

VATICAN Council, 2d. 262.001
The decree on ecumenism of the Second Vatican Council. New tr. by Secretariat for Promoting Christian Unity. Commentary by Thomas F. Stransky. Study-club ed. Glen Rock, N.J., Paulist [c.1965] 86p. 18cm. [BX830. 1962.A45D4?] 65 8641 .50 pap.,
1. Catholic Church—Relations. 2. Christian union—Catholic Church. I. Stransky, Thomas F. II. Title.

VATICAN II on ecumenism. 262.001
Editor: Michael Adams. [1st ed.] Dublin, Chicago, Scepter Books [1966] 117 p. 22 cm. Contents.Contents.—The ecumenical movement, by M. Adams.—Catholic principles on ecumenism, by K. McNamara.—The practice of ecumenism, by E. McDonagh.—The separated churches and ecclesial communities, by T. F. Stransky.—Ecumenism and the missions, by B. Kelly.—Ecumenism in the light of Vatican II, by K. McNamara.—Decretum de oecumenismo—Decree on ecumenism. Includes bibliographical references. [BX830 1962.A45O462] 66-9026
1. Vatican Council. 2d, 1962-1965. Decretum de oecumenismo. 2. Christian union—Catholic Church. I. Adams, Michael, 1937- ed. II. Vatican Council. 2d, 1962-1965. Decretum de oecumenismo. English & Latin. 1966.

VERNEY, Stephen. 262'.001
Into the new age / [by] Stephen Verney. [London] : Fontana, 1976,i.e. 1977 160 p. : ill. ; 18 cm. Includes bibliographical references. [BR121.2.V47] 77-353987 ISBN 0-00-624097-6 pbk. : 1.95
1. Christianity—20th century. I. Title.
Distributed by Collins-World

VIGEVENO, H. S. 262'.001
Sinners anonymous [by] H. S. Vigeveno. Waco, Tex., Word Books [1970] 170 p. 23 cm. Includes bibliographies. [BV600.2.V5] 74-91947 4.95
1. Church. 2. Church renewal. I. Title.

VINCENT, John J. 262'.001
Alternative church / by John J. Vincent. Belfast : Christian Journals Ltd, 1976. 149 p. ; 18 cm. Includes bibliographical references. [BV601.9.V56] 77-357079 ISBN 0-904302-22-9 : £0.90
1. Non-institutional churches. I. Title.

WARD, Hiley H., ed. 262'.001
Documents of dialogue [edited] by Hiley Ward. Englewood Cliffs, N.J., Prentice-Hall [1966] xvi, 525 p. 24 cm. Bibliography: p. 479-490. [BX6.5.W3] 66-22100
1. Christian union—History—Sources. I. Title.

WEBB, Lance. 262'.001
When God comes alive through the Spirit-renewed church. Nashville, Abingdon Press [1968] 223 p. 22 cm. Bibliographical footnotes. [BV600.2.W4] 68-11481
1. Church renewal. I. Title.

WELTGE, Ralph. 262'.001
The church swept out. Philadelphia, Published for the Cooperative Publication Association by United Church Press [1967] 96 p. 20 cm. (Faith for life series) Bibliographical footnotes. [BR115.W6W44] 67-26119
1. Church and the world. 2. Mission of the church. 3. Church renewal. I. Cooperative Publication Association. II. Title.

WHAT unity requires : 262'.001
papers and report of the unity of the Church. Geneva : World Council of Churches, 1976. 74 p. ; 21 cm. (Faith and order paper ; no. 77) Includes bibliographical references. [BX9.W45] 76-378622 ISBN 2-8254-0524-8 : 3.90F
1. Christian union—Addresses, essays, lectures. I. World Council of Churches. II. Title. III. Series.

WHAT'S a nice church 262'.001
like you doing in a place like this? Compiled by Wayne Robinson. Waco, Tex., Word Books [1972] 125 p. 23 cm. Outgrowth of a symposium held at Oklahoma City Univ., May 1971. [BR123.W473] 73-188072 3.50
1. Christianity—20th century—Addresses, essays, lectures. 2. Church renewal—Addresses, essays, lectures. I. Robinson, Wayne, 1937- ed.

WILLIAMS, H. C. N. 262'.001
Nothing to fear [by] H. C. N. Williams. Philadelphia, Pilgrim Press [1968] 95 p. 21 cm. "Grew out of [the author's] presentation of the Paul Jones annual lectures in Winnetka, Illinois, 1966." [BR121.2.W5 1968] 68-54030 2.25
1. Christianity—20th century. I. Title.

WINTER, Michael M. 262'.001
Blueprint for a working church; a study in new pastoral structures [by] Michael M. Winter. St. Meinrad, Ind., Abbey Press, 1973. 143 p. 21 cm. (A Priority edition) British ed. published under title: Mission or maintenance. Includes bibliographical references. [BX1746.W56 1973] 73-85332 2.95
1. Church renewal—Catholic Church. 2. Mission of the Church. I. Title.

WITTE, Paul W. 262'.001
On common ground : Protestant and Catholic evangelicals / Paul W. Witte. Waco, Tex. : Word Books, c1975. 135 p. ; 23 cm. Includes bibliographical references. [BX4818.3.W54] 74-82662 ISBN 0-87680-385-0 : 4.95
1. Catholic Church—Relations—Protestant churches. 2. Protestant churches—Relations—Catholic Church. 3. Evangelicalism. I. Title.

WOODSON, Leslie H., 1929- 262'.001
The church: united or untied? [By] Leslie Woodson. Grand Rapids, Zondervan Pub. House [1974] 156 p. 18 cm. Includes bibliographical references. [BX8.2.W66] 73-13070 1.25
1. Christian union. 2. Christianity and other religions. I. Title.

TONKIN, John. 262'.009'031
The Church and the secular order in Reformation thought. New York, Columbia University Press, 1971. xiv, 219 p. 22 cm. Bibliography: p. [205]-211. [BV598.T65] 73-143390 ISBN 0-231-03374-5 8.00
1. Church—History of doctrines—16th century. I. Title.

ROTH, Alice. 262'.009173'2
Becoming God's people today; the Church's mission in an urban world, by Alice and Willard Roth. Scottdale, Pa., Herald Press

[1966] 144 p. illus. 20 cm. Bibliographical footnotes. [BV637.R62] 66-22241
1. City churches. I. Roth, Willard, joint author. II. Title.

WALKER, G. S. M. 262'.00924
The churchmanship of St. Cyprian, by G. S. M. Walker. Richmond, John Knox Press [1969, c1968] 105 p. 22 cm. (Ecumenical studies in history, no. 9) Includes bibliographical references. [BV598.W3] 69-12121
1. Cyprianus, Saint, Bp. of Carthage. 2. Church—History of doctrines—Early church. I. Title. II. Series.

RODES, Robert E. 262'.00941
Ecclesiastical administration in medieval England : the Anglo-Saxons to the Reformation / Robert E. Rodes, Jr. Notre Dame : University of Notre Dame Press, c1976- p. cm. Includes bibliographical references and index. [KD8605.R6] 73-22584 ISBN 0-268-00903-1 : 19.95
1. Church of England—Government—History. 2. Ecclesiastical law—Great Britain—History. I. Title.

WATT, John A. 262'.009415
The Church and the two nations in medieval Ireland [by J. A. Watt. Cambridge [Eng.] University Press, 1970. xvi, 251 p. 23 cm. (Cambridge studies in medieval life and thought, 3d ser., no. 3) Bibliography: p. 231-240. [BR794.W35] 72-120196 ISBN 0-521-07738-9 85/-
1. Church and state in Ireland. I. Title. II. Series.

TREMPELAS, 262'.01'93
Panagiotes Nikolaou, 1886-
The autocephaly of the Metropolia in America / by Panagiotes N. Trempelas ; translated and edited by George S. Bebis, Robert G. Stephanopoulos, N. M. Vaporis. Brookline, Mass. : Holy Cross Theological School Press, 1973, c1974. 80 p. ; 21 cm. Includes bibliographical references. [BX496.T7313] 75-329980
1. Russian Orthodox Greek Catholic Church of America—Government. I. Title.

BROUCKER, Jose de. 262'.02
The Suenens dossier: the case for collegiality. Notre Dame, Ind., Fides Publishers [1970] ix, 258 p. 20 cm. Translation of Le dossier Suenens. Contents.Contents.—Part 1: The Suenens interview. The impact on world opinion. The Cardinal replies to criticisms. Public opinion in the Church. The symposium at Chur.—Part 2: The logic of Vatican Council II, by P. Muraille. Primacy and collegiality, by G. Thils. Church institutions: a critical interpretation: A. The Roman Curia. B. The College of Cardinals. C. The mission of nuncios. D. The nomination of bishops, by R. Aubert. Legalism and Christian life, by P. Delhaye. Ecumenical hopes. The second Synod: a turning point. Documents: On the doctrinal schema. On the statute of nuncios. [BX1802.B713] 79-120475 3.50
1. Catholic Church—Government. 2. Suenens, Leon Joseph, Cardinal, 1904- 3. Church—Authority. I. Title. II. Title: The case for collegiality.

DANIELOU, Jean. 262'.02
Why the church? / by Jean Cardinal Danielou ; translated from the French by Maurice F. De Lange. Chicago : Franciscan Herald Press, [1975] xiv, 208 p. ; 22 cm. Translation of Pourquoi l'Eglise? [BX1746.D2913] 75-5715 ISBN 0-8199-0562-3 : 6.95
1. Church. I. Title.

GOLLIN, James. 262'.02
Worldly goods; the wealth and power of the American Catholic Church, the Vatican, and the men who control the money. [1st ed.] New York, Random House [1971] xxxiv, 531 p. 22 cm. [BX1950.G6] 72-159345 ISBN 0-394-46330-7
1. Catholic Church—Finance. I. Title.

GRANFIELD, Patrick. 262'.02
Ecclesial cybernetics; a study of democracy in the church. New York, Macmillan [1973] xiii, 280 p. 22 cm. Includes bibliographical references. [BX1802.G67] 72-87158 8.95
1. Catholic Church—Government. 2. Catholic Church—Doctrinal and controversial works—Catholic authors. I. Title.

GRATSCH, Edward J. 262'.02
Where Peter is : a survey of ecclesiology / Edward J. Gratsch. New York : Alba House, [1975] xvii, 283 p. ; 21 cm. Includes index. Bibliography: p. [269]-276. [BV598.G72] 74-34578 ISBN 0-8189-0302-3 : 4.95
1. Church—History of doctrines. I. Title.

KLOPPENBURG, Bonaventure, 262'.02
1919-
The ecclesiology of Vatican II, by Bonaventure Kloppenburg. Translated by Matthew J. O'Connell. Chicago, Franciscan Herald Press [1974] xv, 373 p. 23 cm. Translation of A eclesiologia do Vaticano II. Includes bibliographical references. [BX830 1962.K54313 1974] 74-8035 ISBN 0-8199-0484-8
1. Vatican Council. 2d, 1962-1965. 2. Church—History of doctrines—20th century. I. Title.

MEREDITH, Anthony. 262'.02
The theology of tradition. Notre Dame, Ind., Fides Publishers [1971] 95 p. 19 cm. (Theology today, no. 11) Bibliography: p. 92. [BT90.M46] 77-27746 ISBN 0-85342-257-5 0.95
1. Tradition (Theology) I. Title.

NICODEMUS, Donald E. 262'.02
The democratic church [by] Donald E. Nicodemus. Milwaukee, Bruce Pub. Co. [1969] xi, 145 p. 22 cm. Bibliography: p. 137-145. [BX1802.N5] 69-17320 5.95
1. Catholic Church—Government. I. Title.

O'DONNELL, John Hugh, 262'.02
1895-1947.
The Catholic hierarchy of the United States, 1790-1922. Washington, 1922. [New York, AMS Press, 1974] xiv, 223 p. 23 cm. Reprint of the author's thesis, Catholic University of America, 1922, which was issued as v. 4 of the Catholic University of America. Studies in American church history. Includes bibliographical references. [BX4670.O4 1974] 73-3558 ISBN 0-404-57754-7 9.50
1. Bishops—United States. I. Title. II. Series: Catholic University of America. Studies in American church history, v. 4.

O'DONOGHUE, Joseph. 262.02
Elections in the church. Baltimore, Helicon [c1967] 232 p. 21 cm. Bibliographical footnotes. [BX1802.O3] 66-26480
1. Catholic Church — Government. I. Title.

O'DONOGHUE, Joseph 262.02
Elections in the church. Baltimore, Helicon [c.1967] 232p. 21cm. Bibl. [BX1802.O3] 66-26480 5.95
1. Catholic Church—Government. I. Title.
Distributed by Taplinger, New York.

THE Once & future church: 262'.02
a communion of freedom; studies on unity & collegiality in the church. Editor: James A. Coriden. Contributors: William W. Bassett [and others] Staten Island, N.Y., Alba House [1971] xvi, 310 p. 21 cm. Includes bibliographical references. [BX1802.O5] 73-158568 ISBN 0-8189-0203-5 3.95
1. Catholic Church—Government—Addresses, essays, lectures. I. Coriden, James A., ed. II. Bassett, William W.

PASTORAL reform in church 262.02
government. New York, Paulist Press [1965] viii, 184 p. 24 cm. (Concilium theology in the age of renewal: Canon law, v. 8) Includes bibliographies. [BX1802.P35] 65-28464
1. Catholic Church—Government. 2. Canon law. I. Series: Concilium theology in the age of renewal, v. 8

PASTORAL reform in church 262.02
government New York, Paulist Pr. [c.1965] viii, 184p.24cm. (Concilium theology in the age of renewal: Canon law, v. 8) Includes Bibl. [BX1802.P35] 65-28464 4.50
1. Catholic Church—Government. 2. Canon law. (Series: Councilum theology in the age of renewal, v. 8)

RAHNER, Karl, 1904- 262'.02
Grace in freedom. [Translated and adapted by Hilda Graef. New York] Herder and Herder [1969] 267 p. 21 cm. "Original edition: Gnade als Freiheit." Bibliography: p. [265]-267. [BT810.2.R313 1969b] 75-16564 5.95
1. Catholic Church—Doctrinal and controversial works—Catholic authors. 2. Freedom (Theology) I. Graef, Hilda C. II. Title.

RIGA, Peter J. 262'.02
The church renewed, by Peter J. Riga. New York, Sheed and Ward [1966] x, 246 p. 22 cm. Includes bibliographies. [BX1746.R52] 66-22025
1. Church renewal — Catholic Church. 2. Vatican Council. 2d, 1962-1965. Constitutio de ecclesia. I. Title.

RIGA, Peter J. 262'.02
The church renewed, by Peter J. Riga. New York, Sheed and Ward [1966] x, 246 p. 22 cm. Includes bibliographies. [BX1746.R52] 66-22025
1. Vatican Council. 2d, 1962-1965. Constitutio dogmatica de ecclesia. 2. Church renewal—Catholic Church. I. Title.

SCARPATI, Rosario. 262'.02
Hope or hindrance? The church of the future. Translated by Alba Zizzamia. New York, Sheed and Ward [1967] ix, 179 p. 22 cm. Includes bibliographical references. [BX1746.S2813] 67-21901
1. Church renewal—Catholic Church. I. Title.

SUENENS, Leon Joseph, 262'.02
Cardinal, 1904-
Coresponsibility in the church. Translated by Francis Martin. [New York] Herder and Herder [1968] 218 p. 22 cm. Translation of La coresponsabilite dans l'Eglise d'aujourd'hui. Bibliographical footnotes. [BX1802.S914] 68-29409 4.95
1. Catholic Church—Government. 2. Church renewal—Catholic Church. 3. Church polity. I. Title.

VATICAN Council. 2d, 1962- 262'.02
1965.
Vatican II on the Church. Editor: Austin Flannery. [2d ed.] Dublin, Scepter Books [1967] 363 p. 22 cm. "Constitutio dogmatica de Ecclesia" (p. [173]-335) in Latin and English on opposite pages. First ed. published in 1966 under title: Vatican II: the Church constitution. Includes bibliographical references. [BX830 1962.A45C8233 1967] 70-257873
1. Vatican Council. 2d, 1962-1965. Constitutio dogmatica de Ecclesia. I. Flannery, Austin, ed. II. Vatican Council. 2d, 1962-1965. Constitutio dogmatica de Ecclesia. English & Latin. 1967. III. Title.

WE, the people of God; 262'.02
a study of constitutional government for the church. Edited by James A. Coriden. [Huntington, Ind., Canon Law Society of America [1967 or 8] xvi, 182 p. 23 cm. "Papers prepared by participants or resulting from proceedings of the symposium entitled A constitution for the church, sponsored by the Canon Law Society of America and Fordham University ... [and] held ... in New York City on October 7-9, 1967." Includes bibliographical references. [BX1802.W4] 68-23796
1. Catholic Church—Government. I. Coriden, James A., ed. II. Canon Law Society of America. III. Fordham University, New York.

NOLAN, Hugh Joseph, 262'.02'08
1911- comp.
Pastoral letters of the American hierarchy, 1792-1970. Hugh J. Nolan, editor. Huntington, Ind., Our Sunday Visitor, inc. [1971] xiv, 785 p. 27 cm. Includes bibliographical references. [BX874.A2N63] 74-160366
1. Catholic Church—Pastoral letters and charges. I. Title.

OAKLEY, Francis. 262'.02'09
Council over Pope? Towards a provisional ecclesiology. [New York] Herder and Herder [1969] 190 p. 22 cm. Bibliographical footnotes. [BX1802.O25] 73-80871 5.95
1. Catholic Church—Government. 2. Conciliar theory. I. Title.

CAVALLARI, Alberto, 262'.02'09046
1927-
The changing Vatican. Translated by Raymond T. Kelly. [1st ed.] Garden City, N.Y., Doubleday, 1967. 215 p. 22 cm. Translation of Il Vaticano che cambia. Bibliographical references included in "Notes" (p. 185-215) [BX1802.C313] 67-19075
1. Catholic Church—Government. I. Title.

CUNNINGHAM, Terence 262'.02'415
P., 1922-
The Church since emancipation: Church reorganization [by] Terence P. Cunningham. Church building [by] Thomas P. Kennedy. Ecclesiastical learning [by] John Corkery. Epilogue: Modern Ireland [by] Peter McKevitt. [Dublin] Gill and Macmillan [1970] 32, 36, 33, 29 p. illus. 21 cm. (A History of Irish Catholicism, v. 5, 7/10) At head of title: The Church since emancipation. Includes bibliographical references. [BX1503.H55 vol. 5, no. 7/10] 71-17623 ISBN 0-7171-0267-X 14/-
1. Catholic Church in Ireland—Addresses, essays, lectures. I. Kennedy, Thomas Paul. Church building. 1970. II. Corkery, John, 1918- Ecclesiastical learning. 1970. III. McKevitt, Peter. Modern Ireland. 1970. IV. Title. V. Title: The Church since emancipation. VI. Series.

GODDIJN, Walter, 262'.02'492
1921-
The deferred revolution : a social experiment in church innovation in Holland, 1960-1970 / by Walter Goddijn. Amsterdam ; New York : Elsevier Scientific Pub. Co., 1975, c1974. 202 p. ; 24 cm. Includes indexes. Bibliography: p. 185-193. [BX1551.2.G64 1975] 74-83313 ISBN 0-444-41228-X : 9.50
1. Catholic Church in the Netherlands. 2. Church renewal—Catholic Church. I. Title.

GUILDAY, Peter Keenan, 262'.02'73
1884-1947.
A history of the councils of Baltimore, 1791-1884. New York, Arno Press, 1969. x, 291 p. 22 cm. (Religion in America) Reprint of the 1932 ed. Includes bibliographical references. [BX833.G8 1969] 77-83421
1. Catholic Church in the United States. Councils. 2. Catholic Church in the United States—History. I. Title.

LO BELLO, Nino D 262'.02'73
Vatican, U.S.A. New York, Trident Press [1973, c1972] 237 p. 22 cm. Bibliography: p. 231-237. [BX1407.P8L6 1973] 72-90359 ISBN 0-671-27097-4 6.95
1. Catholic Church in the United States. 2. Church property—United States. I. Title.

A National Pastoral 262'.02'73
Council, pro and con; proceedings of an interdisciplinary consultation August 28-30, 1970, in Chicago, Ill. Washington, Steering Committee, Advisory Council, United States Catholic Conference, 1971. 155 p. 22 cm. [BX833.N38] 72-177245
1. Catholic Church in the United States—Government—Addresses, essays, lectures. I. United States Catholic Conference. Advisory Council. Steering Committee.

CURTIS, William Redmond, 262'.03
1891-
The Lambeth Conferences; the solution for Pan-American organization. New York, AMS Press [1968] 355 p. 23 cm. (Studies in history, economics, and public law, no. 488) Series statement also appears as: Columbia University studies in the social sciences, 488. Reprint of the 1942 ed. Originally presented as the author's thesis, Columbia University. Bibliography: p. 335-341. [BX5021.L5C8 1968] 68-58565
1. Lambeth Conference. 2. Christian union—Anglican Communion. I. Title. II. Series: Columbia studies in the social sciences, no. 488

ERVIN, Spencer, 1886- 262*.03
An introduction to Anglican polity. Ambler, Pa., Trinity Press [1964] xiii, 83 [43] p. 22 cm. "Vol. 1 of a series on the government of the churches of the Anglican Communion." Errata slip inserted. Includes bibliographical references. [BX5008.5.E76] 73-213890
1. Anglican Communion—Government. I. Title.

RIGHTOR, Henry Haskell. 262'.03
The new General Synod of the Church of England; its possible implications for the Protestant Episcopal Church in the U.S.A. Philadelphia, Evangelical Education Society [1972] 29 p. 22 cm. [BX5150.R5] 72-92702 0.50
1. Church of England. General Synod. 2. Protestant Episcopal Church in the U.S.A.—Government. I. Title.

SIMPSON, James Beasley. 262'.03
The long shadows of Lambeth X; a critical, eye-witness account of the tenth decennial conference of 462 bishops of the Anglican Communion [by] James B. Simpson and Edward M. Story. [1st ed.] New York, McGraw-Hill [1969] xiv, 368 p. 22 cm. [BX5021.S5] 75-88891
1. Anglican communion. I. Story, Edward M., joint author. II. Lambeth Conference, 1968. III. Title.

WALLACE, Bob N., 1932- 262'.03
The General Convention of the Episcopal Church / Bob N. Wallace ; foreword by Scott Field Bailey. New York : Seabury Press, c1976. xiii, 105 p. ; 21 cm. "A Crossroad book." [BX5820.W34] 76-10156 ISBN 0-8164-1212-X : 2.95
1. Protestant Episcopal Church in the U.S.A. General Convention. I. Title.

CONTINUITY and change 262'.03'42
: personnel and administration of the Church of England, 1500-1642 / edited by Rosemary O'Day & Felicity Heal. [Leicester] : Leicester University Press, 1976. 303 p. ; 23 cm. "Distributed in North America by Humanities Press Inc., New Jersey." Includes bibliographical references and index. [BX5150.C59] 76-365001 ISBN 0-7185-1138-7 : 18.75
1. Church of England—Government—History—Addresses, essays, lectures. I. O'Day, Rosemary. II. Heal, Felicity.

THOMPSON, Kenneth A. 262'.03'42
Bureaucracy and Church reform: the organizational response of the Church of England to social change 1800-1965, by Kenneth A. Thompson. Oxford, Clarendon P., 1970. xxiii, 264 p. 23 cm. Bibliography: p. [244]-253. [BX5150.T47] 70-457735 55/-
1. Church of England—Government. 2. Sociology, Christian. I. Title.

RADDIN, George Gates, 1906- 262'.03'74822
Centennial survey of the Episcopal Diocese of Bethlehem, 1871-1971. Compiled by George Gates Raddin, Jr. Wilkes-Barre, Pa., King's College Press, 1972. 47 l. 28 cm. [BX5918.B5R3] 73-172399
1. Protestant Episcopal Church in the U.S.A. Bethlehem (Diocese) I. Title.

LUTHERAN Church in America. Northeastern Pennsylvania Synod. 262'.04'1063748
Minutes of the proceedings of the organizing convention of the Northeastern Pennsylvania Synod of the Lutheran Church in America held at Muhlenberg College, Allentown, Pa., October 23, 1968. [Philadelphia, Printed by Board of Publication, Lutheran Church of America, 1968?] 52 p. 23 cm. [BX8061.N87A5] 70-285932

LUTHERAN Church in America. Commission on Function and Structure. 262'.04'133
Function and structure; report. [Philadelphia, Lutheran Church in America, 1972] 90 p. illus. 31 cm. Cover title. [BX8048.2.A45] 72-185609
1. Lutheran Church in America—Government. 2. Mission of the church. I. Title.

LUTHERAN Church in America. Upper New York Synod. 262'.04'1747
Minutes of the organizing convention, October 14-15, 1966, First English Lutheran Church, Syracuse, New York. [Syracuse? N.Y., 1966?] 79 p. 23 cm. [BX8061.U64A5] 74-261674

LUTHERAN Church in America. Southeastern Pennsylvania Synod. 262'.04'1748
Minutes of the proceedings of the organizing convention, held at the Marriott Motor Hotel, Montgomery County, Pa., October 22, 1968. [Philadelphia, 1968?] 56 p. 23 cm. [BX8061.S63A5] 78-261675

KENNEDY, John, 1897- 262.05
Presbyterian authority and discipline. Richmond, Va., Knox [1965, c.1960] viii, 118p. 21cm. (Church officer's lib.) Delivered as the Chalmers lects. Bibl. [BX9190.K4] 65-26743 1.50 pap.,
1. Presbyterian Church—Discipline. 2. Church—Authority. I. Title. II. Series.

PRADERVAND, Marcel. 262'.05
A century of service : a history of the World Alliance of Reformed Churches, 1875-1975 / Marcel Pradervand. Grand Rapids : Eerdmans, c1975. xv, 309 p. ; 23 cm. Includes bibliographical references and index. [BX8905.W63P7 1975] 75-32554 ISBN 0-8028-3466-3 : 8.95
1. World Alliance of Reformed Churches (Presbyterian and Congregational) I. Title.

WILLIAMSON, Lamar, 1887- 262.050207
. . . and a time to laugh; notes from the pen of anuntamed iconoclast. Comp., ed. by Jerry R. Tompkins. Camden, Ark., Hurley Co., 1966. xiv, 49p. 23cm. Excerpts from sessional records of the First Presbyterian Church of Monticello, Ark., written by Lamar Williamson. [BX9211.M78 F58] 66-23532 1.50 pap.,
I. Tompkins, Jerry R., ed. II. Monticello, Ark. First Presbyterian Church. III. Title.

UNITED Presbyterian Church in the U.S.A. 262'.05'131
The constitution of the United Presbyterian Church in the United States of America. Philadelphia, Office of the General Assembly of the United Presbyterian Church in the United States of America [1967] 2 v. 23 cm. Contents Contents.—v. 1. Book of confessions.—v. 2. Book of order. [BX8955.A3 1967] 68-595
1. United Presbyterian Church in the U.S.A.—Catechisms and creeds. I. Title.

UNITED Presbyterian Church in the U.S.A. 262'.05'131
Presbyterian law for presbytery and synod : a manual for ministers and ruling elders, 1976-77 / edited by William P. Thompson. New York : Office of the General Assembly, United Presbyterian Church in the U.S.A., [1976?] 222 p. ; 23 cm. Published in 1967 under title: Presbyterian law for the presbytery. Includes index. [BX8956.U54 1976] 77-150147
1. United Presbyterian Church in the U.S.A.—Government. I. Thompson, William P., 1918- II. Title.

UNITED States Presbyterian Church in the U.S.A. 262'.05'131
Presbyterian law for the local church : a handbook for church officers and members / edited by Eugene Carson Blake. 1976 revision / by William P. Thompson. New York : Office of the General Assembly, United Presbyterian Church in the U.S.A., 1976. 155 p. ; 23 cm. Includes index. [BX8956.U54 1976a] 77-150148
1. United Presbyterian Church in the U.S.A.—Government. I. Thompson, William P., 1918- II. Title.

PRESBYTERIAN Church in the U.S.A. 262.05'132
Presbyterian law for the local church; a handbook for church officers and members, edited by Eugene Carson Blake. 1967 revision by William P. Thompson. Philadelphia, Office of the General Assembly, United Presbyterian Church in the United States of America, 1967 [c1963] 145 p. 23 cm. [BX8956.A6 1967] 68-2613
1. Presbyterian Church in the U.S.A.—Government. I. Blake, Eugene Carson, 1906- ed. II. Thompson, William P., 1918- III. Title.

PRESBYTERIAN Church in the U.S.A. 262.05'132
Presbyterian law for the presbytery; a manual for ministers and ruling elders by Eugene Carson Blake [and] Edward Burns Shaw. 1967 revision by William P. Thompson. Philadelphia, Office of the General Assembly, United Presbyterian Church in the United States of America, 1967 [c1966] 187 p. 23 cm. [BX8956.A5 1967] 63-11693
1. Presbyterian Church in the U.S.A.—Government. I. Blake, Eugene Carson, 1906- II. Shaw, Edward Burns. III. Thompson, William P., 1918- IV. Title.

CUMBERLAND Presbyterian Church. 262'.05'135
The Cumberland Presbyterian digest, 1975 : a compend of the organic law of the Cumberland Presbyterian Church, together with the organic law of its general agencies and judicial deliverances of its General Assembly / [edited] by Charles Hinkley Smartt. Memphis : The Church, 1976. xxii, 225 p. : port. ; 25 cm. Includes index. [BX8976.C85 1976] 77-357853
1. Cumberland Presbyterian Church—Government. I. Smartt, Charles Hinkley. II. Title.

MARTIN 262'.05731
The new revised Church order commentary; a brief explanation of the Church order of the Christian Reformed Church. Grand Rapids, Zondervan [1967] 372p. 24cm. First ed. by Van Dellen & Monsma pub. in 1941 under title: The Church order commentary. [BX6826.A52M6] 66-29829 6.95
1. Christian Reformed Church. Church order. 2. Christian Reformed Church— Government. I. Van Dellen, Idzerd. The Church order commentary. II. Title.

MONSMA, Martin. 262'.05'731
The new revised Church order commentary; a brief explanation of the Church order of the Christian Reformed Church. Grand Rapids, Zondervan Pub. House [1967] 372 p. 24 cm. First ed. by Van Dellen and Monsma published in 1941 under title: The Church order commentary. [BX6826.A52M6] 66-29829
1. Christian Reformed Church. Church order. 2. Christian Reformed Church — Government. I. Van Dellen, Idzerd. The Church order commentary. II. Title.

SPAAN, Howard B. 262'.05'731
Christian Reformed Church government, by Howard B. Spaan. Grand Rapids, Kregel Publications [1968] 237 p. 23 cm. [BX6826.S6] 68-5368
1. Christian Reformed Church—Government. I. Title.

INCREASE Mather vs. 262'.05'8
Solomon Stoddard : two Puritan tracts. New York : Arno Press, 1972. 143, 34 p. ; 24 cm. (Research library of colonial Americana) Reprint of the 1700 editions of Mather's The order of the Gospel, professed and practised by the churches of Christ in New England ... printed by B. Green & F. Allen for N. Buttolph, Boston, and of Stoddard's The doctrine of the instituted churches explained and proved from the Word of God, published by R. Smith, London. [BX7240.I5 1972] 72-141117 ISBN 0-405-03328-1
1. Church discipline. 2. Congregational churches—Government. I. Mather, Increase, 1639-1723. The order of the Gospel ... 1972. II. Stoddard, Solomon, 1643-1729. The doctrine of the instituted churches ... 1972. III. Title. IV. Series.

MATHER, Cotton, 1663-1728. 262'.05'8
Ratio disciplinae fratrum Nov-Anglorum : a faithful acount of the discipline professed and practised in the churches of New-England / Cotton Mather. New York : Arno Press, 1972. iv, 10, 207 p. ; 24 cm. (Research library of colonial Americana) In English. Reprint of the 1726 ed. printed for S. Gerrish in Cornhill, Boston. [BX7240.M28 1972] 71-141114 ISBN 0-405-03327-3
1. Congregational churches—Government. I. Title. II. Title: A faithful account of the discipline professed and practiced in the churches ... III. Series.

NELSON, William Rhame, 1930- 262'.06
Journey toward renewal [by] William R. Nelson [and] William F. Lincoln. Valley Forge [Pa.] Judson Press [1971] 158 p. 22 cm. [BV600.2.N43] 71-163579 ISBN 0-8170-0543-9 3.50
1. Rochester, N.Y. Lake Avenue Memorial Baptist Church. 2. Church renewal—Case studies. I. Lincoln, William F., joint author. II. Title.

WATSON, Emerson Cleveland, 1923- 262'.06
Superintendent of missions for an association [by] E. C. Watson. Atlanta, Home Mission Board, Southern Baptist Convention [1969] 179 p. 20 cm. Includes bibliographical references. [BX6346.W38] 76-9600 3.00
1. Baptists—Government. I. Southern Baptist Convention. Home Mission Board. II. Title.

HEAD, Robert F 262.061
Essentials of church administration [by] Robert F. Head. Poplar Bluff, Mo., General Baptist Press [1966] 197 p. illus., forms. 23 cm. [BV652.H38] 66-31682
1. Church management. 2. Pastoral theology — Baptists. I. Title.

STEWART, Howard R. 262'.06'1
Baptists and local autonomy : the development, distortions, decline and new directions of local autonomy in Baptist churches / Howard R. Stewart ; foreword by Harvey A. Everett. 1st ed. Hicksville, N.Y. : Exposition Press, [1974] 63 p. ; 22 cm. Bibliography: p. 59-63. [BX6340.S73] 74-182287 ISBN 0-682-48030-4 : 3.50
1. Baptists—Government. I. Title.

MARING, Norman Hill, 1914- 262.06131
A short Baptist manual of polity and practice [by] Norman H. Maring, Winthrop S. Hudson. Valley Forge [Pa.] Judson [c.1965] 160p. 18cm. First ed. pub. in 1963 under title: A Baptist manual of polity and practice. Bibl. [BX6342.M3] 65-18356 1.75 pap.,
1. Baptists—Government. I. Hudson, Winthrop Still, 1911- joint author. II. Title.

FOSHEE, Howard B., 1925- 262'.06'132
Broadman church manual [by] Howard B. Foshee. Nashville, Broadman Press [1973] 150 p. illus. 18 cm. [BX6340.F67] 72-94629 ISBN 0-8054-2525-X 3.95
1. Baptists—Government. 2. Baptists—Doctrinal and controversial works. I. Title.

HARRIS, Philip B. 262'.06132
Administering church training [by] Philip B. Harris and staff, Church Training Dept., Baptist Sunday School Board. Nashville, Convention Press [1969] vi, 138 p. 20 cm. "Text for course 6402 of the Training program subject area in the Christian leadership courses of the New church study course." [BV652.1.H25] 71-88062
1. Christian leadership. I. Southern Baptist Convention. Church Training Dept. II. Title.

HOWSE, William Lewis, 1905- 262.06132
A church organized and functioning [by] W.L. Howse and W.O. Thomason. Rev. ed. Nashville, Convention Press [1966] xi, 165 p. 20 cm. "Church study course [of the Sunday School Board of the Southern Baptist Convention] This is number 0105 in category 1, section for adults and young people." [BX6340.H6] 66-20873
1. Baptists—Government. I. Thomason, William O., joint author. II. Southern Baptist Convention. Sunday School Board. III. Title.

SOUTHERN Baptist Convention. Sunday School Board. 262'.06'132
A dynamic church: spirit and structure for the seventies. Nashville, Tenn., Convention Press [1969] xiv, 145 p. 20 cm. At head of title: W. L. Howse/W. O. Thomason. Text for course 6001 in the Christian leadership series, New church study course. Bibliographical footnotes. [BX6340.S64] 79-75399
1. Baptists—Government. 2. Church. I. Howse, William Lewis, 1905- II. Thomason, William O. III. Title.

LAIR, Loren E. 262'.06'6
The Christian Church (Disciples of Christ) and its future [by] Loren E. Lair. St. Louis, Bethany Press [1971] 315 p. 23 cm. On spine: The Christian Church and its future. Bibliography: p. 307-310. [BX7326.L3] 76-150813 ISBN 0-8272-0433-7 7.95
1. Disciples of Christ—Government. I. Title. II. Title: The Christian Church and its future.

SHORT, Roy Hunter, Bp., 1902- 262'.07'6
United Methodism in theory and practice [by] Roy H. Short. Nashville, Abingdon Press [1974] 205 p. 20 cm. [BX8388.S43] 74-13016 ISBN 0-687-43009-7 5.95
1. United Methodist Church (United States)—Government. I. Title.

TUELL, Jack M., 1923- 262'.07'6
The organization of the United Methodist Church [by] Jack M. Tuell. Rev. [ed.] Nashville, Abingdon Press [1973] 175 p. 22 cm. [BX8382.2.T83 1973] 73-1056 ISBN 0-687-29442-8 3.50 (pbk)
1. United Methodist Church (United States)—Government. I. Title.

TUELL, Jack M., 1923- 262'.07'6
The organization of the United Methodist Church / Jack M. Tuell. Rev. ed. Nashville : Abingdon, 1977. 174 p. ; 22 cm. Includes index. [BX8382.2.Z5T83 1977] 76-55784 ISBN 0-687-29443-6 pbk. : 4.95
1. United Methodist Church (United States)—Government. I. Title.

METHODISM'S destiny 262'.07'601
in an ecumenical age. Editor: Paul M. Minus, Jr. Nashville, Abingdon Press [1969] 208 p. 21 cm. "These essays were first presented at a symposium in September, 1968, celebrating the tenth anniversary of the founding of the Methodist Theological School in Ohio." Bibliographical footnotes. [BX8.2.M45] 69-19740 5.00
1. Christian union—Methodist Church. 2. Methodism—History. I. Minus, Paul M., ed.

UNITED Methodist Church (United States) 262'.07'673
The book of discipline of the United Methodist Church, 1972. Nashville, Tenn., United Methodist Pub. House [1973] xi, 653 p. 22 cm. [BX8388.U55 1973] 73-161954 ISBN 0-687-03708-5
1. United Methodist Church (United States)—Government. I. Title.

ELCHINGER, Leon Arthur, Bp., 1908- 262.08
A challenge to the church [by] Leon Arthur Elchinger, Marc Boegner, Francois Perroux. Tr. from French by Sister Marie Celeste. Westminster, Md., Newman, 1965[c.1964, 1965] xiii, 93p. 22cm. [BX885.E413] 65-25984 2.95
1. Christianity—20th cent.—Addresses, essays, lectures. 2. Catholic Church—Addresses, essays, lectures. I. Boegner, Marc, 1881- II. Perroux, Francois, 1903- III. Title.

ERVIN, Spencer, 1886- 262.083
The polity of the Church of Ireland. Ambler, Pa., TrinityPr. [1965] xii, 107p. 22cm. v. 3. of a ser. describing the polities of the major churches of the Anglican Communion. Bibl. [BX5540.E7] 66-6362 4.00
1. Church of Ireland—Government. I. Title.

MCCONKIE, Oscar Walter. 262'.09'3
Aaronic priesthood / Oscar W. McConkie. Salt Lake City : Deseret Book Co., 1977. 134 p. ; 24 cm. Includes index. Bibliography: p. 129-130. [BX8659.5.M3] 77-3609 ISBN 0-87747-631-4 : 4.95
1. Aaronic Priesthood (Mormonism) I. Title.

REORGANIZED Church of Jesus Christ of Latter Day Saints. 262'.09'33
Rules and resolutions / Reorganized Church of Jesus Christ of Latter Day Saints. Independence, Mo. : Herald House, 1975. 304 p. ; 18 cm. (Pastors reference library) Includes index. [BX8671.A5445 1975] 74-84765 ISBN 0-8309-0136-1
1. Reorganized Church of Jesus Christ of Latter-Day Saints—Government. I. Title.

BRUNGS, Robert A., 1931- 262'.1
A priestly people [by] Robert A. Brungs. New York, Sheed and Ward [1968] xii, 179 p. 21 cm. [BX1920.B76] 68-13849
1. Priesthood, Universal. 2. Laity—Catholic Church. I. Title.

CAMPENHAUSEN, Hans, Freiherr von, 1903- 262.1
Jerusalem and Rome; the problem of authority in the early Church, by Hans von Campenhausen, Henry Chadwick. Philadelphia, Fortress [1966] ix, 39p. 20cm. (Facet bks. Hist. ser. 4) [BV648.C28] 66-24859 .85 pap.,
1. Church polity—Early church. I. Chadwick, Henry, 1920- II. Title.
Contents omitted.

CLAASSEN, Willard. 262'.1
Learning to lead. Scottdale, Pa., Herald Press [1963] 107 p. illus. 20 cm. (Christian service training series) (Christian Service training

series) Leader's guide. Scottdale, Pa., Herald Press [1963] 32 p. diagrs. 20 cm. Bibliographical footnotes. [BV652.1.C55] 63-20203
1. Christian leadership — Study and teaching. I. Title.

[CONGAR, Marie Joseph] 262.1
1904-
Power and poverty in the church [by] Yves Congar. Tr. [from French] by Jennifer Nicholson. Helicon [dist. New York, Taplinger, c.]1964. 157p. 21cm. 64-22971 3.50 bds.,
1. Catholic Church—Government. 2. Church—Authority. I. Title. II. Title: Poverty in the church.

CONGAR, Yves Marie Joseph, 262.1
1904-
Power and poverty in the church [by] Yves Congar. Translated by Jennifer Nicholson. Baltimore, Helicon, 1964. 157 p. 21 cm. Translation of Pour une Eglise servante et pauvre. [BX1802.C613] 64-22971
1. Catholic Church—Government. 2. Church—Authority. I. Title. II. Title: Poverty in the church.

GAGARIN, Jean Xavier, 262'.1
1814-1882.
The Russian clergy. Translated from the French of Father Gagarin, by Ch. du Gard Makepeace. New York, AMS Press [1970] vi, 278 p. 18 cm. Translation of Le clerge russe. Reprint of the 1872 ed. Includes bibliographical references. [BX540.G3 1970] 70-131035
1. Clergy—Russia. 2. Orthodox Eastern Church, Russian—Clergy. I. Title.

HANSON, Anthony Tyrrell. 262.1
The pioneer ministry; the relation of church and ministry. Philadelphia, Westminster Press [1961] 176p. 23cm. (The Library of history and doctrine) [BV660.2.H3 1961] 61-6386
1. Clergy—Office. I. Title.

HARRIS, S. L. 262'.1
Leadership unlimited [by] S. L. Harris. Nashville, Tenn., Convention Press [1969] 89 p. 20 cm. Bibliographical references included in "Footnotes" (p. 88-89) [BV652.1.H27] 70-80814
1. Baptist Student Union. 2. Christian leadership. I. Title.

JENKINS, Daniel Thomas, 262.1
1914-
The Protestant ministry. Garden City, N. Y., Doubleday, 1958. 194p. 20cm. [BV660.J42 1958a] 58-8915
1. Clergy—Office. I. Title.

JENSEN, Gustav Margerth, 262.1
1845-1922.
The ministry. Translated by O. E. Brandt. Minneapolis, Augsburg Pub. House [1958] 148p. 20cm. Translation of Indiedning prestetjenesten. [BV660.J453] 58-7685
1. Clergy—Office. I. Title.

LEIFFER, Murray Howard, 262.1
1902-
The role of the district superintendent in the Methodist Church. Evanston, Ill., Bureau of Social and Religious Research [1960] 201p. 21cm. [BX8345.L44] 60-9241
1. Methodist Church (United States)—Government. I. Title.

LLOYD, Kent. 262'.1
The Church executive: building the kingdom through leadership development, by Kent Lloyd [and others. Inglewood, Calif.] Public Executive Development and Research [1967] 90 p. 23 cm. Includes material from the Church Executive Leadership Seminar, a series of 6 weekend meetings organized by the BYU California Center for Continuing Education and held in Pasadena, Santa Monica, and Los Angeles between Feb. 11 and Apr. 30, 1966. Bibliography: p. [185]-86. [BV652.1.C52] 67-30391
1. Christian leadership. 2. Mormans and Mormonism—Government. I. Church Executive Leadership Seminar, Pasadena, Calif., etc., 1966 II. BYU-California Center for Continuing Education. III. Title.

MOHLER, James A. 262'.1
The origin and evolution of the priesthood; a return to the sources [by] James A. Mohler. Staten Island, N.Y., Alba House [1970] xv, 137 p. 22 cm. Bibliography: p. [125]-130. [BV648.M6] 73-110588 ISBN 0-8189-0166-7 3.95
1. Church polity—Early church, ca. 30-600. 2. Priesthood—History of doctrines. I. Title.

OECHSLIN, Raphael Louis, 262.1
1907-
The spirituality of the layman, by R. L. Oechslin. Translated by Michael C. O'Brien. New York, Desclee Co. [1964] 140 p. 21 cm. Bibliography: p. [139]-140. [BX1920.O313] 64-23932
1. Laity — Catholic Church. 2. Catholic action. I. Title.

OECHSLIN, Raphael Louis, 262.1
1907-
The spirituality of the layman. Tr. [from French] by Michael C. O'Brien. New York, Desclee [c.1964] 140p. 21cm. Bibl. 64-23932 3.50
1. Laity—Catholic Church. 2. Catholic action. I. Title.

SANDERS, John Oswald, 262'.1
1902-
Spiritual leadership, by J. Oswald Sanders. Chicago, Moody Press [1967] 160 p. 22 cm. Bibliographical footnotes. [BV652.1.S3] 67-14387
1. Christian leadership. I. Title.

SCHMITHALS, Walter. 262'.1
The office of apostle in the early church. Translated by John E. Steely. Nashville, Abingdon Press [1969] 288 p. 24 cm. Translation of Das kirchliche Apostelamt. Bibliography: p. 11-15. [BS2618.S3513] 73-84724 ISBN 0-687-28399-X 6.50
1. Paul, Saint, apostle. 2. Apostles. 3. Christianity—Early church, ca. 30-600. I. Steely, John E., ed. II. Title.

WOLFF, Richard, 1927- 262'.1
Man at the top; creative leadership. Wheaton, Ill., Tyndale House Publishers [1969] 131 p. 22 cm. Bibliographical footnotes. [BV652.1.W6] 75-79468 3.95
1. Christian leadership. I. Title.

HYDE, Floy (Salls) 262'.1'07
Protestant leadership education schools, by Floy S. Hyde. New York, Bureau of Publications, Teachers College, Columbia University, 1950. [New York, AMS Press, 1972, i.e. 1973] viii, 164 p. 22 cm. Reprint of the 1950 ed., issued in series: Columbia University. Teachers College. Contributions to education, no. 965. Originally presented as the author's thesis, Columbia. Bibliography: p. 151-153. [BV1533.H94 1972] 70-176892 ISBN 0-404-55965-4 10.00
1. Religious education—Teacher training. I. Title. II. Series: Columbia University. Teachers College. Contributions to education, no. 965.

LAYMAN'S church, 262.1082
by J. A. T. Robinson [others] Introd. by Timothy Beaumont. London, Lutterworth Pr. [dist. Naperville, Ill., Alec. R. Allenson, c.1963] 99 p. 20 cm. 63-25796 1.45, pap.
1. Laity. I. Robinson, John Arthur Thomas, Bp., 1919-

NIEBUHR, Helmut Richard, 262.109
1891- ed.
The ministry in historical perspectives, edited by H. Richard Niebuhr and Daniel D. Williams. [1st ed.] New York, Harper [1956] 331p. 22cm. [BV660.N48] 56-10212
1. Clergy—Hist. I. Williams, Daniel Day, 1910- joint ed. II. Title.

NIEBUHR, Helmut Richard, 262.109
1894- ed.
The ministry in historical perspectives, edited by H. Richard Niebuhr and Daniel D. Williams. [1st ed.] New York, Harper [1956] 331p. 22cm. [BV660.N48] 56-102126
1. Clergy—Hist. I. Williams, Daniel Day, 1910- joint ed. II. Title.

APOSTOLIC succession; 262'.11
rethinking a barrier to unity, edited by Hans Kung. New York, Paulist Press [1968] ix, 181 p. 24 cm. (Concilium. Ecumenical theology, v. 34) Bibliographical footnotes. [BV665.A8] 68-25948
1. Apostolic succession—Addresses, essays, lectures. I. Kung, Hans, 1928- ed. II. Series: Concilium (New York) v. 34

JOURNET, Charles. 262.11
The primacy of Peter from the Protestant and from the Catholic point of view; translated from the French by John Chapin. Westminster, Md., Newman Press, 1954. 144p. 22cm. [BX1805.J68] 54-12533
1. Popes—Primacy. 2. Apostolic succession. 3. Catholic Church—Relations—Protestant churches. 4. Protestant churches—Relations—Catholic Church. 5. Cullmann, Oscar. Petrus. I. Title.

KARRER, Otto, 1888- 262.11
Peter and the church; an examination of Cullmann's thesis. [Tr. from German by Ronald Walls. New York] Herder & Herder [1963] 141p. 22cm. (Quaestiones disputatae, 8) 63-10690 2.25 pap.,
1. Peter, Saint, apostle. 2. Church—Foundation. 3. Church—Foundation. I. Title.

KUNG, Hans, 1928- 262.11
Apostolic succession; rethinking a barrier to unity, ed. by Hans Kung. New York, Paulist [1968] ix, 181p. 24cm. (Concilium: theology in the age of renewal. Ecumenical theology, v.34) Bibl. [BV665.K8] 68-25948 4.50
1. Apostolic succession—Addresses, essays, lectures. I. Title. II. Series: Concilium: theology in the age of renewal, v. 34

ANCIAUX, Paul. 262.12
The episcopate in the church. Translated by Thomas F. Murray. Staten Island, N.Y., Alba House [1965] 100 p. 20 cm. Bibliographical footnotes. [BX1905.A513] 65-8659
1. Episcopacy. I. Title.

BERTRAMS, Wilhelm. 262.12
The Papacy, the episcopacy, and collegiality. Translated by Patrick T. Brannan. With a foreword by John J. Reed. Westminster, Md., Newman Press, 1964. xi, 151 p. 23 cm. [BX1905.B4] 64-8771
1. Episcopacy. 2. Bishops (Canon law) I. Title.

BERTRAMS, Wilhelm 262.12
The papacy, the episcopacy, and collegiality. Tr. [from Latin and Italian] by Patrick T. Brannan. Foreword by John J. Reed. Westminster, Md., Newman [c.]1964. xi, 151p. 23cm. 64-8771 3.50
1. Episcopacy. 2. Bishops (Canon law) I. Title.

CARRILLO DE ALBORNOZ, 262.12
Angel Francisco 1905-
Religious liberty, by A. F. Carrillo de Albornoz. Translated by John Drury. New York, Sheed and Ward [1967] xiii, 209 p. 22 cm. Translation of La libertad religiosa y el Concilio Vaticano II. Bibliography: p. 201-209. [BX830.1962.A45L523] 67-21903
1. Vatican Council. 2d, 1962-1965. Declaratio de libatate religiosa. 2. Religious liberty. I. Title.

THE choosing of 262'.12
bishops; historical and theological studies. William W. Bassett, editor. Raymond E. Goedert, introd. Hartford, Canon Law Society of America, 1971. 111 p. 24 cm. "Published as a supplement to the Jurist." Includes bibliographical references. [BV670.2.C46] 70-148684 2.50
1. Bishops—Appointment, call, and election—Addresses, essays, lectures. I. Bassett, William W., ed.

CHRISTIAN Unity 262.12
Conference, St. Pius x Seminary, 1964.
The episcopate and Christian unity; a symposium conducted by the Graymoor Friars . . . Compiled and edited by Titus Cranny. Garrison, N.Y., Chair of Unity Apostolate [1965] 158 p. 22 cm. Includes bibliographical references. [BV670.2.C48 1964] 67-1838
1. Episcopacy and Christian union. I. Cranny, Titus F., 1921- ed. II. St. Pius x Seminary, Garrison, N.Y. III. Friars of the Atonement. IV. Title.

CODE, Joseph Bernard, 262'.12
1899-
American bishops, 1964-1970. St. Louis, Wexford Press [1970?] 25 p. 28 cm. [BX4666.C6] 79-289632 3.00
1. Catholic Church—Clergy. 2. Bishops—U.S. I. Title.

COUGHLIN, Charles Edward, 262'.12
1891-
Bishops versus Pope, by Charles E. Coughlin. [Bloomfield Hills, Mich., Helmet and Sword, [1969] viii, 220 p. 24 cm. Cover title: Bishops versus the Pope. [BX1751.2.C68] 74-12617
1. Catholic Church—Doctrinal and controversial works—Catholic authors. 2. Popes—Primacy. 3. Bishops. I. Title.

ELECTION and consensus in 262'.12
the church. Edited by Giuseppe Alberigo and Anton Weiler. [New York] Herder and Herder [1972] 156 p. 23 cm. (Concilium: religion in the seventies, v. 77: Church history) On cover: The New concilium: religion in the seventies. Includes bibliographical references. [BX1905.E4] 72-3942 ISBN 0-07-073607-3 2.95
1. Catholic Church—Addresses, essays, lectures. 2. Bishops—Appointment, call, and election—Addresses, essays, lectures. I. Alberigo, Giuseppe, ed. II. Weiler, Antonius Gerardus, 1927- ed. III. Series: Concilium: theology in the age of renewal, v. 77.

EPISCOPACY in the 262'.12
Lutheran Church? Studies in the development and definition of the office of church leadership. Edited by Ivar Asheim and Victor R. Gold. With an afterword by Jerald C. Brauer. Philadelphia, Fortress Press [1969, c1970] viii, 261 p. 24 cm. Translation of Kirchenprasident oder Bischof? Contents.Contents.—Church government and the office of the bishop in the first three centuries, by L. Goppelt.—Church government and the office of bishop from the fourth century to the Reformation, by E. Beyreuther.—The development of the offices of leadership in the German Lutheran churches, 1517-1918, by B. Lohse.—The development of offices of leadership in the German Lutheran churches, 1918-present, by K. Schmidt-Clausen.—The post-Reformation developments of the episcopacy in Denmark, Norway, and Iceland, by S. Borregaard.—The post-Reformation developments of the episcopacy in Sweden, Finland, and the Baltic States, by M. Parvio.—The development of the offices of leadership in the Lutheran churches of Eastern Europe, by H.-M. Thimme.—Lutheran ecclesiastical government in the United States of America, by T. G. Tappert.—The derivative churches: Latin American, Africa, Asia, Australia, by A. Sovik. Bibliographical references included in "Notes" (p. 215-251) [BX8065.2.K513] 70-79768 12.00
1. Lutheran Church—Government—Addresses, essays, lectures. I. Asheim, Ivar, ed. II. Gold, Victor R., 1924- ed.

MILTON, John, 1608-1674. 262.12
An apology against a pamphlet called A modest confutation of the animadversions upon the remonstrant against Smectymnuus. Critical ed., by Milford C. Jochums. Urbana, University of Illinois Press, 1950 [i.e. 1951] xii, 255 p. 29 cm. (Illinois studies in language and literature, v. 85, no. 1-2) Pages 9-77 contain a facsimile of the Apology, made from copies in the University of Illinois Library, with original page numbering (59 p.) and t. p. reading: An apology ... London, Printed by. E. G. for John Rothwell, and are to be sold at the signe of the Sunne in Paula Church-yard. 1642. This study, in its original form, was ... [the editor's doctoral dissertation submitted in August, 1948, at the University of Illinois." Bibliography: p. 221-244. [BV669.M47J6] 51-62130
1. Episcopacy — Early works to 1800. I. Jochums, Milford Cyril, 1912- ed. II. Hail, Joseph, Bp. of Norwich, 1574-1656. supposed author. A modest confutation of a slanderous and scurrilous libell, entitled. Animadversions upon the remonstrants defense against Smectyanuus. III. Title. IV. Series: Illinois. University. Illinois studies in language and literature, v. 35, no. 1-2

MOEDE, Gerald F. 262.12
The office of bishop in Methodism, its history and development. Zurich, Pub. House of the Methodist Church; Nashville, Abingdon [1965, c.1964] 277p. 22cm. Bibl. [BX8345.M6] 65-2069 6.50
1. Methodist Church—Bishops. I. Title.

MURPHY, Francis Xavier, 262'.12
1914-
Synod '67; a new sound in Rome [by Francis X. Murphy and Gary MacEoin] Milwaukee, Bruce Pub. Co. [1968] viii, 236 p. 22 cm. Bibliographical footnotes. [BX831 1967.M8] 68-22590
1. Catholic Church. Synodus Episcoporum, 1st, 1967. I. MacEoin, Gary, 1909- joint author. II. Title.

RAHNER, Karl, 1904- 262.12
Bishops: their status and function. Tr. [from German] by Edward Quinn. Helicon [dist. New York, Taplinger, 1965, c.1964] 78p. 21cm. (Challenge bks.) [BX1905.R313] 65-15043 .95 pap.,
1. Bishops. I. Title.

RAHNER, Karl, 1904- 262.12
The episcopate and the primacy [by] Karl Rahner [and] Joseph Ratzinger. [Translated by Kenneth Barker and others. New York] Herder and Herder [1962] 134 p. 22 cm. (Quaestiones disputatae, 4) [BV670.R313] 62-19564
1. Episcopacy. I. Ratzinger, Joseph. II. Title.

SWIDLER, Leonard J., 262'.12
comp.
Bishops and people, by members of the Catholic Theological Faculty of Tubingen: Gunter Biemer [and others] Edited and translated by Leonard Swidler and Arlene Swidler. Philadelphia, Westminster Press [1970] 170 p. 19 cm. Includes 6 articles translated from the Theologische Quartalschrift 2 (1969). Includes bibliographical references. [BX1905.S9] 70-121763 3.25
1. Bishops—Addresses, essays, lectures. 2. Laity—Catholic Church—Addresses, essays, lectures. I. Swidler, Arlene, joint comp. II. Biemer, Gunter. III. Tubingen. Universitat. Katholisch-Theologische Fakultat. IV. Theologische Quartalschrift. V. Title.

TELFER, William, 1886- 262.12
The office of a bishop. London, Darton, Longman & Todd[dist. Westminister, Md., Canterbury, c.1962] 214p. 23cm. Bibl. 63-629 5.95 bds.,
1. Bishops. I. Title.

THE Unifying role of the 262'.12 *bishop,* edited by Edward Schillebeeckx. [New York] Herder and Herder [1972] 156 p. 23 cm. (Concilium: religion in the seventies, 71) On cover: The New concilium: religion in the seventies. Includes bibliographical references. [BX1905.U5] 70-168651 2.95
1. Bishops—Addresses, essays, lectures. I. Schillebeeckx, Edward Cornelis Florentius Alfons, 1914- ed. II. Series: Concilium (New York), v. 71.

URTASUN, Joseph, Abp. 262.12
What is a bishop? Translated from the French by P. J. Hepburne-Scott. [1st ed.] New York, Hawthorn Books [1962] 108 p. 21 cm. The Twentieth century encyclopedia of Catholicism, v. 83. Section 8: The organization of the church) "Except for chapter iii ... by J. M. T. Barton, this work was originally published in France under the title L'eveque dans l'eglise et son diocese." [BX1905.U713] 62-18502
1. Bishops. I. Title.

URTASUN, Joseph, Abp. 262.12
What is a bishop? Tr. from French by P. J. Hepburne-Scott. New York, Hawthorn [c.1962] 108p. 21cm. (Twentieth cent. ency. of Catholicism, v.83. Section 8: The organization of the church) Except for chapter III by J. M. T. Barton. 62-18502 3.50 bds.,
1. Bishops. I. Title.

VATICAN Council. 2d, 1962-1965. 262'.12
The decree on the pastoral office of bishops in the church; Christus Dominus. Commentary by Willy Onclin. Glen Rock, N.J., Paulist Press [1967] vii, 133 p. 18 cm. (Vatican II documents) Translation of Decretum de pastorali episcoporum munere in ecclesia. Bibliographical footnotes. [BX830.1962.A45P33] 67-28693
1. Catholic Church—Government. 2. Bishops. 3. Pastoral theology—Catholic Church. I. Onclin, Willy. II. Title.

STERLING, Chandler W. 262.1208 Bp., 1911-
Little malice in Blunderland; being a not so fanciful account of the adventures of Alfred Chatworthy, D. D., Bishop of Blunderland, in the land of shining mountains and on the rolling plains of the great northwest during the early reign of the mass-man ... by Chandler W. Sterling. With illus. by Bolte Gibson. New York, Morehouse-Barlow [1965] 176 p. illus. 22 cm. [BV4015.S77] 65-27000
1. Pastoral theology—Anecdotes, facetiae, satire, etc. I. Title.

DAHMUS, Joseph Henry, 1909- 262.120924
William Courtenay: Archbishop of Canterbury, 1381-1396, by Joseph Dahmus. University Park, Pennsylvania State University Press, 1966. 341 p. 24 cm. Bibliography: p. [327]-334. [BR754.C66D33] 66-18194
1. Courtenay, William, Abp. of Canterbury, 1342?-1396.

HOGAN, John Joseph, Bp., 1829-1913. 262'.12'0924 B
On the mission in Missouri, 1857-1868. Kansas City, Mo., J. A. Heilmann, 1892. [Westminster, Md., Christian Classics, 1972] ccxxxi [i.e. 211] p. 23 cm. "200 copies reprinted." [BX1415.M8H6 1972] 72-94069 10.00
1. Hogan, John Joseph, Bp., 1829-1913. 2. Catholic Church in Missouri. I. Title.

WEBER, Francis J. 262'.12'0924
Francis Mora; last of the Catalans, by Francis J. Weber. Los Angeles, Westernlore Press, 1967. xiii, 62 p. illus., port. 22 cm. Bibliographical references included in "Notes" (p. 53-62) [BX4705.M712W4] 67-26512
1. Mora, Francis, 1827-1905.

WEBER, Francis J 262.120924
George Thomas Montgomery, California churchman, by Francis J. Weber. Los Angeles. Westernlore, Pr. 1966. xii, 57p. illus., ports. 21cm. Bibl. [BX4705.M654W4] 66-23591 6.00
1. Montgomery, George Thomas, Abp. 1847-1907. I. Title.

BRENTANO, Robert, 1926- 262.12094274
York metropolitan jurisdiction and papal judges delegate(1297-1296) Berkeley, University of California Press, 1959. xv, 293p. illus., facsims. 24cm. (University of California publications in history, v.58) (Series Bibliography: p.239-277. [E173.C15 vol.58] A59
1. Bishops—Gt. Brit.—York. 2. Jurisdiction (Canon law) 3. York (Province)—Hist. 4. Durham, Eng. (Diocese)—Hist. 5. Ecclesiastical courts—York (Province) I. Title. II. Series.

ROSENTHAL, Joel Thomas, 1934- 262'.12'0942
The training of an elite group: English bishops in the fifteenth century. Philadelphia, American Philosophical Society, 1970. 54 p. 30 cm. (Transactions of the American Philosophical Society, new ser. v. 60, pt. 5) Includes bibliographical references. [BX4666.R65 1970] 78-131553 10.00
1. Bishops—England. I. Title. II. Series: American Philosophical Society, Philadelphia. Transactions, new ser. v. 60, pt. 5

LIEDERBACH, Clarence A., 1910- 262'.12'0971
Canada's bishops from 1120 to 1975 ... from Allen to Yelle / Clarence A. Liederbach ; pref. by Philip Pocock. Cleveland : Dillon/Liederbach, [1975] 64 p. : ill. ; 21 cm. (Saint Mary's College historical series) [BX4671.L53] 73-94082 ISBN 0-913228-10-9 pbk. : 3.50
1. Catholic Church in Canada. 2. Bishops—Canada. I. Title.

ARADI, Zsolt 262.13
The popes; the history of how they are chosen. elected, and crowned. New York, Dell [1962, c.1955] 128p. 18cm. (AS175) Bibl. .95 pap.,
1. Popes—Election. I. Title.

ARADI, Zsolt. 262.13
The popes; the history of how they are chosen, elected, and crowned. New York, Farrar, Straus and Cudahy [1955] 192 p. illus. 22 cm. [BX1805.A7] 55-12206
1. Popes—Election.

BANDER, Peter. 262'.13
The prophecies of St. Malachy. Introd. and commentary by Peter Bander. Foreword by Joel Wells. Pref. by Archbishop H. E. Cardinale. Staten Island, N.Y., Alba House [1970, c1969] 96 p. illus. 22 cm. [BX957.B3 1970] 74-125419 ISBN 0-8189-0189-6 2.95
1. Popes—Prophecies. I. Malachy O'Morgair, Saint, 1094?-1148. Prophetia Sancti Malachiae Archipiescopi de summis pontificibus. English and Latin. 1970. II. Title.

BIEL, Gabriel, d.1495. 262'.13
Defensorium obedientiae apostolicae et alia documenta. Edited and translated by Heiko A. Oberman, Daniel E. Zerfoss, and William J. Courtenay. Cambridge, Belknap Press of Harvard University Press, 1968. vii, 387 p. 24 cm. Original Latin text and English translation on facing pages. Bibliography: p. 63-64. [BX1805.B513 1968] 68-14269
1. Popes—Primacy. 2. Conciliar theory. 3. Catholic Church in Germany. I. Oberman, Heiko Augustinus, ed. II. Zerfoss, Daniel E., ed. III. Courtenay, William J., ed. IV. Title.

BREZZI, Paolo. 262.13
The papacy, its origins and historical evolution. Translated by Henry J. Yannone. Westminster, Md., Newman Press, 1958. 225p. 23cm. Includes bibliography. [BX1805.b713] 58-8747
1. Papacy. I. Title.

CATHOLIC Church. Pope, 1073-1085 (Gregorius VII) 262.13
The correspondence of Pope Gregory VII; selected letters from the Registrum. tr. from Latin with introd. by Ephraim Emerton New York, Octagon, 1966[c.1932, 1966] xxxi, 212p. 24cm. (Records of civilization: sources and studies, no. 14) Bibl. [BX1187.A4] 66-16001 8.00
I. Emerton, Ephraim, 1851-1935. ed. & tr. II. Title.

CIOFALO, Andrew C 262.13
The pilgrimage for peace [written by Andrew C. Ciofalo. South Hackensack, N.J. Custombook, inc., 1965] 72 p. illus. (part col.) ports. (part col.) 28 cm. Published to commemorate Pope Paul's visit to the United States, Oct. 4, 1965; includes the texts of his speeches made during the visit. [BX1378.3C52] 65-28655
1. Paulus vi, Pope, 1897- I. Title.

FOURTEEN hours; 262.13
a picture story of the Pope's historic first visit to America. With an introd. by Francis Cardinal Spellman. New York, Dell Pub. Co. [1965] 1 v. (unpaged) illus., ports. 24 cm. [BX1378.3.F6] 65-9199
1. Paulus VI, Pope, 1897-

FOURTEEN hours; 262.13
a picture story of the Pope's historic first visit to America. Introd. by Francis Cardinal Spellman. New York, Dell [c.1965] 1v. (unpaged) illus., ports. 24cm. (8756) [BX1378.3.F6] 65-9199 1.00 pap.,
1. Paulus VI, Pope, 1897-

GARVEY, Jane D. 262.13
The humor and warmth of Pope John XXIII: his anecdotes and legends, by Louis Michaels. New York, Pocket Books, 1965. 96 p. illus. 23 cm. (A Pocket books special) "Originally 'The stories of Pope John XXIII,'" [BX1378.2.G33] 65-29720
1. Joannes XXIII, Pope, 1881-1963 — Anecdotes. I. Title.

GAY, Jules, 1867- 262'.13
Les papes du XIe [i.e. onzieme] siecle et la chretiente. 2. ed. New York, B. Franklin [1974] xvii, 428 p. 21 cm. (Burt Franklin research and source works series. Selected studies in history, economics and social science: n.s. 39 (b) Medieval, Renaissance & Reformation studies.) Reprint of the 1926 ed. published by V. Lecoffre, Paris, in series: Bibliotheque de l'enseignement de l'histoire ecclesiastique. Includes bibliographical references. [BX1178.G3 1974] 74-12220 ISBN 0-8337-1302-7
1. Popes. 2. Church history—Middle Ages, 600-1500. I. Title. II. Series: Bibliotheque de l'enseignement de l'histoire ecclesiastique.

GONZALEZ, James L. 262.13
Chats with Pope Paul. Tr. by Mary F. Ingoldsby. [Boston] St. Paul Ed. [dist. Daughters of St. Paul, c.1965] 217p. illus., ports. 22cm. Bibl. [BX1378.3.G5813] 65-28756 4.00; 3.00 pap.,
1. Paulus VI, Pope, 1897- I. Title.

GONZALEZ, Jose Luis. 262.13 (B)
Chats with Pope Paul by J. L. Gonzalez. Translated by Mary F. Ingoldsby. [Boston] St. Paul Editions [c1965] 217 p. illus. ports. 22 cm. Bibliographical footnotes. [BX1378.3.G5813] 65-28756
1. Paulus vi, Pope, 1897- I. Title.

GRANT, Frederick Clifton, 1891- 262.13
Rome and reunion [by] Frederick C. Grant. New York, Oxford University Press, 1965. ix, 196 p. 21 cm. [BX957.G7] 65-11525
1. Papacy—Hist. 2. Christian union—Catholic Church. 3. Vatican Council, 2d. I. Title.

GRANT, Frederick Clifton, 1891- 262.13
Rome and reunion. New York, Oxford [c.] 1965. ix, 196p. 21cm. [BX957.G7] 65-11525 5.00
1. Papacy—Hist. 2. Christian union—Catholic Church. 3. Vatican Council, 2d. I. Title.

HALES, Edward Elton Young, 1908- 262.13
Pope John and his revolution. London, Eyre & Spottiswoode [Mystic, Conn., Verry, 1966, c.] 1965. xv, 222p. group port. 23cm. Bibl. [BX1378.2.H23] 65-5010 6.00 bds.,
1. Joannes XXIII, Pope, 1881-1963. I. Title.

HATCH, Alden, 1898- 262.13
Pope Paul VI New York. Random [1966] 279p. ports. 22cm. Bibl. [BX1378.3.H3] 66-120062 5.95 bds.,
1. Paulus VI, Pope, 1897- I. Title.

HATCH, Alden, 1898- 262.13
Pope Paul VI New York, Random House [1966] 279 p. ports. 22 cm. Bibliography: p. 267. [BX1378.3.H3] 66-12006
1. Paulus VI, Pope, 1897- I. Title.

HESTON, Edward Louis, 1907- 262.13
The Holy See at work; with a pref. by Samuel Cardinal Stritch. Milwaukee, Bruce [1950] xiv, 188 p. illus., ports. 21 cm. [BX1801.H4] 50-8570
1. Catholic Church. Pope. 2. Catholic Church. Curia Romana. I. Title.

INSTRUMENT of Your peace 262.13
(An); the mission for peace by Pope Paul VI and his momentous visit to America [Ed.: Edward T. Fleming. New York, N.Y. 10017, Commemorative Pubns., 400 Madison Av., 1966, c.1965] 223p. illus. (pt. col.) 29cm. Official documentary report of the visit of His Holiness, Pope Paul VI, to the United Nations and New York. Pub. by Commemorative Pubns. in conjunction with the Archdiocese of New York [BX1378.3.I5] 66-1589 7.95
1. Paulus VI, Pope, 1897- I. Fleming, Edward T., ed. II. Commemorative Publications, inc., New York.

KUHNER, Hans. 262.13
Encyclopedia of the Papacy. [Translated from the German by Kenneth J. Northcott] New York, Philosophical Library [1958] 249p. 22cm. Bibliography: p. 249. [BX955.K853] 58-4521
1. Papacy—Hist. I. Title.

LAMPING, A. J. 262'.13
Ulrichus Velenus (Oldrich Velensky) and his treatise against the papacy / by A. J. Lamping. Leiden : Brill, 1976. viii, 291 p. ; 24 cm. (Studies in medieval and Reformation thought : v. 19) Thesis—Leiden. "In hoc libello ... ": p. [219]-276. Includes indexes. Bibliography: p. [277]-284. [BX1805.V363L35] 76-462277 ISBN 9-00-404397-7 : fl 94.00
1. Velenus, Ulrichus. Petrum Romam non venisse. 2. Popes—Primacy—Controversial literature. I. Velenus, Ulrichus. Petrum Romam non venisse. 1976. II. Title. III. Series.

MCCORMICK, Anne (O'Hare) 262.13
Vatican journal, 1921-1954. Compiled and edited by Marion Turner Sheehan; with an introd. by Clare Booth Luce. New York, Farrar, Straus and Cudahy [1957] 288p. 22cm. [BX1389.M32] 57-11490
1. Papacy—Hist. 2. Catholic Church—Relations (diplomatic) I. Title.

MACGREGOR, Geddes. 262.13
The Vatican revolution. Boston, Beacon Press [1957] xiv, 226p. 22cm. 'The text of the Vatican decrees, with an English translation and notes': p.[163]-197. Bibliography: p.205-216. [BX1806.M25] 57-6524
1. Popes—Infallibility. I. Vatican Council, 1869-1870. Acta et decreta. II. Title.

MCKNIGHT, John P 262.13
The papacy, a new appraisal. New York Rinehart [1952] 487 p. 22 cm. Bibliography: p. 350-360. [BX957.M25] 52-5567
1. Papacy. I. Title.

MAISTRE, Joseph Marie, comte de, 1753-1821. 262'.13
The Pope, considered in his relations with the church, temporal sovereignties, separated churches, and the cause of civilization / by Joseph de Maistre ; translated by Aeneas McD. Dawson ; with an introd. by Richard A. Lebrun. New York : H. Fertig, 1975. xli, 369 p. ; 21 cm. Translation of Du pape. Reprint of the 1850 ed. published by C. Dolman, London. Includes bibliographical references. [BX1805.M3213 1975] 75-5690 16.00
I. Title: The Pope, considered in his relations with the church ...

MALONEY, George A., 1924- 262'.13
Critique of Msgr. Pospishil's The quest for an Ukrainian Catholic Patriarchate, by George A. Maloney and Eva Piddubcheshen. Philadelphia, Society for the Promotion of the Patriarchal System in the Ukrainian Catholic Church, 1972. 17 p. ports. 26 cm. [BX4711.634.M35] 74-151189
1. Catholic Church. Byzantine rite (Ukranian)—Doctrinal and controversial works. 2. Pospishil, Victor J. The quest for an Ukrainian Catholic Patriarchate. I. Piddubcheshen, Eva, joint author. II. Title.

MARCELLO, Cristoford, d 1527; 262'13
Christophori Marcelli De avthoritate Svmmi Pontificis et his qvae ad illam pertinent. adversvs impia Martini Lvtherii dogmata. Ridgewood, N.J., Gregg Pr. 1966. 1451. 20cm. Reproduction of the 1521 Florentine ed. pub. by Haeredes Philippi Iunate. [BX1805.M37 151a] 67-3194 28.00
1. Luther. Martin, 1483-1546. 2. Papacy. I. Title. II. Title: De avthoritate Svmmi Pontificis.

NEW York times. 262.13
The Pope's journey to the United States, written by staff members of the New York times. Edited by A. M. Rosenthal and Arthur Gelb. New York, Bantam Books [1965] 120 p. illus., map, ports. 18 cm. (A Bantam extra, SZ3224) [BX1378.3.N4] 65-28642
1. Paulus VI, Pope, 1897- I. Rosenthal, Abraham Michael, 1922- ed. II. Gelb, Arthur, 1924- ed. III. Title.

OHLIG, Karl-Heinz, 1938- 262'.13
Why we need the Pope : the necessity and limits of Papal primacy / Karl-Heinz Ohlig ; translated by Robert C. Ware. St. Meinrad, Ind. : Abbey Press, 1975. x, 152 p. ; 21 cm. (A Priority edition) Translation of Braucht die Kirche einen Papst? Includes bibliographical references. [BX1805.O3613] 75-19924 ISBN 0-87029-053-3 pbk. : 3.95
1. Popes—Primacy—History. I. Title.

OXFORT, Ursula 262.13
The heresy of Pope John XXIII New York, Exposition [c.1965] 44p. 22cm. Bibl. [BX1779.5.O9] 65-6442 3.00
1. Joannes XXIII, Pope, 1881-1963 2. Catholic Church—Doctrinal and controversial works—Catholic authors. I. Title.

PALLENBERG, Corrado 262.13
Inside the Vatican, [translated from the Italian] New York, Hawthorn Books [c.1960] 273 p. 24 cm. illus. (2 p. bibl. footnotes) 60-5900 4.95 half cloth,
1. Catholic Church—Government. I. Title.

PAPAL ministry in the 262'.13 *Church.* Edited by Hans Kung. [New York] Herder and Herder [1971] 158 p. 23 cm. (Concilium: religion in the seventies. Ecumenism, v. 64) On cover: The New

concilium: religion in the seventies. Includes bibliographical references. [BX955.2.P35] 78-150303 2.95
1. Papacy—Addresses, essays, lectures. I. Kung, Hans, 1928- ed. II. Series: Concilium (New York) v. 64

PAPAL primacy and the 262'.13
universal church / edited by Paul C. Empie and T. Austin Murphy. Minneapolis : Augsburg Pub. House, [1974] 255 p. ; 18 cm. (Lutherans and Catholics in dialogue ; 5) Includes bibliographical references. [BX1805.P24] 74-83329 ISBN 0-8066-1450-1 : 1.95
1. Lutheran Church—Relations—Catholic Church. 2. Catholic Church—Relations—Lutheran Church. 3. Popes—Primacy. I. Empie, Paul C., ed. II. Murphy, Thomas Austin, 1911- ed. III. Title. IV. Series.

A Pope for all 262'.13
Christians? : An inquiry into the role of Peter in the modern church / edited by Peter J. McCord. New York : Paulist Press, c1976. vi, 212 p. ; 23 cm. Includes bibliographical references. [BX1805.P66] 75-32859 ISBN 0-8091-1918-8 pbk. : 7.50
1. Papacy—Addresses, essays, lectures. 2. Authority (Religion)—Addresses, essays, lectures. 3. Church—Authority—Addresses, essays, lectures. I. McCord Peter J.

POPE Paul VI in the Holy 262.13
Land [Tr. from German by Aileen O'Brien. Photos. by Werner Schiller. New York] Herder & Herder [c.1964] 198p. illus. (pt. col.) col. maps, ports. (pt. col.) 31cm. 64-19604 7.50
1. Paulus VI, Pope, 1897- 2. Palestine—Descr. & trav. I. Schiller, Werner.

PRIMACY of Peter (The) 262.13
[by] J. Meyendorff, N. Afanassieff [others. Tr. from French] London, Faith Pr. [dist. Westminster, Md., Canterbury, c.1963] 134p. 23cm. (Lib. of Orthodox theology, no. 1) Bibl. 63-5439 2.50
1. Peter, Saint, apostle. 2. Popes—Primacy. 3. Church—History of doctrines. I. Meyendorff, Jean, 1926- II. Afanas'ev, Nikolai III. Series.

REYNOLDS, Robert L. 262.13
The Story of the Pope. v. 1- [New York, Dell Pub. Co.] 1957- v. illus., ports. 28 cm. Compiler: 1957- R. L. Reynolds. [BX955.S8] 57-3980
1. Popes. I. Title.

RIDLEY, Francis A., 1897- 262'.13
The Papacy and fascism; the crisis of the twentieth century, by F. A. Ridley. London, M. Secker, Warburg, 1937. [New York, AMS Press, 1973] 264 p. 19 cm. Includes bibliographical references. [BX1790.R5 1973] 72-180422 ISBN 0-404-56156-X 13.50
1. Catholic Church—Relations (diplomatic) 2. Papacy—History. 3. Socialism and Catholic Church. 4. Fascism and Catholic Church. I. Title.

SCHILLER, Werner. 262.13
Pope Paul VI in the Holy Land. [Translation by Aileen O'Brien. Photos. by Werner Schiller. New York] Herder and Herder [1964] 198 p. illus. (part col.) col. maps, ports, (part col.) 31 cm. [BX1378.3P6] 64-19604
1. Paulus vi, Pope, 1897- 2. Palestine—Descr. & trav. I. Title.

SHOTWELL, James Thomson, 262.13
1874-1965, ed.
The see of Peter [ed.] by James T. Shotwell, Louise Ropes Loomis. New York, Octagon, 1965[c.1927, 1955] xxvi, 737p. 24cm. (Records of civilization: sources and studies, no.7) Bibl. [BX955.S5] 65-25615 17.50
1. Peter, Saint, apostle. 2. Papacy—Hist. 3. Church history—Primitive and early church. I. Loomis, Louise Ropes, 1874-1958, ed. II. Title. III. Series.

THE Story of the Pope. 262.13
v.1- [New York, Dell Pub. Co.] 1957- v. illus., ports. 28cm. Compiler: 1957- R. L. Reynolds. [BX955.S8] 57-3980
1. Popes. I. Reynolds, Robert L.

TIME, inc. 262.13
The Pope's visit. New York, Author [1966, c.1965] 96p. Illus. (pt. col.) ports. (pt. col.) 29cm. (Time-Life special report bks.) [BX1378.3.T5] 65-28741 1.95 pap.,
1. Paulus VI, Pope, 1897- I. Title.

UNITED Press 262.13
International.
The pilgrim Pope in the New World, the Holy Land, and India. Text and pictures by United Press International. New York, Pocket Books, 1965. 1 v. (unpaged) illus. (part col.) ports. (part col.) 28 cm. (A Pocket book special) Paulus VI, Pope, 1897- [BX1378.3.U5] 65-29641
I. Title.

UNITED Press International 262.13
The pilgrim Pope in the New World, the Holy Land, and India. Text and pictures by United Press International. New York, Pocket Bks. [c.]1965. 1v. (unpaged) illus.(pt. col.) ports. (pt. col.) 28cm. (Pocket bk. special) [BX1378.3.U5] 65-29641 1.95 pap.,
1. Paulus VI, Pope, 1897- I. Title.

WELTIN, Edward George, 262.13
1911-
The ancient Popes, by E. G. Weltin. Westminster, Md., Newman Press, 1964. xv. 369 p. illus., map (on lining papers) 23 cm. (The Popes through history, v. 2) Bibliography: p. 355. [BX970.W4] 64-66033
1. Popes. I. Title. II. Series.

WELTIN, Edward George, 262.13
1911-
The ancient Popes. Westminster, Md., Newman [c.] 1964. xv, 369p. illus., map (on lining papers) 23cm. (The Popes through hist., v.2) Bibl. [BX970.W4] 64-66033 4.50
1. Popes. I. Title. II. Series.

WINTER, Michael M. 262.13
Saint Peter and the Popes. Baltimore, Helicon Press [1960] 236p. Bibl. footnotes. 60-13379 4.50 bds.,
1. Peter, Saint, apostle. 2. Papacy—Hist. I. Title.

BARRACLOUGH, Geoffrey, 262'.13'09
1908-
The medieval papacy. [1st American ed. New York] Harcourt, Brace & World [1968] 216 p. illus., facsims., maps, ports. 22 cm. ([History of European civilization library]) Part of illustrative matter colored. "Bibliographical notes": p. 197-205. [BX955.2.B3 1968b] 68-29667 5.95
1. Papacy—History. I. Title.

CHAPMAN, John, 262'.13'09
Father, 1865-1933.
Studies on the early Papacy. Port Washington, N.Y., Kennikat Press [1971] 238 p. 22 cm. Reprint of the 1928 ed. Includes bibliographical references. [BR162.C45 1971] 76-118517 ISBN 0-8046-1139-4
1. Catholic Church—History. 2. Church history—Primitive and early church, ca. 30-600. 3. Papacy. I. Title.

CORBETT, James Arthur. 262.1309
The papacy, a brief history. Princeton, N.J., Van Nostrand [1956] 192p. 18cm. (An Anvil original, no. 12) [BX955.C66] 56-6881
1. Papacy—Hist. 2. Papacy—Hist.—Sources. I. Title.

FARROW, John, 1904- 262.1309
Pageant of the popes; a frank history of the papacy. St. Paul, Catechetical Guild Educational Society [1955, c1950] 464p. 17cm. Includes bibliography. [BX955] 56-628
1. Papacy—Hist. I. Title.

GONTARD, Friedrich. 262.1309
The Chair of Peter; a history of the papacy. Translated from the German by A. J. and E. F. Peeler. [1st ed.] New York, Holt, Rinehart and Winston [1964] 629 p. coat of arms, map, plates, ports. 25 cm. Translation of Die Papste. [BX955.2.G63] 64-14346
1. Papacy—History. I. Title.

HOLLIS, Christopher, 262.1309
1902- ed.
The Papacy; an illustrated history from St Peter to Paul VI. New York, Macmillan [1964] 304 p. illus. (part col.) facsims., col. maps, ports. (part col.) 33 cm. [BX955.2.H6] 64-12539
1. Papacy — Hist. I. Title.

HOLLIS, Christopher, 262.1309
1902- ed.
The Papacy; an illustrated history from St. Peter to Paul VI. New York, Macmillan [c.1964] 304p. illus. (pt. col.) facsims., col. maps, ports. (pt. col.) 33cm. 64-12539 25.00
1. Papacy—Hist. I. Title.

JOHN, Eric, ed. 262.1309
The Popes, a concise biographical history, Historical surveys by Douglas Woodruff. Biographical articles by J. M. W. Bean [and others. 1st ed.] New York, Hawthorn Books [1964] 496 p. illus., plates (part col.) Ports. 26 cm. Bibliography: p. 481-482. [BX955.2.J58] 64-12422
1. Popes. I. Title.

JOHN, Eric, ed. 262.1309
The Popes, a concise biographical history. Historical surveys by Douglas Woodruff. Biographical articles by J. M. W. Bean [others] New York, Hawthorn [c.1964] 496p. illus., plates (pt. col.) ports. 26cm. Bibl. 64-12422 15.00
1. Popes. I. Title.

LIBER PONTIFICALIS 262.1309
The book of the popes (Liber pontificalis) New York, Octagon, 1965 [c.1916, 1944] 169p. 24cm. (Records of civilization: sources and studies, no.3) Tr. is based upon the text ed. by Mommsen in the Monumenta Germaniae historica. [BX950.E6L6] 7.50
1. Papacy—Hist.—Sources. 2. Catholic church—Hist.—Sources. I. Loomis, Louise Ropes, tr. II. Title.
Contents omitted

MACGREGOR-HASTIE, Roy. 262'.13'09
The throne of Peter; a history of the Papacy. London, New York [etc.] Abelard Schuman, 1966. 192 p. ports. 22 cm. 18/- (B***) [BX955.2.M3] 68-86661
1. Papacy—Hist. I. Title.

MACGREGOR-HASTIE, Roy 262.1309
The throne of Peter; a history of the papacy. New York, Criterion [1966] 192p. ports. 23cm. [BX955.2.M3] 66-15134 3.95
1. Papcy—Hist. I. Title.

MOLLAT, Guillaume, 1877- 262.1309
The popes at Avignon, 1305-1378. Tr. from the 9th French ed., 1949 [by Janet Love] New York, Nelson [c.1963] xxii, 361p. 24cm. Bibl. 63-24639 9.25
1. Papacy—Hist.—1309-1378. 2. Avignon—Hist. I. Title.

MOLLAT, Guillaume, 1877- 262.1309
The popes at Avignon, 1305-1378. Translated from the 9th French ed., 1949 [by Janet Love] London, New York, T. Nelson [1963] xxii, 361 p. 24 cm. Bibliography: p. x. Bibliographical footnotes. [BX1300.M613 1963] 63-24639
1. Papacy — Hist. — 1309-1378. 2. Avignon — Hist. I. Title.

ORMESSON, Wladimir, 262.1309
comte d', 1888-
The papacy. Translated from the French by Michael Derrick. [1st ed.] New York, Hawthorn Books [1959] 142p. 21cm. (The Twentieth century encyclopedia of Catholicism, v.81. Section 8: The organization of the church) Bibliography: p.[141]-142. [BX1805.O713] 59-6740
1. Papacy. I. Title. II. Series: The Twentieth century encyclopedia of Catholicism, v.81

RANKE, Leopold von, 262'.13'09
1795-1886.
History of the Popes; their church and state. [Translated from the German by E. Fowler] New York, F. Ungar Pub. Co. [1966] 3 v. illus., facsims., ports. 22 cm. Translation of Die romischen Papste. Reprint of the 1901 ed. Includes bibliographical references. [BX955.R35 1966] 66-25109
1. Papacy—History. I. Title.

RENOUARD, Yves. 262'.13'09023
The Avignon papacy, 1305-1403. Translated by Denis Bethell. [Hamden, Conn.] Archon Books, 1970. 157 p. maps, port. 23 cm. Translation of La papaute a Avignon. Bibliography: p. 138-150. [BX1270.R413] 70-21164 ISBN 0-208-01156-0 7.50
1. Papacy—History—1309-1378. I. Title.

SMITH, Arthur Lionel 262.130902
Church and state in the Middle Ages New York, Barnes & Noble [1964] 245p. 23cm. 63-4159 7.50
1. Church and state—Hist. 2. Catholic Church—Relations (diplomatic) with Gt. Brit. 3. Gt. Brit.— I. Title.

ULLMANN, Walter, 262'.13'0902
1910-
The papacy and political ideas in the Middle Ages / Walter Ullmann. London : Variorum Reprints, 1976. 406 p. in various pagings : port. ; 23 cm. (Variorum reprint ; CS44) Includes original pagings. Reprints of articles in English or German, originally published between 1952 and 1973. Contents.Contents.—1. Cardinal Humbert and the Roman Ecclesia.—2. Von Canossa nach Pavia.—3. The Pontificate of Adrian IV.—4. Cardinal Roland and Besancon.—5. The significance of Innocent III's decretal Vergentis.—6. Dies ortus imperii.—7. The decline of the Chancellor's authority in medieval Cambridge.—8. The curial exequies for Edward I and Edward III.—9. A decision of the Rota Romana on the benefit of clergy in England.—10. De Bartoli sententia.—11. The University of Cambridge and the Great Schism.—12. The recognition of St Bridget's Rule by Martin V.—13. Eugenius IV, Cardinal Kemp and Archibishop Chichele.—14. Thomas Becket's miraculous oil.—15. The legal validity of the papal electoral pacts.—16. Julius II and the schismatic cardinals.—17. The medieval papal court as an international tribunal.—18. The Papacy as an institution of government in the Middle Ages. Includes bibliographies and index. [BX1068.U44] 76-379934 ISBN 0-902089-87-0 : £13.50
1. Papacy—History—Addresses, essays, lectures. I. Title.

ARETIN, Karl Otmar, 262'.13'09034
Freiherr von, 1923-
The Papacy and the modern world. Translated by Roland Hill. New York, McGraw-Hill [1970] 256 p. illus. (part col.), facsims., col. maps, ports. (part col.) 20 cm. (World university library) Includes bibliographical references. [BX955.2.A73 1970b] 76-77021 4.95
1. Papacy—History. I. Title.

BURY, John Bagnell, 262.130903
1861-1927
History of the papacy in the 19th century; liberty and authority in the Roman Catholic Church. Ed. by R. H. Murray. Augm. ed.: Vatican Council I, Vatican Council II. Introd., epilogue, bibliographical notes by Frederick C. Grant. New York, Schocken [c.1964] xxxiv, 217p. 23cm. Bibl. 64-22610 5.00
1. Pius IX, Pope, 1792-1878. 2. Papacy—Hist. 3. Catholic Church—Hist. I. Title.

BURY, John Bagnell, 262.130903
1861-1927.
History of the papacy in the 19th century liberty and authority in the Roman Catholic Church [by] J. B. Bury. Edited by R. H. Murray. Augm. ed.: Vatican Countil I, Vatican Council II. Introd., epilogue, and bibliographical notes by Frederick C. Grant. New York, Schocken Books [1964] xxxiv, 217 p. 23 cm. "First appeared in 1960." Bibliography: p. 199-207. [BX1386.B8] 64-22610
1. Pius IX, Pope, 1792-1878. 2. Papacu — Hist. 3. Catholic Church — Hist. I. Title.

DELZELL, Charles F., 262'.13'0904
comp.
The Papacy and totalitarianism between the two World Wars, edited by Charles F. Delzell. New York, Wiley [1974] viii, 179 p. 22 cm. (Major issues in history) Bibliography: p. 173-179. [BX1389.D44] 73-16419 ISBN 0-471-20638-5 4.50 (pbk)
1. Papacy—History—20th century. 2. Papal documents. I. Title.

FALCONI, Carlo. 262'.13'0904
The Popes in the twentieth century, from Pius X to John XXIII. Translated from the Italian by Muriel Grindrod. [1st American ed.] Boston, Little, Brown [1968, c1967] xvi, 400 p. illus., ports. 24 cm. Translation of I papi del ventesimo secolo. Bibliography: p. [370]-378. [BX1389.F313 1968b] 68-14744
1. Papacy—History—20th century. I. Title.

FALCONI, Carlo. 262'.13'0904
The Popes in the twentieth century, from Pius X to John XXIII. Translated from the Italian by Muriel Grindrod. [1st American ed.] Boston, Little, Brown [1968, c1967] xvi, 400 p. illus., ports. 24 cm. Translation of I papi del ventesimo secolo. Bibliography: p. [370]-378. [BX1389.F313 1968b] 68-1474
1. Papacy—Hist.—20th cent. I. Title.

NICHOLS, Peter, 262'.13'0904
1928-
The politics of the Vatican. New York, Praeger [1968] ix, 373 p. 8 plates (incl. ports.) 22 cm. Bibliographical footnotes. [BX1389.N5 1968] 68-11321
1. Papacy—History—20th century. I. Title.

BARGRAVE, John, 262'.13'0922 B
1610-1680.
Pope Alexander the Seventh and the College of Cardinals. With a catalogue of Dr. Bargrave's museum. Edited by James Craigie Robertson. [Westminster] Printed for the Camden Society, 1867. New York, AMS Press [1968] xxviii, 144 p. 24 cm. Original ed. issued as no. 92 of the Camden Society publications. [BX4663.B37 1968] 78-160001
1. Alexander VII, Pope, 1599-1667. 2. Bargrave, John, 1610-1680. 3. Cardinals. I. Title. II. Series: Camden Society, London. Publications, no. 92.

CHAMBERLIN, Eric 262'.13'0922
Russell.
The bad Popes [by] E. R. Chamberlin. New York, Dial Press, 1969. 310 p. illus. (part col.) 25 cm. "A Brahmin book." Bibliography: p. 291-296. [BX955.2.C45] 78-83475 12.50
1. Popes. I. Title.

LIBER PONTIFICALIS. 262.130922
The book of the Popes. Liber pontificalis. Translated with an introd. by Louise Ropes Loomis. New York, Octagon Books, 1965- v. 24 cm. (Records of civilization; sources and studies, no. 3 Contents.CONTEnTS. -- [1] To the pontificate of Gregory I. [BX950.E6L612] 65-9020
1. Papacy — Hist. — Sources. 2. Catholic Church — Hist. — Sources. 3. Popes. I. Loomis, Louis Ropes, 1874- tr. II. Title. III. Series.

OLF, Lillian (Browne) 1880- 262'.13'0922 B
Their name is Pius; portraits of five great modern popes [by] Lillian Browne-Olf. Freeport, N.Y., Books for Libraries Press [1970] xv, 382 p. ports. 23 cm. (Essay index reprint series) Reprint of the 1941 ed. Bibliography: p. 371-374. [BX1365.O4 1970] 74-107729
I. Title.

PRINZ, Joachim, 1902- 262.130922
Popes from the ghetto; a view of medieval Christendom. New York, Schocken [1968, c.1966] 256p. 20cm. (SB174) Bibl. [BX1178.P7] 1.95 pap.,
1. Popes. 2. Pierleoni family. I. Title.

PRINZ, Joachim, 1902- 262.130922
Popes from the ghetto; a view of medieval Christendom. New York, Horizon Press [1966] 256 p. illus. 25 cm. Bibliography: p. 251-256. [BX1178.P7] 66-16301
1. Popes. 2. Pierleoni family. I. Title.

PRINZ, Joachim, 1902- 262.130922
Popes from the ghetto; a view of medieval Christendom. New York, Horizon [c.1966] 256p. illus. 25cm. Bibl. [BX1178.P7] 66-16301 6.50
1. Popes. 2. Pierleoni family. I. Title.

PURDY, William Arthur, 1911- 262.130922
The Church on the move; the characters and politics of Pius XII and John XXIII [by] W. A. Purdy. Techny, Ill., Divine Word [1968,c.1966] 352p. 22cm. Bibl. [BX1378.P8 1966] 2.95 pap.,
1. Pius XII, Pope 1876-1958. 2. Joannes XXIII, Pope, 1881-1963. I. Title.

PURDY, William Arthur, 1911- 262.130922
The Church on the move; the characters and policies of Pius XII and John XXIII [by] W. A. Purdy. New York, John Day Co. [1966] 352 p. 22 cm. Bibliography: p. [343]-346. [BX1378.P8 1966] 66-25867
1. Pius XII, Pope, 1876-1958. 2. Joannes XXIII, Pope, 1881-1963. I. Title.

WISEMAN, Nicholas Patrick Stephen, Cardinal, 1802-1865. 262'.13'0922
Recollections of the last four popes and of Rome in their times. New and rev. ed. Freeport, N.Y., Books for Libraries Press [1973] p. (Essay index reprint series) "First published 1858." [BX1386.W5 1973] 72-14111 ISBN 0-518-10032-4
1. Pius VII, Pope, 1742-1823. 2. Leo XII, Pope, 1760-1829. 3. Pius VIII, Pope, 1761-1830. 4. Gregorius XVI, Pope, 1765-1846. I. Title. II. Title: The last four popes.

ADLER, Bill, ed. 262.130924
The Pope John album: his life, his family, his career, his words [edited by] Bill Adler and Savre Ross. [1st ed.] New York, Hawthorn [1966] 97p. illus. (pt. col.) ports. 31cm. [BX1378.2.A5] 66-16220 35.00
1. Joannes XXIII, Pope, 1881-1963. I. Ross, Sayre, joint ed. II. Title.

ADLER, Bill 262.130924
Pope Paul in the United States: his mission for peace on earth, October 4, 1965, by Bill Adler with Sayre Ross. New York, Hawthorn [c.1965] 97p. illus., ports. 29cm. [BX1378.3.A6] 65-28438 2.95
1. Paulus VI, Pope, 1897- I. Title.

ADLER, Bill. 262.130924
Pope Paul in the Unites States: his mission for peace on earth, October 4, 1965, by Bill Adler with Sayre Ross. [1st ed.] New York, Hawthorn Books [1965] 97 p. illus., ports. 29 cm. [BX1378.3.A6] 65-28438
1. Paulus vi, Pope, 1897- I. Title.

ANDREWS, James F., 1936- 262'.13'0924
Paul VI, critical appraisals. Edited by James F. Andrews. New York, Bruce Pub. Co. [1970] 160 p. 22 cm. Includes bibliographical references. [BX1378.3.A75] 78-131474 6.95
1. Paulus VI, Pope, 1897- —Addresses, essays, lectures.

BALDUCCI, Ernesto, 1922- 262.130924
John, 'the transitional Pope.' Tr. [from Italian] by Dorothy White. New York, McGraw [1965, c.1964] xiii, 318p. 23cm. [BX1378.2.B313] 65-23217 7.50 bds.,
1. Johannes XXIII, Pope, 1881-1963. I. Title.

BALDWIN, Marshall Whithed, 1903- 262'.13'0924 B
Alexander III and the twelfth century, by Marshall W. Baldwin Glen Rock, N.J., Newman Press [1968] xi, 228 p. maps (on lining papers) 23 cm. (The Popes through history, v. 3) Includes bibliographical references. [BX1226.B3] 67-15715 6.50
1. Alexander III, Pope, d. 1181. 2. Church and state—History. I. Title. II. Series.

BARRETT, William Edmund, 1900- 262.130924
Shepherd of mankind; a biography of Pope Paul VI. [1st ed.] Garden City, N.Y., Doubleday, 1964. 288 p. illus., ports. 24 cm. [BX1378.3.B6] 64-16869
1. Paulus VI, Pope, 1897- I. Title.

BOSO, Cardinal, d.1178. 262'.13'0924 B
Boso's life of Alexander III. Introd. by Peter Munz. Translated by G. M. Ellis. Totowa, N.J., Rowman and Littlefield [1973] 122 p. 23 cm. Translated from the Liber Pontificalis (edition of L. Duchesne) Includes bibliographical references. [BX1226.B6713 1973] 73-4806 ISBN 0-87471-183-5 8.50
1. Alexander III, Pope, d. 1181. I. Liber Pontificalis. II. Title.

CATHOLIC Church. Pope, 1073-1085 (Gregorius VII) 262'.13'0924
The correspondence of Pope Gregory VII; selected letters from the Registrum. Translated with an introd. by Ephraim Emerton New York, Norton [1969, c1932] xxxi, 212 p. 21 cm. (Records of civilization: sources and studies [14]) Bibliography: p. [196]-197. [BX1187.A4 1969] 70-8470
I. Emerton, Ephraim, 1851-1935, ed. & tr. II. Title. III. Series.

CATHOLIC Church. Pope, 1073-1085 (Gregorius VII) 262'.13'0924 B
The Epistolae vagantes of Pope Gregory VII; edited and translated [from the Latin] by H. E. J. Cowdrey. Oxford, Clarendon Press, 1972. xxi, 175 p. 23 cm. (Oxford medieval texts) English introd. and notes; parallel Latin and English text. Bibliography: p. ix-xv. [BX1187.A4 1972] 72-195673 ISBN 0-19-822220-3
I. Cowdrey, Herbert Edward John, ed. II. Title. III. Series.
Available from Oxford Univ. Pr., 17.00.

CATHOLIC Church, Pope, 1198-1216 (Innocentius III) 262.130924
Das Register Innocenz' III. uber die Reichsfrage 1198-1209. Nach der Ausg. von Baluze, Epistolarum Innocentii III. tomus I, in Auswahl ubers. und erlautert von Georgine Tangl, Leipzig, Verlag der Dykschen Buchhandlung, 1923. Ndw York,1Johnson Reprint [1965] xxxv, 256p. 19cm. (Die Geschichtschreiber der deutschen Vorzeit. 2. Gesamtausg., Bd. 95) Letters not tr. in full are listed in digest form. Bibl. [BX870.1198a] 66-3873 price unreported
1. Holy Roman Empire—Hist.—Otto IV, 1198-1215—Sources. 2. Church history—Middle Ages—Sources. I. Tangl, Georgine, 1893- ed. and tr. II. Title. III. Series.

CHENEY, Christopher Robert, 1906- 262'.13'0924
Pope Innocent III and England / Christopher R. Cheney. 1. Aufl. Stuttgart : Hiersemann, 1976. xii, 433 p. ; 25 cm. (Papste and Papsttum ; Bd. 9 ISSN 0340-7993s) Includes index. Bibliography: p. [409]-416. [BX1236.C45] 77-453416 ISBN 3-7772-7623-5 : DM100.00
1. Innocentius, III, Pope, 1160 or 61-1216. 2. Catholic Church—Relations (diplomatic) with Great Britain. 3. Foreign relations—Catholic Church—Great Britain. 4. Great Britain—Politics and government—1154-1399. I. Title.

COLUMBIA Broadcasting System, inc. CBS News. 262'.13'0924 B
Pope Paul VI, by the staff CBS News Project editor William E. Shapiro New York, F. Watts [1967] 66 p. illus., ports. 23 cm. (The Twentieth century) "Based on the CBS News television series, the Twentieth century." [BX1378.3.C6] 67-25099
1. Paulus VI, Pope, 1897- I. Title.

DE VITO, Albert Conrad, Bp., 1904- 262.130924
Pope Paul VI; glimpses of his life before he became Pope. Allahabad, St Paul Publications [1964] 147 p. ports. 18 cm. "No. 136" [BX1378.3.D4] 65-2870
1. Paulius VI, Pope, 1897- I. Title.

DUDDEN, Frederick Homes, 1874-1955. 262'.13'0924
Gregory the Great, his place in history and thought, by F. Homes Dudden. New York, Russell & Russell [1967] 2 v. port. 22 cm. Reprint of the 1905 ed. Authorities cited in "Preface" (v. 1, p. viii-xv) [BX1076.D8 1967] 66-24687
1. Gregorius I, the Great, Saint, Pope, 540 (ca)-604. I. Title.

THE Earliest life of Gregory the Great, 262'.13'0924 B by an anonymous monk of Whitby. Text, translation & notes by Bertram Colgrave. Lawrence, University of Kansas Press, 1968. ix, 180 p. 22 cm. Cover title: Gregory the Great. Latin text and English translation on opposite pages. The text is based on the only surviving copy of the original MS. which is part of Codex 567 of the Stiftsbibliothek of St. Gall, Switzerland. Bibliography: p. [166]-167. [BX1076.E2] 67-24360
1. Gregorius I, the Great, Saint, Pope, 540 (ca.)-604. I. An anonymous monk of Whitby. II. Colgrave, Bertram. III. St. Gall, Switzerland. Stiftsbibliothek. MSS. (567)

ELLIOTT-BINNS, Leonard Elliott, 1885- 262'.13'0924
Innocent III, by L. Elliott Binns. [Hamden, Conn.] Archon Books, 1968. xi, 212 p. port. 19 cm. Reprint of the 1931 ed. Bibliographical footnotes. [BX1236.E5] 68-15343
1. Innocentius III, Pope, 1160 or 61-1216. I. Title.

ELLIOTT-BINNS, Leonard Elliott, 1885- 262'.13'0924
Innocent III, by L. Elliott Binns. [Hamden, Conn.] Archon Books, 1968. xi, 212 p. port. 19 cm. Reprint of the 1931 ed. Bibliographical footnotes. [BX1236.E5 1968] 68-15343
1. Innocentius III, Pope, 1160 or 61-1216.

ELLIOTT, Lawrence. 262'.13'0924 B
I will be called John; a biography of Pope John XXIII. [1st ed.] New York, Reader's Digest Press, 1973. xii, 338 p. illus. 24 cm. Bibliography: p. 323-325. [BX1378.2.E44] 72-95036 ISBN 0-88349-002-1 10.00
1. Joannes XXIII, Pope, 1881-1963. I. Title.

ERASMUS, Desiderius, d.1536, supposed author. 262'.13'0924 B
The Julius exclusus. Translated by Paul Pascal. Introd. and critical notes by J. Kelly Sowards. Bloomington, Indiana University Press [1968] 141 p. 21 cm. Translation of Julius Secundus. Bibliographical references included in "Notes" (p. 93-141) [BX1314.E713] 68-14600
1. Julius II, Pope, 1443-1513. I. Pascal, Paul, tr. II. Sowards, Jesse Kelley, 1924- III. Title.

FRANCK, Frederick, 1909- 262'.13'0924
"I love life!" said Pope John XXIII. Text and drawings by Frederick Franck New York, St. Martin's Press [1967] 149 p. illus. (part col.), ports. (part col.) 24 cm. [BX1378.2.F7 1967] 67-3434
1. Joannes XXIII, Pope, 1881-1963. I. Title.

FRIEDLANDER, Saul, 1932- 262.130924
Pius XII and the Third Reich; a documentation. Tr. from French and German by Charles Fullman. [1st Amer. ed] New York, Knopf, 1966. xxiv, 238p. 22cm. Bibl. [BX1378.F713] 66-10029 4.95
1. Pius XII, Pope, 1876-1958. 2. Catholic Church—Relations (diplomatic) with Germany. 3. Germany —For. rel.—Catholic Church. I. Title.

GORRESIO, Vittorio, 1910- 262'.13'0924 B
The new mission of Pope John XXIII. Translated by Charles Lam Markmann. New York, Funk & Wagnalls [1970] 330 p. illus., ports. 22 cm. Translation of La nuova missione. [BX1378.2.G613] 79-94820 5.95
1. Joannes XXIII, Pope, 1881-1963. I. Title.

GUITTON, Jean. 262'.13'0924
The Pope speaks: dialogues of Paul VI with Jean Guitton. English translation by Anne and Christopher Fremantle. [1st U.S. ed.] New York, Meredith Press [1968] xiv, 306 p. 24 cm. Translation of Dialogues avec Paul VI. [BX1378.3.G813] 68-15204
1. Paulus VI, Pope, 1897- I. Title.

HALES, Edward Elton Young, 1908- 262.130924
Pope John and his revolution [1st ed. in the U.S.A.] Garden City, N.Y., Doubleday [c.] 1965. xv, 222p. 22cm. Bibl. [BX1378.2.H23] 65-23924 4.95
1. Joannes XXIII, Pope, 1881-1963. I. Title.

HALES, Edward Elton Young, 1908- 262.130924
Pope John and his revolution, by E. E. Y. Hales. [1st ed. in the U. S. A.] Garden City, N. Y., Doubleday, 1965. xv, 222 p. 22 cm. Bibliography: p. 209-213. [BX1378.2.H23 1965a] 65-23924
1. Joannes XXiII, Pope, 1881-1963. I. Title.

JOANNES XXIII Pope, 1881-1963. 262'.13'0924
An invitation to hope. Translated and arranged by John Gregory Clancy. New York, Simon and Schuster [1967] 143 p. 21 cm. (Credo perspectives) [BX891.J58] 67-11705
1. Catholic Church—Addresses, essays, lectures. I. Clancy, John Gregory, ed. and tr. II. Title.

JOANNES XXIII, Pope, 1881-1963. 262'.13'0924 B
Pope John XXIII, letters to his family [1901-1962] Translated by Dorothy White. New York, McGraw-Hill [1970, c1969] xviii, 833 p. group port. 24 cm. Translation of Giovanni XXIII, lettere ai familiari. [BX1378.2.A3833] 70-85160 15.00
I. Title.

JOANNES XXIII, Pope 1881-1963. 262.130924
Mission to France, 1944-1953 [by] Angelo Giuseppe Roncalli, Pope John XXIII. Ed. by Loris Capovilla. Tr. by Dorothy White. New York, McGraw [1966] xsiv, 216p. ports. 25cm. Tr. of Souvenirs d'un nonce; cahiers de France (1944-1953) [BX1378.2.A413] 66-18426 6.95
I. Capovilla, Loris, ed. II. Title.

LERCARO, Giacomo, Cardinal, 1891- 262'.13'0924
John XXIII; simpleton or saint? [By]Giacomo Lercaro and Gabriele De Rosa. Translated by Dorothy White. Chicago, Franciscan Herald Press [1967] 120 p. 23 cm. Translation of Linee per una ricerca storica. "Selected passages from the works of John XXIII": p. [53]-120. Bibliographical footnotes. [BX1378.2.L3813] 68-1884
1. Joannes XXIII, Pope, 1881-1963. I. De Rosa, Gabriele, joint author. II. Joannes XXIII, Pope, 1881-1963. III. Title.

LERCARO, Giacomo, Cardinal, 1891- 262'.13'0924
John XXIII; simpleton or saint? (By] Giacomo Levcaro and Gabriele De Rosa. Translated by Dorothy White. Chicago, Franciscan Herald Press [1967] 120 p. 23 cm. Translation of Linee per una ricerca storica. "Selected passages from the works of John XXIII": p. [53]-120. Bibliographical footnotes. [BX1378.2.L3813 1967] 68-1884
1. Joannes XXIII, Pope, 1881-1963. I. Rosa, Gabriele de, joint author. II. Joannes XXIII, Pope, 1881-1963. III. Title.

LORIT, S C 262'.13'0924 (B)
Everybody's Pope; the life of John xxiii, by S. C. Lorit. [Jamaica, N.Y.] New City Press [1967, c1966] 230 p. 16 cm. [BX1378.2.L6] 67-15775
1. Joannes xxiii, Pope, 1881-1963. I. Title.

LORIT, S. C. 262'.13'0924
Everybody's Pope; the life of John XXIII, by S. C. Lorit. [Jamaica, N.Y.] New City Pr. [1967,c.1966] 230p. 16cm. [BX1378.2.L6] (B) 67-15775 1.00
1. Joannes XXIII, Pope, 1881-1963. I. Title.

MACDONALD, Allan John Macdonald, 1887- 262'.13'0924 B
Hildebrand : a life of Gregory VII / by A. J. Macdonald. Merrick, N.Y. : Richwood Pub. Co., 1976. ix, 254 p. ; 23 cm. Reprint of the 1932 ed. published by Methuen, London, in series: Great medieval churchmen. Includes bibliographical references and index. [BX1187.M25 1976] 76-30354 ISBN 0-915172-26-7 : 15.00
1. Gregorius VII, Saint, Pope, 1015 (ca.)-1085. 2. Popes—Biography. I. Title. II. Series: Great medieval churchmen.

MORLEY, Hugh M. 262'.13'0924
The Pope and the press [by] Hugh Morley. With an introd. by James Doyle. Notre Dame [Ind.] University of Notre Dame Press [1968] xi, 143 p. 21 cm Bibliographical references included in "Notes" (p. 137-143) [BX1378.3.M6] 68-25116 2.45
1. Paulus VI, Pope, 1897- 2. Press. I. Title.

NEVINS, Albert J., 1915- 262.130924 B
The story of Pope John XXIII, written by Albert J. Nevins. New York, Grosset & Dunlap [1966] 48 p. illus. (part col.), coats of arms, facsim., ports. (part col.) 29 cm. [BX1378.2.N4] 65-20015
1. Joannes XXIII, Pope, 1881-1963. I. Title.

O'BRIEN, Felicity. 262'.13'0924 B
St Pius X / by Felicity O'Brien. London : Catholic Truth Society, 1976. 20 p. ; 19 cm. Includes bibliographical references. [BX1375.O18] 77-359057 ISBN 0-85183-183-4 : £0.15
1. Pius X, Saint, Pope, 1835-1914. 2. Popes—Biography. I. Title.

OUR name is Peter : 262'.13'0924 an anthology of key teachings of Pope Paul VI / compiled by Sean O'Reilly. Chicago : Franciscan Herald Press, c1977. xi, 146, [1] p. ; 23 cm. Bibliography: p. [147]. [BX955.2.O95] 77-380 ISBN 0-8199-0666-2 : 6.95
1. Paulus VI, Pope, 1897- —Addresses, essays, lectures. 2. Papacy—Addresses, essays, lectures. I. O'Reilly, Sean, 1922-

PALLENBERG, Corrado, 1912- 262'.13'0924
Pope Paul VI. [Rev. ed.] New York, Putnam [1968] 224p. 22cm. (Lives to remember). First pub. in 1964 under title: The making of a Pope. Bibl. [BX1378.3.P3 1968] (B) 67-14795 3.49 lib. ed.,
1. Paulus VI, Pope, 1897- I. Title.

PALLENBERG, Corrado, 1912- 262'.13'0924 B
Pope Paul VI. [Rev. ed] New York, Putnam [1968] 224 p. 22 cm. (Lives to remember) First published in 1964 under title: The making of a Pope. Bibliography: p. 221-222. A biography of Pope Paul VI, covering his boyhood, education, the positions he held leading to his election as Pope, and the reform movements of his reign. [BX1378.3.P3 1968] 92 AC 68
1. Paulus VI, Pope, 1897- I. Title.

PEPPER, Curtis Bill. 262'.13'0924
An artist and the Pope. Illus. by Manzu. New York, Published in association with Madison Square Press, Grosset & Dunlap [1968] 249 p. illus. (part col.), ports. 25 cm. "A Giniger book." "Based upon the personal recollections of Giacomo Manzu [as well as on other research and original documents]" [BX1378.2.P367] 68-29308 9.95
1. Joannes XXIII, Pope, 1881-1963. I. Manzu Giacomo, 1908- II. Title.

RHOIDES, Emmanouel D., 1835-1904 262.13'0924
Pope Joan. Translated and adapted from the Greek of Emmanuel Royidis. Baltimore, Penguin Books 1974 [158] p. 18 cm. Bibliography: p. [158] [BX958] ISBN 0-1400-3760-8 1.50 (pbk.)
1. Joan, mythical female Pope. I. Durrell, Lawrence. II. Title.

RHOIDES, Emmanouel D., 1835-1904. 262'.13'0924
Pope Joan [by] Lawrence Durrell. Translated and adapted from the Greek of Emmanuel Royidis. [Rev. ed.] Woodstock, N.Y., Overlook Press [1972, c1960] 157 p. 22 cm. Translation of He Papissa Ioanna. Bibliography: p. 151-157. [BX958.F2R56 1972] 72-81088 ISBN 0-87951-002-1 6.50
1. Joan, mythical female Pope. I. Durrell, Lawrence. II. Title.

RICHARDS, Norman. 262'.13'0924 B
Pope John XXIII. Chicago, Childrens Press [1969, c1968] 95 p. illus. 29 cm. (People of destiny: a humanities series) Bibliography: p. 92-93. The life of the Italian peasant who became Pope and instituted many reforms within the Catholic Church including a movement to unite Christian churches. [DX1378.2.R48] 92 68-31307
1. Joannes XXIII, Pope, 1881-1963—Juvenile literature. I. Title.

ROSCOE, William, 1753-1831. 262'.13'0924 B
The life and pontificate of Leo the Tenth, by William Roscoe. 6th ed. Rev. by Thomas Roscoe. London, H. G. Bohn, 1853. [New York, AMS Press, 1973] 2 v. ports. 19 cm. Original ed. issued in series: Bohn's standard library. Includes bibliographical references. [BX1315.R7 1973] 75-174965 ISBN 0-404-05430-7 40.00
1. Leo X, Pope, 1475-1521. I. Roscoe, Thomas, 1791-1871, ed. II. Title.

SHAW, Mark, ed. 262.130924
Messenger of peace; the visit of Pope Paul VI to the United Nations and the United States in the cause of peace. October 4, 1965. Photographed by Magnum. Trinity House; dist. Garden City, N.Y., Doubleday [1965] 63p. (chiefly illus., ports.) 29cm. [BX1378.3.S5] 65-28806 3.30
1. Paulus VI, Pope, 1897- I. Magnum Photos, inc. II. Title.

SHEEHAN, Elizabeth Odell, 1919- 262.130924
Good Pope John. Illustrated by Harry Barton. New York, Vision Books [1966] 178 p. illus. 22 cm. [BX1378.2.S5] 66-14038
1. Joannes XXIII, Pope, 1881-1963. I. Title.

SHEEHAN, Elizabeth Odell, 1919- 262.130924
Good Pope John. Illus. by Harry Barton. New York, Farrar [c.1966] 178p. illus. 22cm. (Vision bk., 69) [BX1378.2.S5] 66-14038 2.25
1. Joannes XXIII, Pope, 1881-1963. I. Title.

SMIT, Jan Olav, Bp., D.D., 1883- 262.130924
St. Pius X, Pope. Tr. by James H. Van der Veldt. Foreword by Richard Cardinal Cushing,Archbishop of Boston. [Boston] St. Paul Eds. [dist. Daughters of St. Paul, c.1965] 185p. illus., facsim., ports. 22cm. [BX1375.S64] 64-7924 4.00; 3.00 pap.,
1. Pius X, Saint, Pope, 1835-1914. I. Title.

SMIT, Jan Olay, Bp., 1883- 262.130924 (B)
St. Pius x, Pope. Translated by James H. Van der Veldt. With a foreword by Richard Cardinal Cushing, Archbishop of Boston. [Boston] St. Paul Editions [1965] 185 p. illus., facsim, ports. 22 cm. [BX1375.S64] 64-7924
1. Plus x, Saint, Pope, 1835-1914. I. Title.

SMITH, Charles Edward, 1905- 262'.13'0924 B
Innocent III, church defender. Westport, Conn., Greenwood Press [1971, c1951] vi, 203 p. 23 cm. Bibliography: p. 189-[192] [BX1236.S6 1971] 79-88939 ISBN 0-8371-3145-6
1. Innocentius III, Pope, 1160 or 61-1216.

STRUCHEN, Jeanette. 262'.13'0924
Pope John XXIII; the gentle shepherd. New York, Watts [1969] xiii, 142 p. illus. 22 cm. (Immortals of philosophy and religion) Bibliography: p. 138-139. The life of the Italian priest who after his election as Pope became an internationally known figure through his efforts to update the Catholic Church. [BX1378.2.S75] 92 B 73-79671 3.95
1. Joannes XXIII, Pope, 1881-1963—Juvenile literature. I. Title.

TREVOR, Meriol. 262'.13'0924
Pope John. Garden City, N.Y., Doubleday [1968, c. 1967] 318p. 18cm. (Image bk. D249) Bibl. [BX1378.2.T7 1967b] (B) 67-19114 1.25 pap.,
1. Joannes XXIII, Pope, 1881-1963. I. Title.

TREVOR, Meriol. 262'.13'0924 (B)
Pope John. London, Melbourne [etc.] Macmillan; New York, St. Martin's P., 1967. x, 329 p. front., 15 plated (incl. ports). 22 1/2 cm. 42/- Bibliography: p. [317]-322. [BX1378.2.T7] 67-90402
1. Joanners xxiii, Pope, 1881-1963. I. Title.

TREVOR, Meriol. 262.130924
Pope John. [1st ed.] Garden City, N. Y., Doubleday, 1967. 312 p. 22 cm. Bibliography: p. [297]-300. [BX1378.2.T7 1967b] 67-19114
1. Joannes XXIII, Pope, 1881-1963. I. Title.

VANASCO, Rocco R. 262'.13'0924 B
The role of Clement VII in Guicciardini's works [by] Rocco R. Vanasco. Strasburg, Mo., E. B. Greene [1969] 24 p. 23 cm. Bibliography: p. 21-24. [BX1317.V3] 73-625749
1. Clemens VII, Pope, 1478-1534. 2. Guicciardini, Francesco, 1483-1540. I. Title.

CHIRICO, Peter. 262'.131
Infallibility : the crossroads of doctrine / by Peter Chirico. Kansas City, [Kan.] : Sheed and Ward, c1977. p. cm. Includes index. [BX1806.C45] 77-3694 ISBN 0-8362-0704-1 : 20.00. ISBN 0-8362-0706-8 pbk. : 6.95
1. Popes—Infallibility. I. Title.

DOYLE, Charles Hugo. 262.131
A day with the Pope. Format by Heyworth. [1st ed.] Garden City, N. Y., Doubleday, 1950. 64 p. illus., ports. 26 cm. [BX1378.D575]
1. Pius XII, Pope, 1876- I. Title.

DVORNIK, Francis, 1893- 262.131
Byzantium and the Roman primacy. New York, Fordham University Press [1966] 176 p. 22 cm. Includes bibliographical references. [BX324.3.D813] 66-14187
1. Catholic Church—Relations—Orthodox Eastern Church—History. 2. Orthodox Eastern Church—Relations—Catholic Church History. 3. Popes—Primacy. I. Title.

KUNG, Hans, 1928- 262'.131
Infallible? An inquiry. Translated by Edward Quinn. Garden City, N.Y., Doubleday, 1971. 262 p. 22 cm. Translation of Unfehlbar? Eine Anfrage. Includes bibliographical references. [BV601.6.I5K813] 77-139784 5.95
1. Catholic Church—Infallibility. I. Title.

MAKRAKES, Apostolos, 1831-1905. 262.131
A scriptural refutation of the Pope's primacy and miscellaneous studies and speeches; translated out of the original Greek by D. Cummings. Chicago, Orthodox Christian Educational Society, 1952. 175p. 22cm. [BX1765.M265] 53-17036
1. Catholic Church—Doctrinal and controversial works—Orthodox Eastern authors. I. Title.

ROWELL, J B 262.131
Papal infallibility: its complete collapse before a factus investigation. Grand Rapids, Kregel Publications, 1963. 171 p. 22 cm. [BX1765.2.R6] 62-22399
1. Catholic Church — Doctrinal and controversial works — Protestant authors. 2. Popes — Infallibility. I. Title.

ROWELL, J. B. 262.131
Papal infallibility: its complete collapse before a factual investigation. Grand Rapids, Mich., Kregel [c.]1963. 171p. 22cm. Bibl. 62-22399 3.50
1. Catholic Church—Doctrinal and controversial works—Protestant authors. 2. Popes—Infallibility. I. Title.

SALMON, George 262.131
The infallibility of the church; lectures delivered in the Divinity School of the University of Dublin. Grand Rapids, Mich., Baker Book House, [c.]1959 xxix, 497p. 23cm. (Bibl. notes) 60-1115 3.95
1. Church—Infallibility. 2. Catholic Church—Infallibility. I. Title.

SHARKEY, Neil. 262.131
Saint Gregory the Great's concept of papal power. Washington, Catholic University of America Press, 1950. vii, 50 p. 23 cm. (The Catholic University of America. Studies in sacred theology, 2d ser., no. 35) Extract from thesis--Catholic University of America. Bibliography: p. 47-50. [BX1076.S5] A 50
1. Gregorius I, the Great, Saint, Pope, 540 (cu.)-604. 2. Popes—Temporal power. I. Title. II. Series: Catholic University of America. School of Sacred Theology. Studies in sacred theology, 2d ser., no. 35

BELLARMINO, Roberto Francesco Romolo, Saint, 1542-1621. 262.132
Extracts on politics and government from the Supreme Pontiff from Third general controversy. [De Summo Pontifice] translated, edited, and published by George Albert Moore. Chevy Chase, Md., Country Dollar Press ['1951] xi, 134 p. port. 28 cm. (The Moore series of English translationsof source books) "Collector's edition ... limited to sixty copies, signed and numbered ... No. 4." [BX1805.B333] 52-27192
1. Papacy. 2. Popes—Temporal power. I. Title.

JEAN de Paris, 1240?-1306. 262'.132
On royal and papal power. A translation, with introd., of the De potestate regia et papali of John of Paris [by] Arthur P. Monahan. New York, Columbia University Press, 1974. xlix, 197 p. 23 cm. (Records of civilization: sources and studies, no. 90) At head of title: John of Paris. Includes bibliographical references. [BX1810.J413 1974] 73-16302 ISBN 0-231-03690-6 9.00
1. Popes—Temporal power. 2. Church and state. I. Monahan, Arthur P., 1928- ed. II. Title. III. Series.

SHARROCK, David John. 262.132
The theological defense of papal power by St. Alphonsus de Liguori. Washington, Catholic University of America Press, 1961. viii, 137 p. 23 cm. (Catholic University of America. Studies in sacred theology, no. 119) Abstract of thesis -- Catholic University of America. Bibliography: p. 128-135. [BX1805.S5] 62-2305
1. Popes — Primacy. 2. Liguori, Alfonso Maria de', Saint, 1696-1787. I. Title. II. Series: Catholic University of America. School of Sacred Theology. Studies in sacred theology, 2d ser., no. 119

VALLA, Lorenzo, 1406-1457. 262'.132
The treatise of Lorenzo Valla on the Donation of Constantine; text and translation into English [by] Christopher B. Coleman. New York, Russell & Russell [1971, c1922] 183 p. facsim. 23 cm. Text of De falso credita et ementita Constantini donatione declamatio, preceded by the abridged text of the Donation of Constantine; in Latin and English. [BX875.D7V3 1971] 71-143561
1. Donation of Constantine. I. Coleman, Christopher Bush, 1875-1944, ed. II. Donation of Constantine. English and Latin. Selections. 1971. III. Title.

WALL, Bernard, 1908- 262.132
The Vatican story. New York, Harper [1957, c1956] 247p. illus. 22cm. Published in London in 1956 under title: Report on the Vatican. [BX957.W3 1957] 56-6036
1. Papacy. 2. Catholic Church. 3. Vatican. I. Title.

WALL, Bernard, 1908- 262.132
The Vatican story. New York, Harper [1957, c1956] 247 p. illus. 22 cm. Published in London in 1956 under title: Report on the Vatican. [BX957.W3 1957] 56-6036
1. Papacy. 2. Catholic Church. 3. Vatican. I. Title.

WATT, John A. 262.132
The theory of papal monarchy in the thirteenth century; the contribution of the canonists. New York, Fordham [1966. c. 1965] viii, 160p. 25cm. Bibl. [BX1810.W3] 65-12886 5.00
1. Popes—Temporal power. I. Title.

WILKS, Michael. 262.132
The problem of sovereignty in the later Middle Ages; the papal monarchy with Augustinus Triumphus and the publicists. Cambridge [Eng.] University Press, 1963. xiii, 619 p. 23 cm. (Cambridge studies in medievel life and thought, new ser., v. 9) Bibliography: p. 560-577. [BX957.W5] 63-3163
1. Papacy. 2. Sovereignty. 3. Trionfo, Agostino, 1243-1328. 4. Political science — Hist. I. Title. II. Series.

WILKS, Michael 262.132
The problem of sovereignty in the later Middle Ages; the papal monarchy with Augustinus Triumphus and the publicists [New York] Cambridge [c.]1963. xiii, 619p. 23cm. (Cambridge studies in medieval life and thought, new ser., v.9) Bibl. 63-3163 12.50
1. Papacy. 2. Sovereignty. 3. Trionfo, Agostino, 1243-1328. 4. Political science—Hist. I. Title. II. Series.

KITTLER, Glenn D 262.135
The papal princes; a history of the Sacred College of Cardinals. New York, Funk & Wagnalls [1960] 369p. 22cm. [BX1815.K38] 60-12750
1. Catholic Church. Collegium Cardinalium. 2. Papacy—Hist. I. Title.

KITTLER, Glenn D. 262.135
The Papal princes; a history of the Sacred College of Cardinals [New York, Dell, 1961, c.1960] 351p. (Chapel bk. S24) Bibl. .60 pap.,
1. Catholic Church. Collegium Cardinalium. 2. Papacy- —Hist. I. Title.

KITTLER, Glenn D. 262.135
The papal princes; a history of the Sacred College of Cardinals. New York, Funk & Wagnalls [c.1960] 369p. p.359-360 22cm. Bibl.: 60-12750 4.95
1. Catholic Church. Collegium Cardinalium. 2. Papacy—Hist. I. Title.

LIERDE, Petrus Canisius van, Bp., 1907- 262.135
What is a cardinal? By P. C. van Lierde and A. Giraud. Translated from the French by A. Manson. [1st ed.] New York, Hawthorn Books [1964] 143 [1] p. 21 cm. (Twentieth century encyclopedia of Catholicism, v. 84. Section 8: the organization of the Church) Translation of Le senat de l'Eglise. Bibliography: p. [144] [BX1815.L513] 64-14161
1. Cardinals. I. Giraud, Alexandre, 1894- joint author. II. Title. III. Series: The Twentieth century encyclopedia of Catholicism, v. 84

LIERDE, Petrus Canisius van, Bp., 1907- 262.135
What is a cardinal? By P. C. van Lierde, A. Giraud. Tr. from French by A. Manson. New York, Hawthorn [c.1964] 143, [1]p. 21cm. (20th cent. ency. of Catholicism, v.84. Sect. 8: The organization of the Church) Bibl. 64-14161 3.50 bds.,
1. Cardinals. I. Giraud, Alexandre, 1894- joint author. II. Title. III. Series: The Twentieth century encyclopedia of Catholicism, v.84

MORGAN, Thomas Brynmor, 1886- 262'.135
Speaking of cardinals, by Thomas B. Morgan. Freeport, N.Y., Books for Libraries Press [1971, c1946] 264 p. 23 cm. (Essay index reprint series) [BX4664.M6 1971] 70-134119 ISBN 0-8369-2002-3
1. Cardinals. I. Title.

PIRIE, Valerie. 262'.135
The triple crown : an account of the papal conclaves from the fifteenth century to the present day / by Valerie Pirie. [Wilmington, N.C.] : Consortium Books, [1976?] xiii, 346 p., [27] leaves of plates : ill. ; 23 cm. Bibliography: p. 345-346. [BX1805.P5 1976] 76-375210 12.00
1. Popes—Election. 2. Papacy—History. I. Title.

SPINA, Tony. 262.135
The making of the Pope. Additional text by Dawson Taylor. With a foreword by John LaFarge. New York, Barnes [1962] 144 p. illus. 31 cm. [BX1378.2.S6] 62-14977
1. Joannes XXIII, Pope, 1881- I. Title.

SPINA, Tony. 262.135
The making of the Pope. Additional text by Dawson Taylor. With a foreword by John LaFarge. New York, Barnes [1962] 144 p. illus. 31 cm. [BX1378.2.S6] 62-14977
1. Joannes XXIII, Pope, 1881- I. Title.

BARRY, Colman James, 1921- 262'.135'0924 B
American nuncio: Cardinal Aloisius Muench [by] Colman J. Barry. Collegeville, Minn., Saint John's University Press, 1969. xii, 379 p. illus. 25 cm. Bibliography: p. 289-293. [BX4705.M755B37] 71-83090

1. Muench, Aloisius Joseph, Abp., 1889-1962. I. Title.

CUSHING, Richard James, Cardinal 1895- 262.1350924
Richard Cardinal Cushing in prose and photos. Comp. by the Daughters of St. Paul. [Boston, Daughters of St. Paul, 1966, c.1965] 139p. ports. 28cm. [BX4705.C8A25 1965] 65-29312 5.00; 4.00 pap.,
1. Cushing, Richard James, Cardinal, 1895- — Portraits, etc. I. Daughters of St. Paul. II. Title.

CUTLER, John Henry, 1910- 262'.135'0924 B
Cardinal Cushing of Boston. New York, Hawthorn Books [1970] xi, 404 p. illus., ports. 24 cm. Includes bibliographical references. [BX4705.C8C9 1970] 70-107898 8.95
1. Cushing, Richard James, Cardinal, 1895- I. Title.

DARK, Sidney, 1874-1947. 262'.135'0924 B
Newman. [Folcroft, Pa.] Folcroft Library Editions, 1973. p. Reprint of the 1934 ed. published by Duckworth, London, which was issued as no. 36 of Great lives. Bibliography: p. [BX4705.N5D3 1973] 73-7641 10.00
1. Newman, John Henry, Cardinal, 1811-1890.

DARK, Sidney, 1874-1947. 262'.135'0924 B
Newman. [Folcroft, Pa.] Folcroft Library Editions, 1973. p. Reprint of the 1934 ed. published by Duckworth, London, which was issued as no. 36 of Great lives. Bibliography: p. [BX4705.N5D3 1973] 73-7641 ISBN 0-8414-1870-5 (lib. bdg.)
1. Newman, John Henry, Cardinal, 1811-1890.

DEVER, Joseph, 1919- 262.1350924 (B)
Cushing of Boston, a candid-portrait. Boston, Bruce Humphries [1965] 287 p. 24 cm. [BX4705.C8D37] 65-20920
1. Cushing, Richard James, Cardinal, 1895- I. Title.

DEVER, Joseph, 1919- 262.1350924
Cushing of Boston, a candid portrait. Boston, BruceHumphries [c.1965] 287p. 24cm. [BX4705.C8D37] 65-20920 5.95
1. Cushing, Richard James, Cardinal, 1895- I. Title.

FABER, Geoffrey Cust, Sir, 1889-1961. 262'.135'0924 B
Oxford apostles : a character study of the Oxford movement / by Geoffrey Faber. New York : AMS Press, [1976] p. cm. Reprint of the 1936 ed. published by Faber and Faber, London. Includes index. Bibliography: p. [BX5100.F3 1976] 75-30022 ISBN 0-404-14027-0 : 32.50
1. Newman, John Henry, Cardinal, 1801-1890. 2. Church of England—Biography. 3. Oxford movement. I. Title.

FENLON, Dermot. 262'.135'0924 B
Heresy and obedience in Tridentine Italy; Cardinal Pole and the counter reformation. Cambridge [Eng.] University Press, 1972. xiii, 300 p. 23 cm. Bibliography: p. 286-296. [DA317.8.P6F46] 72-87177 ISBN 0-521-20005-9 19.50
1. Pole, Reginald, Cardinal, 1500-1558. 2. Trent, Council of, 1545-1563. 3. Counter-Reformation. I. Title.

GARNETT, Emmeline, 1924- 262.1350924 B
Tormented angel; a life of John Henry Newman. New York, Ariel Books [1966] 136 p. 22 cm. Bibliography p. 133. [BX4705.N5G3] 66-18431
1. Newman, John Henry, Cardinal, 1801-1890. I. Title.

GARNETT, Emmeline, 1924- 262.1350924
Tormented angel; a life of John Henry Newman. New York, Ariel Bks. [1966] 136p. 22cm. Bibl. [BX4705.N5G3] 66-18431 3.25
1. Newman, John Henry, Cardinal, 1801-1890. I. Title.
Ages 14-up. Available from Farrar.

HAMILTON, Elizabeth, 1906- 262'.135'0924 B
Suenens : a portrait / Elizabeth Hamilton. 1st ed. in the U.S. of America. Garden City, N.Y. : Doubleday, 1975. 283 p. ; 22 cm. Includes index. [BX4705.S8684H35 1975] 74-32571 ISBN 0-385-09907-X : 7.95
1. Suenens, Leon Joseph, Cardinal, 1904-

HARROLD, Charles Frederick, 1897-1948 262.1350924
John Henry Newman; an expository and critical study of his mind, thought and art. Hamden, Conn., Archon [dist. Shoe String] 1966[c.1945] xv, 472p. 21cm. Bibl. [BX4705.N5H33] 66-16086 11.00

1. Newman, John Henry, Cardinal, 1801-1890. I. Title.

HOLLIS, Christopher, 1902- 262'.135'0924
Newman and the modern world. [1st ed. in the U.S.A.] Garden City, N. Y., Doubleday [1968, c1967] 230 p. 22 cm. Bibliography: p. 222-223. [BX4705.N5H63 1968] 67-11182
1. Newman, John Henry, Cardinal, 1801-1890. I. Title.

HOUPPERT, Joseph W., comp. 262'.135'0924
John Henry Newman, edited by Joseph W. Houppert. Contributors: Northrop Frye [and others] St. Louis, Herder [1968] 108, [1] p. 18 cm. (The Christian critic series) Contents.Contents.—The problem of spiritual authority in the nineteenth century, by N. Frye.—Newman's essays on development in its intellectual milieu, by W. J. Ong.—Newman's idea of literature: a humanist's spectrum, by H. M. Petitpas.—Newman the poet, by J. Pick.—The thinker in the church: the spirit of Newman, by F. O'Malley.—Bibliography (p. [109]) [BX4705.N5H66] 68-25496
1. Newman, John Henry, 1801-1890. I. Frye, Northrop.

HUTTON, Richard Holt, 1826-1897. 262'.135'0924 B
Cardinal Newman / by Richard H. Hutton. 2d ed. New York : AMS Press, 1977. xi, 268 p. : port. ; 18 cm. Reprint of the 1891 ed. published by Methuen, London, in series: English leaders of religion. Includes bibliographical references. [BX4705.N5H8 1977] 75-30029 ISBN 0-404-14033-5 : 16.00
1. Newman, John Henry, Cardinal, 1801-1890. 2. Cardinals—England—Biography. I. Series: English leaders of religion.

IN memoriam: 262'.135'0924
Francis Cardinal Spellman, Archbishop of New York. [New York] Society of the Friendly Sons of Saint Patrick in the City of New York, 1968. 59 p. ports. (part col.) 25 cm. [BX4705.S74I5] 70-268394
1. Spellman, Francis Joseph, Cardinal, 1889-1967. I. Society of the Friendly Sons of St. Patrick in the City of New York.

LAPATI, Americo D. 262'.135'0924
John Henry Newman, by Americo D. Lapati. New York, Twayne Publishers [1972] 161 p. 21 cm. (Twayne's English authors series, TEAS 140) Bibliography: p. 149-155. [BX4705.N5L28] 73-187619 5.500
1. Newman, John Henry, Cardinal, 1801-1890.

LESLIE, Shane, Sir, bart., 1885- 262'.135'0924 B
Henry Edward Manning, his life and labours. Westport, Conn., Greenwood Press [1970] xxiii, 515 p. ports. 23 cm. Reprint of the 1921 ed. [BX4705.M3L4 1970] 78-109767 ISBN 0-8371-4257-1
1. Manning, Henry Edward, Cardinal, 1808-1892.

MIDDLETON, Robert Dudley. 262'.135'0924 B
Newman & Bloxam; an Oxford friendship, by R. D. Middleton. Westport, Conn., Greenwood Press [1971] x, 261 p. illus. 23 cm. Reprint of the 1947 ed. Includes bibliographical references. [BX4705.N5M5 1971] 74-104246 ISBN 0-8371-3986-4
1. Newman, John Henry, Cardinal, 1801-1890. 2. Bloxam, John Rouse, 1807-1891.

MINDSZERTY, Jozsef, Cardinal, 1892- 262'.135'0924 [B]
Memoirs. New York, Macmillan [1974] 341 p. illus. 24 cm. Translation of Erinnerungen. [BX4705.M5565A2813] 74-19494 ISBN 0-02-585050-4 10.00
1. Mindszenty, Jozsef Cardinal, 1892-

POWELL, Jouett Lynn. 262'.135'0924 B
Three uses of Christian discourse in John Henry Newman : an example of nonreductive reflection on the Christian faith / by Jouett Lynn Powell. Missoula, Mont. : Published by Scholars Press for the American Academy of Religion, 1976c1975 x, 232 p. ; 22 cm. (Dissertation series - American Academy of Religion ; no. 10) Originally presented as the author's thesis, Yale, 1972. Bibliography: p. 215-232. [BX4705.N5P65 1975] 75-29423 ISBN 0-89130-042-2 pbk. : 4.50
1. Newman, John Henry, Cardinal, 1801-1890. I. American Academy of Religion. II. Title. III. Series: American Academy of Religion. Dissertation series — American Academy of Religion ; no. 10.

PURCELL, Edmund Sheridan, 1824(?)-1899. 262'.135'0924 B
Life of Cardinal Manning, Archbishop of Westminster. New York, Da Capo Press, 1973. 2 v. ports. 22 cm. (Europe 1815-1945) Reprint of the 1895-96 ed. Includes bibliographical references. [BX4705.M3P872] 70-126605 ISBN 0-306-70050-6 45.00 (set)
1. Manning, Henry Edward, Cardinal, 1808-1892. I. Title. II. Series.

RAYMOND, Father, 1903- 262'.135'0924 B
The man for this moment [by] M. Raymond. Staten Island, N.Y., Alba House [1971] xvii, 345 p. illus. 22 cm. Half-title: The life and death of Aloysius Cardinal Stepinac. [BX4705.S823R39] 77-169142 ISBN 0-8189-0220-5 6.95
1. Stepinac, Aloysius, Cardinal, 1898-1960. I. Title. II. Title: The life and death of Aloysius Cardinal Stepinac.

ROBBINS, William. 262.1350924
The Newman brothers; an essay in comparative intellectual biography. London, Heinemann, 1966. xii, 202 p. front., 6 plates (ports.) 22 1/2 cm. 35/ -- [BX4705.N5R57] 66-71850
1. Newman, John Henry, Cardinal, 1801-1890. 2. Newman, Francis William, 1805-1897. I. Title.

ROBBINS, William. 262.1350924
The Newman brothers; an essay in comparative intellectual biography. Cambridge, Harvard University Press, 1966. xii, 202 p. ports. 23 cm. Bibliographical footnotes. [BX4705.N5R57] 66-4976
1. Newman, John Henry, Cardinal, 1801-1890. 2. Newman, Francis, 1805-1897. I. Title.

ROBBINS, William 262.1350924
The Newman brothers; an essay in comparative intellectual biography. Cambridge, Mass., Harvard [c.]1966. xii, 202p. ports. 23cm. Bibl. [BX4705.N5 R57] 66-4976 6.00
1. Newman, John Henry, Cardinal, 1801-1890. 2. Newman, Francis, 1805-1897. I. Title.

SCHNEIDER, Nicholas A. 262'.135'0924 B
The life of John Cardinal Glennon, Archbishop of St. Louis [by] Nicholas Schneider. Liguori, Mo., Liguori Publications [1971] 224 p. illus. 18 cm. Bibliography: p. 223-224. [BX4705.G557S35] 78-165974 1.75
1. Glennon, John Joseph, 1862-1946. I. Title.

STEIBEL, Warren. 262.1350924
Cardinal Spellman, the man. With an introd. by Francis Cardinal Spellman. [1st ed.] New York, Appleton-Century [1966] 121 p. illus., ports. 27 cm. Adapted from the ABC-Television documentary of Cardinal Spellman: the man. [BX4705.S74S7] 66-27903
1. Spellman, Francis Joseph, Cardinal, 1889- I. American Broadcasting Company. II. Title.

VECSEY, Josef. 262'.135'0924 B
Mindszenty the man, by Joseph Vecsey, as told to Phyllis Schlafly. St. Louis, Cardinal Mindszenty Foundation [1972] 241 p. illus. 21 cm. Bibliography: p. 231-235. [BX4705.M5565V4] 72-93906 2.00
1. Mindszenty, Jozsef, Cardinal, 1892- I. Schlafly, Phyllis. II. Title.

WALLER, Alfred Rayney, 1867-1922. 262'.135'0924 B
John Henry, Cardinal Newman / by A. R. Waller and G. H. S. Burrow [i.e. Barrow]. Norwood, Pa. : Norwood Editions, 1976. xviii, 150 p. ; 23 cm. Reprint of the 1901 ed. published by Kegan Paul, Trench, Trubner, London, in series: The Westminster biographies. Bibliography: p. [148]-150. [BX4705.N5W25 1976] 76-45369 ISBN 0-8482-2954-1 : 17.50
1. Newman, John Henry, Cardinal, 1801-1890. 2. Cardinals—England—Biography. I. Barrow, G. H. S., joint author. II. Series: The Westminster biographies.

WALSH, James Joseph, 1865-1942. 262'.135'0922
Our American cardinals; life stories of the seven American cardinals: McCloskey, Gibbons, Farley, O'Connell, Dougherty, Mundelein, Hayes. Freeport, N.Y., Books for Libraries Press [1969, c1926] xvii, 352 p. ports. 23 cm. (Essay index reprint series) [BX4665.U5W3 1969] 68-58815
1. Cardinals—U.S. I. Title.

WEATHERBY, Harold L., 1934- 262'.135'0924 B
Cardinal Newman in his age; his place in English theology and literature [by] Harold L. Weatherby. Nashville, Vanderbilt University Press, 1973. xv, 296 p. 23 cm. Includes bibliographical references. [BX4705.N5W4] 72-1347 ISBN 0-8265-1182-1 11.50
1. Newman, John Henry, Cardinal, 1801-1890. I. Title.

WEBER, Francis J. 262'.135'0924 B
An historical perspective, elicited by the Holy Father's bestowal of the Cardinalatial Office upon the people of God at Los Angeles in the personage of Archbishop Timothy Manning, 1973. [Compiled by Francis J. Weber. Los Angeles, Printed by Kellow-Brown Co. 1973] 40 p. illus. 23 cm. [BX4705.M313W4] 73-174869
1. Manning, Timothy.

MANZ, James G. 262.136
Vatican II; renewal or reform? St. Louis, Concordia [c. 1966] 142p. 21cm. Bibl. [BX830 1962.M34] 66-20499 1.95 pap.,
1. Vatican Council. 2d, 1962-1965. I. Title.

MANZ, James G. 262.136
Vatican II; renewal or reform? By James G. Manz. St. Louis, Concordia Pub. House [1966] 142 p. 21 cm. Bibliographical references included in "Notes" (p. [137]-142) [BX8301962.M34] 66-20499
1. Vatican Council. 2d, 1962-1965. I. Title.

SCHARP, Heinrich, 1899- 262.136
How the Catholic Church is governed. [1st English ed.] Freiburg, Herder [1960] 167p. illus. 19cm. 'This translation by Annelise Derrick is based on the original German version of 'Wie die Kirche regiert wird'... 4th edition 1954.' [BX1801.S313 1960] 60-6521
1. Catholic Church—Government. I. Title.

ANGLICAN orders and defect of intention. 262.14
London, New York, Longmans, Green [1956] 215p. 23cm. 'Extract from the bull Apootolicae curae of Pope Leo XIII' in Latin and English: p. 1-8. Includes bibliography. [BX5178.C55] 262.17 57-856
1. Anglican orders. I. Clark, Francis, 1919- II. Catholic Church. Pope, 1878-1903 (Leo XIII) Appootolicae curae (13 Sept. 1896) English and Latin.

ANLER, Ludwig, 1882- 262.14
The pastoral companion. Formerly edited by Honoratus Bonzelet. 11th ed., rev. and amplified by Marcian J. Mathis and Clement R. Leahy. Chicago, Franciscan Herald Press [1956] 419p. 20cm. 'A translation and an adaptation of Fr. Louis Anler's German work. Comes pastoralls.' [BX1912.A63 1956] 56-14215
1. Theology. Pastoral—Catholic Church. 2. Canon law. 3. Sacraments—Catholic Church. I. Title.

ANLER, Ludwig, 1882- 262.14
The pastoral companion. Formerly edited by Honoratus Bonzelet. 11th ed., rev. and amplified by Marcian J. Mathis and Clement R. Leahy. Chicago, Franciscan Herald Press [1956] 419p. 20cm. 'A translation and an adaptation of Fr. Louis Anler's German work, Comes pastoralis.' [BX1912.A63 1956] 56-14215
1. Theology. Pastoral—Catholic Church. 2. Canon law. 3. Sacraments—Catholic Church. I. Title.

BROMILEY, Geoffrey, William 262.14
Christian ministry. Grand Rapids, Eerdmans [1960, c.1959] 119p. 19cm. (A Pathway book) 59-14583 1.50 bds.,
1. Clergy—Office. I. Title.

BRUCE, Michael. 262'.14
Why not? : priesthood & the ministry of women : a theological study / edited by Michael Bruce & G. E. Duffield. Revised & augmented ed. / prepared by R. T. Beckwith. Abingdon : Marcham Manor Press, 1976. 174 p. ; 22 cm. Includes bibliographical references. [BV676.B78 1976] 77-355557 ISBN 0 900531-28-2 : £3.50
1. Ordination of women—Church of England—Addresses, essays, lectures. 2. Women in Christianity—Addresses, essays, lectures. I. Duffield, Gervase E., joint author. II. Beckwith, Roger T. III. Title.

BUNNIK, Ruud J. 262'.14
Priests for tomorrow [by] Ruud J. Bunnik. Translated from the Dutch by Frances Wilms. [1st ed.] New York, Holt, Rinehart and Winston [1969] xiii, 224 p. 22 cm. Translation of Dienaren van het aggiornamento. Bibliography: p. [215]-224. [BX1912.B8533] 69-10235 5.95
1. Catholic Church—Clergy. I. Title.

BURNEY, Le Roy P 262.14
Presbyterian elders and deacons serving Christ in the church; a study course for church officers. Richmond, John Knox Press [1954] 59p. 22cm. [BX9195.B84 1954] 262.15 54-3698
1. Presbyterian Church—Government. 2. Church officers. I. Title.

BUTLER, John V 262.14
What is the priesthood? A book on vocation, by John V. Butler and W. Norman Pittenger. New York, Morehouse-Gorham Co., 1954. 221p. 20cm. [BX5965.B8] 54-7264
1. Protestant Episcopal Church in the U. S. A.—Clergy. 2. Clergy—Office. I. Pittenger, William Norman, 1905- II. Title.

CAEMMERER, Richard Rudolph, 1904- 262.14
Feeding and leading. St. Louis, Concordia [c.1962] 112p. 21cm. (Witnessing church ser.) Bibl. 62-10385 1.75 pap.,
1. Clergy—Office. I. Title.

CAMERON, Kenneth Walter, 1908- comp. 262'.14
American Episcopal clergy; registers of ordinations in the Episcopal Church in the United States from 1785 through 1904, with indexes. Hartford, Transcendental Books [1970] 31, 43, 35, 36 l. illus., port. 28 cm. [BX5965.C35] 74-15966
1. Protestant Episcopal Church in the U.S.A.—Clergy. I. Title.

CATHOLIC Church. Pope. 262.14
The Catholic priesthood, according to the teaching of the Church papal documents from Pius x to Pius XII [by] Pierre Veuillot. Pref. by His Excellency Monsignor Montini. Translated by John A. O'Flynn, in collaboration with P. Birch and G. Canon Mitchell. Westminster, Md., Newman Press, 1958. 264, 374p. 22cm. Translation of Notre sacerdoce. [BX1912.A323] 58-1447
1. Priests. 2. Pastoral theology—Catholic Church—Addresses, essays, lectures. I. Veuillot, Pierre, ed. II. Title.

CATHOLIC Church. Pope. 262.14
The Popes and the priesthood; a symposium of papal documents on the priesthood. [Rev. ed.] St. Meinr d, Ind. [1953] 135p. 20cm. 'A Grail publication.' [BX1912.A33 1953] 53-13057
1. Catholic Church—Clergy. I. Title.

CATHOLIC Church. Pope, 1939- (Pius XII) Menti nostrae (23 Sept. 1950) English. 262.14
On promoting the sanctity of the priestly life. [Translation of] Menti nostrae. Apostolic exhortation of Our Holy Father, Pius XII. St. Meinrad, Ind. [1951] 70 p. 20 cm. "Grail publication." [BX1912.A45] 52-18163
1. Catholic Church—Clergy. 2. Clergy—Religious life. I. Title.

CHRYSOSTOMUS, Joannes, Saint, Patriarch of Constantinople, d.407. 262.14
The priesthood; a translation of the Peri hierosynes of St. John Chrysostom, by W. A. Jurgens. New York, Macmillan, 1955. xxv, 133p. 22cm. Bibliography: p. xvii-xviii. [BV4009.C53 1955] 55-14790
1. Clergy—Office. I. Jurgens, W. A., tr. II. Title.

DE JONG, Peter Ymen, 1915- 262.14
The ministry of mercy for today. Grand Rapids, Baker Book House, 1952. 261 p. 21 cm. [BV680.D4] 262.15 52-11972
1. Church officers. 2. Women in church work. I. Title.

DEMAREST, Victoria Booth-Clibborn. 262'.14
Sex & spirit : God, woman, & ministry / by Victoria Booth Demarest. 1st ed. [St. Petersburg, Fla. : Published by Sacred Arts International, in cooperation with Valkyrie Press, c1977] 182 p. : ill., ports. ; 22 cm. Bibliography: p. 181-182. [BV639.W7D4] 76-42915 ISBN 0-912760-29-X pbk. : 4.95 ISBN 0-912760-38-9 : 6.95
1. Demarest, Victoria Booth-Clibborn. 2. United Church of Christ—Clergy—Biography. 3. Women in Christianity. 4. Women as ministers. 5. Clergy—United States—Biography. I. Title.

DEMAREST, Victoria Booth-Clibborn. 262'.14
Sex & spirit : God, woman, & ministry / by Victoria Booth Demarest. 1st ed. [St. Petersburg, Fla. : Published by Sacred Arts International, in cooperation with Valkyrie Press, c1977] 182 p. : ill., ports. ; 22 cm. Bibliography: p. 181-182. [BV639.W7D4] 76-42915 ISBN 0-912760-29-X pbk. : 4.95 ISBN 0-912760-38-9 : 6.95
1. Demarest, Victoria Booth-Clibborn. 2. United Church of Christ—Clergy—Biography. 3. Women in Christianity. 4. Women as ministers. 5. Clergy—United States—Biography. I. Title.

DETROIT Ordination Conference, 1975. 262'.14
Women and Catholic priesthood : an expanded vision : proceedings of the Detroit Ordination Conference / edited by Anne Marie Gardiner. New York : Paulist Press, c1976. vii, 259 p. ; 22 cm. Bibliography: p. 199-208. [BV676.D47 1975] 76-12653 ISBN 0-8091-1955-2 pbk. : 5.95
1. Ordination of women—Catholic Church—Congresses. 2. Women in Christianity—Congresses. I. Gardiner, Anne Marie. II. Title.

DORONZO, Emmanuel, 1903- 262.14
De ordine. Milwaukee, Ex Typographia Bruce [1957- v. 24cm. At head of title: Tractatus dogmaticus. Contents.t.1. De institutions. Includes bibliographies. [BX1912.D65] 57-6322
1. Clergy—Office. 2. Catholic Church—Clergy. I. Title.

THE duties of the ruling elder. 262.14
Philadelphia, Westminster Press [1957] 96p. 20cm. [BX9195.W7] 262.15 57-10765
1. Presbyterian Church—Government. 2. Church officers. I. Wright, Paul S

FENTON, Joseph Clifford, 1906- 262.14
The concept of the diocesan priesthood. Milwaukee, Bruce [1951] 181 p. 22 cm. [BX1912.F42] 51-6988
1. Catholic Church—Clergy. I. Title.

FLOOD, Peter 262.14
The priest in practice; preaching and some other priestly duties. Westminster, Md., Newman [c.1962] 164p. 20cm. Bibl. 62-51095 3.50
1. Catholic Church—Clergy. 2. Pastoral theology—Catholic Church. I. Title.

FOSHEE, Howard B., 1925- 262'.14
The ministry of the deacon, by Howard B. Foshee. Nashville, Convention Press [1968] xi, 115 p. 19 cm. Bibliography: p. 110-113. [BV680.F6] 68-13564
1. Deacons. 2. Baptists—Government. I. Title.

GABRIELE di Santa Maria Maddelena, Father. 262.14
The spiritual director, according to the principles of St. John of the Cross. Translated by a Benedictine of Stanbrook Abbey. Westminster, Md., Newman Press [1952?] 131p. 22cm. [BX1912.G15] 52-14617
1. Juan de la Cruz, Saint, 1542-1591. 2. Spiritual directors. I. Title.

GARESCHE, Edward Francis, 1876- 262.14
The priest. [New ed.] New York, Vista Maria Press [1951] 306 p. 21 cm. [BX1912.G33 1951] 52-16768
1. Catholic Church—Clergy. 2. Priests. I. Title.

GIAQUINTA, Guglielmo, 1914- 262'.14
Tomorrow's priests, by G. Giaquinta. Translated by the Apostolic Oblates of Stanton, California. [Boston] St. Paul Editions [1970] 110 p. 18 cm. [BX1912.G49] 70-114408 0.95
1. Catholic Church—Clergy. I. Title.

GIBSON, Elsie. 262'.14
When the minister is a woman. [1st ed.] New York, Holt, Rinehart and Winston [1970] xviii, 174 p. 22 cm. Includes bibliographical references. [BV676.G5] 75-80361 ISBN 0-03-081846-X 4.95
1. Women clergy. I. Title.

GOEBEL, Bernardin. 262.14
Seven steps to the altar; preparation for priesthood. [English translation by A. V. Littledale and Geoffrey Stevenus] New York, Sheed & Ward [1963] 182 p. 21 cm. [BX2240.G613] 63-10675
1. Ordination — Catholic Church. 2. Tonsure. I. Title.

GOEBEL, Bernardin 262.14
Seven steps to the altar; preparation for priesthood. [Tr. by A. V. Littledale, Geoffrey Stevens] New York, Sheed [c.1963] 182p. 21cm. 63-10675 3.50 bds.,
1. Ordination—Catholic Church. 2. Tonsure. I. Title.

GREELEY, Andrew M., 1928- 262'.14
New horizons for the priesthood, by Andrew M. Greeley. New York, Sheed & Ward [1970] 148 p. 21 cm. [BX1912.G743] 74-103360 4.50
1. Catholic Church—Clergy. I. Title.

HENDERSON, Robert W 262.14
The teaching office in the Reformed tradition; a history of the doctoral ministry. Philadelphia, Westminster Press [1962] 277p. 22cm. [BX9423.C4H4] 62-11995
1. Church— Teaching office. I. Title.

HIMES, Ellvert H. 262'.14
Growing in the priesthood : messages of inspiration and motivation with personal records of fulfillment / by Ellvert H. Himes. Bountiful, Utah : Horizon Publishers, c1975. 128 p. : ill. ; 23 cm. Includes bibliographical references. [BX8659.H55] 75-17103 ISBN 0-88290-052-8 : 4.50
1. Church of Jesus Christ of Latter-Day Saints—Doctrinal and controversial works. 2. Melchizedek Priesthood (Mormonism) 3. Aaronic Priesthood (Mormonism) I. Title.

INSTITUTE of Spirituality. 262'.14
Impact of renewal on priests & religious. Augustine Rock, editor. Chicago, Priory Press [1968] 236 p. 22 cm. (Its Special lectures, v. 2, 1966) Bibliographical footnotes. [BX1912.I5] 68-18373
1. Catholic Church—Clergy. I. Rock, Augustine, ed. II. Title. III. Series.

JUMPER, Andrew A 262.14
The noble task: the elder; a practical manual for the operation of the church session in the Presbyterian Church in the United States, by Andrew A. Jumper. [Rev. ed.] Richmond, John Knox Press [1965] 158 p. 21 cm. Bibliographical footnotes. [BX8966.J8] 65-14420
1. Presbyterian Church in the U.S. — Government. I. Title.

JUMPER, Andrew A. 262.14
The noble task: the elder; a practical manual for the operation of the church session in the Presbyterian Church in the United States, [Rev. ed.] Richmond, Knox [c.1965] 158p. 21cm. Bibl. [BX8966.J8] 65-14420 1.50 pap.,
1. Presbyterian Church in the U.S.—Government. I. Title.

KANE, George Louis, 1911- 262.14
Why I became a priest; with an introd. by James Cardinal McGuigan. Westminister, Md., Newman Press, 1952. 163p. 22cm. [BX1912.K2] 52-12515
1. Catholic Church—Clergy. I. Title.

KUNG, Hans, 1928- 262'.14
Why priests? A proposal for a new church ministry. Translated by Robert C. Collins. Garden City, N.Y., Doubleday, 1972. 118 p. 22 cm. Translation of Wozu Priester? (Eine Hilfe) [BV4011.K7913] 70-186656 5.95
1. Pastoral theology. I. Title.

LECLERCQ, Jacques, 1891- 262'.14
Man of God for others. Translated by Charles Davenport. Westminster, Md., Newman Press [1967, c1968] vi, 169 p. 21 cm. Translation of Le pretre devant Dieu et devant les hommes. [BX1912.L3613] 68-16662
1. Catholic Church—Clergy. 2. Pastoral theology—Catholic Church. I. Title.

LECLERCQ, Jacques, 1891- 262'.14
Man of God for others. Translated by Charles Davenport. Westminster, Md., Newman Press [1967, c1968] vi, 169 p. 21 cm. Translation of Le pretre devant Dieu et devant les hommes. [BX1912.L3613] 68-16662
1. Catholic Church—Clergy. 2. Pastoral theology—Catholic Church. I. Title.

L'HOIR, F X, 1883-1948. 262.14
Alter Christus; meditations for priests. Westminster, Md., Newman Press, 1951. 217 p. 18 cm. [BX1912.L44] 51-12464
1. Clergy—Religious life. I. Title.

LIFE of the spirit. 262.14
The priest of the people; a symposium. Westminster, Md., Newman Press [1956] 95p. 19cm. 'Originally published as a special issue of the Life of the spirit, in April 1951.' [BX1912.L465 1956] 56-3421
1. Catholic Church—Clergy. 2. Clergy—Religious life. I. Title.

MASURE, Eugene, 1882- 262.14
Parish priest; translated by Angeline Bouchard. Chicago, Fides Publishers Association [1955] 255p. 21cm. [BX1912.M345] 55-11502
1. Catholic Church—Clergy. 2. Clergy—Religious life. I. Title.

MINCHIN, Basil 262.14
Every man in his ministry. [New York, Longmans, 1960] xvi, 328p. Includes bibliography. 19cm. (His Worship in the body of Christ) 60-1876 4.25 pap.,
1. Clergy—Office. 2. Episcopacy. 3. Lord's Supper—Celebration. I. Title.

MOORE, William Joseph, 1903- 262.14
New Testament concept of the ministry. St. Louis, Bethany Press [1956] 112p. 21cm. [BV660.M63] 56-13179
1. Clergy—Office. I. Title.

MORRIS, Leon 262.14
Ministers of God. London, Inter-varsity Fellowship [Chicago, Inter-varsity, c.1964] 128p. 19cm. (Great doctrines of the Bible) Bibl. 64-54835 1.50 pap.,
1. Clergy—Office—Biblical teaching. I. Title.

MYERS, Rawley, ed. 262.14
The greatest calling; a presentation of the priesthood by famous Catholics. New York, McMullen Books [1951] 183 p. 21 cm. [BX1912.M87] 51-14228
1. Catholic Church — Clergy. I. Title.

NAYLOR, Robert E 262.14
The Baptist deacon. Nashville, Broadman Press [1955] 138p. 21cm. [BV680.N37] [BV680.N37] 262.15 55-13544 55-13544
1. Deacons. 2. Baptists—Government. I. Title.

NELSON, John Oliver, 1909- 262.14
Opportunities in Protestant religious vocations. New York, Vocational Guidance Manuals [1952] 128 p. 20 cm. (Vocational guidance manuals) [BV660.N38] 52-12240
1. Clergy — Office. 2. Church work. I. Title.

NEVINS, Albert J 1915- 262.14
The making of a priest. Photos, by William H. Lathrop. Westminster, Md., Newman Press [c1957] 141p. illus., ports. 24cm. [BX4705.D5812N4] 57-14760
1. Donnelly, Thomas F. 2. Catholic Church—Clergy—Appointment, call, and election. I. Title.

NOLAN, Richard T. 262'.14
The diaconate now [by] Edmond LaB. Cherbonnier [and others] Edited by Richard T. Nolan. Washington, Corpus Books [1968] 190 p. 21 cm. Bibliographical references included in "Notes" (p. 175-186) [BV680.N6] 68-15781
1. Deacons—Addresses, essays, lectures. I. Cherbonnier, Edmond La Beaume, 1918- II. Title.

PAUL, Robert S 262.14
Ministry, by Robert S. Paul. Grand Rapids, Eerdmans [1965] 252 p. 23 cm. Bibliographical footnotes. [BV660.2.P3] 64-22022
1. Clergy—Office. I. Title.

PAUL, Robert S. 262.14
Ministry. Grand Rapids. Mich., Eerdmans [c.1965] 252p. 23cm. Bibl. [BV660.2.P3] 64-22022 5.00
1. Clergy—Office. I. Title.

PERRIN, Joseph Marie, 1905- 262.14
The minister of Christ [by] J. M. Perrin. Translated by Thomas F. Murray. Dubuque, Iowa, Priory Press [1964] xxiii. 141 p. 23 cm. Translation of Le mystere du pretre. [BX1912.P443] 64-20104
1. Clergy—Office. 2. Catholic Church—Clergy. 3. Priests. I. Title.

PERRIN, Joseph Marie, 1905- 262.14
The minister of Christ, Tr. [from French] Thomas F. Murray. Dubuque, Iowa. Priory Pr. [c.1964] xxiii, 141p. 23cm. 64-20104 2.95
1. Clergy—Office. 2. Catholic Church—Clergy. 3. Priests. I. Title.

POAGE, Godfrey Robert, 1920- 262.14
Opportunities in Catholic religious vocations. New York, Vocational Guidance Manuals [1952] 144 p. 20 cm. (Vocational guidance manuals) [BX2380.P58] 52-12242
1. Catholic Church — Clergy. 2. Monasticism and religious orders. I. Title.

POAGE, Godfrey Robert, 1920- 262.14
Recruiting for Christ. Milwaukee, Bruce [1950] ix, 193 p. 22 cm. (Science and culture series) Bibliography: p. 180-190. [BX2380.P6] 50-58194
1. Clergy — Appointment, call, and election. 2. Vocation (in religious orders, congregations, etc.) I. Title.

RAMING, Ida. 262'.14
The exclusion of women from the priesthood : divine law or sex discrimination? : An historical investigation of the juridical and doctrinal foundations of the code of canon law, canon 968, 1 / by Ida Raming ; translated by Norman R. Adams ; with a pref. by Arlene & Leonard Swidler. Metuchen, N.J. : Scarecrow Press, 1976. xvii, 263 p. ; 23 cm. Translation of Der Ausschluss der Frau vom priesterlichen Amt. Includes index. Bibliography: p. [255]-257. [LAW] 76-23322 ISBN 0-8108-0957-5 : 11.00
1. Women—Legal status, laws, etc. (Canon law) 2. Clergy (Canon law) I. Title.

RASHKE, Richard L. 262'.14
The deacon in search of identity / by Richard L. Rashke. New York : Paulist Press, [1975] v, 104 p. ; 21 cm. Bibliography: p. 101-104. [BX1912.R35] 74-15720 ISBN 0-8091-1851-3 pbk. : 3.50
1. Deacons. I. Title.

SHEEHY, Maurice Stephen, 1898- 262.14
The priestly heart; the last chapter in the life of an old-young priest. New York, Farrar, Straus, and Cudahy [1956] 71p. illus. 22cm. [BX1912.S49] 56-6156
1. Clergy—Religious life. I. Title.

SHEEHY, Maurice Stephen, 1898- 262.14
The priestly heart; the last chapter in the life of an old-young priest. New York, Farrar, Straus, and Cudahy [1956] 71 p. illus. 22 cm. [BX1912.S49] 56-6156
1. Clergy — Religious life. I. Title.

SMEDT, Emile Joseph de, Bp. 262.14
The priesthood of the faithful. Translated by Joseph F. M. Marique. New York, Paulist Press [1962] 126 p. 18 cm. (Paulist Press paperbacks. Deus books) [BX1913.S613] 62-11628
1. Priests. I. Title.

SMEDT, Emile Joseph de, Bp. 262.14
The priesthood of the faithful. Tr. by Joseph F. M. Marique. New York, Paulist [c.1962] 126p. (Deus bks.) 62-11628 .95 pap.,
1. Priests. I. Title.

SMITH, Elwyn Allen, 1919- 262.14
The Presbyterian ministry in American culture, a study in changing concepts, 1700-1900. Philadelphia, Published for the Presbyterian Historical Society by Westminster Press [1962] 269 p. 21 cm. (Presbyterian Historical Society. Studies in Presbyterian history) [BX8936.S4] 62-16251
1. Presbyterian Church in the U.S. — Clergy. 2. Clergy — Office. I. Title.

SMITH, Elwyn Allen, 1919- 262.14
The Presbyterian ministry in American culture, a study in changing concepts, 1700-1900. Philadelphia, Pub. for the Presbyterian Historical Soc. by Westminster [c.1962] 269p. 21cm. (Presbyterian Historical Soc. Studies in Presbyterian hist.) Bibl. 62-16251 4.00
1. Presbyterian Church in the U. S.—Clergy. 2. Clergy—Office. I. Title.

STAUDACHER, Rosemarian V 262.14
Chaplains in action, Illustrated by H. Lawrence Hoffman, New York, Vision Books [1962] 192 p. illus. 22 cm. (Vision books, 53) [BX1914.S75] 62-8841
1. Chaplains — Catholic Church. I. Title.

STAUDACHER, Rosemarian V. 262.14
Chaplains in action. Illus. by H. Lawrence Hoffman. New York, Farrar [c.]1962. 192p. (Vision bks., 53) 62-8841 1.95; 2.25 lib. ed.,
1. Chaplains—Catholic Church. I. Title.

STEPHENSON, Anthony A 262.14
Anglican orders. With appendices by Walton Hannah and Hugh Ross Williamson. Westminster, Md., Newman Press [1956] 76p. 22cm. [BX5178.S8] [BX5178.S8] 262.16 56-9766 56-9766
1. Anglican orders. I. Title.

THORMAN, Donald J 262.14
The emerging layman; the role of the Catholic layman in America. [1st ed.] Garden City, N.Y., Doubleday, 1962. 234 p. 22 cm. [BX1920.T5] 62-15051
1. Laity. I. Title.

THORMAN, Donald J. 262.14
The emerging layman; the role of the Catholic layman in America. [1st ed.] Garden City, N. Y., Doubleday, 1962. 234 p. 22 cm. [BX1920.T5] 62-15051
1. Laity. I. Title.

THORMAN, Donald J. 262.14
The emerging layman; the role of the Catholic layman in America. Garden City, N.Y., Doubleday [1965, c.1957-1962] 238p. 18cm. (Image bk., D186) Bibl. [BX1920T5] .85 pap.,
1. Laity. I. Title.

TO be a priest : 262'.14
perspectives on vocation and ordination / edited by Robert E. Terwilliger, Urban T. Holmes, III ; with a foreword by John M. Allin. New York : Seabury Press, c1975. p. cm. "A Crossroad book." Bibliography: p. [BV662.T6] 75-28248 ISBN 0-8164-2592-2 : 4.95
1. Priests—Addresses, essays, lectures. 2. Priesthood—Addresses, essays, lectures. I. Terwilliger, Robert E. II. Holmes, Urban Tigner, 1930-

TRESE, Leo John, 1902- 262.14
A man approved. New York, Sheed & Ward, 1953. 152p. 20cm. [BX1912.T69] 53-5197
1. Clergy—Religious life. 2. Catholic Church—Clergy. I. Title.

TRESE, Leo John, 1902- 262.14
Tenders of the flock. New York, Sheed and Ward, 1955. 190p. 20cm. [BX1912.T695] 55-7480
1. Clergy— Religious life. 2. Catholic Church—Clergy. I. Title.

TROLLOPE, Anthony, 1815-1882 262'14
Clergymen of the Church of England Leicester, Leicester University Press 1974 [i.e.1975] 65, 130 p. 19 cm. (The Victorian library) Photoreprint of the 1st ed published by Chapman and Hall, London, 1866. [PR5684.C62] 75-315546 ISBN 0-7185-5023-4
1. Church of England—Clergy—Addresses, essays, lectures. I. Title.

Distributed by Humanities Press for 9.00.

TROLLOPE, Anthony, 1815-1882. 262'14
Phineas Redux; with a pref. by R. W. Chapman, illus. by T. L. B. Huskinson. London, New York, Oxford University Press, 1951. 2 v. illus. (part col.) 21 cm. (The Oxford Trollope. Crown ed.) [PR5684.P] A51
I. Title.

TRUEBLOOD, David Elton, 1900- 262.14
Your other vocation. [1st ed.] New York, Harper [1952] 125 p. 20 cm. [BV4525.T75] 52-11078
1. Christian life. 2. Church work. 3. Laity. 4. Vocation. I. Title.

VAN ZELLER, Hubert, 1905- 262.14
The gospel priesthood. New York, Sheed & Ward [1956] 114p. 20cm. 'A series of articles which appeared in Emmanuel throughout the year 1954, with two added from 1955.' [BX1912.V25] 56-6128
1. Clergy—Religious life. I. Title.

VAN ZELLER, Hubert, 1905- 262.14
The gospel priesthood. New York, Sheed & Ward [1956] 114 p. 20 cm. Secular name: Claude Van Zeller. "A series of articles which appeared in Emmanuel throughout the year 1954, with two added from 1955." [BX1912.V25] 56-6128
1. Clergy — Religious life. I. Title. II. Series.

WAGONER, Walter D 262.14
Bachelor of divinity; uncertain servants in seminary and ministry. With drawings by James Crane. New York, Association Press [1963] 150 p. illus. 21 cm. Bibliographical references included in "Notes" (p. 153-159) [BV4030.W3] 63-16044
1. Theology—Study and teaching—U.S. 2. Pastoral theology—Addresses, essays, lectures. 3. Seminarians. I. Title.

WAGONER, Walter D. 262.14
Bachelor of divinity; uncertain servants in seminary and ministry. Drawings by James Crane. New York, Association [c.1963] 159p. illus. 21cm. Bibl. 63-16044 3.50
1. Theology—Study and teaching—U.S. 2. Pastoral theology—Addresses, essays, lectures. 3. Seminarians. I. Title.

WALLACE, Gervias Knox, 1903- 262'.14
Wallace-Ketcherside St. Louis debate, St. Louis, Missouri, October 26-30, 1953, between G. K. Wallace and W. Carl Ketcherside. Tape recorded and transcribed by L. Wesley Jones. 1st ed. Longview, Wash., Telegram Book Co. [1954] ix, 278 p. ports. 22 cm. [BX7077.W34] 74-158337
1. Churches of Christ—Clergy. 2. Churches of Christ—Government. 3. Churches of Christ—Education. I. Ketcherside, W. Carl. II. Title.

WEDEL, Theodore Otto, 1892- ed. 262.14
Ministers of Christ [by] Walter Lowrie [and others] New York, Seabury Press, 1964. 186 p. 22 cm. Contents.Contents. -- Editor's introduction. -- Ministers of Christ, by W. Lowrie. -- Nolo Episcopari, by G. S. Hendry. -- A common ministry, by R. D. Hyslop. -- Apostolicity and restitution, by F. H. Littell. -- The bishop in the church. by J. Meyendorff. -- Editor's epilogue. Bibliographical references included in "Notes" (p. 175-186) [BV660.W33] 64-10140
1. Clergy — Office. I. Lowrie, Walter, 1868-1959. Ministers of Christ. II. Title.

WEDEL, Theodore Otto, 1892- ed. 262.14
Ministers of Christ [by] Walter Lowrie [others] NewYork, Seabury [c.1964] 186p. 22cm. Bibl. 64-10140 3.95
1. Clergy—Office. I. Lowrie, Walter, 1868-1959. Ministers of Christ. II. Title.

WILDER, John B., 1914- 262.14
The young minister, his calling, career, and challenge. Grand Rapids, Mich.,, Zondervan [c.1962] 120p. 21cm. 62-51556 1.95 bds.,
1. Clergy. I. Title.

WILDER, John B 1914- 262.14
The young minister, his calling, career, and challenge. Grand Rapids, Zondervan Pub. House [1962] 120 p. 21 cm. [BV660.2.W5] 62-51556
1. Clergy. I. Title.

WILDER, John Bunyan, 1914- 262.14
The young minister, his calling, career, and challenge. Grant Rapids. Zondervan Pub. House [1962] 120 p. 21 cm. [BV660.2.W5] 62-51556
1. Clergy. I. Title.

CIRCUIT Riders. 262.1405873
A compilation of public records of 658 clergymen and laymen connected with the National Council of Churches. Cincinnati [1962] 230 p. 22 cm. [BR569.C5] 63-44009
1. Clergy — U.S. 2. National Council of Churches of Christ in the United States of America. I. Title.

HOSTIE, Raymond, 1920- 262.14069
The discernment of vocations. Translated by Michael Barry. New York, Sheed & Ward [1963] 160 p. 22 c;. Includes bibliography. [BX2380.H613] 63-10493
1. Vocation, Ecclesiastical. I. Title.

HOSTIE, Raymond, 1920- 262.14069
The discernment of vocations. Tr. by Michael Barry. New York, Sheed [c.1963] 160p. 22cm. Bibl. 63-10493 3.50
1. Vocation, Ecclesiastical. I. Title.

WILLIAMS, Ethel L. 262.140922 B
Biographical directory of Negro ministers, by Ethel L. Williams. New York, Scarecrow Press, 1965. xi, 421 p. 22 cm. Bibliography: p. 407-412. [BR563.N4W5] 65-13562
1. Negro clergy—United States—Biography—Dictionaries. I. Title.

WILLIAMS, Ethel L. 262'.14'0922 B
Biographical directory of Negro ministers, by Ethel L. Williams. 2d ed. Metuchen, N.J., Scarecrow Press, 1970. 605 p. 22 cm. Bibliography: p. 575-580. [BR563.N4W5 1970] 78-18496 ISBN 8-10-803283-
1. Negro clergy—U.S.—Biography—Dictionaries. I. Title.

BOWKER, Margaret. 262'.14'094253
The secular clergy in the Diocese of Lincoln, 1495-1520. London, Cambridge Univ. Pr. 1968. xii, 253p. illus. 23cm. (Cambridge studies in medieval life & thought, new ser., v. 13) Bibl. [BX5107.L5B6] 68-10147 7.50
1. Clergy—Lincoln, Eng. (Diocese) I. Title. II. Series.
Available from publisher's New York office.

CHESTER, Eng. (Diocese) 262'.14'094253
Chester diocesan calendar, clergy list, and year book. Chester, Phillipson and Golder. v. 19cm. Printed and published for the Chester Diocesan Board of Finance. [BX5107.C5A3] 55-32269
1. Chester, Eng.(Diocese)—Yearbooks. I. Title.

MAJOR, Kathleen. 262'.14'094253
A handlist of the records of the Bishop of Lincoln and of the Archdeacons of Lincoln and Stow. London, New York, Oxford University Press, 1953. xiv, 122p. 23cm. [BX5107.L5M3] 54-35837
1. Lincoln, Eng. (Diocese)—Hist.—Sources. 2. Archieves—Lincoln, Eng. (Diocese) I. Title.

FICHTER, Joseph Henry, 1908- 262'.14'0973
America's forgotten priests; what they are saying [by] Joseph H. Fichter. [1st ed.] New York, Harper & Row [1968] 254 p. 22 cm. Includes bibliographical references. [BX1407.C6F5] 68-11735
1. Catholic Church in the U.S.—Clergy. I. Title.

GREELEY, Andrew M., 1928- 262'.14'0973
Uncertain trumpet; the priest in modern America, by Andrew M. Greeley. New York, Sheed and Ward [1968] x, 175 p. 21 cm. [BX1912.G745] 68-13841
1. Catholic Church—Clergy. I. Title.

STEPHENSON, Anthony A 262.14 262.16
Anglican orders. With appendices by Walton Hannah and Hugh Ross Williamson. Westminster, Md., Newman Press [1956] 76 p. 22 cm. [BX5178.S8] 56-9766
1. Anglican orders. I. Title.

WRIGHT, Paul S 262.14 262.15
The duties of the ruling elder. Philadelphia, Westminster Press [1957] 96 p. 20 cm. [BX9195.W7] 57-10765
1. Presbyterian Church — Government. 2. Church officers. I. Title.

ANDERSON, Clifford V. 262'.15
Worthy of the calling; [the layman's vital role] by Clifford V. Anderson. Chicago, Harvest Publications [1968] 146 p. 18 cm. Bibliography: p. 145-146. [BV4525.A5] 68-30884
1. Laity. I. Title.

BLISS, Kathleen. 262.15
We the people: a book about laity. Philadelphia, Fortress Press [1964] 139 p. 29 cm. Bibliographical footnotes. [BV687.B55] 64-18951
1. Laity — Addresses, essays, lectures. I. Title.

BLISS, Kathleen 262.15
We the people: a book about laity. Philadelphia, Fortress [c.1964] 139p. 19cm. Bibl. 64-18951 1.75 pap.,
1. Laity—Addresses, essays, lectures. I. Title.

BRISTER, C. W. 262/.15
People who care [by] C. W. Brister. Nashville, Broadman [1967] 128p. 20cm. Bibl. [BV4400.B73] 67-17424 1.50 bds.,
1. Laity. 2. Church work. I. Title.

BRISTER, C W 262'.15
People who care [by] C. W. Brister. Nashville, Broadman Press [1967] 128 p. 20 cm. Bibliographical references included in "Notes" (p. 125-128) [BV4400.B73] 67-17424
1. Laity. 2. Church work. I. Title.

BUEHNER, Andrew J., ed. 262'.15
Operation theology; the layman and current religious developments. Andrew J. Buehner, editor. St. Louis, Lutheran Academy for Scholarship [1967] 125 p. 21 cm. Papers and addresses of a conference at Concordia Seminary, St. Louis, Mo., held by the Lutheran Academy for Scholarship in cooperation with the Lutheran Laymen's League. Includes bibliographical references. [BR123.O65] 68-1248
1. Christianity—20th cent.—Addresses, essays, lectures. 2. Laity. I. Concordia Theological Seminary, St. Louis. II. Lutheran Academy for Scholarship. III. Lutheran Laymen's League. IV. Title.

CARR, William M. 262'.15
A handbook for lectors, by William M. Carr. Glen Rock, N.J., Paulist Press [1968] vii, 52 p. 17 cm. [BX1915.C3 1968] 68-57878 0.75
1. Lay readers—Handbooks, manuals, etc. I. Title.

CHAFIN, Kenneth. 262.15
Help. I'm a layman. Waco, Tex., Word Books [1966] 131 p. 21 cm. [BV687.C43] 66-22155
1. Laity I. Title.

CHAFIN, Kenneth 262.15
Help! I'm a layman. Waco, Tex., Word Bks. [c.1966] 131p. 21cm. [BV687.C43] 66-22155 3.50
1. Laity. I. Title.

CLEMMONS, Robert S. 262.15
Education for churchmanship [by] Robert S. Clemmon. Nashville, Abingdon [1966] 205 p. 22 cm (151) [bv1488.c5] 66-21968
1. Religious education of adults. Title. I. Title.

CLEMMONS, Robert S 262.15
Education for churchmanship [by] Robert S. Clemmons Nashville, Abingdon Press [1966] 205 p. 22 cm. Includes bibliographies. [BV1488.C5] 66-21968
1. Religious education of adults. I. Title.

CONGAR, Marie Joseph, 1904- 262-.15
Lay people in the church; a study for a theology of laity [by] Yves M. J. Congar. Tr. [from French] by Donald Attwater. [2d] rev. ed., with additions by the author. Westminster, Md., Newman, 1965 [c.1957, 1965] xxi, 498p. 22cm. Bibl. [BX1920.C612] 65-28804 3.50 pap.,
1. Laity—Catholic Church. 2. Catholic Church. 3. Priesthood, Universal. 4. Catholic action. I. Title.

CONSULTATION on the Lay Ministry, Charleston, S.C., 1967. 262'.15
The lay leader in the lead program (laymens' enrichment and devotional program). The study papers presented at, and a report on the considerations and recommendations of, the Consultation on the Lay Ministry. [Washington? 1969] iii, 95 p. 26 cm. "NAVPERS 15156." "Jointly sponsored by Commander, Submarine Force, U.S. Atlantic Fleet [and] Chief of Chaplains, U.S. Navy." Includes bibliographical references. [BV687.C6 1967a] 72-605345
1. Laity—Congresses. I. U.S. Navy. Chaplain Corps. II. U.S. Navy. Atlantic Fleet. Submarine Force. III. Title.

COWLES, S. Macon. 262'.15
Ministers all; an adult resource book [by] S. Macon Cowles, Jr. Boston, United Church Press [1967] 91 p. illus. 21 cm. Bibliography: p. 87-91. [BV4525.C62] 67-10052
1. Laity. I. Title.

FEMIANO, Samuel D. 262'.15
Infallibility of the laity; the legacy of Newman [by] Samuel D. Femiano. [New York] Herder and Herder [1967] xiii, 142 p. 22 cm. Includes bibliographical references. [BX4705.N5F4] 67-27737
1. Newman, John Henry, Cardinal, 1801-1890. 2. Laity—Catholic Church. I. Title.

FEMIANO, Samuel D. 262'.15
Infallibility of the laity; the legacy of Newman [by] Samuel D. Femiano. [New York] Herder and Herder [1967] xiii, 142 p. 22 cm. Includes

bibliographical references. [BX4705.N5F4] 67-27737
1. Newman, John Henry, Cardinal, 1801-1890. 2. Laity—Catholic Church. I. Title.

FEUCHT, Oscar E. 262'.15
Everyone a minister : a guide to churchmanship for laity and clergy / Oscar E. Feucht. St. Louis : Concordia Pub. House, 1974. 158 p. ; 18 cm. Includes bibliographical references. [BV3.F47] 73-90058 ISBN 0-570-03184-2 pbk. : 0.95
1. Theology, Practical. 2. Laity. 3. Christianity—20th century. I. Title.

FIDES Forum, 1st, 262/.15
University of Notre Dame, 1966
Primacy of the person in the church; [papers by M. Aloysius Schaldenbrand, others. Introd. by James V. Cunningham] Notre Dame, Ind., Fides [1967] 132p. form. 20cm. Bibl. [BX1920.F5 1966aa] 67-24814 1.95 pap.,
1. Laity—Catholic Church. 2. Persons. I. Schaldenbrand, Mary Aloysius, Sister. II. Notre Dame, Ind. University. III. Title.
Contents Omitted.

FOSHEE, Howard B., 1925- 262'.15
The ministry of the deacon / Howard B. Foshee. Rev. Nashville : Convention Press, 1974, c1968. 125 p. : ill. ; 21 cm. Bibliography: p. 117-119. [BV680.F6 1974] 75-301352
1. Deacons. 2. Baptists—Government. I. Title.

FOSHEE, Howard B., 1925- 262'.15
Now that you're a deacon / Howard B. Foshee. Nashville : Broadman Press, c1975. 136 p. ; 20 cm. Bibliography: p. 133-136. [BV680.F63] 74-79488 ISBN 0-8054-3506-9 : 2.95
1. Deacons. I. Title.

GIBBS, Mark. 262'.15
God's lively people, by Mark Gibbs and T. Ralph Morton. Philadelphia, Westminster Press [1971] 212 p. 19 cm. Bibliography: p. [205]-212. [BV4525.G5] 77-142997 ISBN 0-664-24914-0 2.65
1. Laity. I. Morton, Thomas Ralph, joint author. II. Title.

GRAEBNER, Alan. 262'.15
Uncertain saints : the laity in the Lutheran Church, Missouri Synod, 1900-1970 / Alan Graebner. Westport, Conn. : Greenwood Press, 1975. xiii, 284 p. ; 22 cm. (Contributions in American history ; no. 42) Includes index. Bibliography: p. 273-278. [BX8061.M7G7] 75-1573 ISBN 0-8371-7963-7 : 15.00
1. Laity—Lutheran Church—Missouri Synod—History. I. Title.

GRAEBNER, Alan. 262'.15
Uncertain saints : the laity in the Lutheran Church, Missouri Synod, 1900-1970 / Alan Graebner. Westport, Conn. : Greenwood Press, 1975. xiii, 284 p. ; 22 cm. (Contributions in American history ; no. 42) Includes index. Bibliography: p. 273-278. [BX8061.M7G7] 75-1573 ISBN 0-8371-7963-7 : 15.00
1. Laity—Lutheran Church—Missouri Synod—History. I. Title.

HALL, Cameron P. 262'.15
Lay action: the church's third force; a strategy for enabling lay ministry in secular institutions [by] Cameron P. Hall. New York, Friendship Press [1974] 144 p. 23 cm. Includes bibliographical references. [BV4400.H25] 74-1455 ISBN 0-377-00018-3 3.50 (pbk.)
1. Laity. I. Title.

HARPER, Howard V 262.15
The vestryman's manual. New York, Seabury Press, 1964. 96 p. 21 cm. [BX5967.5.H3] 64-12940
1. Church officers. 2. Protestant Episcopal Church in the U.S.A. — Government. I. Title.

HARPER, Howard V. 262.15
The vestryman's manual. New York, Seabury [c.]1964. 96p. 21cm. 64-12940 1.95 pap.,
1. Church officers. 2. Protestant Episcopal Church in the U.S.A.—Government. I. Title.

JUMPER, Andrew A. 262.15
Chosen to serve: the deacon; a practical manual for the operation of the board of deacons in the Presbyterian Church in the United States. Richmond, Va., John Knox [c.1961] 128p. 61-18257 1.25 pap.,
1. Presbyterian Church in the United States—Government. 2. Deacons. I. Title.

KENNEDY, Gerald Hamilton, 262'.15
Bp., 1907-
For laymen and other martyrs [by] Gerald Kennedy. [1st ed.] New York, Harper & Row [1969] 122 p. 22 cm. [BV687.K43] 69-17007 3.95
1. Laity—Addresses, essays, lectures. 2. Christianity—20th century—Addresses, essays, lectures. I. Title.

KOLESAR, John. 262'.15
Ministers of life : the role of lay ministers of the Eucharist / by John Kolesar ; foreword by James W. Malone ; introd. by Frederick R. McManus. Revision. Cincinnati : North American Liturgy Resources, 1973. 75 p. : ill. ; 21 cm. Bibliography: p. [70]-72. [BX1915.K64 1973] 75-309105 1.45
1. Lay ministry—Catholic Church. 2. Lord's Supper—Catholic Church. I. Title.

LOEW, Jacques, 1908- 262'.15
As if he had seen the invisible; a portrait of the apostle today. Translated by Marie-Odile Fortier Masek. Notre Dame, Ind., Fides [1967] ix, 175 p. 20 cm. Translation of Comme s'il voyait l'invisible. [BX2348.L6313] 66-30586
1. Catholic action. I. Title.

LOWE, Jacques, 1908- 262'.15
As if he had seen the invisible; a portrait of the apostle today. Translated by Marie-Odile Fortier Masek. Notre Dame, Ind., Fides [1967] ix, 175 p. 20 cm. Translation of Comme s'il voyait l'invisible. [BX2348.L6313] 66-30586
1. Catholic action. I. Title.

LUDLOW, John Malcolm 262'.15
Forbes, 1821-1911.
Woman's work in the church : historical notes on deaconesses and sisterhoods /, by J. M. Ludlow. Washington : Zenger Pub. Co., 1975. p. cm. Reprint of the 1866 ed. published by A. Strahan, London, New York. [BV639.W7L8 1975] 75-33300 ISBN 0-89201-007-X
1. Deaconesses—History. 2. Sisterhoods—History. 3. Monasticism and religious orders for women—History. I. Title.

LYONS, Bernard. 262.1'5
Leaders for parish councils; a handbook of training techniques. Foreword by John P. Donnelly. [Techny, Ill., Divine Word Publications [1971] xv, 151 p. 22 cm. Cover title. [BV652.9.L89] 75-148029 ISBN 0-87298-141-X 2.95
1. Parish councils—Handbooks, manuals, etc. 2. Christian leadership—Handbooks, manuals, etc. I. Title. II. Title: A handbook of training techniques.

MCCARTHY, Timothy. 262'.15
The postconciliar Christian; the meaning of the priesthood of the laity. Foreword by Dorothy Day. New York, P. J. Kenedy [1967] x, 142 p. 22 cm. Bibliography: p. 139-142. [BX1920.M3] 67-18427
1. Priesthood, Universal. 2. Laity—Catholic Church. I. Title.

MARNEY, Carlyle, 1916- 262'.15
Priests to each other. Valley Forge [Pa.] Judson Press [1974] 125 p. 22 cm. (Lake view books) Includes bibliographical references. [BV4525.M37] 73-16787 ISBN 0-8170-0628-1 2.95 (pbk.)
1. Laity. 2. Priesthood, Universal. I. Title.

MIDWESTERN Institute of 262.15
Pastoral Theology. 5th, Sacred Heart Seminary, 1965.
The layman: his Christian witness [Proceedings of the] Fith Annual Institute, August 23-26, 1965. Detroit, 1965 [c1966] 162p. 22cm. Sponsored by Sacred Heart Seminary and St. John's Provincial Seminary. [BX1920.M5 1965] 66-25665 2.00
1. Laity—Catholic Church. I. Detroit. Sacred Heart Seminary. II. St. John's Provincial Seminary, Plymouth, Mich. III. Title.
Available from Sacred Heart Seminary, 2701 W. Chicago Blvd., Detroit, Mich., 48206.

NATIONAL Council of 262'.15
Catholic Men.
The spirit of renewal; [a short course in Vatican II for lay people] Washington [1967] 79 p. illus., ports. 28 cm. [BX830 1962.N33] 68-2447
1. Vatican Council. 2d, 1962-1965. 2. Laity—Catholic Church. I. Title. II. Title: A short course in Vatican II for lay people.

NICHOLS, Harold, 1903- 262.15
The work of the deacon; a deacon talks to deacons [by] Harold Nichols. Valley Forge [Pa.] Judson Press [1964] viii, 118 p. 17 cm. bibliography: p. 116. [BX6346.N5] 64-15799
1. Deacons. 2. Baptists — Clergy. I. Title.

NICHOLS, Harold, 1903- 262.15
The work of the deacon; a deacon talks to deacons. Valley Forge, Pa., Judson [c.1964] viii, 118p. 17cm. Bibl. 64-15799 1.50 pap.,
1. Deacons. 2. Baptists—Clergy. I. Title.

NOWELL, Robert, 1931- 262'.15
The ministry of service: deacons in the contemporary Church. Foreword by Christopher Butler. [New York] Herder and Herder [1968] 127 p. 21 cm. Bibliographical footnotes. [BX1912] 68-8376 3.50
1. Deacons. I. Title.

OPERATION theology; 262'.15
the layman and current religious developments. Andrew J. Buehner, editor. St. Louis, Lutheran Academy for Scholarship [1967] 125 p. 21 cm. Papers and addresses of a conference at Concordia Seminary, St. Louis, Mo., held by the Lutheran Academy for Scholarship in cooperation with the Lutheran Laymen's League. Includes bibliographical references. [BR123.O65] 68-1248
1. Christianity—20th century—Addresses, essays, lectures. 2. Laity. I. Buehner, Andrew J., ed. II. Concordia Theological Seminary, St. Louis. III. Lutheran Academy for Scholarship. IV. Lutheran Laymen's League.

*PIERSON, Roberto H. 262'.15
Para ud. Que quiere ser dirigente. Mountain View, Calif., Pacific Pr. Pub. [1967] 156p 22cm. 2.50 pap.,
I. Title.

SASAKI, Joseph, 1935- 262'.15
The lay apostolate and the hierarchy. Ottawa, St. Paul's University; University of Ottawa Press, 1967. xiv, 199 p. 24 cm. (C 68-234) Bibliography: p. [187]-199. [BX1920.S2] 68-77090 6.00 Can.
1. Laity—Catholic Church. 2. Catholic action. 3. Catholic Church—Government. I. Title.

SCHILLEBEECKX, Edward 262.15
Cornelis Florentius Alfons, 1914-
The layman in the church, and other essays [by] E. H. Schillebeeckx. Staten Island, N. Y., Alba House [1963] 91 p. 19 cm. [BX1920.S3] 63-23157
1. Vatican Council, 2d. 2. Laity—Catholic Church. 3. Death. I. Title.

SCHILLEBEECKX, Edward 262.15
Henricus, 1914-
The layman in the church, and other essays. [Staten Island] N.Y. Alba House [c.1963] 91p. 19cm. 63-23157 2.95
1. Vatican Council, 2d. 2. Laity—Catholic Church. 3. Death. I. Title.

SUPIN, Charles R. 262'.15
Beyond pledging; an informal guide to lay leadership in the Episcopal Church [by] Charles R. Supin. Introd. by Oscar C. Carr, Jr. New York, Seabury Press [1974] x, 173 p. 21 cm. "A Crossroad book." Includes bibliographical references. [BX5968.S9] 74-12315 ISBN 0-8164-2108-0 3.95
1. Laity—Anglican Communion. I. Title.

THOMAS, Donald F. 262'.15
The deacon in a changing church [by] Donald F. Thomas. Valley Forge [Pa.] Judson Press [1969] 125 p. illus. 20 cm. Bibliography: p. 119-122. Bibliographical footnotes. [BV680.T5] 69-16388 1.95
1. Deacons. I. Title.

TODD, John Murray. 262'.15
The laity: The people of God, by John M. Todd. New York [Paulist Press, 1967, c1965] 112 p. 19 cm. (Deus books) Bibliographical footnotes. [BX1920.T55] 67-23603
1. Laity—Catholic Church. I. Title.

VATICAN Council. 2d,1962- 262.15
1965.
De apostolatu laicorum; the decree on the apostolate of the laity promulgated by Pope VI, November 18, 1965. Commentary by John B. Sheerin. [Study-club ed.] Glen Rock, N.J., Paulist Press, 1966. 92 p. 19 cm. (Vatican II documents) Bibliography: p. 91-92. [BX830 1962.A45A63] 66-19149
1. Catholic action. I. Catholic Church. Pope, 1963- (Paulus VI) II. Sheerin, John B., ed. III. Title. IV. Title: The decree on the apostolate of the laity.

VATICAN Council, 2d, 1962- 262.15
1965
De apostolatu laicorum; the decree on the apostolate of the laity promulgated by Pope Paul VI, November 18, 1965. Commentary by John B. Sheerin. [Study-club ed.] Glen Rock, N.J., Paulist [c.]1966. 92p. 19cm. (Vatican II docs.) bBibl. [BX830 1962, A45A63] 66-19149 .75 pap.,
1. Catholic action. I. Catholic Church. Pope, 1963-(Paulus VI) II. Sheerin, John B., ed. III. Title. IV. Title: The decree on the apostolate of the laity.

VATICAN Council, 2d, 1962- 262.15
1965
Laymen; Vatican II's Decree on the Apostolate of the laity. Text, commentary, ed. by Peter Foote [others. Eng. tr. of decree by John Mulholland] Chicago, Ill., 60611, Catholic Action Fedn. [720 N. Rush St., c.1966] 72p. illus. 28cm. Text and commentary on facing pages [BX830 1962.A45A626] 66-4625 1.50 pap.,
1. Catholic action. I. Foote, Peter, ed. II. Title.

VATICAN Council. 2d, 1962- 262'.15
1965.
To burn with the spirit of Christ; daily readings on the role of the laity in the church from the documents of Vatican II [compiled by] Nicholas Schneider. Liguori, Mo., Liguori Publications [1971] 191 p. 18 cm. [BX830 1962.A3S34] 70-183355 1.50
1. Laity—Catholic Church. 2. Devotional calendars. I. Schneider, Nicholas A., comp. II. Title.

WRIGHT, Paul S. 262'.15
The duties of the ruling elder, by Paul S. Wright. Rev. ed. Philadelphia, Westminster Press [1972] 87 p. 19 cm. [BX9195.W7 1972] 72-181899 ISBN 0-664-24952-3 1.50
1. Presbyterian Church—Government. 2. Elders (Church officers) I. Title.

PATTERSON, Webster 262'.15'0924
T.
Newman: pioneer for the layman [by] Webster T. Patterson. Foreword by Robert W. Gleason. Washington, Corpus Books [1968] xxii, 193 p. 21 cm. Bibliography: p. 183-189. [BX4705.N5P3] 68-9475 7.50
1. Newman, John Henry, Cardinal, 1801-1890. 2. Laity. I. Title.

MEYER, Bernard F. 262'.15'0945
1891-.
Your life to share [by] Bernard F. Meyer. Allahabad, St. Paul Publications [1962] 253 p. 18 cm. Bibliography: p. [252]-253. [BX2348.M43] SA65
1. Catholic action. 2. Catholic Church — Missions. I. Title.

POGGI, Gianfranco. 262'.15'0945
Catholic Action in Italy; the sociology of a sponsored organization. Stanford, Calif., Stanford University Press, 1967. xv, 280 p. 24 cm. An enlarged translation of the author's Il clero di riserva, 1963. Bibliography: p. [271]-274. [BX2348.Z8I863] 66-22985
1. Azione cattolica italiana. 2. Catholic action—Italy. I. Title.

MCLAUGHLIN, Francis A 262.17
1881-
The unshattered rock; a study of the invalidity of Anglican and Protestant Episcopal orders, and related subjects; also presentation of ritual ceremonies used in the various Oriental churches not in communion with the See of Peter, yet possessing valid orders. New York, Comet Press Books [1956] 302p. 21cm. Includes bibliography. [BX5178.M3] 56-9420
1. Anglican orders. 2. Ordination. I. Title.

EVERS, Joseph Calvin. 262'.18
The history of the Southern Illinois Conference, the Methodist Church. Nashville, Parthenon Press [1964] 267 p. illus., ports. 24 cm. "Essentially the same as [the author's] doctoral dissertation . . . Boston University." Bibliography: p. 255-258. [BX8382.S62E9] 64-55699
1. Methodist Church (United States) Conferences. Southern Illinois — Hist. I. Title.

JUDY, Marvin T 262'.18
A study of Methodism in the North Arkansas Conference, 1960. In cooperation with Dept. of Research and Survey, Division of National Missions of the Board of Missions of the Methodist Church. Philadelphia [1961] ix, 114p. illus., maps, tables. 28cm. [BX8382.N6J8] 61-65378
1. Methodist Church (United States) Conferences. North Arkansas. I. Title. II. Title: Methodism in the North Arkansas Conference, 1960.

LEIFFER, Murray Howard, 262'.18
1902-
What district superintendents say—about their office and the issues confronting them; a study of professional leadership in the United Methodist Church, by Murray H. Leiffer. Evanston, Ill., Garrett Theological Seminary [1972] 123, 12 p. 23 cm. [BX8382.2.Z5L4] 72-188486 2.50
1. United Methodist Church (United States)—Government. 2. District superintendents (Methodist) I. Title.

NAIL, Olin Webster, 1890- 262'.18
The first hundred years of the Southwest Texas Conference of the Methodist Church, 1858-1958 ... Prepared by Olin W. Nail at the request of the Annual Conference. San Antonio, Southwest Texas Conference, Methodist Church [1958] 246p. illus. 24cm. [BX8382.S635] 58-35743
1. Methodist Church (United States) Conferences. Southwest Texas—Hist. I. Title.

ROSE, Benjamin Lacy, 262'.18
1914-
Confirming your call in church, home, and

vocation, by Ben Lacy Rose. Richmond, John Knox Press [1967] 72 p. 21 cm. [BX9190.R6] 67-12594
1. Presbyterian Church—Government. 2. Christian life—Presbyterian authors. I. Title.

STOCKWELL, Eugene L. 262.19
Claimed by God for mission; the congregation seeks new forms. New York, World Outlook Pr. [1965] 159p. illus. 20cm. Bibl. [BR123.S79] 65-26749 1.00
1. Christianity—20th cent.—Addresses, essays, lectures. 2. Pastoral Theology—Addresses, essays, lectures. 3. Missions-Theory. I. Title. II. Title: Congregation.

AYRES, Francis O. 262.2
The ministry of the laity; a Biblical exposition. Philadelphia, Westminster [c.1962] 139p. 22cm. Bibl. 62-10295 2.50
1. Laity. I. Title.

AYRES, Francis O 262.2
The ministry of the laity; a Biblical exposition. Philadelphia, Westminster Press [1962] 139p. 22cm. Includes bibliography. [BV687.A9] 62-10295
1. Laity. I. Title.

BLOCHLINGER, Alex, 1924- 262.2
The modern parish community. [English translation by Geoffrey Stevens. Adaptation and abridgment by Hilda Graef] New York, P. J. Kennedy [1965] viii, 263 p. 23 cm. [BX1913.B553] 65-14809
1. Parishes. 2. Pastoral theology — Catholic Church. I. Title.

BLOCHLINGER, Alex, 1924- 262.2
The modern parish community. [Tr. from German by Geoffrey Stevens. Adaptation, abridgement by Hilda Graef] New York, Kenedy [c.1965] viii, 263p. 23cm. [BX1913.B553] 65-14809 4.95
1. Parishes. 2. Pastoral theology—Catholic Church. I. Title.

CLARK, Howard Gordon, D. D. 262.2
A handbook for vestrymen; a lay vocation in the service of the church. New York, Morehouse [c.1962] 72p. 19cm. Bibl. 62-19255 1.50 pap.,
1. Church officers. 2. Protestant Episcopal Church in the U. S. A.—Government. I. Title.

THE Commonweal. 262.2
The layman in the Church; edited by James O'Gara [New York, Herder and Herder [1962] 91 p. 22 cm. (Quaestiones disputatae, 6) [BX1920.C58] 62-19563
1. Laity — Catholic Church. I. Essays first published in the Commonweal. II. O'Gara, James, ed. III. Title.

COMMONWEAL (The) 262.2
The layman in the church; ed. by James O'Gara. [New York] Herder & Herder [1962] 91p. 22cm. (Quaestiones disputatae, 6) 62-19563 3.50; 1.75 pap.,
1. Laity—Catholic Church. I. O'Gara, James, ed.

CONGAR, Marie Joseph, 1904- 262.2
Lay people in the church; a study for a theology of the laity, by Yves M. J. Congar. Translated by Donald Attwater. Westminster, Md., Newman Press [1957] 447p. 22cm. Translation of Jalons pour une theologie du Laicat. [BX1920.C612] 56-10002
1. Laity. 2. Catholic Church. 3. Priesthood, Universal. 4. Catholic action. I. Title.

CONGAR, Marie Joseph 262.2
[Secular name: Georges Yves Congar]
Laity, church, and world; three addresses by Yves Congar. Tr. [from German] by Donald Attwater. Baltimore, Helicon Press [1961, c.1960] 87p. Bibl. 60-16436 2.50 bds.,
1. Laity. I. Title.

CONGAR, Yves Marie Joseph, 1904- 262.2
Laity, church, and world; three addresses, by Yves Congar. Translated by Donald Attwater. Baltimore, Helicon Press [1961, c1960] 87 p. 20 cm. Translation of Si vous etes mes temoins. Includes bibliography. [BX1920.C633] 60-16436
1. Laity. I. Title.

CONGAR, Yves Marie Joseph, 1904- 262.2
Lay people in the church; a study for a theology of the laity, by Yves M. J. Congar. Translated by Donald Attwater. Westminster, Md., Newman Press [1957] 447 p. 22 cm. Translation of Jalons pour une theologie du laicat. [BX1920.C612] 56-10002
1. Laity—Catholic Church. 2. Catholic Church. 3. Priesthood, Universal. 4. Catholic action. I. Title.

DE LA BEDOYERE, Michael, 1900- 262.2
The layman in the church. Chicago, H. Regnery Co., 1955. 111p. 22cm. [BX1920] 57-795
1. Laity. 2. Christian life—Catholic authors. I. Title.

ELFORD, Homer J. R. 262.2
A guide to church ushering. Nashville, Abingdon Press [c.1961] 63p. 61-1447 .50 pap.,
1. Church ushers. I. Title.

FOSTER, John, 1898- 262.2
Requiem for a parish; an inquiry into customary practices and procedures in the contemporary parish. Westminster, Md., Newman, [c.]1962. 155p. 21cm. 62-16214 3.00
1. Theology, Pastoral—Catholic Church. I. Title.

GIBBS, Mark. 262.2
God's frozen people; a book for and about Christian laymen, by Mark Gibbs and T. Ralph Morton. Philadelphia, Westminster Press [c1965] 192 p. 19 cm. Bibliography: p. 189-192. [BV 687.G5] 65-10952
1. Laity. I. Morton, Thomas Ralph, joint author. II. Title.

GIBBS, Mark 262.2
God's frozen people; a book for and about Christian laymen, by Mark Gibbs, T. Ralph Morton. Philadelphia, Westminster [c.1965] 192p. 19cm. Bibl. [BV687.G5] 65-10952 1.65
1. Laity. I. Morton, Thomas Ralph, joint author. II. Title.

GRIMES, Howard. 262.2
The rebirth of the laity. New York, Abingdon Press [1962] 176p. 23cm. [BV687.G7] 62-16810
1. Laity. I. Title.

HARKNESS, Georgia Elma, 1891- 262.2
The church and its laity. New York, Abingdon Press [1962] 208 p. 23 cm. Includes bibliography. [BV687.H3] 62-8106
1. Laity. I. Title.

HARRELL, Costen Jordan, 1885- 262.2
The local church in Methodism. Rev. New York, Abingdon Press [1961] 64p. illus. 19cm. [BX8340.H34 1961] 61-65421
1. Methodist Church—Government. I. Title.

KELLEY, Alden Drew, 1903- 262.2
The people of God; a study in the doctrine of the laity. Greenwich, Conn., Seabury [c.]1962. 128p. illus. 20cm. 62-18496 3.00
1. Laity. I. Title.

KRAEMER, Hendrik, 1888- 262.2
A theology of the laity. Philadelphia, Westminster Press [c1958] 191p. 20cm. [BV687.K7] 59-6251
1. Laity. I. Title.

LUFFBERRY, Henry Benner 262.2
Manual for vestrymen. Philadelphia. Muhlenberg Press [c.1960] x, 101p. 19cm. 60-13907 1.50 pap.,
1. Church officers. I. Title.

MARTY, Martin., 1928- 262.2
Death and birth of the parish [by] Martin E. Marty, ed., author, with Paul R. Biegner, Roy Blumhorst, Kenneth R. Young. St. Louis, Concordia [c.1964] vii, 163p. 21cm. Bibl. 64-23370 3.00
1. Pastoral theology—Lutheran Church. 2. Parishes. I. Title.

MILHOUSE, Paul William, 1910- 262.2
Laymen in the church. Anderson, Ind., Warner Press [1957] 80p. 19cm. [BV4525.M5] 57-20842
1. Laity. I. Title.

MOORE, Mark Reynolds, 1916- 262.2
The ministry of ushering. Kansas City, Mo., Beacon Hill Press [1957] 76p. 19cm. 'Text for first series unit 514a. 'Developing church ushers." [BV705.M63] 57-39875
1. Church ushers. I. Title.

NEILL, Stephen Charles, Bp., ed. 262.2
The layman in Christian history; a project of the Department on the Laity of the World Council of Churches, edited by Stephen Charles Neill and Hans-Ruedi Weber. Philadelphia, Westminster Press [1963] 408 p. 23 cm. Includes bibliographical references. [BV687.N4] 63-14640
1. Laity—History. I. Weber, Hans Ruedi, joint ed. II. World Council of Churches. Dept. on the Laity. III. Title.

NEWMAN, Jeremiah. 262.2
The Christian in society; a theological investigation. Baltimore, Helicon Press, 1962. 208p. 22cm. [BX1920.N43] 62-17433
1. Laity. 2. Sociology, Christian (Catholic) I. Title.

NEWMAN, John Henry, Cardinal, 262.2
The Christian in society; a theological investigation. Helicon [dist. New York, Taplinger, c.1962] 208p. 22cm. 62-17433 4.50 bds.,
1. Sociology, Christian (Catholic) I. Title.

NEWMAN, John Henry, Cardinal 1801-1890 262.2
On consulting the faithful in matters of doctrine. Ed., introd. by John Coulson. New York, Sheed & Ward [1962, c.1961] 118p. 62-9877 3.00 bds.,
1. Laity. 2. Dogma, Development of. I. Title.

NUESSE, Celestine Joseph, 1913- ed. 262.2
The sociology of the parish; an introductory symposium, edited by C. J. Nuesse and Thomas J. Harte. Milwaukee, Bruce Pub. Co. [1951] xii, 354 p. illus. 23 cm. Includes bibliographies. [BX1912.N77] 52-86
1. Parishes. 2. Theology, Pastoral—Catholic Church. 3. Church work. 4. Church and social problems—Catholic Church. I. Harte, Thomas Joseph, 1914- joint ed. II. Title.

PARROTT, Leslie, 1922- 262.2
How to usher, by Leslie [and Lora Lee] Parrott. Grand Rapids, Mich., Zondervan Pub. House [1954] 61p. 16cm. (Zondervan's how to do it series) [BV705.P3] 54-3805
1. Church ushers. I. Parrott, Lora Lee (Montgomery) 1923- joint author. II. Title.

PERRIN, Joseph Marie, 1905- 262.2
Forward the layman. Translated by Katherine Gordon. Westminster, Md., Newman Press [1956] 176p. 22cm. Translation of L'heure des laics. [BX1920.P443] 56-14159
1. Laity. 2. sCatholic action. I. Title.

PHILIPS, Gerard, 1899- 262.2
The role of the laity in the church. Translated by John R. Gilbert and James W. Moudry. Chicago, Fides Publishers, 1957. 175p. 22cm. [BX1920.P52] 57-59247
1. Laity. I. Title.

RAHNER, Hugo, 1900- ed. 262.2
The parish, from theology to practice. Translated by Robert Kress. Westminster, Md., Newman Press, 1958. 142p. 23cm. Includes bibliography. [BV700.R213] 58-13640
1. Parishes. 2. Pastoral theology—Catholic Church. I. Title.

RUTHERFORD, Mark. 262.2
The Christian layman and his church. St. Louis, Bethany Press [1958] 71p. 20cm. [BV687.R7] 58-12428
1. Laity. I. Title.

WEDGE, Florence 262.2
Lay sanctity in the parish. Pulaski, Wis., Franciscan Pubs. [1963, c.1962] 60p. 19cm. (Help yourself ser.) .25 pap.,
I. Title.

WENTZ, Frederick K. 262.2
The layman's role today. Garden City, N.Y., Doubleday [c.]1963. 229p. 22cm. Bibl. 63-16274 4.95
1. Christian life—Lutheran authors. 2. Laity. I. Title.

WENTZ, Frederick K. 262.2
The layman's role today [Nashville] Abingdon [1965, c.1963] 229p. 21cm. (Apex bk. V-6) Bibl. [BV4501.2.W42] 1.50 pap.,
1. Christian life—Lutheran authors. 2. Laity. I. Title.

BARRACLOUGH, Geoffrey, 1908- 262'.22
Papal provisions; aspects of church history, constitutional, legal and administrative in the later Middle Ages. Westport, Conn., Greenwood Press [1971] xvi, 187 p. 23 cm. Reprint of the 1935 ed. Bibliography: p. 178-187. [BX1955.B3 1971] 74-109707 ISBN 0-8371-4198-2
1. Catholic Church—Government. 2. Benefices, Ecclesiastical. 3. Papacy. 4. Church history—Middle Ages, 600-1500. I. Title.

CURRIER, Richard. 262'.22
The future parish. Huntington, Ind., Our Sunday Visitor [1971] 74 p. 21 cm. Bibliography: p. 71-74. [BX1913.C87] 79-151291 0.95
1. Parishes. I. Title.

FISHER, Wallace E. 262'.22
Preface to parish renewal [by] Wallace E. Fisher. Nashville, Abingdon Press [1968] 143 p. 20 cm. Bibliographical footnotes. [BV600.2.F5] 68-25358 1.75
1. Church renewal. I. Title.

KILIAN, Sabbas J. 1916- 262'.22
Theological models for the parish / Sabbas J. Kilian. New York : Alba House, c1977. xi, 192 p. ; 22 cm. Bibliography: p. [177]-192. [BX1746.K49 1977] 76-42986 ISBN 0-8189-0337-6 : 5.95
1. Parishes. 2. Church. I. Title.

LANDON, Donald D. 262'.22
For what purpose assembled; a study of the congregation and mission, by Donald D. Landon and Robert L. Smith. [Independence, Mo., Herald Pub. House, 1969] 188 p. illus. 18 cm. Bibliography: p. 187-188. [BX8675.L3] 72-13619 2.95
1. Reorganized Church of Jesus Christ of Latter-Day Saints—Doctrinal and controversial works. I. Smith, Robert L., joint author. II. Title.

LANDON, Donald D. 262'.22
For what purpose assembled; a study of the congregation and mission [by] Donald D. Landon & Robert L. Smith. New York, Family Library [1973, c.1969] 141 p. 19 cm. Bibliography: p. 140-141. [BX8675.L3] ISBN 0-515-03230-1 0.95 (pbk.)
1. Reorganized Church of Jesus Christ of Latter-Day Saints—Doctrinal and controversial works. I. Smith Robert L., joint author. II. Title.
L.C. card no. for the hardbound edition: 72-13619.

O'NEILL, David P. 262'.22
The sharing community; parish councils and their meaning, by David P. O'Neill. Dayton, Ohio, Pflaum Press, 1968. vii, 88 p. 21 cm. [BV652.9.O54] 68-55964 1.50
1. Parish councils. I. Title.

GAMBARI, Elio. 262'.24
Renewal in religious life; general principles, constitutions, formation. Translated by the Daughters of St. Paul. [Boston] St. Paul Editions [1967] 418 p. 22 cm. Bibliography: p. 413-418. [BX2435.G3413] 67-24028
1. Monastic and religious life. I. Title.

EDWARDS, Kathleen. 262/.3
The English secular cathedrals in the Middle Ages: a constitutional study with special reference to the fourteenth century. 2nd ed. Manchester, Manchester Univ. Pr.; New York, Barnes & Noble, 1967. xx, 412p. front., 4 plates (incl. facsims.), tables, 23 cm. Bibl. [BR750.E3 1967] 68-70122 10.00
1. Chapters, Cathedral, collegiate, etc.—England. 2. Cathedrals—England. 3. Gt. Brit.—Church history—Medieval period. I. Title.

*FREIN, George H. 262.3
Seven lesson plans on the constitution on the Church of Vatican Council II. Glen Rock, N.J., Paulist [c.1966] 64p. illus. 21cm. .75 pap.,
I. Title.

HESS, Hamilton. 262.3
The Canons of the Council of Sardica, A. D. 343; a landmark in the early development of Canon law. Oxford, Clarendon Press, 1958. viii, 170p. 22cm. (Oxford theological monographs, v. 1) Bibliography: p. 159-163. 58-1441
1. Sardica, Synod of, 343-344. 2. Bishops (Canon law) I. Title. II. Series.

OSTLING, Richard N. 262'.3
Secrecy in the church; a reporter's case for the Christian's right to know [by] Richard N. Ostling. [1st ed.] New York, Harper & Row [1974] 173 p. 21 cm. Bibliography: p. 169-171. [BV740.O86] 73-18701 ISBN 0-06-066395-2 6.95
1. Catholic Church—Government. 2. Freedom of information in the church. I. Title.

SYKES, Norman, 1897- 262.3
Old priest and new presbyter; [episcopacy and Presbyterianism since the Reformation with especial relation to the Churches of England and Scotland; being the Gunning lectures delivered in the University of Edinburgh 1953-54 and the Edward Cadbury lectures in the University of Birmingham, 1954-55] Cambridge [Eng.] University Press, 1956. 266p. 23cm. [BX5176.S9] 56-2998
1. Church of England—Bishops. 2. Episcopacy. 3. Presbyterianism. 4. Church of England— Relations. I. Title.

SYKES, Norman, 1897- 262.3
Old priest and new presbyter; [episcopacy and Presbyterianism since the Reformation with especial relation to the Churches of England and Scotland; being the Gunning lectures delivered in the University of Edinburgh 1953-54 and the Edward Cadbury lectures in the University of Birmingham, 1954-55] Cambridge [Eng.] University Press, 1956. 266 p. 23 cm. [BX5176.S9] 56-2998
1. Church of England — Bishops. 2.

Episcopacy. 3. Presbyterianism. 4. Church of England — Relations. I. Title.

WHITTEMORE, Lewis Bliss, Bp. 262.3
The care of all the churches; the background, work, and opportunity of the American episcopate. Greenwich, Conn., Seabury Press, 1955. 146p. 20cm. [BX5966.W5] 55-5456
1. Protestant Episcopal Church in the U. S. A.—Bishops. I. Title.

BAPTIST Youth World Conference. 6th, Beirut, 1963. 262.4
Jesus Christ in a changing world; official report. Edited by Cyril E. Bryant. Washington, Baptist World Alliance, Youth Dept. [1963] 151 p. illus., ports. 24 cm. [BX6207.A18] 64-3596
1. Baptists — Congresses. 2. Youth — Congresses. I. Bryant, Cyril E., ed. II. Title.

BEATTY, Frank M 262.4
The office of clerk of session. Richmond, John Knox Press [1956] 78p. 23cm. [BX9195.B4] 56-9342
1. Presbyterian Church—Government. I. Title. II. Title: Clerk of session.

BEATTY, Frank M 262.4
The office of clerk of session. [Rev. ed.] Richmond, John Knox Press [1963] 99 p. 21 cm. [BX9195.B4] 63-13185
1. Presbyterian Church — Government. I. Title. II. Title: Clerk of session

BEATTY, Frank M. 262.4
The office of clerk of session. [Rev. ed.] Richmond, Va., John Knox [c.1956, 1963] 99p. 21cm. 63-13185 1.50 pap.,
1. Presbyterian Church—Government. I. Title. II. Title: Clerk of session.

BOCKELMAN, Wilfred. 262.4
'It will be your duty ...' Columbus, Ohio, Wartburg Press [1956] 74p. illus. 18cm. Includes bibliography. [BV680.B6] 56-3214
1. Church officers. 2. Lutheran Church—Government. I. Title.

CLARK, Harold Glen, 1902- 262.4
Millions of meetings. Salt Lake City, Deseret Book Co. [1955] 118p. illus. 24cm. [BX8657.C55] 55-30108
1. Mormons and Mormonism—Government. I. Title.

DE JONG, Peter Ymen, 1915- 262'.4
Crisis in the reformed churches; essays in commemoration of the great Synod of Dort, 1618-1619. Peter Y. De Jong, editor. Grand Rapids, Mich., Reformed Fellowship, 1968. xi, 266 p. 23 cm. Contents.Contents.—The rise of the reformed churches in the Netherlands, by P. Y. De Jong.—The background of the Arminian controversy (1586-1618), by L. Praamsma.—Leading figures at the Synod of Dort, by S. Kistemaker.—The doctrinal deliverances of Dort, by F. H. Klooster.—The Synod and Bible translation, by M. H. Woudstra.—Preaching and the Synod of Dort, by P. Y. De Jong.—The significance of the canons for pastoral work, by E. H. Palmer.—Calvin, Dort, and Westminister-a comparative study, by J. Murray.—Recent reformed criticisms of the canons, by K. Runia.—The significance of Dort for today, by C. Van Til.—Appendices (p. 197-262):—A. Chronological table.—B. Biographical notes.—C. The remonstrance of 1610.—D. The counter remonstrance of 1611.—E. Political commissioners assigned by the States-General.—F. Delegates to the Synod of Dort.—G. Remonstrants cited to appear at Synod.—H. The opinions of the remonstrants.—I. The canons of Dort. Includes bibliographical references. [BX9478.D4] 76-2685
1. Dort, Synod of, 1618-1619—Addresses, essays, lectures. I. Dort, Synod of, 1618-1619. II. Title.

HARRISON, Paul Mansfield. 262.4
Authority and power in the free church tradition; a social case study of the American Baptist Convention. Princeton, N. J., Princeton University Press, 1959. 248p. 23cm. 'A major portion of this book was a dissertation presented for the degree of doctor of philosophy in Yale University.' Includes bibliography. [BX6207.A36H3] 59-11077
1. American Baptist Convention—Government. 2. Church polity. I. Title.

HEBBLETHWAITE, Peter. 262'.4
Inside the synod, Rome, 1967. New York, Paulist Press [1968] v, 168 p. 18 cm. (Deus books) [BX831 1967.H4] 68-21454
1. Catholic Church. Synodus Episcoporum, 1st, 1967. I. Title.

HEBBLETHWAITE, Peter. 262'.4
Understanding the Synod. Dublin, Sydney, Gill & Son, 1968. 178 p. 19 cm. (Logos books) Includes bibliographies. [BX831 1967.H42] 68-134835 13/6
1. Catholic Church. Synodus Episcoporum, 1st, 1967. I. Title.

KETCHERSIDE, W. Carl. 262.4
The royal priesthood; a plea for the restoration of the priesthood of all believers in the churches of God. St. Louis, Mission Messenger [1956] v, 193 p. 21 cm. [BT769.K44] 57-15264
1. Priesthood, Universal. I. Title.

MURCH, James DeForest, 1892- 262.4
The free church; a treatise on church polity with special relevance to doctrine and practice in Christian Churches and Churches of Christ. [Louisville, Ky.] Restoration Press [1966] vii, 140 p. 21 cm. Bibliography: p. 138-140. [BX7321.2.M8] 66-21559
1. Disciples of Christ — Doctrinal and controversial works. 2. Churches of Christ — Doctrinal and controversial works. I. Title.

NATIONAL Council of the Churches of Christ in the United States of America. 262.4
Growing together; a manual for councils of churches. [New York, c1955] 123p. 24cm. Includes bibliography. [BV626.N338] 55-11909
1. Local church councils. 2. Christian union—Hist. I. Title.

ORTHODOX Eastern Church. Synod of Jerusalem, 1672. 262'.4
The acts and decrees of the Synod of Jerusalem, sometimes called the Council of Bethlehem, holden under Dositheus, Patriarch of Jerusalem in 1672. Translated from the Greek with an appendix containing the confession published with the name of Cyril Lucar condemned by the Synod and with notes by J. N. W. B. Robertson. New York, AMS Press [1969] vii, 215 p. 22 cm. Reprint of the London ed., 1899. Translation of Aspis orthodoxias e apologia kai elenchos pros tous diasyrontas ten Anatoliken Ekklesian (romanized form) [BX220.A4513 1969] 78-81769
1. Orthodox Eastern Church—History—Sources. 2. Councils and synods—Jerusalem. I. Dositheos, Patriarch of Jerusalem, 1641-1707. II. Kyrillos Loukaris, Patriarch of Constantinople, 1572-1638. The Eastern Confession of the Christian faith. III. Robertson, James Nathaniel William Beauchamp, ed. IV. Title.

PRESBYTERIAN Church in the U. S. A. 262.4
Presbyterian law for the presbytery; a manual for ministers and ruling elders [by] Eugene Carson Blake [and] Edward Burns Shaw. Philadelphia, Published for the Office of the General Assembly by the General Division of Publication of the Board of Christian Education of the Presbyterian Church in the United States of America [1958] 157p. 23cm. 60-24677
1. Presbyterian Church in the U. S. A.—Government. I. Blake, Eugene Carson, 1906- II. Shaw, Edward Burns. III. Title.

PRESBYTERIAN Church in the U.S. General Assembly. 262.4
The book of church order of the Presbyterian Church in the United States. Rev. ed. Richmond, Printed for the General Assembly of the Presbyterian Church in the United States by the Board of Christian Education, 1963. 181 p. 21 cm. [BX8966.A45] 63-25949
1. Presbyterian Church in the U.S.—Government. I. Title.

PRESBYTERIAN Church in the U.S. General Assembly. 262.4
The book of church order of the Presbyterian Church in the United States. Rev. ed. Richmond, Va., Printed for the General Assembly of the Presbyterian Church in the United States by the Bd. of Christian Educ. [dist. Knox, c.] 1963. 181p. 21cm. 63-25949 1.00 pap.,
1. Presbyterian Church in the U. S.—Government. I. Title.

STONE, Robert Hamlin, 1896- 262'.4
A history of Orange Presbytery, 1770-1970. Greensboro, N.C. [Orange Presbytery] 1970. xxviii, 430 p. illus., facsims. (part col.), maps (part col.), ports. 25 cm. Bibliography: p. 403-405. [BX8968.O7S75] 78-19371 10.00
1. Presbyterian Church in the U.S. Presbyteries. Orange. I. Title.

2ND Vatican Council (The) 262.5
[Essays. New York, America, c.1962] 96p. illus. 19cm. 62-4976 .50 pap.,
1. Vatican Council, 2d.

ABBOTT, Walter M 262.5
Twelve council fathers. New York, Macmillan [1963] 176 p. 22 cm. [BX830 1962.A53] 63-19434
1. Vatican Council, 2d. I. Title.

ABBOTT, Walter M. 262.5
Twelve council fathers. New York, Macmillan [c.1963] 176p. 22cm. 63-19434 3.50 bds.,
1. Vatican Council, 2d. I. Title.

BARTH, Karl, 1886- 262'.5
Ad limina apostolorum; an appraisal of Vatican II. Translated by Keith R. Crim. Richmond, John Knox Press [1968] 79 p. 19 cm. [BX1765.2.B313] 68-13666
1. Catholic Church—Doctrinal and controversial works—Protestant authors. I. Title.

BASSET, Bernard. 262.5
Priest in the piazza; goal line tribute to a Council. With illus. by Penelope Harter. Fresno, Calif., Academy Guild Press [1963] vi, 111 p. illus. 23 cm. [BX830 1962.B3] 63-23224
1. Vatican Council, 2d. I. Title.

BASSET, Bernard 262.5
Priest in the piazza: goal line tribute to a Council. Illus. by Penelope Harter. Fresno, Calif., Academy Guild [c.1963] vi, 111p. 23cm. 63-23224 3.50
1. Vatican Council, 2d. I. Title.

BEA, Augustin, Cardinal, 1881- 262'.5
The ecumenical council and the laity: The position of Catholics regarding church unity, by Augustin Cardinal Bea. A joint pastoral letter from the Bishops of Holland, December 24, 1960. New York, Paulist Press [1961] 46 p. 19 cm. [BX830.B4] 62-611
1. Vatican Council, 2d. 2. Catholic Church — Relations. I. Catholic Church in the Netherlands. Bishops. A joint pastoral letter from the Bishops of Holland. II. Title. III. Title: The position of Catholics regarding church unity.

BEACH, Bert Beverly. 262.5
Vatican II, bridging the abyss. Washington, Review & Herald [1968] 352p. 22cm. Bibl. [BX830 1962.B424] 67-21871 6.95
1. Vatican Council. 2d, 1962-1965. 2. Catholic Church—Doctrinal and controversial works—Protestant authors. I. Title.

BROWN, Robert McAfee, 1920- 262.5
Observer in Rome; a Protestant report on the Vatican Council. [1st ed.] Garden City, N.Y., Doubleday, 1964. xi, 271 p. 22 cm. [BX830 1962.B7] 64-18495
1. Vatican Council, 2d, 1962-1965. I. Title. II. Title: A Protestant report on the Vatican Council.

BULL, George Anthony. 262.5
Vatican politics at the Second Vatican Council, 1962-5, by George Bull. London, Issued under the auspices of the Royal Institute of International Affairs by Oxford U.P., 1966. vii, 157 p. 18 1/2 cm. (Chatham House essays, 11) 10/6 (B66-6299) [BX830 1962.B8] 66-70757
1. Vatican Counsil. 2d. 1962-1965. I. Royal Institute of International affairs. II. Title.

BULL, George Anthony 262.5
Vatican politics at the Second Vatican Council, 1962-5. London, Issued under the auspices of the Royal Inst. of Intl. Affairs [New York] Oxford [c.]1966. vii, 157p. 19cm. (Chatham House essays, 11) [BX830.1962.B8] 66-70757 1.70 pap.,
1. Vatican Council. 2d, 1962-1965. I. Royal Institute of International affairs. II. Title.

BUTLER, Edward Cuthbert, 1858-1934. 262.5
The Vatican Council, 1869-1870, based on Bishop Ullthorne's letters. Edited by Christopher Butler. Westminster, Md., Newman Press, 1962. 510). 20cm. [BX830 1869.B822] 61-16567
1. Vatican Council, 1869-1870. I. Ullathorne, William Bernard, Abp., 1806-1889. II. Title.

BUTLER, Edward Cuthbert, 1858-1934 262.5
The Vatican Council, 1869-1870, based on Bishop Ullathorne's letter. Ed. by Christopher Butler. Westminster, Md., Newman [c.]1962. 510p. 20cm. 61-16567 5.95; 1.95 pap.,
1. Vatican Council, 1869-1870. I. Ullathorne, William Bernard, Abp., 1806-1889. II. Title.

CAIRD, George Bradford. 262'.5
Our dialogue with Rome; the second Vatican Council and after [by] George B. Caird. [Magnolia, Mass., Peter Smith, 1968, c. 1967] vii, 93p. 21cm. (Congregational lectures, 1966) Oxford paperbacks, no. 124. rebound [BX830 1962.C22] 3.75
1. Vatican Council. 2d, 1962-1965. 2. Christian union. I. Title. II. Series: The Congregational lectures, (London) 1966.

CAIRD, George Bradford. 262'.5
Our dialogue with Rome; the second Vatican Council and after [by] George B. Caird. London, New York, Oxford Univ. Pr., 1967. vii, 93p. 21cm. (Congregational lects., 1966) Oxford paperbacks, no. 124. [BX830 1962.C22] 68-89302 1.75 pap.,
1. Vatican Council. 2d. 1962-1965. 2. Christian union. I. Title. II. Series: The Congregational lectures, (London) 1966.

CAPORALE, Rock 262.5
Vatican II: last of the councils. Foreword by John J. Wright. D.D. Helicon [dist. New York, Taplinger, c.1964] 192p. 21cm. 64-23615 4.95
1. Vatican Council, 2d. I. Title.

CAPORALE, Rock. 262.5
Vatican II; last of the councils. Foreword by John J. Wright. Baltimore, Helicon [1964] 192 p. 21 cm. [BX830 1962.C3] 64-23615
1. Vatican Council, 2d. I. Title.

COMMENTARY on the documents of Vatican II. 262'.5
[Gen. ed.: Herbert Vorgrimler. New York] Herder & Herder [1967- v. 24cm. Tr. of Das zweite Vatikanische Konzil, Dokumente und Kommentare. Contents.v. 2. Decree on ecumenism, by Werner Becker, Johannes Feiner.--Decree on the bishop's pastoral office in the church, by Klaus Morsdorf.--Decree on the appropriate renewal of the religious life, by Friedrich Wolf.--Decree on priestly formation, by Josef Neuner. ibl. [BX830 1962. Z913] 67-22928 10.00
1. Vatican Council. 2d, 1962-1965. I. Vorgrimler, Herbert. ed.

COMMENTARY on the documents of Vatican II. 262'.5
[General editor: Herbert Vorgrimler New York] Herder and Herder [1967- v. 24 cm. Translation of Das zweite Vatikanische Konzil, Dokumente und Kommentare. Contents.Contents.—v. 1. Constitution on the sacred liturgy, by J. A. Jungmann.—Decree on the instruments of social communication, by K. Schmidthus.—Dogmatic constitution on the church.—Decree on Eastern Catholic churches, by J. M. Hoeck. Bibliographical footnotes. [BX830 1962.Z913] 67-22928
1. Vatican Council. 2d, 1962-1965. I. Vorgrimler, Herbert, ed.

CONWAY, John Donald, 1905- 262.5
Times of decision; story of the councils. Notre Dame, Ind., Fides [c.1962] 299p. illus., maps. 22cm. 62-13637 5.95 bds.,
1. Councils and synods, Ecumenical. I. Title.

CROSS Currents 262.5
Looking toward the council, an inquiry among Christians. Ed. by Joseph E. Cunneen. [New York] Herder & Herder [c.1962] 154p. 22cm. (Quaestiones disputatae, 5) 62-19562 3.75; 1.95 pap.,
1. Vatican Council, 2d, 1962- 2. Christian union. I. Cunneen, Joseph E., ed. II. Title.

CULLMANN, Oscar. 262'.5
Vatican Council II; the new direction. Essays selected and arr. by James D. Hester. [1st ed.] New York, Harper & Row [1968] 116 p. 22 cm. (Religious perspectives, v. 19) Translated by J. D. Hester and others. [BX830 1962.C8] 68-11981
1. Vatican Council. 2d, 1962-1965. I. Hester, James D., ed. II. Title. III. Series.

DANIEL-ROPS, Henry [Real name: Henry Jules Charles Petiot] 1901- 262.5
The Second Vatican Council; the story behind the Ecumenical Council of Pope John XXIII. Tr. [from French] by Alastair Guinan. New York, Hawthorn [c.1962] 160p. 21cm. Bibl. 62-9031 3.50
1. Vatican Council, 2d. I. Title.

DERETZ, Jacques, comp. 262'.5
Dictionary of the Council. Edited by J. Deretz and A. Nocent. Washington, Corpus Books [1968] 506 p. 24 cm. "Slightly abridged" translation of Synopse des textes conciliaires. [BX830 1962.A48D43] 69-14374 12.50
1. Vatican Council. 2d, 1962-1965—Indexes. I. Nocent, Adrien, joint comp. II. Vatican Council. 2d, 1962-1965. III. Title.

*DULLES, Avery, 1918- 262.5
Church membership as a Catholic and ecumenical problem. Milwaukee, Marquette University, 1974. iv, 113 p. 18 cm. (The Pere Marquette Theology Lecture, v. 6) [BV720.D78] 4.00 (pbk.)
1. Church. I. Title.
Available from Marquette University Theology Department 1303 W. Wisconsin Ave. Milwaukee, Wisc. 53233.

ECCLESIASTICAL History Society, London. 262'.5
Councils and assemblies; papers read at the Eighth Summer Meeting and the Ninth Winter

Meeting of the Ecclesiastical History Society, edited by G. J. Cuming and Derek Baker. Cambridge [Eng.] University Press, 1971. xiv, 359 p. 23 cm. (Studies in church history, 7) Includes bibliographical references. [BR141.S84 vol. 7] [BV710] 70-132284 ISBN 0-521-08038-X £5.00 ($16.00 U.S.)
1. Councils and synods—Addresses, essays, lectures. I. Cuming, G. J., ed. II. Baker, Derek, ed. III. Title. IV. Series.

FAIRWEATHER, Eugene Rathbone 262.5
The voice of the church, the ecumenical council, by Eugene R. Fairweather, Edward R. Hardy. Greenwich, Conn., Seabury [c.]1962. 127p. 62-8482 3.00 bds.,
1. Councils and synods, Ecumenical. 2. Church—Authority. I. Hardy, Edward Rochie, 1908- II. Title.

FALCONI, Carlo. 262.5
Pope John and the ecumenical council; a diary of the Second Vatican Council, September-December 1962. Translated from the Italian by Muriel Grindrod. [1st ed.] Cleveland, World Pub. Co. [1964] 373 p. plan. 23 cm. Based on the author's diary of the progress of the Council. [BX830 1962.F323] 64-12054
1. Joannes XXIII, Pope, 1881-1963. 2. Vatican Council, 2d, 1962-1965. I. Title.

FESQUET, Henri, 1916- 262'.5
The drama of Vatican II; the Ecumenical Council, June, 1962-December, 1965. Translated by Bernard Murchland. American introd. by Michael Novak. [1st. American ed.] New York, Random House [1967] xviii, 831 p. 25 cm. Translation of Le journal du Concile [Vatican II] [BX830.1962.F3913] 66-21475
1. Vatican Council, 2d, 1962-1965. I. Title.

FESQUET, Henri, 1916- 262'.5
Has Rome converted? New York, J. H. Heineman [1968] 180 p. 21 cm. Translation of Rome, s'est-elle convertie? Bibliographical footnotes. [BX1765.2.F413] 68-15210
1. Catholic Church—Addresses, essays, lectures. 2. Vatican Council. 2d, 1962-1965. I. Title.

FISHER, Desmond. 262'.5
The church in transition. Notre Dame, Ind., Fides Publishers [1967] 168 p. 23 cm. Bibliographical footnotes. [BX830 1962.F563] 67-24803
1. Vatican Council. 2d, 1962-1965. 2. Church renewal—Catholic Church. I. Title.

FISHER, Desmond. 262'.5
The Church in transition. Notre Dame, Ind., Fides Publishers [1967] 168 p. 23 cm. Bibliographical footnotes. [BX830.1962.F563] 67-24803
1. Vatican Council. 2d, 1962-1965. 2. Church renewal—Catholic Church. I. Title.

FROUDE, James Anthony, 1818-1894. 262'.5
Lectures on the Council of Trent, delivered at Oxford 1892-3. Port Washington, N.Y., Kennikat Press [1969] 339 p. 21 cm. Half title: The Council of Trent. "First published 1896; reissued." [BX830 1545.F72] 68-8244
1. Trent, Council of, 1545-1563. I. Title.

FULLAM, Raymond B. 262'.5
Exploring Vatican 2; Christian living today & tomorrow [by] Raymond B. Fullam. Staten Island, N.Y., Alba House [1969] xxiv, 360 p. illus. 22 cm. [BX830 1962.F8] 79-90777 5.95
1. Vatican Council, 2d, 1962-1965. 2. Christian life—Catholic authors. I. Title.

GALLI, Mario von 262.5
The Council and the future. Text by Mario von Galli, Photos. by Bernhard Moosbrugger. New York, McGraw [1966] 299p. illus., ports. 25cm. [BX830 1962.G319] 66-24564 10.95
1. Vatican Council. 2d, 1962-1965. I. Moosbrugger, Bernhard. II. Title.

GUITTON, Jean. 262.5
Guitton at the Council; a layman's appraisal and predictions. With pref. by Fulton J. Sheen. [Translated by Paul Joseph Oligny and Evan Roche] Chicago, Franciscan Herald Press [1964] 62 p. 21 cm. Translation of Regard sur le Concile. [BX8301962.G813] 64-24284
1. Vatican Council, 2d. I. Title.

GUITTON, Jean 262.5
Guitton at the Council; a layman's appraisal and predictions. Pref. by Fulton J. Sheen [Tr. from French by Paul Joseph Oligny, Evan Roche] Chicago, Franciscan Herald [c.1964] 62p. 21cm. 64-24284 1.50 pap.,
1. Vatican Council, 2d. I. Title.

HARING, Bernahrd, 1912- 262.5
The Johannine Council, witness to unity. Translated by Edwin G. Kaiser. [New York] Herder and Herder [1963] 155 p. 21 cm. Translation of Konzil im Zelchen der Einheit. Bibliographical footnotes. [BX830 1962.H313] 63-18151
1. Vatican Council, 2d. I. Title.

HARING, Bernhard, 1912- 262.5
The Johannine Council, witness to unity. Tr. [from German] by Edwin G. Kaiser. [New York] Herder & Herder [c.1963] 155p. 21cm. Bibl. 63-18151 3.50
1. Vatican Council, 2d. I. Title.

HARING, Bernhard, 1912- 262.5
Road to renewal; perspectives of Vatican II [by] Bernard Haring. Staten II Concilio comincia adesso. [BC8301962.H283] 66-27535 3.95
1. Vatican Council, 2d 1962-1965. I. Title.

HARING, Bernhard, 1912- 262.5
Road to Renewal; perspectives of Vatican II [by] Bernard Haring. Staten Island, N.Y., Alba House [1966] 221 p. 19 cm. "Original title: Il Concilio comincia adesso." [BX830 1962.H283] 66-27535
1. Vatican Council. 2d, 1962-1965. I. Title. I. Title.

HEBBLETHWAITE, Peter, ed. and tr. 262'.5
The Council fathers and atheism: the interventions at the fourth session of Vatican Council II. New York. Paulist [1967] 110p. 18cm. (Deus bks.) The definitive text: Pastoral constitution on the Church in the modern world (nn. 19-21) promulgated Dec. 7. 1965: p. 105-110. [BX830.1962.A45C767] 211 67-15724 .95 pap.,
1. Catholic Church and atheism. 2. Vatican Council. 2d. 1962-1965. Constitutio pastoralis de ecclesia in mundo huius temporis. I. Vatican Council 2d. 1962-1965. Pastoral constitution on the Church in the Modern world (nn. 19-21) II. Title.

HEFELE, Karl Joseph von, 1809-1893. 262'.5
A history of the councils of the church, from the original documents, by Charles Joseph Hefele. Edinburgh, T. & T. Clark, 1883-96. [New York, AMS Press, 1972] 5 v. 23 cm. Translation of Conciliengeschichte. Vols. 2-5 reprinted from the 1883-96 ed.; v. 1. from the 2d ed., 1894, published under title: A history of the Christian councils. Contents.Contents.—v. 1. To the close of the Council of Nicaea, A.D. 325.—v. 2. A.D. 326 to A.D. 429.—v. 3. A.D. 431 to A.D. 451.—v. 4. A.D. 451 to A.D. 680.—v. 5. A.D. 626 to the close of the Second Council of Nicaea, A.D. 787. [BX821.H434] 79-39294 ISBN 0-404-03260-5 100.00
1. Councils and synods. I. Title.

HENNESEY, James J 262.5
The First Council of the Vatican; the American experience. [New York] Herder and Herder [1963] 341 p. 22 cm. Bibliographical footnotes. [BX8301869.H4] 63-18150
1. Vatican Council, 1869-1870. I. Title.

HENNESEY, James J. 262.5
The First Council of the Vatican: the American experience. [New York] Herder and Herder [1963] 341 p. 22 cm. Bibliographical footnotes. [BX8301869.H4] 63-18150
1. Vatican Council, 1869-1870.

HENZE, Anton. 262.5
The Pope and the world; an illustrated history of the Ecumenical Councils. Translated from the German by Maurice Michael. New York, Viking Press, 1965. (A Studio book) 133 p. illus., map (on lining papers) ports. 24 cm. Translation of Das grosse Konzillenbuch. [BX825.H413] 65-18143
1. Councils and synods, Ecumenical. I. Title.

HENZE, Anton 262.5
The Pope and the world: an illustrated history of the Ecumenical Councils. Tr. from German by Maurice Michael. New York, Viking [c.1962, 1965] 133p. illus., map (on lining paps.) ports. 24cm. (Studio bk.) [BX825.H413] 65-18143 8.50
1. Councils and synods, Ecumenical. I. Title.

HESTON, Edward Louis, 1907- 262'.5
The press and Vatican II [by] Edward L. Heston Notre Dame, University of Notre Dame Press [1967] 134 p. illus., ports. 21 cm. [BX830.1962.H43] 66-14630
1. Vatican Council. 2d, 1962-1965. 2. Church and the press—Catholic Church. I. Title.

HOLLIS. CHRISTOPHER. 1902- 262'.5
The achievements of Vatican II. [1st ed.] New York, Hawthorn [1967] 119. [2] p. 21cm. (Twentieth cent. ency. of Catholicism; v. 1 Sect. 1: Knowledge and faith) Bibl. [BX830 1962.H58] 67-14865 3.95 bds.,
1. Vatican Council, 2d, 1962-1965. I. Title. II. Series: Twentieth century encyclopedia of Catholicism, v. 1

HORTON, Douglas, 1891- 262.5
Vatican diary; 1962, 1963 [2v.] Philadelphia, United Church Pr. [c.1964] [2v.] 206, 203p. 22cm. Contents.[1] 1962; a Protestant observes the first session of Vatican Council II.--[2] 1963; a Protestant observes the second session of Vatican Council II. 64-23949 4.50; 3.00 ea., pap., ea.,
1. Vatican Council, 2d. I. Title.

HORTON, Douglas, 1891- 262.5
Vatican diary, 1965 Philadelphia, United Church Pr. [1966] 202p. 22cm. [BX830 1962.H6] 64-23949 4.50; 3.00, pap.
1. Vatican Council, 2d. I. Title.

IMPACT of Vatican II 262.5
(The) [by] John Ford [others]. St. Louis, B. Herder. 1966. vi, 88p. 23cm. (Bellarmine Coll. studies). Lects. given before the Bellarmine Coll. Faculty Forum during 1965 and early 1966 Bibl. [BX8301962.I4] 66-19745 1.95 pap.,
1. Vatican Council. 2d. 1962-1965 I. Ford, John H. (Series: Bellarmine College, Louisville Ky. (Studies)

INTERNATIONAL Theological Conference, Notre Dame, Ind., 1966. 262.5
Vatican II; an interfaith appraisal, [Participants] Barnabas Ahern [and others] Edited by John H. Miller. Notre Dame, University of Notre Dame Press [1966] xii, 656 p. 27 cm. Held at the University of Notre Dame. Half title and running title: Theological issues of Vatican II. Includes bibliographical "Notes." [BX830.1962.I5] 66-24920
1. Vatican Council. 2d, 1962-65—Congresses. I. Miller, John H., 1925- ed. II. Notre Dame, Ind. University. III. Title. IV. Title: Theological issues of Vatican II.

JAEGER, Lorenz, Abp. 262.5
The ecumenical council, the church and Christendom. [Tr. by A. V. Littledale] New York, Kenedy [1962, c.1961] Bibl. 61-14294 3.95
1. Vatican Council, 2d. 2. Councils and synods, Ecumenical. 3. Church—History of doctrines. 4. Catholic Church—Relations. I. Title.

JAEGER, Lorenz, Cardinal, 1892- 262.5
The ecumenical council, the church and Christendom; [Translated by A. V. Littledale] New York, P. J. Kenedy [1962, c1961] 194 p. 21 cm. Includes bibliography. [BX830 1962.J313] 61-14294
1. Vatican Council, 2d. 2. Catholic Church—Relations. 3. Councils and synods, Ecumenical. 4. Church—History of doctrines—20th cent. I. Title.

KAISER, Robert Blair. 262.5
Pope, Council, and world; the story of Vatican II. New York, Macmillan [1963] 266 p. 21 cm. [BX830 1962.K3] 63-16122
1. Vatican Council, 2d, 1962-1965. 2. Joannes XXIII, Pope, 1881-1963. I. Title.

KENNY, Denis. 262/.5
The Catholic Church and freedom; the Vatican Council and some modern issues. [St. Lucia, Brisbane] Univ. of Queensland Pr. [1967] 236p. 22cm. Three essays orig. delivered as lects. during Oct.-Nov. 1964 for the Univ. of New England Dept. of Univ. Extension. Bibl. [BX830 1962.K4] 67-102623 6.00 bds.,
1. Vatican Council. 2d, 1962-1965. 2. Marriage—Catholic Church. 3. 3. Religious liberty. I. Title.
American distributor: Tri-Ocean, San Francisco.

KENNY, Denis. 262'.5
The Catholic Church and freedom; the Vatican Council and some modern issues. [St. Lucia, Brisbane] University of Queensland Press [1967] 236 p. 22 cm. $4.00 Aust. (Aus 67-770) Three essays originally delivered as lectures during October-November 1964 for the University of New England Dept. of University Extension. Bibliography: p. 233-236. [BX830 1962.K4] 67-102623
1. Vatican Council. 2d, 1962-1965. 2. Marriage — Catholic Church. 3. Religious liberty. I. Title.

KUNG, Hans, 1928- 262.5
The Council in action; theological reflections on the Second Vatican Council Translated by Cecily Hastings. New York, Sheed and Ward [1963] ix, 276 p. 22 cm. "Published in Great Britian under the title: The living church." Includes bibliographical references. [BX830 1962.K813] 63-17148
1. Vatican Council, 2d. I. Title.

KUNG, Hans, 1928- 262.5
The Council in action; theological reflections on the Second Vatican Council. Translated by Cecily Hastings. New York, Sheed and Ward [1963] ix, 276 p. 22 cm. "Published in Great Britian under the title: The living church." Includes bibliographical references. [BX8301962.K813] 63-17148
1. Vatican Council, 2d, 1962-1965. I. Title.

KUNG, Hans, 1928- 262.5
The Council, reform and reunion. Translated by Cecily Hastings. New York, Sheed and Ward [1962, c1961] 208 p. 22 cm. Translation of Konzil und Wiedervereinigung. [BX1784.K813 1962] 62-9101
1. Vatican Council. 2d, 1962-1965. 2. Catholic Church—Relations. 3. Christian union. I. Title.

KUNG, Hans, 1928- 262'.5
The living church; reflections on the Second Vatican Council Translated by Cecily Hastings and N. D. Smith. London, New York, Sheed and Ward [1963] x, 421 p. 18 cm. (Stagbooks) "Sequel to the Council and reunion." Bibliographical footnotes. [BX830 1963.K813] 63-25274
1. Vatican Council, 2d. I. Title.

LEE, Anthony D ed. 262.5
Vatican II; the theological dimension With introd. by Ferrer E. Smith. [Washington] Thomist Press, 1963. xvi, 621 p. 24 cm. "Originally published as a special issue of the Thomist, volume XXVII (complete) April, July, October, 1963." Bibliographical footnotes. [BX830 1962.L4] 63-21897
1. Vatican Council, 2d. 2. Theology — Addresses, essays, lectures. I. Title.

LEE, Anthony D., ed. 262.5
Vatican II; the theological dimension. Introd. by Ferrer E. Smith. [Washington, D.C.] Thomist [c.]1963. xvi, 621p. 24cm. Orig. pub. as a special issue of the Thomist, vol. XXVII (complete) April, July, Oct., 1963. Bibl. 63-21897 9.75
1. Vatican Council, 2d. 2. Theology—Addresses, essays, lectures. I. Title.

LINDBECK, George A ed. 262.5
Dialogue on the way; Protestants report from Rome on the Vatican Council, edited by George A. Lindbeck. Minneapolis, Augsburg Pub. House [1965] ix, 270 p. 22 cm. "Bibliographical appendix": p. 269-170. [BX8301962.L5] 65-12140
1. Vatican Council, 2d. I. Title.

LINDBECK, George A., ed. 262.5
Dialogue on the way; Protestants report from Rome on the Vatican Council. Minneapolis, Augsburg [c.1965] ix, 270p. 22cm. Bibl. [BX8301962.L5] 65-12140 4.75
1. Vatican Council, 2d. I. Title.

MCDONALD, William Joseph, ed. 262.5
The general council; special studies in doctrinal and historical background. Washington, D.C., Catholic Univ. [c.]1962. viii, 182p. 24cm. Bibl. 62-20329 3.50
1. Councils and synods, Ecumenical. 2. Vatican Council, 2d. I. Title.

MACEOIN, Gary, 1909- 262.5
What happened at Rome? The Council and its implications for the modern world. Introd. by John Cogley. Garden City, N.Y., Doubleday [1967, c.1966] 232p. 18cm. (Echo bk., E38) Bibl. [BX830. 1962. M3] .85 pap.,
1. Vatican Council, 2d, 1962-1965. I. Title.

MACEOIN, Gary, 1909- 262.5
What happened at Rome? The Council and its implications for the modern world. Introd. by John Cogley. [1st ed.] New York, Holt, Rinehart, and Winston [1966] xv, 191 p. 22 cm. Bibliographical footnotes. [BX830 1962.M3] 66-13497
1. Vatican Council. 2d, 1962-1965. I. Title.

MCNALLY, Robert E. 262'.5
The Council of Trent, the Spiritual exercises, and the Catholic reform, by Robert E. McNally. Philadelphia, Fortress Press [1970] vii, 24 p. (p. 22-24 advertisement) 19 cm. (Facet books. Historical series, 15) "First published in Church history, 34 (1965), 36-49." Bibliography: p. 21. [BX830 1545.M3 1970] 70-96863 1.00
1. Trent, Council of, 1545-1563. 2. Loyola, Ignacio de, Saint, 1491-1556. Exercitia spiritualis. I. Title.

MCNAMARA, Kevin, 1926- 262'.5
Vatican II: the constitution on the Church; a theological and pastoral commentary, edited by Kevin McNamara. Chicago, Franciscan Herald Press [1968] 437 p. 23 cm. "Constitutio dogmatica de ecclesia": p. [365]-366. Bibliography: p. [427]-432. Bibliographical footnotes. [BX830 1962.A45C878 1968] 68-29112 7.95
1. Vatican Council. 2d, 1962-1965. Constitutio dogmatica de ecclesia. I. Vatican Council. 2d, 1962-1965. Constitutio dogmatica de ecclesia. 1968. II. Title.

MARGULL, Hans Jochen, ed. 262.5
The councils of the church; history and

analysis [by] Georg Kretschmar [and others] Hans Jochen Margull, editor. Walter F. Bense, translator. Philadelphia, Fortress Press [1966] xvi, 528 p. 23 cm. Includes bibliographical references. [BV720.M313] 66-14793
1. Councils and synods, Ecumenical. I. Kretschmar, Georg, 1925- II. Title.

MATT, Leonard von 262.5
The Councils. Accompanying text by Burkhart Schneider. Chicago, Regnery [c.1961] 20p. plates, maps. 29cm. 61-16239 7.00 bds.,
1. Councils and synods. I. Schneider, Burkhart. II. Title.

NELSON, Claud D. 262.5
The Vatican Council and all Christians. Foreword by Roswell P. Barnes. Epilogue by Edward Duff. New York, Association [c.1962] 126p. 20cm. 62-16876 3.00 bds.,
1. Vatican Council, 2d. I. Title.

NOVAK, Michael. 262.5
The open Church, Vatican II, act II. New York, Macmillan [1964] xiii, 370 p. 22 cm. Includes bibliographical references. [BX830 1962.N63] 64-18270
1. Vatican Council, 2d. I. Title.

NOVAK, Michael 262.5
The open Church, Vatican II, act II. New York, Macmillan [c.1962-1964] xiii, 370p. 22cm. Bibl. 64-18270 6.50
1. Vatican Council, 2d. I. Title.

OUTLER, Albert Cook, 1908- 262'.5
Methodist observer atVatican II by Albert C. Outler westminster [Md.] Newman [1967] 189p. 21cm. [BX8301962.O9] 67-15717 4.50
1. Vatican Council. 2d, 1962-1965. I. Title.

PAGE, Roch. 262'.5
The diocesan pastoral council. Translated by Bernard A. Prince. Paramus, N.J., Newman Press [1970] vi, 170 p. 21 cm. Translation of Le conseil diocesain de pastorale (thesis—University of Ottawa) Includes bibliographical references. [BX838.P313] 76-125098 4.95
1. Diocesan pastoral councils. I. Title.

PAWLEY, Bernard C 262.5
An Anglican view of the VaticanCouncil. [1st American ed.] New York, Morehouse- Barlow Co. [1962] 116p. 20cm. [BX830 1962.P3] 62-20222
1. Vatican Council, 2d. I. Title.

PAWLEY, Bernard C. 262'5
The Second Vatican Council: studies by eight Anglican observers; ed. by Bernard C. Pawley. [Magnolia, Mass., Peter Smith, 1968, c.1967] (Oxford Univ. Pr. bk. rebound Bibl. [BX830 1962.P38] 4.00
1. Vatican Council. 2d, 1962-1965. I. Title.

PAWLEY, Bernard C. 262/.5
The Second Vatican Council: studies by eight Anglican observers; ed. by Bernard C. Pawley. London, New York [etc.] Oxford Univ. Pr., 1967. vi, 262p. 21cm. Bibl. [BX830 1962.P38] 67-112041 3.75 pap.,
1. Vatican Council. 2d, 1962-1965. I. Title.

PIUS II, Pope, 1405-1464. 262'.5
De gestis Concilii Basiliensis commentariorum: libri II; edited and translated [from the Latin] by Denys Hay and W. K. Smith. Oxford, Clarendon P., 1967. xxxviii, 268 p. 22 1/2 cm. (B 67-16737) (Oxford medieval texts) 55/- English and Latin. Bibliography: p. [xxxvii]-xxxviii. [BX830.1431.P5] 67-102198
1. Basel, Council of, 1431-1449. I. Hay, Denys, ed. and tr. II. Smith, W. K. ed. and tr. III. Title. IV. Series.

PIUS II, Pope, 1405-1464 262'.5
De gestis Concilii Basiliensis commentariorum: libri II; ed. & tr. [from Latin] by Denys Hay W. K. Smith. Oxford, Clarendon Pr., 1967. [1], xxxviii, 268p. 23cm. (Oxford medieval texts) English and Latin. Bibl. [BX830.1431.P5] 67-102198 8.80
1. Basel, Council of, 1431-1449. I. Hay, Denys, ed. and tr. II. Smith, W. K., ed. and tr. Iii. III. Title. IV. Series.
American distributor: Oxford Univ. Pr., New York.

QUA-BECK, Warren A., ed. 262'.5
Challenge . . . and response; a Protestant perspective of the Vatican Council ed. by Warren A. Quanbeck with Friedrich Wilhelm Kantzenbach, bBibl. [BX830 1962.Q3] 66-22566 5.00
1. Vatican Council, 2d, 1962-1965. I. Title.
Contents omitted.

QUANBECK, Warren A ed. 262'.5
Challenge .... and response; a Protestant perspective of the Vatican Council, edited by Warren A. Quanbeck in consultation with Frederich Wilhelm Kantzenbach and Vilmos Vajta. Minneapolis, Augsburg Pub. House [c1966] vii, 226 p. 22 cm. Includes bibliographical references. [BX8301962.Q3] 66-22566
1. Vatican Council. 2d, 1962-1965. I. Title.
- contents omitted

RAAB, Clement. 262.5
The twenty ecumenical councils of the Catholic Church. Westminster, Md., Newman Press, 1959 [c1937] 226p. 20cm. [BN825.R25 1959] 60-2894
1. Councils and synods. I. Title. II. Title: Ecumenical councils of the Catholic Church.

RATZINGER, Joseph. 262'.5
Theological highlights of Vatican 11 New York, Paulist Press [1966] vi, 185 p. 18 cm. (Deus books) [BX830.1962.R3] 66-30385
1. Vatican Council. 2d, 1962-1965. I. Title.

RYNNE, Xavier, pseud. 262.5
The fourth session; the debates and decrees of Vatican Council II, September 14 to December 8, 1965. New York, Farrar, Straus and Giroux [1966] xi, 368 p. 22 cm. [BX830 1962.R88] 66-153226
1. Vatican Council. 2d, 1962-1965. I. Vatican Council. 2d, 1962-1965. II. Title.

RYNNE, Xavier pseud pseud. 262.5
The fourth session; the debates and decrees of Vatican Council II, September 14 to December 8, 1965. New York, Farrar [c.1965, 1966] xi, 368p. 22cm. [BX830 1962.R88] 66-15322 5.50
1. Vatican Council. 2d, 1962-1965. I. Vatican Council, 2d, 1962-1965. II. Title.

RYNNE, Xavier, pseud. 262.5
Letters from Vatican City; Vatican Council II, first session: background and debates. Garden City, N.Y., Doubleday [1964, c.1963] 273p. 18cm. (Image bk., D182) .95 pap.,
1. Vatican Council, 2d. I. Title.

RYNNE, Xavier, pseud. 262.5
Letters from Vatican City, Vatican Council II, first session: background and debates. New York, Farrar, Straus [1963] 289 p. illus. 22 cm. [BX830 1962.R9] 63-13197
1. Vatican Council, 2d, 1962-1965. I. Title.

RYNNE, Xavier, pseud. 262.5
The second session; the debates and decrees of Vatican Council II, September 29 to December 4, 1963. New York, Farrar, Straus [1964] xxiii, 390 p. facsims. 22 cm. Facsimiles in Latin. [BX830 1962.R92] 64-17815
1. Vatican Council, 2d, 1962-1965. I. Title. II. Title: The debates and decrees of Vatican Council II.

RYNNE, Xavier pseud 262.5
The third session; the debates and decrees of Vatican Council II, September 14 to November 21, 1964. New York, Farrar [c.1964, 1965] xiii, 399p. facsims. 22cm. [BX830.1962.R93] 65-20915 4.95
1. Vatican Council, 2d. I. Title. II. Title: The debates and decrees of Vatican CouncilII.

RYNNE, Xavier, pseud. 262.5
The third session; the debates and decrees of Vatican Council II, September 14 to November 21, 1964. New York, Farrar, Straus & Giroux [1965] xiii, 399 p. facsims. 22 cm. [BX830 1962.R93] 65-20915
1. Vatican Council, 2d, 1962-1965. I. Title. II. Title: The debates and decrees of Vatican Council II.

RYNNE, Xavier, pseud. 262'.5
Vatican Council II. New York, Farrar, Straus and Giroux [1968] vii, 596 p. 25 cm. A revised version of the author's earlier books covering the 4 sessions of Vatican Council II. [BX830.1962.R94] 67-21527
1. Vatican Council. 2d, 1962-1965.

SCHACHERN, Harold. 262'.5
The meaning of the Second Vatican Council; a newspaperman's report. Notre Dame, Ind., Fides Publishers [1967, c1966] 95 p. 18 cm. (A Fides dome book, D-56) [BX830 1962.S26] 67-24809
1. Vatican Council. 2d, 1962-1965. I. Title.

SCHILLEBEECKX, Edward 262'.5
Cornelis Florentius Alfons, 1914-
The real achievement of Vatican II [by] Eduard Schillebeecky. Translated by H. J. J. Vaughan [New York] Herder and Herder [1967] viii, 99 p. 21 cm. Translation of Het tweede Vaticaans Concilie. Bibliographical footnotes. [BX830 1962.S273b] 67-25884
1. Vatican Council. 2d, 1962-1965. I. Title.

SCHLINK, Edmund, 1903- 262'.5
After the Council. Translated by Herbert J. A. Bouman. Philadelphia, Fortress Press [1968] x, 261 p. 22 cm. Translation of Nach dem Konzil. Bibliographical footnotes. [BX830 1962.S2813] 68-12327
1. Vatican Council. 2d, 1962-1965.

THE 2nd Vatican Council. 262.5
[New York, America Press, 1962] Essays. [BX8301962.S4] 62-4976
1. Vatican Council, 2d.

SPINA, Tony. 262.5
The Pope and the Council. New York, Barnes [1963] 160 p. illus. (part fold., part col.) group ports. (part col.) 31 cm. [BX830 1962.S6] 63-18254
1. Vatican Council, 2d. I. Title.

SPINA, Tony 262.5
The Pope and the Council. New York, A. S. Barnes [c.1963] 160p. illus. (pt. fold., pt. col.) group ports. (pt. col.) 31cm. 63-18254 12.50
1. Vatican Council, 2d. I. Title.

STUBER, Stanley Irving, 262'.5
1903-
Implementing Vatican II in your community; dialogue and action manual based on the sixteen documents of the Second Vatican Council, by Stanley I. Stuber and Claud D Nelson Foword by Walter M. Abbot New York, Guild Press [1967] 239 p. 19 cm. (An Angelus book) Bibliography: p. [230]-232. [BX830.1962.S7] 67-10935
1. Vatican Council. 2d, 1962-1965. I. Nelson, Claud D., joint author. II. Title.

TAVARD, Georges Henri. 262'.5
The Pilgrim Church [by] George H. Tavard. London, Burns & Oates: [New York] Herder & Herder, 1967. 176p. 21cm. Bibl. [BX830 1962.T322] 68-96674 4.95
1. Vatican Council. 2d, 1962-1965. 2. Church. I. Title.

TAVARD, Georges Henri, 262'.5
1922-
The church tomorrow [by] George H. Tavard. [New York] Herder and Herder [1965] 190 p. 21 cm. [BX830 1962.T3] 65-13479
1. Vatican Council, 2d. 2. Theology—20th cent. I. Title.

TAVARD, Georges Henri, 262'.5
1922-
The pilgrim church [by] George H. Tavard. [New York] Herder and Herder [1967] 176 p. 21 cm. [BX830 1962.T32] 67-25886
1. Vatican Council, 2d, 1962-1965. 2. Church. I. Title.

THIELEN, Thoralf Theodore, 262 5
1921-
What is an ecumenical council? A Catholic view. Westminster, Md., Newman Press [c.] 1960. 185p. and bibl. notes. Bibl. p.155-168 60-10732 2.95
1. Councils and synods, Ecumenical. I. Title.

TRACY, Robert E. Bp. 1909- 262.5
American bishop at the Vatican Council; recollections and projections, by Robert E. Tracy. New York, McGraw [1966] viii, 242p. 22cm. [BX8301962.T7] 66-26583 6.50
1. Vatican Council. 2d, 1962-1965. I. Title.

VATICAN Council. 2d,1962- 262'.5
1965.
Declaration on religious liberty (De libertate religiosa). Translation by Thomas Atthill. (London, Catholic Truth Society, 1966. 19 p. 18 1/2 cm. 1/- (B66-10270) Bibliographical footnotes. [BX830 1962.A45D413] 66-76037
1. Religious liberty. I. Title. II. Title: De libertate religiosa.

VATICAN Council. 2d,1962- 262.5
1965.
Preparatory reports: Second Vatican Council. Translated by Aram Berard. Philadelphia, Westminster Press [1965] 225 p. 21 cm. These reports, prepared by the preconciliar commissions and issued in l'Osservatore romano, are here translated from the French version in la Documentation catholique. [BX830 1962.A3B4] 65-19280
I. Berard, Aram, tr. II. Title.

VATICAN Council. 2d,1962- 262.5
1965.
The teachings of the Second Vatican Council; complete texts of the constitutions, decrees, and declarations. Introd. by Gregory Baum. Westminster, Md., Newman Press, 1966. xi, 676 p. 23 cm. Includes bibliographical references. [BX830 1962.A3N4] 66-19960
I. Title.

VATICAN Council. 2d,1962- 262.5
1965.
The Vatican Council and Christian unity; a commentary on the Decree on ecumenism of the Second Vatican Council, together with a translation of the text [by] Bernard Leeming. [1st ed.] New York, Harper & Row [1966] xiv, 333 p. 22 cm. Bibliographical footnotes. [BX830 1962.A45O43] 66-15863
1. Vatican Council. 2d, 1962-1965. De Oecumenismo. I. Leeming, Bernard, ed. and tr. II. Title.

VATICAN council, 2d. 262.5
Preparatory reports: Second Vatican Council. Tr. [from French] by Aram Berard. Philadelphia, Westminster [c.1965] 225p. 21cm. These reports, prepared by the preconciliar commns. and issued in l'Osservatore romano, are here tr. from the French version in la Documentation catholique. [BX8301962.A3B4] 65-19280 5.00
I. Berard, Aram, tr. II. Title.

VATICAN Council, 2d, 1962- 262/.5
1965 1962-1965
American participation in the second Vatican Council. Ed. by Vincent A. Yzermans. New York, Sheed [1967] xvi, 684p. 24cm. Contains the actual texts of the 118 addresses made by the United States' bishops in the Council. Bibl. [BX830 1962.A514] 67-13766 16.50
1. Vatican Council. 2d, 1962-1965. I. Yzermans, Vincent Arthur, 1925- ed. II. Title.

VATICAN Council. 2d, 1962- 262.5
1965.
The documents of Vatican II. Introductions and commentaries by Catholic bishops and experts. Responses by Protestant and Orthodox scholars. Walter M. Abbot, general editor. Joseph Gallagher, translation editor. New York, Guild Press [1966] xxi, 794 p. 19 cm. (An Angelus book, 31185) [BX830 1962.A3G3] 66-20201
I. Abbott, Walter M., ed. II. Title.

VATICAN Council. 2d. 1962- 262.5
1965
The teachings of the Second Vatican Council; complete texts of the constitutions, decree, and declarations. Introd. by Gregory Baum. Westminster, Md., Newman [c.]1966. xi, 676p. 23cm. Bibl. [BX830 1962.A3N4] 66-19960 5.75
I. Title.

VATICAN Council. 2d, 1962- 262.5
1965.
Third session Council speeches of Vatican II. Edited by William K. Leahy and Anthony T. Massimini. Foreword by Lawrence Cardinal Shehan Glen Rock, N.J., Paulist Press [1966] xviii, 334 p. 19 cm. (Deus books) [BX830 1962.A3L4] 66-31290
I. Leahy, William K., ed. II. Massimini, Anthony T., ed. III. Title.

VATICAN Council, 2d, 1962- 262.5
1965
The Vatican Council and Christian unity; a commentary on the Decree on ecumenism of the Second Vatican Council, with a tr. of the text [by] Bernard Leeming. New York, Harper [c.1966] xiv, 333p. 22cm. Bibl. [BX8301962.A45O43] 66-15863 7.95
1. Vatican Council, 2d, 1962-1965. De Oecumenismo. I. Leeming, Bernard, ed. and tr. II. Title.

VATICAN Council II, 262.5
from John XXIII to Paul VI [Rev. ed. New York] America Pr. [c.1963] 96p. 19cm. Cover title. Essays. First pub. in 1962 under title: The 2nd Vatican Council. Bibl. 64-4928 .50 pap.,
1. Vatican Council, 2d.

VATICAN Council 2d, 1962- 262'.5
1965
The sixteen documents of Vatican II and the instruction on the liturgy, with commentaries by the council fathers. [Boston] St. Paul Eds. [1967] 760p. 18cm. (Magister bks.) [BX830 1962. A3N25] 66-19616 1.25 pap.,
I. Title.

VATICAN Council II, from 262.5
John XXIII to Paul VI. [Rev. ed.] New York] America Press [c1963] 96 p. 19 cm. Cover title. Essays. First published in 1962 under title: The 2d Vatican Council. Bibliography: p. 96. [BX830 1962.S42] 64-4928
1. Vatican Council, 2d.

WATKIN, Edward Ingram, 262.5
1888-
The church in council. New York, Sheed & Ward [1961, c.1960] 227p. Bibl. 60-12879 3.95
1. Councils and synods, Ecumenical. I. Title.

WENGER, Antoine. 262'.5
Vatican II. Translated by Robert J. Olsen. Westminster, Md., Newman Press, 1966- v. 24 cm. Contents.Contents.—v. 1. The first session. Includes bibliographical references. [BX830.1962.W413] 66-16573
1. Vatican Council, 2d. I Title.

WILTBEN, Ralph M., 1921- 262'.5
The Rhine flows into the Tiber; the unknown

Council, by Ralph M. Wiltgen. [1st ed.] New York City, Hawthorn [1967] 304p. 24cm. [BX830 1962.W5] 67-17224 6.95
1. Vatican Council. 2d, 1962-1965. I. Title.

WILTGEN, Ralph M., 1921- 262'.5
The Rhine flows into the Tiber; the unknown Council, by Ralph M. Wiltgen. [1st ed.] New York City, Hawthorn Books [1967] 304 p. 24 mc. [BX830 1962.W5] 67-17224
1. Vatican Council. 2d 1962-1965. I. Title.

WOLLEH, Lothar. 262'.5
The Council; the Second Vatican Council [by] Lothar Wolleh with the collaboration of Emil Schmitz. Introd. by Francis Cardinal Spellman. [English translation by Angus Malcolm] New York, Viking Press [1966] 120 p. col. illus., ports. (part col.) 44 cm. (A Studio book) [BX830 1962.W5913] 66-16072
1. Vatican Council. 2d, 1962-1965. I. Schmitz, Emil. II. Title.

YZERMANS, Vincent Arthur, 1925- 262.5
A new Pentecost; Vatican Council II: session 1. Foreword by Gustave Weigel; introd. by Hans Kung. Westminster, Md., Newman Press, 1963. xx, 376 p. illus., ports. 23 cm. "A good portion of this journal ... originally appeared as weekly reports in five Catholic publications." Includes texts of many of the most important documents of the first session. [BX830 1962.Y9] 63-23099
1. Vatican Council, 2d. I. Vatican Council, 2d. II. Title.

YZERMANS, Vincent Arthur, 1925- 262.5
A new Pentecost; Vatican Council II: session 1. Foreword by Gustave Weigel; introd. by Hans Kung. Westminster, Md., Newman [c.] 1963 xx, 376p. illus., ports. 23cm. 63-23099 6.50
1. Vatican Council, 2d. I. Vatican Council, 2d. II. Title.

TIERNEY, Brian. 262'.5'01
Foundations of the conciliar theory; the contribution of the medieval canonists from Gratian to the Great Schism. London, Cambridge U.P., 1968. x, 280 p. 22 cm. (Cambridge University Press. Library editions) Bibliography: p. 264-274. [BX821.T5 1968] 78-376088 9.50
1. Conciliar theory. I. Title.

FRANCK, Frederick, 1909- 262.50904
Outsider in the Vatican. New York, Macmillan [1965] 253 p. illus., ports. 24 cm. Erratum slip inserted. [BX830 1962.F6] 65-22617
1. Vatican Council, 2d. I. Title.

FRANCK, Frederick, 1909- 262.50904
Outsider in the Vatican. New York, Macmillan [c.1965] 253p. illus., ports. 24cm. [BX830. 1962.F7] 65-22617 7.50
1. Vatican Council, 2d. I. Title.

CHEMNITZ, Martin, 1522-1586. 262'.5'2
Examination of the Council of Trent. [St. Louis, Mo.] Concordia Pub. House [1971- v. 24 cm. Vol. 1 translated by Fred Kramer. [BX830 1545.C413] 79-143693 ISBN 0-570-03213-X
1. Trent, Council of, 1545-1563. 2. Catholic Church—Doctrinal and controversial works—Protestant authors. 3. Lutheran Church—Doctrinal and controversial works. I. Title.

CZECH Catholics at the 262'.5'2
41st International Eucharistic Congress held August 1-8, 1976 in Philadelphia, USA / Ludvik Nemec, editor; Oldrich Holubar, design; John J. Sukop, photography [s.l. : s.n.], c1977. 105 p. : ill. ; 28 cm. [BX2215.A116 1977z] 76-52885
1. International Eucharistic Congress, 41st, Philadelphia, 1976—Addresses, essays, lectures. 2. Catholics, Czech—Addresses, essays, lectures. I. Nemec, Ludvik. II. International Eucharistic Congress, 41st, Philadelphia, 1976.

DAVIES, Michael. 262'.5'2
Pope John's Council / by Michael Davies. New Rochelle, N.Y. : Arlington House, c1977. xvi, 336 p. ; 21 cm. (His Liturgical revolution ; pt. 2) Includes index. Bibliography: p. [325]-328. [BX830 1962.D35 1977] 77-1623 ISBN 0-87000-396-8 : 9.95
1. Vatican Council. 2d, 1962-1965. I. Title. II. Series.

DOLLINGER, Johann Joseph Ignaz von, 1799-1890. 262.5'2
Letters from Rome on the Council, by Quirinus. New York, Da Capo Press, 1973. 2 v. 21 cm. (Europe, 1815-1945) Reprint of the 1870 ed. Translation of Romische Briefe vom Concil. [BX830 1869.D63] 78-127193 ISBN 0-306-70040-9 29.50 (Lib. ed.)
1. Vatican Council, 1869-1870. 2. Popes—Infallibility. I. Title. II. Series.

FROUDE, James Anthony, 1818-1894. 262'.5'2
Lectures on the Council of Trent, delivered at Oxford 1892-3. New York, B. Franklin [1972] p. Half title: The Council of Trent. Reprint of the 1896 ed. [BX830 1545.F73] 72-76330 ISBN 0-8337-4121-7 15.00
1. Trent, Council of, 1545-1563. I. Title.

PAWLEY, Bernard C. 262'.5'2
An Anglican view of the Vatican Council, by Bernard C. Pawley. Westport, Conn., Greenwood Press [1973, c1962] vi, 116 p. 20 cm. Includes bibliographical references. [BX830 1962.P32] 72-9368 ISBN 0-8371-6576-8
1. Vatican Council, 2d, 1962-1965. 2. Christian union. I. Title.

TIERNEY, Brian. 262'.5'2
Ockham, the conciliar theory, and the Canonists. Philadelphia, Fortress Press [1971] xxi, 42 p. 20 cm. (Facet books. Historical series, 19 (Medieval)) Includes bibliographical references. [BV720.T53] 74-157547 ISBN 0-8006-3064-5 1.00
1. Ockham, William, d. ca. 1349. 2. Conciliar theory—History of doctrines. I. Title.

UNITY, heresy, and 262'.5'2
reform, 1378-1460 : the conciliar response to the great schism / C. M. D. Crowder. New York : St. Martin's Press, 1977. 212 p. ; 25 cm. (Documents of medieval history ; 3) Includes index. Bibliography: p. 190-205. [BX825.U54 1977] 76-56693 ISBN 0-312-83318-0 : 19.95
1. Councils and synods, Ecumenical—History—Sources. I. Crowder, C. M. D. II. Series.

VATICAN Council. 2d, 1962-1965. 262'.5'2
Documents of Vatican II / Austin P. Flannery, editor Grand Rapids, Mich. : Eerdmans, 1975. xxiv, 1062 p. ; 18 cm. Includes bibliographical references and indexes. [BX830 1962.A3F55] 75-18840 ISBN 0-8028-1623-1 : 2.95
1. Catholic Church—Congresses. I. Flannery, Austin. II. Title.

SIVRIC, Ivo. 262'.5'20924 B
Bishop J. G. Strossmayer; new light on Vatican I. Chicago, Franciscan Herald Press [1974, i.e.1975] p. [BX4705.S845S56] 73-22014 ISBN 0-8199-0491-0 8.95
1. Strossmayer, Josip Juraj, Bp., 1815-1905. 2. Vatican Council, 1869-1870.

LUTHERAN Church in America. Nebraska Synod. 262'.5'41782
Minutes of the centennial convention of the Nebraska Synod, Lutheran Church in America (first organization, Aug. 4, 1870) held at First Lutheran Church, Lincoln, Nebraska, May 18, 19, 20, 21, 1970. [Omaha? 1970] 207, 29 p. 23 cm. Cover title. [BX8061.N2A45] 78-296510
I. Lincoln, Neb. First Lutheran Church.

CHURCH of Scotland. 262'.55'2411
A guide to the General Assembly of the Church of Scotland / [by] Andrew Herron. Edinburgh : St Andrew Press, 1976. [1], v, 34 p. ; 21 cm. [BX9078.C48 1976] 76-374001 ISBN 0-7152-0332-0 : £0.40
1. Church of Scotland. General Assembly. I. Herron, Andrew. II. Title.

BALTHASAR, Hans Urs von, 1905- 262.7
Church and world. Tr. by A. V. Littledale with Alexamder Dru. [New York] Herder & Herder [1967] 176p. 22cm. Translation of Sponsa verbi. [BV600.2.B313] 67-14141 4.95
1. Church. I. Title.

BARCLAY, William lecturer in the University of Glasgow 262.7
Fishers of men. Philadelphia, Westminster Press [1966] 113 p. 20 cm. [BV3790.B323] 66-22246
1. Evangelistic work. I. Title.

BARCLAY, william, lecturer in the University of Glasgow 262.7
Fishers of men. Philadelphia, Westminster [c.1966] 113p. 20cm. [BV3790.B323] 66-22246 2.75
1. Evangelistic work. I. Title.

COLE, Robert Alan 262.7
The body of Christ; a New Testament image of the Church. Philadelphia, Westminster [1965, c.1964] 90p. 19cm. (Christian founds.) [BV600.5.C6] 65-18923 1.25 pap.,
1. Jesus Christ—Mystical body. I. Title.

DEDEN, D. 262.7
The Bible on the church. Tr. by Jos. A. Roessen. [Rev.] De Pere, Wis., St. Norbert Abbey Pr. [c.] 1966. 118, [1]p. 17cm. Bibl. [BS2545.C5D413] 66-22815 .95 pap.,
1. Church—Biblical teaching. I. Title.

DERRICK, Christopher, 1921- 262.7
Trimming the Ark; Catholic attitudes and the cult of change. New York, P. J. Kenedy [1967] vi, 154 p. 22 cm. [BX1746.D4] 67-26803
1. Church renewal—Catholic Church. I. Title.

DULLES, Avery Robert, 1918- 262'.7
Models of the church [by] Avery Dulles. [1st ed.] Garden City, N.Y., Doubleday, 1974. 216 p. 22 cm. Includes bibliographical references. [BV600.2.D78] 73-82245 ISBN 0-385-08069-7 5.95
1. Church. I. Title.

DULLES, Avery Robert, 1918- 262.7
The survival of dogma [by] Avery Dulles. [1st ed.] Garden City, N.Y., Doubleday, 1971. 240 p. 20 cm. Includes bibliographical references. [BT771.2.D77] 76-139016 5.95
1. Catholic Church—Teaching office. 2. Faith. 3. Dogma. I. Title.

DULLES, Avery Robert, 1918- 262.7
The survival of dogma. Garden City, N.Y., Doubleday [1973 c.1971] 238 p. 18 cm. (Image Book, D317) Includes bibliographical references. [BT771.2.D77] ISBN 0-385-08957-0 pap., 1.45
1. Faith. 2. Catholic Church—Teaching office. 3. Dogma. I. Title.

FLANAGAN, Donal, 1929- ed. 262.7
The evolving church. Staten Island, N. Y., Alba House [c.1966,i.e.1967] xvi, 180p. 23cm. Bibl. [BX1746.F55] 67-2109 4.95
1. Church renewal—Catholic Church. I. Title.

FLANAGAN, Donal, 1929- ed. 262.7
The evolving church. Staten Island, N.Y., Alba House [c1966] xvi, 180 p. 23 cm. Bibliographical footnotes. [BX1746.F55] 67-2109
1. Church renewal — Catholic Church. I. Title.

GUARDINI, Romano, 1885- 262.7
The church of the Lord; on the nature and mission of the church. Tr. by Stella Lange. Chicago, Regnery [1967,c.1966] 114p. 21cm. Translation of Die Kirche des Herrn. [BX1796.G813] 67-13492 3.95
1. Church. I. Title.

HAMER, Jerome 262.7
The church is a communion [Eng. tr. by Ronald Matthews] New York, Sheed [1965, c.1964] 240p. 23cm. Bibl. [BX1746.H33] 64-20436 5.00
1. Church—Unity. 2. Jesus Christ—Mystical body. I. Title.

KENNEDY, Eugene C. 262.7
Fashion me a people; man, woman, and the church, by Eugene C. Kennedy. New York, Sheed and Ward [1967] xiii, 176 p. 22 cm. [BX1746.K4] 67-21914
1. Church renewal—Catholic Church. 2. Spiritual life—Catholic authors. 3. Monastic and religious life. I. Title.

KENNEDY, Eugene C. 262.7
The people are the church [by] Eugene C. Kennedy. [1st ed.] New York, Doubleday, 1969. 216 p. 22 cm. [BX1746.K42] 75-86889 4.95
1. Church renewal—Catholic Church. I. Title.

KRUM, Nathaniel. 262'.7
The church triumphant. Washington, Review and Herald Pub. Assn. [1972] 30 p. 14 cm. [BV600.2.K75] 74-190579
1. Church. I. Title.

MCBRIEN, Richard P. 262.7
Do we need the church? [By] Richard P. McBrien. [1st U.S. ed.] New York, Harper & Row [1969] 255 p. 21 cm. Bibliographical references included in "Notes" (p. [231]-248) [BV598.M3 1969] 69-10476 6.50
1. Church—History of doctrines. 2. Mission of the church. I. Title.

MARITAIN, Jacques, 1882- 262.7
Christianity and democracy. [Translated from the French by Doris C. Anson] Freeport, N.Y., Books for Libraries Press [1972, c1944] p. (Essay index reprint series) Translation of Christianisme et democratie. [BR115.P7M3362 1972] 72-6765 ISBN 0-8369-7243-0
1. Christianity and democracy. I. Title.

PATTERSON, Bob E., comp. 262.7
The stirring giant; renewal forces at work in the modern church. Edited by Bob E. Patterson. Waco, Tex., Word Books [1971] 312 p. 25 cm. Bibliography: p. 308-312. [BV600.2.P38] 75-140840 7.95
1. Church renewal. I. Title.

PERSPECTIVES of a political 262.7
ecclesiology. Edited by Johannes B. Metz. [New York] Herder and Herder [1971] 155 p. 23 cm. (Concilium: religion in the seventies. Church and world, v. 66) On cover: The New concilium: religion in the seventies. Includes bibliographical references. [BV603.P445] 79-150306 2.95
1. Church—Addresses, essays, lectures. I. Metz, Johannes Baptist, 1928- ed. II. Series: Concilium (New York) v. 66

POWELL, John Joseph, 1925- 262.7
The mystery of the church, by John Powell. Milwaukee, Bruce Pub. Co. [1967] xvi, 226 p. 23 cm. (Contemporary college theology series) Bibliography: p. 217-222. [BX1746.P6] 67-28214
1. Church. I. Title.

POWELL, John Joseph, 1925- 262.7
The mystery of the church, by John Powell. Milwaukee, Bruce Pub. Co. [1967] xvi, 226 p. 23 cm. (Contemporary college theology series) Bibliography: p. 217-222. [BX1746.P6] 67-28214
1. Church. I. Title.

RAYMOND, Father, 1903- 262.7
Relax and rejoice, for the hand on the tiller is firm, by Father M. Raymond. [San Bernardino, Calif., Culligan Book Co., 1968] xiv, 255 p. illus., port. 22 cm. [BX1390.R37] 73-4326 3.50
1. Church renewal—Catholic Church—Addresses, essays, lectures. I. Title.

RENDTORFF, Trutz. 262.7
Church and theology; the systematic function of the church concept in modern theology. Translated by Reginald H. Fuller. Philadelphia, Westminster Press [1971] 251 p. 24 cm. A revised version of this work was submitted as Habilitationsschrift, Munster/Westf., in 1961. Translation of Kirche und Theologie. Bibliography: p. [243]-251. [BV598.R413] 79-150381 ISBN 0-664-20908-4 10.00
1. Church—History of doctrines—19th century. 2. Church—History of doctrines—20th century. I. Title.

SAUCY, Robert L. 262'.7
The church in God's program, by Robert L. Saucy. Chicago, Moody Press [1972] 254 p. 23 cm. Bibliography: p. 235-245. [BV600.2.S27] 70-175496 ISBN 0-8024-1547-4
1. Church. I. Title.

SCHILLEBEECKX, Edward Cornelis Florentius Alfons, 1914- 262'.7
The mission of the church [by] Edward Schillebeeckx. Translated by N. D. Smith. New York, Seabury Press [1973] ix, 244 p. 22 cm. Translation of De zending van de kerk. "A Crossroad book." Includes bibliographical references. [BX891.S35513] 73-6436 ISBN 0-8164-1144-1 9.75
1. Catholic Church—Addresses, essays, lectures. I. Title.

SCHNACKENBURG, Rudolf, 1914- 262.7
The church in the New Testament. [Tr. from German by W. J. O'Hara] [New York] Herder & Herder [c.1965] 221, [1]p. 23cm. Bibl. [BS2545.C5S383] 4.95
1. Church—Biblical teaching. 2. Bible. N. T.—Theology. I. Title.

SILVEY, D. O. 262'.7
The Lord's unconquerable church; Bible primer [by] D. O. Silvey. [Little Rock, Ark., Baptist Publications Committee, 1972] 255 p. 22 cm. [BV600.2.S53] 72-83960
1. Church. I. Title.

THORNBURY, John. 262.7
The doctrine of the church; a Baptist view. Lewisburg, Pa., Heritage Publishers [1971] 218 p. 21 cm. Bibliography: p. [214]-218. [BV600.2.T49] 72-155780
1. Church. 2. Baptists—Doctrinal and controversial works. I. Title.

TODRANK, Gustave Herman, 1924- 262.7
The secular search for a new Christ, by Gustave H. Todrank. Philadelphia, Westminster Press [1969] 174 p. 21 cm. Bibliographical references included in "Notes" (p. 171-174) [BT83.7.T6] 73-76992 2.65
1. Secularization (Theology) 2. Salvation. I. Title.

COULSON, John, 1919- 262.7'0924
Newman and the common tradition: a study of the Church and society. Oxford, Clarendon, 1970. x, 279 p. 23 cm. Bibliography: p. [256]-265. [BV598.C67 1970] 70-17853 50/-
1. Newman, John Henry, Cardinal, 1801-1890. 2. Church—History of doctrines—19th century. 3. Religion and language. 4. Sociology, Christian. I. Title.

RICHTER, Edward J. 262.7'0973
Jesus and your nice church [by] Ed Richter. Grand Rapids, Eerdmans [1969] 88 p. 20 cm. [BV600.2.R5] 77-88077 1.65
1. Church renewal. I. Title.

BARRETT, Charles Kingsley. 262'.72
The signs of an apostle [by] C. K. Barrett. With an introd. to the American ed. by John Reumann. Philadelphia, Fortress Press [1972, c1970] xvi, 144 p. 18 cm. (The Cato lecture, 1969) Bibliography: p. 1-4. [BS2440.B346 1972] 72-75646 ISBN 0-8006-0116-5 3.25
1. Apostles. 2. Church—Apostolicity. I. Title. II. Series.

BRETSCHER, Paul G. 262.7'2
The holy infection; the mission of the church in parish and community, by Paul G. Bretscher. St. Louis, Concordia Pub. House [1969] 152 p. 22 cm. (The Witnessing church series) Bibliography: p. 150-152. [BV601.8.B7 1969] 74-79997 4.95
1. Holiness. I. Title.

THE Infallibility debate [by] Gregory Baum [and others] Edited by John J. Kirvan. New York, Paulist Press [1971] vi, 154 p. 21 cm. Includes bibliographical references. [BV601.6.I5I525] 76-168745 1.95 262.7'2
1. Catholic Church—Infallibility—Addresses, essays, lectures. I. Baum, Gregory, 1923- II. Kirvan, John J., ed.

NELSON, John Robert, 1920- 262.7'2
Crisis in unity and witness, by J. Robert Nelson. Philadelphia, Geneva Press [1968] 126 p. 21 cm. (Decade books) [BV600.2.N4] 68-10136
1. Church. I. Title.

OVERBECK, Julian Joseph, 1821-1905. 262.7'2
Catholic orthodoxy and Anglo-Catholicism, a word about intercommunion between the English and the Orthodox Churches. New York, AMS Press [1969] viii, 200 p. 22 cm. Reprint of the 1866 ed. Bibliographical footnotes. [BX324.5.O9 1969] 76-81771 10.00
1. Church of England—Relations—Orthodox Eastern Church. 2. Orthodox Eastern Church—Relations—Church of England. I. Title.

EMERY, Pierre Yves. 262.73
The communion of saints. Translated by D. J. and M. Watson. New York, Morehouse-Barlow [1966] xiii, 256 p. 23 cm. Translation of L'unite des croyants au ciel et sur la terre. Bibliographical references included in "Notes" (p. 228-254) [BT972.E413 1966a] 66-9558
1. Communion of saints.

SCHNEEBECK, Harold N., 1942- 262.7'7
The body of Christ [by] Harold N. Scheenbeck, Jr. [Independence? Mo.] Reorganized Church of Jesus Christ of Latter Day Saints [1968] 158 p. 18 cm. Bibliography: p. 156-158. [BV600.2.S33] 68-22581
1. Jesus Christ—Mystical body. I. Title.

BUTLER, Basil Christopher. 262.8
The church and infallibility; a reply to the abridged 'Salmon.' New York, Sheed and Ward, 1954. 230p. 22cm. [BT91.S33B8] 54-6145
1. Satmon, George, 1819-1904. The infallibility of the church. 2. Church—Infallibility. 3. Catholic Church—Infallibility. I. Title.

CAMPENHAUSEN, Hans, Freiherr von, 1903- 262'.8
Ecclesiastical authority and spiritual power in the church of the first three centuries [by] Hans von Campenhausen. Translated by J. A. Baker. Stanford, Calif., Stanford University Press, 1969. vii, 308 p. 23 cm. Translation of Kirchliches Amt und geistliche Vollmacht in den ersten drei Jahrhunderten. Bibliographical footnotes. [BT91.C313] 68-54827 8.95
1. Church—Authority. 2. Church—History of doctrines—Early church. I. Title.

CATHOLIC Church. Pope. 262.8
The papal encyclicals in their historical context, edited by Anne Framantle. With an introd. by Gustave Weigel. New York, Putnam [1956] 317p. 22cm. Bibliography: p. 311-312. [BX860.A36 1956a] 56-14306
1. Encyclicals, Papal. I. Fremantle, Anne (Jackson) 1909- ed. II. Title.

CATHOLIC Church. Pope. 262.8
The papal encyclicals in their historical context [by] Anne Fremantle. With an introd. by Gustave Weigel. [New York] New American Library [1963] 448 p. 18 cm. (A Mentor-Omega book, MQ533) [BX860.A36 1963] 64-2656
1. Encyclicals, Papal. I. Fremantle, Anne (Jackson) 1909- ed. II. Title.

CATHOLIC Church. Pope. 262.8
The papal encyclicals in their historical context, by Anne Fremantle. With an introd. by Gustave Weigel. [New York] New American Library [1956] 317p. 18cm. (A Mentor book, MD177) A Mentor religious classic. Bibliography: p. [311]-[312] [BX860..A36] 56-11328
1. Encyclicals, Papal. I. Fremantle, Anne (Jackson) 1909- ed. II. Title.

CATHOLIC Church. Pope, 1922-1939 (Pius XI) 262.8
Sixteen encyclicals of His Holiness Pope Pius XI, 1926-1937. [Index compiled by Rosabelle Kelp. Washington, National Catholic Welfare Conference, 1955] [567]p. 19cm. Cover title. [BX860.A] A55
I. National Catholic Welfare Conference. II. Title.
Contents omitted.

CURRAN, Charles E., comp. 262'.8
Contraception; authority and dissent. Edited by Charles E. Curran. [New York] Herder and Herder [1969] 237 p. illus. 22 cm. Contents.Contents.—Papal magisterium and the individual Catholic: Living with authority; the nineteenth century, by J. Coulson. The amendment of papal teaching by theologians, by J. T. Noonan. Limits to obedience in the thirteenth century, by B. Tierney. Ordinary papal magisterium and religious assent, by J. A. Komonchak. Moral inquiry and religious assent, by D. C. Maguire.—The encyclical Humanae Vitae: Natural law and contemporary moral theology, by C. E. Curran. The inseparability of the unitive-procreative functions of the marital act, by B. Haring. Humanae Vitae: a Protestant reaction, by R. M. Brown. A Scientist's analysis, by A. E. Hellegers. Bibliographical footnotes. [BX1751.2.A1C8] 69-18902 5.95
1. Catholic Church—Doctrinal and controversial works—Addresses, essays, lectures. 2. Authority (Religion)—Addresses, essays, lectures. 3. Birth control—Religious aspects—Addresses, essays, lectures. I. Title.

*DOMINIAN, Jack. 262'.8
Authority / Jack Dominian. Huntington, Ind. : Our Sunday Visitor, 1977,c1975. 107p. ; 20 cm. Originally published by Burns & Oats. [BV740] 77-82257 ISBN 0-87973-691-7 pbk. : 2.95
1. Church-Authority. I. Title.

*DOMINIAN, Jack. 262'.8
Authority / Jack Dominian. Huntington, Ind. : Our Sunday Visitor, 1977,c1975. 107p. ; 20 cm. Originally published by Burns & Oats. [BV740] 77-82257 ISBN 0-87973-691-7 pbk. : 2.95
1. Church-Authority. I. Title.

DRANE, James F. 262'.8
Authority and institution; a study in Church crisis, [by] James Drane. Milwaukee, Bruce Pub. Co. [1969] ix, 193 p. 21 cm. Bibliographical footnotes. [BX1802.D7] 69-17419
1. Catholic Church—Discipline. 2. Catholic Church—Government. 3. Church—Authority. I. Title.

FLYNN, Leslie B. 262'.8
Great church fights / Leslie B. Flynn. Wheaton, Ill. : Victor Books, c1976. 118 p. ; 21 cm. (An Input book) [BV652.9.F59] 76-14645 ISBN 0-88207-743-0 pbk. : 1.95
1. Church controversies. I. Title.

GOLDINGAY, John. 262'.8
Authority and ministry / by John Goldingay. Bramcote : Grove Books, 1976. 24 p. ; 21 cm. (Grove booklets on ministry and worship ; 46 ISSN 0305-3067s) Includes bibliographical references. [BT88.G65] 77-359490 ISBN 0-901710-99-7 : £0.30
1. Authority (Religion)—Addresses, essays, lectures. I. Title.

HARING, Bernhard, 1912- 262.8
The liberty of the children of God [by] Bernarh Haring. [Translated by Patrick O'Shaughnessy] Staten Island, N.Y., Alba House [1966] 135 p. 19 cm. Translation of Der Christ und die Obrigkeit. [BV741.H283] 66-16472
1. Liberty of conscience. 2. Catholic Church — Discipline. I. Title.

HARING, Bernhard. 1912- 262.8
The liberty of the children of God. [Tr. from German by Patrick O'Shaughnessy] Staten Island. N. Y., Alba [c. 1966] 135p.19cm. [BV741.H283] 66-16472 2.95
I. Liberty of conscience. 2. Catholic Church—Discipline. I. Title.

MCKENZIE, John L. 262.8
Authority in the Church [by] John L. McKenzie. New York, Sheed and Ward [1966] vi, 184 p. 22 cm. Bibliographical footnotes. [BX1802.M23] 66-12270
1. Catholic Church—Discipline. 2. Church—Authority. I. Title.

MANNING, Henry Edward, Cardinal, 1808-1892. 262'.8
The love of Jesus to penitents. Westminster, Md., Newman Press, 1950. 122 p. 16 cm. [[BX2265.M]] A51
1. Confession. I. Title.

MORRISON, Karl Frederick. 262'.8
Tradition and authority in the western church, 300-1140 [by] Karl F. Morrison. Princeton, N.J., Princeton University Press, 1969. xvii, 458 p. 25 cm. Bibliography: p. 409-443. [BT90.M67] 68-20873 ISBN 0-691-07155-1 12.50
1. Tradition (Theology)—History of doctrines. 2. Church—Authority—History of doctrines. 3. Political science—History—Europe. I. Title.

MULLIGAN, James J. 262'.8
The Pope and the theologians; the Humanae vitae controversy, by James J. Mulligan. Emmitsburg, Md., Mount Saint Mary's Seminary Press [1968] 109 p. 18 cm. Includes bibliographical references. [BT91.M8] 74-1867 1.95
1. Catholic Church—Infallibility. 2. Catholic Church. Pope, 1963- (Paulus VI) Humanae vitae. 3. Church—Teaching office. 4. Popes—Infallibility. I. Title.

OBEDIENCE and the church 262'.8
[by] Karl Rahner [and others] Washington, Corpus Books [1968] vi, 250 p. 23 cm. Translation of Studi sull'obedienza. Bibliographical footnotes. [BT91.S713] 68-57777 6.95
1. Catholic Church—Discipline. 2. Church—Authority—Addresses, essays, lectures. 3. Obedience (Canon law) I. Rahner, Karl, 1904-

PIUS XII, Pope, 1876- 262.8
The Pope speaks; the teachings of Pope Pius XII. Compiled and edited with the assistance of the Vatican archives by Michael Chinigo. [New York] Pantheon [1957] 378p. illus. 22cm. 'English translations... [by the editor] unless otherwise mentioned.' [BX890.P58193] 57-7321
1. Catholic Church— Addresses, essays, lectures. I. Title.

RICH, Edward Charles. 262.8
Spiritual authority in the Church of England; an enquiry. London, New York, Longmans, Green [1953] 218p. 23cm. [BX5131.R45] 53-10770
1. Authority (Religion) 2. Church of England—Doctrinal and controversial works. I. Title.

RIGA, Peter J 262'.8
Sin and penance; insights into the mystery of salvation. Milwaukee, Bruce Pub. Co. [1962] 187 p. 23 cm. [BX2265.2.R5] 62-19191
1. Sin. 2. Penance. I. Title.

SCHUTZ, John Howard. 262'.8
Paul and the anatomy of apostolic authority / John Howard Schutz. London ; New York : Cambridge University Press, 1975. xi, 307 p. ; 23 cm. (Monograph series - Society for New Testament studies ; 26) Includes indexes. Bibliography: p. 287-295. [BS2655.A8S38] 74-76573 ISBN 0-521-20464-X : 19.50
1. Bible N.T. Epistles of Paul—Theology. 2. Authority (Religion)—Biblical teaching. I. Title. II. Series: Studiorum Novi Testamenti Societas. Monograph series ; 26.

WHO decides for the Church? 262'.8
Studies in co-responsibility. Edited by James A. Coriden. Hartford, Conn., Cannon Law Society of America [1971] x, 293 p. 24 cm. Papers presented at a symposium sponsored by the Canon Law Society of America in cooperation with Fordham University and held Apr. 3-5, 1970, at Cathedral College, Douglaston, N.Y. Includes bibliographical references. [BV650.2.W48] 77-158455
1. Church polity—Addresses, essays, lectures. I. Coriden, James A., ed. II. Canon Law Society of America. III. Title: Studies in co-responsibility.

WILLS, Garry, 1934- 262.8
Politics and Catholic freedom. Foreword by Will Herberg. Chicago, Regnery Co. [1964] 302 p. 24 cm. Includes bibliographical references. [BV741.W63] 64-19651
1. Liberty of conscience. 2. Catholic Church—Discipline. 3. Church—Teaching office. I. Title. II. Title: Catholic freedom.

TODD, John Murray, ed. 262.8082
Problems of authority; the papers read at an Anglo-French symposium held at the Abbey of Notre-Dame du Bec, in April 1961 ... [Contributors: Elizabeth Anscombs and others] Baltimore, Helicon Press [1962] vii, 260 p. 22 cm. [BT88.T63] 62-10240
1. Authority (Religion) I. Title.

TODD, John Murray, ed. 262.8082
Problems of authority; the papers read at an Anglo-French symposium held at the Abbey of NotreDame du Bec. in April 1961 [Tr. from French by Reginald F. Trevett. Contributors: Elizabeth Anscombe, others] Helicon [dist. New York, Taplinger, c.1962] vii, 260p. 22cm. 62-10240 5.95
1. Authority (Religion) I. Title.

CARLEN, Mary Claudia, 1906- 262.82
Dictionary of papal pronouncements, Leo XIII to Pius xii, 1878-1957. Compiled by Sister M. Claudia New York, P. J. Kenedy [1958] 216p. 24cm. 'Papal document collections':p. 173-177. [BX873.7.C3] 58-12095
1. Papal documents—Indexes. 2. Papal documents—Bibl. I. Title.

CATHOLIC Church. Pope. 262.82
Seven great encyclicals ... Glen Rock, N.J., Paulist Press [1963] vii, 344 p. 20 cm. Includes discussion club outlines by William J. Gibbons and Gerald C. Treacy. [BX860.A4 1963] 63-24169
1. Papal documents. I. Title.
Contents omitted.

CATHOLIC Church Pope 262.82
Seven great encyclicals: labor, education, marriage, reconstructing the social order, atheistic communism, world social problems, world peace. Glen Rock, N.J. Paulist Press [c.1939,1963] vii, 344 p. 20 cm. 63-24169 1.50, pap.
1. Papal documents. I. Title.

CATHOLIC Church. Pope 1939-1958 (Pius XII) 262.82
Four great encyclicals of Pope Pius XII. With Christmas message of 1944: Democracy and peace; and the allocution: The world community and religious tolerance. Discussion club outlines by Rev. Gerald C. Treacy. New York, Deus Books, Paulist Press [c.1961] 224 p. Bibl. 61-8818 .95, pap.
1. Treacy, Gerald Carr, 1883- I. Title.

CATHOLIC Church. Pope. 1958-1963 (Joannes XXIII) 262.82
The encyclicals and other messages of John XXIII. Commentaries by John F. Cronin, Francis X. Murphy, Ferrer Smith. Arr., ed. by the staff of the Pope speaks magazine. Washington 17, D.C., TPS Pr., 3622 12th St. N.E. [c.1964] xi, 522p. coat of arms, ports. 24cm. Bibl. [BX870] 64-66217 8.50
I. Cronin, John Francis, 1908- II. Murphy, Francis Xavier, 1914- III. Smith, Ferrer. IV. The Pope speaks. V. Title.

*CATHOLIC CHURCH, Pope (Paul VI) 262.82
Ecclesiam suam; encyclical letter of His Holiness Pope Paul VI: the paths of the church, commentary by Gregory Baum, with study-club outline. Glen Rock, N. J., Paulist [c.1964] 80p. 18cm. .50 pap.,
I. Title.

WALL, Bernard, 1908- 262.82
Thaw at the Vatican; an account of session two of Vatican II, by Bernard & Barbara Wall. London, Gollancz [Mystic, Conn., Verry, 1965, c.] 1964. 223p. ports. 23cm. [BX830.1962.W3] 65-29695 6.00 bds.
1. Vatican Council, 2d. I. Lucas, Barbara, 1911- joint author. II. Title.

GUNDRY, Patricia. 262.8'34'12
Woman, be free! / Patricia Gundry. Grand Rapids : Zondervan Pub. Co., c1977. 112 p. ; 21 cm. Includes bibliographical references. [BS680.W7G86] 76-30494 4.95
1. Woman (Theology)—Biblical teaching. 2. Women in church work. I. Title.

ABBO, John A 1911- 262.9
The sacred canons; a concise presentation of the current disciplinary norms of the church, by John A. Abbo and Jerome D. Hannan. Rev. ed. St. Louis, Herder [1957, c1952] 2v. 24cm. Contents.v.1. Canons 1-869.--v. 2. Canons 870-2414. Bibliography: v. 2, p. 873-889. 348 57-14869 57-14869
1. Canon law. I. Hannan, Jerome Daniel, 1896- joint author. II. Title.

BAINTON, Roland Herbert, 1894- 262.9
The travail of religious liberty. New York, Harper [1958] 272p. illus., ports. 21cm. (Harper torchbooks TB30) Bibliography: p. [261]-265. [BV741.B] A59
1. Religious liberty. 2. Christian biography. I. Title.

BIECHLER, James E., ed. 262.9
Law for liberty, the role of law in the church today. James E. Biechler, editor. Foreword by Ernest J. Primeau. Baltimore, Helicon [1967] 221 p. 21 cm. Proceedings of a seminar sponsored by the Canon Law Society of

America, held at the Pittsburgh Hilton, Oct. 8-10, 1966. Bibliography: p. 209-213. 67-14646
1. Canon law—Addresses, essays, lectures. I. Canon Law Society of America. II. Title.

THE Bishops' synod : 262.9
(the first synod of St. Patrick) : a symposium with text, translation, and commentary / edited by M. J. Faris. Liverpool : Francis Cairns, 1976. [5], 63, [11] p. : facsims. ; 21 cm. (Parallel Latin text and English translation of ms. 279 of Corpus Christi College, Cambridge; together with a facsimile reprint of the ms., and the papers of a symposium held at Queen's University, Belfast, organized by the Ulster Society for Medieval Latin Studies.) (Arca, classical and medieval texts, papers, and monographs ; 1) Bibliography: p. 61-63. [LAW] 77-375737 ISBN 0-905205-01-4 : £2.50 ($6.00 U.S.)
1. Canon law. 2. Ecclesiastical law—Ireland. I. Patrick, Saint, 373?-463? II. Faris, M. J. III. Cambridge. University. Corpus Christi College. Library. mss. (279) IV. Title. V. Series.

CANON law: 262.9
a text and commentary, by T. Lincoln Bouscaren and Adam C. Ellis. 3d rev. ed. Milwaukee, Bruce Pub. Co. [1957] xviii, 980p. 23cm. Includes bibliographies. 348 57-8314 57-8314
1. Canon law. I. Bouscaren, Timothy Lincoln, 1884- II. Ellis, Adam Charles, 1889- joint author.

CHENEY, Christopher Robert, 1906- 262.9
English synodalia of the thirteenth century, by C. R. Cheney. With a new introd. by the author. London, Oxford University Press, [1968] xvi, 164 p. 23 cm. Bibliography: p. [153]-158. [BR750.C45 1968] 73-3747 ISBN 0-19-821396-4 unpriced
1. England—Church history—Medieval period, 1066-1485. 2. Ecclesiastical law—Great Britain. I. Title.

CONFERENCE of Major Religious Superiors of Women's Institutes in the United States of America. 262.9
Proposed norms for consideration in the revision of the canons concerning religious. [Washington, 1968] vii, 99 p. 23 cm. "As submitted to the Pontifical Commission on Revision of the Code of Canon Law." [LAW] 68-6275
1. Canon law. I. Catholic Church. Codex juris canonici. c. 487-681: De religiosis. II. Title.

THE Future of canon law. 262.9
Edited by Neophytos Edelby, Teodoro Jimenez-Urresti [and] Petrus Huizing. New York, Paulist Press [1969] viii, 180 p. 24 cm. (Concilium: theology in the age of renewal. Canon law, v. 48) Bibliographical footnotes. [LAW] 78-100004 4.50
1. Canon law—Addresses, essays, lectures. I. Edelby, Neophytos, Abp., 1920- ed. II. Jimenez Urresti, Teodoro Ignacio, ed. III. Huizing, Petrus, 1911- ed. IV. Series: Concilium: theology in the age of renewal, v. 48

HAIR, Paul, comp. 262.9
Before the bawdy court; selections from church court and other records relating to the correction of moral offences in England, Scotland, and New England, 1300-1800. New York, Barnes & Noble Books [1972] 271 p. illus. 25 cm. Bibliography: p. [259]-266. [KD8760.H3 1972] 73-156599 ISBN 0-06-492646-X 13.75
1. Offenses against religion—Great Britain. 2. Court records—Great Britain. I. Title.

JESCHKE, Marlin. 262.9
Discipling the brother; congregational discipline according to the Gospel. Scottdale, Pa., Herald Press [1972] 200 p. 18 cm. Bibliography: p. 196-198. [BV760.2.J47] 72-2052 ISBN 0-8361-1671-2 Pap 2.95
1. Church discipline. I. Title.

LYDON, Patrick Joseph, 1883- 262.9
Ready answers in canon law; a practical summary of the Code for the parish clergy. 4th ed., enl. and rev. in accordance with latest decress. New York, Benziger Bros. [1954] xvi, 638p. illus. 22cm. Includes bibliographies. 348 54-2669 54-2669
1. Canon law—Dictionaries. I. Title.

MCMANUS, Martin J. 262.9
American canon law due process [by] Martin J. McManus. [Washington, Law Research Institute, 1971] 55 p. 22 cm. Includes bibliographical references. [KF4765.Z9M3] 72-176243
1. Due process of law—U.S. 2. Canon law. I. Title.

MARCHANT, Ronald Albert. 262.9
The Church under the law: justice, administration and discipline in the diocese of York, 1560-1640 [by] Ronald A. Marchant. London, Cambridge U.P., 1969. xiv, 272 p. maps. 24 cm. Includes material on visitations. Bibliography: p. 255-259. [LAW] 79-80819 75/-
1. Ecclesiastical law—York, Eng. (Diocese) I. Title.

MARSHALL, Nathaniel, d.1730. 262.9
The penitential discipline of the primitive church, for the first four hundred years after Christ; together with its declension from the fifth century, downwards to its present state: impartially represented. Oxford, J. H. Parker, 1844. [New York, AMS Press, 1973] xx, 225 p. 23 cm. (Library of Anglo-Catholic theology, no. 13) [BV648.M3 1973] 74-172846 ISBN 0-404-52105-3 27.50
1. Church discipline—Early church, ca. 30-600. 2. Penance—History. I. Title. II. Series.

MATHIS, Marcian Joseph, 1918- ed. 262.9
The pastoral companion; a handbook of canon llw. 13th ed. by Marcian J. Mathis, Dismas W. Bonner. Chicago, Franciscan Herald Pr. [1967- 1 v. (loose-leaf) 24cm. 66-22158 9.50, loose-leafring binder
1. Canon law. 2. Clergy (Canon law) — Handbooks, manuals, etc. I. Bonner, Dismas W., 1929- joint author. II. Title.

MULLER, Alois, 1924- 262.9
Obedience in the church. Edited and translated by Hilda Graef. Westminster, Md., Newman Press [1966, c1964] 190 p. 21 cm. Translation of Das Problem von Befehl und Gehorsam im Leben der Kirche. Bibliography: p. 171-182. [BX1802.M813] 66-16574
1. Catholic Church — Discipline. I. Title.

MULLER, Alois, 1924- 262.9
Obedience in the church. Edited and translated by Hilda Graef. Westminster, Md., Newman Press [1966, c1964] 190 p. 21 cm. Translation of Das Problem von Befehl und Gehorsam im Leben der Kirche. Bibliography: p. 171-182. [BX1802.M813 1966] 66-16574
1. Catholic Church—Discipline. I. Title.

NAUROIS, Louis de 262.9
Quand l'Eglise juge et condamne [Toulouse] Privat [dist. Philadelphia, Chilton, 1964, c.1960] 112,[7]p. 19cm. (Questions posees aux catholiques) Bibl. 64-9076 1.00 pap.,
1. Catholic Church—Discipline. I. Title.

OAKLEY, Thomas Pollock, 1884-1943. 262.9
English penitential discipline and Anglo-Saxon law in their joint influence. [1st AMS ed.] New York, AMS Press [1969] 226 p. 23 cm. (Studies in history, economics and public law, v. 107, no. 2; whole no. 242) Series statement also appears as: Columbia University studies in the social sciences, 242. Originally presented as the author's thesis, Columbia, 1923. Reprint of the 1923 ed. Bibliography: p. 201-213. [LAW] 71-82243
1. Penitentials. I. Title. II. Series: Columbia studies in the social sciences, 242.

OBERHOLZER, Emil, 1926- 262.9
Delinquent saints; disciplinary action in the early Congregational churches of Massachusetts. New York, Columbia University Press, 1956 [c1955] x, 379p. tables. 24cm. (Columbia studies in the social sciences, no. 590) Issued in microfilm forn in 1954 as thesis, Columbia University, under title: Saints in sin. Bibliography: p. [337]-371. [H31.C7 no. 590] 56-5877
1. Congregational churches in Massachusetts. 2. Puritans. 3. Congregational churches—Discipline. I. Title. II. Series.

OBERHOLZER, Emil, 1926- 262.9
Delinquent saints; disciplinary action in the early Congregational churches of Massachusetts, by Emil Oberholzer, Jr. [1st AMS ed.] New York, AMS Press [1968] x, 379 p. 23 cm. (Columbia studies in the social sciences, no. 590) Reprint of the 1956 ed. Includes bibliographical references. [BX7148.M4O2 1968] 70-76660
1. Congregational churches in Massachusetts. 2. Puritans—Massachusetts. 3. Congregational churches—Discipline. I. Title. II. Series.

POSTCONCILIAR thoughts; 262.9
renewal and reform of canon law. Edited by Neophytos Edelby, Teodoro Jimenez Urresti [and] Petrus Huizing. New York, Paulist Press [1967] viii, 183 p. 24 cm. (Concilium: theology in the age of renewal, v. 28) Contents.Contents.—The theology of canon law, by L. de Echevarria.—Canon law and theology: two different sciences, by T. Jimenez-Urresti.—The new codification of the church order: nature and limits, by P. Huizing.—Unity or plurality of codes: should the eastern churches have a special code? By N. Edelby.—The code of canon law: 1918-1967, by P. Shannon.—Outline of a constitution for the church, by H. Heimerl.—The renewal of canon law and the resolutions of the canon law society of America, 1965, by P. Boyle.—Religious orders in the pastoral work of the diocese and parish, by H. Proesmans.—Episcopal conferences, by C. Munier.—Jewish comments on the conciliar statement about the Jews, by J. Oesterreicher.—Crime and punishment in the Church, by P. Huizing.—Opinions on the future structure of oriental canon law, by I. Zuzek.—Stirrings in religious life, by Concilium General Secretariat.—In memoriam: John Courtney Murray, S.J. Includes bibliographical references. [LAW] 67-30868
1. Canon law—Addresses, essays, lectures. I. Edelby, Neophytos, Abp., 1920- ed. II. Jimenez Urresti, Teodoro Ignacio, ed. III. Huizing, Petrus, 1911- ed.

PRECEPTS. 262.9
Paterson, N. J., St. Anthony Guild Press, 1955. 251p. 24cm. 348 55-14418
1. Precept (Canon law) I. Roelker, Edward George, 1897-

PROBLEMS in canon law: 262.9
classified replies to practical questions. Dublin, Browne and Nolan [1956] 345p. 23cm. 348 57-2183 57-2183
1. Canon law. I. Conway, William.

PROBLEMS in canon law; 262.9
classified replies to practical questions. Westminster, Md., Newman Press [1957] 345p. 23cm. 348 57-13676 57-13676
1. Canon law. I. Conway, William.

RELIGIOUS freedom, canon law. 262.9
[Edited by Neophytos Edelby and Teodoro Jimenez-Urresti] New York, Paulist Press [1966] viii, 183 p. 24 cm. (Concilium, v. 18) "Religious freedom, a bibliographical survey": p. 111-139. Includes bibliographical footnotes. [BV741.R43] 66-29261
1. Catholic Church—Discipline—Addresses, essays, lectures. 2. Religious liberty—Addresses, essays, lectures. I. Edelby, Neophytos, Abp. 1920- ed. II. Jimenez Urresti, Teodoro Ignacio, ed. III. Series: Concilium (New York) v. 18.

RICHSTATTER, Thomas. 262.9
Liturgical law, its spirit and practice / Thomas Richstatter. Chicago : Franciscan Herald Press, [1977] p. cm. Bibliography: p. [LAW] 77-3008 ISBN 0-8199-0672-7 : 7.95
1. Catholic Church. Liturgy and ritual. 2. Canon law. 3. Canon law—History. I. Title.

RITCHIE, Carson IA 262.9
The ecclesiastical courts of York. Arboath, Herald Press, 1956. 245p. 23cm. 348 57-13716
1. Ecclesiastical courts—York, Eng. (Diocese) I. Title.

SAYERS, Jane E. 262.9
Papal judges delegate in the Province of Canterbury, 1198-1254: a study in ecclesiastical jurisdiction and administration, by Jane E. Sayers. London, Oxford University Press, 1971. xxv, 398 p. 23 cm. (Oxford historical monographs) Bibliography: p. [357]-371. [LAW] 72-886518 ISBN 0-19-821836-2 £5.50
1. Ecclesiastical courts—Canterbury, Eng. (Province) I. Title.

SCHWEIZER, Eduard Robert, 1913- 262.9
Church order in the New Testament. [Tr. from German by Frank Clarke] Naperville, Ill., A. R. Allenson [1961] 239p. (Studies in Biblical theology, 32) Bibl. 61-4759 3.50 pap.,
1. Church discipline. 2. Church—Biblical teaching. I. Title.

STOW, Kenneth R. 262.9
Catholic thought and papal Jewry policy, 1555-1593 / by Kenneth R. Stow. New York : Jewish Theological Seminary of America, [1976] p. cm. (Moreshet ; 6) Includes index. Bibliography: p. [LAW] 76-55307 ISBN 0-87334-001-9 : 25.00
1. Susannis, Marquardus de, d. 1578. De Iudaeis. 2. Jews—Legal status, laws, etc. (Canon law) 3. Catholic Church—Relations—Judaism. 4. Judaism—Relations—Catholic Church. I. Title. II. Series: Moreshet (New York) ; 6.

VATICAN Council. 2d, 1962-1965. 262.9
Decree on priestly training of Vatican Council II and Decree on the ministry and life of priests of Vatican Council II. Commentary by Frank B. Norris. Glen Rock, N.J., Paulist Press, 1966. 157 p. 19 cm. (Vatican II documents) Bibliographical footnotes. [BX830 1962.A45D453] 66-29072
1. Vatican Council. 2d, 1962-1965. Decretum de institutione sacerdotali. 2. Vatican Council. 2d, 1962-1965. Decretum de presbyterorum ministerio et vita. I. Norris, Frank B. II. Vatican Council. 2d, 1962-1965. Decree on the ministry and life of priests. III. Title. IV. Title: Decree on the ministry and life of priests.

WESTERN canon law. 262.9
Berkeley, University of California Press, 1953. 92p. 22cm. 348 53-11242
1. Canon law—Hist. 2. Ecclesiastical law—Gt. Brit. I. Mortimer, Robert Cecil, Bp. of Exeter, 1902-

WOODCOCK, Brian Lindsay, 1920-1951. 262.9
Medieval ecclesiastical courts in the Diocese of Canterbury. London, Oxford University Press, 1952. xi, 160 p. map. diagr. 23 cm. (Oxford historical series. British series) Bibliography: p. [138]-145. 52-10596
1. Ecclesiastical courts — Canterbury, Eng. (Diocese) I. Title.

YOUNG, Fred L 262.9
Ministry of reconciliation and church court procedure. Independence, Mo., Herald House, 1960. 200 p. 18 cm. (Pastors' reference library) At head of title: Reorganized Church of Jesus Christ of Latter Day Saints. "The offical court procedures and decisions of the quorums and councils -- have been included." [BX8657.Y57] 60-53060
1. Mormons and Mormonism — Government. I. Reorganized Church of Jesus Christ of Latter-Day Saints. II. Title.

YOUNG, Fred L. 262.9
Ministry of reconciliation and church court procedure. Independence, Mo., Herald House [c.1961, c.]1960. 200p. (Pastor's reference library) 60-53060 2.50
1. Mormons and Mormonism—Government. I. Reorganized Church of Jesus Christ of Latter-Day Saints. II. Title.

MAITLAND, Frederic William, 1850-1906. 262.9'0942
Roman canon law in the Church of England; six essays. New York, B. Franklin [1968] vi, 184 p. 23 cm. (Burt Franklin research and source works series, 340) (History, economics, and social science, 70.) Reprint of the 1898 ed. Contents.Contents.—William Lyndwood.—Church, state, and decretals.—William of Drogheda and the universal ordinary.—Henry II and the criminous clerks.—Execrabilis in the common pleas.—The deacon and the Jewess. Bibliographical footnotes. [LAW] 69-18602
1. Church of England—Addresses, essays, lectures. 2. Ecclesiastical law—Gt. Brit.—Addresses, essays, lectures. I. Title.

OGLE, Arthur, 1871- 262.9'0942
The canon law in mediaeval England; an examination of William Lyndwood's "Provinciale," in reply to the late Professor F. W. Maitland. New York, B. Franklin [1971] xxi, 220 p. 23 cm. (Burt Franklin research and source works series, 731. Selected essays in history, economics and social science, 262) Reprint of the 1912 ed. [LAW] 78-156390 ISBN 0-8337-2603-X
1. Lyndwood, William, Bp. of St. David's, 1375?-1446. Provinciale. 2. Maitland, Frederic William, 1850-1906. Roman canon law in the Church of England. 3. Canon law. 4. Ecclesiastical law—Great Britain. I. Title.

TORPEY, William George, 1913- 262.9'0973
Judicial doctrines of religious rights in America. New York, Da Capo Press, 1970 [c1948] ix, 376 p. 24 cm. (Civil liberties in American history) Bibliography: p. [333]-371. [KF4865.T6 1970] 78-132289
1. Ecclesiastical law—U.S. 2. Religious liberty—U.S. I. Title. II. Series.

INSTITUTE on Religious Freedom, North Aurora, Ill., 1966. 262.91
Religious liberty: an end and a beginning; the Declaration on religious freedom, an ecumenical discussion. Edited by John Courtney Murray. New York, Macmillan [1966] 192 p. 21 cm. Discourses given at the Institute on Religious Freedom, organized by the Bellarmine School of Theology of Loyola University. "Appendix: Declaration on religious freedom": p. 162-189. Bibliographical footnotes. [BX830 1962.A45D423] 66-24891
1. Vatican Council. 2d, 1962-1965. Declaratio de libertate religiosa. 2. Religious liberty — Addresses, essays, lectures. I. Murray, John Courtney, ed. II. Loyola University, Chicago. Bellarmine School of Theology, North Aurora, Ill. III. Vatican Council. 2d, 1962-1965. Declaration on religious freedom. IV. Title.

INSTITUTE on Religious Freedom, North Aurora, Ill., 1966. 262.91
Religious liberty: an end and a beginning; the Declaration on religious freedom.an ecumenical discussion Ed. by John Courtney Murray. New York, Macmillan 1966 192p. 21cm. Discourses given at the Inst. on Religious Freedom. organized by the

Bellarmine School of Theol. of Loyola Univ. Appendix:Declaration on religious freedom': p. 162-189. Bibl. [BX830 1962.A45D423] 66-24891 4.95
1. Vatican Council. 2d. 1962-1965. Declaratio de liberate religious. 2. Religious liberty—Addresses, essays, lectures. I. Murray, John Courtney, ed. II. Vatican Council. 2d, 1962-1965. Declaration on religious freedom. III. Loyola University, Chicago Bellarmine school of Theology, North Aurora, Ill. IV. Loyola University, Chicago. Bellarmine School of Theology, North Aurora, Ill. V. Title.

CHODOROW, Stanley. 262.9'23
Christian political theory and church politics in the mid-twelfth century; the ecclesiology of Gratian's Decretum. Berkeley, University of California Press, 1972. xi, 300 p. 24 cm. (Publications of the Center for Medieval and Renaissance Studies, U.C.L.A., 5) Bibliography: p. 267-292. [LAW] 71-138512 ISBN 0-520-01850-8 15.00
1. Gratianus, the canonist. Decretum. 2. Canon law—History. 3. Church history—12th century. I. Title. II. Series: California. University. University at Los Angeles. Center for Medieval and Renaissance Studies. Publications, 5.

TWO essays on the 262.9'23
Decretum of Gratian, by Hellmut Lehmann-Haupt and Charles McCurry. Together with an original leaf printed on vellum by Peter Schoeffer at Mainz in 1472. Los Angeles, Zeitlin & Ver Brugge, 1971. [17] p. 51 cm. "193 copies printed by Saul & Lillian Marks at the Plantin Press, Los Angeles." Unnumbered copyright deposit copy, without an original leaf. Contents.Contents.—Peter Schoeffer of Gernsheim, printer of the Decretum at Mainz in 1472, by H. Lehmann-Haupt.—The Decretum of Gratian, by C. McCurry. [Z241.G73T95] 73-164721
1. Gratianus, the canonist. Decretum. 2. Schoffer, Peter, ca. 1425-ca. 1502. I. Lehmann-Haupt, Hellmut, 1903- Schoeffer of Gernsheim. 1971. II. McCurry, Charles. The Decretum of Gratian. 1971.

BOUSCAREN, Timothy 262.93
Lincoln, 1884-
Canon law; a text and commentary, by T. Lincoln Bouscaren, Adam C. Ellis, and Francis N. Korth. 4th rev. ed. Milwaukee, Bruce Pub. Co. [1966] xvi, 1011 p. 23 cm. Includes bibliographies. 66-16640
1. Canon law. I. Ellis, Adam Charles, 1889- joint author. II. Korth, Francis N., joint author. III. Title.

BOUSCAREN, Timothy 262.93
Lincoln, 1884-
Canon law; a text and commentary, by T. Lincoln Bouscaren, Adam C. Ellis, Francis N. Korth. 4th rev. ed. Milwaukee, Bruce [c.1966] xvi, 1011p. 23cm. Bibl. 66-16640 12.00
1. sCanon law. I. Ellis, Adam Charles, 1889- joint author. II. Korth, Francis N., joint author. III. Title.

BENSON, Robert Louis, 262.9'32
1925-
The bishop-elect; a study in medieval ecclesiastical office, by Robert L. Benson. Princeton, N.J., Princeton University Press, 1968. xix, 440 p. 23 cm. Bibliography: p. 403-412. [LAW] 65-17130 11.50
1. Bishops (Common law) 2. Middle Ages—History. I. Title.

LAEUCHLI, Samuel. 262.9'32
Power and sexuality; the emergence of canon law at the Synod of Elvira. Philadelphia, Temple University Press [1972] ix, 143 p. 22 cm. Includes bibliographical references. [LAW] 72-83671 ISBN 0-87722-015-8 6.00
1. Council of Elvira, 309? 2. Canon law. 3. Sex crimes (Canon law) I. Title.

CATHOLIC Church. Codex 262.9'33
juris canonici Orientalis. De sacramento matrimonii.
Code of Oriental canon law, the law on marriage; interritual marriage law problems. English translation and differential commentary by Victor J. Pospishil. Chicago, Universe Editions, 1962. 221 p. 24 cm. Bibliography: p. 13-16. [LAW] 73-179691
1. Marriage (Canon law, Oriental) I. Pospishil, Victor J., ed. II. Title.

HERTEL, James R. 262.9'33
When marriage fails, by James R. Hertel. Foreword by Vincent J. Doyle. Paramus, N.J., Paulist Press [1969] v, 121 p. 19 cm. (Paulist Press Deus books) [LAW] 78-92117 1.25
1. Marriage (Canon law) 2. Divorce (Canon law) I. Title.

MAIDA, Adam J. 262.9'33
The tribunal reporter; a comprehensive study of the grounds for the annulment of marriage in the Catholic Church, edited by Adam J. Maida for the Canon Law Society of America. Huntington, Ind., Our Sunday Visitor [1970- v. 27 cm. [LAW] 75-12250
1. Marriage—Annulment (Canon law)—Cases. I. Canon Law Society of America. II. Title.

NOONAN, John Thomas, 262.9'33
1926-
Power to dissolve; lawyers and marriages in the courts of the Roman Curia [by] John T. Noonan, Jr. Cambridge, Belknap Press of Harvard University Press, 1972. xix, 489 p. front. 25 cm. Includes bibliographical references. [LAW] 75-176044 ISBN 0-674-69575-5 15.00
1. Marriage—Annulment (Canon law)—Cases. I. Title.

THE Sacraments in 262.9'33
theology and canon law. Edited by Neophytos Edelby, Teodoro Jimenez-Urresti [and] Petrus Huizing. New York, Paulist Press [1968] viii, 183 p. 24 cm. (Concilium: theology in the age of renewal. Canon law, v. 38) Bibliographical footnotes. [LAW] 68-58308 4.50
1. Catholic Church—Government—Addresses, essays, lectures. 2. Sacraments (Canon law)—Addresses, essays, lectures. I. Edelby, Neophytos, Abp., 1920- ed. II. Jimenez Urresti, Teodoro Ignacio, ed. III. Huizing, Petrus, 1911- ed. IV. Series: Concilium (New York) v. 38

SARPI, Paolo, 1552-1623. 262.9'33
History of benefices; and selections from History of the Council of Trent [by] Sarpi. Newly translated, edited, and with an introd. by Peter Burke. New York, Washington Square Press; [distributed by Simon & Schuster, 1967] xlvi, 322 p. 18 cm. (The Great histories series) Translation of Trattato delle materie beneficiarie, and of selections from Historia del Concilio Tridentino. "The translation follows the text as presented in the standard edition of Sarpi's works (Bari, Laterza, 1935-65)" Bibliography: p. xliii-xliv. [BV775.S32 1967] 67-28145
1. Benefices, Ecclesiastical. I. Burke, Peter, ed. II. Sarpi, Paolo, 1552-1623. Historia del Concilio Tridentino. III. Title.

SIEGLE, Bernard Andrew 262.933
Marriage todav: a commentary of the Code of Canon law Staten Island. N.Y., Alba [1966] 294p. illus. 22cm. Bibl. 66-19716 4.95
1. Marriage (canon law) I. Title.

SIEGLE, Bernard Andrew. 262.9'33
Marriage today; a commentary on the Code of canon law in the light of Vatican II and the ecumenical age. 2d ed. Staten Island, N.Y., Alba House [1973] 347 p. 21 cm. Bibliography: p. [339]-342. [LAW] 72-4055 ISBN 0-8189-0253-1 4.95
1. Marriage (Canon law) I. Title.

WEST, Morris L., 1916- 262.9'33
Scandal in the assembly: a bill of complaints and a proposal for reform in the matrimonial laws and tribunals of the Roman Catholic Church [by] Morris L. West [and] Robert Francis. New York, Morrow, 1970. viii, 182 p. 22 cm. [Law] 72-114190 4.95
1. Marriage (Canon law) I. Francis, Robert, 1919- joint author. II. Title.

ABBO, John A, 1911- *262.9 348
The sacred canons; a concise presentation of the current disciplinary norms of the church, by John A. Abbo and Jerome D. Hannan. St. Louis, Herder, 1952. 2 v. 25 cm. Contents.v. 1. Canons 1-869.--v. 2. Canons 870-2414. Bibliography: v. 2. p. 873-889. 52-10883
1. Canon law. I. Hannan, Jerome Daniel, 1896- joint author. II. Title.

WOYWOD, Stanislaus, *262.9 348
Father, 1880-1941.
A practical commentary on the Code of canon law. Revised by Callistus Smith. [Rev. and enl. ed.] New York, J. F. Wagner [1952] xvii, 833, 905 p. 22 cm. Bibliography: p. 831-835 (2d group) 52-3040
1. Canon law. I. Catholic Church. Codex juris canonici. II. Title.

KELLY, Henry Ansgar, 262.9'35
1934-
The matrimonial trials of Henry VIII / Henry Ansgar Kelly. Stanford, Calif. : Stanford University Press, 1976. xii, 333 p. ; 23 cm. Includes index. Bibliography: p. [299]-307. [KD378.H4K4] 75-7483 ISBN 0-8047-0895-9 : 15.00
1. Henry VIII, King of England, 1491-1547. 2. Catharine of Aragon, consort of Henry VIII, King of England, 1485-1536. 3. Anne Boleyn, consort of Henry VIII, King of England, 1507-1536. 4. Trials (Divorce)—Great Britain. 5. Marriage (Canon law) I. Title.

KELLY, Henry Ansgar, 262.9'35
1934-
The matrimonial trials of Henry VIII / Henry Ansgar Kelly. Stanford, Calif. : Stanford University Press, 1976. xii, 333 p. ; 23 cm. Includes index. Bibliography: p. [299]-307. [KD378.H4K4] 75-7483 ISBN 0-8047-0895-9 : 15.00
1. Henry VIII, King of England, 1491-1547. 2. Catharine of Aragon, consort of Henry VIII, King of England, 1485-1536. 3. Anne Boleyn, consort of Henry VIII, King of England, 1507-1536. 4. Trials (Divorce)—Great Britain. 5. Marriage (Canon law) I. Title.

KREHBIEL, Edward 262.9'35
Benjamin, 1878-
The interdict : its history and its operation, with special attention to the time of Pope Innocent III, 1198-1216 / by Edward B. Krehbiel. Merrick, N.Y. : Richwood Pub. Co., [1977] viii, 184 p. ; 23 cm. Reprint of the 1909 ed. published by the American Historical Association, Washington. Originally presented as the author's thesis, University of Chicago. Includes index. Bibliography: p. 164-173. [LAW] 77-4131 ISBN 0-915172-21-6 lib.bdg. : 17.50
1. Interdict (Canon law) I. Title.

SAKKAS, Basile. 262.9'8'19
The calendar question, by Basile Sakkas. Translated from the French by Holy Transfiguration Monastery in Boston. Jordanville, N.Y., Holy Trinity Monastery, 1973. 94 p. illus. 24 cm. Bibliography; p. 80. [BX323.S213] 72-90868
1. Orthodox Eastern Church—Doctrinal and controversial works. 2. Church calendar. I. Title.

EMMISON, Frederick 262.9'8'3
George, 1907-
Elizabethan life: morals & the church courts [by] F. G. Emmison. Chelmsford, Essex County Council, 1973. xiv, 348 p. illus. 25 cm. "Mainly from Essex archidiaconal records." Includes bibliographical references. [KD8605.E44] 73-181446 £3.50
1. Ecclesiastical law—Great Britain—History. 2. Ecclesiastical courts—Great Britain—History. I. Title.

MOORE, Evelyn 262.9'8'30942
Garth.
An introduction to English canon law, by E. Garth Moore. Oxford, Clarendon P., 1967. xv, 176 p. tables. 22 1/2 cm. (Clarendon law series) Bibliographical footnotes. [LAW] 67-76810
1. Ecclesiastical law—Great Britain. I. Title.

BRYDON, George 262.9'8'373
MacLaren, 1875-
Shall we accept the ancient canons as canon law? : A reply to the pamphlet "The ancient canons and an interpretation of the word discipline in the Book of common prayer" which was published by the Joint Commission on Discipline of the American Church Union and the Clerical Union / G. MacLaren Brydon. Richmond : Virginia Diocesan Library, [1955] 58 p. ; 23 cm. Includes bibliographical references. [LAW] 75-322201
1. Protestant Episcopal Church in the U.S.A. 2. Canon law, Protestant Episcopal. I. Joint Committee on Discipline of the American Church Union and the Clerical Union. The ancient canons and an interpretation of the word discipline in the Book of common prayer. II. Title.

PROTESTANT Episcopal 262.9'83'73
Church in the U.S.A.
Constitution and canons for the government of the Protestant Episcopal Church in the United States of America, otherwise known as the Episcopal Church, adopted in general conventions, 1789-1967. [New York?] Printed for the convention, 1967. xx, 210 p. 23 cm. [BX5955.A5 1967] 74-799
1. Protestant Episcopal Church in the U.S.A.—Government. I. Title.

PRESBYTERIAN Church in 262.9851
the U. S. A. General Assembly.
A digest of the acts and proceedings of the General Assembly of the Presbyterian Church in the United States, 1861-1965. Atlanta, 1966. ix, 489 p. 24 cm. [BX8956.A5] 66-5073
1. Presbyterian Church in the U. S. A.—Discipline. I. Title.

UNITED Presbyterian 262.9851
Church in the U. S. A.
Presbyterian law for the local church; a handbook for church officers and members. Edited by Eugene Carson Blake. Rev. Philadelphia, 1963. 141 p. 22 cm. [BX8956.A6] 68-2705
1. United Presbyterian Church in the U. S. A.—Government. I. Blake, Eugene Carson, 1906- ed. II. Title.

COX, James Taylor, 262.9'8'52411
1865-1948.
Practice and procedure in the Church of Scotland / edited by the late James T. Cox. 6th ed. / edited by D. F. M. MacDonald. [Edinburgh] : Committee on General Administration, Church of Scotland, 1976. [11], 850 p. : forms ; 22 cm. Includes bibliographical references and index. [BX9078.C65 1976] 76-360850 ISBN 0-7152-0326-6 : £5.00
1. Church of Scotland—Government. I. MacDonald, Donald Farquhar Macleod. II. Title.

PETERSEN, Henry, 262.9'8'5731
1915-
The Canons of Dort; a study guide. Grand Rapids, Baker Book House [1968] 115 p. 22 cm. First published as articles in the Banner, official weekly periodical of the Christian Reformed Church. "The Canons of Dort": p. 93-115. [BX9478.P4] 68-5351
1. Dort, Synod of, 1618-1619. 2. Reformed Church—Catechisms and creeds—English. I. Canons of Dort.

UNITED Methodist 262.9'8'76
Church (United States)
The book of discipline of the United Methodist Church, 1976. Nashville : United Methodist Pub. House, c1976. xi, 664 p. ; 23 cm. Errata slip inserted. Includes index. [BX8388.U55 1976] 76-380158 ISBN 0-687-03707-7
1. United Methodist Church (United States)—Government. I. Title.

263 Times & Places Of Religious Observance

FRANCE, Dorothy D. 263
Special days of the church year, by Dorothy D. France. St. Louis, Bethany Press [1969] 279 p. 23 cm. Bibliography: p. 271-275. [BV30.F68] 68-31581
1. Church year. I. Title.

MAERTENS, Thierry, 1921- 263
A feast in honor of Yahweh. Tr. [from French] by Kathryn Sullivan. Foreward by Eugene H. Maly. Notre Dame, Ind., Fides [c.1965] 245p. 21cm. [BV30.M243] 65-13800 3.95
1. Facts and feasts. 2. Fasts and feasts—Judaism. I. Title.

MARTIN, Gerhard M., 1942- 263
Fest : the transformation of everyday / by Gerhard Marcel Martin ; translated and with an introd. by M. Douglas Meeks. Philadelphia : Fortress Press, c1976. xiv, 82 p. : ill. ; 22 cm. Translation of Fest und Alltag. Bibliography: p. 79-82. [BL590.M3713] 76-7865 ISBN 0-8006-1233-7 : 2.95
1. Fasts and feasts. I. Title.

ODOM, Robert Leo, 1901- 263
The Lord's day on a round world. Rev. ed. Nashville, Southern Pub. Association [1970]. 254 p. illus., map. 22 cm. Bibliography: p. 229-241. [BV125.O3 1970] 71-126040
1. Sabbath. I. Title.

PHILIPON, Marie Michel, 1898- 263
The sacraments in the Christian life; translated by John A. Otto. Westminster, Md., Newman Press, 1954. 304p. 22cm. [BX2200.P476] 54-9606
1. Sacraments—Catholic Church. I. Title.

SAUNDERS, Herbert E. 263
The Sabbath: symbol of creation and re-creation [by] Herbert E. Saunders. Plainfield, N.J., American Sabbath Tract Society [1970] 111 p. 22 cm. "Series of lectures delivered at the Seventh Day Baptist Ministers Conference." Includes bibliographical references. [BV111.S37] 73-120460 2.50
1. Sabbath. I. Title.

SHULER, John Lewis, 1887- 263
God's everlasting sign, by J. L. Shuler. Nashville, Southern Pub. Association [1972] 124 p. 21 cm. [BV125.S58] 72-80770
1. Sabbath. I. Title.

THOMSEN, Russel J. 263
Latter-day Saints and the Sabbath, by R. J. Thomsen. Mountain View, Calif., Pacific Press Pub. Association [1971] 150 p. illus., facsims., map, ports. 22 cm. (Dimension 110) Bibliography: p. 147-150. [BX8643.S2T48] 74-130031
1. Church of Jesus Christ of Latter-Day Saints—History. 2. Sabbath. I. Title.

*VANDEMAN, Jorge E. 263
Un dia memorable, Bogota, Ediciones Inter-americanas [1967] 95p. 18cm. .30 pap.,
I. Title.
American distributor: Pacific Pr. Pub. Assn., Mountain View, Calif.

WARD, Hiley H 263
Space-age Sunday. New York, Macmillan, 1960. 160 p. 22 cm. Includes bibliography. [BV130.W3] 60-10617
1. Sunday. I. Title.

WARD, Miley H. 263
Space-age Sunday. New York, Macmillan [c.] 1960. 160p. (Bibl. footnotes) endpaper map 22cm. 60-10617 3.95
1. Sunday. I. Title.

CLARKE, Edith Goreham. 263'.042
Tabernacle talks for young people, by E. Goreham Clarke. New York, Loizeaux Bros. [1954?] 127 p. 17 cm. (Treasury of truth, no. 206) [BM654.C55] 75-304239 0.50
1. Tabernacle. I. Title. II. Series.

PEROWNE, Stewart, 1901- 263'.042
Holy places of Christendom / [by] Stewart Perowne. London : Mowbrays, 1976. 160 p. : ill. (chiefly col.), map ; 27 cm. Ill. on lining papers. Includes index. [BV895.P47] 77-353538 ISBN 0-264-66057-9 : £4.95
1. Christian shrines. I. Title.

ZANDER, Walter. 263'.042'5694
Israel and the holy places of Christendom. New York, Praeger [1971] viii, 248 p. 23 cm. Includes bibliographical references. [DS119.6.Z3] 74-154352 8.50
1. Shrines—Palestine. 2. Israel—Foreign relations. I. Title.

ADAMS, Robert 263'.042'788
Hickman, 1937-
White churches of the Plains; examples from Colorado. Written & photographed by Robert Hickman Adams. With a foreword by Thomas Hornsby Ferril. Boulder, Colorado Associated University Press [1970] [84] p. illus. 27 cm. [F777.A3] 70-119708 ISBN 0-87081-000-6 9.75
1. Churches—Colorado. I. Title.

SOLBERG, Winton U. 263'.0973
Redeem the time : the Puritan Sabbath in early America / Winton U. Solberg. Cambridge : Harvard University Press, 1977. xii, 406 p. ; 24 cm. (A Publication of the Center for the Study of the History of Liberty in America, Harvard University) Includes index. Bibliography: p. 367-383. [BV111.S64] 76-26672 ISBN 0-674-75130-2 : 18.50
1. Sabbath—History. 2. Sunday—History. 3. Puritans. I. Title. II. Series: Harvard University. Center for the Study of the History of Liberty in America. Publication.

ANDREASEN, Niels-Erik A. 263'.1
The Old Testament Sabbath; a tradition-historical investigation, by Niels-Erik A. Andreasen. [Missoula, Mont.] Published by Society of Biblical Literature for the Form Criticism Seminar, 1972. xii, 301 p. 22 cm. (Dissertation series, no. 7) Originally presented as the author's thesis, Vanderbilt University, 1971. Bibliography: p. 275-301. [BS1199.S18A5 1972] 72-88671
1. Bible. O.T.—Criticism, interpretation, etc. 2. Sabbath—Biblical teaching. I. Title. II. Series: Society of Biblical Literature. Dissertation series, no. 7.

JOHNSON, Paul, 263'.13'0924 B
1928-
Pope John XXIII. [1st ed.] Boston, Little, Brown [1974] xiii, 266 p. port. 21 cm. (The Library of world biography) Bibliography: p. [247]-250. [BX1378.2.J66] 74-12325 ISBN 0-316-46755-3 6.95
1. Joannes XXIII, Pope, 1881-1963. I. Title.

JONES, Alonzo T. 263.2
God's sabbath: the only Lord's day. New York, Bx. 87, Cathedral Stat. People's Christian Bulletin, People's Christian Church, [1962] 61p. .50 pap.,
I. Title.

VANDEMAN, George E. 263.2
A day to remember. Mountain View, Calif., Pacific Pr. Pub. [c.1965] 103p. 19cm. [BX6154.V25] 65-24345 .30 pap.,
1. Seventh-Day Adventists—Doctrinal and controversial works. I. Title.

WALKER, Allen. 263.2
The law and the Sabbath. Nashville, Southern Pub. Association [1953] 240p. 21cm. [BX6154.W3] 54-17875
1. Seventh-Day Adventists—Doctrinal and controversial works. 2. Sabbath. I. Title.

ANTI-SABBATH Convention, 263'.3
Boston,
Proceedings. Reported by Henry M. Parkhurst. Port Washington, N.Y., Kennikat Press [1971] 168 p. 21 cm. (Kennikat Press scholarly reprints. Series on literary America in the nineteenth century) "Held in the Melodeon, March 23d and 24th." "First published in 1848." [BM685.A55 1971] 79-122662
1. Sabbath—Addresses, essays, lectures. 2. Sabbath legislation—U.S.—Addresses, essays, lectures. I. Parkhurst, Henry Martyn, 1825-

JEWETT, Paul King. 263'.3
The Lord's day; a theological guide to the Christian day of worship [by] Paul K. Jewett. Grand Rapids, Mich., W. B. Eerdmans Pub. Co. [1971] 174 p. 21 cm. Bibliography: p. 170-171. [BV111.J48] 77-162038 2.95
1. Sabbath. 2. Sunday. I. Title.

KIESLING, Christopher. 263'.3
The future of the Christian Sunday. New York, Sheed & Ward [1970] 142 p. 21 cm. [BV130.K5] 71-106155 ISBN 8-362-12290-4.50
1. Sunday. 2. Christianity—20th century. I. Title.

PORTER, Harry Boone 263.3
The day of light; the Biblical and liturgical meaning of Sunday. Greenwich, Conn., Seabury Press, 1960[ ] 86p. 22cm. Bibl. footnotes, 60-4401 1.75 pap.,
1. Sunday. I. Title.

RORDORF, Willy. 263'.3'09015
Sunday; the history of the day of rest and worship in the earliest centuries of the Christian church. [Translated by A. A. K. Graham from the German] Philadelphia, Westminster Press [1968] xvi, 335 p. 22 cm. Bibliographical footnotes. [BV111.R613] 68-15920
1. Sunday. I. Title.

RORDORF, Willy. 263'.3'09075
Sunday; the history of the day of rest and worship in the earliest centuries of the Christian church. [Translated by A. A. K. Graham from the German] Philadelphia, Westminster Press [1968] xvi, 335 p. 22 cm. Bibliographical footnotes. [BV111.R613] 68-15920
1. Sunday.

COWIE, Leonard W. 263'.9
The Christian calendar: a complete guide to the seasons of the Christian year telling the story of Christ and the saints, from Advent to Pentecost. Text by L. W. Cowie and John Selwyn Gummer. Springfield, Mass., G. & C. Merriam Co. [1974] 256 p. illus. 26 cm. [BV30.C7] 74-955 ISBN 0-87779-040-X 15.00
1. Church year. 2. Christian saints—Calendar. I. Gummer, John Selwyn, joint author. II. Title.

GWYNNE, Walker, 1845-1931. 263'.9
The Christian year; its purpose and its history. New York, Longmans, Green, 1917. Detroit, Grand River Books, 1971. xiv, 143 p. 22 cm. [BV30.G85 1971] 74-89269
1. Church year. I. Title.

KAMPMANN. THEODERICH. 263.9
The year of the church: mystery, fqrm, catechesis. Tr. by Mary Caroline Hemesath. Westminster. Md., Newman Pr. [c.] 1966. x, 96p. 22cm. Bibl. [BV30K313] 66-20035 3.50
1. Church year. I. Title.

KLEINHANS, Theodore J. 263'.9
The year of the Lord; the church year: its customs, growth & ceremonies [by] Theordore J. Kleinhans. St. Louis Concordia Pub. House [1967] xi, 115 p. 21 cm. Church year. [BV30.K55] 67-14768
I. Title.

MARING, Norman Hill, 1914- 263'.9
The Christian calendar in the free churches [by] Norman H. Maring. Valley Forge, Judson Press [1967] 63 p. 16 cm. [BV30.M35] 67-25889
1. Church year. I. Title.

PORTER, Harold Boone. 263'.9
Keeping the church year / Harold Boone Porter, Jr. New York : Seabury Press, 1977. p. cm. Originally published in a monthly column in the magazine The Living church. Includes index. [BV30.P67] 77-13338 ISBN 0-8164-2161-7 : pbk. 3.95
1. Church year—Addresses, essays, lectures. I. The Living church. II. Title.

URLIN, Ethel Lucy 263'.9
Hargreave, 1858-
Festivals, holy days, and saints' days; a study in origins and survivals in church ceremonies & secular customs. London, Simpkin, Marshall, Hamilton, Kent. Ann Arbor, Mich., Gryphon Books, 1971. xv, 271 p. illus. 22 cm. Reprint of the 1915 ed. Bibliography: p. 259-260. [BV43.U74 1971] 70-89301
1. Festivals. 2. Fasts and feasts. I. Title.

BROWN, Handel H. 263.91
Keeping the spirit of Christmas, by Handel H. Brown. Grand Rapids, Eerdmans [1965] 167 p. 22 cm. [BV45.B72] 65-25183
1. Christmas. I. Title.

CELEBRATING advent / 263'.91
edited by Robert Heyer. New York : Paulist Press, 1976c1975 83 p. : ill. ; 19 cm. "A New Catholic world book." "Articles ... originally appeared in the Nov./Dec. 1975 issue of New Catholic world." [BV40.C44] 74-28634 ISBN 0-8091-1864-5 pbk. : 1.45
1. Advent—Addresses, essays, lectures. I. Heyer, Robert J. II. New Catholic world.

DALLEN, James. 263'.91
Liturgical celebration : patterns for Advent and Christmas : presidential prayers and eucharistic prayer models for the Sundays and feast days of Advent and Christmas / by James Dallen. Cincinnati : North American Liturgy Resources, 1974. 76 p. ; 28 cm. [BX2170.A4D26] 75-309863 4.95
1. Advent—Prayer-books and devotions—English. 2. Christmas—Prayer-books and devotions—English. I. Title.

DEKRUYTER, Arthur H. 263'.91
Complete candlelight services for Christmas / by Arthur H. DeKruyter. Grand Rapids : Zondervan Pub. House, c1976. 50 p. ; 21 cm. [BV199.C45D44] 76-25124 pbk. : 2.50
1. Christmas service. I. Title.

IRION, Paul E 263'.91
The funeral: vestige or value? [by] Paul E. Irion. Nashville, Abingdon Press [1966] 240 p. 23 cm. Bibliography: p. 231-235. [BV199.F817] 265 66-11451
1. Funeral service. 2. Church work with the bereaved. I. Title.

*KONZELMAN, Robert 263.91
The talking Christmas tree; family devotions and doings for decorating your Christmas tree on the seven days preceding Christmas. Illus. by George Overlie. [Minneapolis] Augsburg, c.1966. 33p. illus. 20x27p. 1.50 pap.,
1. Christmas. 2. Christmas decorations. I. Title.

TALIAFERRO, Margaret. 263'.91
The real reason for Christmas : letters to children for the twelve nights of Christmas / by Margaret Taliaferro. Garden City, N.Y. : Doubleday, 1977. ca. 150 p. : ill. ; 22 cm. In twelve letters the author explains the reason for celebrating Christmas. [BV45.T33] 76-55080 ISBN 0-385-12414-7 : 5.95
1. Christmas—Juvenile literature. I. Title.

DALLEN, James. 263'.92
Liturgical celebration : patterns for Lent : presidential prayers and eucharistic prayer models for the Sundays of Lent (including Passion/Palm Sunday) developed from the scripture readings for all three years of the lectionary cycle / by James Dallen. Cincinnati : North American Liturgy Resources, 1974, c1973. 68 p. ; 28 cm. [BX2170.L4D34 1974] 75-309864 3.95
1. Lent—Prayer-books and devotions—English. I. Title.

SCHEMANN, Alexander, 1921- 263.92
Great Lent. [Tuckahoe, N.Y.] St. Vladimir's Seminary Press, 1969. 124 p. 22 cm. Bibliography: p. 119-124. [BV85.S35] 72-178338
1. Lent. I. Title.

GRELOT, Pierre, 1917- 263.93
The Paschal feast in the Bible, by P. Grelot, J. Pierron. Baltimore, Helicon [1966] 127p. 18cm. (Living world ser., 3) Tr. of La nuit et les fetes de Paques. [BS680.P33G714] 66-9665 1.25 pap.,
1. Passover— Biblical teaching. I. Pierron, J., joint author. II. Title.
Available from Taplinger, New York.

JOHNSON, Judith Anne. 263'.98
A transformational analysis of the syntax of Alfric's Lives of saints / by J. A. Johnson. The Hague : Mouton, 1976 111 p. ; 26 cm. (Janua linguarum : Series practica ; 212) Bibliography: p. [110]-111. [PR1525.J6] 76-475845 ISBN 9-02-793084-8 pbk. : 14.50
1. Alfric, Abbot of Eynsdam. Homiles. 2. Alfric, Abbot of Eynsdam—Language—Grammar. 3. Anglo-Saxon language—Syntax. 4. Anglo-Saxon language—Grammar, Generative. I. Title. II. Series.
Distributed by Humanities

264 Public Worship

ABBA, Raymond. 264
Principles of Christian worship. New York, Oxford University Press, 1957. 196 p. 21cm. Includes bibliography. [BV15.A15] 57-14051
1. Public worship. I. Title. II. Title: Christian worship.

ALEXANDER, Mary Anna. 264
Begin with these; programs for worship and work [by] Mary Anna Alexander and Beverly Norman. Nashville, Broadman Press [1958] 135p. illus. 21cm. [BV198.A4] [BV198.A4] 268.7 58-8921 58-8921
1. Worship programs. I. Norman, Beverly, joint author. II. Title.

ALLEN, J. P., 1912- 264
Reality in worship [by] J. P. Allen. Nashville, Convention Press [1955] xii, 115 p. 20 cm. [BV10.2.A35] 65-10323
1. Worship. I. Title.

ALLMEN, Jean Jacques von 264
Worship, its theology and practice. New York, Oxford [c.]1965. 317p. 23cm. Bibl. [BV10.2.A44] 65-23571 6.50
1. Worship. I. Title.

ALLMEN, Jean Jacques von. 264
Worship, its theology and practice, by J. J. von Allmen. New York. Oxford University Press, 1965. 317 p. 23 cm. Bibliography: p. 315-317. [BV10.2.A44] 65-23571
1. Worship. I. Title.

ARMES, Woodson, 1912- 264
What is worship? [By] Woodson and Sybil Armes. Nashville, Convention Press [c1965] x, 68 p. 19 cm. [BV10.2.A7] 65-10322
1. Worship. I. Armes, Sybil (Leonard) joint author. II. Title.

ARNOLD, Charlotte E, 1905- 264
Special programs for the Sunday school through the year. Cincinnati, Standard Pub. Co. [1952] 232 p. illus. 21 cm. [BV1572.A1A7] 268.7 52-31847
1. Sunday-schools—Exercises, recitations, etc. I. Title.

BABIN, David E. 264
The celebration of life: our changing liturgy, by David E. Babin. New York, Morehouse-Barlow [1969] viii, 112 p. 21 cm. Bibliographical footnotes. [BV176.B3] 79-97262
1. Liturgies. I. Title.

†BASSETT, S. Denton. 264
Public religious services in the hospital / by S. Denton Bassett ; with a foreword by Myron C. Madden. Springfield, Ill. : Thomas, c1976. xiv, 65 p. ; 24 cm. Includes index. Bibliography: p. 47. [BV4335.B33] 76-2356 ISBN 0-398-03563-6 : 7.50
1. Public worship in hospitals. 2. Church work with the sick. I. Title.

BAUMSTARK, Anton, 1872-1948. 264
Comparative liturgy. Rev. by Bernard Botte. English ed. by F. L. Cross. Westminster, Md., Newman Press [1958] 249p. 23cm. Includes bibliography. [BV175.B293 1958] 58-8754
1. Liturgics—Hist. I. Title.

BAXTER, Edna M 1895- 264
Learning to worship [by] Edna M. Baxter. Valley Forge [Pa.] Judson Press [1965] 255 p. 21 cm. Includes bibliographical references. [BV1522.B28] 64-20502
1. Worship (Religious education) I. Title.

BAXTER, Edna M. 1895- 264
Learning to worship. Valley Forge, Pa. Judson [c.1965] 255p. 21cm. Bibl. [BV1522.B28] 64-20502 3.95
1. Worship (Religious education) I. Title.

BAYNE, Stephen Fielding, 264
Bp., 1908-
Enter with joy. Greenwich, Conn., Seabury Press, 1961. 139p. 22cm. [BV10.2.B35] 61-14368
1. Worship. 2. Preaching. I. Title.

BECQUET, Thomas 264
Missal for young Catholics [by] Thomas Becquet, Alfonso Pereira, Harold Winstone. Glen Rock, N.J., Paulist Pr. [c.1963] 224p. illus. 15cm. price unreported pap.,
I. Title.

BELL, Arthur Donald. 264
Worship programs [by] A. Donald Bell. Grand Rapids, Mich., Zondervan Pub. House [1971] 63 p. 21 cm. [BV198.B43] 78-146562
1. Worship programs.

BENSON, Dennis C. 264
Electric liturgy [by] Dennis C. Benson. Richmond, John Knox Press, 1972. 96 p. 22 cm. Accompanied by 2 phonodiscs (4 s. 8 in. 33 1/3 rpm.) [BV15.B44] 72-175179 ISBN 0-8042-1593-6 4.95
1. Public worship. I. Title.

BLOY, Myron B. 264
Multi-media worship; a model and nine viewpoints. Edited by Myron B. Bloy, Jr. New York, Seabury Press [1969] 144 p. illus. 21 cm. (An Original Seabury paperback SP61) [BV10.2.B57] 78-92204 2.95
1. Worship—Addresses, essays, lectures. 2. Lord's Supper (Liturgy) 3. Youth—Religious life. I. Title.

BONTRAGER, John Kenneth. 264
Sea rations. Nashville, The Upper Room [1964] 88 p. illus. 19 cm. [BV198.B58] 64-14855
1. Worship programs. I. Title.

BOWMAN, Clarice Margurette, 1910- 264
The living art of worship. New York, Association [c.1964] 126p. 15cm. (Reflection bk.) An adaptation of [the author's] Resources for worship, containing part one of that book and special new material. 64-11421 .50 pap.,
1. Worship. I. Title.

BOWMAN, Clarice Margurette, 1910- 264
Restoring worship. New York, Abingdon-Cokesbury Press [1951] 223 p. 21 cm. [BV10.B6] 51-1341
1. Worship. I. Title.

BRAND, Eugene, 1931- 264
The rite thing. Minneapolis, Augsburg Pub. House [1970] 119 p. 20 cm. (A Tower book) Bibliography: p. 119. [BV10.2.B67] 74-101106
1. Worship. I. Title.

BRECK, Flora Elizabeth, 1886- 264
'Makings' of meetings; giving suggestions for meeting-planners Boston, W. A. Wilde Co. [1956] 80p. 20cm. [BV29.B67] 268.7 56-11570 56-11570
1. Young people's meetings (Church work) 2. Worhip programs. I. Title.

BRENNER, Scott Francis, 1903- 264
The art of worship; a guide in corporate worship techniques. New York, Macmillan [c.] 1961. 95p (Oikoumene) Bibl. 61-16541 2.75
1. Public worship. I. Title.

BRENNER, Scott Francis, 1903- 264
Ways of worship for new forms of mission. With action suggestions by Miriam Brattain. New York, Friendship Press [1968] 96 p. 19 cm. Bibliography: p. 95-96. [BV15.B73] 68-24792
1. Public worship. I. Title.

BRILLHART, Florence C 264
Together we praise Him group worship for women. [Westwood, N. J.] Revell [c1956] 144p. 21cm. [BV199.W6B7] 56-5238
1. Worship programs. I. Title.

BRUNNER, Peter, 1900- 264
Worship in the name of Jesus; English edition of a definitive work on Christian worship in the congregation. Translated by M. H. Bertram. St. Louis, Concordia Pub. House [1968] 375 p. 24 cm. Translation of Zur Lehre vom Gottesdienst der im Namen Jesu versammelten Gemeinde, first published in 1954 in v. 1 of Leiturgia, edited by K. F. Muller. Bibliographical references included in "Notes" (p. 313-357) [BV10.2.B753] 68-30965 9.75
1. Worship. I. Title.

BRYANT, Al, 1926- ed. 264
Encyclopedia of devotional programs for women's groups. Grand Rapids, Zondervan Pub. House [1956] 224p. 23cm: [BV199.W6B73] 268.7 56-25037
1. Worship programs. 2. Woman —Religious life. I. Title.

CABANISS, James Allen, 1911- 264
Liturgy and literature; selected essays, by Allen Cabaniss. University, University of Alabama Press [1970] 181 p. 22 cm. Contents.Contents.—The worship of "most primitive" Christianity.—Early Christian nighttime worship.—A fresh exegesis of Mark 2:1-12.—A note on the liturgy of the Apocalypse.—Wisdom 18:14-15; and early Christmas text.—Christmas echoes at Paschaltide.—The harrowing of Hell, Psalm 24, and Pliny the Younger: a note.—Petronius and the gospel before the gospels.—A note on the date of the Great Advent antiphons.—Beowulf and the liturgy.—Joseph of Arimathea and a chalice.—Alleluia; a word and its effect.—Shakespeare and the Holy Rosary. Includes bibliographical references. [PN49.C3] 73-92653 6.00
1. Liturgy and literature. I. Title.

CATHOLIC Church. Liturgy and ritual. Missal. English. 264
The Frere Jacques missal. Illustrated by Leopold Marboeuf. Springfield, Ill., Templegate [1962] 80 p. col. illus. 18 cm. A pamphlet for parents ([16]) p.) inserted. [BX2015.A55M3] 63-2129
1. Children's missals. I. Marboeuf, Leopold, illus. II. Catholic Church. Liturgy and ritual. English. III. Title.

CATHOLIC Church. Liturgy and ritual. Missal. English. 264
The Frere Jacques missal. Illus. by Leopold Marboeuf. Springfield, Ill., Templegate [1963, c.1962] 80p. col. illus. 18cm. A pamphlet for parents ([16]p.) inserted. 63-2129 2.95 bds.,
1. Children's missals. I. Marboeuf, Leopold, illus. II. Catholic Church. Liturgy and ritual. English. III. Title.

CATHOLIC Church. Liturgy and ritual. Missal. English. 264
The Saint Christopher missal; a first missal for children, prepared by the editors of Jubilee. [New York, Herder and Herder c1962] 142 p. illus. 17 cm. [BX2015.A4J8] 63-758
I. Jubilee; a magazine of the Church and her people. II. Catholic Church. Liturgy and ritual. English. III. Title.

CATHOLIC Church. Liturgy and ritual. Missal. English. 264
The Saint Christopher missal; a first missal for children, prepared by the editors of Jubilee. [New York] Herder & Herder [c.1962] 142p. col. illus. 17cm. 63-7586 2.95
I. Jubilee; a magazine of the Church and her people. II. Catholic Church. Liturgy and ritual. English. III. Title.

CATHOLIC Church. Liturgy and Ritual. Ritual. 264
Priest's ritual. Compiled from the Vatican typical ed. of the Rituale Romanum and the Collectio rituum. Psalms from new version. New York, Benziger Bros. [1962] 1v. 13cm. Chiefly Latin and English, with some sacraments in various languages. [BX2035.A4 1962] 62-4864
I. Title.

CHRISTENSEN, James L. 264
Contemporary worship services; a sourcebook [by] James L. Christensen. Old Tappan, N.J., Revell [1971] 256 p. 21 cm. Bibliography: p. 239-241. [BV198.C53] 75-137445 ISBN 0-8007-0432-0 5.95
1. Worship programs. I. Title.

CHRISTENSEN, James L. 264
Creative ways to worship [by] James L. Christensen. Old Tappan, N.J., F. H. Revell Co. [1974] 256 p. 21 cm. Includes bibliographical references. [BV198.C534] 74-3210 ISBN 0-8007-0651-X 5.95
1. Worship programs. I. Title.

CHRISTENSEN, James L. 264
The minister's service handbook. [Westwood, N. J.] Revell [c.1960] 160p. 17cm. Bibl. notes: p. 157-160 60-13092 2.50
1. Pastoral theology—Handbooks, manuals, etc. 2. Liturgies. I. Title.

CHRISTENSEN, James L. 264
New ways to worship; more contemporary worship services. Old Tappan, N.J., Revell [1973] 224 p. 21 cm. Bibliography: p. 217-219. [BV198.C54] 73-933 ISBN 0-8007-0583-1 5.95
1. Worship programs. I. Title.

CLAPP, Mary Constance. 264
The golden quest of worship. [1st ed.] New York, Vantage Press [1957] 106p. 21cm. [BV15.C55] 57-8550
1. Worship. I. Title.

COFFIN, Henry Sloane, 1877-1954. 264
The public worship of God; a source book. Freeport, N.Y., Books for Libraries Press [1972, c1946] 208 p. 22 cm. (Essay index reprint series) Original ed. issued in series: The Westminster source books. Bibliography: p. [199]-205. [BV10.C65 1972] 75-167327 ISBN 0-8369-7272-4
1. Public worship.

COME, let us adore Him; 264
a book of worship services. [Westwood, N. J.] Revell [c1956] 159 p. 21 cm. [BV198.E53] 268.7 56-5239
1. Worship programs. I. Ely, Virginia, 1899-

CONFERENCE on the Layman as a Leader of Worship, Charleston, S.C., 1968. 264
The layman as a leader of worship. The study papers presented at, and a report on the considerations and recommendations of, the Conference on the Layman as a Leader of Worship. [Washington? 1969] v, 82 p. 26 cm. "NAVPERS 15155." "Jointly sponsored by Commander, Submarine Force, U.S. Atlantic Fleet [and] Chief of Chaplains, U.S. Navy." Includes bibliographical references. [BV10.2.C65] 75-605351
1. Public worship—Congresses. 2. Laity—Congresses. I. U.S. Navy. Chaplain Corps. II. U.S. Navy. Atlantic Fleet. Submarine Force. III. Title.

COOK, Virginia D. 264
Guideposts for worship. St. Louis, Bethany [c.1964] 136p. illus. 23cm. 64-12011 3.00
1. Worship programs. I. Title.

COUCH, Helen F., ed. 264
Worship sourcebook for youth [by] Helen F. Couch, Sam S. Barefield. Nashville, Abingdon [c.1962] 304p. Bibl. 62-8104 4.50
1. Worship programs. I. Barefield, Sam S., joint ed. II. Title.

CULLEY, Iris V 264
Christian worship and church education, by Iris V. Cully. Philadelphia, Westminister Press [1967] 187 p. 21 cm. Bibliography: p. [177]-184. [BV10.2.C8] 67-20614
1. Worship. 2. Worship (Religious education) I. Title.

CULLY, Iris V. 264
Christian worship and church education, by Iris V. Cully. Philadelphia, Westminster Press [1967] 187 p. 21 cm. Bibliography: p. [177]-184. [BV10.2.C8] 67-20614
1. Worship. 2. Worship (Religious education) I. Title.

DAVIES, Horton. 264
Christian worship, its history and meaning. New York, Abingdon Press [1957] 128p. 21cm. Includes bibliography. [BV10.D37] 57-9784
1. Worship. I. Title.

DEISS, Lucien. 264
Early sources of the liturgy. Translated by Benet Weatherhead. Staten Island, N.Y., Alba House [1967] xi, 201 p. 22 cm. Translation of Aux sources de la liturgie. Bibliography: p. 200-204. [BV185.D4] 67-6597
1. Liturgies, Early Christian. I. Title.

DEISS, Lucien. 264
Early sources of the liturgy. Translated by Benet Weatherhead. Staten Island, N.Y., Alba House [1967] xi, 204 p. 22 cm. Translation of Aux sources de la liturgie. Bibliography: p. 200-204. [BV185.D4] 67-6597
1. Liturgies, Early Christian. I. Title.

DUNPHY, Mary A. 264
My Mass book: the story of the Mass for young communicants. Illus. by Alan Moyler. New York, Exposition. [c.1964] 46p. illus. 33cm. 64-1498 4.50
1. Mass—Juvenile literature. I. Title.

EASTWOOD, Edna. comp. 264
Let's explore worship; an activity program created by the pupils for church school worship. New York, Morehouse-Gorham Co., 1952. 116 p. 20 cm. [BV1522.E15] 268.7 52-13439
1. Worship (Religious education) I. Title.

EDWARDS, Elizabeth. 264
Sound his glories forth; religious programs for churches and schools, by Elizabeth Edwards and Gladys Besancon. Grand Rapids, Baker Book House, 1965. 172 p. 23 cm. [PN6120.R4E37] 65-2258
1. Religious drama. I. Besancon, Gladys, joint author. II. Title.

EDWARDS, Elizabeth 264
Sound his glories forth; religious programs for churches and schools. by Elizabeth Edwards, Gladys Besancon. Grand Rapids, Mich., Baker Bk. [c.]1965. 172p. 23cm. [PN6120.R4E37] 65-2258 3.95
1. Religious drama. I. Besancon, Gladys, joint author. II. Title.

ELBIN, Paul Nowell, 1905- 264
The improvement of college worship, by Paul N. Elbin. New York, Bureau of Publications, Teachers College, Columbia University, 1932. [New York, AMS Press, 1973, c1972] vii, 154 p. 22 cm. Reprint of the 1932 ed., issued in series: Teachers College, Columbia University. Contributions to education, no. 530. Originally presented as the author's thesis, Columbia. Bibliography: p. 152-154. [BV26.E5 1972] 72-176744 ISBN 0-404-55530-6 10.00
1. Universities and colleges—Chapel exercises. I. Title. II. Series: Columbia University. Teachers College. Contributions to education, no. 530.

ELFORD, Homer J. R. 264
A layman's guide to Protestant worship. Nashville, Abingdon [c.1963] 64p. 17cm. .75 pap.,
I. Title.

EMSWILER, Sharon Neufer. 264
Women and worship; a guide to non-sexist hymns, prayers, and liturgies [by] Sharon Neufer Emswiler and Thomas Neufer Emswiler. [1st ed.] New York, Harper & Row [1974] 115 p. 21 cm. Bibliography: p. 114-115. [BV198.E57] 73-18681 ISBN 0-06-062245-8 5.95
1. Liturgies. 2. Public worship. 3. Women in Christianity. I. Emswiler, Thomas Neufer, joint author. II. Title.
Pbk. 1.95

FAUTH, Robert T. 264
When we worship. Philadelphia [2][1505 Race St., Christian Education Press c.1961] 88p. Bibl. 61-7446 1.50 bds.,
1. Public worship. I. Title.

FOULDS, Elfrida Vipont (Brown) 1902- 264
Some Christian festivals; to which is appended a brief glossary of Christian terminology, by Elfrida Vipont. New York, Roy Publishers [1964, c1963] 194 p. 21 cm. Bibliography: p. 190-194. [BV30.F63] 64-22187
1. Fasts and feasts. I. Title.

FOULDS. ELFRIDA VIPONT (BROWN) 1902- 264
Some Christian festivals: to which is appended a brief glossary of Christian terminology, by Elfrida Vipont. New York, Roy [1964, c.1963] 194p. 21cm. Bibl. 64-22187 4.00
1. Fasts and feasts. I. Title.

FULTON, Mary Beth. 264
Moments of worship; resources for personal and group worship. Philadelphia, Judson Press [1953] 130p. illus. 21cm. [BV198.F8] 268.7 53-7614
1. Worship programs. I. Title.

GARRONE, Gabriel Marie, Abp., 1901- 264
Pourquoi prier? [Toulouse] Privat [dist. Philadelphia, Chilton, 1964, c.1962] 153p. 19cm. (Questions posees aux catholiques) 64-9073 1.50 pap.,
1. Prayer. I. Title.

GIBSON, George Miles, 1896- 264
The story of the Christian year, by George M. Gibson. Illustrated by the author. Freeport, N.Y., Books for Libraries Press [1972, c1945] 238 p. illus. 24 cm. (Essay index reprint series) Bibliography: p. 229-230. [BV30.G5 1972] 71-142635 ISBN 0-8369-2770-2
1. Church year. 2. Festivals. I. Title.

GUDNASON, Kay. 264
Complete worship services for the college age; in which David speaks to youth from the Psalms. Introd. by Eugenia Price. Grand Rapids, Zondervan Pub. House [1956] 153p. 21cm. [BV29.G8] 268.7 56-42839
1. Worship programs. 2. Young people's meetings (Church work) I. Title.

GUNNEMANN, Louis H. 264
The life of worship; an adult resource book [by] Louis H. Gunnemann. Boston. United Church Pr. [1966] 76p. illus. 21cm. Bibl [BV10.2.G78] 66-12054 price unreported pap.,
1. Worship. 2. Religious education—Textbooks for adults—United Church of Christ. I. Title.

GUNNEMANN, Louis H. 264
Worship; a course book for adults [by] Louis H. Gunnemann. Boston, United Church Pr. [1966] 60p. 21cm. Bibl. [BV10.2.G8] 66-12053 price unreported. pap.,
1. Worship—Study and teaching. I. Title.

HADDAM House, inc. 264
The student prayerbook; edited and written by a Haddam House committee, under the chairmanship of John Oliver Nelson, for personal and group devotion. New York, Association Press [1953] 237p. 20cm. (A Haddam House Book) [BV283.C7H3] 53-11972
1. Students—Prayer-books and devotions—English. I. Title.

HAHN, Wilhelm Traugott 264
Worship and congregation. Tr. [from German] by Geoffrey Buswell. Richmond, Va., Knox [1963] 75p. 22cm. (Ecumenical studies in worship, no. 12) Bibl. 63-8699 1.75 pap.,
1. Worship. I. Title. II. Series.

HARDIN, H Grady. 264
The celebration of the gospel; a study in Christian worship [by] H. Grady Hardin, Joseph D. Quillian, Jr. [and] James F. White. Nashville, Abingdon Press [1964] 192 p. 21 cm. Bibliography: p. 175-185. [BV176.H3] 64-15760
1. Liturgies. 2. Liturgical movement — Protestant churches. 3. Public worship. I. Title.

HARDIN, H. Grady 264
The celebration of the gospel; a study in Christian worship [by] H. Grady Hardin, Joseph D. Quillian, Jr., James F. White. Nashville, Abingdon [c.1964] 192p. 21cm. Bibl. 64-15760 3.25
1. Liturgies. 2. Liturgical movement—Protestant churches. 3. Public worship. I. Title.

HARPER, Howard V 264
Days and customs of all faiths. New York, Fleet Pub. Corp. [1957] 399p. 21cm. [GR930.H3] 57-14777
1. Days. 2. Manners and customs. I. Title.

HAUCK, Allan 264
Calendar of Christianity. New York, Association Press [c.1961] 127p. 15cm. (Association Press reflection book, 543) 61-7116 .50 pap.,
1. Church year. 2. Fasts and feasts. I. Title.

HEAD, David 264
Countdown, the launching of prayer in the space age. New York, Macmillan [1964,

c.1963] 184p. 22cm. First pub. in London in 1963 under title: Three, two, one, zero. 64-14970 2.75 bds.,
1. Prayer. I. Title.

HEDLEY, George Percy, 1899- 264
When Protestants worship. Nashville, Pub. for the Cooperative Pubn. Assn. by Abingdon [c.1961] 96p. (Faith for life ser.) 62-16016 1.00 pap.,
1. Public worship. I. Title.

HERRLIN, Olle. 264
Divine service; liturgy in perspective, by Olof Herrlin. Translated by Gene J. Lund. Philadelphia, Fortress Press [1966] 162 p. 21 cm. Translation of Liturgiska perspektiv. Bibliographical references included in "Notes" (p. [155] -- 162) [BV10.2.H4713] 66-10936
1. Worship — Addresses, essays, lectures. I. Title.

HERRLIN, Olle 264
Divine service; liturgy in perspective. Tr. [from Swedish] by Gene J. Lund. Philadelphia, Fortress [c.1966] 162p. 21cm. Bibl. [BV10.2.H4713] 66-10936 3.75
1. Worship—Addresses, essays, lectures. I. Title.

HERSEY, Norman L. 264
Worship services for special occasions. Compiled and edited by Norman L. Hersey. New York, World Pub. Co. [1971, c1970] 214 p. 21 cm. [BV199.O3H4 1971] 70-100002 6.95
1. Worship programs. I. Title.

HIMMELHEBER, Diana (Martin) 264
On paths unknown; a young group's adventure in worship. St. Louis, Bethany [c.1964] 176p. illus. 21cm. Bibl. 64-23621 2.75
1. Worship programs. 2. Youth—Religious life. I. Title.

HITCHCOCK, James. 264
The recovery of the sacred. New York, Seabury Press [1974] xii, 175 p. 22 cm. "A Crossroad book." Includes bibliographical references. [BV176.H57] 73-17899 ISBN 0-8164-1150-6 6.95
1. Liturgics. 2. Rites and ceremonies. 3. Holy, The. I. Title.

HOON, Paul Waitman, 1910- 264
The integrity of worship; ecumenical and pastoral studies in liturgical theology. Nashville, Abingdon Press [1971] 363 p. 24 cm. Includes bibliographical references. [BV176.H66] 70-148861 ISBN 0-687-19108-4 8.50
1. Liturgics. I. Title.

HOPPER, Myron Taggart, 1903- 264
The candle of the Lord. [Rev. ed.] St. Louis, Bethany Press [1957] 240p. 21cm. [BV29.H58 1957] 57-9776
1. Worship programs. 2. Young people's meetings (Church work) I. Title.

HORN, Edward Traill. 264
The Christian year. Philadelphia, Muhlenberg Press [1957] 243p. 22cm. Includes bibliography. [BV30.H6] 57-5753
1. Church year. 2. Lutheran Church. Liturgy and ritual. I. Title.

HORTON, Douglas, 1891- 264
The meaning of worship. New York, Harper [1959] 152p. 20cm. (The Lyman Beecher lectures for 1958) [BV10.2.H6] 59-7151
1. Worship. I. Title.

†HOVDA, Robert W. 264
Strong, loving, and wise : presiding in liturgy / by Robert W. Hovda ; foreword by Godfrey Diekmann. Washington : Liturgical Conference, c1976. ix, 98 p. : ill. ; 28 cm. Bibliography: p. 95-98. [BV178.H68] 76-56474 ISBN 0-918208-12-2 pbk. : 8.25
1. Liturgics. I. Title.

HOW to plan informal 264
worship. New York, Association Press [1955] 64p. 20cm. (Leadership library) [BV259] 55-7407
1. Worship. 2. Worship programs. I. Wygal, Winnifred, 1884-

HOWSE, William Lewis, 1905- 264
In spirit and in truth, a book of worship programs. Rev. and enl. ed. [Westwood, N. J.] F. H. Revell Co. [1955] 96p. 20cm. [BV1522.H67 1955] 268.7 55-5392
1. Worship programs. I. Title.

HOYT, Margaret. 264
Youth looking to Jesus; worship services, by Margaret Hoyt and Eleanor Hoyt Dabney. Illus. by Virginia Templin Gailey. Richmond, John Knox Press [1954] 191p. illus. 25cm. [BV1522.H68] 268.7 53-11765
1. Worship (Religious education) I. Dabney, Eleanor Hoyt, joint author. II. Title.

HUBBARD, David Allan. 264
Church—who needs it? Glendale, Calif., G/L Regal Books [1974] 145 p. 18 cm. [BX6333.H78C48] 73-90622 ISBN 0-8307-0285-7 1.25
1. Baptists—Sermons. 2. Sermons, American. I. Title.

HUCK, Gabe. 264
Liturgy needs community needs liturgy; the possibilities for parish liturgy. New York, Paulist Press [1973] vii, 88 p. illus. 18 cm. (Paulist Press Deus books) [BV176.H82] 73-84360 ISBN 0-8091-1791-6 1.25 (pbk.)
1. Liturgics. I. Title.

HUSS, John Ervin, 1910- 264
Ideas for a successful church program. Grand Rapids, Zondervan Pub. House [1954] 149p. 20cm. [BV652.H8] 54-34232
I. Title.

*HUTTON, Samuel Ward 264
Minister's service manual. Grand Rapids, Mich., Baker Bk., 1964 [c.1958] 224p. 18cm. 2.95
I. Title.

HUTTON, Samuel Ward, 1886- 264
Dedication services. Grand Rapids, Mich., Baker Bk. [1965, c c.1964] 79p. 21cm. (Minister's handbk. ser.) [BV199.D4H8] 64-8349 1.95 bds.,
1. Dedication services. I. Title.

HUXHOLD, Harry N. 264
Bless we the Lord; weekday lessons in the church year for home, church, and school. [Saint Louis] Concordia Pub. House [1963] 123 p. 23 cm. [BV30.H8] 63-18734
1. Church year. 2. Worship programs. I. Title.

HUXHOLD, Harry N. 264
Bless we the Lord; weekday lessons in the church year for home, church, and school. [Saint Louis] Concordia [c.1963] 123p. 23cm. 63-18734 2.00
1. Church year. 2. Worship programs. I. Title.

JAMES, Edwin Oliver, 1886- 264
Christian myth and ritual; a historical study. Cleveland, World [1965] xv, 345p. 21cm. (Living age bks., Meridian bks., LA43) Bibl. [BV175.J3] 65-18001 2.25 pap.,
1. Rites and ceremonies. 2. Christianity and other religions. 3. Catholic Church. Liturgy and ritual—Hist. I. Title.

JAMES, Edwin Oliver, 1886- 264
Christian myth and ritual; a historical study [Gloucester, Mass., P. Smith, 1965] xv, 345p. 21cm. (Living age bks., Meridian bk., La43 rebound) Bibl. [BV175.J3] 4.25
1. Rites and ceremonies. 2. Christianity and other religions. 3. Catholic Church. Liturgy and ritual—History. I. Title.

JENNY, Henri, Bp., 1904- 264
The pascal mystery in the Christian year. Translated by Allan Stehling and John Lundberg. Notre Dame, Ind., Fides Publishers [1962] 112p. 19cm. [BT265.2.J413] 62-4171
1. Jesus Christ—Atonement. 2. Church year. I. Title.

JOINT Liturgical Group. 264
The renewal of worship; essays by members of the Joint Liturgical Group. Edited by Ronald C. D. Jasper. London, New York, Oxford University Press, 1965. viii, 102 p. 19 cm. Contents.The renewal of worship: introduction, by R. C. D. Jasper.--The church at worship, by R. D. Whitehorn.--Liturgy and unity, by J. A. Lamb.--Embodied worship, by S. F. Winward.--Prayer: fixed, free, and extemporary, by J. Huxtable.--Private devotion, by R. E. Davies.--Liturgy and the mission of the church, by R. A. Davies. Bibliographical footnotes. [BV10.2.J6] 66-575
1. Worship—Addresses, essays, lectures. I. Jasper, Ronald Claud Dudley, ed. II. Title.

JOINT Liturgical Group 264
The renewal of worship: essays by members of the Joint Liturgical Group. Ed. by Ronald C. D. Jasper. New York. Oxford [c.] 1965. viii, 102p. 19cm. Bibl. [BV10.2.J6] 66-575 1.55 pap.,
1. Worship—Addresses, essays, lectures. I. Jasper, Ronald Claud Dudley, ed. II. Title.

JONES, Elizabeth Brown, 1907- 264
When we go to church. Pictures by Vera Gohman. Anderson, Ind., Warner Press [1957] unpaged. illus. 23cm. [BV4523] 57-4258
1. Church attendance—Juvenile literature. I. Title.

JONES, Ilion Tingnal, 1889- 264
A historical approach to evangelical worship. Nashville, Abingdon Press [1954] 319p. 24cm. [BV10.J6] 53-11339
1. Public worship. I. Title.

JONES, Paul D. 264
Rediscovering ritual [by] Paul D. Jones. New York, Newman Press [1973] 81 p. illus. 24 cm. [BV176.J66] 73-77392 ISBN 0-8091-0180-7 3.95
1. Liturgies. 2. Ritual. I. Title.

KAY, J Alan. 264
The nature of Christian worship. New York, Philosophical Library [1954] 115p. 20cm. [BV10.K3] 54-2129
1. Worship. I. Title.

KEIR, Thomas H. 264
The word in worship; preaching and its setting in common worship. New York, Oxford [c.] 1962. 150p. 19cm. 62-51116 3.50
1. Public worship. 2. Preaching. I. Title.

KERR, James S. 264
The little liturgy; a children's introduction to Lutheran worship. Illus. by Ollie Jensen. Minneapolis, Augsburg [c.1965] 48p. col. illus. 22cm. [BX8073.K4] 65-12136 2.50
1. Lord's Supper (Liturgy)—Juvenile) literature. 2. Lord's Supper—Lutheran Church—Juvenile literature. I. Lutheran Church. Liturgy and ritual. II. Title.

KILLINGER, John. 264
Leave it to the Spirit; commitment and freedom in the new liturgy. [1st ed.] New York, Harper & Row [1971] xviii, 235 p. 22 cm. Includes bibliographical references. [BV15.K47 1971] 78-149749 6.95
1. Public worship. I. Title.

KNIGHT, Cecil B. 264
Pentecostal worship / edited by Cecil B. Knight. Cleveland, Tenn. : Pathway Press, [1974] 140 p. ; 20 cm. Includes bibliographies. [BV15.K56] 74-83548 ISBN 0-87148-684-9
1. Public worship. 2. Pentecostalism. I. Title.

KOENKER, Ernest Benjamin. 264
Worship in word and sacrament. Saint Louis, Concordia Pub. House [1959] 109p. illus. 19cm. [BV10.2.K6] 59-10270
1. Public worship. 2. Lutheran Church. Liturgy and ritual. I. Title.

LIND, Millard, 1918- 264
Biblical foundations for Christian worship, by Millard C. Lind. Scottdale, Pa., Herald Press, 1973. 61 p. 18 cm. Based on a paper presented at the 1969 Mennonite General Conference. Includes bibliographical references. [BS680.W78L55] 72-7620 ISBN 0-8361-1701-8 0.95 (pbk.)
1. Worship—Biblical teaching. I. Title.

LITURGICAL experience of 264
faith. Edited by Herman Schmidt and David Power. [New York] Herder and Herder [1973] 136 p. 23 cm. (Concilium, 82) Series statement also appears as: The New concilium. Includes bibliographical references. [BV176.L56] 72-12420 ISBN 0-8164-2538-8 3.95
1. Liturgics. 2. Faith. I. Schmidt, Herman A. P., 1912- ed. II. Power, David Noel, ed. III. Title. IV. Series.

LITURGY: self-expression of 264
the church. Edited by Herman Schmidt. [New York] Herder and Herder [1972] 155 p. 23 cm. (Concilium: religion in the seventies, v. 72 Liturgy) On cover: The New concilium: religion in the seventies. Includes bibliographical references. [BV176.L58] 77-168650 pap. 2.95
1. Liturgics—Addresses, essays, lectures. I. Schmidt, Herman A. P., 1912- ed II. Series. Concilium: theology in the age of renewal, v. 72.

LUBIENSKA DE LENVAL, Helene 264
The whole man at worship; the actions of man before God. Tr. [from French] by Rachel Attwater. New York, Desclee [1962, c.]1961. 86p. 20cm. 62-1172 1.95 bds.,
1. Liturgics. I. Title.

MCARTHUR, A Allan. 264
The evolution of the Christian year. Greenwich, Conn., Seabury Press [1953] 192p. 23cm. [BV30] 55-381
1. Church year. I. Title.

MCCABE, Joseph E. 1912- 264
Service book for ministers. New York, McGraw [c.1961] 226p. 61-11392 3.95
1. Liturgiew. I. Title.

MCDORMAND, Thomas Bruce. 264
The art of building worship services. Rev. ed. Nashville, Broadman Press, 1958. 123p. 21cm. Includes bibliography. [BV10.M24 1958] 58-11547
1. Public worship. 2. Worship (Religious education) I. Title.

MCELROY, Paul Simpson, 1902- 264
comp.
A sourcebook for Christian worship. Compiled and edited by Paul S. McElroy. Cleveland, World Pub. Co. [1968] xii, 239 p. 24 cm. [BV198.M33 1968] 68-17647
1. Liturgies. I. Title. II. Title: Christian worship.

MACGREGOR, Geddes. 264
The rhythm of God; a philosophy of worship. New York, Seabury Press [1974] 120 p. 22 cm. "A Crossroad book." [BV15.M28] 74-13598 ISBN 0-8164-1174-3 6.95
1. Public worship. I. Title.

MARSHALL, Romey P. 264
Liturgy and Christian unity [by] Romey P. Marshall, Michael J. Taylor. Englewood Cliffs, N.J., Prentice [c.1965] vi, 186p. 21cm. Bibl. [BV10.2.M3] 65-17534 4.95 bds.,
1. Worship—Comparative studies. 2. Catholic Church—Relations—Protestant churches. 3. Protestant churches—Relations—Catholic Church. 4. Christian union. 5. Liturgical movement. I. Taylor, Michael J. II. Title.

MARTIN, David E. 264
Worship services for special days; forty-four complete services of worship for eighteen great days of the church. Anderson, Ind., Warner [c.1963] 96p. 22cm. 63-10213 1.25 pap.,
1. Worship programs. I. Title.

MARTIN, William Benjamin 264
James.
Acts of worship. New York, Abingdon Press [1960] 192p. 18cm. [BV198.M38] 60-10912
1. Liturgies. I. Title.

MASSEY, James Earl. 264
The worshiping church; a guide to the experience of worship. Anderson, Ind., Warner Press [1961] 106p. 19cm. [BV15.M35] 61-15360
1. Public worship. I. Title.

MAYNARD, Lee Carter. 264
52 worship services (with sermon outlines) / by Lee Carter Maynard. Cincinnati, Ohio : Standard Pub., c1976. 160 p. ; 22 cm. [BV198.M42] 75-27714 pbk. : 3.95
1. Worship programs. I. Title.

MICKS, Marianne H. 264
The future present; the phenomenon of Christian worship [by] Marianne H. Micks. New York, Seabury Press [1974, c1970] xiv, 204 p. 21 cm. "A Crossroad book." [BV15.M52 1974] 74-17343 ISBN 0-8164-2109-9 3.95
1. Public worship. I. Title.

MICKS, Marianne H. 264
The future present; the phenomenon of Christian worship. New York, Seabury Press [1974, c1970] xiv, 204 p. 21 cm. (A Crossroad book) Includes bibliographical references. [BV10.2.M5] 75-103844 ISBN 0-8164-2109-9. 3.95 (pbk.)
1. Worship. I. Title.

MITCHELL, Leonel Lake, 1930- 264
Liturgical change, how much do we need? : With study guide / by Leonel L. Mitchell. New York : Seabury Press, [1975] 122 p. ; 20 cm. "A Crossroad book." Bibliography: p. 119-122. [BV176.M57] 74-26928 ISBN 0-8164-2113-7 pbk. : 3.50
1. Liturgics—Study and teaching. I. Title.

MOORE, Ralph. 264
Toward celebration, with suggestions for using the celebration packet. Philadelphia, Published for Joint Educational Development [by] United Church Press [1973] 126 p. illus. 22 cm. (A Shalom resource book) Part of the Celebration packet which also includes Celebration sharings and sounds, and Liturgical simulation exercise. Bibliography: p. [101]-113. [BV15.M66] 73-6754
1. Public worship. I. Joint Educational Development. II. Title.

MORE children's worship in 264
the church school. [1st ed.] New York, Harper [1953] 250p. 22cm. [BV1522.B76] 268.7 53-5435
1. Worship (Religious education) I. Brown, Jeanette (Perkins) 1887-

MURRELL, Gladys Clarke 264
(Callahan) 1894-
Glimpses of grace; worship services based on women of the Bible. Nashville, Abingdon [1963, c.1941] 107p. 18cm. (Apex bks., M6-69) .69 pap.,
1. Liturgies. 2. Women of the Bible. I. Title. II. Title: Worship services based on women of the Bible.

MURRELL, Gladys Clarke 264
(Callahan) 1894-
Patterns for devotion; twenty-seven story worship services. New York, Abingdon-Cokesbury [1950] 108 p. 18 cm. Bibliography: p. 107-108. [BV198.M83] 50-8419
1. Worship programs. I. Title.

MURRELL, Gladys Clarke (Callahan) 1894- 264
Patterns for devotion; twenty-seven story worship services. Nashville, Abingdon [1967,c.1950] 108p. 17cm. (Apex bks., AA6-95) Bibl. [BV198.M83] 50-8419 .95 pap.,
1. Worship programs. I. Title.

NEALE, John Mason, 1818-1866. 264
Essays on liturgiology and church history / by J. M. Neale ; with an appendix on liturgical quotations from the isapostolic fathers, by Gerard Moultrie. New York : AMS Press, [1976] p. cm. Reprint of the 1863 ed. published by Saunders, Otley, London. Includes bibliographical references. [BV175.N4 1976] 70-173070 ISBN 0-404-04667-3
1. Liturgics—Addresses, essays, lectures. 2. Church history—Addresses, essays, lectures. I. Title.

NELSON, Ruth Youngdahl. 264
The Christian woman; ten programs for women's organizations. Rock Island, Ill., Augustana Book Concern [1951] 96p. 20cm. [BV4527.N4] 51-12981
1. Woman—Religious life. I. Title.

NICHOLLS, William. 264
Jacob's ladder: the meaning of worship. Richmond, John Knox Press [1958] 72p. 22cm. (Ecumenical studies in worship, no.4) [BV10.2.N5] 58-12804
1. Worship. I. Title.

OAKLEY, Austin. 264
The Orthodox liturgy. Alcuin Club ed. London, Mowbray; New York, Morehouse-Gorham [1958] 50p. 22cm. (Studies in Eucharistic faith and practice) Includes bibliography. [BX350.O2] 59-498
1. Orthodox Eastern Church. Liturgy and ritual. I. Title.

O'GUIN, C. M. 264
Special occasion helps. Grand Rapids, Mich., Baker Book [c.]1965. 87p. 21cm. (Minister's handbk. ser.) [BV199.O3O35] 65-18265 1.95
1. Occasional services. I. Title.

ORTHODOX Eastern Church. 264
Liturgy and ritual. Leitourgikon.
The divine liturgy of St. John Chrysostom, in Greek andEnglish, with comparison with others [sic] liturgies and a short explanation of rituals, vestments and short prayers, by A. G. S. Papastefanou. Chicago, Greek Art Print. & Pub. Co., 1928. 159p. front. 16cm. [BX350.A2 1928] 62-56436
I. Orthodox Eastern Church. Liturgy and ritual. English. II. Papastephanos, Alexander George S., 1896- III. Title.

OSBORN, George Edwin, 1897- ed. 264
Christian worship, a service book. St. Louis, Christian Board of Publication, 1953. 598p. 23cm. [BV175.O8] 53-26457
1. Liturgies. 2. Public worship. I. Title.

OSBORN, George Edwin, 1897- ed. 264
Christian worship, a service book. [2d ed.] St. Louis, Christian Board of Publication [c1958] 598p. 22cm. [BV175.O8 1958] 58-10259
1. Liturgies. 2. Public worship. I. Title.

PALMER, Gordon, 1888- 264
A manual of church services; with a summary of State laws governing marriage. Introd. by John W. Bradbury. Rev. ed. New York, Revell [1950] 166 p. diagrs. 21 cm. Bibliography: p. 163-166. [BV198.P32 1950] 50-8688
1. Liturgies. 2. Marriage law — U.S. — States. I. Title.

PAQUIER, Richard. 264
Dynamics of worship; foundations and uses of liturgy. Translated by Donald Macleod. Philadelphia, Fortress Press [1967] xix, 224 p. 23 cm. Translation of Traite de liturgique. Bibliographical footnotes. [BV10.2.P313] 67-19040
1. Worship. I. Title.

PAQUIER, Richard. 264
Dynamics of worship; foundations and uses of liturgy. Translated by Donald Macleod. Philadelphia, Fortress Press [1967] xix, 224 p. 23 cm. Translation of Traite de liturgique. Bibliographical footnotes. [BV10.2.P313] 67-19040
1. Worship. I. Title.

PARROTT, Lora Lee (Montgomery) 1923- 264
Devotional programs for women's groups. Grand Rapids, Zondervan Pub. House [1952-53] 2v. 20cm. [BV198.P36] 268.7 52-7999
1. Worship programs. I. Title.

PEARCE, J. Winston 264
Come, let us worship. Nashville, Broadman [c.1965] 127p. 20cm. Bibl. [BV10.2.P4] 65-11765 1.50 bds.,
1. Worship. I. Title.

PHIFER, Kenneth G. 264
A Protestant case for liturgical renewal. Philadelphia. Westminster [1965] 175p. 21cm. Bibl. [BV10.2.P5] 65-13493 3.95
1. Worship. 2. Liturgical movement—Protestant churches. I. Title.

PICKTHORN, William E., ed. 264
Minister's manual. Springfield, Mo., Gospel Pub. House [1965] 3v. 17cm. Contents.v.1. Services for special occasions.--v.2. Services for weddings and funerals.--v.3. Services for ministers and workers. [BV199.O3P5] 65-13222 price unreported
1. Occasional services. I. Title.

POLITICS and liturgy / 264
edited by Herman Schmidt and David Power. New York : Herder and Herder, 1974. 154 p. ; 23 cm. (Concilium ; new ser., v. 2. no. 10 (92). Liturgy) On cover: The New concilium: religion in the seventies. Includes bibliographical references. [BV178.P64] 73-17910 ISBN 0-8164-2576-0 : 3.95
1. Liturgics. 2. Christianity and politics. 3. Freedom (Theology) I. Schmidt, Herman A. P., 1912- ed. II. Power, David Noel, ed. III. Series: Concilium (New York) ; 92.

POOVEY, William Arthur, 1913- 264
Celebrate with drama : dramas and meditations for six special days, Easter, Ascension Day, Pentecost, Mission Sunday, Fellowship Sunday, Thanksgiving / W. A. Poovey. Minneapolis : Augsburg Pub. House, [1974] c1975. 128 p. ; 20 cm. [BV4254.2.P66] 74-14172 ISBN 0-8066-1456-0 pbk. : 2.95
1. Lutheran Church—Sermons. 2. Occasional sermons. 3. Sermons, American. 4. Christian drama, American. I. Title.

RAND, Christopher 264
Christmas in Bethlehem, and Holy Week at Mount Athos. New York, Oxford [c.]1963. 168p. maps. 21cm. 63-19945 4.00
1. Christmas—Bethlehem. 2. Holy Week. 3. Athos (Monasteries) I. Title.

RAND, Christopher. 264
Christmas in Bethlehem, and Holy Week at Mount Athos. New York, Oxford University Press. 1963. 168 p. maps. 21 cm. "Most of the material in this book appeared originally in the New Yorker." [BV45.R33] 63-19945
1. Christmas — Bethlehem. 2. Holy Week. 3. Athos (Monasteries) I. Title.

*RANDOLPH, David James. 264
Ventures in worship 3. Nashville, Abingdon Press [1973] 223 p. illus. 28 cm. [BV15] ISBN 0-687-43689-3 3.95 (pbk.)
1. Public worship—Methodist authors. I. Title.

RANDOLPH, David James, 1934- 264
God's party: a guide to new forms of worship. Nashville, Abingdon Press [1975] 144 p. illus. 22 cm. Bibliography: p. 135-138. [BV15.R36] 74-18293 ISBN 0-687-15445-6 3.50 (pbk.)
1. Public worship. I. Title.

RANDOLPH, David James, 1934- comp. 264
Peace plus : worship resources for peace and justice / edited by David James Randolph. Nashville : Tidings, [1974] 68 p. ; 21 cm. [BT736.4.R35] 74-80891 pbk. : 1.25
1. Peace (Theology)—Prayer-books and devotions—English. 2. Worship programs. I. Title.

REAM, Guin. 264
Come worship; forty-six short services for young people. St. Louis, Bethany Press [1957] 128p. 21cm. [BV29.R4] 268.7 57-7266
1. Worship programs. 2. Young people's meeting (Church work) I. Title.

REID, Clyde H. 264
Let it happen: creative worship for the emerging church [by] Clyde Reid and Jerry Kerns. [1st ed.] New York, Harper & Row [1973] 86 p. 21 cm. and phonodisc (2 s. 7 in. 33 1/3 rpm.) in pocket. Bibliography: p. 82-86. [BV15.R44 1973] 72-78063 ISBN 0-06-066821-0 4.95
1. Public worship. I. Kerns, Jerry, joint author. II. Title.

REST, Friedrich, 1913- ed. 264
Worship aids for 52 services. Philadelphia, Westminster Press [1951] 247 p. 21 cm. [BV198.R4] 51-12852
1. Worship programs. I. Title.

REST, Friedrich, 1913- 264
Worship services for church groups. Philadelphia, Christian Education Press [1962] 158p. 23cm. Includes bibliography. [BV198.R42] 62-9088
1. Worship programs. I. Title.

REST, Friedrich, 1913- 264
Worship services for church groups. Philadelphia, [United Church Pr., c.1962] 158p. Bibl. 62-9088 3.50
1. Worship programs. I. Title.

RICHARDS, Blair. 264
Come, let us celebrate! : A resource book of contemporary worship services / Blair Richards & Janice Sigmund. New York : Hawthorn Books, c1976. xi, 167 p. ; 26 cm. Bibliography: p. 165-167. [BV198.R54 1976] 75-215 ISBN 0-8015-1457-6 : 5.95
1. Liturgies. I. Sigmund, Janice, joint author. II. Title.

RIVERS, Clarence Joseph. 264
Soulfull worship. [Washington, National Office for Black Catholics, 1974] 160 p. illus. 28 cm. [BX1970.R57] 73-93702
1. Public worship. 2. Liturgies. I. Title.

ROCHELLE, Jay C. 264
Create and celebrate! [by] Jay C. Rochelle. Philadelphia, Fortress Press [1971] iv, 124 p. 22 cm. Includes hymns, with music, and liturgical melodies by the author. Bibliography: p. 114-124. [BV15.R6] 79-139345 2.95
1. Public worship. 2. Worship programs. I. Title.

ROCHELLE, Jay C. 264
The revolutionary year; recapturing the meaning of the church year, by Jay C. Rochelle. Philadelphia, Fortress Press [1973] xiii, 112 p. 22 cm. Bibliography: p. 111-112. [BV30.R6] 72-87065 ISBN 0-8006-0129-7 2.95
1. Church year. 2. Liturgies. I. Title.

THE Roots of ritual. 264
Edited by James D. Shaughnessy. Grand Rapids, Mich., Eerdmans [1973] 251 p. 21 cm. Most of the contributions were first presented at a conference at the University of Notre Dame. Bibliography: p. 235-245. [BL600.R64] 72-96405 ISBN 0-8028-1509-X 3.95
1. Ritual. I. Shaughnessy, James D., ed.

*ROTHERMEL, Bertha M. 264
Seasonal programs for churches. New York, Vantage [c.1965] 102p. 21cm. 2.50 bds.,
I. Title.

SCHALM, Bernard 264
The church at worship. Grand Rapids, Mich., Baker Bk. [c.]1962. 108p. 20cm. [Minister's handbk. ser.] 62-12671 1.95 bds.,
1. Worship. I. Title.

SCHROEDER, Frederick W. 264
Worship in the reformed tradition. Philadelphia, United Church Pr. [c.1966] 157p. 21cm Bibl. [BV10.2.S37] 66-16194 3.50
1. Worship. I. Title.

SCHROEDER, Ruth Jones. 264
Youth programs for Christian growth. New York, Abingdon Press [1957] 256p. 21cm. [BV29.S347] 268.7 57-11016 57-11016
1. Worship programs. 2. Young people's meetings (Church work) I. Title.

SCHROEDER, Ruth Jones. 264
Youth programs for special occasions. New York, Abingdon-Cokesbury Press [1950] 256 p. 21 cm. [BV29.S35] 50-7771
1. Worship programs. 2. Young people's meetings (Church work) I. Title.

SCHROEDER, Ruth Jones. 264
Youth programs on nature themes. New York, Abingdon Press [1959] 192p. 21cm. [BV29.S37] 59-8200
1. Worship programs. 2. Young people's meetings (Church work) I. Title.

SEGLER, Franklin M. 264
Christian worship, its theology and practice [by] Franklin M. Segler. Nashville, Broadman Press [1967] viii, 245 p. 22 cm. Bibliography: p. 221-237. [BV10.2.S4] 67-22034
1. Worship. 2. Public worship. I. Title.

SEIDENSPINNER, Clarence. 264
Great Protestant festivals. N[ew] Y[ork] H. Schuman [1952] 148 p. 23 cm. ([Great religious festivals series]) [BV30.S44] 52-12750
1. Church year. 2. Fasts and feasts. I. Title.

SHEPHERD, Massey Hamilton, Jr. 264
The Paschal liturgy and the Apocalypse. Richmond, John Knox Press [1960] 99p. 22cm. (Ecumenical studies in worship, no. 6) (bibl. footnotes) 60-7041 1.50 pap.,
1. Easter. 2. Bible. N. T.Revelation—Criticism, interpretation, etc. I. Title.

SHEPHERD, Massey Hamilton, 1913- 264
Liturgy and education [by] Massey H. Shepherd, Jr. New York, Seabury Press [1965] 112 p. 20 cm. Bibliographical footnotes. [BX5940.S49] 65-10354
1. Protestant Episcopal Church in the U. S. A. Liturgy and ritual. I. Title.

SHEPHERD, Massey Hamilton, 1913- 264
The liturgy and the Christian faith. Greenwich, Conn., Seabury Press, 1957. 49 p. 19 cm. [BV175.S48] 57-4543
1. Liturgies. I. Title.

SHEPHERD, Massey Hamilton, 1913- 264
The liturgy and the Christian faith. Greenwich, Conn., Seabury Press, 1957. 49p. 19cm. Includes bibliography. [BV175.S48] 54-4543
1. Liturgics. I. Title.

SHEPHERD, Massey Hamilton, 1913- 264
The Psalms in Christian worship : a practical guide / Massey H. Shepherd, Jr. Minneapolis : Augsburg Pub. House, c1976. 128 p. ; 20 cm. Bibliography: p. 118-128. [BS1435.S53] 76-3873 ISBN 0-8066-1533-8 pbk. : 3.95
1. Bible. O.T. Psalms—Liturgical use. I. Title.

SHEPHERD, Massey Hamilton, Jr., 1913- 264
Liturgy and education. New York, Seabury [c.1965] 112p. 20cm. Bibl. [BX5940.S49] 65-10354 3.50
1. Protestant Episcopal Church in the U.S.A. Liturgy and ritual. I. Title.

SKOGLUND, John E. 264
A manual of worship [by] John E. Skoglund. Valley Forge, [Pa.] Judson Press [1968] 315 p. 16 cm. Includes bibliographical references. [BX6337.S56] 68-20431
1. Liturgies. 2. Worship programs. I. Title.

SKOGLUND, John E 264
Worship in the free churches [by] John E. Skoglund. Valley Forge [Pa.] Judson Press [1965] 151 p. illus. 21 cm. [BV176.S56] 65-21999
1. Worship. 2. Liturgical movement—Protestant churches. I. Title. II. Title: Free churches.

SKOGLUND, John R. 264
Worship in the free churches. Valley Forge [Pa.] Judson [c.1965] 151p. illus. 21cm. [BV176.S56] 65-21999 3.95
1. Worship. 2. Liturgical movement—Protestant churches. I. Title. II. Title: Free churches.

SMITH, Lyndsay L., comp. 264
Creative living; fifty worship programmes for use in boys' clubs, girls' clubs, C.E. societies, Sunday Schools, Youth fellowships, compiled and edited by L. L. Smith. [Melbourne, Explorer Boys' Club Auxiliary of the Dept. of Christian Education, Churches of Christ in Victoria and Tasmania, 1968] 112 p. illus., port. 22 cm. [BV25.S6] 74-480171 unpriced
1. Worship programs. I. Churches of Christ in Victoria and Tasmania. Explorer Boys' Club Auxiliary. II. Title.

SNYDER, Ross. 264
Contemporary celebration. Nashville, Abingdon Press [1971] 202 p. 24 cm. [BV15.S56] 74-162458 4.75
1. Public worship. I. Title.

STANFIELD, Vernon L 264
The Christian worshiping [by] V. L. Stanfield. Nashville, Convention Press [1965] ix, 110 p. 19 cm. Bibliography: p. 99-101. [BV10.2.S7] 65-10324
1. Worship. I. Title.

TAYLOR, Michael J., comp. 264
Liturgical renewal in the Christian churches, ed. by Michael J. Taylor. Baltimore, Helicon [1967] 223p. 21cm. Bibl. [BV10.2T35] 67-13794 5.95 bds.,
1. Worship—Addresses, essays, lectures. 2. Liturgical movement—Addresses, essays, lectures. I. Title.
Contents omitted. Distributed by Taplinger, New York.

TAYLOR, Michael J 264
The Protestant liturgical renewal: a Catholic viewpoint. Westminster, Md., Newman Press, 1963. 336 p. 23 cm. [BV182.T3] 62-21494
1. Liturgical movement—Protestant churches. I. Title.

TAYLOR, Michael J. 264
The Protestant liturgical renewal: a Catholic viewpoint. Westminster, Newman [c.]1963. 336). 23cm. Bibl. 62-21494 5.50
1. Liturgical movement—Protestant churches. I. Title.

THOMPSON, Bard, 1925- ed. 264
Liturgies of the Western church. Cleveland, Meridian Books [c1961] xiv, 434 p. 19 cm. (Living age books, LA35) Includes bibliographies. [BV186.5.T5] 61-15750
1. Liturgies. I. Title.

THOMPSON, Bard, 1925- ed. 264
Liturgies of the Western church [Gloucester, Mass., Peter Smith, 1962, c.1961] xiv, 434p. 19cm. (Living age bks., LA35 rebound) Bibl. 4.00
1. Liturgies. I. Title.

THOMPSON, Bard, 1925- ed. 264
Liturgies of the Western church. Cleveland, World [1962, c.1961] xiv, 434p. (Living age books, LA35 Meridian) Bibl. 61-15750 1.95 pap.,
1. Liturgies. I. Title.

TRENT, Robbie, 1894- 264
To church we go. Illustrated by Elizabeth Orton Jones. Chicago, Follett Pub. Co. [1956] unpaged. illus. 27 cm. [BV4523.T7] 56-11219
1. Church attendance — Juvenile literature. I. Title.

TRENT, Robbie, 1894- 264
To church we go. Illustrated by Elizabeth Orton Jones. Chicago, Follett Pub. Co. [1956] unpaged. illus. 27cm. [BV4523.T7 1956] 56-11219
1. Church attendance—Juvenile literature. I. Title.

TURKEL, Roma Rudd 264
Who's zoo in church? [people are likened to animals in their behavior in church]. New York, Paulist Press [c.1959] unpaged illus. (col.) 16cm. .10 pap.,
I. Title.

UNDERHILL, Evelyn 1875-1941 264
Worship. [1st Harper torchbook ed.] New York, Harper [1957, c1936] 350 p. 21 cm. (Harper torchbooks, TB 10) [BV10.U5] 57-3832
1. Worship. I. Title.

UNDERHILL, Evelyn, 1875-1941. 264
Worship. [1st Harper torchbook ed.] New York, Harper [1957, c1936] 350p. 21cm. (Harper torchbooks, TB 10) [BV10.U5 1957] 57-3832
1. Worship. I. Title.

VOGT, Von Ogden, 1879- 264
The primacy of worship. Boston, Starr King Press [1958] 175 p. 21 cm. [BV20.V6] 58-6337
1. Worship. 2. Creeds — Subscription. I. Title.

VONK, Idalee Wolf, 1913- 264
52 primary workshop programs Cincinnati, Standard Pub. Co. [1953] 285p. 21cm. [BV1545.V65] 268.7 53-38202
1. Worship programs. I. Title.

WALLIS, Charles Langworthy, 1921- ed. 264
Worship resources for the Christian year. [1st ed.] New York, Harper [1954] 483p. 25cm. [BV30.W28] 54-8999
1. Church year. I. Title.

WATKINS, Keith. 264
Liturgies in a time when cities burn. Nashville, Abingdon Press [1969] 176 p. 20 cm. "Bibliographical notes": p. 170-173. [BV176.W38] 69-18448 3.75
1. Liturgies. I. Title.

WAYLAND, John T. 264
Planning congregational worship services [by] John T. Wayland. Nashville, Tenn., Broadman Press [1972, c1971] 104 p. 21 cm. [BV198.W35] 72-178067 ISBN 0-8054-2308-7
1. Worship programs. I. Title.

WEISER, Francis Xavier, 1901- 264
Handbook of Christian feasts and customs; the year of the Lord in liturgy and folklore. [1st ed.] New York, Harcourt, Brace [1958] 366 p. 22 cm. Includes bibliography. [BV30.W4] 58-10908
1. Church year. 2. Fasts and feasts. 3. Folklore. I. Title. II. Title: Christian feasts and customs.

WEISER, Francis Xavier, 1901- 264
Handbook of Christian feasts and customs; the year of the Lord in liturgy and folklore. Abridged ed. New York, Paulist Pr. [c.1952-1963] 192p. 18cm. (Deus. bk.) .95 pap.,
1. Church year. 2. Fasts and feasts. 3. Folklore. I. Title. II. Title: Christian feasts and customs.

WHITE, James F. 264
Christian worship in transition / James F. White. Nashville : Abingdon, c1976. 160 p. ; 21 cm. Includes index. [BV15.W46] 76-16848 ISBN 0-687-07659-5 : 6.75
1. Public worship. I. Title.

WHITE, James F. 264
New forms of worship [by] James F. White. Nashville, Abingdon Press [1971] 222 p. 23 cm. Includes bibliographical references. [BV15.W48] 72-160797 ISBN 0-687-27751-5 5.75
1. Public worship. I. Title.

WHITE, James F. 264
The worldliness of worship [by] James F. White. New York, Oxford Univ. Pr., 1967. vii, 181p. 21cm. Bibl. [BV10.2.W45] 67-15136 5.00
1. Worship. I. Title.

WILKIN, Esther 264
The Christ child missal. Pictures by John Johnson. New York, Guild [dist. Golden] c.1963. 29p. col. illus. 20cm. (Catholic child's read-with-me bk.) 1.00 bds.,
I. Title.

WINWARD, Stephen F. 264
The reformation of our worship. Richmond, Va., John Knox [1965] ix, 126p. 22cm. Bibl. [BV10.2.W5] 65-12647 1.75 pap.,
1. Worship. I. Title.

WORLD Conference on Faith and Order. Continuation Committee. 264
Intercommunion: the report of the theological commission appointed by the Continuation Committee of the World Conference on Faith and Order, together with a selection from the material presented to the commission. Edited by Donald Baillie [and] John Marsh. New York, Harper [c1952] 406p. 23cm. Bibliographical footnotes.SIntercommunion. [BX9.5.I5W6 1952a] 52-8459
I. Ballie, Donald Macpherson, 1887- ed. II. Title.

WORLD Council of Churches. Commission on Faith and Order. Commission on Ways of Worship. 264
Ways of worship; the report of a theological commission of faith and order. Edited by Pehr Edwall, Eric Hayman [and] William D. Maxwell. New York, Harper [1951] 362 p. 23 cm. [BV10.W583 1951a] 52-8671
1. Worship. 2. Sacraments. 3. Devotion. I. Edwall, Pehr, ed. II. Title.

WORLD Council of Churches. Commission on Faith and Order. Theological Commission on Intercommunion. 264
Intercommunion; the report of the Theological Commission appointed by the Continuation Committee of the World Conference on Faith and Order, together with a selection from the material presented to the commission. Edited by Donald Baillie, chairman [and] John Marsh, secretary. New York, Harper [1952] 406 p. 23 cm. [BX9.5.I5W6 1952a] 52-8459
1. Intercommunion. I. Ballie, Donald Macpherson, 1887-1954, ed. II. Marsh, John, 1904- ed. III. Title.

WORSHIP for the young in spirit. St. Louis, Bethany Press [1957] 144p. 23cm. [BV198.E52] 268.7 57-12727 264
1. Worship programs. I. Elbin, Paul Nowell, 1905-

WORSHIP services for junior highs. New York, Abingdon Press [1958] 239p. 21cm. [BV29.B353] 268.7 58-10454 264
1. Worship programs. I. Bays, Alice (Anderson) 1892-

YOUTH at worship. 264
Nashville, Broadman Press [1953] 167p. 21cm. [BV1522.B9] 268.7 53-11310
1. Worship programs. I. Byrd, Annie Ward.

ZDENEK, Marilee. 264
Catch the new wind [by] Marilee Zdenek and Marge Champion. Waco, Tex., Word Books [1972] 191 p. illus. 19 x 23 cm. Bibliography: p. 182-187. [BV15.Z39] 77-188073 8.95
1. Public worship. 2. Worship programs. I. Champion, Marge (Belcher) joint author. II. Title.

STEVICK, Daniel B. 264.001'4
Language in worship; reflections on a crisis [by] Daniel B. Stevick. New York, Seabury Press [1970] viii, 184 p. 22 cm. Bibliography: p. [177]-184. [BV15.S7] 76-106518 5.95
1. Public worship. 2. Prayer. 3. Religion and language. I. Title.

ROBERTSON, James Douglas. 264'.002'02
Minister's worship handbook, by James D. Robertson. Grand Rapids, Baker Book House [1974] 136 p. 20 cm. Includes bibliographical references. [BV25.R6] 74-172781 ISBN 0-8010-7619-6 3.95
1. Public worship—Handbooks, manuals, etc. I. Title.

DAVIES, John Gordon, 1919- 264'.003
A dictionary of liturgy and worship. Edited by J. G. Davies. [1st American ed.] New York, Macmillan [1972] ix, 385 p. illus. 24 cm. Includes bibliographical references. [BV173.D28 1972] 72-90276 10.00
1. Liturgics—Dictionaries. I. Title.

DAVIES, John Gordon, 1919- 264.003
A select liturgical lexicon. Richmond, Va., Knox [1966, c.1965] (Ecumenical studies in worship, no. 14) 146p. 22cm. [BV173.D3] 66-10406 2.45
1. Worship—Dictionaries. 2. Liturgies—Dictionaries. I. Title.

PODHRADSKY, Gerhard. 264'.003
New dictionary of the liturgy. Pref. by Joseph Jungmann. Foreword by Clifford Howell. English ed. edited by Lancelot Sheppard. [Original text translated by Ronald Walls and Michael Barry] Staten Island, N.Y., Alba House [1967, c1966] 208 p. illus. 24 cm. Enlarged translation of Lexikon der Liturgie. Bibliography: p. 205-208. [BV173.P613 1967] 67-5547
1. Catholic Church. Liturgy and ritual—Dictionaries. 2. Worship—Dictionaries. I. Title.

HATCHETT, Marion J. 264'.007
Sanctifying life, time, and space : an introduction to liturgical study / Marion J. Hatchett. New York : Seabury Press, c1976. ix, 215 p. ; 22 cm. "A Crossroad book." Includes bibliographical references and index. [BV176.H34] 75-38502 ISBN 0-8164-0290-6 : 8.95
1. Church of England. Book of common prayer. 2. Liturgics. I. Title.

RATCLIFF, Edward Craddock. 264'.008
Liturgical studies [of] E. C. Ratcliff / edited by A. H. Couratin and D. H. Tripp. London : S.P.C.K., 1976. vi, 250 p. ; 23 cm. Includes indexes. Bibliography: p. 1-10. [BV176.R35] 76-374948 ISBN 0-281-02839-7 : 8.50
1. Liturgics—Addresses, essays, lectures. 2. Ratcliff, Edward Craddock—Bibliography. I. Couratin, Arthur Hubert, 1902- II. Tripp, David, 1940- III. Title.

BROWN, Leslie Wilfrid, Abp.,1912- 264.0081
Relevant liturgy [by] L. W. Brown, Archbishop of Uganda and Rwanda-Urundi. New York, Oxford University Press, 1965. vi, 86 p. 19 cm. (Zabriskie lectures, 1964) Bibliographical footnotes. [BV10.2.B7] 65-17432
1. Worship — Addresses, essays, lectures. 2. Liturgical movement — Anglican Communion. I. Title. II. Series.

BROWN, Leslie Wilfrid, Abp., 1912- 264.0081
Relevant liturgy. New York, Oxford [c.]1965. vi, 86p. 19cm. (Zabriskie lects., 1964) Bibl. [BV10.2.B7] 65-17432 1.50 pap.,
1. Worship—Addresses, essays, lectures. 2. Liturgical movement—Anglican Communion. I. Title. II. Series.

REVELL'S minister's annual. 1967 Westwood N. J., Revell [c.1966] 380p. 21cm. Ed.: 1967- D.A. MacLennan [BV4241.R44] 64-20182 3.95 bds., 264.0081
1. Sermons—Yearbooks. I. MacLennan, David Alexander, 1903-ed. II. Title: Minister's annual.

REVELL'S minister's annual. 1966 Westwood, N.J., Revell [c.1965] 363p. 21cm. Ed.: 1966- D. A. MacLennan [BV4241.R44] 64-20182 3.95 bds., 264.0081
1. Sermons—Yearbooks. I. MacLennan, David Alexander, 1903- ed. II. Title: Minister's annual.

REVELL'S minister's annual, 1965. Westwood, N.J., Revell [c.1964] 383p. 21cm. Ed.: 1965- D. A. MacLennan. 64-20182 3.95 bds., 264.0081
1. Sermons—Yearbooks. I. MacLennan, David Alexander, 1903- ed. II. Title: Minister's annual.

HEDLEY, George Percy, 1899- 264.0082
Christina worship, some meanings and means. New York, Macmillan, 1953. 306p. illus. 22cm. [BV10.H37] 264
1. Worship. I. Title.

HOYT, Margaret, ed. 264.0082
My heart an altar; resources for worship, edited by Margaret Hoyt and Eleanor Hoyt Dabney. Richmond, John Knox Press [1959] 189 p. 21 cm. [BV198.H67] 59-13461
1. Worship programs. I. Dabney, Eleanor Hoyt, joint ed. II. Title.

LITURGICAL Conference, Madison, Wis., 1958. 264.0082
The liturgical renewal of the church; addresses by Theodore Otto Wedel [and others] Edited for the Associated Parishes, inc., by Massey Hamilton Shephered, Jr. New York, Oxford University Press, 1960. ix, 160p. 20cm. Sponsored by Grace Episcopal Church, Madison, Wis., and the Associated Parishes. Bibliographical footnotes. [BV182.L5 1958] 60-5277
1. Liturgical movement—Addresses, essays, lectures. I. Shepherd, Massey Hamilton, 1913- ed. II. Wedel, Theodore, Otto, 1892- III. Madison, Wis. Grace Episcopal Church. IV. Associated Parishes. V. Title.

LITURGICAL Conference, San Antonio, 1959. 264.0082
The Eucharist & liturgical renewal; addresses by Stephen Fielding Bayne, Jr. [and others] Foreword by Everett Holland Jones. Edited for the Associated Parishes, Inc., by Massey Hamilton Sheperd, Jr. New York, Oxford University Press [c]1960. xii, 146p. Bibl. footnotes. 60-13205 3.00 bds.,
1. Liturgical movement—Addresses, essays, lectures. 2. Lord's Supper (Liturgy) I. Shepherd, Massey Hamilton, 1913- ed. II. Bayne, Stephen Fielding, Bp., 1908- III. Title.

LITURGICAL Conference, San Antonio, 1959. 264.0082
The Eucharist & liturgical renewal; addresses by Stephen Fielding Bayne, Jr. [and others] Foreword by Everett Holland Jones. Edited for the Associated Parishes, inc., by Massey Hamilton Shephered, Jr. New York, Oxford University Press, 1960. xii, 146p. 20cm. Bibliographical footnotes. [BV182.L5 1959] 60-13205
1. Liturgical movement—Addresses, movement—addresses, essays, lectures. 2. Lord' s Supper (Liturgy) I. Shepherd. Massey Hamilton, 1913- ed. I. Bayne, Stephen Fielding, Bp., 1908- III. Title.

NATIONAL Liturgical Conference. 1st, Madison, Wis., 1958. 264.0082
The liturgical renewal of the church; addresses by Theodore Otto Wedel [and others) Edited for the Associated Parishes, inc., by Massey Hamilton Shepherd, Jr. New York, Oxford University Press, 1960. ix, 160 p. 20 cm. sPonsored by Grace Episcopal Church, Madison, Wis., and the Associated Parishes. Bibliographical footnotes. [BV182.N35] 60-5277
1. Liturgical movement. — Addresses, essays, lectures. I. Shepherd, Massey Hamilton, 1913- ed. II. Wedel, Theodore Otto, 1892- III. Madison, Wis. Grace Episcopal Church. IV. Associated Parishes for Liturgy and Mission. V. Title.

NATIONAL Liturgical Conference, 2d. San Antonio, 1959. 264.0082
The Eucharist & liturgical renewal; addresses by Stephen Fielding Bayne, Jr. [and others] Foreword by Everett Holland Jones. Edited for the Associated Parishes, inc., by Massey Hamilton Shepherd, Jr. New York, Oxford University Press, 1960. xii. 146 p. 20 cm. Sponsored by St. Paul's Episcopal Church, San Antonio, and Associated Parishes. Bibliographical footnotes. [BV182.N35] 60-13205
1. Liturgical movement — Addresses, essays, lectures. 2. Lord's Supper (Liturgy) I. Shepherd, Massey Hamilton, 1913- ed. II. Bayne, Stephen Fielding, Bp., 1908- III. San Antonio. St. Paul's Church. IV. Associated Parishes for Liturgy and Missions. V. Title.

NATIONAL Liturgical Conference. 3d, Wichita, Kan., 1962. 264.0082
Liturgy is mission; [addresses] Edited by Frank Stephen Cellier. New York, Seabury Press, 1964. 159 p. 22 cm. Sponsored by St. James' Church, Wichita, Kan., and the Associated Parishes for Liturgy and Missions. Bibliographical references included in footnotes. [BV182.N35] 64-10141
1. Liturgical movement — Addresses, essays, lectures. I. Cellier, Frank Stephen, ed. II. Wichita, Kan. St. James' Church. III. Associated Parishes for Liturgy and Missions. IV. Title.

NATIONAL Liturgical Conference. 3d, Wichita, Kan., 1962. 264.0082
Liturgy is mission; [addresses] Ed. by Frank Stephen Cellier. New York, Seabury [c.]1964. 159p. 22cm. Sponsored by St. James' Church, Wichita, Kan., and the Associated Parishes for Liturgy and Missions. Bibl. 64-10141 3.95 bds.,
1. Liturgical movement—Addresses, essays, lectures. I. Cellier, Frank Stephen, ed. II. Wichita, Kan. St. James' Church. III. Associated Parishes for Liturgy and Missions. IV. Title.

SHEPHERD, Massey Hamilton, ed. 264.0082
The liturgical renewal of the church; addresses of the liturgical conference held in Grace Church, Madison, May 19-21, 1958, by Theodore Otto Wedel [and others] Edited for the Associated Parishes, inc. New York, Oxford University Press, [c.]1960. ix, 160p.

Bibliographical footnotes. 20cm. 60-5277 3.25 bds.,
1. Liturgical movement—Addresses, essays, lectures. 2. Madison, Wis. Grace Episcopal Church. I. Wedel, Theodore Otto. II. Associated Parishes. III. Title.

SHEPPARD, Lancelot 264.0082
Capel, 1906- ed.
True worship. [Contributors: Irenee-Henri Dalmais, and others] Baltimore, Helicon Press [c1963] xiv, 132 p. 23 cm. "An Anglo-French symposium." Bibliography: p. 129-132. [BV10.2.S5] 63-19674
1. Liturgies—Addresses, essays, lectures. 2. Worship—Addresses, essays, lectures. I. Title.

SHEPPARD, Lancelot 264.0082
Capel, 1906- ed.
True worship [Contributors: Irenee-Henri Dalmais [others] Helicon [dist. New York, Taplinger, 1964, c.1963] xiv, 132p. 23cm. Bibl. 63-19674 3.50
1. Liturgies—Addreses, essays, lectures. 2. Worship—Addresses, essays, lectures. I. Title.

CLARK, Neville 264.009
Call to worship. [stamped: distributed in U. S. by Allenson, Naperville, Ill. 1960] 67p. 22cm. (Studies in ministry and worship, 15) (Bibl. footnotes) 60-3429 1.75 pap.,
1. Liturgics. I. Title.

DELLING, Gerhard 264.009
Worship in the New Testament. Tr. by Percy Scott. Philadelphia, Westminster [c.1962] 191p. Bibl. 62-7733 4.75
1. Worship—Early church. 2. Bible. N.T.—Theology. I. Title.

GARRETT, Thomas Samuel. 264.009
Christian worship: an introductory outline. 2d ed. London, New York, Oxford University Press, 1963. 190 p. 19 cm. Bibliography: p. [182]-183. Bibliographical footnotes. [BV176.G3 1963] 63-25419
1. Liturgics — Hist. I. Title.

GARRETT, Thomas Samuel 264.009
Christian worship, an introductory outline. New York, Oxford [c.]1961[ ] 190p. Bibl. 61-65662 3.50 bds.,
1. Liturgics—Hist. I. Title.

GARRETT, Thomas Samuel 264.009
Christian worship: an introductory outline. 2d ed. New York, Oxford, 1963[c.1961, 1963] 190p. 19cm. Bibl. 63-25419 4.25
1. Liturgics—Hist. I. Title.

MITCHELL, Leonel Lake, 264'.009
1930-
The meaning of ritual / by Leonel L. Mitchell. New York : Paulist Press, c1977. xvi, 139 p. ; 19 cm. (A Deus book) Includes bibliographical references. [BV5.M57] 77-78215 ISBN 0-8091-2035-6 pbk. : 2.45
1. Worship—History. 2. Ritual—History. I. Title.

SPIELMANN, Richard M. 264.009
History of Christian worship [by] Richard M. Spielmann. New York, Seabury [1966] ix, 182p. 22cm. Bibl [BV5.S6] 66-22994 4.95
1. Worship—Hist. I. Title.

CATHOLIC Students' Mission 264.01
Crusade, United States of America
Christians of the East. [Cincinnati, 1962] 79 p. 22 cm. (Five-hour series) [BX324.3.C35] 63-5729
1. Catholic Church — Oriental rites. 2. Orthodox Eastern Church — Relations — Catholic Church. 3. Catholic Church — Relations — Orthodox Eastern Church. I. Title.

HAMMOND, Charles Edward, 264.01
1837-1914, comp.
Liturgies, eastern and western; being the texts, original or translated, of the principal liturgies of the church. Edited with introductions and appendices by F. E. Brightman on the basis of the former work by C. E. Hammond. Vol. 1. Eastern liturgies. Oxford, Clarendon Press [1965] civ, 603 p.23 cm. "No more published."--Brit. Museum general catalogue. Reprint of a work first published in 1896. Includes bibliographical references. [BV175.H3] 66-3857
1. Liturgies. I. Brightman, Frank Edward, 1856-1932, ed. II. Title.

MOULE, Charles Francis 264.01
Digby
Worship in the New Testament. [church] Richmond, Va., JohnKnox [1962] 87p. (Ecumenical studies in worship, no. 9) Bibl. 62-7174 1.75 pap.,
1. Worship—Early church. I. Title.

SAINT SERAPION, Bp. of 264.01
Thmuis
Bishop Sarapion's prayer-book; an Egyptian sacramentary dated probably about A.D. 350-356. Introd., notes, indices by John Wordsworth. Hamden, Conn., Archon [dist. Shoe String] 1964. 104p. 19cm. Reprinted 1964 from the second ed., rev. 1923. 64-9104 3.00
1. Liturgies, Early Christian. I. Wordsworth, John, Bp. of Salisbury, 1843-1911, ed. and tr. II. Title.

SERAPION, Saint, Bp. of 264.01
Thmuis.
Bishop Sarapion's prayer-book; an Egyptian sacramentary dated probably about A. D. 350-356. With introd., notes and indices by John Wordsworth. Hamden, Conn., Archon Books, 1964. 104 p. 19 cm. "Reprinted 1964 from the second edition, revised, 1928." [BV185.S4 1964] 64-9104
1. Liturgies, Early Christian. I. Wordsworth, John, Bp. of Salisbury. 1843-1911, ed. and tr. II. Title.

CATHOLIC Church. Liturgy 264.01'1
and ritual.
The ancient liturgies of the Gallican Church; now first collected, with an introductory dissertation, notes, and various readings, together with parallel passages from the Roman, Ambrosian, and Mozarabic rites, by J. M. Neale and G. H. Forbes. New York, AMS Press [1970] viii, 368 p. 24 cm. Text in Latin. Reprint of the 1855-67 ed. Contents.Contents.—Missale Richenovense.—Missale Gothicum seu Gothico-Gallicanum.—Missale Vesontionense seu Sacramentarium Gallicanum. [BX2037.A3G3 1970] 71-131030 ISBN 0-404-04655-X
I. Neale, John Mason, 1818-1866, ed. II. Forbes, George Hay, 1821-1875, ed. III. Catholic Church. Liturgy and ritual. Gallican rite. IV. [Sacramentary (Gallican)] V. Title.

GRIGASSY, Julius, 1886- 264.011
ed.
Main services of Holy Week and glorious Resurrection in the Greek rite (Byzantine-Slavonic) Catholic Church. [Braddock, Pa., 1950] 319 p. illus. 14 cm. "Based on official editions of Catholic ordinariates ... compiled ... for the use of our American faithful." Church Slavic language in English transcription, with parallel texts' in English translation by Stephen Loya and Joseph Jackanich. [BX1995.B8G66] 50-24451
I. Catholic Church. Byzantine rite. Liturgy and ritual. II. Title.

HAHN, Ferdinand, 1926- 264'.01'1
The worship of the early church. Translated by David E. Green. Edited, with an introd., by John Reumann. Philadelphia, Fortress Press [1973] xxvi, 118 p. 18 cm. Translation of Der urchristliche Gottesdienst. Includes bibliographical references. [BV6.H2713] 72-87063 ISBN 0-8006-0127-0 3.25
1. Worship—Early church. I. Title.

HELIOPOULOS, Demetrius, 264.011
1902-
The morning sacrifice; a brief explanation of the divine liturgy of the Eastern Orthodox Church. Illustrated by Nicholas Nefos. [Pittsburgh? 1955, c1954] 148p. illus. 22cm. [BX350.H4] 55-24285
1. Orthodox Eastern Church. Liturgy and ritual. Leitourgikon. I. Title.

JUNGMANN, Josef Andreas, 264.011
1889-
The early liturgy, to the time of Gregory the Great, Translated by Francis A. Brunner. [Notre Dame, Ind.] University of Notre Dame Press, 1959. 314p. 24cm. (Notre Dame [Ind.] University. Liturgical studies, v. 6) Includes bibliography. [BV185.J813] 58-14182
1. Liturgics—Hist. 2. Worship— Early church. I. Title.

MARTIN, Ralph P. 264'.01'1
Worship in the early church / by Ralph P. Martin. [Rev. ed.] Grand Rapids : Eerdmans, 1974, 1975 printing, c1964. 144 p. ; 22 cm. Includes bibliographical references and index. [BV6.M37 1975] 75-14079 ISBN 0-8028-1613-4 pbk. : 3.45
1. Worship—History—Early church, ca. 30-600. I. Title.

OESTERLEY, William Oscar 264.012
Emil, 1866-
The Jewish background of the Christian liturgy. Gloucester, Mass., P. Smith, 1965. 243p. 22cm. First printed, 1925, by Oxford. Bibl. [BV185.O4] 66-93 4.25
1. Liturgies, Early Christian. 2. Jews. Liturgy and ritual. 3. Christianity and other religions—Judaism. 4. Judaism—Relations—Christianity. I. Title.

WARREN, Frederick 264'.01'3
Edward, 1842-1930.
The liturgy and ritual of the ante-Nicene church. 2d ed., rev. London, Society for Promoting Christian Knowledge; New York, E. S. Gorham, 1912. [New York, AMS Press, 1973] xvi, 317 p. 23 cm. Original ed. issued in series: Side-lights of church history. Bibliography: p. x-xvi. [BV185.W3 1973] 78-177851 ISBN 0-404-06847-2 17.50
1. Liturgies, Early Christian. I. Title. II. Title: Ante-Nicene church.

CATHOLIC Church. 264.015
Byzantine rite (Ruthenian) Liturgy and ritual. Leitourgikon. English.
The liturgy of St. John Chrysostom, Ruthenian form; historical background, introd., and commentary by Basil Shereghy. Collegeville, Minn., Liturgical Press [1961] 64 p. 19 cm. Cover title: The divine liturgy of St. John Chrysostom. [BX4711.665.L4S5] 62-1065
I. Shereghy, Basil, ed. II. Orthodox Eastern Church. Liturgy and ritual. Leitourgikon. English. III. Title. IV. Title: The divine liturgy of St. John Chrysostom.

CATHOLIC Church. Maronite 264.015
rite. Liturgy and ritual. English.
A method for attending the Maronite Mass; calendar for the Maronite rite, holy days of obligations, prayers, pictures with explanations, Epistles, and Gospels. Translated into English from the original Syriac, Aramaic, and Arabic by John Trad. 1st ed. [San Antonio?] '1951. 634 p. illus. 13 cm. [BX1995.M2A42] 51-8757
I. Trad, John. tr. II. Title.

LIESEL, Nikolaus 264.015
The Eucharistic liturgies of the Eastern churches. Tr. [from German]: David Heimann. Photography: Tibor Makula. Art, layout: Brother Placid. Collegevile, Minn., Liturgical Pr. [1963] 310p. illus., maps. 32cm. (Popular liturgical lib.) 63-3837 8.00
1. Liturgies. 2. Lord's Supper (Liturgy) 3. Catholic Church—Oriental rites. I. Title.

SOLOVII, Meletii M., 264'.01'5
Father.
Eastern liturgical theology; general introduction [by] Meletius Michael Solovey. Weston, Ont., Ukrainian Catholic Religion and Culture Society of Etobicoke (Toronto) and Ukrainian Catholic Youth of Canada [1970] 205 p. 23 cm. Bibliography: p. 199-202. [BX127.S63] 72-185096
1. Liturgics—Eastern churches. I. Title.

LIESEL, Nikolaus. 264.0155
The Eastern Catholic liturgies; a study in words and pictures. Photos. by T. Makula. Foreword by Donald Attwater. Westminster, Md., Newman Press, 1960. xx, 168p. illus. 26cm. Translation of Die Liturgien der Ostkirche. [BX4710.63.L513] 60-14814
1. Liturgies. 2. Lord's Supper (Liturgy) 3. Catholic Church—Oriental rites. I. Title.

ARMENIAN Church. Liturgy 264.0162
and ritual.
Divine liturgy of the Armenian Apostolic Orthodox Church. New York, Delphic Press, 1950. 314 p. illus. 27 cm. Title page and text in Armenian and English. Without music. [BX127.A4 1950] 51-36025
I. Title.

COPTIC Church. Liturgy 264'.01'7
and ritual. Euchologion. English.
The Coptic morning service for the Lord's day. Translated into English by John, Marquis of Bute. London, Cope and Fenwick, 1908. [New York, AMS Press 1973] 170 p. illus. 23 cm. Original ed. published in series: Christian liturgies. [BX137.A3 1973] 72-39871 ISBN 0-404-01247-7 9.00
I. Bute, John Patrick Crichton-Stuart, 3d Marquis of, 1847-1900, tr. II. Title. III. Series: Christian liturgies.

MERCER, Samuel Alfred 264.01'7
Browne, 1880-
The Ethiopic liturgy; its sources, development, and present form, by Samuel A. B. Mercer. New York, AMS Press [1970] xvi, 487 p. facsims. 19 cm. (The Hale lectures, 1914-5) English, Ethiopic, or Greek. Reprint of the 1915 ed. Includes bibliographical references. [BX147.A3 1970] 76-131034 ISBN 0-404-04308-9
I. Ya'Ityopya 'ortodoks tawahedo beta kerestiyan. Liturgy and ritual. II. Title. III. Series: Seabury-Western Theological Seminary, Evanston, Ill. The Hale lectures, 1914-15

NESTORIAN Church. 264.01'8
Liturgy and ritual.
The Liturgy of the Holy Apostles Adai and Mari, together with 2 additional liturgies to be said on certain feasts and other days, and the Order of Baptism. Complete and entire; collated from many MSS. from various places. New York, AMS Press [1970] ix, 89 p. 29 cm. Translated from the Syriac ed. published by the Archbishop of Canterbury's Mission to the Assyrian Christians at Urmi. Reprint of the 1893 ed. [BX157.A3 1970] 79-131032 ISBN 0-404-03997-9
I. [Liturgy of the Holy Apostles Adai and Mari. English] II. Title.

BOGOLEPOV, Aleksandr 264.019
Aleksandrovich, 1886-
Orthodox hymns of Christmas, Holy Week, and Easter [by] Alexander A. Bogolepov. New York, Russian Orthodox Theological Fund [1965] 78 p. 23 cm. [BV467.B6] 65-16177
1. Orthodox Eastern Church — Hymns — Hist. & crit. I. Title.

CATHOLIC Church. Liturgy 264'.019
and ritual.
Book of hours. [New Canaan, Conn., Byzantine Franciscans, c1965] 350 p. 19 cm. "An attempt, by way of experiment, to reconstruct the structure and theme of the canonical hours of the Byzantine Church in a logical fashion." Companion volume, including the Lenten and Easter services, to the Horologion published by the Byzantine Franciscans in 1967. Bibliography: p. 345-350. [BX2000.A4B9] 264.02'4 76-19183
I. Franciscans. Custody of St. Mary of the Angels. II. Catholic Church. Liturgy and ritual. Byzantine rite. III. Title.

CATHOLIC Church. 264.019
Byzantine rite. Liturgy and ritual. Leitourgikon. English.
The Byzantine liturgy; a new English translation of the liturgies of St. John Chrysostom and St. Basil the Great [by Clement C. Englert] New York, Fordham Russian Center [1953] 78p. 16cm. [BX1955.B8A28] 53-29338
I. Englert, Clement Cyril, 1910- ed. and tr. II. Title.

CATHOLIC Church. 264.019
Byzantine rite (Ruthenian) Liturgy and ritual. English.
The order for the celebration of vespers, matins, and the divine liturgy, according to the Ruthenian recension. A. translation of 'Ordo celebrationis vesperarum, matutini, et divinae liturgiae, iuxta recensionem Ruthenorum,' published by the Sacred Congregation for the Eastern Church, Rome 1944, by Matthew A. Berko. Washington, 1958 [c1957] 122p. diagrs. 22cm. [BX1995.B8A34] 58-11870
I. Berko, Matthew A, tr. II. Title.

DALMAIS, Irenee Henri 264.019
Eastern liturgies. Translated from the French by Donald Attwater. NewYork, Hawthorn Books [c.1960] 144p. (2p. bibl.) 21cm. (The Twentieth century encyclopedia of Catholicism, v.112. Section 10: The worship of the church) 60-8789 2.95 half cloth,
1. Eastern churches. Liturgy and ritual. I. Title.

GOGOL, Nikolai 264.019
Vasil'evich, 1809-1852.
Meditations on the divine liturgy of the Holy Eastern Orthodox Catholic and Apostolic Church. [New York 27, 537 W. 121 St., Orthodox Book Society, 1960] 56p. 23cm. Translation of (transliterated: Razmyshienii c bozhestvennoi liturgi) 60-2330 1.00
1. Orthodox, Eastern Church. Liturgy and ritual. I. Title.

MIHALY, Joseph, 1907- 264.019
comp.
Under the Cross, Pod Krestom. [Trumbull Conn., 1954] 319p. illus. 12cm. English and Ruthenian-Church Slavic. [BX376.E4M5] 54-27705
1. Orthodox Eastern Church—Prayer-books and devotions—English. I. Title. II. Title: Pod Krestom.

NEALE, John Mason, 1818- 264.01'9
1866, comp.
The liturgies of S. Mark, S. James, S. Clement, S. Chrysostom, and the Church of Malabar. Translated with introd. and appendices, by J. M. Neale. New York, AMS Press [1969] xxxvi, 224 p. illus., plan. 22 cm. Reprint of the London ed., 1859. Appendices (p. [175]-224):—1. The formulae of institution as they occur in every extant liturgy.—2. Prayers for the departed faithful. [BX375.L4N4 1969] 76-83374
I. Orthodox Eastern Church. Liturgy and ritual. Leitourgikon. English. II. Catholic Church. Liturgy and ritual. Malabar rite. English. III. Title.

ORTHODOX Eastern Church. 264.01'9
Liturgy and ritual. Leitourgikon. English.
Anaphora; the divine liturgy of Saint James, the first bishop of Jerusalem, according to the rite of the Syrian Orthodox Church of Antioch. Translated from original Syriac. [Hackensack? N.J.] Metropolitan Mar A. Y. Samuel, 1967. 91 p. 21 cm. Title also in Syriac. "The history of Saint James liturgy, by Dr. M. Moosa": p. 87-91. [BX375.L4A417] 74-6977
I. Samuel, Athanasius Yeshue, Abp., 1907- II. Title. III. Title: The divine liturgy of Saint James.

ORTHODOX Eastern Church. 264.01'9
Liturgy and Ritual. Euchologion. English.
Book of needs of the Holy Orthodox Church, with an appendix containing offices for the laying on of hands. Done into English by G. V. Shann. New York, AMS Press [1969] xxxix, viii, 260, 28 p. 22 cm. "A translation, with some omissions, of the Slavonic service book entitled Trebnik [printed in Moscow, 1882]" Reprinted from the 1894 London ed. [BX375.E75A43] 77-82258
I. Shann, G. V., tr. II. Title.

ORTHODOX Eastern Church. 264.01'9
Liturgy and ritual. Leitourgikon. English.
The divine liturgy of our father among the saints, John Chrysostom, of the Holy Orthodox Catholic and Apostolic Church. Translated by Archimandrite Lazarus. Edited and arranged by John Schneyder. [2d ed. New York?] Holy Orthodox Catholic Apostolic American Church (the Orthodox American Church) [1965] ii, 115 p. 16 cm. [BX375.L4A427 1965] 77-17717
I. Lazarus, Archimandrite, tr. II. Schneyder, John, ed. III. Title.

ORTHODOX Eastern Church. 264.01'9
Liturgy and ritual. Molityoslov. English
Euchology; a manual of prayers of the Holy Orthodox Church done into English by G. V. Shann. New York, AMS Press [1969] xxxi, 524 p. 22 cm. Reprint of the Kidderminster, Eng., ed. of 1891. Bibliography: p. xxv-xxviii. [BX360.A5S5 1969] 75-82260
I. Shann, G. V., tr. II. Title.

ORTHODOX Eastern Church. 264.01'9
Liturgy and ritual. Menaion. English
The ferial Menaion; or, The book of services for the twelve great festivals and the new-year's day. Translated from a Slavonian ed. of last century ... [by N. Orloff] New York, AMS Press [1969] 330 p. 22 cm. Reprint of the 1900 ed. [BX375.M37A4 1969] 72-79155
I. Orloff, Nicolas, tr. II. Title.

ORTHODOX Eastern Church. 264.01'9
Liturgy and ritual. Menaion. English.
The general Menaion; or, The book of services common to the festivals of our Lord Jesus of the Holy Virgin and of the different orders of saints. Translated from the Slavonian 16th ed. of 1862 [by N. Orloff] New York, AMS Press [1969] 287 p. 22 cm. Reprint of the 1899 ed. [BX375.M37A38 1969] 76-79156
I. Orloff, Nicolas, tr. II. Title.

ORTHODOX Eastern Church. 264.01'9
Liturgy and ritual. Horologion. English.
Horologion; a primer for elementary village schools. Translated from the Slavonian ed. of 1894 ... [by N. Orloff] New York, AMS Press [1969] xi, 151 p. 22 cm. Reprint of the 1897 ed. [BX375.H6A4 1969] 79-79154
I. Orloff, Nicolas, tr. II. Title.

ORTHODOX Eastern Church. 264.01'9
Liturgy and ritual. Leitourgikon.
The liturgies of S. Mark, S. James, S. Clement, S. Chrysostom, S. Basil: or according to the use of the churches of Alexandria, Jerusalem, Constantinopole, and the formula of the Apostolic Constitutions. Edited by J. M. Neale. New York, AMS Press [1969] iv, ii, 8-174 p. 23 cm. Title on spine: Primitive liturgies. In Greek. Reprint of London, 1859 ed. [BX350.A2 1969] 79-80721
1. Liturgies, Early Christian. I. Neale, John Mason, 1818-1866, ed. II. Title. III. Title: Primitive liturgies.

ORTHODOX Eastern Church. 264.01'9
Liturgy and ritual. Oktoechos. English.
Octoechos; or, The book of eight tones; a primer containing the Sunday service in eight tones. Translated from the Slavonian 1st ed. of 1891 ... by N. Orloff. New York, AMS Press [1969] 169 p. 22 cm. Reprint of the 1898 ed. [BX375.O3A4 1969] 75-79153
I. Orloff, Nicolas, ed. II. Title.

ORTHODOX Eastern Church. 264.01'9
Liturgy and ritual.
Offices from the service-books of the Holy Eastern Church. With translation, notes, and glossary [by] Richard Frederick Littledale. [1st ed.] New York, AMS Press [1970] xii, 339 p. 23 cm. Reprint of the 1863 ed., London. English and Greek. [BX350.A2 1970] 77-133819 ISBN 0-404-03996-0
I. Title.

ORTHODOX Eastern Church. 264.01'9
Liturgy and ritual. English.
The offices of the Oriental Church, with an historical introd. Edited by Nicholas Bjerring. New York, AMS Press [1969] xxxi, 189 p. 22 cm. Reprint of the 1884 ed. [BX350.A5B5 1969] 73-79805
I. Bjerring, Nicholas, 1831-1900, ed. II. Title.

ORTHODOX Eastern 264'.01'9
Church. Liturgy and ritual. Leitourgikon.
The Orthodox liturgy; the Greek text with a completely new translation followed by notes on the text, the Sunday Gospel and Apostolic readings, together with: tracing the development of the Orthodox liturgy from the 2nd century to this day, by Nicon D. Patrinacos. Foreword by Archbishop Iakovos. [Garwood, N.J., Graphic Arts Press, 1974] 352 p. 18 cm. Text of the divine liturgy of St. John Chrysostom in English and Greek. [BX350.A2 1974] 74-75002
I. Patrinacos, Nicon D., ed. II. Orthodox Eastern Church. Liturgy and ritual. Leitourgikon. English. III. Title.

ORTHODOX Eastern 264'.01'9
Church. Liturgy and ritual. Leitourgikon.
The Orthodox liturgy : the Greek text of the Ecumenical Patriarchate / with a translation into English by the Liturgical Commission of the Greek Orthodox Archdiocese of North and South America. Together with a study of the development of the Orthodox liturgy from the 2nd century to this day / by Nicon D. Patrinacos. Garwood, N.J. : Graphic Arts Press, 1976. 336 p. ; 19 cm. "Authorized to be used within the Greek Orthodox Church of the Americas." [BX350.A2 1976] 76-12252
I. Patrinacos, Nicon D. II. North and South America (Archdiocese, Orthodox). Liturgical Commission. III. Orthodox Eastern Church. Liturgy and ritual. Leitourgikon. English. 1975. IV. Title.

ORTHODOX Eastern 264'.01'9
Church. Liturgy and ritual. Psalter. English.
The Psalter, according to the Seventy, of St. David, the prophet and King : together with the nine odes and an interpretation of how the Psalter should be recited throughout the whole year / translated from the Septuagint version of the Old Testament by the Holy Transfiguration Monastery. Boston : The Monastery, 1974. 296 p. : ill. ; 24 cm. [BX370.A5H64 1974] 74-76941 ISBN 0-913026-09-3
1. Psalters. I. Holy Transfiguration Monastery. II. Title.

ORTHODOX Eastern Church. 264.01'9
Liturgy and ritual. Menaion. English.
The twelve great feasts; or, Festival Menaion of the Holy Orthodox Catholic and Apostolic Church. Translated by the Archimandrite Lazarus. Edited by the American Orthodox Associates. Chicago, American Orthodox Associates, 1965. 187 l. 28 cm. [BX375.M37A47] 71-17875
I. Lazarus, Archimandrite, tr. II. American Orthodox Associates. III. Title. IV. Title: Festival Menaion.

ORTHODOX Eastern Church. 264.019
Liturgy and ritual. English.
Service book of the Holy Orthodox-Catholic Apostolic Church. Compiled, translated, and arr. from the Old Church-Slavonic service books of the Russian Church and collated with the service books of the Greek Church. by Isabel Florence Hapgood. 3d ed. Brooklyn, Syrian Antiochian Orthodox Archdiocese of New York and All North America, 1956. xi, 615 p. illus. 23 cm. "Revised edition with indorsement by Patriarch Tikhon." [BX350.A5H3] 65-44703
I. Hapgood, Isabel Florence, 1850-1928, ed. and tr. II. Title.

ORTHODOX Eastern Church. 264.019
Liturgy and ritual. Euchologion. English.
Liturgy and Catechism of the Eastern Orthodox Church in Albanian and English; translated by Bishop F. S. Noli. Boston, Albanian Orthodox Church in America, 1955. 235p. 19cm. Translation of the Liturgy of St. John Chrysostom from the Euchologion in Greek, and of the Cathechism, Russian version by Metropolitan Philaret. [BX360.A5N6] 55-44675
1. Orthodox Eastern Church—Catechisms and creeds—English. I. Orthodox Eastern Church. Liturgy and ritual. Euchologion. Albanian. II. Filaret, Metropolitan of Moscow, 1782-1867. Catechism. III. Filaret, Metropolitan of Moscow, 1782-1867. Catechism. IV. Noll, Fan Stylian, Bp., 1882- tr. V. Albanian Orthodox Church in America. VI. Title.

ORTHODOX Eastern Church. 264.019
Liturgy and ritual. Leitourgikon.
The divine liturgy of St. John Chrysostom of the Eastern Orthodox Church. Edited and arranged by George Mastrantonis] New York, Greek Orthodox Archdiocese of North and South America [1966] 148 p. illus. 16 cm. Text in English and Greek. [BX375.L4A43] 66-22700
I. Mastrantonis, George, 1906- ed. II. Orthodox Eastern Church. Liturgy and ritual. Leitourgikon. English. III. Title.

ORTHODOX Eastern Church. 264.019
Liturgy and ritual.. Leitourgkon.
The divine liturgy of St. Chrysostom of the Eastern Orthodox Church. [Ed., arranged by George Mastrantonis] New York, Greek Orthodox Archdiocese of North & South America [1966] 148p. illus. 16 cm. Text in English & Greek. [BX375.L4A43 1966] 66-22700 2.00
I. Mastrantonis, George, 1906- ed. II. Orthodox Eastern Church. Liturgy and ritual.. Leitourgikou English. III. Title.
Pub. address: 777 United Nations Plaza, New York, N.Y. 10017

ORTHODOX Eastern Church. 264.01'9
: Liturgy and ritual. : Menaion. : English.
The festal Menaion / translated from the original Greek by Mother Mary and Archimandrite Kallistos Ware ; with an introd. by Georges Florovsky. London : Faber and Faber, 1977. 564p. ; 20 cm. (The Service Books of the Orthodox Church) [BX375.M37A44] ISBN 0-571-11137-8 : 10.95
I. Mary,Mother, tr. II. Ware, Kallistos, 1934- III. Title.
L.C. card no. for 1969 Faber and Faber ed. : 70-518366. Distributed by Faber and Fber, Salem, NH.

POLYZOIDES, Germanos, 264.019
Bp., 1897-
What we see and hear in an Eastern Orthodox Church. New York, D. C. Divry [1961] 92p. illus. 23cm. [BX350.P58] 61-31896
1. Orthodox Eastern Church. Liturgy and ritual. I. Title.

SCHMEMANN, Alexander, 264.019
1921-
Introduction to liturgical theology; translated from the Russian by Asheleigh E. Moorhouse. London, Faith P.; Portland (Maine), American Orthodox P., 1966. 170 p. 22 1/2 cm. (Library of Orthodox theology, no. 4) 37/6 Includes bibliographical references. [BX350.S35] 66-69197
1. Orthodox Eastern Church. Liturgy and ritual. I. Title. II. Series.

SCHMEMANN, Alexander, 264.019
1921-
Introduction to liturgical theology; tr. from Russian by Asheleigh E. Moorhouse. London, Faith Pr.; Portland (Maine), American Orthodox Pr., 1966. 170p. 23cm. (Lib. of Orthodox theol., no. 4) Bibl. [BX350.S35] 66-69197 6.50
1. Orthodox Eastern Church. Liturgy and ritual. I. Title. II. Series.
Publisher's address: Box 1096. Portland, Maine 04104.

SPOER, Hans Henry, 1873- 264.01'9
1951.
An aid for churchmen, Episcopal and Orthodox, toward a mutual understanding, by means of a brief comparison of the rites and ceremonies of the Orthodox Church with those of the Episcopal (Anglican) Church. With a foreword by Frank Gavin. New York, AMSPress [1969] ix, 105 p. 6 illus. 22 cm. Reprint of the 1930 ed. Bibliography: p. 104-105. [BX5927.S7 1969] 71-79152
1. Orthodox Eastern Church—Relations—Anglican Communion. 2. Orthodox Eastern Church. Liturgy and ritual. 3. Anglican Communion—Relations—Orthodox Eastern Church. I. Title.

SWAINSON, Charles 264.01'9
Anthony, 1820-1887.
The Greek liturgies, chiefly from original authorities. With an appendix containing the Coptic ordinary canon of the mass from two manuscripts in the British Museum. Edited and translated by C. Bezold. Hildesheim, New York, G. Olms, 1971. lii, 395 p. 23 cm. Reprint of the ed. published in London in 1884. English, Latin, Greek, or Coptic. Coptic text has English translation. [BX350.S8 1971] 76-886448 ISBN 3-487-04054-9 (Hildesheim)
1. Orthodox Eastern Church. Liturgy and ritual. I. Bezold, Carl, 1859-1922, tr. II. Title.

VERGHESE, Paul. 264.01'9
The joy of freedom; Eastern worship and modern man. Richmond, John Knox Press [1967] 91 p. 22 cm. (Ecumenical studies in worship, no. 17) Bibliographical footnotes. [BX107.V4] 67-15297
1. Eastern churches. Liturgy and ritual. I. Title. II. Series.

NEALE, John Mason, 264.01'9'02
1818-1866, comp.
Hymns of the Eastern Church. New York, AMS Press [1971] xii, 164 p. 19 cm. Reprint of the 1862 ed. [BV467.N52] 77-131029 ISBN 0-404-04666-5
1. Orthodox Eastern Church—Hymns. 2. Hymns, Greek—Translations into English. 3. Hymns, English—Translations from Greek. I. Title.

ORTHODOX Eastern Church. 264.0192
Liturgy and ritual. Apostolos. English.
Epistle lectionary of the Eastern Orthodox Church. Translated by Archbishop Fan Stylian Noli. Boston, Albanian Orthodox Church in America, 1957. 463p. 24cm. [BX375.A65A4 1957] 57-46679
I. Noli, Fan Stylian, Abp., 1882- tr. II. Albanian Orthodox Church in America. III. Title.

ORTHODOX Eastern Church. 264.0192
Liturgy and ritual. Evangelion. English.
Gospel lectionary of the Eastern Orthodox Church. Translated by Bishop Fan Stylian Noli. Boston, Albanian Orthodox Church in America, 1956. 542p. (p.535-542 advertisements) 24cm. [BX375.E78A4] 57-45295
I. Noli, Fan Stylian, Bp., 1882- tr. II. Albanian Orthodox Church in America. III. Title.

CATHOLIC Church. 264'.01'93
Liturgy and ritual.
Office of Christian burial according to the Byzantine rite. Pittsburgh : Byzantine Seminary Press, c1975. iii, 110 p., 74 p. of music ; 23 cm. "Translated by the Inter-Eparchial Liturgical Commission, and the music arranged by the Inter-Eparchial Music Commission of the Byzantine Ruthenian Metropolitan Province." "Approved for the use in the Byzantine Ruthenian Metropolitan Province." [BX4711.665.B87A4 1975] 75-328709
1. Funeral service. I. Catholic Church. Byzantine Ruthenian Metropolitan Province of Munhall, Pa. Inter-Eparchial Liturgical Commission. II. Catholic Church. Byzantine Ruthenian Metropolitan Province of Munhall, Pa. Inter-Eparchial Music Commission. III. Catholic Church. Liturgy and ritual. Byzantine rite. IV. [Burial rite (Ruthenian). English] V. Title.

CATHOLIC Church. 264.0194471
Byzantine rite (Ruthenian) Liturgy and ritual. Leitourgikon. English.
The divine liturgy. [New Canaan, Conn., Byzantine Franciscans, 1965] 101 p. 18 cm. [BX4711.665.L4A4 1965] 65-29649
1. Catholic Church. Byzantine rite (Ruthenian) Liturgy and ritual. Franciscan. I. Orthodox Eastern Church. Liturgy and ritual. Leitourgikon English. II. Franciscans. Custody of St. Mary of the Angels. III. Title.

KING, John Glen, 264'.01'947
1732-1787.
The rites and ceremonies of the Greek church, in Russia; containing an account of its doctrine, worship, and discipline. [1st AMS ed.] London, Printed for W. Owen, 1772. [New York, AMS Press, 1970] xix, 477 p. illus. 23 cm. [BX350.K5 1970] 73-126673 ISBN 0-404-03692-9
1. Orthodox Eastern Church. Liturgy and ritual. I. Title.

AGNES THERESE, Sister. 264.02
Christ in the Mass; our perfect gift to God. Chicago. Loyola University Press [1960] 72p. illus. 21cm. [BX2230.A34] 60-10574
1. Mass—Pictures, illustrations, etc. I. Title.

AGNES THERESE, Sister. 264.02
Christ in the Mass; our perfect gift to God. Chicago, Loyola University Press [c.1960] 72p. illus. (part col.) 21cm. 60-10574 .60 pap.,
1. Mass—Pictures, illustrations, etc. I. Title.

ATHILL, Emmanuel, Mother. 264.02
Teaching liturgy in schools. Chicago, Fides Publishers, 1958 [i. e. 1959] 101p. 19cm. [BX1970 A8] 59-1073
1. Catholic Church. Liturgy and ritual—Study and teaching. I. Title.

ATLING von Geusau, Leo 264.02
George Marie.
Liturgy in development [by] L. G. M. Alting von Geusau [and others] With a foreword by the Bishop of Groningen, Translated by H. J. J. Vaughan. Westminster, Md., Newman Press [1966, c1965] ix, 187 p. 19 cm. (DO-C dossiers, 1) Working papers for the Second Vatican Council. [BX1970.E713] 66-3538
1. Catholic Church. Liturgy and ritual — Addresses, essays, lectures, I. Title.

BARDEN, William. 264.02
What happens at Mass. [1st American ed.] Staten Island, N.Y., Alba House [1963] 159 p. 21 cm. [BX2230.2.B27] 63-14570
1. Mass. I. Title.

BARDEN, William 264.02
What happens at Mass. Staten Island, N. Y., Alba [c.1963] 159p. 21cm. 63-14570 2.95
1. Mass. I. Title.

BAUSCH, William J. 264'.02
A new look at the sacraments / William J. Bausch. Notre Dame, Ind. : Fides/Claretian, c1977. vii, 237 p. ; 20 cm. Includes bibliographical references. [BX2200.B37] 77-2975 ISBN 00-8190-0619-X pbk. : 4.95
1. Sacraments—Catholic Church. I. Title.

BERON, Richard, 1903- ed. 264.02
With the Bible through the church year: around the year from Genesis to Apocalypse, with Psalms and texts on the liturgy; Bible stories retold by Richard Beron. [Translated by Isabel and Florence McHugh] Prefaces on the liturgy by Mary Perkins. Illus. by Brothers of the Benedictine Order. New York, Pantheon Books [1953] 242p. col. illus. 21x28cm. Translation, in part, of Kinder- und Hausbibel. [BS551.B3913] 53-9944
1. Bible stories, English. I. Title.

BEUYER, Louis, 1913- 264.02
Liturgical piety. Notre Dame, Ind., University of Notre Dame Press [1955] x, 284p. 24cm. (Notre Dame [Ind.] University. Liturgical studies, v.1) Erratum slip inserted. Bibliographical footnotes. [BX1970.B68] 54-11103
1. Catholic Church. Liturgy and ritual. I. Title. II. Series.

BISHOP, Patrick. 264'.02
The new mass; a commentary. [Melbourne] Spectrum [Publications, 1970] viii, 88 p. 19 cm. Includes bibliographical references. [BX2230.2.B54] 72-183858 ISBN 0-909837-05-8
1. Mass. I. Title.

BOUMAN, Cornelius Adrianus. 264.02
Key to the Missal [by] Cornelius A. Bouman and Mary Perkins Ryan. Notre Dame, Ind., Fides Publishers Association [1960] 130p. 21cm. [BX2015.B65] 60-8447
1. Catholic Church. Liturgy and ritual. Missal. I. Ryan, Mary Perkins, 1915- joint author. II. Title.

BOUYER, Louis, 1913- 264.02
The liturgy revived; a doctrinal commentary of the Conciliar Constitution on the liturgy. [Notre Dame, Ind.] University of Notre Dame Press, 1964. 107 p. 19 cm. (The Notre Dame pocket library, PL-10) [BX830.1962.A45C62] 64-8174
1. Vatican Council, 2d. Constitute de sacra liturgia. I. Title.

BOUYER, Louis, 1913- 264.02
The liturgy revived; a doctrinal commentary of the Conciliar Constitution on the liturgy. [Notre Dame, Ind.] Univ. of Notre Dame Pr. [c.]1964. 107p. 19cm. (Notre Dame pocket lib., PL-10) 64-8174 .95 pap.,
1. Vatican Council, 2d. Constituto de sacra liturgia. I. Title.

BOUYER, Louis, 1913- 264.02
Rite and man; natural sacredness and Christian liturgy. Translated by M. Joseph Costelloe. [Notre Dame, Ind.] University of Notre Dame Press, 1963. 220 p. 24 cm. (University of Notre Dame. Dept. of Theology. Liturgical studies, v. 7) [BX1970.B66] 62-20224
1. Liturgics — Catholic Church. I. Title.

BOUYER, Louis, 1913- 264.02
Rite and man; natural sacredness and Christian liturgy. Tr. [from French] by M. Joseph Costelloe. [Notre Dame, Ind.] Univ. of Notre Dame Pr. [c.] 1963. 220p. 24cm. (Univ. of Notre Dame. Dept. of Theology. Liturgical studies, v.7) Bibl. 62-20224 6.00 bds.,
1. Liturgics—Catholic Church. I. Title.

BRADLEY, Paul John. 264.02
My Catholic devotions. Gastonia, N. C., Good Will Publishers [c1955] unpaged. illus. 27cm. [BX2110.B82] 55-18058
1. Catholic Church—Prayer-books and devotions—English. I. Title.

BRASO, Gabriel M. 264.02
Liturgy and spirituality. Translated by Leonard J. Doyle. Collegeville, Minn., Liturgical Press [1960] xii, 247 p. 25 cm. "This English translation conforms to the rev. and enl. Italian edition, Liturgia e spiritualita." [BX1970.B693] [BX1970] A 63
1. Catholic Church. Liturgy and ritual. 2. Spirituality. I. Title.

BRINGING the sacraments 264*.02
to the people; a guide to the fruitful use of the English ritual by priests and teachers. Collegeville, Minn., Liturgical Press [1966] 200 p. 24 cm. Bibliography: p. 191-192. [BX2200.B66] 72-177002
1. Sacraments (Liturgy) I. Catholic Church. Liturgy and ritual. Ritual (U.S.). English. Selections.

BRODERICK, Robert C 1913- 264.02
The Catholic layman's book of etiquette. St. Paul, Catechetical Guild Educational Society [1957] 320p. illus. 17cm. [BJ2018.B7] 57-29531
1. Church etiquette. 2. Christian life—Catholic authors. I. Title.

*BRUSSELMANS, Christiane 264.02
I go to mass with God's family. Text by Christi1ne Brusselm1ns. Photogs. by J. A. Fortier and Yan. Milwaukee. Bruce [1967] 1v. (unpaged) illus. (pt. col.) 19cm. 1.75
1. Mass—Juvenile literature. I. Title.

BUCHER, Janet Marie. 264'.02
Run with Him! : a practical source book for planning liturgies for children in primary and intermediate grades / Janet Marie Bucher ; introd. and editorial preparation by Daniel F. Onley. Cincinnati : North American Liturgy Resources, c1974. 251 p. : ill. ; 30 cm. Bibliography: p. 248-249. [BX2150.B8] 75-309862 9.95
1. Children—Prayer-books and devotions—English. I. Title.

[BUCHER, Victor G] 264.02
Franciscan parish prayerbook. [Paterson? N. J., 1953] 258p. illus. 18cm. [BX2050.F7B8 1953] 53-33063
1. Franciscans—Prayer-books and devotions—English. I. Title.

BUGNINI, Annibale. 264.02
The simplification of the rubrics; spirit and practical consequences of the decree of the Sacred Congregation of Rites March 23, 1955. With a pref, by Ferdinando Antonelli. Translated by Leonard J. Doyle. Collegeville, Minn., Doyle and Finegan, 1955. New York] Latin and English. 131p. 21cm. Includes text of the decree in and with comments by George R. Bach [and others. 'Bibliography on the simplification, up to June 28, 1955': p. [125]-126, Bibliographical footnotes. [BX1971.B8] 58-608
1. Catholic Church. Liturgy and ritual—Rubrics. I. Catholic Church. Congregatio Sacrorum Rituum. Cum nostra (23 Mar. 1955) II. Title.

BUISSINK, P J. 264.02
Frequent journeys to Calvary; various exercises for the Way of the Cross. Milwaukee, Bruce [1950] vi, 186 p. 23 cm. [BX2040.B78 1950] 50-6078
1. Stations of the Cross. 2. Catholic Church—Prayer-books and devotions—English. I. Title. II. Title: Various exercises for the Way of the Cross.

BUIST, Werner. 264.02
Come, let us adore; forms for worship Biblically and liturgically oriented, and adapted to the seasons and feats of the church year. Translated by Roland Franz [and] Guerin La Course. Collegeville, Minn., Liturgical Press [c1964] xviii, 253 p. 17 cm. (Popular liturgical library) Translation of Wir beten an. [BX1981.A2] 65-2991
1. Catholic Church — Prayer-books and devotions. 2. Church year — Prayer-books and devotions. I. Catholic Church. Liturgy and ritural. II. Title.

BURGARD, Charles 264.02
Scripture in the liturgy; translated [from the French] by J. Holland Smith. Westminster, Md., Newman Press, 1960[ ] x. 163p. 20cm. ibl. footnotes 60-3204 3.00
1. Catholic Church. Liturgy and ritual. Missal. 2. Bible—Liturgical use. I. Title.

BURGGRAFF, Aloysius John 264.02
Handbook for new Catholics. New York, Paulist Press [c.1960] 189p. illus. 18cm. 60-11596 2.00 bds.,
1. Catholic Church—Ceremonies and practices. I. Title.

BURGGRAFF, Aloysius John, 1898- 264.02
Handbook for new Catholics. New York, Paulist Pr. [1962, c.1960] 189p. illus. (Deus bks.) 60-11596 .95 pap.,
1. Catholic Church—Ceremonies and practices. I. Title.

BUSATO, Daniel, 1927- 264.02
La liturgie, magie, spectacle ou action divine? [Toulouse] Privat. [dist. Philadelphia, Chilton, 1964, c.1962] 142p. 19cm. (Questions posees aux catholiques) Bibl. 64-9072 1.52 pap.,
1. Catholic Church. Liturgy and ritual. I. Title.

CABROL, Fernand, 1855-1937. 264.02
Liturgical prayer, its history & spirit. Translated by a Benedictine of Stanbrook. Westminster, Md., Newman Press, 1950. xiv, 382 p. 23 cm. Translation of Le livre de la priere antique. [BX1970.C22 1950] 50-12131
1. Catholic Church. Liturgy and ritual. I. Title.

CALLAN, Charles Jerome, 1877- 264.02
Blessed be God, a complete Catholic prayer book, by Charles J. Callan and John A. McHugh. New York, Kenedy [1956] 754p. illus. 16cm. Issued in a box. [BX1981.C3 1956] 56-59235
1. Catholic Church—Prayer-books and devotions— English. I. MeHugh, John Ambrose, 1880- joint author. II. Title.

CARTHUSIANS. 264.02
Ancient devotions to the Sacred Heart of Jesus by Carthusian monks of the XIV-XVII centuries. [4th ed.] Westminster, Md., Newman Press [1954] 232p. illus. 16cm. [BX2158.C3 1954] 54-9088
1. Sacred Heart, Devotion to. I. Title.

A Catholic child's missal 264.02
and prayerbook. New York, Published by Guild Press; distributed by Golden Press [1959] 80p. illus. 16cm. (A Catechetical guild book) [BX2150.C24] 59-3912
1. Children—Prayer-books and devotions—English. 2. Catholic Church—Prayer-books and devotions—English.

CATHOLIC Church. 264.02
Liturgy and ritual. Breviary. English. Collegeville, Minn., Liturgical Press [1954] 758p. 16cm. (Popular liturgical library) [BX2000.A4H42] 55-24613
I. Heidt, William George, 1913- ed. II. Catholic Church. Litrrgy and ritual. Benedictine. III. Catholic Church. Liturgy and ritual. English. IV. Title: A short breviary for the religious and the laity, [Abridged ed.]

CATHOLIC Church. Liturgy and ritual. 264'.02
Ceremonies and processions of the cathedral church of Salisbury / edited from the fifteenth century ms. no. 148, with additions from the cathedral records, and woodcuts from the Sarum Processionale of 1502, by Chr. [i.e. Christopher] Wordsworth. New York : AMS Press, [1975] p. cm. Reprint of the 1901 ed. published by University Press, Cambridge. Includes indexes. [BX5142.C3 1975] 78-178544 ISBN 0-404-56626-X : 23.50
I. Wordsworth, Christopher, 1848-1938. II. Salisbury Cathedral. III. Title.

CATHOLIC Church. Liturgy and ritual. 264.02
Horologion. Franciscan edition. [New Canaan, Conn., Byzantine Franciscans, c1967] 692 p. 19 cm. "The present volume contains the canonical hours ... used outside the Great Fast and the Week of Light." "Based on the Chasoslov published at Rome in 1950 at Saint Nilus Monastery at Grotto Ferrata." Companion volume to the Book of hours published by the Byzantine Franciscans in 1965. [BX4711.665.H6A4 1967] 68-26521
I. Franciscans. Custody of St. Mary of the Angels. II. Catholic Church. Liturgy and ritual. Byzantine rite. III. [Horologion. English] IV. Title.

CATHOLIC Church. Byzantine rite (Ruthenian) Liturgy and ritual. Typikon. English. 264.02
Byzantine seraphic typicon; the order of divine services according to the usage of the Custody of St. Mary of the Angels. New Canaan, Franciscan Friars, 1963- v. 24 cm. Contents.--book 1. General norms. Catholic Church. Byzantine rite (Ruthenian). Liturgy and ritual. Franciscan. Bibliography: book 1, p. v. [BX4711.665.T9A4 1963] 63-19454
I. Orthodox Eastern Church. Liturgy and ritual. Typikon. English. II. Franciscans. Custody of St. Mary of the Angels. III. Title.

CATHOLIC Church. Byzantine rite (Ruthenian) Liturgy and ritual. Typikon. English. 264.02
Byzantine seraphic typicon; the order of divine services according to the usage of the Custody of St. Mary of the Angels. New Canaan, Conn., Franciscan Friars, 1963. 24cm. Contents.book. 1. General norms. Bibl. 63-19454 apply.
I. Catholic Church. Byzantine rite (Ruthenian) Liturgy and ritual. Franciscan. II. Orthodox Eastern Church. Liturgy and ritual. Typikon. English. III. Franciscans. Custody of St. Mary of the Angels. IV. Title.

CATHOLIC Church. Liturgy and ritual. Breuiary. English. 264.02
Roman Breviary in English, restored by the Sacred Council of Trent; published by order of the Supreme Pontiff St. Pius v, and carefully revised by other popes. Reformed by order of Pope Pius x. According to the Vatican typical edition, with new Psalter of Pope Pius XII; compiled from approved sources. With "An incentive to prayer" by Francis Cardinal Spellman. Edited by Joseph A. Nelson. New York, Benziger [1950-51, v. 4, 1950] 4v. 18 cm. "General rubrics of the Breviary, according to the typical edition of the jubilee year, 1900" published as suppl. (49 p.) with v. 3. Contents.[v. 1] Winter.--[v. 2] Spring.--[v. 3] Summer.--[v. 4] Autumn. [BX200.A4 1950] 50-2806
I. Nelson, Joseph A. ed. II. Catholic Church. Liturgy and ritual. English. III. Title.

CATHOLIC Church Liturgy and ritual. Breviary. English. 264.02
A short breviary for religious and the laity, edited by William G. Heidt, [abridged ed.] Collegeville, Minn., Liturgical Press [1954] 758p. 16cm. (Popular liturgical library) [BX2000.A4H4] 55-24613
I. Heldt, William George, 1913- ed. II. Catholic Church. Liturgy and ritual. Benedictine. III. Catholic Church. Liturgy and ritual. English. IV. Title.

CATHOLIC Church. Liturgy and ritual. Ceremonial of bishops. 264.02
Manual of episcopal ceremonies, based on the Caeremoniale episcoporum, decrees of the Sacred Congregation of Rites and approved authors, by Aurelius Stehle. Rev. by Emmeran A. Rettger. 5th ed. Latrobe, Pa., Archabbey Press, 1961. 2v. illus., diagrs. 24cm. Includes bibliographies. [BX1971.A25 1961] 61-13124
I. Stehle, Aurelius, 1877-1930. II. Title.

CATHOLIC Church. Liturgy and ritual. Ceremonial of bishops. 264.02
Ordinary Episcopal ceremonies a section of the Manual of episcopal ceremonies, by Aurelius Stehle. Rev. and rearranged to include episcopal ceremonies used frequently in cathedral, abbatial, parish churches, by Emmeran A. Rettger. Latrobe, Pa., Archabbey Press, 1959. viii, 224p. illus., diagrs. 23cm. Bibliography: p. 216-217. [BX1971.A25 1959] 59-13816
I. Stehle, Aurelius, 1877-1930. II. Title.

CATHOLIC Church. Liturgy and ritual English. 264.02
Altar prayers (Enchiridon precum) the most frequently used public prayers and devotions, both those prescribed for liturgical services and those in general use as well as others suitable for various occasions throughout the ecclesiastical year. New York, Benziger Bros. [1962] 105 p. 27 cm. "U.S.A. liturgical editions." Text on lining papers. Some prayers and devotions in Latin. "Revised in accordance with the Enchiridion indulgentiarum, 1950 ed. (The raccolta)" [BX2048.A4A4 1962] 65-1159
1. Altar prayers. I. Title. II. Title: Enchiridion precum.

CATHOLIC Church. Liturgy and ritual. English. 264.02
The book of Catholic worship. Washington, Liturgical Conference [1966] xxii, 807 p. 22 cm. "The hymnal" (with music): p. [413]-554. [BX1981.A3L5] 66-2881
I. Liturgical Conference, inc. II. Title.

CATHOLIC Church. Liturgy and ritual. English 264.02
The book of Catholic worship. Washington, D.C. 20018, Liturgical Conf. [2900 Newton St., N.E., c. 1966] xxii, 807p. 22cm. [BX1981.A3L5] 66-2881 3.50
1. Liturgical Conference, inc. I. Title.

CATHOLIC Church. Liturgy and ritual. English. 264.02
Oremus; the priest's handbook of English prayers for church services and special occasions. New York, J. F. Wagner [1912] vi, 177 p. 23 cm. [BX2048.A4O7] 13-689
1. Altar prayers. I. Title. II. Title: The priest's handbook of English prayers.

CATHOLIC Church. Liturgy and ritual. Missal. 264.02
The Fulton J. Sheen Sunday missal. Arranged and edited by Philip Caraman and James Walsh. New York, Hawthorn Books [1961] ixiii, 630, 630p. illus. 18cm. Latin and English on opposite pages, numbered in duplicate. [BX2015.A4C28] 61-13208
I. Caraman, Philip, 1911- ed. II. Walsh, James, 1920- ed. III. Catholic Church. Liturgy and ritual. Missal. English. IV. Catholic Church. Liturgy and ritual. English. V. Title.

CATHOLIC Church. Liturgy and ritual. Missal. 264.02
The Saint Dominic missal, Latin-English. 1st ed. New York, Saint Dominic Missal [c1959] 1317p. 18cm. [BX2015.A4D6] 60-2956
I. Catholic Church. Liturgy and ritual. English. II. Dominicans. III. Title.

CATHOLIC Church. Liturgy and ritual. Missal. English. 264.02
Layman's daily missal, prayer book & ritual. Baltimore, Helicon Press [c1962] lxxxvi, 1878 p. col. illus., music. 15 cm. Part of the text in Latin and English. "An adaptation of the 'Missel quotidien des fideles' edited by Father Feder, S. J." [BX2015.A4 1962] 63-25564
I. Catholic Church. Liturgy and ritual. English. II. Title.

CATHOLIC Church. Liturgy and ritual. Missal. English. 264.02
Layman's daily missal, prayer book & ritual. Baltimore, Helicon[dist. New York, Taplinger, 1963. c.1962] 1xxxvi, 1878p. col. illus., music.

15cm. Pt. of the text in Latin and English. An adaptation of the Missel quotidien des fideles ed. by Father Feder, 63-25564 10.95
I. Catholic Church. Liturgy and ritual. English. II. Title.

CATHOLIC Church. Liturgy and ritual. Missal. English. 264.02
Saint Joseph daily Mass. Completely rev. ed. in accordance with the latest general decrees of the Sacred Congregation of Rites including new Mass rubrics and the new Holy Week liturgy. Edited by Hugo H. Hoever. Introd. by Richard Kugelman. New York, catholic Book Pub. Co. [1957] 1344p. illus. (part col.) 17cm. [BX2015.A4H63 1957] 57-4750
I. Hoever, Hugo Henry, 1883- ed. II. Catholic Church. Liturgy and ritual English. III. Title.

CATHOLIC Church. Liturgy and ritual. Missal. English. 264.02
Saint Joseph daily missal; the official prayers of the Catholic Church for the celebration of the Sacred Congresgation of Rites. New York, Catholic Book Pub. Co. ,531955] 1344p. illus. (part col.) 17cm. [BX2015.A4H63 1955] 56-514
I. Hoeer, Hugo Henry, 1883- ed. II. Catholic Church. Liturgy and Ritual. English. III. Title.

CATHOLIC Church. Liturgy and ritual. Missal. English. 264.02
Saint Joseph daily missal; the official prayers of the Catholic Church for the celebration of daily Mass, in accordance with the latest Vatican ed. of the "Missale Romanum." Edited by Hugo H. Hoever. Introd. by Richard Kugelman. New York, Catholic Book Pub. Co. [1951] 2 v. illus. 17 cm. [BX2015.A4H63 1951] 51-8113
I. Hoever, Hugo Henry, Father, 1883- ed. II. Catholic Church. Liturgy and ritual. English. III. Title.

CATHOLIC Church. Liturgy and ritual. Missal. English. 264.02
Saint Joseph daily missal; the official prayers of the Catholic Church for the celebration of daily Mass, in accordance with the latest Vatican ed. of the "Missale Romanum." Edited by Hugo H. Hoever. Introd. by Richard Kugelman. New York, Catholic Book Pub. Co. [1950] xxviii, 1312 p. illus. (part col.) 17 cm. [BX2015.A4H63] 51-484
I. Hoever, Hugo Henry, Father, 1883- ed. II. Catholic Church. Liturgy and ritual. English. III. Title.

CATHOLIC Church. Liturgy and ritual. Missal. English. 264.02
Saint Joseph daily missal; the official prayers of the Catholic Church for the celebration of daily Mass. Completely rev. ed. [in accordance with the latest general decrees of the Sacred Congregation of Rites] including new Mass rubrics and the new Holy Week liturgy. Edited by Hugo H. Hoever. Introd. by Richard Kugelman. New York, Catholic Book Pub. Co. [1957] 1344p. illus. (part col.) 17cm. [BX2015.A4H63 1957] 57-4750
I. Hoever, Hugo Henry, 1883- ed. II. Catholic Church. Liturgy and ritual. English. III. Title.

CATHOLIC Church. Liturgy and ritual. Missal. English. 264.02
Saint Paul junior missal, by the Daughters of St. Paul. [Boston?] St. Paul Editions [1961] 253p. illus. (part col.) 14cm. 'Latin and English responses for dialogue Mass.' 'My treasury of prayers: p. [223]-253. [BX2150.C27] 61-66127
1. Children—Prayer-books and devotions—English. 2. Catholic Church—Prayer-books and devotions—English. I. Catholic Church. Liturgy and ritual. English. II. Daughters of St. Paul. III. Title.

CATHOLIC Church. Liturgy and ritual. Missal. English. 264.02
The Sunday missal for young Catholics, by Maurice Le Bas. New York, Guild Pr.; dist. Golden Pr. [1961] 238p. col. illus. 15cm. 61-65901 1.25; 2.00, deluxe ed., bxd.
1. Children—Prayer-books and devotions—English. 2. Catholic Church—Prayer-books and devotions—English. I. La Bas, Maurice. II. Title.

CATHOLIC Church. Liturgy and ritual. Office of the Blessed Virgin Mary. 264.02
The Little Office of the Blessed Virgin Mary. [English translation by Father Aurelian Scharf] Enl. ed. Westminster, Md., Newman Press [1954] xi, 481p. 16cm. English and Latin: added t. p. in Latin. [BX2025.A2 1954a] 54-12450
I. Catholic Church. Liturgy and ritual. Office of the Blessed Virgin Mary. English. II. Catholic Church. Liturgy and ritual. English. III. Title.

CATHOLIC Church. Liturgy and ritual. Office of the Blessed Virgin Mary. 264.02
The Little office of the Blessed Virgin Mary, according to the Roman breviary, together with prayers for the use of the Third Secular Order of Our Blessed Lady of Mount Carmel and St. Teresa of Jesus, with the Latin Psalter of the Pontifical Biblical Institute approved by Pope Pius XII and the English translations of the New Testament and the Psalms made under the patronage of the Episcopal Committee of the Confraternity of Christian Doctrine. Edited by Philip Foley. [Milwaukee, Spiritual Life Press, 1964] 132 p. front. 15 cm. [BX2025.A4 1964] 65-1837
I. Catholic Church. Liturgy and ritual. Office of the Blessed Virgin Mary. Eng. II. Catholic Church. Liturgy and ritual. English. III. Third Secular Order of Our Blessed Lady of Mount Carmel and St. Teresa of Jesus. IV. Foley, Philip, O. C. D., ed. V. Title.

CATHOLIC Church. Liturgy and ritual. Office of the Blessed Virgin Mary. 264.02
The Little office of the Blessed Virgin Mary, in Latin and English, according to the Roman breviary. Containing the Psalms from the new version authorized by Pope Pius XII. For the use of the Sisters of St. Joseph. New York, Benziger [1951] 307 p. 15 cm. [BX2025.A2 1951] 51-5461
I. Catholic Church. Liturgy and ritual. Office of the Blessed Virgin Mary. English. II. Catholic Church. Liturgy and ritual. English. III. Title.

CATHOLIC Church. Liturgy and Ritual. Office of the Blessed Virgin Mary. 264.02
Officium parvum Beatae Mariae Virginis. Editio amplior. Westminster, Md., Newman Press, 1956 [i. e. 1955] 371p. 13cm. [BX2025.A2 1955b] 56-2862
I. Title.

CATHOLIC Church. Liturgy and ritual. Office of the Blessed Virgin Mary. English. 264.02
The Little office of the Blessed Virgin Mary, in English; simply arranged for use by lay people. Psalms translated by Ronald A. Knox. [2d rev. ed.] Chicago, Franciscan Herald Press [1953] 114p. 16cm. [BX2025.A4 1953] 53-4394
I. Catholic Church. Liturgy and ritual. English. II. Title.

CATHOLIC Church. Liturgy and ritual. Ritual. 264.02
Collectio rituum, pro Dioecesibus Civitatum Foederatarum Americae Septentrionalis. Ritual approved by the National Conference of Bishops of the United States of America. Collegeville, Minn., Liturgical Press, 1964. 469 p. 19 cm. Cover title: English ritual. Collectio rituum. [BX2035.A2 1964] 65-3308
I. Catholic Church. Liturgy and ritual. U.S. II. Title.

CATHOLIC Church. Liturgy and ritual. Ritual. 264.02
Collectio rituum, pro Dioecesibus Civitatum Foederatarum Americae Septentrionalis. Ritual approved by the Natl. Conf. of Bishops of the U. S. of Amer. Prep. under the guidance of Walter J. Schmitz. Milwaukee, Bruce, 1964. xiv, 594p. 17cm. Common form of absolution: [1] 1. inserted. 64-7691 5.95
I. Schmitz, Walter J. II. Catholic Church. Liturgy and ritual. U.S. III. Title.

CATHOLIC Church. Liturgy and ritual. Ritual. 264.02
The Roman ritual [by] Philip T. Weller. Completeed. Milwaukee, Bruce [1965] xii, 771p. 22cm. The English version of the Psalms and other passages from the Old Testament are from the Confraternity version. New Testament passages are from the Kleist-Lilly version. [BX2035.A4] 64-8392 red edge ed., 15.00; gold edge ed., 19.00
I. Weller, Philip T., ed. and tr. II. Title.

CATHOLIC Church. Poenitentiaria Apostolica. 264.02
The raccolta; or, A manual of indulgences, prayers, and devotions enriched with indulgences in favor of all the faithful in Christ or of certain groups of persons, and now opportunely revised, edited and in part newly translated into English from the 1950 official edition "Enchiridion indulgentiarum--preces et pia opera" issued by the Sacred Penitentiary Apostolic. By Joseph P. Christopher, Charles E. Spence, and John F. Rowan, by authorization of the Holy See. New York, Benziger Bros., 1952. xvi, 626, xvii-ixxvi p. front. 18 cm. Added t. p., in Latin. [BX2170.I 6A4 1952] 52-8184
1. Catholic Church—Prayer-books and devotions—English. 2. Indulgences. I. Christopher, Joseph Patrick, 1890- ed. and tr. II. Title.

CATHOLIC Church. Pope. 264.02
The Liturgy. Selected, arr. by the Benedictine monks of Solesmes. Tr. by the Daughters of St. Paul. [Boston] St. Paul Eds. [dist. Daughters of St. Paul, c.1962] 664p. 19cm. (Papal teachings) Bibl. 61-17986 5.00; 4.00 pap.,
1. Catholic Church. Liturgy and ritual—Papal documents. I. Solesmes, France. Saint-Pierre (Benedictine abbey) II. Title.

CATHOLIC Church. Pope, 1939- (Pius XII) Mediator Dei (20 Nov. 1947) English. 264.02
On the sacred liturgy. Encyclical letter, Mediator Dei (Nov. 20, 1947) of Pope Pius XII, with introd. and notes by Gerald Ellard. Enl. and rev. ed. New York, America Press, 1954. 108p. 19cm. Includes bibliography. [BX1970.A] A55
1. Catholic Church. Liturgy and ritual. I. Ellard, Gerald, 1894- ed. II. Title. III. Title: The sacred liturgy.

CELEBRATION of the Mass; 264.02
the altar during Holy Mass—Pictures to punch out and assemble. Pictures by Vincent Malta. Planned by Katharine Wood. [New York, Golden Press] c.1960 unpaged col. illus. 36cm. (Guild punchout bk. for Catholic boys and girls 30200) .50 pap.,

CHAMPLIN, Joseph M. 264.02
Christ present and yet to come; the priest and God's people at prayer [by] Joseph M. Champlin. Maryknoll, N.Y., Orbis Books [1971] xiii, 242 p. 21 cm. Includes bibliographical references. [BX1969.C52] 70-151180 2.50
1. Catholic Church—Ceremonies and practices. 2. Worship. I. Title.

CHAPEL, Paul. 264.02
A living liturgy; reflections on the liturgy and on daily life. Translated and adapted by Martin W. Schoenberg. Westminster, Md., Newman Press [1967] 127 p. 21 cm. Translation of Gegeven voor u. [BX1970.C4813] 67-28698
1. Catholic Church. Liturgy and ritual.

CHARMOT, Francois 264.02
The Mass, source of sanctity. Tr. [from French] by M. Angeline Bouchard. Notre Dame, Ind., Fides [c.1964] 349p. 23cm. Bibl. 64-16498 5.50 bds.,
1. Mass. 2. Lord's Supper—Catholic Church. I. Title.

CHURCH and the liturgy 264.02
(The) Glen Rock, N. J., Paulist Pr. [c.1965] viii, 191p. 24cm. (Concilium theology in the age of renewal: Liturgy, v.2) Bibl. [BX830.A45C625] 65-17869 4.50
1. Vatican Council, 2d. Constitutio de sacra liturgia. 2. Catholic Church. Liturgy and ritual. I. Wagner, Johunnes, 1908- (Series: Concilium theology in the age of renewal, v.2)

THE Church at prayer: 264.02
introduction to the liturgy. Edited by A. G. Martimort, with the collaboration of Bernard Botte [and others. Translators: Robert Fisher and others] Editors of the English ed.: Austin Flannery [and] Vincent Ryan. New York, Desclee Co. [1968- v. plates. 22 cm. Translation of L'Eglise en priere. Includes bibliographies. [BV170.E3513] 68-56153 4.95 (v. 1)
1. Liturgies. I. Martimort, Aime Georges, ed. II. Botte, Bernard, 1893-

CLYNES, Raphael. 264.02
Liturgy and Christian life. Paterson, N. J., St. Anthony Guild Press [1960] 428p. 20cm. Includes bibliography. [BX1970.C65] 60-12199
1. Catholic Church. Liturgy and ritual. I. Title.

COCAGNAC, A M 264.02
When I go to Mass, by A. M. Cocagnac. Translated by William Barrow. Illustrated by Jacques Le Scanff. New York, Macmillan [1965] 1 v. (unpaged) col. illus. 21 cm. Translation of Pour compredre ma messe. [BX2230.2.C583 1965] 65-20245
1. Mass — Juvenile literature. I. Title.

COCAGNAC, A. M. 264.02
When I go to Mass. Tr. [from French] by William Barrow Illus. by Jacques Le Scanff. New York, Macmillan [c.1965] 1v. (unpaged) col. illus. 21cm. [BX2230.2.C583] 65-20245 1.45 bds.,
1. Mass—Juvenile literature. I. Title.

CRICHTON, James D 1907- 264.02
Changes in the liturgy; considerations on the Instruction of the Sacred Congregation of Rites for the proper implementation of the Constitution on the sacred liturgy, issued on September 26, 1964 [by] J. D. Crichton. Staten Island, N.Y., Alba House [1965] viii, 131 p. 22 cm. Text of the Instruction translated by F. MacManus and G. Diekmann. [BX1971.C7] 65-8682
1. Catholic Church. Liturgy and ritual. 2. Vatican Council, 2d. Constiutio de sarca litjrgia. I. Catholic Church Congregatio Sacrorum Rituum. Instructio ad executionem Constitutionis de sacra liturgia recte ordinandam (26 Sept. 1964) II. Title.

CRICHTON, James D 1907- 264.02
The church's worship; considerations on the liturgical constitution of the Second Vatican Council [by] J. D. Crichton. New York, Sheed & Ward [1964] x, 246 p. 23 cm. Bibliography: p. 239-242. [BX830 1962.A45C63] 64-22998
1. Vatican Council, 2d. Constituto de sacra liturgis. I. Title.

CRICHTON, James D., 1907- 264.02
The church's worship; considerations on the liturgical constitution of the Second Vatican Council. New York, Sheed [c.1964] x, 246p. 23cm. Bibl. 64-22998 5.00 bds.,
1. Vatican Council, 2d. Constituto de sacra liturgia. I. Title.

CRICHTON, James D. 1907 - ed. 264.02
The liturgy and the future. ed. by J. D. Crichton. [1st Amer. ed.] Techny. Ill ., Divine Word [1966] 173p. music. 18cm. Bibl. [BX1970.C7 1966] 66-8840 1.15 pap.,
1. Catholic Church. Liturgy and ritual. I. Title.

THE Crisis of liturgical 264.02
reform. New York, Paulist Press [1969] viii, 182 p. 24 cm. (Concilium: theology in the age of renewal. Liturgy, v. 42) Bibliographical footnotes. [BX1975.C7] 77-78920 4.50
1. Catholic Church. Liturgy and ritual—Addresses, essays, lectures. 2. Liturgics—History—Addresses, essays, lectures. I. Series: Concilium (New York) v. 42.

DALLEN, James. 264'.02
Liturgical celebration : possible patterns / James Dallen. Cincinnati : North American Liturgy Resources, 1971. 89 p. ; 28 cm. [BX2169.D34] 75-309480
1. Lord's Supper—Prayer-books and devotions—English. 2. Baptism (Liturgy) 3. Marriage service. I. Title.

DALMAIS, Irenee Henri, 1914- 264.02
Introduction to the liturgy. Tr. [from French] by Roger Capel. Pref. by Frederick R. McManus. Baltimore, Helicon Pr. [c.]1961. 208p. Bibl. 61-15959 4.50 bds.,
1. Liturgics—Catholic Church. 2. Catholic Church. Liturgy and ritual. I. Title.

DAUGHTERS of St. Paul, eds. 264.02
Bible vigils; ten celebrations of the word [Boston, Mass.] St. Paul Eds. [dist. Daughters of St. Paul, c.1965] 120p. 21cm. .50 pap.,
I. Title.

DAVIS, Charles 264.02
Liturgy and doctrine; the doctrinal basis of the liturgical movement. New York, Sheed and Ward [1961, c.1960] 123p. 61-7293 2.50
1. Liturgical movement—Catholic Church. I. Title.

DE MARCO, Angelus A. 264.02
A key to the new liturgical constitution; an alphabetical analysis. New York, Desclee [c.] 1964. 132p. 19cm. 64-23899 2.95
1. Vatican Council, 2d. Constituto de sacra liturgia—Indexes. I. Title.

DE MARCO, Angelus A. 264.02
Rome and the vernacular. Westminster, Md., Newman Press [c.]1961. 191p. Bibl. 61-8971 3.25
1. Language question in the church. 2. Liturgical language. I. Title.

DEVINE, George, 1941- 264'.02
Liturgical renewal; an agonizing reappraisal. Staten Island, N.Y., Alba House [1973] ix, 199 p. 21 cm. Includes bibliographical references. [BX1970.D454] 73-12923 ISBN 0-8189-0281-7 3.95 (pbk.)
1. Liturgies—Catholic Church—History. I. Title.

DIAMOND, Wilfrid Joseph, 1913- 264.02
Dictionary of liturgical Latin. Milwaukee, Bruce Pub. Co. [c.1961] 156p. 61-7491 2.50 pap.,
1. Catholic Church. Liturgy and ritual—Dictionaries. 2. Latin lanuage—Church Latin. 3. Latin language, Medieval and modern—Dictionaries. I. Title.

DIEKMANN, Godfrey 264.02
Come, let us worship. Baltimore, Helicon [c.1961] 180p. (Benedictine studies) Bibl. 61-11760 4.50
1. Liturgics—Catholic Church. I. Title.

DIEKMANN, Godfrey 264.02
Come, let us worship. New introd. Garden

City,N.Y. Doubleday [c.1961, 1966] 190p. 18cm. (Image bk., D207) Bibl. [BX1970.D475] .85 pap.,
1. Liturgies—Catholic Church. I. Title.

DIGGES, Mary Laurentia, 1910- 264.02
Transfigured world; design, theme, and symbol in worship. Illustrated by Charlotte Anne Carter. New York, Farrar, Straus and Cudahy [1957] 240p. illus. 22cm. [BX1970.D48] 57-5309
1. Catholic Church. Liturgy and ritual. 2. Christian art and symbolism. I. Title.

*DREZE, A. 264.02
Living in Christ, liturgy and sacraments. Notre Dame, Ind., Fides [1967,c.1966] 209p. illus. 22cm. (Young Christians today, v.2, Fides PBT 25) Orig. pub. as Jesus -Christ Notre Vie, v.2 in the ser. Temoins du Christ. 7th Fremch ed., pub. by Les Editions de Lumen Vitae, Brussels, 1965. Tr. by Geoffrey Chapman. 1.95 pap.,
1. Catholic Church—Sacraments— Study and Teaciphing. 2. Catholic Church—Liturgy—Study and teaching. I. Title. II. Series.

EISENHOFER, Ludwig, 1871-1941. 264.02
The liturgy of the Roman rite [by] Ludwig Eisenhofer, Joseph Lechner. Tr. [from German] by A. J. and E. F. Peeler; ed. by H. E. Winstone. [New York] Herder and Herder [c.1961] 506p. Bibl. 60-13249 8.50
1. Catholic Church. Liturgy and ritual. 2. Liturgics—Catholic Church. I. Lechner, Josef, 1893- II. Title.

FILTHAUT, Theodor 264.02
Learning to worship. Tr. [from German] by Ronald Walls. Westminster, Md., Newman [1966,c.1965] ix. 191p. 21cm. [BX1970.F513] 66-2311 3.95
1. Catholic Church. Liturgy and ritual. I. Title.

FISCHER, Henry. j264.02
Children's book of the Holy Mass. Illustrated by Christa Tewes. Translated by Rosemarie McManus. Baltimore, Helicon [c1965] 39 p. col. illus. 21 cm. Translation of Das Buch von der helligen Messe. [BX2230.2.F5] 66-2685
1. Mass — Juvenile literature. I. Title.

FISCHER, Henry 264.02
Children's book of the Holy Mass. Illus. by Christa Tewes. Tr. [from German]; by Rosemarie McManus. Helicon [dist. New York, Taplinger c.1965] 39p. col. illus. 21cm. [BX2230.2.F5] 66-2685 1.75 bds.,
1. Mass—Juvenile literature. I. Title.

FLICOTEAUX, Emmanuel, 1882- 264.02
The splendor of Pentecost. Tr. from French by Mary Louise Helmer. Baltimore, Helicon Press, [c.]1961 112p. Bibl. 61-11759 3.50
1. Pentecost festival. I. Title.

FLOOD, Edmund 264.02
In memory of me; God's plan for men: present in history, made active in the Eucharist. New York, Sheed [1963, c.1962] 117p. 22cm. First pub. in London in 1962 under title: No small plan. Bibl. 63-17149 3.00
1. Redemption. 2. Mass. I. Title.

GARESCHE, Edward Francis, 1876- 264.02
Moments with God. Milwaukee, Bruce Pub. Co. [c1956] 525p. illus. 16cm. [BX2110.G25 1956] 57-645
1. Catholic Church—Prayer-books and devotions—English. I. Title.

GAUTIER, Leon, 1832-1897. 264.02
Histoire de la poesie liturgique au moyen age; les tropes. Paris, 1886. [Ridgewood, N.J., Gregg Press, 1966] viii, 280 p. illus., facsims., music. 24 cm. On spine: Les tropes. No more published. The bibliographical footnotes include "Table des tropes du Kyrie" (p. 239-243), "Table des tropes du Gloria" (p. 259-266), and "Table des tropes 'Regnum'" (p. 276-278) [BX2043.G3 1966] 67-2466
1. Catholic Church. Liturgy and ritual. Troper. Title: Les tropes. I. Title.

GUIMOND, Jean Claude 264.02
Guide texts for Mass commentators. Tr. [from French] by Kenneth Silvia. Collegeville, Minn., 56321 Liturgical Pr., St. John's Abbey [1965] 128p. 21cm. [BX2015.G813] 65-3387 price unreported
1. Catholic Church. Liturgy and ritual. Missal—Commentaries. 2. Mass—Prayerbooks and devotions—English. I. Title.

HAMMAN, Gauthier Adalbert. 264.02
The grace to act now; liturgy and the apostolate in the light of the early Christian centuries [by] A. Hamman. Translated from the French by Malachy Carroll. Chicago, Franciscan Herald Press [1966] x, 123 p. 21 cm. Translations on Liturgie et apostolat. Includes bibliographies. [BX1970.H2713] 66-17109
1. Catholic Church. Liturgy and ritual. 2. Catholic action. I. Title.

HAMMAN, Gauthier Adalbert 264.02
The grace to act now: liturgy and the apostolate in thelight of the early Christian centuries. Tr. from French by Malachy Carroll. Chicago, Franciscan Herald [c.1966] x, 123p. 21cm. Bibl [BX1970. H2713] 66-17109 3.50
1. Catholic Church. Liturgy and ritual. 2. Catholic action. I. Title.

HARING, Bernhard, 1912- 264'.02
The sacraments and your everyday life / Bernard Haring. Liguori, Mo. : Liguori Publications, 1976. 192 p. ; 22 cm. Includes index. Bibliography: p. 186-187. [BX2200.H23 1976] 76-7824 ISBN 0-89243-053-2 pbk. : 2.95
1. Sacraments—Catholic Church. I. Title.

HAUSMANN, Bernard Andrew, 1899- 264.02
Learning the new breviary. New York, Benziger Bros. [1961] 119p. 20cm. First published in 1932 under title: Learning the breviary. [BX2000.H3 1961] 61-15032
1. Catholic Church. Liturgy and ritual. Breviary. I. Title.

HOEVER, Hugo Henry, 1883- 264.02
Saint Joseph children's missal; an easy way of praying the Mass for boys and girls. New York, Catholic Book Pub. Co. [1954] 128p. illus. 15cm. [BX2150.H6] 56-440
1. Children—Prayer-books and devotions—English. I. Title.

HOFINGER, Johannes. 264.02
Worship: the life of the missions, by Johannes Hofinger [and others] of the Institute of Mission Apologetics, Manila, P. I. Translated by Mary Perkins Ryan. [Notre Dame, Ind.] University of Notre Dame Press, 1958. 342p. 24cm. (Notre Dame [Ind.] University. Liturgical studies,v. 4) [BX2180.H63] 58-11783
1. Catholic Church. Liturgy and ritual. 2. Catholic Church—Missions. I. Institute of Mission Apologetics, Manila. II. Title.

HOVDA, Robert W. 264'.02
Dry bones; living worship guides to good liturgy, by Robert Hovda. Washington, Liturgical Conference, 1973. vi, 152 p. 23 cm. Includes bibliographical references. [BV15.H69] 73-76658 4.95
1. Public worship. I. Title.

HOVDA, Robert W. ed. 264.02
Sunday morning crisis; renewal in Catholic worship. Baltimore, Helicon [1963] 152 p. 23 cm. Bibliography: p. 147-152. [BX1970.H68] 63-19407
1. Liturgical movement — Catholic Church. 2. Liturgics — Catholic Church. I. Title.

HOVDA, Robert W., ed. 264.02
Sunday morning crisis renewal in Catholic worship. Helicon [dist. New York, Taplinger, c.1963] 152p. 23cm. Bibl. 63-19407
1. Liturgical movement—Catholic Church. 2. Liturgics—Catholic Church. I. Title.

INTERNATIONAL Congress of Pastoral Liturgy. 1st, Assisi and Rome, 1956. 264.02
The Assisi papers; proceedings. Collegeville, Minn., Liturgical Press [1957] xviii, 236p. 23cm. 'Published as a supplement to Worship.' Bibliographical footnotes. [BX1970.A1I55 1956] 57-3660
1. Catholic Church. Liturgy and ritual—Congresses. I. Worship (Periodical) II. Title.

INTERNATIONAL Study Week on Mission and Liturgy. 1st, Nimegen and Uden, 1959. 264.02
Liturgy and the missions; the Nijmegen papers. Edited by Johannes Hofinger. New York, P. J. Kenedy [1960] 308p. 22cm. [BX1970.A1I6 1959] 60-8384
1. Catholic Church. Liturgy and ritual—Congresses. 2. Catholic Church—Missions—Congresses. I. Hofinger, Johannes, ed. II. Title.

INTERNATIONAL Study Week on Mission and Liturgy; Nijmegen and Uden, 1959. 264.02
Liturgy and the missions; the Nijmegen papers. Edited by Johannes Hofinger. New York, P. J. Kennedy [c.1960]. xii, 308p. 22cm. 60-8384 5.95
1. Catholic Church. Liturgy and ritual—Congresses. 2. Catholic Church—Missions—Congresses. I. Hofinger, Johannes, ed. II. Title.

JANKAUSKAS, John J. 264.02
Our tongues were loosed; parish experiences in the liturgical renewal. Westminster, Md., Newman [c.] 1965. xvii, 144p. 23cm. [BX1970.J35] 64-66332 3.75
1. Catholic Church. Liturgy and ritual. I. Title.

JEAN-NESMY, Claude. 264.02
Living the liturgy. [Translated by Norah Smaridge] Staten Island, N.Y., Alba House [1966] 216 p. 22 cm. Translation of Pratique de la liturgie. Bibliography: p. 215-216. [BX1970.J413] 66-21812
1. Catholic Church. Liturgy and ritual. I. Title.

JEAN-NESMY, Claude 264.02
Living the liturgy. [Tr. by Norah Smaridge] Staten Staten Island, N.Y., Alba [c.1966] 216p. 22cm. Bibl. [BX1970.J413] 66-21812 3.95
1. Catholic Church. Liturgy and ritual. I. Title.

*JEANNE RENEE, Sister 264.02
Children's Stations of the Cross. Glen Rock, N.J., Paulist [c.1965] 1v. (unpaged) illus. (pt. col.) 10x14cm. .10 pap.,
I. Title.

JONES, Charles Williams, 1905- 264.02
The Saint Nicholas liturgy and its literary relationships (ninth to twelfth centuries) With an essay on the music by Gilbert Reaney. Berkeley, Univ. of Calif. Pr. [c.]1963. x, 151p. music. 24cm. (Univ. of Calif. pubns. Engl. studies, 27) Liturgy ed. from British Museum ms. Cotton Nero E I, pt. II, leaves 153 verso-155 verso. Bibl. 64-63042 3.50 pap.,
1. Nicholas, Saint, Bp. of Myra. I. Catholic Church. Liturgy and ritual. Special Offices. Nicholas, Saint. Bp. of Myra. II. Title. III. Series: California. University. University of California publications in English, 27

JONES, Charles Williams, 1905- 264.02
The Saint Nicholas liturgy and its literary relationships (ninth to twelfth centuries) With an essay on the music by Gilbert Reaney. Berkeley, University of California Press, 1963. x, 151 p. music. 24 cm. (University of California publications. English studies, 27) Liturgy edited from British Museum manuscript Cotton Nero E. I, pt. II, leaves 153 verso-155 verso. "Bibliographic abbreviations": p. ix-x [BX4700.N55J6] 64-63042
1. Nicholas, Saint, Bp. of Myra. I. Catholic Church. Liturgy and ritual. Special Offices. Nicholas, Saint, Bp. of Myra. II. Title. III. Series. IV. Series: California. University. University of California publications. English studies, 27

JOUNEL, Pierre 264.02
The rite of concelebration of Mass and of Communion under both species; history, texts in English, and commentaries. New York, Desclee [1967] 197p. 19cm. Tr. of L1concelebr1tion. Bibl. [BX2231.5.J613] 67-17679 3.50
1. Concelebration. 2. Lord's Supper—Communion in both elements. I. Title.

KAVANAGH, Joseph William. 264.02
The altar boys' ceremonial; with simple and solemn ceremonies of Holy Week according to the new Ordo Hebdomadae Sanctae. New York, Benziger Bros. [1957] 252p. 19cm. [BX1972.K3 1957] 57-1914
1. Altar boys. 2. Catholic Church, Liturgy and ritual. Holy Week rite. I. Title.

KAVANAGH, Joseph William. 264.02
The alter boys' ceremonial. New York, Benziger Bros. [1955] 232p. 19cm. [BX1972.K3] 55-3988
1. Altar boys. I. Title.

KAVANAGH, Joseph William. 264.02
The priests ceremonial. New York, Benziger Bros. [1957] 265p. 19cm. [BX1971.K3] 57-1857
1. Catholic Church, Liturgy and ritual. I. Title.

KIESLING, Christopher 264.02
The spirit and practice of the liturgy. Chicago. Priory Pr. [1966.c.1965] 143p. 20cm. Bibl. [BX1970.K48] 65-28349 2.95
1. Catholic Church. Liturgy and ritual. I. Title.

KILLEEN, B. D. 264'.02
Sacraments in the new liturgy / B. D. Killeen. Huntington, Ind. : Our Sunday Vistor, c1976. 159 p. ; 21 cm. [BX2203.K54] 76-23698 ISBN 0-87973-801-4 pbk. : 3.50
1. Catholic Church. Liturgy and ritual. 2. Sacraments—Catholic Church. I. Title.

KING, Archdale Arthur, 1890- 264.02
Liturgies of the past. Milwaukee, Bruce Pub. Co. [c1959] xii, 487p. illus. 23cm. (His Rites of Western Christendom, v. 4) Includes bibliographies. [BX1995.A1K5 1959] 60-4134
1. Liturgies. I. Title.

KING, Archdale Arthur, 1890- 264.02
Liturgies of the religious orders. London, New York, Longmans, Green [1955] xii, 431p. illus. 23cm. (His Rites of Western Christendom) Includes bibliographies. [BX2049.A1K5 1955] 55-4576
1. Catholic Church. Liturgy and ritual. 2. Monasticism and religious orders. I. Title.

KING, James W. 264.02
The liturgy and the laity. Westminister, Md., Newman Press, 1963. 175 p. 23 cm. Includes bibliography. [BX1970.K52] 63-12254
1. Liturgical movement — Catholic Church. I. Title.

KING, James W. 264.02
The liturgy and the laity. Westminster, Md., Newman [c.1963] 175p. 23cm. Bibl. 63-12254 3.50
1. Liturgical movement—Catholic Church. I. Title.

KIRCHGASSNER, Alfons, 1909- ed. 264.02
Unto the altar; the practice of Catholic worship. [Tr. from German by Rosaleen Brennan. New York] Herder & Herder [1963] 202p. 22cm. 62-19556 4.50
1. Liturgical movement — Catholic Church — Addresses, essays, lectures. I. Title.

KOENIG, John H. 264.02
God's word at Mass, by John Koenig. [1st ed.] New York, Hawthorn [1967] 109p. 21cm. (Twentieth century ency. of Catholicism, v. 64 Sect. 6: The word of Go Bibl. [BX2230.2.K6] 67-13950 3.95 bds.,
1. Mass. 2. Bible—Liturgical use. I. Catholic Church. Liturgy and ritual. II. Title. III. Series: The Twentieth century encyclopedia of Catholicism, v. 64

KOENKER, Ernest Benjamin. 264.02
The liturgical renaissance in the Roman Catholic Church. [2d ed.] Saint Louis, Concordia Pub. House [1966] c1954] xi, 274 p. 21 cm. Bibliography: p. 247-263. [BX1975.K6] 66-4626
1. Liturgical movement—Catholic Church. I. Title.

KOENKER, Ernest Benjamin. 264.02
The liturgical renaissance in the Roman Catholic Church. [Chicago] University of Chicago Press [1954] xi, 271p. 23cm. 'The present study has as its basis a dissertation presented to ... the University of Chicago, in candidacy for the degree of doctor of philosophy.' Bibliography: p. 247-261. [BX1975.K6] 54-12370
1. Liturgical movement—Catholic Church. I. Title.

KOENKER, Ernest Benjamin 264.02
The liturgical renaissance in the Roman Catholic Church. [2d rev. ed.] St. Louis, Concordia [1966,c.1954] xi, 274p. 21cm. Bibl. [BX1975.K6 1966] 66-4626 2.95 pap.,
1. Liturgical movement—Catholic Church. I. Title.

KUGLER, John J 264.02
A commentary on the new Little office, annotated with reflections. Paterson, N. J., Salesiana Publishers [c1955] 209p. 20cm. Includes Psalms from the Pontifical Biblical Institute's Liber Psalmorum cum Canticis Breviaril Romani nova e textibus primigenils interpretatio Latina, with English translations. [BX2025.K8] 58-27468
1. Catholic Church. Liturgy and ritual. Office of the Blessed Virgin Mary. I. Catholic Church. Liturgy and ritual. Psalter. II. Title.

LANE, John Irving, 1892- 264.02
Notes on some ceremonies of the Roman rite. Rev. and enl. Westminster, Md., Newman Bookshop [dist. Newman Pr. c.]1961 124, 164p. illus. Bibl. 61-4705 3.50
1. Catholic Church. Liturgy and ritual. I. Title.

*LAPLANTE, Sister Mary Cosma 264.02
Come to the family meal. Illus. by Sister Mary Josita Baccala. Foreword by Charles H. Helmsing. Milwaukee, Bruce [1966] 62p. col. illus. 21cm. 1.25 bds.,
1. Catholic Church—Liturgy and ritual—juvenile literature. I. Title.

LASANCE, Francis Xavier, 1860-1946, comp. comp. 264.02
Our Lady book; with special prayers and devotions for the Marian year and containing a complete Sunday missal. New York, Benziger Bros. [1954] xxii, 711, 224p. illus. 16cm. [BX2160.L3 1954] 54-1987
1. Mary, Virgin—Prayer-books and devotions—English. 2. Catholic Church—Prayer-books and devotions— English. I. Title.

LAWRENCE, Emeric Anthony, 1908- 264.02
Each month with Christ; insights into the liturgy of the months. Baltimore, Helicon Press [c.]1961. 116p. 61-8100 2.95
1. Catholic Church. Liturgy and ritual. 2. Church year. I. Title.

LEFEBVRE, Gaspar 264.02
The spirit of worship. Translated from the French by Lancelot C. Sheppard. New York, Hawthorn Books [c.1959] 126p. 21cm. (The Twentieth century encyclopedia of Catholicism, v. 108. Section 10: The worship of the church) 59-14520 2.95 bds.,
1. Catholic Church. Liturgy and ritual. 2. Holy Spirit. I. Title.

LEFEBVRE, Gaspar, 1880- 264.02
Catholic liturgy, its fundamental principles; translated by a Benedictine of Stanbrook. New and rev. ed. St. Louis, Herder [1954] 300p. 19cm. Translation of Liturgie. [BX1970.L3913] 54-3881
1. Catholic Church. Liturgy and ritual. I. Title.

LEFEBVRE, Gaspar, 1880- 264.02
The spirit of worship. Translated from the French by Lancelot C. Sheppard. [1st ed.] New York, Hawthorn Books [1959] 126p. 21cm. (The Twentieth century encyclopedia of Catholicism. v. 108. Section 10: The worship of the church) Translation of L esprit de Dieu dans la sainte liturgie. [BX1970.L3843] 50-14520
1. Catholic Church. Liturgy and ritual. 2. Holy Spirit. I. Title.

LEONARD, William J ed. 264.02
Liturgy for the people; essays in honor of Gerald Ellard, s.j., 1894-1963. Milwaukee, Bruce Pub. Co. [1963] xiv, 254 p. 23 cm. Bibliographical footnotes. [BX1970.L414] 63-21155
1. Ellard, Gerald, 1894-1963. 2. Catholic Church. Liturgy and ritual — Addresses, essays, lectures. 3. Liturgical movement — Catholic Church. I. Title.
Contents omitted.

LEONARD, William J., ed. 264.02
Liturgy for the people; essays in honor of Gerald Ellard, S.J., 1894-1963. Milwaukee, Bruce [c.1963] xiv, 254p. 23cm. Bibl. 63-6232 5.50
1. Ellard, Gerald, 1894-1963. 2. Catholic Church. Liturgy and ritual—Addresses, essays, lectures. 3. Liturgical movement—Catholic Church. I. Title.

LERCARO, Giacomo, Cardinal, 1891- 264.02
A small liturgical dictionary. Edited by J. B. O'Connell. [Translation made by J. F. Harwood-Tregear] Collegeville. Minn., Liturgical Press [1959] 248p. 19cm. [BV173.L413 1959] 60-4796
1. Liturgies—Dictionaries. 2. Catholic Church. Liturgy and ritual—Dictionaries. I. Title.

LICHIUS, James, Rev. 264.02
Novena of the Holy Spirit. Tr. from Spanish by Rev. L. M. Dooley. Boston, St. Paul Eds. [dist. Daughters of St. Paul, c.1962] 95p. 17cm. .50 pap.,
1. Catholic Church, Liturgy and ritual. I. Title.

LIGUORI, Alfonso Maria de', Saint, 1696-1787. 264.02
Visits to the Blessed Sacrament. Springfield, Ill., Templegate [1960] 152p. 15cm. [BX2169.L52 1960] 60-4402
1. Catholic Church—Prayer-books and devotions—English. I. Title.

LITTLE, Vilma Gertrude, 1888- 264.02
The sacrifice of praise; an introduction to the meaning and use of the divine office. New York, P. J. Kenedy [c1957] 200p. 20cm. [BX2000.L5] 58-1446
1. Divine office. 2. Catholic Church, Liturgy and ritual. Breviary. I. Title.

LITURGICAL Conference, 1st, Immaculate Heart Seminary, 1967. 264.02
Liturgy, the art of worship; proceedings. [San Diego, Calif., Immaculate Heart Seminary Press, 1968?] 38 p. illus., ports. 25 cm. Cover title. At head of title: Liturgical Commission, Diocese of San Diego, Calif. Bibliography: p. 37. [BX1970.A1L52] 68-4063
1. Catholic Church. Liturgy and ritual—Congresses. I. Catholic Church. Diocese of San Diego, Calif. Liturgical Commission. II. Immaculate Heart Seminary, San Diego, Calif. III. Title.

LITURGICAL Conference, inc. 264.02
Preaching the liturgical renewal; instructional sermons and homilies. Pref. by H. A. Reinhold. Washington [1964] 96 p. 21 cm. (Its The parish worship program) [BX830 1962.A45C65] 64-8256
1. Vatican Council, 2d. Constituto de sacra liturgia. 2. Catholic Church. Liturgy and ritual — Sermons. I. Title.

LITURGICAL Conference, inc. 264.02
Preaching the liturgical renewal; instructural sermons and homilies. Pref. by H. A. Reinhold [Helicon, dist. New York, Taplinger, c.1964] 96p. 21cm. (Its The parish worship program) [BX8301962.A45C65] 64-8256 1.95, pap., wire bdg.
1. Vatican Council, 2d. Constituto de sacra liturgia. 2. Catholic Church. Liturgy and ritual—Sermons. I. Title.

LITURGICAL Conference, inc. 264.02
Priest's guide to parish worship. Pref. by Frederick R. McManus. Introd. by Gerard S. Sloyan. Washington [1964] xiv, 185 p. 22 cm. "Constitutes an explanation of what the Vatican Council's Constitution on the liturgy means in every parish." Bibliography: p. 177-179. [BX1970.L49] 64-20231
1. Catholic Church. Liturgy and ritual. 2. Vatican Council, 2d. Constituto de sacra liturgia. I. Title.

LITURGICAL CONFERENCE, inc. 264.02
Priest's guide to parish worship. Pref. by Frederick R. McManus. Introd. by Gerard S. Sloyan. Washington, D.C., 3428 Ninth St., N.E. Author [c.]1964, xiv, 185p. 22cm. Constitutes an explanation of what Vatican Council's Constitution on the liturgy means in every parish. Bibl. 64-20231 4.50 bds.,
1. Catholic Church. Liturgy and ritual. 2. Vatican Council, 2d. Constituto de sacra liturgia. I. Title.

LITURGY constitution (The); 264.02
a chapter by chapter analysis of the Constitution on the sacred liturgy, with study-club questions. Glen Rock, N.J., Paulist [1965, c.1964] 191p. 18cm. (Deus bks.) Bibl. [BX830 1962.A45C68] 64-8073 .95 pap.,
1. Vatican Council. 2d. Constitutio de sacra liturgia. I. Vatican Council, 2d. Constitutio de sacra liturgia. II. Catholic Church. Pope, 1963- (Paulus VI) Motu proprio sacram liturgiam (25 Jan. 1964) English.

LITURGY in transition. 264.02
Edited by Herman Schmidt. [New York] Herder and Herder [1971] 155 p. 23 cm. (Concilium: religion in the seventies, v. 62: Liturgy) On cover: The New concilium: religion in the seventies. Includes bibliographical references. [BX1970.L53] 70-129761 2.95
1. Liturgical movement—Catholic Church. I. Schmidt, Herman A. P., 1912- ed. II. Series: Concilium (New York) 62

LOMASK, Milton 264.02
The way we worship, by Milton Lomask, Ray Neville. New York, Farrar [c.1961] 126p. illus. 61-11326 2.95 bds.,
1. Catholic Church—Ceremonies and practices. I. Neville, Ray, joint author. II. Title.

LONGLEY, Alfred C 264.02
That they may share; a Mass commentary, by Alfred C. Longley and Frederick R. McManus. New York, Benziger Bros. [1960] 269p. 27cm. Includes bibliography. [BX2015.L6] 60-10174
1. Catholic Church. Liturgy and ritual. Missal. I. McManus, Frederick Richard, 1923- joint author. II. Title.

LORD, Daniel Aloysius, 1888- 264.02
Christ Jesus our King: a Eucharistic prayer book; devotions to Christ in the Blessed Sacrament, written and arranged for those who love or wish to love. [St. Louis? 1951] 495 p. 15 cm. [BX2169.L6] 51-38719
1. Lord's Supper—Prayer-books and devotions—English 2. Catholic Church—Prayer-books and devotions—English. I. Title.

LOVASIK, Lawrence George, 1913- 264.02
Come, Holy Spirit. Milwaukee, Bruce Pub. Co., [1952] 167 p. 10 cm. [BX2170.115L6] 52-1624
1. Holy Spirit—Prayer-books and devotions—English 2. Catholic Church—Prayer-books and devotions—English. I. Title.

LYONS, Hugh Peter Carbery. 264.02
Praying our prayers. Westminster, Md., Newman Press, 1956. 72p. 18cm. [BX2110.L9] 56-9998
1. Catholic Church—Prayer-books and devotions—English. I. Title.

MCCAFFERY, Richard J. 264.02
The liturgy; a discussion course for young people [by] Richard J. McCaffery. Frank X. Smith, artist. Notre Dame, Ind., Fides Publishers [1966 or 7] [32] p. (incl. cover) col. illus. 27 cm. [BX2238.M3] 66-30589
1. Mass—Study and teaching. I. Title.

MCCORRY, Vincent P 1909- 264.02
And cleanse my lips. Garden City, N. Y., McMullen Books [1957] 241p. 20cm. [BX2170.C55M3] 57-1143
1. Church year—Meditations. I. Title.

MCCORRY, Vincent P 1909- 264.02
And cleanse my lips. Garden City, N. Y., McMullen Books [1957] 241p. 20cm. [BX2170.C55M3] 57-1143
1. Church year—Meditations. I. Title.

MCEVOY, Hubert 264.02
Children and priest at Mass. Photos. by Anthony Powell. Westminster, Md., Newman Press, 1960 [c.1959] 95p. 61-425 1.50 bds.,
1. Mass—Juvenile literature. I. Title.

MCGOWAN, Jean Carroll 264.02
Concelebration; sign of the unity of the church. [New York] Herder & Herder [c.1964] xxiii, 13-128p. 21cm. Bibl. 64-19662 3.75
1. Concelebration. I. Title.

MACMANUS, Frederick Richard, 1923- 264.02
Handbook for the new rubrics. Baltimore, Helicon Press [1961] 203p. 23cm. [BX1971.M3] 61-8101
1. Catholic Church. Liturgy and ritual—Rubrics. I. Title.

MCMANUS, Frederick Richard, 1923- ed. 264.02
The revival of the liturgy. [New York] Herder & Herder [c.1963] 224p. 21cm. Bibl. 63-18154 4.50
1. Diekmann, Godfrey. 2. Liturgical movement—Catholic Church—Addresses, essays, lectures. I. Title.

MCMANUS, Frederick Richard, 1923- 264.02
Sacramental liturgy [by] Frederick R. McManus. [New York] Herder and Herder [1967] 256 p. 22 cm. "Text of the constitution on the sacred liturgy": p. [221]-256. [BX830.1962.A45C683] 67-18558
1. Vatican Council. 2d, 1962-1965. Constitutio de sacra liturgia. 2. Catholic Church. Liturgy and ritual. I. Vatican Council. 2d, 1962-1965. Constitutio de sacra liturgia. English. 1967. II. Title.

MCNASPY, C. J. 264.02
Our changing liturgy. Foreword by Godfrey Diekmann. Garden City, N. Y., Doubleday [1967,.1966] 236p. 18cm. (Catholic perspectives, Image bks., D230) Bibl. [BX1970.M265] .95 pap.,
1. Catholic Church. Liturgy and ritual. 2. Vatican Council. 2d, 1962-65. Constituto de sacra litrugia. I. Title.

MCNASPY, Clement J. 264.02
Our changing liturgy, by C. J. McNaspy. With a foreword by Godfrey Diekmann. [1st ed.] New York, Hawthorn Books [1966] 271 p. 22 cm. (Catholic perspectives) Bibliographical reference included in "Notes" (p. 237-258) [BX1970.M265] 66-10175
1. Vatican Council. 2d, 1962-1965. Constitutio de sacra liturgia. 2. Catholic Church. Liturgy and ritual. I. Title.

MAGSAM, Charles M 264.02
The inner life of worship. St. Meinrad, Ind., Grail Publications [1958] 323p. 22cm. [BV10.M29] 58-4739
1. Worship. I. Title.

MANUAL of Catholic prayer (The) 264.02
for all days and seasons and every circumstance of Christian life. Comp. from the Holy Scriptures, the liturgical books of the Latin rite, other Catholic liturgies and the writings of saintly men and women. [Tr. from Dutch] New York, Harper [1962] 599p. 18cm. 62-20255 6.95, bxd.
1. Catholic Church—Prayer-books and devotions—English.

MARTIMORT, Aime Georges. 264.02
In remembrance of Me; the prayer of the church and the sacraments. Translated by Aldhelm Dean. Collegeville, Minn., Liturgical Press [c1958] 217p. 19cm. [BX1970.M343] 60-37394
1. Catholic Church. Liturgy and ritual. 2. Sacraments—Catholic Church. 3. Prayer. I. Title.

MILLER, John H. 264.02
Fundamentals of the liturgy. Notre Dame, Ind., Fides Publishers Association [1960, c.1959] xviii, 531p. Bibl.: p.506-512 and bibl. footnotes 24cm. 60-8444 6.00
1. Catholic Church. Liturgy and ritual. I. Title.

MILLER, John H., 1925- ed. 264.02
Yearbook of liturgical studies. v. 1- Notre Dame, Ind., Fides Publishers Association, 1960- v. 23 cm. Editor 1900- J. H. Miller. [BX1970.A1Y4] 60-15442
1. Catholic Church. Liturgy and ritual — Yearbooks. I. Title.

MISCHKE, Bernard C 264.02
Meditations on the Mass, by Bernard C. Mischke. New York, Sheed and Ward [1964] xvii, 201 p. 22 cm. [BX2230.2.M5] 64-19911
1. Mass — Meditations. I. Title.

MISCHKE, Bernard C. 264.02
Meditations on the Mass. New York, Sheed [c.1964] xvii, 201p. 22cm. 64-19911 4.50 bds.,
1. Mass—Meditations. I. Title.

MODERN liturgy handbook 264'.02
: a study and planning guide for worship / edited by John P. Mossi. New York : Paulist Press, c1976. vii, 228 p. : ill. ; 23 cm. [BX1970.M595] 76-12648 ISBN 0-8091-1952-8 pbk. : 6.95
1. Liturgies—Catholic Church—Handbooks, manuals, etc. I. Mossi, John P.

MONTAGUE, Gerard. 264.02
Problems in the liturgy. Westminster, Md., Newman Press [1958] 451p. 23cm. Includes bibliography. [BX1971.M6] 59-1464
1. Catholic Church. Liturgy and ritual. 2. Questions and answers —Theology. I. Title.

MORETON, Bernard. 264'.02
The eighth-century Gelasian sacramentary : a study in tradition / Bernard Moreton. London; New York Oxford University Press 1976 xii, 222 p. ; 23 cm. (Oxford theological monographs) Includes indexes. Bibliography: p. [206]-218. [BX2037.A3G435] 76-361685 ISBN 0-19-826710-X : 22.00
1. Sacramentaries. I. Title. II. Series.

MULLER, Johann Baptist 1850-1930. 264.02
Handbook of ceremonies for priests and seminariana. 17th English ed. entirely rev. and re-edited by Adam C. Ellis, in conformity with the most recent decress of the Sacred Congregation of Rites of 1955 and 1956. St. Louis, Herder, 1956. 482p. illus. 17cm. [BX1971.M8 1956] 56-11694
1. Catholic Church. Liturgy and ritual. I. Title.

MULLER, Johann Baptist, 1850-1930. 264.02
Handbook of ceremonies for priests and seminarians. 18th English ed., rev. and edited by Adam C. Ellis, in conformity with the most recent decrees of the Sacred Congregation of Rites of 1957 and 1958. St. Louis, Herder, 1958. 482p. illus. 17cm. [BX1971.M8 1958] 58-13340
1. Catholic Church. Liturgy and ritual. I. Title.

MULLER, Johann Baptist, 1850-1930. 264.02
Handbook of ceremonies for priests and seminarians. 17th English ed. entirely rev. and re-edited by Adam C. Ellis, in conformity with the most recent decrees of the Sacred Congregation of Rites of 1955 and 1956. St. Louis, Herder, 1956. 482p. illus. 17cm. [BX1971.M8 1956] 56-11694
1. Catholic Church. Liturgy and ritual. I. Title.

MULLER, Johann Baptist, 1850-1930. 264.02
Handbook of ceremonies for priests and seminarians. 14th English ed. rev. and edited by Adam C. Ellis. St. Louis, B. Herder Book Co., 1950. xiv, 400 p. illus. 17 cm. "Musical supplement": p. 420-440. "The sequence of parts of the divine office" (5 p. on fold. 1.) inserted. [BX1971.M8] 50-14457
1. Catholic Church. Liturgy and ritual. I. Title.

MURPHY, Denis G 264.02
The sacristan's manual. With an introd. by His Grace the Archbishop of Birmingham. Westminster, Md., Newman Press, 1950. xii, 156 p. 23 cm. [BX1972.M8] 50-10984
1. Catholic Church. Liturgy and ritual — Handbooks, manuals, etc. I. Title.

**MY Christian heritage,* 264.02
study book Minneapolis, Augsburg, 1968. (God's church for God's faithful) 1.50 pap.,; 2.25 pap., catechist's gd.,

**MY worship life;* 264.02
a course in liturgy for multiple use, grade 9. Minneapolis, Augsburg, 1968. pap., price unreported

NATIONAL Liturgical Conference. 264.02
A manual for church musicians. Pref. by Paul J. Hallinan. Washington [c1964] 130 p. 21 cm. "Publication in the Parish worship program, a Liturgical Conference Project." Bibliography: p. 127-130. [ML3002.N28] 64-8257
1. Church music — Catholic Church. I. Title.

NATIONAL Liturgical Conference 264.02
A manual for church musicians. Pref. by Paul J. Hallinan [Helicon Pr., dist. New York, Taplinger, c.1964] 130p. 21cm. (Parish worship prog., Liturgical Conference project) Bibl. [ML3002.N28] 64-8257 3.50 bds.,
1. Church music—Catholic Church. I. Title.

NICHOLSON, David. 264.02
Vernacular and music in the missions. Cincinnati, World Library of Sacred Music [1962] 62p. 21cm. Includes unacc. melodies. [ML3007.N5] 62-51318
1. Church music—Catholic Church. 2. Catholic Church—Missions. 3. Missions—Music. I. Title.

NOCENT, Adrien. 264.02
The future of the liturgy. [Translated by Irene Uribe. New York] Herder and Herder [1963] 215 p. 21 cm. Bibliographical references included in footnotes. [BX1970.N613] 63-18155
1. Liturgical movement — Catholic Church. 2. Catholic Church. Liturgy and ritual — Hist. I. Title.

NOCENT, Adrien 264.02
The future of the liturgy. [Tr. from French by Irene Uribe. New York] Herder & Herder [c.1963] 215p. 21cm. Bibl. 63-18155 3.95
1. Liturgical movement—Catholic Church. 2. Catholic. Church. Liturgy and ritual—Hist. I. Title.

*NOYES, Henry Drury 264.02
Bible services for a parish mission and other occasions. Glen Rock, N. J., Paulist [c.1965] 64p. 18cm. .35 pap.,
I. Title.

O'BRIEN, William Alexis, 264.02
1896-
In sacristy and sanctuary; a guide for the sacristan with detailed instructions accompanied by directive schedules and diagrams showing how and what to get ready for the proper carrying out of liturgical functions generally, according to the Roman ceremonial. New ed. with directions for the new Holy Week liturgy. New York, Benzinger Bros. [1958] 101p. illus. 19cm. [BX1972.O26 1958] 58-4933
1. Catholic Church. Liturgy and ritual. I. Title.

O'CONNELL, John Berthram, 264.02
1888-
The celebration of Mass; a study of the rubrics of the Roman missal. 4th ed. rev. throughout in accordance with the new general rubrics of the Codex rubricarum (1960) and the typical ed. of the Roman missal (1962) Milwaukee, Bruce Pub. Co., [1964] xviii, 622 p. illus., diagrs. 24 cm. Bibliography: p. 613-615. 64-14562
1. Mass. 2. Catholic Church. Liturgy and ritual. Missal — Rubrics. I. Title.

O'CONNELL, John Berthram, 264.02
1888-
The celebration of Mass; a study of the rubrics of the Roman missal. 4th ed. rev. throughout in accordance with the new general rubrics of the Codex rubricarum (1960) and the typical ed. of the Roman missal (1962) Milwaukee, Bruce [c.1964] xviii, 622p. illus., diagrs. 24cm. Bibl. 64-14562 8.50
1. Mass. 2. Catholic Church. Liturgy and ritual. Missal—Rubrics. I. Title.

O'MALLEY, John W 264.02
Challenge [by] John W. O'Malley [and others] Chicago, Loyala University Press [1958] 243p. 19cm. Prayers, some of which were written by the authors and many of which were taken from the Raccoita and from other sources. [BX2110.O5] 58-6622
1. Catholic Church—Prayer-books and devotions— English. I. Title.

ORCHARD, William Edwin, 264.02
1877-
Sancta sanctorum; prayers for the holy of holies. New York, Philosophical Library [1955] 210p. 19cm. [BX2182] 55-2917
1. Catholic Church—Prayer-books and devotions—English. I. Title.

O'SHEA, William J 264.02
The worship of the church; a companion to liturgical studies. Westminster, Md. Newman Press, 1957. 646p. illus. 23cm. [BX1970.O7] 56-8428
1. Catholic Church. Liturgy and ritual. I. Title.

PARIS. Saint-Severin 264.02
(Church) Clergy.
The liturgical movement, by the sacerdotal communities of Saint-Severin of Paris and Saint-Joseph of Nice. Tr. from French by Lancelot Sheppard. New York, Hawthorn [c.1964] 139p. 21cm. (Twentieth cent. ency. of Catholicism, v.115 Sect. 10: The worship of the Church) Bibl. 64-14156 3.50 bds.,
1. Liturgical movement—Catholic Church. I. Nice. Saint-Joseph (Church) Clergy. II. Title. III. Series: Twentieth century encyclopedia of Catholicism, v.115

PARSCH, Pius, 1884- 264.02
The breviary explained; translated by William Nayden and Carl Hoegerl. St. Louis, Herder, 1952. 459 p. 22 cm. [BX2000.P313] 52-8708
1. Catholic Church. Liturgy and ritual. Breviary. I. Title.

PEIL, Rudolf, 1901- 264.02
A handbook of the liturgy. Translated [from the German] by H. E. Winstone. [New York] Herder and Herder [1960] xv, 316p. Bibl. footnotes 23cm. 'Based on a completely revised and enlarged version of the first German edition of 'Handbuch der Liturgik fur Katecheten und Lehrer.' 60-11137 5.95
1. Liturgics—Catholic Church. I. Title.

PIUS FRANZISKUS, Father. 264.02
Mother love; a manual for Christian mothers, with instructions for the Archconfraternity of Christian Mothers, by Rev. Pius Franciscus. English revision of 1951 by Bertin Roll. New York, F. Pustet Co. [1951] 691 p. illus. 15 cm. [BX2353.P513 1951] 52-40070
1. Mothers — Prayer-books and devotions — English. 2. Catholic Church — Prayer-books and devotions — English. I. Catholic Church. Liturgy and ritual. English. II. Archconfraternity of Christian Mothers. III. Title.

PORTER, William Stevens. 264.02
The Gallican rite. Alcuin Club ed. London, Mowbray; New York, Morehouse- Gorham Co. [1958] 64p. 22cm. (Studies in Eucharistic faith and practice) [BX1995.G3P6] 60-27434
1. Catholic Church. Liturgy and ritual. Gallican rite. I. Title.

PREMM, Matthias, 1890- 264.02
The year made holy; translated from the German by Colman J. O'Donovan. Milwaukee, Bruce Pub. Co. [1961] 180p. 22cm. Translation of Geheiliqtes Jahr. [BX2230.2.P713 1961] 61-13004
1. Mass. I. Title.

THE Primer set furth by 264'.02
the Kinges Maiestie & his clergie (1545) A facsimile reproduction with an introd. by David Siegenthaler. Delmar, N.Y., Scholars' Facsimiles & Reprints, 1974. vii, [170] p. 23 cm. Original t.p. has imprint: Imprinted at London within the precinct of the late dissolued house of the Graye Friers by Richard Grafton Printer to the Princes grace, the xvii. day of August, the yeare of our Lorde M,D.XLVI. S.T.C. 16044. [BV4831.P7 1545a] 74-5335 ISBN 0-8201-1129-5 10.00
1. Primers (Prayer-books)

RAYMOND, Father, 1903- 264.02
This is love. Milwaukee, Bruce Pub. Co. [c1964] viii, 150 p. 23 cm. [BX2230.2.R3] 64-14802
1. Mass — Meditations. I. Title.

RAYMOND, M., Father, 1903- 264.02
This is love. Milwaukee, Bruce [c.1964] viii, 150p. 23cm. 64-14802 3.50
1. Mass—Meditations. I. Title.

REINHOLD, Hans Ansgar, 264.02
1897-
The American parish and the Roman liturgy; an essay in seven chapters. New York, Macmillan, 1958. 148p. 21cm. [BX1970.R4] 57-12617
1. Catholic Church. Liturgy and ritual. I. Title.

REINHOLD, Hans Ansgar, 264.02
1897-
The dynamics of liturgy. Foreword by Edward G. Murray. New York, Macmillan, 1961[c.1938-1961] 146p. 60-12954 4.75
1. Liturgical movement—Catholic Church. I. Title.

REINHOLD, Hans Ansgar, 264.02
1897- ed.
The soul afire: revelations of the mystics [Magnolia, Mass., P. Smith, 1967, c.1944] xxiii, 413p. 21cm. (Meridinpan living age bk. rebound) [BX1970.R42] 4.00
1. Liturgical movement—Catholic Church. I. Title.

RIEPE, Charles K. 264.02
Living the Christian seasons [New York] Herder & Herder [1964] 95p. 21cm. 64-19734 2.95
1. Fasts and feasts—Catholic Church. I. Title.

ROSAGE, David E ed. 264.02
Hail! The altar boy. Illus. by Carole Knostman. Milwaukee, Bruce Pub. Co. [1954] 64p. illus. 21cm. [BX1972.R63] 54-11043
1. Altar boys. I. Title.

ROSSEAU, Olivier, 1898- 264.02
The progress of the liturgy; an historical sketch from the beginning of the nineteenth century to the pontificate of Pius X. Translated by the Benedictines of Westminister Priory, Vancouver, B.C. Westminster, Md., Newman Press, 1951. 219 p. 20 cm. Translation of Histoire du mouvement liturgique. [BX1975.R613] 51-13740
1. Liturgical movement — Catholic Church. I. Title.

RYAN, John Kenneth, 1897- 264.02
comp.
God and my heart, by Joseph B. Collins and John K. Ryan. Milwaukee, Bruce Pub. Co. [1958] 468p. illus. 15cm. In earlier ed. Ryan's name appeared first on t. p. [BX2110.R9 1958] 58-3991
1. Catholic Church—Prayer-books and devotions— English. I. Collins, Joseph Burns, 1897- joint comp. II. Title.

RYAN, John Kenneth, 1897- 264.02
comp.
The Holy Trinity book of prayers; a spiritual treasury drawn from sacred Scripture, the liturgies, the writings of the saints, and other sources. Illustrated by Sr. Mary of the Compassion. New York, P. J. Kenedy [1952] 304 p. illus. 16 cm. [BX2110.R92] 52-14200
1. Catholic Church — Prayer-books and devotions — English. I. Title.

RYAN, Mary Perkins, 1915- 264.02
Has the new liturgy changed you? New York, Paulist Press [1967] viii, 168 p. 18 cm. (Deus books) [BX2230.2.R9] 67-15721
1. Mass. 2. Catholic Church. Liturgy and ritual. Missal. I. Title.

RYAN, Mery Perkins, 1915- 264.02
Has the new liturgy changed you? New York, Paulist [1967] vii, 168p. 18cm. (Deus bks.) [BX2230.2.Ppr9] 67-15721 .95 pap.,
1. Mass. 2. Catholic Church. Liturgy and ritual. Missal. I. Title.

SCHMITZ, Walter J 264.02
Learning the Mass; manual for seminarians. Milwaukee, Bruce Pub. Co. [1960] 63p. 26cm. [BX2230.2.S35] 60-15482
1. Mass—Study and teaching. I. Title.

SCHMITZ, Walter J 264.02
Learning the Mass; the new liturgy; handbook for priests and seminarians according to the latest decree of the Sacred Congregation of Rites [by] Walter J. Schmitz. Milwaukee, Bruce Pub. Co. [1965] 71 p. 26 cm. English or Latin. Altar card texts included on 2 inserts. [BX2230.2.S352] 65-21499
1. Mass—Study and teaching. I. Title.

SCHMITZ, Walter J. 264.02
Learning the Mass: the new liturgy; handbook for priests and seminarians according to the latest decree of the Sacred Congregation of Rites. Milwaukee, Bruce [c.1965] 71p. 26cm. English or Latin. Altar card texts included on 2 inserts [BX2230.2.S352] 65-21499 2.50, pap., plastic bdg.
1. Mass—Study and teaching. I. Title.

SCHMITZ, Walter J 264.02
Learning the Mass, the new liturgy; handbook for priests and seminarians according to the latest decree of the Sacred Congregation of Rites [by] Walter J. Schmitz. [1966 revision] Milwaukee, Bruce Pub. Co. [1966] 71 p. 26 cm. English or Latin. Altar card texts included on 2 inserts. [BX2230.2.S352] 66-24257
1. Mass—Study and teaching. I. Title.

SCHMITZ, Walter J. 264'.02
Liturgikon : pastoral ministrations / Walter J. Schmitz and Terence E. Tierney. Huntington, Ind. : Our Sunday Visitor, c1977. 240 p. ; 24 cm. Unofficial handbook for priests. Includes selected new rites of Catholic Church in the U.S. Includes index. [BX2035.A4S35] 77-76563 ISBN 0-87973-894-4 deluxe ed. : 9.95
1. Liturgies. 2. Occasional services—Catholic Church. I. Tierney, Terence E., joint author. II. Catholic Church. Liturgy and ritual. Ritual (U.S.). Selections. 1977. III. Title.

SCHMITZ, Walter J. 264.02
Sanctuary manual, prepd. under the guidance of Walter J. Schmitz. Milwaukee, Bruce [1966] 86p. 24cm. Comprised of material taken from the official Collectio Rituum and includes all the liturgical ceremonies performed in the church, except the Mass. 4.00
1. Catholic Church—Liturgy and ritual. I. Title.

SCHULTE, Augustine Joseph, 264.02
1856-
Benedicenda; the rite observed in some of the principal functions of the Roman pontifical and the Roman ritual. New ed. fully rev. and with some additions by J. B. O'Connell. New York, Benziger Bros. [1955] 286p. illus. 22cm. [BX2048.B5S3 1955] 55-12699
1. Benediction. I. Catholic Church. Liturgy and ritual. Pontifical. II. Catholic Church. Liturgy and ritual. Ritual. III. Title.

SEASOLTZ, R. Kevin, ed. 264.02
The new liturgy: a documentation, 1903-1965 [by] R. Kevin Seasoltz. [New York] Herder and Herder [1966] xlvii, 707 p. 23 cm. Bibliographical footnotes. [BX1970.S37] 65-13481
1. Catholic Church. Liturgy and ritual—History—Sources. 2. Catholic Church. Liturgy and ritual—Papal documents. 3. Liturgical movement—Catholic Church—History—Sources. I. Title.

SHEPPARD, Lancelot Capel, 264.02
1906-
Blueprint for worship [by] Lancelot C. Sheppard. With a foreword by John B. Mannion. Westminster, Md., Newman Press, 1964. xxix, 95 p. 22 cm. [BX1970.S46] 64-66282
1. Catholic Church. Liturgy and ritual. 2. Vatican Council, 2d. Constituto de sacra liturgia. I. Title.

SHEPPARD, Lancelot Capel, 264.02
1906-
Blueprint for worship. Foreword by John B. Mannion. Westminster, Md., Newman [c.1964] xxix, 95p. 22cm. [BX1970.S46] 64-66282 2.95
1. Catholic Church. Liturgy and ritual. 2. Vatican Council, 2d. Constituto de sacra liturgia. I. Title.

SISTERS of the 264.02
Presentation of the Blessed Virgin Mary, Fitchburgh, Mass.
Manual of prayers for the Sisters of the Presentation of the Blessed Virgin Mary. New York, P. J. Kenedy [1953] 161p. illus. 15cm. [BX2060.P7A3] 55-28628
1. Sisters of the Presentation of the Blessed Virgin Mary—Prayer-books and devotions—English. I. Title.

SISTERS of the Visitation. 264.02
Baltimore.
The Visitation manual: a collection of prayers and instructions compiled according to the Spiritual directory and spirit of Saint Francis de Sales, founder of the Religious Order of the Visitation of Holy Mary. [Rev. ed.] New York, G. Grady Press, 1955. 508p. 16cm. [BX2060.V5A5 1955] 56-150
1. Sisters of the Visitation—Prayer-books and devotions—English. I. Title.

SLOYAN, Gerard Stephen, 264.02
1919-
Liturgy in focus. Glen Rock, N.J., Paulist [1964] 112p. 19cm. (Deus bks.) Bibl. 64-20244 .95
1. Catholic Church. Liturgy and ritual. I. Title.

SLOYAN, Gerard Stephen, 264.02
1919-
Worship in a new key: what the Council teaches on the liturgy. Garden City, N.Y., Doubleday [1966,c.1965] 152p. 18cm. (Echo bk., E32) [BX1970.S583] .75 pap.,
1. Catholic Church. Liturgy and ritual. 2. Vatican Council, 2d. Constitutio de sacra liturgia. I. Title.

SLOYAN, Gerard Stephen, 264.02
1919-
Worship in a new key: what the Council teaches on the liturgy. Liturgical Conference [dist. New York, Herder & Herder, c.1965] 191p. 21cm. [BX1970.S583] 65-25912 3.95
1. Catholic Church. Liturgy and ritual. 2. Vatican Council, 2d. Constitutio de sacra liturgia. I. Title.

SLOYAN, Gerard Stephen, 264.02
1919-
Worship in a new key: what the Council teaches on the liturgy [by] Gerard S. Sloyan. [Washington] Liturgical Conference [1965] 191 p. 21 cm. [BX1970.S583] 65-25912
1. Vatican Council, 2d Constitutio de sacra liturgia. 2. Catholic Church, Liturgy and rights. I. Title.

SOLOVII, Meletii M., 264.02
Father.
The Byzantine divine liturgy; history and commentary [by] Meletius Michael Solovey. Translated by Demetrius Emil Wysochansky. Washington, Catholic University of America Press, 1970. 346 p. 25 cm. Translation of Bozhestvenna liturhiia (romanized form) Includes bibliographical references. [BX4711.663.S613] 70-119897 ISBN 0-8132-0502-6 12.75
1. Catholic Church. Byzantine rite (Ukrainian). Liturgy and ritual. I. Title.

SORG, Rembert, 1908- 264.02
The Mass for Labor Day; a study of the new mass of St. Joseph the Workman against the background of American labor. St. Louis, Pio Decimo Press [1958] 81 p. 22 cm. "Test of the Mass of St. Joseph, the Workman": p. 80-81. [BX2015.5.J6S6] 60-2339
1. Labor Day Mass. I. Catholic Church. Liturgy and ritual. Missal. Eng. II. Title.

STEHLE, Aurelius, 1877-1930. 264.02
Manual of episcopal ceremonies, based on the Caeremoniale episcoporum, decrees of the Sacred Congregation of Rites, and approved authors. Rev. by Emmeran A. Rettger. 5th ed. Latrobe, Pa. Archabbey Press, 1961. 2 v. illus. diagrs. 24 cm. Includes bibliographies. [BX1971.S] 61-13124
1. Catholic Church. Liturgy and ritual. Ceremonial of bishops. I. Title. II. Title: Episcopal ceremonies.

STEHLE, Aurelius, 1877-1930. 264.02
Ordinary episcopal ceremonies; a section of the Manual of episcopal ceremonies. Rev. and rearranged to include episcopal ceremonies used frequently in cathedral, abbatial, parish churches, by Emmeran A. Rettger. Latrobe, Pa., Archabbey Press, 1959. viii, 224 p. illus. diagrs. 23 cm. Bibliography: p. 216-217. [BX1971.S7] 65-13816
1. Catholic Church. Liturgy and ritual. Ceremonial of bishops. I. Title.

STEUART, Bendict, Father, 1880- 264.02
The development of Christian worship; an outline of liturgical history. With a foreword by J. B. O'Connell. London, New York, Longmans, Green [1953] 290p. 23cm. [BX1970.S84] 54-8824
1. Catholic Church. Liturgy and ritual. I. Title.

STOREY, William George, 1923- 264.02
Morning praise and evensong; a book of common prayer compiled from the Roman Breviary. Musical arrangements by Jerome E. Janssen. Notre Dame, Ind., Fides Publishers [1963] 328 p. music. 18 cm. (A Fides dome book, D-27) [BX2130.S8] 63-12046
1. Catholic Church — Prayer-books and devotions — English. I. Title.

STOREY, William George, 1923- 264.02
Morning praise and evensong; a book of common prayer compiled from the Roman Breviary. Musical arrs. by Jerome E. Janssen. Notre Dame, Ind., Fides [c.1963] 328p. music. 18cm. (Fides dome bk., D-27) 63-12046 1.25; 3.95 pap., deluxe ed.,
1. Catholic Church—Prayer-books and devotions—English. I. Title.

SULLIVAN, John Francis, 1867- 264.02
The externals of the Catholic Church; a handbook of Catholic usage. Completely rev. by John C. O'Leary. 2d ed. New York, Kenedy [c1959] 403 p. illus. 21 cm. [BX1751.S9 1959] 60-2489
1. Catholic Church—Doctrinal and controversial works—Catholic authors. 2. Catholic Church—Government. 3. Sacramentals. I. Title.

SULLIVAN, John Francis, 1867- 264.02
The externals of the Catholic Church; a handbook of Catholic usage. Completely revised by John C. O'Leary. New York, Kenedy, 1951. 403 p. illus. 21 cm. [BX1751.S9 1951] 51-13499
1. Catholic Church — Doctrinal and controversial works — Catholic authors. 2. Catholic Church — Government. 3. Sacramentals. I. Title.

TRETHOWAN, Illtyd, 1907- 264.02
Christ in the liturgy. London, New York, Sheed and Ward [1952] 150 p. 23 cm [BX1970.T7] 52-8883
1. Catholic Church. Liturgy and ritual I. Title.

UNDERSTANDING the liturgy. 264.02
Edited by John P. Bradley. Gastonia, N.C., Good Will Publishers [1970] xiii, 447 p. illus. (part col.), facsims., ports. 25 cm. (The Catholic layman's library, v. 3) [BX1970.U53] 70-92777
1. Liturgies—Catholic Church. I. Bradley, John P., ed. II. Title. III. Series.

VANDENBROUCKE, Francois. 264.02
Liturgical initiation. Translated by Kathryn Sullivan. With study-club questions. Glen Rock, N.J., Paulist Press [1965] 127 p. 18 cm. (Deus books, T890K) Bibliography: p. 123-127. [BX1970.V323] 65-26794
1. Catholic Church. Liturgy and ritual. I. Title.

VANDENBROUCKE, Francois 264.02
Liturgical initiation. Tr. by Kathryn Sullivan. With study-club questions. Glen Rock, N.J., Paulist [c.1965] 127p. 18cm. (Deus bks. T890K) Bibl. [BX1970.V323] 65-26794 .95 pap.,
1. Catholic Church. Liturgy and ritual. I. Title.

VAN DIJK, Stephen Joseph Peter 264.02
The origins of the modern Roman liturgy: the liturgy of the papal court and the Franciscan Order in the thirteenth century, by S. J. P. Van Dijk and J. Hazelden Walker. Westminster, Md., Newman Press [1960] xxxi, 586p. 23cm. Bibl.: p. xiii-xxv. illus., facsims. 59-15212 10.50
1. Catholic Church. Liturgy and ritual. 2. Catholic Church. Curia Romana. 3. Catholic Church. Liturgy and ritual. Franciscan. I. Walker, Joan Hazelden, joint author. II. Title.

VATICAN Council. 2d,1962-1965. 264.02
The constitution on the sacred liturgy of the Second Vatican Council and the Motu proprio of Pope Paul VI. With a commentary by Gerard S. Sloyan. Study-club ed. Glen Rock, N.J., Paulist Press [1964] 86 p. 18 cm. "Selected readings": p. 85-86. [BX830 1962.A45C533] 64-18549
1. Catholic Church. Liturgy and ritual. I. Catholic Church. Pope, 1963- (Paulus VI) Motu proprio sacram liturgiam (25 Jan. 1964) English. II. Sloyan, Gerard Stephen, 1919- III. Title.

VATICAN Council, 2d. 264.02
Constitutio de sacra liturgia.
The Liturgy constitution; a chapter by chapter analysis of the Constitution on the sacred liturgy, with study-club questions. Glen Rock, N.J., Paulist Press [1964] 191 p. 18 cm. (Deus books) "Motu proprio of Pope Paul VI": p. 179-188. Bibliography: p. 189-191. [BX830 1962.A45C68] 64-8078
1. Vatican Council, 2d. Constitutio de sacra liturgia. 2. Catholic Church. Pope, 1963-1978 (Paulus VI) Motu proprio sacram liturgiam (25 Jan. 1964) English. I. Title.

VATICAN COUNCIL, 2d 264.02
The constitution on the sacred liturgy of the Second Vatican Council and the Motu proprio of Pope Paul VI. Commentary by Gerard S. Sloyan. Study-club ed. Glen Rock, N.J., Paulist Pr. [c.1964] 86p. 18cm. Bibl. 64-18549 .50 pap.,
1. Catholic Church. Liturgy and ritual. I. Catholic Church. Pope, 1963- (Paulus VI) Motu proprio sacram liturgiam (25 Jan. 1964) English. II. Sloyan, Gerard Stephen, 1919- III. Title.

VON HILDEBRAND, Dietrich 264.02
Liturgy and personality. Translated from the German. Newly rev. and edited [2d ed.] Baltimore, Helicon Press [c.] 1960. 131p. 23cm. 60-11483 3.50
1. Catholic Church. Liturgy and ritual. 2. Personality. I. Title.

VON HILDEBRAND, Dietrich, 1889- 264.02
Liturgy and personality. Newly rev. and edited [2nd ed.] Balitmore, Helicon Press, 1960. 131 p. 23 cm. Translated from the German. [BX1970.V652 1960] 60-11483
1. Catholic Church. Liturgy and ritual. 2. Personality. I. Title.

WAGNER, Johannes, 1908- 264.02
The Church and the liturgy. Glen Rock, N.J. Paulist Press [1965] viii, 191 p. 24 cm. (Concilium theology in the age of renewal: Liturgy, v. 2) Contents.Preface, by J. Wagner. -- Articles: The bishop and the liturgy, by C. Vagaggini; translated by P. Perfetti. Relation between bishop and priests according to the Liturgy Constitution, by J. Pascher; translated by T. L. Westow.The juridic power of the bishop in the Constitution on the Sacred Liturgy, by F. R. McManus. Liturgy, devotions, and the bishop, by J. A. Jungmann; translated by T. L. Westow. The role of sacred music, by J. Gelineau; translated by T. L Westow. The place of liturgical worship, by G. Diekmann. -- Bibliographical survey: Church music, by H. Hucke; translated by T. L. Westow. Concelebration, by H. Manders; translated by T. L. Westow. Communion under both kinds, by G. Danneels; translated by T. L. Westow. -- DO-C: Documentation concilium: Evolution of the concept of economic expansion, by R. Scarpati; translated by P. Perfitti and A. M. Salerno. -- Chronicle of the living Church: Introduction. International Congress on Education for the Priesthood in Western Europe; translated by T. L. Westow. Includes bibliographical references. [BX830 1962.A45C625] 65-17869
1. Vatican Council, 2d. Constitutio de sacra liturgia. 2. Catholic Church. Liturgy and ritual. I. Title. II. Series. III. Series: Concilium theology in the age of renewal, v. 2

WALKER, James D. 264.02
Commentator's lectionary. Milwaukee, Bruce [1965] 140p. 31cm. [BX2230.2.W3] 65-21500 3.50
1. Mass. I. Title.

WARD, Maisie, 1889- 264.02
The rosary. New York, Sheed and Ward [1957?] 96p. 18cm. (Canterbury books) 'An abridged version of The splendor of the rosary.' [BX2163.W32] 57-4635
1. Rosary. I. Title.

WARD, Maisie, 1889- 264.02
The rosary. New York, Sheed and Ward [1957?] 96 p. 18 cm. (Canterbury books) "An abridged version of The splendor of the rosary." [BX2163.W32] 57-4635
1. Rosary. I. Title.

**WE come to Jesus;* 264.02
first missal for children to prepare them for Holy Mass, in the family circle, at home and at school. Staten Island, Alba [1967] lv. (unpaged) col. illus. 23cm. 1.75
1. Mass—Juvenile literature.

WICKEY, Harold J 264.02
The living Mass. Milwaukee, Bruce Pub. Co. [1961] 186 p. illus. 23 cm. [BX2230.2.W5] 61-13005
1. Mass. I. Title.

WUEST, Joseph, 1834-1924, comp. 264.02
Matters liturgical; the Collectio rerum liturgicarum. Translated by Thomas W. Mullaney; re-arr. and enl. by William T. Barry. 9th ed. New York, F. Pustet Co., 1956. 1171p. 17cm. [BX1970.W83 1956a] 56-14689
1. Catholic Church. Liturgy and ritual. I. Title.

WUEST, Joseph, 1834-1924, comp. 264.02
Matters liturgical; the Collectio rerun liturgicarum. Translated by Thomas W. Mullaney; re-arr. and enl. by William T. Barry. 9th ed. New York, F. Pusteo Co., 1956. 1171 p. 17 cm. [BX1970.W83 1956a] 56-14689
1. Catholic Church. Liturgy and ritual. I. Title.

WUEST, Joseph, 1834-1924, comp. 264.02
Matters liturgical; the Collectio rerun liturgicarum. Translated by Thomas W. Mullaney; re-arr. and enl. by William T. Barry. [8th ed.] New York, F. Pustet Co., 1956. 1171 p. 17 cm. [BX1970.W83 1956] 56-516
1. Catholic Church. Liturgy and ritual. I. Title.

YEARBOOK of liturgical studies. 264.02
v.2. Notre Dame, Ind., Fides [c.1961] 244p. Ed.: 196j J. H. Miller 60-15442 7.00
1. Catholic Church. Liturgy and ritual—Yearbooks. I. Miller, John H., 1925- ed.

LEBLANC, Etienne. 264'.02'00240544
How green is green? 38 eucharistic celebrations for today's youth [by] Etienne LeBlanc and Mary Rose Talbot. Notre Dame, Ind., Ave Maria Press [1973?] 180 p. 26 cm. [BV4850.L4] 73-83350 ISBN 0-87793-061-9 2.95
1. Youth—Prayer-books and devotions—English. 2. Liturgies. I. Talbot, Mary Rose, joint author. II. Title.

BARAUNA. GUILHERME, ed. 264.02008
The liturgy of Vatican II: a symposium; 2 vs. Ed. by William Barauna. English ed. ed. by Jovian Lang. Contributors: Evaristo Paulo Arns [others] Chicago Franciscan Herald [1966] 2v. 24cm. Tr. of A sagrada liturgia renovada per 1o Concilio. Constitution on the sacred liturgy: v.1. p. [4]-31. Bibl. [BX1970.B2913] 65-16674 10.50 bet,
1. Catholic Church. Liturgy and ritual. 2. Vatican Council. 2d. 1962-1965. Constitutio de sacra liturgia. I. Vatican Council. 2d. 1962-1965. Constitution on the sacred liturgy. II. Lang, Jovian, ed. III. Title.

BARAUNA, Gulherme, ed. 264.02008
The liturgy of Vatican II; a symposium. Edited by Wlliam Barauna. English ed. edited by Jovian Lang. Contributors: Evaristo Paulo Arnes and others. Chicago, Franciscan Herald Press [1966] 2 v. 24 cm. Translation of A sagrada liturgia renovada pelo Concilio. "Constitution on the sacred liturgy": v. 1, p. [4]-31. Includes bibliographical references. [BX1970.B2913] 65-16674
1. Catholic Church. Liturgy and ritual. 2. Vatican Council. 2d, 1962-1965. Constitutio de sacra liturgia. I. Vatican Council. 2d, 1962-1965. Constitution on the sacred liturgy. II. Lang, Jovian, ed. III. Title.

THE Church worships. 264.02008
New York, Paulist Press [1966] ix, 175 p. 24 cm. (Concilium theology in the age of renewal: Liturgy, v. 12) Bibliographical footnotes. [BX1970.C58] 66-17730
1. Catholic Church. Liturgy and ritual — Addresses, essays, lectures. I. Series. II. Series: Concilium theology in the age of renewal, v. 12

CHURCH worships (The) 264.02008
New York, Paulist [1966,i.e.1967] xi, 175p. 24cm. (Concilium theology in the age of renewal: Liturgy, v.12) Bibl. [BX1970.C58] 66-17730 4.50
1. Catholic Churhpch. Liturgy and ritual—Addresses. essays, lectures. I. Series: Concilium theology in the age of renewal, v.12

HALLIGAN, Francis Nicholas, 1917- 264'.02'008
The ministry of the celebration of the sacraments [by] Nicholas Halligan. New York, Alba House [1973-74] 3 v. 22 cm. Includes bibliographical references. [BX2200.H25] 73-4203 ISBN 0-8189-0271-X 3.95
1. Sacraments—Catholic Church—Collected works. I. Title.

HALLIGAN, Francis Nicholas, 1917- 264'.02'008 s
Sacraments of community renewal: holy orders, matrimony [by] Nicholas Halligan. New York, Alba House [1974] xvii, 217 p. 21 cm. (His The ministry of the celebration of the sacraments, v. 3) Includes bibliographical references. [BX2200.H25 vol. 3] [BX2240] 265'.4 74-3209 3.95 (pbk.)
1. Ordination—Catholic Church. 2. Marriage—Catholic Church. I. Title. II. Series.

HALLIGAN, Francis Nicholas, 1917- 264'.02'008 s
Sacraments of initiation and union: baptism, confirmation, Eucharist [by] Nicholas Halligan. New York, Alba House [1973] xv, 201 p. 22 cm. (His The ministry of the celebration of the sacraments, v. 1) Includes bibliographical references. [BX2200.H25 vol. 1] [BX2205] 265'.1 73-4222 ISBN 0-8189-0272-8 3.95
1. Baptism—Catholic Church. 2. Confirmation—Catholic Church. 3. Lord's Supper—Catholic Church. I. Title. II. Series.

HALLIGAN, Francis Nicholas, 1917- 264'.02'008 s
Sacraments of reconciliation: penance, anointing of the sick [by] Nicholas Halligan. Staten Island, N.Y., Alba House [1973] xii, 209 p. 21 cm. (His The ministry of the celebration of the sacraments, v. 2) On spine: Penance, anointing of the sick. Includes bibliographical references. [BX2200.H25 vol. 2] [BX2260] 265'.6 73-9604 ISBN 0-8189-0279-5 3.95
1. Penance. 2. Unction. I. Title. II. Title: Penance, anointing of the sick. III. Series.

MERTON, Thomas, 1915- 264.02008
Seasons of celebration. New York, Farrar [c.1950-1965] vi, 248p. 22cm. [BX1970.M47] 65-25837 4.95
1. Catholic Church. Liturgy and ritual—Addresses, essays, lectures. I. Title.

MERTON, Thomas, 1915-1968. 264.02008
Seasons of celebration. New York, Farrar, Straus and Giroux [1965] vi, 248 p. 22 cm. [BX1970.M47] 65-25837
1. Catholic church. Liturgy and ritual—Addresses, essays, lectures. I. Title.

*QUINN, James. 264.02008
The theology of the Eucharist, by James Quinn. Notre Dame, Ind., Fides Publishers [1973] 94 p. 18 cm. (Theology today series, no. 27) [BX2210] ISBN 0-8190-0581-9 0.95 (pbk.)
1. Eucharist. I. Title.

KLAUSER, Theodor, 1894- 264.02'009
A short history of the western liturgy; an account and some reflections. Translated from the German by John Halliburton. London, New York, Oxford U.P., 1969. x, 236 p. 23 cm. Translation of Kleine abendlandische Liturgiegeschichte. Bibliography: p. [173]-228. [BX1970.K5713] 72-446084 unpriced
1. Catholic Church. Liturgy and ritual—History. I. Title.

KUCHAREK, Casimir. 264.02'009
The Byzantine-Slav liturgy of St. John Chrysostom; its origin and evolution. [Allendale, N.J.] Alleluia Press [1971] 836 p. 24 cm. Bibliography: p. [759]-781. [BX4711.163.K8] 74-147735 ISBN 0-911726-06-3
1. Catholic Church. Liturgy and ritual. Byzantine rite. 2. Liturgics—History. I. Catholic Church. Liturgy and ritual. Byzantine rite. II. Title.

SHEPPARD, Lancelot Capel, 1906- ed. 264.02'009
The people worship; a history of the liturgical movement, edited by Lancelot Sheppard. [1st ed.] New York, Hawthorn Books [1967, c1965] 264, [3] p. 22 cm. Bibliography: p. [265-267] [BX1970.S48] 66-22321
1. Liturgical movement—Catholic Church. I. Title.

LEONARD, George R. 264'.02'00924
Light on Archbishop Lefebvre / by George Leonard. London : Catholic Truth Society,

1976. 24 p. ; 19 cm. [BX1755.L48] 77-359991 ISBN 0-85183-178-8 : £0.20
1. Catholic Church—Doctrinal and controversial works—Catholic authors. 2. Lefebvre, Marcel, 1905- 3. Mass. I. Title.

COUGHLAN, Peter, comp. 264'.0201
A prayer book for Holy Year. Edited and arr. by Peter Coughlan, with foreword by the Archbishop of Dublin. Chicago, Franciscan Herald Press [1974] p. cm. [BX2130.C68] 74-17081 ISBN 0-8199-0552-6
1. Catholic Church—Prayer-books and devotions—English. 2. Holy Year, 1975. I. Title.

GROLIMUND, Raphael. 264'.0201
Stand firm in the Lord; thirty-three Scripture celebrations for two or three or more, arr. by Raphael Grolimund, Bernard Frei [and] Hadrian Koch. Edited by Marion A. Habig. Chicago, Franciscan Herald Press [1973] xi, 108 p. 21 cm. Translation of Verkundigung und Feier des Gotteswortes. Bibliography: p. 107-108. [BX2110.G8] 73-10263 ISBN 0-8199-0463-5 2.95
1. Catholic Church—Prayer-books and devotions. I. Frei, Bernard, joint author. II. Koch, Hadrian, joint author. III. Title.

KROSNICKI, Thomas A. 264'.0201
Ancient patterns in modern prayer, by Thomas A. Krosnicki. Washington, Catholic University of America Press, 1973. viii, 309 p. 24 cm. (Catholic University of America. Studies in Christian antiquity, no. 19) Originally presented as the author's thesis, Pontificium Institutum Liturgicum. "Postcommunion prayers and their sources" (p. 151-272) consists of the Latin text of the Postcommunion prayers from the Roman Missal of Paul VI (1970) Bibliography: p. 281-288. [BX2015.74.K76 1973] 74-172790 20.00
1. Post-communion prayers. I. Catholic Church. Liturgy and ritual. Post-Communion. 1973. II. Title. III. Series.

RYAN, John Barry, 1933- 264'.0201
The Eucharistic prayer; a study in contemporary liturgy. New York, Paulist Press [1974] 210 p. 23 cm. Bibliography: p. 201-210. [BX2169.R83] 73-94215 ISBN 0-8091-1834-3 5.95 (pbk.)
1. Eucharistic prayers. I. Title.

CHAGNEAU, Francois. 264.02'01'3
Stay with us. Translated by John Drury. New York, Newman Press [1971] xii, 104 p. illus. 23 cm. Translation of Reste avec nous. [BV245.C4313] 70-152311 1.75
1. Prayers. I. Title.

LET'S pray! / 264'.02013
[compiled] by Brother Charles Reutemann ; illustrated by Brother Dougles Fuchs. Winona, Minn. : St. Mary's College Press, 1974. 198 p. : ill. ; 24 cm. Includes index. [BX2130.L47] 75-197 ISBN 0-9600824-1-7
1. Catholic Church—Prayer-books and devotions—English. I. Reutemann, Charles, Brother, 1919-

LYONS, Hugh Peter 264'.0201'3
Carbery.
Praying our prayers / H. P. C. Lyons. Chicago : Franciscan Herald Press, [1976] p. cm. Reprint of the 1956 ed. published by Newman Press, Westminster, Md. [BX2110.L9 1976] 76-850 ISBN 0-8199-0598-4 : 3.95
1. Catholic Church—Prayer-books and devotions—English. I. Title.

MOSSI, John P., comp. 264'.0201'3
Bread blessed and broken : eucharistic prayers and fraction rites / edited by John P. Mossi. New York : Paulist Press, [1974] vii, 152 p. : ill. ; 23 cm. [BX2169.M65] 74-16844 ISBN 0-8091-1855-6 : 6.95
1. Eucharistic prayers. I. Title.

CHAMPLIN, Joseph M. 264'.0203
The new yet old mass / Joseph M. Champlin. Notre Dame, Ind. : Ave Maria Press, c1977. 111 p. : ill. ; 21 cm. "Originally columns for NC news service Know your faith series." [BX2230.2.C48] 77-72286 ISBN 0-87793-132-1 pbk. : 2.25
1. Mass. I. Title.

DANIEL-ROPS, Henry, 264.0203
1901-
This is the Mass, as described by Henri Daniel-Rops, as celebrated by Fulton J. Sheen, as photographed by Yousuf Karsh. Translated, with annotations, by Alastair Guinan. With an introd. and a foreword by Bishop Sheen. New and rev. New York, Hawthorn Books, [1965] 191 p. illus. 26 cm. Includes bibliographical references. [BX2230.D283 1965] 65-15061
1. Mass — Celebration. I. Karsh, Yousuf, 1908- illus. II. Title.

DANIEL-ROPS, Henry, 264.0203
1901-
This is the Mass, as described by Henri Daniel-Rops, as celebrated by Fulton J. Sheen, as photographed by Yousuf Karsh. Tr., with annotations, by Alastair Guinan. Introd., foreword by Bishop Sheen. New and rev. New York, Doubleday [1967,c.1965] 223p. illus. 18cm. (Image bk., D216) Bibl. [BX2230.D283 1965] 1.25 pap.,
1. Mass—Celebration. I. Karsh, Yousuf, 1908- illus. II. Title.

DANIEL-ROPS, Henry 1901- 264.0203
This is the Mass, as described by Henri Daniel-Rops, as celebrated by Fulton J. Sheen. as photographed by Yousuf Karsh. Tr., with annotations, by Alastair Guinan. Introd., foreword by Bishop Sheen. New and rev. New York, Hawthorn [c. 1958,1965] 191p. illus. 26cm. Bibl. [BX2230.D283] 65-15061 5.95 bds.,
1. Mass—Celebration. I. Karsh, Yousuf, 1908- illus. II. Title.

DUCHARME, Jerome J. 264'.0203
The reader's guide to proclamation for Sundays and major feasts in cycle "A," by Jerome J. DuCharme. Chicago, Franciscan Herald Press [1974] p. cm. [BS391.2.D8] 74-13880 ISBN 0-8199-0577-1
1. Bible—Liturgical lessons, English. 2. Bible—Liturgical use. I. Title.

DUCHARME, Jerome J. 264'.0203
The reader's guide to proclamation for Sundays and major feasts in cycle "B" / by Jerome J. DuCharme. Chicago : Franciscan Herald Press, c1975. 147 p. ; 21 cm. [BS391.2.D83] 75-26816 ISBN 0-8199-0578-X pbk. : 2.95
1. Bible—Liturgical lessons, English. 2. Bible—Liturgical use. I. Title.

DUCHARME, Jerome J. 264'.0203
The reader's guide to proclamation for Sundays and major feasts in cycle "C" / by Jerome J. DuCharme. Chicago : Franciscan Herald Press, [1976] p. cm. [BS391.2.D84] 76-23394 ISBN 0-8199-0579-8 pbk. : 2.95
1. Bible—Liturgical lessons, English. 2. Bible—Liturgical use. I. Title.

MAERTENS, Thierry, 264'.0203
1921-
Guide for the Christian assembly [by] Thierry Maertens [and] Jean Frisque. Rev. ed. Notre Dame, Ind., Fides Publishers [1971-74] 9 v. 20 cm. "A background book of the Mass. Revised to conform to the new Lectionary." Translation of Guide de l'assemblee chretienne. Contents.Contents.—1. Advent.—Christmas.—2. 1st to 8th weeks.—2nd to 8th Sundays.—3. Lent—Easter.—4. Eastertime.—5. 9th to 21st Sundays.—6. 9th to 21st weeks.—7. 22nd to 34th Sundays.—8. 22nd to 34th weeks.—9. Feasts superseding Sundays. Indexes to the new Lectionary. Calendar and biography of saints. General indexes to the guides. [BS391.2.M3313] 72-114245 ISBN 0-8190-0006-X 5.00 (pbk.)
1. Bible—Liturgical lessons, English. 2. Church year—Meditations. I. Frisque, Jean, joint author. II. Title.

MILLER, Walter D 264.0203
Revised ceremonial of the Mass, by Walter D. Miller. Patterson, N.J., St. Anthony Guild Press, 1965. xii, 292 p. illus. 22 cm. "Cantus qui in missali Romano desiderantur luxta instructionem et exsecutionem constitutionis de sacra liturgia recte ordinandam" (Gregorian notation): p. 287-292. [BX2230.2.M47] 65-24924
1. Mass — Celebration. I. Title.

MILLER, Walter D. 264.0203
Revised ceremonial of the Mass. Patterson, N. J., St. Anthony Guild Press [c.]1965. xii, 292p. illus. 22cm. Contains Cantus qui in missali Romano desiderantur iuxta instructionem ad exsecutionem constitutionisde sacra liturgia recte ordinandam (Gregorian notation) [BX2230.2.M47] 65-24924 5.00
1. Mass—Celebration. I. Title.

O'DEA, Paul. 264'.0203
The mass and the passion. Dublin, Clonmore & Reynolds [1965] 152 p. 19 cm. Includes bibliographical references. [BX2230.2.O3] 233 79-219464
1. Mass. I. Title.

THEISEN, Reinold. 264.0203
Mass liturgy and the Council of Trent. Collegeville, Minn., St. John's University Press, 1965. x, 169 p. 23 cm. Includes bibliographies. [BX2230.5.T48] 66-3411
1. Trent, Council of, 1545-1563. 2. Mass — Hist. I. Title.

TIERNEY, Mark 264.0203
The Council and the Mass. [1st Amer. ed.] Wilkes-Barre, Pa., Dimension Bks. [1965] 128p. 20cm. Bibl. [BX2230.2.T5] 65-25561 3.50
1. Mass. 2. Vatican Council, 2d. Constitutio de sacra liturgia. I. Title.

VAN Zeller, Hubert, 1905- 264.0203
The Mass in other words; a presentation for beginners. Springfield, Ill., Templegate [1965] 90 p. 20 cm. [BX2230.2.V3] 65-5198
1. Mass. I. Title.

WATHEN, James F., 1932- 264'.0203
The great sacrilege, by James F. Wathen. Rockford, Ill., Tan Books [1972, c1971] 181 p. 22 cm. Appendixes (p. [173]-181): 1. Apostolic constitution: Quo primum of Pope St. Pius V, 1570.—2. Apostolic constitution: Missale Romanum of Pope Paul VI, 1969.—3. Profession of the Catholic faith taken by all priests at Ordination. Includes bibliographical references. [BX2230.2.W35] 76-183571 5.00
1. Mass. I. Title.

RIVERS, Clarence 264.02'06
Joseph.
Celebration. Designed by William Schickel & Associates. New York, Herder and Herder [1969] 112 p. illus. 21 cm. Includes melodies with words. "Seven celebrations" (a collection of paraliturgical Catholic devotions): p. 41-109. [BV199.O3R58] 76-87767 4.95
1. Occasional services—Catholic Church. I. William Schickel & Associates. II. Title.

CATHOLIC Church. 264.02'09
National Conference of Catholic Bishops. Bishops' Committee on the Liturgy.
The new eucharistic prayers and prefaces. Washington, 1968. 72 p. 23 cm. "The extensive notes to the four eucharistic prayers ... were prepared by the translating body, the International Committee on English in the Liturgy (ICEL)." Bibliography: p. 72. [BX2045.P65A5] 79-4460
1. Prefaces (Liturgy) I. Catholic Church. Liturgy and ritual. Eucharistic prayer II-IV. English. 1968. II. International Committee on English in the Liturgy. III. Title.

JUNGMANN, Josef Andreas, 264.0209
1889-
Pastoral liturgy. New York, Herder & Herder [c.1962] 430p. 23cm. Bibl. 62-17230 6.95
1. Liturgics—Collected works. I. Title.

AVRIL, A M 264.021
The meaning of Christmas. Translated by S.O. Palleske. Chicago, Fides Publishers Association [1957] 153p. 19cm. 'Published in French ... under the title Le dimanche a la radio: le cycle de Noel.' [BX1756.A85D53] 57-4955
1. Church year sermons. 2. Catholic Church—Sermons. 3. Sermons, French—Translations into English. 4. Sermons, English—Translations from French. I. Title.

BOUYER, Louis, 1913- 264.021
The paschal mystery; meditations on the last three days of Holy Week. Translated by Sister Mary Benoit. Chicago, Regnery, 1950. xxiii. 347 p. 22 cm. Bibliographical references included in "Notes" at ends of chapters. [BX2184.B614] 50-6585
1. Meditations. 2. Catholic Church. Liturgy and ritual. Holy Week offices. I. Title.

BOYER, Thomas. 264'.021
More parish liturgies; experiments and resources in Sunday worship. Editorial assistant: Mary Sue Greer. New York, Paulist Press [1973] xiii, 238 p. 23 cm. Companion volume: Parish liturgies. Bibliography: p. 231-236. [BV198.B647] 73-174929 ISBN 0-8091-1777-0 5.95 (pbk.)
1. Liturgies. I. Title.

BOYER, Thomas. 264'.021
Parish liturgies; experiments and resources in Sunday worship. Editorial assistant: Mary Sue Greer. New York, Paulist Press [1973] xvi, 308 p. 23 cm. Companion volume: More parish liturgies. Bibliography: p. 301-306. [BV198.B65] 73-81106 ISBN 0-8091-1776-2 5.95 (pbk.)
1. Liturgies. I. Title.

CATHOLIC Church. Liturgy 264.021
and ritual. Ceremonial of bishops.
Episcopal ceremonies for Holy Week; a section of the Manual of episcopal ceremonies, by Aurelius Stehle. Rev. by Emmeran A. Rettger. Rev. ed. Latrobe, Pa., Archabbey Press, 1958. 79p. illus. 23cm. Includes bibliography. [BX1971.A25 1958] 58-9915
1. Catholic Church. Liturgy and ritual. Holy Week rite. I. Stehle, Aurelius, 1877-1930. II. Title.

CATHOLIC Church. Liturgy 264.021
and ritual. Holy Week rite. English.
The sacred ceremonies of Holy Week, each service from Palm Sunday to Easter as restored in the decree of November 16, 1955 of the Sacred Congregation of Rites;a translation of the Ordo Hebdomadae Sanctae instauratus, edited by F. P. Prucha [and] Gerald Ellard. Rubrics and introductions by John J. Danagher. Washington, National Catholic Welfare Conference [c1956] 186p. illus. 15cm. [BX2045.H7A4 1956] 57-686
I. Prucha, Francis Paul, ed. II. Ellard, Gerard, 1894- ed. III. Catholic Church. Liturgy and ritual. English. IV. Title.

CATHOLIC Church. Liturgy 264.021
and ritual. Martyrology. English.
The Roman martyrology, in which are to be found the eulogies of the saints and blessed approved by the Sacred Congregation of Rites up to 1961. English tr. from the 4th ed. after the typical ed. (1956) approved by Pope Benedict XV (1922) Ed. by J. B. O'Connell. Westminster, Md., Newman [1962] xix, 412p. 24cm. 62-21497 7.95
I. O'Connell, John Berthram, 1888- ed. II. Title.

CATHOLIC Church. Pope, 264.021
1939-1958 (Pius XII) Haurietis aquas (15 May 1956) English.
The Sacred Heart; a commentary on Haurietis aquas [by] Alban J. Dachauer. Milwaukee, Bruce Pub. Co. [1959] 209p. 23cm. 'The translation of Haurietis aquas is taken ... from the Catholic mind of October, 1956.' [BX2157.A45D3] 59-10966
1. Sacred Heart, Devotion to. I. Dachauer, Alban J. II. Title.

CHIRAINELLI, Piero. 264.021
History in miniature of the holy years. [Translated by Vittoria Bonfante and Charles Sleeth] New York, Holy Year Medal and Book Corp. [1950] 60 p. port. 20 cm. [BX961.H6C52] 50-2258
1. Holy Year. I. Title.

CHRISTIAN life calendar 264.021
(The) 1963-1964. by Rev. Lincoln F. Whelan, Rev. George Kolanda. Milwaukee, Bruce, c.1963. unpaged. illus., (pt. col.) 17x17cm. 1.00, pap., plastic bdg.
1. Catholic Church—Calendars. I. Whelan, Lincoln F. The Christian life calendar. II. Kolanda, George, joint author.

DENIS-BOULET, Noele M. 264.021
The Christian calendar. Translated from the French by P. Hepburne-Scott. New York, Hawthorn Books [c.1960] 126 p. 21 cm. (The Twentieth century encyclopedia of Catholicism, v. 113. Section 10: The worship of the church) Bibl.: p. 125-26. 60-13059 2.95
1. Church calendar. I. Title.

DENIS-BOULET, Noele 264.021
Maurice, 1896-
The Christian calendar. Translated from the French by P. Hepburne-Scott. [1st ed.] New York, Hawthorn Books [1960] 126 p. 21 cm. (The Twentieth century encyclopedia of Catholicism, v. 113. Section 10: The worship of the church) Includes bibliography. [BV30.D443] 60-13059
1. Church calendar. I. Title.

FEHREN, Henry 264.021
Christ now; Saturday night thoughts for Sunday Mass. New York, Kenedy [1966] 148p. 22cm. [BX2170.C55F4] 66-25140 3.95
1. Church year—Meditations. I. Title.

GAILLARD, Jean, 1610- 264.021
Holy Week and Easter, a liturgical commentary. William Busch, translator. With a forward [sci] by Peter W. Bartholome. Collegeville, Minn.] Liturgical Press [1954] 163p. 19cm. (Popular liturgical library) [BX2010.A5G3] 55-1281
1. Catholic Church. Liturgy and ritual. Holy Week offices. I. Title.

LOHR, Aemiliana. 264.021
The Great Week; an explanation of the liturgy of Holy Week. Translated by D. T. H. Bridehouse, with a foreword by Ralph Russell. London, Longmans, Green; Westminister, Md., Newman Press [1958] 211p. 19cm. Translation of Die Hellige Woche. [BX2045.H7L613] 58-8748
1. Catholic Church. Liturgy and ritual. Holy Week rite. 2. Holy Week. I. Title.

MCCORRY, Vincent P 1909- 264.021
Cleanse my heart; meditations on the Sunday Gospels. Westminster, Md., Newman Press, 1955. 179p. 21cm. [BX2182.M23] 55-8654
1. Bible. N. T. Epistics and Gospela, Liturgical—Meditations. I. Title.

MCMANUS, Frederick 264.021
Richard, 1923-
The ceremonies of the Easter virgil. Paterson, N. J., St. Anthony Guild Press, 1953. 129p. illus. 19cm. [BX2045.H6M2] 53-8457
1. Catholic Church. Liturgy and ritual. Rite of Holy Saturday. I. Title.

MCMANUS, Frederick 264.021
Richard, 1923-
The rites of Holy Week: ceremonies, preparations, music, commentary. Paterson, N.

J., Saint Anthony Guild Press, 1956. 146p. illus. 23cm. [BX2010.M33] 56-13808
1. Catholic Church. Liturgy and ritual. Holy Week Offices. sHoly Week. I. Title.

MCMANUS, Frederick Richard, 1923- 264.021
The rites of Holy Week: ceremonies, preparations, rules for Holy Week music, commentary. [2d ed.] Paterson, N. J., Saint Anthony Guild Press [1957] 152p. illus. 23cm. [BX2045.H7M2 1957] 57-3830
1. Catholic Church. Liturgy and ritual. Holy Week Rite. 2. Holy Week. I. Title.

MONKS, James Lawrence. 264.021
Great Catholic festivals. New York, H. Schuman [1951] 110 p. illus. 23 cm. (Great religious festivals series) [BV43.M6] 51-10812
1. Fasts and feasts — Catholic Church. I. Title.
Contents omitted.

NEWLAND, Mary (Reed) 264.021
The year and our children; planning the family activities for Christian feasts and seasons. New York, P. J. Kenedy [1956] 328p. illus. 21cm. Includes bibliography. [BV35.N47] 56-6429
1. Church year. 2. Catholic Church—Ceremonies and practices. 3. Rites and ceremonies. I. Title.

NEWLAND, Mary (Reed) 264.021
The year and our children; planning the family activities for Christian feasts and seasons. New York, P. J. Kenedy [1956] 328p. illus. 21cm. Includes bibliography. [BV35.N47] 56-6429
1. Church year. 2. Catholic Church—Ceremonies and practices. 3. Rites and ceremonies. I. Title.

NEWLAND, Mary (Reed) 264.021
The year and our children; planning the family activities for Christian feasts and seasons. Garden City, N.Y., Doubleday [1964, c.1956] 314p. 18cm. (Image bk., D167) Bibl. .95 pap.,
1. Church year. 2. Catholic Church—Ceremonies and practices. 3. Rites and ceremonies. I. Title.

NEWMAN, John Henry, Cardinal, 1801-1890. 264.021
Meditations and devotions. London, New York, Longmans, Green [1954] 348p. 17cm. [BX2182.N5 1954] 54-3865
1. Meditations. I. Title.

NOTRE Dame, Ind. University. 264.021
An analysis of the restored Holy Week rites for pastoral use; a report of the seminar for priests arranged and conducted by the University of Notre Dame, February 7-9, 1956, at the request of the Liturgical Conference. Edited by the Notre Dame Liturgical Committee. Notre Dame, University of Notre Dame Press [1956] ix, 115p. 21cm. Bibliography: p. 112-115. [BX2010.N6 1956] 56-1574
1. Catholic Church. Liturgy and ritual, Holy Week offices. 2. Holy Week. I. Title.

O'CONNELL, John Berthram, 1888- 264.021
The ceremonies of Holy Week, solemn rite and simple rite; a commentary. Westminster, Md., Newman Press [1958] 116p. illus. 22cm. [BX2045.H7O25] 58-8746
1. Catholic Church. Liturgy and ritual. Holy Week rite. I. Title.

RELIGIOUS of Our Lady of the retreat in the cenacle. 264.021
The history of the most wonderful promise ever made. Meditations from Holy Scripture, for God's loving children (to be used by mothers and teachers). . . New York city, The Cenacle of St. Regis [1925] 3p.1., v-xv, 484p. 24cm. 'By the Religious of the cenacle.' On cover: Meditations from Holy Scripture. 'Continuation of the lessons developed in volume i 'Meditations for God's loving children."--Pref. tMeditations from Holy Scripture. [BX2182.R452] 25-24476
I. Title.

SCHMITZ, Walter J 264.021
Holy Week manual for priests. Milwaukee, Bruce Pub. Co. [1956] 227p. illus. 23cm. [BX2010.S35] 56-1688
1. Catholic Church. Liturgy and ritual. Holy Week offices. 2. Holy Week. I. Title.

SCHMITZ, Walter J 264.021
Holy Week manual for priests. Milwaukee, Bruce Pub. Co. [1957] 266p. illus. 23cm. [BX2045.H7S34 1957] 58-70
1. Catholic Church. Liturgy and ritual. Holy Week rite. 2. Holy Week. I. Title.

SCHMITZ, Walter J. 264.021
Holy Week manual for priests. Milwaukee, Bruce [c.1962] 272p. illus. 22cm. 62-3333 4.00
1. Catholic Church. Liturgy and ritual. Holy Week rite. 2. Holy Week. I. Title.

SCHMITZ, Walter J 264.021
Holy Week manual for servers. Milwaukee, Bruce Pub. Co. [1957] 60p. illus. 22cm. [BX2045.H7S35] 57-1999
1. Catholic Church. Liturgy and ritual. Holy Week rite. I. Title.

SHEPHERD, Massey Hamilton, 1913- ed. 264.021
Holy Week offices, edited for the Associated Parishes, incorporated. Greenwich, Conn., Seabury Press, 1958. 6 pts. (viii, 106 p.) in 1 v. illus. 19 cm. "Published under the auspices of the Adult Division of the Department of Christian Education, Protestant Episcopal Church." [BX5147.H6S5] 58-5054
I. Associated Parishes for Liturgy and Mission. II. Protestant Episcopal Church in the U. S. A. Liturgy and ritual. III. Title.

SHEPHERD, Massey Hamilton, 1918- ed. 264.021
Holy Week offices, editred for the Associated Parishes, incorporated. Greenwich, Conn, Seabury Press, 1958. 6 pts. (viii, 106 p.) in 1 v. illus. 19 cm. "Published under the auspices of the Adult Division of the Department of Christian Education, Protestant Episcopal Church." [BX5147.H6S5] 58-5054
I. Associated Parishes. II. Protestant Episcopal Church in the U.S.A. Liturgy and ritual. III. Title.

STEHLE, Aurelius, 1877-1930. 264.021
Episcopal ceremonies for Holy Week; a section of the Manual of episcopal ceremonies. Rev. by Emmeran A. Rettger. Rev. ed. Latrobe, Pa., Archabbey Press, 1958. 79 p. illus. 23 cm. Includes bibliography. [BX1971.S7 1958] 58-9915
1. Catholic Church. Liturgy and ritual. Holy Week rite. I. Title.

STIERLI, Josef, ed. 264.021
Heart of the Saviour; a symposium on devotion to the Sacred Heart. With contributions by Richard Gutzwiller, Hugo Rahner and Karl Rahner. English translation by Paul Andrews. [New York] Herder and Herder [1958] ix, 267 p. 23 cm. Translation of Cor Salvatoris. Bibliography: p. 261-262. [BX2157.S75] 58-5868
1. Sacred Heart, Devotion to. I. Gutzwiller, Richard. II. Title.

STRASSER, Bernard, 1895- 264.021
With Christ through the year; the liturgical year in word symbols. Illustrated by M. A. Justina Knapp. [New ed.] Milwaukee, Bruce Pub. Co. [1958] 381 p. illus. 18 cm. [BV30.S75 1958] 58-1618
1. Church year. I. Title.

SULLIVAN, Walter J 264.021
Thoughts for troubled times. New York, Paulist Press [1961] 128 p. 19 cm. (Deus books) [BX2182.2.S8] 61-17237
1. Devotional literature. I. Title.

SUNDAY liturgy themes 264'.021
for all Sundays and holy days : A, B, C cycles / prepared by the Daughters of St. Paul from conciliar and post-conciliar documents and from addresses of Pope Paul VI. [Boston] : St. Paul Editions, [1975] 300 p. ; 22 cm. The text was originally published in the column, "Sunday liturgy themes," in Strain forward. [BX2170.C55S96] 74-16749 4.95
1. Church year—Meditations. I. Daughters of St. Paul. II. Strain forward.

TRAPP, Maria Augusta. 264.021
Around the year with the Trapp family. Music arr. by Franz Wasner; illus. by Rosemary Trapp and Nikolaus E. Wolff. [New York] Pantheon [1955] 251p. illus. 24cm. [BX2351.T68] 56-11303
1. Family—Religious life. 2. Catholic Church—Ceremonies and practices. I. Title.

WILLIAMS, Margaret Anne, 1902- 264.021
The Sacred Heart in the life of the church. New York, Sheed and Ward [1957] 248p. 22cm. [BX2157.W5] 57-10176
1. Sacred Heart, Devotion to. I. Title.

WILLIAMS, Margaret Anne, 1902- 264.021
The Sacred Heart in the life of the church. New York, Sheed and Ward [1957] 248 p. 22 cm. [BX2157.W5] 57-10176
1. Sacred Heart, Devotion to. I. Title.

WOLFE, Mary Catherine. 264.021
Abba, Father; a continual sacrifice of praise [by] M. Catherine Wolfe. Staten Island,N.Y., Alba House [c1966] 204p. illus. 20 cm. [BX2182.2.W6] 66-27532
1. Meditations I. Title.

WUELLNER, Bernard. 264.021
The graces of Christmas. Milwaukee, Bruce Pub. Co. [1958] 112 p. illus. 24 cm. [BV45.W8] 58-11570
1. Christmas — Meditations. I. Title.

CATHOLIC Church. Liturgy and ritual. Breviary. 264.022
The hours of the divine office in English and Latin; a bilingual edition of the Roman breviary text, together with introductory notes and rubrics in English only. Prepared by the staff of the Liturgical Press. Collegeville, Minn., Liturgical Press [c1963-64] 3 v. 19 cm. Cover title: Divine office. Each vol. with a card, in pocket, with special commonly repeated parts of the office. Contents.-- v. 1. Advent to Passion Sunday. -- v. 2 Passion Sunday to August. -- v. 3. August to Advent. [BX2000.A4 1963] 65-3406
I. Catholic Church. Liturgy and ritual. Breviary. English II. Catholic Church. Liturgy and ritual. English. III. Title. IV. Title: Divine office.

CATHOLIC Church. Liturgy and ritual. Breviary. English. 264.022
The divine office. [1st ed. New York] Herder and Herder [1959] xxxi, 661p. 16cm. 'Based on the original German version of Officium divinum parvum, eighth impression ... 1958 ... Prepared ... by Rev. Hildebrand Fleischmann ... English edition translated and prepared by the Very Rev. Edward E. Malone.' [BX2000.A4M3] 59-7667
I. Fleischmann, Hildebrand, ed. II. Malone, Edward Eugene, 1904- ed. and tr. III. Catholic Church. Liturgy and ritual. English. IV. Title.

CATHOLIC Church. Liturgy and ritual. Breviary. English. 264.022
The little breviary; for the use of both religious and layfolk, containing in simplified form all the offices of the Roman breviary. Haarlem, J. H. Gottmer; Westminster, Md., Newman Press [1957] 1691, 245, 32p. illus. 19cm. [BX2000.A4 1957] 59-2325
I. Catholic Church. Liturgy andritual. English. II. Title.

CATHOLIC Church. Liturgy and ritual. Breviary. English. 264.022
The Roman breviary. An approved English translation complete in one volume from the official text of the Breviarium romanum authorized by the Holy See. [Edited by Bede Babo. Translations of the prayers by Christine Mohrmann] New York, Benziger Bros. [1964] 1 v. (various pagings) 19 cm. [BX2000.A4B3] 65-2633
I. Catholic Church. Liturgy and ritual. English. II. Babo, Bede, 1900- ed. III. Title.

SALMON, Pierre, Aug.23,1896- 264.022
The breviary through the centuries. Translated by Sister David Mary. Collegeville, Minn., Liturgical Press [1962] 163 p. 24 cm. "Authorized English version of L'office divin." [BX2000.S283] 62-52925
1. Catholic Church. Liturgy and ritual. Breviary. I. Title.

SCHMITZ, Walter J 264.022
Follow the rubrics. Edited by Eugene J. Weitzel. Washington, Catholic University of America Press, 1964. x, 166 p. 23 cm. [BX1970.S3] 64-15337
1. Liturgics—Catholic Church. 2. Catholic Church. Liturgy and ritual—Rubrics. I. Title.

SCHMITZ, Walter J. 264.022
Follow the rubrics. Ed. by Eugene J. Weitzel. Washington, D.C., Catholic Univ. [c.]1964. x, 166p. 23cm. 64-15337 4.50
1. Liturgics—Catholic Church. 2. Catholic Church Liturgy and ritual—Rubrics. I. Title.

ANNUAL Catholic missal 264.023
for Sundays and Holydays. 1967- New York. v.16cm. A Dell-Bebziger bk. [BX2015.A4A63] 67-4 1.25 pap.,
1. Catholic Church, Liturgy and ritual, Missal.
Available from Dell.

CATHOLIC Church. Liturgy and ritual. 264.02'3
English-Latin Roman missal for the United States of America, containing the Mass text from the Roman missal and the prayers of the celebrant together with the ordinary of the Mass from the English-Latin sacramentary. New York, Benziger Bros., 1966. xix, 1270, 436, 52 p. 28 cm. On spine: Roman missal. "English translations approved by the National Conference of Bishops of the United States of America and confirmed by the Apostolic See." Includes chants in modern notation. [BX2015.A4 1966d] 73-2731
I. [Missal. English & Latin] II. Title. III. Title: Roman missal.

CATHOLIC Church. Liturgy and ritual. 264.02'3
The English-Latin Sacramentary for the United States of America; the prayers of the celebrant of Mass together with the Ordinary of the Mass. New York, Catholic Book Pub. Co. [1966] xiii, 724 p. 28 cm. On spine: Sacramentary. Rubricated. "English translations approved by the National Conference of Bishops of the United States of America and confirmed by the Apostolic See." Includes chants in modern notation. [BX2037.A4 1966 8 pt.] 70-2820
I. [Sacramentary (U.S.)] II. Title. III. Title: Sacramentary.

CATHOLIC Church. Liturgy and ritual. 264.02'3
Lectionary for Mass. English translation approved by the National Conference of Catholic Bishops and confirmed by the Apostolic See. Bible texts from the Jerusalem Bible. New York, Benziger [1970] xxvii, 976 p. 29 cm. At head of title: The Roman missal revised by decree of the Second Vatican Council and published by authority of Pope Paul VI. [BX2003.A4 1969] 74-23209
I. Catholic Church. National Conference of Catholic Bishops. II. [Lectionary (1969). English] III. Title. IV. Title: The Roman missal revised by decree of the Second Vatican Council and published by authority of Pope Paul VI.

CATHOLIC Church. Liturgy and ritual. 264.02'3
Lectionary for Mass. English translation approved by the National Conference of Catholic Bishops and confirmed by the Apostolic See. With the New American version of Sacred Scripture from the original languages made by members of the Catholic Biblical Association and sponsored by the Bishop's Committee of the Division of Religious Education (Confraternity of Christian Doctrine) New York, Catholic Book Pub. Co., 1970. 1122 p. 29 cm. At head of title: The Roman missal revised by decree of the Second Vatican Council and published by authority of Pope Paul VI. [BX2003.A41969b] 76-23204
I. Catholic Church. National Conference of Catholic Bishops. II. [Lectionary (1969). English] III. Title. IV. Title: The Roman missal revised by decree of the Second Vatican Council and published by authority of Pope Paul VI.

CATHOLIC Church. Liturgy and ritual. 264'.023
Lectionary for Mass for Sundays of year C : arranged for readers : the Roman Missal, revised by decree of the Second Vatican Council and published by authority of Pope Paul VI : English translation approved by the National Conference of Catholic Bishops and confirmed by the Apostolic See : New American Bible / [editor, Stephen J. Hartdegen]. New York : Pueblo Pub. Co., c1973. 441 p. ; 29 cm. Includes chants. [BX2003.A4 1973] 76-351826
I. Hartdegen, Stephen J. II. Catholic Church. National Conference of Catholic Bishops. III. [Lectionary (1969). English. Selections] IV. Title.

CATHOLIC Church. Liturgy and ritual. Missal. English. 264.02'3
The new Catholic family missal. People of God ed. [Charlotte, N.C., Catholic Bible House, 1966] xxii, 1322, 51 p. col. illus. 18 cm. "Official musical settings": p. 1314-1318. Contents.Contents.—Part of the text in Latin and English. [BX2015.A4 1966c] 67-6939
I. Catholic Church. Liturgy and ritual. English. II. Title.

CATHOLIC Church. Liturgy and ritual. 264.02'3
The new Saint Andrew Bible missal. Prepared by a missal commission of Saint Andrew's Abbey. New ed. containing the complete psalter and the mass prayers and readings approved by the bishops of the United States. New York, Benziger Bros. [1966] xiv, 1478 p. 17 cm. [BX2015.A4S3 1966] 67-3503
I. Saint-Andre-lez-Bruges, Belgium (Benedictine abbey) II. [Missal. English] III. Title. IV. Title: Saint Andrew Bible missal.

CATHOLIC Church. Liturgy and ritual. 264.02'3
The Roman missal in Latin and English for Holy Week and Easter Week, including the Mass of the chrism with the blessing of the oils. Collegeville, Minn., Liturgical Press [1966] 268 p. 32 cm. "English translations approved by the National Conference of Bishops of the United States of America and confirmed by the Apostolic See." Includes the chants. [BX2015.8.H6A46] 72-224952
I. [Holy Week rite. English & Latin] II. Title.

CATHOLIC Church. Liturgy and ritual. 264.02'3
Roman Seraphic missal; containing the mass text from the Roman Seraphic missal and the prayers of the celebrant together with the ordinary of the mass from the English-Latin Sacramentary. Paterson, N.J., Saint Anthony

Guild Press, 1968 [c1967] xv, 1468, 306 p. illus., music. 28 cm. "English translations approved by the National Conference of Catholic Bishops of the United States of America and confirmed by the Apostolic See. English translations of mass texts for the three Orders and our Father Francis approved by the Friar Minor Provincials' Conference of the United States and Canada and confirmed by the Apostolic See." [BX2015.A4F7] 68-2826
I. Franciscans. II. [Missal (Franciscan) English & Latin] III. Title.

CATHOLIC Church. Liturgy and ritual. 264.023
The Saint Jerome Sunday missal, with the official liturgical texts approved by the Bishops' Commission on the Liturgical Apostolate. Edited by Thomas B. McDonough, Joseph Marren, and Jex Martin. Chicago, Catholic Press, 1966. x, 660 p. illus. (part col.) 18 cm. (Library of Catholic devotion) [BX2015.A4M24] 66-9048
I. McDonough, Thomas B., ed. II. Marren, Joseph, ed. III. Martin, Jex, ed. IV. [Missal. English. Selections] V. Title.

CATHOLIC Church. Liturgy and ritual. 264'.023
St. Paul daily Mass book. Compiled by the Daughters of St. Paul. [Boston] St. Paul Editions [1972] 1210 p. illus. 16 cm. [BX2015.A4D28] 70-183442
I. Daughters of St. Paul. II. [Missal. English] III. Title.

CATHOLIC Church. Liturgy and ritual. 264.02'3
The Sarum missal, edited from three early manuscripts by J. Wickham Legg. Oxford, Clarendon Press [1969] xxxii, 612 p. 26 1/2 cm. Includes bibliographical references. [BX5142.L4 1969] 75-494640 ISBN 0-19-826428-3
I. Legg, John Wickham, 1843-1921, ed. II. Salisbury, Eng. (Diocese) III. [Missal (Salisbury)]

CATHOLIC Church. Liturgy and ritual. Breviary. 264.023
Daily prime, according to the Roman breviary, with the new Latin version of the Psalms, and the English translation issued by the Confranternity of Christian Doctrine. Edited by Benedict R. Avery. Collegeville, Minn., Litergical Press [1952] 93p. 19cm. (Popularliturgical library) [BX2000.A4A8] 53-19920
1. Catholic Church. Liturgy and ritual. English. I. Avery, Benedict Raymund, 1919- ed. II. Catholic Church. Liturgy and ritual. Breviary. English. III. Title.

CATHOLIC Church. Liturgy and ritual. Missal. English. 264.023
The Maryknoll missal. Formerly published as Daily missal of the mystical body, containing the official texts of masses offered every day of the year and the complete psalter. Edited by the Maryknoll Fathers. [Rev. ed. Vatican II ed.] New York, P. J. Kenedy [1966] 1280, 48 p. 18 cm. "Prayers added at a solemn mass": 48 p. between p. 640 and 641. [BX2015.A4M3 1966] 66-4250
I. Catholic Church. Liturgy and ritual. English. II. Catholic Church. Liturgy and ritual. Psalter. III. Catholic Foreign Mission Society of America. IV. Title.

CATHOLIC Church. Liturgy and ritual. Missal. English. 264.023
The new Catholic family missal: continuous arrangement of masses for Sundays and feast days with approved texts of the mass in English. [Garden City, N. Y.] N. Doubleday [1966] xxii, 1322 p. col. front. 18 cm. Part of the text in Latin and English. "Official musical settings": p. 1314-1318. [BX2015.A4 1966] 66-6795
I. Catholic Church. Liturgy and ritual. English II. Title.

CATHOLIC Church. Liturgy and ritual. [Missal (Franciscan) English & Latin] 264.02'3
Roman Seraphic missal; containing the mass text from the Roman Seraphic missal and the prayers of the celebrant together with the ordinary of the mass from the English-Latin Sacramentary. Paterson, N.J., St. Anthony Guild Pr., 1968 [c1967] xv, 1468, 306p. illus., music. 28cm. English tr. approved by the Natl. Conf. of Catholic Bishops of the U.S. of Amer. and confirmed by the Apostolic See. English trs. of mass texts for the 3 Orders and our Father Francis approved by the Friar Minor Provincials' Conf. of the U.S. and Canada and confirmed by the Apostolic See. [BX2015.A4F7] 68-2826 45.50
I. Franciscans. II. Title.

COUGHLAN, Peter. 264'.023
Commentary on the Sunday lectionary, first Sunday of Advent to last Sunday of the year, year C [by] Peter Coughlan and Peter Purdue. New York, Corpus Books [1970] 198 p. 22 cm. "A Geoffrey Chapman publication." Includes bibliographical references. [BX2003.C68] 78-138353 3.95
1. Catholic Church. Liturgy and ritual. Lectionary (1969) I. Purdue, Peter, joint author. II. Title.

CROSSAN, Dominic M 264.023
Scanning the Sunday Gospel [by] Dominic M. Crossan. Milwaukee, Bruce [1966] xiv, 154 p. 22 cm. [BS2565.Z73C7] 66-16641
1. Bible. N.T. Epistles and Gospels. Liturgical — Commentaries. I. Title.

CROSSAN, Dominic M. 264.023
Scanning the Sunday Gospel. Milwaukee. Bruce [c.1966] xiv, 154p. 22cm. [BS2565.Z73C7] 66-16641 3.50
1. Bible. N.T. Epistles and Gospels. Liturgical—Commentaries. I. Title.

**FRANCISCAN daily missal and hymnal.* 264.02'3 The official prayers for daily mass according to the Roman and Franciscan calendars. With the people's parts of Holy Mass printed in boldface type and arranged for parish participation in accordance with the new revised liturgy as directed by Vatican Council II. With many study helps and extra features. Paterson, N. J., St. Anthony Guild Pr. [1967] 1416, 240p. illus. (col front) music. 17cm. (1-240p.) Contains Franciscan supplement, containing the mass texts for the three orders of our Father Francis 5.95
1. Catholic church—Liturgy and ritual. 2. Missals.

GEISSLER, Eugene S. 264'.023
Together at Mass, with 24 liturgies of the Word [by] Eugene S. Geissler and Kenneth W. Peters. Notre Dame, Ind., Ave Maria Press [1973] 140 p. illus. 23 cm. [BX2169.G4] 72-95962 ISBN 0-87793-051-1 2.50
1. Lord's Supper—Prayer-books and devotions—English. I. Peters, Kenneth W., joint author. II. Title.

HOEY, Robert F., comp. 264.02'3
The experimental liturgy book, collected and edited by Robert F. Hoey. [New York] Herder and Herder [1969] xii, 194 p. 26 cm. Consists of experimental alternates and/or additions chiefly to texts of the Missal. [BV825.5.H6] 79-87757 4.50
1. Mass—Celebration. I. Catholic Church. Liturgy and ritual. Missal. II. Title.

IRWIN, Kevin W. 264'.023
A celebrant's guide to the new sacramentary : a cycle / Kevin W. Irwin. New York : Pueblo Pub. Co., c1975. 230 p. ; 22 cm. [BX2015.I77] 75-322747
1. Catholic Church. Liturgy and ritual. Missal. 2. Bible—Liturgical lessons, English. 3. Church year. I. Title.

LAPLANTE, Mary Cosma. 264'.023
Come to the holy table. Illustrated by Norma T. Baccala. Foreword by Charles H. Helmsing. Huntington, Ind., Our Sunday Visitor, inc. [1973, c1974] 96 p. col. illus. 15 cm. [BX2015.A55L36] 74-156936 ISBN 0-87973-824-3 1.95
1. Children's missals. I. Title.

THE Old Catholic missal and ritual. 264.02'3 Prepared for the use of English-speaking congregations of Old Catholics in communion with the ancient Catholic Archiepiscopal See of Utrecht. New York, AMS Press [1969] xvi, 326 p. 23 cm. "Prepared by ... Arnold H. Mathew." Reprint of the London ed., 1909. [BX4773.A3 1969] 73-84708
I. Mathew, Arnold Harris, 1852-1919.

SKILLIN, Joseph H. 264.02'3
Bread & wine in the now generation, by Joseph H. Skillin. Dayton, Ohio, G. A. Pflaum [1969] 31 p. 28 cm. (What's happening) Prayers. [BX2169.S55] 79-82525 2.00
1. Mass—Prayer-books and devotions—English. I. Title.

SLOYAN, Gerard Stephen, 1919- 264'.023
Commentary on the new lectionary / by Gerard S. Sloyan. New York : Paulist Press, c1975. ix, 428 p. ; 23 cm. Includes index. [BS391.2.S58] 75-22781 ISBN 0-8091-1895-5 : 10.00
1. Bible—Liturgical lessons, English. I. Catholic Church. Liturgy and ritual. Lectionary (1969). English. II. Title.

BEHNKE, John. 264'.024
A children's lectionary : cycle a / John Behnke. New York : Paulist Press, [1974] vii, 183 p. ; 28 cm. [BX2003.B4] 74-22845 ISBN 0-8091-1857-2 pbk. : 8.95
1. Lectionaries. I. Title.

CATHOLIC Church. Liturgy and ritual. 264'.024
Lectionary for Mass for Sundays of Year A, arranged for readers / English translation approved by the National Conference of Catholic Bishops and confirmed by the Apostolic See. New York : Pueblo Pub. Co., c1974. 431 p. : music ; 29 cm. At head of title: The Roman missal revised by decree of the Second Vatican Council and published by authority of Pope Paul VI. "New American Bible." [BX2003.A4 1969c] 75-322212
I. [Lectionary (1969). Selections. English] II. Title. III. Title: The Roman missal revised by decree of the Second Vatican Council.

CATHOLIC Church. Liturgy and ritual. 264'.024
Supplement to the Roman breviary, containing offices proper to the Order of Discalced Carmelites, with an appendix containing some offices proper to certain places. Prepared by Carmel of St. Joseph, Long Beach Calif. [St. Paul, Printed at the North Central Pub. Co., 1966] 134 p. col. front. 18 cm. [BX2049.C2O3513 1966] 73-178814
I. Discalced Carmelites. II. Carmel of St. Joseph, Long Beach, Calif. III. [Officia propria, Discalced Carmelites. English] IV. Title.

CATHOLIC Church. Liturgy and ritual. Breviary. 264.024
Daily compline, according to the Roman bfeviary, arranged for c ongregational singing or recitation, with the new Latin version of the Psalms. Edited by Benedict R. Avery. Collegeville, Minn., Liturgical Press [1952] 104p. 19cm. (Popular liturgical library) Latin and English. With music in modern notation. [BX2000.A4A8] 53-19919
I. Avery, Benedict Raymund, 1919- ed. II. Catholic Church. Liturgy and ritual. Breviary. English. III. Catholic Church. Liturgy and ritual. English. IV. Title.

COCROFT, Ronald Edwin. 264'.024
A study of the Pauline lessons in the Matthean sections of the Greek lectionary, by Ronald E. Cocroft. Salt Lake City, University of Utah Press, 1968. 331 p. 25 cm. (Studies and documents, 32) Bibliography: p. 327-331. [BS2638.C6] 75-313332
1. Epistolaries. I. Title. II. Series.

PREPOSITINUS Cremonensis, d.ca.1210. 264.02'4
Praepositini Cremonensis Tractatus de officiis. Edited by James A. Corbett. Notre Dame [Ind.] University of Notre Dame Press, 1969. xxix, 300 p. 24 cm. (University of Notre Dame. Publications in mediaeval studies, v. 21) Introd. in English. The Latin text is based on 5 MSS. of the work discovered by George Lacombe and his transcription of the British Museum MS. (B. M. Add. MS. 18335 ff. 26-66) Bibliography: p. 293-296. [BX2000.P7 1969] 76-75157
1. Catholic Church. Liturgy and ritual. Breviary—Rubrics. 2. Catholic Church. Liturgy and ritual. Missal—Rubrics. I. Corbett, James Arthur, ed. II. Lacombe, George, d. 1934. III. Title: Tractatus de officiis. IV. Series: Notre Dame, Ind. University. Publications in mediaeval studies, 21

ABELL, William S 264.025
The faithful at Mass. Baltimore, Helicon Press [1958] 116p. 19cm. Includes bibliography. [BX2230.A2] 58-13338
1. Mass. I. Title.

AMERICAN Society for Nocturnal Adoration. 264.025
Office of the Most Blessed Sacrament; official prayer book of the American Society for Nocturnal Adoration. New York, Nocturnal Adoration Society [1956] 126p. 17cm. [BX2055.N6 1956] 60-32617
1. Lord's Supper—Adoration. 2. Lord's Supper—Prayer-books and devotions — English. I. Title.

AMIOT, Francois. 264.025
History of the Mass. Translated from the French by Lancelot C. Sheppard. [1st ed.] New York, Hawthorn Books [1959] 141p. 21cm. (The Twentieth century encyclopedia of Catholicism, v. 110. Section 10: The worship of the church) Bibliography: p. [140]-141. [BX2230.A533] 59-6668
1. Mass—Hist. I. Title. II. Series: The Twentieth century encyclopedia of Catholicism, v. 110

AMIOT, Francois 264.025
History of the Mass. Tr. from French by Lancelot C. Sheppard. New York, Guild Press, dist. Golden Press [1961, c.1958] 212p. (Angelus bk. 31200) Bibl. .85 bds.,
1. Mass—Hist. I. Title.

BAUR, Johannes. 264.025
Liturgical handbook for Holy Mass. Translated by David Heimann. Rev. in accordance with the latest decress of the Sacred Congregation of Rites. Westminister, Md., Newman Press, 1961. 146p. 19cm. Translation of Kleine Liturgik der helligen Messe. [BX2230.2.B313] 60-10730
1. Mass. 2. Lord's Supper (Liturgy) I. Title.

BISKUPEK, Aloysius, 1884-1955. 264.025
Holy Mass and life. New York, Society of Saint Paul [1957] 189p. illus. 21cm. [BX2230.B49] 57-12243
1. Mass. I. Title.

CATHOLIC Church. Liturgy and ritual. 264'.025
Rite of baptism for children. English translation approved by the National Conference of Catholic Bishops and confirmed by the Apostolic See. New York, Corpus Books [1970] 60 p. 29 cm. "The Roman ritual revised by decree of the Second Vatican Ecumenical Council and published by authority of Pope Paul VI." "A Geoffrey Chapman publication." [BX2035.6.B3A4] 75-137461
I. [Baptism for children (1969). English] II. Title.

CATHOLIC Church. Liturgy and ritual. Missal. 264.025
St. Paul daily missal, in Latin and English, with the latest masses and the new Holy Week liturgy, by the Daughters of St. Paul. With pref. by J. Alberione. [Derby? N. Y.] Daughters of St. Paul, Apostolate of the Press [c1955] 2409p. illus. 16cm. [BX2015.A4D3] 59-24353
1. Catholic Church. Liturgy and ritual. English. II. Daughters of St. Paul. III. Title.

CATHOLIC Church. Liturgy and ritual. Missal. English. 264.025
Saint Andrew daily missal, by missal, by Gaspar Lefebvre and the monks of the Abbey of St. Abdrew, Bruges, Belgium. [New regular ed. in accordance with the latest decree issued by the Paul, E. M. Lohamnn Co. 1149p. illus. 17cm. [BX2015.A4L4 1956] 57-24406
I. Catholic Church. Liturgy and ritual. English. II. lefebvre. Gaspear, 1880- III. Saint-Andre-les-Bruges, Belgium (Benedictine abbey) IV. Title.

CATHOLIC Church. Liturgy and ritual. Missal. English. 264.025
Blessed Sacrament missal; an extra-large type Sunday missal with complete new Holy Week services, in conformity with the new decree simplifying the Mass rubrics. Edited by the Fathers of the Blessed Sacrament Raymond A. Tartre, editorial director. With Confraternity text of Old and New Testaments. New York, Benziger Bros. [1958] 608p. illus. 17cm. [BX2015.A4F3] 59-29211
I. Fathers of the Blessed Sacrament. II. Title.

CATHOLIC Church. Liturgy and ritual. Missal. English. 264.025
The cathedral daily missal; the Roman missal adapted to everyday life in conformity with the new decree on the rubrics of the missal and the Ordinationes ad librorum liturgicorum editores, issued by the Sacred Congregation of Rites, January 1, 1961, by Rudolph G. Bandas. Pref. by Pietro C. van Lierde. St. Paul, E. M. Lohmann Co. [1961] 2319 p. illus. (part col.) 16 cm. [BX2015.A4B3] 63-27413
I. Bandas, Rudolph George, 1896- II. Title.

CATHOLIC Church. Liturgy and ritual. Missal. English. 264.025
Catholic girl's manual and Sunday missal; containing spiritual reflections, Sunday missal, and popular indulgenced prayers for Catholic girls; edited by William A. Carroll. New York. Catholic Book Pub. Co. [1952] 541 p. illus. (part col.) 16 cm. [BX2170.W7C64] 52-4506
1. Girls—Religious life. 2. Catholic Church—Prayer-books and dovotions—English. I. Carroll, William A., 1905- ed. II. Title.

CATHOLIC Church. Liturgy and ritual. Missal. English. 264.025
Daily missal of the mystical body. Edited by the Maryknoll Fathers with the collaboration of Charles J. Callan. New York, Kenedy [1957] 1699p. illus. 18cm. [BX2015.A4em3] 57-3223
I. Catholic Church. Liturgy and ritual. English. II. Title.

CATHOLIC Church. Liturgy and ritual. Missal. English. 264.025
The missal; containing all the Masses for Sundays and for holy days of obligation. Edited by John P. O'Connell and Jex Martin. Chicago, Catholic Press [c1954] 944p. illus. 18cm. [BX2015.ea4O34] 55-1076
I. O Connell, John P., ed. II. Martin, Jex., ed. III. Title.

CATHOLIC Church. Liturgy and ritual. Missal. English. 264.025
Perpetual help daily missal. New York,

Perpetual Help Center [1958] 4v. illus. 17cm. [BX2015] 60-684
I. Title.

CATHOLIC Church. Liturgy 264.025
and ritual. Missal. English.
The Roman Missal, compiled by lawful authority from the Missale Romanum. A new ed. agreeable with the Vatican typical ed., with a suppl. containing the additional masses used in English-speaking countries and those for the greater feasts of the principal religious orders. With an introd. by Adrian Fortescue. [10th ed.] New York, Macmillan [1951] 1346 p. 16 cm. [BX2015.A4 1951] 51-13707
I. Catholic Church. Liturgy and ritual. English. II. Title.

CATHOLIC Church. Liturgy 264.025
and ritual. Missal. English.
Saint Andrew daily missal, by Gasper Lefebvre and the monks of Saint Andrew's Abbey. Confraternity version of the Old and New Testaments. Saint Paul, E. M. Lohmann Co. [1958] 4v. illus. 17cm. [BX2015.A4L4 1958] 58-23823
I. Catholic Church. Liturgy and ritual. English. II. Lefebvre, Gaspar, 1880- III. Title.

CATHOLIC Church. Liturgy 264.025
and ritual. Missal. English.
Saint Andrew daily missal, by Gaspar Lefebvre and the monks of the Abbey of St. Andrew, Bruges, Belgium. [New regular ed. in accordance with the latest decree issued by the Sacred Congregation of Rites, effective Jan. 1, 1956] Saint Paul, E. M. Lohmann Co. [c1956] 1149p. illus. 17cm. [BX2015.A4L4 1956] 57-24406
I. Catholic Church. Liturgy and ritual. English. II. Lefebvre, Gaspar, 1880- III. Saint-Andre-lez-Bruges, Belgium (Benedictine abbey) IV. Title.

CATHOLIC Church. Liturgy 264.025
and ritual. Missal. English.
The Saint Jerome daily missal with liturgical commentary. Edited by Thomas B. McDonough and Joseph Marren. London, Virtue & Co.; Chicago, Catholic Press, 1964. 4 v. illus. (part col.) 18 cm. The responses of the people are indented in Latin and English on opposite pages for dialogue Mass. [BX2015.A4 1964] 64-57945
I. McDonough, Thomas B., ed. II. Marren, Joseph, ed. III. Catholic Church. Liturgy and ritual. English. IV. Title.

CATHOLIC Church. Liturgy 264.025
and ritual. Missal. English.
Saint Joseph continuous Sunday missal; a simplified and continuous arrangement of the Mass for all Sundays and feast days, with a treasury of prayers. Edited and compiled from the 'Saint Joseph daily missal' by Hugo Hoever. New York, Catholic Book Pub. Co. [1957] 1279p. illus. (part col.) 17cm. [BX2015.A4H62] 57-4886
I. Hoever, Hugo Henry, 1883- ed. II. Catholic Church. Liturgy and ritual. English. III. Title.

CATHOLIC Church. Liturgy 264.025
and ritual. Missal. English.
Saint Joseph continuous Sunday missal; a simplified and continuous arrangement of the Mass for all Sundays and feast days, with a treasury of prayers. Edited and compiled from the 'Saint Joseph daily missal' by Hugo Hoever. New York, Catholic Book Pub. Co. [c1958] 1279, 16p. illus. (part col.) 17cm. 'Confraternity version.' [BX2015.A4H62 1958] 59-2894
I. Hoever, Hugo Henry, 1883- ed. II. Catholic Church. Liturgy and ritual. English. III. Title.

CATHOLIC Church. Liturgy 264.025
and ritual. Missal. English.
Saint Joseph Sunday missal; a simplified arrangment of praying the mAss on all Sundays and feast days, with a treasury of prayers. Large type Latin-English ed edited by Hugo H. Hoever. New York, Catholic Book Pub. Father, 1883- ed. [BX2015.A4H65] 53-4506
I. Catholic Church. Liturgy and ritual. English. II. Title.

CATHOLIC Church. Liturgy 264.025
and ritual. Missal. English.
Saint Mary, Sunday missal prayers and heritage; the prayers for Sunday Mass to enable the faithful attending the holy sacrifice to follow the exhortation of Pope Pius X: "Pray the Mass." By the monks of St. Mary's Abbey, Newark, N. J., Patrick O'Brien, abbot. Boston, Benziger Bros. [1952] 384 p. illus. 14 cm. [BX2015.A4O32] 52-4813
I. Catholic Church. Liturgy and ritual. English. II. Title.

CATHOLIC Church. Liturgy 264.025
and Ritual. Missal. English.
St. Paul daily missal; with the latest Masses, new Mass rubrics, and the new Holy Week liturgy, musical notation for sung Mass and High Mass for the dead. By the Daughters of St. Paul. With introd. by J. Alberione. Authorized new revision of the New Testament used throughout. [Boston?] St. Paul Editions [c1959] 1608p. illus. (part col.) music. 16cm. Part of the text in Latin and English. [BX2015.A4 1959] 60-22717
I. Catholic Church. Liturgy and ritual. English. II. Daughters of St. Paul. III. Title.

CATHOLIC Church. Liturgy 264.025
and ritual. Missal. English.
St. Paul daily missal with the latest Masses in accordance with the Motu proprio of Pope John XXIII. Musical notation for sung Mass and High Mass for the dead. By the Daughters of St. Paul. Introd. by J. Alberione. Authorized new revision of the New Testament used throughout. 3d rev. ed. [Boston?] St. Paul Editions [1961] 54, 1608p. illus. (part col.) music. 16cm. Part of the text inLatin and English. [BX2015.A4 1961] 61-45729
I. Catholic Church. Liturgy and ritual. English. II. Daughters of St. Paul. III. Title.

CATHOLIC Church. Liturgy 264.025
and ritual. Missal. English.
St. Paul Sunday missal for all Sundays and feast days, in accordance with latest pontifical decrees. Comp., illus. by the Daughters of St. Paul; introd. by J. Alberione. Authorized new rev. of the New Testament used throughout. [Boston] St. Paul Eds. [dist. Daughters of St. Paul, c.1962] 413p. illus. (pt. col.) 16cm. Pt. of the text in Latin and English. Includes music for the sung Mass, in accordance with the directives of the Holy See, Sept. 3, 1958, and the High Mass for the dead 62-14838 2.50; 5.50 leather,
I. Catholic Church. Liturgy and ritual. English. II. Daughters of St. Paul. III. Title.

CATHOLIC Church. Liturgy 264.025
and ritual. Missal. English.
St. Paul Sunday missal for all Sundays and feast days, in acordance with latest pontifical decrees. Compiled and illustrated by the Daughters of St. Paul, with introd. by J. Alberione. Authorized new revision of the New Testament used throughout. [Boston] St. Paul Editions [1962] 413p. illus. (part col.) 16cm. Part of the text in Latin and English Includes music for the sung Mass, in accordance with the directives of the Holy See, Sept. 3, 1958, and the High Mass for the dead. [BX2015.A4D34] 62-14838
I. Catholic Church. Liturgy and ritual. English. II. Daughters of St. Paul. III. Title.

CATHOLIC Church. Liturgy 264.025
and ritual. Missal. English.
St. Paul Sunday missal for teenagers, for all Sundays and feast days, in accordance with latest pontifical decrees. Compiled and illustrated by the Daughters of St. Paul, with introd. by J. Alberione. Authorized new revision of the New Testament used throughout. [Boston] St. Paul Editions [1962] 413p. illus. (part col.) 16cm. Part of the text in Latin and English. Includes music for the sung Mass, in accordance with the directives of the Holy See, Sept. 3, 1958, and the High Mass for the dead. [BX2015.A4D35] 61-10932
I. Catholic Church. Liturgy and ritual. English. II. Daughters of St. Paul. III. Title.

CATHOLIC Church. Liturgy 264.025
and ritual. Missal. English.
Saint Pius X daily missal for Catholic schools; according to the new Holy Week liturgy. Confraternity version of the Epistles and Gospels. Edited by Walter van de Putte. New York, Catholic Book Pub. Co. [1956] 1024p. illus. (part col.) 17cm. 473p. illus. 16cm. [BX2015.A4 1956] 57-4839
I. Van de Co. [1953 II. Hoever, Hugo Henry III. Title. IV. Title: Daiy missal for Catholic schools.

CATHOLIC Church. Liturgy 264.025
and ritual. Missal. English.
Saint Pius x daily missal for Catholic schools; according to the most recent decrees on the simplification of rubrics and the new Holy Week liturgy. Confraternity version of the Epistles and Gospels. Edited by Walter van de Putte. [School ed.] New York, Catholic Book Pub. Co. [1956] 1024p. illus. (part col.) 17cm. [BX2015.A4 1956] 57-4839
I. Van de Putte, Walter, ed. II. Catholic Church. Liturgy and ritual. English. III. Title. IV. Title: Daily missal for Catholic schools.

CATHOLIC Church. Liturgy 264.025
and ritual. Missel. English.
Saint andrew daily missal, by Gaspar Lefebvre. Saint Paul, E. M. Lohmann Co. [1953] xxiv, 1143p. illus., maps. 16cm. [BX2015.A4L4 1953] 53-38200
I. Catholic Church. Liturgy and ritual. English. II. Lefebvrer, Gaspar, 1880- III. Title.

CATHOLIC Church. Liturgy 264.025
and ritual. Pontifical. Ritus ordinum.
The ordination of a subdeacon, a deacon, a priest: the Latin text for the ceremonies of the ordination with a translation into English. [Rev. and expanded] Paterson, N.J., St. Anthony Guild Press [1959] 76p. il. 19cm. 59-65131 .50 pap.,
I. Title.

CATHOLIC Church. Liturgy 264.025
and ritual. Ritual.
Parish ritual, designed to aid parish priests in the regular exercise of the pastoral ministry. Consisting of rites and ceremonies taken from the latest editions of the Collectio rituum and the Rituale Romanum. Supplemented by lawful customary usages proper to the United States. Edited by Frederick R. McManus in association with Bede Babo. New York, Benziger Bros. [1962] 314 p. 21 cm. Latin and English. [BX2035.A2 1962] 63-1087
I. McManus, Frederick Richard, 1923- ed. II. Catholic Church. Liturgy and ritual. English. III. Title.

CATHOLIC Church. Liturgy 264.025
Putie, Walter, ed.
The Sunday missal; the Masses for illus. New York, Benziger Bros. [c1953,54 708p. illus. 15cm. [BD2015.A4L35 1953] 56-339
1. asses and ceremonies for the Forty Hours, in comformity Kelly, with Mass pictures according to te liturgy, and other aLassance(Francis Xavier, 1860-1946, I. Catholic Church. Liturgy and Ritual. Sunday and principal feasts, the Masses for the dead with burial service, the nuptial Mass and marriage service and the English. with the Vatican typical edition of the Missale Romanum (the book used by the priest when saying Massp By F. X. Lasance. With supplement 'Read Mass with the priest' (a study plan) by W. R. and ritual. Missal. English. II. Catholic Church. Liturgy and ritual. English. III. Title.

CATHOLIC Church. Syrian 264.025
rite. Liturgy and ritual. Kthobe Dkhourobo. English.
The Holy Mass according to the the Syrian rite of Antioch, with Anaphora of the Twelve Apostles. Translated into English by Joseph Redlinger. Issued by Andrew C. Shashy for the benefit of Syrians of Oriental rites. Jacksonville, Fla., 1955. 50p. illus., port. 16cm. 'The prayers and responses of the congregation are in Syriac rendered in Roman letters.' [BX1995.S9A26] 55-5779
I. Redinger, Joseph, 1875- ed. and tr. II. Title.

THE Catholic family book 264.025
of novenas. New York, J. J. Crawley, 1956. o71p. illus. 16cm. [BX2170,N7C3] 57-18418
1. Novenas.

CECILIA, Sister, 1892- 264.025
Companion to the missal for Sundays and principal feasts. Milwaukee, Bruce Pub. Co. [1954] 456p. illus. 18cm. [BX2015.C4] 54-10663
1. Catholic Church. Liturgy and ritual. Missal. 2. Church year. I. Title.

CHERY, Henri Charles. 264.025
What is the Mass! By A. [i. e. Henri Charles] Chery. Translated by Lancelot C. Sheppard. 1st ed.] Westminster, Md., Newman Press, 1952. 104 p. 19 cm. Includes bibliography. [BX2230.C527] 52-10598
1. Mass. I. Title.

CRAWLEY-BOEVEY, Mateo, 264.025
1875-1960.
Jesus, King of Love. 5th ed., rev. and enl. Pulaski, Wis., Franciscan Publishers [1963] 318 p. 20 cm. Translation of Versle Roi d'amour. [BX2157.C75 1963] 63-10258
1. Sacred Heart, Devotion to. I. Title.

CRAWLEY-BOEVEY, Mateo, 264.025
1875-1960
Jesus, King of Love [Tr. from French] 5th ed., rev. and enl. Pulaski, Wis., Franciscan [c.1963] 318p. 20cm 63-10258 2.50; 1.25 pap.,
1. Sacred Heart, Devotion to. I. Title.

CROEGAERT, August [Jan 264.025
Marie Josef]
The Mass; a liturgical commentary. Vol. II, the Mass of the faithful [Abridged translation from the French by J. Holland Smith] Westminster, Md., Newman Press [1959. i.e., 1960] ix, 311p. 23cm. (bibl. footnotes) 50-1093 4.75bds.,
1. Catholic Church. Liturgy and ritual. Missal. 2. Mass. 3. Lord's Supper (Liturgy) I. Title.

DANIELOU, Jean. 264.025
The Bible and the liturgy. Notre Dame, Ind., University of Notre Dame Press [1956] 372p. 24cm. (University of Notre Dame. Liturgical studies. v. 3) Includes bibliography. [BX1970.D312] 55-9516
1. Catholic Church. Liturgy and ritual. 2. Sacraments (Liturgy) 3. Sacraments—History of doctrines. 4. Typology (Theology) I. Title.

ELLARD, Gerald, 1894- 264.025
Christian life and workship. Illus. by Ade' de Bethune. [Rev. and enl.] Milwaukee, Bruce Pub. Co. [1953] 426p. illus. 24cm. cScience and culture series) [BX2200.E6 1953] 53-4356
*1. Sacraments (Liturgy) 2. Catholic Church. Liturgy and ritual. 3. Christian life—*catholic authors. I. Title.*

ELLARD, Gerald, 1894- 264.025
Christian life and worship. Illus. by Ade' De Bethune. [Rev. and enl.] Milwaukee, Bruce Pub. Co. [1956] 432p. illus. 24cm. [BX2200.E6 1956] 56-58823
1. Sacraments (Liturgy) 2. Catholic Church. Liturgy and ritual. 3. Christian life—Catholic authors. I. Title.

ELLARD, Gerald, 1894- 264.025
Christian life and worship. Illus. by Ade De Bethune. [Rev. and enl.] Milwaukee, Bruce [1950] xxi, 418 p. illus. 24 cm. (Science and culture series) Includes bibliographies. [BX2200.E6 1950] 51-788
1. Sacraments (Liturgy) 2. Catholic Church. Liturgy and ritual. 3. Christian life—Catholic authors. I. Title.

FREBURGER, William J. 264'.025
Eucharistic prayers for children : with 20 suggested liturgies / William J. Freburger and James E. Haas. Notre Dame, Ind. : Ave Maria Press, c1976. 88 p. ; 26 cm. Bibliography: p. 83-88. [BX2169.F73] 75-39414 ISBN 0-87793-109-7 pbk. : 2.25
1. Children—Prayer-books and devotions—English. 2. Eucharistic prayers. 3. Worship (Religious education) I. Haas, James E., joint author. II. Title.

FREBURGER, William J. 264'.025
The forgiving Christ : a book of penitential celebrations / William J. Freburger, James E. Haas. Notre Dame, Ind. : Ave Maria Press, c1977. 128 p. : ill. ; 23 cm. Includes bibliographical references. [BX2265.2.F7] 76-50442 ISBN 0-87793-125-9 pbk. : 2.95
1. Confession (Liturgy) I. Haas, James E., joint author. II. Title.

FREBURGER, William J. 264'.025
The forgiving Christ : a book of penitential celebrations / William J. Freburger, James E. Haas. Notre Dame, Ind. : Ave Maria Press, c1977. 128 p. : ill. ; 23 cm. Includes bibliographical references. [BX2265.2.F7] 76-50442 ISBN 0-87793-125-9 pbk. : 2.95
1. Confession (Liturgy) I. Haas, James E., joint author. II. Title.

FRENAY, Adolph Dominic, 264.025
1889-
The spirituality of the Mass; in the light of Thomistic theology. Abbreviated ed. St. Paul Ed. [dist. Boston, Daughters of St. Paul, c.1963] 294p. 22cm. 63-21392 3.50; 2.50 pap.,
1. Mass. I. Title.

FRENAY, Adolph Dominic, 264.025
1889-
The spirituality of the Mass in the light of Thomistic theology. St. Louis, Herder, 1952. 296 p. 22 cm. [BX2230.F73] 52-10737
1. Mass. I. Title.

FRENAY, Adolph Dominic, 264.025
1889-
The Spirituality of the Mass in the light of Thomistic theology. Abbreviated ed. [Boston] St. Paul Editions [1963] 294 p. 22 cm. [BX2230.F73 1963] 63-21392
1. Mass. I. Title.

GEARON, Patrick J., D. D. 264.025
The little office of the immaculate conception, with explanation. Downers Grove, Ill., Cass Ave. N. at Route 66 Carmelite Third Order, [1962] 89p. 15cm. .60 pap.,
I. Title.

THE Greatest prayer: 264.025
the Mass. Rev. for use in the new liturgy. Milwaukee, Bruce Pub. Co. [1965] 64 p. illus. 13 cm. [BX2169.G7] 66-795
1. Mass—Prayer-books and devotions.

GUARDINI, Romano, 1885- 264.025
Meditations before Mass; translated from the German by Elinor Castendyk Briefs. Westminster, Md., Newman Press, 1955. 203p. 21cm. Translation of Besinnung vor der Feler der heiligen Messe. [BX2169 g83] 55-10550
1. Mass— Meditations. I. Title.

HOWELL, Clifford, 1902- 264.025
The Mass commentator's handbook. Collegeville, Minn., Liturgical Press [1960] 176p. 22cm. [BX2230.2.H6] 60-37443
1. Mass. I. Title.

JUNGMANN, Josef Andreas, 1889- 264.025
The Mass of the Roman rite: its origins and development (Missarum sollemnia) Translated by Francis A. Brunner. New York, Benziger [1951- v. 25 cm. Bibliography: v. 1, p. x-xvi. [BX2230.J814] 51-4097
1. Mass. 2. Lord's Supper (Liturgy) 3. Catholic Church. Liturgy and ritual. Missal. I. Title.

JUNGMANN, Josef Andreas, 1889- 264.025
The Mass of the Roman rite: its origins and development (Missarum sollemnia) Translated by Francis A. Brunner. New York, Benziger [1951-55] 2v. 25cm. Includes bibliographical references. [BX2230.J814] 51-4097
1. Mass. 2. Lord's Supper (Liturgy) 3. Catholic Church. Liturgy and ritual. Missal. I. Title.

JUNGMANN, Josef Andreas, 1889- 264.025
The Mass of the Roman rite, its origins and development (Missarum sollemnia) Translated by Francis A. Brunner. Rev. by Charles K. Riepe. New rev. and abridged ed. New York, Benziger Bros. [c1961] 567p. 26cm. Includes bibliography. [BX2230.J8142 1962] 62-1137
1. Mass. 2. Lord's Supper (Liturgy) 3. Catholic Church. Liturgy and ritual. Missal. I. Title.

JUNGMANN, Josef Andreas, 1889- 264.025
The Mass of the Roman rite, its origins and development (Missarum sollemnia) Translated by Francis A. Brunner. Rev. by Charles K. Riepe. New rev. and abridged ed. New York, Benziger Bros. [1959] [16]. 567p. 26cm. Bibliography: 11th-12th prelim. pages. [BX2230.J8142] 59-10312
1. Mass. 2. Lord's Supper (Liturgy) 3. Catholic Church. Liturgy and ritual. Missal. I. Title.

KOROLEVSKY, Cyril. 264.025
Living languages in Catholic worship; an historical inquiry. Translated by Donald Attwater. Westminster, Md., Newman Press [1957] 195p. 23cm. [BX1970.K612] 57-11822
1. Liturgical language. I. Title.

LAFERRIERE, M. 264.025
New & eternal testament. Tr. [from French] by Roger Capel. Foreword by C. C. Martindale. Westminster, Md., Newman Press [c.]1961. 287p. 61-8970 3.95
1. Mass. 2. Lord's Supper (Liturgy) I. Title.

LINGS, Albert Ad. 1915. 264.025
Our favorite novenas prayerbook; includes indulgenced novenas and prayers from The raccolta, the book of indulgenced prayers authorized by the Sovereign Pontiff. New York, Benziger Bros. [1956] x, 569p. 17cm. [BX2170.N7L52] 59-33497
1. Novenas. 2. Indulgences. I. Title.

LOHR, Aemiliana. 264.025
The Mass through the year. Translated by I. T. Hale. Foreword by Damasus Winzen. London, Longmans, Green Westminster, Md., Newman Press [1958-59] 2v. 23cm. Translation of Jahr des Herrn. Contents.v.1.Advent to Palm Sunday.--v.2. Holy Week to the last Sunday after Pentecost. [BX2184.L622] 59-338
1. Church year—Meditations. I. Title.

LORD, Daniel Aloysius, 1888- 264.025
Christ in me; prayer book for Communion Mass. Milwaukee, Bruce [1952] 319 p. 16 cm. [BX2169.L58] 52-27189
1. Mass—Prayer-books and devotions—English. 2. Catholic Church—Prayer books and devotions—English. I. Title.

MCCORRY, Vincent P., 1909- 264.025
It is His own blood. Milwaukee, Bruce [c.1962] 157 p. 22 cm. 62-16838 3.75
1. Lord's Supper—Catholic Church. I. Title.

MARY MAGDELA, Sister 264.025
Welcome Jesus Missal. Pictures by Paul and Patricia Karch. Milwaukee, Bruce [c.1962] 160p. col. illus. 14cm. 1.75; 2.50 bds., lib. ed.,
1. Children—Prayer-books and devotions—English. 2. Catholic Church—Prayer-books and devotions—English. I. Title.

MUNSTER, Ludwig. 264.025
Christ in His consecrated virgins; the marriage of the Lamb. Translators: Basil Stegmann [and] Sister M. Margretta. Collegeville, Minn., Liturgical Press, St. John's Abbey [1957] 140p. 19cm. Translation of Hochzelt des Lammes. [BX2305.M813] 58-1888
1. Consecration of virgins. I. Title.

MURPHY, John L 1924- 264.025
The Mass and liturgical reform. Milwaukee, Bruce Pub. Co. [1956] 340p. 23cm. [BX2230.M8] 56-9648
1. Mass. 2. Catholic Church. Liturgy and ritual. Missal. I. Title.

O'CONNELL, John Berthram, 1888- 264.025
The celebration of Mass; a study of the rubrics of the Roman missal. New ed. rev. throughout. Milwaukee, Bruce Pub. Co. [1959] 715p. illus. 24cm. Includes bibliography. [BX2230.O36 1959] 60-459
1. Mass. 2. Catholic Church. Liturgy and ritual. Missal. I. Title.

O'CONNELL, John Berthram, 1888- 264.025
The celebration of Mass; a study of the rubrics of the Roman missal. New ed., rev. throughout. Milwaukee, Bruce Pub. Co. [1956] xviii, 698p. illus. 24cm. Bibliography: p. 689-691. [BX2230.O36 1956] 56-58809
1. Mass. 2. Catholic Church. Liturgy and ritual. Missal. I. Title.

PARIS. Saint-Severin (Church) Clergy. 264.025
The Mass: Christians around the altar, by the community of Saint- Severin. Translated by Margaret Clark. Chicago, Fides Publishers Association [1958] 155p. 20cm. [BX2230.P2513] 58-4707
1. Mass. I. Title.

PARSCH, Pius, 1884- 264.025
Know and live the Mass; a popular explanation of the Holy Sacrifice of the Mass. Translated by Palmer L. Rockey. New York, Catholic Book Pub. Co. [1952] 207p. illus. 16cm. Translation of Lernet die Messe verstehen. [BX2230.P343] 53-607
1. Mass. I. Title.

PARSCH, Pius, 1884- 264.025
The liturgy of the Mass. 3d ed. translated and adapted by H. E. Winstone. Introd. by Clifford Howell. London, St. Louis, B. Herder [c1957] 344p. illus. 23cm. Includes bibliography. [BX2230.P32 1957] 58-482
1. Mass. 2. Catholic Church. Liturgy and ritual. Missal. I. Title.

PLASSMANN, Thomas Bernard, 1879- 264.02'5
From Sunday to Sunday; an interpretation according to the approved vernacular of the Proper of the Mass that seeks to place the venerable liturgy in modern focus, by Thomas Plassmann. [Rev. ed.] Paterson, N.J., St. Anthony Guile Press [1966] vii, 406 p. 19 cm. (Franciscan Institute series v: Spirit and life) [BX2015.P58 1966] 68-323
1. Catholic Church. Liturgy and ritual. Missal. I. Title. II. Series: St. Bonaventure University, St. Bonaventure, N. Y. Franciscan Institute III. Series v: Spirit and life)

PLASSMANN, Thomas Bernard, 1879- 264.02'5
From Sunday to Sunday; an interpretation according to the approved vernacular of the Proper of the Mass that seeks to place the venerable liturgy in modern focus, by Thomas Plassmann. [Rev. ed.] Paterson, N.J., St. Anthony Guild Press [1966] vii, 406 p. 19 cm. (Franciscan Institute series V: Spirit and life) [BX2015.P58 1966] 68-323
1. Catholic Church. Liturgy and ritual. Missal. I. Title. II. Series: St. Bonaventure University, St. Bonaventure, N.Y. Franciscan Institute. Series V: Spirit and life

REINHOLD, Hans Ansgar 264.025
Bringing the Mass to the people, With an introd. by Frederick R. McManus. Baltimore, Helicon Press [c.1960] 114p. 23cm. (Bibl. footnotes) illus. 60-13781 2.95
1. Mass. 2. Catholic Church. Liturgy and ritual. Missal. I. Title.

REINHOLD, Hans Ansgar, 1897- 264.025
Bringing the Mass to the people. With an introd. by Frederick R. McManus. Baltimore, Helicon Press [1960] 114p. illus. 23cm. Includes bibliography. [BX2230.2.R4] 60-13781
1. Mass. 2. Catholic Church. Liturgy and ritual. Missal. I. Title.

ROSS, Williamson, Hugh, 1901- 264.025
The great prayer: concerning the Canon of the Mass. New York, Macmillan, 1956. 164p. 22cm. [BX2015.R6] 56-9364
1. Catholic Church. Liturgy and ritual. Canon of the Mass. 2. Mass. I. Title.

ROSS WILLIAMSON, Hugh, 1901- 264.025
The great prayer: concerning the Canon of the Mass. New York, Macmillan, 1956. 164p. 22cm. [BX2015.R6] 56-9364
1. Catholic Church. Liturgy and ritual. Canon of the Mass. 2. Mass. I. Title.

SCHLITZER, Albert L., 1902- 264.025
The prayer-life of the church. Foreword by Leo A. Pursley. Notre Dame, Ind., Univ. of Notre Dame Pr. [c.]1962 134p. 22cm. Bibl. 62-13610 3.50
1. Mass. 2. Priests. 3. Prayer. I. Title.

SCHMITZ, Walter J 264.025
Learning the Mass; manual for seminarians. Rev. according to the latest decrees of the Sacred Congregation of Rites. Milwaukee, Bruce Pub. Co. [1962] 63 p. 26 cm. [BX2230.8.S3] 62-20565
1. Mass—Celebration. I. Title.

SCHNITZLER, Theodor. 264.025
The Mass in meditation. Translated by Rudolph Kraus. St. Louis, Herder [1959-60] 2v. 21cm. [BX2230.S3413] 59-10354
1. Mass. I. Title.

SCHULTE, Augustine Joseph, 1856- 264.025
Consecranda; the rite observed in some of the principal functions of the Roman pontifical and the Roman ritual. New ed. fully rev. and with some additions by J. B. O'Connell. New York, Benziger Bros. [1956] 246p. illus. 22cm. [BX2302.S35 1956] 56-2584
1. Church dedication. I. Catholic Church. Liturgy and ritual. Pontifical. II. Title.

SCHULTE, Augustine Joseph, 1856- 264.025
Consecranda: the rite observed in some of the principal functions of the Roman pontifical and the Roman ritual. New ed. fully rev. and with some additions by J. B. O'Connell. New York, Benziger Bros. [1956] 246p. illus. 22cm. [BX2302.S35 1956] 56-2584
1. Church dedication. I. Catholic Church. Liturgy and ritual. Pontifical. II. Title.

SHEEN, Fulton John, Bp., 1895- 264.025
These are the sacraments, as described by Fulton J. Sheen, as photographed by Yousuf Karsh. New York, Hawthorn Books [1962] 159 p. illus. 26 cm. [BX2200.S46] 62-9037
1. Sacraments—Catholic Church. I. Karsh, Yousuf, 1908- illus. II. Title.

SHEEN, Fulton John, Bp., 1895- 264.025
These are the sacraments, as described by Fulton J. Sheen, as photographed by Yousuf Karsh. New York, Hawthorn [c.1962] 159p. illus. (pt. col.) 26cm. 62-9037 4.95 bds.,
1. Sacraments—Catholic Church. I. Karsh, Yousuf, 1908- illus. II. Title.

SHEEN, Fulton John, Bp., 1895- 264.025
These are the sacraments, as described by Fulton J. Sheen, as photographed by Yousuf Karsh. Garden City, N. Y., Doubleday [1964, c.1962] 196p. illus. 19cm. (Image bk., D174) .95 pap.,
1. Sacraments—Catholic Church. I. Karsh, Yousuf, 1908—illus. II. Title.

SHEPPARD, Lancelot Capel 1906- 264.025
The liturgical books. [1st ed.?? New York, Hawthorn Books [1962] 112 p. 21 cm. (Twentieth century encyclopedia of Cathollcism, v. 109. Section 10: The worship of the church) [BX1970.S47] 62-21421
1. Catholic Church. Liturgy and ritual — Hist. I. Title.

SHEPPARD, Lancelot Capel, 1906- 264.025
The liturgical books. New York, Hawthorn [c.1962] 112p. 21cm. (Twentieth century ency.. of Catholicism, v.109. Section 10: The worship of the church) Bibl. 62-21421 3.50 bds.,
1. Catholic Church. Liturgy and ritual—Hist. I. Title.

SHEPPARD, Lancelot Capel, 1906- 264.025
The Mass in the West. [1st ed.,] New York, Hawthorn Books [1962] 109 p. 21 cm. (The twentieth century encyclopedia of Catholicism, v. 111. Section 10: The worship of the church) Includes bibliography. [BX1995.A1S5] 62-12212
1. Lord's Supper (Liturgy) 2. Catholic Church. Liturgy and ritual. Missal. I. Title.

SHEPPARD, Lancelot Capel, 1906- 264.025
The Mass in the West. New York, Hawthorn [c.1962] 109p. (Twentieth cent. ency. of Catholicism, v. 111. Sec. 10: The worship of the church) Bibl. 62-12212 3.50 bds.,
1. Lord's Supper (Liturgy) 2. Catholic Church. Liturgy and ritual. Missal. I. Title.

VAGAGGINI, Cipriano, 1909- 264.02'5
The canon of the Mass and liturgical reform. Translation editor: Peter Coughlan. Staten Island, N.Y., Alba House [1967] 200 p. 23 cm. "The present Roman canon" (in Latin and English): p. 34-39. Bibliographical footnotes. [BX2015.6.V313] 67-9310
1. Catholic Church. Liturgy and ritual. Eucharistic prayer I. I. Catholic Church. Liturgy and ritual. Eucharistic prayer I. English & Latin. 1967. II. Title.

HOLASH, Lise M 264.02'5'07
To the house of the Lord, by Lise M. Holash. New York, Paulist Press [1967-] v. 21 cm. v. 21 cm. Parent-teacher initiation, by John T. Doherty, Thierry Maertens [and] Lise M. Holash. Foreword by Vincent M. Novak. New York, [BX1970.H64] 67-28694
1. Catholic Church. Liturgy and ritual—Study and teaching. I. Doherty, John T. II. Maertens, Thierry, 1921- III. Title.

HOLASH, Lise M. 264.02'5'07
To the house of the Lord, by Lise M. Holash. New York, Paulist Press [1967- v. 21 cm. [BX1970.H64] 67-28694
1. Catholic Church. Liturgy and ritual—Study and teaching. I. Doherty, John T. II. Maertens, Thierry, 1921- III. Title.

BIBLE. N. T. Epistles and Gospels, Liturgical. English. 1951. Confraternity version. 264.026
The Epistles and Gospels for pulpit use on Sundays and holy days. Confraternity of Christian Doctrine text. New York, Catholic Book Pub. Co. [1951] 192p. 22cm. [BX2003.A4 1951] 51-6155
I. Title.

CATHOLIC Church. Liturgy and ritual. Lectionary. 264.026
Lectionary of the Roman missal, containing the text for all Epistles, intervening chants, and Gospels as approved for liturgical use by the territorial hierarchy of the United States of America, together with suggested forms for the prayer of the faithful. Collegeville, Minn., 56321, Liturgical Pr. St. John's Abbey [1965] 888p. 24cm. Passages from Sacred Scripture are from the Confraternity of Christian Doctrine version [BX2003.A4] 65-2993 price unreported
I. Bible. N. T. Epistles and Gospels, Liturgical. English. 1965. Confraternity version. II. Title.

CATHOLIC Church. Liturgy and ritual. Lectionary. English. 264.026
Lectionary of the Roman missal, containing the text for all Epistles, intervening chants, and Gospels as approved for liturgical use by the territorial hierarchy of the United States of America, together with suggested forms for the prayer of the faithful. Collegeville, Minn., Liturgical Press [1965] 888 p. 24 cm. The passages from Sacred Scripture are from the Confraternity of Christian Doctrine version. [BX2003.A4 1965] 65-2993
I. Catholic Church. Liturgy and ritual. English. II. Bible. N. T. Epistles and Gospels, Liturgical. English. 1965. Confraternity version. III. Title.

O'SULLIVAN, Kevin. 264.026
My Sunday reading; a popular explanation and application of the Sunday Epistles and Gospels. Milwaukee, Bruce Pub. Co. [1957] 345p. 23cm. [BS2547.A3O8] 57-13119
1. Bible. N. T. Epistles and Gospels, Liturgical—Commentaries. I. Title.

THOMAS Aquinas, Saint, 1225?-1274. 264.026
Sermon matter from St. Thomas Aquinas on the Epistles and Gospels of the Sundays and feast days (Advent to Easter) By C. J. Callan. St. Louis, Herder, 1950. vii, 311 p. 25 cm. "The liturgical texts ... are from the ... Dousy-Challoner version." [BX2003.T5] 50-12334
1. Bible. N. T. Epistles and Gospels, Liturgical — Commentaries. I. Bible. N. T. Epistles and Gospels, Liturgical. English. 1950. Douai. II. Callan, Charles Jerome, Father, 1877- ed. III. Title.

HAMMAN, Adalbert, 1910- ed. 264.02'72
The paschal mystery; ancient liturgies and patristic texts. Editor: A. Hamman. English editorial supervisor: Thomas Halton. [Translated by Thomas Halton] Staten Island, N.Y., Alba House [1969] 230 p. 22 cm. (Alba patristic library, 3) Translation of Le mystere de Paques. Bibliography: p. [225]-227. [BV55.H313] 78-77646 4.95
1. Paschal mystery.

PINSK, Johannes, 1891-1957. 264.0274
Cycle of Christ: the mass texts interpreted in the spirit of the liturgy. Translated by Arthur Gibson. Foreword by Martin B. Hellriegel. New York, Desclee Co. [1966] xxi, 226 p. 22 cm. Translation of Gedanken zum Herrenjahr. [BX2170.C55P5] 66-19225
1. Church year—Meditations. I. Title.

CATHOLIC Church. Liturgy and ritual. Psalter. 264.028
Novum Psalterium Pii XII. An unfinished folio edition of Brother Antoninus, O. P. Los Angeles, 1955. xxviii, 76p. 40cm. 'Number 9 of 48 copies each containing 72 pages [psalmus I-LIII] ... printed by Brother Antoninus, O. P. Preliminary pages printed by Saul & Lillian Marks at the Plantin Press, Los Angeles.' Issued in a case. [BX2033.A2 1955] 57-23831
I. Antonimus, Brother, 1912- II. Bible. C. T. Psalms. Latin. 1955. III. Title.

CATHOLIC Church. Liturgy and ritual. Psalter (Salisbury psalter) 264.028
The Salisbury psalter, edited from Salisbury Cathedral ms. 150 by Celia Sisam and Kenneth Sisam. London, New York, Published for the Early English Text Society by Oxford University Press, 1959. xi, 312p. facsim. 23cm. (Early English Text Society. [Publications] no. 242) Latin, with Old English interlinear translation. Bibliography: p. [ix]-xi. Bibliographical footnotes. [PR1119.A2 no.242] 59-2087
I. Sisam, Celia, ed. II. Sisam, Kenneth, ed. III. Title. IV. Series.

CATHOLIC church. Liturgy and ritual. Psalter (Vespasian psalter) 264.02'8
The Vespasian Psalter. British Museum, Cotton Vespasian A. I. Ed. by David H. Wright. With a contribution on the gloss by Alistair Campbell. Copenhagen, Rosenkilde & Bagger, 1967. Dist. in the U. S. by Hopkins, Baltimore. 101p. facsim. 320p. 7 plates. 38cm. (Early English mss. in facsim., v. 14) [BX2033.A4 1967] 67-101955 326.00; 305.00 pap.,
I. Wright, David Herndon. ed. II. Bible. O. T. Psalms. English (Middle English) Paraphrases. 1967. III. British Museum. MSS. (Cottonian Vespasian A 1) IV. Title. V. Series.

KONUS, William J 264.028
Dictionary of the New Latin Psalter of Pope Pius XII Westminster. Md., Newman Press, 1959. 132p. 20cm. [BX2033.K6] 59-9407
1. Bible. O. T. Psalms. Latin—Glossaries, vocabularies, etc. 2. Catholic Church. Liturgy and ritual. Psalter— Glossaries, vocabularies, etc. 3. Latin language—Glossaries, vocabularies, etc. I. Title.

APPLETON, George, Abp., comp. 264.03
Acts of devotion [2d rev. ed.] Richmond, Va., Knox [1965, c.1963] ix, 78p. 19cm. (Chime paperback) First ed., comp. by F. W. Dwelly, pub. in 1928 in London under the same title [BV4805.A7] 65-10795 1.00 pap.,
1. Devotional exercises. I. Dwelly, Frederick William, 1881- Acts of devotion. II. Title.

BABIN, David E. 264.03
Introduction to the liturgy of the Lord's Supper, by David E. Babin. New York, Morehouse-Barlow Co. [1968] 96 p. 19 cm. [BX5949.C5B25] 68-19700
1. Protestant Episcopal Church in the U.S.A. Book of common prayer. Communion service. 2. Lord's Supper (Liturgy) I. Title.

BUCHANAN, Colin Ogilvie. 264.03
Modern Anglican liturgies 1958-1968; ed. by Colin O. Buchanan. London, New York, Oxford Univ. Pr., 1968. xix, 388p. 2 fold. plates. 23cm. [BV825.5.B8] 68-123240 8.75
1. Lord's Supper (Liturgy) 2. Lord's Supper—Anglican Communion. I. Title.

BUTTERWORTH, Charles C 1894- 264.03
The English primers, 1529-1545; their publication and connection with the English Bible and the Reformation in England Philadelphia, University of Pennsylvania Press, 1953. xiii, 340p. facsims. 24cm. Bibliography: p. 305-325. [BV4818.B85] 53-7051
1. Primers (Prayer-books) 2. Bible. English—Hist. 3. Reformation—England. I. Title.

BUTTERWORTH, Charles C., 1894-1957. 264.03
The English primers (1529-1545): their publication and connection with the English Bible and the Reformation in England. New York, Octagon Books, 1971 [c1953] xiii, 340 p. facsims. 24 cm. Bibliography: p. 305-325. [BV4818.B85 1971] 72-120240
1. Bible. English—History. 2. Primers (Prayer-books) 3. Reformation—England. I. Title.

CATHOLIC Church. Liturgy and ritual. 264'.03
The ancient liturgy of the Church of England, according to the uses of Sarum, York, Hereford, and Bangor, and the Roman liturgy arranged in parallel columns with preface and notes, by William Maskell. 3d ed. Oxford, Clarendon Press, 1882. [New York, AMS Press, 1973] lxxxiv, 338 p. 23 cm. Appendix (p. [279]-333):—Liturgia S. Clementis.—The Order of the Communion, 1548.—The Supper of the Lorde, 1549. [BX5141.A1M3 1973] 71-172848 ISBN 0-404-04196-5 18.00
I. Maskell, William, 1814?-1890. II. Church of England. Book of common prayer. Communion service. The Order of the Communion. 1973. III. Church of England. Book of common prayer. Communion service. The Supper of the Lorde, and the Holy Communion, commonly called the Masse. 1973. IV. [Ordinary of the Mass] V. Title.

CHURCH of England. Book of common prayer. 264'.03
The Book of common prayer, 1559 : the Elizabethan prayer book / edited by John E. Booty. Charlottesville : Published for the Folger Shakespeare Library by the University Press of Virginia, 1976. x, 427 p. ; 23 cm. ([Folger documents of Tudor and Stuart civilization ; no. 22]) Includes index. Bibliography: p. 417-419. [BX5145.A4 1559b] 75-29330 ISBN 0-8139-0503-6 : 15.00 ISBN 0-8139-0696-2 pbk. : 5.95
I. Booty, John E. II. Title. III. Series.

CHURCH of St. Stephen and the Incarnation, Washington, D.C. 264'.03
Celebrations of life. Created by: St. Stephen & the Incarnation. Edited by: Loren B. Mead. Authors & designers: Bibsy Bates [and others] New York, Seabury Press [1974] 182 p. illus. 28 cm. "A Crossroad book." [BX5940.C45 1974] 73-21869 ISBN 0-8164-2092-0 5.95 (pbk.)
1. Liturgies. I. Mead, Loren B., ed. II. Bates, Bibsy. III. Title.

DAVIES, Michael. 264'.03
Cranmer's godly order / Michael Davies. New Rochelle, N.Y. : Arlington House, c1976. p. cm. (His Liturgical revolution ; v. 1) [BV193.G7D38 1976] 77-4266 ISBN 0-87000-395-X : 7.95 (v. 1)
1. Catholic Church. Liturgy and ritual—England—History. 2. Church of England. Liturgy and ritual—History. 3. Cranmer, Thomas, Abp. of Canterbury, 1489-1556. 4. Liturgics—History. I. Title. II. Series.

DEARMER, Percy, 1867-1936 264.03
The parson's handbook; practical directions both for parsons and others according to the Anglican use, as set forth in the Book of common prayer, on the basis of the twelfth edition. 13th ed. New York, Oxford [c.]1965. xx, 192p. illus. 19cm. [BX5141.D38] 4.00
1. Church of England. Liturgy and ritual. 2. Theology, Pastoral—Handbooks, manuals, etc. 3. Theology, Pastoral—Anglican communion. 4. Church vestments. I. Title.

GIFFORD, Frank Dean, 1891- 264.03
The Christian way; a book of instructions and devotions for members of the Episcopal Church. New York, Morehouse-Barlow [c.1961] 136p. 61-12880 2.50; 1.50 pap.,
1. Protestant Episcopal Church in the U.S.A.—Prayer books and devotions. I. Title.

HOOKER, Richard, 1553or4-1600. 264.03
Hooker's theology of common prayer; the fifth book of the Polity paraphrased and expanded into a commentary on the prayer book [by] John S. Marshall. Sewanee, Tenn., University Press at the University of the South, 1956. viii, 186p. 25cm. [BX5145.H64] 56-2695
1. Church of England. Book of common prayer. I. Marshall, John Sedberry, 1898- II. Title.

HOOKER, Richard, 1553or4-1600. 264.03
Hooker's theology of common prayer; the fifth book of the Polity paprahrased and expanded into a commentary on the prayer book [by] John S. Marshall. Sewanee, Tenn., University Press at the University of the South, 1956. viii, 186p. 25cm. [BX5145.H64] 56-2695
1. Church of England, Book of common prayer. I. Marshall, John Sedberry, 1898- II. Title.

*HULL, Eleanor 264.03
Let us worship God, by Eleanor Hull, Elinor G. Galusha, Sarah D. Schear. Illus. by Shirley Hirsch. Philadelphia, United Church Pr. [c.1964] 76p. illus. 22cm. (JH 1-3) 1.15 pap.,
I. Title.

JOHNSON, Frederick A., 1909- 264.03
Brief topical index of the Book of common prayer [by Frederick A. Johnson. Morristown, N.J., 1968] 41 p. 22 cm. [BX5945.J565] 71-257080
1. Protestant Episcopal Church in the U.S.A. Book of common prayer—Indexes. I. Title.

LADD, William Palmer, 1870-1941. 264.03
Prayer book interleaves; some reflections on how the Book of common prayer might by made more influential in our English-speaking world. Foreword by Massey H. Shepherd. Jr. Greenwich, Conn., Seabury Press [c1957] 193p. 19cm. [BX5910.L27 1957] 58-386
1. Protestant Episcopal Church in the U. S. A. Liturgy and ritual. I. Title.

LUXTON, David W. 264.03
Action dramas for the young church, underteens presenting the Prayer Book, written by the Rev. David W. Luxton. [Hamilton, Ont.? 1967?] 35 p. illus., music. 22 cm. [BX5195.L8] 75-350253 unpriced
1. Church of England. Book of common prayer. I. Title.

PELL, Walden, 1902- 264.03
The religion of the prayer book; a course of study designed to review the faith and practice of the Book of common prayer, by Walden Pell, II, and P. M. Dawley. [2d ed.] New York, Morehouse-Gorham Co., 1950. vi, 232 p. 19 cm. Bibliography: p. 232. [BX5930.P4 1950] 50-12570
1. Protestant Episcopal Church in the U.S.A. — Doctrinal and controversial works. 2. Protestant Episcopal Church in the U.S.A. Book of common prayer. I. Dawley, Powel Mills, 1907- joint author. II. Title.

PREGNALL, William S., 1931- 264'.03
Laity and liturgy : a handbook for parish worship / William S. Pregnall. New York : Seabury Press, [1975] p. cm. "A Crossroad book." Includes bibliographical references. [BX5948.P73] 75-22482 ISBN 0-8164-2593-0 pbk. : 3.95
1. Protestant Episcopal Church in the U.S.A.—Prayer books and devotions—English. I. Title.

PRICE, Charles P., 1920- 264'.03
Introducing the proposed Book of common prayer / Charles P. Price. New York : Seabury Press, 1977, c1976. 121 p. ; 21 cm. "A Crossroad book." "Prepared at the request of the Standing Liturgical Commission." [BX5945.P74 1977] 77-6125 ISBN 0-8164-2171-4 pbk. : 1.75
1. Protestant Episcopal Church in the U.S.A. Book of common prayer. I. Protestant Episcopal Church in the U.S.A. Liturgical Commission. II. Title.

PROTESTANT Episcopal Church in the U. S. A. Book of common prayer. 264.03
The children's Book of common prayer, adapted by Virginia Cramp. Foreword by Elbert K. St. Claire. [1st ed.] New York, Exposition Press [1956] 89p. 21cm. (An Exposition-testament book) [BX5943.A4A3] 56-11585
I. Cramp, Virginia. II. Title.

PROTESTANT Episcopal Church in the U. S. A. Book of common prayer. 264.03
Our prayers and praise; the order for daily morning prayer and the order for the administration of the Lord's Supper or Holy Communion, with simplified rubrics and explanatory notes, together with notes on the church year and the collects to be used throughout the year. Illustrated by a Sister of the Community of the Holy Spirit. The notes on morning prayer and Holy Communion were prepared by Massey H. Shepherd, Jr., and Robert N. Rodenmayer. Greenwich, Conn., Seabury Press [1957] 108p. illus. 26cm. (The Seabury series, R-3) [BX5943.A1 1957] 57-8341
I. Shepherd, Massey Hamilton, 1913- ed. II. Title.

PROTESTANT Episcopal Church in the U. S. A. Book of common prayer. 264.03
The prayer book office, Anglican divine service; morning prayer and evening prayer according to the American book of common prayer. With additional invitatories, antiphons for seasons and feasts, the hymns and other enrichments. [Revision of 1963] New York, Morehouse-Barlow, 1963. ixxxvii, 658 p. 17 cm. [BX5943.A4P7] 63-14273
I. Title.

PROTESTANT Episcopal Church in the U. S. A. Liturgy and ritual. 264.03
The Book of offices; services for certain occasions not provided in the Book of common prayer. Compiled by the Standing Liturgical Commission, commended for use by General Convention. 3d ed. New York, Church Pension Fund, 1960. x, 106p. 18cm. [BX5947.B8A3 1960] 60-34864
1. Protestant Episcopal Church in the U. S. A. Liturgical Commission. I. Title.

PROTESTANT Episcopal Church in the U.S.A. Book of common prayer. 264.03
The Oxford American prayer book commentary, by Massey Hamilton Shepherd, Jr. New York, Oxford University Press, 1950. 1 v. (various pagings) 21 cm. Facsimile reproduction of the Book of common prayer [New York, Oxford University Press, 1944) with commentary on opposite pages. Includes bibliography. [BX5945.S5] 50-10192
1. Protestant Episcopal Church in the U.S.A. Book of common prayer. I. Shepherd, Massey Hamilton, 1913- II. Title.

PROTESTANT Episcopal Church in the U.S.A. Committee on the Observance of the Bicentennial. 264'.03
This Nation under God : a book of aids to worship in the bicentennial year 1976 / prepared by the Committee on the Observance of the Bicentennial, in cooperation with the Standing Liturgical Commission ; and recommended for use by the presiding Bishop and the President of the House of Deputies of the General Convention of the Episcopal Church in the United States of America. New York : Seabury Press, c1976. 64 p. ; 21 cm. [BV135.A45P76 1976] 76-378 ISBN 0-8164-7809-0 : 1.00
1. Protestant Episcopal Church in the U.S.A.—Prayer-books and devotions—English. 2. American Revolution Bicentennial, 1776-1976—Prayer-books and devotions—English. 3. Worship programs. I. Protestant Episcopal Church in the U.S.A. Liturgical Commission. II. Title.

PROTESTANT Episcopal Church in the U.S.A. Liturgical Commission. 264'.03
The draft proposed Book of Common Prayer and administration of the sacraments and other rites and ceremonies of the Church : according to the use of the Protestant Episcopal Church in the United States of America, otherwise known as the Episcopal Church, together with the Psalter or Psalms of David : presented to the General Convention of 1976 / by the Standing Liturgical Commission in compliance with the directions of the General Convention of 1973. New York : Church Hymnal Corp., 1976. 1001 p. ; 22 cm. [BX5945.A3 1976] 76-360414
1. Protestant Episcopal Church in the U.S.A. Book of Common Prayer. 2. Protestant Episcopal Church in the U.S.A. Liturgy and ritual. I. Protestant Episcopal Church in the U.S.A. Book of Common Prayer. II. Title: The draft proposed Book of Common Prayer.

PROTESTANT EPISCOPAL CHURCH IN THE U.S.A. BOOK OF COMMON PRAYER 264.03
The prayer book office, Anglican divine service; morning prayer and evening prayer according to the American book of common prayer. With additional invitatories, antiphons for seasons and feasts, the hymns and other enrichments [Revision of 1963] New York, Morehouse, 1963 [c.1944, 1963] lxxxvii, 658p. 17cm. 63-14273 10.95
I. Title.

ROACH, Corwin Carlyle, 1904- 264.03
For all sorts and conditions. Greenwich, Conn., Seabury Press, 1955. 215p. 21cm. [BX5945.R6] 55-6352
1. Protestant Episcopal Church in the U. S. A. Book of common prayer. I. Title.

SHEPHERD, Massey Hamilton, 1913- 264.03
The reform of liturgical worship: perspectives and prospects. New York, Oxford University Press. 1961. 118 p. 20 cm)The Bohein lectures, 1959) [BX5940.S52] 61-8376
1. Liturgical movement — Anglican communion. 2. Protestant Episcopal Church in the U.S.A. Book of common prayer. I. Title.

SHEPHERD, Massey Hamilton, 1913- 264.03
The reform of liturgical worship: perspectives and prospects. New York, Oxford Univ. Press [c.]1961. 118p. Bohlen lectures, 1959) 61-8376 3.00
1. Liturgical movement—Anglican communion. 2. Protestant Episcopal Church in the U. S. A. Book of common prayer. I. Title.

SHEPHERD, Massey Hamilton, 1913- 264.03
The worship of the church [by] Massey H. Shepherd Jr., with the assistance of the Authors' Committee of the Dept. of Christian Education of the Protestant Episcopal Church. Greenwich, Conn., Seabury Press, 1952. ix, 240 p. 22 cm. (The Church's teaching, v. 4) Bibliography: p. 213-236. [BX5945.S52] 52-13444
1. Protestant Episcopal Church in the U.S.A. Book of common prayer. 2. Public worship. I. Title. II. Series.

SIMCOX, Carroll Eugene, 1912- 264.03
The words of our worship; a study in prayer book meanings. Foreword by Horace W. B. Donegan. New York, Morehouse-Gorham,

1955. 239p. 21cm. (Bishop of New York books, 1955) [BX5945.S54] 55-7436
1. Protestant Episcopal Church in the U. S. A. Book of common prayer. 2. Theology—Terminology. I. Title.

VAUX, James Edward. 264'.03
Church folklore; a record of some post-Reformation usages in the English Church, now mostly obsolete, by J. Edward Vaux. [Folcroft, Pa.] Folcroft Library Editions, 1974. p. cm. Reprint of the 1894 ed. published by Griffith Farren, London. [BR136.G7V4 1974] 74-16217 ISBN 0-8414-9172-0 (lib. bdg.)
1. Great Britain—Religious life and customs. I. Title.

WELSBY, Paul A comp. 264.03
Services and prayers for country use. London(New York, Longmans, Green [1955] 99p. 18cm. [BX5147.R8W4] 57-32591
1. Liturgies. I. Church of England. Liturgy and ritual. II. Title.

CARDWELL, Edward, 1787-1861. 264.03'009
A history of conferences and other proceedings connected with the revision of the Book of common prayer; from the year 1558 to the year 1690. 3d ed. Oxford, University Press, 1849. [Ridgewood, N.J., Gregg Press, 1966] xii, 464 p. 20 cm. "Sequel to ... 'The two Books of common prayer, set forth by authority of Parliament in the reign of King Edward VI, compared with each other.' " [BX5145.C35 1966] 67-3157
1. Church of England. Book of common prayer. I. Title.

JOINT Liturgical Group. 264.03'1
The calendar and lectionary: a reconsideration; edited by Ronald C. D. Jasper. London, New York [etc.] Oxford U.P., 1967. xii, 60 p. tables. 18 1/2 cm. [BV30.J6] 67-95575
1. Church year. 2. Lectionaries. I. Jasper, Ronald Claud Dudley, ed. II. Title.

SYDNOR, William. 264.031
Keeping the Christian year, and a Christian year glossary. New York, Morehouse-Barlow Co. [1959] 92 p. 19 cm. [BV30.S9] 59-14083
1. Church year. I. Title.

BROOK, Stella. 264.032
The language of the Book of common prayer. New York, Oxford University Press, 1965. 232 p. 23 cm. (The Language library) Bibliography: p. 220-227. Bibliographical footnotes. [BX5145.B74] 65-20044
1. Church of England. Book of common prayer. I. Title. II. Series.

BROOK, Stella 264.032
The language of the Book of common prayer. New York, Oxford [c.]1965. 232p. 23cm. (Lang. lib.) Bibl. [BX5145.B74] 65-20044 5.50
1. Church of England. Book of common prayer. I. Title.

CHURCH of England. Book of common prayer. 264.032
The Durham Book, being the first draft of the revision of the Book of common prayer in 1661. Edited with an introd. and notes by G. J. Cuming. London, New York, Oxford University Press, 1961. xxxii, 298p. facsims. 26cm. (University of Durham publications) Bibliography: p.[xxvii]-xxx. [BX5145.A4 1661a] 61-66845
I. Cuming. G. J., ed. II. Title. III. Series: Durham, Eng. University. Publications

CHURCH of South India. Liturgy and ritual. Book of common worship. 264.032
The book of common worship, as authorised by the synod, 1962. London, New York, Oxford University Press, 1963 [i. e. 1964] Supplement, as authorised by the synod. [Madras] Published for the Church of South India by the Indian Branch, Oxford University Press, 1964- [BX5671.I55A38] 64-3981
I. Title.

CHURCH of South India. Liturgy and ritual. Book of common worship. 264.032
The book of common worship, as authorised by the synod, 1962. New York, Oxford [1964, c.]1963. xxvi, 213p. 18cm. At head of title: The Church of South India. 64-3981 1.55
I. Title.

CHURCH of South India. Liturgy and ritual. Book of common worship. 264.032
The book of common worship, as authorized by the synod, 1962. London, New York, Oxford University Press, 1963 [i.e. 1964] xxvi, 213 p. 18 cm. At head of title: The Church of South India. [BX5671.I55A38] 64-3981
I. Title.

CHURCH OF ENGLAND. BOOK OF COMMON PRAYER. 264.032
The Durham Book, being the first draft of the revision of the Book of common prayer in 1661. Ed. with introd., notes by G. J. Cuming. New York, Oxford [c.]1961[ ] xxxii, 298p. facsims. 26cm. (Univ. of Durham Pubns.) Bibl. 61-66845 10.10
I. Cuming, G. J., ed. II. Title. III. Series: Durham, Eng. University. Publications

JONES, Bayard Hale, 1887-1957. 264.032
Dynamic redemption; reflections of the Book of common prayer. Greenwich, Conn., Seabury Press, 1961. 147p. 20cm. [BX5945.J58] 61-9107
1. Protestant Episcopal Church In the U.S.A. Book of common prayer. 2. Lords Supper—Anglican Communion. I. Title.

SYDNOR, William. 264.032
How and what the church teaches. [1st ed.] New York, Longmans, Green, 1960. 177 p. 22 cm. [BX5947.L4S9] 60-40536
1. Protestant Episcopal Church in the U.S.A. Book of common prayer. I. Title.

SYDNOR, William 264.032
How and what the church teaches. New York, Longmans, Green [c.]1960. xii, 177p. 22cm. 60-10536 4.00 pap.,
1. Protestant Episcopal Church in the U. S. A. Book of common prayer I. Title.

HIGGINS, John Seville, Bp., 1904- 264.033
The hope of glory. Foreword by Horace W. B. Donegan. New York, Morehouse-Gorham Co., 1953. 146p. 19cm. (Bishop of New York books, 1953) [BX5933.H5] 53-544
1. Protestant Episcopal Church in the U. S. A.—Doctrinal and controversial works. 2. Protestant Episcopal Church in the U. S. A. Book of common prayer. A general thanksgiving. I. Title.

THE American missal; 264.035
the complete liturgy of the American Book of common prayer with additional devotional material appropriate to the same. Revised. Cambridge, Mass., American Missal, 1951. xxx, 624, 145 p. illus. 30 cm. Includes music in plainsong notation. [BX5947.M5A6 1951] 51-6766
I. Protestant Episcopal Church in the U. S. A. Liturgy and ritual.

BABIN, David E. 264.03'5
Doing the Eucharist: a guide to trial use, by David E. Babin. New York, Morehouse-Barlow Co. [1971] 128 p. 19 cm. [BX5949.C5B24] 77-151525 ISBN 0-8192-1125-7
1. Lord's supper (Liturgy) 2. Lord's Supper—Anglican Communion. I. Title.

BERNARDIN, Joseph Buchanan, 1899- comp. 264.035
Burial services. [3d ed.] New York, Morehouse-Gorham, 1958. 128p. 20cm. [BX5947.B9B4 1958] 58-4453
1. Funeral service. I. Protestant Episcopal Church in the U. S. A. Book of common prayer. Order for the burial of the dead. II. Title.

DAVIES, David Richard, 1889- 264.035
Down, peacock's feathers; studies in the contemporary significance of the general confession. Rev. ed. New York, Macmillan, 1961. 204 p. 20 cm. [BX5145.A633D3 1961] 61-10342
1. Church of England. Book of common prayer. General confession. 2. Church and social problems. I. Title.

DELL, Edward Thomas 264.035
A handbook for church weddings. New York, Morehouse-Barlow [c. 1964] 64p. 19cm. 64-16829 1.50 pap.,
1. Wedding etiquette. I. Title.

GARRETT, Thomas Samuel. 264.035
The liturgy of the Church of South India; an introduction to and commentary on 'The service of the Lord's Supper.' [Madras, New York] Indian Branch, Oxford University Press [1952] 92p. 19cm. [BX5671.I 55G3] 53-2272
1. Church of South India. Liturgy and ritual. Service of the Lord's Supper. I. Title.

HIGGINS, John Seville, bp., 1904- 264.035
This means of grace, by John Higgins. New York, Morehouse-Gorham co., 1945. xvii p., 1 l., 168p. 19cm. [BX5949.C5H5] 45-2640
1. Lord's supper—Anglican communion. 2. Protestant Episooal church in the L. S. A. Book of common prayer. Communion service. I. Title.

HUNTER, Leslie Stannard, Bp. of Sheffield, 1890- ed. 264.035
A diocesan service book; services and prayers for various occasions. Ed., ordered by Leslie Stannard Hunter. New York, Oxford [c.]1965. xx, 203p. 20cm. [BX5147.O3H7] 65-1695 3.40
1. Occasional services—Anglican Communton. 2. Pastoral prayers. I. Title.

INGRAM, Ada A. 264.03'5
Off to a good start; installation services for all occasions [by] Ada A. Ingram. Nashville, Abingdon Press [1970] 48 p. 23 cm. [BV199.I5I53] 70-109674
1. Installation service (Church officers) I. Title.

KENNEDY, James William, 1905- 264.035
The celebration of the Eucharist facing the people. Greenwich, Conn. Seabury [c.]1961. 148p. Bibl. 61-11314 3.00 bds.,
1. Lord's Supper—Anglican Communion. I. Title.

KENNEDY, James William, 1905- 264.035
The most comfortable sacrament, a primer of Eucharistic devotion for preparing and guilding the worshipper before, during, and after the Holy Communion. Greenwich, Conn., Seabury Press, 1961. 148p. 18cm. [BX5949.C5K4] 61-11314
1. Lords's Supper-Anglican Communion. I. Title.

MINCHIN, Basil. 264.035
Covenant and sacrifice. London, New York, Longmans, Green [1958] 219p. 19cm. (His Worship in the body of Christ) Includes bibliography. [BX5149.C5M48] 59-16397
1. Lord's Supper (Liturgy) 2. Church of England. Book of common prayer. I. Title.

MINCHIN, Basil 264.035
he celebration of the Eucharist facing the people. [Dist. New York McKay, 1962, c.1961] 53p. illus. 20cm. 62-1494 1.50 pap.,
1. Lord's Supper—Celebration. I. Title.

PARSONS, Donald J., 1922- 264'.035
The Holy Eucharist, rite two : a devotional commentary / Donald J. Parsons. New York : Seabury Press, 1976. 114 p. ; 21 cm. "A Crossroad book." [BX5944.C75P37] 76-15636 ISBN 0-8164-2129-3 pbk. : 3.95
1. Protestant Episcopal Church in the U.S.A. Liturgical Commission. The draft proposed Book of Common Prayer. The Holy Eucharist, rite two. 2. Lord's Supper (Liturgy) I. Title.

ROBINSON, John Arthur Thomas, Bp., 1919- 264.035
Liturgy coming to life. Philadelphia, Westminster [1964, c.1960] xiii, 109 p. 22 cm. An account of liturgical experiment at Clare College, Cambridge. 64-16350 1.45, pap.
1. Lord's Supper (Liturgy). 2. Cambridge. University. Clare College. I. Title.

ROBINSON, John Arthur Thomas, Bp., 1919- 264.035
Liturgy coming to life, by John A. T. Robinson. Philadelphia, Westminster Press [1964, c1960] xiii, 109 p. 22 cm. "An account of liturgical experiment at Clare College, Cambridge." [BX5949.C5R6] 64-16350
1. Lord's Supper (Liturgy) 2. Cambridge. University. Clare College. I. Title.

WIGAN, Bernard, ed. 264.035
The liturgy in English. London, New York, Oxford University Press, 1962. xvi, 250 p. 23 cm. "Comprehensive collection of Anglican and other liturgies -- i.e. forms of the Holy Communion service." -- Dust jacket. [BV825.5.W5] 62-2999
1. Lord's Supper (Liturgy) 2. Lord's Supper — Anglican Communion. I. Title.

WIGAN, Bernard, ed. 264.035
The liturgy in English. New York, Oxford [c.] 1962[ ] xvi, 250p. 62-2999 6.75
1. Lord's Supper (Liturgy). 2. Lord's Supper—Anglican Communion. I. Title.

WIGAN, Bernard, ed. 264.035
The liturgy in English. 2d ed. New York, Oxford, 1964. xvi, 254p. 23cm. 64-56791 5.75
1. Lord's Supper (Liturgy) 2. Lord's Supper—Anglican Communion. I. Title.

WILKINSON, John Donald. 264.035
The Supper and the Eucharist; a layman's guide to Anglican revision, by John Wilkinson. London, Macmillan; New York, St. Martin's Press, 1965. 165 p. illus. 23 cm. [BX5149.C5W53] 66-956
1. Lord's Supper (Liturgy) 2. Lord's Supper — Anglican communion. 3. Church of England. Book of common prayer. Communion service. I. Title.

WILKINSON. JOHN DONALD 264.035
The Supper and the Eucharist: a layman's guide to Anglican revision. London, Macmillan; New York. St. Martin's [1966.c.] 1965. 165p. illus. 23cm. [BX5149.C5W53] 66-956 5.25
1. Lord's Supper (Liturgy) 2. Lord's Supper—Anglican communion. 3. Church of England. Book of common prayer. Communion service. I. Title.

WINCKLEY, Edward. 264.035
The practice of healing evangelism. San Diego, Calif., St. Luke's Press [1963-] v, 19 cm. Contents.Contents. -- V. 1. Preaching and healing. [BX5969.W5] 63-21190
1. Parish missions — Anglican Communion. 2. Faith-cure. I. Title.

WINCKLEY, Edward 264.035
The practice of healing evangelism; v.1. San Diego, Calif., 2243 Front St. St. Luke's Pr., [c.1963] 74p. 19cm. Contents.v.1. Preaching and healing. 63-21190 1.00
1. Parish missions—Anglican Communion. 2. Faith-cure. I. Title.

YATES, Miles Lowell, 1890- 264.035
Our bounden duty, a manual of devotion for communicants. New York, Oxford University Press, 1951. 112 p. 17 cm. [BX5949.C5Y3] 51-10696
1. Lord's Supper — Prayer-books and devotions — English. 2. Protestant Episcopal Church in the U.S.A. — Prayer-books and devotions — English. I. Title.

BRUSH, George Robert, 1871- 264.036
A companion to the prayer book; thoughts on the collects for the Sundays of the Christian year. Boston, Christopher Pub. House [1951] 104 p. 21 cm. [BX5944.C7B7] 51-13294
1. Collects. 2. Protestant Episcopal Church in the U. S. A. Book of common prayer. I. Brussel, James Arnold, 1905- of the Rorschach cards; comprising An introduction to A. Brussel and Kenneth S. Hitch, and A Rorschach compendium, rev. and enl., by Zygmunt A. Piotrowski. 3d ed. II. Title.

CHRISTIAN year (The); 264.036
the prayer book collects, with epistles and gospels as tr. by J. B. Phillips, notes by H. W. Dobson. New York, Macmillan [1963, c.1961] 311p. 21cm. (130) 1.45 pap.,

CHURCH of England. Book of common prayer. 264.036
The Christian year; the prayer book Collects, with Epistles and Gospels; tr. by J. B. Phillips; notes by H. W. Dobson. New York, Macmillan [1963, c.1961] 311p. diagr. 21cm. 63-953 1.45 pap.,
1. Propers (Liturgy) 2. Bible. N. T. Epistles and Gospels, Liturgical—Commentaries. I. Phillips, John Bertram, 1906- tr. II. Title.

FINNIS, H. P. 264.036
Meditations on the Sunday Collects. London, S. P. C. K., [dist. Greenwich, Conn., Seabury, c.] 1962. 103p. 19cm. (Seraph) 63-762 1.25 pap.,
1. Collects—Meditations. I. Title.

MILNER-WHITE, Eric, 1884- comp. 264.036
A procession of Passion prayers. Dist. Greenwich, Conn., Seabury, 1962. 132p. 19cm. 1.50 pap.,
1. Collects. 2. Jesus Christ—Passion. I. Title. II. Title: Passion prayers

ROACH, Corwin Carlyle, 1904- 264.036
In spirit and in truth; the Collects for today. New York, Morehouse- Gorham, 1958. 191p. 21cm. Includes bibliography. [BX5944.C7R6] 58-10302
1. Collects. 2. Protestant Episcopal Church in the U. S. A. Book of common prayer, Collects. I. Title.

CATHOLIC Church. Liturgy and ritual. Psalter (Vitellius psalter) 264.038
The Vitellius psalter, Edited from British Museum Ms. Cotton Vitellius E. xviii, by James L. Rosier. Ithaca, N. Y., Cornell University Press [1962] xxxviii, 397 p. 2 facsims. 22 cm. (Cornell studies in English, v. 42) In Latin, with Old English glosses above the lines of Latin. [BX2033.A3V5 1962] 61-14849
I. Rosier, James L., ed. II. Title. III. Series. IV. Series: Cornell University. Cornell studies in English, v. 42

CHURCH of England. Book of Common Prayer. Psalter. 264.038
The revised Psalter; pointed for use with Anglican chants. London, Cambridge U.P., Eyre & Spottiswoods, Oxford U.P., 1966. viii, 242 p. illus. (music) 16 1/2 cm. 10/6 (Congregation ed. 816; pbk. 6/1-) [BX5146.A1 1966] 66-70596
I. Title.

MORSCH, Vivian Sharp. 264.04
The use of music in Christian education. Philadelphia, Westminster Press [1956] 171p. 21cm. [MT88.M85] 268.73 56-8427
1. Church music—Protestant churches. I. Title.

MORSCH, Vivian Sharp. 264.04
The use of music in Christian education. Philadelphia, Westminster Press [1956] 171 p. 21 cm. [MT88.M85] 268.73 56-8427
1. Church music—Protestant churches. I. Title.

ROLFSRUD, Erling Nicolai, 264.04
1912-
Church etiquette for the layman. Rock Island, Ill,, Augustana Book Concern [1950] 64 p. 16 cm. [BJ2019.R6] 51-18541
1. Church etiquette. I. Title.

BIBLE. N. T. Epistles and 264.041
Gospels,
Raltramiejus Vilentas' Lithuanian translation of the Gospels and Epistles, 1579; v.1. Ed. by Gordon B. Ford, Jr. Louisville, Ky. 40202, Pyramid Pr. 820 Ky. Home Life Bldg., c.1966. 1v. (various p.) 28cm. Includes facsim. of the 1579 Konigsberg ed., prepd. from the Vilnius State Univ. copy (Lr 1387) with t. p. reading: Euangelias bei Epistolas, nedeliu ir schwentuju dienosu skaitomosias, Bazniczosu Chrikszonischkosu, pilnai ir wiernai perguldITAS ant lietuwischkaKaralauczui per J. Osterbergera, 1579. Text in Gothic type, with a transcription in roman type. 'The life and works of Baltramiejus Vilentas' (20 1.) included in v.1 [BS2547.A4L5] 66-1610 36.00
I. Vilentas, Baltromiejus, 1525(ca.)-1587 tr. II. Ford, Gordon B., ed. III. Bible. N. T. Epistles and Gospels, Liturgical. Lithuanian. 1966. IV. Title. V. Title: Euangelias bei Epistolas.

BRANDT, Leslie F. 264'.04'1
Contemporary introits for the revised Church calendar / Leslie F. Brandt. St. Louis : Concordia Pub. House, [1975] 38 p. ; 23 cm. [BX8067.I57B7] 75-25525 ISBN 0-570-03718-2 pbk. 1.95
1. Introits. I. Title.

BROWN, Edgar S 264.041
Living the liturgy. Philadelphia, Muhlenberg Press [1961] 140p. 19cm. [BX8067.A1B7] 61-10279
1. Lutheran Church. Liturgy and ritual. 2. Service book and hymnal of the Lutheran Church in America. I. Title.

*BROWN, Edgar S., Jr. 264.041
Understanding the service. Frank W. Klos, ed. Bernard Sperl, artist. Philadelphia, Lutheran Church Pr. [c.1966] 159p. illus. 21cm. (LCA sch. of religion ser.) 1.50; 1.25 pap., teacher's guide, pap.,
I. Title.

CONCORDIA Publishing 264.041
House, St. Louis.
My prayer book. St. Louis [1957] 239p. 16cm. [BV260.C7] 56-12420
1. Lutheran Church—Prayer-books and devotioes—English. I. Title.

HERSHEY, Robert D. 264'.04'1
Advent landmarks : from a preacher's notebook / Robert D. Hershey. Philadelphia : Fortress Press, c1975. x, 54 p. : ill. ; 19 cm. Includes bibliographical references. [BV40.H47] 75-13034 ISBN 0-8006-1211-6 pbk. : 1.95
1. Advent—Prayer-books and devotions—English. I. Title.

*HERZEL, Catherine 264.041
Christians at worship: helps for using the service book and hymnal in Sunday worship and at home. Ed.: Gustav K. Wiencke. Illus. by Bernhard and Johanna Sperl. Philadelphia, Lutheran Church [c.1964] 128p. illus. (LCA Sunday church sch. ser.) 1.25 bds.,
I. Title.

*HORN, Henry E. 264.041
Liturgy and life. William E. Wendt, ed. Philadelphia. Lutheran Church Pr. [c. 1966] 118p. 21cm. (LCA Sunday church sch. ser.) .90; 1.00 pap., teacher's ed., pap.,
I. Title.

INTER-LUTHERAN 264'.04'1
Conference on Worship, Minneapolis, 1973.
Worship: good news in action. Edited by Mandus A. Egge. Minneapolis, Augsburg Pub. House [1973] 144 p. 20 cm. Lectures presented at the conference. [BV15.I57 1973] 73-88598 ISBN 0-8066-1402-1 3.50
1. Public worship—Congresses. I. Egge, Mandus A., ed. II. Title.

INTER-LUTHERAN 264.04'1
Consultation on Worship, Chicago, 1966.
Liturgical reconnaissance; papers. [Edited by Edgar S. Brown, Jr.] Philadelphia, Fortress Press [1968] viii, 135 p. 23 cm. Includes bibliographical references. [BX8067.A1I5 1966] 68-6652 1.95
1. Lutheran Church. Liturgy and ritual. I. Brown, Edgar S., ed. II. Title.

KALB, Friedrich 264.041
Theology of worship in 17th-century Lutheranism, Tr. [from German] by Henry P. A. Hamann. St. Louis, Concordia [c.1965] xiii, 192p. 24cm. Bibl. [BX8067.A1K33] 65-15934 3.95
1. Worship—Hist. 2. Lutheran Church. Liturgy and ritual—Hist. I. Title.

KALB, Friedrich. 264.041
Theology of worship in 17th-century Lutheranism. Translated by Henry P. A. Hamann. Saint Louis, Concordia Pub. House [1965] xiii, 192 p. 24 cm. Bibliography: p. 189-192. [BX8067.A1K33] 65-15934
1. Worship — Hist. 2. Lutheran Church. Liturgy and ritual — Hist. I. Title.

KRAUS, George, 1924- 264'.04'1
By word and prayer : a pastor's daily prayer and study guide / George Kraus. St. Louis : Concordia Pub. House, c1977. 192 p. ; 18 cm. Includes bibliographical references. [BX8067.P7K7] 76-41809 ISBN 0-570-03045-5 : 6.95
1. Lutheran Church—Prayer-books and devotions—English. 2. Clergy—Prayer-books and devotions—English. I. Title.

LANG, Paul H D 264.041
Ceremony and celebration [by] Paul H. D. Lang. St. Louis, Concordia Pub. House [1965] 191 p. 24 cm. [BX8067.A1L3] 65-13135
1. Lutheran Church. Liturgy and ritual. 2. Liturgics — Lutheran Church. I. Title.

LANG, Paul H. D. 264.041
Ceremony and celebration. St. Louis, Concordia [c.1965] 191p. 24cm. [BX8067.A1L3] 65-13135 4.95
1. Lutheran Church. Liturgy and ritual. 2. Liturgics—Lutheran Church. I. Title.

LINDEMANN, Frederick 264.041
Herman, 1891-
The sermon and the Propers. Saint Louis, Concordia Pub. House [1958-59] 4v. 23cm. Contents.v. 1. The Advent and Epiphany seasons.--v. 2. Pre-Lent to Pentecost.--v. 3. Trinity season, first half.--v. 4. Trinity season, second half. Includes bibliography. [BX8066.L44S4] 57-11909
1. Church year sermons. 2. Lutheran Church—Sermons. 3. Sermons, American. 4. Lutheran Church. Liturgy and ritual. I. Title.

LINDEMANN, Herbert Fred, 264.041
1909- ed.
The daily office: matins and vespers, based on traditional liturgical patterns, with Scripture readings, hymns, canticles, litanies, collects, and the Psalter, designed for Rivate devotion or group orship. Herbert Lindemann, editor. Saint Louis, Concordia Pub. House [1965] xiii, 696 p. 19 cm. Selected prayers included on 2 inserts. Adapted from the breviary for the use of Lutheran and other Protestant denominations. [BV260.L53] 65-26201
1. Lutheran Church — Prayer-books and devotions. I. Catholic Church. Liturgy and ritual. Breviary. English. II. Title.

LINDEMANN, Herbert Fred, 264.04'1
1909-
The new mood in Lutheran worship [by] Herbert F. Lindemann. Minneapolis, Augsburg Pub. House [1971] 109 p. 20 cm. [BX8067.A1L47] 76-159015 ISBN 0-8066-1137-5 2.50
1. Lutheran Church. Liturgy and ritual. I. Title.

LITURGICAL Institute. 264.041
1st, Valparaiso University, 1949.
Essays presented at the First Liturgical Institute, held under the auspices of Valparaiso University at Valparaiso, Indiana, June 7th, 8th, and 9th, 1949. Valparaiso, Valparaiso University Press [1950] 103 p. 24 cm. Addendum slip inserted. Includes bibliographies. [BX8067.A1L5 1949] 50-28566
1. Lutheran Church. Liturgy and ritual. I. Title.
:Contents omitted

LUTHER, Martin, 1483- 264.04'1
1546.
The Magnificat; Luther's commentary. Translated by A. T. W. Steinhaeuser. Minneapolis, Augsburg Pub. House [1967] 77 p. 22 cm. [BV199.C32M3953] 67-25368
1. Magnificat. I. Title.

LUTHER, Martin, 1483- 264.04'1
1546.
The Magnificat; Luther's commentary. Translated by A. T. W. Steinhaeuser. Minneapolis, Augsburg Pub. House [1967] 77 p. 22 cm. [BV199.C32M3953] 67-25368
1. Magnificat.

*LUTHERAN Church in 264.04'1
America, Commission on Worship
Holy Week and Easter; liturgical orders supplementing the Service Book and Hymnal. Prepd. by Commission on Worship, Lutheran Church in America. Philadelphia, Fortress [1968] 58p. 18cm. Bibl. .75 pap.,
1. Lutheran Church—Liturgy and ritual—Easter. I. Title.

LUTHERAN Church. Liturgy 264.041
and ritual.
Altar service book of the Lutheran Church in America. Authorized by the churches cooperating in the Commission on the Liturgy. [Minneapolis, Augsburg Pub. House, 1960] 385p. 30cm. 'The services and all other materials have been taken from the Service book and hymnal of the Lutheran Church in America.' [BX8067.A3A7] 60-4173
I. Title.

LUTHERAN Church Liturgy 264.041
and ritual.
The Lutheran order of services. Saint Louis, Concordia Pub. House [1952] 58 p. illus. 19 cm. [BX8067.A1LS] 52-27461
1. Lutheran Church—Liturgy and ritual I. Title.

NELSON, Clifford Ansgar 264.041
Invitation to worship; a devotional study of the Lutheran liturgy. Rock Island, Ill., Augustana Press [c.1960] xi, 178 p. 20 cm. Includes bibliography 60-9301 3.00
1. Lutheran Church. Liturgy and ritual. I. Title.

OCCASIONAL services from 264.041
the Service book and hymnal (The), together with additional orders and offices. For the use of the Lutheran churches cooperating in the commission on the Liturgy and Hymnal. [Minneapolis, Augsburg, 1962] 215p. 17cm. 62-52506 8.50
1. Lutheran Church. Liturgy and ritual.

OLANDER, Marie Hankla 264.041
My church book. Illus. by Don Wallerstedt. Rock Island, Ill., Augustana Press [c.1960] unpaged. illus. col.) 60-16830 1.00 pap.,
1. Lutheran Church. Liturgy and ritual—Juvenile literature. I. Title.

REED, Luther Dotterer, 264.041
1873-
The Lutheran liturgy; a study of the common liturgy of the Lutheran Church in America. [Rev. ed.] Philadelphia, Muhlenberg Press [1959?] 824p. 24cm. Includes bibliographies. [BX8067.A1R4 1959] 60-15401
1. Lutheran Church. Liturgy and ritual. 2. Service book and hymnal of the Lutheran Church in America. I. Title.

REED, Luther Dotterer, 264.041
1873-
Worship; a study of corporate devotion. Philadelphia, Muhlenberg Press [1959] 437p. illus. 24cm. Includes bibliography. [BX8067.A1R43] 59-105342
1. Liturgics—Lutheran Church. 2. Lutheran Church. Liturgy and ritual. 3. Service book and hymnal of the Lutheran Church in America. 4. Church music—Lutheran Church. I. Title.

REINERTSEN, Peter Amos 264.041
Acolytes and altar guilds: a chancel ministry. Rock Island, Ill., Augustana Press [c.1960] xix, 149 p. 22 cm. Bibliographical references included in 'Notes' (p. 125-129) Bibliography: p. 130-133. 60-9303 3.50
1. Liturgics—Lutheran Church. 2. Altar boys. 3. Altar guilds. I. Title.

SCHALK, Carl. 264.041
The roots of hymnody in the Lutheran Church, Missouri Synod; the story of congregational song, the hymnals and the chorale books from the Saxon immigration to the present. St. Louis, Concordia Pub. House [1965] 61 p. facsims., music, port. 23 cm. (Church music pamphlet series. Hymnology, no. 2) Bibliography: p. 59-61. [ML3100.C5] 65-9403
1. Church music—Lutheran Church—Hist. & crit. 2. Lutheran Church—Hymns—Hist. & crit. I. Title. II. Series.

SENN, Frank C. 264'.04'1
The pastor as worship leader : a manual for corporate worship / Frank C. Senn. Minneapolis : Augsburg Pub. House, c1977. 157 p. : ill. ; 20 cm. Bibliography: p. 151-157. [BX8067.M5S45] 77-72452 ISBN 0-8066-1593-1 : 4.95
1. Liturgics—Lutheran Church. I. Title.

STRENG, William D. 264.041
Toward meaning in worship; an introduction to Lutheran liturgy. Minneapolis, Augsburg Pub. House [1964] xii, 128 p. 20 cm. [BX8067.A1S69] 64-13437
1. Lutheran Church. Liturgy and ritual. 2. Liturgical movement — Lutheran Church. I. Title.

STRENG, William D. 264.041
Toward meaning in worship; an introduction to Lutheran liturgy. Minneapolis, Augsburg [c. 1964] xii, 128p. 20cm. 64-13437 1.95 pap.,
1. Lutheran Church. Liturgy and ritual. 2. Liturgical movement—Lutheran Church. I. Title.

STRODACH, Paul Zeller, 264.041
1876-1947, ed.
Oremus; collects, devotions, litanies, from ancient and modern sources, edited by Paul Zeller Strodach. Minneapolis, Augsburg Pub. House [1966?] 213 p. 18 cm. "Originally published in 1925." "Sources: p. 191-213. [BX8067.A3S8] 66-13049
1. Liturgies. 2. Lutheran Church — Prayer-books and devotions — English. I. Title.

STRODACH, Paul Zeller, 264.041
1876-1947, ed.
Oremus: collects, devotions, litanies, from ancient and modern sources. Minneapolis, Augsburg [1966] 213p. 18cm. Orig. pub. in 1925. Bibl. [BX8067.A3S8] 66-13049 4.50
1. Liturgies. 2. Lutheran Church—Prayer-books and devotions—English. I. Title.

TREASURY of prayers, 264.041
abridged. [28th print., slightly rev.] St. Louis, Concordia Pub. House, 1956. 134p. 16cm. Translation of Der kleine Gebetsschats, an abridgment of Evangelisch- Lutherischer Gebetsschats. [BV257] 57-858
1. Lutheran Church—Prayer-books and devotions— English.

TREASURY of prayers, 264.041
abridged. [28th print., slightly rev.] St. Louis, Concordia Pub. House. 1956. 134 p. 16 cm. Translation of Der kleine Gebetsschatz, an abridgment of Evangelisch-Lutherischer Gebetsschatz. [[BV257]] 57-858
1. Lutheran Church — Prayer-books and devotions — English.

WILLIAMSON, William B. 264.041
ed.
Personal devotions for pastors. Philadelphia, Westminster Press [1961] 202 p. 18 cm. Includes bibliography. [BV260.W44] 61-13305
1. Clergy — Religious life. I. Title.

SKODACEK, August 264.04'1437'3
Adolph, 1913-
Slovak Lutheran liturgy: past and present [by] A. A. Skodacek. [Akron? Ohio, 1968] x, 202 p. front. 22 cm. Includes Liturgicke napevy; liturgical tunes, prepared by Jan Jamnicky (p. 131-177) and Slovenska liturgia; the new Slovak liturgy, 3d ed., 1965 (p. 179-196). With tunes. Bibliography: p. 200-202. [BX8067.A1S55] 68-22457
1. Lutheran Church. Liturgy and ritual. 2. Hymns, Slovak—History and criticism. 3. Lutheran Church in Slovakia. I. Title.

BIBLE. N. T. Epistles 264.0416
and Gospels, Liturgical. English. 1959. Authorized.
Epistles and Gospels together with lessons from the Old Testament, from the Service book and hymnal of the Lutheran Church in America. [Prepared by the Commission on a Common Liturgy] Authorized by the churches cooperating in the Commission on the Liturgy. [Minneapolis, Augsburg Pub. House, 1959] 135p. 22cm. [BS2547 A3 1959] 59-115/
I. Bible. O. T. English. Lessons, Liturgical. 1959, Authorized. II. Lutheran Church. Liturgy and ritual. III. Commission on a Common Liturgy. IV. Title.

†MAXWELL, Jack Martin, 264'.04'2
1939-
Worship and reformed theology : the liturgical lessons of Mercersburg / by Jack Martin Maxwell. Pittsburgh : Pickwick Press, 1976. x, 486 p. ; 22 cm. (Pittsburgh theological monograph series ; no. 10) Includes index. Bibliography: p. 469-486. [BX9427.M39] 75-45492 ISBN 0-915138-12-3 pbk. : 7.50
1. Liturgics—Reformed Church—History. 2. Mercersburg theology. I. Title. II. Series.

NICHOLS, James Hastings, 264.04'2
1915-
Corporate worship in the reformed tradition. Philadelphia, Westminster Press [1968] 190 p. 21 cm. Bibliographical references included in "Notes" (p. 177-182) [BX9427.N5] 68-13957
1. Reformed Church. Liturgy and ritual—History. 2. Worship—History. I. Title.

STOUDT, John Joseph, 264.042
1911- ed. and tr.
Private devotions for home and church. Translated and compiled by John Joseph Stoudt. Philadelphia, Christian Education Press [c1956] 173p. 23cm. [BV260.S85] 56-13071
1. Reformed Church—Prayer-books and devotions—English. I. Title.

STOUDT, John Joseph, 1911- ed. and tr. 264.042
Private devotions for home and church. Translated and compiled by John Joseph Stoudt. Philadelphia, Christian Education Press [1956] 173 p. 23 cm. [BV260.S85] 56-13071
1. Reformed Church — Prayer-books and devotions — English. I. Title.

COMMUNAUTE de Taize. 264.0425
The eucharistic liturgy of Taize. Introductory essay by Max Thurian. Tr. [from French] by John Arnold. London, Faith Pr. [dist. Westminster, Md., Canterbury, c.1959, 1962] 85p. 22cm. 63-726 1.95 pap.,
1. Lord's Supper (Liturgy) I. Thurian, Max. II. Title.

STREET, Julia Montgomery. 264.0461
Candle love feast. Illustrated by Anna Marie Magagna. New York, Coward-McCam [1959] unpaged. illus. 23 cm. [BV45.S86] 59-10998
1. Christmas. 2. Moravians. I. Title.

STREET, Julia Montgomery. 264.0461
Candle love feast. Illustrated by Anna Marie Magagna. New York, Coward-McCann [1959] unpaged. illus 23 cm. [BV45.S86] 59-10998
1. Christmas. 2. Moravians. I. Title.

FERGUSON, James, 1873- ed. 264.05
Prayers for public worship; a service book of morning and evening prayers following the course of the Christian year. Compiled and edited by James Ferguson. American editor: Charles L. Wallis. New York, Harper [1958] 370 p. 22 cm. "A revision of [the author's] Prayers for common worship." Includes bibliography. [BX9185.F4 1958] 58-10369
1. Presbyterian Church—Prayer-books and devotions—English. I. Presbyterian Church. Liturgy and ritual. II. Title.

JONES, James Archibald, 1911-1966 264.05
Prayers for the people; a memorial collection of pulpit prayers [by] James A. Jones. Richmond, Knox [1968, c1967] 127p. port. 24cm. [BV250.J59] 67-31322 4.00 bds.,
1. Prayers. I. Title.

MACLEOD, Donald, 1914- 264.05
Presbyterian worship; its meaning and method. Richmond, Va., Knox [c.1965] 152p. illus. 21cm. Bibl. [BX9185.M23] 65-11499 3.25
1. Public worship. I. Title.

BAIRD, Charles Washington, 1828-1887. 264.051
The Presbyterian liturgies: historical sketches. Grand Rapids, Baker Book House, 1957. 266p. 19cm. First ed. published in 1855 under title: Eutaxiao or, The Presbyterian liturgies: historical sketches. [BX9185.B2 1957] 57-8257
I. Presbyterian Church. Liturgy and ritual. II. Title.

MELTON, Julius. 264.05'1
Presbyterian worship in America: changing patterns since 1787. Richmond, John Knox Press [1967] 173 p. 21 cm. Bibliographical references included in "Notes" (p. 149-163) [BX9185.M4] 67-22003
1. Presbyterian Church. Liturgy and ritual.—Hist. 2. Presbyterian Church in the U.S. (General)—Hist. I. Title.

MELTON, Julius. 264.05'1
Presbyterian worship in America: changing patterns since 1787. Richmond, John Knox Press [1967] 173 p. 21 cm. Bibliographical references included in "Notes" (p. 149-163) [BX9185.M4] 67-22003
1. Presbyterian Church. Liturgy and ritual.—History. 2. Presbyterian Church in the U.S. (General)—History. I. Title.

JOINT Committee on Worship 264.0513
The book of common worship; provisional services and lectionary for the Christian year. Philadelphia, Westminster, 1966. 157p. 22cm. [BX9185.J63] 66-6880 price unreported
1. Presbyterian Church. Liturgy and ritual. I. Title.

SHAFER, Floyd Doud. 264.05131
Liturgy; worship and work. Philadelphia, Board of Christian Education, United Presbyterian Church U.S.A. [1966] xii, [1], 109 p. 19 cm. Bibliography: p. [xiii] [BV10.2.S48] 66-31857
1. Presbyterian Church. Liturgy and ritual. 2. Worship. I. Title.

[BAIRD, Charles Washington] 1828-1887. 264.052
Eutaxia; or, The Presbyterian liturgies: historical sketches, by a minister of the Presbyterian Church. New York, M. W. Dodd, 1855. 260p. 20cm. [BX9185.B2 1855] 57-55352
I. Presbyterian Church. Liturgy and ritual. II. Title. III. Title: The Presbyterian liturgies.

BARKLEY, John Monteith. 264.05'2
The worship of the Reformed Church; an exposition and critical analysis of the eucharistic, baptismal, and confirmation rites in the Scottish, English-Welsh, and Irish liturgies, by John M. Barkley. Richmond, John Knox Press [1967] 132 p. 22 cm. (Ecumenical studies in worship, no. 15) Bibliography: p. 130. [BX9185.B3 1967] 67-10330
1. Presbyterian Church. Liturgy and ritual. I. Title. II. Series.

CHURCH of Scotland. Liturgy and ritual. 264.052
Prayers for the Christian year. 2d ed., rev. and enl. London, New York, Oxford University Press [1952] x, 161 p. 17 cm. 'Prepared by the Committee on Public Worship and Aids to Devotion of the General Assembly of the Church of Scotland.' [BX9185.A] A54
I. Church of Scotland. General Assembly. Committee on Public Worship and Aids to Devotion. II. Title.

MAXWELL, William Delbert. 264.052
A history of worship in the Church of Scotland. London, New York, Oxford University Press, 1955. 190p. 21cm. (The Balrd lectures, 1953) Bibliographical footnotes. [BX9185.M3] 55-2916
1. Church of Scotland. Liturgy and ritual. 2. Worship—Hist. I. Title. II. Title: Worship in the Church of Scotland. III. Series: The Baird lecture, 1953

CHURCH of Scotland. General Assembly. Committee on Public Worship and Aids to Devotion. 264'.05'203
The Divine Service : three orders for the celebration of the Lord's Supper / Committee on Public Worship and Aids to Devotion of the General Assembly of the Church of Scotland. London : Oxford University Press, 1973. iv, 60 p. ; 17 cm. [BX9185.C48 1973] 76-359340
1. Church of Scotland. Liturgy and ritual. 2. Lord's Supper (Liturgy) I. Title.

BURNET, George B. 264.052415
The holy communion in the reformed Church of Scotland, 1560-1960. Edinburgh, Oliver & Boyd [dist. Mystic, Conn., Verry, 1965, c.1960] 329p. illus. 23cm. ibl. [BX9189.C5B8] 60-4767 6.00
1. Lord's Supper—Church of Scotland. I. Title.

HAGEMAN, Howard G. 264.057
Pulpit and table; some chapters in the history of worship in the Reformed churches. Richmond, Va., Knox [c.1962] 139p. 21cm. Bibl. 62-12080 3.00
1. Reformed Church. Liturgy and ritual. I. Title.

MACLEOD, Donald 264.057
Word and sacrament; a preface to preaching and worship. Englewood Cliffs, N. J., Prentice-Hall, [c.]1960. ix, 176p. bibl. notes: p.165-171. 22cm. 60-14662 4.65
1. Reformed Church. 2. Preaching. 3. Public worship. 4. Reformed Church. Liturgy and ritual. I. Title.

MACLEOD, Donald, 1914- 264.057
Word and sacrament; a preface to preaching and worship. Englewood Cliffs, N. J., Prentice-Hall, 1960. 176p. 22cm. Includes bibliography. [BX9422.2.M3] 60-14662
1. Reformed Church. 2. Preaching. 3. Public worship. 4. Reformed Church. Liturgy and ritual. I. Title.

REFORMED Church in America. Liturgy and ritual. 264.05'732
The liturgy of the Reformed Church in America, together with the psalter; selected and arranged for responsive reading. Gerrit T. Vander Lugt, editor. New York, Board of Education, 1968. xi, 518 p. 22 cm. On cover: Liturgy and psalms. [BX9523.A2 1968] 68-5597
I. Vander Lugt, Gerrit T., ed. II. Reformed Church in America. Board of Education. III. Title.

ABERNETHY, William Beaven, 1939- 264'.05'8
A new look for Sunday morning / William Beaven Abernethy. Nashville : Abingdon, [1975] 176 p. ; 20 cm. Includes bibliographical references. [BX7255.M63S682] 74-34387 ISBN 0-687-27805-8 pbk. : 4.50
1. South Congregational Church, Middletown, Conn. 2. Public worship—Case studies. 3. Religious education—Case studies. I. Title.

TODD, James Moody. 264.0581
Prayers and services for Christian festivals. London, New York, Oxford University Press, 1951. 182 p. 18 cm. [BX7237.T6] 52-8525
I. Congregational churches. Liturgy and ritual. II. Title.

THOMAS, E. D., comp. 264.06'1'02
A choice selection of hymns and spiritual songs for the use of the Baptist Church and all lovers of song, by E. D. Thomas. Wayne, W. Va., Arrowood Bros. [1970?] 543, 19 p. 15 cm. Cover title: Hymns and spiritual songs. Without music. First printed in Indianapolis in 1877. [BV380.T48 1970] 70-21439
1. Baptists—Hymns. 2. Hymns, English. I. Title. II. Title: Hymns and spiritual songs.

BRYAN, G. McLeod. 264'.06'1756
Documents concerning baptism and church membership : a controversy among North Carolina Baptists / by G. McLeod Bryan, with contributions by J. William Angell and Carlton T. Mitchell. [Cleveland? Ga.] : Association of Baptist Professors of Religion, 1977. vii, 81 p. ; 23 cm. (Perspectives in religious studies : Special studies series ; no. 1) Includes bibliographical references. [BV814.B78] 76-45687
1. Baptism and church membership. 2. Baptists—Doctrinal and controversial works. 3. Baptists—North Carolina. I. Angell, John William, joint author. II. Mitchell, Carlton T., joint author. III. Title. IV. Series.

CHURCH of the Brethren. General Brothe-hood Board. 264.065
Manual of worship and polity, Church of the Brethren. Elgin, Ill., Brethren Pub. House [1953] 303 p. 19 cm. 'Authorized by the Ministry and Home Mission Commission of the General Brotherhood Board, Church of the Brethren. as a successor to the 1946 Ministers manual [issued by the General Ministerial Board] [BX7825.C47] 53-33064
I. Church of the Brethren. Liturgy and ritual. II. Church of the Brethren. General Ministerial Board. Minister's manual. III. Title.

CHURCH of the Brethren. General Brotherhood Board. 264.065
Manual of worship and polity, Church of the Brethren. Rev. ed. Elgin, Ill., Brethrn Pub. House [c1955] 305 p. 19cm. Authorized by the Ministry and Home Mission Commission of the General Brotherhood Board-Church of the Brethren.' [BX7825.A45 1955] 57-4112
I. Church of the Brethren. Liturgy and ritual. II. Title.

MORSE, Kenneth, 1913- 264'.06'5
Move in our midst : looking at worship in the life of the church / Kenneth Morse. [Elgin, IL] : Brethren Press, c1977. 159 p. ; 18 cm. [BX7825.M67] 77-6411 ISBN 0-87178-583-8 pbk. : 2.95
1. Liturgics—Church of the Brethren. 2. Liturgics. I. Title.

WATKINS, Keith. 264.066
The breaking of bread; an approach to worship for the Christian Churches (Disciples of Christ) St. Louis, Bethany Press [1966] 136 p. 23 cm. Bibliography: p. 131-133. [BX7325.W3] 66-14598
1. Disciples of Christ. Liturgy and ritual. 2. Worship — Hist. 3. Lord's Supper — Disciples of Christ. I. Title.

WATKINS, Keith 264.066
The breaking of bread; an approach to worship for the Christian Churches (Disciples of Christ) St. Louis, Bethany [c.1966] 136p. 23cm. Bibl. [BX7325.W3] 66-14598 3.75
1. Disciples of Christ. Liturgy and ritual. 2. Worship—Hist. 3. Lord's Supper—Disciples of Christ. I. Title.

PEASE, Norval F. 264.06'73
And worship him, by Norval F. Pease. Nashville, Southern Pub. Association [1967] 95 p. 22 cm. Bibliography: p. 95. [BX6154.P37] 67-3208
1. Seventh-Day Adventists. Liturgy and ritual. I. Title.

BEDELL, Kenneth B. 264'.07
Worship in the Methodist tradition / Kenneth B. Bedell. Nashville : Tidings, c1976. 80 p. : ill. ; 19 cm. Includes bibliographical references and index. [BX8337.B4] 75-32723
1. Liturgics—Methodist Church—History. I. Title.

BISHOP, John, 1908- 264'.07
Methodist worship in relation to free church worship / by John Bishop. New York : Scholars Studies Press, [1975] p. cm. A revision of the author's thesis (M.A.), Bristol University, England published under title: The forms and psychology of workship in the free church with special reference to Methodism. Includes indexes. Bibliography: p. [BX8337.B55 1975] 75-20379 ISBN 0-89177-001-1 : 6.95
1. Methodist Church. Liturgy and ritual. 2. Public workship—History. I. Title.

FRENCH, W Maynard, ed. 264.07
The John Wesley prayer book. Commentary by W. Maynard French. Nashville, Parthenon Press [1956] 133p. 22cm. [BX8337.F7] 56-2144
I. Wesley, John, 1708-1791. II. Methodist Church (United States) Liturgy and ritual. III. Title.

WESLEY, John, 1703-1791. 264.07
Devotions and prayers of John Wesley. Compiled and edited by Donald E. Demaray. Grand Rapids, Baker Book House, 1957. 109 p. 16 cm. [BV260.W4] 57-12189
1. Methodist Church — Prayer-books and devotions — English. I. Title.

COMPANION to The book of worship. 264.07'6
Edited for the Commission on Worship of the United Methodist Church by William F. Dunkle, Jr. and Joseph D. Quillian, Jr. Nashville, Abingdon Press [1970] 207 p. 22 cm. Includes bibliographical references. [BX8337.C58] 71-120595 ISBN 0-687-09258-2 4.50
1. Methodist Church (United States) General Conference. Commission on Worship. The book of worship for church and home. I. Dunkle, William Frederick, ed. II. Quillian, Joseph D., 1917- ed. III. United Methodist Church (United States). Commission on Worship.

METHODIST Church (United States) General Conference. Commission on Worship. 264.076
The book of worship for church and home; with orders of worship, services for the administration of sacraments, and aids to worship according to the usages of the Methodist Church. Nashville, Methodist Pub. House 1965. 123 p. 23 cm. "Adopted by the General Conference of 1964." [BX8337.A15] 65-6485
1. Methodist Church (United States) Liturgy and ritual. I. Title.

METHODIST Church (United States) General Conference. Commission on Worship. 264.076
The book of worship for church and home, with orders of worship, services for the administration of sacraments, and aids to worship according to the usages of the Methodist Church. Nashville, Methodist Pub. House [1964] xviii, 437 p. 20 cm. "Report of the Commission on Worship to the General Conference of the Methodist Church, 1964." [BX8337.A15] 64-53543
1. Methodist Church (United States) Liturgy and ritual. I. Title.

METHODIST Church (United States) General Conference. Commission on Worship. 264.076
The book of worship for church and home, with orders of worship, services for the administration of sacraments, and aids to worship according to the usages of the Methodist Church. Nashville, Methodist Pub. House [1964] xviii, 437p. 20cm. Report of the Comm. on Worship to the General Conf. of the Methodist Church, 1964. 64-5354 price unreported
1. Methodist Church (United States) Liturgy and ritual. I. Title.

METHODIST Church (United States) General Conference. Commission on Worship. 264.076
Report. [Nashville] Methodist Pub. House, 1960. 253 p. 20 cm. A proposed revision of The book of worship for church and home. [BN8337.A15] 60-22715
1. Methodist Church (United States) Liturgy and ritual. I. Title. II. Title: Book of worship for church and home.

METHODIST Church (United States) Liturgy and ritual. 264.076
Ritual of the Methodist Church, the general services and occasional offices of the Church, adopted by the General Conference Conference, 1964. Nashville, Methodist Pub. House [c1964] 128 p. 16 cm. [BX8337.A2] 65-3890
1. Occasional services — Methodist Church. I. Title.

VOIGT, Edwin Edgar, 1892- 264.076
Methodist worship in the church universal [by] Edwin Voigt. Nashville, Graded Press [c1965] 160 p. illus. 19 cm. Bibliographical footnotes. [BX8337.V6] 66-563
1. Methodist Church. Liturgy and ritual. 2. Worship. I. Title.

VOIGT. EDWIN EDGAR, 1892- 264.076
Methodist worship in the church universal. Nashville, Graded Pr. [Dist. Abingdon. 1966.c.1965] 160p. illus. 19cm. Bibl. [BX8337.V6] 66-563 1.75 pap.,
1. Methodist Church. Liturgy and ritual. 2. Worship. I. Title.

PATTON, Kenneth Leo, 1911- 264.08'32
Services and songs for the celebration of life,

by Kenneth L. Patton. Boston, Beacon Press [1967] xii, 209 p. 24 cm. [BV198.P38] 67-24897
1. Worship programs. I. Title.

HYMNS, fun songs, worship resources; chapbook 2. Pub. jointly by Bethany and Judson [dist. Valley Forge, Pa., Judson] 1966 1v. (unpaged) music. 15cm. price unreported. pap., ring bdg. 264.086

REORGANIZED Church of Jesus Christ of Latter-Day Saints. 264.093
Armed Forces manual. [Independence, Mo., 1957] 96p. illus. 15cm. [BV4588.R44] 57-4077
1. Armed Forces—Prayer books and devotions—English. I. Title.

WEDDLE, Franklyn S 264.093
O worship the King; a manual of helps and materials for priesthood, ministers of music, and others who assist in worship . . . prepared by Franklyn S. Weddle and Arthur A. Oakman. Independence, Mo., Herald House, Reorganized Church of Jesus Christ of Latterday Saints [1952] 203 p. 21 cm. Appendices (p. [148]-203): A. Bibliography. -- B. Music for weddings. -- C. Music for the prayer meeting. -- D. A selected list of organ music suitable for the church service. -- E. Worship music for the piano. -- F. Graded anthem list. -- G. Epochal hymns. [BX8671.W4] 52-27458
1. Reorganized Church of Jesus Christ of Latter-Day Saints. Liturgy and ritual. 2. Church music — Reorganized Church of Jesus Christ of Latter-Day Saints. I. Oakman, Arthur A., joint author. II. Title.

HATCH, Verena Ursenbach. 264.093'3
Worship in the Church of Jesus Christ of Latter-Day Saints. [Provo, Utah, M. E. Hatch, 1968] xiv, 119 p. 26 cm. Includes bibliographical references. [BX8651.H38] 68-56831
1. Church of Jesus Christ of Latter-Day Saints. 2. Worship I. Title.

BROCKWAY, Charles Edward, 1917- 264.0935
Ordinances and sacraments of the church [by] Charles E. Brockway and Alfred H. Yale, Independence, Mo., Herald House, 1962. 184p. 21cm. [BX8675.B7] 62-15950
1. Sacraments—Reorganized Church of Jesus Christ of Latter-Day Saints. I. Yale, Alfred H., joint author. II. Title.

BEACHY, Alvin J. 264.09'7
Worship as celebration of covenant and incarnation [by] Alvin J. Beachy. Newton, Kan., Faith and Life Press [1968] 73 p. 20 cm. Bibliography: p. 73. [BV10.2.B4] 68-57497
1. Public worship. 2. Liturgics—Mennonites. I. Title.

TOEWS, Abraham Peter 264.097
American Mennonite worship, its roots, development, and application. New York, Exposition Press [c.1960] 193p. 21cm. (An Exposition-university book) Thesis (M.S.T.)--Concordia Theological Seminary. Bibliography: p.186-193. 60-16218 4.00
1. Mennonites. Liturgy and ritual. 2. Mennonites in the U.S. I. Title.

BERKELEY, Calif. Free Church. 264.09'9
The covenant of peace, a liberation prayer book by the Free Church of Berkeley. Compiled by John Pairman Brown and Richard L. York. New York, Morehouse-Barlow Co. [1971] 204 p. 23 cm. [BV176.B47] 72-120338 ISBN 0-8192-1115-X
1. Liturgies. I. Brown, John Pairman, comp. II. York, Richard L., comp. III. Title.

ALLEN, Charles Livingstone, 1913- 264.1
All things are possible through prayer. [Westwood, N. J.] F. H. Revell Co. [1958] 127p. 21cm. [BV220.A4] 58-11022
1. Prayer. I. Title.

ANDREASEN, Milian Lauritz, 1876- 264.1
Prayer. Mountain View, Calif., Pacific Press Pub. Association [1957] 246p. 18cm. (Christian home library) [BV210.A577] 57-7779
1. Prayer. I. Title.

ANDREASEN, Millian Lauritz, 1876- 264.1
Prayer. Mountain View, Calif., Pacific Press Pub. Association [1957] 246p. 18cm. (Christian home library) [BV210.A577] 57-7779
1. Prayer. I. Title.

ARINTERO, Juan Gonzalez, 1860-1928. 264.1
Stages in prayer. Translated by Kathleen Pond. St. Louis, Herder [1957] 178p. 23cm. [BV210.A683] 58-187
1. Prayer. 2. Meditation. I. Title.

BAILEY, James Martin, 1929- 264.1
Worship with youth [by] J. Martin & Betty Jane Bailey. Philadelphia. Christian Education [dist. United Church, c.1962] 247p. 21cm. Bibl. 62-12679 3.95
1. Worship programs. 2. Public worship. 3. Young people's meetings (Church work) I. Bailey, Betty Jane, joint author. II. Title.

BAILEY, James Martin, 1929- 264.1
Worship with youth [by] J. Martin Netty Jane Bailey. Philadelphia, Christian Education Press [1962] 247p. 21cm. Includes bibliography. [BV29.B25] 62-12679
1. Worship programs. 2. Public Worship. 3. Young people's meetings (Church work) I. Bailey, Betty Jane, joint author. II. Title.

BARTH, Karl, 1886- 264.1
Prayer according to the catechisms of the Reformation; stenographic records of three seminars, adapted by A. Roulin. Translated by Sara F. Terrien. Philadelphia, Westminster Press [1952] 78 p. 20 cm. [BV210.B333] 52-9381
1. Prayer. 2. Lord's prayer. I. Title.

BASSET, Bernard. 264'.1
Let's start praying again; field work in meditation. [New York] Herder and Herder [1972] 152 p. 21 cm. [BV210.2.B33] 78-176365 ISBN 0-665-00003-0 4.95
1. Prayer. I. Title.

BASSET, Bernard. 264'.1
Let's start praying again. Garden City, N.Y., Doubleday [1973, c.1972] 118 p. 18 cm. (Image Book, D327) Bibliography: p. [118]-119. [BV210.2.B33] ISBN 0-385-05091-7 1.25 (pbk.)
1. Prayer. I. Title.
L.C. card no. for the hardbound edition: 78-176365.

BAUMAN, Edward W 264.1
Intercessory prayer. Philadelphia, Westminster Press [1958] 112p. 20cm. Includes bibliography. [BV210.B336] 58-5621
1. Prayer. I. Title.

*BISAGNO, John R. 264.1
The power of positive praying. Grand Rapids, Mich., Zondervan [c.1965] 95p. 21cm. (6900 ser.) .69 pap.,
I. Title.

BISHOP, Shelton Hale. 264.1
The wonder of prayer. Greenwich, Conn., Seabury Press, 1959. 95p. 20cm. [BV210.2.B57] 59-5700
1. Prayer. I. Title.

BLACKWOOD, Andrew Watterson, 1882- 264.1
Leading in public prayer. New York, Abingdon Press [1958] 207p. 21cm. Includes bibliography. [BV226.B6] 58-7429
1. Public worship. 2. Pastoral prayers. I. Title.

BLOCKER, Simon, 1881- 264.1
How to achieve personality through prayer. [1st ed.] Grand Rapids, W. B. Eerdmans Pub. Co., 1954. 121p. 23cm. [BV210.B555] 54-14434
1. Prayer. I. Title.

BONNELL, John Sutherland, 1893- 264.1
The practice and power of prayer. Philadelphia, Westminster Press [1954] 93p. 20cm. [BV210.B56] 54-5654
1. Prayer. I. Title.

BOWIE, Walter Russell, 1882- 264.1
Lift up your hearts. Enl. ed. Nashville, Abingdon [1966, c.1939, 1956] 128p. 18cm. [BV245.B62] 56-5370 .95 pap.,
1. Prayers. 2. Liturgies. I. Title.

BRACHER, Marjory Louise, comp. 264.1
Church school prayers. Philadelphia, Muhlenberg Press [c1956] 56p. 16cm. [BV283.S9B7] 55-5640
1. Sunday-schools—Prayers. I. Title.

BRAHER, Marjoyr Louise, comp. 264.1
Church school prayers. Philadelphia, Muhlenberg Press [c1956] 56p. 16cm. [BV283.S9B7] 56-5640
1. Sunday-schools—Prayers. I. Title.

BRINGS, Lawrence Martin, 1897- comp. 264.1
We believe in prayer; a compilation of personal statements by American and world leaders about the value and efficacy of prayer. Minneapolis, T. S. Denison [1958] 616p. 23cm. [BV205.B7] 58-13126
1. Prayer. I. Title.

BRIST, Gladys Z 264.1
The privilege and power of prayer, an inspirational handbook with material adaptable for devotional talks. [1st ed.] New York, Exposition Press [1957] 108p. 21cm. (A Testament book) [BV210.B72] 57-10655
1. Prayer. I. Title.

BRO, Margueritte (Harmon) 1894- 264.1
More than we are. Rev. and enl. ed. New York, Harper & Row [1965] 177 p. 21 cm. (Harper chapel books, CB7) [BV210.B73 1965] 64-20798
1. Prayer. I. Title.

BRO, Margueritte (Harmon) 1894- 264.1
More than we are. Rev., enl. ed. New York, Harper [c.1948, 1965] 177p. 21cm. (Harper chapel bks. CB7) [BV210.B73] 64-20798 1.50 pap.,
1. Prayer. I. Title.

BROWN, James Good. 264.1
I came here to pray. Boston, Christopher Pub. House [1957] 123p. 21cm. [BV260.B83] 57-25844
1. Prayers. I. Title.

BURT, Olive (Woolley) 1894- 264.1
When I pray. Illustrated by Vera Gohman. Anderson, Ind., Warner Press [1956] unpaged. illus. 23cm. [BV265.B8] 56-58351
1. Children—Prayer-books and devotions—English. I. Title.

CAMPBELL, Frank G 1879- 264.1
Prayer--it works. Washington [1953] 89p. illus. 20cm. [BV220.C3] 53-31154
1. Prayer. I. Title.

CARMICHAEL, Alexander, 1832-1912. 264'.1
Celtic invocations : selections from volume I of Carmina gadelica / by Alexander Carmichael. Authorized ed. Noroton, CT. : Vineyard Books, c1977. 127 p. ; 24 cm. Invocations translated from the Gaelic. [PB1645.C3213 1977] 77-373862 ISBN 0-913886-08-4 pbk. : 5.95
1. Hymns, Gaelic—Translations into English. 2. English poetry—Translations from Gaelic. I. Title.

CARROLL, Benajah Harvey, 1843-1914 264.1
Messages on prayer, by B. H. Carroll. Com. by J. W. Crowder, ed. J. B. Cranfill. Nashville, Tenn., Broadman press [1961, c.1942] 167p. (Broadman Starbooks) 1.25 pap.,
1. Prayer—Sermons. 2. Baptists—Sermons. 3. Sermons, American. I. Crowder, Joseph Wade, 1873- comp. II. Cranfill, James Britton, 1858- ed. III. Title.

CARRUTH, Thomas Albert. 264'.1
Prayer, a Christian ministry. Nashville, Tenn., Tidings [1971] 48 p. 19 cm. [BV213.C37] 71-159421
1. Prayer. I. Title.

CARTER, Harold A. 264'.1
The prayer tradition of Black people / Harold A. Carter. Valley Forge, PA : Judson Press, c1976. 142 p. ; 23 cm. Includes index. Bibliography: p. 133-139. [BR563.N4C37] 75-35881 ISBN 0-8170-0698-2 : 6.95
1. Negroes—Religion. 2. Prayer—History. I. Title.

CASTEEL, John Laurence, 1903- 264.1
The promise of prayer. New York, Association Press [1957] 125p. 16cm. (An Association Press reflection book) 'Based on the author's full length book, Rediscovering prayer.' [BV210.C358] 57-11606
1. Prayer. I. Title.

CASTEEL, John Laurence, 1903- 264.1
Rediscovering prayer. New York, Association Press [1955] 242p. 21cm. [BV210.C36] 55-7410
1. Prayer. I. Title.

CAVANAH, Frances. comp. 264.1
Prayers for boys and girls; illustrated by Vera Neville. Racine, Wis., Whitman [1950] [52] p. illus. (part col.) 17 cm. (Story hour series) First published in 1945 under title: Children's prayers. [BV265.C3 1950] 50-12617
1. Children—Prayer-books and devotions—English. I. Neville, Vera. illus. II. Title.

CHANNELS, Lloyd V 264.1
The layman learns to pray. St. Louis, Bethany Press [1957] 96p. 21cm. [BV215.C52] 57-12726
1. Prayer. I. Title.

CHRISTIANSEN, Elmer E. 264.1
A study in prayer [2v.] for home fellowship meetings, organization Bible studies, individual Bible study, by Elmer E. Christiansen, Raymond A. Vogeley. Minneapolis, Augsburg [1963] 2v. (various p.) 20cm. Contents.[1] Leader's guide.--[2] Study guide. 63-16603 .50; .30 v.1, v.2,
1. Prayer—Study and teaching. I. Title.

CLARK, Glenn, 1882- 264.1
On wings of prayer. [1st ed.] Saint Paul, Macalester ParkPub. Co. [1955] 258p. illus. 21cm. [BV220.C54] 55-57984
1. Prayer. 2. Voyages around the world. I. Title.

COBURN, John B 264.1
Prayer and personal religion. Philadelphia, Westminster Press [1957] 96p. 20cm. (Layman's theological library) [BV210.C686] 57-5397
1. Prayer. I. Title.

COE, Albert Buckner, 1888- 264.1
Let us pray. [New York] G. W. Stewart [1952] 157 p. 18 cm. [BV245.C56] 52-1924
1. Prayers. I. Title.

CROSS, Christopher, ed. 264.1
A minute of prayer: prayers of all faiths for every purpose and every occasion. New York, Pocket Books [1954] 339 p. 17 cm. (A Cardinal edition, C-155) [BL560.C75] 54-42575
1. Prayers. I. Title.

CUSHMAN, Ralph Spaulding, Bp., 1879-- 264.1
The prayers of Jesus, with meditations and verse for devotional use. New York, Abingdon Press [1955] 125p. 18cm. [BV229.C8] 55-11444
1. Jesus Christ—Prayers. I. Title.

CUSHMAN, Ralph Spaulding, Bp., 1879- 264.1
The prayers of Jesus, with meditations and verse for devotional use. Nashville, Abingdon [1965, c.1955] 125p. 18cm. (Apex bks., T4) [BV229.C8] .69 pap.,
1. Jesus Christ—Prayers. I. Title.

DAUJAT, Jean. 264.1
Prayer. Tranlsated from the French by Martin Murphy. [1st ed.] New York, Hawthorn Books [1964] 159 [1] p. 21 cm. (The Twentieth century encyclopedia of Catholicism, v. 37. Section 4: The means of redemption) Bibliography: p. [160] [BV210.2.D3513] 64-25386
1. Prayer. I. Title. II. Series. III. Series: The Twentieth century encyclopedia of Catholicism, v. 37

DAUJAT, Jean 264.1
Prayer. Tr. from French by Martin Murphy. New York, Hawthorn [c.1964] 159[1]p. 21cm. (Twentieth cent. ency. of Catholicism, v.37. Sec. 4: The means of redemption) Bibl. [BV210.2.D3513] 64-25386 3.50 bds.,
1. Prayer. (Series: The Twentieth century encyclopedia of Catholicism, v. 37) I. Title.

DAVIES, Arthur Powell. 264.1
The language of the heart; a book of prayers. New York, Farrar, Straus and Cudahy [1956] 117p. 21cm. [BV245.D29] 56-7859
1. Prayers. I. Title.

DAY, Albert Edward, 1884- 264.1
An autobiography of prayer. [1st ed.] New York, Harper [1952] 223 p. 22 cm. Includes bibliography. [BV210.D38] 52-8044
1. Prayer. I. Title.

DAY, Bertram, 1871- 264.1
The power of prayer, the only hope of mankind. Boston, Christopher Pub. House [1954] 376p. 21cm. [BV220.D35] 54-8657
1. Prayer. I. Title.

DICKSON, Louis Klaer, 1890- 264.1
Key in the hand. Mountain View, Calif., Pacific Press Pub. Association [1956] 75p. 19cm. [BV210.D5] 56-35991
1. Prayer. I. Title.

DOBBINS, Gaines Stanley, 1886- 264.1
The church at worship. Nashville, Broadman [1963, c.1962] 147p. 22cm. Bibl. 63-7334 3.25 bds.,
1. Public worship. I. Title.

[DOERFFLER, Alfred] 1887- ed. 264.1
Open the meeting with prayer. Saint Louis, Concordia Pub. House [1955] 94p. 20cm. [BV250.D6] 55-7442
1. Prayers. I. Title.

DONNE, John, 1573-1631. 264.1
Prayers; selected and edited from the earliest sources, with an essay on Donne's idea of

prayer, by Herbert H. Umbach. New York, Bookman Associates [1951] 109 p. 22 cm. Bibliography: p. 93. [BV245.D65] 51-5368
1. Prayers. 2. Prayer. I. Umbach, Herbert Herman, 1908- ed. II. Title.

DONNE, John, 1573-1631 264.1
Prayers; selected, ed. from the earliest sources, with an essay on Donne's idea of prayer, by Herbert H. Umbach. College & Univ. Pr. [dist. New York, Twayne, 1962, c.1961] 109p. 21cm. (L3) 1.25 pap.,
1. Prayers. Prayer. I. Umbach, Herbert Herman, 1908- ed. II. Title.

DOWKONTT, George H 1869- 264.1
Marvel mantel that caused a sweet mother to suffer in silence, and a strong father to sob out a prayer , and other true stories, and a strong father to sob out a prayer, and other true stories, written and edited by George H. Dowkontt. Jacket by F. Sands Brunner. New York, Loizeaux Bros. [194-] 160p. 20cm. Autobiographical. [BV220.D67] 57-15243
1. Prayer. I. Title.

EATON, Kenneth Oxner. 264.1
Men on their knees. New York, Abingdon Press [1956] 96p. 20cm. [BV228.E16] 56-7760
1. Bible. N. T.—Prayers. I. Title.

ESSAYS on prayer; 264'.1
a His reader on conversing with God, by A. W. Tozer and others. Chicago, Inter-Varsity Press [1968] 89, [3] p. illus. 22 cm. A collection of articles that had originally appeared in His magazine. Bibliography: p. [92] [BV205.E8] 68-57740
1. Prayer. I. Tozer, Aiden Wilson, 1897-1963. II. His.

EVELY, Louis, 1910- 264'.1
Our prayer. [Translated by Paul Burns. New York] Herder and Herder [1970] 143 p. 22 cm. Translation of La priere d'un homme moderne. [BV210.2.E8813 1970] 75-110078 4.50
1. Prayer. I. Title.

EVELY, Louis, 1910- 264'.1
Our prayer. [Tr. by Paul Burns.] Garden City, N.Y., Doubleday [1974, c1970] 112 p. 18 cm. (Image books) [BV210.2E8813 1974] ISBN 0-385-03072-X 1.45 (pbk.)
1. Prayer. I. Title.
L.C. card number for original ed.: 75-110078.

EWING, Harold, comp. 264.1
Youth at prayer; a book of prayers for youth, compiled by Harold and Dorothy Ewing. Nashville, Upper Room [1957] 128p. 13cm. [BV245.E94] 57-13008
1. Youth— Prayer-books and devotions—English. I. Ewing, Dorothy, joint comp. II. Title.

FISHER, Fred L. 264.1
Prayer in the New Testament. Philadelphia, Westminster [c.1964] 192p. 21cm. Bibl. 64-11362 4.50
1. Prayer—Biblical teaching. I. Title.

FLEMING, G. Granger 264.1
**The dynamic of all-prayer.* Introd. by Andrew Murray, D.D. Chicago, Moody [1964] 157p. 18cm. (88) .59 pap.,
I. Title.

*FORSYTH, P. T. 264.1
The soul of prayer. Grand Rapids. Mich. Eerdmans [1965] 92p. 20cm. First pub. in 1916. 1.45 pap.,
I. Title.

FORSYTH, Peter Taylor, 264.1
1848-1921.
The soul of prayer. London, Independent Press [1951; label: Chicago, A. R. Allenson] 92p. 21cm. [BV210.F56] 53-33155
1. Prayer. I. Title.

FRAINE, Jean de 264.1
Praying with the Bible; the Biblical bases of great Christian prayers. Tr. [from French] by Jane Wynne Saul. New York, Desclee [c.1964] viii, 182p. 24cm. [BV228.F713] 64-23933 3.75
1. Bible—Prayers. 2. Lord's prayer—Meditations. 3. Magnificat— Meditations. 4. Beatitudes—Meditations. I. Title.

FRAINE, Jean de 264.1
Praying with the Bible: the biblical bases of great Christian prayer. Tr. [from French] by Jane Wynne Saul. Glen Rock, N. J., Paulist [1966. c. 1964] 182p. 18cm. (Deus bk.) [BV228.F713] .95 pap.,
1. Bible—Prayers. 2. Lords prayer—Meditations. 3. Magnificat—Meditations. 4. Beatitudes—Meditations. I. Title.

FREEMAN, James Dillet. 264'.1
Prayer, the master key. [1st ed.] Garden City, N.Y., Doubleday, 1968. 261 p. 22 cm. [BV210.2.F7] 68-11793
1. Prayer. I. Title.

FRIZZELL, John Henry, 1881- 264.1
For days of crisis, a book of prayers. Boston, Christopher Pub. House [1952] 75 p. 21 cm. [BV245.F74] 52-25947
1. Prayers. I. Title.

GARRETT, Constance, 1894- 264.1
Growth in prayer. New York, Macmillan, 1950. viii, 156 p. 21 cm. [BV210.G33] 50-5677
1. Prayer. I. Title.

*GINGER, Helen, comp. 264.1
God still answers prayer; 36 true-life experiences with prayer on the mission field. Cincinnati, Standard Pub. [c.1964] 127p. illus. 22cm. 1.95, pap., plastic bdg.
I. Title.

A Golden treasury of Psalms 264.1
and prayers for all faiths. [Decorations and cover design by Fritz Kredel] Mount Vernon, N. Y., Peter Pauper Press [1952?] 61 p. illus. 18 cm. [BV245.G6] 52-43410
1. Prayers. I. Peter Pauper Press, Mount Vernon, N. Y.

GRAY, Walter G 264.1
Prayers for the pulpit. [West wood, N. J.] F. H. Revell Co. [1957] 127p. 20cm. [BV250.G7] 57-6855
1. Pastoral prayers. I. Title.

GREENE, Wade, ed. 264.1
The importance of prayer; a compilation of the views and experiences of people in all walks of life who confirm the value of prayer in managing their affairs and solving human problems as well as creating a more moral and spiritual world. Minneapolis, T. S. Denison [1958] 284p. 22cm. [BV205.G7] 57-14985
1. Prayer. I. Title.

GRIFFITH, Arthur Leonard, 264'.1
1920-
Hang on to the Lord's prayer, by Leonard Griffith. [Nashville, Tenn.] Upper Room [1973] 87 p. 20 cm. Includes bibliographical references. [BV230.G685] 73-75809
1. Lord's prayer. I. Title.

GROU, Jean Nicolas, 1731- 264.1
1803.
How to pray; the chapters on prayer from The school of Jesus Christ translated by Joseph Dalby. New York, Harper [1955] 154p. 20cm. [BV210.G752] 55-8523
1. Prayer. I. Title.

GUARD, Samuel R 1889- 264.1
The farmer gives thanks. New York, Abingdon Press [1956] 64p. 16cm. [BV283.F3G8] 56-10145
1. Farmers— Prayer-books and devotions—English. I. Title.

GUARDINI, Romano, 1885- 264.1
Prayer in practice. Translated from the German by Prince Leopold of Loewenstein-Wertheim. [New York] Pantheon Books [c1957] 228p. 22cm. Translation of Vorschule des Betens. [BV210.G813] 57-10243
1. Prayer. I. Title.

GUARDINI, Romano, 1885- 264.1
Prayer in practice. Tr. from German by Prince Leopold of Loewenstein-Wertheim. Garden City, N.Y., Doubleday [1963, c.1957] 159p. 18cm. (Image D157) .75 pap.,
1. Prayer. I. Title.

GUIDEPOSTS. 264.1
What prayer can do, by the editors of Guideposts; with photographic commentary by Lucien Aigner. Introd. by Norman Vincent Peale. [1st ed.] Garden City, N. Y., Doubleday, 1953. 95p. illus. 24cm. [BV220.G8] 53-7976
1. Prayer. I. Aigner, Lucien, illus. II. Title.

*GUTZKE, Manford George. 264.1
Plain talk on prayer. Grand Rapids, Mich., Baker Book House [1973] 182 p, 21 cm. [BV215] ISBN 0-8010-3674-7 2.95 (pbk.)
1. Prayer. I. Title.

HACKNEY, Vivian. 264.1
Invitation to prayer. Nashville, Broadman Press [1965] 96 p. 19 cm. Bibliographical footnotes. [BV210.2.H3] 65-10340
1. Prayer. I. Title.

HACKNEY, Vivian 264.1
Invitation to prayer. Nashville, Broadman [c.1965] 96p. 19cm. Bibl. [BV210.2.H3] 65-10340 1.25 pap.,
1. Prayer. I. Title.

HAMMARBERG, Melvin A comp. 264.1
My book of prayers; a personal prayer book, compiled by Melvin A. Hammarberg [and] Clifford Ansgar Nelson. Rock Island, Ill., Augustana Press [1956] 172p. 13cm. [BV260.H25] 56-10134
1. Prayers. 2. Lord's prayer. I. Nelson, Clifford Ansgar, joint comp. II. Title.

HARKNESS, Georgia Elma, 264.1
1891-
Prayer and the common life. Nashville, Abingdon [1962, c.1948] 224 p. (Apex bk. H4) 1.25, pap.
1. Prayer. I. Title.

HARMS, John W 264.1
Prayer in the market place. St. Louis, Mo., Bethany Press [1958] 96p. 21cm. [BV250.H37] 58-10867
1. Prayers. I. Title.

HARRIS, Edward George, 264.1
1917-
Prayers of a university. Philadelphia, Univ. of Pa, Pr. [1962, c.1961] 58p. 61-18520 2.75
1. Universities and colleges—Prayers. I. Title.

*HARTON, Sibyl 264.1
To make intercession [New rev. ed.] New York, Morehouse [c.1964] 125p. 18cm. Previously pub. under title: The Practice of Intercession. 1.00 pap.,
I. Title.

HASKIN, Dorothy (Clark), 264.1
1905-
A practical primer on prayer. Chicago, Moody Press [1950] 127 p. 17 cm. (Colportage library, 206) [BV210.H372] 51-30535
1. Prayer. I. Title.

*HAVERGAL, Frances Ridley, 264.1
1836-1878.
Kept for the master's use. New Canaan, Conn., Keats Publ. Co. [1973] 133 p. 18 cm. (A Pivot family reader) [BV220] 0.95 (pbk)
1. Prayer. 2. Meditations. I. Title.

HAWKINS, Quail, comp. 264.1
A little book of prayers and graces; illustrated by Marguerite de Angeli. Garden City, N. Y., Doubleday [1952] unpaged. illus. 19 cm. First published in 1941 under title: Prayers and graces for little children. [BV265.H35 1952] 52-10124
1. Children—Prayer-books and devotions—English. I. Title.

HEILER, Friedrich, 1892- 264.1
Prayer; a study in the history and psychology of religion. Translated and edited by Samuel McComb with the assistance of J. Edgar Park. New York, Oxford University Press. 1958 [c1932] 376p. 21cm. (A Galaxy book, GB16) Includes bibliography. [BV210.H38 1958] 58-3427
1. Prayer. I. Title.

HENRY, Matthew, 1662-1714. 264.1
The quest for communion with God. Containing the great English Bible commentator's personal and deeply spiritual directions for beginning, spending and closing each day with God. Grand Rapids, Eerdmans, 1954. 110p. 23cm. First published in 1712 in 'Works of Puritan divines' under title: Directions for daily communion with God. [BV213.H4] 54-1601
1. Prayer—Sermons. I. Title.

HENRY, Matthew, 1662-1714. 264.1
The secret of communion with God. Edited by Elisabeth Elliot. [Westwood, N. J.] Revell [1963] 120 p. 21 cm. [BV213.H4] 63-10397
1. "Originally entitled Directions for daily communion with God." 2. Prayer — Sermons. I. Elliot, Elisabeth, ed. II. Title.

HENRY, Matthew, 1662-1714 264.1
The secret of communion with God. Ed. by Elisabeth Elliot. [Westwood, N.J.] Revell [c.1963] 120p. 21cm. 63-10397 2.50 bds.,
1. Prayer—Sermons. I. Elliot, Elisabeth, ed. II. Title.

HEUSS, John, 1908- comp. 264.1
A book of prayers. New York, Morehouse-Gorham Co. [1957] 96p. 19cm. [BV260.H45] 57-5622
1. Prayers. I. Title.

HINNEBUSCH, Paul. 264'.1
Prayer, the search for authenticity. New York, Sheed and Ward [1969] xiii, 271 p. 22 cm. [BV210.2.H55] 77-89476 5.95
1. Prayer. 2. Spiritual life—Catholic authors. I. Title.

HOLLINGS, Michael. 264.1
Hey, you! A call to prayer. Westminster, Md., New-man Press [1955] 127p. 19cm. [BV210.H574] 55-8641
1. Prayer. I. Title.

HORNE, John, writer on 264.1
prayer.
Prayer promptings; an aid in public prayer. Grand Rapids, Baker Book House, 1955. 154p. 21cm. (Minister's hand book series) 'Orginally printed in 1906 under the title: Promptings to devotion.' [BV226.H6 1955] 55-10555
1. Prayer. I. Title.

HOUSE, Anne W comp. 264.1
A girl's prayer book; prayers for everyday and special needs. Greenwich, Conn., Seabury Prss, 1957. 96p. 18cm. [BV283.G5H6] 57-5799
1. Girls—Prayer books and devotions—English. I. Title.

HUEBSCHMANN, John Simon, 264.1
1881-
Alone with God; the shut door. Nashville, Parthenon Press [1956] 95p. illus. 20cm. [BV210.H76] 56-44103
1. Prayer. I. Title.

HUNT, Cecil, 1902- comp. 264.1
Uncommon prayers. American ed. arr, by John Wallace Suter. Greenwich, Conn., Seabury Press, 1955. 182p. 20cm. [BV245.H78] 55-6633
1. Prayers. I. Suter, John Wallace, 1890- II. Title.

HUSS, John Ervin, 1910- 264.1
Paths to power; a guide to dynamic mid-week prayer meetings. Foreword by Roy O. McClain. Grand Rapids, Zondervan Pub. House [1958] 151p. 20cm. [BV285.H83] 58-42581
1. Prayer-meetings. I. Title.

HUXHOLD, Harry N. 264'.1
Open the meeting with prayer. Rev. by Harry N. Huxhold. St. Louis, Concordia Pub. House [1973] 136 p. 16 cm. First ed. by A. Doerffler. [BV250.H85 1973] 73-156263 ISBN 0-570-03147-8
1. Prayers. I. Doerffler, Alfred, 1884- ed. Open the meeting with prayer. II. Title.

INTERNATIONAL Consultation 264'.1
on English Texts.
Prayers we have in common : agreed liturgical texts / prepared by the International Consultation on English Texts. 2d rev. ed. Philadelphia : Fortress Press, 1975. 28 p. ; 22 cm. [BV236.I57 1975] 75-311125 ISBN 0-8006-1207-8 pbk. : 1.25
1. Prayers. 2. Creeds. I. Title.

JACKSON, Edgar Newman. 264'.1
Understanding prayer; an exploration of the nature, disciplines, and growth of the spiritual life [by] Edgar N. Jackson. Cleveland, World Pub. Co. [1968] ix, 212 p. 22 cm. [BV210.2.J3 1968] 68-26842 4.95
1. Prayer. I. Title.

*JOHNSON, Ben C. 264.1
New life for prayer groups. Nashville, Upper Room [c.1964] 64p. 17cm. .35 pap.,
I. Title.

JOHNSON, Samuel, 1709- 264'.1
1784.
Doctor Johnson's prayers / edited by Elton Trueblood. Folcroft, Pa. : Folcroft Library Editions, 1976. p. cm. Reprint of the 1947 ed. published by SCM Press, London. [BV260.J55 1976] 76-25954 ISBN 0-8414-8580-1 lib.bdg. : 10.00
1. Prayers. I. Trueblood, David Elton, 1900- II. Title. III. Title: Prayers.

JONES, Mary, 1898- 264.1
Prayers and graces for a small child, by Mary Alice Jones in collaboration with Kate Smallwood. Illustrated by Elizabeth Webbe. Chicago, Rand McNally, c1955. unpaged. illus. 21cm. (A Rand McNally elf book, 502) [BV265.J59] 55-8188
1. Children— Prayer-books and devotions—English. I. Title.

JORDAN, Gerald Ray, 1896- 264.1
Prayer that prevails. New York, Macmillan, 1958. 157p. 21cm. [BV220.J65] 58-7138
1. Prayer. I. Title.

JUERGENS, Mary, comp. 264.1
My first book of prayers. Pictures by Ruth Ives. New York, Treasure Books [1953] unpaged. illus. 21cm. (Treasure books, 868) [BV265.J8] 54-15471
1. Children—Prayer-books and devotions—English. I. Title.

JUNGMANN, Josef Andreas, 264.1
1889-
The place of Christ in liturgical prayer [by] Joseph Jungmann. 2d rev. ed. Tr. [from German] by A. Peeler. Staten Island, N. Y., Alba [1966, c.1965] xx, 300p. 23cm. Bibl. [BV185.J8313] 66-1294 6.50 bds.,
1. Liturgies, Early Christian. 2. Jesus Christ—History of doctrines. 3. Prayer—Hist. I. Title.

KADEL, William H 264.1
Prayers for every need. Richmond, John Knox Press [1957] 167p. 16cm. [BV260.K2] 57-11747
1. Prayers. I. Title.

KELPIUS, John, 1673-1708. 264.1
A method of prayer; edited, with an introd., by E. Gordon Alderfer. [1st ed.] New York, Published in association with Pendle Hill by Harper [1951] 127 p. 14 cm. Originally published under title: Eine kurtze und begreifilge Anleitung zum stillen Gebet: previous editions in English published under title: A short, easy and comprehensive method of prayer. [BV209.K315 1951] 51-10649
1. Prayer. I. Title.

KIERKEGAARD, Soren Aabye, 1813-1855. 264.1
The prayers of Kierkegaard, edited and with a new interpretation of his life and thought, by Perry D. LeFevre. Chicago, University of Chicago Press [1956] ix, 244p. 23cm. Bibliography: p. 243-[245] [BV260.K5] 56-11000
1. Prayers. I. Title.

KIERKEGAARD, Soren Aabye, 1813-1855 264.1
The prayers of Kierkegaard, ed., new interpretation of his life and thought, by Perry D. LeFevre. Chicago, Univ. of Chic. Pr. [1963, c.1956] ix, 244p. 21cm. (Phoenix bks. P131) Bibl. 1.75 pap.,
1. Prayers. I. Title.

KRETZMANN, Adalbert Raphael Alexander, 1903- ed. 264.1
The pastor at prayer. Minneapolis, Augsburg Pub. House [1957] 49p. 16cm. [BV250.K7] 57-6475
1. Clergy—Prayer-books and devotions—English. I. Title.

LAKE, Alexander. 264.1
You need never walk alone [stories] New York, Messner [1959] 192 p. 22 cm. [BV220.L34] 59-7585
1. Prayer. I. Title.

LAKE, Alexander. 264.1
Your prayers are always answered. [New York] Gilbert Press; distributed by J. Messner [c1956] 248p. 21cm. 'Prayer stories.' [BV220.L35] 56-6791
1. Prayer. I. Title.

LAUBACH, Frank Charles, 1884-1970. 264.1
Prayer, the mightiest force in the world. [Westwood, N. J.] Revell [1959] 127 p. 17 cm. (A Revell inspirational classic) [BV210.L37 1959] 59-11524
1. Prayer.

LEE, Robert Greene, 1886- 264.1
The Bible and prayer. Nashville, Broadman Press ['1950] x, 132 p. 20 cm. [BV214.L4] 51-1504
1. Prayer—Study and teaching. I. Title.

LOCKYER, Herbert. 264.1
How I can make prayer more effective. Grand Rapids, Zondervan Pub. House [1953] 125p. 19cm. [BV220.L6] 53-13072
1. Prayer. I. Title.

LOEHR, Franklin. 264.1
The power of prayer on plants. [1st ed.] Garden City, N. Y., Doubleday, 1959. 144p. illus. 22cm. [BF1031.L77] 58-11320
1. Psychical research. 2. Prayer. 3. Plants, Effect of prayer on. I. Title.

MCBIRNEY, Allegra. 264.1
A compass for prayer. Columbus, Ohio, Wartburg Press [1955] 72p. 18cm. [BV210.M234] 55-4429
1. Prayer. 2. Lutheran Church—Prayer-books and devotions—English. I. Title.

MCCAULEY, Leon, ed. 264.1
The book of prayers, compiled for Protestant worship. Edited by Leon and Elfrieda McCauley. Introd. by Harry Emerson Fosdick. New York, Crown Publishers [1954] viii, 184p. 18cm. [BV245.M22] 54-12401
1. Prayers. I. McCauley, Elfrieda, joint ed. II. Title.

MCCAULEY, Leon, ed. 264.1
The book of prayers, compiled for Protestant worship. Edited by Leon and Elfrieda McCauley. Introd. by Harry Emrson Fosdick. [New York, Dell Pub. Co., 1954] 184p. 17cm. (A Dell first edition, 38) [BV245.M22 1954a] 54-8870
1. Prayers. I. McCauley, Elfrieda, joint ed. II. Title.

MCCOY, Samuel Duff, 1882- ed. 264.1
How prayer helps me. New York, Dial Press, 1955. 143p. 19cm. [BV220.M25] 55-5441
1. Prayer. I. Title.

MACFARLANE, Claire, 1906- 264.1
Prayer for moderns. Jersey City, Mann Publishers, 1956. 64p. illus. 22cm. [BV210.M264] 56-10027
1. Prayer. I. Title.

MCFATRIDGE, Forrest Vernon, 1892- 264.1
Lord, teach us to pray; with Jesus in the school of prayer. Nashville. Broadman Press [1956] 113p. 20cm. [BV215.M25] 56-8674
1. Prayer. 2. Lord's prayer. I. Title.

MACINNES, Gordon A. 264.1
A guide to worship in camp and conference. Philadelphia, Westminster [1963, c.1962] 96p. 21cm. Bibl. 62-17570 1.50 pap.,
1. Worship (Religious education-) I. Title. II. Title: Worship in camp and conference.

MCNABB, Vincent Joseph, 1868-1943. 264.1
Prayers. With a foreword by Donald Proudman. Westminster, Md., Newman Press [1955] 72p. 15cm. [BX2110.M14] 55-4628
1. Catholic Church—Prayer-books and devotions—English. I. Title.

MAGEE, John Benjamin, 1917- 264.1
Reality and prayer; a guide to the meaning and practice of prayer. [1st ed.] New York, Harper [1957] 239 p. 22 cm. [BV210.M288] 57-7350
1. Prayer. I. Title.

MANK, Charles, 1902- comp. 264.1
My favorite prayer; collected from notables chiefly of screen, radio, and television, by Chaw Mank. Introd. by Leo Louis Martello. [1st ed.] New York, Exposition Press [1956] 76p. 21cm. [BV245.M46] 56-9561
1. Prayers. I. Title.

MANSCHRECK, Clyde Leonard, 1917- comp. 264.1
Prayers of the Reformers. [Philadelphia] Muhlenberg Press [1958] 183p. 18cm. [BV245.M465] 58-8944
1. Prayers. I. Title.

MARSHALL, Peter, 1902-1949. 264.1
Prayers; edited and with prefaces by Catherine Marshall. New York, McGraw-Hill [1954] 243 p. illus. 21 cm. [BV245.M48] 54-11762
1. Prayers.

MILLER, Basil William, 1897- 264.1
Remarkable answers to prayer. Kansas City, Mo., Beacon Hill Press [1950] 159 p. 20 cm. [BV220.M5] 50-3937
1. Prayer. I. Title.

MILLER, Samuel Howard, 1900- 264.1
Prayers for daily use. [1st ed.] New York, Harper [1957] 128p. 18cm. [BV260.M49] 57-9880
1. Prayers. I. Title.

MILLER, Samuel Martin, 1890- 264.1
Have faith in God; He answers prayer. Rock Island, Ill., Augustana Book Concern [1952] 156 p. 19 cm. [BV210.M62] 52-14451
1. Prayer. I. Title.

MURCH, James DeForest, 1892- 264.1
Teach me to pray. Cincinnati, Standard Pub. Foundation [1958] 186p. 21cm. [BV215.M84] 58-40063
1. Prayer. I. Title.

NEDONCELLE, Maurice. 264.1
God's encounter with man; a contemporary approach to prayer. [Translation by A. Manson] New York, Sheed and Ward [1964] viii, 183 p. 22 cm. Translation of Priere humaine priere divine. Bibliographical footnotes. [BV210.N413] 64-19898
1. Prayer. I. Title.

NEDONCELLE, Maurice 264.1
God's encounter with man; a contemporary approach to prayer. [Tr. from French by A. Manson] New York, Sheed [c.1962, 1964] viii, 183p. 22cm. Bibl. 64-19898 3.95
1. Prayer. I. Title.

NEWSOME, Dorothy, comp. 264.1
Let there be light; [a book of prayers] chosen and decorated by D. Newsome. London, New York, Warne [1957, c1956] unpaged. illus. 22cm. [BV265] 57-1858
1. Children— Prayer- books and devotions—English. I. Title.

O'CONNELL, John P ed. 264.1
The prayer book; beautiful and helpful prayers from ancient and modern sources. Edited by John P. O'Connell and Jex Martin. Chicago, Catholic Press [c1954] 327p. illus. 18cm. [BX2110.O35] 55-1053
1. Catholic Church—Prayer-books and devotions—English. I. Martin, Jex., joint ed. II. Title.

OMMEN, Lydia. 264.1
God in action. [1st ed.] New York, Vantage Press [1957] 71p. 21cm. 'America's prayer': p.[7] [BR1725.O62A3] 57-8551
I. Title. II. Title: America's prayer.

OMMEN, Lydia. 264.1
God in action. [1st ed.] New York, Vantage Press [1957] 71p. 21cm. 'America's prayer': p.[7] [BR1725.O62A3] 57-8551
1. Title. II. Title: America's prayer.

ORIGENES. 264.1
Prayer. Exhortation to martyrdom. Translated and annotated by John J. O'Meara. Westminster, Md., Newman Press, 1954. vii, 253p. 23cm. (Ancient Christian writers; the works of the Fathers in translation, no. 19) Bibliographical references included in 'Notes' (p. [197]-240) [BR60.A35 no.19] 54-13520
1. Prayer—Early works to 1800. 2. Prayer—Hist. 3. Martyrdom. I. O'Meara, John Joseph, ed. and tr. II. Title. III. Title: Exhortation to martyrdom.

OSBORN, George Edwin, 1897- 264.1
The Glory of Christian worship. Indianapolis, Christian Theological Seminary Press, 1960. 84p. 27cm. 'First appeared in Encounter, vol. xx (1959) 172-243.' Includes bibliography. [BV15.O8] 60-23461
1. Public worship. 2. Worship. I. Title.

PARK, Charles Edwards, 1873- 264.1
Prayers. Boston. The Starr King Press [1955] 71p. 16cm. 'More than half of these prayers are taken from ... [the authors] Beginning the day, which was first published in 1922.' [BV260.P3] 55-11593
1. Prayers. I. Title.

PARKER, Joseph F 264.1
Prayers at sea. Richmond, Press of Whittet and Shepperson, 1956. 192p. 17cm. [BV273.P3] 56-11170
1. Seamen— Prayer-books and devotions—English. I. Title.

PARKER, Joseph F 264.1
Prayers at sea. Richmond, Press of Whittet and Shepperson, 1956[i. e. 1957] 280p. 17cm. [BV273.P3 1957] 57-43690
1. Seamen—Prayer-books and devotions—English. I. Title.

PEARSON, Roy Messer, 1914- 264.1
Hear our prayer; prayers for public worship. [1st ed.] New York, McGraw-Hill [1961] 174p. 21cm. [BV250.P4] 60-53351
1. Pastoral prayers. I. Title.

PEPLER, Conrad 264.1
Sacramental prayer. St. Louis, Herder [c.1959] viii, 148p. 19cm. 60-1253 2.75
1. Catholic Church. Liturgy and ritual. 2. Prayer. I. Title.

PEPLER, Conrad, 1908- 264.1
Sacramental prayer. St. Louis, Herder [c1959] 148p. 19cm. [BX1970.P4] 60-1253
1. Catholic Church. Liturgy and ritual. 2. Prayer. I. Title.

PEYTON, Patrick J 264.1
The ear of God. [1st ed.] Garden City, N.Y., Doubleday, 1951. 226 p. 21 cm. Bibliographical references included in "Notes" (p. [217]-226) [BV210.P47] 51-10036
1. Prayer. 2. Catholic Church — Prayer-books and devotions — English. I. Title.

PIUS XII, Pope, 1876-1958 264.1
Prayers. Translated from the Italian by Martin W. Schoenberg. Westminster, Md., Newman Press, 1957. 115p. 22cm. [BV264.I8P5] 57-5577
1. Prayers. I. Title.

POLING, Daniel Alfred, 1884- ed. 264.1
The Armed Forces prayer book. [1st ed.] New York, Prentice-Hall [1951] ix, 116 p. 16 cm. [BV273.P6] 51-10358
1. Soldiers — Prayer-books and devotions — English. I. Title.

POLING, Daniel Alfred, 1884- 264.1
Faith is power for you. New York, Greenberg [1950] viii, 212 p. 21 cm. [BV220.P6] 50-6842
1. Prayer. I. Title.

POTTS, James Manning, 1895- ed. 264.1
Prayers of the early church. Nashville, The Upper Room [1953] 96p. 15cm. [BX236.P6] 53-39478
1. Prayers, Early Christian. I. Title.

POTTS, James Manning, 1895- ed. 264.1
Prayers of the Middle Ages: light from a thousand years. Nashville, Upper room [c1954] 96p. 15cm. [BV237.P6] 57-3096
1. Prayers, Medieval. I. Title.

POWELL, Cyril H. 264.1
Secrets of answered prayer. New York, T. Y. Crowell [1960, c.1958] 192p. 21cm. (4p. bibl.) 60-5497 3.00 bds.,
1. Prayer. I. Title.

*POWELL, John 264.1
He touched me my pilgrimage of prayer. Niles, Ill., Argus Communications, 1974 95 p. col. illus. 19 cm. [BV215] ISBN 0-913592-47-1 1.50 (pbk.)
1. Prayer. I. Title.

PRANGE, Erwin E. 264'.1
A time for intercession / Erwin Prange. Carol Stream, Ill. : Creation House, c1976. 160 p. ; 22 cm. Bibliography: p. 153-160. [BV210.2.P64] 76-20085 ISBN 0-88419-004-8 pbk. : 2.95
1. Prayer. I. Title.

PRAYERS and other 264'.1
resources for public worship / [compiled by] Horton Davies, Morris D. Slifer. Nashville : Abingdon, [1976] p. cm. [BV245.P82] 76-23251 ISBN 0-687-33495-0 : 4.95
1. Prayers. I. Davies, Horton. II. Slifer, Morris D., 1904-

RADCLIFFE, Lynn James. 264.1
Making prayer real. New York, Abingdon-Cokesbury [1952] 254 p. 23 cm. [BV210.R3] 52-8839
1. Prayer. I. Title.

RADCLIFFE, Lynn James 264.1
Making prayer real. Nashville, Abingdon Press [1961, c.1952] 254p. (Apex Bks. E6) 1.25 pap.,
1. Prayer. I. Title.

RAHNER, Karl, 1904- 264.1
Happiness through prayer. Translated from the German. Westminster [sic] Md., Newman Press [1958] 109p. 19cm. [BV210.R333] 58-2283
1. Prayer. I. Title.

REES, Paul Stromberg. 264.1
Prayer and life's highest. Grand Rapids, Eerdmans, 1956. 128p. 21cm. [BV213] 57-13637
1. Prayer—Sermons. 2. Evangelical Mission Covenant Church of America—Sermons. 3. Sermons, American. I. Title.

REID, Frances P 264.1
None so small: reflections and prayers of a mother. Nashville, Broadman Press [1958] 66p. 19cm. [BV4847.R4] 58-5414
1. Mothers—Prayer-books and devotions—English. I. Title.

*REINBERGER, Francis E. 264.1
How to pray. Ed.: Frank K. Klos. Artist: William H. Campbell. Philadelphia, Lutheran Church Pr. [c.1964] 138p. illus. 21cm. (LCA School of religion ser.) 1.50; 1.25 pap., teacher's guide;
I. Title.

RHYMES, Douglas A. 264'.1
Prayer in the secular city, by Douglas Rhymes. Philadelphia, Westminister [c.1967] 140p. 21cm. Bibl. [BV210.2.R48 1967b] 68-15778 1.65
1. Prayer. I. Title.

ROBERTSON, Josephine. 264.1
New prayers for a woman's day. New York, Abingdon Press [1958] 80p. 12cm. [BV283.W6R58] 58-10461
1. Women —Prayer-books and devotions—English. I. Title. II. Title: Prayers for a woman's day.

ROBERTSON, Josephine. 264.1
Prayers for a woman's day. New York, Abingdon Press [1957] 79p. 12cm. [BV283.W6R6] 57-8355
1. Women—Prayer-books and devotions—English. I. Title.

ROGERS, Dale Evans, comp. 264.1
Prayer book for children. Illustrated by Eleanor Dart. New York, Simon and Schuster [1956] unpaged. illus. 33cm. (A Big golden book, 448) [BV265.R6] 56-14115
1. Children—Prayer-books and devotions—English. I. Title.

ROUNER, Arthur A 264.1
When a man prays. Westwood, N. J., Revell [1953] 160p. 22cm. [BV210.R64] 53-10753
1. Prayer. I. Title.

ROWLAND, Wilmina, comp. 264.1
When we pray. New York, Friendship Press [1955] 63p. illus. 21cm. [BV4850.R69] 55-5766
1. Youth—Prayer-books and devotions—English. I. Title.

RYAN, John Kenneth, 1897- 264.1
The armor of faith; a prayerbook for those in the Armed Services, by John K. Ryan and Joseph B. Bollins. Westminster, Md., Newman Press, 1951. 142 p. illus. 15 cm. [BX2170.S6R85] 52-6137
1. Armed forces — Prayer-books and devotions — English. 2. Catholic Church — Prayer-books and devotions — English. I. Title.

SANDLIN, John Lewis. 264.1
A prayer for every day; 365 daily prayers and table graces, evening prayers for children, prayers for women, prayers for men. [Westwood, N. J.] Revell [1958] 128p. 17cm. [BV4832.S326] 58-8605
1. Devotional calendars. I. Title.

SANFORD, Don, comp. 264.1
Prayers for every occasion. Grand Rapids, Zondervan Pub. House [c1957] 121p. 16cm. [BV260.S3] 58-20214
1. Prayers. I. Title.

SCHMIECHEN, Samuel John. 264.1
Pastoral prayers for the church year. New York, Abingdon Press [1957] 144p. 20cm. [BV250.S35] 57-11015
1. Pastoral prayers. I. Title.

SHEDD, Charlie W. 264.1
How to develop a praying church. Nashville, Abingdon [1964] 111p. 119cm. Bibl. 64-15761 1.25 pap.,
1. Prayer. I. Title.

SHOEMAKER, Helen (Smith) 264.1
The secret of effective prayer. [Westwood, N. J.] Revell [1955] 158p. 22cm. [BV220.S66] 55-6624
1. Prayer. I. Title.

SHOEMAKER, Helen (Smith) 264'.1
The secret of effective prayer. [2d ed.] Waco, Tex., Word Books [1967] 171 p. 22 cm. Bibliography: p. 170-171. [BV220.S66 1967] 67-19306
1. Prayer. I. Title.

SIMPSON, Robert L 264.1
The interpretation of prayer in the early church [by] Robert L. Simpson. Philadelphia, Westminster Press [1965] 189 p. 23 cm. (The Library of history and doctrine) Bibliography: p. [179]-183. [BV207.S5] 65-16147
1. Prayer — Hist. 2. Lord's prayer. I. Title.

SIMPSON, Robert L. 264.1
The interpretation of prayer in the early church. Philadelphia, Westminster [c.1965] 189p. 23cm. (Lib. of hist. and doctrine)BBibl. [BV207.S5] 65-16147 5.00
1. Prayer—Hist. 2. Lord's prayer. I. Title.

SMITH, Bernie, 1920- 264.1
Meditations on prayer. Introd. by Robert G. Lee. Grand Rapids. Baker Bk. [1966] 81p. 20cm. [BV210.2.S6] 66-25396 1.95
1. Prayer. I. Title.

SPICER, Dorothy Gladys. 264.1
Children's prayers from other lands; selected and adapted by Dorothy Gladys Spicer. New York, Association Press [1955] 124p. 16cm. [BV265.S7] 55-9108
1. Children—Prayer-books and devotions—English. I. Title.

STEPHENS, John Underwood, 1901- 264.1
Prayers of the Christian life, for private and public worship. New York, Oxford University Press, 1952. 154 p. 19 cm. [BV245.S67] 52-6171
1. Prayers. I. Title.

STEPHENS, John Underwood, 1901- 264.1
A simple guide to prayer. New York, Abingdon Press [1957] 124p. 20cm. Includes bibliography. [BV215.S75] 57-5281
1. Prayer. I. Title.

STEPHENS, John Underwood, 1901- 264.1
A simple guide to prayer. New York, Abingdon Press [1957] 124 p. 20 cm. Includes bibliography. [BV215.S75] 57-5281
1. Prayer. I. Title.

STOCKDALE, Allen A 264.1
Unconventional prayers. [1st ed.] New York, Comet Press Books, 1955. 64p. illus. 22cm. [BV260.S84] 55-11740
1. Prayers. I. Title.

STROMWALL, Mary W 264.1
A Catholic child's prayer book. Illus. by William De J. Rutherfoord. St. Paul, Catechetical Guild Educational Society [c1956] 56p. illus. 29cm. [BX2150.S73] 57-20299
1. Children—Prayer-books and devotions—English. 2. Catholic Church—Prayer-books and devotions—English. I. Title.

STROMWALL, Mary W 264.1
A Catholic child's prayer book. Illus. by William De J. Rutherfoord. St. Paul, Catechetical Guild Educational Society [1956] 56 p. illus. 29 cm. [BX2150.S73] 57-20299
1. Children — Prayer-books and devotions — English. 2. Catholic Church — Prayer-books and devotions — English. I. Title.

SUTER, John Wallace, 1890- comp. 264.1
A boy's prayer book; prayers for everyday and special needs. Greenwich, Conn., Seabury Press, 1957. 96p. 18cm. [BV283.B7S8] 57-5798
1. Boys—Prayer-books and devotions—English. I. Title.

SUTER, John Wallace, 1890- comp. 264.1
A boy's prayer book; prayers for everyday and special needs. Greenwich, Conn. ,Seabury Press, 1957. 96 p. 18 cm. [BV283.B7S8] 57-5798
1. Boys—Prayer-books and devotions—English. I. Title.

SYMPOSIUM on Prayer, Shrub Oak, N.Y., 1968. 264'.1
Prayer: the problem of dialogue with God. Edited by Christopher F. Mooney. Paramus, N.J., Paulist Press [1969] v, 138 p. 21 cm. (Exploration books) "Papers of the 1968 Bea Institute Symposium." Includes bibliographical references. [BV213.S94 1968] 78-92220 2.95
1. Prayer—Addresses, essays, lectures. I. Mooney, Christopher F., 1925- ed. II. Cardinal Bea Institute. III. Title.

TEEN-AGERS pray. 264.1
Saint Louis, Concordia Pub. House [1956, c1955] 82p. 18cm. [BV283.Y6T4] 55-12193
1. Youth—Prayer-books and devotions—English.

THOMSON, James G S S 264.1
The praying Christ; a study of Jesus' doctrine and practice of prayer. Grand Rapids, Eerdmans [1959] 155 p. 21 cm. Includes bibliography. [BV229.T5] 58-59780
1. Prayer—Biblical teaching. 2. Jesus Christ—Teachings. 3. Lord's prayer. I. Title.

THURSTON, Herbert, 1856-1939. 264.1
Familiar prayers, their origin and history. Selected and arranged by Paul Grosjean. Westminster, Md., Newman Press [1953] 200p. 23cm. 'Appeared originally in The month, between the year 1911 and 1918.' [BX1970.T52] 53-12311
1. Catholic Church. Liturgy and ritual—Addresses, essays, lectures. I. Title.

TITTLE, Ernest Fremont, 1885-1949. 264.1
A book of pastoral prayers; with an essay on the pastoral prayer. New York, Abingdon-Cokesbury Press [1951] 108 p. 18 cm. "The essay 'The pastoral prayer' is reprinted from Religion in life, summer, 1946." [BV250.T5] 51-3220
1. Prayers, Pastoral. I. Title. II. Title: Pastoral prayers.

TORREY, Reuben, Archer D.D. 1856- 264.1
The power of prayer and the prayer of power, by R. A. Torrey, D.D. Grand Rapids, Mich., Zondervan [1964, c.1924] 246p. 21cm. 2.50 pap.,
1. Prayer. I. Title.

*VAN ZELLER, Dom Hubert, 1905- 264.1
Approach to prayer & approach to penance. New York, All Saints [dist. Guild, 1966,c.1958] 288p. 17cm. (AS-251) .75 pap.,
1. Prayer. I. Title.

VAN ZELLER, Hubert, 1905- 264.1
Approach to prayer. New York, Sheed & Ward [1959, c1958] 128 p. 21 cm. Secular name: Claude Van Zeller. [BV210.2.V3] 58-14450
1. Prayer. I. Title. II. Series.

WALKER, George Bilby. 264.1
The quiet time; a collection of prayer-poems. [1st ed.] New York, Vantage Press [1957] 107p. 21cm. [BV260.W27] 56-14383
1. Prayers. I. Title.

WALKER, George Bilby. 264.1
The quiet time; a collection of prayer-poems. [1st ed.] New York, Vantage Press [1957] 107 p. 21 cm. [BV260.W27] 56-14383
1. Prayers. I. Title.

WALKER, William Bruce. 264.1
The power of prayer. Butler, Ind., Higley Press [c1955] 167p. 20cm. [BV210.W22] 56-29296
1. Prayer. I. Title.

WEDGE, Florence. 264.1
Prayer without headaches. Pulaski, Wis., Franciscan Printery, 1956. 173 p. 22 cm. [BV210.W38] 57-37132
1. Prayer. I. Title.

WESLEY, John, 1703-1791. 264.1
Prayers, edited by Frederick C. Gill. New York, Abingdon-Cokesbury Press [1952, c1951] 124 p. 16 cm. [BV245.W4] 52-5381
1. Prayers. I. Title.

WHITE, Reginald E O 264.1
Prayer is the secret; the prayer experience of the apostles and church fathers. New York, Harper [1959, c1958] 143 p. 21 cm. [BV235.W46 1959] 59-7166
1. Prayer — Biblical teaching. I. Title.

WHITE, Reginald E O 264.1
They teach us to pray; a biographical ABC of the prayer life. With a foreword by F. Townley Lord. New York, Harper [1958, c1957] 204 p. 22 cm. [BV235.W47 1958] 58-7106
1. Bible — Prayers. 2. Prayer. I. Title.

WILLIAMSON, Robert L. 264.1
Effective public prayer. Nashville, Broadman Press [1960] 152 p. 21 cm. Includes bibliography. [BV226.W5] 60-9535
1. Pastoral prayers. 2. Prayer. I. Title.

WILSON, Hazel Thorne, comp. 264.1
Prayers for living. With an introd. by Georgia Harkness. New York, Abingdon Press [1955] 128p. 12cm. [BV260.W45] 55-8613
1. Prayers. I. Title.

WITSELL, William Postell, 1874- 264.1
Two vital questions: Why pray? and After death -- what? Boston, Christopher Pub. House [1952] 172 p. 21 cm. [BV210.W56] 52-4878
1. Prayer. 2. Eschatology. I. Title.

WOLCOTT, Carolyn Muller. j264.1
I can talk with God. Pictures by Meg Wohlberg. New York, Abingdon Press, c1962. unpaged. illus. 19 x 23 cm. [BV212.W6] 62-7868
1. Prayer — Juvenile literature. I. Title.

WOLCOTT, Carolyn Muller 264.1
I can talk with God. Pictures by Meg Wholberg. Nashville, Abingdon, c.1962. unpaged. illus. (pt. col.) 19x23cm. 62-7868 1.25
1. Prayer—Juvenile literature. I. Title.

WORLD Council of Churches. Commission on Faith and Order. Theological Commission on Worship. North American Section. 264.1
Worship in Scripture and tradition; essays by members of the Theological Commission on Worship (North American Section) of the Commission on Faith and Order of the World Council of Churches. Ed. by Massey H. Shepherd, Jr. New York, Oxford [c.] 1963 x, 178p. 21cm. Bibl. 63-19947 4.50 bds.,
1. Worship & Hist. I. Shepherd, Massey Hamilton, 1913- ed. II. Title.

WUELLNER, Flora Slosson. 264'.1
Prayer and the living Christ. Nashville, Abingdon Press [1968, c1969] 144 p. 20 cm. Bibliography: p. 142-144. [BV210.2.W8] 69-12015 3.00
1. Prayer. I. Title.

YATES, Elizabeth, 1905- comp. 264.1
Your prayers and mine. Decorations by Nora S. Unwin. Boston, Houghton Mifflin, 1954. 64p. 20cm. [BV260.Y3] 53-10987
1. Prayers. I. Title.

YATES, Elizabeth McGreal, 1905- comp. 264.1
Your prayers and mine. Decorations by Nora S. Unwin. Boston, Houghton Mifflin, 1954. 64 p. 20 cm. [BV260.Y3] 53-10987
1. Prayers. I. Title.

RINKER, Rosalind. 264'.1'07
Teaching conversational prayer; a handbook for groups. Waco, Tex., Word Books [1970] 140 p. 23 cm. Bibliography: p. 125-133. [BV214.R5 1970] 70-91946 3.95
1. Prayer—Study and teaching. 2. Church group work. I. Title.

DONIGER, Simon, ed. 264.1082
Psychological aspects of prayer. Great Neck, N. Y., Pastoral Psychology Press [1954] 63p. 19cm. [BV225.D6] 54-32017
1. Prayer—Psychology. I. Title.

BARCLAY, William 264.13
Prayers for the Christian year. New York, Harper [1965, c.1964] 175p. 21cm. (Harper chapel bks., CB9) [BV30.B3] 65-2489 1.35 pap.,
1. Church year—Prayer-books and devotions. 2. Collects. I. Title.

CHURCH of Scotland. General Assembly. Committee on Public Worship and Aids to Devotion. 264.13
Let us pray; a book of prayers for use in families, schools, and fellowships. London, New York, Oxford University Press, 1959. 95p. 18cm. [BV245.C45] 59-3226
1. Church of Scotland—Prayer-books and devotions—English. I. Title.

CONTEMPORARY prayers for public worship, by Anthony Coates [and others]; edited by Caryl Micklem. [1st American ed.] Grand Rapids, W. B. Eerdmans Pub. Co. [1967] 141 p. 21 cm. [BV250.C6 1967b] 67-28374 264'.13
1. Pastoral prayers. I. Micklem, Caryl, ed. II. Coates, Anthony.

DODEWAARD, J. A. E. van. 264'.13
Mary's titles. Translated from the Dutch "Maria's eretitles" of J. A. E. van Dodewaard by Janine R. Wynholds. [Baltimore, Md., Reparation Society of the Immaculate Heart of Mary, 1969] 65 p. 21 cm. [BT670.T5D613] 70-112785
1. Mary, Virgin—Titles. I. Title.

GARRISON, R. Benjamin. 264'.13
Worldly holiness [by] R. Benjamin Garrison. Nashville, Abingdon Press [1971, c1972] 96 p. 19 cm. Includes bibliographical references. [BV284.F7G37 1972] 72-172808 ISBN 0-687-46336-X
1. Prayer of St. Francis—Meditations. I. Title.

GEFFEN, Roger, comp. 264.13
The handbook of public prayer. New York, Macmillan [1963] 204 p. 21 cm. [BV250.G4] 63-8185
1. Pastoral prayers. I. Title.

GRIFFIN, Christopher P. 264'.13
Prayers offered by the Right Reverend Monsignor Christopher P. Griffin, Chaplain of the Senate of the Commonwealth of Massachusetts, sessions 1963 through 1968. [Boston, Causeway Print, Legislative printers, 1969] 263 p. 23 cm. Cover title: Prayers of the Chaplain of the Senate, 1963-1968. [BV280.G68] 70-629712
1. Legislative bodies—Chaplains' prayers. I. Title. II. Title: Prayers of the Chaplain of the Senate, 1963-1968.

GUARDINI, Romano, 1885- 264.13
Prayers from theology. Translated by Richard Newham. [New York] Herder and Herder [1959] 61p. 19cm. Translation of Theologische Gebete. [BV260.G813 1959a] 58-13656
1. Prayers. I. Title.

GUPTILL, Nathanael M. 264.13
Contemporary pastoral prayers for the Christian year. Philadelphia, Christian Education Press [c.1960] 151p. 60-53182 2.50
1. Pastoral prayers. I. Title.

JONES, George Curtis, 1911- 264.13
Patterns of prayer, by G. Curtis Jones. St. Louis, Bethany Press [1964] 140 p. 23 cm. Bibliographical footnotes. [BV215.J6] 64-20803
1. Prayer. I. Title.

JONES, George Curtis, 1911- 264.13
Patterns of prayer. St. Louis, Bethany [c.1964] 140p. 23cm. Bibl. 64-20803 2.50
1. Prayer. I. Title.

KLOS, Sarah. 264'.13
Prayers alone/together. Philadelphia, Fortress Press [1970] vii, 87 p. 21 cm. [BV245.K55 1970] 71-117977 2.95
1. Prayers. I. Title.

LOCKYER, Herbert. 264.13
All the prayers of the Bible. Grand Rapids, Zondervan Pub. House [1959] 281p. 25cm. Includes bibliography. [BV228.L6] 59-16865
1. Bible—Prayers. I. Title.

LOCKYER, Herbert [Henry John Lockyer] 264.13
All the prayers of the Bible. Grand Rapids, Zondervan Pub. House [c.1959] 281p. 25cm. (bibl.) 59-16865 3.95
1. Bible—Prayers. I. Title.

MCKIM, Audrey, 1909- 264'.13
Children's prayers for today [by] Audrey McKim and Dorothy E. Logan. New York, Association Press [1971] 64 p. illus. 23 cm. Prayers on such themes as death, pain, Christmas, family relationships, and friendship. [BV4870.M2] 78-167881 ISBN 0-8096-1833-8 3.95
1. Children—Prayer-books and devotions—

English—1961- I. Logan, Dorothy E., joint author. II. Title.

ORCHARD, William Edwin, 1877- 264.13
The temple; a book of prayers. Ed., foreword by Marvin Halverson [Rev. ed.] New York, Seabury [1965] xvi, 120p. 17cm. [BV250.O8] 65-22864 3.50
1. Pastoral prayers. I. Halverson, Marvin, 1913- ed. II. Title.

PRAYERS for all occasions. 264.13
Grand Rapids, Baker Book House, 1960. 80p. 20cm. [BV250.P7] 60-16792
1. Pastoral prayers.

PRAYERS for today's church / edited by Dick Williams ; [foreword by Alvin N. Rogness]. 1st U.S. ed. Minneapolis : Augsburg Pub. House, 1977, c1972. 210 p. ; 22 cm. Includes index. [BV245.P85 1977] 76-27081 ISBN 0-8066-1565-6 : 4.95 264'.13
1. Prayers. I. Williams, Dick, 1931-

RODENMAYER, Robert N ed. 264.13
The pastor's prayerbook, selected and arranged for various occasions. New York, Oxford University Press, 1960. 319p. 18cm. [BV250.R6] 60-13210
1. Clergy—Prayer-books and devotions—English. I. Title.

SANDLIN, John Lewis 264.13
Aprayer for every meeting [Westwood, N.J.] Revell [c.1964] 128p. 17cm. 64-16606 2.50 bds.,
1. Pastoral prayers. I. Title.

SANDLIN, John Lewis. 264.13
A prayer for every meeting. [Westwood, N. J.] Revell [1964] 128 p. 17 cm. [BV250.S2] 64-16606
1. Pastoral prayers. I. Title.

TRESCH, John W. 264'.13
A prayer for all seasons [by] John W. Tresch. Nashville, Broadman Press [1971] 128 p. 21 cm. [BV210.2.T73] 78-155681 ISBN 0-8054-8220-2
1. Prayer. 2. Prayers. I. Title.

UEHLING, Carl T. 264'.13
Prayers for public worship, by Carl T. Uehling. Philadelphia, Fortress Press [1972] xi, 163 p. 27 cm. [BV250.U33] 72-75657 ISBN 0-8006-0234-X 10.95
1. Pastoral prayers. I. Title.

WALLACE, Helen Kingsbury. 264.13
Prayers for women's meetings. Westwood, N.J., Revell [1964] 128 p. 21 cm. [BV283.W6W3] 64-20190
1. Women — Prayer-books and devotions — English. I. Title.

WALLACE, Helen Kingsbury 264.13
Prayers for women's meetings. Westwood, N.J., Revell [c.1964] 128p. 21cm. 64-20190 2.50
1. Women—Prayer-books and devotions—English. I. Title.

ZEIDLER, Clemens H. 264.13
Altar prayers for the church year. Minneapolis, Augsburg [c.1962] 200p. 27cm. 62-12925 6.50, bxd.
1. Pastoral prayers. I. Title.

LEE, Elizabeth Meredith 264.15
As among the Methodists; deaconesses yesterday, today, and tomorrow. New York, Woman's Div. of Christian Service, Bd. of Mission, Methodist Church, 1963. 133p. illus. 22cm 63-19354 2.95
1. Deaconesses. I. Title.

GAMBINO, Richard. 264.1'523'0976335
Vendetta : a true story of the worst lynching in America, the mass murder of Italian-Americans in New Orleans in 1891, the vicious motivitations behind it, and the tragic repercussions that linger to this day / Richard Gambino. 1st ed. Garden City, N.Y. : Doubleday, 1977. xi, 198 p., [12] leaves of plates : ill. ; 22 cm. Bibliography: p. 194-198. [HV6534.N45G35] 76-18345 ISBN 0-385-12273-X : 7.95
1. Murder—Louisiana—New Orleans. 2. Italian Americans. 3. Lynching—New Orleans. I. Title.

GAMBINO, Richard. 264.1'523'0976335
Vendetta : a true story of the worst lynching in America, the mass murder of Italian-Americans in New Orleans in 1891, the vicious motivitations behind it, and the tragic repercussions that linger to this day / Richard Gambino. 1st ed. Garden City, N.Y. : Doubleday, 1977. xi, 198 p., [12] leaves of plates : ill. ; 22 cm. Bibliography: p. 194-198. [HV6534.N45G35] 76-18345 ISBN 0-385-12273-X : 7.95
1. Murder—Louisiana—New Orleans. 2. Italian Americans. 3. Lynching—New Orleans. I. Title.

BALES, James D., 1915- 264'.2
Instrumental music and New Testament worship, by James D. Bales. Searcy? Ark. [1973] 299 p. 22 cm. Bibliography: p. 281-294. [ML3001.B2] 73-169351
1. Music in churches. I. Title.

BOOK, Morris Butler, 1907- 264.2
Book-Miller debate on instrumental music in worship, held in Orlando, Florida, March 15-17, 1955 [by] Morris B. Book [and] James P. Miller. [Gainesville, Fla., Phillips Publications, 1955] 140p. group ports. 23cm. [BV290.B63] 55-57985
1. Music in churches. 2. Disciples of Christ—Doctrinal and controversial works. 3. Churches of Christ—Doctrinal and controversial works. I. Miller, James Parker. II. Title.

BRADY, Nicholas, 1659-1726. 264'.2
Church musick vindicated in Estwick, Sampson, d., 1739. The usefulness of church musick, a sermon, 1696 ... Los Angeles, William Andrews Clark Memorial Library, Univ. of California, 1955. [ML3001.E77 1955] 55-3253
I. Title.

BROCK, Earl E., 1890- 264'.2
A devotional interpretation of familiar hymns, by Earl E. Brock. Freeport, N.Y., Books for Libraries Press [1969, c1947] 88 p. 23 cm. (Essay Index reprint series) [BV315.B7 1969] 72-93319
1. Hymns, English—History and criticism. I. Title.

BRUMBACK, Carl, 1917- comp. 264'.2
Holy land hymns, compiled and edited by Carl Brumback. Plainfield, N.J., Logos International [1974] 1 v. (unpaged) 18 cm. [BV459.B75] 73-93792 ISBN 0-88270-087-1 1.45 (pbk.).
1. Hymns, English. I. Title.

BUNTING, Robert H 264.2
Both sides of the music question discussed; a written discussion between Robert H. Bunting of the Church of Christ and J. D. Marion of the Christian Church. Athens, Ala., C. E. I. Store c1957. 61p. 21cm. (Freedom booklets) [ML3001.B9] 59-45627
1. Music in churches. I. Marion, Johnie D. II. Title.

BUTTERWORTH, Hezekiah, 1839-1905. 264.2
The story of the hymns and tunes, by Theron Brown and Hezekiah Butterworth. New York, American Tract Society [c1906] Grosse Pointe, Mich., Scholarly Press, 1968. xvii, 564 p. ports. 22 cm. Based on Butterworth's Story of the hymns, and Story of the tunes. [BV315.B9 1968] 75-8599
1. Hymns—History and criticism. I. Brown, Theron, 1832-1914. II. Title.

CALLAHAN, Daniel J. 264.2
The mind of the Catholic layman. New York, Scribners [c.1963] xiii, 208p. 22cm. Bibl. 63-17937 3.95
1. Laity—Catholic Church. 2. Catholic Church in the U. S. I. Title.

DAHLE, John. 264'.2
Library of Christian hymns / by John Dahle ; English translation by M. Casper Johnshoy. New York : AMS Press, [1975] p. cm. Reprint of the 1924-1928 ed. published by Augsburg Pub. House, Minneapolis. [BV310.D3 1975] 72-1649 ISBN 0-404-13202-2 : 67.50(set)
1. Hymns—History and criticism. I. Title.

HEATON, Charles Huddleston 264.2
A guidebook to worship services of sacred music. St. Louis, Bethany [c.1962] 128p. 62-9375 2.50
1. Church music—Protestant churches. 2. Worship programs. I. Title.

HOLBROOK, David, comp. 264'.2
The Cambridge hymnal; edited by David Holbrook and Elizabeth Poston. Cambridge, Cambridge U.P., 1968. 122 p. 16 cm. Also available with music at 25/- [M2136.H75C3 1968] 68-122324 4/-
1. Hymns, English. I. Poston, Elizabeth, 1905- joint comp. II. Title.

HYMN Society of America. 264'.2
Ten new hymns for the 70's. New York [1970] 12 p. 23 cm. Cover title. [BV350.H9] 72-182742 0.30.
1. Hymns, English. I. Title. II. Title: Hymns for the 70's.

JONES, Francis Arthur. 264'.2
Famous hymns and their authors. Detroit, Singing Tree Press, 1970. xi, 337 p. illus., ports., facsims. 22 cm. Reprint of the 1902 ed. [BV315.J7 1970] 72-99067
1. Hymns—History and criticism. I. Title.

NEW hymns for America, 1976. 264'.2
New York : Hymn Society of America, [1975] 14 p. ; 23 cm. Cover title. Fourteen original hymn texts composed in response to a request by the Hymn Society of America. [BV465.A45N48] 75-319629
1. Hymns, English. 2. American Revolution Bicentennial, 1776-1976—Songs and music. I. Hymn Society of America.

OWENS, James Garfield. 264'.2
All God's chillun; meditations on Negro spirituals [by] J. Garfield Owens. Nashville, Abingdon Press [1971] 144 p. 20 cm. [BV4832.2.O9] 79-134251 ISBN 0-687-01020-9 3.75
1. Negro spirituals—Meditations. I. Title.

PHELPS, Austin, 1820-1890. 264'.2
Hymns and choirs: or, The matter and the manner of the service of song in the house of the Lord, by Austin Phelps, Edwards A. Park, and Daniel L. Furber. Andover [Mass.] W. F. Draper, 1860. [New York, AMS Press, 1971] iv, 425 p. 23 cm. Includes bibliographical references. [BV310.P5 1971] 78-144671 ISBN 0-404-07207-0
1. Park, Edwards Amasa, 1808-1900, ed. The Sabbath hymn book. 2. Hymns—History and criticism. 3. Church music. I. Park, Edwards Amasa, 1808-1900. II. Furber, Daniel Little, 1820-1899. III. Title.

POLING, David, 1928- 264'.2
Songs of faith-signs of hope / David Poling. Waco, Tex. : Word Books, c1976. 124 p. ; 23 cm. [ML3186.P53] 75-36184 5.95
1. Hymns, English—History and criticism. I. Title.

POTEAT, Hubert McNeill, 1886-1958. 264'.2
Practical hymnology / by Hubert McNeill Poteat. New York : AMS Press, [1975] 130 p. ; 19 cm. Reprint of the 1921 ed. published by R. G. Badger, Boston. Includes index. [BV310.P7 1975] 72-1693 ISBN 0-404-09912-2 : 8.00
1. Hymns, English—History and criticism. 2. Church music. I. Title.

PRATT, Waldo Selden, 1857-1939. 264'.2
Musical ministries in the church : studies in the history, theory, and administration of sacred music / by Waldo Selden Pratt. New York : AMS Press, 1976. 213 p. ; 19 cm. Reprint of the 1923 ed. published by Schirmer, New York. Includes bibliographies. [ML3000.P91 1976] 74-24193 ISBN 0-404-13095-X : 12.50
1. Church music. 2. Hymns, English—History and criticism. I. Title.

PUTNAM, Alfred Porter, 1827-1906, comp. 264'.2
Singers and songs of the liberal faith; being selections of hymns and other sacred poems of the Liberal Church in America, with biographical sketches of the writers, and with historical and illustrative notes. Freeport, N.Y., Books for Libraries Press [1973] p. (Essay index reprint series) Reprint of the 1875 ed., published by Roberts Brothers, Boston. [BV403.L53P88 1973] 73-4620 ISBN 0-518-10101-0
1. Liberal Church of America—Hymns. I. Title.

SHAKERS. 264'.2
A collection of millennial hymns adapted to the present order of the church. New York : AMS Press, 1975. 200 p. ; 19 cm. (Communal societies in America) Reprint of the 1847 ed. printed in the United Society, Canterbury, N.H. Includes index. [BV442.S55 1975] 72-2991 ISBN 0-404-10753-2 : 10.50
1. Shakers—Hymns. 2. Hymns, English. I. Title.

SHEPPARD, William John Limmer, 1861- 264'.2
Great hymns and their stories / by W. J. Limmer Sheppard. New York : Gordon Press, [1976] p. cm. Reprint of the 1923 ed. published by the Religious Tract Society, London. Includes indexes. [BV350.S5 1976] 75-44284 ISBN 0-87968-350-3 lib.bdg. : 34.95
1. Hymns, English. I. Title.

SPENCER, Donald Amos, 1945- 264'.2
Hymn and Scripture selection guide : a crossrefernce of scripture and hymns with over 12,000 references for 380 hymns and gospel songs / compiled by Donald A. Spencer. Valley Forge, Pa. : Judson Press, c1977. 176 p. ; 23 cm. Includes index. [BV312.S67] 76-48529 ISBN 0-8170-0705-9 : 6.95
1. Bible—Use in hymns. 2. Hymns, English—History and criticism. I. Title.

TROBIAN, Helen Reed. 264.2
The instrumental ensemble in the church. New York, Abingdon Press [1963] 96 p. 19 cm. (A Basic music book) Includes bibliographies. [ML3001.T86] 62-16125
1. Music in churches. 2. Instrumental music — Hist. & crit. I. Title.

TROBIAN, Helen Reed 264.2
The instrumental ensemble in the church. Nashville, Abingdon [c.1961-1963] 96p. 19cm. (Basic music bk.) Bibl. 62-16125 1.50 pap.,
1. Music in churches. 2. Instrumental music—Hist. & crit. I. Title.

WALLACE, Gervias Knox, 1903- 264.2
Wallace-Hunt debate, held at Ottumwa, Iowa, April 24-27, 1951, between G. K. Wallace and Julian O. Hunt. Tape recorded. Longview, Wash., Telegram Book Co., 1953. 276p. 21cm. [BV290.W28] 54-20984
1. Music in churches. I. Hunt, Julian O. II. Title.

WELLS, Amos Russel, 1862-1933. 264'.2
A treasure of hymns; brief biographies of one hundred and twenty leading hymn-writers with their best hymns. Freeport, N.Y., Books for Libraries Press [1971, c1945] 392 p. 23 cm. (Essay index reprint series) [BV315.W4 1971] 70-128330 ISBN 0-8369-2096-1
1. Hymns, English—History and criticism. I. Title.

WILSON, John F Musician. 264.2
An introduction to church music, by John F. Wilson. Chicago, Moody Press [1965] 207 p. illus., charts, diagrs., music. 23 cm. Includes bibliographies. [ML3100.W54] 65-14612
1. Church music — Protestant churches. I. Title.

WILSON, John F. 264.2
An introduction to church music. Chicago, Moody [c.1965] 207p. illus., charts, diagrs., music. 23cm. Bibl. [ML3100.W54] 65-14612 ISBN MN 2.25 pap.,
1. Church music—Protestant churches. I. Title.

WINKWORTH, Catherine, 1827-1878. 264'.2
Christian singers of Germany. Freeport, N.Y., Books for Libraries Press [1972] xiii, 340 p. ports. 22 cm. (Essay index reprint series) Reprint of the 1869 ed., which was issued as v. 6 of The Sunday library for household reading. [BV480.W5 1972] 72-1295 ISBN 0-8369-2878-4
1. Hymns, German—Bio-bibliography. 2. German literature—History and criticism. I. Title. II. Series: The Sunday library for household reading, v. 6

MCDOWELL, Lowell B. 264.207
Soldiers and servants; a confirmation workbook. New York, Morehouse-Barlow [c.1963] 128p. illus., maps. 27cm. 63-21701 2.25 pap.,
1. Confirmation—Instruction and study. I. Title.

HATFIELD, Edwin Francis, 1807-1883. 264'.2'0922 B
The poets of the church; a series of biographical sketches of hymn-writers with notes on their hymns. Boston, Milford House [1972] vii, 719 p. 22 cm. Reprint of 1884 ed. [BV325.H38 1972] 78-133349
1. Hymn writers. 2. Hymns, English—History and criticism. I. Title.

VONK, Idalee Wolf, 1913- 264 268.7
Fifty-two worship programs on Christian living. Cincinnati, Standard Pub. Co. [1952] 198 p. 21 cm. [BV198.V6] 52-28104
1. Worship programs. I. Title.

HOWARD Mission and Home for Little Wanderers, New York. *264 268.73
The Little wanderers' friend. [New York] no. 24 cm. Issued by Howard Mission and Home for Little Wanderers: numbers for include an account of the mission's work. Includes music. [M2198.L785] 52-52687
1. Hymns, English. I. Title.

TOVEY, Herbert George, 1888- *264 268.73
Music levels in Christian education, a book on Sunday school music. Wheaton, Ill., Van Kampen Press [1952] 143 p. 20 cm. [MT10.T68] 52-1877
1. Religion and music. 2. Religious education of children. I. Title.

FINK, Peter E. 264'.3
Eucharistic liturgies: studies in American

pastoral liturgy. The order of celebration and the liturgical year, by Peter E. Fink, The American days of celebration and Eucharistic prayers, by John R. Hogan. Edited by John Gallen. Paramus, N.J., Newman Press [1969] viii, 215 p. 24 cm. Presented by the Woodstock Center for Religion and Worship. [BX2230.2.F46] 77-94143 6.50
1. Catholic Church. Liturgy and ritual. 2. Mass—Celebration. I. Hogan, John R. II. Gallen, John, ed. III. Woodstock Center for Religion and Worship. IV. Title.

TATE, Judith. 264'.3
Manual for lectors / Judith Tate. Dayton, Ohio : Pflaum Pub., c1975. 52 p. ; 22 cm. [BV677.T37] 75-23848 ISBN 0-8278-0030-4
1. Lay readers—Handbooks, manuals, etc. I. Title.

TOWNSEND, John T. 264'.3
A liturgical interpretation of Our Lord's Passion in narrative form / by John T. Townsend. New York : National Conference of Christians and Jews, 1977. v, 34 p. ; 24 cm. (Occasional papers - Israel Study Group ; no. 1) Includes bibliographical references and index. [BT431.T68] 77-150584
1. Jesus Christ—Passion. 2. Jesus Christ—Passion—Role of Jews. I. Israel Study Group. II. Title. III. Series: Israel Study Group. Occasional papers — Israel Study Group ; no. 1.

BIBLE. English. Selections. 264.4
1955. Revised standard.
Choral readings from the Bible; [selections for groups of all ages] Edited by Helen A. Brown and Harry J. Heltman. Philadelphia, Westminster Press [1955] 63p. 23cm. [BV199.R5B77] 55-8597
1. Responsive worship. 2. Choral speaking. I. Brown, Helen Ada, 1914- ed. II. Heltman, Harry Joseph, 1885- ed. III. Title.

BROWN, Helen Ada, 1914- ed. 264.4
Choral reading for worship and inspiration. [Graded selections for groups of all ages] Edited by Helen A. Brown and Harry J. Heltman. Philadelphia, Westminster Press [1954] 64 p. 23 cm. [BV199.R5B76] 53-12916
1. Responsive worship. 2. Choral speaking. I. Heltman, Harry Joseph, 1885- joint ed. II. Title.

BROWN, Helen Ada, 1914- ed. 264.4
Choral readings for teen-age worship and inspiration, edited by Helen A. Brown and Harry J. Heltman. Philadelphia, Westminster Press [1959] 61p. 23cm. [PN4305.C4B695] 59-9196
1. Choral recitations. I. Heltman, Harry Joseph, 1885- joint ed. II. Title.

SWISHER, Rolla O 264.4
When you lead devotions. Anderson, Ind., Warner Press [1961] 128 p. 21 cm. [BV4832.2.S9] 61-15362
1. Devotional exercises. I. Title.

SWISHER, Rolla O. 264.4
When you lead devotions. Anderson, Ind., Warner Pr. [dist. Gospel Trumpet Pr., C.1961 128p. 61-15362 1.50 pap.,
1. Devotional exercises. I. Title.

[TAYLOR, Kenneth 264'.4
Nathaniel]
Responsive readings from the Living Bible. Wheaton, Ill., Tyndale House Publishers [1973] 1 v. (unpaged) 20 cm. [BV199.R5T32] 72-97658 ISBN 0-8423-5480-8
1. Responsive worship. I. Title.

BIDDLE, Perry H., 1932- 264'.5
Abingdon marriage manual, by Perry H. Biddle, Jr. Nashville, Abingdon Press [1974] 254 p. 16 cm. Bibliography: p. 239-250. [BV199.M3B52] 73-21799 ISBN 0-687-00484-5 4.95
1. Marriage. 2. Marriage service. 3. Marriage law—United States. I. Title.

PRESBYTER ANGLICANUS. 264.5
The Second Vatican Council, an interim report. New York, Morehouse-Barlow [c.1963] iv, 32p. 19cm. 63-24995 .95 pap.,
1. Vatican Council, 2d. I. Title.

*FOUSHEE, Clyde. 264.6
Animated object talks. Grand Rapids, Mich., Baker Book House [1973, c1956] 159 p, 20 cm. (Object lesson series.) [BV4531.2] ISBN 0-8010-3459-0 1.50 (pbk.)
1. Sermons—Study and teaching. I. Title.

AHRENDT, Vivian. 264.7
More prayer meeting topics. Anderson, Ind., Warner Press [1953] 128p. 19cm. [BV285.A34] 53-7375
1. Prayer-meetings. I. Title.

BROWN, John, 1934- 264'.7
New ways in worship for youth. Valley Forge [Pa.] Judson Press [1969] 224 p. illus. 27 cm. [BV29.B73] 68-20435 3.75
1. Worship programs. 2. Young people's meetings (Church work) I. Title.

ENGSTROM, Theodore Wilhelm, 264.7
1916-
Workable prayer meeting programs. Grand Rapids, Zondervan Pub. House [1955] 150 p. 20 cm. [BV285.E5] 55-1345
1. Prayer-meetings. I. Title.

GUNSTOEE, John Thomas 264'.7
Arthur.
The charismatic prayer group / John Gunstone. Minneapolis : Bethany Fellowship, 1976, c1975. 159 p. ; 18 cm. (Dimension books) [BV287.G86 1976] 76-6615 ISBN 0-87123-057-7 pbk. : 1.95
1. Prayer groups. 2. Pentecostalism. I. Title.

MCGINTY, Claudius Lamar 264.7
Sermon outlines for prayer meetings. [Westwood, N. J.] Revell [c.1960] 64p. 21cm. (Revell's sermon outline series) 60-8461 1.00 pap.,
1. Prayer-meetings. I. Title.

MCGINTY, Claudius Lamar, 264.7
1885-
Sermon outlines for prayer meetings. [Westwood, N. Y.] Revell [1960] 64p. 21cm. (Revell's sermon outline series) [BV285.M25] 60-8461
1. Prayer-meetings. I. Title.

MILLER, Milburn H 264.7
Ideas for the midweek service. Anderson, Ind., Warner Press [1956] 128p. 19cm. [BV285.M53] 57-4347
1. Prayer-meetings. 2. Sermons—Outlines. I. Title.

PRAYER meeting talks and 264.7
outlines by David Thomas, Charles Simeon, Charles H. Spurgeon, F. B. Meyer, and others. Grand Rapids, Baker Book House, 1954. 96p. 21cm. (Minister's handbook series) [BV285.P82] 54-3030
1. Prayer-meetings. I. Thomas, David, minister.

RINKER, Rosalind. 264'.7
Praying together. [1st ed.] Grand Rapids, Zondervan [1968] 128 p. 21 cm. [BV285.R55] 68-19841
1. Prayer-meetings. 2. Prayer groups. I. Title.

SHOEMAKER, Helen (Smith) 264.7
Power through prayer groups their why and how. [Westwood, N.J., Revell [1958] 124 p. 21 cm. Includes bibliography. [BV287.S47] 58-8606
1. Prayer groups. 2. Prayer — Bibl. I. Title.

SWISHER, Rolla O. 264.7
When you lead meditations. Anderson, Ind., Warner [c. 1965] 128p. 21cm. [BV4832.2.S92] 65-11353 1.50 pap.,
1. Devotional exercises. I. Title.

GRINDSTAFF, Wilmer E 1912- 264.8
Developing a giving church. [Westwood, N. J.] F. H. Revell Co. [1954] 191p. 21cm. [BV772.G77] 54-9686
1. Christian giving. I. Title.

GUARDINI, Romano, 1885- 264.9
Sacred signs. Translated by Grace Branham; drawings by Wm. V. Cladek. St. Louis, Pio Decimo Press [1956] 106p. 19cm. Translation of Von helligen Zeichen. [BX2295.G817] 56-58164
1. Sacramentals. I. Title.

265 Other Rites, Ceremonies, Ordinances

ALEXANDER, Anthony F., rev. 265
1920-
College sacramental theology. Chicago, Regnery [c.] 1961. 270 p. Bibl. 61-11083 3.00
1. Sacraments—Catholic Church. I. Title.

ALEXANDER, Anthony F 1920- 265
College sacramental theology. Chicago, Regnery, 1961. 270p. 22cm. Includes bibliography. [BX2200.A47] 61-11083
1. Sacraments—Catholic Church. I. Title.

BAILLIE, Donald Macpherson, 265
1887-1954.
The theology of the sacraments, and other papers. With a biographical essay by John Baillie. New York, Scribner [1957] 158p. 22cm. [BV800.B3] 57-7580
1. Sacraments. 2. Free will and determinism. 3. Preaching. I. Title.

BERKOUWER, Gerrit Cornelis, 265
1903-
The sacraments, by G. C. Berkouwer. [Translated by Hugo Bekker] Grand Rapids, Eerdmans [1969] 304 p. 23 cm. (His Studies in dogmatics) Translation of De Sacramenten. Bibliographical footnotes. [BV800.B4713] 66-27410 7.50
1. Sacraments.

BRO, Bernard. 265
The spirituality of the sacraments; doctrine and practice for today. Translated by Theodore DuBois. New York, Sheed and Ward [1968] 250 p. 22 cm. Translation of Faut-il encore pratiquer? Includes bibliographical references. [BV800.B6813] 68-26034 5.00
1. Sacraments. I. Title.

BROMILEY, Geoffrey William. 265
Sacramental teaching and practice in the Reformation churches. Grand Rapids, Eerdmans [1957] 111p. 19cm. (Pathway books) [BV800.B7] 57-14944
1. Sacraments. I. Title.

*BRUSSELMANS, Christiane. 265
I receive God's peace. Orig. photos. by J. A. Fortier. Art & design by Philip Thomas. Milwaukee, Bruce. [1968] 49p. 19cm. 1.50 bds.,
I. Title.

COOKE, Bernard J. 265
Christian sacraments and Christian personality. Introd. by Frederick R. McManus. Garden City, N.Y., Doubleday [1968, c.1965] 278p. 18cm. (Image bk. D246) Bibl. [BX2200.C6] 65-23937 1.25 pap.,
1. Sacraments—Catholic church. I. Title.

COOKE, Bernard J. 265
Christian sacraments and Christian personality [by] Bernard J. Cooke. New York, Holt, Rinehart and Winston [1965] ix, 181 p. 24 cm. Includes bibliographies. [BX2200.C6] 65-23937
1. Sacraments—Catholic Church. I. Title.

COOKE, Bernard J. 265
Christian sacraments and Christian pesonality. New York, Holt [c.1965] ix, 181p. 24cm. Bibl. [BX2200.C6] 65-23937 4.95
1. Sacraments—Catholic Church. I. Title.

CULLY, Kendig Brubaker 265
Sacraments: a language of faith. Philadelphia, Christian Educ. Pr. [c.1961] 83p. Bibl. 61-13243 2.00
1. Sacraments. I. Title.

CURRENT concepts and 265
practices of confirmation in Lutheran churches; a report of a survey conducted for the Joint Commission on the Theology and Practice of Confirmation. The American Lutheran Church, Lutheran Church in America, the Lutheran Church—Missouri Synod. [Philadelphia? 1967] xv, 5, 5, 169 p. illus. 28 cm. [BX8074.C7C8] 67-9383
1. Confirmation—Lutheran Church. I. Joint Lutheran Commission on the Theology and Practice of Confirmation.

CUSHING, Richard James, 265
cardinal
The Sacraments, seven channels of grace for every state in life. [Boston, Daughters of St. Paul, 1960] 218 p. 22 cm. (st. paul editions) 60.50066 3.00; pap., 2.00
1. Sacraments—Catholic Church. I. Title.

CUSHING, Richard James, 265
Cardinal, 1895-
The Sacraments: seven channels of grace for every state in life. [Boston, Daughters of St. Paul, 1961] 218 p. 22 cm. [BX2200.C85 1961] 61-17251
1. Sacraments — Catholic Church. I. Title.

*DAUGHTERS of St. Paul 265
In Christ we live; grade 5. Written by the Daughters of St. Paul under the direction of James Alberione. Illus. by the Daughters of St. Paul under the direction of Guy R. Pennisi. St. Paul Catechetical Ctr. [1966, i.e. 1967] 96p. illus. (pt. col.) 21cm. (The St. Paul way, truth and life ser., 5) Each lesson contains: Sacred scripture, litergy, catechism. .45 pap.,
1. Sacraments—Catholic Church. I. Aberione, James. II. Title.
Available from Daughters of St. Paul, Boston.

DE REEPER, John 265
The Sacraments on the missions a pastoral theological supplement for the missionary. [2d ed.] Dublin, Browne Nolan [dist. Mystic, Conn., Lawrence Verry, 1964] xxiii, 531p. 22cm. Bibl. 64-9586 8.00
1. Sacraments—Catholic Church. 2. Sacraments (Canon law) 3. Missions (Canon law) I. Title.

DILLENSCHNEIDER, Clement 265
The dynamic power of our sacraments. Tr. by Sister M. Renelle. St. Louis, B. Herder [1966] vi. 161p. 24cm. BBibl. [BX2200.D513] 66-17098 4.25
1. Sacraments—Catholic Church. I. Title.

ECUMENCIAL studies: baptism 265
and marriage; edited by Michael Hurley. Dublin, Gill & Son, 1968. 240 p. 22 cm. This book contains for the most part the proceedings of the ecumenical conferences which took place at the Benedictine Abbey of Glenstal, Co. Limerick, in July 1966 and at the Presentation Convent of Greenhills near Drogheda in January 1967. Includes bibliographies. [BV800.E27] 77-393539 21/-
1. Baptism. 2. Marriage. I. Hurley, Michael, 1923- ed.

EVELY, Louis, 1910- 265
Love your neighbor. Translated by Imelda L'Italien. [New York] Herder and Herder [1969] 92 p. 21 cm. Translation of L'Eglise et les sacrements. [BX2200.E7613] 79-81745 3.95
1. Sacraments—Catholic Church. I. Title.

EVELY, Louis, 1910- 265
Love your neighbor. Translated by Imelda L'Italien. Garden City, N.Y.: Image Books, 1975 [c1969] 114 p.; 18 cm. Translation of L'Eglise et les sacrements. [BX2200.E7613] ISBN 0-385-06256-7 1.45 (pbk.)
1. Sacraments—Catholic Church. I. Title.

FEARON, John. 265
Graceful living; a course in the appreciation of the sacraments. Westminster, Md., Newman Press, 1955. 160p. 21cm. [BX2200.F4] 55-9037
1. Sacraments—Catholic Church. I. Title.

FIEDLER, Ernest J. 265
The sacraments; an experiment in ecumenical honesty [by] Ernest J. Fiedler [and] R. Benjamin Garrison. Nashville, Abingdon Press [1969] 144 p. 21 cm. Bibliography: p. 137-139. [BX9.5.S2F5] 70-87027 ISBN 0-687-36726-3 3.50
1. Sacraments and Christian union. I. Garrison, R. Benjamin, joint author. II. Title.

FOLEY, Leonard, 1913- 265
Signs of love. [Cincinnati, St. Anthony Messenger Press, 1971] vii, 168 p. illus. 19 cm. [BX2200.F65] 71-170370 ISBN 0-912228-04-0 1.25
1. Sacraments—Catholic Church. I. Title.

GOLDBRUNNER, Josef 265
Teaching the sacraments. [New York] Herder & Herder [c.1961] 140p. illus. 1.75 pap.,
I. Title.

GOODLOE, Robert Wesley, 1888- 265
The sacraments in Methodism. Nashville, Methodist Pub. House [1953] 160p. 20cm. [BX8338.A1G6] 52-13755
1. Sacraments-Methodist Church. I. Title.

GRENTE, Georges, Abp., 1872- 265
The power of the sacraments; translated by Sister Mary Madonna. New York, P. J. Kenedy [1951] 236 p. 21 cm. Translation of La magnificence des sacrements. [BX2200.G713] 51-10748
1. Sacraments—Catholic Church. I. Title.

HALLIGAN, Francis Nicholas, 265
1917-
The administration of the sacraments; some practical guides for priest and seminarians. [Staten Island] N.Y., Alba House [1963] xxi, 585p. 24cm. Bibl. 63-12676 9.75
1. Sacraments—Catholic Church. 2. Casuistry. 3. Sacraments (Canon law) I. Title.

*HARDIE, Katherine Johnson 265
A very special day. Illus. by Eleanor Mill. Richmond,Va., CLC Pr., 1966. 32p. col. illus. 22cm. 1.45 bds.,
1. Christening—Presbyterian Church—Juvenile literature. I. Title.

HARING, Bernhard, 1912- 265
A sacramental spirituality [by] Bernard Haring. New York ., Sheed and Ward [1965] xi, 281 p. 22 cm. Translation of Gabe und Auftrage der Sakramente. [BX2203.H253 1965] 65-20859
1. Sacraments — Catholic Church. 2. Spiritual life — Catholic authors. I. Title.

HARING, Bernhard, 1912- 265
A sacramental spirituality [Tr. from German by R. A. Wilson] New York, Sheed, c.1962,1965] xi, 281p. [BX2203.H253] 65-20859 5.00
1. Sacraments—Catholic Church. 2. Spiritual life—Catholic authors. I. Title.

HASTINGS, Cecily. 265
The sacraments. London, New York, Sheed and Ward [1961] 217p. 18cm. (Canterbury books, 15) [BX2200.H3 1961a] 61-66075
1. Sacraments—Catholic Church. I. Title.

HASTINGS, Cecily 265
The sacraments. New York, Sheed & Ward [c.1961] 217p. 61-11793 3.50 bds.,
1. Sacraments—Catholic Church. I. Title.

HEALY, Edwin F 1897- 265
Christian guidance; the moral aspects of the sacraments, matrimony excepted. Chicago, Loyola University Press [1958] 240p. 21cm. Includes bibliography. [BX2200.H35 1958] 58-3549
1. Sacraments—Catholic Church. I. Title.

HOWARD, Fred D. 265
Interpreting the Lord's Supper [by] Fred D. Howard. Nashville, Broadman Press [1966] 71, [1] p. 22 cm. (A Broadman theological monograph) Bibliography: p. [72] [BV825.2.H6] 66-19909
1. Lord's Supper. I. Title.

HOWARD, Fred D. 265
Interpreting the Lord's supper. Nashville, Broadman [c.1966] 71, [1]p. 22cm. (Broadman theol. monograph) Bibl. [BV825.2.H6] 66-19909 1.50 pap.,
1. Lord's Supper. I. Title.

HOWELL, Clifford, 1902- 265
Of sacraments and sacrifice. Collegeville, Minn., Liturgical Press [1953, c1952] 171p. illus. 23cm. (Popular liturgical library) [BX2200.H73] 53-712
1. Sacraments—Catholic Church. 2. Catholic Church. Liturgy and ritual. I. Title.

HUGHSON, Shirley Carter, 1867- 265
The seven sacraments. West Park, N. Y., Holy Cross Press, 1950. iv, 73 p. 19 cm. [BX2200.H8] 51-37193
1. Sacraments—Catholic Church. I. Title.

HUGO, of Saint Victor, 1096or7-1141. 265
On the sacraments of the Christian faith (De sacramentis) English version by Roy J. Deferrari. Cambridge, Mass., Mediaeval Academy of America, 1951. xx, 486 p. 27 cm. (The Mediaeval Academy of America. Publication no. 58) "Selected works on Hugh of Saint Victor": p. xx. [BX2200.H843] 51-7939
1. Sacraments—Early works to 1800. I. Title. II. Series.

JANSEN, G. M. A. 265
The sacramental we; an existential approach to the sacramental life [by] G. M. A. Jansen. Milwaukee, Bruce Pub. Co. [1968] xiii, 134 p. 22 cm. (Impact books) "All Biblical citations are taken from the Jerusalem Bible (New York, Doubleday, 1966)" [BX2200.J34] 68-28443
1. Sacraments—Catholic Church. I. Title. II. Title: An existential approach to the sacramental life.

JOYCE, J. Daniel. 265
The place of the sacraments in worship [by] J. Daniel Joyce. St. Louis, Bethany Press [1967] 159 p. 23 cm. Bibliography: p. 157-159. [BV10.2.J65] 67-27122
1. Worship. 2. Sacraments. I. Title.

KEENAN, Alan. 265
Neuroses and sacraments. New York, Sheed and Ward, 1950. xi, 163 p. 20 cm. [BX2203.K4] 50-9858
1. Sacraments—Catholic Church. 2. Psychology, Pastoral. 3. Theology, Pastoral—Catholic Church. I. Title.

KRAABEL, Alf M 265
Ten studies on the sacraments. Minneapolis, Augsburg Pub. House [1954] 116p. 20cm. (Ten-week teacher-training course books) [BX8072.K7] 54-4026
1. Sacraments—Lutheran Church. I. Title.

LANDON, Harold R., ed. 265
Living thankfully; the Christian and the sacraments. Greenwich, Conn., Seabury Pr. [c.]1961. 215p. (Cathedral bk.) Bibl. 61-18037 3.75 bds.,
1. Sacraments—Angelican Communion. I. Title.

LEEMING, Bernard. 265
Principles of sacramental theology. Westminster, Md. Newman Press, 1956. 600p. 23cm. [BX2200.L43] 56-7382
1. Sacraments—Catholic Church. I. Title. II. Title: Sacramental theology.

LINK, Mark J 265
We live in Christ [by] Mark J. Link. Chicago, Loyola University Press [1965] xi, 239 p. illus. 24 cm. [BX930.L486] 65-3098
1. Religious education — Text-books for young people — Catholic. I. Title.

LINK, Mark J. 265
We live in Christ. Chicago, Loyola [c.1965] xi, 239p. illus. 24cm. (New Loyola rel. ser., bk. 2) [BX930.L486] 65-3098 3.00
1. Religious education—Text-books for young people—Catholic. I. Title.

LOUVEL, Francois, 1907- ed. 265
Signs of life [by]Francois Louvel and Louis J. Putz. Chicago, Fides Publishers Association [1953] 134p. 21cm. 'Essays from the current Fides albums ... [with] new material ... added ... Orginally edited under the direction of Father Francois Louvel ... [and] published in French ... Put into English and adapted to the American scence under the direction of Father Louis J. Puts.'--Dust jacket. [BX2200.L68] 53-10870
1. Sacraments—Catholic Church. I. Puts, Louis J. II. Title.

MCAULIFFE, Clarence R. 265
De sacramentis in genere. St. Louis, Mo., B. Herder [c.1960] 224p. 21cm. In Latin Bibl.: p.199-209 60-11797 4.00
1. Sacraments—Catholic Church. I. Title.

MCAULIFFE, Clarence R 265
Sacramental theology; a textbook for advanced students. St. Louis, Herder Herder [1958] 457p. 22cm. Includes bibliography. [BX2200.M27] 58-11740
1. Sacraments—Catholic Church. I. Title.

MCCABE, Herbert, 1926- 265
The peoples of God; the fullness of life in the church. New York, Sheed [c.1964] xvi, 172p. 21cm. Pub. in England under title: The new creation. 64-19905 3.95
1. Church. I. Title.

MCCORMACK, Arthur. 265
Christian initiation. [1st ed.] New York, Hawthorn Books [1969] 192 p. 22 cm. (Twentieth century encyclopedia of Catholicism, v. 50 Section 5: the life of faith) Bibliographical footnotes. [BX2205.M3 1969] 67-14868 4.95
1. Baptism—Catholic Church. 2. Confirmation—Catholic Church. 3. Lord's Supper—Catholic Church. I. Title. II. Series: Twentieth century encyclopedia of Catholicism, v. 50

MCLELLAND, Joseph C 265
The visible words of God; an exposition of the sacramental theology of Peter Martyr Vermigli, A. D. 1500-1562. Grand Rapids, Eerdmans [1957] ix, 291p. 23cm. Bibliography: p. 261-266. [BX9419.V4M35] 58-9551
1. Vermigli, Pietro Martire, 1500-1562. 2. Sacraments—History of doctrines. I. Title.

MADE, not born : 265
new perspectives on Christian initiation and the catechumenate, from the Murphy Center for Liturgical Research. Notre Dame, Ind. : University of Notre Dame Press, [1975] p. cm. (Liturgical studies) Papers presented at a symposium sponsored by the Murphy Center for Liturgical Research. Includes index. Bibliography: [BV812.M27] 75-19874 ISBN 0-268-00708-X : 8.95.
1. Baptism—Addresses, essays, lectures. 2. Confirmation—Addresses, essays, lectures. 3. Lord's Supper—Addresses, essays, lectures. 4. Catechumens—Addresses, essays, lectures. I. Murphy Center for Liturgical Research. II. Series: Notre Dame, Ind. University. Liturgical studies.

MAPLES, Evelyn 265
Norman learns about the sacraments. Illus. by Beverly Logan. Independence, Mo., Herald House. [c.]1961. 40p. illus. 61-9685 1.25
1. Sacraments—Mormons and Mormonism—Juvenile literature. I. Title.

MILLER, John H. 1925- 265
Signs of transformation in Christ. Englewood Cliffs, N.J., Prentice-Hall [1963] x, 117 p. 24 cm. (Foundations of Catholic theology series) Bibliography: p. 103-112. [BX2200.M5] 63-21440
1. Sacraments — Catholic Church. 2. Jesus Christ — Person and offices. I. Title.

MILLER, John H., 1925- 265
Signs of transformation in Christ. Englewood Cliffs, N.J., Prentice [c.1963] x, 117p. 24cm. (Founds. of Catholic theology ser.) Bibl. 63-21440 3.95; 1.50 pap.,
1. Sacraments—Catholic Church. 2. Jesus Christ—Person and offices. I. Title.

MONTGOMERY, David Kemble, 1905- 265
The tree of life. New York, Morehouse-Gorham, 1950. xi, 172 p. front. 21 cm. Bibliographical footnotes. [BX5949.A1M6] 50-6365
1. Sacraments — Angilican Communion. I. Title.

MORK, Wulstan 265
Led by the spirit; a primer of sacramental theology. Milwaukee, Bruce [c.1965] ix, 181p. 22cm. Bibl. [BX2200.M658] 65-18574 3.95
1. Sacraments—Catholic Church. I. Title.

O'NEILL, Colman E 265
Meeting Christ in the sacraments [by] Colman E. O'Neill. Staten Island, New York, Alba House [1964] 371 p. illus. 22 cm. [BX2200.O6] 64-20111
1. Sacraments — Catholic Church. I. Title.

O'NELL, Colman E. 265
Meeting Christ in the sacraments. Staten Island, N.Y., Alba [c.1964] 371p. illus. 22cm. 64-20111 4.95
1. Sacraments—Catholic Church. I. Title.

O'SHEA, William J 265
Sacraments of initiation [by] William J. O'Shea. Englewood Cliffs, N.J., Prentice-Hall [1966] viii, 117 p. illus. 24 cm. (Foundations of Catholic theology series) Bibliography: p. 109. [BX2205.O8] 65-27699
1. Baptism — Catholic Church. 2. Confirmation — Catholic Church. 3. Lord's Supper — Catholic Church. I. Title.

O'SHEA, William J. 265
Sacraments of initiation. Englewood Cliffs, N.J., Prentice [c. 1966] viii, 117p. illus. 24cm. (Founds. of Catholic theol. ser.) Bibl. [BX2205.O8] 65-27699 3.95; 1.75 pap.,
1. Baptism—Catholic Church. 2. Confirmation—Catholic Church. 3. Lord's Supper—Catholic Church. I. Title.

PALMER, Paul F ed. 265
Sacraments and worship; liturgy and doctrinal development of baptism, confirmation, and the Eucharist. Westminster, Md., Newman Press, 1955. xxii, 227p. 23cm. (Sources of Christian theology, v. 1) Includes bibliographical references. [BX1749.S6 vol.1] 54-7546
1. Sacraments—Catholic Church. 2. Sacraments—History of doctrines. I. Title. II. Series.

PALMER, Paul F. 265
Sacraments of healing and of vocation. Englewood Cliffs, N.J. Prentice, 1963 118 p. 23 cm. (Founds. of Catholic theology ser.) Bibl. 63-10939 3.95; pap., 1.50
1. Sacraments—Hist. of doctrines. 2. Sacraments—Catholic Church. I. Title.

PALMER, Paul F 265
Sacraments of healing and of vocation. Englewood Cliffs, N.J., Prentice-Hall, 1963. 118 p. 23 cm. (Foundations of Catholic theology series) Bibliography: p. 109-110. [BV803.P3] 63-10939
1. Sacraments — History of Doctrines. 2. Sacraments — Catholic Church. I. Title.

PIAULT, Bernard. 265
What is a sacrament? Translated from the French by A. Manson. [1st American ed.] New York, Hawthorn Books [1963] 174 p. 21 cm. (The Twentieth century encyclopedia of Catholicism, v. 49, section 5: The life of faith) Bibliography: p. 174. [BX2200.P513] 63-20975
1. Sacraments—Catholic Church. I. Title. II. Series: The Twentieth century encyclopedia of Catholicism, v. 49

PIAULT, Bernard 265
What is a sacrament? Tr. from French by A. Manson. New York, Hawthorn [c.1963] 174p. 21cm. (Twentieth cent. ency. of Catholicism, v.49, sec.5:The life of faith) Bibl. 63-20975 3.50 bds.,
1. Sacraments—Catholic Church. I. Title. II. Series:The Twentieth century encyclopedia of Catholicism, v.49

QUINN, John Richard, 1921- 265
The sacraments of growth and renewal [by] J. Richard Quinn. New York, Bruce Pub. Co. [1969] xv, 196 p. 24 cm. (Contemporary college theology series. Ecclesial theology) Bibliographical footnotes. [BX2200.Q5] 70-78972
1. Catholic Church. Liturgy and ritual. 2. Sacraments—Catholic Church. I. Title.

RAHNER, Karl, 1904- 265
The Church and the sacraments Tr. from German by W. J. O Hara. NewYork] Herder & Herder [1963] 116p. 22cm. (Quaestiones disputatae, 9) 63-10786 2.25 pap.,
1. Sacraments—Catholic Church. 2. Church. I. Title.

RICHARDS, Hubert J 1921- 265
Christ in our world; a study of baptism, Eucharist, penance, and marriage [by] Hubert J. Richards [and] Peter De Rosa. Milwaukee, Bruce Pub. Co. [1966] xi, 208 p. 23 cm. [BX2200.R5] 66-17274
1. Sacraments — Catholic Church. I. De Rosa, Peter, joint author. II. Title.

RICHARDS, Hubert J., 1921- 265
Christ in our world: a study of baptism. Eucharist, penance and marriage [by] Hubert J. Richards. Peter De Rosa. Milwaukee, Bruce [c.1966] xi, 208p. 23cm. [BX2200.R5] 66-17274 3.95 bds.,
1. Sacraments—Catholic Church. I. De Rosa, Peter, joint author. II. Title.

RUTLEDGE, Denys 265
Cosmic theology; the ecclesiastical hierarchy of pseudo-Dionysius, an introduction. Staten Island, N. Y., Alba [1965, c.1964] xi, 212p. 23cm. Bibl. [BR65.D64D5] 65-2802 6.95
1. Dionysius Areopagita. Pseudo- De caelesti hierarchia. I. Title.

THE Sacraments: 265
an ecumenical dilemma. New York, Paulist Press [1967, c1966] x, 178 p. 24 cm. (Concilium theology in the age of renewal: Ecumenical theology, v. 24) Contents.Contents.—Preface, by H. Kung; translated by T. L. Westow.—Articles: Why Baptists do not baptize infants, by J. McClendon. What can Catholics learn from the infant baptism controversy? By M. Hurley. Confession in the Evangelical churches, by M. Thurian; translated by D. Wharton. Confession outside the confessional, by W. Kasper; translated by P. Burns. Ecumenically significant aspects of New Testament eucharistic doctrine, by D. Stanley. Notes on the Orthodox understanding of the Eucharist, by J. Meyendorff. Understanding Protestant teaching on the Lord's Supper, by R. Bertalot; translated by A. M. Buono. Is the Eucharist a sacrifice? By J. Ratzinger; translated by J. Drury. Transubstantiation: how far is this doctrine historically determined? By P. Schoonenberg; translated by T. L. Westow.—Bibliographical survey: Eucharistic developments in the Evangelical church, by W. L. Boelens; translated by T. L. Westow. Divorce and remarriage: east and west, by O. Rousseau; translated by A. M. Buono. Yes, no, and nevertheless, by J. M. Oesterreicher.—DO-C: Documentation concilium: Some results of Catholic education in the United States, by A. Greeley.—Biographical notes. Bibliographical footnotes. [BX9.5.S2S2] 67-23612
1. Sacraments and Christian union. I. Kung, Hans, 1928- II. Series: Concilium (New York) v. 24

THE Sacraments in general: 265
a new perspective. Edited by Edward Schillebeeckx [and] Boniface Willems. New York, Paulist Press [1968] viii, 166 p. 24 cm. (Concilium. Dogma, v. 31) Bibliographical footnotes. [BX2200.S23] 68-20451
1. Sacraments—Catholic Church—Addresses, essays, lectures. I. Schillebeeckx, Edward Cornelis Florentius Alfons, 1914- ed. II. Willems, Boniface A., 1926- ed. III. Series: Concilium (New York) v. 31

SCHANZ, John P 265
The sacraments of life and worship [by] John P. Schanz. Milwaukee, Bruce Pub. Co. [1966] xxii, 310 p. 23 cm. (Contemporary college theology series. Ecclesial theology section) Bibliography: p. 301-306. [BX2200.S33] 66-19748
1. Sacraments—Catholic Church. I. Title.

SCHANZ, John P. 265
The sacraments of life and worship. Milwaukee, Bruce [c.1966] xxii, 310p. 23cm. (Contemp. coll. theol. ser., Ecclesial theol. sect.) Bibl. [BX2200.S33] 66-19748 4.75; p2.50 pap.,
1. Sacraments—Catholic Church. I. Title.

SCHILLEBEECKX, Edward Cornelis Florentius Alfons, 1914- 265
Christ, the sacrament of the encounter with God, by E. Schillebeeckx. [Translation by Paul Barrett. English text rev. by Mark Schoot and Laurence Bright] New York, Sheed and Ward [1963] xvii, 222 p. 22 cm. Bibliographical footnotes. [BX2200.S4143] 63-17144
1. Sacraments—Catholic Church. I. Title.

SCHILLEBEECKX, Edward Cornelis Florentius Alfons, 1914- 265
The sacraments in general: a new perspective. Ed. by Edward Schillebeeckx, Boniface Willems. New York, Paulist [1968] viii, 166p. 24cm. (Concilium theol. in the age of renewal: Dogma, v. 31) Bibl. [BX2200.S4145] 68-20451 4.50
1. Sacraments—Catholic Church—Addresses, essays, lectures. I. Willems, Boniface A., 1926- joint author. II. Title. III. Series: Concilium: theology in the age of renewal, v. 31

SCHILLEBEECKX, Edward Cornelis Florentius Alfons, 1914- 265
The sacraments in general: a new perspective. Edited by Edward Schillebeeckx [and] Boniface Willems. New York, Paulist Press [1968] viii, 166 p. 24 cm. (Concilium theology in the age of renewal: Dogma, v. 31) Bibliographical footnotes. [BX2200.S4145] 68-20451
1. Sacraments—Catholic Church—Addresses, essays, lectures. I. Willems, Boniface A., 1926- joint author. II. Title. III. Series: Concilium: theology in the age of renewal, v. 31

SCHLITZER, Albert L. 1902- 265
Our life in Christ [2v.] the realization of

redemptive incarnation. Notre Dame, Ind., Univ. of Notre Dame Pr. [c.]1962. 2v., 500; 134p. 22cm. (Univ. theology ser.) Bibl. 61-18651 6.50 set,
1. Sacrements—Catholic Church. 2. Christian ethics Catholic authors. 3. Incarnation. I. Title.

SCHMEMANN, Alexander, 1921- 265
Sacraments and orthodoxy. [New York] Herder and Herder [1965] 142 p. 21 cm. [BX350.S36] 65-13482
1. Orthodox Eastern Church. Liturgy and ritual. 2. Sacraments—Orthodox Eastern Church. I. Title.

SCHMEMANN, Alexander, 1921- 265
Sacraments and orthodoxy [New York] Herder & Herder [c.1965] 142p. 21cm. [BX350.S36] 65-13482 3.50
1. Orthodox Eastern Church. Liturgy and ritual. 2. Sacraments—Orthodox Eastern Church. I. Title.

SEMMELROTH, Otto. 265
Church and sacrament. Translated by Emily Schossberger. Notre Dame, Ind., Fides Publishers [c1965] 111 p. 19 cm. Translation of Vom Sinn der Sakramente. [BX2200.S4513] 65-13801
1. Sacraments—Catholic Church. I. Title.

SEMMELROTH, Otto 265
Church and sacrament. Tr. by Emily Schossberger. Notre Dame, Ind., Fides [c.1965] 111p. 19cm. [BX2200.S4513] 65-13801 1.50
1. Sacraments—Catholic Church. I. Title.

SILIGARDAKIS, Titus. 265
The seven sacraments. Brooklyn, Greek Orthodox Community Kimisis Theotokou, 1963. 63 p. illus. 24 cm. [BX377.S5] 63-38386
1. Sacraments—Orthodox Eastern Church. I. Title.

SIMCOX, Carroll Eugene, 1912- 265
Understanding the sacraments. New York, Morehouse-Gorham, 1956. 104p. 21cm. [BX5949.A1S5] 56-12154
1. Sacraments—Anglican Communion. I. Title.

SIMCOX, Carroll Eugene, 1912- 265
Understanding the sacraments. New York, Morehouse-Gorham, 1956. 104 p. 21 cm. [BX5949.A1S5] 56-12154
1. Sacraments — Anglican Communion. I. Title.

TAYMANS D'EYPERNON Fr. 265
The Blessed Trinity and the sacraments Westminster. Md., Newman [c.1961] 150p. 60-14821 3.50 bds.,
1. Sacraments—Catholic Church. I. Title.

TAYMANS D'EYPERNON, Fr 265
The Blessed Trinity and the sacraments. Westminster, Md., Newman Press [1961] 150 p. 21 cm. [BX2200.T313 1961] 60-14821
1. Sacraments — Catholic Church. I. Title.

TONNE, Arthur, 1904- 265
Talks on the sacramentals. [Emporia? Kan., 1950] 126 p. 24 cm. [BX2295.T6] 51-37804
1. Sacramentals. I. Title.

WYLIE, Samuel J. 265
Sacramental living. Prepared under the auspices of the Dept. of Christian Educ., Protestant Episcopal Church. New York, Seabury [c.1965] 61p. 21cm. Bibl. (Senior-High-Sch. Unit) price unreported pap.,
I. Title.

REICHERT, Richard. 265'.07
Teaching Sacraments to youth / by Richard Reichert. New York : Paulist Press, [1975] 136 p. ; 19 cm. [BX2200.R4] 75-9121 ISBN 0-8091-1880-7 pbk. : 1.65
1. Sacraments—Catholic Church—Study and teaching. I. Title.

MAYNOOTH Union Summer 265.082
School, 1963.
Sacraments; the gestures of Christ; [papers] Edited by Denis O'Callaghan. New York, Sheed and Ward [c1964] xii, 194 p. 22 cm. Sponsored by the Maynooth Union. Bibliography: p. [193]-194. [BX2200.M38] 65-12207
1. Sacraments—Catholic Church. I. O'Callaghan, Denis, 1931- ed. II. Maynooth Union. III. Title.

O'CALLAGHAN, Denis, 1931- 265.082
ed.
Sacraments; the gestures of Christ. New York, Sheed [1965, c.1964] xii, 194p. 22cm. (Paps. of the Maynooth Union Summer Schl., 1963) Bibl. [BX2200.O33] 65-12207 4.00
1. Maynooth Union Summer School, 1963. 2. Sacraments—Catholic Church. I. Title.

SULLIVAN, C. Stephen, ed. 265.082
Readings in sacramental theology. Englewood Cliffs, N.J., Prentice [c.1964] viii, 236p. 21cm. Bibl. 64-18183 2.95 pap.,
1. Sacraments—Catholic Church—Addresses, essays, lectures. I. Title.

ALAND, Kurt. 265.1
Did the early church baptize infants? Translated with an introd. by G. R. Beasley-Murray. Pref. by John Frederick Jansen. Philadelphia, Westminster Press [1963] 119 p. 23 cm (The Library of history and doctrine) Translation of Die Sauglingstaufe im Neuen Testament und in der alten Kirche. [BV813.2.A413] 63-8863
I. Infant baptism—Hist. II. Title.

ALAND, Kurt 265.1
Did the early church baptize infants? Tr. [from German], introd. by G. R. Beasley-Murray. Pref. by John Frederick Jansen. Philadelphia, Westminster [c.1963] 119p. 23cm. (Lib. of hist. and doctrine) Bibl. 63-8863 3.50
1. Infant baptism—Hist. I. Title.

ARMOUR, Rollin Stely, 1929- 265.1
Anabaptist baptism; a representative study. Scottdale, Pa., Herald Press [1966] 214 p. 24 cm. (Studies in Anabaptist and Mennonite history, no. 11) Based on thesis, Harvard, entitled: The theology and institution of baptism in sixteenth-century Anabaptism. Bibliography: p. 187-195. [BX4931.2.A7] 66-19026
1. Baptism—Anabaptists. 2. Baptism—History. I. Title. II. Series.

BAILEY, Derrick Sherwin, 265.1
1910-
Sponsors at baptism and confirmation; an historical introduction to Anglican practice. New York, Macmillan [1953] xiii, 162p. 19cm. Bibliography:p. 146-151. [BX5149.B2B2] 53-6323
1. Sponsors. 2. Baptism—Anglican communion. 3. Confirmation—Anglican communion. I. Title.

BANDEY, David Wallis. 265'.1
Baptism reconsidered / David W. Bandey. Cape Town : Methodist Publishing House, 1976. 102 p. ; 18 cm. Includes bibliographical references. [BV811.2.B36] 77-369212 ISBN 0-949942-11-1 : R2.10
1. Baptism. I. Title.

BEASLEY-MURRAY, George 265.1
Raymond, 1916-
Baptism in the New Testament. London, Macmillan; New York, St. Martin's, 1962 424 p. 23 cm. Bibl. 65-51286 4.50.
1. Baptism—Disciples of Christ. 2. Church membership. I. Title.

BEASLEY-MURRAY, George 265.1
Raymond, 1916-
Baptism today and tomorrow [by] G. R. Beasley-Murray. London, Macmillan; New York, St. Martin's P., 1966. viii, 176 p. 19 1/2 cm. (B66-3053) Bibliographical footnotes. [BV811.2.B4] 65-26120
1. Baptism. 2. Baptism and church membership. I. Title.

BEASLEY-MURRAY, George 265.1
Raymond, 1916-
Baptism today and tomorrow. London, Macmillan; New York, St. Martin's [c.]1966. viii, 176p. 19cm. Bibl. [BV811.2.B4] 65-26120 4.95 bds.,
1. Baptism. 2. Baptism and church membership. I. Title.

265.1
Baptism in the New Testament, by G. R. Beasley-Murray. Grand Rapids, Mich., Eerdmans [1973, c.1962] ix, 422 p. Includes bibliographies. [BV806.B4 1962] ISBN 0-8028-1493-X pap., 4.95
1. Baptism. I. Title.
L.C. card no. for original edition: 62-51286.

BELCASTRO, Joseph 265.1
The relationship of baptism to church membership St. Louis, Bethany pr. [c.1963] 224 p. 23 cm. Bibl. 63-20961 4.50
1. Baptism—Disciples of Christ. 2. Church membership. I. Title.

BELCASTRO, Joseph. 265.1
The relationship of baptism to church membership. St. Louis. Bethany Press [1963] 224 p. 23 cm. Bibliography: p. 217-224. [BX7325.5.B3B4] 63-20961
1. Baptism — Disciples of Chriest. 2. Church membership. I. Title.

BROCKETT, Lorna. 265'.1
The theology of baptism. Notre Dame, Ind., Fides Publishers [1971] 94 p. 19 cm. (Theology today, no. 25) Bibliography: p. 91-92. [BV803.B68] 70-30444 ISBN 0-85342-258-3 0.95
1. Baptism—History. I. Title.

BROWN, Kenneth Irving, 265.1
1896-
"... and be baptized"; a minister's handbook on baptism. Philadelphia, Judson Press [1952] 87 p. illus. 20 cm. [BV811.B82] 52-8348
1. Baptism. I. Title.

CARR, Warren. 265.1
Baptism: conscience and clue for the church. [1st ed.] New York, Holt, Rinehart and Winston [1964] xii, 208 p. 22 cm. Bibliographical footnotes. [BV811.2.C3] 63-19468
1. Baptism. 2. Baptism and church membership. I. Title.

CUTTAZ, Francois Joseph 265.1
Baptism: divine birth. Tr. [from French] by Malachy Gerard Carroll. Staten Island, N.Y., Alba House [1964, c.1962] viii, 239p. 19cm. Bibl. 63-21605 3.95
1. Baptism—Catholic Church. I. Title.

DAVIS, Charles 265.1
Sacraments of initiation, baptism and confirmation. New York, Sheed [c.1964] 159p. 21cm. First pub. in London under title: The making of a Christian. Bibl. 64-19910 3.50
1. Baptism—Catholic Church. 2. Confirmation—Catholic Church. I. Title.

DAVIS, Charles, S. T. L. 265.1
Sacraments of initiation, baptism and confirmation. New York, Sheed and Ward [1964] 159 p. 21 cm. First published in London under title: The making of a Christian. Bibliographical footnotes. [BX2205.D3 1964] 64-19910
1. Baptism — Catholic Church. 2. Confirmation — Catholic Church. I. Title.

ENGLAND, Stephen Jackson 265.1
The one baptism; baptism and Christian unity with special reference to Disciples of Christ. St. Louis, Bethany Press [c.1960] 95p. 20cm. (Bibl. Footnotes) 60-9920 1.95; 1.25 pap.,
1. Baptism—Disciples of Christ. I. Title.

EVERY, George 265.1
The baptismal sacrifice. [Naperville, Ill., stamped: distributed by Allenson, 1959, i.e.1960] 112p. 22cm. (Studies in ministry and worship, 14) Bibl. footnotes) 60-16178 2.00 pap.,
1. Baptism. 2. Initiations (in religion, folk-lore, etc.) 3. Lord's Supper. I. Title.

FISHER, John Douglas 265'.1
Close.
The bishop in Christian initiation / [by] J. D. C. Fisher. London : Church Literature Association, 1976. [2], 5 p. ; 21 cm. (Dolphin papers ; 4) Cover title. [BV670.2.F57] 76-381639 ISBN 0-85191-079-3 : £0.18
1. Bishops. 2. Baptism. 3. Confirmation. 4. Lord's Supper. I. Title.

GILMORE, Alec. 265.1
Baptism and Christian unity, by A. Gilmore. Valley Forge [Pa.] Judson Press [1966] 108 p. 23 cm. Bibliographical footnotes. [BV811.2.G49] 66-16677
1. Baptism and Christian union. I. Title.

GILMORE, Alec 265.1
Baptism and Christian unity. Valley Forge [Pa.] Judson [c.1966] 108p. 23cm. Bibl. [BV811.2.G49] 66-16677 3.95
1. Baptism and Christian union. I. Title.

HIELD, Charles R 265.1
Baptism for the dead, by Charles R. Hield and Russell F. Ralston. [Rev. Independence, Mo., Herald Pub. House 1960. 56p. 18cm. [BX8675.H5 1960] 60-4213
1. Reorganized Church of Jesus Christ of Latter-Day Saints—Doctrinal and controversial works. 2. Baptism for the dead. 3. Mormons and Mormonism— Doctrinal and controversial works. I. Ralston, Russell F., joint author. II. Title.

HOWARD, Roy J 1925- 265.1
Liturgical retreat. New York, Sheed and Ward [1959] 145p. 21cm. [BX2375.H66] 59-10657
1. Retreats. I. Title.

HUTCHISON, Harry. 265.1
Why baptize infants? The ancient Christian practice of infant baptism explained for the layman. [1st ed.] New York, Greenwich Book Publishers [c1957] 85p. 21cm. [BV813.H85] 57-13364
1. Infant baptism. I. Title.

JANSEN, John Frederick. 265.1
The meaning of baptism; meditations. Philadelphia, Westminster Press [1958] 125p. 21cm. [BV811.J36] 58-7088
1. Baptism. I. Title.

JEREMIAS, Joachim, 1900- 265.1
Infant baptism in the first four centuries. Tr. [from German] by David Cairns. Philadelphia, Westminster Press [1961, c.1960] 111p. illus. (Library of history and doctrine) Bibl. 61-5625 3.50
1. Infant baptism—Hist. I. Title.

JEREMIAS, Joachim, 1900- 265.1
The origins of infant baptism; a further study in reply to Kurt Aland [Tr. from German by Dorothea M. Barton] Naperville, Ill., A. R. Allenson [1964, c.1963] 91p. 22cm. (Studies in hist. theology, 1) Bibl. 64-753 2.00 pap.,
1. Infant baptism—Hist. I. Aland, Kurt. Die Sauglingstaufe im Neuen Testament und in der alten Kirche. II. Title.

JUNGKUNTZ, Richard. 265'.1
The gospel of baptism. St. Louis, Concordia Pub. House [1968] 137, [2] p. 20 cm. Bibliography: p. [139] [BV811.2.J8] 68-26058 2.50
1. Baptism. I. Title.

KLINE, Meredith G. 265'.1
By oath consigned; a reinterpretation of the covenant signs of circumcision and baptism, by Meredith G. Kline. Grand Rapids, Eerdmans [1968] 110p. 22cm. Rev. version of 2 articles first pub. in the Westminster theological journal, v. 27: 1, Nov. 1964 & v. 27: 2, May 1965. [BT155.K5] 67-19329 3.75
1. Covenants (Theoogy) 2. Baptism. 3. Circumcision. 4. Initiations (in reigion, folklore, etc.) I. Title.

LAMPE, Geoffrey William 265.1
Hugo.
The seal of the Spirit; a study in the doctrine of baptism and confirmation in the New Testament and the Fathers. London, New York, Longmans, Green [1951] 340p. 23cm. [BV803.L3] 52-6697
1. Baptism—Hist. 2. Confirmation— Hist. 3. Holy Spirit. I. Title.

LAVIK, John Rasmus, 1881- 265.1
Baptism and faith; with particular attention to the nature and functions of faith in relation to baptism. [Minneapolis? 1960] 65p. 20cm. 'Published at the request of the district presidents of the Evangelical Lutheran Church.' [BX8073.5.L3] 61-7002
1. Baptism—Lutheran Church. 2. Faith. I. Title.

MARTY, Martin E 1928- 265.1
Baptism. Philadelphia, Muhlenberg Press [1962] 61p. 20cm. (A Fortress book) [BV811.2.M3] 62-20750
I. Title.

MEISTER, John W 265.1
What baptism means. New York, Association Press [1960] 124p. 16cm. (An Association Press reflection book) Includes bibliography. [BV811.2.M4] 60-6565
1. Baptism. I. Title.

NEUNHEUSER, Burkhard, 1903- 265.1
Baptism and confirmation. Translated by John Jay Hughes. [New York] Herder and Herder [1964] x, 251 p. 22 cm. (The Herder history of dogma) Originally published as v. 4, pt. 2, of the Handbuch der Dogmengeschichte. Includes bibliographies. [BX2205] 64-11974
1. Baptism — Hist. 2. Confirmation — Hist. I. Title.

NEUNHEUSER, Burkhard, 1903- 265.1
Baptism and confirmation. Tr. [from German] by John Jay Hughes [New York] Herder & Herder [c.1964] x, 251p. 22cm. (Herder hist. of dogma) Orig. pub. as v.4. pt. 2. of the Handbuch der Dogmenge-schichte. Bibl. 64-11974 6.50
1. Baptism—Hist. 2. Confirmation—Hist. I. Title.

PATRICK, Walter S 1894- 265.1
The true believer complete in Him [Lynbrook, N. Y.] Quick-Set Printers [1963] 131 p. 20 cm. [BX6510.B6551P3] 63-22653
1. Baptism—Bible Protestant Church. I. Title. II. Title: Complete in Him.

PETERSON, Royal F 265.1
Baptized into Christ. Rock Island, Ill., Augustana Press [1959] 53p. 20cm. [BX8073.5.P4] 59-14541
1. Baptism—Lutheran Church. I. Title.

PLUS, Raoul, 1882- 265.1
Baptism and confirmation. [Tr. from French] Westminster, Md., Newman Press [1961, c.1960] 101p. Bibl. 60-14822 1.25 pap.,
1. Baptism—Catholic Church. 2. Confirmation—Catholic Church. I. Title.

RAYBURN, Robert Gibson, 265.1
1915-
What about baptism? St. Louis, Covenant College Press [c1957] 89p. 21cm. [BV811.R36] 57-12377
1. Baptism. I. Title.

REED, Albert A 265.1
The juridical aspect of incorporation into the

church of Christ--Canon 87. Carthagena, Ohio, 1960. 123p. 23cm. 'Dissertatio ad lauream in Facultate Iuris Canonici apud Pontificium Institutum 'Angelicum' de urbe.' 60-42963
1. Baptism (Canon law) 2. Heresy (Canon law) 3. Salvation outside the Catholic Church. I. Title.

RILEY, Hugh M. 265'.1
Christian initiation; a comparative study of the interpretation of the baptismal liturgy in the mystagogical writings of Cyril of Jerusalem, John Chrysostom, Theodore of Mopsuestia, and Ambrose of Milan, by Hugh M. Riley. Washington, Catholic University of America Press, 1974. xxxiii, 481 p. 24 cm. (The Catholic University of America. Studies in Christian antiquity, no. 17) Bibliography: p. xxv-xxxiii. [BV803.R54] 74-11191 ISBN 0-8132-0531-X 21.00
1. Cyrillus, Saint, Bp. of Jerusalem, 315 (ca.)-386. 2. Chrysostomus, Joannes, Saint, Patriarch of Constantinople, d. 407. 3. Theodorus, Bp. of Mopsuestia, d. ca. 428. 4. Ambrosius, Saint, Bp. of Milan. 5. Baptism—History—Early church. I. Title. II. Series.

SAARNIVAARA, Uuras, 1908- 265.1
Scriptural baptism; a dialog between John Bapstead and Martin Childfont ... New York, Vantage Press [c1953] 106p. 23cm. [BV811.S2] 53-6479
1. Baptism. I. Title.

SMALL, Dwight Hervey. 265.1
The Biblical basis for infant baptism; children in God's covenant promises. [Westwood, N.J.] Revell [1959] 191 p. 22 cm. [BV813.S55] 59-11525
1. Infant Baptism I. Title.

SMITH, Benjamin Franklin. 265'.1
Christian baptism, a survey of Christian teaching and practice [by] B. F. Smith. [Rev. ed.] Nashville, Tenn., Broadman Press [1971, c1970] xii, 180 p. 21 cm. Bibliography: p. 173-178. [BV803.S6 1971] 71-136132 4.95
1. Baptism—History. I. Title.

SPRINGER, John. 265.1
The Catholic baby book, by John and Ellen Springer. New York, Paulist Press [1961] 128 p. 18 cm. (Deus books) [BX2205.S65] 61-16663
1. Baptism — Catholic Church. 2. Names, Personal — English. I. Title.

SPRINGER, John 265.1
The Catholic baby book, by John and Ellen Springer. New York, Paulist Pr. [c.1961] 128p. (Deus bks.) 61-16663 .75 pap.,
1. Baptism—Catholic Church. 2. Names, Personal—English. I. Springer, Ellen, joint author. II. Title.

WAINWRIGHT, Geoffrey, 1939- 265'.1
Christian initiation. Richmond, John Knox Press [1969] 107 p. 22 cm. (Ecumenical studies in history no. 10) Includes bibliographical references. [BV811.2.W3 1969b] 75-79922
1. Baptism. I. Title. II. Series.

WHITE, Reginald E. O. 265.1
The Biblical doctrine of initiations; a theology of baptism and evangelism. Grand Rapids, Mich., Eerdmans [1960] 392p. 23cm. (7p. bibl.) 60-9555 6.00
1. Baptism—Biblical teaching. 2. Initiations (in religion, folk-lore, etc.) 3. Evangelistic work. I. Title.

MOSS, Basil S., ed. 265.108
Crisis for baptism. London, SCM Pr. [New York, Morehouse, 1966, c.1965] 189p. 19cm. (Living church bks.) Report of the ecumenical conf. held at Swanwick, Eng., Jan. 4-7, 1965, and sponsored by the Parish and People movement. Bibl. [BV811.2.M6] 66-1714 3.00 pap.,
1. Baptism—Congresses. I. Parish and People. II. Title.

BROWN, Henry F. 265.109
Baptism through the centuries. Mountain View, Calif., Pacific Pr. Pub. [1966. c.1965] 122p. illus. 23cm. Bibl. [BV803.B7] 65-26228 3.95
1. Baptism—Hist. I. Title.

HAMMAN, Adalbert, 1910- comp 265'.1'09
Baptism; ancient liturgies and patristic texts. Ed.: Andre [sic] Hamman. English ed. supervisor: Thomas Halton. Staten Island, N. Y., Alba [1968,c.1967] 240p. 22cm. (Alba patristic lib., 2) Tr. of La bapteme d'apres les peres de l'Eglise. Bibl. [BV807.H2713] 67-16843 4.95
1. Baptism—Hist.—Early church—Sources. 2. Christian literature, Early (Selections: Extracts, etc.) I. Title.

MITCHELL, Leonel Lake, 1930- 265'.1'09
Baptismal anointing / Leonel L. Mitchell. Notre Dame, Ind. : University of Notre Dame Press, 1977, c1966. p. cm. Reprint of the ed. published by S.P.C.K., London, in series: Alcuin Club collections, no. 48. A revision of the author's thesis, General Theological Seminary, New York. Bibliography: p. [BV803.M52 1977] 77-89758 ISBN 0-268-00657-1 : 11.95
1. Baptism (Liturgy)—History. 2. Holy oils. I. Title. II. Series: Alcuin Club. Collections ; no. 48.

AKELEY, T. C. 265'.1'0946
Christian initiation in Spain, c. 300-1100 by] T. C. Akeley. London, Darton, Longman & Todd, 1967. 223p. front. (map) illus., 6 plates (incl. facsim.) tables. 22cm. Bibl. [BV803.A4] 67-78193 5.50
1. Baptism—Hist. I. Title.
Distributed by Hillary House, New York.

PAWSON, David. 265'.12
Infant baptism under cross-examination / by David Pawson and Colin Buchanan. 2nd ed. Bramcote : Grove Books, 1976. 24 p. ; 21 cm. (Grove booklet on ministry and worship ; no. 24 ISSN 0305-3067s) "A sequel to Booklet no. 20. A case for infant baptism." Includes bibliographical references. [BV813.2.P38 1976] 77-350998 ISBN 0-901710-89-X : £0.30
1. Infant baptism. I. Buchanan, Colin Ogilvie, joint author. II. Title.

MOODY, Dale. 265'.12'09
Baptism; foundation for Christian unity. Philadelphia, Westminster Press [1967] 317 p. 24 cm. Bibliographical footnotes. [BV803.M6] 67-19696
1. Baptism—History. 2. Baptism and Christian union. I. Title.

ADULT baptism and the catechumenate. 265'.13 New York, Paulist Press [1967] x, 189 p. 24 cm. (Concilium theology in the age of renewal: Liturgy, v. 22) Contents.Contents.—The relation between baptism and faith, by H. Manders.—The Biblical symbolism of baptism in the Fathers of the Church and the liturgy, by L. Ligier.—Temporal and supra-temporal in the history of the catechumenate and baptism, by A. Stenzel.—Sponsorship, by M. Dujarier.—History and function of the three great pericopes: the Samaritan woman, the man born blind, the raising of Lazarus, by T. Maertens.—Scrutinies and exorcisms, by R. Beraudy.—Blessing of baptismal water in the Roman rite, by E. Lengeling.—The chants of the baptismal liturgy, by J. Gelineau.—The place of catechesis in the catechumenate, by C. Paliard.—Baptism and confirmation: the two sacraments of initiation, by W. Breuning.—Liturgical reform and sacred music in Italy, by L. Borello.—Sacred music in the perspective of liturgical renewal, by D. Cols.—Sacred music in Canada and the United States, by S. Somerville.—Sacred music in South Africa, by M. Kearney.—Sacred music in the liturgical renewal in Brazil, by A. C. de Albuquerque.—Conditional baptism, by R. Kosters.—Evangelization and the catechumenate in the church throughout the world. [BX2205.A3] 67-19979
1. Baptism—Catholic Church—Addresses, essays, lectures. I. Series: Concilium (New York) v. 22.

BAUMAN, William A. 265'.2
Together at confirmation [by] William A. Bauman [and] Therese Randolph. Notre Dame, Ind., Ave Maria Press [1973] 96 p. illus. 22 cm. [BX2210.B38] 72-94177 ISBN 0-87793-052-X 1.50
1. Confirmation—Catholic Church. I. Randolph, Therese, joint author. II. Title.

BOHEN, Marian 265.2
The mystery of confirmation, a theology of the sacrament. [New York] Herder & Herder [c.1963] 192 p. 22 cm. Bibl. 62-9614 4.50
1. Confirmation—Catholic Church. I. Title.

BOHEN, Marian. 265.2
The mystery of confirmation, a theology of the sacrament. [New York] Herder and Herder [1963] 192 p. 22 cm. Includes bibliographies. [BX2210.B6] 63-18147
1. Confirmation — Catholic Church. I. Title.

BOWMAN, S Loren. 265.2
Choosing the Christian way; a manual interpreting church membership in the Church of the Brethren. Elgin, Ill., House of the Church of the Brethren [1951] 128 p. 20 cm. Bibliography: p. 126-128. [BX7826.B6] 51-10473
1. Church of the Brethren—Membership. I. Title.

CONFIRMATION and education. 265'.2 W. Kent Gilbert, editor. [Philadelphia] Fortress Press [1969] 222 p. illus. 23 cm. (Yearbooks in Christian education, v. 1) "A report for study from the Joint Commission on the Theology and Practice of Confirmation": p. [179]-222. Includes bibliographical references. [BX8074.C7C65] 72-4725 4.50 (pbk)
1. Confirmation—Lutheran Church. I. Gilbert, W. Kent, ed. II. Joint Lutheran Commission on the Theology and Practice of Confirmation. III. Title. IV. Series.

CONVIS, Lewis Albert. 265.2
Adventuring into the church; a program for preparing young people for the Christian life and church membership. [1st ed.] New York, Harper [1951] xv, 186 p. 22 cm. [BV820.C58] 51-9578
1. Church membership. I. Title.

CULLY, Kendig Brubaker, ed. 265.2
Confirmation: history, doctrine, and practice. Greenwich, Conn., Seabury [c.]1962. 246p. Bibl. 62-9614 4.75
1. Confirmation—Anglican Communion. I. Title.

DEWEY, Robert D. 265'.2
A manual for confirmation education, by Robert D. Dewey. Boston, United Church Press [1968] iii, 123 p. illus. 22 cm. (Confirmation education series) "Part of the United Church curriculum, prepared and published by the Division of Christian Education and the Division of Publication of the United Church Board for Homeland Ministries." Bibliography: p. 118-123. [BX9886.D4] 68-10039
1. Confirmation—United Church of Christ. I. United Church Board for Homeland Ministries. Division of Christian Education. II. United Church Board for Homeland Ministries. Division of Publication. III. Title.

DOUGLASS, Truman B 265.2
Why go to church? New York, Harper [1957] 118p. 20cm. [BV820.D6] 57-9877
1. Church membership. I. Title.

EVANGELICAL and Reformed Church. Board of Christian Education and Publication. 265.2
My confirmation; a guide for confirmation instruction. [2d ed.] Philadelphia, Christian Education Press [1954] 204p. illus. 23cm. [BX7475.5.C7E9 1954] 54-40328
1. Confirmatiion—Instruction and study. I. Title.

FISHER, John Douglas Close. 265'.2
Baptism, confirmation and commitment / [by] J. D. C. Fisher. London : Church Literature Association, 1976. [2], 11 p. ; 22 cm. [BV803.F57] 76-380510 ISBN 0-85191-072-6 : £0.20
1. Baptism—History. 2. Confirmation—History. I. Title.

GETTYS, Joseph Miller, 1907- 265.2
Meet your church; how Presbyterians think and live. Richmond, John Knox Press [1955] Richmond, John Knox Press [1955] 62p. illus. 22cm. 35p. 22cm. Includes bibliography. [BX9190.G4] 55-6999
1. Presbyterian church—Membership. I. Title. II. Title: —Leader's guide.

**GOD'S grace for God's people;* 265.2 catechist's guide, grade 8, trimester C. [Minneapolis, Augsburg, 1967] v. illus. 28cm (Amer. Lutheran Church: Junior high-confirmation curriculum. Vacation Church sch.) Prepd. for the Bd. of Parish Educ. and the Bd. of Pubns. of the Amer. Lutheran Church. 1.25 pap.,
1. Confirmation—Lutheran Church.

GOD'S word for God's world; 265.2 catechist's guide & study bk. [Prep. for the Bd. of Parish Educ. and the Bd. of Pubn. of the Amer. Lutheran Church. Minneapolis, Augsburg, c.1965] 2v.(151;224p.) 28cm. (Jr. High confirmation, gr. 7, Trimester B; Amer. Lutheran Church curriculum) pap., 2.00; pap., study bk., 2.25

HARTMAN, William Emory. 265.2
Membership manual of the Methodist Church for pastors; a guide for the use of pastors in preparing boys and girls, teen-agers, and young people and adults for membership in the Methodist Church. Prepared under the direction of the Joint Committee on Materials for Training for Church Membership established by the General Conference of the Methodist Church; J. Richard Spann, editor. Baltimore, Methodist Pub. House ['1951] 199 p. illus. 21 cm. [BX8342.H3] 52-525
1. Methodist Church (United States)—Membership. I. Title.

HOLLENSEN, Martin E 265.2
Is it true? Columbus, Ohio, Wartburg Press [1958] 197p. illus. 22cm. 'A series of lectures.' [BX8065.H74] 58-11792
1. Lutheran Church—Membership. 2. Lutheran Church— Doctrinal and controversial works. I. Title.

JONES, Idris W. 265.2
For Christ and the church; a manual for guiding juniors in the meaning of church membership. [1st ed.] Philadelphia, Judson Press [1952, '1951] 102 p. illus. 20 cm. [BX6332.J65] 52-4800
1. Baptists—Membership. 2. Baptists—Doctrinal and controversial works. I. Title.

LUTHERAN World Federation. Commission on Education. 265.2
Confirmation; a study document. Tr. by Walter G. Tillmanns. Minneapolis, Augsburg [1964] 89p. 22cm. Reprint of the major portion of Document no. 16. Commn. on educ., prep. for the Fourth Assembly of the Lutheran World Fed., July 30 to August 11, 1963, in Helsinki, Finland. Bibl. 64-25634 1.50
1. Confirmation—Lutheran Church. I. Title.

MAY, Eugene. 265.2
For better church members. St. Louis, Bethany Press [c1960] 112p. 23cm. [BV820.M42] 60-53144
1. Church membership. 2. Christian life. I. Title.

METHODIST Church (United States) Joint Committee on Materials for Training for Church Membership. 265.2
Membership manual of the Methodist Church for young people and adults. Nashville, Methodist Pub. House, 1960. 91p. 23cm. [BX8342.A35] 61-23398
1. Methodist Church (United States)—Membership. I. Title.

NORWOOD, Frederick Abbott. 265.2
Church membership in the Methodist tradition. Nashville, Methodist Pub. House [1958] 141p. 20cm. Includes bibliography. [BX8342.N6] 58-6594
1. Methodist Church— Membership. I. Title.

PROTESTANT Episcopal Church in the U. S. A. New York (Diocese) Commission on Preparation for Confirmation. 265.2
Ready & desirous; being the report of the Commission on Preparation for Confirmation of the Diocese of New York, 1958-1962. Foreword by Horace W. B. Donegan. New York, Morehouse-Barlow Co. [1962] 84p. 21cm. [BX5949.C7A15] 62-21027
1. Confirmation—Anglican Communion. I. Title.

PROTESTANT Episcopal Church in the U.S.A. New York (Diocese) Commission on Preparation for Confirmation. 265.2
Ready & desirous; being the report of the Commission on Preparation for Confirmation of the Diocese of New York, 1958-1962. Foreword by Horace W. B. Donegan: New York, Morehouse [c.1962] 84p. 21cm. Bibl. 62-21027 2.50 pap.,
1. Confirmation—Anglican Communion. I. Title.

REPP, Arthur Christian, 1906- 265.2
Confirmation in the Lutheran Church. St. Louis, Concordia [c.1964] x, 262p. illus. 24cm. Bibl. 64-19897 5.50
1. Confirmation—Lutheran Church. I. Title.

THURIAN, Max 265.2
Consecration of the layman; new approaches to the sacrament of confirmation. Tr. [from French] by W. J. Kerrigan. Foreword by Frank B. Norris. Helicon [dist. New York, Taplinger, c.1963] x, 118p. 22cm. 63-19400 2.95 bds.,
1. Confirmation. 2. Baptism. I. Title.

20 confirmation sermons, 265.2
by pastors oof the Evangelical Lutheran Church Minneapolis, Augsburg Pub. House [1951] 226 p. 21 cm. [BV4257.7.T8] 51-14656
1. Confirmation sermons. 2. Lutheran Church — Sermons. 3. Sermons, American.

[UNITED Church of Christ] 265.2
My confirmation; a guide for confirmation instruction. Philadelphia, United Church Press [1963] 240 p. illus. 24 cm. [BX7475.5.C7U5] 63-11697
1. Confirmation — Instruction and study. I. Title.

[UNITED Church of Christ] 265.2
My confirmation; a guide for confirmation instruction. Philadelphia, United Church [c.1963] 240p. illus. 24cm. 63-11697 2.25; 1.75 pap.,
1. Confirmation—Instuction and study. I. Title.

UNITED Church of Christ. 265'.2
My confirmation : a guide for confirmation instruction. Rev. ed. Philadelphia : United Church Press, 1977. 240 p. : ill. ; 23 cm. [BX7475.5.C7U5 1977] 77-359184 ISBN 0-8298-0091-3 pbk. : 3.25
1. Confirmation—Instruction and study. I. Title.

WALSH. CHAD. 1914- 265.2
Knock and enter; with illus by Jacqueline Jackson. New York, Morehouse-Gorham Co., 1953. 208p. illus. 21cm. [BX5949C7W2] 53-1246
1. Confinmation Anglicaa communion. I. Title.

WELLBORN, Charles. 265.2
The challenge of church membership. Nashville, Convention Press [1955] 118p. 20cm. [BX6340.W3] 56-1573
1. Baptists—Membership. 2. Church membership. I. Title.

WITSELL, William Postell, 1874- 265.2
Come. Boston, Christopher Pub. House [1955] 127p. 21cm. [BX5950.W55] 55-14258
1. Protestant Episcopal Church in the U.S.A.—Membership. I. Title.

ABELL, William S. 265'.3
The faithful at Mass : a guide to participation by the laity in the liturgy of the post-Vatican Council II Mass / by William S. Abell. Garrett Park, Md. : Georgetown Preparatory School, 1976. 70 p. ; 21 cm. [BX2230.2.A65 1976] 76-27917
1. Mass. I. Title.

ACKEN, Bernhard van. 265.3
The Holy Eucharist, the mystery of faith and the sacrament of love. Translated by H. G. Strauss. Westminster, Md., Newman Press, 1958. 141p. 20cm. [BX2215.A363] 58-13639
1. Lord's Supper—Catholic Church. I. Title.

ALLMEN, Jean Jacques von. 265'.3
The Lord's Supper. Richmond, Va., John Knox Press [1969] 117 p. 22 cm. (Ecumenical studies in worship, no. 19) Translation of Essai sur le repas du Seigneur. Bibliographical footnotes. [BV825.2.A713] 76-79925
1. Lord's Supper. I. Title. II. Series.

AULEN, Gustaf Emanuel Hildebrand, Bp., 1879- 265.3
Eucharist and sacrifice. Translated by Eric H. Wahlstrom. Philadelphia, Muhlenberg Press [1958] 212p. 21cm. 'Translated from For eder utgiven.' [BV825.A843] 58-8946
1. Lord's Supper—Sacrifice. I. Title.

BARCLAY, William, lecturer in the University of Glasgow. 265'.3
The Lord's Supper. Nashville, Abingdon Press [1967] 128 p. 20 cm. Includes bibliographical references. [BV825.2.B3 1967] 68-3913
1. Lord's Supper.

BAYNE, Stephen Fielding, Bp., 1908- 265.3
Mindful of the love; the Holy Communion and daily life. New York, Oxford University Press, 1962. 132 p. 20 cm. [BV825.2.B35] 62-9821
1. Lord's Supper—Sermons. 2. Sermons, American. I. Title.

BEALS, Ivan Anson 265.3
Communion with Christ; the meaning of the Lord's Supper. Kansas City, Mo., Beacon Hill [1964, c.1963] 152p. 20cm. Bibl. 64-10029 1.95
1. Lord's Supper—Church of the Nazarene. I. Title.

BOUQUET, John Alexander, 1875- ed. 265.3
Be ye thankful; thoughts for the Holy Eucharist. London, New York, Longmans, Green [1959] 109p. 17cm. [BV828.B67] 59-16124
1. Lord's Supper—Prayer-books and devotions—English. I. Title.

BOUYER, Louis, 1913- 265'.3
Eucharist: theology and spirituality of the eucharistic prayer. Translated by Charles Underhill Quinn. Notre Dame [Ind.] University of Notre Dame Press [1968] xii, 484 p. 25 cm. Translation of Eucharistie: theologie et spiritualite de la priere eucharistique. Bibliographical footnotes. [BV823.B613] 68-17064 14.00
1. Lord's Supper—History. I. Title.

BOYLAN, Anthony B. 265'.3
The reception of Holy Communion in the hand / [by Anthony B. Boylan ; photographs by Noeline Kelly]. London : Catholic Truth Society, [1976] [28] p. : ill. ; 19 cm. Includes extracts from relevant documents. [BX2235.B69] 76-378401 ISBN 0-85183-166-4 : £0.20
1. Lord's Supper—Bread. I. Title.

BREAD from heaven / 265'.3
edited by Paul Bernier. New York : Paulist Press, c1977. ix, 170 p. ; 19 cm. (Paulist Press/Deus books) [BX2215.2.B69] 77-74581 ISBN 0-8091-2029-1 pbk. : 1.95
1. Lord's Supper—Catholic Church—Addresses, essays, lectures. I. Bernier, Paul, 1937-

THE Breaking of bread. 265'.3
Edited by Pierre Benoit, Roland E. Murphy [and] Bastiaan van Iersel. New York, Paulist Press [1969] viii, 181 p. 24 cm. (Concilium: theology in the age of renewal: Scripture, v. 40) Includes articles translated from several languages by various persons. Bibliographical footnotes. [BX2215.2.B7] 68-59157 4.50
1. Lord's Supper—Catholic Church. I. Benoit, Pierre, Aug. 3, 1906- ed. II. Murphy, Roland Edmund, 1917- ed. III. Iersel, Bastiaan Martinus Franciscus van, ed. IV. Series: Concilium (New York) v. 40

BROOKS, Peter Newman. 265.3
Thomas Cranmer's doctrine of the Eucharist; an essay in historical development, by Peter Brooks. New York, Seabury Press [1965] xviii, 134 p. 20 cm. "Bibliographical note": p. 121-123. Bibliographical footnotes. [BV823.B76] 64-24369
1. Lord's Supper — Hist. 2. Cranmer, Thomas, Abp. of Canterbury, 1489-1556. I. Title.

BROOKS, Peter Newman 265.3
Thomas Cranmer's doctrine of the Eucharist; an essay in historical development. New York, Seabury [c.1965] xviii, 143p. 20cm. Bibl. [BV823.B76] 64-24369 3.75
1. Cranmer, Thomas, Abp. of Canterbury, 1489-1556. 2. Lord's Supper—Hist. I. Title.

BRUCE, Robert, 1554-1631. 265.3
The mystery of the Lord's Supper; sermons of the sacrament preached in the Kirk of Edinburgh in A. D. 1589. Translated and edited by Thomas F. Torrance. Richmond, J. Knox Press [1958] 198p. 20cm. [BX9189.C5B7 1958] 58-11625
1. Lord's Supper—Sermons. 2. Church of Scotland—Sermons. I. Title.

BRUNER, Benjamin Harrison, 1888- 265.3
This sacred hour; communion meditations and prayers. St. Louis, Bethany Press [1953] 105p. 20cm. [BV825.B77] 53-13554
1. Lord's Supper—Meditations. I. Title.

BRYCE, Mary Charles. 265.3
Come let us eat; preparing for first communion. [New York, Herder and Herder, 1964] [New York] Herder and Herder [1964] 64 p. illus. (part col.) 21 cm. 125 p. illus. 21 cm. Includes the musical responses (unacc. melodies) Includes unacc. Catholic hymns and Gregorian chants. Includes bibliographies. [BX2237.B7] 64-13683
1. First communion — Instruction and study. I. Title. II. Title: First communion; III. Title: First communion.

BRYCE, Mary Charles 265.3
Come let us eat; preparing for first communion [New York, Herder & Herder, c.1964] 64p. illus. (pt. col.) 21cm. Includes the musical responses (unacc. melodies) 64-13683 .95 pap.,
1. First communion—Instruction and study. I. Title. II. Title: First communion.

BRYCE, Mary Charles. 265'.3
Come let us eat; preparing for first communion. [Illustrated by Jeanne Heiberg] New ed. [New York] Herder and Herder [1972] 62 p. illus. (part. col.) 23 cm. [BX2237.B7 1972] 70-183075 1.45
1. First communion—Instruction and study. I. Heiberg, Jeanne, illus. II. Title.

BUCK, Carlton C comp. 265.3
At the Lord's table; [meditations, prayers, and poems] St. Louis, Bethany Press [1956] 191p. 17cm. [BV825.B79] 56-13177
1. Lord's Supper—Meditations. I. Title.

CATHOLIC Church. Pope, 1939- (Pius XII) Christus Dominus (6 Jan. 1953) 265.3
The new Eucharistic legislation; a commentary on the Apostolic constitution Christus Dominus and on the Instruction of the Holy Office on the discipline to be observed concerning the Eucharistic fast, by John C. Ford. Forewrod by Richard J. Cushing, Archbishop of Boston. New York, P. J. Kenedy [1953] 129p. 19cm. 'Text and translation':p. [1]-43. [BX2225.A5] 53-11515
1. Lord's Supper—Fasting communion. I. Catholic Church. Congregatio Sancti Officil. II. Ford, John Cuthbert, 1902- III. Title.

CATHOLIC Church. Pope, 1939- (Pius XII) Christus Dominus (6 Jan. 1953) 265.3
The new Eucharistic legislation; a commentary on the Apostolic constitution Christus Dominus and on the Instruction of the Holy Office on the discipline to be observed concerning the Eucharistic fast, by John C. Ford. Foreword by Richard J. Cushing, Abp. of Boston. [2d ed.] New York, P. J. Kenedy [1955] 135p. 19cm. 'Text and translation': p. [1]-43. [BX2225.A5 1955] 55-2843
1. Lord's Supper—Fasting communion. I. Catholic Church. Congregatio Sancti Officil. II. Ford, John Cuthbert, 1902- III. Title.

CLARK, Francis, 1919- 265.3
Eucharistic sacrifice and the Reformation. Westminster, Md., Newman Press [c1960] 582p. 22cm. [BV825.2.C53 1960] 61-8963
1. Lord's Supper—Sacrifice. I. Title.

CLARK, John Guill, 1912-1955. 265.3
Meditations on the Lord's Supper. Nashville, Broadman Press [1958] 124p. 21cm. [BV4257.5.C57] 58-9811
1. Communion sermons. 2. Baptists—Sermons. 3. Sermons, American. I. Title.

CLELAND, James T 265.3
Wherefore art thou come? Meditations on te Lord's Supper. New York, Abingdon Press [1961] 143p. 20cm. [BV825.2.C55] 61-5555
1. Lord's Supper—Meditations. I. Title.

COLLINS, John H. 265.3
When you go to Mass. [Boston] St. Paul Editions [dist. Daughters of St. Paul, c.1961] 100p. illus. 16cm. 61-13306 1.50; 1.00 pap.,
1. Mass. I. Title.

COMMUNION thoughts and prayers / compiled by Carlton C. Buck. 265'.3
St. Louis : Bethany Press, c1976. 160 p. (p. 157-160 blank) ; 17 cm. Includes indexes. [BV826.5.C65] 76-46943 ISBN 0-8272-0440-X : 5.50
1. Lord's Supper—Prayer-books and devotions—English. 2. Elders (Church officers) I. Buck, Carlton C.

CONFERENCE on the Parish Communion, Swanwick, Eng., 1962. 265.3
The parish communion to-day; the report of the 1962 Conference of Parish and People. Ed. by David M. Paton. London, S. P. C. K. [dist. Greenwich, Conn., Seabury, c.]1962. viii. 141p. 19cm. Bibl. 62-52159 2.00 pap.,
1. Lord's Supper—Anglican Communion. I. Paton, David MacDonald, ed. II. Parish and People. III. Title.

CONNIFF, James C G 265.3
The story of the Mass, by James C. G. Conniff in consultation with Paul Bussard. New York, A. A. Wyn [1954] unpaged. illus. 29cm. [BX2230.C686] 54-6947
1. Mass. I. Title.

COUGHLAN, Peter. 265'.3
The new Mass: a pastoral guide. Washington, Corpus Books [1969] vii, 168 p. 21 cm. Includes bibliographical references. [BX2230.2.C68] 74-135464 3.95
1. Lord's Supper (Liturgy) I. Title.

CROFTS, Ambrose M 1894- 265.3
The fulness of sacrifice; doctrinal and devotional synthesis on the Mass, its foretelling, foreshadowing, and fulfilling. Westminster, Md., Newman Press [1953] 296 p. 19 cm. [BX2215.C68] 54-355
1. Lord's Supper— Catholic Church. 2. Lord's Supper—Sacrifice. I. Title.

DANAGHER, John Joseph, 1914- 265.3
Petitions for the indult to reserve the Blessed Sacrament in private oratories; a commentary on section IV of the instruction Quam plurimum given by the Sacred Congregation for the Discipline of the Sacraments on October 1, 1949. Denver, 1954. xii, 111p. 23cm. 'Dissertation ad lauream in Facultate Iuris Canonici apud Pontificium Institutum Angellcum de Urbe. Bibliography: p. ix-x. [BX2215.D33] 55-24352
1. Catholic Church. Congregatio Disciplina Sacramentorum. Quam plurimum (1 Oct. 1949) 2. Lord's Supper—Reservation. I. Title.

DELORME, Jean. 265.3
The Eucharist in the New Testament; a symposium [by] J. Delorme [and others] Translated by E. M. Stewart. Baltimore, Helicon Press, 1964. 160 p. 21 cm. "First published as a special issue of Lumiere et vie, under the title: L'Eucharistie dans le Nouveau Testament, in 1957." Bibliographical footnotes. [BV823.E813] 64-13525
1. Lord's Supper — Biblical teaching. I. Title.

DESPLANQUES, Francois. 265.3
Living the Mass; the Ordinary of the Mass and the ordinary of life. Translated by Sister Maria Constance. Westminster, Md., Newman Press, 1951. xx, 180 p. 24 cm. [BX2230.D395] 51-10475
1. Mass. I. Title.

ECHLIN, Edward P. 265'.3
The Anglican Eucharist in ecumenical perspective; doctrine and rite from Cranmer to Seabury [by] Edward P. Echlin. New York, Seabury Press [1968] viii, 305 p. 22 cm. Bibliography: p. [283]-297. [BX5149.C5E25] 68-11590
1. Lord's Supper—Anglican Communion. 2. Lord's Supper and Christian union. I. Title.

ELERT, Werner, 1885-1954. 265'.3
The Lord's Supper today. Translated by Martin Bertram. St. Louis, Concordia Pub. House [1973] 47 p. 23 cm. (Contemporary theology series) Translated excerpts from Der christliche Glaube. [BV825.2.E42213 1973] 73-80317 ISBN 0-570-06723-5 1.95
1. Lord's Supper. I. Title.

ELLARD, Gerald, 1894- 265.3
The Mass in transition. Milwaukee, Bruce Pub. Co. [1956] 387p. illus. 24cm. Includes bibliographies. [BX2015.E517] 56-10599
1. Mass. 2. Mass-Hist. I. Title.

ELLARD, Gerald, 1894- 265.3
Now, evening Mass, our latest gift. Foreword by Albert R. Zuroweste. Translation of papal constitution and instruction by John C. Ford. [Collegeville, Minn.] Liturgical Press [1954] 90p. illus. 19cm. 90p. illus. 19cm. (Popular liturgical Pres ISSN [1954]e)t(Popular liturgical library) [BX2230.E53] 54-14433
1. Mass. I. Title. II. Title: Evening Mass.

EPPINGA, Jacob D. 265'.3
For sinners only; perspectives on the Lord's Supper drawn from the life of St. Paul, by J. D. Eppinga. Grand Rapids, Eerdmans [1970] 142 p. 19 cm. [BV825.2.E65] 74-127630 3.95
1. Paul, Saint, apostle. 2. Lord's Supper. I. Title.

THE Eucharist as sacrifice. 265'.3
[New York] U.S.A. National Committee of the Lutheran World Federation [1968?] 200 p. 20 cm. (Lutherans and Catholics in dialogue, 3) Result of meetings held Sept. 23-25, 1966 in Washington; Apr. 7-9, 1967 in New York; and Sept. 29-Oct. 1, 1967 in St. Louis between representatives of the U.S. Catholic Bishops' Committee for Ecumenical and Interreligious Affairs and the U.S.A. National Committee of the Lutheran World Federation. Includes bibliographical references. [BV825.2.E83] 74-157730
1. Lord's Supper—Catholic Church—Congresses. 2. Lord's Supper—Lutheran Church—Congresses. I. Catholic Church. National Conference of Catholic Bishops. Bishops' Committee for Ecumenical and Interreligious Affairs. II. Lutheran World Federation. U.S.A. National Committee. III. Title. IV. Series.

EUCHARIST in the New Testament (The); 265.3
a symposium [by] J. Delorme [others] Tr. [from French] by E. M. Stewart. Helicon [dist. New York, Taplinger, c.1964] 160p. 21cm. Bibl. 64-13525 3.50 bds.,
1. Lord's Supper—Biblical teaching. I. Delorme, Jean.

FAHEY, John F 265.3
The eucharistic teaching of Ratramn of Corbie. Mundelein, Ill., Saint Mary of the Lake Seminary, 1951. 176p. 23cm. (Pontificia Facultas Theologica Seminarii Sanctae Mariae ad Lacum. Dissertationes ad lauream, 22) Bibliography: p. 166-176. [BV823.F22] 52-11867
1. Ratramnus, monk of Corble, d. ca. 868. 2. Lord's Supper—Hist. I. Title. II. Series: St. Mary of the Lake Seminary, Mundelein, Ill. Dissertationes ad laurcam, 22

FAY, Bertrand. 265'.3
The church at Eucharist. Milwaukee, Bruce Pub. Co. [1967] x, 115 p. 22 cm. [BX2215.2.F3] 67-29589
1. Lord's Supper—Catholic Church. I. Title.

FAY, Bertrand. 265'.3
The church at Eucharist. Milwaukee, Bruce Pub. Co. [1967] x, 115 p. 22 cm. [BX2215.2.F3] 67-29589
1. Lord's Supper—Catholic Church. I. Title.

FERET, Henricus Maria, 1904- 265'.3
The Eucharist today, by H.-M. Feret. Translated by Aimee Bourneuf. New York [Paulist Press, 1968] ix, 108 p. 18 cm. (Deus books) Translation of L'Eucharistie, paque de l'univers. [BX2215.2.F413] 68-16667
1. Lord's Supper—Catholic Church. I. Title.

*FEY, Harold E. 265.3
The Lord's Supper: seven meanings; memorial, thanksgiving covenant, affirmation, spiritual strength, atonement, immortality. New York, Harper [1965, c.1948] 117p. 21cm. (Chapel bks., CB5) 1.50 pap.,
I. Title.

FIELDS, Wilbert J 265.3
Communion with Christ. Saint Louis, Concordia Pub. House [1964] 111 p. 20 cm. [BX8073.F5] 63-23518
1. Lord's Supper — Lutheran Church. I. Title.

FIELDS, Wilbert J. 265.3
Communion with Christ. St. Louis, Concordia [c.1964] 111p. 20cm. 63-23518 1.50 pap.,
1. Lord's Supper—Lutheran Church. I. Title.

FOOTE, Gaston, 1902- ed. 265.3
Communion meditations. New York, Abingdon-Cokesbury Press [1951] 176 p. 20 cm. [BV4257.5.F6] 51-1342
1. Communion sermons. 2. Sermons, American. I. Title.

FORREST, Michael D. 265.3
Eucharistic chats; a complete explanation of the Catholic doctrine concerning the Holy Eucharist. New York, Sentinel Press [1951] 160 p. 20 cm. [BX2215.F66] 51-3482
1. Lord's Supper—Catholic Church. I. Title.

GEALY, Fred Daniel 265.3
Let us break bread together; communion meditations for the church year. New York, Abingdon Press [1960] 143p. 21cm. 60-6930 2.50
1. Communion sermons. 2. Methodist Church—Sermons. 3. Sermons, American. I. Title.

GREET, Brian A. 265'.3
Broken bread in a broken world [by] Brian A. Greet. Valley Forge, Judson Press [1971, c1970] 121 p. 20 cm. First published in England in 1970 under title: To communion with confidence. Includes bibliographical references. [BV825.2.G7 1971] 70-172826 ISBN 0-8170-0549-8 2.50
1. Lord's Supper. I. Title.

GWYNNE, John Harold, 1899- 265'.3
Communion, meditations, and prayers, by J. Harold Gwynne. Grand Rapids, Zondervan Pub. House [1969] 103 p. 22 cm. [BV4257.5.G9] 71-106419 2.95
1. Communion sermons. 2. Presbyterian Church—Sermons. 3. Sermons, American. I. Title.

HAFFERT, John Mathias. 265/.3
The world's greatest secret, by John M. Haffert. Washington, N. J., Ave Maria Inst. [1967] viii, 310p. illus. 22cm [BV823.H28] 67-9515 4.95
1. Lord's Supper. I. Title.

HARRINGTON, M, 1913- 265.3
Calvary and community: the Passion and the Mass. New York, Sheed and Ward, 1951. 329 p. 22 cm. [BX2230.H33] 51-12462
1. Mass. I. Title.

HARRISON, Russell F., 265'.3
1918-
Brief prayers for Bread and Cup : for elders at the Communion table / Russell F. Harrison. Saint Louis : The Bethany Press, c1976. 78 p. ; 14 cm. [BV826.5.H37] 76-18932 ISBN 0-8272-0211-3 pbk. : 2.95
1. Lord's Supper—Prayer-books and devotions—English. I. Title.

HILDEBRANDT, Franz, 1909- 265'.3
I offered Christ; a Protestant study of the M1ss. Philadelphia, Fortress [1967] x, 34ip. 24cm. Bibl. [BV825.2.H5] 67-30606 5.50
1. Mass. I. Title.

HILDEBRANDT, Franz, 1909- 265'.3
I offered Christ; a Protestant study of the Mass. Philadelphia, Fortress Press [1967] x, 342 p. 24 cm. Bibliographical references included in "Notes" (p. 207-317) [BV825.2.H5] 67-30606
1. Mass. I. Title.

HORSFIELD, L A E 265.3
This our sacrifice [by] L. A. E. Horsfield and H. Riley. [1st American ed. New York, Morehouse-Gorham [1953] 103p. illus. 19cm. [BX5949] 53-13042
1. Lord's Supper— Anglican Communion. I. Riley, Harold, joint author. II. Title.

HUGH, S. S. F. Father 265.3
The burning-glass; a sketch of eucharistic structure. London, Faith Pr. [dist. New York, Morehouse, 1963, c.1962] 68p. illus. 19cm. (Studies in Christian faith and practice, 2) A63 1.00 pap.,
1. Lord's Supper—Anglican Communion. I. Title.

JANSEN, John Frederick. 265.3
Guests of God; meditations for the Lord's Supper. Philadelphia, Westminster Press [1956] 109p. 21cm. [BV825.J35] 56-8420
1. Lord's Supper—Meditations. I. Title.

JEFFREY, George Johnstone, 265.3
ed.
The sacramental table; a series of addresses by representative Scots preachers. New York, Harper [1955] 153p. 21cm. [BV4257.5] 55-14329
1. Communion sermons. 2. Sermons, English—Scotland. I. Title.

JOHNSON, Alan P. 265.3
The sacrament of the Lord's Supper, and doctrines related thereto. Salt Lake City, Desert, 1965. xi, 277p. 24cm. Bibl. [BX8655.L6J6] 65-18577 price unreported
1. Lord's Supper—Mormonism. I. Title.

JORET, Ferdinand Donatien, 265.3
1883-1937.
The Eucharist and the confessional. Westminster, Md., Newman Press [1955?] 192p. 22cm. Translation of Aux sources de l'eau vive. Sequel to Through Jesus Christ Our Lord. [BX2215.J62] 56-2586
1. Lord's Supper—Catholic Church. 2. Penance. I. Title.

JUNGMANN, Josef Andreas, 265.3
1889-
The Sacrifice of the Church; the meaning of the Mass. Translated from the German by Clifford Howell. Collegeville, Minn., Liturgical Press [1956?] 71p. 18cm. Translation of Vom Sinn der Messe als Opfer der Gemeinschaft. [BX2230.J833] 58-2407
1. Mass. I. Title.

JUNGMANN, Josef Andreas, 265'.3
1889-1975.
The Mass : an historical, theological, and pastoral survey / by Josef A. Jungmann ; translated by Julian Fernandes ; edited by Mary Ellen Evans. Collegeville, Minn. : Liturgical Press, c1976. xv, 312 p. ; 24 cm. Includes indexes. Bibliography: p. 291-295. [BV823.J86 1976] 76-357694 ISBN 0-8146-0887-6 : 9.95
1. Lord's Supper. 2. Mass. I. Title.

KEATING, John Fitzstephen, 265'.3
1850-1911.
The agape and the Eucharist in the early church; studies in the history of the Christian love-feasts. [1st ed.] New York, AMS Press [1969] xiii, 207 p. 22 cm. Reprint of the 1901 ed. Bibliographical footnotes. [BV823.K4 1969] 71-79511
1. Lord's Supper—History—Early church, ca. 30-600. 2. Agape. I. Title.

KENNEY, William Joseph, 265.3
1906-
Scenes from the Passion of Our Lord Jesus Christ for meditation during Mass; or, The Most Holy Sacrifice of the Mass explained according to the mysteries of the Passion of Our Lord. A pictorial, symbolical explanation of the Mass. Wakefield, Mass. [1953] unpaged. illus. 22cm. Cover title: The Mass in pictures. [BX2230.K42] 53-711
1. Mass—Pictures, illustrations, etc. I. Title.

KING, Archdale Arthur, 265.3
1890-
Eucharistic reservation in the western church, by Archdale A. King. New York, Sheed and Ward [1965] xiv, 258 p. illus., plates. 22 cm. Bibliography: p. 253-255. Bibliographical footnotes. [BX2233.6.K5] 65-20722
1. Lord's Supper — Reservation. I. Title.

KING, Archdale Arthur, 265.3
1890-
Eucharistic reservation in the western church, by Archdale A. King. New York, Sheed [c.1965] xiv, 258p. illus., plates. 22cm. Bibl. [BX2233.6.K5] 65-20722 6.95
1. Lord's Supper—Reservation. I. Title.

KINN, James W 265.3
The pre-eminence of the Eucharist among the sacraments according to Alexander of Hales, St. Albert the Great. St. Bonaventure and St. Thomas Aquinas. Mundelein, Ill., Saint Mary of the Lake Seminary, 1960. 134p. 23cm. (Pontificia Facultas Theologica, Seminaril Sanctae Mariae ad Lacum. Dissertationes ad lauream, 31) Bibliography: p.142-154. [BV823.K5] 61-25780
1. Lord's Supper— Hist. I. Title. II. Series. III. Series: St. Mary of the Lake Seminary, Mundelein, Ill. Dissertationes and lauream, 31

KNOX, Ronald Arbuthnott, 265.3
1888-
The window in the wall; reflections on the Holy Eucharist. New York, Sheed & Ward [1957, c1956] 130p. 22cm. [BX2215.K63 1957] 57-6044
1. Lord's Supper—Sermons. 2. Catholic Church—Sermons. 3. Sermons, English. I. Title.

LASH, Nicholas. 265'.3
His presence in the world; a study of Eucharistic worship and theology. Dayton, Ohio, Pflaum Press, 1968. x, 214 p. 22 cm. Bibliography: p. [205]-211. [BX2215.2.L3 1968b] 68-22896 5.25
1. Lord's Supper—Catholic Church. I. Title.

LEFEBVRE, Xavier. 265.3
Going to God; preparation for confession, first communion and confirmation [by] Xavier Lefebvre and Louis Perin. Translated by Douglas Lord. New York, P. F. Kenedy [1964] ix, 318 p. 21 cm. Translation of L'appel du Seigneur. [BX2237.L413] 64-21851
1. First communion — Instruction and study. 2. Confession — Instruction and study. 3. Confirmation — Instruction and study. I. Perin, Louis, joint author. II. Title.

LEFEBVRE, Xavier 265.3
Going to God; preparation for confession, first communion and confirmation [by] Xavier Lefebvre, Louis Perin. Tr. [from French] by Douglas Lord. New York. Kenedy [c.1964] ix, 318p. 21cm. 64-21851 4.95 bds.,
1. First communion—Instruction and study. 2. Confession—Instruction and study. 3. Confirmation—Instruction and study. I. Perin, Louis, joint author. II. Title.

LEHMANN, Helmut T., ed. 265.3
Meaning and practice of the Lord's Supper. [By] Robert P. Roth[others] Philadelphia, Muhlenberg Press [c.1961] 210p. Bibl. 60-15402 3.50
1. Lord's Supper—Hist. 2. Lord's Supper—Lutheran Church. I. Title.

L'EUCHARISTIE des premiers chretiens / W. Rordorf ... [et al.]. Paris : Beauchesne, c1976. 214 p. ; 22 cm. (Le Point theologique ; 17) Bibliography: p. [211]-214. [BV823.E93] 77-463957 265'.3
1. Lord's Supper—History—Early church, ca. 30-600. I. Rordorf, Willy.

LIESTING, G. T. H. 265'3
The sacrament of the Eucharist, by G. T. H. Liesting. Translated by James M. Boumans. Glen Rock, N.Y., Newman Press [1968] xi, 194 p. 22 cm. Bibliography: p. 185-191. [BX2215.2.L513] 68-54402 7.50
1. Lord's Supper—Catholic Church. I. Title.

LOVASIK, Lawrence George, 265.3
1913-
The Eucharist in Catholic life. New York, Macmillan [c.]1960. x, 274p. 22cm. 60-14294 4.50
1. Lord's Supper—Catholic authors. 2. Mass. I. Title.

LOWRIE, Walter, 1868- 265.3
Action in the liturgy, essential and unessential. New York, Philosophical Library [1953] 303p. illus. 23cm. Includes bibliography. [BV825.L62] 53-6537
1. Lord's Supper (Liturgy) I. Title.

LUMPKIN, William Latane. 265'.3
Meditations for Communion services. Nashville, Abingdon Press [1968] 111 p. 20 cm. Bibliographical footnotes. [BV826.5.L8] 68-25363 2.95
1. Lord's Supper—Meditations. I. Title.

MCCORMICK, Scott 265.3
The Lord's Supper, a Biblical interpretation. Philadelphia. Westminster [c.1966] 126p. 21cm. Bibl. [BV823.M26] 66-10161 3.00
1. Lord's Supper—Biblical teaching. I. Title.

MCDONNELL, Kilian. 265'.3
John Calvin, the church, and the eucharist. Princeton, N.J., Princeton University Press, 1967. x, 410 p. 21 cm. A revision and expansion of the author's thesis. Treves. Bibliography: p. 383-400. [BX9418.M28] 65-17149
1. Calvin, Jean, 1509-1564—Theology. 2. Lord's Supper—History. I. Title.

MCGLOIN, Joseph T. 265'.3
How to get more out of the mass [by] Joseph T. McGloin. Liguori, Mo., Liguori Publications [1974] 144 p. illus. 18 cm. [BX2230.2.M28] 74-80938 1.75
1. Mass. I. Title.

MCGLOIN, Joseph T. 265'.3
How to get more out of the mass [by] Joseph T. McGloin. Liguori, Mo., Liguori Publications [1974] 144 p. illus. 18 cm. [BX2230.2.M28] 74-80938 1.75 (pbk.)
1. Mass. I. Title.

MCLAREN, Alexander, 1826- 265.3
1910.
Sermons and outlines on the Lord's Supper, by Alexander Maclaren, F. B. Meyer, Charles H. Spurgeon, and others. Grand Rapids, Baker Book House, 1951. 100 p. 21 cm. Prose and poetry. [BV4257.5.S4] 52-6814
1. Communion sermons. I. Title.

MCNIERNEY, Stephen W., 265'.3
comp.
The underground mass book, by Stephen W. McNierney. Baltimore, Helicon [1968] 127 p. 19 cm. Bibliographical footnotes. [BV825.5.M3] 68-58310 1.35
1. Lord's Supper (Liturgy) I. Title.

MANOUSOS, Demetrius. 265.3
First Holy Communion for little Catholics. Illustrated by Catherine Barnes. St. Paul, Catechetical Guild Educational Society, c1955. unpaged. illus. 17cm. (First books for little Catholics, FB071) [BX2217.M26] 56-641
1. First communion. I. Title.

MARY SIMEON Mother, 1894- 265.3
If any man thirst. Milwaukee, Bruce [c.1964] viii, 115p. 22cm. 64-23891 3.25
1. Lord's Supper—Meditations. I. Title.

MEAD, Frank Spencer, 1898- 265.3
ed.
Communion messages. [Westwood, N. J.] Revell [1961] 123p. 21cm. [BV4257.5.A1M4] 61-5929
1. Communion sermons. 2. Sermons, American. I. Title.

MERTON, Thomas, 1915- 265.3
The living bread. New York, Farrar, Straus & Cudahy [1956] 157p. 21cm. [BX2215.M4] 56-6276
1. Lord's Supper—Catholic Church. I. Title.

MEYER, John E ed. 265.3
Our hearts rejoice; communion meditations. Columbus, Ohio, Wartburg Press [1955] 175p. 20cm. [BV4257.5.M49] 55-687
1. Communion sermons. 2. Lutheran Church —Sermons. 3. Sermons, American. I. Title.

MOORE, Farris F. 265.3
Arise and go in peace. Nashville, Abingdon [1966, c.1965] 48p. 24cm. [BV199.C6M6] 66-1495 2.25
1. Lord's Supper (Liturgy) I. Title.

NEVIN, John Williamson, 265.3
1803-1886.
The mystical presence, With an introd., The world of Mercersberg theology, by Richard E. Wentz. Hamden, Conn., Archon Books, 1963. xxiii, 256 p. port. 21 cm. "Facsimile reprint of 1846 edition." Bibliographical footnotes. [BV825.N38] 63-19888
1. Lord's Supper. 2. Mercersberg theology. I. Title.

NEVIN, John Williamson, 265.3
1803-1886.
The mystical presence, and other writings on the Eucharist [by] John W. Nevin. Bard Thompson and George H. Bricker, editors. Philadelphia, United Church Press [1966] 431 p. facsim. 23 cm. (Lancaster series on the Mercersburg theology, v. 4) "Writings of John W. Nevin in the Mercersburg period": p. 423-429. "Selected secondary sources": p. 429-431. [BV825.N38] 66-16193
1. Lord's Supper. 2. Mercersburg theology. I. Title. II. Series.

NEVIN, John Williamson, 265.3
1803-1886
The mystical presence. Introd., The world of Mercersberg theology, by Richard E. Wentz. Hamden, Conn., Archon [dist. Shoe String, c.] 1963. xxiii, 256p. port. 21cm. Bibl. 63-19888 9.00
1. Lord's Supper. 2. Mercersberg theology. I. Title.

NEVIN. JOHN WILLIAMSON. 265.3
1803-1886
The mystical presence, and other writings on the Eucharist. Bard Thompson, George H. Bricker, eds. Philadelphia. United Church Pr. [c.1966] 431p. facsim. 23cm. (Lancaster ser. on the Mercersburg theol., v.4) Writings of John W. Nevin in the Mercersburg period. Bibl. [BV825.N38 1966] 66-16193 6.50 pap.,
1. Lord's Supper 2. Mercersburg theology. I. Title. II. Series.

NICHOL, Charles Ready, 265.3
1876-
The Lord's Supper, prayers: the institution of Lord's Supper, the observance of the Supper, thanks, prayers for all occasions. Clifton, Tex., Nichol Pub. Co., 1957. 164p. 21cm. [BV827.N5] 57-3053
1. Lord's Supper. 2. Prayers. I. Title.

NICHOL, Charles Ready, 265.3
1876-
The Lord's Supper, prayers: the institution of the Lord's Supper, the observance of the Supper, thanks, prayers for all occasions. Clifton, Tex., Nichol Pub. Co., 1957. 164p. 21cm. [BV827.N5] 57-3053
1. Lord's Supper. 2. Prayers. I. Title.

*NICHOLAS, Marie-Joseph 265.3
A new look at the Eucharist (What is the

Eucharist?) Tr. from French by Reginald F. Trevett. Glen Rock, N.J., Paulist Pr. [c.1964] 122p. 18cm. (Deus/Century bk.) .95 pap.,
I. Title.

NICOLAS, Maria Iosephus 265.3
What is the Eucharist? Translated from the French by R. F. Trevett. New York, Hawthorn Books [c.1960] 125p. 21cm. (The Twentieth century encyclopedia of Catholicism, v.52. Section 5: The life of faith) (Bibl., footnotes) 60-13832 2.95 half cloth.,
1. Lord's Supper—Catholic Church. I. Title.

NICOLAS, Maria Iosephus, 1906- 265.3
What is the Eucharist? Translated from the French by R. F. Trevett. [1st ed.] New York, Hawthorn Books [1960] 125p. 21cm. (The Twentieth century encyclopedia of Catholicism, v. 52. Section 5: The life of faith) Translation of L'eucharistie. Includes bibliography. [BX2215.2.N513] 60-13832
1. Lord's Supper—Catholic Church. I. Title.

ON the way to their first Communion : a handbook for parents / [editorial team, Leon Brillon, Doris Gauthier, Reginald Marsolais (team leader)] ; translated by James McGhee ; [photography by John Glaser]. New York : Paulist Press, 1976. 300 p. : ill. ; 18 cm. Translation of Au fils des jours. [BX2237.A813 1976] 76-150863 ISBN 0-8091-1981-1 pbk. 6.95 265'.3
1. First communion—Instruction and study. I. Brillon, Leon. II. Gauthier, Doris. III. Marsolais, Reginald. IV. McGhee, James.

O'NEILL, Colman E. 265'.3
New approaches to the Eucharist [by] Colman O'Neill. Staten Island, N.Y., Alba House [1967] 126 p. 22 cm. Bibliographical footnotes. [BX2215.2.O5] 67-24921
1. Lord's Supper—Catholic Church. I. Title.

PARDUE, Austin, Bp., 1899- 265.3
The Eucharist and you. New York, Morehouse-Barlow Co., 1963. vi. 180 p. 21 cm. Bibliography: p. 180. [BX5949.C5P32] 63-21580
1. Lord's Supper—Anglican Communion. I. Title.

PARDUE, Austin [Henry Austin Pardue] Bp., 1899- 265.3
The Eucharist and you. New York, Morehouse [c.] 1963. vi, 180p. 21cm. Bibl. 63-21580 3.95
1. Lord's Supper—Anglican Communion. I. Title.

PASTORAK, John B 265.3
Sermons for Eucharistic devotions. St. Louis, Herder, 1952. 511 p. 25 cm. [BX1756.P37S4] 52-8932
1. Catholic Church — Sermons. 2. Sermons, American. 3. Lord's Supper — Catholic Church. I. Title.

PHILLIPS, John Bertram, 1906- 265.3
Appointment with God; some thoughts on Holy Communion. New York, Macmillan, 1954. 61p. 21cm. 'A series of Lenten addresses given... at St. John's, Redhill, Surrey.' [BV825.P49] 54-12663
1. Lord's Supper. I. Title.

PIOLANTI, Antonio 265.3
The Holy Eucharist. [Tr. from Italian by Luigi Penzo] New York, Desclee, 1961[ ] 154p. Bibl. 61-15721 2.50
1. Lord's Supper—Catholic Church. I. Title.

PITTENGER, William Norman, 1905- 265.3
The Christian sacrifice; a study of the Eucharist in the life of the Christian Church. New York, Oxford University Press, 1951. 205 p. 21 cm. [BX5949.C5P5] 51-12527
1. Lord's Supper — Anglican Communion. 2. Lord's Supper — Sacrifice. I. Title.

POWERS,Joseph M., 1926- 265.'3
Eucharistic theology [by] Joseph M. Powers. [New York] Herder & [1967] 192p.22cm. Bibl. [BX2215.2.P6] 67-17625 4.95
1. Lord's Supper — Catholic Church. 2. Lord's Supper — Real presence. 3. Transubstantiation. I. Title.

RAHNER, Hugo, 1900- 265.3
Prayers for meditation [by] Hugo Rahner, Karl Rahner. [Tr. by Rosaleen Brennan. New York] Herder & Herder [1962] 70p. 19cm. 62-11035 1.75
1. Lord's Supper—Meditations. I. Rahner, Karl, 1904- II. Title.

RAHNER, Karl, 1904- 265'.3
The celebration of the Eucharist, by Karl Rahner, Angelus Haussling; tr. [from German] by W. J. O'Hara. London, Burns & Oates; New York. Herder & Herder, 1968. x. 132p. 21cm. Orig. pub. as Die vielen Messen und das eine Opfer. Freiburg: Herder, 1966. Bibl. [BX2215.2.R313 1968c] 68-104488 4.50
1. Lord's Supper—Catholic Church—Addresses, essays, lectures. I. Haussling, Angelus. ed. II. Title.

SALA, John Robert, 1905- 265'.3
Command to love; a year of weekly meditations at the table of the Lord. St. Louis, Mo., Bethany Press [1970] 122 p. 20 cm. [BV825.2.S17] 70-127849
1. Lord's Supper—Meditations. I. Title.

SASSE, Hermann, 1895- 265.3
This is my Body; Luther's contention for the real presence in the Sacrament of the Altar. Minneapolis, Augsburg Pub. House [1957] 120p. 22cm. Includes bibliography. [BR333.S3] 57-9725
1. Lord's Supper Hist. 2. Luther, Martin—Theology. 3. Lord's Supper—Real Presence 4. Lord's Supper Lutheran Church. I. Title.

SCHILLEBEECKX, Edward Cornelis Florentius Alfons, 1914- 265'.3
The eucharist [by] E. Schillebeeckx. Translated by N. D. Smith. New York, Sheed and Ward [1968] 160 p. 21 cm. Translation of: Christus' tegenwoordigheid in die eucharistie. Bibliographical footnotes. [BX2220.S3513] 68-13846 3.95
1. Transubstantiation. I. Title.

SCHWEIZER, Eduard, 1913- 265'.3
The Lord's Supper according to the New Testament. Translated by James M. Davis. Philadelphia, Fortress Press [1967] xvi, 48 p. 20 cm. (Facet books. Biblical series 18) "Translated from the third edition of Die Religion in Geschichte und Gegenwart ... with revisions and additions by the author." Includes bibliographies. [BV823.S313] 67-21528
1. Lord's Supper—Biblical teaching. I. Title.

SHEPHERD, Massey Hamilton, 1913- 265.3
'At all times and in all places.' 2d ed., rev. and enl. iGreenwich, Conn., Seabury Press, 1953. 85p. illus. 23cm. [BV823.S49 1953] 53-3739
1. Lord's Supper—Hist. I. Title.

SHEPHERD, Massey Hamilton, 1913- 265.3
At all times and in all places [by] Massey H. Shepherd, Jr. 3d ed., rev. New York, Seabury Press [1965] 96 p. illus. 22 cm. Bibliography: p. 93-96. [BV823.S49] 65-6559
1. Lord's Supper—Hist. I. Title.

SHEPHERD, Massey Hamilton, 1913- ed. 265.3
Before the holy table; a guide to the celebration of the Holy Eucharist, facing the people, according to the Book of common prayer. Edited by Massey H. Shepherd, Jr. [and others] Greenwich, Conn., Seabury Press, 1956. 62p. illus. 21cm. [BX5949.C5S5] 56-7966
1. Lord's Supper—Celebration. I. Title.

SHEPHERD, Massey Hamilton, 1913- ed. 265.3
Before the holy table; a guide to the celebration of the Holy Eucharist, facing the people, according to the Book of common prayer. Edited by Massey H. Shepherd, Jr. [and others] Greenwich, Conn., Seabury Press, 1956. 62 p. illus. 21 cm. [BX5949.C5S5] 56-7966
1. Lord's Supper — Celebration. I. Title.

SHEPHERD, Massey Hamilton, 1913- comp. 265.3
Holy Communion, an anthology of Christian devotion. Greenwich Conn., Seabury Press, 1959. 102 p. 18 cm. [BV826.5S4] 59-12524
1. Lord's Supper — Prayer-books and devotions — English. I. Title.

SHEPHERD, Massey Hamilton, Jr., 1913- 265.3
At all times and in all places. 3d ed., rev. New York, Seabury [c.1955, 1965] 96p. illus. 22cm. Bibl. [BV823.S49] 65-6559 3.95
1. Lord's Supper—Hist. I. Title.

SHULTZ, Joseph R 265.3
The soul of the symbols; a theological study of holy communion, by Joseph R. Shultz. Grand Rapids, W. B. Eerdmans Pub. Co. [1966] 198 p. 21 cm. Bibliography: p. 195-198. [BV825.2.S5] 66-18723
1. Lord's Supper. I. Title.

SHULTZ, Joseph R. 265.3
The soul of the symbols; a theological study of holy communion. Grand Rapids, Mich., Eerdmans [c.1966] 198p. 21cm. Bibl. [BV825.2.S5] 66-18723 3.95
1. Lord's Supper. I. Title.

SPICQ, Ceslaus, 1901- 265.3
Agape in the New Testament [v. 1] Tr. by Marie Aquinas McNamara, Mary Honoria Richter. St. Louis, B. Herder [c.1963] 153p. 21cm. Bibl. 63-21562 3.50
1. Agape. 2. Love (Theology) 3. Bible. N. T.—Criticism, interpretation, etc. I. Title.

SPICQ, Ceslaus, 1901- 265.3
Agape in the New Testament; v.3. Tr. by Sister Marie Aquinas McNamara, Sister Mary Honoria Richter. St. Louis, Herder [c.1966] ix, 262p. 21cm. Contents.v.3. Agape in the Gospel, Epistles and Apocalypse of St. John. Bibl. 63-21562 6.25
1. Agape. 2. Love (Theology) 3. Bible. N.T.—Criticism interpretation. I. Title.

SPICQ, Ceslaus, 1901- 265.3
Agape in the New Testament; v.2. Tr. by Marie Aquinas McNamara, Mary Honoria Richter. St. Louis, Herder [c.1965] 450p. 21cm. Contents.v.2. Agape in the Epistles of St. Paul, the Acts of the Apostles, and the Epistles of St. James, St. Peter, and St. Jude. [BV823.S713] 63-21562 6.95
1. Agape. 2. Love (Theology) 3. Bible. N.T.—Criticism, interpretation, etc. I. Title.

STARENKO, Ronald C. 265'.3
Eat, drink and be merry! [By] Ronald C. Starenko. St. Louis, Concordia Pub. House [1971] 75 p. 19 cm. [BV825.2.S7] 72-157383 ISBN 0-570-03123-0
1. Lord's Supper. 2. Christian life—Lutheran authors. I. Title.

TAPPERT, Theodore Gerhardt, 1904- 265.3
The Lord's Supper, past and present practices. Philadelphia, Muhlenberg Press [1961] 62 p. 20 cm. (A Fortress book) [BV825.2.T3] 61-6752
1. Lord's Supper. I. Title.

TAPPERT, Theodore Gerhartd, 1904- 265.3
The Lord's Supper, past and present practices. Philadelphia, Muhlenberg Press [c.1961] 62p. (Fortress book) 61-6752 1.00 bds.,
1. Lord's Supper. I. Title.

TAYLOR, Edward, 1642-1729 265.3
Treatise concerning the Lord's Supper. Ed. by Norman S. Grabo. [East Lansing] Mich. State Univ. Pr., 1966 [c.1965] lvi. 263p. 24cm. Consists of 8 sermons included in a bound vol. of MSS. in Tavlor's handwriting. now in the Prince Collection, Boston Pub. Lib. Bibl. [BX7239.L6T3] 65-27442 7.50
1. Lord's Supper—Sermons. 2. Congregational churches—Sermons. 3. Sermons, American. I. Grabo, Norman S., ed. II. Title.

THOMAS AQUINAS, Saint, 1225?-1274. 265.3
The Blessed Sacrament and the Mass. Translated, with notes, by F. O'Neill. Westminster, Md., Newman Press [1955] 178p. 20cm. Selections from the Summa theologica, first published in 1965 under title: St. Thomas Aquinas on the Blessed Sacrament and the Mass. [BX2215.T514 1955] 56-9765
1. Lord's Supper—Medieval works. 2. Mass. I. Title.

THURIAN, Max. 265.3
The Eucharistic memorial. Translated by J. G. Davies. Richmond, John Knox Press [1961, v. 1, c1960] 2 v. 22 cm. (Ecumenical studies in worship, no. 7-8) Translation of L'Eucharistie; memorial du Seigneur, Sacrifice d'action de grace et d'intercession. Includes bibliography. [BV825.2.T513] 61-5399
1. Lord's Supper. I. Title.

THURIAN, Max 265.3
The Eucharistic memorial, pt. 1. Richmond, Va., John Knox Pr. [1961] 115p. (Ecumenical studies in worship, no. 7) Contents.pt.1. The Old Testament, tr. [from French] by J. G. Davies (Ecumenical studies in worship, no. 7) Bibl. 1.75 pap.,
1. Lord's Supper. I. Davies, J. G., tr. II. Title.

THURIAN, Max. 265'.3
The one bread. Translated by Theodore DuBois. New York, Sheed and Ward [1969] 159 p. 22 cm. Contents.Contents.—The one bread (translation of Le pain unique)—Crisis of the faith (translation of La foi en crise) [BR121.2.T54313] 69-16988 4.50
1. Lord's Supper and Christian union. 2. Christianity—20th century. I. Thurian, Max. Crisis of the faith. II. Title. III. Title: Crisis of the faith.

TILLARD, J. M. R. 265.3
The Eucharist; Pasch of God's people [by] J. M. R. Tillard. [Translated by Dennis L. Wienk] Staten Island, N.Y., Alba House [1967] 316 p. 22 cm. Bibliographical footnotes. [BX2215.2.T513] 66-17219
1. Lord's Supper—Catholic Church. I. Title.

TURNBULL, Ralph G. 265'.3
At the Lord's table, by Ralph G. Turnbull. Grand Rapids, Baker Bk. [1967] 141p. 20cm. [Minister's handbk. ser.] [BV827.T8] 67-18198 2.50 bds.,
1. Lords Supper—Sermons. 2. Sermons, American. 3. Presbyterian Church —Sermons. I. Title.

TURNBULL, Ralph G. 265'.3
At the Lord's Table, by Ralph G. Turnbull. Grand Rapids, Baker Book House [1974, c1967] 141 p. 20 cm. [BV827.T8] ISBN 0-8010-8822-4. 1.95 (pbk.)
1. Lord's Supper—Sermons. 2. Sermons, American. 3. Presbyterian Church—Sermons. I. Title.
L.C. card number for original ed.: 67-18198.

VAN WYK, William Peter, 1874-1943. 265.3
My sermon notes on the Lord's Supper. Grand Rapids, Mich., Baker's Bk., 1964[c.1945] 117p. 20cm. 45-18657 1.00 pap.,
1. Communion sermons. 2. Sermons—Outlines. 3. Christian Reformed Church—Sermons. I. Title.

VARNER, Chauncey J. 265.3
Can we break bread together? New York, Friendship [1965] 63p. 16cm. (Questions for Christians, no. 2) Bibl. [BX9.5.15V3] 65-11430 .65 pap,
1. Intercommunion. I. Title. II. Series.

VOGEL, Arthur Anton. 265'.3
Is the Last Supper finished? Secular light on a sacred meal, by Arthur A. Vogel. With a pref. by Bernard Cooke. New York, Sheed and Ward [1968] 191 p. 21 cm. [BV825.2.V6] 68-26031 4.50
1. Lord's Supper. 2. Church and the world. I. Title.

VONIER, Anscar, 1875-1938. 265.3
A key to the doctrine of the Eucharist. Westminster, Md., Newman Press, 1956. 209p. 20cm. [BX2215.V6] 57-213
1. Lord's Supper—Catholic Church. I. Title.

VONIER, Anscar, 1875-1938. 265.3
A key to the doctrine of the Eucharist. Westminster, Md., Newman Press, 1956. 269 p. 20 cm. [BX2215.V6] 57-213
1. Lord's Supper — Catholic Church. I. Title.

WALLIS, Charles Langworthy, 1921- ed. 265.3
The table of the Lord; a Communion encyclopedia. [1st ed.] New York, Harper [1958] 228 p. 22 cm. Includes bibliography. [BV199.C6W2] 58-7105
1. Lord's Supper (Liturgy) 2. Lord's Supper — Prayer-books and devotions — English. 3. Communion sermons. I. Title. II. Title: Communion encyclopedia.

WATKINS, Keith. 265'.3
The feast of joy : the Lord's Supper in free churches / Keith Watkins. St. Louis : Bethany Press, c1977. 126 p. : ill. ; 22 cm. [BV825.2.W29] 77-525 pbk. : 4.95
1. Lord's Supper. I. Title.

WENGIER, Francis J. 265.3
The Eucharist-sacrament. Stevens Point, Wis., 1960. 328 p. 23 cm. Includes bibliography. [BX2215.W378] 59-13503
1. Lord's Supper — Catholic Church. I. Title.

WILLIAMS, Thomas David, 1872- 265.3
Little meditations on the Holy Eucharist. Milwaukee, Bruce [1950] viii, 319 p. 23 cm. [BX2169.W53] 50-4666
1. Lord's Supper—Meditations. I. Title.

WISLOFF, Carl Johan Fredrik, 1908- 265.3
The gift of communion; Luther's controversy with Rome on eucharistic sacrifice. Translated by Joseph M. Shaw. Minneapolis, Augsburg Pub. House [1964] vii, 253 p. 23 cm. Translation of Nattverd og messe. Bibliography: p. 241-249. [BV823.W563] 64-13436
1. Luther, Martin — Theology. 2. Lord's Supper — Hist. I. Title.

WISLOFF, Carl Johan Fredrik, 1908- 265.3
The gift of communion; Luther's controversy with Rome on eucharistic sacrifice. Tr. [from Norwegian] by Joseph M. Shaw. Minneapolis, Augsburg [c.1964] vii,253p. 23cm. Bibl. 64-13436 4.75
1. Luther, Martin—Theology. 2. Lord's Supper—Hist. I. Title.

WORD and action; new forms of the liturgy. With an introd. by John C. Kirby. New York, Seabury Press [1969] 199 p. 21 cm. (An Original Seabury paperback SP 57) [BV825.5.W67] 74-76463 2.95 265.3
1. Lord's Supper—Celebration. 2. Mass—Celebration. I. Kirby, John C.

WORSHIP in spirit and truth; papers from a conference entitled Worship in Spirit and Truth, sponsored by and held at the Church of St. Mary the Virgin, New York City, May 20-22, 1970. [New York] Jarrow Press [1970] 75 p. ports. 23 cm. [BX5949.C5W58] 78-133444 265'.3
1. Lord's Supper—Anglican Communion—Addresses, essays, lectures. I. New York (City). Church of St. Mary the Virgin.

WRIGHT, Nathan. 265.3
One bread, one body. Foreword by James A. Pike. Greenwich, Conn., Seabury Press, 1962. 148 p. 22 cm. Includes bibliographies. [BX5949.C5W73] 62-9618
1. Lord's Supper—Anglican Communion. I. Title.

WYON, Olive, 1890- 265.3
The altar fire; reflections on the sacrament of the Lord's Supper. Philadelphia, Westminster Press [1954] 126p. 19cm. [BV825] 54-3509
1. Lord's Supper. I. Title.

YARNOLD, Greville Dennis 265.3
The bread which we break. New York, Oxford Univ. Press [1961, c.]1960 119p. 61-290 2.50 bds.,
1. Lord's Supper. I. Title.

YPERMAN, Joseph. 265'.3
Teaching the Eucharist. Translated by M. D. Leitch. New York, Paulist Press [1968] ix, 83 p. 19 cm. (Deus books) Translation of Gedenken wij dankbaar. Bibliographical footnotes. [BX2215.2.Y613] 68-21457
1. Lord's Supper—Catholic Church. I. Title.

TARTRE, Raymond A comp. 265'.3'08
The Eucharist today; essays on the theology and worship of the real presence, edited by Raymond A. Tartre. New York, P. J. Kenedy [1967] xii, 271 p. 22 cm. Bibliography: p. 251-257. [BX2220.T3] 67-26800
1. Lord's Supper—Real presence. I. Title.

TARTRE, Raymond A., comp. 265'.3'08
The Eucharist today; essays on the theology and worship of the real presence, edited by Raymond A. Tartre. New York, P. J. Kenedy [1967] xii, 271 p. 22 cm. Bibliography: p. 251-257. [BX2220.T3] 67-26800
1. Lord's Supper—Real presence. I. Title.

MARXSEN, Willi, 1919- 265'.3'09
The Lord's Supper as a Christological problem. Translated by Lorenz Nieting. Philadelphia, Fortress Press [1970] xxiv, 40 p. 19 cm. (Facet books. Biblical series, 25) Translation of Das Abendmahl als christologisches Problem. Bibliography: p. 39-40. [BV823.M3713] 79-81528 1.00
1. Jesus Christ—History of doctrines—Early church, 30-600. 2. Lord's Supper—History. I. Title.

ELERT, Werner, 1885-1954. 265.309015
Eucharist and church fellowship in the first four centuries. Translated from the German by N. E. Nagel. St. Louis, Concordia Pub. House [1966] xiv, 231 p. 24 cm. Translation of Abendmahl und Kirchengemeinschaft in der alten Kirche hauptsachlich des Ostens. [BV823.E413] 66-23212
1. Lord's Supper—Hist. I. Title.

ELERT. WERNER, 1885-1955 265.309015
Eucharist and church fellowship in the first four centuries. Tr. from German by N. E. Nagel. St. Louis. Concordia [1966] xiv 231p. 24cm. Tr. of Abendmahl undKirchengemeinschaft in der alten Kirche hauptsachlich des Ostens. [BV823.E413 1966] 66-23212 6.75
1. Lord's Supper—Hist. I. Title.

BLIGH, John. 265.4
Ordination to the priesthood. New York, Sheed and Ward [1956] 189p. illus. 21cm. [BX2240.B56 1956a] 55-9448
1. Ordination—Catholic Church. 2. Catholic Church. Liturgy and ritual. Pontifical. Ritus ordinum. I. Title.

BLIGH, John. 265.4
Ordination to the priesthood. London, New York, Sheed and Ward [1956] 189p. illus. 23cm. [BX2240.B56] 56-3627
1. Ordination—Catholic Church. 2. Catholic Church. Liturgy and Ritual. Pontifical. Ritus ordinum. I. Title.

BLIGH, John. 265.4
Ordination to the priesthood. London, New York, Sheed and Ward [1956] 189p. illus. 23cm. [BX2240.B56] 56-3627
1. Ordination—Catholic Church. 2. Catholic Church. Liturgy and ritual. Pontifical. Ritus ordinum. I. Title.

BLIGH JOHN. 265.4
Ordination to the priesthood. New York, Sheed and Ward [1956] 189p. illus. 21cm. [BX2240.B56 1956a] 55-9448
1. Ordination—Catholic Church. 2. Catholic Church. Liturgy and ritual. Pontifical. Ritus ordinum. I. Title.

CATHOLIC Church. Liturgy and ritual. 265'.4
The ordination of deacons, priests, and bishops : provisional text prepared by the International Committee on English in the Liturgy, approved for interim use by the Bishops' Committee on the Liturgy, National Conference of Catholic Bishops, and confirmed by the Apostolic See. Washington : National Conference of Catholic Bishops, Bishops' Committee on the Liturgy, 1969. 51 p. ; 28 cm. At head of title: The Roman pontifical; restored by decree of the Second Vatican Ecumenical Council and promulgated by authority of Pope Paul VI. Translation of De ordinatione diaconi, presbyteri, et episcopi. [BX2031.R5A4 1969] 75-306712
1. Ordination—Catholic Church. I. International Committee on English in the Liturgy. II. Catholic Church. National Conference of Catholic Bishops. Bishops' Committee on the Liturgy. III. [Rite of ordination. English] IV. Title.

CATHOLIC Church. Liturgy and ritual. 265'.4
The rites of ordination and episcopal consecration. With English translation approved by the National Conference of Catholic Bishops of the United States of America and confirmed by the Apostolic See. Washington, National Conference of Catholic Bishops, Bishops' Committee on the Liturgy, 1967. 78 p. 28 cm. Cover title. Includes the Latin texts. [BX2031.R5A4 1967] 70-7799
I. Catholic Church. Liturgy and ritual. Consecration of a bishop. English & Latin. 1967. II. [Rite of ordination. English & Latin] III. Title.

CENTRE DE PASTORALE LITURGIGUE, Strasbourg 265.4
The sacrament of holy orders; some papers and discussions concerning holy orders at a session of the Centre de pastorale liturgique, 1955. Collegeville, Minn., Liturgical Press [c1962] vi. 358 p. 23 cm. Bibliographical footnotes. [[BX2240]] 64-9052
1. Ordination — Catholic Church. I. Title.

CLANCY, Walter Burroughs, 1926- 265.4
The rites and ceremonies of sacred ordination (canons 1002-1005); a historical conspectus and a canonical commentary. Washington, Catholic University of America Press, 1962. xi, 122 p. 23 cm. (Catholic University of America. Canon law studies, no. 394) Thesis—Catholic University of America. Vita. Bibliography: p. 113-118. [BX2240.C5] 68-7414
1. Ordination. I. Title. II. Series.

DOUGHERTY, John M. 1929- 265.4
Unto the altar of God; a spiritual commentary on the Pontifical by John M. Dougherty. Foreword by Thomas A. Connolly. [1st ed.] New York, Exposition [1966] 274p. 22 cm. (Exposition-Testament bk.) "Ritus Ordinationum": p. [249]-274. [BX2030.D6] 66-17464 5.00
1. Catholic Church. Liturgy and ritual. Pontifical. I. Title.

DOUGHERTY, John M 1929- 265.4
Unto the altar of God; a spiritual commentary on the Pontifical, by John M. Dougherty. Foreword by Thomas A. Connolly. [1st ed.] New York, Exposition Press [1966] 274 p. 22 cm. (An Exposition-Testament book) "Ritus Ordinationum": p. [249]-274. [BX2030.D6] 66-17464
1. Catholic Church. Liturgy and ritual. Pontifical. I. Title.

MAGUIRE, Clyde (Merrill) comp. 265.4
Magnify your office: 33 installation services. Nashville, Broadman Press [1956] 142p. 21cm. [BV199.I5M3] 56-8675
1. Installation service (Church officers) I. Title.

ORZELL, Laurence. 265'.4
Rome and the validity of orders in the Polish National Catholic Church / Laurence Orzell. Scranton, Pa. : Savonarola Theological Seminary Alumni Association, 1977. 49 p. ; 24 cm. Bibliography: p. 46-49. [BX2240.O75] 77-75372
1. Polish National Catholic Church of America. 2. Ordination—Catholic Church. I. Title.

PATTERSON, Roberta Turner, 1908- 265.4
How to conduct an installation service, with installation service programs and ideas. Grand Rapids, Zondervan Pub. House [1954] 95p. 20cm. [BV199.I5P3] 55-201
1. Installation service (Church officers) I. Title.

ACKER, Julius William, comp. 265.5
Wedding addresses. St. Louis, Concordia Pub. House [1956, c1955] 168p. 20cm. [BV4278.A3] 55-11140
1. Marriage—Sermons. 2. Lutheran Church—Sermons. 3. Sermons. American. I. Title.

ACKER, Julius William, comp. 265.5
Wedding addresses. St. Louis, Concordia Pub. House [1956, c1955] 168p. 20cm. [BV4278.A3] 55-11140
1. Marriage—Sermons. 2. Lutheran Church—Sermons. 3. Sermons, American. I. Title.

ARISIAN, Khoren. 265'.5
The new wedding: creating your own marriage ceremony. Photography by Ingbet. [1st ed.] New York, Vintage Books [1973] 175 p. illus. 24 cm. Bibliography: p. [153]-161. [BV199.M3A74 1973b] 72-12126 ISBN 0-394-71919-0 3.50 (pbk.)
1. Marriage service. I. Title.

ARISIAN, Khoren. 265'.5
The new wedding: creating your own marriage ceremony. Photography by Ingbet. New York, Knopf; [distributed by Random House] 1973. 175 p. illus. 25 cm. Bibliography: p. [153]-161. [BV199.M3A74 1973] 72-11029 ISBN 0-394-48334-0 7.95
1. Marriage service. I. Title.

BAINTON, Roland Herbert, 1894- 265.5
What Christianity says about sex, love, and marriage. New York, Association Press [c1957] 124p. 16cm. (An Association Press reflection book) Includes bibliography. [BV835.B3] 57-5497
1. Marriage. I. Title.

BANAHAN, John S 265.5
Instructions for mixed marriages. Milwaukee, Bruce Pub. Co. [1957] 124p. illus. 20cm. [BX1754.B33] 57-6321
1. Marriage, Mixed. 2. Catholic Church—Doctrinal and controversial works, Popular. I. Title.

THE Bond of marriage; 265'.5
an ecumenical and interdisciplinary study. Edited with notes and an introd., by William W. Bassett. Notre Dame [Ind.] University of Notre Dame Press, 1968. xxi, 265 p. 21 cm. Papers delivered at an interdenominational symposium sponsored by the Canon Law Society of America and held at the Center for Continuing Education at the University of Notre Dame, Oct. 15-18, 1967. [BX2250.B6] 68-27588 6.95
1. Marriage—Catholic Church—Societies, etc. I. Bassett, William W., ed. II. Canon Law Society of America. III. Notre Dame, Ind. University. Center for Continuing Education.

BOWMAN, Henry Adelbert, 1903- 265.5
A Christian interpretation of marriage. Philadelphia, Westminster Press [1959] 127p. 21cm. Includes bibliography. [BT705.B6] 59-5913
1. Marriage. I. Title.

CAFFAREL, Henri. 265.5
Love and grace in marriage. Translated by Frederick J. Crosson. Notre Dame, Ind., Fides Publishers Association [1960] 178p. 21cm. Translated from the French, Propos sur l amour et la griace. [BX2250.C213] 60-15440
1. Marriage—Catholic Church. I. Title.

CANA. Conference of Chicago 265.5
The new Cana manual, edited by Walter Imbiorski. Oak Park, Lll., Delaney Publications, 1957. 309p. illus. 26cm. [BX2250.C24] 57-4363
1. Marriage— Catholic Church. I. Imbiorski, Walter, ed. II. Title.

CAPPER, W. Melville. 265.5
Toward Christian marriage; the privileges and responsibilites of sex [by] W. Melville Capper and H. Morgan Williams. Chicago, Inter-varsity Press [1958] 128 p. 21 cm. Published in London in 1948 under title: Heirs together. [BT706.C3 1958] 58-7317
1. Marriage. I. Williams, Hugh Morgan, joint author. II. Title.

CATHOLIC Church. Pope. 265.5
Matrimony. Selected and arr. by the Benedictine monks of Solesmes. Translated by Michael J. Byrnes. [Boston] St. Paul Editions [c1963] 617 p. 19 cm. (Papal teachings) Bibliography: p. 561-562. [BX2250.A4313] 63-13899
1. Marriage — Catholic Church — Papal documents. I. Solesmes, France. Saint-Pierre (Benedictine abbey) II. Byrnes, Michael J., tr. III. Title.

CATHOLIC Church. Pope. 265.5
Matrimony. Selected, arr. by the Benedictine monks of Solesmes. Tr. by Michael J. Byrnes. [Boston] St. Paul Eds. [dist. Daughters of St. Paul, c.1963] 617p. 19cm. (Papal teachings) Bibl. 63-13899 5.00; 4.00 pap.,
1. Marriage—Catholic Church—Papal documents. I. Solesmes, France. Saint-Pierre (Benedictine abbey) II. Byrnes, Michael J., tr. III. Title.

CHRISTENSEN, James L 265.5
The minister's marriage handbook, by James L. Christensen. Westwood, N.J., F. H. Revell Co. [1966] 160 p. 17 cm. Bibliography: p. 154-160. [BV199.M3C5] 66-17045
1. Weddings. 2. Marriage service. 3. Clergy — U.S. — Handbooks, manuals, etc. I. Title.

CHRISTENSEN, James L. 265.5
The minister's marriage handbook. Westwood.N.J., Revell [c.1966] 160p. 17cm. Bibl. [BV199.M3C5] 66-17045 2.95 bds.,
1. Weddings. 2. Marriage service. 3. Clergy—U.S.—Handbooks, manuals, etc. I. Title.

CHRISTENSEN, James L. 265'.5
The minister's marriage handbook / by James L. Christensen. Old Tappan, N.J. : Revell, c1974. 159 p. ; 17 cm. Bibliograph: p. 153-159. [BV199.M3C5 1974] 75-316071 4.95
1. Weddings. 2. Marriage service. 3. Clergy—United States—Handbooks, manuals, etc. I. Title.

CONWAY, James D 1906- 265.5
What they ask about marriage. Chicago, Fides [1955] 322p. 21cm. [BX2250.C62] 55-7774
1. Questions and answers—Marriage. 2. Marriage—Catholic Church. I. Title.

COUTURIER, Marie Alain, Father, 1897-1954. 265.5
Wedding sermons. Translated by Mary Reidy. Washington, Catholic Distributors [1957] 57p. 19cm. Translation of Discours de mariage. [BV4278.C683] 57-2736
1. Marriage—Sermons. I. Title.

DANTEC, Francois. 265.5
Love is life; a Catholic marriage handbook. Rev. and adapted by Albert Schilitzer. Foreword by Theodore M. Hesburgh. (Notre Dame, Ind., University of Ntre Dame Press [1963] 212 p. 22 cm. Translation of Foyers rayonnants. [BX2250.D313 1963] 63-9230
1. Marriage — Catholic Church. I. Title.

DANTEC, Francois 265.5
Love is life; a Catholic marriage handbook. Rev., adapted by Albert Schlitzer. [Tr. from French] Foreword by Theodore M. Hesburgh. [Notre Dame, Ind.] Univ. of Notre Dame Pr. [c.1963] 212pp. 22cm. 63-9230 5.50 bds.,
1. Marriage—Catholic Church. I. Title.

DONLAN, Thomas C 265.5
Toward marriage in Christ; a college text in theology, by Thomas C. Donlan, Francis L. B. Cunningham [and] Augustine Rock. Dubuque, Priory Press, 1957. 199p. 23cm. (College texts in theology) Includes bibliography. [BX2250.D6] 57-12888
1. Marriage—Catholic Church. I. Title.

DRAPER, Maurice L. 265'.5
Marriage in the restoration; a brief historical-doctrinal review, by Maurice L. Draper. [Independence, Mo., Herald Pub. House, 1968] 77 p. 18 cm. Study based on doctrines of the Reorganized Church of Jesus Christ of Latter-Day Saints. Includes bibliographies. [BX8641.D7] 68-13641
1. Marriage—Mormonism. I. Title.

DWYER, Adrian I 265.5
Marriage cases, a handbook for parish priests. Springfield, Ill., Templegate Publishers [1964] x, 100 p. 20 cm. 64-4135
1. Marriage (Cannon law) I. Title.

DWYER, Adrian I. 265.5
Marriage cases, a handbook for parish priests. Springfield, Ill., Templegate [c.1964] x, 100p. 20cm. 64-4135 3.95
1. Marriage (Canon law) I. Title.

EMERSON, James Gordon, jr., 1926- 265.5
Divorce, the church, and remarriage. Philadelphia, WestminsterPr. [c.1961] 190p. Bibl. 61-5228 3.95
1. Divorce. 2. Remarriage. I. Title.

FABREGUES, Jean de. 265.5
Christian marriage. Translated from the French by Rosemary Haughton. New York, Hawthorn Books [c.1959] 109p. 21cm. (The Twentieth century encyclopedia of Catholicism, v.54. Section 5: The life of faith) (bibl.) 59-12171 2.95 bds.,
1. Marriage—Catholic Church. I. Title.

FOREMAN, Kenneth J. 265.5
From this day forward; thoughts about a Christian marriage. Richmond, Outlook Publishers, 1950. xvi, 71 p. 17 cm. [BV835.F6] 50-12336
1. Marriage. 2. Marriage service. I. Title.

FOREMAN, Kenneth Joseph, 1891- 265.5
From this day forward; thoughts about a Christian marriage. Richmond, Outlook Publishers, 1950. xvi, 71p. 17cm. [BV835.F6] 50-12336
1. Marriage. 2. Marriage service. I. Title.

GAGERN, Friedrich Ernst, Freiherr von. 265'.5
New views of sex-marriage-love, by Frederick von Gagern. Translated by Erika Scavillo. Glen Rock, N.J., Paulist Press [1968] vii, 102 p. 19 cm. (Deus books) Translation of Das neue Gesicht der Ehe. [BX2250.G313] 68-54404 1.25
1. Marriage—Catholic Church. I. Title.

GEISSLER, Eugene S. 265.5
The meaning of marriage. Discussion questions by Gerard Pottebaum. Notre Dame, Ind., Fides [c.1962] 159p. (Fides dome bk., D-15) At head of title: Sex, love, and life, 1. 62-1682 .95 pap.,
1. Marriage—Catholic Church. I. Title.

HAAS, Harold. 265.5
Marriage. Philadelphia, Muhlenberg Press [1960] 56p. 20cm. (A Fortress book) Includes bibliography. [BT706.H3] 60-3806
1. Marriage. I. Title.

HARING, Bernhard, 1912- 265'.5
Married love; a modern Christian view of marriage and family life [by] Bernard Haring. Chicago, Argus Communications [1970] 127 p. 23 cm. (Peacock books) [BX2250.H29] 72-113272 2.45
1. Marriage—Catholic Church. I. Title.

HEILLY, Alphonse 265'.5
Love and sacrament. Tr. by Sister Mary Augusta. Notre Dame, Ind., Fides [1966] cix, 118p. 20cm. Bibl. [BX2250.H4513] 65-24106 3o 2.25 pap.,
1. Mrage—Catholic Church. I. Title.

HODSDON, Nick, 1941- 265'.5
The joyful wedding. Nashville, Abingdon Press [1973] 80 p. illus. 28 cm. [BV199.M3H6] 73-8421 ISBN 0-687-20651-0 3.50 (pbk)
1. Marriage service. I. Title.

HUTTON, Samuel Ward, 1886- comp. 265'.5
Minister's marriage manual. Grand Rapids, Baker Bk. [1968] 94p. 18cm. Bibl. [BV199.M3H8] 67-18181 2.95
1. Marriage service. 2. Clergy—U. S.—Handbooks, manuals, etc. I. Title.

KEENAN, Alan, 1920- 265.5
Marriage, a medical and sacramental study, by Alan Keenan and John Ryan. New York, Sheed and Ward, 1955. 337p. illus. 22cm. [BX2250.K38] 55-7486
1. Marriage—Catholic Church. I. Ryan, John, F. B. C. S. K., joint author. II. Title.

KELLY, Philip Christopher M. 265.5
The Catholic book of marriage; the marriage ceremony and counsels for success and happiness in married life. New York, Farrar, Straus & Young [1951] xiii, 297 p. 16 cm. [BX2250.K35] 51-9682
1. Marriage—Catholic Church. I. Catholic Church. Liturgy and ritual. Ritual. De sacramento matrimonil. II. Title.

KINDREGAN, Charles P. 265'.5
A theology of marriage; a doctrinal, moral, and legal study [by] Charles P. Kindregan. Milwaukee, Bruce Pub. Co. [1967] xiv, 162 p. 23 cm. (Contemporary college theology series) Includes bibliographies. [BT706.K5] 67-26508
1. Marriage. I. Title.

KNOX, Ronald Arbuthnott, 1888- 265.5
Bridegroom and bride. New York, Sheed & Ward [1957] 123p. 20cm. [BV4278.K58] 57-6050
1. Marriage—Sermons. I. Title.

KOKKINAKIS, Athenagoras T 265.5
Parents and priests as servants of redemption; an interpretation of the doctrines of the Eastern Orthodox Church on the sacraments of matrimony and priesthood. New York, Morehouse-Gorham Co., 1958. 205p. 23cm. Includes bibliography. [BX378.M2K6] 58-13144
1. Marriage—Orthodox Eastern Church. 2. Orthodox Eastern Church—Clergy. I. Title.

LANGER, Thomas E. 265.5
Christian marriage; a guide for young people. Milwaukee, Bruce [1962] 223p. illus. 22cm. 62-16837 1.95 pap.,
1. Marriage—Catholic Church. I. Title.

LANGER, Thomas E. 265.5
Christian marriage; a guide for young people [by] Thomas E. Langer. Rev. ed. Milwaukee. Bruce [1966] xiii. 225p. illus. 22cm. Bibl. [BX2250.L35 1966] 66-28031 1.95
1. Marriage—Catholic Church. I. Title.

LEACH, William Herman, 1888- ed. 265.5
The Cokesbury marriage manual. Rev. and enl. ed. New York, Abingdon Press [1959] 171 p. 26 cm. Includes bibliography. [BV199.M3L4 1959] 59-10364
1. Marriage. 2. Marriage service. 3. Marriage law—U.S. I. Title.

MCAULEY, Claire, [pseud.] 265.5
Whom God hath not joined. With an introd. by Maisie Ward. New York, Sheed and Ward [c.1961] 159p. 60-12873 3.00 bds.,
1. Marriage—Catholic Church. I. Title.

MCHUGH, James T., comp. 265'.5
Working papers on the theology of marriage. James T. McHugh, editor. [1st ed.] Washington, Family Life Bureau, U.S.C.C., 1967. x, 61 p. 23 cm. Consists of 6 papers compiled from the papers delivered at the Symposium on the Theology of Marriage called by the Family Life Bureau in July 1966, and several subsequent meetings. Includes bibliographies. [BX2250.M2] 67-28978
1. Marriage—Catholic Church. I. United States Catholic Conference. Family life Bureau. II. Symposium on the Theology of Marriage, Washington? D.C., 1966. III. Title. IV. Title: The theology of marriage.

MESSENGER, Ernest Charles, 1888- 265.5
Two in one flesh. [2d ed.] Westminster, Md., Newman Press [1950] xv, 61, viii, 236, 71p. illus. 23cm. 'In three parts: An introduction to sex and marriage. The mystery of sex and marriage. The practice of sex and marriage.' [BX2250.M4 1950] 55-12949
1. Marriage—Catholic Church. 2. Sex. I. Title.

*MILLER, Ella May. 265.5
A woman in her home. Chicago, Moody [1968] 128p. 17cm. (33-531) .50 pap.,
1. Marriage. I. Title.

MURPHY, Thomas J 265.5
The supernatural perfection of conjugal life according to Pope Pius XII. Mundelein, Ill., Saint Mary of the Lake Seminary, 1960. 154p. 23cm. (Pontifica Facultas Theologica Seminaril Sanctae Mariae ad Lacum. Dissertationes ad lauream, 33) Bibliography: p. 138-154. [BX2250.M84] 61-1795
1. Pius XII, Pope, 1876-1958. 2. Marriage—Catholic Church. I. Title. II. Series: St. Mary of the Lake Seminary, Mundele, Ill. Dissertationes ad lauream, 33

NEAL, Emily Gardiner. 265.5
God can heal you now. Englewood Cliffs, N.J., Prentice Hall [1958] 213 p. 21 cm. Includes bibliography. [BT732.4.N4] 58-12861
1. Faith-cure. I. Title.

NUGENT, Vincent Joseph, 1913- ed. 265.5
Christ in marriage; some contemporary problems. Jamaica, N. Y., St. John's University Press [1961] 59p. 23cm. (St. John's University studies. Theological series, 2) [BX2250.N8] 61-9608
1. Marriage—Catholic Church. I. Title.

O MAHONY, Patrick J., [pseud.] 265.5
Catholics and divorce. New York, Nelson [1959.i.e., 1960] ix, 116p. 23cm. Bibliographical footnotes. 60-16084 2.95
1. Divorce. 2. Marriage—Catholic Church. I. Title.

PIUS XII, Pope, 1876-1958. 265.5
Dear newlyweds; Pope Pius XII speaks to young couples. Selected and translated by James F. Murray, Jr., and Bianca M. Murray. New York, Farrar, Straus and Cudahy [1961] 266p. illus. 22cm. [BX2250.P46] 61-5382
1. Marriage—Catholic Church—Papal documents. I. Title.

PIUS XII, Pope, 1876-1958. 265.5
Dear newlyweds; Pope Pius XII speaks to young couples. Selected and translated by James F. Murray, Jr., and Bianca M. Murray. New York, Farrar, Straus and Cudahy [c.]1961 268p. illus. 61-5382 3.95
1. Marriage—Catholic Church—Papal documents. I. Title.

PLANQUE, Daniel. 265.5
The theology of sex in marriage. Translated by Albert J. LaMothe, Jr. Notre Dame, Ind., Fides Publishers Association [1962] 187p. 20cm. (Themes of theology series) Translation of La chastete conjugale. [BX2250.P573] 62-13639
1. Marriage—Catholic Church. I. Title.

POEL, Cornelius J. van der, 1921- 265'.5
God's love in human language; a study of the meaning of marriage and conjugal responsibility [by] Cornelius J. van der Poel. [Pittsburgh] Duquesne University Press, 1969. 142 p. 22 cm. [BX2250.P6] 78-93812 3.25
1. Marriage—Catholic Church. I. Title.

REID, John Calvin, 1901- 265'.5
The marriage covenant. Richmond, Va., John Knox Press [1967] [29] p. 20 cm. [BX9189.M3R4] 67-11305
1. Marriage service. I. Title.

ROBERTS, Rufus Putnam 265.5
Matrimonial legislation in Latin and Oriental canon law: a comparative study. Westminster, Md., Newman Press, [c.]1961. viii, 110p. Canons in Latin. Bibl. 60-14812 2.95
1. Marriage (Canon law,Oriental) 2. Marriage (Canon law) I. Title.

SCHILLEBEECKX. EDWARD CORNELIS FLORENTIUS ALFONS, 1914- 265.5
Marriage: human reality and saving mystery [by] E. Schillebeeckx. Tr. by N. D. Smith. New York, Sheed [1966, c.1965] 415p. 22cm. Bibl. [BX2250.S33513 1966] 66-12263
1. Marriage—Catholic Church. I. Title.
Contents omitted. p7.50

SCHLECK, Charles A 265.5
The sacrament of matrimony, a dogmatic study. Milwaukee, Bruce Pub. Co. [1964] xii, 290 p. 24 cm. Bibliographical footnotes. [BX2250.S34] 64-15488
1. Marriage—Catholic Church. 2. Marriage (Canon law) I. Title.

SCHLEOK, Charles A. 265.5
The sacrament of matrimony, a dogmatic study. Milwaukee, Bruce [c1964] xii, 290p. 24cm. Bibl. 64-15488 5.00
1. Marriage—Catholic Church. 2. Marriage (Canon law) I. Title.

SMITH, Charles Edward, 1905-1959. 265'.5
Papal enforcement of some medieval marriage laws. Port Washington, N.Y., Kennikat Press [1972, c1940] vii, 230 p. 22 cm. A revision of the author's thesis, University of Pennsylvania, 1932. Bibliography: p. 202-211. [LAW] 70-159059 ISBN 0-8046-1682-5
1. Impediments to marriage (Canon law) 2. Marriage—Annulment (Canon law) I. Title.

STANBROUGH, O W 265.5
God's miracle of marriage. Boston, Christopher Pub. House [1954] 51p. 21cm. [BV835.S8] 54-20987
1. Marriage. I. Title.

SWEAZEY, George Edgar. 1905- 265.5
In holy marriage. New York, Harper [c.1966] xii.114p. 22cm. [HQ734.S979] 66-15045 2.95 bds.,
1. Marriage. I. Title.

TERTULLIANUS, Quintus Septimius Florens. 265.5
Treatises on marriage and remarriage: To his wife, An exhortation to chasity, Monogamy. Translated and annotated by William P. Le Saint. Westminster, Md., Newman Press, 1951. vii, 196 p. 23 cm. (Ancient Christian writers: the works of the Fathers in translation, no. 13) Bibliographical references included in "Notes" (p. [109]-170) [BR60.A35] 51-14743
1. Marriage. Catholic Church. 2. Chastity. I. Title. II. Series.

UNION of love (The); 265.5
a Catholic marriage manual for engaged couples. New York, Benziger Bros. [1967] 227p. illus. 20cm. Orig. pub. in French by L'Action Catholique Canadienne, Montreal. 3.50 pap.
1. Marriage—Catholic Church.
Publisher's address: 7 E. 51st St., New York, N.Y. 10022.

WALL, Wendy Somerville. 265'.5
The creative wedding handbook. New York, Newman Press [1973] 163 p. illus. 24 cm. [BV199.M3W34] 72-93983 ISBN 0-8091-0177-7 5.95
1. Marriage service. I. Title.

WASHINGTON, D. C. Founding Church of Scientology. 265'.5
Ceremonies of the Founding Church of Scientology. New ed. East Grinstead (Sx.), Hubbard College of Scientology, 1966. 79 p. 20 1/2 cm. 12/6 (B 67-2805) [BP605.S2A45 1966] 67-89459
1. Scientology. 2. Marriage service. I. Hubbard College of Scientology. II. Title.

WEDGE, Florence 265.5
Hand in hand to holiness. Pulaski, Wis., Franciscan Pubs. [1963, c.1962] 64p. 19cm. .25 pap.,
I. Title.

WINNETT, Arthur Robert, 1910- 265.5
Divorce and remarriage in Anglicanism. London, Macmillan; New York, St. Martin's Press, 1958. xii, 284 p. 23 cm. Bibliography: p. 277-281. Bibliographical footnotes. [BX5149.M3W5 1958] 58-59627
1. Divorce. 2. Remarriage. 3. Church of England — Discipline. I. Title.

WYLIE, William P 265.5
Human nature and Christian marriage. [1st U.S.A. ed.] New York, Association Press [1958] 128 p. 20 cm. Includes bibliography. [BT706.W9 1958] 59-6833
1. Marriage. I. Title.

ANCIAUX, Paul. 265.6
The sacrament of penance. New York, Sheed Ward [1962] 190p. 21cm. [BX2265.A513] 62-52076
1. Penance I. Title.

ANCIAUX, Paul 265.6
The sacrament of penance. [Tr. from French] New York, Sheed [c.1962] 190p. 21cm. 62-52076 3.50
1. Penance. I. Title.

BARRY, David W. 265'.6
Ministry of reconciliation : modern lessons from scripture and sacrament / David W. Barry. New York : Alba House, [1975] xii, 129 p. ; 21 cm. Includes bibliographical references. [BX2260.B28] 75-4630 ISBN 0-8189-0317-1 pbk. : 2.95
1. Penance. I. Title.

BARTON, John Mackintosh Tilney, 1898- 265.6
Penance and absolution. [1st ed.] New York, Hawthorn Books [1961] 159p. 21cm. (The Twentieth century encylopedia of Catholicism, v. 51. Section 5: The life of Faith) Includes bibilography. [BX2260.B3] 61-12987
1. Penance. I. Title.

BELGUM, David Rudolph, 1922- 265.6
Guilt: where religion and psychology meet. Englwood Cliffs, N.J., Prentice-Hall, 1963. 148 p. 22 cm. Bibliography: p. 145-148. [BV845.B37] 63-10669
1. Confession—Psychology. 2. Confession—History. I. Title.

CATHOLIC Theological Society of America. Committee on the Renewal of the Sacrament of Penance. 265'.6
Committee report : the renewal of the sacrament of penance / [CTSA Committee on the Renewal of the Sacrament of Penance]. [Washington] : The Society, 1975. 106 p. ; 23 cm. On spine: CTSA committee report. Bibliography: p. 49-95. [BX2260.C28 1975] 76-354199
1. Penance. I. Title. II. Title: The renewal of the sacrament of penance.

DARCY-BERUBE, Francoise. 265'.6
Sacrament of peace, by Francoise Darcy Berube [and] John Paul Berube. [New York, Paulist Press, 1974] 4 v. illus. (part col.) 22 cm. Contents.Contents.—[1] Book 1, for 7 and 8 year old children.—[2] Book 2, for 9 to 12 year old children.—[3] Director's guide.—[4] Parent guide. Discusses the significance of the Sacrament of Penance. [BX2260.D3] 73-92894 4.00 (pbk.)
1. Penance. 2. Penance—Juvenile literature. I. Berube, John Paul, joint author. II. Title.

DOYLE, Charles Hugo 265.6
Go in peace. Garden City, N. Y., Hanover House [c.1961] 141p. 61-12514 2.95
1. Penance. I. Title.

GRANT, Dorothy (Fremont) 1900- 265.6
'... for I have sinned.' Milwaukee, Bruce Pub. Co. [1952] 89p. 20cm. [BX1754.G69] 53-83
1. Catholic Church—Doctrinal and controversial works, Popular. I. Title.

HARING, Bernhard, 1912- 265'.6
Shalom: peace; the sacrament of reconciliation [by] Bernard Haring. New York, Farrar, Straus and Giroux [1968] xii, 308 p. 22 cm. [BX2260.H18] 68-11424
1. Penance. I. Title.

HARING, Bernhard, 1912- 265'.6
Shalom: peace; the sacrament of reconciliation [by] Bernard Haring. New York, Farrar, Straus and Giroux [1968] xii, 308 p. 22 cm. [BX2260.H18 1968] 68-11424

1. Penance. I. Title.

HARING, Bernhard, 1912- 265'.6
Shalom: peace; the sacrament of reconciliation [by] Bernhard Haring. Rev. ed. Garden City, N.Y., Image Books [1969] 354 p. 19 cm. [BX2260.H18 1969] 72-78750 1.35
1. Penance. I. Title.

LEA, Henry Charles, 1825- 265'.6
1909.
A history of auricular confession and indulgences in the Latin Church. New York, Greenwood Press, 1968. 3 v. facsims. 24 cm. Reprint of the 1896 ed. Contents.Contents.—v. 1-2. Confession and absolution.—v. 3. Indulgences. Bibliographical footnotes. [BX2265.L4 1968] 68-19287
1. Catholic Church—Discipline. 2. Confession—History. 3. Absolution. 4. Penance. 5. Indulgences. I. Title.

PALMER, Paul F., ed. 265.6
Sacraments and forgiveness; history and doctrinal development of penance, extreme unction and indulgences. Edited with commentary by Paul F. Palmer. Westminster, Md., Newman Press [1960, c.1959] 410p. (Sources of Christian theology, v. 2) 59-14809 6.00
1. Sacraments—Catholic Church. 2. Sacraments—History of doctrines. I. Title.

PARIS. Saint-Severin 265.6
(Church) Clergy.
Confession: meaning and practice, by the community of Saint-Severin Translated [from the French] by A. V. Littledale. Chicago, Fides Publishers Association [1960] 128p. 19cm. 60-863 3.25 bds.,
1. Penance. I. Title.

PARIS. Saint-Severin 265'.6
(Church) Clergy.
Confession; meaning and practice, by the community of Saint-Severin. Translated by A. V. Littledale. With and introd. by John E. Corrigan. Notre Dame, Ind., Fides Publishers [1967] 127 p. 18 cm. (A Fides dome book, D-60) [BX2260.P313 1967] 67-24815
1. Penance. I. Title.

RABALAIS, Maria. 265'.6
Come, be reconciled! : Penance celebrations for young Christians / by Maria Rabalais, Howard Hall, David Vavasseur ; [ill., Gloria Ortiz]. New York : Paulist Press, 1975. 148 p. : ill. ; 25 cm. Bibliography: p. 144-148. Devotions on both the elementary and high school level designed to raise one's consciousness of the spirit of forgiveness and prepare one for the sacrament of Penance. [BX2150.R3] 74-33576 ISBN 0-8091-1876-9 pbk. : 4.95
1. Penance—Prayer-books and devotions—English. 2. Children—Prayer-books and devotions—English—1961- 3. Youth—Prayer-books and devotions—English. I. Hall, Howard, 1936- joint author. II. Vavasseur, David, joint author. III. Title.

RICHTER, Stephan. 265'.6
Metanoia: Christian penance and confession. Translated by Raymond T. Kelly. New York, Sheed and Ward [1966] 126 p. 21 cm. Bibliography: p. 124-126. Bibliographical references included in "Notes". [BX2260.R513] 66-22024
1. Penance. 2. Confession. I. Title.

RIGA, Peter, Rev. 265.6
Sin and penance; insights into the mystery of salvation. Milwaukee, Bruce [c.1962] 187p. 23cm. Bibl. 62-19191 4.25
1. Sin. 2. Penance. I. Title.

SACRAMENT of penance, 265.6
(The) by M. B. Carra de Vaux Saint-Cyr. others.[Tr. by R. L. Sullivant. St. Agnes Cunningham. M. Renelle] Glen Rock, N.J. Paulist [1966] v, 122p. 19cm. (Deus bk.) Bibl. [BX2260.S213] 66-22054 .95 pup.,
1. Penance. 2. Confession I. Cana de Vaux Saint-Cyr. M. B.

SHEERIN, John B. 265.6
The sacrament of freedom; a book on confession. Milwaukee, Bruce Pub. Co. [1961] 166 p. 22 cm. [BX2265.2.S5] 61-8015
1. Confession. I. Title.

SHEERIN, John B. 265.6
The sacrament of freedom; a book on confession. Milwaukee, Bruce Pub. Co. [c.1961] 166p 61-8015 3.50
1. Confession. I. Title.

SPEYR, Adrie 265.6
Confession, the encounter with Christ in penance [tr. from german by a. v. littledale. New York] Herder & Herder [c.1964] 234 p. 22 cm. 64-15376 4.75
1. Penance. 2. Confession. I. Title.

SPEYR, Adrienne von. 265.6
Confession, the encounter with Christ in penance. [Translated by A. V. Littledale. New York] Herder and Herder [1964] 234 p. 22 cm. Translation of Die Reichte. [BX2260.S613 1964] 64-15376
1. Penance. 2. Confession. I. Title.

TERTULLIANUS, Quintus 265.6
Septimius Florens.
Treatises on penance: On penitence and On purity. Translated and annotated by William P. LeSaint. Westminster, Md., Newman Press, 1959. vi, 330 p. 23 cm. (Ancient Christian writers; the works of the Fathers in translation, no. 28) Bibliographical references includes in "Notes" (p. [129]-298) [BR60.A35 no.28] 58-10746
1. Penance. 2. Chastity. I. Le Saint, William P., ed. and tr. II. Title. III. Series.

VAN ZELLER, Hubert, 1905- 265.6
Approach to penance. New York, Sheed & Ward [1958] 103 p. 21 cm. Secular name: Claude Van Zeller. [BX2260.V36] 58-5882
1. Penance. I. Title. II. Series.

WEILAND, Duane. 265'.6
Resistance; the sacrament of penance. Dayton, Ohio, G. A. Pflaum, 1969. 128 p. illus. 18 cm. (Christian identity series) (Witness book, CI 1.) Bibliography: p. 123-124. [BX2260.W43] 71-97043 0.95
1. Penance. I. Title.

ZIEGLER, John Henry, 1925- 265.6
The obligation of the confessor to instruct penitents. Washington, Catholic University of America Press, 1959. vi, 60 p. 23 cm. (The Catholic University of America. Studies in sacred theology. 2d ser., no. 121) "An abstract of a dissertation submitted to the ... Catholic University of America." Bibliography: p. 55-58. [BX2265.2.Z5] 61-2102
1. Confessors. I. Title. II. Series: Catholic University of America. School of Sacred Theology. Studies in sacred theology, 2d ser., no. 121

LARSEN, Earnest. 265'.6'07
Will morality make sense to your child? [by] Earnest Larsen [and] Patricia Galvin. Liguori, Mo., Liguori Publications [1971] 165, [4] p. col. illus. 18 cm. Bibliography: p. [167] [BX930.L27] 73-160694 1.75
1. Religious education—Text-books—Catholic. 2. Confession of children. I. Galvin, Patricia, joint author. II. Title.

POSCHMANN, Bernhard. 265.609
1878-1955.
Penance and the anointing of the sick. Translated and rev. by Francis Courtney. [New York] Herder and Herder [1961] cxi, 257 p. 23 cm. (The Herder history of dogma) Includes bibliographies. [BX2262.P613] 64-11976
1. Penance—Hist. 2. Extreme unction—Hist. I. Title.

POSCHMANN, Bernhard, 265.609
1878-1955
Penance and the anointing of the sick. Tr. [from German] and rev. by Francis Courtney [New York] Herder & Herder [c.1964] xi,257p. 23cm. (Herder hist. of dogma) Bibl. 64-11976 6.50
1. Penance—Hist. 2. Extreme unction—Hist. I. Title.

WATKINS, Oscar Daniel, 265'.6'09
1848-1926.
A history of penance; being a study of the authorities. New York, B. Franklin, 1961. 2 v. (xxix, 775 p.) 24 cm. (Burt Franklin research & source works series, #16) Reprint of the 1920 ed. Contents.Contents.—v. 1. The whole church to A.D. 450.—v. 2. The Western church from A.D. 450 to A.D. 1215. Bibliographical footnotes. [BV840.W3 1961] 72-6537
1. Penance—History—Sources. I. Title.

MCNEILL, John Thomas, 265.60902
1885- tr.
Medieval handbooks of penance; a translation of the principal libri poenitentiales and selections from related documents, by John T. McNeill, Helena M. Gamer. New York, Octagon, 1965[c.1938] xiv, 476p. facsims. 24cm. (Records of civilization: sources and studies, no. 29) Bibl. [BX2260.M3] 65-20970 12.50
1. Penitentials. I. Gamer, Helena Margaret, 1900- joint tr. II. Title. III. Series.

FAGES, Raymond 265.61
Examen: the sacraments in our daily life. Prepared in English [from the French] by Kathryn Sullivan. Chicago, H. Regnery Co. [c.]1960. 84p. 15cm. 60-50525 1.45 bds.,
1. Conscience. Examination of. 2. Sacraments—Catholic Church. I. Title.

BAUR, Benedikt 265.62
Frequent confession, its place in the spiritual life;instructions and considerations for the frequent reception of the sacrament of penance. Translated from the 7th German ed. by Patrick C. Barry. Staten Island, N. Y., St. Paul Publications [Society of St. Paul] 1960[ ] 217p. 19cm. 60-15540 3.00 bds.,
1. A Confession—Frequency of confession. I. Title.

BAUSCH, William J. 265'.62
It is the Lord! Sin and confession revisited [by] William J. Bausch. Notre Dame, Ind., Fides Publishers [1970] vii, 157 p. 21 cm. Bibliography: p. 154-157. [BX2265.2.B34] 72-104074 5.00
1. Confession. I. Title.

BETZ, Otto. 265'.62
Making sense of confession; a new approach for parents, teachers, and clergy, edited by Otto Betz. Translated by Hilda Graef. Chicago, Franciscan Herald Press [1968] 142 p. 23 cm. Translation of Beichte im Zwielicht. Bibliographical footnotes. [BX2265.2.B463] 69-11225 4.95
1. Confession—Instruction and study. I. Title.

BOWMAN, George William. 265'.62
The dynamics of confession. Richmond, Va., John Knox Press [1969] 125 p. 21 cm. Bibliography: p. [123]-125. [BV845.B67] 79-79923 3.50
1. Confession. I. Title.

DOYLE, Charles Hugo. 265.62
What to say to the penitent; instructive counsels for use by confessors. Tarrytown, N. Y., Nugent Press [1953] 276p. 24cm. [BX2265.D6] 53-28240
1. Confessors. I. Title.

*FOLEY, Leonard. 265.62
Your confession: using the new ritual. [Cincinnati, St. Anthony Messenger Press, 1975] v, 105 p. ill. 18 cm. [BX2265.2] ISBN 0-912228-17-2 1.50 (pbk.)
1. Confession—Catholic Church. I. Title.

FOLEY, Leonard, 1913- 265'.62
What's happening to confession? [Cincinnati, St. Anthony Messenger Press, 1970] ix, 117 p. illus. 19 cm. [BX2265.2.F6] 79-132545 ISBN 0-912228-00-8 0.95
1. Confession. I. Title.

HEENAN, John Carmel, Bp., 265.62
1905-
Confession. New York, Sheed and Ward [1957?] 95p. 18cm. (Canterbury books) 'An abridged version [i. e. all that is directly on the sacrament of penance from] . . . the same author's Priest and penitent.' [BX2265.H42] 57-4544
1. Penance. I. Title.

HEENAN, John Carmel, 265.62
Cardinal, 1905-
Confession. New York, Sheed and Ward [1957?] 95 p. 18 cm. (Canterbury books) "An abridged version [i.e. all that is directly of the sacrament of penance from] ... the same author's Priest and penitent." [BX2265.H42] 57-4544
1. Penance. I. Title.

HEGGEN, Franz J. 265'.62
Confession and the service of penance [by] F. J. Heggen. Translated by Peter Tomlinson. [1st American ed.] Notre Dame [Ind.] University of Notre Dame Press [1968, c1967] 176 p. 21 cm. Translation of Boeteviering en private biecht. Bibliographical footnotes. [BX2260.H413 1968] 67-31394
1. Penance. I. Title.

JEAN-NESMY, Claude. 265.62
Conscience & confession. Translated by Malachy Carroll. Chicago, Franciscan Herald Press [1965] xvii, 222 p. 21 cm. Bibliography: p. 211. Bibliographical references included in "Notes" (p. 213-222) [BX2265.2.J4] 65-22643
1. Confession. I. Title.

JEAN-NESMY, Claude 265.62
Conscience & confession. Tr. by Malachy Carroll. Chicago, Franciscan Herald [1965] xvii, 222p. 21cm. Bibl. [BX2265.2.J4] 65-22643 4.95
1. Confession. I. Title.

KELLY, Gerald A. 265.62
The good confessor. New York, Sentinel Press [1951] 96 p. 20 cm. [BX2265.K4] 51-33546
1. Confessors. I. Title.

MCGRADE, Francis. 265.62
My confession, for little Catholics. Pictures by Mimi Korach. St. Paul, Catechetical Guild Educational Society, c1953. unpaged. illus. 17cm. [BX2205.M26] 53-23425
1. Confession—Juvenile literature. I. Title.

SAFIEJKO, Joseph Rev. 265.62
Five steps to pardon. St. Paul 2, Minn., Catechetical Guild Educational Society [c.1961] 64p. 16cm. .25 pap.,
I. Title.

SIMON, Alphonse, 1896- 265.62
Fruitful confessions; practical exhortations for the confessor. St. Louis, B. Herder Book Co. [1954] 220p. 22cm. [BX2265.S5] 53-12254
1. Confessors. I. Title.

SNOECK, Andre. 265.62
Confession and pastoral psychology. Translated by Theodore Zuydwijk. Westminster, Md., Newman Press, 1961. 183 p. 21 cm. [BX2265.2.S613] 61-16564
1. Confession — Psychology. 2. Pastoral psychology. I. Title.

SNOECK, Andre 265.62
Confession and pastoral psychology. Tr. by Theodore Zuydwijk. Westminster, Md., Newman [c.]1961. 183p. 61-16564 3.50
1. Confession—Psychology. 2. Pastoral psychology. I. Title.

SNOECK, Andre. 265.62
Confession and psychoanalysis. Translated by Theodore Zuydwijk. Westminster, Md., Newman Press, 1964. viii, 132 p. 21 cm. A companion volume to the author's Confession and pastoral psychology. Includes bibliographical references. [BX2265.2.S623] 63-23493
1. Confession — Psychology. 2. Pastoral psychology. 3. Psychiatry and religion. I. Title.

SNOECK, Andre 265.62
Confession and psychoanalysis. Tr. by Theodore Zuydwijk. Westminster, Md., Newman [c.]1964. viii, 132p. 21cm. Companion vol. to the author's Confession and pastoral psychology. Bibl. 63-23493 3.50
1. Confession—Psychology. 2. Pastoral psychology. 3. Psychiatry and religion. I. Title.

STOTT, John R. W. 265.62
Confess your sins; the way of reconciliation. Philadelphia, Westminster [1965, c.1964] 91, [1]p. 19cm. (Christian founds.) Bibl. [BX5149.C6S7] 65-18922 1.25 pap.,
1. Confession—Anglican Communion. I. Title.

UNITED States Catholic 265'.62
Conference. Division of Religious Education—CCD.
A study paper for first confession. Washington, Publications Office, United States Catholic Conference, 1973. 45 p. 22 cm. [BX2266.C5U54 1973] 73-179249
1. Confession of children. I. Title.

WILSON, Alfred 265.62
Pardon and peace. Garden City, N.Y., Doubleday [1965, c.1947] 274p. 18cm. (Image bks., D196) [BX2265.W55] .95 pap.,
1. Confession. I. Title.

BELGUM, David 265'.62'019
Rudolph, 1922-
Guilt: where religion and psychology meet, by David Belgum. Minneapolis, Augsburg Pub. House [1970] ix, 149 p. 22 cm. Bibliography: p. 145-149. [BV845.B37 1970] 78-10471 2.95
1. Confession—Psychology. 2. Confession—History. I. Title.

HERBST, Winfrid, 1891- 265.66
Indulgences. Milwaukee, Bruce Pub. Co. [c1955] 103p. 19cm. Indulgences. [BX2281.H4] 55-12388
I. Title.

CAMERON, Kenneth 265.660942
Walter, 1908-
The pardoner and his pardons; indulgences circulating in England on the eve of the Reformation. With a historical introd. Hartford, Conn., Transcendental Bks., Drawer 1080 [1965] 80 l. illus., facsims., port. 29cm. Bibl. [BX2281.2.C3] 65-3784 price unreported
1. Indulgences—Hist. I. Title.

ADOLPH, Paul Ernest, 1901- 265.8
Health shall spring forth. Chicago, Moody Press [1956] 127p. 20cm. [BR115.H4A3] 56-14396
1. Faith-cure. 2. Emotions. 3. Conversion. I. Title.

ADOLPH, Paul Ernest, 1904- 265.8
Health shall spring forth. Chicago, Moody Press [1956] 127p. 20cm. [BR115.H4A3] 56-14396
1. Faith-cure. 2. Emotions. 3. Conversion. I. Title.

BAKER, Clara Worth. 265.8
The house God built. [San Diego, Calif., 1951] 162 p. 23 cm. [BR115.H4B27] 51-35109
1. Faith-cure. I. Title.

BALES, James D 1915- 265.8
Miracles or mirages Austin, Tex., Firm

Roundation Pub. House [1956] 279p. 21cm. [BR115.H4B28] 56-30560
1. Faith-cure. 2. Miracles. I. Title.

BECK, Mary Berenice, Sister, 1890- 265.8
Handmaid of the Divine Physician; the religious care of the sick and dying. Milwaukee, Bruce Pub. Co. [1952] 311 p. illus. 17 cm. "A revision of The nurse. handmaid of the Divine Physician ... which first appeared in 1945." [BX2170.S5B4 1952] 52-3595
1. Church work with the sick. I. Title.

BOGGS, Wade H 265.8
Faith healing and the Christian faith. Richmond, John Knox Press [1956] 216p. 21cm. [BR115.H4B57] 56-9210
1. Medicine and religion. 2. Faith-cure. I. Title.

CLARK, Glenn, 1882- 265.8
Be thou made whole. [1st ed.] Saint Paul, Macalester Park Pub. Co. [1953] 161p. 21cm. [BR115.H4C53] 54-34438
1. Faith cure. I. Title.

DAY, Albert Edward, 1884- 265.8
Letters on the healing ministry. Nashville, Methodist Evangelistic Materials [1964] 64p. 19cm. Bibl. 64-8484 price unreported
1. Faith-cure. I. Title.

DIDIER, Jean Charles, 1905- 265.8
Death and the Christian. Tr. from French by P. J. Hepburne-Scott. New York, Hawthorn Books [c.1961] 106p. (Twentieth century encyclopedia of Catholicism, v.55) Bibl. 61-9459 3.50
1. Sacraments—Catholic Church. 2. Church work with the sick. I. Title.

DUNNINGTON, Lewis Le Roy, 1890- 265.8
The inner splendor. New York, Macmillan, 1954. 229p. 20cm. [BR115.H4D83] 54-9059
1. Faith -cure. I. Title.

GROSS, Don H 265.8
The case for spiritual healing. New York, T. Nelson [1958] 263p. 22cm. Includes bibliography. [BR115.H4G73] 58-9037
1. Mental healing. I. Title.

HAMLIN, Howard Harley, 1911- 265.8
From here to maturity; the interaction of spirit, soul, and body in achieving maturity. Kansas City, Mo., Beacon Hill Press [1955] 94p. 19cm. (Aycock lectures, 1953) [BR115] 55-2196
1. Faith-cure. 2. Christian life. I. Title. II. Series.

*HILLIS, Don W. 265.8
Where is the gift of healing. Chicago, Moody [c.1964] 63p. 18cm. (Compact bk., no.47) (Twentieth century encyclopedia of Catholicism v. 55) .29 pap.,
I. Title.

IRION, Paul E 265.8
The funeral and the mourners; pastoral care of the bereaved. Nashville, Abingdon Press [1954] 186p. 23cm. [BV4330.I7] 53-11337
1. Theology, Pastoral. 2. Funeral service. I. Title.

JACKSON, Edgar Newman. 265.8
Understanding grief: its roots, dynamics, and treatment. New York, Abingdon Press [1957] 255 p. 23 cm. [BF575.G7J3] 57-9786
1. Joy and sorrow. 2. Psychotherapy. 3. Pastoral psychology. I. Title.

LARGE, John Ellis. 265.8
The ministry of Healing. Foreword by Horace W. B. Donegan. New York, Morehouse-Gorham Co., 1959. 182p. 21cm. (The Annual Bishop of New York books, 1959) [BT732.4.L3] 59-5850
1. Faith-cure. I. Title.

LEURET, Francois. 265.8
Modern miraculous cures; a documented account of miracles and medicine in the 20th century, by Francois Leuret and Henri Bon. Translated from the French by A. T. Macqueen and John C. Barry. New York, Farrar, Straus and Cudahy [1957] 215p. 22cm. [BR115.H4L452] 57-10317
1. Faith-cure. I. Bon, Henri, 1885- joint author. II. Title.

MARTIN, Bernard, 1905- 265.8
The healing ministry in the church. Richmond, Va., John Knox Press [1960] 125p. Bibl. footnotes 61-5246 3.00 bds.,
1. Mental healing. I. Title.

METHODIST Society for Medical and Pastoral Psychology 265.8
Religion and medicine: essays by members of the Methodist Soc. for Med. and Pastoral Psych. Ed. by John Crowlesmith. London, Epworth Pr. [dist. Mystic, Conn., Verry, 1964, c.1962] 183p. 23cm..) Bibl. 64-5364 5.00 bds.,
1. Faith-cure—Addresses, essays, lectures. 2. Medicine and religion—Addresses, essays, lectures. I. Crowlesmith, John, ed. II. Title.

MILER, Waymon Doyne. 265.8
Modern divine healing. Fort Worth, Tex., Miller Pub. Co. [1956] 334p. illus. 23cm. [BR115.H4M5] 56-32560
1. Daith-cure. I. Title.

MILLER, Paul M. 265.8
How God heals. Scottdale, Pa., Herald Press, [c.1960] 23))p. 20cm. (2p. bibls.) 59-15706 .35 pap.,
1. Faith-cure. I. Title.

MILLER, Waymon Doyne. 265.8
Modern divine healing. Fort Worth, Tex., Miller Pub. Co. [1956] 334p. illus. 23cm. [BR115.H4M5] 56-32560
1. Faith-cure. I. Title.

MORGAN, Edmund Robert, Bp. of Truro, 1888- 265.8
The ordeal of wonder; thoughts on healing, by Edmund R. Morgan. New York, Oxford [c.] 1964. 166p. 20cm. Bibl. 64-5473 4.00
1. Faith-cure. I. Title.

MURPHY, Joseph, 1898- 265.8
How to use your healing power. San Gabriel, Calif., Willing Pub. Co. [1957] 158p. 20cm. [BR115.H4M8] 57-41657
1. Faith-cure. I. Title.

NEAL, Emily Gardiner. 265.8
The Lord is our healer. Englewood Cliffs, N. J., Prentice-Hall [1961] 218 p. 21 cm. [BT732.4.N43] 61-16715
1. Faith-cure. I. Title.

NEAL, Emily Gardiner. 265.8
A reporter finds God through spiritual healing. New York, Morehouse-Gorham Co. [1956] 192 p. 21 cm. Includes bibliography. [BR115.H4N32] 56-9831
1. Faith-cure. I. Title.

OURSLER, William Charles, 1913- 265.8
The healing power of faith. [1st ed.] New York, Hawthorn Books [1957] 366 p. 24 cm. Includes bibliography. [BR115.H4O84] 57-6364
1. Faith-cure. I. Title.

PARKHURST, Genevieve (Cummins) 1894- 265.8
Healing and wholeness are yours! [1st ed.] Saint Paul, Macalester Park Pub. Co. [1957] 206p. 22cm. [BR115.H4P33] 57-41656
1. Faith-cure. I. Title.

ROBERTS, Oral. 265.8
Deliverance from fear and from sickness. Tulsa, Okla, [1954] 94p. illus. 20cm. [BR115.H4R59] 54-40589
1. Mental healing. I. Title.

ROBERTS, Oral. 265.8
Exactly how you may receive your healing--through faith; including a heart-to-heart talk on your salvation. [1st ed.] Tulsa, Okla., Oral Roberts Evangelistic Association, 1958. 64p. 20cm. [BV4501.R575] 58-968
1. Christian life. I. Title.

ROBERTS, Oral. 265.8
If you need healing do these things. [2d , rev. ed.] Tulsa, Okla., Oral Roberts Evangelistic Association [1957] 126p. illus. 20cm. [BR115.H4R592 1957] 58-15903
1. Mental healing. I. Title.

SANFORD. AGNES MARY (WHITE) 265.8
Behold your God. [1st ed.] Saint Paul, Macalester Park Pub. Co. [1958] 201p. illus. 22cm. [BT732.4.S2] 58-44330
1. Faith-cure. I. Title.

SCHERZER, Carl J 265.8
The church and healing. Philadelphia, Westminster Press [1950] 272 p. 21 cm. Bibliography: p. 257-265. [BR115.H4S38] 50-10314
1. Faith-cure. I. Title.

SCHERZER, Carl J. 265.8
Ministering to the dying. Englewood Cliffs, N.J., Prentice [c.1963] 142p. 21cm. (Successful pastoral counseling ser.) Bibl. 63-18143 2.95
1. Church work with the sick. I. Title.

SPIRITUAL Healing Seminar. 265.8
Spiritual Healing Seminar. [Proceedings] 2d-Mar. 1954- Ryen, N. Y., Wainwright House. v. 29cm. [BR115.H4S657] 56-24931
1. Faith-cure. I. Title.

SWAIM, Joseph Carter, 1904- 265.8
Body, soul, and spirit. New York, T. Nelson [c1957] 243 p. 21 cm. [BR115.H4S85] 57-14968
1. Mind and body. 2. Soul. 3. Spirit. 4. Mental healing. I. Title.

TAYLOR, Jeremy, Bp. of Down and Connor, 1613-1667. 265.8
The rule and exercises of holy dying, edited and with an introd. by Thomas S. Kepler. [1st ed.] Cleveland, World Pub. Co. [1952] xxiii. 324p. 16cm. (World devotional classics) [BV4500.T3 1952] 52-10320
1. Christian life. 2. Sick—Prayer-books and devotions—English. I. Title.

WEATHERHEAD, Leslie Dixon, 1893- 265.8
Psychology, religion, and healing. Rev. ed. New York, Abingdon Press [c1952] 543p. 23cm. [BR115.H4W37 1952a] 54-6986
1. Faith-cure. 2. Psychology, Religious. 3. Psychotherapy. I. Title.

WEATHERHEAD, Leslie Dixon, 1893- 265.8
Psychology, religion, and healing; a critical study of all the non-physical methods of healing, with an examination of the principles underlying them and the techniques employed to express them, together with some conclusions regarding further investigation and action in this field. New York, Abingdon-Cokesbury Press [1952, 1951] 543 p. 23 cm. Bibliography: p. 523-532. [BR115.H4W37] 52-5380
1. Faith-cure. 2. Psychology, Religious. 3. Psychotherapy. I. Title.

WINCKLEY, Rev. Edward 265.8
Healing venture [3d ed.] [San Antonio, Tex., Naylor c. 1963] 140p. 19cm. pap., gratis.
I. Title.

DAY, Helen Caldwell, 1926- 265.8062
All the way to heaven. New York, Sheed & Ward [1956] 148p. 20cm. [BX2390.S5D3] 56-9525
1. Catholic Union of the Sick in America. I. Title.

CHURCH of England. Archbishops' Commission on Divins Healing. 265.82
The church's ministry of healing; report. Westminster, Church Information Board 1958. 84p. 22cm. [BT732.4.C47] 59-40382
1. Faith-cure. I. Title.

LESSER, Graham 265.82
Why? Divine healing in medicine and theology. New York, Pageant Press [c.1960] 144p. illus. 21cm. Bibl.: p. 143-144 60-50068 2.75 pap.,
1. Mental healing. I. Title.

LESSER, Graham. 265.82
Why? Divine healing in medicine and theology. [1st ed.] New York, Pageant Press [1960] 144p. illus. 21cm. Includes bibliography. [BT732.4.L4] 60-50068
1. Mental healing. I. Title.

MCKELVEY, Gertrude Delia, 1904- 265.82
Finding God's healing power. Philadelphia, Lippincott [c.1961] 173p. Bibl. 61-8156 3.50 half cloth,
1. Faith-cure. I. Title.

MCKELVEY, Gertrude Della, 1904- 265.82
Finding God's healing power. [1st ed.] Philadelphia, Lippincott [1961] 173p. 21cm. Includes bibliography. [BT732.4.M27] 61-8156
1. Faith-cure. I. Title.

ROBERTS, Oral. 265.82
Seven divine aids for yout health. Tulsa, Okla, 1960. 79p. 20cm. [BT732.4.R6] 60-3652
1. Healing I. Title.

BAERWALD, Reuben C., comp. 265'.85
Hope in grief; address and resources for Christian funerals. Reuben C. Baerwald, ed. St. Louis, Concordia [c.1966] vi, 154p. 20cm. Bibl: [BV4275.A1B3] 67-14950 3.50
1. Funeral sermons. I. Title.

CHRISTENSEN, James L. 265'.85
The complete funeral manual [by] James L. Christensen. Westwood, N.J., Fleming H. Revell Co. [1967] 159 p. 20 cm. Bibliographical references included in "Notes" (p. 149-151) [BV199.F8C48] 67-11065
1. Funeral service. I. Title.

CHRISTENSEN, James L 265.85
Funeral services. [Westwood, N. J.] F. H. Revell Co. [1959] 160p. 17cm. Includes bibliography. [BV199.F8C5] 59-8726
1. Funeral service. I. Title.

CHRISTENSEN, James L. 265'.85
Funeral services for today / James L, Christensen. Old Tappan, N.J. : Revell, c1977. 192 p. ; 17 cm. Includes bibliographical references. [BV199.F8C52] 77-1350 ISBN 0-8007-0856-3 : 6.95
1. Funeral service. I. Title.

GRAHAM, Roscoe 265.85
Remembered with love. New York, American Pr. [c.1961] 106p. 61-8295 2.50
1. Funeral service. 2. Funeral sermons. I. Title.

IRION, Paul E. 265'.85
The funeral : vestige or value ? / Paul E. Irion. New York : Arno Press, 1977, c1966. 240 p. ; 23 cm. (The Literature of death and dying) Reprint of the ed. published by Abingdon Press, Nashville. Includes index. Bibliography: p. [BV199.F8I7 1977] 76-19578 ISBN 0-405-09575-9 : 16.00
1. Funeral service. 2. Church work with the bereaved. I. Title. II. Series.

IRION, Paul E. 265'.85
The funeral : vestige or value ? / Paul E. Irion. New York : Arno Press, 1977, c1966. 240 p. ; 23 cm. (The Literature of death and dying) Reprint of the ed. published by Abingdon Press, Nashville. Includes index. Bibliography: p. [BV199.F8I7 1977] 76-19578 ISBN 0-405-09575-9 : 16.00
1. Funeral service. 2. Church work with the bereaved. I. Title. II. Series.

IRION, Paul E. 265.85
The funeral: vestige or value? Nashville. Abingdon [c.1966] 240p. 23cm. Bibl. [BV199.F817] 66-11451 4.50
1. Funeral service. 2. Church work with the bereaved. I. Title.

LOCKYER, Herbert. 265'.85
The funeral sourcebook. Grand Rapids, Zondervan Pub. House [1967] 187 p. 24 cm. Bibliography: p. 186-187. [BV199.F8L6] 66-25816
1. Funeral service. I. Title.

REFORMING the rites of death, 265'.85 edited by Johannes Wagner. New York, Paulist Press [1968] ix, 180 p. 24 cm. (Concilium: theology in the age of renewal: Liturgy, v. 32) Translations of articles by T. L. Westow and others. Bibliographical footnotes. [BV199.F8R4] 68-20845
1. Funeral service—Addresses, essays, lectures. 2. Funeral rites and ceremonies—Addresses, essays, lectures. I. Wagner, Johannes, 1908- ed. II. Series: Concilium (New York) v. 32

THANATOLOGY course outlines—funeral service 265'.85 / edited by Otto Margolis ... et al., with the editorial assistance of Lillian G. Kutscher. New York : MSS Information Corp., [1975] p. cm. (Continuing series on thanatology) [BV199.F8T47] 75-5795 ISBN 0-8422-7277-1 : 12.50
1. Funeral service—Study and teaching. I. Margolis, Otto Schwarz. II. Series.

BAKER, Roger, 1934- 265'.9
Binding the Devil : exorcism past and present / Roger Baker. New York : Hawthorn Books, 1975, c1974. viii, 187 p. ; 21 cm. Includes index. Bibliography: p. [182]-183. [BV873.E8B34 1975] 74-22920 ISBN 0-8015-0640-9 : 7.95
1. Exorcism. I. Title.

CHURCH management. 265.9
The minister's handbook of dedications. William H. Leach, ed. Nashville, Abingdon Press [1961 c.1958-1961] 144p. 61-5556 2.00
1. Dedication services. I. Leach, William Herman, 1888- ed. II. Title.

ELY, Virginia, 1899- 265.9
Dedication services for all occasions. Westwood, N.J., Revell [1964] 63 p. 20 cm. [BV199.D4E4] 64-16601
1. Dedication services. I. Title.

ELY, Virginia, 1899- 265.9
Dedication services for all occasions. Westwood, N.J., Revell [c.1964] 63p. 20cm. 64-16601 1.75 bds.,
1. Dedication services. I. Title.

FRANCISCANS. Custody of St. Mary of the Angels. 265.9
Making a monk. [New Cannaan, Conn., Byzantine Franciscans, 1965] 65 p. 18 cm. "Translation from the Postrizenije monachov, published in 1952." [BX2049.F7P73] 65-26169
1. Profession (in religious orders, congregations, etc.) I. Title.

HAYES, Norvel. 265'.9 B
Jesus taught me to cast out devils / Norvel Hayes. Greensburg, Pa. : Manna Christian Outreach, c1975. 93 p. ; 18 cm. [BV873.E8H39] 75-23403 ISBN 0-8007-8226-7 pbk. : 1.25
1. Exorcism. I. Title.

MACHOVEC, Frank J. 265'.9
Exorcism : a manual for casting out evil spirits

/ researched by Frank J. MacHovec. Mount Vernon, N.Y. : Peter Pauper Press, c1973. 60 p. ; 19 cm. [BX2340.M3] 75-305039 1.95
1. Exorcism.

A Manual of exorcism, very 265'.9
useful for priests and ministers of the church / [translation from the Spanish, Eunice Beyersdorf, translation from the Latin, J. D. Brady]. [New York] : Hispanic Society of America : distributed by Interbook Inc., [1975] 141 p. ; 19 cm. Translation of an anonymous manuscript found in the Library of the Hispanic Society of America entitled: Tratado de exorcismos, muy util para los sacerdotes y ministros de la iglesia. Includes original Latin phrases, with English translations. [BF1559.M28] 75-12560 ISBN 0-913456-73-X pbk : 2.95
1. Exorcism. I. Beyersdorf, Eunice. II. Brady, J. D. III. Hispanic Society of America.

MARTIN, Malachi. 265'.9
Hostage to the devil : the possession and exorcism of five living Americans/ Malachi Martin. New York : Reader's Digest Press ; distributed by Crowell, 1976. 477 p. ; 24 cm. Includes index. [BX2340.M35 1976] 75-23276 ISBN 0-88349-078-1 : 9.95
1. Exorcism—Case studies. 2. Demoniac possession—Case studies. I. Title.

MILLER, Paul M. 265'.9
The devil did not make me do it / Paul M. Miller ; introd. by Basil Jackson. Scottdale, Pa. : Herald Press, c1977. 233 p. ; 20 cm. Bibliography: p. [221]-233. [BV873.E8M54] 76-57348 ISBN 0-8361-1814-6 pbk. : 4.95
1. Exorcism. 2. Devil—Biblical teaching. 3. Demonology—Biblical teaching. I. Title.

NAUMAN, St. Elmo. 265'.9
Exorcism through the ages / edited by St. Elmo Nauman, Jr. New York : Philosophical Library, [1974] 311 p. : ill. ; 22 cm. Includes bibliographical references. [BV873.E8N38] 74-80275 ISBN 0-8022-2149-1 : 10.00
1. Exorcism—History. I. Title.

PELTON, Robert W., 1934- 265'.9
In My Name shall they cast out devils / Robert W. Pelton and Karen W. Carden. South Brunswick : A. S. Barnes, c1976. p. cm. Includes index. Bibliography: p. [BV873.E8P44 1976] 75-20602 ISBN 0-498-01731-1 : 7.95
1. Exorcism. 2. Demoniac possession. 3. Demonology. 4. Devil. I. Carden, Karen W., joint author. II. Title.

PETITPIERRE, Robert. 265'.9
Exorcising devils / Dom Robert Petitpierre. London : Hale, 1976. 172 p. ; 23 cm. [BV873.E8P47 1976] 76-383584 ISBN 0-7091-5843-2 : £3.95
1. Exorcism. 2. Occult sciences. I. Title.

RICHARDS, John. 265'.9
But deliver us from evil; an introduction to the demonic dimension in pastoral care. New York, Seabury Press [1974] x, 244 p. 22 cm. "A Crossroads book." Bibliography: p. [226]-240. [BV873.E8R52 1974] 74-10845 ISBN 0-8164-1184-0 8.95
1. Exorcism. 2. Demoniac possession. 3. Occult sciences. I. Title.

RODEWYK, Adolf. 265'.9
Possessed by Satan : the church's teaching on the devil, possession, and exorcism / Adolf Rodewyk ; translated by Martin Ebon. 1st ed. Garden City, N.Y. : Doubleday, 1975. 190, [1] p. ; 22 cm. Translation of Die damonische Besessenheit in der Sicht des Rituale Romanum. Bibliography: p. [191] [BX2340.R613] 75-11072 ISBN 0-385-00953-4 : 6.95
1. Demoniac possession. 2. Exorcism. I. Title.

SPICQ, Ceslaus, 1901- 265'.9
Agape in the New Testament. Translated by Marie Aquinas McNamara and Mary Honoria Ricther. St. Louis, B. Herder Book Co. [1963-66] 3 v. 21 cm. Bibliography: v. 3, p. 247-258. Bibliographical footnotes. [BV823.S713] 63-21562
1. Agape. 2. Love (Theology) — Biblical teaching. 3. Bible. N.T. — Criticism, interpretation, etc. I. Title.

WHITE, Elijah. 265'.9
Exorcism as a Christian ministry / by Elijah White. New York : Morehouse-Barlow Co., 1975. 80 p. ; 21 cm. Bibliography: p. [78]-80. [BV873.E8W47] 74-80387 ISBN 0-8192-1183-4 pbk. : 2.50
1. Exorcism. I. Title.

WORLEY, Win. 265'.9
Battling the hosts of hell : diary of an exorcist / by Win Worley. [Lansing, Ill. : H.B.C. Publications, c1976] 243 p. ; 22 cm. Bibliography: p. 243. [BT975.W67] 77-374015
1. Demonology. 2. Exorcism. I. Title.

SUMPTION, Jonathan. 265.909401
Pilgrimage : an image of mediaeval religion. Totowa, NJ. : Rowman and Littlefield [1976c1975] 391p. ; 22 cm. Includes index. Bibliography: p. 355-378. [BX2323.S9] 75-317652 ISBN 0-87471-677-2 : 15.00
1. Christianity-Middle Ages, 600-1500. 2. Christian pilgrims and pilgrimages. I. Title.

266 Missions

ADENEY, David Howard. 266
The unchanging commission. Chicago, Inter-Varsity Press [1955] 94p. 21cm. [BV2063.A3] 55-6884
1. Missions, Foreign. I. Title.

AFRICA'S Bible; [266]
the power of God unto salvation. Introd. by M. A. Darroch. [1st ed. New York] Sudan Interior Mission [1951] 159 p. illus., ports. 18 cm. [BV3625.S8H38] 276.2 51-20741
1. Missions—Sudan. 2. Bible—Publication and distribution. I. Helser, Albert David, 1897-

ALLEN, Roland, 1869-1947 266
Missionary methods; St. Paul's or ours? Grand Rapids, Eerdmans [c.1962] 179p. 22cm. 62-5028 1.65 pap.,
1. Paul, Saint, apostle. 2. Missions, Foreign. I. Title.

ALLEN, Roland. 1869-1947. 266
Missionary methods; St. Paul's or ours? Grand Rapids, Eerdmans [1962] 179p. 22cm. Companion volume to the author's The spontaneous expansion of the church. [BV2110.A5 1962] 62-5028
1. Paul, Saint, apostle. 2. Missions, Foreign. I. Title.

ARMSTRONG, Roger D. 266
Peace Corps and Christian mission, by Roger D. Armstrong. With a foreword by Samuel D. Proctor and a pref. by Charles W. Forman. New York, Friendship Press [1965] 126 p. 19 cm. [HC60.5.A8] 65-11435
1. U.S. Peace Corps. 2. Missions — Theory. I. Title.

ARMSTRONG, Roger D. 266
Peace Corps and Christian mission. Foreword by Samuel D. Proctor. Pref. by Charles W. Forman. New York, Friendship [c.1965] 126p. 19cm. [HC60.5.A8] 65-11435 1.75 pap.,
1. U.S. Peace Corps. 2. Missions—Theory. I. Title.

ASSIGNMENT: 266
Near East. New York, Friendship Press [1950] 119 p. illus., ports., fold. col. map (mounted on p. [3] of cover) 23 cm. Bibliography: p. 119. [BR1070.B3] 275.6 50-3929
1. Christians in the Levant. 2. Missions—Levant. I. Batal, James, 1901-

BALPH, Florence. 266
Beyond romance, a true story from the heart of India Rev. ed. Boston, Christopher Pub. House [1954] 134 p. 21 cm. [BV3269.B35A35 1954] [BV3269.B35A35 1954] 275.4 54-9576 54-9576
1. Missions—India. I. Title.

BARHAM, Marie. 266
Onak and the talkingbox. Chicago Moody Press [1957] 189p. illus. 22cm. [BV3380.B28] [BV3380.B28] 279.14 57-31075 57-31075
1. Missions—Philippine Islands. I. Title.

BARLOW, Sanna Morrison. 266
Light is sown. Chicago, Moody Press [1956] 188p. 22cm. [BV3500.B28] [BV3500.B28] 276 56-14225 56-14225
1. Missions—Africa. 2. Phonorecords in missionary work. 3. Gospel Recordings, inc. I. Title.

BARLOW, Sanna Morrison. 266
Mountains singing; the story of Gospel Recordings in the Philippines. Chicago, Moody Press, 1952. 352p. illus. 22cm. [BV3380.B3] [BV3380.B3] 279.14 53-2338 53-2338
1. Ridderhof, Joy. a Missions—Philippine Islands. 2. Gospel Recordings. inc., Los Angeles. I. Title.

BATCHELOR, Peter G. 266
Theology and rural development in Africa, by Peter G. Batchelor [and] Harry R. Boer. Grand Rapids, W. B. Eerdmans Pub. Co. [1967] 24 p. 21 cm. (A Reformed journal monograph) [S532.B3] 67-19309
1. Agriculture—Moral and religious aspects. 2. Missions—Agricultural work. I. Boer, Harry R., joint author. II. Title.

BAVINCK, Johan Herman, 1895- 266
An introduction to the science of missions. Translated by David Hugh Freeman. Philadelphia, Presbyterian and Reformed Pub. Co., 1960. xxi, 323p. 22cm. Bibliographical references included in 'Notes' (p. 311-323) [BV2060.B383] 60-13465
1. Missions. I. Title. II. Title: The science of missions.

BEARD, Augustus Field, 1833- 266
1934.
A crusade of brotherhood; a history of the American Missionary Association. Boston, Pilgrim Press. [New York, AMS Press, 1972] xii, 334 p. illus. 23 cm. Reprint of the 1909 ed. [BV2360.A8B4 1972] 76-161728 ISBN 0-404-00004-5 12.50
1. American Missionary Association. I. Title.

BEAVER, Robert Pierce, 1906- 266
All loves excelling; American Protestant women in world mission, by R. Pierce Beaver. Grand Rapids, Mich., Eerdmans [1968] 227 p. 20 cm. Includes bibliographical references. [BV2610.B4] 68-18839
1. Women in missionary work. 2. Women as missionaries. 3. Missions, American. 4. Protestant churches—Missions. I. Title.

BEAVER, Robert Pierce, 1906- 266
Envoys of peace; the peace witness in the Christian world mission. Grand Rapids [1964] 133 p. 22 cm. Bibliography: p. 129-130. [BV2080.B4] 64-16582
1. Missions. 2. Christianity and politics. I. Title.

BEAVER, Robert Pierce, 1906- 266
Envoys of peace; the peace witness in the Christian world mission. Grand Rapids, Mich., Eerdmans [c.1964] 133p. 22cm. Bibl. 64-16582 3.00
1. Missions. 2. Christianity and politics. I. Title.

BEYOND the Kikuyu Curtain. 266
Chicago, Moody Press [1956] 267p. illus. 22cm. [BV3625.K4B35] [BV3625.K4B55] 276.76 56-14397 56-14397
1. Missions—Kenya Colony and Protectorate. 2. Kikuyu tribe. I. Blakeslee, Helen Virginia.

BISHOP, Ivyloy. 266
Missions and me [by] Ivyloy and Amelia Bishop. [Teacher's ed.] Nashville, Convention Press [1963] 89 p. 19 cm. [BV2090.B5] 63-8376
1. Missions—Study and teaching. 2. Missions-Theory. I. Bishop, Amelia, joint author. II. Title.

BLAUW, Johannes. 266
The missionary nature of the church; a survey of the Biblical theology of mission. [1st ed.] New York, McGraw-Hill [1962] 182p. 21cm. (Foundations of the Christian mission) [BV2063.B57 1962] 62-8829
1. Missions—Theory. I. Title.

BLAUW, Johannes. 266
The missionary nature of the church; a survey of the Biblical theology of mission. Grand Rapids, Mich., Eerdmans [1974, i.e.1975 c1962] 182 p. 19 cm. Reprint of the ed. published by Lutterworth Press, London, in series: Foundations of the Christian mission. Translation of Gottes Werk in dieser Welt. Bibliography: p. 174. [BV2063.B573 1974] 73-22478 ISBN 0-8028-1577-4 10.95
1. Missions—Theory. I. Title.

BOER, Harry R 266
Pentecost and missions. Grand Rapids, Eerdmans [c1961] 270p. 23cm. Revision of the author's thesis, Free University, Amsterdam, entitled: Pentecost and the missionary witness of the church. Includes bibliography. [BV2063.B6 1961] 61-13664
1. Missions—Theory. 2. Holy Spirit. I. Title.

BOOTH, Esma (Rideout) 266
Bright pathways. Illustrated by Kurt Wiese. New York, Friendship Press [1955] 125p. illus. 20cm. [BV2087.B63] 55-6833
1. Missionary stories. I. Title.

BRACE, Mary Margaret, ed. 266
Now! Everybody needs a church. Editors: Mary Margaret Brace and Lucy M. Eldredge. [New York] Friendship Press, c1951. 128 p. illus. 20 cm. Title from p. [2] of cover. [BV2775.N6] 51-3604
1. Missions—U.S. 2. Missions, Home. 3. U.S.—Religion. I. Eldredge, Lucy M., ed. II. Title.

BRIDSTON, Keith R. 266
Mission, myth and reality [by] Keith Bridston. New York, Friendship Press [1965] 127 p. 19 cm. Bibliographical references included in "Footnotes" (p. 125-127) [BV2063.B73] 65-11426
1. Missions — Theory. I. Title.

BRIDSTON, Keith R. 266
Mission, myth and reality. New York, Friendship [c.1965] 127p. 19cm. Bibl. [BV2063.B73] 65-11426 1.75 pap.,
1. Missions—Theory. I. Title.

BRIDSTON, Keith R comp. 266
Shock and renewal: the Christian mission enters a new era. New York, Published for the Student Volunteer Movement for Christian Missions by Friendship Press [1955] 64p. 19cm. [BV2090] 55-2304
1. Missions—Study and teaching. I. Title.

BROWN, Arthur Judson, 1856- 266
The foreign missionary, today and yesterday; with introd. by Samuel Marinus Zwemer. 20th print. rev. New York, Revell [1950] xxi, 412 p. 20 cm. Bibliography: p. 402A-402C. [BV2060.B8 1950] 51-2737
1. Missions. Foreign. 2. Missionaries. I. Title.

BUCKNER, Jack H, 1891- 266
Jewish evangelism, a study; how to win a son of Abraham to the Son of God. Berne, Ind., Light and Hope Publications, 1950 [i. e. 1951] 111 p. 21 cm. [BV2620.B8] 51-3167
1. Missions—Jews. I. Title.

CAMPBELL, Arch, 1894- 266
The Christ of the Koean heart. Columbus, Ohio, Falco Publishers [1955, c1954] 144p. illus. 20cm. [BV3460.C3] 275.19 55-32268
1. Misssons—Korea. I. Title.

CANNON, Joseph L. 1927- 266
For missionaries only, [by] Joseph L. Cannon. Grand Rapids, Baker Book House, [1975 c1969] 96 p. 21 cm. [BV2061.C3] ISBN 0-8010-2347-5 1.50 (pbk.)
1. Missions. I. Title.
L.C. card no. for original ed.: 70-89619.

CARVER, William Owen, 1868- 266
Missions in the plan of the ages; Bible studies in missions. [4th ed.] Nashville, Broadman Press ['1951] 289 p. 20 cm. [BV2073.C32 1951] 52-7965
1. Missions—Biblical teaching. I. Title.

CATHOLIC Foreign Mission 266
Society of America.
Christianity, a personal mission; a symposium of contemporary Christian thought, edited by Maryknoll Fathers. Maryknoll, N.Y. [Maryknoll Publications] 1964. 60 p. 25 cm. (World horizon reports, report no. 30) Bibliographical references included in "Footnotes" (p. 60) [BV2183.C3] 64-13986
1. Missions — Theory. 2. Catholic action. I. Title. II. Series.

CATHOLIC Foreign Mission 266
Society of America
Christianity, a personal mission; a symposium of contemporary Christian thought, ed. by the Maryknoll Fathers. Maryknoll, N.Y. [Maryknoll Pubns.] 1964. 60 p. 25 cm. (World horizon reports, report no. 30) 64-13986 1.50
1. Missions—Theory. 2. Catholic action. I. Title. II. Series.

CAUTHEN, Baker James. 266
Beyond call. Compiled by Genevieve Greer. Nashville, Broadman Press [1973] 122 p. 21 cm. [BV4501.2.C37] 73-78409 ISBN 0-8054-3613-8 3.95
1. Christian life—Baptist authors. I. Title.

CENTRE national des 266
vocations.
Tomorrow's priest. Raymond Izard, general editor. Translated by Albert J. Lamothe, Jr. Maryknoll, N.Y., Maryknoll Publications, 1968. ix, 140 p. 22 cm. "Reports of the eighteenth session [Lyons, 1965] organized by the National Vocation Center." Translation of Missionaires pour demain. Includes bibliographical references. [BV2180.C413] 68-54386 5.50
1. Catholic Church—Missions. 2. Missionaries—Appointment, call, and election. I. Izard, Raymond, ed. II. Title.

CHRIST the liberator 266
[by] John R. W. Stott and others, Urbana 70. Downers Grove, Ill., Inter Varsity Press [1971] 288 p. 21 cm. Papers addressed to "Urbana 70 conventioneers" attending a four-day conference that ended the year of 1970 for students from 48 states and 72 countries. Includes bibliographical references. [BV970.I6C47] 70-157168 ISBN 0-87784-757-6
1. Inter-Varsity Christian Fellowship of the United States of America. 2. Missions—Congresses. I. Stott, John R. W.

CHURCH growth and group 266
conversion, by J. W. Pickett [and others] Foreword by John R. Mott. [5th ed. South Pasadena, Calif.] William Carey Library [1973] x, 116 p. 22 cm. [BV652.25.C48 1973] 73-80163 ISBN 0-87808-712-5 1.95 (pbk.)
1. Church growth. 2. Missions. I. Pickett, Jarrell Waskom.

COGGINS, Wade T. 266
So that's what missions is all about / Wade T. Coggins. Chicago : Moody Press, [1975] 127 p. 22 cm. Bibliography: p. 125-127.

[BV2061.C63] 74-15357 ISBN 0-8024-8107-8 pbk. : 1.95
1. Missions. I. Title.

COHN, Joseph Hoffman, 1886- 266
1953.
I have fought a good fight; the story of Jewish Mission pioneering in America. New York, American Board of Missions to the Jews [1953] 316p. 21cm. [BV2619.A58C6] 54-780
1. American Board of Missions to the Jews, inc. 2. Missions—Jews. I. Title.

COLINA, Tessa 266
Missionary programs for the church. Cincinnati, Standard Pub. [c.1963] 64p. 22cm. 1.00 pap.,
I. Title.

COLLINS, Marjorie A. 266
Manual for accepted missionary candidates [by] Marjorie A. Collins. South Pasadena, Calif., William Carey Library [1972] xvi, 109 p. 22 cm. Bibliography: p. 97-109. [BV2063.C58] 72-92749 ISBN 0-87808-118-6 2.45
1. Missionaries—Appointment, call, and election. I. Title.

COLLINS, Marjorie A. 266
Manual for missionaries on furlough [by] Marjorie A. Collins. South Pasadena, Calif., William Carey Library [1972] viii, 151 p. 22 cm. [BV2094.C64] 72-92747 ISBN 0-87808-119-4 2.95
1. Missionaries—Leaves and furloughs. I. Title.

COMBLIN, Joseph, 1923- 266
The meaning of mission : Jesus, Christians, and the wayfaring church / Joseph Comblin ; translated by John Drury. Maryknoll, N.Y. : Orbis Books, c1977. vi, 142 p. ; 22 cm. Translation of Teologia de la mision. [BV601.8.C6513] 76-41723 ISBN 0-88344-304-X : 6.95
1. Mission of the church. 2. Missions—Theory. I. Title.

COME wind, come weather; [266]
the story of the year 1950. London, Philadelphia, China Inland Mission, 1951. 77 p. 22 cm. [BV3410.C56H3] 275.1 52-44045
1. China Inland Mission. 2. Missions—China. I. Hazelton, Anne. ed.

THE Conciliar-evangelical 266
debate : the crucial documents, 1964-1976 / edited by Donald McGavran. South Pasadena, Calif. : William Carey Library, [1977] Published in 1972 under title: Eye of the storm, and entered under McGavran. [BV2070.M28 1977] 77-1705 ISBN 0-87808-733-8 pbk. : 7.95
1. Missions—Addresses, essays, lectures. 2. Salvation—Addresses, essays, lectures. 3. Evangelicalism—Addresses, essays, lectures. I. MaGavran, Donald Anderson, 1897- II. McGavran, Donald Anderson, 1897- Eye of the storm.

THE Conciliar-evangelical 266
debate : the crucial documents, 1964-1976 / edited by Donald McGavran. South Pasadena, Calif. : William Carey Library, [1977] p. cm. Published in 1972 under title: Eye of the storm, and entered under McGavran. [BV2070.M28 1977] 77-1196 ISBN 0-87808-733-8 : 7.95
1. Missions—Addresses, essays, lectures. 2. Salvation—Addresses, essays, lectures. 3. Evangelicalism—Addresses, essays, lectures. I. McGavran, Donald Anderson, 1897- II. McGavran, Donald Anderson, 1897- Eye of the storm.

COOK, Harold R 266
An introduction to the study of Christian missions. Chicago, Moody Press [1954] 256p. 22cm. [BV2060.C72] 54-4915
1. Missions. I. Title.

COOK, Harold R. 266
Strategy of missions; an evangelical view. Chicago, Moody [c.1963] 123p. 22cm. 64-555 1.50 pap.,
1. Missions—Theory I. Title.

COOPER, Clay 266
Nothing to win but the world; missions at the crossroad. Foreword by Mark O. Hatfield. Grand Rapids, Mich., Zondervan [c.1965] 152p. 21cm. [BV2063.C645] 64-8848 2.95
1. Missions—Theory. I. Title.

COSBY, Gordon. 266
Handbook for mission groups / Gordon Cosby. Waco, Tex. : Word Books, c1975. 179 p. ; 23 cm. Includes bibliographical references. [BX9999.W383C67] 73-91551 ISBN 0-87680-346-X : 5.95
1. Washington, D.C. Church of the Saviour. 2. Church group work. I. Title.

CRAWLEY, James Winston. 266
New frontiers in an old world. Nashville, Convention Press [1962] 130 p. illus. 19 cm. [BV3400.C7] 62-11538
1. Missions—East (Far East) 2. Southern Baptist Convention—Missions. I. Title.

CROSSROADS in missions. 266
South Pasadena, Calif., William Carey Library [1971?] xxi, 182, 192, 199, 128, xiii, 196 p. 23 cm. (A William Carey multibook) Contents.Contents.—The missionary nature of the church, by J. Blauw.—Missionary, go home! By J. A. Scherer.—The responsible church and the foreign mission, by P. Beyerhaus and H. Lefever.—On the growing edge of the church, by T. W. Street.—The missionary between the times, by R. P. Beaver. Includes bibliographies. [BV2061.C76] 77-171019 ISBN 0-87808-704-4
1. Missions.

CRUCIAL dimensions in world 266
evangelization / [edited by] Arthur F. Glasser ... [et al.]. South Pasadena, Calif. : William Carey Library, c1976. x, 466 p. : ill. ; 22 cm. Includes index. [BV2070.C78] 76-42165 ISBN 0-87808-732-X : 6.95
1. Missions—Addresses, essays, lectures. I. Glasser, Arthur Frederick, 1914-

DANIELOU, Jean. 266
The salvation of the nations; translated by Angeline Bouchard. New York, Sheed & Ward, 1950 ['1949] 1x, 118 p. 20 cm. Translation of Le mystere du salut des nations. Bibliographical footnotes. [BV2180.D32 1950] 50-11978
1. Missions—Theory. 2. Catholic Church—Missions. I. Title.

DANIELOU, Jean 266
The salvation of the nations. Tr. by Angeline Bouchard. Notre Dame, Ind., Univ. of Notre Dame Pr. [c.]1962 118p. (NDP12) Bibl. 1.75 pap.,
1. Missions—Theory. 2. Catholic Church—Missions. I. Title.

DAVIS, Lew A 266
The layman views world missions. St. Louis, Bethany Press [1964] 102 p. 21 cm. [BV2061.D3] 64-13408
1. Missions. I. Title.

DAVIS, Lew A. 266
The layman views world missions. St. Louis, Bethany [c.1964] 102p. 21cm. 64-13408 1.95 bds.,
1. Missions. I. Title.

DAVY, Yvonne. 266
Campfire tales from Africa. Illus. by Homer Norris. Takoma Park, Washington, Review and Herald Pub. Association [1956] 156p. illus. 23cm. [BV2087.D35] 56-14561
1. Missionary stories. I. Title.

DAY after tomorrow. 266
With drawings by Kurt Wiese. New York, Frendship Press [1956] 117p. illus. 21cm. [BV2087.L39] 275.9 56-6579
1. Missionary stories. 2. Missions—Study and teaching (Secondary) I. Lewis, Alice Hudson.

*DEAN, Elizabeth Rice 266
Grandma goes gadding; missionary evangelism with Carrie Reiter Hunsberger in Spain, Ghana and Kenya. New York, Carlton [c.1964] 224p. 21cm. (Reflection bk.) 3.50
I. Title.

DE GROOT, Alfred Thomas, 266
1903-
The Bible on the salvation of nations, by A. De Groot. Translated by F. Vander Heijden. De Pere, Wis., St. Norbert Abbey Press, 1966. 149 p. 17 cm. Translation of De Bijbel over het hell der volken. Bibliography: p. [147]-149. [BV2073.D413] 66-16987
1. Missions — Biblical teaching. I. Title.

DE REEPER, J 266
A missionary companion; a commentary on the apostolic faculties. Dublin, Browne and Nolan [1952] 245p. 19cm. 56-23998
1. Missions (Canon law) I. Title.

DE REEPER, J 266
A missionary companion; a commentary on the apostolic faculties. Westminster, Md., Newman Press, 1952. 245p. 19cm. 53-9202
1. Missions (Canon law) I. Title.

DEWICK, Edward Chisholm, 266
1884-
The Christian attitude to other religions. Cambridge [Eng.] University Press, 1953. 220p. 22cm. (Hulsean lectures, 1949) Includes bibliography. [BR127.D48] 53-10425
1. Christianity and other religions. 2. Apologetics—20th cent. I. Title.

DILLON, William Simon, 1907- 266
God's work in God's way, by William S. Dillon. [Revision] Woodworth, Wis., Brown Gold Publications [1972] x, 296 p. 22 cm. Includes bibliographical references. [BV2082.I5D5 1972] 72-188696
1. Indigenous church administration. I. Title.

DOOLEY, Thomas Anthony, 1927- 266
1961.
The edge of tomorrow. New York, Farrar, Straus and Cudahy [1958] 208 p. illus. 22 cm. [RA390.U5D6 1958] 58-7438
1. Missions, Medical—Laos. 2. Laos—Description and travel. I. Title.

DOUGLASS, Truman B. 266
Mission to America. New York, Friendship Press [1951] 151 p. 19 cm. Bibliography: p. 149-151. [BV2775.D6] 51-4498
1. Missions—U. S. 2. Protestant churches—U. S. 3. U. S.—Religion. I. Title.

DOVEY, J Whitsed. [266]
The gospel in the South Pacific. London, New York, World Dominion Press [1950] 56 p. map. 22 cm. (Post-war survey series, no. 5) [BV3670.D6] 279.9 51-1340
1. Missions—Islands of the Pacific. I. Title. II. Series.

ELLIOT, Elisabeth. 266
Through gates of splendor. Foreword by Abe C. Van Der Puy. Picture editor, Cornell Capa. [1st ed.] New York, Harper [1957] 256 p. illus. 22 cm. [BV2853.E3E5] 278.66* 57-7341
1. Missions—Ecuador. 2. Christian martyrs—Ecuador. I. Title.

EVANGELICAL missions tomorrow 266
/ edited by Wade T. Coggins, E. L. Frizen, Jr. South Pasadena, Calif. : William Carey Library, c1977. vii, 194 p. : ill. ; 22 cm. Papers presented to a joint conference of the Interdenominational Foreign Mission Association of North America, the Evangelical Foreign Missions Association, and the Association of Evangelical Professors of Missions held Sept. 27 to Oct. 1, 1976 at Breech Training Academy, Overland Park, Kansas. Includes bibliographical references. [BV2390.E94] 77-76525 ISBN 0-87808-156-9 : 5.95
1. Missions—Congresses. I. Coggins, Wade T. II. Frizen, E. L. III. Interdenominational Foreign Mission Association of North America. IV. Evangelical Foreign Missions Association. V. Association of Evangelical Professors of Missions.

EVANGELICAL missions tomorrow 266
/ edited by Wade T. Coggins, E. L. Frizen, Jr. South Pasadena, Calif. : William Carey Library, c1977. vii, 194 p. : ill. ; 22 cm. Papers presented to a joint conference of the Interdenominational Foreign Mission Association of North America, the Evangelical Foreign Missions Association, and the Association of Evangelical Professors of Missions held Sept. 27 to Oct. 1, 1976 at Breech Training Academy, Overland Park, Kansas. Includes bibliographical references. [BV2390.E94] 77-76525 ISBN 0-87808-156-9 : 5.95
1. Missions—Congresses. I. Coggins, Wade T. II. Frizen, E. L. III. Interdenominational Foreign Mission Association of North America. IV. Evangelical Foreign Missions Association. V. Association of Evangelical Professors of Missions.

EXPLORING Africa. [266]
Nashville, Broadman Press [1950] xii, 132 p. maps. 19 cm. Includes bibliographies. [BV3500.G6] 276 50-12330
1. Missions—Africa. 2. Missions—Nigeria. I. Goerner, Henry Cornell, 1908-

FACING facts in modern 266
missions; a symposium. Contributors: Milton Baker and others. Chicago, Moody Press [1963] 141 p. 22 cm. "Recommended reading": p. 11. Bibliographical references included in footnotes. [BV2063.F27] 64-313
1. Missions — Theory.

FACING facts in modern 266
missions; a symposium 53Contribs.: Milton Baker, others. Chicago, Moody [c.1963] 141p. 22cm. Bibl. 64-313 1.50 pap.,
1. Missions—Theory.

FERGUSON, Rowena. 266
Hunger and hope. New York, Friendship Press [1955] 64p. 19cm. [BV2064.F4] 55-5765
1. Missions. I. Title.

FIDLER, Marguerite. 266
Can't help wondering. Marguerite and Frank Fidler write about the family in mission. New York, Friendship Press [1967] 96 p. 19 cm. Bibliography: p. 95-96. [BV2063.F44] 67-14317
1. Missions. I. Fidler, Frank P., joint author. II. Title.

FIERS, Alan Dale. 266
The Christian world mission. St. Louis, Pub. for the Co-operative Pubn. Assn. by Bethany Pr. [c.1966] 96p. 19cm. (Faith for life ser.) Bibl. [BV2063.F46] 66-14597 1.25 pap.,
1. Missions—Theory. I. Cooperative Publication Association. II. Title.

FLEMING, Daniel Johnson, 266
1877-
Living as comrades; a study of factors making for "community." New York, Published for the Foreign Missions Conference of North America by Agricultural Missions, 1950. xii, 180 p. 21 cm. (Studies in principles and methods of world missions, no. 13) Bibliographical references included in "Notes" (p. 169-174) [BV625.F6] 50-12075
1. Community life. 2. Christian life. I. Title. II. Series.

FLETCHER, Grace (Nies) 266
The fabulous Flemings of Kathmandu; the story of two doctors in Nepal. [1st ed.] New York, Dutton, 1964. 219 p. illus., map, ports. 21 cm. [R644.N45F56] 64-11095
1. Fleming, Robert Leland, 1905- 2. Fleming, Bethel. 3. Nepal — Descr. & trav. I. Title.

FLETCHER, Grace (Nies) 266
The fabulous Flemings of Kathmandu; the story of two doctors in Nepal. New York, Dutton [c.]1964. 219p. illus., map, ports. 21cm. 64-11095 4.95
1. Fleming, Robert Leland, 1905- 2. Fleming, Bethel. 3. Nepal—Descr. & trav. I. Title.

FOUNDATIONS of mission 266
theology. Edited by SEDOS. Translated by John Drury. Maryknoll, N.Y., Orbis Books [1972] xii, 168 p. 24 cm. (Maryknoll documentation series) Translation of the official French version of a symposium of theologians to study mission questions, held in Rome, Mar. 27-31, 1969. Includes bibliographical references. [BV2020.F68] 70-190168 3.95
1. Missions—Congresses. I. Sedos.

THE Future of the Christian 266
world mission; studies in honor of R. Pierce Beaver. Edited by William J. Danker [and] Wi Jo Kang. Grand Rapids, Eerdmans [1971] 181 p. 23 cm. Contents.Contents.—The oikoumene, by W. R. Hogg.—Dialogue with non-Christian religions, by H.-W. Gensichen.—"Gun" and "ointment" in Asia, by K. Koyama.—The church in northern Sumatra: a look at its past and future, by L. Schreiner.—Aspects of the missionary crisis in Roman Catholicism, by P. Damboriena.—The evangelical missions: the home base, by H. Lindsell.—The evangelicals: world outreach, by A. F. Glasser.—The local church, by F. D. Lueking.—Mission research, writing, and publishing, by G. H. Anderson.—Missions in theological education, by J. A. Scherer.—A piece of the action: a new economic basis for the church, by W. J. Danker.—A tribute to a teacher, by W. J. Kang.—The published work of R. Pierce Beaver: bibliography (p. 171-175)—Messages of appreciation. [BV2070.F88] 76-142900 5.95
1. Missions—Addresses, essays, lectures. I. Beaver, Robert Pierce, 1906- II. Danker, William J., ed. III. Kang, Wi Jo, 1930- ed.

FUTURE of the Missionary 266
Enterprise Seminar/Workshop, Ventnor, N.J., 1974.
In search of mission : an interconfessional and intercultural quest : [proceedings and background readings] : a special issue / prepared by the IDOC Future of the Missionary Enterprise Project. New York : IDOC/North America, 1974. 143 p. ; 28 cm. (The Future of the Missionary Enterprise dossiers ; no. 9) (IDOC/international documentation ; no. 63) Seminar/workshop held jointly by IDOC and the Overseas Ministries Study Center. Includes bibliographical references. [BV2020.F87 1974] 74-12989
1. Missions—Congresses. I. IDOC Future of the Missionary Enterprise Project. II. Idoc. III. Overseas Ministries Study Center. IV. Title. V. Series. VI. Series: IDOC Future of the Missionary Enterprise Project. The Future of the Missionary Enterprise dossiers ; no. 9.

GALLAGHER, Neil, 1941- 266
Don't go overseas until you've read this book / Neil Gallagher. Minneapolis : Bethany Fellowship, c1977. 123 p. ; 21 cm. Includes bibliographical references. [BV2410.G34] 77-2643 ISBN 0-87123-105-0 pbk. : 2.95
1. Missions, American. 2. Americans in foreign countries. I. Title.

GALLAGHER, Neil, 1941- 266
Don't go overseas until you've read this book / Neil Gallagher. Minneapolis : Bethany Fellowship, c1977. 123 p. ; 21 cm. Includes bibliographical references. [BV2410.G34] 77-2643 ISBN 0-87123-105-0 pbk. : 2.95
1. Missions, American. 2. Americans in foreign countries. I. Title.

GARDNER, Elva Babcock. [266]
Sundra Bi, a child bride of India. Washington, Review and Herald Pub. Association [1951] 125 p. illus. 21 cm. [BV2087.G3] 275.4 52-200
1. Missionary stories. I. Title.

GASBARRI, Carlo. 266
A saint for the new India; Father Joseph Vaz, apostle of Kanara and Ceylon, by Charles Gasbarri. With a foreword by L. Raymond. Allahabad, St. Paul Publications [1961] 211 p. illus., facsim., map, port. 18 cm. [BV3277.V3G3] 65-3551
1. Vaz, Jose, 1651-1711. I. Title.

GOLDSMITH, Martin. 266
Don't just stand there! : A first book on Christian mission / Martin Goldsmith. Downers Grove, Ill. : Inter Varsity Press, c1976. 128 p. ; 18 cm. [BV2061.G64 1976] 76-151243 ISBN 0-87784-649-9 : 2.25
1. Missions. 2. Evangelistic work. I. Title.

GOODWIN, R Dean, 1909- 266
There is no end. New York, Friendship Press, 1956. 126p. illus. 23cm. [BR525.G6] 275.3 56-6582
1. U. S.—Soc. condit. 2. U. S.—Religion. 3. Missions, Home. I. Title.

GRASSI, Joseph A 266
A world to win; the missionary methods of Paul the Apostle, by Joseph A. Grassi. Maryknoll, N.Y., Maryknoll Publications, 1965. viii, 184 p. 21 cm. [BS2506.G7] 65-18543
1. Paul, Saint, apostle. 2. Missions—Hist.—Early church. I. Title.

GRASSI, Joseph A. 266
A world to win; the missionary methods of Paul the Apostle. Mary knoll, N. Y., Maryknoll Pubns. [c.]1965. viii, 184p. 21cm. [BS2506.G7] 65-18543 3.95
1. Paul, Saint, apostle. 2. Missions—Hist.—Early church. I. Title.

*GREENWAY, Roger S. ed. 266
A world to win; preaching world missions today, [edited by] Roger S. Greenway Grand Rapids, Baker Book House, [1975] 135 p. 22 cm. [BV2073] ISBN 0-8010-3685-2 3.95 (pbk.)
1. Missions. 2. Evangelistic work. I. Title.

GUY, Harold A 266
A critical introduction to the Gospels. London, Macmillan; New York, St. Martin's Press, 1955. 152p. 19cm. [BS2555.G89 1955] 55-1652
1. Bible. N. T. Gospels—Introductions. I. Title.

HALL, Clarence Wilbur, 1902- 266
Adventurers for God. New York, Harper [1959] 265 p. illus. 22 cm. "Articles which originally appeared in somewhat different form in the Reader's digest." [BV2035.H2] 59-5219
1. Missions—Addresses, essays, lectures. I. Title.

HALL-LINDQUIST, Arthur. 266
The tale of two steamer rugs. Moline, Ill., Christian Service Foundation [c1956] 202p. illus. 23cm. The life and work of the author and his family as missionaries in China. [BV3427.H22A3] 275.1 57-20741
1. Missions—China. I. Title.

HALLOCK, Constance Magee, 1889- 266
East from Burma. New York, Friendship Press [1956] 120p. illus. 21cm. [BV3298.H3] 275.9 56-7953
1. Missions—Asia, Southeastern. I. Title.

HANDY, Robert T 266
We witness together, a history of cooperative home missions. New York, Friendship Press, 1956 [c1957] 273p. 20cm. Includes bibliography. [BV2763.H634] 57-6252
1. Home Missions Council of North America. I. Title.

HARLOW, Robert Edward, 1908- 266
Who is my neighbor? Assembly Missionaries in Africa [by] R. E. Harlow [and] John Smart. New York, The Fields, inc. [c1962] 94 p. illus. 19 cm. [BV3500.H28] 63-32429
1. Missions — Africa. 2. Assemblies of God. General Council — Missions. I. Smart, John, 1906- joint author. II. Title.

HARPER, Irene (Mason) 266
Chand of India; illustrated by Jeanyee Wong. New York, Friendship Press [1954] 117p. illus. 20cm. [BV2087.H32] 275.4 54-6952
1. Missionary stories. I. Title.

HARR, Wilber Christian, 1908- ed. 266
Frontiers of the Christian world mission since 1938; essays in honor of Kenneth Scott Latourette. [1st ed.] New York, Harper [1962] viii, 310p. 22cm. Bibliographical footnotes. [BV2120.H3] 62-7288
1. Latourette, Kenneth Scott, 1884- 2. Missions—Hist. I. Title.
Contents omitted.

HARRINGTON, Fern. 266
Carlos and the green car. Nashville, Convention Press [1958] 102p. illus. 20cm. (Foreign mission series) [BV3380.H36] 279.14 58-8928
1. Missions—Philippine Islands. 2. Missionary stories. I. Title.

HARRINGTON, Janette 266
The shadows they cast. New York, Friendship Press [1958] 161p. 21cm. [BV2087.H36] 58-7036
1. Missionary stories. I. Title.

HASKIN, Dorothy (Clark) 1905- 266
Little hunchback girl of Korea, and other missionary stories. by Dorothy C. Haskin. Grand Rapids. Baker Bk. [1966] 88p. 20cm. (Valor ser., 15) [BV2087.H37] 66-18311 1.95 bds.,
1. Missionary stories. I. Title.

HASKIN, Dorothy (Clark) 1905- 266
Medical missionaries you would like to know. Grand Rapids, Zondervan Pub. House [1957] 89p. illus. 20cm. [R722.H34] 57-38995
1. Missions, Medical. I. Title.

HAZELTON, Anne, ed. [266]
Swords drawn; the story of the year 1955. London, Philadelphia, China Inland Mission, 1956. 79p. 22cm. [BV3410.C56H33] 57-18416
1. China Inland Mission. 2. Missions—China. I. Title.

HAZELTON, Anne, ed. [266]
Swords drawn; the story of the year i955. London, Philadelphia, China Inland Mission, 1956. 79p. 22cm. [BV3410.C56H33] 57-18416
1. China Inland Mission. 2. Missions —China. I. Title.

HENRY, Helga Bender. 266
Mission on Main Street. Boston, W. A. Wilde Co. [1955] 200p. illus. 21cm. [BV2656.L6H4] 55-6704
1. Los Angeles, Union Rescue Mission. I. Title.

*HILLIS, Don W. 266
The Scriptural basis of world evangelization. Edit. assistance from Esther L. Sorensen. Grand Rapids, Mich., Baker Bk. [c.]1965. 59p. 22cm. 1.00 pap.,
I. Title.

HILLMAN, Eugene. 266
The Church as mission. [New York] Herder and Herder [1965] 144 p. 21 cm. Bibliographical footnotes. [BV2063.H48] 65-21946
1. Missions — Theory. I. Title.

HILLMAN, Eugene 266
The Church as mission. [New York] Herder & Herder [c.1965] 144p. 21cm. Bibl. 3.75
1. Missions—Theory. I. Title.

HODGES, Melvin L. 266
The indigenous church and the missionary : a sequel to The indigenous church / Melvin L. Hodges. South Pasadena, Calif. : W. Carey Library, [1977] p. cm. Bibliography: p. [BV2082.I5H6] 77-14519 ISBN 0-87808-151-8 pbk. : 2.95
1. Missions. 2. Indigenous church administration. I. Title.

HODGES, Melvin L. 266
A theology of the church and its mission : a Pentecostal perspective / Melvin L. Hodges. Springfield, Mo. : Gospel Pub. House, c1977. 185 p. ; 21 cm. Includes index. Bibliography: p. 181-182. [BV600.2.H566] 76-20892 ISBN 0-88243-605-8 : 6.95. ISBN 0-88243-607-4 pbk. : 3.95
1. Church. 2. Mission of the church. 3. Missions. I. Title.

HOFFMAN, James W 266
Mission.U. S. A. New York, Friendship Press [1956] 181p. illus. 20cm. [BV2765.H57] 277.3 56-6581
1. Missions—U. S. 2. Missions, Home. I. Title.

HOGG, William Richey 266
One world, one mission. New York, Friendship Press [c.1960] 164p. 20cm. 60-7441 2.95; 1.50 pap.,
1. Missions. 2. Ecumenical movement. I. Title.

HOGG, William Richey, 1921- 266
One world, one mission. New York, Friendship Press [1960] 164p. 20cm. Includes bibliography. [BV2061.H6] 60-7441
1. Missions. 2. Ecumenical movement. I. Title.

HOPKINS, Paul A., 1916- 266
What next in mission? / By Paul A. Hopkins. 1st ed. Philadelphia : Westminster Press, c1977. p. cm. Includes bibliographical references. [BV601.8.H66] 77-21776 ISBN 0-664-24143-3 pbk. : 3.95
1. Mission of the church. I. Title.

HORNER, Norman A 266
Cross and crucifix in mission; a compariston of Protestant-Roman Catholic missionary strategy [by] Norman A. Horner. New York, Abingdon Press [1965] 223 p. 21 cm. Bibliographical footnotes. [BV2184.H6] 65-21974
1. Missions — Comparative studies. 2. Catholic Church — Missions. 3. Protestant churches — Missions. I. Title.

HORNER, Norman A. 266
Cross and crucifix in mission; a comparison of Protestant-Roman Catholic missionary strategy. Nashville, Abingdon [c.1965] 223p. 21cm. Bibl. [BV2184.H6] 65-21974 3.50 bds.,
1. Missions—Comparative studies. 2. Catholic Church—Missions. 3. Protestant churches—Missions. I. Title.

THE hour before sunset. 266
Butler, Ind., Higley Press [c1957] 204p. illus. 20cm. The author's experiences as a pastor in the Philippines. [DS669.M3] 279.14 58-17207
1. Philippine Islands—Hist. 2. Philippine Islands—Church history. I. Mandoriao, Jose N

HOW! 266
Home missions works for human rights. Editor: Betty Stewart. [New York] Friendship Press, '1952. 96 p. illus. 20 cm. [BV2775.H6] 52-2312
1. Missions—U. S. 2. Missions, Home. 3. U. S.—Religion. I. Stewart, Betty. ed.

HUISJEN, Albert. 266
The home front of Jewish missions. Grand Rapids, Baker Book House, 1962. 222p. 23cm. [BV2620.H77] 62-21704
1. Missions— Jews. I. Title.

HUME, Edward Hicks, 1876-1957. 266
Doctors courageous. [1st ed.] New York, Harper [1950] xiv, 297 p. illus., ports., map. 22 cm. Bibliography: p. 285-292. [R722.H8] 50-6813
1. Missions, Medical. I. Title.

INGHAM, Kenneth. 266
Reformers in India, 1793-1833 an account of the work of Christian missionaries on behalf of social reform. Cambridge [Eng.] University Press, 1956. xi, 149p. fold. map. 22cm. Bibliography: p.137-146. [BV3265.I515] 275.4 A56
1. Missions— India. 2. India—Soc. life & cust. 3. Church and social problems—India. 4. Christians in India. I. Title.

INGHAM, Kenneth. 266
Reformers in India, 1793-1833; an account of the work of Christian missionaries on behalf of social reform. Cambridge [Eng.] University Press, 1956. xi, 149p. fold. map. 22cm. Bibliography: p. 137-146. [BV3265.I515] 275.4 A56
1. Missions —India. 2. India—Soc. life & cust. 3. Church and social problems—India. 4. Christians in India. I. Title.

INTERNATIONAL Missionary Council. 266
Missions under the Cross; addresses delivered at the enlarged meeting of the Committee of the International Missionary Council at Willingen, in Germany, 1952; with statements issued by the meeting. Edit d by Norman Good-all. London, Edinburgh House Press; distributed in the U. S. A. by Friendship Press. New York, 1953. 264p. 22cm. [BV2020.I6 1952a] 53-12209
1. Missions, Foreign. I. Goodall, Norman, ed. II. Title.

JACKSON, Herbert C 266
Man reaches out to God; living religions and the Christian missionary obligation. Valley Forge [Pa.] Judson Press [1963] 126 p; 20 cm. Includes bibliographies. [BV2063.J3] 63-13988
1. Religions. 2. Missions. I. Title.

JACKSON, Herbert C. 266
Man reaches out to God; living religions and the Christian missionary obligation. Valley Forge [Pa.] Judson [c.1963] 126p. 20cm. Bibl. 63-13988 1.75 pap.,
1. Religious. 2. Missions. I. Title.

JOHNSON, Carl E., 1937- 266
How in the world? [By] Carl E. Johnson. Old Tappan, N.J., Revell [1969] 125 p. 21 cm. [BV3793.J6] 69-12294 3.50
1. Evangelistic work. 2. Missions. I. Title.

JOHNSON, Roswell Park. 266
Middle East pilgrimage. New York, Friendship Press [1958] 164p. illus. 20cm. [BV3160.J6] 275.6 58-7026
1. Missions—Near East. I. Title.

JONES, Elizabeth Brown 1907- 266
All the children of the world; missionary stories from almost everywhere for boys and girls. Anderson, Ind., Warner Press [1958] 63p. illus. 23cm. [BV2087.J57] 58-10180
1. Missionary stories. I. Title.

JONES, Elizabeth Brown, 1907- 266
When you need a missionary story. Anderson, Ind. Warner Press [1956] 103p. 22cm. [BV2087.J6] 57-16409
1. Missionary stories. I. Title.

JONES, Tracey K. 266
Our mission today; the bGinning of a new age. New York, World Outlook Pr. [1963] 158p. 19cm. Bibl. 63-10784 1.00 pap.,
1. Missions—Theory. I. Title.

THE Jungle Doctor series. 266
[American ed.] Grand Rapids, Eerdmans, 1955- v. illus. 20cm. Each vol. has also special t. p. Contents.no. 1. Jungle Doctor.-- no. 2. Jungle Doctor on safarl.--no. 3. Jungle Doctor operaties. [BV3625] 276.78 55-382
1. Missions—Tanganyika Territory. 2. Missions, medical. I. White, Paul Hamilton Hume.

KANE, J. Herbert. 266
Christian missions in Biblical perspective / by J. Herbert Kane. Grand Rapids, Mich. : Baker Book House, 1976. 328 p. ; 24 cm. Bibliography: p. 325-328. [BV2061.K355] 76-378853 ISBN 0-8010-5370-6 : 9.95
1. Missions. I. Title.

KANE, J. Herbert. 266
Understanding Christian missions / by J. Herbert Kane. Grand Rapids, Mich. : Baker Book House, [1974] 452 p. ; 24 cm. Bibliography: p. 443-452. [BV2061.K36] 74-81783 ISBN 0-8010-5344-7 : 9.95
1. Missions. I. Title.

KANE, J. Herbert. 266
Winds of change in the Christian mission / by J. Herbert Kane. Chicago : Moody Press, 1973. 160 p. ; 22 cm. Includes bibliographical references. [BV2061.K38] 72-95030 ISBN 0-8024-9561-3 : 2.25
1. Missions. I. Title.

KEECH, William J. 266
The church school of missions; a manual. Philadelphia, Judson Press [c.1960] 48p. (Bibl.) diagrs. 19cm. 60-13377 .50 pap.,
1. Missions—Study and teaching. I. Title.

KELLAWAY, William 266
The New England Company, 1649-1776; missionary society to the American Indians. New York, Barnes & Noble [1962, c.1961] 303p. illus. 23cm. Bibl. 62-6232 8.50
1. Indians of North America—Missions. 2. Corporation for the Promoting and Propagating the Gospel of Jesus Christ in New England, London. 3. Company for Propagation of the Gospel in New England and the Parts Adjacent in America, London. I. Title.

KELSEY, Alice (Geer) 266
Many hands in many lands; illustrated by Kurt Wiese. New York, Friendship Press [1953] 120p. illus. 20cm. 12stories for children. [BV2087.K42] 53-10115
1. Missionary stories. I. Title.

KING, Harriette. 266
Ming Li. Nashville, Convention Press [1958] 101p. illus. 19cm. [BV2087.K48] 275.95 58-8930
1. Missionary stories. 2. Missions—Malaya. I. Title.

KOETHER, Luella G 266
Two hundred days as prisoners of the Chinese Communists, by Luella G. Koether and T. Janet Surdam. [Mason City? Iowa, 1956] 248p. 21cm. [BV3427.K6A3] 275.1 56-41458
1. Missions—China. 2. Persecution—China. I. Surdam, T. Janet. joint author. II. Title.

KRAEMER, Hendrik, 1888- 266
The Christian message in a non-Christian world. With a foreword by the late Archbishop of Canterbury. [3d ed.] Grand Rapids, Published for the International Missionary Council by Kregel Publications [1956] 455p. 23cm. [BV2063K7 1956] 56-17032
1. Apologetics, Missionary. 2. Apologetics — 20th cent. 3. Missions, Foreign. I. Title.

KREIDER, Roy 266
Judaism meets Christ; guiding principles for the Christian-Jewish encounter. Scottdale, Pa., Herald Press [c.1960] 77p. 20cm. Includes bibliography. 60-8906 1.00 pap.,
1. Missions—Jews. I. Title.

KUHN, Isobel. 266
Ascent to the tribes; pioneering in north Thailand. Chicago, Moody Press [1956] 315p. illus. 22cm. [BV3315.K8] 275.93 56-3054

1. Missions—Thailand. 2. China Inland Mission. I. Title.

LAMOTT, Willis, 1893- 266
Revolution in missions; from foreign missions to the world mission of the church. New York, Macmillan, 1954. 228p. 22cm. [BV2060.L23] 54-12118
1. Missions. I. Title.

LARSON, Melvin Gunnard, 1916- 266
Skid Row stopgap; the Memphis story. Wheaton, Ill., Van Kampen Press [1950] 112 p. illus., ports, 20 cm. [BV2656.M4L3] 50-4993
1. Memphis. Union Mission. I. Title.

LAUBACH, Frank Charles, 1884- 266
How to teach one and win one for Christ; Christ's plan for winning the world: each one teach and win one, by Frank C. Laubach. Grand Rapids, Mich., Zondervan Pub. House [1964] 90 p. illus., port. 21 cm. [BV2630.L3] 64-7845
1. Missions — Educational work. 2. Illiteracy. I. Title.

LAUBACH, Frank Charles, 1884- 266
-
How to teach one and win one for Christ; Christ's plan for winning the world: each one teach and win one. Grand Rapids. Mich., Zondervan [c.1964] 90p. illus., port. 21cm. 64-7845 1.95 bds.,
1. Missions—Educational work. 2. Illiteracy. I. Title.

LAUBACH, Frank Charles, 1884- 266
Wake up or blow up! America: lift the world or lose it! New York, Revell [1951] 160 p. 20 cm. [BV2063.L313] 51-9911
1. Missions, Foreign. 2. International cooperation. I. Title. II. Title: America: lift the world or lose it!

LAW, Howard W. 266
Winning a hearing; an introduction to missionary anthropology and linguistics. by Howard W. Law. Grand Rapids. Eerdmans [1968] 162p. 23cm. Bibl. [BV2063.L315] 67-19330 3.95 bds.,
1. Missions—Theory. 2. Religion and language. 3. Culture. I. Title.

LEBER, Charles Tudor, 1898- 266
ed.
World faith in action; the unified missionary enterprise of Protestant Christianity. [1st ed.] Indianapolis, Bobbs-Merrill [1951] 345 p. ports. 22 cm. [BV2060.L44] 51-10349
1. Protestant churches—Missions. I. Title.
Contents Omitted.

LIGHT in India's night; 266
true stories of India and her people, written especially for young folk. Springfield, Mo., Gospel Pub. House [c1957] 237p. illus. 20cm. [BV3265.S27] 275.4 58-30007
1. Missions—India. I. Schoonmaker, Violet (Dunham)

LINDSELL, Harold, 1913- 266
Missionary principles and practice. [Westwood, N. J.] Revell [1955] 384p. 21cm. Includes bibliography. [BV2060.L74] 55-7636
I. Title.

LOEWEN, Jacob Abram, 1922- 266
Culture and human values : Christian intervention in anthropological perspective : selections from the writings of Jacob A. Loewen. South Pasadena, Calif. : William Carey Library, [1975] xviii, 443 p. ; 23 cm. (The William Carey Library series on applied cultural anthropology) Papers originally appeared in Practical anthropology, 1961-1970. Includes bibliographical references. [BV2070.L58] 75-12653 ISBN 0-87808-722-2 pbk. : 5.95
1. Missions—Addresses, essays, lectures. 2. Communication (Theology)—Addresses, essays, lectures. 3. Indians of South America—Missions—Addresses, essays, lectures. I. Practical anthropology. II. Title.

LOOKING south. [266]
New York, Friendship Press [1951] 120 p. illus. 23 cm. [BV2830.H26] 278 51-7877
1. Missions—Spanish America. 2. Church work with youth. I. Hallock, Constance Magee, 1889-

LOOMIS, Albertine. [266]
Grapes of Canaan. New York, Dodd, Mead [1951] x, 334 p. map (on lining papers) 22 cm. [BV3680.H3L6] 279.69 51-10030
1. Missions—Hawaiian Islands. I. Title.

LOVEGREN, Alta Lee (Grimes) j266
The big difference. Nashville, Convention Press [1963] 82 p. illus. 21 cm. (1963 Foreign Mission graded series) [BV3210.J6L6] 63-11170
1. Missions — Jordan — Juvenile literature. 2. Baptists — Missions — Juvenile literature. I. Title.

LUDWIG, Charles, 1918- 266
Chuma; a missionary adventure story for girls. Chicago, Scripture Press [1954] 72p. illus. 21cm. [BV2087.L8] 54-9951
1. Missionary stories. I. Title.

LUDWIG, Charles, 1918- 266
Chuma finds a baby; a missionary adventure story for girls. Chicago, Scripture Press [1956] 72p. 21cm. [BV2087.L812] 56-58168
1. Missionary stories. I. Title.

LUDWIG, Charles, 1918- 266
Rogue elephant; a missionary adventure story for boys and girls. (Chicago, Scripture Press [1954] 72p. illus. 21cm. [BV2087.L82] 54-9950
1. Missionary stories. I. Title.

LUDWIG, Charles [Shelton] 266
1918-
Rogue elephant; a missionary adventure story for boys and girls. Wheaton, Ill., Scripture [1963, c.1954] 72p. illus. 20cm. .85 pap.,
1. Missionary stories. I. Title.

MCBETH, Leon. 266
Men who made missions. Nashville, Broadman Press [1967, c1968] 128 p. 20 cm. Bibliography: p. 127-128. Describes briefly the life and dogma of nine Christians who extended the boundaries of their church through missionary work: Gregory, Patrick, Boniface, Ramon Lull, Francis Xavier, David Brainerd, William Carey, Livingstone, and Judson. [BV3700.M24] AC 68
1. Missionaries. I. Title.

MCCONNELL, Dorothy Frances, 266
comp.
Pattern of things to come, compiled by Dorothy McConnell in cooperation with the executive staff of the Division of Foreign Missions, National Council of the Churches of Christ in the U.S. A. New York, Published for the Division of Foreign Missions by Friendship Press, 1955. 80p. 20cm. [BV2120.M27] 55-10430
1. Missions, Foreign. I. Title.

MCCORMICK, Rose Matthew. 266
The global mission of God's people. Maryknoll, N.Y., Maryknoll Publications, 1967. 90 p. 20 cm. Bibliography: p. 85-90. [BV2090.M25] 67-21014
1. Missions—Study and teaching. I. Title.

MCGAVRAN, Donald Anderson, 266
1897-
Crucial issues in missions tomorrow, edited by Donald A. McGavran. Chicago, Moody Press [1972] 272 p. 22 cm. Includes bibliographical references. [BV2070.M276] 72-77944 ISBN 0-8024-1675-6 4.95
1. Missions—Addresses, essays, lectures. I. Title.

MCGAVRAN, Donald Anderson, 266
1897- comp.
Eye of the storm; the great debate in mission. Donald McGavran, editor. Waco, Tex., Word Books [1972] 299 p. 23 cm. Bibliography: p. 297-299. [BV2070.M28] 74-160295 6.95
1. Missions—Addresses, essays, lectures. I. Title.

MCGAVRAN, Donald Anderson, 266
1897-
Understanding church growth, by Donald A. McGavran. Grand Rapids, Eerdmans [1970] 382 p. illus. 23 cm. Bibliography: p. 371-377. [BV2061.M253] 69-12316 7.95
1. Missions. 2. Evangelistic work. 3. Sociology, Christian. I. Title.

MCGAVRAN, Grace Winifred. 266
They live in Bible lands. Illustrated by Weda Yap and Joseph Escourido. [Rev. ed.] New York, Friendship Press [1958] 126p. illus. 20cm. [BV4571.M2 1958] 58-8300
1. Childrens stories. 2. Levant—Descr. & trav. I. Title.

MADDOX, Catherine. [266]
The invincible company. London, Philadelphia, China Inland Mission [1951] 96 p. illus. 19 cm. [BV3415.M323] 275.1 52-43445
1. Missions—China. 2. China Inland Mission. I. Title.

MAEDA, Frances, comp. 266
When we share. New York, Friendship Press [1957] 63p. illus. 21cm. Includes bibliography. [BV2064.M33] 57-11367
1. Missions. I. Title.

MEDITATIONS of a Christian 266
Chinese, by Y. T. Chiu. [1st ed.] New York, Pageant Press [1956] 101p. 21cm. [BV3415.C35] [BV3415.C35] 275.1 56-13118 56-13118
1. Missions—China. I. Chao, En-tz'u, 1890-

MEFFORD, Lila P 266
Sylvia goes to Spain. Nashville, Convention Press [1961] 74p. illus. 21cm. (1961 foreign mission graded series: Europe) 'A publication of the Foreign Mission Board, Richmond, Virginia.' [BX6310.S7M4] 61-7557
1. Baptists—Spain—Juvenile literature. 2. Baptists—Missions—Juvenile literature. I. Title.

METHODIST Church (United 266
States) Board of Missions. Joint Commission on Education and Cultivation.
Crowded ways; a symposium [by] Murray H. Leiffer [and others] New York, Editorial Departments, Joint Section of Education and Cultivation, Board of Mission of the Methodist Church [1954] 112 p. 19 cm. [BV2653.M4] 54-38573
1. City missions. I. Leiffer, Murray Howard, 1902- II. Title.

MEZA, Herbert. 266
"...to serve the present age"; a basic Bible study of Christ's mission and the church's mission in the world today. With study guide and discussion questions for individual and group use. Nashville, Presbyterian U.S. Board of World Missions [c1964] 79 p. 21 cm. "Messages...presented at the World Mission Conference of the Presbyterian Church U.S. in Montreat, North Carolina, July 30 to August 5, 1964." "Footnotes": p. 76-79. [BV2090.M52] 64-66187
1. Missions — Study and teaching. I. Presbyterian Church in the U.S. Board of World Missions. II. Title.

MILLEN, Nina, ed. 266
Missionary stories to play and tell. New York, Friendship Press [1958] 184p. 20cm. [BV2087.M44] 58-12772
1. Missionary stories. I. Title.

MILLEN, Nina, ed. 266
The missionary story hour. New York, Friendship Press [1952] 181p. 20cm. [BV2087.M45] 52-14813
1. Missionary stories. I. Title.

MILLER, Basil William, 1897- 266
Nineteen missionary stories from the Middle East. Grand Rapids, Zondervan [1950] 130 p. 20 cm. [BV2087.M46] 50-4484
1. Missionary stories. I. Title.

MILLER, Basil William, 1897- 266
Twenty missionary stories from Latin America. Grand Rapids, Zondervan [1951] 137 p. 20 cm. [BV2830.M45] 51-2682
1. Missions — Spanish America. 2. Missionary stories. I. Title.

MILLER, Kenneth Dexter, 1887- 266
Man and God in the city. New York, Friendship Press [1954] 179p. 20cm. [BV2805.N5M5] 54-6890
1. City missions. 2. City churches. I. Title.

MIRACLE in Borneo; 266
illustrated by Harold W. Munson. Nashville, Southern Pub. Association [1953] 176p. illus. 21cm. [BV3345.Y6] 279.11 54-430
1. Missionary stories. 2. Missions—Borneo. I. Youngberg, Norma R

THE Miracle of Wu-pao, and 266
other stories. Washington, Review and Herald Pub. Association [1956] 192p. 21cm. [BV2087.M48] 56-58027
1. Missionary stories.

MISSION: 266
New York, Friendship Press [1956] 181p. illus. 20cm. [BV2765.H57] 277.3 56-6581
1. Missions—U. S. 2. Missions, Home. I. Hoffman, James W
. S. A.

MISSION Institute, Chicago, 266
1971.
Mission in the '70s; what direction? Edited by John T. Boberg and James A. Scherer. Chicago, Chicago Cluster of Theological Schools [1972] 208 p. 20 cm. Sponsored by the Chicago Cluster of Theological Schools. [BV2070.M56] 74-187429
1. Missions—Addresses, essays, lectures. I. Boberg, John T., ed. II. Scherer, James A., ed. III. Chicago Cluster of Theological Schools. IV. Title.

MISSIONARY mama; 266
the lighter side of the labors of those who serve the Lord in strange, exotic vineyards, revealed in delightfully realistic letters from India. [1st ed.] New York, Greenwich Book Publishers, 1957. 128p. 21cm. [BV3269.S375A3] 275.4 57-10191
1. Missions—India. I. Seamands, Ruth, 1916-

MOENNICH, Martha L 266
From nation to nation. Grand Rapids, Zondervan Pub. House [1954] 153p. 20cm. [BV2064.M57] 54-34233
1. Missions. I. Title.

MOENNICH, Martha L 266
World missions. Grand Rapids, Zondervan [1950] 181 p. 20 cm. [BV2060.M63] 51-46
1. Missions. I. Title.

MOFFETT, Samuel Hugh. 266
Where'er the sun. Illus. by Kathleen Voute. New York, Friendship Press [1953] 121p. illus. 23cm. [BV2064.M6] 53-1323
1. Missions. I. Title.

MOSS, Zeb V. 266
Missions alive [by] Zeb V. Moss. Nashville, Tenn., Convention Press [1971] 70 p. illus., map, ports. 20 cm. (Foreign mission graded series, 1971) Pages 68-70, blank for "Notes." "Text for course number 3684 of the New church study course." [BV2082.M3M68] 78-139204
1. Mass media in missionary work—Africa, Southern—Study and teaching. I. Title.

MY most unforgettable 266
patients. [1st ed.] New York, Pagent Press [1953] 119p. 21cm. [BV3415.H66] 275.1 53-12685
1. Missions—China. 2. Missions, Medical. I. Holman, Nellie (Pederson)

NEILL, Stephen Charles, Bp. 266
Call to mission, by Stephen Neill. Philadelphia, Fortress Press [1970] v, 113 p. 20 cm. Includes bibliographical references. [BV2061.N4] 77-116460 3.95
1. Missions. I. Title.

NEILL, Stephen Charles, Bp. 266
Colonialism and Christian missions, by Stephen Neill. New York. McGraw [1966] 445p. 22cm. Bibl. [BV2080.N4] 66-21153 7.95
1. Missions. I. Title.

NEILL, Stephen Charles, bp. 266
Colonialism and Christian missions, by Stephen Neill. New York, McGraw-Hill [1966] 445 p. 22 cm. Bibliography: p. 426-429. [BV2080.N4] 66-21153
1. Missions. I. Title.

NEWBIGIN, James Edward 266
Lesslie, Bp.
Trinitarian faith and today's mission. Richmond, Va., Knox [1964, c.1963] 78p. 22cm. (World Council of Churches. Comm. on World Mission and Evangelism. Study pamphlets, no. 2) First pub. in London in 1963 under title: The relevance of trinitarian doctrine for today's mission. Bibl. 64-12261 1.25 pap.,
1. Missions—Theory. 2. Trinity. I. Title.

NISSANKA'S choice. 266
Washington, Review and Herald Pub. Association [1957] 128p. illus. 23cm. [BV2087.R29] 275.48 58-172
1. Missionary stories. I. Rawson, Elsle Lewis.

ODLE, Don, 1920- 266
Venture for victory. Berne, Ind., Light and Hope Publications [1954] 184p. illus. 20cm. [BV3400.O3] [BV3400.O3] 275 54-25223 54-25223
1. Missions—East (Far East) I. Title.

*OOSTERWAL, Gottfried. 266
Mission=possible, the challenge of mission today. Nashville, Southern Publishing Association [1972] 122 p. 22 cm. Bibliography: p. 121-122. [BV2061] 72-95276 ISBN 0-8127-0066-X 2.95
1. Missions. I. Title.

PATTERSON, George Neilson, 266
1920-
God's fool. [1st American ed.] Garden City, N. Y., Doubleday, 1957. 251p. illus. 22cm. [BV3420.T5P34 1957] 275.15 57-7828
1. Missions—Tibet. I. Title.

PETERS, George W. 266
A biblical theology of missions, by George W. Peters. Chicago, Moody Press [1972] 368 p. illus. 24 cm. Bibliography: p. 355-363. [BV2073.P48] 72-77952 ISBN 0-8024-0709-9 6.95
1. Missions—Biblical teaching. 2. Missions—Theory. I. Title.

PHILIPS, Harvey E 1878- 266
Blessed be Egypt my people; life studies from the Land of the Nile. Philadelphia, Judson Press [c1953] 153p. illus. 21cm. [BV2626.3.P48] [BV2626.3.P48] 276.2 54-744 54-744
1. Mohammedans—Converts to Christianity, 2. Missions—Egypt. I. Title.

PHILLIPS, John Bertram, 1906- 266
The church under the Cross. New York, Macmillan, 1956. 111 p. 22 cm. [BV2064.P44 1956a] 56-10964
1. Persecution. 2. Suffering. 3. Missions, Foreign. I. Title.

RANSON, Charles Wesley. 266
That the world may know. New York, Friendship Press [1953] 166p. 20cm. [BV2060.R35] 53-10192
1. Missions. I. Title.

RAWSON, Elsie Lewis. 266
Story of an Indian coin. Washington, Review and Herald Pub. Association [1952] 96 p. illus. 23 cm. [BV2087.R3] 52-66043
1. Missionary stories. I. Title.

REES, Paul Stromberg. 266
Don't sleep through the revolution, by Paul S. Rees. Waco, Tex., Word Books [1969] 130 p. 21 cm. [BV2070.R39] 69-20225 2.95
1. Missions—Addresses, essays, lectures. 2. Christianity—20th century—Addresses, essays, lectures. I. Title.

REISNER, Sherwood. 266
God's troublemakers. Nashville, Presbyterian Church U.S. [1965] 77 p. illus., ports. 21 cm. Prepared for the Joint season of witness, January-March, 1966. [BV2063.R44] 65-27937
1. Missions — Theory. 2. Witness bearing (Christianity) I. Presbyterian Church in the U.S.A. II. Title.

THE rising tide; 266
Christianity challenged in East Africa. Translated by H. Daniel Friberg. Rock Island, Ill., Augustana Press [1957] 70p. 20cm. Translation of Islam och mission 1 Ostafrika. [BV3530.B452] [BV3530.B452] 276.76 57-8755 57-8755
1. Missions—Africa, East. 2. Mohammedans in Africa, East. 3. Missions—Mohammedans. I. Bernander, Gustav Addik, 1888-

ROBINSON, Virgil E. 266
Only in Africa [by] Virgil E. Robinson. Washington, Review and Herald Pub. Association [1965] 160 p. illus. 22 cm. [BV3500.R57] 65-18673
1. Missions—Africa. 2. Missionary stories. I. Title.

ROBINSON, Virgil E. 266
Ye shall reap, by Virgil Robinson. Illustrated by Jim Padgett. Nashville, Southern Pub. Association [1964] 196 p. col. illus. 21 cm. [BV3500.R58] 63-19707
1. Missions—Africa. 2. Seventh-Day Adventists—Missions. 3. Missionary stories. I. Title.

ROWDEN, Marjorie. 266
Three Davids. Pictures by Al J. Stuart. Nashville, Convention Press, 1963. unpaged. illus. 25 cm. [1963 foreign mission graded-series] [BV2065.R68] 63-11173
1. Missions — Juvenile literature. I. Title.

ROY, Andrew T 266
On Asia's rim. New York, Friendship Press [1962] 165p. 20cm. Includes bibliography. [BV3400.R6] 62-7848
1. Missions— East (Far East) 2. East (Far East)—Church history. I. Title.

SALTER, Doris. 266
The story of Bible Christian Union; a work of faith and prayer. [Brooklyn, Bible Christian Union, 1968] 203 p. illus., ports. 20 cm. [BV2360.B48S2] 71-3279
1. Bible Christian Union. I. Title.

SANDS, Audrey Lee. 266
Single and satisfied. Wheaton, Ill., Tyndale House Publishers [1971] 136 p. 18 cm. [BV4596.S5S25] 70-123295 ISBN 0-8423-5890-0
1. Single women—Religious life. I. Title.

SCHERER, James A 266
Missionary, go home! A reappraisal of the Christian world mission. Englewood Cliffs, N. J., Prentice-Hall [1964] 192 p. 21 cm. Bibliography: p. 190-192. [BV2061.S3] 64-12091
1. Missions. I. Title.

SCHERER, James A. 266
Missionary, go home! A reappraisal of the Christian world mission. Englewood Cliffs. N.J., Prentice [c.1964] 192p. 21cm. Bibl. 64-12091 3.95 bds.,
1. Missions. I. Title.

SEABURY, Ruth Isabel. 266
So send I you. Philadelphia, Christian Education Press [1955] 111p. 21cm. [BV2064.S4] 55-9325
1. Missions. I. Title.

SEAMANDS, John T 266
The supreme task of the church; sermons on the mission of the church, by John T. Seamands. Grand Rapids, Eerdmans [1964] 126 p. 21 cm. [BV2075.S36] 64-16593
1. Missions—Sermons. 2. Methodist Church—Sermons. 3. Sermons, American. I. Title. II. Title: Sermons on the mission of the church.

SEAMANDS, John T. 266
The supreme task of the church; sermons on the mission of the church. Grand Rapids, Mich., Eerdmans [c.1964] 126p. 21cm. 64-16593 2.95 bds.,
1. Missions—Sermons. 2. Methodist Church—Sermons. 3. Sermons, American. I. Title. II. Title: Sermons on the mission of the church.

SHEPARD, Walter D. 266
Sent by the sovereign [by] Walter D. Shepard. [Nutley, N.J.] Presbyterian and Reformed Pub. Co., 1968. 108 p. 22 cm. Includes bibliographical references. [BV2070.S49] 68-55451 2.50
1. Missions—Addresses, essays, lectures.

SKOGLUND, John E. 266
They reach for life. Drawings by Joseph Escourido. New York, Friendship Press [1955] 160 p. illus. 21 cm. [BV2063.S55] 55-5761
1. Missions. I. Title.

SKOGLUND, John E. 266
To the whole creation: the church is mission. Valley Forge [Pa.] Judson [c.1962] 128p. 20cm. 62-16996 1.25 pap.,
1. Missions—Theory. I. Title. II. Title: The church is mission.

SMITH, Bradford, 1909- 266
Yankees in paradise; the New England impact on Hawaii. [1st ed] Philadelphia, Lippincott 1956 376p. illus. 22 cm. [BV3680.H3S57] 56-6247 279
1. Missions—Hawaiian Islands. I. Title.

SMITH, Laura Irene (Ivory) 266
Farther into the night, by Mrs. Gordon M. [i.e. H.] Smith. Grand Rapids, Zondervan Pub. House [1954] 247p. illus. 20cm. [BV3300.S555] [BV3300.S555] 275.9 54-34234 54-34234
1. Missions—Indochina, French. I. Title.

SOLTAU, Theodore Stanley, 266
1890-
Missions at the crossroads; the indigenous church--a solution for the unfinished tasks. Wheaton, Ill., Van Kampen Press [1954] 183p. 22cm. [BV2082.I5S6] 55-15149
1. Indigenous church administration. I. Title.

SOLTAU, Theodore Stanley, 266
1890-
Missions at the crossroads; the indigenous church -- a solution for the unfinished task. Grand Rapids, Baker Book House, 1955 [c1954] 188 p. 22 cm; [BV2082.I 5S6 1955] 55-12157
1. Indigenous church administration I. Title.

SOUTH African missions, 266
1800-1950, an anthology compiled by Horton Davies and R. H. W. Shepherd. London, New York, Nelson [1954] 232p. 21cm. Includes bibliography. [BV3555.D35] [BV3555.D35] 276.8 54-4541 54-4541
1. Missions—Africs, South. I. Davies, Horton, ed. II. Shepherd, Robert Henry Wishart, 1888- joint ed.

SOWING God's word in Israel 266
today; personal experiences in the land of Israel. Philadelphia, Million Testaments Campaigns [1953] 137p. illus. 19cm. [BV3200.D3] [BV3200.D3] 275.694 53-12619 53-12619
1. Missions—Palestine. 2. Missions—Jews. I. Davis, George Thompson Brown, 1873-

STEWART, Andrew G 266
Trophies from Cannibal Isles. Washington, Review and Herald Pub. Association [1956] 256p. illus. 21cm. [BV3670.S8] [BV3670.S8] 279.9 57-342 57-342
1. Missions—Islands of the Pacific. I. Title.

STOWE, David M 266
Partners with the Almighty; an adult resource book [by] David M. Stowe. Boston, United Church Press [1966] 123 p. illus. 21 cm. Bibliography: p. 122-123. [BV2061.S7] 66-20545
1. Missions. 2. Church work. I. Title.

STOWE, David M. 266
Partners with the Almighty; an adult resource book [by] David M. Stowe. Boston, United Church Press [1966] 123 p. illus. 21 cm. Bibliography: p. 122-123. [BV2061.S7] 66-20545
1. Missions. 2. Church work. I. Title.

SUNDKLER, Bengt Gustaf 266
Malcolm, 1909-
The world of mission. [Tr. from Swedish by Eric J. Sharpe] Grand Rapids, Mich. Eerdmans [1966, c.1963, 1965] 318p. 21cm. [BV2061.S813] 66-3153 6.95
1. Missions. I. Title.

TECHNICAL assistance by 266
religious agencies in Latin America. [Chicago] University of Chicago Press [1956] 139p. illus. 24cm. [HC60.M24] 278 56-6643
1. Technical assistance, American—Spanish America. 2. Missions—Spanish America. I. Maddox, James Gray, 1907-

THIESSEN, John Caldwell. 266
A survey of world missions. Chicago, Inter-Varsity Press [1955] xii, 504p. 25cm. Bibliography: p. [477]-487. [BV2060.T37] 55-6883
1. Missions. I. Title.

THOMAS, Mary P. 266
Cry in the wilderness: "Hear ye the voice of the Lord," by Tay Thomas. Anchorage, Color Art Printing Co., 1967. 125 p. illus., maps, ports. 22 cm. Bibliography: p. 123-124. [BV2803.A4T5] 67-2683
1. Missions—Alaska. 2. Alaska—Church history. I. Title.

THOMAS, Winburn T 266
The church in Southeast Asia [by] Winburn T. Thomas & Rajah B. Manikam. With an introd. by Frank T. Cartwright. New York, Friendship Press [1956] 171p. illus. 20cm. [BR1178.T45] 275.9 56-7954
1. Asia, Southeastern—Church history. 2. Missions—Asia, South-eastern. I. Manikam, Rajah Bhushanam, 1897- joint author. II. Title.

THOMPSON, May Bel. 266
Chinese teen-agers--and God! [1st ed.] New York, Vantage Press [1956] 206p. 21cm. Autobiographical [BV3427.T45A3] 275.1 56-11201
1. Missions—China. I. Title.

TIPPETT, Alan Richard. 266
Church growth and the word of God; the Biblical basis of the church growth viewpoint, by A. R. Tippett. Grand Rapids, Eerdmans [1970] 82 p. 21 cm. [BV2073.T5] 75-80877 1.95
1. Missions—Biblical teaching. 2. Evangelistic work. 3. Church growth. I. Title.

TOPPENBERG, Valdemar E 266
Africa has my heart. Mountain View, Calif., Pacific Press Pub. Association [1958] 168 p. illus. 23 cm. [BV3505.T6A3] 58-13664
1. Missions — Africa. I. Title.

TRESSEL, Amalia, 1879- 266
Tales truly true; short missionary stories for junior boys and girls. Columbus, Ohio, Wartburg Press [1953] 252p. 20cm. [BV2065.T7] 54-24195
1. Missions—Juvenile literature. I. Title.

TREXLER, Edgar R. 266
Mission in a new world / Edgar R. Trexler. Philadelphia : Fortress Press, c1977. ix, 86 p. : ill. ; 22 cm. [BV2061.T72] 76-62613 ISBN 0-8006-1257-4 pbk. : 2.95
1. Missions. I. Title.

TREXLER, Edgar R. 266
The new face of missions [by] Edgar R. Trexler. St. Louis, Concordia Pub. House [1973] 96 p. illus. 18 cm. (The Christian encounters) Bibliography: p. 94. [BV2061.T73] 72-97344 ISBN 0-570-06259-4 1.50 (pbk.)
1. Missions. I. Title. II. Series.

TRUEBLOOD, David Elton, 1900- 266
The validity of the Christian mission [by] Elton Trueblood. [1st ed.] New York, Harper & Row [1972] xi, 113 p. 22 cm. Includes bibliographical references. [BV2061.T78] 74-160638 ISBN 0-06-068740-1 2.95
1. Missions. I. Title.

TUININGA, Margaret Jean. 266
The "Leopard-man," and other missionary stories; written and illustrated by Margaret Jean Tuininga. Chicago, Moody Press [1951] 64 p. illus. 19 cm. [BV2087.T78] 52-134
1. Missionary stories. I. Title.

TUININGA, Margaret Jean. 266
The wallpaper that talked, and other missionary stories; written and illustrated by Margaret Jean Tuininga. Chicago, Moody Press [1951] 64 p. illus. 19 cm. [BV2087.T8] 52-15612
1. Missionary stories. I. Title.

THE two crosses, where love 266
is, God is; a true story. The drawings in this book were made by Kiyoshi Tamaki. Tokyo; official depository in the U. S. A: Academy Library Guild. Fresno, Calif., 1956 [c1955] 1 v. illus. 27cm. [BV1345] 275.2 56-2219
1. Missions—Japan. I. Nakao, Hiroji, comp.

UNDERHILL, Alice Mertie. 266
Adventures of Kado; illustrated by C. V. Temple. Mountain View, Calif., Pacific Press Pub. Association [1953] 106p. illus. 23cm. [BV2087.U48] 275.4 53-10771
1. Missionary stories. 2. Missions—India. I. Title.

VANDER MEULEN, Arnold J 266
Skid row life line; the story of the Haven of Rest Rescue Mission, Grand Rapids, Michigan. Foreword by S. Franklin Logsdon. Grand Rapids, Zondervan Pub. House [c1956] 96p. illus. 20cm. [BV2656.G7H3] 57-25843
1. Grand Rapids. Haven of Rest Rescue Mission. I. Title.

VANDER MEULEN, Arnold J. 266
Skid row life line; the story of the Haven of Rest Rescue Mission, Grand Rapids, Michigan. Foreword by S. Franklin Logsdon. Grand Rapids, Zondervan Pub. House [c1956] 96 p. illus. 20 cm. [BV2656.G7H3] 57-25843
1. Grand Rapids. Haven of Rest Rescue Mission. I. Title.

VICEDOM, Georg F. 266
The mission of God; an introduction to a theology of mission. Tr. by Gilbert A. Thiele, Dennis Hilgendorf. St. Louis, Concordia [c.1965] xiv, 156p. 22cm. (Witnessing church ser.) Bibl. [BV2063.V473] 65-22814 3.95
1. Missions—Theory. I. Title.

WAGNER, C. Peter. 266
Frontiers in missionary strategy, by C. Peter Wagner. Chicago, Moody Press [1972, c1971] 223 p. 22 cm. Based on lectures delivered at Fuller Theological Seminary School of World Mission during the winter quarters of 1970 and 1971. Bibliography: p. 209-218. [BV2061.W34] 72-181592 ISBN 0-8024-2881-9 4.95
1. Missions. I. Title.

WAGNER, C. Peter. 266
Stop the world, I want to get on [by] C. Peter Wagner. Glendale, Calif., G/L Regal Books [1973, c1974] 136 p. illus. 20 cm. Includes bibliographical references. [BV2061.W35] 73-80093 ISBN 0-8307-0272-5 1.95
1. Missions. I. Title.

WAGNON, Marilyn Simpson. 266
Let's go exploring. [Teacher's ed.] Nashville, Broadman, Press [1953] 115p. 20cm. 'A publication of Woman's Missionary Union, Birmingham, Alabama.' [BV2090.W32] 53-11703
1. Missions—Study and teaching. I. Title.

WAKATAMA, Pius. 266
Independence for the third world church : an African's perspective on missionary work / Pius Wakatama. Downers Gove, Ill. : InterVarsity Press, c1976. 119 p. ; 21 cm. Includes bibliographical references. [BV2061.W36] 76-21462 ISBN 0-87784-719-3 pbk. : 2.95
1. Missions. I. Title.

WARREN, Max Alexander 266
Cunningham, 1904-
Challenge and response; six studies in missionary opportunity. New York, Morehouse-Barlow Co. [1959] 148 p. 19 cm. Includes bibliography. [BV2063.W33] 59-14258
1. Missions. I. Title.

WARREN, Max Alexander 266
Cunningham, 1904-
Perspective in mission [by] Max Warren. New York, Seabury Press [1964] 125 p. 21 cm. (A Seabury paperback) Bibliographical footnotes. [BV2063.W34] 64-7477
1. Missions — Theory. I. Title.

WARREN, Max Alexander 266
Cunningham, 1904-
Perspective in mission. New York, Seabury [c.1964] 125p. 21cm. (SP16) Bibl. 64-7477 1.65 pap.,
1. Missions—Theory. I. Title.

WHEN your home is in the 266
city. Editor: Lucy M. Eldredge. New York, Friendship Press, 1954. 80p. illus. 20cm. [BV2765.W46] 54-6953
1. City missions. I. Eidredge, Lucy M., ed.

WHITE, Amos Jerome. 266
Dawn in Bantuland, an African experiment; or, An account of missionary experiences and observations in South Africa, by Amos Jerome White and Luella Graham White. Boston, Christopher Pub. House [1953] 297p. 21cm. [BV3520.W47] 276.8 53-3803
1. Missions—Africa, Central. I. White, Luella Graham, joint author. II. Title.

WHITE, Paul Hamilton Hume. [266]
The Jungle Doctor series. [Uniform ed. London, Paternoster Press, 1950- v. illus. 20 cm. Each vol. has also special t.p. [BV3625.T3W48] 276.78 51-22652
1. Missions—Tanganyika Territory. 2. Missions, Medical. I. Title.

WHITE, Paul Hamilton Hume. 266
Jungle doctor. With 37 illus. by Joy Griffin. [American ed.] Grand Rapids, Mich., W. B. Eerdmans Pub. Co. [1964] 118 p. illus. 21 cm.

(The Jungle doctor series, no. 1) [Missions -- Tanganyika Territory.] 67-70739
1. Mission, Medical. I. Title.

WHITE, Wallace, 1919- [266]
South to the harvest, as told to Ken Anderson. Grand Rapids, Zondervan [1950] 78 p. illus. 20 cm. [BV2851.W53] 278 50-11973
1. Missions—South America. I. Anderson, Kenneth, 1917- II. Title.

WHO in the world? 266
Edited by Clifford Christians, Earl J. Schipper [and] Wesley Smedes. Grand Rapids, Mich., W. B. Eerdmans Pub. Co. [1972] 163 p. 21 cm. Based on papers presented at a conference called by the Home Missions Board of the Christian Reformed Church in 1970. [BV601.8.W45] 75-184698 ISBN 0-8028-1435-2 1.95
1. Mission of the church—Addresses, essays, lectures. 2. Church—Addresses, essays, lectures. I. Christians, Clifford, ed. II. Schipper, Earl J., ed. III. Smedes, Wesley, ed.

*WILKINSON, Henrietta T. 266
The mystery of missions. Illus. by Raymond Porter. Richmond, Va., CLC Pr. [dist. Knox. 1966, c.1965] 96p. illus. (pt. col.) 21cm. (Covenant life curriculum; elem.: the Church year, 1) 43-9412 1.45 pap.,
I. Title.

WILLIAM S. Carter Symposium 266
on Church Growth, Milligan College, Tenn., 1974.
Christopaganism or indigenous Christianity? / Edited by Tetsunao Yamamori and Charles R. Taber. South Pasadena, Calif. : William Carey Library, [1975] 262 p. ; 23 cm. Consists of 12 lectures delivered at the symposium sponsored by Milligan College. Bibliography: p. [251]-262. [BV2391.M54 1974] 75-6616 ISBN 0-87808-423-1 pbk. : 5.95
1. Missions—Congresses. 2. Christianity and culture—Congresses. I. Yamamori, Tetsunao, 1937- II. Taber, Charles Russell. III. Milligan College, Tenn. College.

WILLIAMS, Rev. Philip. 266
Journey into mission. Illustrated by Mine Okubo. New York, Friendship Press [1957] 180p. 16cm. [BV3457.W53A3] 275.2 57-11366
1. Missions—Japan. I. Title.

WILTGEN, Ralph M 1921- 266
Gold Coast mission history, 1471-1880. Techny, Ill., Divene Word Publications, 1956. 181p. illus. 24cm. [BV3625.G6W5] 276.67 55-6277
1. Missions—Gold Coast. 2. Catholic Church in the Gold Coast—Hist. 3. Gold Coast—Church history. I. Title.

THE Word in the Third 266
World, edited by James P. Cotter. Washington, Corpus Books [1968] 285 p. 21 cm. Papers and discussions of the Woodstock conference held in March, 1967. Bibliographical footnotes. [BV2020.W58 1967aa] 68-15779 7.50
1. Missions—Congresses. I. Cotter, James P., ed.

YAMAMORI, Tetsunao, 1937- 266
Introducing church growth : a textbook in missions / by Tetsunao Yamamori and E. LeRoy Lawson. Cincinnati : New Life Books, [1975] 255 p. ; 22 cm. Includes bibliographical references. [BV652.25.Y35] 74-24577 ISBN 0-87239-000-4 : 7.95
1. Church growth. I. Lawson, E. LeRoy, 1938- joint author. II. Title.

YANKEES in paradise; 266
the New England impact on Hawaii. [1st ed.* Philadelphia, Lippincott [1956] 376p. illus. 22cm. [BV3680.H3S57] [BV3680.H3S57] 279.69 56-6247 56-6247
1. Missions—Hawaiian Islands. I. Smith, Bradford, 1909-

YOUNGBERG, Norma R 266
Jungle thorn; illustrated by Harold W. Munson. Nashville, Southern Pub. Association [1951] 158 p. illus. 20 cm. [BV2087.Y6] 52-16010
1. Missionary stories. I. Title.

ANDERSON, Gerald H., 266'.001
comp.
Crucial issues in mission today, edited by Gerald H. Anderson and Thomas F. Stransky. New York, Paulist Press [1974] ix, 276 p. 19 cm. (Mission trends, no. 1) Includes bibliographical references. [BV2070.A527] 74-182240 ISBN 0-8091-1843-2 2.95
1. Missions—Addresses, essays, lectures. I. Stransky, Thomas F., joint author. II. Title.

BEAVER, Robert Pierce, 266'.001
1906-
The missionary between the times [by] R. Pierce Beaver. [1st ed.] Garden City, N.Y., Doubleday, 1968. xiii, 196 p. 22 cm. Bibliography: p. [193]-196. [BV2063.B4] 65-17225 5.95
1. Missions—Theory. I. Title.

BEYERHAUS, Peter. 266'.001
Shaken foundations; theological foundations for mission. Grand Rapids, Zondervan Pub. House [1972] 105 p. 21 cm. (Contemporary evangelical perspectives) Lectures delivered at the Fuller Theological Seminary School of Missions in the spring of 1972. Includes bibliographical references. [BV2063.B46] 72-85558
1. Missions—Theory. I. Title.

BRAUN, Neil. 266'.001
Laity mobilized; reflections on church growth in Japan and other lands. Grand Rapids, Mich., W. B. Eerdmans Pub. Co. [1971] 224 p. illus., maps. 21 cm. (Church growth series) Bibliography: p. 210-217. [BV2063.B68] 68-56119 3.95
1. Missions—Theory. 2. Church growth. I. Title.

COSTAS, Orlando E. 266'.001
The church and its mission: a shattering critique from the Third World [by] Orlando E. Costas. Wheaton, Ill., Tyndale House Publishers [1974] xviii, 313 p. 22 cm. Includes bibliographical references. [BV600.2.C67] 74-80150 ISBN 0-8423-0275-1 6.95
1. Church. 2. Missions. I. Title.

COSTAS, Orlando E. 266'.001
The church and its mission: a shattering critique from the Third World [by] Orlando E. Costas. Wheaton, Ill., Tyndale House Publishers [1974] xviii, 313 p. 22 cm. Includes bibliographical references. [BV600.2.C67] 74-80150 ISBN 0-8423-0275-1 6.95
1. Church. 2. Missions. I. Title.

DAVIES, John Gordon, 266.001
1919-
Worship and mission [by] J. G. Davies. New York, Association Press [1967] 159 p. 19 cm. Bibliographical footnotes. [BV2063.D27 1967] 67-10550
1. Missions—Theory. I. Title.

GENSICHEN, Hans Werner. 266.001
Living mission; the test of faith. Philadelphia, Fortress Press [1966] xiii, 114 p. 21 cm. (Knubel-Miller-Greever lectures, 1965) "Presented during October 1965 ... in a consultation sponsored jointly by the Board of World Missions and the Board of Theological Education of the Lutheran Church in America." Bibliographical references included in "Notes" (p. 107-112) [BV2063.G4] 66-28661
1. Missions—Theory. I. Lutheran Church in America. Board of World Missions. II. Lutheran Church in America. Board of Theological Education. III. Title. IV. Series.

INTER-VARSITY Missionary 266'.001
Convention, 11th, Urbana, Ill., 1976
Declare his glory among the nations / edited by David M. Howard. Downers Grove, Ill. : InterVarsity Press, c1977. 262 p. ; 21 cm. [BV2390.I5 1976] 77-74847 ISBN 0-87784-784-3 pbk. : 3.95
1. Missions—Congresses. 2. Glory of God—Congresses. I. Howard, David M. II. Title.

INTER-VARSITY Missionary 266'.001
Convention, 11th, Urbana, Ill., 1976
Declare his glory among the nations / edited by David M. Howard. Downers Grove, Ill. : InterVarsity Press, c1977. 262 p. ; 21 cm. [BV2390.I5 1976] 77-74847 ISBN 0-87784-784-3 pbk. : 3.95
1. Missions—Congresses. 2. Glory of God—Congresses. I. Howard, David M. II. Title.

LINDSELL, Harold, 1913- 266'.001
An evangelical theology of missions. [Rev. ed.] Grand Rapids, Mich., Zondervan Pub. House [1970] 234 p. 21 cm. (Contemporary evangelical perspectives) 1949 ed. published under title: A Christian philosophy of missions. [BV2063.L43 1970] 77-95045
1. Missions—Theory. I. Title.

NILES, Daniel 266.001
Thambyrajah.
The message and its messengers [by] Daniel T. Niles. Prepared for the Board of Missions of the Methodist Church. New York, Abingdon Press [1966] 128 p. 20 cm. Lectures delivered at a Methodist consultation, April 1964, at Gatlinburg, Tenn. [BV2063.N5] 66-10922
1. Missions — Theory. I. Methodist Church (United States) Board of Missions. II. Title.

NILES, Daniel Thambyrajah 266.001
The message and its messengers. Prep. for the Board of Missions of the Methodist Church. Nashville, Abingdon [c.1966] 128p. 20cm. Lects. delivered at a Methodist consultation, April 1964. at Gatlinburg, Tenn. [BV2063.N5] 66-10922 2.50 bds.,
1. Missions—Theory. I. Methodist Church (United States) Board of Missions. II. Title.

POWER, John, 1927- 266'.001
Mission theology today. Maryknoll, N.Y., Orbis Books [1971] x, 216 p. 21 cm. [BV2063.P66] 70-156972 3.95
1. Missions—Theory. I. Title.

PROTESTANT crosscurrents 266'.001
in mission; the ecumenical-conservative encounter. Norman A. Horner, editor. Nashville, Abingdon Press [1968] 224 p. 23 cm. Contents.Contents.—Introduction, by N. A. Horner.—The mandates; motivation and responsibility for world mission: Ecumenical mandates for mission, by J. A. Scherer. Missionary imperatives: a conservative evangelical exposition, by H. Lindsell.—The design; objectives in world mission: Toward a reformation of objectives, by M. R. Shaull. The missionary objective: total world evangelization, by J. F. Shepherd.—The process; strategy of world mission: Strategy: The church's response to what God is doing, by D. M. Stowe. Confession, church growth, and authentic unity in missionary strategy, by A. F. Glasser.—The authors. Bibliographical footnotes. [BV2063.P72] 68-17438
1. Missions—Theory—Addresses, essays, lectures. I. Horner, Norman A., ed.

SHORTER, Aylward. 266'.001
Theology of mission. Notre Dame, Ind., Fides Publishers [1972] 92 p. 19 cm. (Theology today, no. 37) Bibliography: p. 91-92. [BV2063.S53] 73-158188 ISBN 0-85342-299-0
1. Missions—Theory. I. Title.

SIMONET, Andre. 266'.001
Apostles for our time : thoughts on apostolic spirituality / Andre Simonet. New York : Alba House, c1977. p. cm. Translation of Apotres pour notre temps. Includes bibliographical references. [BV2061.S52513] 77-8537 ISBN 0-8189-0354-6 pbk. : 4.95
1. Missions. I. Title.

SMALLEY, William Allen, 266'.001
comp.
Readings in missionary anthropology. William A. Smalley, editor. Tarrytown, N.Y., Practical Anthropology, [inc., 1967] x, 368 p. 23 cm. Consists of articles reprinted from Practical anthropology, 1953-1960. Bibliographical footnotes. [BV2063.S58] 67-17463
1. Missions — Theory. I. Practical anthropology. II. Title. III. Title: Missionary anthropology.

SMALLEY, William Allen, 266'.001
comp.
Readings in missionary anthropology. William A. Smalley, editor. South Pasadena, Calif., William Carey Library [1974] vi, 368 p. 23 cm. Articles originally published in Practical anthropology, 1953-1960. Reprint of the 1967 ed. published by Practical Anthropology, inc., Tarrytown, N.Y. Includes bibliographical references. [BV2070.S55 1974] 74-10619 ISBN 0-87808-719-2
1. Missions—Addresses, essays, lectures. I. Practical anthropology. II. Title.

TAYLOR, John Vernon, 266.001
1914-
For all the world; the Christian mission in the modern age, by John V. Taylor. Philadelphia, Westminster Press [1966] 92 p. 19 cm. (Christian foundations) Bibliographical footnotes. [BV2063.T3 1966a] 67-10335
1. Missions—Theory. I. Title.

TIPPETT, Alan Richard. 266'.001
Verdict theology in missionary theory [by] A. R. Tippett. [2d ed.] South Pasadena, Calif., William Carey Library [1973] xix, 195 p. 22 cm. "A collection of addresses and discussions that were prepared for a special week of missionary presentations at Lincoln Christian College and Seminary." Bibliography: p. 181-184. [BV2063.T5 1973] 72-92750 ISBN 0-87808-105-4 4.95
1. Missions—Theory. I. Title.

WARREN, Max, 1904- 266'.001
I believe in the great commission / by Max Warren. Grand Rapids : Eerdmans, [1976] p. cm. Includes index. [BT495.W37] 76-19022 ISBN 0-8028-1659-2 pbk. : 2.95
1. Great Commission (Bible) 2. Missions. I. Title.

WEBSTER, Douglas 266.001
Unchanging mission, Biblical and contemporary. Philadelphia. Fortress [1966.c.1965] xi.75p. 22cm. Bibl. [BV2063.W43] 66-14794 1.50 bds.,
1. Missions—Theory. I. Title.

WEBSTER, Douglas. 266.001
Yes to mission. New York, Seabury Press [1966] 126 p. 20 cm. Bibliographical footnotes. [BV2063.W435] 66-4812
1. Missions — Theory. I. Title.

WEBSTER, Douglas 266.001
Yes to mission. New York, Seabury [c.1966] 126p. 20cm. Bibl. [BV2063.W435] 66-4812 2.50 bds.,
1. Missions—Theory. I. Title.

WEISS, George Christian, 266'.001
1910-
The heart of missionary theology / by G. Christian Weiss. Chicago : Moody Press, 1977, c1976. p. cm. [BV2063.W44 1977] 77-1967 ISBN 0-8024-3483-5 : 1.50
1. Missions—Theory. 2. Missions—Biblical teaching. I. Title.

ECKERT, Fred J ed. 266.00207
What's so funny, Padre? Edited by Fred J. Eckert. Maryknoll, N.Y., Maryknoll Publications, 1965. 79 p. illus. 22 cm. [BV2300.C35E28] 65-28575
1. Catholic Foreign Mission Society of America — Anecdotes, facetiae, satire, etc. 2. Missionary stories. I. Title.

ECKERT, Fred J., ed. 266.00207
What's so funny, Padre? Maryknoll, N. Y., Maryknoll Pubns. [c.]1965. 79p. illus. 22cm. [BV2300.C35E28] 65-28575 2.00 bds.,
1. Catholic Foreign Mission Society of America—Anecdotes, facetiae, satire, etc. 2. Missionary stories. I. Title.

BAILEY, Helen L. 266'.00212
A study of missionary motivation, training, and withdrawal (1953-1962) / by Helen L. Bailey and Herbert C. Jackson. New York : Missionary Research Library, 1965. 99 p. : graphs ; 28 cm. Bibliography: p. 74-76. [BV2063.B28] 266 75-313846
1. Missionaries, Resignation of—Statistics. 2. Protestant churches—Missions—Statistics. I. Jackson, Herbert C., joint author. II. Title.

GRIFFITHS, Michael C. 266'.0023
Give up your small ambitions, by Michael Griffiths. Chicago, Moody Press [1971, c1970] 160 p. 19 cm. Includes bibliographical references. [BV2063.G82] 70-175488 ISBN 0-8024-2970-X 1.95
1. Missionaries—Appointment, call, and election. I. Title.

SoGAARD, Viggo B. 266'.0028
Everything you need to know for a cassette ministry : cassettes in the context of a total Christian communication program / by Viggo B. Sogaard. Minneapolis : Bethany Fellowship, inc., [1975] 221 p. : ill. ; 21 cm. Bibliography: p. 211-214. [BV652.83.S63] 74-20915 ISBN 0-87123-125-5 : 3.95
1. Phonotapes in church work. I. Title.

THE Encyclopedia of 266'.003
missions : descriptive, historical, biographical, statistical / edited under the auspices of the Bureau of Missions by Henry Otis Dwight, H. Allen Tupper, and Edwin Munsell Bliss. 2d ed. Detroit : Gale Research Co., 1975, c1904. xii, 851 p. ; 23 cm. Reprint of the ed. published by Funk & Wagnalls Co., New York. [BV2040.E5 1975] 74-31438 ISBN 0-8103-4205-7 : 37.00
1. Missions—Dictionaries. I. Dwight, Henry Otis, 1843-1917, ed. II. Tupper, Henry Allen, 1856-, ed. III. Bliss, Edwin Munsell, 1848-1919, ed.

THE Encyclopedia of 266'.003
modern Christian missions; the agencies. Burton L. Goddard, editor. William Nigel Kerr [and] William L. Lane, associate editor[s] David M. Scholer, assistant editor. Camden, N.J., T. Nelson [1967] xix, 743 p. 26 cm. "A publication of the faculty of Gordon Divinity School." [BV2040.E53] 67-29099
1. Missions—Dictionaries. I. Goddard, Burton L., ed.

NEILL, Stephen Charles, 266'.003
Bp.
Concise dictionary of the Christian world mission. Edited by Stephen Neill, Gerald H. Anderson [and] John Goodwin. Nashville, Abingdon Press [1971] xxi, 682 p. 23 cm. (World Christian books) Includes bibliographical references. [BV2040.N44] 76-21888 ISBN 0-687-09371-6 10.50
1. Missions—Dictionaries. I. Anderson, Gerald H., joint author. II. Goodwin, John, joint author. III. Title.

ARNOLD, Charlotte E 266'007
Complete missionary programs, by Charlotte E. Arnold. Des Plaines, Ill., Regular Baptist Press [1968] 64 p. 20 cm. [BV2095.A75] 67-25971
1. Missions—Study and teaching I. Title.

ARNOLD, Charlotte E. 266'.007
Complete missionary programs, by Charlotte E. Arnold. Des Plaines, Ill., Regular Baptist Pr. [1968] 64p. 20cm. [BV2095.A75] 67-25971 1.00 pap.,
1. Missions—Study and teaching. I. Title.

BAUER, Arthur O. F., 1925- 266'.007
Making mission happen : year-round program of education for mission in the local church and community / Arthur O. F. Bauer. [New York : Frienship Press, 1974] p. cm. Includes bibliographical references. [BV2090.B28] 74-20517 ISBN 0-377-00019-1
1. Missions—Study and teaching. I. Title.

EASTMAN, Albert Theodore, 1928- 266'.007
Missions: "in" or out? By A. Theodore Eastman. New York, Friendship Press [1967] 64 p. 16 cm. (Questions for Christians, no. 11) Bibliography: p. 62. [BV2090.E2] 67-5530
1. Missions—Study and teaching. I. Title. II. Series.

*HODGES, Melvin L. 266'.007
The indigenous church/ Melvin L. Hodges Rev. Springfield, Mo.: Gospel Pub. House, 1976 c1971. 152 p.; 19 cm. Bibliography: p. 152. [BV602] ISBN 0-88243-527-2 pbk.: 2.00
1. Missions—Study and teaching. 2. Church—Study and teaching. I. Title.

STOWE, David M 266.007
The worldwide mission of the church; a coursebook for leaders of adults [by] David M. Stowe. Boston, United Church Press [1966] 118 p. illus. 21 cm. "Part of the United Church curriculum, prepared and published by the Division of Christian Education and the Division of Publication of the United Church Board for Homeland Ministries." Bibliography: p. 122-123. [BV2090.S85] 66-20544
1. Missions — Study and teaching. I. United Church Board for Homeland Ministries. Division of Christian Education. II. United Church Board for Homeland Ministries. Division of Publication. III. Title.

STOWE, David M. 266.007
The worldwide mission of the church; a coursebook for leaders of adults [by] David M. Stowe. Boston, United Church Press [1966] 118 p. illus. 21 cm. "Part of the United Church curriculum, prepared and published by the Division of Christian Education and the Division of Publication of the United Church Board for Homeland Ministries." Bibliography: p. 122-123. [BV2090.S85] 66-20544
1. Missions—Study and teaching. I. United Church Board for Homeland Ministries. Division of Christian Education. II. United Church Board for Homeland Ministries. Division of Publication. III. Title.

TOWER, Grace Storms. 266.007
Growing up in mission; a leaders handbook on the education of children in the mission of the church. New York, Friendship Press [1966] 175 p. illus. 22 cm. [Leadership library] Bibliography: p. [173]-175. [BV2090.T6] 66-11123
1. Missions. — Study and teaching. I. Title.

TOWER, Grace Storms 266.007
Growing up in mission: a leader's handbook on the education of children in the mission of the church. New York, Friendship [c. 1966] 175p. illus. 22cm. (Leadership lib.]) Bibl. [BV2090.T6] 66-11123 3.95; 2.75 pap.,
1. Missions—Study and teaching. I. Title.

MARTIN, Alvin, 1919- 266'.007'1179493
The means of world evangelization: missiological education at the Fuller School of World Mission, edited by Alvin Martin. Prelim. ed. South Pasadena, Calif., William Carey Library [1974] xix, 518 p. illus. 23 cm. Includes bibliographies. [BV2093.F84M37] 74-9185 ISBN 0-87808-143-7
1. Fuller Theological Seminary, Pasadena, Calif. School of World Mission. 2. Missions—Study and teaching. I. Title.

BEAVER, Robert Pierce 1906- ed. 266.008
Pioneers in mission; the early missionary ordination sermons, charges, and instructions. Source book on the rise of American missions to the heathen, ed.,introd.,notes, by R. Pierce Beaver. Grand Rapids, Eerdmans [1966] vi, 291p. 24cm. Bibl. [BV2410.B4] 66-18730 6.95
1. Missions, American—Hist—Sources. 2. Indians of North America—Missions—Hist.—Sources. I. Title.

CONGRESS on the Church's Worldwide Mission, Wheaton, Ill., 1966. 266.008
The church's worldwide mission: an analysis of the current state of evangelical missions, and a strategy for future activity. Edited by Harold Lindsell. Waco, Tex., Word Books [1966] 289 p. illus., ports. 23 cm. Sponsored by the Evangelical Foreign Missions Association and the Interdenominational Foreign Mission Association. Held Apr. 9-16, 1966 at Wheaton College, Wheaton, Ill. Includes bibliographies. [BV2391.W48 1966] 66-22156
1. Missions—Congresses. I. Lindsell, Harold, 1913- ed. II. Evangelical Foreign Missions Association. III. Interdenominational Foreign Mission Association of North America. IV. Wheaton College, Wheaton, Ill. V. Title.

INTER-VARSITY Missionary Convention. 7th, Urbana, Ill., 1964 266.008
Change, witness, triumph. [Chicago] Inter-varsity Pr., 1519 N. Astor [c.1965] xxxviii, 314p. illus. 21cm. Sponsored by the Inter-varsity Christian Fellowship missionary depart. [BV2390.15] 65-21836 3.00 pap.,
1. Missions—Congresses. 2. Christianity—Congresses. I. Inter-varsity Christian Fellowship of the United States of America. II. Title.

INTER-VARSITY Missionary Convention, 8th, University of Illinois, 1967. 266'.008
God's men, from all nations to all nations. [Chicago] Inter-Varsity Press [1968] 351 p. 21 cm. [BV2390.I5 1967] 68-28079
1. Missions—Congresses. 2. Christianity—Congresses. I. Title.

REES, Paul Stromberg, comp. 266'.008
Nairobi to Berkeley; a bold look at the church in a broken world. Edited by Paul S. Rees. Waco, Tex., Word Books [1967] 176 p. 18 cm. "Chapters in this book originally appeared as articles in World vision magazine." [BV2070.R4] 68-325
1. Missions—Addresses, essays, lectures. I. World vision magazine. II. Title.

VENN, Henry, 1796-1873. 266'.008
To apply the Gospel; selections from the writings of Henry Venn. Edited with an introd. by Max Warren. Grand Rapids, Mich., W. B. Eerdmans Pub. Co. [1971] 243 p. 24 cm. Includes bibliographical references. [BV2035.V45 1971] 79-103451 6.95
1. Missions—Collected works. I. Title.

COOK, Harold R. 266'.009
Highlights of Christian missions, a history and survey [by] Harold R. Cook. Chicago, Moody [1967] 256p. 22cm. Bibl. [BV2100.C6] 67-14385 4.95
1. Missions—Hist. I. Title.

ECCLESIASTICAL History Society, London. 266'.009
The mission of the church and the propagation of the faith. Papers read at the Seventh Summer Meeting and the Eighth Winter Meeting of the Ecclesiastical History Society. Edited by G. J. Cuming. Cambridge [Eng.] University Press, 1970. 170 p. 22 cm. (Studies in church history, 6) Includes bibliographical references. [BR141.S84 vol. 6] 77-108105 ISBN 0-521-07752-4 55/- ($9.50)
1. Missions—History—Addresses, essays, lectures. I. Cuming, G. J., ed. II. Title. III. Series: Studies in church history (London), 6

KANE, J. Herbert. 266'.009
A global view of Christian missions from Pentecost to the present, by J. Herbert Kane. Grand Rapids, Mich., Baker Book House [1971] xi, 590 p. maps. 24 cm. Bibliography: p. 557-576. [BV2100.K24] 77-167688 ISBN 0-8010-5308-0 8.95
1. Missions—History. I. Title.

KEYES, Frances Parkinson (Wheeler) 1885- 266.009
Tongues of fire [by] Frances Parkinson Keyes. New York, Coward [1966] 327p. illus. 22cm. Bibl. [BV2100.K3] 66-20153 6.95
1. Missions—Hist. I. Title.

KEYES, Frances Parkinson Wheeler, 1885-1970. 266.009
Tongues of fire [by] Frances Parkinson Keyes. New York, Coward-McCann [1966] 327 p. illus. 22 cm. Bibliography: p. [299]-302. "Notes and references": p. [303]-318. [BV2100.K3] 66-20153
1. Missions—History. I. Title.

LACY, Creighton. 266'.009
The word-carrying giant : the growth of the American Bible Society / by Creighton B. Lacy. South Pasadena, Calif. : William Carey Library, [1977] p. cm. Includes index. [BV2370.A7L33] 77-22655 ISBN 0-87808-425-8
1. American Bible Society. I. Title.

NEILL, Stephen Charles, Bp. 266.009
Christian missions [by] Stephen Neill. Grand Rapids, Eerdmans [1965, c1964] 622 p. 21 cm. (The Pelican history of the church, v. 6) Bibliography: p. [579]-601. [BV2100.N4 1965] 65-5282
1. Missions—History. I. Title.

SYRDAL, Rolf A. 266'.009
To the end of the earth; mission concept in principle and practice, by Rolf A. Syrdal. Minneapolis, Augsburg Pub. House [1967] xi, 177 p. 22 cm. Bibliographical references included in "Footnotes" (p. 171-177) [BV2100.S9] 67-25365
1. Missions—History. I. Title.

YOUNG, Robert, F.R.S.G.S. 266'.009
Modern missions: their trials and triumphs. With introd. by James H. Wilson. 2d ed. Freeport, N.Y., Books for Libraries Press, 1972. 420 p. illus. 22 cm. (The Black heritage library collection) "First published 1882." [BV2060.Y69 1972] 72-5581 ISBN 0-8369-9153-2
1. Missions—History. I. Title. II. Series.

*KANE, J. Herbert. 266.0092
The making of a missionary, by J. Herbert Kane. Grand Rapids, Baker Book House [1975] 114 p. 23 cm. Bibliography: p. 113-1149 [BV2063] ISBN 0-8010-5358-7 2.95 (pbk.)
1. Missionaries. I. Title.

CREEGAN, Charles Cole, 1850-1939. 266'.00922
Great missionaries of the church, by Charles C. Creegan and Josephine A. B. Goodnow. With an introd. by Francis E. Clark. Freeport, N.Y., Books for Libraries Press [1972] xvi, 404 p. port. 23 cm. (Essay index reprint series) Reprint of the 1895 ed. [BV3700.C67 1972] 73-37522 ISBN 0-8369-2541-6
1. Missionaries. I. Goodnow, Josephine A. B., joint author. II. Title.

EDDY, George Sherwood, 1871- 266'.00922 B
Pathfinders of the world missionary crusade, by Sherwood Eddy. Freeport, N.Y., Books for Libraries Press [1969] 319 p. 23 cm. (Essay index reprint series) Reprint of the 1945 ed. Bibliographical footnotes. [BV2100.E3 1969] 76-84304
1. Missions—History. 2. Missionaries. I. Title.

HILLIS, Dick. 266'.00922
Born to climb. Waco, Tex., Word Books [1967] 157 p. 21 cm. [BV3700.H52] 67-30736
1. Missionaries. I. Title.

HILLIS, Dick. 266'.00922
Born to climb. Waco, Tex., Word Books [1967] 157 p. 21 cm. [BV3700.H52] 67-30736
1. Missionaries. I. Title.

HYATT, Irwin T., 1935- 266'.0092'2 B
Our ordered lives confess : three nineteenth-century American missionaries in East Shantung / Irwin T. Hyatt, Jr. Cambridge : Harvard University Press, 1976. p. cm. (Harvard studies in American-East Asian relations ; 8) Includes index. Bibliography: p. [BV3427.A1H9] 76-7515 ISBN 0-674-64735-1 : 18.50
1. Crawford, Tarleton Perry, 1821-1902. 2. Moon, Charlotte, 1840-1912. 3. Mateer, Calvin Wilson, 1836-1908. I. Title. II. Series.

JARRETT-KERR, Martin, 1912- 266'.0092'2 B
Patterns of Christian acceptance: individual response to the missionary impact, 1550-1950. London, New York, Oxford University Press, 1972. xviii, 342 p. 23 cm. Bibliography: p. [325]-336. [BR1702.J37 1972] 72-178732 ISBN 0-19-213946-0 £4.50
1. Christian biography. 2. Missions. I. Title.

MCBETH, Leon. 266'.00922
Men who made missions. Nashville, Broadman Press [1967, c1968] 128 p. 20 cm. Contents.--Gregory.--Patrick.--Boniface, apostle to Germany.--Ramon Lull, a fool of love.--Francis Xavier.--David Brainerd.--William Carey.--Livingstone.--Judson. Bibliography: p. 127-128. [BV3700.M24] 68-11074
1. Missionaries. I. Title.

MCBETH, Leon. 266'.00922
Men who made missions. Nashville, Broadman Press [1967, c1968] 128 p. 20 cm. Contents.Contents.—Gregory.—Patrick.—Boniface, apostle to Germany.—Ramon Lull, a fool of love.—Francis Xavier.—David Brainerd.—William Carey.—Livingstone.—Judson. Bibliography: p. 127-128. [BV3700.M24] 68-11074
1. Missionaries. I. Title.

MACLEAR, George Frederick, 1833-1902. 266'.0092'2
Apostles of mediaeval Europe. Freeport, N.Y., Books for Libraries Press [1972] vi, 332 p. illus. 23 cm. (Essay index reprint series) Reprint of the 1869 ed. [BV3700.M27 1972] 72-624 ISBN 0-8369-2803-2
1. Missionaries. 2. Missions—Europe. I. Title.

WELCH, Herbert, Bp., 1862-1969. 266'.00922
Men of the outposts; the romance of the modern Christian movement. Freeport, N.Y., Books for Libraries Press [1969, c1937] 261 p. 23 cm. (Drew lectureship in biography) (Essay index reprint series.) [BV3700.W4 1969] 69-17594 ISBN 8-369-11628-
1. Missionaries. I. Title. II. Series: Drew University, Madison, N.J. Drew lectureship in biography

YONGE, Charlotte Mary, 1823-1901. 266'.0092'2 B
Pioneers and founders; or, recent workers in the mission field. Plainview, N.Y., Books for Libraries Press [1974] p. cm. (Essay index reprint series) Reprint of the ed. published by Macmillan, London, in series: The Sunday library for household reading. [BV3700.Y7 1974] 74-4273 ISBN 0-518-10193-2 17.50
1. Missionaries. I. Title. II. Series: The Sunday library for household reading.

ANDREW, Brother. 266'.00924
God's smuggler, by Brother, Andrew with John and Elizabeth Sherrill. [New York] New American Library [1967] 240 p. 22 cm. [BV2372.A7A3] 67-27435
1. Missions—Europe, Eastern. I. Sherrill, John L. II. Sherrill, Elizabeth. III. Title.

ANDREW, Brother. 266'.00924
God's smuggler, by Brother Andrew with John and Elizabeth Sherrill. [New York] New American Library [1967] 240 p. 22 cm. [BV2372.A7A3] 67-27435
1. Missions—Europe, Eastern. I. Sherrill, John L. II. Sherrill, Elizabeth. III. Title.

BREEN, Stephen. 266.00924 (B)
The missionary. Somerset, N. J., Consolata Society for Foreign Missions [1965] xii, 156 p. col. port. 23 cm. [BX4705.A523.B7] 66-6030
1. Allamano, Gluseppe, 1851-1926. 2. Missionaries of the Consolata. I. Title.

CARLSON. LOIS 266.00924
Monganga Paul: the Congo ministry and martvrdom of Paul Carlson, M.D. New York, Harper [c. 1966] viii,197p. illus. 21cm. (Harper jungle missionary classics) [BV3625.C63C34] 66-11482 4.95
1. Missions—Cqngo (Leopoldville) I. Carlson, Paul Earle, 1928-1964. II. Title.

DIMOV, Jim. 266'.0092'4 B
The miraculous escape / Jim Dimov. Old Tappan, N.J. : F. H. Revell Co., [1975] 155 p. ; 21 cm. [BR1725.D55A33] 74-22021 ISBN 0-8007-0694-3 : 4.95
1. Dimov, Jim. I. Title.

*DRURY, Clifford M. 266'.009'24
Nine years with the Spokane indians: the diary, 1838-1848, of Elkanah Walker/ by Clifford M. Drury. Glendale, Calif.: Arthur H. Clark, 1976. 547 p.: ill. (part col.), ports. (part col.); 24 cm. (Northwest historical series; XIII) Includes index. Bibliography: p. [329] [E98.M6] 75-39378 ISBN 0-87062-117-3: 26.50
1. Walker, Elkanah. 2. Indians of North America—Missions. I. Title.

GULICK, Edward Vose. 266'.0092'4 B
Peter Parker and the opening of China [by] Edward V. Gulick. Cambridge, Harvard University Press, 1973. xi, 282 p. illus. 25 cm. (Harvard studies in American-East Asian relations, no. 3) "Works by Peter Parker": p. [253]-256. [BV3427.P29G84] 73-82628 ISBN 0-674-66326-8 12.00
1. Parker, Peter, 1804-1888. 2. Missions—China. I. Title. II. Series.

HITCHCOCK, Ruth. 266'.009'24 B
The good hand of our God / Ruth Hitchcock. Elgin, Ill. : D. C. Cook Pub. Co., c1975. 240 p., [8] leaves of plates : ill. ; 22 cm. [BV3427.H575A33] 75-4177 ISBN 0-912692-65-0 : 6.95
1. Hitchcock, Ruth. 2. Missions—China. I. Title.

MAXEY, Mark, 1918- 266'.0092'4 B
Way down here. San Clemente, Ca[lif.] Go Ye Books [1972] xvi, 492 p. illus. 23 cm. Selections from the author's letters which originally appeared in the Linkletter, 1949-71. [BV3457.M35A4 1972] 72-81341 ISBN 0-87808-950-0 4.95
1. Maxey, Mark, 1918- 2. Missions—Kagoshima, Japan (Prefecture) I. Title.

MORSE, Eugene. 266'.0092'4 B
Exodus to a hidden valley. [1st ed.] New York, Reader's Digest Press; distributed by E. P. Dutton, 1974. 215 p. map. 22 cm. [BV3270.M67] 73-21673 ISBN 0-88349-021-8 7.95
1. Morse, Eugene. 2. Missions—Burma. I. Title.

NEERSKOV, Hans Kristian. 266'.0092'4 B
Mission possible / Hans Kristian, with Dave Hunt. Old Tappan, N.J. : Revell, [1975] 191 p. ; 21 cm. [BV3777.E93N43] 74-26808 ISBN 0-8007-0717-6 pbk. : 2.95

1. Neerskov, Hans Kristian. 2. Evangelistic work—Europe, Eastern. I. Hunt, Dave, joint author. II. Title.

SAINT, Philip. 266'.0092'4
Amazing Saints, by Phil Saint. Plainfield, N.J., Logos International, 1972. vii, 211 p. illus. 21 cm. Autobiographical. [BV3785.S15A3] 71-124480 ISBN 0-912106-24-7 4.95
1. Saint, Philip. I. Title.

STEVENS, George Barker, 1854-1906. 266'.0092'4 B
The life, letters, and journals of the Rev. and Hon. Peter Parker, M.D., missionary, physican, diplomatist ... by George B. Stevens, with the co-operation of W. Fisher Markwick. Wilmington, Del., Scholarly Resources [1972] 362 p. port. 23 cm. [R154.P253S8 1972] 72-79840 ISBN 0-8420-1357-1
1. Parker, Peter, 1804-1888. I. Markwick, William Fisher, 1848-1911, joint author.

TAYLOR, Frederick Howard. 266.00924 (B)
J. Hudson Taylor; a biography, by Dr. and Mrs. Howard Taylor. Foreword by Arthur F. Glasser. Chicago, Moody Press [1965] ix, 366 p. port. 23 cm. (The Tyndale series of great biographies) [BV3427.T3T38] 66-32
1. Taylor, James Hudson, 1832-1905. 2. Missions—China. I. Taylor, Mary Geraldine (Uginness) joint author. II. Title.

TAYLOR, Frederick Howard 266.00924
J. Hudson Taylor; a biography. by Dr. and Mrs. Howard Taylor. Foreword by Arthur F. Glasser. Chicago, Moody [c.1965] xi, 366p. port. 23cm. (Tyndale ser. of great biogs.) [BV3427.T3T38] 66-32 4.95
1. Taylor, James Hudson, 1832-1905. 2. Missions—China. I. Taylor, Mary Geraldine (Guinness) joint author. II. Title.

WATSON, John Thomas. 266.00924 (B)
T. J. Bach; a voice for missions, by Tom Watson, Jr. Chicago, Moody Press [1965] 186 p. 22 cm. [BV2852.B3W3] 65-9729
1. Bach, Thomas John. I. Title.

HARRIS, Walter Stuart, ed. 266.0094
Eyes on Europe, edited by W. Stuart Harris. 2nd impression. Newchurch (Lancs.), European Christian Mission, known in North America as Mission to Europe's Millions, Los Gatos, Calif., 1965. 136 p. Illus. 18 1/2 cm. 5/6 (B.66-7731) [BV2855.H3] 66-73293
1. Missions — Europe. I. Title.

HAAS, Harry, 1925- 266.0095
Christianity in the Asian revolution. Baltimore, Helicon [1966] x, 116p. 18cm. (Helicon paperbk.) [BV3151.H24] 66-24851 1.25 pap.,
1. Missions—Asia. 2. Christianity—Asia. I. Available from Taplinger, New York. II. Title.

MISSIONS Advanced Research and Communication Center. 266'.0095
Church growth and methods of evangelism in Asia-South Pacific. [Monrovia, Calif., c1970] ix, 91 p. illus. 28 cm. Results of a survey of delegates to the Asia-South Pacific Congress on Evangelism, Singapore, 1968. [BV3777.A75M57] 72-170441 2.00
1. Evangelistic work—Asia—Statistics. 2. Evangelistic work—Oceanica—Statistics. I. Title.

SONG, Choan-Seng, 1929- 266'.0095
Christian mission in reconstruction—an Asian analysis / Choan-Seng Song. Maryknoll, N.Y. : Orbis Books, 1977, c1975. 276 p. ; 22 cm. Reprint of the ed. published by the Christian Literature Society, Madras. Includes bibliographical references. [BV3151.S66 1977] 77-23237 ISBN 0-88344-073-3 : 10.00
1. Missions—Asia. I. Title.

SONG, Choan-Seng, 1929- 266'.0095
Christian mission in reconstruction—an Asian analysis / Choan-Seng Song. Maryknoll, N.Y. : Orbis Books, 1977, c1975. 276 p. ; 22 cm. Reprint of the ed. published by the Christian Literature Society, Madras. Includes bibliographical references. [BV3151.S66 1977] 77-23237 ISBN 0-88344-073-3 : 10.00
1. Missions—Asia. I. Title.

CHINA and Christian responsibility; 266'.00951
a symposium. Edited by William J. Richardson. New York, Maryknoll Publications, 1968. vi, 144 p. 19 cm. Bibliographical footnotes. [BV3415.2.C5] 68-23546
1. Missions—China—Addresses, essays, lectures. I. Richardson, William Jerome, 1929- ed.

FORSYTHE, Sidney A., 1920- 266'.00951
An American missionary community in China, 1895-1905, by Sidney A. Forsythe Cambridge, Mass., East Asian Research Center, Harvard University; distributed by Harvard University Press, 1971. viii, 146 p. 26 cm. (Harvard East Asian monographs, 43) Bibliography: p. 129-141. [BV3415.2.F67] 70-178077 ISBN 0-674-02626-8
1. Missions—China. 2. Protestant churches—Missions. 3. Missions, American. I. Title. II. Series.

HONG, Silas. 266'.00951
The dragon net : how God has used Communism to prepare China for the Gospel / Silas Hong. Old Tappan, N.J. : Revell, c1976. 128 p. ; 21 cm. Includes bibliographical references. [BR1285.H65] 75-33773 ISBN 0-8007-0775-3 : 4.95
1. Christianity—China. 2. Missions—China. 3. China—Religion. 4. Communism and Christianity—China. I. Title.

NESTORIAN tablet of Sian-fu 266.00951
The Nestorian monument of Hsi-an Fu in Shen-hsi,China, relation to the diffusion of Christianity in China in the seventh and eighth centuries; with the Chinese text of the inscription, a translation, and notes, and a lecture on the monument with a sketch of subsequent Christian missions in China and their present state, by James Legge. London, Trubner, 1888. New York, Reprinted by Paragon, 1966. iv, 65p. illus. 23cm. [BX154.C4N414 1966] 66-18959 5.00
1. Nestorian tablet of Sian-fu. 2. Missions—China. I. Legge, James, 1815-1897. II. Title.

NESTORIAN tablet of Sian-fu. 266.00951
The Nestorian monument of Hsi-an Fu in Shen-hsi, China, relating to the diffusion of Christianity in China in the seventh and eighth centuries; with the Chinese text of the inscription, a translation, and notes, and a lecture on the monument with a sketch of subsequent Christian missions in China and their present state, by James Legge. London, Trubner, 1888. New York, Reprinted by Paragon Book Reprint Corp., 1966. iv, 65 p. illus. 23 cm. [BX154.C4N414 1966] 66-18959
1. Nestorian tablet of Sian-fu. 2. Missions — China. I. Legge, James, 1815-1897. II. Title.

VARG, Paul A. 266'.00951
Missionaries, Chinese, and diplomats : the American Protestant missionary movement in China, 1890-1952 / by Paul A. Varg. New York : Octagon Books, 1977, c1958. xii, 335 p. ; 23 cm. Reprint of the ed. published by Princeton University Press, Princeton, N.J. Includes bibliographical references and index. [BV3415.2.V37 1977] 76-30301 ISBN 0-374-98071-3 lib.bdg. : 15.75
1. Missions—China—History. 2. China—Relations (general) with the United States. 3. United States—Relations (general) with China. I. Title.

LIU, Kwang-Ching, 1921- ed. 266.00951008
american missionaries in China; papers from Harvard seminars. Ed., introd. by KwangChing Liu. [Cambridge] East Asian Res. Ctr. Harvard Univ., dist. Harvard Univ. Pr., 1966. 31p. 28cm. (Harvard East Asian monographs, 21) 7 articles by Harvard seminar students previously pub. in the annual vols. of Papers on China, 1955-1964. Bibl. [BV3415.L55] 66-31226 4.00 pap.,
1. Missions, American—Addresses, essays, lectures. 2. Missions—China—Addresses, essays, lectures. I. Title. II. Series.

†BOLTON, Robert J., 1929- 266'.00951'249
Treasure Island—church growth among Taiwan's urban Minnan Chinese / by Robert J. Bolton. South Pasadena, Calif. : W. Carey Library, c1976. xxi, 396 p. : ill. ; 21 cm. Includes index. Bibliography: p. 366-381. [BV3430.B64] 76-20828 ISBN 0-87808-315-4 pbk. : 6.95
1. Missions—Taiwan. 2. Church growth—Case studies. I. Title.

LIAO, David C. E. 266'.00951'249
The unresponsive: resistant or neglected? The Hakka Chinese in Taiwan illustrate a common missions problem, by David C. E. Liao. Chicago, Moody Press [1972] 160 p. illus. 22 cm. (Moody church growth series) Bibliography: p. 150-156. [BV3423.H25L5] 73-175494 ISBN 0-8024-9040-9 2.95
1. Missions to Hakkas—Taiwan. 2. Hakkas. I. Title.

OGLE, George E., 1929- 266'.009519'5
Liberty to the captives : the struggle against oppression in South Korea / George E. Ogle. Atlanta : John Knox Press, c1977. 188 p. ; 21 cm. Includes bibliographical references. [BV3462.O34A34] 76-48578 ISBN 0-8042-1494-8 pbk. : 5.95
1. Ogle, George E., 1929- 2. Missionaries—Korea—Biography. 3. Missionaries—United States—Biography. 4. Civil rights—Korea. 5. Christianity and democracy—Korea. 6. Korea—Politics and government—1960- I. Title.

CARY, Otis, 1851-1932. 266'.00952
A history of Christianity in Japan. New York, F. H. Revell, 1970 [c1909] 2 v. 2 fold. maps (1 in pocket) 23 cm. Contents.Contents.—[1] Roman Catholic and Greek Orthodox missions.—[2] Protestant missions. Bibliographical footnotes. [BV3445.C4 1970] 70-107165
1. Missions—Japan. 2. Japan—Church history. I. Title.

CARY, Otis, 1851-1932. 266'.00952
A history of Christianity in Japan : Roman Catholic, Greek Orthodox, and Protestant Missions / by Otis Cary. Rutland, Vt. : C. E. Tuttle Co., 1975 xiii, 431, 367 p. ; 22 cm. Reprint of the 1909 ed. published by F. H. Revell Co., New York. Includes bibliographical references and indexes. [BV3445.C4 1976] 75-28972 ISBN 0-8048-1177-6 : 20.00 (2 v.)
1. Missions—Japan. 2. Japan—Church history. I. Title.

HENDRICKS, Kenneth C. 266'.009'52
Shadow of his hand; the Reiji Takahashi story, by KNneth C. Hendricks. St. Louis, Bethany Pr. [1967] 202p. 22cm. [BV3457.T28H4] 67-15864 3.45 pap.,
1. Takahashi, Reiji, 1930- 2. Missions—Japan. I. Title.

*BADCOCK, D. I. 266.00954
Burma prisoner; the story of Adoniram Judson. Chicago, Moody [1967,c.1962] 63p. 19cm. (Moody arrow: missionary, no. 22) .50 pap.,
1. Judson, Adoniram, d. 1849. 2. Missions—India. I. Title.

INGHAM, Kenneth. 266'.00954
Reformers in India, 1793-1833; an account of the work of Christian missionaries on behalf of social reform. With a new pref. by the author. New York, Octagon Books, 1973. xi, 149 p. 22 cm. Reprint of the 1956 ed. published by University Press, Cambridge. Bibliography: p. 137-146. [BV3265.I515 1973] 73-16425 ISBN 0-374-94112-2 8.00 (lib. bdg.)
1. Missions—India. 2. India—Social life and customs. 3. Church and social problems—India. 4. Christians in India. I. Title.

HEFLEY, James C. 266'.009549'2
Christ in Bangladesh [by] James and Marti Hefley. [1st ed.] New York, Harper & Row [1973] 109 p. illus. 22 cm. [BV3259.H43 1973] 72-79956 4.95
1. Missions—Bangladesh. 2. Charities—Bangladesh. I. Hefley, Marti, joint author. II. Title.

MCNEE, Peter 266'.009549'2
Crucial issues in Bangladesh : making missions more effective in the mosaic of peoples / Peter McNee. South Pasadena, Calif. : William Carey Library, [1976] p. cm. Bibliography: p. [BV3259.M32] 76-27322 ISBN 0-87808-317-0 pbk. : 6.95
1. Missions—Bangladesh. 2. Bangladesh—Religion. I. Title.

HORNE, Shirley. 266'.0095'5
An hour to the stone age. Chicago, Moody Press [1973] 208 p. illus. 22 cm. [BV3680.N5H58] 72-95020 ISBN 0-8024-3690-0 pap. 2.95
1. Missions to Dani (New Guinea people) I. Title.

TRAGER, Helen Gibson. 266.009591
Burma through alien eyes; missionary views of the Burmese in the nineteenth century [by] Helen G. Trager. Bombay, New York, Asia Pub. House [1966] xvi, 239 p. illus. 23 cm. Bibliography: p. [224]-231. [BV3270.T7] SA66
1. Missions — Burma. 2. Burma — Hist. 3. Burmeses. I. Title.

TRAGER, Helen Gibson 266.009591
Burma through alien eyes; missionary views of the Burmese in the nineteenth century. New York. Praeger [1966] xvi. 239p. illus. map (in lining papers) 23cm. Bibl. [BV3270.T7] 66-12480 6.50
1. Missions—Burma. 2. Burma—Hist. 3. Burmese. I. Title.

SMITH, Laura Irene Ivory. 266'.009597
The ten dangerous years / by Mrs. Gordon H. Smith. Chicago : Moody Press, [1975] 255 p. : ill. ; 22 cm. [BV3325.A6S6] 75-14145 ISBN 0-8024-8582-0 pbk. 3.95
1. Missions—Vietnam. I. Title.

EVANS. A. R. 266.0096
Mary Slessor, the white queen of Calabar. Rev. by Ruth I. Johnson. Chicago. Moody [1966, c.1953] 63p. 19cm. (Moody Arrows missionary, no. 15) p.50 pap.,
1. Missions—Africa. I. Title.

JOHNSTON, James. 266'.0096
Missionary landscapes in the Dark Continent. Freeport, N.Y., Books for Libraries Press, 1972 [c1892] 264 p. 22 cm. (The Black heritage library collection) [BV3500.J74 1972] 72-3911 ISBN 0-8369-9100-1
1. Missions—Africa. I. Title. II. Series.

JOHNSTON, James. 266'.0096
Missionary landscapes in the Dark Continent. Freeport, N.Y., Books for Libraries Press, 1972 [c1892] 264 p. 22 cm. (The Black heritage library collection) [BV3500.J74 1972] 72-3911 ISBN 0-8369-9100-1 12.50
1. Missions—Africa. I. Title. II. Series.

MOORHOUSE, Geoffrey, 1931- 266'.0096
The missionaries. Philadelphia, Lippincott [1973] 368 p. illus. 25 cm. Bibliography: p. 351-352. [BV3500.M6] 72-6052 ISBN 0-397-00801-5
1. Missions—Africa—History. I. Title.

SEATS, V. Lavell. 266'.0096
Africa—arrows to atoms [by] V. Lavell Seats. Nashville, Convention Press [1967] 127 p. illus., maps, group port. 19 cm. (1967 Foreign mission graded series) "A publication of the Foreign Mission Board, Richmond, Virginia." Church study course no. 1013, category 10, section for adults. [BV3500.S4] 67-19399
1. Missions—Africa. 2. Missions—Study and teaching. I. Title.

COTTERELL, F. Peter. 266'.00963
Born at midnight, by F. Peter Cotterell. Chicago, Moody Press [1973] 189 p. illus. 22 cm. Bibliography: p. 181-185. [BV3560.C67] 72-95029 ISBN 0-8024-0889-3 3.50
1. Missions—Ethiopia. 2. Ethiopia—Church history. I. Title.

TRIMINGHAM, John Spencer. 266'.00963
The Christian Church and missions in Ethiopia (including Eritrea and the Somalilands) London, New York, World Dominion Press, 1950 [i. e. 1951] viii, 73p. fold. maps. 19cm. [Survey series] [BV3560.T7] 55-44832
1. Missions—Ethiopia. 2. Ethiopic Church. I. Title.

BECKMANN, David M. 266'.009667
Eden Revival : spiritual churches in Ghana / David M. Beckmann ; foreword by William J. Danker. St. Louis : Concordia Pub. House, [1975] 144 p. ; 21 cm. Bibliography: p. 139-144. [BR1463.G5B42] 73-83085 ISBN 0-570-03197-4 : 3.95
1. Eden Revival Church. 2. Independent churches—Ghana. I. Title.

AJAYI, J. F. Ade 266.009669
Christian missions in Nigeria, 1841-1891; the making of a new elite. Evanston [Ill.] Northwestern Univ. Pr. [c.]1965. xvi, 317p. illus., maps. 23cm. (Ibadan hist. ser.) Bibl. [BV3625.N5A7] 65-20800 6.50
1. Missions—Nigeria. I. Title. II. Series.

AJAYI, J F Ade 266.009669
Christian missions in Nigeria, 1841-1891; the making of a new elite [by] J. F. Ade Ajayi. Evanston [Ill.] Northwestern University Press, 1965. xvi, 317 p. illus., maps, 23 cm. (Ibadan history series) Revision of thesis--University of London. Bibliography: p. 278-296. [BV3625.N5A7 1965] 65-20800
1. Missions—Nigeria. I. Title. II. Series.

SWANK, Gerald O. 266'.009669
Frontier peoples in Central Nigeria and a strategy for outreach / Gerald O. Swank. South Pasadena, Calif. : William Carey Library, [1977] p. cm. Translation of Labarin marasa jin bishara a cikin Nigeria ta Tsakiya da dabarun hanyoyin aiki. Bibliography: p. [BV3777.N54S9313] 77-9944 ISBN 0-87808-154-2 pbk. : 5.95
1. Evangelistic work—Nigeria. 2. Ethnology—Nigeria. I. Title.

CHURCH, John Edward. 266'.00967'571
Forgive them; the story of an African martyr, by J. E. Church, and colleagues of the Rwanda Mission (C.M.S.) Chicago, Moody Press [1967, c1966] 126 p. map. 20 cm. [BX5700] 67-4600
1. Kanamuzeyi, Yona, 1918-1964. I. Church Missionary Society. Ruanda Mission. II. Title.

DOWDY, Homer E. 266.009675
Out of the jaws of the lion. New York, Harper [c.1965] 254p. illus., map (on lining paper) ports. 22cm. [BV3625.C63D6] 65-20450 3.95
1. Martyrs—Congo (Leopoldville) 2. Missions—Congo (Leopoldville) I. Title.

DOWDY, Homer E. 266.009675
Out of the jaws of the lion [by] Homer E. Dowdy. [1st ed.] New York, Harper & Row [1965] 254 p. illus., map (on lining paper) ports. 22 cm. [BV3625.C63D6] 65-20450
1. Missions—Congo (Leopoldville) 2. Martyrs—Congo (Leopoldville) I. Title.

FULLER, Millard, 266'.0096751
1935-
Bokotola / Millard Fuller. New York : Association Press, c1977. v, 174 p. ; 22 cm. [BV3625.C6F8] 77-1277 ISBN 0-8096-1924-5 pbk. : 4.25
1. Fuller, Millard, 1935- 2. Missions—Zaire. 3. Labor and laboring classes—Dwellings—Zaire. 4. Missionaries—Zaire—Biography. I. Title.

FULLER, Millard, 266'.0096751
1935-
Bokotola / Millard Fuller. New York : Association Press, c1977. v, 174 p. ; 22 cm. [BV3625.C6F8] 77-1277 ISBN 0-8096-1924-5 pbk. : 4.25
1. Fuller, Millard, 1935- 2. Missions—Zaire. 3. Labor and laboring classes—Dwellings—Zaire. 4. Missionaries—Zaire—Biography. I. Title.

VAN RHEENAN, 266'.009676'1
Gailyn, 1946-
Church planting in Uganda : a comparative study / Gailyn Van Rheenan. South Pasadena, Calif. : William Carey Library, [1976] p. cm. Bibliography: p. [BV3625.U3V36] 76-20461 ISBN 0-87808-314-6 pbk. : 4.95
1. Missions—Uganda. 2. Christianity—Uganda. 3. Church growth. I. Title.

SALES, Jane M. 266'.00968
The planting of the churches in South Africa, by Jane M. Sales. Grand Rapids, Mich., Eerdmans [1971] 170 p. maps. 20 cm. (A Christian world mission book) Bibliography: p. 151-161. [BV3555.S26] 72-127627 3.45
1. Missions—Africa, South. I. Title.

ROTBERG, Robert I 266.0096894
Christian missionaries and the creation of Northern Rhodesia, 1880-1924, by Robert I. Rothberg. Princeton, N.J., Princeton University Press, 1965. xi, 240 p. illus. 21 cm. Includes bibliographies. [BV3625.R52R6] 65-12993
1. Missions — Rhodesia, Northern. I. Title.

ROTBERG, Robert I. 266.0096894
Christian missionaries and the creation of Northern Rhodesia, 1880-1924. Princeton, N. J., Princeton [c.] 1965. xi, 240p. illus. 21cm. Bibl [BV3625.R52R6] 65-12993 6.50
1. Missions—Rhodesia, Northern. I. Title.

PIKE, Eunice V. 266'.00972
An uttermost part, by Eunice V. Pike. Chicago, Moody Press [1971] 192 p. illus. 22 cm. [F1221.M35P5] 79-155692 3.95
1. Mazatec Indians—Missions. I. Title.

BENNETT, Charles, 266'.00972'6
1932-
Tinder in Tabasco; a study of church growth in tropical Mexico. Grand Rapids, Erdmans [1968] 213p. illus., maps. 20cm. (Church growth ser.) Bibl. [BV2837.T3B] 67-28370 2.95 pap.,
1. Presbyterian Church—Missions—Hist. 2. Missions—Tabasco, Mexico. I. Title.

HATLER, Grace 266.0097284
Land of the lighthouse [by] Grace Hatler as told to Dorothy Molan. Drawings by Antonio Fuentes. Valley Forge, Pa., Judson [c.1966] 110p. illus. 22cm. (Amer. Baptist mission bk.) [BV2843.S4H3] 66-18291 1.95 pap.,
1. Missions—Salvador. I. Molan Dorothy Lennon. II. Title.

CHANEY, Charles L., 266'.00973
1934-
The birth of missions in America / Charles L. Chaney. South Pasadena, Calif. : William Carey Library, c1976. xiv, 337 p. ; 23 cm. Bibliography: p. 307-337. [BV2410.C48] 75-26500 ISBN 0-87808-146-1 pbk. : 7.95
1. Missions, American. 2. Protestant churches—Missions. I. Title.

ROSENBERG, Carroll 266'.0097471
Smith.
Religion and the rise of the American city; the New York City mission movement, 1812-1870. Ithaca [N.Y.] Cornell University Press [1971] x, 300 p. 22 cm. Bibliography: p. [283]-293. [BV2805.N5R68 1971] 76-164640 ISBN 0-8014-0659-5 10.50
1. City missions—New York (City) 2. New York (City)—Poor. I. Title.

POSEY, Walter Brownlow, 266.00976
1900-
Frontier mission; a history of religion west of the Southern Appalachians to 1861. Lexington, University of Kentucky Press, 1966. viii, 436 p. illus., map. 23 cm. Bibliographical footnotes. [BV2793.P6] 66-16229
1. Missions—Southern States. I. Title.

POSEY, Walter Brownlow, 266.00976
1900-
Frontier mission; a history of religion west of the Southern Appalachians to 1861. Lexington, Univ. of Ky. Pr. [c.] 1966. viii, 436p. illus., map. 23cm. Bibl. [BV2793.P6] 66-16229 9.00
1. Missions—Southern State. I. Title.

GERHARDT, Alfred C. P. 266'.00978
1665-1965: three hundred years of missionary work among the Sioux Indians; a research project in chronological order on the history of the missionary work that was done among the Sioux Indians. Compiled and edited for the benefit of the churches who have done missionary work among the Sioux Indians by Alfred C. P. Gerhardt, Jr. [Dunmore, Pa., F. Pane Offset Print. Co.] 1969. vii, 103 l. group port. 28 cm. Bibliography: leaves 102-103. [E99.D1G4] 76-83114
1. Dakota Indians—Missions—History. I. Title. II. Title: Three hundred years of missionary work among the Sioux Indians.

*PARSONS, Francis B. 266.0097801
Early 17th century missions of the Southwest, by Francis B. Parsons with historical introduction. Book design and drawings by Harold A. Wolfinbarger, Jr. Tucson, Ariz., Dale Stuart King [1975] viii, 111 p. ill. 22 cm. Includes index. Bibliography: p. 106-107. [BV2800] 74-32368 ISBN 0-912762-21-7 6.50
1. Missions—History. 2. Missions—United States. 3. Indians of North America—Missions. I. Title.
Pbk. 2.95; ISBN: 0-912762-20-9.

FRASER, Gordon Holmes. 266'.00979
Rain on the desert / by Gordon H. Fraser. Chicago : Moody Press, [1975] 156 p. ; 19 cm. [E78.S7F73] 75-15995 ISBN 0-8024-7153-6 : 1.25
1. Indians of North America—Southwest, New—Missions. 2. Missions—Southwest, New. I. Title.

LASUEN, Fermin 266.009794
Francisco de, 1736-1803.
Writings. Translated and edited by Finbar Kenneally. Washington, Academy of American Franciscan History, 1965. 2 v. illus., facsims., map, ports. 26 cm. Bibliography: v. 2, p. [455] -- 456. [F864.L3473] 65-6143
1. California — Hist. — To 1846 — Sources. 2. Missions — California — Hist. — Sources. 3. Franciscans in California — Hist. — Sources. I. Kenneally, Finbar, ed. and tr. II. Title.

LASUEN, Fermin 266.009794
Francisco de, 1736-1803
Writings. Tr., ed. by Finbar Kenneally. Washington, D.C., 20014, Acad. of Amer. Franciscan Hist. Box 5850 [c.1965] 2v. illus., facsims., map, ports. 26cm. Bibl. [F864.L3473] 65-6143 25.00 set,,sCalifornia--Hist.--To 1846--Sources.
1. Missions—California—Hist.—Sources. 2. Franciscans inCalifornia—Hist.—Sources. I. Kenneally, Finbar, ed. and tr. II. Title.

TAYLOR, Clyde Willis, 266'.0098
1904- ed.
Protestant missions in Latin America; a statistical survey, edited by Clyde W. Taylor and Wade T. Coggins. Washington, Evangelical Foreign Missions Association, 1961. xxvi, 314 p. 19 x 24 cm. [BV2831.T35] 62-27216
1. Missions—Latin America—Statistics. 2. Protestant churches—Missions. I. Coggins, Wade T., joint ed. II. Title.

SMITH, W. Douglas, 266'.00984
1932-
Toward continuous mission : strategizing for the evangelization of Bolivia / W. Douglas Smith, Jr. South Pasadena, Calif. : William Carey Library, [1977] p. cm. Includes index. Bibliography: p. [BV2853.B4S54] 77-21490 ISBN 0-87808-321-9 pbk. : 4.95
1. Missions—Bolivia. 2. Missions—Theory. I. Title.

MCCARTHY, Dan B. 266'.00985
Mission to Peru; a story of papal volunteers [by] Dan B. McCarthy. Milwaukee, Bruce Pub. Co. [1967] xi, 164 p. illus., ports. 22 cm. [BV2300.P3M3] 67-28889
1. Papal Volunteers for Latin America. 2. Missions—Peru. I. Title.

KENT, Graeme. 266'.0099
Company of Heaven; early missionaries in the South Seas. Nashville, T. Nelson [1972] 230 p. illus. 22 cm. Bibliography: p. [221]-224. [BV3640.K46] 72-4375 ISBN 0-8407-4036-0
1. Missions—Oceanica—History. I. Title.

TIPPETT, Alan Richard. 266'0099
The deep-sea canoe : the story of Third World missionaries in the South Pacific / Alan R. Tippett. South Pasadena, Calif. : William Carey Library, c1977. xi, 126 p. : ill. ; 22 cm. Includes indexes. [BV3670.T57] 77-8660 ISBN 0-87808-158-5 pbk. : 3.45
1. Missions—Oceanica. I. Title.

BULL, Geoffrey T. 266.0099115
Coral in the sand. Chicago, Moody [1966,. c1962] 125p. map. 17cm. (Colportage lib., 524:MP 39) Bibl. .39 pap.,
1. Missions—North Borneo. I. Title.

PEDERSEN, Paul 266'.00992'1
Bodholdt.
Batak blood and Protestant soul; the development of national Batak churches in North Sumatra. Grand Rapids, Eerdmans [1970] 212 p. map. 20 cm. (A Christian world mission book) Bibliography: p. 197-200. [BV3365.P44] 71-80876 3.95
1. Missions—Sumatra. 2. Batak. I. Title.

MASSOLA, Aldo. 266'.00994'5
Aboriginal mission stations in Victoria: Yelta, Ebenezer, Ramahyuck, Lake Condah. Melbourne, Hawthorn Press, 1970. 120 p. illus. 23 cm. Includes bibliographies. [BV3660.V5M37] 70-865366 ISBN 0-7256-0005-5 4.50
1. Missions—Victoria, Australia. I. Title.

TIPPETT, Alan Richard. 266'.00996
People movements in southern Polynesia; studies in the dynamics of church-planting and growth in Tahiti, New Zealand, Tonga, and Samoa, by Alan R. Tippett. Chicago, Moody Press [1971] 288 p. illus. 22 cm. Bibliography: p. 270-279. [BV3678.5.T56] 75-155691 6.95
1. Missions—Polynesia. I. Title.

ALLEN, Roland, 1869-1947. 266.01
Missionary principles. Grand Rapids, Eerdmans [1964] 168 p. 19 cm. [BV2063.A49] 64-16594
1. Missions — Theory. I. Title.

ALLEN, Roland, 1869-1947 266.01
Missionary principles. Grand Rapids. Mich., Eerdman [c.1964] 168p. 19cm. 64-16584 1.45 pap.,
1. Missions—Theory. I. Title.

DILLISTONE, Frederick 266.01
William, 1903-
Christianity and communication. New York, Scribner [c1956] 156p. 21cm. [BV2063.D5 1956a] 57-6477
1. Missions—Theory. 2. Evangelistic work. 3. Communication. I. Title.

FIFE, Eric S. 266.01
Missions in crisis; rethinking missionary strategy [by] Eric S. Fife. Arthur F. Glasser. [Chicago] Intervarsity Pr. [c.1961] 269p. (IVP ser. in creative Christian living) Bibl. 61-15883 3.75; 2.25 pap.,
1. Missions—Theory. I. Glasser, Arthur Frederick, 1914- joint author. II. Title.

ORCHARD, Ronald Kenneth. 266.01
Missions in a time of testing; thought and practice in contemporary missions, by R. K. Orchard. Philadelphia, Westminster Press [1964] 212 p. 21 cm. Bibliographical references included in "Notes" (p. 199-210) [BV2063.O68] 65-10319
1. Missions — Theory. I. Title.

ORCHARD, Ronald Kenneth 266.01
Missions in a time of testing; thought and practice in contemporary missions. Philadelphia, Westminster [1965, c.1964] 212p. 21cm. Bibl. [BV2063.O68] 65-10319 4.50
1. Missions—Theory. I. Title.

STEWART, James Stuart, 266.01
1896-
Thine is the kingdom. New York, Scribner [1957, c1956] 74p. 23cm. [BV2063] 56-12446
1. Missions—Theory. I. Title.

STEWART, James Stuart, 266.01
1896-
Thine is the kingdom. New York, Scribner [1957, c1956] 74 p. 23 cm. [[BV2063]] 56-12446
1. Missions — Theory. I. Title.

BLESSITT, Arthur. 266'.02
Turned on to Jesus, by Arthur Blessitt, with Walter Wagner. New York, Hawthorn Books [1971] 242 p. 22 cm. [BV3775.L6B55] 76-130700 5.95
1. Evangelistic work—Los Angeles. 2. Los Angeles—Streets—Sunset Boulevard. I. Wagner, Walter, 1927- II. Title.

MATTHEWS, Desmond S. 266.02'0924
The joyful kingdom of Raj Anandpur [by] Desmond S. Matthews. Maryknoll, N. Y., Maryknoll Pubns., 1967. viii, 114p. illus., maps (on lining papers) ports. 21cm. [BV3280.R3M3] 67-15438 3.50
1. Missions — Ranchi, India (District) I. Title.

ALLISON, Carol 266.021
Adventures in other lands; brief missionary stories for boys and girls. Grand Rapids, Mich., Zondervan [c.1962] 120p. 23cm. 2.50 bds.,
I. Title.

ALLSTROM, Elizabeth C 266.021
Here and there with the Bible. Illustrated by Hertha Depper. New York, Friendship Press [1960] 127p. illus. 21cm. [BV2087.A34] 60-7450
1. Missionary stories. I. Title.

ARNOLD, Charlotte E., 266.021
1905-
Missionary stories and illustrations. Grand Rapids, Mich., Baker Bk. House, 1961. 95p. (Minister's handbk. ser.) 61-17543 1.95
1. Missionary stories. 2. Homiletical illustrations. I. Title.

CHRISTIAN, Mary, 1899- 266.021
The talking snowman. Pictures by Janet Smalley. Nashville, Convention Press [1962] 88p. illus. 21cm. (Foreign mission series) [BV2087.C5] 62-11537
1. Missions—Korea. I. Title.

EASTMAN, Frances W. 266.021
We belong together. Illustrated by Joseph Escourido. New York, Friendship Press [c.1960] 125p. illus. 21cm. 60-7446 2.95; 1.50 pap.,
1. Missionary stories. I. Title.

HILLIS, Don W comp. 266.021
Children of the world; true stories from many lands as told by missionaries of the Evangelical Alliance Mission. Grand Rapids, Zondervan Pub. House [c1963] 52 p. illus. 29 cm. [BV2087.H5] 63-15744
1. Missionary stories. I. Title.

HORNER, Esther (Daniels) 266.021
Paths that cross. Illustrated by Robert Pious. New York, Friendship Press [1959] 79p. illus. 21cm. Short stories. [BV2087.H64] 59-6045
1. Missionary stories. I. Title.

*JOHNSTON, Fran 266.021
Rendez-vous with Paris; sketches of Parisians. Chicago, Moody [c.1964] 127p. 17cm. (Colportage lib. 503) .39 pap.,
1. Missions—France. I. Title.

KELSEY, Alice (Geer) 266.021
Adventures with the Bible. Illustrated by William M. Hutchinson. New York, Friendship Press [1960] 128p. illus. 20cm. Short stories. [BV2087.K39] 60-7449
1. Missionary stories. I. Title.

*KIEFER. JAMES S. 266.021
William Carey, the shoemaker who gave India the Bible [a flash card story in five parts] by James S. and Velma B. Kiefer. Illus. by Adrian Beerhorst. Grand Rapids, Mich., Baker Bk., c.1964. unpaged (chiefly col. illus.) 33x43cm. (Baker missionary visuogram ser.) Teacher's manual giving script for the story enclosed in pocket inside front cover. 3.95, bds., plastic bdg.
1. Missionary stories. I. Kiefer, Vlema B., joint author. II. Title. III. Title: The shoemaker who gave India the Bible.

PIERCE, Robert Willard, 266.021
1914-
Orphans of the Orient: stories that will touch your heart, by Bob Pierce, as told to Dorothy C. Haskin. Grand Rapids, Zondervan Pub. House [1964] 96 p. illus. ports. 21 cm. [BV3151.P5] 64-11957
1. Missions—Asia 2. Missionary stories 3. Orphans and orphan asylums—Asia. I. Haskin, Dorothy Clark 1905- II. Title.

PIERCE, Robert Willard, 266.021
1914-
Orphans of the Orient: stories that will touch your heart, by Bob Pierce, as told to Dorothy C. Haskin. Grand Rapids, Mich., Zondervan [c.1964] 96p. illus., ports. 21cm. 64-11957 2.50 bds.,
1. Missions—Asia. 2. Missionary stories. 3. Orphans and orphan-asylums—Asia. I. Haskin, Dorothy Clark, 1905- II. Title.

TERRY, Carol 266.021
Let's go to India, 'Mukti miracles'; missionary stories for boys and girls from life at the Ramabai Mukti Mission. Grand Rapids, Mich., Zondervan [c.1964] 143p. illus., ports. 24cm. 64-11950 2.95
1. Missions—India—Juvenile literature. 2. Missionary stories. I. Title.

*WORMAN, Theresa 266.021
Missionary stories. Chicago, Moody [1965,

c.1948, 1949] 64p. 18cm. (Moody arrows, MP50) .50 pap.,
I. Title.

YOUNGBERG, Norma R. 266.021
Singer on the sand; the true story of an occurrence on the island of Great Sangir, north of the Celebes, more than a hundred years ago, Illus. by Thomas Dunbebin. Washington, D. C., Review ; Herald [c.1964] 128p. illus. 22cm. [BV2087.Y63] 64-17655 3.95
1. Missionary stories. I. Title.

CLOUD, Fred. 266.022
In step with time. Drawings by Rafael D. Palacios. New York, Friendship Press 1960] 127p. illus. 23cm. [BV2650.C55] 60-7443
1. Missions, Home. I. Title.

DUNSTAN. JOHN LESLIE, 266.022
1901-
A light to the city 150 years of the City Missionary Society of Boston. 1816-1966, by J. Leslie Dunstan. Boston, Beacon [1966] xiii, 294p. illus., ports. 21cm. Bibl. [BV2805.B7D8] 66-23785 5.00
1. City Missionary Society, Boston—Hist. I. Title.

ELIZONDO, Virgilio P. 266'.022
Christianity and culture : an introduction to pastoral theology and ministry for the bicultural community / by Virgilio P. Elizondo. Huntington, Ind. : Our Sunday Visitor, inc., c1975. 199 p. ; 21 cm. Bibliography: p. 197-199. [BV2788.M4E44] 75-20718 ISBN 0-87973-863-4 pbk. : 3.95
1. Missions to Mexican Americans. 2. Mexican Americans. 3. Pastoral theology—Catholic Church. I. Title.

GUNTHER, Peter F., ed. 266.022
The fields at home; studies in home missions. Chicago, Moody [1964, c.1963] 283p. illus. 24cm. Bibl. 63-25144 4.50
1. Missions, Home. I. Title.

HASELDEN, Kyle 266.022
Death of a myth, new locus for Spanish American faith. New York, Friendship [c.1964] 175p. 19cm. Bibl. 64-10997 1.75 pap.,
1. Missions—Spanish America. I. Title.

IMPACT, the exploration 266.022
of an idea. [Planned and conducted by Robert A. Elfers, Mae Hurley Ashworth, Bette Virginia Reed. New York, Friendship Press, 1960] 125p. illus. 21cm. [BV2765.I 5] 60-7442
1. Missions, Home—Addresses, essays, lectures. I. Elfers, Robert A.

*JOHNSON, Daniel E. 266.022
Building with buses [by] Daniel E. Johnson Grand Rapids, Baker Book House [1974] [138 p.] illus. 20 cm. [BV638.7] ISBN 0-8010-5059-6 2.95 (pbk.)
1. Rural Churches. I. Title.

LILLIE, Amy Morris 266.022
In unbroken line. Illustrated by John S. Gretzer. New York, FriendshipPress [c.1960] 135p. illus. 21cm. 60-7445 2.95; 1.50 half cloth, pap.,
1. Missions—Juvenile literature. I. Title.

LINDSEY, Hubert. 266'.022 B
Bless your dirty heart. Edited by Howard G. Earl. Plainfield, N.J., Logos International, 1973 [c1972] xi, 205 p. 21 cm. [BV3785.L47A33] 72-93081 1.95
1. Lindsey, Hubert. 2. Church work with students. 3. Evangelistic work—Berkeley, Calif. I. Title.

MILLER, Kenneth Dexter, 266.022
1887-
The people are the city; 150 years of social and religious concern in New York City, by Kenneth D. Miller, Ethel Prince Miller. New York, Macmillan [c.]1962. 258p. illus. 62-7517 3.95
1. New York City Mission Society. I. Miller, Ethel (Prince) 1893- joint author. II. Title.

NATIONAL Council of the 266.022
Churches of Christ in the United States of America. Division of Home Missions and Division of Foreign Missions,
Every tribe and tongue. Reflections from the joint assembly, Division of Home Missions; Division of Foreign Missions; National Council of the Churches of Christ. Atlantic City, N.J., Dec. 8-11, 1959. Ed. Elsie C. Pickhard, Louisa Rossiter Shotwell. [New York] Published by Friendship Press for Division of Home Missions and Division of Foreign Missions, National Council of the Churches of Christ in the U.S.A. [c.] 1960. 127p. Bibl. 60-15507 1.00 pap.,
1. Missions—Congresses. I. Pickhard, Elsie C., ed. II. Shotwell, Louisa Rossiter, ed. III. National Council of the Churches of Christ in the United States of America. Division of Foreign Mission IV. Title.

RIGGS, Stephen Return, 266'.022
1812-1883.
Tah-koo wah-kan; or, The gospel among the Dakotas. New York, Arno Press, 1972 [c1869] p. (Religion in America, series II) [E99.D1R53 1972] 78-38460 ISBN 0-405-04081-4
1. Dakota Indians—Missions. I. Title. II. Title: The gospel among the Dakotas.

SECHLER, Earl Truman, 266'.022
1890-
Our religious heritage; church history of the Ozarks, 1806-1906. Springfield, Mo., Westport Press; [stamped: c1961] 123p. 22cm. Includes bibliography. [BR540.S4] 62-1411
1. Ozark Mountains-Church history. 2. Ozark Mountains— Religion. I. Title.

SPIKE, Robert Warren. 266.022
Safe in bondage; an appraisal of the church's mission to America. New York, Friendship Press, [1960] 165 p. 20 cm. Includes bibliography. [BV2765.S7] 60-7440
1. Missions, Home. 2. U.S. — Civilization. I. Title.

SPIKE, Robert Warren 266.022
Safe in bondage; an appraisal of the church's mission to America. New York, Friendship Press [c.1960] viii, 165p. 20cm. Bibl.: p. 160-165. 60-7440 2.75 1.50 pap.,
1. Missions, Home. 2. U.S.—Civilization. I. Title.

TO win the West; 266'.022
missionary viewpoints, 1814-1815. New York, Arno Press, 1972. 52, 64, 45 p. 24 cm. (Religion in America, series II) Reprint of A correct view of that part of the United States which lies west of the Allegany Mountains, with respect to religion and morals, by J. F. Schermerhorn and S. J. Mills, first published 1814; of Report of a missionary tour through that part of the United States which lies west of the Allegany Mountains, by S. J. Mills and D. Smith, first published 1815; and of Report ... respecting the Indians inhabiting the western parts of the United States, by J. F. Schermerhorn, first published 1814. [BR540.T6 1972] 73-38467 ISBN 0-405-04091-1
1. Mississippi Valley—Church history. 2. Mississippi Valley—Description and travel. 3. Missions—Mississippi Valley. 4. Indians of North America—Mississippi Valley. I. Schermerhorn, John Freeman. A correct view of that part of the United States which lies west of the Allegany Mountains. 1972. II. Mills, Samuel John. 1783-1818. Report of a missionary tour through that part of the United States which lies west of the Allegany Mountains. 1972. III. Schermerhorn, John Freeman. Report ... respecting the Indians inhabiting the western parts of the United States. 1972.

ELLISON, Craig 266'.022'091732
W., 1944-
The urban mission, Edited by Craig W. Ellison. Grand Rapids, Eerdmans [1974] 230 p. 23 cm. Bibliography: p. 229-230. [BV2653.E43] 74-8774 ISBN 0-8028-1560-X
1. City missions. I. Title.

DWIGHT, Edwin 266'.022'0924
Welles, 1789-1841.
Memoirs of Henry Obookiah, a native of Owhyhee and a member of the Foreign Mission School, who died at Cornwall, Connecticut, February 17, 1818, aged 26 years. Honolulu [Woman's Board of Missions for the Pacific Islands] 1968. xiv, 112 p. illus., facsims., map, ports. 21 cm. "150th anniversary edition." [BV3680.H4O33 1968] 68-7300 1.50
1. Obookiah, Henry, 1792?-1818. I. Woman's Board of Missions for the Pacific Islands. II. Title.

FLETCHER, Grace 266'.022'0922
(Nies)
The bridge of love. [1st ed.] New York, Dutton, 1967. 220 p. illus., ports. 21 cm. [BX4827.H5F55] 67-11377
1. Hitotsuyanagi, Makiko, 1884- 2. Vories, William Merrell, 1880-1964. I. Title.

FRANCIS, Convers, 266'.022'0924 B
1795-1863.
Life of John Eliot, the apostle to the Indians. New York, MSS Information Corp. [1972] vi, 184 p. 21 cm. Reprint of the 1854 ed. [E78.M4E523 1972] 72-8081 ISBN 0-13-676387-1 1.95
1. Eliot, John, 1604-1690. I. Title.

HEFLEY, James C. 266'.022'0924 B
God's tribesman; the Rochunga Pudaite story [by] James and Marti Hefley. [1st ed.] Philadelphia, A. J. Holman Co. [1974] 144 p. illus. 21 cm. [BV3269.P8H43] 74-3346 ISBN 0-87981-031-9 5.95
1. Pudaite, Rochunga. I. Hefley, Marti, joint author. II. Title.

PALMER, Bernard 266'.022'0924 B
Alvin, 1914-
So restless, so lonely [by] Bernard Palmer. Minneapolis, Bethany Fellowship [1970] 160 p. 18 cm. (Dimension books) [E99.C88P34] 73-169477 0.95
1. Cree Indians—Missions. 2. Indians of North America—Canada—Missions. I. Title.

SADLER, Robert, 266'.022'0924 B
1911-
The emancipation of Robert Sadler / by Robert Sadler, with Marie Chapian. Minneapolis : Bethany Fellowship, [1975] 254 p. : ill. ; 23 cm. [BR1725.S22A33] 75-14063 ISBN 0-87123-132-8 : 5.95
1. Sadler, Robert, 1911- 2. Slavery in the United States—Personal narratives. I. Chapian, Marie, joint author. II. Title.

SALOFF-ASTAKHOFF, 266'.022'0924 B
Nikita Ignatievich, 1893-
Judith, martyred missionary of Russia; a true story, by N. I. Saloff-Astakhoff. Rev. ed. Grand Rapids, Zondervan Pub. Co. [1971, c1941] 135 p. 18 cm. [BV2623.Z9S3 1971] 78-81052 0.95
1. Converts from Judaism. I. Title.

SEAMANDS, John T. 266'.022'0922
Pioneers of the younger churches [by] John T. Seamands. Nashville, Abingdon Press [1967] 221 p. 23 cm. Bibliography: p. 215-218. [BR1702.S4] 67-22166
1. Christian biography. I. Title.

WALLIS, Ethel 266'.022'0924 B
Emily.
God speaks Navajo. [1st ed.] New York, Harper & Row [1968] x, 146 p. illus., map, ports. 22 cm. [E98.M6W27] 68-29560 4.95
1. Edgerton, Faye, 1889-1968. 2. Navaho Indians—Missions. I. Title.

BERKHOFER, Robert 266'.022'0973
F.
Salvation and the savage : an analysis of Protestant missions and American Indian response, 1787-1862 / Robert F. Berkhofer, Jr. Westport, Conn. : Greenwood Press, 1977, [c1965] p. cm. Reprint of the ed. published by University of Kentucky Press, Lexington. Includes index. Bibliography: p. [E98.M6B37 1977] 77-22857 ISBN 0-8371-9745-7 lib.bdg. : 14.50
1. Indians of North America—Missions. 2. Protestant churches—Missions—History. 3. Missions—United States—History. I. Title.

CHRISTIAN 266'.022'0973
leadership in Indian America / edited by Tom Claus and Dale W. Kietzman. Chicago : Moody Press, c1976. p. cm. Includes bibliographical references. [E59.M65C46] 77-9076 ISBN 0-8024-1417-6 pbk. : 2.50
1. Indians—Missions—Addresses, essays, lectures. 2. Christian leadership—Addresses, essays, lectures. I. Claus, Tom, 1929- II. Kietzman, Dale.

GOODYKOONTZ, Colin 266'.022'0978
Brummitt, 1885-1958.
Home missions on the American frontier, with particular reference to the American Home Missionary Society. New York, Octagon Books, 1971 [c1939] 460 p. 24 cm. "The outgrowth of a doctoral dissertation prepared at Harvard University." Bibliography: p. [429]-452. [BV2765.G62 1971] 76-120619
1. Congregational Home Missionary Society. 2. Missions—The West. 3. Missions, Home. I. Title.

LOGAN, Lorna E. 266'.022'0979461
Ventures in mission : the Cameron House story / by Lorna E. Logan. [s.l. : s.n.], c1976 (Wilson Creek, Wash. : Crawford Hobby Print Shop) 200 p. : ill. ; 20 cm. Bibliography: p. 199-200. [BV2787.L64] 76-365613
1. Donaldina Cameron House. 2. Missions to Chinese—San Francisco. I. Title.

MADDEN, Maude 266'.022'0973
(Whitmore) 1867-
When the East is in the West; Pacific coast sketches. New York, F. H. Revell Co. [San Francisco, R and E Research Associates, 1971, c1923] 153 p. 22 cm. [BV2788.J3M3 1971] 73-138053
1. Missions, Home. 2. Japanese in the United States. I. Title.

PROTESTANT 266'.022'0973
evangelism among Italians in America. New York : Arno Press, 1975. 362 p. in various pagings : ill. ; 24 cm. (The Italian American experience) [BV2788.I8P76 1975] 74-17943 ISBN 0-405-06414-4 : 17.00
1. Missions to Italians—United States—History—Sources. 2. Protestant churches—Missions—History—Sources. I. Series.
Contents omitted

WATERBURY, Maria. 266'.022'0975
Seven years among the freedmen, by M. Waterbury. 2d ed., rev. and enl. Freeport, N.Y., Books for Libraries Press, 1971 [c1890] 198 p. illus. 23 cm. (The Black heritage library collection) [E185.2.W33 1971] 79-178484 ISBN 0-8369-8934-1
1. Freedmen. 2. Missions—Southern States. I. Title.

HERSEY, April. 266'.022'09944
Hooked on God; the Wayside Chapel experiment. Melbourne, Sun Books [1969] 117 p. illus. (part col.) 19 cm. [BV2656.S9W35] 70-508416 0.95
1. King's Cross, Sydney. Wayside Chapel. I. Title.

ALLEN, Roland, 1869-1947 266.023
The spontaneous expansion of the church and the causes which hinder it. Grand Rapids, Mich., Eerdmans [c.1962] 158p. 22cm. 62-52620 1.65 pap.,
1. Missions, Foreign. I. Title.

ALLEN, Roland, 1869-1947. 266.023
The spontaneous expansion of the church and the causes which hinder it. [1st American ed.] Grand Rapids, W. B. Eerdmans Pub. Co. [1962] 158p. 22cm. [BV2063.A55 1962] 62-52620
1. Missions, Foreign. I. Title.

ALMQUIST, Arden. 266'.023
Missionary, come back. New York, World Pub. Co. [1970] xviii, 201 p. 21 cm. Includes bibliographical references. [BV2061.A44] 75-106069 5.95
1. Missions. I. Title.

AMERICAN Society of 266'.023
Missiology.
American missions in Bicentennial perspective : papers presented at the fourth annual meeting of the American Society of Missiology at Trinity Evangelical Divinity School, Deerfield, Illinois, June 18-20, 1976 / R. Pierce Beaver, editor ; contributors, Catherine L. Albanese .. [et al.]. South Pasadena, Calif. : William Carey Library, c1977. viii, 438 p. ; 23 cm. Includes bibliographies. [BV2410.A43 1977] 77-7569 ISBN 0-87808-153-4 pbk. : 8.95
1. Missions, American—History—Congresses. I. Beaver, Robert Pierce, 1906- II. Albanese, Catherine L. III. Title.

ANDERSON, Alpha E 266'.023'
(Almquist)
Pelendo, God's prophet in the Congo. Minneapolis, Free Church Publications [1964] 175 p. illus., ports., maps. 21 cm. [BV3625.C63P4] 64-2732
1. Pelendo, Isaac. 2. Missions — Congo (Leopoldville) I. Title.

ANDERSON, Gerald H., 266'.023
comp.
Mission trends no. 1; crucial issues in mission today. Edited by Gerald H.Anderson and Thomas F. Stransky. New York, Paulist Press [1974] ix, 276 p. 19 cm. Includes bibliographical references. [BV2070.A53] 74-81222 ISBN 0-8028-1483-2 2.95 (pbk.)
1. Missions—Addresses, essays, lectures. I. Stransky, Thomas F., joint comp. II. Title.

ANDERSON, Gerald H., ed. 266.023
The theology of the Christian mission. New York, McGraw-Hill [c.1961] xvii, 341p. Bibl. 60-53347 6.50
1. Missions—Theory. I. Title.

ANDERSON, Gerald H ed. 266.023
The theology of the Christian mission. [1st ed.] New York, McGraw-Hill [1961] xvii, 311p. 22cm. Bibliography: p. 315-336. [BV2063.A73] 60-53317
1. Missions—Theory. I. Title.

BARTLETT, Samuel 266'.023
Colcord, 1817-1898.
Historical sketches of the missions of the American Board. New York, Arno Press, 1972. 1 v. (various pagings) maps. 23 cm. (Religion in America, series II) Reprint of 6 sketches first published separately in 1876. Contents.Contents.—In Africa.—In China.—In India and Ceylon.—Among the North American Indians.—In the Sandwich Islands, Micronesia, and Marquesas.—In Turkey. [BV2750.B37] 78-38436 ISBN 0-405-04057-1
1. Missions. I. American Board of Commissioners for Foreign Missions. II. Title.

BEYERHAUS, Peter. 266'.023
Bangkok '73 : the beginning or end of world mission? / Peter Beyerhaus Grand Rapids : Zondervan Pub. House, [1974] 192 p. : ill. ; 21 cm. (Contemporary evangelical perspectives) Translation of Bangkok '73. Includes selections of the 8th World Missionary Conference, held in Bangkok under the auspices of the World Council of Churches, Dec. 29, 1972-Jan. 8, 1973. Includes bibliographical references. [BV2020.W6513 1973z] 74-4949 pbk. : 3.95
1. World Missionary Conference, 8th,

Bangkok, Thailand, 1972-1973. I. World Missionary Conference, 8th, Bangkok, Thailand, 1972-1973. II. Title.

BEYERHAUS, Peter. 266.023
The responsible church and the foreign mission [by] Peter Beyerhaus and Henry Lefever. Grand Rapids, W. B. Eerdmans Pub. Co. [1964] 199 p. 22 cm. Rev. and condensed version of Die Selbstandigkelt der jungen Kirchen als missionarisches Problem, by Peter Beyerhaus. Bibliography: p. 193-195. [BV2082.I5B43] 64-22027
1. Indigenous church administration. I. Lefever, Henry Charles, 1906- II. Title.

BEYERHAUS, Peter 266.023
The responsible church and the foreign mission [by] Peter Beyerhaus, Henry Lefever. Grand Rapids, Mich., Eerdmans [c.1964] 199p. 22cm. Bibl. 64-22027 1.95 pap.,
1. Indigenous church administration. I. Lefever, Henry Charles, 1906- II. Title.

BUCKINGHAM, Jamie. 266'.023
Into the glory / by Jamie Buckingham. Plainfield, N.J. : Logos International, [1974] xii, 249 p., [10] leaves of plates : ill. ; 22 cm. [BV2082.A9B8] 74-16554 ISBN 0-88270-038-3 : 5.95
1. Jungle Aviation and Radio Service. 2. Aeronautics in missionary work. I. Title.

DANKER, William J. 266.023
Two swords or none; rediscovering missions. St. Louis, Concordia [c.1964] xii, 311p. 21cm. 64-17391 4.50
1. Missions. I. Title.

DANKER, William J 266.023
Two worlds or none; rediscovering missions. Saint Louis, Concordia Pub. House [1964] xii, 311 p. 21 cm. [BV2120.D3] 64-17391
1. Missions. I. Title.

EASTMAN, Albert Theodore, 266.023
1928-
Christian responsibility in one world [by] A. Theodore Eastman. New York, Seabury Press [1965] 128 p. 20 cm. Bibliography: p. 125-128. [BV2500.E3] 64-19626
1. Anglican Communion—Missions. 2. Missions—Theory—Addresses, essays,lectures. I. Title.

EASTMAN, Albert Theodore, 266.023
1928-
Christian responsibility in one world. New York, Seabury [c.1965] 128p. 20cm. Bibl. [BV2500.E3] 64-19626 3.50
1. Anglican Communion—Missions. 2. Missions—Theory—Addresses, essays, lectures. I. Title.

FIFE, Eric S. 266.023
Man's peace, God's glory. Chicago, Inter-varsity Press [c.1961] 144p. (IVP series in creative Christian living) 61-10729 3.50
1. Missions—Theory. 2. Missions—Biblical teaching. 3. Missions, Foreign. I. Title.

FORMAN, Charles W 266'.023
The nation and the kingdom; Christian mission in the new nations. New York, Friendship Press [1964] 174 p. 19 cm. [BV2082.I5F6] 64-10996
1. Nationalism and religion. 2. Indigenous church administration. I. Title.

FORMAN, Charles W 266'.023
The nation and the kingdom; Christian mission in the new nations. New York, Friendship Press [1964] 174 p. 19 cm. Bibliography: p. [173]-174. [BV2082.I5F6] 64-10996
1. Missions. 2. Nationalism and religion. 3. Indigenous church administration. I. Title.

THE Gospel and frontier 266'.023
peoples; a report of a consultation, December 1972. Edited by R. Pierce Beaver. South Pasadena, Calif., William Carey Library [1973] vii, 405 p. illus. 23 cm. Includes bibliographical references. [BV2020.G67] 73-78228 ISBN 0-87808-124-0 2.95
1. Missions—Congresses. I. Beaver, Robert Pierce, 1906- ed.

THE Gospel and frontier 266'.023
peoples; a report of a consultation, December 1972. Edited by R. Pierce Beaver. South Pasadena, Calif., William Carey Library [1973] vii, 405 p. illus. 23 cm. Includes bibliographical references. [BV2020.G67] 73-78228 ISBN 0-87808-124-0 2.95
1. Missions—Congresses. I. Beaver, Robert Pierce, 1906- ed.

GREEN, Ernest L 266'.023'
Congo jungle preachers. Pictures by George S. Pearson. St. Louis, Berean Mission Press [1962] 64p. 18cm. [BV3625.C6G7] 62-52575
1. Clergy—Congo(Leopoldville) 2. Missions—Congo (Leopoldville) 3. Native clergy. I. Title.

HEFLEY, James C. 266'.023
Miracles in Mexico, by James C. Hefley and Hugh Steven. Chicago, Moody Press [1972] 126 p. illus. 19 cm. [F1219.3.M59H4] 76-181585 ISBN 0-8024-5410-0
1. Wycliffe Bible Translators. 2. Indians of Mexico—Missions. I. Steven, Hugh, joint author. II. Title.

HEFLEY, James C. 266'.023
Searchlight on Bible words; unique insights into Biblical word concepts illustrated by "translation treasures" from Wycliffe Bible translators. Compiled by James C. Hefley, with editorial assistance from John Beekman. Grand Rapids, Mich., Zondervan Pub. House [1972] 198 p. 22 cm. [BS450.H38] 75-183047 4.95
1. Bible—Translating. I. Title.

HILLIS, Don W. 266'.023
I don't feel called (thank the Lord!) [by] Don W. Willis. Wheaton, Ill., Tyndale House [1973] 128 p. illus. 18 cm. [BV2063.H47] 72-97651 ISBN 0-8423-1570-5 1.25
1. Missionaries—Appointment, Call and election. I. Title.

HOWARD, David M. 266'.023
Student power in world evangelism [by] David M. Howard. Downers Grove, Ill., Inter-Varsity Press [1970] 129 p. 18 cm. Includes bibliographical references. [BV2073.H69] 79-122918 ISBN 0-87784-539-5
1. Missions—Biblical teaching. 2. College students in missionary work. I. Title.

HUGHES, W., Rev., 266'.023
F.R.G.S.
Dark Africa and the way out; or, A scheme for civilizing and evangelizing the Dark Continent, by W. Hughes. New York, Negro Universities Press [1969] xiv, 155 p. illus., maps, ports. 23 cm. Reprint of the 1892 ed. [BV2093.C66H8 1969] 76-90133
1. Congo Training Institute. 2. Missions—Study and teaching. 3. Missions—Africa. I. Title.

IDOWU, E. Bolaji. 266'.023
Towards an indigenous church [by] E. Bolaji Idowu. London, Oxford University Press, 1965. 60 p. 19 cm. (Students' library 3) Based on the author's 3 broadcast talks given in 1961 on The problems of the indigenization of the church in Nigeria. [BV2082.I 5 I 3] 67-7792
1. Indigenous church administration. 2. Nigeria — Church history. 3. Christianity — Nigeria. I. The problem of the indigenization of the church in Nigeria. II. Title.

INTER-VARSITY Missionary 266'.023
Convention, 10th, Urbana, Ill., 1973.
Jesus Christ: Lord of the universe, hope of the world. Edited by David M. Howard. Downers Grove, Ill., Inter-varsity Press [1974] 252 p. 21 cm. Includes bibliographical references. [BV2391.U72 1973] 74-75454 ISBN 0-87784-763-0 2.95 (pbk.)
1. Jesus Christ—Congresses. 2. Missions—Congresses. I. Howard, David M., ed. II. Title.

ISAIS, Juan M 266'.023
The other side of the coin, by Juan M. Isais. Translated from Spanish by Elisabeth F. Isais. Grand Rapids, W. B. Erdmans Pub. Co. [1966] 104 p. 21 cm. [BV2831.I8] 66-18721
1. Missions — Latin America. I. Title.

ISAIS, Juan M. 266.023
The other side of the coin. Tr. from Spanish by Elisabeth F. Isais. Grand Rapids, Mich., Eerdmans [c.1966] 104p. 21cm. [BV2831.I8] 66-18721 1.45 pap.,
1. Missions—Latin America. I. Title.

*KUHN, Isobel 266.023
Ascent to the tribes; pioneering in North Thailand. Chicago, Moody [1967,c.1956] 315p. 17cm. (Moody diamond ed. no. 15) A China inland mission bk. 1.29 pap.,
1. Missions—Thailand. I. Title.

LYALL, Leslie T., ed. 266.023
Missionary opportunity today, a brief world survey. Chicago, Inter-varsity [c.1963] 160p. maps. 19cm Replaces the previous survey, Mission field today pub. in 1956. 63-25565 1.50 pap.,
1. Missions. I. Title.

LYALL; LESLIE T ed. 266.023
Missionary opportunity today, a brief world survey. [1st ed.] Chicago, Inter-varsity Press [1963] 160 p. maps. 19 cm. Replaces the previous survey, Mission fields today, published in 1956. [[BV2061.L9]] 63-25565
1. Missions. I. Title.

MCGAVRAN, Donald 266.023
Anderson, 1897- ed.
Church growth and Christian mission [by] Donald Anderson McGavran, ed. [others] New York, Harper [c.1965] 252p. illus. 22cm. [BV2063.M2] 65-10702 5.00

1. Missions—Theory. I. Title.

MOODY Bible Institute of 266.023
Chicago.
The indigenous church; a report from many fields. Chicago, Moody Press, c1960. 128p. 17cm. (The Moody colportage library, 398) [BV2082.I5M6] 60-4224
1. Indigenous church administration. I. Title.

MORTENSON, Vernon. 266.023
Light is sprung up. Chicago, Evangelical Alliance Mission [1965] 159 p. (chiefly illus., ports.) 28 cm. [BV2360.E73M6] 66-8250
1. Evangelical Alliance Mission. I. Title.

MOTT, John Raleigh, 266'.023
1865-1955.
The evangelization of the world in this generation. New York, Arno Press, 1972 [c1900] 245 p. 22 cm. (Religion in America, series II) Bibliography: p. 211-234. [BV2060.M84 1972] 76-38457 ISBN 0-405-04078-4
1. Missions, Foreign. I. Title.

NEVIUS, John Livingston, 266.023
1829-1893.
The planting and development of missionary churches. [4th ed.] Philadelphia, Reformed and Presbyterian Pub. Co., 1958. 92p. illus. 21cm. [BV2063.N4 1958] 59-977
1. Missions, Foreign. I. Title.

PETERSEN, William, J. 266'.023'
Another hand on mine; the story of Dr. Carl K. Becker of the Africa Inland Mission, by William J. Petersen. [1st ed.] New York, McGraw [1967] vii. 228p. illus., map. ports. 22cm. [BV3625.C63B37] 9675 67-13515 5.50
1. Becker, Carl K. 2. Missions—Congo. I. Title.

READINGS in Third World 266'.023
missions : a collection of essential documents / edited by Marlin L. Nelson. South Pasadena, Ca. : William Carey Library, [1976] p. cm. Includes index. Bibliography: p. [BV2070.R36] 76-45803 ISBN 0-87808-319-7 pbk. : 5.95
1. Missions—Addresses, essays, lectures. I. Nelson, Marlin L., 1931-

SCHWEITZER, Albert, 266'.023'
1875-1965.
More from the primeval forest. [Translated by C. T. Campion] London, A. and C. Black, 1956. 128 p. 19 cm. Translation of: Mittellungen aus Lambarene. [BV3625] 66-9815
1. Missions—Gabon. 2. Missions, Medical—Gabon. 3. Lambarene, Gabon. I. Campion, Charles Thomas, 1862- tr. II. Title.

SMITH, Eugene Lewis, 266.023
1912-
God's mission -- and ours. New York, Abingdon Press [1961] 169 p. 23 cm. [BV2061.S55] 61-5199
1. Missions, Foreign. I. Title.

SMITH, Eugene Lewis, 266.023
1912-
God's mission--and ours. Nashville, Abingdon Press [c.1961] 169p. 61-5199 3.25
1. Missions, Foreign. I. Title.

SOCIETY for the 266.023
Propagation of the Faith. U.S. Mission Secretariat.
Reappraisal: prelude to change. Edited by William J. Richardson. Maryknoll, N.Y., Maryknoll Publications, 1965. 125 p. 19 cm. (World horizon books) Papers presented at the fifteenth annual meeting of the Mission Secretariat held in Washington, D.C., Sept. 1964. [BV2160.S6 1964a] 65-17640
1. Missions — Congresses. 2. Catholic Church — Missions — Congresses. I. Richardson, William Jerome, 1929- ed. II. Title.

SOCIETY for 266.023
thePropagation of the Faith. U. S. Mission Secretariat
Reappraisal: prelude to change. Ed. by William J. Richardson. Maryknoll. N.Y., Maryknoll [c.]1965. 125p. 19cm. (World horizon bks.) Papers presented at the 15th annual meeting of the Mission Secretariat held in Washington, D.C., Sept. 1964. [BV2160.S6] 65-17640 2.25 pap.,
1. Missions—Congresses. 2. Catholic Church—Missions—Congresses. I. Richardson, William Jerome, 1929- ed. II. Title.

SOLTAU, Theodore Stanley, 266.023
1890-
Facing the field; the foreign missionary and his problems. Grand Rapids, Baker Book House, 1959. 135 p. 21 cm. [Missions, Foreign.] [BV2067.S68] 59-11728
1. Missionaries. I. Title.

STEVEN, Hugh. 266'.023
"You eat bananas!" A collection of fast-moving, contemporary missionary stories that show the high adventure of people in love with God and life. Glendale, Calif., G/L Regal Books [1971] 99 p. illus. 18 cm. [BV2087.S74] 72-161037 ISBN 0-8307-0107-9 1.25
1. Missionary stories. I. Title.

STREET, T Watson. 266.023
On the growing edge of the Church; [new dimensions in world missions, by] T. Watson Street. Richmond, John Knox Press [1965] 128 p. 21 cm. "Acknowledgements" (bibliographical): p. 124-128. [BV2063.S827] 65-12917
1. Missions — Theory. I. Title.

STREET, T. Watson 266.023
On the growing edge of the Church; [new dimensions in world missions] Richmond, Va., Knox [c.1965] 128p. 21cm. Bibl. [BV2063.S827] 65-12917 1.95 pap.,
1. Missions—Theory. I. Title.

TAYLOR, Clyde Willis, 266.023
1904-
A glimpse of world missions; an evangelical view. Chicago, Moody Press [1960] 128 p. illus. 21 cm. Includes bibliography. [BV2061.T3] 60-2491
1. Missions. I. Title.

THIESSEN, John Caldwell. 266.023
A survey of world missions. Rev. [3d] ed. Chicago, Moody Press, 1961. 544 p. 25 cm. [BV2060.T37 1961] 61-65280
1. Missions. I. Title.

TROUTMAN, Charles. 266'.023
Everything you want to know about the mission field, but are afraid you won't learn until you get there : letters to a prospective missionary / Charles Troutman. Downers Grove, Ill. : InterVarsity Press, c1976. 114 p. ; 21 cm. [BV2061.T76] 76-4738 ISBN 0-87784-717-7 pbk. : 2.95
1. Missions. 2. Missionaries—Appointment, call, and election. I. Title: Everything you want to know about the mission field ...

WALLIS, Ethel Emilia. 266.023
Two thousand tongues to go; the story of the Wycliffe Bible Translators [by] Ethel Emily Wallis and Mary Angela Bennett. Drawings by Katherine Voiglander. [1st ed.] New York, Harper [1959] 308 p. illus. 22 cm. [BV2370.W9W3] 59-7146
1. Townsend, William Cameron, 1896- 2. Wycliffe Bible Translators. 3. Missions, Foreign. I. Bennett, Mary Angels, 1906- joint author. II. Title.

WALLIS, Ethel Emilia 266.023
Two thousand tongues to go; the story of the Wycliffe Bible Translators [by] Ethel Emily Wallis, Mary Angela Bennett. Drawings by Katherine Voigtlander. New York, Harper [c.1959, 1964] 308p. illus. 22cm. 1.95 pap.,
1. Townsend. William Cameron, 1896- 2. Wycliffe Bible Translators. 3. Missions, Foreign. I. Bennett, Mary Angela, 1906- joint author. II. Title.

WALLIS, Ethel Emily. 266.023
Two thousand tongues to go; the story of the Wycliffe Bible Translators [by] Ethel Emily Wallis and Mary Angela Bennett. Drawings by Katherine Voigtlander. [1st ed.] New York, Harper [1959] 308 p. illus. 22 cm. [BV2370.W9W3] 59-7146
1. Townsend, William Cameron, 1896- 2. Wycliffe Bible Translators. 3. Missions, Foreign. I. Bennett, Mary Angela, 1906- joint author. II. Title.

WARD, William Ernest 266'.023'
Frank, 1900-
Fraser of Trinity and Achimota [by] W. E. F. Ward. [Accra?] Ghana Universities Press; [sole distributors outside Ghana, Oxford University Press, London] 1965. vii, 328 p. ports. 23 cm. [BV3625.G62F79] 65-2962
1. Fraser, Alexander Garden, 1873-1962. I. Title.

WENZEL, Kristen. 266'.023
Clergymen's attitudes toward Black Africa; role of religious beliefs in shaping them. Washington, Center for Applied Research in the Apostolate, 1971. 183 p. facsims., forms. 23 cm. Bibliography: p. [171]-183. [BR569.W44] 70-28402
1. Clergy—New York (City) 2. Missions—Africa, Sub-Saharan. I. Center for Applied Research in the Apostolate, Washington, D.C. II. Title.

ANDERSON, Rufus, 266'.023'01
1796-1880.
To advance the Gospel; selections from the writings of Rufus Anderson. Edited with an introd. by R. Pierce Beaver. Grand Rapids, Eerdmans [1967] 225 p. 24 cm. "The literary works of Rufus Anderson": p. 39-44. Bibliographical footnotes. [BV2063.A75] 66-22949
1. Missions—Theory—Addresses, essays,

lectures. I. Beaver, Robert Pierce, 1906- ed. II. Title.

MISSIONARY 266'.023'02581
Information Bureau.
Protestant missions in Brasil (sic); MIB/MARC directory of non-Catholic Christian missionary groups. [Monrovia, Calif., Missions Advanced Research & Communication Center] 1968. 24 p. 22 cm. Cover title. [BV2853.B6M54] 73-172214
1. Missions—Brazil—Directories. 2. Protestant churches—Missions—Directories. I. Missions Advanced Research and Communication Center. II. Title. III. Title: MIB/MARC directory of non-Catholic Christian missionary groups.

PHILLIPS, Clifton 266'.023'06273
Jackson.
Protestant America and the pagan world: the first half century of the American Board of Commissioners for Foreign Missions, 1810-1860. [Cambridge, Mass.] East Asian Research Center, Harvard University; distributed by Harvard University Press, 1969 [c1968] viii, 370 p. map. 28 cm. (Harvard East Asian monographs, 32) Thesis—Harvard, 1954. Bibliography: p. [322]-360. [BV2360.A5P48] 70-82303
1. American Board of Commissioners for Foreign Missions. I. Title. II. Series.

PIERCE, Robert Willard, 266.02307
1914-
Emphasizing missions in the local church, by Bob Pierce. Research by Dorothy C. Haskin. Grand Rapids, Zondervan Pub. House [1964] 120 p. illus., group port. 21 cm. Bibliography: p. 112-120. [BV2090.P5] 64-6551
1. Missions—Study and teaching. I. Title.

PIERCE, Robert Willard, 266.02307
1914-
Emphasizing missions in the local church. Research by Dorothy C. Haskin. Grand Rapids, Mich., Zondervan [c.1964] 120p. illus., group port. 21cm. Bibl. 64-6551 2.50 bds.,
1. Missions—Study and teaching. I. Title.

CLARK, Dennis E. 266'.023'091724
The Third World and mission [by] Dennis E. Clark. With a foreword by Paul S. Rees. Waco, Tex., Word Books [1971] 129 p. 23 cm. Includes bibliographical references. [BV2061.C57] 72-134942 3.95
1. Missions. 2. Church and underdeveloped areas. I. Title.

MARSH, Charles 266'.023'0917671
R.
Share your faith with a Muslim / by Charles R. Marsh. Chicago : Moody Press, [1975] 95 p. ; 19 cm. [BV2625.M34] 75-15883 ISBN 0-8024-7900-6 pbk. : 1.95
1. Missions to Muslims. I. Title.

ADVENTURES of a 266'.023'0924 B
missionary; or, Rivers of water in a dry place; being an account of the introduction of the Gospel of Jesus into South Africa and of Mr. Moffat's missionary travels and labors. New York, Carlton & Porter. [n.d.] Miami, Fla., Mnemosyne Pub. Co. [1969] 295 p. illus. 23 cm. Recounts the part played by the nineteenth century English missionary, Robert Moffat, in introducing the Gospel to South Africa. [BV3557.M7A65] 92 70-89387
1. Moffat, Robert, 1795-1883—Juvenile literature. 2. Missions—Africa, South—Juvenile literature. 3. Missionary stories.

AYLWARD, Gladys. 266'.023'0924 B
The small woman of the Inn of the Sixth Happiness, by Gladys Aylward as told to Christine Hunter. Chicago, Moody Press [1970] 153 p. 22 cm. [BV3427.A9A32] 79-104818 3.95
I. Hunter, Christine, joint author. II. Title.

BALLARD, Jerry. 266'.023'0924 B
Never say can't. [1st ed.] Carol Stream, Ill., Creation House [1971] 172 p. illus. 23 cm. [BX6379.W54B34] 72-200870 4.95
1. Willey, Thomas H., 1898-1968. I. Title.

BENSON, David V. 266'.023'0924 B
Miracle in Moscow, by David Benson. Santa Barbara, Calif., Miracle Publications, c1973. xiii, 290 p. illus. 19 cm. [BV3785.B42A35] 74-158968
1. Benson, David V. 2. Evangelistic work—Russia. I. Title.

BENSON, David V. 266'.023'0924 B
Miracle in Moscow / David Benson ; foreword by Harold John Ockenga. Glendale, Calif. : G/L Regal Books, c1975. 303 p. : ill. ; 20 cm. [BV3785.B42A35 1975] 74-32322 ISBN 0-8307-0351-9 pbk. : 2.95
1. Benson, David V. 2. Evangelistic work—Russia. I. Title.

BOCK, Valerie. 266'.023'0924 B
P.S. Please save the stamps / [by] Val Bock. London : Coverdale House, 1976. 128 p. ; 18 cm. [BV3680.N52B623] 77-353518 ISBN 0-902088-89-0 : £0.85
1. Bock, Valerie. 2. Missionaries—Papua New Guinea—Biography. 3. Missionaries—Australia—Biography. 4. Missions—Papua New Guinea. I. Title.

BRISTER, Elaine 266'.023'0922 B
H.
The joy of discovery / Elaine H. Brister. Nashville : Broadman Press, c1976. 153 p., [2] leaves of plates : ports. ; 20 cm. Bibliography: p. [iv] [BV3703.B74] 76-21567 ISBN 0-8054-7217-7 bds. : 3.95
1. Missionaries, Women—Biography. I. Title.

BULL, Geoffrey 266'.023'0924 B
T., 1921-
When iron gates yield / Geoffrey T. Bull. [1st ed. reprinted]. London : Pickering and Inglis, 1976. 254 p. : maps ; 18 cm. [BV3427.B79A3 1976] 77-367631 ISBN 0-7208-0385-3 : £0.90
1. Bull, Geoffrey T., 1921- 2. Missionaries—Tibet—Biography. 3. Missionaries—England—Biography. 4. Missions—Tibet. I. Title.

BURGESS, Alan. 266'.023'0924 B
Daylight must come; the story of a courageous woman doctor in the Congo. New York, Delacorte Press [1975, c1974] vi, 297 p. illus. 22 cm. [BV3625.C63R633 1975] 74-5479 ISBN 0-440-03365-9 6.95
1. Roseveare, Helen. I. Title.

BURGESS, Alan. 266'.023'0924 B
Daylight must come : the story of a courageous woman doctor in the Congo / Alan Burgess. Boston : G. K. Hall, 1975, c1974. 520 p. ; 25 cm. Originally published under title: Hostage. Large print ed. [BV3625.C63R633 1975b] 75-6727 ISBN 0-8161-6281-6 lib.bdg. : 12.95
1. Roseveare, Helen. 2. Sight-saving books. I. Title.

CARLYLE, Gavin. 266'.023'0924
Life and work of the Rev. William Wingate, missionary to the Jews. London, A. Holness [19 --] 299 p. illus. 20 cm. [BV2622.W5C3] 63-45578
1. Wingate, William, 1808-1899. 2. Missions — Jews. 3. Missions — Hungary. I. Title.

CATO, Nancy. 266'.023'0924 B
Mister Maloga : Daniel Matthews and his mission, Murray River, 1864-1902 / [by] Nancy Cato. St. Lucia, Q. : University of Queensland Press, 1976. xiv, 422 p. : ill. ; 23 cm. Includes index. Bibliography: p. [403]-408. [BV3667.M34C37] 77-359982 ISBN 0-7022-1110-9 : 22.80
1. Matthews, Daniel, 1837-1902. 2. Missionaries—Australia—New South Wales—Biography. 3. New South Wales—Biography. 4. Missions to Australian aborigines—Australia—New South Wales. I. Title.
Available from P.Warren 1136 Fifth Ave.,New York,N.Y.10028

CATTAN, Louise 266'.023'0922 B
Armstrong.
Lamps are for lighting; the story of Helen Barrett Montgomery and Lucy Waterbury Peabody. Grand Rapids, Mich., Eerdmans [1972] 123 p. 22 cm. (Christian world mission books) Bibliography: p. 119-120. [BV2610.C37] 72-77184 ISBN 0-8028-1480-8 2.45
1. Montgomery, Helen (Barrett) 1861-1934. 2. Peabody, Lucy (McGill) Waterbury, 1861-1949. I. Title.

CLARK, Edith 266'.023'0924 B
McGill, 1882-
My friends, the Chinese : a missionary in old China / Edith McGill Clark. 1st ed. New York : Vantage Press, [1974] 121 p. : ill. ; 21 cm. Autobiographical. [BV3427.C549A35] 75-316992 ISBN 0-533-01328-3 : 5.95
1. Clark, Edith McGill, 1882- 2. Missionaries—Correspondence, reminiscences, etc. 3. Missions—China. I. Title.

COVELL, Ralph R. 266'.023'0924 B
W. A. P. Martin : pioneer of progress in China / by Ralph Covell. Grand Rapids : Eerdmans, c1977. p. cm. Bibliography: p. [BV3427.M295C68] 77-13321 ISBN 0-8028-1715-7 pbk. : 4.95
1. Martin, William Alexander Parsons, 1827-1916. 2. Missionaries—China—Biography. 3. Missionaries—United States—Biography. 4. Missions—China. I. Title.

COWIE, Vera. 266'.023'0924 B
Girl Friday to Gladys Aylward / [by] Vera Cowie. London : Lakeland, 1976. 156 p., [4] p. of plates : ports. ; 18 cm. [HV887.T28C68] 77-370365 ISBN 0-551-00763-X : £0.95
1. Aylward, Gladys. 2. Orphans and orphan asylums—Taiwan. 3. Missionaries—Biography. I. Title.

DAME, Lawrence. 266'.023'0924
Maya mission. [1st ed.] Garden City, N. Y., Doubleday, 1968. 252 p. 22 cm. [BV2836.L4D3] 67-19101
1. Legters, David. 2. Legters, Elva. 3. Missions—Mexico. 4. Indians of Mexico—Missions. I. Title.

DONOVAN, John F. 266'.023'0924
The pagoda and the cross; the life of Bishop Ford of Maryknoll [by] John F. Donovan. New York, Scribner [1967] xxvii, 223 p. illus., ports. 22 cm. [BX4705.F633D6] 67-17295
1. Ford, Francis Xavier, Bp., 1892-1952. 2. Missions—China. I. Title.

ELLIOT, 266'.023'0924 B
Elisabeth.
Twelve baskets of crumbs / Elisabeth Elliot. 1st ed. Chappaqua, N.Y. : Christian Herald House, c1976. x, 173 p. ; 21 cm. [BR1725.E46A36] 75-45855 ISBN 0-915684-01-2 : 6.95
1. Elliot, Elisabeth. I. Title.

ELLIOT, 266'.023'0924 B
Elisabeth.
Who shall ascend; the life of R. Kenneth Strachan of Costa Rica. [1st ed.] New York, Harper & Row [1968] xii, 171 p. map (on lining paper), ports. 22 cm. [BV2843.C7S75] 68-11732
1. Strachan, Robert Kenneth, 1910-1965. 2. Missions—Costa Rica. I. Title.

ELLIOTT, May. 266'.023'0924 B
Extraordinary blessings of an ordinary Christian / by May Elliott. Independence, Mo. : Herald Pub. House, [1974] 182 p. ; 21 cm. [BX8678.E43A33] 73-90493 ISBN 0-8309-0113-2 : 5.50
1. Elliott, May. I. Title.

EPPERSON, Barbara. 266'.023'0924
Out of Shango's shadow; a biography of James Tanimola Ayorinde. Nashville, Convention Press [1967] 83 p. plates (incl. ports.) 21 cm. (Foreign mission graded series) "Church study course of the Sunday School Board of the Southern Baptist Convention: This book is number 1003 in category 10, section for juniors." 67-16362
1. Ayorinde, James Tanimola, 1907- 2. Missions — Nigeria. I. Title.

ERNY, Edward. 266'.023'0922 B
No guarantee but God; the story of the founders of the Oriental Missionary Society, by Edward and Esther Erny. Greenwood, Ind., Oriental Missionary Society [1969] vii, 116 p. ports. 19 cm. Contents.Contents.—Charles Cowman.—Juji Nakada.—Ernest Kilbourne.—Lettie B. Cowman. [BV2360.O7E7] 78-16999
1. Oriental Missionary Society—Biography. I. Erny, Esther, joint author. II. Title.

FLETCHER, Jesse C. 266'.023'0924
Wimpy Harper of Africa [by] Jesse C. Fletcher. Nashville, Broadman Press [1967] 142 p. 22 cm. [BV3625.T32H338] 67-18170
1. Harper, Winfred Ozell. 2. Missions—Tanganyika. I. Title.

HAWAIIAN Mission 266'.023'0922
Children's Society, Honolulu.
Missionary album; portraits and biographical sketches of the American Protestant missionaries to the Hawaiian Islands. Enl. from the ed. of 1937. Honolulu, 1969. 222 p. illus., facsims., map, ports. 29 cm. "Sesquicentennial edition." First ed. published in 1901 under title: Portraits of American Protestant missionaries to Hawaii. Bibliography: p. 222. [BV3680.H4A2 1969] 74-82312
1. Missions—Hawaii. 2. Missionaries, American. 3. Missions—Micronesia. 4. Missions—Marquesas Islands. I. Title.

HEFLEY, James C. 266'.023'0924
Peril by choice; the story of John and Elaine Beekman, Wycliffe Bible translators in Mexico [by] James C. Hefley. Foreword by W. Cameron Townsend. Introd. by William Culbertson. Grand Rapids, Zondervan Pub. House [1968] 226 p. illus., col. map (on lining papers), ports. 23 cm. [BV2836.B4H4] 68-22837 4.95
1. Beekman, John. 2. Beekman, Elaine. 3. Missions—Mexico. 4. Indians of Mexico. I. Title.

HEFLEY, James C. 266'.023'0924 B
Uncle Cam : the story of William Cameron Townsend, founder of the Wycliffe Bible Translators and the Summer Institute of Linguistics / James & Marti Hefley ; photo editor, Cornell Capa. Waco, Tex. : Word Books, [1974] 272 p. : ports. ; 23 cm. [BV2372.T68H43] 73-91556 6.95
1. Townsend, William Cameron, 1896- 2. Wycliffe Bible Translators. 3. Summer Institute of Linguistics. I. Hefley, Marti, joint author. II. Title.

HOLT, Basil 266'.023'0924 B
Fenelon, 1902-
Greatheart of the border : a life of John Brownlee, pioneer missionary in South Africa / by Basil Holt. King William's Town, S.A. : South African Missionary Museum, 1976. ix, 147, [16] p. : ill. ; 21 cm. Includes index. Bibliography: p. [153]-[155] [BV3557.B73H64] 76-376077
1. Brownlee, John, 1791-1871. 2. Missionaries—South Africa—Biography. I. Title.

HUMPHREY, Peggy. 266'.023'0924
J. H. Ingram, missionary dean. Cleveland, Tenn., Pathway Press [c1966] 100 p. 21 cm. (Missionary series) On cover: Church of God world missions. Bibliographical references included in "References" (p. 145-158) [BX7034.Z8I53] 66-30505
1. Ingram, James Henry, 1893- I. Title.

†HUTLEY, Walter, 266'.023'0924 B
1858-1931.
The Central African diaries of Walter Hutley, 1877 to 1881 / edited by James B. Wolf. [Brookline, Mass.] : African Studies Center, Boston University, 1976. xiv, 299 p. ; 23 cm. (African historical documents series ; no. 4) Bibliography: p. 297-299. [DT351.H87 1976] 77-152578 8.00
1. Hutley, Walter, 1858-1931. 2. London Missionary Society. 3. Africa, Central—Description and travel. 4. Missionaries—Tanzania—Ujiji—Biography. 5. Missionaries—England—Biography. 6. Missions—Tanzania—Ujiji. 7. Ujiji, Tanzania—History—Sources. I. Title. II. Series.

IGLESIAS, 266'.023'0924 B
Margaret G.
Messenger to the golden people; the story of Lonnie Iglesias [by] Margaret G. Iglesias. Nashville, Broadman Press [1967] 64 p. illus., group ports. 19 cm. [BV2843.P4I37] 68-12319
1. Iglesias, Lonnie, d. 1964. I. Title.

JENKINS, David. 266'.023'0922
They led the way: Christian pioneers of central Africa [by] David Jenkins & Dorothy Stebbing. Cape Town, London, Oxford U.P., 1966. [7], 80 p. illus. (Incl. ports.) 19 cm. 64/- [BV3625.R5J4] 67-87883
1. Missions—Rhodesia. I. Stebbing, Dorothy, joint author. II. Title.

JENKINS, David 266'.023'0922
Ernest.
They led the way: Christian pioneers of central Africa [by] David Jenkins & Dorothy Stebbing. Cape Town, London, Oxford U.P., 1966. [7], 80 p. illus. (incl. ports.). 19 cm. [BV3625.R5J4] 67-87883
1. Missions—Rhodesia. I. Stebbing, Dorothy, joint author. II. Title.

JOHNSON, Jean Dye. 266.0230922
God planted five seeds. [1st ed.] New York, Harper & Row [1966] vi, 213 p. illus., map (on lining papers) ports. 22 cm. [F3319.1.C5J6] 66-20779
1. Indians of South America—Bolivia. 2. Indians of South America—Missions. . 3. New Tribes Mission, Chicago. 4. Missions—Chiquitos, Bolivia (Province) I. Title.

JOHNSON, William 266'.023'0924 B
Augustine Bernard, d.1823-
Africa's Mountain Valley; or, The church of Regent's Town, West Africa. Freeport, N.Y., Books for Libraries Press, 1972. vi, 272 p. illus. 22 cm. (The Black heritage library collection) Reprint of the 1856 ed. "Greater part of the materials for the present volume will be found in ... The memoir of the Rev. W. A. B. Johnson [compiled by R. B. Seeley]" [BV3625.S5J58 1972] 72-3995 ISBN 0-8369-9098-6
I. Seeley, Robert Benton, 1798-1886. A memoir of the Rev. W. A. B. Johnson. II. Title. III. Series.

JOHNSON, William 266'.023'0924 B
Augustine Bernard, d.1823-
Africa's Mountain Valley; or, The church of Regent's Town, West Africa. Freeport, N.Y., Books for Libraries Press, 1972. vi, 272 p. illus. 22 cm. (The Black heritage library collection) Reprint of the 1856 ed. "Greater part of the materials for the present volume will be found in ... The memoir of the Rev. W. A. B. Johnson [compiled by R. B. Seeley]" [BV3625.S5J58 1972] 72-3995 ISBN 0-8369-9098-6 13.00
I. Seeley, Robert Benton, 1798-1886. A memoir of the Rev. W. A. B. Johnson. II. Title. III. Series.

JOHNSTON, Fran. 266'.023'0924
More oceans to cross. Chicago, Moody Press [1967] 157 p. 22 cm. [BR1725.J64A3] 67-9298
I. Title.

KEMP, Clarence E. 266'.023'0924
It's a long trip from Shinglehouse to Angmagsalik, by Clarence E. Kemp, Jr. Forward by J. F. Rodriguez. Editings by Freda Hark, Betty Kemp [and] Mary Anne Measer. 1st ed. Lancaster, N.Y., [1969] 114 p. illus., facsims., ports. 24 cm. Title on spine: Shinglehouse to Angmagsalik. Autobiographical. [BX6495.K357A3] 79-10955
I. Title. II. Title: Shinglehouse to Angmagsalik.

LAIRD, Margaret Nicholl. 266'.023'0924 B
They called me Mama / by Margaret Nicholl Laird, with Phil Landrum. Chicago : Moody Press, [1975] 185 p. ; 22 cm. [BV3625.C42L345] 75-15885 ISBN 0-8024-8683-5 pbk. 2.95
1. Laird, Margaret Nicholl. 2. Missions—Central African Republic. I. Landrum, Phil, joint author. II. Title.

LANGMORE, Diane. 266'.023'0924 B
Tamate, a king : James Chalmers in New Guinea, 1877-1901 / [by] Diane Langmore. Carlton, Vic. : Melbourne University Press, 1974. xv, 169 p., [4] leaves of plates : ill. ; 23 cm. Includes index. Bibliography: p. 159-164. [DU740.72.C48L36] 75-308804 ISBN 0-522-84079-5 : 17.80
1. Chalmers, James, 1841-1901. I. Title.
Distributed by International Scholarly Book Services, Beaverton, Or.

LORD, Donald C. 266'.023'0924 B
Mo Bradley and Thailand, by Donald C. Lord. Grand Rapids, Eerdmans [1969] 227 p. 20 cm. (A Christian world mission book) Bibliography: p. 214-220. [BV3317.B7L6] 68-28852 3.95
1. Bradley, Dan Beach, 1804-1873. 2. Missions—Thailand. I. Title.

LOVESTRAND, Harold 266'.023'0924
Hostage in Djakarta. Chicago, Moody [1967] 215p. illus., maps (on lining papers), ports. 22cm. [BV3342.L6A3] 67-17724 3.95
1. Missions—Indonesia. I. Title.

LOVESTRAND, Harold. 266'.023'0924
Hostage in Djakarta. Chicago, Moody Press [1967] 215 p. illus., maps (on lining papers), ports. 22 cm. [BV3342.L6A3] 67-17724
1. Missions — Indonesia. I. Title.

LUDWIG, Charles, 1918- 266'.023'0924 B
Mama was a missionary. Grand Rapids, Zondervan Pub. House [1970, c1963] 192 p. illus., ports. 21 cm. (A Zondervan paperback) [BV3625.K42L8 1970] 77-133354 0.95
1. Ludwig, Twyla I., 1890-1960. 2. Missions—Kenya. I. Title.

LYMAN, Sarah Joiner, 1805-1885. 266'.023'0924
Sarah Joiner Lyman of Hawaii—her own story. Compiled from the journal and letters of Sarah Joiner Lyman by Margaret Greer Martin. [Hilo, Hawaii, Lyman House Memorial Museum, 1970] 201 p. illus., ports. 23 cm. [BV3680.H4L83] 78-12188
1. Missions—Hawaii. I. Martin, Margaret Greer. II. Title.

LYNCH-WATSON, Janet. 266'.023'0924 B
The saffron robe : a life of Sadhu Sundar Singh / by Janet Lynch-Watson. Grand Rapids, Mich. : Zondervan Pub. House, 1976, c1975. 157 p. ; 18 cm. Reprint of the ed. published by Hodder and Stoughton, London, in series: Hodder Christian paperbacks. [BV5095.S5L9 1976] 76-44813 pbk. : 1.75
1. Singh, Sundar, 1889- 2. Christian biography—India. I. Title.

MATHEWS, Winifred, 1894- 266'.023'0922 B
Dauntless women; stories of pioneer wives. Illus. by Rafael Palacios. Freeport, N.Y., Books for Libraries Press [1970, c1947] 164 p. illus. 23 cm. (Biography index reprint series) Contents.Contents.—Ann Judson, comrade of an ambassador in chains.—Mary Moffat, mother of the tribe.—Mary Livingstone, "the main spoke in my wheel."—Christina Coillard, home-maker in the wagon.—Mary Williams, friend of the island women.—Agnes Watt, no ordinary woman.—Lillias Underwood, she followed "a red-maned star." [BV3703.M3 1970] 70-126325
1. Woman—Biography. 2. Missionaries. I. Title.

MEYERS, Robert Rex, 1923- 266'.023'0924
George Borrow: God's picaro, by Robert Meyers. Wichita, Kan., Wichita State University, 1969. 9 p. 23 cm. (University studies, no. 78) (Wichita State University bulletin, v. 45, no. 1.) Includes bibliographical references. [AS36.W62 no. 78] 74-12101
1. Borrow, George Henry, 1803-1881. I. Title. II. Series: Kansas. State University, Wichita. University studies, no. 78

MOFFAT, John Smith, 1835-1918. 266'.023'0924 B
John Smith Moffat, C.M.G. missionary; a memoir [compiled] by his son Robert U. Moffat. New York, Negro Universities Press [1969] xix, 388 p. illus., map, ports. 23 cm. Reprint of the 1921 ed. [DT776.M7A5 1969] 73-88443
I. Moffat, Robert Unwin, 1866-1947, comp.

MOREA, Andre. 266'.023'0924 B
Surrounded by angels : the miraculous story of a Bible courier behind the Iron Curtain / Andre Morea. 1st U.S. ed. Minneapolis : Bethany Fellowship, 1976. 157 p. ; 18 cm. (Dimension books) [BV2369.5.E852M67 1976] 76-22930 ISBN 0-87123-503-X pbk. : 1.95
1. Morea, Andre. 2. Bible—Publication and distribution—Europe, Eastern. I. Title.

MORRISON, James Horne, 1872- 266'.023'0922 B
The missionary heroes of Africa, by J. H. Morrison. New York, Negro Universities Press [1969] xii, 267 p. map. 23 cm. Reprint of the 1922 ed. [BV3503.M6 1969] 79-89010
1. Missionaries. 2. Missions—Africa. I. Title.

MOSS, Charles Frederick Arrowsmith. 266'.023'0924 B
A pioneer in Madagascar, Joseph Pearse of the L.M.S., by C. F. A. Moss. New York, Negro Universities Press [1969] xvi, 261 p. illus., map, ports. 23 cm. Reprint of the 1913 ed. [BV3625.M22P4 1969] 70-98738
1. Pearse, Joseph, 1837-1911. 2. Missions—Madagascar. I. Title.

MUELLER, John Theodore, 1885- 266'.023'0922 B
Great missionaries to China. Freeport, N.Y., Books for Libraries Press [1972, c1947] 135 p. 23 cm. (Biography index reprint series) [BV3427.A1M8 1972] 73-38329 ISBN 0-8369-8124-3
1. Missions—China. 2. Missionaries. I. Title.

MUELLER, John Theodore, 1885- 266'.023'0922 B
Great missionaries to the Orient. Freeport, N.Y., Books for Libraries Press [1972, c1948] 133 p. 23 cm. (Biography index reprint series) Bibliography: p. 133. [BV3150.M8 1972] 78-38330 ISBN 0-8369-8125-1
1. Missions—Asia. 2. Missionaries. I. Title.

PERL, Ruth June. 266'.023'0924
Thy people shall be my people. Foreword by Charles Lee Feinberg. Minneapolis, Bethany Fellowship [1968] 249 p. 21 cm. [BV2622.P4A3] 68-5994
1. Missions to Jews—Israel. 2. Missions—Israel. I. Title.

PRICHARD, Marianna (Nugent) 266.023'0922
Ten against the storm, by Marianna and Norman Prichard. Illus. by Mine Okubo. Rev. ed. New York, Friendship [1967] viii, 165p. illus. 21cm. [BV3457.A1P7] 37-10280 1.75 pap.,
1. Christians in Japan. I. Prichard, Norman Young, joint author. II. Title.

ROBERTS, W. Dayton. 266'.023'0924 B
Strachan of Costa Rica; missionary insights and strategies, by W. Dayton Roberts. Grand Rapids [1971] 187 p. 21 cm. (Christian world mission books) [BV2843.C7S78] 78-163657 2.95
1. Strachan, Robert Kenneth, 1910-1965. I. Title.

ROBINSON, Virgil E 266.0230922 (B)
The Judsons of Burma, by Virgil E. Robinson. Washington, Review and Herald Pub. Association [1966] 94 p. 22 cm [BV3271.J7R6] 66-16551
1. Judson, Adoniram, 1788-1850. 2. Judson, Ann (Hasseltine) 1780-1826. I. Title.

ROBINSON, Virgil E. 266.0230922 (B)
The Judsons of Burma, by Virgil E. Robinson. Washington, Review & Herald [1966] 94p. 22cm. udson, Ann (Hasseltine) 1789-1826. [BV3271.J7R6] 66-16551 2.75
1. Judson, Adoniram, 1788-1850. I. Title. II. Series.

ROBINSON, Virgil E. 266.0230924
The restless missionary [by] Virgil Robinson. Pencil drawings by Fred Collins. Washington. Review & Herald [c.1963] 93p. illus. port. 22cm. [BV3150.W7R6] 66-19419 3.50
1. Wolff, Joseph, 1795-1862. I. Title.

ROBINSON, Virgil E. 266.0230924
The restless missionary [by] Virgil E. Robinson. Pencil drawings by Fred Collins. Washington, Review and Herald Pub. Association [c1963] 93 p. illus., port. 22 cm. [BV3150.W7R6] 66-19419
1. Wolff, Joseph, 1795-1862. I. Title.

ROHRER, Norman B. 266'.023'0924 B
Peter Dynamite, "twice-born" Russian : the story of Peter Deyneka, missionary to the Russian world / Norman B. Rohrer and Peter Deyneka, Jr. Grand Rapids : Baker Book House, c1975. 192 p. : ill. ; 21 cm. [B3785.D45R64] 76-354201 ISBN 0-8010-7639-0 pbk. : 3.95
1. Deyneka, Peter. I. Deyneka, Peter, 1931- joint author. II. Title.

ROSEVEARE, Helen. 266'.023'0924
Give me this mountain; an autobiography. [1st ed.] Grand Rapids, Eerdmans [1966] 166 p. 18 cm. [BV3625.C63R643] 67-3299
1. Missions—Congo. I. Title.

ROSSI, Sanna Barlow. 266'.023'0924 B
God's city in the jungle / Sanna Barlow Rossi. Wheaton, Ill. : Tyndale House Publishers, 1975. 156 p. : ill. ; 22 cm. [F2520.1.T925R67] 74-21968 ISBN 0-8423-1070-3 : 2.95
1. Anderson, Lambert. 2. Wycliffe Bible Translators. 3. Tucuna Indians—Missions. I. Title.

RUFFO, Vinnie. 266'.023'0922
Behind barbed wire. Mountain View, Calif., Pacific Press Pub. Association [1967] v, 121 p. 22 cm. [BV3427.O68R8] 67-27708
1. Oss, John. 2. Oss, Olga Bertine (Osnes) 1897- I. Title.

STEVEN, Hugh. 266'.023'0922 B
The measure of greatness. Old Tappan, N.J., F. H. Revell Co. [1973] 158 p. 21 cm. [BV3680.N52S88] 73-14950 ISBN 0-8007-0634-X 2.50 (pbk.)
1. Steinkraus, Walter. 2. Steinkraus, LaVonne. 3. Missions—New Guinea. I. Title.

THOMPSON, Phyllis. 266'.023'0922 B
Minka and Margaret : the heroic story of two women missionaries martyred by bandits / by Phyllis Thompson. London : Hodder and Stoughton : Overseas Missionary Fellowship, 1976. 188 p. ; 18 cm. (Hodder Christian paperbacks) [R722.3.T49] 77-371656 ISBN 0-340-20741-8 : £0.80
1. Hanskamp, Minka, 1922-1974. 2. Morgan, Margaret, 1934-1974. 3. Missionaries, Medical—Thailand—Biography. 4. Kidnapping—Thailand. I. Title.

THOMPSON, Phyllis. 266'.023'0924 B
A transparent woman; the compelling story of Gladys Aylward, "the small woman" of China whose life was portrayed in "The Inn of the Sixth Happiness." Grand Rapids, Zondervan Pub. House [1972, c1971] 190 p. illus. 18 cm. (Zondervan books) First published in 1971 under title: A London sparrow. [BV3427.A9T48 1972] 72-83876 1.25 (pbk)
1. Aylward, Gladys. I. Title.

TOWNSEND, William Cameron, 1896- 266'.023'0924 B
Remember all the way / by William Cameron Townsend, Richard S. Pittman. Huntington Beach, Calif. : Wycliffe Bible Translators, c1975. 144 p. ; 22 cm. Includes bibliographical references. [BV2372.T68A36] 75-329081
1. Townsend, William Cameron, 1896- I. Pittman, Richard Saunders, 1915- joint author. II. Title.

WAGNER, C. Peter. 266'.023'0924 B
Defeat of the bird god / C. Peter Wagner. South Pasadena, Calif. : William Carey Library, c1975. 256 p. : ill. ; 22 cm. [F3320.2.Z3W3 1975] 75-331578 ISBN 0-87808-721-4 pbk. : 4.95
1. Pencille, Bill. 2. Zamucoan Indians—Missions. 3. Indians of South America—Bolivia—Missions. I. Title.

WAGNER, C. Peter. 266'.023'0924
Defeat of the bird god; the story of missionary Bill Pencille, who risked his life to reach the Ayores of Bolivia [by] C. Peter Wagner. Foreword by Paul S. Rees. Grand Rapids, Zondervan Pub. House [1967] 256 p. illus., map (on lining papers), ports. 23 cm. [F3320.2.Z3W3] 67-11615
1. Pencille, Bill. 2. Zamucoan Indians—Missions. 3. Santa Cruz, Bolivia (Dept.)—Description and travel. I. Title.

WENTWORTH, Elaine. 266'.023'0924 B
Mission to Metlakatla. Boston, Houghton Mifflin, 1968. 194 p. illus., map. 22 cm. Records the missionary work of a nineteenth-century Englishman, who was sent to civilize the Tsimshians, a savage tribe of Alaskan Indians, and who spent a lifetime protecting and helping his adopted people in their endeavor to adjust to the modern world. [E99.T8W54] 92 AC 68
1. Duncan, William, 1832-1918. 2. Tsimshian Indians—Missions. 3. Metlakahtla, Alaska. I. Title.

WILSON, Dorothy Clarke. 266'.023'0924 B
Climb every mountain : the story of Granny Brand / by Dorothy Clarke Wilson. London : Hodder and Stoughton, 1976. 222 p., [8] p. of plates : ill., map, ports. ; 21 cm. American ed. published under title: Granny Brand, her story. [BV3269.B69W54 1976b] 77-356901 ISBN 0-340-20603-9 : £4.50
1. Brand, Evelyn Constance, 1879-1974. 2. Missionaries—India—South India—Biography. 3. Missionaries—England—Biography. I. Title.

WILSON, Dorothy Clarke. 266'.023'0924 B
Granny Brand, her story / Dorothy Clarke Wilson. 1st ed. Chappaqua, N.Y. : Christian Herald Books, c1976. 222 p., [4] leaves of plates : ill. ; 22 cm. [BV3269.B69W54 1976] 76-16721 ISBN 0-915684-11-X : 6.95
1. Brand, Evelyn Constance, 1879-1974. 2. Missionaries—India—South India—Biography. 3. Missionaries—England—Biography. I. Title.

DURASOFF, Steve. 266'.023'0947
Pentecost behind the Iron Curtain. Plainfield, N.J., Logos International, 1972. x, 128 p. 21 cm. [BX8762.Z7E82] 72-93080 ISBN 0-88270-018-9 1.50
1. Pentecostal churches—Europe, Eastern. I. Title.

BARR, Pat, 1934- 266'.023'0951
To China with love; the lives and times of Protestant missionaries in China, 1860-1900. [1st ed. in the U.S.A.] Garden City, N.Y., Doubleday, 1973 [c1972] xiii, 210 p. illus. 22 cm. Bibliography: p. 200-203. [BV3415.2.B37 1973] 72-84888 ISBN 0-385-03864-X 7.95
1. Missions—China. 2. Missionaries, British. 3. Protestant churches—Missions. I. Title.

BILLINGS, Peggy. 266'.023'0959
In no one's pocket. Illustrated by Al Nagy. New York, Friendship Press [1968] 159 p. illus. 19 cm. Bibliography: p. 159. [BR1178.B5] 68-14060
1. Christianity—Asia, Southeastern. I. Title.

CARLSON, Ellsworth C. 266'.023'0951245
The Foochow missionaries, 1847-1880 / by Ellsworth C. Carlson Cambridge : East Asian Research Center, Harvard University : distributed by Harvard University Press, 1974. 259 p. ; 27 cm. (Harvard East Asian monographs ; 51) Includes index. Bibliography: p. [243]-251. [BV3425.F66C37] 72-97832
1. Missions—Foochow, China. 2. Protestant churches—Missions. I. Title. II. Series.

FAIRBANK, John King, 1907- 266'.023'0951
The missionary enterprise in China and America / edited and with an introd. by John K. Fairbank. Cambridge : Harvard University Press, 1974. 442 p. ; 25 cm. (Harvard studies in American-East Asian relations ; 6) Includes bibliographical references and index. [BV3415.2.F34] 74-82191 ISBN 0-674-57655-1 : 15.00
1. Missions—China. 2. Protestant churches—Missions. 3. Missions, American. I. Title. II. Series.

FRANCIS, Mabel. 266'.023'0952
One shall chase a thousand, by Mabel Francis with Gerald B. Smith. Harrisburg, Pa., Christian Publications [1968] 119 p. illus. 21 cm. [BV3457.F7A3] 68-3791
1. Missions—Japan. I. Smith, Gerald B. II. Title.

HAAS, Harry, 1925- 266'.023'095
Christianity in the Asian revolution. Baltimore, Helicon [1966] x, 116 p. 18 cm. (A Helicon paperbook) [BV3151.H24] 66-24851
1. Missions—Asia. 2. Christianity—Asia. I. Title.

HEFLEY, James C. 266'.023'09597
By life or by death; the dramatic story of the valiant missionary martyrs who have lived and died for Christ in war-torn Viet Nam [by] James C. Hefley. [1st ed.] Grand Rapids, Mich., Zondervan Pub. House [1969] 208 p. illus., maps, ports. 23 cm. Bibliographical footnotes. [BV3325.A6H4] 68-58932 4.95
1. Missions—Vietnam. 2. Christian and Missionary Alliance—Missions. 3. Missionaries. I. Title.

HEFLEY, James C. 266'.023'09597
No time for tombstones; life and death in the Vietnamese jungle [by] James and Marti Hefley. Wheaton, Ill., Tyndale House [1974] vii, 125 p. illus. 21 cm. [BV3325.A6H43 1974] 74-80772 ISBN 0-8423-4719-4 2.95 (pbk.)
1. Missions—Vietnam. 2. Persecution—

Vietnam. I. Hefley, Marti, joint author. II. Title.

HIRSCHMANN, Maria Anne. 266'.023'095
Outposts of love / Maria Anne Hirschmann. Old Tappan, N.J. : Revell, c1976. p. cm. [BV2410.H54] 76-45401 ISBN 0-8007-0839-3 pbk. : 3.95
1. Hirschmann, Maria Anne. 2. Missions, American. I. Title.

HOFRENNING, Ralph W. 266'.023'0954162
On the border of Bhutan, by Ralph Hofrenning. [Remer, Minn., 1968] 33 p. illus. 22 cm. Includes music. [BV3280.A8H58] 68-3395
1. Missions—Assam. I. Title.

JONES, Philip Hanson, 1902- 266'.023'0951
The steps of a good man; a missionary's life among the mountain bandits of Southern China. [1st ed.] New York, Exposition Press [1967] 94 p. 21 cm. Autobiographical. [BV3427.J64A3] 67-1297
1. Missions—China. I. Title.

LATOURETTE, Kenneth Scott, 1884- 266'.023'0951
A history of Christian missions in China. New York, Russell & Russell [1967] xii, 930 p. fold. map. 22 cm. "First published in 1929." Bibliography: p. 845-899. [BV3415.L35] 66-24721
1. Missions—China. I. Title.

LATOURETTE, Kenneth Scott, 1884-1968. 266'.023'0951
A history of Christian missions in China. New York, Russell & Russell [1967] xii, 930 p. fold. map. 22 cm. "First published in 1929." Bibliography: p. 845-899. [BV3415.L35 1967] 66-24721
1. Missions—China. I. Title.

LEDYARD, Gleason H. 266'.023'095
Sky waves; the incredible Far East Broadcasting Company story, by Gleason H. Ledyard. Chicago, Moody Press [1968] 227 p. illus., ports. 17 cm. (Moody giants, no. 55) [BV2082.R3L4 1968] 68-3590
1. Far East Broadcasting Company. 2. Radio in missionary work. I. Title.

LOCKERBIE, Jeanette W. 266'.023'09596
When blood flows, the heart grows softer / Jeanette Lockerbie. Wheaton, Ill. : Tyndale House Publishers, 1976. xv, 217 p., [6] leaves of plates : ill. ; 21 cm. [BV3305.L6] 76-8680 ISBN 0-8423-7980-0 pbk. : 3.95
1. Missions—Cambodia. I. Title.

MOULTON, Joseph Langdon. 266'.023'0954
Faith for the future; the American Marathi Mission, India, sesquicentennial, 1963. New York, United Church Board for World Ministries [1967] xix, 228 p. illus., map, ports. 22 cm. [BV3260.A55M6] 68-902
1. American Marathi Mission. 2. Missions—India. I. Title.

MOULTON, Joseph Langdon. 266'.023'0954
Faith for the future; the American Marathi Mission, India, sesquicentennial, 1963. New York, United Church Board for World Ministries [1967] xix, 228 p. illus., map, ports. 22 cm. [BV3260.A55M6] 68-902
1. American Marathi Mission. 2. Missions—India. I. Title.

NELSON, Marlin L., 1931- 266'.023'095
The how and why of third world missions : an Asian case study / Marlin L. Nelson. South Pasadena, Calif. : William Carey Library, [1976] p. cm. Includes index. Bibliography: p. [BV3151.N44] 76-47658 ISBN 0-87808-318-9 : 5.95
1. Missions—Asia. I. Title.

RICHTER, Julius, 1862-1940. 266'.023'0956
A history of Protestant missions in the Near East. New York, AMS Press [1970] 435 p. 23 cm. A translation, with revisions, of Mission und evangelisation im Orient. Reprint of the 1910 ed. [BV3160.R513 1970] 79-133822
1. Missions—Near East. I. Title. II. Title: Protestant missions in the Near East.

ROBBINS, Nancy Estelle. 266'.023'0954
Not forgetting to sing [by] Nancy E. Robbins. Chicago, Moody Press [1968, c1967] x, 179 p. illus., ports. 22 cm. [BV3290.D6] 68-3586
1. Dohnavur Fellowship. I. Title.

SUBBAMMA, B. V. 266'.023'095484
New patterns for discipling Hindus; the next step in Andhra Pradesh, India [by] B. V. Subbamma. South Pasadena, Calif., William Carey Library [1970] xiii, 194 p. illus., maps, ports. 22 cm. Bibliography: p. 175-191. [BV3265.2.S9] 76-128755 ISBN 0-87808-306-5 3.45
1. Missions to Hindus. 2. Missions—Andhra Pradesh, India. I. Title.

TIBAWI, Abdul Latif 266.023095691
American interests in Syria, 1800-1901: a study of educational, literary and religious work, by A. L. Tibawi. Oxford, Clarendon Pr., 1966. xv, 333p. 23cm. Bibl. [BV3200.T5] 66-69456 10.10
1. Missions—Syria. I. Title.
Available from Oxford in New York.

WINTER, Ralph D., comp. 266'.023'09593
The evangelical response to Bangkok, edited by Ralph D. Winter. South Pasadena, Calif., William Carey Library [1973] vii, 153 p. 22 cm. Reports on the "Salvation today" conference, sponsored by the Commission on World Mission and Evangelism of the World Council of Churches, and held in Bangkok, Dec. 29, 1972-Jan. 12, 1973. Includes bibliographical references. [BV2020.W48] 73-80166 ISBN 0-87808-125-9 1.95 (pbk.)
1. Missions—Congresses. 2. Evangelism—Congresses. 3. Evangelicalism. I. World Council of Churches. Commission on World Mission and Evangelism. II. Title.
Contents omitted.

WULFF, Robert M. 266'.023'09593
Village of the outcasts [by] Robert M. Wulff. Foreword by Hubert H. Humphrey. [1st ed.] Garden City, N.Y., Doubleday, 1967. ix, 227 p. 22 cm. "Analysis of leprosy control methods [by] Richard S. Buker": p. 209-226. Bibliography: p. 227. [BV3315.W8] 66-15441
1. Missions—Thailand. 2. Missions to lepers—Thailand. 3. Leprosy—Thailand. I. Title.

ZWEMER, Samuel Marinus, 1867-1952. 266'.023'095
The unoccupied mission fields of Africa and Asia. Freeport, N.Y., Books for Libraries Press, 1972. p. (The Black heritage library collection) Reprint of the 1911 ed. Bibliography: p. [BV3150.Z85 1972] 72-8623 ISBN 0-8369-9197-4
1. Missions—Africa. 2. Missions—Asia. I. Title. II. Series.

ANDERSON, Susan, 1892- 266'.023'09669
May Perry of Africa. Nashville, Broadman Press [1966] 60 p. illus., ports. 19 cm. [BV3625.N6P43] 66-27945
1. Perry, May, 1890- 2. Missions—Nigeria. I. Title.

AYANDELE, Emmanuel Ayankanmi 266'.023'09669
The missionary impact on modern Nigeria, 1842-1914; a political and social analysis [by] E. A. Ayandele. [New York] Humanities [1967] xx, 393p. illus., maps, ports. 23cm. (Ibadan hist. ser.) Bibl. [BV3625.N5] 66-28225 7.50
1. Missions—Hpnigeria. I. Title.
American distributor: Humanities, New York.

BARROW, Alfred Henry. 266'.023'096652
Fifty years in Western Africa; being a record of the work of the West Indian Church on the banks of the Rio Pongo. New York, Negro Universities Press [1969] iv, 157 p. illus., map. 23 cm. Reprint of the 1900 ed. [BV3625.G814B3 1969] 79-92739
1. Missions—Guinea, French. I. Title.

CONGRESS on Africa, Atlanta, 1895. 266'.023'096
Africa and the American Negro; addresses and proceedings. Edited by J. W. E. Bowen. Miami, Fla., Mnemosyne Pub. Inc., 1969. 242 p. illus., ports. 23 cm. Reprint of the 1896 ed. "Held under the auspices of the Stewart Missionary Foundation for Africa of Gammon Theological Seminary in connection with the Cotton States and International Exposition." [BV3500.C7 1895b] 74-79020
1. Missions—Africa. 2. Missions—Congresses. 3. Negroes—Congresses. I. Gammon Theological Seminary, Atlanta. Stewart Missionary Foundation for Africa. II. Bowen, John Wesley Edward, 1855-1933. III. Title.

CRUMMEY, Donald. 266'.023'0963
Priests and politicians: Protestant and Catholic missions in Orthodox Ethiopia, 1830-1868. Oxford, Clarendon Press, 1972. xii, 176 p., 5 leaves. illus., maps, ports. 23 cm. (Oxford studies in African affairs) Based on the author's thesis, University of London. Bibliography: p. [152]-168. [BV3560.A2C78 1972] 73-158506 ISBN 0-19-821677-7 £4.00
1. Missions—Ethiopia. I. Title. II. Series.

CRUMMEY, Donald. 266'.023'0963
Priests and politicians: Protestant and Catholic missions in Orthodox Ethiopia, 1830-1868. Oxford, Clarendon Press, [1973, c1972] xii, 176 p., 5 leaves. illus., maps, ports. 23 cm. (Oxford studies in African affairs) Based on the author's thesis, University of London. Bibliography: p. [152]-168. [BV3560.A2C78 1972] 73-158506 ISBN 0-19-821677-7
1. Missions—Ethiopia. I. Title. II. Series.
Distributed by Oxford University Press, N.Y. 13.00

EKECHI, F. K. 266'.023'096694
Missionary enterprise and rivalry in Igboland, 1857-1914, [by] F. K. Ekechi. London, Cass, 1972. xv, 298, [3] p. illus., maps, ports. 23 cm. (Cass library of African studies. General studies no. 119) A revision of the author's thesis, University of Wisconsin, 1969. Bibliography: p. 277-290. [BV3630.I2E38 1972] 72-170749 2.00
1. Missions to Ibos. I. Title. II. Series.
Distributed by International Scholarly Book Service.

FORSBERG, Malcolm. 266.02309624
Last days on the Nile. [1st ed.] Philadelphia, Lippincott [1966] 216 p. fold. map. 21 cm. [BV3625.S82F6] 66-25409
1. Sudan Interior Mission. 2. Missions—Sudan. I. Title.

FRASER, Donald, 1870-1933. 266'.023'096
The future of Africa. Westport, Conn., Negro Universities Press [1970] x, 309 p. illus., maps, ports. 23 cm. Reprint of the 1911 ed. Bibliography: p. 295-303. [BV3500.F7 1970] 77-137231 ISBN 0-8371-4113-3
1. Missions—Africa—History. I. Title.

FULLER, W. Harold. 266'.023'096
Run while the sun is hot [by] W. Harold Fuller. [New York] Sudan Interior Mission [1966 or 7] 256p. illus., maps. 22cm. Bibl. [BV3500.F8] 67-27564 3.95
1. Missions—Africa. 2. Africa—Descr. & trav. I. Sudan Interior Mission. II. Title.
Publisher's address: 164 W. 74th St., New York, N. Y. 10023.

JONES, Marjorie. 266'.023'09667
Black eagle. Nashville, Convention Press [1967] 71 p. illus., map, port. 21 cm. (Foreign mission graded series, 1967) "A publication of the Foreign Mission Board". "Church study course [of the Sunday School Board of the Southern Baptist Convention] This book is number 1083 in category 10, section for Intermediates." [BV3625.G6J6] 67-19397
1. Missions—Ghana. 2. Baptists—Missions. I. Southern Baptist Convention. Foreign Mission Board. II. Southern Baptist Convention. Sunday School Board. III. Title.

MARKOWITZ, Marvin D. 266'.023'096751
Cross and sword; the political role of Christian missions in the Belgian Congo, 1908-1960 [by] Marvin D. Markowitz. Stanford, Calif., Hoover Institution Press [1973] xiv, 223 p. 29 cm. (Hoover Institution publications, 114) Bibliography: p. 195-210. [BV3625.C6M36] 75-170209 ISBN 0-8179-1141-3
1. Missions—Zaire. 2. Zaire—Politics and government. I. Title. II. Series: Stanford University. Hoover Institution on War, Revolution, and Peace. Publications, 114.

OKWUOSA, V. E. Akubueze. 266'.023'096
In the name of Christianity : the missionaries in Africa / by V. E. Akubueze Okwuosa. Philadelphia : Dorrance, c1977. 50 p. ; 22 cm. Bibliography: p. 49-50. [BV3500.O38] 77-152268 ISBN 0-8059-2420-5 : 4.50
1. Missions—Africa—Influence. 2. Missionaries—Africa. I. Title.

RANDALL, Max Ward. 266'.023'096894
Profile for victory; new proposals for missions in Zambia. South Pasadena, Calif., William Carey Library [1970] xxi, 204 p. illus., maps, port. 23 cm. A revision of the author's thesis (M.A.), Fuller Theological Seminary. Bibliography: p. 194-[202] [BV3625.R52R3 1970] 79-126077 ISBN 0-87808-403-7 3.95
1. Missions—Zambia. I. Title.

TANNER, Ralph E S 266'.023'09678
Transition in African beliefs; traditional religion and Christian change; a study in Sukumaland, Tanzania, East Africa [by] Ralph E. S. Tanner. Maryknoll, N. Y., Maryknoll Publications, 1967. xii, 256 p. 24 cm. [BV3625.T3T3] 67-21411
1. Missions—Tanzania. 2. Suku (African tribe)—Religion. I. Title.

WESTERMANN, Diedrich, 1875-1956. 266'.023'096
Africa and christianity / by Diedrich Westermann. New York : AMS Press, 1977. x, 221 p. ; 19 cm. Reprint of the 1937 ed. published by Oxford University Press, London, which was issued as Duff lectures, 1935. [BV3500.W4 1977] 74-15102 ISBN 0-404-12151-9 : 17.50
1. Missions—Africa. 2. Africa—Religion. 3. Christianity and other religions. 4. Africa—Social life and customs. I. Title. II. Series: Duff missionary lectures, 1935.

WHIRLEY, Carl F. 266'.023'096
So sure of tomorrow [by] Carl F. Whirley. Nashville, Convention Press [1967] vii, 102 p. illus., maps, ports. 19 cm. (Foreign mission graded series) [BV3500.W45] 67-19400
1. Missions—Africa. 2. Missions—Study and teaching (Secondary) I. Title.

WINNINGE, Ingrid, 1934- 266'.023'0963
The international church worker : investigations in Ethiopia / Ingrid and Carol Winninge. [Uppsala : Swedish institute of missionary research, 1976] 197 p. : ill. ; 21 cm. [BV3560.W54] 77-366090 ISBN 9-18-542401-3 : kr10.00
1. Missions—Ethiopia—Case studies. I. Winninge, Carol, 1930- joint author. II. Title.

WOLD, Joseph Conrad. 266'.023'09666
God's impatience in Liberia. Grand Rapids, W. B. Eerdmans Pub. Co. [1968] 227 p. map. 21 cm. (Church growth series) Bibliography: p. 217-221. [BV3625.L5W6] 67-19334
1. Missions—Liberia. I. Title.

GONZALEZ, Justo L. 266'.023'09729
The development of Christianity in the Latin Caribbean, by Justo L. Gonzalez. Grand Rapids, Mich., W. B. Eerdmans Pub. Co. [1969] 136 p. 20 cm. Bibliography: p. 125-129. [BV2845.2.G65] 68-54098 2.65
1. Missions—West Indies. 2. Missions, Spanish. I. Title.

LEE, Allan W. 266'.023'0972
The burro and the Bibles; and other vignettes of a summer in Mexico, by Allan W. Lee. [1st ed.] New York, Exposition Press [1968] 47 p. 22 cm. [BV2369.5.M4L4] 68-24878
1. Bible—Publication and distribution—Mexico. 2. Missions—Mexico. I. Title.

STEVEN, Hugh. 266'.023'09727
They dared to be different / [Hugh Steven]. Irvine, Calif. : Harvest House Publishers, c1976. 160 p. ; 21 cm. [F1221.T9S74] 76-42174 ISBN 0-89081-029-X pbk. : 2.95
1. Tzotzil Indians—Missions. 2. Tzotzil Indians—Social life and customs. 3. Indians of Mexico—Missions. I. Title.

COSTAS, Orlando E. 266'.023'098
Theology of the crossroads in contemporary Latin America : missiology in mainline Protestantism, 1969-1974 / door O. E. Costas. Amsterdam, [Keizersgracht 302-304] : Rodopi, 1976. xiv, 413 p. ; 23 cm. Includes index. Bibliography: p. [359]-408. [BR600.C66] 76-361930 ISBN 9-06-203259-1 pbk. : 19.25
1. Protestant churches—Latin America. 2. Missions—Theory. I. Title.
Distributed by Humanities

EDWARDS, Fred E. 266'.023'0981
The role of the faith mission; a Brazilian case study, by Fred E. Edwards. South Pasadena, Calif., William Carey Library [1971] xxiii, 139 p. illus., maps, port. 22 cm. Bibliography: p. 129-139. [BV2853.B6E39] 79-152406 ISBN 0-87808-406-1 3.45
1. Missions—Brazil. I. Title.

HEFLEY, James C. 266'.023'0985
Dawn over Amazonia; the story of Wycliffe Bible Translators in Peru [by] James and Marti Hefley. Waco, Tex., Word Books [1972] 193 p. illus. 23 cm. Bibliography: p. 193. [F3429.3.M6H38] 71-170914 4.95
1. Wycliffe Bible Translators. 2. Indians of South America—Peru—Missions. 3. Shapra Indians—Missions. I. Hefley, Marti, joint author. II. Title.

HOWARD, David M. 266'.023'098611
The costly harvest / David M. Howard. Wheaton, Ill. : Tyndale House Publishers, 1975, c1969. xv, 207 p. : ill. ; 22 cm. First ed. published in 1969 under title: Hammered as gold. [BV2853.C7H6 1975] 75-310768 ISBN 0-8423-0445-2 pbk. : 2.95
1. Missions—Colombia. I. Title.

HOWARD, David M. 266'.023'098611
Hammered as gold [by] David M. Howard. [1st ed.] New York, Harper & Row [1969] 182 p. illus., map. 22 cm. [BV2853.C7H6] 69-17009 4.95
1. Missions—Colombia. I. Title.

JANK, Margaret, 1939- 266'.023'0987
Culture shock / by Margaret Jank. Chicago : Moody Press, c1977. p. cm. [F2520.1.Y3J36] 77-22658 ISBN 0-8024-1679-9 pbk. : 3.50

1. New Tribes Mission, Chicago. 2. Yanoama Indians—Missions. 3. Indians of South America—Venezuela—Missions. I. Title.

JANK, Margaret, 1939- 266'.023'0987
Culture shock / by Margaret Jank. Chicago : Moody Press, c1977. p. cm. [F2520.1.Y3J36] 77-22658 ISBN 0-8024-1679-9 pbk. : 3.50
1. New Tribes Mission, Chicago. 2. Yanoama Indians—Missions. 3. Indians of South America—Venezuela—Missions. I. Title.

OLSON, Bruce. 266'.023'0987
For this cross I'll kill you. [1st ed.] Carol Stream, Ill., Creation House [1973] 221 p. illus. 24 cm. [F2319.2.M6O44] 73-81494 ISBN 0-88419-038-2 4.95
1. Olson, Bruce. 2. Motilon Indians—Missions. 3. Yuko Indians—Missions. I. Title.

PATTERSON, John Wellington, 1926- 266'.023'098
Look south [by] John W. Patterson. Nashville, Convention Press [1968] 81 p. illus. 21 cm. (Foreign mission graded series) "Church study course [of the Sunday School Board of the Southern Baptist Convention] This book is number 1084 in category 10, section for intermediates." [BV2831.P32] 68-20683
1. Missions—Latin America. 2. Missions—Study and teaching (Secondary) I. Southern Baptist Convention. Sunday School Board. II. Title.

WALL, Martha. 266'.023'09861
As a roaring lion. Foreword by Donald McGavran. Chicago, Moody [1967] 254p. illus., facsim., map (on lining papers), ports. 22cm. [BV2853.C8G67] 67-26296 3.95
1. Gomez, Vicente. 2. Missions—Colombia. I. Title.

CRAWFORD, David Livingston, 1889- 266'.023'09965
Missionary adventures in the South Pacific, by David and Leona Crawford. [1st ed.] Rutland, Vt., Tuttle [1967] 280p. illus., ports. 22cm. [BV3677.C7] 67-15137 5.00
1. Sturges, A. A. 2. Sturges, Susan Thompson, 1820-1893. 3. Missions—Micronesia. I. Crawford, Leona, joint author. II. Title.

CRAWFORD, Davis Livingston, 1889- 266'.023'09965
Missionary adventures in the South Pacific, by david and Lenona Crawford [1st ed] Rutland, Vt., Tuttle [1967] 280 p. illus., ports. 22 cm. [BV3677.C7] 67-15137
1. Sturges, Susan Thompson, 1820-1983. 2. Missions—Micronesia. 3. Sturges, A. A. I. Crawford, Leonora, joint author. II. Title.

DAMON, Ethel Moseley, 1883-1965. 266'.023'099
Samuel Chenery Damon: chaplain and friend of seamen, historian, traveler,diplomat, doctor of divinity, journalist, genial companion, genealogist. Honolulu, Published under the sponsorship of the Hawaiian Mission Children's Society, 1966 141 p. illus., coat-of-arms, fold. geneal, table, ports. 24 cm. [BV3680.H4D34] 67-2589
1. Damon, Samuel Chenery, 1815-1885. I. Title.

HEDGES, Ursula M. 266.0230995
Sasa Rore—Little Warrior, by Ursula M. Hedges. Cover painting by Thomas Dunbebin. Washington, Review and Herald Pub. Association [1966] 96 p. illus., ports. 22 cm. [BV3680.N52R6] 66-19420
1. Rore, Sasa. 2. Seventh-Day Adventists—Missions. 3. Missions—New Guinea. I. Title.

RICHARDSON, Don. 266'.023'09951
Peace child / Don Richardson. Glendale, Calif. : G/L Regal Books, c1974. 287 p. : ill. ; 21 cm. [BV3373.S3R5] 75-26356 ISBN 0-8307-0405-1 : 7.95. ISBN 0-8307-0415-9 pbk. : 3.95
1. Missions to Sawi (Indonesian people) 2. Sawi (Indonesian people) I. Title.

TIPPETT, Alan Richard. 266'.023'09935
Solomon Islands Christianity : a study in growth and obstruction / Alan R. Tippett. South Pasadena, Calif. : William Carey Library, [1975?] c1967. xvii, 407 p., [1] leaf of plates : ill. ; 22 cm. Reprint of the ed. published by Lutterworth Press, London, in series: World studies of churches in mission. Includes indexes. Bibliography: p. 378-393. [BV3680.S6T5 1975] 75-15143 ISBN 0-87808-724-9 pbk. : 5.95
1. Missions—Solomon Islands. 2. Christianity—Solomon Islands. I. Title. II. Series: World studies of churches in mission.

OLSON, Gilbert W. 266'.0234
Church growth in Sierra Leone; a study of church growth in Africa's oldest Protestant mission field, by Gilbert W. Olson. Grand Rapids, W. B. Eerdmans Pub. Co. [1969] 222 p. illus., maps. 21 cm. (Church growth series) Bibliography: p. 213-216. [BV3625.S4O4] 68-28853 3.95
1. Missions—Sierra Leone. 2. Church growth. I. Title.

BARNES, William J. 266.025
Liu Li Ho; the transfiguration of a city, by William J. Barnes. With an introd. by Edward M. Dodd. [1st ed.] New York, Vantage Press [1965] 191 p. 21 cm. [R722.B33] 65-4211
1. Missions, Medical — China. 2. China — Soc. life & cust. I. Title.

BARNES, William J., M.D. 266.025
Liu Li Ho; the transfiguration of a city. Introd. by Edward M. Dodd. New York, Vantage [c.1965] 191p. 21cm. [R722.B33] 65-4211 3.25 bds.,
1. Missions, Medical—China. 2. China—Soc. life & cust. I. Title.

BREWSTER, Dorothy D 266.025
The church and medical missions. Compiled and written by Dorothy D. Brewster *and] Harold N. Brewster. New York, Editorial Dept., Joint Section of Education and Cultivation, Board of Missions of the Methodist Church [1959] 121p. illus. 19cm. [R722.B7] 59-13584
1. Missions, Medical. I. Brewster, Harold N., joint author. II. Title.

DODD, Edward Mills, 1887- 266.025
The gift of the healer; the story of men and medicine in the overseas mission of the Church, by Edward M. Dodd. New York, Friendship Press [1964] 224 p. 21 cm. [R722.D58] 64-11008
1. Missions, Medical — Hist. I. Title.

DODD EDWARD MILLS M. D. 1887- pseud. 266.025
The gift of the healer; the story of men and medicine in the overseas mission of the Church. New York, Friendship [c.1964] 224p. 21cm. 64-11008 2.25 pap.,
1. Missions, Medical—Hist. I. Title.

DOELL, E. W., pseud. 266.025
A mission doctor sees the wind of change. New York City, Archer House [1963, c.1960] 211p. 23cm. 63-14442 4.00
1. Africa, South—Native races. I. Title.

INTERNATIONAL Convention on Missionary Medicine. 1st. Wheaton. Ill. 1959. 266.025
International Convention on Missionary Medicine in review. Oak Park, Ill., Christian Medical Society [1960] 158 p. 21 cm. Organized by the Christian Medical Society. [R722.I57 1959] 60-39264
1. Missions, Medical — Congresses. I. Christian Medical Society. II. Title.

INTERNATIONAL Convention on Missionary Medicine. 2d, Wheaton, Ill., 1961. 266.025
World crisis -- God's opportunity. In review. [Oak Park, Ill., Christian Medical Society, c1962] 143 p. illus., ports. 21 cm. Organized by the Christian Medical Society. Includes bibliographies. [R722.I57 1961] 63-24132
1. Missions, Medical — Congresses. I. Christian Medical Society. II. Title.

INTERNATIONAL Convention on Missionary Medicine. 3d, Wheaton, Ill., 1963. 266.025
Redeemed men redeeming society; transcripts of messages and panel discussions. Oak Park, Ill. [Christian Medical Society, 1963] 154 p. 28 cm. "Sponsored by the Christian Medical Society." [R722.I57 1963] 65-1996
1. Medical missions — Congresses. I. Christian Medical Society. II. Title.

INTERNATIONAL Convention on Missionary Medicine, Wheaton, Ill., 1959. 266.025
International Convention on Missionary Medicine in review. Oak Park, Ill., Christian Medical Society [1960] 158p. 21cm. [R722.I57 1959] 60-39264
1. Missions, Medical—Congresses. I. Title.

MENDELSOHN, Jack, 1918- 266.025
The forest calls back. [1st ed.] Boston, Little Brown [1965] 267 p. illus., map (on lining papers) ports. 22 cm. [R722.M48] 65-10895
1. Binder, Theodor, 1921- 2. Binder, Carmen. I. Title.

MISSIONS Advanced Research and Communication Center. 266'.025
Medicine and missions; a survey of medical missions. Edward R. Dayton, editor. Wheaton, Ill., Medical Assistance Programs [1969] ix, 114 p. illus., forms. 23 cm. An evaluation of the 1968 survey conducted by Medical Assistance Programs, inc. [R722.M57] 70-100664
1. Missions, Medical. 2. Medical statistics. I. Dayton, Edward R., ed. II. Medical Assistance Programs, inc. III. Title.

NEW York. Missionary Research Library. 266.025
Directory of Protestant medical missions, compiled by Arthur W. March [research associate] New York, 1959. 134p. 22x28cm. 'A joint project of the Christian Medical Council for the Christian Medical Council project of the Christian Medical Council for Overseas Work and the Missionary Research Library.' [RA977.A1N4] 59-3373
1. Hospitals— Direct. 2. Missions, Medical. I. March, Arthur W. II. Title. III. Title: Protestant medical missions.

SPENCER, Steven M 266.025
Outposts of medicine, by Steven and Mary Spencer. New York, Friendship Press [1963] 126 p. 19 cm. [R722.S6] 63-8692
1. Missions, Medical. I. Spencer, Mary, joint author. II. Title.

SPENCER, Steven M. 266.025
Outposts of medicine, by Steven and Mary Spencer. New York, Friendship [c.1963] 126p. 19cm. 63-8692 1.25 pap.,
1. Missions, Medical. I. Spencer, Mary, joint author. II. Title.

THE Albert 266'.025'0924
Schweitzer jubilee book, edited by A. A. Roback. With the co-operation of J. S. Bixler [and] George Sarton. Westport, Conn., Greenwood Press [1970] 508 p. illus., facsims., ports. 23 cm. Reprint of the 1945 ed. "A tentative bibliography of Albert Schweitzer": p. [467]-483. [CT1098.S45A5 1970] 79-97392 ISBN 0-8371-2670-3
1. Schweitzer, Albert, 1875-1965. I. Roback, Abraham Aaron, 1890-1965, ed.

ALLEN, Lorna Margaret, 1915- comp. 266'.025'0924 B
Thursday's daughter / Lorna Margaret Allen. 1st ed. New York : Vantage Press, [1974] 306 p. ; 21 cm. Consists of letters of Annie and Harry Colwell. [R722.C58A44] 74-194711 ISBN 0-533-01040-3 : 5.95
1. Colwell, Annie Wallace Andrew, 1885- 2. Colwell, Harry. 3. Missionaries, Medical—India—Correspondence, reminiscences, etc. I. Colwell, Annie Wallace Andrew, 1885- II. Colwell, Harry. III. Title.

ANDERSON, Ken 266.0250924
Himalayan heartbeat; twentieth century stewardship in first century dimension. Waco, Tex., Word Bks [1966, c.1965] vi. 197p. illus., group ports. 23cm. [R722.A47] 66-1300 3.75
1. L5hmann. Geoffrey D. I. Title.

BLUMENSCHEIN, Marian. 266'.025'0924 B
Home in Honduras : the Blumenscheins pioneer in La Suiza / by Marian Blumenschein. Independence, Mo. : Herald Pub. House, [1975] 159 p. : ill. ; 21 cm. Bibliography: p. 159. [BV2843.H7B57] 74-82186 ISBN 0-8309-0125-6 : 6.00
1. Blumenschein, Marian. 2. Blumenschein, John C. 3. Missions—Honduras. I. Title.

BRABAZON, James. 266'.025'0924 B
Albert Schweitzer : a biography / by James Brabazon. New York : Putnam, [1975] 509 p., [8] leaves of plates : ill. ; 24 cm. Includes index. Bibliography: p. 485-488. [CT1098.S45B7 1975] 74-30545 ISBN 0-399-11421-1 : 12.50
1. Schweitzer, Albert, 1875-1965. I. Title.

BRABAZON, James. 266'.025'0924 B
Albert Schweitzer : a biography / James Brabazon. London : Gollancz, 1976. 509 p., [16] p. of plates : ill., plan, ports. ; 24 cm. Includes index. [CT1018.S45B72 1976] 76-383118 ISBN 0-575-02035-0 : £6.95
1. Schweitzer, Albert, 1875-1965. 2. Missionaries, Medical—Gabon—Biography. 3. Theologians—Europe—Biography. 4. Musicians—Europe—Biography.

BRYANT, Cyril E. 266'.025'0924
Operation Brother's Brother, by Cyril E. Bryant. With a foreword by Billy Graham. [1st ed.] Philadelphia, Lippincott [1968] ix, 206 p. illus., ports. 21 cm. [R154.H54B7] 68-17497
1. Hingson, Robert Andrew, 1913- 2. Brother's Brother Foundation. I. Title.

COUSINS, Norman. 266'.025'092'4 B
Dr. Schweitzer of Lambarene. With photos. by Clara Urquhart. Westport, Conn., Greenwood Press [1973, c1960] 254 p. illus. 22 cm. Reprint of the ed. published by Harper, New York. [CT1098.S45C6 1973] 73-7075 ISBN 0-8371-6902-X
1. Schweitzer, Albert, 1875-1965. I. Title.

COUSINS, Norman. 266'.025'092'4 B
Dr. Schweitzer of Lambarene. With photos. by Clara Urquhart. Westport, Conn., Greenwood Press [1973, c1960] 254 p. illus. 22 cm. Reprint of the ed. published by Harper, New York. [CT1098.S45C6 1973] 73-7075 ISBN 0-8371-6902-X 12.50
1. Schweitzer, Albert, 1875-1965. I. Title.

FRANCK, Frederick, 1909- 266'.025'0924 B
Days with Albert Schweitzer; a Lambarene landscape. Illustrated by the author. Westport, Conn., Greenwood Press [1974, c1959] xii, 178 p. illus. 22 cm. Reprint of the ed. published by Holt, Rinehart and Winston, New York. [CT1098.S45F68 1974] 73-22636 ISBN 0-8371-7341-8
1. Schweitzer, Albert, 1875-1965. I. Title.

FRANCK, Frederick, 1909- 266'.025'0924 B
Days with Albert Schweitzer; a Lambarene landscape. Illustrated by the author. Westport, Conn., Greenwood Press [1974, c1959] xii, 178 p. illus. 22 cm. Reprint of the ed. published by Holt, Rinehart and Winston, New York. [CT1098.S45F68 1974] 73-22636 ISBN 0-8371-7341-8 9.50
1. Schweitzer, Albert, 1875-1965. I. Title.

GLEASON, Gene. 266.0250924 B
Joy to my heart. [1st ed.] New York, McGraw-Hill [1966] 215 p. 22 cm. [BV3427.S59G6] 65-28591
1. Skau, Annie Margareth, 1911- 2. Missions—China. I. Title.

HANSEN, Lillian E. 266'.025'0924 B
The double yoke; the Story of William Alexander Noble, M.D., Fellow of the American College of Surgeons, Fellow of the International College of Surgeons, Doctor of Humanities, medical missionary extraordinary to India, his adopted land, by Lillian E. Hansen. Drawings by Ernest L. Reedstrom. New York, Citadel Press [1968] 268 p. illus., col. maps (on lining papers) 21 cm. [BX9743.N6H3 1968] 68-28451 5.95
1. Noble, William Alexander, 1895- 2. Missions, Medical—India. I. Title.

HASSELBLAD, Marva. 266.0250924
Lucky-lucky, by Marva Hasselblad, with Dorothy Brandon. [1st ed.] New York, M. Evans; Distributed in association with Lippincott [1966] 220 p. illus. 22 cm. Autobiographical. [RA390.U5H3] 66-27488
1. Missions, Medical—Vietnam. I. Brandon, Dorothy (Barrett) 1899- II. Title.

HASSOLD, Ernest Christopher, 1896- 266'.025'0924
Albert Schweitzer, E. R. Hagemann, editor. [Louisville, Ky., University of Louisville, 1969] [33] p. facsims., ports. 22 x 28 cm. "The occasion for this symposium, December 6, 1965, was to commemorate Albert Schweitzer (1875-1965) as part of the faculty lectures in the humanities at the University of Louisville." Contents.Contents.—Schweitzer's philosophy of culture, by E. C. Hassold.—Schweitzer and Indian philosophy, by D. P. Patnaik.—Schweitzer, the musician/personal recollections, by G. Herz. Includes bibliographical references. [CT1098.S45H35] 79-230389
1. Schweitzer, Albert, 1875-1965. I. Hagemann, Edward R., ed. II. Louisville, Ky. University. III. Patnaik, Deba Prasad. Schweitzer and Indian philosophy. 1969. IV. Herz, Gerhard, 1911- Schweitzer, the musican/personal recollections. 1969.

HEFLEY, James C. 266'.025'0922 B
The Cross and the scalpel [by] James C. Hefley. Waco, Tex., Word Books [1971] 158 p. illus., ports. 23 cm. [R722.H44] 76-134935 4.95
1. Missions, Medical. I. Title.

KERR, James Lennox, 1899- 266'.025'0924
Wilfred Grenfell, his life and work / by J. Lennox Kerr ; with a foreword by Lord Grenfell of Kilvey. Westport, Conn. : Greenwood Press, 1977, c1959. 272 p. : ill. ; 23 cm. Reprint of the ed. published by Harrap, London. Includes index. Bibliography: p. [261]-262. [R722.32.G75K47 1977] 73-21177 ISBN 0-8371-6068-5 lib.bdg. : 18.75
1. Grenfell, Wilfred Thomason, Sir, 1865-1940. 2. Missionaries, Medical—Newfoundland—Biography. 3. Newfoundland—Description and travel. 4. Labrador—Description and travel. I. Title.

KERR, James Lennox, 1899- 266'.025'0924
Wilfred Grenfell, his life and work / by J. Lennox Kerr ; with a foreword by Lord Grenfell of Kilvey. Westport, Conn. : Greenwood Press, 1977, c1959. 272 p. : ill. ; 23 cm. Reprint of the ed. published by Harrap, London. Includes index. Bibliography: p. [261]-262. [R722.32.G75K47 1977] 73-21177 ISBN 0-8371-6068-5 lib.bdg. : 18.75
1. Grenfell, Wilfred Thomason, Sir, 1865-

1940. 2. Missionaries, Medical—Newfoundland—Biography. 3. Newfoundland—Description and travel. 4. Labrador—Description and travel. I. Title.

MARSHALL, George. 266'.025'0924 B
Schweitzer a biography [by] George Marshall and David Poling. New York, Pillar Books [1975 c1971] 346 p., illus. 18 cm. Includes index. [CT1098.S45M34] 71-130888 ISBN 0-89129-020-6 1.95 (pbk.)
1. Schweitzer, Albert, 1875-1965. I. Poling, David, joint author II. Title.

MONTGOMERY, 266'.025'0924 B
Elizabeth Rider.
Albert Schweitzer, great humanitarian. Illustrated by William Hutchinson. Champaign, Ill., Garrard Pub. Co. [1971] 144 p. illus., ports. 22 cm. ([A People in the arts and sciences book]) A biography of the musician, minister, and teacher who gave up a comfortable teaching career to become a missionary doctor in the African jungle. [CT1098.S45M63] 92 70-132035 ISBN 0-8116-4510-X 2.59
1. Schweitzer, Albert, 1875-1965—Juvenile literature. I. Hutchinson, William M., illus. II. Title.

MOORE, Raymond S. 266'.025'0924 B
China doctor; the life story of Harry Willis Miller, by Raymond S. Moore. Omaha, Pacific Press Pub. Association [1969] vii, 152 p. ports. 22 cm. (A Destiny book, D-128) [R722.M6 1969] 71-76528
1. Miller, Harry Willis, 1879- 2. Missions, Medical—China. I. Title.

MURRAY, Florence 266'.025'0924 B
J., 1894-
At the foot of Dragon Hill / Florence J. Murray. 1st ed. New York : E. P. Dutton, 1975. xiii, 240 p. ; 22 cm. [R722.M8 1975] 75-14424 6.95
1. Murray, Florence J., 1894- 2. Missionaries, Medical—Korea—Correspondence, reminiscences, etc. 3. Women physicians—Correspondence, reminiscences, etc. I. Title.

RICHARDS, Kenneth 266'.025'0924 B
G., 1926-
Albert Schweitzer, by Kenneth G. Richards. Chicago, Childrens Press [1968] 94 p. illus. 29 cm. (People of destiny: a humanities series) Bibliography: p. 90-91. Photographs, drawings, and text trace the life of the famous doctor whose dedicated service to suffering humanity in French Equatorial Africa made him a living symbol of his own philosophy of reverence for life. [CT1098.S45R5] 92 AC 68
1. Schweitzer, Albert, 1875-1965. I. Title.

SCHWEITZER, 266'.025'0924 B
Albert, 1875-1965.
Albert Schweitzer: reverence for life; the inspiring words of a great humanitarian. With a forword [sic] by Norman Cousins. Selected by Peter Seymour. Illustrated by Walter Scott. [Kansas City, Mo., Hallmark Cards, inc., c1971] 62 p. illus. 20 cm. (Hallmark editions) [CT1098.S45A27] 71-147796 ISBN 0-87529-203-8 2.50
I. Title: Reverence for life.

SCHWEITZER, Albert, 266'.025'0924
1875-1965.
My life and thought: an autobiography [by] Albert Schweitzer; translated [from the German] by C. T. Campion. London, Allen & Unwin, 1966. 225 p. 18 1/2 cm. 8/6 (B 66-24082) Translation of Aus meinem Leben und Denken. Bibliographical footnotes. [CT1098.S45A282] 67-105402
I. Title.

SCHWEITZER, 266'.025'0924 B
Albert, 1875-1965.
On the edge of the primeval forest & More form the primeval forest : experiences and observations of a doctor in equatorial Africa / by Albert Schweitzer. New York : AMS Press, [1976] p. cm. Translation by C. T. Campion of the author's Zwischen Wasser und Urwald, and of Mitteilungen aus Lambarene. Reprint of the 1948 ed. published by Macmillan, New York. [BV3625.G3S36 1976] 75-41244 ISBN 0-404-14598-1 : 18.50
1. Schweitzer, Albert, 1875-1965. 2. Missions—Gabon. 3. Missions, Medical—Gabon. 4. Lambarene, Gabon. 5. Missionaries, Medical—Gabon—Biography. 6. Missionaries, Medical—Switzerland—Biography. I. Schweitzer, Albert, 1875-1965. Mitteilungen aus Lambarene. 1976. II. Title.

TURPIN, James W., 266'.025'095
1928-
A faraway country; the continuing story of Project Concern, by James W. Turpin with Al Hirshberg. New York, World Pub. Co. [1970] 228 p. illus., group ports. 22 cm. [R722.T78 1970] 79-115801 6.95
1. Project Concern, inc. I. Hirshberg, Albert, 1909- II. Title.

TURPIN, James W., 266.025095
1928-
Vietnam doctor(the story of Project Concern [by] James W. Turpin, Al Hirshberg. [New York] New Amer. Lib. [1967,c.1966] 175p. illus. map. ports. 18cm. (Signet bk., T3308) [R722.T8] .75 pap.,
1. Project Concern, inc. I. Hirshberg, Albert, 1909- II. Title.

TURPIN, James W., 266.025095
1928-
Vietnam doctor; the story of Project Concern [by] James W. Turpin with Al Hirshberg. [1st ed.] New York, McGraw-Hill [1966] 210 p. illus., map. ports. 23 cm. [R722.T8] 66-28058
1. Project Concern, inc. I. Hirshberg, Albert, 1909- II. Title.

CHRISTIE, Joseph 266.025096894
Wiliam
Medical missionary to Africa. New York, Vantage [c.1966] 140p. illus., ports. 21cm. Autobiographical. [R154.C333A3] 66-18096 3.75 bds.,
I. Title.

CHRISTIE, Joseph 266.025096894
William.
Medical missionary to Africa [by] J. W. Christie. [1st ed.] New York, Vantage Press [1966] 140 p. illus., ports. 21 cm. Autobiographical. [R154.C333A3] 66-18096
I. Title.

CRIPPS, Jean 266.02509681
Donaldson.
The arrow by day. Photos. by P. H. Coetzee and animal drawings by the author. Washington, Review and Herald Pub. Association [1965] 159 p. illus., map (on lining papers) 22 cm. 65-18675
1. 1. Hay, John A. 2. Missions, Medical—Kalahari Desert. 3. Bushmen. I. Title.

CRIPPS, Jean 266.02509681
Donaldson
The arrow by day Photos. by P. H. Coetzee. Animal drawings by the author Washington, D.C., Review & Herald, [1965] Washington, D.C. Review & Herald 1965 159p. illus., map (on lining papers) 22cm. [BV3625.B55H33] 65-18675 3.75
1. Hav. John A. 2. Missions, Medical—Kalahari Desert. 3. Bushmen. I. Title.

REYBURN, William 266'.025'096711
David.
Out of the African night [by] William D. Reyburn. [1st ed.] New York, Harper & Row [1968] 176 p. illus., map, ports. 22 cm. [BV3625.C34R4] 68-29558
1. Missions—Cameroon. 2. Missions, Medical—Cameroon. I. Title.

INTER-VARSITY Missionary 266.04
Convention. 5th, Urbana, Ill., 1957.
One Lord, one church, one world; a missionary compendium. Chicago, Inter-varsity Christian Fellowship [1958] 151 p. ports. 23 cm. "Messages ... given at the Fifth International Student Missionary Convention, sponsored by Inter-varsity Christian Fellowship, Nurses Christian Fellowship, and Student Foreign Mission Fellowship." [BV2390.I5] 58-35839
1. Missions — Congresses. 2. Christianity — Congresses. I. Inter-varsity Christian Fellowship of the United States of America. II. Title.

INTERNATIONAL Student 266.04
Missionary Convention, 5th, University of Illinois, 1957.
One Lord, one church, one world; a missionary compendium. Chicago Inter-varsity Christian Fellowship [1958] 151p. ports. 23cm. [BV2390.I5 1957] 58-35839
1. Christianity— Addresses, essays, lectures. 2. Missions—Addresses, essays, lectures. I. Title.

MOORE, Arthur James, Bp., 266.04
1888-
Immortal tidings in mortal hands. Nashville, Abingdon-Cokesbury Press [1953] 128p. 21cm. [BV2070.M67] 53-8135
1. Missions—Addresses, essays, lectures. I. Title.

WIDBER, Mildred, comp. 266.058
The family looks at one world. Boston, Pilgrim Press [1950] 63 p. illus. 18 x 23 cm. Letters from missionaries. Includes music. [BV2530.W5] 50-21390
1. Congregational churches—Missions. I. Title.

MILLER, Cecille 266.06
Missionary programs for women's meetings. Chicago, Moody [c.1963] 79p. 22cm. 1.25,pap., plastic bdg.
I. Title.

VAWTER, Bruce. 266'.06
The four Gospels; an introduction. [1st ed.] Garden City, N.Y., Doubleday, 1967. 429 p. maps. 24 cm. Bibliography: p. 8. [BS2555.2.V3] 67-10408
1. Bible. N.T. Gospels—Introductions. I. Title.

KANE, J Herbert. 266.0621
Faith, mighty faith; a handbook of the Interdenominational Foreign Mission Association. [New York? c1956] 171p. 19cm. [BV2360.I5K3] 57-790
1. Interdenominational Foreign Mission Association of North America. 2. Missions—Societies, etc. I. Title.

GOODALL, Norman. 266.06242
A history of the London Missionary Society, 1895-1945. London, New York, Oxford University Press, 1954. 640p. illus. 23cm. [BV2361.L8G6] 55-2615
1. London Missionary Society—Hist. I. Title.

AMERICAN Board of 266.06273
Commissioners for Foreign Missions.
The American Board year book and calendar of prayer. Boston. v. 22cm. [BV2360.A373] 57-36353
1. Missions—Yearbooks. I. Title.

NATIONAL Council of the 266.06273
Churches of Christ in the United States of America. Division of Foreign Missions.
Report. 2d- 1952- New York. v. illus. 23-28cm. annual. The Minutes of the division's first meeting are included in v. 57 (1950) of the Report of the Foreign Missions Conference on North America. Includes Report of the 58th- meetings of the Foreign Missions Conference of North America. [BV2390.N273] 55-43961
I. Title.

HOGG, William Richey, 266.0631
1921-
Ecumenical foundations; a history of the International Missionary Council and its nineteenth-century background. [1st ed.] New York, Harper [1952] xi. 406 p. ports. 22 cm. "Presented originally ... as a dissertation for the degree of doctorof philosophy in Yale University." Bibliography: p. 435-449. [BV2020.I 6 1952f] 51-11923
1. International Missionary Council. I. Title.

INTERNATIONAL Missionary 266.0631
Council. Assembly, Accra, 1957-1958.
The Ghana Assembly of the International Missionary Council, 28th December, 1957 to 8th January, 1958; selected papers with an essay on the role of the I. M. C. Edited by Ronald K. Orchard. London, Edinburgh House Press; distributed in the U. S. A. by Friendship Press, New York, 1958. 240p. 23cm. [BV2020.I6 1957] 59-2860
1. Missions—Congresses. I. Orchard, Ronald Kenneth, ed. II. Title.

HIGDON, Elmer Kelso, 266.069
1887-
New missionaries for new days. St. Louis, Bethany Press [1956] 198p. illus. 21cm. [BV2091.H5] 56-62522
1. Missionaries—Appointment, call, and election. I. Title.

JOHNSON, Johnni 266.069
What do missionaries do? Nashville, Broadman [1964] 96p. 21cm. 64-15456 1.75
1. Missionaries—Appointment, call, and election. I. Title.

KANE, George Louis, 1911- 266.069
ed.
Why I became a missioner; with an introd. by Raymond A. Lane. Westminster, Md., Newman Press, 1958. 246p. 22cm. [BV3700.K2] 58-13631
1. Missionaries Appointment, call, and election. 2. Catholic Church—Missions. I. Title.

WALSH, James Edward, 266.069
Bp., 1891-
Blueprint of the missionary vocation. Maryknoll, N.Y., Maryknoll Publications [195-] 134 p. 25 cm. (World horizon reports, report no. 19) [BV2180.W3] 58-14672
1. Missionaries — Appointment, call, and election. I. Title.

ALLSTROM, Elizabeth C 266.07
The singing secret. Illustrated by Dorothy Papy. New York, Friendship Press [1955] New York, Friendship Press, 1955. 127p. illus. 21cm. 64p. 21cm. 'To Bethlehem, come let us go (for plano with interlinear words): p. 21-22.t--A primary teacher's guide on spreading the Gospel today. Includes music. [BV2090.5.A4] 55-6832
1. Missions—Study and teaching (Elementary) 2. Missionary stories. I. Title.

BOLITHO, Axchie A 266.07
At work for a Christian world; a study book on missions. Anderson, Ind., Warner Press [1953] 124p. 19cm. [BV2090.B58] 53-7009
1. Missions—Study and teaching. I. Title.

GRIFFITHS, Louise 266.07
(Benckenstein) 1908-
Wide as the world; junior highs and missions. Illustrated by Mine Okubo. New York, Friendship Press [1958] 167p. illus. 22cm. Includes bibliography. [BV2090.G72] 58-5801
1. Missions—Study and teaching. I. Title.

HARNER, Nevin Cowger, 266.07
1901-
Missionary education in your church, by Nevin C. Harner and David D. Baker. New and rev. ed. New York, Friendship Press [1950] xiii, 176 p. 20 cm. Bibliography: p. [171]-176. [BV2090.H28 1950] 50-10791
1. Missions—Study and teaching. I. Baker, David Dudrow, 1897-1950. joint author. II. Title.

HILL, Frances M 266.07
Missionary education of children. [1st ed.] Philadelphia, Judson Press [1954] 80p. 20cm. [BV2090.5.H5] 54-10160
1. Missions—Study and teaching. I. Title.

HILL, Frances M. 266.07
Missionary education of children, by Frances M. Hill, Florence E. Stansbury. [2d ed.] Valley Forge [Pa.] Judson [1963] 80p. 20cm. 63-13991 apply
1. Missions—Study and teaching (Elementary) 2. Religious education of children. I. Stansbury, Florence, E. II. Title.

HOWSE, William Lewis, 266.07
1905-
The Sunday school and missions. Nashville, Convention Press [1957] 146p. 19cm. [BV2090.H65] 57-12143
1. Missions—Study and teaching. 2. Sunday-schools. I. Title.

RANCK, John Allan, 1912- 266.07
Education for mission. New Yoık, Friendship Press [1961] 159p. 20cm. Includes bibliography. [BV2090.R26] 61-6630
1. Missions—Study and teaching. 2. Missions—Theory. I. Title.

STEVENS, Dorothy A 266.07
Missionary education in a Baptist church. [1st ed.] Philadelphia, Judson Press [1953] 208p. 21cm. [BV2090.S815] 53-8555
1. Missions—Study and teaching. 2. Baptists—Missions—Study and teaching. I. Title.

WYCKOFF, D Campbell. 266.07
In one spirit; senior highs and missions. Illustrated by Joseph Escourido. New York, Friendship Press [1958] 166 p. illus. 22 cm. Includes bibliography. [BV2090.5.W9] 58-5802
1. Missions — Study and teaching. I. Title.

LITTLEJOHN, Carrie U 266.0711769
History of Carver School of Missions and Social Work. Nashville, Broadman Press [1958] 198p. illus. 22cm. Includes bibliography. [BV2093.L6C32] 58-8923
1. Carver School of Missions and Social Work, Louisville, Ky. I. Title.

CONCORDIA PUBLISHING 266.082
HOUSE
89 modern mission stories. St. Louis, Author [c.1962] 94p. 19cm. 61-13458 1.50 pap.,
1. Missionary stories. I. Title.

CONGRESS on World 266.082
Missions, Chicago. 1960.
Facing the unfinished task; messages delivered at the Congress on World Missions. Sponsored by Interdenominational Foreign Missions Assn. of North America. Comp. by J. O. Percy. Ed. by Mary Bennett. Grand Rapids, Mich., Zondervan [c.1961] 281p. illus. 62-104 4.50
1. Missions—Congresses. I. Percy, John Ottley, 1908- comp. II. Bennett, Mary Angela, 1906- ed. III. Title.

INTERNATIONAL Student 266.082
Missionary Convention. 6th, Urbana and Champaign, Ill., 1961.
Commission, conflict, commitment: messages. [Chicago] Inter-varsity [c.1962] xviii, 301p. 22cm. (IVP ser. in creative Christian living) Sponsored by: Inter-varsity Christian Fellowship, U.S.A., others. 62-14847 5.50; 3.25 pap.,
1. Missions—Addresses, essays, lectures. 2. Christianity—Addresses, essay, lecture. I. Inter-varsity Christian Fellowship of the United States of America. II. Title.

INTERNATIONAL Student 266.082
Missionary Convention. 6th, Urbana and Champaign, Ill., 1961.
Commission, conflict, commitment: messages... [Chicago, Inter- varsity Press [1962] xviii, 301p. 22cm. (IVP series in creative Christian living) 'Sponsored by: Inter-varsity Christian Fellowship, U. S. A. [and others]' [BV2390.I5 1961] 62-14847
1. Missions—Addresses, essays, lectures. 2. Christianity—Addresses, essays, lectures. I.

Inter-varsity Christian Fellowship of the United States of America. II. Title.

PICKETT, Jarrell Waskom. 266.082
The dynamics of church growth. New York, Abingdon Press [1963] 124 p. 20 cm. [BV2061.P5] 63-7767
1. Missions—Theory—Addresses, essays, lectures. I. Title.

PICKETT, Jarrell Waskom 266.082
The dynamics of church growth. Nashville, Abingdon [c.1963] 124p. 20cm. 63-7767 2.50
1. Missions—Theory—Addresses, essays, lectures. I. Title.

WEST, Charles C. 266.082
The missionary church in East and West [by] Charles C. West [and others] Edited by Charles C. West & David M. Paton. Naperville, Ill., [stamped distributed by Allenson, 1959, i.e.1960] 133p. 22cm. (Studies in ministry and worship, 13) (bibl. footnotes) 60-16176 2.00 pap.,
1. Missions—Addresses, essays, lectures. I. Title.

WEST, George Allen, 1915- ed. 266.082
Christ for the world. Nashville, Broadman [1963] 146p 22cm. 63-11168 2.95 bds.,
1. Missions—Sermons. 2. Sermons, American. 3. Baptists—Sermons. I. Title.

MACK, Silas Franklin. 266.084
Mission unlimited. New York, Friendship Press, c1955. 96p. illus. 28cm. [BV2064.M3] 55-7564
1. Missions—Pictures, illustrations, etc. I. Title.

BARLOW, Sanna Morrison. 266.0847
Arrows of His bow. Chicago, Moody Press [1960] 208p. illus. 22cm. [BV2082.A8B3] 60-16877
1. Richter, Don. 2. Phonorecords in missionary work. 3. Gospel Recordings, inc. I. Title.

GLOVER, Robert Hall, 1871-1947. 266.09
The progress of world-wide missions. Rev. and enl. by J. Herbert Kane. New York, Harper [1960] x, 502 p. maps. 22 cm. Bibliography: p. 459-480. [BV2100.G5 1960] 60-11775
1. Missions—History. I. Kane, J. Herbert, ed. II. Title.

GOD can do anything; 266'.09
39 incidents relating to Wesleyan missionaries and their work. Compiled and edited by Marie Lind. Marion, Ind., Wesleyan Pub. House [1968] 109 p. illus. 20 cm. [BV2087.G58] 68-7170 1.95
1. Missionary stories. I. Lind, Marie, ed.

HILLIS, Don W., comp. 266'.09
The baboon chase, and other new missionary stories. Compiled by Don W. Hillis. Edited by Esther L. Sorensen. Pictures by Vernon Mortenson. Grand Rapids, Baker Book House [1968] 87 p. illus. 21 cm. (Valor series, 18) [BV2087.H52] 68-19210
1. Missionary stories. I. Sorensen, Esther L., ed. II. Title.

*JOHNSON, Ruth I. 266.09
David Livingstone, rev. by Ruth I. Johnson. Chicago, Moody [c.1962, 1966] 63p. 19cm. (Moody arrows no. 13, MP50) .50 pap.,
1. Livingstone, David, 1813-1873—Juvenile literature. 2. Missions—Africa.—Juvenile literature. I. Title.

*KLEPPER, Harry 266.09
Our little Indians, by Harry and Elsie Klepper. New York, Carlton [c.1965] 45p. 21cm. (Reflection bk.) 2.00
I. Title.

LIND, Marie, ed. 266'.09
God can do anything; 39 incidents relating to Wesleyan missionaries and their work. Compiled and edited by Marie Lind. Marion, Ind., Wesleyan Pub. House G58] 1968] 109 p. illus. 20 cm. $1.95 [BV2087.G58] 68-7170
1. Missionary stories. I. Title.

LIND, Marie, comp. 266'.09
Missionary stories for church programs; 39 incidents relating to missionaries and their work. Grand Rapids, Baker Book House [1968] 109 p. illus. 20 cm. [BV2087.L5] 68-28295 1.95
1. Missionary stories. I. Title.

MATHEWS, Basil Joseph, 1879- 266.09
Forward through the ages. Maps and illus. by Louise Drew. New York, Friendship Press [1951] xii, 275 p. illus., maps. 22 cm. London ed. (Oxford University Press) has title: Disciples of all nations. Bibliography: p. [255]-200. [BV2100.M47 1951] 51-2627
1. Missions—Hist. I. Title.

MATHEWS, Basil Joseph, 1879-1951. 266.09
Forward through the ages. With an epilogue by Kenneth Scott Latourette. Maps and illus. by Louise Drew. New ed. New York, Friendship Press [1960] 276p. illus. 22cm. Includes bibliography. [BV2100.M47 1960] 60-6400
1. Missions—Hist. I. Title.

NEILL, Stephen 266.09
Christian missions [Gloucester, Mass., P. Smith, c.1964] 622p. 19cm. (Pelican bk. A628. Pelican hist. of the Church, v.6 rebound) Bibl. [BV2100.N4] 4.25
1. Missions—Hist. I. Title.

NEILL, Stephen Charles, Bp. 266.09
Christian missions. Baltimore, Penguin [1964] 622p. 19cm. (Pelican hist. of the church, v. 6, A628) Cover title: A history of Christian missions. Bibl. 64-3926 2.25 pap.,
1. Missions—Hist. I. Title.

NEILL, Stephen Charles, Bp. 266.09
Christian missions. Grand Rapids, Mich., Eerdmans [1965, c.1964] 622p. 21cm. (Pelican hist. of the church, v.6) Cover title: A history of Christian missions. Bibl. [BV2100.N4] 7.50
1. Missions—Hist. I. Title.

NEVINS, Albert J., 1915- comp. 266'.09
The Maryknoll book of treasures; an anthology of mission literature, edited and selected by Albert J. Nevins. Maryknoll, N.Y., Maryknoll Publications [1968] 384 p. 22 cm. [BV2300.C35N37] 68-8725
1. Catholic Foreign Mission Society of America. 2. Missionary stories. I. Title.

ROCHE, Aloysius, 1886- 266.09
In the track of the Gospel; an outline of the Christian apostolate from Pentecost to the present. New York, P. J. Kenedy [1953] 200p. 23cm. [BV2185.R6] 53-11514
1. Missions—Hist. 2. CatholicChurch—Missions —Hist. I. Title.

STEVEN, Hugh. 266'.09
It takes time to love / by Hugh Steven. [Glendale, Calif.] : Wycliffe Bible Translators, [1974] 111 p. : ill. ; 21 cm. [BV2087.S72] 74-84490
1. Missionary stories. 2. Missions—Philippine Islands. 3. Missions—Vietnam. I. Title.

*STEWARD, Gwenda R. 266.09
Missionary adventures in the Far East. Chicago, Moody [c.1966] 125p. 17cm. (Colportage lib., 518. MP39) .39 pap.,
I. Title.

UNDERWOOD, Joseph B 266.09
By love compelled [by] Joseph B. Underwood. Nashville, Broadman Press [1966] Boston, Beacon Press [1961, c1957] 127 p. 20 cm. xxi, 484 p. 21 cm. (Beacon paperback, LR 11) [BV2087.U49] 66-12573
1. Missionary stories. I. Underwood, Kenneth Wilson. II. Title. III. Title: Protestant and Catholic;

UNDERWOOD, Joseph B. 266.09
By love compelled. Nashville, Broadman [c.1966] 127p. 20cm. [BV2087.749] 66-12573 1.50 bds.,
1. Missionary stories. I. Title.

WEAD, Doug. 266'.09
The compassionate touch / Douglas Wead. Carol Stream, Ill. : Creation House, c1977. 163 p. : ill. ; 22 cm. [BV2930.C3W42] 76-62694 ISBN 0-88419-015-3 pbk. : 3.50
1. Missions—India—Calcutta. I. Title.

*WORMAN, Theresa 266.09
More missionary stories. Chicago, Moody [1965, c.1961] 64p. 19cm. (Moody arrows,MP50: missionary, no. 7) .50 pap.,
I. Title.

CAMMACK, Phyllis. 266.0909
Missionary moments; sixty diverse "moments" in the life of a South American missionary. With introd. by Jack L. Willcuts. Illus. by the author; her sister, Mignon Pike; and nephew, Ted Pike. Newberg, Or., Barclay Press [c1966] 134 p. illus. 23 cm. [BV2853.P6C3] 66-30364
1. Missions—Peru. 2. Missions—Bolivia. 3. Aymara Indians. I. Title.

DAVIS, Raymond J. 266.090922
Fire on the mountains; the story of a miracle - the Church in Ethiopia [by] Raymond J. Davis. Grand Rapids, Zondervan Pub. House [1966] 253 p. illus., ports. 23 cm. [BV3560.D3] 66-18945
1. Missions—Ethiopia. I. Title.

BAIRD, Mollie Elnora. 266.090954
Sole treading. With illus. by Narcisso Dionson. [Fort Worth, Tex., 1964] 228 p. illus. 22 cm. Stories from the author's experiences as a missionary in India. [BV3277.B3A3] 66-6308
1. Missions—India. I. Title.

MENZIES, Edna O. 266'.09'09669
Little Teny of Nigeria, by Edna O. Menzies. Grand Rapids, Baker Bk. [1968] 72p. illus. 20cm. (Valor ser., no. 16) [BV2087.M39] 67-18186 1.95 bds.,
1. Missionary stories. 2. Missions—Nigeria. I. Title.

YOUNGBERG, Norma R. 266.0909911
Jungle thorn, by Norma R. Youngberg. Illustrated by Harold W. Munson. Mountain View, Calif., Pacific Press Pub. Association [1966] 120 p. illus. 22 cm. (Panda book, P-103) [BV2087.Y6 1966] 66-23434
1. Missionary stories. I. Title.

HITT, Russell T. 266.0924 B
Sensei; the life story of Irene Webster-Smith [by] Russell T. Hitt. [1st ed.] New York, Harper & Row [1965] 240 p. illus., ports. 22 cm. (Harper jungle missionary classics) [BV3457.W4H5] 65-20452
1. Webster-Smith, Irene, 1888- 2. Missions—Japan. I. Title.

HITT, Russell T. 266.0924
Sensie; the life story of Irene Webster-Smith. New York, Harper [c.1965] 240p. illus., ports. 22cm. (Harper jungle missionary classics) [BV3457.WH5] 65-20452 3.95 bds.,
1. Webster-Smith, Irene, 1888- 2. Missions—Japan. I. Title.

WAGNER, C. Peter 266.0924
The condor of the jungle [by] C. Peter Wagner, Joseph S. McCullough. Westwood, N.J., Revell [1966] 158p. illus., maps (on lining papers) ports. 21cm. [BV2853.B5H44] 66-17052 3.95
1. Herron, Walter, 1910-1964. 2. Missions—Bolivia. I. McCullough, Joseph S., joint author. II. Title.

HASKIN, Dorothy (Clark) 1905- 266.095
In spite of dungeon; suffering for Christ in the Orient. Grand Rapids, Zondervan Pub. House [1962] 150 p. illus. 21 cm. [BV3151.H3] 62-53519
1. Missions — Asia. 2. Communism — Asia. I. Title.

HASKIN, Dorothy (Clark) 1905- 266.095
In spite of dungeon; suffering for Christ in the Orient. Grand Rapids, Mich., Zondervan [c.1962] 150p. illus. 21cm. 62-53519 2.50
1. Missions—Asia. 2. Communism—Asia. I. Title.

HOCKIN, Katharine 266.0951
Servants of God in People's China. New York, Friendship [c.1962] 127p. 19cm. 62-7861 1.75 pap.,
1. Christians in China. I. Title.

LYALL, Leslie T. 266.0951
A passion for the impossible; the China Inland Mission, 1865-1965. [London] Hodder and Stoughton; Chicago, Moody [c.1965] 207p. map. 22cm. Bibl. [BV3410.C56L9] 65-9331 3.50
1. China Inland Mission. 2. Missions—China. I. Title.

WILLIAMS, Philip Rev. [266] 175.2
Journey into mission. Illustrated by Mine Okubo. New York, Friendship Press [1957] 180 p. 16 cm. [BV3457.W53A3] 57-11366
1. Missions — Japan. I. Title.

DVORNIK, Francis, 1893- 266.1'9'47
Byzantine missions among the Slavs; SS. Constantine-Cyril and Methodius. New Brunswick, N.J., Rutgers University Press [1970] xviii, 484 p. illus., maps, plans. 25 cm. (Rutgers Byzantine series) Bibliography: p. 419-464. [BV2857.S68D9] 78-75676 17.50
1. Cyrillus, Saint, of Thessalonica, 827(ca.)-869. 2. Methodius, Saint, Abp. of Moravia, d. 885. 3. Missions—Slavs. I. Title.

KUHAR, Aloysius l. 1895-1958. 266.1'9'47
Slovene medieval history; selected studies. New York, Studia Slovenica, 1962. "These eight appendices together with the text published previously under the title: The conversion of the Slovenes and the German-Slav ethnic boundary in the Eastern Alps ... constitute the author's doctoral dissertation ... Cambridge University." Includes bibliographies. [BV2857.S7K82] 65-2942
1. Missions — Slovenia. I. Kuhlar, Aloysius L., 1895-1958. The conversion of the Slovenes, and the German-Slav ethnic boundary in the eastern Alps. II. Title.

KUHAR, Aloysius l. 1895-1958. 266.1'9'47
Slovene medieval history; selected studies. New York, Studia Slovenica, 1962. xv, 143 p. facsim. 24 cm. (Studies Slovenica, 4) "These eight appendices together with the text published previously under the title: The conversion of the Slovenes and the German-Slav ethnic boundary in the Eastern Alps ... constitute the author's doctoral dissertation ... Cambridge University." Includes bibliographies. [BV2857.S7K82] 65-2942
1. Missions — Slovenia. I. Kuhlar, Aloysius L., 1895-1958. The conversion of the Slovenes, and the German-Slav ethnic boundary in the eastern Alps. II. Title. III. Series.

WIDMER, Eric, 1940- 266'.1'9'951
The Russian ecclesiastical mission in Peking during the eighteenth century / by Eric Widmer. Cambridge, Mass. : East Asian Research Center, Harvard University : distributed by Harvard University Press, 1976. xi, 262 p. : map ; 24 cm. (Harvard East Asian monographs ; 69) Includes index. Bibliography: p. 233-250. [BV3417.W46] 76-12575 ISBN 0-674-78129-5 : 15.00
1. Missions—China. 2. Missions, Russian. 3. Russia—Relations (general) with China. 4. China—Relations (general) with Russia. I. Title. II. Series.

ALEXANDER, Calvert. 266'.2
The missionary dimension; Vatican II and the world apostolate. Milwaukee, Bruce Pub. Co. [1967] ix, 117 p. 22 cm. "Appendix: Decree on the missionary activity of the church": p. [69]-117. Bibliographical footnotes. [BX830.1962.A45A45] 67-18212
1. Vatican Council 2d, 1962-1965. Decretum de activitate missionali ecclesiae. 2. Catholic Church—Missions. I. Vatican Council. 2d, 1962-1965. Decree on the missionary activity of the church.

BANE, Martin J. [266.2]
The Catholic story of Liberia. New York, D. X. McMullen Co., 1950. 163 p. illus., ports. maps. 20 cm. Bibliography: p. 157-158. [BV3625.L5B3] 276.66 50-14031
1. Missions—Liberia. 2. Catholic Church in Liberia. I. Title.

BARREAU, Jean Claude. 266.2
The priest today; his mission and witness, by J. C. Barreau and D. Barbe. Translated by Nels Challe. Glen Rock, N.J., Paulist Press [1968] v, 85 p. 18 cm. (Deus books) Translation of Le pretre dans la mission. [BV2063.B3413] 68-55399 1.95
1. Missions—Theory. I. Barbe, Dominique, joint author. II. Title.

BARRES, Oliver 266.2
World mission windows. New York, Alba [c.1963] 209p. 22cm. 63-12677 3.95
1. Missions. 2. Catholic Church—Missions. I. Title.

BISHOP of the winds; 266.2
fifty years in the Arctic regions. Translated from the French by Alan Gordon Smith. New York, Kenedy [1955] 266p. illus. 21cm. Translation of Eveque volant. [BV2813.B7A315] [BV2813.B7A315] 277.1 55-6517 55-6517
I. Breynat, Gabriel Joseph Elie, Abp., 1867-1954.

BRANLEY, Brendan R. 266.2
Christianity and the Japanese [by] Brendan R. Branley. Maryknoll, N. Y., Maryknoll Publications [c1966] x, 271 p. 19 cm. (World horizon books) [BV3445.2.B7] 66-27611
1. Missions — Japan. 2. Catholic Church — Missions. I. Title.

BRANLEY, Brendan R. 266.2
Christianity and the Japanese [by] Brendan R. Branley. Maryknoll, N.Y., Maryknoll Pubns. [c.1966] x, 271p. 19cm. (World horizon bks.) [BV3445.2.B7] 66-27611 2.75 pap.,
1. Missions—Japan. 2. Catholic Church—Missions. I. Title.

BURKE, Thomas J M 1920- ed. 266.2
Sinews of love. [New York] New American Library [1959] 159p. illus. 28cm. [BV2180.B8] 59-14597
1. Catholic Church—Missions—Pictures, illustrations, etc. I. Title.

CACELLA, Joseph, 1882- 266.2
Jungle call. [New York; 1956?] 399p. illus. 21cm. (Catholic action library) Based on the author's experience as a missionary in the jungles of Amazon, Brazil. [BV2853.B6C3] [BV2853.B6C3] 278.1 58-30788 58-30788
1. Missions—Brazil. I. Title.

CATHOLIC Church in the U. S. Commission for Catholic Missionsamong the Colored People and the Indians. 266.2
Our Negro and Indians missions. Report of

the Secretary. [Washington] v. illus. 23 cm. annual. [BV2783.C34] 52-26876
1. Missions—Negroes. 2. Indians of North America—Missions. 3. Catholic Church—Missions. I. Title.

CATHOLIC Church. Pope. 266.2
Catholic missions: four great missionary encyclicals. Edited by Thomas J. M. Burke, with introd., study plans, and topical index. New York, Fordham University Press, 1957. 83p. 23cm. (Fordham University [New York] Institute of Mission Studies, Incidental papers, no. 1) Bibliography: p. 80. [BV2175.A4] 58-2404
1. Catholic Church—Missions. I. Burke, Thomas J. M., 1920- ed. II. Title.
Contents omitted.

CEGIELKA, Francis A 266.2
Life on rocks, among the natives of the Union of South Africa. North Tonawanda, N. Y., Pallottinum [c1957] 187p. illus. 22cm. The author's experiences as a retreat master in the Union of South Africa. [BV3555.C4] [BV3555.C4] 276.8 58-733 58-733
1. Missions—Africa, South. 2. Catholic Church—Missions. I. Title.

CHURCH at work in the world 266.2
(The); selections for a readings course on the theology history and methods of the mission apostolate, contributed by Ronan Hoffman [others]. ed. by Edward A. Freking [others] Cincinnati, 5100 Shattue Ave. Catholic Students' Mission Crusade, [c.1961] 141p. (CSMC five-hour ser.) 1.00 pap.,

COGAN, Mary de Pual, 266'.2
Sister.
Sisters of Maryknoll through troubled waters. Freeport, N.Y., Books for Libraries Press [1972, c1947] vi, 220 p. 23 cm. (Essay index reprint series) [BV2300.M4C64 1972] 72-167329 ISBN 0-8369-2764-8
1. Maryknoll Sisters of St. Dominic. I. Title.

CONSIDINE, Robert Bernard, 266.2
1906-
The Maryknoll story. [1st ed.] New York, Doubleday, 1950. 144 p. illus., ports. 26 cm. [BV2300.C35C62] 50-5305
1. Catholic Foreign Mission Society of America. I. Title.

COUTURIER, Charles 266.2
The mission of the church. Translated from the French by A. V. Littledale. Baltimore, Helicon Press [1960], 146p. 19cm. (2p. bibl.) 59-9914 3.50 bds.,
1. Catholic Church—Missions. I. Title.

DANIEL, Emmett Randolph, 266'.2
1935-
The Franciscan concept of mission in the High Middle Ages / E. Randolph Daniel. Lexington : University Press of Kentucky, [1975] xvi, 168 p. ; 23 cm. Includes index. Bibliography: p. [157]-161. [BV2280.D36] 74-7874 ISBN 0-8131-1315-6 : 11.25
1. Franciscans—Missions—History. I. Title.

DAUGHTERS of St. Paul. 266'.2
Where the Gospel meets the world / by Daughters of St. Paul. Boston : St. Paul Editions, c1977. 470 p., [83] leaves of plates : ill. ; 22 cm. Teatimonials of the American Bishops and episodes of the communications media apostolate of the Daughters of St. Paul. [BX4334.D3 1977] 77-24709 6.95 pbk. : 5.00
1. Daughters of St. Paul. 2. Evangelistic work. I. Title.

DAUGHTERS of St. Paul. 266'.2
Where the Gospel meets the world / by Daughters of St. Paul. Boston : St. Paul Editions, c1977. 470 p., [83] leaves of plates : ill. ; 22 cm. Teatimonials of the American Bishops and episodes of the communications media apostolate of the Daughters of St. Paul. [BX4334.D3 1977] 77-24709 6.95 pbk. : 5.00
1. Daughters of St. Paul. 2. Evangelistic work. I. Title.

DOURNES, Jacques. 266.2
God loves the pagans; a Christian mission on the plateaux of Vietnam. Pref. by Henri de Lubac; translated by Rosemary Sheed. [New York] Herder and Herder [1966] 203 p. map. 22 cm. Translation of Dieu aime les paiens. Bibliographical footnotes. [BV3325.A7D63 1966b] 66-22600
1. Missions — Vietnam. 2. Catholic Church — Missions. I. Title.

FEENEY, Thomas Joseph, [266.2]
1894-
Letters from Likiep. [New York, 1952] 259 p. illus. 20 cm. [BV3680.L52F4] 279.68 52-3492
1. Missions—Likiep Atoll. I. Title.

FLANNERY, Austin. 266.2
Missions and religions: a commentary on the Second Vatican Council's Decree on the Church's missionary Activity and Declaration on the relation of the Church to non-Christian religions. Ed[ited by] Austin Flannery. Dublin, Scepter Publishers Ltd., 1968. 3-163 p. 22 cm. Text of the Decree on the Church's missionary activity (p. [82]-125) Text of the Declaration on the relation of the Church to non-Christian religions (p. [121]-125) Bibliography: p. [152]-160. [BX830 1962.A45E276] 68-134397 21/-
1. Catholic Church—Missions. 2. Christianity and other religions. I. Vatican Council. 2d, 1962-1965. Decretum de activitate missionali ecclesiae. II. Vatican Council. 2d, 1962-1965. Declaratio de Ecclesiae habitudine ad religiones non-Christians. III. Title.

FORD, Francis xavier, Bp., 266.2
1892-1952.
Stone in the King's highway; selections from the writings of Bishop Francis Xavier Ford (1892-1952) with introductory memoir by Raymond A. Lane. New York, McMullen Books, 1953. 297p. 21cm. [BX890.F6417] [BX890.F6417] 275.1 53-8122 53-8122
1. Catholic Church—Collected works. 2. Theology—Collected works—20th cent. I. Title.

GREENE, Robert W 1911- 266.2
Calvary in China. New York, Putnam [1953] 244p. 22cm. Autobiographical. [BV3427.G7A3] 275.1 53-5326
1. Missions—China. I. Title.

GUIDELINES for world 266'.2
evangelism / by George P. Gurganus ... [et al.] ; with a foreword by John C. Stevens ; George P. Gurganus, editor. Abilene, Tex. : Biblical Research Press, c1976. 270 p. : diagrs. ; 22 cm. On spine: World evangelism. Includes bibliographies. [BV2070.G8] 76-56592 ISBN 0-89112-040-8 : 5.95
1. Missions—Addresses, essays, lectures. 2. Evangelistic work—Addresses, essays, lectures. I. Gurganus, George P. II. Title: World evangelism.

HABIG, Marion Alphonse, 266.2
Father, 1901-
In journeyings often; Franciscan pioneers in the Orient. New York, Franciscan Institute, St. Bonaventure University, 1953. 319p. 22cm. [BV2280.H2] 275 53-149
1. Franciscans—Missions. 2. Missions—Asia. 3. Missionaries. I. Title.

HENRY, Antonin Marcel, 266.2
1911-
A mission theology. Tr. [from French] by Albert J. LaMothe, Jr. Notre Dame, Ind., Fides [1963, c.1962] 197p. 20cm. (Themes of theology) 63-12299 3.95
1. Missions—Theory. I. Title.

HICKEY, Edward John, 1893- 266'.2
The Society for the Propagation of the Faith: its foundation, organization, and success (1822-1922). [New York, AMS Press, 1974] x, 195 p. 23 cm. Reprint of the author's thesis, Catholic University of America, 1922, which was issued as v. 3 of the Catholic University of America. Studies in American church history. Includes bibliographical references. [BV2155.S7H5 1974] 73-3557 ISBN 0-404-57753-9 8.50
1. Society for the Propagation of the Faith. 2. Catholic Church—Missions. I. Series: Catholic University of America. Studies in American church history, v. 3.

HOFFMAN, Ronan 266.2
Pioneer theories of missiology; a comparative study of the mission theories of Cardinal Brancati de Laurea, O.F.M. CONV., with those of three of his contemporaries: Jose de Acosta, S.J., Thomas a Jesu, O. CARM., and Dominicus de Gubernatis, O.F.M. With a foreword by Cardinal Cushing. Washington, D.C., Catholic University of America Press [c.] 1960. 182p. 22cm. Bibl.: p. 169-171. 60-2584 3.25 pap.,
1. Brancati, Lorenzo, Cardinal, 1612-1693. 2. Missions—Theory. 3. Catholic Church—Missions. I. Title.

I remember Flores, 266.2
by Mark Tennien and Tasuku Sato. New York, Farrar, Straus [1957] 129p. illus. 21cm. Tusuku Sato's memoirs rewritten by Mark Tennien and Tasuku Sato. [BX1654.F54S3] 279.2 57-6258
1. Catholic Church in Flores (Island) 2. World War, 1939-1945—Flores (Island) I. Sato, Tasuku, 1899- II. Tennien, Mark A., joint author.

JUST, Mary. 266.2
Digest of Catholic mission history. Maryknoll, N. Y., Maryknoll Publications [1958] 136p. illus. 24cm. (World horizon reports. Report no. 20) Includes bibliography. [BV2185.J8] 58-2403
1. Catholic Church—Missions—Hist. 2. Missions—Hist.—Chronology. I. Title.

KELLER, James Gregory, 266.2
1900-
Men of Maryknoll, by James Keller and Meyer Berger. Freeport, N.Y., Books for Libraries Press [1972, c1943] 191 p. 23 cm. (Essay index reprint series) [BV2300.C35K4 1972] 78-142650 ISBN 0-8369-2775-3
1. Catholic Foreign Mission Society of America—Biography. I. Berger, Meyer, 1898-1959, joint author. II. Title.

KENT, Mark Leo. 266.2
The glory of Christ; a pageant of two hundred missionary lives from apostolic times to the present age, by Mark L. Kent and Mary Just. Milwaukee, Bruce Pub. Co. [1955] 285p. 23cm. [BV3700.K3] 55-7863
1. Missionaries. 2. Catholic Church—Missions—Hist. 3. Missions—Hist. I. Just, Mary, joint author. II. Title.

KITTLER, Glenn D 266.2
The White Fathers. Introd. by Bishop Laurian Rugambwa. [1st ed.] New York, Harper [1957] 299p. illus. 22cm. [BV2300.W5K5] 276 57-6134
1. White Fathers. I. Title.

KITTLER, Glenn D 266.2
The White Fathers. Introd. by Bishop Laurian Rugambwa. [1st ed.] New York, Harper [1957] 299p. illus. 22cm. [BV2300.W5K5] 276 57-6134
1. White Fathers. I. Title.

LONG, Richard F. 266.2
Nowhere a stranger, by Richard F. Long. [1st ed.] New York, Vantage Press [1968] 132 p. illus. 22 cm. [BV2300.S53L6] 68-3916
1. Society of Catholic Medical Missionaries. I. Title.

MCCOY, Joseph A. 266.2
Advice from the field. Pref. by Frederick A. McGuire. Baltimore, Helicon[dist. Taplinger, 1963, c.1962] 288p. illus. 22cm. Bibl. 62-18779 4.95
1. Missions—Theory. 2. Catholic Church—Missions. I. Title.

MCDONNELL, Graham P. 266.2
Meaning of a missioner; text and photos. by Graham P. McDonnell. Maryknoll, N.Y., Maryknoll Publications [1967] 93 p. illus., ports. 24 cm. Presents the work of a Catholic missionary in Japan, discussing the work of the Japanese missions in general, and the life of a specific young Maryknoll missioner. Illustrated with photographs. [BV3445.2.M3] AC 67
1. Catholic Church—Missions. 2. Reiley, Robert J. 3. Missionary life. 4. Missions—Japan. I. Title.

MCGLADE, Joseph. 266.2
The Church on mission. Dublin, Gill [1967] xx, 267 p. 21 cm. (Logos books) [BV2180.M26] 75-11734 16/-
1. Catholic Church—Missions. I. Title.

MCGUIRE, Frederick A., 266.2
1905- ed.
Mission to mankind. New York, Random [c.1963] xii, 239p. 22cm. Bibl. 63-15042 4.95
1. Missionary stories. 2. Missionaries, American. 3. Catholic Church—Missions. I. Title.

MCGUIRE, Frederick A., 266.2
1905- ed.
The new missionary church. Helicon [dist. New York, Taplinger, c.1964] 158p. 21cm. 64-16131 3.95
1. Catholic Church—Missions. 2. Missions—Theory. I. Title.

MACLAGAN, Edward Douglas, 266.2
Sir, 1864-
The Jesuits and the Great Mogul, by Sir Edward Maclagan. New York, Octagon Books, 1972. xxi, 433 p. illus. 23 cm. Reprint of the 1932 ed. Bibliography: p. 369-394. [BX3746.I4M3 1972] 71-159212 ISBN 0-374-95248-5
1. Jesuits in India. 2. Jesuits—Missions. 3. Missions—India. 4. Mogul Empire—History. 5. Jesuits in Tibet. 6. Missions—Tibet. I. Title.

MANNA, Paolo. 266.2
Forward with Christ; thoughts and reflections on vocations to the foreign missions, by Paul Manna and Nicholas Maestrini. With a foreword by Edward Cardinal Mooney. Westminster, Md., Newman Press, 1954. 163p. illus. 21cm. Translation of Operaril autem paucis. [BV2180.M353] 54-5897
1. Catholic Church—Missions. 2. Missions, Foreign. 3. Missionaries—Appointment, call, and election. I. Maestrini, Nicholas, ed. and tr. II. Title.

MARIA DEL REY, Sister. 266.2
Dust on my toes; stories of people near and far. New York, Scribner [1959] 191p. 21cm. [BV2087.M34] 59-12006
1. Missionary stories. 2. Foreign Mission Sisters of St. Dominic. I. Title.

MARIA DEL REY, Sister. 266.2
In and out the Andes; mission trails from Yucatan to Chile. New York, Scribner, 1955[i. e. 1954] 281p. illus. 25cm. [BV2830.M35] [BV2830.M35] 278 54-11016 54-11016
1. Missions—Spanish America. 2. Foreign Mission Sisters of St. Dominic. I. Title.

MARTYRS in China. 266.2
Translated by Antonia Pakenham. With a foreword by John C. H. Wu. Chicago, H. Regnery Co. [1956] 288p. illus. 20cm. Translation of Les martyrs de Chine parlent. [BX1665.M642] 275.1 57-13603
1. Catholic Church in China. 2. China—Church history. 3. Persecution—China. I. Monsterleet, Jean, 1912-

MARYGROVE College, Detroit. 266.2
Eternal witness, the missionary apostolate of the Catholic Church. Detroit, 1952. 71p. illus. 31cm. 'A reprint of the commencement number of the Campus reporter. [BV2183.M35] 56-24937
1. Catholic Church— Missions. I. Title.

MARY JUST, Sister. 266.2
Immortal fire; a journey through the centuries with the missionary great. St. Louis, Herder, 1951. vii, 598 p. illus., ports. 24 cm. Secular name: Florence Didies David. Bibliography: p. 565-574. [BV2185.M3] 51-1880
1. Missions—Hist. 2. Catholic Church—Missions—Hist. I. Title.

MILLOT, Rene Pierre. 266.2
Missions in the world today. Translated from the French by J.Holland Smith. [1st ed.] New York, Hawthorn Books [1961] 139p. 21cm. (The Twentieth century encyclopedia of Catholicism, v. 100. Section 9: The church and the modern world) Translation of Missions d'aujourd'hul. Includes bibliography. [BV2185.M513] 61-15608
1. Catholic Church—Missions. I. Title.

MISSION on the Nile. 266.2
New York, Philosophical Library [1956] 247p. illus. 23cm. [BV3625] [BV3625] 276.24 57-868 57-868
1. Missions—Sudan. 2. Shilluks. I. Dempsey, James, 1906-

MISSIONARY academia 266.2
study. New York, Society for the Propagation of the Faith and the Missionary Union of the Clergy. v. 23cm. Title varies: The Missionary academia. [BV2130.M42] 53-23130
1. Catholic Church—Missions—Period. I. Society for the Propagation of the Faith.

MOORE, John Travers. 266.2
Modern crusaders, by John Travers Moore and Rosemarian V. Staudacher. New York, Vision Books [1957] 190p. illus. 22cm. (Vision books, 18) [BV3700.M75] 57-5402
1. Missionaries. 2. Catholic Church—Missions. I. Staudacher, Rosemarian V., joint author. II. Title.

MURPHY, Edward L 266.2
Teach ye all nations; the principles of Catholic missionary work. New York, Benziger Bros. [1958] 234p. 19cm. [BV2180.M84] 58-1590
1. Missions—Theory. 2. Catholic Church—Missions. I. Title.

NEVINS, Albert J 1915- 266.2
Adventures of men of Maryknoll. Illustrated by Albert Schreiner. New York, Dodd, Mead, 1957. 255p. illus. 21cm. [BV2300.C35N35] 56-9312
1. Catholic Foreign Mission Society of America. I. Title.

NEVINS, Albert J., 1915- 266.2
ed.
The Maryknoll golden book; an anthology of mission literature. New York, Book Treasures [1956] 444p. 22cm. [BV2300.C35N38] 56-6277
1. Catholic Foreign Mission Society of America. I. Title.

NEVINS, Albert J 1915- 266.2
The meaning of Maryknoll. New York, McMullen Books [1954] 344p. illus. 22cm. [BV2300.C35N4] 54-10312
1. Catholic Foreign Mission Society of America. I. Title.

NOSOW, Sigmund. 266'.2
Attitudes toward changing organizational goals; an evaluation study of the Eastern Province of the Holy Ghost Fathers [by] Sigmund Nosow [and] Frederick R. Clark. Pittsburgh, Duquesne University Press [1972] xii, 206 p. 26 cm. [BX3682.Z6E25] 74-190710 ISBN 0-8207-0145-9
1. Holy Ghost Fathers. Eastern Province. I. Clark, Frederick Reese, 1928- joint author. II. Title.

PLATTNER, Felix Alfred, 1906- 266.2
Christian India. Introd. by Trevor Huddleston. Photos. by B. Moosbrugger. [Translated from the German by Mollie Seton-Karr] New York, Vanguard Press [1957] 147p. illus. 30cm. [BX1644.P512] [BX1644.P512] 275.4 57-4326 57-4326
1. Catholic Church in India—Pictures, illustrations, etc. I. Title.

REID, Elizabeth. 266.2
I belong where I'm needed. Westminster, Md., Newman Press, 1961. 330p. illus. 24cm. [BX809.G7R4] 61-16570
1. Grail movement (Catholic) I. Title.

RE-THINKING the church's mission. 266.2 New York, Paulist [1966] viii, 152p. 24cm. (Conclium theol. in the age of renewal: Pastoral theol., v. 13) Bibl. [BV2063.R47] 66-20894 4.50
1. Missions—Theory. 2. Catholic Church—Missions. I. Series: Concilium theology in the age of renewal, v. 13

RETIF, Louis 266.2
The church's mission in the world, by Louis and Andre Retif. Tr. from French by Reginald F. Trevett. Glen Rock, N.J., Paulist [c.1964] 121p. 19cm. (Vol. of the 20th Cent. Ency. of Catholicism; Deus/Century bks.) Bibl. .95 pap.,
1. Catholic Church—Missions. 2. Missions—Theory. I. Retif, Andre, joint author. II. Title.

RETIF, Louis 266.2
The church's mission in the world, by Louis and Andre Retif. Tr. from French by Reginald F. Trevett. New York, Hawthorn [c.1962] 156p. (Twentieth cent. ency. of Catholicism, 102. Section 9: The church and the modern world) Bibl. 62-11414 3.50 bds.,
1. Catholic Church—Missions. 2. Missions—Theory. I. Retif, Andre, joint author. II. Title.

RIVELY, William E 266.2
The story of the Romance. New York, Rinehart [1953] 241p. 22cm. [BV3679.C3R5] 279.66 52-14192
1. Missions— Caroline Islands. 2. Catholic Church—Missions. 3. Romance (Brigantine) I. Title.

SATO, Tasuku, 1899- 266.2
I remember Flores by Mark Tennien and Tasuku Sato. New York, Farrar, Straus [1957] 129p. illus. 21cm. Tasuku Sato's memoirs rewritten by Mark Tennien and Tasuku Sato. [BX1654.F54S3] [BX1654.F54S3] 279.2 57-6258 57-6258
1. Catholic Church in Flores (Island) 2. World War, 1939-1945— Flores (Island) I. Tennien, Mark A., joint author. II. Title.

SCHMAIZ, Norbert, 1901- 266.2
Shen-fu's story; the memoirs of two American Missionaries [sic] in the China of yesteryear, by Norbert Schmalz, Boniface Pfeilschifter. Chicago, Franciscan Herald [c.1966] 187p. illus. 21cm. [BV3415.S3] 65-29095 3.50
1. Missions—China. 2. Franciscans in China. I. Pfeilschifter, Boniface, 1900- joint author. II. Title.

SCHMALZ, Norbert, 1901- 266.2
Shen-fu's story; the memoirs of two American missionaries [sic] in the China of yesteryear, by Norbert Schmalz and Boniface Pfeilschifter. Chicago, Franciscan Herald Press [1966] 187 p. illus. 21 cm. [BV3415.S3] 65-29095
1. Missions—China. 2. Franciscans in China. I. Pfeilschifter, Boniface, 1900- joint author. II. Title.

SERRA, Junipero, 1713-1784. 266'.2
A letter of Junipero Serra to the reverend father prencher Fray Fermin Francisco de Lasuen; a bicentennial discovery. Translated and edited by Francis J. Weber. Boston, D. R. Godine, 1970. [15] p. 23 cm. "Five hundred copies ... Copy number 369." Includes bibliographical references. [F864.S39713 1970] 71-107215
1. Serra, Junipero, 1713-1784. 2. Lasuen, Fermin Francisco de, 1736-1803. I. Lasuen, Fermin Francisco de, 1736-1803. II. Title.

SHEEN, Fulton John, Bp., 1895- 266.2
Missions and the world crisis. Milwaukee, Bruce Pub. Co. [1963] viii, 273 p. 22 cm. [BV2180.S5] 63-17493
1. Missions—Theory. 2. Catholic Church—Missions. I. Title.

SHEEN, Fulton John, Bp., 1895- 266.2
Missions and the world crisis. Milwaukee, Bruce [c.1963] viii, 273p. 22cm. 63-17493 4.95
1. Missions—Theory. 2. Catholic Church—Missions. I. Title.

SOCIETY for the Propagation of the Faith. U.S. Mission Secretariat. 266.2
Revolution in missionary thinking; a symp., ed. by William J. Richardson. Marvknoll. N. Y. Marvknoll. 1966. x. 261p. 19cm. (World horizon bks.) Selected papers from the annual meeting of the Mission Secretariat held at Washington, D. C. Bibl. [BV2180.S6] 66-27417 price unreported pap.,
1. Catholic Church—Missions—Addresses, essays, lectures. 2. Missions—Theory—Addresses, essays, lectures. I. Richardson, William Jerome, 1929- ed. II. Title.

SOCIETY for the Propagation of the Faith. U.S. Mission Secretariat. 266.2
Revolution in missionary thinking; a symposium, edited by William J. Richardson. Maryknoll, N.Y., Maryknoll Publications, 1966. x, 261 p. 19 cm. (World horizon books) Selected papers from the annual meeting of the Mission Secretariat held at Washington, D.C. Bibliographical footnotes. [BV2180.S6] 66-27417
1. Catholic Church — Missions — Addresses, essays, lectures. 2. Missions — Theory — Addresses, essays, lectures. I. Richardson, William Jerome, 1929- ed. II. Title.

SOCIETY of Catholic Medical Missionaries. 266.2
If it matters ... [Philadelphia, Medical Mission Sisters, c1967] 210 p. illus. (part col.), maps. 28 cm. [R722.S55] 76-9032
I. Title.

SOCIETY of the Divine Word. 266'.2
The Word in the world : Divine Word missionaries, 1875-1975 / [edited by Divine Word missionaries ; sketches by Ron Berger ; photos. by Steve Dunwell]. Techny, Ill. : The Society, [1975] 191 p., [1] fold. leaf of plates : ill. (some col.) ; 29 cm. [BV2300.S6S6 1975] 75-311879
1. Society of the Divine Word—Missions. I. Title.

STRAELEN, Henricus van, 1903- 266.2
The Catholic encounter with world religions, by H. van Straelen. With a pref. by Paul Cardinal Marella. Westminster, Md., Newman Press [1966] 202 p. 25 cm. [BV2180.S8] 66-9264
1. Catholic Church — Missions. 2. Catholic Church — Relations. I. Title.

STRAELEN, Henricus van, 1903- 266.2
The Catholic encounter with world religions, by H. van Straelen. With a pref. by Paul Cardinal Marella. Westminster, Md., Newman Press [1966] 202 p. 25 cm. [BV2180.S8 1966a] 66-9264
1. Catholic Church—Missions. 2. Catholic Church—Relations. I. Title.

SYLVEST, Edwin Edward. 266'.2
Motifs of Franciscan mission theory in sixteenth century New Spain Province of the Holy Gospel / by Edwin Edward Sylvest, Jr. Washington : Academy of American Franciscan History, 1975. xiv, 148 p. ; 27 cm. (Monograph series - Academy of American Franciscan History ; v. 11) Includes index. Bibliography: p. 135-139. [BV2835.2.S93] 75-324689
1. Franciscans—Missions. 2. Missions—Mexico. 3. Indians of Mexico—Missions. I. Title. II. Series: Academy of American Franciscan History. Monograph series ; v. 11.

TRETTEL, Efrem. 266.2
Rivers, rice fields, souls: memoirs of my mission in China. Translated by Elsa Micallef. Chicago, Franciscan Herald Press [1965] 226 p. maps. (on lining papers) port. 21 cm. [BV3427.T67A33] 65-25842
1. Missions — China (People's Republic of China, 1949-) I. Title.

TRETTEL, Efrem 266.2
Rivers, rice fields, souls: memoirs of my mission in China. Tr. by Elsa Micallef. Chicago, Franciscan Herald [c.1965] 226p. maps (on lining papers) port. 21cm. [BV3427.T67A33] 65-25842 4.50 bds.,
1. Missions—China (People's Republic of China, 1949-) I. Title.

VAULX, Bernard de. 266.2
History of the missions. Translated from the French by Reginald F. Trevett. [1st ed.] New York, Hawthorn Books [1961] 191 p. 21 cm. (The Twentieth century encyclopedia of Catholicism. v. 99. Section 9: The church and the modern world) Translation of Les missions: leur histoire. Includes bibliography. [BV2185.V343] 61-12974
1. Catholic Church — Missions — Hist. 2. Missions — Hist. I. Title.

VAULX, Bernard de 266.2
History of the missions. Tr. from French by Reginald F. Trevett. New York, Hawthorn Books [c.1961] 191p. (Twentieth century encyclopedia of Catholicism, v. 99 Section 9: The church and the modern world) Bibl. 61-12974 3.50 bds.,
1. Catholic Church—Missions—Hist. 2. Missions—Hist. I. Title.

CAMPBELL, Robert Edward, 1924- ed. 266.201
The church in mission. Maryknoll, N. Y., Maryknoll. 1966 [c.1965] x, 278p. 21cm. Bibl. [BV2180.C33] 65-28583 5.95
1. Missions—Theory. I. Title.

SOCIETY for the Propagation of the Faith. U.S. Mission Secretariat. 266.2'025
U. S. Catholics overseas; a statistical directory, January 1, 1968. Washington, 1968. xvi, 79 p. 28 cm. [BV2178.S6] 68-56625
1. Catholic Church—Missions—Directories. I. Title.

KITTLER, Glenn D 266.206273
The Maryknoll Fathers. [1st ed.] Cleveland, World Pub. Co. [1961] 318p. illus. 22cm. [BV2300.C35K5] 61-6648
1. Catholic Foreign Mission Society of America. I. Title.

KITTLER, Glenn D. 266.206273
The Maryknoll Fathers. Cleveland, World Pub. Co. [c.1961] 318p. illus. 61-6648 5.00
1. Catholic Foreign Mission Society of America. I. Title.

KITTLER, Glenn D. 266.206273
The Maryknoll Fathers. New York, All Saints Pr. [1963, c.1961] 310p. illus. 17cm. (AS 705) .75 pap.,
1. Catholic Foreign Mission Society of America. I. Title.

HUNT, Darryl L ed. 266.208
Go, tell it everywhere; modern missioners in action, edited by Darryl L. Hunt. Maryknoll, N.Y., Maryknoll Publications, 1965. 222 p. illus. 21 cm. [BV2300.C35H8] 65-26927
1. Catholic Foreign Mission Society of America. 2. Missionary stories. I. Title.

HUNT, Darryl L., ed. 266.208
Go tell it everywhere; modern missioners in action. Maryknoll, N. Y., Maryknoll [c.] 1965. 222p. illus. 21cm. [BV2300.C35H8] 65-26927 2.00 pap.,
1. Catholic Foreign Mission Society of America. 2. Missionary stories. I. Title.

MARYKNOLL Missioners' Conference, Maryknoll, N.Y., 1963 266.2082
The modern mission apostolate; a symposium. Ed. by William J. Richardson. Maryknoll, N.Y., Maryknoll Pubns. [c.1965] x, 308p. 21cm. Bibl. [BV2160.M3] 65-13702 3.95
1. Missions—Congresses. 2. Catholic Foreign Mission Society of America—Missions. I. Richardson, William Jerome, 1929- ed. II. Catholic Foreign Mission Society of America. III. Title.

FREITAG, Anton, 1882- 266.209
The twentieth century atlas of the Christian world; the expansion of Christianity through the centuries. In collaboration with Heinrich Emmerich, Jakob Buijs. Foreword by Gregory Peter Agagianian [Rev. and up-to-date translation from French] New York, Hawthorn [1964, c.1963] xi, 199p. illus., facsims., maps (pt. col.) ports 35cm. 63-17035 20.00
1. Missions—Hist. 2. Missions—Pictures, illustrations, etc. 3. Missions—Geography—Maps. I. Title.

DUTTON, Charles Judson, 1888- 266.2'0922 B
The samaritans of Molokai; the lives of Father Damien and Brother Dutton among the lepers, by Charles J. Dutton. Freeport, N.Y., Books for Libraries Press [1971] xiv, 286 p. illus., facsim., ports. 23 cm. Reprint of the 1932 ed. Bibliography: p. 281-286. [BX4705.D25D8 1971] 70-152981 ISBN 0-8369-5733-4
1. Damien, Father, 1840-1889. 2. Dutton, Joseph, 1843-1931. 3. Missions to lepers—Hawaii. I. Title.

ANGELINI-LARGHETTI, Ambrose, 1901- 266'.2'0924 B
My Odyssey in China [by] Father Liang (Father Ambrose Angelini-Larghetti) Translated from the Italian by Fr. Raimondo Camilleri. [New York, Printed by Alba House, c1972] 235 p. illus. 21 cm. Translation of I miei ventiquattro anni di vita missionaria in Cina. [BV3427.A52A313] 73-159448
1. Angelini-Larghetti, Ambrose, 1901- I. Title.

BARRETT, William Edmund, 1900- 266.2'0924
The red lacquered gate, by William E. Barrett. New York, Sheed and Ward [1967] xii, 398 p. 22 cm. [BV3427.G25B3] 67-13765
1. Galvin, Edward J., 1882-1956. 2. Missions—China. I. Title.

BEEVERS, John. 266'.2'0924 B
A man for now; the life of Damien de Veuster, friend of lepers. [1st ed.] Garden City, N.Y., Doubleday, 1973. 192 p. 22 cm. [BX4705.D25B36] 73-83584 ISBN 0-385-05574-9 5.95
1. Damien, Father, 1840-1889. I. Title.

BROWN, Evelyn M. 266.2'0924
Edel Quinn, beneath the Southern Cross, by Evelyn M. Brown. Illustrated by Harold Lang. New York, Vision Books [1967] xv, 175 p. illus. 22 cm. [BV3557.Q8B7] 67-3845
1. Quinn, Edel Mary, 1907-1944. 2. Missions — Africa, South. I. Title.

BROWN, Evelyn M. 266.2'092'4 B
Edel Quinn, beneath the Southern Cross, by Evelyn M. Brown. Illustrated by Harold Lang. New York, Vision Books [1967] xv, 175 p. illus. 22 cm. [BV3557.Q8B7] 67-3845
1. Quinn, Edel Mary, 1907-1944. 2. Missions—Africa, South.

BROWNING, Mary Carmel. 266.2'0924 B
Think big; a partial biography of Reverend James Tong, S.J. [1st ed.] Owensboro, Ky., Printed by Winkler Print. Co., 1970. 109 p. illus., ports. 28 cm. [BV3269.T67B76] 76-134943
1. Tong, James. I. Title.

CARTER, Robert F. 266'.2'0924 B
The tarnished halo; story of Fray Francisco Hidalgo, by Robert F. Carter. Chicago, Franciscan Herald Press [1973] p. Bibliography: p. [E78.T4C37] 73-8669 ISBN 0-8199-0457-0
1. Hidalgo, Francisco, 1659?-1726. 2. Indians of North America—Texas—Missions. 3. Indians of Mexico—Missions. I. Title.

CLARKE, Richard Frederick, 1839-1900. 266.2'0924 B
Cardinal Lavigerie and the African slave trade, edited by Richard F. Clarke. New York, Negro Universities Press [1969] viii, 379 p. 23 cm. Reprint of the 1889 ed. [BX4705.L4C5 1969] 74-77199
1. Lavigerie, Charles Martial Allemand, Cardinal, 1825-1892. 2. Catholic Church—Missions. 3. Missions—Africa, Central. 4. Slave trade—Africa.

COLEMAN, Bernard, Sister, 1890- 266'.2'0924 B
Masinaigans: the little book; a biography of Monsignor Joseph F. Buh, Slovenian missionary in America, 1864-1922 [by] Sister Bernard Coleman [and] Sister Verona LaBud. Saint Paul, Minn., North Central Pub. Co., 1972. x, 368 p. illus. 25 cm. Bibliography: p. 261-277. [E78.M7C64] 72-85332
1. Buh, Joseph F., 1833-1922. 2. Indians of North America—Minnesota—Missions. 3. Indians of North America—Nortwest, Old—Missions. I. LaBud, Verona, joint author. II. Title.

DOIG, Desmond. 266'.2'0924 B
Mother Teresa, her people and her work / Desmond Doig ; photos. by Raghu Rai ... [et al.]. 1st. U.S. ed. New York : Harper & Row, c1976. 175 p. : ill. (some col.) ; 25 cm. [BX4406.5.Z8D65 1976] 75-39857 ISBN 0-06-060560-X : 15.00
1. Teresa, Mother, 1910- I. Title.

DOLLEN, Charles. 266.2'0924 B
The cheerful warrior; the life of Charles Garnier. Illustrated by the Daughters of St. Paul, under the direction of Guy R. Pennisi. [Boston] St. Paul Editions [1967] 72 p. illus. 22 cm. A biography of the seventeenth century Catholic martyr who left France to be one of the first Jesuit missionaries to the Huron Indians in New France. [BX705.G247D6] 92 AC 68
1. Garnier, Charles, 1605-1649. I. Title.

DONOVAN, John F. 266'.2'0924 B
A priest named Horse / by John F. Donovan. Huntington, IN : Our Sunday Visitor, c1977. 256 p. : ill. ; 21 cm. [BV3427.M47D66] 76-53703 ISBN 0-87973-748-4 pbk. : 4.95
1. Meyer, Bernard F., 1891-1975. 2. Missionaries—China—Biography. 3. Missionaries—United States—Biography. I. Title.

DONOVAN, John F. 266'.2'0924 B
A priest named Horse / by John F. Donovan. Huntington, IN : Our Sunday Visitor, c1977. 256 p. : ill. ; 21 cm. [BV3427.M47D66] 76-53703 ISBN 0-87973-748-4 pbk. : 4.95
1. Meyer, Bernard F., 1891-1975. 2. Missionaries—China—Biography. 3. Missionaries—United States—Biography. I. Title.

EMERSON, Dorothy. 266'.2'0924 B
Among the Mescalero Apaches; the story of Father Albert Braun, O.F.M. Tucson, Ariz., University of Arizona Press [1973] xiii, 224 p. illus. 24 cm. Bibliography: p. 217-219. [E99.M45E47] 73-76302 ISBN 0-8165-0321-4 7.50
1. Braun, Albert, 1889- 2. Apache Indians—Missions. I. Title.

EMERSON, Dorothy. 266'.2'0924 B
Among the Mescalero Apaches; the story of Father Albert Braun, O.F.M. Tucson, Ariz., University of Arizona Press [1973] xiii, 224 p. illus. 24 cm. Bibliography: p. 217-219. [E99.M45E47] 73-76302 ISBN 0-8165-0321-4 7.50
1. Braun, Albert, 1889- 2. Apache Indians—Missions. I. Title.

FISCHER, Edward. 266'.2'0924 B
Light in the Far East : Archbishop Harold Henry's forty-two years in Korea / Edward Fischer. New York : Seabury Press, c1976. p. cm. "A Crossroad book." [BV3462.H38F57] 76-22466 ISBN 0-8164-0307-4 : 8.95
1. Henry, Harold, 1909- 2. Missions—Korea. I. Title.

GORREE, Georges, 266'.2'0924 B
1908-
Love without boundaries : Mother Teresa of Calcutta / by Georges Gorree and Jean Barbier ; translated by Paula Speakman. Huntington, Ind. : Our Sunday Visitor, c1974. 96 p. : ill. ; 18 cm. Translation of Amour sans frontiere. [BX4406.5.Z8G6713 1974b] 75-37364 ISBN 0-87973-679-8 : 1.50
1. Teresa, Mother, 1910- 2. Missionaries of Charity. I. Barbier, Jean, fl. 1940- joint author. II. Title.

GROELL, Clara, 266'.2'0924 B
1882-
White wings in bamboo land. [Emmitsburg, Md., Saint Joseph's Provincial House Press, 1973] 207 p. illus. 22 cm. Autobiographical. [BV3427.G74A3] 73-83504
1. Groell, Clara, 1882- 2. Daughters of Charity of St. Vincent de Paul, Emmitsburg, Md.—Missions. 3. Missions—China. I. Title.

LOUIS, Sister, 266.2'0924 B
O.S.F.
Love is the answer; the story of Mother Kevin, by Sister M. Louis. [Dublin, Fallon's Educational Supply Co.]; Distributor in the U.S. and Canada: St. Anthony's Guild, Paterson, N.J. [1964] xiv, 254 p. plates, ports. 22 cm. [BX4705.K46L68] 79-250999
1. Kevin, Mother, O.S.F., 1875-1957. I. Title.

LYONS, Letitia 266'.2'0924 B
Mary, Sister, 1903-
Francis Norbert Blanchet and the founding of the Oregon missions (1838-1848). Washington, Catholic University of America Press, 1940. [New York, AMS Press, 1974] p. Reprint of the author's thesis, Catholic University of America, 1940, which was issued as v. 30 [i.e. 31] of the Catholic University of America. Studies in American church history. Bibliography: p. [BX1415.O7L9 1974] 73-3585 ISBN 0-404-57781-4 9.50
1. Catholic Church in Oregon—History. 2. Blanchet, Francis Norbert, Abp., 1795-1883. 3. Portland, Or. (Ecclesiastical province) I. Title. II. Series: Catholic University of America. Studies in American church history, v. 31.

MCAULIFFE, Marius 266'.2'0924 B
Envoy to Africa : the interior life of Edel Quinn / Marius McAuliffe. Chicago : Franciscan Herald Press, [1975] p. cm. [BV3557.Q8M32] 74-31153 ISBN 0-8199-0560-7 pbk. : 1.95
1. Quinn, Edel Mary, 1907-1944. I. Title.

MCDONNELL, Graham P. 266.2'0924
Meaning of a missioner; text and photos. by Graham P. McDonnell. Maryknoll, N.Y., Maryknoll Publications [1967] 93 p. illus., ports. 24 cm. [BV3445.2.M3] 67-21013
1. Catholic Church—Missions. 2. Reiley, Robert J. 3. Missions—Japan. I. Title.

MUGGERIDGE, Malcolm, 266.2'0924 B
1903-
Something beautiful for God; Mother Teresa of Calcutta. New York, Harper & Row [1971] 156 p. illus. 23 cm. [BX4406.5.Z8M8 1971b] 77-155106 5.95
1. Teresa, Mother, 1910- 2. Missionaries of Charity. I. Title.

MUGGERIDGE, 266.2'0924 [B]
Malcolm, 1903-
Something beautiful for God; Mother Teresa of Calcutta. New York, Ballantine [1973, c.1971] 156 p. illus. (1 col.) ports. 21 cm. [BX4406.5.Z8M8] ISBN 0-345-03276-4 2.00 (pbk.)
1. Teresa, Mother, 1910- 2. Missionaries of Charity. I. Title.

L.C. card no. for the hardbound ed.: 77155106.

PIRUS, Betty L. 266'.2'0924 B
Before I sleep / Betty L. Pirus. 1st ed. New York : Vantage Press, c1977. 206 p. ; 21 cm. Bibliography: p. 203-206. [F864.S535] 77-151737 ISBN 0-533-02580-X : 6.95
1. Serra, Junipero, 1713-1784. 2. Missions—California—History. 3. California—History—To 1846. 4. Franciscans—California—History. 5. Franciscans—California—Biography. I. Title.

PITRONE, Jean Maddern. 266.20924
The Great Black Robe. Illustrated by Peggy Worthington Best. Boston, St. Paul Editions, [1965] 121, [2] p. col. illus. 22 cm. Bibliography: p. [123] [F591.S643] 65-17554
1. Smet, Pierre Jean de, 1801-1873—Juvenile literature. 2. Indians of North America—Missions—Juvenile literature. I. Title.

PITRONE, Jean Maddern 266.20924
The Great Black Robe. Illus. by Peggy Worthington Best. [Boston] St. Paul Ed. [dist. Daughters of St. Paul, c.1965] 121, [2]p. col. illus. 22cm. Bibl. [F591.S643] 65-17554 1.50 pap.,
1. Smet, Pierre Jean de, 1801-1873—Juvenile literature. 2. Indians of North America—Missions Juvenile literature. I. Title.

PITRONE, Jean 266.2'0924 B
Maddern.
The touch of his hand; Colombo, a modern day Damien in Burma. Staten Island, Alba House [1970] viii, 161 p. illus., map, port. 22 cm. [BV3271.C58P55] 75-129173 ISBN 0-8189-0195-0 3.95
1. Colombo, Cesare, 1910- 2. Missions to lepers—Burma. I. Title.

POLZER, Charles W. 266.2'0924 B
A Kino guide; a life of Eusebio Francisco Kino, Arizona's first pioneer and a guide to his missions and monuments. Cartography by Donald Bufkin. Tucson, Southwestern Mission Research Center, 1968. 42 p. illus., maps, ports. 29 cm. Bibliography: p. 42. [F799.K632] 68-5133
1. Kino, Eusebio Francisco, 1644-1711. I. Title.

RIOU, Roger, 1909- 266'.2'0924 B
The island of my life : from petty crime to priestly mission / Roger Riou ; translated from the French by Martin Sokolinsky. New York : Delacorte Press, [1975] 300 p., [7] leaves of plates : ill. ; 22 cm. [R722.R56A3313] 75-4980 ISBN 0-440-04559-2 : 7.95
1. Riou, Roger, 1909- 2. Missionaries, Medical—Correspondence, reminiscences, etc. 3. Missions, Medical—Haiti. I. Title.

SERRA, Junipero, 266.2'0924 B
1713-1784.
Diario: the journal of Padre Serra, from Loreto, the capital of Baja California, to San Diego, capital of the new establishments of Alta California, in three months and three days, March 28 to July 1, 1769. A new grass roots translation by Ben F. Dixon. [2d ed.] San Diego, Calif., Don Diego's Libreria, 1967. xi, 116 p. illus., facsims., maps, ports. 22 cm. "The Song of Padre Serra" (unacc.) on inside front cover. Includes San Diego's water rights document. [F864.S393 1967] 71-276685 2.00
1. Missions—California—History—Sources. 2. Franciscans in California—History—Sources. I. Title.

STAGG, Albert. 266'.2'0924 B
The first Bishop of Sonora : Antonio de los Reyes / Albert Stagg. Tucson : University of Arizona Press, c1976. ix, 109 p. : ill. ; 24 cm. Includes index. Bibliography: p. 103-106. [F1219.3.M59R497] 76-379189 ISBN 0-8165-0549-7 : 8.50. ISBN 0-8165-0486-5 pbk. :
1. Reyes, Antonio de los, Bp., 1729-1786. 2. Indians of Mexico—Missions. 3. Franciscans in Mexico. 4. Missionaries—Mexico—Biography. 5. Missionaries—Spain—Biography. I. Title.

STEELE, Harvey, 266'.2'0924 B
1911-
Agent for change; the story of Pablo Steele as told to Gary MacEoin. Maryknoll, N.Y., Orbis Books [1973] xvi, 175 p. 22 cm. [HN32.S79] 72-85797 ISBN 0-88344-006-7 4.50
1. Steele, Harvey, 1911- I. MacEoin, Gary, 1909- II. Title.

STEVENSON, Robert 266.2'0924
Louis, 1850-1894.
Father Damien; an open letter to the Reverend Doctor Hyde of Honolulu, from Robert Louis Stevenson. Foreword by George L. McKay. New York, Cobble Hill Pr. [1968] 56p. port. 17cm. [BX4705.D25S7 1968] 67-27293 2.75
1. Damien, Father, 1840-1889. 2. Hyde, Charles McEwen, 1832-1899. I. Title.
Distributed by Hill & Wang.

WALSH, James 266'.2'0924 B
Edward, Bp., 1891-
Zeal for your house / by James E. Walsh ; edited by Robert E. Sheridan. Huntington, Ind. : Our Sunday Visitor, c1976. 233 p. : ill. ; 23 cm. [BV3427.W32A35] 76-6211 ISBN 0-87973-892-8 : 7.95
1. Walsh, James Edward, Bp., 1891- 2. Missions—China. I. Title.

GELFAND, Michael, 266'.2'096891
comp.
Gubulawayo and beyond; letters and journals of the early Jesuit missionaries to Zambesia (1879-1887). With a foreword by W. F. Rea. New York, Barnes & Noble [1969, c1968] 496 p. illus., maps, ports. 23 cm. Bibliographical footnotes. [BV2290.A5E5 1969] 78-3759 10.00
1. Jesuits in Rhodesia. 2. Missions—Rhodesia. I. Jesuits. Letters from missions. II. Title.

MCCANTS, Dorothea 266.2'09763
Olga, comp.
They came to Louisiana; letters of a Catholic mission, 1854-1882. Translated and edited by Dorothea Olga McCants. Baton Rouge, Louisiana State University Press [1970] xxiii, 263 p. 24 cm. Includes bibliographical references. [BV2803.L8M3] 72-96258 8.50
1. Daughters of the Cross—Missions. 2. Missions—Louisiana. 3. Louisiana—Church history. I. Title.

SIX mission of Texas 266.209764
[by] James Day [and others] Introd. by John Connally. Pref. by Price Daniel. Historical coordinator, Dorman H. Winfrey. [1st ed.] Waco, Tex., Texian Press, 1965. ix, 194 p. 6 col. plates 29 cm. Contents.CONTENTS.—The Alamo, by L. Tinkle.—La Bahia, by J. B. Frantz.—Concepcion, by J. W. Schmitz.—San Francisco de Espada, by D. H. Winfrey.—San Jose, by J. M. Day.—San Juan Capistrano, by B. Procter. [F389.S6] 65-27835
1. Missions—Texas. 2. Spanish missions of Texas. 3. Franciscans in Texas. I. Day, James M.

SIX missions of 266.209764
Texas [by James Day, others] Introd. by John Connally. Pref. by Price Daniel. Hist. coordinator, Dorman H. Winfrey. Waco, Tex., Texian Pr. P.O. Box 1684 [c.]1965. ix, 194p. 6 col. plates. 29cm. [F389.S6] 65-27835 10.00
1. Missions—Texas. 2. Spanish missions of Texas. 3. Franciscans in Texas. I. Day, James M.
Contents omitted.

WEIBEL, Johann 266.2'09767'9
Eugen, 1853-
The Catholic missions of north-east Arkansas, 1867-1893, by John Eugene Weibel. Tr. from German by M. Agnes Voth. Ed. by Lee A. Dew. [State College?] Printed by Arkansas State Univ. Pr. 1967. 109p. facsim., map. 23cm. Tr. of Die katholischen Missionen in nordostlichen Arkansas und das benediktiner Frauenkloster Maria Stein [BX1415.A7W43] 67-7739 1.55
1. Catholic Church in Arkansas. I. Title.

RAUFER. MARIA ILMA 266.20979728
Black robes and Indians on the last frontier, a story of heroism. Milwaukee. Bruce [1966] xiv. 489p. illus,. maps, ports. 23cm. Bibl. [E78.W3R17] 65-29168 7.50
1. St. Mary's Mission. Omak, Wash. 2. Indians of North America—Washington (State)—Hist. 3. Indians of North America—Missions. I. Title.

MARIA DEL REY, [266.2] 275
Sister.
Pacific hopscotch. New York, Scribner, 1951. x, 191 p. illus. 23 cm. [BV2300.F6M3] 51-10254
1. Foreign Mission Sisters of St. Dominic 2. Missions—Asia. Missions—Islands of the Pacific. I. Title.

STRAELEN, Henricus [266.2] 275
van, 1903-
Through Eastern eyes; conferences given at the Lay Mission School, Grailville, Loveland, Ohio. With an introd. by Fulton J. Sheen. [Loveland, Ohio, Grailville, 1951] xiii, 162 p. illus. 22 cm. Full name: Henricus Johannes Josephus Maria van Straelen. Bibliography: p. 158-161. [BX1615.S8] 51-4152
1. Catholic Church in Asia. 2. Christianity and other religions. 3. Asia — Civilization. 4. Civilization. I. Title.

WALSH, James [266.2] 275.1
Edward, Bp., 1891-
The young ones. Illus. by Al Schreiner. New York, Farrar, Straus, and Cudahy [1958] 213 p. illus. 22 cm. [BV3415.W27] 58-12130
1. Missions — China. 2. Children in China. I. Title.

WILLIAMS, Frederick [266.2] 275.2
Vincent, 1890-
The martyrs of Nagasaki. Fresno, Calif., Academy Library Guild, 1956. 145 p. illus. 22 cm, [BV3445.W5] 56-14656
1. Martyrs — Japan. 2. Japan — Church history. I. Title.

ADDISON, James Thayer, 266'.2'4
1887-1953.
The medieval missionary : a study of the conversion of Northern Europe, A.D. 500-1300 / by James Thayer Addison. Philadelphia : Porcupine Press, 1976. xiv, 176 p. ; 22 cm. (Perspectives in European history ; no. 1) Reprint of the 1936 ed. published by International Missionary Council, New York, as no. 2 of Studies in the world mission of Christianity. Includes index. Bibliography: p. [159]-167. [BV2110.A4 1976] 76-7628 ISBN 0-87991-610-9 lib. bdg. : 12.50
1. Missions—History. 2. Missions—Europe. 3. Europe—Church history. 4. Church history—Middle Ages, 600-1500. I. Title. II. Series: Studies in the world mission of Christianity ; no. 2.

WARE, Myrtle (Barber) [266]249
1902-1948.
The home in world missions. Abilene, Tex., Abilene Print. & Stationery Co. [1950] 107 p. group port. 24 cm. [BV4526.W3] 50-29210
1. Family — Religious life. 2. Missions. Foreign. I. Title.

ATTWATER, Rachel. 266.251
Adam Schall, a Jesuit at the court of China, 1592-1666. Adapted from the French of Joseph Duhr. Milwaukee, Bruce Pub. Co. [c1963] 163 p. illus., ports., maps, plans. 21 cm. "Much of the material ... was first published in Un jesuite en Chine, Adam Schall, by Joseph Duhr ... in 1936." [BV3427.S35A8] 63-22843
1. Schall von Bell, Johann Adam, 1952?-1666. 2. Missions — China. I. Duhr, Joseph. Un jesuite en Chine, Adam Schall. II. Title.

DUNNE, George Harold, 266.251
1905-
Generation of giants; the story of the Jesuits in China in the last decades of the Ming dynasty. Notre Dame, Ind., Univ. of Notre Dame Pr. [c.] 1962. 389p. illus. Bibl. 61-18401 5.75
1. Jesuits in China. 2. Missions—China. 3. Chinese rites. I. Title.

ROWBOTHAM, Arnold Horrex, 266.251
1888-
Missionary and mandarin; the Jesuits at the court of China. New York, Russell & Russell, 1966 [c.1942] xi, 374p. illus., ports. 23cm. Bibl. [BX3746.C5R651966] 66-13253 8.50
1. Jesuits in China. 2. Missions—China. 3. Chinese rites. I. Title.

•WEDGE, Florence 266.251
Franciscan nun in China, Sister Mary Joseph Hubrich (1886-1962) Foreword by Most Rev. Rembert C. Kowalski. Pulaski, Wis., Franciscan [1964, c.1963] 64p. 19cm. .25 pap., *I. Title.*

MARCELLINE, Sister, 266'.2'512
O.P.
Sisters carry the gospel, by Sister M. Marcelline, O.P. Maryknoll, N.Y., Maryknoll Publications [1956] 127 p. 25 cm. (World horizon reports, report no. 15) On cover: The Kaying technique developed by the Maryknoll Sisters under the guidance of Bishop Ford. Includes bibliographical references. [BV3423.H25M37] 75-303448
1. Maryknoll Sisters of St. Dominic—Missions. 2. Ford, Francis Xavier, Bp., 1892-1952. 3. Missions to Hakkas. I. Title. II. Series.

SURFACE, Bill 266.25125
Freedom bridge; Maryknoll in Hong Kong, by Bill Surface, Jim Hart. New York, Coward [c.1963] 250p. illus. 22cm. 63-10158 4.95
1. Catholic Foreign Mission Society of America. 2. Missions—Hongkong. I. Hart, Jim, joint author. II. Title.

AIMEE, Julie, Sister 266.252
With dedicated hearts. Foreword by Sister Eleanor Joseph. Sisters of Notre Dame de Namur [dist. New York, Fordham, c.] 1963. 261p. illus. 24cm. 63-14409 4.95
1. Sisters of Notre Dame de Namur—Missions. 2. Missions—Japan. I. Title.

WELFLE, Richard A 266.254
Pieces of India. Chicago, Loyola University Press [1963] 107 p. illus. 24 cm. [BV3265.2.W4] 63-25078
1. Missions — India. 2. Missionary stories. I. Title.

WELFLE, Richard A. 266.254
Pieces of India. Chicago, Loyola [c.1963] 107p. illus. 24cm. 63-25078 2.55
1. Missions—India. 2. Missionary stories. I. Title.

MENGER, Matt J. 266.2'594
In the valley of the Mekong; an American in Laos [by] Matt J. Menger. Foreword by H. Ross Perot. Paterson, N.J., St. Anthony Guild Press [1970] viii, 226 p. illus., ports. 22 cm. [BV3325.L3M4] 79-115966 5.50
1. Catholic Church—Missions. 2. Missions—Laos. I. Title.

DOURISBOURE, Pierre X. 266.2/597
Vietnam; mission on the grand plateaus [by] Pierre Dourisboure. Christian Simonnet. Tr. by Albert J. LaMothe. Jr. Maryknoll. N.Y., Maryknoll [1967] x, 278p. map. 21cm. Tr. and adaptation of P.X. Dourisboure's Les sauvages Bahners. as adapted by C. Simonnet. [BV3325 A7D583] 67-31011 5.95
1. Missions—Vietnam. 2. Catholic Church—Missions. I. Simonnet, Christian. ed. II. Title.

DOURISBOURE, Pierre X 266.2'597
Vietnam; mission on the grand plateaus [by] Pierre Dourisboure [and] Christian Simonnet. Translated by Albert J. LaMothe, Jr. Maryknoll, N.Y., Maryknoll Publications [1967] x, 278 p. map. 21 cm. Translation and adaptation of P. X. Dourisboure's Les sauvages Bahners, as adapted by C. Simonnet. [BV3325.A7D583] 67-31011
1. Missions—Vietnam. 2. Catholic Church—Missions. I. Simonnet, Christian, ed. II. Title.

DOURISBOURE, Pierre X. 266.2'597
Vietnam; mission on the grand plateaus [by] Pierre Dourisboure [and] Christian Simonnet. Translated by Albert J. LaMothe, Jr. Maryknoll, N.Y., Maryknoll Publications [1967] x, 278 p. map. 21 cm. Translation and adaptation of P. X. Dourisboure's Les sauvages Ba-Hnars, as adapted by C. Simonnet. [BV3325.A7D583] 67-31011
1. Catholic Church—Missions. 2. Missions—Vietnam. I. Simonnet, Christian, ed. II. Title.

CATHOLIC Students' Mission 266.26
Crusade, U. S. A.
Africa in five hours. 3d ed. Cincinnati 26, Ohio. 5100 Shattuc Ave. [Author] National Center, 1961 c.1954-1961. 55p. illus., map (CSMC five-hour series) Bibl. 61-521 .50 pap.,
1. Missions—Africa. 2. Catholic Church—Missions—Study and teaching. I. Title.

CATHOLIC Students' Mission 266.26
Crusade, U. S. A. Africa Research Committee.
Africa in five hours; a collection of readings on the presence of the African countries in international affairs and in the life of the church. Contributors: John A. Bell, James Kritzeck, Thomas Patrick Melady [4th ed. Cincinnati, Author 1965] vi, 66p. illus., map. ports. 25cm. (CSMC five-hour ser.) Includes Excerpts: Pope Pius xii, Encyclical 'Fidei donum' and 'The Shield' on current events and a program of apostolic assistance. Bibl. [BV3500.C42] 65-1803 .90 pap.,
1. Missions—Africa. 2. Catholic Church—Missions—Study and teaching. I. Bell. John A. II. Catholic Students' Mission Crusade, U. S. A. Africa in five hours. III. Title.

KITTLER, Glenn D 266.26
The White Fathers. Introd. by Laurian Cardinal Rugambwa. Garden City, N. Y., Image Books [1961, c1957] 318p. 19cm. (Image books, Diii) [BV2300] 61-66032
1. White Fathers. I. Title. II. Series.

BANE, Martin J 266.266
Heroes of the hinterlands; the Bresillac story. With a foreword by Francis Cardinal Spellman. New York, Shamrock Guild [c1959] 112p. illus. 23cm. [BV2300.S5B3] 59-14652
1. Marion-Bresillac, Melchior Marie Joseph de, Bp., 1813-1859. 2. Society of African Missions. I. Title.

BANE, Martin J. 266.266
The Popes and western Africa; an outline of mission history, 1460's-1960's, by Martin J. Bane. Pref. by O. Carlos Stoetzer. Foreword by Sergio Pignedoli. Staten Island, N.Y., Alba House [1968] xv, 187 p. fold. map. 23 cm. Bibliography: p. 183. [BV3540.B3] 68-22134
1. Catholic Church—Missions—Papal documents. 2. Missions—Africa, West. I. Title.

MARY ELEANOR, Mother, 266.266
1903-
Afiong; a story of West Africa. Illustrated by Mother Mary Paschal. Milwaukee, Bruce Pub. Co. [1959] 96p. illus. 22cm. [BV2087.M35] 59-10975
1. Missionary stories. 2. Missions—Africa, West—Juvenile literature. I. Title.

HASTINGS, Adrian. 266.2'67
Church and mission in modern Africa. [New York] Fordham University Press [1967] 263 p. 23 cm. Bibliographical footnotes. [BX1675.H3 1967b] 67-30321
1. Catholic Church in Africa. 2. Missions—Africa. 3. Catholic Church—Missions. I. Title.

HASTINGS, Adrian. 266.2'67
Church and mission in modern Africa. [New York] Fordham University Press [1967] 263 p. 23 cm. Bibliographical footnotes. [BX1675.H3 1967b] 67-30321
1. Catholic Church in Africa. 2. Catholic Church—Missions. 3. Missions—Africa. I. Title.

MISSIONARIES to 266'.2'67
yourselves; African catechists today. Edited by Aylward Shorter and Eugene Kataza. Maryknoll, N.Y., Orbis Books [1972] x, 212 p. 22 cm. "A project of the Pastoral Institute of Eastern Africa, Gaba." Includes bibliographical references. [BX1968.M55 1972] 73-182576 4.50
1. Catechists—Africa, East—Addresses, essays, lectures. I. Shorter, Aylward, ed. II. Kataza, Eugene, ed. III. Pastoral Institute of Eastern Africa.

RATHE, Gerard 266.267
Mud and mosaics; an African missionary journey from the Niger to the Copper Belt. Westminster, Md., Newman [1962] 191p. illus., maps. 62-2119 3.50
1. Missions—Africa, Sub-Saharan. 2. Catholic Church—Missions. I. Title.

MATHESON, Elizabeth Mary 266.2676
African apostles. Staten Island, N.Y., Alba [c.1963] 224p. 20cm. Bibl. 63-12674 3.95
1. White Fathers. 2. Missions—Africa, East. I. Title.

CALKINS, Thomas M 266.2683
Umfundisi, missioner to the Zulus. Milwaukee, Burce Pub. Co. [1959] 173p. illus. 22cm. [BV3625.Z8C3] 59-13564
1. Missions—Africa, South. 2. Zulus. 3. Servites—Missions. I. Title.

SIMON, Jean Marie, Bp., 266.2688
1858-1932.
Bishop for the Hottentots: African memories, 1882-1909. Pref. by Francis Esser. Translated by Angeline Bouchard. New York, Benzinger Bros. [1959] 235 p. illus. 22 cm. [BV3630.H6S53] 59-8083
1. Missions — Hottentots. I. Title.

LINDEN, Ian. 266'.2'6897
Catholics, peasants, and Chewa resistance in Nyasaland, 1889-1939 [by] Ian Linden, with Jane Linden. Berkeley, University of California Press, 1974. xii, 223 p. illus. 26 cm. Includes bibliographical references. [BV3625.N8L47] 73-80823 ISBN 0-520-02500-8 16.00
1. Catholic Church—Missions. 2. Missions—Malawi. 3. Chewa (African tribe) I. Linden, Jane, joint author. II. Title.

KOREN, Henry J. 266.27
Knaves or knights? A history of the Spiritan missionaries in Acadia and North America, 1732-1839. Pittsburgh, Duquesne Univ. Pr., 1962. 211p. illus. maps. (Duguesne studies, Spiritian ser..4) Bibl. 62-8764 4.75
1. Missions—Acadia. 2. Missions—North America. 3. Holy Ghost Fathers—Missions. I. Title.

WEBER, Francis J. 266.27
A historiographical sketch of pioneer Catholicism in the Californias: missions and missionaries. Van Nuys, Calif., California Historical Publications 1961. 56 p. illus. 22 cm. [E98.M6W4] 61-16717
1. Indians of North America — Missions. 2. Catholic Church — Missions. 3. Missions — California. 4. Missions — Baja California. I. Title. II. Title: Pioneer Catholicism in the Californias.

LE CLERCQ, Chretien, 266'.2'71
fl.1641-1695.
First establishment of the faith in New France, by Christian Le Clercq. Now first translated, with notes, by John Gilmary Shea. New York, J. G. Shea, 1881. [New York, AMS Press, 1973] 2 v. illus. 23 cm. Vol. 2 (p. [128]-283) includes the narratives of La Salle's discoveries written by the Recollet missionaries Zenobe Membre and Anastase Douay. Translation of Premier etablissement de la foy. Includes bibliographical references. [BV2810.L413 1973] 77-172312 ISBN 0-404-03914-6 55.00
1. La Salle, Robert Cavelier, sieur de, 1643-1687. 2. Missions—Canada. 3. Recollets (Franciscan) in Canada. 4. New France—Discovery and exploration. 5. Louisiana—History—Colonial period. 6. Jesuits in Canada. I. Shea, John Dawson Gilmary, 1824-1892, tr. II. Membre, Zenobe, 1645?-1687? III. Douay, Anastase. IV. Title.

PRITCHETT, John Perry, 266.271
1902-
Black robe and buckskin; the story of Catholic pioneering in northern North America. Map and illus. by Andrew J. Cosentino. With a foreword by William T. Wood. New York, College and University Press Services [1960] 128p. illus. 23cm. [F1035.C3P7] 60-15684
1. Catholics in Canada. 2. Catholic Church—Missions. 3. Missions—Canada. 4. Frontier and pioneer life—Canada. I. Title.

BECHARD, Henri. 266'.2714
The original Caughnawaga Indians / Henri Bechard. Montreal : International Publishers' Representatives (Canada), 1976. xv, 258 p., [4] leaves of plates : ill. ; 23 cm. Includes index. Bibliography: p. [237]-242. [E99.C27B42] 77-374354 10.00
1. Jesuits—Quebec (Province)—Missions. 2. Caughnawaga Indians—Missions. 3. Indians of North America—Quebec (Province)—Missions. I. Title.

COLLET, Mathieu 266'.2'714
Benoit, 1671-1727.
The Catholic missions in Canada: 1721; a profile for genealogy and microhistory, based on a proces-verbal by procureur-general Collet. Edited and with annotations by Ivanhoe Caron. Index to personal names by Ruth Ortego Berthelot. Cottonport [La.] Polyanthos, 1972. 118 p. illus. 22 cm. An edition of Collet's Proces-verbaux sur la commodite et incommodite dresses dans chacune des paroisses de la Nouvelle-France, in French. "Originally published in Rapport de l'archiviste de la province de Quebec, 1921-1922." Includes bibliographical references. [BV2815.Q3C64] 73-175198
1. Missions—Quebec (Province)—History—Sources. I. Title.
Publisher's Address: Polyanthos Cottonport, La. 71327.

ESPINOSA, Isidro Felix 266.272
de, 1679-1755.
Cronica de los Colegios de Propaganda Fide de la Nueva Espana. New ed. with notes and introd. by Lino G. Canedo. Washington, Academy of American Franciscan History, 1964. cii, 972 p. illus., facsims., maps, ports. 29 cm. (Franciscan historical classics, v. 2) Publications of the Academy of American Franciscan History. Introd. and notes in Spanish. First published in 1746 under title: Chronica apostolica, y seraphica de todos los colegios de propaganda fide de esta Nueva-Espana, parte primera. Includes bibliographies. [BX3612.A1E73] 64-6451
1. Franciscans in Mexico. 2. Queretaro, Mexico (City) Colegio de Misioneros de Propaganda Fide de la Santa Cruz. I. Gomez Canedo, Lino, ed. II. Title. III. Series.

ESPINOSA, Isidro Felix 266.272
de, 1679-1755
Cronica de los Colegios de Propaganda Fide de la Nueva Espana. New ed. Notes, introd. by Lino G. Canedo. Washington 14, D.C., Bx. 5966, Acad. of Amer. Franciscan Hist., 1964. cii, 972p. illus., facsims., maps, ports. 29cm. (Franciscan hist. classics, v.2; Pubns. of the Acad. of Amer. Franciscan Hist.) Introd., notes in Spanish. First pub. in 1746 under title: Chronica apostolica, y seraphica de todos los colegios de propaganda fide de esta Nueva-Espana, parte primera. Bibl. 64-6451 15.00; 35.00; 12.00 deluxe ed., pap.,
1. Franciscans in Mexico. 2. Queretaro, Mexico (City) Colegio de Misioneros de Propaganda Fide de la Santa Cruz. I. Gomez Canedo, Lino, ed. II. Title. III. Series.

POLZER, Charles W. 266'.2'72
Rules and precepts of the Jesuit missions of northwestern New Spain / Charles W. Polzer. Tucson : University of Arizona Press, c1976. x, 141 p. : ill. ; 24 cm. (The Documentary relations of the Southwest ; Jesuit relations) "Rules and precepts for the Mission Rectorate of San Francisco Borja, Sonora, Mexico: translation of documents in the Roman archives of the Society of Jesus": p. [59]-125. Includes index. Bibliography: p. 129-132. [BX3712.A1P64] 75-8456 ISBN 0-8165-0551-9 : 8.50. ISBN 0-8165-0488-1 pbk. : 4.50
1. Jesuits—Missions. 2. Jesuits in Mexico. 3. Missions—Mexico. I. Jesuits. Rectorado de San Francisco Borja. II. Title. III. Series.

PICOLO, Francesco 266.272'2
Maria, 1658-1729.
Informe on the new province of California, 1702, by Francisco Maria Piccolo. Translated and edited by George P. Hammond. Los Angeles, Dawson's Book Shop, 1967. 77 p. facsim. (fold. map in pocket) 22 cm. (Baja California travels series, 10) Includes a facsim. of the Los Angeles Public Library copy, with t. p. reading: Informe del estado de la nueva Christiandad de California, que pidio por auto, la Real Audiencia de Guadalaxara, obedeciendo a la real cedula de n. Rey y Senor, D. Phelipe v, fecha en Madrid, a 17. de Julio, de 1701 ... por el P. Francisco Maria Picolo ... [Mexico, 1702] [F1246.P513] 67-24069
1. Jesuits in Baja California. 2. Baja California—History—Sources. I. Title. II. Series.

PICOLO, Francesco 266.272'2
Maria, 1658-1729.
Informe on the new province of California, 1702. Translated and edited by George P. Hammond. Los Angeles, Dawson's Book Shop, 1967. 77 p. facsim. (fold. map in pocket) 22 cm. (Baja California travels series, 10) Includes facsim. and translation of the copy in the Los Angeles Public Library, with t. p. reading: Informe del estado de la nueva Christiandad de California, que pidio por auto, la Real Audiencia de Guadalaxara, obedeciendo a la real cedula de n. Rey y Senor, D. Phelipe v, fecha en Madrid, a 17. de Julio, de 1701 ... por el P. Francisco Maria Picolo ... [Mexico, 1702] [F1246.P513] 67-24069
1. Jesuits in Baja California. 2. Baja California—Hist.—Sources. I. Title. II. Series.

WEBER, Francis J. 266.2'72'2
The missions & missionaries of Baja California; an historical perspective, by Francis J. Weber. Los Angeles, Dawson's Book Shop, 1968. 92 p. col. front., map (fold. in pocket), ports. 23 cm. (Baja California travels series, 11) "Pastoral visitation of the Right Reverend Buenaventura Portillo y Tejada": p. [77]-92. Bibliographical footnotes. [F864.W43] 67-24070
1. Missions—Baja California. 2. Catholic Church in Baja California—History. I. Title. II. Series.

MARIA del Rey, Sister. 266.27285
Prospero strikes it rich; the growth of a gold town [by] Sister Maria del Rey of Maryknoll. [1st ed.] New York, Harper & Row [1968] x, 182 p. illus. 22 cm. [BV2843.N6M3] 68-17599 5.95
1. Missions—Nicaragua. 2. Prospero—Social life and customs. I. Title.

MARIA DEL REY, Sister. 266.27285
Prospero strikes it rich: the growth of a gold town [by] Sister Maria del Rev of Maryknoll. [1st ed.] New York, Harper [1968] x, 182p. illus. 22cm. [BV2843.N6M3] 68-17599 5.95
1. Missions—Nicaragua. 2. Prospero—Soc. life & cust. I. Title.

CATHOLIC Student's 266.273
Mission Crusade, U.S.A.
U.S.A. in five hours; a symposium. Edited by Limus J. Ryland Cincinnati, CSMC Press [1964] viii, 108 p. illus., ports. 22 cm. (CSMC five-hour series) Bibliography: p. 91-92. [BV2766.C49C32] 65-611
1. Missions, Home. 2. Missions — U.S. I. Ryland, Linus J., ed. II. Title.

CATHOLIC Students' 266.273
Mission Crusade, U.S.A.
U.S.A. in five hours; a symposium. Ed. by Linus J. Ryland. Cincinnati, CSMC Pr. [c.1964] viii, 108p. illus., ports. 22 cm. (CSMC five-hour ser.) Bibl. [BV2766.C49C32] 65-611 1.10 pap.,
1. Missions, Home. 2. Missions—U.S. I. Ryland, Linus J., ed. II. Title.

MULVEY, Mary Doris, 266'.2'73
Sister.
French Catholic missionaries in the present United States (1604-1791). Washington, Catholic University of America, 1936. [New York, AMS Press, 1974] ix, 158 p. 23 cm. Reprint of the author's thesis, Catholic University of America, 1936, which was issued as v. 23 of the Catholic University of America. Studies in American church history. Bibliography: p. 127-133. [BV2770.M8 1974] 73-3578 ISBN 0-404-57773-3 10.00
1. Catholic Church in the United States—Missions. 2. French in the United States. 3. Indians of North America—Missions. 4. United States—History—Colonial period, ca. 1600-1775. I. Title. II. Series: Catholic University of America. Studies in American church history, v. 23.

ROEMER, Theodore, 266'.2'73
Father, 1889-
The Ludwig-missionsverein and the church in the United States (1838-1918). Washington, Catholic University of America, 1933. [New York, AMS Press, 1974] xii, 161 p. 23 cm. Reprint of the author's thesis, Catholic University of America, 1933, which was issued as v. 16 of the Catholic University of America. Studies in American church history. Bibliography: p. 153-156. [BV2155.L8R6 1974] 73-3571 ISBN 0-404-57766-0 8.50
1. Ludwigs-verein. 2. Catholic Church in the United States—History. I. Title. II. Series: Catholic University of America. Studies in American church history, v. 16.

SHEA, John Dawson 266.2'73
Gilmary, 1824-1892.
Catholic missions among the Indian tribes of the United States. New York, Arno Press, 1969. 514, ii (i.e. iv) p. facsims., ports. 23 cm. (Religion in America) Reprint of the 1855 ed. Previous editions have title: History of the

Catholic missions among the Indian tribes of the United States, 1529-1854. Includes bibliographical references. [E98.M6S53 1969] 70-83438
1. Indians of North America—Missions. 2. Catholic Church in the United States—Missions. I. Title.

SHEA, John Dawson 266'.2'73
Gilmary, 1824-1892.
History of the Catholic missions among the Indian tribes of the United States, 1529-1854. New York, E. Dunigan, 1855. [New York, AMS Press, 1973] p. Half title: Catholic missions among the Indian tribes of the United States. [E98.M6S53 1973] 73-175853 ISBN 0-404-07176-7 17.50
1. Catholic Church in the United States—Missions. 2. Indians of North America—Missions. I. Title. II. Title: Catholic missions among the Indian tribes of the United States.

THE Word in the world 266'.2'73
: Divine Word missionaries '76 Black apostolate / [editor, John Boberg, editorial assistants, Patricia Ritter, Terry Steib ; illustrations, Art Haase]. Techny, Ill. : Society of the Divine Word, [1976?] 208 p. : ill. ; 29 cm. [BX1407.N4W65] 77-352490
1. Society of the Divine Word—Addresses, essays, lectures. 2. Afro-American Catholics—Addresses, essays, lectures. I. Boberg, John T. II. Ritter, Patricia. III. Steib, Terry. IV. Society of the Divine Word.

LEGER, Mary Celeste, 266'.2'741
1884-1947.
The Catholic Indian missions in Maine (1611-1820). Washington, Catholic University of America, 1929. [New York, AMS Press, 1974] x, 184 p. illus. 23 cm. Reprint of the author's thesis, Catholic University of America, 1929, which was issued as v. 8 of the Catholic University of America. Studies in American church history. Bibliography: p. 164-178. [E78.M2L43 1974] 73-3563 ISBN 0-404-57758-X 8.00
1. Catholic Church—Missions. 2. Indians of North America—Maine—Missions. 3. Indians of North America—Canada—Missions. I. Title. II. Series: Catholic University of America. Studies in American church history, v. 8.

BROWN, Lenard E. 266.2'741'45
Significance of St. Sauveur Mission, established 1613, Mount Desert Island, by Lenard E. Brown. Washington, Office of History and Historic Architecture, Eastern Service Center, 1970. iv, 57 l. 8 plates (incl. maps) 27 cm. At head of title: Acadia National Park, Maine. Bibliography: leaves 54-56. [F22.B85] 71-612223
1. Saint Sauveur (Colony) I. Title. II. Title: Acadia National Park, Maine.

ODLE, Don J 1920- [266]275
Venture for victory. Berne, Ind., Light and Hope Publications [1954] 184 p. illus. 20 cm. [BV3400.O3] 54-25223
1. Missions — East (Far East) I. Title.

THOMPSON, May Bel. [266] 275.1
Chinese teen-agers -- and God! [1st ed.] New York, Vantage Press [1956] 206 p. 21 cm. Autobiograhical. [BV3427.T45A3] 56-11201
1. Missions — China. I. Title.

CAMPBELL, Archibald, [266] 275.19
1894-
The Christ of the Korean heart. Columbus, Ohio, Falco Publishers [1955, c1954] 144 p. illus. 20 cm. [BV3460.C3] 266 55-32268
1. Missions—Korea. I. Title.

PIERCE, Robert 266 275.19
Willard, 1914-
The untold Korean story, by Bob Pierce, as told to Ken Anderson. Grand Rapids, Zondervan Pub. House [1951] 89 p. illus. 20 cm. [BV3460.P5] 52-345
1. Missions — Korea. 2. Christians in Korea. I. Anderson, Kenneth, 1917- II. Title.

TAKENAKA, Masao, [266] 275.2
1925-
Reconciliation and renewal in Japan. New York, Published jointly by the Student Volunteer Movement for Christian Missions and Friendship Press [1957] 95 p. 19 cm. Includes bibliography. [BR1305.T3] 57-14831
1. Japan — Church history. 2. Church and social problems — Japan. I. Title.

STORM, Ida Paterson. [266] 275.3
Highways in the desert. Nashville, Broadman Press [1950] 135 p. map. 19 cm. [BV3180.S78] 51-197
1. Missions — Arabia. I. Title.

MILLER, Basil [266] 275.4
William, 1897-
Twenty missionary stories from India. Grand Rapids, Zondervan Pub. House [1952] 122 p. 20 cm. [BV3265.M46] 266 52-3532
1. Missions — India. I. Title.

PETTIT, Isabel Lacy. 266 275.4
India, give me thine heart. Boston, W. A. Wilde Co. [1951] 189 p. 21 cm. [BV3265.P43] 51-13865
1. Missions — India. I. Title.

BYERS, David M. 266'.2'755735
Evangelists to the poor : a Catholic ministry in Appalachia / David M. Byers, Bernard Quinn. Washington : Glenmary Research Center, 1975. v, 46 p. ; 28 cm. [BV3774.V8B93] 74-27723 ISBN 0-914422-03-0 : 1.25
1. Evangelistic work—Lee Co., Va. 2. Church and the poor. I. Quinn, Bernard, joint author. II. Glenmary Research Center. III. Title.

THOMAS, Winburn T [266] 275.9
The church in Southeast Asia [by] Winburn T. Thomas & Rajah B. Manikam. With an introd. by Frank T. Cartwright. New York, Friendship Press [1956] 171 p. illus. 20 cm. [BR1178.T45] 56-7954
1. Asia, Southeastern — Church history. 2. Missions — Asia, Southeastern. I. Manikam, Rajah Bhushanam, 1897- joint author. II. Title.

MILLER, Basil William, [266] 276
1897-
Twenty missionary stories from Africa. Grand Rapids, Zondervan Pub. House [1951] 123 p. 20 cm. [BV2087.M47] 266 52-348
1. Missionary stories. 2. Missions — Africa. I. Title.

DELANGLEZ, Jean, 1896- 266'.2'763
1949.
The French Jesuits in lower Louisiana (1700-1763). Washington, Catholic University of America, 1935. [New York, AMS Press, 1974] xxvi, 547 p. 23 cm. Reprint of the author's thesis, Catholic University of America, 1935, which was issued as v. 21 of the Catholic University of America. Studies in American church history. Bibliography: p. ix-xxvi. [BX3709.L8D4 1974] 73-3576 ISBN 0-404-57771-7 24.50
1. Catholic Church in Louisiana. 2. Jesuits in Louisiana. 3. Jesuits—Missions. 4. Missions—Louisiana. I. Title. II. Series: Catholic University of America. Studies in American church history, v. 21.

VOGEL, Claude 266'.2'763
Lawrence, Father, 1894-
The Capuchins in French Louisiana (1722-1766), by Claude L. Vogel. Washington, Catholic University of America, 1928. [New York, AMS Press, 1974] xxiv, 201 p. illus. 23 cm. Reprint of the author's thesis, Catholic University of America, 1928, which was issued as v. 7 of the Catholic University of America. Studies in American church history. Bibliography: p. xiii-xxiv. [BX3109.L68V6 1974] 73-3561 ISBN 0-404-57757-1 9.50
1. Catholic Church in Louisiana. 2. Capuchins in Louisiana. 3. Capuchins—Missions. 4. Missions—Louisiana. 5. Louisiana—History—To 1803. I. Title. II. Series: Catholic University of America. Studies in American church history, v. 7.

WITH valor they serve 266'.2'763
: a sequel to They came to Louisiana / by Dorothea Olga McCants. Baton Rouge, La. : Claitor's Pub. Division, c1975. xvi, 314 p., [6] leaves of plates : ill. ; 23 cm. Selection of letters from the archives of the Daughters of the Cross, translated and edited by D. O. McCants. Includes bibliographical references and index. [BV2803.L8W56] 75-8063 12.50
1. Daughters of the Cross—Missions. 2. Missions—Louisiana. 3. Louisiana—Church history. I. McCants, Dorothea Olga, comp. They came to Louisiana.

OLIVA, Jose Rafael, 266'.2764
d.1809.
Management of the missions in Texas : Fr. Jose Rafael Oliva's views concerning the problem of the temporalities in 1788 / transcript of the Spanish original and English translation by Benedict Leutenegger ; introduction and notes by Marion A. Habig. San Antonio, Tex. : Old Spanish Missions Historical Research Library at San Jose Mission, 1977. 56 leaves ; 28 cm. (Documentary series - Old Spanish Missions Historical Research Library ; no. 2) Comprises one paper and two circular letters. Includes errata for Guidelines for a Texas mission, no. 1 in this series. Includes bibliographical references. [F389.O44 1977] 77-358215
1. Missions—Texas—History—Sources. 2. Indians of North America—Texas—History—Missions—Sources. 3. Texas—History—To 1846—Sources. I. Title. II. Series: Old Spanish Missions Historical Research Library. Documentary series — Old Spanish Missions Historical Research Library ; no. 2.

GUIDELINES for a 266'.2'764351
Texas Mission : instructions for the missionary of Mission Concepcion in San Antonio, ca. 1760 : transcript of the Spanish original and English translation, with notes / by Benedict Leutenegger. San Antonio, Tex. : Old Spanish Missions Historical Research Library at San Jose Mission, 1976. 61 leaves ; 29 cm. ([Documentary series] - Old Spanish Missions Historical Research Library ; 1) English and Spanish. [F394.S2G93] 76-379353
1. Nuestra Senora de la Purisima Concepcion de Acuna Mission. 2. San Antonio—History—Sources. 3. Indians of North America—Missions. 4. Missions—San Antonio. I. Leutenegger, Benedict. II. Series: Old Spanish Missions Historical Research Library. Documentary series — Old Spanish Missions Historical Research Library ; 1.

HABIG, Marion 266.2764'351
Alphonse, 1901-
The Alamo chain of missions; a history of San Antonio's five old missions, by Marion A. Habig. Chicago, Franciscan Herald Press [1968] 304 p. illus., plans. 21 cm. Bibliography: p. 274-293. [F394.S2H26] 68-54397 6.95
1. Missions—San Antonio. I. Title.

WILTGEN, Ralph M. 266 276.67
1921-
Gold Coast missions history, 1471-1880 Techny, Ill., Divine Word Publications, 1956. 181 p. illus. 24 cm. [BV3625.G6W5] 55-6277
1. Missions — Gold Coast. 2. Catholic Church in the Gold Coast — Hist. 3. Gold Coast — Church history. I. Title.

WHITE, Paul Hamilton [266]276.78
Hume.
The Jungle Doctor series [American ed.] Grand Rapids, Eerdmans, 1955- v. illus. 20 cm. Each vol. has also special t.p. [[BV3625]] 55-382
1. Missions, Medical — Tanganyika. I. Title.

BAROUX, Louis, 1817- 266'.2'7745
1897.
Correspondence of Rev. Louis Baroux, missionary apostolic of Michigan, to Rev. M. J. De Neve, superior of the American College at Louvain / translated from the French by E. D. Kelly. [Berrien Springs, Mich. : Hardscrabble Books, 1976] 95 p. : ill. ; 19 cm. Translation of Lettre de M. l'abbe Baroux, missionnaire apostolique du Michigan, a M. J. Deneve. Half-title: An early Indian mission. Added title: History of the Pottawatomies. Photoreprint ed. of the 1913 ed. published by E. D. Kelly, Ann Arbor, Mich. [E99.P8B313 1976] 75-28671 ISBN 0-915056-04-6 : 4.50
1. Catholic Church—Missions. 2. Baroux, Louis, 1817-1897. 3. Deneve, Jean, d. 1898? 4. Potawatomi Indians—Missions. 5. Missions—Michigan. I. Deneve, Jean, d. 1898? II. Title: An early Indian mission. III. Title: History of the Pottawatomies.

WORMAN, Theresa, 1907- [266] 278
Latin American missionary stories. Chicago, Moody Press [c1951] 64 p. 19 cm. [BV2087.W6] 52-805
1. Missionary stories. 2. Missions — Spanish America. I. Title.

STULL, Ruth. [266] 278.5
Sand and stars; missionary adventure on the jungle trail. Los Angeles, Revell [1951] 189 p. 22 cm. [BV2853.P6S8] 51-11699
1. Missions — Peru. I. Title.

FORD, Lillian [266] 278.6
Gertrude (Shafer) 1894-
In the high Andes, by Mrs. Orley Ford. Nashville, Tenn., Southern publishing association, [c1932] 224 p. front., plates, ports. 19 1/2 cm. [BV2853.E2F6] 33-3908
1. Missions—Ecuador. 2. Ecuador—Descr. & trav. I. Title.

MCBRIDE, Genevieve. 266'.2'786
The bird tail / Genevieve McBride. 1st ed. New York : Vantage Press, c1974. 220 p. : ill. ; 21 cm. Bibliography: p. 211-220. [BV2803.M9M3] 75-317815 ISBN 0-533-01042-X : 4.95
1. Missions—Montana. 2. Indians of North America—Montana—Missions. 3. Ursulines—Missions. 4. Montana—History. I. Title.

EVANS, Lucylle H. 266'.2'78689
St. Mary's in the Rocky Mountains : a history of the cradle of Montana's culture / by Lucylle H. Evans. [Stevensville? Mont. : s.n., 1975] viii, 249 leaves ; 28 cm. Bibliography: leaves 245-249. [E99.S2E93] 75-309850
1. St. Mary's Parish, Stevensville, Mont. 2. Salish Indians—Missions. 3. Jesuits—Missions. I. Title.

BENAVIDES, Alonso de fl 266.2789
1630.
The memorial of Fray Alonso de Benavides, 1630. Translated by Mrs. Edward E. Ayer. Annotated by Frederick Webb Hodge and Charles Fletcher Lummis, Albuquerque, N.M., Horn and Wallace [1965] xiii, 309 p. illus. map (on lining papers) 24 cm. Reprint of the 1916 ed. Includes facism, of the original Spanish ed. with t.p. reading: Memorial ... hecho por el padre fray Alsonso de Benavides ... Madrid, Impr. Real., 1630. Bibliographical references included in "Notes" (p. 187-285) [F799.B43] 65-9216
1. New Mexico — Deser. & trav. 2. Missions — New Mexico. 3. Indians of North America — New Mexico. 4. franciscans in New Mexico. I. Hodge, Frederick Webb, 1864-1956. II. Lummis, Charles Fletcher, 1859-1928. III. Title.

BENAVIDES, Alonso de, 266.2789
fl. 1630
The memorial of Fray Alonso de Benavides, 1630. Tr. by Mrs. Edward E. Ayer. Annotated by Frederick Webb Hodge, Charles Fletcher Lummis. Albuquerque, N. M., Horn & Wallace [c.1965] xiii, 309p. illus., map (on lining papers) 24cm. Reprint of the 1916 ed. Includes facsim. of theoriginal Spanish ed. Bibl. [F799.B43] 65-9216 7.00
1. New Mexico—Descr. & trav. 2. Missions—New Mexico. 3. Indians of North America—New Mexico 4. Franciscans in New Mexico. I. Hodge, Frederick Webb, 1864-1956. II. Hodge, Frederick Webb, 1864-1956. III. Lummis, Charles Fletcher, 1859-1928. IV. Title.

ARMITAGE, Merle, 1893- 266.279
Pagans, conquistadores, heroes, and martyrs; the spiritual conquest of America, by Merle Armitage assisted by Peter Ribera Ortega [Fresno, Calif.] Acad. Guild Pr. [1964, c.1960] 99p illus. 21cm. Bibl. 60-11499 7.50 deluxe ed.,
1. Missions, Spanish. 2. Missions—Southwest, New. 3. Missions—Mexico. 4. Indians of North America—Missions. 5. America—Disc. & explor.—Spanish. I. Title.

ARMITAGE, Merle, 1893- 266.279
Pagans, conquistadores, heroes, and martyrs; the spiritual conquest of America, by Merle Armitage assisted by Peter Ribera Ortega. [Santa Fe, 350 anniversary ed. Yucca Valley? Calif.] Manzanita Press stamped: distributors, Academy Library Guid, Fresno, Calif. [1960]; 99p. illus. 18cm. Includes bibliography. [BV2800.A8] 60-11499
1. Missions, Spanish. 2. Missions—Southwest, New. 3. Missions—Mexico, 4. Indians of North America—Missions. 5. America —Disc. & explor.—Spanish. I. Title.

ARMITAGE, Merle, 1893- 266.279
Pagans, conquistadores, heroes, and martyrs; the spiritual conquest of America, by Merle Armitage assisted by Peter Ribera Ortega. [Santa Fe, 350 anniversary ed. Yucca Valley? Calif.] Manzanita Press [c.1960 stamped: distributors, Academy Library Guild, Fresno, Calif.] Fresno, calif. stamped: distributors, Academy Library Guild. 99p. illus. Includes bibl. 60-11499 2.75 pap.,
1. Missions, Spanish. 2. Missions—Southwest, New. 3. Mission—Mexico. 4. Indians of North America—Missions. 5. America—Disc. & explor.—Spanish. I. Title.

KINO, Eusebio Francisco, 266.2'79
1644-1711.
Kino's Historical memoir of Pimeria Alta : a contemporary account of the beginnings of California, Sonora, and Arizona / by Eusebio Francisco Kino ; published for the first time from the original manuscript in the Archives of Mexico translated into English, edited, and annotated by Herbert Eugene Bolton. New York : AMS Press, 1976. 2 v. in 1 : ill. ; 23 cm. Translation of the ms. entitled: Favores celestiales. Reprint of the 1919 ed. published by A. H. Clark Co., Cleveland. Bibliography: p. v. 2, p. 279-296. [F799.K56 1976] 74-7975 ISBN 0-404-11863-1 : 52.50 (2 vols in one)
1. Kino, Eusebio Francisco, 1644-1711. 2. Pimeria Alta. 3. Jesuits in Pimeria Alta. 4. Missions—Pimeria Alta. 5. Pima Indians. I. Title.

PARSONS, Francis B. 266'.2'79
Early 17th century missions of the Southwest : with historical introduction / by Francis B. Parsons; book design and drawings by Harold A. Wolfinbarger, Jr. Tucson, Ariz. : D. S. King, c1975. viii, 111 p. : ill. ; 23 cm. Includes index. Bibliography: p. 106-107. [F799.P35] 74-32368 ISBN 0-912762-21-7. ISBN 0-912762-20-9 pbk.
1. Spanish missions of New Mexico. 2. Spanish missions of Arizona. 3. Franciscans—Missions. 4. New Mexico—History—To 1848. 5. Arizona—History—To 1912. I. Title.

CRUMP, Spencer. 266'.2'794
California's Spanish missions : their yesterdays and todays / by Spencer Crump ; with ill. from historical archives, supplemented by modern photos. 1st ed. Corona del Mar, Calif. : Trans-Anglo Books, [1975] 95 p. : ill. ; 29 cm. Includes index. Bibliography: p. 8-9.

[F864.C93] 73-88320 ISBN 0-87046-028-5 : 6.95
1. Spanish missions of California. 2. Indians of North America—California—Missions. 3. California—History—To 1846. I. Title.

CRUMP, Spencer. 266.2794
California's Spanish missions yesterday and today. [Los Angeles, Trans-Anglo Books, 1964] 64 p. illus. (part col.) maps. 21 cm. (Great American history series) Cover title. [P870.S7C7] 64-23504
1. Spanish missions of California. I. Title.

CRUMP, Spencer 266.2794
California's Spanish missions yesterday and today. [Los Angeles, Trans-Anglc, c.1964] 64p. illus. (pt. col.) maps. 21cm. (Great Amer. hist. ser. Tab. bk.) Cover title. 64-23504 1.00 pap.,
1. Spanish missions of California. I. Title.

ENGLEHARDT, Zephyrin, 266'.2'794
1851-1934.
The missions and missionaries of California. Boston, Milford House [1974] p. Reprint of the 2d ed. of v. 1, first published in 1929 by the Mission Santa Barbara, Santa Barbara, Calif.; and of the 1st ed. of v. 2-[5] first published in 1912-16 by the J. H. Barry Co., San Francisco. Contents.Contents.—v. 1. Lower California.—v. 2-4. Upper California. General history, pts. 1-3.—[5] Index to vols. II-IV. Includes bibliographies. [E78.C15E6 1974] 70-82145 ISBN 0-87821-132-2 150.00
1. Indians of North America—California—Missions. 2. Missions—California. 3. Missions—Baja California. I. Title.

GEARY, Gerald Joseph, 266'.2'794
1905-
The secularization of the California missions (1810-1846), by Gerald J. Geary. Washington, Catholic University of America, 1934. [New York, AMS Press, 1974] p. cm. Reprint of the author's thesis, Catholic University of America, 1934, which was issued as v. 17 of the Catholic University of America. Studies in American church history. Bibliography: p. [BV2803.C2G4 1974] 73-3572 ISBN 0-404-57767-9 9.00
1. Catholic Church in California—Missions. 2. Missions—California. 3. Secularization. 4. Church and state in California. 5. California—History—To 1846. I. Title. II. Series: Catholic University of America. Studies in American church history, v. 17.

KOCHER, Paul H. 266'.2'794
California's old missions : the story of the founding of the 21 Franciscan missions in Spanish Alta California, 1769-1823 / by Paul H. Kocher. Chicago : Franciscan Herald Press, c1976. xi, 177 p. : ill. ; 21 cm. At head of title: A Bicentennial book. Includes index. Bibliography: p. 169-171. [F864.K62] 76-2699 ISBN 0-8199-0601-8 : 6.95
1. Franciscans—Missions. 2. Spanish missions of California. 3. Franciscans in California. 4. Missions—California. 5. California—History—To 1846. I. Title.

LOTH, John H. 266.2794
Catholicism on the march, the California missions. New York, Vantage [c.1961] 93p. illus. Bibl. 61-66083 2.75 bds.,
1. Serra, Junipero, 1713-1784. 2. Missions—California. 3. Franciscans in California. 4. Indians of North America—California. I. Title.

O'NEAL, Margaret. 266'.2'794
California's mission heritage / by Margaret O'Neal. San Diego, Calif. : [O'Neal], 1976. xii, 88, [3] p. : ill. (some col.) ; 23 x 29 cm. "500 copies." Bibliography: p. [91] [F864.O63] 77-151234
1. Catholic Church in California—Missions. 2. Missions—California. 3. Indians of North America—California—Missions. 4. California—History, Local. I. Title.

GEIGER, Maynard J 1901- 266.27949
Mission Santa Barbara, 1782-1965, by Maynard Geiger. Santa Barbara, Calif. [Franciscan Fathers of California] 1965. 285 p. illus., ports. 24 cm. Bibliography: p. [265]-272. [F869.S45G4] 66-6613
1. Santa Barbara Mission. I. Title.

JAYME, Luis, 1740- 266.2'794'98
1775.
Letter of Luis Jayme, O.F.M., San Diego, October 17, 1772. Translated and edited by Maynard Geiger. Los Angeles, Published for San Diego Public Library by Dawson's Book Shop, 1970. 66 p. facsim. 23 cm. (Baja California travels series, 22) Includes the original Spanish letter in facsimile. Includes bibliographical references. [F869.S22J3813] 77-127978
1. San Diego mission. I. Geiger, Maynard J., 1901- ed. II. Title. III. Series.

SMITH, Bradford, [266] 279.69
1909-
Yankees in paradise; the New England impact on Hawaii. [1st ed.] Philadelphia, Lippincott [1956] 376 p. illus. 22 cm. Full name: William Bradford Smith. [BV3680.H3S57] 56-6247
1. Missions — Hawaiian Islands. I. Title.

MENAGER, Francis M., 266.2798
1886-
The kingdom of the seal. Chicago, Loyola Univ. Pr. c.1962. 203p. illus. 62-354 3.00
1. Eskimos—Alaska. 2. Eskimos—Missions. 3. Jesuits—Missions. I. Title.

SAVAGE, Alma Helen 266.2798
The forty-ninth star, Alaska. Illus. by Rus Anderson. New York, Benziger Bros. [c.1959] 180p. illus., map 22cm. (Banner books [6]) 59-15173 2.00
1. Missions—Alaska. 2. Catholic Church in Alaska—Missions. I. Title.

SAVAGE, Alma Helen, 266.2798
1900-
The forty-ninth star, Alaska. Illus. by Rus Anderson. New York, Benziger Bros. [1959] 180p. illus. 22cm. (Banner books [6]) [BV2803.A4S32] 59-15173
1. Missions— Alaska. 2. Catholic Church in Alaska—Missions. I. Title.

STEWARD, Andrew G [266] 279.9
Trophies from Cannibal Isles. Washington, Review and Herald Pub. Association [1956] 256 p. illus. 21 cm. [BV3670.S8] 57-342
1. Missions — Islands of the Pacific. I. Title.

CATHOLIC FOREIGN MISSION 266.28
SOCIETY OF AMERICA
The Christian challenge in Latin America; a symposium, ed. by the Maryknoll Fathers. Maryknoll, N.Y., Maryknoll Pubns., 1964. 86p. 24cm. (World horizon report no. 31) Bibl. 64-16154 1.95
1. Missions—Spanish America. 2. Church and social problems—Spanish America. 3. Church and social problems—Catholic Church. I. Title. II. Series.

GREENWAY, Roger S. 266'.2'8
An urban strategy for Latin America [by] Roger S. Greenway. Grand Rapids, Mich., Baker Book House [1973] 282 p. illus. 21 cm. Bibliography: p. 245-274. [BV2831.G73] 72-93597 ISBN 0-8010-3667-4 4.95 (pbk.)
1. Missions—Latin America. 2. Urbanization—Latin America. I. Title.

PEACE or violence in 266'.2'8
Latin America? Needed: competent personnel for Latin America. [Washington, Papal Volunteers for Latin America, 1968 or 9] 22 p. illus. 22 cm. Special issue of The Papal volunteer, vol. 8, no. 5. [BV2300.P3P4] 74-153076
1. Papal Volunteers for Latin America. I. Papal Volunteers for Latin America. II. The Papal volunteer.

RIPPY, James Fred, 1892- 266.2'8
Crusaders of the jungle, by J. Fred Rippy and Jean Thomas Nelson. Illustrated by Willis Physioc. Westport, Conn., Greenwood Press [1971, c1936] x, 401 p. illus. 23 cm. Bibliography: p. 371-388. [F2230.1.M5R5 1971] 76-136081 ISBN 0-8371-5231-3
1. Catholic Church—Missions. 2. Indians of South America—Missions. 3. Missions—South America. I. Nelson, Jean Thomas, 1905-1933, joint author. II. Title.

RIPPY, James Fred, 1892- 266.2'8
Crusaders of the jungle, by J. Fred Rippy and Jean Thomas Nelson. Illustrated by Willis Physioc. Port Washington, N.Y., Kennikat Press [1971] x, 401 p. illus., map, ports. 23 cm. (Kennikat Press scholarly reprints. Series in Latin-American history and culture) Reprint of the 1936 ed. Includes bibliographical references. [BX1461.R5 1971] 76-123495 ISBN 0-8046-1382-6
1. Catholic Church—Missions. 2. Indians of South America—Missions. 3. Missions—South America. I. Nelson, Jean Thomas, 1905-1933, joint author. II. Title.

WOOD, Robert 266.28
Missionary crisis and challenge in Latin America. St. Louis, B. Herder [c.1964] 96p. 21cm. [BV2831.W6] 64-7634 1.25 pap.,
1. Missions—Latin America. 2. Catholic Church—Missions. 3. Missions—Theory. I. Title.

WOOD, Robert, S. M. 266.28
Missionary crisis and challenge in Latin America. St. Louis, B. Herder [1964] 96 p. 21 cm. [BV2831.W6] 64-7634
1. Missions — Latin America. 2. Catholic Church — Missions. 3. Missions — Theory. I. Title.

MARY LORETTA, Sister 266.281
Amazonia; a study of people and progress in the Amazon jungle. New York, Pageant [c.1963] 212p. illus., map, 24cm. Bibl. 62-22275 5.00
1. Missions—Amazon Valley. 2. Community development—Amazon Valley. 3. Sisters Adorers of the Most Precious Blood—Missions. I. Title.

MICHENFELDER, Joseph. 266.2'85
Gringo volunteers. Photos by Fred Albert [i.e. Allert] Maryknoll, N.Y., Maryknoll Publications, 1969. 96 p. illus., ports. 24 cm. [BV2300.P3M5] 72-11070 4.95
1. Papal Volunteers for Latin America. 2. Missions—Peru. I. Allert, Fred, illus. II. Title.

BONILLA, Victor 266'.2'861
Daniel.
Servants of God or masters of men? the story of a Capuchin mission in Amazonia; translated from French by Rosemary Sheed. Harmondsworth, Penguin, 1972. 304 p. 18 cm. (The Pelican Latin American library) Translated from the French translation of Siervos de Dios y amos de indios. Bibliography: p. 283-290. [F2270.1.M5B6613] 72-169616 ISBN 0-14-021436-4 2.65
1. Indians of South America—Colombia—Missions. 2. Capuchins—Missions. 3. Indians, Treatment of—Colombia. I. Title.
Order from Penguin, Baltimore

HUGENBERG, Joyce A ed. 266.29
Oceania in five hours, a symposium. Contributors: Vincent I. Kennally [and others] Cincinnati, CSMC Press [1963] 71 p. illus., group ports., map. 22 cm. (CSMC five-hour series) [DU28.H8] 63-24566
1. Oceania 2. Missions—Oceania I. Kennally, Vincent I. II. Title.

HUGENBERG, Joyce A., ed. 266.29
Oceania in five hours, a symposium. Contributors: Vincent I. Kennally [others] Cincinnati, CSMC [c.1963] 71p. illus., group ports., map. 22cm. (CSMC five-hour ser.) 63-24566 .75 pap.,
1. Oceanica. 2. Missions—Oceanica. I. Kennally, Vincent I. II. Title.

CATHOLIC Students' 266.291
Mission Crusade, U S A
Indonesia in five hours. [Cincinnati, 1962] 70p. illus. 22cm. (CSMC five-hour series) Includes bibliography. [BX1653.C3] 62-2718
1. Catholic Church in Indonesia 2. Indonesia—Religion. I. Title.

CATHOLIC STUDENTS' 266.291
MISSION CRUSADE,, U.S.A.
Indonesia in five hours. [Cincinnati, Author, c.1962] 70p. illus. (CSMC five-hour ser.) Bibl. 62-2718 .65 pap.,
1. Catholic Church in Indonesia. 2. Indonesia—Religion. I. Title.

WAIKOUAITI, N.Z. St. 266.2'931'57
Anne's Church. Centennial Committee.
The story of a church, its priests and its people; St. Anne's Church, Waikouaiti, 1868-1968. [Dunedin, Printed by Tablet Print, 1968] 28 p. illus. 18 x 25 cm. Cover title. [BX4644.W3S28] 78-865088
1. Waikouaiti, N.Z. St. Anne's Church. I. Title.

LARACY, Hugh M. 266'.2'935
Marists and Melanesians : a history of Catholic missions in the Solomon Islands / Hugh Laracy. Honolulu : University Press of Hawaii, 1975. p. cm. Includes index. Bibliography: p. [BV3680.S6L37 1975] 75-28080 ISBN 0-8248-0361-2 : 12.00
1. Catholic Church—Missions. 2. Catholic Church in the Solomon Islands. 3. Missions—Solomon Islands. I. Title.

BIRT, Henry Norbert, 266.294
1861-1919.
Benedictine pioneers in Australia. London, Herbert & Daniel, 1911. [Melbourne, Polding Press, 1970] 2 v. illus., ports., tables. 23 cm. [BX3048.A1B5 1970] 74-540677 9.55
1. Benedictines in Australia. 2. Missions—Australia. I. Title.

PYE, John. 266'.2'9429
The Port Keats story / by Bro. John Pye. Kensington, N.S.W. : J. Pye, 1973. 52 p. : ill. ; 21 cm. Cover title. [BV3660.N6P93] 75-330136 ISBN 0-9598787-0-X : 1.00
1. Port Keats Mission. 2. Missions to Australian aborigines—Northern Territory, Australia. 3. Missions, Catholic. I. Title.

MARIA DEL REY, Sister, 266.295
Safari by jet: through Africa and Asia. New York, Scribner [1962] 308p. illus. 24cm. [BV2300.F6M32] 62-17726
1. Foreign Mission Sisters of St. Dominic. 2. Missions—East (Far East) I. Title.

[LEDESMA, Andres de] 266'.2'967
d.1684.
Mission in the Marianas : an account of Father Diego Luis de Sanvitores and his companions, 1669-1670 / translated, with commentary by Ward Barrett. Minneapolis : University of Minnesota Press, c1975. vii, 62 p. : ill. ; 23 cm. (A publication from the James Ford Bell Library at the University of Minnesota) Translation of Noticia de los progressos de nuestra Santa Fe, en las Islas Marianas ... desde 15 de mayo de 1669 ... Includes bibliographical references and index. [BV3680.G8L413] 74-27258 ISBN 0-8166-0747-8 : 8.50
1. Sanvitores, Diego Luis de, 1627-1672. 2. Missions—Mariana Islands. 3. Jesuits—Missions. 4. Mariana Islands—History. I. Barrett, Ward J. II. Jesuits. Letters from missions. III. Title. IV. Series: James Ford Bell Library. A publication from the James Ford Bell Library at the University of Minnesota.

ADDISON, James Thayer, 266.3
1887-
Our expanding church; foreword by the presiding bishop. New York, National Council [1951] 132 p. 21 cm. Bibliography: p. 125-132. [BV2575.A8 1951] 51-5327
1. Protestant Episcopal Church in the U. S. A.—Missions. I. Title.

BORNEO, past, 266.3
present and future. Foreword by His Grace the Archbishop of York. Westminster, Society for the Propagation of the Gospel in Foreign Parts, 1953. 60p. illus. 19cm. [BX5672.B65C6] [BX5672.B65C6] 279.11 53-34342 53-34342
1. Church of England. Dioceses (Overseas) Borneo. 2. Labuan. 3. Sarawak (Island) I. Cornwall, Nigel Edmund, Bp., 1903-

CHRISTIAN religion 266.3
explained (The): in a course of twenty-three Anglican sermons. [dist. New York. Morehouse-Barlow, c.1960] 143p. 61-454 1.40 pap.,
1. Church of England—Addresses, essays, Lectures. 2. Christianity—Addresses, essays, lectures.

FRAYSER, Anne Rebecca [266.3]
(Finch).
Missions, by Mrs. Benj. Hobson Frayser. Richmond, Dietz Press, 1951. x, 443 p. port. 21 cm. [BV2803.V5F7] 277.55 51-4150
1. Missions—Virginia. 2. Protestant Episcopal Church in the U. S. A.—Missions. I. Title.

MAYHEW, Jonathan, 1720- 266.3
1766.
Observations on the charter and conduct of the Society for the Propagation of the Gospel in Foreign Parts. New York, Arno Press, 1972. 176 p. 23 cm. (Religion in America, series II) Reprint of the 1763 ed. [BV2763.S8M3 1972] 72-38456 ISBN 0-405-04077-6
1. Society for the Propagation of the Gospel in Foreign Parts, London. 2. Apthorp, East, 1732 or 3-1816. Considerations on the institution and conduct of the Society for the Propagation of the Gospel. 3. Church of England in New England. I. Title.

WEBSTER, Douglas. 266.3
Local church and world mission. Foreword by Kenneth Helm. New York, Seabury Press [1964] 92 p. 21 cm. (A Seabury paperback, SP15) Bibliographical footnotes. [BV2063.W4] 64-19634
1. Missions — Theory. 2. Anglican Communion — Missions. I. Title.

WEBSTER, Douglas 266.3
Local church and world mission. Foreword by Kenneth Heim. New York, Seabury [c.1962.1964] 92p. 21cm. (Seabury paperback, SP 15) Bibl. 64-19634 1.25 pap.,
1. Missions—Theory. 2. Anglican Communion—Missions. I. Title.

WRIGHT, Louis 266.309171242
Booker, 1899-
Religion and empire; the alliance between piety and commerce in English expansion, 1558-1625. New York, Octagon, 1965 [c.1943] ix, 190p. 21cm. (Lects. delivered under the auspices of the Walker-Ames Found. at the Univ. of Wash. April, 1942) Bibl. [BV2420.W7] 65-25894 7.00
1. Missions, British. 2. Gt. Brit.—Colonies—Hist. I. Title. II. Series: Washington (State) University. Walker-Ames Foundation Lectures, 1942

BATTY, Beatrice 266'.3'0924 B
(Stebbing)
Forty-two years amongst the Indians and Eskimo; pictures from the life of the Right Reverend John Horden, first bishop of Moosonee, by Beatrice Batty. With a new series introd. by Sidney Forman. Boston, Gregg Press, 1973. p. (History of minority education) Reprint of the 1893 ed. [E78.C2B38 1973] 73-1811 ISBN 0-8398-0196-3
1. Horden, John, Bp. of Moosonee, 1828-1893.

2. Indians of North America—Canada—Missions. 3. Northwest Territories, Can. I. Title. II. Series.

BOONE, Muriel, 266'.3'0924 B
1893-
The seed of the church in China. Philadelphia, United Church Press [1973] 287 p. illus. 22 cm. "A Pilgrim Press book." [BV3427.B57B66] 73-13815 ISBN 0-8298-0264-9 6.95
1. Boone, William Jones, Bp., 1811-1864. 2. Missions—China. 3. Protestant churches—Missions. I. Title.

BUTLER, Bill, 1914- 266'.3'0924 B
Hill ablaze / by Bill Butler. London : Hodder and Stoughton, 1976. 127 p. ; 18 cm. (Hodder Christian paperbacks) [BV3625.U4B97] 76-372933 ISBN 0-340-20436-2 : £0.70
1. Butler, Bill, 1914- 2. Missionaries—England—Biography. 3. Missionaries—Uganda—Biography. I. Title.

COLE, Edmund Keith, 266'.3'0924 B
1919-
Oenpelli pioneer: a biography of the Reverend Alfred John Dyer; pioneer missionary among the aborigines in Arnhem Land and founder of the Oenpelli Mission. [Melbourne] Church Missionary Historical Publications, 1972. 96 p. illus. 18 cm. (Great Australian missionaries no. 4) [BV3667.D93C64] 79-184183 ISBN 0-909821-07-0
1. Dyer, Alfred John, 1884-1968. I. Title.

COLE, Edmund Keith, 266.3'0924 B
1919-
Sincerity my guide; a biography of the Right Reverend P. W. Stephenson (1888-1962) by Keith Cole. [Melbourne, Church Missionary Historical Publications Trust] 1970. 127 p. illus., ports. 19 cm. (Great Australian missionaries) Includes bibliographical references. [BX5720.S8C64] 72-864218
1. Stephenson, Percival William, 1888-1962. I. Title.

FULLERTON, Arthur 266.3'0924 B
Grey, 1878-
Sunset at midnight; autobiography. [1st ed.] Portland, Or., Professional Pub. Print., inc. [1969] 111 p. illus., ports. 22 cm. Includes Mrs. Fullerton's notebook: p. 78-105. [CT275.F824A3] 74-93479
I. Fullerton, Annie Elizabeth, 1878-1968. II. Title.

HALIBURTON, Gordon 266'.3'0924 B
MacKay.
The prophet Harris; a study of an African prophet and his mass-movement in the Ivory Coast and the Gold Coast, 1913-1915. New York, Oxford University Press, 1973. xv, 155 p. illus. 21 cm. Bibliography: p. 141-143. [BV3785.H348H3 1973] 72-83851 ISBN 0-19-501626-2 7.50
1. Harris, William Wade. I. Title.

HATHAWAY, David. 266'.3'0924 B
Czech mate / David Hathaway. Old Tappan, N.J. : F. H. Revell Co., c1974. 187 p. ; 18 cm. Autobiographical. [BR1725.H245A33 1974] 75-6552 ISBN 0-8007-0742-7 pbk. : 1.95
1. Hathaway, David. 2. Bible—Publication and distribution—Europe, Eastern. 3. Prisoners—Czechoslovak Republic. I. Title.

HEMPHILL, Elizabeth 266.3'0924 B
Anne.
The road to KEEP; the story of Paul Rusch in Japan. With a foreword by Edwin O. Reischauer. [1st ed.] New York, Walker/Weatherhill [1970, c1969] ix, 195 p. illus., ports. 24 cm. Bibliography: p. 190. [BV3457.R8H4 1970] 78-96053 4.95
1. Rusch, Paul, 1897- 2. Protestant Episcopal Church in the U.S.A.—Missions. 3. Missions—Japan. I. Title.

LETTERS from James 266'.3'0924 B
Bay / commentary by James Scanlon ; drawings by Cecil Dunn ; foreword by J. A. Watton. Colbalt, Ont. : Highway Book Shop, 1976. 56 p., [3] p. : ill. ; 22 cm. Bibliography: p. [59] [E99.C88H674] 77-369946 ISBN 0-88954-094-2
1. Horden, John, Bp. of Moosonee, 1828-1893. 2. Missionaries—Canada—Biography. 3. Missionaries—England—Biography. 4. Cree Indians—Missions. 5. Indians of North America—Canada—Missions. I. Scanlon, James.

MEAD, Arthur David, 266.30924
1888-
Richard Taylor, missionary tramper, by A. D. Mead. Wellington, A. H. & A. W. Reed [1966] 272p. illus., maps, port. 23cm. [BV3667.T3M4] 66-7850 6.50
1. Taylor, Richard 1805?-1873. 2. Missions—New Zealand. 3. Maoris. I. Title.
Available from Tri-Ocean in San Francisco.

MERCIER, Anne. 266.3'0924 B
Father Pat; a hero of the Far West, by Mrs. Jerome Mercier. With a pref. by John Dart. Gloucester, Minchin & Gibbs, 1909; [Vernon, B.C.] Okanagan Historical Society, 1968. 109 p. illus., ports. 19 cm. [BX5620.I74M4] 74-478727
1. Irwin, Henry, 1859-1902. I. Okanagan Historical Society, Vernon, B.C. II. Title.

WALMSLEY, Lewis 266'.3'0924 B
Calvin, 1897-
Bishop in Honan : mission and museum in the life of William C. White / Lewis C. Walmsley. Toronto ; Buffalo : University of Toronto Press, [1974] xi, 230 p. : ill. ; 23 cm. "Publications of the Right Reverend W. C. White": p. [217]-220. Includes index. [BV3427.W48W34] 74-82288 ISBN 0-8020-3324-5 : 10.00
1. White, William Charles, Bp., 1873-1960. I. Title.

COLE, Edmund Keith, 266.3'0994'29
1919-
A short history of the C.M.S. Roper River Mission, 1908-1969, by E. K. Cole. [Melbourne, Church Missionary Historical Publications Trust, 1969?] 28 p. illus. 24 cm. Cover title: Roper River Mission. [BV3660.N6C64] 71-859347
1. Roper River Mission. 2. Church of England in Australia—Missions. 3. Missions—Northern Territory, Australia. I. Title.

TYING, Ethel Arens. 266.351
Letters to my grandchildren. Cambridge, Md., Tidewater Pubs. [dist. Cornell Maritime, c.] 1963. 70p. illus., ports., maps. 23cm. 63-23042 2.00 pap.,
1. Missions—China. 2. Protestant Episcopal Church in the U.S.A.—Missions. 3. China—Soc. life & cust. I. Title.

TYNG, Ethel Arens. 266.351
Letters to my grandchildren. Cambridge, Md., Tidewater Publishers, 1963. 70 p. illus., ports., maps 23 cm. [BV3427.T9A4 1963] 63-23042
1. Missions — China. 2. Protestant Episcopal Church in the U.S.A. — Missions. 3. China — Soc. life & cust. I. Title.

JOHNSON, William 266.3'6
Percival, 1854-1928.
My African reminiscences, 1875-1895. Westport, Conn., Negro Universities Press [1970] 236 p. illus., ports. 23 cm. "Originally published in 1924." [BV3625.N82J6 1970] 73-106875
I. Title.

KUMM, Hermann Karl 266.3'63
Wilhelm, 1874-1930.
Khont-hon nofer, the lands of Ethiopia. Westport, Conn., Negro Universities Press [1970] xi, 291 p. illus., fold. map, ports. 23 cm. Reprint of the 1910 ed. Bibliography: p. 255-282. [BV3625.S8K79 1970] 69-18986 ISBN 0-8371-1503-5
1. Missions—Sudan (Region) 2. Sudan (Region)—Description and travel. I. Title.

SCOTT, Anna M. 266.3'66'6
(Steele)
Day dawn in Africa; or, Progress of the Prot. Epis. Mission at Cape Palmas, West Africa, by Anna M. Scott. New York, Negro Universities Press [1969] 314 p. illus., map. 18 cm. Reprint of the 1858 ed. [BV3625.L5S3 1969] 69-18659
1. Protestant Episcopal Church in the U.S.A.—Missions. 2. Missions—Africa, West. I. Title.

TUCKER, Alfred Robert, 266.3'67
Bp., 1849-1914.
Eighteen years in Uganda & East Africa. With illus. from drawings by the author and a map. New ed. Westport, Conn., Negro Universities Press [1970] xvi, 362 p. illus., fold. map, port. 23 cm. Reprint of the 1911 ed. [BV3530.T8 1970] 77-106884
1. Church of England—Missions. 2. Missions—Africa, East. 3. Africa, East—Description and travel. I. Title.

WILSON, George Herbert, 266.3'67
1870-
The history of the Universities' Mission to Central Africa. Freeport, N.Y., Books for Libraries Press [1971] xvi, 278 p. illus. 23 cm. Reprint of the 1936 ed. [BV3520.W5 1971] 71-169781 ISBN 0-8369-6601-5
1. Universities' Mission to Central Africa. 2. Church of England—Missions. 3. Missions—Africa, Central. I. Title.

GIBSON, Alan George 266.3'68'6
Sumner, Bp., 1856-1922.
Eight years in Kaffraria, 1882-1890. New York, Negro Universities Press [1969] 178 p. illus., map. 23 cm. Reprint of the 1891 ed. [BV3625.K3G5 1969] 79-82052
1. Church of England—Missions. 2. Missions—Kaffraria. I. Title.

CALLAWAY, Godfrey, 266.3'68'7
1865or6-1942.
Sketches of Kafir life. With pref. by Alan G. S. Gibson. New York, Negro Universities Press [1969] xv, 154 p. illus. 23 cm. Reprint of the 1905 ed. [DT846.K2C17 1969] 79-77192
1. Kaffraria. 2. Missions—Kaffraria. I. Title.

CHADWICK, Owen 266.36897
Mackenzie's grave. London, Hodder & Stoughton [dist. Mystic, Conn., Verry. 1964, c.1959] 254p. illus., map. 23cm. Bibl. 60-1390 5.00
1. Mackenzie, Charles Frederick, Missionary Bp. of Central Africa, 1825-1862. 2. Missions—Nyasland. I. Title.

HUMPHREYS, David, 1689- 266.3'7
1740.
An historical account of the incorporated Society for the Propagation of the Gospel in Foreign Parts. New York, Arno Press, 1969. xxxi, 356 p. 2 fold. maps. 23 cm. (Religion in America) Reprint of the 1730 ed. [BV2500.A6H9 1969] 75-83426
1. Society for the Propagation of the Gospel in Foreign Parts, London. 2. Missions—North America. I. Title.

COOPER, Donald B. 266.3'7297
The establishment of the Anglican Church in the Leeward Islands [by] Donald B. Cooper. [Stillwater] Oklahoma State University [1966] 45 p. 23 cm. (Oklahoma State University. Monographs in the humanities, social, and biological sciences. Social sciences series, no. 10) Based on the author's thesis (M.A.), University of Texas, 1958. Bibliography: p. 44-45. [H31.O53 no. 10] 66-64970
1. Church of England—Missions. 2. Missions—Leeward Islands. I. Title. II. Series: Oklahoma. State University of Agriculture and Applied Science, Stillwater. Arts and sciences studies. Social studies series, no. 10

HENING, E. F. 266.3'73
History of the African mission of the Protestant Episcopal Church. Freeport, N.Y., Books for Libraries Press, 1971 [c1849] 300 p. map. 23 cm. (The Black heritage library collection) Reprint of the 1850 ed., published under title: History of the African mission of the Protestant Episcopal Church in the United States, with memoirs of deceased missionaries, and notices of native customs. [BV3540.H4 1971] 77-173608 ISBN 0-8369-8900-7
1. Protestant Episcopal Church in the U.S.A.—Missions. 2. Missions—Africa, West. I. Title. II. Series.

RITCHIE, Carson I. A. 266'.3'73
Frontier parish : an account of the Society for the Propagation of the Gospel and the Anglican Church in America : drawn from the records of the Bishop of London / Carson I. A. Ritchie. Rutherford : Fairleigh Dickinson University Press, c1976. xiii, 210 p. ; 22 cm. Includes index. Bibliography: p. 199-200. [BX5881.R57] 75-3564 ISBN 0-8386-1735-2 : 9.50
1. Church of England in America—History—Sources. 2. Society for the Propagation of the Gospel in Foreign Parts, London—History—Sources. 3. Missions—United States—History—Sources. I. Title.

KLINGBERG, Frank 266.3'747
Joseph, 1883-
Anglican humanitarianism in colonial New York, by Frank J. Klingberg. Freeport, N.Y., Books for Libraries Press [1971] x, 295 p. 24 cm. Reprint of the 1940 ed. Contents.Contents.—Leading ideas in the annual S.P.G. sermons, particularly with reference to native peoples.—The noble savage as seen by the S.P.G. missionary.—Sir William Johnson and the S.P.G.—The S.P.G. program for Negroes in colonial New York.—Three notable annual S.P.G. sermons: A plea for humanitarianism for the Negro in the institution of slavery, February 16, 1710-11, by W. Fleetwood. An argument for the Christianization of whites, Negroes, and Indians as sound imperial policy, February 20, 1740-41, by T. Secker. A statement of British manifest destiny, involving aborigines protection and ultimate Negro freedom, February 21, 1766, by W. Warburton.—A select bibliography (p. [251]-265) [BV2500.A6K55 1971] 71-164612 ISBN 0-8369-5896-9
1. Society for the Propagation of the Gospel in Foreign Parts, London. 2. Church of England—Sermons. 3. Missions—New York (State) 4. Indians of North America—Missions. 5. Negroes—New York (State) 6. Missions—Sermons. 7. Sermons, English. I. Title.

COLE, Edmund Keith, 266'.3'94
1919-
A history of the Church Missionary Society of Australia, by Keith Cole. [Melbourne] Church Missionary Historical Publications, 1971. xii, 367 p. illus., maps, tables. 22 cm. Includes bibliographical references. [BV2470.A8C64] 72-176060 ISBN 0-909821-02-X 4.60
1. Church Missionary Society of Australia. 2. Missions, Australian. I. Title.

COLE, Edmund Keith, 266'.3'9429
1919-
Groote Eylandt Mission; a short history of the C. M. S. Groote Eylandt Mission, 1921-1971, by Keith Cole. [Melbourne] Church Missionary Historical Publications, 1971. 87 p. illus., maps, ports. 20 cm. "Companion volume to Groote Eylandt Pioneer, by Keith Cole, Melbourne, 1971." Includes bibliographical references. [BV3660.N6C637] 72-188078 ISBN 0-909821-00-3
1. Groote Eylandt Mission. 2. Missions—Groote Eylandt.

BEAVER, Robert Pierce, 266.4
1906-
From mission to mission; Protestant world mission today and tomorrow. New York, Association [c.1964] 126p. 16cm. (Reflection bk.) 64-11420 .50 pap.,
1. Protestant churches—Missions. I. Title.

BEAVER, Robert Pierce, 266.4
1906-
From missions to mission; Protestant world mission today and tomorrow. New York, Association Press [c1964] 126 p. 16 cm. (A Reflection book) [BV2061.B4] 64-11420
1. Protestant churches — Missions. I. Title.

*BROOKS, Keith L. 266.4
Luke, the gospel of God's man [Chicago] Moody [c.1964] 96p. 22cm. (Teach yourself the Bible ser.) 1.00 pap.,
I. Title.

MALASKA, Hilkka. 266'.4
The challenge for evangelical missions to Europe; a Scandinavian case study. South Pasadena, Calif., William Carey Library [1970] 178 p. illus. 22 cm. Bibliography: p. 161-176. [BV3060.M33] 71-132011 ISBN 0-87808-308-1 2.95
1. Protestant churches—Missions. 2. Missions—Scandinavia. I. Title.

CHRISEMER, Edgar T. 266.40924
The Werner Wedel story, by Edgar T. Chrisemer. Boston, Branden Pr. [1966] 86p. 23cm. [BV3427.W4C5] 66-18428 3.00
1. Wedel, Werner H. O 1903 I. Title.

BEAUCHAMP, William 266'.4'09747
Martin, 1830-1925.
Moravian journals relating to central New York, 1745-66 / arranged and edited by Wm. M. Beauchamp for the Onondaga Historical Association. New York : AMS Press, 1976. 242 p. ; 22 cm. (Communal societies in America) Reprint of the 1916 ed. published by the Dehler Press, Syracuse, N.Y. [E78.N7B37 1976] 72-8246 ISBN 0-404-11000-2 : 14.50
1. Moravian Church—Missions. 2. Indians of North America—New York (State)—Missions. 3. Iroquois Indians—Missions. 4. Moravians in New York (State)—History—Sources. I. Onondaga Historical Association, Syracuse, N.Y. II. Title.
Contents omitted

BURGESS, Andrew Severance, 266.41
1897- ed.
Lutheran world missions; foreign missions of the Lutheran Church in America. Minneapolis, Augsburg Pub. House [1954] 277 p. illus. 22 cm. [BV2540.B85] 55-44
1. Lutheran Church—Missions. I. Title.

EVANGELICAL Lutheran 266.41
Church. Board of Foreign Missions.
Year book. Minneapolis. v. illus., ports. 23 cm. Issues for published by the church under its earlier name: Norwegian Lutheran Church of America. [BV2540.A1E75] 50-41207
1. Lutheran Church—Missions—Yearbooks. I. Title.

FOR the heart of Africa. 266.41
[Minneapolis] Augsburg Pub. House [1956] 271p. illus. 21cm. [BV3625.C34C45] 276.711 56-9459
1. Missions—Cameroons, French. 2. Lutheran Church—Missions. I. Christiansen, Ruth.

HELLAND, Andreas Andersen, 266.41
1870-
The American Santal Mission: notes on its history. Mineapolis, American Santal Mission, 1948. 78p. illus. 21cm. [BV2540.H4] 55-23127
1. American Santal Mission. 2. Missions—Santals. I. Title.

HESTERMAN, Lowell L. 266.4'1
Missionary pioneers of the American Lutheran Church [by] Lowell L. Hesterman. Minneapolis, Augsburg Pub. House [1967] 64 p. illus., maps, ports. 22 cm. A series of articles which originally appeared in One magazine from Feb. 1965 to Apr. 1966. [BV3700.H4] 67-11717

1. American Lutheran Church (1961-)— Missions. 2. Missionaries. I. Title.

KOSCHADE, Alfred. 266.4'1
New branches on the vine; from mission field to church in New Guinea. Minneapolis, Augsburg Pub. House [1967] 175 p. 23 cm. Bibliography:p. 173-175. [BV3680.N5K6] 67-11718
1. Missions — New Guinea. 2. Evangelical Lutheran Church — Missions. I. Title.

LERBERG, Irwin M 266.41
World missions of The American Lutheran Church; 12 capsule studies, by Irwin M. Lerberg. Minneapolis, Augsburg Pub. House [1964] 63 p. illus., maps, ports. 20 cm. [BV2540.L4] 64-21511
1. The American Lutheran Church (1961-) — Missions. I. Title.

LERBERG, Irwin M. 266.41
World missions of The American Lutheran Church; 12 capsule studies. Minneapolis, Augsburg [c.1964] 63p. illus., maps, ports. 20cm. 64-21511 1.00 pap.,
1. The American Lutheran Church (1961-)— Missions. I. Title.

LUEKING, Frederick Dean, 1928- 266.41
Mission in the making; the missionary enterprise among Missouri Synod Lutherans, 1846-1963, by F. Dean Lueking. Saint Louis, Concordia Pub. House [1964] 354 p. 24 cm. Bibliographical references included in "Notes" (p. 315-337) [BV2540.L8] 64-18235
1. Lutheran Church — Missouri Synod — Missions. I. Title.

LUEKING, Frederick Dean, 1928- 266.41
Mission in the making; the missionary enterprise among Missouri Synod Lutherans, 1846-1963. St. Louis. Concordia [c.1964] 354p. 24cm. Bibl. 64-18235 7.50
1. Lutheran Church—Missouri Synod— Missions. I. Title.

LUTHERAN churches in the 266.4'1
third world. Edited by Andrew S. Burgess. Minneapolis, Augsburg Pub. House [1970] 176 p. 22 cm. Includes bibliographical references. [BV2540.L87] 70-101113 3.95
1. Lutheran Church—Missions. 2. Missions— Asia. 3. Missions—Africa. 4. Missions—Latin America. I. Burgess, Andrew Severance, 1897- ed.

LUTHERAN Foreign Missions Conference of America. 266.41
Annual convention. [Minutes] Minneapolis. v. 22 cm. [BV2540.A1L77] 51-30151
1. Lutheran Church—Missions. I. Title.

MEYER, Ruth Fritz. 266.4'1
Women on a mission; the role of women in the church from Bible times up to and including a history of the Lutheran Women's Missionary League during its first twenty-five years. [St. Louis, Printed by Concordia Pub. House, 1967] 300 p. illus., ports. 23 cm. Bibliography: p. [240]-242. [BV2540.A533M4] 67-8141
1. Lutheran Women's Missionary League. I. Title.

SCHERER, James A. 266.4'1
Mission and unity in Lutheranism; a study in confession and ecumenicity [by] James A. Scherer. Philadelphia, Fortress Press [1969] xiv, 258 p. 24 cm. Bibliography: p. 246-254. [BV2540.S3] 71-76808 8.00
1. Lutheran Church—Missions. 2. Christian union—Lutheran Church. I. Title.

SEASE, Rosalyn Summer. 266.41
Missions today in the Lutheran Church in America, by Rosalyn Summer Sease and Erich F. Voehringer. Edited by A. Bonander. Philadelphia, Fortress Press [1963] 128 p. illus., maps (1 fold.) 21 cm. [BV2540.S4] 64-1562
1. Lutheran Church—Missions. I. Voehringer, Erich Frederick, 1905- joint author. II. Title.

SEASE, Rosalyn Summer 266.41
Missions today in the Lutheran Church in America, by Rosalyn Summer Sease, Erich F. Voehringer. Ed. by A. Bonander. Philadelphia, Fortress [c.1963] 128p. illus., maps. (1 fold.) 21cm. 64-1562 .75 pap.,
1. Lutheran Church—Missions. I. Voehringer, Erich Frederick, 1905- joint author. II. Title.

SWANSON, Swan Hjalmar, 1886- 266.41
Foundation for tomorrow; a century of progress in Augustana world missions. Minneapolis, Board of World Missions, Augustana Lutheran Church [1960] 370 p. illus. 24 cm. Includes bibliography. [BV2540.S9] 60-968
1. Lutheran Church — Missions. 2. Augustana Evangelical Lutheran Church — Missions. I. Title.

TROBISCH, Ingrid (Hult) 266.41
On our way rejoicing! [1st ed.] New York, Harper & Row [1964] 254 p. illus., ports. 22 cm. Autobiographical. [BV3505.T7A3] 64-20195
1. Missions — Africa. 2. Hult family. I. Title.

TROBISCH, Ingrid (Hult) 266.41
On our way rejoicing! New York, Harper [c.1964] 254p. illus., ports. 22cm. 64-20195 3.95
1. Hult family 2. Missions—Africa. I. Title.

VOEHRINGER, Erich Frederick, 1905- 266.41
It depends on you; a study of Christian missions. Arthur H. Getz., editor. Philadelphia, Muhelnberg Press [1961] 126 p. illus. 18 cm. [BV2963.V6] 61-4797
1. Missions — Theory. 2. Lutheran Church — Missions. 3. Christianity and other religions. I. Title.

VOEHRINGER, Erich Frederick, 1905- 266.41
It depends on you; a study of Christian missions. Arthur H.Getz, ed. Philadelphia, Muhlenberg [c.1961] 126p. illus. 61-4797 1.25 pap.,
1. Missions—Theory. 2. Lutheran Church— Missions. 3. Christianity and other religions. I. Title.

*VOSBURGH, Adah 266.41
Until everyone knows. Philip R. Hoh, ed. James Heugh, artist. John H. Geiszel, cartographer. Philadelphia, Lutheran Church Pr. [c.1965] 108p. 21cm. (LCA Sunday church sch. ser.) 1; 1.25 pap.,teacher's ed., pap.,
I. Title.

WARNKE, Mabel. 266.41
Partners the world around. St. Louis, Concordia Pub. House [1966] viii, 188 p. illus. 21 cm. Bibliography: p. [187]-188. [BV2540.W3] 66-19975
1. Lutheran Church — Missions. I. Title.

WARNKE, Mabel 266.41
Partners the world around. St. Louis, Concordia [c.1966] viii, 188p. illus, 21cm. Bibl. [BV2540.W3] 66-19975 3.95 pap.,
1. Lutheran Church—Missions. I. Title.

DANIELSON, Elmer R. 266'.4'10924 B
Forty years with Christ in Tanzania, 1928-1968 / Elmer R. Danielson. New York : World Mission Interpretation, Lutheran Church in America, c1977. xii, 236 p. ; 21 cm. Bibliography: p. 236. [BV3625.T42D36] 77-78401 ISBN 0-87808-953-5
1. Danielson, Elmer R. 2. Lutheran Church— Missions. 3. Missionaries—Tanzania— Biography. 4. Missionaries—United States— Biography. 5. Missions—Tanzania. I. Title.

GARNETT, Eve. 266.4'1'0924 B
To Greenland's icy mountains; the story of Hans Egede, explorer, coloniser missionary. With a foreword by Nils Egede Bloch-Hoell. Illustrated with photos. and with drawings by the author. New York, Roy Publishers [1968] xv, 189 p. illus., maps, ports. 23 cm. [G762.E35G3] 69-12999 5.50
1. Egede, Hans Poulsen, 1686-1758. I. Title.

JURGENSEN, Barbara. 266.410924
All the bandits of China; adventures of a missionary in a land by bandits and war lords. Illustrated by Robert Friedericksen. Minneapolis, Augsburg Pub. House [1965] 184 p. illus: 23 cm. [BV3427.H35J8] 65-22839
1. Hellestad, Oscar. 2. Missions — China. I. Title.

JURGENSEN, Barbara 266.410924
All the bandits of China; adventures of a missionary in a land ravaged by bandits and war lords. Illus. by Robert Friedericksen. Minneapolis, Augsburg [c.1965] 184p. illus. 22cm. [BV3427.H35J8] 65-22839 3.95
1. Hellestad, Oscar. 2. Missions—China. I. Title.

WELZ, Justinian 266.4'1'0924 B
Ernst von, Baron von Eberstein, 1621-1668.
Justinian Welz: essays by an early prophet of mission. Translated, annotated, and with an historical introd., by James A. Scherer. Grand Rapids, Mich., Eerdmans [1969] 111 p. 20 cm. (A Christian world mission book) Bibliography: p. 109-111. [BV2853.D9W4] 68-54103 2.45
1. Welz, Justinian Ernst von, Baron von Eberstein, 1621-1668. 2. Lutheran Church— Missions—Collected works. I. Scherer, James A., tr.

SKINSNES, Casper C 1886- [266.41] 275.1
Scalpel and cross in Honan. Minneapolis, Augsburg Pub. House [1952] 254 p. illus. 21 cm. Autobiographical. [BV3420.H6S52] 52-14474
1. Missions—Honan, China (Province) 2. Missions, Medical. I. Title.

MAAHS, Arnold M [266.41] 279.5
Our eyes were opened. Columbus, Ohio, Warthburg Press, 1946. 110 p. plates, maps (on lining-papers) 20 cm. [D811.M17] 48-3468
1. World War, 1939-1945 — Personal narratives, American. 2. Missions — New Guines. 3. American Lutheran Church (1930-1960) — Missions. I. Title.

SCHMIDT, Otto Henry, 1886- 266.415
Globe-trotting for the gospel. New York, Vantage- 53c.1962] 92p. illus. 62-2569 2.75
1. Missions—East (Far East). 2. Lutheran Church—Missouri Synod—Missions. I. Title.

SWENSON, Victor E 266.4151
Parents of many: forty-five years as missionaries in old, new, and divided China; a personal narrative. Rock Island, Ill., Augustana Press [1959] 348 p. illus. 21 cm. [BV3427.S815A3] 59-14543
I. Title.

SWENSON, Victor E. 266.4151
Parents of many: forty-five years as missionaries in old, new, and divided China; a personal narrative. Rock Island, Ill., Augustana Press [c.1959] 348p. illus. 21cm. 59-14543 3.75
I. Title.

NEVE, Lloyd R. 266'.4'152
Japan; God's door to the Far East, by Lloyd R. Neve. Minneapolis, Augsburg Pub. House [1973] 112 p. illus. 19 cm. [BV3445.2.N48] 73-78255 ISBN 0-8066-1321-1 2.50
1. Lutheran Church in Japan. 2. Missions— Japan. 3. Christianity—Japan. I. Nestingen, James A. II. Title.

WENDLAND, Ernst H. 266'.4'16
To Africa with love / by Ernst H. Wendland. Milwaukee, Wis. : Northwestern Pub. House, 1974. xii, 191 p. : ill. ; 22 cm. [BV3520.W38] 74-18631
1. Lutheran Church—Missions. 2. Missions— Africa, Sub-Saharan. I. Title.

WRIGHT, Marcia. 266.4'1'6782
German missions in Tanganyika, 1891-1941: Lutherans and Moravians in the Southern Highlands. Oxford, Clarendon Press, 1971. xiv, 249 p; maps. 23 cm. (Oxford studies in African affairs) Bibliography: p. [227]-240. [BV3625.T3W74] 77-855553 ISBN 0-19-821665-3 £3.25
1. Missions—Tanganyika. 2. Missions, German. I. Title. II. Series.

BOCKELMAN, Wilfred. 266'.4'168
An exercise in compassion; the Lutheran Church in South Africa, by Wilfred and Eleanor Bockelman. Minneapolis, Augsburg Pub. House [1972] 112 p. illus. 19 cm. [BX8063.S7B6] 76-176473 ISBN 0-8066-1204-5 2.50
1. Evangelical Lutheran Church in Southern Africa—South-Eastern Region. 2. Lutheran Church—Missions. 3. Missions—Africa, South. I. Bockelman, Eleanor, joint author. II. Title.

KJOME, June C. 266.41683
Back of beyond; bush nurse in South Africa. Minneapolis, Augsburg Pub. House [1963] 236 p. illus. 21 cm. [RA395.Z8K5] 62-20843
1. Missions, Medical—Zululand. I. Title.

HALVERSON, Alton C. O. 266'.4'1691
Madagascar: footprint at the end of the world, by Alton C. O. Halverson. Minneapolis, Augsburg Pub. House [1973] 112 p. illus. 19 cm. [BV3625.M2H24] 73-78253 ISBN 0-8066-1319-X 2.50
1. Fiangonana Loterana Malagasy. 2. Missions—Madagascar. 3. Madagascar— Church history. I. Ellertson, Carroll F. II. Title.

FRERICHS, Albert C. 266.4'195
Anutu conquers in New Guinea; a story of mission work in New Guinea, by Albert and Sylvia Frerichs. [Rev. ed.] Minneapolis, Augsburg Pub. House [1969] 160 p. illus. 20 cm. [BV3680.N5F68 1969] 69-14178 1.95
1. Missions—New Guinea. I. Frerichs, Sylvia, joint author. II. Title.

KOSCHADE, Alfred. 266.4'1'95
New branches on the vine; from mission field to church in New Guinea. Minneapolis, Augsburg Pub. House [1967] 175 p. 23 cm. Bibliography: p. 173-175. [BV3680.N5K6] 67-11718
1. Evangelical Lutheran Church—Missions. 2. Missions—New Guinea. I. Title.

VICEDOM, Georg F. 266.4195
Church and people in New Guinea. New York, Association [1962] 79p. 19cm. (World Christian bks., no. 38, 2d ser.) 61-7471 1.00 pap.,
1. Missions—New Guinea. 2. Evangelical Lutheran Church of New Guinea. I. Title.

SMIT, Erasmus. 266'.4'20924 B
The diary of Erasmus Smit. Edited by H. F. Schoon. Translated by W. G. A. Mears. Cape Town, C. Struik, 1972. x, 186 p. illus. 22 cm. Translation of Uit het dagboek van Erasmus Smit. [BX9595.S63S613] 72-189813 ISBN 0-86977-013-6 10.00
I. Title.
Available from Verry.

BUCHNER, J. H. 266'.4'6
The Moravians in Jamaica, by J. H. Buchner. Freeport, N.Y., Books for Libraries Press, 1971. 175 p. 23 cm. (The Black heritage library collection) Reprint of the 1854 ed. [BV2848.J2B8 1971] 77-178470 ISBN 0-8369-8918-X
1. Moravian Church—Missions. 2. Missions— Jamaica. I. Title. II. Series.

DANKER, William J. 266.4'6
Profit for the Lord; economic activities in Moravian missions and the Basel Mission Trading Company, by William J. Danker. Grand Rapids, Eerdmans [1971] 183 p. 20 cm. (Christian world mission books) Bibliography: p. 171-174. [BV2560.D35] 77-129850 3.95
1. Moravian Church—Missions. 2. Evangelische Missionsgesellschaft, Basel. 3. Missions—Finance. I. Title.

GRAY, Elma E. 266'.4'6
Wilderness Christians; the Moravian mission to the Delaware Indians, by Elma E. Gray in collaboration with Leslie Robb Gray. Illus. by Clare Bice. New York, Russell & Russell [1973, c1956] xi, 354 p. illus. 24 cm. Reprint of the ed. published by Cornell University Press, Ithaca, N.Y. Includes bibliographical references. [E99.D2G7 1973] 72-84988 ISBN 0-8462-1701-5 22.00
1. Moravian Church—Missions. 2. Delaware Indians—Missions. I. Gray, Leslie Robb., joint author. II. Title.

DE SCHWEINITZ, Edmund Alexander, 1825-1887. 266'.46'0924 B
The life and times of David Zeisberger. [New York] Arno Press [1971] 747 p. 23 cm. (The First America frontier) Reprint of the 1870 ed. "Published works of David Zeisberger": p. 687-692. [E99.M9Z44 1971] 70-146391 ISBN 0-405-02844-X
1. Zeisberger, David, 1721-1808. I. Title. II. Series.

DE SCHWEINITZ, Edmund Alexander, 1825-1887. 266'.46'0924 B
The life and times of David Zeisberger, the Western pioneer and apostle of the Indians. Philadelphia, Lippincott, 1871. New York, Johnson Reprint Corp., 1971. xii, 747 p. 23 cm. (Series in American studies) Includes bibliographical references. [E98.M6Z4 1971] 71-155745
1. Zeisberger, David, 1721-1808. I. Title.

LOSKIEL, George Henry, 1740-1814. 266'.4'60973
The history of the Moravian mission among the Indians in North America, from its commencement to the present time with a preliminary account of the Indians. Compiled from authentic sources by a member of the Brethren's Church. London, T. Allman, 1838. St. Clair Shores, Mich., Scholarly Press, 1973. p. Consists principally of C.I. La Trobe's English translation of Geschichte der Mission der evangelischen Bruder unter den Indianern in Nordamerika, by G. H. Loskiel. [E99.M9L813 1973] 73-108506 ISBN 0-403-00358-X
1. Moravian Indians—Missions. 2. Indians of North America—Missions. I. A member of the Brethren's Church. II. La Trobe, Christian Ignatius, 1758-1836, tr. III. Title.

BURCKHARD, Johann Christian. 266.4'6'701
Partners in the Lord's work; the diary of two Moravian missionaries in the Creek Indian country, 1807-1913. Translated and edited by Carl Mauelshagen and Gerald H. Davis. Atlanta, Georgia State College, 1969. iii, 77 p. illus., facsim., map. 23 cm. (Georgia. State College, Atlanta. School of Arts and Sciences. Research papers, no. 21) [AS36.G378A3 no. 21] 75-633298
1. Moravians in Georgia. 2. Creek Indians— Missions. I. Petersen, Karsten, joint author. II. Mauelshagen, Carl, 1886- ed. III. Davis, Gerald Hinkle, ed. IV. Title. V. Series.

MURPHY, Patricia Shaubah. 266.4'67297'22
The Moravian mission to the African slaves of the Danish West Indies, 1732-1828. [St. Croix,

U.S. Virgin Islands, Prestige Press, c1969] 12, [10] p. illus., maps. 23 cm. "Published under the auspices of the Caribbean Research Institute of the College of the Virgin Islands, St. Thomas." Bibliography: p. [20]-[22] [BV2848.V5M86] 74-633496
1. Moravian Church—Missions. 2. Missions—West Indies, Danish. I. Caribbean Research Institute. II. Title.

MUHLENBERG College, 266.47
Allentown, Pa. Dept. of Sociology.
Inner mission services on the territory of the Ministerium of Pennsylvania; a survey with recommendations and proposals. Philadelphia, Evangelical Lutheran Ministerium of Pennsylvania and the Adjacent States [1951] xv. 198 p. maps, diagrs. tables. 23 cm. Bibliographical footnotes. [BX8061.P4M8] 51-3704
1. Evangelical Lutheran Ministerium of Pennsulvania and Adjacent States — Charities. 2. Inner missions. 3. Missions — Pennsylvania. I. Title.

REISHUS, Martha. 266.47
Hearts and hands uplifted; a history of the Women's Missionary Federation of the Evangelical Lutheran Church. Illus. by Cyrus Running and Lee Mero. Minneapolis. Augsburg Pub. House [1958] 138p. illus. 21cm. [BV2540.R4] 58-10321
1. Evangelical Lutheran Church. women's Missionary Federation. I. Title.

RIGMARK, William, 1913- 266.47
Covenant missions in Japan. Issued under the auspices of the Board of Missions of the Evangelical Covenant Church of America. Chicago, Covenant Press [1959] 118p. illus. 22cm. Includes bibliography. [BV3445.R48] 59-42183
1. Missions—Japan. 2. Evangelical Covenant Church of America—Missions. I. Title.

METHODIST Church 266'.4'97
(United States) Board of Missions. Joint Committee on Missionary Personnel.
Report to the Board of Missions. [New York?] v. 28 cm. [BV2550.A15A43] 64-4645
I. Title.

METHODIST Episcopal 266'.4'97
Church. Woman's Foreign Missionary Society.
Report. Boston. v. ports. 22 cm. annual. [BV2550.A45A5] 50-43184
I. Title.

PEDERICK, Alec W. 266'.4'97
Men on the frontier; a brief history of the Federal Methodist Inland Mission, by A. W. Pederick. Melbourne, Methodist Publishing House (Aldersgate Press) [1970] 72 p. illus. 19 cm. [BV2550.A243P4] 72-189674 ISBN 0-85571-050-0
1. Federal Methodist Inland Mission. 2. Missions—Australia. I. Title.

HALF a lifetime in Korea. 266.5
San Antonio, Naylor Co. [1952] 197p. illus. 22cm. 'Letters to [the author's] ... family and friends.' [BV3462.D6A4] [BV3462.D6A4] 275.19 52-14707 52-14707
1. Missions—Korea. I. Dodson, Mary L

HAYES, Florence (Sooy), 266.5
1895-
Daughters of Dorcas; the story of the work of women for home missions since 1802. New York, Board of National Missions, Presbyterian Church in the U. S. A. [1952] 158 p. 23 cm. [BV2570.H34] 52-11025
1. Women in missionary work. 2. Presbyterian Church—Missions. I. Title.

HEWAT, Elizabeth 266.5
Glendinning Kirkwood.
Vision and achievement, 1796-1956; a history of the foreign missions of the churches united in the Church of Scotland. Foreword by John Baillie. London, New York, Nelson [c1960] 308p. illus. 23cm. [BV2570.H45 1960] 61-2508
1. Missions, Foreign. 2. Church of Scotland—Missions. I. Title.

MCCLURE, William Donald, 266.5
1906-
Red-headed, rash, and religious the story of a pioneer missionary. [Letters] edited and compiled by Marion Fairman. Pittsburgh, Board of Christian Education of the United Presbyterian Church of North America [1954] 142p. illus. 21cm. [BV3625.S8M2] [BV3625.S8M2] 276.24 55-17420 55-17420
1. Missions—Sudan, Egyptian. 2. Missions—Ethiopia. I. Title.

GRIFFITH, Arthur Leonard, 266.506
1920-
The eternal legacy from an upper room. New York, Harper [1964, c.1963] 191p. 21cm. Bibl. 64-10752 3.00
1. Bible. N. T. John XIII-XVII—Criticism, interpretation, etc. I. Title.

BAIRD, Richard H., 266.5'0924 B
1898-
William M. Baird of Korea; a profile. [By Richard H. Baird. Oakland, Calif., 1968] A-D, 241 p. illus., facsims., maps, ports. 29 cm. Cover title. Bibliography: p. 211-212. [BV3462.B3B3] 76-2539 4.75
1. Baird, William M., 1862-1931. 2. Missions—Korea. 3. Presbyterian Church—Missions. 4. Missions—Educational work. I. Title.

HALL, Ralph J., 266.5'0924 B
1891-
The main trail, by Ralph J. Hall. Edited by Vic Jameson. San Antonio, Tex., Naylor [1971] xiii, 193 p. illus. 22 cm. Autobiographical. [BX9225.H312A3] 76-185994 ISBN 0-8111-0448-6 7.95
I. Title.

MACLEAN, Angus Hector, 266.509712
1892-
The galloping Gospel, by Angus H. MacLean. Boston, Beacon Press [1966] 174 p. illus., map. 22 cm. Autobiographical. [BX9969.M3A3] 66-15072
I. Title.

ANDERSON, Llewellyn 266.51
Kennedy, 1900-
Bridge to Africa, by L. K. Anderson & W. Sherman Skinner. Cover design and drawings by Merrill A. Lauck. New York, Board of Foreign Missions of the Presbyterian Church in the United States of America, Foreign Missions and Overseas Interchurch Service [1952] 133 p. illus. 20 cm. [BV3625.C29A7] 52-13953
1. Missions—Cameroons. 2. Presbyterian Church—Missions. I. Title.

DRURY. CLIFFORD MERRILL, [266.51]
1897-
Presbyterian panorama; one hundred and fifty years of National Missions history. Philadelphia, Board of Christian Education, Presbyterian Church in the United States of America, 1952. xvi, 458 p. illus., ports., maps. 24 cm. Bibliography: p. [424]-429. [BV2570.D7] 277.3 52-9984
1. Presbyterian Church—Missions—Hist. 2. Presbyterian Church in the U. S. A. Board of National Missions. I. Title.

HAMILTON, Horace Ernest. 266.51
China two generations ago; a family sketch of Guy and Pauline Ernst Hamilton, Presbyterian medical missionaries in the interior of North China. Denver, Big Mountain Press [1957] 102p. illus. 23cm. [BV3427.H23H25] 275.1 57-3200
1. Hamilton, Guy Wheeler. 2. Hamilton, Pauline (Ernst) I. Title.

LAMBIE, Thomas Alexander, 266.51
1885-1954.
A doctor's great commission. [4th ed., enl.] Wheaton, Ill., Van Kampen Press [1954] 288p. illus. 21cm. [BV3705.L3A3 1954] 276.2 55-14051
1. Missions—Sudan. 2. Missions—Ethiopia. 3. Missions—Palestine. 4. Missions, Medical. I. Title.

RICE, Claton Silas, 1883- 266.51
Ambassador to the saints, by Claton S. Rice. Boston, Christopher Pub. House [1965] 237 p. 21 cm. Autobiographical. [BV2627.R5] 65-16477
1. Missions to Mormons. I. Title.

RICE, Claton Silas, 1883- 266.51
Ambassador to the saints. Boston, Christopher [c.1965] 237p. 21cm. Autobiographical [BV2627.R5] 65-16477 3.95
1. Missions to Mormons. I. Title.

BRAINERD, David, 266'.5'10924 B
1718-1747.
Journey with David Brainerd : forty days or forty nights with David Brainerd. Downers Grove, Ill. : InterVarsity Press, [1975] 120 p. : ill. ; 21 cm. Selections from the author's An account of the life of the late Reverend Mr. David Brainerd; with a prayer by R. A. Hasler following each selection. Includes bibliographical references. [E98.M6M7864 1975] 74-20100 ISBN 0-87784-640-5 pbk. : 2.50
1. Brainerd, David, 1718-1747. 2. Prayers. I. Hasler, Richard A. II. Title.

BRAINERD, David, 266.5'10924 B
1718-1747.
Memoirs of the Rev. David Brainerd, missionary to the Indians on the border of New York, New Jersey, and Pennsylvania; chiefly taken from his own diary, by Jonathan Edwards. Including his journal, now for the first time incorporated with the rest of his diary, in a regular chronological series, by Sereno Edwards Dwight. New Haven, S. Converse, 1822. St. Clair Shores, Mich., Scholarly Press, 1970. 504 p. 22 cm. First ed., 1749, published under title: An account of the life of the late Reverend Mr. David Brainerd. [E98.M6B7863] 70-108477
1. Indians of North America—Missions. I. Edwards, Jonathan, 1703-1758, ed. II. Dwight, Sereno Edwards, 1786-1850. III. Title.

HANSON, Irene. 266'.5'10924 B
The wheelbarrow and the comrade, by Irene Hanson with Bernard Palmer. Chicago, Moody Press [1973] 187 p. illus. 22 cm. [BV3427.H235A3] 72-95015 ISBN 0-8024-9428-5 3.95
1. Hanson, Irene. I. Palmer, Bernard Alvin, 1914- II. Title.

HILLDRUP, Robert 266.5'1'0924 B
Leroy.
An American missionary to Meiji Japan. [Norfolk, Va.] 1970. 138 p. illus., port. 24 cm. Includes bibliographical references. [BV3457.G7H5] 72-17090
1. Grinnan, Randolph Bryan, 1860-1942. 2. Missions—Japan. I. Title.

KINNEAR, Elizabeth 266.5'1'0924 B
Kelsey.
She sat where they sat; a memoir of Anna Young Thompson of Egypt. Grand Rapids, Eerdmans [1971] 112 p. port. 20 cm. (Christian world mission books) [BV3572.T87K55] 76-147363 2.45
1. Thompson, Anna Young, 1851-1932. I. Title.

LAUTENSCHLAGER, 266.5'1'0924 B
Roy S.
On the Dragon Hills, by Roy S. Lautenschlager. Philadelphia, Westminster Press [1970] 217, [2] p. 21 cm. Bibliography: p. [219] [BV3415.2.L3] 72-98382 4.95
1. Missions—China. 2. China—Description and travel. I. Title.

MCNEIL, Marian W. 266'.5'10924 B
Lord, "give me this mountain" / by Marian W. McNeil. Collingswood, N.J. : Christian Beacon Press, 1976. 187 p., [7] leaves of plates : ill. ; 22 cm. [BV3625.K42M285] 76-42948
1. McNeil, Marian W. 2. Missionaries—Kenya—Biography. 3. Missionaries—United States—Biography. I. Title.

SANFORD, Agnes 266'.5'10924 B
Mary (White)
Sealed orders [by] Agnes Sanford. Plainfield, N.J., Logos International, 1972. 313 p. 25 cm. Autobiographical. [BR1725.S27A37] 72-76592 ISBN 0-912106-37-9 5.95
1. Sanford, Agnes Mary (White) I. Title.

STEURT, Marjorie 266'.5'10924 B
Rankin.
Broken bits of old China. [1st ed.] Nashville, T. Nelson [1973] 152 p. 21 cm. Autobiographical. [BV3427.S814A3] 72-12986 ISBN 0-8407-6262-3 4.95
I. Title.

EDWARDS, Charles 266'.5'132
Eugene.
The coming of the Slav. Philadelphia, Westminster Press, 1921. [San Francisco, R and E Research Associates, 1972] 148 p. map. 22 cm. Bibliography: p. 117. [BV2788.S68E4 1972] 71-165782 ISBN 0-88247-158-9 8.00
1. Presbyterian Church in the U.S.A.—Missions. 2. Slavs in the United States. I. Title.

SHALOFF, Stanley, 266.5'133'09675
1939-
Reform in Leopold's Congo. Richmond, Va., John Knox Press [1970] 195 p. illus., map. 21 cm. Bibliography: p. [184]-189. [BV3625.C6S45] 77-103464 5.95
1. Presbyterian Church in the U.S.—Missions. 2. Missions—Kasai, Congo (Province) 3. Kasai, Congo (Province)—History. I. Title.

MITCHELL, James 266.5'136
Erskine.
The emergence of a Mexican church; the Associate Reformed Presbyterian Church of Mexico [by] James E. Mitchell. South Pasadena, Calif., William Carey Library [1970] 183 p. illus. 22 cm. Originally presented as the author's thesis, Fuller Theological Seminary. Bibliography: p. 171-180. [BV2835.2.M52 1970] 74-129189 2.95
1. Associate Reformed Presbyterian Church—Missions. 2. Missions—Mexico. I. Title.

SCOVEL, Myra. 266.5151
Richer by India. Drawings by Joseph Papin. [1st ed.] New York, Harper & Row [1964] 151 p. illus., maps. 21 cm. Autobiographical. [BV3269.S33A3] 64-13746
1. Missions—India. I. Title.

SCOVEL, Myra 266.5151
Richer by India. Drawings by Joseph Papin. New York, Harper [c.1964] 151p. illus., maps. 21cm. 64-13746 3.50
1. Missions—India. I. Title.

CAMPBELL, Archibald, 266.5'1519
1894-
For God's sake, by Arch Campbell. Philadelphia, Dorrance [1970] x, 203 p. illus. 23 cm. [BV3460.C33] 71-105900 4.00
1. Missions—Korea. 2. Presbyterian Church in the U.S.A.—Missions. I. Title.

STEENSMA, Juliana. 266.5'1519
The quality of mercy. Richmond, John Knox Press [1969] 143 p. illus., ports. 21 cm. [HV1559.K8S73] 69-13271 3.95
1. Steensma, John. 2. Physically handicapped—Rehabilitation—Korea. 3. Missions—Korea. I. Title.

STOCK, Frederick, 266'.51'54914
1929-
People movements in the Punjab; with special reference to the United Presbyterian Church, [by] Frederick and Margaret Stock. South Pasadena, Calif., William Carey Library [1974, c1975] xxii, 364 p. illus. 23 cm. Bibliography: p. [341]-357. [BX9151.P18S76] 74-18408 ISBN 0-87808-417-7
1. Presbyterian Church in Punjab, Pakistan (Province) 2. Missions—Punjab, Pakistan (Province) 3. Sects—Pakistan—Punjab (Province) I. Stock, Margaret, 1929- joint author. II. Title.

VANDEVORT, Eleanor. 266.5'1629'3
A leopard tamed; the story of an African pastor, his people, and his problems. Drawings by James Howard. [1st ed.] New York, Harper & Row [1968] xii, 218 p. illus. 22 cm. [BV3625.S83K8] 68-17585
1. Kuac, Moses. 2. Missions—Sudan. 3. Nuer (African tribe) I. Title.

MCKINNON, Arch C. 266.5'1675
Kapitene of the Congo steamship Lapsley [by Arch C. McKinnon] Treasures of darkness [by Fannie W. McKinnon. Boston, Christopher Pub. House, 1968] 295 p. illus., group ports. 21 cm. Cataloged from half-title. Each book has also special t.p. [BV3625.C63M33] 68-21460
1. Lapsley (Steamship) 2. Missions—Congo. I. McKinnon, Fannie W. Treasures of darkness. 1968. II. Title. III. Title: Treasure of darkness.

JACKSON, Sheldon, 266'.5'1798
1834-1909.
Alaska, and missions on the north Pacific coast. With a new series introd. by Sidney Forman. Boston, Gregg Press, 1973 [c1880] p. (History of minority education) [E78.A3J32 1973] 73-1703 ISBN 0-8398-0964-6
1. Presbyterian Church in the United States of America—Missions. 2. Indians of North America—Alaska—Missions. 3. Alaska—Description and travel—1867-1896. I. Title. II. Series.

WRIGHT, Julia 266'.5'1798
(MacNair) 1840-1903.
Among the Alaskans. With a new series introd. by Sidney Forman. Boston, Gregg Press, 1973 [c1883] p. (History of minority education) [E78.A3W74 1973] 73-1701 ISBN 0-8398-2181-6
1. Presbyterian Church in the United States of America—Missions. 2. Indians of North America—Alaska—Missions. 3. Alaska—Description and travel—1867-1896. I. Title. II. Series.

BURNS, Islay, 266'.5'20924 B
1817-1872.
Memoir of the Rev. Wm. C. Burns, M.A., missionary to China from the English Presbyterian Church / by Islay Burns. San Francisco : Chinese Materials Center, 1975. viii, 595 p., [1] leaf of plates : port. ; 20 cm. Reprint of the 1870 ed. published by R. Carter, New York, and J. Nisbet, London. [BV3427.B83B87 1975] 76-351598
1. Burns, William Chalmers, 1815-1868. I. Title: Memoir of the Rev. Wm. C. Burns, M.A., missionary to China ...

CHRISTIAN, Carol, 266'.5'2'0924 B
1923-
God and one redhead: Mary Slessor of Calabar, by Carol Christian and Gladys Plummer. Grand Rapids, Mich., Zondervan Pub. House [1971, c1970] 190 p. illus. 21 cm. Bibliography: p. [185]-186. [BV3625.N6S59 1971] 75-156246 1.95
1. Slessor, Mary Mitchell, 1848-1915. 2. Missions—Calabar, Nigeria. I. Plummer, Gladys, 1891- joint author. II. Title.

*HAGEE, John C. 266'.52'0924
Scandalous saint, by John C. Hagee. Introductions by Merlin R. Carothers and David Coote. Monroeville, Pa. Whitaker House [1974] 178 p. 18 cm. [BV2087] ISBN 0-88368-056-4 1.25 (pbk.)
1. Eils, John. 2. Missionaries. I. Title.

MURPHEY, Cecil B. 266'.5'20924 B
But God has promised / Cecil B. Murphey. Carol Stream, Ill. : Creation House, c1976. 169 p. ; 22 cm. [BV3625.K42M87 1976] 76-16283 ISBN 0-88419-001-3 pbk. : 2.95
1. Murphey, Cecil B. 2. Missionaries—Kenya—Biography. 3. Missionaries—United States—Biography. I. Title.

ROBINSON, Virgil E. 266'.52'0924 B
Mighty Mary; the story of Mary Slessor [by] Virgil E. Robinson. Washington, Review and Herald Pub. Association [1972] 127 p. illus. 22 cm. (Penguin series) [BV3625.N6S647] 79-172787
1. Slessor, Mary Mitchell, 1848-1915. I. Title.

YOUNGBERG, Norma R 266'.52'0924
Singer on the sand; the true story of an occurrence on the island of Great Sangir, north of the Celebes, more than a hundred years ago, by Norma R. Youngberg. Illustrated by Thomas Dunbebin. Washington, Review and Herald Pub. Association [1964] 128 p. illus. 22 cm. [BV2087.Y63] 64-17655
1. Missionary stories. I. Title.

*PEARCE, Winifred M. 266.5'2'0942
Cannibal island; the story of John G. Paton. Chicago, Moody [c.1962,1968] 64p. (Moody arrows: missionary, no. 23) (B) .50 pap.,
1. Missions—New Hebrides islands. I. Paton, John G., 1820-1907. II. Title.

JACK, James William, 1866- 266.5'2689'7
Daybreak in Livingstonia; the story of the Livingstonia-Mission, British Central Africa, by James W. Jack. Rev. with an introd. by Robert Laws. New York, Negro Universities Press [1969] 371 p. illus., plan, ports. 23 cm. Reprint of the 1900 ed. Bibliographical footnotes. [BV3520.J3 1969] 79-77204
1. Missions—Africa, Central. I. Laws, Robert, 1851- II. Title.

FAIRMAN, Marion. 266.54
The tumbling walls, by Marion and Edwin Fairman. [Philadelphia] Board of Foreign Missions of the United Presbyterian Church of N. A. [1957] 192p. illus. 21cm. Includes bibliography. [BV2570.F2] 57-39886
1. United Presbyterian Church of North America—Missions. 2. Missions—Pakistan. 3. Missions—Africa, Northeast. I. Fairman, Edwin, joint author. II. Title.

SYME, Ronald, 1910- 266.54669
Nigerian pioneer; the story of Mary Slessor. Illustrated by Jacqueline Tomes. New York, Morrow, 1964. 189 p. illus. 21 cm. Bibliography: p. 13-14. [BV3625.N6S65] 64-15170
1. Slessor, Mary Mitchell, 1848-1915. 2. Missions—Calabar, Nigeria. I. Title.

PERKINS, Sara, 1892- 266.551
Red China prisoner: my years behind bamboo bars. [Westwood, N.J.] Revell [c.1963] 127p. 21cm. 63-7594 2.50 bds.,
1. Missionaries—Correspondence, reminiscences, etc. 2. Missions—China (People's Republic of China, 1949) 3. Presbyterian Church—Missions. I. Title.

PERKINS, Sra, 1892- 266.551
Red China prisoner; my years behind bamboo bars. [Westwood, N.J.] Revell [1963] 127 p. 21 cm. [BV3415.2.P4] 63-7594
1. Missionaries—Corresondence, reminiscences, etc. 2. Missions—China (People's Republic of China, 1949-) 3. Presbyterian Church—Missions. I. Title.

BROWN, George Thompson. 266.5519
Mission to Korea. Cover design by Logan Bleckley, III. [Richmond?] Board of World Missions, Presbyterian Church U.S. [1962] 252 p. illus. 20 cm. "Adapted from ... doctoral thesis to Union Theological Seminary in Richmond." [BV3460.B7] 63-3828
1. Missions — Korea. 2. Presbyterian Church — Missions. I. Title.

PATON, John Gibson, 1824-1907. 266.55934
Thirty years with South Sea cannibals; autobiography of John G. Paton. Rev. ed. Chicago, Moody [1964] 317p. 18cm. (Moody diamonds, no.10) Adaptation of the author's The story of John G. Paton's thirty years with South Sea cannibals. [BV3680.N6P2] 65-788 1.29
1. Missions—New Hebrides. I. Title.

LONGENECKER, J. Hershey, 1889- 266.5675
Memories of Congo; tales of adventure and work in the heart of Africa; with a final chapter on Congo:past and present, Johnson City, Tenn., Royal Pubs. [1964] 159p. illus., ports. 21cm. 64-55966 2.95
1. Missions—Congo (Leopoldvile) I. Title.

MENNENGA, George H 266.57
All the families of the earth, a study of Christian missions. Grand Rapids, Baker Book House, 1950. 109 p. 21 cm. [BV2580.M4] 51-31453
1. Reformed Church in America — Missions. 2. Missions, Foreign. 3. Missions — Study and teaching. I. Title.

REFORMED Church in America. Board of Domestic Missions. Women's Executive Committee. 266.57
Report 1st-1884- New York [etc.] v. 17-24 cm. annual. Report year for 1884-86 ends Apr. 1; for 1887-19 Apr. 30. Vols. for 1884-93 issued by the committee under a variant name: Women's Executive Committee of Domestic Missions. [BV2580.A2244] 51-38653
1. Reformed Church in America — Missions. I. Title.

DEPREE, Gladys Lenore, 1933- 266.5'7'0924 B
The spring wind, by Gladis DePree. Drawings by James N. Howard. [1st ed.] New York, Harper & Row [1970] 112 p. illus. 22 cm. [BV3427.D35A3 1970] 70-109064 3.95
I. Title.

ABEEL, David, 1804-1846. 266'.5'7320924 B
Memoir of the Rev. David Abeel, D.D. Williamson. Wilmington, Del., Scholarly Resources [1972] 315 p. port. 23 cm. Reprint of the 1848 ed. published by R. Carter, New York. [BV3427.A3A35 1972] 72-79842 ISBN 0-8420-1353-9
1. Abeel, David, 1804-1846. I. Williamson, G. R., comp. II. Title.

BARNETT, Eugene E 1888- 266'.5'7320924
As I look back; recollections of growing up in America's southland and of twenty-six years in pre-Communist China, 1888-1936, by Eugene E. Barnett. [Arlington? Va., 1964?] 346 p. 29 cm. [BV3427.B35A3] 65-79425
1. Missions — China. I. Title.

SCOVEL, Myra. 266'.5'7320924
The Chinese ginger jars [by] Myra Scovel with Nelle Keys Bell. [1st ed.] New York, Harper [1962] 189p. 22cm. Autobiographical. [BV3427.S38A3] 62-7299
I. Title.

VAN ESS, Dorothy. 266'.5'7320924 B
Pioneers in the Arab world, by Dorothy F. Van Ess. Grand Rapids, W. B. Eerdmans Pub. Co. [1974] 188 p. illus. 21 cm. (The Historical series of the Reformed Church in America, no. 3) Bibliography: p. 187-188. [BV2626.V36A36] 74-14964 ISBN 0-8028-1585-5
1. Van Ess, Dorothy. 2. Van Ess, John, 1879- 3. Missions to Muslims—Basra. I. Title. II. Series: Reformed Church in America. The historical series, no. 3.

SMITH, Edgar H., 1907- 266'.5'7669
Nigerian harvest; a Reformed witness to Jesus Christ in Nigeria, West Africa, in the twentieth century, including a detailed history of the missionary ministry of the Christian Reformed Church in the Benue Province from 1940 to 1970, by Edgar H. Smith. Grand Rapids, Baker Book House [1972] 318 p. illus. 23 cm. Includes bibliographical references. [BV3625.N5S64] 72-90326 ISBN 0-8010-7964-0 5.00
1. Christian Reformed Church—Missions. 2. Missions—Nigeria. I. Title.

ANDREW, John A. 266'.5'8
Rebuilding the Christian commonwealth : New England Congregationalists & foreign missions, 1800-1830 / John A. Andrew III. Lexington : University Press of Kentucky, c1976. 232 p. ; 23 cm. Includes index. Bibliography: p. [223]-227. [BV2530.A8] 75-38214 ISBN 0-8131-1333-4 : 14.50
1. American Board of Commissioners for Foreign Missions. 2. Congregational churches—Missions. 3. Congregational churches in New England—History. 4. New England—Church history. I. Title.

GOODSELL, Fred Field, 1880- 266.58
They lived their faith, an almanac of faith, hope and love. Boston, American Board of Commissioners for Foreign Missions [c] 1961. 486p. Front. port. 61-9968 5.50 2.50 pap.,
1. American Board of Commissioners for Foreign Missions. 2. Congregational churches—Missions. I. Title.

STRONG, William Ellsworth, 1860-1934. 266.5'8'06273
The story of the American Board. New York, Arno Press, 1969. xv, 523 p. illus., maps, ports. 23 cm. (Religion in America) Reprint of the 1910 ed. [BV2360.A5S9 1969] 79-83443
1. American Board of Commissioners for Foreign Missions. 2. Missions, Foreign.

*BRAINERD, David. 266.5'8'0924
David Brainerd, his life and diary, ed. by Jonathan Edwards. With a biographical sketch of President Edwards, by Philip E. Howard, Jr. Chicago, Moody [1968, c.1949] 384p. 21cm. (B) 4.95
I. Edwards, Jonathan, 1703-1758. II. Title.

HANCE, Gertrude Rachel, 1844- 266.5'8'09684
The Zulu yesterday and to-day; twenty-nine years in South Africa. New York, Negro Universities Press [1969] 274 p. illus., map, ports. 23 cm. Reprint of the 1916 ed. [BV3625.Z8H3 1969] 79-89002 ISBN 0-8371-1743-7
1. Missions—Africa, South. 2. South Africa—Description and travel,—1901-1950. 3. Zulus. I. Title.

GILLIOM, James O. 266'.5'834
Sent on a mission; a resource and discussion book for youth, by James O. Gilliom. Illustrated by Carol Bachenheimer. [Rev. ed. New York] Herder and Herder [1968] 59 p. illus. 22 cm. (Christian commitment series) Includes bibliographical references. [BX9884.A3G54 1968b] 68-29890 1.20
1. Religious education—Text-books for young people—United Church of Christ. 2. Mission of the church. I. Bachenheimer, Carol, illus. II. Title.

SCHNEIDER, Delano Douglas. 266'.5'8340924 B
Deep the roots of hope / by D. Douglas Schneider. 1st ed. Muskegon, Mich. : Creative Design Books, c1976. xii, 264 p., [16] leaves of plates : ill. ; 22 cm. Autobiographical. [BV3269.S295A3] 75-21171
1. Schneider, Delano Douglas. 2. Missions—Kalahandi, India. 3. Missions—Agricultural work. I. Title.

KETCHUM, Creston Donald. 266.585281
Bread upon the waters. [1st ed.] Rutland, Vt., C. E. Tuttle Co. [1964] 196 p. illus., ports. 22 cm. Autobiographical. Sequel to His path is in the waters. [BV3705.K47A33] 64-13267
I. Title.

DUFF, Alexander, 1806-1878. 266.5'854
India, and India missions, including sketches of the gigantic system of Hinduism, both in theory and practice;also notices of some of the principal agencies employed in conducting the process of Indian evangelization, &c., &c. Edinburgh, J. Johnstone, 1839. 684p. 23cm. [BV3265.D8 1839] 55-45332
1. Missions—India. 2. Hinduism. I. Title.

JONES, Eli Stanley, 1884- 266.5'854
The Christ of the Indian road. London, Hodder and Stoughton [1927, c1925] 254p. 20cm. [BV3265.J65 1927] 54-50523
1. Missions—India. I. Title.

SEYBOLD, Theodore C 1889- 266.5'854
God's guiding hand; a history of the Central India Mission. 1868-1967, by Theodore C. Seybold. [New York] United Church Board for World Ministries of the United Church of Christ [1967] 179 p. illus., ports. 24 cm. Includes bibliographies. [BV3265.2.S4] 68-723
1. Central India Mission. 2. Missions—India. 3. United Church of Christ—Missions. I. Title.

SEYBOLD, Theodore C., 1889- 266.5'854
God's guiding hand; a history of the Central India Mission, 1868-1967, by Theodore C. Seybold. [New York] United Church Board for World Ministries of the United Church of Christ [1967] 179 p. illus., ports. 24 cm. Includes bibliographies. [BV3265.2.S4] 68-723
1. Central India Mission. 2. United Church of Christ—Missions. 3. Missions—India. I. Title.

WILCOX, Mark F 266.5868
Proud endeavorer; the story of a Yankee on a mission to South Africa. New York, Graphic Press [1962] 141 p. 23 cm. [BV3557.W48W5] 62-19484
1. Wilcox, William Cullen, 1850-1928. 2. Missions — Africa, South. I. Title.

WILCOX, Mark F. 266.5868
Proud endeavorer; the story of a Yankee New York, Graphic Pr. [1962] 144p. 23cm. 62-19484 3.00
1. Wilcox, William Cullen, 1850-1928. 2. Missions—Africa, South. I. Title.

HOPKINS, Samuel, 1693-1755. 266'.5'87441
Historical memoirs relating to the Housatonic Indians. Boston, S. Kneeland, 1753. New York, W. Abbatt, 1911. [New York, Johnson Reprint Corp., 1972] 198 p. facsims. 24 cm. Reprint of the 1911 ed., which was issued as Extra number 17 of The Magazine of history with notes and queries. [E99.S8H7 1972] 72-2288 9.00
1. Sergeant, John, 1710-1749. 2. Stockbridge Indians—Missions. I. Title. II. Series: The Magazine of history with notes and queries. Extra numbers, 17.

KELLAWAY, William. 266'.5'90974
The New England Company, 1649-1776 : missionary society to the American Indians / William Kellaway. Westport, Conn. : Greenwood Press, 1975, c1961. 303 p. : map ; 22 cm. Reprint of the ed. published by Longmans, London. Includes index. "List of manuscript sources": p. 284-287. [E98.M6K28 1975] 74-33895 ISBN 0-8371-7995-5
1. Society for Propagation of the Gospel in New England. 2. Indians of North America—Missions. I. Title.

KELLAWAY, William. 266'.5'90974
The New England Company, 1649-1776 : missionary society to the American Indians / William Kellaway. Westport, Conn. : Greenwood Press, 1975, c1961. 303 p. : map ; 22 cm. Reprint of the ed. published by Longmans, London. Includes index. "List of manuscript sources": p. 284-287. [E98.M6K28 1975] 74-33895 ISBN 0-8371-7995-5 : 14.75
1. Society for Propagation of the Gospel in New England. 2. Indians of North America—Missions. I. Title.

SOCIETY for Propagation of the Gospel in New-England. 266'.5'90974
The New England Company of 1649 and John Eliot. The ledger for the years 1650-1660 and the record book of meetings between 1656 and 1686 of the Corporation for the Propagation of the Gospel in New England. Printed from the original manuscripts with an introd., by George Parker Winship. New York, B. Franklin [1967] lxxxv, 219 p. 23 cm. (Burt Franklin research and source works series, 131. American classics in history and social science, 2) On spine: Cooperation for the Gospel of Christ in New England. Reprint of the 1920 ed., issued as v. 36 of the Publications of the Prince Society. Bibliography: p. lxii-lxvi. [E78.N5S6] 72-185593
1. Eliot, John, 1604-1690. 2. Missions—New England. 3. Indians of North America—Missions. I. Company for Propagation of the Gospel in New England and the Parts Adjacent in America. II. Title. III. Title: Cooperation for the Gospel of Christ in New England. IV. Series: Prince Society, Boston. Publications, v. 36.

AITKEN, Dorothy Lockwood. 266.6 (j)
My love, the Amazon, By Dorothy Aitken. Illus. by Jim Padgett. Nashville, Southern Pub. Association [1968] 128 p. illus. 21 cm. [BV2851.A586] 68-24020
1. Seventh-Day Adventists—Missions. 2. Missions—Amazon Valley. 3. Amazon River—Description and travel. I. Title.

BAILEY, Helen L 266.6
Jeep tracks. Drawings by Warren Johnson. New York, Friendship Press [1954] 87p. illus. 21cm. Autobiographical. [BV3269.B33A3] [BV3269.B33A3] 275.4 54-6884 54-6884
1. Missions—India. I. Title.

BRIDGES, Julian C. 266.6
Into Aztec land [by] Julian C. Bridges. Nashville, Convention Press [1968] vi, 104 p. illus., map. 19 cm. (Foreign mission graded series) "Church study course [of the Sunday School Board of the Southern Baptist Convention] This book is number 1074 in category 10, section for young people." [BV2835.2.B7] 68-20668
1. Missions—Mexico. 2. Baptists—Missions. I. Southern Baptist Convention. Sunday School Board. II. Title.

CARTER, Frances (Tunnell) 1922- 266.6
'Tween-age ambassadors. Nashville, Tenn., Convention Press [1970] 93 p. illus., maps, ports. 20 cm. (Foreign mission graded series, 1970) [BV2520.C23] 73-113208
1. Baptists—Missions—Juvenile literature. I. Title.

CRAWLEY, Sadie Tiller. 266.6
World awareness. Nashville, Convention Press [1963] 134 p. 19 cm. Includes bibliography. [BV2520.C67] 63-11174
1. Southern Baptist Convention. Women's Missionary Union. 2. Missions—Theory. I. Title.

CRISWELL, W A. 266.6
Passport to the world, by W. A. Criswell and Duke K. McCall. Nashville, Broadman Press ['1951] 139 p. 21 cm. [BV2520.C7] 52-6218

1. Southern Baptist Convention—Missions. 2. Flights around the world. I. Title.

CRISWELL, Wallie A 266.6
Passport to the world, by W. A. Criswell and Duke K. McCall. Nashville, Broadman Press [1951] 139 p. 21 cm. [BV2520.C7] 52-6218
1. Southern Baptist Convention—Missions. 2. Flights around the world. I. McCall, Duke K., joint author. II. Title.

DOWIS, Solomon F. 266.6
O Jerusalem? Our cities for Christ. Atlanta, Home Mission Board, Southern Baptist Convention [1951] 86 p. 20 cm. (1951 graded series: The urban church serving its community) Bibliography: p. 79. [BV2766.B5D6] 51-2819
1. City missions. I. Title.

DUNCAN, Sylvia. 266.6
Bonganga; experiences of a missionary doctor [by] Sylvia and Peter Duncan. New York, Morrow, 1960. 240 p. illus. 21 cm. [BV3625.C63B7] 59-11700
1. Browne, Stanley George. 2. Yakusu, Belgian Congo. 3. Missions, Medical—Congo, Belgian. I. Duncan, Peter, 1915- joint author.

ECHOES from Indonesia. 266.6
Nashville, Convention Press [1958] 141p. illus. 19cm. [BV3340.N48] 279.1 58-8931
1. Missions—Indonesia. 2. Southern Baptist Convention—Missions. I. Nichols, Buford L

ESTEP, William Roscoe, 1920- 266.6
Colombia; land of conflict and promise [by] William R. Estep, Jr. Nashville, Convention Press [1968] 128 p. illus., map, ports. 19 cm. (Foreign mission graded series) "Church study course [of the Sunday School Board of the Southern Baptist Convention] This book is number 1014 in category 10, section for adults." [BV2853.C7E8] 68-20672
1. Missions—Colombia. 2. Baptists—Missions. I. Southern Baptist Convention. Sunday School Board. II. Title.

FLETCHER, Jesse C. 266.6
The Wimpy Harper story, by Jesse C. Fletcher. Nashville, Broadman [c.1966] 60p. port. (on cover) 19cm. [BV36625.T32H34] 66-27946 .75 pap.,
1. Harper, Winfred Ozell. 2. Missions—Tanganyika. I. Title.

GARNETT, Christine, 1886- 266.6
Through a Cuban window. Atlanta, Home Mission Board, Southern Baptist Convention [1954] 93p. illus. 20cm. (1955 graded series of home mission studies: Home mission outposts) [BV2848.C9G3] [BV2848.C9G3] 277.291 55-16791 55-16791
1. Missions—Cuba. 2. Baptists—Missions. I. Title.

GILL, Everett, 1901- 266.6
Pilgrimage to Spanish America. Nashville, Broadman Press [1951] 142p. illus. 19cm. [BV2830.G5] 278 51-13681
1. Missions—Spanish America. 2. Baptists—Missions. I. Title.

GILL, Everett, 1901-1954. 266.6
Pilgrimage to Brazil. Nashville, Broadman Press [1954] 144p. illus. 19cm. 'A seque to [the author's] Pilgrimage to Spanish America.' [BV2853.B6G47] 278.1 54-12768
1. Missions—Brazil. 2. Baptists—Missions. I. Title.

GOLD in Alaska. 266.6
Atlanta, Home Mission Board, Southern Baptist Convention [1954] 64p. illus. 20cm. (1955 graded series of home mission studies: Home mission outposts) [BV2803.A4D4] [BV2803.A4D4] 277.98 55-16799 55-16799
1. Missions—Alaska. 2. Baptists—Missions. I. De Foore, John Norris, 1919-

HALVARSON, Carl M 266.6
Japan's new Baptists. Nashville, Convention Press [1956] 96p. illus. 19cm. (1956 foreign mission study books, young people) [BX6316.J3H3] 275.2 56-43427
1. Baptists—Japan. 2. Missions—Japan. I. Title.

HOPEWELL, William J. 266.6
The missionary emphasis of the General Association of Regular Baptist Churches, by Wm. J. Hopewell, Jr. Chicago, Regular Baptist Press [1964, c1963] 153 p. 24 cm. Bibliography: p. 144-146. [BV2520.A54H6] 65-462
1. General Association of Regular Baptist Churches — Missions. I. Title.

HUDGINS, Frances E 266.6
Temples of the dawn. Nashville, Convention Press [1958] 91p. illus. 19cm. [BV3315.H8] 275.93 58-8929
1. Missions—Thailand. 2. Southern Baptist Convention—Missions. I. Title.

JACKSON, Joseph Harrison, 1900- 266.6
The eternal flame; the story of a preaching mission in Russia. Philadelphia, Christian Education Press [1956] 125p. illus. 22cm. [BR936.J3] 274.7 56-43423
1. Russia—Church history—1917- 2. Baptists—Russia. I. Title.

JACKSON, Joseph Harrison, 1900- 266.6
The eternal flame; the story of a preaching mission in Russia. Philadelphia, Christian Education Press [1956] 125p. illus. 22cm. [BR936.J3] 274.7 56-43423
1. Russia—Church history—1917- 2. Baptists—Russa. I. Title.

JAPAN Conservative Baptist Mission. Historical Committee. 266.6
Give us this mountain; the story of the ten beginning years with the Conservative Baptist Mission and missionaries in the Tohoku of Japan, 1947-1957. Wheaton, Ill., Conservative Baptist Foreign Mission Society, c1959. 99p. illus. 29cm. [BV3445.2.J3] 60-26937
1. Missions—Japan. 2. Baptists—Missions. I. Conservative Baptist Foreign Mission Society II. Title.

LAWRENCE, John Benjamin, 1873- 266.6
History of the Home Mission Board. Nashville, Broadman Press [1958] 170p. 21cm. Includes bibliography. [BV2766.B5L32] 58-8922
1. Southern Baptist Convention. Home Mission Board. I. Title.

LIPPHARD, William Benjamin, 1886- 266.6
Fifty years an editor. Valley Forge [Pa.] Judson Press [1963] 256 p. 22 cm. [BX6495.L54A3] 63-15817
1. Missions. A Baptist monthly magazine. 2. Journalists — Correspdondence, reminiscences, etc. I. Title.

LIPPHARD, William Benjamin, 1886- 266.6
Fifty years an editor. Valley Forge [Pa.] Judson [c.1963] 256p. 22cm. 63-15817 3.95
1. Missions. A Baptist monthly magazine. 2. Journalists—Correspondence, reminiscences, etc. I. Title.

MCCLELLAN, Albert. [266.6]
Rainbow south. Nashville, Broadman Press [1952] 131 p. illus. 19 cm. [BV2840.M3] 52-2822
1. Missions—Central America. 2. Baptists—Central America. 3. Baptists—Missions. I. Title.

MCRAE, James Thomas, 1920- 266.6
Mission doctor. Nashville, Convention Press [1955] 81p. illus. 20cm. (1955 foreign mission study books, intermediates) A publication of the Foreign Mission Board. [BV3200.M28] [BV3200.M28] 275.69 55-3957 55-3957
1. Missions, Medical—Lebanon. 2. Missions, Medical—Jordan. 3. Missions, Medical—Gaza. I. Title.

MINISTRY to turbulent 266.6
America; a history of the American Baptist Home Mission Society, covering its fifth quarter century, 1932-1957. [1st ed.] Philadelphia, Judson Press [1957] 262p. 22cm. [BV2766.B5B4] [BV2766.B5B4] 277.3 57-7919 57-7919
1. American Baptist Home Mission Society. 2. Baptists—Missions. 3. Missions, Home. I. Beers, George Pitt, 1883-

ROUTH, Eugene Coke, 1874- 266.6
Scattered abroad. Nashville, Broadman Press [1952] 134 p. illus. 19 cm. [BV2520.R68] 52-11931
1. Baptists — Missions. I. Title.

SOUTHERN Baptist Convention. Foreign Mission Board. 266.6
Missionary album. Compiled by Genevieve Greer. [Rev. ed.] Nashville. Convention Press [1959, c1954] 210 p. illus. 28 cm. [Bv2520.S66 1959] 59-9684
1. Baptists — Missions. 2. Missionaries. I. Greer, Genevieve. 1907- II. Title.

TULGA, Chester Earl, 1896- 266.6
The case against modernism in foregin missions. Chicago, Conservative Baptist Fellowship [1950] 64 p. 18 cm. (His Litte books on big subjects) [BV2520.T77] 50-4336
1. Northern Baptist Convention — Missions. 2. Missions, Foreign. 3. Modernist-fundamentalist controversy. I. Title.

TULGA, Chester Earl, 1896- 266.6
The foreign missions controversy in the Northern Baptist Convention, 1919-1949; 30 years of struggle. Chicago, Conservative Baptist Fellowship [1950] 201 p. 19 cm. [BV2520.T773] 50-4205
1. Northern Baptist Convention — Missions. 2. Missions, Foreign. 3. Modernist-fundamentalist controversy. I. Title.

VAN ROYEN, Russell, 1898- 266.6
Tabo in Panama, by Russell and Edith Van Royen. Atlanta, Home Mission Board, Southern Baptist Convention [1954] 56p. illus. 20cm. (1955 graded series of home mission studies: Home mission outposts) [BV2843.P3v3] [BV2843.P3V3] 276.62 55-16790 55-16790
1. Missions—Panama. 2. Baptists—Missions. I. Van Royen, Edith, 1898- joint author. II. Title.

WADSWORTH, Lincoln Burdette, 1909- 266.6
Mission to city multitudes; American Baptists at work. [1st ed.] Philadelphia, Judson Press [1954] 88p. 21cm. [BV2766.B5W3] 54-7988
1. City missions. 2. Baptists—Missions. I. Title.

WEEKS, Dorothy. 266.6
Ten bright eyes. Nashville, Convention Press [1959] 120 p. illus. 19 cm. (1959 foreign mission graded series, junior) Short stories [BV2087.W37] 59-9681
1. Missionary stories I. Title.

WILSON, George, 1927- 266.6
Hong Kong digest. Nashville, Tenn., Convention Press [1970] 88 p. illus., map, ports. 20 cm. (Foreign mission graded series, 1970) [BV3425.H6W5] 75-117308
1. Missions—Hongkong. 2. Baptists—Missions. 3. Refugees—China. I. Title.

WOODSON, Sue Terry. 266.6
Alex and the good news. Nashville, Convention Press [1959] 77 p. illus. 19 cm. (1959 Foreign Mission graded series) [BV2065.W6] 59-9682
1. Missions — Juvenile literature. I. Title.

ALEXANDER, Frances, 1888- 266.6'0924 B
Mary Charlotte Alexander (Au Mo Ling), missionary to China, 1920-1956. [Austin, Tex., Printed by Von Boeckmann-Jones Co., 1968] 93 p. map (on lining papers), ports. 24 cm. Bibliography: p. 93. [BV3427.A42A62] 70-961
1. Alexander, Mary Charlotte, 1886-

FLETCHER, Jesse C. 266.6'0924 B
The search for Blonnye Foreman; the absorbing story of a missionary who found deeper meaning [by] Jesse C. Fletcher. Nashville, Broadman Press [1969] 144 p. 22 cm. [BV2853.B7F64] 69-17895 3.25
1. Foreman, Blonnye. 2. Musgrave, James E. I. Title.

HEFLEY, James C. 266.6'0924
Intrigue in Santo Domingo; the story of Howard Shoemake, missionary to revolution, by James C. Hefley. Waco, Tex., Word Books [1968] 184 p. illus., map, ports. 23 cm. Bibliography: p. 182-183. [BV2848.D7H4 1968] 68-57016 3.95
1. Baptists—Missions. 2. Missions, Medical—Dominican Republic. I. Title.

MUSTAIN, Claud J 266.60924
Wilderness prophet; a biography of Daniel Richard Murphy, pioneer preacher, missionary, colporteur, 1802-1875 [by] Claud J. Mustain. Springfield, Mo., Cain-Service Print. Co. [1966] ii, 54 p. illus. 22 cm. [BX6495.M85M8] 66-6533
1. Murphy, Daniel Richard, 1802-1875. I. Title.

WAGNON, Marilyn Simpson. 266.6'0924 B
Light on the riverfront; the story of Gladys Keith [by] Marilyn S. Wagnon. Nashville, Broadman Press [1967] 64 p. illus., ports. 19 cm. [BX6495.K355W3] 68-12322
1. Keith, Gladys, 1905- I. Title.

REED, Jane. 266.6'0966'6
Voice under every palm; the story of radio station ELWA, by Jane Reed and Jim Grant. Grand Rapids, Zondervan Pub. House [1968] 150 p. illus., ports. 23 cm. [BV2082.R3R4] 68-56089 3.95
1. ELWA (Radio station) Monrovia, Liberia. 2. Radio in missionary work. 3. Missions—Africa. I. Grant, Jim, joint author. II. Title.

BAPTIST General Conference of America. 266.6'1
Our great commission; a manual on missionary education in the local church. Chicago, Harvest Publications [c1966] 117 p. maps. 20 cm. (A Harvest learning-for-serving book) Bibliography: p. 113-117. [BV2520.A33A5] 66-305992
1. Baptist General Conference of America — Missions. 2. Missions — Study and teaching. I. Title.

BAPTIST missionary 266.61
magazine v. 1-89 Jan. 1817-Dec. 1909 89 v. in 83. illus., ports. 23-25cm. Frequency varies [BV2520.A1B3] 57-54674
1. Baptists—Missions—Period. I. Massachusetts Baptist Convention. II. American Baptist Foreign Mission Society. III. ols. 1-6 called new ser. Supersedes Massachusetts Baptist missionary magazine. Title varies: v. 1-4, The American Baptist missionary magazine and missionary intelligencer.—v. 5-15, The American Baptist magazine.—v. 30-52, The Missionary magazine. Issued 1817-26 by the Massachusetts Baptist Convention under its earlier name: Baptist Missionary Society in Massachusetts; 1827-1909 by the American Baptist Foreign Mission Society (called 1827-45, Baptist General Convention; 1846-1909, American Baptist Missionary Union) United with Baptist home mission monthly and Good work to form Missions. Cf. Union list of serials. IV. Title: Boston, V. Title: The American Baptist missionary magazine and missionary intelligencer. VI. Title: The American Baptist magazine. v. VII. Title: The Missionary magazine.

BENNETT, Marjorie. 266.61
Few among many. Nashville, Convention Press [1966] 82 p. illus., map. ports. 21 cm. [BV3257.B4] 66-16374
1. Missions — Pakistan — Juvenile literature. 2. Baptists — Missions — Juvenile literature. I. Title.

BISHOP, Ivyloy. 266.61
Appointment for Andy [by] Ivyloy and Amelia Bishop. Nashville, Convention Press [1959] 104p. illus. 19cm. (1959 Foreign Mission graded series, intermediate) A Publication of the Foreign Mission Board, Richmond, Virginia. [BV2520.B57] 59-9678
1. Southern Baptist Convention—Missions. I. Bishop, Amelia, joint author. II. Title.

CATTAN, Louise Armstrong 266.61
One mark of greatness: American Baptist missions [by] Louise A. Cattan, Helen C. Schmitz. Philadelphia, Judson Pr. [c.1961] 174p. col. map Bibl. 61-11570 1.50 pap.,
1. Baptists—Missions—Hist. I. Schmitz, Helen C., joint author. II. Title. III. Title: American Baptist missions.

CATTAN, Louise Armstrong. 266.61
One mark of greatness: American Baptist missions [by] Louise A. Cattan and Helen C. Schmitz. Philadelphia, Judson Press ,531961] 174p. 21cm. Includes bibliography. [BV2520.C25] 61-11570
1. Baptists—Missions—Hist. I. Schmitz, Helen C., joint author. II. Title. III. Title: American Baptist missions.

CAUTHEN, Baker James. 266.61
By all means, by Baker James Cauthen, and others. Nashville, Convention Press [1959] 148p. illus. 19cm. (1959 Foreign Mission graded series) [BV2520.C27] 59-9679
1. Southern Baptist Convention—Missions. 2. Missions, Foreign. I. Title.

CAYLOR, John, 1894- 266.61
A path of light, by John Caylor and others. Atlanta, Home Mission Board, Southern Baptist Convention [1950] 118 p. 21 cm. [BV2520.C3] 50-12910
1. Southern Baptist Convention—Missions. I. Title.
Contents Omitted.

COGGINS, Ross. 266.61
Missions today. Nashville, Convention Press [1963] 113 p. illus. 20 cm. [BV2063.C57] 63-8377
1. Missions — Theory. 2. Southern Baptist Convention — Missions. I. Title.

DEHONEY, Wayne. 266.61
African diary. Nashville, Broadman Press [1966] 157 p. illus., map, ports. 22 cm. [BV3520.D4] 66-19911
1. Missions — Africa, Sub-Saharan. 2. Baptists — Missions. I. Title.

DEHONEY, Wayne 266.61
African diary. Nashville, Broadman [c.1966] x, 157p. illus., map, ports. 22cm. [BV3520.D4] 66-19911 3.50 bds.,
1. Missions—Africa, Sub-Saharan. 2. Baptists—Missions. I. Title.

EAGLESFIELD, Carrol Frederick. [266.61]
Listen to the drums; Nigeria and its people. Nashville, Broadman Press [1950] 82 p. illus. 19 cm. [DT515.E2] 276.69 50-14398
1. Nigeria—Soc. condit. 2. Missions—Nigeria. 3. Yorubas. I. Title.

HIPPS, John Burder. 266.6'1
Fifty years in Christian missions: an autobiography. [Raleigh. N. C., Printed by Edwards & Broughton Co., c1966] 141 p. port. 24 cm. [BV3427.H57A3] 66-30466
1. Missions—China. I. Title.

HUGHEY, John David. 266'.6'1
Europe—a mission field? By J. D. Hughey. Nashville, Convention Press [1972] 122 p. illus. 20 cm. (Foreign mission graded series) [BV2855.H83] 72-188399
1. Missions—Europe. 2. Baptists—Missions. I. Title.

HUNT, Alma. 266.61
History of Woman's Missionary Union. Nashville, Convention Press [1964] xi, 209 p. 22 cm. Bibliography: p. 199-201. [BV2520.A74H8] 64-19978
1. Southern Baptist Convention. Women's Missionary Union. I. Title.

HUNT, Alma. 266'.6'1
History of Woman's Missionary Union / Alma Hunt. Rev. ed. Nashville : Convention Press, c1976. xiii, 241 p. : ports. ; 21 cm. "Chapters 11-12, Catherine B. Allen." "This is a course in the subject area Missions of the Church study course." Includes bibliographical references and index. [BV2520.A2S6833 1976] 77-359418
1. Southern Baptist Convention. Woman's Missionary Union. I. Title.

JOHNSON, Johnni. 266.61
Missionary assignment: your place in winning the world. Nashville. Convention Press [1959] 143p. illus. 19cm. (Foreign mission grades series) [BV2520.J6] 59-9680
1. Baptists—Missions. 2. Southern Baptist Convention—Missions. I. Title.

MARGRETT, Anne (Sowell) 266.61
Under the Southern Cross. Nashville, Broadman Press [1951] 80p. illus. 19cm. [BX6271.M3] [BX6271.M3] 278 51-12980 51-12980
1. Baptists—South America. 2. Southern Baptist Convention—Missions. 3. Missions—South America. I. Title.

OWENS, Laurella. 266.61
Shalom. Nashville, Convention Press [1963] 110 p. illus. 19 cm. (1963 Foreign mission graded series) [BV3200.O9] 63-11172
1. Missions — Israel. 2. Southern Baptist Convention — Missions. I. Title.

PATTERSON, Roberta Turner, 1908- 266.61
Candle by night; a history of Woman's Missionary Union, Auxiliary to the Baptist General Convention of Texas, 1800-1955. [Dallas?] c1955. 184p. illus. 20cm. [BX6248.T4P3] 55-35794
1. Baptists. Texas. General Convention. Woman's Missionary Union. I. Title.

RUTLEDGE, Don. 266'.6'1
The human touch : crossing barriers in national missions / photographed by Don Rutledge ; written by Elaine Selcraig Furlow. Atlanta : Home Mission Board, Southern Baptist Convention, [1975] 190 p. : ill. ; 28 cm. Includes index. [BV2520.R87] 75-2365 5.95
1. Baptists—Missions. 2. Missionaries, American. 3. Missions, Home. I. Furlow, Elaine Selcraig, 1947- II. Title.

STANTON, William Arthur, 1867- [266.61]
The awakening of India; forty years among the Telugus. Portland, Me., Falmouth Pub. House [1950] 213 p. illus., map, ports. 22 cm. [BV3265.S627] 275.4 5027838
1. Missions — India. 2. Telugus. I. Title.

STEVENS, Dorothy A ed. 266.61
Baptists under the Cross: world-wide witness of American Baptists. [1st ed.] Philadelphia, Judson Press [1953] 96p. 21cm. [BV2520.S72] 53-6231
1. American Baptist Convention—Missions. I. Title.

STEVENS, Dorothy A ed. 266.61
Voices from Japan; Christians speak. Pref. by Jitsuo Morikawa. Drawings contributed by Japanese Christian artists. [1st ed.] Philadelphia, Judson Press [1957] 93p. illus. 21cm. [BX6316.J3S8] [BX6316.J3S8] 275.2 57-8339 57-8339
1. Baptists—Japan. 2. Christmas in Japan. 3. Missions—Japan. I. Title.

TORBET, Robert George, 1912- 266.61
Venture of faith; the story of the American Baptist Foreign Mission Society and the Woman's American Baptist Foreign Mission Society, 1814-1954. With a foreword by Jesse R. Wilson. [1st ed.] Philadelphia, Judson Press [1955] 634p. 22cm. [BV2520.T7] 55-10800
1. American Baptist Foreign Mission Society—Hist. 2. Woman's American Baptist Foreign Mission Society—Hist. I. Title.

FLETCHER, Jesse C. 266'.6'10922 B
Living sacrifices : a missionary odyssey / Jesse C. Fletcher. Nashville : Broadman Press, [1974] 157 p. : ill. ; 21 cm. [BV3427.A33F55] 73-93903 ISBN 0-8054-7210-X : 4.95
1. Abernathy, John Arch. 2. Abernathy, Jewell Leonard. I. Title.

SALLEE, Annie (Jenkins) 266'.6'10922 B
Torchbearers in Honan. Freeport, N.Y., Books for Libraries Press [1972, c1948] 192 p. illus. 22 cm. (Biography index reprint series) Contents.Contents.—Wesley Willingham Lawton.—Mrs. David Wells Herring, mother and missionary.—Viola Humphreys, the courageous.—Zemma Hare, the devoted.—Wang Teh-Lu.—Niu Tsai-Chin. [BV3420.H6S3 1972] 72-5437 ISBN 0-8369-8138-3
1. Missions—Honan, China (Province) I. Title.

BEERS, Richard G. 266.6'1'0924 B
Walk the distant hills; the story of Longri Ao, by Richard G. Beers. New York, Friendship Press [1969] 64 p. port. (on cover) 19 cm. (Bold believers series) [BV3269.A67B4] 76-13810 1.50
1. Ao, Longri, 1906- 2. Missions—India. I. Title.

CARTER, John T. 266.6'1'0924 B
Witness in Israel; the story of Paul Rowden [by] John T. Carter. Nashville, Broadman Press [1969] 64 p. illus., ports. 19 cm. [BV3202.R6C3] 69-19023
1. Rowden, Paul D. 2. Missions—Israel. I. Title.

FLETCHER, Alfred Johnston, 1887- 266.6'1'0924 B
The story of a mountain missionary, Rev. James Floyd Fletcher, 1858-1946, by A. J. Fletcher. Raleigh, N.C., 1966. 39 l. 30 cm. [BX6379.F54F54] 78-17342
1. Fletcher, James Floyd, 1858-1946. I. Title.

HINE, Leland D. 266.6'1'0924 B
Axling: a Christian presence in Japan [by] Leland D. Hine. Valley Forge [Pa.] Judson Press [1969] 205 p. illus., ports. 23 cm. [BV3457.A9H5] 69-16390 5.95
1. Axling, William, 1873-1963. 2. Missions—Japan. 3. Baptists—Missions.

HUBBARD, Ethel Daniels. 266.6'1'0924 B
Ann of Ava. Illustrated by Margaret Ayer. Freeport, N.Y., Books for Libraries Press [1971, c1941] 184 p. illus. 23 cm. (Biography index reprint series) [BV3271.J81H8 1971] 76-160921 ISBN 0-8369-8084-0
1. Judson, Ann (Hasseltine) 1789-1826. I. Title.

LEONARD, Charles Alexander, 1882- 266.6'1'0924 B
Repaid a hundredfold. Grand Rapids, Mich., Eerdmans [1969] 363 p. illus., ports. 23 cm. "Bibliography: Communism in China": p. 362-363. [BV3427.L44A3] 72-75105
1. Missions—China. I. Title.

MCCABA, Joseph 266'.6'10924 B
The teacher who laughs. Des Plaines, Ill., Regular Baptist Press [1973] xi, 148 p. 19 cm. [BV3625.N49M3] 73-80903 2.50 (pbk.)
1. McCaba, Joseph. 2. Missions—Niger. I. Title.

MCELRATH WILLIAM N. 266'.6'10924 B
To be the first : adventures of Adoniram Judson, America's first foreign missionary / William N. McElrath. Nashville : Broadman Press, c1976. 189 p. : ill. ; 21 cm. [BV3271.J7M3] 75-14893 ISBN 0-8054-4318-5 pbk. : 4.95
1. Judson, Adoniram, 1788-1850. 2. Missionaries—United States—Biography. 3. Missionaries—Burma—Biography. I. Title.

MCRAE, Jane Carroll. 266.6'1'0924 B
Photographer in Lebanon; the story of Said Jureidini. Nashville, Broadman Press [1969] 64 p. illus., ports. 19 cm. [BX6495.J95M3] 69-19024
1. Jureidini, Said M., 1866-1952. 2. Baptists—Lebanon. I. Title.

MYERS, John Brown, 1844or45-1915. 266.6'1'0924 B
Thomas J. Comber: missionary pioneer to the Congo. New York, Negro Universities Press [1969] 160 p. illus., map, ports. 23 cm. Reprint of the 1888 ed. [BV3625.C63C64 1969] 74-98739
1. Comber, Thomas J., 1852-1887.

RALEY, Helen Thames. 266.6'1'0924 B
Doctor in an old world; the story of Robert Earl Beddoe, medical missionary to China. Waco, Tex., Word Books [1969] 156 p. illus. 23 cm. [BV3427.B38R3 1969] 69-20222 3.95
1. Beddoe, Robert Earl, 1882-1952. 2. Missions, Medical—China. I. Title.

SUMMERS, Jester. 266.6'1'0924 B
Lottie Moon of China. Illustrated by James Ponter. Nashville, Broadman Press [1970] 62 p. illus., port. 23 cm. A biography of the Virginia-born girl who spent forty years of her life as a Baptist missionary in China. [BV3427.M55S9] 92 70-117304 2.50
1. Moon, Charlotte, 1840-1912—Juvenile literature. I. Ponter, James, illus. II. Title.

WOODWORTH, Ruth A. 266'.6'10924 B
No greater joy / by Ruth A. Woodworth. Des Plaines, Ill. : Regular Baptist Press, [1975] 70 p. : ill. ; 19 cm. [BV3382.W66A36] 74-28952 pbk. : 1.25
1. Woodworth, Ruth A. I. Title.

KWAST, Lloyd Emerson. 266.6'1'0967112
The discipling of West Cameroon; a study of Baptist growth. Grand Rapids, Eerdmans [1971] 205 p. illus., maps. 21 cm. (Church growth series) Bibliography: p. 191-201. [BX6322.C34K88] 71-150643 3.45
1. Baptists—Cameroon. 2. Church growth. I. Title.

STEVENS, Dorothy A ed. [266.61] 275.2
Voices from Japan; Christians speak. Pref. by Jitsuo Morikawa. Drawings contributed by Japanese Christian artists. [1st ed.] Philadelphia, Judson Press [1957] 93 p. illus. 21 cm. [BX6316.J3S8] 57-8339
1. Baptists — Japan. 2. Christmas in Japan. 3. Missions — Japan. I. Title.

EWING, Ruth Grimes. 266'.6'131
Our life with the Garos of Assam, India. Philadelphia, Dorrance [1971] 197 p. 22 cm. [BV3280.A8E93] 77-167294 ISBN 0-8059-1600-8 4.95
1. Missions—Assam. 2. Missions to Garos. I. Title.

HULL, Eleanor Means. 266'.6'131
Women who carried the good news / Eleanor Hull. Valley Forge, Pa. : Judson Press, [1975] 96 p. ; 22 cm. Includes bibliographical references. [BV2766.B48] 74-22520 ISBN 0-8170-0651-6 pbk. : 2.95
1. American Baptist Home Mission Societies. 2. Missionaries, Women. I. Title.

CAUTHEN, Baker James. 266.6'132
Advance: a history of Southern Baptist foreign missions [by] Baker J. Cauthen, and others. Nashville, Broadman Press [1970] 329 p. illus., ports. 22 cm. Bibliography: p. 319-323. [BV2520.C26] 71-117307 4.95
1. Southern Baptist Convention—Missions. 2. Southern Baptist Convention. Foreign Mission Board. I. Title.

FRYER, Ross B 266.6132
My island of Sumatra [by] Ross B. Fryer, Jr. Nashville, Convention Press [1966] 84 p. illus., ports., map. 21 cm. (Foreign mission graded series) [BV3365.F7] 66-14743
1. Missions — Sumatra — Juvenile literature. I. Title.

LOUCKS, Celeste, 1947- 266'.6'132
American montage : the human touch in language missions / written by Celeste Loucks ; photographed by Everett Hullum. Atlanta : Home Mission Board, Southern Baptist Convention, c1976. p. cm. (Human touch photo-text series ; 3) [BV2766.B5L68] 76-41911 6.95
1. Southern Baptist Convention—Missions. 2. Missions, Home. 3. Missions—United States. I. Hullum, Everett, 1942- II. Southern Baptist Convention. Home Mission Board. III. Title. IV. Series.

PARKS, Robert Keith. 266.6132
Crosscurrents, [by] R. Keith Parks. Nashville, Convention Press [1966] vi, 119 p. illus., ports. 19 cm. (1966 Foreign mission graded series) [BV3151.P3] 66-16376
1. Missions—Asia 2. Baptists—Missions. I. Title.

WEBB, Leland. 266'.6'132
How in this world : a consideration of strategy in the foreign missions outreach of Southern Baptists / Leland Webb. Nashville, Tenn. : Convention Press, [1974] viii, 119 p. : ill. ; 21 cm. (Foreign mission graded series, 1974) [BV2520.W4] 75-319215
1. Southern Baptist Convention—Missions. I. Title.

GRAHAM, Finlay M. 266.6'132'09569
Sons of Ishmael; how shall they hear? By Finlay M. Graham. Nashville, Convention Press [1969] 116 p. illus., maps, ports. 19 cm. (1969 foreign mission graded series) "A publication of the Foreign Mission Board." "Church study course [of the Sunday School Board of the Southern Baptist Convention] This book is number 1015 in category 10, section for adults." Includes bibliographical references. [BV2625.G7] 69-17887
1. Missions to Muslims. 2. Baptists—Missions. I. Southern Baptist Convention. Foreign Mission Board. II. Southern Baptist Convention. Sunday School Board. III. Title.

HUNKER, W. Carl. 266.6'1320951249
Taiwan: unfinished revolution [by] W. Carl Hunker. Nashville, Tenn., Convention Press [1970] ix, 127 p. illus., map, port. 20 cm. (Foreign mission graded series) "This book is the text for course 3636 of the missions subject area of the New Church Study Course." Bibliography: p. 126-127. [BV3450.F7H8] 74-113219
1. Missions—Taiwan. I. Title.

JOHNSON, Johnni. 266'.6'1320924 B
The gift of belonging / Johnni Johnson. Nashville : Broadman Press, [1975] 155 p. : ill. ; 18 cm. [BV2626.C6J63] 75-540 ISBN 0-8054-6305-4 pbk. : 1.75
1. Cobb, Virginia. 2. Missions to Muslims—Lebanon. I. Title.

SMITH, Bertha. 266.6151
Go home and tell. Nashville, Broadman Press [c1965] 154 p. 22 cm. Autobiographical. [BV3427.S6A3] 65-10342
1. Missions — China. I. Title.

SMITH, Bertha 266.6151
Go home and tell. Nashville, Broadman [c.1965] 154p. 22cm. [BV3427.S6A3] 65-10342 2.75
1. Missions—China. I. Title.

HEMPHILL, Elizabeth Anne. 266.615211
A treasure to share. Valley Forge, Pa., Judson Press [1964] 160 p. illus., ports. 22 cm. [BV3457.A5H4] 64-20501
1. Allen, Thomasine, 1890- 2. Missions — Japan. I. Title.

HEMPHILL, Elizabeth Anne 266.615211
A treasure to share. Valley Forge, Pa., Judson [c.1964] 160p. illus., ports. 22cm. 64-20501 2.50 pap.,
1. Allen, Thomasine, 1890- 2. Missions—Japan. I. Title.

ALBAUGH, Dana M. 1897- 266.6154
The light in India's hand. Valley Forge, Judson Press [1963] 128 p. illus. 21cm. [BV3265.2.A6] 63-13986
1. Missions—India. 2. American Baptist Convention—Missions. I. Title.

ALBAUGH, Dana M. 1897- 266.6154
The light in India's hand. Valley Forge, Judson [c.1963] 128p. illus. 21cm. Bibl. 63-13986 1.95 pap.,
1. Missions—India. 2. American Baptist Convention—Missions. I. Title.

HARDING, Frederic, 1878- 266'.6'154162
Christ and the hill-men. Lakemont, N.Y., North Country Books [1974] xiii, 186 p. illus. 24 cm. [BV3280.A8H37] 74-174336 6.90
1. Missions to Garos. 2. Missions—Assam. I. Title.

WHATLEY ANNICE. 266.6'15695
Journeyman in Jordan. Nashville, Convention Press [1969] 115 p. illus., map, ports. 19 cm. (1969 foreign mission graded series) "A publication of the Foreign Mission Board." "Church study course [of the Sunday School Board of the Southern Baptist Convention] This books is number 1075 in category 10, section for young people." [BV2087.W45] 69-17894
1. Missionary stories. 2. Missions—Jordan. I. Southern Baptist Convention. Foreign Mission Board. II. Southern Baptist Convention. Sunday School Board. III. Title.

BROWN, Russell E. 266.6'159
Doing the Gospel in Southeast Asia [by] Russell E. Brown. Valley Forge, Pa., Judson Press [1968] 95 p. maps. 22 cm. [BV3298.B7] 68-20432
1. Missions—Asia, Southeastern. I. Title.

JUMP, Chester, 1918- 266.61675
Coming-- ready or not; Congo Baptists advance, by Chester and Margaret Jump. Illustrated by John Savidge. [1st ed.] Philadelphia, Judson Press [1959] 100p. illus. 21cm. Includes bibliography. [BV3625.CJ8] 59-6151
1. Missions—Congo, Belgian. 2. Baptists—Congo, Belgian. I. Jump, Margaret (Savidge) 1920- joint author. II. Title.

DEBORD, Samuel A 266.61676
On the edge of decision. Nashville, Convention Press [1964] 119 p. illus., map. 19 cm. (Foreign mission graded series, 1964) "A publications of the Foreign Mission Board, Richmond, Virginia" [BV3530.D4] 64-12416
1. Missions — Africa, East. 2. Baptists — Missions. I. Title.

CHRISTIAN, Mary, 1899- 266.6'1676'1
Uganda safari. Nashville, Convention Press [1971] 96 p. illus., ports. (p. 89-96 blank for notes) 20 cm. (Foreign mission graded series) [BV3625.U3C5] 74-142065
1. Southern Baptist Convention—Missions—Study and teaching. 2. Missions—Uganda—Study and teaching. I. Title.

DEGOLIER, Florence. 266.6'1'701
Ta-pooth-ka and his descendants; the story of Moses and Eliza Merrill, of Baptist beginnings in Nebraska and of the Nebraska Baptist State Convention, by Florence (Mrs. Maynard R.) DeGolier. Omaha, Nebraska Baptist State Convention, c1967. 18 p. 22 cm. "1967 centennial observance" [BX6248.N2D4] 77-256047
1. Merrill, Moses, 1803-1840. 2. Merrill, Eliza (Wilcox) 1800-1882. 3. Baptists. Nebraska. State Convention. I. Title.

MCCOY, Isaac, 1784-1846. 266.6'1'701
History of Baptist Indian missions. With a new introd. by Robert F. Berkhofer, Jr. New York, Johnson Reprint Corp., 1970 [c1840] xxix, 611 p. 23 cm. (Series in American studies) [E98.M6M2 1970] 70-111997
1. Indians of North America—Missions. 2. Baptists—Missions. 3. Indians of North America—Indian Territory. I. Title. II. Series.

DANIELL, David, 1937- 266'.6'172
Stronger than mushrooms : the various facets of Baptist student work in Mexico / David Daniell. Nashville : Convention Press, c1976. 47 p. : ill. ; 28 cm. (Foreign mission graded series) [BV2835.2.D36] 76-375549
1. Baptists—Missions. 2. Missions—Mexico. 3. Church work with students—Mexico. 4. College students—Mexico—Religious life. I. Title.

PATTERSON, Frank Willard. 266.61729
Caribbean quest. Nashville, Convention Press [1960] 136p. illus. 19cm. (Foreign mission graded series, 1960) 'A publication of the Foreign Mission Board, Richmond, Va.' [BV2831.P3] 60-9541
1. Missions—Caribbean area. 2. Baptists—Missions. I. Title.

MORALES, Adam. 266.6173
American Baptists with a Spanish accent. Valley Forge, Judson Press [1964] 112 p. illus. 22 cm. "Another American Baptist mission book." [BV2831.M6] 64-13126
1. Missions — Spanish America. 2. Baptists — Missions. I. Title.

MORALES, Adam 266.6173
American Baptists with a Spanish accent. Valley Forge, Judson [c.1964] 112p. illus. 22cm. (Amer. Baptist mission bk.) 64-13126 1.95 pap.,
1. Missions—Spanish America. 2. Baptists—Mission. I. Title.

RUTLEDGE, Arthur B. 266.6'173
Mission to America; a century and a quarter of Southern Baptist home missions [by] Arthur B. Rutledge. Nashville, Broadman Press [1969] xiv, 271 p. illus., ports. 22 cm. Includes bibliographical references. [BV2766.B5R84] 78-84499 5.95
1. Southern Baptist Convention. Home Mission Board. 2. Southern Baptist Convention—Missions. 3. Missions, Home. I. Title.

WILLIS, Ron. 266.6'173
A view from the streets. Nashville, Tenn., Broadman Press [1971] 128 p. illus. 21 cm. [BV2653.W53] 77-157407 ISBN 0-8054-4513-7 3.50
1. City missions. I. Title.

CROUCH, Kate C. Maddry. 266'.6'1756
The magnificent nobility : a history of Woman's Missionary Union of North Carolina, 1952-1972 / by Kate C. Maddry Crouch. Raleigh : The Union, c1977. 125 p. : ill. ; 23 cm. Includes index. Bibliography: p. 119. [BV2766.B464C76] 77-153974
1. Baptists. North Carolina. State Convention. Woman's Missionary Union. 2. Women in missionary work. 3. Baptists—Missions. I. Title.

HUNKE, Naomi Ruth. 266.6'1'798
I have planted thee in this land; the story of the first 25 years of Southern Baptist missions in Alaska. Anchorage, Alaska Baptist Convention [1971] 334 p. illus., ports. 23 cm. Title on spine: In this land. Bibliography: p. 334. [BX6248.A25H8] 75-142782 6.50
1. Baptists—Alaska. I. Title. II. Title: In this land.

MEANS, Frank K 266.618
Across the bridge. Nashville, Convention Press [1960] 134p. illus. 19cm. (1960 foreign mission graded series) [BV2830.M38] 60-9540
1. Missions—Spanish America. 2. Baptists—Missions. I. Title.

KIRK, Maxie C. 266.6181
Banner-bearers [by] Maxie C. Kirk. Nashville, Convention Press [1965] 79 p. illus., map, plan, ports. 21 cm. (Foreign mission graded series) [BV2853.B6K5] 65-14933
1. Missions — Brazil — Juvenile literature. 2. Baptists — Missions — Juvenile literature. I. Title.

WISE, Gene H 266.61816
Sao Paulo hears the gospel [by] Gene H. Wise. Nashville, Convention Press [1965] viii, 99 p. illus., maps. ports. 19 cm. (Foreign mission graded series) [BV2853.B6W3] 65-13181
1. Missions — Brazil. 2. Baptists — Missions. I. Title.

SADLER, George W [266.62] 276.69
A century in Nigeria. Nashville, Broadman Press [1950] viii, 151 p. 19 cm. Bibliographical footnotes. [BV3625.N5S3] 51-47
1. Missions — Nigeria. 2. Southern Baptist Convention — Missions. I. Title.

WEEKS, Nan F comp. [266.6]274
Europe, whither bound! A symposium, telling of Southern Baptist missionary work in Italy, Spain, and the Balkan States, Hungary and Yugoslavia. Nashville, Broadman Press [1951] xvi, 144 p. 19 cm. "A publication of the Foreign Mission Board of the Southern Baptist Convention." Contents.Contents. -- Introduction, by G.W. Sadier. -- Europe today, by J.D. Franks. -- Italy, the land of the Book, by W. D. Moore. -- Baptists in Spain, by J.D. Hughey, Jr. -- Hungary, by J.A. Moore. -- Yugoslavia. by J.A. Moore. [BX6275.W4] 51-3483
1. Baptists — Europe. 2. Baptists — Minsione. 3. Missions — Europe. I. Southern Baptist Convention. Foreign Mission Board. II. Title.

ROUTH, Eugene Coke, 1874- [266.6] 275.1
Evening and morning in China. Nashville, Broadman Press [1950] ix, 125 p. illus. 19 cm. [BV3415.R58] 50-12332
1. Missions — China. I. Title.

STEVENS, Dorothy A ed. [266.6] 277
Neighbor voices of representative Baptists. [1st ed.] Philadelphia, Judson Press [1958] 109 p. 21 cm. [BX6233.S77] 58-8807
1. Baptists — America. I. Title.

SCHWEINSBERG, Henry W [266.6] 278
Inca gold. Nashville, Broadman Press [1951] 102 p. illus. 19 cm. [BV2851.S37] 51-12982
1. Missions — South America. 2. Baptists — Missions. I. Title.

CLEVELAND, Clyde C 266.6391
Indonesian adventure for Christ, by Clyde C. Cleveland. Photos, by the author. Washington, Review and Herald Pub. Association [1965] 191 p. illus. ports. 22 cm. [BV3340.C56] 64-24771
1. Missions — Indonesia. I. Title.

CLEVELAND, Clyde C. 266.6391
Indonesian adventure for Christ. Photos. by the author. Washington, D.C., Review & Herald [c.1965] 191p. illus., ports. 22cm. [BV3340.C56] 64-24771 3.75
1. Missions—Indonesia. I. Title.

EVANS, Robert P. 266.64
Transformed Europeans. Chicago, Moody [c.1963] 128p. 17cm. (Colportage lib. 495) .39 pap.,
I. Title.

BOTTS, Eli Daniel 266.6'42
British Baptist missionaries in India, 1793-1837: the history of Serampore and its missions, by E. Daniel Potts. London, Cambridge Univ. Pr., 1967. [12] 276p. map. 23cm. Bibl. [BV3290.S4P6] 67-13806 10.00
1. Missions—Serampore, India. 2. Missions, British. 3. Baptists—Missions. I. Title.
Available from Cambridge Univ. Pr., New York.

POTTS, Eli Daniel. 266.6'42
British Baptist missionaries in India, 1793-1837: the history of Serampore and its missions. by E. Daniel Potts. London. Cambridge U. P., 1967. 12. 276 p. map. 22 1/2 cm. 57/6 Bibliography: p 248-267. [BV3290.S4P6] 67-13806
1. Missions Serampore, India 2. Missions, British 3. Baptists Missions I. Title.

BULL, Geoffrey T., 1921- 266.65
Forbidden land; a saga of Tibet, by Geoffrey T. Bull. Chicago, Moody Press [1967, c1966] 124 p. map. 20 cm. [DS786.B8] 67-2343
1. Tibet. I. Title.

JOBSON, Orville D 266.65
Conquering Oubangui-Chari for Christ. Winona Lake, Ind., Brethren Missionary Herald Co. [1957] 160p. illus., ports., maps. 21cm. (Bauman memorial lectures, 1957) Bibliography: p. 159-160. [BV3625.U2J6] 276.74 57-38254
1. Missions— Ubangi-Shari. I. Title. II. Series.

KULP, Mary Ann Moyer. 266.6'5 B
No longer strangers; a biography of H. Stover Kulp. Elgin, Ill., Brethren Press [1968] 188 p. illus., maps, ports. 21 cm. [BV3625.N6K84] 68-4439
1. Kulp, Harold Stover, 1894-1964. 2. Missions—Nigeria. I. Title.

RONK, Albert T. 266'.65
History of Brethren missionary movements, by Albert T. Ronk. [Ashland, Ohio, Printed by Brethren Pub. Co., c1971] 152 p. illus. 22 cm. Bibliography: p. 137-139. [BV2595.B7R65] 70-184490
1. Brethren Chruch (Ashland, Ohio)—Missions. I. Title.

TO serve the present age 266'.65
: the Brethren Service story / by M. R. Zigler and other former participants ; Donald F. Durnbaugh, editor. Elgin, Ill. : Brethren Press, [1975] 224 p. : ill. ; 22 cm. Includes index. Bibliography: p. 215-218. [BX7827.3.T6] 75-6633 ISBN 0-87178-848-9 pbk. : 4.95
1. Church of the Brethren. Brethren Service Commission. 2. Church of the Brethren—Charities. 3. World War, 1939-1945—Civilian relief. I. Zigler, M. R. II. Durnbaugh, Donald F.

RAY, Rex, 1885-1958 266.651
Cowboy missionary in Kwangsi. Nashville, Broadman [1964] 123p. 20cm. Autobiographical. 64-24025 1.50
1. Missions—China. I. Title.

DUGGAR, John W., comp. 266.651249
Two for God (The Batemans of Formosa) Little Rock, Ark., 716 Main St. Baptist Pubns. Comm., [1962] 91p. illus. 22cm. 1.00 pap.,
1. Missions—Nigeria—Juvenile literature I. Title.

EDDLEMAN, H Leo. 266.656
Mandelbaum Gate. Nashville, Convention Press [1963] 108 p. illus. 19 cm. (1963 foreign mission graded series) "A publication of the [Southern Baptist Convention] Foreign Mission Board, Richmond, Virginia." [BV3160.E3] 63-11169
1. Missions — New East. 2. Southern Baptist Convention — Missions. I. Title.

GRIMLEY, Mildred M 266.65669
Children of the bush country. Illustrated by John B. Grimley. Elgin, Ill., Brethren Press [1959] 89p. illus. 23cm. [BV3625.N5G74] 60-16002
1. Missions—Nigeria—Juvenile literature. 2. Missionary stories. I. Title.

READ, Katherine L (Henderson) 266.6591
Bamboo hospital the story of a missionary family in Burma, by Katherine L. Read with Robert O. Ballou. Foreword by Jesse R. Wilson. [1st ed.] Philadelphia, Lippincott [1961] 224p. 22cm. [R722.R4] 61-8690
1. Henderson, Albert Haley. 2. Missions, Medical—Burma. 3. Missions—Burma. I. Title.

CARR, James Bottorff, 1911- 266.66
The foreign missionary work of the Christian Church. [Manhattan? Kan.] '1950. ix, 156 p. 23 cm. Bibliography: p. vi. [BV2532.C3 1950] 50-11768
1. Disciples of Christ—Missions. I. Title.

FIERS, Alan Dale. 266.66
This is missions; our Christian witness in an unchristian world. St. Louis, Bethany Press [1953] 256p. illus. 23cm. [BV2532.F5] 54-21460
1. Disciples of Christ—Missions. 2. United Christian Missionary Society. I. Title.

GANTA United Methodist Mission. 266'.6666'2
Ganta United Methodist Mission, 1926-1976. [Ganta? Liberia] : The Mission, [1976] 14 p. : ill. ; 22 cm. Cover title. [BV3625.L5G36 1976] 77-369211
1. Methodist Church—Missions. 2. Missions—Liberia.

NELSON, Robert Gilbert. 266.667292
Disciples of Christ in Jamaica, 1858-1958; a centennial of missions in the 'Gem of the Caribbean.' St. Louis, Bethany Press [c1958] 200p. illus. 21cm. Includes bibliography. [BX7319.J25N4] 58-13576
1. Disciples of Christ— Jamaica. I. Title.

HEGE, Ruth. 266.6675
We two alone. New York, Nelson [1965] 192 p. illus., map. 21 cm. [BV3625.C63H35] 65-15407
1. Missions—Congo (Leopoldville) I. Title.

BROWN, Phyllis G. 266'.6'6755
A century with Christian women in Virginia / by Phillis G. Brown. Richmond, Va. : Christian Women's Fellowship, Christian Church (Disciples of Christ) in Virginia, 1975. 48 p. ; 22 cm. Bibliography: p. 47-48. [BV4415.B76] 75-329725
1. Women in church work—Christian Church (Disciples of Christ) 2. Women in church work—Virginia. 3. Virginia—Biography. I. Title.

COMBRIDGE, B. J., 1898- 266.6'694'5
They carried a torch; a history of the Department of Home Missions and Evangelism of Churches of Christ in Victoria and Tasmania [by] B. J. Combridge. Melbourne [Dept. of Home Missions and Evangelism, Churches of Christ Centre] 1967. 87 p. illus., ports. 22 cm. [BV3650.C64] 74-527940
1. Churches of Christ (Australia). Dept. of Home Missions and Evangelism. 2. Missions—Australia. I. Title.

CAMPBELL, Roy G 266.67
Adverturing with gospel literature. Washington*eview and Herald Pub. Association [c1955] 247p. 18cm. [BV2369.C35] 55-19728
1. Religious literature—Publication and distribution. 2. Seventh-Day Adventists. I. Title.

FUZZY-WUZZY tales. [266.67]
Washington, Review and Herald Pub. Association [1950] 191 p. illus., ports., maps. 21 cm. [BV3670.H3] 279.6 50-56691
1. Missions—Islands of the Pacific. 2. Seventh-Day Adventists—Missions. I. Hare, Reuben E.

JACQUES, Oliver, 1920 266.67
Africa called us, by Oliver and Fredonia Jacques. Washington, Review and Herald Pub. Association [1952] 255p. 20cm. [BV3625.T3J28] 276.782 52-67075
1. Missions— Tanganyika Territory. I. Jacques, Fredonia, 1921- joint author. II. Title.

KRUM, Nathaniel. 266.67
The MV story. Washington, Review and Herald Pub. Association [1963] 252 p. illus. 22 cm. [BX6153.K7] 63-17761
1. Seventh-day Adventists. General Conference. Young People's Missionary Volunteer Dept. I. Title.

KRUM, Nathaniel 266.67
The MV story. Washington, D.C., Review & Herald [c.1963] 252p. illus.22cm. 63-17761 4.50
1. Seventh-Day Adventists. General Conference. Young People's Missionary Volunteer Dept. I. Title.

MICHIBIKI; 266.67
the leading of God. Illus. by Stanley Dunlap, Jr. Washington, Review and Herald [1956] 250p. illus. 22cm. [BV3445.M66] 275.2 56-58727
1. Missions— Japan. 2. Seventh-Day Adventists—Missions. 3. Showa, Japan (Chiba Prefecture) Japan Missionary College. I. Moore, Raymond S

SENT . . . because we care 266.67
[Church of God missionary work] Anderson, Ind., Warner [c.1962] 64p. 21cm. .75 pap.,

SHELDON, Robert Lewis 266.67
Daybreak in Korea, by Robert L. Sheldon. Photos. by the author except where otherwise noted. Nashville, Southern Pub. [c.1965] 126p. illus. (pt. col.) map (on lining papers) 26cm. [BV3460.S5] 65-9456 5.95 bds.,
1. Missions—Korea. 2. Seventh-Day Adventists—Missions. I. Title.

WESIPHAL, Barbara Osborne. 266.67
Mexican nuggets; mission stories from south of the border. Cover design by Charles Cook. Washington, Review & Herald Pub. Association [1956] 95p. illus. 23cm. [BV2835.W35] 277.2 56-14487
1. Missions—Mexico. 2. Seventh—Day Adventists—Missions. I. Title.

A white nurse in [266.67]
Africa. Mountain View, Calif., Pacific Press Pub. Association [1951] 134 p. illus. 21 cm. Translation of Als welsse Schwester in Afrikas Wildnis. [BV3562.H3A313] 276 51-6299
I. Haseneder, Maria.

DOWN, Goldie M. 266.6'7'0922
If I have twelve sons, by Goldie Down.

Nashville, Southern Pub. Association [1968] 95 p. 22 cm. [BV2495.D68] 68-55391
1. Seventh-Day Adventists—Missions. 2. Converts, Seventh-Day Adventist. I. Title.

CASON, Mabel (Earp) 266.6'7'0924
1892-
Steering by the star. Nashville, Southern Pub. Association [1968] 134 p. 22 cm. [BV3460.C35] 68-56069
1. Seventh-Day Adventists—Missions. 2. Missions—Korea. I. Title.

COBERLY, Zoral. 266.6'7'0924
Dragon teeth, by Zoral and Elga Coberly. Washington, Review and Herald Pub. Association [1967] 192 p. illus. 22 cm. [DS710.C637] 67-19719
1. China—Description and travel—1901-1948. 2. Missions—China. I. Coberly, Elga, joint author. II. Title.

DAVIS, Thomas A. 266.6'7'0924
Island of forgotten men, by Thomas A. Davis. Photos by Gottfried Oosterwal. Washington, Review Herald [1967] 127p. illus., map (on lining papers), ports. 22cm. [BV3680.N52O6] 67-19717 3.95
1. Oosterwal, Gottfried. 2. Missions—New Guinea. I. Title.

FORD, Herbert. 266.6'7'0924 B
For the love of China. Mountain View, Calif., Pacific Press Pub. Association [1971] 127 p. port. 22 cm. (A Destiny book) [BV3427.R34F67 1971] 73-140084
1. Rebok, Denton Edward, 1897- I. Title.

HARE, Eric B. 266.6'7'0924 B
Fulton's footprints in Fiji [by] Eric B. Hare. Washington, Review and Herald Pub. Association [1969] 252 p. illus., map (on lining papers), ports. 22 cm. [BV3680.F6F8] 77-84993
1. Fulton, John Edwin, 1869-1945. 2. Seventh-Day Adventists—Missions. 3. Seventh-Day Adventists—Missions. 4. Missions—Fiji Islands. I. Title.

HOWELL, John 266'.6'70924 B
Marion, 1893-
Surely God led, by J. M. Howell. Mountain View, Calif., Pacific Press Pub. Association [1973] 125 p. port. 22 cm. (A Destiny book, D-142) Autobiographical. [BX6193.H68A36] 73-86395 2.50 (pbk.).
1. Howell, John Marion, 1893- I. Title.

MARSH, Robert Lee. 266'.6'70924 B
Surgeon in the South Pacific / Robert Lee Marsh. Washington : Review and Herald Pub. Association, c1975. 63 p. ; 19 cm. [R722.32.M37A33] 74-28752
1. Marsh, Robert Lee. 2. Missionaries, Medical—Papua, New Guinea—Correspondence, reminiscences, etc. 3. Oceanica—Description and travel—1951- I. Title.

OGLE, Mary S., 266.6'7'0924 B
1905-
In spite of danger; the story of Thelma Smith in China [by] Mary S. Ogle. Washington, Review and Herald Pub. Association [1969] 159 p. map (on lining papers) 22 cm. [BV3427.S63O35] 74-84995
1. Smith, Thelma, 1904- 2. Seventh-Day Adventists—Missions. 3. Missions—China. I. Title.

STEED, Ernest H. 266.6'7'0924 B
J.
Impaled; the story of Brian Dunn, a twentieth-century medical missionary martyr of the South Pacific, by Ernest H. J. Steed. Mountain View, Calif., Pacific Press Pub. Association [1970] 72, [22] p. illus., ports. 22 cm. (A Destiny book, D-127) [BV3680.S62D87] 76-91331
1. Dunn, Brian Mansfield, 1940-1965. 2. Missions—Solomon Islands. I. Title.

STEWART, Andrew G. 266'.6'70924 B
In letters of gold; heroism for God in the South Seas [by] Andrew G. Stewart. Mountain View, Calif., Pacific Press Pub. Association [1973] 128 p. illus. 22 cm. (A Destiny book, D-143) [BV3676.S8A33] 73-87368
1. Stewart, Andrew G. I. Title.

WANGERIN, Theodora 266.6'7'0924
Scharffenberg.
God sent me to Korea. Cover photo by Robert Sheldon. Washington, Review and Herald Pub. Association [1968] 128 p. 22 cm. [BV3462.W3A3] 68-22281
1. Seventh-Day Adventists—Missions. 2. Missions—Korea. I. Title.

WESTPHAL, Barbara 266.6'7'0924 B
(Osborne)
John, the intrepid, missionary on three continents, by Barbara Westphal. Washington, Review and Herald Pub. Association [1968] 188 p. 22 cm. [BV2831.W43] 68-22280
1. Seventh-Day Adventists—Missions. 2. Missions—Latin America. I. Title.

WHEELER, Ruth Lellah 266.6'7'0924
(Carr) 1899-
Light the paper lantern; the adventures of Merritt and Wilma Warren, missionaries to China, by Ruth Wheeler. Mountain View, Calif., Pacific Press Pub. Association [c1967] v, 122 p. illus. 22 cm. (A Destiny book, D-116) [BV3427.W34W5] 67-31428
1. Warren, Merritt. 2. Warren, Wilma. 3. Missions—China. I. Title.

WESTPHAL, Barbara [266.67] 277.2
Osborne.
Mexican nuggets; mission stories from south of the border. Cover design by Charles Cook. Washington, Review & Herald Pub. Association [1956] 95 p. illus. 23 cm. [BV2835.W35] 56-14487
1. Missions — Mexico. 2. Seventh-Day Adventists — Missions. I. Title.

AITKEN, James J. 266.6'73
White wings, green jungle; the story of the Fernando Stahl, the first Seventh-Day Adventist missionary plane in South America, by James and Dorothy Aitken. Mountain View, Calif., Pacific Pr. Pub. [c.1966] 96p. illus., ports. 22cm. (Destiny bk., D-112) [PBV2495.A94] 66-28099 1.50 pap.,
1. Seventh-Day Adventists—Missions. 2. Aeronautics in missionary work. 3. Missions—South America. I. Aitken, Dorothy Lockwood, joint author. II. Title.

AITKEN, James J 266.6'73
White wings, green jungle; the story of the Fernando Stahl, the first Seventh-Day Adventist missionary plane in South America, by James and Dorothy Aitken. Mountain View, Calif., Pacific Press Pub. Association [1966] 96 p. illus., ports. 22 cm. (A Destiny book, D-112) [BV2495.A94] 66-28099
1. Seventh-Day Adventists—Missions. 2. Aeronautics in Missionsary work. 3. Missions—South America. I. Aitken, Dorothy Lockwood, joint author. II. Title.

MAXWELL, Arthur Stanley, 266.673
1896-
Under the southern cross; the Seventh-Day Adventist story in Australia, New Zealand, and the islands of the South Pacific. Prep. in collaboration with the Australasian Div. of Seventh-Day Adventists. Nashville. Southern Pub. [c.1966] 143p. illus. (pt. col.) col, map (on lining papers) ports. (pt. col.) 26cm. [BV3640.M3] 66-5528 5.95 bds.,
1. Missions—Oceanica. 2. Seventh-Day Adventists—Missions. I. Title.

MOSAIC of adventure : 266'.6'73
a scrapbook of student missionary experiences and documents / by Donna June Evans. Nashville : Southern Pub. Association, c1976. 96 p. ; 23 cm. [BV2495.M67] 76-3876 ISBN 0-8127-0112-7
1. Seventh-Day Adventists—Missions. 2. College students in missionary work. I. Evans, Donna June, 1949-

OLSON, Mildred 266.673 B
Thompson.
Diamondola. Illus. supplied by the author. Cover painting by Nadine Dower. Washington, Review and Herald Pub. Association [1966] 192 p. illus., ports. 22 cm. [BV3177.A8O55] 66-20840
1. Ashod, Diamondola (Keanides) 1894- 2. Seventh-Day Adventists—Missions. 3. Missions—Turkey. I. Title.

PALMER, Blanche 266.673
Pilgrim of the night by Blanche Palmer. Illus. by Don Fields. Nashville, Southern Pub. [c.1966] 157p. illus. 21cm. 3.75 bds.,
I. Title.

†QUIMBY, Paul Elmore. 266'.6'73 B
Yankee on the Yangtze : one missionary's saga in revolutionary China / Paul Quimby with Norma Youngberg. Nashville, Tenn. : Southern Pub. Association, c1976. 176 p. ; 21 cm. [BV3427.Q55A36] 76-49387 ISBN 0-8127-0131-3 pbk. : 4.95
1. Quimby, Paul Elmore. 2. Missionaries—China—Biography. 3. Missionaries—United States—Biography. I. Youngberg, Norma R., joint author. II. Title.

ROBINSON, Virgil E. 266'.6'73 B
Curse of the cannibals / Virgil E. Robinson ; [ill., John Gourley]. Washington : Review and Herald Pub. Association, c1976. 125 p. : ill. ; 21 cm. (Penguin series) "Originally published in Guide magazine under the title King of the cannibals." A biography of the Scottish missionary with emphasis on his work in the New Hebrides. [BV3680.N6P67 1976] 92 76-23025
1. Paton, John Gibson, 1824-1907—Juvenile literature. 2. Missionaries—Scotland—Biography—Juvenile literature. 3. Missionaries—New Hebrides—Biography—Juvenile literature. 4. Missions—New Hebrides—Juvenile literature. I. Title.

SCHWARTZ, Frederick J., 266'.673
comp.
Thailand and the Seventh-Day Adventist medical and missionary work, by Frederick J. Schwartz. Berrien Springs, Mich., Andrews University, 1972. 195 p. illus. 28 cm. "A collection of most of the news releases of the 'Far Eastern Division outlook' as well as articles ... from 'The review and herald'." [BV3315.S37] 72-83283
1. Seventh-Day Adventists—Missions. 2. Missions—Thailand. 3. Missions, Medical—Thailand. I. Title.

COTT, Elizabeth 266'.6'730924 B
(Buhler)
Destination—Green Hell [by] Betty Buhler Cott. Washington, Review and Herald Pub. Association [1972] 160 p. illus. 22 cm. (Penguin series) [BV2853.B9C68] 76-166069 Pap. 1.95
I. Title.

EDWARDS, Josephine 266.6'7'30922
Cunnington.
Pioneers together; a biography of the Roy F. Cottrells. Nashville, Southern Pub. Association [1967] 238 p. port. 21 cm. [BX6193.C6E3] 67-6137
1. Cottrell, Roy Franklin, 1878- 2. Cottrell, Myrtie Ball. 3. Missions—China. I. Title.

RUSSELL, Riley. 266.6'73'0924 B
It came in handy; the story of Riley Russell, M.D., physician extraordinary to the people of Korea, as told to Stella Parker Peterson. Washington, Review and Herald Pub. Association [1969] 160 p. illus., map, ports. 22 cm. [R154.R96A3] 76-81310
1. Missions, Medical—Korea. I. Peterson, Stella Parker. II. Title.

OGLE, Mary S., 266'.6'7510924 B
1905-
Shanghai Wolfe; the Wolfe Ismond story, by Mary S. Ogle. Nashville, Tenn., Southern Pub. Association [1972] 174 p. 22 cm. [BX6193.I74O4] 72-86322 ISBN 0-8127-0065-1
1. Ismond, Wolfe. I. Title.

CHRISTENSEN, Otto 266'.6'75177
H., 1898-
Mission Mongolia; the untold story [by] Otto H. Christensen. Washington, Review and Herald Pub. Association [1974] 123 p. illus. 21 cm. [BV3420.M7C48] 74-182317 3.50
1. Seventh-Day Adventists—Missions. 2. Christensen, Otto H., 1898- 3. Missions—Mongolia (Inner Mongolia) I. Title.

WANGERIN, Theodora 266.67519
Scharffenberg.
High adventure in Korea; illustrated by Howard Larkin. Mountain View, Calif., Pacific Press Pub. Association [c1960] 106 p. illus. 23 cm. [BV3460.W25] 60-16411
1. Missions — Korea — Juvenile literature. 2. Seventh-Day Adventists — Missions — Juvenile literature. I. Title.

JENSEN, Iona (Clark) 266.675281
Adventure for God on Okinawa. Illustrated by Harold Munson. Mountain View, Calif., Pacific Press Pub. Association [1960] 130p. illus. 23cm. [BV3450.O4J4] 60-10102
1. Missons—Okinawa Island. 2. Seventh—Day Adventists—Missions. I. Title.

RAWSON, Elsie Lewis. 266.6754
Sunanda's jewels. Washington, Review and Herald Pub. Association [1960] 127p. illus. 23cm. [BV3265.2.R34] 60-9415
1. Missions—India. 2. Seventh-Day Adventists—Missions. I. Title.

ALLEN, Sydney. 266.6'7599'1
One week with a modern missionary. Washington, Review and Herald Pub. Association [1970] 96 p. illus., ports., map. 22 cm. [BV3380.A45] 76-106498
1. Seventh-Day Adventists—Missions. 2. Missions—Luzon. I. Title.

PIERSON, Robert H. 266'.6'767518
Angels over Elisabethville : a true story of God's providence in time of war / by Robert H. Pierson. Mountain View, Calif. : Pacific Press Pub. Association, c1975. 88 p. : ill. ; 22 cm. (A Destiny book ; D-150) [DT665.E4P53] 74-28684 ISBN pbk. : 2.95
1. Seventh-Day Adventists—Zaire. 2. Pierson, Robert H. 3. Lubumbashi—History. I. Title.

OSMUNSON, Rosemarie. 266.676762
Njoki and the Mau Mau terror. Nashville, Southern Pub. Association [1959] 158p. illus. 21cm. [DT434.E2O69] 59-16954
1. Mau Mau. 2. Missions—Kenya Colony and Protectorate. 3. Kikuyu tribe. I. Title.

GRAYBILL, Ronald D. 266.6'7762
Mission to Black America; the true story of Edson White and the riverboat Morning Star, by Ronald D. Graybill. Illus. [by] Dale Rusch. Mountain View, Calif., Pacific Press Pub. Association [1971] iv, 144 p. illus. 20 cm. [BX6193.W55G7] 75-154982
1. White, James Edson. 2. Morning Star (Riverboat) 3. Missions to Negroes—Mississippi. I. Title.

STIRLING, Betty. 266.6779
Mission to the Navajo. Mountain View, Calif., Pacific Press Pub. Association [1961] 147 p. illus. 23 cm. [E99.N3S82] 61-10880
1. Navajo Indians — Missions. 2. Seventh-Day Adventists — Missions. 3. Missions — Arizona. 4. Missions — New Mexico. I. Title.

STIRLING, Betty 266.6779
Mission to the Navajo. Mountain View, Calif., Pacific Pr. Pub. Assn. [c.1961] 147p. illus. 61-10880 3.50
1. NavajoIndians—Missions. 2. Seventh-Day Adventists—Missions. 3. Missions—Arizona. 4. Missions—New Mexico. I. Title.

COTT, Elizabeth (Buhler) 266.6'78
Jewels from green hell; stories of the Davis Indians of British Guiana [by] Betty Buhler Cott. Washington, Review and Herald Pub. Association [1969] 256 p. illus., map, ports. 22 cm. [BV2087.C68] 71-81309
1. Seventh-Day Adventists—Missions. 2. Missionary stories. 3. Missions—South America. I. Title.

HASELDEN, Kyle. 266.678
Death of a myth, new locus for Spanish American faith. New York, Friendship Press [1964] 175 p. 19 cm. Bibliography: p. [173]-175. [BV2831.H33] 64-10997
1. Missions — Spanish America. I. Title.

TAYLOR, Clyde Willis, 266.678
1904- ed.
Protestant missions in Latin America; a statistical survey, edited by Clyde W. Taylor and Wade T. Coggins. Washington, Evangelical Foreign Missions Association, 1961. xxvi, 314 p. 19 x 24 cm. [BV2831.T35] 62-27216
1. Mission — Spanish America — Stat. 2. Protestant churches — Missions. I. Coggins, Wade T., joint ed. II. Title.

WESTPHAL, Barbara 266.678
(Osborne)
These Fords still run. Mountain View, Calif., Pac. Pr. Pub. [c.1962] 136 p. illus. 23 cm. 62-13527 3.00
1. Ford, Orley. 2. Ford, Lillian Gertrude (Shafer) 1894- 3. Seven-Day Adventists—Missions. 4. Missions—Spanish America. I. Title.

WESTPHAL, Barbara 266.678
(Osborne)
These Fords still run. Mountain View, Calif., Pacific Press Pub. Association [1962] 136 p. illus. 23 cm. [BV2831.W45] 62-13527
1. Ford, Orley. 2. Ford, Lillian Gertrude (Shafer) 1894- 3. Seventh-Day Adventists — Missions. 4. Missions — Spanish America. I. Title.

WILCOX, Elmer Harry, 266.678
1888-
In perils oft. Nashville, Southern Pub. Association [1961] 271 p. illus. 22 cm. [BV2853.P6W5] 61-4438
1. Missions — Peru. 2. Missions — Brazil. 3. Seventh-Day Adventists — Missions. I. Title.

BAERG, John. 266.6'781
Brazil; where the action is. Washington, Review and Herald Pub. Association [1969] 160 p. 22 cm. [BV2853.B6B27] 70-84991
1. Seventh-Day Adventists—Missions. 2. Missions—Brazil. 3. Missionary stories. I. Title.

HALLIWELL, Leo B 266.6781
Light in the jungle; the thirty years' mission of Leo and Jessie Halliwell along the Amazon. Edited and with a foreword by Will Oursler. New York, D. McKay Co. [1959] 269p. illus. 21cm. [BV2853.B6H32] 59-9386
1. Brazil—Descr. & trav. 2. Halliwell, Jessie. I. Title.

JOERS, Lawrence Eugene 266.6785
Claire, 1900-
Mercy rides on wings. Photos by Robert M. Eldridge and by the author. Nashville, Southern Pub. Association [1960] 156p. illus. 21cm. [BV2853.P7J6] 60-36294
1. Missions, Medical—Peru. 2. Seventh-Day Adventists—Missions. I. Title.

MONPUNTAIN, Arthur 266.6'7911'5
Possess your soul in patience; a first-person story of high adventure in Boreno. Nashville, Tenn., Southern Pub. [1967] 304p. illus. 22cm. [BV3345.M6] 67-9026 5.95

1. Missions—Borned. 2. Seventh-Day Adventists—Missions. 3. Borneo — Descr. & trav. I. Title.

MOUNTAIN, Arthur. 266.6'7911'5
Possess your soul in patience; a first-person story of high adventure in Borneo. Nashville, Tenn., Southern Pub. Association [1967] 304 p. illus. 22 cm. [BV3345.M6] 67-9026
1. Missions — Borneo. 2. Seventh-Day Adventists — Missions. 3. Borneo — Descr. & trav. I. Title.

WOOD, Miriam. 266.6'7955
All my dusty babies; one week's visit in New Guinea, November 30-December 7, 1970. Washington, Review & Herald Pub. Co. Assn. [1972] 174 p. illus. 22 cm. [BV3680.N5W66] 79-190580 Pap. 2.95
1. Seventh Day Adventists—Missions. 2. Missions—New Guinea. I. Title.

PALMER, C S 266.679612
Tales of Tonga. Nashville, Southern Pub. Association [1959] 159p. illus. 20cm. [BV3680.T6P3] 59-4789
1. Missions—Tonga Islands. 2. Seventh-Day Adventists—Missions. I. Title.

TAYLOR, Ronald William. 266.679614
Polynesian paradise. Mountain View, Calif., Pacific Press Pub. Association [1960] 136 p. illus. 23 cm. [BV3680.S353] 60-9811
1. Missions — Samoan Islands. I. Title.

TAYLOR, Ronald William 266.679614
Polynesian paradise. Mountain View, Calif., Pacific Press Pub. Association [c.1960] 136p. illus. 23cm. 60-9811 3.50
1. Missions—Samoan Islands. I. Title.

GRIFFIN, Eunice 266.7
The rise of American missions, the African Methodist Episcopal Church. v. 1. [New York, 19] [P.O. Box 255, Radio City Station] Coker Press Books, c1960. 99, 6 unnumbered p. 20cm. 60-2818 3.95
1. African Methodist Episcopal Church—Missions. 2. Missions—Negro race. I. Title.

LAW, Virginia W 266.7
Appointment Congo, by Virginia Law. Chicago, Rand McNally [1966] 289 p. illus., ports. 22 cm. Autobiographical. [BV3625.C63L3] 66-16688
1. Law, Burleight A. 2. Missions — Congo (Leopoidville) I. Title.

LAW, Virginia W. 266.7
Appointment Congo. Chicago, Rand McNally [c.1966] 289p. illus., ports. 22cm. Autobiographical. [BV3625.C63L3] 66-16688 3.95
1. Law, Burleight A. 2. Missions—Congo (Leopoldville) I. Title.

*MARSH, Mabel. 266.7
Service suspended. New York, Carlton [1968] 180p. illus. 21cm. (Reflection bk.) 3.50
1. Missions—Malaysia—Methodist. I. Title.

METHODIST Church (United States) Board of Missions. 266.7
Christian mission in theological perspective; an inquiry by Methodists. Edited by Gerald H. Anderson. Nashville, Abingdon Press [1967] 286 p. 22 cm. Bibliography, compiled and annotated by Gerald H. Anderson": p. 263-286. Bibliographical footnotes. [BV2030.M45] 67-11709
1. Missions — Addresses, essays, lectures. 2. Methodist Church — Missions. I. Anderson, Gerald H., ed. II. Title.

METHODIST Church (United States) Board of Missions. 266.7
Christian mission in theological perspective; an inquiry by Methodists. Edited by Gerald H. Anderson. Nashville, Abingdon Press [1967] 286 p. 22 cm. "Bibliography, compiled and annotated by Gerald H. Anderson": p. 263-286. Bibliographical footnotes. [BV2030.M45] 67-11709
1. Methodist Church—Missions. 2. Missions—Addresses, essays, lectures. I. Anderson, Gerald H., ed. II. Title.

METHODIST Church (United States) Board of Missions and Church Extension. Division of Home Missions and Church Extension. Section of Home Missions. 266.7
Composite annual report. New York. v. illus., ports. 23 cm. [BV2766.M423] 50-49354
1. Methodist Church — Missions. I. Title.

METHODIST Church (United States) Board of Missions and Church Extention. Joint Division of Education and Cultivation. 266.7
The composite report of the secretaries. New York City. v. illus. 23 cm. [BV2550.A15A45] 51-39672
1. Methodist Church (United States) — Missions. I. Title.

METHODIST Church (United States) Board of Missions. Joint Commission on Education and Cultivation. 266.7
The Christian mission today. New York, Abingdon Press [1960] 288 p. 24 cm. "Appraisal by twenty-one contemporary leaders of the church was edited ... upon the request of the Department of Ministerial Training, Board of Education of the Methodist Church." [BV2061.M45] 60-10914
1. Missions. 2. Methodist Church — Missions. I. Title.

METHODIST Church (United States) Board of Missions. Joint Section of Education and Cultivation. 266.7
The Christian mission today. New York, Abingdon Press [1960] 288p. 24cm. 'Appraisal by twenty-one contemporary leaders of the church was edited ... upon the request of the Department of Ministerial Training, Board ofEducation of the Methodist Church.' [BV2061.M45] 60-10914
1. Missions. 2. Methodist Church— Missions. I. Title.

METHODIST Episcopal Church. Woman's Foreign Missionary Society. Pacific Branch. 266.7
Annual session. [Report] Los Angeles. v. ports. 23 cm. annual. [BV2550.A45A85] 50-41545
I. Title.

PRENTICE, Margaret May. 266.7
Unwelcome at the northeast gate. [1st ed. Shawnee Mission? Kan.] Inter-collegiate Press [1966] 207 p. illus., ports., maps (on lining papers) 23 cm. Account of the author's experiences during the period 1924-43 primarily in northeastern China as a missionary and nurse in the Isabella Fisher Hospital. Tientsin, and as a prisoner of the Japanese. [BV3427.P7A3] 66-30541
1. Missions. China. I. Title.

STOCKWELL, Francis Olin. 266.7
With God in Red China; the story of two years in Chinese Communist prisons. [1st ed.] New York, Harper [1953] 256p. 22cm. [BV3427.S825A3] [BV3427.S825A3] 275.1 53-6973 53-6973
I. Title.

WILLIAMS, Walter B 266.7
Adventures with the Krus in West Africa [by] Walter B. Williams and Maude Wigfield Williams. [1st ed.] New York, Vantage Press [cu955] 146p. illus. 21cm. [BV3625.I5W5] 276.66 55-11660
1. Missions—Liberia. I. Williams, Maude Wigfield, joint author. II. Title.

ANDREWS, Charles Freer, 1871-1940. 266'.7'0924 B
John White of Mashonaland. New York, Negro Universities Press [1969] 316 p. 23 cm. Reprint of the 1935 ed. [BV3625.M3A6 1969] 79-91660 ISBN 0-8371-2070-5
1. White, John, 1866 (Jan. 6)-1933.

SEAMANDS, Ruth, 1916- 266.7'0924
House by the bo tree. Waco, Tex., Word Books [1969] 154 p. illus., ports. 23 cm. [BV3269.S375A32] 69-20231 3.95
1. Missions—India. 2. Methodist Church—Missions. I. Title.

MCKENZIE, Maisie. 266'.7'0994
Mission to Arnhem land / [by] Maisie McKenzie. Adelaide : Rigby, 1976. 260 p., [16] leaves of plates : ill. ; 22 cm. [BV3660.N6M3] 77-366086 ISBN 0-7270-0152-3
1. Methodist Church—Missions. 2. Missions to Australian aborigines—Australia—Arnhem Land. 3. Arnhem Land, Australia—History. I. Title.

AN Analysis of the Hawaii Mission of the Methodist Church. 266.7'09969
Philadelphia, Division of National Missions of the Board of Missions of the Methodist Church [1964] xii, 223 p. maps. 28 cm. Report of a study team, composed of staff members of the Division of National Missions and the Woman's Division of Christian Service, to the Strategy Committee for the Hawaii Mission. [BX8248.H38A6] 70-10241
1. Methodist Church (United States)—Missions. 2. Methodist Church in Hawaii. 3. Missions—Hawaii. I. Methodist Church (United States). Woman's Division of Christian Service. II. Methodist Church (United States). Division of National Missions. III. Methodist Church (United States). Strategy Committee for the Hawaii Mission.

PYKE, Frederick Merrill. 266'.7'10924 B
The first of three generations of White Wolves in China; James Howell Pyke's secret. [Timonium, Md., c1973] 109 p. illus. 18 cm. [BV3427.P9P94] 74-157956 1.95
1. Pyke, James Howell. I. Title.

†RANKIN, Molly K. 266'.7'3
I heard singing / by Molly K. Rankin. Mountain View, Calif. : Pacific Press Pub. Association, c1976. 125 p. ; 22 cm. (A Destiny book ; D151) [BV3680.N5R36] 74-27533 pbk. : 3.50
1. Seventh-Day Adventists—Missions. 2. Missions—New Guinea. I. Title.

WHITWELL, Nevada (Miller) 1904- 266.73
At home and abroad; youth worship programs. Cincinnati, Standard Pub. Co. [1952] 216 p. illus. 22 cm. [BV29.W5] 52-27704
1. Worship programs. 2. Young people's meetings (Church work) I. Title.

ROBINSON, Louise A. 266.751
The Chinese in dispersion; Methodism's role, by Louise A. Robinson [and] Frank C. [i.e. T.] Cartwright. Edited by Dorothy McConnell. New York, Joint Section of Education and Cultivation, Board of Missions of the Methodist Church [c1962] 78 p. 19 cm. [BV3300.R65] 62-17537
1. Missions — Asia, Southeastern — To Chinese. 2. Methodist Church — Missions. I. Cartwright, Frank Thomas, 1884- joint author. II. Title.

METHODIST Church (United States) Board of Missions and Church Extension. Division of Foreign Missions. 266.76
Report of the executive secretary ... to the annual meeting. New York. v. 28 cm. [BV2550.A15A4] 50-26326
1. Methodist Church — Missions. I. Title.

METHODIST Church (United States) Board of Missions and Church Extension. Division of Home Missions and Church Extension. 266.76
Mid-century report. [Buck Hill Falls? Pa., 1950?] 241 p. illus., ports. 23 cm. [BV2766.M65] 51-36021
1. Methodist Church — Missions. I. Title.

MURPHY, Bonneau Pernell, 1909- 266.76
The call for new Churches. With an introd. by Bishop Paul Neff Garber. New York, Editoral Dept., joint section of Educatiion and Cultivation, board of Missions of the Methodist Church [1961] Includes bibliography. [BV2766.M7M8] 61-14100
1. Methodist Church (United States)—Missions. 2. Missions, Home. I. Title.

SPRINKLE, Henry Call. 266.76
Spanish doorways; American Methodists and the evangelical mission among Spanish-speaking neighbors. A symposium by Henry C. Sprinkle [and others. 1st ed.] New York, World Outlook Press [1964] 125 p. illus. 19 cm. Contents.Contents. -- Spanish doorways, by H. C. Sprinkle. -- In Santo Domingo, by C. Parkin. -- In Puerto Rico, by J. N. Cintron. -- In the great Southwest, by C. W. Lokey. -- In the American cities, by E. V. May. -- In the local church, by A. B. Rice. [BV2788.L3S6] 64-19520
1. Missions to Spanish-Americans in the U.S. 2. Missions — Latin America. 3. Methodist Church — Missions. I. Title.

TATUM, Noreen (Dunn) 266.76
A crown of service; a story of woman's work in the Methodist Episcopal Church, South, from 1878-1940. Nashville, Parthenon Press, [1960] 418 p. illus. 24 cm. [BV2766.M7T3] 60-34866
1. Methodist Episcopal Church, South. Woman's Missionary Council. 2. Women in church work. 3. Methodist Episcopal Church, South — Missions. I. Title.

WENGATZ, John Christian, 1880- 266.76
Songs in the jungles; forty years in the "white man's grave" and still alive. [Marion, Ind., Wesley Press, 1962] 174 p. illus. 22 cm. [BV3505.W4A3] 62-53677
1. Missions — Africa. 2. Methodist Church — Missions. I. Title.

SCHERER, Frances Schlosser, 1912- 266'.7'60922 B
George and Mary Schlosser : ambassadors for Christ in China / by Frances Schlosser Scherer. Winona Lake, Ind. : Light and Life Press, c1976. xiv, 189 p. : ill. ; 21 cm. [BX8419.S35S34] 76-371953 3.95
1. Schlosser, George, 1875-1936. 2. Schlosser, Mary, 1885-1955. 3. Missionaries—United States—Biography. 4. Missionaries—China—Biography. I. Title: Ambassadors for Christ in China.

BRUMBAUGH, Thoburn Taylor, 1896- 266.7'6'0924 B
My marks and scars I carry; the story of Ernst Kisch, by Thoburn T. Brumbaugh. New York, Friendship Press [1969] 63 p. port. 19 cm. (Bold believers series) [BV3462.K58B75] 72-11334 1.50
1. Kisch, Ernst. I. Title.

GLENN, Layona, 1866- 266.7'6'0924 B
I remember, I remember [by] Layona Glenn with Charlotte Hale Smith. Old Tappan, N.J., F. H. Revell Co. [1969] 158 p. 21 cm. [BV2853.B7G55] 69-20145 3.95
1. Missions—Brazil. I. Smith, Charlotte Hale. II. Title.

GREENE, Ruth Altman, 1896- 266'.7'60924 B
Hsiang-Ya journal / by Ruth Altman Greene. Hamden, Conn. : Archon Books, 1977. xvi, 171 p. : map (on lining papers) ; 22 cm. Includes index. [R722.32.G73A34] 76-28526 ISBN 0-208-01614-7 : 10.00
1. Greene, Ruth Altman, 1896- 2. Hsiang Ya i hsueh yuan, Ch'ang-sha, China. 3. Missionaries' wives—China—Biography. 4. Missions, Medical—China. I. Title.
Distributed by Shoe String Press

GREENE, Ruth Altman, 1896- 266'.7'60924 B
Hsiang-Ya journal / by Ruth Altman Greene. Hamden, Conn. : Archon Books, 1977. xvi, 171 p. : map (on lining papers) ; 22 cm. Includes index. [R722.32.G73A34] 76-28526 ISBN 0-208-01614-7 : 10.00
1. Greene, Ruth Altman, 1896- 2. Hsiang Ya i hsueh yuan, Ch'ang-sha, China. 3. Missionaries' wives—China—Biography. 4. Missions, Medical—China. I. Title.
Distributed by Shoe String Press

LANE, Ortha May, 1894- 266.7'6'0924 B
Under marching orders in North China. [1st ed.] Tyler, Tex., Story-Wright [1971] iii, 276 p. illus., ports. 24 cm. Autobiographical. [BV3427.L325A3] 72-155433
1. Missions—China. 2. Methodist Church—Missions. I. Title.

MABUCE, Ethel, 1886- 266'.7'60924 B
I always wore my topi : the Burma letters of Ethel Mabuce, 1916-1921 / edited and with pref. and introductions by Lucille Griffith. University : University of Alabama Press, [1974] xiv, 336 p. : ill. ; 25 cm. Includes index. [BV3271.M23A4 1974] 73-16956 ISBN 0-8173-5861-7 : 10.00.
1. Mabuce, Ethel, 1886- 2. Missions—Burma. I. Title.

PALMER, Jim, 1929- 266.76'0924 B
Red poncho and big boots; the life of Murray Dickson. Nashville, Abingdon Press [1969] 224 p. port. 21 cm. [BV2853.B5D5] 70-84715 4.50
1. Dickson, Murray. 2. Missions—Bolivia. 3. Methodist Church—Missions. I. Title.

WILSON, Dorothy Clarke. 266.7'6'0924
Palace of healing; the story of Dr. Clara Swain, first woman missionary doctor, and the hospital she founded. [1st ed.] New York, McGraw-Hill [1968] x, 245 p. 22 cm. [R608.S92W5] 68-22771
1. Swain, Clara A., 1834-1910. 2. Clara Swain Hospital. I. Title.

MEEKER, Ruth Esther. 266'.7'6320973
Six decades of service, 1880-1940, a history of the Woman's Home Missionary Society of the Methodist Episcopal Church. [Cincinnati, Ohio, Steinhauser, 1969] v, 405 p. illus., ports. 28 cm. [BV2766.M7M39] 72-14691 4.95
1. Methodist Episcopal Church. Woman's Home Missionary Society. I. Title.

HARRISON, William Pope, 1830-1895. 266'.7'675
The Gospel among the slaves. A short account of missionary operations among the African slaves of the Southern States. Compiled from original sources and edited by W. P. Harrison. Nashville, Pub. House of the M.E. Church, South, 1893. [New York, AMS Press, 1973] 394 p. ports. 23 cm. [BV2783.H3 1973] 70-168249 ISBN 0-404-00263-3 15.50
1. Missions to Negroes—Southern States. 2. Negroes—Religion. I. Title.

SPOTTSWOOD, Curran L 266.76914
Beyond Cotabato. [Westwood, N.J., F. H. Revell Co. [1961] 256 p. 22 cm. [BV3380,S65] 61-5927
1. Missions — Phillippine Islands. I. Title.

SPOTTSWOOD, Curran L. 266.76914
Beyond Cotabato. [Westwood, N.J.] F. H. Revell Co, [c.1961] 256p.p3.50 half cloth, 61-5927
1. Missions—Philippine Islands. I. Title.

PRETYMAN, R. D. 266'.7'6946
A chronicle of Methodism in Van Diemen's Land 1820-1840, compiled by R. D. Pretyman. Melbourne, Aldersgate Press, 1970. 128 p. 22 cm. "Published to commemorate the sesquicentenary of Methodism in Tasmania, 1970." Bibliography: p. 123-128. [BV3660.T2P7] 70-579537 ISBN 0-85571-049-7
1. Missions—Tasmania. 2. Methodist Church—Missions. I. Title.

BENEATH the Southern 266.78
Cross; the story of an American bishop's wife in South Africa. [1st ed.] New York, Exposition Press [1955] 184p. 21cm. [BV3555.W7] 276.8 55-11138
1. Missions—Africa, South. 2. African Methodist Episcopal Church—Missions. I. Wright, Charlotte (Crogman)

EVANGELICAL Church. 266.79
Missionary Society.
Missions of the Evangelical Church; reports. Cleveland. v. illus., ports. 22 cm. annual. [BV2595.E8E8] 51-35681
1. Evangelical Church—Missions. I. Title.

ARCHIBALD, Frank E. 266'.7'92 B
Salute to Sid; the story of Dr. Sidney Gilchrist, by Frank E. Archibald. Windsor, N.S., Lancelot Press [1970] 127 p. illus., ports. 21 cm. [R464.G54A72] 73-177690 2.50
1. Gilchrist, Sidney. 2. Missions, Medical—Angola. I. Title.

*HASTINGS, Adrian 266.82
Mission; the church's number 1 problem: with study-club questions. Glen Rock, N.J., Paulist [c.1965] 62p. 18cm. (Insight ser.) .50 pap.,
1. Missions—Catholic Church. I. Title.

INSPIRATIONAL 266'.8'33
missionary stories / compiled by Leon R. Hartshorn. Salt Lake City : Deseret Book Co., 1976. ix, 206 p. ; 24 cm. Includes index. [BX8661.I57] 76-7300 ISBN 0-87747-588-1 : 5.95
1. Church of Jesus Christ of Latter-Day Saints—Missions. 2. Missionaries—Correspondence, reminiscences, etc. I. Hartshorn, Leon R.

SAUNDERS, Mary Ellen 266'.87'1
Hawk.
Unfinished business in China. Pacific Palisades, Calif., Pan Pacific Centers 1972, [i.e. 1973] xii, 238 p. illus. 20 cm. Bibliography: p. 234-238. [BV3427.H27S28] 73-163413 3.25
1. Hawk, John Chrisman. 2. Hawk, Jean Buchanan. I. Title.

PAULK, Earl P 266.899
Forward in faith sermons; sermons preached on the national radio broadcast 'Forward in faith.' [1st ed.] Cleveland, Tenn., Pathway Press, 1960. 275p. 23cm. [BX7034.Z6P3] 60-14174
1. Church of God (Cleveland, Tenn.)—Sermons. 2. Sermons, American. I. Forward in faith (Radio program) II. Title.

ASTON, Willard A 266.93
Teaching the gospel with prayer and testimony. [San Francisco? 1956] 255p. illus. 24cm. [BX8661.A8] 56-41460
1. Mormons and Mormonism—Missions. I. Title.

BABBEL, Frederick W. 266'.93
On wings of faith, by Frederick W. Babbel. Salt Lake City, Bookcraft, 1972. 195 p. 24 cm. [BX8695.B24A33] 72-88275 3.95
I. Title.

BUTLER, Florence G. 266.93
The art of being a member missionary, by Florence G. Butler. Salt Lake City, Deseret Book Co., 1968. xii, 108 p. 20 cm. Includes bibliographies. [BX8661.B8] 68-25347
1. Mormons and Mormonism—Missions. I. Title.

DAYNES, Robert W 266.9'3
Missionary helps, by Robert W. Daynes. Salt Lake City, Bookcraft [1967] 59 p. 21 cm. [BX8661.D3] 67-17927
1. Mormons and Mormonism — Missions. 2. Evangelistic work. I. Title.

DAYNES, Robert W. 266.9'3
Missionary helps, by Robert W. Daynes. Salt.Lake City, Bookcraft [1967] 59p. 21cm. [BX8661.D3] 67-17927 price unreported
1. Mormons and Mormonism—Missions. 2. Evangelistic work. I. Title.

DYER, Alvin R. 266.93
The challenge. [Salt Lake City] Deseret [1963, c.1962] 216p. 24cm. 63-880 2.75
1. Mormons and Mormonism—Missions. I. Title.

JACOBS, Barbara Tietjen. 266.93
So you're going on a mission! Provo, Utah, Press Pub. Co. [1968] 392 p. illus. 24 cm. [BX8661.J25] 68-3225
1. Mormons and Mormonism—Missions. I. Title.

NIBLEY, Preston, 266'.9'30922 B
comp.
Missionary experiences / compiled under the direction of the Presiding Bishopric for the youth of the church by Preston Nibley. Salt Lake City : Bookcraft, c1975. 320 p. ; 24 cm. [BX8661.N5 1975] 75-327696 4.95
1. Mormons and Mormonism—Missions. I. Title.

GIBBONS, Helen Bay 266.930924
Saint and savage. Salt Lake City, Deseret, 1965. xii, 249p. illus., map, ports. 24cm. Bibl. [E78.S7G32] 65-25452 price unreported
1. Gibbons, Andrew Smith, 1825-1886. 2. Indians of North America—Missions. 3. Indians of North America—Southwest, New. 4. Mormons and Mormonism—Missions. 5. Mormons and Mormonism in the Southwest, New. I. Title.

BROWN, Thomas 266'.9'309701
Dunlop, 1807-1874.
Journal of the Southern Indian Mission; diary of Thomas D. Brown. Edited by Juanita Brooks. Logan, Utah State University Press [1972] xx, 175 p. port. 23 cm. (Western Text Society [series], no. 4) Includes bibliographical references. [E78.U55B7 1972] 74-182832 ISBN 0-87421-047-X
1. Indians of North America—Utah—Missions. 2. Mormons and Mormonism—Missions. I. Brooks, Juanita, 1898- II. Title. III. Series: Western Text Society. Western Text Society series, no. 4.

ZOBELL, Albert L [266.93] 289.348
Under the midnight sun; centennial history of Scandinavian missions. Salt Lake City, Deseret Book Co., 1950. viii, 197 p. illus., port. 23 cm. [BX8617.S3Z6] 50-29209
1. Mormons and Mormonism in Scandinavia. 2. Mormons and Mormonism — Missions. I. Title.

DUNN, Loren C. 266'.9'33
Prepare now to succeed on your mission / Loren C. Dunn. Salt Lake City : Bookcraft, c1976. x, 78 p. ; 24 cm. Includes index. [BX8661.D85] 76-50447 ISBN 0-88494-313-5 : 3.50
1. Church of Jesus Christ of Latter-Day Saints—Missions. 2. Missionaries—Appointment, call, and election. I. Title.

LOVING, Albert L., 266'.9'33 B
1891-
When I put out to sea : autobiography of Albert L. Loving. Independence, Mo. : Herald Pub. House, c1975. 216 p. ; 21 cm. [BX8678.L68A33] 74-82510 ISBN 0-8309-0124-8
1. Loving, Albert L., 1891- I. Title.

PALMER, Spencer J. 266.9'3'5
The church encounters Asia, by Spencer J. Palmer. Salt Lake City, Deseret Book Co., 1970. 201 p. illus., map, ports. 24 cm. Includes bibliographical references. [BV3151.P27] 75-130322 ISBN 0-87747-365-X
1. Church of Jesus Christ of Latter-Day Saints—Missions. 2. Missions—Asia. I. Title.

HATCH, William 266.9'3'75
Whitridge.
There is no law; a history of Mormon civil relations in the Southern States, 1865-1905. [1st ed.] New York, Vantage Press [1968] 133 p. illus., ports. 21 cm. Bibliography: p. 129-133. [BX8661.H3] 78-3018 4.50
1. Mormons and mormonism—Missions. 2. Missions—Southern States—History. 3. Polygamy. I. Title.

HAMBLIN, Jacob, 266.93'792 B
1819-1886.
Jacob Hamblin, a narrative of his personal experience, as a frontiersman, missionary to the Indians and explorer, disclosing interpositions of Providence, severe privations, perilous situations and remarkable escapes, by James A. Little. Freeport, N.Y., Books for Libraries Press [1971] 140 p. 23 cm. Reprint of the 1881 ed. [F826.H19 1971] 72-164615 ISBN 0-8369-5899-3
1. Frontier and pioneer life—Utah. 2. Mormons and Mormonism. 3. Indians of North America—Utah. I. Little, James A.

BUTTERWORTH, F. Edward. 266.9396
The adventures of John Hawkins, Restoration pioneer. Illustrated by Aleah G. Koury. Independence, Mo., Herald House [1963] 264 p. illus. 21 cm. [BV3678.6.H3B8] 63-13244
1. Hawkins, John, b. ca. 1817. 2. Missions—Polynesia. 3. Reorganized Church of Jesus Christ of Latter Day Siants—Missions. I. Title.

BUTTERWORTH, F. Edward 266.9396
The adventures of John Hawkins, Restoration pioneer. illus. by Aleah G. Koury. Independence, Mo., Herald House [c.1963] 264p. illus. 21cm. 63-13244 3.25
1. Hawkins, John, b. ca. 1817. 2. Missions—Polynesia. 3. Reorganized Church of Jesus of Christ of Latter Day Saints—Missions. I. Title.

EMERSON, Elizabeth 266'.96'0924 B
Holaday.
Emory J. Rees language pioneer; a biographical sketch, by Elizabeth H. Emerson. [Gowanda, N.Y., Niagara Frontier Pub. Co., 1958] 25 p. 23 cm. Includes bibliographical references. [BV3625.K42R433] 74-156675
1. Rees, Emory J., 1870-1947. 2. Logooli language. I. Title.

HADLEY, Martha E., 266.9'6'0924 B
1852-1915.
The Alaskan diary of a pioneer Quaker missionary. [Mt. Dora, Fla., Loren S. Hadley, 1969] 210 p. illus., facsims., fold. map, ports. 28 cm. Cover title. [BV2803.A4H26 1969] 73-12622 3.75
1. Friends, Society of—Missions. 2. Missions—Alaska. I. Title.

FRIENDS, Society of. 266'.9'6748
London Yearly Meeting. Meeting for Sufferings. Aborigines' Committee.
Some account of the conduct of the Religious Society of Friends towards the Indian tribes in the settlement of the colonies of East and West Jersey and Pennsylvania: with a brief narrative of their labours for the civilization and Christian instruction of the Indians, from the time of their settlement in America, to the year 1843. With a new series introd. by Sidney Forman. Boston, Gregg Press, 1973. p. (History of minority education) Reprint of the 1844 ed., which was issued as no. 9 of the series: Publications relative to the aborigines. [E78.N6F74 1973] 73-1788 ISBN 0-8398-1890-4
1. Friends, Society of—Missions. 2. Indians of North America—New Jersey. 3. Indians of North America—Pennsylvania. I. Title. II. Series. III. Series: Tracts relative to the aborigines, no. 9.

HIBBS, Iverna. 266'.9'684
From one to multiplication : Oregon Yearly Meeting in Bolivia, 1919-1962 / by Iverna Hibbs. [s.l.] : Hibbs, [1976, c1975] 177 p. : ill. ; 29 cm. Includes bibliographical references. [F2230.2.A9H52 1976] 76-362975
1. Friends, Society of. Oregon Yearly Meeting. 2. Aymara Indians—Missions. 3. Missions—Bolivia. I. Title.

BEILER, Edna. 266.97
Flying high Children's mission study Illustrated by Charles F. Ellis. Scottdale, Pa., Herald Press [1965] 96. L-30 p. illus., maps. 22 cm. "Leader's guide": 30 p. bound in. Includes music. [BV2090.5.B4] 65-22101
1. Missions — Juvenile literature. 2. Missions — Study and teaching (Elementary) I. Title.

CHURCH in mission (The); 266.97
a sixtieth anniversary tribute to J. B. Toews. Ed. by A. J. Klassen. Fresno, Calif., Bd. of Christian Lit., Mennonite Brethren Church [1967] xvi, 417p. 23cm. Bibl. [BV2070.C45] 67-27337 4.50
1. Missions—Addresses, essays, lectures. 2. Mennonite Brethren Church of North America—Missions. I. Toews, J. B. II. Klassen, A. J. ed.

EASTWARD to th e sun. 266.97
Scottdale, Pa., Herald Press [c1953] 220p. illus. 20cm. [BV3265.Y66] 275.4 53-7587
1. Missions—India. 2. Mennonitics—Missions. I. Yoder, Sanford Calgin, Bp., 1879-

ERB, Paul, 1894- 266.97
Our neighbors South and North; a textbook for the study of Mennonite missions on the perimeter of North America. Illustrated by Jan Gleysteen. Scottdale, Pa., Herald Press [1965] 130 p. illus., maps. 20 cm. Leader's guide. Scottdale, Pa., Herald Press [1965] [BV2545.E7] 65-18236
I. Title.

ESHLEMAN, Merle W, 1908- [266.97]
Africa answers. Scottdale, Pa., Mennonite Pub. House, 1951. 179 p. illus. 20 cm. [BV3625.T3E8] 276.78 52-16769
1. Missions—Tanganyika Territory. 2. Mennonites—Missions. I. Title.

GRABER, Joseph Daniel, 266.97
1900-
The church apostolic; adiscussion of modern missions. Scottdale, Pa., Herald Press [c.1960] 137p. (The Conrad Grebel lectures, 1959) Bibl. notes: p.133-135. 60-14171 3.00 bds.,
1. Missions—Theory. 2. Mennonites—Missions. I. Title.

MCCAMMON, Dorothy Snapp, 266.97
1923-
We tried to stay. Scottdale, Pa., Herald Press [1953] 208p. illus. 21cm. Autobiographical. [BV3427.M2A3] [BV3427.M2A3] 275.1 53-1473 53-1473
1. Missions—China. 2. Monnonites—Missions. I. Title.

PANNABECKER, S F ed. 266.97
The Christian mission of the General Conference Mennonite Church. Newton, Kan., Faith and Life Press [1961] 80p. illus., port. 28cm. Bibliography:p. 79-80. [BV2545.P3] 61-2471
1. General Conference Mennonite Church—Missions. I. Title.

SHENK, Wilbert R 266.97
A kingdom of priests; the church in the new nations. Wilbert R. Shenk, editor. Newton, Kan., Faith and Life Press [1967] 144 p. illus. 20 cm. Bibliographical footnotes. [BV2545.S45] 67-23292
1. Mennonite Church—Missions. I. Title.

TOEWS, J. B. 266.97
The Church in mission; a sixtieth anniversary tribute to J. B. Toews. Edited by A. J. Klassen. Fresno, Calif., Board of Christian Literature, Mennonite Brethren Church [1967] xvi, 417 p. 23 cm. Includes bibliographies. [BV2070.C45] 67-27337
1. Missions—Addresses, essays, lectures. 2. Mennonite Brethren Church of North America—Missions. I. Klassen, A. J. ed. II. Title.
-Contents omitted

WENGER, A. Grace. 266.97
God leads us to witness at home, a resource book for the study of Mennonite home missions. Scottdale, Pa., Herald Press [1960] 135 p. illus. 20 cm. Includes bibliography. [BV2545.W4] 60-15707
1. Mennonites — Missions. I. Title.

WENGER, A. Grace 266.97
God leads us to witness at home, a resource book for the study of Mennonite home missions. Scottdale, Pa., Herald pr. [c.1960] 135p. illus Bibl. 60-15707 1.50 pap.,
1. Mennonites—Missions. I. Title.

KRAYBILL, Paul N ed. 266.97082
Called to be sent; essays in honor of the fiftieth anniversary of the founding of the Eastern Mennonite Board of Missions and Charities, 1914-1964. Edited by Paul N. Kraybill. Scottdale, Pa., Herald Press [1964] 238 p. illus., ports, 20 cm. On cover: Called to be sent; fifty years in mission. [BV2545.A385] 64-20136
1. Mennonite Church. Conferences. Lancaster. Eastern Mennonite Board of Missions and Charities. 2. Mennonites — Missions. I. Title. II. Title: Fifty years in mission.

KRAYBILL, Paul N., ed. 266.97082
Called to be sent; essays in honor of the fiftieth anniv. of the founding of the Eastern Mennonite Bd. of Missions and Charities, 1914-1964. Scottdale, Pa., Harald Pr. [c.1964] 238p. illus., ports. 20cm. On cover: Called to be sent fifty years in mission. Bibl. 64-20136 2.95 1.95 pap.,
1. Mennonite Church. Conferences. Lancaster. Eastern Mennonite Board of Missions and Charities. 2. Mennonites—Missions. I. Title. II. Title: Fifty years in mission.

EBY, Omar, 1935- 266.97'0924 B
A whisper in a dry land; a biography of Merlin Grove, martyr for Muslims in Somalia. Scottdale, Pa., Herald Press [1968] 174 p. illus. 21 cm. [BV3625.S62G7] 68-12027
1. Grove, Merlin, 1929-1962. 2. Missions—Somalia. I. Title.

KEIDEL, Levi O. 266'.9'70924 B
War to be one / Levi O. Keidel. Grand Rapids : Zondervan Pub. House, c1977. 239 p. : ill. ; 22 cm. [BV3625.C6K4] 77-6302 ISBN 0-310-35370-X : 7.95 ISBN 0-310-35371-8 pbk. : 4.95
1. Missions—Zaire. 2. Mennonites—Missions. 3. Zaire—History—Civil War, 1960-1965. I. Title.

KEIDEL, Levi O. 266'.9'70924 B
War to be one / Levi O. Keidel. Grand Rapids : Zondervan Pub. House, c1977. 239 p. : ill. ; 22 cm. [BV3625.C6K4] 77-6302 ISBN 0-310-35370-X : 7.95 ISBN 0-310-35371-8 pbk. : 4.95
1. Missions—Zaire. 2. Mennonites—Missions. 3. Zaire—History—Civil War, 1960-1965. I. Title.

WENGER, A Grace. 266.975
God builds the church in South Asia; a resource book for the study of Mennonite missions in South Asia. Illustrated by Jan Gleysteen. Scottdale, Pa., Herald Press [1963] 160 p. illus., 20 cm. [BV3250.W4] 63-17082
1. Missions — South Asia. 2. Mennonites — Missions. I. Title.

WENGER, A. Grace 266.975
God builds the church in South Asia; a resource book for the study of Mennonite missions in South Asia. Illus. by Jan Gleysteen. Scottdale, Pa., Herald [c.1963] 160p. illus. 20cm. 63-17082 1.00 pap.,
1. Missions—South Asia. 2. Mennonites—Missions. I. Title.

KAUFMAN, James Norman, 1880- 266.9754
Walk and Talk in Hindustan. Goshen, Ind., 901 Mervin Ave Author, [c.1963] ix, 173p. illus., ports., map, facsims. 21cm. Memoirs. 63-21175 price unreported
1. Mennonites in India. 2. Missions—India. I. Title.

KAUFMAN, James Norman, 1880- 266.9754
Walks and talks in Hindustan. Goshen, Ind. [c1963] ix, 173 p. illus., ports., map, facsims. 21 cm. Memoirs. [BV3269.K3A3] 63-21175
1. Mennonites in India. 2. Missions — India. I. Title.

LAPP, John Allen. 266'.9'754
The Mennonite Church in India, 1897-1962. Scottdale, Pa., Herald Press [1972] 278 p. illus. 23 cm. (Studies in Anabaptist and Mennonite history, 14) Bibliography: p. [258]-272. [BX8119.I52L36] 73-186445 ISBN 0-8361-1122-2 8.95
1. Mennonite Church—Missions. 2. Mennonites in India. 3. Missions—India. I. Title. II. Series.

CONFERENCE Board of the Associated Research Councils. Committee on International Exchange of Persons. 266'.97'6
United States Government grants under the Fulbright act ... Australia, Burma, Ceylon, India, New Zealand Philippines, Thailand, Union of South Africa. Washington. v. 23cm. annual. [LB2285.U6C64] 55-20203
1. Teachers, Interchange of—U. S. I. Title.

CONFERENCE Board of the Associated Research Councils. Committee on International Exchange of Persons. 266'.97'6
U. S. Government awards under the Fulbright and Smith-Mundt acts. Europe, the Near East, Japan, Pakistan, Latin America, other areas. Washington. v. 22cm. annual. Title varies slightly. [LB2285.U6C63] 55-18791
1. Educational exchanges—U.S. I. Title.

EBY, Omar, 1935- 266'.97'6
How full the river. Scottdale, Pa., Herald Press [1972] 159 p. illus. 21 cm. [LB2285.A35E26] 70-181578 ISBN 0-8361-1617-8
1. American teachers in Africa. I. Title.

INTERNATIONAL Research Associates. 266'.97'6
The effectiveness of the exchange program; Africa; a study in seven African countries. Prepared for the U.S. Advisory Commission on International Educational and Cultural Affairs. New York, 1963. 1 v. (various pagings) 29 cm. [LB2285.U6I55] 63-62088
1. Educational exchanges — U.S. 2. Educational exchanges — Africa. I. U.S. Advisory Commission on International Educational and Cultural Affairs. II. Title.

INTERNATIONAL Research Associates. 266'.97'6
The effectiveness of the exchange program: Europe; a study in three European countries. Prepared for the U.S. Advisory Commission on International Educational and Cultural Affairs. New York, 1963. 1 v. (various pagings) 29 cm. [LB2285.U6I553] 63-61906
1. Educational exchanges — U.S. 2. Educational exchanges — Europe. I. U.S. Advisory Commission on International Educational and Cultural Affairs. II. Title.

INTERNATIONAL Research Associates. 266'.97'6
The effectiveness of the exchange program: the Far East; a study in three Far Eastern countries. Prepared for the U.S. Advisory Commission on International Educational and cultural Affairs. New York, 1963. 1 v. (various pagings) 29 cm. [LB2285.U6I557] 63-62090
1. Educational exchanges — U.S. 2. Educational exchanges — East (Far East) I. U.S. Advisory Commission on International Educational and Cultural Affairs. II. Title.

INTERNATIONAL Research Associates. 266'.97'6
The effectiveness of the exchange program; a study in twenty countries in all regions of the world. Prepared for the U.S. Advisory Commission on International Educational and Cultural Affairs. New York, 1962. 2 v. in 3. 28 cm. Appendix D. Publication by grantees, included in v. 2, pt. 2. [LB2285.U6I54] 63-62156
1. Educational exchanges — U.S. I. U.S. Advisory Commission on International Educational and Cultural Affairs. II. Title.

INTERNATIONAL Research Associates. 266'.97'6
The effectiveness of the exchange program: the Near East; a study in two Near Eastern countries. Prepared for the U.S. Advisory Commission on International Educational and Cultural Affairs. New York, 1963. 1 v. (various pagings) 29 cm. [LB2285.U6I559] 63-61861
1. Educational exchanges — U.S. 2. Educational exchanges — India. 3. Educational exchanges — Turkey. I. U.S. Advisory Commission on International Educational and Cultural Affairs. II. Title.

INTERNATIONAL Research Associates. 266'.97'6
The effectiveness of the exchange program: Latin America; a study in five Latin American countries. Prepared for the U.S. Advisory Commission on International Educational and Cultural Affairs. New York, 1963. 1 v. (various pagings) 29 cm. [LB2285.U6I555] 63-62084
1. Educational exchanges — U.S. 2. Educational exchanges — South America. 3. Educational exchanges — Guatemala. I. U.S. Advisory Commission on International Educational and Cultural Affairs. II. Title.

TENNESSEE. University. Field Unit in Panama. 266'.97'6
Assistance in higher education in Panama, October, 1962-March, 1963. Knoxville, University of Tennessee, 1964. 120 l. 28 cm. "Report to the Agency for International Development." [LB2285.P3T4] 64-64038
1. Educational assistance, American — Panama. I. U.S. Agency for International Development. II. Title.

WEAVER, Edwin, 1903- 266.9'7'6694
The Uyo story, by Edwin and Irene Weaver. Elkhart, Ind., Mennonite Board of Missions, 1970. 127 p. illus., group ports. 22 cm. An abridged version appeared in Gospel herald in 1963. [BV3625.N5W4] 70-261985
1. Missions—Uyo, Nigeria. 2. Mennonites—Missions. I. Weaver, Irene, joint author. II. Title.

EBY, Omar, 1935- 266.976773
Sense and incense. Scottdale, Pa., Herald Pr. [c.1965] 160p. illus., map, ports. 20cm. [BV3625.S62E2] 65-11461 3.00
1. Missions—Somalia. I. Title.

SHENK, David W., 1937- 266'.9'7678
Mennonite safari [by] David W. Shenk. Scottdale, Pa., Herald Press [1974] 135 p. illus. 18 cm. [BV3625.T4S48] 73-21150 ISBN 0-8361-1733-6 1.50 (pbk.)
1. Kanisa la Mennonite, Tanzania. 2. Missions—Tanzania. 3. Mennonites—Missions. I. Title.

LINSCHEID, Ruth C., 1903- 266'.97'78
Red Moon, by Ruth C. Linscheid. [Newton, Kan., Printed by United Printing, 1973] vii, 199 p. illus. 21 cm. Bibliography: p. 198-199. [E99.C53L545] 73-84583
1. Kliewer, Henry J., 1871-1943. 2. Mennonite Church—Missions. 3. Cheyenne Indians—Missions. I. Title.

WENGER, A. Grace. 266.978
God builds the church in Latin America; a resource book for the study of Mennonite missions in Central and South America. Illustrated by Jan Gleysteen. Scottdale, Pa., Herald Press [1961] 142 p. illus. 20 cm. Includes bibliography. [BV2831.W4] 61-14722
1. Missions — Spanish America. 2. Mennonites — Missions. I. Title.

COX, Emmett D. 266.9'9
The Church of the United Brethren in Christ in Sierra Leone [by] Emmett D. Cox. South Pasadena, Calif., William Carey Library [1970] xi, 171 p. illus., maps. 23 cm. Bibliography: p. 166-171. [BV3625.S4C66] 75-126076 ISBN 0-87808-301-4 2.95
1. Church of the United Brethren in Christ (Old constitution)—Missions. 2. Missions—Sierra Leone. 3. Church growth. I. Title.

CUMMINGS, Marjorie J. 266.9'9
Sunrise furlough, by Marjorie J. Cummings. Philadelphia, Dorrance [1969] 183 p. 22 cm. [BV3317.J6C8] 68-54697 4.00
1. Johnson, Paul Leroy, 1923-1952. 2. Missions—Thailand. I. Title.

DONOVAN, Robert O. 266'.99 B
Her door of faith, by Robert O. Donovan. Honolulu, Orovan Books [1971] 112 p. illus. 23 cm. [BV3680.H4B763] 79-172385
1. Brostek, Mildred Johnson. I. Title. II. Title: Door of faith.

DOWDY, Homer E. 266.99
Christ's witchdoctor: from savage sorcerer to jungle missionary. [1st ed.] New York, Harper & Row [1963] 241 p. illus. 22 cm. [BV2853.B9E43] 63-7602
1. Elka, chief of the Wai Wai. 2. Missions—British Guiana. I. Title.

HAITI diary; 266.99
the intimate story of a modern young missionary couple's first two years in a foreign country. Compiled from the letters of Paul Orjala and edited by Kathleen Spell. Kansas City, Mo., Beacon Hill Press [1953] 125p. 19cm. [BV2848.H3O7] [BV2848.H3O7] 277.294 53-10699 53-10699
1. Missions—Haiti. 2. Missionaries, American—Correspondence, reminiscences, etc. 3. Church of the Nazarene—Haiti. I. Orjala, Paul.

HARLOW, Robert Edward. 1908- 266.99
Who is my neighbor? Assmbly missionaries in Latin America [by] R. E. Harlow [and] John Smart. New York, The Fields, Inc. [1960] 71p. illus. 19cm. Includes bibliography. [BV2831.H3] 60-50905
1. Missions—Spanish America. 2. Assemblies of God, General Council—Missions. I. Smart, John, 1906- joint author. II. Title.

HODGES, Serena M ed. 266.99
Look on the fields; a missionary survey. Data supplied by Assemblies of God missionaries. Springfield, Mo., Gospel Pub. House [c1956] 201p. illus. 20cm. [BV2595.A8H6] 57-834
1. Assemblies of God, General Council—Missions. I. Title.

HUNTER, James Hogg, 1890- 266.99
Beside all waters; the story of seventy-five years of world-wide minstry:the Christian and Missionary Alliance. Introd. by Nathan Bailey. Harrisburg, Pa., 1522 N. Third St. Christian Pubns., [1964] 245p. illus., maps (on lining papers) ports. 22cm. 64-21944 price unreported
1. Christian and Missionary Alliance—Missions. I. Title.

LARSON, Melvin Gunnard, 1916- 266.9'9
114 ways to the mission field; testimonies of Evangelical Free Church missionaries [by] Mel Larson. Minneapolis, Free Church Publications [1967] 256 p. 21 cm. [BV3700.L24] 67-9458
1. Missionaries, American. 2. Evangelical Free Church of America — Missions. I. Title.

LARSON, Melvin Gunnard, 1916- 266.9'9
114 ways to the mission field; testimonies of evangelical free church missionaries [by] Mel Larson. Minneapolis, Free Church Pubns. [1967] 256p. 21cm. [BV3700.L24] 67-9458 3.95, 2.50 pap.,
1. Missionaries, American. 2. Evangelical Free Church of America—Missions. I. Title.
Publisher's address: 1515 East 66th St., Minneapolis, Minn. 55423.

*MORRISON, Lavada R. 266.99
Where there is no vision. New York, Carlton [c.1965] 176p. illus. 21cm. (Reflection bk.) 3.50
I. Title.

PERKIN, Noel. 266.99
Our world witness; a survey of Assemblies of God foreign missions by Noel Perkin and John Garlock. Springfield, Mo, Gospel Pb. uHouse [1963] 118 p. diagr. 20 cm. Bibliography: p. 117-118. [BV2595.A8P4] 64-153
1. Assemblies of God, General Council—Missions. I. Garlock, John joint author. II. Title.

REEDER, Hilda. 266.99
A brief history of the Foreign Missionary Department of the Pentecostal Assemblies of the World. [Indianapolis?] Foreign Missionary Dept. [1951] 76 p. illus., ports. 20 cm. [BV2595.P4R4] 51-40440
1. Pentecostal Assemblies of the World. Foreign Missionary Dept. I. Title.

SANDERS, Raymond Ira, 1917-1951. 266.99
Meet the Mossi. [Prepared and edited by Ruby M. Enyart. Memorial ed.] Springfield, Mo., Gospel Pub. House [1953] 103p. illus. 16cm. [BV3625.U72S3 1953] [BV3625.U72S3 1953] 276.625 53-30051 53-30051
1. Missions—Upper Volta. 2. Assemblies of God, General Council—Missions. I. Title.

SCHAEFFER, Sue. 266.9'9 B
Africa is waiting. Grand Rapids, Mich., Baker Book House [1970] 169 p. illus., ports. 22 cm. [BV3625.S352B87] 73-109215 3.95
1. Butler, Talmage, 1928- I. Title.

SPANGENBERG, Alice. 266.99
The Master says, 'Go.' [Kansas City, Mo., Beacon Hill Press, 1955] 144p. 20cm. [BV2595] 55-2163
1. Church of the Nazarene— Missions. I. Title.

TAYLOR, Mendell. 266.99
Fifty years of Nazarene missions. Kansas City, Mo., Beacon Hill Press [1952- v. 23cm. Contents.v. 1. Administration and promotion. [BV2595.C6T3] 54-1307
1. Church of the Nazarene— Missions. I. Title.

TEMPLE, Helen Frances. 266.99
I will build my church; stories about Christians who, under God, made lasting contributions to the cause of foreign missions. Kansas City, Mo., Beacon Hill Press [1955] 96p. 19cm. [BV2595] 55-2197
1. Church of the Nazarene—Missions. I. Title.

TUCKER, Angeline. 266.99 (B)
He is in heaven. [1st ed.] New York, McGraw-Hill [1965] 226 p. illus., maps, parts. 22 cm. [BV3625.C63T8] 65-25521
1. Tucker, J. W., d. 1964. 2. Stanleyville, Congo — Massacre, 1964. 3. Missions — Congo (Leopoldville) I. Title.

TUCKER, Angeline 266.99
He is in heaven. New York, McGraw [c.1965] 226p. illus., maps, parts. 22cm. [BV3625.C63T8] 65-25521 4.95 bds.,
1. Tucker, J. W., d. 1964. 2. Stanleyville, Congo—Massacre, 1964. 3. Missions—Congo (Leopoldville) I. Title.

WILSON, Elizabeth A Galley. 266.99
Making many rich. Springfield, Mo., Gospel Pub. House [c1955] 257p. illus. 20cm. [BV3500.W5] 276 57-20882
1. Missions, Africa. 2. Assemblies of God, General Council—Missions. I. Title.

WILSON, Thomas Ernest, 1902- 266'.99
Angola beloved, by T. Ernest Wilson. Sketches by J. Boyd Nicholson [1st ed.] Neptune, N. J., Loizeaux Bros. [1967] 254 p. illus. maps (on lining papers) 21 cm. Bibliography: p. 246-247. [BV3625.A6W5] 67-31008
1. Missions—Angola I. Title.

WILSON, Thomas Ernest, 1902- 266'.99
Angola beloved, by T. Ernest Wilson. Sketches by J. Boyd Nicholson. [1st ed.] Neptune, N.J., Loizeaux Bros. [1967] 254 p. illus., maps (on lining papers) 21 cm. Bibliography: p. 246-247. [BV3625.A6W5] 67-31008
1. Missions—Angola. I. Title.

267 Associations For Religious Work

ELY, Virginia, 1899- 267
A book of installation services. [Westwood, N. J.] F. H. Revell Co. [1954] 208 p. 22 cm. [BV199.I 5E4] 54-8000
1. Installation service (Church officers)

FREEMAN, Margaret N. 267
Twelve devotional programs for women's meetings. Chicago, Moody [c.1963] 93 p. 22cm. 1.35, pap., plastic bdg.
I. Title.

MELLIS, Charles J. 267
Committed communities : fresh streams for world missions / Charles J. Mellis. South Pasadena, Calif. : William Carey Library, c1976. xix, 138 p. ; 22 cm. Bibliography: p. 129-134. [BV4405.M44] 76-53548 ISBN 0-87808-426-6 pbk. : 3.95
1. Christian communities. 2. Missions. I. Title.

NATIONAL Council of the Churches of Christ in the United States of America. Dept. of Adult Work. 267
A manual for young adults; a guide to program planning for older youth and young adults in the church. [New York, Published for the Division of Christian Education, National Council of the Churches of Christ in the U. S. A., by the Office of Publication and Distribution, c1960] 64p. illus. 23cm. Includes bibliography. [BV4446.N3] 60-53134
1. Church work with young adults. I. Title.

NOVOTNY, Louise Miller 267
Walking the roads with Jesus: programs for women. Cincinnati, Standard Pub. [1963, c. 1962] 112p. 22cm. 1.95, pap., plastic bdg.
I. Title.

SAFFEN, Wayne. 267
Young married couples in the church; a resource book. St. Louis, Concordia Pub. House [c1963] 87 p. 21 cm. [BV4446.S3] 62-22032
1. Church group work with young adults. I. Title.

SAFFEN, Wayne 267
Young married couples in the church; a

resource book. St. Louis, Concordia [c.1963] 87p. 21cm. Bibl. 62-22032 1.25 pap.,
1. Church group work with young adults. I. Title.

*SMITH, Helen Heath 267
Church communications. New York, Vantage [c.1964] 73 p. 21 cm. 2.00
I. Title.

YOUNG Men's Christian Associations. National YMCA Young Adult Assembly. 267
The Y we want; report of the National YMCA Young Adult Assembly, Estes Park, Colorado, July 19-23, 1954. New York, Association Press [1954] 72p. illus. 22cm. [BV1165.A4 1954c] 3056
I. Title.

MACKIE, Robert C. 267.0924
Layman extraordinary: John R. Mott, 1865-1955, by Robert C. Mackie, others, Foreword by W. A. Visser't Hooft [New York] Association [1965] 127p. 18cm. [BV1085.M75M26] 65-27832 1.25 pap.,
1. Mott, John Raleigh 1865-1955. I. Title.

LOCKLEY, Andrew. 267'.094
Christian communes / [by] Andrew Lockley. London : S.C.M. Press, 1976. vii, 119 p. ; 22 cm. Includes bibliographical references and index. [BV4406.E85L6] 76-377647 ISBN 0-334-01927-3 pbk. : £2.25
1. Christian communities—Europe. I. Title.

ARNOLD, Emmy 267.1
Torches together [The beginning and early years of the Bruderhof Communities. Tr. from German at the Society of Brothers, Woodcrest. Woodcrest, Rifton, N.Y., Plough Pub. House, c.1964] 220 p. 21 cm. 63-23426 3.50
1. Bruderhof Communities. I. Title.

ARNOLD, Emmy. 267.1
Torches together. [The beginning and early years of the Burderhof Communities. Translated from the German at the Society of Brothers, Woodcrest. Woodcrest, Rifton, N.Y., Plough Pub. House, 1964] 220 p. 21 cm. [BX8129.B64A8] 63-23426
1. Bruderhof Communities. I. Title.

ARNOLD, Emmy. 267'.1
Torches together; the beginning and early years of the Bruderhof Communities. 2d ed. [Translated from the German by the Society of Brothers] Rifton, N.Y., Plough Pub. House [1971] 231 p. illus. 22 cm. [BX8129.B64A8 1971] 77-166341 ISBN 0-87486-109-8 4.95
1. Bruderhof Communities. I. Title.

CARTER, Isabel Ray, 1916- 267'.1
God and three shillings; the story of the Brotherhood of St. Laurence [by] I. R. Carter. [Melbourne] Lansdowne Press [1967] 173 p. illus. 22 cm. [BX5702.C3] 77-363168 3.25
1. Brotherhood of St. Laurence. I. Title.

BONNER, Arthur. 267'.1'097471
Jerry McAuley and his mission. Neptune, N. J., Loizeaux Bros. [1967] 123 p. illus., plans, ports. 27 cm. Bibliography: p. 120. [BV2657.M3B6] 67-31009
1. McAuley, Jeremiah, 1839-1884. 2. New York. McAuley Water Street Mission. I. Title.

BONNER, Arthur. 267'.1'097471
Jerry McAuley and his mission. Neptune, N.J., Loizeaux Bros. [1967] 123 p. illus., plans, ports. 27 cm. Bibliography: p. 120. [BV2657.M3B6] 67-31009
1. McAuley, Jeremiah, 1839-1884. 2. New York. McAuley Water Street Mission. I. Title.

ADAIR, James R., 1923- 267.10977311
The Old Lighthouse; the story of the Pacific Garden Mission, by James R. Adair. Chicago, Moody Press [1966] 157 p. 22 cm. [BV2656.C4P26] 66-9629
1. Pacific Garden Mission, Chicago. I. Title.

MCCREARY, Alf. 267'.13'0941612
Corrymeela : hill of harmony in Northern Ireland / Alf McCreary. New York : Hawthorn Books, 1976. ix, 116 p., [9] leaves of plates : ill. ; 22 cm. [BV4407.5.M3 1976] 75-41799 ISBN 0-8015-1773-7 : 6.95
1. Corrymeela community. I. Title.

SCHRAMM, John, 1931- 267'.13'09753
Dance in steps of change, by John Schramm and David Earle Anderson. Camden [N.J.] T. Nelson [1970] 119 p. illus. 21 cm. Bibliography: p. 114-115. [BX8076.W3C65] 72-127075 2.95
1. Community of Christ. I. Anderson, David Earle, joint author. II. Title.

HARRIS, William G 267.15
Stuff that makes an army. [New York] Salvation Army Supplies, Print. and Pub. Dept. [1962] 157 p. 23 cm. [BX9721.2H3] 62-21024
1. Salvation Army. I. Title.

HARRIS, William G. 267.15
Stuff that makes an army. [New York] 321 W. 13th St., Salvation Army Supplies. Print. and Pub. Dept., 1962] 157p. 23cm. 62-21024 1.95
1. Salvation Army. I. Title.

SEARCH, Pamela. 267.15
Happy warriors; the story of the social work of the Salvation Army. [1st ed.] London, New York, Arco Publishers [1956] 173p. illus. 23cm. [HV4337.S4] 56-3510
1. Salvation Army. I. Title.

SEARCH, Pamela. 267.15
Happy warriors: the story of the social work of the Salvation Army. [1st ed.] London, New York, Arco Publishers [1956] 173p. illus. 23cm. [HV4337.S4] 56-3510
1. Salvation Army. I. Title.

*STRACHAN, James 267.15 (B)
The Marechale. Foreword by Theodore Booth-Clibborn. Minneapolis. Minn., Bethany Fellowship [1966] xvi. 221p. port 19cm. price unreported. pap.,
1. Booth-Clibborn, Catherine (Booth) 1858-1955. 2. Salvation Army. I. Title.

WISBEY, Herbert Andrew, 1919- 267.15
Soldiers without swords; a history of the Salvation Army in the United States. New York, Macmillan, 1955. 242 p. illus. 22 cm. [BX9716.W5] 55-13783
1. Salvation Army—U.S. I. Title.

COLLIER, Richard, 1924- 267.1509
The general next to God; the story of William Booth and the Salvation Army. [1st ed.] New York, Dutton, 1965. 320 p. illus., ports. 22 cm. Bibliography: p. 293-310. [BX9743.B7C65 1965a] 65-11410
1. Booth, William, 1829-1912. 2. Salvation Army. I. Title.

NEAL, Harry Edward, 1906- 267.1509
The Hallelujah Army. Philadelphia, Chilton [c.1961] 261 p. illus. 61-16619 4.95
1. Salvation Army—Hist. I. Title.

SANDALL, Robert. 267'.15'09 s
Social reform and welfare work; 1883-1953 1883-1953. London, New York, T. Nelson, 1955. xiv, 369 p. illus. 23 cm. (His The History of the Salvation Army, v. 3) Bibliography: p. 361-364. [BX9715.S3 vol. 3] [BX9727.3] 361.7'5 74-171957
1. Salvation Army—Charities. I. Title. II. Series.

LAVINE, Sigmund A. 267.15'0924 B
Evangeline Booth; daughter of Salvation [by] Sigmund A. Lavine. New York, Dodd, Mead [1970] viii, 143 p. illus., facsim., ports. 22 cm. Bibliography: p. 139-140. A biography of the woman who, as head of the Salvation Army, brought practical assistance to many in need throughout the world. [BX9743.B63L38] 92 74-108044 4.00
1. Booth, Evangeline Cory, 1865-1950—Juvenile literature. I. Title.

LINNETT, Arthur. 267'.15'0924 B
Radiant rebel : the story of Ernst Schmidtke / by Arthur Linnett. London : Salvationist, 1976. 97 p. ; 19 cm. [BX9743.S3L56] 77-366233 ISBN 0-85412-292-3
1. Schmidtke, Ernst, 1908- 2. Salvationists—Germany—Biography. 3. Missionaries—China—Biography. 4. Missionaries—Germany—Biography. I. Title.

LUDWIG, Charles, 1918- 267'.15'0924
The lady general. Grand Rapids, Baker Book House, 1962. 93p. illus. 20cm. (Valor series, sBooth, Evangeline Cory, 1865-1950--Juvenile literature:. [BX9743.B63L8] 62-18416
I. Title.

ROBINSON, Virgil E. 267'.15'0924 B
William Booth and his Army / Virgil Robinson. Mountain View, Calif. : Pacific Press Pub. Association, c1976. 112 p. : ill. ; 22 cm. (A Destiny book ; D-163) [BX9743.B7R62] 75-25226 pbk. : 3.50
1. Booth, William, 1829-1912. 2. Salvation Army. 3. Salvationists—England—Biography. I. Title.

STRAHAN, James, 1863-1926. 267'.15'0924
The Marechale, by James Strachan. Foreword by Theodore Booth-Clibborn. Minneapolis, Bethany Fellowship [1966] 221 p. ports. 19 cm. "The cross and the glory, by Theodore Booth-Clibborn": p. 198-221. [BX9743.B8S8] 67-6260
1. Booth-Clibborn, Catherine, 1860-1955. I. Booth-Clibborn, Theodore. II. Title.

STRAHAN, James, 1863-1926. 267'.15'0924 B
The Marechale, by James Strachan. Foreword by Theodore Booth-Clibborn. Minneapolis, Bethany Fellowship [1966] 221 p. ports. 19 cm. "The cross and the glory, by Theodore Booth-Clibborn": p. 198-221. [BX9743.B8S8 1966] 67-6260
1. Booth-Clibborn, Catherine, 1860-1955. I. Booth-Clibborn, Theodore. II. Title.

BOOTH Tucker, Frederick St. George de Lautour, 1853-1929. 267'.15'0973
The Salvation Army in America; selected reports, 1899-1903. New York, Arno Press, 1972. 983-1005, [85], 37, 32 p. illus. 24 cm. (Religion in America, series II) Contents.Contents.—Farm colonies of the Salvation Army [first published in 1903]—The Salvation Army in the United States [first published in 1899]—The social relief work of the Salvation Army in the United States [first published in 1900]—The Salvation Army as a temperance movement. [BX9716.B68 1972] 79-38439 ISBN 0-405-04060-1
1. Salvation Army—United States. I. Title.

CHESHAM, Sallie. 267.150973
Born to battle; the Salvation Army in America. Chicago, Rand McNally [1965] 286 p. illus., ports. 22 cm. [BX9716.C5] 65-18586
1. Salvation Army—U.S. I. Title.

ALONSO, Arthur 267.182
Catholic action and the laity. Tr. by Cornelius J. Crowley. St. Louis, Herder [c.1961] 320p. Bibl. 61-14264 4.50
1. Catholic action. I. Title.

ALONSO, Arthur. 267.182
Catholic action and the laity. Translated by Cornelius J. Crowley. St. Louis, B. Herder Book Co. [1961] 320p. 21cm. Includes bibliography. [BX2348.A713] 61-14264
1. Catholic action. I. Title.

CATHOLIC Church. Pope. 267.182
The lay apostolate. Selected and arr. by the Benedictine monk Translated by a secular priest. [Boston] St. Paul Editions [1961] 727p. 19cm. (Papal teachings) [BX2348.A3A28] 60-16447
1. Catholic action. I. Solesmes, France. Saint-Pierre (Benedictine abbey) II. Title.

CATHOLIC Church. Pope, 1939-1958 (Pius XII) 267.182
Directives to lay apostles. Selected, arr. by the Benedictine monks of Solesmes. Tr. by E. O'Gorman. [Boston] St. Paul Ed.[dist. Daughters of St. Paul, 1964, c.1963] 342p. 19cm. (Papal teachings) Bibl. 63-22753 4.00; 3.00 pap.,
1. Catholic action—Papal documents. I. Solesmes, France. Saint-Pierre (Benedictine abbey) II. Catholic Church. Pope. The lay apostolate. III. Title.

CATHOLIC Students' Mission Crusade, U S A 267.182
Lay apostolate: some fundamental principles from the writings of Our Holy Father, Pope John XXIII, His Holiness, Pope Pius XII, His Eminence Joseph Cardinal Pizzardo, His Eminence Valerian Cardinal Gracias, with applications to the Catholic laity of the United States of America. [Cincinnati, 1960, c1959] 93p. illus. 22cm. (CSMC five-hour series) Includes bibliography. [BX2348.C3] 60-340
1. Catholic action. I. Title.

CATHOLIC Students' Mission Crusade, U S A 267.182
Lay apostolate: some fundamental principles from the writings of Our Holy Father, Pope John xxiii, His Holiness, Pope Pius xii, His Eminence Joseph Cardinal Pizzardo, His Eminence Valerian Cardinal Gracias, with applications to the Catholic laity of the United States of America. [Cincinnati, [Catholic Students' Mission Crusade, U.S.A.] 1960, c.1959] 93 p. (3 p. bibl.) illus. 22 cm. (CSMC five-hour series) 60-340 pap., .45
1. Catholic action. I. Title.

CATHOLIC University of America Institute of Ibero-American Studies, 267.182
The lay apostolate in Latin America today proceedings of the 1959 symposium held under the auspices of the Institute of Ibero American Studies of the Catholic University of America, April 10-11, 1959. Edited by Margaret Bates. Washington, D.C., Catholic University of America Press [c.] 1960. v, 66 p. bibliographical footnotes, 22 cm. 60-1819 pap. 1.25
1. Catholic action—Spanish America. 2. Catholic action—Congresses. I. Bates, Margaret Jane, 1918- ed. II. Title.

CATHOLIC University of America. Institute of Ibero-American Studies. 267.182
The lay apostolate in Latin America today proceedings of the 1959 symposium held under the auspices of the Institute of Ibero American Studies of the Catholic University of America, April 10-11, 1959. Edited by Margaret Bates. Washington, Catholic University of America Press, 1960. Bibliographical footnotes. [BX2348.Z8S6 1959] 60-1819
1. Catholic action—Spanish America. 2. Catholic action- Congresses. I. Bates, Margaret Jane, 1918- ed. II. , 66p. 22cm. III. Title.

CATHOLIC University of America. Institute of Ibero-American Studies. 267.182
The lay apostolate in Latin America today; proceedings of the 1959 symposium held under the auspices of the Institute of Ibero American Studies of the Catholic University Institute of Ibero American Studies of the Margaret Bates. Washington, Catholic University of America action--Spanish America. [BX2348.Z8S6 1959] 60-1819
1. Catholic action—Congresses. I. Bates, Margaret Jane, 1918- ed. II. Title.

CUSHING, Richard James, Abp., 1895-- 267.182
A call to the laity; addresses on the lay apostolate. Compiled by George L. Kane. Westminster, Md., Newman Press, 1957. 237p. 22cm. [BX2348.A3C8] 56-11413
1. Catholic action—Addresses, essays, lectures. I. Title.

DE HUECK, Catherine, 1900- 267.182
Where love is, God is. Milwaukee, Bruce Pub. Co. [1953] 110p. 21cm. [BX2348.D4] 53-485
1. Catholic action. I. Title.

DOHERTY, Edward Joseph, 1890- 267.182
My hay ain't in. Milwaukee, Bruce Pub. Co. [1952] 198 p. 21 cm. [BX2348.Z5D6] 52-10226
1. Catholic action. I. Title.

DUFF, Frank. 267.182
Miracles on tap. Edited by Denis McAuliffe. Bay Shore, N.Y., Montfort Publications [1961?] 286 p. 22 cm. [BX809.L35D8] 61-18118
1. Legion of Mary — Hist. I. Title.

ESTHER, Sister. 267.182
Schoenstatt, an introduction translated by Ulrich J. Proeller. Madison, Wis., New Schoenstatt [1954, c1953] 94p. 25cm. [BX809.A68E83] 54-31525
1. Apostolischer Bund. I. Title.

GIESE, Vincent J 267.182
The apostolic itch. Chicago, Fides Publishers [1954] 126p. 21cm. [BX2348.G5] 54-8124
1. Catholic action. 2. Laity. I. Title.

HALLACK, Cecily Rosemary, 1898-1938. 267.182
The Legion of Mary. New York, Crowell [1950] 240 p. 21 cm. "The Legion from 1938 on: Geometrical progression" by M. O'Carroll: p. 192-235. [BX809.L35H3 1950] 50-9416
1. Legion of Mary. I. Title.

MICHONNEAU, Georges, 1899- 267.182
Catholic action and the parish, by G. Michonneau and R. Meurice. Translated by Edmond Bonin. Westminster, Md., Newman Press, 1955. 116p. 21cm. Translation of Pour use action paroissiale efficace. [BX2348.M512] 55-8652
1. Catholic action. 2. Church work. I. Mourice, R. abbe. II. Title.

MONTCHEUIL, Yves de. 267.182
For men of action. Translated by Charles E. Parnell. South Bend, Fides Publishers [195-?] 162p. 21cm. [BX2348.M653] 51-13836
1. Catholic action. I. Title.

NEWMAN, Jeremiah. 267.182
What is Catholic action? An introduction to the lay apostolate. With a pref. by Leon-Joseph Suenens. West minster, Md., Newman Press, 1958. 164p. 22cm. Includes bibliography. [BX2348.N4] 58-13635
1. Catholic action. I. Title.

PERRIN, Joseph Marie, 1905- 267.182
The fundamentals of Catholic action. Translated by Fegrus Murphy. Chicago, Fides Publishers Association, 1959 [c1958] 74p. 19cm. Translation of Les lois de Laction chretienne. [BX2348.Z8F813] 59-941
1. Catholic action. I. Title.

PERRIN, Joseph Marie, 1905- 267.182
Secular institutes; consecration to God and life in the world. Translated by Lancelot C. Sheppard. New York, P. J. Kenedy [1961] 122p. 19cm. Translation of Conscration Diel et presence au monde. Includes bibliography. [BX818.A1P413] 61-8785
1. Secular institutes I. Title.

PUTZ, Louis J 267.182
The modern apostle. Chicago, Fides Publishers Association [1957] 148p. 21cm. (Fides family readers) 'Essays which appeared originally in the pages of Our Sunday visitor.' [BX2348.P8] 57-13164
1. Catholic action. I. Title.

QUIGLEY, Martin, 1917- 267.182
Catholic action in practice: family life, education, international life [by] Martin Quigley, Jr., and Edward M. Connors. New York, Random House [1963] 240 p. illus. 22 cm. [BX2348.Q5] 63-9351
1. Catholic action. I. Connors, Edward Michael, 1921- joint author. II. Title.

REIDY, Gabriel. 267.182
Secular institutes. [1st ed.] New York, Hawthorn Books [1962] 124p. 21cm. (The Twentieth century encyclopedia of Catholicism, v.87. Section 8: The organization of the church) Includes bibliographies. [BX818.A1R4] 62-12930
1. Secular institutes. I. Title.

RIPLEY, Francis Joseph, 1912- 267.182
Souls at stake, by Francis J. Ripley and F. S. Mitchell [pseud.] With a foreword by Joseph E. Ritter. New York, J. F. Wagner [1948] 198 p. 21 cm. [BX809.c2R5] 48-2237
1. Catholic action. I. Mitchell, F. S., pseud. II. Title.

ROBERTS, Leo. 267.182
Mary in their midst; the legion of Mary in action in China. 1948-1951. Supplement compiled by Aedan MoGrath. Dubin, Clonmore & Reynolds [1960] 75p. 18cm. [BX809.L35R6] 62-6268
1. Legion of Mary. 2. Catholic Church in China. I. Title.

SUENENS, Leon Joseph, B.p., 1904- 267.182
Theology of the apostolate of the Legion of Mary, with letter of papal approbation. Westminster, Md., Newman Press [1954] 159p. 18cm. [BX809.L35S83] 55-14046
1. Legion of Mary. 2. Mary, Virgin—Medication. I. Title.

WORLD Congress of the Lay Apostolate. 2d. Rome, 1957. 267.182
Major documents on Catholic action from the Second World Congress of the Lay Apostolate, Rome, October 6-13, 1957. Notre Dame, Ind., National Catholic Action Study Bureau, National Federal of Catholic College Students [1958] 100 p. 22 cm. At head of title: Apostolle formation. "Third in ... [National Catholic Action Study Bureau, series of studies on the lay apostolate." [BX2348.A2W6 1957] 58-4743
1. Catholic action — Congresses. 2. Catholic action — Study and teaching. I. Title.

STOWE, Walter Herbert 267.183
The Christian Knowledge Society and the revival of the Episcopal Church in New Jersey. [Austin 5, Tex., 606 Rathervue Place, Church Historical Society, 1960] 40p. port., facsims. 22cm. (Church Historical Society. Publication no. 49) Cover title. Bibliographical footnotes. 60-3399 .50 pap.,
1. Protestant Episcopal Church in the U.S.A.—New Jersey. 2. Episcopal Society of New Jersey for the Promotion of Christian Knowledge and Piety. 3. Christian Knowledge Society of New Jersey. I. Title. II. Series.

ALLEN, William Osborne Bird. 267'.18'342
Two hundred years: the history of the Society for Promoting Christian Knowledge, 1698-1898, by W. O. B. Allen and Edmund McClure. New York, B. Franklin [1970] vi, 551 p. 22 cm. (Burt Franklin research & source works series, 622. History, economics and social science, 212) Reprint of the 1898 ed. [BX5013.S6A8 1970] 76-135171 ISBN 0-8337-0044-8
1. Society for Promoting Christian Knowledge, London. I. McClure, Edmund, d. 1922, joint author. II. Title.

JONES, Mary Hoxie. 267'.18'9673
Swords into ploughshares; an account of the American Friends Service Committee, 1917-1937. Westport, Conn., Greenwood Press [1971] xix, 374 p. illus., ports. 23 cm. Reprint of the 1937 ed. [BX7635.A1F65 1971] 70-109757 ISBN 0-8371-4247-4
1. Friends, Society of. American Friends Service Committee. 2. Friends, Society of—Charities. 3. Reconstruction (1914-1939)—Europe. I. Title.

BENDER, Urie A. 267'.23
Soldiers of compassion, by Urie A. Bender. Scottdale, Pa., Herald Press [1969] 319 p. illus., ports. 21 cm. [BX8128.W4B4] 71-76623 4.95
1. Pax (Organization) 2. Conscientious objectors. I. Title.

HOUSTON, Jack, 1937- 267'.23
Wandering Wheels. Grand Rapids, Baker Book House [1970] 173 p. illus. 21 cm. [BV4520.H67] 75-19330 ISBN 0-8010-4009-4 3.95
1. Witness bearing (Christianity) 2. Cycling—U.S. I. Title.

SEATH, William. 267'.23
The challenge of the impossible; the story of the Chicago Christian Industrial League. [1st ed.] New York, Exposition Press [1967] 96 p. 21 cm. [HV4196.C4C55] 67-26397
1. Chicago Christian Industrial League. I. Title.

SEATH, William. 267'.23
The challenge of the impossible; the story of the Chicago Christian Industrial League. [1st ed.] New York, Exposition Press [1967] 96 p. 21 cm. [HV4196.C4C55] 67-26397
1. Chicago Christian Industrial League. I. Title.

SERI, Vernon C. 267'.23
Final report on the Saskatchewan Hutterite program. [n.p., 1958?] 39 l. 22 x 30 cm. [BX8128.C6S4] 61-41987
1. Mennonites — Colonization. 2. Hutterite Brethren — Saskatchewan. I. Title.

WESTBURG, Paul A. 267.23
They stood every man in his place; a 60-year history of the Gideons International, 1899-1959. Chicago, Gideons International [1959] 173 p. illus. 20 cm. [BV1280.G4W4] 59-4364
1. Gideons International. I. Title.

CADA, Joseph, 1896- 267.242
The Catholic Central Union; its contribution to fraternalism and America's cosmopolitan civilization. Chicago, Catholic Central Union [1952] 54p. 23cm. [BX810.C15] 53-15577
1. Catholic Central Union. I. Title.

CATHOLIC Centeral Verein of America. 267.242
Proceedings [of the] convention. v. 23cm. Proceedings of the convention include also Proceedings of the convention of the National Catholic Women's Union. [BX810.C20] 57-20734
I. Title. II. Title: St. Louis.

CATHOLIC Central Union of America. 267.242
Offizieller Bericht uber die Generalversammlung. St. Louis [etc.] v, in 23cm. annual. Title varies: 18- 1906, General-Versammlunp, Reports for issued by the society under an earlier name: Deutscher Romisch-Katholischer Central-Verein von Nord. Amerika (varies slightly) [BX810.C22] 58-53554
I. Title.

CATHOLIC Central Union of America. 267.242
Proceedings [of the] convention. St, Louis. v, 23cm. Proceedings for 1955 issued by the society under an earlier name: Catholic Central Verein of America. Proceedings of the convention include also Proceedings of the convention of the National Catholic Women's Union. [BX810.C2] 57-20734
I. Title.

OBERSTE, William H 267.242
Knights of Columbus in Texas, 1902-1952. Austin, Von Boeckmann-Jones Co., 1952. 298 p. illus. 25 cm. [HS1538.C74O2] 52-29671
1. Knights of Columbus. I. Title.

SWIFT, John Edward. 267.242
Selected addresses. [Boston, 1960] 336 p. illus. 24 cm. [HS1538.C74S85] 60-20880
1. Knights of Columbus. I. Title.

GREEK Catholic Union of the U.S.A. 267'.24'273
Kalendar. Munahall, Pa. v. illus., ports., music. 27cm. [HS1538.G7A15] 59-46167
1. Ukrainians in the U.S.—Societies, etc. I. Title.

LEAGUE of Catholic Slovenian Americans. 267'.24'273
Pravila. By-laws. Cleveland, 1959. 57p. 17cm. [HS1538.L4A5 1959] 59-53835
I. Title.

NAES, Vincent L., 1901- 267'.24'273
Rounding out a century; the Catholic Knights of America, founded April 23, 1877 [by] Vincent L. Naes. [St. Louis, Catholic Knights of America, 1974] 312 p. illus. 23 cm. Includes bibliographical references. [HS1538.C34N33] 73-94009 5.00
1. Catholic Knights of America. 2. Friendly societies—United States. I. Title.

BROWN, Archie E 267.2461
A million men for Christ; the history of the Baptist Brotherhood. Nashville, Convention Press [1956] 179p. 21cm. [BX6207.A40834] 56-10337
1. Southern Baptist Convention. Baptist Brotherhood Commission. I. Title.

SCHROEDER, George W 267.2461
The brotherhood guidebook, a guide for organizing and operating a brotherhood. Nashville, Broadman Press [1950] 152 p. 21 cm. [BX6205.S6S3] 50-12073
1. Southern Baptist Convention. Baptist Brotherhood Commission. I. Title.

SCHROEDER, George W 267.2461
The church brotherhood guidebook; a guide for organizing and operating a church brotherhood. [Rev. Nashville, Broadman Press, 1960] 192 p. illus. 20 cm. First published in 1950 under title: The brotherhood guidebook. [BX6205.B117S3] 60-9894
1. Southern Baptist Convention. Baptist Brotherhood Commission. I. Title.

VILLARET, Emile, 1876-1952. *267 256
Abridged history of the sodalities of Our Lady. Translated by William J. Young. St. Louis, Queen's Work [1957] 181 p: 22 cm. [BX808.V5] 58-17596
1. Confraternities. I. Title. II. Title: Sodalities of Our Lady.

KEITEL, George W 267.3
A topical history of Y'sdom, 1920-1953; the story of the International Association Y's Men's Clubs--the service club of the YMCA. Lawrence, Mass., International Association of Y's Men's Clubs [195-] 354p. illus. 23cm. [BV1160.K4] 58-31868
1. Young Men's Christian Associations. International Association of Y's Men's Clubs. I. Title.

KELLEY, Rex C 267.3
Manual on campaigning for capital funds. New York, Association Press [1956] 117p. illus. 24cm. [BV1100.K4] 56-10662
1. Fund raising. 2. Young Men's Christian Associations—Finance. I. Title. II. Title: Campaigning for capital funds.

LATOURETTE, Kenneth Scott, 1884- 267.3
World service; a history of the foreign work and world service of the Young Men's Christian Associations of the United States and Canada. New York, Association Press [c1957] 489p. illus. 24cm. Includes Bibliography. [BV1125.L3] 57-13143
1. Young Men's Christian Associations I. Title.

LIMBERT, Paul Moyer, 1897- 267.3
New perspectives for the YMCA [by] Paul M. Limbert. New York, Association Press [1964] 255 p. 23 cm. Bibliography: p. 224-231. [BV1090.L5] 64-16124
1. Young Men's Christian Associations. I. Title.

LIMBERT, Paul Moyer, 1897- 267.3
NewPerspectives for the YMCA [by] Paul M. Limbert. New York, Association [c. 1964] 255p. 23cm. Bibl. 64-16124 3.50 pap.,
1. Young Men's Christian Associations. I. Title.

TOMPKINS, Leslie James, 1892- 267.3
Operating ratios in the YMCA. New York, Association Press [1954] 54p. illus. 22cm. [BV1100.T57] 55-12907
1. Young Men's Christian Associations—Management. I. Title.

YOUNG Men's Christian Associations. National Board. 267.3
Association accounting; a guide to financial recording and reporting in the YMCA. Leslie J. Tompkins, editor. New York, Association Press [1954] 80p. illus. 23cm. [BV1100.A7117] 56-147
1. Young Men's Christian Associations—Finance. I. Tompkins, Leslie James, 1892- ed. II. Title.

YOUNG Men's Christian Associations. National Board. 267.3
Association records; the official guide to YMCA program recording and reporting. New York, Association Press [1954] 88p. illus. 23cm. 'Replaces Association records and accounting, published in 1950.' [BV1100.A712] 54-10165
1. Young Men's Christian Associations. I. Title.

YOUNG Men's Christian Associations. Association of Secretaries. 51st conference, Cleveland, 1951. 267.3063771
Professional perspective; the report of the 1951 triennial conference. Clement A. Duran, editor. New York, Association Press, 1951. xi, 209p. 24cm. [BV1100.A44 1951c] 53-1881
1. Young Men's Christian Associations. I. Duran, Clement A., 1902- ed. II. Title.

FATHER and son Y-Indian guides of the Young Men's Christian Association. New York, Association [c.1946-1962] 135p. illus.23cm. 1.50 pap., 267.31
1. Young Men's Chrisian Association—Programs.

HL-Y Tri-Hi-Y adviser's training kit. New York, Association [c.1963] unpaged. 22x28cm. illus. (Natl. Council of Young Men's Christian Assns. pubn.) 2.50, pap., spiral bdg. 267.33

PIERREL, Gren O 267.34
The new executive in the smaller YMCA; developed for the General Secretaries Section of the Association of Secretaries of North America. New York, Association Press [1959] 205p. illus. 24cm. Includes bibliography. [BV1100.P55] 59-65067
1. Young Men's Christian Associations. I. Title.

TURNER, Eugene A ed. 267.34
The CIT in residence camping; a statement of theory and practice. New York, Association Press [1961] 80 p. 22 cm. [GV198.C6T8] 61-14171
1. Camp counselors. I. Title.

PIERREL, Gren O ed. 267.341
The executive role in Y.M.C.A. administration; an analysis and discussion of the administrative process in the North American Y.M.C.A.'s. Financed and supervised by the General Secretaries' Section of the Association of Secretaries. New York, Association Press, 1951. xviii, 540 p. illus. 24 cm. Bibliography; p. [503]-509. [BV1100.P5] 52-1587
1. Young Men's Christian Associations. I. Young Men's Christian Associations. Association of Secretaries. II. Title.

YOUNG Men's Christian Associations. Association of Secretaries. 53d conference, Kansas City, Mo., 1956. 267.341082
A new look at executive responsibilities; report of the 1956 General Secretaries triennial conference of the Association of Secretaries of YMCA's in the United States and Canada, held at Kansas City, Missouri, February 29-March 4, 1956. Ernest M. Ford, editor. New York, Association Press [1956] 71 p. 23 cm. [BV1100.A44 1956c] 57-343
1. Young Men's Christian Associations. I. Ford, Ernest M., ed. II. Title.

PHYSICAL EDUCATION SOCIETY OF THE YOUNG MEN'S CHRISTIAN ASSOCIATIONS OF NORTH AMERICA. LEADERSHIP TRAINING COMMITTEE. 267.343
Training Y.M.C.A. leaders for physical education service. New York, Association Press, 1951. 75 p. illus. 29 cm. [BV1145.A4] 52-3593
1. Young Men's Christian Associations. 2. Physical education and training. I. Title.

HAMLIN, Richard Eugene. 267.35
A new look at YMCA physical education; the report of a national study. New York, Association Press [1959] 220p. illus. 24cm. [GV367.Y7H3] 59-16254
1. Young Men's Christian Associations. 2. Physical education and training—U. S. I. Title.

MOORE, Nan A. 267.35
New program ways with Tri-Gra-Ys; a plan emphasizing personal growth and including story dialogues for devotional periods. A guide for club leaders of preteen girls.By Nan A. Moore, Winifred J. Colton. New York, Association [c.1963] 94p. illus. 23cm. Bibl. 3.00 pap.,
I. Title.

YOUNG Men's Christian Associations. Hi-Y Manual Committee. 267.35
The new Hi-Y manual. New York, Association Press [1960] 63 p. illus. 28 cm. Includes bibliography. [BV1160.A59] 60-50412
1. Boys — Societies and clubs. I. Title.

YOUNG Men's Christian Associations. Hi-Y Manual Committee. 267.35
The new Hi-Y manual. New York, Association Press [c.1960] 63p. illus. 28cm. Bibl. 60-50412 1.25 pap.,

1. Boys—Societies and clubs. I. Title.

YOUNG Men's Christian Associations. Hi-Y Manual Committee. 267.35
The new Tri-Hi-Y manual. New York, Association [c.1961] 63p. illus. 28cm. 1.25 pap.,
1. Boys—Societies and clubs. I. Title.

HAMLIN, Richard E 267.357
Hi-Y today; a report of the national study of the Hi-Y and Tri-Hi-Y movement. New York, Association Press [1955] 150p. illus. 26cm. [BV1160.H3] 55-9119
1. Young Men's Christian Associations. Hi-Y Clubs. 2. Young Men's Christian Associations. Tri-Hi-Y Clubs sBoys—Societies and clubs. I. Title.

HAMLIN, Richard Eugene. 267.357
Hi-Y today; a report of the national study of the Hi-Y and Tri-Hi-Y movement. New York, Association Press [1955] 150p. illus. 26cm. [BV1160.H3] 55-9119
1. Young Men's Christian Associations. Hi-Y Clubs. 2. Young Men's Christian Associations. Tri-Hi-Y Clubs. 3. Boys—Societies and clubs. I. Title.

ROBINSON, Edgar M. 267.357
The early years; the beginnings of work with boys in the Young Men's Christian Association. New York, Association Press, 1950. xi, 127 p. port. 22 cm. [BV1160.R73] 50-14973
1. Boys. 2. Young Men's Christian Associations. I. Title.

YOUNG Men's Christian Associations. National Jr. Hi-Y Commission. 267.357
Jr. Hi-Y, a manual for leaders of Jr. Hi-Y Clubs. New York, Association Press, 1946. 144 p. illus., forms. 22 cm. Bibliography: p. 143-144. [BV1160.A613 1946] 46-7224
1. Boys — Societies and clubs. I. Young Men's Christian Associations. Hi-Y Clubs. II. Title.

HARDY, James M 267'.36
Focus on the family; a national study of work with families in the YMCA [by] James M. Hardy. New York, Association Press [c1966] xii, 146 p. illus., forms. 23 cm. Bibliography: p. 144-146. [BV1172.H37] 66-25378
1. Young Men's Christian Associations. 2. Family. I. Title.

MEYER, William F 267.369
Organization and program of a young men's industrial club, a manual for YMCA young adult leaders. New York, Association Press [1957] 59p. 22cm. [BV1185.M4] 57-1542
1. Young Men's Christian Associations. 2. Labor and laboring classes—U. S.—1914- I. Title.

KEITEL, George W. 267'.39
A topical history of Y'sdom: the story of the International Association of Y's Men's Clubs—The service club of the YMCA. Compiled and written by George W. Keitel. Oak Brook, Ill., International Association of Y's Men's Clubs, 1972. xi, 616 p. illus. 23 cm. Title on cover: History of Y'sdom. "Golden anniversary ed." [BV1160.K4 1972] 73-171331
1. Young Men's Christian Associations. International Association of Y's Men's Clubs. I. Title. II. Title: History of Y'sdom.

MCCONNELL, Joseph J., 1887- 267'.3924
Reminiscences of Joseph J. McConnell, Jr., 1962-1963. [Dallas, 1966] i, 140 p. 28 cm. [BV1085.M32A3] 67-1756
I. Title.

GARRETT, Shirley S. 267'.39'51
Social reformers in urban China; the Chinese Y.M.C.A., 1895-1926 [by] Shirley S. Garrett. Cambridge, Mass., Harvard University Press, 1970. 221 p. 22 cm. (Harvard East Asian series, 56) Bibliography: p. [187]-192. [BV1060.C6G37 1970] 74-133218 ISBN 0-674-81220-4 7.50
1. Young Men's Christian Associations. China. I. Title. II. Series.

HOPKINS, Charles Howard, 1905- 267.3973
History of the Y. M. C. A. in North America. New York, Association Press, 1951. 818 p. illus. 25 cm. [BV1030.H6] 51-11674
1. Young Men's Christian Associations. I. Title.

WORMAN, Eugene Clark, 1878- 267.39747
History of the Brooklyn and Queens Young Men's Christian Association, 1853-1949. New York, Association Press, 1952. 256 p. illus. 24 cm. [BV1050.B8W6] 52-11534
1. Young Men's Christian Associations. Brooklyn and Queens. I. Title.

EICHER, HuBert Clark. 267.39748
A century of service, 1854-1954: the Harrisburg Young Men's Christian Association. Harrisburg, Pa., Printed by the Evangelical Press, c1955. 312 p. illus. 21 cm. [BV1050.H2E5] 55-33685
1. Young Men's Christian Associations. Harrisburg. Pa. I. Title.

MCMILLEN, Theodore Clark, 1905- 267.39771
The Springfiled, Ohio, YMCA, 1854-1954. [Springfield] Ohio, 1954] 172p. illus. 24cm. [BV1050.S83M3] 54-40822
1. Young Men's Christian Associations. Springfield, Ohio. I. Title.

DEDMON, Emmett. 267.39773
Great enterprises; 100 years of the YMCA of Metropolitan Chicago. New York, Rand McNally [1957] 383p. illus. 22cm. [BV1050.C4D4] 57-11669
1. Young Men's Christian Associations. Chicago. I. Title.

HALL, Robert King, 1912- 267.39794
A strategy for the inner city; a report of the program and priority study of the Young Men's Christian Association of Greater New York. [New York] Young Men's Christian Association of Greater New York, 1963. vi, 438 p. diagrs., tables. 25 cm. Bibliography: p. 192-198. [BV1050.N53H3] 64-246
1. Young Men's Christian Associations. Greater New York. I. Title.

SORENSON, Roy, 1900- 267.39794
Designing education in values; a case study in institutional change, by Roy Sorenson and Hedley S.Dimock. New York, Association Press [1955] 365p. illus. 24cm. [BV1050.S4S6] 55-7418
1. Young Men's Christian Association San Francisco. I. Dimock, Hedley Seldon, 1891- joint author. II. Title.

SORENSON, Roy, 1900- 267.39794
Designing education in values; a case study in institutional change, by Roy Sorenson and Hedley S.Dimock. New York, Association Press [1955] 365p. illus. 24cm. [BV1050.S4S6] 55-7418
1. Young Men's Christian Association San Francisco. I. Dimock, Hedley Seldon, 1891- joint author. II. Title.

WHITESIDE, William B 267.39794
The Boston Y.M.C.A. and community need; a century's evolution, 1851-1951. New York, Association Press, 1951. 239 p. illus. 24 cm. [BV1050.B7W5] 267 51-14727
1. Young Men's Christian Associations. Boston. I. Title.

DRURY, Clifford Merrill, 1897- 267.3979461
San Francisco YMCA; 100 years by the Golden Gate, 1853-1953. Glendale, Calif., A. H. Clark Co., 1963. 256 p. illus. 23 cm. [BV1050.S4D7] 63-9295
1. Young Men's Christian Association. San Francisco. I. Title.

DRURY, Clifford Merrill, 1897- 267.3979461
San Francisco YMCA; 100 years by the Golden Gate, 1853-1953. Glendale, Calif., A. H. Clark [c.]1963. 256p. illus. 23cm. Bibl. 63-9295 8.00
1. Young Men's Christian Associations. San Francisco. I. Title.

ALLEN, Gwenfread Elaine, 1904- 267'.39'969
The Y.M.C.A. in Hawaii, 1869-1969, by Gwenfread E. Allen Honolulu, Young Men's Christian Association, 1969. x, 253 p. illus., ports. 24 cm. [BV1045.H3A65] 72-12603
1. Young Men's Christian Associations. Hawaii. I. Young Men's Christian Associations. Honolulu. II. Title.

SHAFFER, Wilma L. 267.4
Church women at work; a manual for church women. Cincinnati, Ohio, Standard Pub. Co. [c.1961] 106p. illus. Bibl. 1.50, pap., plastic binding
I. Title.

WILKERSON, Thelma B. 267'.4
Easy to use installation services, by Thelma B. Wilkerson and Joy B. Crain. Grand Rapids, Mich., Baker Book House [1970] 128 p. 21 cm. [BV199.I5W5] 70-115638 2.95
1. Installation service (Church officers) I. Crain, Joy B., joint author. II. Title.

WORLD Young Women's Christian Association. 267'.4'08 s
Bible study in the YWCA. [Geneva, 1969] 86 p. 32 cm. (YWCA in action programme bulletin, no. 1, 1969) Cover title. Bibliography: p. 81-86. [BV1300.Y14 1969, no. 1] [BS600.2] 73-851206
1. Bible—Study. I. Title. II. Series: YWCA in action

NATIONAL Council of Catholic Women. Nashville Diocesan Council. 267.442
Catholic women of Tennessee, 1937- 1956; a twentieth anniversary history of the Nashville Diocesan Council of the National Council of Catholic Women, edited by Mrs. Herbert Haile, historian. [1st ed. Nashville, 1956] 421p. illus., ports. 23cm. [BX1415.T35N3] 59-45451
1. Catholics in Tennessee. 2. Women in Tennessee. I. Haile, Aloyse. II. Title.

MCGAUGHEY, Janie W 267.4451
On the crest of the present; a history of women's work, Presbyterian Church in the United States. Atlanta, Board of Women's Work, Presbyterian Church in the United States [1961] 204p. illus. 22cm. [BX8966.M3] 61-29014
1. Presbyterian Church in the U. S. Board of Women's Work. I. Title.

HARPER, Elsie Dorothy, 1891- 267'.5
The past is prelude; fifty years of social action in the YWCA. [New York, Bureau of Communications, National Board, YWCA, 1963] 81 p. 23 cm. Cover title. Bibliography: p. 81. [BV1340.H3] 64-829
1. Young Women's Christian Associations — Hist. I. Title. II. Title.

MAINS, Frances Helen. 267'.5
From deep roots : the story of the YWCA's religious dimensions / by Frances Helen Mains and Grace Loucks Elliott. [New York : Communications, National Board. YWCA, 1974] 71 p. ; 23 cm. Bibliography: p. 70. [BV1375.M34] 75-301782 pbk. : 2.00
1. Young Women's Christian Associations. I. Elliott, Grace Loucks, 1891- joint author. II. Title.

MENNONITE Church. Board of Missions and Charities. Girls's Missionary and Service Auxiliary. 267.5
Manual for GMSA leaders, by Winifred Erb Paul. Scottdale, Pa., Herald Pr. [c.1964] 62p. illus. 22cm. 64-17416 1.50, pap., plastic bdg.
1. Church work with children. 2. Creative activities and seat work. I. Paul, Winifred (Erb) II. Title.

ROBINSON, Marion O. 267'.5
YWCA world mutual service; a common quest, by Marion O. Robinson. Pref. by Mary French Rockefeller. New York, National Board of the Young Women's Christian Association of the U.S.A., 1973. 48 p. illus. 22 cm. [BV1340.R6] 73-78017
1. Young Women's Christian Associations. 2. World Young Women's Christian Association. I. Young Women's Christian Associations. United States. National Board. II. Title.

VANCE, Catherine Stuart, 1885- 267'.5
The Girl Reserve movement of the Young Women's Christian Association; an analysis of the educational principles and procedures used throughout its history, by Catherine S. Vance. New York, Bureau of Publications, Teachers College, Columbia University, 1937. [New York, AMS Press, 1972, i.e. 1973] ix, 184 p. 22 cm. Reprint of the 1937 ed., issued in series: Teachers College, Columbia University. Contributions to education, no. 730. Originally presented as the author's thesis, Columbia. Bibliography: p. 164-171. [BV1393.G5V3 1972] 70-177683 ISBN 0-404-55730-9 10.00
1. Girl Reserves. 2. Girls—Societies and clubs. I. Title. II. Series: Columbia University. Teachers College. Contributions to education, no. 730.

YOUNG Women's Christian Associations. U.S. National Board. 267.5
Public affairs in the YWCA. New York, Publications Services, National Board, YWCA [1957] 52 p. 23 cm. [BV1392.P8A5] 58-27492
1. Young Women's Christian Associations. I. Title.

ROBINSON, Marion O. 267.50922
Eight women of the YWCA, by Marion O. Robinson. Pref. by Mary French Rockefeller. New York, Natl. Bd. of the Young Women's Christian Assn. of the U.S.A. 1966. 118p. ports. 25cm. Bibl. [BV1365.R6] 66-27675 3.50
1. Young Women's Christian Associations— Biog. I. Title.
Contents omitted. Publisher's address: 600 lexington Ave., New York, N.Y. 10022.

ROBINSON, Marion O. 267.50922
Eight women of the YWCA, by Marion O. Robinson. Pref. by Mary French Rockefeller. New York, National Board of the Young Women's Christian Association of the U.S.A., 1966. 118 p. ports. 25 cm. Contents.'Should women learn the alphabet?' -- Grace H. Dodge. -- Mabel Cratty.-Emma Ralley Speer.- Mary Billings French.---Vera Scott Cushman.-- Martha Boyden Finley.--Florence Simms.-- Theresa Wilbur Paist. Bibliography: p. [116]-118. [BV1365.R6] 66-27675
1. Young Women's Christian Associations— Biog. I. Title.

SIMS, Mary Sophia Stephens, 1886- 267'.5'9
The purpose widens, 1947-1967, by Mary S. Sims. [New York, Bureau of Communications, National Board, YWCA, 1969] iv, 100 p. 21 cm. [BV1340.S515] 77-12631 2.50
1. Young Women's Christian Associations— History. I. Young Women's Christian Association. U.S. National Board. II. Title.

SIMS, Mary Sophia Stephens, 1886- 267.5973
The YWCA, an unfolding purpose. New York, Woman's Press [1950] xv, 157 p. 21 cm. Bibliography: p. 153. [BV1340.S52] 50-6074
1. Young Women's Christian Associations— Hist. I. Title.

WILSON, Grace Hannah, 1888- 267'.5'973
The religious and educational philosophy of the Young Women's Christian Association; a historical study of the changing religious and social emphases of the association as they relate to changes in its educational philosophy and to observable trends in current religious thought, educational philosophy, and social situations, by Grace H. Wilson. New York, Bureau of Publications, Teachers College, Columbia University, 1933. [New York, AMS Press, 1972, ie 1973] 156 p. 22 cm. Reprint of the 1933 ed., issued in series: Teachers College, Columbia University. Contributions to education, no. 554. Originally presented as the author's thesis, Columbia. Bibliography: p. 149-156. [BV1350.W73 1972] 70-177632 ISBN 0-404-55554-3 10.00
1. Young Women's Christian Associations. United States. 2. Sociology, Christian. 3. United States—Social conditions. I. Title. II. Series: Columbia University. Teachers College. Contributions to education, no. 554.

MOORE, Sidney. 267.5974461
The heart of woman. Published in commemoration of the one hundredth anniversary of the Boston Young Women's Christian Association, March 3, 1966. [Boston? 1966] 62 p. illus. 29 cm. [BV1355.B7M6] 66-6802
1. Young Women's Christian Associations. Boston. I. Title.

SANTA, George Frederick, 1914- 267.6
52 complete young people's programs, by George F. Santa and others. Grand Rapids, Zondervan Pub. House [1955] 226p. illus. 20cm. [BV29.S27] 56-17894
1. Young people's meetings (Church work) 2. Worship programs. I. Title.

SANTA, George Frederick, 1914- 267.6
Youth aid idea handbook, packed with practical tested ideas for youth workers. Grand Rapids, Zondervan Pub. House [1952] 76p. illus. 23cm. [BV29.S3] 52-14267
1. Young people's meetings (Church work) I. Title.

*WILSON, Bill, comp. 267.6
Kid Keepers; a handbook for children's workers and youth leaders [compiled by] Bill Wilson and Paul Tedesco. Grand Rapids, Baker Book House [1975] 83 p. ill. 21 cm. [BV4446] ISBN 0-8010-9574-3 2.95 (pbk.)
1. Church work with youth. I. Tedesco, Paul, joint comp. II. Title.

YAXLEY, Grace 267.6
Let's be different youth meetings. Chicago, Moody [c.1963] 64p. illus. 28cm. 1.25 pap.,
I. Title.

YEAR of youth programs and activities, number 2. Illus. by Bill Granstaff. Cincinnati, Ohio, Standard Pub. [c.1963] 174p. illus. 28cm. 2.95 pap., 267.6

BRIGHT, Bill. 267'.61
Come help change the world. Old Tappan, N.J., F. H. Revell Co. [1970] 207 p. 21 cm. Includes bibliographical references. [BV4427.B73] 70-112462 4.95
1. Campus Crusade for Christ. 2. Students— Religious life. I. Title.

CAILLIET, Emile, 1894- 267.61
Young life. New York, Harper [1964, c.1963] viii, 120p. 22cm. 64-10614 2.95
1. Rayburn, James C. 2. Young Life Campaign. I. Title.

HEFLEY, James C. 267'.61
God goes to high school [by] James Hefley. Waco, Tex., Word Books [1970] 188 p. illus., map, ports. 23 cm. [BV1430.Y6H4] 75-85830 4.95
1. Youth for Christ International. I. Title.

HUMMEL, Charles E. 267.61
Campus Christian Witness; an Inter-Varsity Christian Fellowship manual. Chicago, Inter-varsity [1962, c.1958] 219 p. 21 cm. illus. p pap., 1.95
1. Inter-varsity Christian Fellowship of the United States of America. I. Title.

BOCKELMAN, Wilfred. 267'.61'0924 B
Gothard : the man and his ministry : an evaluation / by Wilfred Bockelman. Santa Barbara, CA : Quill Publications ; Milford, Mich. : distributed by Mott Media, c1976. 150 p., [4] leaves of plates : ill. ; 21 cm. [BR1725.G7B6] 76-43001 ISBN 0-916608-07-7 pbk. : 3.50
1. Gothard, Bill. 2. Clergy—United States—Biography. 3. Church work with youth. 4. Youth—Religious life.

MILLIKEN, Bill. 267'.61'0924
Tough love [by] Bill Milliken, with Char Meredith. Old Tappan, N.J., F. H. Revell Co. [1968] 160 p. 21 cm. [BV4447.M5] 68-17092 3.95
1. Young Life Campaign. 2. Church work with youth. I. Meredith, Char, joint author. II. Title.

YOUNG Christian Workers. 267'.62'2
Time for living. [Melbourne, Young Christian Worker's Movement (Aust.) 1967] 47 p. illus. 21 cm. Cover title. [BX809.Y62A28] 78-444453 unpriced
I. Title.

KLAUSLER, Alfred P 267.6241
Growth in worship; a manual for youth couselors. Saint Louis. Concordia Pub. House [1956] 108p. illus. 19cm. Includes bibliography. [BV29.K55] 55-12479
1. Young people's meetings (Church work) 2. Worship programs. 3. Worship (Religious education) I. Title.

PRESBYTERIAN Church in the U.S.A. Board of Christian Education. 267.625
The manual of Westminster Fellowship. [Rev. ed. Philadelphia, 1950] 106 p. illus.23 cm. [BV1430.W4P7] 50-30595
1. Westminster Fellowship. I. Title.

PRESBYTERIAN Church in the U. S. 267.6251
Handbook, Senior High Fellowship. The adult leaders of youth, The Council, The Commission on Christian Faith, The Commission on Christian Witness, The Commission on Christian Outreach, The Commission on Christian Citizenship. The Commission on Christian Fellowship; a series of manuals for the Senior High Fellowship, Presbyterian Church, U. S. Bettie Currie, editor. Richmond, John Knox Press [1953, c1952] 1v. illus. 23cm. Includes bBibliography. [BV639.Y7P7] 53-29119
1. Church work with youth. 2. Young people's meetings (Church work) I. Title.

AMERICAN Baptist Publication Society. 267.626
Topic; the quarterly for young people's meetings. [Philadelphia, American Baptist Publication Society] v. in 19 cm. [BX6225.T6] 51-31805
1. Religious education — Text-books for young people — Baptist. I. Title.

BAPTIST Youth World Conference. 5th, Tornto, 1958. 267.626
Christ for the world--now Official report. Edited by Cyril E. Bryant. Washington, Baptist World Alliance, Youth Dept. [1958] 211p. illus., ports. 24cm. [BX6207.A18 1958] 59-37511
1. Youth—Congresses. 2. Baptists—Congresses. I. Bryant, Cyril E., ed. II. Title.

BAPTIST Youth World Conference, 7th, Bern, 1968. 267'.62'6
One world, one Lord, one witness; official report. Edited by Cyril E. Bryant. Waco, Tex., Published for the Baptist World Alliance by Word Books [1969] 167 p. illus., ports. 23 cm. [BX6207.A18 1968] 69-20233
1. Baptists—Congresses. 2. Youth—Congresses. I. Bryant, Cyril E., ed. II. Baptist World Congress. III. Title.

SHARP, Margaret, comp. 267.626
Come into His presence; training union assembly programs for intermediates. Nashville, Tenn., Convention Press [1957] 128p. 20cm. [BV29.S4] 57-6333
1. Worship programs. 2. Young people's meetings (Church work) 3. Baptist Training Union. I. Title.

SHARP, Margaret, comp. 267.626
Come into His presence; training union assembly programs for intermediates. Nashville, Tenn., Convention Press [1957] 128 p. 20 cm. [BV29.S4] 57-6333
1. Worship programs. 2. Young people's meetings (Church work) 3. Baptist Training Union. I. Title.

BAIRD, Doyle J. 267'.62'61
Student work administration [by] Doyle J. Baird. Nashville, Convention Press [1969] 44, [36] l. illus. 28 cm. Bibliography: leaf [36] (2d group) [BX6205.B27B25] 76-89875
1. Baptist Student Union. I. Title.

KEEGAN, Gilbert Kearnie, 1907- 267.6261
Baptist Student Union manual [by] G. Kearnie Keegan [and] David K. Alexander. Nashville, Convention Press [1957] 103p. illus. 20cm. 'Successor to Baptist Student Union methods, written by Dr. Frank H. Leavell.' [BX6205.B27K4] 57-36862
1. Baptist Student Union. I. Alexander, David K., joint author. II. Title.

*ASH, David 267.627
Junior highs and their MYF [by] David and Martha Ash. A Christian adventure handbook which may be used for study in church school, Christian adventure week, and special groups. Nashville, The Methodist Pub. House [c.1958, 1963] 72p. illus. 17cm. .25 pap.,
I. Title.

BALES, James D., 1915- 267.7
Understanding communism; a study manual. Grand Rapids, Mich., Baker Bk. [c.]1962. 88p. 22cm. Bibl. 62-6320 1.00 pap.,
1. Communism and religion. 2. Communism—Study and teaching. I. Title.

BALES, James D 1915- 267.7
Understanding communism; a study manual. Grand Rapids, Baker Book-House, 1962. 88p. 22cm. Includes bibliography. [HX536.B25] 62-6320
1. Communism and religion. 2. Communism—Study and teaching. I. Title.

268 Religious Training & Instruction

AASENG, Rolf E. 268
Anyone can teach (they said), by Rolf E. Aaseng. Illustrated by Janna Dory. Minneapolis, Augsburg Pub. House [1965] 108 p. illus. 20 cm. [BV1470.3.A2A3] 65-12137
1. Religious education — Anecdotes, facetiae, satire, etc. I. Title.

AASENG, Rolf E. 268
Anyone can teach (they said). Illus. by Janna Dory. Minneapolis, Augsburg [c,1965] 108p. illus. 20 cm. [BV1470.3.A2A3] 65-12137 1.95 pap.,
1. Religious education—Anecdotes, facetiae, satire, etc. I. Title.

ALL Africa Church Conference, Salisbury, Southern Rhodesia, 1962-63. 268
Christian education in Africa; report. London, Published for All Africa Churches Conference by the Oxford University Press, 1963. vii, 120 p. 20 cm. [BV1463.A4] 67-41827
1. Church and education in Africa — Congresses. I. Title.

ALMA MARIE Sister 268
Witnessing Christ by Sister Alma Marie, Sister Helen Clare. New York, Sadlier [c.1963] 144p. col. illus., music. 22cm. (On our way ser. 7) pap., .72; teacher's guide & key, pap., 1.50
I. Title.

ANDERSON, Phoebe M 268
Living and learning in the church school, by Phoebe M. Anderson. Boxton, Published for the Cooperative Publication Association [by] United Church Press [1965] viii, 102 p. 19 cm. (The Cooperative series) Bibliography: p. 100-102. [BV1471.2.A5] 65-15198
1. Religious education. I. Title.

ANDERSON, Phoebe M. 268
Living and learning in the church school. Boston, Pub. for the Cooperative Pubn. Assn. [by] United Church Pr. [c.1965] viii, 102p. 19cm. (Cooperative ser.) Bibl. [BV1471.2.A5] 65-15198 1.25 pap.,
1. Religious education. I. Title.

ANDERSON, Vernon Ellsworth, 1908- 268
Before you teach children. Philadelphia, Lutheran Church Press [1962] 176p. illus. 22cm. (Leadership education series) [BV1475.2.A5] 62-51866
1. Religious education of children. I. Title.

ANDERSON, Vernon Ellsworth, 1908- 268
Before you teach children. Philadelphia, Lutheran Church [dist. Muhlenberg, c. 1962] 176p. illus. 22cm. (Leadership educ. ser.) 62-51866 1.50
1. Religious education of children. I. Title.

BALLINGER, James L 268
Church conferences for youth and adults; a manual of planning and administration, by James L. Ballinger. St. Louis, Published for Cooperative Publication Association by the Bethany Press [1965] 160 p. forms. 23 cm. Bibliography: p. 155-160. [BV625.15.B3] 65-1756
1. Church meetings. 2. Church work with youth. I. Title.

BALLINGER, James L. 268
Church conferences for youth and adults; a manual of planning and administration. St. Louis, Pub. for Cooperative Pubns. Assn. by Bethany [c.1965] 160p. forms. 23cm. Bibl. [BV625.15.B3] 65-1756 1.95 pap.,
1. Church meetings. 2. Church work with youth. I. Title.

BARNETTE, Jasper Newton, 1887- 268
A church using its Sunday school. [Rev.] Neshville, Convention Press [1957,c1937] 139p. 19cm. [BV1520.B28 1957] 58-13038
1. Sunday-schools. I. Title.

BARNETTE, Jasper Newton, 1887- 268
The place of the Sunday school in evangelism. Nashville, Convention Press [1958] 150p. 19cm. [BV2616.B3 1958] 58-11510
1. Evangelistic work. 2. Sunday-schools. I. Title.

*BELGUM, David 268
Church camp counselor's manual: grades 7-9. Ed.: Walter A. Kortrey. Illus. by Carol Wilde. Philadelphia, Lutheran Church [1964] 52p. 21cm. 1.00 pap.,
I. Title.

BENSON, Clarence Herbert, 1879- 268
Sunday school success. 3d rev. Wheaton, Ill., Evangelical Teacher Training Assn. [1964] 96p. 23cm. (Evangelical Teacher Training Assn. Certificate ser., unit 6) Bibl. 64-13765 price unreported
1. Sunday-schools. I. Title.

BENSON, Dennis C. 268
Gaming: the fine art of creating simulation/learning games for religious education [by] Dennis Benson. Nashville, Abingdon AudioGraphics [1971] 64 p. illus. and phonodiscs (4 s. 8 in. 33 1/3 rpm.) in pocket. 24 cm. [BV1536.3.B45] 79-31994 ISBN 0-687-13995-3 5.95
1. Games in Christian education. I. Title.

BERTHIER, Rene. 268
The good news for children. Translated by Edmond Bonin. Illustrated by Napoli. Introd. by Rosemary Haughton. Dayton, Ohio, Pflaum Press, 1968. ix, [37] p. col. illus. 25 cm. Translation of Evangile pour les enfants. Presents brief excerpts from the New Testament from a Catholic viewpoint and demonstrates how their message may be applied in daily life. [BX1754.5.B413] 68-55965
1. Catholic Church—Juvenile literature. I. Napoli, Guillier, illus. II. Title.

BILLUPS, Ann. 268
Discussion starters for youth groups. Valley Forge [Pa] Judson Press [1966] 224 p. 27 cm. [BV1534.5.B5] 66-18292
1. Discussion in religious education. I. Title.

BILLUPS, Ann 268
Discussion starters for youth groups. Valley Forge [Pa.] Judson [c.1966] 224p. 27cm. [BV1534.5.B5] 66-18292 3.75 pap.,
1. Discussion in religious education. I. Title.

BLAZIER, Kenneth L. 268
Planning Christian education in your church; a guide for boards or committees of Christian education [by] Kenneth D. [i.e. L.] Blazier [and] Evelyn M. Huber. Valley Forge [Pa.] Judson Press [1974] 32 p. illus. 22 cm. Bibliography: p. 31-32. [BV1471.2.B57] 73-19585 ISBN 0-8170-0633-8 1.00 (pbk.).
1. Religious education. I. Huber, Evelyn, joint author. II. Title.

BOEHLKE, Robert R. 268
Theories of learning in Christian education. Philadelphia, Westminister Press [1962] 221 p. 21 cm. [BV1471.2.B6] 62-14049
1. Religious education — Psychology. I. Title.

BOEHLKE, Robert R. 268
Theories of learning in Christian education. Philadelphia, Westminster [c.1962] 221p. 21cm. 62-14049 4.50
1. Religious education—Psychology. I. Title.

BOYER, Leland 268
God's law of love, bk.3 by Leland J. Boyer, William J. Reedy [New York, Sadlier, c.1963] 187p. illus. (pt. col.) col. map. 28cm. (Confraternity high sch. ser. 633) 1.60 pap.,
I. Title.

BRECK, Flora Elizabeth, 1886- 268
Sunday-school ideas (for church and Sunday-school) Boston, W. A. Wilde Co. [1958] 90p. illus. 23cm. [BV1520.B713] 58-12416
1. Sunday-schools. I. Title.

BROWN, Lowell E. 268
Your Sunday school can grow : guidelines for building a better Sunday school / by Lowell E. Brown with Bobbie Reed. Glendale, Calif. : G/L Regal Books, [1974] 120 p. : ill. ; 20 cm. (An ICL insight book) At head of title: Grow. [BV1521.B73] 74-79564 ISBN 0-8307-0309-8 pbk. 2.25
1. Sunday-schools. I. Title. II. Title: Grow.

BRUDERHOF Communities. 268
Children in community. [By the Society of Brothers. Photography & art editor Roswith Arnold. New York, Plough Pub. House, 1963] 103 p. 25 cm. [BX8129.B62A4] 63-19099
1. Religious education of children — Bruderhof Communities. 2. Children — Religious life. I. Title.

BRUDERHOF Communities 268
Children in community. [By the Soc. of Brothers. c.1963] 103p. 25cm. 63-19099 3.00 bds.,
1. Religious education of children—Bruderhof Communities. 2. Children—Religious life. I. Title.

BULTER, James Donald, 1908- 268
Religious education the foundations and practice nature. New York, Harper &Row [1962] 321p. 22cm. [BV147.1.2B8268] 62-10081
1. Religious education. I. Title.

BURKE, Verdia. 268
Building a better Sunday school. St. Louis, Bethany Press [1950] 96 p. 20 cm. Includes bibliographies. [BV1520.B777] 50-2516
1. Sunday-schools. I. Title.

BURNETT, Sibley Curtis. 268
Better vacation Bible schools. Nashville, Convention Press [1957] u50p. 20cm. [BV1585.B816] 57-13894
1. Vacation schools, Religious. I. Title.

BURTON, Janet. 268
52 planned programs for youth and adults. Grand Rapids, Zondervan [1968] 108 p. illus. 21 cm. [BV29.B8] 68-27456
1. Young people's meetings (Church work) 2. Worship programs. I. Title.

BUTLER, James Donald, 1908- 268
Religious education; the foundations and practice of nurture. New York, Harper [c.1962] 321p. 22cm. 62-10081 5.50
I. Title.

BUTT, Elsie Miller. 268
The vacation church school in Christian education. New York, Published for the Cooperative Publication Association by Abingdon Press [1957] 192p. illus. 20cm. (The Cooperative series: leadership training texts) Includes bibliography. [BV1585.B83] 57-6754
1. Vacation schools, Religious. I. Title.

BUTTRICK, George Arthur 268
Biblical thought and the secular university. Baton Rouge, Louisiana State University Press [c. 1960] viii, 83p. 23cm. Bibl. notes: p.[69]-75 60-13168 2.50
1. Religious education. 2. Universities and colleges—Religion. I. Title.

BUTTRICK, George Arthur, 1892- 268
Biblical thought and the secular university. Baton Rouge, Louisiana State University Press [1960] 83p. 23cm. [BV1610.B83] 60-13168
1. Religious education. 2. Universities and colleges—Religion. I. Title.

BYRNE, Herbert W 1917- 268
Christian education for the local church, an evangelical and functional approach. Grand Rapids, Zondervan Pub. House [1963] 355 p. illus. 23 cm. [BV1471.2.B9] 63-9310
1. Religious education. I. Title.

BYRNE, Herbert W., 1917- 268
Christian education for the local church, an evangelical and functional approach. Grand Rapids, Mich., Zondervan [c.1963] 355p. illus. 23cm. 63-9310 5.95
1. Religious education. I. Title.

CARTER, Gerald Emmett, 1912- 268
The modern challenge to religious education; God's message and our response. Contributing ed.: William J. Reedy. New York W. H. Sadlier c.1961 422p. Bibl. 61-3058 5.36
I. Title.

CHAMBERLIN, John Gordon. 268
Freedom and faith; new approaches to

Christian education, by J. Gordon Chamberlin. Philadelphia, Westminster Press [1965] 156 p. 21 cm. Bibliographical references included in "Abbreviations" (p. 9) [BV1471.2.C46] 65-11615
1. Religious education. I. Title.

CHAMBERLIN, John Gordon 268
Freedom and faith; new approaches to Christian education. Philadelphia, Westminster [c.1965] 156p. 21cm. Bibl. [BV1471.2.C46] 65-11615 3.95
1. Religious education. I. Title.

CHAMBERLIN, John Gordon. 268
Parents and religion; a preface to Christian education. Philadelphia, Westminster Press [1961] 111p. 21cm. Includes bibliography. [BV1475.2.C45] 61-5127
1. Religious education of children. 2. Theology, Doctrinal—Hist.—20th cent. I. Title.

CHAPLIN, Dora P. 268
Children and religion. With a foreword by Charles L. Taylor, Jr. Rev. ed. New York, Scribner [1961, c.1948, 1961] 238p. Bibl. 61-6029 3.95 half cloth,
1. Religious education of children. I. Title.

CHAPLIN, Dora P. 268
A leader's guide for use with The privilege of teaching. Prepared by the Rev. Robert W. Renouf. New York, Morehouse [c.1963] 112p. 21cm. 1.75 pap.,
1. Religious education—Teacher training. I. Title.

CHAPLIN, Dora P. 268
The privilege of teaching, its dimension and demand for all who teach the Christian faith. Foreword by Stephen F. Bayne, Jr. New York, Morehouse-Barlow [c.1962] 295p. illus. Bibl. 62-9800 4.50 bds.,
1. Religious education—Teacher training. I. Title.

CHURCH of God (Cleveland, Tenn.) 268
Workers training course. Cleveland, Tenn., Pathway Press [19 v. 20cm. 'Prepared under the auspices of the Church of God, National Sunday School and Youth Board.' [BV1533.C45] 58-40611
1. Religious education—Teacher training. I. Title.

CLEMENT, George H. 268
Versatile object lessons. Grand Rapids, Mich., Zondervan [c.1960] 32p. 20cm. pap., apply
I. Title.

COBER, Kenneth Lorne, 1902- 268
The church's teaching ministry [by] Kenneth L. Cober. Valley Forge [Pa] Judson Press [1964] 143 p. illus. 20 cm. Includes bibliographies. [BV1471.2.C6] 64-13123
1. Religious education. 2. Baptists — Education. I. Title.

COBER, Kenneth Lorne, 1902- 268
The church's teaching ministry. Valley Forge [Pa.] Judson [c.1964] 143p. illus. 20cm. Bibl. 64-13123 1.50 pap.,
1. Religious education. 2. Baptists—Education. I. Title.

CORSON, Fred Pierce, 1896- 268
The Christian imprint. New York, Abingdon Press [1955] 156p. 21cm. [BV1471.C68] 55-6761
1. Religious education. I. Title.

COVE, Mary K. 268
Regarding religious education / Mary K. Cove and Mary Louise Mueller. Mishawaka, Ind. : Religious Education Press, c1977. p. cm. Includes bibliographical references. [BV1471.2.C67] 77-10873 ISBN 0-89135-011-X pbk. : 6.95
1. Christian education. I. Mueller, Mary Louise, joint author. II. Title.

COX, Alva I. 268
Christian education in the church today. Henry M. Bullock, gen. d. Nashville, Graded Pr. [dist. Abingdon, 1966, c.1965] 160p. 19cm. d. Bibl. [BV1471.2.C68] 66-2940 1.75 pap.,
1. Religious education. I. Title.

*CRISCI, Elizabeth W. 268
Creative sunday schools, [by] Elizabeth W. Crisci. Grand Rapids, Baker Book House, [1975] 107 p. 20 cm. [BV1515] ISBN 0-8010-2371-8 1.95 (pbk.)
1. Sunday-schools. 2. Religious education. I. Title.

*CROSS, Luther. 268
Object lessons for children, also usable as story sermons, chalk, picture, puppet, or bedtime stories by Luther Cross. Grand Rapids, Mich., Baker Bk. [1967] 99p. 20cm. 1.50 pap.,
I. Title.

CULLY, Iris V. 268
Change, conflict, and self-determination; next steps in religious education, by Iris V. Cully. Philadelphia, Westminster Press [1972] 191 p. 21 cm. Includes bibliographical references. [BV1464.C85] 72-5582 ISBN 0-664-20954-8 5.95
1. Religious education—Philosophy. I. Title.

CULLY, Iris V. 268
New life for your Sunday school / Iris V. Cully. New York : Hawthorn Books, c1976. viii, 117 p. ; 22 cm. Includes index. [BV1521.C84 1976] 75-28684 ISBN 0-8015-5366-0 : 5.95
1. Sunday-schools. 2. Christian education. I. Title.

CULLY, Kendig Brubaker. 268
The teaching church, an introduction to Christian education for parents and teachers. Philadelphia, United Church Press [1963] 94 p. 20 cm. Includes bibliography. [BV1471.2.C8] 63-12579
1. Religious education. I. Title.

CULLY, Kendig Brubaker 268
The teaching church, an introduction to Christian education for parents and teachers. Philadelphia, United Church [c.1963] 94p. 20cm. Bibl. 63-12579 2.50
1. Religious education. I. Title.

DE WOLF, Lotan Harold, 1905- 268
Teaching our faith in God. New York, Abingdon Press [1963] 188 p. 23 cm. [BV1534.D4] 63-7480
1. Religious education — Study and teaching. 2. Theology — Study and teaching. I. Title.

DE WOLF, Lotan Harold, 1905- 268
Teaching our faith in God. Nashville, Abingdon [1963] 188p. 23cm. Bibl. 63-7480 3.75
1. Religious education—Study and teaching. 2. Theology—Study and teaching. I. Title.

DRINKWATER, Francis Harold 268
Telling the good news; reflections on religion and education. [dist. New York, St. Martin's Press 1960] viii, 228p. 23cm. (bibl. footnotes) 60-2035 4.75
1. Catholic education. 2. Religious education. 3. Catechetics—Catholic Church. I. Title.

DUCKERT, Mary. 268
Help! I run a Sunday school. Illustrated by Donald W. Patterson. Philadelphia, Westminster Press [1971] 128 p. illus. 21 cm. [BV1521.D82] 77-158124 ISBN 0-664-24930-2
1. Sunday-schools. I. Title.

DURKA, Gloria. 268
Modeling God : religious education for tomorrow / by Gloria Durka and Joanmarie Smith. New York : Paulist Press, c1976. v, 92 p. ; 18 cm. (Deus book) Includes bibliographies. [BV1471.2.D87] 75 44595 ISBN 0 8091 1933 1 pbk. : 1.65
1. Christian education. 2. Process theology. I. Smith, Joanmarie, joint author. II. Title.

EASTMAN, Frances W. 268
Reclaiming Christian education / Frances W. Eastman and Carolyn E. Goddard. Philadelphia : United Church Press, c1976. 122 p. : ill. ; 21 cm. "Published by United Church Press for the Division of Evangelism, Church Extension, and Education of the United Church Board for Homeland Ministries." [BV1471.2.E2] 76-26927 ISBN 0-8298-0323-8 pbk. : 2.50
1. Christian education. I. Goddard, Carolyn E., 1918- joint author. II. United Church Board for Homeland Ministries. Division of Evangelism, Church Extension, and Education. III. Title.

EBERSOLE, Eleanor 268
Christian education for socially handicapped children and youth; a manual for chaplains and teachers of persons under custody. Philadelphia. Pub. for the Coop. Pubn. Assn. by United Church [c.1964] 96p. 19cm. (Cooperative ser.: Leadership training texts) [BV1615.S6E2] 64-25579 1.25 pap.,
1. Religious education of socially handicapped children. I. Title.

EL nino que honro a su madre, y otros relato inspiradores [in Spanish dist. Mountain View, Calif., Pacific Pr. c.1962 Pacific Pr. Pub., c.1962] 128p. illus. 20cm. 1.00 pap., 268

EMERGING issues in religious education / edited by Gloria Durka and Joanmarie Smith. New York : Paulist Press, c1976. vi, 211 p. ; 23 cm. Bibliography: p. 209-211. [BV1473.E47] 76-18052 ISBN 0-8091-1971-4 pbk. : 7.95 268
1. Christian education—Addresses, essays, lectures. 2. Theology—Addresses, essays, lectures. I. Durka, Gloria. II. Smith, Joanmarie.

ERB, Alta Mae, 1891- 268
Christian education in the home. Scottdale, Pa., Herald Press [c1963] 92 p. 20 cm. Bibliography: p. 89-92. [BV1475.2F.7] 63-19648
1. Religious education of children. I. Title.

ERB, Alta Mae, 1891- 268
Christian education in the home. Scottdale, Pa., Herald Pr. [c.1963] 92p. 20cm. Bibl. 63-19648 2.50
1. Religious education of children. I. Title.

FAHS, Sophia Blanche (Lyon), 1876- 268
Today's children and yesterday's heritage; a philosophy of creative religious development. With an introd. by Angus H. MacLean. Boston, Beacon Press [1952] 224 p. 22 cm. [BV1475.F3] 52-5242
1. Religious education of children. I. Title.

FALLAW, Wesner 268
Church education for tomorrow. Philadelphia, Westminster Press [c.1960] 219p. 21cm. Bibl. and Bibl. notes p.[209]-215 60-9711 3.75
1. Religious education. 2. Religious education—Curricula. I. Title.

*FINK, Russell E. 268
Church camp program guide: grades 7-9. Walter A. Kortrey, ed. Illus. by Carol Wilde. Philadelphia, Lutheran Church [c.1964] 122p. 28cm. 1.50, pap., wire bdg.
I. Title.

FLAKE, Arthur, 1862-1952. 268
The true functions of the Sunday school. Nashville, Convention Press [1957] 130 p. 20 cm. [BX6223.F62] 62-11837
1. Sunday-schools. 2. Southern Baptist Convention — Education. I. Title.

FOSTER, Virgil E. 268
Christian education where the learning is [by] Virgil E. Foster. Englewood Cliffs, N.J., Prentice-Hall [1968] xii, 147 p. 22 cm. [BV1471.2.F67] 68-15349
1. Religious education. I. Title.

FOSTER, Virgil E 268
How a small church can have good Christian education. [1st ed.] New York, Harper [1956] 127p. 20cm. [BV1520.F57] 56-7028
1. Religious education. 2. Sunday-schools. I. Title.

FULBRIGHT, Robert G. 268
New dimensions in teaching children [by] Robert G. Fulbright. Nashville, Broadman Press [1971] 144 p. illus. 22 cm. Includes bibliographical references. [LB1776.F84] 77-145980 ISBN 0-8054-4917-5 4.95
1. Elementary school teaching. 2. Christian education. I. Title.

GETZ, Gene A. 268
The vacation Bible school in the local church. Chicago, Moody [c.1962] 158p. illus. 62-3051 2.95
1. Vacation schools, Religious. I. Title.

GILBERT, W Kent. 268
As Christians teach [by] W. Kent Gilbert. Philadelphia, Fortress Press [1964, c1962] 167 p. illus. 21 cm. Includes bibliographies. [BV1475.2.G5] 64-23270
1. Religious education — Study and teaching. 2. Lutheran Church — Education. I. Title.

GILBERT W Kent. 268
As Christians teach. Philadelphia, Lutheran Church Press [1962] 160 p. illus. 21 cm. (Leadership education series) Teacher's guide. [n.p., c1962] 32 p. illus. 29 cm. and phonodisc (2 s., 7 in., 33 1/3 rpm) in pocket. (Leadership education series) [BV1475.2.G5] 62-53282
1. Religious education — Study and teaching. 2. Lutheran Church — Education. I. Title.

GILBERT, W. Kent 268
As Christians teach. Philadelphia, Lutheran Church Pr. [dist. Muhlenberg] [c.1962] 160p. illus. 21cm. (Leadership edu. ser.) 62-53282 1.50
1. Religious education—Study and teaching. 2. Lutheran Church—Education. I. Title.

GIORDANI, Francesco, 1896- 268
The Vatican; 64 magnificent photopages of the sights and scenes of Vatican City and its treasures. [Edited by Edward M. Kinney from photos, taken by Francesco Giordani. New York, Vatican Pavilion, New York World's Fair, c1964. [66] p. (chiefly illus. (part col.)) 33 cm. Cover title. "Souvenir of the Vatican Pavilion, New York World's Fair, 1964-1965." [DG800.G45] 64-18301
1. Vatican City. I. Kinney, Edward M;, ed. II. Vatican Pavilion (New York World's Fair) inc. U.S.A. III. Title.

GOSSELINK, Marion Gerard 268
Special day talks for children. Chicago, Moody [1963, c.1962] 79p. 22cm. 1.25, pap., spiral bdg.
I. Title.

HAHN, Hans R. 268
Helping the retarded to know God; a guide for Christian teachers of the mentally handicapped [by] Hans R. Hahn [and] Werner H. Raasch. Saint Louis, Concordia Pub. House [1969] 112 p. 21 cm. (Concordia leadership training series) Includes bibliographies. [BV1615.M37H3] 73-99315 1.95
1. Christian education of the mentally handicapped. I. Raasch, Werner H., joint author. II. Title.

HALL, Arlene Stevens. 268
Teaching children in your church. Anderson, Ind., Warner Press [1951] 118 p. 19 cm. [BV1534.H27] 51-5371
1. Religious education—Teaching methods. I. Title.

HALL, Arlene Stevens 268
Teaching children in your church. Rev. ed. Anderson, Ind., Warner [1962] 96p. 21cm. 62-13336 1.25 pap.,
1. Religious education—Teaching methods. I. Title.

HANSON, Joseph John 268
Our church plans for adults; a manual on adult Christian education. Valley Forge, Pa., Judson [c.1962] 112p. illus. 19cm. Bibl. 62-16999 1.25 pap.,
1. Religious education of adults. I. Title.

HARRIS, Maria. 268
The D.R.E. book : questions and strategies for parish personnel / by Maria Harris. New York : Paulist Press, c1976. v, 190 p. ; 21 cm. Includes bibliographical references. [BV1531.H33] 75-44803 ISBN 0-8091-1938-2 pbk. : 4.95
1. Christian education directors. I. Title.

HAVIGHURST, Robert James, 1900- 268
The educational mission of the church, by Robert J. Havighurst. Philadelphia, Westminster Press [1965] 150 p. 21 cm. "Stone lectures ... 1964 ... form the core of this book." Bibliographical references included in "Notes" (p. [153]-156) [BV1473.H3] 65-10538
1. Religious education — Addresses, essays, lectures. I. Princeton Theological Seminary. Stone lectures, 1964. II. Title.

HAVIGHURST, Robert James, 1900- 268
The educational mission of the church. Philadelphia, Westminster [c.1965] 159p. 21cm. Stone lectures, 1964 form the core of this book. Bibl. [BV1473.H3] 65-10538 4.50
1. Religious education—Addresses, essays, lectures. I. Princeton Theological Seminary. Stone lectures, 1964. II. Title.

HEIM, Ralph Daniel, 1895- 268
Leading a Sunday church school. Philadelphia, Muhlenberg Press [1950] xi, 368 p. 22 cm. [BV1520.H39] 50-9488
1. Sunday-schools. I. Title.

HENDERLITE, Rachel. 268
The Holy Spirit in Christian education. Philadelphia, Westminster Press [1964] 127 p. 21 cm. Bibliographical reference included in "Notes and acknowledgments" (p. 115-122) [BT121.1.H38] 64-14867
1. Holy Spirit. I. Title.

HENDERLITE, Rachel 268
The Holy Spirit in Christian education. Philadelphia, Westminster [c.1964] 127p. 21cm. Bibl. 64-14867 1.95 pap.,
1. Holy Spirit. I. Title.

HENDRIX, John. 268
Experiential education, X-ED : how to get your church started / John & Lela Hendrix. Nashville : Abingdon Press, [1975] 176 p. : ill. ; 21 cm. Bibliography: p. 169-176. [BV1471.2.H45] 75-4722 ISBN 0-687-12421-2 : 6.50
1. Christian education. 2. Church group work. I. Hendrix, Lela, joint author. II. Title.

HERON, Frances (Dunlap) j268
Jay Bain, junior boy. Illustrated by Janet Smalley. New York, Abingdon Press [1963] 144 p. illus. 21 cm. [BV1521.5.H4] 63-15708
1. Sunday-schools — Juvenile literature. I. Title.

HOGAN, Bernice. 268
More from your class meetings. New York, Abingdon Press [1959] 108p. illus. 22cm. Includes bibliography. [BX8346.H6] 59-12782
1. Class meetings, Methodist. I. Title.

HORTON, Roy F 1902- 268
Inspiration Point and its personalities. St. Louis, Bethany Press [1961] 96p. illus. 23cm. [BX7330.I6H6] 61-12217
1. Mowers, Charles. 2. Scoville, Charles Beign, 1869-1938. 3. Inspiration Point, Ark. 4. Disciples of Christ. I. Title.

HOWSE, William Lewis 268
Those treasured hours; the adventure and dividends of Sunday school teaching. Nashville, Broadman Press [c.1960] ix, 67p. 21cm. 60-5630 1.50 bds.,
1. Sunday-schools. 2. Religious education—Teaching methods. I. Title.

HOWSE, William Lewis, 1905- 268
Those treasured hours; the adventure and dividends of Sunday school teaching. Nashville, Broadman Press [c1960] 67p. 21cm. [BV1534.H74] 60-5630
1. Sunday-schools. 2. Religious education—Teaching methods. I. Title.

HOYER, George W. 268
I think I'll be . . . ; a workbook for young people in the church. St. Louis, Concordia, c.1961. 65p. illus. 28cm. .85 pap.,
I. Title.

HUNTER, David R. 1910- 268
Christian education as engagement. New York, Seabury [c.]1963. 128p. 20cm. Bibl. 63-9059 3.00 bds.,
1. Discussion. 2. Religious education. I. Title.

INTERNATIONAL Catechetical Congress, 1st, Rome, 1971. 268
Selected documentation. Edited by William J. Tobin. [Washington] United States Catholic Conference [1972] vi, 148 p. 22 cm. Congress organized by the Sacred Congregation for the Clergy. [BV1463.I46 1971] 72-195517
1. Christian education—Congresses. I. Tobin, William John, 1936- ed. II. Catholic Church. Congregatio pro Clericis.

JACOBS, James Vernon 268
How to increase your Sunday school attendance. Grand Rapids, Michigan, Zondervan [c.1960] 64p. 20cm. (Sunday know-how ser.) 1.00 pap.,
I. Title.

JACOBS, James Vernon, 1898- 268
1,000 plans and ideas for Sunday school workers. Grand Rapids, Zondervan Pub. House [1957] 157p. illus. 20cm. [BV1520.J2] 57-3246
1. Sunday-schools. I. Title.

JONES, Jessie Mae (Orton) 268
The spiritual education of our children. New York, Viking Press [1960] 124p. 21cm. Includes bibliography. [BV1475.2.J6] 60-7673
1. Religious education of children. I. Title.

JONES, Mary Alice, 1898- 268
The pastor and Christian education of children. Nashville, Division of the Local Church, General Board of Education of the Methodist Church [1963] 67 p. illus. 22 cm. "Suggested resources": p. 66-67. [BV1521.J6] 64-56072
1. Church work with children. 2. Religious education of children. I. Title.

JOY, Donald Marvin. 268
Meaningful learning in the church, by Donald M. Joy. Winona Lake, Ind., Light and Life Press [1969] 168 p. illus. 20 cm. "Commissioned as a part of the Aldersgate Graded Curriculum project by the Aldersgate Publications Association." Bibliographical references included in "Notes" (p. 153-162) [BV1521.J65] 72-80801
1. Sunday-schools. 2. Christian education. I. Aldersgate Publications Association. II. Title.

*KNIGHT, Cecil Bertie Howard. 268
Keeping the Sunday school alive, by Cecil B. Knight. Grand Rapids, Mich., Baker Book House [1972, c.1960] 118 p. 19 cm. (Sunday School Workers' Training Course) Bibl.: p. 117-118. [BV1471] ISBN 0-8010-5327-7 pap., 1.75
1. Religious education—Administration. 2. Sunday Schools—Administration. I. Title.

KOULOMZIN, Sophie. 268
Our church and our children / Sophie Koulomzin. [Crestwood, N.Y.] : St. Vladimir's Seminary Press, 1975. 158 p. ; 22 cm. Bibliography: p. 157-158. [BV1475.2.K68] 75-20215 ISBN 0-913836-25-7 pbk. : 4.50
1. Orthodox Eastern Church—Education. 2. Christian education of children. I. Title.

LEAVITT, Guy P 268
How to improve my church's school, an analysis and improvement program. Cincinnati, Standard Pub. Co. [1953] 104p. 19cm. [BV1520.L38] 53-31993
1. Sunday-schools. I. Title.

LE BAR, Lois Emogene, 1907- 268
Education that is Christian. [Westwood, N. J.] Revell [1958] 252p. 22cm. Includes bibliography. [BV1471.L4] 58-8602
1. Religious education. I. Title.

LE BAR, Lois Emogene, 1907- 268
Focus on people in church education [by] Lois E. LeBar. Westwood, N.J., Revell [1968] 256 p. illus. 21 cm. Includes bibliographies. [BV1471.2.L4] 68-17091
1. Religious education. I. Title.

LEDERACH, Paul M. 268
Reshaping the teaching ministry; toward relevant education in the local congregation, by Paul M. Lederach. Scottdale, Pa., Herald Press [1968] 125 p. 20 cm. Includes bibliographical references. [BV1471.2.L42] 68-22266
1. Religious education. I. Title.

LEE, James Michael. 268
The flow of religious instruction: a social-science approach. Dayton, Ohio, Pflaum/Standard [1973] 379 p. illus. 21 cm. Second vol. in a trilogy; the 1st of which is the author's The shape of religious instruction; and the 3d of which is his The content of religious instruction. Includes bibliographical references. [BV1471.2.L442] 72-97171 ISBN 0-8278-9058-3 4.95
1. Religious education. 2. Sociology, Christian. I. Title.

LEE, James Michael. 268
The shape of religious instruction; a social-science approach. Dayton, Ohio, Pflaum, 1971. 330 p. 21 cm. First vol. in a trilogy; the 2d of which is the author's The flow of religious instruction; and the 3d of which is his The content of religious instruction. Includes bibliographical references. [BV1471.2.L443] 78-153802 4.95
1. Christian education. 2. Sociology, Christian. I. Title.

LEWIS, Eve 268
Children and their religion. New York, Sheed [c.1962] 316p. 20cm. 62-15279 4.50
1. Children—Religious life. I. Title.

LINK, Mark J., ed. 268
Teaching the sacraments and morality [by] Stenzel [others. Mark J. Link, ed.] Chicago, Loyola Univ. Pr. [c.]1965. ix, 214p. illus. 24cm. (Loyola pastoral ser.: Lumen vitae studies) Bibl. [BX2203.L5] 64-8102 3.50
1. Sacraments—Study and teaching. 2. Religious education. I. Stenzel, Alois. II. Title.

LITTLE, Gertrude, 1911- 268
Understanding our pupils. Anderson, Ind., Warner Press [1950] 110 p. 19 cm. [BV1471.L56] 50-9995
1. Religious education. I. Title.

LITTLE, Lawrence Calvin, 1897- 268
Foundations for a philosophy of Christian education. [Nashville] Abingdon [c.1962] 240p. Bibl. 62-7440 4.00
1. Religious education. I. Title.

LOBINGIER, John Leslie, 1884- 268
The better church school. Boston, Pilgrim Press [1952] 152 p. 21 cm. [BV1520.L58] 52-1583
1. Sunday schools. 2. Religious education. I. Title.

LONDON, Allie Spencer. 268
The Sunday school challenge. Butler, Ind., Higley Press [1958] 157p. 20cm. [BV1520.L65] 58-1555
1. Sunday-schools. I. Title.

LORENSEN, Larry. 268
Spiritual home training for the child. Chicago, Moody Press [1954] 144p. 22cm. [BV1590.L67] 54-14780
1. Religious education—Home training. I. Title.

LOTZ, Philip Henry, 1889- ed. 268
Orientation in religious education. New York, Abingdon-Cokesbury Press [1950] 618 p. 24 cm. Includes bibliographies. "A selected bibliography of religious education [by] Leonard A. Stidley": p. 567-583. [LC427.L6] 50-7274
1. Religious education—U. S. I. Title.

LYNN, Robert W. 268
The big little school; Sunday child of American Protestantism, by Robert W. Lynn and Elliott Wright. [1st ed.] New York, Harper & Row [1971] xiii, 108 p. 22 cm. Includes bibliographical references. [BV1516.A1L9] 73-124715 3.95
1. Sunday-schools—U.S.—History. I. Wright, H. Elliott, 1937- joint author. II. Title.

MCDONNELL, Lois Eddy 268
The home and church; partners in the Christian education of children. Nashville, Pub. for the Co-operative Pubn. Assn. by Abingdon [1961] 160p. illus. (Cooperative ser.: leadership training texts) Bibl. 62-16020 1.50 pap.,
1. Religious education of children. 2. Religious education—Home training. I. Title.

*MC INTYRE, Ralph L. 268
Big ideas for small sunday schools / by Ralph L.McIntyre Grand Rapids : Baker Book House, 1976c1975. 61.p ; 20 cm. (Teaching helps series) [BV 1521] ISBN 0-8010-6005-2 pbk. : 1.50.
1. Sunday-schools. I. Title.

MCNATT, Elmer E 1908- 268
The Pentecostal Sunday school. [Nashville? 1952] 201p. illus. 20cm. On spine: A Sunday school concordance. [BX3795.P25M32] 53-19913
1. Sunday-schools. 2. United Pentecostal Church—Education. I. Title. II. Title: A Sunday school concordance.

MARY AGNESINE, Sister, 1884- 268
Teaching religion for living. Milwaukee, Bruce Pub. Co. [1953, c1952] 184p. 23cm. [BX925.M33] 53-1999
1. Religious education. 2. Catholic Church—Education. I. Title.

MASON, Harold Carlton, 1888- 268
Abiding values in Christian education. [Westwood, N. J., F. H. Revell Co. [1955] 176p. 21cm. [BV1471.M37] 55-6629
1. Religious education. I. Title.

MASON, Harold Carlton, 1888- 268
The teaching task of the local church. Winona Lake, Ind., Light and Life Press [1960] 214p. 23cm. Includes bibliography. [BV1471.M372] 60-8218
1. Religious education. I. Title.

MASON, Harold Charles, 1889- 268
Abiding values in Christian education. [Westwood, N. J.] F. H. Revell Co. [1955] 176p. 21cm. [BV1471.M37] 55-6629
1. Religious education. I. Title.

MATTSON, Lloyd D. 268
Camping guideposts: Christian camp counselor's handbook. Chicago, Moody [1963, c.1962] 93p. illus. 28cm. 2.50, pap., plastic bdg.
I. Title.

MILLER, Randolph Crump, 1910- 268
Christian nurture and the church. New York, Scribners [c.1961] 208p. Bibl. 61-7226 3.50
1. Church. 2. Religious education. I. Title.

MILLER, Randolph Crump, 1910- 268
Education for Christian living. Englewood Cliffs, N. J., Prentice-Hall, 1956. 418p. 22cm. [BV1471.M49] 56-6985
1. Religious education. I. Title.

MILLER, Randolph Crump, 1910- 268
Education for Christian living. 2d ed. Englewood Cliffs, N.J., Prentice, 1963[c.1956, 1963] 462p. 23cm. Bibl. 63-7923 10.60 bds.,
1. Religious education. I. Title.

MILLER, Randolph Crump, 1910- 268
Your child's religion. [1st ed.] Garden City, N.Y., Doubleday, 1962. 164 p. 22 cm. Includes bibliography. [BV1590.M52] 62-11445
1. Religious education—Home training. 2. Children—Religious life. I. Title.

MILLER, T. Franklin 268
You can have a better Sunday school. Anderson. Ind., Warner Press [dist. Gospel Trumpet Press] [c.1960] 79p. 21cm. 60-13191 1.00 pap.,
1. Sunday-schools. I. Title.

MORRISON, Eleanor Shelton. 268
Creative teaching in the church [by] Eleanor Shelton Morrison and Virgil E. Foster. Englewood Cliffs, N. J., Prentice-Hall [1963] 244 p. 22 cm. [BV1471.2.M6] 63-16578
1. Religious education. I. Foster, Virgil E., joint author. II. Title.

MOW, Anna B 268
Your child from birth to rebirth; how to educate a child to be ready for life with God, a book for parents and teachers. Grand Rapids, Zondervan Pub. House [1963] 152 p. 23 cm. Bibliography: p. 150-152. [BV1475.2.M6] 63-17741
1. Religious education of children. I. Title.

MOW, Anna B. 268
Your child from birth to rebirth; how to educate your child to be ready for a life with God. Grand Rapids, Mich., Zondervan [1972, c.1963] 186 p. 18 cm. Bibliography: p. 183-186. [BV1475.2.M6] 63-17741 pap., 0.95
1. Religious education of children. I. Title.

MUNRO, Harry Clyde, 1890- 268
Protestant nurture; an introduction to Christian education. Englewood Cliffs, N. J., Prentice-Hall, 1956. 270p. 22cm. [BV1471.M76] 56-6111
1. Religious education. I. Title.

MURCH, James DeForest, 1892- 268
Teach or perish! An imperative for Christian education at the localchurch level. Grand Rapids, Mich., Eerdmans [1962, c.1961] 1177p. 21cm. 62-11247 3.00
1. Religious education. I. Title.

MURRAY, Albert Victor, 1890- 268
Education into religion. New York, Harper [1953] xii, 230p. 22cm. [BV1471.M83] 54-7263
1. Religious education. I. Title.

MURRAY, Andrew, 1828-1917. 268
The children for Christ. Chicago, Moody Press [1952] 191p. 20cm. 'A condensation of the author's original work of this title.' [BV1477.M8] 53-30883
1. Religious education—Sermons. 2. Religious education—Home training. I. Title.

NATIONAL Sunday School Association. 268
Sunday school encyclopedia. Edited by Clate A. Risley. Chicago [19 v. illus., ports. 28cm. Includes bibliographies. [BV1521.N3] 61-770
1. Sunday-schools. I. Risley, Clate A., ed. II. Title.

*NEWLAND, Mary Reed, comp. 268.
The resource guide: for adults religious education. Kansas City, Mo., National catholic Reporter, [1974]. 196 p. 28 cm. [BV1550] 9.95 (pbk.)
1. Religious education of adults, (children, etc.). I. Title.
Publisher's address: P.O. Box 281 Kansas City, Mo. 64141

NEWLAND, Mary (Reed) 268
We and our children; molding the child in Christian living. New York, Kenedy [1954] 271p. 21cm. [BV1590.N4] 54-10067
1. Religious education—Home training. 2. Children—Religious life. I. Title.

NEWLAND, Mary (Reed) 268
We and our children; molding the child in Christian living. Garden City, N. Y.., Doubleday [1961, c. 1954] 273p. (Image bk., D123) .85 pap.,
1. Religious education—Home training. 2. Children—Religious life. I. Title.

OLSON, Richard Allan. 268
The pastor's role in educational ministry, edited with introductions by Richard Allan Olson. Philadelphia, Fortress Press [1974] 285 p. illus. 23 cm. (Yearbooks in Christian education, 5) Bibliography: p. 282-285. [BV1473.O43] 74-180255
1. Christian education—Addresses, essays, lectures. 2. Pastoral theology—Addresses, essays, lectures. I. Title. II. Series.

PEACHEY, Laban. 268
Learning to understand people. Scottdale, Pa., Herald Press [1965] 109 p. illus. 20 cm. (Christian service training series) Includes bibliographical references. [BV1471.2.P4] 65-18237
1. Religious education—Psychology. I. Title.

PERSON, Peter P 268
An introduction to Christian education. Grand Rapids, Baker Book House, 1958. 224p. 23cm. Includes bibliography. [BV1471.P4] 59-4465
1. Religious education. I. Title.

PERSON, Peter P 268
The minister in Christian education. Grand Rapids, Baker Book House, 1960. 134p. 20cm. Includes bibliography. [BV4360.P45] 60-10190
1. Religious education. 2. Pastoral theology. I. Title.

POWERS, Edward A. 268
Signs of shalom, by Edward A. Powers. Philadelphia, Published for Joint Educational Development [by] United Church Press [1973] 160 p. illus. 22 cm. (A Shalom resource) Bibliography: p. 152-156. [BV1558.P68] 73-6952
1. Religious education—Curricula. 2. Shalom (The word) 3. Christian life—United Church of Christ authors. I. Title.

PRICE, John Milburn, 1884- 268
Formative factors in Christian character. Nashville, Convention Press [1962, 1959] 137 p. 20 cm. Includes bibliography. [LC268.P67] 59-14427
1. Moral education. 2. Educational psychology. I. Title.

PRICE, John Milburn, 1884- 268
A survey of religious education [by] J. M. Price [and others] 2d ed. New York, Ronald

Press Co. [1959] 466 p. 21 cm. Includes bibliography. [BV1471.P66 1959] 59-6624
1. Religious education.

RANWEZ, Pierre. 268
Together toward God; religious training in the family, by P. Ranwez, J. and M. L. Defossa and J. Gerard-Libois. Translated by Paul Barrett. Westminster, Md., Newman Press, 1959. 200p. 21cm. [BV1590.R313] 59-11339
1. Religious education —Home training. 2. Family—Religious life. I. Title.

REED, William Wellington, 1912- 268
Teaching the church's children; a handbook for teachers and parents. New York, Morehouse-Gorham Co., 1958. 183p. 21cm. Includes bibliography. [BV1475.R4] 58-6842
1. Religious education of children. I. Title.

REIN, Remus C 1905- 268
Building the Sunday School. St. Louis, Concordia Pub. House [1950] v., 116 p. 19 cm. Includes bibliographies. [BV1520.R4] 50-11974
1. Sunday-schools. I. Title.

THE Religious education we need : toward the renewal of Christian education / edited by James Michael Lee ; contributors Alfred McBride ... [et al.]. Mishawaka, Ind. : Religious Education Press, c1977. 174 p. ; 21 cm. Includes indexes. [BV1473.R38] 76-55587 ISBN 0-89135-009-8 lib.bdg. : 8.95 ISBN 0-89135-005-5 pbk. : 5.95 268
1. Christian education—Addresses, essays, lectures. I. Lee, James Michael. II. McBride, Alfred.

REORGANIZED Church of Jesus Christ of Latter Day Saints. Children's Division. 268
Skylark ways; a handbook for Skylark Girls. Independence, Mo., Herald Pub. House [1966] 72 p. illus. 28 cm. [BX8671.A549] 66-17863
1. Religious education of girls. I. Title.

REORGANIZED Church of Jesus of Latter Day Saints. Children's Division 268
Skylark ways; a handbook for Skylark Girls. Independence, Mo., Herald Pub., c.1966. 72p. illus. 28cm. [BX8671.A549] 66-17863 1.95 pap.,
1. Religious education of girls. I. Title.

RICE, Edwin Wilbur, 1831-1929. 268
The Sunday school movement 1780-1917, and the American Sunday-School Union 1817-1917. New York, Arno Press, 1971 [c1917] 501 p. illus. 23 cm. (American education: its men, ideas, and institutions. Series II) [BV1515.R5 1971] 70-165728 ISBN 0-405-03717-1
1. American Sunday-School Union. 2. Sunday-school—United States. I. Title. II. Series.

RIDAY, George Emil, 1912- 268
Understanding the learner [by] George E. Riday. Valley Forge, Judson Press [1964] 125 p. illus. 20 cm. Bibliography: p. 123-125. [LB1053.R5] 64-13124
1. Learning, Psychology of. 2. Religious education — Psychology. I. Title.

RIDAY, George Emil, 1912- 268
Understanding the learner. Valley Forge, Pa., Judson Pr. [c.1964] 125p. illus. 20cm. Bibl. 64-13124 1.50 pap.,
1. Learning, Psychology of. 2. Religious education—Psychology. I. Title.

SANDERSON, Leonard, 1914- 268
Using the Sunday school in evangelism. Vashville, Convention Press [1958] 146p. illus. 20cm. [BV1523.S2] 58-9944
1. Sunday schools. 2. Evangelistic work. I. Title.

SCHISLER, John Quincy. 268
Christian teaching in the churches. Nashville, Abingdon Press [1954] 173p. 21cm. [BV1471.S39] 54-5509
1. Religious education. I. Title.

*SCHMALENBERGER, Jerry L. 268
Church camp counselor's manual: grades 10-12. Art by Andrew Snyder. Ed.: Walter A. Kortrey. Philadelphia, Lutheran Church [c.1964] 60p. 19cm. (LCA church camp ser.) 1.00 pap.,
I. Title.

SCHREYER, George M 1913- 268
Christian education in action. New York, Comet Press Books, 1957. 177p. 21cm. (A Reflection book) [BV1471.S415] 57-8111
1. Religious education. I. Title.

SCHREYER, George M 1913- 268
Christian education in theological focus. Philadelphia, Christian Education Press [1962] 211p. 21cm. [BV1471.2.S3] 62-19192
1. Religious education. I. Title.

SCHULZ, Florence. 268
Summer with nursery children. Illustrated by Lennabelle McBride Reed. Boston, Published for the Cooperative Publication Association [by] Pilgrim Press [1958] 156p. illus. 23cm. (The Cooperative series texts. Vacation church school texts) Includes bibliography. [BV1585.S35] 58-13598
1. Vacation schools, Religious. 2. Religious education of pre-school children. I. Title.

SHAVER, Erwin Leander, 1890- 268
The weekday church school; how to organize and conduct a program of weekday religious education on released time. Boston, Published for the Co-operative Publication Association [by] Pilgrim Press [1956] 154p. 20cm. [BV1580.S49] 56-8213
1. Week-day church schools. I. Title.

SHAVER, Erwin Leander, 1890- 268
The weekday church school: how to organize and conduct a program of weekday religious education on released time. Boston. Published for the Co-operative Publication Association [by] Pilgrim Press [1956] 154 p. 20 cm. [BV1580.S49] 56-8243
1. Week-day church schools. I. Title.

SHERRILL, Lewis Joseph, 1892- 268
The gift of power. New York, Macmillan, 1955. 206p. illus. 22cm. [BV1471.S45] 55-13597
1. Religious education. 2. Church. 3. Psychology, Religious. I. Title.

SILVEY, D O 268
The enlisting Sunday school. Little Rock, Ark., Baptist Publications Committee [c1963] 108 p. diagr. 21 cm. [BV1521.S5] 63-21458
1. Sunday-schools. I. Title.

SILVEY, D. O. 268
The enlisting Sunday school. Little Rock, Ark., Baptist Pubns. Comm. [c.1963] c108p. diagr. 21cm. 63-21458 1.00 pap.,
1. Sunday-chools. I. Title.

SISEMORE, John T 268
The ministry of visitation. Nashville, Broadman Press [1954] 115p. 20cm. [BV1523.S5] 54-2969
1. Visitations (Religious education) I. Title.

SLOYAN, Gerard Stephen, 1919- ed. 268
Modern catechetics; message and method in religious formation. New York, Macmillan [1963] xi, 381 p. 22 cm. Bibliography: p. 361-367. [BX1968.S5] 63-14201
1. Religious education. 2. Catechetics — Catholic Church. I. Title.

SLOYAN, Gerard Stephen, 1919- ed. 268
Modern catechetics: message and method in religious formation. New York, Macmillan [c.1960, 1963] 379p. 22cm. Bibl. 63-12401 5.95
1. Religious education. 2. Catechetics—Catholic Church. I. Title.

SLUSSER, Gerald H 268
A dynamic approach to church education [by] Gerald H. Slusser. Illustrated by Paul Bogdanoff. Philadelphia, Geneva Press [c1968] 124 p. illus. 21 cm. (Decade books) [BV1471.2.S58] 68-10225
1. Religious education. I. Title.

SMART, James D 268
The teaching ministry of the church; an examination of the basic principles of Christian education. Philadelphia, Westminster Press [1954] 207p. 21cm. [BV1471.S57] 54-10569
1. Religious education. I. Title.

*SMITH, Doris J., ed. 268
James goes to vacation church school. Illus. by George Wilde. Philadelphia, Lutheran Church Pr. [c.1966] 1v. (unpaged) col. illus. 22x28cm. .50 pap.,
I. Title.

SMITH, Velma. 268
So you work with nursery children. Rev. ed. Anderson, Ind., Warner Press [1966] 61 p. 21 cm. [BV1540.S6 1966] 66-23607
1. Religious education of preschool children. I. Title.

SPEEDY, Graeme W. 268
Education for Christian living, by Graeme W. Speedy. [Melbourne, Joint Board of Christian Education of Australia and New Zealand, 1968] 40 p. illus. 21 cm. (Christian life curriculum) [BV1471.2.S59] 74-388603 0.30
1. Religious education—Outlines, syllabi, etc. I. Title.

SPOTTS, Charles Dewey, 1899- 268
Called to teach. Philadelphia, United Church Press [1963] 111 p. 20 cm. [BV1471.2.S6] 63-10950
1. Religious education. I. Title.

SPOTTS, Charles Dewey, 1899- 268
Called to teach. Philadelphia, United Church [c.1963] 111p. 20cm. 63-10950 2.50 bds.,
1. Religious education. I. Title.

STEWART, Donald Gordon. 268
Christian education and evangelism. Philadelphia, Westminster Press [1963] 176 p. 21 cm. Bibliography: p. 173-176. [BV1471.2.S8] 63-13356
1. Religious education. 2. Kerygma. I. Title.

STEWART, Donald Gordon 268
Christian education and evangelism. Philadelphia, Westminster [c.1963] 176p. 21cm. Bibl. 63-13356 3.75
1. Religious education. 2. Kerygma. I. Title.

STROMMEN, Merton P. 268
Research on religious development; a comprehensive handbook. A project of the Religious Education Association. Edited by Merton P. Strommen. New York, Hawthorn Books [1971] xxiv, 904 p. 25 cm. Includes bibliographies. [BV1464.S87 1971] 72-115916 24.95
1. Christian education—Collections. I. Religious Education Association. II. Title.

†*SUNDAY school basics /* 268
edited by Floyd D. Carey. Cleveland, Tenn. : Pathway Press, c1976. 142 p. : ill. ; 21 cm. (Church training course ; 130) Bibliography: p. 141-142. [BV1525.S78] 75-31490 ISBN 0-87148-778-0 : 2.50 ISBN 0-87148-777-2 pbk. : 1.95
1. Sunday-schools—Addresses, essays, lectures. I. Carey, Floyd D.

SUTHERLAND, Angelyn B 268
How to run a Sunday school. [Westwood, N. J] Revell [1956] 160p. 20cm. [BV1520.S83] 56-10897
1. Sunday-schools. I. Title.

SUTHERLAND, Angelyn B 268
How to run a Sunday school. [Westwood, N.J.] Revell [1956] 160 p. 20 cm. [BV1520.S83] 56-10897
1. Sunday-schools. I. Title.

SWANSON, Lawrence F 268
Build an approved Sunday Bible school. Chicago, Baptist Conference Press [c1957] 167 p. illus. 20 cm. Includes bibliography. [BV1520.S88] 57-14491
1. Sunday-schools. I. Title.

SWEARINGEN, Tilford Tippett, 1902- 268
The community and Christian education. St Louis, Published for the Cooperative Pub. Association by the Bethany Press [1950] 159 p. 20 cm. Includes, in part, a summary of the findings of the Conference on the Community and Christian Education, Columbus, Ohio, Dec. 2-5, 1947. [BV625.S89] 50-6584
1. Interdenominational cooperation. 2. Religious education — U.S. I. Conference on the Community and Christian Education, Columbus, Ohio, 1947. II. Title.

TAYLOR, Marvin J 1921- ed. 268
An introduction to Christian education. Marvin J. Taylor, editor. Nashville, Abingdon Press [1966] 412 p. 24 cm. Includes bibliographies. [BV1471.2.T3] 66-11452
1. Religious education. I. Christian education. II. Title.

TAYLOR, Marvin J. 1921- ed. 268
An introduction to Christian education. Nashville, Abingdon [c.1966] 412p. 24cm. Bibl. [BV1471.2.T3] 66-11452 6.50
1. Religious education. I. Title. II. Title: Christian education.

TODD, Floyd 268
Camping for Christian youth; a guide to methods and principles for evangelical camps [by] Floyd and Pauline Todd. New York, Harper [c.1963] 198p. 22cm. 63-14972 3.95
1. Church camps. I. Todd, Pauline, joint author. II. Title.

TODD, Galbraith Hall 268
The torch and the flag. Philadelphia, Amer. Sunday-School Union [1966] vii, 104p. illus. (pt. col.) port. 24cm. Bibl. [BV1503.A75T6] 66-23139 2.00
1. American Sunday-School Union I. Title.
816 Chestnut St., Philadelphia Pa. 19103.

TOWNER, Walter. 268
Guiding a church school. New York, Abingdon Press [1963] 192 p. 23 cm. [BV1521.T6] 63-19032
1. Sunday-schools. I. Title.

TOWNER, Walter 268
Guiding a church school. Nashville, Abingdon [c.1961, 1963] 192p. 23cm. 63-19032 2.00 pap.,
1. Sunday-schools. I. Title.

TOWNS, Elmer L. 268
The bright future of Sunday School. Minneapolis, Minn., F. C. Publications [1969] 171 p. 22 cm. [BV1471.2.T68] 75-82279 2.50
1. Christian education. I. Title.

TOWNS, Elmer L. 268
The successful Sunday school and teachers guidebook / Elmer Towns. Carol Stream, Ill. : Creation House, 1976. 400 p. : ill. ; 24 cm. Includes index. [BV1521.T628 1976] 75-23009 ISBN 0-88419-118-4 pbk. : 6.95
1. Sunday-schools. 2. Christian education. I. Title.

TRENT, Robbie, 1894- 268
Your child and God. [Rev. ed.] New York Harper [1952] 157 p. 20 cm. [BV1590.T7] 52-5476
1. Religious education — Home training. I. Title.

U.S. Dept. of Defense. Armed Forces Chaplains' Board. 268
Teaching in the Armed Forces; Protestant religious education program. Rev. [Washington, U.S. Govt. Print. Off., 1967] 73 p. 24 cm. Cover title. Bibliography: p. 66-73. [BV1533.U53 1967] 68-61133
1. Religious education—Teacher training. I. Title.

VATICAN Council. 2d,1962-1965. 268
De educatione Christiana. The declaration on Christian education of Vatican Council II, promulgated by Pope Paul VI, October 28, 1965. Commentary by Mark J. Hurley. [Study-club ed.] Glen Rock, N.J., Paulist Press, 1966. 158 p. 18 cm. (Vatican II documents) Bibliographical footnotes. [BX830 1962.A45E33] 66-19151
1. Religious education. I. Hurley, Mark Joseph, 1917- II. Title. III. Title: The declaration on Christian education of Vatican Council II.

VATICAN COUNCIL. 2D, 1962-1965 268
De educatione Christiana. The declaration on Christian education of Vatican Council II, promulgated by Pope Paul VI. October 28, 1965. Commentary by Mark J. Hurley. [Study-club ed.] Glen Rock, N.J., Paulist, 1966. 158p. 18cm. (Vatican II docs.) Bibl. [BX8301962.A45E33] 66-19151 .75 pap.,
1. Religious education. I. Hurley. Mark Joseph, 1917. II. Title. III. Title: The declaration on Christian education of Vatican Council II.

VENABLE, Mary E 268
God at work in His world; a program guidance manual for leaders in church day camps or resident camps for juniors. Stories by Mabel Brehm. Illus. by Oscar Bergesen. [Junior camp manual] Nashville, Published for the Co-operative Publication Association by Abingdon Press [1955] Nashville, Abingdon Press [1955] 153p. illus. 23cm. 31p. illus. 18x26cm. (The Cooperative series) Includes bibliography. [BV1650.V4] 55-5421
1. Camping. 2. Religious education of children. I. Title. II. Title: —Junior camper's book;

VIETH, Paul Herman, 1895- 268
The church school: the organization, administration, and supervision of Christian education in the local church. Philadelphia, Christian Education Press [c1957] 179 p. illus. 22 cm. [BV1520.V45] 57-14607
1. Sunday-schools. I. Title.

WARFORD, Malcolm L., 1942- 268
The necessary illusion : church culture and educational change / Malcolm L. Warford. Philadelphia : United Church Press, c1976. 95 p. ; 22 cm. "A Pilgrim Press book." Includes bibliographical references. [BV1467.W37 1976] 76-18840 ISBN 0-8298-0311-4 : 5.95
1. Christian education—United States. I. Title.

WASHBURN, Alphonso V., comp. 268
The Sunday School at work. 1967-68. A. V. Washburn, compiler. Nashville, Tenn. Convention Press [1967] x. 142 p. 20 cm. "Church study course [of the Sunday School Board of the Southern Baptist Convention] This book is number 1732 in category 17, section for adults and young people." Includes bibliographical references. [BX6223.W34] 67-5603
1. Sunday schools. 2. Southern Baptist Convention — Education. I. Southern Baptist Convention. Sunday School Board. II. Title.

WATERINK, Jan, 1890- 268
Leading little ones to Jesus; a book for mothers. Translated from the Dutch by Betty Vredevoogd. Grand Rapids, Zondervan Pub. House [1962] 119 p. illus. 22 cm. Translation of Aan moeders hand tot Jesus. [BV1590.W353] 62-4374
1. Religious education — Home training. I. Title.

WATERINK, Jan, 1890- 268
Leading little ones to Jesus; a book for mothers. Tr. from Dutch by Betty Vredvoogd. Grand Rapids, Mich., Zondervan [c.1962] 119p. illus. 22cm. 62-4374 2.50
1. Religious education—Home training. I. Title.

WESTERHOFF, John H. 268
Will our children have faith? / John H. Westerhoff III. New York : Seabury Press, c1976. p. cm. "A Crossroad book." [BV1471.2.W48] 76-21258 ISBN 0-8164-0319-8 : 6.95
1. Christian education. I. Title.

WHITEHOUSE, Elizabeth Scott, 1893- 268
The children we teach. [1st ed.] Philadelphia, Judson Press [1950] 304 p. 21 cm. Includes bibliographies. [BV1475.W47] 50-9200
1. Religious education of children. I. Title.

WORKSHOP on Home, Church, and School Relations in the Religious Education of Children and Youth, University of Chicago, 1954. 268
Home, church, and school relations in the religious education of children and youth; [lectures] Edited by Harold A. Anderson and Rolfe Lanier Hunt. [Chicago, 1963; 1 v. (unpaged) 28 cm. Sponsored by the Dept. of Education, University of Chicago, and the Dept. of Religion and Public Education, National Council of the Churches of Christ in the United States of America. "40 copies." Bibliographical footnotes. [BV1463.W6 1954] 66-7944
1. Religious education — Congresses. 2. Church and education — Congresses. I. Anderson, Harold A, ed. II. Hunt, Rolfe Lanier, 1903- ed. III. Chicago. University. Department of Education. National Council of the Churches of Christ in the United States of America. Office of Public Education. IV. Title.

WORKSHOP on the Curriculum of Christian Education for Adults. University of Pittsburgh, 1961. 268
Wider horizons in Christian adult education; selected addresses and papers. Conducted by the School of Education, University of Pittsburgh. Edited by Lawrence C. Little. [Pittsburgh] University of Pittsburgh Press, 1962. x, 338 p. diagr., tables. 24 cm. Bibliography: p. 806-831. [BV1550.W68 1961a] 62-14381
1. Religious education of adults. I. Pittsburgh. University. School of Education. II. Little, Lawrence Calvin, 1897- ed. III. Title.

WORKSHOP on the Curriculum of Christian Education for Adults, University of Pittsburgh, 1961. 268
Wider horizons in Christian adult education; selected addresses and papers. Conducted by the Sch. of Educ., Univ. of Pittsburgh .Ed. by Lawrence C. Little. [Pittsburgh] Univ. of Pittsburgh Pr. [c.]1962. x, 338p. illus. 24cm. Bibl. 62-14381 6.00
1. Religious education of adults. I. Pittsburgh. University. School of Education. II. Little, Lawrence Calvin, 1897- ed. III. Title.

WYCKOFF, D. Campbell. 268
The gospel and Christian education; a theory of Christian education for our times. Philadelphia, Westminster Press [1958, c1959] 191 p. 21 cm. [BV1471.W88] 59-5128
1. Religious education. I. Title.

WYCKOFF, D Campbell. 268
How to evaluate your Christian education program. Philadelphia, Published for the Cooperative Publication Association, by Westminster Press [1962] 103 p. 28 cm. (The Cooperative series) Includes bibliography. [BV1471.2.W9] 62-8080
1. Religious education. I. Title.

WYCKOFF, D. Campbell 268
How to evaluate your Christian education program. Philadelphia, Pub. for the Cooperative Pubn. Assn., by Westminster [c.1962] 103p. 28cm. (Cooperative ser.) Bibl. 62-8082 3.50 pap.,
1. Religious education. I. Title.

WYCKOFF, D Campbell. 268
The task of Christian education. Philadelphia, Westminster Press [1955] 172p. 21cm. [BV1471.W9] 55-5074
1. Religious education. I. Title.

WYNN, John Charles, 1920- 268
Christian education for liberation and other upsetting ideas / J. C. Wynn. Nashville : Abingdon, c1977. 111 p. ; 19 cm. Includes index. Bibliography: p. 101-106. [BV1471.2.W96] 76-57926 pbk. : 3.95
1. Christian education. I. Title.

YOUNG, Lois Horton. 268
God and His world; a cooperative vacation school course for use with kindergarten children. Teacher's guide. Drawings by Carol Roach. Dayton, Ohio, Published for the Cooperative Publication Association by Otterbein Press [c1958] 96 p. illus. 23 cm. (The Cooperative series: vacation church school texts) Includes hymns, with music, by the author. To be used with the pupil's book, God and His world. [BV1585.Y66] 58-13374
1. Vacation schools, Religious — Teachers' manuals. I. Title.

YOUNG, Lois Horton. j268
God's world of wonder. [Illustrated by Paul Behrens and Terry Hitt. Dayton, Ohio, Otterbein Press, c1964] Rev. Dayton, Ohio, Published for the Cooperative Publication Association by the Otterbein Press [1967] 16 p. col. illus. 18 x 23 cm. 104 p. illus., music. 23 cm. (The Cooperative series, vacation church school texts) Cover title. Includes hymns with music. "A cooperative vacation church school course for use with kindergarten children." [BV1585.Y67] 64-22741
1. Vacation schools, Religious — Text-books. 2. Religious education of pre-school children. I. Cooperative Publication Association. II. Title. III. Title: Teacher's guide.

ZIEGLER, Jesse H 268
Psychology and the teaching church. New York, Abingdon Press [1962] 125 p. illus. 20 cm. [BV147.Z5] 62-16813
1. Religious education—Psychology. I. Title.

ZIEGLER, Jesse H. 268
Psychology and the teaching church. Nashville, Abingdon [c.1962] 125p. illus. 20cm. 62-16813 2.75
1. Religous education—Psychology. I. Title.

ZUCK, Roy B 268
The Holy Spirit in your teaching. Wheaton, Ill., Scripture Press Publications [1963] xiii, 189 p. 24 cm. Bibliography: p. 171-179. [BV1471.2.Z8] 63-21391
1. Religious education. 2. Holy Spirit. I. Title.

ZUCK, Roy B. 268
The Holy Spirit in your teaching. Wheaton, Ill., Scripture Pr. [c.1963] xiii, 189p. 24cm. Bibl. 63-21391 3.95 bds.,
1. Religious education. 2. Holy Spirit. I. Title.

BAN, Joseph D 268'.01
Education for change [by] Joseph D. Ban. Valley Forge, Pa., Judson Press [1968] 126 p. illus. 22 cm. Bibliography: p. 123-126. [BV1471.B23] 68-14562
1. Religious education. I. Title.

BAN, Joseph D. 268'.01
Education for change [by] Joseph D. Ban. Valley Forge, Pa., Judson Press [1968] 126 p. illus. 22 cm. Bibliography: p. 123-126. [BV1471.B23] 68-14562
1. Religious education. I. Title.

COE, George Albert, 1862-1951. 268'.01
A social theory of religious education. New York, Arno Press, 1969. xiii, 361 p. 23 cm. (American education: its men, ideas, and institutions) Reprint of the 1917 ed. Bibliography: p. 343-355. [BV1475.C6 1969] 78-89164
1. Christian education. I. Title. II. Series.

KNOX, Ian P. 268'.01
Above or within? : The supernatural in religious education / Ian Knox. Mishawaka, Ind. : Religious Education Press, 1977,c1976 xii, 164 p. ; 24 cm. Includes bibliographical references and index. [BV1464.K57] 76-55589 ISBN 0-89135-010-1 lib.bdg. : 9.95 ISBN 0-89135-006-3 pbk. : 7.95
1. Christian education (Theology) 2. Transcendence of God. 3. God—Immanence. I. Title.

LO, Samuel E. 268'.01
Tillichian theology and educational philosophy, by Samuel E. Lo. New York, Philosophical Library [1970] 126 p. 22 cm. Bibliography: p. 117-126. [BX4827.T53L6] 70-124516 6.95
1. Tillich, Paul, 1886-1965. 2. Religious education—Philosophy. I. Title.

ORAISON, Marc M. D. 268.01
Love or constraint? Some psychological aspects of religious education. Tr. from French. New York, Paulist Pr. [c.1959, 1961] 160p. (Deus bks.) 95 pap.,
1. Religious education—Psychology. I. Title.

ORAISON, Marc. 268.01
Love or constraint? Some psychological aspects of religious education. Translated from the French by Una Morrissy. New York, P. J. Kenedy [1959] 172 p. 21 cm. [BV1471.O543] 59-12899
1. Religious education—Psychology. I. Title.

ROOD, Wayne R. 268'.01
Understanding Christian education, by Wayne R. Rood. Nashville, Tenn., Abingdon Press [1970] 406 p. 25 cm. [BV1464.R63] 71-97575 ISBN 0-687-42844-0 8.50
1. Christian education (Theology)—History. 2. Christian education—Philosophy—History. I. Title.

WILLIAMSON, William Bedford, 1918- 268'.01
Language and concepts in Christian education. Philadelphia, Westminster Press [1969, c1970] 173 p. 21 cm. Based on the author's thesis, Temple University, 1966. Bibliography: p. [165]-169. [BV1464.W5 1970] 72-85859 6.50
1. Religious education—Philosophy. 2. Religion and language. I. Title.

GRIFFIN, Dale E., comp. 268'.01'9
The subject is persons; psychological perspectives in Christian education. Edited by Dale E. Griffin. Saint Louis, Concordia Pub. House [1970] 85 p. 19 cm. (Church teachers library) [BV1471.2.G67] 78-107423
1. Religious education—Psychology—Addresses, essays, lectures. I. Title.

COBER, Kenneth Lorne, 1902- 268'.02'02
Shaping the church's educational ministry; a manual for the board of Christian education [by] Kenneth L. Cober. Valley Forge [Pa.] Judson Press [1971] 47 p. illus. 28 cm. Bibliography: p. 46-47. [BV1471.2.C62] 75-139502 ISBN 0-8170-0519-6 1.50
1. Christian education—Handbooks, manuals, etc. I. Title.

MCNULTY, Edward N., 1936- 268'.028
Gadgets, gimmicks, and grace : a handbook on multimedia in church and school / Edward N. McNulty. St. Meinrad, Ind. : Abbey Press, c1976. xi, 130 p. : ill. ; 21 cm. Bibliography: p. 121-130. [BV1535.M3] 76-12094 ISBN 0-87029-060-6 pbk. : 3.50
1. Christian education—Audio-visual aids. I. Title.

CULLY, Kendig Brubaker, ed. 268.03
The Westminster dictionary of Christian education. Philadelphia, Westminster [c. 1963] 812p. 24cm. Bibl. 63-11083 6.00
1. Religious education—Dictionaries. I. Title. II. Title: Dictionary of Christian education.

CULLY, Kendig Brubaker, ed. 268.03
The Westmister dictionary of Christian education. Philadelphia, Westminster Press [1963] 812 p. 24 cm. Bibliography: p. [756]-797. [BV1461.C8] 63-11083
1. Religious education — Dictionaries. I. Title. II. Title: Dictionary of Christian education.

YOUTH ministry notebook. 1967-1968. New York, Seabury [1967] v. illus. 28cm. Bibl. 3.00 pap., 268.05

ORGANIZED Bible Class Association. 268.06273
Bible class directory. Washington. v. 23cm. annual. Title varies: 19-47, Directory. [BV1503.O69] 53-17014
1. Sunday-schools—Direct. I. Title.

ORGANIZED Bible Class Association. 268.06273
Report [of the] conference. Washington. v. 28 cm. annual. [BV1503.O7] 52-17242
1. Sunday-schools—Societies. I. Title.

WILLIAMSON, E. Stanley. 268.06273
Helping churches through associational Sunday school work. Nashville, Convention Press [c1959] 146 p. 29 cm. [BX6222.A1W5] 59-9966
1. Sunday schools — Societies, etc. 2. Baptist associations. I. Title.

MCCOMB, Louise 268.069
D. C. E., a challenging career in Christian education. Richmond, Va., Knox [c.1963] 79p. 21cm. 63-12091 1.50 pap.,
1. Religious education as a profession. 2. Directors of religious education. I. Title.

CHURCH educational agencies. [1st ed.] Wheaton, Ill., Evangelical Teacher Training Association [1968] 96 p. illus. 23 cm. (Advanced specialized certificate series) Includes bibliographical references. [BV1471.2.C53] 67-27288 268'.07
1. Religious education. I. Evangelical Teacher Training Association.

*GANGEL, Kenneth O. 268.07
Sunday School Evangelism; A guide of practical helps for teaching teachers and leaders in the church educational program. Wheaton, Ill., Box 327, Evangelical Teacher Trng. Assoc., c. 1964. (various p.) Bibl. 1.35, pap., plastic bdg.
I. Title.

GOODYKOONTZ, Harry G. 268.07
Training to teach, a basic cource in Christian education [by] Harry G. and Betty L. Goodykoontz. Philadelphia, Westminster Pr. [c. 1961] 141p. illus. Bibl. 61-10293 3.50
1. Religious education—Teacher training. I. Goodykoontz, Betty L., joint author. II. Title.

GRIFFIN, Dale E., comp. 268'.07
New ways to learn; practical methods for Christian teaching. Edited by Dale E. Griffin. Saint Louis, Concordia Pub. House [1970] 91 p. illus. 19 cm. (Church teachers library) [BV1534.G73] 74-107422
1. Religious education—Teaching methods—Addresses, essays, lectures. I. Title.

ROOD, Wayne R. 268'.07
The art of teaching Christianity; enabling the loving revolution [by] Wayne R. Rood. Photos. by Robert D. Fitch. Nashville, Abingdon Press [1968] 224 p. illus. 20 cm. [BV1534.R627] 68-11472
1. Religious education—Teaching methods. I. Title.

DOHERTY, Mary Michael. 268'.071'2
Dynamic approaches to teaching high school religion [by] M. Michael Doherty. Staten Island, N.Y., Alba House [1969] 326 p. 22 cm. Includes bibliographies. [BX926.D6] 69-11492 6.95
1. Catholic Church—Education. 2. Christian education of adolescents. I. Title.

SULLIVAN, Jessie P. 268.077
Exciting object lessons and ideas for children's sermons [by] Jessie Sullivan Grand Rapids, Baker Book House [1975 c1970] 124 p. 19 cm. [BV1475.2.S9] ISBN 0-8010-7909-8 1.95 (pbk.
1. Worship (religious education) I. Title.
L.C. card no. for original edition: 70-129816.

GRIFFIN, Dale E., comp. 268'.08
What has God done lately? Christian perspectives for the church school teacher. Edited by Dale E. Griffin. Saint Louis, Concordia Pub. House [1970] 106 p. 19 cm. (Church teachers library) [BV4319.G7] 77-107420
1. Communication (Theology)—Addresses, essays, lectures. 2. Christian education—Addresses, essays, lectures. I. Title.

NEIGHBOR, Russell J., comp. 268'.08
There's more than one way; new programs and possibilities for out-of-school religious education, edited by Russell J. Neighbor and Mary Perkins Ryan. Paramus, N.J., Paulist Press [1970] viii, 311 p. 21 cm. Title on spine: There's more than one way to teach religion. [BV1473.N4] 74-101540 4.95
1. Christian education—Addresses, essays, lectures. I. Ryan, Mary Perkins, 1915- joint comp. II. Title. III. Title: There's more than one way to teach religion.

SISEMORE, John T comp. 268.08
Vital principles in religious education, compiled by John T. Sisemore. Nashville, Broadman Press [c1966] 128 p. 21 cm. Includes bibliographies. [BV1473.S5] 66-10709
1. Religious education — Addresses, essays, lectures. I. Title.

SISEMORE, John T., comp. 268.08
Vital principles in religious education. Nashville. Broadman [c.1966] 128p. 21cm. Bibl. [BV1473.S5] 66-10709 2.75 bds.,
1. Religious education—Addresses, essays, lectures. I. Title.

DENDY, Marshall C. 268.081
Changing patterns in Christian education. Richmond, Va., Knox Pr. [1965, c.1964] 96p. 21cm. Bibl. [BV1473.D4] 65-10715 1.50 pap.,
1. Religious education—Addresses, essays, lectures. I. Title.

JACOBS, J. Vernon 268.081
24 talks for Sunday School workers' conferences. Grand Rapids, Mich., Zondervan [c.1961] 64p. (Sunday school know-how ser.) 1.00 pap.,
I. Title.

JACOBS, J. Vernon 268.081
Teaching tools for Sunday schools; teaching methods, types of lessons, and teaching materials. Grand Rapids, Mich., Zondervan [c.1963] 64p. diagrs. 21p. (Sunday school know-how ser.) 1.00 pap.,
I. Title.

HAKES, J Edward, 1917- ed. 268.082
An introduction to evangelical Christian education. Edited by J. Edward Hakes. Chicago, Moody Press [1964] 423 p. illus. 24 cm. Includes bibliographies. [BV1471.2.H3] 64-20989
1. Religious education. I. Title.

HAKES, J. Edward, 1917- ed. 268.082
An introduction to evangelical Christian education. Chicago, Moody [c.1964] 423p. illus. 24cm. Bibl. 64-20989 5.95
1. Religious education. I. Title.

SLOYAN, Gerard Stephen, 1919- ed. 268.082
Shaping the Christian message; essays in religious education. Contributors: Andre Boyer [and others] New York, Macmillan, 1958. 327 p. 22 cm. [BX925.S6] 58-11545
1. Religious education. 2. Catholic Church — Education. I. Boyer, Andre. II. Title.

SLOYAN, Gerard Stephen, 1919- ed. 268.082
Shaping the Christian message; essays in religious education. Abridged ed. Contributors: Andre Boyer [and others] Glen Rock, N.J. Paulist Press [1963] 256 p. 18 cm. (Deus books) Bibliography: p. 245. [BX921.S5 1963] 63-20215
1. Religious education. 2. Catholic Church — Education. I. Boyer, Andre 1889- II. Title.

SLOYAN, Gerard Stephen, 1919- ed. 268.082
Shaping the Christian message; essays in religious education. Abridged ed. Contribs.: Andre Boyer [others] Glen Rock, N. J., Paulist Pr. [c.1958, 1963] 256p. 18cm. (Deus bks) Bibl. 63-20215 .95 pap.,
1. Religious education. 2. Catholic Church—Education. I. Boyer, Andre, 1889- II. Title.

TAYLOR, Marvin J 1921- ed. 268.082
Religious education: a comprehensive survey. New York, Abingdon Press [1960] 446 p. 24 cm. Includes bibliographies. [BV1471.T35] 60-5477
1. Religious education. I. Title.

TAYLOR, Marvin J., 1921- ed. 268.082
Religious education: a comprehensive survey. New York, Abingdon Press [1960] 446 p. 24 cm. Includes bibliographies. [BV1471.T35] 60-5477
1. Religious education.

WALDRUP, Earl W 1920- 268.084
Teaching and training with audio-visuals. Nashville, Convention Press, 1962] 114 p. illus. 19 cm. [BV1535.W3] 62-7975
1. Church work — Audio-visual aids. I. Title.

WILLIAMS, Maxine. 268.084
The eyes have it; a handbook on the use of visual materials in Christian teaching. Springfield, Mo., Gospel Pub. House [1962] 145 p. 19 cm. [BV1535.W4] 62-15648
1. Religious education — Audio-visual aids. I. Title.

YOUR guide to church and church school supplies. 268.085 Rock Island, Ill., Augustana [1961] 238p. illus. (pt. col.) 28cm. (Catalog 162, 1962) 1.00 pap.,

EAVEY, Charles Benton, 1889- 268.09
History of Christian education. Chicago, Moody [c.1964] 430p. illus., ports.24cm. Bibl. 5.50
1. Religious education—Hist. I. Title. II. Title: Christian education.

KINLOCH, Tom Fleming, 1874- 268'.09
Pioneers of religious education, by T. F. Kinloch. With a foreword by J. S. Whale. Freeport, N.Y., Books for Libraries Press [1969] vii, 144 p. 22 cm. (Essay index reprint series) Reprint of the 1939 ed. Bibliography: p. 142-144. [BV1465.K5 1969] 69-18929
1. Religious education—History. I. Title.

ULICH, Robert, 1890- 268'.09
A history of religious education; documents and interpretations from the Judaeo-Christian tradition. New York, New York University press, 1968. viii, 302 p. 24 cm. "Bibliographical references included in "Notes" (p. 283-298) [BV1465.U4] 68-29433
1. Religious education—History. I. Title.

MILLER, Minor Cline, 1889- 268'.0924 (B)
These things I remember, by Minor C. Miller. Philadelphia, Dorrance [1968] 226 p. 21 cm. [BV1470.3.M5A3] 67-18237
1. Sunday-schools—Virginia. I. Title.

MILLER, Minor Cline, 1889- 268'.0924
These things I remember, by Minor C. Miller, Philadelphia, Dorrance [1968] 226p. 21cm. [BV1470.3.M5A3] (B) 67-18237 4.50
1. Sunday-schools—Virginia. I. Title.

*BARLOW, Fred S. 268.0973
Reap ten tips for Sunday school enlargement campaigns by Fred M. Barlow. Des Plaines, Ill., Regular Baptist Press, 1974 60 p. illus. 19 cm. [BV1516] 1.50 (pbk.)
1. Sunday-schools. I. Title.

JONES, Charles Colcock, 1804-1863. 268'.0973
The religious instruction of the Negroes in the United States. New York, Negro Universities Press [1969] xiii, 277 p. 23 cm. Reprint of the 1842 ed. [LC2751.J7 1969] 73-82466 ISBN 0-8371-1645-7
1. Negroes—Education. 2. Christian education. I. Title.

JONES, Charles Colcock, 1804-1863. 268'.0973
The religious instruction of the Negroes in the United States. Freeport, N.Y., Books for Libraries Press, 1971. xiii, 277 p. 23 cm. (The Black heritage library collection) Reprint of the 1842 ed. [LC2751.J7 1971] 70-149869 ISBN 0-8369-8718-7
1. Negroes—Education. 2. Christian education. I. Title. II. Series.

SKELTON, Eugene. 268'.0973
10 fastest-growing Southern Baptist Sunday Schools. Nashville, Broadman Press [1974] 152 p. illus. 21 cm. [BV1516.A1S56] 73-83831 ISBN 0-8054-6515-4 1.50 (pbk.)
1. Sunday-schools—United States. 2. Church growth—Case studies. I. Title.

TOWNS, Elmer L. 268'.0973
The ten largest Sunday schools and what makes them grow, by Elmer L. Towns. Grand Rapids, Baker Book House [1969] 163 p. illus. 20 cm. Bibliographical footnotes. [BV1521.T63] 74-98554 1.95
1. Sunday-schools—U.S.—Case studies. I. Title.

STEWART, George, 1892- 268'.09746
A history of religious education in Connecticut. New York, Arno Press, 1969. xiv, 402 p. facsims. 24 cm. (American education: its men, ideas, and educations) Reprint of the 1924 ed., which was published under title: A history of religious education in Connecticut to the middle of the nineteenth century. Originally presented as the author's thesis, Yale University, and published as Yale studies in the history and theory of religious education, 1. Bibliography: p. [371]-384. [BV1468.C8S7 1969] 79-89238
1. Christian education—Connecticut. I. Title. II. Series.

TOWNS, Elmer L. 268'.09772'99
World's largest Sunday school [by] Elmer L. Towns. Nashville, T. Nelson [1974] 189 p. front. 22 cm. [BX6480.H317F577] 74-985 5.95
1. First Baptist Church, Hammond, Ind. 2. Hyles, Jack, 1926- I. Title.

ADMINISTERING a vacation Bible school. 268'.1 A. V. Washburn, compiler. Nashville, Convention Press [1970] viii, 136 p. illus. 20 cm. "Text for course 6305 in the subject area Bible teaching program of the New church study course." [BV1585.A44] 76-128049
1. Vacation schools, Christian. I. Washburn, Alphonso V., ed.

BARNETTE, Jasper Newton, 1887- 268.1
The Sunday school and the church budget. Nashville, Convention Press [1960] 146p. 19cm. 'Church study course for teaching and training ... number 1725 in category 17, section A.' Includes bibliography. [BV772.B28] 59-14428
1. Christian giving. 2. Church finance. 3. Sunday-schools. I. Title.

BLAZIER, Kenneth D. 268'.1
Building an effective church school : guide for the superintendent and board of Christian education / Kenneth D. Blazier. Valley Forge, Pa. : Judson Press, c1976. 64 p. : ill. ; 22 cm. Includes bibliographical references. [BV1521.B5] 75-42018 ISBN 0-8170-0708-3 pbk. : 1.95
1. Sunday-schools. I. Title.

BOWER, Robert K. 268.1
Administering Christian education; principles of administration for ministers and Christian leaders, by Robert K. Bower. Grand Rapids, W. B. Eerdmans Pub. Co. [1964] 227 p. illus., forms. 24 cm. Bibliography: p. 219-223. [BV1521.B6] 64-22018
1. Sunday-schools. 2. Religious education. I. Title.

BOWER, Robert K. 268.1
Administering Christian education; principles of administration for ministers and Christian leaders. Grand Rapids, Mich., Eerdmans [c.1964] 227p. illus., forms. 24cm. Bibl. 64-22018 3.95
1. Sunday-schools. 2. Religious education. I. Title.

HANSON, Joseph John. 268'.1
Launching the church school year [by] Joseph John Hanson [and] Kenneth D. Blazier. Valley Forge, Judson Press [1972] 48 p. 22 cm. Bibliography: p. 46-48. [BV1471.2.H38] 75-181558 ISBN 0-8170-0553-6 1.25
1. Christian education. I. Blazier, Kenneth D., joint author. II. Title.

HEIM, Ralph Daniel, 1895- 268'.1
Leading a church school, by Ralph D. Heim. Philadelphia, Fortress Press [1968] x, 358 p. 23 cm. Bibliographical footnotes. [BV1521.H4] 68-16262 6.95
1. Sunday-schools. I. Title.

*HUGHES, Ray H. 268.1
Sunday school workers' training course, no. 1., introd. course. Grand Rapids, Mich., Baker Bk. [1964, c.1955] 110p. 20cm. 1.50 pap.,
I. Title.

IT'S a great time to be a Christian; 268.1 experiences and experiments with parish programs of lay Christian eduction. New York. Seabury [1968] 71p. illus. 21cm. 1.50 pap.,
1. Religious education—Programming.

*RANEY, L. H. 268.1
Blueprint for a balanced Sunday school, by L. H. Raney, others. Grand Rapiopds, Baker Bk. [1967] 89p. 20cm. Bibl. 1.50 pap.,
1. Sunday schools, Protestant—Administration. I. Title.

WASHBURN, Alphonso V. 268'.1
Administering the Bible teaching program; Sunday school work, by A. V. Washburn and Melva Cook. Nashville, Convention Press [1969] x, 128 p. 20 cm. "This book is the text for course 6301 in the subject area Bible teaching program of the new church study course." [BS600.2.W33] 71-79195
1. Bible—Study. 2. Sunday-schools. I. Cook, Melva, joint author. II. Title.

WESTING, Harold J. 268'.1
Make your Sunday school grow through evaluation / Harold J. Westing. Wheaton, Ill. : Victor Books, c1976. 117 p. : forms ; 21 cm. [BV1521.W4 1976] 76-9216 ISBN 0-88207-464-4 : 1.95
1. Sunday-schools. I. Title.

BACKUS, Isaac, 1724-1806. 268'.174
A history of New England, with particular reference to the Baptists. New York, Arno Press, 1969. 2 v. in 1. 24 cm. (Religion in America) Title on spine: History of New England Baptists. Reprint of the "Second edition, with notes by David Weston" 1871. Includes bibliographical references. [BX6239.B3 1969] 76-83410
1. Baptists—New England. 2. New England—Church history. I. Weston, David, 1836-1875, ed. II. Title. III. Title: History of New England Baptists.

ADAIR, Thelma. 268.2
How to make chruch school equipment: it's easier than you think! By Thelma Adair and Elizabeth McCort. Philadelphia, Westminster Press [1955] 96p. illus. 23cm. [BV1528.A3] 55-7707
1. Schools—Furniture, equipment, etc. 2. Religious education. I. McCort, Elizabeth, joint author. II. Title.

ADAIR, Thelma C 268.2
How to make church school equipment: it's easier than you think! By Thelma Adair and Elizabeth McCort. Philadelphia, Westminster Press [1955] 96 p. illus. 23 cm. [BV1528.A3] 55-7707
1. Schools — Furniture, equipment, etc. 2. Religious education. I. McCort, Elizabeth, joint author. II. Title.

ATKINSON, Charles Harry, 1894- 268.2
Building and equipping for Christian education. New York, Published for the Bureau of Church Building and the Dept. of Administration and Leadership of the National Council of the Churches of Christ in the U. S. A., by the Office of Publication and Distribution [c1956] 87p. illus. 30cm. [BV1528.A8] 56-12731
1. Sunday-school buildings. I. Title.

BASICS for teaching in the church 268'.3 [by] T. Franklin Miller [and others] Study guidance by Kenneth F. Hall. Anderson, Ind., Warner Press [1968] 224 p. illus. 26 cm. (Foundations for teaching) Bibliographical footnotes. [BV1533.B36] 68-23026
1. Religious education—Teacher training. I. Miller, T. Franklin.

EAVEY, Charles Benton, 1889- 268'.3
History of Christian education. Chicago, Moody Press [1964] 430 p. illus., ports. 24 cm. Includes bibliographies. [BV1465.E2] 64-1860
1. Religious education—Hist. I. Title. II. Title: Christian education.

EDWARDS, Mary Alice Douty 268'.3
Leadership development and the workers conference. Nashville, Abingdon [1967] 224p. 23cm. Bibl. [BV1533.E3] 67-15637 4.50
1. Christian leadership. 2. Religious education—Teacher training. I. Title.

FIDLER, James E. 268.3
Our church plans for leadership education; a manual on enlisting and developing workers. Valley Forge [Pa.] Judson [c.1962] 112p. illus. 20cm. 62-17001 1.25 pap.,
1. Religious education—Teacher training. 2. Leadership. 3. American Baptist Convention—Education. I. Title.

GRASSI, Joseph A. 268'.3
The teacher in the primitive church and the teacher today [by] Joseph A. Grassi. Santa Clara, Calif., University of Santa Clara Press [1973] v, 132 p. 22 cm. Includes bibliographical references. [BV1465.G7] 73-78011 2.95
1. Christian education—History. 2. Education—History. I. Title.

GRASSI, Joseph A. 268'.3
The teacher in the primitive church and the teacher today [by] Joseph A. Grassi. Santa Clara, Calif., University of Santa Clara Press [1973] v, 132 p. 22 cm. Includes bibliographical references. [BV1465.G7] 73-78011 2.95
1. Religious education—History. 2. Teaching—History. I. Title.

GWYNN, Price Henderson, 1892- 268.3
Leadership education in the local church. Philadelphia, Published for the Cooperative Publishing Association by the Westminster Press [1952] 157 p. 21 cm. [BV1533.G8] 52-7051
1. Religious education—Teacher training. I. Title.

HAMMACK, Mary L. 268.3
How to train the Sunday school Grand Rapids, Mich., Zondervan [c.1961] 63p. illus. (Sunday school 'Know-how' ser.) Bibl. 62-1132 1.00 pap.,
1. Religious education—Teacher training. I. Title.

HAMMACK, Mary L 268.3
How to train the Sunday school teacher. Grand Rapids, Zondervan Pub. House [1961] 63p. illus. 21cm. (Sunday school 'Know-how' series) Includes bibliography. [BV1533.H28] 62-1132
1. Religious education—Teacher training. I. Title.

HYDE, Floy (Salls). 268.3
Protestant leadership education schools. New York, Bureau of Publications, Teachers College, Columbia University, 1950. viii, 164 p. tables. 24 cm. (Columbia University. Teachers College. Contributions to education, no. 965) Issued also as thesis, Columbia University. Bibliography: p. [149]-153. [BV1533.H94] 50-9189
1. Religious education—Teacher training. I. Title. II. Series.

JACOBS, James Vernon, 1898- 268.3
Ten steps to leadership. Cincinnati, Standard Pub. Foundation [1956] 172p. illus. 20cm. [BF637.L4J3] 56-37351
1. Leadership. I. Title.

KECKLEY, Weldon 268.3
The church school superintendent: the person and the job. St. Louis, Pub. for Co-op. Pubn. Assn. by Bethany [c.1963] 144p. illus. 21cm. (Co-op. text) 63-3167 2.50
1. Sunday-school superintendents. I. Title.

LEAVITT, Guy P. 268.3
Superintend with success. Illustrated by Robert E. Huffman. Cincinnati, Standard Pub. Co. [c.1960] 143p. illus. 28cm. 61-1 2.95, pap., plastic binding
1. Sunday-school superintendents. I. Title.

PLUMMER, L. Flora (Fait) 1862-1945. 268'.3
The spirit of the teacher. Rev. and enl. by G. R. Nash. Takoma Park, Washington, Review and Herald Pub. Association [1967] 128 p. 22 cm. Bibliographical footnotes. [BV1534.P58 1967] 67-30827
1. Sunday-schools. 2. Teachers. I. Nash, Gerald R. II. Title.

PLUMMER, L. Flora (Fait) 268'.3
1862-1945.
The spirit of the teacher. Rev. by G. R. Nash. Takoma Park, Review and Herald Pub. Association [1967] 128 p. 22 cm. Bibliographical footnotes. [BV1534.P58 1967] 67-30827
1. Sunday-schools. 2. Teachers. I. Nash, Gerald R. II. Title.

PRIEST, James Eugene, 1923- 268.3
The educational work of the church. 1st ed. Tyler, Tex., Wilmeth Publications [1960] 165p. illus. 21cm. Includes bibliography. [BV1531.P7] 60-23553
1. Directors of religious education. I. Title.

SCOTFORD, John Ryland, 268.3
1888-
How to recruit and keep Sunday school teachers. [Westwood, N. J.] Revell [c.1962] 62p. 22cm. (Revell's better church ser.) 62-17110 1.00 pap.,
1. Religious education—Teacher recruitment. I. Title.

THAT men may live in 268.3
Christ; a course on Why we teach, by Elaine Tracy, Harlen Norem. Minneapolis, Augsburg, c.1963. 48p. 28cm. (Leadership educ. ser. course 11a. 5; senior high school dept.) 1.25 pap.,
1. Religious education—Teacher training. I. Tracy, Elaine. II. Norem, Harlan.

BROWN, Elmore. 268'.3'0924
The struggle for trained teachers; the story of John W. Shackford's early efforts to provide trained teachers in the church. [Nashville? 1966] xii, 87 p. illus., port. 21 cm. Without thesis statement. Thesis (M.A.)—Boston University School of Theology. Bibliographical footnotes. [BX8495.S48B7] 67-2036
1. Shackford, John Walter, 1878- I. Title.

KRAFT, Vernon Robert. 268.32
The director of Christian education in the local church. Chicago, Moody Press [1957] 128p. 19cm. Includes bibliography. [BV1531.K7] 57-3578
1. Directors of religious education. I. Title.

JONES, Idris W 268.333
The superintendent plans his work. Philadelphia, Judson Press [1956] 88p. 19cm. [BV1531.J58] 56-13457
1. Sunday-school superintendents. I. Title.

*PURDHAM, Betty Mae 268.342
Followers of Jesus. Ed. by Margaret J. Irvin. Illus. by John Gretzer. Philadelphia, Lutheran Church Pr. [c.1966] 32p. 23x28cm. (LCA vacation church sch. ser.) .50; .90 pap., teacher's ed., pap.,
1. Religious education—Elementary—Lutheran Church. I. Title.

MCKIBBEN, Frank 268.372
Melbourne, 1889-
Guiding workers in Christian education. Nashville, Published for the Cooperative Publication Association by Abingdon-Cokesbury Press [1953] 160p. 20cm. (The Cooperative series leadership training textbooks) [BV1533.M32] 53-5397
1. Religious education—Teacher training. I. Title.

NOLDE, Otto Frederick, 268.372
1899-
God's master builders; methods of leading group sessions, by O. Frederick Nolde and Paul J. Hoh. Philadelphia, Muhlenberg Press [1950] 95 p. illus. 18 cm. "Based on an earlier book, My group sessions, by the same authors." Bibliography: p. 94. "Audio-visual aids": p. 95. [BV1533.N55] 50-1757
1. Religious education — Teacher training. I. Hoh, Paul Jacob, 1893- joint author. II. Title.

ANDERSEN, Richard, 1931- 268'.4
Devotions for church school teachers / Richard Andersen. St. Louis : Concordia Pub. House, c1976. p. cm. [BV4596.S9A5] 76-2158 ISBN 0-570-03722-0 pbk. : 1.75
1. Sunday-school teachers—Prayer-books and devotions—English. I. Title.

ASPER, Wallace J 268.4
How to organize the education program of your church: a planbook for the Committee on Parish Education. Minneapolis, Augsburg Pub. Co. [1959] 67p. illus. 20cm. Includes bibliography. [BV1471.A67] 59-12117
1. Religious education. I. Title.

CARROLL, John L. 268'.4
Youth ministry: Sunday, Monday, and every day [by] John L. Carroll and Keith L. Ignatius. Valley Forge [Pa.] Judson Press [1972] 62 p. 22 cm. $1.65 [BV4447.C37] 72-3236 ISBN 0-8170-0577-3
1. Church work with youth. I. Ignatius, Keith L., joint author. II. Title.

CHRISTIAN education 268.4
handbook; 157 outlines on various on various phases of the church's teaching program, organization, and personnel. Cincinnati, Standard Pub. Co., c.1960. 176p. 28cm. Includes bibl. 2.95 pap.,
1. Religious education. 2. Sunday-schools.

FRITZ, Dorothy B. 268.4
Activity programs for junior groups; a guide for adult advisers, including four expandable units of creative discovery, concerning the making and use of the Bible, worship, stewardship, and the world church. Philadelphia, Westminster Press [c.1961] 208p. illus. 2.75 pap.,
I. Title.

HARRIS, Philip B 268.4
The training program of a church [by] Philip B. Harris and staff, Training Union Dept., Baptist Sunday School Board. Nashville, Convention Press [1966] xviii, 137 p. 20 cm. "Church study course [of the Sunday School Board of the Southern Baptist Convention] This book si number 1812 in category 18, section for adults and young people." Bibliography: p. 132-134. [BX6223.H3] 66-13313
1. Religious education. 2. Baptists. — Education. I. Southern Baptist Convention. Sunday School Board. Baptist Training Union Dept. II. Title.

JEEP, Elizabeth. 268'.4
Classroom creativity; an idea book for religion teachers. [New York] Herder and Herder [1970] vii, 148 p. illus. 28 cm. Includes bibliographies. [BV1534.J4] 73-114150 2.45
1. Religious education—Teaching methods. I. Title.

*JOHNSON, Jerry Don 268.4
Learning to know God; a resource book for use with retarded persons by Jerry Don Johnson and Martha Jones. St. Louis, Mo., Bethany Pr. [c.1966] 128p. 23cm. 2.50 pap.,
I. Title.

LEYPOLDT, Martha M. 268'.4
40 ways to teach in groups [by] Martha M. Leypold. Valley Forge, Judson Press [1967] 125 p. illus. (part col.) 24 cm. Bibliography: p. 121-123. [LC6519.L45] 67-22215
1. Forums (Discussion and debate) I. Title.

LUBIENSKA DE LENVAL, 268'.4
Helene,
How to teach religion. Translated by Paul Joseph Oligny. Chicago, Franciscan Herald Press [1967] 104 p. 19 cm. Translation of Pedagogie sacree. [BX926.L813] 67-19967
1. Christian education. I. Title.

MCCRAW, Mildred C 268.4
The extension department; lifting through love. Nashville, Convention Press [1958] 150p. illus. 19cm. [BV1523.M3 1958] 59-3674
1. Sunday-schools. I. Title.

MERLAUD, Andre. 268'.4
Children and adolescents, our teachers. Translated by Theodore DuBois. Paramus, N.J. [Paulist Press, 1969] vii, 101 p. 19 cm. (Paulist Press Deus books) Translation of Enfants et adolescents, nos maitres. Bibliographical footnotes. [BV1475.2.M5613] 77-92043 1.25
1. Religious education of children. I. Title.

RESPOND. 268'.4
Valley Forge, PA : Judson Press.
Vol. 5, Resources for Senior Highs in the church, c1977 and edited by Robert Howard, is available for 5.95 (pbk.) ISBN 0-8170-0767-9. L.C. card no.: 77-159050.

RESPOND; 268'.4
a resource book for youth ministry [edited by] Keith L. Ignatius. Valley Forge [Pa.] Judson Press [1971-73] 3 v. illus., music. 28 cm. Vol. 2 edited by J. M. Corbett; v. 3 by M. L. Brown. Includes bibliographies. [BX6225.R47] 77-159050 ISBN 0-8170-0542-0 (v. 1) 3.95 per vol.
1. Religious education—Text-books for young people—Baptist. I. Ignatius, Keith L., ed. II. Corbett, Janice M., ed. III. Brown, Mason L., ed.

RICE, Kenneth S 268.4
The department supervisor. Kansas City, Mo., Beacon Hill Press [1955] 124p. illus. 20cm. [BV1532] 55-14616
1. Sunday-schools. I. Title.

WOODWORTH, Reginald O 268.4
How to operate a Sunday school; a handbook of practical Sunday school methods. Introd. by G. Beauchamp Vick. Grand Rapids, Zondervan Pub. House [1961] 160 p. 23 cm. [BV1521.W65] 61-1489
1. Sunday-schools. I. Title.

WOODWORTH, Reginald O. 268.4
How to operate a Sunday school; a handbook of practical Sunday school methods. Grand Rapids, Mich., Zondervan [c.1961] 160p. 61-1489 2.95
1. Sunday-schools. I. Title.

*PFEIFFER, Marie Venard 268.42
Mother
In Christ Jesus, gr. 3. New York, Sadlier, c.1965. col. illus. music. 28cm. (Our life with God ser., Vatican II ed.) 1.08 pap.,
1. Religious education (Elementary) Catholic. I. Title.

MCCRAW, Mildred C 268.422
The extension department; lifting through love. Nashville, Broadman Press [1952] 146 p. illus. 20 cm. [BV1523.M3] 52-11929
1. Sunday-schools I. Title.

GRAHAM, Margaret Althea, 268.424
1924-
How to win a Sunday school contest; a gold mine of successful ideas for building larger Sunday school attendance through the contest method, chosen from the many entires in the National Christian life magazine contest. Compiled and written by Margaret Graham and Nancy Bates. Wheaton, Ill., Scripture Press [1958] 108 p. illus. 26 cm. [BV1520.G67] 58-42569
1. Sunday-schools. I. Bates, Nancy, joint author. II. Title.

ADAMS, Rachel Swann. 268.43
The small church and Christian education. Philadelphia, Westminster Press [1961] 75p. illus. 23cm. [BV1471.2.A3] 61-8764
1. Religious education. I. Title.

ADAMS, Rachel Swann 268.43
The small church and Christian education. Philadelphia, Westminster Press [c.1961] 75p. illus. Bibl. 61-8764 1.00 pap.,
1. Religious education. I. Title.

**I believe in God* 268.43
[5 bxd. kits] Minneapolis, Augsburg [c.1962, 1965] 5 kits (unpaged) 29cm. (Vacation church school ser.) Series: Vacation church school series. [1] Nursery activities.--[2] Kindergarten activities.--[3] Primary activities.--[4] Junior activities.--[5] Intermediate activities. .95 box, ea.,
1. Religious education of children. I. Series.

JACOBS, J. Vernon 268.43
Teaching problems and how to solve them; a question and answer book. Grand Rapids, Mich., Zondervan [c.1962] 64p. 21cm. (Sunday sch. know-how ser.) 1.00 pap.,
I. Title.

**JUNIOR-HI kit,* 268.43
22. Program resources for advisers of junior high groups. Ed.: James E. Simpson. Ed.-in-chief, Norman F. Langford. Exec. Ed.: Donald L. Leonard. Philadelphia, Geneva Pr. [dist. Westminster, c1965] 160p. illus. 28cm. 3.00 pap.,

LAZARETH, William Henry, 268.43
1928-
Helping children know doctrine [by] William H. Lazareth and Marjorie F. Garhart. Philadelphia, Lutheran Church Press, c1962. 176 p. illus. 22 cm. (Leadership education series) [BV1545.L3] 63-1180
1. Religious education of children. I. Garhart, Marjorie F. II. Title.

LAZARETH, William Henry, 268.43
1928-
Helping children know doctrine [by] William H. Lazareth, Marjorie F. Garhart. Philadelphia. Fortress [1963, c.1962] 176p. illus. 22cm. (Leadership educa. ser.) 63-1180 1.50
1. Religious education of children. I. Garhart, Marjorie F. II. Title.

*MESSINGER, C. F. 268.43
Seeking meaning with junior highs in camp, by C. F. Messinger, J. E. Simpson, G. F. Ulrich. Philadelphia, Geneva Pr [Dist. Westminster, 1966] 192p. 23cm. 1.85 pap.,
I. Title.

*STACKEL, Robert W. 268.43
I believe in the holy spirit and the church. Philadelphia, Lutheran Church Pr. [c.1966] 191p. col. illus. music. 22cm. (LCA weekday church sch. ser.) 2.25; 2.50 teacher's ed.,
1. Religious education—Textbooks for children—Lutheran Church. I. Title.

STRENG, William D. 268.43
The faith we teach, by William D. Streng, others. Minneapolis, Augsburg [c.1962] 160p. 22cm. 1.25 pap.,
I. Title.

WILKINSON, Henrietta T. 268'.43
Free as the wind; teacher's book, grades 5 and 6 [by] Henrietta T. Wilkinson. Richmond, Published for the Cooperative Publication Association by John Knox Press [1970] 192 p. 22 cm. (Through-the-week series) Bibliography: p. 190-191. [HM271.W54] 73-103463 3.45
1. Liberty—Study and teaching. I. Cooperative Publication Association. II. Title.

**YOUTH kit,* 268.43
23 (formerly Youth fellowship kit) varied resources for study, discussion, action by church groups. Ed.: John C. Purdy. Ed.-in-chief: Norman F. Langford. Exec. ed.: Donald L. Leonard. Philadelphia, Geneva Pr. [dist. Westminister, c.1965] 232p. illus. 28cm. 3.50

ADAIR, Thelma C. 268.432
When we teach 4's & 5's, by Thelma C. Adair, Rachel S. Adams. Philadelphia, Geneva Pr. [dist. Westminster, 1963, c.1962] 96p. illus. 23cm. 63-598 1.25 pap.,
1. Religious education of pre-school children. I. Adams, Rachel Swann, joint author. II. Title.

ADVENTURE of growing 268.432
(The) (The) Prepared by the Children's Div., Dept. of Christian Educ., Protestant Episcopal Church. Greenwich, Conn., Seabury [c.1962] 64p. 28cm. (Vocation church sch. primary bk. 2) 1.90 pap.,

ADVENTURES in Christian 268'.432
living and learning; a resource book for use with retarded persons, ages 6-10. Jessie B. Carlson, editor. Martha Jones, supervisory editor. St. Louis, Published for the Cooperative Publication Association, by the Bethany Press [1969- v. illus. 22 cm. (The Cooperative series: Curriculum materials for the mentally retarded) Includes music. Includes bibliographical references. [BV1615.M4A36] 78-86154
1. Religious education—Text-books for mentally handicapped children. I. Carlson, Jessie B., ed. II. Cooperative Publication Association.

ALBUS, Harry James, 1920- 268.432
225 stories for the children's hour. Grand Rapids, Zondervan Pub. House [c1957] 120p. 20cm. [BV4315.A38] 58-19315
1. Children's stories. 2. Homiletical illustrations. I. Title.

**AMERICAN Lutheran Church* 268.432
elementary curriculum; weekday, grades 1-5; Sunday, grades 1-5. Minneapolis, Augsburg [1968] Materials included for each grade: pupil's bk., teacher's gd., & a packet of assorted learning aids. pap., apply

ANDERSON, Phoebe M 268.432
Religious living with nursery children in church and home. Boston, Published for the Co-operative Publication Association[by] Pilgrim Press [1956] 179p. 20cm. [BV1540.A62] 56-9758
1. Religious education of pre-school children. I. Title.

ANDERSON, Phoebe M 268.432
Religious living with nursery children in church and home. Boston, Published for the Co-operative Publication Association [by] Pilgrim Press [1956] 179p. 20cm. [BV1540.A62] 56-9758
1. Religious education of pre-school children. I. Title.

*ANDREWS, Dorothy 268.432
Westlake
A boy with a song. Illus. by Alex Kenne. Richmond, Va., CLC Pr. [dist. Knox] c.1965. 1v. (unpaged) col. illus. 22cm. 1.45 bds.,
1. Religious education (Elementary)—Presbyterian. I. Title.

*ANDREWS, Dorothy 268.432
Westlake
Everywhere I go [by] Dorothy Westlake Andrews, Virginia Barksdale Lancaster. Illus. by Robert William Hinds. Richmond, Va., CLC Pr. [dist. Knox] c.1965. 1v. (unpaged) col. illus. 22cm. 1.45 bds.,
1. Religious education (Elementary)—Presbyterian. I. Lancaster, Virginia Barksdale, joint author. II. Title.

*ANDREWS, Dorothy 268.432
Westlake
He has done marvelous things. Illus. by David K. Stone. Richmond, Va., CLC Pr. [dist. Knox] c.1965. 1v. (unpaged) col. illus. 22cm. 1.45 bds.,
1. Religious education (Elementary)—Presbyterian. I. Title.

*ANDREWS, Dorothy 268.432
Westlake
When I think of Jesus. Illus. by Elizabeth Dauber. Richmond, Va., CLC Pr. [dist. Knox] c.1965. 1v. (unpaged) col. illus. 22cm. 1.45 bds.,

1. Religious education (Elementary)—Presbyterian. I. Title.

ARNOLD, Arnold. 268'.432
The Arnold Arnold book of toy soldiers. Text and pictures by Arnold Arnold. New York, Random House [c1963] 8, [47] p. col. illus. 33 cm. Includes toy soldiers to push out and stand up, together with battle games. [GV1218.T55A7] 63-8998
1. Military miniatures. 2. War games. I. Title.

ARNOTE, Thelma. 268.432
Understanding nursery children. Nashville, Convention Press [1963] viii, 103 p. illus. 19 cm. "Church study course [of the Sunday School Board of the Southern Baptist Convention] This book is number 1505 in category 15, section for adults and young people." Bibliography: p. 96-99. [BV1475.7.A7] 63-13396
1. Religious education of pre-school children. I. Southern Baptist Convention. Sunday School Board. II. Title.

ASHBY. LAVERNE. 268.432
The primary leadership manual [by] LaVerne Ashby and Doris Monrde. Nashville, Convention Press [1959] 154p. illus. 19cm. Includes bibliography. [BV1545.A7] 59-3136
1. Religious education of children. 2. Religious education— Teaching methods. I. Monroe, Doris, joint author. II. Title.

AUTRY, Lola M. 268'.432
52 devotional programs for primary children [by Lola M. Autry Grand Rapids, Baker Book House [1970] 111 p. 20 cm. Includes a song to be used with each program. [BV4870.A9] 71-115633 1.95
1. Children—Prayer-books and devotions—1961- 2. Worship programs. I. Title.

AYCOCK, Martha B., 1920- 268'.432 s
Understanding: a resource book for use with persons who have learning difficulties. Martha B. Aycock, editor. Richmond, Va., Published for Cooperative Publication Association by John Knox Press [1972] 107 p. music. 23 cm. (Exploring life, ages 7-12, pt. 2) "The resources for use with this teacher's guide ... include pupil's books: Hey, somebody look. God created it all. My big friends. We remember Jesus." Includes bibliographies. [BV1615.M4A9] [BV1615.M4] 248'.82'07 72-519 ISBN 0-8042-1195-7
1. Religious education—Text-books for mentally handicapped children. I. Title. II. Series: Exploring life.

*AYMES, Maria de la Cruz Sister 268.432
Jesus. New York, Sadlier [1968] (On our way ser.; Vatican II ed.) .96 Elem. pap.,; .52 home workbk., pap.,; teacher's gd., price unreported
I. Title.

BABIN, Pierre. 268'.432
Methods; approaches for the catechesis of adolescents. Translated and adapted by John F. Murphy. [New York] Herder and Herder [1967] 187 p. 21 cm. Bibliographical footnotes. [BX926.B2813] 67-25875
1. Catechetics—Catholic Church. 2. Christian education of children. I. Title.

BAKER, Cosette. 268'.432
God's outdoors; a unit for use with nursery children in the church study course. [Nashville, Convention Press, 1968] x, 78 p. illus. 19 cm. Includes melodies with words. [BV1475.7.B3] 68-11675
1. Religious education of preschool children. I. Title.

BEILER, Edna. 268'.432
Uhuru! freedom! Children's mission study. [Leader's guide] Scottdale, Pa., Herald Press [1967] 96 p. illus., map, ports. 22 cm. Includes bibliographies. [BV2090.5.B43] 67-20984
1. Missions—Study and teaching (Elementary) 2. Missionary stories. 3. Tanzania—Description and travel. 4. Congo—Description and travel. 5. Nigeria—Description and travel. I. Title.

**BIBLE, life and worship series;* 268.432
bk. 1 Boston, Allyn, 1966. 133p. music. 23cm. (Guide bk. Confraternity ed.)
I. Johnice, M. Sister II. Elizabeth, M. Sister
Contents omitted.

**BIBLE, life and worship series;* 268.432
bk.4 Boston, Allyn, 1966 [c.1960, 1966] 191p. col. illus. 23cm. 1.64 pap.,
1. Religious education—Textbooks for children (Elementary) I. Johnice, M. II. Elizabeth, M., joint author. III. Cooke, Bernard J., joint author. IV. Title: Children of the Kingdom.
Contents omitted.

**BIBLE, life and worship series;* 268.432
bks. 2 & 3. Boston, Allyn [c.]1965. 2v. (160; 174p.) col. illus. 23cm. Bk. 2.--Come, Lord Jesus, by Sister M. Johnice, Sister M. Elizabeth. Illus. by A. and M. Provensen.--Bk. 3. The Lord Jesus says, by Sister M. Elizabeth, Sister M. Johnice. Illus. by A. and M. Provenson. pap., bk. 2, 1.40; bk. 3, 1.60
1. Religious education—Text-books for children (Elementary) I. Johnice, M. II. Elizabeth, M., joint authors.

BLANKENSHIP, Lois. 268.432
Our church plans for children; a manual on administration. Philadelphia, Judson Press, '1951. 94 p. illus. 20 cm. [BV1475.B53] 52-315
1. Religious education of children. I. Title.

BLANKINSHIP, Carribel. 268.432
Programs and plans for the Cradle Roll department. Nashville, Sunday School Board of the Southern Baptist Convention [1954] 51p. illus. 26 cm. [BV1537.B55] 55-18043
1. Religious education of pre-school children. 2. Sunday-schools. I. Title.

BOLER, James E., 1943- 268'.432
Why people fight : teachers' book : a shalom resource for use with eight- to twelve-year olds / by James E. Boler. Philadelphia : Published for Joint Educational Development by United Church Press, [1975] p. cm. (A Shalom resource) Bibliography: p. [LC311.B6] 75-16196 ISBN 0-8298-0297-5 pbk. : 2.95
1. Moral education—Handbooks, manuals, etc. 2. Christian education—Text-books. 3. Social conflict—Study and teaching. I. Joint Educational Development. II. Title.

BOLTON, Barbara J. 268'.432
Bible learning activities: children, grades 1 to 6 [by] Barbara J. Bolton and Charles T. Smith. Glendale, Calif., G/L Regal Books [1973] 154 p. illus. 20 cm. (ICL teacher's/leader's success handbook) (An ICL insight book) Bibliography: p. 151-152. [BV1475.2.B63] 73-85021 ISBN 0-8307-0240-7 2.25
1. Religious education of children. 2. Religious education—Text-books. I. Smith, Charles T., joint author. II. Title.

BOLTON, Barbara J. 268'.432
Ways to help them learn: children, grades 1 to 6 [by] Barbara J. Bolton. Glendale, Calif., International Center for Learning [1973, c1972] 149 p. illus. 20 cm. (ICL teacher's/leader's success handbook) (An ICL insight book) Bibliography: p. 149. [BV1475.2.B64] 77-168843 ISBN 0-8307-0119-2 1.95
1. Religious education of children. I. Title.

**BOOK of the Convenant people (The).* 268.432
Illus. by Gordon Laite. Richmond, Va., CLC Pr. [dist. Knox, 1966] 95p. illus. (pt. col.) 21cm. (Covenant life curriculum, elementary; The Bible, year 2) 1.45 pap.,
1. Religious education (Elementary) — Lutheran.

*BORAAS, Roger S. 268.432
A letter from Paul. Philip R. Hoh, ed. Karl Wurzer, ed. Philadelphia, Lutheran Church Pr. [c.1965] 102p. illus. 21cm. (LCA Sunday Church sch. ser.) With a teacher's guide. pap., 1.00; teacher's guide, pap., 1.25
1. Religious education of children—Lutheran I. Title.

*BOTHWELL, Sister Mary de Angelis. 268'.432
Good is good [by] Sister Mary de Angelis Bothwell and other Sisters of Notre Dame. Art: Sister Mary Megan Dull [&] Sister Mary Leon Wilhelmy. Theological advisor: John A. Hardon. Consultant: Daniel L. Flaherty. Chicago, Loyola University Press [1973] 138 p. col. illus. 28 cm. (Christ our life series: perform-a-text, 1) [BX930] ISBN 0-8294-0218-7 1.48 (pbk.)
1. Religious education—Textbooks for young people—Catholic. I. Hardon, John A. II. Flaherty, Daniel L. III. Title. IV. Series.

*BREAM, Gerry 268.432
God cares: kindergarten, teacher's guide. Ed.: Margaret J. Irvin. Philadelphia, Lutheran Church [1964, c.1965] 80p. 23cm. (LCA vacation church sch. ser.) .90 pap.,
I. Title.

BRECK, Flora Elizabeth, 1886- 268.432
Church school chats for primary teaching. Boston, Wilde [1950] 155 p. 20 cm. Includes hymns. [BV1545.B59] 50-12736
1. Religious education of children. I. Title.

BREHM, Mabel. 268.432
The church around the world, junior vacation school manual. Teacher's book. New York, Published for the Cooperative Publication Association by Abingdon-Cokes-bury Press [1951] 125 p. illus. 20 cm. [The Cooperative series; vacation church school texts] [BR151.B7] 51-2780
1. Church history—Juvenile literature. 2. Vacation schools, Religious—Text-books. I. Title.

BREHM, Mabel 268.432
The church around the world; junior pupil's book, vacation church school. Nashville, Published for Cooperative Publication Association by Abingdon Press [c.1959] 32p. illus. (col.) 23x18cm. .30 pap.,
1. Church history—Juvenile literature. 2. Vacation schools, Religious—Textbooks. I. Title.

BREHM, Mabel 268.432
The church around the world; rev. ed. Teacher's text, for use with juniors in vacation church school. Nashville, Published for the Cooperative Publication Association by Abingdon Press [c.1951, 1959] 128p. 23cm. (The Cooperative series; vacation church school texts) 51-2780 1.00 pap.,
1. Church history—Juvenile literature. 2. Vacation schools, Religious—Text-books. I. Title.

BRUMLEY, Mary Cureton. 268.432
Stories about Jesus; vacation church school unit for kindergarten children. New York, Abingdon-Cokesbury Press [1950] 96 p. illus. 23 cm. [BV1585.B73] 51-5981
1. Vacation schools, Religious—Text-books. I. Title.

CARLSON, Jessie B 268.432
The nursery department of the church. St. Louis, Bethany Press [1958] 128p. illus. 20cm. Includes bibliography. [BV1540.C315] 58-14386
1. Religious education of pre-school children. I. Title.

CARLSON, Jessie B 268.432
Teaching nursery children. Philadelphia, Judson Press [c1957] 112p. illus. 20cm. Includes bibliography. [BV1540.C32] 58-1134
1. Religious education of pre-school children. I. Title.

CARLSON, Jessie B. 268.432
Toddlers at church. Illus. by Dorothy Grider. St. Louis, Bethany [c.1961] 80p. illus. Bibl. 61-11104 1.00 pap.,
1. Religious education of pre-school children. I. Title.

CATON, Dorothy Webber. 268.432
Let's teach through group relations; one of a series of guides on using the out-of-doors in Christian education, for leaders and parents of six- to twelve-year-olds. [Illus. by P. Nowell Yamron. New York, Published for the Division of Christian Education, National Council of the Churches of Christ in the U. S. A. by the Office of Publication and Distribution, 1959] 64p. illus. 23cm. Includes bibliography. [BV1538.C3] 59-11638
1. Religious education of children. 2. Social group work. I. Title.

*CATON, Dorothy Webber 268.432
Light from my Bible for today. Teacher's guide. Nashville, Abingdon [1961] 128p. 23cm. (Co-op. ser.& Vacation Church sch. texts) A coop. vacation church sch. course for use with junior children. 1.25 pap.,
1. Religious education (Elementary)—Protestant. I. Title.

CAVALLETTI, Sofia. 268.432
Teaching doctrine and liturgy, the Montessori approach [by] Sofia Cavalletti and Gianna Gobbi. [Translated by Sister M. Juliana] Staten Island, N.Y., Alba House [1964] 132 p. illus. 20 cm. Translation of Educazione religiosa, liturgia e metodo Montessori. [BX926.C343] 64-15370
1. Religious education of children. 2. Catholic Church. Liturgy and ritual — Study and teaching (Elementary) I. Gobbi, Gianna, joint author. II. Title.

CAVALLETTI, Sofia 268.432
Teaching doctrine and liturgy, the Montessori approach [by] Sofia Cavalletti, Gianna Gobbi [Tr. from Italian by Sister M. Juliana] Staten Island, N.Y., Alba [c.1964] 132p. illus. 20cm. 64-15370 2.95
1. Religious education of children. 2. Catholic Church. Liturgy and ritual—Study and teaching (Elementary) I. Gobbi, Gianna, joint author. II. Title.

CHAMBERLAIN, Eugene. 268'.432
Children's Sunday school work [by] Eugene Chamberlain [and] Robert G. Fulbright. Nashville, Tenn., Convention Press [1969] 172 p. illus. 21 cm. [BV1475.2.C453] 79-98042
1. Religious education of children. I. Fulbright, Robert G., joint author. II. Title.

CHAPMAN, June R. 268.432
Primary worship programs. Grand Rapids, Mich., Zondervan [c.1962] 64p. 21cm. 1.00 pap.,
I. Title.

CHILDHOOD education in the church / 268'.432
edited by Roy B. Zuck and Robert E. Clark. Chicago : Moody Press, [1975] p. cm. Includes bibliographical references and index. [BV1475.2.C47] 74-15350 ISBN 0-8024-1249-1 : 7.95
1. Religious education of children. I. Zuck, Roy B. II. Clark, Robert E.

**CHURCH'S teaching for small church schools (The)* 268.432
Unit Bks. B, C [Drawings by Maurice Rawson, others] Prep. by the Dept. of Christian Educ. of the Protestant Episcopal Church at the direction of Gen. Convention. New York, Seabury, c.1964. 2v. (95; 96p.) illus. 28cm. (Church's teaching ser.) 2.00 pap.,
Contents omitted.

**CHURCH'S teaching in the [closely graded church schools (The)* 268.432
2d grade. Photos by Ken Heyman; drawings by Randolph Chirwood] Materials for Christian educ. prep. [by the Dept. of Christian Educ. of the Protestant Episcopal Church] at the direction of Gen. Convention. New York, Seabury [c.1955-1964] 98p. illus. 28cm. (Church's teaching ser.) 2.10 pap.,
Contents omitted.

COLINA, Tessa 268.432
A year of programs for children's church. Drawings by John Ham. Cincinnati, Ohio, Standard [c.1962] 175p. illus. 28cm. 2.95 pap.,
I. Title.

**COME to the Father;* 268.432
pupil's text, grade 1. Glen Rock, N.Y., Paulist [1966] 127p. col. illus. 23cm. (Come to the Father ser., 1) English version of the Catechism 'Viens vers le Pere,' written by the Office Catechistique Provincial, Montreal, Canada. 1.25 pap.,
1. Religious education (Elementary)—Catholic. I. Office Catechistique Provincial, Montreal, Canada.

CONNOLE, Roger Joseph. 268'.432
The Christian inheritance. Book 1- [Authors: Roger J. Connole, Sister Judith Stodola, and Sister Aline Baumgartner. Illus.: Sister Ansgar Holmberg. Rev. ed.] Saint Paul, North Central Pub. Co.; distributed by the Liturgical Press, Collegeville, Minn. [1968- v. illus. (part col.) 26 cm. [BX930.C6332] 68-55351
1. Religious education—Text-books for children—Catholic. I. Stodola, Judith, joint author. II. Baumgartner, Aline, joint author. III. Holmberg, Ansgar, illus. IV. Shields, Kathleen Marie. V. Confraternity of Christian Doctrine. VI. Title.

CULLY, Iris V. 268.432
Children in the church. Philadelphia, Westminster Press [c.1960] 204p. 21cm. (6p. bibl. and 2p. bibl. notes) 60-5125 3.75
1. Religious education of children. I. Title.

CULLY, Iris V 268.432
Ways to teach children, by Iris V. Cully. Illustrated by Harry Eaby. [Rev.] Philadelphia, Fortress Press [1966, c1965] 135, [1] p. illus. 20 cm. Bibliography: p. 134-[136] [BV1475.2C82 1966] 66-24201
1. Religious education of children. I. Title.

CULLY, Iris V 268.432
Ways to teach children, by Iris V. Cully. Edited by Philip R. Hoh. Illustrated by Harry Eaby. Philadelphia, Lutheran Church Press [1965] 136 p. illus. 22 cm. (Leadership education series) Teacher's guide, by Iris V. Cully. Edited by Philip R. Hoh, Philadelphia Lutheran Church Press [1965] 48 p. 21 cm. Leadership education series) Bibliography: p. 134-136. [BV1475.2.C82] 65-2631
1. Religious education of children. I. Title.

CULLY, Iris V. 268.432
Ways to teach children. by Iris V. Cully. Illus. by Harry Eaby. [Rev.] Philadelphia, Fortress [1966, c.1965] 135,[1]p. illus. 20cm. Bibl. [BV1475.2.C821966] 66-24201 2.50 bds.,
1. Religious education of children I. Title.

CULLY, Iris V 268.432
Ways to teach children, Ed. by Philip R. Hoh. Illus. by Harry Eaby. Philadelphia, Lutheran Church Pr. [c.1965] 136p. illus. 22cm. (Leadership educ. ser.) Bibl. [BV1475.2.C82] 65-2631 1.50; teacher's guide, pap., .50
1. Religious education of children. I. Title.

*CURRIE, Stuart D. 268.432
The beginnings of the church. Illus. by Kathleen Elgin. Richmond, Va., CLC Pr. dist. Knox [1966] 143p. illus. (pt. col.) 21cm. (Covenant life curriculum, elementary; the church year, 2) 1.95 pap.,
1. Religious education (Elementary)—Lutheran. I. Title.

*D becker, Pat 268.432
Finding out about God(teachings guide: kindergarten, age 4. Joseph W. Inslee, ed. Philadelphia, Lutheran Church Pr. [1966] 176p. 22cm. (LCA weekday church sch. ser.) 2.50
1. Religious education (Elementary)—Lutheran. I. Inslee, Joseph W., ed. II. Title.

DOAN, Eleanor Lloyd, 268.432
1914-
How to plan and conduct a primary church, with a special section for kindergarten church leaders, by Eleanor L. Doan and Frances Blankenbaker. Grand Rapids, Zondervan Pub. House [1961] 112 p. illus. 26 cm. [BV199.C4D6] 61-66783
1. Worship (Reglious education) 2. Church work with children. I. Blankenbaker, Frances, joint author. II. Title. III. Title: Primary church.

DOAN, Eleanor Lloyd, 268.432
1914-
How to plan and conduct a primary church, with a special section for kindergarten church leaders, by Eleanor L. Doan, Frances Blankenbaker. Grand Rapids, Mich., Zondervan [c.1961] 112p. illus. 26cm. Bibl. 61-66783 1.95 pap.,
1. Worship (Religious education) 2. Church work with children. I. Blankenbaker, Frances, joint author. II. Title. III. Title: Primary church.

DODDER, G Clyde. 268.432
Becoming a Christian person, a course for ninth and tenth grades. Illus. by Mark Kelley. Boston, United Church Press [1963] 127 p. illus. 26 cm. [BX9884.A3D6] 62-15302
1. Religious education — Text-books for adolescents — United Church of Christ. I. Title.

DODDER, G. Clyde 268.432
Becoming a Christian person, a course for ninth and tenth grades. Illus. by Mark Kelley. Philadelphia, United Church [c.1963] 127p. illus. 26cm. 62-15302 1.50 pap.,
1. Religous education—Text-books for adolescents—United Church of Christ. I. Title.

DOMINGOS, Ann Maria. 268.432
Working with children in the small church. Issued by Dept. of Christian Education of Children [and] the Division of the Local Church, the General Board of Education of the Methodist Church. Nashville, Methodist Pub. House [1952] 63 p. illus. 20 cm. [BV1475.D64] 53-16589
1. Religious education of children. I. Title.

DREW, Louise C. 268'.432
Nursery manual; a manual for administrators in the church school nursery department, by Louise C. Drew. Photos. by Sheldon Brody. Illustrated by Walter Lorraine. [Rev. ed.] Boston, United Church Press [1969] 63 p. illus. 26 cm. Bibliography: p. 60-62. [BV1539.D7 1969] 68-10417
1. Religious education of pre-school children. I. Title.

DUBUISSON, Odile. 268'.432
Children, crayons, and Christ; understanding the religious art of children. Translated by M. Angeline Bouchard. Paramus, N.J., Newman Press [1969] vii, 149 p. col. illus. 23 cm. Translation of Le dessin au catechisme. Bibliography: p. 149. [BV1536.D813] 74-81228 4.95
1. Creative activities and seat work. 2. Christian education of children. I. Title.

DUCKERT, Mary. 268'.432
Help! I'm a Sunday school teacher. Illustrated by Don Patterson. Philadelphia, Westminster Press [1969] 125 p. illus. 21 cm. [BV1534.D82] 77-83133 1.85
1. Sunday-school teachers. I. Title.

DUNCAN, Cleo. 268.432
The mark of Christians; a course for the first and second grades. Boston, United Church Press [1964] 124 p. illus. 26 cm. "Part of the United Church curriculum, prepared and published by the Division of Christian Education and the Division of Publication of the United Church Board for Homeland Ministries." Bibliography: p. 123. [] bX9884.A3D8] 64-19458
1. Religious education — Textbooks for children — United Church of Christ. I. United Church Board for Homeland Ministries. Division of Christian Education. II. United Church Board for Homeland Ministries. Division of Publication. III. Title.

ECKEL, Fred L 268.432
The cathedral series; a series of Christian education courses and materials. Atlanta, c1957. 1 v. (various pagings) illus., port., plan. 29cm. Includes 'Bell ringer arrangements.' Includes bibliographical references. [BV1585.E25] 57-44560
1. Vacation schools, Religious—Text-books. I. Title.

EDWARDS, Charlotte 268'.432
Walrath.
Let yourself go; try creative Sunday school. New York, Morehouse-Barlow Co. [1969] 122 p. 21 cm. [BV1534.E36] 77-88121
1. Religious education—Teaching methods. I. Title.

*ELIZABETH, M. Sister 268.432
Growing as Christians. Boston, Allyn [1968] Bible, life, and worship ser., bk. 6) 1.68 pap.,
I. Title.

*ELIZABETH, M. Sister 268.432
The Lord Jesus says, by Sister M. Elizabeth, Sister M. Johnice. Confraternity ed. Consultant: Bernard J. Cooke. Illus. by A. and M. Provensen. Boston, Allyn, 1967. 126p. illus. (pt. col.) 23cm. (Bible, life, and worship ser.; bk. 3) Adapted from The Lord has said, by Andre Boyer, orig. pub. by Les Editions de 1 Ecole, Paris, in 1960. 1.20 pap.,
1. Religious education—Elementary (Catholic) I. Johnice, Sister M., joint author. II. Title. III. Series: Bible, life, and worship series. Book 3

*ELIZABETH, Sister M. 268.432
The Lord Jesus says; guidebook, by Sister M. Elizabeth, Sister M. Johnice. Consultant: Reverend Bernard J. Cooke. Boston, Allyn [c.1961, 1965] 268p. music. 23cm. (Bible, life and worship ser., bk. 3) Adapted from Practical guide for the Christian initiation of young children, by Andre Boyer, pub. in Paris in 1961. .88 pap.,
I. Title.

*ELIZABETH. SISTER M. 268.432
Let us give thanks by Sister M. Elizabeth. Sister M. Johnice. Consultant: Reverend Bernard J. Cooke. Illus. by Joyce Winkel. Boston. Allyn, 1966. 191p. illus. (pt. col.) 23cm. (Bible, life and worship ser., bk. 5) 1.64 pap.,
I. Title.

*ELIZABETH SISTER M. 268.432
The Lord Jesus By Sister M. Elizabeth, Sister M. Johnice. Consultant: Rev. Bernard J. Cooke, S. J. Boston, Allyn [c.1958, 1966] 96p. col. illus. 23cm. (Bible, life and worship ser., confraternity ed., bk. 1) Adapted from The Lord Jesus, by Andre Boyer, pub. in Paris in 1958. .96 pap.,
I. Title.

*ELLIS, Mary Leith 268.432
Jesus Christ, Son of God. Illus. by Leonard Weisgard. Richmond Va., CLC Pr. [dist. Knox, 1966] 191p. illus. 21cm. (Covenant life curriculum, elementary; The Bible, year 2) Adapted from The Son of God, by Edric A. Weld, William Sydnor. 2.45 sReligious education (Elementary)--Lutheran.
I. Title.

ERB, Bessie Pehotsky. 268.432
In awe and wonder; a weekday church school course for boys and girls of grades five and six. Boston, Published for the Co-operative Publication Association by Pilgrim Press [1956] 64 p. illus. 20 cm. 140 p. illus. 20 cm. (The Co-operative series texts for weekday religious education classes and released-time religious education instruction) -- -- Teacher's book. Boston, Published for the Co-operative Publication Association [by] Pilgrim Press [BV1583.E7] 56-9757
1. Week-day church schools. 2. Religious education—Text-books for children. I. Title.

EXPLORING life. 268'.432 s
Richmond, Va., Published for Cooperative Publication Association by John Knox Press [197 p. Curriculum materials for persons who have learning difficulties. Includes bibliographies. [BV1615.M4E9] 72-520
1. Religious education—Text-books for mentally handicapped children. I. Cooperative Publication Association.

FAHS, Sophia Blanche 268.432
(Lyon) 1876-
Worshipping together with questioning minds, by Sophia Lyon Fahs. Boston, Beacon Press [1965] cx. 240 p. 21 cm. Bibliographical references included in "Notes" (p. 239-240) [BV1522.F3] 65-12241
1. Worship (Religious education) 2. Universalism — Education. I. Title.

FAHS, Sophia Blanche 268.432
(Lyon) 1876-
Worshipping together with questioning minds. Boston, Beacon [c.1965] x, 240p. 21cm. Bibl. [BV1522.F3] 65-12241 4.95
1. Worship (Religious education) 2. Universalism—Education. I. Title.

FARGUES, Marie. 268.432
Our children and the Lord; religious education for young children Translated by Geraldine McIntosh. Notre Dame, Ind., Fides Publishers [1965] Viii, 212 p. 20 cm. [BV1475.2.F313] 65-23117
1. Religious education of children. I. Title.

FARQUES, Marie 268.432
Our children and the Lord; religious education for young children. Tr. [from French] by Geraldine McIntosh. Notre Dame, Ind., Fides [c.1965] viii, 212p. 20cm. [BV1475.2.F313] 65-23117 2.95 pap.,
1. Religious education of children. I. Title.

FAUCHER, W. Thomas. 268'.432
Touching God : a book about children's liturgies, [including 17 model liturgies for grades one through six] / W. Thomas Faucher and Ione C. Nieland. Notre Dame, Ind. : Ave Maria Press, [1975] 157 p. : ill. ; 26 cm. Includes bibliographical references. [BX2015.A55F38] 74-26313 ISBN 0-87793-085-6 pbk. : 3.50
1. Children's missals. I. Nieland, Ione C., joint author. II. Title.

FENNER, Mabel B. 268.432
Guiding the nursery class; edited by Theodore K. Finck. Philadelphia, Muhlenberg Press [1950] viii, 248 p. illus. 20 cm. Includes music. Bibliography: p. 244-245. [BV1540.F38] 50-9483
1. Religious education of pre-school children. 2. Sunday-Schools. I. Title.

FLOYD, Pat, 1929- 268'.432
God made me ... to be responsible : leader's guide / by Pat Floyd ; [photos. by Barbara Withers]. Philadelphia : Published for the Cooperative Publication Association by United Church Press, [1975] 64 p. : ill. ; 28 cm. (Vacation ventures series) Bibliography: p. 56-62. [BV1585.F5] 75-14030 ISBN 0-8298-0295-9 pbk. : 1.95
1. Vacation schools, Christian. 2. Christian education—Text-books. I. Title.

FOUNTAIN, Rosanna B. 268'.432
God loves all people : teacher's course guide / Rosanna B. Fountain, Madeline H. Beck. Atlanta : John Knox Press, [1975] p. cm. Includes bibliographies and index. [BV1561.F68] 75-12645 ISBN 0-8042-9428-3 pbk. : 3.95
1. Christian education—Text-books. I. Beck, Madeline H., joint author. II. Title.

FOUNTAIN, Rosanna B. 268.432
Learning from Jesus. Illus. by Huntley Brown. Richmond, Va., CLC Pr. [dist. Knox, 1966] 63p. illus. (pt. col.) 21cm. (Covenant life curriculum, elementary; The Christian life, year, 2) 1.25 pap.,
1. Religious education (Elementary)—Lutheran. I. Title.

*FRANCIS, Mary Grace 268.432
Sister
Christ in His church(grade 8, home workbook. New York, Sadlier, 1967. v. 22cm. (On our way ser.) .44; .14 pap.,keys,
1. Religious education—Elementary—Catholic. I. Title. II. Series.

*FRANCIS, Mary Grace 268.432
Sister
Fulfillment in Christ(grade 6, home workbook. New York, Sadlier, 1967. v. 22cm. (On our way ser.) .44 pap.,
1. Religious education—Elementary—Catholic. I. Title. II. Series.

**FRIENDS of Jesus;* 268.432
teacher's guide, grade 2. Philadelphia, Lutheran Church Pr. [1967] v. illus. 24cm. (LCA Sunday chruch sch. ser.) Teacher's guide grade 3, by Lawrie Hamilton, Evelyn Byerly, Kathryn Orso. 2.50
1. Religious edication—Elementary—Lutheran. I. Hamilton, Lawrie. II. Byerly, Evelyn, joint author. III. Orso, Kathryn.

*FRITZ, Dorothy Bertolet 268.432
Christian teaching of kindergarten children. Richmond, Va., Covenant Life Curriculum [dist. Knox, c.1964] 96p. illus. 28cm. 2.00 pap.,
I. Title.

FROHNE, Marydel D 268.432
Understanding the church; a course for the third and fourth grades, by Marydel D. and Victor M. Frohne. Boston, United Church Press [1964] iii, 124 p. illus. (part col.) 26 cm. "Part of the United Church curriculum, prepared and published by the Division of Christian Education and the Division of Publication of the United Church Board for Homeland Ministries." Bibliography: p. 122-123. [BX9884.A3F7] 64-19459
1. Religious education — Textbooks for children — United Church of Christ. 2. Church — Study and teaching. I. Frohne, Victor M., joint author. II. United Church Board for Homeland Ministries. Division of Christian Education. III. United Church Board for Homeland Ministries. Division of Publication. IV. Title.

GALE, Elizabeth Wright 268.432
Have you tried this? Activities for preschool groups at church. Photos. by M. Edward Clark. Philadelphia, Judson Press [c.1960] 64p. illus. 28cm. 60-4518 pap., apply
1. Religious education of pre-school children. I. Title.

GAMM, David B. 268'.432
On cloud nine : 24 model liturgies and 4 penance services for grades one through four, thematically arranged for the school year with emphasis on the liturgical seasons / David B. Gamm. Notre Dame, Ind. : Ave Maria Press, c1976. 126 p. : ill. ; 26 cm. [BX2015.A55G35] 76-718 ISBN 0-87793-110-0 : 2.95
1. Children—Prayer-books and devotions—English. 2. Worship (Religious education) 3. Children's missals. I. Title.

GARDNER, Ann 268.432
Seek to serve, by Ann Gardner, Lois Burford. Murfreesboro, Tenn., DeHoff Pubns., 1963. 128p. illus. 21cm. Bibl. 63-12320 price unreported
1. Religious education of children. 2. Creative activities and seat work. I. Burford, Lois, joint author. II. Title.

GARDNER, Elizabeth. 268.432
The 2's at church; teaching material for the year for use with two-year-olds Philadelphia, Judson Press [1953] 132p. illus. 23cm. (Judson graded series. Judson nursery series) [BV1540.G33] 53-3853
1. Religious education of pre-school children. I. Title.

*GARHART, Marjorie 268.432
The book of the promises of God, work book, term 3. Illus. by Bert Marsh. Ed.: Gustav K. Wiencke. [Philadelphia] Lutheran Church Pr., c.1965. 32p. col. illus. 28cm. (LCA Sunday church school ser.) .40 pap.,
I. Title.

*GARHART, Marjorie 268.432
The book of the promises of God; term 4. Illus. by Tom Irons. Gustav K. Wiencke, ed. Philadelphia, Lutheran Church Pr., c.1965. 304p. 21cm. (LCA Sunday church sch. ser.) With teacher's guide and workbook. bds., 2.50; teacher's guide, 2.50; workbook, pap., .70
1. Religious education—Textbooks for children—Lutheran Church. I. Title.

*GARHART, Marjorie 268.432
The book of the promises of God; term 1, work-book. Illus. by Bert Marsh. Gustave K. Wiencke, ed. Philadelphia, Lutheran Church Pr., c.1965. 48p. illus. (pt. col.) map. 28cm. (LCA Sunday church sch. ser.) Flexible vinyl 34 record, 'a talking book of Psalms and prayers' in pocket on back cover. .70 pap.,
1. Religious education—Textbooks for Children—Lutheran Church. I. Title.

**GOD is in many places;* 268.432
a manual to use through the week and in summertime with kindergarten children. New York, Seabury [1968] 1.95 pap.,

GOD is with us. 268.432
Illus. by Kreigh Collins. Rev. teacher's manual replacing Wonder and faith in the first grade. Greenwich, Conn., Seabury [c.1955-1962] 105p. 27cm. (The church's teaching in the 1st grade) 2.00 pap.,

GODDARD, Carrie Lou. 268.432
Learning to live with others, junior camp manual [by] Carrie Lou Goddard in cooperation with the Special Committee on Camps and Conferences, Division of Christian Education, National Council of the Churches of Christ in the U. S. A. Illus. by Edwin N. Goddard. Nashville, Published for the Cooperative Publication Association by Abingdon-Cokesbury Press [1953] 160p. illus. 23cm. [BV1650.G6] 53-6351
1. Camping. I. Title.

**GOD'S word for God's* 268.432
world; catechist's guide grade 7, trimester C, unit 9. Prepd. for the Bd. of Parish Educ., and the Bd. of Pubn. of the Amer. Lutheran Church. 1v. (unpaged) 28cm. (Amer Lutheran Church curriculum: junior-high confirmation) 1.35 pap.,
1. Religious education (Elementary) Lutheran.

GOOD news; 268.432
workbook, by James Burtness T. J. Vinger. Produced by the Bd. of Parish Educ. and the Bd. of Pubn. of the Amer. Lutheran Church. Minneapolis, Augsburg, c.1962. 111p. col. illus. 23cm. 76 pap.,

GRIFFITHS, Louise 268.432
(Benckenstein) 1908-
Becoming a person: teacher's book. Rev. ed. Philadelphia, Published for Cooperative

Publication Association by the Westminster Press [1959] 187p. 21cm. (The Cooperative series texts) [BV1583.G7 1959] 59-6402
1. Week-day church schools—Teachers' manuals. 2. Religious education—Textbooks for adolescents. I. Title.

*GROOMER, Vera MacKinnon 268.432
Illustrating Sabbath songs for tiny tots--cradle roll. Mountain View Calif. Pacific Pr. Pub. [1967] 119p. illus. 28cm. 3.25, pap., wire bdg.
I. Title.

HALEY, Mary Jane 268.432
Bible personalities, teacher's book for use with 10 year olds. James C. Barry, ed Nashville, Broadman [c.1963] 192p. illus. 21cm. (Weekday Bible study ser.) 63-17523 2.75; 1.00 pap., pupil's ed.,
1. Bible—Study. I. Title.

HALEY, Mary Jane. 268.432
Bible personalities, teacher's book for use with 10 year olds. James C. Barry, editor. Nashville, Broadman Press [1963] 192 p. illus. 21 cm. (The Weekday Bible study series) [BS600.2.H3] 63-17523
1. Bible—Study. I. Title.

*HAMILTON, Lawrie 268.432
Sunday church school for 4's; class activity packet for terms 2 & 3. Lawrie Hamilton, course author; Gisela Jordan, packet illustrator; Gustav K. Wiencke, ser. ed. Philadelphia. Lutheran Church Pr. [1967] v. col. illus. 26x34cm. (LCA Sunday church sch. ser.) pap., term 2, 5.25; term 3, 1.25
1. Religious education—Elementary—Lutheran. I. Title. II. Series.

HARRIS, Jane Bowerman. 268.432
When we teach junior; a junior guidance manual. Philadelphia, Board of Christian Education of the Presbyterian Church in the United States of America [1957] 89p. illus. 23cm. [BV1546.H344] 57-7594
1. Religious education of children. I. Title.

HARRIS, Jane Bowerman. 268.432
When we teach juniors; a junior guidance manual. Philadelphia, Baord of Christian Education of the Presbyterian Church in the United States of America [1957] 80p. illus. 23cm. [BV1546.H344] 57-7594
1. Religious education of children. I. Title.

HARRIS, William J. 268.432
Our priceless primaries; making child teaching more child reaching for primary leaders and teachers. Mountain View, Calif., Pacific Press Pub. Association [c.1959] 195p. illus. (part col.) 24cm. 59-13496 4.00
1. Religious education of children. I. Title.

HATHAWAY, Lulu. 268'.432
Partners in teaching older children. Valley Forge [Pa.] Judson Press [1971] 55 p. illus. 28 cm. "Manual for middler and junior workers." Bibliography: p. 55. [BV1475.9.H38] 74-147849 ISBN 0-8170-0531-5 2.50
1. Religious education—Text-books for youth. I. Title.

HAXTON, Jennie Norman. 268.432
The two-year-old at home; a quarterly guide for parents of two-year-olds. Parents' manual. Nashville, The Graded Press ['1950- v. illus. 23 cm. "Closely graded courses." Bibliography: v. 1, p. 46. [BV1540.H33] 51-3349
1. Religious education of pre-school children. I. Title.

HAXTON, Jennie Norman. 268.432
When the two-year-old comes to church; a teachers' guide for use in church schools where two-Year-olds meet in separate groups. C. A. Bowen, general editor. Nashville. Graded Press ['1950] 128 p. illus. 20 cm. "Listening music [for piano]": p. 127. "Closely graded courses." Bibliography: p. 128. [BV1540.H34] 51-3350
1. Religious education of pre-school children. I. Title.

HAYNES, Marjorie. 268.432
When we teach primary children; a primary guidance manual. Philadelphia, Board of Christian Education of the Presbyterian Church in the United States of America [1957] 78p. illus. 23cm. Includes bibliography. [BV1545.H35] 57-8931
1. Religious education of children. I. Title.

HAYSTEAD, Wesley. 268'.432
Ways to plan & organize your Sunday school: early childhood, birth to 5 yrs. Glendale, Calif., International Center for Learning [1973, c1971] 127 p. illus. 20 cm. (ICL teacher's/leader's success handbook) (An ICL insight book) Bibliography: p. 127. [BV1475.8.H38] 78-168838 ISBN 0-8307-0122-2 1.95 (pbk.)
1. Religious education of preschool children. I. Title.

HAZZARD, Lowell Brestel. 268.432
Fairest Lord Jesus; a course for intermediate of junior high school groups in vacation church schools: teacher's book [by] Lowell Brestel Hazzard and Stella Tombaugh Hazzard. New York, Published for the Cooperative Publication Association by Abingdon Press [1957] 128p. illus: 20cm. (The Cooperative series: vacation church school texts) [BV1585.H39] 57-7096
1. Vacation schools, Religious— Teachers' manuals. I. Hazzard, Stella Tombaugh., joint author. II. Title.

HEARN, Florence Conner. 268'.432
Guiding preschoolers. Nashville, Convention Press [1969] 181 p. illus. 21 cm. (Basic preschool books) "Text for course 6107 of the subject area 1 of the New church study course." Bibliography: p. 163-169. [BV1475.8.H4] 70-97868
1. Christian education of preschool children. I. Title.

HEATON, Ada Beth, 1918- 268.432
The 3's at church; teaching material for the year for use with three-year olds in the church school. With methods sections by Helen Cann Rounds. Philadelphia, Judson Press [1953] 296p. illus. 23cm. (Judson graded series, Judson nursery series) [BV1540.H4] 53-3852
1. Religious education of pre-school children. I. Title.

HEMPHILL, Martha Locke. 268'.432
Partners in teaching young children; [manual for kindergarten primary workers] Valley Forge, Judson Press [1972] 64 p. illus. 28 cm. Bibliography: p. 63-64. [LB1511.H45] 79-147850 ISBN 0-8170-0532-3 3.50
1. Education, Primary—Handbooks, manuals, etc. 2. Christian education. I. Title.

HEMPHILL, Martha Locke. 268'.432
Weekday ministry with young children. Valley Forge [Pa.] Judson Press [1973] 95 p. music. 22 cm. Includes bibliographies. [BV1475.7.H45] 72-7594 ISBN 0-8170-0573-0 2.50
1. Religious education of preschool children. I. Title.

HERON, Frances Dunlap. 268.432
Kathy Ann, kindergartner. Illustrated by Janet Smalley. New York, Abingdon Press [1955] 128 p. illus. 20 cm. [BV1540.H45] 55-6763
1. Religious education of pre-school children. I. Title.

HERZEL, Catherine 268.432
Our Christian response and witness. Teacher's guide. Gustav K. Wiencke, ed. Philadelphia, Lutheran Church Pr. [c.1964] 320p. 24cm. 2.50
I. Title.

*HILL, Dorothy La Croix 268.432
The church teaches nines to twelves. Illus. by Ann Doyle. Nashville, pub. for the Coop. Pub. Assn. by Abingdon [c.1965] 192p. 19cm. 1.75 pap.,
I. Title.

HILL, Dorothy La Croix. 268.432
Working with juniors at church. Henry M. Bullock, general editor. Nashville, Abingdon Press [c1955] 160p. 20cm. [BV1546.H5] 55-6764
1. Religious education of children. I. Title.

HILL, Dorothy LaCroix. 268.432
The church teaches nines to twelves. Illus. by Ann Doyle. New York, Published for the Cooperative Publication Association by Abingdon Press [1965] 192 p. illus. 19 cm. (The Cooperative series) Bibliography: p. 187-188. [BV1475.2.H5] 65-8476
1. Religious education of children. I. Title.

*HILL, Elmira D., ed. 268.432
First Bible lessons, for beginners. For use in Sunday Schools, children's church, week-day church, week-day church schools child evangelism classes, and the home. Chicago, Moody [1965, c.1963] 140p. illus. 26cm. 3.50
I. Title.

HILLS, Hannah Brummitt. 268.432
The cradle roll department visitor. Nashville, Convention Press [c1959] 137p. 20cm. Includes bibliography. [BV1537.H5] 59-14358
1. Religious education of pre-school children. 2. Visitations (Church work) 3. Sunday-schools. I. Title.

HODGSON, Natalie. 268'.432
Pieces of the puzzle. St. Louis, Published for the Cooperative Publication Association by Bethany Press [1969] 191 p. 22 cm. (The Cooperative through-the-week series) "One of two courses available for grades 7 and 8. Teacher's book." Bibliography: p. 189-191. [BV1559.H6] 69-20438
1. Religious education—Text-books. I. Cooperative Publication Association. II. Title.

HOYER, George W. 268'.432
Child of God, the Lord be with you / by George W. Hoyer. St. Louis : Clayton Pub. House, c1977. 294 p. ; 23 cm. On spine: The Lord be with you. [BV1522.H677] 77-85172 ISBN 0-915644-11-8 : 8.50
1. Worship (Religious education) I. Title. II. Title: The Lord be with you.

HUNTER, Edith Fisher, 268.432
1919-
Conversation with children. Boston, Beacon Press [1961] 192p. illus. 23cm. Includes bibliography. [BX9821.H8] 61-10571
1. Religious education—Text-books for children. I. Title.

HUNTER, Edith Fisher, 268.432
1919-
The questioning child and religion. Boston, Starr King Press [1956] 209 p. 22 cm. [BV1475.H85] 56-10076
1. Children's questions and answers. 2. Questions and answers—Theology. 3. Religious education of children. I. Title.

HUNTER, Elizabeth M 268.432
God's wonderful world, a course for the church school kindergarten. Photos. by Sheldon Brody. Drawings by Calvin Burnett. Boston, United Church Press [1963] 64 p. illus. 26 cm. [BX9884.A3H8] 63-7295
1. Religious education — Text-books for pre-school children — United Church of Christ. I. Title.

HUNTER, Elizabeth M. 268.432
God's wonderful world, a course for the church school kindergarten. Photos.by Sheldon Brody. Drawings by Calvin Burnett. Philadelphia, United Church [c.1963] 64p. illus. 26cm. 63-7295 1.15 pap.
1. Religious education—Text-books for pre-school children—United Church of Christ. I. Title.

HUNTER, Elizabeth M 268.432
Learning to live with others; a course for the church school kindergarten. Photos. by Sheldon Brody. Boston, United Church Press [1962] 64p. illus. 26cm. Includes bibliography. [BV1540.H8] 62-7222
1. Religions education of pre-school children. I. Title.

HUNTER, Elizabeth M. 268.432
Learning to live with others; a course for the church school kindergarten. Photos. by Sheldon Brody. Philadelphia, United Church [c.1962] 64p. illus. 23cm. Bibl. 62-7222 .75 pap.,
1. Religious education of pre-school children. I. Title.

*HURTY, Kathleen 268.432
God's children at work and play; teachers guide: kindergarten [by] Kathleen Hurty, Kathryn Swanson. Doris J. Smith, ed. Marjorie F. Garhart, ser. ed. Philadelphia, Lutheran Church Pr. [1967] 96p. 23cm. (LCA vacation church sch. ser.) Third year of three-year cycle: God and my life. .90 pap.,
1. Religious education (Elementary)—Lutheran. I. Swanson, Kathryn, joint author. II. Garhart, Marjorie F., ed. III. Title.

*HURTY, Kathleen 268.432
Michael Martin and his friends, by Kathleen Hurty, Kathryn Swanson. Illus. by June Goldsborough. 1v. (unpaged) col. illus. 22x28cm. (LCA vacation church sch. ser. Third year of 3-year cycle: God and my life.) .50 pap.,
1. Religious education—Elementary Lutheran. I. Swanson, Kathryn, joint author. II. Title.

HUTTAR, Leora W. 268'.432
Church time for preschoolers / by Leora W. Huttar ; drawings by Doris L. Hedsten. Denver : Accent Books, c1975. 123 p. : ill. ; 28 cm. Includes index. [BV1475.8.H83] 75-17368 5.95
1. Christian education of preschool children. 2. Christian education—Text-books. I. Title.

*HUTTAR, Leora W. 268.432
Jack and Jill stay for church; how to lead a churchtime nursery. Drawings by Doris L. Hedsten. Chicago, Moody [c.1965] 112p. illus. 28cm. (MP295) 2.95, pap., plastic bdg.
1. Religious education—Elementary. I. Title.

I learn about the 268.432
Bible; primary activity book. Prepared for the Board of Parish Educ. and The Board of Pubn. of the Amer. Lutheran Church. Based on materials furnished by Ella M. Osten. Illus. by Robert Ed, Melva Mickelson. Minneapolis, Minn., Augsburg, c.1965. 48p. illus. 28cm. (Jr. Lutheran ser., grs. 1-3) pap., 1.00; leader's guide, pap., 1.25

*ILLWITZER, Elinor G. 268.432
For you and me. New York, Sadlier [1968] (Kindergarten religion program) 3.96 Elem. pap.,; teacher's gd., pap., price unreported.
I. Title.

INGRAM, Tolbert Robert, 268.432
1913-
Sacred studies; foundations of our common heritage. [Bellaire, Tex.] St. Thomas Press, 1958. 124p. 24cm. [BX5875.I5] 58-14390
1. Religious education—Text -books for children—Anglican. I. Title.

ISHAM, Linda. 268'.432
On behalf of children / by Linda Isham. Valley Forge, Pa. : Judson Press, [1975] 48 p. : ill. ; 22 cm. Bibliography: p. 45-47. [BV639.C4I8] 74-17842 ISBN 0-8170-0666-4 pbk. : 1.50
1. Church work with children. I. Title.

*JOHNICE, M. Sister 268.432
Children of the kingdom, by Sister M. Johnice, Sister M. Elizabeth. Consultant: Bernard J. Cooke. Illus. by H. and R. Shekerjian. Boston, Allyn [1967] v. illus. (pt. col.) 23cm. (Bible, life, and worship ser., bk. 4, confraternity ed.) Adapted from Our history as children of God, by Andre Boyer. 1.32 pap.,
1. Religious education—Elementary (Catholic) I. Elizabeth, M., Sister joint author. II. Title.

*JOHNICE, M. Sister 268.432
Come, Lord Jesus, by Sister M. Johnice, Sister M. Elizabeth. Consultant: Bernard J. Cooke. Illus. by A. and M. Provensen. Confraternity ed. Boston, Allyn. 1967. 128p. p. illus. (pt. col.) 23cm. (Bible, life and worship ser.; bk. 2) Adapted from Come Lord, by Andre Boyer, orig. pub. by Les Editions de l'Ecole, Paris, in 1960. 1.20 pap.,
1. Religious education—Elementary (Catholic) I. Elizabeth, M., Sister joint author. II. Title. III. Series: Bible, life and worship series. Book 2

*JOHNICE, M. Sister 268.432
Growing as Christians, by Sister M. Johnice Sister M. Elizabeth. Consultant: Bernard J. Cooke. Illus. by Mary and Maurice Kirchoff. Boston, Allyn 1967. v. illus. (pt. col.) 23cm. (Bible, life, and worship ser., bk. 6) 2.04 pap.,
1. Religious education—Elementary (Catholic. I. Elizabeth, Mary, Sister joint author. II. Title.

*JOHNICE, M. Sister 268.432
Let us give thanks. By Sister M. Johnice, Sister M. Elizabeth, assistant, Barton & Joan DeMerchant consultants. Bernard J. Cooke. Boston, Allyn 1968. xvi. illus. (Bible, life and worship ser. bks.) guidebook, .56 pap.,
1. Religious education—Elementary (Catholic) I. Elizabeth, M. Sister Joint author. II. Title.

*JOHNSON, Margery 268.432
Mallard.
Hand in hand. Richmond, Va., Knox [1968] (CLC Pr. bk.: Covenant life curriculum) 1.45 Elem. pap.,
I. Title.

JONES, Elizabeth Norton. 268.432
Nursery children and our church; nursery superintendent's book. Philadelphia, Judson Press [1955] 96p. illus. 23cm. (Judson nursery series) 'An official publication of the Board of Education and Publication of the American Baptist Convention.' [BV1540.J56] 56-4677
1. Religious education of pre-school children I. Title.

KELSEY, Alice (Geer) 268.432
Living and working together as Christians; a vacation church school course for girls & boys of grades 4, 5 & 6. Teacher's book. Boston, Published for the Co-operative Publication Association by Pilgrim Press [1954] 172p. 20cm. (The Co-operative series: vacation church school texts) [BV1585.K38] 55-20520
1. Vacation schools, Religious—Teachers' manuals. 2. Christian life—Study and teaching. I. Title.

KELSEY, Alice Geer 268.432
Living and working together as Christians; rev. ed. A Vacation Church School course for girls and boys of grades 4, 5, and 6. Teacher's book. Boston, 14 Beacon St., Published for the Cooperative Publication Association by Pilgrim Press, [c.1960] 128p. Bibl. p.126-127. 1.00 pap.,
I. Title.

*KIDD, Elizabeth 268.432
A Christian decides, by Elizabeth Kidd, Margaret. J. Irvin. Illus. by Tom Irons, Philadelphia, Lutheran Church Pr. [c.1966] 64p. illus. (pt. col.) 23cm. (LCA vacation church sch. ser.) With teacher's guide. .50; .90 pap., teacher's guide,
1. Religious education (Elementary)—Lutheran. I. Irvin, Margaret J., joint author. II. Title.

KLEIN, Sarah Guss, 1911- 268.432
When they are three; nursery children in the church and home, by Sara G. Klein and Elizabeth C. Gardner. Illustrated by Jacqueline C. Stone. Philadelphia, Westminster Press [c1956] 255p. illus. 24cm. [BV1540.K57] 56-11766
1. Religious education of pre-school children. I. Gardner, Elizabeth, joint author. II. Title.

KLINK, Johanna Louise. 268'.432
Teaching children to pray / Johanna Klink ; [translated by John Bowden]. Philadelphia : Westminster Press, [1975] c1974. 78 p. ; 20 cm. Translation of Niet in de wind niet in het vuur. [BV4870.K5313 1975] 74-34591 ISBN 0-664-24766-0 pbk. : 1.95
1. Children—Prayer-books and devotions—English. 2. Children—Religious life. I. Title.

KRAMER, William Albert, 1900- 268'.432
God's people : devotions for Christian schools / by William A. Kramer. Milwaukee : Northwestern Pub. House, 1975. 159 p. ; 20 cm. Devotions for school and family on a wide range of topics, e.g.: "How Important Are We?", "God Can Do Everything," and "Sweet Revenge." [BV4870.K67] 75-16790
1. Children—Prayer-books and devotions—English. I. Title.

KUIPER, Barend Klass, 1877- 268.432
The church in history, by B. K. Kuiper. [Rev. ed.] [BR151.K8 1964] 65-4954
1. Church history — Juvenile literature. I. Title.

KUIPER, Barend Klass, 1877- 268.432
The church in history, by B. K. Kuiper. [Rev. ed.] Grand Rapids, National Union of Christian Schools [1964] 412 p. illus., facsims., col. maps, ports. 24 cm. [BR151.K8 1964] 65-4954
1. Church history — Juvenile literature. I. Title.

LACHAPELLE, Dolores. 268'.432
First steps in faith ... [by] Dolores LaChapelle, Janet Bourque, and Pat McCauley. [New York] Herder and Herder [1969] 3 v. illus., music. 28 cm. Contents.Contents.—[1] First steps in faith; an introduction for parents and teachers.—[2] Learning about God's world; first steps in faith for four-year olds.—[3] Learning to love God; first steps in faith for five-year olds. Bibliographical footnotes. [BX930.L18] 69-12678 5.95 (v. 1) 4.95 (v. 2) 6.95 (v. 3)
1. Religious education—Text-books for pre-school children—Catholic. I. Bourque, Janet, joint author. II. McCauley, Pat, 1940- joint author. III. Title. IV. Title: Learning about God's world. V. Title: Learning to love God.

LE BAR, Lois Emogene, 1907- 268.432
Children in the Bible school; the how of Christian education. Westwood, N. J., Revell [1952] 382 p. illus. 21 cm. Includes bibliography. [BV1475.L43] 52-9635
1. Religious education of children. I. Title.

LE BAR, Mary Evelyn, 1910- 268'.432
Children can worship meaningfully at church and home / Mary E. LeBar. Wheaton, Ill. : Victor Books, c1976. 119 p. : ill. ; 21 cm. [BV1522.L4] 75-32884 ISBN 0-88207-173-4 : 1.95
1. Worship (Religious education) I. Title.

LE BAR, Mary Evelyn, 1910 268'.432
Children can worship meaningfully at church and home / Mary E. LeBar. Wheaton, Ill. : Victor Books, c1976. 119 p. : ill. ; 21 cm. [BV1522.L4] 75-32884 ISBN 0-88207-173-4 pbk. : 1.95
1. Worship (Religious education) I. Title.

LEE, Florence B. 268.432
Primary children in the church. Illus. by Louis Segal. Philadelphia, Pub. for the Cooperative Pubn. Assn. by Judson Pr. [c.1961] 160p. illus. (Cooperative ser.) 61-11996 3.00
1. Religious education of children. I. Title.

LEFEBVRE, Xavier. 268.432
Bringing your child to God; the religious education of the pre-school child [by] Xavier Lefebvre and Louis Perin. Translated by Marta Gondos. New York, P. J. Kenedy [1963] 178 p. 21 cm. Translation of L'enfant devant Dieu. [BV1475.8.L413] 63-20401
1. Religious education of pre-school children. 2. Children — Religious life. I. Perin, Louis, joint author. II. Title.

LEFEBVRE, Xavier 268.432
Bringing your child to God; the religious education of the pre-school child [by] Xavier Lefebvre, Louis Perin. Tr. [from French] by Marta Gondos. New York, Kenedy [c.1963] 178p. 21cm. 63-20401 3.95 bds.,
1. Religious education of pre-school children. 2. Children—Religious life. I. Perin, Louis, joint author. II. Title.

LEROY, Jean 268.432
Children in our urban world: children's mission study, 1963-1964, primary and junior leader'sguides. Drawings by Joseph Edcourido. Prepared for the children's div. Dept. of Christian Educ. Protestant Episcopal Church. New York, Seabury [c.1963] 62p. illus. 28cm. 1.25 pap.,
I. Title.

LEWIS, Hazel Asenath, 1886- 268.432
The primary church school Rev. ed. St. Louis, Published for the Cooperative Publication Association by the Bethany Press [1951] 149 p. 20 cm. [BV1545.L47 1951] 51-11140
1. Religious education of children. 2. Sunday-schools. I. Title.

LIVING in the church. 268.432
Rev. teacher's manual replacing Discovering the holy fellowship. Illus. by Frank Giusto. New York, Seabury [c.1964] 216p. illus. 21cm. (Church's teaching in the 5th gr.) 2.10 pap.,

LUTHERAN Church -- 268.432
Missouri Synod. Board for Parish Education. *Memory book for Lutheran schools,* published under the auspices of the Board of Christian Education, Evangelical Lutheran Synod of Missouri, Ohio, and Other States. St. Louis, Mo., Concordia Pub. House, 1944. 172 p. illus. 19 cm. At head of title: Grades I to VIII, number 18. "Source books used": p.8. [BX8015.A3 1944b] 62-56774
1. Religious education — Text-books for children — Lutheran. I. Title.

MCCUTCHAN, Marjorie Munn 268.432
The church guides children's work. Richmond, Va., Pub. for the Cooperative Pubn. Assn. by John Knox [c.1963] 99p. illus. 21cm. (Cooperative ser.) 63-7518 1.50 pap.,
1. Church work with children. I. Title.

MCDANIEL, Elsiebeth. 268'.432
You and children, by Elsiebeth McDaniel, with Lawrence O. Richards. Chicago, Moody Press [1973] 125 p. 22 cm. (Effective teaching series) Bibliography: p. 124-125. [BV1475.2.M33] 72-95032 ISBN 0-8024-9831-0 1.95
1. Religious education of children. I. Richards, Lawrence O., joint author. II. Title.

MCDANIEL, Elsiebeth. 268'.432
You and preschoolers / by Elsiebeth McDaniel and Lawrence O. Richards. Chicago : Moody Press, 1976 126 p. : ill. ; 22 cm. (Effective teaching series) Bibliography: p. 125-126. [BV1475.8.M3] 74-15353 ISBN 0-8024-9834-5 : 1.95
1. Religious education of preschool children. I. Richards, Lawrence O., joint author. II. Title.

MCDANIEL, Myrtle Arlene. 268.432
Boys and girls of the Bible; a weekday church school course for boys and girls of grades 1 and 2. Philadelphia. Published for the Cooperative Publication Association [by] Christian Education Press [1957] 147p. 20cm. [BV1583.M15] 57-11775
1. Week-day church schools—Teachers' manuals. 2. Children in the Bible. I. Title.

MCDANIEL, Myrtle Arlene. 268.432
Boys and girls of the Bible; a weekday church school course for boys and girls of grades 1 and 2. Philadelphia, Published for the cooperative Publication Association [by] Christian Education Press [1957] 147p. 20cm. [BV1583.M15] 57-11775
1. Week-day church schools—Teachers' manuals. 2. Children in the Bible. I. Title.

*MCFADYEN, Mary Jean 268.432
The earth is the Lord's; camp leader's guide, grades 5 and 6. Illus. by Ruth S. Ensign. Richmond, Va., CLC Pr. [dist. Knox, 1966] 158p. illus. 23cm. (Covenant life curriculum; camping and confs.) 3.00 pap.,
1. Religious education (Elementary)—Lutheran. I. Title.

MCGINNIS, Joanna V. 268.432
The gift of God, parent-teacher guidebook; bk. 3, by the Religious of the Cenacle: Joanne V. McGinnis, Florence Sweetin. New York, Paulist Pr. [c.1963] 59p. 24cm. price unreported pap.,
I. Title.

*MCGLOIN, Joseph T. 268.432
Life of man in Christ. Milwaukee, Bruce [1967] pap., price unreported
I. Title.

MCINTYRE, Marie, comp. 268'.432
Aids for grade school religion teachers: organization and procedures, edited by Marie McIntyre. Huntington, Ind., Our Sunday Visitor [1972] 128 p. 18 cm. [BV1534.M18] 72-84253 ISBN 0-87973-756-5 pap., 1.25
1. Religious education—Teaching methods. I. Title.

MANSO, Leo, 1914- 268'.432
The Wild West. Cleveland, World Pub. Co. [1950] 1 v. (unpaged) col. illus. 27 cm. (A Rainbow playbook) Part of the illus. are cut outs. [GV1218.C7M3] 50-8287
1. Paper work. I. Title.

MARTIN, Florence, 1904- 268'.432
Observing national holidays and church festivals; a weekday church school unit in Christian citizenship series for grades three and four. Printed for the International Committee on Co-operative Publication of Weekday Church School Curriculum. St. Louis, Mo., Bethany Press. Ann Arbor, Mich., Gryphon Books, 1971 [c1940] 279 p. illus. 22 cm. Includes bibliographies. [BV1583.M3 1971] 76-174077
1. Week-day church schools—Teacher's manuals. I. International Council of Religious Education. Interdenominational Committee on Co-operative Publication of Vacation and Church School Curriculum. II. Title.

*MARY MAURIANA, Sister 268.432
Christ our Savior(grades 3, home workbook. New York, Sadlier, 1967. v. 22cm. (On our way ser.) .44; .14 pap.,key,
1. Religious education — Elementary — Catholic. I. Title. II. Series.

*MATHEWS, Eleanor Muth 268.432
God's way in the Old Testament; grade 5 workbk. Illus.: Davis Meltzer. Ed.: Joseph W. Inslee. Philadelphia, Lutheran Church Pr. [c.1964] 64p. col. illus. 28cm. (LCA weekday church sch. ser.) .40 pap.,
I. Title.

*MATHEWS, Eleanor Muth 268.432
Lives that praise God; teacher's guide: grades 3 8 4. Marjorie F. Garhart, ed. Philadelphia, Lutheran Church Pr. [1967] 80p. 23cm. (LCA vacation church sch. ser.) Third year of three-year cycle: God and my life. .90 pap.,
1. Religious education (Young adults)—Lutheran. I. Garhart, Mrrjorie F., ed. II. Title.

*MEEK, Pauline Palmer 268.432
All day long. Illus. by Kelly Oechsli. Richmond, Va., CLC Pr. [dist. Knox] c.1965. 1v. (unpaged) col. illus. 22cm. 1.45 bds.,
1. Religious education (Elementary)—Presbyterian. I. Title.

*MEEK, Pauline Palmer 268.432
The broken vase. Illus. by Ati Forberg. Richmond, Va., CLC Pr. [dist. Knox] c.1965. 1v. (unpaged) col. illus. 22cm. 1.45 bds.,
1. Religious education (Elementary)—Presbyterian. I. Title.

*MEEK, Pauline Palmer 268.432
God sent his son. Illus. by Jo Polseno. Richmond, Va., CLC Pr. [dist. Knox] c.1965. 1v. (unpaged) col. illus. 22cm. 1.45 bds.,
1. Religious education (Elementary)—Presbyterian. I. Title.

*MEEK, Pauline Palmer 268.432
Hop, skip, hop. Illus. by June Goldsborough. Richmond, Va., CLC Pr. [dist. Knox] c.1965. 1v. (unpaged) col. illus. 22cm. 1.45 bds.,
1. Religious education (Elementary)—Presbyterian. I. Title.

*MEEK, Pauline Palmer 268.432
Knock!knock! Illus. by Richard Powers. Richmond, Va., CLC Pr. [dist. Knox] c.1965. 1v. (unpaged) col. illus. 22cm. 1.45 bds.,
1. Religious education (Elementary)—Presbyterian. I. Title.

*MEEK, Pauline Palmer 268.432
Who is Debbie? Illus. by June Goldsborough. Richmond, Va., CLC Pr. [dist. Knox] c.1965. 1v. (unpaged) col. illus. 22cm. 1.45 bds.,
1. Religious education (Elementary)—Presbyterian. I. Title.

MEYER, Kathleen Louise. 268'.432
Teaching tiny tots; a guide for workers in cradle-roll and kindergarten divisions. Photos by D. Tank. Mountain View, Calif., Pacific Press Pub. Association [1967] 157 p. illus. (part col.) 22 cm. [LB1169.M55] 66-18296
1. Kindergarten—Methods and manuals. I. Title.

MOLAN, Dorothy Lennon. 268.432
Teaching middlers. Valley Forge, Judson Press [1963] 94 p. illus. 22 cm. [BV1546.M6] 63-9447
1. Religious education of children. I. Title.

MOLAN, Dorothy Lennon 268.432
Teaching middlers. Valley Forge, Judson [c.1963] 94p. illus. 22cm. Bibl. 63-9447 1.00 pap.,
1. Religious education of children. I. Title.

MOON, Mary Hazel (Ford) 268.432
A boy named Nelson [by] Mary Hazel Moon. Nashville, Convention Press [1965] 87 p. illus., map, ports. 21 cm. (Foreign mission graded series) [BX2853.B6M58] 65-14932
1. Missions — Brazil — Juvenile literature. 2. Baptists — Missions — Juvenile literature. I. Title.

MULLINS, Beverly Schultz 268.432
Why Jesus came, by Beverly Schultz Mullins. Bonny Vaught. Illus. by Isa Barnett. Gustav K. Wiencke, ed. Philadelphia, Lutheran Church Pr. [c.1966] 126p. illus. (pt. col.) 21cm. 1.25
1. Religious education of children—Lutheran Church. I. Title.

MY way to God. 268'.432
Huntington, Ind., Our Sunday Visitor, inc. [1971] 4 v. col. illus. 25 cm. "North America edition." [BX930.M9 1971] 71-153783
1. Christian education—Text-books for children—Catholic.

NARRAMORE, Clyde Maurice, 1916- 268.432
How to understand and influence children, ages five, six, seven, and eight. Illus. by by Sam Pollach. Grand Rapids, Zondervan Pub. House [1957] 93p. illus. 21cm. [BV1475.N3] 57-3369
1. Religious education of children. I. Title.

NATIONAL Sunday School Association. 268'.432
Annual lesson commentary [on the] National Sunday School Association uniform lessons. Springfield, Mo., Gospel Publishing House. v. illus. 23 cm. Began publication in 1958. [BV1561.A65] 64-28482
1. Religious education — Text-books — Series. I. Title.

NAUGHTON. IRENE MARY 268.432
Make ready the way of the Lord. Milwaukee. Bruce [1966] xxv. 267p. 23cm. Music appendix: p.263-267 [BX930.N3] 66-19972 3.95
1. Religious education—Textbooks for children—Catholic. 2. Church year—Study and teaching. I. Title.

NEFF, Herbert B. 268'.432
Meaningful religious experiences for the bright or gifted child [by] Herbert B. Neff. New York, Association Press [1968] 160 p. 21 cm. Bibliography: p. 158-160. [BV1475.2.N4] 68-17777
1. Religious education of exceptional children. I. Title.

*NEWBURY, Josepephine 268.432
Church kindergarten resource book. Richmond, Va., Covenant Life Curriculum [dist. Knox, c.1964] 253p. music. 28cm. Bibl. 4.00 pap.,
I. Title.

NEWBURY, Josephine. 268.432
Nursery-kindergarten weekday education in the church. Richmond, Va., Published for the Cooperative Publication Association by John Knox Press [c.1960] 203p. illus. 21cm. (Cooperative Publication Association. The cooperative series) (Bibls.) 60-13496 3.50
1. Church schools. 2. Nursery schools. I. Title.

NICHOLSON, Dorothy. 268'.432
I can choose: leader's guide; a cooperative vacation ventures series course for use in nursery. Philadelphia, Published for the Cooperative Publication Association by United Church Press [1974] 64 p. illus. 28 cm. (Vacation ventures series) Bibliography: p. 60-61. [BV1585.N5] 74-8043 ISBN 0-8298-0280-0
1. Vacation schools, Christian—Text-books. 2. Christian education of preschool children. I. Cooperative Publication Association. II. Title.

NICHOLSON, Dorothy. 268.432
So you work with kindergartners. Anderson, Ind., Warner Press [1960] 64p. 21cm. [BV1540.N53] 60-13193
1. Religious education of pre-school children. I. Title.

OSTEN, Ella M. 268.432
Adventure with Christ. Illus. by Terry Kennard Hitt. Minneapolis, Augsburg [1963] c.1957. 63p. col. illus. 28cm. (Jr. Lutherans weekday church sch. ser.) 1.00 pap.,
I. Title.

*OSTWALT, Adeline Hill 268.432
God so loved the world. Illus. by Jo Polseno. Richmond, Va., CLC Pr. [dist. Knox, 1966] 128p. illus. (pt. col.) 21cm. (Covenant life curriculum, elementary, The Bible, year 2) 1.95 pap.,

1. Religious education (Elementary)—Lutheran. I. Title.

PAULS, Ferdinand. 268'.432
Building juniors / Ferdinand & Florence Pauls. Elgin, Ill. : D. C. Cook Pub. Co., c1975. 158 p. : ill. ; 18 cm. (Christian education series) [BV1475.9.P39] 75-4178 ISBN 0-912692-66-9 pbk. : 1.95
1. Christian education of adolescents. I. Pauls, Florence, joint author. II. Title.

*PAULSON, Donna 268.432
God speaks, grade 6; teacher's guide. Illus. by Mae Gerhard. Gustav K. Wiencke, ed. Philadelphia, Lutheran Church [c.1965] 318p. illus. 24cm. (LCA Sunday church sch. ser.) 2.50
I. Title.

*PAULSON, Donna 268.432
God speaks in my life [term 2] Illus. by William K. Plummer. Gustav K. Wiencke, ed. Philadelphia, Lutheran Church [c.1965] 318p. illus. (pt. col.) 22cm. (LCA Sunday church sch. ser.) 1.25; workbk., pap., .50
I. Title.

*PAULSON, Donna 268.432
The way of the Christian; teacher's guide: grades 5 & 6. Marjorie F. Garhart, ed. Philadelphia, Lutheran Church Pr. [1967] 86p. 23cm. (LCA vacation church sch. ser.) Third year of three-year cycle: God and my life. .90 pap.,
1. Religious education (Elementary)—Lutheran. I. Garhart, Marjorie F., ed. II. Title.

PECK, Kathryn (Blackburn) 268.432
1904-
Better primary teaching. Kansas City, Mo., Beacon Hill Press [1957] 128p. illus. 19cm. 'Text for first series unit 242a, 'Planning for primary children." Includes bibliography. [BV1545.P39] 57-3560
1. Religious education of children. I. Title.

*PEIFFER, Marie Venard 268.432
Mother
God loves us; teacher's guide [for] grade 1. Advisory comm., Rev. John B. McDowell [others] New York, Sadlier [c.1965] 288p. 22x20cm. With 2 34 rpm phono-discs in pocket (Our life with God ser.; Vatican II ed., 011) Appended is Musical booklet entitled Sing to the Lord, by Mother Marie Venard, Margaret Land with words and piano accompaniment. 2.00 pap.,
1. Religious education (elementary) Catholic. I. Title.

*PENNELL, Lucy 268.432
Our church at work in the world [by] Lucy Pennell, Jack Smith. Illus. by Don Bolognese. Richmond, Va., CLC Pr. [dist. Knox, 1966] 112p. illus. (pt. col.) 21cm. Covenant life curriculum elementary The Christian life, year 2) 1.45 pap.,
1. Religious education (Elementary)—Lutheran. I. Title.

*PEOPLE *of God;* 268.432
grade 7. New York, Sadlier, 1967. v. (pt. col.) music. 21cm. (Our life with God ser., Vatican II ed.) Grade 7 by Sister Edward Mary Magill, Sister M. Celine Lhota. 1.44 pap.,
1. Religious education—Elementary—Catholic. I. Magill, Sister Edward Mary. II. Lotha, M. Celine, Sister joint author.

*PETERSON, Edward. 268.432
Doors--not fences: a teacher's guide to accompany The case of the door-openers vs the fence-builders. New York, Friendship [1967] 1.50 pap.,
I. Title.

*PFEIFFER, Marie Venard. 268.432
Sister
Alive in Christ. Gr. 5. New York, Sadlier [1968] (Our life with God ser.; Vatican II ed. CCD version) 1.28 Elem. pap.,; 2.67 teacher's gd., pap.,
I. Title.

*PFEIFFER, Marie Venard 268.432
Sister
Christ with us; teacher's guide,by Sister Marie Venard Pfeiffer, Sister Mary Gerald Carroll. New York, Sadlier [1967] v. 22cm. (Out life with God ser., Vatican II ed.) Recording, Selections for Unit II, CSM 34 rpm in pocket on back cover. 2.00 pap.,
1. Religious education—Elementary—Catholic. I. Carroll, Mary Gerald, Sister joint author. II. Title. III. Series.

*PFEIFFER, Marie Venard 268.432
Mother
God's gifts to us; teacher's guide [for] gr. 2. Advisory comm.: Rev. John B. McDowell [others] New York, Sadlier [c.1965] 220p. illus. 22x20cm. With a 33 1/3 phonodisc in pocket. (Our life with God ser.; Vatican 22 ed., 012) Appended is music booklet entitled Sing joyfully to God, all the earth by Mother Marie Venard Pfeiffer, Margaret Lang with words and piano accompaniment. 2.00 pap.,
1. Religious education (Elementary) Catholic. I. Title.

*PFEIFFER, Mother Marie 268.432
Love the Lord, with all your heart, and with all your soul, and with all your mind [by] Mother Marie Pfeiffer, Mother Mary Laiiatte. New York, Sadlier, 1966. 191p. illus. (pt. col.) 21cm. (Our life with God ser., Vatican II ed., Grade 4) 1.20 pap.,
1. Religious education study and teaching, (Elementary)—Catholic. I. Carroll, Mary, Mother jipoint author. II. Title. III. Series.

*PFFIFFER, Marie Venard 268.432
Mother
Alive in Christ; Grade 5 [by] Marie Venard Mother Pfeiffer, Mother Mary Gerald Carrol. Advisory comm.: John B. McDowell [others] New York, Sadlier [1966] 191p. illus. (pt. col.) 22x21cm. Cover title. T. P. reads: It is no longer I who live, but Christ who lives in me (Our life with God ser.: Vatican II ed., 006) pap., 1.20; teacher58s ed., 2.00
1. Religious education (Elementary) Catholic. I. Carroll, Mother Mary Gerald, joint author. II. Title.

PHILLIPS, Ethel M. 268.432
So you work with primaries. Anderson, Ind., Warner Press [dist. Gospel Trumpet Press, c.1960] 64p. 21cm. 60-13192 1.00 pap.,
1. Religious education of children. I. Title.

PHILLIPS, Ethel M 1916- 268.432
So you work with primaries. Anderson, Ind., Warner Press [1960] 64p. 21cm. [BV1545.P5] 60-13192
1. Religious education of children. I. Title.

*POTTEBAUM, George A. 268.432
Little people's paperbacks [3v.] Illus. by Robert Strobridge. Dayton, Ohio, Pflaum. c.1965. 3v. (unpaged) chiefly col. illus. 18cm. (LPP13-15) .35 pap., ea.,
1. Religious education (Elementary)—Catholic. I. Title.
Contents omitted.

*POTTEBAUM, George A. 268.432
Little people's paperbacks [2v.] Illus. by Robert Strobridge. Dayton, Ohio, Pflaum [c.1964] 2v. (unpaged) col. illus. 18cm. (LPP—10) Contents.[1] The good samaritan.--[2] The king and the servant. (LPP9-10) .35 pap., ea.,
1. Religious education (Elementary)—Catholic. I. Title.

*POTTEBAUM, Gerard A. 268.432
Little people's paperbacks [3v.] Illus. by Robert Strobridge. Dayton, Ohio, Pflaum [c.1964] 3v. col. illus. 18cm. (LLP6-8) Contents.[1] The little grain of wheat.--[2] He obeyed.--[3] The Easter lamb. .35 pap., ea.,
1. Religious education (Elementary)—Catholic. I. Title.

*PRESENTINA, Mary Sister 268.432
Christ leads the way grade 4, home workbook. New York, Sadlier, 1967. v. 22cm. (On our way ser.) .44 pap.,
1. Religious education—Elementary — Catholic. I. Title. II. Series.

*PRESENTINA, Mary Sister 268.432
With Christ the Father; home workbook. New York, Sadlier, 1967. v. illus. 22cm. (On our way ser., Vatican II ed.) .52 pap.,
1. Religious education — Elementary — Catholic. I. Title. II. Series.

*PRESENTINA, Mary Sister 268.432
Witnessing Christ; grade 7, home workbook New York, Sadlier, 1967. v. 22cm. (On our way ser.) .44; .14 pap.,key,
1. Religious education — Elementary — Catholic. I. Title. II. Series.

PRFRANCIS, Mary Grace 268.432
Sister
One in Christ(grade 5, home workbook. New York, Sadlier, 1967, v. 22cm. (On our way ser.) .44; .14 pap.,key,
1. Religious education—Elementary — Catholic. I. Title. II. Series.

*PRIESTER, Gertrude 268.432
Teaching primary children in the church. Philadelphia, Geneva Pr. [dist.] Westminster [c.1964] 96p. 23cm. Bibl. 1.25 pap.,
I. Title.

PROTESTANT Episcopal 268.432
Church in the U. S. A. National Council. Dept. of Christian Education.
Apostles in the home; a manual for use with classes of parents and godparents, with special reference to church school grades 2, 5, and 8, and kindergarten (five-year-olds) Illustrated by Maurice Rawson. Greenwich, Conn., Seabury Press [1956] 179p. illus. 21cm. (The Seabury series, P-11) [BV1475.P7] 56-7856
1. Religious education of children. 2. Religious education—Home training. I. Title.

PROTESTANT Episcopal 268.432
Church in the U. S. A. National Council. Dept. of Christian Education.
Deciding for myself; teacher's manual, grade 6. Illustrated by Susan Perl. Greenwich, Conn., Seabury Press [1957] 181p. illus. 21cm. (The Seabury series, T-6) Includes bibliography. [BV1546.P68] 57-8344
1. Religious education of children. I. Title.

PROTESTANT Episcopal 268.432
Church in the U. S. A. National Council. Dept. of Christian Education.
Five-year-olds in the church; revised kindergarten teacher's manual. Prepared at the direction of General Convention. Greenwich, Conn., Seabury Press [1960] 121p. illus. 28cm. (The Seabury series, T-KB) First published in 1956 under title: Receiving the five-year-old. Includes bibliography. [BV1540.P7 1960] 60-2708
1. Religious education of pre-school children. I. Title.

PROTESTANT Episcopal 268.432
Church in the U. S. A. National Council. Dept. of Christian Education.
God's world and mine, revised teacher's manual, grade 2. Prepared at the direction of General Convention. Greenwich, Conn., Seabury Press [1960] 121p. illus. 28cm. (The Seabury series, T-2B) First published in 1956 under title: My place in God's world. Includes bibliography. [BV1545.P699 1960] 60-2707
1. Religious education of children. I. Title.

PROTESTANT Episcopal 268.432
Church in the U. S. A. National Council. Dept. of Christian Education.
The goodly company; teacher's manual, grade 5. Illustrated by William Sharp. Greenwich, Conn., Seabury Press [1956] 182p. illus. 21cm. (The Seabury series, T-5) [BV1546.P69] 56-7854
1. Religious education of children. 2. Protestant Episcopal Church in the U. S. A.—Education. I. Title.

PROTESTANT Episcopal 268.432
Church in the U. S. A. National Council. Dept. of Christian Education.
Growing in faith; teacher's manual, grade 9. Greenwich, Conn., Seabury Press [1957] 88p. 28cm. (The Seabury series, F-9) [BV1548.P68] 57-8346
1. Religious education of adolescents. I. Title.

PROTESTANT Episcopal 268.432
Church in the U. S. A. National Council. Dept. of Christian Education.
My place in God's world; teacher's manual, grade 2. Illustrated by Mary Stevens. Greenwich, Conn., Seabury Press [1956] 87p. illus. 28cm. (The Seabury series, T-2) [BV1545.P699] 56-7853
1. Religious education of children. I. Title.

PROTESTANT Episcopal 268.432
Church in the U. S. A. National Council. Dept. of Christian Education.
Receiving the five- year-old; kindergarten teacher's kit. Illustrated by Alice Golden; flannelboard section by Dellwyn Cunningham. Greenwich, Conn., Seabury Press [1956] 85p. illus. 28cm. (The Seabury series, T-K1) [BV1540.P7] 56-7852
1. Religious education of pre-school children. I. Title.

PROTESTANT Episcopal 268.432
Church in the U. S. A. National Council. Dept. of Christian Education.
Receiving the nursery child; a manual for teaching children three and four years old. Illustrated by Sally Michel. Greenwich, Conn., Seabury Press [1957] 92p. illus. 28cm. (The Seabury series, T-N) Includes bibliography. [BV1540.P72] 57-8340
1. Religious education of pre-school children. I. Title.

PROTESTANT Episcopal 268.432
Church in the U. S. A. National Council. Dept. of Christian Education.
Throughout the whole wide earth: teacher's manual, grade 3. Illustrated by Beatrice and Leonard Derwinski. Greenwich, Conn., Seabury Press [1957] 83p. illus. 28cm. (The Seabury series, T-3) [BV1545.P6993] 57-8342
1. Religious education of children. I. Title.

PROTESTANT Episcopal 268.432
Church in the U. S. A. National Council. Dept. of Christian Education.
What about us? Teacher's manual, grade 8. Greenwich, Conn., Seabury Press [1956] 103p. 28cm. (The Seabury series, T-8) [BV1548.P69] 56-7855
1. Religious education of adolescents. I. Title.

PROTESTANT Episcopal 268.432
Church in the U. S. A. National Council. Dept. of Christian Education.
What is Christian Education. Greenwich, Conn., Seabury Press [1956] 177p. illus. 22cm. (The Seabury series, R-8) [BV1548.P694] 56-7851
1. Religious education—Text-books for adolescents—Anglican. I. Title. II. Title: What is Christian courage?

PROTESTANT Episcopal 268.432
Church in the U. S. A. National Council. Dept. of Christian Education.
Wonder and faith in the first grade; revised teacher's manual, grade 1. Illustrated by Randolph Chitwood. Greenwich, Conn., Seabury Press [1958] 89p. illus. 28cm. (The Seabury series, T-1B) Includes bibliography. [BV1545.P6995 1958] 58-9259
1. Religious education of children. I. Title.

REEVES, Katherine 268.432
When we teach 3's. Philadelphia, Geneva [dist. Westminster, c.1962] 63-836 1.25 pap.,
1. Religious education of pre-school children. I. Title.

*RENFRD, Jean Marie 268.432
Sister
We are risen in the Lord; teacher's guide, [by] Sister Jean Marie Renfro, Jane Moore. Consultant: William J. Reedy. New York, Sadlier [1967] v. 22cm. (*summer sch. of religion ser., grade 5) .25 pap.,
1. Religious education—Elementary—Catholic. I. Moore, Jane, joint author. II. Title. III. Series.

*RENFRD. JEAN MARIE 268.432
Sister
Freedom in Christ; teacher's ed. [by] Sister Jean Marie Renfro, Jane Moore. Consultant: William J. Reedy. New York, Sadlier [1967] v. 22cm. (Summer sch. of religion ser., grade 6) .25 pap.,
1. Religious education—Elementary—Catholic. I. Moore, Jane, joint author. II. Title. III. Series.

*RENFRO, Jean Marie 268.432
Sister
We are the people of God; grade 3, teacher's ed. [by] Sister Jean Marie Renfro. Jane Moore. Consultant: William J. Reedy. New York, Sadlier [1966] 112p. music. 22x21cm. (Summer sch. of religion ser., 048) .25 pap.,
1. Religious education (Elementary) I. Moore, Jane, joint author. II. Title. III. Series.

*RENFRO, Sister Jean 268.432
Marie
Children of our Father; teacher's guide [for] grade 2 [by] Sister Jean Marie Renfro, Jean Moore. Consultant: William J. Reedy. New York, Sadlier [c.1965] 96p. music. 22cm. (Summer sch. of Religion ser., 047) .25 pap.,
1. Religious education (Elementary)—Catholic. I. Moore, Jean, joint author. II. Title.

*RENFRO, Sister Jean 268.432
Marie
Going to God our Father; teacher's guide [for] grade 1 [by] Sister Jean Marie Renfro, Jane Moore. Consultant: William J. Reedy. New York, Sadlier [c.1965] 96p. music. 22x20cm. (Summer sch. of religion ser., 046) .25 pap.,
1. Religious education (Elementary) Catholic. I. Moore, Jane, joint author. II. Title.

RICE, Lillian (Moore) 268.432
How to work with juniors in the Sunday school. Nashville, Convention Press [1956] 143p. 19cm. [BV1546.R485] 56-42688
1. Religious education of children. I. Title.

RICE, Rebecca, 1899- 268.432
The earth is full of His riches; a vacation church school course for primary groups. Teacher's book. Boston, Published for the Co-operative Publication Association [by] Pilgrim Press [1953] 136p. 21cm. [The Co-operative series, vacation church school texts] [BV1585.R52] 53-2016
1. Vacation schools, Religious—Text-books. I. Title. II. Series.

RICHTER, Dolle. 268.432
Primaries at worship, by Dolle Richter and Barbara Wade. Cincinnati, Standard Pub. Foundation, c1956. 128p. illus. 20cm. (Religious education) [BV1522.R52] 56-41916
1. Worship. I. Wade, Barbara, joint author. II. Title.

*RINGLAND, Elinor 268.432
Loving others: grades 1 & 2: teacher's guide. Marjorie F. Garhart, ed. Philadelphia, Lutheran Church Pr. [1967] 86p. 23cm. (LCA vacation church sch. ser.) Third year of three-year cycle: God and my life. .90 pap.,
1. Religious education (Elementary)—Lutheran. I. Garhart, Marjorie F., ed. II. Title.

RITTENHOUSE, Laurence 268.432
God created me. Illus. by Trina Schart Hyman. Philadelphia, United Church [c.1963] 95p. col. illus. 23cm. Part of the United Church curriculum. 63-4252 1.50
1. Religious education—Text-books for children—United Church of Christ. I. Title.

RIVES, Elsie. 268'.432
Guiding children [by] Elsie Rives [and] Margaret Sharp. Nashville, Convention Press [1969] 217 p. illus. 21 cm. (Basic books for persons who guide children, first through sixth grades) Includes musical examples. "Text for course 6108 subject area 1 of the New church study course." Includes bibliographies. [BV1475.2.R56] 76-98044
1. Christian education of children. I. Sharp, Margaret, joint author. II. Title.

RIVES, Elsie. 268.432
My family, a unit for use with nursery children in the Church study course. [By] Elsie Rives and Hazel Rowe Luck. [Nashville, Convention Press, c1962] 79 p. illus. 19 cm. "B.S.S.B. [1. i.e. the Sunday School Board of the Southern Baptist Convention] Church nursery program." [BV1539.R5] 62-21681
1. Religious education of pre-school children. I. Luck, Hazel Rowe, joint author. II. Southern Baptist Convention. Sunday School Board. III. Title.

ROORBACH, Harriet A. 268.432
Jesus, the Friend; a vacation church school unit for primary girls and boys. New York, Abingdon-Cokesbury [1950] 93 p. 23 cm. Hymns with music: p. [91]-93. [BV1585.R65] 50-2069
1. Vacation schools, Religious — Teachers' manuals. I. Title.

ROORBACH, Rosemary K 268.432
Teaching children in the church. New York, Abingdon Press [1959] 159p. 19cm. Includes bibliography. [BV1534.R63] 59-1746
1. Religious education—Teaching methods. I. Title.

ROWEN, Dolores. 268'.432
Ways to help them learn: early childhood, birth to 5 yrs. Glendale, Calif., International Center for Learning [1973, c1972] 152 p. illus. 20 cm. (ICL Teacher's/leader's success handbook) (An ICL insight book) Bibliography: p. 151-152. [BV1475.8.R68 1973] 73-168842 ISBN 0-8307-0118-4 1.95
1. Religious education of preschool children. I. Title.

*RUDOLPH, L. C. 268.432
Story of the church. Illus. by Lewis Parker. Richmond, Va., CLC Pr. [dist. Knox, 1966] 191p. illus. (pt. col.) map (pt. col.) 21cm. (Covenant life curriculum, elementary; The church year 2) 2.45 pap.,
1. Religious education (Elementary)—Lutheran. I. Title.

*RUDOLPH, Mary Baine 268.432
The church teaching children grades one through six. [dist.] Richmond, Va. [Knox, CLC Pr. c.1964] 104p. 28cm. (Covenant life curriculum) 2.00 pap.,
I. Title.

RUMBOUGH, Constance 268.432
Hickey.
Living as Christian Americans; a weekday church school course for grades 5 and 6. Teacher's book. New York, Published for Cooperative Publication Association by Abingdon Press [1958] 220p. 20cm. (The Cooperative series) [BV1583.R8] 57-13181
1. Week-day church schools—Teachers' manuals. 2. Christian life— Study and teaching. I. Title.

RUSSELL, Howard H., 268'.432
1934-
Growing in love; a course for the first and second grades, by Howard H. Russell. Philadelphia, United Church Press [1972] 128 p. illus. 26 cm. "Part of the United Church curriculum, prepared and published by the Division of Christian Education and the Division of Publication of the United Church Board for Homeland Ministries." Bibliography: p. 125-126. [BX9884.A3R87] 72-7378 2.20
1. Religious education—Text-books—Congregational. I. United Church Board for Homeland Ministries. Division of Christian Education. II. United Church Board for Homeland Ministries. Division of Publication. III. Title.

SAPP, Phyllis Woodruff, 268'.432
1908-
Creative teaching in the church school. Nashville, Broadman Press [1967] vi, 120 p. illus. 22 cm. [BV1534.S2] 67-22033
1. Religious education—Teaching methods. 2. Religious education of children. I. Title.

SAPP, Phyllis Woodruff, 268'.432
1908-
59 programs for pre-teens. Nashville, Tenn., Broadman Press [1969] 144 p. 21 cm. [BV1546.S26] 78-84500 3.50
1. Christian education of children. I. Title.

*SCHLENKER, Elizabeth D. 268.432
God's way in his world [term 1] Illus. by Ruth Van Sciver. Ed., JosephW. Inslee. Philadelphia. Luthern Church [c.1965] 137p. col. illus. 22cm. (LCA weekday church sch. ser.) 1.25; teacher's guide, 2.50; workbk., pap., .50
I. Title.

SCHOENFELD, Elizabeth. 268.432
Please tell me; answers to gospel questions children ask [by] Elizabeth Schoenfeld and J. Stanley Schoenfeld. Salt Lake City, Deseret Book Co., 1966. 168 p. illus. 24 cm. [BX8610.S34] 66-20707
1. Religious education—Text-books for children—Mormon. I. Schoenfeld, J. Stanley, joint author. II. Title.

SCHOONMAKER, Hazel K. 268'.432
Creation and me; by Hazel K. Schoonmaker. Philadelphia, Published for the Cooperative Publication Association by United Church Press [1970] iii, 92 p. illus., music. 28 cm. (The Cooperative vacation church school series) "A cooperative vacation church school course for use with kindergarten children/Teacher's course book." Bibliography: p. 90-91. [BV1585.S324] 77-132862 ISBN 0-8298-0191-X
1. Vacation schools, Christian—Text-books. 2. Christian education of pre-school children. I. Cooperative Publication Association. II. Title. III. Series.

SCHOONMAKER, Hazel K 268.432
Kindergarten manual for administrators and teachers in the church school kindergarten. With photos by Sheldon Brody and drawings by Shirley Hirsch. Boston, United Church Press [1961]*0p. illus. 26cm. Includes bibliography. [BV1540.S3] 61-9724
1. Religious education of pre-school children. I. Title.

SCHOONMAKER, Hazel K. 268'.432
Kindergarten manual for administrators and teachers in the church school kindergarten [by] Hazel K. Schoonmaker. With photos. by Sheldon Brody and drawings by Shirley Hirsch. [Rev. ed.] Boston, United Church Press [1969] 80 p. illus. 26 cm. Bibliography: p. 76-78. [BV1540.S3 1969] 68-13123
1. Religious education of pre-school children. I. Title.

*SCHULZ, Florence 268.432
Families and friends. Illus. by Tom O'Sullivan. Richmond, Va., CLC Pr. [dist. Knox] c.1965. 1v. (unpaged) col. illus. 22cm. 1.45 bds.,
1. Religious education (Elementary)—Presbyterian. I. Title.

SCHULZ, Florence 268.432
Friends and neighbors; a resource book for ministering to primary and junior boys and girls in inner-city areas Boston, 14 Beacon St. Pub. for the Cooperative Pubn. Assn. [by] Pilgrim Pr. [c.1962] 118p. 23cm. (Cooperative vacation church sch. texts) 62-21605 1.50 pap.,
1. Vacation schools, Religions. 2. Church work with children. I. Title.

SCHULZ, Florence. 268.432
Growing in the fellowship; a course for the church school kindergarten. Phtos. by Sheldon Brody; drawings by Laurence Scott. Boston, United Church Press [c1960] 128p. illus. 26cm. Includes singing games (unace.) [BV1540.S32] 60-53133
1. Religious education of pre-school children. I. Title.

*SCHULZ, Florence 268.432
I am Andrew. Illus. by Lucy and John Hawkinson. Richmond, Va, CLC Pr. [dist. Knox] c.1965. 1v. (unpaged) col. illus. 22cm. 1.45 bds.,
1. Religious education (Elementary) Presbyterian. I. Title.

SCHULZ, Florence. 268.432
Living in the Christian community, a course for the church school kindergarten. Photos. by Sheldon Brody. Drawings by Shirley Hirsch. Boston, United Church Press [1962] 128p. illus. 26cm. [BV1475.8.S3] 61-17818
1. Religious education of pre-school children. I. Title.

*SCHULZ, Florence 268.432
Sunday morning. Illus. by Erica Merkling. Richmond, Va., CLC Pr. [dist. Knox] c.1965. 1v. (unpaged) col. illus. 22cm. 1.45 bds.,
1. Religious education (Elementary)—Presbyterian. I. Title.

*SCHULZ, Florence 268.432
Who is Jesus? Illus. by Eleanor Mill. Richmond, Va., CLC Pr. [dist. Knox] c.1965. 1v. (unpaged) col. illus. 22cm. 1.45 bds.,
1. Religious education (Elementary)—Presbyterian. I. Title.

SEVENTH Day Adventists. 268.432
General Conference. Dept. of Education.
All the way with God, Bible stories for grades 3 and 4; illustrated by John Lear. [Teacher's ed.] Mountain View, Calif., Pacific Press Pub. Association [1951] 128, 320 p. illus. 21 cm. "Series IIa, even year." The main work, also issued separately, is preceded by "Teacher's guide and key for All the way with God" with special t.p. [BS551.S433] 51-37198
1. Bible stories, English. I. Title.

SEVENTH-DAY Adventists. 268.432
General Conference. Dept. of Education.
Teacher's guide for Bible, grades one and two. Mountain View, Calif., Pacific Press Pub. Association [1954- v. illus. 21cm. 'Designed to be used with the Listen and do companion books for the first and second grades.' Includes bibliography. [BS546.S45] 54-40590
1. Bible stories. I. Title.

SHARP, Margaret. 268.432
A church training juniors. Nashville, Convention Press [1966] xiv, 145 p. 20 cm. "Church study course [of the Sunday School Board of the Southern Baptist Convention] This book is number 1816 in category 18, section for adults and young people." [BV1547.S5] 66-13317
1. Religious education of children. I. Southern Baptist Convention. Sunday School Board. II. Title.

SHERWICK, Winston M 268.432
Bible doctrine, by Winston M. Sherwick. Chicago, Harvest Publications [c1964] 103 p. illus. (part col.) 26 cm. ("Tell me, please," book 1) [BX6225.S5] 64-8448
1. Religious education—Textbooks for adolescents—Baptist. I. Title.

SHIELDS, Elizabeth 268.432
McEwen, 1879-
Guiding kindergarten children in the church school. Rev. by Dorothae G. Mallard. Richmond, Published for the Co-operative Pub. Association by John Knox Press [1955] 174p. illus. 19cm. (A Cooperative text) [BV1540.S518 1955] 54-10894
1. Religious education of pre-school children. 2. Religious education—Teacher training. I. Title.

SMITH, Ada (Wilcox) 1885- 268.432
Learning to know the Bible; junior vacation school manual. Teacher's book. New York, Published for the Cooperative Publication Association by Abingdon-Cokesbury Press [1951] 160 p. illus. 20 cm. (The Cooperative series of vacation church school texts] Full name: Ada Littleton (Wilcox) Smith. Bibliography: p. 10-11. [BV1585.S57] 51-4278
1. Vacation schools, Religious—Text-books. 2. Bible—Study. I. Title.

SMITH, Clarence T. 268'.432
Ways to plan & organize your Sunday school: children, grades 1 to 6 [by] Charles T. Smith. Glendale, Calif., International Center for Learning [1973, c1971] 127 p. illus. 20 cm. (ICL teacher's/leader's success handbook) (An ICL insight book) Bibliography: p. 125-127. [BV1475.2.S63] 71-168839 ISBN 0-8307-0123-0 1.95
1. Religious education of children. I. Title.

*SMITH, Doris J. 268.432
God loves and plans for me: teacher's guide: nursery. Margaret J. Irvin, ed. William C. Kautz, designer. Philadelphia, Lutheran Church Pr. [1967] 96p. 23cm. (LCA vacation church sch. ser.) .90 pap.,
1. Religious education (Elementary)—Lutheran. I. Irvin, Margaret J., ed. II. Title.

*SMITH, Doris J. 268.432
God loves me [pupil bk., nursery ed.] Margaret J. Irvin, ed. William C. Kautz, designer. Joy Troth Friedman, illus. Philadelphia, Lutheran Church Pr. [c.1965] 32p. col. illus. 22x28cm. (Vacation church sch. ser.) With teacher's guide God loves and plans for me. pupil's bk., pap., .50; teacher's guide, pap., .90
I. Title.

SMITH, Velma. 268.432
So you work with nursery children. Anderson, Ind., Warner Press [1960] 64 p. 21 cm. [BV1540.S6] 60-13194
1. Religious education of pre-school children. I. Title.

SMITH, Velma 268.432
So you work with nursery children. Anderson, Ind., Warner Press [dist. Gospel Trumpet Press, c.1960] 64p. 21cm. 60-13194 1.00 pap.,
1. Religious education of pre-school children. I. Title.

*SODERHOLM, Marjorie 268'.432
Elaine.
The junior; a handbook for the Sunday school teacher. Grand Rapids, Mich., Baker Bk. House [1968,c.1955] 95p. illus. 20cm. 1.50 pap.,
I. Title.

SODERHOLM, Marjorie 268.432
Elaine.
Understanding the pupil. Grand Rapids, Baker Book House [1956]-57 [v.1, 1957, c1955] 3v. illus. 23cm. [LB1115.S7] 57-2407
1. Child study. 2. Religions education. I. Title.

*SQUILLER, Cecelia 268.432
This is my church; teacher's guide. Ed.: Doris J. Smith, designer: John Gretzer. Philadelphia, Lutheran Church Pr. [c.1966] 96p. 23cm. (Vacations Church Sch. ser. kindergarten, 2d yr.) .90 pap.,
I. Title.

STINSON, Roddy. 268.432
My church helps me learn. [Teacher's ed.] Nashville, Convention Press [1967] vi, 89 p. illus. 19 cm. [BX6225.S7] 67-10004
1. Religious education — Text-books for children — Baptist. I. Title.

STRIPLIN, Clara M 268.432
Those tiny tots; a manual for leaders and teachers in the Cradle Roll and Kindergarten Divisions of the Sabbath School. Rev. ed. Mountain View, Calif., Pacific Press Pub. Association [1954] 268p. illus. 24cm. [BV1537.S75 1954] 54-12717
1. Religious education of pre-school children. I. Title.

SUITER, Helene Moore, 268.432
1913-
Man at work in God's world; a cooperative text for use with grades three and four, weekday church school classes. Teacher's book. Pittsburgh, Published for the Cooperative Publication Association by Geneva Press [1956] 189p. illus. 21cm. [BV1583.S8] 56-42687
1. Week-day church schools— Teachers' manuals. I. Title.

SUITER, Helene Moore, 268.432
1913-
Man at work in God's world; a cooperative text for use with grades three and four, weekday church school classes. Teacher's book. Pittsburgh, Published for the Cooperative Publication Association by Geneva Press [1956] 189 p. illus. 21 cm. [BV1583.S8] 56-42687
1. Week-day church schools—Teachers' manuals. I. Title.

**SUNDAY Church school for* 268.432
4's; class activity packet, term 1. Gerry Bream, course ed. Gisela Jordan, packet illus. Gustav K. Wiencke, ser. ed. Philadelphia, Lutheran Church Pr. [c.1966] 1v. (chiefly col. illus.) 26x34cm. (LCA Sunday church sch. ser.) 5.75 pap.,

TALTAVULL, Frances. 268.432
Our families; a vacation school course for primary boys and girls. Philadelphia, Published for the Cooperative Publication Association [by] the Christian Education Press [1957, c1956] 137p. 20cm. (The Cooperative series: vacation church texts) Includes bibliography. [BV1585.T23] 56-12721
1. Family—Religious life— Study and teaching. 2. Vacation schools, Religious—Text-books. I. Title.

TALTAVULL, Frances. 268.432
Our families;a vacation school course for primary boys and girls. Philadelphia, Published for the Cooperative Publication Association [by] the Christian Education Press [1957, c1956] 137 p. 20 cm. (The Cooperative series: vacation church texts) Includes bibliography. [BV1585.T23] 56-12721
1. Family — Religious life — Study and teaching. 2. Vacation schools, Religious — Text-books. I. Title.

THOMPSON, Jean A 268.432
Before they are three; infants and two-year-olds in the home and church, by Jean A. Thompson, Sara G. Klein [and] Elizabeth Cringan Gardner. Illustrated by Janet Smalley. Philadelphia, Westminster Press [1954] 217p. illus. 24cm. Bibliography: p. 213-216. [BV1540.T53] 54-7370
1. Religious education of pre-schoolchildren. I. Title.

TILLEY, Ethel. 268.432
Jesus is His name; a vacation school course for junior groups. Illustrated by Harold Kihl. Teacher's book. Philadelphia, Published for the Cooperative Publication Association by the Westminster Press [1957] 96p. illus. 23cm.

(The Cooperative series: vacation church school texts) [BV1585.T5] 57-11101
1. Vacation schools, Religious—Text-books. I. Title.

TILLEY, Ethel. 268.432
Jesus is His name; a vacation school course for junior groups. Illustrated by Harold Kihl. Teacher's book. Philadelphia, Published for the Cooperative Publication Association by the Westminster Press [1957] 96 p. illus. 23 cm. (The Cooperative series: vacation church school texts) [BV1585.T5] 57-11101
1. Vacation schools, Religious—Text-books. I. Title.

*TINY thoughts books 268.432
[4v.] Written by Ruth McNaughton Hinds. Illus. by Richard Mlodock, Faith McNaughton Hinds [Wheaton, Ill.] Scripture Pr., c.1963. [4v.] col. illus. 20cm. (Tiny thoughts bks. for pre-schoolers, 71x2029-2032) Contents.[1] God gives us night-time.--[2] God gives us sunlight.--[3] God gives us water.--[4] God gave us Jesus .50 pap., ea.,
1. Religious education—Pre-school. I. Hinds. Ruth McNaughton. Tiny thought books.

*TOBEY, Kathrene McLandress 268.432
The church and children under two; nurturing infants through groups at church. Richmond, Va., Covenant Life Curriculum [dist. Knox, c.1964] 63p. 22cm. .90 pap.,
I. Title.

TOBEY, Kathrene McLandress. 268.432
The church plans for kindergarten children. Philadelphia, Published for Cooperative Publication Association by Westminster Press [1959] 192 p. 20 cm. Includes bibliography. [BV1540.T57] 59-13436
1. Religious education of pre-school children. I. Title.

TOBEY, Kathrene McLandress 268.432
The church plans for kindergarten children. Philadelphia, Published for Cooperative Publication Association by Westminster Press [c.1959] 192p. Includes bibliography. 20cm. 50-13436 2.75
1. Religious education of pre-school children. I. Title.

TOBEY, Kathrene McLandress. 268.432
When we teach kindergarten children; a kindergarten guidance manual. Philadelphia, Board of Christian Education of the Presbyterian Church in the United States of America [1957] 70p. illus. 23cm. [BV1540.T58] 57-8942
1. Religious education of pre-school children. I. Title.

TOBEY, Kathrene McLandress. 268.432
When we teach kindergarten children; a kindergarten guidance manual. Philadelphia, Board of Christian Education of the Presbyterian Church in the United States of America [1957] 70 p. illus. 23 cm. [BV1540.T58] 57-8942
1. Religious education of pre-school children. I. Title.

TOWER, Grace Storms. 268.432
What is the church? A course for fifth and sixth grades. Boston, United Church Press [1964] 124 p. illus. (part col.) 26 cm. "Part of the United Church curriculum prepared and published by the Division of Christian Education and the Division of Publication of the United Church Board for Homeland Ministries." Bibliography: p. 123. [BX9884.A3T6] 64-19460
1. Religious education — Textbooks for children — United Church of Christ. 2. Church — Study and teaching. I. United Church Board for Homeland Ministries. Division of Christian Education. United Church Board for Homeland Ministries Division of Publication. II. Title.

TRENT, Robbie, 1894- 268.432
A year of junior programs. Nashville, Broadman Press [1950] ix, 201 p. illus., music. 21 cm. [BV1546.T75] 50-12072
1. Religious education of children. 2. Worship (Religious education) I. Title.

TRICKEY, Edna Butler 268.432
Our Christian community; a course for the first and second grades. Illus. by Robert Hanson. Philadelphia, United Church [1964] 124p. illus. (pt. col.) 26cm. Pt. of the United Church curriculum, prepared, pub. by the Div. of Christian Educ. and the Div. of Pubn. of the United Church Bd. for Homeland Ministries. Bibl. 64-14492 price unreported
1. Religious education—Text-books for children—United Church of Christ. I. United Church Board for Homeland Ministries. Division of Christian Education. II. United Church Board for Homeland Ministries. Division of Publication. III. Title.

TRIMMER, Ellen McKay 268.432
Tiny tales 'n tunes. Pictures by Joanne Brubaker. Chicago, Moody [c.1963] 55p. illus. 28cm. 1.50, pap., plastic bdg.
1. Religious education of pre-school children. I. Title.

UNIT book A for the primary course 268.432
God in our widening world, to be used with the manual for primary teachers. Greenwich, Conn., Seabury [c.1962] 96p. illus. 28cm. (The church's teaching for small church schs.) 2.00 pap.,
I. Title.

VAN METER, Harriet D 268.432
Hands, hands, hands, thank you, God for hands. Photos., music, and words by Harriet D. Van Meter. Richmond, John Knox Press [1958] unpaged. illus. 19 x 25 cm. [BV1590.V3] 58-9823
1. Religious education — Home training. I. Title.

*VAUGHT, Bonny 268.432
Chosen to serve; term 1 workbk. Illus.: William K. Plummer. Ed.: Joseph W. Inslee. Philadelphia, Luthern Church Pr. [c.1964] 32p. col. illus. 28cm. (LCA weekday church sch. ser.) .40 pap.,
I. Title.

VONK, Idalee Iolf, 1913- 268.432
Growing in stature; 52 junior worship programs with object lessons, stories, playlets, and poems. Cincinnati, Standard Pub. Co. [1951] 255 p. 22 cm. [BV1546.V6] 51-25527
1. Worship programs. 2. Worship (Religious education) I. Title.

*WE haven seen the Lord, 268.432
grade 4. Glen Rock, N.J., Paulist [1968] 1.35 pap.,

WELKER, Edith Frances. 268.432
Friends with all the world; illustrated by Janet Smalley. New York, Friendship Press [1954] 167p. illus. 22cm. [BV1475.W44] 54-6188
1. Religious education of children. I. Title.

WELLER, Katharine J. 268.432
Here am I; primary leader's guide. Minneapolis, Augsburg [c.1963] 63p. 22cm. 1.25 pap.,
1. Religious education of pre-school children. I. Title.

*WHITE, Louise. 268.432
God lives in his city. Teacher's manual. [Philadelphia, Westminster, 1968] Geneva Pr. pubn.) 1.35 pap.,
I. Title.

*WHITE, Marian 268.432
Through the Bible with finger plays. Illus. by Robert Winter. Grand Rapids, Mich., Baker Bk. [c.]1965. 60p. illus. 22cm. 1.00 pap.,
I. Title.

WHITLOCK, Pamela, ed. 268.432
The open book; a collection of stories, essays, poems, songs and music for girls and boys and every member of all Christian families. Drawings by Marcia Lane Foster. New York, P. J. Kenedy [1956] xii, 222p. illus. map. 22cm. 'Songs to sing' (for 1-4 voices): p.[187]-222. [BX930.W47] 56-10357
1. Religious education—Text-books for children—Catholic. 2. Children's songs. I. Title.

WHITLOCK, Pamela, ed. 268.432
The open book; a collection of stories, essays, poems, songs and music for girls and boys and every member of all Christian families. Drawings by Marcia Lane Foster. New York, P. J. Kenedy [1956] xii, 222 p. illus., map. 22 cm. "Songs to sing" (for 1-4 voices): p. [187]-222. [BX930.W47] 56-10357
1. Religious education — Text-books for children — Catholic. 2. Children's songs. I. Title.

WILLIAMS, Jessie (Tandy) 1876-1948. 268.432
The junior workers' manual, including helps for Bible study, worship themes, projects, special selections for junior workers in Sunday school, worship services, vacation Bible schools, week-day religious schools [and] the home circle. Butler, Ind., Higley Press [1950] 160 p. 20 cm. [BV1546.W52] 50-13813
1. Religious education of children. Full name: Jessie Martha (Tandy) Williams Earhart. I. Title.

*WOODARD, Carol J. 268.432
Ways to teach 3's to 5's. Ed.: Doris J. Smith. Philadelphia, Lutheran Church [c.1965] 142p. illus. 21cm. Bibl. 1.50; teacher's guide, pap., .50
I. Title.

*WORK and worship. 268.432
Rev. teacher's manual replacing Many messengers. New York, Seabury [1968] (Church's teaching in the third grade) 2.30 pap.,

WORSHIP in my church: 268.432
junior leader's manual. Minneapolis, Minn. Augsburg [c.1963] 64p. 21cm. 1.00 pap.,

WRIGHT, Kathryn S. 268'.432
Let the children sing; music in religious education [by] Kathryn S. Wright. New York, Seabury Press [1974] p. cm. "A Crossroad book." [BV1534.8.W74] 73-17915 ISBN 0-8164-0256-6 5.95
1. Music in religious education. I. Title.

YODER, Glee 268.432
The church and infants and toddlers [Elgin, Ill., Brethren Pr.: 1966] 127p. illus., diagrs. 23cm. Bibl. 1.50 pap.,
I. Title.

YOUNG, Lois Horton. 268.432
Kindergarten story time. Illus. by Alcy Kendrick., Cover by James Koscis. Valley Forge [Pa.] Judson Pr. [1962] 269p. illus. 27cm. 62-52107 3.95
1. Religious education—Text-books for children—Baptists. I. Title.

ZIMMERMAN, Eleanor. 268.432
Doctrine for 3's to 5's. [Philadelphia, Lutheran Church Press, 1963] 160 p. illus. 21 cm. (LCA leadership education series) Includes bibliography. [BV1475.8.Z5] 63-6199
1. Religious education of pre-school children. I. Title.

ZIMMERMAN, Eleanor 268.432
Doctrine for 3's to 5's. [Philadelphia, Lutheran Church Pr., c.1963] 160p. illus. 21cm. (LCA leadership educ. ser.) Bibl. 63-6199 1.50
1. Religious education of pre-school children. I. Title.

*ZIMMERMAN, Eleanor 268.432
Fellow workers for God. Illus. by Joyce Hewitt. Ed.: Gustav K. Weincke. Philadelphia, Lutheran Church [c.1964] 127p. 21cm. (LCA Sunday sch. ser.) 1.25; 2.50 teacher's guide, bds.,
I. Title.

*ZIMMERMAN, Eleanor 268.432
Fellow workers for God in the church around the world; workbk. [term 2] Ed.: Gustav K. Wiencke. Illus. Joyce Hewitt. Philadelphia, Lutheran Church [c.1964] 48p. illus. (pt. col.) 28cm. (LCA Sunday Church sch. ser.) .40 pap.,
I. Title.

ZIMMERMAN, Eleanor. 268.432
Now we are three. Joseph W. Inslee, editor. Philadelphia, Muhlenberg Press [1960] 252 p. illus. 24 cm. Includes bibliography. [BV1540.Z5] 60-51022
1. Religious education of pre-school children. I. Title.

BRITISH Council of Churches. Working Party on the Child in the Church. 268'.432'0941
Report of the Working Party on the Child in the Church / [presented to the] British Council of Churches, Consultative Group on Ministry among Children. [London] : [British Council of Churches, 1976] [1], iv, 52 p. ; 21 cm. [BV1475.2.B74 1976] 76-376814
1. Christian education of children. 2. Christian education—Great Britain.

*ANDERSON, Marbury E. 268.433
I believe in Jesus Christ, by Marbury E. Anderson, Frank W. Klos. Illus. by Albert Machini. Philadelphia, Lutheran Church Pr. [c.1965] 207p. illus. (pt. col.) 22cm. (LCA weekday church sch. ser.) With teacher's guide. 2.25; 2.50 teacher's ed.,
1. Religious education— Textbooks for children—Lutheran Church. I. Klos, Frank W., joint author. II. Title.

BABIN, Pierre. 268'.433
Adolescents in search of a new church. Translated and adapted by Nancy Hennessy and Carol White. [New York] Herder and Herder [1969] 89 p. 21 cm. Translation of L'Eglise. Includes bibliographical references. [BV1485.B2713] 71-87747
1. Christian education of young people. I. Title.

BABIN, Pierre. 268.433
Crisis of faith; the religious psychology of adolescence. [Translation and adaptation by Eva Fleischner. New York] Herder and Herder [1963] 251 p. 22 cm. Translation of Les jeunes et la foi. Bibliographical footnotes. [BV1475.9.B313] 63-18148
1. Religious education of adolescents. 2. Adolescence. I. Title.

BALY, Denis 268.433
Isms of the modern world. Greenwich, Conn., Seabury [c.1962] 62p. illus. 21cm. (Senior-high-sch. unit) .75 pap.,
I. Title.

BARGER, R. Curtis. 268'.433
Tomorrow in your hand; a guide for the Christian leader and teacher of earliteens and youth [by] R. Curtis Barger. Washington, Review and Herald Pub. Association [1966] 176 p. illus. 22 cm. Bibliography: p. 175-176. [BV1485.B3] 66-28651
1. Seventh-Day Adventists—Education. 2. Christian education of young people. I. Title.

BIBLE lessons for youth; 268.433
teacher's quarterly. [Cincinnati, Methodist Pub. House, etc.] v. 23 cm. Prepared by the Editorial Division of the General Board of Education of the Methodist Church. [BX8225.A1B5151] 51-17109
1. Religious education—Text-books for young people—Methodist. I. Methodist Church (United States) Board of Education. Editorial Division.

BOWMAN, Clarice Margurette, 1910- 268.433
Ways youth learn. [1st ed.] New York, Harper [1952] 189 p. 20 cm. [BV1600.B6] 52-8462
1. Religious education of youth. I. Title.

BOWMAN, Locke E. 268.433
How to teach senior highs. Philadelphia, Westminister Press [1963] 191 p. 21 cm. [BV1549.78.B6] 63-8065
1. Religious education of young people. I. Title.

BOWMAN, Locke E. 268.433
How to teach senior highs. Philadelphia, Westminster [c.1963] 191p. 21cm. 63-8065 3.50
1. Religious education of young people. I. Title.

BROKHOFF, John R. 268.433
Defending my faith. Ed. by Philip R. Hoh, illus by Thomas Lulevitch. Philadelphia, Lutheran Church Pr. [c1966] 144p. illus. 21 cm.
I. Hoh, Philip R., ed. II. Lulevitch, Thomas, ill. III. Title.

BROWNING, Robert L. 268'.433
Communicating with junior highs [by] Robert L. Browning. Illus. by Tom Armstrong. Henry M. Bullock, general editor. Nashville, Graded Press [1968] 208 p. illus. 23 cm. Bibliography: p. 207-208. [BV1475.9.B7] 68-3726
1. Religious education of adolescents. 2. Communication (Theology) I. Title.

BRUNK, Ada Zimmerman. 268.433
The Christian nurture of youth; a guide for leaders of youth [by] Ada Zimmerman Brunk [and] Ethel Yake Metzler. Scottdale, Pa., Herald Press [1960] 158p. 21cm. Includes bibliography. [BV1547.B7] 60-5890
1. Religious education of adolescents. I. Metzler, Ethel Yake. II. Title.

BUETOW, Harold A 268.433
Joy to my youth; a religious guide for Catholic youth, with instructions for altar servers. Illustrated by Carl Pfeufer. [1st ed.] New York, Dutton [1961] 208p. illus. 22cm. [BX930.B86] 61-6010
1. Religious education—Text-books for young people—Catholic. 2. Altar boys. I. Title.

BURKHALTER, Frank Elisha, 1880- 268.433
Intermediate fishers. Nashville, Broadman Press [1951] 104 p. illus. 20 cm. [BV1548.B8] 51-3472
1. Religious education—Text-books for adolescents—Baptist. 2. Evangelistic work—Study and teaching. I. Title.

BURTON, Janet. 268'.433
Guiding youth. Nashville, Convention Press [1969] viii, 212 p. illus. 21 cm. "Text for course 09 of subject area 61 of the Christian leadership courses, New church study course." Bibliography: p. 208-212. [BV1485.B85] 72-107041
1. Christian education of young people. I. Title.

BYRD, Annie Ward. 268.433
Better Bible teaching for intermediates. Nashville, Convention Press [1959] 127p. 19cm. Includes bibliography. [BV1548.B9] 59-9968
1. Religious education of adolescents. I. Title.

CARTER, Carlton, 1926- 268.433
.
A church training young people. Nashville, Convention Press [1966] x. 118 p. 20 cm. "Church study course [of the Sunday School board of the Southern Baptist Convention] This book is number 1814 in category 18, section for adults and young people." "Replaces Baptist young people's union administration by Arthur Flake." Bibliography: p. 116-118. [BV1549.2.C3] 66-13315
1. Religious education of young people. I. Southern Baptist Convention. Sunday School. Board. II. Title.

*CHENEY, Ruth G. 268.433
Transition; an overview of twelve- to fourteen-year-olds in the church. Illus. by Randolph Chitwood. New York, Seabury [1967] 127p. 21cm. Prepd. under the auspices of the Dept. of Christian Educ.,Executive Council of the Protestant Episcopal Church. 1.95 pap.,
1. Religious education—Protestant Episcopal. I. Title.

CHEVILLE, Roy Arthur, 268.433
1879-
Growing up in religion; a text for explorers who are in the quest for spiritual development. Independence, Mo., Herald Pub. House [1951] 176 p. 21 cm. [BV4531.C45] 51-7974
1. Youth—Religious life. 2. Mormons and Mormonism. I. Title.

**CHURCH'S teaching in the* 268.433
[closely graded church schools (The) 7th grade. Photos by Edward Wallowitch, Wayne Miller] Materials for Christian educ. prep. [by the Dept. of Christian Educ. of the Protestant Episcopal Church] at the direction of Gen. Convention. New York, Seabury [c.1955-1964] 96p. illus. 28cm. (Church's teaching ser.) 2.10 pap.,
Contents omitted.

COME alive. 268'.433
[Editor. Sister M. St. Thomas. North American ed. Huntington, Ind., Our Sunday Visitor, 1971- v. illus. (part col.) 28 cm. Cover title. Contents.Contents.—v. 1. To be a man.—v. 2. Patterns.—v. 3. I am not a rock.—v. 4. Life's like that.—v. 5. Wide angle.—v. 6. Turned off.—v. 7. The now.—v. 8. The shape of things to come.—v. 9. The big rethink. [BX930.C58] 74-153781
1. Religious education—Text-books for young people—Catholic. I. St. Thomas, Sister, R.S.M., ed.

CORBETT, Janice M. 268'.433
Explore; resources for junior highs in the Church, edited by Janice M. Corbett. [Valley Forge, Pa., Judson Press, 1974] 142 p. illus. 28 cm. Includes bibliographies. [BV639.C4C66] 74-8574 ISBN 0-8170-0646-X 5.95 (pbk.).
1. Church work with children. 2. Children—Religious life. I. Title.

CUMMINGS, Oliver De Wolf, 268.433
1900--
Guiding youth in Christian growth. Philadelphia, Published for the Cooperative Publication Association by the Judson Press [1954] 192p. 20cm. [BV1600.C8] 54-6177
1. Religions education of young people. I. Title.

*DAEHLING, Edythe 268.433
Together: doing our part as Christians. Writers: Edy-the Daehling, Marjorie F. Garhart, John Stevens Kerr. Designer: Peggy Powell. Photos: John Kerr [others] Philadelphia, Lutheran Church Pr., 1967. 49p. illus. 28cm. (Vacation church sch. ser.) Third year of three-year cycle: God and my life. .50 pap.,
1. Religious education (Young adults)—Lutheran. I. Garhart, Marjorie F. II. Kerr, John Stevens. III. Title.

DOWLING, Enos E. 268.433
The restoration movement; study course for youth and adults. Cincinnatti, Standard [c.1964] 128p. 22cm. Bibl. pap., price unreported.
I. Title.

EGLY, Alan 268.433
So you work with junior highs. Anderson, Ind., Warner Press [Gospel Trumpet Press c.1960] 62p. 21cm. 60-10184 pap., apply
1. Religious education of adolescents. I. Title.

EPISCOPAL young 268.433
churchmen's notebook. For use with senior-high young people [New York, Seabury, 1964] 95p. illus. 28cm. (Prep. under the auspices of the Dept. of Christian Educ., Protestant Episcopal Church) 2.50 pap.,

ERB, Paul, 1894- 268'.433
We believe; an interpretation of the 1963 Mennonite confession of faith for the younger generation. Scottdale, Pa., Herald Press [1969] 111 p. 20 cm. "First published in 1967 as a series of articles in Youth's Christian companion." "Mennonite confession of faith": p. 91-108. Bibliography: p. 109. [BX8124.E7] 69-15831
1. Mennonites—Catechisms and creeds—English. 2. Religious education—Text-books for young people—Mennonites. I. Mennonite Church. General Conference. Mennonite confession of faith. II. Title.

EXPANDING life in the 268'.433
Christian faith with junior highs. Nancy B. Geyer, editor. New York, Seabury Press [1972] 80 p. illus. 28 cm. "Prepared from materials developed under the direction of Robert G. Nesbit at St. Mary's Episcopal Church, Park Ridge, Ill." [BX5875.E9] 75-189103 ISBN 0-8164-5697-6
1. Religious education—Text-books—Anglican. I. Geyer, Nancy, ed.

*FAGERLIN, Elsie 268.433
The Gospel story of Jesus, terms 1 and 2: As one who serves, term 3. Teacher's guide, grade 7. Ed.: Gustav K. Wiencke. Philadelphia, Lutheran Church [c.1964] 320p. 24cm. (LCA Sunday church sch. ser.) 2.50
I. Title.

*FAGERLIN, Elsie 268.433
The Gospel story of Jesus; Bible notebook 1. Illus. by Alex Stein. Gustav K. Wiencke, ed. Philadelphia, Lutheran Church Pr. [c.1964] unpaged. (col. illus.) col. map. 23cm. (LCA Sunday sch. church ser.) .35 pap.,
I. Title.

*FOGELMAN, William J. 268.433
I live in the world, Art by Bill McKibben. Richmond, Va., CLC Pr. [dist. Knox, 1966] 223p. illus. (pt. col.) 24cm. (Covenant life curriculum, youth The Christan life, year3) 2.95pap.,
1. Religious education (Intermediate) — Lutheran. I. Title.

FRIENDSHIP; 268'.433
teaching units for the religious education of adolescents. Directed by Pierre Babin. [Written by] Nancy Hennessy, Carol White, Joan Lark. [New York] Herder & Herder [1967] 144p. illus. 21cm. (Faith and the world) Orig. ed.: Amite. Where charity and love prevail [unacc. song by] J. Clifford Evers, Dom Paul Benoit, O.S.B. : p. 114 [BV1485.A413] 67-17620 1.95 pap. sReligious education of youth.
1. Friendship — Study and teaching. I. Babin, Pierre. II. Hennessy, Nancy. III. White, Carol. IV. Lark, Joan.

GARRISON, Karl Claudius, 268.433
1900-
Before you teach teen-agers. [Philadelphia, Lutheran Church Press, 1962] Philadelphia, Lutheran Church Press [c1962] 174 p. illus. 22 cm. 64 p. 21 cm. (Leadership education series) (Leadership education series) [BV1547.G3] 63-799
1. Religious education of adolescents. I. Title. II. Title: Teacher's guide.

GARRISON, Karl Claudius, 268.433
1900-
Before you teach teen-agers. [Philadelphia, Lutheran Church. dist. Fortress, c.1962] 174p. illus. 22cm. (Leadership educ. ser.) Bibl. 63-799 1.50
1. Religious education of adolescents. I. Title.

GRABER, Edith 268.433
Choice; a study guide on teenage issues. Drawings by Robert W. Regier. Newton, Kans., Faith & Life Pr., [c.1963] 144p. 23cm. Bibl. .75 pap.,
I. Title.

GRAF, Arthur E. 268'.433
God's claim on you; a Bible study guide on the dedicated life, by Arthur E. Graf. Jefferson City, Mo., Faith Publications [1969] 41 p. 19 cm. Includes bibliographies. [BX8015.G72] 70-81748 0.40
1. Religious education—Text-books for young people—Lutheran. I. Title.

GRIFFITHS, Louise 268.433
(Benckenstein) 1908-
The teacher and young teens; illustrated by Chris Pearson. St. Louis, Bethany Press [1954] 176p. illus. 22cm. [BV1548.G73] 54-14350
1. Religious education of adolescents. I. Title.

HAAS, James E. 268'.433
Praise the Lord! / By James E. Haas. New York : Morehouse-Barlow Co., [1974] 32 p. ; 28 cm. [BV1522.H25] 74-80388 ISBN 0-8192-1176-1 pbk. : 2.25
1. Worship (Religious education) 2. Youth—Religious life. I. Title.

*HALL, B. Frank 268.433
This company of new men; a study of the Thessalonian church. Richmond. Va., CLC Pr. [dist. John Knox. 1967] 80p. 23cm. (Covenant life curriculum; leaders' bklet. for sr. high conf.) 1.50 pap.,
I. Title.

HALL, Kenneth, 1926- 268.433
So you work with senior high youth. Anderson, Ind., Warner Press [1959] 64p. 21cm. [BV1480.H3] 59-1115
1. Religious education of young people. I. Title.

HALL, Kenneth F 1926- 268.433
So you work with senior high youth. Anderson, Ind., Warner Press [1959] 64 p. 21 cm. [BV1480.H3] 59-1115
1. Religious education of young people. I. Title.

*HAMILTON, Darlene 268.433
What God is like, by Darlene Hamilton, Beverly Schultz Mullins. Illus. by David K. Stone. Gustav K. Wiencke, ed. Philadelphia, Lutheran Church Pr. [1966] 128p. col. illus. 21cm. 1.25
1. Relgious education (Elementary) Lutheran. I. Mullins, Beverly Schultz, joint author. II. Title.

HASTINGS, Robert J 268.433
The Christian faith and life [by] Robert J. Hastings. Teacher's book for use with 15- and 16-year-olds, may be adapted for other ages. Nashville, Broadman Press [1965] 192 p. 21 cm. (The Weekday Bible study series) [BV1549.2.H3] 65-16572
1. Religious eduction — Text-books for young people — Baptist. I. Title.

HASTINGS, Robert J. 268.433
The Christian faith and life. Teacher's bk. for use with 15- and 16-year-olds, may be adapted for other ages. Nashville, Broadman [c.1964, 1965] 192p. 21cm. (Weekday Bible study ser.) [BV1549.2.H3] 65-16572 pap., 2.75; student's bk., pap., 1.00
1. Religious education—Text-books for young people—Baptist. I. Title.

*HAZZARD, Lowell Brestel 268.433
Come, follow me; a course for junior high youth in vacation church schools, youth week programs, and other settings [by] Lowell Brestel [and] Stella Tombaugh Hazzard. Illus. by Murray McKeehan. Nashville, Abingdon [c.1957, c.1963] 48p. illus. (pt. col.) music. 23cm. Rev. of Fairest Lord Jesus, pub. 1957. .40; 1.25 pap., teacher's ed.,
1. Religious education—Textbooks. I. Hazzard, Stella Tombaugh, joint author. II. Title.

*HEIN, Lucille E. 268.433
Living in Christ, by Lucille E. Hein, Walter A. Kortrey. Art. by Jeff Zinggler. Philadelphia, Lutheran Church Pr. [1967] 49p. illus. 21cm. (LCA church camp ser.) .65 pap.,
1. Religious education (Young adults)—Lutheran. I. Kortrey, Walter A., joint author. II. Title.

HILTON, Patricia A. 268'.433
God reveals himself, by Patricia A. Hilton. Layout and design by William C. Diesinger, Jr. [Valley Forge, Pa., American Baptist Board of Education and Publication, 1969] 175 p. illus. (part col.) 21 cm. (Judson graded series) "Student's book, first semester, senior high (grades 11-12) Perspective 1." "A curriculum resource developed by the American Baptist Board of Education and Publication in cooperation with the Christian Churches (Disciples of Christ) [and others]" [BT108.H5] 74-7197
1. God—Study and teaching. 2. Religious education—Text-books—Baptists. I. American Baptist Convention. Board of Education and Publication. II. Title.

HOLDERNESS, Ginny Ward, 268'.433
1946-
The exuberant years : a guide for junior high leaders / Ginny Ward Holderness. Atlanta : John Knox Press, c1976. ix, 215 p. ; 23 cm. Includes bibliographical references. [BV1475.9.H64] 75-13458 ISBN 0-8042-1225-2 pbk. : 3.95
1. Church work with adolescents. 2. Christian education of adolescents. I. Title.

*HORN, William M. 268.433
Challenge and witness. Ed. by Wilbur G. Volker. Illus. by Stan Tusan. Philadelphia, Lutheran Church Pr. [c.1966] 320p. illus. (pt. col.) 24cm. (LCA Sunday church sch. ser.) Accompanied by a Teacher's guide. 2.25; 2.50 text, teacher's guide,
1. Relgious education (Young adults)—Lutheran. I. Title.

*HORN, William M. 268.433
I believe in God the Father. Ed. by Frank W. Klos. Illus. by Rey Abruzzi. Philadelphia, Lutheran Church Pr. [c.1964] 191p. illus. 22cm. (LCA week day sch. ser., gr. 7) 2.00; 2.50 teacher's guide,
I. Title.

HUBERTUS ALBERT, Brother. 268.433
Teaching in the CCD high school [by] H. Albert. Chicago, H. Regnery Co. [c1964] xvi, 397 p. illus. 25 cm. Includes bibliographies. [BX1968.H8] 64-66117
1. Catechetics—Catholic Church. 2. Religious education—Teacher training. 3. Confraternity of Christian doctrine. I. Title.

**IN communication with* 268.433
God; student's book [Minneapolis] Augsburg [1967] v. illus. (pt. col.) 14x21cm. (Amer. Lutheran Church curriculum: Senior high sch.) Prepd. for the Bd. of Parish Educ. and the Bd. of Pubn. of the Amer. Lutheran Church based on materials provided by Norman Landvik. pap., 1.35; teacher's combined ed., 2.25
1. Religious education — Intermediate — Lutheran.

IRVING, Roy G. 268'.433
Youth and the church; a survey of the church's ministry to youth, ed. by Roy G. Irving, Roy B. Zuck. Chicago, Moody [1968] 422p. illus. 24cm. Bibl. [BV1475.9.17] 67-14388 5.95
I. Title.

**IT'S my congregation,* 268.433
too! Student's book [Minneapolis, Augsburg, c.1965] 80p. 22cm. [Based on material prep. by Clifton Anderson, others] (Amer. Lutheran Church curriculum: senior high) With teacher's guide. pap., 1.00; teacher's guide, pap., 2.00
1. Religious education (Young adults) Lutheran.

JEMISON, T Housel. 268.433
Facing life; guidance for Christian youth. [Mountain View, Calif.] Printed for the Dept. of Education, General Conference of Seventh-Day Adventists [by] Pacific Press Pub. Association [1958] 645p. illus. 24cm. 'A survey of the instruction contained in the writings of Ellen G. White.' [BV4531.J42] 58-10585
1. Youth— Religious life. 2. Religious education—Text-books for young people—Seventh-Day Adventists. I. White, Ellen Gould (Harmon) 1827-1915. II. Seventh-Day Adventists. General Conference. Dept. of Education. III. Title.

JOHNSON, Olive L. 268.433
One church for one world; a course for intermediate or junior high school groups in vacation church schools. Teacher's book. [By] Olive L. Johnson and Frances M. Nall. New York, Published for the Cooperative Publication Association by Abingdon-Cokesbury Press [1951] 128 p. 20 cm. (Cooperative texts for vacation church schools) Bibliography: p. 124-127. [BV1585.J6] 51-2781
1. Vacation schools, Religious—Text-books. 2. Christian union—Study and teaching. I. Nall, Frances (Mabaffie), 1902- joint author. II. Title.

JOHNSON, Rex E. 268'.433
Ways to plan & organize your Sunday school; youth, grades 7 to 12 [by] Rex E. Johnson. Glendale, Calif., International Center for Learning [1972] 104 p. illus. 20 cm. (ICL teacher's/leader's success handbook) (An ICL insight book)) Bibliography: p. 103-104. [BV1485.J64] 76-168840 ISBN 0-8307-0124-9 1.95
1. Religious education of young people. I. Title.

**JOUNIOR-HI kit,* 268.433
program resources for advisers of junior high groups, no. 21. Ed. [of this v.] James E. Simpson. Ed.-in-chief: Norman F. Langford. Exec. ed.: Donald L. Leonard. Philadelphia, Geneva Pr. [dist. Westminster, c.1964] 160p. illus. 28cm. 3.00 pap.,

**JUNIOR Hi kit, no. 23;* 268.433
resources for adults who work with junior highs. Philadelphia. Geneva Pr [dist. Westminster [c.1958- 1966] 10 pts. (various p.) 16x21cm. 4.75 pap.,

KIRK, Mary Virginia (Lee) 268.433
1888-
Effective work with intermediates in the Sunday school. Nashville, Broadman Press [1952] 148 p. 20 cm. [BV1548.K55 1952] 52-4584
1. Religious education of adolescents. 2. Religious education — Teacher training. 3. Sunday-schools. I. Title.

KIRK, Mary Virginia (Lee) 268.433
1888-
Effective work with intermediates in the Sunday school. [Rev. ed., 1955] Nashville, Convention Press [1959, c1952] 134p. 20cm. [BV1548.K55 1959] 60-53103
1. Religious education of adolescents. 2. Religious education—Teacher training. 3. Sunday-schools. I. Title.

KIRK, Mary Virginia (Lee) 1888- 268.433
Intermediate Sunday school work. Nashville, Sunday School Board of the Southern Baptist Convention [1937] 159 p. 19 cm. [BV1548.K56] 37-38550
1. Religious education of adolescents. I. Title.

KRAMER, William Albert, 1900- ed. 268.433
Units in religion [for Lutheran schools. (Intermediate and upper grades)] Saint Louis, Concordia Pub. House, c19 v. illus. 28cm. [BX8015] 57-4029
1. Religious education—Text-books—Series. 2. Religious education—Text-books—Lutheran. I. Concordia Publishing House, St. Louis. II. Title.
Contents omitted.

LACKEY,James Vernon. 268.433
Understanding and developing young people. Nashville, Convention Press [1959] 146p. 20cm. Includes bibliography. [BV1485.L3] 59-5626
1. Religious education of young people. I. Title.

LACKEY, James Vernon. 268.433
Young people and the Sunday school challenge. Nashville, Convention Press [1960] 144p. illus. 19cm. 'Church study course for teaching and training ... number 1771 in category 17, section B.' [BV1485.L33] 60-9743
1. Religious education of young people. 2. Sunday-schools. I. Title.

*LAUBACH, Eugene E. 268.433
World without end: a worship anthology; for use by junior high youth in vacation church schools, youth week programs and other settings. Illus. by Linda Richmond. Nashville, Pub. for the Coop. Pubn. Assn. by Abingdon [1965, c.1964] 48p. col. illus., music 25cm. pap., .30; teacher's bk., pap., 1.75
I. Title.

LAZARETH, William Henry, 1928- 268.433
Helping youth and adults know doctrine [by] William H. Lazareth and Ralph O. Hjelm. Philadelphia, Lutheran Church Press, c1963. 176 p. illus. 22 cm. (Leadership education series) Teacher's guide [by] Ralph O. Hjelm and William H. Lazareth. Philadelphia, Lutheran Church Press, c1963. 48 p. 21 cm. (Leadership education series) [BV1549.2.L3] 63-3305
1. Religious education of young people. I. Hjelm, Ralph O. II. Title.

LIBBEY, Scott 268.433
God's restless servants, a course for seventh and eighth grades. Illus. by Larry Channing [Philadelphia] United Church [1964] 124p. illus. (pt. col.) 26cm. Pt. of the United Church curriculum, prepared, pub. by the Div. of Christian Educ. and the Div. of Pubn. of the United Church Bd. for Homeland Ministries. Bibl. 64-14493 2.25
1. Religious education—Text-books for children—United Church of Christ. I. United Church Board for Homeland Ministries. Division of Christian Education. II. United Church Board for Homeland Ministries. Division of Publication. III. Title.

*LINK, Mark J. 268.433
Man in the modern world. Chicago, Loyola Univ. Pr. [1967] x, 255p. illus. 24cm. 3.00
1. Religious education—Intermediate—Catholic. I. Title.

MCCLANAHAN, John H., 1929- 268'.433
A call to contemporary discipleship [by] John H. McClanahan. Nashville, Convention Press [1969] xiii, 129 p. 20 cm. Bibliographical references included in "Notes" (p. 114-119) [BV4511.M26] 69-10014
1. Christian life—Study and teaching. 2. Religious education—Text-books for young people—Baptist. I. Title.

MCCLELLAND, Margaret Tyrrell. 268.433
Intermediates in action, through the Sunday school. [Teacher's ed.] Nashville, Convention Press [c1960] 104p. illus. 19cm. [BV1549.65.M25] 60-15526
1. Religious education—Text-books for adolescents. I. Title.

MCDONELL, Ruth. 268'.433
So you're having an adolescent: insights for parents and others on the religious education of teen-agers. Edited by Ruth McDonell. Authors: Ruth McDonell [and others] Design/photography by Patricia Ellen Ricci. [Chicago] Peacock Books [1970] 130 p. illus., facsim. 22 cm. (Peacock paperbacks) [BV1485.M23] 76-113273 1.95
1. Christian education of young people—Addresses, essays, lectures. I. Title.

*MASHECK, Charles L. 268.433
We serve. Art by Frank P. Grobelny. Walter A. Kortery, ed. Philadelphia, Lutheran Church Pr. [1967] 61p. illus. 19cm. (LCA church camp ser.) .85 pap.,
1. Religious education (Young adults)—Lutheran. I. K. Kortrey, Walter A., ed. II. Title.

MAYER, Herbert Carleton. 268.433
Young people in your church; on building a program. Westwood, N. J., F. H. Revell Co. [1953] 226 p. 21 cm. Includes bibliography. [BV4447.M35] 53-10526
1. Church work with youth. 2. Religious education of young people. I. Title.

**ME, my self, and God;* 268.433
teachers guide [Writer: Harlan Norem] Minneapolis, Augsburg [c.1965] 80p. 28cm. Senior high sch. course prep. for the Div. of Parish Educ., and the Div. of Pubn. of the Amer. Lutheran Church 1.75 pap.,
1. Religious education—Text-books for children—Lutheran Church. I. Norem, Harlan.

**MEMBERS one of* 268.433
another; the church's teaching in the eighth grade. New York, Seabury [c.1965] 122p. illus. 28cm. Rev. teacher's manual replacing Strength to grow. Prep. by the Dept. of Christian Educ. of the Executive Council of the Protestant Church at the direction of the General Convention (Seabury ser., the church's teaching for closely graded church schs.) 2.10 pap.,

METHODIST Church (United States) Board of Education. Editorial division. 268.433
Program quarterly; for youth meetings in small churches. [Nashville, Methodist Pub. House] v. in 23 cm. Prepared by the General Board of Education of the Methodist Church through the Editorial Division. [BV29.P7] 52-19204
1. Young People's meetings (Church work) 2. Worship programs. I. Title.

MIX, Rex. 268'.433
Toward effective teaching; youth, by Rex and Susan Mix. Anderson, Ind., Warner Press [1970] 112 p. (p. 110-112 blank and advertisements) 26 cm. (Foundations for teaching) Includes bibliographical references. [BV1485.M55] 70-99936
1. Religious education of young people. 2. Religious education—Text-books. I. Mix, Susan, joint author. II. Title.

*MORENTZ, Ethel Irene 268.433
Life's mystery and meaning. Ed.: Philip R. Hoh. Philadelphia, Lutheran Church Pr. [c.1965] 110p. illus. 20cm. pap., 1.15; teacher's guide, pap., 1.50
I. Title.

MORTON, Nelle. 268.433
Making our group Christian; a text for leaders of boys and girls of junior high school age ... Teacher's book. [Rev. ed.] Richmond, Published for the Cooperative Publication Association by John Knox Press [1961] 104p. illus. 23cm. Includes bibliography. [BV1585.M58 1961] 61-6342
1. Vacation schools, Religious—Teachers' manuals. 2. Social group work (Church work) I. Title.

MURRAY, Jane Marie, 1896- 268.433
The Christian life series. Chicago, Fides Publishers Association [1957- v. illus. 24cm. [BX930.M8] 57-11577
1. Religious education—Text-books for adolescents—Catholic. I. Title.
Contents omitted.

*NELSON, Lawrence E. 268.433
Ways to teach teens. Ed. by Robert W. Schmeding. Photographs by Ed Eckstein, Philadelphia, Lutheran Church [c.1965] 141p. illus. 21cm. (LCA Leadership educ. ser.) 1.50; teacher's guide, pap., .70
I. Title.

*NILSSEN, Jerome 268.433
Wise as serpents, innocent as doves, by Jerome Nilssen. John Kerr, ed. Andrew A. Snyder, illus. Philadelphia, Lutheran Church Pr. [1967] 126p. illus. 21cm. (LCA Sunday church sch. ser., 16-192) With accompanying teacher's guide, My world, my church and I, by Jerome Nilssen; John Kerr, ed. (LCA Sunday church sch. ser., 16-193) 1.00; 1.25 pap.,teach.guide, pap.,
1. Religious education — Intermediate — Lutheran. I. Title. II. Title: My world, my Church and I.

OATES, Wayne Edward, 1917- 268'.433
On becoming children of God, by Wayne E. Oates. Philadelphia, Published for the Cooperative Publication Association by Westminster Press [1968, c1969] 124 p. 22 cm. Bibliographical references included in "Notes" (p. [121]-124) [BV1475.9.O2] 68-20149 ISBN 0-664-21281-6
1. Religious education of young people. 2. Child study. I. Cooperative Publication Association. II. Title.

O'KEEFE, Thomas. 268'.433
The signs of the times. North Easton, Mass., Holy Cross Press [1969] 76 p. illus. 22 cm. [BX930.O45] 74-89845 2.25
1. Religious education—Text-books for adolescents—Catholic. I. Title.

OLSON, Virgil A 268.433
Church history, by Virgil A. Olson. Chicago, Harvest Publications [1955] 115 p. illus. (part col.) 26 cm. ("Tell me, please," book 2) [BX6225.O4] 65-25400
1. Religious education — Text-books for adolescents — Baptist. 2. Church history. I. Title.

OUR quest for 268.433
happiness; the story of divine love. High school religion. By ClarenceE. Elwell [and others] Chicago, Mentzer, Bush, 1955- v. illus. 23cm. [BX930.O866] 55-28233
1. Religious education—Text-books for young people—Catholic. I. Elwell, Clarence Edward, 1904-

OUR quest for 268.433
happiness; the story of divine love. High school religion. [By] Clarence E. Elwell [and others. Rev.] Chicago, Mentzer, Bush, 1955-58. 4 v. illus. 23cm. [BX930.O866] 55-28233
1. Religious education—Text-books for young people—Catholic. I. Elwell, Clarence Edward, 1904-

*PETERMAN, Richard 268.433
Who is Jesus? by Richard Peterman, John Kerr. Design/ illus.: Charles Light. Philadelphia, Lutheran Church Pr. [1967] 104p. illus. 21cm. (LCA Sunday church sch. ser.) 1.00 pap.,
1. Religious education (Intermediate)—Lutheran. I. Kerr, John, joint author. II. Title.

*PETULLA, Joseph. 268.433
All over the world. New York, Sadlier [1968] (Life and light ser.) HS pap., price unreported
I. Title.

*PETULLA, Joseph 268.433
The friendship of Christ, by Joseph Petulla. William J. Reedy. New York, Sadlier [1966] 94p. 22cm. (Life & light ser., bk. 2) 1.00 pap.,
1. Religious education—Study and teaching (Intermediate)— Catholic. I. Reedy, William J., joint author. II. Title. III. Series.

PINSON, William M. 268'.433
No greater challenge [by] William M. Pinson, Jr. [Teacher's ed.] Nashville, Convention Press [1969] xiii, 82 p. 19 cm. "Church study course [of the Sunday School Board of the Southern Baptist Convention] This book is number 1484 in category 4, section for intermediates." "Teacher's helps": [16] p. bound in between p. 34-35. Bibliography: p. 76-79. [BX6225.P5] 69-10015
1. Religious education—Text-books for adolescents—Baptist. I. Southern Baptist Convention. Sunday School Board. II. Title.

PODSIADLO, Jack, comp. 268'.433
Discovery in celebration; a teacher source book [by] Jack Podsiadlo and Robert Heyer. Designed by Judith Savard and Marion Faller. New York, Paulist Press [1970] 124 p. illus. (part col.) 20 cm. (Discovery series) [BX930.P6] 75-133470 4.50
1. Religious education—Text-books—Catholic. I. Heyer, Robert J., joint comp. II. Title.

POWERS, Edward A 268.433
Journey into faith; a course for eleventh and twelfth grades [by] Edward A. Powers. Boston, United Church Press [1964] 124 p. illus. 26 cm. "Part of the United Church curriculum, prepared and published by the Division of Christian Education and the Division of Publication of the United Church Board for Homeland Ministries." Bibliography: p. 15. Bibliographical references included in "Notes and acknowledgments" (p. 123-124) [BX9884.A3P6] 64-19465
1. Religious education—Textbooks for yount people—United Church of Christ. I. United Church Board for Homeland Ministries. Division of Christian Education II. United Church Board for Homeland Ministries. Division of Publication. III. Title.

PRICHARD MARIANNA (NUGENT) 268.433
My Christian heritage; a course for ninth and tenth grades. by Marianna Nugent Prichard and Norman Young Prichard. Boston, United Church Press,[1964] 124 p. illus., col., maps. 26 cm. "Part of the United Church curriculum, prepared and published by the Division of Christian Education and the Division of Publication of the United Church Board for Homeland Ministries." Bibliography: p. 122-123. [BX9884.A3P7] 64-19463
1. Religious education—Textbooks for adolescents—United Church of Christ. I. Prichard, Norman Young, joint author. II. United Church Board for Homeland Ministries. Division of Christian Education. III. United Church Board for Homeland Ministries. Division of Publications. IV. Title.

PROTESTANT Episcopal Church in the U. S. A. National Council. Dept. of Christian Education. 268.433
Why should I? Teacher's manual, grade 7. Rev. ed. Greenwich, Conn., Seabury Press [1958] 106p. illus. 28cm. (The Seabury series, T-7B) Includes bibliography. [BV1548.P7 1958] 58-9263
1. Religious education of adolescents. I. Title.

PROTESTANT Episcopal Church in the U.S.A. National Council. Dept. of Chrisian Education. 268.433
It's your choice. Illus. by Randolph Chitwood. Greenwich, Conn., Seabury [c.1962] 105p. illus. (The church's teaching inthe 11th grade, teacher's manual) 2.10 pap.,
I. Title.

**QUESTIONS about the* 268.433
Bible; student's bk. Minneapolis, Minn., Augsburg [c.1965] 22cm. (Amer. Lutheran Church curriculum: senior high) pap., 1.25 Teacher's guide, pap., 1.75
1. Religious education (Young adults) Lutheran.

*RAMSEY, William M. 268.433
The meaning of Jesus Christ. [dist. Richmond, Va., John Knox, c.1964] CLC Press 200p. illus. (pt. col.) 24cm. (Convenant life curriculum, 9220) 2.95 pap.,
I. Title.

*REEDY, William J. 268.433
The story of salvation [by] William J. Reedy. Consultants: Brother Bartholomew Albert [others] New York. Sadlier [1966] 449p. illus. 22cm. (Life & light ser., bk. 2) pap., 2.16; teacher's guide, pap., 1.50
1. Religious education—Study & teaching (Intermediate)—Catholic. I. Title. II. Series.

REYNOLDS, Lillian Richter 268.433
How big is your world: a text for leaders of young people of Junior high school age . . . usable in vacation church schools, youth week programs, and other settings. Teacher's bk. Pub. for the Cooperative Pubn. Assn. by Richmond, Va., Knox [c.1962] 99p. 23cm. 1.25 pap.,
I. Title.

REYNOLDS, Lillian Richter. 268.433
A Pioneer handbook, for leaders of junior high school boys and girls. With illus. by Anne Newbold. Richmond, John Knox Press [1951] 109 p. illus. 23 cm. [BV1548.R4] 51-28813
1. Religious education of adolescents. I. Title.

RICE, Lillian (Moore) 268.433
Better Bible teaching for juniors in the Sunday school. Nashville, Broadman Press [1952] 143 p. illus. 20 cm. [BV1546.R48] 52-13859
1. Religious education of children. 2. Bible — Study. 3. Sunday-schools. I. Title.

RICHARDS, Lawrence O. 268'.433
You and youth / by Lawrence O. Richards. Chicago : Moody Press, c1973, 1974 printing. 128 p. : ill. ; 22 cm. (Effective teaching series) Includes bibliographical references. [BV1485.R5] 72-95018 ISBN 0-8024-9830-2 : 1.95
1. Christian education of young people. I. Title.

**RIGHT and wrong;* 268.433
student's book. Minneapolis, Augsburg, 1966. 72p. illus. (pt. col.) 22cm (Amer. Lutheran Church curriculum: senior high student's bk.) 1.00; 2.00 pap., teacher's guide,
1. Religious education (Young adults) Lutheran.

RUSSO, Anthony. 268'.433
The God of the deaf adolescent : an inside view / by Anthony Russo. New York : Paulist Press, [1975] vii, 278 p. : ill. ; 23 cm. Includes index. Bibliography: p. 270-273. [BV1615.D4R87] 74-27902 ISBN 0-8091-1868-8 pbk. : 6.95
1. Christian education of the deaf. I. Title.

SEELY, Edward D. 268'.433
Teaching early adolescents creatively: a manual for church school teachers, by Edward D. Seely. Philadelphia, Westminster Press [1971] 222 p. 19 cm. Bibliography: p. [211]-213. [BV1475.9.S42] 71-155903 ISBN 0-664-24927-2 2.95
1. Christian education of adolescents. I. Title.

*SHRIVER, Donald W., Jr. 268.433
How do you do, and why? An introduction to Christian ethics. Illus. by Martha Meeks, Richmond, Va., CLC Pr. [dist. Knox, 1966] 224p. illus. 24cm. (Covenant life curriculum, youth; The Christian life, year 3) 2.95 pap.,
1. Religious education (Intermediate)—Lutheran. I. Title.

SIMPSON, James E. 268.433
Junior-hi kit no. 19: annual program resources for advisers of junior high groups, ed. by James E. Simpson, Norman F. Langford, Donald L. Leonard. Philadelphia, Westminster [c.1962] 160p. illus. 28cm. Bibl. 3.00 pap.,
I. Title.

SKOGLUND, John E 268.433
Come and see, a cooperative text; an invitation to older youth and young adults. Philadelphia, Published for the Cooperative Publication Association by the Judson Press [1956] 96p. 19cm. (Faith for life series) [BV1603.S5] 57-44912
1. Religious education — Text-books for young people. 2. Jesus Christ—Biog.—Study. I. Title.

SKOGLUND, John E 268.433
Come and see, a cooperative text; an invitation to older youth and young adults. Philadelphia, Published for the Cooperative Publication Association by the Judson Press [1956] 96 p. 19 cm. (Faith for life series) [BV1603.S5] 57-44912
1. Religious education — Text-books for young people. 2. Jesus Christ — Biog. — Study. I. Title.

SMITH, Barbara, 1922- 268.433
How to teach junior high. Philadelphia, Westminster [c.1965] 224p. 22cm. [BV1548.S55] 65-12101 3.95
1. Religious education of adolescents. I. Title.

SMITH, Barbara, 1922- 268.433
How to teach junior highs. Philadelphia, Westminster Press [1965] 224 p. 22 cm. [BV1548.S55] 65-12101
1. Religious education of adolescents. I. Title.

STOOP, David A. 268'.433
Ways to help them learn: youth, grades 7 to 12 [by] David A. Stoop. Glendale, Calif., International Center for Learning [1973, c1971] 141, [3] p. illus. 20 cm. (ICL teacher's/leader's success handbook) (An ICL insight book) Bibliography: p. [143]-[144] [BV1485.S77] 70-168844 ISBN 0-8307-0120-6 1.95
1. Religious education of young people. I. Title.

SWAIM, Dorothy G 268.433
Christian citizens in school and community, a cooperative text. Teacher's book. Chicago, Published for the Cooperative Publication Association by Judson Press [1958] Chicago, Published for the Cooperative Publication Association by Judson Press [1958] 128 p. 20 cm. 63 p. illus. 23 cm. (The Cooperative series of texts for weekday religious education) -- Pupil's book. [BV1583.S85] 58-6759
1. Week-day church schools—Teachers' manuals. 2. Church and social problems—Study and teaching. I. Title.

TARPLEE, Cornelius C. 268.433
Racial prejudice. Preface by Gordon Allport. Greenwich, Conn., Seabury [c.1962] 67p. illus. 21cm. (Senior-high-sch. unit) .75 pap.,
I. Title.

TAYLOR, Bob R 1935- 268.433
A church training intermediates, by Bob R. Taylor. Nashville, Convention Press [1966] xii, 145 p. illus. 19 cm. "Church study course [of the Sunday School Board of the Southern Baptist Convention]. This book is numbered 1815 in category 18, section for adults and young people." Includes bibliographical references. [BV1548.T3] 66-13316
1. Religious education of young people. 2. Baptist training union. I. Southern Baptist Convention. Sunday School Board. II. Title.

TEACHING with Witness 268'.433
junior high: handbook for use in 1969-1970. [Dayton, Ohio, G. A. Pflaum, 1969] 72 p. illus. 21 cm. Cover title. Intended for use with the "Witness program—student magazine, filmstrips, guide, resources, and doctrinal topics." "Resource guide": p. 61-72. [BX930.T38] 75-95906
1. Religious education—Text-books—Catholic. I. Title: Witness junior high.

TILLEY, Ethel 268.433
Book of the ages; a course for junior high groups in the vacation church school. Teacher's book. Rev. ed. [Nashville] Pub. for the Cooperative Pubn. Assn. by Abingdon [c.1956, 1962] 110p. illus. 23cm. (Cooperative ser.: vacation church sch. texts) 62-10417 1.00 pap.,
1. Bible—Study—Text-books. 2. Vacation schools, Religious—Textbooks. I. Title.

*TILLEY, Ethel 268.433
He was called Jesus; a vacation Church school course for junior groups: teacher's bk. Philadelphia, Pub. for the Cooperative Pubn. Assn. by Westminster [c.1963] 96p. illus. 23cm. Based on Jesus in his name. Pupil's bk. illus. by Robert Jefferson. With activities packet. pap., 1.25; pupil's bk., pap., .35; activities packet, .35
1. Religious education—Textbooks. I. Title.

VANGUARDS for change; 268'.433
an action-reflection handbook. Robert L. Burt, editor. Philadelphia, United Church Press [1971] 95 p. illus. 26 cm. [BX9884.A3V35] 70-151862
1. Religious education—Text-books for young people—United Church of Christ. I. Burt, Robert L., ed.

WALSH, Edward, 1941- 268'.433
What do you think of Christ? [Dayton, Ohio] Pflaum [1971] 108 p. illus. 17 cm. (Christian experience series. Witness book 16) Bibliography: p. 106-108. [BT202.W29] 71-153803 0.95
1. Jesus Christ—Person and offices. I. Title.

WARREN, Michael. 268'.433
A future for youth catechesis / by Michael Warren. New York : Paulist Press, [1975] v, 113 p. ; 18 cm. (Deus book) Contents.Contents.—New directions.—The catechetical presupposition.—Role of adult models.—Adolescent crises.—Models for youth catechesis.—A program that worked.—Teenage catechetical programs.—Education for service.—Religious values in church schools. Includes bibliographies. [BV1485.W37] 75-9234 ISBN 0-8091-1883-1 pbk. : 1.65
1. Christian education of young people. I. Title.

*WATSON, Stanley J. 268'.433
Youth work in the church. Nashville, Broadman Press [1973] 61 p. 22 cm. Bibliography: p. 59-61. [BV4447] ISBN 0-8054-3210-8 1.95 (pbk.)
1. Church work with youth—Baptist authors. I. Title.

WESTON, Sidney A. 268.433
Jesus' teachings for young people: a discussion unit for high school ages and young adults. [rev. ed.] Boston, Whittemore [c.]1962. 93p. 19cm. .75 pap.,
I. Title.

**WHAT is a Christian?* 268.433
[Minneapolis, Augsburg, 1968] HS 1.15 pap.,; 2.25 teacher's gd., pap.,

**WHAT is my purpose?* 268.433
[Senior high. Based on material prep. by Eqald Bash, Milo Brekke. Art work by Clyde Ricks, Kurt Carlson. Minneapolis, Augsburg, 1965, c.1964] 111p. col. illus. 25cm. (Amer. Lutheran church curriculum) ap., 1.35; teacher's guide, pap., 2.00

**WHY doesn't God . . .?* 268.433
student's book. Minneapolis, Augsberg, c.1965. 64p. illus. (pt. col.) 28cm. Prep. for the Bd. of Parish Educ., and the Bd. of Pubn. of the Amer. Lutheran Church. Based on material prep. by Paul Gabrielsen, Lena Seidel, Janet Woodcock (Amer. Lutheran church curriculum; senior high students bk.) With teacher's guide. pap., 1.50;teacher's guide, pap., 1.75
1. Religious education (young adults) Lutheran. I. Gabrielsen, Paul. II. Deidel, Lena, joint author.

WILKINS, Ronald J. 268'.433
Focus on life [by] Ronald J. Wilkins and John T. Bettin. Dubuque, Iowa, W.C. Brown Co. [1971] 204 p. illus. (part col.) 16 x 23 cm. (To live is Christ. Focus book 3) [BX930.W485] 72-160431
1. Religious education—Text-books for adolescents—Catholic. I. Bettin, John T., joint author. II. Title.

*WINN, Albert Curry 268.433
The worry and wonder of being human. Drawings by Jim Crane. Richmond, Va., CLC Pr. [dist. Knox, 1966] 224p. illus. 24cm. (Covenant life curriculum, youth; The Christian life, year 3) 2.95 pap.,
1. Religious education (Intermediate)—Lutheran. I. Title.

WOODS, Sheila D 268.433
Youth ventures toward a vital church [by] Sheila D. Woods. New York, Abingdon Press [1965] 238 p. 23 cm. Bibliography: p. 231-234. Bibliographical references included in "Notes" (p. 223-229) [BV1522.W58] 65-21978
1. Worship (Religious education) I. Title.

WOODS, Sheila D. 268.433
Youth ventures toward a vital church. Nashville, Abingdon [c.1965] 238p. 23cm. Bibl. [BV1522.W58] 65-21978 3.95
1. Worship (Religious education) I. Title.

**WORLD religions and* 268.433
Christian mission; senior high students book [Minneapolis, Augsburg, 1967] v. illus., maps. 21x29cm. (Amer. Lutheran Church curriculum) Prepd. for the Bd. of Parish Educ. and the Bd. of Pubn. of the Amer. Lutheran Church based on material prepd. by Lowell G. Almen, Waldemar Gies. Ed. by Lawrence W. Denef. pap., 1.75; teacher's guide, 1.75
1. Religious education—Intermediate Lutheran.

YOUNG adolescent in the 268.433
church (The) a guide for workers with Junior Highs. Geneva Pr. [dist. Philadelphia, Westminster, 1963, c.1962] 96p. 22cm. 1.00 pap.,

**YOUR responses to God.* 268.433
Co.-pub. by Priory Pr., & Webster-McGraw [1966] xi, 516p. illus. 24cm. Authors: Reginald Doherty, others. General ed.: Reginald Doherty (Challenge of Christ, 2) 5.24
1. Religious education—Catholic authors. I. Doherty, Reginald, ed.

**YOUTH kit,* 268.433
24: study, discussion, action resources. Philadelphia, Geneva Pr. [dist. Westminster. c.1946-1966] 16pts. (various p.) illus. 21cm. 5.00 pap.,

**YOUTH kit,* 268.433
22(formerly youth fellowship kit) varied resources for study, discussion, action by church groups. Ed.[of this v.] John C. Purdy. Ed.-in-chief: Norman F. Langford. Exec. ed.: Donald L. Leonard. Philadelphia, Geneva Pr. [dist. Westminster, c.1964] 232p. illus. 28cm. 3.50 pap.,

GREER, Virginia. 268'.433'0924
Give them their dignity. Richmond, John Knox Press [1968] 127 p. 21 cm. [BV4447.G67] 68-11683
1. Church work with youth—Personal narratives. I. Title.

ADULT education in the 268'.434
church. Edited by Roy B. Zuck and Gene A. Getz. Chicago, Moody Press [1970] 383 p. illus. 24 cm. Includes bibliographies. [BV1488.A33] 79-123154 5.95
1. Christian education of adults—Addresses, essays, lectures. 2. Family—Religious life—Addresses, essays, lectures. I. Zuck, Roy B., ed. II. Getz, Gene A., ed.

ADULT Sunday school 268'.434
work. Charles R. Livingstone, compiler. Nashville, Convention Press [1969] 155 p. illus. 20 cm. "Text for course 6304 of subject area 3 of the Christian leadership series, New church study course [of the Sunday School Board of the Southern Baptist Convention]" [BV1488.A35] 70-90819
1. Christian education of adults. I. Livingstone, Charles R. II. Southern Baptist Convention. Sunday School Board.

AGNEW, Marie. 268'.434
Future shapes of adult religious education : a Delphi study / by Sister Marie Agnew. New York : Paulist Press, c1976. xiv, 259 p. ; 28 cm. Bibliography: p. 253-259. [BV1488.A37] 75-39116 ISBN 0-8091-1929-3 pbk. : 7.50
1. Christian education of adults. I. Title.

AMMERMAN, Leila Tremaine. 268.434
Inspiring develotional programs for women's groups. Natick, Mass., W. A. Wilde Co. [1960] 62p. 20cm. [BV199.W6A6] 60-15264
1. Worship programs. 2. Woman—Religious life. I. Title.

AMMERMAN, Leila Tremaine 268.434
Inspiring devotional programs for women's groups. Natick, Mass., W. A. Wilde Co. [c.1960] 62p. 20cm. 60-15264 1.95 bds.,
1. Worship programs. 2. Woman—Religious life. I. Title.

APPS, Jerold W., 1934- 268'.434
How to improve adult education in your church [by] Jerold W. Apps. Minneapolis, Augsburg Pub. House [1972] 110 p. 20 cm. Includes bibliographical references. [BV1488.A65] 72-78560 ISBN 0-8066-1226-6 2.95
1. Religious education of adults. I. Title.

BERGEVIN, Paul Emile. 268.434
Design for adult education in the church [by] Paul Bergevin [and] John McKinley. Greenwich, Conn., Seabury Press, 1958. 320p. 22cm. [BV1550.B4] 58-6061
1. Religious education of adults. I. McKinley, John, 1921- joint author. II. Title.

*BRATT, John H. 268'.434
Springboards for discussion no. 2 [by] John H. Bratt. Grand Rapids, Baker Book House [1974] 126 p. 18 cm. [BV652] ISBN 0-8010-0627-9 1.45 (pbk.)
1. Church group work. I. Title.

**BOOK of good news* 268.434
(The): pupil's book grade 4, trimester A, weekday. Minneapolis, Augsburg 1967 v. illus. (pt. col.) 22x28cm. (Elementary curriculum, Amer. Lutheran Church) Prepd. for the Bd. of Parish Educ. and the Bd. of Pubn. of the Amer. Lutheran Church based on materials provided by Alice L. Schimpf and The Bible for all people. 1.25; 1.25 pap.,teacher's guide,
1. Religious education—Elementary—Lutheran.

CALDWELL, Irene Catherine (Smith) 1919- 268.434
Responsible adults in the church school program. Anderson, Ind., Published for the Co-operative Publication Association [by] Warner Press [dist. Gospel Trumpet Press, c.1961] 96p. illus. Bibl. notes 61-5283 1.25 pap.,
1. Religious education of adults. I. Title.

*CALLEN, Barry. 268'.434
Where life begins! Anderson, Ind., Warner Press [1973] 128 p. 19 cm. Includes

bibliographical references. [BV1488] ISBN 0-87162-146-0 2.50 (pbk)
1. Religious education of adults. 2. Religious education—Text-books for adults. I. Title.

CLEMMONS, Robert S 268.434
Dynamics of Christian adult education. New York, Abingdon Press [1958] 143p. illus. 20cm. Includes bibliography. [BV1550.C53] 58-8122
1. Religious education of adults. I. Title.

COLE, Clifford Adair, 1915- 268.434
The revelation in Christ. [Independence, Mo., Herald Pub. House, 1963] 346 p. 20 cm. Originally prepared for senior high youth under title: Jesus the Christ: now adapted for adult study by the Dept. of Religious Education, Reorganized Church of Christ of Latter Day Saints. [BX8672.C6] 63-19113
1. Religious education — Text-books for adults — Mormon. 2. Jesus Christ — Mormon interpretation. I. Title.

COLE, Clifford Adair, 1915- 268.434
The revelation in Christ. [Independence, Mo., Herald Pub. House, c.1963] 346p. 20cm. Orig. prep. for senior high youth under title: Jesus the Christ; now adapted for adult study by the Dept. of Religious Educ., Reorganized Church of Jesus Christ of Latter Day Saints. 63-19113 3.25
1. Religious education—Text-books for adults—Mormon. 2. Jesus Christ—Mormon interpretations. I. Title.

COOK, Thomas C. 268'.434
"So even in old age ..." : final report on a planning conference project for aging education in the religious sector / by Thomas C. Cook, Jr., Donna L. McGinty. [Athens, Ga.] : National Interfaith Coalition on Aging, 1977. iv, 131 p. ; 29 cm. Appendices (p. 58-131): A. National Planning Conference on Gerontological Education in the Religious Sector.—B. National Intra-decade Conference on Spiritual Well-being of the Elderly.—C. Miscellaneous. [BV4435.C67] 77-153861
1. Church work with the aged—Congresses. 2. Education of the aged—Congresses. 3. Aged—Religious life—Congresses. I. McGinty, Donna L. II. National Interfaith Coalition on Aging. III. National Planning Conference on Gerontological Education in the Religious Sector, Erlanger, Ky., 1977. IV. National Intra-decade Conference on Spiritual Well-being of the Elderly, Atlanta, Ga., 1977. V. Title.

DAVIES, Archibald Donald. 268'.434
Adventure in renewal / A. Donald Davies. New York : Morehouse-Barlow Co., [1974] 115 p. ; 22 cm. Includes bibliographies. [BV4400.D37] 74-80384 ISBN 0-8192-1170-2 pbk. : 2.95
1. Church work. 2. Religious education of adults. I. Title.

DEES, Norman. ed. 268.434
Approaches to adult teaching. [1st ed.] Oxford, New York, Pergamon Press [1965] viii, 190 p. 20 cm. (The Commonwealth and international library of science, technology, engineering and liberal studies. Education and education research division) Bibliography: p. 182-185. [LC5215.D44] 64-66142
1. Adult education — Addresses, essays, lectures. I. Title. II. Series.

DEKKER, K M 268.434
Het onderwijs en het beroep van boerenzoons en boerendochters in het noorden des lands. [Door] K. M. Dekker [en] L. Tjoonk. 's-Gravenhage, 1967. 26 p. 28 1/2 cm. (Studies Landbouw-Economisch Instituut, no. 49) fl 3.-Ne67-46 Bibliographical footnotes. [HD1407.H3 no.49] 68-81514
1. Rural schools—German, Northern. 2. Education, Rural—Curricula. I. Tjoonk, L., joint author. II. Title. III. Series: Hague. Landbouw-Economisch Instituut. Studie no. 49

DONNELLAN, Michael. 268'.434
We together; a series of thought-provoking ideas that bring people together on common ground to discuss changes in religion today. [Techny, Ill., Divine Word Publications, 1971] 1 v. (various pagings) illus. 30 cm. Includes bibliographical references. [BV1488.D65] 71-148028 ISBN 0-87298-122-3
1. Christian education—Text-books for adults—Catholic Church. I. Title.

EICKMANN, Paul E. 268'.434
The wonderful works of God, by Paul E. Eickmann. Milwaukee, Northwestern Pub. House [1970] 88 p. 27 cm. [BX8015.E34] 70-123728
1. Religious education—Text-books—Lutheran. I. Title.

FAIR, Harold L., 1924- 268'.434
Class devotions : for use with the 1976-77 International lessons / Harold L. Fair. Nashville : Abingdon, c1976. 127 p. ; 20 cm. [BV4832.2.F35] 76-224 ISBN 0-687-08615-9 pbk. : 2.95
1. Devotional exercises. I. The International lesson annual. II. Title.

FAIR, Harold L., 1924- 268'.434
Class devotions : for use with the 1975-76 International lessons / Harold L. Fair. Nashville : Abingdon Press, [1975] 127 p. ; 20 cm. [BV4832.2.F34] 75-1371 ISBN 0-687-08617-5
1. Devotional exercises. I. The international lesson annual. II. Title.

*FROM bondage to freedom. 268.434
Richmond, Va., Covenant Life Curriculum, 1967. v. illus. 21cm. Contents.v. 4. God's varied voices. 2.95 pap.,
1. Religious education—Adult—Presbyterian authors.

FRY, John R. 268.434
A hard look at adult Christian education. Philadelphia, Westminster Pr. [c.1961] 150p. 61-7708 3.50
1. Religious education of adults. I. Title.

*GOD'S Church and my life; 268.434
student's book. Minneapolis, Augsburg [1967] v. illus. (pt. col.) 22cm. (Core curriculum--adult educ.) Prepd. for the Bd. of Parish Educ. and the Bd. of Pubn. of the Amer. Lutheran Church, based on materials provided by Orvis M. Hanson, others. 2.50;2.00 pap., teacher's guide.
1. Religious education—Adult—Lutheran.

*GOD'S grace and my need; 268.434
student's book [Prepd. for the Bd. of Parish Educ., and the Bd. of Pubn. of the Amer. Lutheran Church, 1966. Minneapolis, Augsburg, 1966] 240p. illus. (pt. col) 22cm. (Core curriculum, adult educ.) pap., 2.50; teacher's guide, pap., 2.00
1. Religious education (Adult)—Lutheran.

HART, Lee O., 1924- 268'.434
Adult ministries in the church and the world / by Lee O. Hart ; with contributions from Jim Cable ... [et al.]. Independence, Mo. : Herald Pub. House, c1976. 267 p. : ill. ; 20 cm. Bibliography: p. 266-267. [BV4400.H313] 76-773 ISBN 0-8309-0160-4
1. Church work—Reorganized Church of Jesus Christ of Latter-Day Saints. I. Title.

IVERSON, Gerald D. 268'.434
Ways to plan & organize your Sunday school: adult [by] Gerald D. Iverson. Glendale, Calif., International Center for Learning [1973, c1971] 109 p. illus. 20 cm. (ICL teacher's/leader's success handbook) (An ICL insight book) Bibliography: p. 99-100. [BV1488.I9] 70-168841 ISBN 0-8307-0125-7 1.95
1. Religious education of adults. I. Title.

JACOBSEN, Henry, 1908- 268'.434
You can teach adults more effectively. Rev. ed. Wheaton, Ill., Scripture Press [1968] 48 p. 22 cm. (The Successful Sunday school series) 1957 ed. published under title: How to teach adults. [BV1488.J3 1968] 79-3053
1. Christian education of adults. 2. Christian education—Teaching methods. I. Title.

JONES, Idris W. 268.434
Our church plans for adult education; a manual on administration. Philadelphia, Judson Press [1952] 76 p. illus. 19 cm. Includes bibliography. [BV1550.J6] 52-10370
1. Religious education of adults. I. Title.

KHOOBYAR, Helen 268.434
Facing adult problems in Christian education. Philadelphia, Westminster [c.1963] 140p. 21cm. Bibl. 63-15467 2.95
1. Religious education. I. Title.

LENTZ, Richard E 268.434
Making the adult class vital; illustrated by Janice Lovett. St. Louis, Published for the Cooperative Publication Association by Bethany Press [1954] 112p. illus. 20cm. [BV1550.L4] 54-9472
1. Religious education of adults. I. Title.

LEYPOLDT, Martha M. 268'.434
Learning is change [by] Martha M. Leypoldt. Valley Forge, Pa., Judson Press [1971] 158 p. illus. 22 cm. Bibliography: p. 151-158. [BV1488.L48] 70-144082 ISBN 0-8170-0526-9 2.95
1. Christian education of adults. I. Title.

LIFE and work lesson annual. 268.434
1966/67- Nashville, Convention Press. v. 21 cm. [BX6225.L5] 66-19916
1. Religious education — Text-books for young adults — Baptist. 2. Religious education — Text-books for adults — Baptist.

LOESSNER, Ernest J. 268.434
Adults continuing to learn [by] Ernest J. Loessner. Nashville, Convention Press [1967] viii, 135 p. 19 cm. Includes bibliographical references. [BV1488.L6] 67-10001
1. Religious education of adults. I. Title.

MCKINLEY, John 268.434
Creative methods for adult classes. St. Louis, Bethany Press [c.1960] 96p. illus. 20cm. 60-9919 1.50 pap.,
1. Religious education of adults. I. Title.

MCKINLEY, John, 1921- 268.434
Creative methods for adult classes. St. Louis, Bethany Press [1960] 96p. illus. 20cm. [BV1550.M25] 60-9919
1. Religious education of adults. I. Title.

MILLER, Cyr N. 268'.434
Christians are not for lions; adult religious education today [by] Cyr N. Miller. New York, Bruce Pub. Co. [1971] vii, 130 p. 21 cm. Includes bibliographies. [BV1488.M54] 70-151159
1. Christian education of adults. I. Title.

MINOR, Harold D., comp. 268'.434
Creative procedures for adult groups. Harold D. Minor, editor. Nashville, Abingdon Press [1968] 176 p. forms. 20 cm. Selected from Adult teacher. Bibliography: p. 173-176. [BV1534.M52] 68-27624 2.00
1. Religious education of adults. 2. Religious education—Teaching methods. I. Adult teacher. II. Title.

MINOR, Harold D. 268'.434
Techniques and resources for guiding adult groups. Harold D. Minor, editor. Nashville, Abingdon Press [1972] 159 p. illus. 20 cm. Bibliography: p. 157-159. [BV4446.M5] 72-2564 ISBN 0-687-41186-6
1. Church group work with young adults. I. Title.

*NEWLAND, Mary (Reed) 268.434
Religion in the home; a parents' guide to the Our life with God series for use with In Christ Jesus, gr. 3. New York, Sadlier [1968] .80 pap.,
I. Title.

*PANZARELLA, Andrew. Brother 268.434
Growth in Christ. New York, Sadlier [1968] (Life and light ser., gr. 11) 2.32 pap.,
I. Title.

*PANZARELLA, Andrew. Brother 268.434
Growth in Christ. Teacher's ed. New York, Sadlier [1968] HS pap., price unreported
I. Title.

*PANZARELLA, Andrew Brother 268.434
Growth in Christ. New York, Sadlier [1967] 371p. 22cm. (Life and light ser., bk. 3) 1.00 pap.,
1. Religious education—Adult—Catholic. I. Title. II. Series.

PARTRIDGE, Edmund B., 1932- 268'.434
The church in perspective; standard lay readers' training course, by Edmund B. Partridge. New York, Morehouse-Barlow Co. [1969] 142 p. 24 cm. [BX5875.P3] 68-56918
1. Religious education—Text-books for adults—Anglican. 2. Lay readers. I. Title.

PROTESTANT Episcopal Church in the U. S. A. National Council. 268.434
Leading adult classes; a handbook. Greenwich, Conn., Seabury Press [1958] 80p. 21cm. (The Seabury series, P-L2) Includes bibliography. [BV1550.P78] 58-2642
1. Religious education of adults. I. Title.

PROTESTANT Episcopal Church in the U. S. A. National Council. Dept. of Christian Education. 268.434
Faith is a family affair; a manual for use with classes of parents and godparents with special reference to church school grades 3, 6, and 9, and nursery children three and four years old. Illustrated by Seymour Fleishman. Greenwich, Conn., Seabury Press [1957] 151p. illus. 21cm. (The Seabury series, P-3) Includes bibliography. [BV1550.P8] 57-8347
1. Religious education—Text-books for adults—Anglican. I. Title.

RAMSAY, William M. 268'.434
Cycles and renewal trends in Protestant lay education [by] William M. Ramsay. Nashville, Abingdon Press [1969] 159 p. 20 cm. Bibliographical references included in "Notes" (p. 153-159) [BV1488.R3] 69-12023
1. Christian education of adults. I. Title.

REINHART, Bruce. 268.434
The institutional nature of adult Christian education. Philadelphia, Westminster Press [1962] 242p. 21cm. Includes bibliography. [BV1550.R4] 62-9809
1. Religious education of adults. I. Title.

RICHARDS, Lawrence O. 268'.434
69 ways to start a study group and keep it growing. Grand Rapids, Zondervan Pub. House [1973] 144 p. illus. 18 cm. [BV652.2.R52] 73-8443 1.25 (pbk.)
1. Church group work. I. Title.

ROTH, Robert M ed. 268.434
A conspectus to the self-study project of University College, the University of Chicago. Edited by Robert M. Roth. [Chicago] Center for the Study of Liberal Education for Adults [1964] xi, 94 p. 23 cm. (CSLEA reports) [LC5301.C5R6] 64-4945
1. Chicago. University. University College. I. Title. II. Series: Center for the Study of Liberal Education for adults. CSLEA reports

SCHAEFER, James R. 268'.434
Program planning for adult Christian education, by James R. Schaefer. With a foreword by D. Campbell Wyckoff. New York, Newman Press [1972] x, 262 p. 23 cm. A revision of the author's thesis, Catholic University of America, 1971, with title: A proposed curriculum design for adult Christian education for use in Catholic dioceses. Bibliography: p. 232-251. [BV1488.S3 1972] 72-88324 ISBN 0-8091-0175-0 4.95
1. Religious education of adults. I. Title.

SISEMORE, John T 268.434
The Sunday school ministry to adults. Nashville, Convention Press [1959] 148 p. 20 cm. Includes bibliography. [BV1550.S56] 59-5870
1. Religious education of adults. I. Title.

SNYDER, Alton G 268.434
Teaching adults. Philadelphia, Judson Press [1959] 96 p. illus. 20 cm. Includes bibliography. [BV1550.S58] 59-12888
1. Religious education of adults. I. Title.

TRENTHAM, Charles Arthur, 1919- 268'.434
Daring discipleship [by] Charles A. Trentham. Nashville, Convention Press [1969] xiii, 123 p. 20 cm. "Church study course [of the Sunday School Board of the Southern Baptist Convention] This book is number 0412 in category 4, section for adults and young people." Includes bibliographies. [BV4511.T7] 69-10013
1. Religious education—Text-books for adults—Baptist. 2. Christian life—Baptist authors. I. Southern Baptist Convention. Sunday School Board. II. Title.

*WEAVER, J. Bruce 268.434
Belonging to the people of God; a short-term study course for adults. Teacher's guide. By J. Bruce Weaver, Frank W. Klos. Philadelphia, Lutheran Church Pr. [1966] 127p. 21cm. price unreported pap.,
I. Title.

WIGAL, Donald. 268'.434
A presence of love. Edited by Donald Wigal and Charles Murphy. [New York] Herder and Herder [1969] 127 p. illus., ports. 21 cm. (Experiences in faith, book 2) Bibliography: p. 126-127. [BX930.W48] 72-87774 1.95
1. Religious education—Text-books for adults—Catholic. I. Murphy, Charles, joint author. II. Title. III. Series.

WORKSHOP on the Christian Education of Adults, University of Pittsburgh, 1958. 268.434
The future course of Christian adult education; selected addresses and papers. Editor: Lawrence C. Little. [Pittsburgh] University of Pittsburgh Press [1959] xi, 322 p. diagrs. 24 cm. Revision of "Charting the future course of Christian adult education in America." "A selected bibliography compiled by Lawrence C. Little": p. 300-322. [BV1550.W67 1958a] 59-11642
1. Religious education of adults. I. Little, Lawrence Calvin, 1897- ed. II. Title.

WRIGHT, H. Norman. 268'.434
Ways to help them learn: adult [by] H. Norman Wright. Glendale, Calif., International Center for Learning [1972, c1971] 150 p. illus. 20 cm. (ICL teacher's/leader's success handbook) (An ICL insight book) Bibliography: p. 150. [BV1488.W74] 74-168845 ISBN 0-8307-0121-4 1.95
1. Christian education of adults. I. Title.

ZEIGLER, Earl Frederick, 1889- 268.434
Christian education of adults. Philadelphia, Published for the Cooperative Pub. Association by Westminster Press [1958] 142 p. 21 cm. [BV1550.Z39] 58-5517
1. Religious education of adults. I. Title.

WORKSHOP on the Christian Education of Adults, University of Pittsburgh, 1958. 268.4341
Charting the future course of Christian adult education in America; selected addresses and papers. Lawrence C. Little, editor. [Pittsburgh] Dept. of Religious Education, University of Pittsburgh, c1958. 195 l. 20 cm. Bibliography:leaves 185-195. [BV1550.W67 1958] 59-17821
1. Religious education of adults. I. Little, Lawrence Calvin, 1897- ed. II. Title.

MCCRAW, Mildred C 268.435
The teaching ministry of the extension visitor. Nashville, Convention Press [1959] 141p. 19cm. [BV1523.M33] 59-7079
1. Sunday-schools. I. Title.

NOLAND, Emma. 268.5
The six point record system and its use. [Rev. ed., 1955] Nashville, Convention Press [1958, c1941] 139p. 20cm. [BV1527.N6 1958] 60-15018
1. Sunday-schools—Records. I. Title.

ACHESON, Edna Lucile, 1891- 268'.6
The construction of junior church school curricula. New York, Bureau of Publications, Teachers College, Columbia University, 1929. [New York, AMS Press, 1973, c1972] viii, 185 p. 22 cm. Reprint of the 1929 ed., issued in series: Teachers College, Columbia University. Contributions to education, no. 331. Originally presented as the author's thesis, Columbia. Includes bibliographical references. [BV1475.A33 1972] 73-176503 ISBN 0-404-55331-1 10.00
1. Religious education of children. 2. Religious education—Curricula. I. Title. II. Series: Columbia University. Teachers College. Contributions to education, no. 331.

ADVENTURE with Christ: 268.6
leader's guide. Minneapolis, Augsburg [c.1963] 64p. illus. 21cm. (Jr. Lutheran ser.) 1.25 pap.,

ANDERSEN, Karen. 268.6
Ways of teaching. Philadelphia, Muhlenberg Press [c1952] 144p. illus. 20cm. [BV1534.A63] 52-11416
1. Religious education—Teaching methods. 2. Sunday-schools. I. Title.

ANDERSON, Vernon E. 268.6
Before you teach children: teacher's guide. Philadelphia, Lutheran Church Pr. [dist.] Muhlenberg [c.1962] 64p. 21cm. (Leadership educ. ser.) .60 pap.,
I. Title.

AUDINET, Jacques. 268'.6
Forming the faith of adolescents. Pref. by Gabriel Moran. [New York] Herder and Herder [1968] 88 p. 23 cm. Translation of Vers une catechese des adolescents. Bibliographical footnotes. [BV1475.9.A7813] 68-4530
1. Religious education of adolescents. I. Title.

BAKER, Dolores. 268.6
Teaching the Bible to primaries [by] Dolores Baker and Elsie Rives. Nashville, Convention Press [1964] vii, 150 p. 19 cm. [BV1475.2.B3] 64-24947
1. Religious education of children. I. Rives, Elsie, joint author. II. Title.

BENSON, Clarence Herbert, 1879- 268.6
The Christian teacher. Chicago, Moody Press [1950] 288 p. 21 cm. Bibliography: p. 287-288. [BV1534.B35] 50-9203
1. Religious education—Teaching methods. 2. Sunday schools. I. Title.

BENSON, Erwin George, 1905- 268.6
Planning church school workers' conferences. Boston, W. A. Wilde Co. [1952] 104 p. 20 cm. [BV1533.B43] 52-12580
1. Religious education—Teacher training. 2. Sunday-schools. I. Title.

BINGHAM, Robert E. 268'.6
New ways of teaching the old story [by] Robert E. Bingham. Nashville, Broadman Press [1970] 125 p. 21 cm. Bibliography: p. 123-125. [BV1471.2.B54] 77-117303 3.50
1. Christian education. I. Title.

BOGARDUS, LaDonna. 268.6
Christian education for retarded children and youth. Illus. by Pat Roper. New York, Published for the Cooperative Publication Association by Abingdon Press [c1963] 108 p. illus. 19 cm. (The Cooperative series: Leadership training texts) Bibliography: p. 105-108. [BV1615.M4B6] 63-23612
1. Religious education of mentally handicapped children. I. Title.

BOGARDUS, LaDonna 268.6
Christian education for retarded children and youth. Illus. by Pat Roper. Nashville Pub. for the Cooperative Pubn. Assn. by Abingdon, [c.1963] 108p. illus. 19cm. (Cooperative ser.: Leadership training texts) Bibl. 63-23612 1.25 pap.,
1. Religious education of mentally handicapped children. I. Title.

BOWMAN, Locke E. 268'.6
Straight talk about teaching in today's church, by Locke E. Bowman, Jr. Philadelphia, Westminster [1967] 151p. 21cm. Bibl. [BV1534.B6] 67-11764 1.95 pap.,
1. Religious education— Teaching methods. I. Title.

BOWMAN, Locke E. 268'.6
Straight talk about teaching in today's church, by Locke E. Bowman, Jr. Philadelphia, Westminister Press [1967] 151 p. 21 cm. Bibliographical references included in "Notes" (p. 149-151) [BV1534.B6] 67-11764
1. Religious education — Teaching methods. I. Title.

*BROWN, Harsh J. 268.6
The church--for everyone. St. Louis, Bethany [c.1965] 128p. 23cm. (Cooperative ser., vacation church sch.
I. Title. II. Title: exts p1.75 pap.,

BURKHARDT, Edward C. 268'.6
Guidelines for high school CCD teachers [by] Edward C. Burkhardt. [1st ed.] New York, Benziger Bros., 1968. 45 p. 28 cm. [BX926.B8] 68-18699
1. Confraternity of Christian Doctrine. 2. Religious education—Teaching methods. 3. Catechetics—Catholic Church. I. Title.

CALDWELL, Irene Catherine (Smith) 1919- 268'.6
Basics for communication in the church, by Irene S. Caldwell, Richard A. Hatch [and] Beverly Welton. Anderson, Ind., Warner Press [1971] 224 p. illus. 26 cm. (Foundations for teaching) [BV1534.C237] 78-150370 ISBN 0-87162-121-5
1. Religious education—Teaching methods. I. Hatch, Richard A. II. Welton, Beverly. III. Title.

CALDWELL, Irene Catherine (Smith), 1919- 268.6
Teaching that makes a difference. Anderson, Ind., Warner Press [1950] 111 p. 19 cm. Includes bibliographies. [BV1534.C24] 50-9989
1. Religious education—Teaching methods. I. Title.

CALDWELL, Irene Catherine (Smith) 1919- 268.6
Teaching that makes a difference. [Rev. ed.] Anderson, Ind., Warner [c.1958, 1962] 95p. illus. 21cm. 62-13334 1.25 pap.,
1. Religious education—Teaching methods. I. Title.

CAMPBELL, Doak Sheridan, 1888- 268.6
When do teachers teach? Nashville, Convention Press [1958, c1935] 107p. 20cm. [BV1534.C25 1958] 58-10181
1. Religious education—Teaching methods. 2. Sunday-schools. I. Title.

CARLTON, Anna Lee. 268.6
Blessed are they who teach. Anderson, Ind., Warner Press [1961] 112p. 21cm. [BV1534.C28] 61-9719
1. Religious education—Teaching methods. 2. Sunday -schools. I. Title.

CARROLL, James P. 268'.6
Feed my lambs; a beginner's guide for parents who want to prepare their children for the Eucharist and penance [by] James P. Carroll. Dayton, Ohio, G. A. Pflaum [1967, c1966] 126 p. illus. 17 cm. (Parent education series, no. 2) (Witness books, 5) Bibliography: p. 121-126. [BV1590.C3 1967] 67-19684
1. Christian education of children. 2. Christian education—Home training. I. Title.

CATHOLIC Church. Congregatio pro Clericis. 268'.6
General catechetical directory. Washington, Publications Office, United States Catholic Conference, 1971. 112 p. 22 cm. At head of title: Sacred Congregation for the Clergy. Translation of Directorium catechisticum generale. [BV1471.2.C3513] 72-196137
1. Christian education. 2. Pastoral theology—Catholic Church. I. Title.

CHAPMAN, Marie M. 268.6
Practical methods for Sunday School teachers. Grand Rapids, Mich., Zondervan [c.1962] 64p. 21cm. (Sunday School know-how ser.) 1.00 pap.,
I. Title.

CHAPMAN, Marie M. 268'.6
Successful teaching ideas / by Marie M. Chapman ; illustrated by Kathryn Hutton. Cincinnati : Standard Pub., [1975] 96 p. : ill. ; 28 cm. Bibliography: p. 92-96. [BV1534.C45] 74-82558 pbk. : 3.95
1. Christian education—Teaching methods. I. Title.

COLLINS, Joseph Burns, 1897.- 268.6
CCD methods in modern catechetics for use in leadership courses in the catechetical renewal S. 103: Catechetical procedures in CCD elementary school. S. 104: Catechetical procedures in CCD high school. [By] Joseph B. Collins. Milwaukee. Bruce [1966] xi, 139p. forms. 23cm. Bibl. [BV1534.C58] 66-22584 2.95
1. Religious education—Teaching methods I. Confraternity of Christian Doctrine. II. Title.

COLSON, Howard P., 1910- 268'.6
Understanding your church's curriculum, by Howard P. Colson [and] Raymond M. Rigdon. Nashville, Broadman Press [1969] 160 p. illus. 21 cm. Includes bibliographical references. [BV1558.C6] 77-93915
1. Religious education—Curricula. I. Rigdon, Raymond M., joint author. II. Title.

COOPERATIVE Curriculum Development 268'.6
Tools of curriculum development for the church's educational ministry; the work of Cooperative Curriculum Development. Anderson. Ind., Warner [1967] 224p. 24cm. Bibl. [BV1559.C66] 67-19936 10.50
1. Religious education—Curricula. I. Title.

COOPERATIVE Curriculum Project. 268'.6
A design for teaching-learning. St. Louis, Bethany Press [1967] xxxii, 317 p. 23 cm. "An abridged edition of The church's educational ministry: a curriculum plan." [BV1559.C672] 67-24194
1. Religious education—Curricula. I. Title.

CORZINE, Jesse Lynn, 1892- 268.6
Teaching to win and develop. Nashville, Sunday School Board of the Southern Baptist Convention [1954] 152p. 20cm. [BV1534.C66] 54-36206
1. Religious education—Teaching methods. I. Title.

COTTRELL, Ralph. 268'.6
Go ye and teach. Grand Rapids, Mich., Baker Book House [1971] 133 p. 20 cm. [BV1471.2.C655] 79-172298 ISBN 0-8010-2325-4 1.95
1. Christian education. I. Title.

DUCKERT, Mary. 268'.6
Open education goes to church / by Mary Duckert ; illustrated by Lee DeGroot. Philadelphia : Westminster Press, c1976. 140 p. : ill. ; 21 cm. [BV1536.5.D8] 75-45195 ISBN 0-664-24796-2 pbk. : 3.25
1. Christian education—Teaching methods. 2. Open plan schools. I. Title.

DUCKERT, Mary. 268'.6
Tailor-made teaching in the church school. Illustrated by Lee DeGroot. Philadelphia, Westminster Press [1974] 124 p. illus. 21 cm. [BV1558.D82] 73-21904 ISBN 0-664-24985-X 2.85 (pbk.)
1. Religious education—Curricula. 2. Religious education. I. Title.

DUNN, Paul H 268.6
You too can teach; a how to book for the lay teacher on methods and techniques of teaching the gospel, by Paul H. Dunn in collaboration with Cherie B. Parker. With illus. by Hal T. Sperry. Salt Lake City, Bookcraft [1962] 226 p. illus. 24 cm. [BV1534.D84] 62-53281
1. Religious education — Teacher training. 2. Mormons and Mormonism.-Education. I. Title.

EDGE, Findley B 1916- 268.6
Teaching for results. Nashville, Broadman Press [1956] 230p. 22cm. [BV1534.E34] 56-1640
1. Religious education—Teaching methods. 2. Sunday-schools. I. Title.

EGGLESTON, George Teeple, 1906- ed. 268.6
A treasury of Christian teaching. [1st ed.] New York, Harcourt, Brace [1958] 306 p. 22 cm. [BV1561.E4] 58-10912
1. Religious education—Text-books. I. Title.

EUCHARISTIC Missionaries of St. Dominic. 268.6
Heralds of the good news. [2d ed.] St. Paul, Catechetical Guild Educational Society [1965] 126 p. illus. 23 cm. Bibliography: p. 10-11. [BX921.E9] 65-28317
1. Religious education. I. Title.

EUCHARISTIC Missionaries of St. Dominic. 268.6
Heralds of the good news [2d ed.] St. Paul, Minn., 55101, 262 E. Fourth St. Catechetical Guild Educational Soc., 1965 126p. illus. 23cm. Bibl. [BX921.E9] 65-28317 2.00
1. Religious education. I. Title.

EZELL, Mancil. 268'.6
Youth in Bible study/new dynamics. Nashville, Convention Press [1970] 126 p. illus. 20 cm. Includes bibliographical references. [BS592.E95] 77-110747
1. Bible—Study—Outlines, syllabi, etc. 2. Religious education of young people. I. Title.

FARGUES, Marie. 268'.6
How to teach religion. Translated by Sister Gertrude. Glen Rock, N.J., Paulist Press [1968] v, 122 p. 19 cm. (Deus books) Translation of D'hier a demain, le catechisme. [BX926.F313] 68-31050 1.45
1. Catechetics—Catholic Church. 2. Religious education of children. 3. Religious education—Teaching methods. I. Title.

FEUCHT, Oscar E. 268.6
Building better Bible classes. St. Louis, Concordia Pub. House [1951] iv, 117 p. 19 cm. "Practical library for Bible teachers": p. 45-50. [BV1533.F4] 51-5178
1. Religious education—Teacher training. 2. Sunday-schools. I. Title.

FRITZ, Dorothy Bertolet. 268.6
Ways of teaching; a book concerning approaches to and techniques of teaching, with an emphasis on the learner. For teachers, group leaders and Philadelphia, Published for the Cooperative Publication Association by the Westminster Press [1965] 111 p. 21 cm. [LB1025.F86] 65-17002
1. Teaching. I. Title.

FRITZ, Dorothy Bertolet 268.6
Ways of teaching; a book concerning approaches to and techniques of teaching, with an emphasis on the learner. For teachers, group leaders and those who train teachers of any age group and possibly for the parents of children and youth. Philadelphia, Pub. for the Cooperative Pub. Assn. by Westminster [c.1965] 111p. 21cm. [LB1025.F86] 65-17002 1.75 pap.,
1. Teaching. I. Title.

GANGEL, Kenneth O. 268'.6
Understanding teaching, by Kenneth O. Gangel. [1st ed.] Wheaton, Ill., Evangelical Teacher Training Association [1968] 95 p. illus. 22 cm. (E.T.T.A. preliminary (foundational) certificate series) Includes bibliographical references. [BV1534.G33] 68-24579
1. Religious education—Teaching methods. I. Title.

GOLDBRUNNER, Josef, ed. 268.6
New catechetical methods. Translated by M. Veronica Riedl. Notre Dame, Ind. University of Notre Dame Press, 1965. 134 p. illus. 18 cm. (Contemporary catechetics series) Translation of Katechetische Methoden heute. Bibliographical footnotes. [BX926.G643] 65-23518
1. Religious education. 2. Catechetics — Catholic Church. I. Title.

GOLDBRUNNER, Josef, ed. 268.6
New catechetical methods. Tr. [from German] by M. Veronica Riedl [Notre Dame, Ind.] Univ. of Notre Dame Pr. [c.]1965. 134p. illus. 18cm. (Contemporary catechetics ser.) Bibl. [BX926.G643] 65-23518 3.00; 1.25 pap.,
1. Religious education. 2. Catechetics—Catholic Church. I. Title.

*GREATER Chicago Sunday School Association (The) 268.6
The key to Sunday school achievement, ed. by Lawrence O. Richards. Chicago, Moody [c.1965] 110p. diagrs. 28cm. 2.95 pap., plastic bdg.
1. Religious education—Sunday schools. I. Richards, Lawrence O., ed. II. Title.

GRIFFIN, Dale E., comp. 268'.6
Well, what is teaching? Perspectives on the teaching-learning process. Edited by Dale E. Griffin. Saint Louis, Concordia Pub. House [1970] 79 p. 19 cm. (Church teachers library) [BV1473.G73] 70-107421
1. Christian education—Addresses, essays, lectures. 2. Teaching—Addresses, essays, lectures. I. Title.

HAAS, James E. 268'.6
Make a joyful noise! By James E. and Lynne M. Haas. New York, Morehouse-Barlow Co. [1973] 40 p. illus., music. 29 cm. Includes bibliographical references. [BV1522.H24] 73-84089 ISBN 0-8192-1146-X 1.95 (pbk.)
1. Worship (Religious education) I. Haas, Lynne M., joint author. II. Title.

HALBFAS, Hubertus. 268'.6
Theory of catechetics; language and experience in religious education [by] Hubert Halbfas. [New York] Herder and Herder [1971] 211 p. 22 cm. Translation of Fundamentalkatechetik. Includes bibliographical references. [BV1471.2.H3313 1971] 74-114153 6.95
1. Christian education. I. Title.

HARPER, Albert Foster, 1907- 268.6
The Sunday-school teacher. Kansas City, Mo., Beacon Hill Press [1956] 115p. illus. 19cm. (Christian service training course) [BV1534.H358] 56-2200
1. Religious education- -Teaching methods. 2. Sunday-schools. I. Title.

HEFLEY, James C 268'.6
Illustrate! The Sunday school lessons. Grand Rapids, Zondervan Pub. House. 1966- v. 22 cm. annual. "Current illustrations on Biblical truth for the international Sunday school lessons." Title varies slightly. [BV1560.H38] 67-17515
1. International Sunday school lessons. 2. Homiletical illustrations. I. Title.

HEFLEY, James C. 268.6
Illustrate! The 1966 Sunday school lesson; current illustrations on Biblical truth for the 1966 International Sunday school lessons (also indexed topically) Grand Rapids, Mich., Zondervan [c.1965] 128p. 22cm. [BV1560.H38] 65-19503 1.50 pap.,
1. International Sunday school lessons. 2. Homiletical illustrations. I. Title.

HEFLEY, James C. 268.6
Illustrate! The 1967 Sunday school lesson; current illustrations on Biblical truth for the 1967 International Sunday school lessons (also indexed topically) By James C. Hefley. Grand Rapids. Zondervan [c.1966] 128p. 22cm. Indexes for the 1967 ed. include: topical for use with other curriculums; weekly for use with the 1967 International Sunday School Lessons; index of names. [BV1560.H38] 65-19503 1.50 pap.,
1. International Sunday School lessons. 2. Homiletical illustrations. I. Title.

HEFLEY, James C. 268.6
Illustrate! The 1968 Sunday school lessons; current illustrations on biblical truth for the 1968 International Sunday school lessons, by James C. hefley Grand Rapids, Mich. Zondervan [1967]. v. 22cm. Indexes for the 1968 ed. include: weekly, topical, and index of names [BV1560.H38] 65-19503 1.95 pap.,
1. International Sunday school lessons. 2. Homiletical illustrations. I. Title.

HELD, Ronald G. 268'.6
Learning together / Ronald G. Held. Springfield, Mo. : Gospel Pub. House, c1976. 126, [1] p. : ill. ; 20 cm. Bibliography: p. [127] [BV1471.2.H44] 76-9515 ISBN 0-88243-571-X pbk. : 1.25
1. Christian education. 2. Christian education—Teaching methods. I. Title.

HENDERSON, Caroline D 268.6
Sunday school training plans and recognitions. Nashville, Convention Press [1957] unpaged. illus. 22cm. [BV1533.H43] 57-8662
1. Religious education— Teacher training. I. Title.

HOAG, [Frank] Victor 268.6
The ladder of learning; new ways of teaching in the church school. Greenwich, Conn., Seabury Press, [c.]1960. viii, 152p. 22cm. 60-11085 3.75
1. Religious education—Teaching methods. I. Title.

HOAG, Frank Victor, 1891- 268.6
It's fun to teach; a book for folks who wish to help children in the church school, but don't know how to start. [Abridged ed.] New York, Morehouse-Gorham Co., 1951. 150 p. 21 cm. [BV1534.H57] 51-8611
1. Religious education—Teaching methods. 2. Sunday-schools. I. Title.

HOAG, Frank Victor, 1891- 268.6
The ladder of learning; new ways of teaching in the church school. Greenwich, Conn., Seabury Press, 1960. 152p. 22cm. [BV1534.H58] 60-11085
1. Religious education— Teaching methods. I. Title.

HOBBS, Charles R 268.6
Teaching with new techniques. Illus. by Dick and Mary Scopes [and] Charles R. Hobbs. Salt Lake City, Utah, Deseret Book Co., 1964. xiv, 256 p. illus., music. 24 cm. "Teaching methods chart" (fold. leaf) in pocket. Bibliography: p. [248]-249. [BV1534.H58] 64-5019
1. Religious education of children. I. Title.

HOBBS, Charles R. 268.6
Teaching with new techniques. Illus. by Dick and Mary Scopes, Charles R. Hobbs. Salt Lake City, Utah, Deseret [c.]1964. xiv, 256p. illus., music. 24cm. Bibl. 64-5049 3.75
1. Religious education of children. I. Title.

HOFINGER, Johannes. 268'.6
The good news and its proclamation. Post-Vatican II ed. of The art of teaching Christian doctrine. In collaboration with Francis J. Buckley. Notre Dame [Ind.] University of Notre Dame Press [1968] xiii, 354 p. 24 cm. First and 2d editions published under title: The art of teaching Christian doctrine. Bibliography: p. 344-346. [BX1968.H58 1968] 68-17065
1. Catechetics—Catholic Church. I. Title.

HOH, Philip Richard, 1921- 268.6
Called to be Christian. Terence Y. Mullins, editor. Roland Shutts, artist. Philadelphia, Muhlenberg Press [1961] Philadelphia, Muhlenberg Press [1961] 192p. illus. 23cm. 80p. 23cm. [BX8015.H6] 61-19961
1. Religious education—Text-books for young people—Lutheran. I. Title. II. Title: — Teacher's guide.

HOLCOMB, Jerry. 268'.6
Team teaching with the Scotts and Bartons. Valley Forge [Pa.] Judson Press [1968] 127 p. illus. 20 cm. [BV1534.H59] 68-22753 2.50
1. Religious education—Teaching methods. 2. Teaching teams. I. Title.

HOY, David. 268.6
Magic with a message. Illustrated by Sid Couchey. [Westwood, N. J.] Revell [1956] 72p. illus. 23cm. [BV1472.H67] 56-5241
1. Religious education. 2. Conjuring. I. Title.

INTERNATIONAL Council of Religious Education. 268.6
The curriculum guide for the local church, developed cooperatively by Protestant evangelical forces of the United States and Canada through the International Council of Religious Education. [Rev.] Chicago [1950] 99 p. 23 cm. Bibliography: p. 86-87. [BV1558.I 5 1950] 51-862
1. Religious education—Curricula. I. Title.

INTRODUCTION to catechetics. 268'.6 Edited by Peter De Rosa. Milwaukee, Bruce Pub. Co. [1968] ix, 198 p. 22 cm. Includes bibliographical references. [BX1968.I65 1968] 68-22453 2.75 (pbk)
1. Catechetics—Catholic Church. I. De Rosa, Peter, ed.

JAHSMANN, Allan Hart. 268.6
How you too can teach, reading text of a basic training course for church school teachers. St. Louis, Concordia Pub. House [1963] St. Louis, Concordia Pub. House, 1963. 85 p. 21 cm. 40 p. 28 cm. (Concordia leadership training series) "22-1177." "22-1179." BV1533.J3 Manual Includes bibliography. [BV1533.J3] 63-18733
1. Religious education—Teacher training. I. Title. II. Title: Trainer's manual.

JAHSMANN, Allan Hart 268.6
How you too can teach, reading text of a basic training course for church school teachers. St. Louis, Concordia [c.1963] 85p. 21cm. (Concordia leadership training ser.; 22-1177) Bibl. 63-18733 pap., .75; Trainers manual, pap., 1.50
1. Religious education—Teacher training. I. Title.

JAHSMANN, Allan Hart. 268'.6
Power beyond words; communication systems of the spirit and ways of teaching religion. Saint Louis, Concordia Pub. House [1969] 180 p. 22 cm. Bibliographical references included in "Notes" (p. 177-180) [BV1471.2.J3 1969] 73-76574
1. Christian education. 2. Communication (Theology) I. Title.

JEEP, Elizabeth. 268'.6
Classroom creativity : an idea book for religion teachers / Elizabeth Jeep. New rev. ed. New York : Seabury Press, 1977. p. cm. "A Crossroad book." Bibliography: p. [BV1534.J4 1977] 77-24719 ISBN 0-8164-21609 pbk. : 4.95
1. Christian education—Teaching methods. I. Title.

JEEP, Elizabeth. 268'.6
Classroom creativity : an idea book for religion teachers / Elizabeth Jeep. New rev. ed. New York : Seabury Press, 1977. p. cm. "A Crossroad book." Bibliography: p. [BV1534.J4 1977] 77-24719 ISBN 0-8164-21609 pbk. : 4.95
1. Christian education—Teaching methods. I. Title.

JOINT Board of Christian Education of Australia and New Zealand. 268'.6
The Christian life curriculum; a plan for Christian education in local churches. Melbourne [1968] 48 p. diagrs., tables. 24 cm. [BV1559.J64] 76-494564 unpriced
1. Religious education—Curricula. I. Title.

KEISER, Armilda Brome. 268.6
Here's how and when; illustrated by Janet Smalley. New York, Friendship Press [1952] 174 p. illus. 22 cm. [BV1536.K4] 52-7624
1. Religious education of children—Occupations and busy work. I. Title.

KEMP, Charles F 1912- 268.6
The church: the gifted and the retarded child. St. Louis, Bethany Press [1958, c1957] 189p. illus. 22cm. Includes bibliography. [BV639.C4K4] 58-6596
1. Church Work with children. 2. Exceptional children. I. Title.

KIRKENDALL, Norma Anne. 268.6
Let's do something about our teaching. Independence, Mo., Herald House [1958] 237p. 18cm. At head of title: Reorganized Church of Jesus Christ of Latter Day Saints. [BX8672.K5] 58-8200
1. Religious education—Teaching methods. 2. Reorganized Church of Jesus Christ of Latter-Day Saints—Education. I. Title.

LEAVITT, Guy P 268.6
Teach with success. Illustrated by Robert E. Huffman. Cincinnati, Standard Pub. Foundation [1956] 160p. illus. 28cm. [BV1534.L43] 66-47552
1. Religious education—Teaching methods. I. Title.

LEDERACH, Paul M 268.6
Learning to teach, by Paul M. Lederach. Newton, Kan., Faith and Life Press [1964] 103 p. illus. 20 cm. 36 p. 20 cm. (Christian service training series) (Christian service training series) Leader's guide. [Newton, Kan., Faith and Life Press, 1964] Cover title. Bibliographical footnotes. [BV1475.2.L4] 64-24359
1. Religious education. 2. Mennonites — Education. I. Title.

LE DU, Jean. 268'.6
Experiential catechetics, by Jean Le Du and Marcel van Caster. Translated by Denis Barrett. Paramus, N.J., Newman Press [1969] v, 247 p. 22 cm. Translation of Ervaring en catechese. Bibliographical footnotes. [BV1471.2.L4413] 71-100005 5.95
1. Christian education. 2. Experience. I. Caster, Marcel van. II. Title.

LESTER, Mildred E 268.6
Exploring Beginnings, by Mildred E. Lester and Lucile H. Lindberg. With illus. by Jannette Spitzer. Boston, Beacon Press [1960] 136p. illus. 21cm. 'A guide to Beginnings: earth, sky, life, death, by Sophia L. Fahs and Dorothy Spoerl, Beacon Press, 1958.' [BV1561.F23L4] 61-523
1. Fahs, Sophia Blanche (Lyon) 1876- Beginnings. I. Lindberg(Lucile H., joint author. II. Title.

LIFE in God's love series; 268.6 Catholic programmed instruction. Program ed.: Julian May. Content ed.:Louis B. Antl. Chicago, Franciscan Herald [1963] 28cm. 63-17251 teacher's ed., 2.95; student's ed., 1.50
1. Religious education—Text-books—Catholic Church. I. May, Julian, ed.

LITTLE, Sara. 268.6
Learning together in the Christian fellowship. Richard, John Knox Press [1956] 104p. illus. 21cm. [BV1534.L5] 56-9220
1. Religious education—Teaching method I. Title.

LOBINGIER, John Leslie, 1884- 268.6
If teaching is your job. Boston, Pilgrim Press [1956] 154p. 21cm. [BV1534.L6] 56-8212
1. Religious education—Teaching methods. I. Title.

MCCONKIE, Joseph F 268'.6
Teach & reach / Joseph Fielding McConkie. Salt Lake City : Bookcraft, 1975. 61 p. ; 24 cm. Includes bibliographical references and index. [BX8610.M27] 75-31080 ISBN 0-88494-289-9 : 2.95
1. Christian education. 2. Mormons and Mormonism—Study and teaching. I. Title.

MCCONKIE, Joseph F. 268'.6
Teach & reach / Joseph Fielding McConkie. Salt Lake City : Bookcraft, 1975. 61 p. ; 24

cm. Includes bibliographical references and index. [BX8610.M27] 75-31080 ISBN 0-88494-289-9 : 2.95
1. Christian education. 2. Mormons and Mormonism—Study and teaching. I. Title.

MCKENZIE, Leon. 268'.6
Christian education in the 70's; modern perspectives and approaches in the teaching of religion. Staten Island, N.Y., Alba House [1971] 153 p. illus. 21 cm. Bibliography: p. 145-150. [BV1471.2.M27] 70-169140 ISBN 0-8189-0216-7 2.95
1. Christian education. I. Title.

*MCLAREN, Rosemary 268'.6
Collyer, 1916-
St. Michael the Archangel and the holy terror, memoirs, by Rosemary Collyer McLaren. [First ed.] New York, Exposition Press [1973] 61 p. 21 cm. [BV1471] ISBN 0-682-47828-8. 3.50
1. Religious education. I. Title.

MCLESTER, Frances Cole. 268.6
Teaching in the church school. Henry M. Bullock, general editor. Rev. ed. New York, Abingdon Press [1961] 158p. 19cm. Includes bibliography. [BV1534.M286 1961] 61-2653
1. Religious education—Teaching methods. I. Title.

MCLESTER, Frances Cole. 268.6
What is teaching? Suggestions on how to teach in the church school. 3d ed., rev. Nashville, Abingdon-Cokesbury Press [1953] 125p. 19cm. [BV1534.M287 1953] 52-13758
1. Religious education—Teaching methods. 2. Sunday-schools. 3. Teaching. I. Title.

MCMILLIN, Joseph L. 268.6
How to make your teaching count. Nashville, Broadman [c.1965] 55p. 22cm. [BV1471.2.M3] 65-10337 .75 pap.,
1. Religious education. I. Title.

MCRAE, Glenn, 1887- 268.6
Teaching youth in the church. [Rev. ed.] St. Louis, Bethany Press [1957, c1940] 119p. 18cm. [BV1534.M288 1957] 56-12428
1. Religious education—Teaching methods. I. Title.

MARTHALER, Berard L. 268'.6
Catechetics in context; notes and commentary on the General catechetical directory issued by the Sacred Congregation for the Clergy, by Berard L. Marthaler. Huntington, Ind., Our Sunday Visitor [1973] xxxi, 293 p. 23 cm. Includes bibliographical references. [BV1471.2.M347] 72-90557 ISBN 0-87973-842-1 pap. 4.95
1. Religious education. 2. Pastoral theology—Catholic Church. I. Catholic Church. Congregatio pro Clericis. Directorium catechisticum generale. English. 1973. II. Title. Cloth 7.95; ISBN 0-87973-842-1.

MARY Vincenza, Sister, 268'.6
S.S.N.D.
Creative religion involvement programs [by] M. Vincenza. Staten Island, N.Y., Alba House [1973] viii, 169 p. 21 cm. Bibliography: p. [145]-162. [BV1485.M28] 73-10212 ISBN 0-8189-0277-9 2.95 (pbk)
1. Religious education of young people. I. Title.

MEADOWS, Thomas Burton, 268.6
1881-
Psychology of learning and teaching Christian education; psychology for Christian workers. With Teacher's manual supplement. [1st ed.] New York, Pageant Press [1958] 2 v. illus. 24cm. [BV1471.M38] 57-9934
1. Learning, Psychology of. 2. Religious education—Psychology. I. Title.

METHODIST Church (United 268.6
States) Curriculum Committee.
Educational principles in the curriculum; a report to the Curriculum Committee of the Methodist Church. [Statement by Committee on Educational Principles in the Curriculum. Nashville, Pierce and Smith, c1951. 104 l. 28 cm. [BV1471.M4] 52-23366
1. Religious education. I. Title.

METHODIST Church (United 268.6
States) Curriculum Committee.
Educational principles in the curriculum; a report to the Curriculum Committee of the Methodist Church [by the Committee on Educational Principles in the Curriculum. Nashville, Pierce and Smith, c1952. 50 p. 23 cm. "A supplement to the Report of the Curriculum Committee of the General Board of Education, the Methodist Church. Approved January 3, 1952." [BV1471.M4] 52-38086
1. Religious education. I. Methodist Church (United States) Curriculum Committee. Report. Supplement. II. Title.

MILLER, Randolph Crump, 268.6
1910-
Biblical theology and Christian education. New York, Scribner [1956] 226p. 21cm. [BV1471.M47] 56-10349
1. Bible—Study. 2. Religious education. I. Title.

MILLER, Randolph Crump, 268.6
1910-
The clue to Christian education. New York, Scribner, 1950. xi, 211 p. 21 cm. Bibliography: p. 203-204. [BV1471.M48] 50-11377
1. Religious education. I. Title.

NASH, Gerald R 268.6
Sabbath school special days, by Gerald R. Nash. Mountain View Calif., Pacific Press Pub. Association [1966] 178 p. illus. 22 cm. Includes music. [BX6113.N32] 66-20342
1. Sunday schools — Exercises, recitations, etc. 2. Seventh-Day Adventists — Education. I. Title.

NASH, Gerald R. 268.6
Sabbath school special days. Mountain View, Calif., Pacific Pr. Pub [c.1966] 178p. illus. 22cm. Includes music. [BX6113.N32] 66-20342 3.25
1. Sunday-schools—Exercises, recitations, etc. 2. Seventh-Day Adventists—Education. I. Title.

NIJMEGEN, Netherlands. 268.6
Hoger Katechetisch Instituut
Fundamentals and programs of a new catechesis. [Tr. from Duth by Walter van de Putte] Pittsburgh, Duquesne [c.1966] 312p. 22cm. Bibl. [BX926.N53] 66-15157 6.95
1. Catechetics—Catholic Church. 2. Religious education. I. Title.

*PEACE, Richard. 268'.6
Learning to love people. Grand Rapids, Zondervan [1968] In the same ser.: Learning to love God; Learning to love ourselves. 1.00 pap.,
I. Title.

PIERCE, Rice Alexander, 268'.6
1916-
Leading dynamic Bible study [by] Rice A. Pierce. Forword by Gaines S. Dobbins. Nashville, Broadman Press [1969] 128 p. 21 cm. Bibliographical footnotes. [BS600.2.P5] 74-78835 2.95
1. Bible—Study. I. Title.

*POGANSKI, Donald J. 268'.6
50 object lessons; the Gospel visualized for children St. Louis, Concordia [1967] 152p. illus. 18cm. 2.75 pap.,
I. Title.

POTTS, Edwin James. 268.6
How to teach the word of God. Chicago, Harvest Publications [c1963] 104 p. illus. 20 cm. (A Harvest leadership training book) [BV1471.2.P6] 63-11151
1. Religious education I. Title.

POTTS, Edwin James 268.6
How to teach the word of God. Chicago 26 5750 N. Ashland Ave. Harvest Pubns., [c.1963] 104p. illus. 20cm. (Harvest leadership training bks.) 63-11151 price unreported
1. Religious education. I. Title.

REICHERT, Richard. 268'.6
A learning process for religious education / Richard Reichert. Dayton, Ohio : Pflaum Pub., [1974] c1975. vii, 151 p. ; 21 cm. Bibliography: p. 99-104. [BV1471.2.R43] 74-14308 ISBN 0-8278-0001-0 pbk. : 5.25
1. Religious education. I. Title.

REICHERT, Richard. 268'.6
Simulation games for religious education / by Richard Reichert ; [ill. by R. G. Davis]. Winona, Minn. : St. Mary's College Press, [1975] 106 p. : ill. ; 22 cm. [BV1536.3.R44] 75-142 ISBN 0-88489-060-0 pbk. : 4.50
1. Games in Christian education. I. Title.

*REISZ, Kathryn 268.6
Look at teaching, by Kathryn and Howard Reisz. Ed.: Margaret J. Irvin. Illus.: Robert L. Jefferson. Philadelphia, Lutheran Church [c.1965] 62p. 23cm. (LCA vacation church sch. ser.) pap., .50; teacher's guide, pap., .90
I. Title.

REYNOLDS, Ferris E 268.6
An adventure with people; the 'reading, writing, and arithmetic' of teaching religion. Philadelphia, Christian Education Press [1954] 96p. 20cm. [BV1534.R4] 54-7072
1. Religious education—Teaching methods. I. Title.

RICHARDS, Lawrence O. 268'.6
You, the teacher, by Lawrence O. Richards. Chicago, Moody Press [1972] 124 p. illus. 22 cm. (Effective teaching series) [BV1534.R43] 72-77942 ISBN 0-8024-9829-9 1.95
1. Sunday-school teachers. I. Title.

*RIDENOUR, Fritz. 268'.6
How to be Christian without being religious; the Book of Romans in living letters paraphrase combined with illustrated contemporary comment. Glendale, Calif. Gospel Light Pubs. [1967] (G/L Regal bks.) HS In kit containing various teaching aids. 4.35 pap., set,
I. Title.

ROZELL. RAY 268.6
The Sunday school teacher as counselor. Grand Rapids, Mich., Zondervan Pub. House [c.1960] 94p. 21cm. Bibl: p.89. 60-4172 1.50 pap.,
1. Counseling. 2. Sunday-schools. 3. Pastoral counseling. I. Title.

ROZELL, Ray 268.6
Talks on Sunday school teaching, [3d ed.] Grand Rapids, Zondervan Pub. House [1960, c.1956] 150p. 21cm. 60-4173 1.50 pap.,
1. Religious education—Teaching methods. 2. Sunday-schools. I. Title.

RUSSELL, Ruth W. 268.6
Learning how to live with others: for use with Grades Three and Four. Teacher's book. Published for the Cooperative Publication Association by The Judson Press. Philadelphia. [c.1959] 157p. illus. (A Cooperative Text) 19cm. 2.50
I. Title.

SCHAAL, John H. 268'.6
Feed my sheep; a manual for Sunday school teachers, superintendents, and leaders. Compiled and edited by John H. Schaal. Grand Rapids, Baker Book House [1972] 162 p. 21 cm. Includes bibliographies. [BV1521.S3] 72-85717 ISBN 0-8010-7958-6 1.95
1. Sunday-schools. 2. Christian education. I. Title.

SCHMIEDING, Alfred, 1888- 268.6
Teaching the Bible story, [4th ed.] Saint Louis, Concordia Pub. House [1951] 152 p. 20 cm. [BS546.S35 1951] 51-6990
1. Bible stories. 2. Bible — Study — Textbooks. 3. Religious education. I. Title.

SCHROEDER, Theodore W 268.6
49 worship stories for children; an aid to all who are concerned with the spiritual welfare of children: pastors, Sunday school workers, teachers, and parents. Saint Louis, Concordia Pub. House [1957] 132p. 20cm. [BV4315.S34] 57-9734
1. Children's stories. I. Title.

SCHROEDER, Theodore W 268.6
49 worship stories for children; an aide to all who are concerned with the spiritual welfare of children: pastors, Sunday school workers, teachers, and parents. Saint Louis, Concordia Pub. House [1957] 132p. 20cm. [BV4315.S34] 57-9734
1. Children's stories. I. Title.

SHAMON, Albert J. 268'.6
Catching up on catechetics, by Albert J. Shamon. New York, Paulist Press [1972] 73 p. 18 cm. (Deus books) [BV1471.2.S48] 72-85698 ISBN 0-8091-1739-8 0.95 (pbk.)
1. Religious education. I. Title.

SHINN, Roger Lincoln. 268.6
The educational mission of our church. Boston, United Church Press [1962] 176 p. 21cm. Includes bibliographies. [BX9884.A3S4] 62-13797
1. Religious education. 2. United Church of Christ — Education I. Title.

SHINN, Roger Lincoln 268.6
The educational mission of our church. Philadelphia, United Church [c.1962] 176p. 21cm. Bibl. 62-13797 2.00; 1.00 pap.,
1. Religious education. 2. United Church of Christ—Education. I. Title.

SISEMORE, John T 268.6
Blueprint for teaching. Nashville, Broadman Press [1964] 103 p. forms. 21 cm. Bibliographical footnotes. [BV1534.S55] 64-12413
1. Religious education — Teaching methods. I. Title.

SISEMORE, John T. 268.6
Blueprint for teaching. Nashville, Broadman [c.1964] 103p. forms. 21cm. Bibl. 64-12413 1.95 bds.,
1. Religious education—Teaching methods. I. Title.

SISEMORE, John T. 268'.6
Rejoice, you're a Sunday school teacher! / John T. Sisemore ; [ill. by Ron Hester]. Nashville : Broadman Press, c1977. 94 p. : ill. ; 20 cm. [BV1534.S553] 76-20053 ISBN 0-8054-5147-1 : 3.25
1. Sunday-school teachers. I. Title.

SONS and heirs. 268.6
Rev. teacher's manual replacing Deciding for myself. Illus. by Maurice Rawson. Greenwich,Conn., Seabury [c.1957-1962] 222p. 21cm. (The church's teaching in the sixth grade) 2.10 pap.,

SOUTHERN Baptist 268.6
Convention. Sunday School Board.
The curriculum guide. 1960- Nashville, Tenn., Convention Press. v. 20 cm. annual. Editors: 1960- C. J. Allen and W. I. Howse. Includes bibliography. [BV1559.S6] 60-9536
1. Religious education — Curricula. I. Allen, Clifton J. 1901- ed. II. Howse, William Lewis, 1965- ed. III. Title.

SOUTHERN Baptist 268.6
Convention. Sunday School Board.
The curriculum guide. 1960-1963/4. Nashville, Tenn., Convention Press. 4 v. 20 cm. annual. Edited by C. J. Allen and W. L. Howse. Superseded by Church program guidebook issued by the convention's Baptist Brotherhood Commission. [BV1559.S6] 60-9536
1. Religious education—Curricula. I. Allen, Clifton J., 1901- ed. II. Howse, William Lewis, 1905- ed. III. Title.

*STAINBACK, Arthur House 268.6
Illustrating the lesson. 1965 ed. Westwood, N.J., Revell [c.1964] 122p. 22cm. 1.50 pap.,
I. Title.

*STAINBACK, Arthur House 268.6
Illustrating the lesson. 1967 ed. Westwood, N.J., Revell [c.1966] 120p. 22cm. 400 illustrations to complement the weekly Intl. uniform Sunday-school lessons. 1.95 pap.,
1. International Sunday-school lessons. I. Title.

*STAINBACK, Arthur House 268.6
Illustrating the lesson. 1966 ed. Westwood, N.J., Revell [c.1965] 121p. 22cm. 400 illustrations to complement the weekly Intl. uniform Sunday-school lessons. 1.50 pap.,
1. International Sunday-school lessons. I. Title.

STEELE, Eileen Aultman. 268'.6
In behalf of children: a guide to challenge the bit of God in us. Philadelphia, Dorrance [1974] 85 p. 22 cm. [BV1475.2.S77] 73-87873 ISBN 0-8059-1948-1 4.95
1. Religious education of children. I. Title.

SWAIN, Dorothy G 268.6
Teach me to teach [by] Dorothy G. Swain. Valley Forge [Pa.] Judson Press [1964] 127 p. 20 cm. Bibliography: p. 123-127. [BV1533.S8] 64-13125
1. Religious education — Teacher training. I. Title.

SWAIN, Dorothy G. 268.6
Teach me to teach. Valley Forge [Pa.] Judson [c.1964] 127p. 20cm. Bibl. 64-13125 1.50 pap.,
1. Religious education—Teacher training. I. Title.

TALBOT, Gladys Mary, comp; 268.6
40 stories for you to tell Chicago, Moody Press [1952] 192 p. 20 cm. [BV4571.T3] 52-4450
1. Children's stories. 2. Children — Religious life. I. Title.

TAYLOR, Margaret Fisk 268.6
Time for discovery. Illus. by Ruth Baldwin. Philadelphia, United Church [1964] 76p. illus. 28cm. Includes hymns, with music. Bibl. 64-24444 3.25, pap., plastic bdg.
1. Religious education of children. 2. Dancing (in religion, folklore, etc.) I. Title.

WEBER, Gerard P., 1918- 268'.6
Parents' guide; the word and worship program [by] Gerard P. Weber, James J. Killgallon [and] Sr. M. Michael O'Shaughnessy. [1st ed.] New York, Benziger Brothers, 1968. xii, 169 p. 18 cm. Bibliography: p. 161-164. [BX929.W4] 68-58714
1. Catholic Church—Education. 2. Religious education—Curricula. I. Killgallon, James J., 1914- joint author. II. O'Shaughnessy, Mary Michael, joint author. III. Title.

WILLIS, Wayne. 268'.6
Communicating Christ in the inner city; a handbook for teachers of disadvantaged children. Austin, Tex., Sweet Pub. Co. [1970] 128 p. illus. 20 cm. Bibliography: p. 127-128. [BV1615.S6W5] 70-107390 ISBN 0-8344-0059-6
1. Christian education of socially handicapped children. 2. Religious education—Text-books. I. Title.

WRIGHT, Kathryn S 268.6
Let the children paint; art in religious education [by] Kathryn S. Wright. New York, Seabury Press [1966] 168 p. illus. 22 cm. Includes bibliographies. [BV1536.W75] 66-16651

1. Religious education. 2. Object teaching. I. Title. II. Title: Art in religious education.

WRIGHT, Kathryn S. 268.6
Let the children paint; art in religious education. New York, Seabury [c.1966] 168p. illus. 22cm. Bibl. [BV1536.W75] 66-16651 4.50
1. Religious education. 2. Object teaching. I. Title. II. Title: Art in religious education.

WYCKOFF, D Campbell. 268.6
Theory and design of Christian education curriculum. Philadelphia, Westminster Press [1961] 219 p. 22 cm. Includes bibliography. [BV1559.W9] 61-6103
1. Religious education-Curricula. I. Title. II. Title: Christian education curriculum.

WYCKOFF, D. Campbell 268.6
Theory and design of Christian education curriculum. Philadelphia, Westminster Press [c.1961] 219p. Bibl. 61-6103 4.50
1. Religious education—Curricula. I. Title. II. Title: Christian education curriculum.

YODER, Glee. 268'.6
Take it from here; suggestions for creative activities. Valley Forge [Pa.] Judson Press [1973] 62 p. illus. 28 cm. [BV1536.Y63] 72-9570 ISBN 0-8170-0584-6 2.50
1. Creative activities and seat work. 2. Religious education. I. Title.

YODER, Glee. 268'.6
Take it from here, series two : suggestions for creative activities / Glee Yoder ; page layout by Linda Beher. Valley Forge, Pa. : Judson Press, [1975] 64 p. : ill. ; 28 cm. Includes index. [BV1536.Y62] 75-2334 ISBN 0-8170-0662-1 pbk. : 3.50
1. Creative activities and seat work. 2. Religious education. I. Title.

YOUNG, Lois Horton. 268'.6
Dimensions for happening. Valley Forge [Pa.] Judson Press [1971] 96 p. illus. 22 cm. Bibliography: p. 77-82. [BV1536.Y68] 76-144081 ISBN 0-8170-0506-4
1. Bible—Study. 2. Religious education—Teaching methods. I. Title.

ZOBELL, Albert L. 268'.6
Talks to see. Compiled by Albert L. Zobell, Jr. Salt Lake City, Deseret Book Co., 1971. 127 p. 20 cm. [BV4227.Z6] 77-155236 ISBN 0-87747-436-2 3.25
1. Object-teaching. 2. Homiletical illustrations. I. Title.

TOBEY, Kathrene McLandress. 268'.6'019
Learning and teaching through the senses. Philadelphia, Westminster Press [1970] 128 p. illus. 23 cm. Bibliography: p. [127]-128. [LB1067.T6] 70-92899 2.45
1. Perceptual learning. I. Title.

AGNEW, Milton S., 1905- 268'.61
Manual of salvationism, by Milton S. Agnew. [New York] Salvation Army [1968] 72, 72a-b p. illus., map. 22 cm. Includes bibliographies. [BX9714.A37] 68-22790
1. Religious education—Text-books for young people—Salvation Army. I. Title.

BARBER, Estelle Bianton. 268.61
God in our lives; a course for intermediates or junior high school groups in vacation church school. Teacher's book. New York, Published for the Cooperative Publication Associationby Abingdon-Cokesbury Press [1952] 128 p. 20 cm. (Cooperative texts for vacation church schools) [BV1585.B356] 268.432 52-2161
1. Vacation schools, Religious—Text-books. I. Title.

BEERS, Lorna Doone. 268'.61
My brothers, my country, my world. Teacher's book [grades 5 and 6] by Lorna Beers. Philadelphia, Published for the Cooperative Publication Association by United Church Press [1969] 192 p. illus. 22 cm. (Through-the-week series) Includes bibliographical references. [LC331.B4] 69-17640
1. Christian education—Handbooks, manuals, etc. I. Cooperative Publication Association. II. Title.

BROADMAN comments on the 268.61
International Bible lessons for Christian teaching. Uniform ser.
The 1969 edition is now available from Broadman Pr., Nashville, Tenn. for $3.25. L.C. card order no.: 45-437.

BROADMAN comments on the 268.61
International Bible lessons for Christian teaching; 1968, by Edward A. McDowell [others] Nashville, Broadman [1967] v. 22cm. (Uniform ser.) [BV1520.B725] 45-437 3.25 bds.,
1. International Sunday school lessons.

BROADMAN comments on the 268.61
International Bible lessons for Christian teaching. Uniform series. 1962. [By] H. I. Hester, J. Winston Pearce. Nashville Broadman [c.1961] 437p. 2.95 bds.,

BROADMAN comments on the 268.61
International Bible lessons for Christian teaching. Uniform ser. 1964 [by] H. I. Hester, J. Winston Pearce. Nashville, Broadman [c.1963] 438p. 21cm: 2.95 bds.,

BROADMAN comments on the 268.61
International Bible lessons for Christian teaching. Uniform ser. 1963. [By] H. I. Hester, J. Winston Pearce. Nashville, Broadman [c.1962] 437p. 21cm. 2.95 bds.,

BROADMAN comments on the 268.61
International Bible lessons for Christian teaching, by Hugh R. Peterson [others] Uniform ed. Nashville, Broadman [c.1965] 437p. 22cm. [BV1520.B725] 45-437 2.95
1. International Sunday-school lessons. I. Peterson, Hugh R.

BROADMAN comments on the 268.61
international Bible Lessons for Christian Teaching; 1967, by Hugh R. Peterson [others] Nashville, Broadman [c.1966] 437p. 22cm. (Uniform ser.) [BV1520.B725] 45-437 2.95 bds.,
1. International Sunday-school lessons. I. Peterson, Hugh R.

BROWN, Henry Clifton. 268'.61
Biblical Sunday school commentary. H. C. Brown, Jr., editor-in-chief. Waco, Tex., Word Books [1968] 422 p. 23 cm. [BV1560.B73] 68-31107 3.95
1. International Sunday-school lessons. I. Title.

BRUEGGEMANN, Walter. 268'.61
Confronting the Bible; a resource and discussion book for youth. [Rev. ed. New York] Herder and Herder [1968] 75 p. illus. 22 cm. (Christian commitment series) Bibliography: p. 73-75. [BS605.2.B78] 68-29888 1.20
1. Bible—Study—Text-books. 2. Religious education—Text-books for young people—United Church of Christ. I. Title.

CALDWELL, Irene Catherine (Smith) 1919- 268.61
Adults learn and like it; how to teach adults in the church. Anderson, Ind., Warner Press [1955] 112p. illus. 20cm. [BV1550.C3] 268.434 55-58705
1. Religious education of adults. I. Title.

CAMPBELL, Elizabeth W. 268.61
Security for young children, the foundation for spiritual values; a booklet for teachers and parents who live with three-year-old children in home, church, and school. Boston, Pilgrim Press [1952] 99 p. illus. 23 cm. [HQ784.S43C3] 268.432 52-10166
1. Security (Psychology) 2. Child study. I. Title.

CHILCOTE, Thomas F. 268.61
Man's spiritual pilgrimage; an adventure into elementary theology for laymen, by Thomas F. Chilcote, Jr. Nashville, Methodist Evangelistic Materials, [1965] 88 p. col. front. 14 x 22 cm. Bibliography: p. 86-87. [BX8225.C5] 65-20492
1. Religious education — Text-books for adults — Methodist. I. Title.

THE Christian in the 268'.61
world. General editor, Reginald Doherty. Rev. ed. Chicago, Priory Press [1968] 536 p. illus., maps. 24 cm. (The Challenge of Christ, 4) [BV1549.94.C5 1968] 68-7269
1. Religious education—Text-books for young people—Catholic. I. Doherty, Reginald, ed. II. Title. III. Series.

**COMMENTARIES on* 268'.61
doctrinal themes, according to the catechetical program of Come to the Father series. Grades 1 & 2. Glen Rock, N.J., Paulist [1967] 1.50 pap.,

DISCOVERY patterns 268'.61
[edited by] Robert J. Heyer [and] Richard J. Payne. Paramus, N.J., Paulist Press [1969] 3 v. illus., facsims., ports. 28 cm. Contents.Contents.—book 1. Patterns of situations.—book 2. Patterns of dynamics and strategies.—book 3. Patterns of techniques. [BX930.D53] 77-103003
1. Religious education—Text-books—Catholic. I. Heyer, Robert J. II. Payne, Richard J., ed.

DOUGLASS Sunday school 268.61
lessons 1961 (The);1practical expositions of the International Sunday school lessons. Edited by Earl L. Douglass. New York, Macmillan Co. [c.1960] 494p. annual, Subtitle varies slightly. 21-13506 3.25
1. International Sunday-school lessons. I. Douglass, Earl Leroy, 1888- ed.

DOUGLASS Sunday school 268.61
lessons 1962 (The); practical expositions of the International Sunday school lessons. New York, Macmillan [c.1961] xii, 475p. annual. Title varies. Ed.: 1961--Earl L. Douglass. 21-13506 3.25
1. International Sunday-school lessons. I. Snowden, James Henry, 1852-1936, ed. II. Douglass, Earl Leroy, 1888- ed.

DOUGLASS Sunday school 268.61
lessons, 1964 (The) Practical expositions of the international Sunday school lessons, by Earl L. Douglass, Gordon L. Roberts. New York, Macmillan [c.1963] 475p. 20cm. Title varies. 21-13506 2.95
1. International Sunday-school lessons. I. Douglass, Earl Leroy, 1888- ed.

DOUGLASS Sunday school 268.61
lessons, 1965 (The) Practical expositions of the international Sunday school lessons, by Earl L. Douglass, Gordon L. Roberts. New York, Macmillan [c.1964] 475p. 20cm. Title varies. 3.25
1. International Sunday-school lessons. I. Douglass, Earl Leroy, 1888- ed.

DOUGLASS Sunday school 268.61
lessons (The); practical expositions of the International Sunday school lessons, 1963. New York, Macmillan [c.1962] 478p. 20cm. annual. title varies. Ed.: 1963, E. L. Douglass. 21-13506 3.25
1. International Sunday-school lessons. I. Douglass, Earl Leroy, 1888- ed.

DOUGLASS Sunday School 268.61
lessons (The) 1967; practical expositions of the International Sunday school lessons, by Earl L. Douglass. assisted by Gordon L. Roberts. New York, Macmillan [c.1966] xxiii, 386p. 22cm. Title varies. 21-13506 3.95
1. International Sunday-school lessons. I. Douglass, Earl Leroy, 1888- ed. II. Roberts, Gordon L., joint ed.

DOUGLASS SUNDAY SCHOOL LESSONS. 1966(The) 268.61
Practical expositions of the International Sunday School lesson, by Earl L. Douglass, Gordon L. Roberts. New York, Macmillan [c.1965] 392p. 22cm. Title varies. 3.25 bds.,
1. International Sunday-school lessons. I. Douglass, Earl Leroy, 1888- ed. II. Title.

EARLY Old Testament 268.61
times; a textbook for fifth and sixth grades. Nashville, Published for the Cooperative Publication Association by Abingdon-Cokesbury Press [1952] 215 p. 20 cm. [The Co-operative series: weekday church school texts] [BV1583.H3] 268.432 52-30631
1. Week-day church schools—Teachers' manuals. 2. Bible stories—O. T. I. Hazelwood, Lola, 1897-

EVANGELICAL Sunday school 268.61
lesson commentary on the Uniform Bible lesson series of the National Sunday School Association for 1960; 8th annual volume. Butler, Ind., Higley Press. c.1959 320p. maps 22cm. 53-33415 2.50
1. Religious education—Text-books—Series.

*FUERST, Wesley J. 268.61
Key Bible words. Philadelphia, Lutheran Church Pr. [c.1965] 96p. 21cm. pap., 1.25; teacher's ed., 1.35
I. Title.

GALUSHA, Elinor G. 268'.61
Lift up your hearts; a resource and discussion book for youth. Elinor G. Galusha, editor. [Rev. ed. New York] Herder and Herder [1968] 73 p. illus. 22 cm. (Christian commitment series) [BV10.2.G33 1968b] 68-29891 1.20
1. Worship. 2. Religious education—Text-books for young people. I. Title.

GALUSHA, Elinor G. 268'.61
Lift up your hearts; a resource and discussion book for youth. Elinor G. Galusha, editor. Boston, United Church Press [1968] 76 p. illus. 22 cm. (Confirmation education series) "Part of the United Church curriculum, prepared and published by the Division of Christian Education and the Division of Publication of the United Church Board for Homeland Ministries." Includes unacc. melodies with words. [BX9884.A3G3] 68-10313
1. Worship. 2. Religious education—Text-books for young people—United Church of Christ. I. United Church Board for Homeland Ministries. Division of Christian Education. II. United Church Board for Homeland Ministries. Division of Publication. III. Title.

GILBERT, W Kent, ed. 268.61
The weekday church school series. Philadelphia, Muhlenberg Press [1952- v. illus. 28cm. In each vol. the main work, also published separately, is preceded by a Teacher's guide with special t. p. [BV1583.G5] 53-23897
1. Week-day church schools—Text-books. I. Title.
Contents omitted.

GILLILAND, Anne Hitchcock. 268'.61
Understanding preschoolers. Nashville, Convention Press [1969] viii, 180 p. illus. 21 cm. (Basic preschool books) Text for course 6101 of subject area: Understanding work with age level and special groups in a church, of the New church study course. Bibliography: p. 158-163. [HQ772.G475] 76-97867
1. Child study. I. Title.

GLASS, Esther Eby. 268.61
Our city neighbors; children's mission study. Illustrated by Charles F. Ellis. Scottdale, Pa., Herald Press [1966] 96, L-32 p. illus., map, ports. 22 cm. Includes hymns, with music. "Leader's guide": L-32 p. inserted. [BX8114.G5] 66-25427
1. Religious education — Text-books for children — pmennonite. 2. City missions. I. Title.

GOOD news; 268.61
teacher's guide, by T. J. Vinger. Produced by the Bd. of Parish Educ. and the Bd. of Pubn. of the Amer. Lutheran Church. Minneapolis, Augsburg, c. 1962. 111p. 28cm. 2.00 pap.,

GOUKER, Loice. 268.61
God in my world; illustrated by Janet Smalley. W. Kent Gilbert, editor. Philadelphia, Muhlenberg Press [1954] 112, 127p. illus. 23cm. (The Weekday church school series. grade 1) The main work is preceded by the 'Teacher's guide' (112 p.) with special t. p. [BV1580.G57] 54-14415
1. Week-day church schools— Teachers' manuals. I. Title.

HIGHLEY commentary [for] 268.61
1964; international uniform Sunday school lessons, 31st v. Winona, Ind., Lambert Huffman [c.1963] 528p. illus. 23cm. Jasper A. Huffman, ed.-in-chief; Knute Larson, ed. 2.95
1. International Sunday-School lessons.

**HIGHLEY commentary [for]* 268.61
1965 international uniform Sunday school lessons; 32d. v. Winona Lake, Ind., Lambert Huffman [c.1964] 526p. illus. 23cm. Jasper A. Huffman, ed.-in-chief; Knute Larson, ed. 2.95 bds.,
1. International Sunday-school lessons.

**HIGHLEY commentary [for]* 268.61
1966; international uniform Sunday school lessons; 33d v. Winona Lake, Ind., Lambert Huffman [c.1965] 526p. illus. 24cm. Jasper A. Huffman, ed.-in-chief; Knut Larson, ed. p3.25 bds.,
1. International Sunday-school lessons.

HIGHLEY'S Sunday school 268.61
lesson commentary. International Sunday school lessons. uniform ser. 1962. 29th annual vol. Winona Lake, Ind., Lamberg Huffman [c.1961] 527p. 'Founder: L. H. Higley.' 41-18790 2.95
1. International Sunday-school lessons.

HIGHLEY'S Sunday school 268.61
lesson commentary on the International Sunday school lessons, uniform series for 1960; the 27th annual v. Butler, Ind., Highley Press [c.1959] 320p. map 23cm. 'Founder: L. H. Higley.' 41-18970 2.50
1. International Sunday school lessons.

HIGLEY commentary, 268.61
1968. International uniform Sunday school lessons. 35th v. Winowa Lake, Ind. Lambert Huffman Pubs., [1967] 531, 49p. illus. col. maps. Eds.: 1967-Jasper A. Huffman, ed.-in chief: Knute Larson, ed. Cover title: Higley verse by verse Sunday school lesson commentary (Intl. Sunday school lesson ser., [BV1560.H53] 41-18790 3.25
1. International Sunday school lessons. I. Huffman, Jasper A., ed.

**HIGLEY commentary,* 268.61
1967. International uniform Sunday school lessons. 34th v. Winona Lake, Ind., Lambert Huffman Pubs. [1966] 541, 48p. illus. 8 col. maps. Eds.: 1967-Jasper A. Huffman, ed.-in-chief: Knute Larson, ed. Cover title: Higley verse by verse Sunday school lesson commentary (Intl. Sunday school lesson ser.) 3.25
1. International Sunday school lessons. I. Huffman, Jasper A., ed.

HOWSE, William Lewis, 1905- 268.61
Guiding young people in Bible study. Nashville, Convention Press [1955] 144p. 20cm. [BV1534.H73] 268.433 55-14855
1. Religious education—Teaching methods. 2. Bible— Study. I. Title.

INTERNATIONAL Council of Religious Education. 268.61
International Sunday school lessons; the international Bible lessons for Christian teaching. Uniform ser. Chicago. v. 23 cm. [BV1560.I 625] 51-36085
1. International Sunday-school lessons. 2. Religious education—Curricula. I. Title.

INTERNATIONAL lesson annual (the) 1968 Nashville, [1967] v. illus., maps. 24cm. Editor: 1956-;C. M. Laymon-- 1966-;H. R. Weaver. -- 1968- Lesson analysis by C. M. Layman. 1968 v. has as subtitleA comprehensive commentary on the International Sunday school lessons. uniform ser. [BV1560.164] 55 6961 3.25 268.61
1. International Sunday-School lessons. I. Laymon Charles M., ed.

INTERNATIONAL Lesson annual 1960 (The) a comprehensive commentary on the International Sunday School lessons, uniform ser. Edited by Charles M. Laymon. Lesson analysis by Roy L. Smith, Nashville, Abingdon Press [c.1959] 448p. illus., maps. 24cm. (Bibl. foot notes). 55-6961 2.95 268.61
1. International Sunday-school lessons. I. Laymon, Charles M., ed.

THE International lesson annual. 1956- New York, Abingdon Press. v. illus., maps. 24cm. Editor: 1956- C. M. Laymon. [BV1560.I64] 55-6961 268.61
1. International Sunday-school lessons. I. Laymon, Charles M., ed.

INTERNATIONAL lesson annual (The) Nashville, Abingdon v. illus., maps. 24cm. Ed.: 1956- C. M. Laymon; 1969- H. R. Weaver; Lesson analysis by C. M. Laymon [BV1560.I 64] 55-6961 3.25 268.61
1. International Sunday-school lessons. I. Laymon Charles M., d. II. Weaver, Horace R. ed.

INTERNATIONAL lesson annual (The) 1964. A comprehensive commentary on The International Sunday school lessons, uniform ser. Ed. by Horace R. Weaver. Lesson analysis by Roy L. Smith. Nashville, Abingdon [c.1963] 24cm. 55-6961 2.95 268.61
1. International Sunday school lessons. I. Weaver, Horace R., ed.

INTERNATIONAL lesson annual, The. 1962. A comprehensive commentary on The international Sunday School Lessons, uniform series. Ed. by Charles M. Laymon; lesson analysis by Roy L. Smith. Nashville, Abingdon [c.1961] illus. 55-6961 2.95 268.61
1. International Sunday-school lessons I. Laymon, Charles M., ed.

INTERNATIONAL lesson annual (the) 1967 A Comprehensive commentary on The International Sunday School Lessons. Uniform ser. Ed. by Horace R Weaver. Lesson analysis by Charles M. Laymon Nashville, Abingdon [c.1966] 448p. 24cm. annual. 55-6961 2.95 268.61
1. International Sunday school lessions. I. Weaver, Horace R., ed.

INTERNATIONAL Lesson annual (The) 1961. A comprensive commentary on the International Sunday School lessons, uniform series. Edited by Charles M. Laymon; lesson analysis by Roy L. Smith. Nashville, Abingdon Press [c.1960] 448p. illus. 24cm. (Bibl. foonotes) 55-6961 2.95 268.61
1. International Sunday-school lessons. I. Laymon, Charles M., ed.

INTERNATIONAL lesson annual (The) 1963. A comprehensive commentary on The international Sunday School Lessons, uniform series. Ed. by Horace R. Weaver. Lesson analysis by Roy L. Smith. Nashville, Abingdon [c.1962] 447p. 24cm. illus. 55-6961 2.95 268.61
1. International Sunday-school lessons. I. Weaver, Horace R., ed.

INTERNATIONAL lesson annual (The) 1965 A comprehensive commentary on the International Sunday School lessons, uniform ser. by Horace R. Weaver. Lesson analysis by Roy L. Smith. Nashville, Abingdon [c.1964] 445p. 24cm. annual. 55-6961 2.95 268.61
1. International Sunday school lessons. I. Weaver, Horace R., ed.

INTERNATIONAL Sunday School Lesson 268.61
The gist of the lesson; a concise exposition of the International Sunday school lessons for 1967. 68th [New enlarged ed.] Originated by R. A. Torrey. Ed. by Donald T. Kaufman. Westwood. N. J., Revell [1966] 127p. 18cm. .95 pap.,
1. International Sunday school lessons. I. Torrey, R. A. II. Kauffman, Donald T., ed. III. Title.

INTERNATIONAL Sunday school lessons; uniform lesson commentary. 1954- Philadelphia, Muhlenberg Press. v. illus. 22cm. annual. Editor: 1954- W. M. Horn. [BV1560.I68] 54-37263 268.61
1. International Sunday-school lessons. I. Horn, William M., ed.

INTERNATIONAL Sunday School lessons; uniform lesson commentary. 1965. Philadelphia, Fortress [c.1964] 320p. illus. 22cm. annual. 54-37263 3.75 268.61
1. International Sunday-school lessons.

INTERNATIONAL Sunday school lessons; uniform lesson commentary. 1964. Philadelphia, Fortress Pr. [c.1963] 319p. illus. 22cm. annual. 54-37263 2.95 268.61
1. International Sunday-school lessons.

INTERNATIONAL Sunday school lessons; uniform lesson commentary. Philadelphia, Muhlenberg. 1963. 320p. illus. 22cm. annual. Eds. 1963--A. H. Getz, T. K. Finck. 54-37263 2.95 268.61
1. International Sunday-school lessons. I. Getz, Arthur H., ed. II. Finck, Theodore K., ed.

ISHEE, John A. 268'.61
Adults in church training [by] John A. Ishee. Nashville, Convention Press [1969] ix, 131 p. illus. 20 cm. "Text for course 6403 of subject area 64, Christian leadership series, New church study course." Bibliography: p. 113-114. [BX6225.I8] 79-85882
1. Religious education—Text-books for adults—Baptists. 2. Church group work. I. Title.

KALT, William J. 268'.61
The emerging church [by] William J. Kalt and Ronald J. Wilkins. With the special assistance of Raymond Schmandt. Chicago, Regnery [1968] 2 v. (v, 243 p.) illus., maps, ports. 23 cm. (To live is Christ. Dicusssion booklet 4-5) Includes bibliographical footnotes. [BX930.K25] 68-55750
1. Religious education—Text-books for adolescents—Catholic. I. Wilkins, Ronald J., joint author. II. Title.

KALT, William J. 268'.61
Mankind's search for meaning [by] William J. Kalt and Ronald J. Wilkins. Chicago, Regnery [1968] v, 106 p. illus. 23 cm. (To live is Christ. Discussion booklet 7) [BX930.K255] 68-55752
I. Wilkins, Ronald J., joint author. II. Title.

KALT, William J 268'.61
To live is Christ [by] William J. Kalt and Ronald J. Wilkins. Chicago, Regnery [1965- v. 23 cm. Contents.--v. 1. An overview.--v. 2. The mystery of Christ. Bibliographical footnotes. [BX930.K26] 65-21900
1. Religious education—Text-books for youth—Catholic Church. I. Wilkins, Ronald J., joint author. II. Title.

KINNEY, Dorothy W 268.61
Sore spots in society, a course for young people [by] Dorothy W. Kinney and Charles B. Kinney, Jr. Drawings by Allen M. Johson. Teacher's ed. Boston, Pilgrim Press [1953] 74p, 84p. illus. 19cm. (Pilgrim series) [BV1549.K5 1953] 268.433 53-20860
1. Religious education—Text-books for young people—Congregational. 2. Church and social problems—Study and teaching. I. Kinney, Charles B., joint author. II. Title.

KOONTZ, Ida Matilda. 268.61
Making our community friendly; a weekday church school unit in Christian citizenship series for grades one and two, [2d ed., rev.] Dayton, Ohio, Printed for the International Committee on Cooperative Publication of Weekday Church School Curriculum, by the Otterbein Press [1952] 239 p. illus. 28 cm. [BV1583.K6 1952] 52-64328
1. Week-day church schools—Teachers' manuals. 2. Church and social problems—Study and teaching. I. Title.

LE BAR, Mary Evelyn, 1910- 268.61
Patty goes to the nursery class; a year's course in twelve units for 2- and 3-year-old children. Illustrated by Faith M. Lowell. Chicago, Scripture Press, c1952. 256p. illus. 22cm. [All-Bible graded series of Sunday school lessons] [BV1540.L4 1952] [BV1540.L4 1952] 268.432 53-1723 53-1723
1. Religious education of pre-school children. I. Title.

LINK, Mark J. 268'.61
Youth in the modern world; literature, friends, Christ, action [by] Mark J. Link. Chicago, Loyola University Press [1969] xi, 243 p. illus. 23 cm. [BX930.L4863] 73-3337 2.80
1. Religious education—Text-books for young people—Catholic. I. Title.

MCDONNELL, Lois Eddy 268.61
Everyone needs a church; for use in vacation church schools; primary pupil's book. Nashville, Published for the Cooperative Publication Association [by] Abingdon Press. 23p. illus. (col.) 23cm. .25 pap.,
1. Church—Study and teaching. 2. Vacation schools, Religious—Pupil's manuals. I. Title.

MCDONNELL, Lois Eddy 268.61
Everyone needs a church; rev. ed. a cooperative vacation school text for use with primary children, teacher's textbook to accompany pupil's book by the same title. Nashville, Published for the Cooperative Pub. Association [by] Abingdon Press [c.1951, 1959] 128p. 23cm. (The Cooperative series) vacation church school texts) 51-790 1.00 pap.,
1. Church—Study and teaching. 2. Vacation schools, Religious—Teachers'manuals. I. Title.

MCKEE, Rose Knisley. 268'.61
The Christian way. Nashville, Tenn., Broadman Press [1969] 96 p. illus. 21 cm. (The Weekday Bible study series) "Student's book." [BX6225.M35] 69-10831
1. Religious education—Text-books for children—Baptist. I. Title.

MARIELLA, Sister, M.H.S.H. 268'.61
What have they done to the catechism? Paramus, N.J., Paulist Press. [1970] 30 p. illus. 19 cm. Reprinted from Pittsburgh Catholic. [BV1471.2.M34 1970] 71-112658 0.35
1. Christian education. I. Title.

MAXFIELD, Heln Adell, 1894- 268.61
The Tabernacle; director's manual. Grand Rapids, Zondervan [1950] 180 p. 20 cm. [BM654.M36] 50-4560
1. Paton, John Gibson, 2. Tabernacle—Study and teaching. I. Title.

MEIBURG, Albert L. 268'.61
Called to minister [by] Albert L. Meiburg. Nashville, Convention Press [1968] ix, 111 p. 19 cm. "Church study course [of the Sunday School Board of the Southern Baptist Convention] This book is number 0411 in category 4, section for adults and young people." Includes bibliographical references. [BX6225.M42] 68-11670
1. Service (Theology)—Study and teaching. 2. Religious education—Text-books for adults—Baptist. 3. Religious education—Text-books for young people—Baptist. I. Southern Baptist Convention. Sunday School Board. II. Title.

METHODIST Church (United States) Curriculum Committee. 268.61
Outlines of curriculum. [Nashville?] Editorial Division of the General Board of Education of the Methodist Church. v. 23 cm. annual. "A supplement to the Report of the Curriculum Committee of the General Board of Education." [BX8219.A37] 52-36210
1. Religious education — Curricula. 2. Methodist Church — Education. I. Methodist Church (United States) Board of Education. Editorial Division. II. Methodist Church (United States) Curriculum Committee. Report. Supplement. III. Title.

METHODIST Church (United States) Dept. of Children's Publications. 268.61
Resources for leaders of children. [Nashville, Methodist Pub. House] v. 23 cm. annual. Prepared by the Department of Children's Publications and the Department of Christian Education of Children. [BX8225.A1M38] 64-5644
1. Religious education — Text-books — Methodist. I. Methodist Church (United States) Dept. of Christian Education of Children. II. Title.

MONTREAL (Ecclesiastical Province) Office catechistique provincial. 268.61
Come to the Father series. 1- New York, Paulist Press [1966-] v. illus. 23 cm. Prepared by the Office catechistique provincial, Montreal. [BX930.C59] 66-24234
1. Religious education — Text-books for children — Catholic. I. Title.

NALL. FRANCES (MAHAFFIE) 1902- 268.61
It happened this way. Illustrated by John Gretzer. New York, Friendship Press [1956] 117p. illus. 21cm. [BV1548N3] 268.433 56-6580
1. Religious education—Text-books for adolescents. I. Title.

OPENING doors of faith; guidance for the Christian home children are one to five. Kansas City, Mo., Beacon Hill Press [1953] 154p. illus. 19cm. (Christian home series) [BV1590] [BV1590] 268.432 55-2957 55-2957 268.61
1. Religious education of pre-school children. I. Edwards, Mildred Speakes, 1904-

**PELOUBET'S notes.* 268.'61
Grand Rapids : Baker Books.
The 103rd annual vol. for 1976-77 is available for 4.95(pbk.)ISBN 0-8010-3345-4.

PELOUBET'S select notes on the International Bible lessons for Christian living, uniform series, v. 88-1962. Natick, Mass., Wilde [1961] xiii, 500p. illus., maps. annual. Title varies. Comp.: 1961- Wilbur M. Smith. 98-1063 2.95 bds., 268.61
1. International Sunday-school lessons. I. Peloubet, Francis Nathan, 1831-1920, comp.

PELOUBET'S select notes on the International Bible lessons for Christian teaching uniform series 1967. Natick, Mass., Wilde [1966] 436p. 22cm. annual, Pt. of the illustrative matter is colored. Title varies: 1875-1907. 19-36. 1939, Select notes on the intl. Sunday school lessons. improved uniform ser. (varies slightly).--1908- 1937-38. 1940- Peloubet's select notes on the Intl. Bible lessons for Christian teaching, uniform ser. (varies slightly) 93rd annual v. by Wilbur M. Smith [BV1560.P5] 98-1063 3.25 268.61
1. International Sunday-school lessons. I. Peloubet, Francis Nathan. 1831-1920, comp. II. Wells, Amos Russell, 1862-1933, Comp. III. Smith, Wilbur Moorehead. 1894- comp.

PELOUBET'S select notes on the International Bible lessons for Christian living; uniform ser., 1961, by Wilbur M. Smith. Natick, Mass., 10 Huron Dr. W. A. Wilde Co., [c.1960] 444p. Annual. 98-1063 2.95 268.61
1. International Sunday school lessons. I. Peloubet, Francis Nathan, 1831-1920, comp.

PELOUBET'S select notes on the International Bible lessons for Christian living, uniform ser., 1965. Natick, Mass., Wilde [c.1964] 499p. 22cm. annual. title varies. Comp.: 1965, W. M. Smith. 98-1063 2.95 bds., 268.61
1. International Sunday-School lessons. I. Smith, Wilbur Moorehead, 1894- comp.

PELOUBET'S select notes on the International Bible lessons for Christian living, uniform series;v.89. 1963. Natick, Mass., Wilde [c.1962] 447p. 22cm. annual. Title varies. Corp.: 1963, W. M. Smith. 98-1063 2.95 268.61
1. International Sunday-school lessons. I. Smith, Wilbur Moorehead, 1894- comp.

PELOUBET'S select notes on the International Bible lessons for Christian living, uniform series. 1964. Natick, Mass., Wilde [c.1963] 419p. 22cm. annual. title varies. Comp.: 1964, W. M. Smith. 98-1063 2.95 bds., 268.61
1. International Sunday-school lessons. I. Smith, Wilbur Moorehead, 1894- comp.

POINTS for emphasis; a pocket commentary. The Intl. Sunday school lessons, improved uniform ser. 1968 51st annual v. Nashville, Broadman [1967] v. 14cm. Ed.: H. C. Moore. Ed.: 1965- C. J. Allen [BV1560.P65] 35-3640 .95 268.61
1. International Sunday-School lessons. I. Moore, Hight C., 1871- II. Clifton J., ed.

POINTS for emphasis a pocket commentary [on] the international Bible lessons for Christian teaching, uniform series. 45th annual vol., 1962. [by] Clifton J. Allen. Nashville, Broadman Pr. [c.1961] 215p. 14cm. 35-3640 .95 268.61
1. International Sunday-school lessons.

POINTS for emphasis; a pocket commentary [on] the International Bible lessons for Christian teaching, uniform series. 1966. 49th annual v. [by] Clifton J. Allen. Nashville, Broadman [c.1965] 215p. 14cm. 35-3640 .95 268.61
1. International Sunday-school lessons. I. Allen, Clifton J.

POINTS for emphasis a pocket commentary. The International Bible lessons for Christian teaching, uniform series; 1961. 44th annual volume [by] Clifton J. Allen. Nashville, Tenn., Broadman Press [c.1960] 216p. map annual 14cm. 35-3640 .95 flex. lea. cl., 268.61
1. International Sunday-school lessons.

PRETE, Anthony. 268'.61
Witness catechist's handbook; theme material. Dayton, Ohio, G. A. Pflaum [1968] xvii, 78 p. illus. 21 cm. "Teacher material for Witness-Plus a doctrinal course 'The life of the Church—today and tomorrow' combined with Witness junior high 1968-1969."

Bibliographical references included in "Weekly resource guide" (p. 69-78) [BV1549.77.P7] 68-55340
1. Religious education—Text-books for adolescents—Catholic. I. Title.

PROTESTANT Episcopal 268.61
Church in the U. S. A. National Council. Dept. of Christian Education.
Right or wrong? Teacher's manual, grade 4. Rev. ed. Illus. by Gregor Thompson Goethals. Greenwich, Conn., Seabury Press [1958] 157p. illus. 21cm. (The Seabury series, T-4B) Includes bibliographies. [BV1546.P7 1958] 268.432 58-9261
1. Religious education of children. I. Title.

ROZELL, Ray. 268.61
Complete lessons, based on the International Bible lessons for Christian teaching. Uniform series, 1952. Fort Worth, Tex., Rozell [1951, c1952] 243 p. 23 cm. [BV1560.R6] 52-347
1. International Sunday-school lessons. I. An International Council of Religious Education. International Sunday School lessons. Uniform ser., 1952. II. Title.

ROZELL'S complete 268.61
lessons. 1968. Commentary on International Bible lessons uniform series. 21st annual v. Grand Rapids, Mich., Zondervan [1967] v. 23cm. Ed.: 1965- B. Ramsey [BV1560.R6] 52-347 2.95 bds.,
1. International Sunday- school lessons. I. Rozell, Lydia E. II. Ramsey, Brooks, ed.

ROZELL'S complete 268.61
lessons. 1969. Commentary on International Bible lessons uniform series. 22nd annual vol. Grand Rapids, Mich., Zondervan [1968] v. 23cm. Ed.: 1965- B. Ramsey [BV1560.R6] 52-347 3.25 bds.,
1. International Sunday-school lessons. I. Rozell, Lydia E. II. Ramsey, Brooks. ed.

ROZELL'S complete 268.61
lessons commentary on International Bible lessons uniform series, 16th v., 1963. Fort Worth, Tex., Box 11 Rozell, [c.]1963. 322p. 23cm. annual. Subtitle varies slightly. 52-347 2.95 bds.,
1. International Sunday school lessons.

ROZELL'S complete 268.61
lessons. 15th annual volume, 1962; commentary on International Bible lessons uniform series, by Ray Rozell. Fort Worth, Tex., P. O. Box 11 Rozell 318p. annual. subtitle varies. 52-347 2.95 bds.,
1. International Sunday-school lessons. I. Rozell, Ray.

ROZELL'S complete 268.61
lessons; commentary on International Bible lessons uniform series: 14th annual volume, by Ray Rozell. Fort Worth, Tex., Rozell and Co. [c.]1960. 320p. 23cm. annual. Subtitle varies slightly 52-347 2.95 bds.,
1. International Sunday-school lessons. I. Rozell. Ray.

ROZELL'S complete 268.61
lessons; commentary on International Bible lessons uniform series; v.19, 1966, by William Austin. Grand Rapids, Mich., Zondervan [c.1965] 318p. 23cm. annual. Subtitle varies. 53-347 2.95 bds.,
1. International Sunday-school lessons. I. Rozell, Lydia E., II. Austin, William.

ROZELL'S complete 268.61
lessons; commentary on International Bible lessons uniform series, 1967. 20th annual v. Grand Rapids, Mich., Zondervan [c.1966] 317p. 23cm. Ed.: 1967--Rev. Brooks Ramsey [BV1560.R6] 52-347 2.95 bds.,
1. International Sunday-school lessons. I. Rozell, Lydia E. II. Ramsey, Brooks, ed.

ROZELL'S complete 268.61
lessons commentary on International Bible lessons uniform series; v.17, 1964. Continued by Lydia E. Rozell, managing ed., Rev. Bill Austin, ed. Fort Worth, Texas, Rozell [1963, c.1964] 320p. 23cm. annual. Subtitle varies slightly. 52-347 2.95 bds.,
1. International Sunday-school lessons. I. Rozell, Lydia E. II. Austin, Bill.

ROZELL'S complete 268.61
lessons commentary on International Bible lessons uniforms series; v.18, 1965. Continued by Lydia E. Rozell, managing ed., Rev. Bill Austin, ed. Rozell & Co. [dist. Grand Rapids, Mich., Zondervan, 1964, c.1965] 319p. 23cm. annual. Subtitle varies slightly. 53-347 2.95 bds.,
1. International Sunday-school lessons. I. Rozell, Lydia E. II. Austin, Bill.

SEVENTH-DAY Adventists. 268.61
General Conference. Dept. of Education.
Witness s for Jesus; Bible lessons for grades 7 and 8. [Teacher's ed.] Mountain View, Calif., Pacific Press Pub. Association for the Dept. of Education, General Conference of Seventh-Day Adventists [1952] 134, 520p. illus. 24cm. 'Series IV degree, odd year.' The main work, also issued separately, is preceded by 'Teacher's guide and key for Witnesses for Jesus,' with special t.p. [BX6155.S45 1952a] [BX6155.S45 1952a] 268.432 56-17682 56-17682
1. Religious education— Text-books for children—Seventh-Day Adventists. I. Title.

SEVENTH-DAY Adventists. 268.61
General Conferences. Dept. of Education.
Witnesses for Jesus; Bible lessons for grades 7 and 8. Mountain View, Calif., Pacific Press Pub. Association for the Dept. of Education, General Conference of Seventh-Day Adventists [1952] 520p. illus. 24cm. 'Series IVdegree, odd year.' [BX6155.S45] [BX6155.S45] 268.432 52-14730 52-14730
1. Religions education—Text-books for children—Seventh-Day Adventists. I. Title.

STANDARD lesson 268.61
commentary, v. 1- 1954- Cincinnati. Standard Pub. Co. v. illus., maps. 28cm. [BV1560.S747] 54-17065
1. International Sunday-school lessons.

STANDARD lesson 268.61
commentary; v. 8, 1961. International Sunday School Lessons. Orrin Root, ed.-in-chief. Cincinnati, Standard Pub. Co. c.1960 448p. illus., maps. 25cm. 54-17065 2.95
1. International Sunday-school lessons.

STANDARD lesson 268.61
commentary, 1962. v.9. Ed.-in-chief: Orrin Root; Ed.: John W. Wade. Cincinnati, Standard Pub. Co. [1961, c.1958] viii, 448p. illus., maps. 25cm. annual. 54-17065 2.95 bds.,
1. International Sunday-school lessons.

STANDARD lesson 268.61
commentary, v. 10, 1963. International Sunday School Lessons. Orrin Root, ed.-in-chief; John W. Wade, ed. Cincinnati, Standard Pub. Co., c.1962. 447p. illus., maps. 28cm. annual. 54-17065 2.95 bds.,
1. International Sunday-school lessons.

STANDARD lesson 268.61
commentary; v. 13, 1966. International Sunday School Lessons. Orrin Root. ed.-in-chief; J. W. Yarbrough, James I. Fehl, eds. Cincinnati, Ohio, Standard Pub. Co., c.1965. 448p. illus. 25cm. annual. 54-17065 3.25 bds.,
1. International Sunday-School lessons.

STANDARD lesson 268.61
commentary; v.11, 1964. International Sunday School Lessons. Orrin Root, ed.-in-chief; John W. Wade, John M. Carter, Sr., eds. Cincinnati, Ohio, Standard Pub. Co., c.1963. 4448p. illus., maps. 25cm. annual. 54-17065 2.95 bds.,
1. International Sunday-school lessons.

STITH, Marjorie M. 268'.61
Understanding children [by] Marjorie Stith. Nashville, Convention Press [1969] 172 p. illus. 21 cm. (Basic books for persons who guide children, first through sixth grades) "Text for course 2102 of subject area 1 of the New church study course." Bibliography: p. 156-163. [HQ772.S756] 70-98045
1. Child psychology. I. Title.

TARBELL'S teacher's 268.61
guide to the International Bible Lessons for Christian teaching of the Uniform course for 1969.
This, the 64th annual vol. is now available from Revell, Westwood, N.J. for $3.25, bds. L.C. card order no.: 5-40811 rev*

TARBELL'S teacher's 268.61
guide to the International Bible Lessons for Christian teaching of the uniform courses for 1962. 57th v. [Westwood, N.J.] Revell [c.1961] 384p. illus. annual. Title varies slightly. Ed.: 1961--Frank S. Mead. 5-40811 2.95 bds.,
I. International Sunday-school lessons.

TARBELL'S Teachers' 268.61
guide to the International Bible lessons for Christian teaching of the uniform courses for 1964; v.59. [Westwood, N.J.] Revell [c.1963] 382p. 22cm. annual. Ed.: 1963--Frank S. Mead. Bibl. 5-40811 2.95 bds.,
1. International Sunday-school lessons. I. Mead, Frank Spencer, 1898- ed.

TARBELL'S teachers' 268.61
guide to the International Bible Lessons for Christian teaching of the uniform courses for 1963; v. 58. [Westwood, N.J.] Revell [c.1962] 384p. illus. 23cm. annual. Title varies slightly. Ed.: 1962--Frank S. Mead. 5-40811 2.95 bds.,
1. International Sunday-school lessons. I. Mead, Frank Spencer, ed. ed.

TARBELL'S teacher's guide 268.61
to the International Bible lessons for Christian teaching of the uniform course for 1966. Ed. by Frank, S. Mead. 61st annual v. Westwood, N.J., Revell [c.1965] 384p. 22cm. annual. Bibl. 5-40811 2.95 bds.,
1. International Sunday-school lessons. I. Mead, Frank Spencer, 1898- ed.

TARBELL'S teacher's guide 268.61
to the International Bible lessons for Christian teaching of the uniform course for 1957. Ed. by Frank S. Mead. 62d annual v. Westwood, N.J., Revell [c.1966] xv, 376p. 22cm. annual. Bibl. 5-40811 3.25 bds.,
1. International Sunday-school lessons. I. Mead, Frank Spencer, 1898- ed.

TARBELL'S teachers guide 268.61
to the International Bible Lessons for Christian teaching of the uniform course for 1961. Edited by Frank S. Mead. 56th annual volume. [Westwood, N.J.] Fleming H. Revell Co. [c.1960] 384p. endpaper maps. 22cm. annual. Title varies slightly. Editors: 1906-49, M. Tarbell (with W. G. Chanter, 1948-49)- 1951- F. S. Mead. 5-40811 2.95 bds.,
1. International Sunday-school lessons. I. Tarbell, Martha, ed. II. Mead, Frank Spencer, ed.

TORREY, Reuben Archer 268.61
The gist of the lesson; a concise exposition of the International Sunday school lessons for 1960. Originated by R. A. Torrey. Edited by Donald T. Kauffman. Westwood, N.J. Fleming H. Revell Co. c.1959 160p. 13 x 9 cm. 0-5600 1.00 bds.,
1. International Sunday-school lessons. I. Title.

TORREY, Reuben Archer, 268.61
1856-1928
The gist of the lesson; a concise exposition of the International Sunday school lessons for the year 1962. Ed. by Donald T. Kauffman. [Westwood, N.J.] Revell [c.1961] 128p. 14cm. 0-5600 1.25
1. International Sunday-school lessons. I. Title.

TORREY, Reuben Archer, 268.61
1856-1928
The gist of the lesson; a concise exposition of the International Sunday School Lessons for 1964. Originated by R. A. Torrey. Ed. by Donald T. Kaufmann [Westwood, N.J.] Revell [c.1963] 125p. 14cm. 0-5600 1.25 bds.,
1. International Sunday School Lessons. I. Title.

WEST, Richard F. 268'.61
Christian decision and action; a resource and discussion book for youth [by] Richard F. West. Illustrated by Don Herzbach. [Rev. ed. New York] Herder and Herder [1968] 76 p. illus. 22 cm. (Christian commitment series) [BJ1261.W43 1968b] 68-29887 1.20
1. Christian ethics. 2. Religious education—Text-books for young people—United Church of Christ. I. Herzbach, Don, illus. II. Title.

WILLIAMS, Alfred E 268'.61
Dilemmas and decisions; a resource and discussion book for youth [by] Alfred E. Williams, Jr. Boston, United Church Press [1968] 76 p. illus. 22 cm. (Confirmation education series) "Part of the United Church curriculum, prepared and published by the Division of Christian Education and the Division of Publication of the United Church Board for homeland Ministries. Bibliographical references included in "Notes and acknowledgements" (p. 74-76) [BV4531.2.W54] 68-10314
1. Christian life—United Church of Christ authors. 2. Religious education—Text-books for young people—United Church of Christ. I. United Church Board for Homeland Ministries. Division of Christian Education. II. United Church Board for Homeland Ministries. Division of Publication. III. Title.

WILLIAMS, Alfred E. 268'.61
Dilemmas and decisions; a resource and discussion book for youth [by] Alfred E. Williams, Jr. [Rev. ed. New York] Herder and Herder [1968] 76 p. illus. 22 cm. (Christian commitment series) Bibliography: p. 73-74. [BV4531.2.W54 1968b] 68-29892 1.20
1. Youth—Religious life. 2. Religious education—Text-books for young people—United Church of Christ. I. Title.

WILLIAMS, Alfred E. 268'.61
Dilemmas and decisions; a resource and discussion book for youth [by] Alfred E. Williams, Jr. Boston, United Church Press [1968] 76 p. illus. 22 cm. (Confirmation education series) "Part of the United Church curriculum, prepared and published by the Division of Christian Education and the Division of Christian Education and the Division of Publication of the United Church Board for Homeland Ministries." Bibliographical references included in "Notes and acknowledgements" (p. 74-76) [BV4531.2.W54] 68-10314
1. Youth—Religious life. 2. Religious education—Text-books for young people—United Church of Christ. I. United Church Board for Homeland Ministries. Division of Christian Education. II. United Church Board for Homeland Ministries. Division of Publication. III. Title.

TARBELL'S 268.61-5-40811 rev*
teacher's guide, to the International Bible Lessons for Christian Teaching of the uniform course for 1964; v.60. Westwood, N.J., Revell [c.1964] 382p. 22cm. annual. Ed.: 1964--Frank S. Mead. Bibl. 2.95 bds.,
1. International Sunday-School lessons. I. Mead, Frank Spencer, 1898- ed.

GREEN, Hollis L. 268.62
Dynamics of Christian discipleship. an adventure in Christian living. Cleveland, Tenn., Pathway, c.1962. 112p. 21cm. Bibl. 1.50
I. Title.

JENKINS, David L. 268'.62
Openings to understandings; (student's book for use primarily by older youth) Writers: David L. Jenkins, Floyd A. Craig, and Val Harvey. Editor: Thomas L. Clark. Nashville, Convention Press, c1971. 98 p. illus. 28 x 11 cm. At head of title: Learning at home and church. [BX6225.J45] 72-185016
1. Religious education—Text-books for young people—Baptist. I. Craig, Floyd A. II. Harvey, Val. III. Title.

LUTHERAN Church. Missouri 268.62
Synod. Board for Parish Education
Graded memory course for Lutheran Sunday-schools and other institutions. Dr. Martin Luther's Small catechism with correlated Bible-passages, hymn stanzas, prayers, and Bible-story references. Published by the Board of Christian St. Louis, Mo., Concordia publishing house, 1933. 63 p. 18 1/2 cm. [BX8015.L8] 39-1484
1. Religious education — Text books for children — Lutheran. I. Title.

LUTHERAN Church. Missouri 268.62
Synod. Board for Parish Education
Graded memory course for Lutheran Sunday-schools and other institutions. Dr. Martin Luther's Small catechism with correlated Bible-passages, hymn stanzas, prayers, and Bible-story references. Published by the Board of Christian education of the Evangelical Lutheran synod of Missouri, Ohio, and other states. St. Louis, Mo., Concordia publishing house, 1933. 63 p. 18 1/2 cm. [BX8015.L8] 39-1484
1. Religious education — Text books for children — Lutheran. I. Title.

FORD, LeRoy. 268'.632
Using the lecture in teaching and training. Illustrated by Doug Dillard. Nashville, Broadman Press [1968] 127 p. illus. 21 cm. [BV1534.F6] 68-20673
1. Religious education—Teaching methods. 2. Lecture method in teaching. I. Dillard, Samuel D., illus. II. Title.

THE Audio-visual man. 268'.635
Edited by Pierre Babin. Translated by C. Belisle [and others] Dayton, Ohio, Pflaum, 1970. v, 218 p. illus. 24 cm. Translation of Audio-visuel et foi. Bibliography: p. 216-217. [BV1535.A7613] 70-133407 5.95
1. Religious education—Audio-visual aids—Addresses, essays, lectures. 2. Audio-visual education—Addresses, essays, lectures. I. Babin, Pierre, ed.

BARNETT, Stella Odell, 268.635
1903-
Better chalk talks. With devotions by Quentin M. Perreault and Reve Stewart Perreault. [Westwood, N. J.] Revell [1958] 127p. illus. 20cm. [BV4227.B29] 58-5345
1. Chalk-talks. 2. Worship programs. I. Title.

BISHOP, David S. 268'.635
Effective communication / David S. Bishop. Cleveland, Tenn. : Pathway Press, c1977. 112 p. : ill. ; 21 cm. (Church training course ; 704) Bibliography: p. 111-112. [BV4319.B57] 76-58043 ISBN 0-87148-285-1 : 2.50 pbk. : 1.95
1. Communication (Theology) 2. Christian education—Audio-visual aids. I. Title.

DALGLISH, William A. 268'.635
Media for Christian formation; a guide to audio-visual resources. William A. Dalglish, editor; Roger E. Beaubien [and] Walter R. Laude, associate editors. Dayton, Ohio, G. A. Pflaum, 1969. xix, 393 p. illus. 23 cm. [BV1535.Z9D3] 78-79711 7.50
1. Religious education—Audio-visual aids—Catalogs. I. Beaubien, Roger E., joint author. II. Laude, Walter R., joint author. III. Title.

FORD, LeRoy. 268'.635
Using audiovisuals in religious education / LeRoy Ford. Nashville : Convention Press, [1974] 128 p. : ill. ; 20 cm. "This book is the text for course 6912 of subject area 69,

Program and Administrative Services of the Church Study Course [Sunday School Board, Southern Baptist Convention]" Bibliography: p. 121-125. [BV1535.F65] 75-302520
1. Religious education—Audio-visual aids. I. Southern Baptist Convention. Sunday School Board. II. Title.

GETZ, Gene A. 268'.635
Audiovisual media in Christian education, by Gene A. Getz. Chicago, Moody Press [1972] 236 p. illus. 27 cm. Published in 1959 under title: Audio-visuals in the church. Bibliography: p. 231-232. [BV1535.G46 1972] 73-181587 ISBN 0-8024-0365-4 5.95
1. Church work—Audio-visual aids. I. Title.

HARRELL, John Grinnell, 268.635
1922-
Teaching is communicating; an audio-visual handbook for church use, by John Harrell. New York, Seabury Press [1965] 142 p. illus. 20 cm. [BV1535.H3] 64-19631
1. Religious education — Audio-visual aids. I. Title.

HARRELL, John Grinnell, 268.635
1922-
Teaching is communicating; an audio-visual handbook for church use. New York, Seabury [c.1965] 142p. illus. 20cm. Bibl. [BV1535.H3] 64-19631 3.95
1. Religious education—Audio-visual aids. I. Title.

MCNULTY, Edward N., 268'.635
1936-
Television, a guide for Christians / Ed McNulty. Nashville : Abingdon, c1976. 96 p. : ill. ; 21 cm. Bibliography: p. 94-96. [BV656.3.M3] 76-1990 ISBN 0-687-41220-X pbk. : 3.50
1. Television in religion. I. Title.

ROBINSON, James Herman. 268'.635
Bulletin board ideas; for weekday and Sunday school teachers [by] James H. and Rowena D. Robinson. St. Louis, Concordia Pub. House [1973] 61 p. illus. 28 cm. [BV1535.25.R6] 72-94108 ISBN 0-570-03141-9 1.75 (pbk.)
1. Bulletin boards in religious education. I. Robinson, Rowena D., joint author. II. Title.

RUMPF, Oscar, 1903- 268.635
The use of audio-visuals in the church. Illustrated by Anna R. Atene. Philadelphia, Christian Education Press [1958] 150p. illus. 21cm. Includes bibliography. [BV1535.R8] 58-11703
1. Religious education—Audio-visual aids. I. Title.

TOWER, Howard E 268.635
Church use of audio-visuals. New York, Abingdon-Cokesbury Press [c1950] 152 p. illus. 21 cm. Bibliography: p. 152. [BV1643.T6] 51-9632
1. Audio-visual education. I. Title.

THE use and misuse of 268'.635
visual arts in religious education / edited by Celia T. Hubbard ; introd. by Mary Perkins Ryan. Glen Rock, N.J. : Paulist Press, 1966. 96 p. : ill. ; 21 cm. (Let's see ; no. 1) Includes bibliographical references. [BV150.U76] 66-18517
1. Christian art and symbolism. 2. Religious education—Audio-visual aids. I. Hubbard, Celia T.

PARKER, Everett C 268.6353
Film use in the church, by Everett C. Parker [and others] New York, Broadcasting and Film Commission, National Council of the Churches of Christ in the United States [c1955] 78p. 28cm. (Studies in the mass media of communication) [BV1643.P3] 56-786
1. Religious education—Audio-visual aids. I. Title.

WORLD Council of 268.63530838
Christian Education and Sunday School Association. North American Administrative Committee.
Slide and film strip evaluations for use in Christian churches around the world. Published cooperatively by the North American Administrative Committee, World Council of Chirstian Education and Sunday School Association, and Committee on Radio, Audio Visual Education and Mass Communication, Division of Foreign Missions, National Council of Churches of Christ in the U. S. A. New York [1953- v. illus. 22cm. Introd. to pt. 1 signed: Erich F. Voehringer. [BV1643.W62] 53-34243
1. Moving pictures—Catalogs. I. National Council of the Churches of Christ in the United States of America Division of Foreign Missions. Committee on Radio Audio Visual Education and Mass Communication. II. Voehringer. Erich Frederick, 1905- III. Title.

BARNETT, Stella Odell, 268.6357
1903-
How to make chalk talk. Westwood, N. J., Revell ['1951] 96 p. illus. 20 cm. [BV4227.B3] 52-6688
1. Chalk-talks. I. Title.

BRECK, Flora Elizabeth, 268.67
1886-
Playlets and poems for church school (for teaching Bible truths) Boston, W. A. Wilde Co. [1954] 50p. 22cm. [BV1573.B7] 54-10180
1. Sunday-schools—Exercises, recitations, etc. I. Title.

BRUCE, Violet Rose 268.67
Lord of the dance: an approach to religious education. by Violet R. Bruce. Joan D. Tooke. [1st ed.] Oxford. New York, Pergamon [1966] xi, 112p. illus. 20cm. (Commonwealth & intl. lib.) Bibl. [BV1536.5.B7 1966] 66-23844 2.95 pap.,
1. Dancing in religious education. I. Tooke. Joan D., joint author. II. Title.

EDYVEAN, Alfred R. 268'.67
This dramatic world; using contemporary drama in the church [by] Alfred R. Edyvean. New York, Friendship Press [1970] 96 p. 18 cm. Bibliography: p. [86]-94. [PS351.E3] 77-102948 1.50
1. American drama—20th century—History and criticism. 2. Religion in drama. I. Title.

MYERS, Galene J 268.67
Puppets can teach too; using puppetry in religious education, By Galene J. Myers. Illus. adapted by Betty Ellingboe. Minneapolis, Augsburg Pub. House [1966] 64 p. illus., ports. 26 cm. Bibliography: p. 61. [BV1535.9.P8M9] 66-13058
1. Puppets and puppet-plays in religious education. I. Title.

MYERS, Galene J. 268.67
Puppets can teach too; using puppetry in religious education. Illus. adapted by Betty Ellingboe. Minneapolis. Augsburg [c.1966] 64p. illus., ports. 26cm. Bibl. [BV1535.9.P8.M9] 66-13058 3.50, pap., plastic bdg.
1. Puppets and puppet-plays in religious education. I. Title.

REYNOLDS, Joyce. 268'.67
Puppet shows that reach & teach children. Springfield, Mo., Gospel Pub. House [1972-74] 2 v. illus. 29 cm. [BV1535.9.P8R48] 73-185586 5.90
1. Puppets and puppet-plays in Christian education. I. Title.

REYNOLDS, Joyce. 268'.67
Puppet shows that reach & teach children. Springfield, Mo., Gospel Pub. House [1972] 62 p. illus. 29 cm. [BV1535.9.P8R48] 73-185586 2.95
1. Puppets and puppet-plays in religious education. I. Title.

*SEGER, Doris Louise. 268.67
Teen programs that click. Chicago, Moody [1967] 93p. illus. 22cm. 1.77 pap.,
1. Drama in religious education. 2. Games in religious education. I. Title.

SYLWESTER, Roland. 268'.67
Teaching Bible stories more effectively with puppets / Roland Sylwester. St. Louis : Concordia Pub. House, c1976. p. cm. Bibliography: p. [BS546.S9] 76-10179 ISBN 0-570-03261-X pbk. : 2.50
1. Bible stories. 2. Puppets and puppet-plays in Christian education. I. Title.

WARGO, Dan 268.67
Dramatics in the Christian school. by Dan and Dorothy Wargo, Photos, by Robert Hochstaetter. St. Louis, Concordia 1966. viii, 124p. illus. 28cm. Bibl. [BV1534.4.W3] 66-22354 5.25
1. Drama in religious education. I. Wargo, Dorothy, joint author. II. Title.

ADCOCK, Mabel. 268.68
Creative activities, by Mabel Adcock and Elsie Blackwell. Illus. by Vera Gohman. Anderson, Ind., Warner Press [1964] 64 p. illus. 28 cm. [BV1536.A3] 64-12624
1. Creative activities and seat work. 2. Religious education of children. I. Blackwell, Elsie, joint author. II. Title.

ADCOCK, Mabel 268.68
Creative activities, by Mabel Adcock, Elsie Blackwell. Illus. by Vera Gohman. Anderson, Ind., Warner [c.1964] 64p. illus. 28cm. 64-12624 1.95, pap., plastic bdg.
1. Creative activities and seat work. 2. Religious education of children. I. Blackwell, Elsie, joint author. II. Title.

LEE, Carvel 268.68
The Sunday school bulletin board guide, by Carvel and Lorita Lee. Illus. by the authors. Minneapolis, Denison [c.1963] 63p. col. illus. 28 cm. 1.85 pap.,
I. Title.

LOBINGIER, Elizabeth Erwin 268.68
(Miller) 1889-
Activities in child education for the church school teacher. With drawings by children. Boston, Pilgrim Press [1950] xiv, 226 p. illus. 23 cm. Bibliography: p. 221-224. [BV1535.L55] 50-7946
1. Religious education of children—Occupations and busy work. I. Title.

*MAUCH, Theodor 268.68
David, a Bible study; pts. A & B; pupil's program booklet 1. Programed by Elizabeth Rooney, New York, Seabury [c.1965] 54p. 27cm. (Seabury ser.; the Church's teaching for closely graded schs.) price unreported. pap.,
I. Title.

MILLER, Elfrieda, 1905- 268.68
Religious arts and crafts for children. Saint Louis, Concordia [1966] xvi, 269p. illus., maps. 27cm. Bibl. [BV1536.M48] 66-14568 7.50
1. Creative activities and seat work. 2. Religious education of children. I. Title.

BROWN, Jeanette (Perkins), 268.69
1887-
The storyteller in religious education; how to tell stories to children and young people. Boston, Pilgrim Press [1951] x, 165 p. illus. 20 cm. A Co-operative book published for the Co-operative Publication Association. Bibliography: p. 157-163. [BV1472.B7] 51-3076
1. Religious education. 2. Story-telling. I. Title.

ROYAL, Claudia. 268.69
Storytelling. Nashville, Broadman Press [1956, c1955] 132p. illus. 21cm. [BV1472.R66] 56-1570
1. Story-telling. 2. Religious education. I. Title.

APPLEGARTH, Margaret Tyson, 268.7
1886-
Right here, right now ! [1st ed.] New York, Harper [1950] vii, 269 p. 22 cm. [BV198.A63] 50-9843
1. Worship programs. I. Title.

BAYS, Alice (Anderson) 268.7
Worship programs for juniors [by] Alice Anderson Bays and Elizabeth Jones Oakberg. Nashville, Abingdon Press [c.1960] 206p. 21cm. Bibl.: p.199-204. 60-12065 3.00
1. Worship programs. 2. Worship (Religious education) I. Oakberg, Elizabeth Jones, joint author. II. Title.

BAYS, Alice (Anderson) 268.7
1892-
Worship programs for juniors [by] Alice Anderson Bays and Elizabeth Jones Oakberg. New York, Abingdon Press [1960] 206p. 21cm. Includes bibliography. [BV1522.B29] 60-12065
1. Worship programs. 2. Worship (Religious education) I. Oakberg, Elizabeth Jones, joint author. II. Title.

BAYS, Alice (Anderson) 268.7
1892-
Worship services for life planning. Nashville, Abingdon-Cokesbury Press [c1958] 256p. 21cm. [BV29.B355] 52-11311
1. Worship programs. 2. Young people's meetings (Church work) I. Title.

BRYANT, Al [Thomas Alton 268.7
Bryant] 1926- ed.
Encyclopedia of devotional programs for women's groups, no. 2. Grand Rapids, Mich., Zondervan [c.1961] 224p. 1.95 pap.,
1. Worship programs. 2. Woman—Religious life I. Title.

ENGSTROM, Theodore Wilhelm 268.7
Fifty-two workable junior high programs, by Ted W. Engstrom and Warren W. Wiersbe, Grand Rapids, Mich., Zondervan Pub. House. [c.1960] 116p. 20cm. 2.00 bds.,
1. Worship programs. 2. Young people's meetings (Church work) I. Title.

ENGSTROM, Theodore Wilhelm, 268.7
1916-
52 workable young people's programs. Grand Rapids, Zondervan [1950] 177 p. 20 cm. [BV29.E5] 51-16
1. Worship programs. 2. Young people's meetings (church work) I. Title.

HALL, Donald E 1923- 268.7
Tested youth programs; 52 different young people's programs. Grand Rapids, Zondervan Pub. House [c1958] 121p. illus. 20cm. [BV29.H32] 59-29219
1. Worship programs. 2. Young peoples' meetings (Church work) I. Title.

HERZEL, Catherine B. 268.7
Helping children worship [Philadelphia, Lutheran Church Pr., 1964, c.1963] 142p. col. illus. 21cm. (LCA leadership educa. ser.) 64-4213 1.50; .50 teacher's guide, pap.,
I. Title.

*JACOBS, J. Vernon 268.7
How to plan and conduct Sunday school worship services. Grand Rapids, Mich., Zondervan [c.1964] 63p. 20cm. (Sunday sch. know-how ser.) 1.00 pap.,
I. Title.

JACOBS, James Vernon, 1898- 268.7
How to plan and conduct Sunday school worship services, by J. Veronon Jacobs. Grand Rapids, Zondervan Pub. House [1964] 63 p. 21 cm. (Sunday school know-how series) "No. 9947p;" [BV1522.J3] 64-5210
1. Worship (Religious education) I. Title.

LILYERS, Jean 268.7
Sing of Christmas, a Christmas service for church school. Rock Island, Ill., Augustana Press [c.1960] 16p. illus., diagrs. 21cm. .10 pap.,
I. Title.

MCGAVRAN, Grace Winifred 268.7
Learning how children worship. Illus. by James A. Scott. St. Louis. Pub. for the Cooperative Pubn. Assn. by Bethany [c.1964] 192p. illus. 20cm. (Cooperative ser.) Bibl. 64-21304 2.95 bds.,
1. Worship (Religious education) I. Title.

NOVOTNY, Louise (Miller) 268.7
1889-
52 practical programs for young people Grand Rapids, Zondervan Pub. House [1957] 147p. 20cm. [BV29.N6] 57-2400
1. Worship programs. 2. Young people's meetings (Church work) I. Title.

RABALAIS, Maria. 268'.7
Children, celebrate! Resources for youth liturgy, by Maria Rabalais [and] Howard Hall. New York, Paulist Press [1974] 137 p. 25 cm. Bibliography: p. 131-137. [BV1522.R25] 73-94212 ISBN 0-8091-1820-3 3.95 (pbk.).
1. Worship (Religious education) I. Hall, Howard, 1936- joint author. II. Title.

ROCKWELL, Katharine 268'.7
Lambert (Richards) 1891-
How Christmas came to the Sunday-schools; the observance of Christmas in the Protestant church schools of the United States, an historical study, by Katharine Lambert Richards. New York, Dodd, Mead, 1934. Ann Arbor, Mich., Gryphon Books, 1971. ix, 292 p. 22 cm. Originally presented as the author's thesis, Columbia University, 1934. Includes bibliographical references. [BV1572.C5R5 1971] 70-159860
1. Christmas. 2. Sunday-schools—U.S. I. Title.

VIETH, Paul Herman, 1895- 268.7
Worship in Christian education [by] Paul H. Vieth. Philadelphia, United Church Press [1965] 174 p. 21 cm. Bibliographical footnotes. [BV1522.V5] 65-18875
1. Worship (Religious education) I. Title.

VIETH, Paul Herman, 1895- 268.7
Worship in Christian education. Philadelphia, United Church [c.1965] 174p. 21cm.bBibl. [BV1522.V5] 65-18875 3.00
1. Worship (Religious education) I. Title.

WOOD, Letitia W 268.7
Dynamic worship programs for young people. Boston, Wilde [1950] 198 p. 20 cm. [BV29.W6] 51-747
1. Worship programs. 2. Young people's meetings (Church work) I. Title.

COON, Zula Evelyn. 268.73
O worship the King; services in song. Nashville, Broadman Press [1951] 237 p. 23 cm. [BV198.C83] 51-6898
1. Worship programs. I. Title.

*DELAFIELD, D. A. 268.73
Elena G. de White y la Iglesia Adventista del Septimo Dia. Mountain View, Calif., Pacific Pr. Pub. Co. [c.1965] 96p. illus. (pt. col.) 18cm. Spanish tr. .50 pap.,
I. Title.

VERKUYL, Gerrit, 1872- 268.73
Teen-age worship; with a chapter on teaching the elements of worship, by Harold E. Garner. Chicago, Moody Press, 1950. 192 p. illus. 20cm. Includes bibliographies. [BV1522.V4] 50-10998
1. Worship (Religious education) 2. Adolescence. I. Garner, Harold Eugene, 1907- II. Title.

BRECK, Flora Elizabeth, 268.76
1886-
Special day programs and selections, for church and Sunday school. Boston, W. A.

Wilde Co. [1951] 142 p. illus. 20 cm. [BV1572.A1B7] 51-14489
1. Sunday-schools—Exercises, recitations, etc. I. Title.

BRILLHART, Florence C 268.76
Worshiping with women of the Bible a book of devotions. [Westwood, N. J.] Revell [1958] 150p. 21cm. [BV199.W6B72] 58-5341
1. Worship programs. 2. Women in the Bible. I. Title.

SUNDELOF-ASBRAND, Karin. 268.76
Easy programs for church holidays. Boston, Baker's Plays [1953] 104 p. illus. 19 cm. [BV1572.A1S8] 55-3990
1. Festivals. I. Title.

MAC LEAN, Angus Hector, 268'.8'04
1892-
The idea of God in Protestant religious education. New York, Bureau of Publications, Teachers College, Columbia University, 1930. [New York, AMS Press, 1973, c1972] vi, 150 p. illus. 22 cm. Reprint of the 1930 ed., issued in series: Teachers College, Columbia University. Contributions to education, no. 410. Originally presented as the author's thesis, Columbia. Bibliography: p. 149-150. [BT108.M3 1972] 75-177033 ISBN 0-404-55410-5 10.00
1. God. 2. Religious education—Curricula. 3. Children—Religious life. I. Title. II. Series: Columbia University. Teachers College. Contributions to education, no. 410.

IMBAKOM Kalewold, 1917- 268'.8'17
Traditional Ethiopian church education. Translated by Menghestu Lemma. New York, Teachers College press [1970] xiv, 41 p. maps. 23 cm. (Publications of the Center for Education in Africa) Includes bibliographical references. [BV1470.E8I413] 70-93506
1. Ethiopic Church—Education. 2. Christian education—Ethiopia. I. Title. II. Series: Columbia University. Center for Education in Africa. Publications

NEUSER, Heinz. 268'.8'17
Religiose Erziehung in berufsbildenden Schulen : Aspekte z. didakt. u. theolog. Begrundung u. Rechtfertigung / Heinz Neuser. Als Ms. vervielf. Munster : Dt. Inst. f. Wiss. Padagogik, 1975. 460 p. ; 30 cm. (D.I.P.-Studien ; Nr. 1) Originally presented as the author's thesis, Ratisbon, 1974. Bibliography: p. 425-459. [BV1470.G3N48 1975] 75-522639
1. Christian education—Germany, West. 2. Vocational education—Germany, West. 3. Trade schools—Germany, West. I. Title. II. Series: Munster. Deutsches Institut fur Wissenschaftliche Padagogok. D.I.P.-Studien ; Nr. 1.

BECKER, Antoinette 268.82
Children ask about God and everything; a book for mothers and teachers [Tr. from German by M. Dolores Sablone. New York] Herder & Herder [c.1966] 221p. 21cm. [BV1475.2.B413] 66-13078 4.50
1. Children's questions and answers. 2. Religious education of children. I. Title.

BECKER, Antoinette. 268.82
Children ask about God and everything; a book for mothers and teachers. [Translation by M. Dolores Sablone. New York] Herder and Herder [1966] 221 p. 21 cm. [BV1475.2.B413] 66-13078
1. Children's questions and answers. 2. Religious education of children. I. Title.

CATECHESIS, realities 268'.8'2
and visions : a symposium on the catechesis of children and youth. Washington : Dept. of Education, United States Catholic Conference, c1977. 194 p. ; 27 cm. Cover title. [BV1475.2.C33] 77-155726
1. Christian education of children—Congresses. 2. Christian education of adolescents—Congresses. 3. Christian education of young people—Congresses. I. United States Catholic Conference. Dept. of Education.

CATHOLIC Church. Diocese 268'.82
of Green Bay, Wis. Dept. of Education.
The Green Bay Plan. [Green Bay] 1971. 239 p. 29 cm. [BX929.A47] 77-175854
1. Religious education—Curricula. 2. Religious education—Philosophy. I. Title.

CATHOLIC University of 268.82
America. Workshop on Religious Education through the Confraternity of Christian Doctrine, 1960.
Religious education through CCD the proceedings of the Workshop on Religious Education through the Confraternity of Christian Doctrine, conducted at the Catholic University of America, June 10 to 21, 1960. Edited by Joseph B. Collins. Washington, Catholic University of America Press, 1961. vii, 164p. 22cm. Includes bibliographies. [BX926.C3 1960] 61-1944
1. Catholic Church—Education. 2. Confraternity of Christian Doctrine. I. Collins, Joseph Burns, 1897- ed. II. Title.

CONFRATERNITY of Christian 268.82
Doctrine.
Manual of the parish Confraternity of Christian Doctrine for priests, religious, seminarians and laity promoting Confraternity activities 8th ed. With discussion aids based on the content of each section. [Washington, 1952, c1950] 122p. 19cm. [BX809.C6A35 1952] 53-26417
I. Title.

THE Confratternity comes 268.82
of age, a historical symposium. Paterson. N. J., Confraternity Publications, 1956. xiii, 310p. 24cm. Includes bibliographies. [BX809.C6C63 1956] 56-58928
1. Confratenity of Christian Doctrine.

COONEY, Eugene J. 268.8'2
A murmur within me; theological themes of Come to the Father, by Eugene J. Cooney. New York, Paulist Press [1973] 134 p. 23 cm. Bibliography: p. 131-134. [BX930.C64] 72-94110 ISBN 0-8091-1762-2 4.50
1. Religious education—Text-books for adults—Catholic. I. Title.

COUDREAU, Francois 268.82
The child and the problem of faith. Tr. by Sister Gertrude. With discussion questions. Glen Rock, N.J., Paulist [1966] 92p. 18cm. (Deus bks.) [BX925.C6813] 66-22052 .75 pap.,
1. Religious education of children. 2. Catholic Church—Education. I. Title.

*GLYNN, Jeanne Davis 268.82
If I were an angel. Pictures by Irene Otani. New York, Guild, c.1965. 1v. (unpaged) col. illus. 19cm. (Little angel bk., 30910) .25 pap.,
1. Religious instruction—Catholic authors. I. Title.

*HENNESSY, Denys 268.82
Hear me; bk. 1. Consultants: Charles M. Walsh, John P. Wodarski, David J. Coffey. Morristown, N.J., Silver Burdett [c.1964] 172p. col. illus. 28cm. (Learn of me ser.) Contents.bk. 1. The Creed. 1.20 pap.,
I. Title.

LITTLE children praise 268.82
the Lord. Adapted from the Book of Daniel, chapter 3. Pictures by Idellette Dordigoni. New York, Guild, c.1965. 1v. (unpaged) col. illus. 19cm. (Little angel bk., 30905) .25 pap.,
1. Religious instruction—Catholic authors.

THE Living light, 268'.8'2
helping adolescents grow up in Christ. Ed. by Mary Perkins ryan. New York, Paul 1st [1967] x, 246p. 18cm. (Deus bks.) Articles which orig. appeared in the Living light. Bibl. [BX926.L54] 67-15722 1.45 pap.,
1. Religious education of adolescents. 2. Catechetics—Catholic Church. I. Ryan, Mary Perkins, 1915- ed.

THE Living light. 268'.8'2
Helping adolescents grow up in Christ. Edited by Mary Perkins Ryan. New York, Paulist Press [1967] x. 246 p. 18 cm. (Deus books) Articles which originally appeared in the Living light. Includes bibliographical references. [BX926.L54] 67-15722
1. Religious education of adolescents. 2. Catechetics — Catholic Church. I. Ryan, Mary Perkins, 1915- ed. II. Title.

MCBRIDE, Alfred 268.82
Catechetics: a theology of proclamation. Milwaukee, Bruce [c.1966] ix, 154p. 22cm. (Impact bks.) [BX921.M25] 66-16639 3.75; 2.00 pap.,
1. Religious educat9on. 2. Kerygma. I. Title.

MCBRIDE, Alfred. 268'.8'2
The human dimension of catechetics. Milwaukee, Bruce Pub. Co. [1969] xi, 186 p. 22 cm. Bibliography: p. [185]-186. [BX921.M253] 72-75708 4.95
1. Christian education. 2. Communication (Theology) I. Title.

MARY ROSALIA, Sister, 268.82
1896-
The adaptive way of teaching confraternity classes. St. Paul, Catechetical Guild Educational Society, 1955. 308p. 20cm. Revision of the author's Teaching confraternity classes (the adaptive way) published 1944. [BX1968.M41955] 56-640
1. Catechetics—Catholic Church. I. Title.

ROSALIA, Sister, 1896- 268.82
The adaptive way of teaching confraternity classes. St. Paul, Catechetical Guild Educational Society. 1955. 308p. 20cm. Revision of the author's Teaching confruternity classes (the adaptive why) published in 1944. [BX1968.R66 1955] 56-640
1. Catechetics I. Title.

*ROUKE, Eve 268.82
I like Christmas. Pictures by Betsy J. Roosen. New York, Guild, c.1965. 1v. (unpaged) col. illus. 19cm. (Little angel bk., 30906) .25 pap.,
1. Religious instruction—Catholic authors. I. Title.

SEMMELROTH, Otto 268.82
The church and Christian belief. Tr. by Thomas R. Milligan. Study-club questions. Glen Rock, N. J., Paulist [1966] 156p. 19cm. (Deus bks.) Tr. of articles which were orig. pub. separately. [BX930.S4] 66-26962 .95 pap.,
1. Religious education—Text-books for adults—Catholic. I. Title.

SMARIDGE, Norah 268.82
I do my best. Pitcures by Trina Hyman. New York, Guild, c.1965. 1v. (unpaged) col. illus. 19cm. (Little angel bk., 30908) .25 pap.,
1. Religious instruction—Catholic authors. I. Title.

*VAL, Sue 268.82
Why? Pictures by Christiane Cassan. New York, Guild, c.1965. 1v. (unpaged) col. illus. 19cm. (Little angel bk., 30907) .25 pap.,
1. Religious instruction—Catholic authors. I. Title.

WHERE there's life 268'.8'2
[by] Gabriel Moran [others] Dayton, Ohio, Pflaum [1967] 126p. illus. 17cm. (Trends in religious educ., no. 1) Witness bks., 7. [BX921.W5] 67-20744 .75 pap.,
1. Religious education—Addresses, essays, lectures. 2. Catholic Church—Education—Addresses, essays,lectures. I. Moran, Gabriel. Contents omitted.

SLOYAN, Gerard 268'.8'208
Stephen, 1919-
Speaking of religious education [by] Gerard S. Sloyan. [New York] Herder and Herder [1968] 235 p. 22 cm. Bibliographical footnotes. [BV1473.S55] 68-21485 5.95
1. Catholic Church—Doctrinal and controversial works. 2. Christian education—Addresses, essays, lectures. I. Title.

SANDT, Eleanor E., comp. 268'.8'3
Variations on the Sunday church school, edited by Eleanor E. Sandt. New York, Seabury Press [1967] 89 p. illus. 24 cm. Consists chiefly of articles adapted from the magazine Christian education findings. [BV1475.2.S25] 68-1300
1. Religious education of children. 2. Sunday-schools. I. Christian education findings. II. Title.

SANDT, Eleanor E comp. 268'.8'3
Variations on the Sunday church school, edited by Eleanor E. Sandt. New York, Seabury Press [1967] 89 p. illus. 24 cm. Consists chiefly of articles adapted from the magazine Christian education findings. [BV1475.2.S25] 68-1300
1. Religious education of children. 2. Sunday-schools. I. Christian education findings. II. Title.

BREWER, Clifton 268'.8'373
Hartwell, 1876-1947.
The history of religious education in the Episcopal Church to 1835. New York, Arno Press, 1969. xi, 362 p. facsims. 23 cm. (American education: its men, ideas, and institutions) On spine: Religious education in the Episcopal Church. Reprint of the 1924 ed., first published as Yale studies in the history and theory of religious education, 2. Bibliography: p. [331]-348. [BX5850.B8 1969] 73-89152
1 Protestant Episcopal Church in the U.S.A.—Education. 2. Christian education—United States. I. Title. II. Title: Religious education in the Episcopal Church. III. Series.

AMERICAN Evangelical 268.841
Lutheran Church Board of Parish Education.
The functional objectives for Christian education; prepared in connection with the long-range program of Lutheran boards of parish education [by the Board of Parish Education of the American Evangelical Lutheran Church, and others. n. p., 1959] 2v. forms. tables. 29cm. Cover title. Bibliography: v.1.p.423-429. [BX8013.A6] 60-22707
1. Lutheran Church—Education. 2. Religious education. I. Title.

BECK, Walter Herman, 268.841
1898-
Lutheran elementary schools in the United States; a history of the development of parochial schools and synodical educational policies and programs, by Walter H. Beck, [2d ed.] St. Louis, Concordia Pub. House, 1939 [i.e. 1965] xv, 511 p. 23 cm. (A Concordia paperback) Imprint covered by label: Second edition, c1965, Concordia Publishing House, St. Louis. Bibliography: p. 477-494. [LC574.B4 1965] 65-6086
1. Lutheran Church in the U.S. — Education. 2. Church schools — U.S. Education — U.S. — Hist. I. Title.

BECK, Walter Herman, 268.841
1898-
Lutheran elementary schools in the United States; a history of the development of parochial schools and synodical educational policies and programs. St. Louis, Concordia [c.1939, 1965] xv, 511p. 23cm. Bibl. [LC574.B4] 65-6086 4.95 pap.,
1. Lutheran Church in the U. S.—Education. 2. Church schools—U. S. 3. Education—U. S.—Hist. I. Title.

FOUNDATIONS for 268'.8'41
educational ministry. C. Richard Evenson, editor. [Philadelphia] Fortress Press [1971] 308 p. 23 cm. (Yearbooks in Christian education, v. 3) Includes bibliographical references. [BV1473.F68] 78-29727
1. Lutheran Church—Education—Addresses, essays, lectures. 2. Christian education—Addresses, essays, lectures. I. Evenson, C. Richard, 1922- ed. II. Title. III. Series.

LUTHERAN Church--Missouri 268.841
Synod.
Katalog der Lehranstalten. St. Louis. v. 23 cm. Title varies: 18 Synodal-Bericht. Katalog der Lehranstalten. Issued 18 by the synod under its earlier name: Deutsche Evangelisch-Lutherische Synode von Missouri, Ohio und Anderen Staaten. [LC574.L8] 51-25272
1. Lutheran Church in the U. S.—Education. I. Title.

WICKEY, Gould, 1891- 268.841
A study of needs and possibilities for Lutheran higher education in Wisconsin. [N.p.] 1954. 87 p. illus. 23 cm. [LC574.W52] 65-46496
1. Lutheran Church In Wisconsin — Education. I. Title. II. Title: Lutheran higher education in Wisconsin.

*LUCKHARDT, Mildred Corell 268.85
The church at work and worship; teacher's book. Philadelphia, pub. for the Cooperative Pubn. Assn. by Westminster [c.1965] 111p. 23cm. (Coop. ser., Vacation church sch. texts) A vacation church sch. course for junior groups. Accompanied by Pupil's book, and Activity sheets. pap., 1.25; pupil's bk., pap., .35; activity sheets, .45 per packet.
1. Religious education of children—Presbyterian. I. Title.

UNITED 268'.8'51310977311
Presbyterian Church in the U. S. A. Board of Christian Education.
Education in the city church; the city church project, 1964-1967; a report on an experimental project and its analysis. Philadelphia [1967] 235 p. 29 cm. Bibliographical footnotes. [BV637.U5] 68-1273
1. City churches—Chicago. 2. Religious education—Illinois—Chicago. I. Title.

UNITED 268'.8'51310977311
Presbyterian Church in the U.S.A. Board of Christian Education.
Education in the city church: the city church project, 1964-1967; a report on an experimental project and its analysis. Philadelphia [1967] 235 p. 29 cm. Bibliographical footnotes. [BV637.U5] 68-1273
1. City churches—Chicago. 2. Religious education—Illinois—Chicago. I. Title.

HARNER, Nevin Cowger, 268'.8'5733
1901-1951.
Factors related to Sunday school growth and decline in the Eastern Synod of the Reformed Church in the United States. New York, Bureau of Publications, Teachers College, Columbia University, 1931. [New York, AMS Press, 1973, c1972] vi, 101 p. illus. 22 cm. Reprint of the 1931 ed., issued in series: Teachers College, Columbia University. Contributions to education, no. 479. Originally presented as the author's thesis, Columbia. Bibliography: p. 101. [BX9563.H3 1972] 71-176839 ISBN 0-404-55479-2 10.00
1. Reformed Church in the United States. Eastern Synod. 2. Sunday schools—Pennsylvania. 3. Churches—Pennsylvania. I. Title. II. Series: Columbia University. Teachers College. Contributions to education, no. 479.

FACKRE, Gabriel J. 268'.8'5834
Conversation in faith; a resource and discussion book for adults, by Gabriel Fackre. Illustrated by Reed Champion. Boston, United Church Press [1968] 92 p. illus. 22 cm. (Confirmation education series) "Part of the United Church curriculum, prepared and published by the Division of Christian Education and the Division of Publication of the United Church Board for Homeland Ministries." Bibliography: p. 90-91. [BV4501.2.F27] 68-10312
1. Christian life—United Church of Christ authors. 2. Religious education—Textbooks for adults—United Church of Christ. I. United Church Board for Homeland Ministries.

Division of Christian Education. II. United Church Board for Homeland Ministries. Division of Publication. III. Title.

BELL, Arthur Donald. 268'.8'6
In Christian love [by] A. Donald Bell. Nashville, Convention Press [1968] x, 128 p. illus. 19 cm. "Church study course [of the Sunday School Board of the Southern Baptist Convention] This book is number 0474 in category 4, section for adults and young people." Includes bibliographical references. [BX6225.B48] 68-11671
1. Service (Theology)—Study and teaching. 2. Religious education—Text-books for adults—Baptist. 3. Religious education—Text-books for young people—Baptist. I. Southern Baptist Convention. Sunday School Board. II. Title.

CONNELLY, H. Walton. 268.86
Learning for living [by] H. Walton Connelly, Jr. Nashville, Convention Press [1967] xi, 129 p. 19 cm. Includes bibliographical references. [BV1471.2.C64] 67-10002
1. Religious education. I. Title.

EUTING, George L. 268.86
Missionary education for Baptist men; a guide for organizing and operating a Baptist men's unit, by George L. Euting. [Memphis, Brotherhood Commn., 1966] 154p. 20cm. [BX6225.E9] 66-27808 1.00
1. Religious education—Text-books for adults—Baptist. 2. Southern Baptists Convention—Education. I. Title.
548 Poplar Ave., Memphis, Tenn. 38104

MCELRATH, William N. 268'.8'6
Me, myself, and others, by William N. McElrath. [Teacher's ed.] Nashville, Convention Press [1968] vi, 93 p. illus. 19 cm. [BX6225.M3] 68-11673
1. Religious education—Text-books for children—Baptist. I. Title.

MCKAY, Richard W. 268'.8'6
Helping people in need [by] Richard W. McKay. [Teacher's ed.] Nashville, Convention Press [1968] xii, 78 p. illus. 19 cm. "Church study course [of the Sunday School Board of the Southern Baptist Convention] This book is number 0483 in category 4, section for intermediates." Includes bibliographical references. [BX6225.M33] 68-11672
1. Religious education—Text-books for adolescents—Baptist. I. Title.

SHARP, Margaret. 268'.8'6
Juniors in training. [Teacher's ed.] Nashville, Convention Press [1968] 104, [16] p. illus. 19 cm. "Church study course [of the Sunday School Board of the Southern Baptist Convention] This book is number 1893 in category 18, section for juniors." "Helps for the teacher": [16] p. (2d group) [BX6225.S45] 69-10016
1. Religious education—Text-books for children—Baptist. I. Southern Baptist Convention. Sunday School Board. II. Title.

WASHBURN, Alphonso V. 268.86
comp.
Reaching all prospects for the church. A. V.Washburn, compiler. Nashville, Convention Press [1964] xi, 145 p. 19 cm. [BV1471.2.W3] 64-17644
1. Religious education. 2. Baptists — Education. I. Title.

ANDERSON, Andy, 1927- 268'.8'6132
Where action is / Andy Anderson with Eugene Skelton. Nashville : Broadman Press, c1976. 158 p. : ill. ; 21 cm. [BV1523.A7A52] 76-11988 ISBN 0-8054-6212-0 : 4.95
1. Anderson, Andy, 1927- 2. Bible—Study. 3. Sunday—schools. 4. Church growth. I. Skelton, Eugene, joint author. II. Title.

BAKER, Robert Andrew. 268.86132
The story of the Sunday School Board [by] Robert A. Baker. Nashville, Convention Press [1966] vi, 254 p. illus., ports. 22 cm. Includes bibliographical references. [BX6222.A48B3] 66-12886
1. Southern Baptist Convention Sunday School Board I. Title.

BRIGHAM, Judith, 268'.8'6132
1915-
A historical study of the educational agencies of the Southern Baptist Convention, 1845-1945. New York, Bureau of Publications, Teachers College, Columbia University, 1951. [New York, AMS Press, 1972, i.e. 1973] xi, 161 p. 22 cm. Reprint of the 1951 ed., issued in series: Teachers College, Columbia University. Contributions to education, no. 974. Originally presented as the author's thesis, Columbia. Bibliography: p. 139-152. [LC561.S63B7 1972] 77-177047 ISBN 0-404-55974-3 10.00
1. Southern Baptist Convention—Education—History. I. Title. II. Series: Columbia University. Teachers College. Contributions to education, no. 974.

STUART, George Wilse, 268'.8'6132
1911-
A guide to Sunday School enlargement. George W. Stuart, comp. Nashville, Convention Press [1968] x, 142 p. 20 cm. "Church study course [of the Sunday School Board of the Southern Baptist Convention] This book is number 1734 in category 17, section for adults and young people." Bibliographical footnotes. [BV1521.S7] 68-28773
1. Sunday-schools. I. Southern Baptist Convention. Sunday School Board. II. Title.

STUART, George Wilse, 268'.8'6132
1911-
A guide to Sunday School enlargement. George W. Stuart, compiler. [Rev.] Nashville, Convention Press [1970] vii, 134 p. illus. 20 cm. "New church study course [of the Sunday School Board of the Southern Baptist Convention] ... number 6311 in Subject area 63, Bible teaching program." Includes bibliographical references. [BV1521.S7 1970] 77-21036
1. Sunday-schools. I. Southern Baptist Convention. Sunday School Board. II. Title.

TAYLOR, Bob R., 1935- 268'.8'6132
Intermediates in training [by] Bob R. Taylor. [Teacher's ed.] Nashville, Convention Press [1968] vi, 106 p. illus. 19 cm. "Church study course [of the Sunday School Board of the Southern Baptist Convention] This book is number 1882 in category 18, section for intermediates." Includes bibliographies. [BX6225.T35] 68-11674
1. Religious education—Text-books for adolescents—Baptist. I. Southern Baptist Convention. Sunday School Board. II. Title.

WALDRUP, Earl W 1920- 268.86132
New church member orientation manual [by] Earl Waldrup. Nashville, Convention Press [1965] xvi, 141 p. 19 cm. [BV4520.W24] 851
1. Church membership—Study and teaching. I. Title.

WALDRUP, Earl W., 268'.8'6132
1920-
New church member orientation manual [by] Earl Waldrup. Rev. Nashville, Convention Press [1970, c1965] viii, 135 p. 20 cm. "This book is the text for course 6406 of the New church study course." [BV4520.W24 1970] 77-14427
1. Church membership—Study and teachings. I. Title.

WASHBURN, Alphonso V., 268'86'132
comp.
The Sunday School at work, 1966-67 Nashville, Convention Press. v. in 19 cm. annual. (Vols. for 1968/69- issued as series: Crusade of the Americas resource.) Vols. for 1968/69- issued in different editions, e. g. Adult, extension, cradle roll workers' edition. Compiler: 1966/67- A. V. Washburn. [BX6223.S85] 68-25544
1. Sunday-schools. 2. Southern Baptist Convention—Education. I. Title. II. Series: Crusade of the Americas resource

WASHBURN, Alphonso V. 268.86132
comp.
The Sunday school at work, 1966-67. Compiler: A. V. Washburn. Nashville, Convention Press [1966] x, 134 p. 20 cm. "Church study course [of the Sunday School Board of the Southern Baptist Convention] This book is number 1730 in category 17, section for adults and young people." Includes bibliographical references. [BX6223.W33] 66-20896
1. Sunday schools. 2. Southern Baptist Convention — Education. I. Southern Baptist Convention. Sunday School Board. II. Title.

WASHBURN, Alphonso V. 268.86132
The sunday school program of a church [by] A. V. Washburn and staff. Nashville, Convention Press [1966] ix, 150 p. 19 cm. "Church study course [of the Sunday School Board of the Southern Baptist Convention] This book is number 31 in category 17, section for adults and young people." Bibliographical footnotes. [BV1521.W3] 66-23089
1. Sunday-schools. I. Southern Baptist Convention. Sunday School Board. II. Title.

TYMS, James Daniel 268.86133
The rise of religious education among Negro Baptists; a historical case study, by James D. Tyms. New York, Exposition, 1966, c.1965] xiv, 408p. 21cm. (Exposition-univ. bk.) Bibl. [BX6450.T93] 66-1120 7.50
1. Baptists, Negro—Education. I. Title.

HARRIS, William J. 268'.8'67
The challenge of vacation Bible school evangelism; the story of the beginning, growth, and effectiveness of Seventh-Day Adventist vacation Bible school evangelism, by William J. Harris. Nashville, Published for the Sabbath School Dept., General Conference of Seventh-Day Adventists, by Southern Pub. Association [1967] 214 p. illus. 22 cm. [BX6113.H3] 67-2208
1. Vacation schools, Seventh-Day Adventist. 2. Vacation schools, Religious. I. Seventh-Day Adventists. General Conference. Sabbath School Dept. II. Title.

NASH, Gerald R. 268.867
Evangelism through the Sabbath school. Washington, D.C., Review & Herald [1964] 192p. 22cm. 64-17652 price unreported
1. Seventh-Day Adventists—Education. 2. Evangelistic work. I. Title.

SEVENTH-DAY Adventists. 268.867
General Conference. Dept: of Education.
The wonderful way; Bible lessons for grades 7 and 8. Mountain View, Calif., Pacific Pub. Association [1955] Mountain View, Calif., Pacific Press Pub. Association [1956] 556p. illus. 24cm. 135p. 24cm. 'Series IV degree, even) year. [BX6113.S45] 55-11540
1. Secenth-Day Adventists—Doctrinal and controversial works. I. Title. II. Title: — Teacher's guide and key.

SEVENTH-DAY Adventists. 268.867
General Conference. Sabbath School Dept.
Sabbath school manual; official handbook for Sabbath school officers and teachers. Nashville, Southern Pub. Association [1956] 167p. illus. 18cm. [BX6113.S47] 56-27806
1. Seventh-Day Adventists—Education. I. Title.

NASH, Gerald R 268.8673
Planning better Sabbath schools, by Gerald R. Nash. Washington, Review and Herald Pub. Association [1965] 190 p. 22 cm. [BX6113.N316] 65-18672
1. Seventh-Day Adventists — Education. 2. Religious education. I. Title.

WILL, Stanley S. 268'.8'673
Teach : a guide to effective Sabbath school teaching / by Stanley S. Will ; ill. by Jim Padgett. Rev. ed. Nashville : Southern Pub. Association, c1974. 220 p. : ill. ; 21 cm. Bibliography: p. 219-220. [BX6155.W54 1974] 74-18927 ISBN 0-8127-0087-2 pbk. : 2.95
1. Seventh-Day Adventists—Education. 2. Christian education—Teaching methods. I. Title.

BOWEN, Cawthon Asbury, 268.87
1885-
Child and church; a history of Methodist church-school curriculum. New York, Abington Press [1960] 253p. 23cm. Includes bibliography. [BX8223.B65] 60-12068
1. Methodist Church—Education. 2. Religious education—Curricula. I. Title.

SCHISLER, John 268'.8'7'673
Quincy.
Christian education in local Methodist churches. Nashville, Abingdon Press [1969] 272 p. 23 cm. Bibliographical footnotes. [BX8223.S38] 69-18446 6.00
1. Methodist Church—Education—History. I. Title.

MERJANIAN, Pepronia. 268.88
The joy of teaching. Philadelphia, United Church Press [1966] 143 p. 20 cm. Bibliography: p. 136-143. [BV1475.2.M45] 66-23991
1. Religious education of children. I. Title.

HOOLE, Daryl (Van Dam) 268.893
With sugar 'n spice, by Daryl V. Hoole, Donette V. Ockey, Illus. by Aurelia P. Richards. Salt Lake City, Deseret, 1966. vii, 146p. illus., ports. 27cm. [BX8610.H69] 65-28862 price unreported.
1. Religious education—Text-books—Mormon. I. Ockey, Donette V., joint author. II. Title.

THE Instructor (Salt Lake 268.893
City)
A reader for the teacher; an anthology of ideas and teaching helps taken from the Instructor, the teacher's magazine of the church. Compiled by A. Hamer Reiser. Salt Lake City, Deseret Book Co., 1960. 362p. 24cm. Includes bibliography. [BX8610.I5] 60-29868
1. Mormons and Mormonism—Education. 2. Religious education. I. Reiser, A. Hamer, comp. II. Title.

WENGER, John Christian, 268.897
1910-
The church nurtures faith, 1683-1963. Scottdale, Pa., Herald Pr. [c.1963] 104p. ports. 20cm. 63-17083 1.00 pap.,
1. Mennonites in the U.S.—Education. I. Title.

269 Organized Spiritual Renewal

ALLAN, Tom. 269
The face of my parish. New York, Harper [1957] 120p. 20cm. [BV3793] [BV3793] 253 57-9874 57-9874
1. Evangellstic work. I. Title.

APPELMAN, Hyman Jedidiah, 269
1902-
When the world is on fire, and other evangelistic messages. Grand Rapids, Zondervan Pub. House [c1962] 117 p. 21 cm. [BV3797.A594] 63-1367
1. Evangelistic sermons. 2. Sermons, American. I. Title.

APPLEMAN, Hyman Jedidiah, 269
1902-
When the world is on fire, and other evangelistic messages. Grand Rapids, Mich., Zondervan [1963, c.1962] 117p. 21cm. 63-1367 1.95
1. Evangelistic sermons. 2. Sermons, American. I. Title.

THE art of soul-winning. 269
Grand Rapids, Baker Book House, 1957. 176p. 23cm. Includes bibliography. [BV3790.D68] [BV3790.D68] 253 57-9523 57-9523
1. Evangelistic work. I. Downey, Murray W

AYER, William Ward. 269
Flame for the altar. Grand Rapids, Zondervan Pub. House [c1952] 198p. 20cm. (The Bob Jones University lectures on evangelism for 1952) [BV3790.A9] [BV3790.A9] 243 53-16585 53-16585
1. Evangelistic work. I. Title.

BARLOW, Walter, 1883- 269
God so loved; the spiritual basis of evangelism. Introd. by John A. Mackay. Westwood, N. J., Revell [1952] 159 p. 21 cm. [BV3790.B324] 253 52-3494
1. Evangelistic work. 2. Conversion. I. Title.

BARNETTE, Jasper Newton, 269
1887-
One to eight. Nashville, Sunday School Board of the Southern Baptist Convention [1954] 127 p. 19 cm. [BV3795.B34] [BV3795.B34] 253 54-35834 54-35834
1. Evangelistic work—Study and teaching. I. Title.

BAYLESS, C. Gordon. 269
And be ye saved; a book of revival sermons. Westwood, N. J., F. H. Revell Co. [1952] 159 p. 21 cm. [BV3797.B35] 243 52-4965
1. Evangelistic sermons. 2. Sermons, American. I. Title.

BAYLESS, C. Gordon. 269
God at your door; sermons for salvation. [Westwood, N.J.] F.H. Revell Co, [c1955] 158p. 21cm. [BV3797.B36] 55-5387 343 55-5387
1. Evangellstic sermons. 2. Baptists—Sermons. 3. Sermons, American. I. Title.

BAYLY, Joseph. 269
The gospel blimp. Havertown, Pa., Windward Press [1960] 85p. 22cm. [BV3795.B36] 60-53018
1. Evangelistic work. I. Title.

BAYLY, Joseph 269
The gospel blimp [Reissue] Grand Rapids, Mich., Zondervan [1964, c.1960] 85p. 22cm. 1.95
1. Evangelistic work. I. Title.

BAYLY, Joseph T 269
The gospel blimp. Havertown, Pa., Windward Press [1960] 85 p. 22 cm. [BV3795.B36] 60-53018
1. Evangelistic work. I. Title.

BOYD, Malcolm. 269
Focus; rethinking the meaning of our evangelism. New York, Morehouse-Barlow Co. [1960] 112p. 19cm. [BV3790.B62] 60-6319
1. Evangelistic work. I. Title.

BOYD, Malcolm, 1923- 269
Focus; rethinking the meaning of our evangelism. NewYork, Morehouse-Barlow Co. [1960] 112 p. 19 cm. [BV3790.B62] 60-6319
1. Evangelistic work. I. Title.

BRADSHAW, Malcolm R. 269
Church growth through Evangelism-in-depth [by] Malcolm R. Bradshaw. South Pasadena, Calif., William Carey Library [1969] xvi, 127 p. illus. 23 cm. Bibliography: p. 121-127. [BV3790.B647] 75-96753 2.75
1. Evangelistic work. 2. Missions. 3. Church growth. I. Title.

BRYANT, Al, 1926- ed. 269
Revival sermon outlines. Grand Rapids, Zondervan Pub. House [1955] 93p. 22cm. [BV3797.B67] 243 55-14894
1. Evangelistic sermons—Outlines. I. Title.

BUILDING church membership through evangelism. New York, Abingdon-Cokesbury Press [1952] 188 p. 20 cm. [BV3793.B7] 253 52-5376 269
1. Evangelistic work. 2. Church membership. I. Bryan, Dawson Charles, 1900-

THE call of the harvest. 269
Nashville, Convention Press [1956] 132p. 20cm. [BV3795.M27] 253 56-58499
1. Evangelistic work—Study and teaching. I. McKay, Charles Lloyd, 1908-

CALVARY covers it all. 269
Foreword by Hugh Redwood. Westwood, N. J., F. H. Revell Co. [1957] 120p. 20cm. [BV2655.J39] 253 58-1082
1. Evangelistic work. I. Jennings, Frank Leonard, 1890-

CATHOLIC Church. Pope. 269
The popes on youth; principles for forming and guiding youth from Popes Leo XIII to Pius XII, compiled and edited by Raymond B. Fullam. New York, D. McKay Co. [c1956] 442p. 24cm. [BX2390.Y7A4 1956a] 57-4398
1. Church work with youth. 2. Youth—Religious life. 3. Religious education of young people. I. Fullam, Raymond B., ed. II. Title.

DEAN, Horace F 269
Operation Evangelism. Grand Rapids, Zondervan Pub. House [1957] 170p. 21cm. (The Bob Jones University lectures on evangelism, 1957) [BV3795.D4] 57-3367
1. Evangelistic work—Addresses, essays, lectures. I. Title.

ESTABLISHING the converts; 269
what pastors and church members can do to conserve the results of their evangelistic efforts. With a foreword by Dores Robinson Sharpe. Philadelphia, Judson Press [1952] 108 p. 21 cm. [BV3790.A68] 253 52-11056
1. Evangelistic work. 2. Church work. I. Archibald, Arthur Crawley, 1878-

EVANGELISM in a changing America. St. Louis, Bethany Press [1957] 192p. 21cm. [BV3790.B23] [BV3790.B23] 253 57-8364 57-8364 269
1. Evangelistic work. I. Bader, Jesse Moren, 1886-

EVANGELISM in the Sunday church school. Philadelphia, Judson Press [1955] 95p. 20cm. [BV1475.C56] [BV1475.C56] 253 55-8634 55-8634 269
1. Evangelistic work. 2. Sunday-schools. I. Cober, Kenneth Lorne, 1902-

EXUM, Jack. 269
How to win souls today. Old Tappan, N.J., Revell [1970] 157, [2] p. 21 cm. Bibliography: p. [159] [BV3790.E9] 79-96249 3.95
1. Evangelistic work. I. Title.

FRAKES, Margaret 269
Bridges to understanding: the 'academy movement' in Europe and North America. Philadelphia, Muhlenberg Press [c.1960] 134p. illus. 21cm. Bibl.: p.130-131. 60-13906 2.50
1. Evangelical academies. I. Title.

FULLER, Ellis Adams, 1891-1950. 269
Evangelistic sermons. Nashville, Broadman Press [1953] 144p. 20cm. [BV3797.F8] 243 53-8495
1. Evangelistic sermons. 2. Baptists—Sermons. 3. Sermons, American. I. Title.

GABLE, Lee J. 269
Church and world encounter [the evangelical academies in Germany and their meaning for the ecumenical church] Philadelphia, United Church Pr. [c.1964] 111p. map. 21cm. Bibl. 64-16623 1.60 pap.,
1. Evangelical academies. I. Title.

GOD in His World. 269
New York, Abingdon Press [1956] 176p. 21cm. [BT77] 253 56-7759
1. Theology, Doctrinal. 2. Evangelistic work. I. Duthie, Charles S

GOFORTH, Jonathan, 1859-1936 269
'By my spirit.' Foreword by Mrs. Rosalind Goforth. Minneapolis, 6820 Auto Club Rd. Bethany Fellowship, [1964, c.1942] 138p. 19cm. 1.50 pap.,
1. Missions—China. 2. Evangelistic work. I. Title.

GRAHAM, William Franklin, 1918- 269
Revival in our time [by Billy Graham and others] The story of the Billy Graham evangelistic campaigns, including six of his sermons. Wheaton, Ill., Van Kampen Press [1950] 140 p. illus., ports. 20 cm. [BV3785.G69A3] 50-7766
1. Revivals—U. S. 2. Evangelistic sermons. 3. Sermons, American. I. Title.

GRINDSTAFF, Wilmer E 1912- 269
Ways to win; methods of evangelism for the local church. Nashville, Broadman Press [c1957] 212p. 22cm. [BV3790.G86] 253 57-6323
1. Evangelistic work. I. Title.

HALE, Joe, 1935- 269
Design for evangelism. Nashville, Tidings [1969] 119 p. illus. 22 cm. Includes bibliographical references. [BV3790.H28] 72-100643
1. Evangelistic work. I. Title.

HARRISON, Eugene Myers, 1900- 269
How to win souls; a manual of personal evangelism, by E. Myers Harrison, Walter L. Wilson. Wheaton, Ill., Scripture Pr. [1963, c.1952] 155p. 20cm. 2.00 pap.,
1. Evangelistic work. I. Title.

HARTT, Julian Norris. 269
Toward a theology of evangelism. Nashville, Abingdon Press [c1955] 123p. 20cm. [BV3793.H35] 253 55-5396
1. Evangelistic work. I. Title.

HAYDEN, Eric W. 269
Spurgeon on revival; a Biblical and theological approach. Grand Rapids, Mich., Zondervan [c.1962] 144p. 23cm. 62-52736 2.95
1. Spurgeon, Charles Haddon, 1834-1892. 2. Evangelistic work. I. Title.

HEARTS afire. 269
Westwood, N. J., Revell [1952] 160 p. 20 cm. [BV3790.H374] 253 52-10954
1. Evangelistic work. I. Havner, Vance, 1901-

HENRY, Carl Ferdinand Howard, 1913- 269
Evangelical responsibility in contemporary theology. Grand Rapids, Eerdmans [1957] 89p. 19cm. (Pathway books; aseries of contemporary evangelical studies) [BR479.H44] 253 57-13036
1. Theology—20th cent. 2. Evangelicalism. I. Title.

HENRY, Carl Ferdinand Howard, 1913- 269
Evangelicals at the brink of crisis; significance of the World Congress on Evangelism, by Carl F. H. Henry. Waco, Tex., Word Books [1967] 120 p. 19 cm. [BR1640.H4] 67-21104
1. World Congress on Evangelism, Berlin, 1966. 2. Evangelicalism. I. Title.

HOW to win souls: 269
a manual of personal evangelism, by E. Myers Harrison and Walter L. Wilson. Wheaton, Ill., Van Kampen Press [1952] 155 p. 20 cm. [BV3790.H358] 253 52-64330
1. Evangelistic work. I. Harrison, Eugene Myers, 1900-

HOWARD, Walden. 269
Nine roads to renewal. Waco Tex., Word Books [1967] 162 p. 21 cm. [BV600.2.H66] 67-29860
1. Church renewal—Case studies. I. Title.

HOWARD, Walden. 269
Nine roads to renewal. Waco, Tex., Word Books [1967] 162 p. 21 cm. [BV600.2.H66] 67-29860
1. Church renewal—Case studies. I. Title.

HUNT, Lionel A. 269
Mass child evangelism. Chicago, Moody Press [1951] 192 p. 20 cm. [BV4925.H76] 51-11135
1. Children—Conversion to Christianity. I. Title.

HURST, Duane v 1923- 269
Ye shall be witnesses. Springfield, Mo., Gospel Pub. House [1952] 190p. 19cm. [BV3793.H85] 253 54-36881
1. Evangelistic work. 2. Witness bearing (Christianity) I. Title.

JENNINGS, Frank Leonard, 1890- 269
The Gospel on Skid Row. Westood, N. J., F. H. Revell Co. [1953] 159p. 20cm. [BV2655.J4] 253 53-2019
1. Evangelistic work. I. Title.

KANTONEN, Taito Almar, 1900- 269
The theology of evangelism. Philadelphia, Muhlenberg Press [c1954] 98p. 20cm. [BV3790.K3] 253 54-534
1. Evangelistic work. I. Title.

KILLINGER, John. 269
All you lonely people, all you lovely people. Waco, Tex., Word Books [1973] 153 p. 23 cm. [BV652.2.K54] 72-96357 4.95
1. Church group work—Case studies. I. Title.

KRAEMER, Hendrik, 1888- 269
The communication of the Christian faith. Philadelphia, Westminster Press [1956] 128p. 20cm. [BV3793.K7] 253 56-10046
1. Evangelistic work. 2. Missions. 3. Communication. I. Title.

LAURIE, David James. 269
Sound the trumpet. Grand Rapids, Zondervan Pub. House [1956] 89p. 20cm. (The Bob Jones University lectures on evangelism for 1955) [BV3790.L254] 253 56-41459
1. Evangelistic work. I. Title.

LEAVELL, Roland Quinche, 1891- 269
Evangelism, Christ's imperative commission. Nashville, Broadman Press ['1951] 234 p. 21 cm. [BV3790.L26] 253 52-6828
1. Evangelistic work. I. Title.

MACAULAY, Joseph Cordner, 1900- 269
Personal evangelism, by J. C. Macaulay and Robert H. Belton. Chicago Moody Press [1956] 255p. 22cm. [BV3790.M22] 253 56-14230
1. Evangelistic work. I. Belton, Robert H., joint author. II. Title.

MCLOUGHLIN, William Gerald, comp. 269
The American evangelicals, 1800-1900; an anthology. Edited by William G. McLoughlin New York, Harper & Row [1968] 213 p. 21 cm. (American perspectives) (Harper torchbooks, TB/1382.) Contents.Contents.—Introduction, by W. G. McLoughlin.—The battle hymn of the Republic, by J. W. Howe.—Religion in America, by R. Baird.—Autobiography, by P. Cartwright.—The faith once delivered, by L. Beecher.—A revival of religion, by C. G. Finney.—Moral science, and Political economy, by F. Wayland.—Preaching Christ, by H. W. Beecher.—Obligations to the dead, by H. Bushnell.—The law of growth, by P. Brooks.—Non church goers, To reformed men, and Return of our Lord, by D. L. Moody.—Personal Consecration, by S. P. Jones.—Our country, by J. Strong. Bibliographical footnotes. [BR1642.U5M3] 68-26894 2.75
1. Evangelicalism—United States. 2. Theology—Collections. 3. United States—Religion—19th century. I. Title.

MAIN, Robert L., 1918- 269
Encountering Christ; lay witness ... one key to renewal, by Robert L. Main. Nashville, Tidings [1970] 95 p. 22 cm. [BV4400.M366] 72-129550
1. Laity. 2. Witness bearing (Christianity) 3. Church renewal. I. Title.

MAN to man; 269
ten sermons on visitation evangelism. Nashville, Broadman Press [1956, c1955] ix, 123p. 20cm. [BV3797.A67] 253 56-25342
1. Evangelistic sermons. 2. Evangelistic work. I. Archibald, Arthur Crawley, 1878-

MARTINEZ, Angel, 1921or2- 269
The fountain of youth, and other revival sermons. Grand Rapids, Zondervan Pub. House [1957] 120p. 20cm. [BV3797.M315] 243 58-15403
1. Evangelistic sermons. 2. Sermons, American. I. Title.

MARTINEZ, Angel, 1921or2- 269
The logic of tragedy, and other sermons. Grand Rapids, Zondervan Pub. House [1958] 121p. 20cm. [BV3797.M3155] 243 58-42576
1. Evangelistic sermons. 2. Baptists—Sermons. 3. Sermons, American. I. Title.

MARTY, Martin E. 1928- 269
The improper opinion: mass media and the Christian faith. Philadelphia, Westminster Pr. [c.1961] 144p. 21cm. (Westminster studies in Christian communication) Bibl. 61-10298 3.50
1. Evangelistic work. 2. Public relations—Churches. 3. Communication. I. Title.

MATTHEWS, David. 269
I saw the Welsh revival. Chicago, Moody Press [1951] 126 p. 17 cm. (Colportage library, 205) [BV3777.G85M3] 51-9654
1. Revivals—Wales. I. Title.

METHODS of evangelism 269
Independence, Mo., Herald House [1953] 84p. 20cm. At head of title: The Reorganized Church of Jesus Christ of Latter Day Saints. [BV3790.D7] 253 53-8843
1. Evangelistic work. 2. Reorganized Church of Jesus Christ of Letter-Day Saints—Missions. I. Draper, Maurice L.

MILLER, Paul M 269
Group dynamics in evangelism. Scottdale, Pa., Herald Press [1958] 202p. 21cm. [BV3793.M5] 253 58-8517
1. Evangelistic work. 2. Social group work. I. Title.

MOTTE, Jean Francois. 1913- 269
The new parish mission; the work of the church, by Jean-Francois Motte and Medard Dourmap. Translated by Paul J. Oligny. Chicago, Franciscan Herald Press [1962] 100 p. 19 cm. "Translated and condensed ... from Mission generale, oeuvre d'englise [sic]" [BX2375.M633] 62-15826
1. Parish missions. I. Dourmap, Medard, joint author. II. Title.

MUNRO, Harry Clyde, 1890- 269
Fellowship evangelism through church groups; an adaptation of the National Christian Teaching Mission program for use by the local church that may not have an opportunity to participate in the larger project. St. Louis, Published for the Cooperative Association by the Bethany Press [1951] 159 p. 20 cm. [BV3790.M845] 51-9889
1. Evangelistic work. I. National Christian Teaching Mission. II. Title.

NEELLEY, Elizabeth. 269
The eternal hills, by Mrs. C. L. Neeley. San Antonio, Naylor Co. [1956] 53p. illus. 20cm. [CT275.N418A3] 56-3411
I. Title.

O'BRIEN, John Anthony, 1893- ed. 269
Bringing souls to Christ; methods of sharing the faith with others. With an introd. by Francis Cardinal Spellman. [1st ed.] Garden City, N. Y., Hanover House [c1955] 223p. 22cm. [BX2374.O28] [BX2374.O28] 253 55-5595 55-5595
1. Evangelistic work. I. Title.

O'BRIEN, John Anthony, 1893- ed. 269
The white harvest; a symposium on methods of convert making. With a pref. by Francis C. Kelley. Westminster, Md., Newman Press, 1952. 358p. illus. 21cm. [BX2374.O3 1952] [BX2374.O3 1952] 253 52-14476 52-14476
1. Evangelistic work. 2. Theology, Pastoral—Catholic Church. I. Title.

O'BRIEN, John Anthony, 1893- ed. 269
Winning converts; a symposium on methods of convert making for priests and lay people. [Rev. and enl.] Notre Dame, Ind., Notre Dame Books [1957] 250p. illus. 17cm. [BX2374.O32 1957] 253 57-12041
1. Vangelistic work. 2. Pastoral theology—Catholic Church. I. Title.

O'BRIEN, John Anthony, 1893- 269
You too can win souls; intimate personal stories of Catholics who shared their faith. New York, Macmillan, 1955. 240p. 22cm. [BX2374.O33] [BX2374.O33] 253 55-1502 55-1502
1. Evangelistic work. I. Title.

ORAL Roberts' best sermons 269
and stories, as presented in his great evangelistic campaigns around the world. Tulsa, Okla., 1956. 124p. 20cm. [BV3797.R59] 243 56-8451
1. Evangelistic sermons. 2. Pentecostal Holiness Church— Sermons. 3. Sermons, American. I. Roberts, Oral.

ORR, James Edwin, 1912- 269
Good news in bad times: signs of revival. Grand Rapids, Zondervan Pub. House [1953] 259p. 20cm. [BV3770.O7] 54-743
1. Revivals. I. Title.

OUR children and evangelism 269
Philadelphia, Judson Press [1955] 80p. illus. 20cm. [BV639.C4H43] 253 55-8633
1. Church work with children. 2. Evangelistic work. I. Henderson, Phillips.

PREUS, David W. 269
Go with the gospel / David W. Preus. Minneapolis : Augsburg Pub. House, c1977. 112 p. ; 20 cm. [BV2074.P73] 76-27075 ISBN 0-8066-1560-5 pbk. : 2.95
1. Great Commission (Bible)—Sermons. 2. Lutheran Church—Sermons. 3. Sermons, American. 4. Evangelistic work. I. Title.

PURKISER, W. T. 269
The message of evangelism: the saving power of God. Kansas City, Mo., Beacon Hill Pr. [1963] 112p. 20cm. Bibl. 63-14516 2.00
1. Evangelistic work. I. Title.

*RHODES, Rev. D. L. 269
Revival now. New York, Vantage [c.1964] 78p. 22cm. 2.00 bds.,

I. Title.

ROBERSON, Lee. 269
It's dynamite; gospel sermons that helped build the greatest soul-winning church in the world. Wheaton, Ill., Sword of the Lord Publishers [1953] 130p. illus. 21cm. [BV3797.R56] 243 53-39865
1. Evangelistic sermons. 2. Baptists — Sermons. 3. Sermons, American. I. Title.

ROBERTS, Oral. 269
Oral Roberts' best sermons and stories, as presented in his great evangelistic campaigns around the world. Tulsa, Okla, 1956. 124p. 20cm. [BV3797.R59] 243 56-8451
1. Evangelistic sermons. 2. Pentecostal Holiness Church—Sermons. 3. Sermons, American. I. Title.

SCARBOUROUGH, Lee Rutland, 269
1870-
With Christ after the lost; a search for souls. Rev. and expanded by E. D. Head. Nashville, Broadman Press [1953,c1952] 291p. 22cm. Includes bibliography. [BV3790.S2 1953] 253 53-7946
1. Evangelistic work. I. Title.

SHELLEY, Bruce Leon, 1927- 269
Evangelicalism in America, by Bruce L. Shelley. Grand Rapids, Eerdmans [1967] 134 p. 21 cm. Bibliographical references included in "Notes" (p. 133-134) [BR513.S5] 67-21466
1. National Association of Evangelicals. 2. Evangelicalism—United States. I. Title.

SHOEMAKER, Samuel Moor, 269
1893-
The experiment of faith; a handbook for beginners. [1st ed.] New York, Harper [1957] 64p. 22cm. [BV3793.S45] 253 57-7345
1. Evangelistic work. I. Title.

SHORT, Roy Hunter, 269
Bp., 1902-
Evangelism through the local church. New York, Abingdon Press [1956] 126p. 20cm. [BV3790.S54] 253 56-10149
1. Evangelistic work. I. Title.

SMITH, Harry R 1900- 269
Apart with Him; fifty years of the Mount Hermon conference. Oakland, Calif., Western Book & Tract Co. [1956] 137p. illus. 21cm. [BV3799.M6S56] 56-36225
1. Mount Hermon Association. I. Title.

SMITH, Harry R 1900- 269
Apart with Him; fifty years of the Mount Hermon conference. Oakland, Calif., Western Book & Tract Co. [1956] 137 p. illus. 21 cm. [BV3799.M6S56] 56-36225
1. Mount Hermon Association. I. Title.

SMITH, Oswald J 269
The consuming fire. Grand Rapids, Zondervan Pub. House [c1954] 151p. 20cm. (The Bob Jones University lectures on evangelism. 1953) [BV3790.S64] [BV3790.S64] 253 57-2301 57-2301
1. Evangelistic work. I. Title. II. Series.

STAGG, Paul L. 269
The converted church; from escape to engagement [by] Paul L. Stagg. Valley Forge [Pa.] Judson [1967] 160p. 22cm. Bibl. [BV3790.S757] 67-14362 2.75 pap.,
1. Evangelistic work. I. Title.

STEWART, James Alexander 269
Evangelism without apology. Grand Rapids, Mich., Kregel Publications [c.] 1960. 129p. front. 20cm. (The Bob Jones University lectures on evangelism, 1959) 59-13641 2.25
1. Evangelistic work. I. Title.

STEWART, James Alexander, 269
1910-
Evangelism without apology. Grand Rapids, Kregel Publications, 1960. 129 p. illus. 20 cm. (The Bob Jones University lectures on evangelism, 1959) [BV3790.S776] 59-13641
1. Evangelistic work. I. Title.

SUENENS, Leon Joseph, Bp., 269
1904-
The Gospel to every creature. With a pref. by John Baptist Montini, Archibishop of Milan. [Translation by Louise Gavan Duffy] Westminster, Md., Newman Press, 1957. 163p. 19cm. Translation of L'Eglise on etat de mission. [BV3790.S892] 253 57-8609
1. Evangelistic work. 2. Catholic Church—Missions. I. Title.

SWEAZEY, George Edgar, 1905- 269
Effective evangelism: the greatest work in the world. 1st. ed [1st ed.] New York, Harper [1953] 284p. 22cm. [BV3790.S92] 253 53-5990
1. Evangelistic work. 2. Church work. I. Title.

SWEET, William Warren, 1881- 269
Revivalism in America [its origin, growth and decline] Nashville, Abingdon [1965, c.1944] xv, 192p. 19cm. (Apex bks., V3) [BV3773.S8] 1.50 pap.,
I. Title.

TAYLOR, Mendell 269
Exploring evangelism: history, methods, theology. Kansas City, Mo., Nazarene Pub. House [1964] 647p. 23cm. Bibl. 64-18587 5.95
1. Evangelistic work. I. Title.

TECHNIQUES of torchbearing. 269
Foreword by Bob Jones, Jr. Grand Rapids, Zondervan Pub. House [1957] 153p. 20cm. (The Bob Jones University lectures on evangelism for 1956) [BV3790.D25] 253 57-3454
1. Evangelistic work. I. Daniels, Elam J

TEMPLETON, Charles Bradley, *269
1915-
Evangelism for tomorrow. [1st ed.] New York, Harper [1957] 175p. 22cm. [BV3790.T4] 253 57-10530
1. Evangelistic work. I. Title.

THAT my house may be 269
filled; a study of Evangelism in the Christian Reformed Church. Grand Rapids, W. B. Eerdmans [1957] 128p. 21cm. [BV3793.B55] 253 57-4518
1. Evangelistic work. 2. Christian Reformed Church —Missions. I. Boer, Harry R

VISITATION evangelism made 269
practical; reaching your community for Christ and the church. Grand Rapids, Zondervan Pub. House [1957] 93p. illus. 20cm. [BV3793.D4] 253 57-28032
1. Visitations (Church work) 2. Evangelistic work. I. Dean, Horace F

WAKE up and lift. 269
Kansas City, Mo., Beacon Hill Press [1955] 72p. 20cm. [BV3795] 253 55-2161
1. Evangellstic work. I. Fisher, C William.

WALKER, Alan. 269
The whole gospel for the whole world. With an introd. by E. G. Homrighausen. New York, Abingdon Press [1957] 128p. 20cm. (The Wieand lectures in evangelism) [BV3790.W316] 253 57-5283
1. Evangelistic work. I. Title.

WE can win others, 269
a program of of evangelism for presentday churches. Philadelphia, Judson Press [1953] 115p. 21cm. Includes bibliography. [BV3790.C5614] 253 53-9664
1. Evangelistic work. I. Chastain, Theron, 1906-

WEST Virginia Baptist 269
Convention.
The sound of the trumpet [by Randolph F. Johnson and others. Parkersburg, W. Va.] 1969. 96 p. 22 cm. Bibliography: p. 93-95. [BV3790.W465] 72-85327
1. Evangelistic work. I. Johnson, Randolph F., 1931- II. Title.

WILLIAMS, Colin Wilbur, 1917- 269
What in the world? [New York, Dist. Office of Pubn. & Dist.,Natl. Council of the Churches of Christ in the U. S. A., 1964] xxi, 105p. 19cm. Bibl. 64-23080 .75 pap.,
1. Evangelistic work. 2. Missions—Theory. I. Title.

WILLIAMS, Colin Wilbur, 1917- 269
Where in the world? changing forms of the church's witness. [New York, Dist. by Natl. Council of the Churches of Christ in the U.S.A., 1963] x, 116p. 19cm. Bibl. 63-25199 .75 pap.,
1. Evangelistic work. 2. Missions—Theory. I. Title.

WITH Him in glory; 269
the chief function of the parish minister for effective evangelism in the modern Christian church [1st ed.] New York, Vantage Press [1955] 91p. 21cm. Includes bibliography. [BV3790.D8] 254 55-7183
1. Evangelistic work. I. Durbney, Clydrow J

WITHROW, Pat B 1880- comp. 269
Soup soap, and salvation; God's changing power. Winona Lake, Ind. Rodeheaver, Hall-Mack Co. [1952] 139p. illus. 23cm. 'Testimonies of ... converts ... through the ministry of the Union Mission [Charleston, W. Va.]' [BV2656.C38U5] 53-17737
1. Charleston, W. Va. Union Mission. I. Title.

WORLD Congress on Evangelism, 269
Berlin, 1966.
One race, one gospel, one task; official reference volumes: papers and reports. Edited by Carl F. H. Henry and W. Stanley Mooneyham. Minneapolis, World Wide Publications [1967] 2 v. illus. 24 cm. [BV3755.W6 1966c] 67-22479
1. Evangelistic work—Congresses. I. Henry, Carl Ferdinand Howard, 1913- ed. II. Mooneyham, Walter Stanley, 1926- ed. III. Title.

MOSELEY, Joseph Edward, 269.08
1910- ed.
Evangelism --commitment and involvement. St. Louis, Bethany [c.1965] 94p. port. 20cm. (N. E. A. lects. on evangelism) N. E. A. lectures for 1964 pub. in memory of Jesse M. Bader. [BV3795.M6] 65-18203 1.00 pap.,
1. Evangelistic work—Addresses, essays, lectures. I. Bader, Jesse Moren, 1886-1963. II. National Evangelistic Association of the Disciples of Christ. III. Title. IV. Series.

MOSELEY, Joseph Edward, 269.08
1910- ed.
Evangelism -- commitment and involvement, edited by J. Edward Moseley. St. Louis, Bethany Press [1965] 94 p. port. 20 cm. (N. E. A. lectures on evangelism) N. E. A. lectures for 1964 published in memory of Jesse M. Bader. [BV3795.M6] 65-18203
1. Evangelistic work — Addresses, essays, lectures. I. Bader, Jesse Moren, 1886-1963. II. National Evangelistic Association of the Disciples of Christ. III. Title. IV. Series.
Contents Omitted.

SCHARPFF, Paulus, 1885- 269.09
1965
History of evangelism; three hundred years of evangelism in Germany, Great Britain, and the United States of America. Tr. by Helga Bender Henry. Grand Rapids. Eerdmans [1966] xviii, 373p. 23cm. Bibl. [BV3770.S313] 66-18731 5.75
1. Evangelistic work—Hist. 2. Reyivals—Hist. I. Title.

GEWEHR, Wesley Marsh, 269.09755
1888-
The great awakening in Virginia, 1740-1790, by Wesley M. Gewehr. Gloucester, Mass., P. Smith, 1965 [c1930] viii, 292 p. maps, ports. 21 cm. (Duke University publications) Bibliography: p. 263-279. [BR555.V8G4 1965] 66-1635
1. Revivals — Virginia. 2. Great awakening. 3. Virginia — Church history. I. Title. II. Series.

GEWEHR, Wesley Marsh, 269.09755
1888-
The great awakening in Virginia, 1740-1790. Gloucester, Mass., P. Smith [1966, c.1930] vii, 292p. maps, ports. 21cm. (Duke Univ. pubns.) Orig. pub. by Duke in 1930 Bibl. [BR555.V8G4] 66-1635 4.50
1. Revivals—Virginia. 2. Great awakening. 3. Virginia—Church history. I. Title.

ARMENIAN Missionary 269'.2
Association of America.
To the memory of Puzant H. Kalfayan, 1913-1959. New York, 1960. 55p. illus. 25cm. [BX6194.A98K3] 62-32734
1. Kalfayan, Puzant H., 1913-1959. I. Title.

ARMSTRONG, James, 1924- 269'.2 s
The public servant and the pastor, by A. James Armstrong. Nashville, Tidings [1972] 56 p. 19 cm. (Denman lectures [1972]) Includes bibliographical references. [BV3760.H3 1972] [BR115.P7] 261.7 72-79499 1.00
1. Christianity and politics. I. Title. II. Series: Harry Denman lectures on evangelism, 1972.

AUTREY, C. E. 269.2
Revivals of the Old Testament. Grand Rapids, Zondervan Pub. House [c.1960] 160p. 23cm. (5p. bibl. notes) 60-147 2.95
1. Revivals—Hist. 2. Bible. O.T.—History of Biblical events. I. Title.

AUTREY, C E 269.2
Revivals of the Old Testament. Grand Rapids, Zondervan Pub. House [1960] 160p. 23cm. Includes bibliography. [BV3770.A8] 60-147
1. Revivals—Hist. 2. Bible. O. T.—History of Biblical events. I. Title.

BABBAGE, Stuart Barton 269.2
Light beneath the Cross, by Stuart Barton Babbage and Ian Siggins. Garden City, N. Y., Doubleday [c.]1960. 161p. illus. 22cm. 60-11374 2.95 half cloth,
1. Graham, William Franklin. 2. Revivals—Australia. 3. Revivals—New Zealand. I. Siggins, Ian, joint author. II. Title.

BABBAGE, Stuart Barton. 269.2
Light beneath the Cross, by Stuart Barton Babbage and Ian Siggins. [1st ed.] Garden City, N. Y., Doubleday, 1960. 161p. illus. 22cm. [BV3785.G69B23] 60-11374
1. Graham. William Franklin. 1918- 2. Revivals— Australia. 3. Revivals—New Zealand. I. Siggins, Ian. joint author. II. Title.

BARNHART, Joe E., 1931- 269'.2
The Billy Graham religion, by Joe E. Barnhart. Philadelphia, United Church Press [1972] 255 p. 22 cm. "A Pilgrim Press book." Includes bibliographical references. [BV3785.G69B28] 72-8447 ISBN 0-8298-0242-8 6.95
1. Graham, William Franklin, 1918- 2. Evangelicalism—United States. 3. United States—Religion. I. Title.

BENSON, Dennis C. 269'.2
Electric evangelism [by] Dennis C. Benson. Nashville, Abingdon Press [1973] 144 p. illus. 23 cm. [BV656.B45] 72-7425 ISBN 0-687-11633-3 3.95
1. Radio in religion. 2. Television in religion. I. Title.

BISAGNO, John R. 269'.2
The power of positive evangelism [by] John R. Bisagno. Nashville, Broadman Press [1968] 64 p. 19 cm. [BV3790.B487] 68-26918
1. Evangelistic work. 2. Revivals. I. Title.

BLOESCH, Donald G., 1928- 269'.2
The evangelical renaissance, by Donald G. Bloesch. Grand Rapids, Eerdmans [1973] 165 p. 21 cm. Includes bibliographical references. [BR1640.B55] 72-96407 ISBN 0-8028-1527-8 2.45
1. Evangelicalism. 2. Pietism. I. Title.

BORCHERT, Gerald L. 269'.2
Dynamics of evangelism / Gerald L. Borchert ; foreword by Leighton Ford. Waco, Tex. : Word Books, c1976. 146 p. : ill. ; 23 cm. Includes bibliographical references. [BV3790.B615] 76-2866 ISBN 0-87680-468-7 : 5.95
1. Evangelistic work. I. Title.

BROOKS, W. Hal. 269'.2
Follow up evangelism [by] W. Hal Brooks. Nashville, Broadman Press [1972] xiii, 128 p. 21 cm. Bibliography: p. 121-124. [BV3790.B715] 72-187475 ISBN 0-8054-2519-5
1. Evangelistic work. I. Title.

CANNON, William Ragsdale, 269'.2
1916-
Evangelism in a contemporary context, by William R. Cannon. Nashville, Tenn., Tidings [1974] 110 p. 19 cm. Includes bibliographical references. [BV3790.C25] 73-90152 1.25 (pbk.)
1. Evangelistic work. I. Title.

*CARL, Paul E. 269.2
Church camp program guide; grades ten through twelve, Illus. by Unada Gliewe. Walter A. Kortrey, ed. Philadelphia, Lutheran Church in Amer., Bd. of Parish Education, 2900 Queen Lane [c.1965] 90p. illus. 28cm. (LCA church camp ser.) Bibl. 1.50 pap., wire bdg.
I. Title.

CATHOLIC Church. Pope, 269'.2
1963- (Paulus VI)
Apostolic exhortation = Evangelii nuntiandi of His Holiness Pope Paul VI to the episcopate, to the clergy and to all the faithful of the entire world on evangelization in the modern world / [translated from the Latin]. London : Catholic Truth Society, [1976] 125 p. ; 19 cm. Cover title: Evangelization in the modern world. "S 312." Includes bibliographical references. [BV3790.C36 1976] 77-359058 ISBN 0-85183-158-3 : £0.45
1. Evangelistic work. I. [Evangelii nuntiandi. English] II. Title. III. Title: Evangelization in the modern world.

CHAFER, Lewis Sperry, 269'.2
1871-1952.
True evangelism; or, Winning souls by prayer. Rev. ed. Grand Rapids, Zondervan Pub. House [1971, c1919] xi, 143 p. 21 cm. "A Dunham publication." [BV3790.C47 1971] 79-81047
1. Evangelistic work. I. Title.

CHAPPELL, Clovis Gilham, 269'.2
1882-1972.
Evangelistic sermons of Clovis G. Chappell. Nashville, Abingdon Press [1973] 144 p. 20 cm. Contents.Contents.—Great things.—His thrilling program.—Bought with a price.—The work of the evangelist.—When God came back.—A glimpse of the afterlife.—The heroic highwayman.—A winsome invitation.—God's endless quest.—What happened at Pentecost.—The victory.—The supreme questions.—Being decisive. [BV3797.C554] 73-320 ISBN 0-687-12182-5 2.95
1. Methodist Church—Sermons. 2. Evangelistic sermons. 3. Sermons, American.

COLEMAN, Robert Emerson, 269'.2
1928-
Dry bones can live again; revival in the local church [by] Robert E. Coleman. Old Tappan, N.J., Revell [1969] 127 p. illus. 21 cm. Bibliographical footnotes. [BV3793.C62] 68-56092 3.50
1. Evangelistic work. I. Title.

CUSTER, Chester E., comp. 269'.2
All things new; perspectives on evangelism. Edited by Chester E. Custer. Nashville, Tidings [1972] 72 p. 19 cm. [BV3795.C9] 72-89660 1.25
1. Evangelistic work. I. Title.

DALABA, Oliver V. 269'.2
That none be lost / Oliver V. Dalaba. Springfield, Mo. : Gospel Pub. House, c1977. 127 p. ; 19 cm. Bibliography: p. 126-127. [BV3790.D23] 77-74553 ISBN 0-88243-621-X pbk. : 1.25
1. Evangelistic work. I. Title.

DALABA, Oliver V. 269'.2
That none be lost / Oliver V. Dalaba. Springfield, Mo. : Gospel Pub. House, c1977. 127 p. ; 19 cm. Bibliography: p. 126-127. [BV3790.D23] 77-74553 ISBN 0-88243-621-X pbk. : 1.25
1. Evangelistic work. I. Title.

DAVENPORT, Frederick Morgan, 1866-1956. 269'.2
Primitive traits in religious revivals; a study in mental and social evolution. New York, Negro Universities Press [1968, c1905] 323 p. 23 cm. Thesis—Columbia University. Bibliographical footnotes. [BV3790.D4 1968] 68-58053
1. Revivals. 2. Psychology, Religious. I. Title.

DAVENPORT, Frederick Morgan, 1866-1956. 269'.2
Primitive traits in religious revivals; a study in mental and social evolution. New York, Macmillan, 1905. [New York, AMS Press, 1972] xii, 323 p. 19 cm. Expansion of the author's thesis, Columbia, 1905. Includes bibliographical references. [BV3790.D4 1972] 72-163669 ISBN 0-404-01929-3 15.00
1. Revivals. 2. Psychology, Religious. I. Title.

DRUMMOND, Lewis A. 269'.2
Leading your church in evangelism / Lewis A. Drummond. Nashville : Broadman Press, c1975. 165 p. ; 19 cm. First published in 1972 under title: Evangelism: the counter revolution. Includes bibliographical references. [BV3790.D75 1975] 75-30135 ISBN 0-8054-6210-4 pbk. : 2.95
1. Evangelistic work. I. Title.

ELLWOOD, Robert S., 1933- 269'.2
One way: the Jesus movement and its meaning [by] Robert S. Ellwood, Jr. Englewood Cliffs, N.J., Prentice-Hall [1973] x, 150 p. 24 cm. Bibliography: p. 145-146. [BV4531.2.E44 1973] 73-3108 ISBN 0-13-636100-5 6.95
1. Jesus People. 2. Evangelicalism—United States. I. Title.
Pbk. 3.95.

ENGEL, James F. 269'.2
What's gone wrong with the harvest? : A communication strategy for the church and world evangelization / James F. Engel and H. Wilbert Norton. Grand Rapids : Zondervan Pub. House, c1975. 171 p. : ill. ; 21 cm. (Contemporary evangelical perspectives) Includes index. Bibliography: p. 161-164. [BV4319.E53] 75-6174 3.95
1. Communication (Theology) 2. Evangelistic work. I. Norton, Hugo Wilbert, joint author. II. Title.

ENROTH, Ronald M. 269'.2
The Jesus People; old-time religion in the age of Aquarius [by] Ronald M. Enroth, Edward E. Ericson, Jr. [and] C. Breckinridge Peters. Grand Rapids, Mich., Eerdmans [1972] 249 p. illus. 21 cm. [BV3793.E56] 73-188249 ISBN 0-8028-1443-3 2.95
1. Jesus People. I. Ericson, Edward E., joint author. II. Peters, C. Breckinridge, joint author.

ESHLEMAN, Paul. 269'.2
The Explo story; a plan to change the world, by Paul Eshleman with Norman Rohrer. Glendale Calif., G/L Regal Books [1972] 111 p. illus. 20 cm. [BV3755.E83] 72-89436 1.45
1. International Student Congress on Evangelism. 2. Evangelistic work—Congresses. 3. Youth—Religious life—Congresses. I. Rohrer, Norman B. II. Title.

ESHLEMAN, Paul. 269'.2
The Explo story; a plan to change the world, by Paul Eshleman with Norman Rohrer. Glenda'e, Calif., G/L Regal Books [1972] 111 p. illus. 20 cm. [BV3755.E83] 72-98436 ISBN 0-8307-0198-2 1.45
1. International Student Congress on Evangelism. 2. Evangelistic work—Congresses. 3. Youth—Religious life—Congresses. I. Rohrer, Norman B. II. Title.

ESHLEMAN, Paul. 269'.2
The Explo story; a plan to change the world, by Paul Eshleman with Norman Rohrer. Glendale Calif., G/L Regal Books [1972] 111 p. illus. 20 cm. [BV3755.E83] 72-98436 ISBN 0-8307-0198-2 1.45
1. International Student Congress on Evangelism. 2. Evangelistic work—Congresses. 3. Youth—Religious life—Congresses. I. Rohrer, Norman B. II. Title.

EVANGELISM : 269'.2
mandates for action / edited by James T. Laney. New York : Hawthorn Books, [1975] viii, 128 p. ; 21 cm. Based on a series of lectures delivered at the Candler School of Theology, Emory University. Includes bibliographical references. [BV3795.E9 1975] 74-22917 ISBN 0-8015-2410-5 : 3.50
1. Evangelistic work—Addresses, essays, lectures. I. Laney, James T.

EVANGELIZATION / 269'.2
edited by Gerald H. Anderson and Thomas F. Stransky. New York : Paulist Press, c1975. vii, 279 p. ; 19 cm. (Mission trends ; no. 2) Includes bibliographical references. [BV3795.E93] 75-29836 ISBN 0-8091-1900-5 pbk. : 2.95
1. Evangelistic work—Addresses, essays, lectures. I. Anderson, Gerald H. II. Stransky, Thomas F.

EVANGELIZATION in the 269'.2
American context / David B. Burrell and Franzita Kane, editors. Notre Dame, Ind. : University of Notre Dame, c1976. p. cm. Proceedings of a symposium held at the University of Notre Dame, Jan. 11-13, 1976. [BX1913.E9] 76-22403 ISBN 0-268-00901-5 : 7.95. ISBN 0-268-00902-3 pbk. : 2.95
1. Catholic Church in the United States—Congresses. 2. Pastoral theology—Catholic Church—Congresses. 3. Catholic learning and scholarship—Congresses. I. Burrell, David B. II. Kane, Franzita, 1909- III. Notre Dame, Ind. University.

FACKRE, Gabriel J. 269'.2
Do and tell: engagement evangelism in the '70s, by Gabriel Fackre. Grand Rapids, Eerdmans [1973] 106 p. 18 cm. Includes bibliographical references. [BV3790.F25] 72-93619 ISBN 0-8028-1494-8 1.45
1. Evangelistic work. I. Title.

FACKRE, Gabriel J. 269'.2
Word in deed : theological themes in evangelism / by Gabriel Fackre. Grand Rapids : Eerdmans, [1975] 109 p. : ill. ; 18 cm. Bibliography: p. 106-109. [BV3793.F32] 74-30328 ISBN 0-8028-1605-3 pbk. : 1.95
1. Evangelistic work (Christian theology) I. Title.

FISH, Roy J. 269'.2
Every member evangelism for today / Roy J. Fish, J. E. Conant. 1st ed. New York : Harper & Row, c1976. vii, 111 p. ; 21 cm. "An updating of J. E. Conant's classic, Every member evangelism." [BV3790.C59 1976] 75-12289 ISBN 0-06-061551-6 pbk. : 2.95
1. Evangelistic work. I. Conant, Judson E., joint author. II. Conant, Judson E. Every-member evangelism. III. Title.

FISHER, Wallace E. 269'.2
Because we have good news [by] Wallace E. Fisher. Nashville, Abingdon Press [1974] 128 p. 19 cm. Includes bibliographical references. [BV3790.F543] 73-12233 ISBN 0-687-02532-X 2.50 (pbk.).
1. Evangelistic work. I. Title.

FORD, Leighton. 269'.2
New man ... new world. Waco, Tex., Word Books [1972] 119 p. 23 cm. [BV3797.F557] 72-88642 3.95
1. Evangelistic sermons. 2. Sermons, American. I. Title.

FORD, Leighton. 269'.2
New man ... new world. Waco, Tex., Word Books [1972] 119 p. 23 cm. [BV3797.F557] 72-88642 3.95
1. Evangelistic sermons. 2. Sermons, American. I. Title.

FORD, William Herschel, 1900- 269'.2
Simple sermons on conversion and commitment, by W. Herschel Ford. Grand Rapids, Mich., Zondervan Pub. House [1972] 127 p. 22 cm. [BV3797.F56] 76-189575 2.95
1. Evangelistic sermons. 2. Baptists—Sermons. 3. Sermons, American. I. Title.

FOUST, Paul J. 269'.2
Reborn to multiply; tested techniques for personal evangelism, by Paul J. Foust. St. Louis, Concordia Pub. House [1973] 56 p. 23 cm. [BV3795.F68] 73-9110 ISBN 0-570-03170-2 1.35 (pbk.)
1. Evangelistic work. I. Title.

FROHLICH, Samuel Heinrich, 1803-1857. 269'.2
The mystery of godliness and the mystery of ungodliness, their essence and the contract between them viewed in the light of the Word of God. [Syracuse, N.Y., Translators' Pub. Co., 1908] viii, 65 p. 22 cm. Cover title: A protest against infant baptism and the falling away of the established churches viewed in the light of the Word of God. Also issued with the German original. [BX6194.A6F72] 8-35969
1. Apostolic Christian Church — Doctrinal and controversial works. I. Title. II. Title: A protest against infant baptism and the falling away of the established churches.

FROHLICH, Samuel Heinrich, 1803-1857. 269'.2
The mystery of godliness and the mystery of ungodliness, their essence and the contract between them viewed in the light of the Word of God. [Syracuse, N.Y., Translators' Pub. Co., 1908] viii, 65 p. 22 cm. Cover title: A protest against infant baptism and the falling away of the established churches viewed in the light of the Word of God. Also issued with the German original. [BX6194.A6F72] 8-35969
1. Apostolic Christian Church — Doctrinal and controversial works. I. Title. II. Title: A protest against infant baptism and the falling away of the established churches.

GODFREY, George. 269'.2
How to win souls and influence people for heaven. Grand Rapids, Baker Book House [1973] 160 p. port. 22 cm. Bibliography: p. 157-158. [BV4520.G6] 72-85673 ISBN 0-8010-3666-6 2.95
1. Witness bearing (Christianity) 2. Evangelistic work. I. Title.

GREEN, Edward Michael Bankes. 269'.2
Evangelism in the early Church, by Michael Green. Grand Rapids, Eerdmans [1970] 349 p. illus. 23 cm. Includes bibliographical references. [BR195.E9G7 1970b] 75-127633 ISBN 0-340-10707-3 6.95
1. Evangelistic work—History. 2. Church history—Primitive and early church, ca. 30-600. I. Title.

HAGGAI, John Edmund. 269'.2
New hope for planet Earth [by] John Haggai. Nashville, T. Nelson [1974] 160 p. illus. 21 cm. [BV3790.H26] 73-21518 5.95
1. Evangelistic work. 2. Missions. I. Title.

HARING, Bernhard, 1912- 269'.2
Evangelization today / Bernard Haring ; [translated by Albert Kuuire]. Notre Dame, Ind. : Fides Publishers, [1975,] c1974 ix, 182 p. ; 22 cm. Includes bibliographical references. [BV3790.H2413] 75-313212 ISBN 0-8190-0557-6 pbk. : 4.00
1. Evangelistic work. 2. Christian ethics—Catholic authors. I. Title.

HARRINGTON, Bob, 1927- 269'.2
Bring them in! Nashville, Broadman Press [1974] 158 p. illus. 21 cm. [BV3790.H356] 74-77358 ISBN 0-8054-5544-2 4.95
1. Evangelistic work. I. Title.

HARRINGTON, Bob, 1927- 269'.2
God's super salesman. Nashville, Broadman Press [1970] 176 p. illus., ports. 21 cm. [BV3785.H346A3] 73-117310 4.95
1. Evangelists—Correspondence, reminiscences, etc. 2. Evangelistic work. I. Title.

HAVLIK, John F. 269'.2
People-centered evangelism [by] John F. Havlik. Nashville, Broadman Press [1970, c1971] 91 p. 20 cm. [BV3790.H373 1971] 74-136130
1. Evangelistic work. I. Title.

HENDRICK, John R., 1927- 269'.2
Opening the door of faith : the why and when of evangelism / John R. Hendrick. Atlanta : John Knox Press, c1977. p. cm. Includes bibliographical references. [BV3790.H388] 76-12404 ISBN 0-8042-0675-9 : 4.50
1. Evangelistic work. 2. Faith. I. Title.

HENRICHSEN, Walter A. 269'.2
Disciples are made-not born [by] Walter A. Henrichsen. Wheaton, Ill., Victor Books [1974] 160 p. illus. 18 cm. (An Input book) [BV4501.2.H374] 74-79162 ISBN 0-88207-706-6 1.75 (pbk.).
1. Christian life—1960- 2. Evangelistic work. I. Title.

HINDSON, Edward E. 269'.2
Glory in the church : the coming Bicentennial revival / by Edward E. Hindson. New York : T. Nelson, [1975] p. cm. [BV3790.H48] 75-17883 ISBN 0-8407-5600-3 pbk.
1. Revivals. I. Title.

HIS guide to evangelism 269'.2
/ Paul E. Little & others. Downers Grove, Ill. : InterVarsity Press, c1977. 157 p. : ill. ; 18 cm. Articles reprinted from His magazine. Includes bibliographical references. [BV3795.H48] 77-72523 ISBN 0-87784-488-7 pbk. : 2.50
1. Evangelistic work—Addresses, essays, lectures. 2. College students—Religious life—Addresses, essays, lectures. I. Little, Paul E. II. His. III. Title: Guide to evangelism.

HOFFMAN, Fred W 269.2
Revival times in America. Boston, W. A. Wilde Co. [1956] 189p. 20cm. [BV3773.H6] 56-11245
1. Revivals— U. S. I. Title.

HOFINGER, Johannes. 269'.2
Evangelization and catechesis / by Johannes Hofinger. New York : Paulist Press, 1976. v, 153 p. ; 21 cm. Includes index. [BV3790.H59] 75-36171 ISBN 0-8091-1928-5 pbk. : pbk. : 4.95
1. Evangelistic work. I. Title.

HOGUE, C. Bill. 269'.2
Love leaves no choice : life-style evangelism / C. B. Hogue. Waco, Tex. : Word Books, c1976. 160 p. ; 23 cm. Bibliography: p. 160. [BV3790.H598] 76-5720 ISBN 0-87680-471-7 : 5.95
1. Evangelistic work. I. Title.

HOW to win them 269'.2
[by] John R. Bisagno, Kenneth L. Chafin, C. Wade Freeman, and others. Nashville, Broadman Press [1971, c1970] 158 p. 21 cm. Contents.Contents.—Jacob's substitutes for prayer, by J. R. Bisagno.—Evangelism in the 70's, by K. L. Chafin.—Preparing for evangelism, by J. E. Coggin.—The road to renewal, by R. J. Fish.—Difficult days for the church, by C. W. Freeman.—On really following Jesus, by R. H. Langley.—Baptists united in evangelism, by L. P. Leavell.—Punching holes in the darkness, by P. McLeod.—The object of a New Testament church, by P. A. Meigs.—Rolling away the stones, by R. E. Roberts.—Winning words, by L. Sanderson.—Different ways to believe in Jesus, by H. Shannon.—Regeneration, by W. E. Ward. [BV3795.H67] 75-136133 3.95
1. Evangelistic work—Addresses, essays, lectures. I. Bisagno, John R.

HUNTER, Charles, 1920- 269'.2
Since Jesus passed by, by Charles [and] Frances Hunter. Old Tappan, N.J., F. H. Revell Co. [1974, c1973] 148 p. 18 cm. (Spire books) [BV3785.H78A37 1973] 74-155357 1.45
1. Revivals—United States. 2. Faith-cure. 3. Pentecostalism. I. Hunter, Frances Gardner, 1916- joint author. II. Title.

HUNTER, George G., comp. 269'.2
Rethinking evangelism. Edited by George G. Hunter III. Nashville, Tidings [1971] 94 p. 22 cm. [BV3795.H85] 77-185264 1.50
1. Evangelistic work—Addresses, essays, lectures. I. Title.

INCH, Morris A., 1925- 269'.2
Paced by God [by] Morris A. Inch. Waco, Tex., Word Books [1973] 129 p. 23 cm. Bibliography: p. 128-129. [BR1640.I5] 72-84163 4.95
1. Evangelicalism. 2. God. 3. Man (Theology) I. Title.

INTERNATIONAL Congress on World Evangelization, Lausanne, 1974. 269'.2
Let the earth hear His voice : official reference volume, papers and responses / International Congress on World Evangelization, Lausanne, Switzerland ; edited by J. D. Douglas. Minneapolis : World Wide Publications, c1975. vii, 1471 p. : ill. ; 23 cm. Includes bibliographical references. [BV3755.I55 1974] 74-24847 12.95
1. Evangelistic work—Congresses. I. Douglas, James Dixon. II. Title.

JAUNCEY, James H. 269'.2
Psychology for successful evangelism, by James H. Jauncey. Foreword by Leighton Ford. Chicago, Moody Press [1972] 126 p. 22 cm. [BV3793.J38] 71-175499 ISBN 0-8024-6940-X 3.95
1. Evangelistic work. 2. Salvation—Psychology. I. Title.

JOB, Rueben P. 269'.2
Issue one: evangelism, edited by Rueben P. Job and Harold K. Bales. Nashville, Tidings [1970] 116 p. 22 cm. [BV3795.J6] 70-120777 1.75
1. Evangelistic work—Addresses, essays, lectures. I. Bales, Harold K., joint author. II. Title.

JOHNSTON, Arthur P. 269'.2
World evangelism and the word of God [by] Arthur P. Johnston. Foreword by Billy Graham. Minneapolis, Bethany Fellowship [1974] 301 p. 22 cm. Bibliography: p. 285-301. [BV3793.J63] 74-13788 ISBN 0-87123-600-1 3.95 (pbk.).
1. International Missionary Council. 2. Evangelistic work. I. Title.

JORSTAD, Erling, 1930- 269'.2
comp.
The Holy Spirit in today's church; a handbook of the new pentecostalism. Nashville, Abingdon Press [1973] 160 p. 20 cm. Bibliography: p. 157-160. [BX8763.J67] 73-8691 ISBN 0-687-17293-4 2.75
1. Pentecostalism. I. Title.

JORSTAD, Erling, 1930- 269'.2
That new-time religion; the Jesus revival in America. Minneapolis, Augsburg Pub. House [1972] 143 p. 20 cm. Bibliography: p. 139-141. [BV3773.J67] 72-78553 ISBN 0-8066-1221-5 2.95
1. Revivals—United States. 2. Jesus People—United States. I. Title.

JULES-ROSETTE, Bennetta. 269'.2
African apostles : ritual and conversion in the Church of John Maranke / Bennetta Jules-Rosette. Ithaca, N.Y. : Cornell University Press, 1975. 302 p. : ill. ; 22 cm. (Symbol, myth, and ritual series) Includes index. Bibliography: p. [290]-298. [BX6194.A63J84] 75-8437 ISBN 0-8014-0846-6
1. Apostolic Church of John Maranke. 2. Jules-Rosette, Bennetta. 3. Rites and ceremonies—Africa, Sub-Saharan. I. Title.

JULES-ROSETTE, Bennetta. 269'.2
African apostles : ritual and conversion in the Church of John Maranke / Bennetta Jules-Rosette. Ithaca, N.Y. : Cornell University Press, 1975. 302 p. : ill. ; 22 cm. (Symbol, myth, and ritual series) Includes index. Bibliography: p. [290]-298. [BX6194.A63J84] 75-8437 ISBN 0-8014-0846-6 : 17.50
1. Apostolic Church of John Maranke. 2. Jules-Rosette, Bennetta. 3. Rites and ceremonies—Africa, Sub-Saharan. I. Title.

KENNEDY, Dennis James, 269'.2
1930-
Evangelism explosion [by] D. James Kennedy. Foreword by Billy Graham. [3d ed.] Wheaton, Ill., Tyndale House Publishers [1970] v, 187, [3] p. illus. 27 cm. Bibliography: p. [189]-[190] [BV3790.K46 1970] 71-116480 ISBN 0-8423-0780-X
1. Evangelistic work. I. Title.

KENNEDY, Dennis James, 269'.2
1930-
Evangelism explosion / [by] D. James Kennedy ; foreword by Billy Graham. Revised British ed. London : Coverdale House, 1976. [11], 164 p. : ill., forms ; 23 cm. Includes index. Bibliography: p. 159-160. [BV3790.K46 1976] 76-374947 ISBN 0-902088-80-7 : £1.95
1. Evangelistic work. I. Title.

KEUCHER, William F. 269'.2
Good news people in action / by William F. Keucher. Valley Forge, Pa. : Judson Press, [1975] 96 p. : ill. ; 22 cm. Includes bibliographical references. [BV3790.K493] 74-30039 ISBN 0-8170-0671-0 pbk. : 2.50
1. Evangelistic work. 2. Witness bearing (Christianity) I. Title.

KNIGHT, Walker L., 1924- 269'.2
comp.
Jesus people come alive. Compiled by Walker L. Knight. Wheaton, Ill., Tyndale House Publishers [1971] 127 p. illus. 18 cm. Contents.Contents.—"It's so wild ... praise the Lord!" By E. Hullum, Jr., and D. Lee.—The Jesus explosion, by B. Price and E. Hullum, Jr.—Communes for Christ, by W. L. Knight.—Stirrings in the churches, by D. Lee.—Reverberations from Asbury, by F. Ashley.—Coast-to-coast echoes, by T. Druin.—The new sound, by M. V. Burns.—Faddists or disciples? By W. L. Knight. [BV3773.K58] 75-179070 1.25
1. Revivals—United States. 2. Jesus People—United States. I. Title.

KOOIMAN, Helen W. 269'.2
Transformed; behind the scenes with Billy Graham [by] Helen W. Kooiman. Wheaton, Ill., Tyndale House Publishers [1970] 145 p. illus., port. 22 cm. [BV3775.A5K6] 70-112663 3.95
1. Graham, William Franklin, 1918- 2. Revivals—Anaheim, Calif. I. Title.

KRASS, Alfred C. 269'.2
Beyond the either-or church; notes toward the recovery of the wholeness of evangelism [by] Alfred C. Krass. Nashville, Tidings [1973] 104 p. 19 cm. Includes bibliographical references. [BV3790.K67] 73-86695 1.50 (pbk.)
1. Evangelistic work. I. Title.

LOUD, Grover Cleveland, 269'.2
1890-1968.
Evangelized America. Freeport, N.Y., Books for Libraries Press [1971] xvi, 373 p. illus. 23 cm. Reprint of the 1928 ed. Bibliography: p. 369-373. [BV3773.L6 1971] 70-169770 ISBN 0-8369-5990-6
1. Evangelistic work. 2. Revivals—U.S. 3. Evangelists—U.S. I. Title.

MCDILL, Wayne. 269'.2
Evangelism in a tangled world / Wayne McDill. Nashville : Broadman Press, 1977, c1976. 181 p. ; 19 cm. Includes bibliographical references. [BV3790.M225] 76-39712 ISBN 0-8054-6214-7 pbk. : 3.95
1. Evangelistic work. I. Title.

MCKAY, Charles Lloyd, 269'.2
1908-
The call of the harvest / Charles L. McKay. Nashville : Convention Press, 1976. 129 p. ; 22 cm. [BV3796.M28 1976] 76-151693
1. Evangelistic work—Study and teaching. I. Title.

MCNAMARA, William. 269.2
Manual for retreat masters. Milwaukee, Bruce Pub. Co. [1960] 94p. 20cm. [BX2375.W5] 60-12649
1. Retrents. I. Title.

MATTHEWS, Charles Evert, 269.2
1887-
A church revival. Nashville, Broadman Press [c1955] 119p. illus. 20cm. [BV3790.M445] 55-14118
1. Revivals. I. Title.

MAYFIELD, William H. 269'.2
Restoring first century evangelism : for an effective program in soul-winning through the rediscovery of the witnessing power of the early church : evangelism text book and training manual / by William H. Mayfield. Cincinnati : New Life Books, [1974] 103 p. : ill. ; 27 cm. Includes index. [BV3790.M47] 74-81096 ISBN 0-87239-015-2 : 3.95
1. Evangelistic work. I. Title.

MORRIS, George E. 269'.2
Shalom : a vision of a new world / edited by George Morris. Nashville : Tidings, [1974] ix, 85 p. ; 19 cm. Includes bibliographical references. [BV3795.M57] 74-21903 pbk. : 1.75
1. Evangelistic work—Addresses, essays, lectures. I. Title.

MORSE, Tom. 269'.2
When the music stops [by] Tom Morse, with Bobbie Lauster. Old Tappan, N.J., Revell [1971] 125 p. 21 cm. [BV4470.M67] 75-160271 ISBN 0-8007-0463-0 3.95
1. Church work with narcotic addicts—Miami, Fla. I. Title.

NATIONAL Conference on New 269'.2
Styles in Cooperative Evangelism, New Orleans, 1971.
Bridges to the world. Edited by Harold K. Bales. Nashville, Tidings [1971] 109 p. 21 cm. "Key 73." Chapters in this volume are portions of addresses presented at the conference. [BV3795.N37 1971] 75-171884
1. Evangelistic work—Addresses, essays, lectures. I. Bales, Harold K., ed. II. Title.

NEIGHBOUR, Ralph Webster, 269'.2
1929-
Target-group evangelism / Ralph W. Neighbour, Jr. and Cal Thomas. Nashville : Broadman Press, [1975] 132 p. : ill. ; 21 cm. Includes bibliographical references. [BV3790.N286] 74-20309 ISBN 0-8054-5551-5 : 3.95
1. Evangelistic work. I. Thomas, Cal, joint author. II. Title.

NEIGHBOUR, Ralph Webster, 269'.2
1929-
The touch of the spirit [by] Ralph W. Neighbour, Jr. Nashville, Tenn., Broadman Press [1972] x, 160 p. illus. 21 cm. Bibliography: p. 157-160. [BV3790.N29] 72-84243 ISBN 0-8054-5130-7 4.95
1. Evangelistic work. I. Title.

THE New face of 269'.2
evangelicalism : an international symposium on the Lausanne covenant / edited by C. Rene Padilla. Downers Grove, Ill. : InterVarsity Press, 1976, i.e.1977 282 p. ; 21 cm. Includes bibliographical references. [BV3795.N48 1976b] 76-12301 ISBN 0-87784-779-7 pbk. : 4.95
1. Lausanne covenant—Addresses, essays, lectures. 2. Evangelistic work—Addresses, essays, lectures. 3. Evangelicalism—Addresses, essays, lectures. I. Rene Padilla, C.

NIGHTINGALE, Reuben H. 269'.2
Crossing Jordan at flood tide / [R. H. Nightingale]. Mountain View, Calif. : Pacific Press Pub. Association, [1975] 155 p. ; 19 cm. [BV3790.N48] 75-16541 pbk. : 2.95
1. Seventh-Day Adventists—Doctrinal and controversial works. 2. Evangelistic work. I. Title.

NORTHEY, James E. 269'.2
Outreach : toward effective open-air evangelism / by James Northey. London : Salvationist Publishing and Supplies, 1976. [6], ii, 86 p. ; 22 cm. Includes index. Bibliography: p. 81-84. [BV3790.N63] 76-365345 ISBN 0-85412-264-8 : £0.75
1. Evangelistic work. I. Title.

ORR, James Edwin, 1912- 269'.2
Campus aflame; dynamic of student religious revolution, by J. Edwin Orr. Glendale, Calif., Regal Books [1972, c1971] v, 277 p. 20 cm. Bibliography: p. 265-277. [BV639.C6O77] 71-185801 ISBN 0-8307-0157-5 2.95
1. College students—Religious life. 2. Revivals. 3. Evangelicalism. I. Title.

ORR, James Edwin, 1912- 269'.2
The fervent prayer: the worldwide impact of the Great Awakening of 1858, by J. Edwin Orr. Chicago, Moody Press [1974] xx, 236 p. 24 cm. Bibliography: p. 225-233. [BV3770.O67] 74-2938 ISBN 0-8024-2615-8 5.95
1. Revivals. I. Title.

ORR, James Edwin, 1912- 269'.2
The flaming tongue; the impact of twentieth century revivals, by J. Edwin Orr. Chicago, Moody Press [1973] xiv, 241 p. 24 cm. Bibliography: p. 231-237. [BV3770.O68] 72-95016 ISBN 0-8024-2801-0 4.95
1. Revivals—History. I. Title.

PENTECOST, Edward C. 269'.2
Reaching the unreached; an introductory study on developing an overall strategy for world evangelization, by Edward C. Pentecost. South Pasadena, Calif., William Carey Library [1974] xiv, 149, [85] p. illus. 22 cm. Bibliography: p. [135]-141. [BV3790.P45] 74-11270 ISBN 0-87808-418-5 5.95
1. Evangelistic work. 2. Christianity—Statistics. I. Title.

PETERS, George W. 269'.2
Saturation evangelism [by] George W. Peters. Grand Rapids, Zondervan Pub. House [1970] 237 p. illus. 22 cm. (Contemporary evangelical perspectives) Bibliography: p. 224-237. [BV3790.P46] 74-106433
1. Evangelistic work. I. Title.

PICKERING, Ernest D. 269'.2
The theology of evangelism / by Ernest D. Pickering. 1st ed. Clarks Summit, Pa. : Baptist Bible College Press, 1974. 68 p. ; 17 cm. [BV3793.P47] 74-18174
1. Evangelistic work. I. Title.

POTTER, C. Burtt. 269'.2
The church reaching out / Burtt Potter ; foreword by Owen Cooper. Durham, N.C. : Moore Pub. Co., c1976. 164 p. ; 24 cm. Includes bibliographical references. [BV3790.P656] 76-12219 ISBN 0-87716-062-7 : 5.00
1. Evangelistic work. I. Title.

QUEBEDEAUX, Richard. 269'.2
The young evangelicals; revolution in orthodoxy. [1st ed.] New York, Harper & Row [1974] xii, 157 p. 21 cm. Bibliography: p. 154-157. [BR1640.Q42] 73-6344 ISBN 0-06-066725-7 2.50 (pbk.)
1. Evangelicalism. I. Title.

RAMM, Bernard L., 1916- 269'.2
The Evangelical heritage, by Bernard L. Ramm. Waco, Tex., Word Books [1973] 180 p. 23 cm. Includes bibliographical references. [BR1640.R35] 72-96359 5.95
1. Evangelicalism—History. I. Title.

RENDALL, Ted S. 269'.2
Fire in the church / Ted S. Rendall ; foreword by Theodore H. Epp. Chicago : Moody Press, [1974] 160 p. ; 22 cm. Bibliography: p. 152-160. [BV3790.R4] 74-193336 ISBN 0-8024-2635-2 pbk. : 2.95
1. Revivals. I. Title.

RICHARDSON, J. Spurgeon. 269*.2
The Kiamichi Baptist Assembly, its origin and early development, by J. S. (Spurgeon) Richardson. [Talihina, Okla., 1965] 52 p. illus., ports. 22 cm. [BV3799.K5R53] 72-218362
1. Kiamichi Baptist Assembly. 2. Camp-meetings.

ROBERTS, W. Dayton. 269'.2
Revolution in evangelism; the story of Evangelism-in-depth in Latin America. [by] W. Dayton Roberts. Foreword by Leighton Ford. Chicago, Moody [1967] 127p. 18cm. (Christian forum bks.) [BV3777.L3R6] 67-26295 1.25 pap.,
1. Strachan, Robert Kenneth, 1910-1965. 2. Evangelistic work—Latin American. 3. Latin America Mission. I. Title. II. Title: Evangelism-in-depth.

ROBINSON, Paul M., 1914- 269'.2
Call the witnesses: perspectives on evangelism in the Church of the Brethren. Edited by Paul M. Robinson. Elgin, Ill., Brethren Press [1974] 144 p. ports. 18 cm. [BV3770.R6] 74-1480 ISBN 0-87178-124-7 2.95 (pbk.)
1. Evangelistic work. I. Title.

SMITH, Timothy Lawrence, 269.2
1924-
Revivalism and social reform; American Protestantism on the eve of the Civil War [Gloucester, Mass., P. Smith, 1966, c.1957] 253p. 21cm. (Harper torch-bks. Acad. lib., TB1229L rebound) First pub. by Abingdon in 1957. Bibl. [BR525.S6] 4.00
1. U.S.—Church history. 2. Revivals—U.S. 3. Church and social problems—U.S. I. Title.

SMITH, Timothy Lawrence, *269.2
1924-
Revivalism and social reform in mid-nineteenth-century America. Chapters I-XI and XIV comprise the Frank S. and Elizabeth D. Brewer prize essay for 1955, the American Society of Church History. New York, Abingdon Press [1957] 253 p. 24 cm. "Critical essay on the sources of information": p. 238-248. [BR525.S6] 57-6757
1. U.S. — Church history. 2. Revivals — U.S. 3. Church and social problems — U.S. I. Title.

SMITH, Timothy Lawrence, 269.2*
1924-
Revivalism and social reform in mid-nineteenth-century America. Chapters I-XI and XIV comprise the Frank S. and Elizabeth D. Brewer prize essay for 1955, the American Society of Church History. New York, Abingdon Press [1957] 253 p. 24 cm. "Critical essay on the sources of information": p. 238-248. [BR525.S6] 57-6757
1. United States—Church history. 2. Revivals—United States. 3. Church and social problems—United States. I. Title.

STEWART, Don. 269'.2
Fakes, frauds, and fools. Miracle Valley, Ariz., Don Stewart Evangelistic Assoc. [1972] 53 p. illus. 18 cm. Bibliography: p. 53. [BT1105.S78] 72-171030
1. Apologetics—20th century. I. Title.

STOTT, John R. W. 269'.2
Christian mission in the modern world / John R. W. Stott. Downers Grove, Ill. : InterVarsity Press, 1975. 128 p. ; 22 cm. [BV601.8.S8 1975] 75-21455 ISBN 0-87784-485-2 : 2.95
1. Mission of the church—Addresses, essays, lectures. 2. Evangelistic work—Addresses, essays, lectures. 3. Christianity and other religions—Addresses, essays, lectures. 4. Salvation—Addresses, essays, lectures. 5. Conversion—Addresses, essays, lectures. I. Title.

STOTT, John R. W. 269'.2
Our guilty silence [by] John R. W. Stott. [1st U.S.A. ed.] Grand Rapids, Eerdmans [1969, c1967] 119 p. 18 cm. Cover title: Our guilty silence: the Church, the gospel and the world. Bibliographical footnotes. [BV3790.S884 1969] 75-3986 1.45
1. Evangelistic work. I. Title.

SWEET, William Warren, 269.2
1881-1959
Revivalism in America, its origin, growth, and decline. Gloucester, Mass., P. Smith, 1965[c.1944] xv, 192p. 21cm. First pub. in 1944 by Scribners. Bibl. [BV3773.S8] 66-3246 3.75
I. Title.

SYRDAL, Rolf A. 269'.2
Go, make disciples / Rolf A. Syrdal. Minneapolis : Augsburg Pub. House, c1977. 128 p. ; 20 cm. Bibliography: p. 128. [BV3770.S97] 77-84077 ISBN 0-8066-1603-2 : 3.50
1. Evangelistic work. 2. Mission of the church. 3. Witness bearing (Christianity) I. Title.

TARI, Mel. 269'.2
Like a mighty wind, by Mel Tari as told to Cliff Dudley. [1st ed.] Carol Stream, Ill., Creation House [1971] 161 p. 23 cm. [BV3785.T25A3] 76-182854 3.95
1. Evangelistic work—Indonesia. I. Dudley, Cliff. II. Title.

TORREY, Reuben Archer, 269'.2
1856-1928.
How to bring men to Christ / R. A. Torrey. Minneapolis : Bethany Fellowship, 1977. 121 p. ; 18 cm. (Dimension books) Reprint of the 1893 ed. published by F. H. Revell Co., New York. [BV3790.T58 1977] 76-57111 ISBN 0-87123-230-8 pbk. : 1.50
1. Evangelistic work. I. Title.

TOWNS, Elmer L. 269'.2
Evangelize thru Christian education, by Elmer L. Towns. [1st ed.] Wheaton, Ill., Evangelical Teacher Training Association [1970] 96 p. 23 cm. (Courses in the advanced (specialized) certificate program) Includes bibliographical references. [BV3790.T67] 78-97811 ISBN 9-10-566089-
1. Evangelistic work—Study and teaching. I. Title.

TURNBULL, Ralph G. 269'.2
Evangelism now. Ralph G. Turnbull, editor. Grand Rapids, Baker Book House [1972] 112 p. 22 cm. Bibliography: p. 110-112. [BV3795.T87] 72-75551 ISBN 0-8010-8778-3 1.95
1. Evangelistic work—Addresses, essays, lectures. I. Title.

VOELKEL, Jack. 269'.2
Student evangelism in a world of revolution / Jack Voelkel ; foreword by David M. Howard. Grand Rapids : Zondervan Pub. House, c1974. 254 p. ; 21 cm. (Contemporary evangelical perspectives) Includes index. Bibliography: p. 240-247. [BV3777.L3V63] 73-13074
1. Church work with students. 2. Evangelistic work—Latin America. I. Title.

WALKER, Alan, 1911- 269'.2
The new evangelism / Alan Walker. Nashville : Abingdon Press, [1975] 112 p. ; 19 cm. [BV3790.W314] 74-28016 ISBN 0-687-27736-1 pbk. : 3.25.
1. Evangelistic work. I. Title.

WATSON, David C. K., 1933- 269'.2
I believe in evangelism / by David Watson. 1st American ed. Grand Rapids : Eerdmans, 1977, c1976. 188 p. ; 21 cm. [BV3790.W327 1977] 77-2229 ISBN 0-8028-1687-8 : 2.95
1. Evangelistic work. I. Title.

WEBER, Jaroy. 269'.2
Winning America to Christ / Jaroy Weber. Nashville : Broadman Press, [1975] 125 p. ; 21 cm. [BV3773.W36] 74-24668 ISBN 0-8054-6518-9 : 3.95
1. Evangelistic work—United States. I. Title.

WEEKS, Howard B. 269'.2
Adventist evangelism in the twentieth century [by] Howard B. Weeks. Washington, Review & Herald Pub. Association [1969] 320 p. illus., facsims., ports. 24 cm. Includes bibliographies. [BX6154.W43] 68-25111
1. Seventh-day Adventists—Doctrinal and controversial works. 2. Evangelistic work. I. Title.

WEISBERGER, Bernard A., 1922- 269.2
They gathered at the river; the story of the great revivalists and their impact upon religion in America [Magnolia, Mass., Peter Smith, 1968,c.1958] xi, 345p. (Quadrangle paperback rebound) Bibl. [BU3773.W4] 5.00
1. Revivals—U.S. 2. Evangelists. I. Title.

WEISBERGER, Bernard A., 1922- 269.2
They gathered at the river; the story of the great revivalists and their impact upon religion in America. [1st ed.] Boston, Little, Brown [1958] 345 p. illus. 22 cm. Includes bibliography. [BV377.W4] 58-7848
1. Revivals—United States. 2. Evangelists. I. Title.

WHITE, John Wesley. 269'.2
Future hope. Carol Stream, Ill., Creation House [1974] 149 p. 23 cm. [BV3797.W424] 73-86952 ISBN 0-88419-067-6 4.95
1. Evangelistic sermons. 2. Sermons, English—Canada. I. Title.

WILLIAM, Father 269.2
Manual for retreat masters. Milwaukee, Bruce Pub. Co. [1961, c.1960] 94p. 60-12649 1.50 pap.,
1. Retreats. I. Title.

WOMACK, David A. 269'.2
Breaking the stained-glass barrier [by] David A. Womack. [1st ed.] New York, Harper & Row [1973] 167 p. 21 cm. [BV3790.W56 1973] 72-11366 ISBN 0-06-069680-X 5.95
1. Evangelistic work. I. Title.

WOODSON, Leslie H., 1929- 269'.2
Evangelism for today's church; meaning, motivation, method, mobilization, by Leslie H. Woodson. Grand Rapids, Zondervan Pub. House [1973] 159 p. 18 cm. Includes bibliographical references. [BV3790.W62] 72-85569 1.25 (pbk.)
1. Evangelistic work. I. Title.

WOOLSEY, Raymond H. 269'.2
Evangelism handbook [by] Raymond H. Woolsey. Washington, Review and Herald Pub. Association [1972] 320 p. illus. 23 cm. Includes bibliographical references. [BV3790.W63] 76-178163
1. Evangelistic work. I. Title.

WORLD Methodist Council 269'.2
Consultation on Evangelism, Jerusalem, 1974.
Beginning in Jerusalem / edited by Rueben P. Job. Nashville : Tidings, c1975. viii, 120 p. ; 22 cm. "Addresses presented at the World Methodist Council Consultation on Evangelism held in Jerusalem in late November 1974." [BV3755.W64 1974] 75-10373
1. Evangelistic work—Congresses. 2. Church and the world—Congresses. I. Job, Rueben P. II. World Methodist Council. III. Title.

GREEN, Hollis L. 269'.2'0202
Why wait till Sunday? : An action approach to local evangelism / by Hollis L. Green. Minneapolis : Bethany Fellowship, [1975] 112 p. : ill. ; 20 cm. Bibliography: p. 108-109. [BV3790.G78] 75-6773 ISBN 0-87123-601-X pbk. : 1.75
1. Evangelistic work—Handbooks, manuals, etc. I. Title.

TENNESSEE Temple 269.2058
College, Chattanooga.
Annual lecture on revival and evangelism, Tennessee Temple schools, Chattanooga, Tennessee. 1st-1954- Wheaton, Ill., Sword of the Lord Publishers. v. 21cm. [BV3760.T4] 55-37454
1. Revivals. 2. Evangelistic work. I. Title.

MARTIN, Dorothy 269'.2'06277311
McKay, 1921-
Moody Bible Institute : God's power in action / by Dorothy Martin. Chicago : Moody Press, c1977. 187 p. : ports. ; 22 cm. Includes bibliographical references. [BV4070.M76M37] 76-49492 ISBN 0-8024-5518-2 pbk. : 2.95
1. Moody Bible Institute of Chicago. I. Title.

AUTREY, C E 269'.2'09
Renewals before Pentecost [by] C. E. Autrey. Nashville, Broadman Press [1968] 144 p. 20 cm. 1960 ed. published under title: Revivals of the Old Testament. Bibliographical references included in "Notes" (p. 141-144) [BV3770.A8 1968] 68-9025
1. Revivals—Hist. 2. Bible. Q. T.—History of Biblical events. I. Title.

AUTREY, C. E. 269'.2'09
Renewals before Pentecost [by] C. E. Autrey. Nashville, Broadman Press [1968] 144 p. 20 cm. 1960 ed. published under title: Revivals of the Old Testament. Bibliographical references included in "Notes" (p. 141-144) [BV3770.A8 1968] 68-9025
1. Bible. O.T.—History of Biblical events. 2. Revivals—History. I. Title.

BURNS, James, 1865-1948. 269.209
Revivals, their laws and leaders. Two additional chapters by Andrew W. Blackwood, Sr. Grand Rapids, Baker Book House, 1960. 353p. 21cm. [BV3770.B8 1960] 60-2791
1. Revivals— Hist. 2. Reformers. I. Title.

ORR, James Edwin, 1912- 269'.2'09034
The eager feet : Evangelical awakenings, 1790-1830 / by J. Edwin Orr. Chicago : Moody Press, [1975] viii, 248 p. ; 24 cm. Includes index. Bibliography: p. 230-244. [BV3770.O66] 75-315875 ISBN 0-8024-2287-X : 5.95
1. Revivals—History. I. Title.

CLARKE, Charles. 269'.2'0922 B
Pioneers of revival. London and New Jersey (Central Hall, Durnsford Rd, SW19 8ED), Fountain Trust-Watchung Books, 1971. 71 p. 18 cm. [BV3780.C57] 72-190434 ISBN 0-901398-21-7 £0.35
1. Evangelists. 2. Revivals. I. Title.

EVANS, William 269'.2'0922 B
Glyn.
Profiles of revival leaders / W. Glyn Evans. Nashville : Broadman Press, c1976. 128 p. ; 21 cm. Includes bibliographical references. [BV3780.E82] 76-4368 ISBN 0-8054-8604-6 : 2.50
1. Evangelists—United States—Biography. 2. Revivals—United States. I. Title.
Contents omitted

GOODSPEED, Edgar 269'.2'0922 B
Johnson, 1833-1881.
A full history of the wonderful career of Moody and Sankey in Great Britain and America. New York, H. S. Goodspeed, 1876. [New York, AMS Press, 1973] 617 p. illus. 23 cm. [BV3785.M7G6 1973] 70-168154 ISBN 0-404-07227-5 25.00
1. Moody, Dwight Lyman, 1837-1899. 2. Sankey, Ira David, 1840-1908. 3. Evangelistic work. I. Title.

MORRIS, James, 1926- 269'.2'0922 B
The preachers. Illus. by Tom Huffman. New York, St. Martin's Press [1973] x, 418 p. illus. 25 cm. Includes bibliographical references. [BV3780.M67] 72-93927 8.95
1. Evangelists—United States. 2. Clergy—United States. I. Title.

ALLEN, Asa Alonso, 1911-1970. 269'.2'0924 B
Born to lose, bound to win; an autobiography [by] A. A. Allen, with Walter Wagner. [1st ed.] Garden City, N.Y., Doubleday, 1970. 202 p. 22 cm. [BV3785.A43A3] 70-132493
I. Wagner, Walter, 1927- II. Title.

ASHMAN, Chuck. 269'.2092'4 B
The gospel according to Billy / by Chuck Ashman ; with an introd. by Rod McKuen. 1st ed. Secaucus, N.J. : Lyle Stuart, c1977. 240 p. ; 24 cm. [BV3785.G69A8 1977] 77-23027 ISBN 0-8184-0251-2 : 8.95
1. Graham, William Franklin, 1918- I. Title.

BAKKER, Jim. 269'.2'0924 B
Move that mountain / by Jim Bakker with Robert Paul Lamb. 1st ed. Plainfield, N.J. : Logos International, 1976. vii, 183 p., [4] leaves of plates : ill. ; 21 cm. [BV3785.B3A35] 76-10532 ISBN 0-88270-164-9 : 5.95
1. Bakker, Jim. 2. Evangelists—United States—Biography. 3. Television in religion. I. Lamb, Robert Paul, joint author. II. Title.

BRABHAM, Lewis F. 269'.2'0924
A new song in the South; the story of the Billy Graham Greenville, S.C. Crusade [by] Lewis F. Brabham. Introd. by Billy Graham. Grand Rapids, Zondervan Pub. House [1966] 155 p. illus., ports. 21 cm. [BV3785.G69B66] 66-29033
1. Graham, William Franklin, 1918- 2. Revivals—Greenville, S.C. I. Title.

BRADFORD, Gamaliel, 1863-1932. 269'.2'0924 B
D. L. Moody; a worker in souls. Freeport, N.Y., Books for Libraries Press [1972] 320 p. illus. 22 cm. Reprint of the 1927 ed. Bibliography: p. 305-308. [BV3785.M7B7 1972] 72-1275 ISBN 0-8369-6821-2
1. Moody, Dwight Lyman, 1837-1899.

BRISCOE, Jill. 269'.2'0924 B
There's a snake in my garden / Jill Briscoe. Grand Rapids : Zondervan Pub. House, [1975] 143 p. ; 22 cm. [BR1725.B684A37] 74-25328 4.95
1. Briscoe, Jill. I. Title.

BUCKINGHAM, Jamie. 269'.2'0924 B
Daughter of destiny : Kathryn Kuhlman, her story / by Jamie Buckingham. Plainfield, N.J. : Logos International, c1976. ix, 309 p., [8] leaves of plates : ill. ; 22 cm. [BV3785.K84B8] 76-12034 ISBN 0-88270-078-2 : 6.95
1. Kuhlman, Kathryn. 2. Evangelists—Pennsylvania—Pittsburgh—Biography. 3. Healers—Pennsylvania—Pittsburgh—Biography. 4. Pittsburgh—Biography. I. Title.

BUMSTED, J. M. 269'.2'0924 B
Henry Alline 1748-1784. [Toronto] University of Toronto Press [1971] [ix], 116 p. 22 cm. (Canadian biographical studies) Bibliography: p. [107]-112. [BV3785.A46B8] 73-24664 ISBN 0-8020-3247-8 4.50
1. Alline, Henry, 1748-1784.

CHANDLER, E. 269'.2'0924 B
Russell.
The Kennedy explosion; the story of Dr. D. James Kennedy ... by E. Russell Chandler. Elgin, Ill., D. C. Cook Pub. Co. [1972, c1971] 125 p. 18 cm. Bibliography: p. 125. [BV3775.F67C48] 79-178886 ISBN 0-912692-02-2 0.95
1. Kennedy, Dennis James, 1930- 2. Evangelistic work—Fort Lauderdale, Fla. I. Title.

CLAUS, Tom, 1929- 269'.2'0924 B
On eagles' wings / by Tom Claus. [Orange?, CA] : Thunderbird Indian Co., c1976. 162 p. : ill. ; 22 cm. [E99.M8C53] 77-354780 3.95
1. Claus, Tom, 1929- 2. Claus family. 3. Mohawk Indians—Biography. 4. Evangelists—United States—Biography. 5. Indians of North America—Missions. I. Title.

DOUGLAS, James 269'.2'0924 B
Dixon.
Completing the course : the story of Lindsay Glegg / by J. D. Douglas. London : Pickering and Inglis, 1976. 128 p., [8] p. of plates : ill., ports. ; 19 cm. [BV3785.G54D68] 77-350974 ISBN 0-7208-0386-1 : £1.00
1. Glegg, Lindsay, 1882-1975. 2. Evangelists—England—Biography. I. Title.

DULLEA, Charles W. 269'.2'0924 B
A Catholic looks at Billy Graham, by Charles W. Dullea. New York, Paulist Press [1973] 149 p. 19 cm. (Deus books) Based on the author's thesis, Gregorian University, Rome, with title: W. F. "Billy" Graham's "Decision for Christ." Bibliography: p. 147-149. [BV3785.G69D84] 73-88904 ISBN 0-8091-1804-1 1.65
1. Graham, William Franklin, 1918- I. Title.

ELLIS, James 269'.2'0924 B
Benton, 1870-1946.
Blazing the Gospel trail / by James B. Ellis. Plainfield, N.J. : Logos International, c1976. 127 p. ; 21 cm. (A Logos classic) [BX7034.Z8E43] 76-2329 ISBN 0-88270-165-7 pbk. : 2.50
1. Ellis, James Benton, 1870-1946. I. Title.

ENGLISH, Eugene 269'.2'0924 B
Schuyler, 1899-
Ordained of the Lord, H. A. Ironside / by E. Schuyler English. Neptune, N.J. : Loizeaux Brothers, [1976] p. cm. Published in 1946 under title: H. A. Ironside, ordained of the Lord. Includes index. "The complete writings of H. A. Ironside": p. [BV3785.I68E5 1976] 76-13873 ISBN 0-87213-141-6
1. Ironside, Henry Allan, 1876-1951. I. Title.

FINDLAY, James F., 269'.2'0924
1930-
Dwight L. Moody, American evangelist, 1837-1899 [by] James F. Findlay, Jr. With a foreword by Martin E. Marty. Chicago, University of Chicago Press [1969] ix, 440 p. 23 cm. "A note on sources": p. 422-426. Bibliographical footnotes. [BV3785.M7F47] 69-13200 10.00
1. Moody, Dwight Lyman, 1837-1899. I. Title.

FISHER, Lee. 269'.2'0924 B
A funny thing happened on the way to the crusade. Carol Stream, Ill., Creation House [1974] 102 p. illus. 22 cm. [BV3785.G69F57 1974] 73-81981 ISBN 0-88419-043-9 4.95
1. Graham, William Franklin, 1918- — Anecdotes. I. Title.

FISHER, Lee. 269'.2'0924 B
Out of this world; the story of the greatest character I have ever known. With art work by Al Petrick. Plainfield, N.J., Logos International [1970] xiii, 173 p. illus. 21 cm. [BV3785.F49F5] 74-100578 3.95
1. Fisher, Charles Arthur, 1888- I. Title.

FRIEND, J. B. B. 269'.2'0924 B
Gipsy for Jesus / [by] J. B. B. Friend. Stoke-on-Trent : M.O.V.E. Press, 1976. 67 p. ; 19 cm. [BR1725.F63A33] 76-380849 ISBN 0-9504136-3-1 : £0.50
1. Friend, J. B. B. 2. Christian biography—South Africa. I. Title.

FULLER, Daniel P. 269'.2'0924 B
Give the winds a mighty voice; the story of Charles E. Fuller, by Daniel P. Fuller. Waco, Tex., Word Books [1972] 247 p. illus. 23 cm. [BV3785.F8F84] 72-83342 5.95
1. Fuller, Charles Edward, 1887-1968. I. Title.

GAINES, Stephen S. 269'.2'0924
Marjoe [by] Stephen S. Gaines. [New York, Dell, 1974 c.1973] 236 p. 18 cm. [BV3785.G64G34] [[B]] 1.50 (pbk.)
1. Gortner, Marjoe. I. Title.
L.C. number for hardbound ed.: 72-9118.

GAINES, Steven S. 269'.2'0924 B
Marjoe: the life of Marjoe Gortner [by] Steven S. Gaines. [1st ed.] New York, Harper & Row [1973] 238 p. illus. 22 cm. [BV3785.G64G34] 72-9118 ISBN 0-06-011401-0 6.95
1. Gortner, Marjoe. I. Title.

*GRAHAM, Billy. 269'.2'0924 B
Blow, wind of God! : selecting writings of Billy Graham / Edited by Donald E. Demaray. New York : New American Library, 1977c1975. 121p. ; 18 cm. (A Signet Book) [BV3785.G69] ISBN 0-451-07380-0 pbk. : 1.50
1. Graham, William Franklin, 1918- I. Demaray, Donald E. ed. II. Title.

*GRAHAM, Billy. 269'.2'0924
Blow, wind of God! : selecting writings of Billy Graham / Edited by Donald E. Demaray. New York : New American Library, 1977c1975. 121p. ; 18 cm. (A Signet Book) [BV3785.G69] ISBN 0-451-07380-0 pbk. : 1.50
1. Graham, William Franklin, 1918- I. Demaray, Donald E. ed. II. Title.

GRAHAM, Morrow C., 269'.2'0924 B
1892-
They call me Mother Graham / Morrow C. Graham. Old Tappan, N.J. : F. H. Revell Co., c1977. 64 p. : ports. ; 18 cm. (New life ventures) Autobiographical. [BX6495.G663A35] 77-5617 ISBN 0-8007-9000-6 pbk. : 0.95
1. Graham, Morrow C., 1892- 2. Graham, William Franklin, 1918- 3. Baptists—North Carolina—Charlotte—Biography. 4. Charlotte, N.C.—Biography. I. Title.

GRAHAM, Morrow C., 269'.2'0924 B
1892-
They call me Mother Graham / Morrow C. Graham. Old Tappan, N.J. : F. H. Revell Co., c1977. 64 p. : ports. ; 18 cm. (New life ventures) Autobiographical. [BX6495.G663A35] 77-5617 ISBN 0-8007-9000-6 pbk. : 0.95
1. Graham, Morrow C., 1892- 2. Graham, William Franklin, 1918- 3. Baptists—North

Carolina—Charlotte—Biography. 4. Charlotte, N.C.—Biography. I. Title.

GUNDRY, Stanley N. 269'.2'0924 B
Love them in : the proclamation theology of D. L. Moody / by Stanley N. Gundry ; foreword by Frank E. Gaebelein. Chicago : Moody Press, c1976. 252 p. ; 24 cm. A revision of the author's thesis, Lutheran School of Theology, Chicago. Includes indexes. Bibliography: p. 223-248. [BV3785.M7G86 1976] 76-20731 ISBN 0-8024-5026-1 : 6.95
1. Moody, Dwight Lyman, 1837-1899. I. Title.

HALL, Douglas, 269'.2'0924 B
Not made for defeat; the authorized biography of Oswald J. Smith. With a foreword by Billy Graham and an introd. by John Wesley White. Grand Rapids, Zondervan [1969] 192 p. illus. 21 cm. [BX9225.S54H3] 77-81068
1. Smith, Oswald J. I. Title.

HARGIS, Billy James, 1925- 269'.2'0924 B
Why I fight for a Christian America. Nashville, T. Nelson [1974] 179 p. 18 cm. [BR1725.H237A37] 74-14714 ISBN 0-8407-5557-0
1. Hargis, Billy James, 1925- I. Title.

HARRISON, Tank. 269'.2'0924 B
I've been had. Nashville, Abingdon Press [1974] 62 p. 19 cm. [BR1725.H24A34] 74-3479 ISBN 0-687-19789-9 1.25 (pbk.)
1. Harrison, Tank. I. Title.

HOSIER, Helen Kooiman. 269'.2'0924 B
Kathryn Kuhlman : the life she led, the legacy she left / Helen Kooiman Hosier. Boston : G. K. Hall, 1976. p. cm. Large print ed. Includes bibliographical references. [BV3785.K84H67 1976] 76-41341 ISBN 0-8161-6411-8 : 10.95
1. Kuhlman, Kathryn. 2. Evangelists—United States—Biography. 3. Sight-saving books.

HOSIER, Helen Kooiman. 269'.2'0924 B
Kathyrn Kuhlman : the life she led, the legacy she left / Helen Kooiman Hosier. Old Tappan, N.J. : F. H. Revell, Co., c1976. 160 p. : ill. ; 21 cm. Includes bibliographical references. [BV3785.K84H67] 76-18277 ISBN 0-8007-0827-X : 5.95 pbk. : 3.95
1. Kuhlman, Kathyrn.

HUMBARD, Martha Childers. 269'.2'0924 B
Give me that old-time religion / Martha Childers Humbard, with Bill Armstrong. Plainfield, N.J. : Logos International, c1977. 156 p. : ill. ; 21 cm. On spine: Old-time religion. [BV3785.H76A33] 77-80161 ISBN 0-88270-227-0 : 2.95
1. Humbard, Martha Childers. 2. Evangelists—United States—Biography. I. Armstrong, Bill, 1921- joint author. II. Title.

HUMBARD, Rex, 1919- 269'.2'0924 B
Miracles in my life; Rex Humbard's own story. Old Tappan, N.J., Revell [1971] 125 p. 22 cm. [BV3785.H77A3] 70-175524 ISBN 0-8007-0494-0 3.95
I. Title.

HUMBARD, Rex, 1919- 269'.2'0924 B
To tell the world / Rex Humbard. Englewood Cliffs, N.J. : Prentice-Hall, [1975] 211 p. ; 22 cm. [BV3785.H77A33] 75-19273 ISBN 0-13-477158-3 : 6.95
1. Humbard, Rex, 1919- 2. Cathedral of Tomorrow, Cuyahoga Falls, Ohio. I. Title.

*HUNTER, Jack D. 269'.2'0924 B
Word of life by Jack D. Hunter. New York, Pocket Books [1976] 192 p. 18 cm. [BV3785] ISBN 0-671-80169-4 1.95 (pbk.)
1. Wyrtzen, Jack. I. Title.

JOHNSTON, Faith, 1902- 269'.2'0924 B
Anchor post / by Faith Johnston. [Mount Pleasant] : Clarke Historical Library, Central Michigan University, c1975. 354 p., [9] leaves of plates : ill., ports. ; 24 cm. [BX7990.H62J634] 75-329981
1. Johnston, John Young, 1857-1931. I. Title.

KILGORE, James E 269'.2'0924
Billy Graham, the preacher, by James E. Kilgore. [1st ed.] New York, Exposition Press [1968] 70 p. 21 cm. Bibliographical footnotes. [BV3785.G69K5] 68-13258
1. Graham, William Franklin, 1918- I. Title.

KILGORE, James E. 269'.2'0924
Billy Graham, the preacher, by James E. Kilgore. [1st ed.] New York, Exposition Press [1968] 70 p. 21 cm. Bibliographical footnotes. [BV3785.G69K5] 68-13258
1. Graham, William Franklin, 1918-

LATIN American Mission. 269'.2'0924
Evangelism-in-depth; experimenting with a new type of evangelism, as told by team members of the Latin America Mission Chicago, Moody Press [1961] 126 p. 20 cm. "Experiences in Evangelism-in-depth in Nicaragua." [BV3777.N5L3] 64-3822
1. Evangelistic work — Nicaragua. I. Title.

LAZELL, David. 269'.2'0924[B]
Gipsy Smith: from the forest I came. Chicago, Moody [1973, c.1970] 256 p. illus., ports. 18 cm. First published in London under title: From the forest I came: the story of Gipsy Rodney Smith. [BV3785] ISBN 0-8024-2959-9 pap., 0.95
1. Smith, Rodney, 1860-1947. I. Title. II. Title: From the forest I came.
L.C. card no. for the London edition: 74-516965.

LEVY, Alan. 269'.2'0924
God bless you real good; my crusade with Billy Graham. New York, [Essandess Special Editions, 1969] 128 p. illus., ports. 22 cm. [BV3785.G69L48] 73-6103 1.00
1. Graham, William Franklin, 1918- I. Title.

LOCKARD, David. 269'.2'0924
The unheard Billy Graham. Waco, Tex., Word Books [1971] 166 p. 23 cm. Includes bibliographical references. [BV3785.G69L6] 74-151263 4.95
1. Graham, William Franklin, 1918- I. Title.

LOCKERBIE, D. Bruce 269.20924
Billy Sunday [Waco. Tex., Word Bks., 1966, c.1965] 64p. illus., ports. 29cm. Based on the motion picture by Sacred Cinema [BV3785.S8L6] 66-1560 3.50 bds.,
I. Sunday, William Ashley, 1862-1935. II. Title.

MITCHELL, Curtis. 269.20924
Billy Graham; the making of a crusader. Foreword by George M. Wilson. [1st ed.] Philadelphia, Chilton Books [1966] x, 288 p. 21 cm. [BV3785.G69M47] 65-25659
1. Graham, William Franklin, 1918-

MITCHELL, Curtis. 269'.2'0924
The Billy Graham London crusade. Official photographer: Vincent Hayhurst. [Minneapolis? c1966] 128 p. illus., ports. 28 cm. [BV3785.G69M48] 67-5692
1. Graham, William Franklin, 1918- 2. Revivals—London. I. Title.

MURCH, James DeForest, 1892- 269'.2'0924 B
Adventuring for Christ in changing times; an autobiography of James DeForest Murch. [Louisville, Ky.] Restoration Press, 1973. 348 p. port. 25 cm. [BX7343.M8A33] 73-84633
1. Murch, James DeForest, 1892- I. Title.

†MURPHY, Willie, 1933- 269'.2'0924 B
Black and trying / by Willie Murphy. Harrison, Ark. : New Leaf Press, c1976. 165 p. : port. ; 23 cm. Written by W. Murphy with C. Dudley. [BV4935.M86A33] 76-22272 ISBN 0-89221-023-0 : 5.95
1. Murphy, Willie, 1933- 2. Converts—United States—Biography. 3. Evangelists—United States—Biography. I. Dudley, Cliff, joint author. II. Title.

OLDHAM, Dale. 269'.2'0924 B
Giants along my path; my fifty years in the ministry. Anderson, Ind., Warner Press [1973] 288 p. illus. 21 cm. [BX7027.Z8O4] 73-16413 ISBN 0-87162-165-7 10.00
1. Oldham, Dale. I. Title.
Pbk. 3.95; ISBN 0-87162-162-2.

PANOS, Chris. 269'.2'0924 B
God's spy / by Chris Panos. 1st ed. Plainfield, N.J. : Logos International, 1976. xiii, 270 p. ; 22 cm. [BV3785.P33A33] 76-55451 ISBN 0-88270-213-0 : 6.95. pbk. : 3.50
1. Panos, Chris. 2. Evangelists—United States—Biography. I. Title.

POLING, David, 1928- 269'.2'0924 B
Why Billy Graham? / By David Poling. Grand Rapids, Mich. : Zondervan Pub. House, c1977. p. cm. [BV3785.G69P59] 77-13195 ISBN 0-310-36350-0 : 6.95
1. Graham, William Franklin, 1918- 2. Evangelists—United States—Biography. I. Title.

POLLOCK, John Charles. 269'.2'0924
Billy Graham; the authorized biography, by John Pollock. Grand Rapids, Zondervan [1967, c.1966] ix, 277p. illus., ports. 18cm. Bibl. [BV3785.G69P6 1967] 67-17236 .95 pap.,
1. Graham, William Franklin, 1918- I. Title.

POLLOCK, John Charles. 269'.2'0924
Billy Graham; the authorized biography, by John Pollock. Grand Rapids, Zondervan Pub. House [1967, c1966] ix, 277 p. illus., ports. 18 cm. "Notes on sources": p. 270. [BV3785.G69P6] 67-17236
1. Graham, William Franklin, 1918- I. Title.

POLLOCK, John Charles. 269.20924 B
Billy Graham; the authorized biography, by John Pollock. New York, McGraw-Hill [1966] ix, 277 p. 21 cm. "Notes on sources": p. 270. [BV3785.G69P6 1966a] 66-19465
1. Graham, William Franklin, 1918-

POLLOCK, John Charles. 269'.2'0924 B
Moody; a biographical portrait of the pacesetter in modern mass evangelism [by] J. C. Pollock. Grand Rapids, Zondervan Pub. House [1967, c1963] xii, 336 p. illus., ports. 21 cm. Bibliography: p. 319-325. [BV3785.M7P6 1967] 67-22692
1. Moody, Dwight Lyman, 1837-1899.

ROBERTS, Cecil A. 269'.2'0924 B
Vic Coburn : man with the healing touch / by C. A. Roberts. Nashville : T. Nelson, [1975] 204 p., [4] leaves of plates : ill. ; 21 cm. "Sermons by Vic Coburn": p. 163-204. [BV3785.C554R6] 75-12931 ISBN 0-8407-5597-X pbk. : 3.50
1. Coburn, Vic. 2. Faith-cure. 3. Sermons, American. I. Coburn, Vic.

ROBERTS, Evelyn, 1917- 269'.2'0924 B
His darling wife, Evelyn : the autobiography of Mrs. Oral Roberts / by Evelyn Roberts. New York : Dial Press, 1976. x, 273 p., [8] leaves of plates : ill. ; 22 cm. "A Damascus House book." [BX8495.R52A3] 76-23429 ISBN 0-8037-3601-0 : 6.95
1. Roberts, Evelyn, 1917- 2. Roberts, Oral. I. Title.

ROBERTS, Evelyn, 1917- 269'.2'0924 B
His darling wife, Evelyn : the autobiography of Mrs. Oral Roberts / Evelyn Roberts. Boston : G. K. Hall, 1977, c1976. 418 p. ; 25 cm. Large print ed. [BX8495.R52A3 1977] 77-1416 ISBN 0-8161-6469-X lib.bdg. : 11.95
1. Roberts, Evelyn, 1917- 2. Roberts, Oral. 3. Methodist Church—Clergy—Biography. 4. Clergymen's wives—Oklahoma—Tulsa—Biography. 5. Tulsa, Okla.—Biography. 6. Clergy—Oklahoma—Tulsa—Biography. 7. Large type books. I. Title.

ROBERTS, Oral. 269'.2'0924 B
The call; an autobiography. [1st ed.] Garden City, N.Y., Doubleday, 1972 [c1971] 216 p. 22 cm. [BV3785.R58A23] 79-139057 4.95
I. Title.

ROBERTS, Oral. 269'.2'0924
My twenty years of a miracle ministry. [Tulsa? Okla., 1967] 96 p. illus. (part col.), ports. (part col.) 28 cm. [BV3785.R58A29] 72-9283
1. Evangelists—Correspondence, reminiscences, etc. I. Title.

ROBERTS, Oral. 269'.2'0924 B
Twelve greatest miracles of my ministry / by Oral Roberts. 1st published ed. [Tulsa, Okla. : Pinoak Publications], 1974. 174 p. : ill. ; 21 cm. [BV3785.R58A35] 75-308770
1. Roberts, Oral. 2. Miracles. 3. Faith-cure. I. Title.

ROBERTSON, Pat. 269'.2'0924 B
Shout it from the housetops, by Pat Robertson, with Jamie Buckingham. Plainfield, N.J., Logos International, 1972. xi, 238 p. 22 cm. [BR1725.R62A3] 72-76591 ISBN 0-912106-30-1 4.95
1. Robertson, Pat. 2. Mass media in religion. I. Buckingham, Jamie. II. Title.

ROBINSON, Virgil E. 269'.2'0924 B
Magnificent missionary; the story of Dwight L. Moody, by Virgil E. Robinson. Nashville, Southern Pub. Association [1969] 96 p. illus. 21 cm. A biography of the nineteenth-century evangelist who traveled extensively gathering converts to Christianity. [BV3785.M7R62] 69-19418 2.95
1. Moody, Dwight Lyman, 1837-1899—Juvenile literature. I. Title.

ROBINSON, Wayne, 1937- 269'.2'0924 B
Oral : the warm, intimate, unauthorized portrait of a man of God / Wayne A. Robinson. Los Angeles : Acton House, c1976. xi, 154 p. ; 23 cm. [BX8495.R528R62] 76-151756 ISBN 0-89202-003-2 : 5.95
1. Roberts, Oral. 2. Methodist Church—Clergy—Biography. 3. Clergy—Oklahoma—Tulsa—Biography. 4. Tulsa, Okla.—Biography. I. Title.

ROGERS, Jack Bartlett. 269'.2'0924 B
Confessions of a conservative Evangelical, by Jack Rogers. Philadelphia, Westminster Press [1974] 144 p. 20 cm. [BX9225.R73A33] 74-12249 ISBN 0-664-24996-5 2.65 (pbk.)
1. Rogers, Jack Bartlett. 2. Evangelicalism. I. Title.

SKINNER, Tom, 1942- 269'.2'0924
Black and free. Grand Rapids, Zondervan Pub. House [1968] 154 p. illus. 21 cm. [BV3785.S512A3] 68-27459
1. Evangelistic work—United States. I. Title.

SMITH, Amanda (Berry) 1837-1915. 269'.2'0924 B
An autobiography: the story of the Lord's dealings with Mrs. Amanda Smith, the colored evangelist; containing an account of her life work of faith, and her travels in America, England, Ireland, Scotland, India, and Africa, as an independent missionary. With an introd. by Bishop Thoburn, of India. Chicago, Afro-Am Press, 1969. 506 p. illus., ports. 22 cm. Reprint of the 1893 ed. Running title: Autobiography of Amanda Smith. [BV3785.S56A3 1969] 71-99407
1. Evangelistic work. I. Title: Autobiography of Amanda Smith.

†SMITH, Malcolm, 1938- 269'.2'0924 B
Follow me! : The apprenticing of disciples / Malcolm Smith. Plainfield, N.J. : Logos International, c1976. 168 p. ; 22 cm. [BR1725.S54A33] 76-41065 5.95. pbk. : 5.95
1. Smith, Malcolm, 1938- 2. Clergy—New Jersey—Biography. 3. Christian life—1960- I. Title.

SONG, Ben. 269'.2'0924 B
Born out of conflict; the autobiography of Ben Song as told to Cliff Christians. Foreword by Dale Evans Rogers. Grand Rapids, Zondervan Pub. House [1970] 141 p. illus., ports. 22 cm. [BV3785.S65A3] 79-106429 2.95
I. Christians, Clifford. II. Title.

SPILLMAN, Sandy. 269'.2'0924 B
Billy Graham : a photobiography / written by Sandy Spillman. Houston : Epps-Praxis Publishers, c1976. [80] p. : chiefly ill. ; 28 cm. [BV3785.G69S68] 76-151099 2.95
1. Graham, William Franklin, 1918- — Portraits, etc. 2. Evangelists—United States—Portraits, etc.

STEBBINS, George Coles, 1846-1945. 269'.2'0924 B
George C. Stebbins: reminiscences and gospel hymn stories. With an introd. by Charles H. Gabriel. New York, G. H. Doran Co. [New York, AMS Press, 1971] 327 p. illus., ports. 19 cm. Includes hymns, with music. Reprint of the 1924 ed. "First AMS edition." [BV3780.S7 1971] 74-144689 ISBN 0-404-07203-8
1. Evangelists. 2. Hymn writers. I. Title.

STONE, Robert B. 269'.2'0924 B
Jesus has a man in Waikiki; the story of Bob Turnbull [by] Robert B. Stone. Old Tappan, N.J., F. H. Revell Co. [1973] 128 p. illus. 21 cm. [BV4447.S72] 73-3311 ISBN 0-8007-0599-8 1.95 (pbk)
1. Turnbull, Bob, 1936- 2. Church work with youth—Honolulu. I. Title.

STOREY, Del. 269'.2'0924 B
Collision course / by Del Storey, with Laura Watson. Plainfield, N.J. : Logos International, c1977. xiv, 123 p. ; 21 cm. [BR1725.S825A34] 77-71143 ISBN 0-88270-230-0 pbk. : 2.95
1. Storey, Del. 2. Clergy—United States—Biography. I. Watson, Laura, joint author. II. Title.

STREIKER, Lowell D. 269'.2'0924 B
Religion and the new majority: Billy Graham, Middle America, and the politics of the 70s [by] Lowell D. Streiker and Gerald S. Strober. New York, Association Press [1972] 202 p. 22 cm. Includes bibliographical references. [BR515.S76] 79-189009 ISBN 0-8096-1844-3 5.95
1. Graham, William Franklin, 1918- 2. United States—Religion—1945- 3. Fundamentalism. 4. United States—Politics and government—1969-1974. I. Strober, Gerald S., joint author. II. Title.

STROBER, Gerald S. 269'.2'0924 B
Billy Graham, his life and faith / Gerald S. Strober. Waco, Tex. : Word Books, c1977. 144 p. ; 23 cm. A biography of the world-famous evangelist who has advised presidents and kings. [BV3785.G69S86] 92 76-56484 ISBN 0-87680-445-8 : 4.95
1. Graham, William Franklin, 1918- —Juvenile literature. 2. Evangelists—United States—Biography—Juvenile literature. I. Title.

STROBER, Gerald S. 269'.2'0924 B
Graham : a day in Billy's life / Gerald S. Strober. 1st ed. Garden City, N.Y. :

Doubleday, 1976. p. cm. [BV3785.G69S87] 75-40745 ISBN 0-385-11373-0 : 4.95
1. Graham, William Franklin, 1918-

STROBER, Gerald S. 269'.2'0924 B
Graham : a day in Billy's life / Gerald S. Strober. Boston : G. K. Hall, 1977, c1976. 294 p. ; 24 cm. Large print ed. [BV3782.G69S87 1977] 77-598 ISBN 0-8161-6468-1 : 10.95
1. Graham, William Franklin, 1918- 2. Sight-saving books.

*STROBER, Gerald S. 269.20924
Graham : a day in Billy's life / Gerald S. Strober. New York : Dell Pub. Co., 1977,c1976. 206p. : ill. ; 18 cm. (A Dell Book) [BV3785.G69 S87] ISBN 0-440-12870-6pbk. : 1.95
1. Graham, William Franklin, 1918- I. Title.
L.C. card no. for 1976 Doubleday ed.:75-40745.

TALBOT, Carol. 269'.2'0924 B
For this I was born / by Carol Talbot. Chicago : Moody Press, c1977. p. cm. Bibliography & filmography: p. [BR1725.T23T34] 77-10537 ISBN 0-8024-2822-3 pbk. : 4.95
1. Talbot, Louis Thompson, 1889-1976. 2. Clergy—United States—Biography. I. Title.

TALBOT, Carol. 269'.2'0924 B
For this I was born / by Carol Talbot. Chicago : Moody Press, c1977. p. cm. Bibliography & filmography: p. [BR1725.T23T34] 77-10537 ISBN 0-8024-2822-3 pbk. : 4.95
1. Talbot, Louis Thompson, 1889-1976. 2. Clergy—United States—Biography. I. Title.

TARR, Charles R., 269.20924
A new wind blowing! [by] Charles R. Tarr. Anderson, Ind., Warner Press [1974, c1972] 126 p. illus. 19 cm. "A Portal Book" [BV3775.A53T37] ISBN 0-87162-175-4 1.50 (pbk.)
I. Title.
L.C. card number for original edition: 72-10912

TARR, Charles R., 269'.2'0924 B
1932-
A new wind blowing! [by] Charles R. Tarr. [Anderson, Ind.] Warner Press [1972] 123 p. illus. 19 cm. Includes bibliographical references. [BV3775.A53T37] 72-10912 ISBN 0-87162-147-9 2.50 (pbk.)
1. Revivals—Anderson, Ind. 2. Revivals—Wilmore, Ky. I. Title.

TEN BOOM, Corrie. 269'.2'0924 B
In my father's house / by Corrie ten Boom, with C. C. Carlson. Old Tappan, N.J. : F. H. Revell Co., c1976. p. cm. [BR1725.T35A34] 75-45373 ISBN 0-8007-0783-4 : 6.95
1. Ten Boom, Corrie. I. Carlson, Carole C., joint author. II. Title.

TEN BOOM, Corrie. 269'.2'0924 B
Tramp for the Lord / by Corrie ten Boom, with Jamie Buckingham. Boston : G. K. Hall, 1974. xx, 305 p. 25 cm. Large print ed. [BR1725.T35A37 1974b] 74-20672 ISBN 0-8161-6259-X
1. Ten Boom, Corrie. 2. Sight-saving books. I. Buckingham, Jamie, joint author. II. Title.

TEN BOOM, Corrie. 269'.2'0924 B
Tramp for the Lord [by] Corrie ten Boom, with Jamie Buckingham. Fort Washington, Pa., Christian Literature Crusade [1974] 192 p. illus. 21 cm. [BR1725.T35A37] 74-5205 ISBN 0-8007-0665-X 5.95
1. Ten Boom, Corrie. I. Buckingham, Jamie, joint author. II. Title.

THROWER, Bob, 1927- 269'.2'0924 B
About face; the story of why Bob Thrower changed churches, as told to Don Christman. Washington, Review and Herald Pub. Association [1972] 128 p. illus. 21 cm. (Discovery paperbacks) [BX6189.T48A3] 72-77021
1. Thrower, Bob, 1927- I. Christman, Don R. II. Title.

TIPPIT, Sammy. 269'.2'0924 B
Sammy Tippit: God's love in action, as told to Jerry B. Jenkins. Nashville, Broadman Press [1973] 121 p. illus. 20 cm. [BR1725.T56A33] 73-78216 ISBN 0-8054-5542-6 3.95
1. Tippit, Sammy. I. Jenkins, Jerry B. II. Title. III. Title: God's love in action.

WALLACE, Wendell. 269'.2'0924 B
Born to burn, by Wendell Wallace with Pat King. [Special Charisma ed.] Watchung, N.J., Charisma Books [1972, c1970] 103 p. ports. 18 cm. [BR1725.W29A32 1972] 77-131116 0.95
1. Wallace, Wendell. I. King, Pat, joint author. II. Title.

WIRT, Sherwood 269'.2'0924 B
Eliot.
Afterglow : the excitement of being filled with the spirit / by Sherwood Eliot Wirt. Grand Rapids, Mich. : Zondervan Pub. House, c1975. p. cm. [BR1725.W56A32] 75-21122 4.95 pbk. : 2.95
1. Wirt, Sherwood Eliot. 2. Revivals—Canada. I. Title.

WOODARD, Arvle, 269'.2'0924 B
1908-
The Mexico Kid: from an outlaw to a preacher; the life story of evangelist Arvle Woodard. New York, Carlton Press [1968] 77 p. 21 cm. (A Hearthstone book) [BV3785.W62A3] 71-226 2.50
I. Title.

WOODWARD, David B. 269'.2'0924(B)
Aflame for God: biography of Fredrik Franson, founder of The Evengelical ,alliance Mission, by David B. Woodward. Chicago. Moody [1966] 190p. 22cm. [BV3705.F7W6] 66-16225 3.50
1. Franson, Fredrik, 1852- 1908. 2. The Evangelical Alliance Mission. I. Title.

FOSTER, Dave. 269'.2'094
Billy Graham, Euro '70; eight days when the miracle of modern technology projected the Christian message across Europe. [Minneapolis, World Wide Publications, 1971] 138 p. illus. (part col.), col. map, ports. (part col.) 28 cm. [BV3785.G69F67] 71-150990
1. Graham, William Franklin, 1918- 2. Revivals—Europe. I. Title.

MITCHELL, Curtis. 269'.2'0942
The all-Britain crusade of 1967. Minneapolis, World Wide Publications [1968] 139 p. illus., ports. 28 cm. [BV3785.G69M46] 68-5661
1. Graham, William Franklin, 1918- 2. Revivals—Great Britain. I. Title.

*POLLOCK, John 269'.2'09421
Crusade '66; Britain hears Billy Graham Grand Rapids, Mich., Zondervan [1966] 96p. 18cm. 1.00 pap.,
1. Graham, William Franklin, 1918. 2. Evangelistic work. I. Title.

OWEN, Bob. 269'.2'094336
To Munich with love. Chino, Calif., Chick Publications [1972] 126 p. illus. 18 cm. [BV3777.G3O93] 72-92737 0.95
1. Evangelistic work—Munich. 2. Witness bearing (Christianity) 3. Jesus People—Munich. I. Title.

SAVOCA, Nick. 269'.2'0947
Roadblock to Moscow [by] Nick Savoca with Dick Schneider. Sketches by William Mather. Old Tappan, N.J., F. H. Revell Co. [1974] 157 p. illus. 21 cm. [BV3777.R8S35] 74-2313 ISBN 0-8007-0658-7 4.95
1. Evangelistic work—Russia. 2. Witness bearing (Christianity) I. Schneider, Dick. II. Title.
Pbk. 2.95; ISBN 0-8007-0659-5

ORR, James Edwin, 269'.2'095
1912-
Evangelical awakenings in Eastern Asia / J. Edwin Orr. Minneapolis : Bethany Fellowship, [1975] x, 180 p. ; 22 cm. Includes index. Bibliography: p. 175-178. [BV3777.E18O77] 74-30353 ISBN 0-87123-126-3 pbk. : 2.95
1. Revivals—East (Far East)—History. I. Title.

CULPEPPER, C. L., 269'.2'095114
1895-
The Shantung revival, by C. L. Culpepper. [Dallas, Tex., Crescendo Book Publications, c1971] 79 p. illus. 21 cm. Cover title. [BV3777.C5C8] 73-81143
1. Revivals—Shantung, China. I. Title.

KOCH, Kurt E. 269'.2'09519
Victory through persecution, by Kurt Koch. Translated by Anthea Bell. With a foreword by Billy Graham. [1st American ed.] Grand Rapids, Kregel Publications [1972, c1971] 62 p. 18 cm. Translation of Koreas Beter. [BV3777.K6K613 1972] 72-77231 ISBN 0-8254-3009-7 1.00
1. Revivals—Korea. I. Title.

A Lantern in 269'.2'0952135
Tokyo. [Reporting and editing: J. D. Douglas and others; photography: Russell Busby] Minneapolis, World Wide Publications [1968] 79 p. illus. (part col.), ports. 21 cm. On cover: The Billy Graham Tokyo crusade. [BV3785.G69L3] 68-4524
1. Graham, William Franklin, 1918- 2. Revivals—Tokyo. I. Douglas, James Dixon. II. Title: The Billy Graham Tokyo crusade.

ORR, James Edwin, 269'.2'0954
1912-
Evangelical awakenings in southern Asia / J. Edwin Orr. Minneapolis : Bethany Fellowship, [1975] x, 240 p. ; 22 cm. Published in New Delhi, 1970, under title: Evangelical awakenings in India. Includes index. Bibliography: p. 227-236. [BV3777.I4O77 1975] 74-32019 ISBN 0-87123-127-1 pbk. : 2.95
1. Revivals—India—History. 2. Revivals—South Asia—History. I. Title.

CRAWFORD, Don, 1929- 269'.2'09598
Miracles in Indonesia; God's power builds his church! Wheaton, Ill., Tyndale House Publishers [1972] 160 p. illus. 18 cm. [BV3777.I5C7] 72-75962 ISBN 0-8423-4350-4 1.25 (pbk.)
1. Revivals—Indonesia. I. Title.

TARI, Mel. 269'.2'095986
The gentle breeze of Jesus [by] Mel and Nona Tari. Carol Stream, Ill., Creation House [1974] 191 p. illus. 23 cm. [BV3777.I5T37] 74-82507 ISBN 0-88419-057-9 4.95
1. Revivals—Timor. I. Tari, Nona, joint author. II. Title.

ARTHUR, Joseph, 269'.2'09599
1935-
The sleeping giant : a strategy for a student program of evangelism and church planting in the Philippines / by Joseph Arthur. Pasadena, Ca. : William Carey Library, [1976] p. cm. Thesis—Fuller Theological Seminary, Pasadena, Calif., 1974. Bibliography: p. [BV3777.P5A77] 75-42212 ISBN 0-87808-419-3
1. Christian and Missionary Alliance—Missions. 2. Evangelistic work—Philippine Islands. 3. Church work with students—Philippine Islands. 4. College students—Philippine Islands. 5. Philippine Islands—Civilization. I. Title.

MCMAHAN, Tom. 269.2096
Safari for souls: with Billy Graham in Africa. Columbia, S. C., State-Record Co. [1960] 111p. illus. 22cm. [BV3785.G69M33] 60-14979
1. Graham, William Franklin, 1918- 2. Revivals—Africa. I. Title.

ORR, James Edwin, 269'.2'0967
1912-
Evangelical awakenings in Africa / J. Edwin Orr. Rev. and expanded. Minneapolis : Bethany Fellowship, [1975] x, 245 p. ; 22 cm. Published in 1970 under title: Evangelical awakenings in South Africa. Includes index. Bibliography: p. 231-242. [BV3777.A4O77 1975] 74-32018 ISBN 0-87123-128-X pbk. : 2.95
1. Revivals—Africa, Sub-Saharan—History. I. Title.

KOCH, Kurt E. 269'.2'0971
Revival fires in Canada, by Kurt E. Koch. [1st ed.] Grand Rapids, Kregel Publications [1973] 102 p. 18 cm. Translation of Die Erweckung in Kanada. [BV3777.C36K613] 72-93352 ISBN 0-8254-3015-1 pap. 1.00
1. Revivals—Canada. I. Title.

BESTIC, Alan. 269'.2'0973
Praise the Lord and pass the contribution. New York, Taplinger Pub. Co. [1971] xii, 259 p. 22 cm. [BR516.2.B47 1971b] 77-155804 ISBN 0-8008-6460-3 6.50
1. Sects—U.S. 2. Evangelists—U.S. 3. Church finance—U.S. I. Title.

BRUCE, Dickson D., 269'.2'0973
1946-
And they all sang hallelujah; plain-folk camp-meeting religion, 1800-1845 [by] Dickson D. Bruce, Jr. [1st ed.] Knoxville, University of Tennessee Press [1974] xii, 155 p. illus. 22 cm. Bibliography: p. 137-150. [BV3798.B78] 74-11344 ISBN 0-87049-157-1 7.50
1. Camp-meetings. 2. Southern States—Religion. 3. Frontier and pioneer life—United States—Southern States. I. Title.

CANNON, William S. 269'.2'0973
The Jesus revolution; new inspiration for evangelicals [by] William S. Cannon. Nashville, Tenn., Broadman Press [1971] 144 p. illus., ports. 21 cm. [BV3773.C33] 76-172423 ISBN 0-8054-5516-7 4.95
1. Revivals—United States. 2. Jesus People—United States. I. Title.

COHEN, Daniel. 269'.2'0973
The spirit of the Lord : revivalism in America / Daniel Cohen. New York : Four Winds Press, [1975] 220 p. : ill. ; 23 cm. Includes index. Bibliography: p. 210-212. Traces the causes and progression of revival movements in the United States from the eighteenth century to the present. [BV3773.C56] 74-28056 ISBN 0-590-07292-7 : 7.95
1. Revivals—United States—Juvenile literature. I. Title.

COLTON, Calvin, 1789- 269'.2'0973
1857.
History and character of American revivals of religion. London, F. Westley and A. H. Davis, 1832. [New York, AMS Press, 1973] xvi, 294 p. 19 cm. On spine: American revivals of religion. [BV3773.C6 1973] 72-1008 ISBN 0-404-00018-5 12.00
1. Revivals—United States. I. Title. II. Title: American revivals of religion.

DAYTON, Donald W. 269'.2'0973
Discovering an evangelical heritage / Donald W. Dayton. 1st ed. New York : Harper & Row, c1976. 147 p. : ill. ; 21 cm. Bibliography: p. [143]-147. [BR1642.U5D39 1976] 75-36750 ISBN 0-06-061781-0 : 8.95. ISBN 0-06-061780-2 pbk. : 3.95
1. Evangelicalism—United States. I. Title.

HARRELL, David Edwin. 269'.2'0973
All things are possible : the healing and charismatic revivals in modern America / David Edwin Harrell, Jr. Bloomington : Indiana University Press, [1975] p. cm. Bibliography: p. [BV3773.H37 1975] 75-1937 ISBN 0-253-10090-9 : 10.95
1. Revivals—United States. 2. Faith-cure—History. 3. Pentecostalism—History. I. Title.

MCLOUGHLIN, William 269.20973
Gerald.
Modern revivalism: Charles Grandison Finney to Billy Graham. New York, Ronald Press Co. [1959] 551p. 22cm. Includes bibliography. [BV3773.M3] 58-12959
1. Revivals—U. S. I. Title.

RUTMAN, Darrett 269'.2'0973
Bruce, comp.
The Great Awakening; event and exegesis. Edited by Darrett B. Rutman. New York, Wiley [1970] viii, 200 p. 22 cm. (Problems in American history) Includes bibliographical references. [BR520.R88 1970] 79-110174
1. Great Awakening—Addresses, essays, lectures. I. Title.

RUTMAN, Darrett 269'.2'0973
Bruce, comp.
The Great Awakening : event and exegesis / edited by Darrett B. Rutman. Huntington, N.Y. : R. E. Krieger Pub. Co., 1977, c1970. p. cm. Reprint of the ed. published by Wiley, New York, in series: Problems in American history. Includes bibliographical references. [[BR520.R88 1977]] 77-10540 ISBN 0-88275-605-2 pbk. : 4.50
1. Great Awakening—Addresses, essays, lectures. I. Title.

VACHON, Brian, 1941- 269'.2'0973
A time to be born ... Photographed by Jack and Betty Cheetham. Englewood Cliffs, N.J., Prentice-Hall [1972] 138 p. illus. 28 cm. [BV3774.C3V3] 75-37623 ISBN 0-13-922021-6 (pbk) 3.95
1. Evangelistic work—California. 2. Revivals—California. 3. Youth—Religious life. I. Cheetham, Jack, 1931- illus. II. Cheetham, Betty, 1919- illus. III. Title.

DICKINSON, Eleanor, 269'.2'0974
1931-
Revival. Text by Barbara Benziger. Introd. by Walter Hopps. [1st ed.] New York, Harper & Row [1974] p. cm. [BV3774.A66D5] 73-18697 ISBN 0-06-061920-1. 7.95
1. Revivals—Appalachian Mountains, Southern. I. Benziger, Barbara. II. Title.
Pbk. 5.95, ISBN 0-06-061921-X.

*FINNEY, Charles 269.2'0974
Grandison
Finney on revival the highlights of the sermons on revival Minneapolis, Dimension Books, [1974] v., 120 p. 18 cm. [BV3774] ISBN 0-87123-151-4 0.95 (pbk.)
1. Revivals. I. Title.

BELL, Marion L. 269'.2'0974811
Crusade in the city : revivalism in nineteenth-century Philadelphia / Marion L. Bell. Lewisburg, Pa. : Bucknell University Press, c1977. p. cm. "The original version of this work was a doctoral dissertation at Temple University." Includes index. Bibliography: p. [BV3775.P5B44 1977] 76-759 ISBN 0-8387-1929-5 : 15.00
1. Revivals—Pennsylvania—Philadelphia. 2. Philadelphia—Social life and customs. I. Title.

BOLES, John B. 269'.2'0975
The Great Revival, 1787-1805: the origins of the Southern evangelical mind [by] John B. Boles. [Lexington] University Press of Kentucky [1972] xiii, 236 p. illus. 24 cm. Bibliography: p. [205]-221. [BV3773.B65] 77-183349 ISBN 0-8131-1260-5 10.00
1. Revivals—Southern States. I. Title.

DOROUGH, C. Dwight, 269'.2'0975
1912-
The Bible belt mystique, by C. Dwight Dorough. Philadelphia, Westminster Press [1974] 217 p. 22 cm. Includes bibliographical references. [BR535.D67] 74-11395 ISBN 0-664-20709-X
1. Southern States—Religion. I. Title.

GUDNASON, Kay. 269'.2'0979465
Rings in the redwoods; the story of Mount Hermon. Mount Hermon, Calif., Mount

Hermon Association, 1972. 439 p. illus. 31 cm. [BV3799.M6G82] 73-160698
1. Mount Hermon Association. I. Title.

WIRT, Sherwood Eliot. 269.20979461
Crusade at the Golden Gate. Foreword and keynote sermon by Billy Graham. [1st ed.] New York, Harper [1959] 176 p. illus. 21 cm. A report on Billy Graham's evangelistic campaign in San Francisco, April 27-June 22, 1958. [BV3785.G69W5] 59-7163
1. Graham, William Franklin, 1918- 2. Revivals — San Francisco. I. Title.

COPPIN, Ezra. 269'.2'0982
Guns, guts, and God! / By Ezra Coppin. San Diego, Calif. : Production House Publishers, c1976. 159 p. ; 22 cm. [BV3777.A7C66] 76-2214 2.95
1. Coppin, Ezra. 2. Cabrera, Omar Hugo, 1936- 3. Cabrera, Marfa. 4. Evangelistic work—Argentine Republic. 5. Faith-cure. I. Title.

ORR, James Edwin, 1912- 269'.2'099
Evangelical awakenings in the South Seas / by J. Edwin Orr. Minneapolis : Bethany Fellowship, c1976. p. cm. Includes index. Bibliography: p. [BV3777.O26O77] 76-26966 ISBN 0-87123-129-8 pbk. : 2.95
1. Revivals—Oceanica—History. 2. Revivals—Madagascar—History. I. Title.

LLOYD, Marjorie Lewis. 269 243
Love on fire. Decorations by Iris Johnson. Washington Review and Herald Pub. Association [1952] 127 p. illus. 18 cm. Prose and poems. [PS3523.L67L6] 52-32440
I. Title.

LUTHERAN Evangelism Council. 269 243
Share Christ today; sermons and addresses from the Lutheran Evangelism Conference, the Armory, Minneapolis, January 23-27, 1952. Minneapolis, c1952. 112 p. illus. 28 cm. [BV3755.L8] 52-40069
1. Evangelistic work. Evangelistic sermons. Title I. Title.

POWELL, Sidney Waterbury, 1889- 269.253
Where are the converts? Nashville, Broadman Press [1958] 165p. 21cm. [BV3793.P6] 58-5413
1. Evangelistic work. 2. Church work. I. Title.

REES, Paul Stromberg. *269 253
Stir up the gift. Grand Rapids, Zondervan Pub. House [1952] 158 p. 21 cm. (The Bob Jones University lectures on evangelism for 1951) [BV3790.R356] 52-8001
1. Evangelistic work. I. Title.

SHOEMAKER, Samuel Moor, 1893- *269 253
The experiment of faith; a handbook for beginners. [1st ed.] New York, Harper [1957] 64 p. 22 cm. [BV3793.S45] 57-7345
1. Evangelistic work. I. Title.

SHORT, Roy Hunter, bp., 1902-. *269 253
Evangelism through the local church. New York, Abingdon Press [1956] 126 p. 20 cm. [BV3790.S54] 56-10149
1. Evangelistic work. I. Title.

SUENENS, Leon Joseph, Cardinal. 1904- *269 253
The Gospel to every creature. With a pref. by John Baptist Montini, Archbishop of Milan [Translation by Louise Gavan Duffy] Westminister, Md., Newman Press, 1957. 163 p. 19 cm. Translation of L'Englise en etat de mission. [BV3790.S892] 57-8609
1. Evangelistic work. 2. Catholic Church—Missions. I. Title.

TEMPLETON, Charles Bradley, 1915- *269 253
Evangelism for tomorrow. [1st ed;] New York, Harper [1957] 175 p. 22 cm. [BV3790.T4] 57-10530
1. Evangelistic work. I. Title.

WALKER, Alan. *269 253
The whole gospel for the whole world. With an introd. by E. G. Homrighausen. New York, Abingdon Press [1957] 128 p. 20 cm. (The Wieand lectures is evangelism) [BV3790.W316] 57-5283
1. Evangelistic work. I. Title.

YATES, John Clyde, 1898- *269 253
Our marching orders in evangelism, a practical guidebook. [1st ed.] New York, American Press, 1957 [i.e. 1958] 152 p. 21 cm. [BV3790.Y3] 57-12055
1. Evangelistic work. I. Title.

CENTRAL Conference of American Rabbis. 269.4
Rabbi's manual., Rev. ed. New York 40 W. 68th St., [Author, c.]1961. 156p. 61-10418 4.00
1. Rabbis—Handbooks, manuals, etc. I. Title.

CASTEEL, John Laurence, 1903- 269.6
Renewal in retreats. New York, Association Press [1959] 250p. 20cm. [BV5068.R4C3] 59-12107
1. Retreats. I. Title.

GARRETT, Constance, 1894- 269.6
I give myself unto prayer; addresses and meditations for a retreat, together with a timetable, prayers and readings. [Cincinnati, Literature Headquarters, Woman's Division of Christian Service, Board of Missions of the Methodist Church, 1962] 64 p. 20 cm. [BV5068.R4G3] 62-16513
1. Retreats. I. Title.

GENNE, Elizabeth 269.6
Church family camps and conferences; an administrative and program manual [by] Elizabeth and William H. Genne. Philadelphia, Christian Educ. [dist. United Church, c.1962] 95p. illus. 62-9970 1.40 pap.,
1. Church camps. I. Genne, William H., joint author. II. Title.

HARRINGTON, Wilfrid J. 269'.6
Come, Lord Jesus; a Biblical retreat [by] Wilfrid J. Harrington. Staten Island, N.Y., Alba House [1968] 207 p. 22 cm. [BX2375.H35] 68-31512 4.95
1. Retreats. 2. Meditations. I. Title.

HENNESSY, Thomas C ed. 269.6
The inner crusade; the closed retreat in the United States. Thomas C. Hennessy, editor. With a foreword by John J. Wright. Chicago, Loyola University Press, 1965. x, 207 p. 23 cm. Bibliographical footnotes. [BX2375.H38] 65-28325
1. Retreats. I. Title.

HENNESSY, Thomas C. ed. 269.6
The inner crusade; the closed retreat in the United States. Foreword by John J. Wright. Chicago, Loyola Univ. Pr. [c.]1965. x, 207p. 23cm. Bibl. [BX2375.H38] 65-28325 3.00 pap.,
1. Retreats. I. Title.

IPARRAGUIRRE, Ignacio. 269.6
How to give a retreat; practical notes. [Translation by Angelo Benedetti] Westminster, Md., Newman Press, 1959. 188p. 19cm. [BX2375.A3I63] 61-484
1. Retreats. I. Title.

JUD, Gerald John. 269'.6
Training in the art of loving; the church and the human potential movement [by] Gerald J. and Elisabeth Jud. Philadelphia, Pilgrim Press [1972] 191 p. 22 cm. Bibliography: p. 190-191. [BV5068.R4J83] 79-184455 ISBN 0-8298-0223-1 7.95
1. Retreats. 2. Love. I. Jud, Elisabeth, joint author. II. Title.

KNOX, Ronald Arbuthnott, 1888-1957. 269.6
Retreat for beginners. New York, Sheed and Ward [c.1960] 234p. 21cm. 60-11680 3.50
1. Retreats—Addresses, essays, lectures. 2. Boys—Religious life. I. Title.

KNOX, Ronald Arbuthnott, 1888-1957 269.6
Retreat for beginners. Glen Rock, N.J., Paulist [1964, c.1960] 192p. 18cm. (Deus bks.) 64-20246 .95 pap.,
1. Retreats—Addresses, essays, lectures. 2. Boys—Religious life. I. Title.

LEEN. EDWARD, 1885-1944. 269.6
Retreat notes for religious. Edited with a biographical note by R. F. Walker. New York, Kenedy [1959] 142p. 22cm. [BX2435.L44] 59-86849
1. Monastic and religious life. I. Title.

MAGEE, Raymond J., ed. 269'.6
Call to adventure; the retreat as religious experience, edited by Raymond J. Magee. Nashville, Abingdon Press [1967] 160 p. 20 cm. Bibliography: p. 153-155. [BX2375.A3M2] 67-11013
1. Retreats. I. Title.

SIMONS, Joseph B. 269'.6
Retreat dynamics [by] Joseph B. Simons. Notre Dame, Ind., Fides Publishers [1967] 189 p. 23 cm. Includes bibliographies. [BX2375.A3S5] 67-24812
1. Retreats. I. Title.

WALCHARS, John. 269.6
The call from beyond; thoughts for a retreat. St. Paul, North Central Pub. Co., 1960. 172 p. 23 cm. [BX2375.W3] 60-40203
1. Retreats — Addresses, essays, lectures. I. Title.

NELSON, Virgil. 269'.6'0202
Retreat handbook : a-way to meaning / Virgil and Lynn Nelson. Valley Forge, Pa. : Judson Press, c1976. 129 p. : ill. ; 28 cm. Includes bibliographical references. [BV5068.R4N44] 75-23468 ISBN 0-8170-0694-X : 5.95
1. Retreats—Handbooks, manuals, etc. I. Nelson, Lynn, joint author. II. Title.

DEEMER, Philip. 269'.6'02573
Ecumenical directory of retreat and conference centers. Philip Deemer, editor. Boston, Jarrow Press [1974- v. 25 cm. [BV1652.D43] 74-76974 ISBN 0-912190-10-8 15.00
1. Church conference centers—United States—Directories. 2. Church conference centers—Canada—Directories. I. Title.

RETREAT resources : 269'.6'08
designs and strategies for spiritual growth / general editor, Maury Smith ; assistant editor, E. Jackie Kenney. New York : Paulist Press, [1975- v. : ill. ; 28 cm. Includes bibliographies and indexes. [BX2375.A3R47] 75-307051
1. Retreats—Collected works. I. Smith, Maury. II. Kenney, E. Jackie.

RETREATS for adults. 269.6'08 s
New York : Paulist Press, c1976. xix, 265 p. ; 28 cm. (Retreat resources ; v. 2) Includes bibliographies and index. [BX2375.A3R47 vol. 2] 269'.6 76-372449 ISBN 0-8091-1911-0 : 11.50
1. Retreats. I. Series.

RETREATS for clergy and religious. 269'.6'08 s
New York : Paulist Press, [1975] x, 181 p. : ill. ; 28 cm. (Retreat resources ; v. 1) Includes bibliographies and indexes. [BX2375.A3R47 vol. 1] 269'.6'9 74-83719 ISBN 0-8091-1850-5 : 9.50
1. Retreats. I. Title. II. Series.

RETREATS for youth / 269.6'08 s
general editor, Maury Smith, assistant editor, E. Jackie Kenney. New York : Paulist Press, c1976. xix, 202 p. ; 28 cm. (Retreat resources ; v. 3) Includes index. [BX2375.A3R47 vol. 3] [BX2376.Y73] 269'.6'3 76-360813 ISBN 0-8091-1910-2 : 10.50
1. Retreats for youth. I. Smith, Maury. II. Kenney, E. Jackie. III. Series.

GRANNAN, Dick. 269'.6'3
Youth quake; a radical restructuring of the high school retreat ... Dayton, Ohio, G. A. Pflaum [1969] 55 p. 28 cm. (What's happening) Based on a program conducted by staff members of the Renewal Centre, Windsor, Ont. [BX2376.S7G7] 78-82522 2.50
1. Retreats. 2. Students—Religious life. I. Renewal Centre. II. Title.

270 HISTORY & GEOGRAPHY OF CHURCH

ABRECHT, Paul. 270
The churches and rapid social change. [1st ed.] Garden City, N. Y., Doubleday, 1961. 216 p. 22 cm. Bibliography: p. [208]-216. [HN31.A2] 61-12488
1. Christianity and politics. I. Title.

*ALLISON, Frances Harris. 270
For people who fidget in church; or, Religion and how to enjoy it. Illus. by Donn Camden Allison. With a foreword by James G. Long. New York, Exposition Pr. [1973] 112 p. illus. 21 cm. [BR148] ISBN 0-682-47704-4 5.00
1. Church history—Popular works. I. Title.

*ANDERSON, H. George 270
The story of the church. James Heugh, illustrator. Philip R. Hoh. ed. Philadelphia, Lutheran Church Pr. [1966] 128p. illus. 20cm. (LCA Sunday church sch. ser.) Bibl. 1.00 pap.,
1. Church history. I. Hoh, Philip R., ed. II. Title.

ATKINS, Gaius Glenn, 1868-1956. 270
Pilgrims of the lonely road. Freeport, N.Y., Books for Libraries Press [1967] 339 p. 22 cm. (Essay index reprint series) "First published 1913." Bibliographical footnotes. [BR148.A8 1967] 67-28741
1. Christian biography. 2. Church history. I. Title.

ATKINS, Gaius Glenn, 1868-1956. 270
Pilgrims of the lonely road. Freeport, N.Y., Books for Libraries Press [1967] 339 p. 22 cm. (Essay index reprint series) "First published 1913." Bibliographical footnotes. [BR148.A8 1967] 67-28741
1. Christian biography. 2. Church history. I. Title.

BACKMAN, Milton Vaughn. 270
American religions and the rise of Mormonism, by Milton V. Backman, Jr. Salt Lake City, Deseret Book Book Co., 1965. xiii, 466 p. illus., maps (on lining papers) ports. 24 cm. Bibliography: p. 431-442. [BX8611.B314] 65-27488
1. Mormons and Mormonism—Hist. 2. Church history. 3. U.S.—Church history. I. Title.

BAINTON, Roland Herbert, 1894- 270
Christendom; a short history of Christianity and its impact on Western civilization [by] Roland H. Bainton. New York, Harper & Row [1966] 2 v. illus. 21 cm. (Harper torchbooks. The Cloister library, TB13N, TB132) "The text of this book was first published in [the author's] The Horizon history of Christianity in 1964." Contents.v. 1. From the birth of Christ to the Reformation.--v. 2. From the Reformation to the present. Includes bibliographies. [BR145.2.B31966] 66-7003
1. Church history. I. Title.

BAINTON, Roland Herbert, 1894- 270
Christendom; a short history of Christianity and its impact on Western civilization, v.1. New York, Harper [c.1964, 1966] 274p. illus. 21cm. (Torchbk. TB 131N Cloister lib.) Contents.v.1. From the birth of Christ to the Reformation. Bibl. [BR145.2.B3] 2.45 pap.,
1. Church history. I. Title.

BAINTON, Roland Herbert, 1894- 270
Christendom; a short history of Christianity and its impact on Western civilization. v.2 [by] Roland H. Bainton. New York, Harper [1966, c.1964] vi, 216p. illus. 21cm. (Harper torchbks. Cloister lib. TB131N) The text of this bk. was first pub. in the author's The Horizon history of Christianity in 1964. Contents.v.2. From the Reformation to the present. [BR145.2.B33] 66-7003 2.45 pap.,
1. Church history. I. Title.

BAINTON, Roland Herbert, 1894- 270
The church of our fathers. Philadelphia, Westminster Press [1950] 219 p. illus. 24 cm. [BR151.B3 1950] 50-14399
1. Church history—Juvenile literature. I. Title.

BAINTON, Roland Herbert, 1894- 270
The church of our fathers. [New rev. ed.] New York, Scribner, 1950 [c1950] 222p. illus. 24cm. [BR151.B3 1953] 53-12416
1. Church history—Juvenile literature. I. Title.

BAINTON, Roland Herbert, 1894- 270
The Horizon history of Christianity [New York] Avon [c.1964, 1966] 430p. 18cm. (Avon lib. bk. W 109) [BR145.2.B3] 1.25 pap.,
1. Church history. I. Horizon (New York, 1958-) II. Title.

BAINTON, Roland Herbert, 1894- 270
The Horizon history of Christianity, by the editors of Horizon magazine. Editor in charge: Marshall B. Davidson. Author: Roland H. Bainton. New York, American Heritage Pub. Co.; book trade distribution by Harper & Row [1964] 432 p. illus., ports. 31 cm. Part of the illustrative matter is colored. [BR145.2.B3] 64-19638
1. Church history. I. Horizon (New York, 1958-) II. Title.

BAKER, Archibald Gillies, 1875- ed. 270
A short history of Christianity. Written in collaboration by Archibald G. Baker, ed. [others] Chicago, Univ. of Chic. Pr. [1962, c.1960] 278p. (Phoenix bks., P95) Bibl. 1.50 pap.,
1. Church history. I. Title.

BAKER, Robert Andrew. 270
A summary of Christian history. Nashville, Broadman Press [1959] 391p. illus. 24cm. [BR146.B2] 59-5852
1. Church history. I. Title. II. Title: Christian history.

BALDWIN, Marshall Whithed, 1903- comp. 270
Christianity through the thirteenth century. Edited by Marshall W. Baldwin. New York, Harper & Row [1970] ix, 431 p. 21 cm. (Documentary history of Western civilization) Includes bibliographies. [BR141.B23 1970] 72-122470 3.95
1. Church history—Sources. I. Title.

BALDWIN, Marshall Whithed, 1903- comp. 270
Christianity through the thirteenth century. Edited by Marshall W. Baldwin. New York, Walker [1971, c1970] 431 p. 24 cm. (Documentary history of Western civilization)

Includes bibliographies. [BR162.2.B34 1971] 77-103858 ISBN 0-8027-2003-X 10.00
1. Church history—Primitive and early church, ca. 30-600—Sources. 2. Church history—Middle Ages, 600-1500—Sources. I. Title.

BARRY, Colman James, ed. 270
Readings in church history, v.1 Westminster, Md., Newman Press [c.1960] xx, 633p. 'Reference table to standard textbooks in church history': v. 1, p.633. 25cm. Contents.v. 1. From Pentecost to the Protestant revolt. 59-14755 2.95
1. Church history—Sources. I. Title.

BARRY, Colman James, 1921- ed. 270
Readings in church history. v.2. Westminster, Md., Newman [c.]1965. 393p. 24cm. Contents.v.2. The Reformation and the absolute states, 1517-1789. [BR141.B27] 59-14755 7.50; 3.75 pap.,
1. Church history—Sources. I. Title.

BARRY, Colman James, 1921- ed. 270
Readings in church history, v. 3 Westminister, Md., Newman [c.]1965. 575p. 24cm. Contents.v. 1. From Pentecost to the Protestant revolt.--v. 2. The Reformation and the absolute states.--v. 3. The Modern era, 1789 to the present. [BR141.B27] 59-14755 7.50; 3.75 pap.,
1. Church history—Sources. I. Title.

BATTEN. JOSEPH MINTON, 1893- 270
Protestant backgrounds in history. New York, Abingdon-CokesburyPress [1951] 160 p. 19 cm. [BX4805.B3] 51-10322
1. Protestantism—Hist. I. Title.

BAUR, Ferdinand Christian, 1792-1860. 270
Ferdinand Christian Baur on the writing of church history. Edited and translated by Peter C. Hodgson. New York, Oxford University Press, 1968. xii, 380 p. 24 cm. (A Library of Protestant thought) Contents.Contents.—The epochs of church historiography.—Introduction to Lectures on the history of Christian dogma. Includes bibliographical references. [BR138.B32] 68-8582 8.00
1. Church history—Historiography. I. Hodgson, Peter Crafts, 1934- ed. II. Title. III. Series.

BAYNES, Helton Godwin, 1882-1943. 270
Mythology of the soul; a research into the unconscious from schizophrenic dreams and drawings. New York, Humanities Press, 1955. xiii, 939p. illus., plates (part col.) 23cm. [RC628.B] A 56
1. Schizophrenia. 2. Subconsciouness. 3. Dreams. I. Title.

BESANT, Annie (Wood) 1847-1933. 270
Christianity: its evidences, its origin, its morality, its history. 3d ed. New York, Arno Press, 1972. 194-478 p. 22 cm. (The Freethinker's text-book, pt. 2) Reprint of the 1881(?) ed. [BL2775.B447 1972] 77-169205 ISBN 0-405-03803-8
1. Christianity—Controversial literature. I. Title. II. Series. III. The Atheist viewpoint

BETTENSON, Henry Scowcroft, ed. 270
Documents of the Christian Church. 2d ed. London, New York, Oxford University Press, 1963. xx, 489 p. 18 cm. Bibliography: p. 474-475. [BR141.B4] 63-6298
1. Church history — Sources. I. Title.

BETTENSON, Henry Scowcroft. ed. 270
Documents of the Christian Church; selected, ed. by Henry Bettenson. 2nd ed. London, New York [etc.] Oxford Univ. Pr. xvii, 343p. 21cm. (Oxford paperbacks, no. 125) Bibl. [BR141.B4 1967] 68-109402 2.75 pap.,
1. Church history—Sources. I. Title.

BETTENSON, Henry Scowcroft, ed. 270
Documents of the Christian Church; selected and edited by Henry Bettenson. 2nd ed. London, New York [etc.] Oxford U. P., 1967. xvii, 343 p. 20 1/2 cm. (Oxford paperbacks, no. 125) 12/6 (B 67-23384) Bibliography: p. 335-336. [BR141.B4 1967] 68-109402
1. Church history—Sources. I. Title.

BETTENSON, Henry Scowcroft, ed. 270
Documents of the Christian Church. 2d ed. New York, Oxford [c.]1963 xx, 489p. 18cm. Bibl. 63-6298 3.00
1. Church history—Sources. I. Title.

BIGGS, Wilfred W 270
Introduction to the history of the Christian church, by Wilfred W. Biggs. New York, St. Martin's Press, 1965. 238 p. maps. 23 cm. Includes bibliographical references. [BR145.2.B5] 65-20814
1. Church history. I. Title. II. Title: The history of the Christian Church.

BIGGS, Wilfred W. 270
Introduction to the history of the Christian church, New York, St. Martin's [c.] 1965 238p. maps. 23cm. Bibl. [BR145.2.B5] 65-20814 4.95 bds.,
1. Church history. I. Title. II. Title: The history of the Christian church.

BIHLMEYER, Karl, 1874-1942 270
Church history. Rev. by Hermann Tuchle. Tr. from 13th German ed. by Victor E. Mills. Westminster, Md., Newman [c.1963] 534p. 24cm. Contents.v.2. The Middle Ages. Bibl. 58-8753 9.50
1. Church history. I. Tuchle, Hermann. II. Title.

BIHLMEYER, Karl, 1874-1942 270
Church history, v.3. Rev. by Hermann Tuchle. Tr. from the 13th German ed. by Victor E. Mills. Westminster, Md., Newman 1966 xiv, 585p. 24cm. Contents.v. 3. Modern and recent times. Bibl. [BR145.B5732] 58-8753 12.00
1. Church history. I. Tuchle, Hermann. II. Title.

BIHLMEYER, Karl, 1874-1942. 270
The obese patient. New York, Intercontinental Medical Book Corp. [1962] 151p. 23cm. Includes bibliography. [BR145.B5732] 58-8753
1. anagement of the obese patient, by Frank L. Bigsby and Cayetano Muniz. 2. Corpulence. I. Muniz, Cayetano, joint author. II. Title.

BOWIE, Walter Russell, 1882-1969. 270
The story of the church. Illustrated by Clifford Johnston. New York, Abingdon Press [1955] 208 p. illus. 24 cm. [BR150.B6] 55-9137
1. Church history—Popular works. I. Title.

BRODRICK, James, 1891- 270 B
A procession of saints. Freeport, N.Y., Books for Libraries Press [1972, c1949] p. (Biography index reprint series) Includes bibliographical references. [BX4655.B7 1972] 72-5436 ISBN 0-8369-8134-0
1. Saints. I. Title.

BRUMBACK, Robert H 1892- 270
History of the church through the ages, from the apostolic age, through the apostasies, the Dark Ages, the Reformation, and the restoration. St. Louis, Mission Messenger [1957] 428p. illus. 24cm. Includes bibliography. [BR145.B78] 57-24407
1. Church history. 2. Disciples of Christ—Hist. 3. Churches of Christ—Hist. I. Title.

BULTMANN, Rudolf Karl, 1884- 270
History and eschatology; the presence of eternity. New York, Harper [1962, c.1957] 21cm. (Gifford lectures 1955; Harper torchbks., Cloister lib. TB91) 1.25 pap.,
1. History—Philosophy. 2. Eschatology. I. Title. II. Series.

BULTMANN, Rudolf Karl, 1884- 270
History and eschatology [by] Rudolph Bultmann, Edinburgh; Totowa, NJ University Press 1975 c1957 ix, 170 p. 21 cm. (The Gifford lectures 1955) Includes indexes Includes bibliographical references [BR115.H5B78] ISBN 0-85224-103-8 8.00.
*1. History*Philosophy. 2. Eschatology. I. Title. II. Series.*
L.C. card no. for original edition: A58-1988.

BURGESS, John H. 270
The Christian pagan; a naturalistic survey of Christian history, by John H. Burgess. [1st ed.] Madison, Wis., Mimir [1969] xv, 352 p. maps. 24 cm. Includes bibliographies. [BL2775.2.B85] 78-6698
1. Christianity—Controversial literature. I. Title.

BURKE, J. Bruce. 270
Foundations of Christianity; from the beginnings to 1650 [by] J. Bruce Burke [and] James B. Wiggins. New York, Ronald Press Co. [1970] ix, 316 p. maps. 24 cm. Bibliography: p. 307. [BR145.2.B87] 73-110545
1. Church history. I. Wiggins, James B., 1935- joint author. II. Title.

BUTTERFIELD, Herbert, 1900- 270
Christianity in European history. London, New York, Oxford University Press, 1951. 63 p. 23 cm. (Riddell memorial lectures, 23d ser.) At head of title: University of Durham. [BR735.B8 1951] 52-1669
1. Europe—Church history. I. Title. II. Series.

CAIRNS, Earle Edwin, 1910- 270
Christianity through the centuries; a history of the Christian church. Grand Rapids, Zondervan Pub. House [1954] 511 p. illus. 23 cm. [BR145.C3] 54-33303
1. Church history. I. Title.

CAIRNS, Fred I, 1907- 270
Progress is unorthodox. With a foreword by M. C. Otto. Boston, Beacon Press, 1950. x, 185 p. 22 cm. [BR1615.C25] 50-10949
1. Liberalism (Religion) I. Title.

CAMPENHAUSEN, Hans, Freiherr von, 1903- 270
Tradition and life in the church; essays and lectures in church history. Translated by A. V. Littledale. Philadelphia, Fortress Press [1968] 254 p. 23 cm. Translation of Tradition und Leben, Krafte der Kirchengeschichte. Bibliography: p. 253-254. [BR155.C273] 68-27859 4.50
1. Church history—Addresses, essays, lectures. 2. Christianity—Addresses, essays, lectures. I. Title.

CASE, Shirley Jackson, 1872-1947. 270 B
Makers of Christianity; from Jesus to Charlemagne. Port Washington, N.Y., Kennikat Press [1971, c1934] xii, 256 p. 22 cm. (Essay and general literature index reprint series) Originally issued as the first volume of Makers of Christianity. Bibliography: p. 241-249. [BR145.C35 1971] 79-118460
1. Church history. 2. Christian biography. I. Title.

CATHOLIC Church. Pope, 1963. (Paulus VI) 270
The apostolic letter, Sabaudiae gemma, of Pope Paul VI to the cardinals, archbishops, bishops, and other ordinaries of France, Switzerland and the Piedmont Region commemorating the four-hundredth anniversary of the birth of Saint Francis de Sales. Translated by Neil Kilty. Hyattsville, Md., Institute of Salesian Studies [1967] 15, [1] p. 19 cm. Bibliographical references included in "Notes" (p. [16]) [BX4700.F85C313] 68-6901
I. Francois de Sales, Saint, Bp. of Geneva, 1567-1622. II. [Sabaudiae gemma] III. Title. IV. Title: Sabaudiae gemma.

CHADWICK, Henry, 1920- 270
The early Church. Harmondsworth, Baltimore. Penguin, 1967 [i.e. 1968] 304p. 18 cm. (Pelican hist. of the Church, 1, A502) Bibl. [BR165.C48 1968] 68-92647 1.45 pap.,
1. Church history—Primitive and early church. I. Title.

CHESTERTON, Gilbert Keith, 1874-1936. 270
St. Francis of Assisi. Garden City, N.Y., Image Books [1957, c1924] 158 p. 19 cm. (A Doubleday image book, D50) [BX4700] 57-1230
1. Francesco d'Assisi, Saint, 1182-1226. I. Title.

CHURCH history in future perspective. 270
Edited by Roger Aubert. [New York] Herder and Herder [1970] 160 p. 23 cm. (Concilium: theology in the age of renewal. Church history, v. 57) [BR138.C53] 70-129756 2.95
1. Church history—Historiography—Addresses, essays, lectures. I. Aubert, Roger, ed. II. Series: Concilium (New York) v. 57

CLARKE, Charles Philip Stewart, 1871-1947. 270 B
Everyman's book of saints, by C. P. S. Clarke. Rev. by Rosemary Edisford. New York, Philosophical Society [1969, c1968] 346 p. 21 cm. "List of authorities": p. 343-344. [BR1710.C6 1969] 72-4847
1. Christian saints. I. Edisford, Rosemary, ed. II. Title.

CLARKE, James Everitt, 1868- 270
Youth and the church simplicity in Christ. Boston, Christopher Pub. House [1956] 79p. 21cm. [BR150.C55] 56-26189
1. Church history—Popular works. I. Title.

COLGRAVE, Bertram. 270
The earliest saints' lives written in England / by Bertram Colgrave. Norwood, Pa. : Norwood Editions, 1975. p. cm. Reprint of the 1958 ed. published by the British Academy, London, which was issued in v. 44 (1959) of the Academy's Proceedings as the Sir Israel Gollancz memorial lecture, 1958. Reprint of the 1958 ed. published by the British Academy, London which was issued in v. 44 (1959) of the Academy's Proceedings as the Sir Israel Gollancz memorial lecture, 1958. Bibliography: p. [BX4662.C65 1975] 75-28247 ISBN 0-88305-136-2 : 5.00
1. Christian hagiography. 2. Anglo-Saxon literature—History and criticism. I. Title. II. Series: British Academy, London (Founded 1901). Sir Israel Gollancz memorial lecture ; 1958.

COLLEDGE, Edmund. 270 B
Following the saints, by Edmund Colledge and James Walsh. Gastonia, N.C., Good Will Publishers [1970] 3 v. (xvii, 959, xiii p.) col. illus., col. ports. 25 cm. (The Catholic layman's library, v. 4-6) Contents.Contents.—[1] January 1st through April 30th.—[2] May 1st through August 31st.—[3] September 1st through December 31. Includes bibliographies. [BX4655.2.C6] 74-92778
1. Christian saints—Calendar. I. Walsh, James, 1920- joint author. II. Title. III. Series.

CONSTABLE, John W., 1922- 270
The church since Pentecost [by] John W. Constable. Edited by Oscar E. Feucht. Saint Louis, Concordia Pub. House [1969] 101 p. maps. 21 cm. (The Discipleship series) Includes bibliographies. [BR146.C65] 70-91808
1. Church history—Study and teaching. I. Title.

CORPUS scriptorum ecclesiasticorum latinorum. 270
Editum consilio et impensis Academiae litterarum caesareae vindobonensis . . . Vindobonae, apud C. Geroldi filium; [etc., etc.] 1866-19; New York, Johnson Reprint [1967] v. in 24cm. Each has also special t.-p. Imprint varies: vol. [16] Mediolani [etc.] Vlricys Hoeplivs edidit. v. 17-35. 37-42, Vindobonae, Pragae, F. Tempsky; Lipsiae, G. Freytag. -- v. 36, 43-57, 59-60, 62, 64-65: Vindobonae, F. Tempsky; Lipsiae. G. Freytag. -- v. 58, 61, 63: Vindobonae, Lipsiae, Holder-Pichler-Tempsky, a.g. [BR60.C6] 7-26284 25.00 pap.,ea.,
1. Fathers of the church (Collections) 2. Fathers of the church, Latin (Collections) I. Akademie der wissenschaften, Vienna.

COWAN, Henry, 1844-1932. 270
Landmarks of church history, to the Reformation. New ed., rev. and enl. New York, A. D. F. Randolph, 1896. [New York, AMS Press, 1973] x, 188 p. 19 cm. [BR145.C68 1973] 70-144590 ISBN 0-404-01787-8 6.50
1. Church history. I. Title.

COWIE, Leonard W. 270
The march of the cross. New York, McGraw-Hill [1962] 213 p. illus. (part col.) ports. (part col.) col. maps, facsims. 28 cm. [BR150.C59 1962] 61-8853
1. Church history. I. Title.

COX, John Dee, 1907- 270
A concise account, of church history, with questions for group study. Murfreesboro, Tenn., De Hoff Publications, 1951. [BR150.C6] 51-27494
1. Church history. 2. Churches of Christ—Hist. I. Title.

CUSHING, Richard James, Abp., 1895-- 270
That they may know Thee; selected writings on vocations. Compiled by George L. Kane. Westminster, Md., Newman Press, 1956. 217p. 22cm. [BX2380.C8] 56-8136
1. Vocation (in religious orders, congregations, etc.) 2. Catholic Church—Clergy—Appointment, call, and election. I. Title.

*DAMETZ, Maurice Gordon 270
The focal points of Christian history. New York, Carlton [1967] 167p. 21cm. A thesis presented to the Faculty of the Graduate Coll., Univ. of Denver in partial fulfillment of the requirements for the degree of Master of Arts. Bibl. 3.75
1. Church history. I. Title.

DANIEL-ROPS, Henry [Real name: Henry Jules Charles Petiot] 1901- 270
The church in the Dark Ages [2v.] Tr. from French by Audrey Butler. Garden City, N.Y., Doubleday [1962, c.1960. 2v.] 431;437p. 18cm. (Image bks., D143A, D143B) Bibl. 1.35 pap., ea.,
1. Church history—Middle Ages. I. Title.

D'ARCY, Mary Ryan. 270
The saints of Ireland : a chronological account of the lives and works of Ireland's saints and missionaries at home and abroad / by Mary Ryan D'Arcy. St. Paul : Irish American Cultural Institute, c1974. xi, 241 p. ; 25 cm. Includes index. Bibliography: p. 230-233. [BX4659.I7D37] 74-83242 7.50
1. Christian saints—Ireland. 2. Christian martyrs—Ireland. 3. Missionaries, Irish. I. Title.

DAVIS, Charles, 1923- 270
God's grade in history. New York, Sheed [1967,c.1966] 128p. 21cm. [BR115.W6D36 1967b] 67-14816 3.50
1. Church and the world. I. Title.

DAWLEY, Powel Mills, 1907- 270
Chapters in church history, by Powel Mills Dawley with the assistance of the Author's [sic] Committee of the Department of Christian Education. New York, The National Council, Protestant Episcopal Church, 1950. 278 p. 22 cm. (The Church's teaching, v. 2)

Bibliography: p. 255-272. [BR150.D35] 50-8279
1. Church history. I. Title. II. Series.

DAWLEY, Powel Mills, 1907- 270
Chapters in church history [by] Powel Mills Dawley, with the Authors' Comm. of the Dept. of Christian Educ. of the Protestant Episcopal Church. Rev. ed. New York, Seabury [1963] 274p. 22cm. (Church's teaching, 2) Bibl. 63-16290 3.50; 2.00 pap.,
1. Church history—Addresses, essays, lectures. I. Title.

DAWSON, Christopher Henry, 1889- 270
Religion and the rise of Western culture. New York, Sheed & Ward, 1950. xvi, 286 p. illus., ports. 22 cm. (Gifford lectures, 1948-1949) Bibliographical footnotes. [BR115.C5D37] 50-6539
1. Civilization, Christian. 2. Civilization, Occidental. I. Title. II. Series.

DELEHAYE, Hippolyte, 1859-1941. 270 B
Les legendes grecques des saints militaires / Hippolyte Delehaye. New York : Arno Press, 1975. ix, 270 p. ; 23 cm. (Roman history) French or Greek. Reprint of the 1909 ed. published by Librairie Alphonse Picard, Paris. Includes bibliographical references. [BR1710.D44 1975] 75-7314 ISBN 0-405-07196-5
1. Christian saints. 2. Hagiography. I. Title. II. Series.

DE WAAL, Victor. 270
What is the church? Valley Forge [Pa.] Judson Press [1970, c1969] 128 p. 19 cm. Bibliography: p. 124. [BV600.2.D47 1970] 70-121057 1.95
1. Church. I. Title.

DOBSCHUTZ, Ernst [Adolf Alfred Oskar Adalbert] von 270
The influence of the Bible on civilisation. New York, F. Ungar Pub. Co. [1959] 190p. illus. 19cm. 58-5869 3.50
1. Bible—Influence. I. Title.

D'SOUZA, Jerome. 270
The Church and civilization. [1st ed.] Garden City, N.Y., Doubleday, 1967. 191 p. 22 cm. Bibliography: p. [189]-191. [BR148.D68] 67-11156
1. Christianity and culture—History. I. Title.

DUNCAN, Pope A 270
The pilgrimage of Christianity [by] Pope A. Duncan. Nashville, Broadman Press [1965] 128 p. 20 cm. [BR150.D8] 65-11766
1. Church history. I. Title.

DUNCAN, Pope A. 270
The pilgrimage of Christianity. Nashville, Broadman [c.1965] 128p. 20cm. [BR150.D8] 65-11766 1.50 bds.,
1. Church history. I. Title.

DUNNEY, Joseph Aloysius, 1881- 270 B
Church history in the light of the saints, by Joseph A. Dunney. Plainview, N.Y., Books for Libraries Press [1974] p. cm. (Essay index reprint series) Reprint of the 1944 ed. published by Macmillan, New York. Bibliography: p. [BR145.D86 1974] 74-2196 ISBN 0-518-10162-2 21.50
1. Catholic Church—History. 2. Church history. 3. Christian saints. I. Title.

EERDMANS' handbook to 270
Christian history / by Tim Dowley, organizing editor. Grand Rapids : Eerdmans, c1977. p. cm. Includes index. [BR146.E35] 77-5616 ISBN 0-8028-3450-7 : 19.95
1. Church history—Handbooks, manuals, etc. I. Dowley, Tim. II. Title: Handbook to Christian history.

EMMRICH, Kurt 270
The kingdoms of Christ from the days of the apostles to the Middle Ages [by] Peter Bamm [pseud. Translated and adapted by Christopher Holme New York, McGraw-Hill [1959i.e., 1960] 367p. illus. (part col.), maps 25cm. 60-3737 8.95 buck.,
1. Church history—Primitive and early works—Pictures, illustrations, etc. 2. Church history—Middle Ages—Pictures, illustrations, etc. I. Title.

FISHER, George Park, 1827-1909. 270
History of the Christian Church / by George Park Fisher. New York : AMS Press, [1976] p. cm. Reprint of the 1904 ed. published by Scribner, New York. Includes index. [BR145.F5 1976] 75-41094 ISBN 0-404-14662-7 : 20.00
1. Church history. I. Title.

FLICK, Alexander Clarence, 1869-1942. 270
The rise of the mediaeval church and its influence on the civilisation of Western Europe from the first to the thirteenth century. New York, B. Franklin [1964, c1909] xiii, 623 p. 24 cm. (Burt Franklin bibliography and reference series #60) Includes bibliographical references. [BR252.F6 1964] 79-6595
1. Church history—Middle Ages, 600-1500. I. Title.

FLOOD, Joseph Mary, 1882- 270 B
Ireland; its saints and scholars, by J. M. Flood. Port Washington, N.Y., Kennikat Press [1970] x, 118 p. illus. 19 cm. (Series in Irish history and culture) (Kennikat Press scholarly reprints.) Reprint of the 1918 ed. [BX4659.I7F6 1970] 79-102604 ISBN 0-8046-0781-8
1. Christian saints—Ireland. I. Title.

FORRISTAL, Desmond. 270
The Christian heritage / Desmond Forristal. Dublin : Veritas Publications, 1976. 192 p., [4] leaves of plates : ill. ; 25 cm. [BR145.2.F66] 77-360468 ISBN 0-905092-20-1 : £6.00
1. Catholic Church—History. 2. Church history. 3. Christianity and culture—History. I. Title.

FOSTER, John, 1898- 270
Beginning from Jerusalem; Christian expansion through seventeen centuries. New York, Association Press [1956] 92p. illus. 20cm. (World Christian books) [BR150.F6 1956a] 56-6456
1. Church history—Popular works. I. Title.

FOX, Robert Joseph, 1927- 270 B
Saints & heroes speak / by Robert J. Fox. Huntington, Ind. : Our Sunday Visitor, c1977. 512 p. : ports. ; 21 cm. [BX1751.2.F68] 77-70206 ISBN 0-87973-640-2 pbk. : 7.50
1. Catholic Church—Doctrinal and controversial works—Catholic authors. 2. Christian saints—Biography. 3. Catholics—Biography. I. Title.

FOX, Robert Joseph, 1927- 270 B
Saints & heroes speak / by Robert J. Fox. Huntington, Ind. : Our Sunday Visitor, c1977. 512 p. : ports. ; 21 cm. [BX1751.2.F68] 77-70206 ISBN 0-87973-640-2 pbk. : 7.50
1. Catholic Church—Doctrinal and controversial works—Catholic authors. 2. Christian saints—Biography. 3. Catholics—Biography. I. Title.

FRANKFORTER, A. Daniel. 270
A history of the Christian movement : an essay on the development of Christian institutions / by A. Daniel Frankforter. Chicago : Nelson-Hall, [1977] p. cm. Includes index. Bibliography: p. [BR145.2.F69] 77-8071 ISBN 0-88229-292-7 : 17.95
1. Church history. I. Title.

FRANKFORTER, A. Daniel. 270
A history of the Christian movement : an essay on the development of Christian institutions / by A. Daniel Frankforter. Chicago : Nelson-Hall, [1977] p. cm. Includes index. Bibliography: p. [BR145.2.F69] 77-8071 ISBN 0-88229-292-7 : 17.95
1. Church history. I. Title.

FRANZEN, August. 270
A history of the church. Rev. and edited by John P. Dolan. Translated from the German by Peter Becker. [New York] Herder and Herder [1969] xii, 461, [1] p. 22 cm. Translation of Kleine Kirchengeschichte. "Chronological table of the Popes": p. 459-[462] [BR145.2.F713 1969b] 78-79825 9.50
1. Church history. I. Title.

GARRETT, Arthur. 270
AmeriChristendom. [1st American ed. Portland, Or., printed at GraphicArts Center, for A. Garrett, 1967] 250 p. illus. 28 cm. [BR153.A5 1967] 67-30333
1. Church history. I. Title.

GARVEY, John. 270 B
Saints for confused times / by John Garvey. Chicago : Thomas More Press, c1976. 176 p. ; 21 cm. [BX4655.2.G35] 76-370967 ISBN 0-88347-066-7 : 8.50
1. Christian saints—Biography. I. Title.

GIBBON, Edward, 1737-1794. 270
History of Christianity: comprising all that relates to the progress of the Christian religion in "The history of the decline and fall of the Roman Empire," and A vindication of some passages in the 15th and 16th chapters. With a life of the author, pref., and notes by the editor, including variorum notes by Guizot, Wenck, Milman, an English churchman, and other scholars. New York, Arno Press, 1972 [c1882] 778, 86 p. illus. 21 cm. (The Atheist viewpoint) Includes bibliographical references. [BR170.G4 1972] 79-169227 ISBN 0-405-03796-1
1. Church history—Primitive and early church, ca. 30-600. I. Gibbon, Edward, 1737-1794. A vindication of some passages in the 15th and 16th chapters of The history of the decline and fall of the Roman Empire. 1972. II. Title. III. Series.

GREEN, Vivian Hubert Howard. 270 B
From St. Augustine to William Temple; eight studies in Christian leadership, by Vivian H. H. Green. Freeport, N.Y., Books for Libraries Press [1971] 172 p. 23 cm. (Biography index reprint series) Reprint of the 1948 ed. Includes bibliographies. [BR1700.G7 1971] 72-148213 ISBN 0-8369-8060-3
1. Christian biography. I. Title.

GUIGNEBERT, Charles Alfred Honore, 1867-1939. 270
Ancient, medieval, and modern Christianity; the evolution of a religion. New Hyde Park, N. Y., University Books [1961] 507p. 22cm. First published in 1927 under title: Christianity, past and present. A translation of the author's Le christianisme antique and Le christianisme medieval et moderne. [BR145.G95 1961] 61-15334
1. Church history. I. Title.

GUIGNEBERT, Charles Alfred Honore, 1867-1939 270
The Christ. Tr. by Peter Ouzts, Phyllis Cooperman. Ed. & rev. by Sonia Volochova. New Hyde Park. N.Y., University Bks. [1968] xxv, 321p. 24cm. Bibl. [BR129.G813] 66-24067 10.00
1. Christianity—Origin. 2. Church history—Primitive and early church. I. Title.

*HAGEMAN, Howard G. 270
That the world may know [by] Howard G. Hageman, with Ruth Douglas See. Illus. by Hans Zander. Richmond, Va., CLC Pr. [dist. Knox, 1966, c.1965] 225p. illus. col. maps, 24cm. 2.95 pap.,
I. Title.

HAM, Wayne. 270
Yesterday's horizons : exploring the history of Christianity / by Wayne Ham. Independence, Mo. : Herald Pub. House, [1975] p. cm. [BR145.2.H35] 75-22455
1. Church history. I. Title.

HEALY, Martin J 1909- 270
The whole story; God and man through the ages. Brooklyn, Confraternity of the Precious Blood, 1959. 690p. 13cm. [BR147.H4] 59-50052
1. Church history. I. Title. II. Title: God and man through the ages.

HERRICK, Samuel Edward, 1841-1904. 270 B
Some heretics of yesterday. Freeport, N.Y., Books for Libraries Press [1973] p. (Essay index reprint series) Reprint of the 1884 ed. Contents.Contents.—Tauler and the mystics.—Wiclif.—Hus.—Savonarola.—Latimer.—Cranmer.—Melancthon.—Knox.—Calvin.—Coligny.—William Brewster.—Wesley. [BR1700.H47 1973] 72-14160 ISBN 0-518-10013-8
1. Christian biography. I. Title.

HISTORY: self-understanding 270
of the Church. Edited by Roger Aubert. [New York] Herder and Herder [1971] 144 p. 23 cm. (Concilium: religion in the seventies, v. 67) On cover: The New concilium: religion in the seventies. Includes bibliographical references. [BV603.H58] 75-168655 2.95
1. Church—Addresses, essays, lectures. 2. Church history—Addresses, essays, lectures. I. Aubert, Roger, ed. II. Series: Concilium (New York) v. 67.

HUDSON, Winthrop Still, 1911- 270
The story of the Christian church. New York, Harper [1958] 107p. illus. 20cm. Includes bibliography. [BR150.H82] 58-7475
1. Church history—Popular works. I. Title. II. Title: The Christian church.

HUGHES, Philip, 1895- 270
The church in crisis: a history of the general councils, 325-1870. [1st ed.] Garden City, N.Y., Hanover House [1961] 384 p. 22 cm. Includes bibliography. [BX825.H8] 61-6511
1. Councils and synods, Ecumenical. I. Title.

HUGHES, Philip, 1895- 270
A popular history of the Catholic Church. Garden City, N. Y., Image Books [1954, c1947] 309p. 19cm. (A Doubleday image book, D 4) First published under title: A popular history of the Church. [BX948] 54-13001
1. Catholic Church—Hist. 2. Church history. I. Title.

HURLBUT, Jesse Lyman, 1843-1930. 270
The story of the Christian church. New and rev. ed. Grand Rapids, Zondervan Pub. House [1967] 254 p. illus., ports. 21 cm. [BR146] 67-7978
1. Church history. I. Title.

HURLBUT, Jesse Lyman, 1843-1930. 270
The story of the Christian church. Latest rev. ed. Grand Rapids, Mich., Zondervan Pub. House [1970] 192 p. illus., ports. 22 cm. Includes bibliographies. [BR146.H65 1970] 75-16757 4.95
1. Church history. I. Title.

HURREY, Marjory 270
The great adventure; adventures of the apostles. Illus. Prue Theobalds. New York, Kenedy [1964] 128p. illus., maps. 22cm. 64-21856 2.95
1. Apostles—Juvenile literature. I. Title.

HUTCHINSON, Paul, 1890-1955. 270
20 centuries of Christianity; a concise history [by] Paul Hutchinson and Winfred E. Garrison. [1st. ed.] New York, Harcourt, Brace [1959] 306p. 25cm. Includes bibliography. [BR150.H87] 59-6424
1. Church history. I. Garrison, Winfred Ernest, 1874- II. Title.

HUTCHINSON, Paul, 1890-1956. 270
20 centuries of Christianity; a concise history [by] Paul Hutchinson [and] Winfred E. Garrison. [1st ed.] New York, Harcourt, Brace [1959] 306 p. 25 cm. Includes bibliography. [BR150.H87] 59-6424
1. Church history. I. Garrison, Winfred Ernest, 1874- . Title. II. Title.

THE Impact of the church upon 270
its culture; reappraisals of the history of Christianity, by Quirinus Breen [and others] Edited by Jerald C. Brauer. Chicago, University of Chicago Press [1968] x, 396 p. 24 cm. (Essays in divinity, v. 2) Most of the papers were presented at the Alumni Conference of the Field of History of Christianity, Oct. 6-8, 1966, celebrating the 75th anniversary of the University of Chicago and the 100th anniversary of its Divinity School. Bibliographical footnotes. [BR155.I5] 67-30155
1. Church history—Addresses, essays, lectures. I. Brauer, Jerald C., ed. II. Breen, Quirinus, 1896- III. Chicago. University. Divinity School. IV. Title. V. Series.

JACOBUS de Varagine. 270 B
The golden legend of Jacobus de Voragine. Translated and adapted from the Latin by Granger Ryan and Helmut Ripperger. New York, Arno Press, 1969 [c1941] xxiv, 800 p. illus. 23 cm. [BX4654.J334 1969] 72-88826
1. Christian saints. I. Title.

JANE MARIE, Sister, 1896- 270
Christ in His church. Milwaukee, Bruce Pub. Co. [1952] 656 p. illus. 23 cm. (The Christian religion series for high schools) [BR147.J3] 52-12826
1. Church history. 2. Catholic Church—Hist. I. Title.

JEDIN, Hubert, 1900- ed. 270
Handbook of church history, edited by Hubert Jedin and John Dolan. [New York] Herder and Herder [1965- v. 25 cm. Contents.Contents.—v. 1 From the apostolic community to Constantine, by K. Baus. Includes bibliographies. [BR145.2.J413] 64-15929
1. Church history. I. Dolan, John Patrick, joint ed. II. Title.

JOHNSON, George, 1889-1944. 270
The story of the Church; [a textbook for the upper grades, by] George Johnson, Jerome D. Hannan [and] Sister m. Dominica. [New rev. ed. by David Sharrock] New York, Benziger Bros. [c1963] xii, 398 p. col. illus. 23 cm. First published in 1935 under title: The story of the Church, her founding, mission, and progress. [BX948.J6 1963] 63-17043
1. Catholic Church — Hist. — Textbooks. I. Sharrock, David John. II. Title.

KINDER, Ernst. 270
Evangelical; what does it really mean? Translated by Edward and Marie Schroeder. St. Louis, Concordia Pub. House [1968] 105 p. 21 cm. Translation of Was ist eigentlich evangelisch? [BR1640.K513] 68-20729
1. Evangelicalism. I. Title.

KLEEBERG, Irene Cumming. 270
Christianity / Irene Cumming Kleeberg. New York : F. Watts, 1976. 87 p. : ill. ; 23 cm. (A First book) Includes index. Bibliography: p. 84. Traces the history of Christianity from the time of Jesus to the present, and discusses the major Christian beliefs and holidays, individual Protestant denominations, and trends in

modern Christianity. [BR151.K53] 75-37743 ISBN 0-531-00843-6 lib.bdg. : 3.90
1. Church history—Juvenile literature. 2. Sects—Juvenile literature. I. Title.

KUIPER, Barend Klaas, 1877- 270
The church in history. Grand Rapids, National Union of Christian Schools [1951] 499 p. illus., ports., maps. 25 cm. [BR151.K8] 51-10567
1. Church history—Juvenile literature. I. Title.

LANGFORD, Norman F., 1914- 270
Fire upon the earth, the story of the Christian church; illustrated by John Lear. Philadelphia, Westminster Press [1950] 207 p. illus. 22 cm. [BR151.L3] 50-10943
1. Church history. I. Title.

LATOURETT, Kenneth Scott, 1884- 270
Christianity through the ages. [1st ed.] New York, Harper & Row [1965] xiii, 321 p. 21 cm. (Harper chapel books, CB1) Bibliography: p. 310-311. [BR146.L3] 65-11348
1. Church history. I. Title.

LATOURETTE, Kenneth Scott, 1884-1968. 270
A history of Christianity. [1st ed.] New York, Harper [1953] xxvii, 1516 p. maps (part fold.) 24 cm. Includes bibliographies. [BR145.L28] 53-5004
1. Church history.

LATOURETTE, Kenneth Scott, 1884-1968. 270
A history of Christianity / Kenneth Scott Latourette. Rev. ed. New York : Harper & Row, 1975. 2 v. : maps ; 21 cm. Includes bibliographies and index. [BR145.2.L35 1975] 74-25693 ISBN 0-06-064952-6 (v. 1) : 6.95 per. vol.
1. Church history. I. Title.

LILLIE, Amy Morris. 270
I will build my church; illustrated by Norman Guthrie Rudolph. Philadelphia, Westminster Press [1950] 192 p. illus. (part col.) 21 cm. [BR151.L75] 50-10401
1. Church history—Juvenile literature. I. Title.

LIPTAK, David Q. 270 B
Saints for our time / David Q. Liptak. New York : Arena Lettres, 1977,c1976 xiii, 169 p. ; 18 cm. Bibliography: p. 169. [BX4655.2.L55] 76-45725 ISBN 0-88479-002-9 : 1.75
1. Christian saints—Biography. I. Title.

LOTZ, Philip Henry, 1889- ed. 270 B
Founders of Christian movements. Freeport, N.Y., Books for Libraries Press [1970, c1941] x, 160 p. 23 cm. (Essay index reprint series) "Originally published as v. 3 of the [author's] Creative personality series." Contents.Contents.—Robert Raikes, founder of the Sunday School, by A. J. W. Myers.—William Booth, founder of the Salvation Army, by F. G. Lankard.—Walter Rauschenbusch, prophet of social justice, by G. W. Fiske.—John Calvin, man of iron will who lived for God's glory, by G. Harkness.—St. Paul, the man who dared, by L. R. Robison.—Nicolaus Ludwig von Zinzendorf, founder of the Moravian Church, by H. H. Meyer.—St. Benedict, founder of western monasticism, by L. B. Hazzard.—St. Francis of Assisi, saint of the Middle Ages, by W. D. Schermerhorn.—Horace Bushnell, pioneer in religious education, by A. J. W. Myers.—Martin Luther, saint or devil, by J. V. Thompson.—Alexander Campbell, adventurer in freedom, by E. J. Wrather.—Ignatius Loyola, author of "A spiritual manual of arms," by L. H. Wild.—William Ellery Channing, founder of Unitarianism, by L. R. Robison.—George Fox, founder of the Society of Friends, by T. R. Kelly.—John Wesley, founder of Methodism, by J. W. Prince. Includes bibliographies. [BR1700.L67 1970] 71-111843 ISBN 0-8369-1672-7
1. Christian biography. 2. Reformers—Biography. I. Title.

LUCKHARDT, Mildred Madeleine (Corell), 1898- 270
The church through the ages; a primer of church history. New York, Association Press, 1951. 244 p. 21 cm. [BR150.L8] 51-11113
1. Church history. I. Title.

MACCULLOCH, John Arnott, 1868-1950. 270
Medieval faith and fable. With a foreword by Sir J. G. Frazer. Freeport, N.Y., Books for Libraries Press [1973] Reprint of the 1932 ed. Bibliography: p. [BR253.M3 1973] 72-10612 ISBN 0-8369-7118-3
1. Church history—Middle Ages. 2. Civilization, Medieval. 3. Sects, Medieval. I. Title.

MACCULLOCH, John Arnott, 1868-1950. 270
Medieval faith and fable. With a foreword by Sir J. G. Frazer. [Folcroft, Pa.] Folcroft Library Editions, 1973. p. Reprint of the 1932 ed. published by Harrap, London. Bibliography: p. [BR253.M3 1973b] 73-12549 35.00
1. Church history—Middle Ages. 2. Civilization, Medieval. 3. Sects, Medieval. I. Title.

MCGINLEY, Phyllis, 1905- 270
Saint-watching. New York, Viking Press [1969] x, 243 p. 22 cm. Bibliographical references included in "Afterword" (p. 223-277) [BR1710.M23] 79-83242 ISBN 0-670-16775-4 5.95
1. Christian saints. 2. Heroes. I. Title.

MACGREGOR, Geddes. [John Geddes MacGregor] 270
The hemlock and the cross; humanism, Socrates, and Christ. Philadelphia, Lippincott [c.1963] 225p. 22cm. Bibl. 63-7284 5.50
1. Humanism—Hist. 2. Christianity. I. Title.

MACKAY, Henry Falconar Barclay, 1864-1936. 270 B
Followers in the way. Freeport, N.Y., Books for Libraries Press [1969] 207 p. 23 cm. (Essay index reprint series) Reprint of the 1934 ed. Contents.Contents.—Gaius.—Demas.—Diotrephes.—Antipas.—The martyrdoms at Lyons and Vienne.—Phocas.—Constantine.—The life and death of St. John Chrysostom.—St. Edward the Confessor.—St. Thomas of Canterbury.—The life and death of Blessed Thomas More.—St. Francis de Sales.—Hurrell Froude.—The martyrdom of Bishop John Colerdige Patteson.—A hundred years in Margaret Street. [BR1700.M265 1969] 71-93359
1. Church of England—Biography. 2. Christian biography. 3. Fathers of the church. I. Title.

MCNEILL, John Thomas, 1885- 270
Modern Christian movements [by] John T. McNeill. New York, Harper & Row [1968] 201 p. 20 cm. (Harper torchbooks, TB1402) Bibliography: p. 179-191. [BR290] 79-331 1.75
1. Church history—Modern period, 1500- I. Title.

MANSCHRECK, Clyde Leonard, 1917- 270
A history of Christianity in the world; from persecution to uncertainty [by] Clyde L. Manschreck. Englewood Cliffs, N.J., Prentice-Hall [1974] v, 378 p. 23 cm. Bibliography: p. 361-370. [BR145.2.M3] 73-22206 ISBN 0-13-389346-4 7.95
1. Church history. I. Title.

MARCHANT, James, Sir, 1867-1956, ed. 270
The coming-of-age of Christianity [by] John Foster [and others] Westport, Conn., Greenwood Press [1971] xvii, 190 p. 23 cm. Reprint of the 1950 ed. Includes bibliographical references. [BR155.M3 1971] 70-106673 ISBN 0-8371-3424-2
1. Church history—Addresses, essays, lectures. I. Foster, John, 1898- II. Title.

MARTY, Martin E., 1928- 270
A short history of Christianity. New York, Meridian Books [1959] 384 p. 19 cm. (Living age books [LA24]) Includes bibliography. [BR146.M28] 59-7187
1. Church history. I. Title.

MAYNARD, Theodore, 1890-1956. 270 B
Pillars of the church. Freeport, N.Y., Books for Libraries Press [1970, c1945] xi, 308 p. 23 cm. (Essay index reprint series) Bibliography: p. 301-308. [BX4651.M38 1970] 76-136763
1. Catholic Church—Biography. I. Title.

MEAD, Frank Spencer, 1898- 270
The march of eleven men. [Westwood. N. J.] Revell [1963, c.1932] 236p. 21cm. 63-3164 2.95 bds.,
1. Church history. 2. Civilization, Christian. I. Title.

MEAD, Frank Spencer, 1898- 270
The ten decisive battles of Christianity. Freeport, N.Y., Books for Libraries Press [1970, c1937] 151 p. 23 cm. (Essay index reprint series) Contents.Contents.—The Resurrection.—The Council of Jerusalem.—Constantine and the Edict of Milan.—Augustine and The city of God.—The battle of Tours.—The battle of Worms: Martin Luther.—The battle of Boston: Roger Williams.—Street battle: George Whitehead.—The battle for missions: William Carey.—The battle with society. [BR148.M4 1970] 72-117823
1. Church history. 2. Civilization, Christian. I. Title.

*MEEKS, Wayne A. 270
Go from your father's house: a college student's introduction to the Christian faith Illus by Martha F. Meeks [dist.] Richmond, Va. [Knox, c.1964] CLC Pr. 356p. 21cm. (Covenant life curriculum) 2.95 pap.,
I. Title.

MIGNE, Jacques Paul, 1800-1875 270
J. P. Migne: Index alphabeticus omnium Doctorum-Patrum scriptorumque ecclesiasticorum quorum opera scriptaque vel minima Latina reperiuntur. J. B. Pearson: Conspectus auctorum quorum nomina indicibus Patrologiae Graeco-Latinae a J. P. Migne editae continentur. [Ridgewood, N. J., Gregg Pr., 1966] [42] p. 28cm. The Index alphabeticus is extracted from v. 218 of Migne's Patrologia Latina, published 1844-64. The Conspectus auctorum is a reprint of a separate work, first pub. in 1882. [BR60.M37 1844a] 67-3656 9.80
1. Migne, Jacques Paul, 1800-1875. Patrologiae cursus completus. Series Graeca. (Indexes) I. Migne, Jacques Paul, 1800-1875. Patrologiae cursus completus. Series Latina. (Indexes) II. Pearson, John Batteridge. Conspectus auctorum quorum nomina indicibus Patrologiae Graeco-Latinae . . . continentur. III. Title. IV. Title: Index alphabeticus omnium Doctorum-Patrum, scriptorumque ecclesiasticorum.

MOORE, Ralph Westwood, 1906- 270
The furtherance of the gospel. London, New York, Oxford University Press, 1950. 168 p. 20 cm. (A Primer of Christianity, pt. 2) Bibliography: p. [160]-162. [BR146.M75] 50-12103
1. Church history. I. Title. II. Series.

MURPHY, John L. 270
The general councils of the church. Milwaukee, Bruce Pub. Co. [c.1960] ix, 193p. illus., map 22cm. 60-8237 3.50
1. Councils and synods, Ecumenical. I. Title.

MURPHY, John L 1924- 270
The general councils of the church. Milwaukee, Bruce Pub. Co. [1960] 193p. illus. 22cm. [BX825.M8] 60-8237
1. Councils and synods, Ecumenical. I. Title.

MURRAY, Jane Marie, 1896- 270
Christ in His church. Milwaukee, Bruce Pub. Co. [1952] 656p. illus. 23cm. (The Christian religion series for high schools) [BR147.M8] 52-12826
1. Church history. 2. Catholic Church—Hist. I. Title.

MURRAY, Robert Henry, 1874-1947. 270
Group movements throughout the ages. Freeport, N.Y., Books for Libraries Press [1972] 377 p. illus. 23 cm. (Essay index reprint series) Reprint of the 1935 ed. Contents.Contents.—The Montanists; or, The priest versus the prophet.—The Franciscans; or, The realisation of the ideal.—The Friends of God; or, The quest of the ideal under difficulties.—Port Royal; or, The group in miniature.—The Methodists; with a reference to the Evangelicals.—The Oxford group movement; with a reference to the Tractarians. Includes bibliographies. [BV4487.O9M87 1972] 72-301 ISBN 0-8369-2810-5
1. Oxford Group. 2. Sects. 3. Revivals—History. I. Title.

NEILL, Stephen Charles, Bp. 270
The Christian society. New York, Harper [1953, c1952] 334p. 22cm. (The Library of constructive theology) [BR148.N4 1953] 53-7764
1. Church history. I. Title.

NEILL, Stephen Charles, Bp. 270
The Christian society. Westport, Conn., Greenwood Press [1972] xv, 334 p. 22 cm. Reprint of the 1952 ed., issued in series: The Library of constructive theology. [BR148.N4 1972] 76-141280 ISBN 0-8371-5877-X
1. Church history. I. Title.

NORWOOD, Frederick Abbott. 270
Great in church history. New York, Abingdon Press [1962] 128p. 20cm. [BR146.N6] 62-52341
1. Church history—Outlines, syllabi, etc. I. Title.

NORWOOD, Frederick Abbott. 270
Great moments in church history. Nashville, Greaded Press [c1962] 128 p. 20 cm. (Basic Christian books) [BR146.N6] 63-5912
1. Church history — Outlines, syllabi, etc. I. Title.

NORWOOD, Frederick Abbott 270
Great moments in church history. Nashville, Abingdon [c.1962] 128p. 20cm. Bibl. 62-52341 1.00
1. Church history—Outlines, syllabi, etc. I. Title.

O'BRIEN, John M. 270
Medieval church, by John M. O'Brien. Totowa, N.J., Littlefield, Adams, 1968. vii, 120 p. 21 cm. (A Littlefield, Adams quality paperback no. 227) Includes bibliographies. [BR252.O2] 68-19397 1.50
1. Church history—Middle Ages, 600-1500. I. Title.

OLSON, John Frederick, ed. 270
Our religious heritage; documents and readings in the Judaeo-Christian, tradition. [Syracuse, N. Y.,] Syracuse University Press [1953] 272p. 22cm. [BR141.O4] 53-3776
1. Church history—Sources. I. Title.

ORDERICUS Vitalis, 1075-1143? 270
The ecclesiastical history of England and Normandy. Translated, with notes, and the introd. of Guizot, by Thomas Forester. London, H. G. Bohn, 1853-56. New York, AMS Press [1968] 4 v. 22 cm. Original ed. issued in series: Bohn's antiquarian library. Translation of Historiae ecclesiasticae libri XIII. Includes bibliographical references. [BR252.O632] 68-57872
1. Church history. 2. Normandy—History—To 1461. 3. Great Britain—History—To 1485. 4. Normans. 5. Crusades. I. Title.

PALANQUE, Jean Remy 270
The dawn of the Middle Ages; translated from the French by Finbar Murphy. New York, Hawthorn Books [c.1960] 126p. 21cm. (The Twentieth century encyclopedia of Catholicism, v. 75. Section 7: The history of the church) Bibl.: p.125-126 60-16685 2.95 half cloth,
1. Church history—Primitive and early church. 2. Church history—Middle Ages. I. Title.

PASCHASIUS Radbertus, Saint, Abbot of Corbie, d.ca.860. 270 B
Charlemagne's cousins; contemporary lives of Adalard and Wala. Translated, with introd. and notes, by Allen Cabaniss. [1st ed. Syracuse, N.Y.] Syracuse University Press [1967] vii, 266 p. 24 cm. Translation of Vita sancti Adalhardi and Vita Walae seu Epitaphium Arsenii. Bibliographical references included in "Notes" (p. 205-223) [BX4700.A19P313] 67-26919
1. Adalard, Saint, Abbott of Corbie, d. 826. 2. Wala, Saint, Abbot of Corbie, d. 836. I. Paschasius Radbertus, Saint, Abbot of Corbie, d. ca. 860. Vita Walae. English. 1967. II. Title

PASCHASIUS RADBERTUS, Saint, Abbot of Corbie, d.ca.860. 270 (B)
Charlemagne's cousins; contemporary lives of Adalard and Wala. Translated, with introd. and notes, by Allen Cabaniss. [1st ed. Syracuse, N. Y.] Syracuse University Press [1967 vii, 266 p. 24 cm. Translation of Vita sancti Adalhardi and Vita Walae seu Epitaphium Arsenii. Bibliographical references included in "Notes" (p. 205-223) [BX4700.A19P313] 67-26919
1. Adalard, Saint, Abbot of Corbie, d. 826. 2. Wala, Saint, Abbot of Corbie, d. 836. I. Title.

PETRELLI, Giuseppe. 270
From darkness to light. [New York, Van Rees Press, 1957] 243p. 21cm. [BR125.P418] 57-7339
1. Christianity— 20th cent. I. Title.

PETRY, Ann (Lane) 1911- 270 B
Legends of the saints, by Ann Petry. Illustrated by Anne Rockwell. New York, Crowell [1970] 47 p. illus. (part col.) 24 cm. Retells the legends of ten saints: Christopher, Genesius, George, Blaise, Catherine of Alexandria, Nicholas, Francis of Assisi, Joan of Arc, Thomas More, and Martin de Porres. [BX4658.P44 1970] 920 72-106576 4.50
1. Christian saints—Juvenile literature. I. Rockwell, Anne F., illus. II. Title.

POPE, Richard Martin, 1916- 270
The Church and its culture; a history of the Church in changing cultures, by Richard M. Pope. St. Louis, Bethany Press [1965] 618 p. 23 cm. Bibliography: p. 603-612. [BR121.2.P6] 65-12292
1. Church history. I. Title.

POPE, Richard Martin, 1916- 270
The Church and its culture; a history of the Church in changing cultures. St. Louis, Bethany [c.1965] 618p. 23cm. Bibl. [BR121.2.P6] 65-12292 8.95
1. Church history. I. Title.

PRICHARD, Marianna (Nugent) 270
Back to the sources, by Marianna Nugent Prichard and Norman Young Prichard. Boston, United Church Press [1964] 124 p. illus., col. maps. 21 cm. "Part of the United Church curriculum, prepared and published by the Division of Christian Education and the Division of Publication of the United Church Board for Homeland Ministries." Bibliographical references included in "Footnotes and acknowledgments" (p 123) [BR149.P7] 64-19464
1. Church history—Outlines, syllabi, etc. I. Prichard, Norman Young, joint author. II. United Church Board for Homeland Ministries. Division of Christian Education. United Church Board for Homeland Ministries. Division of Publications III. Title.

PROGRESS and decline in the 270
history of church renewal. Ed. by Roger Aubert. New York, Paulist [1967] viii, 183p. 24cm. (Concilium: theol. in the age of renewal; Church hist., v. 27) Series: Concilium: theology in the age of renewal, v. 27) Includes articles tr. from several langs. by various persons. Bibl. [BR155.P7] 67-30136 4.50
1. Church history— Addresses, essays, lectures. I. Aubert, Roger, ed. II. Series.
Contents omitted.

QUALBEN, Lars Pederson, 1891- 270
A history of the Christian church. Rev. and enl. New York, T. Nelson [1958] 649 p. illus. 21 cm. Includes bibliography. [BR146.Q3 1958] 58-4171
1. Church history. I. Title: The Christian church.

REID, Clyde H 270
The God-evaders [by] Clyde Reid [1st ed.] New York, Harper & Row [1966] x, 118 p. 22 cm. Bibliography: p. 111-112. [BR123.R43] 66-15044
1. Christianity — 20th cent. — Addresses, essays, lectures. I. Title.

REID, Clyde H. 270
The God-evaders. New York, Harper [c.1966] x, 118p. 22cm. Bibl. [BR123.R43] 66-15044 3.50 bds.,
1. Christianity—20th cent.—Addresses, essays, lectures. I. Title.

RENWICK, A M 270
The story of the church. Grand Rapids, Eerdmans [1958] 222p. 18cm. (Eerdmans pocket editions) Includes bibliography. [BR150.R4 1958] 59-6955
1. Church history. I. Title.

ROUSE, Ruth. 270
A history of the ecumenical movement, 1517-1948, edited by Ruth Rouse and Stephen Charles Neill. 2d ed. with rev. bibliography. Philadelphia, Westminster Press, 1967. xxiv, 838 p. 23 cm. Bibliography: p. 747-801. [BX6.5.R6 1967a] 67-14834
1. Ecumenical movement. 2. Church history—Modern period. I. Neill, Stephen Charles, Bp., joint ed. II. Title.

RUPP, Ernest Gordon. 270
The old Reformation and the new [by] Gordon Rupp. Philadelphia, Fortress Press [1967] 68 p. 18 cm. (The Cato lecture, 1966) [BR305.2.R8 1967b] 67-21530
1. Reformation. 2. Christianity—20th cent. 3. Church renewal. I. Title. II. Series.

RUPP, Ernest Gordon. 270
The old Reformation and the new [by] Gordon Rupp. Philadelphia, Fortress Press [1967] 68 p. 18 cm. (The Cato lecture 1966) [BR305.2.R8 1967b] 67-21530
1. Reformation. 2. Christianity—20th century. 3. Church renewal. I. Title. II. Series.

RUSSELL, Jeffrey Burton. 270
A history of medieval Christianity; prophesy and order. New York, Crowell [1968] vii, 216 p. 22 cm. Bibliography: p. 197-206. [BR252.R8] 68-9743 5.95
1. Church history—Middle ages. I. Title.

SCHAFF, Philip, 1819-1893. 270
History of the Christian church. Grand Rapids Mich., W. B. Eerdmans Pub. Co. 19 v. 23 cm. Contents.Contents. -- v. 5. The Middle Ages from Gregory vii., 1049, to Boniface viii., 1294, by D. S. Schaff. 1949. [[BR145.S)] A51
1. Church history. 2. Reformation. I. Schaff, David Schley, 1852-1941. II. Title.

SHERIDAN, John V. 270 B
Saints in times of turmoil / by John V. Sheridan ; foreword by Timothy Manning. New York : Paulist Press, c1977. v, 130 p. ; 19 cm. (A Deus book) [BX4655.2.S49] 76-39774 ISBN 0-8091-2005-4 pbk. : 2.45
1. Christian saints—Biography. 2. Catholics—Biography. I. Title.

SIMPSON, Robert L comp. 270
Our Christian heritage; a reading book. Robert L. Simpson and Donald F. Heath, editors. Enid, Okla., Phillips University Press, 1967- v. 24 cm. [BR141.S5] 67-30775
1. Church history—Sources. I. Heath, Donald F., joint comp. II. Title.

*SMYLIE, James H. 270
Into all the world. Illus. by Hans Zander. Richmond, Va., CLC Pr. [dist. Knox. 1966, c.1965] 96p. col. illus. 21cm. Bibl. 1.45 pap.,
I. Title.

SNIADOFF, Peter, 1893- 270
The historical catalyst; a critical analysis of history to prove the inadequacy of popular belief. [1st ed.] Los Angeles [1972] xiv, 226 p. 22 cm. [BR145.2.S64] 74-173167
1. Church history. 2. Religions—History. 3. History—Philosophy. I. Title.

SOUTH English legendary. 270 B
The South English legendary. Edited from Corpus Christi College, Cambridge, MS. 145 and British Museum MS. Harley 2277, with variants from Bodley MS. Ashmole 43 and British Museum MS. Cotton Julius D. IX, by Charlotte D'Evelyn and Anna J. Mill. London, New York, Published for the Early English Text Society by the Oxford University Press [1967- v. facsims. 23 cm. (Early English Text Society. [Publications. Original series] no. 235) Reprint of the 1956-59 ed. [PR1119.A2 no. 235, etc., 1967] 77-825 50/- per vol.
1. Saints—Legends. I. D'Evelyn, Charlotte, 1889- ed. II. Mill, Anna Jean, ed. III. Series: Early English Text Society. Publications. Original series, no. 235 [etc.]

SOUTHERN, Richard William. 270
Western society and the Church in the Middle Ages [by] R. W. Southern. [Harmondsworth, Eng.] Penguin Books [1970] 376 p. maps. 18 cm. (The Pelican history of the Church, 2) (Pelican books) Includes bibliographical references. [BR252.S6] 75-21956 ISBN 0-14-020503-9 2.25 (U.S.)
1. Church history—Middle Ages, 600-1500. 2. Civilization, Medieval. I. Title.

SPENCER, Bonnell. 270
Ye are the Body; a people's history of the Church. West Park, N.Y., Holy Cross Press [1950] xiii, 378 p. illus., maps. 24 cm. Bibliography: p. 368-370. [BR150.S6] 50-56379
1. Church history. I. Title.

SPINKA, Matthew, 1890- 270
Selected articles. [Claremont? Calif., 1968] 4 v. 26-28 cm. Vol. 4 has title: Selected articles and speeches. Contains 59 pamphlets, typescripts, extracts from periodicals, photocopies of articles, etc. Contents.Contents.—1920-1933.—2. 1935-1949.—3. 1953-1968.—4. 1919-1967. Includes bibliographies. [BR142.S65] 71-171
1. Church history—Addresses, essays, lectures.

STUBER, Stanley Irving, 1903- 270
How we got our denominations; a primer on church history, by Stanley I. Stuber, [Rev. ed.] New York, Association Press [1965] 254 p. 20 cm. Bibliography: p. 251-254. [BR157.S77] 65-23134
1. Sects. 2. Church history. I. Title.

SYKES, Norman, 1897- 270
Man as churchman. Cambridge [Eng.] University Press, 1960 i.e. 1961] 202 p. 21 cm. (The Wiles lectures, 1959) Includes bibliography. [BR155.S9] 61-1029
1. Church history — Addresses, essays, lectures. I. Title.

SYKES, Norman, 1897- 270
Man as churchman. [New York] Cambridge Univ. Press, 1960[c.1961] 202p. (Wiles lectures, 1959) Bibl. 61-1029 4.00
1. Church history—Addresses, essays, lectures. I. Title.

*THOMPSON, Ernest Trice 270
Through the ages; a history of the Christian Church. Richmond, Va., CLC Pr. [dist. Knox, 1966, c.1965] 447p. illus. 21cm. Bibl. 2.95 pap.,
I. Title.

TOLIVER, Ralph 270
They found the way of victory. Chicago, Moody [c.1963] 77p. 18cm. (Compact bks., 27) Bibl. .29 pap.,
I. Title.

TOWNS, Elmer L. 270 B
The Christian Hall of Fame [by] Elmer L. Towns. Grand Rapids, Baker Book House [1971] 223 p. ports. 22 cm. [BR1700.2.T68] 72-159668 ISBN 0-8010-8770-8 2.95
1. Christian biography. I. Title.

TYDINGS, Judith. 270
Gathering a people / Judith Tydings. Plainfield, N.J. : Logos International, c1977. 327 p. ; 21 cm. Includes bibliographical references. [BX4651.2.T92] 76-28680 ISBN 0-88270-187-8 : 6.95. ISBN 0-88270-188-6 pbk. : 3.50
1. Christian saints. I. Title.

VATH, Mary Loyola, Sister. 270
Visualized church history. New Ed. New York, Oxford Book Co. 1952. 350 p. illus. 19 cm. [BR147.V3 1952] 52-25584
1. Church history. 2. Catholic Church — Hist. 3. Catholic Church in the U.S. I. Title.

VOS, Howard Frederic, 1925- 270
Beginnings in church history / by Howard F. Vos. Rev. ed. Chicago : Moody Press, c1977. p. cm. Bibliography: p. [BR145.2.V67 1977] 77-21991 ISBN 0-8024-0607-6 pbk. : 2.95
1. Church history. I. Title.

WADDAMS, Herbert Montague. 270
The struggle for Christian unity [by] Herbert Waddams. New York, Walker [1968] xii, 268 p. illus., map, ports. 21 cm. ([Problems of history]) London ed. (Blandford) has title: The church and man's struggle for unity. Includes bibliographical references. [BR145.2.W3 1968b] 68-14000 6.50
1. Church history. 2. Christian union—History. I. Title.

WALKER, Williston, 1860-1922. 270
A history of the Christian church. Rev. by Cyril C. Richardson, Wilhelm Pauck [and] Robert T. Handy. New York, Scribner [1959] 585 p. illus. 25 cm. Includes bibliography. [BR146.W3 1959] 58-12494
1. Church history. I. Title.

WASHBURN, Henry Bradford, 270 B
1869-1962.
Men of conviction. Freeport, N.Y., Books for Libraries Press [1971, c1931] viii, 250 p. illus. 22 cm. (Essay index reprint series) Originally published as The Bohlen lectures, 1931. Contents.Contents.—Autobiographic.—Athanasius.—Benedict of Nursia.—Hildebrand.—Francis of Assisi.—Ignatius Loyola.—Pius IX. "A list of recommended books": p. 243-244. [BR1700.W33 1971] 74-134152 ISBN 0-8369-2081-3
1. Christian biography. I. Title.

WENDELL, Claus August, 1866- j270
1950.
Little journeys in His kingdom. With revisions by Reynold N. Johnson. [2d rev. ed.] Philadelphia, Fortress Press [c1963] 147 p. maps. 16 cm. [BR151.W4] 63-22224
1. Church history — Juvenile literature. I. Johnson, Reynold N. II. Title.

WENDELL, Claus August, 1866- 270
1950
Little journeys in His kingdom. Revs. by Reynold N. Johnson [2d rev. ed.] Philadelphia, Fortress [c.1963] 147p. maps. 16cm. 63-22224 1.00 bds.,
1. Church history—Juvenile literature. I. Johnson, Reynold N. II. Title.

WENGER, John Christian, 1910- 270
The Christian faith; glimpses of church history, by J. C. Wenger. Scottdale, Pa., Herald Press [1971] 116 p. 18 cm. Includes bibliographical references. [BR145.2.W43] 71-153968 ISBN 0-8361-1646-1
1. Church history. I. Title.

WILLIAMS, Charles, 1886-1945. 270
The descent of the Dove; a short history of the Holy Spirit in the church. New York, Pellegrini and Cudahy [1950] ix, 245 p. front. 23 cm. [BR148.W55] 50-7637
1. Church history. I. Title.

WILLIAMS, Charles, 1886-1945. 270
The descent of the Dove; a history of the Holy Spirit in the church. Introd. by W. H. Auden. New York, Meridian Books, 1956. xv, 240p. 19cm. (Living age books, 5) [BR148.W55 1956] 56-9241
1. Church history. I. Title.

WILLIAMS, Charles, 1886-1945. 270
The descent of the Dove; a history of the Holy Spirit in the church. Introd. by W. H. Auden New York, Meridian Books, 1956. xv. 240 p. 19 cm. (Living age books, 5) [BR148W55 1956] 56-9241
1. Church history. I. Title.

WILLIAMS, Charles Walter 270
Stansby, 1886-
The descent of the Dove; a short history of the Holy Spirit in the church. Grand Rapids, Mich., Eerdmans [1965, c.1939] 245p. front. 20cm. 1.95 pap.,
1. Church history. I. Title.

WILLIAMS, Glanmor. 270
Reformation views of church history. Richmond, Va., John Knox Press [1970] 85 p. 22 cm. (Ecumenical studies in history, no. 11) Includes bibliographical references. [BR138.W56 1970] 70-107323
1. Church history—Historiography. I. Title. II. Series.

WRIGHT, Robert Roy. 270
The church's first thousand years. New York, Published for the Cooperative Publication Association by Abingdon Press [1960] 96 p. 19 cm. (Faith for life series) [BR162.2.W7] 60-1589
1. Church history — Primitive and early church. 2. Church history — Middle Ages. I. Title.

WRIGHT, Robert Roy 270
The church's first thousand years. Nashville, Published for the Cooperative Publication Association by Abingdon Press [c.1960] 96p. 20cm. (Faith for life series) 60-1589 1.00 pap.,
1. Church history—Primitive and early church. 2. Church history—Middle Ages. I. Title.

YOUNGMAN, Bernard R. 270
Into all the world; the story of Christianity to 1066 A.D. Maps by Pierre Savoie. New York, St Martin's. 1965[c.1963] 222p. illus., maps, ports. 23cm. Bibl. [BR162.2.Y6] 65-18315 5.95 bds.,
1. Church history—Primitive and early church. 2. Church history—Middle Ages. I. Title.

RATZINGER, Joseph. 270'.01
The theology of history in St. Bonaventure. [Translated by Zachary Hayes. Chicago, Ill.] Franciscan Herald Press [1971] xv, 268 p. 22 cm. Originally presented as the author's Habilitationsschrift, Munich, 1959, under title: Die Geschichtstheologie des heiligen Bonaventura. Bibliography: p. 241-253. [BR115.H5R3513] 71-85509 ISBN 0-8199-0415-5 12.50
1. Bonaventura, Saint, Cardinal, 1221-1274. 2. History (Theology)—History of doctrines. I. Title.

SMITH, Charles 270'.02'07
Merrill.
The Pearly Gates Syndicate; or, How to sell real estate in heaven. [1st ed.] Garden City, N.Y., Doubleday, 1971. xiv, 220 p. 22 cm. [BR145.2.S6] 77-105619 4.95
1. Church history. I. Title.

SMITH, William, Sir 1813- 270'.03
1893, ed.
A dictionary of Christian antiquities. Being a continuation of the Dictionary of the. Bibl. Ed. by William Smith, Samuel Cheetham. Illus. by engravings on wood. Hartford, the J. B. Burr Pub. Co., 1880; New York, Kraus Reprint, 1968. 2v. illus. (incl. music) 23cm. [BR95.S6 1880] 17-21174 85.00 set,
1. Christian antiquities—Dictionaries. I. Cheetham, Samuel, 1827-1908, joint ed. II. Title.

THE Westminster 270'.03
dictionary of church history. Editor: Jerald C. Brauer. Associate editors: Brian Gerrish [and others] Philadelphia, Westminster Press [1971] xii, 887 p. 25 cm. Includes bibliographical references. [BR95.W496] 69-11071 ISBN 0-664-21285-9 17.50
1. Church history—Dictionaries. I. Brauer, Jerald C., ed. II. Gerrish, Brian Albert, 1931- ed. III. Title: Dictionary of Church history.

JOURNAL of ecclesiastical 270.05
history (The) s. 1-12. London, Faber and Faber; New York, Johnson Reprint [1967] v. 25cm. semiannual. Began pubn. with Apr. 1950 issue. Cf. New serial titles, 1955. Ed.: C.W. Dugmore [BR140.J6] 58-20553 180.00 set,
1. Church history—Period. I. Dugmore, Clifford William, ed.

JOURNAL of ecclesiastical 270.05
history (The). v. 1-12, 1950-1961. London, Faber and Faber, 1950-1961; New York, Johnson Reprint, 1966. 12v. (various p.) 25cm. semiannual. Began pub. with Apr. 1950 issue. Cf. New serial titles, 1955, Ed.: C. W. Dugmore [BR140.J6] set, 180.00; set, pap., 150.00; ea., pap., 12.50
1. Church history—Period. I. Dugmore, Clifford William, ed.

REVUE de l Drient 270.05
chretien. 1.-3. ser., to 1-30; 1896-1936 [i.e. 1946] New York, JohnsonReprint 1966. 30v. illus. 23cm. Each ser. also numbered separately. Vol. 30 covers 1935-46. Vols. 1-25 issued as photoreproduction of the periodical pub. with imprint: Paris, Au Bureau des oeuvres d'Orient (and others); v. 26-30 of the L.C. set are the original ed. Vol. 1-2 called Supplement trimestriel Eds.: 1911-36, R. Graffin (with F. Nau, 1911-19) Indexes: Vols. 1-10, 1896-1905 in v. 10. Vols. 11-20, 1906-17 in v. 20. Vols 21-30, 1918-46 in v. 30. Vols. 21-30, 1918-46 in v. 30. [BR140.R48] 67-5486 price unreported.
1. Church history—Period. I. Graffin, Rene, 1858- ed. II. Nau, Francois Nicolas, 1864-1931, ed.

YEARBOOK of American 270.05873
churches; information on all faiths in the U.S.A. Thirty-third issue; ed. for 1965. Ed. by Benson Y. Landis. New York, Natl. Council of the Churches of Christ [c.1965] 314p. 23cm. annual. 16-5726 7.50; 6.25 pap.,
1. Sects—U.S. I. Landis, Benson Y., ed.

ECCLESIASTICAL History 270'.07'2
Society, London.
The materials, sources, and methods of ecclesiastical history : papers read at the twelfth summer meeting and the thirteenth winter meeting of the Ecclesiastical History Society / edited by Derek Baker. New York : Barnes & Noble Books, 1975. xii, 370 p. ; 23 cm. (Studies in church history ; 11) Includes bibliographical references. [BR140.5.E27 1975] 74-12561 ISBN 0-06-490286-2 : 20.00
1. Church history—Historiography—Congresses. I. Baker, Derek. II. Title. III. Series.

ECCLESIASTICAL History 270'.08 s
Society, London.
Popular belief and practice; papers read at the ninth summer meeting and the tenth winter meeting of the Ecclesiastical History Society. Edited by G. J. Cuming and Derek Baker. Cambridge [Eng.] University Press, 1972. xii, 330 p. 23 cm. (Studies in church history, 8) Includes bibliographical references. [BR141.S84 vol. 8] [BR50] 201'.1 77-155583 ISBN 0-521-08220-X
1. Theology—Addresses, essays, lectures. 2. Religion—Addresses, essays, lectures. I. Cuming, G. J., ed. II. Baker, Derek, ed. III. Title. IV. Series: Studies in church history (London), 8.

ECCLESIASTICAL History 270'.08 s
Society, London.
Schism, heresy and religious protest; papers read at the tenth summer meeting and the eleventh winter meeting of the Ecclesiastical History Society. Edited by Derek Baker. Cambridge [Eng] University Press, 1972. xv, 404 p. 23 cm. (Studies in church history, 9) Includes bibliographical references. [BR141.S84 vol. 9] [BT1318] 273 75-184899 ISBN 0-521-08486-5
1. Heresies and heretics—Addresses, essays, lectures. 2. Church history—Addresses, essays, lectures. I. Baker, Derek, ed. II. Title. III. Series: Studies in church history (London) 9.

FREND, W. H. C. 270'.08
Religion, popular and unpopular in the early Christian centuries / W. H. C. Frend. London : Variorum Reprints, 1976. 390 p. in various pagings : port. ; 23 cm. (Variorum reprint ; CS45) Includes original pagings. Reprints of articles, originally published between 1942 and 1975. Includes bibliographical references and index. [BR162.2.F73] 76-379939 ISBN 0-902089-89-7 : £3.50
1. Church history—Primitive and early church, ca. 30-600—Addresses, essays, lectures. I. Title.

HISTORICAL 270.08
investigations New York, Paulist [1966, ie. 1967] viii, 184p. 24cm. (Concilium theol. in the age of renewal: Church hist. v. 17) [BR155.H5] 66-29260 4.50
1. Church history—Addresses, essays, lectures. I. Series: Concilium theology in the age of renewal, v.17

HISTORICAL 270.08
investigations. New York, Paulist Press [1966] viii, 184 p. 24 cm. (Concilium theology in the age of renewal: Church history, v. 17) Bibliographical footnotes. [BR155.H5] 66-29260
1. Church history — Addresses, essays, lectures. I. Series: Concilium theology in the age of renewal, v. 17

MIRGELER, Albert. 270.081
Mutations of Western Christianity. Translated by Edward Quinn. With a foreword by David Knowles. [New York] Herder and Herder [1964] x, 158 p. 22 cm. Translation of Ruckblick auf das abendiandische Christentum. Bibliographical references included in "Notes" (p. 151-158) [BR148.M513] 64-11599
1. Church history — Addresses, essays, lectures. I. Title.

MIRGELER, Albert 270.081
Mutations of Western Christianity. Tr. [from German] by Edward Quinn. Foreword by David Knowles [New York] Herder & Herder [c.1961, 1964] x, 158p. 22cm. Bibl. 64-11599 4.50
1. Church history—Addresses, essays, lectures. I. Title.

BAINTON, Roland Herbert, 270.082
1894-
Early and medieval Christianity. Boston, Beacon Press [1962] iv, 261 p. 21 cm. (His collected papers in church history, ser. 1) Includes bibliographies. [BR162.B25] 62-7894
1. Church history—Primitive and early church, ca. 30-600—Addresses, essays, lectures. 2. Church history—Middle Ages, 600-1500—Addresses, essays, lectures. I. Title.

A History of 270.082
Christianity. [Englewood Cliffs, N.J., Prentice-Hall, 1962-64. 2 v. illus. 26 cm. Contents.Contents.—[1] Readings in the history of the early and medieval church, edited by R. C. Petry.—[2] Readings in the history of the church from the Reformation to the present, edited by C. L. Manschreck. [BR141.H53] 62-19679
1. Church history—Sources. I. Petry, Ray C., 1903- ed. II. Manschreck, Clyde Leonard, 1917- ed.

KING, Grace Hamilton, 270.082
1903- ed.
An anthology of Christian literature. Glendale, Calif. [1951] 223 l. 29 cm. [BR53.K63] 51-6860
1. Religious literature (Selections: Extracts, etc.) I. Title.

KNOWLES, David, 1896- 270.082
The historian and character, and other essays by David Knowles, collected and presented to him by his friends, pupils and colleagues on the occasion of his retirement ... University of Cambridge. Cambridge [Eng.] University Press, 1963. 387 p. illus. 23 cm. Includes bibliography. [BX941.K6] 63-4449
1. Church history—Collected works. 2. Monasticism and religious orders—Hist.—Collected works. I. Title.

KNOWLES, David [Secular 270.082
name: Michael Clive Knowles] 1896-
The historian and character, and other essays by David Knowles, collected, presented to him by his friends, pupils, colleagues on the occasion of his retirement [from the] Univ. of Cambridge [New York] Cambridge [c.]1963. 387p. illus. 23cm. Bibl. 63-4449 8.50
1. Church history—Collected works. 2. Monasticism and religious orders—Hist.—Collected works. I. Title.

MAUS, Cynthia Pearl, 270.082
1880- comp.
The church and the fine arts; an anthology of pictures, poetry, music, and stories portraying the growth and development of the church through the centuries, by Cynthia Pearl Maus, in collaboration with John P. Cavarnos [and others] New York, Harper [1960] 902 p. illus. 24 cm. [BR148.M35] 60-7956
1. Church history. 2. Christian art and symbolism. 3. Religious poetry, English. I. Title.

VAN DUSEN, Henry Pitney, 270.082
1897- ed.
Christianity on the march [by] Cyril C. Richardson [and others] [1st ed.] New York, Harper & Row [1963] xii, 176 p. 22 cm. "These chapters were given originally as lectures in the 'January Monday morning lecture series' sponsored by the Women's Committee of Union Theological Seminary, New York City." Bibliographical references included in "Notes" (p. 169-172) Bibliography: p. 173-176. [BR123.V28] 63-14973
1. Church history—Addresses, essays, lectures. 2. Christianity and other religions—Addresses, essays, lectures. I. Richardson, Cyril Charles, 1909- II. Title.

BOWDEN, Henry Warner. 270'.09
Church history in the age of science; historiographical patterns in the United States, 1876-1918. Chapel Hill, University of North Carolina Press [1971] xvi, 269 p. 24 cm. Bibliography: p. [247]-266. [BR138.B68] 72-156134 ISBN 0-8078-1176-9 10.00
1. Church history—Historiography. 2. Church historians, American. I. Title.

DELEHAYE, Hippolyte, 270'.09
1859-1941.
The legends of the saints; an introduction to hagiography, from the French of H. Delehaye. Translated by Mrs. V. M. Crawford. [Norwood, Pa.] Norwood Editions, 1974. p. cm. Reprint of the 1907 ed. published by Longmans, Green, London, in series: The Westminster library, a series of manuals for Catholic priests and students. Translation of Les legendes hagiographiques. Bibliography: p. [BX4662.D343 1974] 74-13653 ISBN 0-88305-166-4 (lib. bdg.)
1. Christian hagiography. I. Title. II. Series: The Westminster library, a series of manuals for Catholic priests and students.

DELEHAYE, Hippolyte, 270'.09
1859-1941.
The legends of the saints; an introduction to hagiography, from the French of H. Delehaye. Translated by Mrs. V. M. Crawford. [Norwood, Pa.] Norwood Editions, 1974. p. cm. Reprint of the 1907 ed. published by Longmans, Green, London, in series: The Westminster library, a series of manuals for Catholic priests and students. Translation of Les legendes hagiographiques. Bibliography: p. [BX4662.D343 1974] 74-13653 15.00 (lib. bdg.).
1. Christian hagiography. I. Title. II. Series: The Westminster library, a series of manuals for Catholic priests and students.

MCCLOY, Shelby Thomas, 270.09
1898-
Gibbon's antagonism to Christianity, by Shelby T. McCloy. New York, B. Franklin [196-?] 400 p. 24 cm. (Burt Franklin research & source works series, no. 144) (Selected essays in history and social science series, no. 3.) Reprint of the 1933 ed. Bibliography: p. [369]-381. [BL2773.G5M3 1960] 149'.7 68-1849
1. Gibbon, Edward, 1737-1794. The history of the decline and fall of the Roman Empire. 2. Christianity—Controversial literature. 3. Church history—Historiography. I. Title.

PULLAPILLY, Cyriac K. 270'.09 B
Caesar Baronius, Counter-Reformation historian / Cyriac K. Pullapilly. Notre Dame, Ind. : University of Notre Dame Press, [1975] xiv, 222 p. : port., facsim. (on lining papers) ; 24 cm. Includes index. Bibliography: p. 207-216. [BX4705.B2P8] 74-12567 ISBN 0-268-00501-X : 12.95
1. Baronio, Cesare, Cardinal, 1538-1607. I. Title.

BAUMGARTEN, Paul 270'.092'4
Maria, 1860-
Henry Charles Lea's historical writings : a critical inquiry into their method and merit / by Paul Maria Baumgarten. New York : Gordon Press, [1975] p. cm. Reprint of the 1909 ed. published by J. F. Wagner, New York. [BR139.L4B3 1975] 75-26910 34.95
1. Lea, Henry Charles, 1825-1909. I. Title.

FAIRFIELD, Leslie P. 270'.092'4 B
John Bale, mythmaker for the English Reformation / by Leslie P. Fairfield. West Lafayette, Ind. : Purdue University Press, 1976. x, 240 p. ; 24 cm. Includes index. Bibliography: p. 221-233. [BX5199.B254F34] 75-19953 ISBN 0-911198-42-3 : 9.75
1. Bale, John, Bp. of Ossory, 1495-1563. I. Title.

ARNOLD, Eberhard, 1883-1935 270.1
Lectures and writings: v. 2 & 4 [Rifton, N.Y.] Plough [1962] 123;96p. 18cm. Contents.2. The early Christians, after the death of the apostles [Tr. from German by J. S. Hoyland E. Wilms, K. E. Hasenberg] 4. The peace of God [Tr. from German by K. E. Hasenberg] Bibl. pap., v.2, 1.50; v.4, 1.25, plastic bdg.
1. Theology—Collected works—20th cent. I. Title.

AYER, Joseph Cullen, 1866- 270.1
1944.
A source book for ancient church history from the apostolic age to the close of the conciliar period. [1st AMS ed.] New York, AMS Press [1970] xxi, 707 p. 23 cm. Originally published in 1913. Bibliography: p. xix-xxi. [BR160.A2A9 1970] 70-113546
1. Church history—Primitive and early church, ca. 30-600—Sources. I. Title.

BARCLAY, William, lecturer 270.1
in the University of Glasgow.
God's young church. Philadelphia, Westminster Press [1970] 120 p. 19 cm. [BR165.B277] 70-110082 ISBN 0-664-24884-5 1.85
1. Bible. N.T.—Biography. 2. Church history—Primitive and early church, ca. 30-600. 3. Christian life—1960- I. Title.

BARNES, Arthur Stapylton, 270.1
1861-1936.
Christianity at Rome in the apostolic age; an attempt at reconstruction of history. Westport, Conn., Greenwood Press [1971] xiii, 222 p. 23 cm. Reprint of the 1938 ed. Includes bibliographical references. [BR165.B285 1971] 72-114462 ISBN 0-8371-4760-3
1. Peter, Saint, apostle. 2. Paul, Saint, apostle. 3. John, Saint, apostle. 4. Rome (City)—Church history. 5. Church history—Primitive and early church, ca. 30-600. I. Title.

BAYNES, Norman Hepburn, 270.1
1877-1961.
Constantine the Great and the Christian Church. 2nd ed. (i.e. 1st ed. reprinted) with a preface by Henry Chadwick. London, Oxford University Press for the British Academy, 1972. viii, 107 p. 23 cm. Reprint of the 1930 ed., issued in series: The Raleigh lecture on history, 1929. Includes bibliographical references. [BR180.B3 1972] 72-188266 ISBN 0-19-725672-4 £1.00
1. Constantinus I, the Great, Emperor of Rome, d. 337. 2. Church history—Primitive and early church, ca. 30-600. I. Title. II. Series: British Academy, London (Founded 1901) Annual Raleigh lecture, 1929.

BOER, Harry R. 270.1
A short history of the early church / by Harry R. Boer. Grand Rapids : Eerdmans, c1976. xiv, 184 p. : maps ; 22 cm. Includes index. Bibliography: p. 178-179. [BR165.B645] 75-25742 ISBN 0-8028-1339-9 pbk. : 2.95
1. Church history—Primitive and early church, ca. 30-600. I. Title.

BRUCE, Frederick Fyvie, 270.1
1910-
The spreading flame; the rise and progress of Christianity. Grand Rapids, W. B. Eerdmans Pub. Co., 1953. 191, 192, 160 p. 23 cm. Contents.Contents.—The dawn of Christianity.—The growing day.—Light in the West. [BR165.B715 1953] 53-9739
1. Church history—Primitive and early church. 2. Gt. Brit.—Church history—Early period. 3. Gt. Brit.—Church history—Anglo-Saxon period. I. Title.

CARLETON, William Augustus, 270.1
1905-
The growth of the early church [by] W. A. Carleton. Nashville, Convention Press [1970] v, 212 p. maps. 21 cm. (Bible survey series, v. 7) "Text for course 3209 of subject area Biblical revelation of the New church study course." Bibliography: p. 203-204. [BR168.C37] 73-124565
1. Bible. N.T. Acts—Study—Text-books. 2. Church history—Primitive and early church, ca. 30-600—Study and teaching. I. Title. II. Series.

CASE, Shirley Jackson 270.1
The evolution of early Christianity; a genetic study of first-century Christianity in relation to its religious environment, by Shirley Jackson Case. Ill., The University of Chicago Press [1960, c.1942] ix, 385p. 22cm. (Chicago reprint series) Bibl. footnotes 6.00
1. Church history—Primitive and early church. I. Title.

CHADWICK, Henry, 1920- 270.1
The early Church. Harmondsworth, Penguin, 1967 [i.e. 1968] 304 p. 18 cm. (The Pelican history of the Church, 1) Bibliography: p. 290-295. [BR165.C48 1968] 68-92647 7/6
1. Church history—Primitive and early church, ca. 30-600. I. Title.

CHADWICK, Henry, 1920- 270.1
The early church. Grand Rapids, Mich., Eerdmans [1968, c1967] 304 p. 22 cm. (The Pelican history of the church, v.1) Bibliography: p. [290]-295. [BR165.C48 1968b] 72-4670 6.95
1. Church history—Primitive and early church, ca. 30-600. I. Title.

THE Church in the Christian 270.1
Roman Empire, by J. R.
Palanque translated from the French by Ernest C. Messenger New York, Macmillan, 1953- v. in 23cm. A sequel to The history of the primitive church [by J. Lebrdon and J. Zeiller]' Vols. 1 and 2 are a translation of J. R. Palanque's De la paix constantinlenne a ia mort de Theodose. Contents.v. 1. The church and the Arian crisis.--V. 2. The life of the church in the fourth century. Includes bibliographies. [BR165.C53] 53-12983
1. Church history—Primitive and early church. I. Palanque.Jean Remy, 1898- De la paix constantinlenne a la mort de Theodose. II. Title.

COCHRANE, Charles Norris, 270.1
1889-1945.
Christianity and classical culture; a study of thought and action from Augustus to Augustine. New York, Oxford University Press, 1957. vii, 523p. 21cm. (A Galaxy book, GB7) Bibliographical footnotes. [BR170.C6 1957] 57-13990
1. Civilization, Christian. 2. Civilization, Greco-Roman. 3. Church history—Primitive and early church. I. Title.

COLGRAVE, Bertram. 270.1
The earliest saints' lives written in England. Folcroft, Pa., Folcroft Press [1969] [35]-60 p. 29 cm. Reprint of the Sir Israel Gollancz memorial lecture for 1958 from the Proceedings of the British Academy, London, v. 44 (1959), p. [35]-60. Includes bibliographical references. [BX4662.C65 1969] 72-193175
1. Christian hagiography. 2. Anglo-saxon literature—History and criticism. I. Title. II. Series: British Academy, London (Founded 1901). Sir Israel Gollancz memorial lecture, 1958.

CONZELMANN, Hans. 270.1
History of primitive Christianity. Translated by John E. Steely. Nashville, Abingdon Press [1973] 190 p. 24 cm. Translation of Geschichte des Urchristentums. Bibliography:

p. 179-180. [BR165.C6613] 72-8818 ISBN 0-687-17251-9 8.50
1. Church history—Primitive and early church. I. Title.

DANIEL-ROPS, Henry [Henry Jules Charles Petiot] 270.1
The church of apostles and martyrs. Translated from the French by Audrey Butler. London, Dent; New York, Dutton [1960] xi, 623p. illus. 22cm. Includes bibliography. 60-2918 10.00
1. Church history—Primitive and early church. I. Title.

DANIELOU, Jean. 270.1
The first six hundred years, by Jean Danielou and Henri Marrou. Translated by Vincent Cronin, with illus. selected and annotated by Peter Ludlow. New York, McGraw-Hill [1964] xxx, 522 p. illus., maps (1 fold.) ports. 23 cm. (The Christian centuries, v. 1) Contents.Contents.—General introduction, by J. T. Ellis.—The origins to the end of the third century, by J. Danielou.—The great persecution to the emergence of medieval Christianity, by H. Marrou. Bibliography: p. [463]-494. [BR145.2.C46 vol. 1] 63-22123
1. Church history—Primitive and early church, ca. 30-600. I. Marrou, Henri Irenee. II. Title.

DANIEL-ROPS, Henry [Henry Jules Charles Petiot] 1904- 270.1
The church of apostles and martyrs. [2vs.] Tr. from French by Audrey Butler. Garden City, N.Y., Doubleday [1962, c.1960] 2v. 388; 397p. (Image bk., D128A;D128B) Bibl. 1.35 pap., ea.,
1. Church history—Primitive and early church. I. Title.

DAVIES, John Gordon, 1919- 270.1
Daily life of early Christians. [1st American ed.] New York, Duell, Sloan and Pearce [1953] 268 p. 22 cm. First published in London in 1952 under title: Daily life in the early church. [BR195.C5D3 1953] 53-5255
1. Christian life—Early church. 2. Christian biography. I. Title.

DAVIES, John Gordon, 1919- 270.1
The early Christian church / J. G. Davies. Westport, Conn. : Greenwood Press, 1976, c1965. p. cm. Reprint of the ed. published by Holt, Rinehart and Winston, New York, in History of religion series. Includes index. Bibliography: p. [BR165.D37 1976] 75-3989 ISBN 0-8371-7696-4
1. Church history—Primitive and early church, ca. 30-600. I. Title.

DAVIES, John Gordon, 1919- 270.1
The early Christian church / J. G. Davies. Westport, Conn. : Greenwood Press, 1976, c1965. xiii, 314 p., [12] leaves of plates : ill. ; 24 cm. Reprint of the ed. published by Holt, Rinehart and Winston, New York, in History of religion series. Includes index. Bibliography: p. 299-303. [BR165.D37 1976] 75-3989 ISBN 0-8371-7696-4 lib.bdg. : 22.00
1. Church history—Primitive and early church, ca. 30-600. I. Title.

DAVIES, Russell P 270.1
The doubting Thomas today. New York, Philosophical Library [1953] 344p. illus. 23cm. [BR165.D38] 53-10045
1. Church history-Primitive and early church. I. Title.

DAVIES, William David, 1911- 270.1
Christian origins and Judaism [by] W. D. Davies. New York, Arno Press, 1973 [c1962] 261 p. 23 cm. (The Jewish people: history, religion, literature) Reprint of the ed. published by Westminster Press, Philadelphia. Includes bibliographical references. [BR165.D39 1973] 73-2192 ISBN 0-405-05258-8 14.00
1. Church history—Primitive and early church. 2. Christianity and other religions—Judaism. 3. Judaism—Relations—Christianity. I. Title. II. Series.

DIX, Gregory, Father. 270.1
Jew and Greek; a study in the primitive church. New York, Harper [c1953] 119p. 22cm. [BR165] 54-1348
1. Church history—Primitive and early church. I. Title.

DIX, Gregory, Father. 270.1
Jew and Greek a study in the primitive church. Westminster, Dacre Press [1953] 119p. 23cm. [BR165.D5 1953] 54-484
1. Church history—Primitive and early church. I. Title.

DIX, Gregory, Father 270.1
Jew and Greek; a study in the primitive church. Westminster [Eng.] Dacre Pr. [dist. Chester Springs. Pa., Dufour, 1964] 119p. 22cm. 3.50 bds.,
1. Church history—Primitive and early church. I. Title.

EDWARDS, Otis Carl, 1928- 270.1
How it all began; origins of the Christian Church [by] O. C. Edwards, Jr. New York, Seabury Press [1973] 156 p. illus. 22 cm. "A Crossroad book." Bibliography: p. 147-156. [BR129.E34] 73-77767 ISBN 0-8164-2082-3 5.95
1. Christianity—Origin. I. Title.

EDWARDS, Otis Carl, 1928- 270.1
How it all began : origins of the Christian Church : with study guide / O. C. Edwards, Jr. New York : Seabury Press, 1977. p. cm. "This book had its origins in a series of lectures delivered at Trinity Episcopal Church in Wauwatosa, Wisconsin." "A Crossroad book." Bibliography: p. [BR129.E34 1977] 77-20782 ISBN 0-8164-2164-1 pbk. : 3.95
1. Christianity—Origin. I. Title.

ENSLIN, Morton Scott, 1897- 270.1
From Jesus to Christianity [by] Morton S. Enslin. Boston, Beacon Press [1964] 75 p. 21 cm. "Lectures ... delivered in all Souls Unitarian Church, Tulsa, Oklahoma, as the Winter lectures for 1964." [BR129.E5] 64-20495
1. Christianity — Origin — Addresses, essays, lectures. I. Title.

ENSLIN, Morton Scott, 1897- 270.1
From Jesus to Christianity. Boston, Beacon [c.1964] 75p. 21cm. 64-20495 3.00
1. Christianity—Origin—Addresses, essays, lectures. I. Title.

EUSEBIUS, Pamphili, Bp. of Caesarea 270.1
The history of the church from Christ to Constantine. Tr., introd. by G. A. Williamson. [New York] N.Y.U., 1966[c.1965] 429p. map. 24cm. Bibl. [BR160.E5E6] 6.00
1. Church history—Primitive and early church. I. Williamson, Geoffrey Arthur, 1895- ed. and tr. II. Title.

EUSEBIUS PAMPHILI, Bp. of Casarea. 270.1
Ecclesiastical history; translated by Roy J. Deferrari. New York, Fathers of the Church, 1953-55 [i. e. 1953-56] 2v. 22cm. (The Fathers of the church a new translation. v.19, 29) Includes bibliographies. [BR60.F3E87] 53-2838
1. Church history—Primitive and early church. I. Title. II. Series.

EUSEBIUS PAMPHILI, Bp. of Casarea. 270.1
Ecclesiastical history. Translated from the original with an introd. by Christian Frederick Cruse and An historical view of the Council of Nice by Isaac Boyle. Grand Rapids, Baker Book House, 1955. xxxviii, 13-480, 59p. 23cm. 'Popular edition.'--Dust jacket. 'A historical view of the Council of Nice, with a translation of documents' (Philadelphia, Lippincott, 1879) has special t. p. and separate paging. Bibliographical footnotes. [BR160.E5E45 1955] 55-10437
1. Church history— Primitive and early church. I. Boyle, Isaac. A historical view of the Council of Nice. II. Title.

EUSEBIUS PAMPHILI, Bp. of Caesaria. 270.1
Ecclesiastical history; translated by Roy J. Deferrari. Washington, Catholic University of America Press [1965, c1953- v. 22 cm. (The Fathers of the Church, a new translation, v. 19, [etc.]) Contents.Contents.—[1] Books 1-5. Includes bibliographical references. [BR60.F3E873] 65-27501
1. Church history—Primitive and early church. I. Title. II. Series.

EUSEBIUS PAMPHILI, Bp. of Caesarea 270.1
The essential Eusebius. Selected, newly tr., introd., commentary, by Colm Luibheid. New York, New Amer. Lib. [1966] 236p. 18cm. (Mentor-Omega bk., MT671) Selections from the Preparation for the gospel, the Proof of the gospel, the Ecclesiastical history, and the Life of Constantine, together with the complete Letter to the church at Caesarea. Bibl. [PR160.E5E55] 66-20243 .75 pap.,
1. Church history—Primitive and early church. I. Luibheid, Colm, ed. and tr. II. Title.

FERGUSON, Everett, 1933- 270.1
Early Christians speak. Austin, Tex., Sweet Pub. Co. [1971] 258 p. illus. 23 cm. Includes bibliographical references. [BR165.F37] 78-163874 ISBN 0-8344-0075-8 7.95
1. Church history—Primitive and early church, ca. 30-600. 2. Liturgics—History. 3. Christian life—Early church, ca. 30-600. I. Title.

FREND, W. H. C. 270.1
The early church. Philadelphia, Lippincott, 1966 [c.1965] 288p. 21cm. (Knowing Christianity) Bibl. [BR165.F75] 66-13364 3.50 bds.,
1. Church history—Primitive and early church. I. Title.

GAGER, John G. 270.1
Kingdom and community : the social world of early Christianity / John G. Gager. Englewood Cliffs, N.J. : Prentice-Hall, [1975] xiii, 158 p. ; 24 cm. (Prentice-Hall studies in religion series) Includes bibliographical references and index. [BR166.G33] 74-28199 ISBN 0-13-516211-4 : 6.95
1. Sociology, Christian—Early church, ca. 30-600. I. Title.

GLOVER, Terrot Reaveley 270.1
The conflict of religions in the early Roman Empire. Boston, Beacon Press [1960] 359p. 21cm. (Beacon paperback, BP94) Includes bibliography. 4.40 1.75 pap.,
1. Church history—Primitive and early church. 2. Christianity and other religions. 3. Rome—Religion. I. Title.

GOGUEL, Maurice, 1880- 270.1
The birth of Christianity; translated from the French by H. C. Snape. New York, Macmillan, 1954 [c1953] xviii, 558p. 22cm. A translation of the 2d vol. of a trilogy entitled Jesus et les origines du christianisme. The English translation of the 1st vol. has title: The life of Jesus. Bibliography: p. xi-xiv, 555-556. [BR165.K633 1954] 54-7175
1. Church history— Primitive and early church. I. Title.

GOGUEL, Maurice, 1880- 270.1
The primitive church. Translated from the French by H. C. Snape. New York, Macmillan [1964] 610 p. 22 cm. Translation of vol. 3 of the author's trilogy entitled: Jesus et les origines du christianisme. The English translation of the 1st vol. has title: The life of Jesus, the 2d vol. has title: The birth of Christianity. Includes bibliographical references. [BR165.G643] 64-10226
1. Chruch history-Primitive and early church. I. Title.

GOGUEL, Maurice, 1880- 270.1
The primitive church. Tr. from French by H. C. Snape. New York, Macmillan [c.1947, 1964] 610p. 22cm. Tr. of v.3 of the author's trilogy. Eng. tr. of the 1st vol. has title: The life of Jesus, the 2d vol. has title: The birth of Christianity. Bibl. 64-10226 14.95
1. Church history—Primitive and early church. I. Title.

GOODENOUGH, Erwin Ramsdell, 1893-1965. 270.1
The church in the Roman Empire. New York, Cooper Square Publishers, 1970 [c1931] xii, 132 p. 23 cm. (The Berkshire studies in European history) "Bibliographical note": p. 127-129. [BR170.G63 1970] 77-122754 ISBN 0-8154-0337-2
1. Church history—Primitive and early church, 30-600. I. Title. II. Series.

GOUGH, Michael 270.1
The early Christians, New York, Praeger [c.1961] 268p. illus., map. (Ancient peoples and places, v.19) Bibl. 61-9981 6.50
1. Christianity—Early church. 2. Church architecture—Hist. 3. Christian art and symbolism—Hist. I. Title.

GRANT, Robert McQueen, 1917- 270.1
The sword and the cross. New York, Macmillan, 1955. 144 p. 22 cm. [BL805.G7] 55-806
1. Nationalism and religion—Rome. 2. Rome—Religion. 3. Church history—Primitive and early church. I. Title.

GRASSI, Joseph A. 270.1
Underground Christians in the earliest church / Joseph A. Grassi. Santa Clara, Calif. : Diakonia Press, [1975] 142 p. ; 22 cm. Includes bibliographical references. [BS2410.G69] 74-18990 3.95
1. Christianity—Early church, ca. 30-600. I. Title.

GUIGNEBERT, Charles Alfred Honore, 1867-1939 270.1
The early history of Christianity, covering the period from 300 B.C. to the origin of the Papacy. New York, Twayne [1962, c.1927] 255p. 62-238 4.50
1. Church history—Primitive and early church. 2. Church history—Middle Ages. I. Title.

GWATKIN, Henry Melvill, 1844-1916. 270.1
Early church history to A.D. 313. London, Macmillan, 1909. [New York, AMS Press, 1974] 2 v. illus. 22 cm. Includes bibliographical references. [BR165.G9 1974] 77-168216 ISBN 0-404-02966-3 45.00
1. Church history—Primitive and early church, ca. 30-600. I. Title.

HAHN, Ferdinand, 1926- 270.1
The beginnings of the Church in the New Testament; essays by Ferdinand Hahn, August Strobel [and] Eduard Schweizer. Translated by Iain and Ute Nicol. Minneapolis, Augsburg Pub. House [1970] 104 p. 19 cm. Translation of Die Anfange der Kirche im Neuen Testament. Includes bibliographical references. [BR195.C5H33 1970b] 79-121046 2.25
1. Christian life—Early church, ca. 30-600—Addresses, essays, lectures. I. Strobel, August. II. Schweizer, Eduard, 1913- III. Title.

HARINGTON, Joy 270.1
Paul of Tarsus. Cleveland, World [1965, c.1961] 216p. illus. (pt. col.) fold. map. 23cm. (Shepherd Bks.) [BS2506.5.H3] 65-15121 3.95
1. Paul, Saint, Apostle—Juvenile literature. I. Title.

HARNACK, Adolf von, 1851-1930. 270.1
The expansion of Christianity in the first three centuries. Translated and edited by James Moffatt. Freeport, N.Y., Books for Libraries Press [1972] 2 v. 22 cm. Reprint of the 1904-05 ed., a translation of Die Mission und Ausbreitung des Christentums, and which was issued as no. 19-20 of Theological translation library. Includes bibliographical references. [BR165.H4 1972] 72-4163 ISBN 0-8369-6882-4
1. Church history—Primitive and early church, ca. 30-600. 2. Missions—History—Early church, ca. 30-600. I. Moffatt, James, 1870-1944, ed. II. Title. III. Series: Theological translation library, v. 98 [etc.]

HARNACK, Adolf von, 1851-1930. 270.1
The mission and expansion of Christianity in the first three centuries. Translated and edited by James Moffatt. New York, Harper [1962] 527p. illus. 21cm. (Harper torchbooks. The cloister library, TB92) First ed. in English published in 1904 under title: The expansion of Christianity in the first three centuries. Torchbook ed. consists of v. 1 of the 2d English ed. Includes bibliography. [BR165.H4 1962] 62-4721
1. Church history— Primitive and early church. I. Moffatt, James, 1870-1944. tr. II. Title.

HARNACK, Adolf von [Carl Gustav Adolf von Harnack] 1851-1930 270.1
The mission and expansion of Christianity in the first three centuries. Tr. [from German] ed. by James Moffatt [new intro. by Jaroslav Penlika] New York, Harper & Row [1962, c.1961] 527p. 21cm. (Harper torchbks.; Cloister lib., TB92) Bibl. 2.25 pap.,
1. Church history—Primitive and early church. I. Moffatt, James, 1870- tr. II. Title.

HARNACK, Adolf von [Carl Gustav Adolf von Harnack] 1851-1930 270.1
The mission and expansion of Christianity in the first three centuries. Tr. [from German] ed. by James Moffatt. [Gloucester, Mass., P. Smith, 1963, c.1961] 527p. illus. 21cm. First ed. in Eng. pub. in 1904 under title: The expansion of Christianity in the first three centuries. Torchbook ed. consists of v.1 of the 2d Eng. ed. Bibl. (Harper torchbks. Cloister lib. TB92 rebound). Bibl. 4.25
1. Church history—Primitive and early church. I. Moffatt, James, 1870-1944, tr. II. Title.

HARNACK, Carl Gustav Adolf von, 1851-1930. 270.1
The mission and expansion of Christianity in the first three centuries, by Adolf Harnack. Trans. & ed. by James Moffatt. [New York] [Harper] [1962] Gloucester, Mass., Peter Smith, 1972 x, 527 p. illus. 22 cm. First ed. in English pub. in 1904 under title: The expansion of Christianity in the first three centuries. Bibl. [BR165.H4] 6.75
1. Church history—Primitive and early church. I. Moffat, James, 1870-1944, tr. II. Title.
L.C. card no. for the Harper ed.: 62-4721.

HATCH, Edwin, 1835-1889. 270.1
The influence of Greek ideas on Christianity. Foreword with new notes and a bibliography by Frederick C. Grant. [1st Harper torchbook ed.] New York, Harper [1957] xxxv, 359p. 21cm. (The Library of religion and culture) Harper torchbooks, TB18. First published in 1890 under title: The influence of Greek ideas and usages upon the Christian church. [BR128.G8H3 1957] 57-7535
1. Church history—Primitive and early church. 2. Philosophy—Hist. 3. Theology Doctrinal. I. Title.

HAZELTINE, Rachel C 270.1
How did it happen? A history of the early Christian churches written by deduction; deduction means just a remaking of events from all the data collected. [Santa Cruz, Calif., Voice in the Wilderness] c1958. 371p. 23cm. [BR165.H42] 58-49286

1. Church history—Primitive and earl church. I. Title.

HUTTMAN, Maude Aline, 1872- 270.1
The establishment of Christianity and the proscription of paganism, by Maude Aline Huttmann. New York, AMS Press, 1967. 257 p. 23 cm. (Studies in history, economics and public law, v. 60, no. 2; whole no. 147) Reprint of the 1914 ed. Originally presented as the author's thesis, Columbia, 1914. Bibliography: p. 250-257. [BR180.H87 1967] 78-29881
1. Constantinus I, the Great, Emperor of Rome, d. 337. 2. Church history—Primitive and early church, ca. 30-600. 3. Paganism. I. Title. II. Title: Paganism, Proscription of. III. Series: Columbia studies in the social sciences, no. 147.

HYDE, Walter Woodburn, 1871-1966. 270.1
Paganism to Christianity in the Roman Empire. New York, Octagon Books, 1970 [c1946] vii, 296 p. 25 cm. Includes bibliographical references. [BR170.H9 1970] 79-120633
1. Church history—Primitive and early church, ca. 30-600. 2. Christianity and other religions. I. Title.

KAUTSKY, Karl, 1854-1938. 270.1
Foundations of Christianity, translated by Henry F. Mins. New York, S. A. Russell, 1953. 401 p. 22 cm. [BR129.K37 1953] 53-8294
1. Jesus Christ—Historicity. 2. Christianity—Origin. I. Title.

KAUTSKY, Karl, 1854-1938 270.1
Foundations of Christianity, translated by Henry F. Mins. New York, Russell and Russell [1960, c.1953] xx, 401p. 22cm. (Russell & Russell Scholars Classics. RP1) (Bibl. footnotes) 1.95 pap.,
1. Christianity—Origin. 2. Jesus Christ—Historicity. I. Title.

KAUTSKY, Karl, 1854-1938. 270.1
Foundations of Christianity; a study in Christian origins. Authorized translation from the 13th German ed. New York, Monthly Review Press [1972, c1925] 480 p. 21 cm. (Modern reader, PB-262) Translation of Der Ursprung des Christentums. Includes bibliographical references. [BR129.K37 1972] 72-81774 4.95
1. Jews—Political and social conditions—To 70 A.D. 2. Christianity—Origin. 3. Rome—Social conditions. I. Title.

KEALY, John P. 270.1
The early church and Africa : a school certificate course based on the East African syllabus for Christian religious education / John P. Kealy, David W. Shenk. Nairobi : Oxford University Press, 1975. xxiii, 345 p. : ill. ; 21 cm. Includes index. Bibliography: p. 336-338. [BR165.K36] 76-365628 ISBN 0-19-572279-5 : 7.50
1. Bible. N.T. Acts—Commentaries. 2. Church history—Primitive and early church, ca. 30-600. 3. Africa—Church history. I. Shenk, David W., 1937- joint author. II. Title.
Distributed by Oxford, New York.

KIDD, Beresford James, 1863-1948. 270.1
A history of the church to A.D. 461 / by B.J. Kidd New York : AMS Press, [1976] p. cm. Reprint of the 1922 ed. published at the Clarendon Press, Oxford. Includes indexes. Contents.Contents.—v. 1. To A.D. 313.—v. 2. A.D. 313-408.—v. 3. A.D. 408-461. [BR165.K46 1976] 75-41165 ISBN 0-404-15010-1 : 82.50 (3 vols.)
1. Church history—Primitive and early church, ca. 30-600. I. Title.

KNOX, John, 1900- 270.1
The early church and the coming great church. New York, Abingdon Press [1955] 160p. 21cm. (Hoover lectures [1955]) [BR165.K63] 55-6765
1. Church history—Primitive and early church. 2. Christian union. I. Title.

LAEUCHLI, Samuel 270.1
The language of faith; an introduction to the semantic dilemma of the early church. Nashville, Abingdon [c.1962] 269p. Bibl. 62-8107 5.50
1. Language question in the church. 2. Theology—Terminology. 3. Theology—Early church. 4. Gnosticism. I. Title.

LEBRETON, Jules 270.1
A history of the early church, bk.4, by Jules Lebreton, Jacques Zeiller. Tr. from French by Ernest C. Messenger. Foreword by Augustin Fliche, Mgr. Victor Martin. New York, Collier [1962, c.1946, 1947] 383p. 21cm. (BS80V) Orig. pub. as The history of the primitive church, v.2, bk.4: The church in the third century, pt.2. Contents.bk.4. The triumph of Christianity. (BS80V) 1.50 pap.,
1. Church history—Primitive and early church. 2. Christianity—Origin. I. Zeiller, Jacques, 1878- joint author. II. Title.

LEBRETON, Jules, 1873-1956 270.1
A history of the early church, bk. 1, by Jules Lebreton, Jacques Zeiller. Tr. from French by Ernest C. Messenger. Foreword by Augustin Fliche, Mgr. Victor Martin. New York, Collier [1962, c.1942, 1944] 352p. 18cm. (BS77V) Orig. pub. as bk. 1, v.1, of The history of the primitive church. Contents.bk. 1. The church in the New Testament. (BS77V) Bibl. 1.50 pap.,
1. Church history—Primitive and early church. 2. Christianity—Origin. I. Zeiller, Jacques, 1878- joint author. II. Title.

LEBRETON, Jules Marie Leon, 1873-1956 270.1
The emergence of the church in the Roman world [by] Jules Lebreton, Jacques Zeiller. Tr. from French by Ernest C. Messenger. Foreword by Augustin Fliche, Victor Martin. New York, Collier [1962, c.1942, 1944] 317p. 18cm. (Collier Catholic readers ser., BS78V) Book ii of A history of the early church Bibl. A62 1.50 pap.,
1. Church history—Primitive and early church. I. Zeiller, Jacques, 1878- joint author. II. Title.

LIETZMANN, Hans, 1875-1942. 270.1
The era of the church fathers. Translated by Bertram Lee Woolf. New York, Scribner's, 1952. 212p. 22cm. (His A history of the early church, v. 4) 'Literature': p. [203]-205. [BR205.L493] A53
1. Church history—Primitive and early church. I. Title.

LIETZMANN, Hans, 1875-1942. 270.1
The founding of the church universal; a history of the early church: volume II. Translated by Bertram Lee Woolf. [2d ed.] New York, Scribner, 1950. 828p. 23cm. Includes bibliographies. [BR165.L483 1950] 53-1474
1. Church history—Primitive and early church. 2. Christian literature, Early—Hist. & crit. I. Title.

LIETZMANN, Hans [Johannes Carl Alexander Lietzmann] 1875-1942. 270.1
A history of the early church. 2v. Tr. by Bertram Lee Woolf. Cleveland, World Pub. Co. [1961] 4v. in 2, 328 212p. (Meridian bks., MG26A-B) Previously pub. as 4 separate works. Contents.v.1. The beginnings of the Christian church.--v.2. The foundling of the church universal.--v.3. From Constantine to Julian.--v.4. The era of the church fathers. Bibl. 61-15602 2.25 pap., ea.,
1. Church history—Primitive and early church. I. Title.

LOISY, Alfred Firmin, 1857-1940 270.1
The birth of the Christian religion (La naissance du christianisme) and The origins of the New Testament (Les origines du Nouveau Testament) Authorized tr. from French by L. P. Jacks. New Hyde Park, N.Y., University Bks. [c.1962] xix, 413, 332p. 24cm. 62-18073 10.00
1. Church history—Primitive and early church. 2. Bible. N. T.—Criticism, interpretation, etc. I. Loisy, Alfred Firmin, 1857-1940. The origins of the New Testament. (Les origines du Nouveau Testament. Eng. 1962) II. Title. III. Title: The origins of the New Testament.

MAIER, Paul L. 270.1
First Christians : Pentecost and the spread of Christianity / Paul L. Maier. 1st ed. New York : Harper & Row, c1976. 160 p., [2] leaves of plates : ill. ; 22 cm. Includes bibliographical references. [BR165.M26 1976] 75-36751 ISBN 0-06-065399-X : 6.95
1. Church history—Primitive and early church, ca. 30-600. I. Title.

MARKUS, Robert Austin, 1924- 270.1
Christianity in the Roman world / R. A. Markus. New York : Scribner, c1974. 192 p. : 74 ill., map ; 23 cm. Includes index. Bibliography: p. 187-192. [BR170.M36 1974b] 74-16823 ISBN 0-684-14129-9 : 10.00
1. Church history—Primitive and early church, ca. 30-600. I. Title.

MILBURN, Robert Leslie Pollington. 270.1
Early Christian interpretations of history. New York, Harper [1954] ix, 221p. 22cm. (The Bampton lectures of 1952) Bibliographical references included in 'Notes' (p. 193-214) [BR115.H5M5 1954a] 54-11663
1. History—Philosophy. 2. Church history—Primitive and early church. 3. Mary, Virgin—Assumption. I. Title. II. Series: Bampton lectures, 1952

MOMIGLIANO, Arnaldo, ed. 270.1
The conflict between paganism and Christianity in the fourth century; essays. Oxford, Clarendon Press, 1963. 222 p. plates, port., geneal. table. 24 cm. (Oxford-Warburg studies) Lectures given at the Warburg Institute of the University of London, 1958-59. Errata slip mounted on p. [1] Includes bibliographical references. [BR205.M6] 63-2454
1. Church history — Primitive and early church. 2. Christianity and other religions. I. Title.

MOMIGLIANO, Arnaldo, ed. 270.1
The conflict between paganism and Christianity in the fourth century; essays. Oxford, Clarendon Pr. [New York, Oxford, c.] 1963. 222p. plates, port., geneal. table. 24cm. (Oxford-Warburg studies) Lectures given at the Warburg Inst. of the Univ. of London, 1958-59. 63-2454 5.60
1. Church history—Primitive and early church. 2. Christianity and other religions. I. Title.

MORRISON, Hugh Tucker, 1877- 270.1
Mysterious omissions; an interpretation of certain unresolved issues in the New Testament Church, by Hugh T. Morrison. [Chicago] Disciples Divinity House of the University of Chicago, 1969. vi, 56 p. 22 cm. [BT308.M65 1969] 70-18361
1. Jesus Christ—Biography. 2. Essenes. 3. Pharisees. 4. Church history—Primitive and early church, ca. 30-600. I. Title.

MOULE, Charles Francis Digby. 270.1
The birth of the New Testament. [1st ed.] New York, Harper & Row [1962] 252 p. 22 cm. (Harper's New Testament commentaries) [BS2330.2.M6] 62-14579
1. Church history—Primitive and early church. 2. Bible, N. T.—Canon. I. Title.

NOCK, Arthur Darby, 1902- 270.1
Early gentile Christianity and its Hellenistic background. Introd. by the author, 1962, and two additional essays, A note on the resurrection and Hellenistic mysteries and Christian sacraments. New York, Harper [c.1964] xxi, 155p. 21cm. (Harper torchbks. Cloister lib. TB111) Bibl. 64-330 1.45 pap.,
1. Christianity and other religions—Greek. 2. Church history—Primitive and early church. I. Title.

O'BRIEN, Isidore, Father, 1895- 270.1
Peter and Paul, apostles, an account of the early years of the Church. Paterson, N.J., St. Anthony Guild Press. 1950. vii, 432 p. col. illus., map (on lining papers) 29 cm. [BS2410.O2] 50-10486
1. Bible. N. T.—History of Biblical events. 2. Peter, Saint, apostle. 3. Paul, Saint, apostle. I. Title.

O'BRIEN, Isidore, 1895-1953. 270.1
Peter and Paul, apostles; an account of the early years of the Church. Paterson, N. J., St. Anthony Guild Press, 1950. vii, 432p. col. illus., map (on lining papers) 20cm. [BS2410.O2] 50-10486
1. Bible. N. T.—History of Biblical events, 2. Peter, Saint, apostle. 3. Paul, Saint, Apostle. I. Title.

OETTING, Walter, W 270.1
The church of the catacombs; the introduction to the surging life of the early church from the apostles to A.D. 250, based on firsthand accounts, by Walter W. Oetting. St. Louis, Concordia Pub. House [1964] 131 p. map. 21 cm. (Church in history series) Bibliography: p. [127]-128 [BR162.2.O4] 64-24277
1. Church history — Primitive and early church. I. Title. II. Series.

OETTING, Walter W. 270.1
The church of the catacombs; the introduction to the surging life of the early church from the apostles to A.D. 250, based on firsthand accounts. St. Louis, Concordia [c.1964] 131p. map. 21cm. (Church in hist. ser.) Bibl. 64-24277 1.95 pap.,
1. Church history—Primitive and early church. I. Title. II. Series.

PETERSEN, Emma Marr. 270.1
The church that Jesus built. Salt Lake City, Bookcraft, 1971. vi, 104 p. illus. 24 cm. [BR165.P47] 78-169748
1. Church history—Primitive and early church, ca. 30-600. I. Title.

PHILLIPS, John Bertram, 1906- 270.1
New Testament Christianity. New York, Macmillan, 1956. 107p. 20cm. [BR121.P517 1956a] 56-8203
1. Christianity—Essence, genius, nature. I. Title.

PURVES, George Tybout, 1852-1901. 270.1
Christianity in the apostolic age. Grand Rapids, Baker Book House, 1955. 343p. 20cm. [BS2410] 55-9473
1. Church history—Primitive and early church. I. Title.

RAMSAY, William Mitchell, Sir 1851-1939. 270.1
Luke, the physician, and other studies in the history of religion. Grand Rapids, Baker Book House, 1956. 418p. illus. 23cm. [BP142.R3 1956] 56-7583
1. Lake, Saint. 2. Church history—Addresses, essays, lectures. I. Title.

RAMSAY, William Mitchell, Sir 1851-1939. 270.1
Luke, the physician, and other studies in the history of religion. Grand Rapids, Baker Book House, 1956. 418p. illus. 23cm. [BR142.R3 1956] 56-7583
1. Luke, Saint. 2. Church history —Addresses, essays, lectures. I. Title.

ROBERTSON, Archibald, 1886- 270.1
The origins of Christianity. New York, International Publishers [1954] 216p. 21cm. [BR129.R65 1954] 54-12222
1. Christianity—Origin. I. Title.

ROBERTSON, Archibald Horace Mann, 1886- 270.1
The origins of Christianity. With an appendix on the Dead Sea scrolls. [Rev. ed.] New York, Intl. Pubs. [1962, c.1954] 224p. 22cm. 62-53124 3.75; 1.65 pap.,
1. Christianity—Origin. I. Title.

SCHOFIELD, Guy, 1902- 270.1
It began on the cross; the historical sequel to the New Testament, A. D. 39-155. [1st American ed.] New York, Hawthorn Books [1960, c1959] 255p. illus. 24cm. 'Originally published in Great Britain as The purple and the scarlet.58 [BR165.S39 1960] 60-5896
1. Church history Primitive and early church. I. Title.

SCHOFIELD, Guy [Edward Guy Schofield] 270.1
It began on the cross; the historical sequel to the New Testament, A. D. 39-155. New York, Hawthorn Books [1960, c.1959] 255p. illus., map 24cm. (3p. bibl.) 60-5896 5.00
1. Church history—Primitive and early church. I. Title.

SCHONFIELD, Hugh Joseph, 1901- 270.1
Those incredible Christians [by] Hugh J. Schonfield. [New York] B. Geis Associates; Distributed by Grove Press [1968] xx, 266 p. 22 cm. Bibliography: p. 256-262. [BR165.S395 1968b] 68-16148
1. Church history—Primitive and early church, ca. 30-600. I. Title.

SIMON, Edith, 1917- 270.1
The saints. [New York, Delacorte Press [1969, c1968] 127 p. illus. 22 cm. (Pageant of history series) Bibliography: p. [123] [BR1710.S52 1969] 70-75098 3.95
1. Saints. 2. Church history—Primitive and early church.

STAUFFER, Ethelbert, 1902- 270.1
Christ and the Caesars; historical sketches. Translated by K. and R. Gregor Smith. Philadelphia, Westminster Press [1955] 293 p. illus. 23 cm. [BR165.S792 1955] 55-7708
1. Church history—Primitive and early church. I. Title.

TAAFFE, Thomas 270.1
The writings of the early Church Fathers, by Thomas P. Taaffe. New York, Monarch Pr. [c.1966] 108p. 22cm. (Monarch notes & study gds., 826-8) Bibl. [BR67] 66-27277 1.50 pap.,
1. Christian literature, Early— Outlines, syllabi, etc. I. Title.

THERON, Daniel Johannes, ed. 270.1
Evidence of tradition; selected source material for the study of the history of the early church, the New Testament books, the New Testament canon. Grand Rapids, Baker Book House, 1958 [c1957] xiv, 135 p. 23 cm. Greek and Latin texts, with parallel English translations. Includes bibliographies. [BR160.A2T5 1958] 58-13188
1. Church history — Primitive and early church — Sources. 2. Christian literature. Early (Selections: Extracts, etc.) 3. Bible. N.T. — Hist. — Sources. I. Title.

WEST, Franklin Lorenzo Richards, 1885- 270.1
The apostles and the primitive church. Salt Lake City, Deseret 1964. vii, 191p. col. illus., maps. 24cm. [BS2407.W36] 65-1371 price unreported

1. Bible. N.T.—History of Biblical events. I. Title.

WESTBURY-JONES, John. 270.1
Roman and Christian imperialism, by J. Westbury-Jones. Port Washington, N.Y., Kennikat Press [1971] xxxvii, 374 p. 22 cm. Reprint of the 1939 ed. Bibliography: p. [xxxv] -xxxvii. [BR170.W44 1971] 78-118555 ISBN 0-8046-1180-7
1. Church history—Primitive and early church, ca. 30-600. 2. Rome—History—Empire, 30 B.C.-476 A.D. 3. Religion and law. I. Title.

ZEHNLE, Richard F. 270.1
The making of the Christian church. Notre Dame, Ind., Fides Publishers [1969] xii, 168 p. 20 cm. Includes bibliographical footnotes. [BR165.Z38] 70-95638 ISBN 0-8190-0517-7 2.50
1. Sociology, Christian—Early church, ca. 30-600. I. Title.

ZEILLER, Jacques [Marie Joseph Charles Jacques Zeiller] 1878- 270.1
Christian beginnings; tr. [from French] by P. J. Hepburne-Scott. New York, Hawthorne Books [c.1960] 184p. (Twentieth century encyclopedia of Catholicism, v. 74. Section 7: The history of the church) Bibl. 60-53118 2.95 bds.,
1. Church history—Primitive and early church. I. Title.

ARNOLD, Eberhard, 1883-1935, comp. 270.1'08
The early Christians after the death of the apostles; selected and edited from all the sources of the first centuries. [Translated and edited by the Society of Brothers at Rifton, N.Y.] Rifton, N.Y., Plough Pub. House [1970] xii, 469 p. illus. 23 cm. Originally published in 1926 under title: Die ersten Christen nach dem Tode der Apostel. Bibliography: p. [452]-466. [BR63.A713] 70-115839 ISBN 0-87486-107-1 10.00
1. Christian literature, Early. I. Bruderhof Communities. II. Title.

ARNOLD, Eberhard, 1883-1935. 270.1'08
The early Christians after the death of the Apostles; selected and edited from all the sources of the first centuries. [Translated and edited by the Society of Brothers at Rifton, N.Y.] [2d ed.] Rifton, N.Y., Plough Pub. House [1972] xii, 469 p. illus. 23 cm. Originally published in 1926 under title: Die ersten Christen nach dem Tode der Apostel. Bibliography: p. [452]-466. [BR63.A713 1972] 71-31629 ISBN 0-87486-110-1 10.00
1. Christian literature, Early. I. Bruderhof Communities. II. Title.

RAMSAY, William Mitchell, Sir., 1851-1939. 270.1'08
Pauline and other studies in early Christian history, by W. M. Ramsay. Grand Rapids, Mich., Baker Book House [1970] xi, 415 p. illus., maps. 23 cm. ([Limited editions library]) Reprint of the 1906 ed. Contents.Contents.—Shall we hear evidence or not?—The charm of Paul.—The statesmanship of Paul.—Pagan revivalism and the persecutions of the early church. —The worship of the Virgin Mary at Ephesus.—The permanence of religion at holy places in Western Asia.—The Acts of the apostles.—The lawfull assembly.—The olive-tree and the wild-olive.—Questions: with a memory of Dr. Hort.—St. Paul's road from Cilicia to Iconium. —The authorship of the Acts.—A study of St. Paul by Mr. Baring-Gould. —The Pauline chronology.—Life in the days of St. Basil the Great. Includes bibliographical references. [BS2650.R3 1970] 72-14344 6.95
I. Title.

RECORDS of 270.1'08
Christianity. New York, Barnes & Noble, 1971- v. illus., facsims., maps, ports. 23 cm. Contents.Contents.—v. 1. In the Roman Empire, by D. Ayerst and A. S. T. Fisher. [BR142.R4] 70-28480 ISBN 0-389-01345-5 (v. 1)
1. Church history—Sources.

ALAND, Kurt. 270.1'0922 B
Saints and sinners; men and ideas in the early church. Translated by Wilhelm C. Linss. Philadelphia, Fortress Press [1970] vi, 250 p. 19 cm. Translation of Kirchengeschichte in Lebensbildern dargestellt, v. 1, Die Fruhzeit. [BR1706.A413] 76-123507 3.95
1. Christian biography. 2. Fathers of the church. I. Title.

DAVIES, John Gordon, 1919- 270.1'0922 B
Daily life of early Christians, by J. G. Davies. New York, Greenwood Press [1969, c1953] xvi, 268 p. 23 cm. First published in London in 1952 under title: Daily life in the early church. Bibliographical footnotes. [BR195.C5D3 1969] 75-91757
1. Christian life—Early church. 2. Christian biography. I. Title.

BAYNES, Norman Hepburn, 1877-1961. 270.1'092'4 B
Constantine the Great and the Christian church / by Norman H. Baynes. New York : Haskell House, 1975. 102 p. ; 21 cm. Reprint of the 1930 ed. published by H. Milford, London, which was issued as the Raleigh lecture on history, 1930. Includes bibliographical references. [BR180.B3 1975] 74-34500 ISBN 0-8383-0131-2 : 7.95
1. Constantinus I, the Great, Emperor of Rome, d. 337. 2. Church history—Primitive and early church, ca. 30-600. I. Title. II. Series: British Academy, London (Founded 1901). Annual Raleigh lecture ; 1930.

DORRIES, Hermann, 1895- 270.1'0924
Constantine the Great. Translated by Roland H. Bainton. New York, Harper & Row [1972] xi, 250 p. 21 cm. (Harper torchbooks, HR 1567) Bibliography: p. [235]-245. [DG315.D613 1972] 72-179281
1. Constantinus I, the Great, Emperor of Rome, d. 337. 2. Church history—Primitive and early church, ca. 30-600.

HIERONYMUS, Saint. 270.1'0924 B
The first desert hero: St. Jerome's Vita Pauli. With introd., notes, and vocabulary by Ignatius S. Kozik. Mount Vernon, N.Y., King Lithographers [1968] x, 67 p. illus. 22 cm. Text in Latin. "The Migne edition is the one mainly followed ... The following sections of the Vita have been omitted: Prologue (PL 23. 17-18), the story of the two martyrs (ibid. 19-20), and Anthony's journey through the desert (ibid. 22-24)." Bibliography: p. 12-14. Bibliographical footnotes. [BR1720.P28H5] 68-56001
1. Paulus, Thebaeus, Saint. I. Kozik, Ignatius S., ed. II. Title. III. Title: Vita Pauli.

THE life of 270.1'092'4 B
Pachomius : vita prima Graeca / translated by Apostolos N. Athanassakis ; introd. by Birger A. Pearson. Missoula, Mont. : Published by Scholars Press for the Society of Biblical Literature, c1975. xi, 201 p. : 24 cm. (Texts and translations - Society of Biblical Literature ; 7) (Early Christian literature series ; 2) English and Greek. "Contains the text of G1 [i.e. the Vita prima Graeca] as edited by F. Halkin." Bibliography: p. xi. [BR1720.P23V5613] 75-37766 ISBN 0-89130-065-1 : 2.80
1. Pachomius, Saint. I. Athanassakis, Apostolos N. II. Title. III. Series. IV. Series: Society of Biblical Literature. Texts and translations ; 7.

SAGE, Michael M. 270.1'092'4 B
Cyprian / by Michael M. Sage. Cambridge, Mass. : Philadelphia Patristic Foundation : [sole distributors, Greeno, Hadden], 1975. v, 439 p. ; 24 cm. (Patristic monograph series ; no. 1) Includes index. Bibliography: p. 411-429. [BR1720.C8S23] 75-11008 ISBN 0-915646-00-5
1. Cyprianus, Saint, Bp. of Carthage. I. Title. II. Series.

CANNON, William Ragsdale 270.2
History of Christianity in the Middle Ages: from the fall of Rome to the fall of Constantinople. Nashville, Abingdon Press [c.1960] 352p. (bibl. footnotes) 24cm. 60-6928 4.50
1. Church history—Middle Ages. I. Title.

CANNON, William Ragsdale, 1916- 270.2
History of Christianity in the Middle Ages: from the fall of Rome to the fall of Constantinople. New York, Abingdon Press [1960] 352p. 24cm. [BR162.2.C3] 60-6928
1. Church history—Middle Ages. I. Title.

COHN, Norman Rufus Colin 270.2
The pursuit of the millennium revolutionary messianism in medieval and Reformation Europe and its bearing on modern totalitarian movements. 2nd ed. New York, Harper [c.1961] 481p. illus., (Harper torchbooks: Academy lib. TB 1037) Bibl. 2.25 pap.,
1. Church history—Middle Ages. 2. Sects, Medieval. I. Title.

FOUSEK, Marianka S. 270.2
The church in a changing world; events and trends from 250 to 600, by Marianka S. Fousek. St. Louis, Concordia Pub. House [1971] 176 p. map. 22 cm. (Church in history series) Bibliography: p. [172]-173. [BR160.F68] 77-139331 ISBN 0-570-06272-1
1. Church history—Primitive and early church, ca. 30-600. I. Title. II. Series.

HONIGMANN, Ernst, 1892- 270.2
Juvenal of Jerusalem. (In Dumbarten Oaks papers. Cambridge, Mass., 1950. 30 cm. no. 5, p. [209]-279) Includes bibliographies. [N5970.D8 no. 5] 51-4862
1. Juvenalis, Patriarch of Jerusalem, d. 458? I. Title. II. Series: Dumbarton Oaks papers, no. 5, p. [209]-279

KING, Noel Quinton 270.2
The Emperor Theodosius and the establishment of Christianity. Philadelphia, Westminster Pr. [1961, c.1960] 135p. map. (Lib. of hist. and doctrine) Bibl. 61-11847 4.00
1. Theodosius I, the Great, Emperor of Rome, 346?-395. 2. Church history—Primitive and early church. 3. Church and state—Hist. I. Title.

LAISTNER, Max Ludwig Wolfram, 1890- 270.2
Christianity and pagan culture in the later Roman Empire; together with an English translation of John Chrysostom's Address on vainglory and the right way for parents to bring up their children. Ithaca, Cornell University Press [1951] vi, 145 p. 23 cm. (The James W. Richard lectures in history for 1950-1951) Bibliographical references included in "Notes" (p. [123]-140) [BR203.L27] 51-10283
1. Church history—Primitive and early church. 2. Paganism. 3. Pride and vanity. 4. Religous education of children. I. Chrysostomus, Joannes, Saint, Patriarch of Constantinople, d. 407. II. Title. III. Title: Address on vainglory and the right way for parents to bring up their children. IV. Series.

SMITH, Michael Auckland. 270.2
The church under siege / M. A. Smith. Downers Grove, Ill. : Inter-Varsity Press, 1976. 277 p. : ill. ; 20 cm. Includes bibliographical references and index. [BR200.S55] 76-12304 ISBN 0-87784-855-6 : 5.95
1. Church history—Primitive and early church, ca. 30-600. 2. Church history—Middle Ages, 600-1500. I. Title.

STEVENSON, James, lecturer, ed. 270.2
Creeds, councils, and controversies; documents illustrative of the history of the church A.D. 337-461. Edited by J. Stevenson. New York, Seabury Press [1966] xix, 390 p. map (on lining papers) 23 cm. "Based upon the collection edited by the late B. J. Kidd." "Intended to be a successor to vol. II of the late B. J. Kidd's Documents, published in 1923." [BR160.A2S7 1966a] 66-16652
1. Church history—Primitive and early church, ca. 30-600—Sources. 2. Christian literature, Early. I. Kidd, Beresford James, 1863-1948, ed. Documents illustrative of the history of the church. II. Title.

*VAN DER MEER, F. 270.2
Augustine the bishop; Religion and society at the dawn of The Middle Ages, Tr. by Brian Battershaw, G. R. Lamb. New York, Harper [1965, c.1961] xviii, 679p. illus. 21cm. (Harper torchbks., TB304) 3.75 pap.,
I. Title.

VOLZ, Carl A. 270.2
The church of the Middle Ages; growth and change from 600 to 1400, by Carl A. Volz. Saint Louis, Concordia Pub. House [1970] 198 p. map. 22 cm. (Church in history series) Includes bibliographies. [BR162.2.V6] 72-99217
1. Church history—Middle Ages, 600-1500. I. Title. II. Series.

BROWN, Peter Robert Lamont. 270.2'08
Religion and society in the age of Saint Augustine [by] Peter Brown. [1st U.S. ed.] New York, Harper & Row [1972] 351 p. 23 cm. Includes bibliographical references. [BL60.B75 1972b] 70-181609 ISBN 0-06-010554-2 12.00
1. Augustinus, Aurelius, Saint, Bp. of Hippo—Sociology—Addresses, essays, lectures. 2. Religion and sociology—History—Addresses, essays, lectures. I. Title.

WATT, William Montgomery. 270.2'08
Truth in the religions, a sociological and psychological approach. Edinburgh, University Press;[U.S. & Canadian agent: Aldine Pub. Co., Chicago, 1963] viii, 190 p. 24 cm. Bibliographical references included in "Notes" (p. [176]-179) [BL60.W37] 63-22839
1. Religion and sociology. 2. Psychology, Religious. I. Title.

JONES, Charles Williams, 1905- 270.2'0922
Saints' lives and chronicles in early England. Together with first English translations of The oldest life of Pope St. Gregory the Great by a monk of Whitby and The life of St. Guthlac of Crowland by Felix. By Charles W. Jones. [Hamden, Conn.] Archon Books, 1968 [c1947] xiii, 232 p. facsims. 23 cm. The translation of the life of Gregory the Great is from Cardinal Gasquet's transcription of the original MS. which is part of Codex 567 of the Stiftsbibliothek of St. Gall, Switzerland. Bibliographical references included in "Notes" (p. [200]-220) [BX4662.J6 1968] 68-26934
1. Gregorius I, the Great, Saint, Pope, 540 (ca.)-604. 2. Guthlac, Saint, 673?-714. 3. Hagiography. I. Felix, 8th cent. Vita Sancti Guthlaci. English. 1968. II. The Oldest life of Pope St. Gregory the Great. Vita Sancti Gregorii I Popae. English. 1968. III. Title.

BEEBE, Catherine, 1898- 270.20924 B
Saint Patrick, apostle of Ireland. Drawings by S. Ohrvel Carlson. Paterson, N.J., Saint Anthony Guild Press [1968] 40 p. col. illus. 23 cm. Relates what is known of St. Patrick, whose feast day is celebrated March 17th, describing his servitude in Ireland, his journey to England and freedom, and his return to Ireland to teach Christianity. [BX4700.P3B4] 92 AC 68
1. Patrick, Saint, 373?-463? I. Carlson, S. Ohrvel, illus. II. Title.

BONIFACIUS, originally Winfried, Saint, Abp. of Mainz, 680-755. 270'.2'0924 B
The letters of Saint Boniface. Translated with an introd. by Ephraim Emerton. New York, Octagon Books, 1973 [c1940] 204 p. 24 cm. Translation of the author's Epistolae. Reprint of the ed. published by Columbia University Press, New York, which was issued as no. 331 of Records of civilization: sources and studies. Bibliography: p. [193]-195. [BX4700.B7A43 1973] 79-147408 ISBN 0-374-92584-4 10.00
1. Bonifacius, originally Winfried, Saint, Abp. of Mainz, 680-755. I. Emerton, Ephraim, 1851-1935, tr. II. Series: Records of civilization: sources and studies, no. 331.

†BONIFACIUS, originally Winfried, Saint, Abp. of Mainz, 680-755. 270.2'092'4 B
The letters of Saint Boniface / translated with an introd. by Ephraim Emerton. New York : Norton, 1976, c1940. 204 p. ; 20 cm. Reprint of the ed. published by Columbia University Press, New York, which was issued as no. 31 of Records of civilization, sources and studies. Includes index. Bibliography: p. [193]-195. [BX4700.B7A413 1976] 76-18847 ISBN 0-393-09147-3 pbk. : 3.95
1. Bonifacius, originally Winfried, Saint, Abp. of Mainz, 680-755. 2. Christian saints—Germany, West—Mainz—Biography. 3. Mainz—Biography. I. Emerton, Ephraim, 1851-1935. II. Title. III. Series: Records of civilization, sources and studies ; no. 31.

BONIFACIUS, originally Winifried Saint, Abp. of Mainz 680-755 270.2'0924
The English correspondence of Saint Boniface: being for the most part letters exchanged between the apostle of the Germans and his English friends, translated and edited with an introductory sketch of the saint's life by Edward Kylie. New York, Cooper Square Publishers, 1966. xiv, 212 p. front. 17 cm. (The Medieval library) [BX4700.B7A5] 66-30729
I. Kylie, Edward Joseph, 1880- tr. II. Title.

BROWN, Peter Robert Lamont 270.2'0924
Augustine of Hippo; a biography, by Peter Brown. Berkeley. Univ. of Calif. Pr., 1967. 463p. 23cm. Bibl. [BR1720.A9B7 1967b] 67-13137 10.00
1. Augustinus, Aurelius, Saint, Bp. of Hippo. I. Title.

BROWN, Peter Robert Lamont. 270.2'0924
Augustine of Hippo; a biography, by Peter Brown. Berkeley, University of California Press, 1967. 463 p. 23 cm. Bibliography: p. 435-452. [BR1720.A9B7 1967b] 67-13137
1. Augustinus, Aurelius, Saint, Bp. of Hippo. I. Title.

BURY, John Bagnell, 1861-1927. 270.20924 B
The life of St. Patrick and his place in history. Freeport, N.Y., Books for Libraries Press [1971] xv, 404 p. maps. 23 cm. Reprint of the 1905 ed. Includes bibliographical references. [BX4700.P3B8 1971] 79-175691 ISBN 0-8369-6606-6
1. Patrick, Saint, 373?-463? I. Title.

COLGRAVE, Bertram, ed. and tr. 270.2'0924 B
Two lives of Saint Cuthbert; a life by an anonymous monk of Lindisfarne and Bede's prose life. Texts, translation, and notes by Bertram Colgrave. New York, Greenwood Press [1969] xiii, 375 p. 23 cm. Reprint of the 1940 ed. Latin and English on opposite pages. "Manuscripts": p. [17]-50. "Previous editions": p. [51]-55. [BX4700.C8C6 1969] 69-13862
1. Cuthbert, Saint, d. 687. I. A monk of Lindisfarne. Vita sancti Cuthberti. II. Beda

Venerabilis, 673-735. Vita sancti Cuthberti. III. Title.

CRISTIANI, Leon, 1879- 270.2'092'4 B
Saint Monica (331-387 A.D.) : a biography / by Leon Cristiani; translated by M. Angeline Bouchard Boston : Daughters of St. Paul, c1975. p. cm. Translation of Sainte Monique, 331-387. [BX4700.M63C7413] 75-43832
1. Monica, Saint, d. 387. I. Title.

HANSEL, Robert R. 270.2'0924 B
The life of Saint Augustine, by Robert R. Hansel. New York, F. Watts [1968, c1969] xii, 116 p. port. 22 cm. (Immortals of religion) Biography of Aurelius Augustinus, who grew up during the decay and fall of the Roman Empire and whose writings had particular significance to Christians and their church at this time. [BR1720.A9H33] 92 69-11687
1. Augustinus, Aurelius, Saint, Bp. of Hippo—Juvenile literature. I. Title.

HANSON, Richard Patrick Crosland. 270.2'0924
Saint Patrick, his origins and career, by R. P. C. Hanson. New York, Oxford University Press, 1968. 248 p. 22 cm. Bibliography: p. [230]-235. [BX4700.P3H27] 68-20360
1. Patrick, Saint, 373?-463? I. Title.

HARNEY, Martin Patrick, 1896- 270.2'092'4 B
The legacy of Saint Patrick as found in his own writings [by] Martin P. Harney. [Boston] St. Paul Editions [1972] 144 p. illus. 22 cm. Includes bibliographical references. [BX4700.P3H29] 76-183441 3.00
1. Patrick, Saint, 373?-463? I. Title.

HATZFELD, Adolphe, 1824-1900. 270.2'092'4 B
Saint Augustine / by Ad. Hatzfeld ; translated by E. Holt ; with a pref. and notes by George Tyrrell. New York : AMS Press, 1975. x, 155 p. ; 18 cm. Reprint of the 1903 ed. published by Duckworth, London, in series: The Saints. [BR1720.A9H3413 1975] 71-168252 ISBN 0-404-03155-2 : 11.00
1. Augustinus, Aurelius, Saint, Bp. of Hippo. I. Series: The Saints.

HAYS, Wilma Pitchford. 270.2'0924 B
Patrick of Ireland. Illustrated by Peter Burchard. New York, Coward-McCann [1970] 64 p. illus. (part col.) 23 cm. A biography of the fifth-century monk who brought Christianity to Ireland. [BX4700.P3H36] 92 71-87885 3.29
1. Patrick, Saint, 373?-463?—Juvenile literature. I. Burchard, Peter, illus. II. Title.

KELLY, John Norman Davidson. 270.2'092'4 B
Jerome : his life, writings, and controversies / J. N. D. Kelly. 1st U.S. ed. New York : Harper & Row, c1975. xi, 353 p. : map (on lining papers) ; 24 cm. Includes bibliographical references and index. [BR1720.J5K44 1975b] 75-36732 ISBN 0-06-064333-1 : 15.00
1. Hieronymus, Saint. I. Title.

PALANCA, Louis, 1921- 270.2'092'4
Prose artistry and birth of rhyme in St. Zeno of Verona. [2d ed. rev. and enl.] New York, Exposition Press [1972] 112 p. 22 cm. (An Exposition-university book) Based on the author's thesis, Catholic University of America. [PA2310.Z4P3 1972] 71-164864 ISBN 0-682-47334-0 5.00
1. Zeno, Saint, Bp. of Verona, 4th cent. Tractatus. 2. Latin language, Postclassical Figures of speech. 3. Latin language, Postclassical—Metrics and rhythmics (Prose) I. Title.

PATRICK, Saint, 373?-463? 270.2'092'4 B
Patrick in his own words. [Translated and with commentary by] Joseph Duffy. [Dublin] Veritas Publications [1972] 97 p. 19 cm. English translation and Latin original of the author's Confessio. Includes bibliographical references. [BX4700.P3P3713] 74-152587 £0.50
1. Patrick, Saint, 373?-463? I. Duffy, Joseph A. II. Title.

PAULINUS, Saint, Bp. of Nola, 353-431. 270.2'0924
Letters of St. Paulinus of Nola. Translated and annotated by P. G. Walsh. Westminster, Md., Newmann Press, 1966-67. 2 v. 23 cm. (Ancient Christian writers; the works of the Fathers in translation, no. 35-36) Contents.Contents.—v. 1. Letter 1-22.—v. 2. Letters 23-51. Includes bibliographical references. [BR60.A35 no. 35-36] 66-28933
I. Walsh, Patrick Gerard, ed. and tr. II. Title. III. Series.

REYNOLDS, Quentin James, 1902-1965. 270.2'0924 B
The life of Saint Patrick, by Quentin Reynolds. Illustrated by Douglas Gorsline. New York, Random House [1955] 182 p. illus. 22 cm. (World landmark books [W-17]) A biography of the British boy, captured by raiding Irish warriors at age sixteen, who performed miracles, ended the power of the Druid priests over the Irish people, and converted the Irish kings and their people to Christianity. [BX4700.P3R4] 92 AC 68
1. Patrick, Saint, 373?-463? I. Gorsline, Douglas W., 1913- illus. II. Title.

SAINT Wilfrid at Hexham / D. P. Kirby, editor. Newcastle upon Tyne [Eng.] : Oriel Press, 1974. xi, 196, 31 p. : ill. ; 24 cm. Includes bibliographical references and index. [BX4700.W5S24] 75-308585 ISBN 0-85362-155-1 : £5.50 270.2'092'4 B
1. Wilfred, Saint, Bp. of York, 634-709. 2. Art—Hexham, Eng. 3. Art, Anglo-Saxon—Hexham, Eng. 4. Hexham, Eng.—History. I. Kirby, D. P.

MURPHY, Francis Xavier, 1914- 270.24
Peter speaks through Leo; the Council of Chalcedon, A. D. 451. Washington, Catholic University of America Press [1952] xii, 132p. 23cm. Bibliographical references included in 'Notes' (p. 117-128) [BR225.M85] A52
1. Chalcedon, Council of, 451. 2. Jesus Christ—Divinity. 3. Hypostatic union] I. Title.

BALDWIN, Marshall Whithed, 1903- 270.3
The medieval church. Ithaca, Cornell University Press, 1953. 124 p. 22 cm. (The Development of Western civilization; narrative essays in the history of our tradition from the time of the ancient Greeks and Hebrews to the present) [BR252.B28] 53-13133
1. Church history—Middle Ages, 600-1500. I. Title.

BALDWIN, Summerfield, 1896- 270.3
The organization of medieval Christianity, by Summerfield Baldwin [Gloucester, Mass., Peter Smith, 1962, c.1929] x, 105p. (Berkshire studies in European hist.) Bibl. 3.00
1. Church history—Middle ages. 2. Catholic church—Hist. I. Title. II. Title: Medieval Christianity.

DANIEL-ROPS, Henry, 1901- 270.3
Cathedral and crusade, studies of the medieval church, 1050-1350. Translated by John Warrington. London, Dent; New York, Dutton [1957] xi, 644p. maps. 22cm. Translation of L Eglise de la cathedrale et de la croisade. [BR270.D312 1957] 57-10100
1. Church history—Middle Ages. I. Title.

DANIEL-ROPS, Henry, 1901-1965. 270.3
Cathedral and crusade; studies of the medieval church, 1050-1350. Translated by John Warrington. New York, Dutton, 1957. 644 p. illus. 22 cm. Translation of L'Eglise de la cathedrale et de la croisade. [BR270.D312 1957a] 57-3659
1. Church history—Middle Ages, 600-1500. I. Title.

DANIEL-ROPS, Henry [Name orig.: Henry Jules Charles Petiot] 1901- 270.3
Cathedral and crusade, studies of the medieval church, 1050-1350[2v.] Tr. [from French] by John Warrington. Garden City, N.Y., Doubleday [1963, c.1957] 2v. (381; 430p.) 18cm. (Image bks., DB154A; D154B) 1.35 pap., ea.,
1. Church history—Middle Ages. I. Title.

DAWSON, Christopher Henry, 1889- 270.3
Medieval essays. New York, Sheed and Ward, 1954 271p. 21cm. founded upon...[the authors] Medieval religion" [CB353.D32] 54-6353
1. Civilization, Medieval. I. Title.

DAWSON, Christopher Henry, 1889- 270.3
Medieval essays. London and New York, Sheed andWard [1953] 271p. 22cm. 'Founded upon [the author's] ... Medieval religion.' [BR253.D357] 54-1161
1. Civilization, Christian. 2. Civilization, Medieval. I. Title.

GREENSLADE, Stanley Lawrence. 270.3
Schism in the early church. New York, Harper [1953] 247p. 23cm. (Edward Cadbury lectures, 1949-50) Bibliography: p. [231]-235. [BT1317.G7] 53-1118
1. Schism. 2. Church history—Primitive and early church. 3. Theology, Doctrinal—Hist.—Early church. I. Title. II. Series.

JOHN OF SALISBURY, Bp. of Chapters(d.1180. 270.3
Memoirs of the Papal Court translated from the Latin with introd. and notes by Marjorie Chibnall. London, New York, Nelson [1956] 1, 89, 109p. 23cm. (Medieval texts) Added t. p.: Historia pontificalis. Paged, in part, in duplicate. Latin and English. Reginald L. Poole's edition of the text was used as a basis for this edition, the original ms., which came from the Monastery of Fleury, is now ms. 367 in the Library of Berne. [BX953.J613] 270.46 56-4947
1. Eugenius III, Pope, d. 153. 2. Papacy—Hist. 3. Catholic Church—Hist. I. Chibnall, Marjorie, ed. and tr. II. Title. III. Title: Historia pontificalis. IV. Series: Medieval classics (London)

LAISTNER, Max Ludwig Wolfram, 1890- 270.3
Thought and letters in western Europe, A. D. 500 to 900. [New ed., rev. and re-set] Ithaca, N. Y., Cornell University Press [1957] 416p. 22cm. Bibliography: p. 398-402. [CB351.L] A57
1. Civilization, Medieval. 2. Literature, Medieval—Hist. & crit. 3. Learning and scholarship. I. Title.

LAISTNER, Max Ludwig Wolfram, 1890- 270.3
Thought and letters in western Europe, A.D. 500 to 900. [new ed., rev. and re-set] Ihaea N. Y., Cornell University Press [1957] 416p. 22cm. Bibliography: p. 398-402. [CB351.L] A57
1. Civilization, Medieval. 2. Literature, Medieval—Hist. & crit. 3. Learning and scholarship. I. Title.

LEVEQUE, Andre, 1904- 270.3
Histoire de la civilisation francaise. 3 ed. New York, Holt, Rinehart and Winston, [1966] vii, 499 p. illus., facsims,. maps, ports. 25 cm. [DC33.L63 1966] 66-22847
1. France — Civilization — Hist. I. Title.

MELLONE, Sydney Herbert, 1869- 270.3
Western Christian thought in the middle ages; an essay in interpretation. Edinburgh and London, W. Blackwood [Mystic, Conn., Verry, 1965] viii p., 1 1,304p. 19cm. [BR252.M4] 3.00 bds.,
1. Religious thought—Middle ages. 2. Philosophy, Medieval. 3. Middle ages—Hist. I. Title.

SCHNURER, Gustav, 1860-1941. 270.3
Church and culture in the Middle Ages. Translated by George J. Undreiner from the German. Paterson, N. J., St. Anthony Guild Press, 1956- v. 24cm. Contents.v.1.350-814. Bibliography: v.1, p.547-574. [BR253.S412] 57-13717
1. Church history—Middle Ages. 2. Civilization, Medieval. 3. Civilization, Christian. I. Title.

THRUPP, Sylvia Lettice, 1903- ed. 270.3
Change in medieval society, Europe north of the Alps, 1050-1500, edited by Sylvia L. Thrupp. New York, Appleton-Century-Crofts [1964] xii,324 p. 24 cm. Includes bibliographical references. [CB351.T55] 64-13697
1. Civilization, Mediaeval — Addresses, essays, lectures. I. Title.

WALLACH, Luitpold. 270.3
Diplomatic studies in Latin and Greek documents from the Carolingian Age / Luitpold Wallach. Ithaca, N.Y. : Cornell University Press, 1977. p. cm. Includes index. Bibliography: p. [BX830787.W34] 76-28027 27.50
1. Council of Nicaea, 2d, 787. 2. Leo III, Saint, pope, d. 816. 3. Libri Carolini. 4. Idols and images—Worship. I. Title.

EARLE, John, 1824-1903, comp. 270.3'092'4 B
Gloucester fragments. [Folcroft, Pa.] Folcroft Library Editions, 1974. vii, 4, 116 p. 34 cm. Reprint of the 1861 ed. published by Longman, Green, Longman, and Roberts, London. Contents.Contents.—Facsimile of some leaves in Saxon handwriting on Saint SwiEhun, copied by photozincography.—Leaves from an Anglosaxon translation of the life of S. Maria Agyptiaca, with a translation and notes, and a photozincography facsimile. [BX4700.S86E2 1974] 74-18301 ISBN 0-8414-3989-3 (lib. bdg.)
1. Swithun, Saint, Bp. of Winchester, d. 862. I. Title.

CONGAR, Yves Marie Joseph, 1904- 270.38
After nine hundred years; the background of the schism between the Eastern and Western churches [by] Yves Congar. New York, Fordham University Press [1959] 150 p. 23 cm. 613 270.3 59-15643rev "A translation of Neuf cents ans apres, originally published as part of 1054-1954, 1 Eglise et les Eglises." Includes bibliography. [BX303.]
1. Schism—Eastern and Western Church. I. Title.

EVERY, George. 270.38
Misunderstandings between East and West. Richmond, John Knox Press [1966, c1965] 70 p. 22 cm. (Ecumenical studies in history, no. 4) Bibliographical footnotes. [BX303.E9] 66-12355
1. Schism — Eastern and Western Church. I. Title. II. Series.

EVERY, George 270.38
Misunderstandings between East and West. Richmond, Va., Knox [1966, c.1965] 70p. 22cm. (Ecumenical studies in hist., no. 4) Bibl. [BX303.E9] 66-12355 1.75 pap.,
1. Schism—Eastern and Western Church. I. Title. II. Series.

GAIL, Marzieh. 270.3'8
The three Popes; an account of the great schism when rival Popes in Rome, Avignon, and Pisa vied for the rule of Christendom. New York, Simon and Schuster [1969] 320 p. illus. 25 cm. Bibliography: p. 307-310. [BX1301.G25] 79-75861 7.95
1. Schism, The Great Western, 1378-1417. I. Title.

GEANAKOPLOS, Deno John 270.3'8
Bvzantine east and Latin west: two worlds of Christendom in Middle Ages and Renaissance; studies in ecclesiastical and cultural history [by] Deno J. Geanakoplos. New York, Harper [1966] x, 206, 6p. illus., maps. 21cm. (Harper torchbks.) Bibl: [BX303.G4 1966] 66-29030 1.95 pap.,
1. Schism—Eastern and Western Church. 2. Ferrara- Florence, Council of 1438-1439. 3. Byzantine Empire—Relations (general) with Europe. 4. Europe—Relations (general) with the Byzantine Empire. I. Title.

GEANAKOPLOS, Deno John. 270.3'8
Byzantine East and Latin West : two worlds of Christendom in Middle Ages and Renaissance : studies in ecclesiastical and cultural history / Deno J. Geanakoplos. Hamden, Conn. : Archon Books, 1976, c1966. xii, 206 p., [8] leaves of plates : ill. ; 23 cm. Reprint of the ed. published by Blackwell, Oxford. Includes index. Bibliography: p. [194]-200. [BX303.G4 1976] 76-20685 ISBN 0-208-01615-5 : 10.00
1. Ferrara-Florence, Council of 1438-1439. 2. Byzantine Empire—Relations (general) with Europe. 3. Schism—Eastern and Western Church. 4. Europe—Relations (general) with the Byzantine Empire. I. Title.

GEANAKOPLOS, Deno John. 270.38
Byzantine East and Latin West: two worlds of Christendom in Middle Ages and Renaissance; studies in ecclesiastical and cultural history [essays, by] Deno J. Geanakoplos. New York, Barnes & Noble, 1966. x, 206 p. illus., maps (part fold.) ports. 22 cm. Bibliography: p. [194] -200. [BX303.G4] 66-31413
1. Ferrara-Florence, Council of, 1438-1439. 2. Schism—Eastern and Western Church. 3. Byzantine Empire—Relations (general) with Europe. 4. Europe—Relations (general) with the Byzantine Empire. I. Title.

SHERRARD, Philip. 270.38
The Greek East and the Latin West; a study in the Christian tradition. London, New York, Oxford University Press, 1959. 202 p. 22 cm. Includes bibliography. [BX303.S5] 59-65256
1. Schism — Eastern and Western church. 2. Religious thought — Hist. 3. Philosophy — Hist. I. Title.

BACHRACH, Bernard S., 1939- comp. 270.4
The medieval church: success or failure? Edited by Bernard S. Bachrach. New York, Holt, Rinehart and Winston [1971, c1972] 120 p. illus. 24 cm. (European problem studies) Contents.Contents.—Europe becomes Christian, by C. Dawson.—How the people create a saint, by H. Delehaye.—Charlemagne's church, by H. Fichtenau.—The church takes the offensive, by G. Tellenbach.—What did the crusades accomplish? By S. Runciman.—The knight and the church, by S. Painter.—The universities of Northern Europe, by C. H. Haskins.—The church and the medieval economy, by J. Gilchrist.—The peasants' search for salvation, by G. G. Coulton.—The image of religion, by J. Huizinga. Includes bibliographical references. [BR252.B2] 76-162863 ISBN 0-03-085185-8
1. Church history—Middle Ages, 600-1500—Addresses, essays, lectures. 2. Middle Ages—Addresses, essays, lectures. I. Title.

BAINTON, Roland Herbert, 1894- 270.4
The medieval church. Princeton, N.J., Van Nostrand [c1962] 192 p. 19 cm. (An Anvil original) "Readings": p. 89-187. [BR252.B26] 63-1686
1. Church history—Middle ages. I. Title.

GUILLEMAIN, Bernard 270.4
The early Middle Ages. Translated from the French by S. Taylor. New York, Hawthorn Books [c.1960] 128p. maps 21cm. (The Twentieth century encyclopedia of Catholicism, v. 76. Section 7: The history of the church) Bibl.: p.127-128. 60-15103 2.95 bds.
1. Church history—Middle Ages. I. Title.

GUILLEMAIN, Bernard, 1917- 270.4
The early Middle Ages. Translated from the French by S. Taylor. [1st ed.] New York, Hawthorn Books [1960] 128p. illus. 21cm. (The Twentieth century encyclopedia of Catholicism, v. 76. Section 7: The history of the church) 'Originally published in France under the title La chretiente, sa grandeur et sa ruine.' Includes bibliography. [BR270.G793] 60-15103
1. Church history—Middle Ages. I. Title.

MCNALLY, Robert E. 270.4
Reform of the church; crisis and criticism in historical perspective. [NewYork] Herder & Herder [c.1963] 140p. 21cm. Bibl. 63-18153 3.50
1. Reformation—Early movements. 2. Papacy—Hist.—1309-1378. I. Title.

MORRISON, Karl Frederick, comp. 270.4
The investiture controversy; issues, ideas, and results. Edited by Karl F. Morrison. New York, Holt, Rinehart and Winston [1971] xi, 132 p. map. 24 cm. (European problem studies) Contents.Contents.—The issue of law: conflict of churches, by Z. N. Brooke.—The issue of government: conflict of church and empire, by P. Joachimsen.—The issue of property: difficulties within the Roman See, by D. B. Zema.—Gregory VII's position: Dictatus papae (1075) Gregory's second letter to Bishop Herman of Metz (1081) Encyclical letter of Gregory VII (1084)—Henry IV's position: Henry's letter condemning Gregory VII (1076) Decree of the Synod of Brixen (1080)—Gregory sought to revive the ancient spirit of the church, by G. B. Ladner.—Tradition: a skeleton in the Gregorians' closet, by K. F. Morrison.—Text: Paschal II's Privilegia in favor of Henry V (1111)—Recovery of Apostolic ideals, by F. Gregorovius.—Papal weakness, by P. R. McKeon.—Text: The Concordat of Worms (1122)—The papacy master of the field, by J. Bryce.—The agreement of London: a distinct victory for the lay power, by J. T. Ellis.—The Concordat of Worms: a limited victory for the emperor, by R. L. Benson.—The downfall of the papacy, by A. Toynbee.—Suggestions for additional reading (p. 131-132) [BX1198.M67] 74-124777 ISBN 0-03-085156-4
1. Investiture—Addresses, essays, lectures. I. Title.

NICHOLL, Donald, 1923- 270.4
Thurstan, Archibishop of York, 1114-1140. York, Stonegate Pr., 1964. xi, 277p. 23cm. Bibl. [BR754.T57N5] 66-6700 7.00
1. Thurstan, Abp. of York, 1070 (ca.)-1140. I. Title.
American distributor: Dufour in Chester Springs, Pa.

ORDERICUS Vitalis, 1075-1143? 270.4
The ecclesiastical history of Orderic Vitalis; edited and translated with introduction and notes by Marjorie Chibnall. Oxford, Clarendon P., 1969- v. 23 cm. (Oxford medieval texts) Translation of Historiae ecclesiasticae libri xiii, vol. II, books III and IV. [BR252.O634] 70-25316 ISBN 0-19-822204-1 90/- (v. 2)
1. Church history. 2. Normandy—History—To 1461. 3. Great Britain—History—To 1485. 4. Normans. 5. Crusades. I. Chibnall, Marjorie, ed. II. Title. III. Series.

SLESSAREV, Vsevolod. 270.4
Prester John; the letter and the legend. Minneapolis, University of Minnesota Press [1959] 127 p. map. 21 cm. Includes facsim. ([12] p. 19 cm.) of the French edition of Prester John's letter preserved in the James Ford Bell Collection of the University of Minnesota Library. "The translation [of the letter]": p. 67-79. Bibliographical references included in "Notes" (p. 95-122) [BR275.J7S5 1959] 59-13651
1. John, Prester.

TIERNEY, Brian. 270.4
The crisis of church & state, 1050-1300. With selected documents. Englewood Cliffs, N.J., Prentice-Hall [1964] xi, 211 p. 21 cm. (A Spectrum book) Bibliography: p. 211. [BV630.2.T5] 64-23072
1. Church and state—History. I. Title.

TREECE, Henry, 1911-1966. 270.4 (j)
Know about the Crusades. [Chester Springs, Pa.] Dufour, 1967 [c1963] 62 p. illus. (part col.) 21 cm. Bibliography: p. 62. [D158.T8] 67-4854
1. Crusades—Juvenile literature. I. Title.

WALKER, G. S. M. 270.4
The growing storm; sketches of church history from A. D. 600 to A. D. 1350. Grand Rapids, Mich., Eerdmans [1962, c.1961] 252p. (Advance of Christianity through the centuries, v. 2) Bibl. 62-3001 3.75
1. Church history—Middle Ages. I. Title.

WILLIAMS, Schafer, ed. 270.4
The Gregorian epoch: reformation, revolution, reaction? Boston, Heath [1964] xiv, 110 p. 24 cm. (Problems in European civilization) Bibliography: p. 109-110. [BX1178.W5] 63-20378
1. Gregorius VII, Saint, Pope, 1015 (ca.)-1085. 2. Church history—11th century. I. Title. II. Series.

BROOKE, Christopher Nugent Lawrence. 270.4'08
Medieval church and society; collected essays [by] Christopher Brooke. [New York] New York University Press [1972] 256 p. illus. 23 cm. Includes bibliographical references. [BR252.B75 1972] 72-166506 ISBN 0-8147-0968-0
1. Church history—Middle Ages, 600-1500—Addresses, essays, lectures. I. Title.

FIEHLER, Rudolph 270.40924
The strange history of Sir John Oldcastle, [1st ed.] New York, American Pr. [c.1965] 243p. 21cm. Bibl. [BX4906.O6G5] 65-25021 3.50
1. Oldcastle, John, styled Lord Cobham, d. Sir 1417. I. Title.

BAINTON, Roland Herbert, 1894- 270.463
The medieval church. Princeton, N.J., Van Nostrand [c.1962] 192 p. 19 cm. (Anvil orig. 64) Bibl. pap., 1.45
1. Church history—Middle Ages. I. Title.

BLOCK, Edward A. 270.5
John Wyclif, radical dissenter. [San Diego] San Diego State College Press, 1962. 58 p. 23 cm. (Humanities monograph series, v. 1, no. 1) Bibliographical footnotes. [BX4905.B58] 63-3841
1. Wycliffe, John, d. 1384. I. Title. II. Series.

BURNS, J. H. 270.5
Scottish churchmen and the Council of Basle. [Chester Springs, Pa., Dufour, 1964, c.1962] Glasgow J. S. Burns 98p. facsim., plates, ports. 25cm. Bibl. 64-7472 5.00
1. Basel, Council of, 1431-1449. 2. Scotland—Church history—Medieval period. I. Title.

CHENEY, Christopher Robert, 1906- 270.5
Medieval texts and studies [by] C. R. Cheney. Oxford, Clarendon Press, 1973. viii, 371 p. 23 cm. Includes bibliographical references. [BR750.C464] 73-180967 ISBN 0-19-822399-4
1. Great Britain—Church history—Addresses, essays, lectures. I. Title.
Distributed by Oxford University Press, New York, 19.25.

COHN, Norman Rufus Colin. 270.5
The pursuit of the millennium. Fairlawn [i. e. Fair Lawn] N. J., Essential Books, 1957. 476 p. illus. 23 cm. [BR270.C6] 57-4259
1. Church history—Middle Ages. 2. Sects, Medieval. I. Title.

COHN, Norman Rufus Colin. 270.5
The pursuit of the millennium; revolutionary millenarians and mystical anarchists of the Middle Ages [by] Norman Cohn. Rev. and expanded ed. New York, Oxford University Press, 1970. 412 p. illus., port. 24 cm. Bibliography: p. 372-399. [BR270.C6 1970b] 79-12811 9.50
1. Church history—Middle Ages, 600-1500. 2. Sects, Medieval. 3. Millennium—History of doctrines. I. Title.

COULTON, George Gordon, 1858-1947. 270.5
Ten medieval studies, by G. G. Coulton. Gloucester, Mass., P. Smith, 1967. xi, 297 p. 21 cm. First ed. published in 1906 under title: Mediaeval studies. Bibliographical footnotes. [BR252.C652 1967] 67-8880
1. Church history—Middle Ages, 600-1500. 2. Great Britain—Church History—Medieval period, 1066-1485. 3. Monasticism and religious orders—Middle Ages, 600-1500. I. Title.

FLICK, Alexander Clarence, 1869-1942. 270.5
The decline of the Medieval Church. New York, B. Franklin [1967] 2 v. 23 cm. (Burt Franklin bibliography & reference series, 133) (Essays in history, economics & social science, 7.) Reprint of the 1930 ed. Includes bibliographies. [BR252.F58 1967] 73-6284
1. Church history—Middle Ages, 600-1500. I. Title.

GILL, Joseph, 1901- 270.5
Personalities of the Council of Florence, and other essays. New York, Barnes & Noble [1965, c.1964] viii, 297p. 23cm. Bibl. [BX830.1438.G5] 65-2068 7.50
1. Ferrara-Florence, Council of, 1438-1439. I. Title.

GUILLEMAIN, Bernard 270.5
The later Middle Ages. Translated from the French by S. Taylor. New York, Hawthorn Books [c.1960] 122p. map 21cm. (The Twentieth century encyclopedia of Catholicism, v. 77. Section 7: The history of the church) (bibl.) 60-8788 2.95 half cloth,
1. Church history—Middle Ages. I. Title.

GUILLEMAIN, Bernard, 1917- 270.5
The later Middle Ages. Translated from the French by S. Taylor. [1st ed.] New York, Hawthorn Books [1960] 122p. illus. 21cm. (The Twentieth century encyclopedia of Catholicism, v. 77. Section 7: The history of the church) Translation of La chretiente, sa grandeur et sa ruine. Includes bibliography. [BR270.G813] 60-8788
1. Church history—Middle Ages. I. Title.

HYMA, Albert, 1893- 270.5
Renaissance to Reformation. Grand Rapids, Eerdmans, 1951. 591 p. 24 cm. Bibliographical footnotes. [BR280.H9] 51-11560
1. Renaissance. 2. Reformation. I. Title.

JACK Upland. 270.5
Jack Upland; Friar Daw's reply; and, Upland's rejoinder; edited by P. L. Heyworth. London, Oxford U.P., 1968. xii, 176 p. plate, facsim. 23 cm. (Oxford English monographs) Bibliography: p. [174]-176. [PR1999.J3 1968] 76-530008 ISBN 0-19-811712-4 35/-
I. Heyworth, P. L., ed. II. Friar Daw's reply. 1968. III. Upland's rejoinder. 1968.

JACOB, Ernest Fraser, 1894- 270.5
Essays in the conciliar epoch. [Rev. ed. Notre Dame, Ind.] Univ. of Notre Dame Pr., 1963. viii, 264p. 22cm. Bibl. 63-15295 4.75
1. Church history—Middle Ages. 2. Councils and synods. I. Title. II. Title: Conciliar epoch.

LEA, Henry Charles, 1825-1909. 270.5
A history of the Inquisition in the Middle Ages. New York, Harbor Press [1955] 3 v. 23 cm. (The Harbor scholars' classics edition) [BX1711.L4 1955] 272.2 55-3956
1. Inquisition—History.

LOOMIS, Louise Ropes, 1874-1958, tr. 270.5
The Council of Constance: the unification of the church. Ed., annotated by John Hine Mundy, Kennerly M. Woody. New York, Columbia, 1961. xiii, 562p. (Records of civilization: sources and studies, 63) Includes Richental's Chronicle of the Council of Constance, Fillastre's Diary of the Council of Constance, and Cerretano's Journal. Bibl. 61-9659 10.00
1. Constance, Council of, 1414-1418. I. Mundy, John Hine, 1917- ed. II. Woody, Kennerly M., ed. III. Title. IV. Series.

*MCFARLANE, K. B. 270.5
The origins of religious dissent in England (Title orig.: John Wycliffe and the beginnings of English nonconformity.) New York, Collier [1966] 220p. 18cm. (03464) Bibl. 1.25 pap.,
I. Title.

OSTROUMOV, Ivan N. 270.5
The history of the Council of Florence [by] Ivan N. Ostroumoff. Translated from the Russian by Basil Popoff. Boston, Mass., Holy Transfiguration Monastery, 1971. ix, 311 p. ports. 20 cm. Translation of Istoriia Florentiiskago sobora. Bibliography: p. [231]-311. [BX830 1438.O7813] 72-179163
1. Ferrara-Florence Council of, 1438-1439. I. Title.

PARKER, Geoffrey Henry William. 270.5
The morning star; Wycliffe and the dawn of the Reformation, by G. H. W. Parker. Grand Rapids, W. B. Eerdmans Pub. Co. [1966, c1965] 248 p. 23 cm. (The Advance of Christianity throught the centturies, v. 3) Bibliography: p. 235-240. [BR270.P3] 66-1534
1. Church history—Middle Ages. I. Title. II. Series.

ROGERS, Francis Millet. 270.5
The quest for Eastern Christians travels and rumor in the Age of Discovery. Minneapolis, University of Minnesota Press [1962] 221p. illus. 23cm. [BX6.5.R57] 62-18138
1. Eastern churches—Relations—Catholic Church. 2. Catholic Church —Relations—Eastern churches. 3. Christian union—Hist. 4. Church history— 15th cent. I. Title.

SMITH, John Holland. 270.5
The Great Schism, 1378. New York, Weybright and Talley [1970] vii, 280 p. illus., ports. 23 cm. (Turning points in history) [BX1301.S6 1970b] 75-99006 7.50
1. Schism, The Great Western, 1378-1417. I. Title.

SPINKA, Matthew, 1890- ed. 270.5
Advocates of reform, from Wyclif to Erasmus. Philadelphia, Westminster Press [1953] 399 p. 24 cm. (The Library of Christian classics, v. 14) Bibliography: p. 380-382. [BR301.S65] 53-13092
1. Reformation—Sources. 2. Reformation—Early movements. I. Title. II. Series: The Library of Christian classics (Philadelphia) v. 14

STACEY, John 270.5
John Wycif and reform Philadelphia, Westminster [c.1964] 169p. 22cm. Bibl. 64-19147 3.75
1. Wycliffe, John, d. 1384. I. Title.

STACEY, John. 270.5
John Wyclif and reform. Philadelphia, Westminster Press [1964] 169 p. 22 cm. Includes bibliographies. [BX4905.S68] 64-19147
1. Wycliffe, John, d. 1384. I. Title.

TURBERVILLE, Arthur Stanley, 1888-1945 270.5
Mediaeval heresy & the Inquisition. Hamden [Conn.] Archon [dist. Shoe String, 1964] vi, 264p. 22cm. Bibl. 64-11061 6.00
1. Sects, Medieval. 2. Heresy. 3. Inquisition. I. Title.

ULLMANN, Walter, 1910- 270.5
The origins of the Great Schism; a study in fourteenth-century ecclesiastical history. [Hamden, Conn.] Archon Books, 1967. xiii, 244 p. illus., ports. 22 cm. Reprint of the 1948 ed. Bibliographical footnotes. [BX1301.U55 1967] 67-12982
1. Schism, The Great Western, 1378-1417. I. Title.

WILLIAMS, George Huntston, 1914- 270.5
The Radical Reformation. Philadelphia, Westminster Press [1962] xxxi, 924 p. map (on lining paper) 24 cm. Bibliographical footnotes. [BR307.W5] 62-7066
1. Reformation. 2. Anabaptists. I. Title.

WORKMAN, Herbert Brook, 1862- 270.5 (B)
John Wyclif; a study of the English medieval church, by Herbert B. Workman. Hamden, Conn., Archon Books, 1966. 2 v. in 1. illus., facsims., ports. 23 cm. "Originally published . . . 1926." "Abbreviations and editions": v. 1, p. [xxvii]-[xxxv] [BX4905.W6 1966] 66-14608
1. Wycliffe, John, d. 1384. I. Title.

JACOB, Ernest Fraser, 1894- comp 270.5'08
Essays in later medieval history, comp. by E. F. Jacob. Manchester, Manchester Univ. Pr., New York, Barnes & Noble, 1968. [8], 223p. facsims. 23cm. Bibl. footnotes. [BR270.J29 1968] 68-118252 6.00
1. Church history—15th cent.—Addresses, essays, lectures. I. Title.

SEEBOHM, Frederic, 1833-1912. 270.5'0922 B
The Oxford reformers: John Colet, Erasmus, and Thomas More. Being a history of their fellow-work. London, New York, Longmans,

Green, 1913. [New York, AMS Press, 1971] xvi, 551 p. 23 cm. [BR378.S4 1971] 70-147115 ISBN 0-404-05696-2
1. Colet, John, 1467?-1519. 2. Erasmus, Desiderius, d. 1536. 3. More, Thomas, Sir, Saint, 1478-1535. 4. Reformation. 5. Education—England—History. I. Title.

DAHMUS, Joseph Henry, 1909- 270.5'0924
The prosecution of John Wyclyf, by Joseph H. Dahmus. [Hamden, Conn.] Archon Books, 1970 [c1952] xi, 167 p. 23 cm. Bibliography: p. 158-161. [BX4905.D2 1970] 76-120371
1. Wycliffe, John, d. 1384. I. Title.

FIEHLER, Rudolph. 270.50924 (B)
The strange history of Sir John Oldcastle. [1st ed.] New York, American Press [c1965] 243 p. 21 cm. "Notes on the sources": p. 239-243. [BX4906.O6F5] 65-25021
1. Oldcastle, Sir John, styled Lord Cobham, d. 1417. I. Title.

GLASFURD, Alexander Lamont, 1907- 270.50924
The antipope, Peter de Luna, 1342-1423; a study in obstinacy [by] Alec Glasfurd. New York, Roy [1966, c.1965] 287p. illus., map (on lining papers) ports. 23cm. Bibl. [BX1286.G5 1966] 66-21800 6.95
1. Benedictus XIII, antipope, 1342-1423? I. Title.

LEWIS, John, 1675-1747. 270.5'092'4 B
The history of the life and sufferings of the Reverend and learned John Wiclif, D.D. ... Together with a collection of papers and records relating to the said history. A new ed., corr. and enl. by the author. Oxford, Clarendon Press, 1820. [New York, AMS Press, 1973] xxxii, 389 p. port. 23 cm. [BX4905.L45 1973] 74-178543 ISBN 0-404-56625-1 21.00
1. Wycliffe, John, d. 1384. I. Title.

MCFARLANE, Kenneth Bruce. 270.5'0924
John Wycliffe and the beginnings of English noncomformity [by] K. B. McFarlane [London] English Universities Pr. [1972, c.1952] xiii, 188 p. maps. 23 cm. ([Men & their times]) Bibliography: p. [174]-175 [BX4905.M3] A53 ISBN 0-340-16648-7
1. Wycliffe, John, d. 1384. 2. Reformation—Early movements. 3. Reformation—England. I. Title. II. Title: English nonconformity. III. Series.
Available from Verry, Mystic, Conn., for 5.00.

MCFARLANE, Kenneth Bruce. 270.5'092'4
Wycliffe and English nonconformity [by] K. B. McFarlane. Harmondsworth, Penguin, 1972. xvii, 188 p. maps. 19 cm. (A Pelican book) (Teach yourself history) Originally published in 1952 under title: John Wycliffe and the beginnings of English nonconformity. Bibliography: p. [174]-175. [BX4905.M2 1972] 73-164247 ISBN 0-14-021377-5 £0.35
1. Wycliffe, John, d. 1384. I. Title.

SERGEANT, Lewis, d.1902. 270.5'092'4 B
John Wyclif, last of the schoolmen and first of the English reformers. Freeport, N.Y., Books for Libraries Press [1973] p. (Essay index reprint series) Reprint of the 1893 ed., issued in series: Heroes of the nations. [BX4905.S4 1973] 72-14162 ISBN 0-518-10022-7
1. Wycliffe, John, d. 1384. I. Series: Heroes of the nations.

VAUGHAN, Robert, 1795-1868. 270.5'092'4 B
The life and opinions of John de Wycliffe, D. D. Illustrated principally from his unpublished manuscripts; with a preliminary view of the papal system, and of the state of the Protestant doctrine in Europe, to the commencement of the fourteenth century. 2d ed. much improved. London, Holdsworth and Ball, 1831. [New York, AMS Press, 1973] 2 v. port. 23 cm. Includes bibliographical references. [BX4905.V36 1973] 71-178561 ISBN 0-404-56678-2
1. Wycliffe, John, d. 1384. I. Title.

ADAM, Karl, 1876- 270.6
The roots of the Reformation. Translated by Cecily Hastings. New York, Sheed & Ward [1957?] 95p. 18cm. (Canterbury books) 'A large part of One and holy, a translation of Una Sacta in katholischer Sicht.' [BR307.A314] 57-4639
1. Luther, Martin, 1483-1546. 2. Catholic Church—Doctrinal and controversial works—Catholic authors. I. Title.

ANDERSON, Charles S. 270.6
The Reformation ... then and now [by] Charles S. Anderson. Minneapolis, Augsburg Pub. House [1966] 119, [1] p. 20 cm. (A Tower book) Bibliography: p. [120] [BR305.2.A5] 66-9710
1. Reformation. 2. Christianity—20th century. I. Title.

ATKINSON, James, 1914- 270.6
The great light; Luther and Reformation. Grand Rapids, W. B. Eerdmans Pub. Co. [1968] 287 p. 23 cm. (The Advance of Christianity through the centuries, v. 4) Bibliography: p. 266-276. [BR305.2.A73] 68-20590
1. Reformation. I. Title. II. Series.

AULEN. GUSTAF EMANUEL HILDEBRAND, Bp., 1879- 270.6
Reformation and catholicity. Tr. [from Swedish] by Eric H. Wahlstrom. Philadelphia, Muhlenberg [c.1961] 203p. Bibl. 61-10281 3.75
1. Reformation. 2. Justification—History of doctrines. 3. Authority (Religion) 4. Catholicity. I. Title.

BABINGTON, John Albert, 1843- 270.6
The Reformation; a religious and historical sketch. Port Washington, N.Y., Kennikat Press [1971] x, 362 p. 22 cm. Reprint of the 1901 ed. [BR305.B3 1971] 71-118513
1. Reformation.

BAINTON, Roland Herbert, 1894- 270.6
The age of the Reformation. Princeton, N.J., Van Nostrand [1956] 192 p. 18 cm. (An Anvil original, no. 13) [BR305.B33] 56-6880
1. Reformation. I. Title.

BAINTON, Roland Herbert, 1894- 270.6
The Reformation of the sixteenth century [Gloucester, Mass. Peter Smith 1962, c.1952] 278p. illus. 21cm. (Beacon Pr. bk. rebound) Bibl. 3.75
1. Reformation. I. Title.

BAINTON, Roland Herbert, 1894- 270.6
The Reformation of the sixteenth century. Boston, Beacon Press [1952] xi, 276 p. illus. 22 cm. Bibliography: p. 262-268. [BR305.B35] 52-5244
1. Reformation. I. Title.

BAINTON, Roland Herbert, 1894- 270.6
Studies on the Reformation. Boston, Beacon Press [1963] 289 p. illus. 21 cm. (His Collected papers in church history, ser. 2) Includes bibliographies. [BR305.2.B3] 63-17527
1. Reformation. I. Title.

BAINTON, Roland Herbert, 1894- 270.6
Studies on the Reformation. Boston, Beacon [c.1963] 289p. illus. 21cm. (His Collected papers in church hist., ser. 2) Bibl. 63-17527 6.00 bds.,
1. Reformation. I. Title.

BEARD, Charles, 1827-1888. 270.6
The Reformation of the 16th century in its relation to modern thought and knowledge. Foreword by Joseph Dorfman. Introd. by Ernest Barker. [Ann Arbor] University of Michigan Press [1962] 450 p. 20 cm. (Ann Arbor paperbacks, AA61) [BR305.B45 1962] 62-53003
1. Reformation.

BELLOC, Hilaire, 1870-1953. 270.6
Characters of the Reformation. New York, Image Books [1958] 200 p. 19 cm. (Image books, D71) [BR315.B35 1958] 58-9384
1. Reformation—Biography. I. Title.

BELLOC, Hilaire [Joseph Hilaire Pierre Belloc] 1870-1953. 270.6
How the Reformation happened [New York 16, Apollo Eds. Inc. 425 Park Ave., S. 1961, c.1928] 290p. (A-10) 1.95 pap.,
1. Reformation. I. Title.

BLAYNEY, Ida Walz. 270.6
The age of Luther; the spirit of Renaissance-humanism and the Reformation. [1st ed.] New York, Vantage Press [1957] 499p. illus. 21cm. Includes bibliography. [BR280.B5] 56-12321
1. Luther, Martin, 1483-1586. 2. Renaissance. 3. Humanism. 4. Reformation. I. Title.

BOHNSTEDT, John Wolfgang. 270.6
The infidel scourge of God; the Turkish menace as seen by German pamphleteers of the Reformation era [by] John W. Bohnstedt. Philadelphia, American Philosophical Society, 1968. 58 p. illus. 30 cm. (Transactions of the American Philosophical Society, new ser., v. 58, pt. 9) Bibliography: p. 52-56. [Q11.P6 ns., vol. 58, pt. 9] 68-59177 2.00
1. Turkey—Foreign opinion, German. 2. Islam—Relations—Christianity. 3. Christianity and other religions—Islam. I. Title. II. Series: American Philosophical Society, Philadelphia. Transactions, new ser., v. 58, pt. 9

BOYER, Merle William, 1910- 270.6
Luther in Protestantism today. New York, Association Press [1958] 188p. 20cm. [BX4817.B68] 58-6468
1. Protestantism. 2. Luther, Martin—Influence. I. Title.

BURNS, Edward McNall, 1897- 270.6
The Counter Reformation. Princeton, N.J., Van Nostrand [1964] 186 p. 19 cm. (An Anvil original) Van Nostrand anvil books, 69. Bibliography: p. 180-182. [BR430.B8] 64-2411
1. Counter Reformation.

CALVIN, Jean, 1509-1564 270.6
A Reformation debate; Sadoleto's letter to the Genevans and Calvin's reply. [By] John Calvin, Jacopo Sadoleto. With an appendix on the justification controversy Ed., introd., by John C. Olin. New York, Harper [c.1966] 136p. 21cm. (Torchbk. TB1239G. Acad. lib.) Bibl. [BR301.C3] 66-10529 1.25 pap.,
1. Reformation—Sources. 2. Church—Authority. 3. Justification. I. Sadoleto, Jacopo, Cardinal, 1477-1547. II. Olin, John C., ed. III. Title.

CALVIN, Jean, 1509-1564 270.6
A Reformation debate; Sadoleto's letter to the Genevans and Calvin's reply [by] John Calvin, Jacopo Sadoleto. With an appendix on the justification of controversy. Ed., introd. by John C. Olin [Gloucester, Mass., P. Smith, c.1966] 136p. 21cm. (Harper torchbk., TB1239G, Acad. lib. rebound) Bibl. [BR301.C3 1966] 3.25
1. Reformation—Sources. 2. Church—Authority. 3. Justification. I. Sadoleto, Jacopo, Cardinal, 1477-1547. II. Olin, John C., ed. III. Title.

CALVIN, Jean, 1509-1964. 270.6
A Reformation debate; Sadoleto's letter to the Genevans and Calvin's reply. [By] John Calvin & Jacopo Sadoleto. With an appendix on the justification controversy. Edited, with an introd., by John C. Olin. [1st ed.] New York, Harper & Row [1966] 136 p. 21 cm. (Harper Torchbooks. The academy library, TB 1239 G) Bibliographical footnotes. 66-10529
1. Reformation—Sources. 2. Church—Authority. 3. Justification. I. Sadoleto, Jacopo, Cardinal, 1477-1547. II. Olin, John C., ed. III. III. Title.

CHADWICK, Owen 270.6
The Reformation. Grand Rapids, Mich., Eerdmans [1965, c,1964] 463p. maps. 22cm. Bibl. [BR305.2.C5] 5.95
1. Reformation. I. Title.

CHADWICK, Owen 270.6
The Reformation [Gloucester, Mass., P. Smith, c.1964] 463p. 19cm. (Pelican bk. A504. Pelican hist. of the Church v. 3) Bibl. 4.00
1. Reformation. I. Title.

CHADWICK, Owen 270.6
The Reformation. Baltimore, Penguin [1964] 463p. maps. 19cm. (Pelican hist. of the church, v. 3, A504) Bibl. 64-3925 1.95 pap.,
1. Reformation. I. Title.

CHADWICK, Owen. 270.6
The Reformation. Grand Rapids, Eerdmans [1965, c1964] 463 p. 22 cm. (The Pelican history of the church, v. 3) "Suggestions for further reading": p. [446]-449. [BR305.2.C5 1965] 65-5283
1. Reformation.

CHADWICK, Owen. 270.6
The Reformation. [1st ed.], reprinted with revisions. Harmondsworth, Penguin, 1972. 463 p. 18 cm. (The Pelican history of the church, v. 3) (Pelican books) Bibliography: p. [446]-449. [BR305.2.C5 1972] 73-331082 ISBN 0-14-020504-7 £0.50
1. Reformation.

CHRISTIANITY and revolution : radical Christian testimonies, 1520-1650 / edited by Lowell H. Zuck. Philadelphia : Temple University Press, 1975. xiv, 310 p. ; 23 cm. (Documents in free church history) Includes indexes. Bibliography: p. 287-297. [BR301.C45] 74-25355 ISBN 0-87722-040-9 : 20.00 ISBN 0-87722-044-1 pbk. : 5.00 270.6
1. Reformation—Sources. 2. Anabaptists—History—Sources. I. Zuck, Lowell H. II. Title. III. Series.

COMPAGNIE des pasteurs et professeurs de Geneve. 270.6
The register of the Company of Pastors of Geneva in the time of Calvin, Ed., tr. [from French & Latin] by Philip Edgcumbe Hughes. Grand Rapids, Mich., Eerdmans [c.1966] xvi, 380p. 24cm. Bibl. [BR410.C6] 65-18095 12.50
1. Reformation—Switzerland—Geneva—Sources. I. Hughes, Philip Edgcumbe ed. and tr. II. Title.

COURVOISIER, Jaques. 270.6
Reformation and politics. Translated from the French by Grace A. Gibson. [Newcastle upon Tyne, University of Newcastle upon Tyne, 1971] 20 p. 21 cm. (Earl Grey memorial lecture, 50) [BR309.C6313] 73-157357 ISBN 0-900565-37-3 £0.25
1. Reformation. 2. Christianity and politics—History. I. Title. II. Series.

COWIE, Leonard W. 270.6
The Reformation [by] Leonard W. Cowie. Drawings by Elizabeth Hammond. [1st American ed.] New York, John Day Co. [1968] 112 p. illus., maps, ports. 23 cm. (Young historian books) [BR308.C6 1968] 68-11309
1. Reformation.

COWIE, Leonard W. 270.6
The Reformation [by] Leonard W. Cowie. Drawings by Elizabeth Hammond. [1st American ed.] New York, John Day Co. [1968] 112 p. illus., maps, ports. 23 cm. (Young historian books) Traces the events leading to the Reformation, the movements of Luther and Calvin, the reforms within the Catholic Church itself, the unique course of the reform movement in England, and the influence of the Reformation on New World settlements. [BR308.C6 1968] AC 68
1. Reformation. I. Hammond, Elizabeth, illus. II. Title.

COWIE, Leonard W. 270.6
The Reformation of the sixteenth century, by Leonard W. Cowie. New York, Putnam [1970] 128 p. illus., ports. 24 cm. (The Putnam documentary history series) Includes bibliographical references. [BR305.2.C65 1970b] 75-116150 4.95
1. Reformation. I. Title.

CRISTIANI, Leon [Augustin Louis Leon Pierre Cristiani] 270.6
The revolt against the church. Tr.from French by R. F. Trevett. New York, Hawthorn [c.1962] 142p. 21cm. (Twentieth century ency. of Catholicism, v.78. Sect. 7: The hist. of the church) Bibl. 62-12933 3.50 bds.,
1. Reformation. 2. Counter-Reformation. I. Title.

CROSBY, Ernest S. 270.6
Reformation and the reformers; a layman's story for laymen [Hartford 3, Conn., South Congregational Church, 1964] vii, 622p. illus., ports. 21cm. Bibl. 64-633 4.95
1. Reformation. I. Title.

DANIEL-ROPS, Henry, 1901- 270.6
The church in the seventeenth century. Translated by J. J. Buckingham. London, Dent; New York, Dutton [1963] 466 p. illus. 23 cm. (His History of the Church of Christ, 6) Translation of Le grand siecle des ames, published as v. 1 of the Author's L'Eglise des temps classiques. Includes bibliographies. [BR440.D313] 63-5909
1. Church history — 17th cent. I. Title.

DANIEL-ROPS, Henry 1901- 270.6
The church in the seventeenth century; 2v. Tr. [from French] by J. J. Buckingham. Garden City, N.Y., Doubleday [1965, c.1963] 2v. 320;318p. 18cm. (His Hist. of the Church of Christ (Image bks., D191A/B) Bibl. 1.25 pap., ea.,
1. Church history—17th cent. I. Title.

DANIEL-ROPS, Henry [Henry Jules Charles Petiot] 1901- 270.6
The church in the seventeenth century. Tr. [from French] by J. J. Buckingham. London, Dent; New York, Dutton [1963] 466p. map. 23cm. (His Hist. of the Church of Christ, 6) Bibl. 63-5909 10.00
1. Church history—17th cent. I. Title.

DANIEL-ROPS, Henry [Henry Jules Charles Petiot] 1901- 270.6
The Protestant Reformation. Tr. from French by Audrey Butler. New York, Dutton [c.1961] 560p. (His Hist. of the Church of Christ, 4) Bibl. 61-65905 10.00
1. Church history—Middle Ages. 2. Renaissance. 3. Reformation. I. Title.

DANIEL-ROPS, Henry [Real name: Henry Jules Charles Petiot] 1901- 270.6
The Catholic Reformation. Tr. from French by John Warrington. New York, Dutton [c.1962] 435p. illus., maps. 22cm. (His History of the Church of Christ, 5) Bibl. 62-6532 10.00
1. Counter-Reformation. I. Title.

DANIEL-ROPS, Henry [Henry Jules Charles Petiot] 1901- 270.6
The Catholic Reformation [2v.] Tr. from French by John Warrington. Garden City, N.Y., Doubleday [1964, c.1962] 2v. (360; 280p.) 18cm. (Image bks. D179A, B) 1.25 pap., ea.,
1. Counter-Reformation. I. Title.

DANIEL-ROPS, Henry [Real 270.6
name: Henry Jules Charles Petiot] 1901-
The Protestant Reformation; 2v. Tr. from French by Audrey Butler. Garden City. N.Y., Doubleday [1963, c.1961] 359; 393p. 18cm. (His History of the Church of Christ, 4. Image bks., DB159A & B) Bibl. 1.35 pap., ea.,
1. Church history—Middle Ages. 2. Renaissance. 3. Reformation. I. Title.

DANNENFELDT, Karl H. 270.6
The church of the Renaissance and Reformation; decline and reform from 1300 to 1600, by Karl H. Dannenfeldt. Saint Louis, Concordia Pub. House [1970] 145 p. 21 cm. (Church in history series) Includes bibliographical references. [BR280.D33] 77-98300
1. Renaissance. 2. Reformation. I. Title. II. Series.

*D'AUBIGNE, J. H. Merle 270.'6
History of the reformation of the sixteenth century / by J. H. Merle D'Aubigne ; translated by H. White. Grand Rapids : Baker Book House, 1976. xxi, 867 p. ; 23 cm. (Religious heritage library) Contents.Vol. 1-5. [BR305.2] ISBN 0-8010-2859-0 : 14.95
1. Reformation. 2. Church history—Modern period, 1500- I. White, H. tr. II. Title.

DAWSON, Christopher Henry 270.6
The dividing of Christendom. Foreword by Douglas Horton. New York, Doubleday [1967, c.1965] 237p. 18cm. (Image bks. R229) Bibl. [BR148.D3] .95 pap.,
1. Schism. 2. Reformation—Addresses, essays, lectures. 3. Church history—Addresses, essays, lectures. I. Title.

DAWSON, Christopher Henry, 270.6
1889-
The dividing of Christendom [by] Christopher Dawson. Foreword by Douglas Horton. New York, Sheed and Ward [1965] x, 304 p. 22 cm. "Drawn, in considerable part, from the lectures which . . . [the] author gave while occupying the Charles Chauncey Stillman Chair of Roman Catholic Theological Studies at the Divinity School of Harvard University." Bibliographical footnotes. [BR148.D3] 65-12208
1. Schism. 2. Reformation — Addresses, essays, lectures. 3. Church history — Addresses, essays, lectures. I. Title.

DAWSON, Christopher Henry, 270.6
1889-
The dividing of Christendom. Foreword by Douglas Horton. New York, Sheed [c.1965] x, 304p. 22cm. Bibl. [BR148.D3] 65-12208 5.95
1. Schism. 2. Reformation—Addresses, essays, lectures. 3. Church history—Addresses, essays, lectures. I. Title.

DICKENS, Arthur Geoffrey. 270.6
The Counter Reformation [by] A. G. Dickens. [New York] Harcourt, Brace & World [1969] 215 p. illus., ports. (both part col.) 22 cm. Bibliography: p. 203-206. [BR430.D5 1969] 69-15442 5.95
1. Counter-Reformation.

DICKENS, Arthur Geoffrey. 270.6
Reformation and society in sixteenth-century Europe [by] A. G. Dickens. [1st American ed. New York] Harcourt, Brace & World [1966] 216 p. illus. (part col.) facsims., maps (1 fold.) ports. (part col.) 21 cm. (History of European civilization library) Bibliography: p. 203-206. [BR305.2.D5 1966a] 66-19863
1. Reformation. I. Title.

DOLAN, John Patrick 270.6
History of the Reformation; a concilliatory assessment of opposite views. Introd. by Jaroslav Pelikan. New York, New Amer. Lib. [1967, c.1965] xv, 366p. 18cm. (Mentor-Omega MQ712) [BR305.2D6] .95 pap.,
1. Reformation. I. Title.

DOLAN, John Patrick 270.6
History of the Reformation; a conciliatory assessment of opposite views. New York, Desclee [1965] xvii, 417p. 22cm. [BR305.2.D6] 65-22364 6.75
1. Reformation. I. Title.

DOLLINGER, Johann Joseph 270.6
Ignaz von, 1799-1890.
Lectures on the reunion of the churches. [Translated with pref. by Henry Nutcombe Oxenham] Naperville, Ill., Aleph Press, 1973. xliv, 165 p. 20 cm. (Sources in the history of interpretation, 2) Reprint of the 1872 ed. published by Rivingtons, London. Includes bibliographical references. [BX8.D59 1973] 74-131579 ISBN 0-8401-0567-3
1. Christian union. I. Title.

EVENNETT, Henry Outram, 270.6
1901-1964.
The spirit of the Counter-Reformation: the Birkbeck lectures in ecclesiastical history given in the University of Cambridge in May 1951, by the late H. Outram Evennett; edited with a postscript by John Bossy. Cambridge, London, Cambridge U.P., 1968. xiii, 159 p. plate, port. 23 cm. Bibliography: p. 146-153. [BR430.E95] 68-11282 35/-
1. Counter-Reformation. I. Bossy, John, ed. II. Title.

FORELL, George Walfgang 270.6
Faith active in love; an investigation of the principles underlying Luther's social ethics. Minneapolis, Augsburg Pub. House [1960, c.1954] 198p. port. 20cm. Bibliography: p.190-198 2.00 pap.,
1. Luther, Martin, 1483-1546. 2. Sociology, Christian (Lutheran) 3. Social ethics. I. Title.

FORELL, George Wolfgang. 270.6
Faith active in love; an investigation of principles underlying Luther's social ethics. [1st ed.] New York, American Press [1954] 198p. port. 21cm. Bibliography: p. 190-198. [BR333.F58] 54-10896
1. Luther, Martin, 1483-1546. 2. Sociology, Christian (Lutheran) 3. Social ethics. I. Title.

FOSDICK, Harry Emerson, 270.6
1878- ed.
Great voices of the Reformation; an anthology. Edited, with an introd. and commentaries. New York, Modern Library [1954, c1952] 546p. 21cm. (The Modern library of the world's best books.[A Modern library giant, G-9]) [BX4801] 54-9973
1. Protestantism—Hist.—Sources. 2. Reformation— Sources. 3. Theology—Collections. I. Title.

FOSDICK, Harry Emerson, 270.6
1878-1969. ed.
Great voices of the Reformation, an anthology. New York, Random House [1952] xxx, 548 p. 22 cm. [BX4801.F6] 52-5550
1. Protestantism—History—Sources. 2. Reformation—Sources. 3. Theology—Collected works. I. Title.

GELDER, Herman Arend Enno 270.6
van, 1889-
The two reformations in the 16th century: a study of the religious aspects and consequences of Renaissance and humanism. [Tr. from Dutch by Jan F. Finlay, Alison Hanham] The Hague, M. Nijhoff [dist. New York, Heinman, 1962, c.]1961. x, 406p. 25cm. Bibl. 63-228 12.50
1. Reformation. 2. Humanism. I. Title.

GENSICHEN, Hans Werner 270.6
We condemn; how Luther and 16th-century Lutheranism condemned false doctrine. Tr. by Herbert J. A. Bouman. St. Louis, Concordia [1967] x, 213p. 24cm. Tr. of the author'sHabilitationsschrift. Gottingen, published in 1955 under title: Damnamus. Bibl. [BR333.G413] 67-17792 7.50
1. Luther, Martin, 1483-1546—Theology. 2. Heresies and heretics. 3. Reformation. I. Title.

GENSICHEN, Hans Werner. 270.6
We condemn: how Luther and 16th-century Lutheranism condemned false doctrine. Translated by Herbert J. A. Bouman. Saint Louis, Concordia Pub. House [1967] x, 213 p. 24 cm. A translation of the author's Habilitationsschrift, Gottingen, published in 1955 under title: Damnamus. Includes bibliographical references. [BR333.G413] 67-17792
1. Luther, Martin, 1483-1546—Theology. 2. Heresies and heretics. I. Title.

GRIMM, Harold John, 1901- 270.6
The Reformation [by] Harold J. Grimm. Washington, American Historical Association [1972] 34 p. 23 cm. (AHA pamphlets, 403) First published in 1964 under title: The Reformation in recent historical thought. Bibliography: p. 32-34. [BR309.G74 1972] 72-76717
1. Reformation. I. Series: American Historical Association. AHA pamphlets, 403.

GRIMM, Harold John, 1901- 270.6
The Reformation era, 1500-1650 [by] Harold J. Grimm. 2d ed. New York, Macmillan [1973] xiii, 594 p. illus. 24 cm. Bibliography: p. 509-580. [BR305.2.G74 1973] 72-91167 10.95
1. Reformation. I. Title.

GRIMM, Harold John, 1901- 270.6
The Reformation era, 1500-1650 New York, Macmillan [1954] 675 p. illus. 22 cm. [BR305.G74] 54-12610
1. Reformation. I. Title.

GRIMM, Harold John, 1901- 270.6
The Reformation era, 1500-1650; with a revised and expanded bibliography [by] Harold J. Grimm New York, Macmillan [1965] xiii, 703 p. maps. 22 cm. Bibliography: p. 617-684. [BR305.2.G74 1965] 65-25864
1. Reformation. I. Title.

HAGSTOTZ, Gideon David, 270.6
1896-
Heroes of the Reformation [by] Gideon David Hagstotz and Hilda Boettcher Hagstotz. Mountain View, Calif., Pacific Press Pub. Association [1951] 307 p. 23 cm. [BR315.H3] 51-7544
1. Reformers. 2. Reformation. I. Title.

HILLERBRAND, Hans Joachim. 270.6
Christendom divided; the Protestant Reformation [by] Hans J. Hillerbrand. New York, Corpus [1971] xiii, 344 p. 24 cm. (Theological resources) Bibliography: p. 321-336. [BR305.2.H49 1971] 70-93573 ISBN 0-664-20912-2 9.95
1. Reformation. I. Title.

HILLERBRAND, Hans Joachim. 270.6
The world of the Reformation [by] Hans J. Hillerbrand. New York, Scribner [1973] x, 229 p. map. 24 cm. Bibliography: p. 215-220. [BR305.2.H53 1973] 73-5175 ISBN 0-684-13534-5 10.00
1. Reformation. I. Title.

HOLL, Karl, 1866-1926. 270.6
The cultural significance of the Reformation. Introd. by Wilhelm Pauck. Translated by Karl and Barbara Hertz and John H. Lichtblau. New York, Meridian Books [1959] 191 p. 19 cm. (Living age books [LA25]) [BR307.H643] 59-7188
1. Reformation. I. Title.

HUGHES, Philip, 1895- 270.6
A popular history of the Reformation. [1st ed.] Garden City, N. Y., Hanover House [1957] 343 p. 22 cm. [BR305.H68] 57-5788
1. Reformation. I. Title.

ILLUSTRATED history of the 270.6
Reformation. Edited by Oskar Thulin. Translators: Jalo E. Nopola [and others] St. Louis, Concordia Pub. House [1967] 327 p. illus., facsims., maps, ports. 23 cm. Translation of Reformation in Europa. Bibliography: p. 319-321. [BR305.2.R413] 67-20941
1. Reformation. I. Thulin, Oskar, ed.

INTERNATIONALER Kongress 270.6
fur Lutherforschung. 2d Munster, 1960.
Luther and Melanchthon in the history and theology of the Reformation. Edited by Vilmos Vajta. Philadelphia, Muhlenberg Press [1961] 198p. 25cm. 'Published in Germany under the title Luther und Melanchthon.' Papers in English or German. Bibliographical footnotes. [BR300.I5 1960] 61-9253
1. Melanchthon, Phillip 1497-1560. 2. Luther, Martin—Congresses. I. Vajta, Vilmos, ed. II. Title.

JANELLE, Pierre 270.6
The Catholic reformation. Milwaukee, Bruce [1964, c.1963] 311p. 22cm. 63-21050 4.95; 2.25 pap.,
1. Counter-Reformation. I. Title.

JEDIN, Hubert, 1900- 270.6
A history of the Council of Trent. Tr. from German by Ernest Graf. St. Louis, Herder [1962, c.1957, 1961] 562p. illus. 25cm. Contents.v. 2, The first sessions at Trent, 1545-47. Bibl. A58 15.00
1. Trent, Council of, 1545-1563. I. Title.

JONES, Alonzo T. 270.6
Lessons from the Reformation. Boston, Forum [1961] 404p. 3.00
I. Title.

LAZARETH, William Henry, 270.6
1928-
Luther on the Christian home; an application of the social ethics of the Reformation. Philadelphia, Muhlenberg Press [1960] 244p. 22cm. 'A condensed adaptation of a doctoral dissertation approved in 1958 by the joint faculties of Columbia University and Union Theological Seminary.' Includes bibliography. [BR333.L32] 60-6184
1. Luther, Martin—Ethics. I. Title.

LENTZ, Harold H 270.6
Reformation crossroads; a comparison of the theology of Luther and Melanchthon. Minneapolis, Augsburg Pub. House [1958] 92p. 20cm. [BR333.L36] 58-11863
1. Mclanchthon, Philipp, 1497-1560. 2. Luther, Martin—Theology. I. Title.

LILJE, Hanns, 1899- 270.6
Luther now; translated by Carl J. Schindler. Philadelphia, Muhlenberg Press [1952] 190 p. 20 cm. Translation of Luther; Anbruch und Krise der Neuzeit. [BR325.L473] 52-9119
1. Luther, Martin, 1483-1546. 2. Reformation. I. Title.

LITTELL, Franklin Hamlin, 270.6
ed.
Reformation studies; essays in honor of Roland H. Bainton. Richmond, Va., Knox [c.1962] 285p. front. 25cm. Bibl. 62-16259 5.50
1. Bainton, Roland Herbert, 1894- 2. Reformation-Addresses, essays, lectures. I. Title.

LITTELL, Franklin Hamlin, 270.6
ed.
Reformation studies; essays in honor of Roland H. Bainton. Richmond, John Knox Press [1962] 285p. port. 25cm. Bibliographical references included in 'Notes and acknowledgments' (p. [254]-285) [BR309.L5] 62-16259
1. Bainton, Roland Herbert, 1894- 2. Reformation—Ad- dresses, essays, lectures. I. Title.
Contents omitted.

LORTZ, Joseph, 1887- 270.6
How the Reformation came. [Tr. from German by Ott M. Knab. New York] Herder [c.1964] 115 p. 21 cm. 63-18152 2.95
1. Reformation—Causes. I. Title.

LORTZ, Joseph, 1887- 270.6
The Reformation: a problem for today. Translated by John C. Dwyer. Westminster, Md., Newman Press, 1964. 261 p. 23 cm. Translation of Die Reformation als religioses Anliegen heute. Bibliographical footnotes. [BR305.2.L613] 63-12239
1. Reformation. I. Title.

LUTHER, Erasmus, and the 270.6
Reformation; a Catholic-Protestant reappraisal. Edited by John C. Olin, James D. Smart [and] Robert E. McNally. New York, Fordham University Press, 1969. x, 150 p. ports. (on lining papers) 22 cm. Essays presented at a conference held Oct. 20-21, 1967, and sponsored by Union Theological Seminary and Fordham University. Includes bibliographical references. [BR309.L84] 68-8749 6.00
1. Luther, Martin, 1483-1546. 2. Erasmus, Desiderius, d. 1536. 3. Reformation—Addresses, essays, lectures. I. Olin, John C., ed. II. Smart, James D., ed. III. McNally, Robert E., ed. IV. New York. Union Theological Seminary. V. Fordham University, New York.

MCLELLAND, Joseph C. 270.6
The Reformation and its significance today. Philadelphia, Westminster Press [1962] 238 p. 21 cm. Includes bibliography. [BR305.2.M3] 62-9810
1. Reformation. I. Title.

MOSSE, George Lachmann 270.6
The Reformation. 3d ed. [Gloucester, Mass., P. Smith, 1964, c.1953, 1963] 136p. 18cm. (Berkshire studies in European hist. rebound) Bibl. 2.50
1. Reformation. I. Title.

MOSSE, George Lachmann. 270.6
The Reformation. 3d ed. New York, Holt, Rinehart and Winston [1963] 136 p. 19 cm. (Berkshire studies in European history) [BR305.M96 1963] 63-11339
1. Reformation.

NICKERSON, Hoffman, 1888- 270.6
The loss of unity. Garden City, N. Y., Doubleday [1961] 360p. 61-12562 4.95
1. Reformation. I. Title.

NORWOOD, Frederick Abbott 270.6
The development of modern Christianity since 1500. Nashville, Abingdon [1964, c.1956] 256p. maps., diagrs. 23cm. (Apex bk., R3-195) Bibl. 1.95 pap.,
1. Church history—Modern period. I. Title.

NORWOOD, Frederick Abbott. 270.6
The development of modern Christianity since 1500 New York, Abingdon Press [c1956] 256p. maps. diagrs. 24cm. Includes bibliographies. [BR290.N6] 56-5371
1. Church history—Modern period. I. Title.

*O'CONNELL, Marvin R. 270.6
The counter reformation 1559-1610, by Marvin R. O'Connell. New York, Harper Torchbooks, [1974]. xv, 390 p. illus. 21 cm. [BR304] ISBN 0-06-131825-6. 3.95 (pbk.)
1. Counter-reformation. I. Title.

OZMENT, Steven E., comp. 270.6
The Reformation in medieval perspective. Edited with an introd. by Steven E. Ozment. Chicago, Quadrangle Books, 1971. xiv, 267 p. 22 cm. (Modern scholarship on European history) Contents.Contents.—Romantic and revolutionary elements in German theology on the eve of the Reformation, by G. Ritter.—Piety in Germany around 1500, by B. Moeller.—The crisis of the Middle Ages and the Hussites, by F. Graus.—On Luther and Ockham, bv P. Vignaux.—Facientibus quod in se est Deus non denegat gratiam: Robert Holcot O. P. and the beginnings of Luther's theology, by H. A. Oberman.—Home viator: Luther and late medieval theology, by S. E.

Ozment.—The Windesheimers after c. 1485: confrontation with the reformation and humanism, by R. R. Post.—Paracelsus, by A. Koyre.—Simul gemitus et raptus: Luther and mysticism, by H. A. Oberman.—Bibliography (p. 253-256) [BR309.O93] 72-152100 ISBN 0-8129-0194-0 12.50
1. Reformation—Addresses, essays, lectures. I. Title.

PELIKAN, Jaroslav Jan, 1923- 270.6
Obedient rebels; Catholic substance and Protestant principle in Luther's Reformation. [1st ed.] New York, Harper & Row [1964] 212 p. 24 cm. Bibliographical footnotes. [BR307.P4] 64-20200
1. Reformation. 2. Catholic Church—Relations—Protestant churches. 3. Protestant church—Relations—Catholic Church. I. Title.

PELIKAN, Jaroslaw, 1923- 270.6
Obedient rebels; Catholic substance and Protestant principle in Luther's Reformation. New York, Harper [c.1964] 212p. 24cm. Bibl. 64-20200 5.00
1. Reformation. 2. Catholic Church—Relations—Protestant churches. 3. Protestant church—Relations—Catholic Church. I. Title.

PORTEOUS, David. 270.6
Calendar of the Reformation. Pref. by Joseph Zacchello. New York, Loizeaux Bros. [1960] 96p. 21cm. Includes bibliography. [BR307.P65] 60-51665
1. Reformation. 2. Calendars. I. Title.

PRENTER, Regin, 1907- 270.6
Spiritus Creator; translated by John M. Jensen. Philadelphia, Muhlenberg Press [1953] 311p. 22cm. [BR333.P714] 53-8256
1. Luther, Martin, 1483-1546. 2. Holy Spirit—History of doctrines. I. Title.

REID, William Stanford, 1913- comp. 270.6
The Reformation: revival or revolution? Edited by W. Stanford Reid. New York, Holt, Rinehart and Winston [1968] 122 p. illus. 24 cm. (European problem studies) Bibliography: p. 119-122. [BR309.R4] 68-28181
1. Reformation—Addresses, essays, lectures. I. Title.

ROBINSON, William Childs, 1897- 270.6
The Reformation; a rediscovery of grace. Grand Rapids, Eerdmans [1962] 189 p. 23 cm. [BT27.R6] 62-21373
1. Reformation. 2. Theology, Doctrinal—History—16th cen.

SANDSTROM, Peter G. 270.6
Luther's sense of himself. as an interpreter of the Word to the world. Amherst, Mass., Amhherst Coll. Pr. [dist. Jeffrey Amherst Bkshop., [c.]1961. 63p. (Amherst Coll. honors thesis no. 8) Bibl. 61-16137 .95 pap.,
1. Luther, Martin—Theology. I. Title.

SEARLE, Graham William. 270.6
The Counter Reformation / G. W. Searle. Totowa, N.J. : Rowman and Littlefield, 1974 [i.e. 1975] c1973. 189 p. : ill. ; 22 cm. Includes index. Bibliography: p. [182]-184. [BR430.S42 1975] 75-305055 ISBN 0-87471-528-8 : 7.50. ISBN 0-87471-529-6 pbk. : 3.75
1. Counter-Reformation.

SEEBOHM, Frederic, 1833-1912. 270.6
The era of the Protestant revolution. 2d ed. New York, AMS Press [1971] xv, 250 p. maps. 19 cm. Reprint of the 1903 ed. Bibliography: p. 239 246. [D228.S4 1971] 77-147114 ISBN 0-404-05695-4
1. Reformation. I. Title.

SIMON, Edith. 270.6
Luther alive; Martin Luther and the making of the Reformation. [1st ed.] Garden City, N.Y., Doubleday, 1968. xi, 371 p. col. map (on lining papers) 24 cm. (The Crossroads of world history series) Bibliography: p. [361]-364. [BR325.S49] 68-14194
1. Luther, Martin, 1483-1546. 2. Reformation. I. Title.

SIMON, Edith, 1917- 270.6
The Reformation, by Edith Simon and the editors of Time-Life books. New York, Time, inc. [1966] 191 p. illus. (part col.) facsims., col. maps, ports. (part col.) 28 cm. (Great ages of man) Bibliography: p. 186. [BR305.2.S5] 66-22782
1. Reformation.

THE Social history of the Reformation. 270.6 Edited by Lawrence P. Buck and Jonathan W. Zophy. Columbus, Ohio State University Press [1972] xxiv, 397 p. 24 cm. "In honor of Harold J. Grimm." [BR307.S6] 72-5952 ISBN 0-8142-0174-1 12.50
1. Grimm, Harold John, 1901- 2. Reformation—Addresses, essays, lectures. I. Grimm, Harold John, 1901- II. Buck, Lawrence P., 1944- ed. III. Zophy, Jonathan W., 1945- ed.

SPIRITUAL and Anabaptist writers. 270.6 Documents illustrative of the Radical Reformation, edited by George Huntston Williams, and Evangelical Catholicism as represented by Juan de Valdes, edited by Angel M. Mergal. Philadelphia, West-minster Press [1957] 421 p. 24 cm. (The Library of Christian classics, v. 25) [BR301.S67] 57-5003
1. Reformation—Sources. 2. Anabaptists. I. Williams, George Hunston, 1914- ed. II. Valdes, Juan de, d. 1541.

SPITZ, Lewis William, 1922- ed. 270.6
The Protestant Reformation. Edited by Lewis W. Spitz. Englewood Cliffs, N.J., Prentice-Hall [1966] viii, 178 p. 21 cm. (A Spectrum book, S-140.) (Sources of civilization in the West) Bibliography: p. 177-178. [BR301.S68] 66-16344
1. Reformation—Sources. I. Title. II. Series.

SPITZ, Lewis William, 1922- ed. 270.6
The Reformation; basic interpretations. Edited and with an introd. by Lewis W. Spitz. 2d ed. Lexington, Mass., Heath [1972] xxi, 221 p. 21 cm. (Problems in European civilization) Contents.Contents.—Bainton, R. H. Interpretations of the Reformation.—Dilthey, W. The interpretation and analysis of man in the 15th and 16th centuries.—Troeltsch, E. Renaissance and Reformation.—Spitz, L. W. The third generation of German Renaissance humanists.—Walker, P. C. G. Capitalism and the Reformation.—Holborn, H. The social basis of the German Reformation.—Grimm, H. J. Social forces in the German Reformation.—Lea, H. C. The eve of the Reformation.—Lortz, J. Why did the Reformation happen?—Ritter, G. Why the Reformation occured in Germany.—Barth, K. Reformation as decision.—Luther, M. Luther's road to the Reformation.—Erikson, E. H. Young man Luther.—Bainton, R. H. Luther's struggle for faith.—Bibliography (p. 213-221) [CB359.S64 1972] 72-2273 ISBN 0-669-81620-5
1. Reformation—Addresses, essays, lectures. I. Title. II. Series.

STEVENSON, William, 1901- 270.6
The story of the Reformation. Richmond, John Knox Press [1959] 206 p. 21 cm. Includes bibliography. [BR305.2.S8] 59-10517
1. Reformation. I. Title.

STEVENSON, William, 1901- 270.6
The story of the Reformation. Richmond, John Knox Press [1959] 206 p. 21 cm. Includes bibliography. [BR305.2.S8] 59-10517
1. Reformation.

SWANSON, Guy E. 270.6
Religion and regime; a sociological account of the reformation, by Guy E. Swanson. Ann Arbor, University of Michigan Press [1967] x, 295 p. 21 cm. Bibliographical references included in "Notes" (p. 263-291) [BR307.S9] 67-11979
1. Reformation. 2. Protestantism. 3. Religion and sociology. I. Title.

*SYKES, Norman 270.6
The crisis of the Reformation. New York, Norton [1967, c.1946] 122p. 20cm. (Norton lib., N380) 4.00; 1.25 pap.,
1. Reformation. I. Title.

SYKES, Norman, 1897-1961. 270.6
The crisis of the Reformation. New York, W. W. Norton [1967, c1946] 122 p. 21 cm. [BR305.S8 1967] 67-3850
1. Reformation. I. Title.

TAVARD, Georges Henri 270.6
Protestantism. Translated from the French by Rachel Attwater. New York, Hawthorn Books [c.1959] 139p. 21cm. (The Twentieth century encyclopedia of Catholicism, v.137. Section 13: Outside the church) (2p. bibl.) 59-12170 2.95 bds.,
1. Protestantism. I. Title.

TAVARD, Georges Henri, 1922- 270.6
Protestantism. Translated from the French by Rachel Attwater. [1st ed.] New York, Hawthorn Books [1959] 139 p. 21 cm. (The Twentieth century encyclopedia of Catholicism, v. 137. Section 13: Outside the church) Includes bibliography. [BX4817.T313] 59-12170
1. Protestantism. I. Title.

TILLMANNS, Walter G 270.6
The world and men around Luther. Illus. by Edmund Kopietz. Minneapolis, Augsburg Pub. House [1959] 384 p. illus. 23 cm. Includes bibliography. [BR305.2.T54] 59-11714
1. Luther, Martin, 1483-1546. 2. Reformation. 3. Reformation—Biog. I. Title.

TJERNAGEL, Neelak Serawlook, 1906- 270.6
Henry VIII and the Lutherans; a study in Anglo-Lutheran relations from 1521 to 1547. St. Louis, Concordia [c.]1965. xii, 326p. 24cm. Bibl. [DA332.T55] 63-12302 6.95
1. Henry VIII, King of England, 1491-1547. 2. Church of England—Relations—Lutheran Church. 3. Lutheran Church—Relations—Church of England. 4. Reformation—England. I. Title.

TODD, John Murray. 270.6
Reformation [by] John M. Todd. Garden City, N.Y., Doubleday, 1971. 377 p. 22 cm. Bibliography: p. [360]-371. [BR305.2.T58] 75-157629 7.95
1. Reformation.

TORBET, Robert George, 1912- 270.6
The Protestant Reformation, a cooperative text. Philadelphia, Published for the Cooperative Publication Association, by the Judson Press [1961] 96 p. 19 cm. (Faith for life series) [BR306.T65] 61-19282
1. Reformation — Hist. I. Title.

TORBET, Robert George, 1912- 270.6
The Protestant Reformation, a cooperative text. Philadelphia, Published for the Cooperative Publication Assn., by Judson Pr. [c.1961] 96p. e(Faith for life ser.) 61-19282 1.00 pap.,
1. Reformation—Hist. I. Title.

VAN TIL, Henry R 270.6
The Calvinistic concept of culture. Grand Rapids, Baker Book House, 1959. 245 p. 23 cm. Includes bibliography. [BR115.C8V3] 00-1114
1. Culture. 2. Calvinism. I. Title.

VAN TIL, Henry R. 270.6
The Calvinistic concept of culture. Grand Rapids, Baker Bk. House [1972, c.1959] 245 p. 22 cm. (Twin books ser.) Bibl. refs. [BR118C8V3] 60-1114 ISBN 0-8010-9258-2 pap., 3.95
1. Culture. 2. Calvinism. I. Title.

VERDUIN, Leonard. 270.6
The reformers and their stepchildren. Grand Rapids, Mich., Eerdmans [1964] 292 p. 24 cm. "Bibliographical footnotes": p. 282-288. [BR307.V4] 64-16595
1. Reformation. 2. Church — History of doctrines — 16th cent. 3. Church and state — Hist. I. Title.

VERDUIN, Leonard 270.6
The reformers and their stepchildren. Grand Rapids, Mich., Eerdmans [c.1964] 292p. 24cm. Bibl. [BR307.V4] 64-16595 5.75
1. Reformation. 2. Church—History of doctrines—16th cent. 3. Church and state—Hist. I. Title.

ZEEDEN, Ernst Walter. 270.6
The legacy of Luther; Martin Luther and the Reformation in the estimation of the German Lutherans from Luther's death to the beginning of the age of Goethe. [Translation from the original German by Ruth Mary Bethell] Westminster, Md., Newman Press [1954] xiii, 221p. ports. 22cm. Translation of v. 1 of Martin Luther und die Reformation im Urteil des deutschen Luthertums. 'In the German edition a second volume has been prepared reproducing the texts of the more important documents on which the work is based ... For the English edition this second volume has not been translated.' [BR325.Z43] 54-97533
1. Luther, Martin, 1483-1546. 2. Lutheran Church—Hist. I. Title.

ZWINGLI. ULRICH, 1484-1531. 270.6
Zwingli and Bullinger: selected translations with introductions and notes by G. W. Bromiley. Philadelphia, Westmister Press [1953] 364p. 24cm. (The Library of Christian classics, v. 24) Bibliography: p. 353-357. [BR346.A24] 53-1533
1. Reformed Church—Collected works. 2. Theology—Collected works—16th cent. I. Bullinger, Heinrich, 1504-1575. II. Bromiley, G. W., ed. and tr. III. Title. IV. Series.

MARTIN Luther lectures. 270.604
Decorah, Iowa, Luther College Press [1957- v. 22 cm. Lectures, sponsored by Luther College, were inaugurated in 1956. [BR326.M34] 57-9726
1. Luther, Martin—Addresses, essays, lectures. I. Luther College, Decorah, Iowa.

HILLERBRAND, Hans Joachim, comp. 270.6'08
The Protestant Reformation, edited by Hans J. Hillerbrand. New York, Walker [1968] xxvii, 290 p. 24 cm. (Documentary history of Western civilization) Includes bibliographical references. [BR301.H64 1968b] 68-3924
1. Reformation—Sources. I. Title.

HILLERBRAND, Hans Joachim, comp. 270.6'08
The Protestant Reformation, edited by Hans J. Hillerbrand. [1st ed.] New York, Harper & Row [1968] xxvii, 290 p. 21 cm. (Documentary history of Western civilization) (Harper torchbooks, TB1342.) Includes bibliographical references. [BR301.H64 1968] 68-13328
1. Reformation—Sources. I. Title.

HURSTFIELD, Joel, ed. 270.608
The Reformation crisis. New York, Barnes & Noble [1966, c1965] ix, 126 p. 21 cm. Consists chiefly of talks broadcast by the B. B. C. in 1962, here revised with two new chapters added. Bibliography: p. [119]-120. [BR309.H77 1966] 66-3534
1. Reformation — Addresses, essays, lectures. Title. I. Title.

HURSTFIELD, Joel, ed. 270.608
The Reformation crisis. New York, Barnes & Noble [1966, c.1965] ix, 126p. 21cm. Bibl. [BR309.H77] 66-3534 3.00 bds.,
1. Reformation—Addresses, essays, lectures. I. Title.

KIDD, Beresford James, 1863-1948. 270.6'08
Documents illustrative of the Continental Reformation; edited by B. J. Kidd. 1st ed. reprinted. Oxford, Clarendon P., 1967. xix, 743 p. 20 cm. Contributions in English, Latin and French. [BR301.K4 1967] 68-75422 50/-
1. Reformation—Sources. I. Title.

KOHLER, Hans-Joachim. 270.6'08 s
Obrigkeitliche Konfessionsanderung in Kondominaten : eine Fallstudie uber ihre Bedingungen und Methoden am Beispiel der Baden-Badischen Religionspolitik unter der Regierung Markgraf Wilhelms (1622-1677) / von Hans-Joachim Kohler. Munster : Aschendorff, 1975. viii, 240 p. : col. maps ; 23 cm. (Reformationsgeschichtliche Studien und Texte ; Heft 110) Originally presented as the author's thesis, Tubingen, 1973. Includes index. Bibliography: p. [222]-232. [BR302.R4 Heft 110] [BR857.B3] 274.3'46 76-460411 ISBN 3-402-03717-3
1. Wilhelm, Margraf von Baden, 1593-1677. 2. Baden—Church history. 3. Baden—Politics and government. I. Title. II. Series.

OLIN, John C., comp. 270.6'08
The Catholic reformation: Savonarola to Ignatius Loyola; reform in the Church 1495-1540 [by] John C. Olin. [1st ed.] New York, Harper & Row [1969] xxvi, 220 p. illus., facsims., ports. 25 cm. A selection of documents in English translation with background material. Contents.Contents.—Savonarola On the renovation of the Church, 1495.—The oratory of divine love, 1497.—Colet's Convocation sermon, 1512.—Egidio da Viterbo's Address to the Fifth Lateran Council, 1512.—The reform bull Supernae dispositionis arbitrio, 1514.—Erasmus' Sileni Alcibiadis, 1515.—Contarini's De officio episcopi, 1516.—Lefevre's Preface to his Commentaries on the Four Gospels, 1521.—Adrian VI's Instruction to Chieregati, 1522.—The Theatine rule of 1526.—Giberti's Constitutions, after 1527.—The Capuchin Constitutions of 1536.—The Consilium de emendanda ecclesia, 1537.—St. Ignatius Loyola and the founding of the Jesuits. "Bibliographical postscript": p. [212]-214. Bibliographical footnotes. [BR430.O4] 69-17021 8.50
1. Counter-Reformation—Sources. I. Title.

HILLERBRAND, Hans Joachim, ed. 270.6082
The Reformation; a narrative history related by contemporary observers and participants [edited by] Hans J. Hillerbrand. [1st ed.] New York, Harper & Row [1964] 495 p. illus., facsims., ports. 25 cm. London ed. (Student Christian Movement Press) has title: The Reformation in its own words. Includes bibliographies. [BR305.2.H5 1964] 64-15480
1. Reformation.

BAINTON, Roland Herbert, 1894- 270.6'092'2 B
Women of the Reformation in France and England [by] Roland H. Bainton. Minneapolis, Augsburg Pub. House [1973] 287 p. illus. 23 cm. Bibliography: p. 277. [BR317.B29] 73-78269 ISBN 0-8066-1333-5 8.95
1. Reformation—Biography. 2. Woman—Biography. I. Title.

BAINTON, Roland Herbert, 1894- 270.6'092'2 B
Women of the Reformation in France and England / Roland H. Bainton. Boston : Beacon Press, 1975, c1973. 287 p. : ill. ; 20 cm. Reprint of the ed. published by Augsburg Pub. House, Minneapolis. Includes index.

Bibliography: p. 277. [BR317.B29 1975] 75-19393 ISBN 0-8070-5649-9 pbk. : 4.45
1. Reformation—Biography. 2. Women—Biography. I. Title.

BAINTON, Roland 270.6'0922 B
Herbert, 1894-
Women of the Reformation in Germany and Italy, by Roland H. Bainton. Minneapolis, Augsburg Pub. House [1971] 279 p. illus., facsims., geneal. table, maps, ports. 23 cm. Includes bibliographies. [BR317.B3 1971] 70-135235 7.95
1. Reformation—Biography. 2. Woman—Biography. I. Title.

BAINTON, Roland 270.6'092'2 B
Herbert, 1894-
Women of the Reformation in Germany and Italy, by Roland H. Bainton. Boston, Beacon Press [1974, c1971] 279 p. illus. 21 cm. (Beacon paperback, 485) Reprint of the ed. published by Augsburg Pub. House, Minneapolis. Includes bibliographies. [BR317.B3 1974] 74-6085 ISBN 0-8070-5651-0 3.95
1. Reformation—Biography. 2. Woman—Biography. I. Title.

GARVER, Isobel M. 270.6'092'2 B
Our Christian heritage. Artist: Isobel M. Garver. Author: Stuart P. Garver. Hackensack, N.J., Christ's Mission [1973] 103 p. illus. (part col.) 29 cm. [BR315.G3] 73-77907
1. Reformation—Biography. I. Garver, Stuart P. II. Title.

GARVER, Isobel M. 270.6'092'2 B
Our Christian heritage. Artist: Isobel M. Garver. Author: Stuart P. Garver. Hackensack, N.J., Christ's Mission [1973] 103 p. illus. (part col.) 29 cm. [BR315.G3] 73-77907
1. Reformation—Biography. I. Garver, Stuart P. II. Title.
Publisher's address: 275 State, Hackensack, N.J. 07304.

GERRISH, Brian Albert, 270.6'0922
1931-
Reformers in profile. Ed. by B. A. Gerrish. Philadelphia, Fortress [1967] vii, 264p. 23cm. Bibl. [BR315.G4] 67-27134 5.95
1. Reformation—Biog. I. Title.
Contents Omitted.

JONES, Rosemary 270.6'0922
Devonshire.
Erasmus and Luther, by R. Devonshire Jones. London, Oxford U.P., 1968. 96 p. 12 plates, illus., facsims., map (on lining paper), ports. 21 cm. (The Clarendon biographies, 13) Bibliography: p. 91-93. [BR350.E7J58] 74-355482 12/6
1. Erasmus, Desiderius, d. 1536. 2. Luther, Martin, 1483-1546.

RUPP, Ernest Gordon. 270.6'0922
Patterns of reformation, by Gordon Rupp. Philadelphia, Fortress Press [1969] xxiii, 427 p. illus. 26 cm. Contents.Contents.—Johannes Oecolampadius; the reformer as scholar.—Andrew Karlstadt; the reformer as Puritan.—Thomas Muntzer; the reformer as rebel.—A sixteenth-century Dr. Johnson and his Boswell; the reformer as layman. Bibliographical footnotes. [BR315.R86] 69-14626 9.50
1. Oecolampadius, Joannes, 1482-1531. 2. Karlstadt, Andreas Rudolf, 1480 (ca.)-1541. 3. Munzer, Thomas, 1490 (ca.)-1525. 4. Vadianus, Joachim, 1484-1551. 5. Kessler, Johannes, 1502?-1574. I. Title.

STEINMETZ, David 270.6'0922 B
Curtis.
Reformers in the wings [by] David C. Steinmetz. Philadelphia, Fortress Press [1971] viii, 240 p. 23 cm. Includes bibliographies. [BR315.S83] 75-135266 ISBN 0-8006-0051-7 8.50
1. Reformation—Biography. I. Title.

MCNAIR, Philip 270.6'09224(B)
Murray Jourdan
Peter Martyr in Italy; an anatomy of apostacy, by Philip McNair. Oxford, Clarendon Pr., 1967. xxii, 325p. front. (port.) table. 23cm. Bibl. [BR350.V37M3] 67-78940 8.80
1. Vermigli, Pietro Martire, 1499-1562. I. Title.
Available from Oxford Univ. Pr. in New York.

ATKINSON, James, 1914- 270.6'0924
Martin Luther and the birth of Protestantism. Harmondsworth, Penguin, 1968. 352 p. 2 maps. 19 cm. (Pelican books, A865) 7/6 Bibliography: p. [337]-340. [BR325.A8] 68-115719
1. Luther, Martin, 1483-1546. I. Title.

ATKINSON, James, 1914- 270.6'0924
The trial of Luther. New York, Stein and Day [1971] 212 p. illus., facsims., ports. 23 cm. (Historic trials series) Bibliography: p. [203] [BR326.5.A8] 72-104626 ISBN 0-8128-1361-8 7.95
1. Luther, Martin, 1483-1546. 2. Worms, Diet of, 1521. I. Title.

EDWARDS, Mark U. 270.6'092'4
Luther and the false brethren / Mark U. Edwards, Jr. Stanford, Calif. : Stanford University Press, 1975. viii, 242 p. ; 23 cm. Includes bibliographical references and index. [BR325.E34] 75-181 ISBN 0-8047-0883-5 : 10.00
1. Luther, Martin, 1483-1546. I. Title.

ERASMUS, 270.6'092'4 B
Desiderius, d.1536.
Christian humanism and the Reformation : selected writings of Erasmus, with The life of Erasmus by Beatus Rhenanus / edited by John C. Olin. 2d rev. ed. New York : Fordham University Press, 1975. x, 202 p. : ill. ; 22 cm. Includes index. Bibliography: p. 195-199. [BR75.E743 1975] 76-353637 ISBN 0-8232-0987-3. pbk. : 5.00
1. Erasmus, Desiderius, d. 1536. I. Rhenanus, Beatus, 1485-1547. II. Olin, John C. III. Title.
Contents omitted

FARNER, Oskar, 1884- 270.6'0924 B
Zwingli the reformer; his life and work. Translated by D. G. Sear. [Hamden, Conn.] Archon Books, 1968. 135 p. facsims., ports. 18 cm. Reprint of the 1952 ed. Translation of Huldrych Zwingli, der schweizerische Reformator. [BR345.F295 1968] 68-8017 ISBN 0-208-00694-X
1. Zwingli, Ulrich, 1484-1531. I. Title.

FIFE, Robert 270.6'0924 B
Herndon, 1871-1958.
Young Luther; the intellectual and religious development of Martin Luther to 1518. New York, AMS Press [1970] 232 p. 19 cm. Reprint of the 1928 ed. Includes bibliographical references. [BR325.F54 1970] 79-131040
1. Luther, Martin, 1483-1546. I. Title.

FREYTAG, Gustav, 270.6'092'4 B
1816-1895.
Martin Luther. Translated by Henry E. O. Heinemann. Chicago, Open Court Pub. Co., 1897. [New York, AMS Press, 1972] vi, 130 p. illus. 23 cm. Translation of Doktor Luther. [BR325.F73 1972] 78-144612 ISBN 0-404-02577-3 10.00
1. Luther, Martin, 1483-1546.

FRIEDENTHAL, Richard, 270.6'0924
1896-
Luther; his life and times. Translated from the German by John Nowell. [1st American ed.] New York, Harcourt, Brace, Jovanovich [1970] viii, 566 p. illus., ports. 24 cm. "A Helen and Kurt Wolff book." Includes bibliographical references. [BR325.F7713 1970] 72-124834 ISBN 1-515-47858-
1. Luther, Martin, 1483-1546.

ISERLOH, Erwin. 270.6'0924
The theses were not posted; Luther between reform and Reformation. Introd. by Martin E. Marty. [Translated by Jared Wicks] Boston, Beacon Press [1968] xx, 116 p. facsims. 21 cm. Translation of Luther zwischen Reform und Reformation. Bibliography: p. 111-112. [BR325.I813] 68-14706
1. Luther, Martin, 1483-1546. I. Title.

JACKSON, Samuel 270.6'0924 B
Macauley, 1851-1912.
Huldreich Zwingli, 1484-1531, the reformer of German Switzerland. Together with an historical survey of Switzerland before the Reformation, by Prof. John Martin Vincent ... and a chapter on Zwingli's theology, by Prof. Frank Hugh Foster. New York, Putnam, 1901. St. Clair Shores, Mich., Scholarly Press [1969] xxvi, 519 p. illus., facsims., plan, ports. 22 cm. (Heroes of the Reformation [v. 5]) Bibliography: p. xxi-xxvi. [BR345.J3 1969] 70-8883
1. Zwingli, Ulrich, 1484-1531. 2. Reformation—Switzerland. I. Vincent, John Martin, 1857-1939. II. Foster, Frank Hugh, 1851-1935.

JACKSON, Samuel 270.6'092'4 B
Macauley, 1851-1912.
Huldreich Zwingli, the reformer of German Switzerland, 1484-1531. Together with an historical survey of Switzerland before the Reformation, by John Martin Vincent; and a chapter on Zwingli's theology by Frank Hugh Foster. 2d ed. rev. New York, Putnam. [New York, AMS Press, 1972] xxvi, 519 p. illus. 19 cm. Reprint of the 1901 ed., which was issued as v. 5 of Heroes of the Reformation. Bibliography: p. xxi-xxvi. [BR345.J3 1972] 75-170836 ISBN 0-404-03543-4
1. Zwingli, Ulrich, 1484-1531. 2. Reformation—Switzerland. I. Vincent, John Martin, 1857-1939. II. Foster, Frank Hugh, 1851-1935. III. Title.

THE last days of 270.6'0924 B
Luther, by Justus Jonas, Michael Coelius, and others. Translated and annotated by Martin Ebon. With an introd. by Theodore G. Tappert. [1st ed.] Garden City, N.Y., Doubleday, 1970. 120 p. 3 fold. maps. 22 cm. Translation of Vom christlichen Abschied aus diesem todlichen Leben des Ehrwerdigen Herrn D. M. Lutheri, originally published in Wittenberg in 1546. Facsim. of the German text and English translation on opposite pages (p. 45-103). Contents.Contents.—Luther and death, by T. G. Tappert.—Only thirty-one days, by M. Ebon.—Biographical notes.—Concerning the Christian departure from this mortal life of the Reverend Dr. Martin Luther, by J. Jonas, M. Coelius, and others who were present.—Martin Luther-life chronology.—Chronology: January 23 to February 22, 1546.—Bibliography (p. 117-120) [BR325.V57] 74-120743 5.00
1. Luther, Martin, 1483-1546. I. Jonas, Justus, 1493-1555. II. Caelius, Michael, 1492-1559. III. Ebon, Martin, tr.

LILJE, Hanns, Bp., 270.6'0924
1899-
Luther and the Reformation; an illustrated review, by Hanns Lilje in collaboration with Karl F. Reinking. American ed. Translated and eidted by Martin O. Dietrich. Philadelphia, Fortress Press,[1967] 223 p. illus., facsims., ports. 23 cm. Translation of Martin Luther; eine Bildmonographie. [BR325.L4743] 67-24339
1. Luther, Martin, 1483-1546. I. Reinking, Karl Frans. II. Title.

LILJE, Hanns, Bp., 270.6'0924
1899-
Luther and the Reformation; an illustrated review, by Hanns Lilje in collaboration with Karl F. Reinking. American ed. Translated and edited by Martin O. Dietrich. Philadelphia, Fortress Press [1967] 223 p. illus., facsims., ports. 23 cm. Translation of Martin Luther: eine Bildmonographie. [BR325.L4743] 67-24339
1. Luther, Martin, 1483-1546. I. Reinking, Karl Franz. II. Title.

LINDSAY, Thomas 270.6'0924 B
Martin, 1843-1914.
Luther and the German Reformation. Freeport, N.Y., Books for Libraries Press [1970] xii, 300 p. 23 cm. Reprint of the 1900 ed. "Chronological summary of the history of the Reformation": p. 267-291. Bibliography: p. 293-296. [BR325.L48 1970] 71-133524
1. Luther, Martin, 1483-1546. 2. Reformation—Germany. I. Title.

MANSCHRECK, Clyde 270.6'092'4 B
Leonard, 1917-
Melanchthon, the quiet reformer / Clyde Leonard Manschreck. Westport, Conn. : Greenwood Press, 1975, c1958. 350 p., [1] leaf of plates : ill. ; 23 cm. Reprint of the ed. published by Abingdon Press, New York. Includes index. Includes bibliographical references. [BR335.M3 1975] 73-21263 ISBN 0-8371-6131-2 : 17.50
1. Melanchthon, Philipp, 1497-1560. I. Title.

MATHESON, Peter. 270.6'092'4 B
Cardinal Contarini at Regensburg. Oxford, Clarendon Press, 1972. x, 193 p. 23 cm. Bibliography: p. [183]-190. [BX4705.C774M38] 72-180270 ISBN 0-19-826431-3 £3.25
1. Contarini, Gasparo, Cardinal, 1484-1542. 2. Ratisbon, Colloquy of, 1941. I. Title.

MEE, Charles L. 270.6'092'4 B
White robe, black robe [by] Charles L. Mee, Jr. New York, Putnam [1972] 316 p. 22 cm. Bibliography: p. 301-303. [BR325.M4125 1972] 76-183547 7.95
1. Luther, Martin, 1483-1546. 2. Leo X, Pope, 1475-1521. 3. Reformation. I. Title.

OLSEN, Viggo Norskov. 270'.6'0924
John Foxe and the Elizabethan church [by] V. Norskov Olsen. Berkeley, University of California Press, 1973. xii, 264 p. 23 cm. Based on the author's thesis, University of London. Bibliography: p. 224-248. [BR754.F6O58 1973] 70-165231 ISBN 0-520-02075-8 11.50
1. Foxe, John, 1516-1587. 2. Church—History of doctrines—16th century. I. Title.

PELIKAN, Jaroslav Jan, 270.6'0924
1923-
Spirit versus structure; Luther and the institutions of the church [by] Jaroslav Pelikan. [1st ed.] New York, Harper & Row [1968] x, 149 p. 21 cm. Bibliographical references included in "Notes" (p. 140-149) [BR325.P45] 68-29557
1. Luther, Martin, 1483-1546. 2. Reformation. I. Title.

PITTENGER, William 270.6'0924
Norman, 1905-
Martin Luther: the great reformer, by W. Norman Pittenger. [1st ed.] New York, Watts [1969] ix, 182 p. 22 cm. (Immortals of philosophy and religion) Bibliography: p. 175-176. [BR325.P53] 69-11189
1. Luther, Martin, 1483-1546.

POTTER, George 270.6'092'4 B
Richard, 1900-
Zwingli / G. R. Potter. Cambridge ; New York : Cambridge University Press, 1976. p. cm. Includes index. [BR345.P68] 75-46136 ISBN 0-521-20939-0 ; 43.50
1. Zwingli, Ulrich, 1484-1531.

RICHARD, James 270.6'092'4 B
William, 1843-1909.
Philip Melanchthon, the Protestant preceptor of Germany, 1497-1560. New York, B. Franklin Reprint [1974] xv, 399 p. illus. 23 cm. (Burt Franklin research & source work series, 139. Philosophy and religious history monographs) Reprint of the 1898 ed. published by Putnam, New York, which was issued as v. 2 of the series, Heroes of the Reformation. Includes bibliographical references. [BR335.R5 1974] 72-82414 ISBN 0-8337-4341-4 18.50
1. Melanchthon, Philipp, 1497-1560.

RUPP, Ernest Gordon, 270.6'0924 B
comp.
Martin Luther. Edited by E. G. Rupp and Benjamin Drewery. New York, St. Martin's Press [1970] xii, 179, [1] p. 21 cm. (Documents of modern history) Bibliography: p. [180] [BR331.E5R86 1970b] 79-124955 6.00
1. Lutheran Church—Collected works. 2. Theology—Collected works—16th century. I. Drewery, Benjamin, joint comp. II. Luther, Martin, 1483-1546.

SMITH, Preserved, 270.6'0924
1880-1941.
The life and letters of Martin Luther. New York, Barnes & Noble [1968] xvi, 490 p. illus., facsim., ports. 23 cm. Reprint of the 1911 ed. Bibliography: p. [433]-470. [BR325.S6 1968] 68-20697
1. Luther, Martin, 1483-1546. I. Title.

URBAN, Georg, ed. 270.6'092'4
Philipp Melanchthon, 1497-1560; Gedenkschrift zum 400. Todestag des Reformators 19. April 1560/1560. 2. erweiterte Aufl. Bretten, Melanchthonverein, 1960. 224 p. illus., ports., facsims. 24 cm. Includes bibliographies. [BR335.U6] 61-42769
I. Melanchthon, Philipp, 1497-1560. II. Title.

ZWINGLI, Ulrich, 270.6'092'4
1484-1531.
Selected works. Edited by Samuel Macauley Jackson. Introd. by Edward Peters [Translations from the German by Lawrence A. McLouth; translations from the Latin by Henry Preble and George W. Gilmore] Philadelphia, University of Pennsylvania Press [1972, c1901] xxx, 258 p. 21 cm. Original ed. issued as v. 1 of Translations and reprints from the original sources of European history, ser. 2. Bibliography: p. xxx. [BR410.Z87 1972b] 73-151482 ISBN 0-8122-7670-1 12.50
1. Reformation—Switzerland. I. Series: Pennsylvania. University. Dept. of History. Translations and reprints from the original sources of history, ser. 2, v. 1.

DICKENS, Arthur 270.6'0942
Geoffrey. comp.
The Reformation in England: to the accession of Elizabeth 1; edited by A. G. Dickens, Dorothy Carr. New York, St. Martins, 1968 [c. 1967] viii, 168p. 21cm. (Documents of modern hist.) Bibl. [BR375.D52] 2.00 pap.,
1. Gt. Brit.—Hist.—Henry VIII, 1509-1547—Sources. 2. Reformation—England. I. Carr, Dorothy. joint comp. II. Title.

DICKENS, Arthur 270.6'0942
Geoffrey.
The Reformation in England, to the accession of Elizabeth I. edited by A. G. Dickens and Dorothy Carr. New York, St. Martin's Press, 1968 [c1967] vii, 167, [1] p. 20 cm. (Documents of modern history) Bibliography: p. [168] [BR375.D52 1968] 67-29568
1. Reformation—England—Sources. I. Carr, Dorothy, joint author. II. Title.

GAIRDNER, James, 1828- 270.6'0942
1912.
Lollardy and the Reformation in England; an historical survey. New York, B. Franklin [1968] 4 v. 24 cm. (Burt Franklin research and source work series, no. 84) Reprint of the 1908-13 ed. Vol. 4 edited by William Hunt. Bibliographical footnotes. [BR375.G3 1968] 76-6834
1. Lollards. 2. Reformation—England. I. Hunt, William, 1842-1931, ed. II. Title.

CRAGG, Gerald Robertson 270.7
The church and the age of reason, 1648-1789. Grand Rapids, Mich., Eerdmans [1964, c.1960] 299p. 21cm. Bibl. 5.00 bds.,

1. Church history—17th cent. 2. Church history—18th cent. I. Title.

CRAGG, Gerald Robertson 270.7
The church and the age of reason, 1648-1789. New York, Atheneum, 1961 [c.1960] 299p. (Pelican history of the church, v. 4) (Faith for life ser.) 61-12784 4.50
1. Church history—17th cent. 2. Church history—18th cent. I. Title.

CRAGG, Gerald Robertson 270.7
The church and the age of reason, 1648-1789. Penguin Books [dist. New York, Athenuem, 1961, c.1960] 299p. (Pelican history of the church, v.4, Pelican books, A505) Bibl. 61-3977 1.25 pap.,
1. Church history—17th cent. 2. Church history—18th cent. 3. Enlightenment. I. Title.

DANIEL-ROPS, Henry, 1901- 270.7
The church in the eighteenth century, by H. Daniel-Rops. Translated from the French by John Warrington. London, Dent; New York, Dutton [1964] ix, 373 p. 23 cm. (His History of the Church of Christ, v. 7) Translation of L'ere des grands craquements, published as v. 2 of the author's L'Elise des temps classiques. Bibliography: p. 348-350. [BR470.D323] 64-6258
1. Church history — 18th cent. 2. Catholic Church — Hist. I. Title.

DANIEL-ROPS, Henry, 1901- 270.7
The church in the eighteenth century. Tr. from French by John Warrington. London, Dent; New York, Dutton [c.1964] ix, 373p. 23cm. (His Hist. of the Church of Christ, v.7) Bibl. 64-6258 10.00
1. Church history—18th cent. 2. Catholic Church—Hist. I. Title.

DANIEL-ROPS, Henry 1901- 270.7
The church in the eighteenth century. Tr. from French by John Warrington. Garden City, N. Y., Doubleday [1966, c.1964] 478p. 18cm. (His Hist. of the Church of Christ, v.7; Image bk. D201) Bibl. [BR470.D323] 1.45 pap.,
1. Church history—18th cent. 2. Catholic Church—Hist. I. Title.

NICHOLS, James Hastings, 270.7
1915-
History of Christianity, 1650-1950; secularization of the West New York, Ronald Press Co. [1956] 493p. 22cm. [BR450.N5] 56-6268
1. Church history— Modern period. I. Title.

WOOD, Arthur Skevington. 270.7
The inextinguishable blaze; spiritual renewal and advance in the eighteenth century. Grand Rapids, Eerdmans [1960] 256 p. 23 cm. (Advance of Christianity, v. 6) Bibliography: p. [247]-249. [BR470.W65 1960] 61-1302
1. Church history—18th cent. 2. Revivals—History. 3. Eighteenth century. I. Title. II. Series.

BATES, Miner Searle, 1897- 270.8
ed.
The prospects of Christianity throughout the world. Edited by M. Searle Bates and Wilhelm Pauck. New York, Scribner [1964] 286 p. 22 cm. "A series of essays dedicated to Henry Pitney Van Dusen." Bibliographical footnotes. [BR481.B33] 64-14660
1. Christianity — 20th cent. I. Pauck, Wilhelm, 1901- joint ed. II. Van Dusen, Henry Pitney, 1897- III. Title.

BATES, Miner Searle, 1897- 270.8
ed.
The prospects of Christianity throughout the world. Ed. by M. Searle Bates, Wilhelm Pauck. New York, Scribners [c.1964] 286p. 22cm. Bibl. 64-14660 4.95
1. Christianity—20th cent. I. Pauck, Wilhelm, 1901- joint ed. II. Van Dusen, Henry Pitney, 1897- III. Title.

BEACH, Bert Beverly. 270.8
Ecumenism: boon or bane? Washington, Review and Herald Pub. Association [1974] 314 p. 22 cm. Bibliography: p. 297-314. [BX8.2.B385] 73-87678 8.95
1. Christian union. I. Title.

DANIEL-ROPS, Henry, 1901- 270.8
1965
Our brothers in Christ. 1870-1959, by H. Daniel-Rops; tr. from French by J. M. Orpen. John Warrington, ed. by A. Cox J. Hetherington. London, Dent; New York, Dutton. 1967. x. 496p. tables, diagrs. 23cm. (His History of the church of Christ, 10) Orig. pub. as L'Eglise des revolutions: ces chretiens nos freres. Paris, Fayard, 1965. [BX4805.2.D313] 68-86851 10.00
1. Protestantism—Hist. 2. Eastern churches—Hist. 3. Christian union—Catholic Church I. Title.

DONDEYNE, Albert, 1901- 270.8
Faith and the world [tr. from Dutch by Father Walter van de Putte] Pittsburgh, Duquesne Univ. Pr. [c.]1963. xi, 324p. 23cm. (Duquesne studies. Theological ser., 1) Bibl. 63-8795 5.00
1. Christianity—20th cent. 2. Sociology, Christian (Catholic) I. Title. II. Series.

FOSTER, John, 1898- 270.8
To all nations; Christian expansion from 1700 to today. New York, Association Press [1961] 86p. illus., maps (World Christian books, no. 35, 2d ser.) 61-7468 1.00 pap.,
1. Church history—Modern period. I. Title.

HROMADKA, Josef Lukl, 1889- 270.8
Theology between yesterday and tomorrow. Philadelphia, Westminster Press [1957] 106p. 20cm. (Laidlaw lectures, 1956) [BR481.H7] 57-9717
1. Church history—1945- 2. Theology—20th cent. 3. World politics—1945- I. Title. II. Series.

HUTCHINSON, Paul, 1890- 270.8
1955.
The new ordeal of Christianity. New York, Association Press [1957] 128p. 20cm. [BR481.H8] 57-6887
1. Church history—20th cent. I. Title.

HUTCHINSON, Paul, 1890- 270.8
1956.
The new ordeal of Christianity. New York, Association Press [1957] 128 p. 20 cm. [BR481.H8] 57-6887
1. Church history — 20th cent. I. Title.

JORDAN, Gerald Ray, 1896- 270.8
Christ, communism, and the clock. Anderson, Ind., Warner Press [1963] 128 p. 21 cm. [BR481.J64] 63-7920
1. Communism and religion. 2. Christianity—20th cent. I. Title.

JORDAN, Gerlad Ray, 1896- 270.8
Christ, communism, and the clock. Anderson, Ind., Warner [c.1963] 128p. 21cm. 63-7920 1.50 pap.,
1. Communism and religion. 2. Christianity—20th cent. I. Title.

LATOURETTE, Kenneth Scott, 270.8
1884-
The Christian world mission in our day. [1st ed.] New York, Harper [1954] 192p. 22cm. [BR475.L3] 54-5852
1. Church history—Modern period. 2. Missions. I. Title.

LATOURETTE, Kenneth Scott, 270.8
1884-
Christianity in a revolutionary age; a history of Christianity in the nineteenth and twentieth centuries. [1st ed.] New York, Harper [1958- v. 25 cm. Contents.Contents.—v. 1. The nineteenth century in Europe; background and The Roman Catholic phase.—v. 2. The Protestant and Eastern Churches.—v. 3. 19th century outside Europe.—v. 4. 20th century in Europe.—v. 5. 20th Bibliography: v. 1, p. 469-486. [BR477.L3] 58-10370
1. Church history—19th cent. 2. Catholic Church in Europe. I. Title.

LATOURETTE, Kenneth Scott, 270.8
1884-1968.
Christianity in a revolutionary age; a history of Christianity in the nineteenth and twentieth centuries. Westport, Conn., Greenwood Press [1973- c1958- v. 23 cm. Bibliography: p. v. 1, p. 469-486. [BR475.L33] 77-138141 ISBN 0-8371-5700-5 95.00 (5 vol.)
1. Church history—19th century. 2. Church history—20th century. I. Title.

LATOURETTE, Kenneth 270.8 s
Scott, 1884-1968.
The nineteenth century in Europe: background and the Roman Catholic phase. Westport, Conn., Greenwood Press [1973, c1958] xiv, 498 p. 23 cm. (His Christianity in a revolutionary age, v. 1) Bibliography: p. 469-486. [BX475.L33 vol. 1] [BX1490] 282'.4 72-11976 ISBN 0-8371-5701-3
1. Catholic Church in Europe. 2. Europe—History—1789-1900. I. Title. II. Series.

LATOURETTE, Kenneth 270.8 s
Scott, 1884-1968.
The nineteenth century in Europe: the Protestant and Eastern churches. Westport, Conn., Greenwood Press [1973, c1959] viii, 532 p. 23 cm. (His Christianity in a revolutionary age, v. 2) Bibliography: p. 495-512. [BR475.L33 vol. 2] [BX4837] 280'.4'094 72-11977 ISBN 0-8371-5702-1 95.00, 5 vol. set
1. Orthodox Eastern Church—Europe. 2. Protestant churches—Europe. I. Title. II. Series.

LATOURETTE, Kenneth 270.8 s
Scott, 1884-1968.
The nineteenth century outside Europe: the Americas, the Pacific, Asia, and Africa. Westport, Conn., Greenwood Press, [1973, c1961] viii, 527 p. 23 cm. (His Christianity in a revolutionary age, v. 3) Bibliography: p. 497-514. [BR475.L33 vol. 3] [BR477] 270.8'1 72-11978 ISBN 0-8371-5703-X 95.00 (part of 5 vol. set)
1. Church history—19th century. I. Title. II. Series.

LATOURETTE, Kenneth 270.8 s
Scott, 1884-1968.
The twentieth century in Europe: the Roman Catholic, Protestant, and Eastern churches. Westport, Conn., Greenwood Press [1973, c1961] vii, 568 p. 24 cm. (His Christianity in a revolutionary age, v. 4) Bibliography: p. 545-560. [BR475.L33 vol. 4] [BR735] 274 72-11979 ISBN 0-8371-5704-8 95.00, 5 vol. set
1. Europe—Church history. 2. Church history—20th century. I. Title. II. Series.

LATOURETTE, Kenneth 270.8 s
Scott, 1884-1968.
The twentieth century outside Europe: the Americas, the Pacific, Asia, and Africa: the emerging world Christian community. Westport, Conn., Greenwood Press [1973, c1962] vi, 568 p. 23 cm. (His Christianity in a revolutionary age, v. 5) Bibliography: p. 535-552. [BR475.L33 vol. 5] [BR479] 270.8'2 72-11980 ISBN 0-8371-5705-6 95.00, 5 vol. set
1. Church history—20th century. I. Title. II. Series.

MACGREGOR, Geddes. 270.8
From a Christian ghetto; letters of ghostly wit, written A. D. .2453. London, New York, Longmans, Green [1954] 140p. 19cm. [BR125.M29] 54-11940
1. Christianity—20th cent. I. Title.

MCNEILL, John Thomas, 1885- 270.8
Modern Christian movements. New York. Harper [1968,c.1954] 201p. 20cm. (Torch bks., TB1402) [BR290.M25] 1.75 pap.,
1. Church history—Modern period. I. Title.

MCNEILL, John Thomas, 1885- 270.8
Modern Christian movements. Philadelphia, Westminster Press [1954] 197 p. 21 cm. [BR290.M26] 54-8839
1. Church history—Modern period. I. Title.

MURRAY, George Lewis, 1896- 270.8
Our hope of survival. Grand Rapids, Baker Book House, 1951. 133 p. 20 cm. Bibliographical footnotes. [BR481.M8] 51-9694
1. Church history — 1945- 2. Christianity — 20th cent. I. Title.

NEBORAK, Sonja. 270.8
Thoughts in the atomic age. New York, Philosophical Library [1951] 157 p. 21 cm. [BR126.N37] 52-6324
I. Title.

NEILL, Stephen Charles, 270.8
Bp., ed.
Twentieth century Christianity; a survey of modern religious trends by leading churchmen. New, rev. ed. [1st ed. in the United States] Garden City, N. Y., Doubleday [1963] 432 p. 19 cm. (A Dolphin book) [BR479.N4 1963] 63-11255
1. Church history—20th century. 2. Theology—20th cent. 3. Christian union. I. Title.

RAUGHLEY, Ralph C ed. 270.8
New frontiers of Christianity. New York, Association Press [c1962] 254p. 21cm. [BR481.R3] 62-9395
1. Christianity—20th cent.—Addresses, essays, lectures. I. Title.

TILLICH, Paul, 1886- 270.8
The religious situation. Translated by H. Richard Niebuhr. New York, Meridian Books, 1956 [c1932] 219p. 19cm. (Living age books, LA6) Translation of Die religlose Lage der Gegenwart. [BR479] 56-9242
1. Religious thought—20th cent. I. Title.

TILLICH, Paul, 1886- 270.8
The religious situation. Translated by H. Richard Niebuhr. New York, Meridian Books, 1956 [c1932] 219 p. 19cm. (Living age books, LA 6) Translation of Die religiose Lage der Gegenwart. [BR479] 56-9242
1. Religious thought -20th cent. I. Title.

VIDLER, Alexander Roper, 270.8
1899-
The church in an age of revolution: 1789 to the present day. Grand Rapids, Mich., Eerdmans [1964, c.1961] 287p. 19cm. Bibl. 5.00 bds.,
1. Church history—Modern period. I. Title.

VIDLER, Alexander Roper, 270.8
1899-
The church in an age of revolution 1789 to the present. Penguin [dist. Boston Houghton 1962, c.1961] 287p. (Pelican hist. of the church, v.5; Pelican bks., A506) Bibl. 62-783 1.25 pap.,
1. Church history—Modern period. I. Title.

VIDLER, Alexander Roper, 270.8
1899-
The Church in an age of revolution: 1789 to the present day [by] Alec R. Vidler. [Harmondsworth, Eng.] Penguin Books [1971] 302 p. 18 cm. (Pelican history of the church, v. 5) (Pelican books, A506) Bibliography: p. [287]-293. [BR475.V5 1971] 79-24234 ISBN 0-14-020506-3 2.65 (U.S.)
1. Church history—Modern period, 1500- I. Title.

WENTZ, Frederick K 270.8
The times test the church. Philadelphia, Muhlenberg Press [1956,54 154p. 20cm. [BR481.W4] 56-9339
1. Christianity—20th cent. 2. U.S.—Religion. I. Title.

WENTZ, Frederick K. 270.8
The times test the church. Philadelphia, Muhlenberg Press [1956] 154 p. 20 cm. [BR481.W4] 56-9339
1. Christianity — 20th cent. 2. U.S. — Religion. I. Title.

ALTHOLZ, Josef Lewis, 270.8'1
1933-
The churches in the nineteenth century [by] Josef L. Altholz. Indianapolis, Bobbs-Merrill [1967] x, 248 p. map. 21cm. Bibliography: p. 227-229. [BR477.A73] 66-30446
1. Church history—19th cent. I. Title.

ALTHOLZ, Josef Lewis, 270.8'1
1933-
The churches in the nineteenth century [by] Josef L. Altholz. Indianapolis, Bobbs-Merrill [1967] x, 248 p. map. 21 cm. Bibliography: p. 227-229. [BR477.A73] 66-30446
1. Church history—19th century. I. Title.

ORR, James Edwin, 1912- 270.81
The light of the nations; evangelical renewal and advance in the nineteenth century. Grand Rapids, Mich., Eerdmans [1966, c.1965] 302p. 23cm. (Advance of Christianity through the centuries, v. 8) Bibl. [BR477.O7 1966a] 66-5059 5.00
1. Church history—19th cent. I. Title.

ATTWATER, Donald, 270.8'1'0922
1892- ed.
Modern Christian revolutionaries; an introduction to the lives and thought of: Kierkegaard, Eric Gill, G. K. Chesterton, C. F. Andrews [and] Berdyaev. Edited by Donald Attwater. Freeport, N.Y., Books for Libraries Press [1971, c1947] xiii, 390 p. illus., ports. 23 cm. (Essay index reprint series) Contents.Contents.—Soren Kierkegaard, by M. Chaning-Pearce.—G. K. Chesterton, by F. A. Lea.—Eric Gill, by D. Attwater.—C. F. Andrews, by N. MacNichol.—Nicolas Berdyaev, by E. Lampert.—Bibliography (p. [383]-390) [BR1700.A8 1971] 76-156608 ISBN 0-8369-2304-9
1. Kierkegaard, Soren Aabye, 1813-1855. 2. Chesterton, Gilbert Keith, 1874-1936. 3. Gill, Eric, 1882-1940. 4. Andrews, Charles Freer, 1871-1940. 5. Berdiaev, Nikolai Aleksandrovich, 1874-1948. I. Title.

AGRIMSON, J. Elmo. 270.8'2
Gifts of the spirit and the body of Christ; perspectives on the charismatic movement. Edited by J. Elmo Agrimson. Minneapolis, Augsburg Pub. House [1974] 112 p. 20 cm. Includes bibliographies. [BX8763.A15] 73-88608 ISBN 0-8066-1411-0 2.95 (pbk.)
1. Pentecostalism. I. Title.

ASPECTS of pentecostal- 270.8'2
charismatic origins / Vinson Synan, editor. Plainfield, N.J. : Logos International, c1975. iv, 252 p. ; 21 cm. Papers delivered at the 3d annual meeting of the Society for Pentecostal Studies at Lee College, Cleveland, Tenn., in 1973. Includes bibliographical references and index. [BX8762.A72] 75-2802 ISBN 0-88270-110-X : 5.95. ISBN 0-88270-111-8 pbk. : 3.50
1. Pentecostalism—History—Congresses. I. Synan, Vinson. II. Society for Pentecostal Studies.

BRUMBACK, Carl, 1917- 270.8'2
A sound from heaven / Carl Brumback. Springfield, Mo. : Gospel Pub. House, c1977. iii, 153 p. : ill. ; 22 cm. Includes index. Bibliography: p. 147-149. [BR1644.5.U6B76] 76-58781 ISBN 0-88243-560-4 : 2.95
1. Pentecostalism—United States—History. I. Title.

BURI, Fritz, 1907- 270.82
Christian faith in our time. Translated by Edward Allen Kent. New York, Macmillan [1966] 128 p. 22 cm. [BR481.B813] 64-12862
1. Christianity — 20th cent. I. Title.

BURI, Fritz, 1907- 270.82
Christian faith in our time. Tr. [from German] by Edward Allen Kent. New York, Macmillan [c.1952, 1966] 128p. 22cm. [BR481.B813] 64-12862 3.95
1. Christianity—20th cent. I. Title.

CAVERT, Samuel McCrea, 1888- 270.8'2
Church cooperation and unity in America; a historical review: 1900-1970. New York, Association Press [1970] 400 p. 26 cm. Bibliography: p. 354-396. [BX6.5.C38] 79-122488 15.00
1. Christian union—U.S. 2. Ecumenical movement—History. I. Title.

COOK, Harold R. 270.8'2
Historic patterns of church growth; a study of five churches [by] Harold R. Cook. Chicago, Moody Press [1971] 128 p. 22 cm. Bibliography: p. 119-128. [BV652.25.C66] 71-143466 1.95
1. Church growth—Case studies. 2. Church history. I. Title.

CULPEPPER, Robert H. 270.8'2
Evaluating the charismatic movement : a theological and Biblical appraisal / by Robert H. Culpepper. Valley Forge, Pa. : Judson Press, c1977. 192 p. ; 22 cm. Includes index. Bibliography: p. 185-189. [BR1644.C84] 77-1197 ISBN 0-8170-0743-1 pbk. : 6.95
1. Pentecostalism. I. Title.

CULPEPPER, Robert H. 270.8'2
Evaluating the charismatic movement : a theological and Biblical appraisal / by Robert H. Culpepper. Valley Forge, Pa. : Judson Press, c1977. 192 p. ; 22 cm. Includes index. Bibliography: p. 185-189. [BR1644.C84] 77-1197 ISBN 0-8170-0743-1 pbk. : 6.95
1. Pentecostalism. I. Title.

GOODALL, Norman. 270.8'2
Ecumenical progress: a decade of change in the ecumenical movement, 1961-71. London, Oxford University Press, 1972. x, 173 p. 23 cm. Bibliography: p. 137-138. [BX8.2.G653] 72-192724 ISBN 0-19-213954-1 £3.00
1. Ecumenical movement. I. Title.

THE Gospel and unity. 270.8'2
Edited by Vilmos Vajta. Minneapolis, Augsburg Pub. House [1971] 207 p. 22 cm. (The Gospel encounters history series) Includes bibliographical references. [BX9.G67] 72-135233 ISBN 0-8066-9430-0 5.95
1. Christian union—Addresses, essays, lectures. 2. Theology—Addresses, essays, lectures. I. Vajta, Vilmos, ed. II. Title. III. Series.

HAMILTON, Michael Pollock, 1927- 270.8'2
The charismatic movement, edited by Michael P. Hamilton. Grand Rapids, Eerdmans [1975] 196 p. 23 cm. and phonodisc (2 s. 5 1/2 in. 33 1/3 rpm. microgroove) in pocket. Bibliography: p. 195-196. [BX8764.Z6A2] 74-14865 ISBN 0-8028-3453-1 6.95
1. Pentecostalism—Addresses, essays, lectures. I. Title.

HEGSTAD, Roland R. 270.8'2
Rattling the gates [by] Roland R. Hegstad. Washington, Review and Herald Pub. Association [1974] 253 p. illus. 21 cm. Includes bibliographical references. [BX8763.H43] 73-87488 4.95; 3.50 (pbk.).
1. Pentecostalism. I. Title.

*KUNG, Hans. 270.'82
The Church / Hans Kung. Garden City, N.Y. : Doubleday, 1976c1967. 655p. ; 18 cm. (Image books edition) Originally published 1967 with title, Die Kirche. Includes index. [BV601] ISBN 0-385-11367-6 pbk. : 3.50
1. Catholic Church-History-Modern period, 1500- 2. Catholic renewal-Catholic Church. I. Title.

LARSON, Bruce. 270.8'2
The emerging church [by] Bruce Larson and Ralph Osborne. Edited by Richard Engquist. Waco, Tex., Word Books [1970] 160 p. 23 cm. Bibliography: p. 157-160. [BR121.2.L28 1970] 77-118264 3.95
1. Christianity—20th century. I. Osborne, Ralph, joint author. II. Title.

†LORIT, Sergio C. 270.8'2
Focolare after 30 years / by S. C. Lorit & N. Grimaldi ; [translated by New City Press staff] . English ed./prepared by Nuzzo Grimaldi [Brooklyn] : New City Press, [c1976] 198 p., [36] leaves of plates : ill. ; 21 cm. [BX809.F6L67] 76-18456 ISBN 0-911782-27-3 pbk. : 4.50
1. Focolare Movement. I. Grimaldi, Nuzzo, joint author. II. Title.

LUBICH, Chiara, 1920- 270.8'2
When our love is charity. [Translated from the Italian by Julian Stead] New York, New City Press [1972] 81 p. 19 cm. Translation of La carita come ideale. [BX809.F6L8213] 72-85632 0.75
1. Focolare Movement. I. Title.

MCDONNELL, Kilian. 270.8'2
Charismatic renewal / Kilian McDonnell. New York : Seabury Press, c1976. p. cm. "A Crossroad book." Includes index. Bibliography: p. [BX8763.M28] 76-896 ISBN 0-8164-0293-0 : 6.95
1. Pentecostalism. 2. Glossolalia—Psychology. I. Title.

NORTHBOURNE, Walter Ernest Christopher James baron 1896- 270.82
Religion in the modern world. London, J. M. Dent [New York, Hillary House, 1966, c.1963] ix, 110p. 21cm. [BT60.N6] 66-1657 3.00
1. Christianity—Essence, genius, nature. 2. Religion. I. Title.

OLIVER, Revilo Pendleton, 1910- 270.8'2
Christianity and the survival of the West, by Revilo P. Oliver. Sterling, Va., Sterling Enterprises, 1973. viii, 85 p. port. 23 cm. Includes bibliographical references. [BR121.2.O44] 73-77357
1. Christianity—20th century. 2. Civilization, Modern—1950- I. Title.

PETRY, Ray C., 1903- ed. 270.82
A History of Christianity. [Englewood Cliffs, N.J., Prentice-Hall, 1962-64. 2 v. illus. 26 cm. Contents.CONTENTS. -- [1] Readings in the history of the early and medieval church, edited by R. C. Petry. -- [2] Readings in the history of the church from the Reformation to the present, edited by C. L. Manschreck. [BR141.H53] 62-19679
1. Church history — Sources. I. Manschreck, Clyde Leonard, 1917- ed. II. Title.

QUEBEDEAUX, Richard. 270.8'2
The new charismatics : the origins, development, and significance of neo-pentecostalism / Richard Quebedeaux. 1st ed. Garden City, N.Y. : Doubleday, 1976. xii, 252 p. ; 22 cm. A revision of the author's thesis, Oxford University, 1975. Includes index. Bibliography: p. [233]-242. [BX8762.Q4 1976] 75-21242 ISBN 0-385-11007-3 : 7.95
1. Pentecostalism—History. I. Title.

RAMSEY, Arthur Michael, Abp. of Canterbury, 1904- 270.8'2
The future of the Christian Church, by Michael Ramsey and Leon-Joseph Cardinal Suenens. New York, Morehouse-Barlow [1970] 128 p. 19 cm. Includes bibliographical references. [BR123.R29] 79-138033 ISBN 0-8192-1124-9
1. Christianity—20th century—Addresses, essays, lectures. I. Suenens, Leon-Joseph, Cardinal, 1904- II. Title.

ROGNESS, Michael. 270.8'2
The church nobody knows; the shaping of the future church. Minneapolis, Augsburg Pub. House [1971] 126 p. 20 cm. Includes bibliographical references. [BX8.2.R57] 71-135230 ISBN 0-8066-1112-X 2.75
1. Christian union. I. Title.

VISSER 't Hooft, Willem Adolph, 1900- 270.8'2
Has the ecumenical movement a future? / Willem Visser 't Hooft ; [translated from the Dutch by Annebeth Mackie]. Atlanta : John Knox Press, [1976] c1974. 97 p. ; 21 cm. Translation of Heeft de oecumenische beweging toekomst? Original Dutch version was delivered in May 1972 in the Netherlands as the Berkelbach van der Sprenkel lecture. Reprint of the ed. published by Christian Journals Limited, Dublin. [BX8.2.V53913 1976] 75-32947 ISBN 0-8042-0917-0 : 5.50
1. Ecumenical movement. I. Title.

WARNER, Harvey C. ed. 270.82
Why -- in the world? A symposium on the dynamics of spiritual renewal. Compiled and edited by Harvey C. Warner. Waco, Tex., Word Books [c1965] vii, 115 p. 21 cm. [BR123.W34] 66-1655
1. Christianity — 20th cent. — Addresses, essays, lectures. I. Title.

WARNER, Harvey C. ed. 270.82
Why--in the world? A symposium on the dynamics of spiritual renewal. Comp. & ed. by Harvey C. Warner. Waco, Tex., World Bks. [c.1965] vii, 115p. 21cm. [BR123.W34] 66-1655 2.95
1. Christianity—20th cent.—Addresses, essays, lectures. I. Title.

THE Commentary on the Constitution and on the Instruction on the sacred liturgy, 270.8'2*6 by a committee of liturgical experts. Edited by A. Bugnini and C. Braga. Translated by Vincent P. Mallon. New York, Benziger Bros., 1965. xi, 441 p. 24 cm. Half title: Commentary on the sacred liturgy. On spine: The Commentary and the Instruction on the sacred liturgy. Includes the English text of the Constitution on the sacred liturgy, a commentary on each section of it, and an English translation of the Instruction for the proper implementation of the Constitution on the sacred liturgy. Bibliography: p. 439-441. [BX830 1962.A45C627] 71-2988
1. Vatican Council. 2d, 1962-1965. Constitutio de sacra liturgia. 2. Catholic Church. Congregatio Sacrorum Rituum. Instructio ad exsecutionem Constitutionis de sacra liturgia recte ordinandam (26 Sept. 1964) I. Bugnini, Annibale. II. Braga, Carlo. III. Vatican Council. 2d, 1962-1965. Constitutio de sacra liturgia. IV. Catholic Church. Congregatio Sacrorum Rituum. Instructio ad exsecutionem Constitutionis de sacra liturgia recte ordinandam (26 Sept. 1964) English. V. Title: Commentary on the sacred liturgy. VI. Title: The Commentary and the Instruction on the sacred liturgy.

MARTY, Martin E., 1928- 270.8'2'6
The fire we can light; the role of religion in a suddenly different world [by] Martin E. Marty. [1st ed.] Garden City, N.Y., Doubleday, 1973. 240 p. 22 cm. "A Christian century projection for the 1970s." Includes bibliographical references. [BR515.M28] 73-83601 ISBN 0-385-07602-9 5.95
1. United States—Religion. I. Title.

271 Religious Congregations & Orders

AEBY, Gervais. 271
Call to commitment in the school of St. Francis; a manual of instructions for Franciscan Tertiaries, by Gervais Aeby, Hubert Delesty [and] Basile Chaignat. Translated by Michael D. Meilach. Chicago, Franciscan Herald Press [c1964] 192 p. 21 cm. Translation of A l'ecole de Saint Francois. [BX3651.A683] 64-19597
1. Franciscans. Third Order. I. Delesty, Hubert, joint author. II. Chaignat, Basile, joint author. III. Title.

ANONYMOUS apostle; 271(B)
the life of Jean Claude Colin, Marist, by Stanley W. Hosie. New York, Morrow, 1967. xi, 302p. maps. 22cm. Bibl. [BX4705.C687H6] 67-29842 1922- 6.50
1. Colin, Jean Claude Marie, 1790-1875.

BIOT, Francois. 271
The rise of Protestant monasticism. Translated by W. J. Kerrigan. [1st ed.] Baltimore, Helicon [c1963] 161 p. 23 cm. Translation of Communautes protestantes. Bibliographical footnotes. [BV4405.B513] 63-19410
1. Monasticism and religious orders, Protestant. 2. Monastic and religious life—History of doctrines. I. Title.

BIOT, Francois 271
The rise of Protestant monasticism. Tr. [from French] by W. J. Kerrigan. Helicon 161 p. 23 cm. Bibl. 63-19410 3.95 bds.,
1. Monasticism and religious orders, Protestant. 2. Monastic and religious life—History of doctrines. I. Title.

BIOT, Rene, 1889- 271
Medical guide to vocations, by Rene Biot and Pierre Galimard. Translated from the French and adapted into English by Robert P. Odenwald. Westminster, Md., Newman Press, 1955. 303p. 22cm. Translation of Guide medical des vocations sacerdotales et religieuses. [BX2380.B512] 54-5659
1. Vocation (in religious orders, congregations, etc.) I. Galimard. Pierre, 1912- joint author. II. Title.

BISKUPEK, Aloysius, 1884-1955. 271
Conferences on the religious life. Milwaukee, Bruce Pub. Co., [1957] 204p. 22cm. [BX2435.B5] 57-12344
1. Monastic and religious life. I. Title.

BLOESCH, Donald G. 1928- 271
Centers of Christian renewal [by] Donald G. Bloesch. Philadelphia, United Church Press [1964] 173 p. 21 cm. Bibliographical references included in "Notes" (p. 155-173) [BV4405.B55] 64-14140
1. Monasticism and religious orders, Protestant. I. Title.

BOUYER, Louis, 1913- 271
The meaning of the monastic life. [Translation by Kathleen Pond. New York, P. J. Kenedy [1955?] 209p. 23cm. [BX2435] 55-9394
1. Monastic and religious life. I. Title.

CALLAHAN, Mary T 271
Meet the Vincentian Fathers, the Holy Cross Fathers, the Jesuit Fathers, the Passionist Fathers, the Redemptorist Fathers, the Dominican Fathers, the Marist fathers. St. Meinrad, Ind. [c1952] 92p. 19cm. 'Grail publication.' On cover: Meet these priests. [BX2431.C25] 53-20712
1. Monasticism and religious orders. I. Title. II. Title: Meet these priests.

CANU, Jean 271
Religious orders of men. Translated from the French by P. J. Hepburne-Scott. New York, Hawthorn Books [c.1960] 144p. 21cm. (Twentieth century encyclopedia of Catholicism, 85. Section 8: The organization of the church) Includes bibliography. 60-8781 2.95 half cloth,
1. Monasticism and religious orders. I. Title.

CANU, Jean, 1898- 271
Religious orders of men. Translated from the French by P. J. Hepburne-Scott. [1st ed.] New York, Hawthorn Books [1960] 144p. 21cm. (Twentieth century encyclopedia of Catholicism, 85. Section 8: The organization of the church) Includes bibliography. [BX2432.C313] 60-8781
1. Monasticism and religious orders. I. Title.

CARR, John, 1878- 271
Why hast thou come? Westminster, Md., Newman Press [1956] 221p. 20cm. [BX2435.C28] 57-8608
1. Monastic and religious life. I. Title.

CARY-ELWES, Columba, 1903- 271
The sheepfold and the shepherd. London, New York, Longmans, Green [1956] 259p. 19cm. [BX1754.C27 1956] 56-35692
1. Catholic Church. I. Title.

CATECHISM of the religious profession, 271 translated from the French and rev. in conformity with the new code of canon law. New ed. Metuchen, N. J., Brothers of the Sacred Heart [1954] 158p. 19cm. [BX2437.C32 1954] 54-39028
1. Monasticism and religious orders—Discipline. 2. Vows. I. Brothers of the Sacred Heart, Metuchen, N. J.

CATHOLIC University Conference of Clerics and Religious of the Catholic Students' Mission Crusade, Washington, 1948. 271
The guidepost; religious vocation manual for young men, compiled by the Catholic University Conference of Clerics and Religious. [4th ed.] Washington [1964] xxvii, 244 p. illus., ports. 27 cm. [BX2505.C3 1948hd] 64-19577
1. Monasticism and religious orders — U.S. 2. Vocation, Ecclesiastical. I. Title.

CATHOLIC University Conference of Clerics and Religious of the Catholic Students' Mission Crusade, Washington, 1948 271
The guidepost; religious vocation manual for young men, comp. by the Catholic Univ. Conf. of Clerics and religious [4th ed.] Washington, D.C., Author [c.1964] xxvii, 244p. illus., ports. 27cm. 64-19577 3.95; 2.50 pap.,
1. Monasticism and religious orders—U.S. 2. Vocation, Ecclesiastical. I. Title.

CHADWICK, Owen. 271
John Cassian; a study in primitive monasticism. Cambridge [Eng.] University Press, 1950. xi, 212 p. 23 cm. Bibliography: p. 204-208. [BR1720.C3C47] 51-5543
1. Cassianus, Joannes, ca. 370-ca. 435. 2. Monasticism and religious orders. I. Title.

CHADWICK, Owen. 271
John Cassian. 2nd ed. London, Cambridge U.P., 1968. viii, 171 p. 22 cm. Includes bibliographical references. [BR1720.C3C47 1968] 67-24936 ISBN 0-521-04607-6 40/-
1. Cassianus, Joannes, ca. 370-ca. 435. 2. Monasticism and religious orders—Early church.

COLIN, Louis, 1884- 271
The practice of the rules. Translated from the French by David Heimann. Westminster, Md., Newman Press, 1957. 250p. 23cm. Translation of Gulte de la regle. [BX2435.C617] 57-11807
1. Monasticism and religious orders—Discipline. I. Title.

COLIN, Louis, 1884- 271
The practice of the vows. Translated by Suzanne Rickman. Chicago, H. Regnery Co., 1955. 276p. 22cm. [BX2435.C62] 55-5993
1. Vows. I. Title.

COLIN, Louis, 1884- 271
The superior's handbook. Translated from the French by Fergus Murphy. Chicago, Regnery, 1955 [i. e. 1956] 144p. 23cm. [BX2438.C6] 56-4461
1. Superiors, Religious. I. Title.

COMMUNAL life; 271
being the English version of La Vie commune. Translated by a Religious of the Sacred Heart. [Edited under the direction of A. Ple]

Westminster, Md., Newman Press [1957] 320p. 22cm. (Religious life, 8) [BX2435.C643] 57-11808
1. Monastic and religious life.

CREUSEN, Joseph. 271
Religious men and women in the Code. 5th English ed., rev. and edited to conform with the 6th French ed. by Adam C. Ellis. Milwaukee, Bruce Pub. Co. [1953] xiv, 322 p. 23 cm. 'Authorised translation of Religieux at religieuses d'apre's le droit ecclesiastique, 6th edition.' Bibliography: p. vii-vii. 53-2804
1. Monasticism and religious orders (Canon law) I. Title.

DIRKS, Walter, 1901- 271
The monk and the world; translated by Daniel Coogan. New York, D. McKay Co. [1954] 234p. 21cm. [BX2431.D513] 53-11381
1. Monasticism and religious orders. I. Title.

DOYLE, Charles Hugo. 271
Leaven of holiness; conferNces for religious. Westminster, Md., Newman Press, 1955. 242p. 21cm. [BX4210.D67] 56-306
1. Monastic and religious life of women. I. Title.

DOYLE, Charles Hugo. 271
Little steps to great holiness. Westminster, Md., Newman Press, 1956. 265p. 22cm. [BX2435.D67] 56-13248
1. Monastic and religious life. I. Title.

DUBAY, Thomas. 271
The seminary rule: an explanation of the purposes behind it and how best to carry it out. With a foreword by Joseph Francis Rummel. Westminster, Md., Newman Press, 1954. 140p. 23cm. [BX903.D8] 54-5896
1. Seminarians. I. Title.

DUFFEY, Felix D 1903- 271
Manual for novices. St. Louis, Herder [1957] 232p. 21cm. [BX2438.D79] 57-10689
1. Novitlate. I. Title.

EDWARDS, Tudor. 271
Worlds apart; a journey to the great living monastaries [sic] of Europe. [1st American ed.] New York, Coward-McCann [1958] 232 p. illus. (1 item in pocket) 22 cm. [BX2590.E3] 58-12120
1. Monasteries—Europe. I. Title.

ENGEMAN, Jack 271
The Catholic priest, his training and ministry; a picture story. Foreword by Richard Cardinal Cushing, Archbishop of Boston. New York, Lothrop [c.1961] 127p. illus. 28cm. 61-15445 3.50 bds.,
1. Catholic Church—Clergy—Pictures, illustrations, etc. I. Title.

ERASMUS, Desiderius, d.1536. 271
De contemptu mundi, 1488? Translated by Thomas Paynell. A more production of the Berthelet ed. of 1533 with an introd. by William James Hirten Gainesville, Fla., Scholars' Facsimiles & Reprints, 1967. xiiv, 178 p. 21 cm. "Reproduced from an copy in ... [the] Princeton University Library." [BX2430.E713 1533a] 67-18715
1. Monasticism and religious orders. I. Paynell, Thomas, fl. 1528-1567. II. Hirten, William James. III. Title.

ERASMUS, Desiderius. d. 1536 271
De contemptu mundi, 1488? Tr. by Thomas Paynell. A facsim. reprod. of the Berthelet ed. of 1533 with an introd. by William James Hirten Gainesville, Fla., Scholars' Facsimiles, 1967. xliv, 178p. 21cm. Reproduced from a cony in . . . [the] Princeton Univ. Lib. [BX2430.E713 1533a] 67-18715 7.50
1. Monasticism and religious orders. I. Paynell, Thomas, fl. 1528-1567. II. Hirten, William James. III. Title.

FANFANI, Lodovico Giuseppe, 1876-1955. 271
Catechism on the religious state in conformity with the Code of canon law; translated by Paul C. Perrotta. St. Louis, B. Herder Book Co. [1956] 184p. 20cm. [BX2385.F3] 56-7080
1. Monastic and religious life. I. Title.

FARRELL, Edward P. 271
The theology of religious vocation. St. Louis, Herder, 1951. 228 p. 22 cm. [BX2380.F3] 51-8076
1. Vocation (in religious orders, congregations, etc.) I. Title.

FISH, Simon, d.1531. 271
A supplication for the beggars. <Spring of 1529.> Edited by Edward Arber. London, 1878. [New York, AMS Press, 1967] xviii, 14 p. 23 cm. (The English scholar's library of old and modern works [v. 1] no. 4) "Bibliography of Simon Fish's works": p. [vi] [PR1121.A72 no. 4] [BX2592] 225'.05'2 72-194940
1. Monasticism and religious orders—England. 2. Friars—Controversial literature. I. Title. II. Series.

FROSSARD, Andre. 271
The salt of the earth. Translated by Marjorie Villers. New York, Kenedy [1954] 160p. illus. 19cm. [BX2431.F715] 55-7852
1. Monasticism and religious orders. I. Title.

GASQUET, Francis Aidan, Cardinal, 1846-1929. 271
Religio religiosi; the object and scope of the religious life. [1st American ed.] St. Meinrad, Ind., Grail Publication[s] 1955] 120 p. 21 cm. [BX2385.G3] 56-1836
1. Monastic and religious life. I. Title.

HALEY, Joseph Edmund, ed. 271
Apostolic sanctity in the world; a symposium on total dedication in the world and secular institutes. [Notre Dame, Ind., University of Notre Dame Press, 1957. xiv, 210p. 24cm. 'Presented as a proceedings of ... various conferences held from 1952-1956. Selected papers from these meetings, reports on the various groups existing in the United States and Canada, the basic church documents regarding secular institutes, and an exhaustive bibliography [p. 197-210] have been integrated into a whole.' [BX808.H3] 57-7491
1. Secular institutes. I. Title.

HARNETT, Cynthia 271
Monasteries & monks. London, Batsford [New Rochelle, N. Y., Leisure Time Bks., 1965, c.1963] 176p. illus., map, plans. 22cm. [BX2592.H3] 64-3271 4.25 bds.,
1. Monasteries—England. 2. Monasticism and religious orders—England. I. Title.

HERR, Vincent V. 271
Screening candidates for the priesthood and religious life [by] Vincent V. Herr [and others] Chicago, Loyola University Press [1964] vii, 203 p. illus. 24 cm. Includes bibliographies. [BX2380.H44] 248'.894 68-1770
1. Vocation (in religious orders, congregations, etc.) I. Title.

HERZEL, Catherine B 271
On call; deaconesses across the world. Illustrated by Dorothy Bayley Morse. [1st ed.] New York, Holt, Rinehart and Winston [1961] 121p. illus. 22cm. [BV4423.H4] 61-14970
1. Deaconesses—Juvenile literature. I. Title.

HOEGER, Frederick T, 1888- 271
The convent mirror; a series of conferences for religious. New York, F. Pustet Co., 1951. 246 p. 21 cm. [BX4214.H6] 51-12065
1. Monasticism and religious orders for women. 2. Retreats. I. Title.

HOFFER, Paul. 271
Guide for religious administrators. Translated by Gabriel J. Rus. Milwaukee, Bruce Pub. Co. [1959] 171p. 22cm. [BX2435.H613] 59-8635
1. Monasticism and religious orders—Government. I. Title.

HOMAN, Helen (Walker) 1893- 271
Knights of Christ. Englewood Cliffs, N. J., Prentice-Hall [1957] 486p. illus. 26cm. Includes bibliography. [BX2431.H6] 57-10677
1. Monasticism and religious orders. I. Title.

HOSIE, Stanley W 1922- 271 (B)
Anonymous apostle; the life of Jean Claude Colin, Marist, by Stanley W. Hosie. New York, Morrow, 1967. xi, 302 p. maps. 22 cm. Bibliography: p. 295-296. [BX4705.C687H6] 67-29842
1. Colin, Jean Claude Marie, 1790-1875. I. Title.

[JUSTIN LUCIAN, Brother] 1925- 271
Everybody calls me Brother; the diary of a teaching Brother. Winona, Minn., St. Mary's College Press [1954] 60p. illus. 21cm. [BX2835.J8] 55-17421
1. Monasticism and religious orders—Brothers. I. Title.

KANE, George Louis, 1911- ed. 271
Meeting the vocation crisis. Westminster, Md., Newman Press [1956] 204p. 21cm. [BX2380.K3] 56-7858
1. Vocation (in religious orders, congregations, etc.) I. Title.

KANE, George Louis, 1911- ed. 271
Why I became a brother; with an introd. by Daniel A. Lord. Westminster, Md., Newman Press, 1954. 173p. 22cm. [BX2835.K3] 54-12081
1. Monasticism and religious orders—Brothers. 2. Monasticism and religious orders—Lay brothers. I. Title.

KELLY, Bernard J 271
Progress in the religious life. Westminster, Md., Newman Press [1953] 128p. 19cm. [BX2385.K4] 53-11047
1. Monasticism and religious orders. I. Title.

KELLY, Gerald A 271
Guidance for religious. Westminster, Md., Newman Press, 1956. 321p. 22cm. [BX2438.K4] 56-11420
1. Spiritual direction. 2. Monastic and religious life. I. Title.

KNOWLES, David, 1896- 271
Christian monasticism. New York, McGraw-Hill [1969] 253 p. illus. (part col.), col. maps. 19 cm. (World university library) Bibliography: p. 249-252. [BX2461.2.K55] 68-25148 2.45
1. Monasticism and religious orders—History. 2. Monastic and religious life. I. Title.

KNOWLES, David, 1896- 271
The religious orders in England. Cambridge [Eng.] University Press, 1948- v. fronts. 26cm. Contents.[v.1] The old orders, 1216-1340. The friars, 1216-1340. The monasteries and their world.-- v.2. The end of the Middle Ages. Includes bibliographies. [BX2592.K583] 48-10465
1. Monasticism and religious orders—England. I. Title.

KNOWLES, David [Secular name: Michael Clive Knowles] 271
The religious orders in England, v.3, The Tudor age. [New York], Cambridge University Press 1959[ ] xiv, 522p. fronts. 26cm. Includes bibliographies. 48-10465 10.00 25.00 set of 3v.,
1. Monasticism and religious orders—England I. Title.

LAVAUD, Benoit, 1890- 271
The meaning of the religious life. Translated by Walter Mitchell. Westminster, Md., Newman Press, 1955. 81p. 19cm. [BX2385.L364] 55-8665
1. Monastic and religious life. I. Title.

LECLERCQ, Jacques, 1891- 271
The religious vocation. Translated by the Earl of Wicklow. New York, Kenedy [1955] 184p. 23cm. [BX2380] 54-5656
1. Vocation (in religious orders, congregations, etc.) I. Title.

LYNCH, Joseph H., 1943- 271
Simoniacal entry into religious life from 1000 to 1260 : a social, economic, and legal study / Joseph H. Lynch Columbus : Ohio State University Press, [1976] p. cm. Includes index. Bibliography: p. [BX2470.L95] 76-22670 ISBN 0-8142-0222-5 : 15.00
1. Monasticism and religious orders—Middle Ages, 600-1500. 2. Simony—History. I. Title.

MCDONNELL, Ernest W 271
The Beguines and Beghards in medieval culture, with special emphasis on the Belgian scene. New Brunswick, N. J., Rutgers University Press, 1954. xvii, 643p. 25cm. Bibliography:p.575-612. [BX4270.B5M2] 54-6842
1. Beguines. 2. Beghards. I. Title.

MCDONNELL, Ernest W. 271
The Beguines and Beghards in medieval culture, with special emphasis on the Belgian scene [by] Ernest W. McDonnell. New York, Octagon Books, 1969. xvii, 643 p. 24 cm. Reprint of the 1954 ed. Bibliography: p. 575-612. [BX4272.M3 1969] 72-96187
1. Beguines. 2. Beghards. I. Title.

MCELHONE, James Francis, 1890- 271
Spirituality for postulate, novitiate, scholasticate. Notre Dame, Ind., Ave Maria Press [1955] 196p. 22cm. [BX2350.M146] 55-9482
1. Spiritual life—Catholic Church. 2. Monastic and religious life. I. Title.

MARY FRANCIS, Mother, 1921- 271
Strange gods before me. New York, Sheed [c.1965] 214p. 22cm. [BX4230.M3] 65-12209 4.50
1. Contemplative orders. 2. Poor Clares. I. Title.

MERTON, Thomas, 1915- 271
Monastic peace. [Trappist P. O., Ky.] Abbey of Gethsemani [1958] 57p. illus. 24cm. [BX2435.M47] 58-2120
1. Monastic and religious life. I. Title.

MERTON, Thomas, 1915- 271
The silent life. New York, Farrar, Straus & Cudahy [1957] 178p. illus. 21cm. [BX2431.M4] 56-6164
1. Monasticism and religious orders. 2. Monastic and religious life. I. Title.

MYERS, Rawley. 271
This is the seminary. Milwaukee, Bruce Pub. Co. [1953] 123p. 21cm. [BX903.M43] 53-2191
1. Seminarians. I. Title.

NIGG, Walter, 1903- 271
Warriors of God; the great religious orders and their founders. Edited and translated from the German by Mary Ilford. [1st American ed.] New York, Knopf, 1959. 353 p. illus. 25 cm. Translation of Vom Geheimnis der Monche. [BX2432.N513] 59-5429
1. Monasticism and religious orders—History. 2. Monasticism and religious orders—Biography. I. Title.

NOTRE Dame, Ind. University. Vocation Institute. 271
Proceedings of the annual convocation. Notre Dame, University of Notre Dame Press. v. 22cm. 'Under the auspices of the Holy Cross Fathers, Notre Dame, Indiana.' [BX2380.N6] 55-2302
1. Vocation (in religious orders, congregations, etc.) I. Title.

O'LEARY, Mary Florence Margaret. 271
Our time is now; a study of some modern congregations and secular institutes. With an introd. by T. D. Roberts. Westminster, Md., Newman Press, 1956. 120p. 19cm. [BX2440.O4 1956] 56-11419
1. Monasticism and religious orders. 2. Secular Institutes. I. Title.

O'LEARY, Mary Florence Margaret. 271
Our time is now; a study of some modern congregations and secular institutes. With an introd. by T. D. Roberts. Westminster, Md., Newman Press, 1956. 120p. 19cm. [BX2440.O4 1956] 56-11419
1. Monasticism and religious orders. 2. Secular institutes. I. Title.

PARKER, Thomas William, 1921- 271
The Knights Templars in England. Tucson, Univ. of Ariz. Pr. [c.]1963. 195p. 24cm. Bibl. 63-11983 5.00
1. Templars in England. I. Title.

PERINELLE, Joseph, 1880- 271
God's highways; the religious life and secular institutes. Translated by Donald Attwater. Westminster, Md., Newman Press [1958] 339p. 22cm. [BX2385.P4413] 58-13645
1. Monastic and religious life. I. Title.

POVERTY. 271
Translated by Lancelot C. Sheppard. Westminster, Md., Newman Press [1954] viii, 253p. 22cm. (Religious life, 4) 'Papers read at the ... annual conference held in Paris to consider the needs of French nuns.' Bibliographical footnotes. [BX2435.P313] 54-4812
1. Poverty. 2. Monasticism and religious orders. I. Sheppard, Lancelot Capel, 1906- tr.

SAINT-LEGER-VAUBAN, France. Pierre-qui- Vire (Benedictine abbey) 271
Silence in heaven; a book of the monastic life. Text by Thomas Merton, with 90 photos. and many texts from religious writings [selected and arranged by the monks of La Pierre-qui-Vire. Translated by Phyllis Cummins] New York, Studio Publications [1956] 68p. illus. 26cm. Thomas Merton's In silentio: p. 17-30. [BX2435.S312] 57-4866
1. Monastic and religious life. I. Merton, Thomas, 1915- In silentio. II. Title.

SIMONEAUX, Henry J 271
Spiritual guidance and the varieties of character. [1st ed.] New York, Pageant Press [1956] 248p. 24cm. [BX903.S5] 56-11344
1. Spiritual directors. 2. Seminarians—Religious life. I. Title.

SIMONEAUX, Henry J 271
Spiritual guidance and the varieties of character. [1st ed.] New York, Pageant Press [1956] 248 p. 24 cm. [BX903.S5] 56-11344
1. Spiritual directos. 2. Seminarians — Religious life. I. Title.

VON HILDEBRAND, Dietrich, 1889- 271
Not as the world gives; St. Francis' message to laymen today. Chicago, Franciscan Herald Press [1963] [BX3651.V6] 63-21389
1. 93 p. port. 21 cm. 2. Franciscans. Third Order. 3. Francesco d'Assisi, Saint, 1182-1226. I. Title.

VON HILDEBRAND, Dietrich. 1889- 271
Not as the world gives; St. Francis' message to laymen today. Chicago, Franciscan Herald [c.1963] 93p. port. 21cm. 63-21389 3.00
1. Francesco d'Assisi, Saint,1182-1226. 2. Franciscans. Third Order. I. Title.

WATTEROTT, Ignaz, 1869-1922. 271
Guidance of religious; considerations on the duties of religious superiors. Translated by A. Simon. St. Louis, Herder, 1950. x, 426 p. 24 cm. Translation of Ordensieitung. [BX2438.W312] 50-12287
1. Monasticism and religious orders. I. Title.

WOOD, Susan. 271
English monasteries and their patrons in the thirteenth century. London, Oxford University Press, 1955. viii, 191p. 23cm. (Oxford historical series. British series) Bibliography: p. [171]-177. Bibliographical footnotes. [BX2592.W65] 55-3230
1. Monasteries—England. 2. Patronage, Eccleslastical—Gt. Brit. I. Title.

WORKMAN, Herbert B. 271
The evolution of the monastic ideal, from the earliest times down to the coming of the friars. Second chapter in the history of Christian renunciation. Boston, Beacon [1962] 368p. 21cm. (BP147) 2.25pap.,
1. Monasticism and religious orders. I. Title.

WORKMAN, Herbert B. 271
The evolution of the monastic ideal from the earliest times down to the coming of the friars. A second chapter in the history of Christian renunciation [Gloucester, Mass., P. Smith. 1963] 368p. 21cm. (Beacon paperback rebound) Bibl. 4.25
1. Monasticism and religious orders. I. Title.

ZARNECKI, George. 271
The monastic achievement. New York, McGraw-Hill [1972] 144 p. illus. 22 cm. (Library of medieval civilization) Bibliography: p. 138-139. [BX2432.Z37 1972] 79-175186 ISBN 0-07-072736-8 5.95
1. Monasticism and religious orders. I. Title.

'ANAN Isho', 271'.00932
7thcent., comp.
The paradise or garden of the holy fathers; being histories of the anchorites, recluses, monks, Coenobites, and ascetic fathers of the deserts of Egypt between A.D. CCL and A.D. CCCC circiter, compiled by Athanasius, Archbishop of Alexandria, Palladius, Bishop of Helenopolis, Saint Jerome, and others. Now translated out of the Syriac, with notes & introd., by Ernest A. Wallis Budge. New York, B. Franklin [1972] 2 v. 2 facsims. 23 cm. (Burt Franklin research and source works series. Philosophy & religious history monographs, 112) Reprint of the 1907 ed., which was a rev. translation of The book of paradise, as compiled by 'Anan Isho, and published in 1904. "The life of Saint Anthony, by Athanasius, Archbishop of Alexandria": v. 1, p. 3-76. [BX2734.A619 1972] 72-85099 ISBN 0-8337-4011-3 25.00
1. Antonius, the Great, Saint. 2. Monasticism and religious orders—Egypt. 3. Asceticism. I. Athanasius, Saint, Patriarch of Alexandria, d. 373. II. Palladius, successively Bp. of Helenopolis and of Aspona, d. ca. 430. III. Hieronymus, Saint. IV. Budge, Ernest Alfred Thompson Wallis, Sir, 1857-1934, ed. V. Title.

GAVIN, Frank Stanton 271'.00932
Burns, 1890-1938.
Aphraates and the Jews; a study of the controversial homilies of the Persian sage in their relation to Jewish thought. New York, AMS Press, 1966. xvi, 74 p. 23 cm. Reprint of the 1923 ed., which was issued as v. 9 of Contributions to oriental history and philology. Bibliography: p. [xi]-xvi. [BR1720.A65G3 1966] 72-185388
1. Aphraates, the Persian sage, fl. 337-345. 2. Judaism—Relations—Christianity. 3. Christianity and other religions—Judaism. 4. Preaching—History—Early church, ca. 30-600. I. Title. II. Series: Contributions to oriental history and philology, v. 9.

BROOKE, Christopher 271'.0094
Nugent Lawrence.
The monastic world, 1000-1300 [by] Christopher Brooke. Photos. by Wim Swaan. New York, Random House [1974] 272 p. illus. 32 cm. Includes bibliographical references. [BX2470.B76 1974] 74-5368 ISBN 0-394-47478-3
1. Monasticism and religious orders—Middle Ages, 600-1500. I. Title.

COWAN, Ian Borthwick. 271'.009411
Medieval religious houses, Scotland : with an appendix on the houses in the Isle of Man / by Ian B. Cowan and David E. Easson ; with a foreword by David Knowles ; and maps by R. Neville Hadcock. 2d ed. London ; New York : Longman, 1976. p. cm. Edition for 1957 entered under D. E. Easson. Includes index. [BX2597.E2 1976] 75-42083 ISBN 0-582-12069-1 : £13.00
1. Monasteries—Scotland. I. Easson, David Edward, 1897- Medieval religious houses, Scotland. II. Title.

COWAN, Ian Borthwick. 271'.009411
Medieval religious houses, Scotland : with an appendix on the houses in the Isle of Man / by Ian B. Cowan and David E. Easson ; with a foreword by David Knowles ; and maps by R. Neville Hadcock. 2d ed. London ; New York : Longman, 1976. xxviii, 246 p., [4] fold. leaves of plates : 4 maps ; 22 cm. Edition for 1957 entered under D. E. Easson. Includes index. [BX2597.E2 1976] 75-42083 ISBN 0-582-12069-1 : 35.00
1. Monasteries—Scotland. I. Easson, David Edward, 1897- Medieval religious houses, Scotland. II. Title.

BRADSHAW, Brendan. 271'.009415
The dissolution of the religious orders in Ireland under Henry VIII. [London, New York] Cambridge University Press [1974] viii, 276 p. illus. 23 cm. Bibliography: p. 256-261. [BX2600.B72] 73-83104 16.50
1. Henry VIII, King of England, 1491-1547. 2. Monasticism and religious orders—Ireland. I. Title.

MOULD, Daphne Desiree 271'.009415
Charlotte Pochin.
The monasteries of Ireland : an introduction / Daphne D. C. Pochin Mould. London : B. T. Batsford, 1976. 188 p., [12] leaves of plates : ill. ; 23 cm. Bibliography: p. 184-188. [BX2600.M68] 76-363595 ISBN 0-7134-3090-7 : £4.95
1. Monasticism and religious orders—Ireland. 2. Monasteries—Ireland. I. Title.

RYAN, John, 1894- 271'.009415
Irish monasticism: origins and early development. New introd. and bibliography. Ithaca, N.Y., Cornell University Press [1972] viii, xv, 481, xiv p. 25 cm. Reprint of the 1931 ed., with a new introd. and bibliography. [BX2600.R8 1972] 70-137677 ISBN 0-8014-0613-7 12.50
1. Monasticism and religious orders—Ireland. I. Title.

GASQUET, Francis 271'.00942
Aidan, Cardinal, 1846-1929.
English monastic life. Port Washington, N.Y., Kennikat Press [1971] xix, 326 p. illus., maps, plans, ports. 22 cm. Reprint of the 1904 ed. Bibliography: p. xv-xix. [BS2592.G3 1971] 76-118470 ISBN 0-8046-1219-6
1. Monasticism and religious orders—England. I. Title.

GASQUET, Francis 271'.00942
Aidan, Cardinal, 1846-1929.
English monastic life. Freeport, N.Y., Books for Libraries Press [1971] xix, 326 p. illus., maps, plans, ports. 23 cm. Reprint of the 1904 ed. Includes bibliographical references. [BX2592.G3 1971b] 77-157336 ISBN 0-8369-5796-2
1. Monasticism and religious orders—England. I. Title.

KELLY, J. Thomas. 271'.00942
Thorns on the Tudor rose : monks, rogues, vagabonds, and sturdy beggars / by J. Thomas Kelly. Jackson : University Press of Mississippi, 1977. p. cm. Includes index. Bibliography: p. [BX2592.K44] 76-58547 ISBN 0-87805-029-9 : 12.00
1. Monasteries—England. 2. Secularization—England. 3. Great Britain—Politics and government—1485-1603. 4. Poor laws—Great Britain—History. 5. Poor—England—History. I. Title.

KELLY, J. Thomas. 271'.00942
Thorns on the Tudor rose : monks, rogues, vagabonds, and sturdy beggars / by J. Thomas Kelly. Jackson : University Press of Mississippi, 1977. p. cm. Includes index. Bibliography: p. [BX2592.K44] 76-58547 ISBN 0-87805-029-9 : 12.00
1. Monasteries—England. 2. Secularization—England. 3. Great Britain—Politics and government—1485-1603. 4. Poor laws—Great Britain—History. 5. Poor—England—History. I. Title.

KNOWLES, David, 1896- 271'.00942
Bare ruined choirs : the dissolution of the English monasteries / David Knowles. Cambridge [Eng.] ; New York : Cambridge University Press, 1975 329 p. : ill. ; 26 cm. Abridged ed. of The Religious orders in England, v. 3 : The Tudor age ; first published in 1959. Includes index. Bibliography: p. [321] [BX2592.K5832 1976] 76-363067 ISBN 0-521-20712-6 : 16.95
1. Monasticism and religious orders—England. I. Knowles, David, 1896- The religious orders in England. II. Title.

KNOWLES, David, 1896- 271'.00942
The heads of religious houses, England and Wales, 940-1216; edited by David Knowles, C. N. L. Brooke [and] Vera C. M. London. Cambridge [Eng.] University Press, 1972. xlviii, 277 p. 24 cm. Bibliography: p. xix-xlvii. [BX2592.K55] 79-171676 ISBN 0-521-08367-2
1. Monasticism and religious orders—Great Britain—Registers. 2. Superiors, Religious—Great Britain. I. Brooke, Christopher Nugent Lawrence, joint author. II. London, Vera C. M., joint author. III. Title.

KNOWLES, David, 1896- 271'.00942
Medieval religious houses, England and Wales, by David Knowles and R. Neville Hadcock. New York, St. Martin's Press [1972, c1971] xv, 565 p. fold. maps. 24 cm. Includes bibliographical references. [BX2592.K56 1972] 76-167756
1. Monasticism and religious orders—England. 2. Monasticism and religious orders—Wales. I. Hadcock, Richard Neville, joint author. II. Title.

MILLIKEN, Ernest 271/.00942
Kenneth.
English monasticism yesterday and today, by E. K. Milliken. London, Toronto, Harrap, 1967. 123p. illus., plans, facsims. (incl. ports.), diagrs. 23cm. Maps on endpapers. Bibl. [BX2592.M5] 68-71352 4.00 bds.,
1. Monasticism and religious orders—England. I. Title.
American distributor: Verry, Mystic, Conn.

SNAPE, Robert Hugh. 271'.00942
English monastic finances in the later Middle Ages, by R. H. Snape. New York, Barnes & Noble [1968] ix, 190 p. 22 cm. Reprint of the 1926 ed. Includes bibliographical references. [BX2592.S64 1968] 68-23757
1. Monasticism and religious orders—England—Finance. I. Title.

WOODWARD, George 271'.009'42
William Otway
The dissolution of the monasteries [by] G. W. O. Woodward. New York, Walker [c1966] ix, 186p. illus. 22cm. (Blandford hist. ser. Problems of hist) Bibl. [BX2592.W67 1966a] 67-13243 5.95
1. Monasticism and religious orders—England. 2. Secularization—Gt. Brit. I. Title.

WOODWARD, George 271'.009'42
William Otway.
The dissolution of the monasteries [by] G. W. O. Woodward. New York, Walker [c1966] ix, 186 p. illus. 22 cm. (Blandford history series. Problems of history) "Bibliographical note": p. 174-175. [BX2592.W67] 67-13243
1. Monasticism and religious orders — England. 2. Secularisation — Gt. Brit. I. Title.

CONFERENCE of Major 271'.0097
Religious Superiors of Women's Institutes of the United States of America. Research Committee.
Final report on the survey for contemplatives, submitted by Marie Augusta Neal. Dubuque, Iowa, The Scriptory, New Melleray Abbey [1970] 47 p. illus. 28 cm. Cover title. "Sponsored by the Conference of Major Religious Superiors of Women's Institutes of the United States of America." [BX2440.C64] 72-127860 2.00
1. Monastic and religious life—Statistics. I. Neal, Marie Augusta. II. Conference of Major Religious Superiors of Women's Institutes in the United States of America. III. Title. IV. Title: Survey for contemplatives.

DARWIN, Francis 271'.02'0942
Darwin Swift.
The English mediaeval recluse, by Francis D. S. Darwin. [Folcroft, Pa.] Folcroft Library Editions, 1974. vi, 90 p. 24 cm. Reprint of the 1944 ed. published by Society for Promoting Christian Knowledge, London. Includes bibliographical references. [BX2847.G7D3 1974] 73-4825 ISBN 0-8414-1865-9 (lib. bdg.)
1. Hermits—England. I. Title.

KAPSNER, Oliver Leonard, 271.03
1902-
Catholic religious orders; listing conventional and full names in English, foreign language, and Latin, also abbreviations, date and country of origin and founders. 2d ed., enl. Collegeville, Minn., St. John's Abbey Press, 1957. xxxviii, 594 p. 24 cm. Bibliography: p. xxvii-xxxvii. [BX2420.K3 1957] 57-1997
1. Monasticism and religious orders—Dictionaries. I. Title.

JAMES, George 271'.0'3109794
Wharton, 1858-1923.
The old Franciscan missions of California. Boston, Milford House [1973] xvi, 287 p. illus. 22 cm. A condensation of the author's In and out of the old missions of California. Reprint of the 1913 ed. published by Little, Brown, Boston. [F864.J23 1973] 73-4860 ISBN 0-87821-116-0 25.00 (lib. bdg.)
1. Spanish missions of California. 2. Franciscans in California. I. Title.

SEWARD, Desmond, 1935- 271'.05
The monks of war; the military religious orders. [Hamden, Conn.] Archon Books, 1972. ix, 346 p. illus. 22 cm. Bibliography: p. [316]-335. [CR4701.S48 1972] 73-39239 ISBN 0-208-01266-4 13.50
1. Military religious orders—History. I. Title.

WOODHOUSE, 271'.05'00902
Frederick Charles, 1827-1905.
The military religious orders of the Middle Ages: the Hospitallers, the Templars, the Teutonic knights, and others. With an appendix of other orders of knighthood: legendary, honorary, and modern. Freeport, N.Y., Books for Libraries Press [1973] p. (Essay index reprint series) Reprint of the 1879 ed. published by Society for Promoting Christian knowledge, London, in series: The Home library. [CR4701.W6 1973] 73-4572 ISBN 0-518-10107-X
1. Military religious orders. I. Title. II. Series: The Home library (London)

ALBERIONE, Giacomo 271.069
Giuseppe, 1884-
Religious life: life of courageous souls. Extracts from meditations and conferences of Very Rev. James Alberione, S. S. P., S. T. D. to the religious of his five congregations. Compiled and translated from the Italian by Daughters of St. Paul. [Boston?] St. Paul Editions [c1957] 107p. illus. 22cm. [BX2385.A6] 59-28518
1. Monastic and religious life. I. Title.

APOSTOLIC life, 271.069
being the English version of L'apostolat. Translated by Ronald Halstead. Westminster, Md., Newman Press [c1958] 206p. 23cm. (Religious life, 10) Papers edited by Albert Pie. Includes bibliography. [BX2435.A613 1958] 59-2070
1. Monastic and religious life. I. Pie, Albert, ed.

BULLETIN de spiritualite 271.069
monastique.
The message of monastic spirituality, by Andre Louf and the staff of the Collectanea OCR. Translated by Luke Stevens. New York, Desclee Co., 1964. xv. 304 p. 22 cm. A translation of the 1962 Bulletin de spiritualite monastique. "Notes" (bibilographical): p. [281] -297. [Z7839.B8] 64-19816
1. Monasticism and religious orders — Bibl. I. Louf, Andre, comp. II. Trappists. Collectanea Ordinis Cisterciensium Reformatorum. III. Title.

BULLETIN de spiritualite 271.069
monastique
The message of monastic spirituality, by Andre Louf and the staff of the Collectanea OCR. Tr. [from French] by Luke Stevens. New York, Desclee [c.] 1964. xv, 304p. 22cm. Bibl. 64-19816 4.95
1. Monasticism and religious orders—Bibl. I. Louf, Andre, comp. II. Trappists. Collectanea Ordinis Cisterciensium Reformatorum. III. Title.

CASSIODORES, Flavius 271.069
Magnus, Aurelius Senator ca.487-ca.580.
Happiness in the cloister. Westminster, Md., Newman [1962] 152p. 62-16058 3.50
1. Monastic and religious life. I. Title.

CASSIODOROS SENATOR, 271.069
Flavius Magnus Aurelius, ca. 487-ca. 280.
Cassiodori Senatoris Institutiones, ed. from the manuscripts by R.A.B. Mynors. [New York] Oxford Univ. Press [1961] 193p. 3.40
1. Theology—Methodology. 2. Classification of sciences. I. Mynors, Roger Aubrey Baskerville, ed. II. Title.

CATHOLIC University of 271.069
America. Institute in Catholic Pastoral Counseling.
Psychological aspects of spiritual development; Proceedings of the Institutes of Catholic Pastoral Counseling and of the Conferences for Religious Superiors of Men under the auspices of the director of summer session and workshops, the Catholic University of America. Edited by Michael J. O'Brien and Raymond J. Steimel. Washington, Catholic University of America Press [cover 1964, c1965] vii, 234 p. 22 cm. Includes bibliographies. [BV4012.C34] 65-12987
1. Psychology. Religious — Congresses. 2. Pastoral psychology — Congresses. 3. Monastic and religious life. I. O'Brien, Michael J., ed. II. Steimel, Raymond J., ed. III. Catholic University of America. Conference for Superiors on the Psychological Aspects of the Religious Life. IV. Title.

CATHOLIC CHURCH. POPE. 271.069
The states of perfection according to the teaching of the church; papal documents from Leo XIII to Pius XII [ed. by] Gaston Courtois. Pref. by Valerio Cardinal Valeri. Tr. [from French] by John A. O'Flynn. Westminster, Md., Newman [1962, c.]1961. xviii, 400p. Bibl. 62-16059 8.75
1. Monastic and religious life—Papal documents. I. Courtois, Gaston, ed. II. Title.

CATHOLIC UNIVERSITY OF 271.069
AMERICA. INSTITUTE IN CATHOLIC PASTORAL COUNSELING.
Psychological aspects of spiritual development; proceedings of the Insts. of Catholic Pastoral Counseling and of the Confs. for Religious Superiors of Men under the auspices of the director of summer session and workshops, the Catholic Univ. of Amer. Ed. by Michael J.

O'Brien, Raymond J. Steimel. Washington, D.C., Catholic Univ. of Amer. Pr. [c.1965] vii, 234p. 22cm. Bibl. [BV4012.C34] 65-12987 3.75 pap.,
1. Psychology, Religious—Congresses. 2. Pastoral psychology—Congresses. 3. Monastic and religious life. I. O'Brien, Michael J., ed. II. Steimel, Raymond J., ed. III. Catholic University of America. Conference for Superiors on the Psychological Aspects of the Religious Life. IV. Title.

COLIN, Louis. 1884- 271.069
The novitiate. Tr. from the French by Una Morrissy. Westminster. Md., Newman [c.] 1961. 447p. Bibl. 61-16566 4.95
1. Novitiate. I. Title.

CONNELL, Francis Jeremiah, 1888- 271.069
Spiritual and pastoral conferences to priests. Westminster, Md., Newman [c.]1962. 349p. 23cm. Bibl. 62-21496 4.95
1. Clergy—Religious life. 2. Pastoral theology—Catholic Church—Addresses, essays, lectures. 3. Christian ethics—Catholic authors. I. Title.

DICKINSON, John Compton. 271.069
Monastic life in medieval England. With 57 photos. and 6 plans. New York, Barnes & Noble [1962, c1961] xiii, 160 p. illus. 26 cm. Bibliography: p. 151-153. [BX2592.D48 1962] 62-934
1. Monasticism and religious orders—England. 2. Monasteries—England. I. Title.

DUFFEY, Felix D., 1903- 271.069
With anxious care. St. Louis, B. Herder [c.1961] 125p. 61-7244 2.75
1. Monastic and religious life. I. Title.

FLINN, Robert J 271.069
Admission to vows; recent directives and trends [by] Robert J. Flinn. Techny, Ill., Divine Word Publications, 1965. xi, 157 p. 24 cm. "Represents somewhat more than two thirds of the author's doctoral dissertation presented to the Pontifical Gregorian University. Bibliography: p. 143-150. 65-16595
1. Vows (Canon law) I. Title.

FLINN, Robert J. 271.069
Admission to vows; recent directives and trends [by] Robert J. Flinn. Techny, Ill., 60082 Divine Word Pubns. [c.]1965 xi, 157p. 24cm. Bibl. 65-16595 5.00
1. Vows (Canon law) I. Title.

FORD, John Cuthbert, 1902- 271.069
Religious superiors, subjects, and psychiatrists. Westminster, Md., Newman Press, 1963. 101 p. 21 cm. Bibliographical footnotes. [BX2440.F6] 63-23097
1. Monasticism and religious life. 2. Psychiatry and religion. 3. Manifestation of conscience. 4. Superiors, Religious. I. Title.

FORD, John Cuthbert, 1902- 271.069
Religious superiors, subjects, and psychiatrists. Westminster, Md., Newman [c.]1963. 101p. 21cm. Bibl. 63-23097 1.50 pap.,
1. Monasticism and religious life. 2. Psychiatry and religion. 3. Manifestation of conscience. 4. Superiors, Religious. I. Title.

GAIANI, Vito, 1912-ed 271.069
For a better religious life. Tr by Father Patrick. New York, St. Paul Pubs. [dist. Alba House, c.1962] 212 p. 21 cm. Digest of the Report of the Intl. Congress of the States of Perfection held in Rome, 1950. 62-20956 3.95
1. Monastic and religious life. I. Congressus Generalis de Statibus Perfectionis, Rome, 1950. II. Title.

GLEASON, Robert W. 271.069
To live is Christ; nature and grace in the religious life. New York, Sheed and Ward [c.1961] 180p. Bibl. 61-7287 3.00 half cloth,
1. Monastic and religious life. I. Title.

HELBO, Florent 271.069
Ces inutiles; propos sur la vie religieuse. Sous la direction de Florent Helbo, avec Norbert Capelle, Charles Cossee de Maulde, Georges Nossent. Realisation de Pierre Defoux. Gembloux [Belgium] J. Duculot [dist. Philadelphia, Chilton, 1964]c.1962. 363p. illus. 25cm. 64-9256 2.98 pap.,
1. Monasticism and religious orders—Anedotes, facetiae, satire, etc. 2. Monasticism and religious orders—Caricatures and cartoons. I. Title.

LACARRIERE, Jacques, 1925- 271.069
Men possessed by God; the story of the desert monks of ancient Christendom. Translated by Roy Monkcom. [1st ed. in the U.S.A.] Garden City, N. Y., Doubleday, 1964 [c1963] 237 p. illus., maps. 22 cm. Translation of Les hommes ivres de Dieu. Bibliography: p. 229-231. [BX2465.L293 1964] 64-13885
1. Monasticism and religious orders—Early church. 2. Hermits. I. Title.

LECLERCQ, Jean, 1911- 271.069
The life of perfection; points of view on the essence of the religious state. Translated by Leonard J. Doyle. Collegeville, Minn., Liturgical Press [c1961] 125 p. 22 cm. [BX2435.L423] 63-348
1. Monastic and religious life. I. Title.

LUCAS OF ST. JOSEPH. Father 271.069
The secret of sanctity of St. John of the Cross. Tr. by SisterMary Alberto. Milwaukee, Bruce [c.1962] 166p. 23cm. 62-13664 3.75
1. Juan de la Cruz, Saint, 1542-1591. 2. Monastic and religious life. 3. Spiritual life—Catholic authors. I. Title.

MCLAUGHLIN, Barry. 271.069
Nature, grace, and religious development. Glen Rock, N. J., Paulist [1968,c.1964] ix, 164p. 18cm. (Deus bks.) [BR110M33] 1.45 pap.,
1. Psychology, Religious. 2. Spiritual life—Catholic authors. I. Title.

MCLAUGHLIN, Barry 271.069
Nature, grace, and religious development. Westminster, Md., Newman [c.]1964. ix, 164p. 22cm. 63-12253 3.95
1. Psychology, Religious. 2. Spiritual life—Catholic authors. I. Title.

MAHER, Trafford Patrick, 1914- 271.069
Lest we build on sand; a study of the natural basis for supernatural formation. St. Louis, Catholic Hospital Assn. of the U.S. and Canada [1962] 273p. illus. 23cm. 62-52149 4.50
1. Monastic and religious life. I. Title.

MASON, Mary Elizabeth 271.069
Active life and contemplative life, a study of the concepts from Plato to the present. Ed., foreword by George E. Ganss. Milwaukee, Marquette Univ. Pr. [c.]1961. 137p. Bibl. 60-16598 2.50 pap.,
1. Perfection (Catholic)—History of doctrines. I. Title.

MASON, Mary Elizabeth. 271.069
Active life and contemplative life, a study of the concepts from Plato to the present. Edited, with a foreword by George E. Ganss. Milwaukee, Marquette University Press, 1961. 137p. 23cm. Includes bibliography. [BX2350.5.M3] 60-16598
1. Perfection (Catholic)—History of doctrines. I. Title.

MERTON, Thomas Name in religion: Father Louis 1915- 271.069
The solitary life. [Lexington, Ky.] [220 Market St.] Stamperia del Santuccio c.1960. 21p. 26cm. (Opus XVI of which there are 60 copies signed by the author) 'Pro manuscripto.' 60-34568 25.00
1. Hermits. 2. Solitude. I. Title.

NATIONAL Congress of Religious of the United States. 2d, University of Notre Dame, 1961. 271.069
Proceedings of the Second National Congress of Religious of the United States: Men's Section. Edited by Celsus R. Wheeler [and others. Notre Dame, Ind.] University of Notre Dame Press, 1962. vi, 166p. 23cm. Includes bibliographical references. [BX2435.N3 1961] 62-51168
1. Monastic and religious life Congresses. I. Wheeler, Celsus R., ed. II. Title.

NATIONAL Congress of Religious of the United States. University of Notre Dame, 1961. 271.069
Proceedings of the Second National Congress of Religious of the United States: Men's Section. Ed. by Celsus R. Wheeler [others. Notre Dame, Ind.] Univ. of Notre Dame Pr. [c.]1962. vi, 166p. 23cm. Bibl. 62-51168 4.00
1. Monastic and religious life—Congresses. I. Wheeler, Celsus R., ed. II. Title.

NOTRE Dame, Ind. University. Sisters' Institute of Spirituality. 271.069
Prayer and sacrifice [by] Albert E. Bourke [and others. Notre Dame] University of Notre Dame Press, 1962. 249p. 21cm. (Religious life in the modern world: selections from the Notre Dame Institute of Spirituality, v. 4) [Notre Dame paperbooks] NDP17. 'Articles . . . previously published in the Proceeding s of the Sisters' Institute of Spirituality 1953, 1955 and 1956.' Bibliographical footnotes. [BX2385.N6] 62-6148
1. Spiritual life—Catholic authors. I. Bourke, Albert E. II. Title. III. Series.

PROVERA, Paolo 271.069
Live your vocation. Translated from the Italian by Thomas F. Murray. St. Louis, B. Herder Book Co. [1959, i.e.1960] 260p. 22cm. 60-2639 3.75
1. Monastic and religious life. I. Title.

REVIEW for religious. 271.069
Questions on religious life St. Marys, Kan., St. Mary's Coll. Author, [c.]1964. xiii, 337p. 24cm. Bibl. 64-3733 6.00
1. Monasticism and religious orders. 2. Monasticism and religious orders (Canon law) 3. Questions and answers—Monasticism and religious orders. I. Title.

SCHLECK, Charles A 271.069
The theology of vocations. Milwaukee, Bruce Pub. co. [1963] 357 p. 24 cm. [BX2380.S33] 62-20960
1. Vocation, Ecclesiastical. I. Title.

SCHLECK, Charles A. 271.069
The theology of vocations. Milwaukee, Bruce [c.1963] 357p. 24cm. 62-20960 7.00
1. Vocation, Ecclesiastical. I. Title.

SHEEN, Fulton John, Bp., 1895- 271.069
The priest is not his own. [1st ed.] New York, McGraw-Hill [1963] 276 p. 21 cm. [BX1912.5.S4] 63-15896
1. Priests. 2. Meditations. 3. Catholic Church—Clergy. I. Title.

SHEEN, Fulton John, Bp., 1895- 271.069
The priest is not his own. New York, McGraw [c.1963] 276p. 21cm. 63-15896 4.95 bds.,
1. Priests. 2. Meditations. 3. Catholic Church—Clergy. I. Title.

THEOLOGICAL Institute for Local Superiors, University of Notre Dame. 271.069
Prayer and sacrifice [by] Albert E. Bourke [and others. Notre Dame] University of Notre Dame Press, 1962. 249 p. 21 cm. (Religious life in the modern world, v. 4) "Articles ... previously published in the Proceedings of the Sisters' Institute of Spirituality 1953, 1955, and 1956." Bibliographical footnotes. [BX2385.T45] 62-6148
1. Spiritual life — Catholic authors. I. Bourke, Albert M. II. Notre Dame, Ind. University. III. Title. IV. Series.

VAN ZELLER, Hubert, 1905- 271.069
Approach to monasticism. New York, Sheed and Ward [1960] 182 p. 21 cm. Secular name: Calude Van Zeller. Includes bibliography. [BX2435.V3] 60-7309
1. Monastic and religious life. I. Title. II. Series.

VAN ZELLER, Hubert [secular name: Claude Van Zeller] 271.069
Approach to monasticism. New York, Sheed and Ward [c.1960] 182p. 21cm. Includes bibliography. 60-7309. 3.00
1. Monastic and religious life. I. Title.

WOLTER, Marius, 1825-1900 271.069
The principles of monasticism. Tr [from Latin] ed., annotated by Bernard A. Sause. St. Louis, Herder [c.1962] xx, 789 p. 24 cm. (Studies in ascetical theology, n.1) Bibl. 62-105071 12.00
1. Monastic and religious life. 2. Monasticism and religious orders—Rules. I. Sause, bernard austin, 1901- ed. and tr. II. Title. III. Series.

WOLTER, Maurus, 1825-1900. 271.069
The principles of monasticism. Translated, edited, and annotated by Bernard A. sause. St. Louis, Herder [1962] xx, 789 p. 24 cm. (Studies in ascetical theology, no. 1) Translation of Praecipua ordinis monastici elementa. Bibliography: p. 765-776. [BX2435.W613] 62-10507
1. Monastic and religious life. 2. Monasticism and religious orders — Rules. I. Sause, Bernard Austin, 1901- ed. and tr. II. Title. III. Series.

BUTLER, Richard, 1918- 271.0692
Religious vocation: an unnecessary mystery. Foreword by Edwin Vincent Byrne. [Chicago] H. Regnery Co., 1961. 167p. 21cm. [BX2380.B83] 61-7961
1. Vocation (in religious orders, congregations, etc.) I. Title.

FICHTER, Joseph Henry, 1908- 271.0692
Religion as an occupation; a study in the sociology of professions. [Notre Dame, Ind] Univ. of Notre Dame Press [c.]1961 295p. Bibl. 61-10846 6.50
1. Vocation (in religious orders, congregations, etc.) 2. Catholic Church—Clergy—Appointment, call, and election. I. Title.

FRISON, Basil M., Rev. 1912- 271.0692
Selection and incorporation of candidates for the religious life. Milwaukee, Bruce [c.1962] 186p. 23cm. Bibl. 62-13665 5.75
1. Monasticism and religious orders—Education. 2. Vocation (in religious orders, congregations, etc.) I. Title.

*GILLESE, John Patrick 271.0692
About your state in life. Pulaski, Wis., Franciscan [c.1964] 56p. 20cm. .25 pap.,
I. Title.

INTERNATIONAL Congress on Vocations to the States of Perfection. 1st, Rome, 1961. 271.0692
Today's vocation crisis; a summary of the studies and discussions. Translated and edited by Godfrey Poage and Germain Lievin. Westminister, Md., Newman Press for Pontifical Organization for Religious Vocations, Vatican City, 1962. vii, 435 p. tables. 21 cm. Sponsored by Sacra Congregazione del Religiosi. Bibliography: p. 407-435. [BX2380.I5] 63-1449
1. Vocation (in religious orders, congregations, etc.) 2. Catholic Church — Clergy — Appointment, call and election. I. Catholic Church. Congregatio de Religiosis. II. Poage, Godfrey Robert, 1920- ed. and tr. III. Lievin. IV. Title.

POAGE, Godfrey Robert, 1920- 271.0692
Parents' role in vocations, by Godfrey Poage and John P. Treacy. Milwaukee, Bruce Pub. Co. [1959] 132p. 23cm. [BX2380.P59] 59-9540
1. Vocation. 2. Vocational guidance. 3. Clergy—Appointment, call. and election. 4. Vocation (in religious orders, congregations, etc.) I. Treacy, John Patrick, joint author. II. Title.

POAGE, Godfrey Robert, 1920- 271.0692
Secrets of successful recruiting; the principles of religious vocational guidance and tested techniques of America's most successful religious recruiters. Foreword by Germain Lievin. Westminster, Md., Newman Press, 1961. 219p. 22cm. Includes bibliography. [BX2380.P63] 61-8972
1. Vocation (in religions orders, congregations, etc.) I. Title.

PRIEST and vocations *(The).* 271.0692
Tr. [from French] by Ronald Halstead. Westminster, Md., Newman, 1962 [c.1961] ix, 181p. 22cm. (Religious life, 11) 62-3808 4.75
1. Vocation (in religious orders, congregations, etc.)

SCREENING candidates for 271.0692
the priesthood and religious life [by] Magda B. Arnold [and others] Pref. by Vincent V. Herr. Chicago, Loyola University Press [1962] 203p. illus. 24cm. [BX2380.S35] 62-20462
1. Vocation (in religious orders, congregations, etc.) 2. Catholic Church—Clergy—Appointment, call, and election. 3. Mental tests. I. Arnold, Magda B.

THERESE CATHERINE Sister 271.0692
Let's talk it over: a student's text in vocational guidance. Foreword by Very Rev. Godfrey Poage. New York, Noble & Noble [c.1962] 92p. illus. (pt. col.) 22cm. 1.25 pap.,
I. Title.

BARRINGTON, Leo 271.0698
Go forth; considerations for religious brothers and other religious teachers in their first years of community. dist. New York St. Martin's Press, c.]1961[ ] 140p. 61-3963 2.00
1. Monasticism and religious orders—Brothers. I. Title.

LEEMING, Bernard. 271.0698
The mysticism of obedience. [Boston?] St. Paul Editions [1964] 71 p. 19 cm. [BX2435.L43] 64-16827
1. Obedience. I. Title.

LEEMING, Bernard 271.0698
The mysticism of obedience. St. Paul Eds. [dist. Boston, Daughters of St. Paul, c.1964] 71p. 19cm. 64-16827 2.00; 1.00 pap.,
1. Obedience. I. Title.

ROSMINI SERBATI, Antonio, 1797-1855. 2710.698
Counsels to religious superiors. Selected, edited, and translated by Claude Leetham. Westminster, Md., Newman Press [1961] 177p. 23cm. [BX2438.R6] 60-14829
1. Spiritual I. Title.

SCHUSTER, I'defonso [Alfredo I'defonso Schusters Cardinal 1880-1954. 271.0698
Historical notes on St. Benedict's Rule for monks. Tr. by Leonard J. Doyle, Hamden, Conn., Shoe String Pr., 1962 [c.1961] 102 p. Bibl. 61-18384 3.50
1. Benedictus, Saint, Abbot of Monte Cassino. Regula. I. Title.

KAUFFMAN, Christopher J., 1936- 271'.07
Tamers of death : the history of the Alexian Brothers / Christopher J. Kauffman. New York : Seabury Press, c1976- v. : ill. ; 24 cm. "A crossroad book." Contents.Contents.—v. 1. From 1300 to 1789. Includes bibliographical references and index. [BX2890.K38] 76-24469 ISBN 0-8164-0314-7 : 15.95
1. Alexian Brothers—History. I. Title.

ECCLESINE, Margaret Wyvill. 271.07'0924
A touch of radiance; Sister Honorat of the Bon Secours Sisters. Milwaukee, Bruce Pub. Co. [1966] xiv, 226 p. illus., ports. 22 cm. [BX4705.H742E25] 67-1650
1. Honorat, Sister, 1898-1961. I. Title.

CONSTABLE, Giles 271.09
Monastic tithes, from their origins to the twelfth century. [New York] Cambridge. 1964. xxi, 346p. 23cm. (Cambridge studies in medieval life and thought, new ser., v.10) Bibl. 64-24317 9.50
1. Tithes—Hist. 2. Monasticism and religious orders—Finance—Hist. 3. Monasticism and religious orders—Middle Ages. I. Title. II. Series.

MOSS, Doley C 271.09
Of cell and cloister; Catholic religious orders through the ages. Illustrated by Virginia Broderick. Milwaukee, Bruce Pub. Co. [1957] 248p. illus. 23cm. Includes bibliography. [BX2461.M63] 57-8941
1. Monasticism and religious orders—Hist. I. Title.

DECARREAUX, Jean, 1899- 271.0902
Monks and civilization, from the barbarian invasions to the reign of Charlemagne. Translated by Charlotee Haldane. [1st ed. in the U.S.A.] Garden City, N.Y., Doubleday, 1964. 397 p. maps (part fold.) 22 cm. Translation of Les moines et la civilisation en Occident. Bibliography: p. 376-387. [BX2465.D413 1964] 64-19287
1. Monasticism and religious orders — Early church. 2. Civilization, Christian. 3. Civilization, Occidental. I. Title.

DECARREAUX, Jean, 1899- 271.0902
Monks and civilization, From the barbarian invasions to the reign of Charlemagne. Translated by Charlotte Haldane. [1st ed. in the U. S. A.] Garden City, N. Y., Doubleday, 1964. 397 p. maps (part fold.) 22 cm. Translation of Les moines et la civilisation en Occident. Bibliography: p. 376-387. [BX2465.D413 1964] 64-19287
1. Monasticism and religious orders—Early church. 2. Civilization, Christian. 3. Civilization, Occidental. I. Title.

LECLERCQ, Jean, 1911- 271.0902
The love of learning and the desire for God; a study of monastic culture. Tr. by Catharine Misrahi. New York, New Amer. Lib. [1962, c.1961] 336p. 18cm. (Mentor Omega, MT432) Bibl. .75 pap.,
1. Monasticism and religious orders—Middle Ages. 2. Christian literature, Early—Hist. & crit. 3. Theology—Middle Ages. I. Title.

LECLERCQ, Jean, 1911- 271.0902
The love of learning and the desire for God; a study of monastic culture. Translated by Catharine Misrahi. New York, Fordham University Press [1961] 415 p. 23 cm. Includes bibliography. [BX2470.L413] 60-53004
1. Monasticism and religious orders—Middle Ages, 600-1500. 2. Christian literature, Early—History and criticism. 3. Theology—Middle Ages, 600-1500. I. Title.

CASHIN, Edward L., 1927- 271.092
Your calling as a brother [by] Edward L. Cashin. [1st ed.] New York, R. Rosen Press [1966] 159 p. 22 cm. (Careers in depth, 62) Bibliography: p. 156-159. [BX2835.C3] 66-12894
1. Brothers (in religious orders, congregations, etc.) 2. Vocation (in religious orders, congregations, etc.) I. Title.

WEIGLE, Marta. 271'.093'0789
Brothers of light, brothers of blood : the Penitentes of the Southwest / Marta Weigle. 1st ed. Albuquerque : University of New Mexico Press, c1976. xix, 300 p., [7] leaves of plates : ill. ; 25 cm. Includes index. Bibliography: p. 276-287. [BX3653.U6W39] 75-21188 12.95
1. Hermanos Penitentes. I. Title.

PALLADIUS, successively Bp. of Helenopolis and of Aspons d.ca.430 271.0932
Palladius: the Lausiac history. Tr., annotated by Robert T. Meyer. Westminster, Md., Newman [c.]1965. vii, 265p. 23cm. (Ancient Christian writers; the works of the Fathers in translation, no.34) Bibl. [BR60.A35 no.34] 65-18184 4.50
1. Monasticism and religious orders—Egypt. 2. Monasticism and religious orders—Early church. I. Meyer, Robert T., 1911- ed. and tr. II. Title. III. Title: Title: The Lausiac history. (Series)

MATTHEW, Donald 271.094
The Norman monasteries and their English possessions. New York] Oxford [c.]1962. x, 200p. 23cm. (Oxford historical ser., 2d ser.) Bibl. 62-5886 4.40
1. Monasteries—Normandy. 2. Monasteries—Gt. Brit. I. Title.

MATTHEW, Donald James Alexander, 1930- 271.094
The Norman monasteries and their English possessions. [London] Oxford University Press, 1962. x, 200 p. 23 cm. (Oxford historical series, 2d ser.) [BX2592.M3] 62-5886
1. Monasteries—Normandy. 2. Monasteries—Gt. Brit. I. Title.

COOK, George Henry, ed. 271.0942
Letters to Cromwell on the suppression of the monasteries. London, John Baker [Mystic, Conn., Verry, c.1965] viii, 272p. port. 22cm. [BX2592.C6] 65-4152 9.00
1. Monasteries—England. 2. Gt.Brit.—Hist.—Henry VIII, 1509-1547—Sources. 3. Monasticism and religious orders—England. I. Cromwell, Thomas, Earl of Essex, 1485?-1540. II. Title. III. Title: The suppression of the monasteries.

COOK, George Henry, ed. 271.0942
Letters to Cromwell on the suppression of the monasteries. London, J. Baker [New York, Hillary House, c.1965] viii, 272p. port. 22cm. [BX2592.C6] 65-4152 7.50
1. Monasteries—England. 2. Gt. Brit.—Hist.—Henry VIII, 1509-1547—Sources. 3. Monasticism and religious orders—England. I. Cromwell, Thomas, earl of Essex, 1485?-1540. II. Title. III. Title: The suppression of the monasteries.

KNOWLES, David, 1896- 271.0942
The monastic order in England; a history of its development from the times of St. Dunstan to the Fourth Lateran Council, 940-1216. 2d ed. [New York] Cambridge, 1963. xxi, 780p. plate, diagrs. 26cm. Bibl. 64-29 13.15
1. Monasticism and religious orders—England. I. Title.

EMERY, Richard Wilder, 1912- 271.0944
The friars in medieval France; a catalogue of French mendicant convents, 1200-1550. New York, Columbia, 1962. xix, 130p. maps. 21cm. Bibl. 62-16689 4.00
1. Friars. 2. Monasticism and religious orders—France. I. Title.

ANSON, Peter F., ed. 271.1
The brothers of Braemore. London, Campion Press [dist. New York, Taplinger, 1960] 61p. 19cm. 1.50 pap.,
I. Title.

BARRY, Colman James, 1921- 271.1
Worship and work; Saint John's Abbey and University, 1856-1956. Collegeville, Minn., Saint John's Abbey, 1956. 447p. illus. 27cm. (American Benedictine Academy. Historical studies, no. 11) [BX2525.C6S3] 56-10530
1. St. John's Abbey, Collegeville, Minn. 2. St. John's University, Collegeville, Minn. I. Title.

BECKMAN, Peter, 1911- 271.1
Kansas monks; a history of St. Benedict's Abbey. Atchison, Kan, Abbey Student Press [1957] 362p. illus. 24cm. (American Benedictine Academy. Historical studies. Monasteries and convents, 3) [BX2525.A8S22] 57-44042
1. St. Benedict's Abbey, Atchison, Kan. 2. St. Benedict's College, Atchison, Kan. I. Title.

BENEDICTUS, Saint, Abbot of Monte Cassino. 271.1
The rule of Saint Benedict, in Latin and English, edited translated by Justin McCann. Westminster, Md., Newman Press, 1952. xxiv, 214p. facsim. 20cm. (The Orchard books) [BX3004.E6 1952] 53-863
1. Benedictiones. I. Title. II. Series.

BENEDICTUS Saint, Abbot of Monte Cassino 271'.1
The rule of Saint Benedict. Translated with an introd. by Cardinal Gasquet. New York, Cooper Square Publishers, 1966. xxviii, 130 p. port. 17 cm. (The Medieval library) [BX3004.E6 1966] 66-30730
1. Monasticism and religious orders—Rules. 2. Benedictines I. Gasquet, Francis Aldan, Cardinal, 1846-1929, tr. II. Title.

BENEDICTUS, Saint, Abbot of Monte Cassino. 271'.1
The rule of Saint Benedict. Translated with an introd. by Cardinal Gasquet. New York, Cooper Square Publishers, 1966. xxviii, 130 p. port. 17 cm. (The Medieval library) [BX3004.E6 1966] 66-30730
I. Gasquet, Francis Aidan, Cardinal, 1846-1929, tr. II. Title.

BUTLER, Edward Cuthbert, 1858-1934. 271.1
Benedictine monachism; studies in Benedictine life and rule. New foreword by David Knowles. New York, Barnes & Noble [1962] [12], 424p. 22cm. Bibl. 62-4053 7.00
1. Benedictines. 2. Benedictus, Saint, Abbot of Monte Cassino. I. Title.

COWDREY, Herbert Edward John. 271'.1
The Cluniacs and the Gregorian reform, by H. E. J. Cowdrey. Oxford, Clarendon P., 1970. xxvii, 289 p. 23 cm. Bibliography: p. [274]-282. [BX3460.C68] 73-525044 75/-
1. Cluniacs. 2. Gregorius VII, Saint, Pope, 1015 (ca.)-1085. I. Title.

DALY, Lowrie John. 271.1
Benedictine monasticism, its formation and development through the 12th century [by] Lowrie J. Daly. New York, Sheed and Ward [1965] xv, 375 p. 22 cm. Includes bibliographies. [BX3006.2.D3] 65-12201
1. Benedictines — Hist. 2. Monasticism and religious orders — Middle Ages. I. Title.

DALY, Lowrie John 271.1
Benedictine monasticism, its formation and development through the 12th century. New York, Sheed [c.1965] xv, 375p. 22cm. Bibl. [BX3006.2.D3] 65-12201 7.50
1. Benedictines—Hist. 2. Monasticism and religious orders—Middle Ages. I. Title.

EVANS, Joan, 1893- 271'.1
Monastic life at Cluny, 910-1157. [Hamden, Conn.] Archon Books, 1968. xix, 137 p. illus., facsims. maps. 22 cm. Includes music. Bibliography: p. [xiii]-xix. [BX2615.C63E8 1968] 68-20376
1. Cluny, France (Benedictine abbey) I. Title.

GRIFFITHS, Bede, 1906- 271.1
The golden string. New York, Kenedy [1954?] 168p. 22cm. Autobiography [BX4668.G74] 55-5191
1. Converts, Catholic. I. Title.

GRIFFITHS, Bede, 1906- 271.1
The golden string. Garden City, N.Y., Doubleday [1964, c.1955] 187p. 18cm. (Image bk. D173) .75 pap.,
1. Converts, Catholic. I. Title.

HILPISCH, Stephanus, 1894- 271.1
Benedictinism through changing centuries. Translated from the German by Leonard J. Doyle. Collegeville, Minn., St. John's Abbey Press, 1958. 172p. illus. 23cm. Includes bibliography. [BX3006.H513] 60-37319
1. Benedictines—Hist. I. Title.

HOUTRYVE, Idesbald van, 1886- 271.1
Benedictine peace. Translated from the 2d French ed. (1946) by Leonard J. Doyle. Westminster, Md., Newman Press, 1950. xiv, 235 p. 22 cm. Bibliographical footnotes. [BX3003.H62] 50-8737
1. Benedictines. I. Title.

HUNT, Noreen, comp. 271'.1
Cluniac monasticism in the central Middle Ages. [Hamden, Conn.] Archon Books, 1971. x, 248 p. 23 cm. Bibliography: p. [238]-242. [BX2615.C63H79 1971b] 76-32307 ISBN 0-208-01247-8
1. Monasticism and religious orders—France—Cluny—Addresses, essays, lectures. 2. Cluniacs—Addresses, essays, lectures. I. Title.

MORIN, Germain, 1861-1946. 271.1
Ideal of the monastic life found in the apostolic age. Translated from the French by C. Gunning, with a pref. by Bede Camm. Westminster, Md., Newman Press, 1950. xvi, 200 p. 19 cm. [BX3003.M62] 50-14971
1. Benedictines. 2. Monasticism. I. Title.

RYELANDT, Idesbald 271.1
The quest for God; a study in Benedictine spirituality. Translated from the French by Matthew Dillon. London, St. Louis, Herder [1959] 207p. 21cm. 60-1232 3.25
1. Benedictines. I. Title.

SORG, Rembert, 1908- 271.1
Holy work; towards a Benedictine theology of manual labor. [Rev. & enl. ed.] St. Louis, Pio Decimo Press [1953] 124p. 24cm. Published in 1949 under title: Towards a Benedictine theology of manual labor. [BX3003.S6 1953] 54-2593
1. Benedictus, Saint, Abbot of Monte Cassino. Regula. 2. Benedictines. 3. Church and labor. I. Title.

TUNINK, Wilfrid. 271.1
Vision of peace, a study of Benedictine monastic life. With a foreword by Joseph Cardinal Ritter. New York, Farrar, Straus [1963] 332 p. 22 cm. Includes bibliography. [BX3004.Z5T8] 63-10565
1. Benedictus, Siant, Abbot of Monte Cassino. Regula. 2. Monastic and religious life. I. Title.

TUNINK, Wilfrid 271.1
Vision of peace, a study of Benedictine monastic life. Foreword by Joseph Cardinal Ritter. New York, Farrar [c.1963] 332p. 22cm. Bibl. 63-10565 4.95 bds.,
1. Benedictus, Saint, Abbot of Monte Cassino, Regula. 2. Monastic and religious life. I. Title.

VAN ZELLER, Hubert, 1905- 271.1
The holy rule; notes on St. Benedict's legislation for monks. New York, Sheed and Ward [1958] 476 p. 20 cm. Includes bibliographies. [BX3004.Z5V3] 58-10554
1. Benedictus, Saint, Abbot of Monte Cassino. Regula. I. Title.

CHAPMAN, John, Father, 1865-1933. 271'.1'024 B
Saint Benedict and the sixth century. Westport, Conn., Greenwood Press [1971] vi, 239 p. 23 cm. Reprint of the 1929 ed. Includes bibliographical references. [BX4700.B3C5 1971] 79-109719 ISBN 0-8371-4209-1
1. Benedictus, Saint, Abbot of Monte Cassino. 2. Benedictus, Saint, Abbot of Monte Cassino. Regula. 3. Monasticism and religious orders. I. Title.

HURT, James, 1934- 271'.1'024
Alfric. New York Twayne Publishers [1972] 152 p. 21 cm. (Twayne's English authors series, 131) Bibliography: p. 145-150. [PR1533.H8] 76-162871
1. Aelfric, Abbot of Eynsham.

REYNOLDS, Bede, 1892- 271'.1'024 B
A rebel from riches : the autobiography of an unpremeditated monk / Bede Reynolds (ne Kenyon L. Reynolds). Canfield, Ohio : Alba Books, [1975] 150 p., [11] leaves of plates : ill. ; 18 cm. [BX4705.R446A34] 74-27608 pbk. : 1.65
1. Reynolds, Bede, 1892- I. Title.

RYAN, George E. 271'.1'024 B
Botolph of Boston, by George E. Ryan. Foreword by Richard Cardinal Cushing. [North Quincy, Mass., Christopher Pub. House, 1971] 268 p. illus., facsims. 25 cm. Includes bibliographical references. [BX4700.B76R9] 76-136030 ISBN 0-8158-0252-8 10.00
1. Botolph, Saint, d. 680. 2. Boston. I. Title.

DILWORTH, Mark. 271'.1'04333
The Scots in Franconia : a century of monastic life / Mark Dilworth. Totowa, N.J. : Rowman and Littlefield, 1974. 301 p. : ill. ; 23 cm. Includes index. Bibliography: p. 282-289. [BX2618.S3117D54 1974b] 74-195058 ISBN 0-87471-453-2 : 13.50
1. Sankt Jakob (Monastery), Wurzburg. 2. Scotch in Franconia. I. Title.

WISPLINGHOFF, Erich. 271'.1'04333
Die Benediktinerabtei Siegburg / im Auftr. d. Max-Planck-Inst. f. Geschichte bearb. von Erich Wisplinghoff. Berlin ; New York : de Gruyter, 1975. ix, 263 p. ; 25 cm. (His Das Erzbistum Koln ; 2) (Die Bistumer der Kirchenprovinz Koln) (Germania sacra ; n. F., 9) (Series: Wisplinghoff, Erich. Das Erzbistum Koln ; 2.) Includes index. Bibliography: p. 2-5. [BX1534.A1G53 n.F. 9, pt. 2] [BX2618.S5] 75-512994 ISBN 3-11-005752-2 : DM110.00
1. Siegburg, Ger. St. Michael (Benedictine abbey) I. Title. II. Series.

MURPHY, Joseph F. 271'.1'0766
Tenacious monks : the Oklahoma Benedictines, 1875-1975 : Indian missionaries, Catholic founders, educators, agriculturists / by Joseph F. Murphy. Shawnee, Okla. : Benedictine Color Press, [1974] x, 465 p. : ill. ; 25 cm. Includes bibliographical references. [BX3009.O5M87] 74-84770
1. St. Gregory's Abbey, Shawnee, Okla. 2. Benedictines in Oklahoma. 3. Indians of North America—Oklahoma—Missions. I. Title.

VAN ZELLER, Hubert, 1905- 271.109
The Benedictine idea. Springfield, Ill., Templegate [c1959] 297 p. 23 cm. Secular name: Claude Van Zeller. Includes bibliography. [BX3006.2.V3] 60-4420
1. Benedictines — Hist. I. Title. II. Series.

DELFORGE, Thomas 271.10924
Columba Marmion, servant of God. Tr. by Richard L. Stewart. St. Louis, B. Herder [1966, c.1965] viii, 71p. 19cm. Bibl. [BX4705.M411D4] 66-3546 1.50 pap.,
I. Marmion, Columba, Abbott, 1858-1923. II. Title.

GREGORIUS I, the 271'.1'0924
Great, Saint, Pope, 540(ca.)-604.
The dialogues of Gregory the Great. Book two: Saint Benedict. Translated, with an introd. and notes, by Myra L. Uhlfelder. Indianapolis, Bobbs-Merrill [1967] xxiv, 49 p. 20 cm. (The Library of liberal arts, 216) Translation of Book 2 of Dialogi de vita. [BX4700.B3G718] 66-30611
1. Benedictus, Saint, Abbot of Monte Cassino. I. Uhlfelder, Myra L., ed. & tr. II. Title.

ROCKWELL, Anne F. 271'.1'0924' B
Glass, stones & crown; the Abbe Suger and the building of St. Denis [by] Anne Rockwell. [1st ed.] New York, Atheneum, 1968. 80 p. illus. 25 cm. [DC89.7.S8R6] 68-12241
1. Suger, Abbot of Saint Denis, 1081-1151—Juvenile literature. 2. Saint-Denis, France (Benedictine abbey)—Juvenile literature. I. Title.

BEACH, Peter. 271.1096431
Benedictine and Moor; a Christian adventure in Moslem Morocco, by Peter Beach and William Dunphy. Introd. by John LaFarge. [1st ed.] New York, Holt, Rinehart and Winston [1960] 214p. illus. 22cm. [BX2740.M8B4] 60-12011
1. Toumililine. Morocco. Monastere benediction. I. Dunphy, William, joint author. II. Title.

BOUYER, Louis, 1913- 271.12
The Cistercian heritage. [1st English ed.] Westminster, Md., Newman Press [1958] 207p. 23cm. 'A translation of La spiritualite de Citeaux, by Elizabeth A. Livingstone.' Includes bibliography. [BX3403.B613] 58-13637
1. Cistercians. I. Title.

CISTERCIAN Studies 271'.12
Conference, 2d, Kalamazoo, Mich., 1972.
Studies in medieval Cistercian history, II; [papers] edited by John R. Sommerfeldt. [Spencer, Mass.] Cistercian Publications; [distributed by] Consortium Press, Washington, 1974 [c1973] p. cm. (Cistercian studies series, no. 24) Conference held Apr. 30-May 3, 1972. Includes bibliographical references. [BX3401.C575 1972] 74-8625 ISBN 0-87907-824-3 12.75
1. Cistercians—Congresses. I. Sommerfeldt, John R., ed. II. Title. III. Series.

LEKAI, Louis Julius, 271'.12
1916-
The Cistercians : ideals and reality / Louis J. Lekai. Kent, Ohio : Kent State University Press, c1977. p. cm. Includes index. Bibliography: p. [BX3402.2.L44] 77-3692 ISBN 0-87338-201-3 : 20.00
1. Cisterians. I. Title.

ORTHODOX-CISTERCIAN 271'.12
Symposium, Oxford University, 1973.
One yet two : monastic tradition, East and West : Orthodox-Cistercian Symposium, Oxford University, 26 August-1 September, 1973 / edited by M. Basil Pennington. Kalamazoo, Mich. : Cistercian Publications, 1976. 509 p. ; 23 cm. (Cistercian studies series ; no. 29) Includes bibliographical references. [BX3401.O77 1973] 75-26146 ISBN 0-87907-829-4 : 14.95
1. Cistercians—Congresses. 2. Monasticism and religious orders, Orthodox Eastern—Congresses. 3. Monastic and religious life—Congresses. I. Pennington, M. Basil. II. Title. III. Series.

STUDIES in medieval 271'.12
Cistercian history. Presented to Jeremiah F. O'Sullivan. Spencer, Mass., Cistercian Publications, 1971. xi, 204, [1] p. 23 cm. (Cistercian studies series, no. 13) Contents.Contents.—O'Callaghan, J. F. Preface.—Donnelly, J. S. Dedication.—Lackner, B. K. The liturgy of early Citeaux.—Sommerfeldt, J. R. The social theory of Bernard of Clairvaux.—Constable, G. A report of a lost sermon by St. Bernard on the failure of the Second Crusade.—Brundage, J. A. A transformed angel (X 3.31.18): the problem of the crusading monk.—O'Callaghan, J. F. The Order of Calatrava and the archbishops of Toledo, 1147-1245.—Buczek, D. S. "Pro defendendis ordinis": the French Cistercians and their enemies.—Hays, R. W. The Welsh monasteries and the Edwardian conquest.—Desmond, L. A. The statute of Carlisle and the Cistercians, 1298-1369.—Telesca, W. J. The Cistercian dilemma at the close of the Middle Ages: Gallicanism or Rome.—Volz, C. Martin Luther's attitude toward Bernard of Clairvaux.—Bibliography of studies by Jeremiah F. O'Sullivan (p. [205]) [BX3402.2.S78 1971b] 77-152486 ISBN 0-87907-813-8 7.95
1. O'Sullivan, Jeremiah Francis, 1903- 2. O'Sullivan, Jeremiah Francis, 1903—Bibliography. 3. Cistercians—Addresses, essays, lectures. I. O'Sullivan, Jeremiah Francis, 1903- II. Title. III. Series.

ADAM de Perseigne, 271'.12'024 B
d.1221.
The letters of Adam of Perseigne / translated by Grace Perigo ; introduction by Thomas Merton. Kalamazoo, Mich. : Cistercian Publication, c1976- v. ; 23 cm. (Cistercian Fathers series ; no. 21) "The feast of freedom, by Thomas Merton": p. 3-48. Includes index. [BX4705.A27A4313 1976] 76-15486 ISBN 0-87907-621-6 : 12.50.
1. Adam de Perseigne, d. 1221. 2. Cistercians—Biography. I. Merton, Thomas, 1915-1968. The feast of freedom. 1976.

BERNARD of 271'.12'024 B
Clairvaux: studies presented to Dom Jean Leclercq. Washington, Cistercian Publications, 1973. xii, 264 p. illus. 23 cm. (Cistercian studies series, no. 23) [BX4700.B5B47] 73-8099 ISBN 0-87907-823-5 11.95
1. Bernard de Clairvaux, Saint, 1091?-1153—Addresses, essays, lectures. 2. Leclercq, Jean, 1911- 3. Leclercq, Jean, 1911-—Bibliography. I. Leclercq, Jean, 1911- II. Title. III. Series.
Contents omitted.

CRISTIANI, Leon, 271'.12'024 B
1879-
St. Bernard of Clairvaux, 1090-1153 / by Leon Cristiani ; translated from the french by M. Angeline Bouchard. Boston : St. Paul Editions, c1977. 172 p. ; 21 cm. Tranlation of Saint Bernard de Clairvaux. [BX4700.B5C6913] 77-4942 3.95 pbk. : 2.95
1. Bernard de Clairvaux, Saint, 1091?-1153. 2. Christian saints—France—Clairvaux—Biography. 3. Clairvaux, France—Biography.

THE Influence of 271'.12'024
Saint Bernard : Anglican essays / with an introduction by Jean Leclercq ; edited by Benedicta Ward. Oxford : S.L.G. Press, 1976. xviii, 144 p. : ill., facsim. ; 21 cm. (Fairacres publication ; no. 60 ISSN 0307-1405s) Includes bibliographical references. [BX4700.B5I48] 77-362806 £1.75
1. Bernard de Clairvaux, Saint, 1091?-1153—Addresses, essays, lectures. I. Ward, Benedicta, 1933-

MERTON, Thomas, 271'.12'024 B
1915-1968.
The last of the Fathers; Saint Bernard of Clairvaux and the encyclical letter, Doctor Mellifluus. Westport, Conn., Greenwood Press [1970, c1954] 123 p. 23 cm. Bibliography: p. 119. [BX4700.B5M4 1970] 77-110049 ISBN 0-8371-4434-5
1. Bernard de Clairvaux, Saint, 1091?-1153. I. Title.

WARE, Gwen. 271'.12'042219
The White Monks of Waverley / by Gwen Ware. Farnham [Eng.] : Farnham & District Museum Society, c1976. 39, [3] p. : ill., plan (on lining paper) ; 18 cm. Bibliography: p. [42] [BX2596.F37W37] 77-354226 ISBN 0-901638-06-4 : £1.10
1. Waverley Abbey. I. Title.

LEWIS, John Masters. 271'.12'0429
The white monks in Wales ... [catalogue] of an exhibition held at the National Museum of Wales 24 April-23 May 1976 to mark the 750th anniversary of the foundation of Grace Dieu Abbey, Gwent, on 24 April 1226 / compiled by J. M. Lewis and David H. Williams. Cardiff : National Museum of Wales, 1976. 39 p. : ill., facsims., maps, plan, port. ; 15 x 23 cm. Includes index. [BX3425.L48] 76-381839 ISBN 0-7200-0093-9 : £0.30
1. Cistercians in Wales—Exhibitions. I. Williams, David Henry, joint author. II. Cardiff, Wales. National Museum of Wales. III. Title.

LACKNER, Bede K. 271'.12'04442
The eleventh-century background of Citeaux [by] Bede K. Lackner. Washington, Cistercian Publications, 1972. xxii, 309 p. 23 cm. (Cistercian studies series, no. 8) Bibliography: p. 277-296. [BX2615.C48L3] 70-152484 ISBN 0-87907-808-1 15.95
1. Citeaux, France (Cistercian Abbey) I. Title. II. Series.

MCGUIRE, Brian 271'.12'04895
Patrick.
Conflict and continuity at m abbey : a Cistercian experience in medieval Denmark / Brian Patrick McGuire. Copenhagen : Museum Tusculanum : [Institut for klassisk filologi, Fiolstrade 10], 1976. 151 p., [4] leaves of plates : ill. ; 23 cm. (Opuscula Graecolatina ; v. 8) Includes index. Bibliography: p. [137]-141. [BX2644.O4M32] 77-457250 kr35.00
1. m (Cistercian abbey), Aarhus, Denmark (Province) I. Title. II. Series.

LEKAI, Louis Julius, 271.1209
1916-
The White Monks; a history of the Cistercian Order. Okauchee, Wis., Cistercian Fathers, Our Lady of Spring Bank, 1953. vi, 328 p. illus., maps. 21 cm. 'Bibliographical notes': p. 287-304. [BX3406.L4] 53-7711
1. Cistercians—Hist. I. Title.

VITA prima 271'.12'0924 B
Bernardi. Books 1-3. Portuguese. Selections.
The Old Portuguese Vida de Sam Bernardo, edited from Alcobaca manuscript CCXCI/200, with introd., linguistic study, notes, table of proper names, and glossary, by Lawrence A. Sharpe. Chapel Hill, University of North Carolina Press [1971] 183 p. 24 cm. (Studies in the Romance languages and literatures, no. 103) An edition of a fourteenth or fifteenth century Portuguese translation of the first three books of the Vita prima Bernardi. Book 1 was written by Guillaume de Saint-Thierry; book 2, by Arnaldus Abbas Bonaevallis; book 3, by Gaufridus Claraevallensis. Bibliography: p. [181]-183. [BX4700.B5V5662 1971] 73-31379
1. Bernard de Clairvaux, Saint, 1091?-1153. I. Sharpe, Lawrence A., 1920- ed. II. Guillaume de Saint-Thierry, 1085 (ca.)-1148? III. Arnaldus Abbas Bonaevallis, d. ca. 1156. IV. Gaufridus Claraevallensis, ca. 1120-1194. V. Title. VI. Series: North Carolina. University. Studies in the Romance languages and literatures, no. 103

HILL, Bennett D. 271'.12'0942
English Cistercian monasteries and their patrons in the twelfth century [by] Bennett D. Hill. Urbana, University of Illinois Press, 1968. xi, 188 p. illus. 22 cm. Bibliography: p. 162-172. [BX3416.H5] 68-11029
1. Cistercians in England. I. Title.

LEKAI, Louis Julius, 271'.12'0944
1916-
The rise of the Cistercian strict observance in seventeenth century France, by Louis J. Lekai. Washington, D.C. Catholic University of America Press [1968] vii, 261 p. illus., map, ports. 24 cm. Bibliography: p. 241-254. [BX3431.L4] 67-27074
1. Cistercians in France. 2. Trappists in France. I. Title.

BURDEN, Shirley. 271.125
God is my life; the story of Our Lady of Gethsemani. Photos. by Shirley Burden, introd. by Thomas Merton. New York, Reynal [1960] unpaged. il6us. 29cm. [BX2525.N35G38] 60-9227
1. Gethsemani (Trappist abbey) Nelson Co., Ky. I. Title.

HOFFMAN, Mathias Martin, 271.125
1889-
Arms and the monk! The Trappist saga in Mid-America. Dubuque, Iowa, W. C. Brown Co. [1952] 233p. illus. 24cm. [BX2525.N4H6] 53-1677
1. New Melleray, Iowa (Trappist abbey) I. Title.

*MERTON, Thomas, 1915- 271.125(B)
[Nameinreligion:FatherLouis]
The seven storey mountain [New York] New Amer. Lib. [1967, c.1948] 412p. 18cm. (Signet bk., Q2857) .95 pap.,
I. Title.

MERTON, Thomas, 1915- 271.125
The sign of Jonas. [1st ed.] New York, Harcourt, Brace [c1953] 362p. 22cm. 'A collection of personal notes and meditations set down during about five years ... in the monastery of Gethsemani.' [BX4705.M542A32] 52-9857
I. Title.

MERTON, Thomas [Name in 271.125
religion: Father Louis] 1915
The waters of Siloe. Garden City, N.Y., Doubleday [1962, c.1949] 399p. 18cm. (Image bk., D144) Bibl. 1.25 pap.,
1. Trappists. I. Title.

BAKER, James 271'.125'024 B
Thomas.
Thomas Merton, social critic; a study. [Lexington] University Press of Kentucky [1971] ix, 173 p. 25 cm. Bibliography: p. [149]-155. [BX4705.M542B3] 76-132827 ISBN 0-8131-1238-9 8.00
1. Merton, Thomas, 1915-1968. I. Title.

HART, Patrick, 271'.125'024 B
Brother, comp.
Thomas Merton, monk; a monastic tribute. [New York] Sheed and Ward [1974] 230 p. illus. 25 cm. [BX4705.M542H37] 74-1533 8.95
1. Merton, Thomas, 1915-1968.
Contents omitted.

KRAILSHEIMER, A. 271'.125'024 B
J.
Armand-Jean de Rance, Abbot of La Trappe : his influence in the cloister and the world / by A. J. Krailsheimer. Oxford : Clarendon Press, 1974. xvi, 376 p., [5] leaves of plates : ill. ; 23 cm. Includes index. Bibliography: p. [345]-362. [BX4705.R3K7] 74-186609 ISBN 0-19-815744-4 : 25.00
1. Rance, Armand Jean Le Bouthillier de, 1626-1700.
Distributed by Oxford University Press, New York.

MCINERNY, Dennis 271'.125'024 B
Q.
Thomas Merton; the man and his work [by] Dennis Q. McInerny. [Spencer, Mass.] Cistercian Publications; [distributed by] Consortium Press, Washington, 1974. xii, 128 p. 23 cm. (Cistercian studies series, no. 27) [BX4705.M542M3] 74-4319 ISBN 0-87907-827-8
1. Merton, Thomas, 1915-1968. I. Title. II. Series.

SUSSMAN, Cornelia 271'.125'024 B
Silver.
Thomas Merton : the daring young man on the flying belltower / Cornelia & Irving Sussman. New York : Macmillan, c1976. 177 p. : port. ; 22 cm. Includes index. Bibliography: p. 169-171. A biography of the Trappist monk and Zen mystic who gained fame as a writer, social critic, and radical peace activist. [BX4705.M542S9] 92 76-34236 ISBN 0-02-788630-1 : 6.95
1. Merton, Thomas, 1915-1968—Juvenile literature. I. Sussman, Irving, joint author.

THE Thomas Merton 271'.125'024 B
Studies Center, by Thomas Merton, John Howard Griffin & Monsignor Horrigan. Santa Barbara [Calif.] Unicorn Press, 1971. 24 p. 25 cm. (Merton Studies Center. [Publications] v. 1) Contents.Contents.—Thomas Merton Studies Center, by Msgr. Horrigan.—Concerning the collection in the Bellarmine College Library, by T. Merton.—In search of Thomas Merton, by J. H. Griffin. [BX4705.M542T5] 72-189292
1. Merton, Thomas, 1915-1968. 2. Bellarmine College, Louisville, Ky. Library. 3. Thomas Merton Studies Center. I. Horrigan, Alfred Frederick, 1914- Thomas Merton Studies Center. 1971. II. Merton, Thomas, 1915-1968. Concerning the collection in the Bellarmine College Library. 1971. III. Griffin, John Howard, 1920- In search of Thomas Merton. 1971. IV. Series: Thomas Merton Studies Center. Publications, v. 1.

HART, Patrick, comp. 271.1250924
Thomas Merton, monk : a monastic tribute. Garden City, N.Y. : Doubleday [1976c1974] 232p. ; 18 cm. (Image books) [BX4705.M542H37] ISBN 0-385-11244-0 pbk. : 1.95
1. Merton, Thomas, 1915-1968. I. Title.
L. C. card no. for original edition: 74-1533.

*VOTH, M. Agnes, 271.13073
Sister.
Green Olive Branch by Sister M. Agnes Voth, ed. by Father M. Raymond, illus. by Sister M. Louise Frankenberger, and Sister M. Michelle Bullock. Chicago, Franciscan Herald Press [1973] xii, 351 p. illus., 21 cm. Bibliography: p. [315]-326. [BX9766]
1. Benedictions. I. Title.

BENNETT, Ralph Francis. 271'.2
The early Dominicans; studies in thirteenth-century Dominican history, by R. F. Bennett. New York, Russell & Russell [1971] xii, 189 p. 23 cm. (Cambridge studies in medieval life and thought) Reprint of the 1937 ed. Bibliography: p. [182]-186. [BX3506.B4 1971] 71-139903
1. Dominicans. I. Title. II. Series.

DOMINICANS. Third Order. 271.2
Dominican tertiaries' manual, completely revised. For the daily use of private and fraternity tertiaries of the Third Order of St. Dominic. 1st ed. New York [1952] 364 p. illus. 14 cm. [BX3552.E6 1952] 52-44398
1. Dominicans. Third order. I. Catholic Church. Liturgy and ritual. Dominican. II. Title.

HINNEBUSCH, William A. 271'.2
The Dominicans : a short history / William A. Hinnebusch. New York : Alba House, [1975] 185 p. ; 21 cm. Bibliography: p. [183]-185. [BX3506.2.H48] 74-26562 ISBN 0-8189-0301-5 pbk. : 3.95
1. Dominicans—History.

HINNEBUSCH, William A. 271.2
The history of the Dominican Order [by] William A. Hinnebusch. Staten Island, N.Y., Alba House [1966- v. 24 cm. Contents.Contents.—v. 1. Origins and growth to 1500.—v. 2. The intellectual and cultural life to 1500. Bibliography: v. 1, p. [417]-422, v. 2, p. [449]-461. [BX3506.2.H5] 65-17977 ISBN 0-8189-0266-3 (v. 1)
1. Dominicans. I. Title.

JORET, Ferdinand Donatien, 271.2
1883-1937.
Dominican life. With a foreword by Bernard Delany. Westminster, Md., Newman Press [1958?] 311p. 22cm. Translation of Notre vie dominicaine. [BX3551.J6 1958] 58-2870
1. Dominicans. Third Order. I. Title.

QUETIF, Jacques 271.2
Scriptores Ordinis Praedicatorum recensiti, notisque historicis et criticis. Inchoavit Jacobus Quetif absolvit Jacobus Echard. New York, B. Franklin [1959] v.1, 2 pts.: xxvii, 954p. v.2, 2 pts.: xxxii, 1000, 8p. illus. 34cm. (Burt Franklin bibliographical and reference series no.16) 60-1099 175.00 buck.,
1. Dominicans— Bio-bibl. I. Echard, Jacques, 1644-1724, joint author. II. Title.

WALGRAVE, V. 271'.2
Dominican self-appraisal in the light of the council [by] Valentine Walgrave. Chicago, Priory Press [1968] xxxiv, 346 p. 24 cm. Translation of Essai d'autocritique d'un ordre religieux; les Dominicains en fin de concile. Bibliographical footnotes. [BX3502.2.W313] 68-29600
1. Vatican Council. 2d, 1962-1965. 2. Dominicans. 3. Church renewal. I. Title.

DESMOND, Cecelia. 271'.2'00924 B
Blessed James Salomoni; patron of cancer patients apostle of the afflicted. [Boston] St. Paul Editions [1971] 76, [1] p. illus. 20 cm. Bibliography: p. [77] [BX4705.S142D4] 70-150719 2.00
1. Salomoni, Giacomo, 1231-1314. I. Title.

RIDOLFI, Roberto, 271'.2'00924 B
1899-
The life of Girolamo Savonarola / by Roberto Ridolfi ; translated from the Italian by Cecil Grayson. Westport, Conn. : Greenwood Press, 1976, c1959. x, 325 p., [1] leaf of plates : port. ; 24 cm. Reprint of the ed. published by Knopf, New York. Translation of Vita di Girolamo Savonarola. Includes index. [DG737.97.R533 1976] 76-8001 ISBN 0-8371-8873-3 lib.bdg. : 21.00
1. Savonarola, Girolamo Maria Francesco Matteo, 1452-1498.

BENZIGER, Marieli G. 271'.2'024 B
Saint Martin de Porres: many sided Martin; the first Negro saint of the Western Hemisphere, by Marieli and Rita Benziger. Altadena, Calif., Benziger Sisters [1973] 134 p. port. 21 cm. [BX4700.M397B38] 73-86681
1. Martin de Porres, Saint, 1579-1639. I. Benziger, Rita, joint author. II. Title.

MOORE, John Aiken, 271'.2'024
1920-
Fray Luis de Granada / by John A. Moore. Boston : Twayne Publishers, c1977. p. cm. (Twayne's world authors series ; TWAS 438 : Spain) Includes index. Bibliography: p. [PQ6412.L8Z75] 76-55365 ISBN 0-8057-6276-0 lib.bdg. : 8.50
1. Luis de Granada, 1504-1588. 2. Authors, Spanish—16th century—Biography.

REYES, Gabriel de los. 271'.2'024
Estudio etimologico y semantico del vocabulario contenido en los "Lucidarios" espanoles / Gabriel de los Reyes. Miami, Fla. : Ediciones Universal, 1975, c1974. 196 p. ; 21 cm. (Coleccion Polymita) Bibliography: p. 195-196. [PQ6412.L733Z49 1975] 73-94179
1. Lucidario—Dictionaries. I. Title.

VILLARI, Pasquale, 271'.2'024 B
1827-1917.
Life and times of Girolamo Savonarola. Translated by Linda Villari. New York, Scribner and Welford, 1888. St. Clair Shores, Mich., Scholarly Press, 1972. 2 v. illus. 22 cm. Translation of La storia di Girolamo Savonarola e de suoi tempi. Includes bibliographical references. [DG737.97.V7 1972] 79-115284 ISBN 0-403-00265-6 25.00
1. Savonarola, Girolamo Maria Francesco Matteo, 1452-1498. I. Title.

NEWLAND, Mary 271'.2'0924 B
(Reed)
St. Thomas Aquinas; a concise biography. Foreword by J. M. Donahue. New York, American R.D.M. Corp. [1967] 62 p. port. 21 cm. (A Study master publication, 961) Bibliography: p. 62. [BX4700.T6N4] 66-28705
1. Thomas Aquinas, Saint, 1225?-1274.

PITTENGER, William 271'.2'0924 B
Norman, 1905-
Saint Thomas Aquinas; the angelic doctor, by Norman Pittenger. New York, F. Watts [1969] vii, 150 p. map. 22 cm. (Immortals of philosophy and religion) Bibliography: p. 146-148. A biography of the thirteenth-century philosopher best known for his ability to reconcile the basic principles of Christian and Aristotelian thought. [BX4700.T6P565] 92 77-79849
1. Thomas Aquinas, Saint, 1225?-1274— Juvenile literature. I. Title.

VILLARI, Pasquale, 271'.2'0924 B
1827-1917.
Life and times of Girolamo Savonarola. Translated by Linda Villari. New York, Haskell House Publishers, 1969. 2 v. illus., facsim., plates, ports. 23 cm. Translation of La storia di Girolamo Savonarola e de suoi tempi. Reprint of the 1888 ed. Bibliographical footnotes. [DG737.97.V7 1969] 68-25276
1. Savonarola, Girolamo Maria Francesco Matteo, 1452-1498. I. Title.

COFFEY, Reginald 271'.2'0973
Mary.
The American Dominicans; a history of Saint Joseph's Province [by] Reginald M. Coffey. New York, Saint Martin de Porres Guild [1970] v, 701 p. illus., ports. 24 cm. Includes bibliographical references. [BX3508.C63] 70-116646
1. Dominicans. Province of St. Joseph. I. Title.

LEDYARD, Gleason 271.22
Adrift on Hudson Bay: a true story of the Canadian Arctic. Chicago, Moody [c.1963] 63p. 19cm. .50 pap.,
I. Title.

LEDYARD, Gleason 271.22
Arctic school days: true stories of the Canadian Arctic. Chicago, Moody [c.1963] 20cm. .50 pap.,
I. Title.

ARCHIVUM franciscanum 271.3
historicum. Periodica publicatio trimestris cura pp. Collegii D. Bonaventura, annus 1-3 1908-1910 Ad Claras Aquas prope Florentiam, 1908-; New York, Johnson Reprint, 1967. v. plates. 25cm. [BX3601.A7] 10-2408 set; pap.; 75.00; ea., pap., 27.50
1. Quaracchi, Italy. Collegium S. Bonaventura.

BETTONI, Efrem. 271.3
Nothing for your journey. Translated by Bruce Malina. [2d ed.] Chicago, Franciscan Herald Press [1959] 165p. 22cm. Includes bibliography. [BX3603.B413 1959] 59-9335
1. Franciscans. I. Title.

BONAVENTURA, Saint, 271.3
Cardinal, 1221-1274.
A Franciscan view of the spiritual and religious life. Edited by Titus Cranny. Garrison, N. Y., Franciscan Friars of the Atonement [c1962] 96 p. 22 cm. [BX2430.B57] 62-21889
1. Monastic and religious life. I. Cranny, Titus F., 1921- ed. II. Title.

BRETON, Valentin Marie, 271.3
1877-
Franciscan spirituality: synthesis, antithesis. Translated from the French by Flavian Frey. Chicago, Franciscan Herald Press [1957] 70p. 19cm. [BX3603.B732] 57-3069
1. Franciscans. 2. Spiritual life—Catholic authors. I. Title.

BRETON, Valentin Marie, 271.3
1877-
Lady poverty. Translated from the French by Paul J. Oligny. Chicago, Franciscan Herald Press [1963] 104 p. 21 cm. Translation of La pauvrete. Secular name: Henri Breton. [BX3603.B713] 63-12855
1. Poverty. 2. Franciscans. I. Title.

BRETON, Valentin Marie 271.3
1877-
Lady poverty. Tr. from French by Paul J. Oligny. Chicago, Franciscan Herald [c.1963] 104p. 21cm. 63-12855 2.50
1. Poverty. 2. Franciscans. I. Title.

BROPHY, Liam. 271.3
Echoes of Assisi. Chicago, Franciscan Herald Press [c1958] 208p. 21cm. [BX3602.B7] 58-13685
1. Francesco d'Assisi, Saint, 1182-1226. 2. Franciscans. I. Title.

CESAIRE DE TOURS, Father, 271.3
d. 1922.
Franciscan perfection; translated by Paul Barrett. Westminster, Md., Newman Press, 1956. 193p. 23cm. Translation of La perfection seraphique d'apres Saint Francois. [BX3603.C415] 55-12309
1. Francesco d'Assisi, Saint, 1182-1226. 2. Franciscans. 3. Perfection—Catholic Church. I. Title.

CORSTANJE, Auspicius van. 271'.3
The Third Order for our times. Chicago, Franciscan Herald Press [1974] ix, 127 p. 22 cm. Essays and addresses, two translated from the Dutch. [BX3651.C67] 73-20436 ISBN 0-8199-0487-2 2.50 (pbk.)
1. Franciscans. Third Order. 2. Francesco d'Assisi, Saint, 1182-1226. I. Title.
Contents omitted.

CRANE, John de Murinelly 271.3
Cirne, 1900-
The Franciscan monastery, memorial church of the Holy Land. Washington, '1951. 1 v. (unpaged) illus., map. 26 cm. [BX2525.W3M64] 51-5369
1. Washington, D. C. Mt. St. Sepulchre (Franciscan monastery) I. Title.

CROSBY, Jeremiah. 271.3
Bearing witness; the place of the Franciscan family in the church. Chicago, Franciscan Herald Press [1966] 183 p. 21 cm. Bibliographical references included in "Notes" (p. 159-176) [BX3603.C7] 65-16675
1. Franciscans. I. Title.

CROSBY, Jeremiah 271.3
Bearing witness; the place of the Franciscan family in the church. Chicago Franciscan Herald [c.1966] 183p. 21cm. Bibl. [BX3603.C7] 65-16675 3.75
1. Franciscans. I. Title.

ESSER, Kajetan, 1913- 271.3
The Order of St. Francis, its spirit and its mission in the kingdom of God. Translated by Ignatius Brady. Chicago, Franciscan Herald Press [1959] 60 p. illus. 19 cm. (FHP text series) Includes bibliography. [BX3603.E813] 59-9331
1. Franciscans. I. Title.

ESSER, Kajetan, 1913- 271.3
Repair my house. Edited by Luc Mely. Translated by Michael D. Meilach. Chicago, Franciscan Herald Press [1963] 222 p. 21 cm. Translation of Themes spirituels. [BX3603.E8333] 63-12854
1. Francesco d'Assisi, Saint, 1182-1226. 2. Franciscans. I. Title.

ESSER, Kajetan, 1913- 271.3
Repair my house. Ed. by Luc Mely. Tr. [from French] by Michael D. Meilach. Chicago, Franciscan Herald [c.1963] 222p. 21cm. 63-12854 3.95
1. Francesco d'Assisi, Saint, 1182-1226. 2. Franciscans. I. Title.

FOLEY, Theodosius, 1884- 271.3
Spiritual conferences for religious based on the Franciscan ideal. [2d ed.] Milwaukee, Bruce Pub. Co. [1951] x, 386 p. 24 cm. [BX3603.F6 1951] 51-1916
1. Francesco d'Assisl, Saint, 1182-1226. 2. Franciscans. I. Title.

FRANCISCAN Education 271.3
Conference
Report of the annual meeting, 43rd, 1962. [Chicago, FranciscanHerald, c.1963] 310p. illus. 23cm. Contents.v.43. The Holy Eucharist and Christian unity. Bibl. 22-7378 4.50 pap.,
1. Catholic Church—Societies, etc. 2. Catholic Church in the U.S.—Education. I. Title.

GEMELLI, Agostino, 1878- 271.3
1959
The message of St. Francis. Tr. by Paul J. Oligny. Chicago, Franciscan Herald [1964, c.1963] ix, 197p. 22cm. Bibl. 63-21386 3.95
1. Francesco d'Assisi, Saint, 1182-1226. 2. Franciscans. I. Title.

HABIG, Marion Alphonse, 271.3
1901-
New catechism of the Third Order. Chicago, Franciscan Herald Press, 1962. 94p. 23cm. Includes bibliography. [BX3652.H3] 61-18901
1. Franciscans Third Order. I. Title. II. Title: Catechism of the Third Order.

HABIG, Marion Alphonse, 271'.3
1901- comp.
St. Francis of Assisi: writings and early biographies; English omnibus of the sources for the life of St. Francis, edited by Marion A. Habig. Chicago, Franciscan Herald Press [1973] xx, 1808 p. maps (on lining papers) 22 cm. "Translations by Raphael Brown, Benen Fahy, Placid Hermann, Paul Oligny, Nesta de Robeck, Leo Sherley-Price, with a research bibliography by R. Brown." Bibliography: p. 1667-1760. [BX4700.F6H27] 72-11257 ISBN 0-8199-0440-6 18.95
1. Francesco d'Assisi, Saint, 1182-1226.

HABIG, Marion Alphonse 271.3
[Secular name: John Alphonse Habig]
A short history of the Third Order, by Marion A. Habig, Mark Hegener. Chicago, Franciscan [c.1963] 104p. illus. 18cm. Bibl. 62-22289 .95 pap.,
1. Franciscan. Third Order—Hist. I. Hegener, Mark, joint author. II. Title.

HANLEY, Boniface 271.3
The Franciscans: love at work [by] Boniface Hanley, Salvator Fink. Garden City, N.Y., Doubleday [1966, c.1962] 249p. illus. 19cm. (Image bk., D205) [BX3602.2.H3] .95 pap.,
1. Franciscans. I. Fink, Salvator, joint author. II. Title.

HANLEY, Boniface. 271.3
The Franciscans: love at work [by] Boniface Hanley [and] Salvator Fink. Paterson, N. J., St. Anthony Guild Press [1962] 247 p. illus. 24 cm. [BX3602.2.H3] 61-18713
1. Franciscans. I. Fink, Salvator, joint author.

HORKA-FOLLICK, Lorayne 271'.3
Ann, 1940-
Los Hermanos Penitentes; a vestige of medievalism in Southwestern United States. Los Angeles, Westernlore Press, 1969. xi, 226 p. illus. 22 cm. (Great West and Indian series, 38) Thesis—London, 1968. Bibliography: p. 187-200. [BX3653.U6H67] 71-97000 7.50
1. Hermanos Penitentes. I. Title. II. Series.

THE Marrow of the Gospel; 271.3
a study of the rule of Saint Francis of Assisi, by the Franciscans of Germany. Translated and edited by Ignatius Brady. Chicago, Franciscan Herald Press, 1958. xiv, 346p. 22cm. Translation of Werkbuch zur Regel des heiligen Franziskus von Assisi. Includes bibliography. [BX3604.Z5W43] 58-8688
1. Francesco d'Assisi, Saint, 1182-1226. Regula. 2. Franciscans. 3. Monasticism and religious orders—Rules. I. Brady, Ignatius, ed. and tr.

MASSERON, Alexandre, 1880- 271.3
1959.
The Franciscans; St. Francis of Assisi and his three orders, by Alexandre Masseron and Marion A. Habig. Chicago, Franciscan Herald Press [c1959] xxi, 518p. illus., ports. 22cm. Includes bibliographical references. Appendices (p. 433-506): The Franciscan orders and congregations in the world.--Bibliography of English Franciscana. [BX3602.M33 1959] 59-15747
1. Franciscans. I. Habig, Marion Alphonse, 1901- II. Title.

MASSERON, Alexandre [Marie 271.3
Joseph]
The Franciscans; St. Francis of Assisi and his three orders, by Alexandre Masseron and Marion A. Habig. Chicago, Franciscan Herald Press [c.1959] xxi, 518p. illus., ports. 22cm. (28 p. bibl. and bibliographical references) 59-15747 5.95 half cloth,
1. Franciscans. I. Habig, Marion Alphonse. II. Title.

MOORMAN, John Richard 271.3
Humpidge.
The Grey Friars in Cambridge, 1225-1538. Cambridge [Eng.] University Press, 1952. viii, 277p. illus., maps. 22cm. (The Birkbeck lectures, 1948-9) 'Biographical notes on Cambridge Franciscans': p. 146- 226. Bibliographical footnotes. [BX3618.C2M6] 52-10898
1. Franciscans in Cambridge. 2. Cambridge. University. I. Title. II. Series.

MOTTE, Jean Francois, 1913- 271.3
Face to the world: the Third Order in modern society. Translated by Margaret Sullivan. Chicago, Franciscan Herald Press [1960] 103 p. 19 cm. [BX3651.M563] 60-10696
1. Franciscans. Third Order. I. Title.

MOTTE, John Francis 271.3
Face to the world: the Third Order in modern society. Translated by Margaret Sullivan. Chicago, Franciscan Herald Press [c.1960] x, 103p. 19cm. 60-10696 1.75 bds.,
1. Franciscans. Third Order. I. Title.

O'BRIEN, Joachim. 271.3
Franciscan formation conferences. Chicago, Franciscan Herald Press [1959- v. 24cm. [BX3603.O2] 59-9334
1. Franciscans. I. Title.

O'ROURKE, Daniel. 271.3
How to live in a layman's order. Chicago, Franciscan Herald Press [1964] vi, 67 p. 21 cm. (A Tertiary's library of Franciscan books) [BX3651.O75] 64-24287
1. Franciscans. Third Order. I. Title.

O'ROURKE, Daniel 271.3
How to live in a layman's order. Chicago. Franciscan Herald [c.1964] vi, 67p. 21cm. (Tertiary's lib. of Franciscan bks.) [BX3651.O75] 64-24287 1.50 pap.,
1. Franciscans. Third Order. I. Title.

PECKHAM, John, Abp. of 271'.3
Canterbury, d. 1292
Fratris Johannnis Pecham . . . Tractatus tres de paupertate. Cum bibliographia ediderunt C. L. Kingsford, A. G. Little, F. Tocco. Aberdoniae, Typis Academicis, 1910. ix, 198p. 23cm. Texts in Latin; bd. matter in English. Photo-offset. Farnborough, Eng., Greggpr., 1966. 20cm. Bibl. [BX3601.P41910a] 67-3607 9.80
1. Kilwardby, Robert, Cardinal, Abp. of Canterbury, d. 1279. 2. Friars. 3. Franciscans. 4. Dominicans. I. Kingsford, Charles Lethbridge, 1862-1926, ed. II. Little, Andrew

George, 1863-1946, ed. III. Tocco, Felice, 1845-1911, ed. IV. Title.
American distributor: Gregg Pr., Ridgewood, N. J.

THE Penitentes of New 271'.3
Mexico. New York, Arno Press, 1974. 85, 126, xiv, 359 p. illus. 24 cm. (The Mexican American) Reprint of The Passionists of the Southwest, by A. M. Darley, first published 1893 in Pueblo, Colo.; of Brothers of light, by A. C. Henderson, first published 1937 by Harcourt, Brace, New York; and of The Penitentes of New Mexico, by D. Woodward, first published 1935 in New Haven. Includes bibliographical references. [BX3653.U6P4] 73-14212 ISBN 0-405-05686-9 30.00
1. Hermanos Penitentes. I. Darley, Alexander M. The Passionists of the Southwest. 1974. II. Henderson, Alice (Corbin) 1881-1949. Brothers of light. 1974. III. Woodward, Dorothy, 1895- The Penitentes of New Mexico. 1974. IV. Title. V. Series.

ROMB, Anselm William, 271'.3
1929-
The Franciscan charism in the church [by] Anselm W. Romb. Paterson, N.J., St. Anthony Guild Press [1969] ix, 112 p. 22 cm. Bibliographical footnotes. [BX4700.F6R63] 79-91837 3.00
1. Francesco d'Assisi, Saint, 1182-1226. 2. Franciscans—Spiritual life. I. Title.

ROYER, Fanchon, 1902- 271.3
The Franciscans came first. Paterson, N.J., St. Anthony Guild Press, 1951. xi, 195 p. illus., ports., map (on lining papers) 23 cm. Bibliography: p. 188-190. [BX3612.A1R6] 51-5413
1. Franciscans in Mexico. 2. Franciscans — Missions. 3. Franciscans — Biog. I. Title.
CONTENTS. -- First schoolteacher: Pedro de Gante. -- First great victory for God: Toribio de Motolinia. -- The boy martyrs of Tiaxcala: Martin de Valencia. -- The fighting first bishop's reward: Juan de Zumarraga. -- The first American Republics: Don Vasco de Quiroga. -- The saintly first road builder: Sebastian de Aparicio. -- "First in the hearts of his countrymen": Pedro de Betancourt. -- First among God's walkers: Antonio Margil de Jesus. -- The first California: Junipero Serra.

STIER, Mark. 271.3
Franciscan life in Christ. Paterson, N. J., St. Anthony Guild Press, 1953. 290p. 23cm. [BX3603.S75] 53-4495
1. Franciscans. I. Title.

TAMARON Y ROMERAL, Pedro, 271.3
Bp., 1695-1768.
Bishop Tamaron's visitation of New Mexico, 1760, Edited by Eleanor B. Adams. Albuquerque, N. M., 1954. 113p. 23cm. (New Mexico. Historical Society. Publications in history, v. 15) 'Translation ... based on Vito Alessio Robles' edition ... [of Demostracion del vastisimo obispado de la Nueva Vizcaya] published in Mexico in 1937.' Bibliographical footnotes. [F791.N45 vol.15] 57-62563
1. Visitations, Ecclesiastical—New Mexico. 2. Franciscans in New Mexico. I. Adams, Eleanor Burnham, ed. II. Title. III. Series.

TIBESAR, Antonine, 1909- 271.3
Franciscan beginnings in colonial Peru. Washington, Academy of American Franciscan History, 1953. xviii, 162p. illus., facsims. 26cm. (Publications of the Academy of American Franciscan History. Monograph series, v. 1) 'Originally written and published as a doctoral thesis ... Catholic University of America [in microcard form] ... Revised and enlarged.' Bibliography: p. 143-151. [BX3614.P4T5 1953] 53-13222
1. Franciscans in Peru. 2. Missions—Peru. 3. Indians of South America—Missions. I. Title. II. Series: Academy of American Franciscan History. Monograph series, v. 1

VEUTHEY, Leon. 271.3
Union with Christ; lessons in Franciscan asceticism. Translated by James Meyer. Chicago, Franciscan Herald Press [1954] ix, 96p. illus. 21cm. (Franciscan spirituality, no.1) [BX3603.V43] 54-14706
1. Franciscans. 2. Asceticism—Catholic Church. I. Title.

WOLTER, Allan Bernard, 271.3
1913-
Life in God's love. Chicago, Franciscan Herald Press [1958] 157 p. 21 cm. [BX3603.W6] 58-13983
1. Franciscans. 2. Monastic and religious life. 3. God — Worship and love. I. Title.

WROBLEWSKI, Sergius 271.3
Following Francis; commentary on the Third Order general constitutions. Chicago, Franciscan Herald Pr., c.1961. 63p. .50 pap.,
1. Roman Catholic Church—Religious orders—Franciscans. 2. Roman Catholic Church—The Third Order. 3. Third Order. I. Title.

WROBLEWSKI, Sergius. 271.3
Updating Franciscan communities. Pulaski, Wis., Franciscan Publishers [1966] 128 p. 19 cm. Bibliographical footnotes. [BX3602.2.W7] 66-6539
1. Franciscans. I. Title.

WROBLEWSKI, Serguis 271.3
Updating Franciscan communities. Pulaski, Wis., Franciscan Pubs. [c.1966] 128p. 19cm. Bibl. [BX3602.2.W7] 66-6539 .75 pap.,
1. Franciscans. I. Title.

OROZ, Pedro. 271'.3'022 B
The Oroz codex; the Oroz Relacion, or Relation of the description of the Holy Gospel Province in New Spain, and the lives of the founders and other noteworthy men of said province, composed by fray Pedro Oroz, 1584-1586. Translated and edited by Angelico Chavez. Washington, Academy of American Franciscan History, 1972. xiv, 393 p. facsim. 26 cm. (Publications of the Academy of American Franciscan History. Documentary series, v. 10) Translation of a portion of the ms. in Latin American Library at Tulane University, New Orleans, with caption title: Relacion de la descripcion de la Provincia del Santo Evangelio que es en las Indias Occidentales que llaman la Nueva Espana hecha el ano de 1585. Bibliography: p. 376-380. [BX3612.A1O76] 72-184964
1. Franciscans—Biography. 2. Franciscans in Mexico—History—Sources. I. Title. II. Title: Relation of the description of the Province of the Holy Gospel. III. Title: Relacion de la descripcion de la Provincia del Santo Evangelio. IV. Series: Academy of American Franciscan History. Documentary series, v. 10.

ARMSTRONG, Edward 271'.3'024 B
Allworthy.
Saint Francis: nature mystic; the derivation and significance of the nature stories in the Franciscan Legend [by] Edward A. Armstrong. Berkeley, University of California Press, 1973. 270 p. illus. 24 cm. (Hermeneutics studies in the history of religions, v. 2) Bibliography: p. 253-254. [BX4700.F6A78] 74-149949 ISBN 0-520-01966-0 12.00
1. Francesco d'Assisi, Saint, 1182-1226. Legend. 2. Francesco d'Assisi, Saint, 1182-1226—Legends—History and criticism. 3. Animals, Legends and stories of. I. Title. II. Series.

BOWDEN, Dina Moore. 271'.3'024 B
Junipero Serra in his native isle (1713-1749) / text, Dina Moore Bowden ; photos., Stefan Laszlo ; drawings, Xam. Palma [Majorca] : s.n., 1976. 170 p. : ill. ; 30 cm. Includes bibliographical references. [F864.S44B68] 77-372391 ISBN 8-440-01725-1
1. Serra, Junipero, 1713-1784. 2. Majorca—Church history. 3. Franciscans—Balearic Islands—Majorca—Biography. I. Laszlo, Stefan. II. Title.

BULLA, Clyde Robert. 271'.3'024 B
Song of St. Francis; illustrated by Valenti Angelo. New York, Crowell [1952] 71 p. illus. 21 cm. A short biography of St. Francis telling how his father wanted him to become a rich prince but how Francis became a princely person who cared for the sick and needy and loved all animals. [PZ7.B912So] 92 AC 68
1. Francesco d'Assisi, Saint, 1182-1226. I. Angelo, Valenti, 1897- illus. II. Title.

BURR, David, 1934- 271'.3'024 B
The persecution of Peter Olivi / David Burr. Philadelphia : American Philosophical Society, 1976. 98 p. ; 30 cm. (Transactions of the American Philosophical Society ; new ser., v. 66, pt. 5 ISSN 0065-9746s) Includes index.IBibliography: p. 93-96.I[BX4705.O48543B87].76-24254 ISBN 0-87169-665-7 pbk. : 6.00
1. Olivi, Pierre Jean, 1248 or 9-1298. 2. Franciscans in France—Biography. I. Title. II. Series: American Philosophical Society, Philadelphia. Transactions ; new ser., v. 66, pt. 5.

[CARLETTI, Giuseppe] 271'.3'024 B
Life of St. Benedict. Translated from the French of M. Allibert. Freeport, N.Y., Books For Libraries Press, 1971. 213 p. 23 cm. (The Black heritage library collection) "First published 1835." Translation of Vita di S. Benedetto da S. Filadelfo, detto il moro. [BX4700.B33C32 1971] 70-168505 ISBN 0-8369-8859-0
1. Benedetto da San Filadelfo, Saint, 1526-1589. I. Title. II. Series.

CHAVEZ, Angelico, 271'.3'024 B
1910-
The song of Francis. Illus. by Judy Graese. [1st ed.] Flagstaff, Ariz., Northland Press [1973] 59 p. illus. (part col.) 21 cm. Recounts the life of St. Francis of Assisi, who gave all his riches to the poor and devoted the rest of his life to the service of Lady Poverty. [BX4700.F69C47] 92 73-75205 ISBN 0-87358-105-9 6.50
1. Franceso d'Assisi, Saint, 1182-1226—Juvenile literature. I. Graese, Judy, illus. II. Title.

CORSTANJE, Auspicius 271'3'024 B
van.
Francis, Bible of the poor / by Auspicius van Corstanje ; translated by David Smith ; introd. by L. A. M. Goossens. Chicago : Franciscan Herald Press, [1977] p. cm. Translation of Franciscus, Bijbel der armen. Includes bibliographical references. [BX4700.F6C77313] 77-24188 ISBN 0-8199-0661-1 : 5.95
1. Francesco d'Assisi, Saint, 1182-1226. 2. Christian saints—Italy—Assisi—Biography. 3. Assisi—Biography. I. Title.

CORSTANJE, Auspicius 271'3'024 B
van.
Francis, Bible of the poor / by Auspicius van Corstanje ; translated by David Smith ; introd. by L. A. M. Goossens. Chicago : Franciscan Herald Press, [1977] p. cm. Translation of Franciscus, Bijbel der armen. Includes bibliographical references. [BX4700.F6C77313] 77-24188 ISBN 0-8199-0661-1 : 5.95
1. Francesco d'Assisi, Saint, 1182-1226. 2. Christian saints—Italy—Assisi—Biography. 3. Assisi—Biography. I. Title.

COULTON, George 271'.3'024 B
Gordon, 1858-1947.
From St. Francis to Dante; translations from the chronicle of the Franciscan Salimbene (1221-1288), with notes and illustrations from other medieval sources. 2d ed., rev and enl. Philadelphia, University of Pennsylvania Press [1972] xlii, 446 p. 21 cm. Reprint of the 1907 ed., with a new introd. by Edward Peters. Bibliography: p. [414]-415. [BX4705.S24C7 1972] 73-150704 ISBN 0-8122-7672-8 15.00
1. Salimbene, Ognibene di Guido di Adamo, Brother, b. 1221. I. Salimbene, Ognibene di Guido di Adamo, Brother, b. 1221. II. Title.

CRISTIANI, Leon, 271'.3'024 B
1879-
Saint Francis of Assisi, 1182-1226 / by Leon Cristiani; translated from the French by M. Angeline Bouchard. Boston : St. Paul Editions, c1975. 164 p., [12] leaves of plates : ill. ; 22 cm. Translation of Saint Francois d'Assise, 1182-1226. [BX4700.F6C77913] 74-79802 4.95
1. Francesco d'Assisi, Saint, 1182-1226. 2. Franciscans.

CUNNINGHAM, 271'.3'024 B
Lawrence, comp.
Brother Francis; an anthology of writings by and about St. Francis of Assisi. [1st ed.] New York, Harper & Row [1972] xxii, 201 p. illus. 22 cm. [BX4700.F6C784 1972] 72-78080 ISBN 0-06-061647-4 5.95
1. Francesco d'Assisi, Saint, 1182-1226. I. Title.

CUNNINGHAM, 271'.3'024 B
Lawrence.
Saint Francis of Assisi / by Lawrence S. Cunningham. Boston : Twayne Publishers, c1976. p. cm. (Twayne's world authors series ; TWAS 409) Includes index. Bibliography: p. [BX4700.F6C785] 76-14219 ISBN 0-8057-6249-3 lib. bdg. : 7.95
1. Francesco d'Assisi, Saint, 1182-1226.

FRANCIS of Assisi 271'.3'024 B
: an essay / by Walter Nigg, with extracts from the lives of Bonaventure, Thomas of Celano, and the Three Companions ; and 71 color photos. by Toni Schneiders ; translated by William Neil. Chicago : Franciscan Herald Press, 1975. 132 p. : ill. ; 25 cm. Translation of Der Mann von Assisi. The extracts constitute captions for tho photos. [BX4700.F6N5413] 75-25662 ISBN 0-8199-0586-0 : 12.95
1. Francesco d'Assisi, Saint, 1182-1226. I. Schneiders, Toni.

GALLI, Mario von. 271'.3'024 B
Living our future: Francis of Assisi and the Church tomorrow. With color photos by Dennis Stock. Translated by Maureen Sullivan and John Drury. Chicago, Franciscan Herald Press [1972] 234 p. illus. (part col.) 21 cm. Translation of Gelebte Zukunft: Franz von Assisi. Bibliography: p. 236-239. [BX4700.F6G2513] 72-77444 ISBN 0-8199-0439-2 6.95
1. Francesco d'Assisi, Saint, 1182-1226. I. Stock, Dennis, illus. II. Title.

GONZALO de Jesus, 271'.3'024 B
fray, O.F.M.
Fray Jose G. Mojica, O.F.M., mi guia y mi estrella / por fray Gonzalo de Jesus, O.F.M. Chicago: Franciscan Herald Press, [1975] p. cm. [BX4705.M5965G66] 75-9951 ISBN 0-8199-0570-4
1. Mojica, Jose, 1895-1974. I. Title: Mi guia y mi estrella.

GUEST, Francis F. 271'.3'024 B
Fermin Francisco de Lasuen (1736-1803); a biography, by Francis F. Guest. Washington, Academy of American Franciscan History, 1973. xx, 374 p. illus. 27 cm. (Publications of the Academy of American Franciscan History. Monograph series, v. 9) Bibliography: p. 359-366. [F864.G93] 73-159539
1. Lasuen, Fermin Francisco de, 1736-1803. 2. California—History—To 1846. 3. Missions—California—History. 4. Franciscans in California—History. I. Title. II. Series: Academy of American Franciscan History. Monograph series, v. 9.

HABIG, Marion 271'.3'024 B
Alphonse, 1901- comp.
St. Francis of Assisi : writings and early biographies : English omnibus of the sources for the life of St. Francis / edited by Marion A. Habig ; translations by Raphael Brown ... [et al.]. 3d rev. ed., including A new Fioretti / by John R. H. Moorman. Chicago : Franciscan Herald Press, [1977] p. cm. Bibliography: p. [BX4700.F6H27 1977] 76-58903 ISBN 0-8199-0658-1 : 18.95
1. Francesco d'Assisi, Saint, 1182-1226. 2. Christian saints—Italy-Assisi—Biography. 3. Assisi—Biography. I. Moorman, John Richard Humpidge, Bp. of Ripon. A new Fioretti. 1977. II. Title.

MCMAHON, Thomas S. 271'.3'024 B
What, you a priest! : Father Tom, Pastor / by Thomas S. McMahon. Chicago : Franciscan Herald Press, 1976. p. cm. [BX4705.M2524A38] 76-16805 ISBN 0-8199-0612-3 : 4.90
1. McMahon, Thomas S. 2. Catholic Church—Clergy—Correspondence, reminiscences, etc. I. Title. II. Title: Father Tom, Pastor.

MARGIL de Jesus, 271'.3'024 B
Antonio, Father, 1657-1726.
Nothingness itself : selected writings of Ven. Fr. Antonio Margil / collected and translated by Benedict Leutenegger ; edited and annotated by Marion A. Habig. Chicago : Franciscan Herald Press, [1976] p. cm. "A Bicentennial book." Includes index. Bibliography: p. [BX4705.M3252A25 1976] 75-45128 ISBN 0-8199-0595-X : 9.95
1. Margil de Jesus, Antonio, Father, 1657-1726. I. Title.

MOORMAN, John 271'.3'024 B
Richard Humpidge, Bp. of Ripon.
Saint Francis of Assisi / [by] John R. H. Moorman. New ed. London : S.P.C.K., 1976. x, 118 p. ; 19 cm. Bibliography: p. 117-118. [BX4700.F6M648 1976] 76-384065 ISBN 0-281-02946-6 : £0.95
1. Francesco d'Assisi, Saint, 1182-1226. 2. Christian saints—Italy—Assisi—Biography. 3. Assisi—Biography.

MOORSELAAR, Corinne 271'.3'024 B
van.
Francis and the animals / by Corinne van Moorselaar. Chicago : Franciscan Herald Press, [1977] p. cm. Translation of Franciscus en de dieren. Recounts the life of St. Francis of Assisi and his special relationship with animals. [BX4700.F69M6613] 92 77-7391 ISBN 0-8199-0677-8 : 2.95
1. Francesco d'Assisi, Saint—Juvenile literature. 2. Christian saints—Italy—Assisi—Biography. 3. Assisi—Biography—Juvenile literature. I. Title.

OBERSTE, William 271'.3'024 B
Herman, 1899-
The restless friar: Venerable Fray Antonio Margil de Jesus, missionary to the Americas—Apostle of Texas, by William H. Oberste. [Austin, Tex., Printed by Von Boeckman-Jones Co., c1970] 145 p. illus., port. 24 cm. Bibliography: p. [144]-145. [BX4705.M3252O23] 72-185199
1. Margil de Jesus, Antonio, Father, 1657-1726. I. Title.

RAYMOND, Ernest, 271'.3'024 B
1888-
In the steps of St. Francis. Illustrated with photos. by the author. Chicago, Franciscan Herald Press [1975] p. cm. Reprint of the 1939 ed. published by H. C. Kinsey, New York. [BX4700.F6R3 1975] 74-17076 ISBN 0-8199-0551-8
1. Francesco d'Assisi, Saint, 1182-1226. 2. Franciscans. 3. Italy—Description and travel—1901-1944. 4. Levant—Description and travel. I. Title.

RODINO, Amedeo. 271'3'024 B
Music master; the story of Herman Cohen. Illustrated by the Daughters of St. Paul with the cooperation of Guy B. Pennisi. [Boston, Mass.] St. Paul Editions [1968] 99 p. illus. 22 cm. (Encounter books) A biography of the Jewish boy who became a famous pianist while

still a child, but later converted to Catholicism and spent the rest of his life serving in the Carmelite Order. [BX4705.A785R6] 92 AC 68
1. Augustin Marie du Tres Saint Sacrement pere, 1821-1871. I. Title.

SMITH, John 271'.3'024 [B]
Holland.
Francis of Assisi. New York, Scribner [1974 c1972] 210 p. illus. 21 cm. Bibliography: [p. 204]-206. [BX4700.F6S56] 72-1439 ISBN 0-684-13697-X. 2.95 (pbk.)
1. Francesco d'Assisi, Saint, 1182-1226. I. Title.

TRETTEL, Efrem. 271'.3'024 B
Francis, Saint of Assisi and of the world / by Efrem Trettel. Chicago : Franciscan Herald Press, c1975. xxii, 224 p., [19] leaves of plates : ill. ; 21 cm. Translation of Francesco d'Assisi. [BX4700.F6T6513] 75-23336 ISBN 0-8199-0587-9 pbk. : 4.95
1. Francesco d'Assisi, Saint, 1182-1226. I. Title.

NYHUS, Paul L. 271'.3'0433
The Franciscans in South Germany, 1400-1530 : reform and revolution / Paul L. Nyhus. Philadelphia : American Philosophical Society, 1975, c1976. 47 p. ; 30 cm. (Transactions of the American Philosophical Society ; new ser., v. 65, pt. 8 ISSN 0065-9746s) Includes index.IBibliography: p. 44-46.I[BX3634.N9] .75-32621 ISBN 0-87169-658-4 pbk. : 3.00
1. Franciscans in southern Germany. I. Title. II. Series: American Philosophical Society, Philadelphia. Transactions ; new ser., v. 65, pt. 8.

MORALES, Francisco, 271'.3'072
1937-
Ethnic and social background of the Franciscan Friars in seventeenth century Mexico. Washington, Academy of American Franciscan History, 1973. ix, 166 p. 27 cm. (Publications of the Academy of American Franciscan History. Monograph series, v. 10) Appendices (p. 132-146) contain selections from original Spanish documents. Bibliography: p. 147-158. [BX3612.A1M6] 73-180285
1. Franciscans in Mexico. 2. Indians in Mexico—Missions. I. Title. II. Series: Academy of American Franciscan History. Monograph series, v. 10.

BACIGALUPO, Leonard. 271'.3'073
The Franciscans and Italian immigration in America / Leonard Bacigalupo. 1st ed. Hicksville, N.Y. : Exposition Press, c1977. 80 p., [1] leaf of plates : port. ; 22 cm. (An Exposition-university book) Bibliography: p. 49-56. [BX3608.B32] 76-50676 ISBN 0-682-48741-4 : 4.50
1. Franciscans—United States. 2. Italian Americans—History. 3. Church work with foreigners. I. Title.

O'ROURKE, Thomas 271'.3'0764
Patrick, 1889-
The Franciscan missions in Texas (1690-1793), by Thomas P. O'Rourke. Washington, 1927. [New York, AMS Press, 1974] iv, 107 p. 23 cm. Reprint of the author's thesis, Catholic University of America, 1927, which was issued as v. 5 of the Catholic University of America. Studies in American church history. Bibliography: p. 94-101. [BV2803.T4O76 1974] 73-3559 ISBN 0-404-57755-5 5.00
1. Franciscans—Missions. 2. Missions—Texas. I. Title. II. Series: Catholic University of America. Studies in American church history, v. 5.

LITTLE, Andrew George, 271'.3'08
1863-1945. ed.
Collectanea Franciscana. Typis Academicis, 1914-22. 2 v. facsims. 20-23 cm. Vol. 1 edited by A. G. Little, M. R. James, and H. M. Bannister: v. 2 by C. L. Kingsford and others. Vol. 2 has imprint: Manchester, University Press. Photoreproduction. Ridgewood, N.J., Gregg Press. 1965-66 [BX3601.C6] 67-5529
1. Franciscans — Collections. I. Kingsford, Charles Lethbridge, 1862-1926, ed. II. Title.

FRANCISCANS. Province of 271.3082
Saint Barbara.
Early Franciscan classics. Tr. by the Friars Minor of the Franciscan Province of Saint Barbara, Oakland, Cal. Paterson, N. J., St. Anthony [c.1962] vii, 275p. front. 61-11252 3.50
1. Francesco d'Assisi, Saint, 1182-1226. 2. Franciscans—Collections. I. Title.

BROOKE, Rosalind B 271.309
Early Franciscan government; Elias to Bonaventure. Cambridge [Eng.] University Press, 1959. xv, 313p. illus., port. 23cm. (Cambridge studies in medieval life and thought, New ser., v. 7) Bibliography: p. xi-xiv. Bibliographical footnotes. [BX3606.B76] 59-3290
1. Elia da Cortona, Brother, d. 1253. 2. Franciscans—Hist. I. Title. II. Series.

HERMANN, Placid, tr. 271.309
XIIIth century chronicles Translated fromthe Latin. With introd. and notes by Marie-Therese Laureilhe. Chicago, Franciscan Herald Press [1961] xvii, 302p. maps. 22cm. [BX3606.A2H4] 61-11198
1. Franciscans—Hist.—Sources. I. Jordanus de Yano, fl. 1220-1262. Chronicle. II. Thomas of Eccleston, fl. 1250. Chronicle. III. Salimbene, Ognibene di Guido di Adamo, Brother, b. 1221. Chronicle. IV. Title.
Contents omitted.

MOORMAN, John Richard 271'.3'09
Humpidge, Bp. of Ripon.
A history of the Franciscan Order from its origins to the year 1517 [by] John Moorman. Oxford, Clarendon P., 1968. xiii, 641 p. 24 cm. Bibliography: p. [595]-613. [BX3606.2.M6] 68-101796 ISBN 0-19-826425-9 £5.
1. Franciscans—History. I. Title.

GEIGER, Maynard J., 271'.30922
1901-
Franciscan missionaries in Hispanic California, 1769-1848; a biographical dictionary, by Maynard Geiger. San Marino [Calif.] Huntington Library, 1969. xiv, 304 p. 24 cm. Includes bibliographical references. [F864.G38] 74-79607 12.50
1. Franciscans in California. I. Title.

ALMEDINGEN, Martha 271'.3'0924 B
Edith, 1898-
St. Francis of Assisi; a great life in brief, by E. M. Almedingen. New York, A. A. Knopf, 1967. ix, 229, ix p. 19 cm. (Great lives in brief) First published in London in 1967 under title: Francis of Assisi; a portrait. Bibliography: p. 227-229. [BX4700.F6A725 1967b] 67-11143
1. Francesco d'Assisi, Saint, 1182-1226.

ARMSTRONG, April 271.30924 B
(Oursler)
St. Francis of Assisi; a concise biography. New York, American R.D.M. Corp. [1966] 70 p. port. 21 cm. (A Study master publication, 960) Bibliography: p. 70. [BX4700.F6A77] 66-28702
1. Francesco d'Assisi, Saint, 1182-1226.

BOASE, Thomas 271'.3'0924 B
Sherrer Ross, 1898-
St. Francis of Assisi [by] T. S. R. Boase. With 16 lithographs by Arthur Boyd. Bloomington, Indiana University Press [1968] 120 p. illus. 25 cm. Bibliography: p. [117] [BX4700.F6B55 1968b] 68-15550
1. Francesco d'Assisi, Saint, 1182-1226. I. Boyd, Arthur, 1920- illus. II. Title.

CAPOZZI, Francis 271'.3'0924(B)
Clement, 1885-
A new portrait of Francis of Assisi, by Francis C. Capozzi. Northridge, Calif., Voice Christian Publications [1967] 222 p. 22 cm. First published in 1956 under title: God's fool. [BX4700.F6C326] 67-8551
1. Francesco d'Assisi, Saint, 1182-1226. I. Title.

COULTON, George 271'.3'0924 B
Gordon, 1858-1947.
From St. Francis to Dante; translations from the chronicle of the Franciscan Salimbene, 1221-1288, with notes and illus. from other medieval sources, by G. G. Coulton. 2d ed., rev. and enl. New York, Russell & Russell [1968] xiv, 446 p. front. 23 cm. A reprint of the 1907 ed. Bibliography: p. [414]-415. [BX4705.S24C7 1968] 68-10910
1. Salimbene, Ognibene di Guido di Adamo, Brother, b. 1221. I. Salimbene, Ognibene di Guido di Adamo, Brother, b. 1221. II. Title.

ENGLEBERT, Omer, 1893- 271.30924
Saint Francis of Assisi; a biography New tr. [from French] by Eve Marie Cooper. 2d English ed., rev., augm. by Ignatius Brady, Raphael Brown. Chicago, Franciscan Herald [1966, c.1965] xii, 616p. 21cm. Bibl. [BX4700.F6E612] 64-14252 8.50
1. Francesco d'Assisi, Saint, 1182-1226. 2. Francesco d'Assisi, Saint, 1182-1226—Bibl. I. Brown, Beverly Holladay, 1912- II. Title.

ERIKSON, Joan Mowat. 271'.3'0924
Saint Francis et his four ladies. [1st ed.] New York, Norton [1970] 140 p. illus. 25 cm. Includes bibliographical references. [BX4700.F6E74 1970] 71-127178 5.00
1. Francesco d'Assisi, Saint, 1182-1226. I. Title.

FRANCESCO D'ASSISI, 271.30924
Saint. Legend Fioretti
The little flowers of Saint Francis of Assisi. in the 1st Eng. tr., rev., emended by Roger Hudleston; Introd. by Arthur Livingston. New York, Heritage [Dist. Dial, c.1965] xviii, 261p. illus. 29cm. [BX4700.F63E5] 66-829 6.50
I. Hudleston, Gilbert Roger, 1874- ed. II. Title.

FRANCESCO D'ASSISI, 271.30924 (B)
Saint. Legend. Fioretti.
The little flowers of Saint Francis of Assisi, in the 1st English translation, rev. & emended by Roger Hudleston; with an introd. by Arthur Livingston. New York, Heritage Press [c1965] xviii, 261 p. illus. 29 cm. [BX4700.F63E5] 66-829
I. Hudleston, Gilbert Roger, 1874- ed. II. Title.

GHILARDI, Agostino. 271'.3'0924 B
The life and times of St Francis; text by Agostino Ghilardi; translator [from the Italian] Salvator Attanasio. Revised ed. London, New York, Hamlyn, 1969. 2-75 p. illus. (some col.), facsims. (some col.), ports. 30 cm. (Portraits of greatness) Col. illus. on lining papers. [BX4700.F69G49 1969] 79-541923 ISBN 0-600-03140-3 17/6
1. Francesco d'Assisi, Saint, 1182-1226. 2. Francesco d'Assisi, Saint, 1182-1226—Art. I. Title.

LIVERSIDGE, 271'.3'0924 B
Douglas, 1913-
Saint Francis of Assisi. New York, F. Watts [1968] v, 164 p. map. 22 cm. (Immortals of philosophy and religion) A biography of the man whose life and deeds were a quiet protest against man's inhumanity to man and to animals. [BX4700.F6L62] 92 AC 68
1. Francesco d'Assisi, Saint, 1182-1226. I. Title.

LUDWIG, Mileta, 271'.3'0924 (B)
Sister.
Right-hand glove uplifted; a biography of Archbishop Michael Heiss, by Sister M. Mileta Ludwig. [1st ed.] New York, Pageant Press [1968] 567 p. illus., ports. 24 cm. $7.50 Includes bibliographical references. [BX4705.H4527L8] 67-30506
1. Heiss, Michael, Abp., 1818-1890. I. Title.

A new portrait of 271'.3'0924
Francis of Assisi, by Francis C. Capozzi. Northridge, Calif., Voice Christian Pubns. [1967] 222p. 22cm. First pub. in 1956 under title: God's fool. [BX4700.F6C326 1967] (B) 67-8551 3.95
1. Francesco d'Assisi, Saint, 1182-1226. I. Capozzi, Francis Clement, 1885-

POLITI, Leo, 1908- 271'.3'0924 B
Saint Francis and the animals. New York, Scribner, c1959. [32] p. illus. 26 cm. Tells of St. Francis' friendship with various animals—birds, a little hare, doves, a pheasant, a fish, a lamb, and the wolf of Gubbio. [BX4700.F69P6] 92 AC 68
1. Francesco d'Assisi, Saint, 1182-1226. I. Title.

SETON, Walter Warren, 271'.3'0924
1882-1927
Blessed Giles of Assisi. Manchester [Eng.] Univ. Pr., 1918. Farnborough, Eng., Gregg Pr., 1966. vii, 94p. 20cm. The short Life of Giles of Assisi which forms the basis of the present work is found in Codex Canonici misc. 528 in the Bodleian Library, Oxford. It is attributed to Brother Leo. 'Text of Canonici misc. 528 and tr.' p. 51-89. Photoreproduction. Bibl. [BX4705.A319S47 1918a] 67-4915 9.80
1. Aegidius, of Assisi, d. 1262. I. Leo, Franciscan, 13th cent. II. Title.
American distributor: Gregg Pr., Ridgewood, N. J.

WROBLEWSKI, 271'.3'0924 (B)
Sergius.
The real Francis, Poetry by M. Angela Sassak. Pulaski, Wis., Franciscan Publishers [1967] 128 p. 19 cm. Bibliographical references included in "Notes" (p. 125-128) [BX4700.F6W7] 67-7411
1. Francesco of Assisi, Saint, 1182-1226. 2. Franciscans — Spiritual life. I. Title.

CUTHBERT, Father, 1866- 271'.36
1939.
The Capuchins; a contribution to the history of the Counter-Reformation. Port Washington, N.Y., Kennikat Press [1971] 2 v. (475 p.) illus., ports. 22 cm. Reprint of the 1928 ed. Includes bibliographical references. [BX3115.C8 1971] 70-118518
1. Capuchins. 2. Counter-Reformation.

*GIGLIOZZI, Giovanni 271.36
Padre Pio, a pictorial biography. Tr. [from Italian] by Oscar DeLiso. New York, Pocket Bks. [1966, c.1965] 128p. illus., ports. 18cm. (75177) First pub. in 1965 by Phaedra under the title: I monili dello sposo (Cardinal ed., 75177) .75 pap.,
1. Guiseppe, Francesco, 1887- 2. Stigmata. I. Title.

GAUDIOSE, Dorothy 271'.36'024 B
M., 1920-
Prophet of the people; a biography of Padre Pio, by Dorothy M. Gaudiose. Illustrated by George Lallas. New York, Alba House [1974] xviii, 237 p. illus. 22 cm. [BX4705.P49G38] 74-7123 ISBN 0-8189-0290-6
1. Pio da Pietrelcina, Father. I. Title.

SCHUG, John A. 271'.36'024 B
Padre Pio / John A. Schug. Huntington, Ind. : Our Sunday Visitor, 1976. 256 p. : port. ; 21 cm. [BX4705.P49S38] 76-17953 ISBN 0-87973-856-1 pbk. : 4.95
1. Pio da Pietrelcina, father. 2. Capuchins—Biography. I. Title.

DERUM, James 271'.36'0924 B
Patrick.
The porter of Saint Bonaventure's; the life of Father Solanus Casey, Capuchin. Detroit, Fidelity Press [1968] 279 p. illus., ports. 23 cm. [BX4705.C33573D4] 78-1230 4.95
1. Casey, Solanus, 1870-1957. I. Title.

GIGLIOZZI, Giovanni. 271.360924 B
Padre Pio; a pictorial biography. Translation by Oscar DeLiso. [New York] Phaedra, 1965. 84 p. illus., map, ports. 23 cm. Translation of I monilli dello sposo. [BX4705.P49G53] 65-23441
1. Pio da Pietrelcina, Father. I. Title.

O'DONNELL, Clement 271'.37'045634
Maria.
The Friars Minor Conventual Penitentiaries in the Basilica of St. Peter in the Vatican / Clement M. O'Donnell. Albany, N.Y. : O'Donnell, 1975. 125 p. : ill. ; 24 cm. Translation of Frati Minori Conventuali, Penitenzieri nella Basilica di S. Pietro in Vaticano. Includes index. Bibliography: p. 15. [BX1862.O3613] 76-358227
1. Catholic Church. Poenitentiaria Apostolica. 2. Conventuals. I. Title.

AUGUSTINUS, Aurelius, 271.4
Saint, Bp. of Hippo.
The rule of Saint Augustine. Commentary by Blessed Alphonsus Orozco. Translation by Thomas A. Hand. Westminster, Md., Newman Press, 1956. xxii, 84p. port. 19cm. [BX2904.Z5O7] 56-11410
1. Monasticism and religious orders—Rules. I. Orozco, Alonso de, 1500-1591. II. Title.

COLVIN, Howard Montagu. 271.4
The White Canons in England. Oxford, Clarendon Press, 1951. viii, 459 p. front., fold. map. 23 cm. Bibliography: p. [369]-388. [BX3916.C6] 52-2460
1. Premonstratensians in Gt. Brit. I. Title.

CREAKE, Abbey 271.4
A cartulary of Creake Abbey; with an introduction by A. L. Bedingfeld [based on the translation by K. C. Newton]. Norwich, Norfolk Record Society, 1966. xxxvi, 146 p. plates (incl. facsims.). 26 cm. (Norfolk Record Society. Publications v. 35) Bibliography: p. xxxiv-xxxvi. [DA670.N59N863 vol. 35] 67-85745 N.T.
1. Creake Abbey—Charters, grants, privileges. I. Bedingfeld, A. L. II. Title. III. Series.

DARWIN, Francis 271'.4'00942
Darwin Swift.
The English mediaeval recluse / by Francis D. S. Darwin. Norwood, Pa. : Norwood Editions, 1976. vi, 90 p. ; 24 cm. Reprint of the 1944 ed. published by the Society for Promoting Christian Knowledge, London. Includes bibliographical references and index. [BX2847.G7D3 1976] 76-2006 ISBN 0-88305-216-4 lib. bdg. : 10.00
1. Hermits—England. I. Title.

ROTH, Francis Xavier, 271'.4'042
1900-
Collectanea Anglicana Ordinis Fratrum Eremitarum S. Augustini; a source book for the history of the Austin Friars in England, with a biographical index of over 1,000 names, by Francis Roth. Philadelphia [1952?] 1 v. (unpaged) 29 cm. "Completed August 31, 1952." [BX2916.R67] 74-172561
1. Augustinians in England—History—Sources. I. Title.

BURKE, Thomas J M 1920- ed. 271.5
Beyond all horizons; Jesuits and the missions. Pref. by Anne Fremantle. [1st ed.] Garden City, N. Y., Hanover House [1957] 288p. 22cm. [BV2290.B8] 57-7378
1. Jesuits—Missions. I. Title.

BURKE, Thomas J M 1920- ed. 271.5
Beyond all horizons; Jesuits and the missions. Pref. by Anne Fremantle. [1st ed.] Garden City, N. Y., Hanover House [1957] 288p. 22cm. [BV2290.B8] 57-7378
1. Jesuits-Missions. I. Title.

DONNE, John, 1572-1631. 271'.5
Ignatius his conclave; an edition of the Latin

and English texts with introduction and commentary by T. S. Healy. Oxford, Clarendon P., 1969. lii, 175 p., plate. port. 23 cm. Includes bibliographical references. [BX3705.A2D6 1969] 70-465939 ISBN 0-19-812405-8 50/-
1. Loyola, Ignacio de, Saint, 1491-1556. 2. Jesuits—Controversial literature. I. Healy, Timothy Stafford, ed. II. Title.

FOSS, Michael. 271'.5
The founding of the Jesuits, 1540. New York, Weybright and Talley [1969] vii, 307 p. illus., ports. 23 cm. (Turning points in history) Bibliography: p. 295-296. [BX3706.2.F6 1969b] 69-17199 7.50
1. Jesuits—History. I. Title.

FULOP-MILLER, Rene, 1891- 271.5
The power and secret of the Jesuits. Translated by F. S. Flint and D. F. Tait. New York, G. Braziller, 1956. ix, 499p. 22cm. [BX3702.F8 1956] 56-2481
1. Jesuits. I. Title.

GUIBERT, Joseph de 271.5
The Jesuits: their spiritual doctrine and practice; a historical study. William J. Young, tr. [from French] George E. Ganss, ed. Chicago, Inst. of Jesuit Sources [dist.] Loyola Univ. [c.]1964. xxv, 692p. 24cm. Bibl. 64-21430 14.00
1. Loyola, Ignacio de, Saint, 1491-1556. 2. Loyola, Ignacio de, Saint, 1491-1556. Exercitia spiritualia. 3. Jesuits. I. Title.

GUIBERT, Joseph de. 271.5
The Jesuits: their spiritual doctrine and practice; a historical study. William J. Young, Translator. George E. Ganss, editor. Chicago, Institute of Jesuit Sources, 1964. xxv, 692 p. 24 cm. Translation of La spiritualite de la Compagnie de Jesus; esquisse historique. List of Joseph de Guibert's writings": p. xxi-xxv. Bibliography: p. 617-625. Bibliographical footnotes. [BX3703.G813] 64-21430
1. Jesuits. 2. Loyola, Ignacio de, Saint, 1491-1556. 3. Loyola, Ignacio de, Saint, 1491-1556. Exercitia spiritualia. I. Title.

LA FARGE, John, 1880- 271.5
A report on the American Jesuits. Photos. by Margaret Bourke-White. New York, Farrar, Straus and Cudahy [1956] 236p. illus. 25cm. [BX3708.L3] 56-5756
1. Jesuits in the U. S. I. Title.

LA'FARGE, Johv, 1880- 271.5
A report on the American Jesuits. Photos. by Margaret Bourke-White. New York, Farrar, Straus and Cudahy [1956] 236p. illus. 25cm. [BX3708.L3] 56-5756
1. Jesuits in the U. S. I. Title.

LEARY, John P, 1919- ed. 271.5
Better a day. New York, Macmillan, 1951. vii, 341 p. map (on lining paper) 21 cm. [BX3755.L4] 51-10456
1. Jesuits—Biog. I. Title.

LEARY, John P 1919- ed. 271.5
I lift my lamp; Jesuits in America. Westminster, Md., Newman Press, 1955. 383p. 24cm. [BX3708.L4] 54-12449
1. Jesuits in the U. S. I. Title.

LEWIS, Clifford Merle, 1911- 271.5
The Spanish Jesuit Mission in Virginia, 1570-1572, by Clifford M. Lewis and Albert J. Loomie. Chapel Hill, Published for the Virginia Historical Society by the University of North Carolina Press, 1953. [F229.L6] 53-12911
1. Jesuit in Virginia. 2. Jesuit—Missions. 3. Virginia—Hist.—Colonial period—Sources. I. Loomle, Albert Joseph, 1922- joint author. II. Virginia Historical Society, Richmond. III. Title.
Contents omitted.

LIPPERT, Peter, 1879-1936. 271.5
The Jesuits; a self-portrait. Translated by John Murray. [1st ed.] Freiburg] Herder [1958] 130p. 19cm. Translation of Zur Psychologie des Jesuitenordens. [BX3703.L51o] 58-5852
1. Jesuits. I. Title.

LIPPERT, Peter, 1879-1936. 271.5
The Jesuits, a self-portrait. Translated by John Murray. [New York] Herder and Herder [1958] 130p. 19cm. 'The English translation is based on the original German version of 'Zur Psychologie des Jesuitenordens." [BX3703.L513 1958a] 58-5865
1. Jesuits. I. Title.

MCGLOIN, Joseph T 271.5
I'll die laughing! Illustrated by Don Baumgart. Milwaukee, Bruce Pub. Co. [1955] 178p. illus. 21cm. Reminiscences of days spent in a Jesult seminary. [BX4705.M197A3] 55-9764
1. Jesults—Education. I. Title.

MCGLOIN, Joseph T. 271.5
I'll die laughing! New York, All Saints Pr. [1962, c.1955] 145p. illus. (Bruce paperback, AS215) .50 pap.,
1. Roman Catholic Church—Religious orders—Jesuits. 2. Roman Catholic Church—Clergy—Humor. I. Title.

MEADOWS, Denis. 271.5
Obedient men. New York, Appleton-Century-Crofts [c1954] 308p. 21cm. Autobiographical. [BX4705.M477A3] 53-10090
I. Title.

PASCAL, Blaise, 1623-1662. 271'.5
The provincial letters. Translated, with an introd., by A. J. Krailsheimer. Baltimore, Penguin Books [1967] 300 p. 18 cm. (The Penguin classics) [BX4720.P3K7 1967b] 68-4495
1. Jesuits. 2. Port Royal. 3. Jansenists. I. Title.

PASCAL, Blaise, 1623-1662. 271.5
The provincial letters. [Translated by Thomas M'Crie] Pensees. [Translated by W. F. Trotter] Scientific treatises. [Translated by Richard Scofield] Chicago, Encyclopaedia Britannica [1955, c1952] vi, 487 p. illus. 25 cm. (Great books of the Western World, v. 33) [AC1.G72 vol. 33] 284.84 55-10340
1. Jesuits. 2. Port Royal. 3. Jansenists. I. McCrie, Thomas, 1797-1875, tr. II. Trotter, William Finlayson, 1871- tr. III. Scofield, Richard, tr. IV. Pascal, Blaise, 1623-1662. Pensees. 1955. V. Pascal, Blaise, 1623-1662. Scientific treatises. 1955. VI. Title. VII. Title: Pensees.

PLATTNER, Felix Alfred, 1906- 271.5
Jesuits go East. Translated from the German by Lord Sudley and Oscar Blobel. Westminster, Md., Newman Press, 1952. 283 p. illus. 22 cm. "A record of missionary activity in the East, 1541-1786." -- Dust Jacket. [BV2290.P513 1952] 52-10539
1. Jesuits — Missions. 2. Jesuits in Asia. 3. Asia — Descr. & trav. I. Title.

RICCI, Matteo, 1552-1610. 271.5
China in the sixteenth century: the journals of Matthew Ricci, 1583-1610; translated from the Latin by Louis J. Gallagher. With a foreword by Richard J. Cushing, Archbishop of Boston. New York, Random House [1953] xxii, 616p. ports. 24cm. 'Translation of Trigault's 1615 Latin version of the Ricci commentaries [entitled De Christiana expeditione apud Sinas suscepta ab Socielate Jesut] [BX3746.C5R473] 53-9708
1. Jesults in China. 2. Missione—China. 3. Jesults—Missions. I. Trigault, Nicolas, 1577-1628. II. Title.

PENNING de Vries, Piet. 271'.5'024
Discernment of spirits, according to the life and teachings of St. Ignatius of Loyola. Translated by W. Dudok Van Heel. [1st ed.] New York, Exposition Press [1973] 252 p. 22 cm. (An Exposition-Testament book) Bibliography: p. 247-248. [BX2350.2.P4193] 72-90063 ISBN 0-682-47592-0 8.00
1. Loyola, Ignacio de, Saint, 1491-1556. 2. Spiritual life—History of doctrines. I. Title.

BEITZELL, Edwin Warfield, 1905- 271'.5'075241
The Jesuit missions of St. Mary's County, Maryland / by Edwin Warfield Beitzell ; sponsored by the St. Mary's County Bicentennial Commission. 2d ed. Abell, Md. : Beitzell, 1976. xiii, 422 p. : ill. ; 29 cm. Includes bibliographical references and index. [DX3709.M3B4 1976] 77-75320 15.00
1. Jesuits—Maryland—St. Mary's Co. 2. Jesuits—Missions. I. Title.

HOLLIS, Christopher, 1902- 271'.5'09
The Jesuits; a history. [1st American ed.] New York, Macmillan [1968] 284 p. illus., facsims., ports. 23 cm. London ed. (Weidenfeld and Nicolson) has title: A history of the Jesuits. Bibliography: p. [272]-274. [BX3706.2.H64 1968] 68-54474
1. Jesuits—History.

MAYNARD, Theodore, 1890- 271.509
Saint Ignatius and the Jesuits. New York, P. J. Kenedy [1956] i13p. 22cm. [BX3706.M38] 56-5751
1. Loyola, Ignatius de, Saint, 1491-1556. 2. Jesuits—Hist. I. Title.

MEADOWS, Denis. 271.509
A popular history of the Jesuits. New York, Macmillan, 1958. 160p. 21cm. Includes bibliography. [BX3706.M4] 57-12945
1. Jesuits—Hist. I. Title.

BERRIGAN DANIEL. 271'.5'0924 B
No bars to manhood. [1st ed.] Garden City, N.Y., Doubleday, 1970. 215 p. 22 cm. [BX4705.B3845A3] 77-97650 5.95
I. Title.

JOHNSON, Joseph Mitchell. 271'.5'0924
The story of a county pastor [by] J. M. Johnson. [1st ed.] New York, Vantage Press [1967] 260 p. 21 cm. [BX4705.J672A3] 68-6250
1. Hollywood, Md. St. John's Church. I. Title.

JOHNSON, Joseph Mitchell. 271'.5'0924
The story of a county pastor [by] J. M. Johnson. [1st ed.] New York, Vantage Press [1967] 260 p. 21 cm. [BX4705.J672A3] 68-6250
1. Hollywood, Md. St. John's Church. I. Title.

LIVERSIDGE, Douglas, 1913- 271.5'0924 B
Ignatius of Loyola; the soldier-saint. New York, F. Watts [1970] 150 p. map. 22 cm. (Immortals of philosophy and religion) A biography of the man who turned from a military life to God's service, becoming famous for writing Spiritual Exercises and founding the Society of Jesus. [BX4700.L7L55] 92 70-103098
1. Loyola, Ignacio de, Saint, 1491-1556—Juvenile literature. I. Title.

MULLER, Gerald Francis, 1927- 271'.5'0924 B
With life and laughter; the life of Father Miguel Agustin Pro, by Gerald F. Muller. Notre Dame [Ind.] Dujarie Press [1969] 128 p. illus., ports. 22 cm. First ed. published in 1954 under title: The martyr laughed. [BX4705.P72M8 1969] 70-76774
1. Pro Juarez, Miguel Agustin, 1891-1927. I. Title.

ONE of a kind; 271'.5'0924
essays in tribute to Gustave Weigel. With an introd. by John Courtney Murray. Wilkes-Barre, Pa., Dimension Books [1967] 111 p. 21 cm. Contents.Contents.—A memorable man, by J. C. Murray.—The gringo, by J. Ochagavia.—An uncommon ecumenist, by A. C. Outler.—A living epistle of Christ, by D. Horton.—One of a kind, by J. B. Sheerin.—Unstucknes, by H. M. Jenkins.—A figure in transition, by E. Burke.—An ocumenical pioneer, by M. Brown.—Liquidator of prejudices, by R. Balkam. [BX4705.W415O5] 67-27131
1. Weigel, Gustave, 1906-1964. I. Murray, John Courtney.

SMET, Pierre Jean de, 1801-1873. 271'.5'0924 B
Life, letters, and travels of Father de Smet. [Edited by] Hiram Martin Chittenden and Alfred Talbot Richardson. New York, Arno Press, 1969. 4 v. (xv, 1624 p.) illus., facsims., fold. map, ports. 23 cm. (Religion in America) Reprint of the 1905, c1904 ed. Bibliography: v. 1, p. 144-146. [F591.S63 1969] 75-83418
1. Indians of North America. 2. The West—Description and travel—To 1848. 3. Northwestern States—Description and travel. 4. Northwest, Canadian—Description and travel. I. Chittenden, Hiram Martin, 1858-1917, ed. II. Richardson, Alfred Talbot, ed.

STROUSSE, Flora, 1897- 271'.5'0924 (B)
John La Farge, gentle Jesuit. Illustrated by Salem Tamer. New York, P.J. Kenedy [1968, c1967] 188 p. illus., ports. 22 cm. (American background books, 33) [BX4705.L237S7] 67-26801 2.50
1. La Farge, John, 1880-1963. I. Title. II. Series.

TEILHARD de Chardin, Pierre. 271'.5'0924
Letters from Hastings, 1908-1912. Introd. by Henri de Lubac.(Translated by Judith de Stefano New York] Herder and Herder [1968] 206 p. 21 cm. Translation of 70 letters from the 1st part of the author's Lettres d'Hastings et de Paris, 1908-1914. Bibliographical footnotes. [B2430.T374A413] 68-9137 4.95
I. Title.

TEILHARD de Chardin, Pierre. 271'.5'0924
Letters from Paris, 1912-1914. Introd. by Henri de Luba.(Annotation by Auguste Demoment and Henri de Lubac.(Translated by Michael Mazzarese [New York] Herder and Herder [1967] 157 p. 21 cm. Portion of the author's Lettres d'Hastings et de Paris, 1908-1914, published in 1965. Bibliographical footnotes. [B2430.T374A42] 67-17626
I. Lubac, Henri de, 1896- ed. II. Title.

TEILHARD de Chardin, Pierre. 271'.5'0924
Letters to Leontine Zanta. Introd. by Robert Garric and Henri de Lubac. Translated by Bernard Wall. [1st U.S. ed.] New York, Harper & Row [1969] 127 p. 21 cm. Bibliographical footnotes. [B2430.T374A493 1969b] 69-17020 4.00
1. Zanta, Leontine. I. Title.

VAN DYKE, Paul, 1859-1933. 271'.5'0924
Ignatius Loyola, the founder of the Jesuits. Port Washington, N.Y., Kennikat Press [1968, c1926] vi, 381 p. 21 cm. Bibliography: p. 364-368. [BX4700.L7V3 1968] 67-27659
1. Loyola, Ignacio de, Saint, 1491-1556.

BASSET, Bernard. 271'.5'0942
The English Jesuits: from Campion to Martindale. Pref. by Terence Corrigan. [New York] Herder & Herder [1968,c.1967] xv, 477p. illus., ports. 22cm. Bibl. [BX3716.B32 1968] 67-29671 9.50
1. Jesuits in England. I. Title.

BASSET, Bernard. 271'.5'0942
The English Jesuits: from Campion to Martindale. With a pref. by Terence Corrigan. [New York] Herder and Herder [1968, c1967] xv, 477 p. illus., ports. 22 cm. Bibliography: p. 465-468. [BX3716.B32 1968] 67-29671
1. Jesuits in England. I. Title.

O'BRIEN, John A. 271.5097
The first martyrs of North America. New York, All Saints [1963, c.1953] 208p. 17cm. (As.238) .50 pap.,
I. Title.

CURRAN, Francis Xavier, 1914- 271.50973
The return of the Jesuits; chapters in the history of the Society of Jesus in nineteenth century America [by] Francis X. Curran. Chicago, Loyola University Press [1966] 155 p. 24 cm. Bibliographical footnotes. [BX3708.C8] 66-29559
1. Jesuits in the United States—History. I. Title.

WALSH, James Joseph, 1865-1942. 271'.5'0973
American Jesuits. Freeport, N.Y., Books for Libraries Press [1968] ix, 336 p. 23 cm. (Essay index reprint series) Reprint of the 1934 ed. [BX3708.W3 1968] 68-29251
1. Jesuits in the United States. 2. Catholic Church in the United States. I. Title.

SCHOENBERG, Wilfred P 271.509786
Jesuits in Montana, 1840-1960. [Portland, Oregon-Jesuit, 1960] 120p. illus. 21cm. [BX3709.M9S33] 61-664
1. Jesuits in Montana. I. Title.

SCHOENBERG, Wilfred P 271.509795
Jesuits in Oregon, 1844-1959. [Portland, Oregon-Jesuit, 1959] 64p. illus. 21cm. [BX3709.O7S35] 59-43543
1. Jesuits in Oregon. I. Title.

MORNER, Magnus, ed. 271.5098
The expulsion of the Jesuits from Latin America. [1st ed.] New York, Knopf [1967] 207p. 19cm. (Borzoi bks. on Latin Amer.) Bibl. [BX3714.A1M6] 64-23730 3.95
1. Jesuits in Latin America—Hist.—Collections. I. Title.

MORNER, Magnus, ed. 271.5098
The expulsion of the Jesuits from Latin America. [1st ed.] New York, Knopf, 1965. 207 p. 19 cm. (Borzol books on Latin America) "A bibliographical note": p. [199]-207. [BX3714.A1M6] 64-23730
1. Jesuits in Latin America — Hist. — Collections. I. Title.

COSTA, Horacio de la 271.509914
The Jesuits in the Philippines, 1581-1768. Cambridge, Mass., Harvard Univ. Press [c.] 1961. 702p. illus. 25cm. Bibl. 60-10036 12.50
1. Jesuits in the Philippine Islands. I. Title.

BOEHMER, Heinrich, 1869-1927. 271'.53
The Jesuits : an historical study / by H. Boehmer ; translated from the 4th rev. ed. by Paul Zeller Strodach. New York : Gordon Press, 1975. 192 p. ; 24 cm. Translation of Die Jesuiten. First published in 1928. Bibliography: p. 191-192. [BX3706.B62 1975] 75-3885 ISBN 0-87968-199-3 lib.bdg. : 34.95
1. Loyola, Ignacio de, Saint, 1491-1556. 2. Jesuits. I. Title.

BRODRICK, James, 1891- 271'.53
The origin of the Jesuits. Westport, Conn., Greenwood Press [1971] vii, 274 p. port. 23 cm. Reprint of the 1940 ed. Includes bibliographical references. [BX3706.B7 1971] 70-138604 ISBN 0-8371-5523-1
1. Loyola, Ignacio de, Saint, 1491-1556. 2. Jesuits—History. I. Title.

CAMPBELL, Thomas Joseph, 1848-1925. 271'.53
The Jesuits, 1534-1921; a history of the Society of Jesus from its foundation to the present time. Boston, Milford House [1971]

xvi, 937 p. 23 cm. Reprint of the 1921 ed. Bibliography: p. xi-xii. [BX3706.C28 1971] 77-82144 ISBN 0-87821-018-0
1. Jesuits—History. I. Title.

CLANCY, Thomas H. 271'.53
An introduction to Jesuit life : the constitutions and history through 435 years / Thomas H. Clancy. St. Louis : Institute of Jesuit Sources, 1976. xiii, 407 p. ; 23 cm. (Study aids on Jesuit topics ; no. 3) Includes index. Bibliography: p. 336-344. [BX3706.2.C55] 75-46080 ISBN 0-912422-12-2 : 5.50
1. Jesuits—History. I. Title. II. Series.

HASTINGS, Macdonald. 271'.53
Jesuit child. New York, St. Martin's Press [1972, c1971] 251 p. illus. 23 cm. Autobiographical. Bibliography: p. 241-242. [BX3702.2.H35 1972] 74-175001 7.95
1. Jesuits. I. Title.

BANGERT, William V. 271'.53'009
A history of the Society of Jesus [by] William V. Bangert. St. Louis, Institute of Jesuit Sources, 1972. xii, 558 p. maps. 24 cm. [BX3706.2.B33] 78-188687 ISBN 0-912422-05-X 14.75
1. Jesuits—History. I. Title.
Publishers Address: Institute of Jesuit Sources, 3700 West Pine Blvd., St. Louis, Mo. 63108

O'MALLEY, William J. 271'.53'022 B
The fifth week / William J. O'Malley. Chicago : Loyola University Press, c1976. 216 p. ; 21 cm. Bibliography: p. 210-212. [BX3755.O65] 75-43583 ISBN 0-8294-0248-9 : 4.50
1. Jesuits—Biography. 2. Jesuits. I. Title.

CISZEK, Walter J., 1904- 271'.5'3024B
He leadeth me [by] Walter J. Ciszek, with Daniel L. Flaherty. Garden City, N.Y., Image Books 1975 [c1973] 232 p., 18 cm. [BX4705.C546A34] ISBN 0-385-02805-9 1.75 (pbk.)
1. Ciszek, Walter J., 1904- 2. World War, 1939-1945—Prisoners and prisons, Russian. 3. World War, 1939-1945—Personal narratives, American. I. Flaherty, Daniel L., joint author. II. Title.
L.C. card no. for original ed.: 73-79654.

COOPER, Michael, S.J. 271'.53'024 B
Rodrigues the interpreter; an early Jesuit in Japan and China. [1st ed.] New York, Weatherhill [1974] 416 p. illus. 24 cm. Bibliography: p. 385-395. [BX4705.R619C66] 73-88466 ISBN 0-8348-0094-2 13.50
1. Rodrigues, Joao, 1561 (ca.)-1634. I. Title.

†GAVIN, Thomas F. 271'.53'024 B
Champion of youth : biography of Father Daniel A. Lord, S. J. / by Thomas F. Gavin. Boston : St. Paul Editions, c1977. p. cm. Bibliography: p. [BX4705.L742G38] 77-70827 6.50 pbk. : 5.00
1. Lord, Daniel Aloysius, 1888-1955. 2. Jesuits—United States—Biography. I. Title.

†GAVIN, Thomas F. 271'.53'024 B
Champion of youth : biography of Father Daniel A. Lord, S. J. / by Thomas F. Gavin. Boston : St. Paul Editions, c1977. p. cm. Bibliography: p. [BX4705.L742G38] 77-70827 6.50 pbk. : 5.00
1. Lord, Daniel Aloysius, 1888-1955. 2. Jesuits—United States—Biography. I. Title.

JOLY, Henri, 1839-1925. 271'.53'024 B
Saint Ignatius of Loyola / by Henri Joly ; translated by Mildred Partridge ; with a pref. by George Tyrrell. New York : AMS Press, [1976] p. cm. Translation of Saint Ignace de Loyola. Reprint of the 1899 ed. published by Duckworth, London, which was issued in series: The Saints. [BX4700.L7J6 1976] 70-170821 ISBN 0-404-03597-3
1. Loyola, Ignacio de, Saint, 1491-1556. I. Title. II. Series: The Saints.

MCGLOIN, Joseph T. 271'.53'024 B
Living to beat hell! By Joseph T. McGloin. Illustrated by Don Baumgart. Englewood Cliffs, N.J., Prentice-Hall [1972] 325 p. illus. 24 cm. [BX4705.M197A34] 79-141498 ISBN 0-13-538496-6 6.95
I. Title.

ROBERTS, Kenneth J., 1930- 271'.53'024 B
Playboy to priest [by] Kenneth J. Roberts. Staten Island, N.Y., Alba House [1971] ix, 290 p. 22 cm. [BX4705.R58A3] 78-169145 ISBN 0-8189-0234-5 4.95
I. Title.

POLLARD, Albert Frederick, 1869-1948. 271'.53'0438
The Jesuits in Poland. New York, Haskell House Publishers, 1971. viii, 98 p. 22 cm. (Lothian essay, 1892) Reprint of the 1892 ed. Includes bibliographical references. [BX3745.P6P6 1971] 76-116799 ISBN 0-8383-1041-9
1. Jesuits in Poland. 2. Poland—Church history. I. Title. II. Series.

PARKMAN, Francis, 1823-1893. 271'.53'071
The Jesuits in North America in the seventeenth century / by Francis Parkman. St. Clair Shores, Mich. : Scholarly Press, [1976] p. cm. (His France and England in North America ; pt. 2) Reprint of the 1900 ed. published by Little, Brown, Boston. Includes bibliographical references. [F1030.7.P24 1976] 76-8483 ISBN 0-403-03104-4
1. Jesuits in New France. 2. Missions—New France. 3. Jesuits—Missions. 4. Canada—History—To 1763 (New France) I. Title. II. Series.

RIEMER, George R. 271'.53'073
The new Jesuits [by] George Riemer. [1st ed.] Boston, Little, Brown [1971] xviii, 333 p. ports. 21 cm. [BX3708.R54] 79-135433 6.95
1. Jesuits in the United States—Addresses, essays, lectures. I. Title.

MCGLOIN, John Bernard. 271'.53'079461
Jesuits by the Golden Gate; the Society of Jesus in San Francisco, 1849-1969. [San Francisco] University of San Francisco, 1972. 309 p. illus. 24 cm. Includes bibliographical references. [BX3710.S36M36] 74-173134 8.50
1. San Francisco. University. 2. Jesuits in San Francisco. I. Title.

CARAMAN, Philip, 1911- 271'.53'0892
The lost paradise : the Jesuit Republic in South America / Philip Caraman. New York : Seabury Press, 1976, c1975. 341 p., [7] leaves of plates : ill. ; 22 cm. (A Continuum book) Includes index. Bibliography: p. 319-324. [F2684.C25 1976] 76-25948 ISBN 0-8164-9295-6 : 14.95
1. Jesuits in Paraguay. 2. Guarani Indians—Missions. 3. Missions—Paraguay. 4. Paraguay—History—To 1811. I. Title.

MARCUSE, Ludwig, 1894- 271'.53'0924 B
Soldier of the church; the life of Ignatius Loyola. Translated from the German and edited by Christopher Lazare. New York, Simon and Schuster, 1939. [New York, AMS Press, 1972] vi, 352 p. 23 cm. Translation of Ignatius von Loyola. [BX4700.L7M37 1972] 70-172842 ISBN 0-404-04187-6 12.50
1. Loyola, Ignacio de, Saint, 1491-1556. I. Title.

KNOX, Ronald Arbuthnott, 1888- 271.6
Enthusiasm; a chapter in the history of religion, with special reference to the XVII and XVIII centuries. New York, Oxford [1961, c1950] viii, 622p. (Galaxy bk. GB59) Bibl. 2.95 pap.,
1. Enthusiasm. 2. Church history—17th cent. 3. Church history—18th cent. I. Title.

TETTEMER, John Moynihan, 1876-1949. 271.6
I was a monk; the autobiography of John Tettemer, edited by Janet Mabie, with a foreword by Jean Burden and an introd. by John Burton. [1st ed.] New York, Knopf, 1951. 289 p. illus. 22 cm. [BX1765.T28] 51-11062
1. Catholic Church—Doctrinal and controversial works—Miscellaneous authors. I. Title.

INTERNATIONAL Congress on Vocations to the States of Perfection. 1st. Rome, 1961. 271.6092
Today's vocation crisis; a summary of the studies and discussions. Tr., ed. by Godfrey Poage, Germain Lievin. Westminster, Md., Newman for Pontifical Organization for Religious Vocations, Vatican City. [1963] vii, 435p. tables. 21cm. Bibl. 63-1449 5.95
1. Vocation (in religious orders, congregations, etc.) 2. Catholic Church—Clergy—Appointment, call, and election. I. Catholic. Church. Congregatio de Religiosis. II. Poage, Godfrey Robert, 1920- ed. and tr. III. Lievin, Germain, ed. and tr. IV. Title.

YUHAUS, Cassian J. 271'.62
Compelled to speak; the Passionists in America, origin and apostolate, by Cassian J. Yuhaus. Pref. by John J. Wright. Westminster, Md., Newman [1967] xxii, 343p. illus., facsim., ports. 24cm. Centenary ed. canonization of St. Paul of the Cross. [BX3880.Y8] 67-23610 5.95
1. Passionists in the U.S. I. Title.
Publisher's new address: 21 Harristown Rd., Glen Rock, N.J. 07452.

PAOLO della Croce, Saint, 1694-1775. 271'.62'024 B
Words from the heart : a selection from the personal letters of Saint Paul of the Cross / translated [from the Italian] and annotated by Edmund Burke ; [edited by] Roger Mercurio, Silvan Rouse. Dublin : Gill and Macmillan, 1976. viii, 168 p. ; 23 cm. Includes index. [BX4700.P25A4 1976] 77-363539 ISBN 0-7171-0806-6 : £7.00
1. Paolo della Croce, Saint, 1694-1775. I. Burke, Edmund, 1904-1975. II. Mercurio, Roger. III. Rouse, Silvan. IV. Title.

TETTEMER, John Moynihan, 1876-1949. 271'.62'024 B
I was a monk; the autobiography of John Tettemer. Edited by Janet Mabie, with a foreword by Jean Burden and an introd. by John Burton. Wheaton, Ill. [Published by Pyramid Publications for the Theosophical Pub. House, 1974, c1951] 255 p. 18 cm. (Re-quest books) [BX4668.3.T47A34 1974] 73-89888 ISBN 0-8356-0300-8 1.25 (pbk.)
1. Tettemer, John Moyniahn, 1876-1949. I. Title.

VYTELL, Virginia Marie. 271'.62'024 B
Praise the Lord, all you nations : Lithuania's historical and cultural development form a background for the life story of Rev. Alphonsus Maria, CP, missionary and founder of the Poor Sisters of Jesus Crucified and of the Sorrowful Mother / Virginia Marie Vytell. Eimhurst [i.e. Elmhurst] Pa. : Sisters of Jesus Crucified and the Sorrowful Mother, c1976. 351 p. : ill. ; 22 cm. Includes bibliographical references and index. [BX4705.A5554V95] 76-21454
1. Alphonsus Maria, Father, CP, 1884-1949. 2. Passionists in Lithuania—Biography. 3. Lithuania—History. I. Title.

MEAD, Jude. 271'.62'0924 B
Shepherd of the second spring; the life of Blessed Dominic Barberi, C. P., 1792-1849. Paterson, N.J., St. Anthony Guild Press [1968] vii, 240 p. illus., port. 24 cm. Bibliography: p. 233-235. [BX4705.D583M4] 68-22313
1. Dominic of the Mother of God, Father, 1792-1849. I. Title.

ELLIOTT, Walter, 1842-1928. 271'.64'024 B
The life of Father Hecker. New York, Arno Press, 1972. xvii, 428 p. port. 24 cm. (Religion in America, series II) Reprint of the 1891 ed. [BX4705.H4E6 1972] 75-38446 ISBN 0-405-04065-2
1. Hecker, Isaac Thomas, 1819-1888. I. Title.

HOLDEN, Vincent F. 271'.64'024
The early years of Isaac Thomas Hecker (1819-1844), by Vincent F. Holden. Washington, Catholic University of America Press, 1939. [New York, AMS Press, 1974] ix, 257 p. 23 cm. Reprint of the author's thesis, Catholic University of America, 1939, which was issued as v. 29 of the Catholic University of America. Studies in American church history. Bibliography: p. 247-252. [BX4705.H4H6 1974] 73-3583 ISBN 0-404-57779-2 11.00
1. Hecker, Isaac Thomas, 1819-1888. I. Title. II. Series: Catholic University of America. Studies in American church history, v. 29.

†BALSKUS, Pat. 271'.7 B
Trailblazer for the Sacred Heart / by Pat Balskus. Boston : St. Paul Editions, c1976. 120 p., [8] leaves of plates : ill. ; 22 cm. The life of the founder of the Enthronement of the Sacred Heart of Jesus. [BX4705.C7817B34] 92 75-37947 pbk. : 3.00
1. Crawley-Boevey, Mateo, 1875-1960—Juvenile literature. I. Title.

CHAVEZ, Angelico, 1910- 271'.7
My Penitente land : reflections on Spanish New Mexico / Angelico Chavez. 1st ed. Albuquerque : University of New Mexico Press, [1974] xiv, 272 p. ; 26 cm. [BR555.N6C48] 74-83380 ISBN 0-8263-0334-X : 12.00
1. Hermanos Penitentes. 2. New Mexico—Religion. I. Title.

KRAMER, Herbert George. 271'.7 B
Brother Norbert's masterpiece : biography of Brother Norbert A. Kramer, S.M., 1910-1959 / by Herbert George Kramer. St. Louis : : Marianist Provincialate, 1975. vi, 172 p. ; 22 cm. [BX4705.K692K7] 75-25179
1. Kramer, Norbert A., 1910-1959. I. Title.

TREVOR, Meriol. 271.7 (B)
Apostle of Rome; a life of PhilipNeri, 1515-1595. London, Melbourne [etc.] Macmillan, 1966. xviii, 380 p. front., 7 plates (incl. ports) 22 1/2 cm. 55/- "Notes on sources:" p. 354-358. [BX4700.F33T7] 66-74518
1. Flippo Neri, Saint, 1515-1595. I. Title.

THE Carthusians: 271.71
origin, spirit, family life. 2d rev. ed. Westminster, Md., Newman Press, 1952. 107p. 22cm. [BX3302.C29 1952] 53-47
1. Carthusians.

CARTWRIGHT, John K. 271.73
The Catholic shrines of Europe; with photos. by Alfred Wagg. Foreword by Martin J. O'Connor. New York, McGraw-Hill [1955] 212 p. illus. 26 cm. [BX2320.C37] 54-11259
1. Shrines—Europe. I. Title.

JAMART, Francois. 271.73
The spirit and prayer of Carmel; translated by E. J. Ross. Westminster, Md., Newman Press, 1951. 85 p. 19 cm. Translation of Le Carmel. [BX3203.J313] 51-8925
1. Carmelites. I. Title.

LYNCH, Edward Kilian, 1902- 271.73
Your brown scapular; with a preface by Francis Cardinal Spellman. Westminster, Md., Newman Press, 1950. xv, 141 p. 20 cm. [BX2310.S3L9] 50-9760
1. Scapulars I. Title.

MADDEN, Richard C 271.73
Men in sandals. Milwaukee, Bruce Pub. Co. [1954] 154p. illus. 21cm. [BX3203.M25] 54-12550
1. Carmelltes. I. Title.

PEERS, Edgar Allison. 271.73
Handbook to the life and times of St. Teresa and St. John of the Cross. Westminster, Md., Newman Press [1954] vii, 277p. 23cm. Bibliographical footnotes. [BX3206] 54-10164
1. Teresa, Saint, 1515-1582. 2. Juan de la Cruz, Saint, 1542-1591. 3. Camelites—Hist. I. Title.

BRENAN, Gerald. 271'.73'024 B
St John of the Cross; his life and poetry. With a translation of his poetry by Lynda Nicholson. Cambridge [Eng.] University Press, 1973. xii, 232 p. illus. 23 cm. Includes the poems of Juan de la Cruz in the original Spanish with parallel English translations. Bibliography: p. 224-227. [BX4700.J7B64] 72-83577 ISBN 0-521-20006-7
1. Juan de la Cruz, Saint, 1542-1591. I. Nicholson, Lynda, tr. II. Juan de la Cruz, Saint, 1542-1591. Poems. English & Spanish. 1973.
Distributed by Cambridge University Press N.Y; 11.95.

GICOVATE, Bernard, 1922- 271'.73'024
San Juan de la Cruz (Saint John of the Cross), by Bernard Gicovate. New York, Twayne Publishers [1971] 153 p. 21 cm. (Twayne's world authors series, TWAS 141. Spain) Includes poems by Saint John of the Cross in Spanish and English (p. 121-149) Bibliography: p. 115-120. [PQ6400.J8Z6] 71-120481
1. Juan de la Cruz, Saint, 1542-1591.

PEERS, Edgar Allison. 271'.73'024 B
Spirit of flame : a study of St. John of the Cross / by E. Allison Peers. Folcroft, Pa. : Folcroft Library Editions, 1976. p. cm. Reprint of the 1943 ed. published by Student Christian Movement Press, London. Includes bibliographical references and index. [BX4700.J7P43 1976] 76-40107 ISBN 0-8414-6784-6 lib. bdg. : 17.50
1. Juan de la Cruz, Saint, 1542-1591. 2. Christian saints—Spain—Biography. I. Title.

CARR, William J. 271'.73'07471
The Irish Carmelites of New York City and the fight for Irish independence, 1916-1919 / by William J. Carr. Middletown, N.Y. : Vestigium Press, St. Albert's Jr. Seminary, [1973?] 68 p. ; 28 cm. Bibliography: p. 57-58. [BX3210.N48C37] 75-318667
1. Carmelites in New York (City) 2. Irish in New York (City) 3. Ireland—History—1910-1921. I. Title: The Irish Carmelites of New York City ...

ROHRBACH, Peter Thomas 271.7309
Journey to Carith: the story of the Carmelite Order. [1st ed.] Garden City, N. Y., Doubleday, 1966. 381p. 22cm. Bibl. [BX3206.2.R6] 66-20942 5.95
1. Carmelites—Hist. I. Title.

WEBER, Francis J. 271'.75'0924 B
Thomas James Conaty, pastor-educator-bishop, by Francis J. Weber. Los Angeles, Westernlore Press [1969] xiv, 81 p. illus., port. 22 cm. 250 copies printed. Bibliographical references included in "Notes" (p. 73-81) [BX4705.C737W4] 70-77980
1. Conaty, Thomas James, Bp., 1847-1915.

DOYON, Bernard. 271.76
The Cavalry of Christ on the Rio Grande, 1849-1883. Milwaukee, Bruce Press [1956]

252p. illus. 23cm. (Catholic life publications) [BX3820.M3D6] 56-4137
1. Oblates of Mary Immaculate—Texas. I. Title.

WILD, Joseph Charles. 271'.76'09
Men of hope; the background and history of the Oblate Province of Our Lady of Hope (Eastern American Province), by JosephC. Wild. [Boston?] Missionary Oblates of Mary Immaculate, 1967. x,324 p. 21 cm. Includes bibliographical references. [BX3821.Z6088] 67-30024
1. Oblates of Mary Immaculate. Our Lady of Hope Province—Hist. I. Title.

PURCELL, Mary, 1906- 271'.77'041
The story of the Vincentians; a record of the achievements in Ireland and Britain of the priests and lay-brothers of the Congregation of the Mission, founded by St. Vincent de Paul. Dublin, All Hallows College [1973] 214 p. 22 cm. Includes bibliographical references. [BX3770.Z5I77] 75-303854 £1.50
1. Vincentians in Ireland. 2. Vincentians in Great Britain. 3. Vincentians—Missions. I. Title.

ROBERTO, Brother, 271.780924
1927-
Boys and Brothers; a life of Saint John Baptist de la Salle, Illus. by Carolyn Lee Jagodits. Notre Dame, Ind., 46556, Dujarie Pr. [1965] 95p. illus. 24cm. [LB475.L22R6] 65-27762 2.25
1. La. Salle, Jean Baptiste de, Saint, 1651-1719—Juvenile literature. I. Title.

BROTHERS of the 271'.78'0994
Christian Schools, Australasian Province.
Christian Brothers 1868-1968. [Melbourne?] 1968. 68 p. illus. 26 cm. [BX3060.Z5A84] 79-461410 unpriced
1. Brothers of the Christian Schools in Australia. I. Title.

BARROSSE, Thomas. 271'.79 B
Moreau; portrait of a founder. Notre Dame, Ind., Fides Publishers [1969] viii 392 p. 23 cm. Includes bibliographical references. [BX4705.M72B37] 75-92021
1. Moreau, Basile Antoine Marie, 1799-1873. 2. Congregation of Holy Cross.

BEIRNE, Kilian, 1896- 271.79
From sea to shining sea; the Holy Cross Brothers in the United States. Valatie, N. Y., Holy Cross Pr. [1966] 396p. illus., ports. 23cm. [BX3475.Z5U52] 66-9024 4.50
1. Congregation of Holy Cross—U. S. I. Title.

BERRIGAN, Philip. 271'.79 B
Prison journals of a priest revolutionary. Compiled and edited by Vincent McGee. Introd. by Daniel Berrigan. [1st ed.] New York, Holt, Rinehart and Winston [1970] xxii, 198 p. 22 cm. [BX4705.B3846A3 1970] 77-102136 5.95
I. Title.

BOCQUET, Marcel. 271'.79 (B)
The firebrand; the life of Father Mateo Crawley-Boevey, ss. cc. Translated by Francis Larkin. Washington, Corda Press [c1966] xxiv, 368 p. illus., ports. 23 cm. Translation of Le Pere Mateo, ss. cc.; l'amour present au monde, with adaptation and augmentation by the translator. Bibliography: p. 367-368. [BX4705.C7817B63] 66-19642
1. Crawley-Boevey, Mateo, 1875-1960. I. Title.

BRADFORD, Ernle Dusgate 271'.79
Selby.
The shield and the sword; the Knights of St. John, Jerusalem, Rhodes, and Malta [by] Ernle Bradford. [1st ed.] New York, Dutton, 1973 [c1972] 245 p. illus. 25 cm. Bibliography: p. [233]-234. [CR4723.B78 1973] 72-94687 ISBN 0-525-20313-3 7.95
1. Knights of Malta. I. Title.

BRUNNER, Francis de Sales, 271.79
1795-1859.
Four historical booklets regarding the American Province of the Most Precious Blood. A translation from the original German. Carthagena, Ohio, Messenger Press, 1957. 304p. 23cm. [BX3960.P7B72] 57-33578
1. Priests of the Most Precious Blood. American Province. I. Title.

BUTLER, Lionel Harry, ed. 271'.79
A History of the Order of the Hospital of St. John of Jerusalem. General editor: Lionel Butler. London, Macmillan; New York, St. Martin's P., 1967- v. illus. 23 cm. unpriced (B***) [CR4723.H5] 68-4010
1. Knights of Malta—Hist. I. Title.

CENTER, Allen H ed. 271'.79
Public relations ideas in action; 500 tested public relations programs and techniques. New York, McGraw-Hill, 1957. 327p. 24cm. [HM263.C33] 56-11045
1. Public relations. I. Title.

CIRENCESTER, Abbey. 271.79
The cartulary of Cirencester Abbey, Gloucestershire, edited by C.D. Ross, London, Oxford University Press, 1964- v. facsims., port. 26 cm. "Based upon the two abbey registers now in the possession of the present Lord Vestey at Stowell Park, near Cirencester." Bibliographical footnotes. [DA690.C61C5] 64-55757
I. Ross, Charles Derek, ed. II. Title.

CIRENCESTER ABBEY 271.79
The cartulary of Cirencester Abbey, Gloucestershire [2v.] Ed. by C. D. Ross [New York] Oxford [c.]1964. 2v. (736p.) facsims., port. 26cm. Based upon the two abbey registers now in the possession of the present Lord Vestey at Stowell Park, near Cirencester. Bibl. 64-55757 20.20 set,
I. Ross, Charles Derek, ed. II. Title.

CRISTIANI, Leon, 1879- 271'.79 B
Saint Vincent de Paul, 1581-1660 / by Leon Cristiani; translated by John R. Gregoli Boston : St. Paul Editions, c1977. p. cm. [BX4700.V6C7413] 77-4377 3.95 pbk. : 2.95
1. Vincent de Paul, Saint, 1581-1660. 2. Christian saints—France—Biography.

CRISTIANI, Leon, 1879- 271'.79 B
Saint Vincent de Paul, 1581-1660 / by Leon Cristiani; translated by John R. Gregoli Boston : St. Paul Editions, c1977. p. cm. [BX4700.V6C7413] 77-4377 3.95 pbk. : 2.95
1. Vincent de Paul, Saint, 1581-1660. 2. Christian saints—France—Biography.

FOREY, Alan John. 271'.79
The Templars in the Corona de Aragon [by] A. J. Forey. London, Oxford University Press, 1973. xi, 498 p. maps. 23 cm. (University of Durham. Publications) Bibliography: p. 455-470. [CR4755.S6A724 1973] 73-163691 ISBN 0-19-713137-9 £7.50
1. Templars—Spain—Aragon. I. Title. II. Series: Durham, Eng. University. Publications.

FOREY, Alan John. 271'.79
The Templars in the Corona de Aragon [by] A. J. Forey. London, Oxford University Press, 1973. xi, 498 p. maps. 23 cm. (University of Durham. Publications) Bibliography: p. 455-470. [CR4755.S6A724 1973] 73-163691 ISBN 0-19-713137-9
1. Templars in Aragon. I. Title. II. Series: Durham, Eng. University. Publications.
Distributed by Oxford University Press N.Y. 30.00.

HENDERSON, Alice (Corbin) 271.79
1881-1949.
Brothers of light; the Penitentes of the Southwest. [Chicago, Rio Grande Pr., 1963] 126p. illus. 24cm. (Rio Grande classic) Reproduction of the 1st ed., pub. in 1937, by Harcourt, New York. 62-21940 7.00
1. Hermanos Penitentes. I. Title.

HYMA, Albert, 1893- 271.79
The Brethren of the Common Life. Grand Rapids, Eerdmans, 1950. 222 p. facsims. 23 cm. Bibliography: p. 213-220. [BX3070.H9] 50-11233
1. Brothers of the Common Life. 2. Imitatio Christl. I. Title.

KNAPKE, Paul Justin, 1910- 271.79
History of the American Province of the Society of the Precious Blood. Carthagena, Ohio, Messenger Press, 1958- v. illus., port., fold. map. 22cm. Bibliography: v. 1, p. 8-13. [BX3958.Z5A5] 60-22716
1. Priests of the Most Precious Blood. American Province. I. Title.

KOREN, Henry J 271.79
The Spiritans; a history of the Congregation of the Holy Ghost. Pittsburgh, Duquesne University, 1958. xxix, 641p. illus., ports., maps. 26cm. (Duquesne studies. Spiritan series, 1) Bibliography: p. 601-612. [BX3680.H6K6] 58-34812
1. Holy Ghost Fathers—Hist. I. Title. II. Series.

MCAVOY, Thomas Timothy, 271'.79
1903-1969.
Father O'Hara of Notre Dame, the Cardinal-Archbishop of Philadelphia [by] Thomas T. McAvoy. Notre Dame, Ind., University of Notre Dame Press [1967] xi, 514 p. ports. 24 cm. "Footnotes": p. 492-505. [BX4705.O44M3] 66-14627
1. O'Hara, John Francis, 1888-1960. I. Title.

MACEOIN, Gary, 1909- 271.79
Nothing is quite enough. [1st ed.] New York, Holt [1953] 306p. 22cm. Autobiographical. [BX1777.M25A3] 53-5268
I. Title.

MCLAUGHLIN, Arthur 271.79
St. Vincent de Paul, servant of the poor. Milwaukee, Bruce [c.1965] 109p. 21cm. [BX4700.V6M46] 65-24241 2.95
1. Vincent de Paul, Saint, 1581-1660. I. Title.

MCMAHON, Norbert. 271.79
The story of the Hospitallers of St. John of God. Pref. by the Bishop of Middlesbrough. Westminster, Md., Newman Press, 1959 [c1958] 194p. illus. 22cm. [BX3058.3.M3] 58-13636
1. Brothers Hospitallers of St. John of God. I. Title.

MARCUS, Sheldon. 271'.79 B
Father Coughlin; the tumultuous life of the priest of the Little Flower. [1st ed.] Boston, Little, Brown [1973] 317 p. illus. 22 cm. Bibliography: p. 261-272. [BX4705.C7795M37] 73-186969 ISBN 0-316-54596-1 8.95
1. Coughlin, Charles Edward, 1891- I. Title.

MATT, Leonard von. 271'.79 B
Don Bosco [by] Leonard von Matt and Henri Bosco. [Translated from the Italian by John Bennett. 1st American ed.] New York, Universe Books [1967] 228 p. illus., facsims., ports. 25 cm. [BX4700.B75M343] 67-12505
1. Bosco, Giovanni, Saint, 1815-1888. I. Bosco, Henri, 1888- joint author. II. Title.

PAULIN, Eugene, 1882- 271.79
New wars; the history of the Brothers of Mary (Marianists) in Hawaii. 1883-1958 [by] Eugene Paulin and Joseph A. Becker. Milwaukee, Catholic Life Publications [1959] 189p. illus. 23cm. [BX3784.P3] 60-199
1. Marianists in the Hawaiian Islands. I. Becker, Joseph A., joint author. II. Title.

PICHEL, Charles Louis 271'.79
Thourot, 1890-
History of the hereditary government of the Sovereign Order of Saint John of Jerusalem, Knights of Malta: Jerusalem 1050-1291, Cyprus 1292-1310, Rhodes 1311-1523, Malta 1530-1798, Russia 1798-1907, U.S.A. 1908-[1970] by Thourot Pichel. 2d ed. Shickshinny, Pa., Maltese Cross Press [1970] 200 p. illus., ports. 23 cm. First published in 1957 under title: History of the Sovereign Order of Saint John of Jerusalem. Bibliography: p. 89-91. [CR4723.P5 1970] 76-19550
1. Knights of Malta—History. I. Title.

RAUSCH, Jerome W 271.79
The Crosier family; history of the Crosier Fathers in the United States. With contributions from confreres Lawrence J. Kerich, Francis P. Pitka, and Bernard C. Mischke. Onamia, Minn., Crosier Press, 1960. 384p. illus. 24cm. Includes bibliography. [BX3493.Z6U5] 60-12554
1. Crosier Fathers in the U. S. I. Title.

REILE, Louis. 271.79
The battle and Brother Louis. Foreword by Richard Cardinal Cushing. Westminster, Md., Newman Press, 1959. 171p. 23cm. [BX2835.R4] 59-14805
1. Monasticism and religious orders—Brothers. I. Title.

RILEY-SMITH, Jonathan, 271'.79
1938-
The Knights of St. John in Jerusalem and Cyprus, c. 1050-1310. London, Macmillan; New York, St. Martin's Pr., 1967. xv, 553p. illus., maps. 23cm. (Hist. of the Order of the Hospital of St. John of Jerusalem, v 1) Bibl. [CR4723.H5 vol.1] 68-11359 14.50
1. Knights of Malta—Hist. I. Title.

SCHMITZ, Joseph William. 271.79
The Society of Mary in Texas. San Antonio, Naylor, 1951. 261 p. illus. 23 cm. [BX3780.M35S4] 52-6270
1. Marianists in Texas. I. Title.

*SWEENEY, Joseph W. 271.79
Lilies in service; the nun and her offering. New York, Exposition [1967] 186p. 21cm. (Exposition-Testament bk., EP45679) 5.00
1. Monastic and religious life of women. I. Title.

TATE, Bill 271'.79
The Penitentes of the Sangre de Cristos; an American tragedy. 2d ed. [Truchas, N.M., Tate Gallery] 1967. 53p. illus., facsims. 24cm. Bibl. [BX3653.U6T3 1967] 67-8133 pap.,price unreported.
1. Hermanos penitentes. I. Title.
Publisher's address: Box 428, Truchas, N.M. 87578

VOILLAUME, Rene. 271.79
Brothers of men; letters to the Petits Freres. Edited, with an introd., by Lancelot Sheppard. [Translation by A. Manson] Baltimore, Helicon Press [1966] 222 p. 19 cm. (A Helicon paperbook) Translation of extracts from the author's Lettres aux fraternites. [BX3775.V613] 66-17082
1. Foucauld, Charles Eugene, vicomte de, 1858-1916. 2. Little Brothers of Jesus. I. Title.

VOILLAUME, Rene. 271.79
In the midst of men; seeds of the desert, II. Translated and adapted by Willard Hill. Notre Dame, Ind., Fides Publishers [1966] 160 p. 18 cm. (A Fides dome book, D-51) "Extracts from Seeds of the desert ... [published in 1955] including passages hitherto unpublished from Au coeur des masses: la vie religieuse des Petits Freres du Peere Foucauld." [BX3775.V623] 66-20178
1. Foucauld, Charles Eugene, vicomte de, 1858-1916. 2. Little Brothers of Jesus. I. Title.

VOILLAUME, Rene. 271.79
Seeds of the desert; the legacy of Charles de Foucauld. With a pref. by John LaFarge. Chicago, Fides Publishers Association [1955] 308p. illus. 19cm. 'Translation and adaptation of Au coeur des masses: la vie religieuse des

Petits Freres du Pere de Founcauld ... by Willard Hill.' [BX3775] 55-14675
1. Foucauld, Charles Eugene, vicomte de, 1858-1916. 2. Little Brothers of Jesus. I. Title.

VOSBURGH, Joseph Mary, 1892- 271.79
The vine of seven branches; a history of the Order of Servants of Mary, 1233-1955. Chicago, Stabat Mater Press [1955] 221p. 21cm. [BX4040.S5V6] 57-20295
1. Servites—Hist. I. Title.

WEIGLE, Marta. 271'.79
The Penitentes of the Southwest. With etchings by Eli Levin. Santa Fe, N.M., Ancient City Press [1970] 46 p. illus. 22 cm. Bibliography: p. 45-46. [BX3653.U6W4] 78-131971
1. Hermanos Penitentes. I. Title.

ALLCHIN, A. M. 271.8
The silent rebellion; Anglican religious communities, 1845-1900. London, SCM Pr. [dist. Westminister, Md., Canterbury, 1964, c.1958] 256p. 23cm. Bibl. 59-1298 2.50
1. Monasticism and religious orders, Anglican. I. Title.

ANTONY, Abp. of San Francisco. 271'.8 B
The young elder : a biography of blessed Archimandrite Ambrose of Milkovo / by Archbishop Antony (Medvedev) of San Francisco ; translated from the Russian by Deacon Lev Puhalo and Vasili Novakshonoff. Jordanville, N.Y. : Holy Trinity Orthodox Monastery, 1974. 70 p. ; 23 cm. (Great ascetics of Russia ; book 3) [BX597.A624A5713] 74-79070 pbk. : 1.50
1. Amvrosii, Archimandrite of Milkovo, 1894-1933. I. Title. II. Series.

BOZARTH, Rene. 271'.8
The single eye; lectures on the life of the Society of St. Paul, a religious order within the Episcopal Church. 2d ed. Gresham, Or., St. Paul's Press [1968] 220 p. 22 cm. [BX5971.S6B6 1968] 70-1287
1. Society of St. Paul. I. Title.

CAVARNOS, Constantine. 271.8
Anchored in God; an inside account of life, art and thought on the Holy Mountain of Athos. Athens, Astir Pub. Co. [1959] 230p. illus. 22cm. [BX385.A8C3] 60-16248
1. Athos (Monasteries) I. Title.

CAVARNOS, Constantine. 271'.8
Anchored in God : an inside account of life, art, and thought on the Holy Mountain of Athos / by Constantine Cavarnos. 2d ed. Belmont, Mass. : Institute for Byzantine and Modern Greek Studies, 1975. 230 p., [2] leaves of plates : ill. ; 21 cm. Includes index. [BX385.A8C3 1975] 75-35432 ISBN 0-914744-30-5. pbk. : 4.95
1. Athos (Monasteries) I. Title.

DJOBADZE, Wachtang Z. 271.8
Materials for the study of Georgian monasteries in the Western environs of Antioch on the Orontes / by Wachtang Z. Djobadze. Louvain : Corpussco, 1976. vii, 114 p., [7] leaves of plates : ill. ; 26 cm. (Corpus Scriptorum Christianorum orientalium ; v. 372 : Subsidia ; t. 48) English and/or Georgian. Includes bibliographical references. [BR60.C5S85 t.48] [BX385.A57] 281.1 77-359105 ISBN 2-8017-0031-2
1. Antioch—Monasteries. I. Title. II. Series: Corpus scriptorum Christianorum orientalium ; v. 327.

SCHUTZ, Roger. 271.8
Living today for God. Translated by Stephen McNierney and Louis Evrard. Baltimore, Helicon Press [1962] 128p. 23cm. [BV4405.S313] 60-15712
1. Monastic and religious life. 2. Monasticism and religious others, Protestant. I. Title.

SHERRARD, Philip 271.8
Athos, the mountain of silence. With colour-photos. by Paul du Marchie v. Vorthuysen. New York, Oxford University Press, 1960. [ ] vii, 110p. illus. (part mounted col.) map. 30cm. Bibl.: p.107-108 60-50070 12.50
1. Athos (Monasteries) 2. Athos, Mount—Descr. & trav. I. Title.

WYON, Olive, 1890- 271.8
Living springs: new religious movements in Western Europe. Philadelphia, Westminster Press [1962?] 128 p. illus. 20 cm. Includes bibliography. [BV4405.W9] 63-14642
1. Monasticism and religious orders, Protestant. 2. Monasticism and religious orders — Europe. I. Title.

WYON, Olive, 1890- 271.8
Living springs: new religious movements in Western Europe. Philadelphia, Westminster Press [1962?] 128 p. illus. 20 cm. Includes bibliography. [BV4405.W9] 63-14642
1. Monasticism and religious orders, Protestant. 2. Monasticism and religious orders—Europe. I. Title.

ZNOSKO, Vladimir. 271'.8 B
Hieroschemamonk Feofil, fool-for-Christ's-sake; ascetic and visionary of the Kievo-Pecherskaya lavra. Translated from the Russian by Lev Puhalo and Vassili Novakshonoff. Jordanville, N.Y., Holy Trinity Russian Orthodox Monastery, 1972. 134 p. illus. 23 cm. (Great ascetics of Russia, book 1) Includes bibliographical references. [BX597.F43Z58] 72-90866
1. Feofil, ieroskhimonakh, 1788-1853. I. Title. II. Series.

NORWICH, John Julius Cooper, 2d viscount 1929- 271.8'094956
Mount Athos, by John Julius Norwich, Reres by Sitwell. Photos, by the authors and A. Costa. New York, Harper [1966, i.e.1967] 191p. illus. (pt. col.) facsims., maps (on lining papers) ports. (pt. col.) 29cm. Bibl. [BX3852A8N6 1966a] 66-20306 20.00
1. Athos (Monasteries) 2. Athos, Mount—Descr. & trav. I. Sitwell, Reresby, 1927- joint author. II. Title.

NORWICH, John Julius Cooper, 2d viscount, 1929- 271'.8'094956
Mount Athos, by John Julius Norwich and Reresby Sitwell. With photos. by the authors and A. Costa. New York, Harper & Row [1966] 191 p. illus. (part col.) facsims., maps (on lining papers) ports. (part col.) 29 cm. Bibliography: p. [183] [BX385.A8N6] 66-20306
1. Athos (Monasteries) 2. Athos, Mount — Descr. & trav. I. Sitwell, Reresby, 1927- joint author. II. Title.

ANCREEN riwle 271.9
The English text of the Ancrene riwle, edited from British Museums ms. Royal 8lC.I, by A. C. Baugh. London, Published for the Early English Text Society by Oxford University Press, 1956. xi, 58p. facsim. 22 cm. (Early English Text Society. [Publications. Original series] no. 232, 1956 (for 1949)) [PR1119.A2 no. 229] 55-14162
1. Monasticism and religious orders for women. 2. Monasticism and religious orders—Rules. I. Baugh, Albert Croll, 1891- ed. II. Title. III. Series.

ANCREN RIWLE. 271.9
The Ancrene riwle, (the Corpus ms.: Ancrene wisse), Translated into modern English by M. B. Salu. With an introd. by Gerard Sitwell and a pref. by J.R.R. Tolkien [ist American ed.] Notre Dame, Ind., University of Notre Dame Press [1956] xxvii, 196 p. 21cm. Bibliographical footnotes. [PR1808] 57-13685
1. Monasticism and religious orders for women. 2. Monasticism and religious orders—Rules. I. Salu, M. B. tr. II. Title.

ANCREN RIWLE. 271.9
The English text of the Ancrene riwle, edited from Gonville and Caius College ms. 234/120 by R. M. Wilson. With an introd. by N. R. Ker. London, Published for the Early English Text Society by Oxford University Press, 1954. xiii, 87 p. facsim. 23 cm. (Early English Text Society. [Publications] Original series, no. 229. 1954 (for 1948)) [PR1119.A2 no.229] 55-14162
1. Monasticism and religious orders for women. 2. Monasticism and religious orders—Rules. I. Wilson, Richard Middlewood, ed. II. Title. III. Series.

BALDWIN, Monica. 271.9
I leap over the wall; contrasts and impressions after twenty-eight years in a convent. New York, Rinehart [1950] vi, 313 p. 22 cm. [BX4210.B25 1950] 50-5148
1. Monasticism and religious orders for women. I. Title.

BERNSTEIN, Marcelle. 271'.9
Nuns / Marcelle Bernstein. London : Collins, 1976. 361 p. ; 22 cm. Includes index. [BX4210.B377 1976b] 76-365019 ISBN 0-00-215579-6 : £4.95
1. Nuns. 2. Monastic and religious life of women. I. Title.

BERNSTEIN, Marcelle. 271'.9
The nuns / Marcelle Bernstein. 1st ed. Philadelphia : Lippincott, c1976. 326 p. ; 24 cm. Includes index. [BX4210.B377] 76-14794 ISBN 0-397-01135-0 : 9.95
1. Nuns. 2. Monastic and religious life of women. I. Title.

BERTSCHE, Leopold. 271.9
Directorium sponsae; short addresses for nuns. [Translated by Marie Heffernan] Westminster, Md., Newman Press [c1958-60] 2v. 16cm. [BX4210.B383] 58-13643
1. Monastic and religious life of women—Addresses, essays, lectures. I. Title.

BERTSCHE, Leopold. 271.9
Directorium sponsae; short meditations for each day of the year. v.5Tr. by Maria H. Arndt. Westminster, Md., Newman [c1958-] 401p. 16 cm. V3 tr. by Colman J. O'donovan, has subtitle: A rosary bk. for nuns. V.4, tr. by Marie Heffernan, has subtitle: Short addresses for nuns. [BX4210.B383] 58-13643 3.75
1. Monastic and religious life of women—Addresses, essays, lectures. 2. Rosary—Meditations. I. Title.

BERTSCHE, Leopold 271.9
Directorium sponsae; v.3. Westminster, Md., Newman [1963, c.1962] 156p. 16cm. Contents.v.3. A Rosary book for nuns, tr. [from German] by Colman J. O'Donovan. 58-13643 2.75
1. Monastic and religious life of women—Addresses, essays, lectures. 2. Rosary—Meditations. I. Title.

BLOCKER, Hyacinth. 271.9
Good morning, good people; retreat reflections for religious. Cincinnati, St. Francis Book Shop [1950] vi, 341 p. 21 cm. [BX4210.B5] 50-36842
1. Monasticism and religious orders for women. I. Title.

CATHERINE FREDERIC, Sister, 1902- 271.9
... and spare me not in the making; pages from a novice's diary. Milwaukee, Bruce Pub. Co. [1953] 96p. illus. 21cm. [BX4210.C27] 53-3302
1. Monasticism and religious orders for women. I. Title.

CHASTITY, 271.9
being the English version of La Chastete in Problemes de la religieuse d'aujourd'hui; translated by Lancelot C. Sheppard. Westminster, Md., Newman Press, 1955. x, 267p. 22cm. (Religious life, 5) Bibliographical footnotes. [BX4210.C442] 55-7045
1. Chastity, Vow of. 2. Monastic and religious life of women.

COURTOIS, Gaston. 271.9
An hour with Jesus; meditations for religious. Translated from the French by Sister Helen Madeleine. Foreword by Richard J. Cushing, Archbishop of Boston. Westminster, Md., Newman Press, 1955-56. 2 v. 21cm. [BX4210.C615] 55-8655
1. Monastic and religious life of women. 2. Meditations. I. Title.

DE HUECK, Catherine, 1900- 271.9
Dear Sister ... Milwaukee, Bruce Pub. Co. [1953] 80p. 19cm. [BX4210.D4] 53-963
1. Monasticism and religious orders for women. I. Title.

THE Direction of nuns; 271.9
being the English version of Directoire des pretres charges des religieuses. Translated by Lancelot C. Sheppard. Westminster, Md., Newman Press, 1957. x, 259p. 22cm. (Religious life, 7) Bibliographical footnotes. [BX4210.D482] 57-2892
1. Monastic and religious life of women. 2. Spiritual directions.

THE Doctrinal instruction of religious sisters: 271.9
being the English version of Formation doctrinale des religieuses. Translated by a religious of the Retreat of the Sacred Heart. Westminster, Md., Newman Press, 1956. x, 192p. 22cm. (Religious life, 6) Les Editions du Cerf, who published the original French edition. the authors of the various chapters, and Pere Ple, the editor, have all ... assisted in the production of this English version.' [BX4210.5.F63] 56-9996
1. Monasticism and religious orders for women. 2. Catholic Church—Education. I. A religious of the Retreat of the Sacred Heart, tr.

DORCY, Mary Jean, Sister. 1914- 271.9
Shepherd's tartan. New York, All Saints Pr. [1961, c.1953] 149p. (AS 211) .50 pap.,
1. Monasticism and religious orders for women. I. Title.

DORCY, Mary Jean, 1914- 271.9
Shepherd's tartan. New York, Sheed and Ward, 1953. 179 p. illus. 21 cm. Autobiographical. [BX4210.D65] 53-9631
1. Monasticism and religious orders for women. I. Title.

ELGIN, Kathleen, 1923- 271.9
Nun; a gallery of Sisters. Foreword by Sister Maria del Ray. New York, Random House [1964] 141 p. illus. 29 cm. [BX4225.E55] 64-18931
1. Monasticism and religious orders for women — Biog. I. Title. II. Title: A gallery of Sisters.

ELGIN, Kathleen, 1923- 271.9
Nun; a gallery of Sisters. Foreword by Sister Maria del Ray. New York, Random [c.1964] 141p. illus. 29cm. 64-18931 4.95
1. Monasticism and religious orders for women—Biog. I. Title. II. Title: A gallery of Sisters.

FARRELL, Ambrose. 271.9
The education of the novice [by] Ambrose Farrell, Henry St. John [and] F. B. Elkisch. With an introd. by Conrad Pepler. Westminster, Md., Newman Press [1956] 73p. 19cm. 'The essays in this volume represent some of the papers read to ... novice mistresses gathered at Spode House in Staffordshire in January 1955.' [BX4213.F34] 56-43424
1. Novitiate. 2. Monastic and religious life of women. I. Title.

FERRARO, Norma Downey. 271.9
Few are chosen. [1st ed.] New York, Harper [1953] 307 p. 22 cm. Autobiographical. [BX4216.F4A3] 53-5367
I. Title.

GAMBARI, Elio 271.9
The religious-apostolic formation of Sisters. Foreword by Arcadio Cardinal Larraona. New York, Fordham [c.1964] xii, 188p. 24cm. Bibl. 63-23173 4.00
1. Monasticism and religious orders for women—Education. I. Title.

HAGSPIEL, Bruno, 1885- 271.9
Live in the Holy Spirit. Milwaukee, Bruce Pub. Co. [1957] 170p. 23cm. [BX4210.H3] 57-13411
1. Monastic and religious life of women. I. Title.

HASPIEL, Brund Martin, 1885- 271.9
Milwaukee, Bruce Pub. Co. [1957] 170p. 23cm. [BX4210.H3] 57-13411
1. Monastic and religious life of women. I. Title.

HERBST, Winfrid, 1891- 271.9
The sisters are asking. Westminster, Md., Newman Press, 1956. 190p. 21cm. [BX4210.H4] 56-9383
1. Monastic and religious life of women. 2. Questions and answers—Theology. I. Title.

KANE, George Louis, 1911- ed. 271.9
Melody in your hearts; a sequel to Why I entered the convent. With an introd. by Richard J. Cushing. Westminster, Md., Newman Press, 1958. 173p. 22cm. [BX4210.K3] 57-11818
1. Monastic and religious life of women. I. Title.

KANE, George Louis, 1911- ed. 271.9
A seal upon my heart; autobiographies of twenty sisters. Introd. by Godfrey Poage. Milwaukee, Bruce Pub. Co. [1957] 170p. 22cm. [BX4225.K28] 57-6658
1. Monasticism and religious orders for women—Biog. I. Title.

KANE, George Louis, 1911- ed. 271.9
Why I entered the convent. [Autobiographies] With an introd. by Richard J. Cushing, Archbishop of Boston. Westminster, Md., Newman Press, 1953. 214p. 22cm. [BX4225.K3] 53-10463
1. Monasticism and religious orders for women—Biog. I. Title.

KANE, Harnett Thomas, 1910- 271.9
The Ursulines, nuns of adventure; the story of the New Orleans community. Illustrated by James J. Spanfeller. New York, Vision Books [1959] 188 p. illus. 22 cm. (Vision books, 42) [BX4544.N4K3] 59-6063
1. Ursulines in New Orleans.

LORD, Daniel Aloysius, 1888- 271.9
Everynun; a modern morality play. Illus. by Lee Hines. St. Louis, Eucharistic Crusade of the Knights and Handmaids of the Blessed Sacrament [1952] 163p. 22cm. [BX4205.L65] 52-66377
I. Title.

LOWERY, Kathleen. 271'.9 B
Up among the stars / by Kathleen Lowery. 1st ed. Port Washington, N.Y. : Ashley Books, c1974. 233 p. ; 22 cm. [BX4668.3.L68A35 1974] 73-83922 ISBN 0-87949-022-5
1. Lowery, Kathleen. 2. Ex-nuns—Personal narratives. I. Title.

LUCARINI, Spartaco. 271'.9 B
A woman for our time: the servant of God, Mother Thecla Merlo, co-foundress of the Daughters of St. Paul. Translated by the Daughters of St. Paul. [Boston] St. Paul Editions [1974] 253 p. illus. 22 cm. [BX4334.Z8L8] 74-77253 3.95

1. Merlo, Thecla, 1894-1964. 2. Daughters of St. Paul. I. Title.

MCCARTHY, Thomas Patrick, 1920- comp. 271.9
Guide to the Catholic sisterhoods in the United States. Washington, Catholic University of America Press, 1952. viii, 281 p. illus. 23 cm. [BX4220.U6M3] A52
1. Monasticism and religious orders for women. 2. Monasticism and religious orders—U. S. I. Title.

MCCARTHY, Thomas Patrick, 1920- comp. 271.9
Guide to the Catholic sisterhoods in the United States. With foreword by Amleto Giovanni Cicognani. Washington, Catholic University of America Press, 1952 [i.e. 1953] viii, 319p. illus. 23cm. [BX4220.U6M3 1953] A 53
1. Monasticism and religious orders for women. 2. Monasticism and religious orders—U.S. I. Title.

MCCARTHY, Thomas Patrick, 1920- 271.9
Guide to the Catholic sisterhoods in the United States. With foreword by Amleto Giovanni Cicognani. [3d ed., rev. and enl.] Washington, Catholic University of America Press, 1955. viii, 367p. illus. 23cm. [BX4220.U6M3 1955] 56-3967
1. Monasticism and religious orders for women. 2. Monasticism and religious orders—U.S. I. Title.

MCCARTHY, Thomas Patrick, 1920- 271.9
Guide to the Catholic sisterhoods in the United States. With a foreword by Amleto Giovanni Cicognani. [4th ed.] rev. and enl. Washington, Catholic University of America Press, 1958. viii, 881 p. illus. 24 cm. [BX4220.U6M3 1958] 58-4741
1. Monasticism and religious orders for women. 2. Monasticism and religious orders—U.S. I. Title.

MCDONALD, Grace. 271.9
With lamps burning. Saint Joseph, Minn., Saint Benedict's Priory Press, 1957. 329p. illus. 24cm. (American Benedictine Academy. Historical studies. Monasteries and convents, 4) [BX4278.S25M27] 57-13066
1. St. Joseph, Minn. Convent of St. Benedict. I. Title.

MCKENNA, Mary Lawrence. 271'.9
Women of the church; role and renewal. Foreword by Jean Danielon. New York, P.J. Kenedy [1967] xvi, 192 p. 22 cm. Includes bibliographical references. [BR195.W6M3] 67-26804
1. Women in Christianity—Early church. 2. Widows. 3. Deaconesses. 4. Virginity. I. Title.

MCKENNA, Mary Lawrence. 271'.9
Women of the church; role and renewal. Foreword by Jean Danielou. New York, P. J. Kenedy [1967] xvi, 192 p. 22 cm. Includes bibliographical references. [BR195.W6M3] 67-26804
1. Women in Christianity—Early church, ca. 30-600. 2. Widows. 3. Deaconesses. 4. Virginity. I. Title.

MAFFATT, John Edward, 1894- 271.9
Listen, Sister Superior. New York, McMullen Books [1953] 208p. 20cm. [BX4210.M64] 53-11800
1. Monasticism and religious orders for women. I. Title.

MARIA DEL REY, Sister. 271.9
Bernie becomes a nun. Photos. by George Barria. New York, Farrar, Straus & Cudahy [1956] 117p. illus. 24cm. [BX4210.M24] 56-6155
1. Monastic and religious life of women. I. Title.

MARIA DEL REY, Sister. 271.9
Bernie becomes a nun. Photos. by George Barris. New York, Farrar, Straus & Cudahy [1956] 117p. illus. 24cm. [BX4210.M24] 56-6155
1. Monastic and religious life of women. I. Title.

MARY LAURENCE, Sister. 271.9
The convent and the world. Westminster, Md., Newman Press [1954] 199p. 19cm. 'Divided into three parts: She takes the veil: Within the walls: and They live the life, which were originally published in England as separate booklets.' [BX4210.M32] 54-4863
1. Monasticism and religious orders for women. I. Title.

MARY LAURENCE, Sister. 271.9
Nuns are real people. Westminster, Md., Newman Press [1955] 181p. 19cm. [BX4210.M325] 56-13836

1. Monastic and religious life of women. I. Title.

MARY VIANNEY, Sister. 271.9
And Nora said yes. New York, McMullen Books [1953] 150p. 21cm. [BX4210.M33] 53-2271
1. Monasticism and religious orders for women. I. Title.

MEEHAN, Thomas A ed. 271.9
Christ's career woman; the story of religious communities of women in the province of Chicago. Chicago, New World Pub. Co., c1950. 128 p. illus. 24 cm. [BX4220.U6M4] 52-1201
1. Monasticism and religious orders for women. 2. Monsaticism and religious orders — Illinois. I. Title.

MOFFATT, John Edward, 1894- 271.9
As I was saying, Sister ... More thoughts for nuns. New York, McMullen Books [c1954] 264p. 21cm. [BX4210.M62] 55-14132
1. Monasticism and religious orders for women. I. Title.

MOFFATT, John Edward, 1894- 271.9
By the way, Sister; obiter dicta for nuns. New York, McMullen Books [1958] 246p. 22cm. [BX4210.M624] 58-12983
1. Monastic and religious life of women. I. Title.

MOFFATT, John Edward, 1894- 271.9
Listen, Sister. New York, McMullen Books [1952] 210p. 20cm. [BX4210.M63] 52-13508
1. Monasticism and religious orders for women. I. Title.

MOFFATT, John Edward, 1894- 271.9
Look, Sister. New York, McMullen Books [1956] 256p. 22cm. [BX4210.M65] 56-9311
1. Monastic and religious life of women. I. Title.

NASH, Robert. 271.9
The nun at her prie-dieu. Westminster, Md., Newman Press, 1950. 298 p. 23 cm. [BX4210.N3] 50-10406
1. Monasticism and religious orders for women. I. Title.

NOTRE Dame, Ind. University. Institute for Local Superiors. 271.9
Proceedings, 1962. Ed.: Robert S. Pelton. [Notre Dame] Univ. of Notre Dame Pr. [c.] 1963 393p. 23cm. Bibl. 63-12511 5.00
1. Monasticism and religious orders of women—Congresses. 2. Superiors, Religious. I. Pelton, Robert S., ed. II. Notre Dame, Ind. University. Dept. of Theology. III. Title.

NOTRE Dame, Ind. University. Institute for Local Superiors. 271.9
Proceedings 1963 Ed. by Robert D. Pelton [Notre Dame] Univ. of Notre Dame Pr. [c.] 1964. 236p. 23cm. Sponsored by the Theology Dept. of the Univ. of Notre Dame in coop. with Conf. of Major Supericrs of Women in the United States, and the Sister Formation Conf. Bibl. 63-12511 5.00
1. Monasticism and religious orders of women—Congresses. sSuperiors, Religious. I. Pelton, Robert S., ed. II. Notre Dame, Ind. University. Dept. of Theology. III. Title.

O'CONNOR, Mary Paschala, Sister, 1882- 271.9
Five decades; history of the Congregation of the Most Holy Rosary, Sinsinawa, Wisconsin, 1849-1899. Sinsinawa, Wis., Sinsinawa Press, 1954. 370p. illus. 24cm. [BX4510.S93O25] 54-37083
1. Sisters of the Order of St. Dominic, Sinsinawa, Wis. I. Title.

REILLY, Mary Paul, Sister, 1920- 271.9
What must I do? Milwaukee, Bruce [1950] 96 p. 21 cm. Bibliography: p. 95-96. [BX4210.R4] 50-7362
1. Monasticism and religious orders for women. I. Title.

RITAMARY, Sister, ed. 271.9
The mind of the church in the formation of sisters; selections from addresses given during the six regional conferences and the first national meeting of the sister formation conference, 1954-1955 [of the National Catholic Educational Association] New York, Fordham University Press, 1956. xxxi, 282p. 24cm. Includes bibliographies. [BX4210.R5] 56-9888
1. Monastic and religious life of women. 2. Monastic and religious life. 3. Catholic Church—Education. I. Title. II. Title: Sister formation conference.

RITAMARY, Sister, ed. 271.9
Spiritual and intellectual elements in the formation of sisters; selections from addresses and communications on discussion topics from the six regional meetings of the sister formation conference, 1955-1956 [of the College and University Dept. of the National Catholic Educational Association] Foreword by Francis Cardinal Spellman. New York, Fordham University Press, 1957. xxv, 261p. 24cm. [BX4210.R52] 57-9099
1. Monastic and religious life of women. 2. Catholic Church—Education. I. Title. II. Title: Sister formation conference.

RONSIN, F X 271.9
To govern is to love; addressed to superiors of religious communities of women. Translated by Eugenia Logan [American ed.] New York, Society of Saint Paul [1955, c1953] 287p. 21cm. Resume of the author's Pour mieux gouverner. [BX4200.R593] 57-34668
1. Monastic and religious life of women. I. Title.

SISTER Formation Conferences 271.9
Proceedings., 1965. New York, Fordham Univ. Pr. [1966] 287p. 24cm. annual. Vs. for 1954/55-1955/56 lack title. Each v. has also distinctive title: 1965, Program for progress; proceedings and communications of regional meetings, ed. by Sister Mary Hester Valentine. Foreward by Edwin A. Quain. [BX4210.S5] 58-10465 5.50
1. Monastic and religious life of women. 2. Catholic Church—Education. I. Ritamary, Sister, ed. II. Title. III. Title: The mind of the church in the formation of Sisters. IV. Title: Spiritual and intellectual elements in the formation of Sisters. V. Title: Planning for the formation of Sisters.

SISTER Formation Conferences. 271.9
Proceedings. 1954/55- New York, Fordham University Press v.24 cm. annual. vols.for 1954/55 -- 1955/56 lack title. Each vol. has also distinctive title: 1954/55, The mind of the church in the formation of Sisters. -- 1955/56, Spiritual and intellectual elements in the formation of Sisters. -- 1955/56, Spiritual and intellectual elements in the formation of Sisters. -- 1956/57, Planning for the formation of Sisters. Editor: 1954/55- Sister Ritamary. [BX4210.S5] 58-10465
1. Monastic and religious life of women. 2. Catholic Church — Education. I. Ritamary, Sister, ed. II. Title. III. Title: The mind of the church in the formation of Sisters. IV. Title: Spiritual and intellectual elements in the formation of Sisters. V. Title: Planning for the formation of Sisters.

STOLZ, Benedict, 1895- ed. 271.9
The voice of the Beloved; an appeal to consecrated souls. Collegeville, Minn., St. John's Abbey Press, 1954. 176p. 17cm. Translation of Maria als Vorbild und Mutter meiner Braeute. [BX4210.S812] 55-1236
1. Monastic and religious life of women. I. Title.

VALENTINE, Ferdinand. 271.9
Religious obedience; a practical exposition for religious sisters. Westminster, Md., Newman Press, 1952. xiv, 128p. 19cm. [BX4210.V28] 51-13501
1. Obedience. 2. Monasticism and religious orders for women. I. Title.

VICTORINE, Sister. 271.9
Christlikeness; conferences for religious on spiritual transformation through a Christocentric life. Westminster, Md., Newman Press, 1951. xi, 181 p. 21 cm. Bibliography: p. 179-181. [BX4210.V5] 51-10490
1. Monasticism and religious orders for women. 2. Spiritual life — Catholic authors. I. Title.

WALSH, James Joseph, 1865-1942, comp. 271'.9 B
These splendid Sisters, compiled by James Joseph Walsh with introd. Freeport, N.Y., Books for Libraries Press [1970] 252 p. 23 cm. (Essay index reprint series) Reprint of the 1927 ed. Contents.Contents.—St. Bridget: pioneer feminine educator.—St. Hilda: abbess of streoneshalh (Whitby).—St. Scholastica and her Benedictine nuns. By J. J. Walsh.—St. Clare: founder of the Franciscan nuns, by Friar Thomas of Celano.—Mother Marie de L'Incarnation, by F. Parkman and W. Wood.—Mother Seton: founder of the American Sisters of Charity, by C. I. White.—The Irish Sisters of Charity and Mercy, by J. J. Walsh.—Sisters in the Crimean War, by Sister Mary Aloysius.—Mother Angela and the Sisters of the Civil War, by J. J. Walsh.—The nuns of the battlefield, by A. Kennedy.—Mother Cabrini: an apostle of the Italians, by J. J. Walsh.—Mother Mary, of the sick poor, by T. M. Schwertner.—Mother Alphonsa Lathrop, by J. J. Walsh.—Twenty five years among New York's cancerous poor, by H. A. Gillis. [BX4225.W3 1970] 75-128326 ISBN 0-8369-1856-8
1. Nuns. I. Title.

WATTEROTT, Ignaz, 1869-1922. 271.9
Religious life and spirit; translated by A. Simon. St. Louis, Herder, 1950. x, 426 p. 24 cm. Translation of Ordensieitung. [BX4210.W314] 51-442
1. Monasticism and religious orders for women. I. Title.

MORRIS, Joan. 271'.9'009
The lady was a bishop; the hidden history of women with clerical ordination and the jurisdiction of bishops. New York, Macmillan [1973] xii, 192 p. 22 cm. [BV639.W7M63] 72-89049 6.95
1. Women in Christianity. 2. Monasticism and religious orders for women. I. Title.

WOODLEY, Janice 271.900924
Not in this way. Adelaide, Rigby [San Francisco, Tri-Ocean, 1966, c.1965] 135p. 22cm. [BX4705.W7A3] 66-10440 3.95 bds.,
I. Title.

MCCARTHY, Thomas Patrick, 1920- 271.905873
Guide to the Catholic sisterhoods in the United States. With foreword by Amleto Giovanni Cardinal Cicognani and introd. by Egidio Vagnozzi. [5th ed.] rev. and enl. Washington, Catholic University of America Press, 1964. xii, 404 p. illus., ports. 24 cm. [BX4220.U6M3 1964] 64-15336
1. Monasticism and religious orders for women. 2. Monasticism and religious orders—U.S. I. Title.

BRO, Bernard, ed. 271.9069
Contemplative nuns speak; Benedictine, Carmelite, Poor Clare, Dominican, Trappistine, and Visitation nuns reply to a questionnaire. Presented by Bernard Bro. Tr. [from French] by Isabel and Florence McHugh. Helicon [dist. New York, Taplinger] 1964 c.1963] 286p. 23cm. 64-13526 4.95
1. Contemplative orders. 2. Monastic and religious life of women. I. La Vie Spirituelle. II. Title.

COURTOIS, Gaston 271.9069
An hour with Jesus; meditations for religious. Tr. from French by Sister Helen Madeleleine. Foreword by Richard J. Cushing, Archbishop of Boston. Westminster, Md., Newman [c.] 1962. 155p. 21cm. 55-8655 3.00
1. Monastic and religious life of women. 2. Meditations. I. Title.

DONNELLY, Gertrude Joseph. 271.9069
The Sister apostle. With a foreword by Sister M. Charles Borromeo. Notre Dame, Ind., Fides Publishers [1964] 181 p. 21 cm. [BX4205.D6] 64-22891
1. Monastic and religious life of women. 2. Women in church work. I. Title.

DONNELLY, Gertrude Joseph, Sister 271.9069
The Sister apostle. Foreword by Sister M. Charles Borromeo. Notre Dame, Ind., Fides [c.1964] 181p. 21cm. 64-22891 3.95; 1.95 pap.,
1. Monastic and religious life of women. 2. Women in church work. I. Title.

DUBAY, Thomas. 271.9069
Sisters' retreats, a guide for priests and sisters. Westminster, Md., Newman Press, 1963. 226 p. 22 cm. [BX4214.D8] 62-21501
1. Retreats for members of religious orders. I. Title.

DUBAY, Thomas 271.9069
Sisters' retreats, a guide for priests and sisters. Westminster, Md., Newman, [c.]1963. 226p. 22cm. 62-21501 4.50
1. Retreats for members of religious orders. I. Title.

ECKENSTEIN, Lina d.1931 271.9069
Woman under monasticism; chapters on saint-lore and convent life between A.D. 500 and A.D. 1500. New York, Russell, 1963. 496p. 25cm. Bibl. 63-11028 10.00
1. Convents and nunneries. 2. Monasticism and religious orders for women—Hist. I. Title.

EVOY, John J 271.9069
Personality development in the religious life, by John J. Evoy and Van F. Christoph. New York, Sheed and Ward [1963] 247 p. 22 cm. [BX4205.E9] 62-15285
1. Monastic and religious life of women. I. Christoph, Van Francis. II. Title.

EVOY, John J. 271.9069
Personality development in the religious life, by John J. Evoy, Van F. Christoph. New York, Sheed & Ward [c.1963] 247p. 22cm. 62-15285 3.95
1. Monastic and religious life of women. I. Christoph, Van Francis. II. Title.

HAGSPIEL, Brund Martin, 1885- 271.9069
Spiritual highlights for Sisters. Milwaukee, Bruce Pub. Co. [1960] 228p. 23cm. [BX4210.H32] 60-8903
1. Monastic and religious life of women. I. Title.

HAGSPIEL, Bruno Martin, 1885- 271.9069
Convent readings and reflections. Milwaukee, Bruce Pub. Co. [1959] 274p. 23cm. [BX4210.H27] 59-7944
1. Monastic and religious life of women. I. Title.

HERBST, Winfrid, 1891- 271.9069
Question box for Sisters. New York, St. Paul Publication [1961] 192p. 21cm. [BX4210.H38] 61-13712
1. Monastic and religious life of women. I. Title.

HERBST, Winfrid, 1891- 271.9069
Sisters want to know. Collegeville, Minn., Liturgical Press [c1958] 288p. 19cm. [BX4210.H43] 60-4768
1. Monastic and religious life of women. 2. Questions and answers—Theology. I. Title.

IMMACULATA, Sister M., 1913- 271.9069
Witness to Christ. Westminster, Md., Newman [c.]1964. xvii, 191p. 23cm. 64-25014 3.95
1. Monastic and religious life of women. I. Title.

KEAN, Claude, Father, 1903- 271.9069
As one of them: letters to a sister superior, by Claude Kean. Westminster, Md., Newman Press, 1965. v, 153 p. 22 cm. [BX4210.K37] 64-66335
1. Monastic and religious life of women. I. Title.

KEAN, Claude, Father 1903- 271.9069
As one of them; letters to a sister superior. Westminister, Md., Newman [c.]1965. v, 153p. 22cm. [BX4210.K37] 64-66335 3.50
1. Monastic and religious life of women. I. Title.

KENRICK, Edward F. 271.9069
The spirituality of the teaching sister. St. Louis, Herder [1962] 243p. 22cm. 62-10508 4.50
1. Spiritual life—Catholic authors. 2. Monastic and religious life of women. I. Title.

KLIMISCH, Mary Jane, Sister 271.9069
The one bride: the church and consecrated virginity. Pref. by Ignatius Hunt. New York, Sheed [c.1965] xviii, 235p. 22cm. Bibl. [BV4647.C5K55] 65-12211 4.95
1. Virginity. I. Title.

KLMISCH, Mary Jane. 271.9069
The one bride: the church and consecrated virginity. Pref. by Ignatius Hunt. New York, Sheed and Ward [1965] xvii, 235 p. 22 cm. Includes bibliographical references. [BV4647.C5K55] 65-12211
1. Virginity. I. Title.

LEXAU, Joan M., ed. 271.9069
Convent life; Roman Catholic religious orders for women in North America, edited, and with an introd., by Joan M. Lexau. Forward [i.e. Foreword] by Sister Maria del Rey of Maryknoll. New York, Dial Press, 1964. xviii, 398 p. 22 cm. [BX4210.L48] 64-15224
1. Monastic and religious life of women. 2. Monasticism and religious orders for women—Dictionaries. I. Title.

MCGOEY, John H. 271.9069
The sins of the just. Milwaukee, Bruce [c.1963] 224p. 22cm. 63-14922 3.75
1. Monastic and religious life of women. I. Title.

MCGOLDRICK, Desmond F. 271.9069
Holy restraint; simple talks to sister novices on the formation of the religious personality. Pittsburgh, Duquesne Univ. Pr. [c.]1962. 198p. 19cm. (Duquesne sister formation ser., 2) 62-21189 3.75
1. Monastic and religious life of women. I. Title.

MCGOLDRICK, Desmond F 271.9069
The martyrdom of change; simple talks to postulant sisters on the religious mentality and ideal. Pittsburgh, Duquesne University Press, 1961. xvi, 123p. 19cm. (Duquesne sister formation series, 1) [BX4210.M22] 61-14767
1. Monastic and religious life of women—Addresses, essays, lectures. I. Title. II. Series.

MCKENNA, Alice Glendon 271.9069
After rain. New York, Vantage Press [c.1960] 72p. illus. 22cm. 2.00 bds.,
I. Title.

MALARD, Suzanne, 1907- 271.9069
Religious orders of women, by Suzanne Cita-Malard. Tr. from French by George J. Robinson. New York, Hawthorn [c.1964] 110, [1] p. 21cm. (Twentieth cent. ency. of Catholicism, v.86. Sect. 8: The organizations of the church) Bibl. 64-14165 3.50 bds.,
1. Monasticism and religious orders for women. 2. Monastic and religious life of women. I. Title. II. Series: The Twentieth century encyclopedia of Catholicism, v. 86

MARY LAURENCE, Sister. 271.9069
One nun to another. St. Louis, Herder [1959] 129p. 19cm. [BX4210.M326] 59-3673
1. Monastic and religious life of women. I. Title.

MEYERS, Bertrande. 271.9069
Sisters for the 21st century. With a pref. by Cardinal Ritter. New York, Sheed and Ward [1965] xix, 364 p. 22 cm. Bibliographical footnotes. [BX4210.M46] 65-12196
1. Monastic and religious life of women. I. Title.

MEYERS, Bertrande. 271.9069
Sisters for the 21st century. With a pref. by Cardinal Ritter. New York, Sheed and Ward [1965] xix, 304 p. 22 cm. Bibliiographical footnotes. [BX4210.M46] 65-12196
1. Monastic and religious life of women. I. Title.

MEYERS, Sister Bertrande 271.9069
Sisters for the 21st century. Pref. by Cardinal Ritter. New York, Sheed [c.1965] xix, 364p. 22cm. Bibl. [BX4210.M46] 65-12196 5.00
1. Monastic and religious life of women. I. Title.

MOFFATT, John Edward, 1894- 271.9069
Pray, Sister; prie-dieu thoughts for nuns. New York, McMullen Books [1959] 172p. 22cm. [BX4210.M66] 59-13181
1. Monastic and religious life of women. I. Title.

MOFFATT, John Edward, 1894- 271.9069
Step this way, Sister; reflections for nuns, young and less young. New York, Farrar, Straus and Cudahy [1960] 203p. 22cm. [BX4210.M68] 60-12698
1. Monastic and religious life of women. I. Title.

MOFFATT, John Edward, 1894- 271.9069
Think, Sister; thoughts in a convent garden. New York, Farrar, Straus and Cudahy [1962] 189p. 22cm. [BX4210.M69] 62-7772
1. Monastic and religious life of women. I. Title.

MONK, Maria, d.ca.1850. 271.9069
Awful disclosures of the Hotel Dieu Nunnery. With an introd. by Ray Allen Billington. Facsim. of 1836 ed. Hamden, Conn., Archon Books, 1962. 376p. 17cm. Previous editions published under title: Awful disclosures. [BX4216.M6A3 1836aa] 62-16004
I. Title.

MONTGOMERY, Ruth (Shick) 1912- 271.9069
Once there was a nun; Mary McCarran's years as Sister Mary Mercy. New York, Putnam [1962] 317p. 22cm. [BX4705.M136M6] 62-10976
1. McCarran, Mary L. I. Title.

MONTGOMERY, Ruth (Shick) 1912- 271.9069
Once there was a nun; Mary McCarran's years as Sister Mary Mercy [New York] Avon [1963, c.1962] 256p. 18cm. (S-136) .60 pap.,
1. McCarran, Mary L. I. Title.

NOTRE Dame, Ind. University. Sisters' Institute of Spirituality. 271.9069
Adaptation of the religious life to modern conditions [by] A. Ple [and others. Notre Dame] University of Notre Dame Press, 1961. 160p. 21cm. (Religious life in the modern world: selections from the Notre Dame Institutes of Spirituality, v. 1) 'Articles . . . previously published in the Proceedings of the Sisters' Institute of Spirituality, 1953, 1954, and 1956 respectively. bBibliographical footnotes. [BX4210.N58] 61-65519
1. Monastic and religious life of women. I. Ple, Albert. II. Title. III. Series.

O'KEEFE, Maureen. 271.9069
The convent in the modern world; a philosophy of conventual living. Chicago, H. Regnery Co., 1963. 143 p. 21 cm. [BX4210.O67] 63-12861
1. Monastic and religious life of women. I. Title.

O'KEEFE, Maureen 271.9069
The convent in the modern world; a philosophy of conventual living. Chicago, Regnery [c.]1963. 143p. 21cm. 63-12861 3.75
1. Monastic and religious life of women. I. Title.

PHILIPPE, Paul, 1905- 271.9069
The movitiate. [Notre Dame, Ind.] Univ. of Notre Dame Pr. [c.]1961 169p. (Religious life in the modern world; selections from the Notre Dame Insts. of Spirituality, v.2; NDP4) 61-655172 1.95 pap.,
1. Novitiate. 2. Spiritual direction. I. Title.

PHILIPPE, Paul, 1905- 271.9069
The novitiate. [Notre Dame, Ind.] University of Notre Dame Press, 1961. 169p. 21cm. (Religious life in the modern world; selections from the Notre Dame Institutes of Spirituallty, v. 2) 'Articles ... previously published in the Proceedings of the Sisters' Institute of Spirituality, 1953, 1954, and 1955 respectively.' [BX4213.P5] 61-65517
1. Novitiate. 2. Spiritual direction. I. Title.

RITA AGNES [SECULAR NAME: MARIE WENNERBERG] Sister 1890- 271.9069
Dear atoms; [story-essays] Boston, Humphries [c.1962] 139p. 22cm. 62-51417 3.75
I. Title.

RONSIN, F X 271.9069
To obey is to reign; the beauty and grandeur of the religious life. Translated from the French by Eugenia Logan. New York, St. Paul Publications [c1961] 234p. 21cm. [BX4210.R64] 61-14113
1. Monastic and religious life of women. I. Title.

SUENENS, Leon Joseph, Cardinal, 1904- 271.9069
The nun in the world; new dimensions in the modern apostolate. [Tr. from French by Geoffrey Stevens] Westminster, Md., Newman [1963, c.1962] 175p. 19cm. 63-1829 1.95 pap.,
1. Monastic and religious life of women. 2. Women as missionaries. I. Title.

THEOLOGICAL INSTITUTE FOR LOCAL SUPERIORS, University of Notre Dame. 271.9069
Adaptation of the religious life to modern conditions [by] A. Ple [and others. Notre Dame] University of Notre Dame Press, 1961. 160 p. 21 cm. (Religious life in the modern world, v. 1) "Articles ... previously published in the Proceedings of the Sisters' Institute of Spirituality, 1953, 1954, and 1956 respectively." Bibliographical footnotes. [BX4210.T46] 61-65519
1. Monastic and religious life of women. I. Ple, Albert. II. Notre Dame, Ind. University. III. Title. IV. Series.

THEOLOGICAL INSTITUTE FOR LOCAL SUPERIORS, University of Notre Dame. 271.9069
The novitiate, by Paul Philippe. [Notre Dame] University of Notre Dame Press, 1961. 169 p. 21 cm. (Religious life in the modern world, v. 2) "Articles ... previously published in the Proceedings of the Sisters' Institute of Spirituality, 1953, 1954, and 1955 respectively." [BX4213.T45] 61-65517
1. Novitiate. 2. Spiritual direction. I. Philippe, Paul, 1905- . II. Notre Dame, Ind. University. III. Title. IV. Series.

KINZEL, Margaret Mary. 271.90692
The metaphysical basis of certain principles of the religious life in the light of Thomistic principles. Washington, Catholic University of America Press, 1959. 51p. 23cm. (Catholic University of America. Philosophical studies, no. 189. Abstract no. 40) Abstract of thesis--Catholic University of America. Bibliography: p.33-42. [BX4210.K55] 61-2870
1. Monastic and religious life of women. 2. Thomas Aquinas, Saint—Metaphysics. I. Title. II. Series.

ANCREN riwle. 271.90698
The English text of the Ancrene riwle. Ed. from Cotton MS. Titus D. XVIII, by Frances M. Mack. Together with the Lanhydrock fragment, Bodleian MS. Eng. th. c. 70, ed. by A. Zettersten. New York, Pub. for the Early Eng. Text Soc., by Oxford [1964, c.]1963 xvii, 171p. facsims. 23cm. (Early Eng. Text Soc. Pubns. Orig. ser. no. 252) 64-1597 6.40
1. Monasticism and religious orders for women. 2. Monasticism and religious orders—Rules. I. Mack, Frances May, ed. II. Series.

ANCREN riwle. 271.90698
Ancrene wisse; the English text of the Ancrene riwle, ed. from ms. Corpus Christi College, Cambridge 402, by J. R. R. Tolkien. Introd. by N. R. Ker. New York, Pub. for the Early English Text Society by Oxford [1963, c.]1962. xviii, 222p. facsims. 22cm. (Early Eng. Text Soc. [Pubns. Original ser.] no. 249, 1962 (for 1960)) 63-2235 4.80
1. Monasticism and religious orders for women. 2. Monasticism and religious orders—Rules. I. Tolkien. John Ronald Renel, 1892- ed. II. Title. III. Series: Early English Text Society. Publications, no. 249

ANCREN RIWLE. 271.90698
Ancrene wisse; the English text of the Ancrene Riwie, edited from ms. Corpus Christi College, Cambridge 402, by J. R. R. Tolkien. With an introd. by N. R. Ker. London, New York, Published for the Early English Text Society by the Oxford University Press, 1962. xviii, 222 p. fascims. 22 cm. (Early English Text Society. [Publications. Original series, no. 249, 1962 (for 1960)) [PR1119.A2] 63-2235
1. Monasticism and religious orders for women. 2. Monasticism and religious orders — Rules. I. Tolkien, John Ronald Renei, 1892- ed. II. Title. III. Series: Early English Text Society. Publications. Original series, no. 249

ANCREN RIWLE 271.90698
Ancrene wisse: parts six and seven. Edited by Geoffrey Shephered. London, T. Nelson [dist. New York, Barnes &Noble, 1959, i.e., 1960] 1xxiii, 116p. 19cm. (Nelson's medieval and Renaissance library) 'The present edition of parts 6 and 7 . . . is based upon . . . Ms. 402 of Corpus Christi College, Cambridge (CCCC Ms. 402)' Bibliography: p. 73-77. 60-2665 2.50
1. Monasticism and religious orders for women. 2. Monasticism and religious orders—Rules. I. Shepherd, Geoffrey, ed. II. Title.

ANCREN RIWLE. 271.90698
The English text of the Ancrene riwle. Edited from Cotton MS. Titus D. XVIII, by Frances M. Mack. Together with the Lahydrock fragment, Bodleian MS. Eng. th. c. 70, edited by A. Zettersten. London, New York, Published for the Early English Text Society, by the Oxford University Press, 1963. xvii, 171 p. facisms. 23 cm. (Early English Text Society. [Publications. Original series] no. 252) [PR1119.A2] 64=1597
1. Monasticism and religious orders for women. 2. Monasticism and religious orders — Rules. I. Mack, Frances May, ed. II. Title. III. Series.

CATHOLIC Church. Pope, 1939-1958 (Pius XII) Sponsa Christi (21 Nov. 1950) English. 271.90698
Apostolic constitution 'Sponsa Christi' and instruction of the Sacred Congregation of Religious. [Derby, N. Y.] Daughters of St. Paul, Apostolate of the Press [c1955] 75p. 17cm. 59-24927
1. Monasticism and religious orders for women (Canonlaw) I. Catholic Church. Congregatio de Religiosis. Inter praeclara (23 Nov. 1950) II. Title.

FANFANI, Lodovico Giuseppe 1876-1955 271.90698
Canon law for religious women, by Louis G. Fanfani, Kevin D. O'Rourke. Dubuque, Iowa, Priory Press [c.1961] 393p. 60-53079 4.95
1. Monasticism and religious orders for women (Canon law) I. O'Rourke, Kevin D., ed. and tr. II. Title.

NOTRE Dame, Ind. University. Sisters' Institute of Spirituality. 271.90698
The vows and perfection [by] Bernard I. Mullahy [others, Notre Dame] Univ. of Notre Dame Pr. [c.] 1962 vii, 232 p. (religious life in the modern world; selections from the Notre Dame Inst. of Spirituality, v. 3, NDp15) Articles...previously pub. inthe Proceedings of the Sisters' Inst. of Spirituality, 1953, 1954, and 1955 respectively. Bibl. 62-1570 pap., 1.95
1. Vows. 2. Perfection (Catholic). 3. Monastic and religious life of women. I. Mullahy, Bernard II. Title. III. Series.

THEOLOGICAL INSTITUTE FOR LOCAL SUPERIORS, University of Notre Dame. 271.90698
The vows and perfection [by] Bernard I. Mullahy [and others. Notre Dame] University of Notre Dame Press, 1962. vii, 232 p. 21 cm. (Religious life in the modern world, v. 3) "Articles ... previously published in the Proceedings of the Sisters' Institute of Spirituality 1953, 1954, and 1955 respectively." Bibliographical footnotes. [BX2435.T45] 62-1570
1. Vows. 2. Perfection (Catholic) 3. Monastic and religious life of women. I. Mullahy, Bernard I. II. Notre Dame, Ind. University. III. Title. IV. Series.

VALENTINE, Ferdinand. 271.90698
All for the King's delight; a treatise on Christian chastity, principally for religious sisters. Westminster, Md., Newman Press [c1958] 280 p. 23 cm. [BV4647.C5V28] 58-13648
1. Chastity. 2. Monastic and religious life of women. I. Title.

HALEY, Joseph Edmund, ed. 271.9082
Proceedings of the 1960 Sisters' Institute of Spirituality; the superior and the common good of the religious community [8th ser.] Notre Dame, Ind., Univ. of Notre Dame Pr. [c.]1961. xiii, 345p. Bibl. 4.25
1. Monasticism and religious orders for women. 2. Spiritual life—Catholic authors. I. Haley, Joseph Edmund, ed. II. Title.

NATIONAL Congress of Religious of the United States. 2d, University of Notre Dame, 1961. 271.9082
Religious life in the Church today: prospect and retrospect. Proceedings of the Women's Section of the Second Natl. Congress of Religious in the United States, under the auspices of the Conferences of Major Religious Superiors., Univ. of Notre Dame, Ind., Aug. 16-19, 1961. Ed. by Mother Mary Florence, S.L. [Notre Dame, Ind.] Univ. of Notre Dame Pr. [c.] 1962. Bibl. 62-12468 4.00
1. Monastic and religious life of women—Congresses. I. Mary, Florence Mother, S. L. ed. II. Title.

NOTRE Dame, Ind. University. Sisters' Institute of Spirituality. 271.9082
Proceedings. 1953- Notre Dame, University of Notre Dame Press. v. illus., ports. 24cm. Editor: 1953- J. E. Haley. [BX4210.N6] 54-11413
1. Monasticism and religious orders for women. 2. Spiritual life— Catholic authors. I. Haley, Joseph Edmund, ed. II. Title.

POWER, Eileen Edna, 1889-1940 271.90942
Medieval English nunneries, c.1275 to 1535. New York, Biblo & Tannen, 1964. xiv, 724p. illus., map. 24cm. (Biblo & Tannen's archives of civilization) Bibl. 64-13393 20.00 lim. ed.,
1. Convents and nunneries—England. 2. Monastic and religious life of women—Hist. I. Title.

COOGAN, Jane. 271'.91
The price of our heritage : history of the Sisters of Charity of the Blessed Virgin Mary / M. Jane Coogan. Dubuque, Iowa : Mount Carmel Press, 1975- v. : ill. ; 23 cm. Includes index. Contents.Contents.—v. 1. 1831-1869. Bibliography: v. 1, p. 471-490. [BX4467.C66] 75-318954 4.00 (v. 1)
1. Sisters of Charity of the Blessed Virgin Mary, Dubuque, Iowa. I. Title.

DAUGHTERS of the church: 271'.91
proceedings of two inter-province institutes on renewal and adaptation. St. Louis, Daughters of Charity of St. Vincent de Paul [1967] 122 p. illus. 28 cm. Proceedings of meetings held Oct. 14-19, 1966, at Marillac Province House, St. Louis, and sponsored by the Daughters of Charity of St. Vincent de Paul, Emmitsburg, Md., and St. Louis, Mo. Bibliography: p. 121-122. [BX809.S6D3] 67-21935
1. Daughters of Charity of St. Vincent de Paul—Congresses. I. Daughters of Charity of St. Vincent de Paul, Emmitsburg, Md. II. Daughters of Charity of St. Vincent de Paul, St. Louis.

GRIFFIN, Mary Annarose, Sister. 271'.91 B
The courage to choose : an American nun's story / by Mary Griffin. 1st ed. Boston : Little, Brown, [1975] ix, 214 p. ; 22 cm. Autobiographical. Includes bibliographical references. [BX4705.G62245A33] 75-9636 ISBN 0-316-32864-2 : 7.95
1. Griffin, Mary Annarose, Sister. 2. Monastic and religious life of women. 3. Ex-nuns—Personal narratives. I. Title.

JAMESON, Anna Brownell Murphy, 1794-1860. 271'.9'1
Sisters of charity, Catholic and Protestant and The communion of labor / by Mrs. Jameson. Westport, Conn. : Hyperion Press, 1976. p. cm. (Pioneers of the woman's movement ; 8) Reprint of the 1857 ed. published by Ticknor and Fields, Boston. [BX4237.J35 1976] 75-15087 ISBN 0-88355-268-X : 19.75
1. Sisters of Charity—Addresses, essays, lectures. 2. Women in charitable work—Addresses, essays, lectures. 3. Nursing—Moral and religious aspects—Addresses, essays, lectures. I. Jameson, Anna Brownell Murphy, 1794-1860. The communion of labor. 1976. II. Title.

VINCENT DE PAUL, Saint, 1576?-1660. 271.91
The conferences of St. Vincent de Paul to the Sisters of Charity. Translated from the French by Joseph Leonard. Westminster, Md., Newman Press, 1952. 4 v. 22 cm. [BX4462.V513] 52-3073
1. Sisters of Charity of St. Vincent de Paul. 2. Spiritual life — Catholic authors. I. Title.

VINCENT DE PAUL, Saint, 1581-1660. 271.91
The conferences of St. Vincent de Paul to the Sisters of Charity. Translated from the French by Joseph Leonard. Westminster, Md., Newman Press 1952. 4 v. 22 cm. Translation of Conferences spirituelles pour l'explication des regles des Soeurs de charite. [BX4462.V513] 52-3073
1. Sisters of Charity of St. Vincent de Paul. 2. Spiritual life — Catholic authors. I. Title.

WALSH, Marie de Lourdes. 271.91
The Sisters of Charity of New York, 1809-1959. Foreword by Francis Cardinal Spellman. New York, Fordham University Press [1960] 3 v. illus. 24 cm. Includes bibliography. [BX4463.6.N5W3] 60-10735
1. Sisters of Charity of St. Vincent de Paul of New York — Hist. I. Title.

WALSH, Marie de Lourdes 271.91
The Sisters of Charity of New York, 1809-1959 [3v.] Foreword by Francis Cardinal Spellman. New York, Fordham University [c.1960] 3v. various p. illus. Bibl. 60-10735 15.00
1. Sisters of Charity of St. Vincent de Paul of New York—Hist. I. Title.

DAUGHTERS of St. Paul. 271.91024 B
Mother Seton : wife, mother, educator, foundress, saint : profile by the Daughters of St. Paul, based on "Elizabeth Seton" by Msgr. Joseph Bardi. Spiritual gems of Mother Seton. Boston : St. Paul Editions, 1975. 140 p. : ill. ; 22 cm. [BX4705.S57D3 1975] 75-6861 3.95 pbk. : 2.95
1. Seaton, Elizabeth Ann, 1774-1821. I. Bardi, Giuseppe, Mons. Elisabetta Anna Seton. II. Seton, Elizabeth Ann, 1774-1821. Spiritual gems. 1975. III. Title.

DIRVIN, Joseph I. 271'.91'024 B
Mrs. Seton, foundress of the American Sisters of Charity / Joseph I. Dirvin. New canonization ed. New York : Farrar, Straus and Giroux, 1975. xix, 498 p., [8] leaves of plates : ill. ; 21 cm. Includes index. Bibliography: p. [465]-469. [BX4705.S57D5 1975] 75-321767 ISBN 0-374-51255-8 : 4.95
1. Seton, Elizabeth Ann, 1774-1821. 2. Sisters of Charity of St. Vincent de Paul. I. Title.

ELIZABETH Seton's 271'.91'024 B
two Bibles, her notes and markings / compiled and edited by Ellin M. Kelly. Huntington, Ind. : Our Sunday Visitor, c1977. 184 p. : ill. ; 21 cm. Includes bibliographical references and indexes. [BX4700.S4E43] 77-80539 ISBN 0-87973-741-7 pbk. : 3.95
1. Seton, Elizabeth Ann, Saint, 1774-1821. 2. Bible—Influence. 3. Christian saints—United States—Biography. I. Seton, Elizabeth Ann, Saint, 1774-1821. II. Kelly, Ellin M. III. Bible. English. Douai. Selections. 1805.

†HINDMAN, Jane F. 271'.91'024 B
Elizabeth Ann Seton, mother, teacher, saint for our time / by Jane F. Hindman. New York : Arena Lettres, c1976. vii, 82, [1] p. ; 18 cm. Bibliography: p. [83] A brief biography of the Catholic convert who founded a religious order and the first parochial school in the United States. She was proclaimed a saint in 1975. [BX4700.S4H56] 92 76-15327 pbk. : 1.50
1. Seton, Elizabeth Ann, Saint, 1774-1821—Juvenile literature. 2. Christian saints—United States—Biography—Juvenile literature. I. Title.

MADELEINE, Sister. 271'.91'024 B
Chasing rainbows. Sketches by Charles Blaze Vukovich. Englewood Cliffs, N.J., Englewood Cliffs College Press [1973] xi, 205 p. illus. 23 cm. Autobiographical. [BX4705.M2566A33] 73-75173 4.95 (pbk.)
1. Madeleine, Sister. I. Title.

MELVILLE, Annabelle McConnell, 1910- 271'.91'024 B
Elizabeth Bayley Seton, 1774-1821 / by Annabelle M. Melville. New York : Scribner, [1976] c1951. xix, 411 p., [4] leaves of plates : ill. ; 22 cm. "Hudson River editions." Includes index. Bibliography: p. 383-391. [BX4700.S4M44 1976] 76-8053 ISBN 0-684-14735-1 lib.bdg. : 12.50
1. Seton, Elizabeth Ann, Saint, 1774-1821. 2. Christian saints—United States—Biography.

SPILLANE, James Maria. 271'.91'0924
Kentucky spring. St. Meinrad, Ind., Abbey Press [1968] 293 p. 18 cm. Bibliography: p. 291-293. [BX4705.S715S65] 68-29322
1. Spalding, Catherine, 1790-1850. 2. Sisters of Charity of Nazareth, Nazareth, Ky. I. Title.

GARNETT, Emmeline, 1924- 271.92
Florence Nightingale's nuns. Illus. by Anne Marie Jauss. New York, Vision Books [dist. Farrar, Straus & Cudahy, c.1961] 185p. (Vision books, 49) 61-5896 1.95
1. Sisters of Mercy. England—Juvenile literature. 2. Nightingale, Florence, 1820-1910—Juvenile literature. 3. Crimean War, 1853-1856—Hospitals, charities, etc.—Juvenile literature. I. Title.

MCAULEY, Mary Catherine, 1778-1841. 271.92
Retreat instructions of Mother Mary Catherine McAuley, by Sister Mary Teresa Purcell; edited by Sisiters of Mercy, Albany, New York. Westminster, Md., Newman Press, 1952. 213p. illus. 20cm. [BX4210.M15] 53-654
1. Monastic and religious life of women. 2. Sisters of Mercy. I. Title.

MCAULEY, Mary Catherine, Mother, 1787-1841. 271.92
Retreat instructions of Mother Mary Catherine McAuley, by Sister Mary Teresa Purcell; edited by Sisters of Mercy, Albany, New York. Westminster, Md., Newman Press, 1952. 243p. illus. 20cm. [BX4210.M15] 53-654
1. Monasticism and religious orders for women. 2. Sisters of Mercy. I. Title.

O'CONNOR, Mary Loretto, Sister, 1911- 271.92
Mercy marks the century. Providence, Sisters of Mercy [1951] 161 p. illus., ports. 28 cm. Bibliography: p. 147. [BX4484.P703] 51-28812
1. Sisters of Mercy. Providence. I. Title.

HEALY, Kathleen. 271'.92'024 B
Frances Warde: American founder of the Sisters of Mercy. New York, Seabury Press [1973] x, 535 p. 21 cm. "A Crossroad book." Bibliography: p. 509-517. [BX4705.W32H42] 73-6433 ISBN 0-8164-1139-5 14.50
1. Warde, Mary Francis Xavier, 1810?-1884. 2. Sisters of Mercy.

SABOURIN, Justine. 271'.92'073
The amalgamation : a history of the union of the Religious Sisters of Mercy of the United States of America / Justine Sabourin. Saint Meinrad, Ind. : Abbey Press, c1976. p. cm. Includes index. Bibliography: p. [BX4482.2.S2] 75-19927 ISBN 0-87029-059-2 : 12.95
1. Sisters of Mercy. United States.—History. I. Title.

FOX, Mary Loyola. 271'.92'09768
A return of love; the story of the Sisters of Mercy in Tennessee, 1866-1966. [Milwaukee?] Bruce Pub. Co. [1967] xii, 188 p. illus., ports. 22 cm. Bibliography: p. 179. [BX4483.6.T4F6] 67-28892
1. Sisters of Mercy, Tennessee—History. I. Title.

MORGAN, Mary Evangelist. 271.920979454
Mercy, generation to generation; history of the first century of the Sisters of Mercy, Diocese of Sacramento, California. Foreword by Joseph T. McGucken. San Francisco, Fearon Publishers [c1957] 278p. illus. 22cm. [BX4484.S14M6] 57-9844
1. Sisters of Mercy. Sacramento, Calif. (Diocese) I. Title.

TURK, Midge. 271'.93
The buried life; a nun's journey. New York, World Pub. Co. [1971] 196 p. 22 cm. [BX4668.3.T87A3] 77-149415 6.95
1. Ex-nuns—Personal narratives. I. Title.

WILLIAMS, Margaret Anne, 1902- 271.93
St. Madeleine Sophie; her life and letters. [New York] Herder & Herder [1966, c.1965] 662p. port. 23cm. Bibl. [BX4700.M2W5] 65-13478 14.50
1. Madeleine Sophie, Saint, 1779-1865. I. Title.

*DE MEJO, Oscar 271.9452
Diary of a nun. New York, Pyramid [1964, c.1955] 144p. 18cm. (F959) Bibl. .40 pap.,
1. Monasticism and religious orders for women—Italy. I. De Vincentiis, Cara. II. Title.

MCSHANE, John Francis. 271.95
Little beggars of Christ: an appreciation and a tribute. Photos. by the author. [Paterson? N. J.] 1954. 147p. illus. 22cm. [BX4402.M3] 54-27852
1. Little Sisters of the Poor. I. Title.

BURNS, Katherine. 271.97
Symbolized by a shrine; the story of the Nursing Sisters of the Sick Poor. [Brooklyn? 1955] 271p. 22cm. [BX4510.S84B8] 56-4692
1. Sisters of the Infant Jesus. I. Title.

CALLAHAN, Mary Geneosa, 1901- 271.97
The history of the Sisters of Divine Providence, San Antonio, Texas. Milwaukee, Bruce Press [1955] 304p. illus. 24cm. (Catholic life publications) [BX4475.S43C3] 56-3366
1. Sisters of Divine Providence of San Antonio, Texas—Hist. I. Title.

CEGIELKA, Francis A. 271.97
"Nazareth" spirituality [by] Francis A. Cegielka. Authorized translation from Polish by Sister M. Theophame and Mother M. Laurence. Milwaukee, Bruce Pub. Co. [1966] viii, 175 p. 22 cm. [BX4497.Z7C413] 66-5051
1. Sisters of the Holy Family of Nazareth. I. Title.

CLIMB along the cutting 271'.97
edge : an analysis of change in religious life / Joan Chittister ... [et al.]. New York : Paulist Press, c1977. xiv, 304 p. ; 23 cm. Includes bibliographical references and index. [BX4276.C64] 77-80802 ISBN 0-8091-2038-0 pbk. : 7.95
1. Benedictine nuns—Addresses, essays, lectures. 2. Monastic and religious life of women—Addresses, essays, lectures. 3. Church renewal—Addresses, essays, lectures. I. Chittister, Joan.

DECHANTAL, Sister. 271'.97
Out of Nazareth; a centenary of the Sisters of the Holy Family of Nazareth in the service of the Church [by] M. DeChantal. Foreword by John Cardinal Krol. [1st ed.] New York, Exposition Press [1974] xii, 375 p. 24 cm. (An Exposition-testament book) Bibliography: p. 359-363. [BX4497.D4] 74-174483 ISBN 0-682-47820-2 17.50
1. Sisters of the Holy Family of Nazareth. I. Title.

FELICIAN Sisters of the Order of St. Francis. 271.97
Magnificat; a centennial record of the Congregation of the Sisters of Saint Felix (the Felician Sisters) 1855, November, 1955. [Buffalo, 1955] 155p. illus. 29cm. [BX4350.F4A23] 56-28907
1. Felician Sisters of the Order of St. Francis—Hist. I. Title.

GAVIN, Donald Phillip, 1911- 271.97
In all things charity; history of the Sisters of Charity of St. Augustine, Cleveland, Ohio, 1851-1954. Milwaukee, Bruce Press [1955] 164 p. illus. 23 cm. (Catholic life publications) [BX4470.C54G3] 56-59131
1. Sisters of Charity of St. Augustine. I. Title.

GUIDRY, Mary Gabriella, 1914- 271'.97 B
The Southern Negro nun : an autobiography / by Mary Gabriella Guidry. 1st ed. New York : Exposition Press, c1974. 156 p., [4] leaves of plates : ill. ; 22 cm. [BX4705.G717A35] 75-321162 ISBN 0-682-47888-1 : 6.50
1. Guidry, Mary Gabriella, 1914- I. Title.

HOLLAND, Mary Ildephonse, Sister, 1884- 271.97
Lengthened shadows, a history of the Sisters of Mercy, Cedar Rapids, Iowa. New York, Bookman Associates, 1952. 337 p. illus. 24 cm. [BX4484.C4H6] 52-4509
1. Sisters of Mercy. Cedar Rapids, Iowa. I. Title.

HURLEY, Helen Angela, Sister. 271.97
On good ground; the story of the Sisters of St. Joseph in St. Paul. Minneapolis, University of Minnesota Press [1951] xiii, 312 p. illus., ports., map. 23 cm. "Bibliographical notes": p. 289-301. [BX4490.S3H8] 51-14167
1. Sisters of St. Joseph of Carondelet. Province of St. Paul. I. Title.

MARY Bernard, Sister, 1917- 271'.97 B
I leap for joy / by Sister Mary Bernard ; edited by Howard Earl. Plainfield, N.J. : Logos International, [1974] 241 p. ; 18 cm. [BX4705.M4138A34] 74-75798 ISBN 0-88270-101-0 pbk. : 1.45
1. Mary Bernard, Sister, 1917- I. Title.

MARY Francis, Mother, 1921- 271'.9'7
Strange gods before me / Mother Mary Francis. Chicago : Franciscan Herald Press, 1965, c1976. 214 p. ; 21 cm. Reprint of the ed. published by Sheed and Ward, New York. [BX4230.M3 1976] 76-875 ISBN 0-8199-0599-2 pbk. : 4.50
1. Poor Clares. 2. Contemplative orders. I. Title.

MARY Francis, Sister, P.C. 271.97
A right to be merry. New York, Sheed & Ward [1956] 212 p. 21 cm. [BX4362.M3] 56-9528
1. Poor Clares. 2. Monastic and religious life of women. I. Title.

MARY CHARITAS, Sister, 1893- 271.97
A new superior generation. Boston, Bruce Humphries [c1951] 143p. 21cm. [BX4410.P58M3] 53-11992
1. Poor School Sisters de Notre Dame. 2. Education of woman. I. Title.

MARY FRANCIS, Sister, P. C. 271.97
A right to be merry. New York, Sheed & Ward [1956] 212p. 21cm. [BX4362.M3] 56-9528
1. Poor Clares. 2. Monastic and religious life of women. I. Title.

MARY HESTER, Sister, 1909- 271.97
Canticle for the harvest, New York, Kenedy [1951] 196 p. 21 cm. Includes bibliographies. [BX4443.U6M3] 51-4895
1. School Sisters of Notre Dame. I. Title.

MARY VINCENTIA, Sister, S. N. D. 271.97
Their quiet tread; growth and spirit of the Congregation of the Sisters of Notre Dame through its first one hundred years, 1850-1950. Milwaukee, Bruce Press [1955] 555p. illus. 23cm. [BX4485.S49M3] 56-3367
1. Sisters of Notre Dame—Hist. I. Title.

MONK, Maria, d.ca.1850. 271'.97 B
Awful disclosures of the Hotel Dieu Nunnery of Montreal / Maria Monk. New York : Arno Press, 1977. 376 p. ; 21 cm. (Anti-movements in America) Maria Monk's personal narrative as related to T. Dwight. Has also been ascribed to J. J. Slocum and to W. K. Hoyte. Cf. New York herald, Aug. 12, 1836, p. 2, column 1; The Colophon, pt. 17, 1934; Sabin and Gagnon, P. Essai de bibl. can. Reprint of the rev. ed. published in 1836 for M. Monk by Hoisington & Trow, New York. [BX4216.M6A3 1977] 76-46089 ISBN 0-405-09962-2 : 21.00
1. Monk, Maria d. ca. 1850. 2. Nuns—Quebec (Province)—Montreal—Biography. 3. Montreal, Que.—Biography. I. Dwight, Theodore, 1796-1866. II. Slocum John Jay, 1803-1863. III. Hoyte, William K. IV. Title. V. Series.

MOUSEL, Eunice, Sister, 1896- 271.97
They have taken root; the Sisters of the Third Order of St. Francis of the Holy Family. New York, Bookman Associates [1954] 384p. illus. 24cm. [BX4515.S3M6] 54-13447
1. Sisters of the Third Order of St. Francis of the Holy Family. I. Title.

SAINT Joseph, Mother, 1756-1838. 271'.97 B
The memoirs of Mother Frances Blin de Bourdon, S.N.D. / [translated by Sister Mary Godfrey ... et al.]. Westminster, Md. : Christian Classics, [1975] xxxi, 299 p., [1] leaf of plates : ports. ; 23 cm. Bibliography: p. [297]-299. [BX4485.3.Z8B5813 1975] 75-311256 6.50
1. Billiart, Julie, 1751-1816. 2. Saint Joseph, Mother, 1756-1838. I. Title.

SCHLINK, Basilea. 271'.97 B
I found the key to the heart of God : my personal story / Basilea Schlink. Minneapolis : Bethany Fellowship, 1975. 412 p., [8] leaves of plates : ill. ; 18 cm. (Dimension books) Translation of Wie ich Gott erlebte. [BX8080.S248A3613 1975] 75-23920 ISBN 0-87123-239-1 pbk. : 2.95
1. Schlink, Basilea. I. Title.

SISTERS of the Holy Names of Jesus and Mary. Province of Oregon. 271.97
Gleanings of fifty years; the Sisters of the Holy Names of Jesus and Mary in the Northwest, 1859-1909. [Portland! Or. 1909] xvi, 230 p. illus., ports. 19 cm. [BX4499.Z607] 31-35764
1. Blanchet, Francis Norbert. Abp., 1795-1883. 2. Catholic Church in Oregon — Education. I. Title.

SOCIETY of the Holy Child Jesus. American Province. 271.97
Annals of the Society of the Holy Child Jesus, American Province, 1862-1882 [by] Mother M Mildred. Colldale, Pa., Bailey Print Co. [1950] 113 p. 23 cm. [BX4515.S83A7 1862/1882] 52-17587
I. Title.

VILLET, Barbara 271.97
Those whom God chooses, by Barbara and Grey Villet. New York, Viking [c.1963, 1966] 124p. illus., ports. 29cm. (Sudtio bk.) [BX4408.5.V5] 66-15417 6.95
1. Missionary Sisters of the Society of Mary. I. Villet, Grey, illus. II. Title.

VOTH, M. Agnes. 271'.97
Green olive branch, by M. Agnes Voth. Edited by M. Raymond. Illus. by M. Louise Frankenberger and M. Michelle Bullock. Chicago, Franciscan Herald Press [1973] xii, 351 p. illus. 21 cm. Includes bibliographical references. [BX4412.7.Z5U58] 74-166216
1. Olivetan Benedictine Sisters (U.S.) I. Title.

WORDLEY, Dick. 271'.97 B
No one dies alone / [by] Dick Wordley, with assisted creative research by Sister Jeanne Hyland and Frank S. Greenop. [Sydney] : Australian Creative Workshop for The Little Company of Mary, 1976. 244 p., [16] p. of col. plates : ill. ; 25 cm. [BX4390.Z8W67] 77-373919 ISBN 0-909246-33-5 : 14.95
1. Potter, Mary, 1847-1913. 2. Little Company of Mary—History. 3. Nuns—Australia—Biography. I. Hyland, Jeanne, joint author. II. Greenop, Frank Sydney, joint author. III. Title.

BURTON, Katherine (Kurz) 1890- 271.971
With God and two ducats; the story of the Corpus Christi Carmelites in three countries, 1908-1958. Chicago, Carmelite Press, 1958. 214p. illus. 21cm. [BX4310.C82B8] 58-13985
1. Carmelite Sisters of Corpus Christi. I. Title.

CATCH us those little foxes, 271.971
by a Carmelite nun. Chicago, H. Regnery Co. [1955] 95p. 20cm. [BX4322] 55-13818
1. Camelite nuns. I. A Carmelite nun.

EACH hour remains, 271.971
by a Carmelite nun. Westminster, Md. Newman Press, 1952. 232p. 20cm. [BX4210.E2 1952] 52-10391
1. Monasticism and religious orders for women. I. A Carmelite nun.

THE nun's answer, 271.971
by a Carmelite nun. Chicago, H. Regnery Co. [1958] 174p. 19cm. [BX4322.N8] 58-173
1. Carmelite nuns. I. A Carmelite nun.

LOWRY, Walker. 271'.971'024 B
Teresa de Jesus : a secular appreciation / Walker Lowry. [New York : Lowry], 1977. 91 p. ; 27 cm. 125 copies. [BX4700.T4L68] 77-150320
1. Teresa, Saint, 1515-1582. 2. Christian saints—Spain—Avila—Biography. 3. Avila, Spain—Biography. I. Title.

THERESE, Saint, 1873-1897. 271'.971'024 B
Story of a soul : the autobiography of St. Therese of Lisieux ; a new translation from the original manuscripts by John Clarke. Washington : ICS Publications, 1975. xviii, 288 p., [4] leaves of plates : ill. ; 22 cm. Translation of Histoire d'une ame. Includes bibliographical references. [BX4700.T5A5 1975] 74-12777 3.95
1. Therese, Saint, 1873-1897. I. Title.

THERESE, Saint, 1873-1897. 271'.971'024 B
Story of a soul : the autobiography of St. Therese of Lisieux / a new translation from the original manuscripts by John Clarke. 2d ed. Washington : ICS Publications, 1976. xviii, 299 p., [4] leaves of plates : ill. ; 22 cm. Translation of Histoire d'une ame. Includes bibliographical references and index. [BX4700.T5A5 1976] 76-43620 ISBN 0-9600876-4-8 pbk. : 4.95
1. Therese, Saint, 1873-1897. 2. Christian saints—France—Lisieux—Biography. 3. Lisieux, France—Biography. I. Title.

BOEHLKE, Frederick J 1926- 271.9710924 (B)
Pierre de Thomas, scholar, diplomat, and crusader [by] Frederick J. Boehlke, Jr. Philadelphia, University of Pennsylvania Press [1966] 360 p. 22 cm. Based on thesis, University of Pennsylvania. Bibliography: p. 328-352. [BX4700.P466B6 1966] 65-23579
1. Petrus Thomasius, Saint, 1305-1306. I. Title.

BOEHLKE, Frederick J., Jr., 1926- 271.9710924
Pierre de Thomas, scholar, diplomat, and crusader. Philadelphia, Univ. of Pa. Pr. [c.1966] 360p. 22cm. Bibl. [BX4700.P466B6] 65-23579 7.50
1. Petrus Thomasius, Saint, 1305-1366. I. Title.

GABRIELE DI SANTA MARIA MADDALENA, Father 271.9710924 (B)
From the Sacred Heart to the Trinity; [the spiritual itinerary of St. Teresa Margaret of the Sacred Heart] by Father Gabriel of St. Mary Magdalene. Translated by Sebastian V. Ramge. Milwaukee, Spiritual Life Press, 1965. 75 p. 22 cm. "The original French, Du sacre-Coeur a la Trinite, appeared in Ephemerides carmeliticae, vol. III (1949) pp. 337-296." [BX4700.T43G33] 65-24751
1. Teresa Margherita del Sacro Cuore di Gesu. Saint, 1747-1770. I. Title.

GABRIELE DI SANTA MARIA MADDALENA. Father 271.9710924
The way of prayer; a commentary on St. Teresa's "Way of perfection," by Father Gabriel of St. Mary Magdalen. Translated by the Carmel of Baltimore. Milwaukee, Spiritual Life Press, 1965. 143 p. 22 cm. [BX2179.T4C373] 65-24750
1. Teresa, Saint, 1515-1582. Camino de perfeccion. I. Title.

HAUGHTON, Rosemary. 271'.971'0924 (B)
Therese Martin; the story of St. Therese of Lisieux. [Rev. Ed.] New York, Macmillan [1967] 218 p. illus., ports. 22 cm. [BX4700.T5H3] 67-21249
1. Therese, Saint, 1873-1897. I. Title.

HAUGHTON, Rosemary 271'.971'0924(B)
Therese Martin; the story of St. Therese of Lisieux. [Rev. ed.] New York, Macmillan [1967] 218p. illus., ports. 22cm. [BX4700.T5H3 1967] 67-21349 4.50
1. Therese, Saint, 1873-1897. I. Title.

HAUGHTON, Rosemary. 271'.971'0924 B
Therese Martin; the story of St. Therese of Lisieux. [Rev. ed.] New York, Macmillan [1967] 218 p. illus., ports. 22 cm. A biography of the French woman who entered the Carmelite order at the age of fifteen, died of tuberculosis at twenty-four, and was canonized in 1925. [BX4700.T5H3 1967] 92 AC 68
1. Therese, Saint, 1873-1897. I. Title.

WUST, Louis. 271'.971'0924 B
Zelie Martin, mother of St. Therese, by Louis and Marjorie Wust. With an introd. by Martin J. O'Connor. [Boston?] St. Paul Editions [1969] 336 p. 22 cm. Bibliography: p. 331-336. [BX4705.M41235W8] 68-28103 4.00
1. Martin, Zelie Marie (Guerin) 1831-1877. 2. Therese, Saint, 1873-1897. I. Wust, Marjorie, joint author. II. Title.

ATLANTA. Our Lady of Perpetual Help Free Cancer Home. 271.972
A memoir of Mary Ann, by the Dominican nuns of Our Lady of Perpetual Help Home. Atlanta, Georgia. Introd. by Flannery O'Connor. New York, Farrar [c.1961] 134p. 61-13682 3.50
1. Long, Mary Ann, 1946-1959. I. O'Connor, Flannery, ed. II. Title.

BARRY, Mary Gerald. 271.972
The charity of Christ presses us; letters to her community [by] Mother Mary Gerald Barry, Mother general of the Sisters of St. Dominic, Congregation of the Most Holy Rosary, Adrian, Michigan. Milwaukee, Bruce Press [1962] 483 p. illus. 23 cm. (Catholic life publications) [BX4337.38.B3] 62-53408
1. Monastic and religious life of women. I. Dominican Sisters. Congregation of the Most Holy Rosary, Adrian, Mich. II. Title.

BURTON, Katherine (Kurz) 1890- 271.972
Make the way known; the history of the Dominican Congregation of St. Mary of the Springs, 1822 to 1957. New York, Farrar, Straus & Cudahy [1959] 291p. 22cm. [BX4337.3.B8] 59-11637
1. Dominican Sisters. Congregation of St. Mary of the Springs. I. Title.

GELFAND, Michael, ed. 271.972
Mother Patrick and her nursing sisters; based on extracts of letters and journals in Rhodesia of the Dominican Sisterhood, 1890-1901. Capetown, Juta [dist. Mystic, Conn., Verry, 1965] 281p. illus., map, ports. 23cm. [BV3625.R5G4] 65-9765 10.00
1. Dominican Missionary Sisters of the Most Sacred Heart of Jesus, Rhodesia. 2. Dominicans (Women) in Rhodesia. 3. Missions—Rhodesia. I. Patrick, Mother, 1863-1900. II. Title.

MCCARTY, Mary Eva, Sister. 271.972
The Sinsinawa Dominicans; outlines of twentieth century development, 1901-1949. Dubuque, Iowa, Printed by the Hoermann Press [1952] 591p. illus. 24cm. [BX4510.S93M2] 53-17039
1. Sisters of the Order of St. Dominic, Sinsinawa, Wis. I. Title.

MARY Thomas, Sister, O.P. 271'.972
The Lord may be in a hurry; the Congregation of Dominican Sisters of St. Catherine of Siena of Kenosha, Wisconsin. Milwaukee, Bruce Pub. Co. [1967] xvi, 219 p. illus., ports. 23 cm. Bibliography: p. 214. [BX4337.5.W5M3] 76-3213
1. Dominican Sisters. Congregation of St. Catherine of Siena, Kenosha, Wis. I. Title.

MARY ALOYSIUS, of Jesus Mother. 271.972
History of the Dominican Sisters of the Perpetual Rosary; commemorating the diamond jubilee of the Perpetual Rosary branch of the Dominican Order, 1880-1955. Union City, N.J. Perpetual Rosary Monastery 1959. 271p. illus. 24cm. [BX4331.8.M3] 59-48869
1. Congregation of the Dominican Sisters of the Perpetual Rosary. I. Title.

MARY FRANCIS LOUISE, Sister. 271.972
Maryknoll Sisters, a pictorial history. [1st ed.] New York, Dutton, 1962. 184p. illus. 28cm. [BV2300.M4M3] 62-14731
1. Maryknoll Sisters of St. Dominic. I. Title.

MARY JOSEPH, Sister, O.P. 271.972
Out of many hearts. Hawthorne, N.Y., Servants of Relief for Incurable Cancer [1965] 309p. illus., ports. 22cm. [BX4446.8.Z8M3] 65-3823 price unreported
1. Lathrop, Rose (Hawthorne) 1851-1926. 2. Servants of Relief for Incurable Cancer. I. Title.

MARY OF THE IMMACULATE HEART, Sister 1914- 271.972
Inside out [by] Sister Ann Edward [pseud.] Fresno, Calif., Acad. Lib. [c.1962] 170p. 22cm. 62-20461 4.00
I. Title.

GIORDANI, Igino, 1894- 271'.972'024 B
Saint Catherine of Siena, doctor of the Church / by Igino Giordani ; translated from the Italian by Thomas J. Tobin. Boston : St. Paul Editions, [1975] 258 p., [12] leaves of plates : ill. ; 24 cm. Translation of Vita di santa Caterina da Siena. Includes bibliographical references. [BX4700.C4G5613] 75-1624 5.95
1. Caterina da Siena, Saint, 1347-1380. I. Title.

COLLINS, Mary Lucille. 271'.972'074728
The vision is tremendous / Mary Lucille Collins. Sparkill, N.Y. : Dominican Sisters, c1975. 327 p., [6] leaves of plates : ill. ; 24 cm. Bibliography: p. 321-323. [BX4337.23.C64] 74-30986 5.00
1. Dominican Sisters. Congregation of Our Lady of the Rosary. I. Title.

WINTERBAUER, Thomas Aquinas. 271'.972'077356
Lest we forget; the first hundred years of the Dominican Sisters, Springfield, Illinois. Chicago, Adams Press [1973] xi, 385 p. illus. 24 cm. Cover title: Springfield Dominicans, 1873-1973. Includes bibliographical references. [BX4337.25.W56] 72-90886
1. Dominican Sisters. Congregation of Our Lady of the Sacred Heart, Springfield, Ill. I. Title. II. Title: Springfield Dominicans, 1873-1973.

MARY Alphonsus, Sister, O.SS.R. 271'.972'0924 B
St. Rose of Lima, patroness of the Americas. St. Louis, Herder [1968] xiii, 304 p. 21 cm. (Cross and crown series of spirituality, no. 36) [BX4700.R6M27] 68-8925 5.50
1. Rosa, of Lima, Saint, 1586-1617. I. Title. II. Series.

THERESE Catherine, Sister, O.P. 271'.972'0924 B
An emerging woman [by] S. Therese Catherine. Staten Island, N.Y., Alba House [1970] xiv, 97 p., illus., coat of arms, geneal. table. 20 cm. Includes bibliographical references. [BX4705.W66T5] 71-129172 2.95
1. Witzlhofer, Josepha, 1817-1864. I. Title.

CRAWFORD, Eugene Joseph, 1900- 271.9720974721
The Daughters of Dominic on Long Island, the Brooklyn Sisters of Saint Dominic the history of the American Congregation of the Holy Cross, Sisters of the Third Order of Saint Dominic of the Diocese of Brooklyn. With a foreword by Thomas E. Molloy. New York, Benziger Bros, 1938-53. 2v. illus., ports. 24cm. Bibliography: v.1. p.372-376; v.2,p. 291-312. [BX4344.B7C7] 38-14463
1. Sisters of the Order of St. Dominic, Brooklyn. I. Title.

MCCARTHY, Mary Augustine. 271'.972'09931
Star in the South: the centennial history of the New Zealand Dominican Sisters. Dunedin, St Dominic's Priory, 1970. 341 p. illus., ports. 22 cm. Bibliography: p. [330]-331. [BX4343.N45M3] 76-865074 5.25
1. Dominicans (Women) in New Zealand. I. Title.

BURTON, Katherine (Kruz) 1890- 271.973
The Bernardines, by Katherine Burton. Villanova, Pa., Maryview Press [1964] x, 229 p. illus., map (on lining papers) ports. 24 cm. [BX4284.B8] 64-24724
1. Bernardines (Franciscan Nuns) 2. Bernadines (Franciscan Nuns) — Missions. I. Title.

BURTON, Katherine (Kurz) 271.973
1890-
Cry jubilee! Allegany, N. Y., Sisters of St. Francis of the Third Order Regular [1960] 227p. illus. 22cm. [BX4520.2.B8] 60-51670
1. Sisters of the Third Order Regular of St. Francis of Allegany, New York. I. Title.

FELICIAN Sisters of the 271.973
Order of St. Francis. Province of Buffalo.
The golden harvest (Zlote zniwa); a memoir of the fifty years of the Immaculate Heart of Mary Province of the Felician Sisters, O. S. F., 1900-1950. Buffalo, 1950. xxxiv, 190 p. (p. 165-190 advertisements) illus., ports. 27 cm. English and Polish. [BX4350.F4A26] 51-1387
I. Title.

FELICITY, Sister 271.973
Barefoot journey; autobiography of a Poor Clare. Illus. by Brother Placid. Staten Island, N.Y., Alba [1964, c.1963] xi, 169p. illus. 21cm. 63-20225 3.50
1. Colettines. I. Title.

FRANCISCAN women : 271'.973
the dynamics of Christian fidelity. Chicago : Franciscan Herald Press, c1975. 57 p. ; 18 cm. [BX4361.F7] 75-41389 ISBN 0-8199-0593-3 : 0.65
1. Poor Clares—Congresses.

KENDRICK, Thomas 271'.973
Downing. Sir
Mary of Agreda: the life and legend of a Spanish nun [by] T. D. Kendrick. London, Routledge & K. Paul, 1967. xii, 178p. 8 plates (incl. ports., facsims.), diagrs. 22cm. Bibl. [BX4705.M3255K4] (B) 67-109481 4.50
1. Maria, de Jesus de Agreda, Mother, 1602-1665. I. Title.
Distributed by Fernhill House, 162 E. 23 St., New York, N. Y. 10010.

LUDWIG, Mileta, Sister. 271.973
A chapter of Franciscan history; the Sisters of the Third Order of Saint Francis of Perpetual Adoration, 1849-1949. New York, Bookman Associates [1950] 455 p. illus. ports. map. 24 cm. Bibliographical footnotes. "Author's commentary as sources and procedures". p.[443]-446. [BX4515.S33L83] 50-10952
1. Sisters of the Third Order of St. Francis of the Perpetual Adoration. I. Title.

MARY FRANCIS, Sister 271.973
A right to be merry. New York, All Saints [1962, c.1956] 180p. (AS216) .50 pap.,
1. Monastic and religious life of women. 2. Poor Clares—Order. 3. Spiritual life—Catholic authors. I. Title.

MARY FRANCIS BORGIA, 271.973
Sister, 1922-
He sent two; the story of the bargaining of the School Sisters of St. Francis. Bruce in coop. with Seraphic Pr. [dist.] Milwaukee, Bruce [c.] 1965. xiii, 224p. illus., ports. 24cm. Bibl. [BX4446.M3] 65-6845 5.00
1. Alexia, Mutter, 1839-1918. 2. Alfons, Mutter, d. 1929. 3. School Sisters of St. Francis, Milwaukee, Wis. I. Title.

MAZURE, M. Adeline. 271'.973
One step and then another; Franciscan Sisters of the Sacred Heart, 1866-1971 [by] M. Adeline Mazure. Chicago, Franciscan Herald Press [1973] xxiii, 136 p. illus. 22 cm. Includes bibliographical references. [BX4358.5.M39] 73-10182 ISBN 0-8199-0455-4
1. Franciscan Sisters of the Sacred Heart. I. Title.

NUGENT, Rosamond. 271.973
Poor little millionaires. [1st ed.] New York, Pageant Press [1959] 67p. illus. 21cm. [BX4360.C5N8] 59-12300
1. Franciscan Sisters of Christian Charity, Manitowoc, Wis. I. Title.

FAHRNER, Mary, 271'.973'024 B
1904-
Way of the cross—where it led me : the story of a Franciscan nun / Mary Fahrner. Mountain View, Calif. : Pacific Press Pub. Association, c1977. 56 p., [2] leaves of plates : ports ; 18 cm. [BX6189.F33A38] 76-5072 pbk. : 0.75
1. Fahrner, Mary, 1904- 2. Converts, Seventh-Day Adventist—United States—Biography. 3. Ex-nuns—United States—Biography. I. Title.

FAHRNER, Mary, 271'.973'024 B
1904-
Way of the cross—where it led me : the story of a Franciscan nun / Mary Fahrner. Mountain View, Calif. : Pacific Press Pub. Association, c1977. 56 p., [2] leaves of plates : ports ; 18 cm. [BX6189.F33A38] 76-5072 pbk. : 0.75
1. Fahrner, Mary, 1904- 2. Converts, Seventh-Day Adventist—United States—Biography. 3. Ex-nuns—United States—Biography. I. Title.

HARDICK, Lothar. 271'.973'024 B
He leads, I follow; the life of Mother Maria Theresia Bonzel, foundress of the Sisters of St. Francis of Perpetual Adoration. Translated from the German by M. Honora Hau and M. Clarahilda Fischer. Colorado Springs, Sisters of St. Francis of Perpetual Adoration [1971] xi, 344 p. port. 23 cm. [BX4519.Z8H37] 72-177750 8.50
1. Bonzel, Maria Theresia, Mother, 1830-1905. 2. Sisters of the Third order of St. Francis of the Perpetual Adoration. I. Title.

MARY Francis, 271'.973'024 B
Mother, 1921-
A right to be merry. Chicago, Franciscan Herald Press [1973] 180 p. 17 cm. Reprint of the 1956 ed. published by Sheed & Ward, New York. [BX4362.M3 1973] 73-6850 1.95
1. Poor Clares. 2. Monastic and religious life of women. I. Title.

WILLMANN, Agnes. 271'.973'024 B
Everywhere people waiting; the life of Helen de Chappotin de Neuville (Mother Mary of the Passion) 1839-1904, foundress of the Franciscan Missionaries of Mary. North Quincy, Mass., Christopher Pub. House [1973] 376 p. port. 23 cm. Bibliography: p. 375-376. [BX4351.Z8W44] 72-94708 ISBN 0-8158-0294-3 5.95
1. Maria de Passione, Mere, 1839-1904. I. Title.

BACKES, James 271.9730924(B)
Adam.
If the grain does not die: a portrait of the life of the servant of God, Mother Mary Rose Flesch, foundress of the Franciscan Sisters of the Blessed Virgin Mary of the Angels. Translated by Isidore A. McCarthy. Chicago, Franciscan Herald Press [c1965] 61 p. illus. 18 cm. [BX4355.Z8B313] 65-16671
1. Flesche, Mary Rose, 1824-1906. 2. Franciscan Sisters of Our Lady of the Angels. I. Title.

NUGENT, Rosamond. 271'.973'0924 B
Buried wheat. Milwaukee, Bruce Publishing Co. [1967] vii, 165 p. 22 cm. Bibliography: p. 161-162. [BX4354.N8] 70-4822
1. Franciscan Sisters of Christian Charity, Manitowoc, Wis.—History. 2. Gabriel, Mother, 1842-1914. I. Title.

ROGGEN, Heribert. 271'.973'0924 B
The spirit of St. Clare. Translated by Paul Joseph Oligny. [Chicago] Franciscan Herald Press [1971] xiii, 93 p. 21 cm. Translation from German ed. (1970) of the work first published in Dutch under title: Franciscaans evangelische levensstijl volgens de H. Clara van Assisi. Includes bibliographical references. [BX4700.C6R6413] 74-123595 ISBN 0-8199-0410-4 3.95
1. Clara, of Assisi, Saint, d. 1253. I. Title.

MARY GERTRUDE, Sister, 271.974
O. S. U., 1899-
Ursulines in training; a study based upon the counsels of Saint Angela Merici. Toledo [1956] 172p. illus. 22cm. [BX4542.M25] 57-15266
1. Ursulines. I. Angela Merici, Saint, 1474-1540. II. Title.

HACHARD, Marie 271'.974'024 B
Madeleine.
The letters of Marie Madeleine Hachard, 1727-28 / translated by Myldred Masson Costa. 1st ed. New Orleans : [s.n.], 1974. 66 p. ; 19 cm. Translation of Relation du voyage des dames religieuses Ursulines de Rouen a la Nouvelle Orleans. On spine: Letters of an Ursuline, 1727-1728. [BX4705.H13A413 1974] 74-193362
1. Hachard, Marie Madeleine. 2. New Orleans—History. I. Title: Letters of an Ursuline, 1727-1728.

SALVATORI, Filippo 271'.974'024 B
Maria.
Angela. [Translated] by Marie di Mercurio. A translation from the original Italian: Vita della Santa Madre Angela Merici, by Filippo Maria Salvatori. Saint Martin, Ohio, Ursulines of Brown County [1970] xv, 238 p. illus., coat of arms. 24 cm. Includes bibliographies. [BX4700.A45S3313] 72-274482
1. Angela Merici, Saint, 1474-1540. I. Title.

JOHNSTON, Sue 271'.974'0764139
Mildred Lee, 1900-1970.
Builders by the sea; history of the Ursuline community of Galveston, Texas [by] S. M. Johnston. [1st ed.] New York, Exposition Press [1971] 286 p. illus. 22 cm. (An Exposition-testament book) [BX4544.G34J64 1971] 78-164863 ISBN 0-682-47341-3 7.50
1. Ursulines in Galveston. I. Title.

[WILLETT, Franciscus] 271.9740924
The promise to Angela; the story of St. Angela Merici [by] Pat McKern. Illus. by Suzanne Atkinson. Valatie, N. Y., Holy Cross Pr. [1966] 82p. illus. 23cm. [BX4700.A45W5] 66-8606 2.50
1. Angela Merici, Saint, 1474-1540.—Juvenile literature. 2. Ursulines—Juvenile literature. I. Title.

BURTON, Katherine (Kruz) 271.975
1890-
Bells on two rivers; the history of the Sisters of the Visitation of Rock Island, Illinois [by] Katherine Burton. Milwaukee,Burce Pub. Co. [1965] viii, 118 p. illus. 23 cm. [BX4549.R6M63] 66-6381
1. Rock Island, Ill. Monastery of the Visitation. I. Title.

NEW York. Monastery of 271.975
the Visitation.
Story of a monastery; the story of the monastery of cloistered Visitandines of Riverdale, Bronx, N.Y., December 18, 1864 -- December 18, 1964. with a foreword by Francis Cardinal Spellman. New York, 1964. xviii, 146 p. illus. 21 cm. Bibliography: p. 145-146. [BX4549.N5M6] 64-22783
I. Title.

A. Sister of Saint 271.976
Joseph.
Sisters of Saint Joseph of Rochester, by a Sister of Saint Joseph. [Rochester? N.Y.] 1950. vii, 163 p. illus., port. 20 cm. Bibliography: p. 159-160. [BX4490.R6S5] 50-12942
1. Sisters of St. Joseph of Carondelet. Rochester, N.Y. I. Title.

DOUGHERTY, Dolorita 271.976
Marie, 1909-
Sisters of St. Joseph of Carondelet, by Sister Dolorita Marie Dougherty [and others] With a foreword by Joseph Cardinal Ritter. St. Louis, B. Herder Book Co., 1966. x, 509 p. illus., map, ports. 24 cm. Bibliography: p. 487-493. [BX4489.6.C3S5] 66-17097
1. Sisters of St. Joseph of Carondelet. I. Title.

IMMACULATA, Sister, 1913- 271.976
Like a swarm of bees: Sisters of Saint Joseph of Buffalo. Designs by Sister M. Dorothy. Buffalo, Mount Saint Joseph [1957] 213p. 22cm. Includes bibliography. [BX4490.B8 I5] 58-20660
1. Sisters of St. Joseph, Buffalo. I. Title.

MARIA HESTKA, Sister, 271.976
1883-
Sisters of St. Joseph of Philadelphia: a century of growth and development, 1847-1947. Westminster, Md., Newman Press, 1950. xii, 380 p. illus., ports. 22 cm. Secular name: Mary Elizabeth Logue. Bibliography: p. [297]-318. "Translations of Mother St. John Fourrier": p. 359. [BX4490.P5M3] 50-8164
1. Sisters of St. Joseph, Philadelphia. I. Title.

MEANY, Mary Ignatius 271.976
By railway or rainbow; a history of the Sisters of St. Joseph of Brentwood. Brentwood, N.Y., Pine Pr., 1964. xii, 336p. illus., map (on lining papers) ports. 24cm. Bibl. 63-23383 price unreported
1. Sisters of St. Joseph, Brentwood, N.Y. I. Title.

MEDAILLE, Jean Pierre, 271.976
1610-1669.
The spiritual legacy of John Peter Medaille, S. J.; an intercongregational publication of the Sisters of St. Joseph. [Paterson? N. J.] 1959. 95p. 22cm. 'Members of only ten of the twenty-one congregations which stemmed from the original foundation of the Sisters of St. Joseph at Carondelet constituted the 'working committee.' [BX4488.M4] 60-17893
1. Sisters of St. Joseph. I. Sisters of St. Joseph of Carondelet. II. Title.

SISTERS of St. Joseph of 271.976
Carondelet, by Sister Dolorita Marie Dougherty [others] foreword by Joseph Cardinal Ritter. St. Louis. B. Herder. 1966. x, 509p. illus. map ports. 24cm. Bibl. [BX4489.6.C3S5] 66-17097 7.00
1. Sisters of St. Joseph of Carondelet. I. Dougherty, Dolorita Marie, 1909-

SISTERS of Saint Joseph, 271.976
Wichita, Kan.
Sisters of Saint Joseph of Wichita, Kansas, 1888-1963. [Wichita, 1963?] 1 v. (unpaged) illus., ports. 25 cm. Cover title. [BX4489.6.W5S5] 66-85343
I. Title.

SISTERS OF ST. JOSEPH. 271.976
Return to the fountainhead; addresses at the tercentenary celebration of the Sisters of St. Joseph, Le Puy, France, July 17, 18, 19. 20, 1950. by His Eminence, Cardinal Gerlier, and other French churchmen. En amont, in an English edition by the Sisters of St. Joseph of Carondelet, Fontbonne College, St. Louis. Translators and editors: Sister Mary Berchmans Fournier [and others] St. Louis, Sisters of St. Joseph of Carondelet, 1952. 143p. illus. 21cm. Includes bibliography. [BX4487.S5E53] 53-19922
1. Sisters of St. Joseph. 2. Sisters of St. Joseph of Carondelet. I. Title.

VIDULICH, Dorothy. 271'.976 B
Peace pays a price : a study of Margaret Anna Cusack, the nun of Kenmare, foundress of the Sisters of St. Joseph of Peace / by Sister Dorothy Vidulich ; photos. by Ray Gora. Englewood Cliffs, N.J. : Center for Peace and Justice, 1975. 80, [3] p. : ill. ; 23 cm. Bibliography: p. [82] [BX4490.5.Z8C878] 75-32628 pbk. : 4.95
1. Cusack, Mary Francis, 1829 or 30-1899. 2. Sisters of St. Joseph of Newark. I. Title.

QUIN, Eleanor. 271'.976'0924 B
Last on the menu, by Sister Eleanor Quin (Sister M. Vincent dePaul, C.S.J.) Englewood Cliffs, N.J., Prentice-Hall [1969] 182 p. 22 cm. Autobiographical. [BX4210.Q5] 78-80997 ISBN 0-13-524033-6 4.95
1. Nuns—Correspondence, reminiscences, etc. I. Title.

KANE, Kathleen 271'.977'094
Dunlop.
Adventure in faith : the Presentation sisters / [by] Kathleen Dunlop Kane. [Melbourne] : Congregation of the Presentation of the Blessed Virgin Mary, 1974. xi, 303, xxix p. : ill., diagrs., facsims., ports. ; 25 cm. Includes index. [BX4511.Z5 A84] 75-327894 ISBN 0-909246-05-X
1. Presentation Sisters in Victoria. 2. Victoria, Australia—Religion. I. Title.

O'CALLAGHAN, 271'.977'094
Rosaria.
Flame of love; a biography of Nano Nagle, foundress of the Presentation Order, 1718-1784. Milwaukee, Bruce Press [1960] 192p. illus. 23cm. (Catholic life publications) Includes bibliography. [BX4511.Z8N3] 61-1445
1. Nagle, Nano, 1718-1784. 2. Sisters of the Presentation of the Blessed Virgin Mary—Hist. I. Title.

BURTON, Katherine (Kurz) 271.979
1890-
Lily and sword and crown; the history of the congregation of the Sisters of St. Casimir, Chicago, Illinois, 1907-1957. Milwaukee, Bruce Press [1958] 178p. illus. 23cm. (Catholic life publications) [BX4486.5.B85] 59-4019
1. Sisters of St. Casimir. I. Title.

BUTKOVICH, Anthony, 271'.979 B
1921-
Anima eroica; St. Brigitte of Sweden. [Los Angeles?] Ecumenical Foundation of America, 1968. vii, 87 p. illus., ports. 27 cm. Sequel: Iconography: St. Birgitta of Sweden. Bibliography: p. 87. [BX4700.B6B8] 68-26139
1. Birgitta, Saint, of Sweden, d. 1373. I. Title.

BUTKOVICH, Anthony, 271'.979 B
1921-
Iconography: St. Birgitta of Sweden. [Los Angeles?] Ecumenical Foundation of America, 1969. viii, 102 p. illus., ports. (part col.) 27 cm. Sequel to Anima eroica. Sequel: The revelations. Bibliography: p. 101-102. [BX4700.B6B83] 72-107679
1. Birgitta, Saint, of Sweden, d. 1373. I. Title.

BUTKOVICH, Anthony, 271'.979 B
1921-
Revelations; Saint Birgitta of Sweden. Los Angeles, Ecumenical Foundation of America, 1972. xvi, 110 p. illus. 28 cm. Bibliography: p. 108-110. [BX4700.B6B85] 74-187358
1. Birgitta, Saint, of Sweden, d. 1373. I. Title.

CAMPBELL, Stephanie. 271'.979
Chosen for peace; the history of the Benedictine Sisters of Elizabeth, New Jersey. [Paterson, N.J., Printed by Saint Anthony Guild Press, 1968] ix, 246 p. illus., ports. 24 cm. Includes bibliographical references. [BX4278.E4C3] 68-4798
1. Benedictine Sisters of Elizabeth, New Jersey—History. I. Title.

DAUGHTERS of St. Paul 271.979
Christ is here; the life of the Daughters of St. Paul reflected in pictures and prose [Boston] St. Paul Eds. [dist. Author, c.1964] [87]p. illus., map, ports. 28cm. 64-21601 2.00; 1.00 pap.,
1. Daughters of St. Paul. I. Title.

DAUGHTERS of St. Paul. 271'.979
Communicators for Christ; the story of the Daughters of St. Paul in the U.S.A. [Boston] St. Paul Editions [1972] 360 p. illus. 22 cm. [BX4334.Z5U5] 67-31595
1. Daughters of St. Paul in the United States. I. Title.

DAUGHTERS of St. Paul 271.979
Women of faith; a profile of Mother Thecla Merlo, confoundress of the Daughters of St.

Paul. [Boston, Author, 1966, c.1965] 226p. illus. 21cm. [BX4334.Z8A5] 65-29133 3.00, 2.00 pap.,
1. Merlo, Thecla, 1894-1964. 2. Daughters of St. Paul. I. Title.

DUDINE, M. Frederica. 271'.979
The castle on the hill; centennial history of the Convent of the Immaculate Conception, Ferdinand, Indiana, 1867-1967 [by] Sister M. Frederica Dudine. Milwaukee, Bruce Pub. Co., 1967. xvi, 330 p. illus., maps, ports. 24 cm. (American Benedictine Academy. Historical studies, no. 5) Bibliography: p. 316-319. [BX4278.F4D8] 67-28890
1. Ferdinand, Ind. Convent of the Immaculate Conception. I. Title. II. Series: American Benedictine Academy, Latrobe, Pa. Historical studies, no. 5

DUDINE, M. Frederica. 271'.979
The castle on the hill; centennial history of the Convent of the Immaculate Conception, Ferdinand, Indiana, 1867-1967 [by] Sister M. Frederica Dudine. Milwaukee, Bruce Pub. Co., 1967. xvi, 330 p. illus., maps, ports. 24 cm. (American Benedictine Academy. Historical studies, no. 5) Bibliography: p. 316-319. [BX4278.F4D8] 67-28890
1. Ferdinand, Ind. Convent of the Immaculate Conception. I. Title. II. Series: American Benedictine Academy, Latrobe, Pa. Historical studies, no. 5.

DUFFY, Consuela Marie. 271'.979
Katharine Drexel; a biography. With an introd. by Richard Cardinal Cushing. Philadelphia, P. Reilly Co. [c1966] 434 p. ports. 23 cm. Bibliographical references included in "Footnotes" (p. 400-421) [BX4705.D755D8] 66-29382
1. Drexel, Katharine, 1858-1955. I. Title.

FITTS, Mary Pauline. 271'.979 B
Hands to the needy; Blessed Marguerite d'Youville, apostle to the poor. Garden City, N.Y., Doubleday, 1971. xiii, 332 p. 21 cm. Bibliography: p. 323-326. [BX4705.Y6F5 1971] 79-182572
1. Youville, Marie Marguerite (Dufrost de La Jemmerais) d', 1701-1771. 2. Grey nuns. I. Title.

HAMILTON, Elizabeth, 1906- 271.979 B
Heloise. [1st ed. in the U.S.] Garden City, N. Y., Doubleday, 1967. 234 p. map (on lining papers) 22 cm. Bibliography: p. [213] Bibliographical references included in "Notes" (p. [215]-219) [BX4705.H463H3 1967] 67-10380
1. Heloise, 1101-1164.

HILPISCH, Stephanus, 1894- 271.979
History of Benedictine nuns. Translated by M. Joanne Muggli, edited by Leonard J. Doyle. Collegeville, Minn., St. John's Abbey Press, 1958. 122p. illus. 23cm. Includes bibliography. [BX4276.H513] 60-37396
1. Benedictine nuns—Hist. 2. Monasticism and religious orders for women. I. Title.

JOSEPH, Eleanor, Sister, S.P. 271'.979 B
Call to courage; a story of Mother Theodore Guerin. Illustrated by Carolyn Lee Jagodits. Notre Dame, Dujarie Press [1968] 94 p. port. 22 cm. [BX4705.G65J6] 68-23381
1. Guerin, Theodore, Mother, 1798-1856. I. Title.

KALKSTEIN, Teresa. 271'.979 (B)
Witness to the resurrection; the servant of God, Mother Celine Borzecka, foundress of the Congregation, Sisters of the Resurrection of our Lord Jesus Christ. Translated by Sisters Celine and Mary Gertrude Maleska. Castleton-on-Hudson, N. Y., Sisters of the Resurrection [1967] xiii, 212 p. illus., facsim., ports. 23 cm. "An enlarged version of the first edition, written by the author, in Polish and Italian." Bibliography: p. 211-212. [BX4705.B675K33] 67-29594
1. Borzecka, Celina, 1833-1913. I. Title.

KALKSTEIN, Teresa. 271'.979 B
Witness to the resurrection; the servant of God, Mother Celine Bőrzecka, foundress of the Congregation, Sisters of the Resurrection of our Lord Jesus Christ. Translated by Sisters Celine and Mary Gertrude Maleska. Castleton-on-Hudson, N.Y., Sisters of the Resurrection [1967] xiii, 212 p. illus., facsim., ports. 23 cm. "An enlarged version of the first edition, written by the author, in Polish and Italian." Bibliography: p. 211-212. [BX4705.B675K33] 67-29594
1. Borzocka, Celina, 1833-1913. I. Title.

MCNAMEE, Mary Dominica. 271.979
Willamette interlude. Palo Alto, Calif., Pacific Books [1959] 302 p. illus. 23 cm. Includes bibliography. [BX4485.3.M33] 59-9810
1. Sisters of Notre Dame de Namur. I. Title.

MARIA Alma, Sister, 1887- 271'.979
Sisters, Servants of the Immaculate Heart of Mary, 1845-1967, by Mother Maria Alma. Introd. by John Cardinal Krol. Lancaster, Pa., Dolphin Press, 1967. xiv, 463 p. illus., ports. 24 cm. Bibliographical footnotes. [BX4522.M3] 67-8841
1. Sisters, Servants of the Immaculate Heart of Mary—History.

MARIA DEL REY, Sister 271.979
No two alike: those Maryknoll sisters. Garden City, N.Y., Doubleday [1966, c.1965] 199p. illus. 18cm. (Echo bks., E30) [BV2300.M4M27] .85 pap.,
1. Maryknoll Sisters of St. Dominic. 2. Missionary stories. I. Title.

MARIA DEL REY, Sister 271.979
No two alike: those Maryknoll Sisters! New York, Dodd [c.1965] x, 240p. illus. 24cm. [BV2300.M4M27] 65-23534 5.00
1. Maryknoll Sisters of St. Dominic. 2. Missionary stories. I. Title.

MARIE Jean de Pathmos, Sister. 271.979
A history of the Sisters of Saint Anne. Translated from the French by Sister Marie Anne Eva. [1st American ed.] New York, Vantage Press [1962- c1961- v. illus. 21 cm. Contents.Contents.—v. 1. 1850-1900. Includes bibliography. [BX4486.4.M3] 61-14779
1. Sisters of Saint Ann. 2. Marie Anne, Mother, 1809-1890. I. Marie Anne Eva, Sister, tr.

MARY Bernadita, Sister, S.A.C., 1932- 271'.979
A house built on rock, by Sister Mary Bernadita [and] Sister Mary Anthony. Philadelphia, Dorrance [1967] 136 p. illus., ports. 21 cm. Bibliography: p. 134. [BX4415.8.M3] 67-13052
1. Pallottine Missionary Sisters. I. Mary Anthony, Sister, S.A.C., joint author. II. Title.

MARY Paul, Sister. 271'.979
An American nun in Taiwan [by] Sister Mary Paul with C. Edmund Fisher. [1st ed.] Garden City, N.Y., Doubleday, 1967. 240 p. illus., ports. 22 cm. [BX4327.5.M3] 67-11150
1. Chung-hua sheng mu hui. I. Fisher, C. Edmund, joint author. II. Title.

MARY ELEANOR, Mother, 1903- 271.979
His by choice; the Sisters of the Holy Child Jesus. With a pref. by Fulton J. Sheen. Photos. by Thomas C. Walsh. Milwaukee, Bruce Press [c1960] 115p. illus. 22cm. (Catholic life publications) [BX4527.M35] 61-3446
1. Society of the Holy Child Jesus. I. Title.

MARY PAULINE, Sister 271.979
God wills it; centenary story of the Sisters of St. Louis. With a pref. by Rev. Dr. O'Callaghan. Fresno, Calif., Academy Guild Press [1960] x, 320p. illus. 23cm. (bibl. footnotes) 60-9247 6.00
1. Sisters of St. Louis. I. Title.

MASTERSON, Mary Adrian. 271'.979 B
Smiling Maria: Blessed Maria de Mattias; the girl who gave everything for love. Illustrator: Margaret Holt Griffith. Ruma, Ill., Sisters Adorers of the Most Precious Blood [1966] 74 p. illus. (part col.) 21 cm. A brief biography of Maria de Mattias whose schools in nineteenth-century Italy made many friends for the Catholic Church. [BX4700.M3984M37] 92 70-20344
1. Mattias, Maria de, 1805-1866. I. Griffith, Margaret Holt, illus. II. Title.

MEAD, Jude. 271'.979 B
Dove in the cleft; the life of Mother Mary Crucified of Jesus, C.P., the first Passionist nun, 1713-1787. [1st ed.] New York, Exposition Press [1971] 248 p. port. 21 cm. (An Exposition-testament book) Bibliography: p. [235]-241. [BX4705.M32545143M4] 78-156078 ISBN 0-682-47263-8 6.00
1. Maria Crocifissa di Gesu, madre, 1713-1787. I. Title.

MULLER, Gerald Francis, 1927- 271'.979 B
Diamond in the dust; a story of blessed Therese Couderc, by Brother Roberto. With front. by Carolyn Lee Jagodits. Notre Dame [Ind.] Dujarie Press [1968] 94 p. port. 22 cm. The life of the nineteenth-century French nun who founded the order called the Religious of the Cenacle which provides places of retreat for women. [BX4705.C7794M8] 92 68-23380
1. Couderc, Therese, 1805-1885—Juvenile literature. I. Title.

NABER, Vera 271.979
With all devotedness; chronicles of the Sisters of St. Agnes, Fond du Lac, Wisconsin. New York, Kenedy [c.1959] vi, 312p. illus. 22cm. 60-5904 3.95
1. Sisters of St. Agnes, Fond du Lac. I. Salvation II. Title.

NABER, Vera, 1885- 271.979
With all devotedness; chronicles of the Sisters of St. Agnes, Fond du Lac, Wisconsin. New York, Kenedy [1959] 312p. illus. 22cm. [BX4486.3.N3] 60-5904
1. Sisters of St. Agnes, Fond du Lac. I. Title.

PASSERO, Louise. 271'.979 B
Hands for others. [Boston] St. Paul Editions [1971] 78 p. 18 cm. [BX4700.M43P37] 72-183440 0.50
1. Mazzarello, Maria Domenica, Saint, 1837-1881. 2. Daughters of Mary, Help of Christians. I. Title.

RICHMOND. Monastery of the Visitation. 271'.979
Sentinel on the hill: Monte Maria and one hundred years. [Richmond, 1966] xii, 220 p. illus. 19 x 27 cm. [BX4549.R5M6] 67-6609
I. Title.

ROBERTO, Brother, 1927- 271'.979
Diamond in the dust; a story of blessed Therese Couderc. Frontispiece by Carolyn Lee Jagodits. Notre Dame, Dujarie [1968] 94p. port. 22cm. [BX4705.C7794R6] (B) 68-23380 2.75
1. Couderc, Therese, 1805-1885. I. Title.

SISTERS Marianites of Holy Cross. Louisiana Province. 271.979
Marianite centennial in Louisiana, 1848-1948. New Orleans, Marianites of Holy Cross [1948] 330 p. illus. 23 cm. [BX4448.5.A44] 60-23552
1. Sisters Marianites of Holy Cross — Hist. I. Title.

SISTERS of Saints Cyril and Methodius. 271.979
Adveniat regnum tuum. Sisters of SS. Cyril and Methodius, Danville, Pennsylvania, 1909-1959. [Danville 1959] 80 p. illus. 32 cm. "Golden jubilee program [Sept. 7, 1959]" inserted. [BX4491.8.A42] 60-23459
I. Title.

TOWNE, Carola, 1897- 271'.979 B
Keys and pedals; an autobiography, by Sister M. Carola Towne, C.S.A. Philadelphia, Dorrance [1972] 173 p. 22 cm. [BX4705.T735A3] 72-81634 ISBN 0-8059-1719-5 4.95
I. Title.

TURLEY, Mary Immaculata. 271'.979 B
Mother Margaret Mary Healy-Murphy; a biography. San Antonio, Tex., Naylor Co. [1969] xviii, 228 p. illus., maps (on lining paper), ports. 22 cm. Bibliography: p. 219-223. [BX4705.H383T87] 74-92518 7.95
1. Healy-Murphy, Margaret Mary, 1833-1907. I. Title.

VAN Zeller, Hubert, 1905- 271.979
The Benedictine nun, her story and aim. Baltimore, Helicon [1965] 271 p. 22 cm. Bibliography: p. 265-266. [BX4276.V3] 65-15036
1. Benedictine nuns. I. Title.

VAN ZELLER, Huber, 1905- 271.979
The Benedictine nun, her story and aim. Helicon [dist. New York, Taplinger, c.1965] 271p. 22cm. Bibl. [BX4276.V3] 65-15036 4.95 bds.,
1. Benedictine nuns. I. Title.

ZIMMERMANN, Mary Theola. 271'.979
As a magnet; life of Mother Caroline, S.S.N.D. illustrated by Jo Polseno. New York, Regina Press [1967] xi, 129 p. illus. 21 cm. [BX4705.C315Z5] 67-28216
1. Caroline, Mother, 1824-1892. I. Title.

MEYERS, Bertrande. 271'.979'0924 B
Always springtime. Saint Louis, Marillac Towers Press [1969] 174 p. 22 cm. [BX4705.S869M4] 79-102726
1. Sullivan, Catherine, 1886-1969. I. Title.

SCHUSTER, Mary Faith 271.9790978136
The meaning of the mountain; a history of the first century at Mount St. Scholastica. Helicon [dist. New York Taplinger c.1963] 329p. illus., ports., 23cm. (Benedictine studies, 6) Bibl. 63-19401 6.00
1. Mount Scholastica Convent, Atchison, Kan. 2. Mount St. Scholastica College, Atchison, Kan. I. Title. II. Series.

ALMEDINGEN, Martha Edith, 1898- 271.98
An unbroken unity; a memoir of Grand-Duchess Serge of Russia, 1864-1918. London, Bodley Head [Westminster, Md. 21157, Canterbury Pr., Court Place, 1965, c.1964] 144p. illus., ports. 23cm. [DK254.E6A7] 66-2779 3.95 bds.,
1. Elizabeth, Grand Duchess of Russia, 1864-1918. I. Title.

MARY HILARY, Sister. 271.98
Ten decades of praise; the story of the Community of Saint Mary during its first century, 1865-1965. Racine, Wis., DeKoven Found. [1967, c.1965] 226, [8]p. illus., maps, ports. 21cm. Bibl. [BX5973.S47M3] [i71.98] 65-4002 1.65 pap.,
1. Sisterhood of St. Mary. I. Title.

MARY HILARY, Sister. 271.98
Ten decades of praise; the story of the Community of Saint Mary during its first century, 1865-1965. Racine, Wis., DeKoven Found. for Church Work [dist. Sisters of St. Mary, Box 311, c.1965] 226, [8]p. illus., map. ports. 22cm. Bibl. [BX5973.S47M3] 65-4002 4.00
1. Sistenhood of St. Mary. I. Title.

SCHLINK, Basilea. 271.98
Realities; the miracles of God experienced today [by] M. Basilea Schlink. Translated by Larry Christenson and William Castell. Grand Rapids, Zondervan Pub. House [1966] 128 p. 21 cm. [BX8071.5.S3313] 66-18951
1. Okumenische Marienschwesternschaft. I. Title.

SCHLINK, Basilea 271.98
Realities; the miracles of God experienced today [by] M. Basilea Schlink. Tr. [from German] by Larry Christenson, William Castell. Grand Rapids, Mich Zondervan [c.1966] 128p. 21cm. [BX8071.5.S3313] 66-18951 1.50 pap.,
1. Okumenische Marienschwesternschaft. I. Title.

SCHLINK, Basilea [Secular name: Klara Schlink] 271.98
God is always greater. Foreword by Olive Wyon. Tr. from German by N. B. Cryer] London, Faith Pr. [dist. Westminister, M.D., Centerbury, c.1963 130p. illus. group port. 19cm. (Ecumenical Sisterhood of Mary, Darmstadt. Pub. 2) 63-4128 2.00 pap.,
1. Okumemsche Marienschwesternschaft. I. Title.

SMITH, T. Stratton. 271.98
The rebel nun; the moving story of Mother Maria of Paris. Springfield, Ill., Templegate [c.1965] 252p. illus., ports. 23cm. First pub. in England by Souvenir Pr. in 1965 [BX597.S53S6] 65-29349 4.95
1. Skobtsova, Evgeniia Iur'evna (Pilenko) d. 1945. II. Title.

WEISER, Frederick Sheely, 1935- 271.98
Love's response: a story of Lutheran deaconesses in America. introd. by F. Eppling Reinartz. Illus. by Robert L. Jefferson. Philadelphia, [2900] W. Queen La. Bd. of Pubn., United Lutheran Church in America, [c.1962] 164p. illus. 23cm. Bibl. 62-14824 3.00
1. Deaconesses. 2. Lutheran Church in the U. S.—Hist. I. Title.

PAYE, Anne. 271'.992'00974837
Heritage of faith : century of Mercy in the Diocese of Scranton, 1874-1975 / Anne Paye. Dallas, Pa. : Mercy Information Center, c1976. ix, 76 p., [8] leaf of plates : ill. ; 22 cm. "First appeared as a year-long series of articles in the diocesan newspaper, 'The Catholic light'." [BX4483.6.S38P39] 77-372818
1. Sisters of Mercy. Scranton. I. Title.

272 Persecutions

AIDA of Leningrad: 272 B
the story of Aida Skripnikova; edited by Xenia Howard-Johnston and Michael Bourdeaux. [Reading, Eng.] Gateway Outreach [1972] [8], 121 p. port. 23 cm. [BX6495.S52A75 1972] 73-160416 ISBN 0-901644-09-9 £1.50
1. Skripnikova, Aida Mikhailovna, 1942- 2. Persecution—Russia. I. Howard-Johnston, Xenia, ed. II. Bourdeaux, Michael, ed.

ATTWATER, Donald, 1892- 272
Martyrs, from St. Stephen to John Tung. New York, Sheed & Ward [1957] 236p. 22cm. Includes bibliography. [BR1601.A8] 57-10180
1. Martyrs. I. Title.

ATTWATER, Donald, 1892- 272
Martyrs, from St. Stephen to John Tung. New York, Sheed & Ward [1957] 236 p. 22 cm. Includes bibliography. [BR1601.A8] 57-10180
1. Martyrs. I. Title.

BAINTON, Roland Herbert, 1894- 272
The travail of religious liberty; nine biographical studies. Philadelphia, Westminster Press [1951] Philadelphia, Westminster Press

[1951] 272 p. illus. 21 cm. 272 p. illus. 21 cm. [BV741.B26] 51-11705
1. Religious liberty. 2. Christian biography. I. Title.

BOURDEAUX, Michael. 272
Faith on trial in Russia. [1st U.S. ed.] New York, Harper & Row [1971] 192 p. 22 cm. Bibliography: p. 190. [BR1608.R85B68 1971] 70-160642 ISBN 0-06-060985-0 5.95
1. Persecution—Russia. 2. Baptists—Russia. I. Title.

BOURDEAUX, Michael. 272
Patriarch and prophets; persecution of the Russian Orthodox Church today. New York, Praeger [1970] 359 p. 23 cm. Includes bibliographical references. [BR1608.R8B67 1970] 79-106201 10.00
1. Orthodox Eastern Church, Russian. 2. Persecution—Russia. I. Title.

CHATEILLON, Sebastien, 1515-1563 272
Concerning heretics, whether they are to be persecuted and how they are to be treated; a collection of the opinions of learned men both ancient and modern; an anonymous work attributed to Sebastian Castellio, now first done into English, together with excerpts from other works of Sebastian Castellio and David Joris on religious liberty, by Roland H. Bainton. New York, Octagon, 1965 [c.1935, 1963] xiv, 346p. facsims., ports. 24cm. (Records of civilization: sources and studies, no. 22) Finding list of the works of Sebastian Frank [sic] in American libraries, by Philip L. Kintner: p.313-320. Bibl. [BT1313.C45] 65-25617 10.00
1. Heresy. 2. Religious liberty. I. Joris, David, 1501 or 2-1556. II. Bainton, Roland Herbert, 1894- tr. III. Title. IV. Series.

COWAN, Ian Borthwick. 272
The Scottish Covenanters, 1660-1688 / by Ian B. Cowan London : V. Gollancz, 1976. 191 p. ; 22 cm. Includes index. Bibliography: p. [167]-171. [BX9081.C68] 76-366906 ISBN 0-575-02105-5 : 16.50
1. Covenanters. 2. Persecution—Scotland. 3. Scotland—Church history—17th century. I. Title.
Distributed by Verry.

DEYNEKA, Anita. 272
A song in Siberia : [the true story of a Russian church that could not be silenced] / Anita and Peter Deyneka, Jr. Elgin, Ill. : D. C. Cook Pub. Co., c1977. 235 p., [4] leaves of plates : ill. ; 22 cm. [BR1608.R8D49] 77-70790 ISBN 0-89191-065-4 pbk. : 3.95
1. Persecution—Russia—Barnaul, Siberia. 2. Baptists—Russia—Barnaul, Siberia. I. Deyneka, Peter, 1931- joint author. II. Title.

THE Evidence that convicted 272 B
Aida Skripnikova [edited] by [Xenia Howard-Johnson and] Michael Bourdeaux. Elgin, Il[l.] D. C. Cook [1973, c1972] 154 p. 18 cm. First published under title: Aida of Leningrad. [BX6495.S52A75 1973] 73-78712 ISBN 0-912692-22-7 1.25
1. Skripnikova, Aida Mikhailovna, 1942- 2. Persecution—Russia. I. Howard-Johnson, Xenia, ed. II. Bourdeaux, Michael, ed.

THE Evidence that convicted 272 B
Aida Skripnikova [edited] by [Xenia Howard-Johnson and] Michael Bourdeaux. Elgin, Il[l.] D. C. Cook [1973, c1972] 154 p. 18 cm. First published under title: Aida of Leningrad. [BX6495.S52A75 1973] 73-78712 ISBN 0-912692-22-7 1.25 (pbk.)
1. Skripnikova, Aida Mikhailovna, 1942- 2. Persecution—Russia. I. Howard-Johnson, Xenia, ed. II. Bourdeaux, Michael, ed.

FOXE, John, 1516-1587. 272
The acts and monuments of John Foxe; with a life of the martyrologist, and vindication of the work, by George Townsend. New York, AMS Press, 1965. 8 v. illus. 24 cm. Reprint of the 1843-49? ed. First complete English ed. published in 1563 under title: Actes and monuments of these latter and perillous dayes, touching matters of the church. [BR1600.F6 1965] 72-185708
1. Martyrs. 2. Persecution. 3. Church history. I. Townsend, George, 1788-1857. II. Title.

FOXE, John, 1516-1587 272
Book of martyrs. Ed. [abridged] by Marie Gentert King. New York, Pyramid [1968] 396p. 18cm. (N1751) First complete version pub. in 1563 under title: Actes and monuments of these latter and perillous dayes. [BR1600.F62 1966] .95 pap.,
1. Martyrs. 2. Persecution. 3. Church history. I. Williamson, Geoffrey Arthur, 1895- ed. II. Title.

FOXE, John, 1516-1587 272
Book of martyrs. Ed. &abridged by G. A. Williamson [1st Amer. ed.] Boston, Little [1966, c.1965] xliv, 475p. illus. 23cm. First complete version pub. in 1563 under title: Actes and monuments of these latter and perillous dayes. [BR1600.F62] 66-11277 7.50 bds.,
1. Martyrs. 2. Persecution. 3. Church history. I. Williamson. Geoffey Arthur, 1895- ed. II. Title.

FOXE, John, 1516-1587. 272
Christian martyrs of the world, from the celebrated work by John Foxe, and other eminent authorities. Newly rev. and illustrated. Chicago, Moody Press [1963?] vi, 590 p. illus. 23 cm. First complete version published in 1563 under title: Actes and monuments of these latter and perilous dayes. [[BR1607]] 63-22993
1. Martyrs. 2. Persecution. 3. Church history. I. Title.

FOXE, John, 1516-1587. 272
Fox's Book of martyrs; a history of the lives, sufferings, and triumphant deaths of the early Christian and the Protestant martyrs. Edited by William Byron Forbush. Grand Rapids, Zondervan Pub. House [1955?c1926] xiv, 370p. 22cm. First published in Latin at Basle in 1554, and in English in 1563 [under title: Actes and monuments of these latter and perillous dayes]' [BR1600] 53-11161
1. Martyrs. 2. Persecution. 3. Church history. I. Title. II. Title: Book of martyrs.

GALLONIO, Antonio Father 272
Torture of the Christian martyrs. No. Hollywood, Calif., Brandon House [1966] 235p. illus. 17cm. (1012) 1.25 pap.,
I. Title.

GROSSU, Sergiu, comp. 272
The church in today's catacombs / edited by Sergiu Grossu ; translated from the French by Janet L. Johnson. New Rochelle, N.Y. : Arlington House Publishers, [1975] 224 p. ; 24 cm. "Originally published in France in 1973 as a supplement to the journal Catacombes." Bibliography: p. 224. [BR1608.C7G7613] 74-32251 ISBN 0-87000-260-0 : 8.95
1. Persecution—Communist countries—Collected works. 2. Communism and Christianity—Communist countries—Collected works. I. Title.

HARE, Douglas R A 272
The theme of Jewish persecution of Christians in the Gospel according to St. Matthew, by Douglas R.A. Hare. Cambridge, Cambridge U.P., 1967. xiv, 204 p. 23 cm. (Society for New Testament Studies. Monograph series, 6) 50/- Bibliography: p. 180-189. [BS2575.2.H28] 67-19502
1. Bible. N. T. Matthew—Criticism, interpretation, etc. 2. Persecution—Eary church. 3. Judaism—Relations—Christianity. 4. Christianity and other religions—Judaism. I. Title. II. Series: Studiorum Novi Testamenti Societas. Monograph series, 6

HARE, Douglas R. A. 272
The theme of Jewish persecution of Christians in the Gospel according to St. Matthew, by Douglas R. A. Hare. Cambridge, Cambridge Univ. Pr., 1967. xiv, 204p. 23cm. (Soc. for New Testament Studies. Monograph ser., 6) Bibl. [BS2575.2.H28] 67-19502 8.50
1. Bible. N. T. Matthew—Criticism, interpretation, etc. 2. Persecution—Early church. 3. Judaism—Relations—Christianity. 4. Christianity and other religions—Judaism. I. Title. II. Series: Studiorum Novi Testamenti Societas. Monograph Series, 6
Available from the publisher's New York office.

HODGES, Tony. 272
Jehovah's Witnesses in Central Africa / by Tony Hodges. London : Minority Rights Group, 1976. 16 p. : map ; 30 cm. (Report - Minority Rights Group ; no. 29 ISSN 0305-6252s) Bibliography: p. 16..[BX8525.8.A35H63] 76-380509 ISBN 0-903114-31-3 : £0.45
1. Jehovah's Witnesses in Central Africa. I. Title. II. Series: Minority Rights Group. Report ; no. 29.

HOMAN, Helen (Walker), 1893- 272
Letters to the martyrs. [1st ed.] New York, McKay [1951] 236 p. 21 cm. [BR1601.H66] 51-12033
1. Martyrs. I. Title.

HOMAN, Helen (Walker) 1893- 272
Letters to the martyrs. Freeport, N.Y., Books for Libraries Press [1971, c1951] xii, 236 p. 23 cm. (Biography index reprint series) Bibliography: p. 235-236. [BR1601.2.H6 1971] 79-148220 ISBN 0-8369-8067-0
1. Christian martyrs. I. Title.

HUNTER, Allan Armstrong, 1893- 272
Christians in the arena. Nyack, N. Y., Fellowship Publications, 1958. 108p. 19cm. [BR1601.H8] 58-2873
1. Persecution. I. Title.

LOCKE, John, 1632-1704. 272
Epistola de tolerantia. A letter on toleration; Latin text edited with a preface by Raymond Klibansky; English translation with an introduction and notes by J. W. Gough. Oxford, Clarendon P., 1968. xliv, 171 p. 2 plates, 2 facsims. 23 cm. Parallel texts in English and Latin. [BR1610.L823] 70-373959 40/-
1. Toleration. I. Klibansky, Raymond, 1905- ed. II. Gough, John Weidhofft. III. Title. IV. Title: A letter on toleration.

SHELLEY, Bruce Leon, 1927- 272
The cross and flame; chapters in the history of martyrdom, by Bruce L. Shelley. Grand Rapids, Eerdmans [1968, c1967] 191 p. 21 cm. Bibliographical footnotes. [BR1601.2.S5] 67-13985
1. Martyrdom. 2. Martyrs. I. Title.

SINISHTA, Gjon, 1929- 272
The fulfilled promise : a documentary account of religious persecution in Albania / by Gjon Sinishta. Santa Clara, Calif. : Sinishta, 1976. 248 p. : ill. ; 22 cm. Bibliography: p. 242-247. [BR1608.A38S57] 76-57433 7.95
1. Persecution—Albania—Miscellanea. 2. Martyrs—Albania—Miscellanea. 3. Albania—Church history—Miscellanea. I. Title.

WADDY, J. Leonard. 272
The bitter sacred cup : the Wednesbury riots, 1743-44 / [by] J. Leonard Waddy. London : Pinhorns for the World Methodist Historical Society (British Section), 1976. viii [i.e. ix], 46 p. : map ; 21 cm. (The Wesley Historical Society lecture ; no. 36) Includes bibliographical references and index. [BX8277.B55W3] 77-367629 ISBN 0-901262-18-8 : £0.60
1. Methodists in Black Country, Eng.—History. 2. Persecution—England—Black Country. 3. Black Country, Eng.—History. I. Title. II. Series: Wesley Historical Society. The Wesley Historical Society lectures ; no. 36.

WURMBRAND, Sabina. 272
The pastor's wife. Edited by Charles Foley. [1st American ed.] New York, John Day Co. [1971, c1970] 218 p. 24 cm. [BR1608.R8W85 1971] 79-143216 5.95
1. Persecution—Romania. I. Title.

NORWOOD, Frederick Abbott. 272'.09
Strangers and exiles; a history of religious refugees [by] Frederick A. Norwood. Nashville, Abingdon Press [1969] 2 v. illus., maps. 25 cm. Bibliography: v. 2, p. 479-511. [BR1601.2.N6] 75-86164 25.00
1. Persecution—History. 2. Refugees, Religious. 3. Dissenters, Religious. I. Title.

GREENLEAF, Richard E 272.0972
Zumarraga and the Mexican Inquisition, 1536-1543. Washington, Academy of American Franciscan History, 1961 [c1962] viii, 155 p. illus., port., facsims. 27 cm. (Academy of American Franciscan History. Monograph series, v. 4) Bibliography: p. 133-148. [BX4705.Z8G7 1962] 63-1181
1. Zumarraga, Juan de, Abp., 1468-1548. 2. Inquisition. Mexico. I. Title. II. Series.

GREENLEAF, Richard E. 272.0972
Zumarraga and the Mexican Inquisition, 1536-1543. Washington, D.C., Acad. of Amer. Franciscan Hist., 1961[c.1962] viii, 155p. illus. 27cm. (Acad. of Amer. Franciscan Hist. Monograph ser., v. 4) Bibl. 63-1181 6.50
1. Zumarraga, Juan de, Abp, 1468-1548. 2. Inquisition. Mexico. I. Title. II. Series.

CRAWFORD, Don, 1929- 272'.097291
Red star over Cuba, by Don Crawford and Brother Andrew. Wheaton, Ill., Tyndale House Publishers [1971] 112 p. illus. 18 cm. [BR1608.C9C7] 76-123286 ISBN 0-8423-5350-X
1. Persecution—Cuba. 2. Refugees, Religious. I. Andrew, Brother, joint author. II. Title.

CANFIELD, Leon Hardy, 1886- 272'.1
The early persecutions of the Christians. New York, AMS Press [1968] 215 p. 22 cm. (Studies in history, economics, and public law, v. 55, no. 2, whole no. 136) Reprint of the 1913 ed. Bibliography: p. 210-215. [BR1604.C32 1968] 68-54259
1. Persecution—Early church. I. Title. II. Series: Columbia studies in the social sciences, no. 136

FREND, W. H. C. 272'.1
Martyrdom and persecution in the early church; a study of a conflict from the Maccabees to Donatus. by W. H. C. Frend [New York] N.Y.U. Pr., 1967. xviii, 577p. 24cm. Bibl. [BR1604.2.F7 1967] 8.00
1. Persecution—Early church. I. Title.

FREND, W. H. C. 272'.1
Martyrdom and persecution in the early church; a study of a conflict from the Maccabees to Donatus, by W. H. C. Frend. Garden City, N.Y., Anchor Books, 1967 [c1965] xviii, 577 p. 18 cm. Bibliography: p. [527]-557. [BR1604.2.F7 1967] 66-24325
1. Persecution—Early church. I. Title.

REYMOND, Eve A. E., comp. 272'.1
Four martyrdoms from the Pierpont Morgan Coptic codices, edited by E. A. E. Reymond and J. W. B. Barns. Oxford, Clarendon Press, 1973. xii, 278 p. 24 cm. Coptic and/or English. Bibliography: p. [ix]-xii. [BR1608.E3R49] 74-159108 ISBN 0-19-815448-8 £7.50
1. Christian martyrs—Egypt. I. Barns, John Wintour Baldwin, joint comp. II. Pierpont Morgan Library, New York. III. Title.

REYMOND, Eve A. E., comp. 272'.1
Four martyrdoms from the Pierpont Morgan Coptic codices, edited by E. A. E. Reymond and J. W. B. Barns. Oxford, Clarendon Press, 1973. xii, 278 p. 24 cm. Coptic and/or English. Bibliography: p. [ix]-xii. [BR1608.E3R49] 74-159108 ISBN 0-19-815448-8
1. Christian martyrs—Egypt. I. Barns, John Wintour Baldwin, joint comp. II. Pierpont Morgan Library, New York. III. Title.
Distributed by Oxford University Press, New York; 24.00.

RICCIOTTI, Giuseppe, 1890- 272.1
The age of martyrs; Christianity from Diocletian to Constantine. Translated by Anthony Bull. Milwaukee, Bruce Pub. Co. [1959] 305p. illus. 25cm. Includes bibliography. [BR165.R553] 59-10532
1. Martyrs. 2. Persecution—Early church. I. Title.

RUSSO-ALESI, Anthony Ignatius, 1896- 272'.1
Martyrology pronouncing dictionary. It contains the proper pronunciation of over 5,000 names of martyrs, confessors, virgins, emperors, cities, and places occurring in the Roman martyrology with a daily calendar and a list of the patron saints, by Anthony I. Russo-Alesi. New York, E. O'Toole Co., 1939. Detroit, Gale Research Co., 1973. xiv, 177 p. 18 cm. Bibliography: p. ix. [BX4661.R8 1973] 79-167151
1. Martyrs—Dictionaries. 2. Names, Latin—Pronunciation. 3. Latin language—Church Latin. I. Title.

WORKMAN, Herbert Brook 272.1
Persecutions in the early church. Nashville, Abingdon [1961, c.1960] 155p. (Apex bks., G4) 1.00 pap.,
1. Persecution. 2. Church history—Primitive and early church. I. Title.

WORKMAN, Herbert Brook, 1862- 272'.1
Persecution in the early church. New York, Abingdon Press [1960] 155 p. 17 cm. [Apex books, G4) [BR1604.W8 1960] 62-762
1. Persecution — Early church. I. Title.

MUSURILLO, Herbert Anthony, comp. 272'.1'0922 B
The acts of the Christian martyrs; introduction, texts and translations by Herbert Musurillo. Oxford, Clarendon Press, 1972. lxxiii, 379 p. 21 cm. (Oxford early Christian texts) Parallel Greek or Latin texts with English translations. Includes bibliographical references [BR1603.A1M87] 72-177389 ISBN 0-19-826806-8 £6.00
1. Martyrs. 2. Persecution—Early church, ca. 30-1600. I. Title. II. Series.

MUSURILLO, Herbert Anthony, comp. 272'.1'0922 B
The acts of the Christian martyrs; introduction, texts and translations by Herbert Musurillo. Oxford, Clarendon Press, 1972. lxxiii, 379 p. 21 cm. (Oxford early Christian texts) Parallel Greek or Latin texts with English translations. Includes bibliographical references. [BR1603.A1M87] 72-177389 ISBN 0-19-826806-8
1. Martyrs. 2. Persecution—Early church. I. Title. II. Series.
Distributed by Oxford University Press N.Y. 19.25.

CHADWICK, Henry, 1920- 272'.1'0924 B
Priscillian of Avila : the occult and the charismatic in the early church / Henry Chadwick. Oxford : Clarendon Press, 1976. viii, 250 p. ; 23 cm. Includes index. Bibliography: 11th prelim. page. [BT1465.C44] 76-370521 ISBN 0-19-826643-X : 22.00
1. Priscillianus, Bp. of Avila, d. 385. 2. Christian martyrs—Biography.
Dist. by Oxford University Press NY NY

COULTON, George Gordon, 1858-1947. 272'.2
The Inquisition. [Folcroft, Pa.] Folcroft Library Editions, 1974. 79, [1] p. 23 cm. Reprint of the 1929 ed. published by E. Benn, London, which was issued as no. 71 of Benn's sixpenny library. Bibliography: p. [80] [BX1711.C6 1974] 74-18020 10.00
1. Inquisition. 2. Heresy. I. Title.

COULTON, George Gordon, 1858-1947. 272'.2
The Inquisition. [Folcroft, Pa.] Folcroft Library Editions, 1974. 79, [1] p. 23 cm. Reprint of the 1929 ed. published by E. Benn, London, which was issued as no. 71 of Benn's sixpenny library. Bibliography: p. [80] [BX1711.C6 1974] 74-18020 ISBN 0-8414-3647-9 (lib. bdg.)
1. Inquisition. 2. Heresy. I. Title.

COULTON, George Gordon, 1858-1947. 272'.2
Inquisition and liberty. Gloucester, Mass., P. Smith, 1969. 354 p. illus. 21 cm. Reprint of the 1959 ed. Bibliographical references included in "Notes" (p. 329-337) [BX1711.C62 1969] 71-7515
1. Inquisition. 2. Heresy. I. Title.

HAYWARD, Fernand, 1888- 272.2
The Inquisition. [Translated by Malachy Carroll. New York, Alba House, 1966] 176 p. 22 cm. Translation of Que faut -- Il penser de l'Inquisition? [BX1712.H313] 65-13733
1. Inquisition. I. Title.

HAYWARD, Fernand, 1888- 272.2
The Inquisition. [Tr. from French by Malachy Carroll. Staten Island, N.Y., Alba, c.1966] 176p. 22cm. [BX1712.H313] 65-15733 3.95
1. Inquisition. I. Title.

HERCULANO de Carvalho e Araujo, Alexandre, 1810-1877. 272'.2
History of the origin and establishment of the Inquisition in Portugal. Translated from the Portuguese, by John C. Branner. Prolegomenon by Yosef Hayim Yerushalmi. New York, Ktav Pub. House, 1973 504 p. illus. 24 cm. (Studia Sephardica) Translation of Historia da origem e estabelecimento da Inquisicao em Portugal. First published in 1926 as vol. 1, no. 2 of Stanford University publications, University series: History, economics, and political science. Includes bibliographical references. [BX1730.H43 1971] 77-113852 ISBN 0-87068-153-2 19.95
1. Inquisition. Portugal. I. Title. II. Series. III. Series: Stanford studies in history, economics, and political science, v. 1, no. 2.

INQUISITION. Albi, France. 272'.2
The Inquisition at Albi, 1299-1300; text of register and analysis, by Georgene Webber Davis. New York, Octagon Books, 1974 [c1948] p. cm. Text transcribed from ms. lat. 11847 of the Bibliotheque nationale. Reprint of the ed. published by Columbia University Press, New York, which was issued as no. 538 of Studies in history, economics, and public law. Bibliography: p. [BX1720.I5 1974] 74-5269 ISBN 0-374-92075-3 13.00
1. Inquisition. Albi, France. I. Davis, Georgene Webber, 1900- II. Title. III. Series: Columbia studies in the social sciences, no. 538.

LEA, Henry Charles, 1825-1909. 272.2
A history of the Inquisition of the Middle Ages. New York, Russell & Russell [1958] 3v. 21cm. (Russell scholars' classics edition) [BX1711.L4 1958] 58-9830
1. Inquisition—Hist. I. Title.

LEA, Henry Charles, 1825-1909. 272'.2
The Inquisition in the Spanish dependencies : Sicily-Naples-Sardinia-Milan-the Canaries-Mexico-Peru-New Granada / by Henry Charles Lea. New York : Gordon Press, [1975] c1908. p. cm. Reprint of the 1922 ed. published by Macmillan, New York. [BX1735.L48 1975] 75-20123 ISBN 0-87968-242-6
1. Inquisition—History. I. Title.

LEA, Henry Charles, 1825-1909 272.2
The Inquisition of the Middle Ages; its organization and operation. With hist. introd. by Walter Ullmann. London, Eyre & Spottiswoode [dist. New York, Barnes & Noble, 1965, c.1963] 326p. 23cm. Consists of chapts. 7-14 of v.1. of the author's Hist. of the Inquisition of the Middle Ages, pub. in 1887. Bibl. [BX1711.L415] 65-1333 4.50
1. Inquisition—Hist. I. Title.

LEA, Henry Charles, 1825-1909. 272'.2
The Inquisition of the Middle Ages; its organization and operation. With an historical introd. by Walter Ullmann. New York, Harper & Row [1969, c1963] 326, 10 p. 21 cm. (Harper torchbooks, TB1456) Consists of chapters 7-14 of v. 1. of the author's History of the Inquisition of the Middle Ages, published in 1887. Bibliography: p. [319]-320. [BX1711.L415 1969] 70-5507 1.95
1. Inquisition—History. I. Title.

MAYCOCK, Alan Lawson. 272'.2
The Inquisition from its establishment to the Great Schism; an introductory study, by A. L. Maycock. With an introd. by Ronald Knox. New York, Harper & Row [1969] xxiii, 276 p. illus., facsim., ports. 22 cm. (J. & J. Harper editions) Reprint of the 1927 London ed. Bibliographical footnotes. [BX1711.M3 1969] 75-81866
1. Inquisition—History. 2. Church history—Middle Ages, 600-1500. I. Title.

MOCATTA, Frederic David, 1828-1905. 272'.2
The Jews of Spain and Portugal and the Inquisition. With an introd. and supplementary chronological tables by David Bortin. New York, Cooper Square, 1973. xxi, 106 p. illus. 22 cm. (Illustrated Jewish historical series) "A Marandell book." Reprint of the 1933 ed. of a work originally published in 1877 by Longmans, Green, London. Includes bibliographical references. [DS135.S7M6 1973] 72-88016 ISBN 0-8154-0440-9 5.00
1. Inquisition. 2. Jews in Spain. 3. Jews in Portugal. I. Title.

O'BRIEN, John Anthony, 1893- 272'.2
The Inquisition [by] John A. O'Brien. New York, Macmillan [1973] xiii, 233 p. 22 cm. Bibliography: p. 223-226. [BX1712.O27] 73-1962 6.95
1. Inquisition.

VACANDARD, Elphege, 1849-1927. 272'.2
The Inquisition : a critical and historical study of the coercive power of the church / by E. Vacandard ; translated from the second edition by Bertrand L. Conway. Merrick, N.Y. : Richwood Pub. Co., [1977] p. cm. Translation of L'Inquisition. Reprint of the new ed. published in 1915 by Longmans, Green, London. Includes index. Bibliography: p. [BX1712.V3213 1977] 76-1127 ISBN 0-915172-09-7 lib.bdg. : 20.00
1. Inquisition—History. I. Title.

WALSH, William Thomas, 1891-1949. 272'.2
Characters of the Inquisition. Port Washington, N.Y., Kennikat Press [1969, c1940] xi, 301 p. 22 cm. (Essay and general literature index reprint series) Bibliographical footnotes. [BX1711.W3 1969] 68-8192
1. Catholic Church—Biography. 2. Inquisition—History. I. Title.

WILLETT, Franciscus. 272'.2
Understanding the Inquisition. No. Easton, Mass., Holy Cross Press [1968] 93 p. illus. 23 cm. [BX1712.W54] 68-30958 2.95
1. Inquisition. I. Title.

NICKERSON, Hoffman, 1888-1965 272'.2'09
The Inquisition; a political and military study of its establishment. Pref. by Hilaire Belloc. 2d ed. with a new pref. on the Battle of Muret. Port Washington, N. Y., Kennikat [1968,c.1932] xli, 268p. maps, plans. 22cm. Bibl. [BX1711.N5 1968] 67-27630 8.50
1. Inquisition—Hist. 2. Albigenses. 3. Prohibition. I. Title.

COHEN, Martin A. 272'.2'0924 B
The martyr; the story of a secret Jew and the Mexican Inquisition in the sixteenth century [by] Martin A. Cohen. [1st ed.] Philadelphia, Jewish Publication Society of America, 1973. xv, 373 p. illus. 25 cm. Bibliography: p. [335]-357. [F1231.C32C63] 72-14055 ISBN 0-8276-0011-9 7.95
1. Carvajal, Luis de, 1567?-1596. 2. Inquisition. Mexico. 3. Jews in Mexico. I. Title.

HAUBEN, Paul J. 272'.2'0946
The Spanish Inquisition, edited by Paul J. Hauben. New York, Wiley [1969] xiii, 140 p. 22 cm. (Major issues in history) "Bibliographical essay": p. 138-140. [BX1735.H38] 71-91161
1. Inquisition. Spain. I. Title.

HIBBERT, Eleanor, 1906- 272.20946
The Spanish Inquisition: its rise, growth, and end [by] Jean Plaidy. [1st American ed.] New York, Citadel Press [1967] 3 v. in 1. illus., ports. 22 cm. First published 1959-61 as three monographs with titles: The rise of the Spanish Inquisition, The growth of the Spanish Inquisition, and The end of the Spanish Inquisition. Includes bibliographies. [BX1735.H52] 67-12374
1. Inquisition, Spain. I. Title.

KAMEN, Henry. 272.2'0946
The Spanish Inquisition. New York, New Amer. Lib. [1968, c.1965] 334p. illus. 18cm. (Mentor bk., MY817) Bibl. [BX1735.H313] 1.25 pap.,
1. Inquisition. I. Title.

KAMEN, Henry Arthur Francis 272.20946
The Spanish Inquisition. [New York] New Amer. Lib. [1966, c.1965] x, 339p. illus., map. 22cm. Bibl. [BX1735.K3] 66-17728 5.95
1. Inquisition. Spain. I. Title.

LEA, Henry Charles, 1825-1909. 272.2*0946
A history of the Inquisition of Spain. New York, AMS Press, 1966. 4 v. 23 cm. Reprint of the 1906-07 ed. Includes bibliographical references. [BX1735.L462] 72-181943
1. Inquisition. Spain. I. Title.

LEA, Henry Charles, 1825-1909 272.20946
A history of the inquisition of Spain. New York, Amer. Scholar Pubns., 1966. 4 v. 23cm. Reprint of 1906-07 ed. Bibl. [BX175.L46] 65-24237 60.00 set.,
1. Inquisition. Spain. I. Title.
0 E. 11th St. New York, N. Y., 10003

LONGHURST, John Edward, 1918- 272.20946
The age of Torquemada, 2d ed. Lawrence, Kan., Bx. 32 Coronado Pr. [1964, c.1962] 146p. illus. 23cm. 3.95
1. Torquemada, Tomas de, 1420-1498. 2. Jews in Spain—Persecutions. 3. Inquisition. Spain. I. Title.

ROTH, Cecil, 1899- 272.20946
The Spanish Inquisition. New York, Norton [1964] vi, 316p. illus., facsims., ports. 20cm. (Norton lib.) Bibl. 64-55951 1.75 pap.,
1. Inquisition. Spain. 2. Jews in Spain. 3. Jews—Persecutions. I. Title.

TURBERVILLE, Arthur Stanley, 1888-1945. 272'.2'0946
The Spanish Inquisition. [Hamden, Conn.] Archon Books, 1968. v, 249 p. 19 cm. Reprint of the 1932 ed. Bibliography: p. 239-243. [BX1735.T8 1968] 68-11257
1. Inquisition. Spain.

BRAUNSTEIN, Baruch, 1906- 272'.2'094675
The Chuetas of Majorca; conversos and the Inquisition of Majorca. New York, Ktav Pub. House, 1972 [i.e. 1973] xxxii, 227 p. 24 cm. (Studia Sephardica) Reprint of the 1936 ed. published by Mennonite Pub. House, Scottdale, Pa., which was issued as v. 29 of Columbia University oriental series. Originally presented as the author's thesis, Columbia University. Bibliography: p. 205-220. [BX1743.M2B7 1973] 71-139465 ISBN 0-87068-147-8 12.50
1. Inquisition. Majorca. I. Title. II. Series. III. Series: Columbia University oriental studies, v. 29.

HERCULANO de Carvalho e Araujo, Alexandre, 1810-1877. 272'.2'09469
History of the origin and establishment of the Inquisition in Portugal. Translated by John C. Branner. New York, AMS Press [1968] 189-636 p. illus. 22 cm. Translation of Historia da origem e estabelecimento da Inquisacao em Portugal. Reprint of the 1926 ed., which was issued as v. 1, no. 2 of Stanford University publications. University series: history, economics, and political science. Includes bibliographical references. [BX1730.H43 1968] 68-54274
1. Inquisition. Portugal. I. Title. II. Series: Stanford studies in history, economics, and political science, v. 1, no. 2

GREENLEAF, Richard E. 272'.2'0972
The Mexican Inquisition of the sixteenth century [by] Richard E. Greenleaf. [1st ed.] Albuquerque, University of New Mexico Press [1969] x, 242 p. facsim. 22 cm. Bibliography: p. 215-231. [BX1740.M6G73] 77-78553 8.95
1. Inquisition. Mexico. I. Title.

LIEBMAN, Seymour B., 1907- 272'.2'098
The inquisitors and the Jews in the New World : summaries of procesos, 1500-1810 : and bibliographical guide / by Seymour B. Liebman. Coral Gables, Fla. : University of Miami Press, [1975] c1974. 224 p. : ill. ; 23 cm. Bibliography: p. [218]-224. [F1419.J4L52 1975] 72-85110 ISBN 0-87024-245-8 : 10.95
1. Inquisition. Latin America. 2. Maranos in Latin America. 3. Latin America—Religion. I. Title.

EMERY, Richard Wilder, 1912- 272'.3
Heresy and inquisition in Narbonne. New York, AMS Press, 1967 [c1941] 184 p. 2 maps. 23 cm. (Studies in history, economics, and public law, no. 480) Originally was presented as the author's thesis, Columbia University. Bibliography: p. 176-178. [BX1720.E5 1967] 75-166031
1. Inquisition. Languedoc. 2. Albigenses. 3. Narbonne—History. I. Title. II. Series: Columbia studies in the social sciences, 480.

OLDENBOURG, Zoe, 1916- 272.3
Massacre at Monsegur; a history of the Albigensian Crusade. Tr. from French by Peter Green. [New York] Pantheon [1962, c.1961] 420p. illus. Bibl. 62-11076 6.95
1. Albigenses. 2. Languedoc—Hist. 3. Montsegur. I. Title.

SIMONDE de Sismondi, Jean Charles Leonard, 1773-1842. 272'.3
History of the crusades against the Albigenses, in the thirteenth century ... With an introductory essay by the translator. London, Wightman and Cramp, 1826. [New York, AMS Press, 1973] xl, 266 p. 23 cm. Translated from parts of v. 6 and 7 of the author's Histoire des Francais published in 1823 and 1826 respectively. Includes bibliographical references. [DC83.3.S58 1973] 72-178564 ISBN 0-404-56672-3 16.00
1. Albigenses. I. Title.

BIEN, David D. 272.4
The Calas affair; persecution, toleration, and heresy in eighteenth-century Toulouse. Princeton, N. J., Princeton University Press [c.]1960. ix, 199p. 23cm. Bibl.: p.181-194 and bibl. footnotes 60-12228 4.00
1. Calas, Jean, 1698-1762. 2. Huguenots in France. 3. Toleration. I. Title.

BIEN, David D 272.4
The Calas affair; persecution, toleration, and heresy in eighteenth-century Toulouse. Princeton, N. J., Princeton University Press, 1960. 199p. 23cm. [BX9459.C3B5] 60-12228
1. Calas, Jean, 1698—1762. 2. Huguenots in France. 3. Toleration. I. Title.

OLIVER, Alfred Cookman, 1885- 272.4
A Paris rosary, Boston, Christopher Pub. House [1952] 64 p. illus. 21 cm. [BR848.P304] 52-4810
1. Paris—Churches. I. Title.

SCOVILLE, Warren Candler 272.4
The persecution of Huguenots and French economic development, 1680-1720. Berkeley, University of California Press [c.]1960. x, 497p. 25cm. (Publications of the Bureau of Business and Economic Research, University of California) Bibl.: p.451-476 and Bibl. footnotes) 60-7083 6.50
1. Huguenots in France. 2. France—Econ, condit. I. Title. II. Series: California. University. Bureau of Business and Economic Research. Publications

SCOVILLE, Warren Candler, 1913- 272.4
The persecution of Huguenots and French economic development. 1680-1720. Berkeley, University of California Press, 1960. x, 497p. 25cm. (Publications of the Bureau of Business and Economic Research, University of California) Bibliography: p. 451-476. [HC275.S37] 60-7083
1. Huguenots in France. 2. France—Econ. condit. I. Title. II. Series: California. University. Bureau of Business and Economic Research, Publications

ZWEIG, Stefan, 1881-1942. 272.4
The right to heresy: Castellio against Calvin. Translated by Eden and Cedar Paul. Boston, Beacon Press. 1951. 238p. plates. 22cm. Translation of Castellio gegen Calvin. [BX9459.C] A53
1. Chateillon. Sebastien. 1515-1563. 2. Calvin, Jean, 1509-1564. 3. Servetus, Michael, 1509 or 11-1553. I. Title.

HALLER, William, 1885- 272.6
The elect nation; the meaning and relevance of Foxe's Book of martyrs. New York, Harper [1964, c.1963] 258p. ports., facsims. 22cm. London ed. (J. Cape) has title: Foxe's Book of martyrs and the elect nation. Bibl. 64-10456 5.00
1. Foxe, John, 1516-1587. Actes and monuments. I. Title.

LOADES, D. M. 272'.6
The Oxford martyrs [by] D. M. Loades. New York, Stein and Day [1970] 296 p. illus., map, ports. 23 cm. (Historic trials series) Bibliography: p. [277]-284. [BR1607.L63 1970b] 77-127028 ISBN 0-8128-1340-5 7.95
1. Christian martyrs—England. I. Title.

KANE, Liza, 1929- 272.7
The Devil's greatest counterfeit: the Roman Catholic Church. New York, Greenwich [c.1961] 29p. illus. Bibl. 61-14515 2.50
1. Catholic Church—Doctrinal and

controversial works—Protestant authors. I. Title.

WUERL, Donald W. 272'.7
The forty Martyrs; new saints of England and Wales, by Donald W. Wuerl. With a pref. by John Wright. Huntington, Ind., Our Sunday Visitor [1971] 79 p. illus., port. 21 cm. [BR1607.W8] 70-160365 1.25
1. Christian martyrs—England. 2. Christian martyrs—Wales. I. Title.

DICKINSON, Alice. 272'.8
The Salem witchcraft delusion 1692. New York, Watts, 1974. 64 p. illus. 22 cm. (A Focus book) Bibliography: p. 63. Discusses the social and religious climate that led to the Salem witch hunts and describes the trials and their aftermath. [BF1576.D5] 73-12085 ISBN 0-531-01049-X 3.95 (lib. bdg.)
1. Witchcraft—Massachusetts—Juvenile literature. I. Title.

MONTER, E. William. 272'.8'09445
Witchcraft in France and Switzerland : the borderlands during the Reformation / E. William Monter. Ithaca, N.Y. : Cornell University Press, 1976. 232 p. : ill. ; 23 cm. Includes index. Bibliography: p. 201-206. [BF1582.M6] 75-31449 ISBN 0-8014-0963-2 : 15.00
1. Witchcraft—Jura Mountain region. I. Title.

MARY VERONICA, Sister, O. S. F. 272.8917
Lands of the Western Hemisphere. Geography editor, Kenneth J. Bertrand; consulting editor, Joseph F. X. Mc-Carthy. [Teachers ed.] Garden City, N. Y., Doubleday, Catholic Textbook Division [1960] 367p. illus. 29cm. [E27.M36] 60-51005
1. America—Descr.& trav. I. Title.

REBAGLIATO FONT, Juan. 272.8917
Georgrafía universal. 2d ed. Barcelona, De Gasso Hnos [1960] 511p. illus. 20cm. (Enciclopedias De Gasso) [G126.R36 1960] 61-41998
1. Geography—Text-books—1945- I. Title.

MYERS, Gustavus, 1872-1942 272.9
History of bigotry in the United States, by Gustavus Myers. Edited and revised by Henry M. Christman. New York, Capricorn Books [dist. Putnam, 1960, c.1943, 1960] xii, 474p. 19cm. (A Putnam Capricorn bk. CAP42) (Bibl. footnotes) 1.65 pap.,
1. Religious liberty—U. S. 2. Persecution. 3. Toleration. 4. U. S.—Race question. I. Title. II. Title: Bigotry in the United States.

UNITED States. Congress. Senate. Committee on the Judiciary. Subcommittee to Investigate the Administration of the Internal Security Act and Other Internal Security Laws. 272'.9
Communist exploitation of religion. Hearing, Eighty-ninth Congress, second session, May 6, 1966: testimony of Rev. Richard Wurmbrand. Washington, U.S. Govt. Print. Off., 1966. ii, 42, ii p. 24 cm. [BR1608.R8U5] 66-61649
1. Persecution—Rumania. 2. Communism and religion. I. Wurmbrand, Richard. II. Title.

WURMBRAND, Richard. 272'.9
Christ in the communist prisons. Edited by Charles Foley. [1st American ed.] New York, Coward-McCann [1968] 255 p. 22 cm. [BR1608.R8W8 1968] 68-11879
1. Persecution—Romania. 2. Prisoners—Romania—Personal narratives. I. Title.

273 Doctrinal Controversies & Heresies

BELLOC, Hilaire, 1870-1953. 273
The great heresies. Freeport, N.Y., Books for Libraries Press [1968] 277 p. 22 cm. (Essay index reprint series) Reprint of the 1938 ed. Contents.Contents.—The Arian heresy.—The great and enduring heresy of Mohammed.—The Albigensian attack.—What was the Reformation?—The modern phase. [BT1315.B4 1968] 68-16908
1. Heresies and heretics. I. Title.

THE Birth of popular heresy 273
/ [compiled by] R. I. Moore. New York : St. Martin's Press, 1976, c1975. viii, 166 p. ; 25 cm. (Documents of medieval history ; 1) Consists of translated passages from medieval documents. Includes index. Bibliography: p. 157-161. [BT1319.B57 1976] 75-32934 19.95
1. Heresies and heretics—Middle Ages, 600-1500—Sources. I. Moore, Robert Ian, 1941- II. Series.

CHRISTIE-MURRAY, David, 273
A history of heresy / [by] David Christie-Murray. London : New English Library, 1976. viii, 243 p. ; 22 cm. Includes index. Bibliography: p. 227-229. [BT1315.2.C48 1976] 76-376213 ISBN 0-450-02843-7 : £6.00
1. Heresies and heretics—History. 2. Sects—History. I. Title.

THE Dissenting tradition : 273
essays for Leland H. Carlson / edited by C. Robert Cole and Michael E. Moody. Athens : Ohio University Press, c1975. xxiii, 272 p. : port. ; 25 cm. Includes bibliographical references. [BX5203.2.D57] 74-27706 ISBN 0-8214-0176-9 lib.bdg. : 13.50
1. Carlson, Leland Henry, 1908- 2. Carlson, Leland Henry, 1908- —Bibliography. 3. Dissenters, Religious—England—Addresses, essays, lectures. I. Carlson, Leland Henry, 1908- II. Cole, Charles Robert, 1939- III. Moody, Michael E.
Contents omitted

GUITTON, Jean. 273
Great heresies and church councils. [English translation by F. D. Wieck] New York, Harper & Row [1965] 191 p. 22 cm. Translation of Le Christ ecartele; crises et consiles dans l'Eglise. [BX949.G813] 64-20198
1. Church history — Addresses, essays, lectures. 2. Theology, Doctrinal — Hist. — Addresses, essays, lectures. I. Title.

GUITTON, Jean 273
Great heresies and church councils [Tr. by F. D. Wieck] New York, Harper [c.1965] 191p. 22cm. [BX949.G813] 64-20198 4.00
1. Church history—Addresses, essays, lectures. 2. Theology, Doctrinal—Hist.—Addresses, essays, lectures. I. Title.

GUITTON, Jean. 273
Great heresies and church councils. [English translation by F. D. Wieck] Freeport, N.Y., Books for Libraries Press [1971, c1965] 191 p. 23 cm. (Essay index reprint series) Translation of Le Christ ecartele; crises et consiles dans l'Eglise. [BR155.G813 1971] 73-117798 ISBN 0-8369-2502-5
1. Church history—Addresses, essays, lectures. 2. Theology, Doctrinal—History—Addresses, essays, lectures. 3. Heresies and heretics—Addresses, essays, lectures. I. Title.

HEATH, Carl, 1869- 273
Social and religious heretics in five centuries. With a new introd. for the Garland ed. by Sylvia Strauss. New York, Garland Pub., 1972. 12, 158 p. 22 cm. (The Garland library of war and peace) Reprint of the 1936 ed. [BR157.H4 1972] 78-147622 ISBN 0-8240-0397-7
1. Sects. 2. Heresies and heretics. I. Title. II. Series.

JONES, Arnold Hugh Martin, 1904- 273
Were ancient heresies disquised social movement? by A. H. M. Jones. Philadelphia, Fortress Press [1966] xi, 36 p. 19 cm. (Facet books. Historical series, 1) "Appeared originally under the title 'Were ancient heresies national or social movements in disguise'? in the Journal of theological studies, new series, vol. x, part 2 (1959) pp. 280-297." Bibliography: p. 34. [BT1317.J57] 66-11534
1. Heresies and heretics—Early church. I. Title. II. Series.

KRUMM, John McGill, 1913- 273
Modern heresies. Greenwich, Conn., Seabury Press, 1961. 182 p. 22 cm. Includes bibliography. [BT1315.2.K7] 61-5797
1. Heresies and heretics. I. Title.

NIGG, Walter, 1903- 273
The heretics. Edited and translated by Richard and Clara Winston. [1st American ed.] New York, Knopf, 1962. 411p. 22cm. Translation of Das Buch der Ketzer. [BT1315.N513 1962] 62-8684
1. Heresies and heretics. I. Title.

ROWE, John Franklin, 1827-1897. 273
The history of apostasies. Re-evaluated and augm. by John Allen Hudson. Rosemead. Calif., Old Paths Book Club [1956] 312p. 23cm. First published as part of the author's History of reformatory movements. [BR148.R83] 56-33918
1. Church history. 2. Heresies and heretics. 3. Mormons and Mormonism. I. Title.

ROWE, John Franklin, 1827-1897. 273
A history of reformatory movements resulting in a restoration of the Apostolic Church; to which is appended a history of the nineteen general church councils, also a history of all innovations, from the third century down. 9th ed., rev. and enl. Rosemead, Calif., Old Paths Book Club [c1957] 278p. 23cm. A revision of the authors The Apostolic Church restored. [BR148.R8 1957] 58-27401
1. Church history. 2. Heresies and heretics. 3. Councils and synods. 4. Disciples of Christ—Hist. I. Title. II. Title: Reformatory movements resulting in a restoration of the Apostolic Church.

WALLINGTON, Nellie (Urner) 1847-1933. 273
Historic churches of America. Introd. by Edward Everett Hale. Boston, Milford House [1974] xxv, 259 p. illus. 22 cm. Reprint of the 1907 ed. published by Duffield, New York. [BR565.W3 1974] 73-9898 ISBN 0-87821-154-3
1. Churches—United States. I. Title.

WAND, John William Charles, Bp. of London, 1885- 273
The four great heresies. London, Mowbray; New York, Morehouse-Gorham [1955] 139p. 19cm. [BT1315.W3] 56-710
1. Heresies and heretics—Early church. I. Title.

LEFF, Gordon. 273/.09/02
Heresy in the later Middle Ages: the relation of heterodoxy to dissent, c. 1250-c. 1450. Manchester, Manchester Univ. Pr.; New York, Barnes & Noble [1967] 2v. 25cm. Bibl. [BT1315.2.L4 1967] 67-113563 15.00 set,
1. Sects, Medieval. 2. Theology, Doctrinal—Hist.—Middle Ages. 3. Heresies and heretics. I. Title.

RUSSELL, Jeffrey Burton. 273.09021
Dissent and reform in the early Middle Ages. Berkeley, University of California Press, 1965. 323 p. 24 cm. (Publications of the Center for Medieval and Renaissance Studies, 1) Bibliographical references included in "Notes" (p. 273-311) [BT1315.2.R8] 65-22422
1. Heresies and heretics. 2. Sects, Medieval. I. Title. II. Series: California. University. University at Los Angeles. Center for Medieval and Renaissance Studies Publications, 1)

WAKEFIELD, Walter Leggett, comp. 273'.09'021
Heresies of the high Middle Ages. Selected sources translated and annotated by Walter L. Wakefield and Austin P. Evans. New York, Columbia University Press, 1969. xiv, 865 p. 24 cm. (Records of civilization: sources and studies, no. 81) Includes bibliographical references. [BT1315.2.W32] 68-28402 22.50
1. Sects, Medieval. I. Evans, Austin Patterson, joint comp. II. Title. III. Series.

ALLEN, Don Cameron, 1904- 273.0903
Doubt's boundless sea: skepticism and faith in the Renaissance. Baltimore Johns Hopkins Press, 1964. xi, 272 p. 22 cm. Bibliography: p. 244-261. [CB361.A48] 64-10939
1. Renaissance. 2. Religious thought — 16th cent. 3. Skepticism. I. Title.

ALLEN, Don Cameron, 1904- 273.0903
Doubt's boundless sea; skepticism and faith in the Renaissance. Baltimore, Johns Hopkins [c.] 1964. xi, 272p. 22cm. Bibl. 64-10939 5.95
1. Renaissance. 2. Religious thought—16th cent. 3. Skepticism. I. Title.

SHRIVER, George H., ed. 273.0922
American religious heretics; formal and informal trials, edited by George H. Shriver. Nashville, Abingdon Press [1966] 240 p. 23 cm. Includes bibliographical references. [BR517.S44] 66-21972
1. Heresies and heretics. 2. Trials (Heresy)—United States. 3. United States—Church history. I. Title.

BAUER, Walter, 1877-1960. 273'.1
Orthodoxy and heresy in earliest Christianity. Translated by a team from the Philadelphia Seminar on Christian Origins, and edited by Robert A. Kraft and Gerhard Krodel. Philadelphia, Fortress Press [1971] xxv, 326 p. 24 cm. Translation of Rechtglaubigkeit und Ketzerei im altesten Christentum. Includes bibliographical references. [BT1315.B313 1971] 71-141252 ISBN 0-8006-0055-X 12.50
1. Heresies and heretics—Early church, ca. 30-600. 2. Church history—Primitive and early church, ca. 30-600. 3. Apologetics—Early church, ca. 30-600. I. Kraft, Robert A., ed. II. Krodel, Gerhard, 1926- ed. III. Title.

CENTER for Hermeneutical Studies in Hellenistic and Modern Culture. 273'.1
The Thunder = perfect mind (Nag Hammadi Codex VI, tractate 2) : protocol of the fifth colloquy, 11 March 1973 / The Center for Hermeneutical Studies in Hellenistic and Modern Culture ; George W. MacRae. Berkeley, CA : The Center, c1975. p. cm. (Protocol series of the colloquies of the Center for Hermeneutical Studies in Hellenistic and Modern Culture ; no. 5) Includes English translation of The Thunder and bibliographical references. [BT1390.C36 1975] 75-44028 ISBN 0-89242-004-9 : 2.00
1. The Thunder—Congresses. 2. Gnosticism—Congresses. I. MacRae, George W. II. The Thunder. English. 1975. III. Title. IV. Series: Center for Hermeneutical Studies in Hellenistic and Modern Culture. Protocol series of the colloquies ; no. 5.

DART, John, 1936- 273'.1
The laughing Savior : the discovery and significance of the Nag Hammadi gnostic library / John Dart. 1st ed. New York : Harper & Row, c1976. xxi, 154 p. : ill. ; 22 cm. Includes index. Bibliography: p. 142-147. [BT1390.D35 1976] 75-36749 ISBN 0-06-061692-X : 8.95
1. Chenoboskion manuscripts. 2. Gnosticism. I. Title.

DORESSE, Jean, 1917- 273'.1
The secret books of the Egyptian Gnostics; an introduction to the Gnostic Coptic manuscripts discovered at Chenoboskion. With an English translation and critical evaluation of the Gospel according to Thomas. New York, Viking Press. [New York, AMS Press, 1972, c1960] xvii, 445 p. illus. 23 cm. Translation of Les livres secrets des gnostiques d'Egypte. Includes bibliographical references. [BT1390.D613 1972] 79-153316 ISBN 0-404-04646-0 19.50
1. Gnosticism. I. Bible. N.T. Apocryphyl books. Coptic Gospel of Thomas. English. Johnston. 1972. II. Title.

DORESSE, Jean, 1917- 273.1
The secret books of the Egyptian Gnostics; an introduction to the Gnostic Coptic manuscripts discovered at Chenoboskion. [Translation by Philip Mairet] With an English translation and critical evaluation of the Gospel according to Thomas. New York, Viking Press [1960] xvii, 445 p. illus., ports., facsims. 22 cm. "The Gospel according to Thomas; or, The secret words of Jesus, from the Coptic. Originally translated into French, with introduction and notes, by Jean Doresse, and now rendered into English from the French by the Rev. Leonard Johnston, L. S. S., in collaboration with Jean Doresse": p. 333-383. Bibliographical footnotes. [BT1390.D613] 60-6161
1. Gnosticism. I. Mairet, Philippe, 1886- tr. II. Johnston, Leonard, tr. III. Bible. N. T. Apocryphal Books. Coptic Gospel of Thomas. English. Johnston. 1960. IV. Title.

FOERSTER, Werner, 1897- comp. 273'.1
Gnosis; a selection of Gnostic texts. English translation edited by R. McL. Wilson. Oxford, Clarendon Press, 1972- v. 22 cm. Translation of Die Gnosis. Contents.Contents.—1. Patristic evidence. Bibliography: v. 1, p. [365]-367. [BT1390.F613] 73-156488
1. Gnosticism. I. Wilson, Robert MacLachlan, ed. II. Title.
Distributed by Oxford University Press N.Y; 12.95.

GOSPEL of the Egyptians. English & Coptic. 273'.1
Nag Hammadi codices III, 2 and IV, 2 : The gospel of the Egyptians (The holy book of the great invisible spirit) / edited with translation and commentary by Alexander Bohlig and Frederik Wisse, in cooperation with Pahor Labib. Grand Rapids, Mich. : W. B. Eerdmans, 1975. xii, 234 p. ; 25 cm. (Nag Hammadi studies ; 4) Includes indexes. Bibliography: p. [208]-210. [BT1390.G6713 1975] 75-316868 27.50
1. Gnosticism. I. Bohlig, Alexander. II. Wisse, Frederik. III. Labib, Pahor. IV. Title. V. Series. VI. The Coptic gnostic library

GRANT, Robert McQueen, 1917- ed. 273.1
Gnosticism; a source book of heretical writings from the early Christian period. New York, Harper [c.1961] 254p. Bibl. 61-7341 4.00
1. Gnosticism. I. Title.

GRANT, Robert McQueen, 1917- 273.1
Gnosticism and early Christianity, by R. M. Grant. Rev. ed. New York, Harper & Row [1966] viii, 241 p. 21 cm. (Harper Torchbooks. The Cloister library) Lectures delivered under the auspices of the Committee on the History of Religions of the American Council of Learned Societies, 1957-58. Bibliography: p. [226]-232. [BT1390.G72] 66-31751
1. Gnosticism. I. Title.

GRANT, Robert McQueen, 1917- 273.1
Gnosticism and early Christianity. Rev. ed. New York, Harper [c.1959, 1966] 241p. 21cm. (Torchbk. TB136K Cloister lib.) Bibl. [BL25.L4] 7.00
1. Gnosticism. I. Title.

GRANT, Robert McQueen, 1917- 273.1
Gnosticism and early Christianity. 2d ed. New York, Columbia, 1966 [c.1959] viii, 241p. 21cm. (Lect. on the hist. of religions. New ser., no. 5) Bibl. [BL25.G7] 7.00

1. Gnosticism. I. Title.

GRANT, Robert McQueen, 1917- 273.1
Gnosticism and early Christianity, by R. M. Grant. 2d ed. New York, Columbia University Press, 1966. viii, 241 p. 21 cm. Bibliography: p. [226]-232. [BT1390.G72 1966a] 66-31334
1. Gnosticism. I. Title.

GRANT, Robert McQueen, 1917- 273.1
Gnosticism and early Christianity, by R. M. Grant. Rev. ed. New York, Harper & Row [1966] viii, 241 p. 21 cm. (Harper Torchbooks. The Cloister library) Lectures delivered under the auspices of the Committee on the History of Religions of the American Council of Learned Societies, 1957-58. Bibliography: p. [226]-232. [BT1390.G72] 66-31751
1. Gnosticism. I. Title.

HELMBOLD, Andrew K. 273'.1
The Nag Hammadi Gnostic texts and the Bible, by Andrew K. Helmbold. Grand Rapids, Baker Book House, 1967. 106 p. illus., maps. 22 cm. (Baker studies in Biblical archaeology, 5) Includes bibliographies. [BT1390.H4] 67-18178
1. Gnosticism. 2. Chenoboskion manuscripts. I. Title.

JONAS, Hans, 1903- 273.1
The gnostic religion; the message of the alien God and the beginnings of Christianity. Boston, Beacon Press [1958] xviii, 302p. 21cm. Bibliography: p. 291-299. [BT1390.J62] 58-6246
1. Gnosticism. I. Title.

JONAS, Hans, 1903- 273.1
The gnostic religion; the message of the alien God and the beginnings of Christianity. 2d ed., rev. Boston, Beacon Press [1963] 355 p. 21 cm. (Beacon paperback) [BT1390.J62] 63-8950
1. Ghosticism. I. Title.

JONAS, Hans, 1903- 273.1
The gnostic religion; the message of the alien God and the beginnings of Christianity. 2d ed. rev. [Gloucester, Mass., P. Smith, 1964, c.1958, 1963] 355p. 21cm. (Beacon paperback LR18 rebound) Bibl. 4.50
1. Gnosticism. I. Title.

JONAS HANS 1903- 273.1
The gnostic religion; the message of the alien God and the beginnings of Christianity. 2d ed., rev. Boston, Beacon [c.1958, 1963] 355p. 21cm. (Beacon paperback, LR 18) Bibl. 63-8950 2.45 pap.,
1. Gnosticism. I. Title.

KING, Charles William, 1818-1888. 273'.1
The Gnostics and their remains, ancient and mediaeval. Minneapolis, Wizards Bookshelf, 1973. xxiii, 472 p. illus. 23 cm. (Secret doctrine reference series) "Verbatim with the second enlarged edition 1887. Bibliography: p. [449]-461. [BT1390.K5 1973] 73-76092 ISBN 0-913510-04-1 15.00
1. Gnosticism. I. Title.

MEAD, George Robert Stow, 1863-1933. 273.1
Fragments of a faith forgotten; the Gnostics, a contribution to the study of the origins of Christianity. Introd. by Kenneth Rexroth. New Hyde Park, N. Y., University Books [1960] ixvii, 633p. 24cm. Bibliography: p. 609-633. [BT1390.M45 1960] 60-15310
1. Gnosticism. I. Title.

MEAD, George Robert Stow, 1863-1933 273.1
Fragments of a faith forgotten; the Gnostics, a contribution to the study of the origins of Christianity. Introd. by Kenneth Rexroth. New Hyde Park, N. Y., University Books [c.1960] 1xvii, 633p. 24cm. Bibl.: p. 609-633. 60-15310 10.00 half cloth,
1. Gnosticism. I. Title.

SCHMITHALS, Walter. 273'.1
The apocalyptic movement, introduction & interpretation / Walter Schmithals ; translated by John E. Steely. Nashville : Abingdon Press, [1975] 255 p. ; 23 cm. Translation of Die Apokalyptik. Bibliography: p. 255. [BS646.S3413] 74-34242 ISBN 0-687-01630-4 : 8.95
1. Apocalyptic literature. I. Title.

SCHMITHALS, Walter. 273'.1
Gnosticism in Corinth; an investigation of the letters to the Corinthians. Translated by John E. Steely. Nashville, Abingdon Press [1971] 412 p. 25 cm. Translation of Die Gnosis in Korinth. Bibliography: p. 15-21. [BS2675.2.S3513] 70-158670 ISBN 0-687-14887-1 12.95
1. Bible. N.T. Corinthians—Criticism, interpretation, etc. 2. Gnosticism. 3. Corinth, Greece—Religion. I. Title.

TURNER, John Douglas. 273'.1
The Book of Thomas the Contender, from Codex II of the Cairo gnostic library from Nag Hammadi (CG II, 7) : the Coptic text, with translation, introd., and commentary / by John Douglas Turner. Missoula, Mont. : Society of Biblical Literature : Distributed by Scholars Press, University of Montana, 1975. (Dissertation series ; no. 23) Thesis - Duke University, 1970. Includes index. Bibliography: p. [BS2970.T8] 75-22446 ISBN 0-89130-017-1
1. Book of Thomas the Contender. 2. Gnosticism—History—Sources. 3. Coptic language—Texts. I. Chenoboskion manuscripts. II. Book of Thomas the Contender. English & Coptic. 1975. III. Series: Society of Biblical Literature. Dissertation series ; no. 18.

UNNIK, Willem Cornelis van. 273.1
Newly discovered gnostic writings; a preliminary survey of the Nag-Hammadi find. [1st English ed.] Naperville, Ill., A. R. Allenson [1960] 96 p. 22 cm. (Studies in Biblical theology, no. 30) Translation of Openbaringen uit Egyptisch Zand. Bibliography: p. 94. [BT1390.U533] 60-4220
1. Gnosticism. 2. Manuscripts, Coptic (Papyri) I. Title. II. Series.

UNNIK, Willem Cornelis van. 273.1
Newly discovered gnostic writings; a preliminary survy of the Nag-Hammadi find. [Translated from the Dutch] Naperville, Ill., A. R. Allenson [1960] 96 p.: p. 94. 22 cm. (Studies in Biblical theology, no. 30) Bibl. 60-1220 1.75 pap.,
1. Gnosticism. 2. Manuscripts, Coptic (Papyri) I. Title. II. Series.

WIDENGREN, Geo, 1907- 273'.1
The gnostic attitude. Translated from the Swedish and edited by Birger A. Pearson. Santa Barbara, Institute of Religious Studies, University of California [1973] ix, 75 p. 22 cm. Translation of chapter 16, Den gnostiska installningen in the author's Religionens varld. Includes bibliographical references. [B638.W523] 73-159697
1. Gnosticism. I. Title.

YAMAUCHI, Edwin M. 273'.1
Gnostic ethics and Mandaean origins [by] Edwin M. Yamauchi. Cambridge, Harvard University Press, 1970. 102 p. 24 cm. (Harvard theological studies, 24) Bibliography: p. 94-102. [BT1405.Y3] 70-23074
1. Mandaeans. 2. Gnostic ethics. I. Title. II. Series.

YAMAUCHI, Edwin M., 1937- 273'.1
Pre-Christian Gnosticism; a survey of the proposed evidences, by Edwin M. Yamauchi. [1st ed.] Grand Rapids, Eerdmans [1973] 208 p. 23 cm. "An expansion of the Tyndale lecture for Biblical archaeology presented ... in July 1970." Bibliography: p. [187]-194. [BT1390.Y35] 72-94668 ISBN 0-8028-3429-9 7.95
1. Gnosticism. I. Title.

WILSON, Robert McLachlan. 273'.1'08
Gnosis and the New Testament [by] R. McL. Wilson. Philadelphia, Fortress Press [1968] viii, 149 p. 23 cm. Bibliographical footnotes. [BT1390.W48 1968] 68-13446
1. Bible. N.T.—Criticism, interpretation, etc. 2. Gnosticism. I. Title.

ASMUSSEN, Jes Peter, comp. 273'.2
Manichaean literature : representative texts chiefly from Middle Persian and Parthian writings / selected, introduced, and partly translated by Jes P. Asmussen. Delmar, N.Y. : Scholars' Facsimiles & Reprints, 1975. p. cm. (UNESCO collection of representative works, Persian heritage series ; no.) Includes index. Bibliography: p. [BT1410.A72] 74-22063 ISBN 0-8201-1141-4 lib.bdg. : 10.00
1. Manichaeism—History—Sources. I. Title. II. Series. III. UNESCO collection of representative works, Persian series

LEA, Henry Charles, 1825-1909. 273.2
The Inquisition of the Middle Ages. An abridgment by Margaret Nicholson. New York, Macmillan, 1961. 906 p. 22 cm. "Abridged from A history of the Inquisition of the Middle Ages." [BX1711.L413] 61-10024
1. Inquistion—History.

OBOLENSKY, Dimitri, 1918- 273.2
The Bogomils, a study in Balkan neo-Manichaeism. Cambridge [Eng.] University Press, 1948. xiv, 317 p. fold. map. 23 cm. Bibliography: p. [290]-304. [BT1355.Os] A51
1. Bogomolies. 2. Manichaeism. I. Title.

RUNCIMAN, Stevan [James Cochran Stevenson Runciman] 1903- 273.2
The medieval Manichee; a study of the Christian dualist heresy. New York, Viking [1961] 212p. (Compass bk. C86) Bibl. 1.45 pap.,
1. Sects, Medieval. I. Title.

AUGUSTINUS, Aurelius, Saint, Bp. of Hippo. 273.23
The Catholic and Manichaen ways of life. De moribus ecclesiae Catholicae et de moribus Manichaeorum. Translated by Donald A. Gallagher and Idella J. Gallagher. Washington, Catholic University of America Press [1966] xx, 135 p. 22 cm. (The Fathers of the Church; a new translation, v. 56) Bibliography: p. xix-xx. [BR60.F3A8143] 66-11337
1. Manichaeism. I. Title. II. Series.

AUGUSTINUS AURELIUS, Saint, Bp. of Hippo 273.23
The Catholic and Manichaean ways of life. De moribus ecclesiae Catholicae et de moribus Manichaeorum. Tr. by Donald A. Gallagher, Idella J. Gallgher. Washington, D.C., Catholic Univ. of Amer. Pr. [c.1966] xx, 135p. 22cm. (Fathers of the Church; a new tr. v.56) Bibl. [BR60.F3A8143] 66-11337 4.45
1. Manichaeism. I. Title. II. Series.

WIDENGREN, Geo, 1907- 273.23
Mani and manichaeism. Translation by Charles Kessler, [1st ed.] New York, Holt, Rinehart and Winston [c1965] 167 p. illus., facsims. 25 cm. (History of religion series) Bibliography: p. 145-158. [BT1410.W543] 65-22455
1. Manichaeism. I. Title.

FREND, W. H. C. 273'.4
The Donatist Church: a movement of protest in Roman North Africa, by W. H. C. Frend. Oxford, Clarendon Press, 1971. xviii, 361 p., 3 fold. plates; 3 maps. 23 cm. Bibliography: p. [339]-352. [BT1370.F7 1971] 75-595861 ISBN 0-19-826408-9 £5.00
1. Donatists. I. Title.

NEWMAN, John Henry, Cardinal, 1801-1890. 273'.4
The Arians of the fourth century. New ed. Westminster, Md., Christian Classics, 1968. xix, 474 p. 21 cm. (The works of Cardinal Newman) Reprint of the 1871 ed. Bibliographical footnotes. [BT1350.N4 1968] 68-24081
1. Arianism. I. Title.

REISMAN, Frederick W. 273.4
A layman speaks out loud. Boston, Christopher Pub. House [c.1961] 128p. illus. Bibl. 61-18077 3.00
1. Arianism. I. Title.

EVANS, Robert F. 273'.5
Four letters of Pelagius [by] Robert F. Evans. New York, Seabury Press [1968] 134 p. 24 cm. (Studies in Pelagius) Bibliographical references included in "Notes" (p. 120-132) [BT1450.E88] 68-11594
1. Pelagius. I. Pelagius. II. Title.

EVANS, Robert F 273'.5
Pelagius; inquiries and reappraisals [by] Robert F. Evans. New York, Seabury Press [1968] xvi, 171 p. 22 cm. Bibliographical references included in ""Notes" (p. [123]-167) [BT1450.E9] 67-20939
1. Pelagius. I. Title.

EVANS, Robert F. 273'.5
Pelagius; inquiries and reappraisals [by] Robert F. Evans. New York, Seabury Press [1968] xvi, 171 p. 22 cm. Bibliographical references included in "Notes" (p. [123]-167) [BT1450.E9 1968] 67-20939
1. Pelagius.

FERGUSON, John, 1921- 273.5
Pelagius; a historical and theological study. Cambridge [Eng.] W. Heffer, 1956. 206p. 22cm. Includes bibliography. [BT1450.F4] 57-4262
1. Pelagius. I. Title.

LEFF, Gordon. 273.5
Bradwardine and the Pelagians; a study of his 'De causa Dei' and its opponents. Cambridge [Eng.] University Press, 1957. 282p. 23cm. (Cambridge studies in medieval life and thought, new ser., v. 5) Bibliography: p. [269]-273. [BT1450.B73L4] 57-2511
1. Bradwardine, Thomas, Abp. of Canterbury, 1290-1349. De causa Dei. 2. Pelagianism. I. Title. II. Series.

LAMBERT, Malcolm. 273'.6
Medieval heresy : popular movements from Bogomil to Hus / Malcolm Lambert. New York : Holmes & Meier Publishers, 1977, c1976. xvi, 430 p. : ill. ; 24 cm. Includes index. Bibliography: p. [388]-391. [BT1319.L35 1977] 76-49949 ISBN 0-8419-0298-4 : 27.50
1. Heresies and heretics—Middle Ages, 600-1500. I. Title.

LERNER, Robert E. 273'.6
The heresy of the free spirit in the later Middle Ages [by] Robert E. Lerner. Berkeley, University of California Press, 1972. xv, 257 p. 24 cm. Bibliography: p. [244]-246. [BT1358.L47 1972] 78-145790 ISBN 0-520-01908-3 10.00
1. Brethren of the Free Spirit. 2. Heresies and heretics—Middle Ages, 600-1500. I. Title.

OZMENT, Steven E. 273'.6
Mysticism and dissent; religious ideology and social protest in the sixteenth century, by Steven E. Ozment. New Haven, Yale University Press, 1973. xii, 270 p. 25 cm. Bibliography: p. 248-263. [BX4817.O96 1973] 72-91316 ISBN 0-300-01576-3 10.00
1. Dissenters, Religious. 2. Mysticism—Middle Ages. I. Title.

RUSSELL, Jeffrey Burton, comp. 273'.6
Religious dissent in the Middle Ages. Edited by Jeffrey B. Russell. New York, Wiley [1971] xi, 161 p. 23 cm. (Major issues in history) Bibliography: p. 159-161. [BT1315.2.R83] 73-136722 ISBN 0-471-74555-3
1. Dissenters, Religious—Collections. 2. Sects, Medieval—Collections. 3. Heresies and heretics—Middle Ages, 600-1500—Collections. I. Title.

FABER, Doris, 1924- 273.6'0924 B
A colony leader: Anne Hutchinson. Illustrated by Frank Vaughn. Champaign, Ill., Garrard Pub. Co. [1970] 64 p. col. illus., col. map. 24 cm. (Colony leaders) A biography of the woman banished from the Massachusetts Bay Colony for disagreeing with the prevailing religious practices. [F67.H92F3] 92 75-111907 2.39
1. Hutchinson, Anne (Marbury) 1591-1643—Juvenile literature. I. Vaughn, Frank, 1915- illus. II. Title.

RUGG, Winnifred King. 273'.6'0924 B
Unafraid; a life of Anne Hutchinson. Freeport, N.Y., Books for Libraries Press [1970] xii, 263 p. front. 23 cm. Reprint of the 1930 ed. Bibliography: p. [255]-257. [F67.H92R8 1970] 73-114891 ISBN 0-8369-5295-2
1. Hutchinson, Anne (Marbury) 1591-1643. I. Title.

HALL, David D., comp. 273'.6'09744
The Antinomian controversy, 1636-1638; a documentary history, edited, with introd. and notes, by David D. Hall. [1st ed.] Middletown, Conn., Wesleyan University Press [1968] viii, 447 p. 24 cm. Includes bibliographical references. [F67.H92H3] 68-17148
1. Hutchinson, Anne (Marbury) 1591-1643. 2. Antinomianism. I. Title.

SIMMONS, Frederick Johnson, 1884- 273'.6'09744
Emanuel Downing. [Montclair, N.J.] 1958. 93 p. illus. 23 cm. Includes bibliography [F67.D69D5] 60-39974
1. Downing, Emanuel, 1585-1660. I. Title.

STRANDNESS, Theodore Benson. 273'.6'09744
Samuel Sewall; a Puritan portrait, by T. B. Strandness. [East Lansing?] Michigan State University Press, 1967. xiv, 234 p. map (on lining papers) 24 cm. Bibliography: p. 209-226. [F67.S546] 67-28876
1. Sewall, Samuel, 1652-1730. I. Title.

FERGUSON, James P. 273'.8
Dr. Samuel Clarke : an eighteenth century heretic / [by] J. P. Ferguson. Kineton : Roundwood Press, 1976. vii, 255 p., [5] leaves of plates : 1 ill., ports. ; 24 cm. Includes index. Bibliography: p. 230-241. [BX5199.C52F47] 77-353989 ISBN 0-900093-59-5 : £7.50
1. Clarke, Samuel, 1675-1729.

EVERITT, Alan Milner. 273'.9
The pattern of rural dissent; the nineteenth century, by Alan Everitt. Leicester, Leicester University Press, 1972. 90 p. 25 cm.

(University of Leicester. Department of English Local History. Occasional papers, second series, no. 4) Distributed in North America by Humanities Press, New York. Includes bibliographical references. [BX5203.2.E95] 72-194002 ISBN 0-7185-2028-9 3.50
1. Dissenters, Religious—England. I. Title. II. Series: Leicester, Eng. University. Dept. of English Local History. Occasional papers, second series, no. 4.

GARSOIAN, Nina G., 1923- 273'.9
The Paulician heresy. A study of the origin and development of Paulicianism in Armenia and the eastern provinces of the Byzantine empire. By Nina G. Garsoian. The Hague, Paris, Mouton, 1967 [1968] 296p. fold. map. 24cm. (Columbia Univ. Pubns. in Near & Middle East studies. Ser. A, 6) Bibl. [BT1445. G3] 67-24377 15.50
1. Paulicians. I. Title. II. Series.
Distributed by Humanities, New York.

HUTCHISON, William R. 273'.9
The modernist impulse in American Protestantism / William R. Hutchison. Cambridge, Mass. : Harvard University Press, 1976. x, 347 p. : ports. ; 25 cm. Includes index. Bibliography: p. [325]-340. [BT82.H87] 75-20190 ISBN 0-674-58058-3 : 15.00
1. Modernism. I. Title.

ROTONDO, Antonio. 273'.9
Calvin and the Italian anti-Trinitarians. Translated by John and Anne Tedeschi. St. Louis, Mo., Foundation for Reformation Research, 1968. 28 p. 23 cm. (Reformation essays & studies, 2) Bibliographical footnotes. [BT109.R6] 70-3056 1.00
1. Calvin, Jean, 1509-1564—Theology. 2. Antitrinitarianism—Italy. I. Title. II. Series.

274 Christian Church In Europe

BRENTANO, Robert, 1926- 274
Two churches; England and Italy in the thirteenth century. Princeton, N.J., Princeton University Press, 1968. xvi, 372 p. illus., maps. 22 cm. Bibliographical footnotes. [BR750.B755] 68-11438 11.00
1. Great Britain—Church history—Medieval period, 1066-1485. 2. Italy—Church history. I. Title.

BURRELL, Sidney Alexander, 274
1912- ed.
The role of religion in modern European history. New York, Macmillan [c.1964] ix, 147p. 22cm. (Main themes in Eur. hist. 31723) Bibl. 64-16853 1.50 pap.,
1. Church history—Modern period—Addresses, essays, lectures. I. Title.

BURRELL, Sidney Alexander, 274
1917- ed.
The role of religion in modern European history. New York, Macmillan [1964] ix, 147 p. 22 cm. (Main themes in European history) Includes bibliographical references. [BR290.B8] 64-16853
1. Church history — Modern Period — Addresses, essays, lectures. I. Title.

CRAWFORD, Samuel John, 1884- 274
1931.
Anglo-Saxon influence on Western Christendom, 600-800 Cambridge [Eng.] Speculum Historiale; New York, Barnes & Noble [1966] 109 p. 19 cm. "Lectures, delivered under the auspices of the University of London at University College in April and May 1931." Contents. The position of the papacy in the sixth and seventh centuries.--The Anglo-Saxons on the continent in the later seventh and eighth centuries.--Anglo-Saxon England and the transmission of ancient culture. [BR253.C75 1966] 66-8736
1. Church history—Middle Ages. 2. Gt. Brit.—Church history—Anglo-Saxon period. I. Title.

CRAWFORD, Samuel John, 1884- 274
1931
Anglo-Saxon influence on Western Christendom, 600-800 Cambridge [Eng.] Speculum Historiale; New York, Barnes &Noble [1966] 109p. 19cm. Lects. delivered under the auspices of the Univ. of London at Univ. Coll. in April and May 1931. [BR253.C75 1966] 66-8736 3.00
1. Church history—Middle Ages. 2. Gt. Brit.—Church history—Anglo-Saxon period. I. Title.
Contents omitted.

DEMAREST, Victoria Booth- 274
Clibborn.
What I saw in Europe; a challenge to Christians every-where. Introd. by Paul Christopher Warren. New York, Vantage Press [1953] 160p. 23cm. [BR735.D43] 53-6467
1. Europe—Religion. 2. Europe—Soc. condit. I. Title.

EVANS, Robert P 274
Let Europe hear; the spiritual plight of Europe. A survey of sixteen countries of free, western Europe, stressing the conditions which have made them mission fields in our generation. Chicago, Moody Press [1963] 528 p. illus. 25 cm. Bibliographical references included in "Notes": p. 509-520. [BR735.E9] 63-14562
1. Europe — Religion. I. Title.

EVANS, Robert P. 274
Let Europe hear; the spiritual plight of Europe. A survey of sixteen countries of free, western Europe, stressing the conditions which have made them mission fields in our generation. Chicago, Moody [c.1963] 528p. illus. 25cm. Bibl. 63-14562 5.95
1. Europe—Religion. I. Title.

HARNEY, Martin Patrick, 1896- 274
Medieval ties between Italy and Ireland. [Boston] St. Paul Eds. [dist. Daughters of St. Paul, c.1963] 74p. illus. 22cm. 63-14891 1.50; 1.00 pap.,
1. Ireland—Church history. 2. Italy—Church history. 3. Ireland—Relations (general) with Italy. 4. Italy—Relations (general) with Ireland. I. Title.

HERMAN, Stewart Winfield, 274
1909-
Report from Christian Europe. New York, Friendship Press [1953] 211p. 21cm. [BR735.H45] 53-1046
1. Europe—Church history. 2. Europe—Religion. 3. Europe—Politics—1945- 4. Church and state in Europe. I. Title.

HILLGARTH, J. N., comp. 274
The conversion of Western Europe, 350-750. Edited by J. N. Hillgarth. Englewood Cliffs, N.J., Prentice-Hall [1969] xi, 147 p. map. 22 cm. (A Spectrum book.) (Sources of civilization in the West) Includes bibliographical references. [BR200.H5] 69-17378 ISBN 0-13-172163-1 4.95
1. Church history—Middle Ages, 600-1500—Sources. I. Title. II. Series.

HULL, Eleanor (Means) 274
The church not made with hands [by] Eleanor Hull. Valley Forge [Pa.] Judson Press [1965] 110 p. illus., ports. 22 cm. "Another American Baptist mission book." Bibliographical footnotes. [BR481.H76] 65-15008
1. Christianity—20th cent. I. Title.

HULL, Eleanor (Means) 274
The church not made with hands. Valley Forge [Pa.] Judson [c.1965] 110p. illus., ports. 22cm. (Amer. Baptist mission bk.) Bibl. [BR481.H76] 65-15008 1.95 pap.,
1. Christianity—20th cent. I. Title.

KINGTON-OLIPHANT, Thomas 274
Laurence, 1831-1902.
Rome and reform. Port Washington, N.Y., Kennikat Press [1971] 2 v. 22 cm. Reprint of the 1902 ed. Includes bibliographical references. [BX1304.K5 1971] 76-118541
1. Catholic Church—History. 2. Protestantism—History. 3. Europe—Church history. I. Title.

MCNEILL, John Thomas, 1885- 274
The Celtic churches; a history A.D. 200 to 1200 [by] John T. McNeill. Chicago, University of Chicago Press [1974] xii, 289 p. 24 cm. Bibliography: p. 273-279. [BR748.M33] 73-84193 ISBN 0-226-56095-3 10.00
1. Celtic Church—History. I. Title.

MEYER, Carl Stamm, 1907- 274
A history of Western Christianity [by] Carl S. Meyer [and] Neelak S. Tjernagel. Edited by Harold W. Rast. St. Louis, Concordia Pub. House [1971] 287 p. illus. 22 cm. [BR145.2.M455] 70-164503 ISBN 0-570-01505-7
1. Church history. I. Tjernagel, Neelak Serawlook, 1906- joint author. II. Title.

RENNA, Thomas J. 274
Church and state in medieval Europe, 1050-1314 / Thomas J. Renna. Dubuque, Iowa : Kendall/Hunt Pub. Co., [1974] xiii, 205 p. ; 22 cm. Bibliography: p. 203-205. [BR735.R46] 74-81660 ISBN 0-8403-0959-7
1. Church and state in Europe. 2. Middle Ages. I. Title.

SHUSTER, George Nauman, 1894- 274
Religion behind the Iron Curtain. New York, MacMillan, 1954. 281p. 22cm. [BR738.6.S48] 54-10354
1. Europe, Eastern—Religion. I. Title.

TOBIAS, Robert. 274
Communist-Christian encounter in East Europe. Indianapolis, School of Religion Press, 1956. vi, 567p. 25cm. Bibliography: p. 557-560. [BR738.6.T6] 56-35689
1. Europe, Eastern—Religion. 2. Communism and religion. I. Title.

TOBIAS, Robert. 274
Communist-Christian encounter in East Europe. Indianapolis, School of Religion Press. 1956. vi, 567 p. 25 cm. Bibliography: p. 557-560. [BR738.6.T6] 56-35689
1. Europe, Eastern — Religion. 2. Communism and religion. I. Title.

CREIGHTON, Mandell, Bp. 274/.08
of London, 1843-1901
Historical lectures and addresses. Ed. by Louise Creighton. Freeport, N. Y., Bks. for Libs. Pr. [1967] vii, 346p. 22cm. (Essay index reprint ser.) Reprint of the 1904 ed. [D7.C9 1967] 67-26730 9.50
1. History—Addresses, essays, lectures. 2. Gt. Brit.—Church history. I. Creighton, Louise (von Glehn) 1850-1936, ed. II. Title.

BURLEIGH, John H. S. 274.1
A church history of Scotland. London, New York, Oxford University Press, 1960[ ] 456p. illus. (maps) Bibl.: p.[423]-424 and bibl. notes 60-50629 6.75
1. Scotland—Church history. I. Title.

DONALDSON, Gordon. 274.1
Scotland: church and nation through sixteen centuries. New York Barnes & Noble [1974, c1972] 128 p. 23 cm. Bibliography p 124-125. [BR782.D57] ISBN 0-06-491738-X 5.00
1. Scotland—Church history. I. Title.
L.C. card number for original edition: 60-4701.

DONALDSON, Gordon 274.1
The Scottish Reformation. [New York] Cambridge University Press, 1960[ ] 242p. illus. 'Based on the Birkbeck lectures delivered in the University of Cambridge in 1957-8. bIncludes bibl. 60-16183 5.50
1. Reformation—Scotland. 2. Scotland—Church history—16th cent. 3. Church of Scotland—Hist. 4. Scotland—Soc. life & cust. I. Title.

FREE Presbyterian Church of 274.1
Scotland. Synod.
Quater-centenary of the Scottish Reformation, as commemorated by the Synod of the Free Presbyterian Church of Scotland, at Edinburgh, May, 1960, by the reading of papers on the Reformation of 1560 [Inverness, Free Presbyterian Church of Scotland (Synod) 1967]. 3-68 p. front. (port.). 22 cm. Includes bibliographical references. [BR385.F7] 68-119620 6/-
1. Reformation—Scotland. I. Title.

HIGHET, John 274.1
The Scottish churches; a review of their state 400 years after the Reformation. [dist. New York, Humantites Pr., 1961, c.1960] 224p. 61-2868 6.00
1. Scotland—Religion. 2. Scotland—Church history. I. Title.

INNES review (The) 274.1
Essays on the Scottish Reformation, 1513-1625. Ed. by David McRoberts. Glasgow, Burns [dist. Chester Springs, Dufour, 1964] xxix, 496p. illus., ports., maps, facsims. 25cm. Essays which appeared in the Innes review. Bibl. 63-24324 15.00
1. Reformation—Scotland. I. McRoberts, David, ed. II. Title.

KELLET, Ernest Edward, 274.1
1864-1950.
Religion and life in the early Victorian age / by E. E. Kellett. Folcroft, Pa. : Folcroft Library Editions, 1976. 168 p. ; 23 cm. Reprint of the 1938 ed. published by Epworth Press (E. C. Barton), London, in series: THe Lincoln library. [BR759.K4 1976] 76-6509 ISBN 0-8414-5522-8 lib. bdg. : 20.00
1. England—Religion—19th century. 2. England—Social life and customs—19th century. I. Title. II. Series: The Lincoln library.

KELLET, Ernest Edward, 274.1
1864-1950.
Religion and life in the early Victorian age / by E. E. Kellett. Folcroft, Pa. : Folcroft Library Editions, 1976. 168 p. ; 23 cm. Reprint of the 1938 ed. published by Epworth Press (E. C. Barton), London, in series: THe Lincoln library. [BR759.K4 1976] 76-6509 ISBN 0-8414-5522-8 lib. bdg. : 20.00
1. England—Religion—19th century. 2. England—Social life and customs—19th century. I. Title. II. Series: The Lincoln library.

LOWE, Harry William. 274.1
Scottish heroes; tales of the Covenanters. Mountain View, Calif., Pacific Press Pub. Association [1950] xvi, 192 p. 21 cm. Bibliography: p. 189-190. [BX9081.L6] 51-337
1. Covenanters. I. Title.

PAWLEY, Bernard C. 274.1
Rome and Canterbury, through four centuries; a study of the relations between the Church of Rome and the Anglican churches, 1530-1973, by Bernard and Margaret Pawley. With an American epilogue by Arthur A. Vogel. New York, Seabury Press [1975] xii, 419 p. illus. 22 cm. "A Crossroad book." Bibliography: p. 388-403. [BX5129.P37] 74-19253 ISBN 0-8164-1178-6 13.50
1. Church of England—Relations—Catholic Church. 2. Catholic Church—Relations—Church of England. I. Pawley, Margaret, joint author. II. Title.

RENWICK, A. M. 274.1
The story of the Scottish Reformation. Grand Rapids, Mich., Eerdmans [1960] 176p. 18cm. (Eerdmans pocket editions) Includes bibliography. 60-2957 1.25
1. Reformation—Scotland. I. Title. II. Title: Scottish Reformation.

SOCIETY of American 274'.1
Archivists. Church Records Committee.
Directory of religious archival and historical depositories in America. 1962- [St. Louis?] v. 28 cm. Title varies: 1962, Directory of religious archivists and historians in America. [BR133.U5S6] 64-5361
1. Church records and registers — U.S. 2. Archives — Direct. 3. Archives, Diocesan — Direct. I. Title. II. Title: Directory of religious archivists and historians in America.

SPOTTISWOOD, John, Abp. of 274.1
St. Andrews, 1565-1639.
The history of the Church of Scotland. New York, AMS Press [1973] 3 v. 24 cm. Reprint of the 1847-51 ed. printed for the Spottiswoode Society, Edinburgh, which was issued as no. 93 of Bannatyne Club Publications. With biographical sketches and notes by M. Russell. [BR785.S682] 76-176004 ISBN 0-404-52840-6 70.00
1. Scotland—Church history. I. Title. II. Series: Bannatyne Club, Edinburgh. Publications no. 93.

THOMAS, Charles, 1928- 274'.1
The early Christian archaeology of North Britain: the Hunter Marshall lectures delivered at the University of Glasgow in January and February 1968. London, New York, Oxford University Press for the University of Glasgow, 1971. xvi, 253 p., 8 plates; illus., maps, plans. 23 cm. (The Hunter Marshall lectures) Bibliography: p. [229]-245. [BR133.G6T48] 75-858359 ISBN 0-19-214102-3 £3.00
1. Christian antiquities—Gt. Brit. I. Title. II. Series.

TOWILL, Edwin Sprott. 274.11
People and places in the story of the Scottish Church / [by] Edwin Sprott Towill ; illustrated by Colin Gibson. Edinburgh : St. Andrew Press, 1976. xix, 99 p. : ill., ports. ; 24 cm. [BR781.T68] 77-367785 ISBN 0-7152-0322-3 : £3.25. pbk.
1. Scotland—Church history—Dictionaries. 2. Christian biography—Scotland. I. Title.

COCKBURN, James 274.132
Hutchison, 1882-
The medieval bishops of Dunblane and their church. Edinburgh, Pub. for the Soc. of Friends of Dunblane Cathedral by Oliver & Boyd [dist. Mystic. Conn., Verry, 1965, c.1959] 282p. illus. 23cm. [BX1501.D8C6] 59-2608 6.50
1. Dunblane, Scot (Diocese)—Hist. 2. Bishops—Scotland—Dunblane. 3. Dunblane Cathedral. I. Title.

BIELER, Ludwig. 274.15
Ireland, harbinger of the Middle Ages. [1st English ed.] London, New York, Oxford Univeristy Press, 1963. viii, 148 p. illus. (part col., part mounted) maps, facsims. 30 cm. "First published in German." Bibliography: p. 145. [BR794.B513 1963] 63-6010
1. Ireland—Church history. 2. Monasticism and religious orders—Ireland. 3. Missionaries, Irish. 4. Art, Irish. I. Title.

CARTY, Xavier. 274.15
The churches in Ireland; facts about: Church of Ireland, Presbyterians, Methodists, Jews, Society of Friends. [Dublin] Catholic Truth Society of Ireland [1968] 35 p. 18 cm. "These articles were first published in the Redemptorist record ... [Jan.-July 1966]" [BR793.C37] 70-281664
1. Sects—Ireland. I. Catholic Truth Society of Ireland. II. Title.

CHADWICK, Nora (Kershaw) 274.15
1891-
The age of the saints in the early Celtic Church. New York, Oxford [1962, c.1961] 166p. 19cm. (Riddell memorial lects. 32d ser., Univ. of Durham pubn.) Bibl. 62-6872 2.00 bds.,
1. Celtic Church. 2. Asceticism—Early church. I. Title.

HUGHES, Kathleen. 274.15
The church in early Irish society. Ithaca, N. Y., Cornell University Press [1966] xii, 303 p. illus., fold. col. map. 23 cm. Bibliography: p. 284-292. [BR794.H8] 66-25052
1. Ireland—Church history. 2. Ireland—Hist.—To 1172. 3. Celtic Church. I. Title.

HUGHES, Kathleen. 274.15
The church in early Irish society. Ithaca, N.Y., Cornell University Press [1966] xii, 303 p. illus., fold. col. map. 23 cm. Bibliography: p. 284-292. [BR794.H8 1966a] 66-25052
1. Ireland—Church history. 2. Ireland—History—To 1172. 3. Celtic church. I. Title.

LEHANE, Brendan. 274.15
The quest of three abbots. New York, Viking Press [1968] 240 p. illus., map (on lining papers) 22 cm. [BR794.L4 1968b] 67-20300
1. Ireland—Church history. 2. Ireland—History—To 1172. I. Title.

LYNCH, Patricia, 1898- 274.15 B
Knights of God; tales and legends of the Irish saints. Illustrated by Victor Ambrus. [1st ed.] New York, Holt, Rinehart and Winston [1969] xix, 219 p. illus. 24 cm. Contents.Contents.—Introduction.—Saint Ciaran, the first of them all.—Saint Patrick, the Roman slave.—Enda of Aran.—Saint Brigid, the light of Kildare.—Brendan the voyager.—Columcille, dove of the church.—Kevin of Glendalough.—Lawrence O'Toole, captive prince.—There were other saints.—List of books (p. 219) [BX4659.I7L9 1969] 920 69-11811 4.50
1. Saints, Irish—Juvenile literature. I. Ambrus, Victor G., illus. II. Title.

ARBER, Edward, 1835-1912. 274.2
An introductory sketch to the Martin Marprelate controversy. 1588-1590. New York, B. Franklin [1967] 200 p. 24 cm. (The English scholar's library of old and modern works, no. 8) Burt Franklin research and source works series, #54. Originally published in 1895. "A provisional chronological list of the works comprising this controversy": p. [197]-200. [PR1121.A7] 67-7546
1. Marprelate controversy. I. Title. II. Series.

ARBER, Edward, 1836-1912 274.2
An introductory sketch to the Martin Marprelate controversy, 1588-1590. New York, B. Franklin [1967] 200p. 24cm. (English scholar's lib. of old and modern works, no. 8) Burt Franklin res. and source works ser., No. 54. Orig. pub. in 1895. A provisional chronological list of the works comprising this controversy: p. [197]-200. [PR1121.A7 no.8 1967] 67-7546 12.50
1. Marprelate controversy. I. Title. II. Series.

BARLOW, Frank 274.2
The English church, 1000-1066; a constitutional history [Hamden, Conn.] Archon [dist. Shoe String, c.1963] xii, 324p. maps, diagrs., geneal tables. 23cm. Bibl. 63-22885 12.00
1. Gt. Brit.—Church history—Anglo-Saxon period. I. Title.

BARLOW, Frank. 274.2
The English church, 1000-1066; a constitutional history [Hamden, Conn.] Archon Books [1963] xii, 324 p. maps, diagrs., geneal. tables. 23 cm. Bibliographical footnotes. [BR749.B3] 63-22885
1. Gt. Brit. — Church history — Anglo-Saxon period. I. Title.

BARLOW, Richard Burgess, 274.2
1927-
Citizenship and conscience; a study in the theory and practice of religious toleration in England during the eighteenth century. Philadelphia, University of Pennsylvania Press [1963, c1962] 348 p. 22 cm. [BR1610.B35] 62-7197
1. Toleration. 2. Gt. Brit. — Church history — 18th cent. I. Title.

BARLOW, William, Bp. of 274.2
Lincoln, d.1613.
The summe and substance of the conference which it pleased His Excellent Majestie to have with the lords, bishops, and other of his clergie at Hampton Court, January 14, 1603 (1604) A facsimile reprod. with an introd. by William T. Costello, Hcarles Keenan. Gainesville, Fla., Scholars' Facsmiles, 1965. viii, 103p. 23cm. Reproduced from a copy in Crosby Lib., Gonzaga Univ. [BR757.B3] 65-10395 6.00
1. Hampton Court Conference, 1604. I. Title.

BEDA Venerabilis, 673-735. 274.2
The ecclesiastical history of the English people, and other selections from the writings of the Venerable Bede. Edited, and with an introd., by James Campbell. New York, Washington Square Press [1968] xl, 422 p. maps. 18 cm. (The Great histories) "Bibliographical note": p. xxxvii. [BR746.B5 1968] 68-29672
1. Great Britain—Church history—Anglo-Saxon period, 449-1066. I. Campbell, James, 1935- ed. II. Title.

BEDA Venerabilis, 673-735. 274.2
Ecclesiastical history of the English nation. Introd. by David Knowles. London, J. M. Dent; New York, E. P. Dutton [1954] xiii, 382p. 19cm. (Everyman's library. History, 479) 'The text of this transiation, which also includes The life and miracles of St. Cuthbert and The lives of the bbots of Wearmouth and Jarrow, is that by John Stevenson (1870) revised with notes by L. C. Jane (1903)' Bibliograhy: p. xii. [BR746.B] A55
1. Cuthbert, Saint, d. 687. 2. Gt. Brit.—Church history—Angio-Saxon period. I. Title. II. Series.

BEDA Venerabilis, 673-735. 274.2
A history of the English church and people. Translated and with an introd. by Lee Sherley-Price. [Harmonds-worth, Middlesex] Penguin Books [1955] 340p. 18cm. (The Penguin classics, L42) [BR746.B5 1955] 56-289
1. Gt. Brit.—Church history—Angio-Saxon period. I. Title. II. Title: The English church and people.

BEDA Venerabilis, 673-735. 274.2
The Venerable Bedes Ecclesiastical history of England. Also the Anglo-Saxon chronicle. Edited by J. A. Giles. 2d ed. London, H. G. Bohn, 1849. [New York, AMS Press, 1971] xliv, 515 p. fold. map. 23 cm. (Bohn's antiquarian library) Translation of Historia ecclesiastica gentis Anglorum. [BR746.B5 1971] 78-136367 ISBN 0-404-50001-3
1. Great Britain—Church history—Anglo-Saxon period, 449-1066. 2. Great Britain—History—Anglo-Saxon period, 449-1066—Sources. I. Giles, John Allen, 1808-1884, ed. II. Anglo-Saxon chronicle. English. 1971. III. Title.

BEDA VENERABILIS, 673-735. 274.2
A history of the English Church and people [by] Bede; translated [from the Latin] and with an introduction by Leo Sherley-Price. Revised ed.; revised by R. E. Latham. Harmondsworth, Penguin, 1968. 364 p. tables. 18 cm. (The Penguin classics, L42) Translation of Historia ecclesiastica gentis Angolorum. [BR746.B5 1968b] 76-369430 7/-
1. Great Britain—Church history—Anglo-Saxon period, 449-1066. I. Title: The English church and people.

BENNETT, Gareth Vaughan, 274.2
ed.
Essays in modern English church history, in memory of Norman Sykes, ed. by G. V. Bennett, J. D. Walsh. New York, Oxford [c.] 1966. x, 227p. 23cm. Bibl. [BR755.B4] 66-10794 5.75
1. Sykes, Norman, 1897-1961. 2. Gt. Brit.—Church history—Modern Period—Addresses. essays, lectures. I. Walsh, John Dixon, joint author. II. Title.

BENNETT, Gareth Vaughan, 274.2
ed.
Essays in modern English church history, in memory of Norman Sykes, edited by G. V. Bennett & J. D. Walsh. New York, Oxford University Press, 1966. x. 227 p. 23 cm. Bibliographical footnotes. [BR755.B4] 66-10794
1. Gt. Brit. — Church history — Modern period — Addresses, essays, lectures. 2. Sykes, Norman, 1897-1961. I. Walsh, John Dixon, joint author. II. Walsh, John Dixon, joint author. III. Title.
Contents Omitted

BREADY, John Wesley, 1887- 274.2
1953.
England: before and after Wesley; the evangelical revival and social reform. New York, Russell & Russell [1971] 463 p. illus., ports. 22 cm. Reprint of the 1938 ed. [BR755.B7 1971] 72-139906
1. Wesley, John, 1703-1791. 2. Great Britain—Church history—Modern period, 1485- 3. Great Britain—Social conditions. 4. Evangelical revival. I. Title.

BURRAGE, Champlin, 1874- 274.2
1951
The early English dissenters in the light of recent research (1550-1641). New York, Russell & Russell [1967] 2v. facsims. 23cm. First pub. in 1912. Bibl. [BX5203.B9 1967] 66-27048 22.00 set,
1. Dissenters, Religious—England. I. Title.

BUTTERWORTH, Charles C., 274.2
1894-1957.
George Joye, 1495?-1553; a chapter in the history of the English Bible and the English Reformation, by Charles C. Butterworth, Allan G. Chester. Philadelphia, Univ. of Pa. Pr. [c.1962] 293p. 22cm. Bibl. 62-7198 6.00
1. Joye, George, 1495?-1553. I. Chester, Allan Griffith, 1900- joint author. II. Title.

CAMPBELL, William Edward, 274.2
1875-
Erasmus, Tyndale, and More. Milwaukee, Bruce Pub. Co. [1950] 288 p. plate, ports. 22 cm. Bibliography: p. 280-281. [B R378. C3 1950] 49-539
1. Erasmus, Desiderius, d. 1536. 2. Tyndale, William, d. 1536. 3. More, Sir Thomas, Saint, 1478-1535. 4. Reformation—England. I. Title.

CANTERBURY, Eng. (Province) 274.2
Archbishop, 1207-1228(StephcnLangton)
Acta Stephani Langton Cantuariensis Archiepiscopi A. D. 1207-1228.Collected, transcribed, and edited by Kathleen Major. Oxford, Printed at the University Press, 1950. Oxford, University Press, 1952- ii, 200 p. 4 facsims. 27 cm. (Canterbury and York series, v. 50) Cover title: Diocesis Cantuariensis. Acta Stephani Langton. [BX5013.C3A5 vol.50] A 51
1. Gt. Brit.—Church history—Sources. I. Major, Kathleen. ed. II. Title. III. Series: Canterbury and York Society. Canterbury and York series, v. 50

CANTERBURY, Eng. (Province) 274.2
Archbishop, 1366-1368 (Simon Langham)
Registrum Simonis Langham cantuariensis archiepiscopi, Transcribed and edited by A. C. Wood. Oxford, Printed at the University Press, 1956. viii, 458p. 26cm. (Canterbury and York series, v. 53) Cover title: Dioceals cantuariensis. Registrum Simonis de Langham. Issued in 3 parts, 1948-56. [BX5013.C3A5 vol. 53] A58
1. Gt. Brit.—Church history—Sources. I. Wood, Alfred Cecll, ed. II. Title. III. Series: Canterbury and York Society. Canterbury and York series, v. 53

CANTERBURY, Eng. (Provine) 274.2
Archbishop, 1151-1186 (Thomas Bourchier)
Registrum Thome Bourgcher, Cantuariensis archiepiscopi, A. D. 1454-1486. Transcribed and edited by F. R. H. Du Boulay Oxford, University Press, 1957. xivi, 569p. 26cm. (The Canterbury and York series, v. 54) Cover title: Diocels Cantuariensis. Registrum Thome Bourghiea Issued in 2 parts, 1948-57. [BX5013.C3A5] A58
1. Gt. Brit.—Church history—Sources. I. Du Boulay, F. R. H., ed. II. Title. III. Series: Canterbury and York Society. Canterbury and York series, v. 54

CARLSON, Leland Henry, 274.2
1908-
English satire; papers read at a Clark Library Seminar, January 15, 1972, by Leland H. Carlson and Ronald Paulson. Los Angeles, William Andrews Clark Memorial Library, University of California, 1972. v, 112 p. facsims. 24 cm. (William Andrews Clark Memorial Library seminar papers) Includes bibliographical references. [BR757.C26] 73-161452
1. Pope, Alexander, 1688-1744. 2. Marprelate controversy. 3. Satire, English. I. Paulson, Roland. II. California. University. University at Los Angeles. William Andrews Clark Memorial Library. III. Title. IV. Series.

CHADWICK, Nora (Kershaw) 274.2
1891-
Studies in the early British church, by Nora K. Chadwick [and others] Cambridge [Eng.] University Press, 1958. vii,374 p. 23 cm. Bibliographical footnotes. [BR748.S87] 58-14971
1. Celtic Church. I. Title.

CHADWICK, Nora (Kershaw) 274.2
1891-
Studies in the early British church, by Nora K. Chadwick [and others] Cambridge [Eng.] University Press, 1958. vii, 374p. 23cm. Bibliographical footnotes. [BR748.C45 1958] 58-14971
1. Celtic Church. I. Title. II. Title: Early British church.

CHAMBERS, David Sanderson. 274.2
Cardinal Bainbridge in the court of Rome, 1509-1514 by D. S. Chambers. [London] Oxford University Press, 1965. xii, 178 p. illus., maps. 23 cm. (Oxford historical series, 2d ser.) Errata slip inserted. "Originally formed part of a D. Phil. thesis entitled English representation at the court of Rome in the early Tudor period." "List of Bainbridge's correspondence": p. [152]-154. "Unpublished letters in foreign archieves": p. [155]-165. Bibliography: p. [166]-170. [BR754.B3C5] 65-3740
1. Bainbridge, Christopher, Cardinal, 1464?-1514. I. Title.

CHURCH and society in 274.2
England : Henry VIII to James I / edited by Felicity Heal and Rosemary O'Day. Hamden, Conn. : Archon Books, c1977. 206 p. ; 23 cm. Includes bibliographical references and index. [BR756.C54 1977b] 76-51723 ISBN 0-208-01649-X : 12.50
1. England—Church history—16th century—Addresses, essays, lectures. I. Heal, Felicity. II. O'Day, Rosemary.

CLARK, Henry William, 1869- 274.2
1949
History of English nonconformity from Wiclif to the close of the nineteenth century; v.1 &2. New York, Russell &Russell, 1965. 2v. (439; 458p.) 23cm. First pub. in 1911-1913 in London. Contents.v.1. From Wiclif to the Restoration.--v.2. From the Restoration to the close of the nineteenth century. [BX5203.C6] 65-18797 17.50 set,
1. Dissenters, Religious—England. 2. Reformation—England. 3. Gt. Brit.—Church history. I. Title. II. Title: English nonconformity from Wichf to the close of the nineteenth century.

CLEBSCH, William A 274.2
England's earliest Protestants, 1520-1535, by William A. Clebsch. New Haven, Yale University Press, 1964. xvi, 358 p. illus. 25 cm. (Yale publications in religion, 11) Bibliography: p. 319-345. [BR375.C58] 64-20912
1. Reformation — England. I. Title. II. Series.

CLEBSCH, William A. 274.2
England's earliest Protestants, 1520-1535 New Haven, Conn., Yale [c.]1964. xvi, 358p. illus. 25cm. (Yale pubns. in religion, 11) Bibl. [BR375.C58] 64-20912 7.50
1. Reformation—England. I. Title. II. Series.

CONSTANT, Gustave Leon 274.2
Marie Joseph, 1869-1940
The Reformation in England; [v.1. Tr. from French] New York, Harper [1966] 531p. 21cm. (Torchbk. TB314S. Cathedral lib.) Reprint of the Eng. ed. pub. in 1934. First French ed. pub in 1929. [BR375.C76] 66-4630 3.45 pap.,
1. Reformation—England. 2. Gt. Brit—Pol &govt.—1485-1603. I. Scantlebury, Robert Elliott, tr. II. Title.
Contents omitted.

CROSS, Claire. 274.2
Church and people, 1450-1660 : the triumph of the laity in the English church / Claire Cross. Atlantic Highlands, N.J. : Humanities Press, c1976. p. cm. (Fontana library of English history) [BR756.C76 1976] 76-25005 ISBN 0-391-00649-5 : 17.50
1. England—Church history. 2. Laity—England. I. Title.

CURTIS, Lewis Perry, 1900- 274.2
Anglican moods of the eighteenth century, by L. P. Curris. [Hamden Conn.] Archon Books, 1966. 84 p. 22 cm. Bibliographical footnotes. [BR756.C8] 66-19325
1. Religious thought — England. 2. Religious thought — 18th cent. 3. Church of England — Parties and movements. I. Title.

CURTIS, Lewis Perry, 1900- 274.2
Anglican moods of the eighteenth century. [Hamden, Conn.] Archon [dist. Shoe String, c.]1966. 84p. 22cm. Bibl. [BR756.C8] 66-19325 4.00
1. Religious thought—England. 2. Religious thought—18th cent. 3. Church of England—Parties and movements. I. Title.

DAVIES, Horton. 274.2
The English Free Churches. London, New York, Oxford University Press, 1952. 208 p. 17 cm. (The Home university library of modern knowledge, 220) [BX5203.D25] 52-8906
1. Dissenters—England. I. Title.

DAVIES, Horton. 274.2
The English Free Churches. 2d ed. London, New York, Oxford University Press, 1963. viii, 208 p. 17 cm. (The Home university library of modern knowledge, 220) Bibliography: p. [201] -204. [BX5203.D25 1963] 63-25030
1. Dissenters, Religious — England. I. Title.

DAVIES, Horton 274.2
The English Free Churches. 2d ed. New York, Oxford [c.]1963. viii, 208p.17cm. (Home univ. lib. of mod. knowledge, 220) Bibl. 63-25030 1.70
1. Dissenters, Religious—England. I. Title.

DAVIES, Horton 274.2
Worship and theology in England; from Newman to Martineau, 1850-1900 [v.4.] Princeton, N.J., Princeton [c:]1962. 390p. illus. Bibl. 61-7402 7.50
1. Gt. Brit.—Church history—Modern period. 2. Public worship—Hist. 3. Worship—Hist. 4. Theology, Doctrinal—Hist.—Gt. Brit. I. Title.

DAVIES, Horton 274.2
Worship and theology in England [v.5] Princeton, N.J., Princeton [c.]1965. xix, 493p. plates. 25cm. Bibl. [BR755.D35] 61-7402 10.00
1. Gt. Brit.—Church history—Modern period.

2. Public worship—Hist. 3. Worship—Hist. 4. Theology, Doctrinal—Hist.—Gt. Brit. I. Title. Contents omitted.,

DAVIES, Horton 274.2
Worship and theology in England; from Watts and Wesley to Maurice, 1690-1850. Princeton, N. J., Princeton University Press, [c.]1961. xiv, 355p. illus. Bibl. 61-7402 7.50
1. Gt. Brit.—Church history—Modern period. 2. Public worship—Hist. 3. Worship—Hist. 4. Theology, Doctrinal—Hist.—Gt. Brit. I. Title.

DEANESLY, Margaret 274.2
Sidelights on the Anglo-Saxon church. [Dist. New York, Oxford, c.1962] vii, 187p. front. 24cm. Bibl. 62-6075 4.00
1. Gt. Brit.—Church history—Anglo-Saxon period. I. Title.

DEANSLEY, Margaret 274.2
The pre-conquest church in England. New York, Oxford [c.1961] vii, 374p. facsim. 25cm. (Ecclesiastical hist. of England, 1) Bibl. 61-65214 6.00
1. Gt. Brit.—Church history—Early period. 2. Gt. Brit.—Church history—Anglo-saxton period. 3. Celtic Church. I. Title. II. Series.

DICKENS, Arthur Geoffrey. 274.2
The English Reformation [by] A. G. Dickens. New York, Schocken [1968,c.1964] x, 374p. 20cm. (SB177) Bibl. [BR375.D5] 64-22987 2.45 pap.,
1. Reformation—England. I. Title.

DONNE, John, 1572-1631. 274.2
Pseudo-martyr. A facsimilie reproduction with an introd. by Francis Jacques Sypher. Delmar, N.Y., Scholar's Facsimiles & Reprints, 1974. 392 p. 23 cm. Original t.p. has imprint: London, Printed by W. Stansby for Walter Burre, 1610. [BX1492.D66 1610a] 74-16215 ISBN 0-8201-1140-6
1. James I, King of Great Britain, 1566-1625. 2. Catholics in England. 3. Oaths—England. I. Title.

DONNE, John, 1572-1631. 274.2
Pseudo-martyr. A facsimilie reproduction with an introd. by Francis Jacques Sypher. Delmar, N.Y., Scholar's Facsimiles & Reprints, 1974. 392 p. 23 cm. Original t.p. has imprint: London, Printed by W. Stansby for Walter Burre, 1610. [BX1492.D66 1610a] 74-16215 ISBN 0-8201-1140-6 25.00
1. James I, King of Great Britain, 1566-1625. 2. Catholics in England. 3. Oaths—England. I. Title.

DUCKETT, Eleanor Shipley. 274.2
Anglo-Saxon saints and scholars Hamden, Conn., Archon Books, 1967 [c1947] x, 484 p. 22 cm. Contents.Contents. -- Aldheim of Malmesbury. -- Wilfrid of York. -- Bede of Jarrow. -- Boniface of Devon. -- Bibliogrpahy and abbreviations (p. 456-473) [BR754.A1D8] 67-11473
1. Aldheim, Saint, Bp. of Sherborne, 640?-709. 2. Wilfrid, Saint, Bp. of York, 634-709. 3. Beda Venerabilis, 673-735. 4. Boniface, originally Winfrid, Saint, Bp. of Mainz, 680-755. I. Title.

DUCKETT, Eleanor Shipley. 274.2
Anglo-Saxon saints and scholars Hamden, Conn., Archon Books, 1967 [c1947] x, 484 p. 22 cm. Contents.Contents.—Aldheim of Malmesbury.—Wilfrid of York.—Bede of Jarrow.—Boniface of Devon.—Bibliography and abbreviations (p. 456-473) [BR754.A1D8 1967] 67-11473
1. Aldheim, Saint, Bp. of Sherborne, 640?-709. 2. Wilfrid, Saint, Bp. of York, 634-709. 3. Beda Venerabilis, 673-735. 4. Bonifacius, originally Winfrid, Saint, Bp. of Mainz, 680-755. I. Title.

DUKE, John Alexander, 1873-1935 274.2
The Columban church [Reissue] Edinburgh, Oliver and Boyd [Mystic, Conn., Verry, 1965] xii, 200p. 22cm. Bibl. [BR747] 65-29935 4.00 bds.,
1. Ireland—Church history. 2. Scotland—Church history. 3. Gt. Brit.—Church history—Anglo-Saxon period. 4. Columba, Saint, 521-597. 5. Celtic Church. I. Title.

DU LEAVY, Gareth W. 274.2
Colum's other island; the Irish at Lindisfarne. Madison. University of Wisconsin Press [c.] 1960. x, 149p. illus., map. 23cm. Bibl. and bibl. notes: p. 101-143 60-5657 4.50
1. Gt. Brit.—Church history—Anglo-Saxon period. 2. Missionaries, Irish. 3. Lindisfarne Abbey. 4. Holy Island. I. Title.

EDWARDS, Maxwell D 274.2
The Tudors and the church, 1509-1553. [n. p.] 1957. 58 p. 24 cm. (Utah State Agricultural College. Monograph series, 5, no.2p [BR375.E3] 57-62995
1. Reformation—England. 2. Church and state in Great Britain. 3. Gt. Brit.—Hist.—Tudors, 1485-1603. I. Title.

ELLIOTT-BINNS, Leonard Elliott, 1885- 274.2
The development of English theology in the later nineteenth century. London, New York, Longmans, Green [1952] 137p. 19cm. (The Burroughs memorial lectures for 1950) [BR759.E49] 52-9175
1. Gt. Brit.-Church history—19th cent. 2. Theology—19th cent. in the later nineteenth century. I. Title.

ELLIOTT-BINNS, Leonard Elliott. 1885- 274.2
The Reformation in England. Hamden, Conn., Archon [dist. Shoe String] 1966. 244p. 19cm. First pub. in 1937. Bibl. [BR375.E5] 66-18644 6.00
1. Reformation—England. I. Title.

ELLIOTT-BINNS, Leonard Elliott, 1885- 274.2
The Reformation in England, by L. Elliott-Binns. Hamden, Conn., Archon Books, 1966. 244 p. 19 cm. First published in 1937. Bibliography: p. 235-238. [BR375.E5 1966] 66-18644
1. Reformation — England. I. Title.

ELLIOTT-BINNS, Leonard Elliott, 1885- 274.2
Religion in the Victorian era. Greenwich, Conn., Seabury Press [1953] 525p. 22cm. [BR759.E5 1953] 55-14273
1. Gt. Brit-Religion. 2. Religious thought—19th cent. 3. Gt. Brit.—Intellectual life. 4. Gt. Brit—Soc. condit. I. Title.

FLETCHER, Joseph Smith, 1863-1935. 274.2
The Reformation in northern England, six lectures. Port Washington, N.Y., Kennikat Press [1971] 191 p. 22 cm. Reprint of the 1921 ed. Bibliography: p. 181-188. [BR375.F5 1971] 71-118469
1. Reformation—England. I. Title.

FOLIOT, Gilbert, Bp. of London, 1107(ca.)-1187. 274.2
The letters and charters of Gilbert Foliot, Abbot of Gloucester (1139-48), Bishop of Hereford (1148-63), and London (1163-87): an edition projected by the late Z. N. Brooke and completed by Dom Adrian Morey and C. N. L. Brooke. London, Cambridge U. P., 1967. liv, 576 p. 4 plates (incl. 3 facsims.) 24 1/2 cm. Bibliography: p. xi-xxviii. [BR754.F55A4] 66-11623
1. Great Britain—Church history—Medieval period, 1066-1485—Sources. I. Brooke, Zachary Nugent, 1883-1946. II. Morey, Adrian, 1904- III. Brooke, Christopher Nugent Lawrence. IV. Title.

FOSTER, Charles I. 274.2
An errand of mercy; the Evangelical united front, 1790-1837. Chapel Hill, University of North Cardolina Press [c.1960] 320p. 24cm. bibl. 60-16048 6.50
1. Evangelicalism. 2. Gt. Brit.—Church history—19th cent. 3. U. S.—Church history. I. Title.

GAIRDNER, James, 1828-1912. 274.2
The English church in the sixteenth century from the accession of Henry VIII to the death of Mary. New York, AMS Press [1971?] xv, 430 p. map. 23 cm. Reprint of the 1902 ed., which was issued as v. 4 of A History of the English church. Includes bibliographical references. [BR375.G29 1971] 72-168089
1. Great Britain—Church history—16th century. 2. Reformation—England. I. Title. II. Series: A History of the English church, no. 4.

GASQUET, Francis Aidan, Cardinal, 1846-1929. 274.2
The eve of the Reformation; studies in the religious life and thought of the English people in the period preceding the rejection of the Roman jurisdiction by Henry VIII. Port Washington, N.Y., Kennikat Press [1971] 460 p. 22 cm. Reprint of the 1900 ed. Includes bibliographical references. [BR750.G3 1971] 75-118522 ISBN 0-8046-1144-0
1. England—Church history—Medieval period, 1066-1485. 2. Reformation—England. I. Title.

GASQUET, Francis Aidan, Cardinal, 1846-1929. 274.2
Henry VIII and the English monasteries; an attempt to illustrate the history of their suppression. Freeport, N.Y., Books for Libraries Press [1972] 2 v. fold. maps. 23 cm. "First published 1887-1888." [BX2592.G35 1972] 74-39467 ISBN 0-8369-9905-3
1. Monasticism and religious orders—Great Britain. 2. Church and state in Great Britain. 3. Secularization—Great Britain. I. Title.

GASQUET, Francis Aidan, Cardinal, 1846-1929. 274.2
Parish life in mediaeval England. Freeport, N.Y., Books for Libraries Press [1973] p. Reprint of the 1906 ed. published by Methuen, in series: The Antiquary's books. [BR747.G3 1973] 73-6567 ISBN 0-518-19045-5
1. Great Britain—Church history—Medieval period. 2. Great Britain—Social life and customs—Medieval period, 1066-1485. I. Title. II. Series: The Antiquary's books.

GEE, Henry, 1858-1938 274.2
Documents illustrative of English church history. Comp. from original sources by ,henry Gee, William Johm Hardy. London, Macmillan, 1910. New York, Kraus Reprint 1966. xii, 670p. 24cm. First pub. in 1896. [BR741.G3 1966] 67-447 15.00
1. Gt. Brit.—Church history—Sources. I. Hardy, William John, 1857-1819, joint author. II. Title.

GEE, Henry, 1858-1938. 274.2
Documents illustrative of English church history. Compiled from original sources by Henry Gee and William John Hardy. London, Macmillan, 1910. New York, Kraus Reprint Corp., 1966. xii, 670 p. 24 cm. First published in 1896. [BR741.G8 1966] 67-447
1. Gt. Brit. — Church history — Sources. I. Hardy, William John, 1857-1919, joint author. II. Title.

GEORGE, Charles H. 274.2
The Protestant mind of the English Reformation, 1570-1640, by Charles H. George, Katherine George. Princeton, N.J., Princeton Univ. Press [c.]1961. x, 452p. front. port. 25cm. Bibl. 61-7399 8.50
1. Reformation—England. 2. Gt. Brit.—Church history—16th cent 3. Gt. Brit.—Church history—17th cent. 4. Church and social problems—Gt. Brit. I. George, Katherine, joint author. II. Title.

GIBBS, Margaret. 274.2 B
Saints beyond the White Cliffs; stories of English saints. Illustrated by T. H. Robinson. Freeport, N.Y., Books for Libraries Press [1971] vii, 213 p. illus. 23 cm. (Biography index reprint series) Reprint of the 1947 ed. [BX4659.G7G5 1971] 75-148211 ISBN 0-8369-8058-1
1. Christian saints—England. I. Robinson, Thomas Heath, 1869-1950, illus. II. Title.

GODFREY, John 274.2
The church in Anglo-Saxon England. [New York] Cambridge [c.]1962 529p. illus. maps. 24cm. 62-52074 10.00
1. Gt. Brit.—Church history—Anglo-Saxon period. I. Title.

HALLER, William, 1885- 274.2
Liberty and reformation in the Puritan Revolution. New York, Columbia [1963, c.1955] 410p. 21cm. (47) Bibl. 2.45 pap.,
1. Puritans. 2. Gt. Brit.—Church history—17th cent. 3. Church and state in Great Britain. 4. Gt. Brit.—Pol. & govt.—1625-1649. I. Title.

HALLER, William, 1885- 274.2
Liberty and reformation in the Puritan Revolution [Gloucester, Mass., P. Smith, 1964, c.1955] xv, 410p. 21cm. (Columbia Univ. Pr. bk. rebound) Bibl. 4.50
1. Puritans. 2. Gt. Brit.—Church history—17th cent. 3. Church and state in Great Britain. 4. Gt. Brit.—Pol. & govt.—1625-1649. I. Title.

HANNA, James Arthur MacClannahan, 1925- 274.2
A history of the Celtic Church from its inception to 1153 [Ann Arbor? Mich., 1963] xix. 104 p. illus., port., maps. 29 cm. Bibliography: p. 75-80. [BR748.H3] 63-36808
1. Gt. Brit. — Church history — Early period. 2. Celtic Church. I. Title.

HARDINGE, Leslie. 274.2
The Celtic church in Britain. London, S.P.C.K. for the Church Historical Society, 1972. xx, 265 p., [2] leaves. illus., 2 facsims., map. 23 cm. (Church Historical Society series, no. 91) Bibliography: p. [235]-257. [BR748.H37] 72-195611 ISBN 0-281-02483-9
1. Celtic Church. I. Title. II. Series: Church historical series, no. 91.
Distributed by Allenson, Naperville, Ill. 60540 16.00.

HART, Arthur Tindal 274.2
The man in the pew, 1558-1660 [by] A. Tindal Hart. New York, Humanities [c1966] 221p. illus., port. 23cm. [BR756.H5 1966a] 66-28388 6.00
1. Gt. Brit.—Religious life and customs. 2. Gt. Brit.—Church history—16th cent. 3. Gt. Brit.—Church history—17th cent. I. Title.

HART, Arthur Tindal. 274.2
The man in the pew, 1558-1660 [by] A. Tindal Hart. New York, Humanities Press [c1966] 221 p. illus. port. 23 cm. Bibliography: p. 207-213. [BR756.H3] 66-28388
1. Gt. Brit. — Religious life and customs. 2. Gt. Brit. — Church history — 16th cent. 3. Gt. Brit. — Church history — 17th cent. I. Title.

HENRIQUES, Ursula. 274.2
Religious toleration in England, 1787-1833. Toronto, University of Toronto Press, 1961. vii, 294p. 23cm. (Studies in social history) Based on thesis, Manchester University. Bibliography: p. 278-288. [BR755.H44 1961] 62-792
1. Gt. Brit.— Church history—Modern period. 2. Toleration. 3. Gt. Brit.—Pol. & govt. 4. Religious liberty—Gt. Brit. I. Title.

HUDSON, Winthrop Still, 1911- 274.2
Theology in sixteenth- and seventeenth-century England; papers read at a Clark Library seminar, February 6, 1971, by Winthrop S. Hudson and Leonard J. Trinterud. Los Angeles, William Andrews Clark Memorial Library, University of California, 1971. iv, 55 p. 24 cm. (William Andrews Clark Memorial Library seminar papers) Includes bibliographical references. [BR756.H8] 78-31908
1. Gt. Brit.—Religion—Addresses, essays, lectures. I. Trinterud, Leonard J., 1904- II. Title. III. Series.

HUGHES, Philip, 1895- 274.2
The Reformation in England. Rev. [i. e. 5th] ed. New York, Macmillan [1963] 3 v. in 1 illus., ports., maps, facsims. 24 cm. Contents.Contents.—"The King's proceedings."—Religio depopulata.—"True religion now established." "Bibliographical note to the revised edition": p. [vi] Includes bibliographies. [BR375.H752] 63-16363
1. Reformation—England. 2. Catholic Church in England—History. 3. Gt. brit.—Church history—16th century.

HUNT, John, 1827-ca.1908. 274.2
Religious thought in England, from the Reformation to the end of last century; a contribution to the history of theology. London, Strahan, 1870-73. [New York, AMS Press, 1973] 3 v. 23 cm. Includes bibliographies. [BR755.H832] 72-153593 ISBN 0-404-09480-5
1. Great Britain—Church history—Modern period, 1485- 2. Religious thought—Great Britain. I. Title.

HUTCHINSON, Francis Ernest, 1871- 274.2
Cranmer and the English Reformation. New York, Collier [1962] 128p. 18cm. (Men & hist., AS266V) .95 pap.,
1. Cranmer, Thomas, Abp. of Canterbury, 1489-1556. 2. Reformation—England. I. Title.

INNOCENTIUS III, Pope, 1160or61-1216. 274.2
The letters of Pope Innocent III (1198-1216) concerning England and Wales: a calendar with an appendix of texts; ed. by C. R. Cheney, Mary G. Cheney. Oxford, Clarendon Pr., 1967. xxxv, 308p. 28cm. Facsim. as insert. Bibl. [BR750.I 5] 68-89026 26.90
1. Gt. Brit.—Church history—Medieval period—Sources. I. Cheney, Christopher Robert, 1906- ed. II. Cheney, Mary G. ed. III. Title.
Order from Oxford Univ. Pr., New York.

JONES, Rufus Matthew, 1863-1948 274.2
Mysticism and democracy in the English Commonwealth; being the William Belden Noble lectures delivered in Harvard University, 1930-1931. New York, Octagon, 1965[c.1932] xi, 184p. 21cm. Bibl. [BV5077.G7J6] 65-16774 6.00
1. Dissenters, Religious—England. 2. Mysticism. 3. Gt. Brit.—Church history—17th cent. 4. Religious liberty—Gt. Brit. 5. Gt. Brit.—Pol. & govt.—1649-1660 6. Seekers (Sect.) I. Title.

JORDAN, Wilbur Kitchener, 1902- 274.2
The development of religious toleration in England: 4v. Gloucester, Mass., P. Smith. 1965. 4v. (various p.) 21cm. Reprint of work first pub. in England in 1932 by Allen & Unwin, and previously pub. in the U.S.A. by Harvard. Bibl. [BR756.J6] 66-1454 6.75 ea.,
1. Gt. Brit.—Church history—16th cent. 2. Gt. Brit.—Church history—17th cent. 3. Toleration. 4. Religious liberty—Gt Brit. I. Title.
Contents omitted.

MCALPINE, Robert George. 274.2
Celtic Christianity: the story of the Celtic religion in the British Isles, by R. G. McAlpine. Harrogate (Yorks.), Merrythought P., 1967. 118 p. 19 cm. [BR748.M3] 68-114617 10/-
1. Celtic Church. 2. Great Britain—Church history—To 449. I. Title.

MCGINN, Donald Joseph 274.2
John Penry and the Marprelate controversy. New Brunswick, N.J., Rutgers [c.1966] xi, 274p. facsims. 22cm. Bibl. [BR757.M16] 65-28212 9.00
1. Penry, John, 1563-1593. 2. Marprelate controversy. I. Title.

MANNING, Bernard Lord, 274.2
1892-1941.
The Protestant dissenting deputies. Edited by Ormerod Greenwood. Cambridge [Eng.] University Press, 1952. ix, 497p. facsim. 23cm. Bibliography: p. 488-489. [BX5203.M32] 52-13946
1. Dissenters—England. I. Title.

MARTIN, David A 274.2
A sociology of English religion, by David Martin. Introd. by D. G. MacRae. New York, Basic Books [1967] 158 p. 23 cm. Bibliography: p. 145-153. [BR759.M35] 67-22385
1. Gt. Brit.—Religion. I. Title.

MARTIN, David A. 274.2
A sociology of English religion, by David Martin. Introd. by D. G. MacRae. New York, Basic Books [1967] 158 p. 23 cm. Bibliography: p. 145-153. [BR759.M35 1967b] 67-22385
1. Great Britain—Religion. I. Title.

MAYR-HARTING, Henry. 274.2
The coming of Christianity to England. New York, Schocken Books [1972] 334 p. illus. 23 cm. Includes bibliographical references. [BR748.M38 1972] 74-169818 12.50
1. Great Britain—Church history—To 449. 2. Great Britain—Church history—Anglo-Saxon period, 449-1066. I. Title.

MEYER, Carl Stamm 274.2
Elizabeth I and the religious settlement of 1559. Saint Louis, Concordia Pub. House [c.1960] 182p. 24cm. (Bibl. footnotes) 60-11413 4.95
1. Elizabeth, Queen of England 1533-1603. 2. Gt. Brit.—Church history—16th cent. 3. Church and state in Great Britain. 4. Church of England—Hist. I. Title.

MEYER, Carl Stamm, 1907- 274.2
Elizabeth I and the religious settlement of 1559. Saint Louis, Concordia Pub. House [1960] 182p. 24cm. Includes bibliography. [BR756.M46] 60-11413
1. Elizabeth, Queen of England, 1533-1603. 2. Gt. Brit.—Church history—16th cent. 3. Church and state in Great Britain. 4. Church of England—Hist. I. Title.

MOORMAN, John Richard 274.2
Humpidge.
A history of the church in England. [1st American ed.] New York, Morehouse-Gorham, 1954. 460p. 24cm. [BR743] 55-3135
1. Gt. Brit.—Church history. I. Title.

MOREY, Adrian, 1904- ed. 274.2
Gilbert Foliot and his letters [by] Adrian Morey and C. N. L. Brooke. Cambridge [Eng] University Press, 1965. xv, 312 p. 23 cm. (Cambridge studies in medieval life and thought, new ser., v. 11) "List of abbreviations" (bibliography): p. xi-xv. [BR754.F55M6] 65-17204
1. Foliot, Gilbert, Bp. of London, 1107 (ca.)-1187. I. Brooke, Christopher Nugent Lawrence, joint ed. II. Title. III. Series.

NEWSOME, David 274.2
The Wilberforces and Henry Manning; the parting of friends. Cambridge, Mass., Belknap Pr. of Harvard, 1966. xiii, 486p. illus., geneal table, ports. 24cm. Bibl. [BR759.N4] 67-2 12.00
1. Manning, Henry Edward, Cardinal, 1808-1892. 2. Gt. Brit.—Church history—19th cent. 3. Evangelicalism—Church of England. 4. Oxford movement. 5. Wilberforce family. I. Title.

NEWSOME, David, 1929- 274.2
The Wilberforces and Henry Manning; the parting of friends. Cambridge, Mass., Belknap Press of Harvard University Press, 1966. xiii, 486 p. illus., geneal. table, ports. 24 cm. Bibliography: p. 455-465. [BR759.N4] 67-2
1. Manning, Henry Edward, Cardinal, 1808-1892. 2. Wilberforce family. 3. Gt. Brit. — Church history — 19th cent. 4. Evangelicalism — Church of England. 5. Oxford movement. I. Title.

NORMAN, Edward R. 274.2
Anti-Catholicism in Victorian England [by] E. R. Norman New York, Barnes & Noble [1968] 240 p. 23 cm. (Historical problems: studies and documents, 1) Bibliographical footnotes. [BX1766.N6] 68-5997
1. Anti-Catholicism—Great Britain. 2. Great Britain—Church history—19th century. I. Title. II. Series.

O'CONNELL, Marvin Richard. 274.2
Thomas Stapleton and the Counter Reformation. New Haven, Yale University Press, 1964. xii, 221 p. 23 cm. (Yale publications in religion,9) "Bibliographical note": p. [211]-213. [BX4705.S812O2] 64-12656
1. Stapleton, Thomas, 1535-1598. 2. Counter-Reformation — England. I. Title. II. Series.

O'CONNELL, Marvin Richard 274.2
Thomas Stapleton and the Counter Reformation. New Haven, Conn., Yale [c.] 1964. xx, 221p. 23cm. (Yale pubns. in religion, 9) Bibl. 64-12656 6.00
1. Stapleton, Thomas, 1535-1598. 2. Counter-Reformation—England. I. Title. II. Series.

O'NEIL, Maud. 274.2
They took John's torch, Sequel to the book of Acts. Illus. by James Converse Mountain View, Calif., Pacific Pr. Pub. [c.1962] 134p. illus. 21cm. 62-19055 4.00
1. Gt. Brit.—Church history—Early period—Juvenile literature. I. Title.

OWEN, John, 1616-1683. 274.2
The correspondence of John Owen (1616-1683): with an account of his life and work; edited by Peter Toon, foreword by Geoffrey F. Nuttall Cambridge, James Clarke, 1970. xv, 190 p. 23 cm. Bibliography: p. 187-188. [BX5207.O88A4 1970] 73-582713 ISBN 0-227-67736-6 £1.50
I. Toon, Peter, 1939- ed.

PANTIN, William Abel, 1902- 274.2
The English church in the fourteenth century. Based on the Birkbeck lectures, 1948. Cambridge [Eng.] University Press, 1955. 291p. 22cm. [BR750.P3] 55-2044
1. Gt. Brit.—Church history—Medieval period. I. Title.

PANTIN, William Abel, 1902- 274.2
The English church in the fourteenth century. Foreword by Paul E. Beichner. [Notre Dame, Ind.] University of Notre Dame Press, 1962, [c1963] 291 p. 21 cm. [BR750.P3] 63-727
1. Gt. Brit. — Church history — Medieval period. I. Title.

PANTIN, William Abel, 1902- 274.2
The English church in the fourteenth century. Foreword by Paul E. Beichner. [Notre Dame, Ind.] Univ. of Notre Dame Pr. [c.1963] 291p. 21cm. 63-727 1.95 pap.,
1. Gt. Brit.—Church history—Medieval period. I. Title.

PARKER, Thomas Henry Louis, 274.2
ed.
English reformers, edited by T. H. L. Parker. Philadelphia, Westminster Press [1966] xxiv, 360 p. 24 cm. (The Library of Christian classics, v. 26) Includes bibliographies. [BR375.P26 1966] 66-10354
1. Reformation—England—Collections. I. Title.

PARKER, Thomas Maynard, 274.2
1906-
The English Reformation to 1558 London, New York, Oxford University Press, 1950. viii, 200 p. 18 cm. (The Home university library of modern knowledge, 217) Bibliography: p. 189-195. [BR375.P3] 50-9769
1. Reformation — England. I. Title.

PARKER, Thomas Maynard, 274.2
1906-
The English Reformation to 1558 [by] T. M. Parker. 2d ed. London iNew York, Oxford Univ. Pr. 1966. vi, 168p. 20cm. (Oxford paperbacks univ. ser., opus 2) Bibl. [BR375.P3 1966] 66-8422 1.85 pap.,
1. Reformation—England. I. Title.

PARSONS, Robert, 1546-1610. 274.2
The judgment of a Catholicke English-man living in banishment for his religion (1608) by Robert Persons. A facsimile reproduction with an introd. by William T. Costello. Gainesville, Fla., Scholars' Facsimiles & Reprints, 1957. xvii p., facsim.: 128p. 23cm. 'Reproduced from a copy in ... Crosby Memorial Library of Gonzaga University.' [BR757.P37 1608a] 57-9033
1. James I, King of Great Britain, 1566-1625. Triplici nodo, triplex cuneus. 2. Catholic Church in England. 3. Oath of allegiance, 1606. I. Title.

PIERCE, William. 274.2
An historical introduction to the Marprelate tracts; a chapter in the evolution of religious and civil liberty in England. New York, B. Franklin [1964] xix, 350 p. illus., port. 24 cm. (Burt Franklin research & source works series, 58) Reprint of the 1908 ed. [BR757.P6 1964] 77-6364
1. Gt. Brit.—Church history—16th century. 2. Reformation—England. I. Title. II. Title: Marprelate tracts.

PILL, David H. 274.2
The English Reformation, 1529-58 [by] David H. Pill. Totowa, N.J., Rowman and Littlefield [1973] 224 p. 22 cm. Includes bibliographies. [BR375.P54 1973] 72-11733 ISBN 0-87471-159-2 7.00
1. Reformation—England. I. Title.

PLUM, Harry Grant, 1868- 274.2
1956.
Restoration puritanism; a study of the growth of English liberty. Port Washington, N.Y., Kennikat Press [1972, c1943] ix, 129 p. 22 cm. Bibliography: p. [103]-123. [BX9334.P55 1972] 72-159101 ISBN 0-8046-1644-2
1. Puritans—England. 2. Great Britain—Church history—17th century. 3. Great Britain—Politics and government—1660-1714. I. Title.

POWICKE, Frederick Maurice, 274.2
Sir 1819-
The Reformation in England. [New York] Oxford Univ. Press [1961] 153p. (Oxford paperbacks, no. 24) Bibl. 1.25 pap.,
1. Reformation—England. I. Title.

READ, Conyers, 1881- 274.2
Social and political forces in the English reformation. Houston [Tex.] Elsevier Press, 1953. 87p. 22cm. (The Rockwell lectures) [BR375.R4] 53-5960
1. Reformation—England. 2. Gt. Brit.—Pol. & govt.—1485-1606. I. Title.

ROSS WILLIAMSON, Hugh, 274.2
1901-
The beginning of the English Reformation. New York, Sheed and Ward [1957] 113p. 20cm. [BR375.R7] 57-10179
1. Reformation—England. I. Title.

ROUTLEY, Erik. 274.2
English religious dissent. Cambridge [Eng.] University Press, 1960. 213p. illus. 21cm. (English institutions) [BX5203.2.R65 1960] 60-51970
1. Dissenters—England. I. Title.

RUPP, Ernest Gordon. 274.2
Six makers of English religion, 1500-1700. New York, Harper [c1957] 125p. 19cm. [BR767.R8 1957a] 58-7102
1. Gt. Brit.—Biog. 2. Christian biography. I. Title.

RUPP, Ernest Gordon. 274.2 B
Six makers of English religion, 1500-1700, by Gordon Rupp. Plainview, N.Y., Books for Libraries Press [1974, c1957] p. cm. (Essay index reprint series) Reprint of the ed. published by Harper, New York. [BR767.R8 1974] 74-849 ISBN 0-518-10159-2 9.75
1. Great Britain—Biography. 2. Christian biography. I. Title.
Contents omitted.

RUPP, Ernest Gordon 274.2
Studies in the making of the English Protestant tradition, mainlv in the reign of Henrv VIII. Cambridge [eng.] Univ. Pr. 1966. xvi. 220p. 19cm. Bibl. [BR375.R8] 48-15338 1.75 pap.,
1. Reformation—England. I. Title.

SAKLATVALA, Beram. 274.2
The Christian island. [1st American ed.] Rutherford [N.J.] Fairleigh Dickinson University Press [1970, c1969] xi, 150 p. illus. 22 cm. Includes bibliographical references. [BR748.S23 1970] 75-92561 ISBN 0-8386-7571-9 6.50
1. Great Britain—Church history—To 449. I. Title.

SEATON, Alexander Adam. 274.2
The theory of toleration under the later Stuarts, by A. A. Seaton. New York, Octagon Books, 1972. vii, 364 p. 23 cm. Reprint of the 1911 ed., which was issued as no. 19 of the Cambridge historical essays. Bibliography: p. [346]-350. [BR757.S4 1972] 72-7443 ISBN 0-374-97233-8 12.25
1. Religious tolerance. 2. Great Britain—Church history—Modern period. 3. Religious liberty—Great Britain. I. Title. II. Series: Cambridge historical essays, no. 19.

SELBY-LOWNDES, Joan 274.2
Your book of the English church. Illus. by John Turner. London, Faber & Faber [dist. Hollywood-by-the-Sea. Fla., Transatlantic, 1964, c.1963] 64p. illus., plan. 22cm. [BX5057] 64-57291 3.00
1. Gt. Brit.—Church history. 2. Church of England—Hist. I. Title. II. Title: The English church.

SMITH, Herbert Maynard, 274.2
1869-1949.
Pre-Reformation England. PreReformation England New York, Russell & Russell, 1963. xv, 556 p. 23 cm. Bibliography: p. 527-540. [BR746.S63 1963] 63-15182
1. Gt. Brit.—Church history—Medieval period. 2. Gt. Brit.—Religion. 3. Gt. Brit.—Civilization. I. Title.

SMITH, Lacey Baldwin. 274.2
Tudor prelates and politics, 1536-1558. Princeton, Princeton University Press, 1953. viii, 333p. 23cm. (Princeton studies in history, v. 8) Bibliography: p. 309-318. [BR755.S62] 52-13146
1. Gt. Brit.—Church history—16th cent. 2. Reformation—England. 3. Gt. Brit.—Pol. & govt.—1509-1547. 4. Gt. Brit.—Pol. & govt.—1553-1558. I. Title. II. Series: Princeton University. Princeton studies in history, v. 8

SMYTH, Charles Hugh 274.2
Egerton, 1903-
The church and the nation; six studies in the Anglican tradition. Introd. by the sermon preached by Archbishop Lord Fisher at his enthronement in Canterbury Cathedral in 1945. New York, Morehouse [1963, c.]1962 191 [1] p. illus., ports. 23 cm. Bibl. 63-24878 3.75 bds.,
1. Gt. Brit.—Church history—Addresses, essays, lectures. I. Title.

SMYTH, Charles Hugh 274.2
Egerton, 1903-
Cranmer & the Reformation under Edward VI, by C. H. Smyth Westport, Conn., Greenwood Press [1970] x, 315 p. 23 cm. Reprint of the 1926 ed. Bibliography: p. [303]-306. [BR375.S6 1970] 75-100842 ISBN 0-8371-4025-0
1. Cranmer, Thomas, Abp. of Canterbury, 1489-1556. 2. Reformation—England. I. Title.

SOUTHWELL CATHEDRAL 274.2
Visitations and memorials of Southwell minster. Ed. by Arthur Francis Leach. [Westminster] Printed for the Camden Soc., 1891. New York, Johnson Reprint, 1965 cxi, 234, 10p. incl. front. 22cm. (Camden Soc. Pubns. with Camden Soc. reps., list of members [DA20.C17 New Ser., No. 48] A17 13.50
1. Visitations, Ecclesiastical—Southwell, Eng. I. Leach, Arthur Francis, 1851-1915, ed. II. Title.

STROMBERG, Ronald N 1916- 274.2
Religious liberalism in eighteenth-century England. [London] Oxford University Press, 1954. xi, 192p. 23cm. Bibliography: p.[175]-185. [BR758.S85] 54-2970
1. Religious thought—England. 2. Liberalism (Religion) I. Title.

STRYPE, John, 1643-1737 274.2
Annals of the Reformation and establishment of religion and other various occurrences in the Church of England during Queen Elizabeth's happy reign, together with an appendix of original papers of state, records, and letters. New York, Burt Franklin (res. & source works ser.: no. 122) New ed. 1st pub. in London 1708-09. Bibl. refs. [BR756.S88] 66-20694 125.00
1. Gt. Brit.—Church history—16th cent.—Sources. 2. Gt. Brit.—Hist.—Elizabeth, 1558-1603—Sources. I. Title.

STUDIES in the early 274.2
British church, by Nora K. Chadwick [and others] [Hamden, Conn.] Archon Books, 1973 [c1958] vii, 374 p. 22 cm. Contents.Contents.—Chadwick, N. K. Introduction.—Chadwick, N. K. Early culture and learning in North Wales.—Chadwick, N. K. Intellectual life in West Wales in the last days of the Celtic Church.—Hughes, K. British Museum Ms. Cotton Vespasian A. XIV ('Vitae Sanctorum Wallensium'): its purpose and provenance.—Brooke, C. The archbishops of St. David's, Llandaff, and Caerleon-on-Usk.—Hughes, K. The distribution of Irish scriptoria and centres of learning from 730 to 1111.—Jackson, K. H. The sources for the Life of St. Kentigern. Includes bibliographical references. [BR748.S87 1973] 73-673 ISBN 0-208-01315-6
1. Celtic Church. I. Chadwick, Nora (Kershaw), 1891-

SYKES, Norman, 1897- 274.2
From Sheldon to Secker; aspects of English church history, 1660-1768. Cambridge [Eng.] University Press, 1959. 237 p. 22 cm. (The Ford lectures, 1958) Includes bibliography. [BR756.S96 1959] 59-2371
1. Sheldon, Gilbert, Abp. of Canterbury, 1508-1677. 2. Secker, Thomas of Canterbury, Abp. 1693-1768. 3. Gt. Brit. — Church history — 17th cent. 4. Gt. Brit. — Church history — 18th cent. I. Title.

THOMPSON, Craig Ringwalt, 274.2
1911-
The English church in the sixteenth century. Washington, Folger Shakespeare Library, 1958. 57 p. illus., facsims. 22 cm. (Folger booklets on Tudor and Stuart civilization.) Bibliography: p. 17-18. [BR756.T44] 59-1243
1. Gt. Brit. — Church history — 16th cent. 2.

Church of England — Hist. 3. Reformation — England. I. Title. II. Series.

TOOTELL, Hugh, 1672-1743. 274.2
Dodd's Church history of England, from the commencement of the sixteenth century to the revolution in 1688. With notes, additions, and a continuation by M. A. Tierney. New York, AMS Press [1971] 5 v. fold. facsims. 23 cm. Reprint of the 1839-43 ed. "A list of the historians and manuscripts made use of by the author": v. 1, p. xxix-xxxviii. [BR756.T62] 75-119152 ISBN 0-404-02150-6
1. Great Britain—Church history—16th century. 2. Great Britain—Church history—17th century. 3. Reformation—England. 4. Catholics in England. I. Tierney, Mark Aloysius, 1795-1862, ed. II. Title.

TULLOCH, John, 1823-1886. 274.2
Rational theology and Christian philosophy in England in the seventeenth century. 2d ed. New York, B. Franklin [1972] 2 v. 21 cm. (Burt Franklin research & source works series. Philosophy & religious history monographs, 114) Reprint of the 1874 ed. Contents.Contents.—v. 1. Liberal churchmen.—v. 2. The Cambridge Platonists. Includes bibliographical references. [BR756.T9 1972] 72-80399 ISBN 0-8337-3577-2 35.00
1. Cambridge Platonists. 2. Great Britain—Church history—17th century. 3. Religious thought—England. 4. Philosophy, English—17th century. I. Title.

WALZER, Michael. 274.2
The revolution of the saints; a study in the origins of radical politics. Cambridge, Harvard University Press, 1965. x., 334 p. 24 cm. "Bibliographical note": p. [323]-328. Bibliographical footnotes. [BR756.W34] 65-22048
1. Gt. Brit. — Church history — Modern period. 2. Puritans. 3. Calvinism. 4. Christianity and politics — Hist. I. Title.

WALZER, Michael 274.2
The revolution of the saints; a study in the origins of radical politics. Cambridge, Mass., Harvard [c.]1965. x, 334p. 24cm. Bibl. [BR756.W34] 65-22048 6.95
1. Gt. Brit.—Church history—Modern period. 2. Puritans. 3. Calvinism. 4. Christianity and politics—Hist. I. Title.

WARD, Nathaniel, 1578?-1652. 274.2
The simple cobler of Aggawam in America. Edited by P. M. Zall. Lincoln, University of Nebraska Press [1969] xviii, 81 p. map (on lining papers) 22 cm. Bibliographical footnotes. [PS858.W2S5 1969] 69-19107 3.95
1. Religious liberty—Gt. Brit. 2. Gt. Brit.—Church history—17th century. 3. Gt. Brit.—Politics and government—1642-1649. I. Zall, Paul M., ed. II. Title.

WATSON, Edward William, 1859-1936. 274.2
The Church of England. Epilogue by Alwyn Williams. 3d ed. London, New York, Oxford University Press, 1961. 192 p. 17 cm. (The Home university library of modern knowledge, 90) Includes bibliography. [BX5057.W3 1961] 61-19932
1. Church of England — Hist. 2. Gt. Brit. — Church history. I. Williams, Alwyn Terrell Petre, Bp. of Durham, 1888- II. Title.

WATSON, Edward William, 1859-1936 274.2
The Church of England. Epilogue by Alwyn Williams. 3d ed. New York. Oxford [c.]1961[ ] 192 p. 17 cm. (Home univ. lib. of modern knowledge, 90) Bibl. 61-19932 1.40
1. Church of England—Hist. 2. Gt. Brit.—Church history. I. Williams, Alwyn Terrell Petre, Bp. of Durham, 1888- II. Title.

WHITE, Helen Constance, 1896- 274.2
Social criticism in popular religious literature of the sixteenth century. New York, Octagon, 1965[c.1944] ix, 330p. 24cm. Bibl. [BR757.W45] 65-25892 8.00
1. Gt. Brit.—Church history—16th cent. 2. Religious thought—Gt. Brit. 3. Gt. Brit.—Soc. condit. 4. English literature—Early modern(to 1700)—Hist. & crit. 5. Religious literature, English—Hist. & crit. 6. Reformation—England. I. Title.

WHITING, Charles Edwin, 1871- 274.2
Studies in English Puritanism from the Restoration to the Revolution, 1660-1688, by C. E. Whiting. New York, A. M. Kelley, 1968. xvi, 584 p. illus., facsims., ports. 23 cm. (Reprints of economic classics) Reprint of the 1931 ed. Bibliography: p. ix-xvi. [BX9334.W5 1968b] 68-56060 ISBN 0-7146-1382-7
1. Dissenters, Religious—England. 2. Great Britain—Church history—17th century. 3. Church and state in Great Britain. 4. English literature—Early modern, 1500-1700—History and criticism. I. Title.

*WILLIAM OF MALMESBURY, c.1095-1143 274.2
Willelmi Malmesbiriensis Monachi De gestis ponticum Anglorum libri quinque. Ed. by N.E.S.A. Hamilton. New York, Kraus Reprint, 1964. 680p. 25cm. (Rerum Britannicarum Medii Aevi Scriptores: Rolls ser. 52) 25.00
I. Title.

WILLIS, Anthony Armstrong, 1897- 274.2
The Church of England, the Methodists and society, 1700-1850. Totowa, N.J., Rowman and Littlefield [1973] 224 p. 22 cm. Includes bibliographies. [BR758.W54 1973] 72-11862 ISBN 0-87471-160-6 7.00
1. Great Britain—Church history—18th century. 2. Great Britain—Church history—19th century. I. Title.

WILSON, Derek A. 274.2
The people and the Book : the revolutionary impact of the English Bible, 1380-1611 / [by] Derek Wilson. London : Barrie and Jenkins, 1976. x, 182 p. ; 23 cm. B76-24851 Includes index. Bibliography: p. 173-175. [BS538.7.W54] 76-377183 ISBN 0-214-20072-8 : £3.95
1. Bible—Influence—England. I. Title.

WILSON, Derek A. 274.2
A Tudor tapestry; men, women and society in Reformation England [by] Derek Wilson. [Pittsburgh] University of Pittsburgh Press [1972] viii, 287 p. illus. 23 cm. Bibliography: p. [273]-278. [BR375.W74 1972] 71-158187 ISBN 0-8229-3242-3 9.95
1. Reformation—England. I. Title.

WILSON, John Dover, 1881-1969. 274.2
Martin Marprelate and Shakespeare's Fluellen; a new theory of the authorship of the Marprelate tracts. [Folcroft, Pa.] Folcroft Library Editons (sic) 1971. 74 p. 26 cm. Reprint of the 1912 ed. Includes bibliographical references. [BR757.W5 1971] 72-194068 10.00
1. Williams, Roger, Sir, 1540?-1595. 2. Shakespeare, William, 1564-1616. King Henry V. 3. Marprelate controversy. I. Title.

POWICKE, Frederick Maurice, Sir 1879-1963 ed. 274.2082
Councils & synods, with other documents relating to the English Church [v.2. pts. 1 & 2] ed. by F. M. Powicke, C. R. Cheney. Oxford, Clarendon Pr. [dist. New York, Oxford [c.] 1964. 2v. (1450p.) 25cm. Continue [s] the English section of the Councils and ecclesiastical documents of Hadden and Stubbs (1869-78) from King Alfred to King Henry VIII. Contents.contents—v. 2. A.D. 1203-1313 (pt. 1., 1205-1265. Pt. 2., 1265-1313 Bibl. 64-55341 50.40 set,
1. Councils and synods—Gt. Brit.—Collections. 2. Gt. Brit.—Church history—Sources. I. Cheney, Christopher Robert, 1906- joint ed. II. Hadden, Arthur West, 1816-1873. Councils and ecclesiastical documents relating to Great Britain and Ireland. III. Title.

BEGBIE, Harold, 1871-1929. 274.2'0922 B
Painted windows; a study in religious personality, by Harold Begbie (a gentleman with a duster) Port Washington, N.Y., Kennikat Press [1970] 204 p. 21 cm. (Essay and general literature index reprint series) Reprint of the 1922 ed. Contents.Contents.—Bishop Gore.—Dean Inge.—Father Knox.—Dr. L. P. Jacks.—Bishop Hensley Henson.—Miss Maude Royden.—Canon E. W. Barnes.—General Bramwell Booth.—Dr. W. E. Orchard.—Bishop Temple.—Dr. W. B. Selbie.—Archbishop Randall Davidson. [BR767.B4 1970] 77-108696
1. Clergy—England. I. Title.

WARNE, Arthur. 274.23'5
Church and society in eighteenth-century Devon. New York, A. M. Kelley [1969] 184 p. illus., ports. 23 cm. Bibliographical references included in "Notes and bibliography" (p. 169-178) [BR763.D6W3] 69-16764
1. Devon, Eng.—Church history. I. Title.

CHRISTIANITY in Somerset / edited by Robert W. Dunning. 274.23'8
[Bridgwater] : Somerset County Council, 1976. xii, 132 p. : ill., maps, music, plans, ports. ; 21 x 22 cm. Includes index. Bibliography: p. 126-127. [BR763.S5C48] 76-379389 ISBN 0-9503615-2-6 : £1.60
1. Somerset, Eng.—Church history. I. Dunning, Robert William, 1916-

OXLEY, James Edwin 274.267
The Reformation in Essex to the death of Mary [Manchester. Eng.] Manchester Univ. Pr. [New York, Barnes & Noble, 1966, c.1965] xii, 320p. fold. map. 23cm. Bibl. [BR377.5.E8O9] 66-879 8.00
1. Reformation—England—Essex. I. Title.

SOTTOVAGINA, Hugh, d. 1139? 1139? 274.274
The history of the church of York, 1066-1127 [by] Hugh the chantor. Tr. from Latin with introd. by Charles Johnson. New York [dist. Oxford Univ. Press, 1961] various p. (Medieval texts) Bibl. 61-3331 6.75
1. Gt. Brit.—Church history. 2. York, Eng. (Province)—Hist. I. Title. II. Series: Medieval classics (London)

HAIGH, Christopher. 274.27'6
Reformation and resistance in Tudor Lancashire / Christopher Haigh. London ; New York : Cambridge University Press, 1975. xiii, 377 p. ; 22 cm. Includes index. Bibliography: p. 336-348. [BR377.5.L36H34] 73-88308 ISBN 0-521-20367-8 : 23.50
1. Reformation—England—Lancashire. 2. Lancashire, Eng.—Church history. I. Title.

CHADWICK, Owen. 274.281
The Victorian church. New York, Oxford University Press, 1966-70. 2 v. 24 cm. (An Ecclesiastical history of England, 5 [i.e. 7], 8) Series no. 5 in pt. 1 given as no. 7 in pt. 2. Contents.Contents.—pt. 1. 1829-1859.—pt. 2. 1860-1901. Includes bibliographies. [BR743.2.E3 no. 5 [i.e.7] etc.] 66-14976
1. Great Britain—Church history—19th century. I. Title. II. Series.

PARBURY, Kathleen. 274.28'2
The saints of Lindisfarne. Newcastle upon Tyne, Graham, 1970. 60 p. illus., facsims. 22 cm. (Northern history booklets, no. 5) [BX4659.G7P37] 70-871464 ISBN 0-900409-46-0 10/6
1. Lindisfarne Abbey. 2. Christian saints—Holy Island. I. Title. II. Series.

BOWEN, Emrys George, 1900- 274.29
The settlements of the Celtic saints in Wales. Cardiff, University of Wales Press, 1954. x, 175p. illus., maps. 22cm. Bibliography: p. 161-165. [BR774.B68] 55-23134
1. Wales—Church history. 2. Celtic Church. 3. Wales—Historical geography. I. Title.

BOWEN, Emrys George, 1900- 274.29
The settlements of the Celtic Saints in Wales. [2d ed.] Cardiff, Univ. of Wales Pr. [Mystic, Conn., Verry, 1966] xi, 175p. illus., maps. 22cm. First and 2d eds. Orig. pub. 1954 and 1956. Bibl. [BR774.B68] 3.50 bds.,
1. Wales—Church history. 2. Celtic Church. 3. Wales—Historical geography. I. Title.

DAVIES, Ebenezer Thomas 274.29
Religion in the industrial revolution in South Wales Cardiff, Univ. of Wales Pr. [dist. Mystic, Conn., Verry, 1965] viii, 202p. 23cm. (Pantyfedwen lects., 1962) Bibl. [BR776.D3] 65-8766 4.50
1. Wales, South—Church history. I. Title. II. Series.

A history of the Church in Wales / edited by David Walker ; foreword by the Archbishop of Wales. 274.29
Penarth : Church in Wales Publications for the Historical Society of the Church in Wales, 1976. xv, 221 p., 8 p. of plates : ill., facsim., ports. ; 23 cm. Includes index. Bibliography: p. [191]-200. [BR772.H57] 77-364750 ISBN 0-85326-010-9 : £1.75. ISBN 0-85326-011-7 pbk.
1. Wales—Church history. I. Walker, David, 1923-

WILLIAMS, Glanmor 274.29
The Welsh church from Conquest to Reformation. Cardiff, Univ. of Wales Pr. [Mystic, Conn., Verry, 1965] 602p. illus. 23cm. Bibl. [BR774.W58] 12.50
1. Wales—Church history. I. Title.

WILLIAMS, Glanmor 274.29
The Welsh church from Conquest to Reformation. Cardiff, Univ. of Wales Pr. [dist. Chester Springs, Pa., Dufour, 1963] 602p. tables (pt. fold.) 23cm. Bibl. 63-3625 12.50
1. Wales—Church history. I. Title.

WILLIAMS, Glanmor. 274.29
The Welsh church from Conquest to Reformation / by Glanmor Williams. Revised ed. Cardiff : University of Wales Press, 1976. xiv, 612 p., fold. leaf ; 23 cm. Includes index. Bibliography: p. [569]-591. [BR774.W58 1976] 77-357648 ISBN 0-7083-0084-7 : £12.00
1. Wales—Church history. I. Title.

WILLIAMS, Glanmor. comp. 274.29
Welsh Reformation essays. Cardiff. Univ. of Wales Pr., 1967. 232p. 23cm. Bibl. [BR775.W5] 68-82089 5.00 bds.,
1. Reformation—England—Wales. 2. Wales—Church history. I. Title.
Distributed by Verry, Mystic. Conn.

ADAMUS BREMENSIS 11thcentury 274.3
History of the archbishops of Hamburg-Bremen [by] Adam of Bremen. Translated with an introd. and notes by Francis J. Tschan. New York, Columbia University Press, 1959. xxxiv, 253p. diagr. 24cm. (Records of civilization: sources and studies, no. 53) Bibliography: p. [230]-238. [BR854.A313 1959] 56-7363
1. Germany—Church history. 2. Church history—Middle Ages. 3. Hamburg—Church history. 4. Bremen—Church history. I. Title. II. Title: Archbishops of Hamburg-Bremen. III. Series.

BARTH, Karl, 1886- 274.3
The German church conflict. [Translated by P.T.A. Parker] Richmond, John Knox Press [1965] 77 p. 22 cm. (Ecumenical studies in history, no. 1) Translation of Karl Barth sum Kirchenkampf. Bibliographical footnotes. [BR856.B2513] 65-15427
1. Germany — Church history — 1938-1945. I. Title. II. Series.

BARTH, Karl, 1886- 274.3
The German church conflict [Tr. from German by P. T. A. Paker] Richmond, Va., Knox [c.1965] 77p. 22cm. (Ecumenical studies in hist., no.1) Bibl. [BR856.B2513] 65-15427 1.75 pap.,
1. Germany—Church history—1933-1945. I. Title. II. Series.

BARTH, Karl, 1886- 274.3
How to serve God in a Marxist land, by Karl Barth and Johannes Hamel. With an introductory essay by Robert McAfee Brown. New York, Association Press [1959] 126p. 20cm. [BR738.6.B35] 59-14237
1. Christians in Europe, Eastern. 2. Europe, Eastern—Religion. I. Hamel, Johannes. II. Title.
Contents omitted.

COCHRANE, Arthur C 274.3
The church's confession under Hitler. Philadelphia, Westminster Press [1962] 317p. 24cm. Bibliographical references included in 'Notes' (p. 281-297) Biblipgraphy: p. 299-311. [BR856.C6] 62-7939
1. Barmer bekenntnis. 2. Church and state in Germany—1933-1945. 3. Germany—Religion—1933-1945. I. Title.

COCHRANE, Arthur C. 274.3
The church's confession under Hitler / by Arthur C. Cochrane. 2d ed. Pittsburgh : Pickwick Press, 1976[i.e.1977] 325 p. ; 22 cm. (Pittsburgh reprint series ; no. 4) Includes index. Bibliography: p. 307-320. [BR856.C6 1976] 76-57655 ISBN 0-915138-28-X pbk. : 7.50
1. Barmer Bekenntnis. 2. Church and state in Germany—1933-1945. I. Title.

JACKSON, Joseph Harrison, 1900- 274.3
Stars in the night; report on a visit to Germany. Philadelphia, Christian Education Press [1950] 72 p. illus., ports. 22 cm. [BR856.3.J3] 50-39049
1. Germany—Church history—1945- I. Title.

LITTELL, Franklin Hamlin 274.3
The German phoenix; men and movements in the in Germany Garden City, N. Y., Doubleday [c.]1960. xv, 226p. 22cm. Bibl. notes: p.211-223 60-13542 3.95
1. Germany—Church history—20th cent. 2. Deutscher Evangelischer Kirchentag. 3. Evangelical academies. I. Title.

LITTELL, Franklin Hamlin. 274.3
The German phoenix; men and movements in the church in Germany. [1st ed.] Garden City, N. Y., Doubleday, 1960. 226p. illus. 22cm. Includes bibliography. [BR856.L55] 60-13542
1. Germany—Church history—20th cent. 2. Deutscher Evangellncher Kirchentag. 3. Evangelical academies. I. Title.

MOELLER, Bernd, 1931- 274.3
Imperial cities and the Reformation; three essays. Edited and translated by H. C. Erik Midelfort and Mark U. Edwards, Jr. Philadelphia, Fortress Press [1972] xi, 115 p. illus. 22 cm. "Translated from the expanded French version of 1966 [of Reichsstadt und Reformation]" Includes Problems of Reformation research (translation of Probleme der Reformationsgeschichtsforschung) and The German humanists and the beginnings of the Reformation (translation of Die deutschen Humanisten und die Anfange der Reformation). Includes bibliographical references. [BR307.M613] 72-75660 ISBN 0-8006-0121-1 3.25
1. Reformation—Germany. 2. Imperial cities (Holy Roman Empire) I. Moeller, Bernd, 1931- Probleme der Reformationsgeschichtsforschung. English. 1972. II. Moeller, Bernd, 1931- Die deutschen

Humanisten und die Anfange der Reformation. English. 1972. III. Title.

RANKE, Leopold von, 1795- 1886. 274.3
History of the Reformation in Germany. [Translated by Sarah Austin. Edited by Robert A. Johnson] New York, F. Unger Pub. Co. [1966] 2 v. (xx, 792 p.) 27 cm. "Reprinted from the edition of 1905." Bibliographical footnotes. [BR305.R4 1966] 66-26513
1. Reformation—Germany. I. Austin, Sarah (Taylor) 1793-1867, tr. II. Johnson, Robert A., ed.

SOLBERG, Richard W 1917- 274.3
God and Caesar in East Germany; the conflicts of church and state in East Germany since 1945. Foreword by Bishop Otto Dibelius. New York, Macmillan, 1961. 294 p. illus. 22 cm. [BR856.35.S6] 61-8759
1. Germany (Democratic Republic, 1949-) — Church history. 2. Germany (Democratic Republic, 1949-) — Religion. I. Title.

SOLBERG, Richard W., 1917- 274.3
God and Caesar in East Germany; the conflicts of church and state in East Germany since 1945. Foreword by Bishop Otto Dibelius. New York, Macmillan [c.]1961. 294p. illus. 61-8759 4.95
1. Germany (Democratic Republic, 1949-)—Church history. 2. Germany (Democratic Republic, 1949-)—Religion. I. Title.

WESTERMEYER, H E 274.3
The fall of the German gods. Mountain View, Calif., Pacific Press Pub. Association [1950] xv,328 p. illus., ports. 23 cm. Bibliography: p. 295-303. [BR856.W5] 50-3140
1. Germany — Religion — 1932-1945. I. Title.

PREUS, James Samuel. 274.3'18
Carlstadt's ordinaciones and Luther's liberty : a study of the Wittenberg Movement, 1521-22 / James S. Preus. Cambridge, Mass. : Harvard University Press, 1974. 88 p. ; 24 cm. (Harvard theological studies ; 26 [i.e. 27]) Includes bibliographical references. [BR359.W57P73] 74-190635 4.50
1. Karlstadt, Andreas Rudolf, 1480 (ca.)-1541. 2. Luther, Martin, 1483-1546. 3. Reformation—Germany—Wittenberg. I. Title. II. Series: Harvard theological studies ; 27.

SOCIETY for Promoting Christian Knowledge, London. 274.363
Henry Newman's Salzburger letterbooks. Transcribed, ed. by George Fenwick Jones. Athens, Univ. of Ga. Pr. [1966] xi, 626p. illus., maps. 25cm. (Wormsloe Found. Pubns., no. 8) Based on Xerox copies from microfilms of letterbks., preserved in the archives of the soc., consisting of correspondence, chiefly between Henry Newman, secretary, & Samuel Urlsperger about the soc. efforts to aid Protestant exiles from Salzburg who wished to settle in colonial Ga. Bibl. [BR817.S3S6] 66-25848 12.00
1. Salzburgers—Emigration. 1731-1735. I. Newman, Henry, 1670-1743. II. Urlsperger, Samuel, 1685-1772. III. Jones, George Fenwick, 1916- ed. IV. Title. V. Title: Salzburger letterbooks. VI. Series.

DYGGVE, Ejnar, 1887- 274.369
History of Salonitan Christianity. Oslo, Aschenhoug; Cambridge, Harvard University Press, 1951. xiii, 163 p. plates, maps. 22 cm. (Instituttet for sammenlignende kulturforskning. Serie A: Forelesninger, 21) Includes bibliographical references. [BR133.Y8S3] A 52
1. Church history—Primitive and early church. 2. Salona, Dalmatia—Antiq. I. Title. II. Series: Instituttet for sammenlignende kulturforskning, Oslo. Serie A: Forelesninger, 21

FOX, Paul, 1874- 274.38
The Reformation in Poland: some social and economic aspects. Baltimore, Johns Hopkins Press, 1924. [New York, AMS Press, 1971] viii, 153 p. 23 cm. (Johns Hopkins University. Studies in historical and political science, ser. 42, no. 4) Originally presented as the author's thesis, Johns Hopkins University. Includes bibliographical references. [BR420.P7F6 1971b] 72-136395 ISBN 0-404-02544-7
1. Reformation—Poland. 2. Poland—Social conditions. 3. Poland—Economic conditions. I. Title. II. Series.

KRASINSKI, Walerjan Skorobohaty, d.1855. 274.38
Historical sketch of the rise, progress, and decline of the Reformation in Poland, and of the influence which the scriptural doctrines have exercised on that country in literary, moral, and political respects, by Count Valerian Krasinski. New York, B. Franklin [1974] p. cm. Reprint of the 1838-40 ed. [BR420.P7K8 1974] 72-82255 ISBN 0-8337-1957-2 42.50
1. Reformation—Poland. 2. Poland—Church history. I. Title.

KUHAR, Aloysius L 1895- 1958. 274.39
The conversion of the Slovenes, and the German-Slav ethnic boundary in the eastern Alps. New York, League of C. S. A., 1959 231p. illus. 23cm. (Studia Slovenica, 2) Part of thesis, Cambridge University. Includes bibliographies. [BV2857.S7K8 1959] 60-23462
1. Missions—Slovenes. I. Title.

CHATEILLON, Sebastien, 1515-1563. 274.4
Advice to a desolate France : in the course of which the reason for the present war is outlined, as well as the possible remedy and, in the main, advice is given as to whether consciences should be forced, the year 1562 / Sebastian Castellio [i.e. S. Chateillon]. New ed., with an introd. and explanatory notes / by Marius F. Valkhoff ; English translation by Wouter Valkhoff ; pref. to the English translation by Albert Geyser. Shepherdstown, W. Va. : Patmos Press, 1975. xiii, 50 p., [1] leaf of plates : facsim. ; 22 cm. Translation of Conseil a la France desolee. "Limited edition of 500." Includes bibliographical references. [BV741.C4713 1975] 75-16650 ISBN 0-915762-00-5 : 7.95
1. Liberty of conscience. 2. Religious liberty—France. 3. Religious tolerance—France. I. Title.

NUGENT, Donald, 1930- 274.4
Ecumenism in the age of the Reformation: the Colloquy of Poissy. Cambridge, Mass., Harvard University Press, 1974. xi, 258 p. front. 22 cm. (Harvard historical studies, v. 89) Originally presented as the author's thesis, University of Iowa, 1965. Bibliography: p. 241-254. [BR355.P64N8 1974] 73-80026 ISBN 0-674-23725-0 14.00
1. Poissy, Colloquy of, 1561. 2. Christian union—History. I. Title. II. Series.

ROBINET, Jean Francois Eugene, 1825-1899. 274.4
Le mouvement religieux a Paris pendant la Revolution (1789-1801). Paris, L. Cerf, 1896-98. [New York, AMS Press, 1974] p. cm. Original ed. issued in series: Collection de documents relatifs a l'histoire de Paris pendant la Revolution francaise. No more published. Contents.Contents.—t. 1. La revolution dans l'Eglise, juillet 1789 a septembre 1791.—t. 2. Preliminaires de la dechristianisation, septembre 1791 a septembre 1793. Includes bibliographical references. [DC194.A2R6 1974] 70-174331 ISBN 0-404-52567-9
1. France—History—Revolution, 1789-1799—Religious history—Sources. I. Title. II. Series: Collection de documents relatifs a l'histoire de Paris pendant la Revolution francaise.

SYLVESTER II, Pope d.1003 274.4
The letters of Gerbert, with his papal privileges as Sylvester II. Translated with an introd. by Harriet Pratt Lattin. New York, Columbia University Press, 1961. x, 412 p. illus. 24 cm. (Records of civilization: sources and studies, no. 60) Bibliography: p. [393]-399. [BX1158.A413 1961] 60-5012
1. Catholic Church in France. 2. France — Church history — Middle Ages. I. Title. II. Series.

SYLVESTER I I Pope 1003 Sylvester the second 274.4
The letters of Gerbert, with his papal privileges as Sylvester II. Tr., introd. by Harriet Pratt Lattin. New York, Columbia, 1961. x, 412p. illus. (Records of civilization: sources and studies, no. 60) Bibl. 61-19432 7.50
1. Catholic Church in France. 2. France—Church history—Middle Ages. I. Lattin, Harriet (Pratt) 1898- II. Title. III. Series.

WAKEFIELD, Walter Leggett. 274.4
Heresy, crusade, and inquisition in southern France, 1100-1250 [by] Walter L. Wakefield Berkeley, University of California Press, 1974. 288 p. maps. 23 cm. Bibliography: p. [259]-276. [DC59.5.W34 1974b] 72-93524 ISBN 0-520-02380-3 14.00
1. Inquisition. France. 2. France—Church history—Middle Ages, 987-1515. 3. Albigenses. 4. Waldenses in France. I. Title.

WOOD, Charles T., comp. 274.4
Philip the Fair and Boniface VIII : state vs. papacy / edited by Charles T. Wood. 2d ed. Huntington, N.Y. : R. E. Krieger Pub. Co., 1976, c1971. vii, 116 p. ; 23 cm. Reprint of the ed. published by Holt, Rinehart and Winston, New York, in series: European problem studies. Bibliography: p. 113-116. [BX1253.W6 1976] 76-23207 ISBN 0-88275-454-8 pbk. : 3.95
1. Bonifacius VIII, Pope, d. 1303. 2. Philippe IV, le Bel, King of France, 1268-1314. 3. France—Church history—Middle Ages, 987-1515. 4. Popes—Biography. 5. France—Kings and rulers—Biography. I. Title.

WOOD, Charles T., comp. 274.4
Philip the Fair and Boniface VIII; state vs. papacy, edited by Charles T. Wood. New York, Holt, Rinehart and Winston [1967] viii, 116 p. 24 cm. (European problem studies) Bibliography: p. 113-116. [BX1253.W6] 67-11806
1. Bonifacius VIII, Pope, 1303, d. 2. Philippe IV, le Bel, King of France, 1268-1314. 3. France—Church history—Middle Ages, 987-1515. I. Title.

WOOD, Charles T., comp. 274.4
Philip the Fair and Boniface VIII; state vs. papacy, edited by Charles T. Wood. 2d ed. New York, Holt, Rinehart and Winston [1971] vii, 116 p. 24 cm. (European problem studies) Includes bibliographical references. [BX1253.W6 1971] 78-135126 ISBN 0-03-085412-1
1. Bonifacius VIII, Pope, d. 1303. 2. Philippe IV, le Bel, King of France, 1268-1314. 3. France—Church history—Middle Ages, 987-1515. I. Title.

GOFFART, Walter A. 274.4'17
The Le Mans forgeries; a chapter from the history of church property in the ninth century [by] Walter Goffart. Cambridge, Harvard University Press, 1966 [i.e. 1967] xv, 382 p. 22 cm. (Harvard historical studies v. 76) Appendices (p. [255]-366): A. The charters of the Actus and Gesta, a critical survey.—B. The textual transmission of the cartulary of St. Calais.—C. Hagiographical notes. Bibliographical footnotes. [BR848.L4G6] 66-18246
1. Le Mans—Church history—Sources—History and criticism. I. Title. II. Series.

CHRISMAN, Miriam Usher 274.4'3835
Strasbourg and the Reform; a study in the process of change. New Haven, Yale, 1967. xii, 351p. illus., map. 22cm. (Yale hist. pubns. Miscellany, 87) (Series) Covers the period from 1523 to1533. Bibl. [BR848.S7C45] 67-13431 8.75
1. Reformation—Germany—Strassburg. 2. Strassburg—Church history. I. Title. II. Series.

CHRISMAN, Miriam Usher. 274.4'3835
Strasbourg and the Reform; a study in the process of change. New Haven, Yale University Press, 1967. xii, 351 p. illus., map. 22 cm. (Yale historical publications. Miscellany, 87) "Bibliographical note": p. 319-322. Bibliography: p. 323-333. [BR848.S7C45] 67-13431
1. Reformation — Germany — Strassburg. 2. Strassburg — Church history. I. Title. II. Series.

STAFFORD, William S. 274.4'3835
Domesticating the clergy : the inception of the Reformation in Strasbourg, 1522-1524 / by William S. Stafford. Missoula, Mont. : Published by Scholars Press for the American Academy of Religion, c1976. vii, 296 p. ; 21 cm. (Dissertation series - American Academy of Religion ; no. 17) Originally presented as the author's thesis, Yale, 1974. Bibliography: p. 289-296. [BR372.S8S8 1976] 76-15567 ISBN 0-89130-109-7 : 3.00
1. Reformation—France—Strasbourg. 2. Clergy—France—Strasbourg. 3. Strasbourg—Church history. I. Title. II. Series: American Academy of Religion. Dissertation series — American Academy of Religion ; no. 17.

STAFFORD, William S. 274.4'3835
Domesticating the clergy : the inception of the Reformation in Strasbourg, 1522-1524 / by William S. Stafford. Missoula, Mont. : Published by Scholars Press for the American Academy of Religion, c1976. p. cm. (Dissertation series - American Academy of Religion ; no. 17) Originally presented as the author's thesis, Yale, 1974. Includes bibliographical references. [BR372.S8S8 1976] 76-15567 ISBN 0-89130-109-7 : 3.00
1. Reformation—France—Strasbourg. 2. Clergy—France—Strasbourg. 3. Strasbourg—Church history. I. Title. II. Series: American Academy of Religion. Dissertation series — American Academy of Religion ; no. 17.

HUNTER, Leslie Stannard, Bp. of Sheffield, 1890- ed. 274.48
Scandinavian churches; a picture of the development and life of the churches of Denmark, Finland, Iceland, Norway, and Sweden. [London, Faber &Faber] Minneapolis, Augsburg [1966, c.1965] 200p. illus., ports. 23cm. Bibl. [BR973.H8] 66-3693 4.50
1. Scandinavia—Religion. 2. Sects—Scandinavia. I. Title.

BROWN, George Kenneth. 274.5
Italy and the Reformation to 1550, by G. K. Brown. New York, Russell & Russell [1971] vii, 324 p. 23 cm. A reprint of the 1933 modification of the author's thesis, University of Edinburgh. Bibliography: p. 299-309. [BR390.B7 1971] 70-139908
1. Reformation—Italy. 2. Italy—Church history. I. Title.

CHURCH, Frederic Corss. 274.5
The Italian reformers, 1534-1564, by Frederic C. Church. New York, Octagon Books, 1974 [c1932] xii, 428 p. 23 cm. Reprint of the ed. published by Columbia University Press, New York. Bibliography: p. [387]-399. [BR390.C5 1974] 73-19934 ISBN 0-374-91595-4 14.50
1. Reformation—Italy. 2. Counter-Reformation. I. Title.

MCCRIE, Thomas, 1772-1835. 274.5
History of the progress and suppression of the Reformation in Italy in the sixteenth century; including a sketch of the history of the Reformation in the Grisons. A new ed. edited by his son. Edinburgh, W. Blackwood, 1856. [New York, AMS Press, 1974] xiv, 266 p. port. 23 cm. Includes bibliographical references. [BR390.M29 1974] 72-1006 ISBN 0-404-04118-3 13.00
1. Reformation—Italy. 2. Reformation—Switzerland—Grisons. I. Title.

WRIGHT, Anthony David. 274.5
Federico Borromeo and Baronius : a turning-point in the development of the Counter-Reformation Church / by A. D. Wright. [Reading] : University of Reading, Department of Italian Studies, 1974. 27 p. ; 22 cm. (Occasional papers - Centre for the Advanced Study of Italian Society ; no. 6) Includes bibliographical references. [BX4705.B67W74] 75-323797 ISBN 0-7049-0401-2 : £0.80
1. Borromeo, Federico, Cardinal, 1564-1631. 2. Baronio, Cesare, Cardinal, 1538-1607. 3. Counter-Reformation—Italy. I. Title. II. Series: Reading, Eng. University. Centre for the Advanced Study of Italian Society. Occasional papers ; no. 6.

GRENDLER, Paul F. 274.5'31
The Roman Inquisition and the Venetian press, 1540-1605/ Paul F. Grendler Princeton, N.J. : Princeton University Press, c1977. xxiii, 374 p. : ill. ; 25 cm. Includes index. Bibliography: p. 325-348. [BX1723.G73] 76-45900 ISBN 0-691-05245-X : 21.50
1. Inquisition. Venice. 2. Press—Italy—Venice. 3. Counter-Reformation. I. Title.

LEA, Henry Charles, 1825- 1900. 274.6
Chapters from the religions history of Spain connected with the Inquisition. New York, Burt Franklin [1967] 522 p. 23 cm. (Burt Franklin research & source work series, 245) Selected essays [in] history and social science, 31. Title on spine: Religious history of Spain. Reprint of the 1890 ed. English with Spanish appendix. Bibliographical footnotes. [BX1735.L4] 68-56760
1. Spain—Church history. 2. Inquisition. Spain—Hist. 3. Liberty of the press. I. Title. II. Title: Religious history of Spain.
Contents Ommitted

LEA, Henry Charles, 1825- 1900. 274.6
Chapters from the religious history of Spain connected with the Inquisition. New York, Burt Franklin [1967] 522 p. 23 cm. (Burt Franklin research & source work series, 245) (Selected essays [in] history and social science, 31.) Title on spine: Religious history of Spain. Reprint of the 1890 ed. English with Spanish appendix. Contents.Contents.—Censorship of the press.—Mystics and illuminati.—Endemoniadas.—El Santo Nino de la Guardia.—Brianda de Bardaxi.—Appendix of documents. Bibliographical footnotes. [BX1735.L4 1967] 68-56760
1. Inquisition. Spain—History. 2. Spain—Church history. 3. Liberty of the press. I. Title. II. Title: Religious history of Spain.

MCCRIE, Thomas, 1772-1835. 274'.6
History of the progress and suppression of the Reformation in Spain in the sixteenth century, by Thomas M'Crie. New York, AMS Press [1971] viii, 424 p. 23 cm. Reprint of the 1829 ed. Includes bibliographical references. [BR405.M3 1971] 75-120206 ISBN 0-404-04117-5
1. Reformation—Spain. I. Title.

MARIQUE, Joseph Marie Felix, ed. 274.6
Leaders of Iberean Christianity, 50-650 A.D. [Boston] St. Paul Eds. [dist. Daughters of St. Paul, c.1962] 163p. 22cm. Bibl. 62-22008 3.00 bds.,
1. Christians in Spain. 2. Spain—Church history—Sources. I. Title.

BACH, Marcus, 1906- 274.7
God and the Soviets. New York, Crowell [1958] 214 p. illus. 21 cm. [BR936.B15] 58-12287
1. Russia—Religion—1917- 2. Communism and religion. I. Title.

BACH, Marcus, 1906- 274.7
God and the Soviets. [New York 16, 425 Park Ave., S., Apollo Editions, Inc., 1961, c.1958] 214p. (Apollo ed. A-2) 1.25 pap.,
1. Russia—Religion—1917- 2. Communism and religion. I. Title.

BOLSHAKOFF, Serge. 274.7
Russian nonconformity; the story of "unofficial" religion in Russia. Philadelphia, Westminster Press [1950] 192 p. 21 cm. Bibliography: p. 187-192. [BX599.B58] 50-10296
1. Dissenters—Russia. 2. Sects—Russia. 3. Russia—Church history. I. Title.

BOLSHAKOFF, Serge. 274.7
Russian nonconformity; the story of "unofficial" religion in Russia. Philadelphia, Westminster Press, 1950. [New York, AMS Press, 1973] 192 p. 23 cm. Bibliography: p. 187-192. [BX599.B58 1973] 74-153304 ISBN 0-404-00933-6 10.00
1. Dissenters, Religious—Russia. 2. Sects—Russia. 3. Russia—Church history. I. Title.

BOURDEAUX, Michael. 274.7
Opium of the people; the Christian religion in the U.S.S.R. Indianapolis, Bobbs-Merrill [1966] 244 p. illus., map, ports. 22 cm. "Notes for further reading": p. 235-240. [BR936.B65] 66-15532
1. Russia — Religion — 1917- . 2. Church and state in Russia — 1917- . I. Title. II. Title: The Christian religion in the U.S.S.R.

BOURDEAUX, Michael 274.7
Opium of the people; the Christian religion in the U. S. S. R. Indianapolis, Bobbs [c.1966] 244p. illus., map, ports. 22cm. Bibl. [BR936.B65] 66-15532 5.00 bds.,
1. Russia—Religion—1917- 2. Church and state in Russia—1917- I. Title. II. Title: The Christian religion in the U. S. S. R.

BRUNELLO, Aristide. 274.7
The silent church; facts and documents concerning religious persecution behind the Iron Curtain, by Lino Gussoni and Aristede Brunello. [1st ed. in English] New York, Veritas [1954] 391p. illus. 21cm. A translation of Brunello's La chiesa del silenzio. Includes bibliography. [BR738.6.B73] 54-10337
1. Persecution —Europe, Eastern. 2. Europe, Eastern—Religion. I. Gussoni, Lino, 1920- tr. II. Title.

CONQUEST, Robert. 274.7
Religion in the U.S.S.R. New York, Praeger [1968] 135 p. 23 cm. (Praeger publications in Russian history and world communism, no. 201.) (The Contemporary Soviet Union series: institutions and policies) Bibliography: p. 128-135. [BR936.C6 1968] 68-17377
1. Russia—Religion—1917- I. Title. II. Series.

GRUNWALD, Constantin de 274.7
The churches and the Soviet Union. Tr. by G. J. Robinson-Paskevsky. New York, Macmillan, 1962 [c.1961] 255p. illus. Bibl. 62-1974 4.00
1. Russia—Church history—1917- 2. Russia—Religion—1917- I. Title.

HECKER, Julius Friedrich, 274.7
1881-
Religion and communism; a study of religion and atheism in Soviet Russia, by Julius F. Hecker. Westport, Conn., Hyperion Press [1973] p. Reprint of the 1934 ed. published by Wiley, New York. [BR936.H28 1973] 73-842 ISBN 0-88355-037-7 14.75
1. Russia—Religion—1917- 2. Church and state in Russia—1917- 3. Communism and religion. I. Title.

JOHNSON, Joseph, 1907- 274.7
God's secret armies within the Soviet Empire. New York, Putnam [1954] 268p. 21cm. [BR936.J63] 54-5488
1. Christians in Russia. 2. Russia—Church history—1917- 3. Anti-communist underground—Russia. I. Title.

PASTOR Nicoli. 274.7
Persecuted but not forsaken : the story of a church behind the iron curtain / by Pastor Nicoli. Valley Forge, Pa. : Judson Press, c1977. 172 p. ; 22 cm. [BR1608.E8P37] 77-7114 ISBN 0-8170-0749-0 pbk. : 3.95
1. Persecution—Europe, Eastern. I. Title.

POLLOCK, John Charles. 274.7
The faith of the Russian Evangelicals, by J. C. Pollock. New York, McGraw-Hill [1964] 190 p. 21 cm. London ed. (Hodder and Stoughton) has title: The Christians from Siberia. Bibliography: p. 187-190. [BX4849.P6] 64-25603
1. Protestants in Russia. 2. Baptists—Russia. 3. Persecution—Russia. I. Title.

POLLOCK, John Charles 274.7
The faith of the Russian Evangelicals. New York, McGraw [c.1964] 190p. 21cm. London ed. (Hodder and Stoughton) has title: The Christians from Siberia. Bibl. 64-25603 3.95 bds.,
1. Protestants in Russia. 2. Baptists—Russia. 3. Persecution—Russia. I. Title.

SOLOVIEV, Alexandre V. 274.7
Holy Russia; the history of a religious-social idea [tr. from the Russian]. 's-Gaevenhage, Mouton. [dist. New York, Humanities Press, 1959, i.e., 1960] 61 p. 23 cm. (Musagets contributtions to the history of Slavic literature and culture 12) This article was written in 1927 and printed in the Sbornik Russkogo archeologiceskogo obscstva'v Korolevste SHS in Belgrade. Bibliographical footnotes A60 2.00 pap.,
1. Orthodox Eastern Church, Russian—Hist. 2. Religious thought—Russia. 3. Russia—Church history. I. Title. II. Series.

STRUVE, Nikita. 274.7
Christians in contemporary Russia. Translated by Lancelot Sheppard and A. Manson from the 2d rev. and augmented ed. New York, Scribner [1967] 464 p. 22 cm. Translation of Les chretiens en U.R. S. S. Bibliographical references included in "Notes" (p. 421-455) [BR936.S8613] 67-17298
1. Church and state in Russia — 1917- 2. Russia — Church history — 1917- I. Title.

STRUVE, Nikita. 274.7
Christians in contemporary Russia. Translated by Lancelot Sheppard and A. Manson from the 2d rev. and augmented ed. New York, Scribner [1967] 464 p. 22 cm. Translation of Les chretiens en U. R. S. S. Bibliographical references included in "Notes" (p. 421-455) [BR936.S8613 1967] 67-17298
1. Church and state in Russia—1917- 2. Russia—Church history—1917- . I. Title.

SZCZESNIAK, Boleslaw ed. 274.7
and tr.
The Russian revolution and religion; a collection of docuemnts concerning the suppression of religion by the Communists, 1917-1925. With introductory essays, appendices, and a selective bibliography. [Ntre Dame, Ind. University of Notre Dame Press 1959. xx, 289 p. 24 cm. (International studies of the Committee on International Relations, University of Notre Dame) Notre Dame, Ind. University. Committee on International Relations. International studies) Bibliography: p. 253-269. Bibliographical footnotes. [BR936.S94] 58-14180
1. Russia — Church history — 1917- I. Title. II. Series.

SZCZESNIAK, Boleslaw, ed. 274.7
and tr.
The Russian revolution and religion; a collection of documents concerning the suppression of religion by the Communists, 1917-1925. With introductory essay, appendices, and a selective bibliography. [Notre Dame, Ind.] University of Notre Dame Press [c.]1959. xx, 289p. 24cm. (International studies of the Committee on International Relations, University of Notre Dame) (Bibl.: p.253-269. Bibl. footnotes.) 58-14180 6.75
1. Russia—Church history—1917- I. Title. II. Series: Notre Dame, Ind. University. Committee on International Relations. International studies

VAN PAASSEN, Pierre, 1895- 274.7
Visions rise and change. New York, Dial Press, 1955. 400 p. 22 cm. [BR936.V34] 55-11199
1. Russia—Religion—1917- I. Title.

ZERNOV, Nicolas 274.7
The Russian religious renaissance of the twentieth century. New York, Harper [1964, c.1963] xi, 410p. ports. 23cm. Bibl. 64-10768 7.00
1. Russia—Church history—1917- I. Title.

MEZEZERS, Valdis. 274.7'4
The Herrnhuterian pietism in the Baltic, and its outreach into America and elsewhere in the world / by Valdis Mezezers. North Quincy, Mass. : Christopher Pub. House, c1975. 151 p., [1] leaf of plates : ill. ; 20 cm. Bibliography: p. 147-151. [BR1652.B34M49] 74-28646 ISBN 0-8158-0322-2 : 6.95
1. Zinzendorf, Nicolaus Ludwig, Graf von, 1700-1760. 2. Pietism—Baltic States. I. Title: The Herrnhuterian pietism in the Baltic ...

SAVASIS, J. pseud. 274.75
The war against God in Lithuania Pref. by Ed ward E. Swanstrom. New York, Manyland [c.1966] 134p. illus., map, ports. 23cm. Bibl. [BL2747.3.S3613] 66-15367 3.00
1. Atheism—Lithuania. I. Title.

SAVASIS, J pseud. 274.75
The war against God in Lithuania, by J. Savasis. Pref. by Edward E. Swanstrom. New York, Manyland Books [1966] 134 p. illus., map, ports. 23 cm. Bibliographical footnotes. [BL2747.3.S3613] 66-15367
1. Atheism—Lithuania. I. Title.

MOLLAND, Einar, 1908- 274.81
Church life in Norway, 1800-1950. Translated by Harris Kaasa. Minneapolis, Augsburg Pub. House [1957] 120 p. 21 cm. [BR1006.M6] 57-6474
1. Norway—Church history. I. Title.

BERGENDOFF, Conrad John 274.85
Immanuel, 1895-
Olavus Petri and the ecclesiastical transformation in Sweden, 1521-1552; a study in the Swedish Reformation [New introd. by the author] Philadelphia, Fortress [c.1965] xvi, 267p. 20cm. Orig. pub. in 1928. Bibl. [BR350.P4B4] 3.75
1. Petri, Olavus, 1493-1552. 2. Reformation—Sweden. 3. Sweden—Church history. 4. Church and state in Sweden. I. Title.

RUNCIMAN, Steven, Sir, 274.95
1903-
The Byzantine theocracy / Steven Runciman. Cambridge ; New York : Cambridge University Press, 1977. viii, 197 p. ; 20 cm. (The Weil lectures ; 1973) Includes bibliographical references and index. [BX300.R86] 76-47405 ISBN 0-521-21401-7 : 9.95
1. Church and state in the Byzantine Empire—History—Addresses, essays, lectures. I. Title. II. Series.

MOREA, Andre. 274.98
The book they couldn't ban : the miraculous experiences of a Bible courier in Romania / [by] Andre Morea. London : Lakeland, 1976. 157 p. ; 18 cm. [BV2369.5.E852M66] 77-353521 ISBN 0-551-00589-0 : £0.75
1. Morea, Andre. 2. Bible—Publication and distribution—Europe, Eastern. I. Title.

275 Christian Church In Asia

BROWNE, Laurence Edward, 275
1887-
The eclipse of Christianity in Asia, from the time of Muhammad till the fourteenth century, by Laurence E. Browne. New York, H. Fertig, 1967. 198p. map. 24cm. First pub. in 1933. Bibl. [BR1065.B7 1967] 67-13640 6.50
1. Asia—Church history. 2. Islam—Relations—Christianity. 3. Christianity and other religions—Islam. I. Title.

BROWNE, Laurence Edward, 275
1887-
The eclipse of Christianity in Asia, from the time of Muhammad till the fourteenth century, by Laurence E. Browne. New York, H. Fertig, 1967. 108 p. map. 24 cm. First published in 1933. Bibliography: p. [187]-192. [BR1065.B7] 67-13640
1. Asia — Church history. 2. Islam — Relations — Christianity. 3. Christianity and other religions — Islam. I. Title.

DEVANANDAN, Paul David. 275
Christian issues in southern Asia. New York, Friendship Press, [1963] 174 p. 19 cm. Includes bibliography. [BV3250.D4] 63-8682
1. Christianity — South Asia. 2. Missions — South Asia. I. Title.

DEVANANDAN, Paul David 275
Christian issues in southern Asia. New York, Friendship [c.1963] 174p. 19cm. Bibl. 63-8682 1.75 pap.,
1. Christianity—South Asia. 2. Missions—South Asia. I. Title.

EASTMAN, Addison J ed. 275
Branches of the banyan; observations on the church in southern Asia. New York, Friendship Press [1963] 160 p. illus. 21 cm. [BV3250.E2] 63-8683
1. Missions—South Asia. 2. Christianity—South Asia. I. Title.

EASTMAN, Addison J., ed. 275
Branches of the banyan; observations on the church in southern Asia. New York, Friendship [c.1963] 160p. illus. col. map. 21cm. 63-8633 1.95 pap.,
1. Missions—South Asia. 2. Christianity—South Asia. I. Title.

GEHMAN, Richard 275
Let my heart be broken with the things that break the heart of God. Photos. by Richard Reinhold. Grand Rapids, Mich., Zondervan [1966, c.1960] 245p. illus. 21cm. [BV2360.W88G4] .98 pap.,
1. Pierce, Robert Willard, 1914- 2. World Vision, Inc. 3. Missions—Asia. I. Title.

GEHMAN, Richard. 275
Let my heart be broken with the things that break the heart of God. Photos. by Richard Reinhold. New York, McGraw-Hill [1960] 245 p. illus. 22 cm. [BV2360.W88G4] 60-15687
1. World Vision, inc. 2. Pierce, Robert Willard, 1914- 3. Missions—Asia. I. Title.

LEDYARD, Gleason H 275
Sky waves; the incredible Far East Broadcasting Company story. Chicago, Moody Press [c1963] 208 p. illus., ports. 22 cm. [BV2082.R3L4] 63-23170
1. Far East Broadcasting Company. 2. Radio in religion. I. Title.

LEDYARD, Gleason H. 275
Sky waves; the incredible Far East Broadcasting Company story. Chicago, Moody [1968, c.1963] 208p. illus., ports. 22cm. [BV2082.R3L4] 63-23170 .89 pap.,
1. Far East Broadcasting Company. 2. Radio in religion. I. Title.

LEDYARD, Gleason H. 275
Sky waves; the incredible Far East Broadcasting Company story. Chicago, Moody [c.1963] 208p. illus., ports. 22cm. 63-23170 3.50
1. Far East Broadcasting Company. 2. Radio in religion. I. Title.

OHM, Thomas, 1892- 275
Asia looks at Western Christianity. [English translation by Irene Marinoff. New York] Herder and Herder [1959] 251p. 19cm. Includes bibliography. [BR127.O313 1959a] 59-11368
1. Christianity and other religions. 2. Missions—Asia. I. Title.

ADENEY, David Howard. 275'.1
China; Christian students face the revolution [by] David H. Adeney. Downers Grove, Ill., InterVarsity Press [1973] 130 p. map. 18 cm. [BR1288.A3] 72-96067 ISBN 0-87784-354-6 1.50 (pbk.)
1. Christianity—China. 2. Students—China. I. Title.

CARY-ELWES, Columba, 1903- 275.1
China and the cross; a survey of missionary history. New York, P. J. Kenedy [1957] 323p. illus. 21cm. Includes bibliography. [BR1285.C3] 57-5760
1. China—Church history. 2. Missions—China. I. Title.

CHAN, Wing-tsit, 1901- 275.1
Religious trends in modern China. New York, Columbia University Press, 1953. xiii, 327p. 23cm. (Lectures on the history of religions sponsored by the American Council of Learned Societies. New series, no.3) The Haskell lectures at the University of Chicago, 1950. Bibliography: p. [265]-281. [BL25.L4 no.3] 53-7012
1. China—Religion. 2. Religious thought—China. I. Title. II. Series: Haskell lectures in comparative religion, University of Chicago, 1950

FERRIS, Helen. 275.1
The Christian church in Communist China, to 1952. Produced under Contract no. AF 33(038)-25075. Research accomplished under contract with Human Resources Research Institute, Maxwell Air Force Base, Alabama. Lackland Air Force Base, Texas, Air Force Personnel and Training Research Center, Air Research and Development Command, 1956. xi, 76p. map. 27cm. ([U. S.] Human Resources Research Institute. Research Memorandum no. 45) (Series. Studies in Chinese communism, ser. 2, no. 5) Studies in Chinese communism, ser. 2, no. 5. On cover: HRRI Project 'Chinese Documents Project.' Bibliographical footnotes. [BR1285.F4 1956] 57-61199
1. Church and state in China. 2. China—Religion. I. Title. II. Series.

HILLIS, Dick 275.1
Unlock the heavens. Chicago, Moody [c.1963] 62p. 18cm. (Compact bks., 33) .29 pap.,
I. Title.

JONES, Francis Price. 275.1
The church in Communist China; a Protestant appraisal. New York, Friendship Press [1962] 180p. 19cm. Includes bibliography. [BR1285.J6] 62-7859
1. Protestant churches—China (People's Republic of China, 1949-) 2. Communism and religion—1946- I. Title.

KUHN, Isobel 275.1
Nests above the abyss. Chicago, Moody [1964, c.1947] 254p. illus. 22cm. (China Inland Mission bk.) 64-9081 3.75
1. Missions—Yunnan, China. I. Title. II. Series.

*KUHN, Isobel 275.1
Precious things of the lasting hills. Rev. ed. Chicago, Moody [c.1963] 64p. 18cm. .29 pap.,
I. Title.

LUTZ, Jessie Gregory, 1925- 275.1
ed.
Christian missions in China; evangelists of what? Edited with an introd. by Jessie G. Lutz. Boston, Heath [1965] xx, 108 p. 24 cm.

(Problems in Asian civilizations) Bibliography, p. 104-108. [BV3415.2.L8] 64-8155
1. Missions — China. I. Title. II. Series.

LUTZ, Jessie Gregory, 1925- ed. 275.1
Christian missions in China; evangelists of what?Ed., introd. by Jessie G. Lutz. Boston, Heath [c.1965] xx, 108p. 24cm. (Probs. in Asian civilizations) Bibl. [BV3415.2.L8] 64-8155 1.75 pap.,
1. Missions—China. I. Title. II. Series.

LYALL, Leslie T. 275.1
Come wind, come weather; the present experience of the church in China. Chicago, Moody Press [c.1960] 95p. 60-51514 2.00
1. China—Church history. I. Title.

OSS, John. 275.1
Mission advance in China. Nashville, Southern Pub. Association [1950, c1949] 284 p. illus., ports., map (on lining paper) 20 cm. "One of a series of study books on the great mission fields of the world." Includes bibliographies. [BV3415.O76] [266.67] 275.1 50-714
1. Missions—China. 2. Seventh-Day Adventists—Missions. I. Title.

OUTERBRIDGE, Leonard M 275.1
The lost churches of China. Philadelphia, Westminster Press [1952] 237 p. 21 cm. [BR1285.O87] 52-8859
1. China — Church history. I. Title.

PATTERSON, George Neilson, 1920- 275.1
Christianity in Communist China [by] George N. Patterson. Waco, Tex., Word Books [1969] xii, 174 p. 23 cm. Bibliographical references included in "Notes" (p. 160-166) [BR1288.P33] 69-12818 4.95
1. Christianity—China. I. Title.

ROY, Andrew T. 275.1
On Asia's rim. New York, Friendship [c.1962] 165p. 20cm. Bibl. 62-7848 2.95
1. Missions—East (Far East) 2. East (Far East)—Church history. I. Title.

T'IEN FENG. 275.1
Selected translations of religious articles on Communist China from T'ien-feng, nos. 6 and 7, 1958. New York, U.S. Joint Publications Research Service, 1959. a, 51 p. 27 cm. (JPRS: 1313-N) "CSO: 2267-N." [AS36.U57 no. 1313] 59-60697
1. China—Church history. I. Title. II. Series: U.S. Joint Publications Research Service. JPRS/NY report 1313

U.S. Joint Publications Research Service. 275.1
Religion in Communist China. NY-59/1 -- Apr. 19, 1958- New York. no. 28 cm. (Its JPRS/NY report) Reports are based on Chinese Communist publications issued 1956- [AS36.U57] 58-60898
1. China (People's Republic of China, 1949-) — Religion. I. Title. II. Series.

VARGE, Paul A 275.1
Missionaries, Chinese, and diplomats; the American Protestant missionary movement in China, 1890-1952. Princeton, N.J., Princeton University Press, 1958. 335 p. 23 cm. [BV3415.V35] 58-7134
1. Missions — China. 2. China — Relations (general) with the U.S. 3. U.S. — Relations (general) with China. I. Title.

WANG, Mary. 275.1
The Chinese church that will not die [by] Mary Wang, with Gwen and Edward England. Wheaton, Ill., Tyndale House Publishers [1972] 201 p. illus. 18 cm. [BR1297.W28A3 1972] 79-188533 ISBN 0-8423-0235-2 1.25
1. Wang, Mary. 2. Christianity—China. 3. Persecution—China. I. England, Gwen, joint author. II. England, Edward O., joint author. III. Title.

SWANSON, Allen J. 275.1'249
Taiwan: mainline versus independent church growth; a study in contrasts [by] Allen J. Swanson. South Pasadena, Calif., William Carey Library [1973?] 300 p. 21 cm. Adaptation of the author's thesis (M.A.), Fuller Theological Seminary, 1968. Bibliography: p. 288-297. [BR1298.S93] 74-126424 ISBN 0-87808-404-5
1. Christianity—Taiwan. 2. Church growth. I. Title.

BULL, Geoffrey T., 1921- 275.15
When iron gates yield [London, Hodder & Stoughton; dist. Chicago, Moody, 1965] 254p. 18cm. Account of the author's missionary work in Tibet and his imprisonment by the Chinese Communists. [BV3427.B79A3] .89 pap.,
1. Missions—Tibet. I. Title.

AN, Yong-jun. 275.19 B
The triumph of Pastor Son; from Korea ... a true story of faith under persecution [by] Yong Choon Ahn with Phyllis Thompson. Downers Grove, Ill., InterVarsity Press [1974, c1973] 96 p. 18 cm. [BX9225.S62A83 1974] 73-93140 ISBN 0-87784-555-7 1.50 (pbk.)
1. Son, Yang-won. I. Thompson, Phyllis, joint author. II. Title.

MOFFETT, Samuel Hugh. 275.19
The Christians of Korea. New York, Friendship Press [1962] 174p. illus. 19cm. [BR1320.M6] 62-17527
1. Christians in Korea. I. Title.

MOFFETT, Samuel Hugh 275.19
The Christians of Korea. New York, Friendship [c.1962] 174p. illus. 19cm. Bibl. 62-17527 2.95; 1.95 pap.,
1. Christians in Korea. I. Title.

SHEARER, Roy E 275.19
Wildfire: church growth in Korea, by Roy E. Shearer. Grand Rapids, W. B. Eerdmans Pub. Co. [1966] 242 p. illus., maps. 21 cm. (Church growth series) Bibliography: p. 229-236. [BR1320.S45] 65-18085
1. Protestant churches—Korea. 2. Missions—Korea. I. Title.

SHEARER, Roy E. 275.19
Wildfire: church growth in Korea. Grand Rapids, Mich., Eerdmans [c.1966] 242p. illus., maps. 21cm. (Church growth ser.) Bibl. [BR1320.S45] 65-18085 2.95 pap.,
1. Protestant churches—Korea. 2. Missions—Korea. I. Title.

VOELKEL, Harold, 1898- 275.19
Open door to Korea. Grand Rapids, Zondervan Pub. House [1958] 62 p. 21 cm. [BV3460.V6] 58-49283
1. Missions — Korea. I. Title.

AIKAWA, Takaaki, 1905- 275.2
The mind of Japan; a Christian perspective [by] Takaaki Aikawa, Lynn Leavenworth. Valley Forge [Pa.] Judson [1967] 159p. 23cm. Bibl. [BR1305.A4] 67-17169 4.95 bds.,
1. Christianity—Japan. 2. National characteristics, Japanese. 3. Japan—Civilization. I. Leavenworth, Lynn, joint author. II. Title.

*BECKER, Vivian Bergsrud 275.2
Christians near and far by Vivian Bergsrud Becker, Margaret J. Irvin. Designer: John Gretzer. Illus.: Tom Hall. Philadelphia, Lutheran Church Pr. [c.1966] 47p. illus. (pt. col.) 22cm. (LCA vacation church school ser.) .50;.90 pap., teacher's ed.,
I. Title.

BELLAH, Robert Neelly, 1927- 275.2
Tokugawa religion; the values of pre-industrial Japan. Glencoe, Ill., Free Press [1957] 249 p. 22 cm. [BL2210.B4] 57-6748
1. Japan—Religion. 2. Japan—Social conditions. 3. Religion and sociology. I. Title.

BOXER, Charles Ralph, 1904- 275.2
The Christian century in Japan, 1549-1650. Berkeley, University of California Press, 1951. xv. 535 p. illus., ports., maps (1 fold inserted) 24 cm. Bibliography: p. [501]-516. [BR1305.B6] 51-11017
1. Japan—Church history. 2. Japan—Hist.—To 1867. 3. Catholic Church in Japan. I. Title.

*BOXER, Charles Ralph 1904 275.2
The Christian century in Japan, 1549-1650, by C. R. Boxer. Berkeley, University of California Press [1974] xv, 535 p. illus., map. 25 cm. (California library reprint series, no. 51) Bibliography: p. 503-517. [BR1305.B6 1974] ISBN 0-520-02702-7 16.75
1. Japan—Church history. 2. Japan—Hist.—To 1867. 3. Catholic Church in Japan. I. Title.
L.C. card no. for original ed.: 51-11017.

ELISON, George. 275.2
Deus destroyed; the image of Christianity in early modern Japan. Cambridge, Harvard University Press, 1973. xiv, 542 p. illus. 24 cm. (Harvard East Asian series 72) Translations (p. [255]-389) Fabian, F. Deus destroyed (Ha Daiusu).—Ferreira, C. sive Sawano, C. Deceit disclosed (Kengiroku).—Kirishitan monogatari, anonymous chapbook.—Suzuki, S. Christians countered (Ha Kirishitan) Bibliography: p. 495-514. [BR1306.E4] 72-97833 ISBN 0-674-19961-8 18.00
1. Christianity—Japan. 2. Christianity—Controversial literature. 3. Japan—Politics and government. I. Fabian, Fucan, fl. 1583-1607. Ha Daiusu. English. 1973. II. Ferreira, Christovao, 1580-ca. 1652. Kengiroku. English. 1973. III. Suzuki, Shosan, 1579-1655. Ha Kirishitan. English. 1973. IV. Kirishitan monogatari. English. 1973. V. Title. VI. Series.

GERMANY, Charles Hugh, 1922- 275.2
The response of the church in changing Japan. Edited by Charles H. Germany. New York, Friendship Press [1967] 175 p. 19 cm. Bibliography: p. 172. [BR1305.G4] 67-11855
1. Japan—Church history. I. Title.

IGLEHART, Charles W 275.2
Cross and crisis in Japan. New York, Friendship Press [1957] 166p. illus. 20cm. Includes bibliography. [BR1305.I35] 57-6159
1. Japan—Church history. I. Title.

*LEE, Robert 275.2
Stranger in the land; a study of the church in Japan. Dist. in the U.S.A. [on behalf of the Commn. on World Mission & Evangelism of the World Council of Churches] by Friendship, New York [1967] xiv, 216p. (World studies of churches in mission) 2.95 pap.,
1. Missions—Japan. 2. Christianity and other religions—Japan. I. Title.

SPAE, Joseph John, 1913- 275.2
Christian corridors to Japan [by] Joseph J. Spae. Tokyo, Oriens Institute for Religious Research, 1965. 265 p. 27 cm. On label mounted on t. p.: Sole distributors in the U.S.A.: Paragon Book Gallery, New York. Pt. 1 first published in 1964 under title: Precatechetics for Japan. Bibliographical footnotes. [BV3445.2.S65] 65-29804
1. Missions — Japan. 2. Christianity and other religions — Japanese. I. Title.

SPAE, Joseph John, 1913- 275.2
Christian corridors tq Japan. Tokyo, Oriens Inst. for Religious Res. [Austin, Tex., Perkins Oriental] 1965. 265p. 27cm. Pt. I first pub. in 1964 under title: Precatechetics for Japan. Bibl. [BV3445.2.S65] 65-29804 6.00
1. Missions—Japan. 2. Christianity and other religions—Japanese. I. Title.

SUPREME Commander for the Allied Powers. Civil Information and Education Section. 275.2
Religions in Japan: Buddhism, Shinto, Christianity; from the report prepared by the Religions and Cultural Resources Division, Civil Information and Education Section, General Headquarters of the Supreme Commander for the Allied Powers, Tokyo, March, 1948, under the editorial direction of William K. Bunce. [1st ed.] Rutland, Vt., C. E. Tuttle Co. [1955] xi, 194 p. 22 cm. Bibliography: p. 187-189. [BL2201.S82] 55-14727
1. Japan—Religion. 2. Sects—Japan.

TAKENAKA, Masao, 1925- 275.2
Reconciliation and renewal in Japan. Rev. ed. New York, Friendship Press [1967] 126 p. 19 cm. Bibliographical references included in "Footnotes" (p. 125-126) [BR1305.T3 1967] 67-11859
1. Japan—Church history—1945- 2. Church and social problems—Japan. I. Title.

NELSON, Dorothy (Nelson) 275.249
Treasures of Taiwan, by Ruth Kipp Nelson. Washington, Review and Herald Pub. Association [1964] 191 p. illus., ports. 22 cm. Letters from Dorothy and Wilbur Nelson to Mrs. Ruth Kipp Nelson, who prepared them for publication. [BV3450.F7N4] 64-17661
1. Missions — Formosa. I. Nelson, Wilbur K. II. Nelson, Ruth Kipp, ed. III. Title.

[NELSON, Dorothy (Nelson)] 275.249
Treasures of Taiwan, by Ruth Kipp Nelson. Washington, D.C., Review & Herald [c.1964] 191p. illus., ports. 22cm. Letters from Dorothy and Wilbur Nelson to Mrs. Ruth Kipp Nelson, who prep. them for pubn. [BV3450.F7N4] 64-17661 3.95
1. Missions—Formosa. I. Nelson, Wilbur K. II. Nelson, Ruth Kipp, ed. III. Title.

EIDLITZ, Walther, 1892- 275.4
Unknown India; a pilgrimage into a forgotten world. London, New York, Rider [1952] 192 p. illus. 22 cm. [BL2003.E4] 52-3451
1. India—Religion. I. Title.

FUCHS, Stephen 275.4
Rebellious prophets; a study of messianic movements in Indian religions. New York, Asia Pub. [dist., Taplinger, 1966, c.1965] vix, 304p. 23cm. (Pubns. of the Indian branch of the Anthropos Inst., no. 1) Title. (Series: Anthropos Institute. Indian Branch. Publications, no. 1) Bibl. [BL2015.N3F8] 66-3997 10.75
1. Nativistic movements—India. 2. India—Religion. I. Title. II. Series.

HAGEN, Kristofer. 275.4
Bells still are calling; church and mission in India today. Illustrated by Bert Baumann. Minneapolis, Augsburg Pub. House [1964] 175 p. illus. 20 cm. Bibliographical footnotes. [BV3265.2.H3] 64-13441
1. Missions — India. I. Title.

HAGEN, Kristofer 275.4
Bells still are calling; church and mission in India today. Illus. by Bert Baumann. Minneapolis, Augsburg [c.1964] 175p. illus. 20cm. Bibl. 64-13441 3.00 pap.,
1. Missions—India. I. Title.

HOLLIS, Michael, Bp. 275.4
Paternalism and the church; a study of south Indian church history. London, New York, Oxford University Press, 1962. 114p. 20cm. Includes bibliography. [BR1155.H65] 62-1493
1. India—Church history. 2. Indigenous church administration. I. Title.

HOLLIS, Michael [Arthur Michael Hollis] Bp. 275.4
Paternalism and the church; a study of south Indian church history. New York, Oxford [c.] 1962[ ] 114p. Bibl. 62-1493 1.55
1. India—Church history. 2. Indigenous church administration. I. Title.

MUELLER, John Theodore, 1885- 275.4
Great missionaries to India. Grand Rapids, Zondervan Pub. House [1952] 186 p. 20 cm. [BV3269.A1M8] 52-33804
1. Missions — India. 2. Missionaries. I. Title.

NEILL, Stephen Charles, Bp. 275.4
The story of the Christian church in India and Pakistan, by Stephen Neill. Grand Rapids, Eerdmans [1970] 183 p. 20 cm. (Christian world mission books) (Discipling the nations.) Bibliography: p. 170-173. [BR1155.N4] 76-75106 3.95
1. India—Church history. 2. Pakistan—Church history. I. Title.

HOLLIS, Michael, Bp. 275.4'8
The significance of South India. Richmond, J. Knox Press [1966] 82 p. 22 cm. (Ecumenical studies in history no. 5) Bibliography: p. 11-13. [BX5671.I54H6 1966a] 66-24093
1. Church of South India. I. Title. II. Series.

WILDER, Harriet 275.482
A century in the Madura mission, South India, 1834-1934. New York, Vantage [1962, c.1961] 352p. illus. map. 61-8184 4.50
1. Missions—Madura, India (City) I. Title.

WATERFIELD, Robin Everard. 275.5
Christians in Persia: Assyrians, Armenians, Roman Catholics and Protestants, by Robin E. Waterfield. New York, Barnes & Noble [1973] 192 p. illus. 23 cm. Bibliography: p. 182-188. [BR1115.I7W37 1973b] 73-171090 ISBN 0-06-497488-X 11.75
1. Iran—Church history. 2. Missions—Iran. 3. Christians in Iran. I. Title.

GEREN, Paul Francis, 1913- 275.6
New voices, old worlds. New York, Friendship Press [1958] 166 p. 21 cm. [BR1070.G4] 58-7028
1. Christians in the Near East. I. Title.

WARD, Harold B. 275.61
The seven golden candlesticks, by Harold B. Ward. New York, Carlton Press [1972] 123 p. 21 cm. (A Hearthstone book) [BR185.W37] 72-172300 3.75
1. The seven churches. I. Title.

ECKARDT, Arthur Roy, 1918- comp. 275.694
Christianity in Israel. Edited by A. Roy Eckardt. New York, American Academic Association for Peace in the Middle East [1972] c1971. 51 p. 23 cm. (Middle East area studies, ser. 6) Contents.Contents.—Introduction, by A. R. Eckardt.—The early centuries, by S. Colbi.—The holy land of Christianity, by J. Parkes.—The churches of Israel: some recent developments, by S. Colbi.—Catholic teaching in Israel, from SIDIC.—Some reflections on reactions to the crisis of 1967, by Christian members, Jerusalem Rainbow Group.—Current Jewish-Christian relations in Israel, by P. Schneider. Includes bibliographical references. [BR1110.E3] 72-179648
1. Christianity—Israel—Addresses, essays, lectures. I. Title. II. Series.

FOLEY, Rolla. 275.694
Song of the Arab; the religious ceremonies, shrines, and folk music of the Holy Land Christian Arab. New York, Macmillan, 1953. 170p. illus. 22cm. [BR1110.F6] 53-8481
1. Christians in Palestine. 2. Arabs in Palestine. I. Title.

KUHN, Isobel. 275.9
Stones of fire. Chicago, Moody Press [1960] 224p. 22cm. [BV3423.L5K8] 60-51966
1. Missions—Lisic (Tibeto- Burman tribe) I. Title.

LYALL, Leslie T. 275.9
Urgent harvest; partnership with the church in Asia. Chicago, Moody [1964] 191p. maps.

22cm. (China Inland Mission bk.) Bibl. 64-3982 1.75 pap.,
1. Missions—Asia, Southeastern. I. China Inland Mission. II. Title.

DOOLEY, Thomas A., M. D. 275.94
1927-1961
The edge of tomorrow. [New York] New American Library [1961, c.1958] 144p. illus. (Signet bk. D1993) .50 pap.,
1. Missions, Medical—Laos (Kingdom) 2. Laos (Kingdom)—Descr. & trav. I. Title.

DOWDY, Homer E. 275.97
The bamboo cross; Christian witness in the jungles of Viet Nam, by Homer E. Dowdy. [1st ed.] New York, Harper & Row [1964] 239 p. illus., map (on lining paper) ports. 22 cm. (Harper jungle missionary classics) [BV3325.A6D6] 64-14376
1. Missions—Vietnam. I. Title.

SMITH, Laura Irene (Ivory) 275.97
Victory in Viet Nam, by Mrs. Gordon H.Smith. Grand Rapids, Zondervan Pub. House [1965] 246 p. illus., map, ports. 25 cm. [BV3325.A7S5] 64-8838
1. Missions — Vietnam. I. Title.

SMITH, Laura Irene (Ivory) 275.97
Victory in Viet Nam, by Mrs. Gordon H. Smith. Grand Rapids, Mich., Zondervan [c.1965] 264p. illus., map, ports. 25cm. [BV3325.A7S5] 64-8838 3.95 bds.,
1. Missions—Vietnam. I. Title.

SMITH, Ebbie C. 275.98
God's miracles; Indonesian church growth [by] Ebbie C. Smith. South Pasadena, Calif., William Carey Library [1970] xv, 217 p. illus. 22 cm. Bibliography: p. 201-214. [BR1220.S63] 78-132010 ISBN 0-87808-302-2 3.45
1. Christianity—Indonesia. 2. Church growth. 3. Baptists—Indonesia. I. Title.

WILLIS, Avery T. 275.98'2
Indonesian revival : why two million came / Avery T. Willis, Jr. South Pasadena, Calif. : William Carey Library, 1977. p. cm. Bibliography: p. [BR1235.W54] 77-12811 ISBN 0-87808-428-2 pbk. : 6.95
1. Church growth—Java. 2. Sociology, Christian—Java. I. Title.

TUGGY, Arthur Leonard. 275'.99
The Philippine church: growth in a changing society. Grand Rapids, Eerdmans [1971] 191 p. map. 21 cm. (Church growth series) Bibliography: p. 175-184. [BV3380.T8] 75-150644 3.45
1. Missions—Philippine Islands. I. Title.

276 Christian Church In Africa

BEETHAM, Thomas Allan 276
Christianity and the new Africa [by] T. A. Beetham. New York, Praeger [1967] x, 206p. maps. 22cm. (Praeger lib. of African affairs) Bibl. [BR1360.B4] 67-14705 5.00
1. Christianity—Africa. 2. Africa—Church history. I. Title.

BEETHAM, Thomas Allan. 276
Christianity and the new Africa [by] T. A. Beetham. New York, Praeger [1967] x, 206 p. maps. 22 cm. (Praeger library of African affairs) Bibliography: p. 183-186. [BR1360.B4] 67-14705
1. Christianity — Africa. 2. Africa — Church history. I. Title.

CLEMES, Gene (Phillips) 276
Drum call of hope. Text and photos. by Gene Phillips Clemes. New York, Published for American Leprosy Missions by Friendship Press [1960, c1959] 96p. illus. 21cm. [BV2637.C55] 59-15036
1. Missions—Lepers. I. Title.

COLLINS, Robert O 276
Americans in Africa; a preliminary guide to American missionary archives and library manuscript collections on Africa, by Robert Collins and Peter Duignan. [Stanford, Calif.] Hoover Institution on War, Revolution, and Peace, Stanford University, 1963. vii, 96 p. 26 cm. (Hoover Institution bibliographical series, 12) [DT1.C57] 63-16262
1. Americans in Africa — Hist. — Sources. 2. Missions — Africa — Hist. — Sources. 3. Archives — U.S. — Inventories, calendars, etc. I. Duignan, Peter, joint author. II. Title. III. Series. IV. Series: Stanford University. Hoover Institution on War, Revolution, and Peace. Bibliographical series, 12

COLLINS, Robert O. 276
Americans in Africa; a preliminary guide to American missionary archives and library manuscript collections on Africa, by Robert Collins and Peter Duignan. [Stanford, Calif.] Hoover Inst. on War, Revolution, and Peace, Stanford [c.]1963. vii, 96p. 26cm. (Hoover Inst. Bibl. ser., 12) 63-16262 2.00 pap.,
1. Americans in Africa—Hist.—Sources. 2. Missions—Africa—Hist.—Sources. 3. Archives—U.S.—Inventories, calendars, etc. I. Duignan, Peter, joint author. II. Title. III. Series: Stanford University. Hoover Institution on War, Revolution, and Peace. Bibliographical series, 12

DODGE, Ralph Edward 276
The unpopular missionary. [Westwood, N. J.] Revell [1964, c.1946, 1952] 167p. 21cm. 64-12204 3.50 bds.,
1. Missions—Africa, Sub-Saharan. I. Title.

GROVES, Charles Pelham 276
The planting of Christianity in Africa [4v.] London, Lutterworth [dist. New York, Humanities [1965] 4v. (various p.) maps. 23cm. First pub. 1948--[58] reprinted 1964. Contents.v.1 to 1840.--v.2. 1840-1878.--v.3. 1878-1914.--v.4. 1914-1954. Bibl. [BR1360] 65-7593 7.00; 25.00 ea., set,
1. Africa—Church history. 2. Missions—Africa. I. Title.

HOLLAND, Frederick E., 1891- 276
Kulikuwa hatari: a way, a walk, and a warfare of faith; forty-three years in Africa as nimrod, nomad, and missionary. New York, Exposition [c.1963] 85p. illus. 21cm. 63-2455 3.50
1. Missions—Africa, East. I. Title.

HOLLAND, Frederick E 1891- 276
Kulikuwa hatari: a way, a walk, and a warfare of faith; forty-three years in Africa as nimrod, nomad, and missionary. [1st ed.] New York, Exposition Press [1963] 85 p. illus. 21 cm. [BV3532.H58A3] 63-2455
1. Missions — Africa, East. I. Title.

KAREFA-SMART, John. 276
The halting kingdom; Christianity and the African revolution. by John and Rena Karefa-Smart. New York, Friendship Press [1959] 86p. 19cm. Includes bibliography. [BR1360.K3] 59-6044
1. Africa—Church history. 2. Missions—Africa. 3. Africa—Civilization. I. Karefa-Smart, Rena, joint author. II. Title.

KING, Noel Quinton. 276
Christian and Muslim in Africa [by] Noel Q. King. [1st ed.] New York, Harper & Row [1971] xiv, 153 p. 22 cm. Includes bibliographical references. [BR1360.K55 1971] 71-148438 ISBN 0-06-064709-4 5.95
1. Christianity—Africa. 2. Islam—Africa. 3. Islam—Relations—Christianity. 4. Christianity and other religions—Islam. I. Title.

NORTHCOTT, William Cecil, 276
1902-
Christianity in Africa. Philadelphia, Westminster [c.1963] 125p. illus. 19cm. Bibl. 63-10421 2.95
1. Christianity—Africa. 2. Africa, West—Religion 3. Missionaries—Correspondence, reminiscence, etc. I. Title.

*WOLD, Joseph Conrad. 276
God's impatience in Liberia, by Joseph Conrad Wold. Grand Rapids, Mich. Eerdmans [1968] 227p. 20cm. (Church growth ser.) 67-19334 2.95 pap.,
I. Title.

GATEWOOD, Richard Duncan, 276.083
1910-
Some American Protestant constributions to the welfare of African countries in 1963 [by] R. D. Gatewood. New York, National Council of the Churches of Christ, 1964. x. 88 p. 28 cm. [BV3500.G3] 65-3783
1. Missions — Africa — Stat. 2. Protestant churches — Missions — Stat. I. Title.

HOLME, Leonard Ralph. 276.1
The extinction of the Christian churches in North Africa, by L. R. Holme. New York, B. Franklin [1969] vi, 263 p. fold. map. 23 cm. (Burt Franklin research & source works series, 372. Medieval & Byzantine series, 26) Reprint of the 1898 ed. Bibliography: p. [257]-259. [BR1390.H6 1969] 71-80265
1. Church history—Africa, North. I. Title.

HARDY, Edward Rochie, 1908- 276.2
Christian Egypt: church and people; Christianity and nationalism in the patriarchate of Alexandria. New York, Oxford University Press, 1952. viii, 241 p. map. 22 cm. Bibliography: p. 205-213. [BR1380.H3] 52-6166
1. Egypt—Church history. 2. Alexandria, Egypt (Patriarchate) 3. Nationalism and religion—Egypt. I. Title.

FORSBERG, Malcolm. 276.24
Land beyond the Nile. Chicago, Moody [1967, c. 1958] 232p. illus. 17cm. (Moody giants, 53) [BV3625.S8F64] .89 pap.,
1. Missions—Sudan. I. Title.

HAITZ, Linn. 276.6
Juju gods of West Africa. [Drawings by Angela Zabransky] Saint Louis, Concordia Pub. House [1961] 113p. illus. 20cm. [BV3542.H3A3] 60-53152
1. Missions—Africa, West. 2. Missionaries—Correspondence, reminiscences, etc. 3. Africa, West— Religion. I. Title.

HUNTER, James Hogg, 1890- 276.6
A flame of fire; the life and work of R. V. Bingham. Foreword by Donald M. Fleming, introd. by Albert D. Helser. Sudan Interior Mission [dist. Chicago, Moody Pr., c.]1961 320p. illus. maps. 61-66182 3.50
1. Bingham, Rowland Victor, 1872-1942. 2. Sudan Interior Mission. I. Title.

WALL, Martha. 276.61
Splinters from an African log. Chicago, Moody Press [1960] 319 p. illus. 22 cm. Autobiographical. [BV3542.W3A3] 60-16878
1. Missions — Africa, West. 2. Sudan Interior Mission. I. Title.

WALL, Martha. 276.61
Splinters from an African log. Drawings by Al Fabrizio, from photographs. Chicago, Moody [1968,c.1960] 319p. illus. 18cm. (Moody Diamonds, 20) Autobiographical. [BV3542.W3A3] 60-16878 1.29 pap.,
1. Sudan Interior Mission. 2. Missions—Africa, West. I. Title.

OLIVER, Roland Anthony. 276.676
The missionary factor in East Africa [2d ed.] London, New York, Longmans, Green [1967] xv. 302p. maps on lining paps. 19cm. Bibl. [BV3530.O4] 3.50 pap.,
1. Missions—Africa, East. 2. Africa, East—Hist. I. Title.
Distributed by Humanities, New York.

GRIMLEY, John B 276.69
Church growth in central and southern Nigeria, by John B. Grimley [and] Gordon E. Robinson. Grand Rapids, Eerdmans [1966] 386 p. illus., maps. 21 cm. (Church growth series) Includes bibliographies. [BV3625.N5G76] 65-18084
1. Missions — Nigeria. 2. Nigeria — Religion. I. Robinson, Gordon E., joint author. II. Title.

GRIMLEY, John B. 276.69
Church growth in central and southern Nigeria, by John B. Grimley, Gordon E. Robinson. Grand Rapids, Mich., Eerdmans [c.1966] 386p. illus., maps. 21cm. (Church growth ser.) Bibl. [BV3625.N5G76] 65-18084 3.25 pap.,
1. Missions—Nigeria. 2. Nigeria—Religion. I. Robinson, Gordon E., joint author. II. Title.

WEBSTER, James Bertin 276.69
The African churches among the Yoruba 1888-1922. [New York] Oxford [c.]1964. xvii, 217p. illus., map, ports. 23cm. (Oxford studies in African affairs) Bibl. [BV3625.Y6W4] 65-80 4.80
1. Missions—Yoruba. I. Title. II. Series.

WEBSTER, James Bertin. 276.69
The African churches among the Yoruba, 1888-1922 Oxford, Clarendon Press, 1964. xvii, 217 p. illus., map, ports. 23 cm. (Oxford studies in African affairs) Bibliography: p. [199]-210. [BV3625.Y6W4] 65-80
1. Missions — Yoruba. I. Title. II. Series.

MENDELSOHN, Jack, 1918- 276.7
God, Allah, and Ju Ju; religion in Africa today. Boston, Beacon [1965, c.1962] 245p. 21cm. (BP196) Bibl. [BR1430.M4] 1.95 pap.,
1. Africa, Sub-Saharan—Religion. I. Title.

MENDELSOHN, Jack, 1918- 276.7
God, Allah, and Ju Ju; religion in Africa today. New York, Nelson [1962] 245 p. 22 cm. Includes bibliography. [BR1430.M4] 62-10370
1. Africa, Sub-Saharan—Religion. I. Title.

OOSTHUIZEN, Gerhardus 276.7
Cornelis.
Post-Christianity in Africa; a theological and anthropological study, by G. C. Oosthuizen. Grand Rapids, W. B. Eerdmans Pub. Co. [1968] xiv, 273 p. illus. 23 cm. Includes bibliographies. [BR1360.O58 1968] 69-12489 7.95
1. Christianity—Africa. 2. Nativistic movements—Africa. I. Title.

SCHWEITZER, Albert 276.721
The primeval forest (Including On the edge of the primeval forest and More from the primeval forest) [Tr. from German by C. T. Campion] New York, Pyramid [1963, c.1931] 239p. map. diagr. 19cm. (R-8560) .50 pap.,
1. Missions—Gabon. 2. Missions, Medical. 3. Lambarene, Gabon. I. Campion, Charles Thomas, 1862 -tr. II. Title. III. Title: More from the primeval forest.

COLES, Samuel B., d.1957. 276.73
Preacher with a plow. Boston, Houghton Mifflin [1957] 241 p. illus. 21 cm. [BV3625.A6C57] 266.58 57-8223
1. Missions—Angola. I. Title.

ANDERSON, Alpha E. 276.75
(Almquist)
Pelendo, God's prophet in the Congo. Minneapolis, 1515 E. 66 St. Free Church Pubns., [c.1964] 175p. illus., ports., maps. 21cm. 64-2732 3.45; 1.95 pap.,
1. Pelendo, Isaac. 2. Missions—Congo (Leopoldville) I. Title.

ANDERSON, Alpha E. 276.75
(Almquist)
Pelendo, God's prophet in the Congo. Chicago, Moody [1967, c.1964] 160p. 18cm. [BV3625.C36P4] .59 pap.,
1. Pelendo, Isaac. 2. Missions—Congo (Leopoldville) I. Title.

DEANS, William Alexander 276.75
Muffled drumbeats in the Congo. Chicago, Moody [c.1961] 126p. 61-4456 2.25
1. Missions—Congo, Belgian. 2. Religious literature—Publication and distribution. I. Title.

GREEN, Ernest L. 276.75
Congo jungle preachers. Pictures by George S. Pearson. St. Louis, 3536 Russell Blvd. Berean Mission Pr., [1963, c.1962] 64p. 18cm. 62-52575 1.00 pap.,
1. Clergy—Congo (Leopoldville) 2. Missions—Congo (Leopoldville) 3. Native clergy. I. Title.

NELSON, Robert Gilbert 276.75
Congo crisis and Christian mission. St. Louis, Bethany [c.1961] 112p. illus. 61-12218 2.50 pap.,
1. Missions—Congo, Belgian. 2. Congo, Belgian—Pol. & govt. I. Title.

FAUPEL, John Francis, 276.761
1906-
African holocaust; the story of the Uganda martyrs. New York, Kenedy [c.1962] 242p. illus. 23cm. 62-18003 4.95
1. Martyrs—Uganda. I. Title.

LUDWIG, Charles, 1918- 276.762
Mama was a missionary. Anderson, Ind., Warner Press [1963] 192 p. illus., group ports. 21 cm. [BV3625.K42L8] 63-17431
1. Ludwig, Twyla I., 1890-1960. 2. Missions — Kenya Colony and Protectorate. I. Title.

LUDWIG, Charles Shelton, 276.762
1918-
Mama was a missionary. Anderson, Ind., Warner [c.1963] 192p. illus., group ports. 21cm. 63-17431 2.95
1. Ludwig, Twyla I., 1890-1960. 2. Missions—Kenya Colony and Protectorate. I. Title.

WELBOURN, Frederick 276.762
Burkewood.
A place to feel at home: a study of two independent churches in Western Kenya [by] F. B. Welbourn [and] B. A. Ogot. London, Nairobi [etc.] Oxford U.P., 1966. xv, 157 p. front. (map) 4 plates (incl. ports.) diagrs. 22 1/2 cm. 35/- (B66-18667) Bibliography: p. [149]-151. [BR1443.K4W4] 66-77111
1. Church of Christ in Africa. 2. African Israel Church Nineveh. 3. Kenya — Church history. I. Ogot, B. A., joint author. II. Title.

WHITE, Paul Hamilton Hume 276.78
The Jungle Doctor series. [American ed.] Grand Rapids, Eerdmans, 1955-[c.1959] 120p. illus. 20cm. 55-382 1.50 bds.,
1. Missions— Tanganyika Territory. 2. Missions, Medical. I. Title.
Contents omitted.

WHITE, Paul Hamilton Hume 276.78
The Jungle Doctor series [Amer. ed.] Grand Rapids, Mich., Eerdmans [1964, c.1963] 120p. illus. 20cm. Each vol. has also special t.p.; this vol.--Jungle Doctor sports a leopard [by] Paul White. Illus. by Graham Wade. 55-382 1.25 pap.,
1. Missions, Medical—Tanganyika. I. Title.

SAYRE, Leslie C. 276.8
Africans on safari; illustrated by William F. P. Burton, New York, Friendship Press [1952] 164 p. illus. 21 cm. [BV3555.S37 [266]] 52-8540
1. Missions — Africa, South. I. Title.

SUNDKLER, Bengt Gustaf 276.8
Malcolm, 1909-
Bantu prophets in South Africa. 2d ed. London, New York, Published for the International African Institute by the Oxford University Press, 1961. 381 p. illus. 23 cm. Includes bibliography. [SB1367.Z8S8] 61-65161
1. Zulus—Church history. 2. Sects—Africa, South. I. Title.

SUNDKLER, Bengt Gustaf 276.8
Malcolm, 1909-
Bantu prophets in South Africa. 2d ed. New York, Pub. for the Internatl. African Inst. by Oxford [c.]1961 381p. illus. Bibl. 61-65161 4.80
1. Zulus—Church history. 2. Sects—Africa, South. I. Title.

BARKER, Anthony, full 276.83
name: Eric Anthony Barker M.D.
The man next to me; an adventure in African medical practice. New York, Harper [1960, c.1959] 175p. illus. 22cm. 60-11768 3.50 half cloth,
1. Missions, Medical—Zululand. I. Title.

PAUW, Berthold Adolf 276.87
Religion in a Tswana chiefdom. New York, Published for the International African Institute by Oxford University Press, 1960[ ] 258 p. illus., maps. tables (1 fold. col. in pocket) tables. 'A condensation of . . . [the author's] thesis accepted by the University of Cape Town for the Ph.D. degree in 1955. Bibl.: p.[249]-252. 60-3296 6.10
1. Twana (Bantu tribe)—Church history. 2. Sects—Cape of Good Hope. I. Title.

277 Christian Church In North America

HANDY, Robert T. 277
A history of the churches in the United States and Canada / Robert T. Handy. New York : Oxford University Press, 1977, c1976. ix, 471 p. : maps ; 24 cm. (Oxford history of the Christian Church) Includes index. Bibliography: p. 428-449. [BR510.H35 1977] 77-151281 ISBN 0-19-826910-2 : 19.95
1. North America—Church history. I. Title. II. Series.

HOFFMAN, James W ed. 277
Concerns of a continent. With contributions by the editor and [others] New York, Friendship Press, 1958. 166p. illus. 20cm. [BR510.H6] 58-7035
1. North America—Church history. I. Title.

WEIGEL, Gustav, 1906- 277
Churches in North America: an introduction. New York, Schocken [c.1961, 1965] 152p. 21cm. (SB95) [BR516.5.W4] 1.75 pap.,
1. Sects—U. S. 2. Protestant churches—U.S. I. Title.

WEIGEL, Gustave, 1906- 277
Churches in North America: an introduction. Baltimore, Helicon Press [1961] 152 p. 23 cm. [BR516.5.W4] 61-17627
1. Sects—U.S. 2. Protestant churches—U.S. I. Title.

PINK, Arthur Walkington, 277'.06
1886-1952
Gleanings from Paul; studies in the prayers of the Apostle, by Arthur W. Pink. Chicago, Moody [1967] 351p. 24cm. [B 235.P5] 67-14379 4.95
1. Bible. N. T. Epistles of Paul—Prayers. I. Title.

GRANT, John Webster. 277.1 s
The Church in the Canadian era: the first century of confederation. Toronto, New York, McGraw-Hill Ryerson [1972] xi, 241 p. 25 cm. (A History of the Christian church in Canada, v. 3) "Bibliographical note": p. 227-234. [BR570.H5 vol. 3] 277.1 70-37320 ISBN 0-07-092997-1
1. Canada—Church history. I. Title. II. Series.

MOIR, John S. 277.1
The Church in the British era, from the British conquest to confederation [by] John S. Moir. Toronto, New York, McGraw-Hill Ryerson [1972] xiii, 230 p. 25 cm. (A History of the Christian church in Canada, v. 2) Bibliography: p. 215-222. [BR570.H5 vol. 2] 73-37321 ISBN 0-07-092959-9
1. Canada—Church history. I. Title. II. Series.

ROUSTANG, Francois, ed. 277.1
An autobiography of martyrdom; spiritual writings of the Jesuits in New France. Texts selected & presented by Francois Roustang. Translated by Sister M. Renelle. [St. Louis] Herder [1964] x, 342 p. 24 cm. "The selection of texts and the introductory essays preceding the groups of writings of the individual men, as well as the General Introduction, are those of Father Francois Roustang, s. j. They are translated from his book Jesuites de la Nouvelle-France ... The selections that were written originally in Latin, however, are here translated directly from that language ... Passages that are included in The Jesuit relations and allied documents, edited by Rueben Gold Thwaites ... have also been completely retranslated into English." Bibliography: p. 341-342. [F1030.7.R873] 63-23156
1. Jesuits in Canada. 2. Indians of North America — Canada. 3. Canada — Hist. — To 1763 (New France) I. Roustang, Francois, ed. Jesuites de la Nouvelle-France. II. Title.

ROUSTANG, Francois, ed. 277.1
An autobiography of martyrdom; spiritual writings of the Jesuits in New France. Texts selected, presented by Francois Roustand. Tr. [from Latin] by Sister M. Renelle [St. Louis] B. Herder [c.1964] x, 342p. 24cm. Bibl. 63-23156 5.75
1. Jesuits in Canada. 2. Indians of North America—Canada 3. Canada—Hist.—To 1763 (New France) I. Roustang, Francois, ed. Jesuites de la Nouvelle-France. II. Title.

WILSON, Douglas James, 277.1
1904-
The Church grows in Canada. Toronto, Committee on Missionary Education, Canadian Council of Churches; distributed in the United States of America by Firiendship Press, New York [c1966] x, 224 p. illus., fold. col. map. 20 cm. $1.75 Can. (C66-3659) Bibliographical references included in "Notes" (p. 211-222) [BR570.W5] 67-72574
1. Canada — Church history. I. Canadian Council of Churches. Committee on Missionary Education. II. Title.

ADAMS, Ada E. 277.1'07
A primary leader's guide on the contribution of the Church to the development of Canada, by Ada Admas. Toronto, Canadian Council of Churches, Dept. of Christian Education: distributed in the United States of America by Friendship Press, New York, 1966. 56 p. music. 21 cm. "Printed resources": p. 47-50. [BR570.A6] 67-102619
1. Canada — Church history — Study and teaching. I. Canadian Council of Churches. Dept. of Christian Education. II. Title.

KELLER, Weldon Phillip, 277.1134
1911-
Splendour from the sea; the saga of the Shantymen. Chicago, Moody [c.1963] 237p. illus., col. front., ports. 24cm. 64-1856 3.95
1. Missions—Vancouver Island. I. Title.

LEDYARD, Gleason H. 277.126
And to the Eskimos. Chicago, Moody Press [1958] 254 p. illus. 22 cm. [E99.E7L4] 58-4778
1. Eskimos—Keewatin. 2. Missions—Keewatin. I. Title.

HARDER, Leland, 1926- 277.127'4
Steinbach and its churches. Elkhart, Ind., Work of the Church Dept., Mennonite Biblical Seminary, 1970. vi, 109 p. illus., maps. 28 cm. [BR580.S7H3] 73-263850
1. Sociology, Christian—Manitoba—Steinbach. 2. Steinbach, Manitoba—Church history. I. Title.

STEWART, Gordon, 1945- 277.16
A people highly favoured of God; the Nova Scotia Yankees and the American Revolution [by] Gordon Stewart and George Rawlyk. [Hamden, Conn.] Archon Books [1972] xxii, 219 p. map. 24 cm. "A revised version of Gordon Stewart's doctoral dissertation, 'Religion and the Yankee mind of Nova Scotia during the American Revolution' ... Queen's University." Includes bibliographical references. [BV3777.N6S73 1972] 78-38968 ISBN 0-208-01283-4 13.00
1. Alline, Henry, 1748-1784. 2. Revivals—Nova Scotia. 3. Nova Scotia—History. 4. United States—History—Revolution, 1775-1783—Foreign public opinion. 5. New Englanders in Nova Scotia. I. Rawlyk, George A., joint author. II. Title.

SCHNEIDER, Herbert Wallace, 277.2
1892-
Religion in 20th century America. Rev. ed. New York, Atheneum, 1964 [c.1963, 1952] 285p. 19cm. (52) Bibl. 1.75 pap.,
1. U. S.—Religion. 2. U. S.—Church history—20th cent. I. Title.

JAMAICA Christian 277.292
Council.
Christ for Jamaica; a symposium of religious activities. Edited by J. A. Crabb. Pref. by John Poxon. [1st ed.] Kingston, Pioneer Press [1951] 102 p. illus. 19 cm. [BR645.J3J3] 51-38120
1. Jamaica—Church history. I. Crabb, J. A. ed. II. Title.

MISSIONS Advanced 277.294
Research and Communication Center.
Haiti, status of Christianity. [Monrovia, Calif.] 1971. vi, 27 p. illus. 28 cm. On cover: MARC country data file. Bibliography: p. 27. [BR645.H2M57] 72-183110
1. Christianity—Haiti (Republic) I. Title.

ABELL, Aaron Ignatius, 277.3
1903-
The urban impact on American Protestantism, 1865-1900. Hamden [Conn.] Archon [dist. Shoe String] 1962[c.1943] 273p. 22cm. Bibl. A62 7.00
1. City churches. 2. Church and social problems—U.S. 3. Protestant churches—U.S. 4. Church work. 5. Theology, Doctrinal—Hist.—U.S. 6. Missions—U.S. I. Title.

BAILEY, Raymond, 1938- 277.3
Destiny and disappointment / Raymond Bailey. Wilmington, N.C. : Consortium Books, [1977] p. cm. (Faith of our fathers ; v. 7) [BR525.B34] 77-9549 ISBN 0-8434-0626-7 : 9.50
1. United States—Church history—20th century. I. Title. II. Series.

BAILEY, Wilfred M. 277.3
Christ's suburban body [by] Wilfred M. Bailey & William K. McElvaney. Nashville, Abingdon Press [1970] 208 p. 21 cm. Includes bibliographical references. [BV637.7.B3] 79-109672 4.95
1. Mission of the church. 2. Suburban churches. I. McElvaney, William K., 1928- joint author. II. Title.

BAIRD, Robert, 1798-1863. 277.3
Religion in the United States of America. New York, Arno Press, 1969. xix, 736 p. map. 23 cm. (Religion in America) Reprint of the 1844 ed. Includes bibliographical references. [BR515.B3 1969] 70-83411
1. United States—Church history. I. Title.

BERKHOFER, Robert F. 277.3
Salvation and the savage; an analysis of Protestant missions and American Indian response, 1787-1862. [Lexington] University of Kentucky Press [1965] xiv. 186 p. 23 cm. "Bibliographical essay": p. [161]-180. [E98.M6B37] 65-11826
1. Indians of North America — Missions. 2. Protestant churches — Missions — Hist. 3. Missions — U.S. — Hist. I. Title.

BERKHOFER, Robert F. 277.3
Salvation and the savage; an analysis of Protestant missions and American Indian response, 1787-1862 [Lexington] Univ. of Ky. Pr. [c.1965] xiv, 186p. 23cm. Bibl. [E98.M6B37] 65-11826 6.00
1. Indians of North America—Missions. 2. Protestant churches—Missions—Hist. 3. Missions—U.S.—Hist. I. Title.

BOYD, Malcolm, 1923- 277.3
The underground church. Edited by Malcolm Boyd. New York, Sheed and Ward [1968] x, 246 p. 21 cm. Bibliographical footnotes. [BV601.9.B6] 68-17361
1. Non-institutional churches. 2. Christianity—20th century. I. Title.

BRADEN, Charles Samuel, 277.3
1887- ed.
Varieties of American religion; the goal of religion as interpreted by representative exponents of seventeen distinctive types of religious thought. Edited by Charles Samuel Braden. Freeport, N.Y., Books for Libraries Press [1971, c1936] viii, 294 p. 23 cm. (Essay index reprint series) Contents.Contents.—Fundamentalism, by W. B. Riley.—Orthodox protestantism, by W. H. Foulkes.—Liberal protestantism, by E. F. Tittle.—Radical protestantism, by E. S. Ames.—Sacramentarianism, by G. C. Stewart.—Barthianism, by E. G. Homrighausen.—Roman Catholicism, by F. J. Sheen.—Mormonism, by J. A. Widtsoe.—Unity, by C. Fillmore.—Christian Science, by A. F. Gilmore.—Ethical culture, by H. J. Bridges.—Humanism, by J. H. Dietrich.—Spiritualism, by M. A. Barwise.—Theosophy, by A. P. Warrington.—Orthodox Judaism, by L. Jung.—National Judaism, by S. Goldman.—Reform Judaism, by F. A. Levy. Includes bibliographical references. [BR516.5.B7 1971] 76-156616 ISBN 0-8369-2307-3
1. Sects—U.S. 2. U.S.—Religion—1901-1945. I. Title.

BRAUER, Jerald C. 277.3
Protestantism in America; a narrative history, by Jerald C. Brauer. Rev. ed. Philadelphia, Westminister Press [1965] 320 p. 21 cm. "Sources": p. [305]-308. "Suggestions for further reading": p. [309]-314. [BR515.B7] 66-12686
1. Protestant churches — U.S. 2. U.S. — Church history. I. Title.

BRAUER, Jerald C. 277.3
Protestantism in America; a narrative history. Philadelphia, Westminster Press [1953] 307 p. 21 cm. [BR515.B7] 53-6778
1. Protestant churches—U.S. 2. U.S.—Church history. I. Title.

BRAUER, Jerald C. 277.3
Protestantism in America; a narrative history. Rev. ed. Philadelphia, Westminster [c.1965] 320p. 21cm. Bibl. [BR515.B7] 66-12686 3.95
1. Protestant churches—U.S. 2. U.S.—Church history I. Title.

BUMSTED, J. M. 277.3
What must I do to be saved? : The great awakening in colonial America / J. M. Bumsted, John E. Van de Wetering. Hinsdale, Ill. : Dryden Press, c1976. vi, 184 p. ; 21 cm. (Berkshire studies in history) Includes index. Bibliography: p. [166]-176. [BR520.B93] 74-25535 ISBN 0-03-086651-0 pbk. : 3.50
1. Great Awakening. I. Van de Wetering, John Edward, 1927- joint author. II. Title.

BUXBAUM, Melvin H. 277.3
Benjamin Franklin and the zealous Presbyterians [by] Melvin H. Buxbaum. University Park, Pennsylvania State University Press [1975] 265 p. ports. 24 cm. Includes bibliographical references. [E302.6.F8B94] 74-14932 ISBN 0-271-01176-9
1. Franklin, Benjamin, 1706-1790. 2. Presbyterians in the United States. I. Title.

CAIRNS, Earle Edwin, 1910- 277.3
Christianity in the United States. Chicago, Moody [c.1964] 192p. illus. 22cm. (Christian handbks.) Bibl. 64-20990 1.75 pap.,
1. U.S.—Church history. I. Title.

CHANEY, Elmer V 277.3
The unity of science, theology, and doubt; a plea for social progress. [1st ed.] New York, Exposition Press [1957] 126p. illus. 21cm. [BR516.C45] 56-12365
1. U. S.—Religion. I. Title.

CHANEY, Elmer V 277.3
The unity of science, theology, and doubt; a plea for social progress. [1st ed.] New York, Exposition Press [1957] 126p. illus. 21cm. [BR516.C45] 56-12365
1. U. S.— Religion. I. Title.

COX, Claire 277.3
The new-time religion. Englewood Cliffs, N.J., Prentice-Hall [c.1961] 248p. 61-9430 3.95 bds.,
1. U.S.—Religion. I. Title.

ELSON, Edward Lee Roy, 277.3
1906-
Americas spiritual recovery Introd. by J. Edgar Hoover [Westwood, N. J.] F. H. Revell Co. [1954] 189p. 21cm. [BR516.E45] 53-10969
1. U. S.—Religion. I. Title.

FOGDE, Myron Jean, 1934- 277.3
The church goes West / Myron Jean Fogde. Wilmington, N.C. : Consortium Books, c1977. 231 p. ; 23 cm. (Faith of our fathers ; v. 6) Bibliography: p. 226-231. [BR525.F63] 77-74856 ISBN 0-8434-0625-9 : 9.50
1. United States—Church history—19th century. I. Title. II. Series.

FOGDE, Myron Jean, 1934- 277.3
The church goes West / Myron Jean Fogde. Wilmington, N.C. : Consortium Books, c1977. 231 p. ; 23 cm. (Faith of our fathers ; v. 6) Bibliography: p. 226-231. [BR525.F63] 77-74856 ISBN 0-8434-0625-9 : 9.50
1. United States—Church history—19th century. I. Title. II. Series.

FRAZIER, Edward Franklin, 277.3
1894-1962
The Negro church in America. New York, Schocken [1966, c.1963] xii, 92p. 21cm. (SB135) Bibl. 1.45 pap.,
1. Negroes—Religion. I. Title.

FRAZIER, Edward Franklin, 277.3
1894-1962.
The Negro church in America. New York, Schocken Books [1964, c1963] xii, 92 p. 23 cm. (Studies in sociology) Bibliographical footnotes. [BR563.N4F7] 62-19390
1. Negro churches. I. Title.

GARRISON, Winfred Ernest, 277.3
1874-1969.
The march of faith; the story of religion in America since 1865. Westport, Conn., Greenwood Press [1971, c1933] viii, 332 p. 23 cm. Bibliography: p. 309-316. [BR525.G3 1971] 79-138112 ISBN 0-8371-5688-2
1. U.S.—Religion. 2. U.S.—Church history. 3. Protestant churches—U.S. I. Title.

GATES, John Alexander, 277.3
1898-
Christendom revisited; a Kierkegaardian view of the church today. Philadelphia, Westminster Press [1963] 176 p. 21 cm. "Selected bibliography": p. 175-176. [BX4827.K5G3] 63-10496
1. Kierkegaard, Soren Aabye, 1813-1855. 2. U.S.—Religion. I. Title.

GAUSTAD, Edwin Scott. 277.3
A religious history of America. [1st ed.] New York, Harper & Row [1966] xxiii, 421 p. illus. (part col.) maps, ports. 24 cm. Includes bibliographical references. 66-11488
1. U.S. — Church history. I. Title.

GAUSTAD, Edwin Scott 277.3
A religious history of America. New York, Harper [c.1966] xxiii, 421p. illus. (pt. col.) maps, ports. 24cm. Bibl. [BR515.G3] 66-11488 8.95
1. U. S.—Church history. I. Title.

GAUSTAD, Edwin Scott. 277.3
A religious history of America. New York, Harper and Row [1974, c.1966] xxiii, 421 p. illus., maps, ports. 21 cm. Includes bibliographical references. [BR513.G3] 66-11488 ISBN 0-06-063093-0 3.95 (pbk.)
1. U.S.—Church history. I. Title.

HALL, Thomas Cuming, 1858-1936. 277.3
The religious background of American culture. New York, Ungar [1959] 354p. 22cm. (American classics) Includes bibliography. [BR515.H28 1959] 58-59870
1. U. S.—Church history, 2. U. S.—Religion. 3. Dissenters—England. 4. Protestantism. I. Title.

HANLEY, Thomas O'Brien. 277.3
The American Revolution and religion; Maryland 1770-1800. Washington, Catholic University of America Press [1971] 260 p. 24 cm. Bibliography: p. 249-256. [BR555.M3H28] 72-4742 ISBN 0-8132-0524-7
1. Maryland—Church history. 2. United States—History—Revolution, 1775-1783—Religious aspects. I. Title.

HEDLEY, George Percy, 1899- 277.3
The superstitions of the irreligious. New York, Macmillan, 1951. 140 p. 21 cm. [BR525.H4] 51-13953
1. U.S.—Religion. I. Title.

HENRY, Carl Ferdinand Howard, 1913- 277.3
Evangelicals in search of identity / Carl F. H. Henry. Waco, Tex. : Word Books, c1976. 96 p. ; 20 cm. [BR1642.U5H46] 76-2856 ISBN 0-87680-461-X pbk. : 3.95
1. Evangelicalism—United States. I. Title.

HENRY, Stuart Clark, ed. 277.3
A miscellany of American Christianity; essays in honor of H. Shelton Smith. Durham, N. C., Duke University Press, 1963. viii, 390 p. port. 24 cm. Bibliographical footnotes. [BR515.H46] 63-14288
I. Title.
Contents omitted.

HENRY, Stuart Clark, ed. 277.3
A miscellany of American Christianity; essays in honor of H. Shelton Smith. Durham, N.C., Duke [c.]1963. viii, 390p. port. 24cm. Bibl. 63-14288 10.00
1. Smith, Hilrie Shelton, 1893- 2. U.S.—Religion—Addresses, essays, lectures. 3. Theology, Doctrinal—Hist.—U.S. I. Title.
Contents omitted.

HERBERG, Will. 277.3
Protestant, Catholic, Jew; an essay in American religious sociology. New ed., completely rev. Garden City, N.Y., Anchor Books, 1960. 309 p. 18 cm. (A Doubleday Anchor book, A195) Includes bibliography. [BR526.H4 1960] 60-5931
1. United States—Religion—1945- 2. United States—Civilization—1945- I. Title.

HERTZBERG, Arthur. 277.3
The outbursts that await us, three essays on religion and culture in the United States [by] Arthur Hertzberg, Martin E. Marty [and] Joseph N. Moody. New York, Macmillan [1963] 181 p. 21 cm. [BR526.H45] 63-15684
1. U.S.—Religion. I. Title.

HERZOG, Arthur. 277.3
The church trap. New York, Macmillan [1968] 185 p. 22 cm. [BR526.H47] 68-23064
1. United States—Religion—1946- I. Title.

HITT, Russell T ed. 277.3
Heroic colonial Christians [by] Courtney Anderson [and others] Edited with an introd. by Russell T. Hitt. [1st ed.] Philadelphia, Lippincott [1966] 255 p. 22 cm. Contents.CONTENTS. -- Jonathan Edwards, by C. Anderson. -- Gilbert Tennent, by R. T. Hitt. -- David Brainerd, by C. S. Kilby. -- John Witherspoon, by H. W. Coray. Includes bibliographical references. [BR569.H5] 66-19987
1. U.S. — Church history — Colonial period — Biog. I. Anderson, Courtney. II. Title.

HITT, Russell T., ed. 277.3
Heroic colonial Christians [by] Courtney Anderson [others] Ed. introd. by Russell T. Hitt. Philadelphia, Lippincott [c.1966] 255p. 22cm. Bibl. [BR569.H5] 66-19987 4.95 bds.,
1. U. S.—Church history—Colonial period—Biog. I. Anderson, Courtney. II. Title.
Contents omitted.

HUDSON, Winthrop Still, 1911- 277.3
American Protestantism. [Chicago] University of Chicago Press [1961] 198 p. 21 cm. (The Chicago history of American civilization) Includes bibliography. [BR515.H78] 61-15936
1. Protestant churches—United States. 2. United States—Church history. I. Title.

INSTITUTE for Religious and Social Studies. Jewish Theological Seminary of America. 277.3
Patterns of faith in America today. Ed. by Ernest Johnson. New York, Collier [1962, c.1957] 192p. 18cm. (AS203) Bibl. .95 pap.,
1. U.S.—Religion. I. Johnson, Frederick Ernest, 1884- ed. II. Title.

INSTITUTE for Religious and Social Studies, Jewish Theological Seminary of America. 277.3
Patterns of faith in America today, edited by F. Ernest Johnson. New York, Institute for Religious and Social Studies; distributed by Harper [1957] 192 p. 21 cm. (Religion and civilization series) "A symposium based on lectures given at the institute ... during the winter of 1954-1955." Contents.Contents.—Classical Protestantism, by R. M. Brown.—Liberal Protestantism, by E. E. Aubrey.—Roman Catholicism, by C. Donahue.—Judaism, by S. Greenberg.—Naturalistic humanism, by J. H. Randall, Jr. Includes bibliographies. [BR515.I5 1954] 57-11160
1. U.S.—Religion. I. Johnson, Frederick Ernest, 1884- ed. II. Title. III. Series.

JOHNSTON, Ruby Funchess. 277.3
The development of Negro religion. New York, Philosophical Library [1954] 202p. illus. 23cm. [BR563.N4J6] 54-7966
1. Negroes—Religion. I. Title.

JOHNSTON, Ruby Funchess. 277.3
The religion of Negro Protestants; changing religious attitudes and practices. New York, Philosophical Library [1956] xxvi, 224p. tables. 24cm. Bibliography:p. 214-217. [BR563.N4J62] 56-13828
1. Negroes—Religion. 2. Protestant churches-U.S. I. Title.

JONES, Kenneth, 1920- 277.3
Strange new faiths. Anderson, Ind., Gospel Trumpet Co. [1954] 127p. 20cm. [BR516.J76] 54-31765
1. Sects—U. S. I. Title.

JOYCE, Lester Douglas. 277.3
Church and clergy in the American Revolution; a study in group behavior. [1st ed.] New York, Exposition Press [1966] 224 p. 22 cm. Bibliography: p. [216]-224. [BR520.J6] 66-3990
1. U.S. — Church history. 2. Clergy — U.S. U.S. — Hist. — Revolution — Religious aspects. I. Title.

JOYCE, Lester Douglas 277.3
Church and clergy in the American Revolution; a study in group behavior. New York, Exposition [c.1966] 224p. 22cm. Bibl. [BR520.J6] 66-3990 6.00
1. U.S.—Church history. 2. Clergy—U.S. 3. U.S.—Hist.—Revolution—Religious aspects. I. Title.

LITTELL, Franklin Hamlin. 277.3
The church and the body politic [by] Franklin H. Littell. New York, Seabury Press [1969] vii, 175 p. 22 cm. Bibliographical references included in "Notes" (p. 165-170) [BR526.L5] 69-13888 5.95
1 United States Religion—1945- I. Title.

LITTELL, Franklin Hamlin. 277.3
From State church to pluralism: a Prostestant interpretation of religion in American history. New York, Macmillan [1971] xxvii, 225 p. 19 cm. Includes bibliographical references. [BR515.L55 1971] 73-127461
1. U.S.—Church history. 2. U.S.—Religion. 3. Sects—U.S. I. Title.

LOVEJOY, David Sherman, 1919- 277.3
Religious enthusiasm and the Great Awakening [by] David S. Lovejoy. Englewood Cliffs, N.J., Prentice-Hall [1969] ix, 115 p. 22 cm. (American historical sources series: research and interpretation) Includes bibliographical references. [BR520.L63] 70-86519 ISBN 1-377-32759- 4.25
1. Great Awakening. I. Title.

MCCALL, Emmanuel L., comp. 277*.3
The Black Christian experience. Emmanuel L. McCall, compiler. Nashville, Broadman Press [1972] 126 p. 21 cm. [BR563.N4M23] 72-79173 ISBN 0-8054-6514-6 3.95
1. Negroes—Religion—Addresses, essays, lectures. I. Title.

MARTY, Martin E 1928- 277.3
Infidel free thought and American religion Cleveland, Meridian Books [1961] 224p. 19cm. (Living age books, LA34) Includes bibliography. [BR515.M3] 61-15604
1. Religious thought—U. S. 2. Free thought—Hist. 3. U. S.—Church history. I. Title.

MARTY, Martin E., 1928- 277.3
The infidel; free thought and American religion [Magnolia, Mass., P. Smith, 1967, c.1961] 244p. 20cm. (Living age bk., LA34: Meridian bk. rebound) Bibl. [BR515.M3] 3.50
1. Religious thought—U. S. 2. Free thought—Hist. 3. U. S.—Church history. I. Title.

MARTY, Martin E., 1928- 277.3
The infidel; freethought and American religion. Cleveland, World Pub. Co. [c.1961] 224p. (Meridian Living Age bk., LA34) 61-15604 3.75; 1.45 pap.,
1. Religious thought—U. S. 2. Free thought—Hist. 3. U. S.—Church history. I. Title.

MARTY, Myron A. 277.3
Lutherans and Roman Catholicism; the changing conflict, 1917-1963 [by] Myron A. Marty. Notre Dame, University of Notre Dame Press [1968] xi, 245 p. 22 cm. Bibliography: p. 227-232. [BX4817.M35] 68-25117 6.95
1. Lutheran Church—Relations—Catholic Church. 2. Catholic Church—Relations—Lutheran Church. I. Title.

MAYS, Benjamin Elijah, 1895- 277.3
The Negro's church, by Benjamin Elijah Mays and Joseph William Nicholson. New York, Russell & Russell [1969] xiii, 321 p. maps. 20 cm. Reprint of the 1933 ed. Bibliographical footnotes. [BR563.N4M3 1969] 68-15142
1. Negro churches. I. Nicholson, Joseph William, joint author. II. Title.

MAYS, Benjamin Elijah, 1895- 277'.3
The Negro's church [by] Benjamin Elijah Mays & Joseph William Nicholson. New York, Arno Press, 1969. xiii, 321 p. map, plans. 22 cm. (Religion in America) Reprint of the 1933 ed. Includes bibliographical references. [BR563.N4M3 1969c] 70-83430
1. Negro churches. I. Nicholson, Joseph William, joint author. II. Title.

MEAD, Sidney Earl, 1904- 277.3
The lively experiment: the shaping of Christianity in America. [1st ed.] New York, Harper & Row [1963] 220 p. 22 cm. [BR515.M43] 63-10750
1. U.S.—Church history. I. Title.

MEAD, Sidney Earl, 1904-. 277.3
The lively experiment : the shaping of Christianity in America. / Sidney E. Mead. New York : Harper & Row, 1976 c1963. xiii, 220 p. ; 20 cm. Includes bibliographical references and index. [BR515.M43] pbk. : 4.95
1. U.S.—Church history. I. Title.
L.C. no. for 1963 edition: 63-10750.

MECKLIN, John Moffatt, 1871-1956. 277.3
The story of American dissent. Port Washington, N.Y., Kennikat Press [1970, c1962] 381 p. 23 cm. Includes bibliographical references. [BR516.M4 1970] 70-86570
1. Dissenters, Religious—U.S. 2. U.S.—Church history. 3. Religious liberty—U.S. 4. Sects—U.S. 5. Revivals—U.S. I. Title.

MILLER, Karl Palmer, 1889- 277.3
How in the world do Americans? A biographical inquiry. [1st ed.] New York, Pageant Press [1957] 240p. 21cm. [BR569.M5] 57-8232
1. U. S.—Biog. 2. U. S.—Religion. I. Title.

NEDERHOOD, Joel H. 277.3
The church's mission to the educated American. Grand Rapids, Mich., Eerdmans [1960] 163p. Includes bibliography. 60-51054 2.50
1. Missions—U.S. 2. Apologetics—20th cent. 3. Church work with students. I. Title.

NEWLIN, Claude Milton. 277.3
Philosophy and religion in colonial America. New York, Philosophical Library [1962] 212 p. 22 cm. [BR520.N4] 61-15245
1. Religious thought—New England. 2. Philosophy and religion. I. Title.

NOLL, Mark A., 1946- 277.3
Christians in the American Revolution / Mark A. Noll. Grand Rapids : Eerdmans, [1977] p. cm. Bibliography: p. [E209.N64] 77-23354 ISBN 0-8028-1706-8 pbk. : 4.95
1. United States—History—Revolution, 1775-1783—Religious aspects. 2. United States—Church history—Colonial period, ca. 1600-1775. I. Title.

NOYCE, Gaylord B. 277.3
The responsible suburban church, by Gaylord B. Noyce. Philadelphia, Westminster Press [1970] 176 p. illus. 21 cm. Includes bibliographical references. [BV637.7.N68] 71-110724 3.50
1. Suburban churches. I. Title.

OSBORN, Ronald E 277.3
The spirit of America Christianity. [1st ed.] New York, Harper [1958] 241p. 22cm. Includes bibliography. [BR516.O74] 57-9881
1. U. S.—Religion. 2. Religious thought—U. S. I. Title.

*OSBORN, Ronald E. 277.3
The spirit of American Christianity. Abbott Bks. [dist.] St. Louis, Bethany [1964, c.1958] 241p. 22cm. 2.00 pap.,
I. Title.

POWELL, Milton, comp. 277.3
The voluntary church: American religious life, 1740-1865, seen through the eyes of European visitors New York, Macmillan [1967] xix, 197 p. 22 cm. Bibliography: p. 193-197. [BR515.P6] 67-19678
1. United States—Religion—To 1800. 2. United States—Religion—19th century. I. Title.

ROBERTSON, Archibald Thomas. 277.3
That old-time religion. Boston, Houghton Mifflin, 1950. 282 p. 22 cm. [BR516.R6] 50-5680
1. U.S.—Religion. I. Title.

ROWLAND, Stanley J 277.3
Land in search of God. New York, Random House [1958] 242p. illus. 21cm. [BR517.R6] 58-9883
1. U. S.— Religion. I. Title.

ROY, Ralph Lord. 277.3
Apostles of discord, a study of organized bigotry and disruption on the fringes of Protestantism. Boston, Beacon Press [1953] 437p. 22cm. (Beacon studies in church and state) 'Originally ... [the author's] thesis.' [BR516.R68] 53-6616
1. U. S.—Religion. 2. Protestant churches—U. S. I. Title.

SALISBURY, William Seward. 277.3
Religion in America. New York, Oxford Book Co., 1951. iv, 60 p. illus. 19 cm. (Oxford social studies pamphlets, no. 7) Includes bibliographics. [BR515.S23] 51-4458
1. U.S. — Church history. 2. U.S. — Religion. I. Title.

SCHAFF, Philip, 1819-1893 277.3
America, a sketch of its political, social, and religious character. [Tr. from German] Ed. by Perry Miller. Cambridge, Belknap Press of Harvard University Press [c.]1961. 241p. (John Harvard Library) 61-8871 4.25
1. U. S.—Religion 2. U. S.—Church history. 3. U. S.—Civilization. I. Title.

SCHNEIDER, Herbert Wallace, 1892- 277.3
Religion in 20th century America. Cambridge, Harvard University Press, 1952. x, 244 p. illus. 22 cm. (The Library of Congress series in American civilization) Bibliographical references included in "Notes" (p. [200]-221) [BR525.S34] 52-8219
1. U.S. — Religion. 2. U.S. — Church history — 20th cent. I. Title. II. Series.

SMITH, Hilrie Shelton, 1893- 277.3
American Christianity; an historical interpretation with representative documents, by H. Shelton Smith, Robert T. Handy [and] Lefferts A. Loetscher. New York, Scribner [1960-63] 2 v. illus., ports. 24 cm. Contents.Contents. -- v. 1. 1607-1820. -- v. 2. 1820-1900. Includes bibliographical references. [BR514.S55] 60-8117
1. U.S. — Church history — Sources. 2. U.S. — Church history. I. Title.

SMITH, Hilrie Shelton, 1893- 277.3
American Christianity; an historical interpretation with representative documents, by H. Shelton Smith, Robert T. Handy [and] Lefferts A. Loetscher. New York, Scribner [1960-63] 2 v. illus., ports. 24 cm. Includes bibliographical references. [BR514.S55] 60-8117
1. U.S.—Church history—Sources. 2. U.S.—Church history. I. Title.

SMITH, James Ward, 1917- ed. 277.3
Religion in American life. Editors: James Ward Smith and A. Leland Jamison. Princeton, N.J., Princeton University Press, 1961- v. in illus., plans. 22 cm. (Princeton studies in American civilization, no. 5) Vol. 4 by Nelson R. Burr in collaboration with the editors. Contents.-- 1. The shaping of American religion. -- 2. Religious perspectives in American culture. -- 4. A critical

bibliography of religion in America. 2 v. [BR515.S6] 61-5383
1. U.S. — Religion. 2. U.S. — Civilization. I. Jamison, Albert Leland, 1911- joint ed. II. Burr, Nelson Rollin, 1904- III. Title. IV. Series.

SMITH, James Ward, 1917- ed. 277.3
Religion in American life. 4v. Ed.: James Ward Smith, A. Leland Jamison. Princeton, N.J., Princeton Univ. Press [c.]1961. 4v. (various p.) illus. (Princeton studies in American civilization, no. 5) Vol. 4 (2v) by Nelson R. Burr in collaboration with the editors. Contents.1. The shaping of American religion.--2. Religious perspectives in American culture.--4. A critical bibliography of religion in America. 2v. 61-5383 v.1, 8.50; v.2, 7.50; v.4, (2v) 17.50
1. U.S.—Religion. 2. U. S.—Civilization. I. Jamison, Albert Leland, 1911- joint ed. II. Burr, Nelson Rollin, 1904- III. Title. IV. Series.

SMOOT, Dan. 277.3
The hope of the world. [1st ed. Dallas, Miller Pub. Co., 1958] 57 p. illus. 23 cm. [BR517.S47] 59-19517
1. U.S. — Religion. I. Title.

SPERRY, Willard Learoyd, 1882- 277.3
Religion in America, by Willard L. Sperry. Appendices comp. by Ralph Lazzaro. Boston, Beacon [1963] 317p. 21cm. (BP162) Bibl. 2.25 pap.,
1. U. S.—Church history. 2. U. S.—Religion. I. Lazzaro, Ralph. II. Title.

STARK, Rodney. 277.3
Patterns of religious commitment [by Rodney Stark and Charles Y. Glock. Berkeley, University of California Press, 1968- v. illus. 24 cm. Each vol. has also special t.p. "A publication from the Research Program in Religion and Society of the Survey Research Center, University of California, Berkeley." Contents.Contents.—v. 1. American piety: the nature of religious commitment. Bibliographical footnotes. [BR517.S73] 68-12792
1. United States—Religion—1945- I. Glock, Charles Y., joint author. II. California. University. Survey Research Center. III. Title. IV. Title: American piety: the nature of religious commitment.

STEPHENSON, George Malcolm, 1883- 277.3
The Puritan heritage. New York, Macmillan, 1952. 282 p. 21 cm. Bibliography: p. 271-273. [BR515.S73] 52-1108
1. U.S. — Church history. 2. U.S. — Religion. I. Title.

STRONG, Josiah, 1847-1916 277.3
Our country. Ed. by Jurgen Herbst. Cambridge, Mass., Belknap Pr.of Harvard [c.] 1963 xxvi, 265p. illus., map, facsim. 22cm. (John Harvard lib.) Reproduction, with special t.p., of the 'revised edition of 1891, except for the forms of citation and quotations, which have been modernized.' Bible. 63-19148 4.95
1. Missions, Home. 2. U. S.—Moral conditions. 3. U. S.—Econ. condit. I. Title. II. Series.

STRONG, Josiah, 1847-1916. 277.3
Our country, Edited by Jurgen Herbst. Cambridge, Belknap Press of Harvard University Press, 1963. xxvi, 265 p. illus., map, facsim. 22 cm. (The John Harvard library). Reproduction, with special t. p., of the "revised edition of 1891 except for the forms of citation and quotations, which have been modernized." Bibliographical references included in footnotes. [BV2775.S8] 63-19148
1. Missions, Home. 2. U.S. — Moral conditions. 3. U.S. — Econ. condit. I. Title. II. Series.

SWEET, William Warren, 1881- 277.3
American culture and religion; six essays. Dallas, Southern Methodist University Press, 1951. 114 p. 21 cm. (The Southwestern University lectures for 1947) Contents.Contents. -- Cultural pluralism in the American tradition. -- Protestantism and democracy. -- Natural religion and religious liberty. -- Methodist unification. -- The church, the sect, and the cult in America. -- Ecumenicity begins at home. [BR516.S95] 51-2143
1. U.S. — Religion. 2. U.S. — Civilization. I. Title. II. Series: Georgetown, Tex. Southwestern University. Southwestern University lectures. 1947

SWEET, William Warren, 1881- 277.3
Religion in colonial America, by William Warren Sweet. New York, Cooper Square Publishers, 1965. xiii p., 1 1., 367 p. 24 cm. "Selected bibliography": p. 341-356. [BR520.S88] 42-19309
1. U.S.—Church history—Colonial period. I. Title.

SWEET, William Warren, 1881- 277.3
Religion in the development of American culture, 1765-1840. New York, Scribner, 1952. xiv, 338 p. 22 cm. Bibliography: p. 315-332. [BR520.S882] 52-9960
1. U.S. — Church history. 2. U.S. — Civilization. I. Title.

SWEET, William Warren, 1881- 277.3
Religion in the development of American culture, 1765-1840. Gloucester, Mass., P. Smith [1964, c.1962] xiv, 338p. 22cm. (Scribners bk. rebound) Bibl. 5.00
1. U.S.—Church history. 2. U.S.—Civilization. I. Title.

SWEET, William Warren, 1881-1959. 277.3
American culture and religion; six essays. New York, Cooper Square Publishers, 1972. 114 p. 23 cm. Reprint of the 1951 ed., which was issued as the Southwestern University lectures for 1947. Contents.Contents.—Cultural pluralism in the American tradition.—Protestantism and democracy.—Natural religion and religious liberty.—Methodist unification.—The church, the sect, and the cult in America.—Ecumenicity begins at home. Includes bibliographical references. [BR517.S95 1972] 72-78372 ISBN 0-8154-0421-2
1. United States—Religion. 2. United States—Civilization. I. Title. II. Series: Georgetown, Tex. Southwestern University. Southwestern University lectures, 1947.

SWEET, William Warren, 1881-1959. 277.3
The story of religion in America. [2d rev. ed.] New York, Harper [1950] ix, 492 p. 22 cm. First ed. (1930) has title: The story of religions in America. Bibliography: p. 453-472. [BR515.S82 1950] 50-10239
1. United States—Church history. 2. United States—Religion.

THOMAS, John Lawrence. 277.3
Religion and the American people. Westminster, Md., Newman Press, 1963. 307 p. illus. 23 cm. [BR526.T5] 63-12247
1. U.S.—Religion. I. Title.

TOWARD creative urban strategy, compiled by George A. Torney. 277.3 Waco, Tex., Word Books [1970] 249 p. 23 cm. "Results from the combined efforts of the Departments of Metropolitan Missions and editorial services of the Home Mission Board of the Southern Baptist Convention." Bibliography: p. 245-249. [BV637.T68] 72-128352 5.95
1. City churches—U.S.—Addresses, essays, lectures. I. Torney, George A., ed.

TYLER, Alice Felt, 1892- 277.3
Freedom's ferment; phases of American social history from the colonial period to the outbreak of the Civil War. New York, Harper & Row [1962, c.1944] 608p. illus. 21cm. (Harper Torchbk., Acad. Lib. TB/1074) Bibl. 2.75 pap.,
1. Sects—U.S. 2. U.S.—Hist.—1815-1861. 3. U.S.—Soc life & cust. I. Title.

TYLER, Alice (Felt) 1892- 277.3
Freedom's ferment; phases of American social history from the Colonial period to the outbreak of the Civil War. [Gloucester, Mass., P. Smith, 1963, c.1944] 608p. 21cm. (Harper torchbks., TB1074 Acad. lib. rebound) Bibl. 4.75
1. Sects—U.S. 2. U.S.—Hist.—1815-1861. 3. U.S.—Soc. life & cust. I. Title.

WALDROP, W. Earl. 277.3
What makes America great? St. Louis, Bethany Press [1957] 96p. 21cm. [BR516.W3] 57-8365
1. U.S.—Religion. I. Title.

WALDROP, W Earl. 277.3
What makes America great? St. Louis, Bethany Press [1957] 96 p. 21 cm. [BR516.W3] 57-8365
1. U.S. — Religion. I. Title.

WALLACE, Dewey D. 277.3
The Pilgrims / Dewey D. Wallace, Jr. Wilmington, N.C. : Consortium Books, c1977. iii, 240 p. ; 22 cm. (Faith of our fathers ; v. 3) [BR520.W26] 77-9507 ISBN 0-8434-0622-4 : 9.50
1. United States—Church history—Colonial period, ca. 1600-1775. I. Title. II. Series.

WALLINGTON, Nellie Urner, 1847-1933. 277'.3
Historic churches of America / by Nellie Urner Wallington ; introd. by Edward Everett Hale. Boston : Longwood Press, 1977. p. cm. Reprint of the 1907 ed. published by Duffield, New York. [BR565.W3 1977] 77-85628 ISBN 0-89341-227-9 lib.bdg. : 25.00
1. Churches—United States. I. Title.

WASHINGTON, Joseph R. 277.3
Black religion; the Negro and Christianity in the United States [by] Joseph R. Washington, Jr. Boston, Beacon Press [1964] ix, 308 p. 22 cm. Bibliographical references included in "Notes" (p. 298-303) [BR563.N4W3] 64-13529
1. Negroes—Religion. I. Title. II. Title: The Negro and Christianity in the United States.

WEISENBURGER, Francis Phelps, 1900- 277.3
Ordeal of faith; the crisis of church-going America, 1865-1900. New York, Philosophical Library [1959] 380 p. 22 cm. [BR525.W37] 59-16373
1. U.S. — Church history. 2. U.S. — Hist. — 1835-1898. 3. Church attendance. I. Title.

WEISENBURGER, Francis Phelps, 1900- 277.3
Triumph of faith; contributions of the church to American life, 1865-1900. [Richmond?] 1962. 221 p. 24 cm. Includes bibliography. [BR525.W38] 62-2042
1. U.S. — Religion. 2. U.S. — Civilization. I. Title.

WRIGHT, Conrad, comp. 277.3
Religion in American life; selected readings. Boston, Houghton Mifflin [1972] x, 182 p. illus. 21 cm. (Houghton Mifflin history program) (Life in America series) Includes bibliographical references. [BR515.W75] 72-180481 ISBN 0-395-03145-1 pap. 2.60
1. United States—Religion—Collections. I. Title. II. Series.

EARLE, Alice (Morse) 1851-1911. 277.4
The Sabbath in Puritan New England. Williamstown, Mass., Corner House Publishers, 1969. viii, 335 p. 22 cm. Reprint of the 1891 ed. [F7.E14 1969] 76-15961 8.50
1. Sunday. 2. New England—Social life and customs—Colonial period, ca. 1600-1775. I. Title.

EARLE, Alice (Morse) 1851-1911. 277.4
The Sabbath in Puritan New England. Detroit, Singing Tree Press, 1968. viii, 335 p. 21 cm. Title page includes original imprint: New York, Scribner, 1891. Reprint of the 1891 ed. [F7.E14 1968] 68-17961
1. Sunday. 2. New England—Social life and customs—Colonial period, ca. 1600-1775. I. Title.

GAUSTAD, Edwin Scott. 277.4
The Great Awakening in New England. Chicago, Quadrangle [1968,c.1957] 173p. 21cm. (QP46) Bibl. [BR520.G2 1965] 2.25 pap.,
1. Great Awakening. I. Title.

GAUSTAD, Edwin Scott. 277.4
The Great Awakening in New England. New York, Harper [1957] 173 p. illus. 22 cm. [BR520.G2] 57-9888
1. Great Awakening.

GAUSTAD, Edwin Scott 277.4
The Great Awakening in New England. Gloucester, Mass., P. Smith, 1965 [c.1957] 173p. illus., maps. 21cm. Bibl. [BR520.G2] 65-4750 3.75
1. Great Awakening. I. Title.

GOEN, C. C. 277.4
Revivalism and separatism in New England, 1740-1800; Strict Congregationalists and Separate Baptists in the Great Awakening. New Haven, Conn., Yale [c.]1962. x, 370p. maps. 24cm. (Yale pubns. in religion, 2) Bibl. 62-8246 7.50
1. Dissenters—New England. 2. New England—Church history. I. Title. II. Series.

GOEN, C. C. 277.4
Revivalism and separatism in New England, 1740-1800; Strict Congregationalists and Separate Baptists in the Great Awakening, by C. C. Goen. With a new preface by the author. [Hamden, Conn.] Archon Books, 1969 [c1962] xii, 370 p. 23 cm. Bibliography: p. 328-346. [BR520.G6 1969] 69-19225
1. Dissenters, Religious—New England. 2. New England—Church history. I. Title.

LATHROP, Elise L 277.4
Old New England churches. Illustrated by Welsh. Rutland, Vt C. E. Tuttle Co [c1963] 171 p. illus. 27 cm. Bibliography: p. 167-171. [NA5215.L3 1963] 63-22540
1. Churches — New England. 2. Church architecture — New England. I. Title.

LATHROP, Elise L. 277.4
Old New England churches. Illus. by Welsh. Rutland, Vt., Tuttle [c.1963] 171p. illus. 27cm. Bibl. 63-22540 5.00
1. Churches—New England. 2. Church architecture—New England. I. Title.

MATHER, Cotton, 1663-1728 277.4
Magnalia Christi Americana; or, The ecclesiastical history of New-England from its first planting in the year 1620 unto the year of Our Lord 1698, in seven books. With an introd. and occasional notes, by Thomas Robbins and translations of the Hebrew, Greek and Latin quotations, by Lucius F. Robinson. To which is added a memoir of Cotton Mather, by Samuel G. Drake. Also, a comprehensive index by another hand. New York, Russell & Russell [1967] 2 v. ports. 25cm. Reissue of the text of the 1853-55 ed., each bk. having special t.p. Contents.v.1 Book 1. Antiquities. Book 2. Ecclesiarum clypei. Book 3. Polybius.--v. 2. Book 4. Sal gentium. Book 5. Acts and monuments Book 6. Thaumaturgus. Book 7. Ecclesiarum praelia. [BR520.M4 1967] 66-24730 35.00 set,
1. Mather, Cotton, 1663-1728. 2. New England—Church history. 3. New England—Biog. 4. New England—Hist.—Colonial period. I. Title.

MATHER, Cotton, 1663-1728. 277.4
Magnalia Christi Americana : or, The ecclesiastical history of New-England from its first planting in the year 1620 unto the year of our Lord 1698 / Cotton Mather. New York : Arno Press, 1972. 7 v. in 1 : ill. ; 27 cm. (Research library of colonial Americana) Reprint of the 1702 ed. printed for T. Parkhurst, London. [BR530.M34 1972] 74-141092 ISBN 0-405-03297-8
1. New England—Church history. 2. New England—History—Colonial period, ca. 1600-1775. 3. New England—Biography. I. Title. II. Series.

NEWLIN, Claude Milton. 277.4
Philosophy and religion in colonial America [by] Claude M. Newlin. New York, Greenwood Press, 1968 [c1962] ix, 212 p. 22 cm. [BR520.N4 1968] 68-23317
1. Religious thought—New England. 2. Philosophy and religion. I. Title.

TRACY, Joseph, 1793?-1874. 277'.4
The Great Awakening. New York, Arno Press, 1969. xviii, 433 p. ports. 23 cm. (Religion in America) Reprint of the 1841 ed. [BR520.T7 1969] 72-83444
1. Great Awakening. 2. Revivals—United States. 3. United States—Church history—Colonial period, ca. 1600-1775.

WILLIAMS, Roger, 1604?-1683. 277.4
Complete writings. New York, Russell & Russell, 1963. 7 v. facsims. 27 cm. "The new matter ... will be found in volume seven ... in order to retain the original pagination of the first six volumes ... [of] the Narragansett edition." "Limited edition of four hundred sets." [BX6495.W55A2] 63-11034
I. Title.

WILLIAMS, Roger, 1604?-1683. 277.4
Complete writings; 7v. New York, Russell [c.] 1963. 7v. (various p.) facsims. 27cm. 63-11034 100.00 lim. ed., set,
I. Title.

WINSLOW, Ola Elizabeth. 277.4
Meetinghouse Hill, 1630-1783. New York, Macmillan, 1952. 344 p. illus. 22 cm. [BR530.W5] 52-11102
1. New England—Church history. I. Title.

WINSLOW, Ola Elizabeth. 277.4
Meetinghouse Hill, 1630-1783. With a new pref. New York, Norton [1972] x, 344 p. illus. 20 cm. (The Norton library, N632) Reprint of the 1952 ed., with a new pref. [BR530.W5 1972] 79-39172 ISBN 0-393-00632-8 2.95
1. New England—Church history. I. Title.

BUDD, Nancy J. 277.4'14
History of Lake Shore Chapel, Douglas, Michigan / by Nancy J. Budd. Ann Arbor, Mich. : Malloy Lithographers, 1974. 182 p. : ill. ; 28 cm. Cover title: Lake Shore Chapel : "The little church in the wooods," 1904-1974. Includes indexes. [BX9999.D68L342] 74-186461
1. Lake Shore Chapel, Douglas, Mich. I. Title.

SKINNER, Ralph Burgess. 277.418
Historically speaking on Lewiston-Auburn, Maine, churches; an historical study of the origin and development of religious organizations in a two-city community from its date of settlement to and including the ecumenical year 1964, by Ralph Skinner. Lewiston, Me., printed by Twin City Printery [1965] v, [vi] 176 p. illus. 24 cm. [BR555.M2S5] 66-7099

1. Lewiston. Me. — Church history. 2. Auburn, Me. — Church history. I. Title.

ADAMS, Charles Francis, 1835-1915. 277.44
The Antinomian controversy : from his Three episodes in Massachusetts history / by Charles Francis Adams ; edited and with an introd. by Emery Battis. New York : DaCapo Press, 1976. lxvii, 216 p. ; 22 cm. Reprint of pt. 2. of the 1892 ed. published by Houghton Mifflin, Boston. Bibliography: p. [lxiii]-lxvii. [BR555.M4A3 1976] 74-164507 ISBN 0-306-70290-8 : 12.50
1. Hutchinson, Anne (Marbury) 1591-1643. 2. Massachusetts—Church history. 3. Antinomianism. I. Title.

MEYER, Jacob Conrad. 277.44
Church and state in Massachusetts from 1740 to 1833; a chapter in the history of the development of individual freedom, by Jacob C. Meyer. New York, Russell & Russell [1968] vii, 276 p. 22 cm. Reprint of the 1930 ed. Bibliography: p. 244-261. [BR555.M4M4 1968] 68-25043
1. Church and state in Massachusetts. 2. Massachusetts—Church history.

MILLER, Perry, 1905- 277.44
Orthodoxy in Massachusetts, 1630-1650. With a New pref. by the author. Boston, Beacon Press [1959] 319p. 21cm. (Beacon paperback no. 89) Includes bibliography. [BR520.M57 1959] 59-10735
1. Massachusetts—Church history. 2. Puritans. 3. Massachusetts— Hist.—Colonial period. 4. Congregational churches in Massachusetts—Hist. —Colonial period. 5. Congregational churches in Massachusetts. 6. Gt. Brit.—Church history—17th cent. I. Title.

MILLER, Perry, 1905-1963. 277.44
Orthodoxy in Massachusetts, 1630-1650. Introd. to the Torchbook ed. by David D. Hall. New York, Harper & Row [1970, c1933] xxxiv, 316 p. 21 cm. (Harper torchbook, TB 1525) Bibliography: p. [314]-316. [BR520.M57 1970] 73-154595 2.75 (pbk.)
1. Massachusetts—Church history. 2. Puritans—Massachusetts. 3. Massachusetts—History—Colonial period, ca. 1600-1775. 4. Congregational churches in Massachusetts. 5. Great Britain—Church history—17th century. I. Title.

UNDERWOOD, Kenneth Wilson. 277.44
Protestant and Catholic: religious and social interaction in an industrial community. Boston, Beacon Press [1957] xxi, 484 p. digrrs., tables. 22 cm. Bibliography: p. 409-417. [BR560.H7U5] 57-6529
1. Holyoke, Mass. — Church history. 2. Protestant churches — Relations — Catholic Church. 3. Catholic Church — Relations — Protestant churches. I. Title.

UNDERWOOD, Kenneth Wilson 277.44
Protestant and Catholic; religious and social interaction in an industrial community. Boston, Beacon Press [1961, c.1957] xxi, 484p. (Beacon paperback 11) Bibl. 2.45 pap.,
1. Holyoke. Mass.—Church history. 2. Protestant churches—Relations—Catholic Church. 3. Catholic Church—Relations—Protestant churches. I. Title.

SLAFTER, Edmund Farwell, 1816-1906, ed. 277.44*092*4
John Checkley; or, The evolution of religious tolerance in Massachusetts Bay ... With historical illus. and a memoir by Edmund F. Slafter. New York, B. Franklin [1967] 2 v. illus. 23 cm. (Burt Franklin research and source works series, 131. American classics in history and social science, 2) On spine: Religious tolerance in Mass. Bay, 1719-1774. Reprint of the 1897 ed., issued as v. 22-23 of the publications of the Prince Society. [BX5995.C52S55 1967] 72-184808
1. Checkley, John, 1680-1754. 2. Checkley family. 3. Episcopacy—Bibliography. I. Title. II. Title: Religious tolerance in Mass. Bay, 1719-1774. III. Series: Prince Society, Boston. Publications, v. 22-23.

LUCAS, Paul R. 277.44'2
Valley of discord : church and society along the Connecticut River, 1636-1725 / Paul R. Lucas. Hanover, N.H. : University Press of New England, 1976. xiv, 275 p. ; 25 cm. Includes index. Bibliography: p. 207-214. [BR520.L8] 75-22520 ISBN 0-87451-121-6 : 12.00
1. Sociology, Christian—Connecticut Valley. 2. Connecticut Valley—Church history. I. Title.

KELLER, Charles Roy, 1901- 277.46
The second great awakening in Connecticut. [Hamden, Conn.] Archon Books, 1968 [c1942] ix, 275 p. 22 cm. (Yale historical publications. Miscellany, 40) "Bibliographical note": p. [240]-258. [BR555.C8K4 1968] 68-26923
1. Connecticut—Church history. 2. Revivals—Connecticut. I. Title. II. Series.

NISSENBAUM, Stephen, comp. 277.46'8
The great awakening at Yale College. Stephen Nissenbaum, editor. Belmont, Calif., Wadsworth Pub. Co. [1972] xii, 263 p. 23 cm. (The American history research series) Bibliography: p. 261-263. [BR520.N73] 74-167899 ISBN 0-534-00101-7
1. Yale University—History—Sources. 2. Great Awakening—History—Sources. I. Title.

STOKES, Charles J. 277.46'9
Historic churches of Fairfield County, by Charles J. Stokes. Photography by Dave Nadig. [Westport, Conn.] County Books [1969] 95 p. illus. (part col.) 28 cm. Bibliography: p. 95. [F102.F2S84] 78-12827
1. Churches—Connecticut—Fairfield County. I. Title.

CROSS, Whitney R. 277.47
The Burned-over District; the social and intellectual history of enthusiastic religion in western New York, 1800-1850. New York, Harper [1965, c.1950] xiii, 383p. maps. 21cm. (Torchbk., TB1242 N. Acad. lib.) Bibl. [BR555.N7C7] 2.45 pap.,
1. New York (State)—Church history. 2. Enthusiasm. I. Title.

CROSS, Whitney R. 277.47
The burned-over district; the social and intellectual history of enthusiastic religion in western New York, 1800-1850 [Gloucester, Mass., P. Smith, 1966, c. 1950] xii, 383p. maps. 21cm. (Harper torchbk., Acad. lib., TB1242N rebound) Bibl. [BR555.N7C7] 4.50
1. New York (State)—Church history. 2. Enthusiasm. I. Title.

ZWIERLEIN, Frederick James, 1881-1960. 277.47
Religion in New Netherland, 1623-1664. New York, Da Capo Press, 1971. vii, 351 p. map. 23 cm. (Civil liberties in American history) Thesis—University of Louvain. Reprint of the 1910 ed. Bibliography: p. 331-351. [F122.1.Z98 1971] 72-120851 ISBN 0-306-71960-6
1. New York (State)—History—Colonial period, ca. 1600-1775. 2. New York (State)—Church history. I. Title. II. Series.

DES GRANGE, Jane, ed. 277.4721
Long Island's religious history; compiled by Jane des Grange, director, Suffolk Museum. Stony Brook, L.I., Suffolk Museum; distributed by I. J. Friedman, Port Washington, N.Y. c1963. 54 p. illus. 21 cm. 64-3500
1. Long Island — Church history. 2. Sects — New York — Long Island. I. Suffolk Museum. Stony Brook, N.Y. II. Title.

DES GRANGE, Jane, ed. 277.4721
Long Island's religious history; comp. by Jane des Grange, director, Suffolk Museum. Suffolk Mus; Friedman [1964] c.1963. dist. Port Washington, N.Y., Friedman 1964 [c.1963] 54p. illus. 21cm. 64-3500 3.25
1. Long Island—Church history. 2. Sects—New York—Long Island. I. Suffolk Museum, Stony Brook, N.Y. II. Title.

MCNAMARA, Robert Francis, 1910- 277.47*89
History of Sacred Heart Cathedral, Rochester, New York, 1911-1961; a historical sketch, by Robert F. McNamara. Rochester, The Cathedral, 1961. 78 p. illus. 23 cm. Cover title: History of Sacred Heart Parish. [BX4603.R58S24] 72-204321
1. Rochester, N.Y. Sacred Heart Cathedral. I. Title. II. Title: History of Sacred Heart Parish.

WILSON, David L., 1913- 277.48*11
Through two hundred years, 1765-1965: Saint Paul's Lutheran Church, Ardmore, Pennsylvania. Donald Goodyear Doll, pastor, David L. Wilson, church historian Philadelphia, Clark Print. House [1965] x, 93 p. illus. 24 cm. [BX8076.A7S368] 72-208245
1. Ardmore, Pa. Saint Paul's Lutheran Church. I. Title.

KAUFMAN, Jean Troxell. 277.48'81
Salem X Roads' churches in the nineteenth century / by Jean Troxell Kaufman. Greensburg, Pa. : Research Committee, Westmoreland County Historical Society, 1977. 7 leaves ; 29 cm. (Westmoreland Co. church & cemetery history ; no. 2) Bibliography: leaf 7. [BR560.N38K38] 77-152585
1. New Salem, Pa.—Church history. I. Title. II. Series.

KAUFMAN, Jean Troxell. 277.48'81
Westmoreland County's pioneer ministers, 1758-1800 / by Jean Troxell Kaufman. Greensburg, Pa. : Research Committee, Westmoreland County Historical Society, 1977. 14 leaves ; 29 cm. (Westmoreland Co. church & cemetery history ; no. 1) Bibliography: leaves 13-14. [BR555.P5W474] 77-152583
1. Westmoreland Co., Pa.—Church history. 2. Clergy—Pennsylvania—Westmoreland Co.—Biography. I. Title. II. Series.

STEELMAN, Robert Bevis. 277.4994
Cumberland's hallowed heritage; our country's religious history, including records of beautiful edifices builded by our forefathers, some bearing imprints of colonialism. Bridgeton, N.J. Cumberland Mutual Fire Insurance Co. [1965] 55 p. illus., maps, port. 23 cm. (Cumberland County Historical Society, 1965 series, no. 1) (Cumberland County (N.J.) Historical Society. Series, 1965, no. 1) Bibliography: p. 55. [F142.C9C8 1965, no. 1] 66-5876
1. Cumberland Co., N.J.—Church history. I. Title. II. Series.

CALDWELL, Erskine, 1903- 277.5
Deep South; memory and observation. New York, Weybright and Talley [1968] 257 p. 24 cm. "Part 1 of Deep South was first published in England under the title In the shadow of the steeple." [BR535.C29] 68-12867
1. Caldwell, Erskine, 1903- 2. Southern States—Religion. 3. Protestant churches—Southern States. I. Title. II. Title: In the shadow of the steeple.

FELTON, Ralph Almon, 1882- 277.5
These my brethren; a study of 570 Negro churches and 1542 Negro homes in the rural South. Madison, N. J., Dept. of the Rural Church, Drew Theological Seminary [1950] 102 p. 23 cm. Cover title. [BR563.N4F4] 50-2257
1. Negroes—Religion. 2. Negroes—Moral and social conditions. 3. Rural churches—Southern States. I. Title.

HILL, Samuel S. 277.5
Religion and the solid South [by] Samuel S. Hill, Jr. with Edgar T. Thompson [and others] Nashville, Abingdon Press [1972] 208 p. maps. 22 cm. (An Abingdon original paperback) Includes bibliographical references. [BR535.H49] 72-175282 ISBN 0-687-36003-X
1. Southern States—Religion—Addresses, essays, lectures. I. Title.

HOLLAND'S, the magazine of the South. 277.5
Historic churches of the South, a collection of articles published in Holland's, the magazine of the South. Selected and edited by Mary Lorraine Smith. Atlanta, Tupper & Love [1952] 125p. illus. 23cm. [BR535.H58] 52-14974
1. Churches—Southern States. I. Smith, Mary Lorraine, 1920- ed. II. Title.

MATHEWS, Donald G. 277.5
Religion in the old South / Donald G. Mathews. Chicago : University of Chicago Press, 1977. xx, 274 p. ; 21 cm. (Chicago history of American religion) Includes index. Bibliography: p. 265-268. [BR535.M37] 77-587 ISBN 0-226-51001-8 : 10.95
1. Christianity—United States—Southern States. 2. Evangelicalism—United States—Southern States. I. Title.

BROWN, Lillian Brooks. 277.53
Churches of the Presidents, a television series. Presented under the auspices of the Dept. of Radio and Television of the Washington Federation of Churches. [Washington? 1955] unpaged. illus. 22cm. [F203.2.A1B7] 55-4016
1. Washington, D. C.— Churches. 2. Presidents—U. S.—Religion. I. Churches of the Presidents (Television program) II. Title.

JONES, Olga Anna. 277.53
Churches of the Presidents in Washington; visits to sixteen national shrines. Foreword by Edward L. P. Elson. [2d enl. ed.] New York, Exposition Press [1961] 128p. illus. 21cm. [F203.2.A1J63 1961] 61-66359
1. Washington, D. C.—Churches. 2. Presidents—U. S.—Religion. I. Title.

JONES, Olga Anna 277.53
Churches of the Presidents in Washington; visits to sixteen national shrines. Foreword by Edward L. R. Elson. [2d enl. ed.] New York, Exposition [c.1954, 1961] 128p. illus. 61-66359 3.00
1. Washington, D.C.—Churches. 2. Presidents—U.S.—Religion. I. Title.

RICHMOND (Diocese). Synod, 4th, 1966. 277.55451
Fourth Synod of the Diocese of Richmond. Celebrated by John J. Russell, Bishop of Richmond, together with the clergy, religious, and laity of the Diocese in Sacred Heart Cathedral, Richmond, Virginia, December 5, 1966. [Richmond, Diocese of Richmond, 1967? c1966] x, 86 p. 23 cm. [BX1417.R5A47 1966] 70-259761
I. Richmond (Diocese). Bishop, 1958- (J. J. Russell) II. Richmond (Diocese)

HOLLOWAY, Jerry Lloyd. 277.5547
The churches of Fluvanna County, Virginia. Compiled and edited by Jerry L. Holloway. [1st ed. Richmond? 1966] vi, 161 p. illus., fold. map. 21 cm. [BR555.V8H6] 66-6606
1. Fluvanna Co., Va. — Church history. I. Title.

MARTIN, Thomas L 277.56
Churches of Davie County, North Carolina; a photographic study. [Charlotte? N. C., 1957] 68p. illus. 22x29cm. [BR555.N79D3] 57-47819
1. Churches—North Carolina— Davie Co. I. Title.

POSEY, Walter Brownlow, 1900- 277.6
Religious strife on the Southern frontier. [Baton Rouge] Louisiana State University Press, 1965. xviii, 112 p. 21 cm. (The Walter Lynwood Fleming lectures in Southern history) [BR535.P6] 65-16509
1. Southwest, Old—Religion. 2. Sects—Southwest, Old. I. Title. II. Series. III. Series: Louisiana. State University and Agricultural and Mechanical College. Walter Lynwood Fleming lectures in Southern history

POSEY, Walter Brownlow, 1900- 277.6
Religious strife on the Southern frontier. [Baton Rouge] La. State Univ. Pr. [c.]1965. xviii, 112p. 21cm. (Walter Lynwood Fleming lects. in Southern hist.) Title. (Series: Louisiana. State University and Agricultural and Mechanical College. Walter Lynwood Fleming lectures in Southern history) [BR535.P6] 65-16509 4.00
1. Southwest, Old—Religion. 2. Sects—Southwest, Old. I. Title. II. Series.

GRAYSTON, Kenneth. 277'6'077
The letters of Paul to the Philippians and to the Thessalonians; commentary by Kenneth Grayston. London, Cambridge, U. P., 1967. viii, 116 p. 2 maps. 21 cm. (Cambridge Bible commentary: New English Bible) 17/6 "A note on books": p. 113. [BS2705.3.G68] 67-18312
1. Bible. N. T. Philippians—Commentaries. 2. Bible. N. T. Thessalonians—Commentaries. I. Bible. N.T. Epistles of Paul. English. 1967 II. Title.

GRAYSTON, Kenneth. 277'.6'077
The letters of Paul to the Philippians and to the Thessalonians; commentary by Kenneth Grayston. London, Cambridge U.P., 1967 viii, 116 p. 2 maps. 21 cm. (Cambridge Bible commentary: New English Bible) "A note on books": p. 113. [BS2705.3.G68] 67-18312
1. Bible. N.T. Philippians—Commentaries. 2. Bible. N.T. Thessalonians—Commentaries. I. Bible. N.T. Epistles of Paul. English. 1967. II. Title.

BAINTON, Roland Herbert, 1894- 277.6'0922 B
Women of the Reformation, from Spain to Scandinavia / Roland H. Bainton. Minneapolis : Augsburg Pub. House, c1977. 240 p. : ill. ; 22 cm. Includes bibliographies and index. [BR317.B28] 76-27089 ISBN 0-8066-1568-0 : 9.95
1. Reformation—Biography. 2. Women—Biography. I. Title.

PARKER, Donald Dean, 1899- 277.61
Early churches and towns in South Dakota. [Brookings? S. D., 1964?] 132 p. map. 18 x 22 cm. Bibliography: p. 132. [BR555.S62P29] 66-64965
1. South Dakota—Church history. 2. Cities and towns—South Dakota. I. Title.

PARKER, Donald Dean, 1899- 277.61
Founding the church in South Dakota. [Brookings, S.D., pref. 1962] 116, [27] p. map. 18 x 22 cm. Bibliography: p. [133] [BR555.S62P3] 62-64111
1. South Dakota—Church history. I. Title.

ROUSE, Jordan K 277.61
Some interesting colonial churches in North Carolina. Kannapolis, N. C. [1961] 123p. illus. 28cm. Includes bibliography. [BR555.N78R6] 62-101
1. Churches—North Carolina. I. Title. II. Title: Colonial churches in North Carolina.

STUDENT Writers Club of Selma. 277.61
Some old churches of the black belt. Illustrated by Nancy E. Bell. Birmingham, Ala., Banner Press [c1962] 73 p. illus. 21 cm. (A Banner book) [BR555.A4S7] 62-22346
1. Churches — Alabama. I. Title.

STUDENT Writers Club of Selma. 277.61
Some old churches of the black belt. Illus. by Nancy E. Bell. Birmingham, Ala., Banner [1963, c.1962] 62-22346 3.00
1. Churches—Alabama. I. Title.

WILSON, Mabel Ponder. 277.61
Some early Alabama churches (established before 1870). Compiled by Mabel Ponder Wilson, Dorothy Youngblood Woodyerd [and] Rosa Lee Busby. [Birmingham] Alabama Society, Daughters of the American Revolution [1973] 293 p. 24 cm. "Commemorating the bicentennial of the United States of America." [BR555.A4W54] 73-174902 ISBN 0-88428-029-2
1. Alabama—Church history. I. Woodyerd, Dorothy Youngblood, joint author. II. Busby, Rosa Lee, joint author. III. Daughters of the American Revolution. Alabama. IV. Title.

SMITH, Jesse Guy. 277.64
Heroes of the saddle bags; a history of Christian denominations in the Republic of Texas. San Antonio, Naylor Co. [1951] ix, 234 p. map (on lining papers) 22 cm. Bibliography: p. 210-227. [BR555.T4S6] 51-4527
1. Texas—Church history. 2. Texas—Hist.—Revolution, 1835-1836. 3. Texas—Hist.—Republic, 1836-1846. 4. Sects—Texas. I. Title.

OBENHAUS, Victor 277.7
The church and faith in Mid-America. Philadelphia, Westminster [c.1963] 174p. illus. 21cm. 62-13873 3.75
1. Middle West—Religious life and customs. I. Title.

MOULE, Handley Carr 277'.7'077
Glyn, Bp. of Durham, 1841-1920.
Colossian and Philemon studies; lessons in faith and holiness. Grand Rapids, Mich., Zondervan Pub. House [1962] xi, 318 p. 22 cm. [BS2715.M63 1962] 74-187522
1. Bible. N.T. Colossians—Commentaries. 2. Bible. N.T. Philemon—Commentaries. I. Title.

HOLT, Harry Quentin, 1896- 277.72
ed.
Churches of Martin County, Indiana. Paoli, Ind., Stout's Print Shop [1951] 100 p. 20 cm. [BR555.I 6H6] 51-4623
1. Churches—Indiana—Martin Co. 2. Martin Co., Ind.—Church history. I. Title.

CHURCH Directory 277.73
Publications, Chicago.
Directory of churches in Chicago and suburbs. [Chicago] W. W. Hoffmeister [1952] 115 p. 24 x 11 cm. [BR560.C4C45] 52-67072
1. Chicago—Churches— Direct. I. Title.

ILLINOIS. Sesquicentennial 277'73
Commission.
Illinois believes; a guide to activities of churches and religious groups of all faiths in the observance of the sesquicentennial anniversary of the State of Illinois, December 4, 1967-December 3, 1968. [Springfield, 1968] 1 v. (unpaged) 28 cm. Cover title. Includes bibliography. [BR555.I314] 77-625707
1. Illinois—Religion. 2. Illinois—Centennial celebration, etc. I. Title.

SMITH, Chard Powers, 1894- 277.74
Yankees and God. [1st ed.] New York, Hermitage House [1954] 528 p. 22 cm. [BR530.S6] 54-11978
1. New England—Church history. 2. New England—Intellectual life. 3. Puritans. 4. Religious thought—U.S. 5. Philosophy, American. I. Title.

MAST, Dolorita 277.740924
Always the priest; the life of Gabriel Richard, S.S. Helicon [dist New York, Taplinger, c.1965] 368p. 21cm. Bibl. [F574.D4R517] 64-20229 6.95
1. Richard. Gabriel, 1767-1832. I. Title.

YOUNG, A. Beatrice 277.78883
The Epiphany story, 1895-1965 [by] A. Beatrice Young. [Denver] Pub. by Big Mountain Pr. for Epiphany Episcopal Church, 1966. 123p. illus. (pt. col.) ports. 23cm. [BX5980.D42Y63] 67-1679 3.50
1. Denver. Epiphany Episcopal Church—Hist. I. Title.

MIYAKAWA, Tetsuo Scott. 277.8
Protestants and pioneers; individualism and conformity on the American frontier [by] T. Scott Miyakawa. Chicago, University of Chicago Press [1964] 306 p. 23 cm. Bibliography: p. 275-293. [BR545.M5] 64-22247
1. The West—Religion. 2. Protestants in The West. I. Title.

*HIEBERT, D. Edmond 277'.83'07
First Timothy. Chicago, Moody [1967,c.1957] 127p. 21cm. (Everyman's Bible commentary) Bibl. .95 pap.,
1. Bible. N.T. Timothy—Commentaries. I. Title.

SIMMONDS, A. J. 277.92'12
The gentile comes to Cache Valley : a study of the Logan apostacies of 1874 and the establishment of non-Mormon churches in Cache Valley, 1873-1913 / A. J. Simmonds. Logan : Utah State University Press, 1976. p. cm. Bibliography: p. [BX8611.S5] 76-28513 ISBN 0-87421-088-7 : 5.00
1. Mormons and Mormonism in Cache Co., Utah. 2. Cache, Co., Utah—Church history. 3. Cache, Co., Utah—History. I. Title.

LOOFBOUROW, Leonidas 277.93
Latimer, 1877-
Steeples among the sage; a centennial story of Nevada's churches, by Leon L. Loofbourow. [Oakland, Calif., Lake Park Press, 1964] 160 p. illus., ports. 22 cm. 'A Nevada centennial book." [BR555.N76L6] 64-56952
1. Nevada — Church history. I. Title.

LOOFBOUROW, Leonidas 277.93
Latimer, 1877-
Steeples among the sage: a centennial story of Nevada's churches. Lake Park Pr. dist. Richmond, Calif. 3016 Barrett, Author, c.1964. 160p. illus., ports. 22cm. A Nevada centennial book. 64-56952 2.50 pap.,
1. Nevada—Church history. I. Title.

ACADEMY of California 277.94
Church History.
Academy scrapbook. Fresno. v. illus. 23cm. 10 no. a year. [BR555.C2A25] 54-36878
1. California—Church history—Period. 2. Catholic Church in California—Hist.—Period. I. Title.

ACADEMY of California 277.94
Church History
Academy scrapbook. [volume 5] Fresno, Cal., Academy Guild Press [c.1959] 312p. illus. 23cm. (bibl. notes) 54-36878 12.00 lea. cl.,
1. California—Church history—Period. 2. Catholic Church in California—Hist.—Period. I. Title.

FISK, Elinor Williams. 277'.94
Some of the early churches of California; a survey, by Elinor Williams Fisk and Harriet Trumbull Parsons, for the Historical Activities Committee of the National Society of Colonial Dames of America, resident in the State of California. [n.p.] 1968. 23 p. 23 cm. Includes bibliographies. [BR555.C2F58] 74-290331
1. California—Church history. I. Parsons, Harriet Trumbull, joint author. II. National Society of the Colonial Dames of America. California. Historical Activities Committee. III. Title.

SHIM, Steve S. 277.94'9
Korean immigrant churches today in Southern California / by Steve S. Shim. San Francisco : R and E Research Associates, 1977. x, 83 p. ; 28 cm. Bibliography: p. 78-83. [BV4468.2.K6S54] 76-24724 ISBN 0-88247-426-X pbk. : 9.00
1. Church work with Korean Americans—California—California, Southern. 2. California, Southern—Church history. 3. Korean Americans—California, Southern—History. I. Title.

HUNTINGTON Park, Calif. 277.94*93
St. Matthias' Parish.
Golden jubilee, St. Matthias' Parish, 1913-1963. [Huntington Park, Calif., Alhambra Review Print. Co., 1963] 103 p. illus. 28 cm. Cover title. [BX4603.H85S34] 72-202944
1. Huntington Park, Calif. St. Matthias' Parish. I. Title.

SCAFF, Marilee K ed. 277.9493
Perspectives on a college church; a report of the College Church study in Claremont, California. [By] Theodore M. Greene [and others] New York, Association Press [1961] 239p. 20cm. [BR561.C5S3] 61-14179
1. Claremont. Calif. College Church. I. Title.

FREDERICK, Arthur L, 1894- 277.97
The Columbia basin project area and its churches; a report to the Department of Church Planning and Strategy of the Washington and Northern Idaho Council of Churches and Christian Education, Seattle, Washington, September 3 and 4, 1950, by Arthur L. Frederick and Ross W. Sanderson. [Seattle] Washington State Council of Churches, '1950. 63 p., 64-65 (i. e. 66), 3 l. maps. 28 cm. "State of Washington highway map, Department of Highways, State of Washington, 1950": fold. col. map inserted. Bibliography: p. 63. [BR555.W3F7] 50-12911
1. Social surveys—Columbia River Valley. 2. Churches—Location. I. Sanderson, Ross Warren, 1884- joint author. II. Washington and Northern Idaho Council of Churches and Christian Education. III. Title.

FREDERICK, Arthur Lester, 277.97
1894-
Churches in the State of Washington; a statistical analysis. Seattle, Washington State Council of Churches, 1967, c1968. iv, 36 p. 28 cm. [BR555.W3F67] 70-3276
1. Church statistics—Washington (State) I. Title.

FREDERICK, Arthur Lester, 277.97
1894-
The Columbia basin project area and its churches; a report to the Department of Church Planning and Strategy of the Washington and Northern Idaho Council of Churches and Christian Education, Seattle, Washington, September 3 and 4, 1950, by Arthur L. Frederick and Ross W. Sanderson. [Seattle] Washington State Council of Churches, c1950. 63p. 64-65 (i. e. 66), 3 l. maps. 28cm. 'State of Washington highway map, Department of Highways, State of Washington, 1950': fold. col. map inserted. -- The Columbia basin and its churches. Supplement. [Seattle] Bibliography: p. 63. [BR555.W3F7] 50-12911
1. Social surveys—Columbia River Valley. 2. Churches—Location. I. Sanderson, Ross Warren, 1884- joint author. II. Washington and Northern Idaho Council of Churches and Christian Education. III. Title.

278 Christian Church In South America

CONVERSE, Hyla Stuntz, comp. 278
Raise a signal; God's action and the church's task in Latin America today, a symposium. New York, Friendship Pr. [c.]1961. 126p. 61-6629 1.75 pap.,
1. Missions—Spanish America. I. Title.

HOWARD, George Parkinson, 278
1882-
We Americans: North and South. New York, Friendship Press [1951] x, 148 p. fold. col. map (inserted) 20 cm. Bibliography: p. 144-148. [BR600.H72] 51-3605
1. Protestant churches—Spanish America. I. Title.

LEE, Elizabeth Meredith. 278
He wears orchids, & other Latin American stories. With an epilogue by W. Stanley Rycroft. Drawings by Rafael Palacios. Freeport, N.Y., Books for Libraries Press [1970, c1951] x, 178 p. illus. 23 cm. (Biography index reprint series) Includes bibliographical references. [BR600.L4 1970] 76-117327 ISBN 8-369-80190-
1. Protestants in Latin America. 2. Latin America—Religion. I. Title.

LEE, Elizabeth Meredith. 278
He wears orchids, & other Latin American stories; with an epilogue by W. Stanley Rycroft. Drawings by Rafael Palacios. New York, Friendship Press [1951] x, 181 p. illus. 22 cm. Bibliography: p. 179-180. [BR600.L4] 51-5044
1. Protestants in Spanish America. 2. Spanish America—Religion. I. Title.

MCCORKLE, Henry L. 278
The quiet crusaders. New York, Friendship Press [c.1961] 175p. illus. 61-6631 2.95
1. Missions—Spanish America. I. Title.

RYCROFT, William Stanley. 278
Religion and faith in Latin America. With a foreword by Alberto Rembao. Philadelphia, Westminster Press [1958] 208p. 21cm. Includes bibliography. [BR600.R82] 58-5838
1. Spanish America—Religion. 2. Protestant churches—Spanish America. I. Title.

GATES, Charles W. 278.1
Industrialization: Brazil's catalyst for church growth; a study of the Rio area, by C. W. Gates. South Pasadena, Calif., William Carey Library [1972] xi, 78 p. illus. 22 cm. Bibliography: p. 68-72. [BX4836.B8G38] 72-81342 ISBN 0-87808-413-4 1.95
1. Protestant churches—Brazil. 2. Church growth. I. Title.

GATES, Charles W. 278.1
Industrialization: Brazil's catalyst for church growth; a study of the Rio area, by C. W. Gates. South Pasadena, Calif., William Carey Library [1972] xi, 78 p. illus. 22 cm. Bibliography: p. 68-72. [BX4836.B8G38] 72-81342 ISBN 0-87808-413-4 1.95
1. Protestant churches—Brazil. 2. Church growth. I. Title.

READ, William R 1923- 278.1
New patterns of church growth in Brazil, by William R. Read. Grand Rapids, W. B. Eerdmans Pub. Co. [1965] 240 p. illus., maps. 21 cm. (Church growth series) Bibliography: p. 232-237. [BV2853.B6R35] 65-18086
1. Missions — Brazil. 2. Brazil — Religion. I. Title.

READ, William R., 1923- 278.1
New patterns of church growth in Brazil. Grand Rapids, Mich., Eerdmans [c.1965] 240p. illus., maps. 21cm. (Church growth ser.) Bibl. [BV2853.B6R35] 65-18086 2.45 pap.,
1. Missions—Brazil. 2. Brazil—Religion. I. Title.

ENNS, Arno W. 278.2
Man, milieu, and mission in Argentina; a close look at Church growth, by Arno W. Enns. Grand Rapids, Mich., W. B. Eerdmans Pub. Co. [1971] 258 p. illus., map. 21 cm. Bibliography: p. 243-254. [BV2853.A7E55] 78-80875 3.95
1. Missions—Argentine Republic. I. Title.

GEYER, Robert Raine 278.4
Death trails in Bolivia to faith triumphant. New York. Vantage [c.1963] 124p.21cm. 2.50
I. Title.

PORTERFIELD, Bruce E. 278.4
Commandos for Christ; the Gospel witness in Bolivia's "Green Hell." [1st ed.] New York, Harper & Row [1963] 238 p. illus. 22 cm. [BV2853.B4P65] 63-15953
1. Missions—Bolivia. 2. Indians of South America—Bolivia. I. Title.

TARIRI, Shapra chief. 278.5
My story; from jungle killer to Christian missionary, as told to Ethel Emily Wallis. [1st ed.] New York, Harper & Row [1965] 126 p. illus. (part col.) map, ports. 25 cm. (Harper jungle missionary classics) [F3430.1.S47T3] 65-15394
1. Shapra Indians—Missions. 2. Missions—Peru. 3. Wycliffe Bible Translators. I. Wallis, Ethel Emily. II. Title. III. Title: From jungle killer to Christian missionary.

FLORA, Cornelia Butler, 278'.61
1943-
Pentecostalism in Colombia : baptism by fire and spirit / Cornelia Butler Flora. Rutherford, N.J. : Fairleigh Dickinson University Press, [1976] p. cm. Includes index. Bibliography: p. [BX8762.Z7C643] 74-4974 ISBN 0-8386-1578-3 : 13.50
1. Pentecostal churches—Colombia. 2. Sociology, Christian—Colombia. 3. Social classes—Colombia. I. Title.

FLORA, Cornelia Butler, 278'.61
1943-
Pentecostalism in Colombia : baptism by fire and spirit / Cornelia Butler Flora. Rutherford, [N.J.] : Fairleigh Dickinson University Press, c1976. 288 p. : ill. ; 22 cm. Includes index. Bibliography: p. 263-282. [BX8762.Z7C643 1976] 74-4974 ISBN 0-8386-1578-3 : 13.50
1. Pentecostal churches—Colombia. 2. Sociology, Christian—Colombia. 3. Social classes—Colombia. I. Title.

*DROWN, Frank. 278.66
Mission to the head-hunters [by] Frank and Marie Drown. Grand Rapids, Mich. Zondervan [1973 c.1961] 252. 18 cm. Glossary: p. 249-252. [F3722.1J5] 61-12825 pap. 1.25
1. Jivaro Indians—Missions. 2. Ecuador—Social life and customs. I. Drown, Marie, joint author. II. Title.

*ELLIOT, Elisabeth 278.66
Through gates of splendor. New York, Harper [1965, c.1957, 1958] 258p. illus. 21cm. (Chapel bks., CB101) 1.75 pap.,
I. Title.

WALLIS, Ethel Emily. 278.66
The Dayuma story; life under Auca spears. [1st ed.] New York, Harper [1960] 288 p. illus. 22 cm. [BV2853.E3D3] 60-11789
1. Dayuma, Auca Indian. 2. Missions — Ecuador. 3. Indians of South America — Missions. I. Title.

WALLIS, Ethel Emily. 278.66
The Dayuma story; life under Auca spears. [1st ed.] New York, Harper [1960] 288 p. illus. 22 cm. [BV2853.E3D3] 60-11789
1. Dayuma, Auca Indian. 2. Missions—Ecuador. 3. Indians of South America—Missions. I. Title.

279 Christian Church In Other Areas

TRIMINGHAM, John 279.09676
Spencer.
Islam in east Africa, by J. Spencer Trimingham. Oxford, Clarendon Press, 1964. xii, 108 p. maps (1 fold.) 23 cm. Bibliographical footnotes. [BP64.A4E27] 64-6991
1. Islam — Africa, East. 2. Africa, East — Religious life and customs. I. Title.

ANDERSON, Gerald H. 279.14
Studies in Philippine church history. Edited by Gerald H. Anderson. Ithaca [N.Y.] Cornell University Press [1969] xiv, 421 p. 24 cm. [BR1260.A5] 69-18208 14.50
1. Philippine Islands—Church history—Addresses, essays, lectures. I. Title.

BARLOW, Sanna Morrison. 279.14
Mountains singing; the story of Gospel Recordings in the Philippines. Chicago,

Moody [1968,c.1952] 352p. illus. 17cm. [BV3380.B3] 53-2338 1.29 pap.,
1. Gospel Recordings, inc. 2. Ridderhof, Joy. 3. Missions—Philippine Islands. 4. Phonorecords in missionary work. I. Title.

DEATS, Richard L. 279.14
Nationalism and Christianity in the Philippines [by] Richard L. Deats. Dallas, Southern Methodist University Press [1968, c1967] ix, 207 p. 24 cm. Bibliography: p. [181]-200. [BR1260.D4] 67-28035
1. Nationalism and religion—Philippine Islands. 2. Missions—Philippine Islands. 3. Indigenous church administration. 4. Philippine Islands—Church history. I. Title.

WHITTEMORE, Lewis Bliss, Bp. 279.14
Struggle for freedom; history of the Philippine Independent Church. Greenwich, Conn. [Seabury Press, 1961] 228 p. 22 cm. Includes bibliography. [BX4795.I5W5 1961] 61-10457
1. Iglesia Filipina Independiente. 2. Philippine Islands — Church history. I. Title.

WHITTEMORE, Lewis Bliss, Bp. 279.14
Struggle for freedom; history of the Philippine Independent Church. Greenwich, Conn. [Seabury Pr., c.1961] 228p. Bibl. 61-10457 5.50
1. Iglesia Filipina Independiente. 2. Philippine Islands—Church history. I. Title.

RELIGION in early Australia 279.4
: the problem of church and state / edited with an introduction by Jean Woolmington. Stanmore, N.S.W. : Cassell Australia, 1976. xiii, 174 p. ; 23 cm. (Problems in Australian history) Includes index. Bibliography: p. 170. [BR1480.R44] 76-379102 ISBN 0-7269-9257-7
1. Australia—Church history—Sources. 2. Church and state in Australia—History—Sources. I. Woolmington, Jean Clara.

SOUTHALL, Ivan, ed. 279.4
The challenge: is the Church obsolete? An Australian response to the challenge of modern society. [Melbourne] Lansdowne Pr. in assn. with the Australian Council of Churches [1966] Stamped on t.p.: Dist. SportShelf, New Rochelle, N.Y. x, 264p. 23cm. Bibl. [BR115.W6S57] 67-72590 10.50
1. Church and the world—Addresses, essays, lectures. 2. Australia—Church history—Addresses, essays, lectures. 3. Australian Council of Churches. I. Title.

TURNER, Naomi. 279.44
Sinews of sectarian warfare? State aid in New South Wales 1836-1862. Canberra, Australian National University Press, 1972. xiv, 272 p. 23 cm. Bibliography: p. 251-265. [BR1483.N5T87] 72-187596 11.50
1. Church and state in New South Wales. I. Title.

FRY, Peter. 279'.6
Spirits of protest : spirit-mediums and the articulation of consensus among the Zezuru of Southern Rhodesia (Zimbabwe) / Peter Fry. Cambridge, Eng. ; New York : Cambridge University Press, c1976. viii, 145 p. ; 24 cm. (Cambridge studies in social anthropology ; 14) Includes index. Bibliography: p. 133-136. [BL2480.Z4F79] 75-20832 ISBN 0-521-21052-6 : 10.95
1. Zezuru (Bantu people)—Religion. 2. Spiritualism—Zimbabwe African People's Union. I. Title.

DAVIES, John, 1772-1855. 279.6211
The history of the Tahitian Mission, 1799-1830. Supplementary papers from the correspondence of the missionaries. Ed. by C. W. Newbury. [New York] Cambridge [c.] 1961[ ] liv, 392p. illus., fold. maps (1 in pocket) geneal. table. (Hakluyt Soc. Works, 2d ser., no. 116) Bibl. 61-19740 7.50
1. Missions—Tahiti—Hist. I. Newbury, Colin W., ed. II. Title. III. Series.

HALFORD, Francis John, 1902-1953. 279.69
9 doctors & God. Illus. by Keichi Kimura. Honolulu, University of Hawaii, 1954. xiv, 322 p. illus., ports. 24 cm. Bibliography: p. 315-322. [R722.H23] 266 54-10046
1. Missions—Hawaiian Islands. I. Title.

FLEMING, Archibald Lang, Bp., 1883-1953. 279.8
Archibald the Arctic. New York, Appleton-Century-Crofts [1956] 399 p. illus. 22 cm. [BV3695.F5A3] 266.3 56-11934
1. Eskimos—Missions. 2. Missionaries—Correspondence, reminiscences, etc.

MORGAN, Bernice Bangs. 279.8
The very thought of Thee; adventures of an Arctic missionary. Grand Rapids, Zondervan Pub. House [1952] 136 p. illus. 20 cm. [BV2803.A4M6] 266 52-2162
1. Missions—Alaska. I. Title.

RODLI, Agnes Sylvia. 279.8
North of heaven; a teaching ministry among the Alaskan Indians. Chicago, Moody Press [1963] 189 p. 22 cm. [BV2803.A4R6] 63-5735
1. Athapascan Indians—Missions. 2. Missions—Nikolai, Alaska. I. Title.

BULL, Geoffrey T., 1921- 279.9115
Coral in the sand. Chicago, Moody [1963, c.1962] 125p. map (on lining papers) 20cm. Bibl. 64-2945 1.95 bds.,
1. Missions—North Borneo. I. Title.

ACHUTEGUI, Pedro S. de. 279.914
Religious revolution in the Philippines; the life and church of Gregorio Aglipay, 1860-1960 v.1, by Pedro S. de Achutegui, Miguel A. Bernad. Manila, Ateneo de Manila[dist. Detroit 21, Mich., Box 6, Coll. Park Sta., Cellar Bk. Shop, 1964, c.1960] 578p. illus. 26cm. Bibl. 60-15094 7.00
1. Aglipay y Labayan, Gregorio, Abp., 1870-1940. 2. Iglesia Filipina Independiente. I. Bernad, Miguel Anselmo, joint author. II. Title.

ACHUTEGUI, Pedro S de 279.914
Religious revolution in the Philippines; the life and church of Gregorio Aglipay, 1860-1960, by Pedro S. de Achutegui, Miguel A. Bernad, v.2. Manila, Ateneo de Manila, 1966. xvi, 502p. illus., ports. facsims. 26cm. Contents.v.2. From 1940 to the present. Bibl. [BX4795.I5A43] 61-16948 7.00
1. Aglipay y Labayan, Gregorio, Abp., 1860-1940. 2. Iglesia Filipina Independiente. I. Bernad, Miguel Anselmo, joint author. II. Title.
Available from Cellar Bk. Shop, Detroit.

FOX, Paul, 1874- 279.914
The polish National Catholic Church. Scranton, School of Christian Living [1961?] 144 p. col. illus., ports. 23 cm. Includes bibliographical references. [BX4795.P63F6] 66-53641
1. Polish National Catholic Church of America. I. Title.

FOX, Paul, 1874- 279.914
The Polish National Catholic Church. Scranton, School of Christian Living [1961?] 144 p. col. illus., ports. 23 cm. Includes bibliographical references. [BX4795.P63F6] 66-53641
1. Polish National Catholic Church of America. I. Title.

DE WAARD, Nellie 279.921
Pioneer in Sumatra: the story of Ludwig Nommensen. Chicago, Moody [1963] 63p. (Compact bk. no. 29) .29 pap.,
I. Title.

HETHERINGTON, John Aikman, 1907- 279.94'5
Pillars of the faith; churchmen and their churches in early Victoria [by] John Hetherington. Melbourne, Canberra [etc.] Cheshire [1966] xii, 110 p. illus., ports. 25 cm. Bibliography: p. 107-108. [BR1483.V5H4] 66-25774
1. Victoria, Australia—Church history. I. Title.

HITT, Russell T. 279.95
Cannibal valley. [1st ed.] New York, Harper & Row [1962] 253 p. illus. 22 cm. [BV3680.N5H5] 62-14577
1. Missions—New Guinea. I. Title.

280 CHRISTIAN DENOMINATIONS & SECTS

ALGERMISSEN, Konrad, 1889- 280
Christian sects. Tr. from German by J. R. Foster. New York, Hawthorn [c.1962] 128p. 21cm. (Twentieth cent. encyclopedia of Catholicism, v.139. Sect. 14: Outside the church) Bibl. 62-12932 3.50 bds.,
1. Sects. I. Title.

ANSON, Peter Frederick, 1889- 280
Bishops at large, by Peter F. Anson. With an introd. by Henry St. John. New York, October House [1965, c1964] 593 p. illus., ports. 23 cm. Bibliography: p. 545-572. [BR157.A56] 65-11510
1. Sects. I. Title.

BOUYER, Louis, 1913- 280
The Word, church, and sacraments in Protestantism and Catholicism. [Translated by A. V. Littledale] New York, Desclee Co., 1961. 80p. 20cm. [BT88.B633] 61-11030
1. Authority (Religion) 2. Sacraments. 3. Catholic Church—Relations—Protestant churches. 4. Protestant churches—Relations—Catholic Church. I. Title.

BOUYER, Louis, 1913- 280
The Word, church, and sacraments in Protestantism and Catholicism. [Tr. from French by A. V. Littledale] New York, Desclee Co. [c.]1961 80p. 61-11030 2.00 bds.,
1. Authority (Religion) 2. Sacraments. 3. Catholic Church—Relations—Protestant churches. 4. Protestant churches—Relations—Catholic Church. I. Title.

BOYER, Charles, 1884- 280
One shepherd, the problem of Christian reunion; translated by Angeline Bouchard. New York, P. J. Kenedy [1952] 142 p. 17 cm. [BX1753.B653] 52-9473
1. Christian union. 2. Catholic Church—Relations. I. Title.

BROMILEY, Geoffrey William. 280
The unity and disunity of the church. Grand Rapids, Eerdmans [1958] 104p. 19cm. (Pathway books) [BX8.B718] 58-13062
1. Christian union. 2. Church—Unity. I. Title.

BROWN, Robert McAfee, 1920- ed. 280
The challenge to reunion, compiled and edited by Robert McAfee Brown and David H. Scott. [1st ed.] New York, McGraw-Hill [1963] 292 p. 22 cm. Includes bibliography. [BX8.2.A1B7] 63-12125
1. Christian union—Protestant churches. I. Scott, David H., joint ed. II. Title.

CHANDLER, Daniel Ross, 1937- 280 B
The official, authorized biography of the Reverend Dr. Preston Bradley. [1st ed.] New York, Exposition Press [1971] 115, [2] p. 21 cm. (An Exposition-testament book) Bibliography: p. [117] [BR1725.B68C48] 78-166186 ISBN 0-682-47333-2 4.50
1. Bradley, Preston, 1888- 2. Sermons, American. I. Title.

CHRISTIANS in conversation; 280
[papers] With a pref. by Peter W. Bartholome. Westminster, Md., Newman Press, 1962. x, 112p. 21cm. 'A colloquy between American Catholics and Protestants ... held at St.John's Abbey, Collegeville, Minnesota, on 1, 2, 3 December, 1960.' 'Organized by the American Benedictine Academy.' Includes bibliographical references. [BX1779.C45] 62-17186
1. Catholic Church—Doctrinal and controversial works—Debates, etc. I. American Benedictine Academy, Latrobe, Pa.

CONFRONTING the cults, 280
by Gordon R. Lewis [Philadelphia, Presbyterian & Reformed Pub. Co.] 1966. 198p. 22cm. Bibl. [BR516.5.L4] 66-26791 1926- 2.95
1. Sects—U.S.

CRAIG, Clarence Tucker, 1895- 280
The one church, in the light of the New Testament. New York, Abingdon-Cokesbury Press [1951] 155 p. 21 cm. [BX8.C7] 51-12193
1. Ecumenical movement. I. Title.

FERM, Vergilius Ture Anselm, 1896- ed. 280
The American church of the Protestant heritage. New York, Philosophical Library [1953] 481p. 21cm. Includes bibliographies. [BR516.F45] 53-7607
1. Sects—U. S. 2. Protestant churches—U. S. I. Title.
Contents omitted.

HOWELLS, Rulon Stanley, 1902- 280
His many mansions; a compilation of Christian beliefs, by Rulon S. Howells. With a comparative chart of ten Christian denominations on twenty-three important doctrinal questions. Illustrated with diagrams of the intricate and interesting organizations of the leading Christian churches which have been condensed into an authoritative and understandable form. New York, World Pub. [1972, c1967] 225 p. illus. 22 cm. Includes bibliographical references. [BR157.H62 1972] 76-159843 5.95
1. Sects. 2. Sects—United States. 3. Creeds—Comparative studies. I. Title.

IRVINE, William C., comp. 280
Heresies exposed; a brief critical examination in the light of the Holy Scriptures of some of the prevailing heresies and false teachings of today. New York, Loizeaux Bros. [1953] 225p. 20cm. First ed. published in 1917 under title: Timely warnings. [BR157.I7 1953] 54-36212
1. Sects. 2. Heresies and heretics. I. Title.

JENKINS, Daniel Thomas, 1914- 280
Europe and America, their contributions to the world church. Philadelphia, Westminster Press [1951] 72 p. 20 cm. [BX8.J4] 51-10029
1. Ecumenical movement. I. Title.

LAMPRECHT, Sterling Power, 1890- 280
Our religious traditions. Cambridge, Harvard University Press, 1950. viii, 99 p. 22 cm. [BL85.L32 1950] 50-5745
1. Jews—Religion. 2. Catholic Church. 3. Protestantism. I. Title.

LATOURETTE, Kenneth Scott, 1884- 280
The emergence of a world Christian community. New Haven, Published for the Rice Institute by Yale University Press, 1949. iv, 91 p. 21 cm. (The Rockwell lectures on religion at the Rice Institute, Houston, Texas) [BX8.L37] 49-7529
1. Christian union. I. Title. II. Series. III. Series: Rockwell lectures

LEENHARDT, Franz J 1902- 280
Two Biblical faiths: Protestant and Catholic, by Franz J. Leenhardt. Translated by Harold Knight. Philadelphia, Westminster Press [1964] 120 p. 23 cm. Translation of La parole et le buisson de feu. Bibliographical footnotes. [BX8.2.L443] 64-19149
1. Christian union. 2. Catholic Church — Relations — Protestant churches. 3. Protestant churches — Relations — Catholic Church. I. Title.

LEENHARDT, Franz J., 1902- 280
Two Biblical faiths; Protestant and Catholic. Tr. [from French] by Harold Knight. Philadelphia, Westminster [c.1962-1964] 120p. 23cm. Bibl. 64-19149 2.75
1. Christian union. 2. Catholic Church—Relations—Protestant churches. 3. Protestant churches—Relations—Catholic Church. I. Title.

LEHRBURGER, Egon, 1904- 280
Strange sects and cults: a study of their origins and influence [by] Egon Larsen. New York, Hart Pub. Co. [1972, c1971] 245 p. 21 cm. Bibliography: p. 231-232. [BR157.L44 1972] 79-189636 ISBN 0-8055-1044-3 5.95
1. Sects. I. Title.

LEWIS, Gordon Russell, 1926- 280
Confronting the cults, by Gordon R. Lewis. Philadelphia, Presbyterian and Reformed Pub. Co., 1966. 198 p. 22 cm. Includes bibliographical references. [BR516.5.L4] 66-26791
1. Sects—United States. I. Title.

MANWELL, Reginald Dickinson, 1897- 280
The church across the street; an introduction to the ways and beliefs of fifteen different faiths, by Reginald D. Manwell, Sophia Lyon Fahs. Rev. ed. Boston, Beacon [1963, c.1962] 318p. illus. 22cm. Bibl. 62-13635 3.95
1. Sects. I. Fahs, Sophia Blanche (Lyon) 1876- joint author. II. Title.

MARTIN, Walter Ralston, 1928- 280
The Christian and the cults; answering the cultist from the Bible. Grand Rapids, Division of Cult Apologetics, Zondervan Pub. House [1956] 152p. 21cm. (The Modern cult library series) Includes bibliography. [BR516.M25] 57-17619
1. Sects—U. S. 2. Religions. I. Title.

MAYER, Frederick Emanuel, 1892- 280
The religious bodies of America. St. Louis, Concordia Pub. House [1954] 587p. 26cm. Includes bibliography. [BR516.M37] 54-2818
1. Sects—U. S. 2. Creeds— Comparative studies. 3. Lutheran Church—Doctrinal and controversial works. I. Title

MAYER, Frederick Emanuel, 1892-1954. 280
The religious bodies of America. 2d ed. Saint Louis, Concordia Pub. House, 1956. xiii, 591p. 25cm. Includes bibliographies. [BR516.M37 1956] 56-4924
1. Sects—U. S. 2. Creeds—Comparative studies. 3. Lutheran Church—Doctrinal and controversial works. I. Title.

MAYER, Frederick Emanuel, 1892-1954. 280
The religious bodies of America. 3d ed. Saint Louis, Concordia Pub. House, 1958. xiii, 591p. 25cm. Includes bibliographies. [BR516.5.M3 1958] 58-4617
1. Sects—U. S. 2. Creeds—Comparative studies. 3. Lutheran Church—Doctrinal and controversial works. I. Title.

MAYER, Frederick Emanuel, 1892-1954. 280
The religious bodies of America. 4th ed., rev. by Arthur Carl Piepkorn. Saint Louis, Concordia Pub. House, 1961. xiii, 598p. 25cm. Includes bibliographies. [BR516.5.M3 1961] 61-15535
1. Sects—U. S. 2. Creeds—Comparative studies. 3. Lutheran Church—Doctrinal and controversial works. I. Piepkorn, Arthur Carl, 1907- II. Title.

MOLLAND, Einar 280
Christendom; the Christian churches, their doctrines, constitutional forms, and ways of worship. [Translated from the Norwegian] New York, Philosophical Library [1959] xiv, 418p. 23cm. (16p.bibl.) 59-65285 10.00
1. Sects. I. Title.

NELSON, John Robert, 1920- ed. 280
Christian unity in North America, a symposium. St. Louis, Bethany Press [1958] 208p. 23cm. Bibliographical footnotes. [BX8.N44] 58-10866
1. Christian union. I. Title.

NICHOLS, James Hastings, 1915- 280
A short primer for Protestants; an abridgement of his full length Haddam House book. New York, Association Press [c1957] 127p. 16cm. (An Association Press reflection book) [BX4810.N52] 57-5492
1. Protestantism. I. Title.

NIEBUHR, Heimut Richard, 1894- 280
The social sources of denominationalism [Gloucester. Mass., Peter Smith, 1963, c.1929] 304p. 18cm. (Meridian living age bk., LA11 rebound) Bibl. 3.50
1. Sociology, Christian. 2. Sects. I. Title.

NIEBUHR, Helmut Richard, 1894-1962. 280
The social sources of denominationalism. New York, Meridian Books, 1957. 304 p. 18 cm. (Living age books, LA11) [BR115] 57-6685
1. Sociology, Christian. 2. Sects. I. Title.

NIEBUHR. HELMUT RICHARD, 1894- 280
The social sources of denominationalism. New York, Meridian Books, 1957. 304p. 18cm. (Living age books, LA11) [BR115] 57-6685
1. Sociology, Christian. 2. Sects. I. Title.

NIESEL, Wilhelm. 280
The gospel and the churches; a comparison of Catholicism, Orthodoxy, and Protestantism. Translated by David Lewis. Philadelphia, Westminster Press [1962] c384p. 23cm. [BR157.N513] 62-17753
1. Catholic Church—Doctrinal and controversial works— Protestant authors. 2. Orthodox Eastern Church—Doctrinal and controversial works—Protestant authors. 3. Protestant churches. I. Title.

NOSS, John Boyer. 280
Living religions. Philadelphia, United Church Press [1962] 111 p. 19 cm. (A Pilgrim book) [BL95.N6] 62-19786
1. Religions. I. Title.

NOSS, John Boyer 280
Living religions. Philadelphia, United Church [c.1957, 1962] 111p. 19cm. (Pilgrim bk.) 62-19786 1.45 pap.,
1. Religions. I. Title.

OHRING, George. 280
Planetary meteorology, by George Ohring, Wen Tang, and Joseph Mariano. Springfield, Va., For sale by the Clearinghouse for Federal Scientific and Technical Information [1965] vi, 88 p. illus. 27 cm. (NASA contractor report NASA CR-280) "Prepared under contract no. NASw-975 by GCA Corporation, Bedford, Mass., for National Aeronautics and Space Administration." Bibliography: p. 85-88. [TL521.3.C6A3] 65-62662
1. Poanetary meteorology. I. Tang, Wen, 1921- joint auhtor. II. Mariano, Joseph, joint author. III. GCA Corporation. IV. U.S. National Aeronautics and Space Administration. V. Title. VI. Series. VII. Series: U.S. National Aeronautics and Space Administration. NASA contractor report CR-280

OXNAM, Garfield Bromley, Bp., 1891- 280
On this rock; an appeal for Christian unity. [1st ed.] New York, Harper [1951] 117 p. 20 cm. (The William Henry Hoover Lectureship on Christian Unity, 3d ser.) [BX8.O9] 51-9375
1. Christian union. I. Title. II. Series: Disciples Divinity House, University of Chicago Hoover lectures on Christian unity)

PACHE, Rene. 280
The ecumenical movement. [Dallas, Dallas Theological Seminary, 1951 c 1950] 130, [2] p. 19 cm. (W. H. Griffith Thomas Memorial Lectureship [lectures 1950] Bibliography: p. [131]-[132] [BX8.P2] 51-2745
1. Ecumenical movement. I. Title. II. Series: Griffith Thomas memorial lectures, 1950

PFEFFER, Leo, 1910- 280
Creeds in competition: a creative force in American culture. [New York] Harper [1958] 176p. 22cm. [BR516.5.P43] 58-10373
1. Sects—U. S. 2. Church and state in the U. S. I. Title.

POTTER, Charles Francis, 1885-1962. 280
The faiths men live by. New York, Prentice-Hall [1954] 323 p. 22 cm. [BL80.P59] 54-5679
1. Religions. 2. Sects—U.S. I. Title.

PROTESTANT Episcopal Church in the U. S. A. Joint Commission on Ecumenical Relations. 280
Empty shoes; a study of the Church of South India. New York, National Council, Protestant Episcopal Church, 1956. 153p. illus. 22cm. Includes bibliography. [BX5671.I53P7] 57-34188
1. Church of South India—Hist. I. Title.

RHODES, Arnold Black, ed. 280
The church faces the isms [by] the members of the faculty of the Louisville Presbyterian Theological Seminary, Louisville, Kentucky. Arnold Black Rhodes, editor. Associate editors: Frank H. Caldwell and L.C. Rudolph. New York, Abingdon Press [1958] 304p. 24cm. Includes bibliographies. [BR157.R48] 58-5392
1. Sects. I. Louisville Presbyterian Theological Seminary (1901-) II. Title.

RHODES, Arnold Black, ed. 280
The church faces the isms [by] the members of the faculty of the Louisville Presbyterian Theological Seminary, Louisville, Kentucky. Assoc. eds.: Frank H. Caldwell, L. C. Rudolph. Nashville, Abingdon [1964, c.1958] 304p. 23cm. (Apex bks., R4) Bibl. 2.25 pap.,
1. Sects. I. Louisville Preyterian Theological Seminary (1901-) II. Title.

ROUTH, Eugene Coke, 1874- 280
Who are they? Shawnee, Printed by O[klahoma] B[aptist] U[niversity] Press [1951] 71 p. 18 cm. [BR157.R6] 51-3097
1. Sects. 2. Baptists — Doctrinal and controversial works. I. Title.

SANDERS, John Oswald, 1902- 280
Cults and isms ancient and modern. [8th] rev., enl. [ed.] Grand Rapids, Mich., Zondervan [1963, c.1948] 167p. 21cm. Firt ed. pub. in 1948 under title: Heresies ancient and modern. Bibl. 63-17746 2.50
1. Sects. I. Title.

SHEEDER, Franklin I 280
The story of the denominations; a course for older young peopleand adults. Teacher's ed. Boston, Pilgrim Press [1953] 65, 92p. illus. 21cm. (Pilgrim series) [BR516.S47 1953] 53-33411
1. Sects—U. S. I. Title.

SNARE, J P 1870- 280
A new look at religion. [1st ed.] New York, Greenwich Book Publishers [c1956] 60p. 21cm. [BL390.S64] 56-12843
1. Religions (PropOsed, unlversal, etc.) I. Title.

SNARE, J P 1870- 280
A new look at religion. [1st ed.] New York, Greenwich Book Publishers [c1956] 60 p. 21 cm. [BL390.S64] 56-12843
1. Religious (Proposed, universal, etc.) I. Title.

SPERRY, Willard Learoyd, 1882-1954, ed. 280
Religion and our divided denominations. By Willard L. Sperry [and others] Freeport, N.Y., Books for Libraries Press [1971, c1945] ix, 115 p. 23 cm. (Essay index reprint series) "Originally published as v. 1. of [the editor's] Religion in the post-war world." Contents.Contents.—Our present disunity, by W. L. Sperry.—Roman Catholicism, by J. LaFarge.—Protestantism, by J. T. McNeill.—Judaism, by L. Finkelstein.—Humanism, by A. MacLeish. Includes bibliographical references. [BR516.S76 1971] 74-128315 ISBN 0-8369-2201-8
1. Sects. 2. U.S.—Religion—1901-1945. I. Title.

SPITTLER, Russell P. 280
Cults and isms; twenty alternates to evangelical Christianity. Grand Rapids, Baker Bk. [1963, c.1962] 143p. 23cm. Bibl. 62-21702 2.95
1. Religions. I. Title.

STUBER, Stanley Irvin, 1903- 280
How we got our denominations; a primer on church history. [Rev. ed.] New York, Association Press [1959] 254 p. 20 cm. Includes bibliography. [BR157.S77 1959] 59-12104
1. Sects. 2. Church history. I. Title.

STUBER, Stanley Irving, 1903- 280
Denominations -- how we got them. New York, Association Press [1958] 127 p. 16 cm. (An Association Press reflection book) "Condensed and revised from How we got our denominations." Includes bibliography. [BR157.S775] 58-6474
1. Sects. 2. Church history. I. Title.

STUBER, Stanley Irving, 1903- 280
How we got our denominations; a primer on church history. [Rev. ed.] New York, Association Press [1959] 254 p. 20 cm. Includes bibliography. [BR159.S77 1959] 59-12104
1. Sects. 2. Church history. I. Title.

TANIS, Edward J 280
What the sects teach; Jehovah's Witnesses, Seventh- Day Adventists, Christian Science [and] Spiritism. Grand Rapids, Baker Book House, 1958. 89 p. 22 cm. [BR157.T2] 59-184
1. Sects. I. Title.

TYLER, Gladys Beckwith. 280
This, too, can happen in Miami. Miami Shores, Fla., 1956. 183 p. illus. 23 cm. [BX9999.M53C6] 57-23158
1. Miami Shores, Fla. Community Church. I. Title.

V8ALGERMISSEA, Konrad. 1889- 280
Christian seets, Translat*d from the German by J. R. Foster, [1st ed.] New York, Hawthron Books [1962] 128p. 24cmcm. (The Twentieth century encyclopedia of Catholicism, v. 139. Section 11: Outside the church) Translation of Das Sektenwesen der Gegenwart. Includes bibliography. [BR157.A473] 62-12932
1. Sects. I. Title.

VAN BAALEN, Jay Karel, 1890- 280
Christianity versus the cults. Grand Rapids, Eerdmans [1958] 136 p. 22 cm. [BR157.V3] 58-9530
1. Sects. I. Title.

WASHINGTON, Joseph R. 280
Black sects and cults, by Joseph R. Washington, Jr. [1st ed.] Garden City, N.Y., Doubleday, 1972. xii, 176 p. 22 cm. (The C. Eric Lincoln series on Black religion) Bibliography: p. [167]-170. [BR563.N4W32] 72-86649 ISBN 0-385-00209-2 5.95
1. Negroes—Religion. I. Title. II. Series.

WASHINGTON, Joseph R. 280
Black sects and cults, by Joseph R. Washington, Jr. Garden City, N.Y., Anchor Press/Doubleday, 1973 [c.1972] xii, 176 p. 21 cm. (Anchor Book, A0-102) (C. Eric Lincoln series on Black religion) [BR563.N4W32] -72 ISBN 0-385-00252-1 2.95 (pbk.)
1. Negroes—Religion. I. Title. II. Series.

WENTZ, Frederick W. 280
Lutherans and other denominations. Philip R. Hoh, ed. illus. by Harry Eaby. Philadelphia, Lutheran Church Pr. [c.1964] 117p. illus. 22cm. (LCA Sunday church sch. ser.) 1.25; 1.50 pap., teacher's gd., pap.,
I. Title.

WENTZEL, Fred De Hart, 1895- 280
Once there were two churches. Illustrated by Kathleen Voute. New York, Friendship Press [1950] viii, 117 p. illus. 23 cm. Bibliography: p. 115-116. [BV636.W4] 50-8263
1. Community churches. I. Title.

WESTIN, Gunnar, 1890- 280
The free church through the ages. Translated from the Swedish by Virgil A. Olson. Nashville, Broadman Press [1958] 380 p. 22 cm. [BR157.W352] 58-8926
1. Sects. I. Title.

WHALEN, William Joseph. 280
Faiths for the few; a study of minority religions. Milwaukee, Bruce Pub. Co. [1963] x, 201 p. 22 cm. Bibliography: p. 189-194. [BR516.5.W436] 63-19634
1. Sects — U.S. I. Title.

WHALEN, William Joseph 280
Faiths for the few; a study of minority religions. Milwaukee. Bruce [c.1963] x, 201p. 22cm. Bibl. 63-19634 3.75
1. Sects—U. S. I. Title.

WHALEN, William Joseph. 280
Separated brethren; a survey of non-Catholic Christian denominations in the United States. Milwaukee, Bruce Pub. Co. [1958] 284 p. illus. 23 cm. Includes bibliography. [BR516.W44] 57-13118
1. Sects — U.S. I. Title.

WILLIAMS, John Paul, 1900- 280
What Americans believe and how they worship. [1st ed.] New York, Harper [1952] 400 p. 22 cm. [BR516.W47] 52-5477
1. U.S.—Religion. 2. Sects.—U.S. I. Title.

WILLIAMS, John Paul, 1900- 280
What Americans believe and how they worship. Rev. ed. New York, Harper & Row [1962] 530 p. 22 cm. [BR516.5.W5 1962] 62-7308
1. U.S.—Religion. 2. Sects—U.S. I. Title.

WILLIAMS, John Paul, 1900- 280
What Americans believe and how they worship. [1st ed.] New York, Harper [1952] 400 p. 22 cm. [BR516.W47] 52-5477
1. United States—Religion—1945- 2. Sects—United States. I. Title.

WOLF, William J ed. 280
Protestant churches and reform today [by] Lawrence L. Durgin [and others] William J. Wolf, editor. New York, Seabury Press [1964] 155 p. 22 cm. Bibliographical references included in "Contributors' notes" (p. [151]-155) [BX4818.3.W6] 64-19633
1. Catholic Church — Relations — Protestant churches. 2. Protestant churches — Relations — Catholic Church. I. Durgin, Lawrence L. II. Title.

WOLF, William J., ed. 280
Protestant churches and reform today [by] Lawrence L. Durgin [others] William J. Wolf, ed. New York, Seabury [c.1964] 155p. 22cm. Bibl. 64-19633 3.95
1. Catholic Church—Relations—Protestant churches. 2. Protestant churches—Relations—Catholic Church. I. Durgin, Lawrence L. II. Title.

WORLD Council of Churches. Commission on Faith and Order. 280
The church in the purpose of God; an introduction to the work of the Commission on Faith and Order of the World Council of Churches, in preparation for the Third World Conference on Faith and Order to be held at Lund, Sweden, in 1952. Oliver S. Tomkins, secretary to the commission. New York [1951] 118 p. 21 cm. Bibliography: p. 102-100. [BX6.W775F3] 51-36438
1. Christian union. I. Tomkins, Oliver S. II. Title.

ECUMENISM Research Agency. 280'.025'73
The state of the churches in the U.S.A., 1973, as shown in their own official yearbooks : a study resource / by Ecumenism Research Agency. Sun City, Ariz. : The Agency, [1973] 24 p. ; 23 cm. [BR516.5.E28 1973] 75-311308
1. Sects—United States—Directories. 2. United States—Religion—1945- I. Title.

ROMAN Catholic/Presbyterian-Reformed Consultation. 280'.042
The unity we seek : a statement by the Roman Catholic/Presbyterian-Reformed Consultation / edited by Ernest L. Unterkoefler, Andrew Harsanyi. New York : Paulist Press, c1977. v, 135 p. : ill. ; 21 cm. "Background papers": p. 53-134. Includes bibliographical references. [BX1789.P73R65 1977] 77-74579 ISBN 0-8091-2027-5 pbk. : 4.95
1. Catholic Church—Relations—Presbyterian Church. 2. Catholic Church—Relations—Reformed Church. 3. Presbyterian Church—Relations—Catholic Church. 4. Reformed Church—Relations—Catholic Church. I. Unterkoefler, Ernest L. II. Harsanyi, Andrew. III. Title.

WOOLLEY, Davis C., 1908- 280'.072'2
Guide for writing the history of a church [by] Davis C. Woolley. Nashville, Broadman Press [1969] 60 p. 19 cm. [BR138.W6] 70-87728
1. Church history—Historiography. I. Title.

TOWNS, Elmer L. 280'.07'73
Is the day of the denomination dead? By Elmer L. Towns. Nashville, T. Nelson [1973] 160 p. illus. 21 cm. Includes bibliographical references. [BR516.5.T68] 73-6993 ISBN 0-8407-5052-8 5.95
1. Sects—United States. 2. United States—Religion. 3. Independent churches—United States. I. Title.

STEPHENSON, George Malcolm, 1883-1958. 280'.09174'397
The religious aspects of Swedish immigration. New York, Arno Press, 1969. viii, 542 p. 24 cm. (The American immigration collection) Reprint of the 1932 ed. Bibliography: p. 479-510. [BR563.S8S7 1969] 69-18790
1. Swedish Americans. 2. Sects—United States. I. Title.

JOHNSON, Pierce. 280'.092'2 B
Dying into life; a study in Christian life styles. Nashville, Abingdon Press [1972] 176 p. 22 cm. Includes bibliographical references. [BV4501.2.J57] 72-186828 ISBN 0-687-11279-6 4.95
1. Christian life—Methodist authors. 2. Christian biography. I. Title.

STEPHEN, James, Sir, 1789-1859. 280'.092'2 B
Essays in ecclesiastical biography. New ed. Freeport, N.Y., Books for Libraries Press [1973] p. (Essay index reprint series) Reprint of the 1875 ed. published by Longmans, Green, Reader, and Dyer, London. Contents.Contents.—Hildebrand.—Saint Francis of Assisi.—The founders of

Jesuitism.—Martin Luther.—The French Benedictines.—The Port-Royalists.—Richard Baxter.—The "evangelical" succession.—William Wilberforce.—The Clapham sect.—The historian of enthusiasm.—The epilogue. [BR1700.S8 1973] 73-5593 ISBN 0-518-10134-7
1. Christian biography. I. Title.

TUCKER, David M., 1937- 280'.092'2 B
Black pastors and leaders : Memphis, 1819-1972 / David M. Tucker. [Memphis] : Memphis State University Press, [1975] xi, 158 p. ; 22 cm. Includes bibliographical references and index. [BR563.N4T78] 75-1248 ISBN 0-87870-024-2 : 8.50
1. Afro-American clergy—Tennessee—Memphis. 2. Afro-Americans—Tennessee—Memphis. 3. Memphis—Biography. I. Title.

TWELVE modern apostles and their creeds, 280'.0922 by Gilbert K. Chesterton [and others] With an introd. by William Ralph Inge. Freeport, N.Y., Books for Libraries Press [1968] 209 p. 22 cm. (Essay index reprint series) Reprint of 1926 ed. Contents.Contents.—The future of Christianity, by W. R. Inge.—Why I am a Catholic, by G. K. Chesterton.—Why I am an Episcopalian, by C. L. Slattery.—Why I am a Presbyterian, by H. S. Coffin.—Why I am a Lutheran, by N. Soderblom.—Why I am a Baptist, by E. Y. Mullins.—Why I am a Quaker, by R. M. Jones.—Why I am a Methodist, by F. M. North.—Why I am a Congregationalist, by C. E. Jefferson.—Why I am a Unitarian, by S. M. Crothers.—Why I am a Mormon, by R. Smoot.—Why I am a Christian Scientist, by C. Smith.—Why I am an unbeliever, by C. Van Doren. [BR157.T8 1968] 68-16982
1. Sects. I. Chesterton, Gilbert Keith, 1874-1936. II. Inge, William Ralph, 1860-1954. III. Title: Modern apostles and their creeds.

WAGENKNECHT, Edward Charles, 1900- 280'.092'2 B
Ambassadors for Christ; seven American preachers [by] Edward Wagenknecht. New York, Oxford University Press, 1972. 310 p. illus. 22 cm. Contents.Contents.—Lyman Beecher: great by his religion.—William Ellery Channing: messages from the Spirit.—Henry Ward Beecher: God was in Christ.—Phillips Brooks: the Lord our God is a sun.—D. L. Moody: whosoever will may come.—Washington Gladden: where does the sky begin?—Lyman Abbott: the life of God in the soul of man.—Appendix: a postscript on the Beecher-Tilton scandal (p. [249]-254) Includes bibliographical references. [BV4208.U6W34 1972] 76-179361 8.50
1. Preaching—History—U.S. I. Title.

WATERBURY, Jared Bell, 1799-1876. 280'.092'2 B
Sketches eloquent preachers. Freeport, N.Y., Books for Libraries Press [1973] p. (Essay index reprint series) Reprint of the 1864 ed. published by American Tract Society, New York. Contents.Contents.—Dr. John M. Mason.—Dr. Archibald Alexander.—Rev. John Summerfield.—Rev. Sylvester Larned.—Dr. Asahel Nettleton.—Dr. Lyman Beecher.—Dr. Henry B. Bascom.—Dr. Edward Payson.—Dr. Edward Dorr Griffin.—Dr. Robert Hall.—Dr. Thomas Chalmers.—Rev. Henry Melvill.—Rev. Rowland Hill.—Rev. Legh Richmond.—Dr. Timothy Dwight.—Rev. Jonathan Edwards.—Rev. George Whitefield—Rev. Richard Baxter.—Rev. John Bunyan.—Rev. James Saurin.—John Baptist Massillon.—Martin Luther.—The Apostle Paul. [BR1700.W35 1973] 73-3394 ISBN 0-518-10138-X
1. Christian biography. 2. Clergy. I. Title.

WIERSBE, Warren W. 280'.092'2 B
Walking with the giants : a minister's guide to good reading and great preaching / Warren Wiersbe. Grand Rapids : Baker Book House, c1976. 289 p. : ports. ; 24 cm. Includes bibliographies and index. [BR1700.2.W49] 76-22989 ISBN 0-8010-9578-6 : 7.95
1. Clergy—Biography. 2. Preaching—History—Bibliography. 3. Pastoral theology—Bibliography. I. Title.

WILLIAMS, Ethel L. 280'.092'2 B
Biographical directory of Negro ministers / by Ethel L. Williams. 3d ed. Boston : G. K. Hall, 1975. p. cm. Includes index. Bibliography: p. [BR563.N4W5 1975] 74-34109 ISBN 0-8161-1183-9 lib.bdg. : 28.00
1. Negro clergy—United States—Biography—Dictionaries. I. Title.

THOMAS, Abraham Vazhayil, 1934- 280'.0954
Christians in secular India. Rutherford, Fairleigh Dickinson University Press [1974] 246 p. 25 cm. Bibliography: p. 229-241. [BR1155.T46] 72-420 ISBN 0-8386-1021-8
1. Christians in India. 2. Church and state in India. I. Title.

HOHENSEE, Donald, 1939- 280'.0967'572
Church growth in Burundi / by Donald Hohensee. South Pasadena, Calif. : William Carey Library, c1977. vi, 153 p. : ill. ; 22 cm. Includes index. Bibliography: p. [145]-151. [BR1443.B86H64] 76-54342 ISBN 0-87808-316-2 pbk. : 4.95
1. Sects—Burundi. 2. Church growth—Burundi. I. Title.

WISHLADE, R. L. 280.096897
Sectarianism in southern Nyasaland. New York, Pub. for the Intl. African Inst. by Oxford [c.]1965. 162p. illus., map. 23cm. Bibl. [BR1443.N9W5] 65-5669 5.20
1. Sects—Nyasaland. 2. Nyasaland—Church history. I. International African Institute. II. Title.

WISHLADE, R L 280.096897
Sectarianism in southern Nyassland [by] R. L. Wishlade. London, New York, Published for the International African Institute by the Oxford University Press, 1965. 162 p. illus., map. 28 cm. Bibliography: p. 157-159. [BR1443.N9W5] 65-5669
1. Sects — Nyassaland. 2. Nyassland — Church history. I. International African Institute. II. Title.

BACKMAN, Milton Vaughn. 280'.0973
Christian churches of America : origins and beliefs / Milton V. Backman, Jr. Provo, Utah : Brigham Young University Press, [1976] xvii, 230 p. : ill. ; 23 cm. Includes index. Bibliography: p. 215-219. [BR516.5.B33] 75-30772 ISBN 0-8425-0028-6 : 11.95 ISBN 0-8425-0029-4 pbk. : 7.95
1. Sects—Religion. 2. United States—Religion. I. Title.

CONTINENTAL pietism and early American Christianity / 280'.0973 edited by F. Ernest Stoeffler. Grand Rapids : Eerdmans, c1976. 276 p. ; 21 cm. Includes bibliographies and index. [BR1652.U6C66] 75-46511 ISBN 0-8028-1641-X pbk. : 4.50
1. Pietism—United States—Addresses, essays, lectures. 2. Sects—United States—Addresses, essays, lectures. I. Stoeffler, F. Ernest.

DENOMINATIONALISM / 280'.0973 edited by Russell E. Richey. Nashville : Abingdon, c1977. 288 p. ; 22 cm. [BR516.5.D45] 76-49103 ISBN 0-687-10469-6 : 15.95 ISBN 0-687-10470-X pbk. : 6.95
1. Sects—United States—Addresses, essays, lectures. I. Richey, Russell E.

DENOMINATIONALISM / 280'.0973 edited by Russell E. Richey. Nashville : Abingdon, c1977. 288 p. ; 22 cm. [BR516.5.D45] 76-49103 ISBN 0-687-10469-6 : 15.95 ISBN 0-687-10470-X pbk. : 6.95
1. Sects—United States—Addresses, essays, lectures. I. Richey, Russell E.

FLOOD, Robert. 280'.0973
America, God shed His grace on thee / Robert Flood ; illustrated by Tom Fawell. Chicago : Moody Press, c1975. 192 p. : ill. ; 29 cm. Traces the growth of christianity throughout the history of the United States. [BR515.F56] 76-356230 ISBN 0-8024-0208-9 : 9.95
1. United States—Religion—Juvenile literature. 2. Evangelicalism—United States—Juvenile literature. 3. United States—History—Juvenile literature. I. Fawell, Tom. II. Title.

GILMORE, Jan, comp. 280'.0973
That old-time religion; the humor, reverence, and joy of American religion in an earlier time, with just a touch of nostalgia. Edited by Jan Gilmore and Ginny Jacoby. [Kansas City, Mo.] Hallmark Editions [1972] 61 p. illus. 20 cm. [BR515.G53] 77-179715 ISBN 0-87529-259-3 2.50
1. United States—Religion. 2. Revivals—United States. I. Jacoby, Ginny, joint comp. II. Title.

JOHNSON, Douglas W., 1934- 280'.0973
Churches & church membership in the United States: an enumeration by region, state, and county; 1971 [by] Douglas W. Johnson, Paul R. Picard [and] Bernard Quinn. Washington, Glenmary Research Center [1974] xiv, 237 p. maps (1 fold. in pocket) 29 cm. [BR526.J64] 73-94224 ISBN 0-914422-01-4 15.00
1. Church statistics—United States. I. Picard, Paul R., joint author. II. Quinn, Bernard, 1928- joint author. III. Title.

JUDAH, J. Stillson. 280'.0973
The history and philosophy of the metaphysical movements in America, by J. Stillson Judah. Philadelphia, Westminster Press [1967] 317 p. 24 cm. Bibliographical footnotes. [BR516.J8] 67-11672
1. Sects—United States. I. Title.

MARTIN, Walter Ralston, 1928- 280'.0973
The kingdom of the cults; an analysis of the major cult systems in the present Christian era, by Walter R. Martin. [Rev. ed.] Minneapolis, Bethany Fellowship [1968] 443 p. 23 cm. Bibliography: p. 435-440. [BR516.5.M283 1968] 70-192
1. Sects—U.S. I. Title.

MEAD, Frank Spencer, 1898- 280.0973
Handbook of denominations in the United States [by] Frank S. Mead. New 4th ed. New York, Abingdon Press [1965] 271 p. 24 cm. Bibliography: p. 246-256. [BR516.5.M38 1965] 65-21980
1. Sects—United States. I. Title. II. Title: Denominations in the United States.

MEAD, Frank Spencer, 1898- 280'.0973
Handbook of denominations in the United States [by] Frank S. Mead. New 5th ed. Nashville, Abingdon Press [1970] 265 p. 24 cm. Bibliography: p. 235-245. [BR516.5.M38 1970] 70-109675 3.95
1. Sects—U.S. I. Title. II. Title: Denominations in the United States.

RELIGIOUS denominations in the United States, their past history, present condition, and doctrines, accurately set forth in fifty-three ... articles written by eminent clerical and lay authors ... together with complete and well-digested statistics. To which is added a historical summary of religious denominations in England and Scotland. 280'.0973 New York : AMS Press, 1975. 656, 208 p., [24] leaves of plates : ill. ; 24 cm. (Communal societies in America) The first section is a revision of He pasa ekklesia, compiled by I. D. Rupp and published in 1844. The second section (which has special t.p.: History of religious denominations in England and Scotland) is apparently an abridgment of Cyclopaedia of religious denominations, published in 1853 by J. J. Griffin, London. Reprint of the 1861 ed. published by C. Desilver, Philadelphia. [BR516.5.R46 1975] 72-2943 ISBN 0-404-10709-5 : 67.50
1. Sects—United States. 2. Church statistics—United States. 3. Sects—Great Britain. I. Rupp, Israel Daniel, 1803-1878, ed. He pasa ekklesia. II. Desilver, Charles, firm, Philadelphia. III. Cyclopaedia of religious denominations. IV. Title: History of religious denominations in England and Scotland.

ROSTEN, Leo Calvin, 1908- comp. 280'.0973
Religions of America : ferment and faith in an age of crisis : a new guide and almanac / edited with extensive comments and essays, by Leo Rosten. New York : Simon and Schuster, [1975] 672 p. ; 22 cm. Expanded version of the work first published in 1955 under title: A guide to the religions of America; and in 1963 under title: Religions in America. Includes bibliographical references and index. [BR516.5.R67 1975] 74-11703 ISBN 0-671-21970-7 : 12.95 ISBN 0-671-21971-5 pbk. : 5.95 pbk.
1. Sects—United States. 2. United States—Religion. I. Title.

SMITH, Hannah Whitall, 1832-1911. 280'.0973
Religious fanaticism : extracts from the papers of Hannah Whitall Smith / edited with an introd. by Ray Strachey, consisting of an account of the author of these papers, and of the times in which she lived, together with a description of the curious religious sects and communities of America during the early and middle years of the nineteenth century. New York : AMS Press, 1976. p. cm. (Communal societies in America) Reprint of the 1928 ed. published by Faber & Gwyer, London. Includes index. [BR516.5.S55 1976] 72-8252 ISBN 0-404-11005-3 : 16.50
1. Smith, Hannah Whitall, 1832-1911. 2. Sects—United States. 3. Fanaticism. I. Title.

STARKES, M. Thomas. 280'.0973
Confronting popular cults [by] M. Thomas Starkes. Nashville, Broadman Press [1972] 122 p. 19 cm. Includes bibliographical references. [BR516.5.S74] 72-79177 ISBN 0-8054-1805-9
1. Sects—United States. I. Title.

STEPHENSON, George Malcolm, 1883-1958. 280'.0973
The religious aspects of Swedish immigration; a study of immigrant churches. Minneapolis, University of Minnesota Press, 1932. [New York, AMS Press, 1972] viii, 542 p. illus. 23 cm. Bibliography: p. 479-510. [BR563.S8S7 1972] 71-137294 ISBN 0-404-06257-1
1. Swedish Americans. 2. Sects—United States. I. Title.

WHALEN, William Joseph 280.0973
Separated brethren; a survey of non-Catholic Christian denominations in the United States [by] William J. Whalen. 2d rev. ed. Milwaukee, Bruce [1966] x, 288p. illus. 22cm. Bibl. [BR516.5.W44 1966] 66-15845 1.95 pap.,
1. Sects—U. S. I. Title.

WHALEN, William Joseph. 280'.0973
Separated brethren; a survey of Protestant, Anglican, Orthodox, Old Catholic, and other denominations in the United States, by William J. Whalen. Rev. and enl. Huntington, Ind., Our Sunday visitor [1972] 302 p. 21 cm. Bibliography: p. 293-294. [BR516.5.W44 1972] 70-177998
1. Sects—U.S. I. Title.

FELLOWSHIP of Solanco Churches. 280'.09748'15
Churches of today and yesterday in southern Lancaster County. Raymond L. Dunlap, editor, assisted by George E. Herbert [and] Richard G. Yates, Sr. [Lancaster? Pa., 1968] xvii, 204 p. illus., port. 24 cm. Bibliography: p. 192. [BR555.P4F4] 68-55934
1. Churches—Pennsylvania—Lancaster Co. 2. Lancaster Co., Pa.—History. I. Dunlap, Raymond L., ed. II. Herbert, George E., ed. III. Yates, Richard G., ed. IV. Title.

FREEMAN, Olga Samuelson. 280'.09795
A guide to early Oregon churches / by Olga Samuelson Freeman. Eugene, Or. : Freeman, 1976. 88 p. : ill. ; 22 cm. Bibliography: p. 86-88. [BR555.O7F73] 76-372452 5.50
1. Churches—Oregon. 2. Oregon—Church history. I. Title.

FREEMAN, Olga Samuelson. 280'.09795
A guide to early Oregon churches / by Olga Samuelson Freeman. Eugene, Or. : Freeman, 1976. 88 p. : ill. ; 22 cm. Bibliography: p. 86-88. [BR555.O7F73] 76-372452 5.50
1. Churches—Oregon. 2. Oregon—Church history. I. Title.

VAN SOMMERS, Tess 280.0994
Religions in Australia; the Pix series extended to 41 beliefs. Adelaide, Rigby [San Francisco, Tri-Ocean, c.1966] 248p. illus. 25cm. Articles orig. pub. in Pix. [BR1480.V3] 65-191376 6.45 bds.,
1. Sects—Australia. I. Title.

ALL-AFRICA Church Conference, Ibadan, Nigeria, 1958. 280.1
The church in changing Africa; report. New York, International Missionary Council [1958] 106p. 23cm. [BX6.A46A3 1958c] 58-42577
1. Christian union—Africa—Congresses. 2. Missions—Africa—Congresses. I. Title.

ASMUSSEN, Hans, 1898- 280.1
The Unfinished Reformation [by] Hans Asmussen [and others] Translated by Robert J. Olsen. Foreword to the English ed. by John P. Dolan. Notre Dame, Ind., Fides Publishers Association [1961] 213 p. 21 cm. Translation of Katholische Reformation. Includes bibliography. [BX4818.3.K313] 61-10368
1. Lutheran Church — Relations — Catholic Church. 2. Catholic Church — Relations — Lutheran Church. I. Title.

BAINTON, Roland Herbert, 1894- 280.1
Christian unity and religion in New England. Boston, Beacon Press [1964] 294 p. illus., maps. 21 cm. (His Collected papers in church history, ser. 3) Bibliography: p. [283]-289. [BR530.B34] 64-13530
1. New England—Church history. 2. Christian union—New England. 3. Sects—New England. I. Title.

BAINTON, Roland Herbert, 1894- 280.1
Christian unity and religion in New England. Boston, Beacon [c.1964] 294p. illus., maps. 21cm. (His Collected papers in church hist., ser. 3) Bibl. 64-13530 6.00
1. New England—Church history. 2. Christian union—New England. 3. Sects—New England. I. Title.

BAUM, Gregory, 1923- 280.1
The Catholic quest for Christian unity. Glen Rock, N. J., Paulist [1965, c.1962] 252p. 18cm. (Deus bks.) First ed. pub. in 1962 under title: Progress and perspectives. Bibl. [BX1785.B28] 65-4087 .95 pap.,
1. Catholic Church—Relations. 2. Christian union—Catholic Church. 3. Ecumenical movement. I. Title.

BAUM, Gregory, 1923- 280.1
Ecumenical theology today. Glen Rock, N.J., Paulist Press [1964] 256 p. 19 cm. (An Original Deus book) Bibliography: p. 245-256. [BX9.B34] 64-24514
1. Christian unity — Addresses, essays, lectures. I. Title.

BAUM, Gregory, 1923- ed. 280.1
Ecumenical theology today. no. 2 Glen Rock, N. J., Paulist [1967] v. 19cm. (Orig. Deus bk.) No. 2 Entitled Ecumenical theology. [BX9.B34] 64-24514 1.95 pap.,
1. Christian unity—Addresses,essays, lectures. I. Title.

BAUM, Gregory, 1923- 280.1
Progress and perspectives; the Catholic quest for Christian unity. New York, Sheed [c.1962] 245p. 22cm. Bibl. 62-15283 3.95
1. Catholic Church—Relations. 2. Christian union. 3. Ecumenical movement. I. Title.

BAUM, Gregory, 1923- 280.1
That they may be one; a study of papal doctrine (Leo xiii-Pius xii) Westminster, Md., Newman Press, 1958. 181p. 23cm. Includes bibliography. [BX1785.B3 1958] 58-13633
1. Catholic Church—Relations. 2. Ecumenical movement. I. Title.

BEA, Augustin, 280.1
Cardinal,1881-
Unity in freedom; reflections on the human family. New York, Harper & Row [1964] v. 272 p. 22 cm. (Religious perspectives, v. 11) Bibliographical footnotes. [BX8.2.B36] 64-20199
1. Christian union. I. Title. II. Series.

BEA, Augustin Cardinal, 280.1
1881-
Unity in freedom; reflections on the human family. New York, Harper [c.1964] v, 272p. 22cm. (Religious perspectives, v.11) Bibl. 64-20199 5.00
1. Christian union. I. Title. II. Series.

BEA, Augustin, Cardinal, 280.1
1881-
The unity of Christians. Edited by Bernard Leeming. Introd. by Gerald P. O'Hara. [New York] Herder and Herder [1963] 231 p. 23 cm. Includes bibliography. [BX8.2.B37] 63-11307
1. Christian union—Addresses, essays, lectures. I. Title.

BEAVER, Robert Pierce, 280.1
1906-
Ecumenical beginnings in Protestant world mission; a history of comity. New York, Nelson [1962] 356 p. 22 cm. Includes bibliographies. [BV2120.B4] 62-19597
1. Interdenominational cooperation. 2. Protestant churches — Missions. I. Title.

BEAVER, Robert Pierce, 280.1
1906-
Ecumenical beginnings in Protestant world mission; a history of comity. New York, Nelson [c.1962] 356p. 22cm. Bibl. 62-19597 5.00
1. Interdenominational cooperation. 2. Protestant churches—Missions. I. Title.

BELL, George Kennedy Allen, 280.1
Bp. of Chichester, 1883- ed.
Documents on Christian unity; a selection from the first and second series, 1920-30. London, New York, Oxford University Press, 1955. xi, 271p. 19cm. [BX8.A1B4 1st-2d series] 56-1457
1. Christian union. I. Title.

BELL, George Kennedy Allen, 280.1
Bp. of Chichester, 1883-
The kingship of Christ the story of the World Council of Churches. [Harmondsworth, Middlesex, Baltimore] Penguin Books [1954] 181p. illus. 18cm. (A Penguin special, S161) [BX6.W78B4] 55-849
1. World Council of Churches. 2. Ecumenical movement—Hist. I. Title.

BERGENDOFF, Conrad John 280.1
Immanuel, 1895-
The one holy catholic apostolic church. Rock Island, Ill., Augustana Book Concern [1954] 99p. 20cm. (The Hoover lectures, 1953) [BV600.B42] 54-35839
1. Church—Marks. I. Title.

BEVAN, R J W ed. 280.1
The churches and Christian unity. London, New York, Oxford University Press, 1963. xvii, 263 p. illus. 19 cm. Bibliographical footnotes. [BX8.2.B4] 63-4426
1. Christian union — Addresses, essays, lectures. I. Title.

BEVAN, R. J. W. ed. 280.1
The churches and Christian unity. New York, Oxford [c.]1963. xvii, 263p. illus. 19cm. Bibl. 63-4426 4.00
1. Christian union—Addresses, essays, lectures. I. Title.

BILHEIMER, Robert S 1917- 280.1
The quest for Christian unity. New York, Association Press [1952] 181p. 20cm. (A Haddam House book) [BR516.B47] 52-14564
1. U. S.—Church history. 2. Sects—U. S. 3. Christian union—U. S. I. Title.

BLAKEMORE, William Barnett, 280.1
1912-
The challenge of Christian unity. St. Louis. Bethany [1964, c.1963] 144p. 21cm. (William Henry Hoover lects. on Christian unity for 1961) 64-12008 3.00
1. Ecumenical movement—Addresses, essays, lectures. I. Title. II. Series: Disciples Divinity House, University of Chicago. Hoover lectures on Christian unity, 1961

BOSC, Jean 280.1
The Catholic Protestant dialogue. [by] Jean Bosc, Jean Guitton, Jean Danielou. Foreword by Gustave Weigel; pref. by Jacques Madaule. Tr. [from French] by Robert J. Olsen. Baltimore, Helicon Press, [c.]1960. 138p. Bibl. 60-15632 3.50 bds.,
1. Catholic Church—Doctrinal and controversial works—Debates, etc. I. Title.

BOYER, Charles, 1884- 280.1
Christian unity. Translated from the Italian by Jill Dean. [1st ed.] New York, Hawthorn Books [1962] 131p. 21cm. (The Twentieth century encyclopedia of Catholicism, v. 138. Section 14: Outside the church) 'A revision of the book originally published ... under the title Unita cristianae movimento ecumenico.' Includes bibliographies. [BX1784.B613] 62-12931
1. Christian union. 2. Catholic Church—Relations. I. Title.

BOYER, Charles Emile George 280.1
Augustin 1884-
Christian unity. Tr. from Italian by Jill Dean. New York, Hawthorn [c.1962] 131p. 21cm. (Twentieth century ency. of Catholicism. v. 138. Sect. 14: Outside the church) Bibl. 62-12931 3.50 bds.,
1. Christian union. 2. Catholic Church—Relations. I. Title.

BRADSHAW, Marion John, 280.1
1886-
Free churches and Christian unity; a critical view of the ecumenical movement and the World Council of Churches. Boston, Beacon Press [1954] 225p. 22cm. [BX8.B68] 54-6659
1. Ecumenical movement. 2. World Council of Churches. I. Title.

BUNDY, Edgar C 280.1
Collectivism in the churches; a documented account of the political activities of the Federal, National, and World Councils of Churches. Wheaton, Ill., Church League of America, 1958. 354p. 22cm. Includes bibliography. [BR516.B82] [BR516.B82] 280.6273 57- 57-13355
1. Protestant churches—U. S. 2. Federal Council of the Churches of Christ in America. 3. National Council of the Churches of Christ in the United States of America. 4. World Council of Churches. 5. Socialism in the U. S. I. Title.

CATE, William B. 1924- 280.1
The ecumenical scandal on Main Street [by] William B. Cate. New York, Association Press [1965] 126 p. 20 cm. Bibliography: p. 125-126. [BX8.2.C28] 65-11092
1. Christian union. 2. Interdenominational cooperation. I. Title.

CATE, William B., 1924- 280.1
The ecumenical scandal on Main Street. New York, Association [c.1965] 126p. 20cm. Bibl. [BX8.2.C28] 65-11092 3.50
1. Christian union. 2. Interdenominational cooperation. I. Title.

CAVERT, Samuel McCrea, 280.1
1888-
On the road to Christian unity; an appraisal of the ecumenical movement. [1st ed.] New York, Harper [1961] 192p. 22cm. Includes bibliography. [BX8.2.C3] 61-12823
1. Ecumenical movement. I. Title.

CHAMPION, L. G. 280.1
Baptists and unity. [Dist. New York, Morehouse, c.1962] 93p. 20cm. (Star bks. on reunion) 1.00 pap.,
I. Title.

COOPERATION without 280.1
compromise; a history of the National Association of Evangelicals. Grand Rapids, Eerdmans, 1956. 220p. 23cm. [BR513.M8] 280.6273 56-12876
I. Murch, James DeForest, 1892- II. National Association of Evangelicals.

CULLMANN. OSCAR 280.1
Message to Catholics and Protestants. Translated [from the German] by Joseph A. Burgess. Grand Rapids, Eerdmans [1959] 57p. 20cm. 59-14590 1.50
1. Protestant churches—Relations—Catholic Church. 2. Catholic Church—Relations—Protestant churches. I. Title.

DANA, Ellis Huntington. 280.1
Protestant strategy in the making; modern Protestantism, strugling for greater influence agaainst the swirling tides of secular ideas and methods in a dangerous world, faces an imperative need for a more dynamic counciliar approach. [Boston, Distributed by Beacon Press, 1950?] 121 p illus., ports. 23 cm. Cover title. [BX8.D25] 54-29661
1. Christian union. 2. Protestant churches—U.S. I. Title.

DAVIES, Rupert Eric, 1909- 280.1
Methodists and unity. London, A. R. Mowbray; New York, Morehouse-Barlow [c1962] 100 p. 20 cm. (Star books on reunion) [BX8.2.D27] 63-1269
1. Christian union — Methodist Church. I. Title.

DAVIES, Rupert Eric, 1909- 280.1
Methodists and unity. London. A. R. Mowbray; New York, Morehouse [c.1962] 100p. 20cm. (Star bks. on reunion) 63-1269 1.00 pap.,
1. Christian union—Methodist Church. I. Title.

DAY, Peter. 280.1
Strangers no longer. Foreword by Frederick C. Grant. New York, Morehouse-Barlow Co., 1962. 174 p. 21 cm. [BX8.2.D3] 62-20516
1. Christian union. 2. Kingdom of God. I. Title.

DUFF, Edward. 280.1
The social thought of the World Council of Churches. New York, Association Press [1956] xii, 339p. diagr. 23cm. Bibliography: p. 321-331. [BX6.W78D8] 56-10665
1. World Council of Churches. 2. Church and social problems. I. Title.

DUMONT, Christophe Jean 280.1
Approaches to Christian unity; doctrine and prayer. Translated [from the French] with an introd. by Henry St. John. Baltimore, Helicon Press [1959] ix, 226p. 23cm. 59-65038 4.50 bds.,
1. Ecumenical movement. 2. Christian union. 3. Catholic Church—Relations. 4. Church—Unity. I. Title.

ENGLERT, Clement Cyril, 280.1
1910-
Catholics and Orthodox: can they unite? New York, Paulist Pr. [c.1961] 127p. (Deus bks.) Bibl. 61-16662 .75 pap.,
1. Catholic Church—Relations—Orthodox Eastern Church. 2. Orthodox Eastern Church—Relations—Catholic Church. I. Title.

FLETCHER, Grace (Nies) 280.1
The whole world's in His hand. New York, Dutton [c.]1962. 219p. illus. 21cm. 62-18690 4.50
1. World Council of Churches. 3d Assembly, Delhi, 1961. 2. Christianity—20th cent. I. Title.

GARRISON, Winfred Ernest, 280.1
1874-
Christian unity and Disciples of Christ. St. Louis. Bethany Press [1955] 286p. 23cm. [BX8.G33] 55-9664
1. Ecumenical movement. 2. Disciples of Christ—Relations. I. Title.

GARRISON, Winfred Ernest, 280.1
1874-
The quest and character of a united church. Nashville, Abingdon Press [1957] 238p. 22cm. [BX6.5.G3] 57-9785
1. Christian union—Hist. 2. Ecumenical movement. I. Title.

GLOVER, Christopher. 280.1
The church for the new age; a disertation on church unity. With forewords by Arthur H. Howe Browne and Walter J. Carey. [1st ed.] New York, Exposition Press [1956] 205p. 21cm. (An Exposition-testament book) [BX8.G64] 55-12126
1. Church—Unity. 2. Christian union. 3. Episcopacy. I. Title.

GOOD, James 280.1
The Church of England and the ecumenical movement. London, Cork Univ. Pr.[dist. Mystic, Conn., Verry, 1964] 163p. 23cm. 63-265 4.00 bds.,
1. Christian union—Anglican Communion. I. Title.

GOODALL, Norman 280.1
The ecumenical movement. what it is and what it does. New York, Oxford [c.]1961[ ] 240p. illus. Bibl. 61-19171 4.50
1. Ecumenical movement. I. Title.

GRAY, Albert Frederick 280.1
The nature of the church. Anderson, Ind., Warner Press [dist. Gospel Trumpet Press] [c.1960] 80p. 19cm. 60-10185 1.00 pap.,
1. Church. 2. Christian union. I. Title.

GUITTON, Jean 280.1
Unity through love, essays in ecumenism. [Tr. from French by Brian Thompson. New York] Herder & Herder [c.1964] 152p. 21cm. Bibl. 64-19728 3.95
1. Christian union—Addresses, essays, lectures. I. Title.

GUITTON, Jean. 280.1
Unity through love, essays in ecumenism Translated by Brian Thompson. New York] Herder and Herder [1964] 152 p. 21 cm. Translation of Vers l'unite dans l'amour. Bibliographical footnotes. [BX8.2.G813] 64-19728
1. Christian union — Addresses, essays, lectures. I. Title.

HANAHOE, Edward Francis, 280.1
1913- ed.
One fold; essays and documents to commemorate the golden jubilee of the Chair of Unity Octave, 1908-1958. Edited by Edward F. Hanahoe [and] Titus F. Cranny. Graymoor, Garrison, N. Y., Chair of Unity Apostolate, Franciscan Friars of the Atonement, 1959. 384p. illus. 22cm. Includes bibliography. [BX1786.H3] 50-15736
1. Paul James Francis, Father, 1863-1940. 2. Chair of Unity Octave. 3. Friars of the Atonement. I. Cranny, Titus F., 1921- joint ed. II. Title.

HEBERT, Arthur Gabriel, 280.1
1886-
Apostle and bishop, a study of the Gospel, the ministry and the church-community. New York, Seabury [c.1963] 159p. 23cm. 4.00
I. Title.

HEUFELDER, Emmanuel Maria, 280.1
1898- ed.
In the hope of His coming; studies in Christian unity. Translated by Otto M. Knab. Notre Dame, Ind., Fides Publishers [c1964] 261 p. 21 cm. "A translation of the series Das[s] alle eins seien, published from 1959 to 1962." Bibliographical footnotes. [BX8.2.A1H43] 64-23520
1. Christian union — Addresses, essays, lectures. I. Title.

HEUFELDER, Emmanuel Maria, 280.1
1898- ed.
In the hope of His coming; studies in Christian unity. Tr. [from German] by Otto M. Knab. Notre Dame, Ind., Fides [c.1964] 261p. 21cm. Bibl. [BX8.2.A1H43] 64-23520 4.95
1. Christian union—Addresses, essays, lectures. I. Title.

HODGSON, Leonard, 1889- 280.1
The ecumenical movement; three lectures given at the University of the South, Sewanee, Tenn., in March, 1950. Sewanee, University Press, University of the South, 1951. 50 p. 24 cm. Errata slip inserted. [BX8.H6] A 52
1. Ecumenical movement. 2. World Council of Churches. I. Title.

HOPE, Norman Victor, 1908- 280.1
One Christ, one world, one church; a short introduction to the ecumenical movement. Philadelphia, Church Historical Society [1953] 96p. 23cm. (Church Historical Society Publication no. 37) Includes bibliography. [BX8.H67] 53-3953
1. Ecumenical movement. I. Title.

HUNT, George Laird. 280.1
A guide to Christian unity. St. Louis, Bethany Press [1958] 96p. 22cm. Includes bibliography. [BX8.H85] 58-10258
1. Christian union—Study and teaching. 2. North American Conference on Faith and Order, Oberlin College, 1957. I. Title. II. Title: Christian unity.

HUNT, George Laird, ed. 280.1
Where we are in church union; a report on the present accomplishments of the Consultation on Church Union, edited by George L. Hunt and Paul A. Crow, Jr. New York, Association Press [1965] 126 p. 16 cm. (A Reflection book) Includes bibliographies. [BX6.C63H8] 65-11099
1. Christian union — U.S. 2. Consultation on Church Union. I. Crow, Paul A., joint ed. II. Title.

JACKSON, Joseph Harrison, 280.1
1900-
Many but one; the ecumenics of charity [by] J. H. Jackson. New York, Sheed and Ward [1964] xii, 211 p. 22 cm. Bibliography: p. 203-2-5. [BX8.2.J3] 64-19899
1. Christian union. I. Title.

JACKSON, Joseph Harrison. 280.1
1900-
Many but one; the ecumenics of charity New

York, Sheed & Ward [c.1964] xii, 211p. 22cm. Bibl. 64-19899 4.50
1. Christian union. I. Title.

JOHNSON, Olive L 280.1
The church in today's world (a revision of One church for one world); a course for junior high school groups in vacation church schools [by] Olive L. Johnson and Frances Nall. Teacher's book. New York, Published for the Cooperative Publication Assoication by Abingdon Press [c1959] 128p. illus. 23cm. (The Cooperative series: vacation church school texts. Includes bibliography. [BV1585] 60-785
1. Vacation schools, Religious—Text-books. 2. Christian union—Study and teaching. I. Nall, Frances (Mahaffle) 1902- joint author. II. Title.

JOHNSON. OLIVE L. 280.1
The church in today's world (a revision of One church for one world): a course for junior high school groups in vacation church schools [by] Olive L. Johnson and Frances Nall. Teacher's book. New York. Published for the Cooperative Publication Association by Abingdon Press [c.1959] 128p. illus. 23cm. (The Cooperative series: vacation church school texts) (5p. bibl.) 60-7850 1.00 pap.,
1. Vacation schools. Religious—Text-books. 2. Christian union—Study and teaching. I. Nall, Frances (Mahaffie) joint author. II. Title.

KEAN, Charles Duell, 1910- 280.1
Ecumenical encounters in Christian unity; background information. New York, Seabury Press [c1963] 80 p. 21 cm. Bibliographical footnotes. [BX8.2K4] 63-25955
1. Ecumenical movement. I. Title.

KEAN, Charles Duell, 1910- 280.1
Ecumenical encounters in Christian unity; background information. New York, Seabury [c.1963] 80p. 21cm. Bibl. 63-25955 .95 pap.,
1. Ecumenical movement. I. Title.

KEAN. CHARLES DUELL, 1910- 280.1
The road to reunion. Greenwich, Conn., Seabury Press, 1958. 145p. 20cm. [BX5926.K4] 58-5507
1. Protestant Episcopal Church in the U. S. A.—Relations. 2. Ecumenical movement. I. Title.

KENNEDY, James William, 1905- 280.1
No darkness at all; a report and study guide on the Third Assembly of the World Council of Churches. New Delhi, India, November 19-December 5, 1961. Introd. by Roswell P. Barnes. St. Louis, Bethany [c.1962] 128p. 22cm.illus. Bibl. 62-12917 1.50 pap.,
1. World Council of Churches. 3d Assembly, Delhi, 1961. I. Title.

KIK, Jacob Marcellus, 1903- 280.1
Ecumenism and the evangelical. Philadelphia, Presbyterian and Reformed Pub. Co., 1958 [c1957] 152p. 21cm. [BX8.K5] 57-12171
1. Ecumenical movement. 2. Church. 3. Church—Unity. 4. Evangelicalism. I. Title.

KNOFF, Gerald E. 280.1
Churches working together: an elective unit for adults. With leader's guide by Frank R.Snavely and Bob J. Golter. The Methodist Publishing House 48p. 23cm. (bibl. .50 pap.,
I. Title.

KUNG, Hans, 1928- 280.1
The Council and reunion. Translated by Cecily Hastings. London, New York, Sheed and Ward [1961] 307p. 18cm. (Stagbooks) [BX1784.K813 1961] 62-3233
1. Catholic Church—Relations. 2. Christian union. 3. Vatican Council, 2d. I. Title.

LEE, Robert 280.1
The social sources of church unity; an interpretation of unitive movements in American Protestantism. Nashville, Abingdon Press [c.1960] 238p. 23cm. (6p. bibl. and bibl. footnotes) 60-9199 4.50
1. Christian union—U.S. 2. Sects—U.S. 3. Church and social problems—U.S. I. Title.

LEEMING, Bernard. 280.1
The churches and the church; a study of ecumenism developed from the Lauriston lectures for 1957. London, Darton, Longman & Todd [1960] [dist.] Westminster, Md. Newman Press x, 340p. 23cm. Bibl.: p.312-324 60-14819 6.50
1. Catholic Church—Relations. 2. Ecumenical movement. I. Title.

LLOYD-JONES, D. Martyn 280.1
The basis of Christian unity: an exposition of John 17 and Ephesians 4. Grand Rapids, Mich., Eerdmans [1963, c.1962] 64p. 18cm. .50 pap.,
I. Title.

MCDONAGH, Enda 280.1
Roman Catholic and unity. London, A. R. Mowbray New York, Morehouse [c.1962] 98p. 20cm. (Star bks., on reunion) 63-594 1.00 pap.,
1. Christian union—Catholic Church. I. Title.

MCINTIRE, Carl, 1906- 280.1
Servants of apostasy. Collingswood, N. J., Christian Beacon Press, 1955. 414p. 22cm. [BX6.I63M33] 55-4958
1. International Council of Christian Churches. 2. World Council of Churches. 2d Assembly. Evanston, Ill., 1954. 3. Modernist-fundamentalist controversy. I. Title.

MACKIE, Robert C., ed. 280.1
The sufficiency of God; essays on the ecumenical hope in honor of W. A. Visser 't Hooft. Ed. by Robert C. Mackie, Charles C. West. Philadelphia, Westminster [c.1963] 240p. group ports. 23cm. Bibl. 64-10049 5.50
1. Visser 't Hooft, Willem Adolph, 1900- 2. Ecumenical movement—Addresses, essays, lectures. 3. Christian union — Addresses, essays, lecture. I. West, Charles C., joint ed. II. Title.

MCNEILL, John Thomas, 1885- 280.1
Unitive Protestantism; the ecumenical spirit and its persistent expression. [Rev. ed.] Richmond, Va., Knox [c.1964] 352p. 21cm. Bibl. 64-10527 4.50
1. Christian union. 2. Protestantism. I. Title.

MACY, Paul Griswold, 1888- 280.1
If it be of God; the story of the World Council of Churches. St. Louis, Bethany Press [1960] 191 p. 23 cm. Includes bibliography. [BX6.W78M28] 60-9918
1. Christian union—History. I. Title.

MARTY, Martin E., 1928- 280.1
Church unity and church mission. Grand Rapids, Mich., Eerdmans [c.1964] 139p. 22cm. Bibl. 63-17781 3.00
1. Christian union. I. Title.

MAXIMOS IV, Patriarch of Antioch 1878- ed. 280.1
The Eastern churches and Catholic unity. [Tr. from French by John Dingle, others] New York, Herder & Herder [c.1963] 236p. 21cm. Bibl. 63-11310 4.95
1. Christian union—Eastern churches. I. Title.

MILLER, Joseph Quinter. 280.1
Christian unity: its relevance to the community. [Strasburg, Va., Shenandoah Pub. House] 1957. 122p. 24cm. [BV625.M5] 57-31087
1. Interdenominational cooperation. 2. Ecumenical movement. 3. Local church councils. I. Title.

MILLER, Joseph Quinter. 280.1
Christian unity: its relevance to the community. [Strasburg, Va., Shenandoah Pub. House] 1957. 122p. 24cm. [BV625.M5] 57-31087
1. Interdenominational cooperation. 2. Ecumenical movement. 3. Local church councils. I. Title.

MILLER, Samuel Jefferson Thomas, 1919- 280.1
Cristobal Rojas y Spinola, cameralist and irenicist, 1626-1695 [by] Samuel J. T. Miller and John P. Spielman, Jr. Philadelphia, American Philosophical Society, 1962. 108p. 30cm. (Transactions of the American Philosophical Society, new ser., v. 52, pt. 5) Bibliography: p. 101-105. [Q11.P6 n.s., vol. 52, pt. 5] 62-21092
1. Spinola. Christoph Rojas de, Bp., 1626-1995. 2. Christian union—Hist. I. Spielman, John Philip, 1930- II. Title. III. Series: American Philosophical Society, Transactions, new ser., v. 52, pt. 5

MILLER, William A. 280.1
Some boast of Chariots. Tahlequah, Okla., Pan Press [c.1960] xi, 89p. 22cm. 60-6383 3.00; 2.50 pap.,
1. Christianity—Essence, genius, nature. I. Title.

MOONEYHAM, Walter Stanley, 1926- ed. 280.1
The dynamics of Christian unity; a symposium on the ecumenical movement. Grand Rapids, Zondervan Pub. House [1963] 116 p. 21 cm. Messages given at conferences on Christian unity sponsored by the National Association of Evangelicals. Bibliographical references: p. 114-116. [BX8.2A1M6] 63-19721
1. Ecumenical movement — Congresses. I. National Association of Evangelicals. II. Title.

MOONEYHAM, Walter Stanley, 1926- ed. 280.1
The dynamics of Christian unity; a symposium on the ecumenical movement. Grand Rapids, Mich., Zondervan [c.1963] 116p. 21cm. Bibl. 63-19721 2.50
1. Ecumenical movement—Congresses. 2. National Association of Evangelicals. I. Title.

MORRIS, William Sparkes, 1916- ed. 280.1
The unity we seek; lectures on the church and the churches. New York, Oxford University Press, 1963 [c1962] 150 p. 21 cm. [BX8.2.M6 1963] 63-13711
1. Church unity. 2. Church. I. Title.

MORRIS, William Sparkes, 1916- ed. 280.1
The unity we seek; lectures on the church and the churches. New York, Oxford, 1963[c.1962] 150p. 21cm. Bibl. 63-13711 1.75 pap.,
1. Church unity. 2. Church. I. Title.

MORRISON, Charles Clayton, 1874- 280.1
The unfinished Reformation. [1st ed.] New York, Harper [1953] 236p. 22cm. (The Hoover lectures, 1951) [BX8.M65] 52-11079
1. Ecumenical movement. I. Title.

MUDGE, Lewis Seymour 280.1
One church: Catholic and Reformed; toward a theology for ecumenical decision. Philadelphia, Westminster [1963] 96p. 20cm. 63-11561 1.75 pap.,
1. Ecumenical movement. I. Title.

MUDGE, Lewis Seymour. 280.1
One church: Catholic and Reformed; toward a theology for ecumenical decision. Philadelphia, Westminster Press [1963] 96 p. 20 cm. [BX8.2.M8] 63-11561
1. Ecumenical movement. I. Title.

NEILL, Stephen Charles, Bp. 280.1
Brothers of the faith. Nashville, Abingdon Press [c.1960[192p. 23cm. Includes bibliography. 60-9201 4.00
1. Ecumenical movement—Biog. I. Title.

NELSON, John Robert, 1920- 280.1
One Lord, one church. New York, Association Press [1958] 93p. 20cm. (World Christian books) [BX8N46] 58-11535
1. Ecumenical movement. 2. Christian union—Hist. 3. Church—Unity. I. Title.

NELSON, John Robert, 1920- 280.1
Overcoming Christian divisions. Rev. ed. of the World Christian book: One Lord, one church New York, Association [c.1962] 126p. 16cm. (Reflection bk.) 62-10267 .50 pap.,
1. Ecumenical movement. 2. Christian union—Hist. 3. Church—Unity. I. Title.

NEWBIGIN, James Edward Lesslie, Bp. 280.1
Is Christ divided? A plea for Christian unity in a revolutionary age. Grand Rapids, Mich., Eerdmans [c.1961] 41p. 61-10855 1.25 bds.,
1. Christian union. 2. Missions—Theory. I. Title.

NICHOLS, James Hastings, 1915- 280.1
Evanston, an interpretation. [1st ed.] New York, Harper [1954] 155p. 20cm. [BX6.W77 1954j] 54-12332
1. World Council of Churches. 2d Assembly, Evanston, Ill. I. Title.

NORTH American Conference on Faith and Order, Oberlin College. 1957. 280.1
The nature of the unity we seek; official report of the North American Conference on Faith and Order, September 3-10, 1957, Oberlin, Ohio. Edited by Paul S. Minear St Louis, Bethany Press [1958] 304p. 23cm. [BX6.N57A3 1957] 58-7477
1. Christian union— Congresses. I. Minear, Paul Sevier, 1906- ed. II. Title.

NORTH American Conference on Faith and Order, Oberlin College, 1957. 280.1
The nature of the unity we seek; official report of the North American Conference on Faith and Order, September 3-10, 1957, Oberlin, Ohio. Ed. by Paul S. Minear. St. Louis Bethany [1963, c.1958] 304p. 22cm. (Abbott Bks.) 1.75 pap.,
1. Christian union—Congresses. I. Minear, Paul Sevier, 1906- ed. II. Title.

O'NEILL, Charles A ed. 280.1
Ecumenism and Vatican II. Edited by Charles O'Neill. Essays by Bernard Cooke [and others] With a foreword by Vincent T. O'Keefe. Milwaukee, Bruce Pub. Co. [1964] xii, 146 p. 22 cm. Bibliographical footnotes. [BX830 1962.O5] 64-23892
1. Vatican Council, 2d. 2. Ecumenical movement. I. Cooke, Bernard. II. Title.

O'NEILL, Charles A., ed. 280.1
Ecumenism and Vatican II Essays by Bernard Cooke [others] Foreword by Vincent T O'Keefe. Milwaukee, Bruce [c.1964] xii, 146p. 22cm. Bibl. 64-23892 3.75
1. Vatican Council, 2d. 2. Ecumenical movement. I. Cooke, Bernard. II. Title.

OUTLER, Albert Cook, 1908- 280.1
The Christian tradition and the unity we seek. New York, Oxford University Press, 1957. 165p. 20cm. (Richard lectures, 1955) [BX8.O8] 57-10386
1. Ecumenical movement. I. Title.

PATON, David MacDonald. 280.1
Anglicans and unity. London, A. R. Mowbray; New York, Morehouse-Barlow [1963, 1962] 115 p. 20 cm. (Star books on reunion) [BX8.2P3] 63-1270
1. Christian union—Anglican Communion. I. Title.

PATON, David MacDonald 280.1
Anglicans and unity. London, A. R. Mowbray, New York, Morehouse [1963, c.1962] 115p. 20cm. (Star bks. on reunion) 63-1270 1.00 pap.,
1. Christian union—Anglican Communion. I. Title.

POL, Willem Hendrick van de, 1897- 280.1
Anglicanism in ecumenical perspective [Tr. by Walter van de Putte] Pittsburgh, Duquesne, 1965. x, 293p. 22cm. (Duquesne studies. Theological ser., 4) Bibl. [BX8.2.P613] 65-10053 6.75
1. Christian union—Anglican Communion. I. Title. II. Series.

REID, John Kelman Sutherland 280.1
Presbyterian and unity. London, A. R. Mowbray, New York, Morehouse [c.1962] 99p. 20cm. (Star bks. on reunion) 63-592 1.00 pap.,
1. Christian union—Presbyterian Church. I. Title.

REID, John Kelman Sutherland. 280.1
Presbyterians and unity. London, A. R. Mowbray; New York, Morehouse-Barlow Co. [1962] 99 p. 20 cm. (Star books on reunion) [BX8.2.R4] 63-592
1. Christian union — Presbyterian Church. I. Title.

ROUTLEY, Erik 280.1
Congregationalists and unity. London, A. R. Mowbray [dist. New York, Morehouse, c.1962] 94p. 20cm. (Star bks. on reunion) 63-593 1.00 pap.,
1. Christian union—Congregational churches. I. Title.

ST. JOHN, Henry. 280.1
Essays in Christian unity, 1928-1954. Westminster, Md., Newman Press [1955] 144p. 22cm. [BX8.S3] 55-7041
1. Christian union. 2. Ecumenical movement. 3. Catholic Church—Relations. I. Title. II. Title: Christian unity, 1928-1954.

SANDERSON, Ross Warren, 1884- 280.1
Church cooperation in the United States; the nation-wide backgrounds and ecumenical significance of state and local councils of churches in their historical perspective. [New York] Association of Council Secretaries, 1960. 272p. 25cm. Includes bibliography. [BV626.S3] 60-13189
1. Local church councils. 2. Interdenominational cooperation. 3. Christian union—Hist. I. Title.

SARTORY, Thomas A. 280.1
Westminster, Md., Newman [c.]1963. xx, 290p. 23cm. Bibl. 62-21502 5.75
1. Ecumenical movement. 2. Church. 3. Christian union. I. Title.

SARTORY, Thomas A 280.1
The oecumenical movement and the unity of the church. Translated by Hilda C. Graef. Westminster, Md., Newman Press, 1963. xx, 290 p. 23 cm. "Sources and literature": p. [251]-256. Bibliographical footnotes. [BX8.2.S253] 62-21502
1. Ecumenical movement. 2. Church. 3. Christian union. I. Title.

SCHMUCKER, Samuel Simon, 1799-1873 280.1
Fraternal appeal to the American churches, with a plan for catholic union on apostolic principles. Ed., introd. by Frederick K. Wentz. Philadelphia, Fortress Pr. [c.1965] vii, 229p. 21cm. (Seminar eds.) First ed. pub. in 1838 under title: Appeal to the American churches. Bibl. [BX8.S37] 65-13255 2.25 pap.,
1. Christian union—U.S. I. Wentz, Frederick K., ed. II. Title.

SCHMUCKER, Samuel Simon, 1799-1873. 280.1
Fraternal appeal to the American churches, with a plan for catholic union on apostolic

principles. Edited and with an introd. by Frederick K. Wentz. Philadelphia, Fortress Press [1965] vii, 229 p. 21 cm. (Seminar editions) First ed. published in 1838 under title: Appeal to the American churches. Bibliographical footnotes. [BX8.S37] 65-13255
1. Christian union—U. S. I. Wentz, Frederick K., ed. II. Title.

SCHUTZ, Roger 280.1
Unity: man's tomorrow. [Tr. from French. New York] Herder & Herder [c.1963] 94p. 21cm. 63-8518 2.95
1. Christian union. I. Title.

SHELFORD, Paul K 280.1
Protestant cooperation in northern California; the historical background of the federation and counciliar movement, written in preparation for the golden anniversary of the founding, 1913-1963. [San Franciso, Northern California-Nevada Council of Churches, 1962] 115 p. illus. 22 cm. [BV626.S5] 63-3365
1. Interdenominational cooperation. 2. California—Church history. I. Title.

SHERWOOD, Polycarp, ed. and tr. 280.1
The unity of the churches of God. Helicon New York Taplinger, c.1963 227p. 23cm. Bibl. 62-18778 4.95 bds.,
1. Christian union. 2. Catholic Church—Relations—Orthodox Eastern Church. 3. Orthodox Eastern Church—Relations—Catholic Church. I. Title.
Contents omitted.

SHERWOOD, Polycarp, ed. and tr. 280.1
The unity of the churches of God. Baltimore, Helicon [1963] 227 p. 23 cm. Includes bibliography. [BX8.2.S5] 62-18778
1. Christian union. 2. Catholic Church—Relations—Orthodox Eastern Church. 3. Orthodox Eastern Church—Relations—Catholic Church. I. Title.
Contents omitted

SHORT, Howard Elmo. 280.1
Christian unity is our business; disciples of Christ within the ecumenical fellowship. [St. Louis] Published for the Association for the Promotion of Christian Unity by Bethany Press [1953] 59p. 18cm. [BX8.S46] 53-32886
1. Christian union. 2. Disciples of Christ—Relations. I. Title.

SKOGLUND, John E. 280.1
Fifty years of Faith and Order; an interpretation of the Faith and Order movement [by] John E. Skoglund, J. Robert Nelson. St. Louis, Pub. for Abbott Bks. by Bethany [1964, c.1963] 159p. 20cm. Bibl. [BX6.W7S5] 65-274 1.75 pap.,
1. World Conference on Faith and Order. I. Nelson, John Robert, 1920- II. Title.

SKYDSGAARD, K E 280.1
One in Christ; translated by Axel C. Kildegaard. Philadelphia, Muhlenberg Press [1957] 220p. 20cm. [BX4817.S5] 57-9596
1. Protestant churches— Relations—Catholic Church. 2. Catholic Church—Relations—Protestant churches. I. Title.

SKYDSGAARD, Kristen E 280.1
One in Christ; translated by Axel C. Kildegaard. Philadelphia, Muhlenberg Press [1957] 220 p. 20 cm. [BX4818.3.S54] 57-9596
1. Protestant churches — Relations — Catholic Church. 2. Catholic Church — Relations — Protestant churches. I. Title.

SKYDSGAARD, Kristen E ed. 280.1
The papal council and the gospel; Protestant theologians evaluate the coming Vatican Council. Minneapolis, Augsburg Pub. House [1961] vii, 213 p. 22 cm. Bibliography: p. 211-213. Includes bibliographical references. [BX830 1962.S5] 61-17915
1. Vatican Council, 2d. 2. Catholic Church — Relations — Lutheran Church. 3. Lutheran Church — Relations — Catholic Church. I. Title.

SKYDSGAARD, Kristen E., ed. 280.1
The papal council and the gospel: Protestant theologians evaluate the coming Vatican Council Minneapolis, Augsburg [c.1961] vii, 213p. Bibl. 61-17915 3.95
1. Vatican Council, 2d, 2. Catholic Church—Relations—Lutheran Church. 3. Lutheran Church—Relations—Catholic Church. I. Title.

SPAETH, J. Paul, ed. 280.1
Ecumenism, unity, and peace; a collection of commentaries and readings. Foreword from pastoral letter of Richard Cardinal Cushing. Contributors: George Eldarov, Edward A. Freking, Edward L. Murphy [Cincinnati 26. 5100 Shattuc Ave., Catholic Students' Mission Crusade, c.1963] 43p. ports. 22cm. (CSMC five-hour ser.) Bibl. 63-24598 .40 pap.,
1. Christian union—Addresses, essays, lectures. I. Title.

SPINKA, Matthew 280.1
The quest for church unity. New York, Macmillan, [c.]1960. 85p. 21cm. (bibl. footnotes) 60-5287 2.50
1. Christian union. 2. Ecumenical movement—Hist. I. Title.

SPINKA, Matthew, 1890- 280.1
The quest for church unity. New York, Macmillan, 1960. 85 p. 21 cm. Includes bibliography. [BX8.2S6] 60-5287
1. Christian union. 2. Ecumenical movement — Hist. I. Title.

SWIDLER, Leonard J ed. 280.1
Dialogue for reunion; the Catholic premises, edited by Leonard Swidler. New York, Herder and Herder [1962] 88 p. 22 cm. (Quaestiones disputatae, 7) Contents.Contents. -- Introduction, by L. Snidler. -- The impact of the ecumenical movement, by J. J. Wright. -- Liturgy and ecumenism, by H. A. Reinhold. -- The holy tradition, by G. H. Tavard. Bibliographical footnotes. [BX8.2.S9] 62-20963
1. Christian union. I. Title.

TAVARD, Georges Henri 280.1
Protestant hopes and the Catholic responsibility. Notre Dame, Ind., Fides Publishers [1960] 63p. 18cm. (2p. bibl.) 60-723 .75 pap.,
1. Catholic Church—Relations. 2. Ecumenical movement. I. Title.

TAVARD, Georges Henri, 1922- *280.1
The Catholic approach to Protestantism. Translated from the French by the author. Foreword by George N. Shuster. [1st ed.] New York, Harper [1955] 160p. 20cm. Translation of A la rencontre du protestantisme. [BX8.T255] 55-8528
1. Ecumenical movement. 2. Protestantism. I. Title.

TAVARD, Georges Henri, 1922- 280.1
Protestant hopes and the Catholic responsibility. Notre Dame, Ind., Fides Publishers [1960] 63 p. 18 cm. [BX1785.T35] 60-723
1. Catholic Church — Relations. 2. Ecumenical movement. I. Title.

TAVARD, Georges Henri, 1922- 280.1
Protestant hopes and the Catholic responsibility, by George Tavard. Notre Dame, Ind., Fides Publishers [1964] 91 p. 18 cm. [A Fides dome book, D-40] "An enlarged edition of the original [1960] to which has been added Part III. Reforming the Church." Bibliography: p. 89-91. [BX1785.T35] 65-1250
1. Catholic Church—Relations. 2. Ecumenical movement. I. Title.

TAVARD, Georges Henri, 1922- 280.1
Two centuries of ecumenism: the search for unity. Tr. by Royce W. Hughes [New York] New Amer. Lib. [1962, c.1960] 192p. 18cm. (Mentor-Omega bk., MT465) Bibl. .75 pap.,
1. Ecumenical council. I. Title.

TAVARD GEORGES HENRI, 1922- 280.1
Two centuries of ecumenism. Translated by Royce W. Hughes. Notre Dame, Ind., Fides Publishers Association [c1960] 129 p. 24 cm. Includes bibliography. [BX8.2T313] 60-15441
1. Ecumenical movement. I. Title.

THOMPSON, Betty. 280.1
Turning world. New York, Friendship Press [1960] 128 p. illus. 23 cm. [BX8.2.T5] 60-7444
1. Christian union. I. Title.

THOMPSON, Betty 280.1
Turning world. New York, Friendship Press [c.1960] 128p. illus. 23cm. 60-7444 2.95; 1.50 pap.,
1. Christian union. I. Title.

THURIAN, Max 280.1
Visible unity and tradition. Tr. [from French] by W. J. Kerrigan. Baltimore, Helicon [dist. New York, Taplinger, 1962, c.1961] Bibl. 62-18771 3.50
1. Church—Unity. 2. Tradition (Theology) 3. Christian union. I. Title.

TOBIAS, Robert, ed. *280.1
Preaching on Christian unity. St. Louis, Bethany Press [1958] 160 p. 21 cm. [BX9.T6] 58-12742
1. Christian union — Sermons. 2. Sermons, English I. Title.

TOMKINS, Oliver S 280.1
A time for unity [by] Oliver Tomkins, New York, Morehouse-Barlow Co. [1964] 127 p. 19 cm. Bibliographical footnotes. [BX8.2.T62] 64-5178
1. Christian union — Addresses, essays, lectures. I. Title.

TOMKINS, Oliver S. 280.1
A time for unity. New York, Morehouse [c.1964] 127p. 19cm. Bibl. 64-5178 1.75 pap.,
1. Christian union—Addresses, essays, lectures. I. Title.

VAJTA, Vilmos, ed. 280.1
Church in fellowship; pulpit and altar fellowship among Lutherans. Essays by Fred W. Meuser [and others] Minneapolis, Augsburg Pub. House [1963] 279 p. 23 cm. [BX8.2.V3] 62-21820
1. Christian union — Lutheran Church. 2. Lutheran Church — Discipline. I. Meuser, Fred W. II. Title.

VAJTA, Vilmos, ed. 280.1
Church in fellowship; pulpit and altar fellowship among Lutherans. Essays by Fred W. Meuser [others] Minneapolis, Augsburg [c.1963] 279p. 23cm. Bibl. 62-21820 5.95
1. Christian union—Lutheran Church. 2. Lutheran Church—Discipline. I. Meuser, Fred W. II. Title.

VAN DUSEN, Henry Pitney, 1897- 280.1
One great ground of hope; Christian missions and Christian unity. Philadelphia, Westminster Pr. [1961] 205p. 61-8496 3.95 bds.,
1. Christian union—Hist. 2. Missions—Theory. I. Title.

VILLAIN, Maurice, 1900- 280.1
Unity; a history and some reflections, Tr. [from French] by J. R. Foster from 3d rev., augm. ed Baltimore, Helicon[dist. New York, Taplinger, c.1961, 1963] 381p. 22cm. Bibl. 63-19675 5.95
1. Christian union. 2. Ecumenical movement—Hist. I. Title.

VISSER'T HOOFT, Willem Adolph, 1900- 280.1
The pressure of our common calling. [1st ed.] Garden City, N.Y., Doubleday [1959] 90 p. 22 cm. Includes bibliography. [BX8.2.V56] 59-12655
1. Ecumenical movement. I. Title.

WEIGEL, Gustave, 1906- *280.1
A Catholic primer on the ecumenical movement. Westminister, Md., Newman Press, 1957. 79 p. 22 cm. (Woodstock papers; occasional essays for theology, no.1) [BX1785.W4] 57-14814
1. Ecumenical movement. 2. Catholic Church — Relations. I. Title.

WOOD, Robert, s.m. 280.1
The unity of faith. St. Louis, Herder [1962] 124 p. 21 cm. [BX1784.W6] 62-21623
1. Christian union. 2. Religions. I. Title.

WOOD, Robert 280.1
The unity of faith. St. Louis, B. Herder [c.1962] 124p. 21cm. 62-21623 2.75
1. Christian union. 2. Religions. I. Title.

WORLD Council of Churches. 280.1
Six ecumenical surveys: preparatory material for the Second Assembly of the World Council of Churches, North western University, Evanston, Illinois, U. S. A., 1954. New York, Harper [1954] 1v. 21cm. [BX6.W77 1954i] 54-2808
1. World Council of Churches. 2d Assembly. Evanston, Ill., 1954 (Proposed) 2. Christianity—20th cent. I. Title. II. Title: Ecumenical surveys.

WORLD Council of Churches. 280.1
2d Assembly, Evanston, Ill., 1954.
The Christian hope and the task of the church; six ecumenical surveys and the report of the Assembly, prepared by the Advisory Commission on the Main Theme. New York, Harper, 1954. 1v. (various pagings) 22cm. Includes bibliographical references. [BX6.W77 1954c] 54-9005
1. Church. 2. Christian union—Congresses. I. Title.

WORLD Council of Churches. 280.1
2d Assembly, Evanston, Ill., 1954.
The Evanston report, the Second Assembly of the World Council of Churches, 1954. [W. A. Visser't Hooft, editor] London, SCM Press [1955] viii, 360p. 23cm. [BX6.W77 1954] 55-3616
I. Title.

WORLD Council of Churches. 280.1
3d Assembly, Delhi, 1961.
New Delhi speaks about Christian witness, service, and unity; the message, appeal, and section reports. Edited by W. A. Visser 't Hooft. New York, Association Press [1962] 124 p. 16 cm. (An Association Press reflection book) [BX6.W77 1961b] 62-11031
1. Ecumenical movement. 2. Evangelistic work. 3. Church and social problems. 4. Church — Unity. I. Viser 't Hooft, Willem Adolph, 1900- ed. II. Title.

WORLD Council of Churches. 280.1
3d Assembly, Delhi, 1961
New Delhi speaks about Christian witness, service, and unity; the message, appeal, and section reports. Ed. by W. A. Visser 't Hooft. New York, Association [c.1962] 124p. 16cm. (Association reflection bk.) 62-11031 .50 pap.,
1. Ecumenical movement. 2. Evangelistic work. 3. Church and social problems. 4. Church—Unity. I. Visser 't Hooft, Willem Adolph, 1900- ed. II. Title.

WORLD Council of Churches. 280.1
3rd Assembly,Dehli, 1961.
The New Delhi report. New York, Association [1962] viii, 448p. 23cm. 62-51170 6.50
I. Title.

WORLD Council of Churches. 280.1
Commission on Faith and Order Study Commission on Institutionalism.
Institutionalism and church unity; a symposium. Ed. by Nils Ehrenstrom, Walter G. Muelder. New York, Association [c.1963] 378p. diagrs. 21cm. Bibl. 63-8883 6.50
1. Institutionalism (Religion)—Addresses, essays, lectures. 2. Christian Union—Addresses, essays. I. Ehrenstrom, Nils, ed. II. Muelder, Walter George, 1907- ed. III. Title.

WORLD Council of Churcles. 280.1
Advisory Commission on the Main Theme of the Second Assembly.
Report: Christ-- the hope of the world. New York, Harper [1954] 51p. 21cm. [BX6.W77 1954h] 54-2807
1. World Council of Churches. 2d Assembly, Evanston, Ill., 1954 (Proposed) 2. Hope. I. Title. II. Title: Christ—the hope of the world.

WYLIE, Samuel J 280.1
New patterns for Christian action. Greenwich, Conn., Seabury Press, 1959. 96 p. 21 cm. Includes bibliography. [BX8.2.W9] 59-7289
1. Christian union. I. Title.

IN the unity of the 280.104
faith; twenty-seven sermons and meditations. Foreword by Edwin T. Dahlberg. Philadelphia, Christian Education Press [1960] 187p. 21cm. [BX9.I 5] 60-13799
1. Christian union— Sermons. I. Christian Education Press, Philadelphia.

JURJI, Edward Jabra, 1907- ed. 280.104
The ecumenical era in church and society; a symposium in honor of John A. Mackay [by] Hugh T. Kerr [and others] New York, Macmillan, 1959. ix, 238p. port. 22cm. [BX9.J8 1959] 59-7444
1. Mackay, John Alexander. 1889- 2. Ecumenical movement—Addresses, essays, lectures. I. Title.
Contents omitted.

BRIDSTON, Keith R., ed. 280.1082
Unity in mid-career: an ecumenical critique, ed. by Keith R. Bridston, Walter D. Wagoner. New York, Macmillan [1963] 211p. 22cm. 63-15050 4.95
1. Ecumenical movement. I. Wagoner, Walter D., joint ed. II. Title.

CATHOLIC Students' 280.1082
Mission Crusade, U. S. A. National Center.
Ecumenism and universalism; a collection of readings on world outlooks for the 'sixties. Pref., Karl J. Alter. Contributors, Paul Broadhurst [others] Ed. by J. Paul Spaeth. Chincinnati, Author [c.1963] xi, 89p. illus., ports. 22cm. (World cultures and religion ser.) Bibl. 64-247 1.10 pap.,
1. Christian union. 2. Christianity—20th cent. 3. Missions—Theory. I. Spaeth, J. Paul, ed. II. Title.

CHURCH and ecumenism 280.1082
(The) Glen Rock, N.J., Paulist [1965] viii, 215p. 24cm. (Concilium theology in the age of renewal: Ecumenical theology, v.4) Edit. director: Hans Kung. Bibl. [BX1785.C5] 65-21762 4.50
1. Ecumenical movement. 2. Catholic Church—Relations. I. Kung, Hans, 1928- II. Series: concilium theology in the age of renewal, v.4

KUNG, Hans, 1928- 280.1082
The Church and ecumenism. New York, Paulist Press [1965] viii, 215 p. 24 cm. (Concilium theology in the age of renewal: Ecumenical theology, v. 4) Contents.Preface, by H. Kung. -- Articles: Mission: obstacle or stimulus to ecumenism? By M. J. Le Guillou; translated by K. Sullivan. Communicatio in sacris, by W. de Vries; translated by J. F. McCue. The charismatic structure of the church, by H. Kung; translated by T. L. Westow. The ecclesial reality of the other churches, by G. Baum. The church under the Word of God, by W. Kasper; translated by E. O'Gorman. The World Council of Churches and Christian unity: a Catholic view, by J. Groot; translated by T. L. Westow. The World

Council of Churches and Christian unity: a Protestant view, by L. Vischer; translated by G. C. Thormann. Mixed marriages: a Protestant view, by H. Dombois; translated by T. L. Westow. Mixed marriages: a Catholic view, by F. Bockle; translated by T. L. Westow. How to promote reunion in a diocese: practical considerations, by P. Nierman; translated by T. L Westow. -- Bibliographical survey: The dialogue with the orthodox, by H. J. Schulz; translated by T. Rattler. The dialogue with Protestant theology, by W. Kasper: translated by T. Rattler. -- DO-C: Documentation concilium: Collegial character of the priesthood and the episcopate, by B. Botte; translated by R. Dowd. The problem of the Catholic school and Christian education, by G. Gozzer; translated by T. J. Clarkson. -- Chronicle of the living Church. -- Chronicle of the living church: Pastoral discussions on confession. Catechesis in Africa. Actual situation of sociology in Spain, by R. E. Ysturiz; translated by C. Ingram. Biographical notes. Includes bibliographical references. [BX1785.C5] 65-21762
1. Ecumenical movement. 2. Catholic Church — Relations. I. Title. II. Series. III. Series: Concilium theology in the age of renewal, v. 4

O'BRIEN, John Anthony, 1893- ed. 280.1082
Steps to Christian unity, edited by John A. O'Brien. [1st ed.] Garden City, N. Y., Doubleday, 1964. 321 p. 22 cm. [BX8.2.A1O2] 64-19310
1. Christian union—Collected works. I. Title.

PROBLEMS before unity 280.1082
[by] J. G. M. Willebrands [others] Foreword by Augustine Cardinal Bea. Helicon New York, Taplinger, 1963, c.1962 149p. illus. 23cm. 62-18781 3.50 bds.,
1. Christian union—Addresses, essays, lectures. I. Willebrands, J. G. M. II. Friars of the Atonement.

ROMAN Catholic-Protestant Colloquium, Harvard University, 1963 280.1082
Ecumenical dialogue at Harvard; the Roman Catholic-Protestant Colloquium. Ed. by Samuel H. Miller, G. Ernest Wright. Cambridge, Mass., Belknap Pr. of Harvard [c.] 1964. xi, 385p. 22cm. Bibl. 64-19583 4.95
1. Christian union—Congresses. I. Miller, Samuel Howard, 1900- ed. II. Wright, George Ernest, 1909- ed. III. Harvard University. Divinity School. IV. Title.

WORLD Conference on Faith and Order. 4th, Montreal, 1963. 280.1082
Report, ed. by P. C. Rodger, Lukas Vischer. New York, Association [c.1964] 126p. 23cm. Held by the World Council of Churches. Bibl. 64-19477 3.95
1. Christian union—Congresses. I. Rodger, Patrick Campbell, ed. II. Vischer, Lukas, ed. III. World Council of Churches. IV. Title.

*WINTZ, Jack. comp. 280.2
Keeping up with our Catholic faith; explaining changes in Catholic thinking since Vatican II. Edited by Jack Wintz. [Cincinnati, Ohio, St. Anthony Messenger Press, 1975] v. ill. 20 cm. (Catholic Update Series v.1) [BX2347] ISBN 0-912228-19-9 1.75 (pbk.)
1. Catholicism. I. Title.

STEWART, Ora (Pate) 1910- 280.3
Dear land of home. Salt Lake City, Deseret Book Co. [1960] 94 p. 16 cm. [BX8627.A2S7] 61-22321
1. Book of Mormon stories. I. Title.

BIBLE Sabbath Association. 280'.4
Directory of Sabbath-observing groups. 4th ed. Fairview, Okla. : Bible Sabbath Association, 1974. 258 p. ; 21 cm. Previously published under title: Sabbath handbook and directory of Sabbath-observing organizations. Includes indexes. [BV125.B5 1974] 74-196036
1. Sabbath. 2. Sunday. 3. Sabbatarians. 4. Sects—Directories. I. Title.

BRIGGS, John, 1938- comp. 280'.4
Victorian nonconformity. Edited by John Briggs and Ian Sellers. New York, St. Martin's Press [1974] vii, 180 p. 21 cm. (Documents of modern history) Bibliography: p. [175]-176. [BR759.B68 1974] 73-89997 10.95
1. Dissenters, Religious—England. 2. Great Britain—Religion—19th century. I. Sellers, Ian, joint comp. II. Title.

BROWN, Robert McAfee, 1920- 280.4
The spirit of Protestantism. New York, Oxford University Press, 1965 [i.e. 1966] xxx, 270 p. 21 cm. (A Galaxy book, GB 151) Bibliographical references included in "Notes" (p. 227-254) "Supplementary bibliography": p. 255-259. [BX4811.B74 1966] 67-732
1. Protestantism. I. Title.

CAMPBELL, Robert, 1919- 280'.4
Spectrum of Protestant beliefs, edited by Robert Campbell. Contributors: William Hamilton [and others] Milwaukee, Bruce Pub. Co. [1968] xiv, 106 p. 22 cm. [BX4811.C3] 68-17118
1. Theology, Protestant—United States. 2. Protestantism—20th century. I. Hamilton, William, 1924- II. Title.

CARPENTER, Delburn. 280'.4
The radical pietists : celibate communal societies established in the United States before 1820 / by Delburn Carpenter. New York : AMS Press, 1975. x, 261 p. : ill. ; 24 cm. (Communal societies in America) Originally presented as the author's thesis, University of Northern Iowa, 1972. Bibliography: p. 253-259. [BV4406.U6C35 1975] 72-13586 ISBN 0-404-11008-8 : 15.00
1. Christian communities—United States. 2. Pietism—United States. I. Title.

CLABAUGH, Gary K. 280'.4
Thunder on the right; the Protestant fundamentalists [by] Gary K. Clabaugh. Chicago, Nelson-Hall Co. [1974] xx, 261 p. illus. 23 cm. Includes bibliographical references. [BT82.2.C53] 74-9551 ISBN 0-88229-108-4 8.95
1. Fundamentalism. 2. Radicalism—United States. I. Title.

DENBEAUX, Fred J. 280'.4
The premature death of protestantism; an invitation to a future [by] Fred J. Denbeaux. [1st ed.] Philadelphia, Lippincott [1967] 155 p. 19 cm. Bibliographical footnotes. [BX4811.D4] 67-25897
1. Protestantism—20th century. I. Title.

DOLLAR, George W. 280'.4
A history of fundamentalism in America, by George W. Dollar. Greenville, S.C., Bob Jones University Press [1973] xiii, 415 p. 23 cm. Pages 412-415, blank for "Notes." Bibliography: p. [387]-395. [BT82.2.D64] 73-176063
1. Fundamentalism—History. I. Title.

DURNBAUGH, Donald F. 280'.4
The believers' church; the history and character of radical Protestantism [by] Donald F. Durnbaugh. New York, Macmillan [1968] xi, 315 p. 21 cm. Bibliographical footnotes. [BX4817.D8] 68-23631
1. Protestantism. 2. Dissenters, Religious. I. Title.

DURNBAUGH, Donald F., comp. 280'.4
Every need supplied : mutual aid and Christian community in the free churches, 1525-1675 / edited by Donald F. Durnbaugh. Philadelphia : Temple University Press, 1974. xiv, 258 p. : ill. ; 23 cm. (Documents in free church history) Includes documents translated from German and Dutch. Includes indexes. Bibliography: p. [235]-242. [BR157.D86] 73-94279 ISBN 0-87722-031-X : 15.00
1. Sects—History—Sources. 2. Church charities—History—Sources. I. Title. II. Series.

KEGERREIS, Robert B 280.4
[Catalogue of the Poe collection of Robert B. Kegerreis. Richland, Pa., 1965] New York, Harper & Row [1965] 1 v. (various pagings) 36 cm. v. 282 p. 22 cm. Bibliographical footnotes. [BX4811.K35] 66-81401 65-20453
1. Poe, Edgar Allan, 1809-1849 — Bibl. 2. Protestantism — 20th cent. I. Kegley, Charles W II. Title. III. Title: Protestantism in transition

KEGLEY, Charles W. 280.4
Protestantism in transition. New York, Harper [c.1965] v, 282p. 22cm. Bibl. [BX4811.K35] 65-20453 5.75
1. Protestantism—20th cent. I. Title.

MARTY, Martin E., 1928- 280'.4
Protestantism [by] Martin E. Marty. [1st ed.] New York, Holt, Rinehart and Winston [1972] xii, 368 p. 25 cm. (History of religion series) Includes bibliographical references. [BX4811.M347] 76-182759 ISBN 0-03-091353-5 8.95
1. Protestantism.

MARTY, Martin E., 1928- 280'.4
Protestantism. Garden City, N.Y., Doubleday [1974, c1972] 440 p. 18 cm. (Image books, D334) Includes bibliographical references. [BX4811.M347] ISBN 0-385-07610-X 2.45 (pbk.)
1. Protestantism. I. Title.
L.C. card no. for the hardbound edition: 76-182759.

NICHOLS, James Hastings, 1915- 280'.4
Primer for Protestants. Westport, Conn., Greenwood Press [1971, c1947] 151 p. 23 cm. Includes bibliographical references. [BX4810.N5 1971] 78-152620 ISBN 0-8371-6019-7
1. Protestantism. I. Title.

PAUCK, Wilhelm, 1901- 280'.4
The heritage of the Reformation. Rev., enl. ed. London New York, Oxford Univ. Pr. [1968] x, 399p. 21cm. (Galaxy bk. GB251) Bibl. refs. [BX4810.P3 1968] 68-115753 2.75 pap.,
1. Protestantism. I. Title.

PROTESTANTISM / 280'.4
Hugh T. Kerr, editor. Woodbury, N.Y. : Barron's Educational Series, [1976] p. cm. Includes bibliographies. [BX4815.P74] 76-16065 ISBN 0-8120-0665-8 pbk. : 2.95
1. Protestantism—Addresses, essays, lectures. I. Kerr, Hugh Thomson, 1909-

SANDEEN, Ernest Robert, 1931- 280'.4
The roots of fundamentalism; British and American millenarianism, 1800-1930 [by] Ernest R. Sandeen. Chicago, University of Chicago Press [1970] xix, 328 p. 23 cm. Bibliography: p. [283]-310. [BT82.2.S18] 79-112739 ISBN 0-226-73467-6
1. Fundamentalism. 2. Millennialism. I. Title.

SPECTRUM of Protestant beliefs, 280'.4
ed. by Robert Campbell. Contributors: William Hamilton [& others] Milwaukee, Bruce [1968] xiv, 106p. 22cm. Statements illustrating the religious, moral, and political attitudes of Amer. Protestantism, by B. Jones, Jr., representing the fundamentalist; C.F.H. Henry, the new evangelical; J. W. Montgomery, the confessional; J. A. Pike, the liberal; and W. Hamilton, the radical theologian position. [BX4811.S65] 68-17118 3.95
1. Theology, Protestant—U. S. 2. Protestantism—20th cent. I. Hamilton, William, 1924- II. Campbell, Robert, 1919- ed.

THOMPSON, David Michael, comp. 280'.4
Nonconformity in the nineteenth century; edited by David M. Thompson. London, Boston, Routledge and K. Paul, 1972. xiv, 281 p. 22 cm. (Birth of modern Britain series) Bibliography: p. 275-278. [BX5203.2.T48] 72-196402 ISBN 0-7100-7274-0 10.00
1. Dissenters, Religious—England—History—Sources. I. Title.

VON ROHR, John Robert. 280'.4
Profile of Protestantism; an introduction to its faith and life [by] John Von Rohr. Belmont, Calif., Dickenson Pub. Co. [1969] 240 p. 22 cm. Bibliography: p. 226-230. [BX4811.V6] 70-76139
1. Protestantism. I. Title.

BOWIE, Walter Russell, 1882- ed. 280.408
What is Protestantism? ed. by Walter Russell Bowie Kenneth Seeman Giniger. New York, Watts [c.1965] xiii, 190p. 25cm. [BX4801.B6] 65-11755 5.95; 4.46 lib. ed.,
1. Protestantism—Collections. I. Giniger, Kenneth Seeman, 1919- joint ed. II. Title.

BOWIE, Walter Russell, 1882-1969. ed. 280.408
What is Protestantism? edited by Walter Russell Bowie and Kenneth Seeman Giniger. New York, F. Watts [1965] xiii, 190 p. 25 cm. [BX4801.B6] 65-11755
1. Protestantism—Collected works. I. Giniger, Kenneth Seeman, 1919- joint ed. II. Title.

HAVERSTICK, John. 280'.4'09
The progress of the Protestant; a pictorial history from the early reformers to present-day ecumenism. Design by Al Corchia, Jr. [1st ed.] New York, Holt, Rinehart and Winston [1968] 273 p. illus., ports. 31 cm. [BX4805.2.H3] 66-22065
1. Protestantism—History—Pictures, illustrations, etc. I. Title.

LEONARD, Emile G., 1891- 280'.4'09
A history of Protestantism [by] Emile G. Leonard. Edited by H. H. Rowley. Translated by Joyce M. H. Reid. Indianapolis, Bobbs-Merrill [1968- v. maps. 24 cm. Translation of Histoire generale du protestantisme. Contents.Contents.—v. 1. The Reformation. Includes bibliographical references. [BX4805.2.L4133] 68-12987
1. Protestantism—History. I. Title.

MURCH, James DeForest, 1892- 280'.4'09B
The Protestant revolt; road to freedom for American churches. Foreword by Edmund A. Opitz. Arlington, Va., Crestwood Books, 1967. 326 p. ports. 21 cm. [BR516.M82] 67-21695
1. National Council of the Churches of Christ in the United States of America. 2. Protestant churches—United States. I. Title.

ADAIR, James R., 1923- 280'.4'0922
Saints alive, by James R. Adair. Introd. by A. W. Tozer. Freeport, N.Y., Books for Libraries Press [1970, c1951] 159 p. illus. 23 cm. (Biography index reprint series) [BR1700.2.A3 1970] 76-117319
1. Christian biography. I. Title.

FOSTER, John W. 280'.4'0922 B
Four Northwest fundamentalists / by John W. Foster. Portland, Or. : Foster, [1975] 128 p. : ill. ; 21 cm. Contents.Contents.—The great Northwest country.—Fundamentalism.—Dr. John James Staub.—Dr. Mark Allison Matthews.—Dr. Walter Benwell Hinson.—Dr. Albert Garfield Johnson.—Neo-fundamentalism? Appendix. [BR550.F67] 75-309309 2.95
1. Clergy—Northwestern States—Biography. 2. Fundamentalism. I. Title.

HARPER, Howard V. 280'.4'0922
Profiles of Protestant saints, by Howard V. Harper. Foreword by Richard Cardinal Cushing. New York, Fleet Press Corp. [1968] 231 p. 21 cm. [BX4825.H3] 67-24071
1. Protestant churches—Biography. I. Title.

HILL, David C. 280'.4'0922 B
Messengers of the King, by David C. Hill. Illustrated by Paul Konsterlie. Minneapolis, Augsburg Pub. House [1968] 167 p. illus. 21 cm. Contents.Contents.—Francis of Assisi, God's laughing beggar.—John Wycliffe, battling scholar.—John Huss, flame of truth from Bohemia.—John Calvin, master of Geneva.—John Knox, stern saint of the Scots.—John Milton, Puritan prophet.—Roger Williams, disciple of liberty.—George Fox, apostle of peace.—David Brainerd, aflame for God.—Johann Sebastian Bach: "Sing to the Lord."—John Wesley, minister to millions.—Isaac Watts, the father of hymns.—George Whitefield, evangelist extraordinary.—Dorothea Dix, angel of mercy.—William Booth, general for God.—Fanny Crosby, sweet blind singer.—Billy Sunday, battlin' Billy.—Wilfred Grenfell, the man who did things.—Dietrich Bonhoeffer, witness for today.—C. S. Lewis, unwilling apostle. [BR1700.2.H5] 68-25802 3.95
1. Christian biography. I. Title.

MCCLENDON, James William. 280'.4'0922
Pacemakers of Christian thought. Nashville, Broadman Press [1962] 68p. 20cm. (A Broadman starbook) Includes bibliography. [BX4825.M3] 62-9198
1. Theology—20th cent. 2. Theologians. I. Title.

SPRAGUE, William Buell, 1795-1876. 280'.4'0922 B
Annals of the American pulpit. [Reprint ed.] New York, Arno Press, 1969. 9 v. ports. 24 cm. (Religion in America) The volumes for each denomination were originally issued separately, with special t.p. Contents.Contents.—v. 1-2. Trinitarian Congregational. 1866.—v. 3-4. Presbyterian. 1868.—v. 5. Episcopalian. 1861.—v. 6. Baptist. 1865.—v. 7. Methodist. 1865.—v. 8. Unitarian Congregational. 1865.—v. 9. Lutheran, Reformed Dutch, Associate, Associate Reformed, Reformed Presbyterian. 1869. [BR569.S72] 75-83442
1. Clergy—U.S. I. Title.

WEIS, Frederick Lewis, 1895-1966. 280'.4'0922 B
The colonial clergy of Virginia, North Carolina, and South Carolina / by Frederick Lewis Weis. Baltimore : Genealogical Pub. Co., 1976, c1955. p. cm. Reprint of the ed. published by the Society of the Descendants of the Colonial Clergy, Boston, which was issued as no. 7 of the Society's Publications. [BR569.W42 1976] 76-22493 ISBN 0-8063-0731-5 : 10.00
1. Clergy—Virginia. 2. Clergy—North Carolina. 3. Clergy—South Carolina. I. Title. II. Series: Society of the Descendants of the Colonial Clergy. Publications ; 7.

WHITE, Jack, 1920- 280'.4'09417
Minority report : the Protestant community in the Irish Republic / Jack White. Dublin : Gill and Macmillan, 1975. 208 p. ; 23 cm. Includes bibliographical references and index. [BX4839.W45] 75-332310 ISBN 0-7171-0766-3 : £6.50
1. Protestants in Ireland. I. Title.

OZMENT, Steven E. 280'.4'0943
The Reformation in the cities : the appeal of Protestantism to sixteenth-century Germany and Switzerland / Steven E. Ozment. New Haven : Yale University Press, 1975. xi, 237 p. ; 22 cm. Includes bibliographical references and index. [BR305.2.O9] 75-8444 ISBN 0-300-01898-3 : 12.50
1. Reformation—Germany. 2. Reformation—Switzerland. 3. Protestantism. I. Title.

UJSZASZY, Kalman. 280'.4'094391
Hungarian Protestantism yesterday and today.

[Denville, N.J., Pannonia Press, 196-] 48 p. 23 cm. [BX4854.H8U38] 67-30022
1. Protestant churches—Hungary. 2. Protestants in Hungary. I. Title.

IRIZARRY, Carmen. 280.40946
The thirty thousand; modern Spain and Protestantism. [1st ed.] New York, Harcourt, Brace & World [1966] x, 399 p. illus., facsims. 22 cm. Bibliography: p. 383-385. [BX4851.I7] 66-22276
1. Protestants in Spain. 2. Religious liberty—Spain. I. Title.

VOUGHT, Dale G., 1937- 280'.4'0946
Protestants in modern Spain; the struggle for religious pluralism [by] Dale G. Vought. South Pasadena, Calif., William Carey Library [1973] xiv, 153 p. illus. 23 cm. Originally presented as the author's thesis (M.A. in Missions), Fuller Theological Seminary. Bibliography: p. 141-153. [BX4851.V68 1973] 73-9744 ISBN 0-87808-311-1 3.45
1. Protestants in Spain. 2. Protestant churches—Spain. I. Title.

BRANDENBURG, Hans, 1895- 280'.4'0947
The meek and the mighty : the emergence of the evangelical movement in Russia / [by] Hans Brandenburg ; [translated from the German]. London : Mowbrays, 1976. xii, 210 p. ; 22 cm. (Keston book ; no. 7) Translation of Christen im Schatten der Macht. Includes index. Bibliography: p. 206. [BX9798.S8B713] 77-364637 ISBN 0-264-66349-7 : £3.75
1. Stundists. 2. Russia—Church history. 3. Church and state in Russia. I. Title.

DURASOFF, Steve. 280'.4'0947
The Russian Protestants; evangelicals in the Soviet Union, 1944-1964. Rutherford, Fairleigh Dickinson University Press [1969] 312 p. 22 cm. Bibliography: p. 293-306. [BX4849.D87] 72-76843 ISBN 8-386-74658-10.00
1. Protestant churches—Russia. I. Title.

HEBLY, J A. 280'.4'0947
Protestants in Russia / by J. A. Hebly ; translated [from the Dutch] by John Pott. Belfast : Christian Journals Limited, 1976. 192 p. ; 18 cm. Translation of Protestanten in Rusland. [BX4849.H413 1976] 76-369830 ISBN 0-904302-14-8 : £1.50
1. Protestant churches—Russia. I. Title.

HEBLY, J. A. 280'.4'0947
Protestants in Russia / by J. A. Hebly ; translated by John Pott. 1st American ed. Grand Rapids : Eerdmans, c1976. 192 p. ; 18 cm. Translation of Protestanten in Rusland. Includes bibliographical references. [BX4849.H413 1976b] 76-149 ISBN 0-8028-1614-2 : 2.45
1. Protestant churches—Russia. I. Title.

YAMAMORI, Tetsunao, 1937- 280'.4'0952
Church growth in Japan; a study in the development of eight denominations, 1859-1939. South Pasadena, Calif., William Carey Library [1974] xi, 185 p. illus. 23 cm. Revised version of the author's thesis, Duke University. Bibliography: p. [175]-185. [BR1305.Y35] 74-4009 ISBN 0-87808-412-6
1. Protestant churches—Japan. 2. Church growth—Case studies. I. Title.

NELSON, Amirtharaj, 1934- 280'.4'095482
A new day in Madras : a study of Protestant churches in Madras / Amirtharaj Nelson. Pasadena, Calif. : William Carey Library, [1974, i.e.1975] xxvi, 340 p. : ill. ; 23 cm. Bibliography: p. [311]-340. [BR1175.M3N44] 74-23951 ISBN 0-87808-420-7 pbk. : 7.95
1. Protestant churches—India—Madras. I. Title.

BUMSTED, J. M., comp. 280'.4'0973
The Great Awakening; the beginnings of evangelical pietism in America. Edited by J. M. Bumsted. Waltham, Mass., Blaisdell Pub. Co. [1970] ix, 180 p. 21 cm. (Primary sources in American history) Bibliography: p. 179-180. [BR520.B9] 73-93240
1. Great Awakening.

DODGE, Ralph Edward. 280'.4'0973
The pagan church; the Protestant failure in America [by] Ralph E. Dodge. [1st ed.] Philadelphia, Lippincott [1968] 144 p. 21 cm. Bibliographical footnotes. [BR526.D6] 68-54413 2.25
1. Protestantism—20th century. 2. United States—Religion—1945- I. Title.

THE Evangelicals : 280'.4'0973
what they believe, who they are, where they are changing / edited by David F. Wells and John D. Woodbridge. Nashville : Abingdon Press, [1975] 304 p. ; 23 cm. Includes index. Bibliography: p. 290-297. [BR1640.E9] 75-15574 ISBN 0-687-12181-7 : 8.95
1. Evangelicalism. I. Wells, David F. II. Woodbridge, John D., 1941-

THE Evangelicals : 280'.4'0973
what they believe, who they are, where they are changing / edited by David F. Wells and John D. Woodbridge. Rev. ed. Grand Rapids : Baker Book House, 1977. 325 p. ; 22 cm. Includes bibliographical references and index. [BR1642.U5E9 1977] 77-152613 ISBN 0-8010-9543-3 : 4.95
1. Evangelicalism—United States—Addresses, essays, lectures. I. Wells, David F. II. Woodbridge, John D., 1941-

THE Evangelicals : 280'.4'0973
what they believe, who they are, where they are changing / edited by David F. Wells and John D. Woodbridge. Rev. ed. Grand Rapids : Baker Book House, 1977. 325 p. ; 22 cm. Includes bibliographical references and index. [BR1642.U5E9 1977] 77-152613 ISBN 0-8010-9543-3 : 4.95
1. Evangelicalism—United States—Addresses, essays, lectures. I. Wells, David F. II. Woodbridge, John D., 1941-

FERM, Robert L., comp. 280'.4'0973
Issues in American Protestantism; a documentary history from the Puritans to the present. Edited with an introd. and notes by Robert L. Ferm. Garden City, N.Y., Anchor Books [1969] xxii, 418 p. 18 cm. Includes bibliographical references. [BX4801.F43] 69-11012 1.95
1. Protestantism—Collections. 2. Protestant churches—U.S. 3. U.S.—Church history—Sources. I. Title.

FERM, Vergilius Ture Anselm, 1896- ed. 280'.4'0973
The American church of the Protestant heritage. Westport, Conn., Greenwood Press [1972, c1953] 481 p. chart. 22 cm. Contents.Contents.—The Moravian Church, by J. R. Weinlick.—The Lutheran Church in America, by V. Ferm.—The Mennonites, by J. C. Wenger.—The Presbyterian Church in America, by C. M. Drury.—The Protestant Episcopal Church in the United States of America, by W. H. Stowe.—The Reformed Church in America, by M. J. Hoffman.—Unitarianism, by E. T. Buehrer.—The Congregational Christian churches, by M. M. Deems.—Baptist churches in America, by R. G. Torbet.—The United Presbyterian Church in America, by W. E. McCulloch.—The Society of Friends in America (Quakers) by W. E. Berry.—The Evangelical Mission Covenant Church and the free churches of Swedish background, by K. A. Olsson.—The Church of the Brethren, by D. W. Bittinger.—The Evangelical and Reformed Church, by D. Dunn.—Methodism, by E. T. Clark.—The Universalist Church of America, by R. Cummins.—The Evangelical United Brethren Church, by P. H. Eller.—Seventh-Day Adventists, by L. E. Froom.—Disciples of Christ, by R. E. Osborn.—Churches of Christ, by E. West.—The Church of God (Anderson, Indiana) by C. E. Brown. Includes bibliographies. [BR516.5.F47 1972] 76-138228 ISBN 0-8371-5585-1
1. Sects—United States. 2. Protestant churches—United States. I. Title.

HANDY, Robert T. 280'.4'0973
A Christian America; Protestant hopes and historical realities [by] Robert T. Handy. New York, Oxford University Press, 1971. x, 282 p. 22 cm. Bibliography: p. 227-236. [BR515.H354] 78-161888 ISBN 0-19-501453-7 7.95
1. U.S.—Church history. 2. Protestant churches—U.S. 3. Christianity and culture. I. Title.

HANDY, Robert T. 280'.4'0973
A christian America; protestant hopes and historical realities. New York, Oxford University Press [1974, c1971] x, 282 p., 21 cm. Bibliography: p. 227-236 [BR515.H354] ISBN 0-19-501784-6 2.95 (pbk.)
1. United States Church history. 2. Protestant churches—United States 3. Christianity and culture. I. Title.

HARDON, John A. 280'.4'0973
The Protestant churches of America [by] John A. Hardon. Rev. ed. Garden City, N.Y., Image Books [1969] 439 p. 19 cm. Includes bibliographical references. [BR516.5.H3 1969] 69-12858 1.45
1. Sects—U.S. 2. Protestant churches—U.S. 3. U.S.—Religion—1945- I. Title.

HEFLEY, James C. 280'.4'0973
Unique evangelical churches / James C. Hefley. Waco, Tex. : Word Books, c1977. 164 p. : ill. ; 23 cm. [BR1642.U5H43] 76-48515 ISBN 0-87680-319-2 : 5.95
1. Evangelicalism—United States. 2. Church growth—United States. I. Title.

HOGE, Dean R., 1937- 280'.4'0973
Division in the Protestant house : the basic reasons behind intra-church conflicts / by Dean R. Hoge, with the research assistance of Everett L. Perry, Dudley E. Sarfaty, and John E. Dyble ; with the editorial assistance of Grace Ann Goodman. Philadelphia : Westminster Press, c1976. 166 p. : ill. ; 23 cm. Includes bibliographical references. [BR516.5.H64] 76-1022 ISBN 0-664-24793-8 pbk. : 3.95
1. United Presbyterian Church in the U.S.A.—Doctrinal and controversial works. 2. Theology, Protestant—United States. 3. Sociology, Christian—United States. I. Title.

HUTCHISON, William R., comp. 280'.4'0973
American Protestant thought: the liberal era. Edited by William R. Hutchison. [1st ed.] New York, Harper & Row [1968] vii, 243 p. 21 cm. (American perspectives) (Harper torchbooks, TB1385.) Includes bibliographical references. [BR1615.H8] 68-27286 2.75
1. Liberalism (Religion)—United States—Collections. 2. Religious thought—United States. I. Title.

MARTY, Martin E., 1928- 280'.4'0973
Righteous empire; the Protestant experience in America [by] Martin E. Marty. New York, Dial Press [1970] 295 p. 24 cm. (Two centuries of American life: a bicentennial series) Includes bibliographical references. [BR515.M33] 72-120468 8.95
1. Protestant churches—U.S. 2. U.S.—Church history. I. Title.

MARTY, Martin E., 1928- 280'.4'0973
Rightous empire : the protestant experience in America / Martin E. Marty. New York : Harper & Row, 1977,c1970. 95p. ; 21 cm. (Harper Torchbooks) Includes bibliographical references and index. [BR515.M33] ISBN 0-06-131931-7 pbk. : 4.95
1. Protestant churches-United States. 2. United States-Church history. I. Title.
L.C. card no. for c1970 Dial Press ed.:72-120468.

MILLER, William Robert, comp. 280'.4'0973
Contemporary American Protestant thought, 1900-1970. Indianapolis, Bobbs-Merrill [1973] xc, 567 p. 21 cm. (The American heritage series, 84) Includes bibliographical references. [BX4811.M53] 70-151613 9.50
1. Theology, Protestant—United States—Collections. I. Title.
pap 4.75.

MURCH, James DeForest, 1892- 280'.4'0973
The Protestant revolt; road to freedom for American churches. Foreword by Edmund A. Opitz. Arlington, Va., Crestwood Books, 1967. 326 p. ports. 21 cm. [BR516.M82] 67-21695
1. Protestant churches—U. S. 2. National Council of the Churches of Christ in the United States of America. I. Title.

NATIONAL Council of the Churches of Christ in the United States of America. 280'.4'0973
American churchmen visit the Soviet Union; who went and what was achieved. [New York, 1956?] 24 p. illus., ports. 31 cm. [BX4817.N37] 73-253261
1. Orthodox Eastern Church, Russian—Relations—Protestant churches. 2. Protestant churches—Relations—Orthodox. I. Title.

STEARNS, Monroe. 280'.4'0973
The Great Awakening, 1720-1760; religious revival rouses Americans' sense of individual liberties. New York, Watts [1970] 60 p. illus., ports. 23 cm. (A Focus book) Bibliography: p. 56-58. Discusses that period in American history when ministers such as Theodorus Frelinghuysen and Jonathan Edwards stirred in men a sense of worth and dignity which eventually produced the movement for independence. [BR520.S82] 73-93224 ISBN 0-531-01008-2
1. Great Awakening.

STEWART, John T. 280.40973
The deacon wore spats; profiles from America's changing religious scene [by] John T. Stewart. [1st ed.] New York, Holt, Rinehart and Winston [1965] xii, 191 p. 22 cm. [BR515.S75] 65-15059
1. U.S.—Religion. 2. Clergy—Correspondence, reminiscences, etc. 3. Preaching—U.S. I. Title.

BAILEY, Kenneth Kyle, 1923- 280'.4'0975
Southern white Protestantism in the twentieth century [by] Kenneth K. Bailey. Gloucester, Mass., P. Smith, 1968 [c1964] ix, 180 p. 21 cm. Includes bibliographical references. [BR535.B3 1968] 68-3689
1. Southern States—Church history. 2. Protestantism—Southern States. I. Title.

HILL, Samuel S. 280'.4'0975
Southern churches in crisis [by] Samuel S. Hill. [1st ed.] New York, Holt, Rinehart and Winston [1967] xvii, 234 p. 22 cm. Bibliographical references included in "Notes" (p. 121-229) [BR535.H5] 66-10211
1. Protestant churches—Southern States. 2. Southern States—Church history. I. Title.

SERNETT, Milton C., 1942- 280'.4'0975
Black religion and American evangelicalism : white Protestants, plantation missions, and the flowering of Negro Christianity, 1787-1865 / by Milton C. Sernett ; with a foreword by Martin E. Marty. Metuchen, N.J. : Scarecrow Press, 1975. 320 p. : ill. ; 23 cm. (ATLA monograph series ; no. 7) A revision of the author's thesis, University of Delaware. Includes index. Bibliography: p. 239-288. [BR563.N4S47 1975] 75-4754 ISBN 0-8108-0803-X : 16.50
1. Negroes—Religion. 2. Evangelicalism—Southern States. I. Title. II. Series: American Theological Library Association. ATLA monograph series ; no. 7.

RYLAND, John A. 280.4'09755'352
King and Queen County, Virginia; its churches and religious life, 1691-1791, by John A. Ryland. [West Point? Va., 1967?] iv, 20 p. 23 cm. "An address delivered before the King and Queen County Historical Society at King and Queen Court House, Virginia on April 25, 1967." Bibliography: p. 20. [BR555.V9K567] 75-304391
1. King and Queen Co., Va.—Church history. 2. Churches—Virginia—King and Queen Co.

DOUGLASS, Harlan Paul, 1871-1953. 280'.4'0977866
The St. Louis church survey. New York, Arno Press, 1970 [c1924] 327 p. illus., forms, maps. 23 cm. (The Rise of urban America) [BR560.S2D6 1970] 77-112540 ISBN 4-05-024495-
1. St. Louis—Religious life and customs—Statistics. 2. St. Louis—Social conditions—Statistics. I. Title. II. Series.

HOLLAND, Clifton L., 1939- 280'.4'0979494
The religious dimension in Hispanic Los Angeles; a Protestant case study [by] Clifton L. Holland. South Pasadena, Calif., William Carey Library [1974] xxxii, 541 p. illus. 23 cm. Thesis (M.A.)—Fuller Theological Seminary. Bibliography: p. [509]-541. [BR563.M49H64] 74-5123 ISBN 0-87808-309-X
1. Mexican Americans—Religion—Los Angeles. 2. Mexican Americans—Los Angeles. 3. Los Angeles—Religion. I. Title.

READ, William R., 1923- 280'.4'098
Latin American church growth, by William R. Read, Victor M. Monterroso [and] Harmon A. Johnson. Grand Rapids, Eerdmans [1969] xxiv, 421 p. illus., maps. 24 cm. (Church growth series) Bibliography: p. 387-417. [BR600.R37] 79-75104 8.95
1. Latin America—Church history. I. Monterroso, Victor M., joint author. II. Johnson, Harmon A., joint author. III. Title.

WILLEMS, Emilio. 280/.4/098
Followers of the new faith; culture change and the rise of Protestantism in Brazil and Chile. [Nashville] Vanderbilt Univ. Pr., 1967. x, 290p. 24cm. Bibl. [BX4836.B8W5] 67-27517 7.50
1. Protestant churches—Brazil. 2. Protestant churches—Chile. 3. Brazil—Soc. condit. 4. Chile—Soc. condit. I. Title.

MISSIONS Advanced Research and Communication Center. 280'.4'0981
Continuing evangelism in Brazil; a MARC/MIB study project. Monrovia, Calif. [1971] xi, 107 p. illus. 28 cm. (Its Interpretive bulletin 1) Bibliography: p. 100-106. [BX4836.B8M57 1971] 73-180295
1. Protestant churches—Brazil—Statistics. 2. Evangelistic work—Brazil. I. Missionary Information Bureau. II. Title. III. Series.

READ, William R., 1923- 280'.4'0981
Brazil 1980: the Protestant handbook; the dynamics of church growth in the 1950's and 60's, and the tremendous potential for the 70's [by] William R. Read & Frank A. Ineson. Monrovia, Calif., MARC [1973] xxx, 405 p. illus. 23 cm. Bibliography: p. [368]-396. [BX4836.B8R4] 73-84887 ISBN 0-912552-04-2
1. Protestant churches—Brazil—Statistics. 2. Church growth. 3. Religious and ecclesiastical

institutions—Brazil—Directories. I. Ineson, Frank Avery, 1902- joint author. II. Title.

READ, William R., 1923- 280'.4'0981
Brazil 1980: the Protestant handbook; the dynamics of church growth in the 1950's and 60's, and the tremendous potential for the 70's [by] William R. Read and Frank A. Ineson. Monrovia, Calif., MARC [1973] xxx, 405 p. illus. 23 cm. Bibliography: p. [368]-396. [BX4836.B8R4] 73-84887 ISBN 0-912552-04-2
1. Protestant churches—Brazil—Statistics. 2. Church growth. 3. Religious and ecclesiastical institutions—Brazil—Directories. I. Ineson, Frank Avery, 1902- joint author. II. Title.
Publisher's address: 919 W. Huntington Drive, Monrovia, Calif. 91016.

FEDERAL Council of the Churches of Christ in America. 280.6273
Annual report. New York. v. 23cm. [BX6.F4A3] 54-16306
I. Title.

NATIONAL Council of the Churches of Christ in the United States of America. General Board. National Lay Committee. 280.6273
The chairman's final report to the members of the National Lay Committee. June 16, 1950-June 30, 1955. [J. Howard Pew, chairman. Philadelphia? 1955?] xi, 316p. 24cm. [BX6.N2A457] 60-19256
I. Pew, John Howard. 1882- II. Title.

TULGA, Chester Earl, 1896- 280.6273
The case against the National Council of Churches. Chicago, Conservative Baptist Fellowship [1951] 60 p. 18 cm. (His Little books on big subjects) [BX6.N218T8] 51-7432
1. National Council of the Churches of Christ in the United States of America. I. Title.

*[SEIDEL, Lena] 280.7
Your neighbor's faith; teacher's guide. Minneapolis, Augsburg [c.1964] 63p. 28cm. (Amer. Lutheran church curriculum: sen. high) 1.25 pap.,
I. Title.

MUNRO, William Fraser, 1894- 280.97
A brief dictionary of the denominations. Nashville, Tidings, 1908 Grand Ave. [1964] 64p. 19cm. [BR516.5.M8] 64-25536 .60
1. Sects—U. S. I. Title.

BISHOP, Charles Cager, 1898- 280.973
Churches, 253,762; their doctrines, history, government. Wellington? Tex., '1951. 84 p. 23 cm. [BR516.B5 1951] 51-4621
1. Sects—U. S. 2. U. S.—Religion. I. Title.

THE Christian century. 280.973
What's ahead for the churches; a report. Edited by Kyle Haselden and Martin E. Marty. New York, Sheed and Ward [1964] vi, 214 p. 22 cm. Includes 16 articles, some revised and expanded, originally published in the Christian century during 1963, and 2 new chapters. [BR481.C49] 64-20407
1. Christianity — 20th cent. — Addresses, essays, lectures. I. Haselden, Kyle, ed. II. Marty, Martin E., 1928- ed. III. Title.

CLARK, Elmer Talmage, 1886- 280.973
The small sects in America. Rev. ed. [Gloucester, Mass., P. Smith 1964, c.1937, 1949] 256p. 22cm. (Abingdon bk. rebound) Bibl. 3.25
1. Sects—U.S. 2. U.S.—Religion. I. Title.

LANDIS, Benson Young, 1897- 280.973
Religion in the United States [by] Benson Y. Landis. New York, Barnes & Noble [1965] viii, 120 p. 22 cm. (Everyday handbooks) [BR516.5.L3] 65-14270
1. Sects—U.S. I. Title.

LOOK. 280.973
A guide to the religions of America; the famous Look magazine series on religion, plus facts, figures, tables, charts, articles, and comprehensive reference material on churches and religious groups in the United States. Edited by Leo Rosten. [New York] Simon and Schuster, 1955. xiii, 282 p. 23 cm. "Contains the complete series of articles on religion published in Look from 1952-1955." [BR516.L77] 55-7133
1. Sects—United States. I. Rosten, Leo Calvin, 1908- ed. II. Title: Religions of America.

LOOK 280.973
Religions in America; a completely revised and up-to-date guide to churches and religious groups in the United States. The famous Look magazine series on religion, plus facts, figures, tables, charts, articles, and comprehensive reference material. Ed. by Leo Rosten. New York, S. & S., 1963 [c.1952-1963] 414p. 21cm. (Essandess) 5.95; 1.95 pap.,
1. Sects—U.S. 2. U.S.—Religion. I. Rosten, Leo Calvin, 1908- ed. II. Title. III. Title: Religions of America.

MARTY, Martin E., 280.973
What's ahead for the churches: New York, Sheed [c.1963, 1964] vi, 214p. 22cm. Includes 16 articles, some rev. and expanded, orig. pub. in the Christian century during 1963, and 2 new chapters. 64-20407 4.50
1. Christianity—20th cent.—Addresses, essays, lectures. I. Haselden, Kyle, ed. II. Christian century (The) III. Title.

MAYER, Frederick Emanuel, 1892- 280.973
American churches, beliefs practices, by F. E. Mayer ... St. Louis, Mo., Concordia publishing house, 1946. xiii, 102p. 19cm. (Concordia teacher training series) 'Suggested bibliography': p.100-102. [BR516.M36] 46-18835
1. Sects—U. S. 2. Creeds—Comparative studies. I. Title.

MEAD, Frank Spencer, 1898- 280.973
Handbook of denominations in the United States. 2d rev. ed. New York, Abingdon Press [1961] 272p. 24cm. Bibliography: p. 249-257. [BR516.5.M38 1961] 61-8412
1. Sects—U. S. 2. U. S.—Religion. I. Title.

MEAD, Frank Spencer, 1898- 280.973
Handbook of denominations in the United States. Rev. and enl. ed. New York, Abingdon Press [c1956] 255p. 24cm. Bibliography: p. 229-237. [BR516.M38 1956] 55-10270
1. Sects—U. S. 2. U. S.—Religion. I. Title.

MEAD, Frank Spencer, 1898- 280.973
Handbook of denominations in the United States. New York, Abingdon-Cokesbury Press [1951] 207 p. 24 cm. [BR516.M38] 51-11298
1. Sects—U.S. 2. U.S.—Religion. I. Title.

POOVEY, William Arthur, 1913- 280.973
Your neighbor's faith; a Lutheran looks at other churches. Minneapolis, Augsburg Pub. House [1961] 139p. illus. 20cm. 'Reprint of articles that appeared in One magazine from May 1959 to November 1960.' [BR516.5.P6] 61-6998
1. Sects—U. S. 2. Lutheran Church—Doctrinal and controversial works. I. Title.

ROBERTS, Waldemar 280.973
Jesus Christ, Light of the World: Protestant and Orthooox Center, New York World's Fair, 1964-1965. New York, Nelson [c.1964] 96p. illus. (1 col.) facsims., plan, ports. 26cm. 64-17739 1.95 bds.,
1. Sects—U.S. I. Title.

ROBERTS, Waldemar. 280.973
Jesus Christ, Light of the World: Protestant and Orthodox Center, New York World's Fair, 1964-1965. New York, T. Nelson [1964] 96 p. illus. (1 col.) facsims., plan, ports. 26 cm. [BR516.5.R6] 64-17739
1. Sects — U.S. I. Title.

TAPPERT, Theodore Gerhardt, 1904- 280.973
Our neighbors' churches. [Philadelphia] Muhlenberg Press [1954] 96p. illus. 18cm. (Faith and action series) [BR516.T35] 54-4810
1. Sects—U. S. I. Title.

VAN BAALEN, Jan Karel, 1890- 280.973
The chaos of cults; a study in present-day isms. 2d rev. and enl. ed. Grand Rapids, Mich., Eerdmans, 1956. 409 p. 23 cm. [BR516.V3] 56-58880
1. Sects — U.S. 2. U.S. — Religion. I. Title.

VAN BAALEN, Jan Karel, 1890- 280.973
The chaos of cults; a study in present-day isms. 2d rev. and enl. ed. Grand Rapids, Mich., Eerdmans, 1956. 409p. 23cm. [BR516.V3 1956] 56-58880
1. Sects—U.S. 2. U. S.—Religion. I. Title.

VAN BAALEN, Jan Karel, 1890- 280.973
The chaos of cults; a study in present-day isms. 3d rev. and enl. ed. Grand Rapids, Eerdmans [1960] 444 p. 23 cm. Includes bibliography. [BR516.5.V3] 00-50834
1. Sects — U.S. 2. U.S. — Religion. I. Title.

WHALEN, William Joseph. 280.973
Separated brethren; a survey of non-Catholic Christian denominations in the United States. Rev. ed. Milwaukee, Bruce Pub. Co. [1961] 284 p. illus. 22 cm. Includes bibliography. [BR516.5.W44 1961] 61-8014
1. Sects — U.S. I. Title.

WHALEN, William Joseph 280.973
Separated brethren; a survey of non-Catholic Christian denominations in the United States. Rev. ed. Milwaukee, Bruce Pub. Co. [c.1961] 284p. illus. Bibl. 61-8014 1.95 pap.,
1. Sects—U. S. I. Title.

281 Primitive & Oriental Churches

ADENEY, Walter Frederic, 1849-1920. 281
The Greek and Eastern churches [by] Walter F. Adeney. Clifton, N.J., Reference Book Publishers, 1965. 634 p. 23 cm. (Library of religious and philosphic thought) First published in 1908. Bibliographical footnotes. [BX106.A3 1965] 65-22087
1. Eastern churches I. Title.

BARNARD, Leslie William. 281
Studies in the Apostolic Fathers and their background [by] L. W. Barnard. New York, Schocken Books [1967, c1966] 177 p. 23 cm. Bibliographical footnotes. [BR67.B366 1967] 66-24902
1. Apostolic Fathers—Addresses, essays, lectures. I. Title.

COMBALUZIER, Charles, 1903- 281
God tomorrow. Translated by Matthew J. O'Connell. New York, Paulist Press [1974] vi, 182 p. 21 cm. Translation of Dieu demain. Includes bibliographical references. [BL263.C72513] 74-78419 ISBN 0-8091-1835-1 4.50
1. Evolution. 2. God. I. Title.

FORTESCUE, Adrian, 1874-1923. 281
The lesser eastern churches. New York, AMS Press [1972] xv, 468 p. illus. 23 cm. Reprint of the 1913 ed. [BX106.F67 1972] 79-168124 ISBN 0-404-02517-X
1. Eastern churches. I. Title.

SCHMEMANN, Alexander, 1921- 281.
The historical road of Eastern Orthodoxy. Tr. by Lydia W. Kesich. Chicago, Regnery [1966, c.1963] viii, 343p. 18cm. (Logos ed., 51L-713) Bibl. [BX290.S373] 1.95 pap.,
1. Orthodox Eastern Church—Hist. I. Title.

UPSON, Stephen H R 281.
Orthodox church history, by Stephen H. R. Upson. 3d ed. [Batavia? N.Y., c1954] 96 p. 18 cm. [BX290.U6] 65-2714
1. Orthodox Eastern Church — Hist. I. Title.

VIELHAUER, Philipp, 1914- 281
Geschichte der urchristlichen Literatur : Einl. in d. Neue Testament, d. Apokryphen u. d. Apostol. Vater / Philipp Vielhauer. Berlin ; New York : de Gruyter, 1975. xix, 813 p. ; 22 cm. (De Gruyter Lehrbuch) Errata slip inserted. Includes bibliographical references and indexes. [BR67.V5] 76-456872 ISBN 3-11-002447-0 : DM68.00
1. Bible. N.T.—Criticism, interpretation, etc. 2. Christian literature, Early—History and criticism. I. Title.

WETZEL, Willard W. ed. 281
The church fathers speak; a course-book for leaders of adults. Willard W. Wetzel, editor. Boston, United Church press [c1965] 124 p. illus. 21 cm. "Part of the United Church curriculum, prepared and published by the Division of Christian Education and the Division of Publication of the United Church Board for Homeland Ministries." Includes bibliographical references. [BR67.W38] 65-28088
1. Fathers of the church. I. United Church Board for Homeland Ministeries. Division of Christian Education. II. United Church Board for Homeland Ministeries. Division of Publication. III. Title.

WETZEL, Willard W ed. 281
The fathers of the early church; an adult resource book. Willard W. Wetzel, editor. Boston, United Church Press [c1965] 124 p. illus., map. 21 cm. "Part of the United Church curriculum, prepared and published by the Division of Christian Education and the Division of Publication of the United Church Board of Homeland Ministries." Includes bibliographical references. [BR67.W4] 65-28089
1. Christian literature, Early. I. United Church Board for Homeland Ministries. Division of Christian Education. II. United Church Board for Homeland Ministries. Divison of Publication. III. Title.

MINUCIUS Felix, Marcus. 281'.08 s
The Octavius of Marcus Minucius Felix. Translated and annotated by G. W. Clarke. New York, Newman Press, 1974. v, 414 p. 22 cm. (Ancient Christian writers; the works of the Fathers in translation, no. 39) Includes bibliographical references. [BR60.A35 no. 39] [BT1116.M7] 239'.1 74-75994 8.95
1. Apologetics—Early church, ca. 30-600. I. Clarke, Graeme Wilbur, ed. II. Title. III. Series.

PAULINUS, Saint, Bp. of Nola, 353-431. 281'.08 s
The poems of St. Paulinus of Nola / translated and annotated P. G. Walsh. New York : Newman Press, 1975. vi, 443 p. ; 23 cm. (Ancient Christian writers : The works of the Fathers in translation ; no. 40) Includes bibliographical references and indexes. [BR60.A35 no. 40] [PA6554.P5] 871'.1 74-77484 12.95
I. Title. II. Series.

HAMELL, Patrick J. 281'.0922
Handbook of patrology [by] Patrick J. Hamell. Staten Island, N.Y., Alba House [1968] 170 p. 21 cm. Includes bibliographical references. [BR67.H27] 76-325 1.95
1. Fathers of the church—Bio-bibliography. 2. Christian literature, Early—History and criticism. I. Title.

ALTANER, Berthold, 1885- 281.1
Patrology; translated by Hilda C. Graef. [1st ed.] Freiburg, Herder [1960] xxiv, 659p. 23cm. [BR67.A373] 57-12030
1. Christian literature, Early—Hist. & crit. 2. Fathers of the church—Bio-bibl. 3. Church history—Primitive and early church—Bibl. I. Title.

ALTANER, Berthold, 1885- 281.1
Patrology. Translated by Hilda C. Graef. [New York] Herder and Herder [1960] xxiv, 659p. 23cm. 'Based on the fifth German edition of Patrologie.' Includes bibliographical references. [BR67.A373 1960a] 58-5869
1. Christian literature, Early—Hist. & crit. 2. Fathers of the church—Bio-bibl. 3. Church history— Primitive and early church—Bibl. I. Title.

APOSTOLIC Fathers. 281.1
The Apostolic Fathers, by J. B. Lightfoot. Edited and completed by J. R. Harmer. Grand Rapids, Baker Book House, 1956. 288p. map. 23cm. 'This English translation ... is reprinted from the edition published in 1891 by Macmillan and Company, London.' [BR60.A62L52 1956] 56-11603
1. Christian literature, Early (Collections) I. Lightfoot, Joseph Barker, Bp. of Durham, 1828-1889, ed. and tr. II. Title.
Contents omitted.

APOSTOLIC Fathers 281.1
The Apostolic Fathers; a new translation and commentary; v.1 [Ed. by Robert M. Grant] New York, Nelson [c.1964] 193p. 22cm. Contents.v.1. An introduction, by R. M. Grant. Bibl. 64-11546 4.00
1. Christian literature, Early (Collections) 2. Apostolic Fathers. I. Grant, Robert McQueen, 1917- ed. II. Title.

APOSTOLIC Fathers. 281'.1
The Apostolic Fathers. A revised text with introductions, notes, dissertations, and translations, by Joseph Barber Lightfoot. Hildesheim, New York, G. Olms, 1973. 2 v. in 5. 20 cm. Reprint of the 1889 ed. published by MacMillan, London. "An autotype of the Constantinople manuscript": pt. I, vol. 1, p. [421]-474. Contents.Contents.—pt. I, 1-2. S. Clement of Rome.—pt. II, 1-3. S. Ignatius; S. Polycarp. Includes bibliographical references. [BR60.A62L52 1973] 73-173713 ISBN 3-487-04688-1
1. Christian literature, Early. I. Clemens Romanus. II. Ignatius, Saint, Bp. of Antioch, 1st cent. III. Polycarpus, Saint, Bp. of Smyrna. IV. Lightfoot, Joseph Barber, Bp. of Durham, 1828-1889, ed.

APOSTOLIC Fathers 281.1
The Apostolic Fathers; a new translation and commentary.
I. Title.
Volume 6, The shepherd of Hermas, by Graydon F. Snyder, is now available from Nelson, Camden, N.J., for $5.00. L.C. card order no.: 64-11546.

APOSTOLIC FATHERS 281.1
The Apostolic Fathers; a new translation and commentary,ed. by Robert M. Grant, London, Camden, N. J., Nelson [1967] v. 22cm. Contents.v.5. Polycarp, Martyrdom of Polycarp, Fragments of Papias, by William R. Schoedel. Bibl. [BR60.A62G7] 64-11546 5.00
1. Christian literature, Early (Collections) 2. Apostolic Fathers. I. Grant, Robert Mc-Queen, 1917- ed. II. Title.

APOSTOLIC FATHERS 281.1
The Apostolic Fathers; a new translation and commentary, v.2&3. New York, Nelson [c.1965] 2vs. (138;188p.) 22cm. Contents.v.2. First and second Clement by Robert M. Grant, Holt H. Graham--v.3. The Didache and Barnabas by Robert A. Kraft. Bibl. [BR60.A62G7] 64-11546 v.2, 4.00; v.3, 5.00

1. Christian literature, Early (Collections) 2. Apostolic Fathers. I. Title.

AUGUSTINUS, Aurelius Bp. of Hippo 281.1
Continence. Tr. by Sister Mary Francis McDonald. Foreword by Roy J. Defarrari [Boston] St. Paul Eds. [dist. Daughters of St. Paul, 1962] 54p. 18cm. (Selections from the Works of the Fathers of the Church. Reprinted from v.16 of the ser. Pamph. no. 6) .35 pap.,
I. Daughters of St. Paul. II. The Fathers of the Church, a new translation. III. Title.

AUGUSTINUS, Aurelius Bp. of Hippo 281.1
The good of marriage, Tr. by Charles T. Wilcox, Foreword by Roy J. Deferrari [Boston] St. Paul Eds. [dist. Daughters of St. Paul, 1962] 55p. 18cm. (Selections from the Works of the Fathers of the Church. Reprinted from v. 27 of the ser. Pamph. no.10) .50 pap.,
I. Daughters of St. Paul. II. The Fathers of the Church, a new translation. III. Title.

AUGUSTINUS, Aurelius Bp. of Hippo 281.1
On taming the tongue [etc.] Tr. by Denis J. Kavanagh. Foreword by Roy J. Defarrari [Boston] St. Paul Eds. [Dist. Daughters of St. Paul, 1962] 55p. 18cm. (Selections from the Works of the Fathers of the Church. Reprinted from v.11 of the ser. Pamph. no. 9) .35 pap.,
I. Daughters of St. Paul. II. The Fathers of the Church, a new translation. III. Title.

AUGUSTINUS, Aurelius Bp. of Hippo 281.1
The work of Religious. Tr. by Sister Mary Sarah Muldowney, Foreword by Roy J. Defarrari [Boston] St. Paul Eds. [dist. Daughters of St. Paul, 1962] 79p. 18cm. (Selections from the Works of the Fathers of the Church. Reprinted from v.16 of the ser. Pamph. no. 8) .50 pap.,
I. Daughters of St. Paul. II. The Fathers of the Church, a new translation. III. Title.

BAINTON, Roland Herbert, 1894- 281.1
Early Christianity. Princeton, N. J., Van Nostrand [1960] 192 p. 18 cm. (An Anvil original, 49) Includes bibliography. [BR162.2.B3] 60-13457
1. Church history—Primitive and early church. 2. Church history—Primitive and early church—Sources. I. Title.

BERNARD DE CLAIRVAUX, Saint, 1091?-1153 281.1
Saint Bernard on the Christian year; selections from his sermons. Tr., ed. by a religious of C. S. M. V. London, A. R. Mowbray [dist. Chester Springs, Pa., Dufour, 1964] 167p. illus. 20cm. [BX1756.B42S45] 2.95 bds.,
1. Church year sermons. 2. Catholic Church—Sermons. 3. Sermons, Latin—Translations into English. 4. Sermons, English—Translations from Latin. I. Title.

BETTENSON, Henry Scowcroft, ed. and tr. 281.1
The early Christian fathers; a selection from the writings of the fathers from St. Clement of Rome to St. Athanasius. London, New York, Oxford University Press, 1956. 424p. 19cm. [BR63.B4] 56-58236
1. Christian literature, Early (Selections:' extracts, etc.) I. Title.

BEVENOT, Maurice, 1897- 281.1
The tradition of manuscripts; a study in the transmission of St. Cyprian's treatises. Oxford, Clarendon Press, 1961. viii, 163 p. diagrs. 24 cm. "The treatise chosen to represent them all is the De ecclesiae catholicae unitate." "De ecclesiae catholicae unitate: the resultant text": p. 96-123. Bibliography: p. [151]-153. [BR65.C86B43] 61-19227
1. Cyprianus, Saint, Bp. of Carthage—Manuscripts. 2. Transmission of texts. I. Cyprianus, Saint, Bp. of Carthage. De ecclesiae catholi

CARMODY, James M., ed. 281.1
Word and Redeemer; Christology in the Fathers, prepd., ed., introd., commentary by James M. Carmody, Thomas E. Clarke. Glen Rock, N. J., Paulist [1966] vii, 136p. 21cm. (Guide to the Fathers of the church, 2) Bibl. [BR63.C3] 66-17731 1.45 pap.,
1. Jesus Christ—History of doctrines—Early church. 2. Christian literature, Early (Selections: Extracts, etc.) I. Clarke, Thomas E., joint ed. II. Title.

CAYRE, Fulbert. 281.1
Spiritual writers of the early church. Translated from the French by W. Webster Wilson. [1st ed.] New York, Hawthorn Books [1959] 126, [1]p. 21cm.. (The Twentieth century encyclopedia of Catholicism, v. 39. Section 4: The means of redemption) Translation of Spirituels et mystiques des premiers temps. Bibliography: p. [127] [BV5075.C313] 59-6725
1. Mysticism—Early church. I. Title. II. Series: The Twentieth century encyclopedia of Catholicism, v. 39

CHADWICK, Henry, 1920- 281.1
Early Christian thought and the classical tradition: studies in Justin, Clement, and Origen. Oxford, Clarendon P., 1966. [7], 174 p. 19 1/2 cm. 25/- [BR67.C43 1966a] 66-71158
1. Justinianus I, Emperor of the East, 4837-565. 2. Clemens, Titus Flavius, Alexandrinus 3. Origenes. I. Title.

CHADWICK, Henry, 1920- 281.1
Early Christian thought and the classical tradition, studies in Justin Clement, and Origen. New York, Oxford University Press, 1966. 174 p. 19 cm. Bibliographical reference included in "Notes" (p. [124]-170) [BR67.C43 1966] 66-15011
1. Clemens, Titus Flavius, Alexandrinus. 2. Justinus Martyr. Saint. 3. Origenes I. Title.

CHADWICK, Henry, 1920- 281.1
Early Christian thought and the classical tradition; studies in Justin, Clement, and Origen. New York, Oxford [c.]1966 174p. 19cm. Bibl. [BR67.C43] 66-15011 4.00
1. Clemens, Titus Flavius, Alexandrinus. 2. Justinus Martyr, Saint. 3. Origenes. I. Title.

CHRYSOSTOMUS, Joanne, Saint, Patriarch of Constantinople d.407 281.1
Baptismal instructions. Tr., annotated by Paul W. Harkins. Westminster, Md., Newman [c.] 1963. vi, 375p. 23cm. (Ancient Christian writers: the works of the Fathers in tr., no. 31) Bibl. 62-21489 4.50
1. Baptism—Early works to 1800. I. Harkins, Paul William, 1911- ed. and tr. II. Title. III. Series.

CHRYSOSTOMUS, Joannes, Saint, Patriarch of Constaninople, d. 407. 281.1
Baptismal instructions. Translated and annotated by Paul W. Harkins. Westminster, Md., Newman Press, 1963. vi, 375 p. 23 cm. (Ancient Christian writers; the works of the Fathers in translation, no. 31) Bibliographical references included in "Notes" (p. 199-338) [BR60.A35 no.31] 62-21489
1. Baptism — Early works to 1800. I. Harkins, Paul William, 1911- ed. and tr. II. Title. III. Series.

CHYSOSTOMUS, Joanne Saint Patriarch of Constantinople d.407 281.1
Chrysostomus and his message, a selection from the sermons of St. John Chrysostom of Antioch and Constantinople by Stephen Neill. New York Association [1963] 80p. 19cm. (World Christian bks., no. 44, 2d ser.) 63-3222 1.00 pap.,
I. Neill, Stephen Charles, Bp., comp. and tr. II. Title.

CLEMENS, Titus Flavius, Alexandrinus. 281.1
Selections from the Protreptikos. An essay and translation by Thomas Merton. [Norfolk, Conn.] New Directions [1963] 27 p. 19 cm. [BR65.C64P73] 63-621
1. Apologetics—Early church. I. Merton, Thomas, 1915-1968.

*CORPUS Scriptorium 281.1
Ecclesiasticorum Latinorum; 10v. New York, Johnson Reprint, 1964. 10v. (various p.) 22cm. Contents.v.12. S. Aureli Augustini. Sect. 3, pars 1: Liber qui appellatur Speculum et liber De divinis scriptoris . . .--v.36. S. Aureli Augustini. Sect. 1, pars 2: Retractationum libri II.--v.37. Flavii Iosephi. Opera. Rec C. Boysen, Pars 4.--v.39. Itinera Hierosolymitana. Saeculi 4-8.--v.43. S. Aureli Augustini. Sect.3, pars 4. De consensu evangelistarum libri. 4.--v.50. Pseudo-Augustini. Quaestiones Veteris et Novi Testamenti, 127. v.51. S. Aureli Augustini. Sect 7, pars 1. Scripta contra Donatistas.--v.52. S. Aureli Augustini. Sect 7, pars 2. Scriptorum contra Donatistas, pars 2, etc. v.67. Boethius, pars 4: Philosophiae consolationis libri V Rec. Guil. Weinberger, 1934. v.69. Tertulliani. Apologeticum secundum utramque libri recensionem ed. Henr. Hoppe, 1939. v.12, pap., 25.00; v.36, 37,43, 50-52,67,69 ea., pap., 15.00; v.39, 20.00

DAVIES, John Gordon, 1919- 281.1
The early Christian church. Garden City, N.Y., Doubleday [1967.c.1965] xvii, 412p. illus. 18cm. (Anchor bk., A566) Bibl. [BR165.D37] 1.75 pap.,
1. Church history—Primitive and early church. I. Title.

DAVIES, John Gordon, 1919- 281.1
The early Christian church [by] J. G. Davies. [1st ed.] New York, Holt, Rinehart and Winston [1965] xiii, 314 p. illus., plans. 25 cm. (History of religion series) Bibliography: p. 299-303. [BR165.D37 1965] 65-12074
1. Church history—Primitive and early church. I. Title.

DOCUMENTS in early 281'.1
Christian thought / Maurice Wiles, Mark Santer. Cambridge ; New York : Cambridge University Press, 1975. p. cm. [BR60.A62D62] 74-31807 ISBN 0-521-20669-3. pbk. : 22.50
1. Christian literature, Early—Collected works. 2. Theology—Collected works—Early church, ca. 30-600. I. Wiles, Maurice F. II. Santer, Mark.

FOLLOWING Saint Francis; 281.1
no. 1--Commandments. Pulaski, Wis., Franciscan, c.1964. 79p. 19cm. .50 pap.,

GOODSPEED, Edgar Johnson, 1871-1962. 281.1
A history of early Christian literature. Rev. and enl. by Robert M. Grant. [Chicago] University of Chicago Press)[1966] ix. 214 p. 22 cm. Bibliography: p. 203-210. [BR67.G58 1966] 66-13871
1. Christian literature, Early — Hist. & crit. I. Grant, Robert McQueen, 1917 — II. Title.

GOODSPEED, Edgar Johnson, 1871-1962 281.1
A history of early Christian literature. Rev. enl. by Robert M. Grant. [Chicago] Univ. of Chic Pr [c.1942, 1966] ix, 214p. 21cm. (Phoenix, P220) Bibl. [BR67.G58] 66-13871 5.95; 1.95 pap.,
1. Christian literature, Early—Hist. &crit. I. Grant, Robert McQueen, 1917- II. Title.

GRANT, Robert McQueen, 1917- 281'.1
Augustus to Constantine; the thrust of the Christian movement into the Roman world [by] Robert M. Grant. [1st ed.] New York, Harper & Row [1970] xiv, 334 p. ports. 25 cm. Includes bibliographical references. [BR165.G66 1970] 73-109065 10.00
1. Church history—Primitive and early church. I. Title.

HAGENDAHL, Harald, 1889- 281.1
Augustine and the Latin classics. Goteborg, Universitetet; Stockholm, Almqvist & Wiksell (distr.) 1967. 2 v. in I (769 p.) 23cm. (Studia Graeca et Latina Gothoburgensia, 20) Contents.v. 1. Testimonia. With a contribution on Varro by B. Cardauns.--v. 2. Augustine's attitude. Bibl. [BR1720.A9H28] 67-110256 25.00
1. Augustinus, Aurelius, Saint, Bp. of Hippo—Knowledge—Classical literature. I. Title. II. Series.
Distributed by Humanities, New York.

HERTLING, Ludwig, Freiherr von, 1892- 281'.1
Communio: church and papacy in early Christianity. Translated with an introd. by Jared Wicks. Chicago, Loyola University Press [1972] 86 p. 23 cm. Originally appeared in German in Miscellanea historiae pontificis, v. 7, 1943; present translation was made from a later German version, Communio und primat, issued in Una sancta, v. 17, 1962. Includes bibliographical references. [BR166.H47] 75-38777 ISBN 0-8294-0212-8 2.95
1. Church history—Primitive and early church, ca. 30-600. 2. Papacy—History—To 1309. I. Title.

HERVEY, James W 281.1
Highlights of early church history; essays on the beginning and development of the old Catholic Church (A.D. 101-1226) Foreword by Leroy Nixon. [1st ed.] New York, Exposition Press [1962] 86p. 21cm. (An Exposition- Testament book) [BR162.2.H4] 62-17037
1. Church history—Addresses, essays, lectures. I. Title.

HERVEY, Rev. James W. 281.1
Highlights of early church history; essays on the beginning and development of the old Catholic Church (A.D. 101-1226) Foreword by Leroy Nixon. New York, Exposition [c.1962] 86p. 21cm. (Exposition-Testament bk.) 62-17037 3.50
1. Church history—Addresses, essays, lectures. I. Title.

JURGENS, W. A. 281'.1
The faith of the early fathers; a source-book of theological and historical passages from the Christian writings of the pre-Nicene and Nicene eras, selected and translated by W. A. Jurgens. Collegeville, Minn., Liturgical Press [1970] xxiv, 450 p. 25 cm. Includes bibliographical references. [BR63.J87] 74-157871
1. Christian literature, Early. I. Title.

LACTANTIUS, Lucius Caecilius Firmianus. 281.1
The divine institutes, books I-VII. Translated by Sister Mary Francis McDonald. Washington, Catholic University of America Press [1964] xxv, 561 p. 22 cm. (The Fathers of the Church, a new translation, v. 49) Bibliography: p. xxiv-xxv. Bibliographical footnotes. [BR60.F3L3] 64-18669
1. Apologetics—Early church, 600-1500. 2. Theology, Doctrinal. I. McDonald, Mary Francis, Sister, 1920- tr. II. Title. III. Series.

LAWSON, John. 281.1
A theological and historical introduction to the Apostolic Fathers. New York, Macmillan, 1961. 334p. 22cm. [BR1705.L3] 61-6893
1. Apostolic fathers. I. Title.

MARTIN, Ira Jay, 1911- 281.1
Glossolalia in the Apostolic church, a survey study of tongue-speech. Berea, Ky., 1960. 100p. 23cm. Includes bibliography. [BL54.M35] 60-40200
1. Glossolalia. I. Title.

MUSURILLO, Herbert Anthony, ed. and tr. 281.1
The fathers of the primitive church [selected and translated] by Herbert Musurillo. New York, New American Library [1966] 272 p. illus. 18 cm. (A Mento-Omega book, MT629) Bibliography: p. 266-267. [BR63.M8] 65-22036
1. Christian literature, Early (Selections: Extracts, etc.) I. Title.

MUSURILLO, Herbert Anthony, ed. and tr. 281.1
The fathers of the primitive church [selected, tr.] by Herbert Musurillo. New York, New Amer. Lib. [c.1966] 272p. illus. 18cm. (Mentor-Omega bk., MT629) Bibl. [BR63.M8] 65-22036 .75 pap.,
1. Christian literature, Early (Selections Extracts, etc.) I. Title.

NICETAS, Saint, Bp. of Remesiana, 4thcent. 281'.1
Niceta of Remesiana: Writings, translated by Gerald G. Walsh. Sulpicius Severus: Writings, translated by Bernard M. Peebles. Vincent of Lerins: Commonitories, translated by Rudolph E. Morris. Prosper of Aquitaine: Grace and free will, translated by J. Reginald O'Donnell. Washington, the Catholic University of America Press [1970, c1949] 443 p. 22 cm. (The Fathers of the church, a new translation, v. 7) Includes bibliographies. [BR60.F3N5 1970] 73-23947 ISBN 0-8132-0007-5 9.75
1. Christian literature, Early. I. Severus, Sulpicius. Selected works. English. 1970. II. Vincentius Lerinensis, Saint, 5th cent. Commonitoria. English. 1970. III. Prosper, Tiro, Aquitanus, Saint. De gratia Dei. English. 1970. IV. Title. V. Series.

PHILLIPS, Gordon Lewis. 281.1
Flame in the mind; an introduction to some early Christian writings. With a foreword by the Bishop of London. London. New York. Longmans, Green [1957] 118p. 18cm. Includes bibliography. [BR1705.P5 1957] 57-794
1. Fathers of the church. I. Title.

PROSPER, Tiro, Aguitanus, Saint 281.1
Defense of St. Augustine. Tr. [from Latin] annotated by P. DeLetter Westminster, Md., Newman [c.]1963. v, 248p. 23cm. (Ancient Christian writers; works of the Fathers in tr., no. 32) Bibl. 62-21490 3.75
1. Augustinus, Aurelius, Saint Bp. of Hippo Bp. of Hippo. 2. Semi-Pelagianism. I. Letter, Prudentius de, ed. and tr. II. Title. III. Series.

PROSPER, Tiro Aquitanus, Saint. 281.1
Defense of St. Augustine. Translated and annotated by P. De Letter. Westminster, Md, Newman Press, 1963. v. 248 p. 23 cm. (Ancient Christian writters; the works of the Fathers in translation, no. 32) Bibliographical references included in "Notes": p. [187]-235. [BR60.A35] 62-21490
1. Augustinus, Aurelius, Saint. Bp. of Hippo. Semi-Pelagianism. I. Letter, Prudentius de, ed. and tr. II. Title. III. Series.

QUASTEN, Johannes, 1900- 281.1
Patrology. Westminster, Md., Newman Press, 1950- v. 23 cm. Contents.Contents. -- v. 1. The beginnings of patristic literature. Includes Bibliographies. [BR67.Q3] 51-622
1. Christian literature, Early — Hist. & crit. I. Title.

QUASTEN, Johannes, 1900- 281.1
Patrology. Westminster, Md., Newman Press 1960[ ] 605p. Contents.v. 3. The golden age of Greek patristic literature, from the Council of Nicaea to the Council of Chalcedon. Includes bibls. 51-622 6.57
1. Christian literature, Early—Hist. & Crit. I. Title.

STRACHEY, Marjorie Colvile. 281.1
The Fathers without theology. New York, G. Braziller, 1958 [1957] 235 p. illus. 22 cm. [BR67.S72 1958] 58-6625

1. Christian literature, Early — Hist. & crit. 2. Church history — Primitive and early church. I. Title.

TARDIF, Henri 281.1
Qu est-ce que la patrologie? [Toulouse] Privat [Toulouse] Privat [dist. Philadelphia, Chilton 1964, c.1963] 122p. 19cm. (Questions posees aux catholiques) 64-9077 1.00 pap.,
1. Fathers of the church. I. Title.

TERTULLIANUS, Quintus 281.1
Septimius Florens.
Disciplinary, moral, and ascetical works. Translated by Rudolph Arbesmann, Sister Emily Joseph Daly [and] Edwin A. Quain. New York, Fathers of the Church, inc., 1959. 323 p. 22 cm. (The Fathers of the church, a new translation, v. 40) Includes bibliographies. [BR60.F3T38] 60-281
1. Theology — Collected works — Early church. I. Title. II. Series.
Contents omitted.

TERTULLIANUS, Quintus 281.1
Septimius Florens.
Disciplinary, moral, and ascetical works. Translated by Rudolph Arbesmann, Sister Emily Joseph Daly [and] Edwin A. Quain. New York, Fathers of the Church, inc., 1959. 323 p. 22 cm. (The Fathers of the church, a new translation, v. 40) Contents.Contents.—Foreword, by R. J. Deferrari.—To the martyrs.—Spectacles.—The apparel of women.—Prayer.—Patience.—The chaplet.—Flight in time of persecution. Includes bibliographies. [BR60.F3T38] 60-281
1. Theology—Collected works—Early church. I. Title. II. Series.

VERBA Seniorum. English. 281.1
The wisdom of the desert: sayings from the Desert Fathers of the fourth centyry. Tr. [from Latin] by Thomas Merton [New York] New Directions [1961, c.1960] ix, 81p. 59-15021 3.50
1. Christian literature, Early (Selections: Extracts, etc.) I. Merton, Thomas, 1915- tr. II. Title.

WARD, Maisie, 1889- 281.1
Early church portrait gallery. London, New York, Sheed and Ward [1959] 377 p. 23 cm. Includes bibliography. [BR1705.W3 1959] 60-2535
1. Fathers of the church. 2. Church history — Primitive and early church. I. Title.

WILLIAMS, Robert R. 281.1
A guide to the teachings of the early church Fathers. Grand Rapids, Eerdmans [1960] 224 p. 23 cm. Includes bibliography. [BT25.W5] 60-6401
1. Theology, Doctrinal — Hist. — Early church. 2. Fathers of the church. I. Title.

WILLIAMS, Robert R. 281.1
A guide to the teachings of the early church Fathers. Grand Rapids, Mich., Eerdmans [c.1960] 224p. 23cm. bibl. 60-6401 4.00
1. Theology, Doctrinal—Hist.—Early church. 2. Fathers of the church. I. Title.

WILLIS, John Randolph, 281'.1
comp.
The teachings of the Church Fathers. Edited by John R. Willis. [New York] Herder and Herder [1966] 537 p. 22 cm. Based on the Enchiridion patristicum of Rouet de Journel. Bibliographical references included in "Introduction" (p. 7-9) [BR63.W5] 66-13067
1. Christian literature, Early. 2. Christian literature, Early—Indexes, Topical. I. Title.

RICHARDSON, Cyril 281'.1'08
Charles, 1909- ed. and tr.
Early Christian fathers, newly translated and edited by Cyril C. Richardson, in collaboration with Eugene R. Fairweather, Edward Rochie Hardy [and] Massey Hamilton Shepherd. [New York] Macmillan [1970] 415 p. 21 cm. (The Library of Christian classics, v. 1) Includes bibliographies. [BR60.R5 1970] 72-123888 2.95
1. Christian literature, Early. I. Title. II. Series.

EUGIPPIUS. 281.1'080
Evgippii Vita Sancti Severini. Recensvit en commentario critico instrvxit Pivs Knoell. Vindobonae, apvd C. Geroldi filivm, 1886; New York, Johnson Reprint, 1968. 3 p. 1., xiii, [2], 102p. 1 I. 23cm. (Added t.-p.: Corpys scriptorvm ecclesiasticorvm latinorvm . . . vol. 8 [Pars II] Evgippii Opera, pars II) [BR60.C6 vol. 9] AC 34 15.00 pap.,
1. Severinus, Saint, d. 482. I. Knoll, Pius. ed. II. Title.

AMBROSIUS, Saint, Bp. 281.1'082
of Milan.
Hexameron, Paradise, and Cain and Abel. Translated by John J. Savage. New York, Fathers of the Church, 1961. xi. 449 p. 22 cm. Bibliography: p. xi. [[BR60.F3]] A 63
1. (The Fathers of the church, a new translation, v. 42) I. Title. II. Title: Cain and Abel.

THE Ante-Nicene 281.1'082
Fathers; translations of the writings of the Fathers down to A. P. 325. Alexander Roberts and James Donaldson, editors. American reprint of the Edinburgh ed., rev. and chronologically arr., with brief prefaces and occasional notes by A. Cleveland Coxe. Grand Rapids, W. B. Eerdmans Pub. Co., 1950- v. 25 cm. First published under title: Ante Nicene Christian library. [BR60.A] A 52
1. Christian literature, Early (Collections) 2. Christian literature, Early—Bibl. I. Roberts. Alexander, 1826-1901, ed. II. Donaldson, James, Sir 1831-1915, ed.

APOSTOLIC FATHERS. 281.1082
The Apostolic Fathers, an American translation by Edgar J. Goodspeed. [1st ed.] New York, Harper [1950] xi, 321 p. 22 cm. [BR60.A62] 50-5878
1. Christian literature, Early (Collections) I. Goodspeed, Edgar Johnson, 1871- ed. and tr. II. Title.
Contents Omitted.

AUGUSTINUS, Aurelius, 281.1'082
Saint, Bp. of Hippo.
Letters; translated by Sister Wilfrid Parsons. Washington, Catholic University of America Press [1964- c1951- v. 22 cm. (Writings of Saint Augustine, v. 9- The Fathers of the church, a new translation, v. 12, [BR60.F3A8 vol. 9, etc. 1964] 64-19948
I. Title. II. Series: The Fathers of the church, a new translation, 12

AUGUSTINUS, Aurelius, 281.1'082
Saint, bp. of Hippo.
Sancti Avren Avgvstini Scripta contra donatistas . . . Recensvit M. Petschenig. Vindobonae, F. Tempsky; Lipsiae, G. Freytag (g. m. b. h.) 1908-10; New York, Johnson Reprint; 1968. 3v. diagr. 23cm. (Added t.-p.: Corpys scriptorvm eccelsiasticorvm latinorvm . . . vol. LI-LIII. Sanct Avgvstini Opera (sect. VII, pars I-III)) [BR60.C6 vol. 51-53] AC34 25.00 set, pap.,
1. Donatists. I. Petschenig, Michael, 1845- ed. II. Title.

AUGUSTINUS, Aurelius, 281.1'082
Saint, Bp. of Hippo.
Treatises on various subjects. Translated by Mary Sarah Muldowney [and others] Edited by Roy J. Deferrari. Washington, Catholic University of America Press [1965, c1952] viii, 479 p. 22 cm. (The Fathers of the church, a new translation, v. 16) At head of title: Volume 14. Includes bibliographies. [BR60.F3A833] 65-18319
1. Theology—Collected works—Early chruch. I. Title. II. Series: The Fathers of the church, a new translation, v. 16
Contents omitted

BASILIUS, Saint, the 281.1'082
Great, Abp. of Caesarea, 330(ca.)-379.
Letters; volume 1 (1-185) [by] Saint Basil. Translated by Sister Agens Clare Way, with notes by Roy J. Deferrari. Washington, Catholic University of America Press [1965, 1951] xviii, 345 p. 22 cm. (The Fathers of the church, a new translation, v. 13) Bibliography: p. xviii. [BR60.F3B28] 65-18318
I. Title. II. Series.

DEFERRARI, Roy Joseph, 281.1'082
1890- ed.
Early Christian biographies: lives of St. Cyprian, by Pontius; St. Ambrose, by Paulinus; St. Augustine, by Possidius; St. Anthony, by St. Athanasius; St. Paul the first hermit, St. Hilarion, and Malchus, by St. Jerome; St. Epiphanius, by Ennodius; with a sermon on the life of St. Honoratus, by St. Hilary. Translated by Roy J. Deferrari [and others] Edited by Roy J. Deferrari. Washington, Catholic University of America Press [1964, c1952] xiv, 407 p. 22 cm. (The Fathers of the church, a new translation, v. 15) [BR60.F3D4] 64-19949
1. Fathers of the church. 2. Christian literature, Early (Selections: Extracts, Etc. I. Title. II. Series.

EUGIPPIUS. 281.1'082
Evgippii Excerpta ex operibus S. Avgvstini. Recensvit et commentario critico instrvxit Pivs Knoell. Vindobonae, apvd C. Geroldi filivm, 1885; New York, Johnson Reprint 1968. 2 p. 1., xxxii, [2], 1149, [1] p. 23cm. (Added t.p.: Corpvs scriptorvm eccesiasticorvm latinorvm . . . vol. 8, [pars I] Evgippii Opera, pars I) [BR60.C6 Vol. 9] AC 34 30.00 pap.,
I. Augustinus, Aurelius, Saint, bp. of Hippo. II. Knoll, Pius. ed. III. Title.

FREMANTLE, Anne 281.1082
(Jackson) 1909- ed.
A treasury of early Christianity. New York, Viking Press, 1953. 625p. 22cm. [BR63.F73] 53-7952
1. Christian literature, Early (Selections: Extracts, etc.) I. Title.

FREMANTLE, Anne 281.1082
(Jackson) [Anne Marie Huth (Jackson) Fremantle], ed.
A treasury of early Christianity. [New York] New American Library [1960, c.1953] 511p. 19cm. (Mentor bk. MT285) (bibl. p. 505-507) .75 pap.,
1. Christian literature, Early (Selections: Extracts, etc.) I. Title.

JUSTINUS Martyr, Saint. 281.1'082
Saint Justin Martyr: The first apology, the second apology, dialogue with Trypho, exhortation to the Greeks, discourse to the Greeks, the monarchy, or the rule of God, by Thomas B. Falls. Washington, Catholic University of America Press [1965, c1948] 486 p. 22 cm. (The Fathers of the church, a new translation, v. 6) Bibliographical footnotes. [BR60.F3J8] 65-18317
1. Theology — Collected works — Early church. I. Falls, Thomas B. II. Title. III. Series.

RICHARDSON, Cyril 281.1082
Charles, 1909- ed. and tr.
Early Christian fathers; newly translated and edited by Cyril C. Richardson, in collaboration with Eugene R. Fairweather, Edward Rochie Hardy [and] Massey Hamilton Shepherd, Jr. Philadelphia, Westminster Press [1953] 415p. 24cm. (The Library of Christian classics, v. 1) Includes bibliographies. [BR60.R5] 53-8963
1. Christian literature (Collections) I. Title. II. Series.

VICTOR, Saint, bp. of 281.1'082
Vita, fl484
Victoris episcopi vitensis Historia persecutionis africanae provinciae. Recensuit Michael Petschenig. Accedit incerti auctoris Passio septem monachorum et Notitia quae vocatur. Vindobonae, apud C. Geroldi filium, 1881; New York, Johnson Reprint, 1968. 3 p. 1., xiii p., 1 1., 174p. diagr. 23cm. (Added t.-p.: Corpus scriptorum ecclesiasticorum latinorum . . . vol. VII) [BR60.C6 Vol. 7] AC34 15.00 pap.,
1. Africa, North—History—To 647. 2. Rome—Provinces—Africa. 3. Church history—Primitive and early church. 4. Persecution. I. Passio septem monachorum. II. Petschenig, Michael, 1845- ed. III. Title.

VOOBUS, Arthur. 281.1'082
Studies in the history of the Gospel text in Syriac. Louvain. L. Durbecq, 1951. xxv, 218p. (Cropus scriptorum Christianorum orientallum, v. 128. Subsidla, t. 3) Bibliography: p. [v]-xxv. [BR60.C5S85 vol.3] A53
1. Bible. N. T. Gospels. Syriac—Hist. I. Title. II. Series.

BROWN, Milton Perry 281.2
The authentic writings of Ignatius; a study of linguistic criteria. Durham,N.C., Duke Univ. Pr., 1963. xv, 159p. 25cm. (Duke studies in religion, 2) Bibl. 63-19458 7.50
1. Ignatius, Saint, Bp. of Antioch, 1st cent. I. Title. II. Series.

FAW, Chalmer Ernest, 1910- 281'.2
When the way is new [by] Chalmer Faw. Elgin, Ill., Brethren Press [1974] 144 p. 18 cm. Includes bibliographical references. [BR165.F28] 74-2034 ISBN 0-87178-929-9
1. Church history—Primitive and early church, ca. 30-600. I. Title.

FAW, Chalmer Ernest, 1910- 281'.2
When the way is new [by] Chalmer Faw. Elgin, Ill., Brethren Press [1974] 144 p. 18 cm. Includes bibliographical references. [BR165.F28] 74-2034 ISBN 0-87178-929-9 2.45 (pbk.)
1. Church history—Primitive and early church. I. Title.

GWATKIN, Henry Melvill, 281.2
1844-1916.
Selections from early writers, illustrative of church history to the time of Constantine. Westwood, N. J., Revell [1961] 196p. 61-825 3.00
1. Church history—Primitive and early church—Sources. I. Title.

HOTH, Iva. 281'.2
The church: Acts-Revelation. Script by Iva Hoth. Illus. by Andere Le Blanc. Bible editor: C. Elvan Olmstead. Elgin, Il., D. C. Cook Pub. Co. [1973] 160 p. illus. 18 cm. (Her The picture Bible for all ages, v. 6) [BS2410.H64] 73-78173 ISBN 0-912692-18-9 0.95 (pbk.)
1. Church history—Primitive and early church—Juvenile literature. I. Title.

TYSON, Joseph B. 281'.2
A study of early Christianity [by] Joseph B. Tyson. New York, Macmillan [1973] xv, 447 p. illus. 24 cm. Bibliography: p. 401-417. [BR165.T9 1973] 74-190674
1. Jesus Christ—History of doctrines—Early church, ca. 30-600. 2. Church history—Primitive and early church, ca. 30-600. 3. Christian literature, Early—History and criticism. I. Title.

SALVIANUS, 5thcent. 281.2'082
Salviani presbyteri massiliensis Opera omnia. Recensvit et commentario critico instrvxit Franciscvs Pavly. Vindobonae, apvd. C. Geroldi filivm, 1883; New York, Johnson Reprint 1968 xvi, 359, [1] p. 23cm. (Added t.-p.: Corpvs scriptorvm eccelsiasticorvm latinorvm. . . vol. VIII) [BR60.C6vol. 8] AC34 20.00 pap.,
1. Theology—Collected works—Early church. I. Pauly, Franz, 1827- ed. II. Title.

SEDULIUS, 5thcent. 281.2'082
Sedvlii Opera omnia. Recensvit et commentario critico instrvxit Iohannes Huemer. Accedvnt excerpta ex Remigii Expositione in Sedvlii Paschale carmen. Vindobonae, apvd C. Geroldi filivm, 1885; New York, Johnson Reprint. 1968. 2p. 1., xlvii, [1] p., 1 1., [2] 414p. diagr. 23cm. (Added t.-p.: Corpvs scriptorvm ecclesiasticorvm latinorvm . . . vol. x) [BR60C6 vol.10] AC34 25.00 pap.,
1. Theology—Collectedworks—Early church. I. Remigius, of Auxerre, 9th cent. II. Huemer, Johann, 1849-1915, ed. III. Title.

CYPRIANUS, Saint, Bp. of 281.3
Carthage.
he lapsed. The unity of the Catholic Church. Translated and annotated by Maurice Bevenot. Westminster, Md., Newman Press, 1957. 133p. 23cm. (Ancient Christian writers; the works of the Fathers in translation, no. 25) Bibliographical references included in 'Notes' (p. [69]-124) [BR60.A35 no.25] 57-7364
1. Church discipline—Early church. 2. Church—Unity. I. Bevenot, Maurice. ed. and tr. II. Title. III. Title: The unity of the Catholic Church. IV. Series.

CYPRIANUS, Saint, Bp. of 281.3
Carthage.
Letters (1-81) [by] Saint Cyprian. Tr. [from Latin] by Sister Rose Bernard Donna. Washington, D.C., Catholic Univ. of Amer. [1965, c.1964] xxvi, 358p. 22cm. (Fathers of the Church: a new tr. v.51) Bibl. [BR60.F3C87] 65-12906 6.40
I. Donna, Rose Bernard, Sister, 1909- tr. II. Title. III. Series.

DANIELOU, Jean. 281.3
Origen; translated by Walter Mitchell. New York, Sheed and Ward [1955] 343p. 22cm. [BR1720.O7D315] 55-7487
1. Origenks. I. Title.

EARLY Christian 281'.3
writings: the Apostolic Fathers; translated [from the Greek] by Maxwell Staniforth. Harmondsworth, Penguin, 1968. 237 p. map. 19 cm. (The Penguin classics, L197) Bibliographical footnotes. [BR60.A62E2] 71-350149 6/-
1. Christian literature, Early. I. Staniforth, Maxwell, tr.

EARLY Christian 281'.3
writings; the apostolic fathers, translated by Maxwell Staniforth. [Harmondsworth, Eng.] Penguin Books [1975, c1968] 236 p. 19 cm. (The Penguin classics) [BR60.A62E2] ISBN 0-14-044197-2 2.95 (pbk.)
1. Christian literature, Early (Collections) I. Staniforth, Maxwell, trans.
L.C. card number for original ed.: 71-350149. Distributed by Penguin, Baltimore.

GREENSLADE, Stanley 281.3
Lawrence, ed. and tr.
Early Latin theology; selections from Tertullian, Cyprian, Ambrose, and Jerome. Philadelphia, Westminster Press [1956] 415p. 24cm. (The Library of Christian classics, v. 5) Bibliography: p. 391-899. [BR60.G64] 56-5229
1. Christian literature, Early—Latin authors. 2. Theology—Early church. I. Title. II. Series.

IRENAEUS, Saint, Bp. of 281.3
Lyons.
Proof of the apostolic preaching; translated and annotated by Joseph P. Smith. Westminster, Md., Newman Press, 1952. viii, 233p. 23cm. (Ancient Christian writers; the works of the Fathers in translation, no. 16) Bibliographical references included in 'Notes' (p. [111]-219) [BR60.A35 no. 16] 52-14882
1. Apologetics—Early church. I. Title. II. Series.

KELCHER, James P 281.3
Saint Augustine's notion of schism in the Donatist controversy. Mundelein, Ill., Saint Mary of the Lake Seminary, 1961. 147 p. 23 cm. (Pontificia Facultas Theologica Seminarii Sanctae Marise ad Lacum. Dissertationes ad lauream, 34) Bibliography: p. 141-147. [BR1720.A9K44] 63-3918

1. Augustinus, Aurelius, Saint, Bp. of Hippo. 2. Schism. 3. Donatists. I. Title. II. Series. III. Series: St. Mary of the Lake Seminary, Mundelein, Ill. Dissertationes ad lauream, 34

LACTANTIUS, Lucius Caecilius Firmianus. 281.3
Minor works. Translated by Sister Mary Francis McDonald. Washington, Catholic University of America Press [1965] x, 248 p. 22 cm. (The Fathers of the church, a new translation. v. 54) Bibliographical footnotes. [BR60.F3L33] 65-6715
1. Theology — Collected works — Early church. I. McDonald, Mary Francis, Sister, 1920- tr. II. Title. III. Series.

LACTANTIUS, Lucius Caecilius Firmianus 281.3
Minor works. Tr. by Sister Mary Francis McDonald. Washington, D.C., Catholic Univ. of Amer Pr. [c.1965] x, 248p. 22cm. (Fathers of the church, a new tr., v.54) Bibl. [BR60.F3L33] 65-6715 5.80
1. Theology—Collected works—Early church. I. McDonald, Mary Francis, Sister, 1920- tr. (Series) II. Title.

MCDONALD, Mary Francis, Sister 1920- tr. 281.3
Minor works. Translated by Sister Mary Francis McDonald. Washington, Catholic University of America Press [1965] x, 248 p. 22 cm. (The Fathers of the church, a new translation. v. 54) Bibliographical footnotes. [BR60.F3L33] 65-6715
1. Theology — Collected works — Early church. I. Title. II. Series.

OSBORN, Eric Francis. 281.3
The philosophy of Clement of Alexandria. Cambridge, University Press, 1957. xi, 205p. 22cm. (Texts and studies: contributions to Biblical and patristic literature, new ser.,3) Bibliography: p.195-199. [BR45.T43 n.s.3] 58-813
1. Clemens, Titus Flavius, Alexandrinus. I. Title. II. Series.

OULTON, John Ernest Leonard, 1886- ed. 281.3
Alexandrian Christianity; selected translations of Clement and Origen with introductions and notes by John Ernest Leonard Oulton and Henry Chadwick. Philadelphia, Westminster Press [1954] 475p. 24cm. (The Library of Christian classics. v.2) Bibliographical footnotes. [BR65.C65S8 1954] 54-10257
1. Christian literature, Early (Selections: Extracts, etc.) I. Clemens, Titus Flavius, Alexandrinus. Stromateis aOrigenes. II. Chadwick, Henry, 1920- joint ed. III. Title. IV. Series: The Library of Christian classics (Philadelphia) v.2
Contents omitted.

TERTULLIANUS, Quintus Septimius Florens. 281.3
Tertullian: Apologetical works, and Minucius Felix: Octavius; translated by Rudolph Arbesmann, Sister Emily Joseph Daly [and] Edwin A. Quain. New York, Fathers of the Church, inc., 1950. xix, 430 p. 22 cm. (The Fathers of the Church, a new translation, v. 10) Includes bibliographies. [BR60.F3T4] 51-9180
1. Theology—Collected works—Early church. 2. Apologetics—Early church. I. Minucius Felix, Marcus. Octavius. II. Series.

TERTULLIANUS, Quintus Septimius Florens. 281.3
The treatise against Hermogenes. Translated and annotated by J. H. Waszink. Westminster, Md., Newman Press, 1956 [i. e. 1957] vi. 178p. 23cm. (Ancient Christian writers: the works of the Fathers in translation, no. 24) Translation of Adversus Hermogenem. [BR60.A35 no.24] 56-13257
1. Hermogenes, the heretic, fl. ca. 200. 2. Creation—Early works to 1800. I. Title. II. Series.

TERTULLIANUS, Quintus Septimius Florens. 281.3
The treatise against Hermogenes. Translated and annotated by J. J. Waszink. Westminster, Md., Newman Press, 1956 [i.e. 1957] vi, 178 p. 23 cm. (Ancient Christian writers; the works of the Fathers in translation, no. 24) Translations of Adversus Hermogenem. [BR60.A35 no.24] 56-13257
1. Hermogenes, the heretic, fl. ca. 200. 2. Creation — Early works to 1800. I. Title. II. Series.

ROUTLEY, Erik. 281.3082
The wisdom of the Fathers. Philadelphia, Westminster Press [1957] 128p. 20cm. [BR63.R68] 57-9568
1. Christian literature. Early (Selections: Extracts, etc.) 2. Theology—Early church. I. Title.

LAEUCHLI, Samuel 281.309
The serpent and the dove; five essays on early Christianity. Nashville, Abingdon [1966] 256p. 23cm. Bibl. [BR165.L234] 66-21193 5.95
1. Church history—Primitive and early church—Addresses, essays, lectures. I. Title.

CAMPENHAUSEN, Hans, Freiherr von, 1903- 281'.3'0922 B
The fathers of the Latin Church. Translated by Manfred Hoffman. Stanford, Calif., Stanford University Press [1969, c1964] vii, 328 p. 23 cm. Translation of Lateinische Kirchenvater. Contents.Contents.—Tertullian.—Cyprian.—Lactantius.—Ambrose.—Jerome.—Augustine.—Boethius.—Bibliography (p. 317-325) [BR1706.C313 1969] 76-75260 6.50
1. Fathers of the Church, Latin. I. Title.

HORT, Fenton John Anthony, 1828-1892. 281'.3'0922 B
Six lectures on the ante-Nicene fathers. Freeport, N.Y., Books for Libraries Press [1972] vi, 138 p. 23 cm. (Essay index reprint series) Reprint of the 1895 ed. Contents.Contents.—Clement of Rome and Hermas.—Ignatius and Polycarp.—Justin and Irenaus.—Hippolytus and Clement of Alexandria.—Tertullian and Cyprian.—Origen. [BR1705.H8 1972] 79-37789 ISBN 0-8369-2596-3
1. Fathers of the church. 2. Apostolic Fathers. I. Title.

FERGUSON, John, 1921- 281'.3'0924 B
Clement of Alexandria. New York, Twayne Publishers [1974, c1973] p. cm. (Twayne's world authors series, TWAS 289) Bibliography: p. [BR1720.C6F4 1974] 73-15745 ISBN 0-8057-2231-9 5.95
1. Clemens, Titus Flavius, Alexandrinus. I. Title.

HARRIS, Carl Vernon, 1922- 281'.3'0924
Origen of Alexandria's interpretation of the teacher's function in the early Christian hierarchy and community. [1st ed.] New York, American Press [c1966] 278 p. 22 cm. Bibliography: p. 267-278. [BR65.O68H32] 66-28803
1. Origenes. 2. Religious education—Hist.—Early church. I. Title.

LILLA, Salvatore R. C. 281'.3'0924 B
Clement of Alexandria: a study in Christian Platonism and Gnosticism, by Salvatore R. C. Lilla. [London] Oxford University Press, 1971. xiv, 266 p. 23 cm. (Oxford theological monographs) Revision of thesis, Oxford. Bibliography: p. [235]-245. [B666.Z7L54 1971] 77-881314 ISBN 0-19-826706-1 £3.50
1. Clemens, Titus Flavius, Alexandrinus. I. Title. II. Series.

AMBROSIUS, Saint, Bp. of Milan. 281.4
Letters; translated by Sister Mary Melchior Beyenka. New York, Fathers of the Church, inc., 1954. xviii, 515p. 21cm. (The Fathers of the church, a new translation, v.26) 'Select bibliography': p.xiv. [BR60.F3A56] A55
I. Title. II. Series.
Contents omitted.

AMBROSIUS, Saint, Bp. of Milan. 281.4
Saint Ambrose: theological and dogmatic works. Translated by Roy J. Deferrari. Washington, Catholic University of America Press, 1963. xxiii. 343 p. 22 cm. (The Fathers of the church, a new translation, v. 44) Bibliography: p. xxii-xxiii. [BR60.F3A57] 63-2801
1. Holy Spirit — Early works to 1800. 2. Sacraments — Early works to 1800. I. Deferrari, Roy Joseph, 1800- tr. II. Title. III. Series.

AMBROSIUS, Salnt, Bp. of Milan. 281.4
Saint Ambrose: theological and dogmatic works. Tr. by Roy J. Deferrari. Washington. D.C., Catholic Univ. [c.]1963. xxiii, 343p. 22cm. (Fathers of the church, a new tr., v.44) Bibl. 63-2801 5.50
1. Holy Spirit—Early works to 1800. 2. Sacraments—Early works to 1800. I. Deferrari, Roy Joseph, 1890- tr. II. Duff, James, Rev. III. Title.

AUGUSTINUS, Aurelius, Saint, Bp. of Hippo. 281.4
An Augustine sunthesis, arranged by Erich Przywara. New York, Harper [1958] xii, 495p. 21cm. (Harper torchbooks, TB35. Cathedral library) [BR65.A52E6 1958] 58-7110
1. Theology—Collected works—Early church. I. Przywara, Erich, 1889- comp. II. Title.

AUGUSTINUS, Aurelius, Saint, Bp. of Hippo. 281.4
Earlier writings; selected and translated with introductions by John H. S. Burleigh. Philadelphia, Westminster Press [1953] 413p. 24cm. (The Library of Christian classics, v. 6) Bibliography: p.407. [BR65.A52E6 1953] 53-13043
1. Theology—Collected works—Early church. I. Title. II. Series.

AUGUSTINUS, Aurelius, Saint. Bp. of Hippo. 281.4
Letters; translated by Sister Wilfrid Parsons. New York, Fathers of the Church, inc., 1951-55 [i. e. 1951-56] 4v. 22cm. (Writings of Saint Augustine, v. 9-12) The Fathers of the Church, a new translation, v. 12, 18, 20, 30. [BR60.F3A8 vol. 9, etc.] 51-12720
I. Title.

AUGUSTINUS Aurelius Bp. of Hippo 281.4
St. Augustine [pamphs. 12-13 Boston] St. Paul eds. [dist. Daughters of St. Paul, 1963] 2v. 18cm. Selections from the works of the Fathers in pamphlet form. 63-23668 .50 pap., ea.,
1. Theology—Collected works—Early church. I. Title.
Contents omitted.

AUGUSTINUS, Aurelius, Bp. of Hippo 281.4
Selected writings. Ed., introd. by Roger Hazelton. Cleveland, World [c.1962] 312p. 18cm. (Meridian Living age bks., LA37) Bibl. 62-13383 1.65 pap.,
1. Theology—Collected works—Early church. I. Hazelton, Roger, 1909- ed. II. Title.

AUGUSTINUS, Aurelius, Saint, Bp. of Hippo. 281.4
Selected writings. Edited and with an introd. by Roger Hazelton. Cleveland, Meridian Books [1962] 312p. 18cm. (Living age books, LA37) Bibliography: p. 311-312. [BR65.A52E6 1962] 62-13383
1. Theology— Collected works—Early church. I. Hazelton, Roger, 1909- ed. II. Title.

AUGUSTINUS, Aurelius, Saint, Bp. of Hippo. 281.4
Treatises on various subjects; translated by Mary Sarah Muldowney [and others] Edited by Roy J. Deferrari. New York, Fathers of the Church, inc., 1952. viii, 479p. 22cm. (The Fathers of the church, a new translation, v. 16) [BR60.F3A83] 53-287
1. Theology—Collected works—Early church. I. Title.
Contents omitted.

AUGUSTINUS, Aurelius, Saint, Bp. of Hippo. 281.4
Autobiography; an abridged form of the Latin text of Saint Augustine's Confessions, ed., introd., commentary by James Duff. Dublin, Browne and Nolan[dist. Mystic, Conn., Lawrence Verry, 1964] xlix, 113p. 22cm. 64-838 2.25 bds.,
I. Duff, Rev. James, ed. II. Title.

AUGUSTINUS, Aurelius, Saint, Bp. of Hippo. 281.4
Later works. Selected and translated with introductions by John Burnaby. Philadelphia, Westminster Press [1955] 359 p. 24 cm. (The Library of Christian classics, v. 8) Contents.Contents.—The Trinity.—The Spirit and the letter.—Ten homilies on the First epistle general of St. John.—Select bibliography (p. 349-351) [BR65.A52E6 1955] 55-5022
1. Theology—Collected works—Early church. I. Burnaby, John, ed. and tr. II. Series: The Library of Christian classics (Philadelphia) v. 8

AUGUSTINUS, Aurelius, Saint, Bp. of Hippo. 281.4
Sermons for Christmas and Epiphany; translated and annotated by Thomas Comerford Lawler. Westminster, Md., Newman Press, 1952. 249 p. 23 cm. (Ancient Christian writers; the works of Fathers in translation, no. 15) Selections from Sermones ad populum. Bibliographical references included in "Notes" (p. [183]-231) [BR60.A35 no. 15] 52-4901
1. Christmas sermons. 2. Sermons, Latin—Translations into English. 3. Sermons, English—Translations from Latin. I. Lawler, Thomas Comerford, ed. and tr. II. Title. III. Series.

BARLOW, Claude W., comp. 281.4
Iberian fathers. Translated by Claude W. Barlow. Washington, Catholic University of America Press [1969- v. 22 cm. (The Fathers of the church, a new translation, v. 62) Contents.Contents.—v. 1. Martin of Braga. Paschasius of Dumium. Leander of Seville. Includes bibliographical references. [BR60.F3I2] 70-80270 8.60 (v. 1)
1. Christian literature, Early. I. Title.

BARRACHINA, Ignatius 281.4
Spiritual doctrine of St. Augustine. Tr. [from Spanish] by Edward James Schuster. St. Louis, B. Herder [c.1963] xvi, 264p. 21cm. (Cross & crown ser. of spirituality, no. 25) Bibl. 63-19829 4.75
1. Augustinus Aurelius, Saint Bp. of Hippo Bp. of Hippo. 2. Spiritual life—History of doctrines. I. Title. II. Series.

BASILIUS, Saint, the Great, Abp. of Caesarea, 330(ca.)-379. 281.4
Writings. [New York, Fathers of the Church, inc., 1950- v. 22 cm. (The Fathers of the Church, a new translation. v. 9 Contents.v. 1. Ascetical works, translated by Sister M. Monica Wagner. Bibliography: v. 1, p. 6. [BR60.F3B3] 50-10735
1. Theology—Collected works—Early church. I. Title. II. Series.

BASILIUS, Saint, the Great, Abp. of Caesarea, 330(ca.)-379 281.4
Exegetic homilies. Tr. [from Greek] by Agnes Clare Way. Washington, D.C., Catholic Univ. [c.1963] xvi, 378p. 22cm. (Fathers of the church, a new tr. v. 46) Bibl. 63-12483 6.25
1. Bible. O. T. Genesis I-II, 3—Sermons. 2. Bible. O. T. Psalms—Sermons. 3. Sermons, Greek—Translations into English. 4. Sermons, English—Translations from Greek. I. Way, Agnes Clare, tr. II. Title. III. Series.

BASILIUS, Saint, the Great, Abp. of Caesarea, 330(ca.)-379 281.4
St. Basil. [Boston, Daughters of St. Paul, 1963] 3v. (various p.) 18cm. (Selections from the works of the Fathers of the church in pamphlet form) Vols. 1-3 translated by Sister M. Monica Wagner. Selections from St. Basilius' Writings issued in the ser.: The Fathers of the church, a new translation. 62-16942 v.1, pap., .35; v.2,3, ea., .50
1. Theology—Collected works—Early church. I. Title.
Contents omitted.

BATTENHOUSE, Roy Wesley, 1912- ed. 281.4
A companion to the study of St. Augustine. New York, Oxford University Press, 1955. 425p. 22cm. [BR1720.A9B33] 55-6253
1. Augustinus, Aurellus, Saint, Bp. of Hippo. I. Title.

BRIGHT, William, 1824-1901. 281'.4
The age of the fathers, being chapters in the history of the church during the fourth and fifth centuries. New York, AMS Press [1970] 2 v. 23 cm. Reprint of the 1903 ed. [BR205.B7 1970] 77-113564 ISBN 0-404-01078-4 (v. 1)
1. Church history—Primitive and early church, ca. 30-600. I. Title.

BROWN, Clifton F., 1943- 281'.4
The conversion experience in Axum during the fourth and fifth centuries, by Clifton F. Brown. [Washington] Dept. of History, Howard University [1973] 30 p. 23 cm. (Second series of historical publications, Dept. of History, Howard University) Bibliography: p. 27-30. [BR1370.B76] 73-164609
1. Aksum (Kingdom)—Church history. 2. Church history—Primitive and early church, 30-600. I. Title. II. Series: Howard University, Washington, D.C. Dept. of History. Second series of historical publications.

CAESARIUS, Saint, Bp. of Arles, 470?-543. 281.4
Sermons; translated by Mary Magdeleine Mueller. New York, Fathers of the Church, inc., 1956- v. 22cm. (The Fathers of the church, a new translation, v. 31) Bibliography: v. 1, p. xxvi-xxvii. [BR60.F3C3] 56-3628
1. Sermons, Latin—Translation into English. 2. Sermons, English—Translations from Latin. I. Title. II. Series.

CAESARIUS, Saint, Bp. of Arles, 470?-543. 281.4
Sermons; translated by Mary Magdeleine Mueller. New York, Fathers of the Church, inc., 1956- v. 22 cm. (The Fathers of the church, a new translation, v. 31) Bibliography: v. 1, p. xxvi-xxvii. [BR60.F3C3] 56-3628
1. Sermons, Latin—Translations into English. 2. Sermons, English—Translations from Latin. I. Series.

CANTOR, Norman F., comp. 281'.4
Medieval thought; Augustine & Thomas Aquinas, edited by Norman F. Cantor and Peter L. Klein. Waltham, Mass., Blaisdell Pub. Co. [1969] viii, 199 p. 23 cm. (Monuments of Western thought, v. 2) Contents.—The historical context.—An introduction to the life and work of Augustine and Thomas Aquinas.—Selections from Augustine's work (p. 18-99)—Selections from Thomas Aquinas' work (p. 101-171)—Modern commentary on Augustine, by F. Van der Meer and others.—Modern commentary on Thomas Aquinas, by M. D. Knowles and others. [BR65.A52E6 1969] 68-21146

I. Klein, Peter L., joint comp. II. Augustinus, Aurelius, Saint, Bp. of Hippo. III. Thomas Aquinas, Saint, 1225?-1274. IV. Title. V. Title: Augustine & Thomas Aquinas. VI. Series.

CHROSCIECHOWSKI, Julian. 281.4
God's infinite mercy. Stockbridge, Mass., Marian Fathers, Mercy of God Apostolate [1959] 140p. 19cm. Includes bibliography. [BT153.M4c5 1959] 60-20388
1. God— Mercy. I. Title.

CYRILLUS, Saint, Bp. of Jerusalem, 315(ca.)-386. 281.4
Catechetical lectures in Telfer, William, 1886- ed. and tr. Cyril of Jerusalem and Nemesius of Emesa. Philadelphia, Westminster Press [1955] [BR65.C93C45] 55-7709
I. Title.

CYRILLUS, Saint, Bp. of Jerusalem, 315(ca.)-386. 281'.4
The works of Saint Cyril of Jerusalem. Translated by Leo P. McCauley and Anthony A. Stephenson. Washington, Catholic University of America Press [1969-70] 2 v. 22 cm. (The Fathers of the church, a new translation, v. 61, 64) Contents.Contents.—v. 1. General introduction. The introductory lecture (Procatechesis). Lenten lectures (Catecheses).—v. 2. Lenten lectures (Katecheseis). Mystagogical lectures (Katecheseis mystagogikai). Sermon on the paralytic (Homilia eis ton paralytikon ton epi ten Kolymbethran). Letter to Constantius (Epistole pros Konstantion). Fragments. Indices. Includes bibliographical references. [BR60.F3C92] 68-55980 ISBN 0-8132-0061-X (v. 1) 8.50 (v. 1) 8.65 (v. 2)
1. Theology—Collected works—Early church, ca. 30-600. I. Series: The fathers of the church, a new translation, v. 61, [etc.]

DIONYSIUS Areopagita, Pseudo- 281'.4
The works of Dionysius the Areopagite / now first translated into English from the original Greek by John Parker. Merrick, N.Y. : Richwood Pub. Co., 1976. 2 v. in 1 ; 21 cm. Reprint of the 1897-1899 ed. published by James Parker & Co., London. Includes bibliographical references and index. [BR65.D62E5 1976] 76-15013 ISBN 0-915172-13-5 lib.bdg. : 25.00
1. Theology—Collected works—Early church, ca. 30-600. I. Parker, John, Rev. II. Title.

FREND, W H C. 281.4
The Donatist Church; a movement of protest in Roman North Africa. Oxford, Clarendon Press, 1952. xvi, 360 p. fold. maps. 23 cm. Bibliography: p. 339-351. [BT1370.F7] 52-4301
1. Donatists. I. Title.

GREGORIUS, Saint, Bp. of Nyssa, fl.379-394. 281.4
The Lord's prayer. The Beatitudes. Translated and annotated by Hilda C. Graef. Westminster, Md., Newman Press, 1954. v, 210p. 23cm. (Ancient Christian writers; the works of the Fathers in translation, no. 18) Bibliographical references included in 'Notes' (p. [117]-198) [BR60.A35 no. 18] 54-9263
1. Lord's prayer. 2. Beatitudes. I. Title. II. Series.

GREGORIUS I, the Great, Saint, Pope, 540(ca.)-604. 281.4
Dialogues; translated by Odo John Zimmerman. New York, Fathers of the Church, inc., 1959. xvi, 287 p. 22 cm. (The Fathers of the church, a new translation, v. 39) Bibliography: p. viii. [BR60.F3G7] 59-4637
1. Benedictus, Saint, Abbot of Monte Cassino. 2. Saints, Italian. 3. Miracles—Early works to 1800. 4. Immortality. I. Title. II. Series.

GREGORIUS I, the Great, Saint, Pope, 540(ca.)-604. 281.4
Dialogues; translated by Odo John Zimmerman. New York, Fathers of the Church, inc., 1959. xvi, 287p. 22cm. (The Fathers of the church, a new translation, v. 39) Bibliography: p. viii. [BR60.F3G7] 59-4637
1. Saints, Italian. 2. Benedictus, Saint, Albot of Monte Cassino. 3. Miracles—Early works to 1800. 4. Immortality. I. Title. II. Series.

HIERONYMUS, Saint. 281.4
Letters. Translated by Charles Christopher Mierow. Intro. and notes by Thomas Comerford Lawler. Westminster, Md., Newman Press, 1963- v. 23 cm. (Ancient Christian writers; the works of the Fathers in translation, no. 33 "The text followed ... is that provided by I. Hilberg, Sancti Eusebil Hieronymi Epistulae (Corpus scriptorum ecclesiasticorum latinorum 54 [Vienna-Leipzig 1910] 1-211)" Contents.CONTENTS. -- v. 1. Letters 1-22. [BR60.A35] 63-22028
I. Mierow, Charles Christopher, 1883- II. Lawler, Thomas Comerford. III. Title. IV. Series.

HIERONYMUS, Saint. 281.4
The satirical letters of St. Jerome. Translated into English and with an introd. by Paul Carroll. Chicago, Gateway Editions; distributed by H. Regnery Co. [1956] 198p. 18cm. (A Gateway edition, 6020) [BR1720.J5A42] 57-646
I. Title.

HIERONYMUS, Saint 281.4
Letters; v.1. Tr. [from Latin] by Charles Christopher Mierow. Introd., notes by Thomas Comerford Lawler. Westminster, Md., Newman [c.]1963. 281p. 23cm. (Corpus scriptorum ecclesiasticorum latinorum 54 Vienna-Leipzig 1910 1-2111) (Ancient Christian writers; works of the Fathers in tr., no. 33) The text followed is that provided by I. Hilberg, Sanctii Eusebii Hieronymi Epistulae Contents.v.1. Letters 1-22. 63-22028 4.00
I. Mierow, Charles Christopher, 1883- tr. II. Lawler, Thomas Comerford. III. Title. IV. Series.

JOANNES, of Damascus, Saint 281.4
Writings: [The fount of knowledge] Translated by Frederic H. Chase, Jr. New York, Fathers of the Church, inc., 1958. 1, 426 p. 22 cm. (The Fathers of the church, a new translation, v. 37) Contents.—Philosophical chapters.—On heresies.—An exact exposition of the orthodox faith. Bibliography: p. xxxviii. [BR60.F3J6] 59-792
1. Christian literature, Early (Collections) I. Chase, Frederic Hathaway, 1904- tr. II. Title: The fount of knowledge. III. Series.

KRUEGER, Arthur F. 281.4
Synthesis of sacrifice according to Saint Augustine; a study of the sacramentality of sacrifice. Mundelein, Ill., Apud Aedes Seminarii Sanctae Mariae ad Lacum, 1950. 171 p. 23 cm. (Poutificia Facultas Theologica Seminaril SanctaeMariae ad Lacum. Dissertationes ad lauream, 19) Bibliography: p. 165-171. [BR65.A9K7] 50-32946
1. Sacrifice. 2. Augustinus, Aurelius, Saint, Bp. of Hippo. I. Title. II. Series: St. Mary of the Lake Seminary, Mundelein, Ill. Dissertationes ad lauream, 19

LEO I, the Great, Saint, Pope, d.461. 281.4
Letters; translated by Edmund Hunt. New York, Fathers of the Church, inc., 1957. 312 p. 22 cm. (The Fathers of the church, a new translation, v. 34) Bibliography: p. 12. [BR60.F3L4] 57-3021
I. Series.

LEO I, the Great, Saint, Pope, d.461 281.4
Letters. Tr. by Edmund Hunt. Washington, D.C., Catholic Univ. of America Pr. [1963, c.1957] 312p. 22cm. (Fathers of the church; a new translation, v. 34) Bibl. 63-18827 5.00
I. Title.

LEO I, the Great, Saint, Pope, d. 461. 281.4
Letters; translated by Edmund Hunt. New York, Fathers of the Church, inc., 1957. 312p. 22cm. (The Fathers of the church, a new translation, v. 34) Bibliography: p. 12. [BR60.F3L4] 57-3021
I. Title. II. Series.

MARROU, Henri Irenee. 281.4
St. Augustine and his influence through the ages. Translated by Patrick Hepburne-Scott. Texts of St. Augustine translated by Edmund Hill. New York, Harper Torchbooks [c1957] 191p. illus. 18cm. (Men of wisdom, 2) Translation of Saint Augustin et l'augustinisme. Includes bibliography. [BR1720.A9M333] 58-5219
1. Augustinus, Aurelius, Saint, Bp. of Hippo. I. Title.

MARTINUS, Saint, Abp. of Braga, d.580 281.4
Opera omnia; edidit Claude W. Barlow. Published for the American Academy in Rome. New Haven, Yale University Press, 1950. xii, 328 p. diagrs. 25 cm. (Papers and monographs of the American Academy in Rome, v. 12) Bibliography: p. 305-306. [BR65.M39] 50-10338
1. Theology—Collected works—Early church. I. Barlow, Claude W., ed. II. Title. III. Series: American Academy in Rome. Papers and monographs, v. 12

NEMESIUS, William, Bp. of Emesa. 1886- ed. and tr. 281.4
on the nature of man in Telfer,On the nature of man in Telfer, 1886- ed. and tr. Philadelphia, Westminster Press [1955] [BR65.C93C45] 55-7709
I. Title. II. Title: Cyril of Jerusalem amd Nemesius of Emesa.

PELIKAN, Jaroslav, 1923- 281.4
The Light of the World; a basic image in early Christian thought. [1st ed.] New York, Harper [1962] 128p. 20cm. Includes bibliography. [BR65.A47P4] 62-7298
1. Light and darkness (in religion, folk-lore, etc.) 2. Athanasius, Saint, Patriarch of Alexandria, d. 373. I. Title.

PELIKAN, Jarslav Jan, 1923- 281.4
The Light of the World; a basic image in early Christian thought, [1st ed.] New York, Harper [1962] 128 p. 20 cm. (Gray lectures, 11th ser., 1960) Includes bibliography. [BR65.A47P4] 62-7298
1. Athanasius, Saint, Patriarch of Alexandria, d. 373. 2. Light and darkness (in religion, folk-lore, etc.) I. Title. II. Series. III. Series: The James A. Gray lectures at Duke University, 11th ser., 1960

PETRUS CHRYSOLOGUS, Saint, Bp. of Ravenna. 281.4
Saint Peter Chrysologus: Selected sermons; and Saint valerian: Homillies. Translated by George E. Ganss. New York, Father[s] of the Church, inc., 1953. viii, 454p. 22cm. (The Fathers of the church, a new translation, v. 17) Bibliography: p. 24. [BR60.F3P47] 53-9297
1. Sermons, Latin—Translations into English. 2. Sermons, English—Translations from Latin. I. Valerianus, Saint, Bp. of Cimies, fl. 439-455. Homilies. II. Title. III. Series.

PORTALIE, Eugene, 1852-1909. 281.4
A guide to the thought of Saint Augustine. With an introd. by Vernon J. Bourke. Translated by Ralph J. Bastian. Chicago, H. Hegnery Co., 1960. 428p. 22cm. (Library of living Catholic thought) 'Translation from the article, 'Saint Augustin' ... in the Dictionaire de theologie catholique, published by Editions Letouzey et Ane, Paris.' Includes bibliography. [BR65.A9P63] 60-50387
1. Augustinus, Aurelius, Saint, Bp. of Hippo—Theology. 2. Augustinus, Aurelius, Saint, Bp. of Hippo—Philosophy. I. Title.

TELFER, William, 1886- ed. and tr. 281.4
Cyril of Jerusalem and Nemesius of Emesa. Philadelphia, Westminster Press [1955] 466 p. plans. 24 cm. (The Library of Christian classics, v. 4) Contents.Contents.—Selections from the Catechetical lectures.—A letter of Cyril to Constantius.—On the nature of man.—Bibliography (p. 454-455) [BR65.C93C45] 55-7709
1. Catechetics. 2. Psychology—Early works to 1850. I. Cyrillus, Saint, Bp. of Jerusalem, 815 (ca.)-386. Catechetical lectures. II. Nemesius, Bp. of Emesa. On the nature of man. III. Series.

WILD, Philip Theodore, 1921- 281.4
The divinization of man according to Saint Hilary of Poitiers. Mundelein, Ill., Saint Mary of the Lake Seminary, 1950. 168 p. 23 cm. (Pontificia Facultas Theologica, Seminarii Sanctae Marie ad Lacum. Dissertationes ad lauream, 21) Bibliography: p. 161-168. [BR1720.H7W5] 51-4791
1. Hillarius, Saint, Bp. of Poitiers, d. 367: 2. Mystical union—History of doctrines. I. Title. II. Series: St.Mary of the Oake Seminary, Mundelein, Ill. Dissertationes ad lauream, 21

*WORKS of St. Augustine (The) 281.4
[notes] by Leo C. Daley. Edit. bd. of consultants: Stanley Cooperman,Charles Leavitt, Unicio J. Violi. New York, Monarch Pr. [c.1965] 89p. 22cm. (Monarch notes and study guides, 537-1) Cover title. Bibl. 1.00 pap.,

AUGUSTINUS, Aurelius, Saint, Bp. of Hippo. 281'.4'0924
The retractations. Translated by Mary Inez Bogan. Washington, Catholic University of America Press [1968] xxvi, 321 p. 22 cm. (The Fathers of the church, a new translation, v. 60) Includes bibliographical references. [BR60.F3A8253] 67-30513 7.80
1. Augustinus, Aurelius, Saint, Bp. of Hippo—Bio-bibliography. I. Title. II. Series.

BENOIT, Alphonse. 281'.4'0924 B
Saint Gregoire de Nazianze; sa vie, ses ouvres et son epoque. Hildesheim, New York, G. Olms, 1973. vi, 788 p. port. 20 cm. "Nachdruck der Ausgabe Marseille und Paris 1876." Includes bibliographical references. [BR1720.G7B46 1973] 73-168647 ISBN 3-487-04695-4
1. Gregorius Nazianzenus, Saint, Patriarch of Constaninople. I. Title.

BUDGE, Ernest Alfred Thompson Wallis, 1857-1834, ed. 281'.4'0924 B
The histories of Rabban Hormizd the Persian and Rabban Bar-'Idta : the Syriac texts edited with English translations / by E. A. Wallis Budge. New York : AMS Press, 1976. 2 v. ; 23 cm. Reprint of the 1902 ed. published by Luzac, London. The life of Hormizd was written by Rabban Mar Simon, the disciple of Mar Yozadhak. The life of Bar-'Idta was written by Abraham, a priest, at the command of 'Abhd-Isho, metropolitan of Adiabene, and is based upon that which was written by Mar John, a disciple of Bar-'Idta, who flourished about A.D. 660. Contents.Contents.—[v. 1] The Syriac texts.—v. 2, pt. 1. English translations. pt. 2. The metrical life of Rabban Hormizd by Mar Sergius of Adhorbijaijan. [BR1720.H82B8 1976] 73-18847 ISBN 0-404-11336-2 : 46.00 (2 vol set)
1. Hormizd, Rabban, 7th cent. 2. Bar-'Idta, ca. 509-612. I. Shem'on, Rabban Mar, 7th cent. Tash'ita de-'amlauhi alahaye ve-dubbarauhi temihe de-Rabban Hormizd. English & Syriac. 1976. II. Abraham, a priest. Tash'ita mekallasta de-abun zahya ve-kaddisha Rabban Bar 'Idta. English & Syriac. 1976. III. Sargis bar Wahle. Memerona. English. 1976. IV. Title.

EUGIPPIUS 281.40924
Leben des heiligen Severin. Ubersetzt von Carl Rodenberg. 3.,neubearb. Aufl. Leipzig, Verlag der Dykschen Buchhandlung [1884]. New York, Johnson Reprint [1965] 88p. 19cm. (Die Geschichtschreiber der deutschen Vorzeit. 2. Gesamtausg., Bd. 4) Tr. from T. Mommsen's ed. pub. in the Scriptores rerum Germanicarum in 1898 [BR1720.S4 E85 1965] 66-3872 Price unreported
1. Severinus, Saint, d. 482. I. Rodenberg, Carl, 1854-1926, ed. and tr. II. Title.

EUGIPPIUS 281.40924
The life of Saint Severin. Tr. by Ludwig Bieler with Ludmilla Krestan. Washington, Catholic Univ. of Amer. [c.1965] x, 139p. map. 22cm. (Fathers of the church, a new tr. v. 55) Bibl. [BR60.F3E853] 65-12908 4.40
1. Severinus, Saint, d. 482. I. Bieler, Ludwig, tr. II. Title. III. Series.

GNAYALLOOR, Jacob 281.40924
Augustine, saint for today. Milwaukee, Bruce [c.1965] v, 113p. 22cm. [BR1720.A9G58] 65-21893 2.95
1. Augustinus, Aurelius, Saint, Bp. of Hippo. I. Title.

GNAYALLOOR, Jacob. 281.40924 (B)
Augustine, saint for today. Milwaukee, Bruce Pub. Co. [1965] v. 113 p. 22 cm. [BR1720.A9G58] 65-21893
1. Augustinus, Aurelius, Saint, Bp. of Hippo. I. Title.

PAULINUS, Saint, Bp. of Nola, 353-431 281.40924
Letters of St. Paulinus of Nola. Tr., annotated by P. G. Walsh. Westminster, Md., Newman, 1967. v. 23cm. (Ancient Christian writers: the works of the Fathers in tr. no. 36) Contents.v.2.--Letters 23-51. [BR60.A35 No. 35, etc.] 66-28933 8.95
I. Walsh, Patrick Gerard. ed. and tr. II. Title. III. Series.

PAULINUS, Saint, Bp. of Nola 353-431 281.40924
Letters of St. Paulinus of Nola [v.1] Tr. annotated by P. G. Walsh. Westminster, Md., Newman, 1966. v 277p. 23cm. (Ancient Christian writers: the works of the Fathers in tr. no. 35) [BR60.A35 No. 35, etc.] 66-28933 4.75
I. Walsh, Patrick Gerard, ed. and tr. II. Title. III. Series.

YAMAMORI, Tetsunao, 1937- 281'.4'0952
Church growth in Japan; a study in the development of eight denominations, 1859-1939. South Pasadena, Calif., William Carey Library [1974] xi, 185 p. illus. 23 cm. Revised version of the author's thesis, Duke University. Bibliography: p. [175]-185. [BR1305.Y35] 74-4009 ISBN 0-87808-412-6 4.95
1. Protestant churches—Japan. 2. Church growth—Case studies. I. Title.

DICK, Ignace. 281'.5
What is the Christian Orient? Translated by C. Gerard Guertin. Westminster, Md., Newman Press, 1967. x, 176 p. 22 cm. Translation of Qu'est-ce que l'Orient chretien. Bibliographical footnotes. [BX106.2.D513] 66-28936
1. Eastern churches. I. Title.

EMHARDT, William Chauncey, 1874- 281'.5
The eastern church in the Western World, by Wm. Chauncey Emhardt, Thomas Burgess [and] Robert Frederick Lau. New York, AMS Press [1970] x, 149 p. illus., ports. 19 cm. Reprint of the 1928 ed. "These chapters were delivered as a series of lectures in St. Paul's Chapel, Trinity parish, New York City, daily at noon in the Advent season of 1926." [BX733.E5 1970] 74-131039 ISBN 0-404-02329-0

1. Eastern churches. I. Burgess, Thomas, 1880-1955, joint author. II. Lau, Robert Frederick, 1885-1943, joint author. III. Title.

KING, Archdale Arthur, 1890- 281'.5
The rites of Eastern Christendom, by Archdale A. King. With a foreword by His Grace the Apostolic Delegate to Great Britain. Rome, Catholic Book Agency, 1947-48. [New York, AMS Press, 1972] 2 v. illus. 23 cm. Includes bibliographies. [BX4710.33.K552] 70-142246 ISBN 0-404-03677-5 70.00
1. Catholic Church—Oriental rites. I. Title.

KUZYK, Daria. 281'.5
Death verdict for a church. [Trenton, N.J., Society for the Promotion of the Patriarchal System in the Ukrainian Catholic Church, 1972] 11 p. illus. 22 cm. Caption title. [BX4711.623.K89] 74-151139
1. Catholic Church. Byzantine rite (Ukranian) I. Title.

LENTSYK, Vasyl'. 281'.5
The Eastern Catholic Church and Czar Nicholas I, by Wasyl Lencyk. Romae, New York, 1966. xiii, 148 p. 25 cm. Added t.p.: in Ukranian. Prefatory matter in English and Ukrainian. Bibliography: p. 145-148. [BX4711.622.L43] 74-151975
1. Catholic Church. Byzantine rite (Ukrainian) 2. Nicholas I, Emperor of Russia, 1796-1855. I. Title. II. Title: Skhidna Katolyts'ka tserkva i tsar Mykola Pershyi. III. Series: Rome (City). Ukrains'kyi katolyts'kyi universytet. Vydannia. IV. Series: Rome (City). Ukrains'kyi katolyts'kyi universytet. Filosofichno-filolohichnyi fakul'tet. Pratsi, t. 2.

POTHAN, S G 1905- 281.5
The Syrian Christians of Kerala. New York, Asia Pub. House [1963] 119 p. illus. 23 cm. [BX163.2.P6] 63-1869
1. St. Thomas Christians 2. Kerala—Church history. I. Title.

POTHAN, S. G. 1905- 281.5
The Syrian Christians of Kerala. Bombay, New York, Asia, Pub, House [1963] 119 p. illus., plates. 23 cm. Bibliography: p. 111-112 [BX163.2] 63-4051
1. St. Thomas Christians. 2. Kerala—Church history. I. Title.

POTHAN, S. G., 1905- 281.5
The Syrian Christians of Kerala. New York, Asia Pub. [dist. Taplinger, c.1963] 119p. illus. 23cm. 63-1869 6.50
1. St. Thomas Christians. 2. Kerala—Church history. I. Title.

RABBATH, Antoine, 1867-1913, comp. 281'.5
Documents inedits pour servir a l'histoire du christianisme en Orient. New York, AMS Press [1973] 2 v. 23 cm. Texts in French and/or Italian, Latin, Arabic, Portuguese; some summaries in French. Reprint of the 1905?-1911? ed. published by A. Picard, Paris. [BR1070.R3 1973] 72-174293 ISBN 0-404-05202-9
1. Near East—Church history—Sources. I. Title.

SCHOEPS, Hans Joachim. 281'.5
Jewish Christianity; factional disputes in the early church. Translated by Douglas R. A. Hare. Philadelphia, Fortress Press [1969] xi, 163 p. 20 cm. Translation of Das Judenchristentum. Includes bibliographical references. [BT1375.S313] 69-12994 3.50
1. Ebionism. I. Title.

FREND, W. H. C. 281'.6
The rise of the monophysite movement; chapters in the history of the church in the fifth and sixth centuries [by] W. H. C. Frend. Cambridge, [Eng.] University Press, 1972. xvii, 405 p. 24 cm. Revised ed. of the Birkbeck lectures for 1968 on the Rise of the monophysite empire. Bibliography: p. 369-392. [BT1425.F73] 72-75302 ISBN 0-521-08130-0
1. Monophysites. 2. Church history—Primitive and early church, ca. 30-600. I. Title.

BOYAJIAN, Dickran H 281.62
A light through the Iron Curtain. [1st ed.] New York, Vantage Press [1958, c1957] 75p. illus. 21cm. [BX123.B6] 58-401
1. Armenian Church. 2. Armenia—Descr. & trav. I. Title.

DOWLING, Theodore Edward, 1837-1921. 281'.62
The Armenian Church. With an introd. by the Lord Bishop of Salisbury. New York, AMS Press [1970] 160 p. illus. 19 cm. Reprint of the 1910 ed. Bibliography: p. xvi. [BX126.D7 1970] 71-131511 ISBN 0-404-02167-0
1. Armenian Church.

FORTESCUE, Edward Francis Knottesford. 281'.62
The Armenian Church, founded by St. Gregory the Illuminator; being a sketch of the history, liturgy, doctrine, and ceremonies of this ancient national church, by E. F. K. Fortescue. With an appendix by S. C. Malan. [1st AMS ed.] New York, AMS Press [1970] 336 p. illus. 19 cm. "The confession of faith of the Orthodox Armenian Church; together with The rite of holy baptism as it is administered in that church, translated from the originals by ... S. C. Malan": p. [245]-321. Reprint of the 1892 ed. Includes bibliographical references. [BX126.F6 1970] 76-131507 ISBN 0-404-02518-8
1. Armenian Church. I. Malan, Solomon Casar, 1812-1894. II. Title.

KIWLESERIAN, Babgen, 1868-1936. 281'.62
The Armenian Church, by Papken Catholicos Gulesserian. Translated by Terenig Vartabed Poladian. 2d ed. New York, AMS Press [1970] xii, 61 p. 18 cm. Reprint of the 1939 ed. [BX126.K5 1970] 70-131508 ISBN 0-404-02949-3
1. Armenian Church.

MANOOGIAN, Sion, 1906- 281'.62
The Armenian Church and her teachings. [Detroit? 1951?] 53 p. illus., ports. 22 cm. Cover title. [BX126.2.M35] 77-2602
1. Armenian Church—Doctrinal and controversial works. I. Title.

NERSOYAN, Hagop. 281'.62
A history of the Armenian Church; with thirty-five stories. New York, Council for Religious Education, Diocese of the Armenian Church of North America [c1963] xiv, 287 p. 23 cm. [BX123.2.N4] 64-4015
1. Armenian Church — Hist. I. Title.

NERSOYAN, Hagop. 281'.62
Stories from the history of the Armenian Church. Illustrated by Joseph Kalemkerian. New York, Council for Religious Education, Diocese of the Armenian Church of North America [c1963] vii, 214 p. illus. 23 cm. [BX123.2.N42] 64-4054
1. Armenian Church — Hist. I. Title.

SARKISSIAN, Karekin, Bp. 281'.62
The Council of Chalcedon and the Armenian Church / Karekin Sarkissian. [2d ed.] New York : Armenian Church Prelacy, 1975. p. cm. Includes indexes. Bibliography: p. [BX126.2.S25 1975] 75-28381
1. Armenian Church. 2. Chalcedon, Council of, 451. I. Title.

ST. Mary's Armenian Apostolic Church, Washington, D.C. Booklet Committee. 281'.62'09753
Saint Mary's Armenian Apostolic Church; commemorative booklet. [Washington] 1968. 64 p. illus. 28 cm. Cover title. [BX128.W37S347 1968] 75-303574
1. St. Mary's Armenian Apostolic Church, Washington, D.C.

MANOUKIAN, Serovpe. 281.62569
Album of the Armenian Monastery of Jerusalem. New York, Delphic Press [1950] 59 p. illus., ports. 26 x 34 cm. Armenian and English; translation by Charles Vertanes and Mrs. Arlin K. Shallan. [BX128.J4S3] 51-23621
1. Jerusalem. St. James (Armenian monastery) 2. Jerusalem (Patriarchate, Armenian) I. Title.

BROWN, Leslie Wilfrid, Bp., 1912- 281.63
The Indian Christians of St. Thomas; an account of the ancient Syrian Church of Malabar. Cambridge [Eng.] University Press, 1956. 315p. illus. 22cm. [BX163.B7] 57-544
1. St. Thomas Christians. I. Title.

TISSERANT, Eugene, Cardinal, 1884- 281.63
Eastern Christianity in India; a history of the Syro-Malabar Church from the earliest time to the present day. Authorized adaptation from the French by E. R. Hambye. [1st ed.] Westminster, Md., Newman Press, 1957. 266 p. illus. 22 cm. Translation, with corrections and additions, of Syro-Malabare (Eglise) published in 1941 as a section of v. 14, pt. 2, of Dictionnaire de theologie catholique. [BX1644.T5] 57-11830
1. Catholic Church. Syro-Malabar rite—Hist. 2. Catholic Church. Syro-Malankara rite—Hist. 3. St. Thomas Christians. 4. Catholic Church in India—Hist. I. Hambye, E. R., ed. and tr. II. Full name: Eugene Gabriel Gervais Laurent Tisserant. III. Title.

GIDADA Solon, 1901- 281'.7 B
The other side of darkness, by Gidada Solon. As told to and recorded by: Ruth McCreery and Martha M. Vandevort. Edited by: Marion Fairman. New York, Friendship Press [1972] 116 p. 23 cm. Bibliography: p. 114-116. [BX6510.B44G5] 75-187807
I. McCreery, Ruth. II. Vandevort, Martha M. III. Title.

ISAAC, Ephraim. 281'.7
The Ethiopian Church. Boston, H. N. Sawyer Co., 1967. 60 p. illus., col. plates. 24 x 27 cm. [BX146.2.I8] 68-2579
1. Ya' Ityopya 'ortodoks tawahedo beta kerestiyan. I. Title.

JOSEPH, John. 281.8
The Nestorians and their Muslim neighbors, a study of western influence on their relations. Princeton, Princeton University Press, 1961. xv, 281p. maps. 23cm. (Princeton Oriental studies, 20) Bibliography: p. 239-269. [DS39.J6] 61-7417
1. Nestorians— Hist. I. Title. II. Series.

JOSEPH, John Benjamin 281.8
The Nestorians and their Muslim neighbors. a study of western influence on their relations. Princeton, N. J., Princeton [c.]1961. xv, 281p. maps (Princeton Oriental studies. 20) Bibl. 61-7417 6.00
1. Nestorians—Hist. I. Title. II. Series.

EMHARDT, William Chauncey, 1874- 281'.8'09
The oldest Christian people; a brief account of the history and traditions of the Assyrian people and the fateful history of the Nestorian church, by William Chauncey Emhardt and George M. Lamsa. Introd. by John Gardiner Murray. New York, AMS Press [1970] 141 p. map. 23 cm. Reprint of the 1926 ed. Bibliography: p. 137-138. [BX153.E6 1970] 71-126651 ISBN 4-04-023398-
1. Nestorians. I. Lamsa, George Mamishisho, 1893- joint author. II. Title.

THE Monks of Kublai Khan, Emperor of China; or, The history of the life and travels of Rabban Sawma, envoy and plenipotentiary of the Mongol khans to the kings of Europe, and Markos who as Mar Yahbh-Allaha III became Patriarch of the Nestorian Church in Asia. Translated from the Syriac by E. A. Wallis Budge. With 16 plates and 6 illus. in the text. London, Religious Tract Society, 1928. [New York, AMS Press, 1973] xvi, 335 p. illus. 23 cm. Translation of Yish'iata demar Yahbalaha vderaban Sauma. Bibliography: p. [307]-313. [DS752.Y5513 1973] 71-38051 ISBN 0-404-56905-6 20.00 281'.8'0922 B
1. Sauma, Rabban, d. 1293? 2. Yabhalaha III, Patriarch of the Nestorians, 1244?-1317. 3. Voyages and travels. 4. Nestorians. I. Budge, Ernest Alfred Thompson Wallis, Sir, 1857-1934, tr.

BENZ, Ernst, 1907- 281.9
The Eastern Orthodox Church, its thought and life. Translated from the German by Richard and Clara Winston. [1st ed.] Garden City, N.Y., Anchor Books, 1963. 230 p. 18 cm. (Anchor, A332) Translation of Geist und Leben der Ostkirche. Bibliography: p. [218]-230. [BX320.2.B413] 63-7690
1. Orthodox Eastern Church.

BENZ, Ernst Wilhelm, 1907- 281.9
The Eastern Orthodox Church, its thought and life. Tr. from German by Richard and Clara Winston. Chicago, Aldine [c.1963] 230p. 22cm. Bibl. 5.00
1. Orthodox Eastern Church. I. Title.

CALIAN, Carnegie Samuel. 281.9
Icon and pulpit; the Protestant-Orthodox encounter. Philadelphia, Westminster Press [1968] 220 p. 21 cm. Bibliography: p. 171-181. Bibliographical references included in "Notes" (p. 183-214) [BX324.5.C3] 68-23798 6.50
1. Orthodox Eastern Church—Doctrinal and controversial works—Protestant authors. 2. Orthodox Eastern Church—Relations—Protestant Churches. 3. Christian union—Orthodox Eastern Church. 4. Protestant churches—Relations—Orthodox Eastern Church. I. Title.

CONSTANTELOS, Demetrios J. 281.9
The Greek Orthodox Church: faith, history, and practice [by] Demetrios J. Constantelos. Foreword by Archbishop Iakovos. New York, Seabury Press [1967] 127 p. 21 cm. (A Seabury paperback, SP38) Bibliography: p. 125-127. [BX320.2.C64] 67-11468
1. Orthodox Eastern Church. 2. Orthodox Eastern Church, Greek. I. Title.

ENGLERT, Clement Cyril, 1910- 281.9
An appreciation of Eastern Christianity [by] Clement O. Englert. [Rev. and updated ed.] Liguori, Mo., Liguori Publications [1972] 128 p. 18 cm. First ed. published in 1961 under title: Catholics and Orthodox: can they unite? Bibliography: p. 126-128. [BX324.3.E5 1972] 78-189073 1.75
1. Catholic Church—Relations—Orthodox Eastern Church. 2. Orthodox Eastern Church—Relations—Catholic Church. I. Title.

ETTELDORF, Raymond. 281.9
The soul of Greece. Westminster, Md., Newman Press, 1963. xiv, 235 p. illus. 23 cm. Bibliography: p. 225-228. [BX320.2.E8] 63-23098
1. Orthodox Eastern Church. 2. Orthodox Eastern Church, Greek. I. Title.

ETTELDORF, Raymond 281.9
The sould of Greece. Westminster, Md., Newman [c.]1963. xiv, 235p. illus. 23cm. Bibl. 63-23098 4.75
1. Orthodox Eastern Church. 2. Orthodox Eastern Church, Greek. I. Title.

EVERY, George 281.9
The Byzantine patriarchate, 451-1204. [2d ed., rev. dist. Greenwich, Conn., Seabury, c.]1962. 204p. illus. 22cm. Bibl. 62-51093 5.00
1. Orthodox Eastern Church—Hist. 2. Schism—Eaetern and Western Church. I. Title.

FEDOTOV, Georgii Petrovich 281.9
The Russian religious mind; Kievan Christianity: the 10th to the 13th centuries. New York, Harper [1960, c.1946] xvi, 431p. Bibl.: p.413-422 21cm. (Harper Torchbooks/The Cloister Library/TB 70) 1.95 pap.,
1. Religious thought—Russia. 2. Russia—Church history. 3. Orthodox Eastern church, Russian—Hist. 4. Spirituality. I. Title.

FEDOTOV, Georgii Petrovich 281.9
The Russian religious mind, by George P. Fedotov [Gloucester, Mass., Peter Smith. 1960, c.1946] xvi, 431p. 'Selected literature'; v. 1, p.[413]-422. 21cm. (Harper Torchbook/The Cloister library, rebound in cloth) Contents.[1] Kievan Christianity. The tenth to the thirteenth centuries. 4.00
1. Religious thought—Russia. 2. Russia—Church history. 3. Orthodox Eastern church, Russian—Hist. 4. Spirituality. I. Title.

FEDOTOV, Georgii Petrovich, 1886-1951 281.9
The Russian religious mind; 2v. Cambridge, Mass., Harvard [c.1946, 1966] 2v. (431; 423) 24cm. Contents.v.1. Kievan Christianity.--v2. The Middle Ages. Bibl. [BX485.F4] A47 v.1, 10.00; v.2, 12.00
1. Orthodox Eastern church, Russian—Hist. 2. Religious thought—Russia. 3. Russia—Church history. 4. Spirituality. I. Title.

FINN, Edward E. 281.9
Brothers East and West : a Catholic examines for Catholics the proposed Pan-Orthodox Synod / by Edward Finn. Collegeville, Minn. : Liturgical Press, c1975. 172 p. : maps ; 18 cm. Includes index. Bibliography: p. 164-165. [BX324.3.F56] 76-353847 ISBN 0-8146-0876-0
1. Orthodox Eastern Church—Relations—Catholic Church. 2. Catholic Church—Relations—Orthodox Eastern Church. I. Title.

FORTESCUE, Adrian, 1874-1923. 281.9
The Orthodox Eastern Church. Freeport, N.Y., Books for Libraries Press [1971] xxxiii, 451 p. illus. 23 cm. Reprint of the 1920 ed. Bibliography: p. xxi-xxxiii. [BX320.F6 1971] 70-179520 ISBN 0-8369-6649-X
1. Orthodox Eastern Church.

FORTESCUE, Adrian, 1874-1923. 281.9
The Orthodox Eastern Church. With illus. by the author. New York, B. Franklin [1969] xxvii, 451 p. illus., map. 22 cm. (Medieval & Byzantine series 2) (Burt Franklin research & source works series 380.) Reprint of the 1907 ed. Bibliography: p. xv-xxvii. [BX320.F6 1969] 79-80232
1. Orthodox Eastern Church.

FORTESCUE, Adrian, 1874-1926. 281.9
The Uniate Eastern Churches; the Byzantine rite in Italy, Sicily, Syria, and Egypt. Edited by George D. Smith. New York, Ungar [1957] xxiii, 244p. 24cm. Bibliography: p. xi-xxi. [BX4713.F6 1957] 57-6424
1. Catholic Church. Byzantine rite—Hist. I. Title.

FOUYAS, Mathodios. 281.9
Orthodoxy, Roman Catholicism and Anglicanism. London, New York, Oxford University Press, 1972. xxi, 280 p. 23 cm. Bibliography: p. 260-272. [BX320.2.F68] 72-195672 ISBN 0-19-213947-9 £4.50
1. Orthodox Eastern Church—Doctrinal and controversial works. 2. Catholic Church—Doctrinal and controversial works—Orthodox Eastern authors. 3. Church of England—Doctrinal and controversial works. 4. Christian union. I. Title.

FOUYAS, Mathodios. 281.9
Orthodoxy, Roman Catholicism and Anglicanism. London, New York, Oxford University Press, 1972. xxi, 280 p. 23 cm.

Bibliography: p. 260-272. [BX320.2.F68] 72-195672 ISBN 0-19-213947-9
1. Orthodox Eastern Church—Doctrinal and controversial works. 2. Catholic Church—Doctrinal and controversial works—Orthodox Eastern authors. 3. Church of England—Doctrinal and controversial works. 4. Christian union. I. Title.
Available from Oxford University Press, New York, 15.25.

FRENCH, Reginald Michael, 1884- 281.9
The Eastern Orthodox Church. London, New York, Hutchinson's University Library, 1951. 186 p. 19 cm. (Hutchinson's university library. Christian religion) [BX290.F7] 51-11318
1. Orthodox Eastern Church—Hist. I. Title.

HALECKI, Oskar, 1891- 281.9
From Florence to Brest (1439-1596) [by] Oscar Halecki. 2d. ed. [Hamden, Conn.] Archon Books, 1968. 456 p. 25 cm. Includes bibliographical references. [BX830 1596.H3 1968] 68-26103 ISBN 0-208-00702-4
1. Orthodox Eastern Church—Relations—Catholic Church. 2. Ferrara-Florence, Council of, 1438-1439. 3. Brest-Litovsk, Council of, 1596. 4. Catholic Church—Relations—Orthodox Eastern Church. I. Title.

HERSEY, Merle Williams, 1888- 281.9
75th anniversary of the Lily Dale Assembly, 1879-1954 ... Condensed history Lily Dale, N. Y., Lily Dale Book Shop, c1954. 63p. illus. 19cm. [BX9798.S7H46] 54-28237
1. Lily Dale Assembly. I. Title.

JOSEPHSON, Emanuel Mann, 1895- 281.9
The unheeded teachings of Jesus; or, Christ rejected; the strangest story never told. Illustrated by Andre Michaillot. New York, Chedney Press [c1959] 96p. illus. 19cm. ('Blacked-out' history series) Includes bibliography. [BX9798.S47J6] 59-15870
1. Skoptsi. I. Title.

KIDD, Beresford James, 1863-1948. 281.9
The churches of eastern Christendom from A.D. 451 to the present time. New York, B. Franklin [1974] 541 p. illus. 23 cm. (Burt Franklin research & source works series. Philosophy & religious history monographs, 134) Reprint of the 1927 ed. published by Faith Press, London. Includes bibliographical references. [BX103.K5 1974] 73-16359 ISBN 0-8337-5168-9 23.50
1. Catholic Church—Oriental rites. 2. Eastern churches—History. 3. Byzantine Empire—Church history. I. Title.

KORPER, Ruth. 281.9
The candlelight kingdom; a meeting with the Russian Church. New York, Macmillan, 1955. 83 p. 22 cm. [BX510.K65] 55-1152
1. Orthodox Eastern Church, Russian. I. Title.

LE GUILLOU, M. J. 281.9
The spirit of Eastern Orthodoxy, Tr. from French by Donald Attwater. Glen Rock,N.J., Paulist [c.1964] 121p. 18cm. (Vol. of the 20th cent. ency. of Catholicism; Deus/Century bks.) Bibl. 1.00 pap.,
1. Orthodox Eastern Church. 2. Orthodox Eastern Church—Relations—Catholic Church. 3. Catholic Church—Relations—Orthodox Eastern Church. I. Title.

LE GUILLOU, M. J. 281.9
The spirit of Eastern Orthodoxy. Tr. from French by Donald Attwater. New York, Hawthorn [c.1962] 144p. (Twentieth cent. ency. of Catholicism, v. 135. Section 14: Outside the church) Bibl. 62-11413 3.50 bds.,
1. Orthodox Eastern Church. 2. Orthodox Easternern Church—Relations—Catholic Church. 3. Catholic Church—Relations—Orthodox Eastern Church. I. Title.

MAKRAKES, Apostolos, 1831-1905. 281.9
An Orthodox-Protestant dialogue. Translated from the Greek by Denver Cummings. [2d ed.] Chicago, Orthodox Christian Educational Society [1966] 127 p. 23 cm. [BX324.5.M313] 67-9736
1. Orthodox Eastern Church—Relations—Protestant churches. 2. Protestant churches—Relations—Orthodox Eastern Church. I. Title.

MAKRAKES, Apostolos, 1831-1905. 281.9
An Orthodox-Protestant dialogue. Translated from the Greek by Denver Cummings. [2d ed.] Chicago, Orthodox Christian Educational Society [1966] 127 p. 23 cm. [BX324.5.M313 1966] 67-9736
1. Orthodox Eastern Church—Relations—Protestant churches. 2. Protestant churches—Relations—Orthodox Eastern Church. I. Title.

MEYENDORFF, Jean, 1926- 281.9
The Orthodox Church, its past and its role in the world today. Translated from the French by John Chapin. [New York] Pantheon Books [1962] 244 p. 21 cm. Translation of L'Eglise orthodoxe: hier et aujourd'hui. Includes bibliographies. [BX290.M413] 62-14260
1. Orthodox Eastern Church—History. I. Title.

NATIONAL Spiritualist Association. 281.9
Proceedings of the annual convention. Washington. v. 23cm. Proceedings for 18 issued by the association under an earlier name: National Spiritualists Association. Published 1893-1905? Cf. Union list of serials. [BX9798.S7A15] 57-54693
I. Title.

NATIONAL Spiritualist Association of Churches. 281.9
Proceedings of the annual convention Washington. v. 23 cm. Proceedings for 18 issued by the association under an earlier name: National Spiritualists Association. Published 1893-19059 Cf. Union list of serials. [BX9798.S7A15] 57-54693
1. Spiritualism — Congresses. I. Title.

NATIONAL Spiritualist Association of Churches. 281.9
Spiritualist manual. [1st- ed.; Washington. 1911. v. illus., ports. 23 cm. Vols. for 1911- issued by the association under an earlier name: National Spiritualist Association of the United States of America. [BX9798.S7N35] 52-46465
1. Spiritualism. I. Title.

NATIONAL Spiritualist Association of Churches. 281.9
Year book. [Chicago, etc.] v.illus., ports. 16 cm. Vols. for issued by the assocaition under an earlier name: National Spiritualist Association of the United States of America. [BX9798.S7A16] 40-16569
1. Spiritualism — Yearbooks. I. Title.

NEALE, John Mason, 1818-1866, comp. 281.9
Voices from the East; documents on the present state and working of the Oriental Church. Translated from the original Russ, Slavonic, and French, with notes. London, J. Masters, 1859. [New York, AMS Press, 1974] xii, 215 p. 19 cm. Includes six essays and letters by Andrew Nicolaievitch Mouravieff and the Acathiston by Innocent, Archbishop of Odessa. [BX320.N4 1974] 75-173069 ISBN 0-404-04659-2 12.50
1. Orthodox Eastern Church. I. Murav'ev, Andrei Nikolaevich, 1806-1874. II. Innokentii, Abp. of Kherson, 1800-1857. III. Title.

ORTHODOXY and the religion of the future : can the Orthodox Church enter a "dialogue" with non-Christian religions? / By the editors of The Orthodox word. Platina, Calif. : Saint Herman of Alaska Brotherhood, 1975. xii, 92 p. ; 21 cm. Includes bibliographical references and index. [BX324.O77] 75-16940 2.00 281.9
1. Christian union—Orthodox Eastern Church. 2. Christianity and other religions. 3. Pentecostalism—Controversial literature. I. The Orthodox word.

PATRINACOS, Nicon D. 281.9
The individual and his Orthodox Church [by] Nicon D. Patrinacos. [New York] Orthodox Observer Press [1970] xii, 152 p. 22 cm. [BX320.2.P35] 73-128773
1. Orthodox Eastern Church—Doctrinal and controversial works. I. Title.

POLYZOIDES, Germanos, 1897- 281.9
The history and teachings of the Eastern Greek Orthodox church. New York, D. C. Divry [1969] 95 p. illus., ports. 23 cm. [BX290.P63 1969] 77-243091
1. Orthodox Eastern Church—History. I. Title.

THE Religious world of Russian culture / Andrew Blane, editor. The Hague : Mouton, 1976 359 p. ; 25 cm. (Russia and Orthodoxy ; v. 2) English, French, German or Russian. Includes bibliographical references and index. [BX250.R87 vol. 2] [BR932] 281.9'47 72-94520 40.00 281.9 s
1. Florovskii, Georgii Vasil'evich, 1893- 2. Russia—Religion—Addresses, essays, lectures. I. Blane, Andrew. II. Series. III. Slavistic printings and reprintings ; 260/2
Distributed by Humanities

RUNCIMAN, Steven, Sir, 1903- 281.9
The Great Church in captivity: a study of the Patriarchate of Constantinople from the eve of the Turkish conquest to the Greek War of Independence. London, Cambridge U.P., 1968. x, 455 p. 22 cm. Bibliography: p. 413-434. [BX410.R8] 68-29330 ISBN 0-521-07188-7 55/-
1. Constantinople (Patriarchate)—History. 2. Constantinople (Patriarchate)—Relations. I. Title.

SCHMEMANN, Alexander, 1921- 281.9
The historical road of Eastern Orthodoxy. Tr. by Lydia W. Kesich. New York, Holt [1963] viii, 343p. 22cm. Bibl. 63-11873 6.50
1. Orthodox Eastern Church—Hist. I. Title.

SOROKA, Leonid, 1916- 281.9
Faith of our fathers; the Eastern Orthodox religion, by Leonid Soroka and Stan W. Carlson. Minneapolis, Olympic Press [1954] 160p. illus. 27cm. [BX325.S67] 55-21996
1. Orthodox Eastern Church. I. Carlson, Stanley Waldo, 1909- joint author. II. Title.

SOROKA, Leonid, 1916- 281.9
Faith of our fathers; the Eastern Orthodox religion, by Stan W. Carlson and Leonid Soroka. Rev. ed. Minneapolis, Olympic Press [1958] 176 p, illus. 27 cm. In the earlier ed. Soroka's name appeared first on t. p. [BX325.S67 1958] 58-42572
1. Orthodox Eastern Church. I. Carlson, Stanley Waldo, 1909- joint author. II. Title.

WARE, Timothy, 1934- 281.9
The Orthodox Church. Baltimore, Penguin Books [1963] 352 p. 18 cm. (A Pelican original, A592) [BX106.W3] 63-4018
1. Orthodox Eastern Church. I. Title.

WARE, Timothy, 1934- 281.9
The orthodox church [Gloucester, Mass., P. Smith, 1964, c.1963] 352p. 19cm. (Pelican bk., A592 rebound) Bibl. 3.25
1. Orthodox Eastern Church. I. Title.

WARE, Timothy, 1934- 281.9
The Orthodox Church. Baltimore, Penguin [c.1963] 352p. map. 18cm. (Pelican orig., A592) Bibl. 63-4018 1.25 pap.,
1. Orthodox Eastern Church. I. Title.

ZERNOV, Nicolas. 281.9
Eastern Christendom, a study of the origin and development of the Eastern Orthodox Church, 1st American ed.,] New York, Putnam [1961] 326 p. illus. 24 cm. (The Putnam history of religion) Includes bibliography. [BX320.2.Z45 1961] 61-5715
1. Orthodox Eastern Church. I. Title.

ZERNOV, Nicolas 281.9
Eastern Christendom, a study of the origin and development of the Eastern Orthodox Church. New York, Putnam [c.1961] 326p. illus. (Putnam hist. of religion) Bibl. 61-5715 7.50
1. Orthodox Eastern Church. I. Title.

BESPUDA, Anastasia. 281.9*025*1812
Guide to Orthodox America. Pref. by Alexander Schmemann. [Tuckahoe, N.Y.] St. Vladimir's Seminary Press [1965] 150 p. illus. 23 cm. Bibliography: p. 8. [BX240.B47] 72-177219
1. Orthodox Eastern Church—United States—Directories. 2. Orthodox Eastern Church—Canada—Directories. 3. Orthodox Eastern Church—South America—Directories. I. Title.

DEMETRAKOPOULOS, George H. 281.903
Dictionary of Orthodox theology: a summary of the beliefs, practices and history of the Eastern Orthodox Church. Introd. by John E. Rexine. New York, Philosophical [c.1964] xv, 187p. 21cm. 63-13346 5.00 bds.,
1. Orthodox Eastern Church—Dictionaries. 2. Theology, Dictionaries. I. Title.

LANGFORD-JAMES, Richard Lloyd. 281.9'03
A dictionary of the Eastern Orthodox Church / by R. Ll. Langford-James ; with a pref. by Joannes Gennadius. New York : B. Franklin, [1976] p. cm. Reprint of the 1923 ed. published by the Faith Press, London. Bibliography: p. [BX230.L3 1975] 72-82261 ISBN 0-8337-4210-8 : 18.00
1. Orthodox Eastern Church—Dictionaries. I. Title.

ORIENS Christianus: 281.906
new ser. v.1-14, 1911-1924. New York, Johnson Reprint 1965. 14v. (various) p.) illus., facsims. 23cm. From the orig. which began pubn. in 1901 in Rome (later published in Leipzig, and Wiesbaden) Begrundet vom Priesterkollegium des Deutschen Campo Santo in Rom. Im Auftrage der Gorresgesellschaft herausgegeben. Chiefly in German [BX100] 65-7912 set 175.00; set, pap., 150.00
1. Eastern churches—Period. I. Baumstark, Anton, 1872- ed.

KOULOMZIN, Sophie. 281.909
The Orthodox Christian Church through the ages. New York, Metropolitan Council Publications Committee, Russian Orthodox Greek Catholic Church of America, 1956. 239p. illus. 21cm. (The Advanced Sunday school series for teen-agers) [BX290.K65] 57-24411
1. Orthodox Eastern Church—Hist. 2. Orthodox Eastern Church, Russian—Hist. 3. Russian Orthodox Greek Catholic Church of North America—Hist. I. Title.

NEALE, John Mason, 1818-1866. 281.9'09
A history of the Holy Eastern Church. London, J. Masters, 1850-73. [New York, AMS Press, 1973] p. [BX320.2.N42 1973] 74-144662 ISBN 0-404-04670-3 (set)
1. Orthodox Eastern Church. I. Title.

PARASKEVAS, John E. 281.9'09
The Eastern Orthodox Church; a brief history, including a church directory and prominent orthodox laymen, by John E. Paraskevas and Frederick Reinstein. [1st ed.] Washington, El Greco Press [1969] vii, 131 p., illus., map, ports. 21 cm. Bibliography: p. 127. [BX290.P36] 73-10983 5.95
1. Orthodox Eastern Church—History. I. Reinstein, Frederick, joint author. II. Title.

POLYZOIDES, Germanos, 1897- 281.9'09
The history and teachings of the Eastern Greek Orthodox Church / by Germanos Polizoides. New York : D.C. Divry, c1977. 95 p. : ill. ; 23 cm. [BX732.5.P64 1977] 77-152803
1. Orthodox Eastern Church—History. 2. Christian education—Text-books—Orthodox Eastern. I. Title.

WILLIAMS, George, comp. 281.9'09'033
The Orthodox Church of the East in the eighteenth century, being the correspondence between the Eastern patriarchs and the Nonjuring bishops. With an introduction on various projects of reunion between the Eastern Church and the Anglican Communion. [1st AMS ed.] New York, AMS Press [1970] lxxi, 180 p. port. 23 cm. Reprint of the 1868 ed. [BX310.W54 1970] 73-131028 ISBN 0-404-06977-0
1. Orthodox Eastern Church—History—Sources. I. Title.

FOR the glory of the Father, Son, and Holy Spirit: a history of Eastern Orthodox saints, by Michael James Fochios. Translations from [Megas synaxaristes and Vioi ton hagion (romanized form)] Edited by Aristides Isidoros Cederakis. Illustrated by Michael James Fochios [and] Harry Constantine Maistros. [Baltimore, Phanari Publications, 1974] 175 p. plates. 22 cm. [BX393.F67] 74-174410 281.9'092'2 B
1. Orthodox Eastern Church—Biography. 2. Christian saints. I. Fochios, Michael James, tr. II. Cederakis, Aristides Isidoros, ed. III. Doukakes, K. Megas synaxaristes. Selections. English. 1974. IV. Vioi ton hagion. Selections. English. 1974. V. Title: A history of Eastern Orthodox saints.

CAVARNOS, Constantine, comp. 281.9'0924 B
St. Cosmas Aitolos: great missionary, illuminator, and martyr of Greece; an account of his life, character, and message, together with selections from his teachings. Belmont, Mass., Institute for Byzantine and Modern Greek Studies [1971] 71 p. port. 21 cm. (Modern Orthodox Saints, 1) The introduction is a revision of an article by the compiler originally published in St. Vladimir's Seminary Quarterly in 1966. The biography of the Saint is by Saphiros Christodoulidis. [BX395.K67C38] 73-157457 1.50
1. Kosmas ho Aitolos, Saint, 1714-1779.

CAVARNOS, Constantine. 281.9'092'4 B
St. Macarios of Corinth, Archbishop of Corinth ... an account of his life, character, and message, together with selections from three of his publications. Belmont, Mass., Institute for Byzantine and Modern Greek Studies [1972] 118 p. port. 21 cm. (His Modern Orthodox saints, 2) Includes bibliographical references. [BX619.M26C38] 72-85116 2.75
1. Makarios, Saint, Metropolitan of Corinth, d. 1805.

CAVARNOS, Constantine. 281.9'092'4 B
St. Macarios of Corinth, Archbishop of Corinth ... an account of his life, character, and message, together with selections three of his publications. Belmont, Mass., Institute for Byzantine and Modern Greek Studies [1972] 118 p. port. 21 cm. (His Modern Orthodox saints, 2) Includes bibliographical references. [BX619.M26C38] 72-85116 2.75
1. Makarios, Saint, Metropolitan of Corinth, d. 1805.

CAVARNOS, Constantine. 281.9'092'4 B
St. Nicodemos the Hagiorite, great theologian and teacher of the Orthodox Church ... : an account of his life, character, and message ... / by Constantine Cavarnos. Belmont, Mass. : Institute for Byzantine and Modern Greek Studies, [1974] 167 p. : port. ; 21 cm. (His Modern Orthodox saints ; 3) Includes index. Bibliography: p. 157-158. [BX619.N5C38] 74-79388 ISBN 0-914744-17-8. ISBN 0-914744-18-6 pbk.
1. Nikodemos Hagioreites, 1748 or 9-1809. I. Title: St. Nicodemos the Hagiorite, great theologian and teacher ...

CAVARNOS, Constantine. 281.9'092'4 B
St. Nicodemos the Hagiorite, great theologian and teacher of the Orthodox Church ... : an account of his life, character, and message ... / by Constantine Cavarnos. Belmont, Mass. : Institute for Byzantine and Modern Greek Studies, [1974] 167 p. : port. ; 21 cm. (His Modern Orthodox saints ; 3) Includes index. Bibliography: p. 157-158. [BX619.N5C38] 74-79388 ISBN 0-914744-17-8 : 6.00 ISBN 0-914744-18-6 pbk. : 3.95
1. Nikodemos Hagioreites, 1748 or 9-1809. I. Title: St. Nicodemos the Hagiorite, great theologian and teacher ...

CAVARNOS, Constantine. 281.9'092'4 B
St. Nikephoros of Chios, outstanding writer of liturgical poetry and lives of saints, educator, spiritual striver, and trainer of martyrs : an account of his life, character, and message, together with a comprehensive list of his publications, selections from them, and brief biographies of eleven neomartyrs and other Orthodox saints who are treated in his works / by Constantine Cavarnos. Belmont, Mass. : Institute for Byzantine and Modern Greek Studies, c1976. 124 p. : port. ; 21 cm. (His Modern Orthodox saints ; 4) Includes index. Bibliography: p. 111-114. [BX395.N46C38] 76-3152 ISBN 0-914744-32-1 : 6.50. ISBN 0-914744-33-X pbk. : 3.95
1. Nikephoros of Chios, Saint. 2. Christian saints—Biography. I. Title: St. Nikephoros of Chios, outstanding writer of liturgical poetry ...

AN Early Soviet saint : the life of Father Zachariah / translated [from the Russian MS.] by Jane Ellis ; and with an introduction by Sir John Lawrence. London : Mowbrays, 1976. xiv, 111 p. ; 23 cm. (Modern Russian spirituality series) (Keston books ; no. 6) [BX597.Z3E17] 77-361317 ISBN 0-264-66334-9 : £4.25 281.9'092'4 B
1. Zachariah, Father, 1850-1936. 2. Orthodox (Orthodox Eastern Church)—Biography. I. Ellis, Jane, 1951- II. Series: Modern Russian spirituality series.

FLETCHER, William C. 281.9'0924 B
Nikolai; portrait of a dilemma, by William C. Fletcher. New York, Macmillan [1968] ix, 230 p. 22 cm. Includes bibliographical references. [BX597.N49F55 1968] 68-13209
1. Nikolai, Metropolitan of Krutitsy and Kolomna, 1892-1961.

GARDNER, Alice, 1854-1927. 281.9'092'4 B
Theodore of Studium; his life and times. New York, B. Franklin Reprints [1974] xiii, 284 p. illus. 23 cm. (Burt Franklin research & source works series. Philosophy & religious history monographs, 151) Reprint of the 1905 ed. published by E. Arnold, London. "The published works of Theodore": p. 271-277. Includes bibliographical references. [BR1720.T38G3 1974] 72-82007 ISBN 0-8337-1280-2 12.00
1. Theodorus Studita, Saint, 759?-826. 2. Byzantine Empire—Politics and government.

GOLDER, Frank Alfred, 1877-1929. 281.9'092'4 B
Father Herman, Alaska's saint; a preliminary account of the life and miracles of blessed Father Herman. Willits, Calif., Eastern Orthodox Books [1972, c1968] 66 p. illus. 20 cm. Reprint of the ed. published by Orthodox Christian Books & Icons, Platina, Calif. [BX597.G47G64 1972] 74-166116
1. German Aliaskinskii, Saint, 1756-1837. 2. Orthodox Eastern Church, Russian, in Alaska. I. Title.

HILL, Ida Carleton Thallon. 281.9'092'4
A mediaeval humanist: Michael Akominatos. New York, Burt Franklin Reprints [1973] 44 p. 23 cm. (Burt Franklin research and source works series. Philosophy and religious history monographs, 127) First published in 1923 in Vassar mediaeval studies, edited by C. F. Fiske, p. 275-314. Bibliography: p. [43]-44. [PA5301.A36Z7] 73-3164 ISBN 0-8337-3497-0
1. Acominatus, Michael, Choniates, Abp. of Athens, d. ca. 1220. I. Title.

JUDAS, Elizabeth, 1897- 281.90924
Rasputin, neither devil nor saint, [2d ed.] Miami, Fla., Allied Publishers [1965] 216 p. illus. ports. 21 cm. [DK254.R3J8] 65-8566
1. Rasputin, Grigorii Efimovich, 1871-1916. I. Title.

JUDAS, Elizabeth, 1897- 281.90924
Rasputin, neither devil nor saint. [2d ed.] Miami, Fla. 33127, Allied Pubs. 220 N.W. 47 St. [c.1942-1965] 216p. illus. ports. 21cm. [DK254.R3J8] 65-8566 3.95
1. Rasputin, Grigorii Efimovich, 1871-1916. I. Title.

LUCIW, Theodore. 281.9'0924 B
Father Agapius Honcharenko; first Ukrainian priest in America. Introd. by Walter Dushnyck. New York, Ukrainian Congress Committee of America, 1970. xx, 223 p. illus., facsims., ports. 24 cm. Bibliography: p. 209-216. [E184.U5L77] 78-115892 7.50
1. Honcharenko, Ahapius, 1832-1916. 2. Ukrainians in the United States. I. Title.

MEININGER, Thomas A. 281.9'0924
Ignatiev and the establishment of the Bulgarian Exarchate, 1864-1872; a study in personal diplomacy [by] Thomas A. Meininger. Madison [Prepared by] State Historical Society of Wisconsin for the Dept. of History, University of Wisconsin, 1970. xii, 251 p. 24 cm. Bibliography: p. 198-229. [BX653.M43] 70-630135
1. Ignat'ev, Nikolai Pavlovich, graf, 1832-1908. 2. Orthodox Eastern Church, Bulgarian—History. I. Title.

PAPADEMETRIOU, George C. 281.9'092'4
Introduction to Saint Gregory Palamas, by George C. Papademetriou. New York, Philosophical Library [1973] 103 p. 22 cm. Bibliography: p. 81-83. [BX395.P3P36] 73-77406 ISBN 0-8022-2120-3 5.00
1. Palamas, Gregorius, Saint, Abp. of Thessalonica, ca. 1296-ca. 1359. I. Title.

ZANDER, Valentine. 281.9'092'4 B
St. Seraphim of Sarov / Valentine Zander ; translated by Sister Gabriel Anne ; introd. by Boris Bobrinskoy. Crestwood, N.Y. : St. Vladimir's Seminary Press, 1975. p. cm. German translation has title: Seraphim von Sarow. Bibliography: p. [BX597.S37Z33 1975] 75-42136 ISBN 0-913836-28-1 : 4.95
1. Serafim, Saint, 1759-1833. I. Title.

CONSTANTINOPLE (Patriarchate). MSS.(Codex gamma). English. 281.9'3
Codex (G) gamma of the Ecumenical Patriarchate of Constantinople / [edited] by Nomikos Michael Vaporis. Brookline, Mass. : Holy Cross Theological School Press, 1974. 156 p. ; 23 cm. (The Archbishop Iakovos library of ecclesiastical and historical sources ; no. 2) First published in the Greek Orthodox theological review, v. 18, no. 1-2 (1973) and v. 19, no. 1 (1974). Includes bibliographical references and index. [BX410.C66 1974] 75-316532
1. Constantinople (Patriarchate)—History—Sources. I. Vaporis, Nomikos Michael. II. Title. III. Series.

DUSHNYCK, Walter. 281.9'3
The Ukrainian-rite Catholic Church at the Ecumenical Council. 1962-1965; a collection of articles, book reviews, editorials, reports, and commentaries with special emphasis on Ukrainian-rite and other Eastern churches. New York, Shevchenko Scientific Society, 1967. 191 p. illus., ports. 26 cm. (Shevchenko Scientific Society. Ukrainian studies. English section, v. 5 (23)) Bibliography: p. [157]. [BX8301962.D78] 67-28417
1. Vatican Council. 2d, 1962-1965. 2. Catholic church. Byzantine rite (Ukrainian) I. Shevchenko Scientific Society (U. S.) II. Title.

FLETCHER, William C. 281.9'3
The Russian Orthodox Church underground, 1917-1970, [by William C. Fletcher] London, New York, Oxford University Press, 1971. x, 314 p. 23 cm. Bibliography: p. [293]-308. [BX492.F49] 70-868518 ISBN 0-19-213952-5 £3.75
1. Orthodox Eastern Church, Russian. 2. Church and state in Russia—1917- 3. Persecution—Russia. I. Title.

FREEZE, Gregory L., 1945- 281.9'3
The Russian Levites : parish clergy in the eighteenth century / Gregory L. Freeze. Cambridge, Mass. : Harvard University Press, 1977. xi, 325 p. ; 25 cm. (Russian Research Center studies ; 78) Includes index. Bibliography: p. [298]-317. [BX540.F73] 76-30764 ISBN 0-674-78175-9 : 15.00
1. Orthodox Eastern Church, Russian—Clergy—History. 2. Clergy—Russia—History. I. Title. II. Series: Harvard University. Russian Research Center. Studies ; 78.

FREEZE, Gregory L., 1945- 281.9'3
The Russian Levites : parish clergy in the eighteenth century / Gregory L. Freeze. Cambridge, Mass. : Harvard University Press, 1977. xi, 325 p. ; 25 cm. (Russian Research Center studies ; 78) Includes index. Bibliography: p. [298]-317. [BX540.F73] 76-30764 ISBN 0-674-78175-9 : 15.00
1. Orthodox Eastern Church, Russian—Clergy—History. 2. Clergy—Russia—History. I. Title. II. Series: Harvard University. Russian Research Center. Studies ; 78.

KOVALEVSKY, Pierre. 281.9'3 B
Saint Sergius and Russian spirituality / by Pierre Kovalevsky ; translation by W. Elias Jones. Crestwood, N.Y. : St. Vladimir's Seminary Press, 1976. p. cm. Translation of Saint Serge et la spiritualite russe. Includes index. Bibliography: p. [BX597.S45K6913] 76-13018 ISBN 0-913836-24-9 : 5.50
1. Sergii Radonezhskii, Saint, 1314?-1392. 2. Russia—Religious life and customs. I. Title.

MAGOULIAS, Harry J. 281.9'3
Byzantine Christianity: emperor, church, and the West [by] Harry J. Magoulias. Chicago, Rand McNally [1970] x, 196 p. map. 21 cm. (The Rand McNally European history series) Bibliography: p. 181-185. [BX290.M3] 70-75615
1. Orthodox Eastern Church—History. I. Title.

THE New man: an Orthodox and Reformed dialogue. Edited by John Meyendorff and Joseph McLelland. [New Brunswick, N.J.] Agora Books, 1973. 170 p. 22 cm. Papers and summaries from a 3-year cycle of theological conversations, 1968-70, between representatives of the Standing Conference of Canonical Orthodox Bishops in America and the World Alliance of Reformed Churches, North America Area. "A short Orthodox bibliography in English, prepared by Prof. Nomikos M. Vaporis ...": p. 167-170. [BX324.5.N48] 73-78229 281.9'3
1. Orthodox Eastern Church—Relations—Reformed Church. 2. Reformed Church—Relations—Orthodox Eastern Church. I. Meyendorff, Jean, 1926- ed. II. McLelland, Joseph C., ed. III. Standing Conference of Canonical Orthodox Bishops in America. IV. Alliance of Reformed Churches throughout the World Holding the Presbyterian System. North America Area.

RODZIANKO, M. 281.9'3
The truth about the Russian Church abroad : the Russian Orthodox Church outside of Russia / by M. Rodzianko ; translated from the Russian by Michael P. Hilko. [Jordanville, N.Y. : Holy Trinity Monastery], 1975. 48 p. : ports. ; 24 cm. [BX495.5.R613] 74-29321 ISBN 0-88465-004-9 pbk. : 1.50
1. Russkaia pravoslavnaia tserkov' zagranitsei. I. Title.

RYCAUT, Paul, Sir, 1628-1700. 281.9'3
The present state of the Greek and Armenian churches, anno Christi, 1678. Written at the command of His Majesty. London, J. Starkey, 1679. [New York, AMS Press, 1970] 452 p. 23 cm. [BX320.R9 1970] 75-133821 ISBN 0-404-05476-5
1. Orthodox Eastern Church—Doctrinal and controversial works. 2. Armenian Church—Doctrinal and controversial works. I. Title.

VAPORIS, Nomikos Michael. 281.9'3
Some aspects of the history of the ecumenical patriarchate of Constantinople in the seventeenth and eighteenth centuries; a study of the Ziskind MS. no. 22 of the Yale University Library. [New York? Greek Orthodox Archdiocese of North and South America] 1969. vi, 151 p. 6 facsims. 23 cm. (The Archbishop Iakovos library of ecclesiastical and historical sources, no. 1) Includes 85 documents, dated Jan. 1655-May 10, 1763, in English translation with annotations, and 12 texts transcribed from the Greek MS. Based on the author's thesis (M.A.) Columbia. Bibliography: p. 147-151. [BX410.V36] 76-17304
1. Constantinople (Patriarchate) I. Yale University. Library. MSS. (Ziskind 22) II. Title. III. Series.

WARZESKI, Walter C., 1929- 281.9'3
Byzantine rite Rusins in Carpatho-Ruthenia and America, by Walter C. Warzeski. [Pittsburgh, Byzantine Seminary Press, 1971] x, 332 p. illus. 23 cm. Bibliography: p. 285-315. [DB355.W37] 70-30058
1. Catholic Church. Byzantine rite (Ruthenian) 2. Zakarpatskaia oblast'—History. 3. Ruthenians in the United States. I. Title.

HOLY Transfiguration Monastery. 281.9'3'09
A history of the Russian Church abroad and the events leading to the American Metropolia's autocephaly. Seattle, Wa., St Nectarios Press, c1972. 210 p. 29 cm. Bibliography: p. 210. [BX495.5.H64] 72-79507 ISBN 0-913026-04-2
1. Russkaia pravoslavnaia tserkov' zagranitsei. 2. Avtokefal'naia Amerikanskaia pravoslavnaia tserkov'. 3. Orthodox Eastern Church, Russian. I. Title.

NEWMAN-NORTON, Seraphim. 281.9'41
Fitly framed together : a summary of the history, beliefs, and mission of the Orthodox Church of the British Isles / by Seraphim Newman-Norton. Glastonbury : Metropolitical Press, 1976. 20 p. : ill., port. ; 22 cm. Bibliography: p. 19-20. [BX747.5.N48] 77-360456 ISBN 0-905146-02-6 : £0.50
1. Orthodox Church of the British Isles. I. Title.

CARPATHIAN Alliance. 281.9'437
The tragedy of the Greek Catholic Church in Czechoslovakia. New York, 1971. 68 p. illus. 24 cm. Includes bibliographical references. [BX4711.77.C95C37 1971] 74-157552 2.00
1. Catholic Church. Byzantine rite (Ukrainian)—Czechoslovak Republic. 2. Ukrainians in the Czechoslovak Republic. I. Title. II. Title: The Greek Catholic Church in Czechoslovakia.

BOGOLEPOV, Aleksandr Aleksandrovich, 1886- 281.947
Church reforms in Russia, 1905-1918, in commemoration of the 50th anniversary of the All-Russian Church Council of 1917-1918 [by] Alexander A. Bogolepov. [Translated by A. E. Moorhouse] Bridgeport, Conn., Publications Committee of the Metropolitan Council of the Russian Orthodox Church of America [1966] 59 p. 23 cm. Bibliography: p. 57-59. [BX491.B613] 66-28385
1. Orthodox Eastern Church, Russian. Pomestnyi sobor. Moscow, 1917-1918. 2. Councils and synods—Russia. I. Title.

CONYBEARE, Frederick Cornwallis, 1856-1924 281.947
Russian dissenters. New York, Russell & Russell, 1962 [c.1921] 370p. (Harvard theological studies, 10) Bibl. 61-13779 7.50
1. Sects—Russia. 2. Dissenters—Russia. I. Title.

CRACRAFT, James. 281.9'47
The church reform of Peter the Great. Stanford, Calif., Stanford University Press, 1971. xii, 336 p. 23 cm. Based on the author's thesis, University of Oxford. Bibliography: p. [308]-322. [BR935.C7 1971] 70-130823 ISBN 0-8047-0747-2 13.50
1. Peter I, the Great, Emperor of Russia, 1672-1725. 2. Church and state in Russia. 3. Russia—Church history. I. Title.

CURTISS, John Shelton, 1899- 281.947
Church and state in Russia; the last years of the Empire, 1900-1917. New York, Octagon, 1965[c.1940] ix, 442p. 24cm. [BX491.C8] 65-16770 9.50
1. Church and state in Russia. 2. Russia—Church history. I. Title.

ESHLIMAN, Nikolai. 281.9'47
A cry of despair from Moscow churchmen [by Nicholas Eshliman and Gleb Yakunin] An open letter of two Moscow priests to Patriarch Alexis of Moscow and to the chairman of the Presidium of the Supreme Soviet of the USSR about the persecution of religion. With an introd. by George Grabbe. New York, Synod of Bishops of the Russian Orthodox Church Outside of Russia, 1966. 65 p. 23 cm. Cover title. [BX492.E8] 67-8584
1. Orthodox Eastern Church. Russian. 2. Church and state in Russia — 1917- 3. Persecution — Russia I. Iakunin, Gleb P., joint author. II. Title.

*FEDOTOV, G. P., comp. 281.947
A treasury of Russian spirituality [Gloucester, Mass., P. Smith, 1965] xviii, 501p. (Harper torchbk., Acad. lib. rebound) Bibl. 5.00
I. Title.

*FEDOTOV, G. P., comp. 281.947
A treasury of Russian spirituality. New York, Harper [1965] xviii, 501p. illus. 21cm. (Harper torchbk.; Cathedral lib., TB303) Bibl. 2.95 pap.,
I. Title.

FEDOTOV, Georgii Petrovich, 1886-1951. 281.947
The Russian religious mind. Cambridge, Harvard University Press, 1946-66. 2 v. 13 1/2 cm. "Selected literature": v. 1. p. [413]-424. "Bibliography of the writings of George P. Fedotov (1886-1951) compiled and edited by Thomas E. Bird": v. 2, p. [397]-413. Bibliographical footnotes. Contents.[I] Klevan Christianity--II. The Middle Ages, the thirteenth to the fifteenth centuries, edited, with a foreword, by John Meyendorff. [BX485.F4] A 47

1. Religious thought—Russia. 2. Russia—Church history. 3. Orthodox Eastern church, Russian—Hist. 4. Spirituality. I. Title.

FLETCHER, William C 281.947
A study in survival: the church in Russia, 1927-1943 [by] William C. Fletcher [1st American ed.] New York, Macmillan [1965] 168 p. 21 cm. Bibliography: p. [158]-165. [BX492.F5] 65-28240
1. Orthodox Eastern Church, Russian — Hist. 2. Russia — Church history — 1917- I. Title.

FLETCHER, William C. 281.947
A study in survival: the church in Russia, 1927-1943 [1st Amer. ed.] New York, Macmillan [c.1965] 168p. 21cm. Bibl. [BX492.F5] 65-28240 4.95
1. Orthodox Eastern Church, Russian—Hist. 2. Russia—Church history—1917- I. Title.

HEARD, Albert F. 281.9'47
The Russian church and Russian dissent, comprising orthodoxy, dissent, and erratic sects, by Albert F. Heard. New York, Harper, 1887. [New York, AMS Press, 1971] ix, 310 p. 23 cm. Bibliography: p. [vii]-ix. [BX510.H4 1971] 70-127909 ISBN 0-404-03198-6
1. Orthodox Eastern Church, Russian. 2. Raskolniks. 3. Sects—Russia. I. Title.

ISWOLSKY, Helene. 281.947
Christ in Russia; the history, tradition, and life of the Russian Church. Includes bibliography. [BX485.I8] 60-12648
1. Orthodox Eastern Church, Russian— Hist. I. Title.

MARY JUST, Sister. 281.947
Rome and Russia, a tragedy of errors. Westminster, Md., Newman Press, 1954. 223p. 22cm. [BX323.M3] 54-12078
1. Orthodox Eastern Church, Russian—Relations—Catholic Church. 2. Catholic Church—Relations—Orthodox Eastern Church, Russian. I. Title.

MURAV'EV, Andrei Nikolaevich, 1806-1874. 281.9'47
A history of the Church of Russia, by A. N. Mouravieff. Tanslated by R. W. Blackmore. New York, AMS Press [1971] xix, 448 p. 24 cm. Translation of Istoriia Rossiiskoi tserkvi (romanized form) [BX485.M813 1971] 76-133816 ISBN 0-404-04541-3
1. Orthodox Eastern Church, Russian—History. I. Title.

ZERNOV, Nicolas. 281.9'47
Moscow, the third Rome. New York, AMS Press [1971] 94 p. 19 cm. Reprint of the 1938 ed. A history of the Russian Orthodox Eastern church. [BR932.Z4 1971] 76-149664 ISBN 0-404-07075-2
1. Orthodox Eastern Church. Russian. 2. Russia—Church history. I. Title.

CRUMMEY, Robert O. 281.9'47'2
The Old Believers & the world of Antichrist; the Vyg community & the Russian State, 1694-1855 [by] Robert O. Crummey. Madison, University of Wisconsin Press, 1970. xix, 258 p. illus., maps. 25 cm. Bibliography: p. 227-247. [BX601.C78 1970] 79-98121 ISBN 0-299-05560-4 10.00
1. Raskolniks. I. Title.

LACKO, Michael. 281.9'47'71
The Union of Uzhorod / Michael Lacko. Cleveland : Slovak Institute, 1966 [i.e. 1969?] 190 p., [2] leaves of plates : ill., maps ; 25 cm. "This dissertation appeared in Slovak studies vol. VI with the same pagination." Translation of Unio Uzhorodensis Ruthenorum Carpaticorum cum Ecclesia Catholica, by Joseph Gill. Bibliography: p. 11-14. [BX4711.62.L313] 75-316503
1. Catholic Church. Byzantine rite (Ruthenian) 2. Ruthenia—Church history. I. Title.

PAPADOPOULLOS, Theodore H. 281.9'495
Studies and documents relating to the history of the Greek Church and people under Turkish domination, by Theodore H. Papadopoullos. Brussels, 1952. [New York, AMS Press, 1973] xxiv, 507 p. 23 cm. Original ed. issued as no. 1 of Bibliotheca Graeca aevi posterioris. "[Planosparaktes (romanized form)], a document in political verse, edited from British Museum manuscript Additional 10077" (summary, text, and notes): p. [265]-392. Bibliography: p. [xi]-xxiv. [BX613.P3 1973] 70-180302 ISBN 0-404-56314-7 27.50
1. Orthodox Eastern Church, Greek. 2. Orthodox Eastern Church—History—Sources. I. Planosparaktes. 1973. II. Title. III. Series: Bibliotheca Graeca aevi posterioris, 1.

RINVOLUCRI, Mario. 281.9495
Anatomy of a church; Greek Orthodoxy today. With a foreword by Peter Hammond. [Bronx, N.Y.] Fordham University Press [1966] 192 p. 21 cm. Bibliography: p. 187-188. [BX615.R5 1966] 66-30071
1. Orthodox Eastern Church, Greek. I. Title.

PSOMIADES, Harry J. 281.9*561
The ecumenical patriarchate under the Turkish Republic: the first ten years, by Harry J. Psomiades. [New York] Reprinted by the Greek Archdiocese of North and South America [1964?] 56-80 p. port. 22 cm. Cover title. "Reprinted from The Greek Orthodox theological review, vol. VI, no. 1." [BX410.P74] 70-299797
1. Constantinople (Patriarchate). 2. Church and state in Turkey. 3. Turkey—Relations (general) with Greece. 4. Greece, Modern—Relations (general) with Turkey. I. Title.

MOLNAR, Enrico S., 1913- 281.9'63
The Ethiopian Orthodox Church; a contribution to the ecumenical study of less known Eastern Churches, by Enrico S. Molnar. Pasadena [Calif.] Bloy House Theological School, 1969. 25 p. illus., map. 24 cm. Cover title. Bibliography: p. 24-25. [BX143.2.M6] 70-7764
1. Ya' Ityopya 'ortodoks tawahedo beta kerestiyan. I. Title.

BOGOLEPOV, Aleksandr Aleksandrovich, 1886- 281.973
Toward an American Orthodox Church; the establishment of an autocephalous Orthodox Church. New York, Morehouse-Barlow Co. [c1963] 124 p. 21 cm. Bibliography: p. 105-108. [BX735.B6] 63-21703
1. Orthodox Eastern Church — U.S. 2. Orthodox Eastern Church, Russian, in the U.S. I. Title.

BOGOLEPOV, Aleksandr Aleksandrovich, 1886- 281.973
Toward an American Orthodox Church; the establishment of an autocephalous Orthodox Church. New York, Morehouse [c.1963] 124p. 21cm. Bibl. 63-21703 3.00
1. Orthodox Eastern Church—U.S. 2. Orthodox Eastern Church, Russian, in the U.S. I. Title.

ETEROVICH, Adam S. 281.9'73
Eastern Orthodox Church directory of the United States, 1968. Editor: Adam S. Eterovich. Saratoga, Calif., R & E Research Associates [1968?] 32 l. 29 cm. [BX731.E8] 73-23143
1. Orthodox Eastern Church—U.S.—Directories. I. Title.

FEDOROVICH, Nicholas. 281.9'73
My Church and my faith. [So. Bound Brook, N.J.] Ukrainian Orthodox Church of USA, 1969. 40 p. illus. map, ports. 26 cm. Enlarged and revised ed. of the author's The great Prince St. Vladimir. [BX738.U45F4 1969] 78-256441
1. Ukrainian Orthodox Church of the United States of America. 2. Vladimir, Saint, called the Great, Grand Duke of Kiev, 956 (ca.)-1015. I. Title.

NOLI, Fan Stylian, Abp., 1882 comp. 281.973
Fiftieth anniversary book of the Albanian Orthodox Church in America, 1908-1958. Boston, Albanian Orthodox Church in America, 1960. 265p. illus. 24cm. [BX738.A53N6] 60-35413
1. Albanian Orthodox Church in America—Hist. I. Title.

SERAFIM, Archimandrite. 281.9'73
The quest for Orthodox Church unity in America; a history of the Orthodox Church in North America in the twentieth century. New York, Saints Boris and Gleb Press, 1973. 187 p. 24 cm. Errata slip inserted. Bibliography: p. 176-187. [BX735.S47] 73-82540
1. Orthodox Eastern Church—North America. 2. Christian union—Orthodox Eastern Church. I. Title.

ST. Nicholas Cathedral Study Group. 281.9'7471
St. Nicholas Cathedral of New York; history and legacy, edited by M. Pokrovsky. [1st ed.] New York, 1968. 103 p. illus., ports. 23 cm. [BX591.N57S2] 68-56203
1. New York (City) St. Nicholas Cathedral. I. Pokrovsky, M., ed. II. Title.

PEKAR, Atanasii V. 281.9'748'85
Our past and present : historical outlines of the Byzantine Ruthenian metropolitan province / by A. Pekar. Pittsburgh, Pa. : Byzantine Seminary Press, 1974. viii, 60 p. ; 18 cm. [BX4711.72.P44] 75-307945
1. Catholic Church. Byzantine Ruthenian Metropolitan Province of Munhall, Pa. I. Title.

ALEUTIAN Islands and North America (Archdiocese) 281.9798
Year book. New York, Exarchal Council. v. illus. 21cm. [BX496.A5L55] 53-33367
1. Orthodox Eastern Church—U. S.—Yearbooks. 2. Orthodox Eastern Church, Russian—Yearbooks. I. Title.

282 Roman Catholic Church

ACKER, William G 282
You are God's chosen people; a study of the real you. New York, St. Paul Publications [1961, c.1960] 102p. Bibl. 61-8202 2.25
1. Catholics. 2. Christian life—Catholic authors. I. Title.

ACTON, John Emerich Edward Dalberg Acton, baron, 1834-1902. 282
Essays on church and state. Edited and introduced by Douglas Woodruff. New York, Viking Press, 1953. 518p. 23cm. [BV630.A3 1953] 53-5863
1. Church and state. I. Woodruff, Douglas, 1897- ed. II. Title.

ADOLFS, Robert, 1922- 282
The church is different. Translated by Hubert Hoskins. [1st ed.] New York, Harper & Row [1966] 149, [1] p. 22 cm. Bibliographical references included in "Notes" (p. 146-[150]) [BX891.A213 1966a] 66-15862
1. Catholic Church—Addresses, essays, lectures. I. Title.

ADOLFS, Robert, 1922- 282
The church is different. Tr. [from Dutch] by Hubert Hoskins. New York, Harper [c.1964, 1966] x, 149, [1]p. 22cm. Bibl. [BX891.A213] 66-15862 3.95 bds.,
1. Catholic Church—Addresses, essays, lectures. I. Title.

ARMSTRONG, April (Oursler) 282
What's happening to the Catholic Church? [By] April Armstrong. [1st ed.] Garden City, N.Y., Doubelday, 1966. 267 p. 22 cm. Bibliography: p. 205-207. [BX891.A7] 65-19943
1. Catholic Church — Addresses, essays, lectures. I. Title.

ARMSTRONG, April (Outsler) 282
What's happening to the Catholic Church? Garden City, N.Y. Doubleday [c.] 1966. 207p. 22cm. Bibl. [BX891.A7] 65-19943 4.50
1. Catholic Church—Addresses, essays, lectures. I. Title.

ARRIEN, Rose Fe Narro. 282
I married a priest. Brooklyn [1951] 128 p. illus. 19 cm. [BX1777.A7A7] 51-8317
1. Arrien, John Joseph Uriarte. 2. Catholic Church—Doctrinal and controversial works—Protestant authors. I. Title.

AS the spirit leads us. 282
Edited by Kevin and Dorothy Ranaghan. Paramus, N.J., Paulist Press [1971] vi, 250 p. 19 cm. (Deus books) Includes bibliographical references. [BT123.A8] 77-152573 1.45
1. Baptism in the Holy Spirit—Addresses, essays, lectures. 2. Pentecostalism—Addresses, essays, lectures. I. Ranaghan, Kevin, ed. II. Ranaghan, Dorothy, ed.

ATTWATER, Donald, 1892- 282
The Christian churches of the East. v.2. Milwaukee, Bruce [c.1962] 260p. illus. 22cm. (Religion and culture ser.) Contents.v.2. Churches not in communion with Rome. Bibl. 7.50
1. Eastern churches. 2. Catholic Church-Oriental rites. I. Title. II. Series.

BACKUS, Isaac, 1724-1806. 282
A fish caught in his own net; an examination of nine sermons, from Matt. 16. 18, published last year, by Mr. Joseph Fish of Stonington; wherein he labours to prove, that those called standing churches in New-England are built upon the Rock and upon the same principles with the first Fathers of this country and that separates and Baptists are joining with the gates of hell against them. In answer to which many of his mistakes are corrected; the constitution of those churches opened; the testimonies of prophets and apostles, and also of many of those Fathers are produced, which as plainly condemn his plan, as any separate or Baptist can do. Boston, Printed by Edes and Gill, 1768. 129p. 19cm. Bibliographical footnotes. [BV600.A2F57] 59-56226
1. Fish, Joseph, 1707-1781. The church of Christ a firm and durable house. 2. Baptists—Doctrinal and controversial works. I. Title.

BALLANTYNE, Murray, 1909- 282
All or nothing. New York, Sheed & Ward [1956] 216p. 21cm. [BX4668.B27] 56-9521
1. Converts, Catholic. I. Title.

BALY, Denis. 282
Chosen peoples. Philadelphia, Christian Education Press [1956] 147p. 19cm. [BV600.B33] 56-9207
1. Church. I. Title.

BALY, Denis. 282
Shosen peoples. Philadelphia, Christian Education Press [1956] 147p. 19cm. [BV600.B33] 56-9207
1. Church. I. Title.

BAUMANN, Richard, 1899- 282
To see Peter, a Lutheran minister's journey to the Eternal City; translated by John M. Oesterreicher. New York, D. McKay Co. [1953] 192p. 21cm. Translation of Evangellsche Romfahrt. [BX4817.B32] 53-11352
1. Lutheran Church—Relations—Catholic Church. 2. Catholic Church— Relations—Lutheran Church. I. Title.

BEHM, Ernst Gustav, 1892- 282
The papacy evaluated. [2d ed. rev.] Milwaukee, Northwestern Pub. House [c1962] 168 p. 21 cm. [BX1765.B43] 63-4130
1. Catholic Church — Doctrinal and controversial works — Protestant authors. I. Title.

BERKOUWER, Gerrit Cornelis, 1903- 282
Recent developments in Roman Catholic thought. [Translated from the Dutch by J. J. Lamberts. Grand Rapids, Eerdmans [1958] 81p. 19cm. (A Pathway book) [BX4817.B433] 58-9543
1. Catholic Church—Relations—Protestant churches. 2. Protestant churches—Relations—Catholic Church. I. Title.

BERRIGAN, Daniel. 282
They call us dead men; reflections on life and conscience. Introd. by William Stringfellow. New York, Macmillan [1966] 192 p. 22 cm. [BX891.B47 1966] 66-11689
1. Catholic Church — Addresses, essays, lectures. I. Title.

BERRIGAN, Daniel 282
They call us dead men; reflections on life and conscience. Introd. by William Stringfellow. New York, Macmillan [c.1966] 192p. 22cm. [BX891.B47] 66-11689 4.95
1. Catholic Church—Addresses, essays, lectures. I. Title.

BIANCHI, Eugene C. 282
John XXIII and American Protestants, by Eugene C. Bianchi. With a foreword by Albert C. Outler. Washington, Corpus Books [1968] 287 p. 21 cm. Bibliography: p. 269-277. [BX4818.3.B5] 67-17520
1. Catholic Church—Relations—Protestant churches. 2. Joannes XXIII, Pope, 1881-1963. 3. Protestant churches—Relations—Catholic Church. I. Title.

BILSEN, Bertrand van. 282
The changing church. Adapted by Henry J. Koren. Pittsburgh, Duquesne University Press [1966] 440 p. 22 cm. (Duquesne studies. Theological series, 6) Translation of Kerk in heweging. Bibliographical footnotes. [BX891.B513] 66-18451
1. Catholic Church—Addresses, essays, lectures. I. Title. II. Series.

BILSEN, Bertrand van 282
The changing church. Adapted by Henry J. Koren. Pittsburgh, Duquesne Univ. Pr. [c.1966] 440p. 22cm. (Duquesne studies. Theological ser., 6) Bibl. [BX891.B513] 66-18451 7.95
1. Catholic Church—Addresses, essays, lectures. I. Title. II. Series.

BLANSHARD, Paul, 1892- 282
Paul, Blanshard on Vatican Boston, Bcacon [1966] 371p. 21cm. Bibl. [BX830 1962.B5] 66-23783 5.95 bds.,
1. Vatican Council. 2d, 1962-1965. I. Title. II. Title: On Vatican II.

BLANSHARD, Paul, 1892- 282
Paul Blanshard on Vatican II. Boston, Beacon [1967, c.1966] 371p. 21cm. (BP260) Bibl. [BX830.1962.B5] 66-23783 2.45 pap.,
1. Vatican Council. 2d, 1962-1965. I. Title. II. Title: On Vatican II.

BOETTNER, Loraine. 282
Roman Catholicism. Philadelphia, Presbyterian and Reformed Pub. Co., 1962. 466p. 24cm. [BX1765.2.B6] 61-16943
1. Catholic Church—Doctrinal and controversial works—Protestant authors. I. Title.

BROWN, Robert McAfee, 1920- 282
An American dialogue: a Protestant looks at Catholicism and a Catholic looks at Protestantism, by Robert McAfee Brown and Gustave Weigel. With a foreword by Will Herberg. [1st ed.] Garden City, N. Y., Doubleday, 1960. 216 p. 22 cm. Includes bibliography. [BX4818.3.B7] 60-13750
1. Protestant churches—Relations—Catholic Church. 2. Catholic Church—Relations—

Protestant churches. I. Weigel, Gustave, 1906- joint author. II. Title.

BUDDY, Charles Francis, Bp. 282
"Going, therefore, teach ..." [San Diego Calif., c1965] ix, 373 p. 21 cm. [BX891.B8] 66-95908
1. Catholic Church — Collected works. I. Title.

BUHLMANN, Walbert. 282
The coming of the third church : an analysis of the present and future of the church / Walbert Buhlmann. Maryknoll, N.Y. : Orbis Books, 1977, c1976. xi, 419 p. ; 22 cm. Translation of Es kommt die dritte Kirche. Includes index. Bibliography: p. 408-413. [BX1390.B8313 1977] 76-23237 ISBN 0-88344-069-5 : 12.95 ISBN 0-88344-070-9 pbk. : 6.95
1. Catholic Church—History—1965- 2. Catholic Church—Doctrinal and controversial works—Catholic authors. 3. Church and underdeveloped areas. I. Title.

BULLOUGH, Sebastian 282
Roman Catholicism. Baltimore, Penguin [1963] 330p. 18cm. (Pelican bks., A610) Bibl. 64-834 1.25 pap.,
1. Catholic Church. I. Title.

BULLOUGH, Sebastian 282
Roman Catholicism [Gloucester, Mass., P. Smith, 1964, c.1963] 330p. 18cm. (Pelican bk. A610 rebound) Bibl. 3.25
1. Catholic Church. I. Title.

BURGHARDT, Walter J ed. 282
The idea of Catholicism; an introduction to the thought and worship of the Church. Edited by Walter J. Burghardt and William F. Lynch. Expanded ed. Cleveland, Merridian Books [1964] 518 p. 21 cm. Bibliographical footnotes. [BX1747.5B8] 64-15322
1. Catholic Church. I. Lynch, William F., 1908- joint ed. II. Title.

BURGHARDT, Walter J., ed. 282
The idea of Catholicism; an introduction to the thought and worship of the church. Ed. by Walter J. Burghardt, William F. Lynch. Expanded ed. [Gloucester, Mass., P. Smith, 1965, c.1960, 1964] 518p. 21cm. (Meridian bk., M173 rebound) Bibl. [BX1747.5.B8] 5.00
1. Catholic Church. I. Lynch, William F., 1908- joint ed. II. Title.

BURGHARDT, Walter J., ed. 282
The idea of Catholicism; an introduction to the thought and worship of the Church [2d ed.] Ed. by Walter J. Burghardt, William F. Lynch. Expanded ed. Cleveland, World [c.1960, 1964] 518p. 21cm. (Meridian bks., M173) Bibl. [BX1747.5.B8] 64-15322 2.95 pap.,
1. Catholic Church. I. Lynch, William F., 1908- joint ed. II. Title.

BURGHARDT. WALTER J., ed. 282
The idea of, Catholicism: an introduction to the thought and worship of the Church. Ed. by Walter J. Burghardt. William F. Lynch. Expanded ed. [Gloucester, Mass., P. Smith, 1966. c.1960, 1964] 518p. 21cm. (Meridian bk. rebound) Bibl. [BX1747.5.B8] 5.00
1. Catholic Church. I. Lynch,. William F., 1908- joint ed. II. Title.

BURN-MURDOCH, Hector, 1881- 282
The development of the papacy. New York, Praeger [1954] 432p. 23cm. (Books that matter) Bibliographical footnotes. [BX955.B88 1954a] 54-12063
1. Papacy—Hist. I. Title.

CALLAHAN, Daniel J ed. 282
Generation of the third eye. Edited with an introd. by Daniel Callahan. New York, Sheed and Ward [1965] vi, 249 p. 22 cm. [BX1406.2C3] 65-12198
1. Catholic Church in the U.S.—Addresses, essays, lectures. I. Title.

CALLAHAN, Daniel J. ed. 282
Generation of the third eye. New York, Sheed & Ward [c.1965] vi, 249p. 22cm. [BX 1406.2.C3] 65-12198 4.95
1. Catholic Church in the U. S.—Addresses, essays, lectures. I. Title.

CALLAHAN, Daniel J. 282
Honesty in the church. New York, Scribners [1966, c.1965] 188p. 21cm. (SL128) [BV741.C28] 1.45 pap.,
1. Liberty of conscience. 2. Religious liberty. I. Title.

CALLAHAN, Daniel J. 282
The new church; essays in Catholic reform [by] Daniel Callahan. New York, Scribner [1966] xvi, 222 p. 22 cm. Bibliographical footnotes. [BX891.C25] 66-24497
1. Catholic Church—Addresses, essays, lectures. I. Title.

CARSON, Herbert M. 282
Roman Catholicism today, by H. M. Carson [1st American ed.] Grand Rapids, Eerdmans [1965] 128 p. 18 cm. Bibliographical footnotes. [BX891.C34] 65-3897
1. Catholic Church — Addresses, essays, lectures. I. Title.

CARSON, Herbert M. 282
Roman Catholicism today [1st Amer. ed.] Grand Rapids, Mich., Eerdmans [c.1965] 128p. 18cm. Bibl. [BX891.C34] 65-3897 1.45 pap.,
1. Catholic Church—Addresses, essays, lectures. I. Title.

CATHOLIC Students' Missionn 282
Crusade, U. S. A.
Christians of the East. [Cincinnati, Author, 1963] 79p. illus. 22cm. (CSMC five-hour ser.) Bibl. .90 pap.,
I. Title.

CAVANAUGH, Joseph Hubert, 282
1917-
Evidence for our faith. Notre Dame, University of Notre Dame Press [1952] 340 p. illus. 24 cm. (University religion series. Texts in theology for the layman) [BX1751.C34] 52-2580
1. Apologetics—20th cent. 2. Catholic Church—Apologetic works. I. Title.

CAVANAUGH, Joseph Hubert, 282
1917-1953.
Evidence for our faith. [3d ed.] Notre Dame, Ind., University of Notre Dame Press [1959] 256p. 24cm. (University religion series. Theology for the layman) Includes bibliography. [BX1751.2.C35 1959] 59-10456
1. Apologetics—20th cent. 2. Catholic Church—Apologetic works. I. Title.

CHEVILLE, Roy Arthur, 1897- 282
Did the light go out? A study of the process of apostasy. [Independence, Mo.] Dept. of Religious Education, Reorganized Church of Jesus Christ of Latter Day Saints [dist. Herald Pub. House, c.1962] 261p. 20cm. 62-21344 2.75
1. Catholic Church—Doctrinal and controversial works—Protestant authors. I. Title.

COLOMER, Luis, 1880- 282
The Catholic Church, the mystical body of Christ; translated from the Spanish by Palmer L. Rockey. Paterson, N. J., St. Anthony Guild Press, 1952- Brooklyn. v. 23 cm. v. illus., ports. 25 cm. [BX1751.C553] 52-12845
1. Catholic Church. I. Title.

CONTESTATION in the church. 282
Edited by Teodoro Jimenez Urresti. [New York] Herder and Herder [1971] 152 p. 23 cm. (Concilium: religion in the seventies, v. 68. Canon law) On cover: The New concilium: religion in the seventies. Includes bibliographical references. [BX1390.C65] 71-168654 2.95
1. Catholic Church—History—1965- I. Jimenez Urresti, Teodoro Ignacio, ed. II. Series: Concilium (New York) v. 68.

*CONWAY, J. D. 282
What the Church teaches. Garden City, N.Y., Doubleday [1965, c.1962] 320p. 19cm. (Echo bk., E10) .95 pap.,
I. Title.

CONWAY, John Donald, 1905- 282
What the church teaches. New York, Harper & Row [c.1962] 336p. 22cm. 62-11125 4.95
1. Catholic Church—Doctrinal and controversial works, Popular. I. Title.

CORBISHLEY, Thomas 282
Roman Catholicism. New York, Harper [c.1964] 150p. 21cm. (Harper torchbks., Cloister lib., TB112) Bibl. 64-333 .95 pap.,
1. Catholic Church—Addresses, essays, lectures. I. Title.

CRONIN, John Francis, 1908- 282
The Catholic as citizen. Baltimore, Helicon [1963] 176 p. 23 cm. Includes bibliography. [BX1793.C7] 63-120944
1. Christianity and politics. 2. Catholics in the U.S. I. Title.

D'ARCH, Martin Cyril, 1888- 282
Dialogue with myself. New York, Trident [c.] 1966. xlii, 179p. 21cm. (Credo ser.) [BX891.D3] 66-15723 4.95
1. Catholic Church—Addresses, essays, lectures. I. Title.

D'ARCY, Martin Cyril, 1888- 282
Catholicism. Dublin, Clonmore & Reynolds[dist. Wilkes-Barre, Pa., Dimension Bks., 1964] 92p. 16cm. Bibl. 1.25 pap.,
1. Catholic church. I. Title.

D'ARCY, Martin Cyril, 1888- 282
Dialogue with myself, by Martin C. D'Arcy. New York, Trident Press, 1966. xiii, 179 p. 21 cm. (The Credo series) [BX891.D3] 66-15723
1. Catholic Church — Addresses, essays, lectures. I. Title.

DE LA BEDOYERE, Michael, 282
1900- ed.
Objections to Roman Catholicism [by] Magdalen Goffin [others] Philadelphia, Lippincott, 1965[c.1964] 184p. 20cm. Bibl. [BX891.D4] 65-14339 3.95 bds.,
1. Catholic Church—Addresses, essays, lectures. 2. Catholic Church—Apologetic works. I. Goffin, Magdalen (Watkin) II. Title.

DE LA BEDOYERE, Michael, 282
1900- ed.
Objections to Roman Catholicism [by] Magdalen Goffin [others. New York] New Amer. Lib. [1966, c.1964] xvi, 172p. 18cm. (Signet bk., T2965) Bibl. [BX891.D4 1965] .75 pap.,
1. Catholic Church—Addresses, essays, lectures. 2. Catholic Church—Apologetic works. I. Goffin, Magdalen (Watkin) II. Title.

DOESWICK, Peter J., 1907- 282
The Roman way of salvation; its origin and development; or, History of dogma. Long Beach, Calif., Knights of Christ [1963] 176p. 21cm. (His Hist. of dogma, v.3) 63-8582 apply
1. Catholic Church—Doctrinal and controversial works—Protestant authors. I. Title.

DOMENICA, Angelo di 282
A Protestant primer on Roman Catholicism [new ed.] Minneapolis, Minn., 4500 W. Bway, Osterhus Publishing House, 1960 [c.1949] 168p. 19cm. 49-2671 2.00, pap., plastic binding
1. Catholic Church—Doctrinal and controversial works—Protestant authors. I. Title.

DOORNIK, Nicolaas Gerardus 282
Maria van.
A handbook of the Catholic faith (The triptych of the kingdom) [by] N. G. M. van Doornik, S. Jelsma [and] A. van de Lisdonk. Edited by John Greenwood. Translated from the Dutch. Garden City, N. Y., Image Books [1956] 514p. 18cm. (A Doubleday image book, D38) [BX1751] 56-4863
1. Catolic Church—Apologetic works. I. Title. II. Title: The triptych of the kingdom.

DOORNIK, Nicolaas Gerardus 282
Maria van.
The triptych of the kingdom; a handbook of the Catholic faith, by N. G. M. van Doornik, S. Jelsma [and] A. van de Lisdonk. Translated from the Dutch; edited by John Greenwood. Westminster, Md., Newman Press [1954] 490p. 23cm. [BX1751] 54-11090
1. Catholic Church—Apologetic works. I. Title.

DOWNEY, Richard, Abp., 1881- 282
Critical and constructive essays, by Archbishop Downey. Freeport, N.Y., Bks. for Libs. Pr. [1968] 239p. 23cm. (Essay index reprint ser.) Reprint of 1934 ed. Bibl. footnotes. [BX1756.D7C7 1968] 68-8455 7.75
1. Catholic Church—Addresses, essays, lectures. 2. Psychology—Addresses, essays, lectures. I. Title.

DOWNEY, Richard, Abp., 1881- 282
Critical and constructive essays, by Archbishop Downey. Freeport, N. Y., Books for Libraries Press [1968] 239 p. 23 cm. (Essay index reprint series) Reprint of 1934 edition. Contents.--Where did the world come from?--Rationalising the gods.--Personal immortality.--Catholic exegesis.--Rationalist criticism of the Incarnation.--St. Thomas Aquinas and Aristotle.--Psychoanalysis.--Adventures in psychology.--The question of reunion. Bibliographical footnotes. [BX1756.D7C7] 68-8455
1. Catholic Church—Addresses, essays, lectures. 2. Psychology—Addresses, essays, lectures. I. Title.

DUBAY, William H. 282
The human church [by] William H. DuBay. [1st ed.] Garden City, N. Y., Doubleday, 1966. 192 p. 22 cm. Bibliography: p. [183]-192. [BX891.D8] 65-23792
1. Catholic Church—Addresses, essays, lectures. I. Title.

DUQUOC, Christian, ed. 282
Opportunities for belief and behavior, edited by Christian Duquoc. New York, Paulist Press [1967] x, 176 p. 24 cm. (Concilium: theology in the age of renewal. Spirituality, v. 29) Translated by Theodore L. Westow and others. Bibliographical footnotes. [BX880.O58] 67-31523
1. Catholic Church—Addresses, essays, lectures. I. Title. II. Series: Concilium: theology in the age of renewal, v. 29
Contents omitted

DVORNIK, Francis, 1893- 282
The ecumenical councils. New York, Hawthorn Books [c.1961] 112p. (Twentieth century encyclopedia of Catholicism, v. 82. Section 8: The organization of the church) Bibl. 61-9455 3.50 half cloth,
1. Councils and synods, Ecumenical. I. Title.

ELDERKIN, George Wicker, 282
1879-
The Roman Catholic problem. New York, Vantage Press [1954] 267p. 23cm. [BX1765.E37] 54-7413
1. Catholic Church—Doctrinal and controversial works—Protestant authors. I. Title.

EVANS, Illtud, ed. 282
The New library of Catholic knowledge, Advisory editors: Illtud Evans [and others. 1st ed.] New York, Hawthorn Books [1963-64] 12 v. (1216 p.) illus. (part col.) facsims., maps, plans, ports. 26 cm. Vol. 12 has imprint: London, Burns & Oates. Contents.V. 1. Preparing the way, by M. E. Odell. -- v. 2. The New Testament, by A. Mullins. -- v. 3. The story of the church, by G. Albion. -- v. 4. The church in the modern world, by G. Albion and R. Nowell. -- v. 5. Great saints and saintly figures, by B. Lucas. -- v. 6. The organization of the church, by S. G. A. Luff. -- v. 7. The doctrinal teaching of the church, by Q. de la Bedoyere. -- v. 8. The moral and social teaching of the church, by C. Derrick. -- v. 9. The worship of the church, by . Milner. -- v. 10. The building of churches, by P. F. Anson. -- v. 11. The art of the church, by I. Conlay and P. F. Anson. -- v. 12. Dictionary-index; a guide to selected Christian topics. Includes bibliographies. [BX885.N4] 63-11044
1. Catholic Church. I. Title.

FABIAN, Johannes. 282
Jamaa; a charismatic movement in Katanga. Evanston, Ill., Northwestern University Press, 1971. xi, 284 p. 23 cm. Bibliography: p. [268]-277. [BL2470.C6F3] 74-134345 ISBN 0-8101-0339-7
1. Jamaa movement. I. Title.

FESQUET, Henri, 1916- 282
Catholicism: religion of tomorrow? Translated by Irene Uribe. [1st ed.] New York, Holt, Rinehart and Winston [c1964] viii, 216 p. 22 cm. Bibliographical footnotes. [BX891.F413] 64-21931
1. Catholic Church—Addresses, essays, lectures. I. Title.

FESQUET, Henri, 1916- 282
Catholicism: religion of tomorrow? Tr. [from French] by Irene Uribe. New York, Holt [c.1962, 1964] viii, 216p. 22cm. Bibl. [BX891.F413] 64-21931 4.95 bds.,
1. Catholic Church—Addresses, essays, lectures. I. Title.

FRAIGNEUX, Maurice. 282
Christianity is revolutionary. With a pref. by Gonzague De Reynold. Translated from the French by Emma Craufurd. Westminster, Md., Newman Press, 1955 [c1954] 163p. 21cm. [BX946.F7] 55-7044
1. Catholic Church—Hist. I. Title.

FRIES, Heinrich 282
Aspects ofthe church. Tr. [from German] by Thomas O'meara. Westminster. Md., Newman [1966, c.1965] 174p. 19cm. [BX1746.F713] 66-3194 4.50
1. Church. I. Title.

GEANEY, Dennis J. 282
On the road to renewal ... breakthrough [by] Dennis J. Geaney. Notre Dame, Ind., Fides Publishers [1968] viii, 201 p. illus. 22 cm. [BX891.G37] 68-15358
1. Catholic Church—Addresses, essays, lectures. I. Title.

GIBBONS, James, Cardinal, 282
1834-1921.
Outlines of The faith of our fathers, by Edward J. Kelly. Boise, Idaho [Diocese of Boise] Chancery Office [1951] xvi, 149 p. 24 cm. On cover: High school junior year apologetics. [BX1751.G512] 51-2144
1. Catholic Church—Doctrinal and controversial works—Catholic authors. I. Gibbons, James, Cardinal, 1834-1921. II. Kelly, Edward J., Bp., 1890- III. Title. IV. Title: The faith of our fathers.

GILBERT, Arthur. 282
The Vatican Council and the Jews. Cleveland, World Pub. Co. [1968] xiv, 322 p. 22 cm. Bibliographical references included in "Notes" (p. 243-261) [BX830 1962.A45G5] 68-26843 6.95
1. Vatican Council. 2d, 1962-1965. Declaratio de ecclesiae habitudine ad religiones non-christianas. 2. Catholic Church—Relations—Judaism. 3. Judaism—Relations—Catholic Church. I. Title.

GRACE, William Joseph, 1882- 282
The Catholic Church and you. Milwaukee, Bruce Pub. Co. [1955] 246p. 22cm. [BX1754.G684] 55-7111
1. Catholic Church—Doctrinal and controversial works, Popular. I. Title.

GRACE, William Joseph, 1882- 282
The Catholic Church and you. Rev. by Francis N. Korth. Milwaukee, Bruce Pub. Co. [1964] viii, 261 p. 22 cm. [BX1754.G684 1964] 64-15440
1. Catholic Church — Doctrinal and controversial works, Popular. I. Title.

GRACE, William Joseph, 1882- 282
The Catholic Church and you. Rev. by Francis N. Korth. Milwaukee, Bruce [c.1964] viii, 261p. 22cm. 64-15440 1.75 pap.,
1. Catholic Church—Doctrinal and controversial works, Popular. I. Title.

GRAHAM, Aelred, 1907- 282
Catholicism and the world today. New York, D. McKay Co. [1952] 234 p. 21 cm. [BX1754.G685] 52-7929
1. Blanshard, Paul, 1892- 2. Catholic Church—Apologetic works. I. Title.

GRANDI, Domenico 282
The story of the church [by] Domenico Grandi and Antonio Galli. Translated and edited by John Chapin. Garden City, N. Y., Hanover House [c.1960] 336p. 22cm. 60-15175 4.95
1. Catholic Church—Hist. I. Galli, Antonio, joint author. II. Title.

HALES, E. E. Y. 282
Revolution and papacy; 1769-1846. Notre Dame. Ind., Univ. of Notre Dame [1966.c.1960] 320p. map. 21cm. (NDP49) Bibl. [BX1361.H3 1960] 2.50 pap.,
1. Catholic Church—Hist.—18th cent. 2. Catholic Church—Hist.—19th cent. I. Title.

HALES, Edward Elton Young, 1908- 282
Pio Nono, a study in European politics and religion in the nineteenth century. Garden City, N.Y., Doubleday [1962, c.1954] 402p. map. (Image bk., D133) Bibl. 1.25 pap.,
1. Pius IX, Pope, 1792-1878. 2. Europe—Politics—1848-1871. I. Title.

HALES, Edward Elton Young, 1908- 282
Revolution and Papacy, 1769-1846. Garden City. N.Y., Hanover House [c.]1960. 320p. Front. map. 22cm. Includes bibliography. 60-13527 4.50
1. Catholic Church—Hist.—18th cent. 2. Catholic Church—Hist.—19th cent. I. Title.

HALES, Edward Elton Young, 1908- 282
Revolution and Papacy. 1769-1846. London, Eyre & Spottiswoode [Chester Springs Pa., Dufour, 1966, c.1960] 320p. illus. 23cm. Bibl. [BX1361.H3] 61-194 6.00
1. Catholic Church—Hist.—18th cent. 2. Catholic Church—Hist.—19th cent. I. Title.

HALES, Edward Elton Young, 1908- 282
Revolution and Papacy, 1769-1846. [1st ed.] Garden City, N. Y., Hanover House, 1960. 320p. illus. 22cm. Includes bibliography. [BX1361.H3] 60-13527
1. Catholic Church—Hist.—18th cent. 2. Catholic Church—Hist.— 19th cent. I. Title.

HALLETT, Paul H. 282
What is a Catholic? New York, Macmillan [1966, c.1955] 191p. 18cm. Bibl. [BX1754.H18] 55-8253 .95
1. Catholic Church—Doctrinal and controversial works, Popular. I. Title.

HALLETT, Paul H. 282
What is Catholicity? [1st ed.] Cleveland, World Pub. Co. [1955] 254 p. 22 cm. Includes bibliography. [BX1754.H18] 55-8253
1. Catholic Church—Doctrinal and controversial works, Popular. I. Title.

HANSON, Richard Patrick Crosland. 282
The Church of Rome; a dissuasive [by] R. P. C. Hanson [and] R. H. Fuller. [Rev. ed.] Greenwich, Conn., Seabury Press [1960] 160p. 19cm. 60-2919 1.50 pap.,
1. Catholic Church—Doctrinal and controversial works — Protestant authors. I. Fuller, Reginald Horace, joint author. II. Title.

HASSEVELDT, Roger, 1917- 282
The church, a divine mystery. Translated by William Storey. Chicago, Fides Publishers [1954] 263p. 21cm. 'Published originally...under the title, Le mystere de l'eglise.' [BX1751.H313] 54-11023
1. Church. 2. Catholic Church. I. Title.

HASSEVELDT, Roger, 1917- 282
The church in the world; the nature and mission of the church. Translated by William Storey. Notre Dame, Ind., Fides Publishers [1964? c1954] 133 p. 22 cm. "Drawn from [the author's] The church, a divine mystery . . . originally published under the title, Le mystere de l'eglise." Bibliographical references included in "Footnotes" (p. 131-133) [BX1746] 65-7257
1. Church. I. Title.

HASTINGS, Adrian, ed. 282
The church and the nations; a study of minority Catholicism in England, India, Norway, America, Lebanon, Australia, Wales, Japan, the Netherlands, Vietnam, Brazil, Egypt, southern Africa and among the Lele of the Congo. London, New York, Sheed and Ward [1959] 238 p. 23 cm. [BX1401.A1H3] 60-16056
1. Catholics in non-Catholic countries. I. Title.

HEALEY, John B. 282
Charismatic renewal : reflections of a pastor / by John B. Healey. New York : Paulist Press, c1976. vi, 109 p. ; 18 cm. (Deus book) [BX2350.57.H4] 76-9368 ISBN 0-8091-1948-X pbk. : 1.95
1. Pentecostalism. I. Title.

HELLWIG, Monika. 282
Tradition : the Catholic story today / Monika Hellwig. Dayton, Ohio : Pflaum Pub., [1974] 89 p. ; 21 cm. Includes bibliographical references. [BX1752.H425] 74-14305 ISBN 0-8278-9060-5
1. Catholic Church—Apologetic works. I. Title.

HENDERSON, E Harold. 282
Roman dogma versus Bible doctrine, by E. Harold Henderson. Little Rock, Ark., Baptist Publications Committee, [1964] 152 p. 20 cm. Messages "originally delivered to listeners of 'The central Baptist hour' ... station KFYO, Lubbock, Texas." Includes bibliographies. [BX1765.2.H4] 64-18768
1. Baptists — Doctrinal and controversial works. 2. Catholic Church — Doctrinal and controversial works — Protestant authors. I. Title.

HENDERSON, E. Harold 282
Roman dogma versus Bible doctrine. Little Rock, Ark., 716 Main St. Baptist Pubns. Comm., [c.1964] 152p. 20cm. Messages orig. delivered to listeners of The central Baptist hour station KFYO, Lubbock, Texas. Bibl. 64-18768 1.00 pap.,
1. Baptists—Doctrinal and controversial works. 2. Catholic Church—Doctrinal and controversial works—Protestants authors. I. Title.

HIGGINS, Thomas J 1899- 282
Dogma for the layman. Milwaukee, Bruce Pub. Co. [1961] 218p. 23cm. [BX1754.H53] 61-17437
1. Catholic Church—Doctrinal and controversial works, Popular. I. Title.

HOEVER, Hugo Henry, 1883- ed. 282
Saint Joseph Catholic manual; a complete manual of Christian doctrine with popular indulgenced prayers and devotions and lives of the saints. New York, Catholic Book Pub. Co. [1955] 797p. illus. (part col.) 17cm. [BX1754.H58] 56-441
1. Catholic Church—Doctrinal and controversial works, Popular. 2. Catholic Church—Prayer-books and devotions—English. 3. Saints— Calendar. 4. Catholic Church—Dictionaries. I. Title.

HOLT, Edd, 1906- 282
If Brother Paul were there: answering Who is teaching heresy? showing Rome's roaming--the Catholischism; being twenty seven radio sermons delivered in 1950 (here revised and supplemented)... Montgomery, Ala. [1954, 201p. illus. 23cm. [BX1765.H65] 54-2012
1. Catholic Church—Doctrinal and controversial works—Protestant authors. I. Title.

HOUTART, Francois, 1925- 282
The eleventh hour; explosion of a church. Edited by Mary Anne Chouteau, with an introd. by Harvey Cox. New York, Sheed and Ward [1968] 192 p. 21 cm. "Edited from lectures [by the author] ... given during a Pastoral Institute for Priests at Conception Abbey, Missouri, in July and August of 1966, and completed from notes in the course on the Sociology of pastoral work by the author at Louvain University, Belgium, in 1966-67." [BX1746.H62] 68-13856
1. Church renewal—Catholic Church. I. Title.

HUDSON, Winthrop Still, 1911- 282
Understanding Roman Catholicism; a guide to papal teaching for Protestants. Philadelphia, Westminster Press [1959] 192p. 21cm. Indludes bibliography. [BX1765.2.H8] 59-6964
1. Catholic Church—Doctrinal and controversial works—Protestant authors. I. Title.

ISSUES. 282
Edited by Urban H. Fleege. Glen Rock, N.J., Paulist Press [1968] vi, 167 p. 19 cm. (Deus books) Consists chiefly of contributions to a conference sponsored by the Charles Carroll Forum of De Paul University. [BX885.I84] 68-24812 1.95
1. Catholic Church—Addresses, essays, lectures. I. Fleege, Urban H., 1908- ed.

ISSUES that divide the church. 282
Edited by Robert G. Hoyt. New York, Macmillan [1967] xx, 168 p. 22 cm. Consists of working papers, edited transcript, and final position papers of a discussion meeting organized by the National Catholic reporter and held in Kansas City, Mo., in Jan. 1967. First published in the National Catholic reporter during Lent 1967. [BX885.I85 1967] 67-28576
1. Catholic Church—Addresses, essays, lectures. I. Hoyt, Robert G., ed. II. National Catholic reporter.

JEDIN, Hubert 282
Ecumenical councils of the Catholic Church; an historical outline. [Translation [from the German] by Ernest Graf. New York] Herder and Herder [1960] 253p. 19cm. (9p. bibl.) 59-15483 3.95
1. Councils and synods, Ecumenical. I. Title.

JEDIN, Hubert, 1900- 282
Ecumenical councils of the Catholic Church; an historical survey. [Tr. by Ernest Graf] New York, Paulist Pr. [1962, c.1960] 192p. (Deus bks.) Bibl. .95 pap.,
1. Councils and synods, Ecumenical. I. Title.

JEFFRIES, Betty Jean. 282
From the other side; a look into the Catholic Church. Milwaukee, Bruce Pub. Co. [1955] 128p. 21cm. [BX1751.J44] 55-8483
1. Catholic Church. I. Title.

JOHNSON, Frederick A 1909- 282
Christ and Catholicism. New York, Vantage Press [1954] 284p. 23cm. [BX1765.J64] 54-7415
1. Catholic Church—Doctrinal and controversial works—Protestant authors. I. Title.

JONES, Ilion Tingal 282
A Protestant speaks his mind. Philadelphia, Westminster Press [c.1960] 237p. 21cm. (9p. bibl.) 60-5095 3.95
1. Catholic Church—Doctrinal and controversial works—Protestant authors. I. Title.

JONES, Ilion Tingnal, 1889- 282
A Protestant speaks his mind. Philadelphia, Westminster Press [1960] 237p. 21cm. Includes bibliography. [BX1765.2.J64] 60-5095
1. Catholic Church—Doctrinal and controversial works—Protestant authors. I. Title.

KARRER, Otto, 1888- 282
The kingdom of God today. [Translated by Rosaleen Ockenden. New York, Herder and Herder 1964] 254 p. 21 cm. [[BX8.2.K313]] 64-14108
1. Christian union. 2. Kingdom of God. I. Title.

KARRER, Otto, 1888- 282
The kingdom of God today [Tr. from German by Rosaleen Ockenden. New York] Herder & Herder [c.1964] 254p. 21cm. [BX8.2.K313] 64-14108 4.95
1. Christian union. 2. Kingdom of God. I. Title.

KELLY, James Patrick, 1901- 282
What the church givesus by James P. Kelly and Mary T. Ellis New York, Kenedy [1955] 152p. 20cm. [BX1754.K35] 55-9334
1. Catholic Church—Doctrinal and controversial works, Popular. I. Ellis, Mary T., joint author. II. Title.

KELLY, Virgil A 282
The truth about Catholics. New York, Dial Press, 1954. 173p. 20cm. [BX1754.K38] 54-10538
1. Catholic Church— Doctrinal and controversial works—Catholic authors. I. Title.

KING, Betty. 282
The wall between us; a Protestant-Catholic dialogue, by Betty King and Lorraine Juliana. With a foreword by Dale Francis. Milwaukee, Bruce Pub. Co. [1964] viii, 173 p. 22 cm. [BX1754.K5195] 64-17331
1. Catholic Church — Relations — Protestant Episcopal Church in the U.S.A. 2. Protestant Episcopal Church in the U.S.A. — Relations — Catholic Church. I. Juliana, Lorraine. II. Title.

KING, Betty 282
The wall between us; a Protestant-Catholic dialogue, by Betty King, Lorraine Juliana. Foreword by Dale Francis. Milwaukee, Bruce [c.1964] viii, 173p. 22cm. 64-17331 3.75
1. Catholic Church—Relations—Protestant Episcopal Church in the U.S.A. 2. Protestant Episcopal Church in the U.S.A.—Relations—Catholic Church. I. Juliana, Lorraine. II. Title.

KNOX, Ronald Arbuthnott, 1888- 282
Off the record. New York, Sheed and Ward, 1954. 176p. 21cm. [BX1754.K58] 54-6138
1. Catholic Church—Doctrinal and controversial work,s Popular. I. Title.

LAURENTIN, Rene. 282
Catholic pentecostalism / Rene Laurentin ; translated by Matthew J. O'Connell. 1st ed. Garden City, N.Y. : Doubleday, 1977. 239 p. ; 22 cm. Translation of Pentecotisme chez les catholiques. Bibliography: p. [204]-222. [BX2350.57.L3613] 76-18358 ISBN 0-385-12129-6 : 6.95
1. Pentecostalism—Catholic Church. I. Title.

LEHMANN, Leo Herbert, 1895- 282
Out of the labyrinth. Grand Rapids, Mich., Baker Bk., 1964 [c.1947] 252p. map. 23cm. Bibl. 64-16942 2.95
1. Catholic Church—Doctrinal and controversial works—Protestant authors. I. Title.

LIEBLER, H. B. 282
When we look around us; a little book about God and what he has done for us. Illus., Gertrude Van Allen. New York, Exposition Press [c.1960] 86p. (Exposition-Testament bk.) 2.50
1. Roman Catholic Church. I. Title.

LIERDE, Petrus Canisius van, Bp., 1907- 282
The Holy See at work: how the Catholic Church is governed. Translated by James Tucek. [1st ed.] New York, Hawthorn Books [1962] 254p. 24cm. Translation of Achter de bronzen poort. [BX1802.L513] 62-9042
1. Catholic Church—Government. I. Title.

LINDEN, James V 282
The Catholic Church invites you. St. Louis, Herder [1959] 118p. 20cm. [BX1784.L5] 59-8461
1. Catholic Church— Relations. 2. Church—Unity. I. Title.

LOEWENICH, Walther von 282
Modern Catholicism. Translated by Reginald H. Fuller. New York, St. Martin's Press. 1959 [ ] viii, 378p. 23cm. (4p. bibl.) 59-65290 9.00
1. Protestant churches—Relations—Catholic Church. 2. Catholic Church—Relations—Protestant churches. 3. Catholic Church—Doctrinal and controversial works—Protestant authors. 4. Catholic Church—Hist.—Modern period. I. Title.

LOEWENICH, Walther von, 1903- 282
Modern Catholicism. Translated by Reginald H. Fuller. New York, St Martin's Press, 1959. 378p. 23cm. Includes bibliography. [BX4817.L613 1959] 59-65290
1. Protestant churches—Relations—Catholic Church. 2. Catholic Church—Relations—Protestant churches. 3. Catholic Church—Doctrinal and controversial works —Protestant authors. 4. Catholic Church—Hist.—Modern period. I. Title.

LOGAL, Nelson William, 1910- 282
The font of truth. [Derby? N. Y.] St. Paul Editions [c1956] 448p. illus. 22cm. [BX1754.L58] 59-25205
1. Catholic Church—Doctrinal and controversial works, Popular. I. Title.

LUBAC, Henri de 282
The Catholic and his church. [Trans. from the French by Michael Mason.] New York, Sheed & Ward [c.1956] 90p. (Canterbury bk.) "From the splendour of the Church." .75 pap.,
I. Title.

LUBAC, Henri de, 1896- 282
Catholicism; a study of dogma in relation to the corporate destiny of mankind. New York, Sheed and Ward, 1958. 283p. 23cm. Translated from the 4th French ed. by Lancelot C. Sheppard. [BX1751.L913 1958] 58-14969
1. Catholic Church—Doctrinal and controversial works. 2. Sociology, Christian (Catholic) I. Title.

LUBAC, Henri de, 1896- 282
Catholicism; a study of dogma in relation to the corporate destiny of mankind [Tr. from French by Lamcelot C. Sheppard] New York, New Amer. Lib. [1964] 280p. 18cm. (Mentor-Omega MT573) .75 pap.,
1. Catholic Church—Doctrinal and

controversial works. 2. Sociology, Christian (Catholic) I. Title.

MCBRIDE, Alfred. 282
The pearl and the seed. Consultants: Sister M. Johnice Cohan and Sister M. Elizabeth Fowkes. Illustrated by Mary and Morris Kirchoff. Boston, Allyn and Bacon [1971] 4 v. illus. (part col.) 27 cm. (Bible, life, and worship series) Short stories, Bible stories, and historical anecdotes trace the history of the Catholic Church with emphasis on the Church's approach to the modern problems of a changing world. [BX948.M22] 74-145600
1. Catholic Church—History—Juvenile literature. I. Kirchoff, Mary, illus. II. Kirchoff, Morris, illus. III. Title.

MCCARRON, Hugh Michael, 1893- 282
The family of God; a study of the Catholic Church. New York, McMullen Books, 1951. 196 p. 21 cm. [BX1751.M13] 51-10912
1. Catholic Church. I. Title.

MCDERMOTT, Thomas, 1917- 282
Certainly, I'm a Catholic! Milwaukee, Bruce [1950] vii. 154 p. 21 cm. [BX1754.M183] 50-5746
1. Catholic Church—Doctrinal and controversial works, Popular. I. Title.

MCGLOIN, Joseph T. 282
Friends. Romans, Protestants . . . Milwaukee, Bruce [c.1963] x, 159p. 22cm. Bibl. 63-20699 3.50
1. Apologetics—20th cent. 2. Catholic Church—Apologetic works. I. Title.

MCGOEY, John H. 282
The uncertain sound, by John H. McGoey. Milwaukee, Bruce Pub. Co. [1967] ix, 224 p. 22 cm. [BX891.M26] 67-18434
1. Catholic Church—Addresses, essays, lectures. I. Title.

MCGOVERN, James O., 1936- 282
The church in the churches, by James O. McGovern. Washington, Corpus Books [1968] 172 p. 21 cm. Bibliography: p. 161-170. [BX1746.M23] 68-18710
1. Catholic Church. 2. Church—History of doctrines—20th century. 3. Christian union—Catholic Church. I. Title.

MCGURN, Barrett 282
A reporter looks at the Vatican. New York, Coward [c.1962] 316p. 22cm. 62-10952 5.00
1. Pius XX, Pope, 1876-1958. 2. Joannes XXIII, Pope, 1881- 3. Popes—Court. I. Title.

MCKENZIE, John L. 282
The Roman Catholic Church [by] John L. McKenzie. [1st ed.] New York, Holt, Rinehart and Winston [1969] xiv, 288 p. illus., facsims., ports. 25 cm. (History of religion series) Bibliographical references included in "Notes" (p. 272-280) [BX945.2.M33] 69-16188 6.95
1. Catholic Church. 2. Catholic Church—History. I. Title.

MCLOUGHLIN, Emmett, 1907- ed. 282
Letters to an ex-priest. New York, L., Stuart [c.1965] 288p. 22cm. [BX1765.2.M32] 64-13875 4.95 bds.,
1. Catholic Church—Doctrinal and controversial works—Miscellaneous authors. I. Title.

MCNABB, Vincent Joseph, 1868-1943. 282
Francis Thompson, & other essays. Introd. by Gilbert K. Chesterton. Freeport, N.Y., Books for Libraries Press [1968] xi, 106 p. port. 22 cm. (Essay index reprint series) Reprint of the 1936 ed. [BX890.M23 1968] 68-22117
1. Catholic Church—Addresses, essays, lectures. 2. Thompson, Francis, 1859-1907. I. Title.

MANHATTAN, Avro. 282
Catholic imperialism and world freedom. New York, Arno Press, 1972. xvii, 510 p. 23 cm. (The Atheist viewpoint) Reprint of the 1952 ed. Bibliography: p. 504-505. [BX1765.2.M348 1972] 73-161336 ISBN 0-405-03810-0
1. Catholic Church—Doctrinal and controversial works—Miscellaneous authors. I. Title. II. Series.

MANHATTAN, Avro 282
Catholic power today. New York, Lyle Stuart [1967] 288p. 21cm. Bibl. [BX1765.2.M35] 67-15886 6.00 bds.,
1. Catholic Church—Doctrinal and controversial works—Miscellaneous authors. I. Title.

MANHATTAN, Avro 282
Vatican imperialism in the twentieth century [3rd ed.] Grand Rapids, Mich., Zondervan [c.1965] 414p. 24cm. Bibl. [BX1765.M2763] 64-8844 5.95
1. Catholic Church—Doctrinal and controversial works—Miscellaneous authors. 2. Catholic Church—Relations (diplomatic) I. Title.

MARITAIN, Jacques, 1882- 282
The peasant of the Garonne; an old layman questions himself about the present time. Translated by Michael Cuddihy and Elizabeth Hughes. [1st ed.] New York, Holt, Rinehart and Winston [1968] vii, 277 p. 22 cm. Bibliographical footnotes. [BR115.W6M313] 68-10182
1. Church and the world. 2. Church. I. Title.

MARTIN, Malachi. 282
Three Popes and the Cardinal. New York, Popular Lib. [1973? c.1972] 414 p. 18 cm. [BX1389.M37 1972] pap., 1.50
1. Papacy—History—20th century. 2. Catholic Church—History—1965- 3. Civilization, Modern—1950- I. Title.

MARTIN, Malachi. 282
Three Popes and the Cardinal. New York, Farrar, Straus and Giroux [1972] xiv, 300 p. 23 cm. [BX1389.M37 1972] 74-181756 ISBN 0-374-27675-7 7.95
1. Catholic Church—History—1965- 2. Papacy—History—20th century. 3. Civilization, Modern—1950- I. Title.

MAURIAC, Francois, 1885- 282
What I believe. Tr., introd. by Wallace Fowlie. New York, Farrar [c.1963] xviii, 139p. 21cm. Bibl. 63-21591 3.95
1. Catholic Church—Apologetic works. 2. Apologetics—20th cent. I. Title.

MEADOWS, Denis. 282
A short history of the Catholic Church. New York, Devin-Adair, 1959. 246p. 22cm. [BX945.2.M4] 59-13555
1. Catholic Church—Hist. I. Title.

MEADOWS, Denis [George Denis Meadows] 282
A short history of the Catholic Church. New York, All Saints Press [dist. Pocket Bks.] [1960, c.1959] 246p. (AS2) .60 pap.,
1. Catholic Church—Hist. I. Title.

MEIER, Jacob H 282
What Catholics and Protestants should know. Mountain View, Calif., Pacific Press Pub. Association [1953] 200p. 28cm. Includes bibliography. [BX1765.M4] 53-8823
1. Catholic Church—Doctrinal and controversial works—Protestant authors. I. Title.

MILLS, Betty. 282
Mind if I differ? A Catholic-Unitarian dialogue [by] Betty Mills and Lucile Hasley. With a note, Ecumenism at the grass roots, by F. J. Sheed. New York, Sheed and Ward [1964] x, 210 p. 22 cm. [BX1754.M57] 64-13577
1. Catholic Church—Relations—Unitarian churches. 2. Unitarian churches—Relations—Catholic Church. I. Hasley, Lucile. II. Title.

MONTANO, Walter Manuel. 282
Behind the purple curtain. Los Angeles, Cowman Publications [1950] xviii, 327 p. 21 cm. Bibliography: p. 321-327. [BX1773.M6] 50-4204
1. Catholic Church — Doctrinal and controversial works — Protestant authors. I. Title.

MOULD, Daphne Desiree Charlotte Pochin. 282
The rock of truth. London, New York, Sheed and Ward [1953] vii, 216p. 22cm. Autobiographical. [BX4668.M63] 53-12808
1. Converts, Catholic. I. Title.

MUCKENHIRN, Charles Borromeo, Sister. 282
The implications of renewal. Notre Dame, Ind., Fides Publishers [1967] vi, 299 p. 20 cm. Bibliography: p. 295-299. [BX1746.M8] 66-30588
1. Church renewal—Catholic Church. 2. Monastic and religious life of women. I. Title.

NEUVECELLE, Jean, 1912- 282
The Vatican; its organization, customs, and way of life. Translated from the French by George Libaire. New York, Criterion Books [1955] 250 p. illus. 22 cm. Translation of Eglise, capitale Vatican. [BX1801.N445] 55-11025
1. Catholic Church. Curia Romana. 2. Catholic Church—Government. I. Title.

NEVILLE, Robert. 282
The world of the Vatican, [1st ed.] New York, Harper & Row [1962] 256 p. illus. 22 cm. [BX1802.N4] 62-7295
1. Vatican. 2. Papacy. I. Title.

NEVILLE, Robert 282
The world of the Vatican. New York, Harper [1962] 256p. illus. 22cm. 62-7295 4.95
1. Vatican. 2. Papacy. I. Title.

NEWMAN Foundation at the University of Minnesota. 282
The Newman annual. Minneapolis, Newman Foundation at the University of Minnesota. v. 21 cm. [BX810.N48N4] 51-39049
1. Catholic Church — Addresses, essays, lectures. I. Title.

NEWMAN, Jeremiah 282
Change and the Catholic Church; an essay in sociological ecclesiology. Helicon [dist. New York, Taplinger 1966c.1965] 349p. 21cm. Bibl. [BX891.N4] 65-24128 5.95
1. Catholic Church—Addresses, essays, lectures. I. Title.

NOORE, Gerardus Cornelis van, 1861-1946. 282
Dogmatic theology; translated and revised by John J. Castelot [and] William R. Murphy. Westminster, Md., Newman Press, 1955- v. 24cm. Contents.v.1. The true religion; from the 5th ed. edited by J. P. Verhaar. Includes bibliographies. [BX1751.N7] 55-10552
1. Theology, Doctrinal. 2. Catholic Church—Doctrinal and controversial works. I. Title.

NOORT, Gerardus Cornelis van, 1861-1946. 282
Dogmatic theology; translated and revised by John J. Castelot [and] William R. Murphy. Westminster, Md., Newman Press, 1955- v. 24cm. Contents.v. 1. The true religion.-- v. 2. Christ's church. Includes bibliographies. [BX1751.N7] 55-10552
1. Theology, Doctrinal. 2. Catholic Church—Doctrinal and controversial works. I. Title.

NOORT, Gerardus Cornelis van, 1861-1946. 282
Dogmatic theology, v. 3. tr. and rev. by John J. Castelot, William R. Murphy. Westminster, Md., Newman Press [c.]1961. 420p. Contents.v. 3. The sources of revelation; Divine Faith. Bibl. 55-10552 7.50 rev
1. Theology, Doctrinal. 2. Catholic Church—Doctrinal and controversial works. I. Title.

NORRIS, Frank B 282
God's own people: an introductory study of the church. Baltimore, Helicon Press [1962] 122p. 23cm. [BX1746.N6] 62-11186
1. Church. I. Title.

NOVAK, Michael. 282
A new generation, American and Catholic. [New York] Herder and Herder [1964] 250 p. 21 cm. [BX1406.2.N6] 64-13688
1. Catholics in the U.S. I. Title.

O'BRIEN, John Anthony, 1893- 282
Catching up with the Church: Catholic faith and practice today [by] John A. O'Brien. London, Burns & Oates; Herder & Herder, 1967 [i.e. 1968] 188p. 23cm. [BX1754.O16 1968] 68-98948 4.50
1. Vatican Council. 2d, 1962-1965. 2. Catholic Church—Doctrinal and controversial works, Popular. I. Title.

O'BRIEN, John Anthony, 1893- 282
Catching up with the church; Catholic faith and practice today [by) John A. O'Brien. [New York] Herder and Herder [1967] 188 p. 21 cm. Includes bibliographical references. [BX1754.O16] 67-18559
1. Catholic Church — Doctrinal and controversial works, Popular. 2. Vatican Council, 2d, 1962-1965. I. Title.

O'BRIEN, John Anthony, 1893- 282
Catching up with the church: Catholic faith and practice today [by] John A. O'Brien. [New York] Herder and Herder [1967] 188 p. 21 cm. Includes bibliographical references. [BX1754.O16] 67-18559
1. Catholic Church—Doctrinal and controversial works, Popular. 2. Vatican Council, 2d, 1962-1965. I. Title.

O'BRIEN, John Anthony, 1893- 282
The faith of millions; the credentials of the Catholic religion. With a pref. by William Cardinal O'Connell and an introd. by Dennis Cardinal Dougherty. 14th ed., rev. and enl. [Huntington, Ind., Our Sunday visitor] 1958 [c1938] 498p. illus. 20cm. Includes bibliography. [BX1751.O17 1958] 61-23517
1. Catholic Church—Doctrinal and controversial works. I. Title.

O'BRIEN, John Anthony, 1893- 282
The faith of millions : the credentials of the Catholic religion / John A. O'Brien. New and rev. ed. Huntington, Ind. : Our Sunday Visitor, [1974] 438 p. : ill. ; 21 cm. Includes bibliographical references and index. [BX1751.O17 1974] 74-82119 ISBN 0-87973-830-8 pbk. : 4.95
1. Catholic Church—Doctrinal and controversial works—Catholic authors. I. Title.

O'BRIEN, John Anthony, 1893- ed. 282
Sharing the faith; winning the churchless millions for Christ. Huntington, Ind., Our Sunday Visitor Press, 1951. 246p. illus. 19cm. [BX1754.O18] 52-7369
1. Catholic Church—Doctrinal and controversial works, Popular. I. Title.

O'BRIEN, John Anthony, 1893- 282
What's the truth about Catholics? Why 400 million people profess the Catholic faith; an exposition of Catholic belief and practice. [Huntington? Ind., c1950] 304p. illus. 19cm. [BX1754.O2] 53-36890
1. Catholic Church—Doctrinal and controversial works, Popular. I. Title.

O'CONNOR, Edward Dennis. 282
The pentecostal movement in the Catholic Church, by Edward D. O'Connor. Notre Dame, Ind., Ave Maria Press [1971] 301 p. 22 cm. Bibliography: p. 295-301. [BX8763.O25] 70-153878 5.95
1. Catholic Church. 2. Pentecostalism. I. Title.

O'CONNOR, John, 1921- 282
The pain of renewal. Glen Rock, N.J., Paulist Press [1968] v, 88 p. 18 cm. (Deus books) [BX891.O25] 68-31052 0.95
1. Catholic Church—Addresses, essays, lectures. I. Title.

O'DEA, Thomas F. 282
The Catholic crisis [by] Thomas F. O'Dea. Boston, Beacon Press [1968] 267 p. 22 cm. Bibliographical references included in "Notes" (p. 253-261) [BX1746.O3] 68-14707
1. Vatican Council, 2d, 1962-1965. 2. Church renewal—Catholic Church. I. Title.

OESTERREICHER, John M., 1904- 282
The rediscovery of Judaism; a re-examination of the conciliar statement on the Jews, by John M. Oesterreicher. [South Orange, N.J.] Institute of Judaeo-Christian Studies, Seton Hall University [1971] 59 p. 23 cm. [BM535.O44] 79-156318
1. Catholic Church—Relations—Judaism. 2. Vatican Council. 2d., 1962-1965. Declaratio de ecclesiae habitudine ad religiones non-christianas. 3. Judaism—Relations—Catholic Church. I. Title.

O'HARA, Constance Marie. 282
Heaven was not enough. [1st ed.] Philadelphia, Lippincott [1955] 381 p. 21 cm. Autobiography. [BX4668.O5] 55-6308
1. Converts, Catholic. I. Title.

OPPORTUNITIES for belief and behavior, edited by Christian Duquoc. New York, Paulist Press [1967] 1, 176 p. 24 cm. (Concilium: theology in the age of renewal. Spirituality, v. 29) Translated by Theodore L. Westow and others. Contents.Contents.—Preface, by C. Duquoc.—Articles: The real challenge of atheistic humanism, by J. Y. Jolif. Brotherly love in the church as the sign of the kingdom, by H. J. Feret. Immediate relationship with God, by H. U. von Balthasar. Christian conscience in America and the war in Vietnam, by P. Steinfels. The Christian conscience of Brazil, by F. Lepargneur. Racism in Central and South Africa, M. Ekwa. French Canada: a challenge to the Christian conscience, by P. M. Lemaire. A note on radical theology, by W. Hamilton.—Bibliographical survey: A discussion: the Bishop of Woolwich's book The new Reformation, by J. E. Crouzet. The present position in Mariology, by S. Napiorkowski.—Documentation concilium: The encounter with Buddhism, by G. Siegmund. A dialogue with Zen Buddhists, by H. Dumoulin. Biographical notes. Bibliographical footnotes. [BX880.O58] 67-31523 282
1. Catholic Church—Addresses, essays, lectures. I. Duquoc, Christian, ed. II. Series: Concilium (New York) v. 29.

PASTOR, Ludwig, freiherr von, [Full name: Ludwig Friedrich August, freiherr von Pastor von Camperfelden], 1854-1928 282
The history of the popes, from the Middle Ages. Drawn from the secret archives of the Vatican and other orig. sources. From the German of Dr. Ludwig Pastor. London, J. Hodges. 1891. Nendeln, Liechtenstein, Kraus-Thomson. 1968. 40v. 1891-1961. 23 cm. Half-title: Catholic standard library. Vs. 1-6 ed. by F. I. Antrobus: v. 7-24 by R. F. Kerr; v. 25-34 by Ernest Graf; v. 35-40 by K. F. Peeler. Imprint varies . . . Bibl. 24-12249 600.00
1. Papacy—Hist. 2. Catholic church—Hist. I. Title.
Order from Kraus-Thomson Org., 9491 Nendeln, Liechtenstein.

PAUL, Raymond James 282
A Catholic's Ripley's believe it or not! [New York] Dell [1964, c.1963] unpaged illus. 17cm. (1142) .45 pap.,
I. Title.

PELIKAN, Jaroslav, 1923- 282
The riddle of Roman Catholicism. New York,

Abingdon Press [1959] 272p. 24cm. Includes bibliography. [BX1765.2.P4] 59-10367
1. Catholic Church—Doctrinal and controversial works—Protestant authors. 2. Catholic Church—Relations—Protestant Churches. 3. Protestant churches—Relations—Catholic Church. I. Title.

PELIKAN, Jaroslav Jan, 1923- 282
The riddle of Roman Catholicism. New York, Abingdon Press [1959] 272 p. 24 cm. Includes bibliography. [BX1765.2.P4] 59-10367
1. Catholic Church—Doctrinal and controversial works—Protestant authors. 2. Catholic Church—Relations—Protestant churches. 3. Protestant churches—Relations—Catholic Church. I. Title.

PERSSON, Per Erik, 1923- 282
Roman & evangelical; Gospel and ministry: an ecumenical issue. Tr. by Eric H. Wahlstrom. Philadelphia, Fortress [c.1964] 89p. 21cm. Bibl. 64-24080 2.00
1. Lutheran Church—Doctrinal and controversial works. 2. Catholic Church—Doctrinal and controversial works—Protestant authors. 3. Theology—20th cent. 4. Christian union—Catholic Church. 5. Christian union—Lutheran Church. I. Title.

PERSSON, Per Erik, 1923- 282
Roman & evangelical Gospel and ministry, an ecumenical issue. Translated by Eric H. Wahlstrom. Philadelphia, Fortress press [1964] 89 p. 21 cm. Bibliogrpahical footnotes [BX8065.2.P413] 64-24080
1. Lutheran Church—Doctrinal and controversial works. 2. Catholic Church—Doctrinal and controversial works—Protestant authors. 3. Theology—20th cent. 4. Christian union—Catholic Church 5. Christian union—Lutheran Church I. Title.

PIEPER, Josef, 1904- 282
What Catholics believe [by] Josef Pieper, Heinz Raskop. Introd. by Gerald B. Phelan; tr. [from German] by Christopher Huntington. Chicago, Regnery [1966, c.1951] 112p. 17cm. (Logos ed., 51L-712) [BX1754.P523] 1.25 pap.,
1. Catholic Church—Doctrinal and controversial works, Popular. I. Title.

PIEPER, Josef, 1904- 282
What Catholics believe [by] Josef Pieper and Heinz Raskop. Introd. by Gerald B. Phelan; translation by Christopher Huntington. [New York] Pantheon [1951] 112 p. 21 cm. Translation of Katholische Christenfibel. [BX1754.P523] 51-12297
1. Catholic Church—Doctrinal and controversial works, Popular. I. Title.

QUINLAN, David 282
Roman Catholicism. London, English Univ. Pr. [1966] ix, 195p. 19cm. (Teach yourself bks.) Bibl. [BX1754.Q5] 66-74266 1.75 bds.,
1. Catholic Church. I. Title.

RAHNER, Karl 282
Free speech in the church. [Translated from the German] New York, Sheed & Ward [1960, c.1959] 112p. 20cm. 60-7313 2.75
1. Liberty of speech in the church. 2. Public opinion. 3. Christianity—20th cent. I. Title.

RAHNER, Karl, 1904- 282
Free speech in the church. [Translated by G. R. Lamb] London, New York, Sheed and Ward [1959] 82p. 18cm. [BV740.R313 1959] 60-2606
1. Liberty of speech in the church. 2. Public opinion. 3. Christianity—20th cent. I. Title. Contents omitted.

RAHNER, Karl, 1904- 282
The shape of the church to come. Translation and introd. by Edward Quinn. New York, Seabury Press [1974] 136 p. 22 cm. "A Crossroad book." [BV600.2.R3613 1974] 73-17907 ISBN 0-8164-1181-6 6.95
1. Church. I. Title.

*RAMER, Ernest L. 282
The Catholic Church of the future, [by] Ernest L. Ramer. Hicksville, N.Y., Exposition [1974] 63 p. 21 cm. [BX1751] ISBN 0-682-48078-9 4.50
1. Catholic Church—Doctrinal and controversial work. I. Title.

RANAGHAN, Kevin. 282
Catholic pentecostals, by Kevin and Dorothy Ranaghan. Paramus, N.J., Paulist Press [1969] v, 266 p. 18 cm. (Deus books) Bibliography: p. 263-266. [BX8763.R3] 73-79919
1. Pentecostalism. I. Ranaghan, Dorothy, joint author. II. Title.

RANCHETTI, Michele. 282
The Catholic modernists, a study of the religious reform movement, 1864-1907; translated by Isabel Quigly. London, New York, Oxford University Press, 1969. x, 230 p. 23 cm. Includes bibliographical references. [BX1396.R2713 1969b] 70-452364 unpriced
1. Modernism—Catholic Church. I. Title.

REICHERT, Florian, Sister, 1900- 282
Chamber music. [1st ed.] New York, Pageant Press [1958] 142p. 21cm. [BX4668.R4] 58-3230
1. Converts, Catholic. I. Title.

RICE, Charles E. 282
Authority and rebellion; the case for orthodoxy in the Catholic Church [by] Charles E. Rice. [1st ed.] Garden City, N.Y., Doubleday, 1971. 252 p. 22 cm. Includes bibliographical references. [BX1751.2.R485] 72-140065 5.95
1. Catholic Church—Doctrinal and controversial works—Catholic authors. I. Title.

RICKABY, Joseph John, 1845-1932. 282
The Lord my light, with an introd. by I. C. Scoles. Westminster, Md., Newman Press [1954] 248p. 22cm. [BX890.R48] 54-9091
1. Catholic Church—Addresses, essays, lectures. I. Title.

ROENSCH, Roger C 282
The Mass and sacraments for teenagers, by Roger C. Roensch. Glen Rock, N.J., Paulist Press [1966] 224 p. 18 cm. (Deus books) [BX930.R57] 66-16554
1. Religious education—Text-books for young people—Catholic. I. Title.

ROENSCH, Roger C. 282
The Mass and sacraments for teenagers. Glen Rock, N.J., PaulistPr., [c.1966] 224p. 18cm. (Deus bks.) [BX930.R57] 66-16554 .95 pap.,
1. Religious education—Text-books for young people—Catholic. I. Title.

SCHEETZ, Leo A., 1896- 282
God's rules for the game of life; how to get to heaven [by] Leo A. Scheetz. [1st ed.] New York, Exposition Press [1971] 190 p. 22 cm. (An Exposition-testament book) [BX1754.S277] 76-171714 ISBN 0-682-47346-4 5.00
1. Catholic Church—Doctrinal and controversial works—Catholic authors. I. Title.

SCHEIBER, Richard B. 282
Wine & gall / Richard B. Scheiber. Huntington, Ind. : Our Sunday Visitor, 1977. 336 p. : ill. ; 22 cm. [BX891.S345] 76-57862 ISBN 0-87973-746-8 : 7.50
1. Catholic Church—Addresses, essays, lectures. I. Title.

SCHEIBER, Richard B. 282
Wine & gall / Richard B. Scheiber. Huntington, Ind. : Our Sunday Visitor, 1977. 336 p. : ill. ; 22 cm. [BX891.S345] 76-57862 ISBN 0-87973-746-8 : 7.50
1. Catholic Church—Addresses, essays, lectures. I. Title.

SCHMITT, Patricia Ann. 282
First picture dictionary for little Catholics, by Patricia Ann Schmitt and Ruth Hannon. Illus. by Decie Merwin. St. Paul, Catechetical Guild Educational Society [c1955] unpaged. illus. 17cm. (First books for little Catholics, FB070) [BX841.S35] 56-642
1. Catholic Church—Dictionaries, Juvenile. I. Hannon, Ruth, joint author. II. Title.

SERAFIAN, Michael, pseud. 282
The pilgrim. New York, Farrar, Straus [1964] xix, 281 p. 22 cm. [BX1378.3.S4] 64-19805
1. Paulus VI, Pope, 1897- 2. Vatican Council, 2d. I. Title.

SERAFIAN, Michael, pseud. 282
The pilgrim. New York, Farrar [c.1964] xix, 281p. 22cm. 64-19805 4.50
1. Paulus VI, Pope, 1897- 2. Vatican Council, 2d. I. Title.

SHEEN, Fulton John, Bp., 1895- 282
The cross and the crisis. Freeport, N.Y., Books for Libraries Press [1969] xi, 219 p. 23 cm. (Essay index reprint series) Reprint of the 1938 ed. Bibliographical footnotes. [BX1753.S52 1969] 73-99725
1. Catholic Church. 2. Christianity—20th century. 3. Civilization, Christian. 4. Communism. I. Title.

SIMON, Paul, 1882-1946. 282
The human element in the church of Christ. Translated from the German by Meyrick Booth. Westminster, Md., Newman Press, 1954. 166p. 23cm. [BX1751.S5753] 54-10905
1. Catholic Church. I. Title.

SIMONS, Francis, 1908- 282
Infallibility and the evidence. Springfield, Ill., Templegate [1968] 120 p. 22 cm. Bibliographical footnotes. [BT88.S55] 68-55376 4.95
1. Catholic Church—Infallibility. I. Title.

SLONIM, Reuben. 282
In the steps of Pope Paul; a rabbi's impression of the Pope in the Holy Land. Introd. by Archibishop Philip F. Pocock. Baltimore, Helicon [1965] 126 p. 23 cm. [BX1378.3.S55] 65-18648
1. Paulus VI, Pope, 1897- I. Title.

SLONIM, Reuben 282
In the steps of Pope Paul; a rebbi's impression of the Pope in the Holy Land. Introd. by Archbishop Philip F. Pocock. Helicon [dist. New York, Taplinger, c.1965] 126p. 23cm. [BX1378.3.S55] 65-18648 3.50
1. Paulus VI, Pope, 1897- I. Title.

SOURCES of Christian theology; v. 3 Westminster, Md., Newman, 1966. 328p. 23cm. Contents.v. 3. Christ and his mission; Christology and soteriology, Ed., commentary by James M. Carmody, S.J., Thomas E. Clarke, S.J. Bibl. [BX1747.S6] 55-1503 6.75 282
1. Catholic Church—Doctrinal and controversial works. 2. Theology, Doctrinal—Hist.

THE Spirit and the church : a personal and documentary record of the charismatic renewal and the ways it is bursting to life in the Catholic Church / compiled by Ralph Martin. New York : Paulist Press, c1976. viii, 341 p. ; 18 cm. [BX2350.57.S64] 76-9366 ISBN 0-8091-1947-1 pbk. : 2.95 282
1. Pentecostalism—Addresses, essays, lectures. 2. Church renewal—Catholic Church—Addresses, essays, lectures. I. Martin, Ralph, 1942-

SUBILIA, Vittorio. 282
The problem of Catholicism. Translated by Reginald Kissack. Philadelphia, Westminster Press [1964] 190 p. 23 cm. (The Library of history and doctrine) Bibliographical footnotes. [BX1765.2.S853] 64-12392
1. Vatican Council, 2d, 1962-1965. 2. Catholic Church—Doctrinal and controversial works—Protestant authors. I. Title.

THOMAS OF STRASSBURG, d 1357. 282
Thomae ab Argentina . . . Commentaria in IIII libros sententiarvm, hac postrema editione a mendis . . . repurgata. Vna cvm avctoris vita. Venetiis, Ex Officina Stellae, 1564. 202, 217 l. Commentary on Petrus Lombarous Sententiarum libri quattuor, edited by Simon Brazzolato. Photooffset. Ridgewood, N. J., Gregg Pr., 1966. 34cm. [BX1749.P4T5 1564a] 67-3777 84.00
1. Petrus Lombardus, Bp. of Parts, 12th cent. Sententiarum libri quattuor. I. Brazzolato, Simon, 16th cent., ed. II. Title.

THOMSON, Paul van Kuykendall, 1916- 282
Why I am a Catholic. New York, T. Nelson [1959] 204 p. 21 cm. [BX4668.T53] 59-7639
1. Converts, Catholic. 2. Catholic Church. I. Title.

THOMSON, Paul van Kuykendall, 1916- 282
Why I am a Catholic [Gloucester, Mass., P. Smith, 1965, c.1959] 204p. 21cm. (Beacon paperback, BP201 rebound) [BX4668.T53] 3.25
1. Converts, Catholic. 2. Catholic Church. I. Title.

THOMSON, Paul van Kuykendall, 1916- 282
Why I am a Catholic. New York, T. Nelson [1959] 204 p. 21 cm. [BX4668.T53] 59-7639
1. Catholic Church. 2. Converts, Catholic. I. Title.

TIMMERMAN, Samuel Federick, 1918- 282
Lectures on Catholicism, delivered as a part of the 1952 series of the annual Denver lectures of the Churches of Christ of Denver, Colorado. Denver, Sherman Street Church of Christ [c1952] 116p. 21cm. [BX1765.T5] 53-22459
1. Catholic Church—Doctrinal and controversial works—Protestant authors. I. Title.

TODD, Paul, 1911- 282
Do you really know the Church? / Paul Todd. Canfield, Ohio : Alba Books, c1977. 94 p. ; 18 cm. On cover: Do you know th Church? [BX1752.T623] 76-27402 ISBN 0-8189-1140-9 : 1.75
1. Catholic Church—Apologetic works—Miscellanea. I. Title.

ULLMANN, Walter, 1910- 282
The growth of papal government in the Middle Ages; a study in the ideological relation of clerical to lay power. [2 ed.] London, Methuen [dist. New York, Barnes & Noble, 1963] xxiv, 492p. 23cm. Bibl. 63-4507 8.50
1. Papacy—Hist. 2. Popes—Temporal power. 3. Church and state—Hist. I. Title.

VAZ, August Mark. 282
To sow in tears; religious essays. New York, Exposition Press [1951, c1952] 78 p. 23 cm. [BX1755.V25] 51-12348
1. Catholic Church — Doctrinal and controversial works — Catholic authors. I. Title.

VIDLER, Alexander Roper, 1899- 282
The modernist movement in the Roman Church, its origins & outcome / by Alec R. Vidler. New York : Gordon Press, 1976. Reprint of the 1934 ed. published by the University Press, Cambridge, which was issued as the Norrisian prize essay, Cambridge University, 1933. Includes index. Bibliography: p. [BX1396.V5 1976] 76-12999 lib.bdg. : 39.95
1. Loisy, Alfred Firmin, 1857-1940. 2. Tyrell, George, 1861-1909. 3. Modernism—Catholic Church. I. Title. II. Series: The Norrisian prize essay ; 1933.

WALSH, John, 1916- 282
This is Catholicism. Garden City, N.Y., Image Books [1959] 398 p. 19 cm. (A Doubleday image book, D85) Includes bibliography. [BX1754.W29] 59-12050
1. Catholic Church — Doctrinal and controversial works, Popular. I. Title.

WELLS, Herbert George, 1866-1946. 282
Crux ansata; an indictment of the Roman Catholic Church. New York, Arno Press, 1972 [c1944] 113 p. port. 23 cm. (The Atheist viewpoint) [BX1765.W44 1972] 73-161344 ISBN 0-405-03798-8
1. Catholic Church—Doctrinal and controversial works—Miscellaneous authors. I. Title. II. Series.

WELLS, Joel, comp. 282
A funny thing happened to the church; humor, cartoons, satire, and fiction from the pages of the Critic. [New York] Macmillan [1969] ix, 209 p. illus. 22 cm. [BV600.2.W44] 71-76587 5.95
1. Catholic Church—Caricatures and cartoons. 2. Church renewal—Catholic Church. I. The Critic. II. Title.

WHITE, Arthur Kent, 1889- 282
Protestant ideals. Zarephath, N.J., Pillar of Fire, 1951. 265 p. illus. 20 cm. [BX1765.W54] 52-17586
1. Catholic Church—Doctrinal and controversial works—Protestant authors. I. Title.

WILDER, John B 1914- 282
The other side of Rome. Grand Rapids, Zondervan Pub. House [1959] 159 p. 21 cm. Includes bibliography. [BX1765.2.W5] 59-1510
1. Catholic Church — Doctrinal and controversial works — Protestant authors. I. Title.

WILDER, John Bunyan, 1914- 282
The other side of Rome. Grand Rapids, Zondervan Pub. House [1959] 159 p. 21 cm. Includes bibliography. [BX1765.2.W5] 59-1510
1. Catholic Church — Doctrinal and controversial works — Protestant authors. I. Title.

WILDER, John Bunyan, 1914- 282
The shadow of Rome; a survey of Roman intolerance and persecution over the years, and the implications of Romanist activity today in the political, economic and social fields. Grand Rapids, Zondervan Pub. House [1960] 128 p. 21 cm. Includes bibliography. [BX1765.2.W52] 60-51205
1. Catholic Church — Doctrinal and controversial works — Protestant authors. I. Title.

WILHELM, Anthony J. 282
Christ among us; a modern presentation of the Catholic faith, by Anthony J. Wilhelm. Westminster, Md., Newman Press [1967] v, 393 p. 22 cm. Includes bibliographies. [BX1754.W47] 67-28697
1. Catholic Church—Doctrinal and controversial works, Popular. I. Title.

WILLIAMS, Michael, 1878-1950. 282
The Catholic Church in action, by Michael Williams, with the collaboration of Julia Kernan. Completely rev. by Zsolt Aradi. New York, P. J. Kennedy [1958] 350 p. illus. 22 cm. [BX1751.W58 1958] 58-5790
1. Catholic Church. I. Title.

WILLIAMS, Walter Dakin, 1919- 282
Nails of protest; a critical comparison of modern Protestant and Catholic beliefs, by Walter Dakin Williams and Walter Robert

Stewart. [1st ed.] New York, Exposition Press [1955] 102p. 21cm. [BX1780.W48] 55-11137
1. Catholic Church—Doctrinal and controversial works—Catholic authors. I. Stewart, Walter Robert, 1925- joint author. II. Title.

WINCOFF, John Eugene Lee, 1863- 282
Fair play the Christian way. Boston, Meador Pub. Co. [1952] 118 p. 21 cm. [BX1765.W786] 52-8542
1. Catholic Church—Doctrinal and controversial works—Protestant authors. I. Title.

CATHERINE FREDERIC, Sister, 1902- 282.02
The handbook of Catholic practices. With a foreword by Winfrid Herbst. [1st ed.] New York, Hawthorn Books [1964] 319 p. 22 cm. Bibliography: p. 303-308. [BX842.C29] 64-10670
1. Catholic Church — Handbooks, manuals, etc. 2. Catholic Church — Ceremonies and practices. I. Title.

CATHERINE FREDERIC, Sister, 1902- 282.02
The handbook of Catholic practices. Foreword by Winfrid Herbst. New York, Hawthorn [c.1964] 319p. 22cm. Bibl. 64-10670 4.95
1. Catholic Church—Handbooks, manuals, etc. 2. CatholicChurch—Ceremonies and practices. I. Title.

ARMSTRONG, William, 1918- 282'.02'07
The angels must have smiled; gems of gayety, by Wm. Armstrong. Cover and cartoons by Art Hargrave. [Spokane, Gonzaga University Press, 1969] 143 p. illus. 18 cm. [PN6231.C22A7] 70-101346
1. Catholic wit and humor. I. Title.

HOYT, Robert G., comp. 282'.02'07
The best of Cry pax! Edited and introduced by Robert G. Hoyt. Kansas City, Mo., National Catholic reporter [1969] 128 p. illus. 18 cm. (NCR paperback) Consists chiefly of material first published in the National Catholic reporter. [PN6231.C22H6] 73-107036 1.45
1. Catholic wit and humor. I. National Catholic reporter. II. Title. III. Title: Cry pax!

ADDIS, William Edward, 1844-1917. 282.03
A Catholic dictionary, containing some account of the doctrine, discipline, rites, ceremonies, councils, and religious orders of the Catholic Church, by William E. Addis and Thomas Arnold. Rev. by T. B. Scannell, P. E. Hallett [and] Gordon Albion; further rev. by members of the staff of St. John's Seminary, Wonersh. 16th ed., rev. London, Routledge & Paul, 1957. viii, 860 p. 26 cm. [BX841.A3 1957] 57-4607
1. Catholic Church—Dictionaries. I. Arnold, Thomas, 1823-1900, joint author.

BOWDEN, Charles Henry. 282.03
Short dictionary of Catholicism. New York, Philosophical Library [1958] 158 p. 20 cm. [BX841.B6] 58-14832
1. Catholic Church—Dictionaries. I. Title.

BRODERICK, Robert C 1913- 282.03
Catholic concise dictionary, compiled by Robert C. Broderick. Rev. by Placid Hermann and Marion A. Habig. Chicago, Franciscan Herald Press [1966] xi, 330 p. 21 cm. First published in 1944 under title: Concise Catholic dictionary. [BX841.B7 1966] 66-14726
1. Catholic Church — Dictionaries. I. Hermann, Placid, ed. II. Habig, Marion Alphonse, 1901- ed. III. Title.

BRODERICK, Robert C., 1913- comp 282.03
Catholic concise dictionary. Rev. by Placid Hermann, Marion A. Habig. Chicago, Franciscan Herald [c.1966] Chicago, Franciscan Herald c.1966 xi, 330p. 21cm. First pub. in 1944 under title: Concise Catholic dictionary [BX841.B7] 66-14762 4.50
1. Catholic Church—Dictionaries. I. Hermann, Placid, ed. II. Habig, Marion Alphonse, 1901- ed. III. Title.

BRODERICK, Robert C 1913- ed. 282.03
The Catholic concise encyclopedia. Line drawings by Ade de Bethune. St. Paul, Catechetical Guild Educational Society;general trade distribution by Simon and Schuster, New York [1957] 330p. illus. 23cm. [BX841.B69] 57-2635
1. Catholic Church—Dictionaries. I. Title.

BRODERICK, Robert C., 1913- 282'.03
The Catholic encyclopedia / by Robert C. Broderick ; ill. by Virginia Broderick. Nashville : T. Nelson, [1976] p. cm. [BX841.B695] 76-10976 ISBN 0-8407-5096-X 24.00
1. Catholic Church—Dictionaries. I. Title.

A Catholic dictionary 282.03
(The Catholic encyclopadic dictionary.) Edited by Donald Attwater. 3d ed. New York, Macmillan, 1958. vii, 552 p. 25 cm. "Originally published under the title, 'The Catholic encyclopadic dictionary.'" [BX841.C35 1958] 58-5797
1. Catholic Church—Dictionaries. I. Attwater, Donald, 1892- ed.

CATHOLIC dictionary (A); 282.03
the Catholic encyclopaedic dictionary, ed. by Donald Attwater. 3d ed. New York, Macmillan, 1961 [c.1931-1958] 552p. (Macmillan paperback 53) Originally published under title: The Catholic encyclopaedic dictionary 2.45 pap.,
1. Catholic Church—Dictionaries. I. Attwater, Donald, 1892- ed.

HANNON, Ruth. 282.03
A Catholic child's picture dictionary; illustrated by Ted Chaiko. St. Paul, Catechetical Guild Educational Society [1956] 58p. illus. 29cm. [BX841.H34] 56-3819
1. Catholic Church- -Dictionaries, Juvenile. I. Title.

HANON, Ruth. 282.03
A Catholic child's picture dictionary; illustrated by Ted Chaiko. St. Paul, Catechetical Guild Educational Society [1956] 58p. illus. 29cm. [BX841.H34] 56-3819
1. Catholic Church— Dictionaries, Juvenile. I. Title.

MARYKNOLL Catholic 282.03
dictionary (The) Comp., ed. by Albert J. Nevins. Pref. by Donald Attwater [1st Amer. ed. Dimension Bks. [dist. New York] Grosset [c.1965] xvii, 710p. 24cm. [BX841.M36] 65-15436 9.95
1. Catholic Church—Dictionaries. I. Nevins, Albert J., 1915-

NEW Catholic 282'.03
encyclopedia. Prepared by an editorial staff at the Catholic University of America. New York, McGraw-Hill [1967] 15 v. illus. (part col.), facsims., maps, ports. (part col.) 29 cm. Includes bibliographies. [BX841.N44 1967] 66-22292
1. Catholic Church—Dictionaries. I. Catholic University of America. II. Title: Catholic Encyclopedia.

PEGIS, Jessie Corrigan. 282.03
A practical Catholic dictionary. [1st ed.] Garden City, N. Y., Hanover House [1957] 258p. 22cm. [BX841.P36] 57-6297
1. Catholic Church—Dictionaries. I. Title.

PEGIS, Jessie Corrigan 282.03
A practical Catholic dictionary. New York, All Saints Pr. [1961, c.1957] 260p. (AS207) .50 pap.,
1. Catholic Church—Dictionaries. I. Title.

PEGIS, Jessie Corrigan. 282.03
A practical Catholic dictionary. [1st ed.] Garden City, N.Y., Hanover House [1957] 258 p. 22 cm. [BX841.P36] 57-6297
1. Catholic Church—Dictionaries. I. Title.

SATO, Seitaro 282.03
Ecclesiastical Japanese, v.1, A-M. [dist. Los Angeles, Perkins Oriental Books, 1960] 783 p. 27 cm. English and Japanese. 60-4901 13.00
1. Catholic Church—Dictionaries. 2. Theology—Dictionaries. 3. English language—Dictionaries—Japanese. I. Title. II. Title: Kyokaigo jiten.

THE Catholic digest. 282.04
Catholic digest reader; selected by the editors. [1st ed.] Garden City, N. Y., Doubleday, 1952. 500 p. 22 cm. [BX880.C28] 52-11011
1. Catholic Church—Addresses, essays, lectures. I. Title.

THE Catholic mind. 282.04
The Catholic mind through fifty years, 1903-1953. New York, America Press [1953] xxii, 681p. 22cm. [BX801.C3643] 52-13404
1. Catholic Church—Addresses, essays, lectures. I. Masse, Benjamin Louis, 1905- ed. II. Title.

CAVANAUGH, John, 1870-1935. 282.04
The conquest of life; conferences on timeless truths. Edited with a biographical sketch by John A. O'Brien. Paterson, N. J., St. Anthony Guild Press, 1952. 212 p. 24 cm. [BX890.C367] 52-12084
1. Catholic Church—Addresses, essays, lectures. I. Title.

HERR, Dan, ed. 282.04
Realities; significant writing from the Catholic press, edited by Dan Herr and Clem Lane. Milwaukee, Bruce Pub. Co. [1958] 296p. 22cm. [BX885.H46] 58-7669
1. Catholic Church— Addresses, essays, lectures. 2. Press, Catholic. I. Lane, Clem, joint ed. II. Title.

LA FARGE, John, 1880- 282.04
A John La Farge reader; selected and edited by Thurston N.Davis [and] Joseph Small. Introd. by Harold C. Gardiner. New York, America Press, 1956. 272p. 24cm. [BX890.L26] 56-7626
1. Catholic Church— Addresses, essays, lectures. I. Title.

LAWLER, Justus George. 282.04
The Christian imagination; studies in religious thought. With an introd. by John M. Oesterreicher. Westminster, Md. Newman Press, 1955. 199p. 21cm. [BX890.L29] 55-7047
1. Catholic Church—Addresses, essays, lectures. I. Title.

LONG, Valentine. 282.04
Fountain of living waters; a collection of essays having as a common denominator the faith: as shown in the yearning of poets, the lives of the heroic, and the needs of daily life. Paterson, N. J., St. Anthony Guild Press [c1957] 338p. 20cm. [BX890.L58] 58-14558
1. Catholic Church—Addresses, essays, lectures. I. Title.

LONGFORD, Elizabeth (Harman) Pakenham, countess of, 1906- ed. 282.04
Catholic approaches to modern dilemmas and eternal truths, edited by Elizabeth Pakenham. New York, Frarar, Straus, and Cudahy [1955] 240 p. 21 cm. London ed. (Weldenfeld and Nicolson) has title: Catholic approaches. [BX885.L6 1955a] 55-8461
1. Catholic Church — Addresses, essays, lectures. I. Title.

LONGFORD, Elizabeth (Harman) Pakenham, countess of 1906- ed. 282.04
Catholic approaches to modern dilemmas and eternal truths, edited by Elizabeth Pakenham. New York, Farrar, Straus, and Cudahy [1955] London ed. (Weidenfeld and Nicolson) has title: Catholic approaches. [BX885.L6 1955a] 55-8461
1. Catholic Church — Addresses, essays, lectures. I. Title.

MERTON, Thomas, 1915- 282.04
Disputed questions. New York, Farrar, Staus and Cudahy [1960] 297 p. 21 cm. [BX891.M45] 60-12636
1. Catholic Church—Addresses, essays, lectures. I. Title.

MERTON, Thomas, 1915- [Nameinreligion:FatherLouis] 282.04
Disputed questions [New York] New Amer. Lib. [1965, c.1953-1960] xi, 222p. 18cm. (Mentor-omega bk., MT622) [BX891.M45] .75 pap.,
1. Catholic Church—Addresses, essays, lectures. I. Title.

PAKENHAM, Elizabeth (Harman) Pakenham, baroness, ed. 282.04
Catholic approaches to modern dilemmas and eternal truths. New York, Farrar, Straus, and Cudahy [1955] 240p. 21cm. London ed. (Weidenfeld and Nicolson) has title: Catholic approaches. [BX885.P27 1955a] 55-8461
1. Catholic Church—Addresses, essays, lectures. I. Title.

PIUS XII, Pope. 1876-1958. 282.04
Pius XII and the American people, by Vincent A. Yzermans. Baltimore, Helicaon Press [1958] 159p. illus. 27cm. Addresses delivered to American audiences. [BX890.P5665] 58-59504
1. Catholic Church—Addresses, essays, lectures. I. Vzermans, Vincent Arthur, 1925- ed. II. Title.

TOWARDS a living 282.04
tradition. Foreword by Dietrich von Hildebrand. Saint Louis, Pio Decimo Press [1953] 105p. 21cm. (Ecclesia sancta, 1) Bibliographical references included in 'Notes' (p. 100-105) [BX885.T6] 54-30218
1. Catholic Church—Addresses, essays, lectures. I. Series.
Contents omitted.

VON HILDEBRAND, Dietrich, 1889- 282.04
The new Tower of Babel, essays. New York, P. J. Kenedy [1953] 243p. 21cm. [BX890.V65] 53-12221
1. Catholic Church—Addresses, essays, lectures. 2. Civilization, Modern. I. Title.

WHITE, Victor. 282.04
God the unknown, and other essays. New York, Harper [1956] 205p. 22cm. [BX890] 56-14152
1. Catholic Church—Addresses, essays, lectures. I. Title.

WHITE, Victor, 1902-1960. 282.04
God the unknown, and other essays. New York, Harper [1956] 205 p. 22 cm. [[BX890]] 56-14152
1. Catholic Church — Addresses, essays, lectures. I. Title.

COMMISSION on Journals Academic and Professional. 282.05
Publisher's guide: Catholic journals academic and professional, compiled by Stanley J. Gaines, chairman. River Forest, Ill. [1961] ix, 85 p. 21 cm. [Z6951.C72] 61-48824
1. Catholic Church—Periodicals—Directories. I. Gaines, Stanley J., comp. II. Title.

**REVUE Thomiste;* 282.05
revue doctrinale de theologie et de philosophie; v.1-48. New York, Kraus Reprint, 1965. 48v. (various p.) 23cm. For the years 1893-1948, excluding 1915-1917 and 1940-1945 when pubn. was suspended. set, 1,100.00; set, pap., 990.00; ea., pap., 22.50

TWENTIETH century 282.05
Catholicism; a periodic supplement to The Twentieth Century Encyclopedia of Catholicism, no.3. Ed. [by] Lancelot Sheppard. Managing ed. Paul Fargis. New York, Hawthorn [c.1966] 237p. 21cm. [BX801.T9] 65-3716 6.00 bds.,
1. Catholic Church—Period. I. Sheppard, Lancelot Capel, 1906- ed. II. The Twentieth century encyclopedia of Catholicism. Supplement.

CATHOLIC life annual. 282.058
1958- Milwaukee Bruce Pub. Co. v. illus. .part col.) ports 28cm. Editor: 1958- E. P. Willging. [AY81.R6C37] 58-4
1. Catholic Church—Yearbooks. I. Willging. Eugene Paul, 1909- ed.

OFFICIAL Catholic 282.058
directory (The) 1963. Giving status of the Catholic church as of Jan. 1, 1963. Containing ecclesiastical stats. of the United States, the Canal Zone, Puerto Rico, the Virgin Islands. Guam, Carolina and Marshall islands, Jamaic, W.I., foreign missionary activities, Canada, Ireland. England, Scotland, Wales, Australia, New Zealand, Oceania, Cuba, Mexico and the Philippines. [Thomas B. Kenedy, ed., Charles R. Cunningham, managing ed.] Complete ed. New York, Kenedy [c.1963] various p. illus. (pt. col.) 29cm. 1-30961 15.00
1. Catholic Church—Direct.

CATHOLIC almanac. 282'.059
Huntington, Ind. : Our Sunday Visitor.
The 1977 ed., edited by Felician A Foy, is availab le for 10.95; pbk., 6.95. L.C. card no.: 73-641001. ISBN 0-87973-873-1; 0-87973-821-9 (pbk.)

NATIONAL Catholic almanac 282.059
(The). 64th year of publication; 1904- Paterson, N.J., St. Anthony's Guild Pr. Garden City, N.Y., Doubleday [1968] v. illus. (incl. ports., maps, music) plates (pt. col.) tables. 20-27cm. 1931-33 issued as no. 1, v. 11-13 of the Franciscan. No volumes issued for the years 1930, 1934-35. Title varies: 1904-1910, St. Antony's almanac. 1911, Franciscan almanac. 1912-1926, St. Antony's almanac. 1927-1929, St. Anthony's almanac. 1931-1933, The Franciscan . . . almanac edition. 1936-1939, The . . . Franciscan almanac. 1940- The National Catholic almanac. Editors: 1904-1929, Published by the Franciscan fathers of the Province of the most holy name.--1940- compiled by the Franciscan clerics of Holy name college, Washington, D. C. Imprint varies: 1904-1907, Callicoon Depot, N.Y., St. Joseph's college.--1908-1929, Paterson, N.J. [etc.] St. Anthony's almanac.--1931-1933, Paterson, N.J., The Franciscan magazine.--1936- Paterson, N.J., St. Anthony's guild. Ed. 1968 F. Foy. [AY81.R6N3] A43 3.95
1. Almanacs, American. 2. Catholic Church—Yearbooks. I. Franciscans. Province of the most holy name of Jesus. II. Washington, D.C. Holy name college. III. St. Anthony's guild, Paterson, N.J.

CATHOLIC Theological Society of America. 282.06273
Proceedings of the annual convention. [Washington] v. 23cm. Title varies slightly. [BX810.C285] 53-17016
1. Theology— Addresses, essays, lectures. 2. Catholic Church—Addresses, essays, lectures. I. Title.

WEBER, Francis J. 282'.07'2024 B
Maynard J. Geiger, O.F.M., Franciscan & historian: a 70th birthday tribute, by Francis J. Weber and Doyce B. Nunis, Jr. Foreword by W. W. Robinson. Santa Barbara, Friends of the Santa Barbara Mission Archive-Library, 1971. viii, 53 p. ports. 23 cm. 300 copies

printed. "A Geiger bibliography": p. 19-52. [E175.5.G4W4] 71-173908
1. Geiger, Maynard J., 1901- I. Nunis, Doyce Blackman.

THORNTON, Francis Beauchesne, 1898- 282.076
What is your Catholic I. Q., by Francis Beauchesne Thornton and Timothy Murphy Rowe. New York, P. J. Kenedy [1951] 216 p. 20 cm. [BX1754.T5] 51-14705
1. Questions and answers — Theology. 2. Catholic Church — Doctrinal and controversial works, Popular. I. Title.

AMERICA (New York, 1909-) 282.08
American Catholic horizons, ed. by Eugene K. Culhane. Garden City, N.Y., Doubleday, 1966 [c.1964-1966] 304p. 22cm. Reprint of selected articles which appeared in the 1961-1965 issues of America. [BX885.A58] 66-12176 4.95
1. Catholic Church—Addresses, essays, lectures. I. Culhane, Eugene K., ed.

AMERICA (New York, 1909-) 282.08
American Catholic horizons, edited by Eugene K. Culhane. [1st ed.] Garden City, N. Y., Doubleday, 1966. 304 p. 22 cm. A reprint of selected articles which appeared in the 1961-1965 issues of America. [BX885.A58 1966] 66-12176
1. Catholic Church—Addresses, essays, lectures. I. Culhane, Eugene K., ed. II. Title.

BARRY, Colman James, 1921- ed. 282.08
Readings in church history. Westminster, Md., Newman Press [1960]-65. 3 v. 24 cm. "Reference table to standard textbooks in church history": v. 1, p. 633. Contents.CONTENTS. -- v. 1. From Pentecost to the Protestant revolt. -- v. 2. The Reformation and the absolute states. -- v. 3. The modern ear; 1789 to the present. [BR141.B27] 59-14755
1. Church history — Sources. I. Title.

BARRY, William Francis, 1849-1930. 282'.08
Roma Sacra; essays on Christian Rome. Freeport, N.Y., Books for Libraries Press [1968] vi, 250 p. 22 cm. (Essay index reprint series) Reprint of the 1927 ed. Bibliographical footnotes. [BX890.B33 1968] 68-14896
1. Catholic Church—Addresses, essays, lectures. I. Title.

BEKKERS, W. M. 282.08
God's people on the march; a modern bishop speaks to his people. Tr. from Dutch by Catherine Jarrott. Introd. by Michel van der Plas. New York, Holt [c.1964, 1966] xi, 180p. 22cm. [BX891.B413] 66-13495 4.95
1. Catholic Church—Addresses, essays, lectures. I. Title.

BEKKERS, Willem Marinus, Bp., 1908-1966. 282.08
God's people on the march; a modern bishop speaks to his people, by W. M. Bekkers. Translated from the Dutch by Catherine Jarrott. With an introd. by Michel van der Plas. [1st ed.] New York, Holt, Rinehart and Winston [1966] xi, 180 p. 22 cm. [BX891.B413] 66-13495
1. Catholic Church—Addresses, essays, lectures. I. Title.

BEKKERS, Willem Marinus, Bp., 1908-1966. 282.08
God's people on the march; a modern bishop speaks to his people, by W. M. Bekkers. Translated from the Dutch by Catherine Jarrott. With an introd. by Michel van der Plas. [1st ed.] New York, Holt, Rinehart and Winston [1966] xi, 180 p. 22 cm. [BX891.B413] 66-13495
1. Catholic Church—Addresses, essays, lectures. I. Title.

BELLOC, Hilaire, 1870-1953 282'.08
Essays of a Catholic. Freeport, N. Y., Bks. for Libs. Pr. [1967] 319p. 22cm. (Essay index reprint ser.) Reprint of the 1931 New York ed. [BX890.B43 1967] 67-26713 8.50
1. Catholic Church—Addresses essays, lectures. I. Title.

BICKERSTAFFE-DREW, Francis Browning Drew, Count, 1858-1928. 282'.08
Discourses and essays. Freeport, N.Y., Books for Libraries Press [1970] 220 p. 23 cm. (Essay index reprint series) Reprint of the 1922 ed. [BX890.B6 1970] 78-107683
1. Catholic Church—Addresses, essays, lectures. I. Title.

CLAUDEL, Paul, 1868-1955. 282'.08
Ways and crossways. Translated by John O'Connor with the collaboration of the author. Freeport, N. Y., Books for Libraries Press [1967] vii, 260 p. 22 cm. (Essay index reprint series) Reprint of the 1933 ed. [BX890.C45] 67-28732
1. Catholic Church—Addresses, essays, lectures. I. Title.

CLAUDEL, Paul, 1868-1955. 282'.08
Ways and crossways. Translated by John O'Connor with the collaboration of the author. Freeport, N.Y., Books for Libraries Press [1967] vii, 260 p. 22 cm. (Essay index reprint series) Reprint of the 1933 ed. [BX890.C45 1967] 67-28732
1. Catholic Church—Addresses, essays, lectures. I. Title.

CLAUDEL, Paul, 1868-1955. 282'.08
Ways and crossways. Translated by John O'Connor with the collaboration of the author. Port Washington, N.Y., Kennikat Press [1968] vii, 260 p. 21 cm. (Essay and general literature index reprint series) Reprint of the 1933 ed. Contents.Contents.—Religion and poetry.—To the Catholic actors of New York.—Propositions on justice.—On evil and liberty.—Letter to Madame E.—The physics of the Eucharist.—Five unsuccessful letters.—On the track of God.—Two letters to Arthur Fontaine.—What thinkest thou of Christ?—On turning the other cheek.—My childhood's winsome faith.—Letter to Alexander Cingria.—On art.—Postscript.—An underground church.—Ecce sto ad ostium et pulso.—Two letters about St. Joseph.—The third meeting.—The presence of God. [BX890.C45 1968] 68-15820
1. Catholic Church—Addresses, essays, lectures. I. Title.

DE LA BEDOYERE,Michael, 1900- ed. 282.08
The future of Catholic Christianity [by] Yvonne Lubbock [others] Ed., introd. by Michael de la Bedoyere. Philadelphia, Lippincott [1966] xiii, 313p. 20 cm. Bibl. [BR123.D44 1966] 66-23144 4.95 bds.
1. Christianity—20th cent.—Addresses, essays, lectures. I. Lubbock, Yvonne. II. Title.

DE LA BEDOYERE, Michael, 1900- ed. 282.08
The future of Catholic Christianity [by] Yvonne Lubbock [and others] Edited with an introd. by Micahel de la Bedoyere. Philadelphia, Lippincott [1966] xiii, 313 p. 20 cm. Bibliographical footnotes. [BR123.D44 1966] 66-23144
1. Christianity — 20th cetn. — Addresses, essays, lectures. I. Lubbock, Yvonee. II. Title.

FALCONER, John, 1577-1656. 282'.08 s
The mirrour of created perfection, 1632, [by] John Falconer; [and] S. Peters complaint and Saint Mary Magdalens funerall teares, 1616, [by] Robert Southwell. Menston, Scolar Press, 1971. [21], 150, [8], 170 p. 20 cm. (English recusant literature, 1558-1640, v. 76) (Series: Rogers, David Morrison, comp. English recusant literature, 1558-1640, v. 76.) Facsimile reprints. The mirrour of created perfection, originally published St. Omer, 1632. This ed. of S. Peters complaint and Saint Mary Magdalens funerall teares originally published, St. Omer, 1616. [BX1750.A1E5 vol. 76] [BT605.2] 232.91 72-196481 ISBN 0-85417-578-4 £1850.00 for the series
1. Mary, Virgin. 2. Mary Magdalene, Saint. I. Southwell, Robert, 1561?-1595. S[aint] Peters complaint. 1971. II. Southwell, Robert, 1561?-1595. Saint Mary Magdalens funerall teares. 1971. III. Title. IV. Title: S[aint] Peters complaint. V. Title: Saint Mary Magdalens funerall teares. VI. Series.
Available from DaCapo, 50.00

FRISBIE, Richard P. 282'.08
Who put the bomb in Father Murphy's chowder? Irreverent essays, by Richard Frisbie. [1st ed.] Garden City, N.Y., Doubleday, 1968. 206 p. 22 cm. [BX891.F7] 68-12772
1. Catholic Church—Addresses, essays, lectures. I. Title.

JOANNES XXIII, Pope, 1881-1963- 282'.08
The voice of John. Commemorating the dedication of the John XXIII Library, St. Mary's Dominican College, New Orleans, March 5, 1967. [New Orleans, c1967] 55 p. illus. 24 cm. "Selected from the spoken word of John XXIII, by Reverend Anselm M. Townsend." Includes bibliographical references. [BX891.J64] 68-3843
1. Catholic Church—Addresses, essays, lectures. I. Townsend, Anselm Mary, father, 1901- II. John XXIII Library. III. Title.

JOANNES XXIII, Pope, 1881-1963. 282'.08
The voice of John. Commemorating the dedication of the John XXIII Library, St. Mary's Dominican College, New Orleans, March 5, 1967. [New Orleans, c1967] 55 p. illus. 24 cm. "Selected from the spoken word of John XXIII, by Reverend Anselm M. Townsend." Includes bibliographical references. [BX891.J64] 68-3843
1. Catholic Church—Addresses, essays, lectures. I. Townsend, Anselm Mary, father, 1901- II. John XXIII Library. III. Title.

MCNALLY, Robert E. 282.08
The unreformed church. New York, Sheed [c.1965] 216p. 22cm. Bibl. [BX891.M28] 65-20852 4.50
1. Catholic Church—Addresses, essays, lectures. 2. Catholic Church—Hist.—Addresses, essays, lectures. I. Title.

RAHNER, Karl, 1904- 282'.08
The Christian of the future. [Translated by W. J. O'Hara. New York] Herder and Herder [1967] 104 p. 22 cm. (Quaestiones disputatae, 18) Translation of four chapters of Schriften zur Theologie, v. 6, 1965. [BX891.R27] 66-28290
1. Catholic Church—Addresses, essays, lectures. I. Title.

SUHARD, Emmanuel Celestin, Cardinal, 1874-1949. 282'.08
The responsible church; selected texts of Cardinal Suhard. Compiled by Olivier de la Brosse. Notre Dame, Ind., Fides Publishers [1967] 258 p. 23 cm. Abridged translation of Vers une eglise en etat de mission. Bibliographical footnotes. [BX890.S843 1967b] 68-15355
1. Catholic Church—Collected works. 2. Theology—Collected works—20th century. I. Title.

VATICAN Council. 2d,1962-1965. 282.08
The documents of Vatican 2; introductions and commentaries by Catholic bishops and experts, responses by Protestant and Orthodox scholars, Walter M. Abbott, general editor, Very Rev. Msgr. Joseph Gallagher, translation editor. Documents of Vatican two London, Dublin, G. Chapman, 1966. xxii, 794 p. table 18 1/2 cm. (An Angelus book) (B 66-7734) Bibliographical footnotes. [BX830 1962.A3G3] 66-74439
I. Abbott, Walter M., ed. II. Title.

AGHAJANIAN, Krikor Bedros, Cardinal, 1895- 282.081
The man of the missions: an American visit. 1960: Gregory Peter XV Cardinal Agagianian [Boston, Daughters of St. Paul, 1963] 60p. 18cm. Addresses delivered during the author's visit to the United States, 1960. 60-16446 50 pap.,
1. Catholic Church—Education—Addresses, essays, lectures. 2. Missions—Addresses, essays, lectures. I. Title.

DOPFNER, Julius, Cardinal, 1913- 282.081
The questioning church [Addresses tr. from German by Barbara Waldstein-Wartenberg] Westminster, Md., Newman [1965, c.1964] x, 83p. 29cm. [BX891.D613] 65-1334 1.50 pap.,
1. Catholic Church—Addresses, essays, lectures. I. Title.

FRANCESCO d'Assisi, Saint 282.081
St. Francis of Assisi, his life and writings as recorded by his contemporaries. A new version of The mirror of perfection, together with a complete collection of all the known writings of the Saint. Translated [from the Italian] by Leo Sherley Price. New York, Harper [1960, c.1959] 234p. plates, port. 22cm. 60-8137 4.50 half cloth,
1. Catholic Church—Collected works. 2. Theology—Collected works—Middle Ages. I. Francesco d'Assisi, Saint. Legend. Speculum perfectionis. II. Sherley-Price, Lionel Digby, tr. III. Title.

FRANCIS, Dale 282.081
Kneeling in the bean patch. Foreword by Frank Scully. New York, P. J. Kenedy [c.1960] xv, 207p. 22cm. 60-14107 3.95
1. Catholic Church—Addresses, essays, lectures. I. Title.

GETLEIN, Frank. 282.081
"The trouble with Catholics ... " Baltimore, Helicon [1964] 224 p. 21 cm. [BX891.G4] 64-20228
1. Catholic Church — Addresses, essays, lectures. 2. Catholics in the U.S. I. Title.

GETLEIN, Frank 282.081
'The trouble with Catholics . . . New York, Helicon dist. Taplinger, c.1964. 224p. 21cm. 64-20228 4.95
1. Catholic Church—Addresses, essays, lectures. 2. Catholics in the U.S. I. Title.

GILLIS, James Martin 1876- 282.081
On almost everything. From the syndicated column Sursum corda. New York, Dodd, Mead, 1955. 177p. 21cm. [BX1395.G47] 55-11793
1. Catholic Church—Addresses, essays, lectures. I. Title.

NICOLAUS Cusanus, Cardinal, 1401-1464. 282.081
Unity and reform; selected writings. Edited by John Patrick Dolan. [Notre Dame, Ind.] University of Notre Dame Press [c1962] viii, 260 p. port. 24 cm. Name originally: Nicolaus Krebs (Khrypffs, Chrypffs) of Cues or Cusa. Bibliographical footnotes. [BX890.N52] 62-19019
I. Dolan, John Patrick, ed. II. Title.

NICOLAUS CUSANUS, Cardinal, [Name orig.: Nicolaus Krebs (Khrypffs, Chrypffs) of Cues or Cusa] 1401-1464. 282.081
Unity and reform; selected writings. Ed. by John Patrick Dolan. [Notre Dame, Ind.] Univ. of Notre Came Pr. [c.1962] viii, 260p. port. 24cm. Bibl. 62-19019 6.50
I. Title.

PAULUS VI, Pope, 1897- 282.081
The Church, by Giovanni Battista Cardinal Montini. [Translated by Alfred Di Lascia] Baltimore, Helicon [1964] 232 p. 21 cm. Translation of Discorsi su in Chiesa. Bibliographical footnotes. "Bibliographical note": p. 232. [BX891.P313] 64-14667
1. Catholic Church—Addresses, essays, lectures. 2. Church—Addresses, essays, lectures. 3. Vatican Council, 2d. I. Title.

PIUS XII, Pope, 1876-1958. 282.081
Major addresses. Edited by Vincent A. Yzermans. St. Paul, North Central Pub. Co., 1961. 2 v. 24 cm. Contents.v. Selected addresses.--v. Christmas messages, Bibliography: v. 2, p. 248-261. [BX890.P5813] 64-55962
1. Catholic Church—Addresses, essays, lectures. I. Yzermans, Vincent Arthur 1925- ed. II. Title.

RAHNER, Karl. 1904- 282.081
Nature and grace; dilemmas in the modern church. New York, Sheed and Ward [1964] 149 p. 21 cm. [BX1746.R3] 64-13574
1. Catholic Church—Addresses, essays, lectures. I. Title.

SUENENS, Leon Joseph, Cardinal, 1904- 282.081
The church in dialogue; five talks in America. Ed. by Arthur McCormack. Notre Dame, Ind., Fides [c.1965] 128p. 20cm. [BX891.S8] 65-13802 1.50 pap.,
1. Catholic Church—Addresses, essays, lectures. I. Title.

SUHARD, Emmanuel Celestin, Cardinal 282.081
The church today, the collected writings of Emmanuel Cardinal Suhard. Introd. by John J. Wright. Chicago, Fides Publishers [1953] 371p. illus. 21cm. [BX890.S83] 53-9911
1. Catholic Church—Collected works. 2. Theology—Collected works—20th cent. I. Title.

CATHOLIC Church. Pope. 282.082
The Church. Selected and arr. by the Benedictine monks of Solesmes. Translated by E. O'Gorman. [Boston] St. Paul Editions [c1962] 927 p. 19 cm. (Papal teachings) Includes bibliographical references. [BX1746.A45] 62-12454
1. Church — Papal documents. I. Solesmes, France. Saint-Pierre (Benedictine abbey) II. Title.

CHAPIN, John, ed. 282.082
A treasury of Catholic reading. New York, Farrar, Straus and Cudahy [1957] 656p. 22cm. [BX885.C52] 57-7700
1. Catholic literature. I. Title.

GLEASON, Robert W 282.082
In the eyes of others. Edited by Robert W. Gleason. New York, Macmillan [1962] 168 p. 22 cm. [BX1780.G5] 62-19753
1. Catholic Church — Doctrinal and controversial works — Catholic authors. I. Title.

PAULUS VI, Pope, 1897- 282.082
The mind of Paul VI on the church and the world. Introd. by Augustin, Cardinal Bea. Edited from the works of Cardinal Montini by James Walsh. Translated by Archibald Colguhoun. Milwaukee, Bruce Pub. Co. [1964] xvi, 267 p. 23 cm. Bibliographical footnotes. [BX891.P343] 64-6368
1. Catholic Church—Addresses, essays, lectures. I. Title.

PAULUS VI, Pope, 1897- 282.082
The mind of Paul VI on the church and the world. Introd. by Augustin, Cardinal Bea. Ed. from the works of Cardinal Montini by James

Walsh. Tr. by Archibald Colquhoun. Milwaukee, Bruce [c.1964] xvi, 267p. 23cm. Bibl. 64-6368 5.50
1. Catholic Church—Addresses, essays, lectures. I. Title.

ULANOV, Barry, ed. 282.082
Contemporary Catholic thought; faith, hope and love in the modern world. New York, Sheed and Ward [1963] 310 p. 22 cm. Includes bibliography. [BX885.U4] 62-15276
1. Christianity — 20th cent. — Addresses, essays, lectures. 2. Catholic Church — Addresses, essays, lectures. I. Title.

ULANOV, Barry, ed. 282.082
Contemporary Catholic thought; faith, hope and love in the modern world. New York, Sheed [c.1963] 310p. 22cm. Bibl. 62-15276 6.00
1. Christianity—20th cent.—Addresses, essays, lectures. 2. Catholic Church—Addresses, essays, lectures. I. Title.

VATICAN Council. 2d,1962- 1965. 282.082
Council speeches of Vatican II. Edited by Hans Kung, Yves Congar [and] Daniel O'Hanlon. Glen Rock, N.J. Paulist Press [c1964] 288 p. 19 cm. (Deus books) [BX830 1962.A3K8] 64-18548
1. Catholic Church — Addresses, essays, lectures. I. Kung, Hans, 1928- ed. II. Title.

VATICAN COUNCIL, 2d 282.082
Council speeches of Vatican II. Ed. by Hans Kung, Yves Congar, Daniel O'Hanlon. Glen Rock, N.J., Paulist Pr. [c.1964] 288p. 19cm. (Deus bks.) 64-18548 1.25 pap.,
1. Catholic Church—Addresses, essays, lectures. I. Kung, Hans, 1928- ed. II. Title.

WOLF, Donald J., ed. 282.082
Current trends in theology, ed. by Donald J. Wolf, James V. Schall. Garden City, N.Y., Doubleday [c.]1965. 285p. 22cm. Bibl. [BT28.W6] 65-12362 4.95
1. Theology—20th cent. 2. Catholic Church—Addresses, essays, lectures. I. Schall, James V., joint ed. II. Title.

WOLF, Donald J., ed: 282.082
Current trends in theology, ed. by Donald J. Wolf, James V. Schall. Garden City, N.Y., Doubleday [1966, c.19658] 274p. 18cm. (Image bks., D202) Bibl. [BT28.W6] 65-12362 .85 pap.,
1. Theology—20th cent. 2. Catholic Church—Addresses, essays, lectures. I. Schall, James V., joint ed. II. Title.

MCKENNA, Marian Cecelia, 1926- 282.084
Concise history of Catholicism. Paterson, N.J., Little-field [c.]1962. 285p. 21cm. (143) Bibl. 61-12622 1.95 pap.,
1. Catholic Church—Hist. I. Title.

RICE, Edward E 1918- 282.084
The church, a pictorial history. New York, Farrar, Straus & Cudahy [1961] 268p. illus. 30cm. [BX945.2.R5 1961] 61-6989
1. Catholic Church—Hist.—Pictorial works. I. Title.

RICE, Edward E 1918- j 282.084
A young people's pictorial history of the church. Text adapted by Blanche Jennings Thompson from The church; a pictorial history. New York, Farrar, Straus [1963] 4 v. illus. 24 cm. Contents.v. 1. The early Christians. -- v. 2. The Age of Charlemagne. -- v. 3. The high Middle Ages. -- v. 4. The church today. [BX945.2.R52] 63-9926
1. Catholic Church — Hist. — Juvenile literature. I. Thompson, Blanche Jennings, 1887- II. Title.

RICE, Edward E., 1918- 282.084
A young people's pictorial history of the church, 2 v. Text adapted by Blanche Jennings Thompson from The church; a pictorial history. New York, Farrar [c.1954-1963] 2v. (128;112p.) illus. 24cm. Contents.v. 1. The early Christians.--v. 2. The Age of Charlemagne. 63-9926 2.95 ea.,
1. Catholic Church—Hist.—Pictorial works. I. Thompson, Blanche Jennings, 1887- II. Title.

RICE. EDWARD E., 1918- 282.084
The church. a pictorial history. New York, Farrar [c.1954-1961] 268p. illus. 30cm. 61-6989 10.00
1. Catholic Church—Hist.—Pictorial works. I. Title.

BAUSCH, William J. 282'.09
Pilgrim church; a popular history of Catholic Christianity [by] William J. Bausch. Notre Dame, Ind., Fides Publishers [1973] 529 p. 21 cm. Bibliography: p. 523-524. [BR145.2.B37] 73-6608 ISBN 0-8190-0598-3 9.95
1. Catholic Church—History. 2. Church history. I. Title.

BOKENKOTTER, Thomas S. 282'.09
A concise history of the Catholic Church / Thomas Bokenkotter. 1st ed. Garden City, N.Y. : Doubleday, 1977. 431 p. ; 22 cm. Includes bibliographical references and index. [BX945.2.B64] 77-75382 ISBN 0-516-03902-4 lib.bdg. : 6.60
1. Catholic Church—History. 2. Church history. I. Title.

BRAURE, Maurice 282.09
The age of absolutism [tr. from French] New York, Hawthorn [c.1963] 138p. 21cm. (20th cent. ency. of Catholicism, v.79. Sect. 7: Hist. of the church) Bibl. 63-23327 3.50 bds.,
1. Catholic Church—Hist. I. Title. II. Series: The Twentieth century encyclopedia of Catholicism, v. 79

CREIGHTON, Mandell, Bp. of London, 1843-1901. 282'.09
A history of the papacy from the great schism to the sack of Rome. New ed. London, New York, Longmans, Green, 1897. [New York, AMS Press, 1969] 6 v. 22 cm. Includes bibliographical references. [BX955.C8 1969] 74-77897
1. Catholic Church—History. 2. Papacy—History. I. Title.

DAUGHTERS of St. Paul. 282'.09
The Church's amazing story. Written and illsutrated by a team of Daughters of St. Paul. [Boston] St. Paul Editions [1969] 268 p. illus. (part col.) 24 cm. [BX945.2.D36] 68-59043
1. Catholic Church—History. I. Title.

DAY, Edward, Father. 282'.09
The Catholic Church story, changing and changeless / Edward Day. Liguori, Mo. : Liguori Publications, 1975. 187 p. : ill. ; 22 cm. Includes index. Bibliography: p. 187. [BR147.D39] 75-27612 ISBN 0-89243-004-4 pbk. : 2.95
1. Catholic Church—History. 2. Church history. I. Title.

DE WOHL, Louis, 1903-1961 282.09
Founded on a rock; a history of the Catholic Church. Philadelphia, Lippincott [c.1961] 249p. 61-8674 3.95
1. Catholic Church—Hist. I. Title.

DOLAN, John Patrick. 282'.09
Catholicism; an historical survey, by John P. Dolan. Woodbury, N.Y., Barron's Educational Series, inc. [1968] vi, 250 p. 21 cm. (Barron's compact studies of world religions) Includes bibliographical references. [BX945.2.D6] 65-25674
1. Catholic Church—History. I. Title.

EBERHARDT, Newman C. 282.09
A summary of Catholic history; v.2. St. Louis, B. Herder [c.1962] viii, 911p. Contents.v.2. Modern History. Bibl. 61-8059 13.00
1. Catholic Church—Hist. I. Title.

EBERHARDT, Newman C. 282.09
A summary of Catholic history; v. 1. St. Louis, B. Herder [c.1961] 879p. Contents.v. 1. Ancient & medieval history. 61-8059 12.00; 9.00 student ed.,
1. Catholic Church—Hist. I. Title.

FENICHELL, Stephen S. 282.09
The Vatican and Holy Year, by Stephen S. Fenichell and Phillip Andrews. [1st ed.] Garden City, N.Y., Halcyon House [1950] 115 p. illus., ports. 23 cm. [BX961.H6F4] 50-7621
1. Holy Year. 2. Vatican. I. Andrews, Phillip, 1911- joint author. II. Title.

FUNK, Franz Xaver von, 1840-1907. 282'.09
A manual of church history. Authorised translation from the 5th German ed. by Luigi Cappadelta. London, K. Paul, Trench, Trubner, 1910. [New York, AMS Press, 1973] 2 v. 23 cm. Translation of Lehrbuch der Kirchengeschichte. Includes bibliographical references. [BR145.2.F8613 1973] 78-168077 ISBN 0-404-02646-X 26.00
1. Catholic Church—History. 2. Church history. I. Title.

GRANDI, Domenico. 282.09
The story of the church [by] Domenico Grandi and Antonio Galli. Rev. ed. Translated and edited by John Chapin. Garden City, N.Y., Image Books [1966] 358 p. 19 cm. [BX945.2.G7 1966] 66-11569
1. Catholic Church — Hist. I. I. Galli, Antonio, joint author. II. Title.

GRANDI, Domenico 282.09
The story of the church [by] Domenico Grandi, Antonio Galli. Rev. ed. Tr., ed. by John Chapin. Garden City, N. Y., Doubleday [c.1960, 1966] 358p. 19cm. (Image bk., D206) [BX945.2.G7] 66-11569 1.25 pap.,
1. Catholic Church—Hist. I. Galli, Antonio, joint author. II. Title.

GURIAN, Waldemar, 1902- ed. 282.09
The Catholic Church in world affairs, edited by Waldemar Gurian and M. A. Fitzsimons. Notre Dame, University of Notre Dame Press [1954] ix, 420p. 24cm. (International studies of the Committee on International Relations, University of Notre Dame) Bibliographical footnotes. [BX1389.G8] 53-7351
1. Catholic—Church—Hist. I. Fitzsimons, Matthew A., 1912- joint ed. II. Title. III. Series: Notre Dame, Ind. University. Committee on International Relations. International studies

HARNEY, Martin Patrick, 1896- 282'.09
The Catholic Church through the ages / Martin P. Harney. Boston : St. Paul Editions, 1974. 601 p. : ill. ; 22 cm. Includes indexes. [BX945.2.H35] 73-76312 8.95
1. Catholic Church—History. 2. Church history. I. Title.

HERTLING, Ludwig, Freiherr von, 1892- 282.09
A history of the Catholic Church. Translated from the German by Anselm Gordon Biggs. Westminster, Md., Newman Press, 1957. 643 p. 23 cm. Includes bibliography. [BX945.H472] 56-13468
1. Catholic Church—History.

HERTLING. LUDWIG, Freiherr von, 1892- 282.09
A history of the Catholic Church. Translated from the German by Anselm Gordon Biggs. Westminster, Md., Newman Press, 1957. 643p. 23cm. Includes bibliography. [BX945.H472] 56-13468
1. Catholic Church—Hist. I. Title.

HISTORICAL problems of church renewal. 282.09 Glen Rock, N.J., Paulist Press [1965] ix, 179 p. 24 cm. (Concilium theology in the age of renewal: Church history, v. 7) Bibliographical footnotes. [BR148.H55] 65-26792
1. Church history — Addresses, essays, lectures. I. Series: Concilium theology in the age of renewal, v. 7

HISTORICAL problems of church renewal. 282.09 Glen Rock, N. J., Paulist [c.1965] ix, 179p. 24cm. (Concillium theology in the age of renewal: Church hist., v.7) Bibl. [BR148.H55] 65-26792 4.50
1. Church history—Addresses, essays, lectures. (Series: Concilium theology in the age of renewal, v.7)

JOHNSON, George, 1889-1944 282.09
The story of the Church [a textbook for the upper grades, by] George Johnson, Jerome D. Hannan, Sister M. Dominica [New rev. ed. by David Sharrock] New York, Benziger [c.1963] xii, 398p. col. illus. 23cm. 63-17043 3.72 bds.,
1. Catholic Church—Hist.—Text-books. I. Sharrock, David John. II. Title.

LEROUX, Jean Marie, 1918- 282.09
The new people of God; a short history of the church. Tr. [from French] by Jex Martin. Notre Dame, Ind., Fides [1964, c.1963] 301p. 21cm. 63-20802 4.95
1. Catholic Church—Hist. I. Title.

MAHONY, Jerome. 282.09
A short history of the Catholic Church. [Library ed.] Dublin, Talbot Press [1951] 2v. illus. 19cm. [BX945.M34] 52-67020
1. Catholic Church—Hist. I. Title.

MARITAIN, Jacques, 1882-1973. 282'.09
On the church of Christ; the person of the church and her personnel. Translated by Joseph W. Evans. Notre Dame [Ind.] University of Notre Dame Press [1973] xiii, 302 p. 24 cm. Translation of De l'Eglise du Christ. Includes bibliographical references. [BX1746.M3513] 73-11559 ISBN 0-268-00519-2 9.95
1. Church. 2. Church history. I. Title.
Pbk. 3.95.

MOODY, Joseph Nestor, 1904- ed. 282.09
Church and society; Catholic social and political thought and movements, 1789-1950. Edited by Joseph N. Moody in collaboration with: Edgar Alexander [and others] New York, Arts, inc. [c1953] 914p. 24cm. Includes bibliographical references. [BX1365.M6] 53-10712
1. Catholic Church—Hist. 2. Church and social problems—Catholic Church. 3. Church and state—Catholic Church. I. Title.

NEILL, Thomas Patrick, 1915- 282.09
History of the Catholic Church [by] Thomas P. Neil and Raymond H. Schmandt. Milwaukee, Bruce Pub. Co. [1957] 684p. illus. 24cm. [BX945.N4] 57-8837
1. Catholic Church—Hist. I. Schmandt, Raymond Henry, 1925- joint author. II. Title.

NEILL, Thomas Patrick, 1915- 282.09
History of the Catholic Church [by] Thomas P. Neill and Raymond H. Schmandt. 2d ed. Milwaukee, Bruce Pub. Co., 1965. xx, 696 p. illus., maps, ports. 24 cm. Includes bibliographical references. [BX945.2.N4 1965] 65-17468
1. Catholic Church — Hist. I. Schmandt, Raymond H, joint author. II. Title.

PALLOTTI, Vincenzo, Saint, 1795-1850. 282'.09
Complete writings. Baltimore, Pallottine Fathers & Brothers Press, 1968- v. 24 cm. Contents.Contents.—v. 1. Pious Society of the Catholic Apostolate. Bibliographical footnotes. [BX890.P25] 68-7190
1. Catholic Church—Collected works. 2. Theology—Collected works—19th century.

PICHON, Charles, 1893- 282.09
The Vatican and its role in world affairs; translated from the French by Jean Misrahi. [1st ed.] New York, Dutton, 1950. 382 p. illus., ports. 23 cm. Translation of Histoire du Vatican. [BX946.P514] 50-9872
1. Catholic Church — Hist. 2. Catholic Church — Relations. 3. Catholic Church — Relations (diplomatic) I. Title.

PIUS XI, Pope, 1857-1939. 282'.09
Essays in history, written between the years 1896-1912, by Achille Ratti, now Pope Pius XI. Freeport, N. Y., Books for Libraries Press [1967] xvii, 312 p. illus., plates, ports. 22 cm. (Essay index reprint series) Reprint of the 1934 ed. Translation of Scritti storici. [BX890.P55 1967] 67-26771
1. Carlo Borromeo, Saint, 1538-1584. 2. History—Addresses, essays, lectures. 3. Catholic Church—Hist. 4. Milan—Hist. 5. Milan. Biblioteca ambrosiana. I. Title.
:Contents omitted

SANCHEZ, Jose Mariano, 1932- 282'.09
Anticlericalism; a brief history [by] Jose Sanchez. Notre Dame [Ind.] University of Notre Dame Press [1972] xi, 244 p. 22 cm. Bibliography: p. 225-234. [BX1766.S25] 72-3504 ISBN 0-268-00471-4 8.95
1. Anti-clericalism—History. 2. Anti-catholicism—History. I. Title.

WERNER, Karl, 1821-1888 282.09
Geschichte der katholischen theologie. Seit dem Trienter konzil bis zur gegenwart. Von dr. Karl Werner ... 2. Aufl. Munchen und Leipzig, R. Oldenbourg 1889; New York, Johnson Reprint. 1966 2p. 1., viii, 656p. 22cm. (Added t.-p.: Geschichte der wissenschaften in Deutschland. Neuere zeit. 6. bd.) [BX1747.W4] 25.00
1. Theology—Hist. 2. Catholic church—Hist. I. Title.

ELLIOTT-BINNS, Leonard Elliott, 1885- 282'.09'02
The history of the decline and fall of the medieval Papacy, by L. Elliott Binns. [Hamden, Conn.] Archon Books, 1967. xv, 388 p. 22 cm. Reprint of the 1934 ed. Bibliographical footnotes. [BX1068.E5 1967] 67-19514
1. Papacy — Hist. 2. Catholic Church — Hist. 3. Church history — Middle Ages. I. Title.

ELLIOTT-BINNS, Leonard Elliott, 1885- 282'.09'02
The history of the decline and fall of the medieval Papacy, by L. Elliott-Binns. [Hamden, Conn.] Archon Books, 1967. xv, 388 p. 22 cm. Reprint of the 1934 ed. Bibliographical footnotes. [BX1068.E5 1967] 67-19514
1. Catholic Church—History. 2. Papacy—History. 3. Church history—Middle Ages. I. Title.

JORDAN, George Jefferis, 1890- 282'.09'023
The inner history of the Great Schism of the West; a problem in Church unity, by G. J. Jordan. New York, B. Franklin [1972] 216 p. 23 cm. (Burt Franklin research and source works series. Philosophy & religious history monographs, 105) Reprint of the 1930 ed. Bibliography: p. 210-211. [BX1301.J6 1972] 72-80392 ISBN 0-8337-4193-4 13.50
1. Schism, The Great Western, 1378-1417. I. Title.

ULLMANN, Walter, 1910- 282'.09'023
The origins of the great schism; a study in fourteenth-century ecclesiastical history. With a 1972 pref. by the author. [Hamden, Conn.] Archon Books, 1972. xxvii, 244 p. illus. 22 cm. Reprint of the 1948 ed. published by Burns, Oates, & Washbourne, London. Includes bibliographical references.

[BX1301.U55 1972] 79-39365 ISBN 0-208-01277-X
1. Schism, The Great Western, 1378-1417. I. Title.

HALES, Edward Elton Young, 1908- 282.0903
The Catholic Church in the modern world; a survey from the French revolution to the present. [1st ed.] Garden City, N. Y., Manover House, 1958. 312p. 22cm. Includes bibliography. [BX1386.H3] 58-5943
1. Catholic Church—Hist. 2. Church history—19th cent. 3. Church history—20th cent. I. Title.

MACCAFFREY, James, 1875-1935. 282'.09'03
History of the Catholic Church from the Renaissance to the French Revolution. Freeport, Books for Libraries Press [1970] 2 v. 23 cm. Reprint of the 1915 ed. Includes bibliographical references. [BX1330.M3 1970] 75-130558 ISBN 0-8369-5531-5
1. Catholic Church—History—Modern period, 1500- I. Title.

TREVOR, Meriol. 282'.09'03
Prophets and guardians; renewal and tradition in the church. Garden City, N.Y., Doubleday, 1969. 221 p. 22 cm. "Bibliographical note": p. 211-214. [BX1396.2.T7] 74-84384 5.95
1. Catholic Church—History—Modern period, 1500- 2. Liberalism (Religion)—Catholic Church. I. Title.

DANIEL-ROPS, Henry, 1901- 282.09034
The church in an age of revolution. 1789-1870. Tr. from French by John Warrington. Garden City, N. Y., Doubleday 1967[c.1965] 2v. (311; 359p.) map. 18cm. (His Hist. of the Church of Christ). Image bk., D217A/B) Bibl. [BR290.D313] 1.35 pap., ea,
1. Church history—Modern period. 2. Catholic Church—Hist.—Modern period. I. Title.

DANIEL-ROPS, Henry, 1901- 282.09034
The church in an age of revolution, 1789-1870. Tr. from French by John Warrington. London, J. M. Dent; New York, Dutton [c.1965] x, 509p. map. 23cm. (His Hist.of the church of Christ, v.8) Bibl. [BR290.D313] 65-5178 10.00
1. Church history—Modern period. 2. Catholic Church—Hist.—Modern period. I. Title.

DANIEL-ROPS, Henry, 1901- 282.09034
The church in an age of revolution, 1789-1870, by H. Daniel-Rops. Translated from the French by John Warrington. London, J. M. Dent; New York, Dutton [1965] x, 509 p. map. 23 cm. (His History of the church of Christ, v. 8) Translation of En face des n veaux destins, published as v. 1 of the author's L'Eglise des revolutions. Bibliography: p. 479-481. [BR290.D313 1965] 65-5178
1. Church history — Modern period. 2. Catholic Church — Hist. — Modern period. I. Title.

RANCHETTI, Michele. 282'.09'034
The Catholic modernists: a study of the religious reform movement, 1864-1907; translated [from the Italian] by Isabel Quigly. London, Oxford U.P., 1969. x, 230 p. 23 cm. Originally published as Cultura e riforma religiosa nella storia del modernismo, Torino, G. Einaudi, 1963. Includes bibliographical references. [BX1396.R2713] 77-453711 45/-
1. Modernism—Catholic Church. I. Title.

REARDON, Bernard M. G., comp. 282'.09'034
Roman Catholic modernism, edited and introduced by Bernard M. G. Reardon. Stanford, Calif., Stanford University Press [1970] 251 p. 23 cm. (A Library of modern religious thought) Includes bibliographical references. [BX1396.R4 1970] 77-130825 ISBN 0-8047-0750-2 7.95
1. Modernism—Catholic Church. I. Title. II. Series.

BAUM, Gregory, 1923- 282'.09'04
The credibility of the church today; a reply to Charles Davis. [New York] Herder and Herder [1968] 222 p. 21 cm. Bibliographical references included in "Notes" (p. 211-219) [BX1780.B28 1968b] 68-26509
1. Catholic Church—Doctrinal and controversial works—Catholic authors. 2. Davis, Charles, 1923- A question of conscience. I. Title.

BAUSCH, William J. 282'.09'04
Renewal and the middle Catholic [by] William J. Bausch. Notre Dame, Ind., Fides Publishers [1971] ix, 221 p. 20 cm. Bibliography: p. 218-221. [BX1746.B37] 71-129460 ISBN 0-8190-0563-0 2.95
1. Church renewal—Catholic Church. I. Title.

BOUYER, Louis, 1913- 282'.09'04
The decomposition of Catholicism, by Louis C. Bouyer. Translated and with a foreword by Charles Underhill Quinn. [Chicago] Franciscan Herald Press [1969] vii, 110 p. 21 cm. Translation of La decomposition du catholicisme. [BX1389.B613] 79-95292 3.95
1. Catholic Church—History—20th century. 2. Church renewal—Catholic Church. I. Title.

CAMPBELL, Robert, 1919- 282'.09'04
Spectrum of Catholic attitudes, edited by Robert Campbell. Contributors: William F. Buckley, Jr. [and others] Milwaukee, Bruce Pub. Co. [1969] xxx, 191 p. 22 cm. [BX1751.2.C33] 77-77154 4.95
1. Catholic Church—Doctrinal and controversial works—Catholic authors. I. Buckley, William Frank, 1925- II. Title.

CROWE, Frederick E. 282'.09'04
A time of change; guidelines for the perplexed Catholic [by] Frederick E. Crowe. Milwaukee, Bruce Pub. Co. [1968] xvi, 168 p. 23 cm. [BX1746.C7] 68-23898
1. Church renewal—Catholic Church. I. Title.

THE Crucial questions on problems facing the church today [by] Yves Congar [and others. Edited by Frank Fehmers] New York, Newman Press, 1969. 172 p. ports. 20 cm. Includes bibliographies. [BX885.C77] 79-92215 3.95 282'.09'04
1. Catholic Church—Addresses, essays, lectures. I. Congar, Yves Marie Joseph, 1904-

DANIEL-ROPS, Henry, 1901-1965 282.0904
A fight for God, 1870-1939. Tr. From French by John Warrington. Garden City, N. Y., Doubleday [1967, c.1965] 1v. in 2. 18cm. (Image bks., D224/D224B) Tr. of Un combat pour Dieu, pub. as v. 2 of the author's L'Eglise des revolutions. Bibl. [BR477.D2713 1966] 1.45 pap., ea.,
1. Catholic Church—Hist. I. Title.

DANIEL-ROPS, Henry 1901-1965 282.0904
A fight for God. 1870-1939. Tr. from French by John Warrington. London, Dent; New York, Dutton [1966.c.1965] x, 452p. 23cm. (His Hist. of the church of Christ. 9) Tr. of Un combat pour Dieu. pub. as v. 2 of the author's L'Eglise des revolutions. Bibl. [BR477.D2713 1966] 66-31970 10.00
1. Catholic Church—Hist. I. Title.

DANIEL-ROPS, Henry, 1901-1965. 282.0904
A fight for God, 1870-1939. Translated from the French by John Warrington London, Dent; New York, Dutton [1966, c1965] x, 452 p. 22 cm. (His History of the church of Christ, 9) Translation of Un combat pour Dieu, published as v. 2 of the author's L'Eglise des revolutions. Bibliography: p. 432-434. [BR477.D2713 1966] 66-31979
1. Catholic Church — Hist. I. Title.

DEEDY, John G. 282'.0904
The Vatican, by John Deedy. New York, Watts [1970] 66 p. illus., ports. 23 cm. (A First book) An introduction to the history, art, and people of the world's smallest nation, with special emphasis on the duties of the Pope. [DG800.D4] 70-102275 ISBN 5-310-06972-3.25
1. Catholic Church—Juvenile literature. 2. Vatican City—Juvenile literature. I. Title.

DOTY, William Lodewick, 1919- 282'.09'04
A view from the middle; a centrist commentary on current trends in the American church, by William Doty. Liguori, Mo., Liguori Publications [1972] 192 p. 18 cm. [BX1390.D68] 72-87325 2.00
1. Catholic Church—History—1965-

FOLLIET, Joseph 282.0904
World Catholicism today. [Tr. from French by Edmond Bonin] Westminster, Md., Newman Press [c.]1961. 214p. 61-8968 3.25
1. Catholic Church—Hist.—20th cent. I. Title.

GALTER, Alberte. 282.0904
The red book of the persecuted church. Westminster, Md., Newman Press, 1957. 491p. 22cm. 'Translation ... published by arrangement with the proprictors, Editions Fleurus, Paris.' [BX1378.G312] 57-14025
1. Persecution. 2. Catholic Church—Hist.—20th cent. 3. Communism and religion. I. Title.

HERDER correspondence 282.0904
John XXIII; Pope Paul on his predecessor, and a documentation by the editors of Herder correspondence. [New York] Herder & Herder [c.1965] 200p. illus., ports. 21cm. Bibl. [BX1378.2.H4] 64-19731 4.50
1. Joannes XXIII, Pope, 1881-1963. I. Paulus VI, Pope, 1897- II. Title. III. Title: Pope Paul on his predecessor.

HERDER CORRESPONDENCE. 282.0904
John XXIII; Pope Pual on his predecessor, and a documentation by the editors of Herder correspondence. [New York] Herder and Herder [1965] 200 p. illus., ports. 21 cm. Includes bibliographies. [BX1378.2.H4] 64-19731
1. Joannes XXIII, Pope, 1881-1963. 2. Paulus VI, Pope, 1897- I. Title.

MOLNAR, Thomas Steven. 282'.09'04
Ecumenism or new reformation? [By] Thomas Molnar. New York, Funk & Wagnalls [1968] 169 p. 22 cm. Bibliographical footnotes. [BX1746.M64] 68-21723
1. Catholic Church—History—20th century. 2. Church renewal—Catholic Church. I. Title.

O'HANLON, Daniel, 1919- 282'.09'04
What's happening to the church? Daniel O'Hanlon. [Cincinnati] : St. Anthony Messenger Press, [1974] iv, 171 p. : ill. ; 19 cm. [BX1751.2.O33] 74-193284 ISBN 0-912228-14-8 pbk. : 1.85
1. Catholic Church—Doctrinal and controversial works—Catholic authors. I. Title.

ROCHE, Douglas J. 282'.09'04
The Catholic revolution, by Douglas J. Roche. New York, D. McKay Co. [1968] xxiii, 325 p. 21 cm. Bibliography: p. 311-316. [BX1390.R6] 68-31283 6.50
1. Catholic Church—History—1965- 2. Church renewal—Catholic Church. I. Title.

ROCHE, Douglas J. 282'.09'04
Man to man; a frank talk between a layman and a bishop, by Douglas J. Roche and Remi DeRoo. Edited and with an introd. by Gary MacEoin. Milwaukee, Bruce Pub. Co. [1969] xiii, 240 p. 22 cm. [BX1751.2.R62] 77-76812
1. Catholic Church—Doctrinal and controversial works—Catholic authors. 2. Catholic Church—Government. 3. Laity—Catholic Church. I. DeRoo, Remi. II. Title.

SHEED, Francis Joseph, 1897- 282'.09'04
Is this the same church? [By] F. J. Sheed Dayton, Ohio, Pflaum, 1968. xv, 224p. 18cm. [BX1389.S4 1968b] 68-55966 1.75 pap.,
1. Catholic Church—Hist.—20th cent. 2. Church renewal—Catholic Church. I. Title.

VON HILDEBRAND, Dietrich, 1889- 282'.09'04
Trojan horse in the city of God. Chicago, Franciscan Herald Press [1967] xiii, 233 p. 21 cm. Bibliographical references included in "Notes" (p. 227-233) [BX1755.V6] 67-22202
1. Catholic Church—Doctrinal and controversial works. 2. Secularism. I. Title.

WILLIS, Garry, 1934- 282'.09'04
Bare ruined choirs; doubt, prophecy, and radical religion. [New York, Dell, 1974, c1972] 272 p. 21 cm. (A Delta book) [BX1389.W53] 2.95 (pbk.)
1. Catholic Church—History—20th century. I. Title.
L.C. card number for hardbound ed.: 75-175406.

WILLS, Garry, 1934- 282'.09'04
Bare ruined choirs; doubt, prophecy, and radical religion. [1st ed.] Garden City, N.Y., Doubleday, 1972. x, 272 p. 22 cm. [BX1389.W53] 75-175406 ISBN 0-385-08970-8 7.95
1. Catholic Church—History—20th century. I. Title.

HAUGHTON, Rosemary. 282'.09'046
Dialogue; the state of the church today [by] Rosemary Haughton and Cardinal Heenan. New York, Sheed and Ward [1968, c1967] ix, 182 p. 23 cm. [BX1390] 68-17362
1. Catholic Church—History—1965- I. Heenan, John Carmel, Cardinal, 1905- joint author. II. Title.

WESTOW, Theodore L. 282'.09'046
Introducing contemporary Catholicism, by Theo Westow. With a profile of Catholicism in America, by Leonard Swidler. Philadelphia, Westminster [c.1967] 127p. 19cm. Bibl. [BX1389.W4 1967b] 68-14959 1.65 pap.,
1. Catholic Church—Hist.—20th cent. I. Title.

WESTOW, Theodore L 282'.09'046
Introducing contemporary Catholicism, by Theo Westow. With a profile of Catholicism in America, by Leonard Swidler. Philadelphia, Westminster Press [1967] 127 p. 19 cm. Bibliography: p. 123-124. [BX1389.W4] 68-14959
1. Catholic Church—Hist.—20th cent. I. Title.

GILKEY, Langdon Brown, 1919- 282'.09'047
Catholicism confronts modernity; a Protestant view [by] Langdon Gilkey. New York, Seabury Press [1975] 211 p. 22 cm. "A Crossroad book." [BX1396.G54] 74-19167 ISBN 0-8164-1163-8 8.95
1. Catholic Church—Doctrinal and controversial works—Protestant authors. 2. Catholic Church—History—20th century. 3. Modernism—Catholic Church. I. Title.

HEBBLETHWAITE, Peter. 282'.09'047
The runaway Church : post-conciliar growth or decline / Peter Hebblethwaite. New York : Seabury Press, c1975. p. cm. "A crossroad book." Includes index. Bibliography: p. [BX1751.2.H4] 75-44474 ISBN 0-8164-0291-4 : 8.95
1. Catholic Church—Doctrinal and controversial works. 2. Catholic Church—History—1965- I. Title.

ALLAN, Alfred K. 282.0922
Catholics courageous. Foreword by Richard Cardinal Cushing. Garden City, N.Y., Doubleday [1966, c.1965] 196p. 18cm. (Echo bk., E31) .75 pap.,
1. Catholic Church—Biog. I. Title.

ALLAN, Alfred K. 282.0922
Catholics courageous. Foreword by Richard Cardinal Cushing. New York, Citadel [c.1965] xi, 240p. illus., ports. 21cm. [BX4651.2.A4] 65-27091 4.95
1. Catholic Church—Biog. I. Title.

ALLIES, Mary Helen Agnes, 1852-1927. 282'.0922 B
Three Catholic reformers of the fifteenth century. Freeport, N.Y., Books for Libraries Press [1972] xii, 235 p. 23 cm. (Essay index reprint series) Reprint of the 1878 ed. Includes bibliographical references. [BX1302.A63 1972] 73-38755 ISBN 0-8369-2633-1 9.75
1. Vincentius Ferrerius, Saint, 1350 (ca.)-1419. 2. Bernardino da Siena, Saint, 1380-1444. 3. Giovanni da Capistrano, Saint, 1385 or 6-1456. 4. Church history—15th century. I. Title.

BLUNT, Hugh Francis, 1877- 282'.0922
The great Magdalens. Freeport, N.Y., Books for Libraries Press [1969] ix, 335 p. 23 cm. (Essay index reprint series) Reprint of the 1928 ed. Contents.Contents.—Penitents of the stage.—Voices from the desert.—Magdalens of the ages of penance.—The woman Augustine loved.—Rosamond Clifford.—Saint Margaret of Cortona.—Blessed Angela of Foligno.—Blessed Clare of Rimini.—Saint Hyacintha of Mariscotti.—Cataline de Cardona, "the sinner."—Beatrice Cenci.—The Princess Palatine.—Madame de Longueville.—Louise de la Valliere.—Madame de Montespan.—Madame de la Sabliere.—Madame Pompadour.—Madame Tiquet. [BX4667.B5 1969] 71-86731
1. Catholic Church—Biography. 2. Woman—Biography. I. Title.

CLARK, Mary Ann. 282'.092'2 B
Great American Catholics / by Mary Ann Clark, Jerri Pogue, Diane Rickard ; ill. by Robert L. Mutchler. Notre Dame, Ind. : Ave Maria Press, c1976. 191 p. : ill. ; 23 cm. Includes bibliographical references. [BX4670.C48] 76-7278 ISBN 0-87793-111-9 pbk. : 3.50
1. Catholic Church in the United States—Biography—Study and teaching. 2. Catholic Church in the United States—Biography. 3. United States—Biography—Study and teaching. I. Pogue, Jerri, joint author. II. Rickard, Diane, joint author. III. Title.

COLAIANNI, James F., 1922- 282'.0922
Married priests & married nuns, ed., introd. by James F. Colaianni. [1st ed.] New York, McGraw [1968] xvi, 230p. 22cm. Ramparts bk. [BV4390.C62] 67-26169 6.95
1. Celibacy. 2. Catholic Church—Clergy. I. Title.

COULTON, George Gordon, 1858-1947. 282'.092'2 B
Two saints: St. Bernard & St. Francis. [Folcroft, Pa.] Folcroft Library Editions, 1974. p. cm. Reprint of the 1932 ed. published by the University Press, Cambridge, which was issued as v. 4 of The Cambridge miscellany. Originally published as v. 1-2 of the author's Five centuries of religion. Includes bibliographical references. [BX4700.B5C6 1974] 74-9549 10.00
1. Bernard de Clairvaux, Saint, 1091-1153. 2. Francesco d'Assisi, Saint, 1182-1226. I. Title. II. Series: The Cambridge miscellany, v. 4.

COULTON, George Gordon, 1858-1947. 282'.092'2 B
Two saints, St. Bernard & St. Francis / by G. G. Coulton. Norwood, Pa. : Norwood Editions, 1976. vii, 129 p. : ill. ; 24 cm. Originally published as v. 1-2 of the author's Five centuries of religion. Reprint of the 1932

ed. published by the University Press, Cambridge, which was issued as v. 4 of the Cambridge miscellany. Includes bibliographical references and index. [BX4700.B5C6 1976] 76-11806 ISBN 0-8482-0355-0 lib. bdg. : 12.50
1. Bernard de Clairvaux, Saint, 1091?-1153. 2. Francesco d'Assisi, Saint, 1182-1226. I. Title. II. Series: The Cambridge miscellany ; v. 4.

DAUGHTERS of St. Paul. 282'.092'2 B
Moments of decision / by the Daughters of St. Paul. Boston : St. Paul Editions, c1975. p. cm. [BX4655.2.D3 1975] 75-25893
1. Christian saints. I. Title.

DELANY, Selden Peabody, 1874-1935. 282'.0922
Married saints. Freeport, N.Y., Books for Libraries Press [1969] x, 338 p. 23 cm. (Essay index reprint series) Reprint of the 1935 ed. Bibliographical footnotes. [BX4661D38 1969] 69-17573
1. Catholic Church—Biography. 2. Christian saints. I. Title.

FOLEY, Albert Sidney, 1912- 282'.0922
God's men of color [by] Albert S. Foley. New York, Arno Press, 1969. x, 322 p. 23 cm. (The American Negro: his history and literature) Reprint of the 1955 ed. [BX4670.F6 1969] 69-18569
1. Catholics, Negro. 2. Catholic Church in the United States—Biography. I. Title. II. Series.

FRANCESCO D'ASSISI, Saint. Legend. Fioretti. 282'.0922
Flowers from St. Francis. Selected by Hilda Noel Schroetter. Illustrated by Irene Aronson. New York, Golden Press [1967] 63 p. illus. 17 cm. (The Golden library of faith & inspiration) "A Giniger book." Selections from the Raphael Brown translation of The little flowers of St. Francis, published by Image Books in 1958. [BX4700.F63E445] 67-13731
I. Schroetter, Hilda (Noel) comp. II. Title.

FRANCESCO D'ASSISI, Saint. Legend. Fioretti. 282'.0922
Flowers from St. Francis. Selected by Hilda Noel Schroetter. Illus. by Irene Aronson. New York, Golden Pr. [1967] 63p. illus. 17cm. (Golden lib. of faith & inspiration) A Giniger bk. Selections from the Raphael Brown tr. of The little flowers of St. Francis, pub. by Image Bks. in 1958. [BX4700.F63E445] 67-13731 1.00 bds.,
I. Schroetter. Hilda (Noel) comp. II. Title.

GOODIER, Alban, Abp., 1869-1939. 282'.0922 B
Saints for sinners. Freeport, N.Y., Books for Libraries Press [1970] vi, 200 p. 23 cm. (Essay index reprint series) Reprint of the 1943 ed. [BX4655.G6 1970] 70-99637 ISBN 0-8369-1504-6
1. Christian saints. I. Title.

GRAY, Francine du Plessix. 282'.0922
Divine disobedience: profiles in Catholic radicalism. [1st ed.] New York, Knopf, 1970. xii, 322, vii p. 22 cm. [BX4669.G68] 78-106627 6.95
1. Catholic Church—Biography. 2. Catholic Church—Doctrinal and controversial works—Catholic authors. 3. Dissenters, Religious. I. Title.

GUMBLEY, Walter, 1887- 282'.0922 B
Parish priests among the saints; canonized or beatified parish priests. Foreword by Vincent McNabb. Freeport, N.Y., Books for Libraries Press [1971] 105 p. 23 cm. (Biography index reprint series) Originally published in 1947. Includes bibliographical references. [BX4655.G84 1971] 76-148214 ISBN 0-8369-8061-1
1. Christian saints. 2. Clergy—Religious life. I. Title.

HABIG, Marion Alphonse, 1901- 282'.092'2 B
Saints of the Americas / M. A. Habig. Huntington, Ind. : Our Sunday Visitor, 1974. 384 p. : ill. ; 24 cm. Includes index. Bibliography: p. 378-380. [BX4659.A45H3] 74-15269 ISBN 0-87973-880-4 : 9.95
1. Christian saints—America. I. Title.

HODGES, George, 1856-1919. 282'.0922
Saints and heroes to the end of the Middle Ages. Freeport, N. Y., Books for Libraries Press [1967] 268 p. ports. 22 cm. (Essay index reprint series) Reprint of the 1911 ed. Contents.--Cyprian, 200-258.--Athanasius, 296-373.--Ambrose, 340-397.--Chrysostom, 347-407.--Jerome, 340-420.--Augustine, 354-430.--Benedict, 480-543.--Gregory the Great, 540-604.--Columba, 521-597.--Charlemagne, 742-814.--Hildebrand, 1020-1085.--Anselm, 1033-1109.--Bernard, 1091-1153.--Becket, 1118-1170.--Langton, 1170-1228.--Dominic, 1170-1221.--Francis, 1182-1226.--Wycliffe, 1320-1384.--Hus, 1373-1415.--Savonarola, 1452-1498. [BR1703.H6 1967] 67-26749
1. Christian biography. I. Title.

HODGES, George, 1856-1919. 282'.0922
Saints and heroes to the end of the Middle Ages. Freeport, N.Y., Books for Libraries Press [1967] 268 p. ports. 22 cm. (Essay index reprint series) Reprint of the 1911 ed. Contents.Contents.—Cyprian, 200-258.—Athanasius, 296-373.—Ambrose, 340-397.—Chrysostom, 347-407.—Jerome, 340-420.—Augustine, 354-430.—Benedict, 480-543.—Gregory the Great, 540-604.—Columba, 521-597.—Charlemagne, 742-814.—Hildebrand, 1020-1085.—Anselm, 1033-1109.—Bernard, 1091-1153.—Becket, 1118-1170.—Langton, 1170-1228.—Dominic, 1170-1221.—Francis, 1182-1226.—Wycliffe, 1320-1384.—Hus, 1373-1415.—Savonarola, 1452-1498. [BR1703.H6 1967] 67-26749
1. Christian biography. I. Title.

HOGAN, John Gerard, 1896- 282'.0922
Heralds of the king, by John G. Hogan. Freeport, N.Y., Books for Libraries Press [1970] ii, 190 p. 23 cm. (Essay index reprint series) "First published 1934." Contents.Contents.—St. Francis of Assisi.—St. Dominic.—St. Ignatius Loyola.—St. Teresa of Avila.—St. Jane Frances de Chantal.—Mother Elizabeth Ann Seton. [BX4655.H55 1970] 79-107714 ISBN 0-8369-1516-X
1. Catholic Church—Biography. 2. Christian saints. I. Title.

HOLWECK, Frederick George, 1856-1927. 282'.0922
A biographical dictionary of the saints, with a general introduction on hagiology. St. Louis, Herder, 1924. Detroit, Gale Research Co., 1969. xxix, 1053 p. 23 cm. [BX4655.H6 1969] 68-30625
1. Christian saints—Dictionaries. I. Title.

JACOBI, Andrea. 282'.092'2 B
The saints of the Benedictine Order of Montefano, by Andrew Jacobi. Clifton, N.J., Holy Face Monastery [1972] 268 p. illus. 21 cm. Translations of Latin mss. by Francis Fattorini. Contents.Contents.—Guzzolini, Sylvester, Saint. The life of Blessed Bonfil, bishop and confessor of Christ.—Jacobi, A. The life of Saint Sylvester Guzzolini, founder of the Benedictine Order of Montefano.—Jacobi, A. The life of Saint John of the Staff, O. S. B. Syl.—The Life of Blessed Hugo, O. S. B. Syl., by an anonymous Sylvestrine monk, O. S. B. Syl. Includes bibliographical references. [BX4659.I8J3] 72-171246
1. Christian saints—Italy. I. Guzzolini, Silvestro, Saint, 1177-1267. The life of Blessed Bonfil, bishop and confessor of Christ. 1972. II. The Life of Blessed Hugo, O. S. B. Syl. 1972. III. Title.

JACOBUS de Varagine. 282'.092'2 B
The golden legend; or, Lives of the saints, as Englished by William Caxton. London, J. M. Dent, 1900-39. [v. 1, 1931. New York, AMS Press, 1973] 7 v. cm. Original ed. issued in series: The Temple classics. [BX4654.J33 1973] 76-170839 ISBN 0-404-06770-0 92.50
1. Saints. I. Caxton, William, ca. 1422-1491, tr. II. Title.

KALBERER, Augustine. 282'.092'2 B
Lives of the saints; daily readings. Chicago, Franciscan Herald Press [1975] p. cm. [BX4655.2.K34] 74-10761 ISBN 0-8199-0539-9 10.95
1. Christian saints. 2. Devotional calendars—Catholic Church. I. Title.

KAYE-SMITH, Sheila, 1887-1956. 282'.0922 B
Quartet in heaven. Freeport, N.Y., Books for Libraries Press [1970, c1952] viii, 244 p. 23 cm. (Biography index reprint series) Contents.Contents.—The matrons: Caterina Fiesca Adorna. Cornelia Connelly.—The maidens: Isabella Rosa de Santa Maria de Flores. Therese Martin.—Some notes on the nature of sanctity. [BX4667.K3 1970] 75-136649
1. Caterina da Genova, Saint, 1447-1510. 2. Connelly, Cornelia Augusta (Peacock) 1809-1879. 3. Rosa, of Lima, Saint, 1586-1617. 4. Therese, Saint, 1873-1897. I. Title.

KITTLER, Glenn D. 282.0922
The wings of eagles. Garden City, N.Y., Doubleday [1967, c.1966] 197p. 19cm. (Echo bks., E37) [BX4651.2K5] .85 pap.,
I. Catholic Church—Biog. II. Title.

KITTLER, Glenn D. 282.0922 B
The wings of eagles [by] Glenn D. Kittler. [1st ed.] Garden City, N.Y., Doubleday [1966] 215 p. 22 cm. [BX4651.2.K5] 66-12246
1. Catholic Church—Biography. I. Title.

LIEDERBACH, Clarence A., 1910- 282'.092'2 B
America's thousand bishops: from 1513 to 1974 ... from Abramowicz to Zuroweste [by] Clarence A. Liederbach. Cleveland, Dillon/Liederbach, 1974. 67 p. 22 cm. (Saint Mary's College historical series) [BX4670.L5] 73-94081 ISBN 0-913228-09-5 2.95 (pbk.)
1. Catholic Church—Clergy. 2. Bishops—United States. I. Title.

LUSCOMBE, T. R. 282'.0922
Builders and crusaders, [by] T. R. Luscombe. [Melbourne] Landsdowne Press [1967] xi, 253 p. 22 cm. Stamped on t.p.: Distributed by Sportshelf, New Rochelle, New York. [BX1685.L83] 68-98953 4.50 Aust.
1. Catholic Church in Australia. 2. Catholics in Australia. I. Title.

MCLOUGHLIN, Emmett, 1907- 282'.0922
Famous ex-priests. New York, L. Stuart [1968] 224 p. 21 cm. Bibliography: p. 221-224. [BX4669.M3] 68-18759 4.95
1. Ex-priests, Catholic. I. Title.

MCNAMARA, Robert Francis, 1910- 282'.092'2 B
Catholic Bicentennial profiles / by Robert F. McNamara. [Rochester, N.Y. : Christopher Press], c1975. 31 p. ; 18 cm. [BX4670.M25] 76-359391
1. Catholic Church in the United States—Biography. 2. United States—Biography. I. Title.

MARBACH, Ethel. 282'.092'2 B
Once-upon-a-time saints : faith-tales for children / by Ethel Marbach ; with ill. by Victoria Brzustowicz. [Cincinnati, OH] : St. Anthony Messenger Press, c1977. vii, 72 p. : ill. ; 21 cm. Relates briefly the lives and deeds of nineteen saints including Germaine, Swithin, Clement, and Bridgid. [BX4658.M415] 920 77-153145 ISBN 0-912228-37-7 pbk. : 1.95
1. Christian saints—Biography—Juvenile literature. I. Brzustowicz, Victoria. II. Title.

MARTINDALE, Cyril Charlie, 1879-1963. 282'.0922
What are saints? Fifteen chapters in sanctity, broadcast by C. C. Martindale. Freeport, N.Y., Books for Libraries Press [1968] 157 p. 22 cm. (Essay index reprint series) Biographical sketches. "First published 1932." [BX4655.M35 1968] 68-16954
1. Christian saints. I. Title.

MELVILLE, Thomas. 282'.0922 B
Whose heaven, whose earth? [By] Thomas and Marjorie Melville. [1st ed.] New York, Knopf, 1971 [c1970] 303 p. illus., ports. 22 cm. [BX4705.M4847A3 1971] 70-118719 6.95
I. Melville, Marjorie, 1929- II. Title.

MELVILLE, Thomas. 282'.0922 [B]
Whose heaven, whose earth? By Thomas and Marjorie Melville. New York, Pocket Books [1973, c.1971] xii, 274 p. ports. 18 cm. [BX4705.M4847A3] ISBN 0-671-78347-5 1.25 (pbk)
I. Melville, Marjorie, 1929- II. Title.
L.C. card no. for the hardbound edition: 70-118719.

MONRO, Margaret Theodora, 1896- 282'.0922 B
A book of unlikely saints, by Margaret T. Monro. Freeport, N.Y., Books for Libraries Press [1970, c1943] vii, 220 p. 23 cm. (Essay index reprint series) "Note on sources": p. 9-12. [BX4655.2.M6 1970] 77-107727 ISBN 0-8369-1528-3
1. Christian saints. I. Title.

PERNOUD, Regine, 1909- 282'.092'2 B
Heloise and Abelard. Translated by Peter Wiles. New York, Stein and Day [1973] 256 p. illus. 24 cm. Bibliography: p. 246-247. [BX4705.H463P4613 1973] 72-95915 ISBN 0-8128-1558-0 8.95
1. Heloise, 1101-1164. 2. Abailard, Pierre, 1079-1142. I. Title.

RATTE, John,(1936- 282'.0922
Three modernists; Alfred Loisy, George Tyrrell, William L. Sullivan. New York, Sheed [1967] viii. 370p. 22cm. Bibl. [BX1396.R3] 67-13763 6.95
1. Loisy, Alfred Firmin, 2. Sullivan, William Laurence, 1872-1935. 3. Tyrell, George, 1861-1909. 4. Modernism—Catholic Church. I. Title.

SCHAMONI, Wilhelm, 1905- 282'.0922 B
The face of the saints. Translation by Anne Fremantle. Freeport, N.Y., Books for Libraries Press [1972, c1947] 278 p. illus., ports. 24 cm. (Biography index reprint series) Translation of Das wahre Gesicht der Heiligen. [BX4655.S342 1972] 70-38328 ISBN 0-8369-8128-6
1. Christian saints. 2. Christian saints in art. I. Title.

SCHEURING, Tom. 282'.092'2 B
Two for joy : spirit-led journey of a husband and wife through Jesus to the Father / by Tom and Lyn Scheuring. New York : Paulist Press, c1976. v, 183 p. : ill. ; 21 cm. [BX2350.2.S32] 76-28274 ISBN 0-8091-1985-4 pbk. : 4.95
1. Scheuring, Tom. 2. Scheuring, Lyn. 3. Spiritual life—Catholic authors. 4. Christian communities. 5. Catholics in the United States—Biography. I. Scheuring, Lyn, joint author. II. Title.

SLAVES of the Immaculate Heart of Mary. 282'.0922 B
The communion of saints: sanctity through the centuries. Still River [Mass., 1967] v, 121 p. illus. (part col.) 24 cm. [BX4655.2.S54] 72-191281
1. Saints. I. Title.

STEUART, Robert Henry Joseph, 1874-1948. 282'.0922
Diversity in holiness. Freeport, N. Y., Books for Libraries Press [1967] vii, 221 p. 22 cm. (Essay index reprint series) Reprint of the 1937 ed. [BX4651.S7] 67-28770
1. Catholic Church—Biog. I. Title.
Contents omitted

STEUART, Robert Henry Joseph, 1874-1948. 282'.0922
Diversity in holiness. Freeport, N.Y., Books for Libraries Press [1967] vii, 221 p. 22 cm. (Essay index reprint series) Reprint of the 1937 ed. Contents.Contents.—Mother Julian of Norwich.—St. Francis de Sales.—Brother Lawrence.—St. Benedict Joseph Labre.—The holy man of Tours.—St. Catherine of Genoa.—Marie-Eustelle Harpain.—St. Teresa of Lisieux.—The Abbe Huvelin.—St. Bernadette Soubirous.—St. John-Baptist Vianney, cure d'Ars.—St. Ignatius Loyola. [BX4651.S7 1967] 67-28770
1. Catholic Church—Biography. I. Title.

STEVENS, Clifford J. 282'.092'2 B
Portraits of faith / Clifford Stevens. Huntington, Ind. : Our Sunday Visitor, c1975. 176 p. ; 18 cm. [BX4651.2.S8] 74-21891 ISBN 0-87973-764-6 pbk. : 2.25
1. Catholic Church—Biography. I. Title.

THREE studies in simplicity, by Malachy Carroll and Pol de Leon Albaret. [Pol de Leon Albaret's Sainte Benedict l'Africain translated from the French by Malachy Carroll] Chicago, Franciscan Herald Press [1974] vii, 201 p. 21 cm. [BX4655.2.T45] 74-8284 ISBN 0-8199-0533-X 5.95 282'.092'2 B
1. Pio da Pietrelcina, Father. 2. Martin de Porres, Saint, 1579-1639. 3. Benedetto da San Filadelfo, Saint, 1526-1589. I. Carroll, Malachy Gerard, 1918- Padre Pio. 1974. II. Carroll, Malachy Gerard, 1918- St. Martin de Porres. 1974. III. Albaret, Pol de Leon, Father, 1906- Benedict l'Africain. English. 1974.
Contents omitted.

UNDSET, Sigrid, 1882-1949. 282'.0922
Saga of saints. Translated by E. C. Ramsden. Freeport, N.Y., Books for Libraries Press [1968, c1934] xii, 321 p. illus., map, ports. 22 cm. (Essay index reprint series) Translation of Norske helgener. Contents.Contents.—The coming of Christianity.—St. Sunniva and the Seljemen.—St. Olav, Norway's king to all eternity.—St. Hallvard.—St. Magnus, Earl of the Orkney Islands.—St. Eystein, Archbishop of Nidaros.—St. Thorfinn, Bishop of Hamar.—Father Karl Schilling, Barnabite. [BX4659.N8U7 1968] 68-22952
1. Saints, Norwegian. 2. Norway—Church history. I. Title.

UNDSET, Sigrid, 1882-1949. 282'.0922 B
Stages on the road. Translated from the Norwegian for the first time by Arthur G. Chater. Freeport, N.Y., Books for Libraries Press [1969, c1934] ix, 266 p. 23 cm. (Essay index reprint series) Translation of Etapper. Ny rakke. [BX4651.U52 1969] 74-80405
1. Catholic Church—Biography. 2. Catholic Church—Doctrinal and controversial works—Catholic authors. I. Title.

VIDLER, Alexander Roper, 1899- 282'.0922
A variety of Catholic modernists, by Alex R. Vidler. [London] Cambridge University Press, 1970. viii, 232 p. illus., ports. 22 cm. (The Sarum lectures, 1968-69) Bibliography: p. 221-226. [BX1396.V52 1970] 70-93712 50/- ($8.50)
1. Catholic Church—Biography. 2.

Modernism—Catholic Church. I. Title. II. Series.

WALSH, James Joseph, 1865-1942, comp. 282'.0922
These splendid priests. Freeport, N.Y., Books for Libraries Press [1968] 248 p. 22 cm. (Essay index reprint series) Reprint of the 1926 ed. Contents.Contents.—St. Benedict, founder of the Rule of St. Benedict, by C. F. de Tryon, Comte de Montalembert.—Friar William de Rubruquis, explorer and traveler in the Orient; his journal, translated by J. Mandeville.—Friar Odoric, missionary traveler in the East; his journal, translated by J. Mandeville.—St. Ignatius Loyola, founder of the Society of Jesus; from the Life by Father Bouhours, translated by J. Dryden. Life work of Ignatius Loyola.—St. Francis Xavier, apostle to the Indies; from the Life by Father Bouhours, translated by J. Dryden. Missionary labors of St. Francis Xavier, by J. Schurhammer.—Father James Marquette, explorer of the Mississippi and missionary to the Indians of North America, by J. G. Shea.—St. Vincent de Paul, founder of charitable orders, by F. Goldie.—Father Isaac Jogues, missionary to the Iroquois, by C. J. Devine.—Father Jerome Lobo, missionary to Abyssinia; account of his voyages, translated by S. Johnson.—Friar Junipero Serra, founder of the missions of California, by H. H. Bancroft. The work of Friar Junipero Serra, by Z. Engelhardt.—Father John MacEnery, pioneer palaeontologist, by J. J. Walsh. Other priest anthropologists, by H. G. Osborn. [BX4651.W3 1968] 68-29252
1. Catholic Church—Clergy—Biography. 2. Priests. I. Title.

WARD, Maisie, 1889- ed. 282'.0922
The English way; studies in English sanctity, from St. Bede to Newman, by M. C. D'Arcy [and others] Freeport, N.Y., Books for Libraries Press [1968] 328 p. 22 cm. (Essay index reprint series) Reprint of the 1933 ed. Contents.Contents.—St. Bede, by G. Mathew.—St. Boniface, by A. Manson.—Alcuin, by D. Woodruff.—Alfred the Great, by G. K. Chesterton.—St. Wulstan of Worcester, by D. Knowles.—St. Aelred of Rievaulx, by B. Jarrett.—St. Thomas of Canterbury, by H. Belloc.—Dame Julian of Norwich, by E. I. Watkin.—William Langland, by C. Dawson.—John Fisher, by D. Mathew.—Thomas More, by G. K. Chesterton.—Edmund Campion, by C. C. Martindale.—Mary Ward, by M. Ward.—Richard Crashaw, by E. I. Watkin.—Bishop Challoner, by M. Trappes-Lomax.—Cardinal Newman, by M. C. D'Arcy. Includes bibliographical references. [BX4676.W3 1968] 68-29253
1. Catholic Church—Biography. 2. Catholics in England. I. D'Arcy, Martin Cyril, 1888- II. Title.

ABELOE, William N. 282'.092'4 B
To the top of the mountain : the life of Father Umberto Olivieri, "Padre of the Otomis" / William N. Abeloe ; with a foreword by Miguel Dario Cardinal Miranda. 1st ed. Hicksville, N.Y. : Exposition Press, c1976. 160 p., [11] leaves of plates : ill. ; 22 cm. [BX4705.O48545A63] 76-7187 ISBN 0-682-48558-6 : 8.00
1. Olivieri, Umberto, 1884-1973. 2. Catholic Church—Clergy—Biography. 3. Clergy—United States—Biography. I. Title.

AINSWORTH, Katherine, 1908- 282'.0924 B
In the shade of the juniper tree; a life of Fray Junipero Serra [by] Katherine Ainsworth and Edward M. Ainsworth. With a pref. by Salvador Garcia. [1st ed.] Garden City, N.Y., Doubleday, 1970. xii, 199 p. 22 cm. Bibliography: p. [189]-190. [F864.S417] 76-98541 5.95
1. Serra, Junipero, 1713-1784. I. Ainsworth, Edward Maddin, 1902-1968, joint author. II. Title.

ALDERSON, Jo Bartels. 282'.092'4 B
The man Mazzuchelli, pioneer priest [by] Jo Bartels Alderson and J. Michael Alderson. [1st ed. Madison, Wisconsin House, 1974] 1 v. (unpaged) illus. 24 cm. Includes bibliography. [BX4705.M475] 73-89029 ISBN 0-88361-026-4
1. Mazzuchelli, Samuel Charles, 1806-1864. I. Alderson, Jim Michael, joint author. II. Title.

ANDRADE, Laurinda C., 1899- 282'.0924 B
The open door, by Laurinda C. Andrade. New Bedford, Mass. [Reynolds-De Walt] 1968. 240 p. 22 cm. [BX4705.A575A3] 68-57506 4.95
I. Title.

BALSKUS, Pat. 282'.092'4 B
Mary's pilgrim; life of St. Peregrine. Illustrated by the Daughters of St. Paul. [Boston] St. Paul Editions [1972] 92 p. illus. 22 cm. (Encounter books) The life of the thirteenth-century Italian priest who became the patron against cancer after being miraculously cured of that disease. [BX4700.L43B34] 92 68-58160 1.50
1. Laziosi, Pellegrino, Saint, 1265-1345—Juvenile literature. I. Daughters of St. Paul. II. Title.

BASSET, Bernard 282.0924
Priest in paradise; with God to Illinois. [New York] Herder & Herder [1966] 107p. illus. 21cm. [BX4705.B2518A3] 66-22599 3.50 3.50
1. Catholic Church—Clergy—Correspondence, reminisences, etc. I. Title.

BAYLEY, James Roosevelt, Abp., 1814-1877. 282'.0924 B
Frontier bishop; the life of Bishop Simon Brute. Edited by Albert J. Nevins. Huntington, Ind., Our Sunday Visitor, inc. [1971] 92 p. illus., maps, port. 21 cm. Originally published in 1861 as the introd. to Memoirs of the Right Reverend Simon Wm. Gabriel Brute. [BX4705.B88B34 1971] 70-147935 1.95 (pbk)
1. Brute de Remur, Simon Guillaume Gabriel, Bp., 1779-1839. I. Title.

BELL, Stephen, 1864- 282'.092'4 B
Rebel, priest, and prophet : a biography of Dr. Edward McGlynn / by Stephen Bell. Westport, Conn. : Hyperion Press, 1975, c1937. p. cm. (The Radical tradition in America) Reprint of the ed. published by Devin-Adair, New York. [BX4705.M2B4 1975] 75-301 ISBN 0-88355-206-X : 18.00
1. McGlynn, Edward, 1837-1900. I. Title.

BENSON, Robert Hugh, 1871-1914. 282'.0924
A book of essays. With a memoir by Allan Ross and a foreword by C. C. Martindale. Freeport, N.Y., Books for Libraries Press [1968] 1 v. (various pagings) port. 22 cm. (Essay index reprint series) Reprint of the 1916 ed. A collection of reprinted pamphlets. Contents.Contents.—Monsignor Hugh Benson.—Infallibility and tradition.—The deathbeds of Bloody Mary and Good Queen Bess.—Christian science.—Spiritualism.—Catholicism.—Catholicism and the future.—The conversion of England. Includes bibliographical references. [BX1756.B4 1968] 68-54325
1. Benson, Robert Hugh, 1871-1914. 2. Catholic Church—Addresses, essays, lectures.

BENSON, Robert Hugh, 1871-1914. 282'.0924
Papers of a pariah. Freeport, N.Y., Books for Libraries Press [1967] x, 211 p. 22 cm. (Essay index reprint series) First published in 1907. Contents.Contents.—At a requiem.—On the dulness of irreligious people.—Intellectual slavery.—A father in God.—The sense of the supernatural.—The mystical sense.—Holy Week.—On the dance as a religious exercise.—Religious persecution.—Science and faith.—Low mass.—Benediction.—The personality of the church.—Death. [BX1751.B38 1967] 67-23176
1. Catholic Church—Addresses, essays, lectures. I. Title.

BENZIGER, Marieli G. 282'.092'4 B
Mamma Margherita: St. John Bosco's mother, by Marieli and Rita Benziger. [2d ed.] Altadena, Calif., Benziger Sisters [1973, c1958] ix, 213 p. 21 cm. Bibliography: p. 213. [BX4705.B68B46 1973] 73-84375
1. Bosco, Margherita (Occhiena) 1788-1856. 2. Bosco, Giovanni, Saint, 1815-1888. I. Benziger, Rita, joint author. II. Title.

BISHOP, Morris, 1893-1973. 282'.092'4 B
Saint Francis of Assisi. [1st ed.] Boston, Little, Brown [1974] xii, 227 p. port. 21 cm. (The Library of world biography) Bibliography: p. [215]-217. [BX4700.F6B52 1974] 74-10757 ISBN 0-316-09665-2 6.95
1. Francesco d'Assisi, Saint, 1182-1226.

BONIFAZI, Flavian. 282'.0924
Our Pallottine heritage; for the infinite glory of God. Baltimore, Pallottine Fathers & Brothers Press, 1968. x, 48 p. 23 cm. Bibliography: p. ix-x. [BX4700.P23B58] 68-29101
1. Pallotti, Vincenzo, Saint, 1795-1850. 2. Pallottines. I. Title.

BROUCKER, Jose de. 282'.0924 B
Dom Helder Camara; the violence of a peacemaker. Translated from the French by Herma Briffault. Maryknoll, N.Y., Orbis Books [1970] xiii, 154 p. illus., ports. 24 cm. Includes bibliographical references. [BX4705.C2625B7613] 78-135536 4.95
1. Camara, Helder, 1908-

BUCZEK, Daniel S. 282'.092'4 B
Immigrant pastor; the life of the Right Reverend Monsignor Lucyan Bojnowski of New Britain, Connecticut [by] Daniel S. Buczek. Waterbury, Conn., Heminway Corp., 1974. ix, 184 p. illus. 23 cm. Bibliography: p. 174-176. [BX4705.B5724B8] 74-81981 2.95
1. Bojnowski, Lucyan, 1868-1960. I. Title.

CALIARO, Marco. 282'.092'4 B
John Baptist Scalabrini, apostle to emigrants / Marco Caliaro and Mario Francesconi ; [translation by Alba I. Zizzamia]. 1st ed. New York : Center for Migration Studies, 1977. xi, 555 p. : ill. ; 24 cm. Translation of L'apostolo degli emigranti. Includes indexes. Bibliography: p. 453-469. [BX4705.S38C313] 76-44922 ISBN 0--913256-24-2 : 15.00
1. Scalabrini, Giovanni Battista, Bp., 1839-1905. 2. Catholic Church—Bishops—Biography. 3. Bishops—Italy—Biography. 4. Church work with emigrants—Italy. I. Francesconi, Mario, joint author. II. Title.

CALLAHAN, Nelson J. 282'.0924 B
A case for due process in the church; Father Eugene O'Callaghan American pioneer of dissent [by] Nelson J. Callahan. Staten Island, N.Y., Alba House [1971] x, 133 p. illus. 22 cm. Includes bibliographical references. [BX4705.O25C33] 71-158570 ISBN 0-8189-0214-0 3.95
1. O'Callaghan, Eugene, 1831-1891. 2. Catholic Church—Government. I. Title.

CANTONI, Louise Bellucci. 282'.0924 B
The girl in the stable; the life of St. Germaine. Illustrated by the Daughters of St. Paul under the direction of Guy R. Pennisi. [Boston] St. Paul Editions [1967] 55 p. illus. 22 cm. A brief biography of the young shepherd girl who, in spite of poor health and a cruel stepmother, showed great love and charity to all she met and is remembered for these qualities more than for the miracles attributed to her. [BX4700.G5C3] 92 AC 68
1. Germaine Cousin, Saint, 1579-1601. I. Title.

CARRILLO, Emilia E. 282.0924 B
The bishop has kept his word, by Emilia E. Carrillo. New York, Carlton Press [1966] 64 p. 21 cm. (A Reflection book) [BX4705.M547C3] 66-9031
1. Metzger, Sidney Matthew, Bp., 1902- 2. El Paso, Tex. (Diocese) I. Title.

CARROLL, James. 282'.092'4 B
The winter name of God / by James Carroll. New York : Sheed and Ward, c1975. 187 p. ; 22 cm. [BX4705.C327A37] 74-34556 ISBN 0-8362-0615-0 : 6.95
1. Carroll, James. I. Title.

CARROLL, John, Abp., 1735-1815. 282'.092'4 B
The John Carroll papers / Thomas O'Brien Hanley, editor. Notre Dame : University of Notre Dame Press, 1976 c1975. p. cm. Includes index. Bibliography: p. [BX4705.C33A34] 75-19879 ISBN 0-268-01186-9 : 75.00(3 vols.)
1. Carroll, John, Abp., 1735-1815. 2. Catholic Church in the United States—Collected works. 3. United States—Politics and government—Revolution, 1775-1783—Collected works. I. Hanley, Thomas O'Brien.

CHANTAL, Jeanne Francoise (Fremiot) de Rabutin, Baronne de, Saint, 1572-1641. 282'.0924
St. Francis de Sales; a testimony, by St. Chantal. Newly edited in translation with an introd. by Elisabeth Stopp. Hyattsville, Md. Institute of Salesian Studies [1967] 181 p. illus., port. 23 cm. Bibliography: p 175-176. [BX4700.F85C53 1967a] 67-6454
1. Francois de Sales, Saint, Bp. of Geneva, 1567-1622. I. Stoop, Elisabeth, ed. II. Title.

CHANTAL, Jeanne Francoise (Fremiot) de Rabutin, Baronne de, 1572-1641 282'.0924
St. Francis de Sales; a testimony, by St. Chantal. Newly ed. in tr. with an introd. by Elisabeth Stopp. Hyattsville, Md. Inst. of Salesian Studies [1967] 181p. illus., port. 23cm. Bibl. [BX4700.F85C53 1967a] 67-6454 3.75
1. Francois de Sales, Saint, Bp. of Geneva, 1567-1622. I. Stopp, Elizabeth, ed. II. Title.

CLARIDGE, Mary 282.0924
Margaret Clitherow. 1556?-1586. Foreword by Philip Caraman. New York, Frrdham [1966] x, 196p. port. 23cm. Bibl. [BX4705.C64C5 1966a] 66-19228 5.00
1. Clitherow, Margaret (Middleton) 1556(ca.)-1586. I. Title.

CONGAR, Yves Marie Joseph, 1904- 282'.092'4
Challenge to the Church : the case of Archbishop Lefebvre / Yves Congar ; pref. by George Patrick Dwyer ; [English translation by Paul Inwood]. Huntington, Ind. : Our Sunday Visitor, 1977c1976 96 p. ; 19 cm. Translation of La crise dans l'Eglise et Mgr. Lefebvre. Includes bibliographical references. [BX1390.C6413] 76-53715 ISBN 0-87973-689-5 pbk. : 1.95
1. Catholic Church in France. 2. Catholic Church in Switzerland. 3. Lefebvre, Marcel, 1905- 4. Catholic traditionalist movement. I. Title.

CURLEY, Michael Joseph, 1900- 282'.0924 B
Cheerful ascetic: the life of Francis Xavier Seelos, C.SS.R., by Michael J. Curley. New Orleans, Redemptorist Fathers, 1969. ix, 436 p. illus., ports. 24 cm. Bibliography: p. [405]-420. [BX4705.S517C85] 76-12639
1. Seelos, Franz Xaver, 1819-1867. I. Title.

DAUGHTERS of St. Paul. 282'.092'4 B
Mother Cabrini / by Daughters of St. Paul. Boston : St. Paul Editions, c1977. p. cm. [BX4700.C13D35 1977] 77-10878 3.25 pbk. : 2.25
1. Cabrini, Frances Xavier, Saint, 1850-1917. 2. Christian saints—United States—Biography. I. Title.

DAUGHTERS of St. Paul. 282'.092'4 B
Mother Cabrini / by Daughters of St. Paul. Boston : St. Paul Editions, c1977. p. cm. [BX4700.C13D35 1977] 77-10878 3.25 pbk. : 2.25
1. Cabrini, Frances Xavier, Saint, 1850-1917. 2. Christian saints—United States—Biography. I. Title.

DAWS, Gavan. 282'.092'4 B
Holy man: Father Damien of Molokai. [1st ed.] New York, Harper & Row [1973] xi, 293 p. illus. 22 cm. Bibliography: p. 281-288. [BX4705.D25D38] 73-4075 8.95
1. Damien, Father, 1840-1889. I. Title.

DE HUECK, Catherine, 1900- 282'.092'4 B
Poustinia : Christian spirituality of the East for western man / Catherine de Hueck Doherty. Notre Dame, Ind. : Ave Maria Press, [1975] 216 p. ; 21 cm. [BX2350.2.D4] 74-19961 ISBN 0-87793-084-8 : 5.95 ISBN 0-87793-083-X pbk. : 3.50
1. De Hueck, Catherine, 1900- 2. Spiritual life—Catholic authors. I. Title.

DELFELD, Paula. 282'.092'4 B
The Indian priest, Father Philip B. Gordon, 1885-1948 / by Paula Delfeld. Chicago : Franciscan Herald Press, [1977] p. cm. [E99.C6G643] 76-44869 ISBN 0-8199-0650-6 : 5.95
1. Gordon, Philip B., 1885-1948. 2. Catholic Church—Clergy—Biography. 3. Chippewa Indians—Biography. 4. Clergy—United States—Biography. I. Title.

DELFELD, Paula. 282'.092'4 B
The Indian priest, Father Philip B. Gordon, 1885-1948 / by Paula Delfeld. Chicago : Franciscan Herald Press, [1977] p. cm. [E99.C6G643] 76-44869 ISBN 0-8199-0650-6 : 5.95
1. Gordon, Philip B., 1885-1948. 2. Catholic Church—Clergy—Biography. 3. Chippewa Indians—Biography. 4. Clergy—United States—Biography. I. Title.

DE PAUW, Gommar Albert, 1918- 282'.0924 B
The 'rebel' priest of the Catholic Traditionalist Movement [by] Gommar A. DePauw. [New York, Catholic Traditionalist Movement, 1967] 16 p. illus., ports. 22 cm. Cover title. [BX1390.D45] 79-12235
1. Catholic Traditionalist Movement. I. Title.

DIRVIN, Joseph I. 282'.092'4 B
Louise de Marillac [by] Joseph I. Dirvin. New York, Farrar, Straus & Giroux [1970] xi, 468 p. 22 cm. Bibliography: p. [415]-418. [BX4700.L66D57] 73-115750 10.00
1. Louise de Marillac, Saint, 1591-1660.

DOLLEN, Charles. 282'.0924 B
African triumph; life of Charles Lwanga. Illustrated by the Daughters of St. Paul under the direction of Guy R. Pennisi. [Boston] St. Paul Editions [1967] 70 p. illus., map. 22 cm. A biography of an early Uganda convert to Christianity who became martyr for his faith. [BX4705.L8D6] 92 AC 68
1. Lwanga, Charles, d. 1866. 2. Martyrs—Uganda.

DONNELLY, Joseph Peter, 1905- 282'.092'4 B
Jean de Brebeuf, 1593-1649 / Joseph P. Donnelly. Chicago : Loyola University Press, 1975. xii, 346 p. : maps ; 23 cm. Includes index. Bibliography: p. 313-323. [E99.H9B743] 75-5682 ISBN 0-8294-0233-0 : 5.95
1. Brebeuf, Jean de, Saint, 1593-1649. 2. Huron Indians—Missions.

DWYER, John T. 282'.092'4 B
Condemned to the mines : the life of Eugene

O'Connell, 1815-1891, pioneer bishop of Northern California and Nevada / by John T. Dwyer. 1st ed. New York : Vantage Press, c1976. xxiii, 302 p. : ill., ports. ; 21 cm. Includes bibliographical references and index. [BX4705.O293D88] 76-150322 ISBN 0-533-02130-8 : 8.95
1. O'Connell, Eugene, 1815-1891. 2. Catholic Church—Bishops—Biography. 3. Bishops—California—Biography. I. Title.

EADMER, d.1124? 282'.0924 B
The life of St Anselm, Archbishop of Canterbury, edited with introduction, notes and translation by R. W. Southern. Oxford, Clarendon Press [1972, c1962] 1 v. (various pagings) 23 cm. (Oxford medieval texts) Parallel Latin text and English translation. Translation of Vita D. Anselmi archiepiscopi Cantuariensis. Includes bibliographical references. [BX4700.A58E2 1972] 72-190762 ISBN 0-19-822225-4 £4.50
1. Anselm, Saint, Abp. of Canterbury, 1033-1109. I. Title. II. Series.

EASTERLY, Frederick 282'.092'4 B
John, 1910-
The life of Rt. Rev. Joseph Rosati, C.M., first bishop of St. Louis, 1789-1843. Washington, Catholic University of America Press, 1942. [New York, AMS Press, 1974] xi, 203 p. 23 cm. Reprint of the author's thesis, Catholic University of America, 1942, which was issued as v. 33 of the Catholic University of America. Studies in American church history. Bibliography: p. 191-197. [BX4705.R723E3 1974] 73-3587 ISBN 0-404-57783-0 9.00
1. Rosati, Joseph, Bp., 1789-1843. 2. Catholic Church in St. Louis—History. 3. St. Louis, Mo. (Archdiocese)—History. I. Series: Catholic University of America. Studies in American church history, v. 33.

EBON, Martin. 282'.092'4 B
Saint Nicholas : life and legend / Martin Ebon. 1st ed. New York : Harper & Row, [1975] p. cm. Bibliography: p. [BX4700.N55E26 1975] 75-9329 ISBN 0-06-062113-3 : 8.95
1. Nicholas, Saint, Bp. of Myra. 2. Santa Claus.

ENGLEBERT, Omer, 282'.092'4 B
1893-
The last of the conquistadors, Junipero Serra, 1713-1784. Translated from the French by Katherine Woods. Westport, Conn., Greenwood Press [1974, c1956] ix, 368 p. illus. 23 cm. Reprint of the ed. published by Harcourt, Brace, New York. Bibliography: p. 355-359. [F864.S442 1974] 74-5924 ISBN 0-8371-7523-2
1. Serra, Junipero, 1713-1784. I. Title.

ESTERKA, Peter. 282'.0924
Never say Comrade, by Peter Esterka, assisted by Mary Butschek. Rome, Tipolitografia PRO [1967] 253 p. illus., ports. 22 cm. [BX4705.E7315A3] 67-4542
I. Butschek, Mary. II. Title.

FEARON, Nancy. 282'.092'4 B
Never stop walking : the life and spirit of St. Alphonsus Liguori / Nancy Fearon. Monroe, Mich. : Sisters, Servants of the Immaculate Heart of Mary, c1977. 180 p. ; 22 cm. [BX4700.L6F4] 77-358212
1. Liguori, Alfonso Maria de', Saint, 1696-1787. 2. Christian saints—Italy—Biography. I. Title.

FEENEY, John, 1948- 282'.092'4 B
John Charles McQuaid : the man and the mask / by John Feeney. Dublin : Mercier Press, 1974. 88 p. ; 18 cm. [BX4705.M2555F43] 75-304534 ISBN 0-85342-377-6 : 0.75
1. McQuaid, John Charles.

*FEENEY, Leonard, 282'092'4 B
1897-
Elizabeth Seton: an American woman Huntington, In., Our Sunday Visitor [1975] 304 p. frontis. 18 cm. [BX4705.S] 75-21599 ISBN 0-87973-861-8 3.50 (pbk.)
1. Seton, Elizabeth Ann, 1774-1821. I. Title.

FEENEY, Leonard, 282'.092'4 B
1897-
Mother Seton : Saint Elizabeth of New York (1774-1821) / Leonard Feeney. Rev. ed. Cambridge [Mass.] : Ravengate Press, [1975] p. cm. [BX4705.S57F4 1975] 75-23224 ISBN 0-911218-06-8 pbk. : 2.95
1. Seton, Elizabeth Ann, 1774-1821. I. Title.

FISHER, Lillian 282'.0924 B
Estelle, 1891-
Champion of reform, Manuel Abad y Queipo. New York, Russell & Russell [1971, c1955] 314 p. 23 cm. Bibliography: p. 279-301. [F123.F57 1971] 76-151549
1. Abad Queipo, Manuel, Bp., 1751-1825. I. Title.

FOLEY, Albert Sidney, 282'.0924 B
1912-
Bishop Healy: beloved outcaste [by] Albert S. Foley. New York, Arno Press, 1969 [c1954] viii, 248 p. port. 21 cm. (The American Negro, his history and literature) [BX4705.H37F6 1969] 79-94130
1. Healy, James Augustine, Bp., 1830-1900. I. Title. II. Series.

FOLEY, Albert 282'.092'4 B
Sidney, 1912-
A modern Galahad, St. John Berchmans, by Albert S. Foley. Mobile, Spring Hill College Press [1973] xvii, 241 p. illus. 18 cm. Reprint of the 1937 ed. published by The Bruce Pub. Co., Milwaukee in series: Science and culture series. "Berchmansiana": p. 231-235. [BX4700.B4F6 1973] 73-176466
1. Berchmans, Jan, Saint, 1599-1621. I. Title.

FORD, George Barry. 282'.0924 B
A degree of difference. New York, Farrar, Straus & Giroux [1969] 271 p. 22 cm. [BX4705.F635A3] 73-97136 5.95
I. Title.

FOSTER, John J., 282'.0924 B
1912-
A priest for all men; the life of Henry B. Strickland, by John J. Foster. Lebanon, Penn., Holy Name Society, Assumption B.V.M. Church [1971] 160 p. illus., facsim., ports. 23 cm. Bibliography: p. 160. [BX4705.S8433F68] 77-158664 3.00
1. Strickland, Henry Benjamin, 1884-1944. I. Title.

FULBERT, Bp. of 282'.092'4 B
Chartres, 960(ca.)-1028.
The letters and poems of Fulbert of Chartres / edited and translated by Frederick Behrends. Oxford : Clarendon Press, 1976. xciii, 297 p. ; 22 cm. (Oxford medieval texts) Introd. and notes in English, parallel text in English and Latin. Includes indexes. Bibliography: p. [x]-xii. [BX4705.F88A4 1976] 76-379876 ISBN 0-19-822233-5 : 27.50
1. Fulbert, Bp. of Chartres, 960 (ca.)-1028. 2. Bishops—France—Chartres—Correspondence. 3. Chartres, France—Biography. I. Behrends, Frederick. II. Title. III. Series.
Dist. by Oxford University Press NY NY

GAFFEY, James P. 282'.092'4 B
Citizen of no mean city: Archbishop Patrick Riordan of San Francisco (1841-1914) [by] James P. Gaffey. [Washington, Catholic University of America Press, 1974] p. cm. Includes bibliographical references. [BX4705.R555G33] 74-5435 ISBN 0-8132-0537-9
1. Riordan, Patrick William, Abp., 1841-1914. I. Title.

GALLET, Paul. 282'.092'4 B
Freedom to starve. With an introd. by Michel Quoist and Rosemary Sheed. Translated by Rosemary Sheed. [Harmondsworth, Eng., Baltimore] Penguin Books [1972, c1970] 249 p. 18 cm. (The Pelican Latin American library) Translation of El Padre. [BX4705.G16A313 1972] 73-156286 ISBN 0-14-021519-0 2.45 (U.S.)
1. Gallet, Paul. 2. Catholic Church in Brazil. 3. Brazil—Social conditions. I. Title.

GALLET, Paul. 282'.092'4 B
Freedom to starve. With an introd. by Michel Quoist and Rosemary Sheed. Translated by Rosemary Sheed. [Harmondsworth, Eng., Baltimore] Penguin Books [1972, c1970] 249 p. 18 cm. (The Pelican Latin American library) Translation of El Padre. [BX4705.G16A313 1972] 73-156286 ISBN 0-14-021519-0 2.45 (U.S.)
1. Gallet, Paul. 2. Catholic Church in Brazil. 3. Brazil—Social conditions. I. Title.

GARCIA Diego y 282'.092'4 B
Moreno, Francisco, Bp., 1785-1846.
The writings of Francisco Garcia Diego y Moreno, Obispo de Ambas Californias / translated and edited by Francis J. Weber. Los Angeles : Weber, 1976. xiii, 192 p. : group port. ; 27 cm. Includes bibliographical references. [BX4705.G244.G37] 76-21434
1. Garcia Diego y Moreno, Francisco, Bp., 1785-1846. 2. Catholic Church—Bishops—Biography. 3. Catholic Church in California—History—Sources. 4. Bishops—California—Biography.

GARCIA Diego y 282'.092'4 B
Moreno, Francisco, Bp., 1785-1846.
The writings of Francisco Garcia Diego y Moreno, Obispo de Ambas Californias / translated and edited by Francis J. Weber. Los Angeles : Weber, 1976. xiii, 192 p. : group port. ; 27 cm. Includes bibliographical references. [BX4705.G244.G37] 76-21434
1. Garcia Diego y Moreno, Francisco, Bp., 1785-1846. 2. Catholic Church—Bishops—Biography. 3. Catholic Church in California—History—Sources. 4. Bishops—California—Biography.

GIESE, Frank S. 282'.092'4 B
Artus Desire: priest and pamphleteer of the sixteenth century, by Frank S. Giese. Chapel Hill [N.C.] UNC Dept. of Romance Languages; [distributed by International Scholarly Book Service, Portland, Or.] 1973. 188 p. 24 cm. (North Carolina studies in the Romance languages and literatures, no. 136) "Bibliography of sources containing information on Artus Desire and on his times; and on works by, or attributed to, him": p. [15]-17. [BX4705.D439G53] 73-14987 ISBN 0-88438-936-7
1. Desire, Artus. 2. Desire, Artus—Bibliography. I. Title. II. Title: Priest and pamphleteer of the sixteenth century. III. Series.

GIESE, Vincent J. 282.0924
Journal of a late vocation [by] Vincent J. Giese. Notre Dame, Ind. Fides [1966] 159p. 18cm. (Fides dome bk., D-53) Autobiographical. [BX4705.G513 A3] 66-28038 .95 pap.,
1. Catholic Church—Clergy—Correspondence, reminiscences, etc. I. Title.

GIRANDOLA, Anthony, 282'.0924
1924-
The most defiant priest; the story of the priest who married. New York, Crown Publishers [1968] 277 p. 24 cm. [BX1765.2.G57 1968] 68-31204 5.95
1. Catholic Church—Doctrinal and controversial works. I. Title.

GREENE, Ellis 282'.0924(B)
Champion of the apostolate; the life of St. Vincent Pallotti. Illustrated by Dorothy Koch. North Easton, Mass., Holy Cross Pr., 1967. 111p. illus. 22cm. [BX4700.P23G7] 67-25215 2.50
1. Pallotti, Vincenzo, Saint, 1795-1850 I. Title.

GRIFFIN, Robert, 282'.092'4 B
1925-
In the kingdom of the lonely God. New York, Paulist Press [1973] 128 p. illus. 18 cm. Autobiographical. [BX4705.G6225A33] 72-94181 ISBN 0-8091-1747-9 2.95
1. Griffin, Robert. I. Title.

GUILDAY, Peter 282'.0924 B
Keenan, 1884-1947.
The life & times of John England. New York, Arno Press, 1969 [c1927] x, 596, 577 p. 24 cm. (Thought foundation: historical series, no. 1) Includes bibliographical references. [BX4705.E66G5 1969] 70-83422
1. England, John, Bp., 1786-1842. 2. Catholic Church in the United States. I. Title. II. Series.

HABIG, Marion 282'.092'4 B
Alphonse, 1901- comp.
A modern Saint Anthony; a novena in honor of the servant of God Brother Jordan Mai, with a sketch of the saintly American Brother Simon Van Ackeren, and a novena prayer to obtain his help [compiled by] Marion A. Habig. Chicago, Franciscan Herald Press [1974] p. cm. [BX4705.M2614H3] 74-18313 ISBN 0-8199-0553-4 0.65 (pbk.)
1. Mai, Jordan, 1866-1922. 2. Van Ackeren, Simon, 1918-1938. 3. Novenas. I. Title.

HASSARD, John Rose 282'.0924 B
Greene, 1836-1888.
Life of John Hughes, first archbishop of New York. New York, Arno Press, 1969. 519 p. facsim., port. 22 cm. (Religion in America) Reprint of the 1866 ed., which was published under title: Life of the Most Reverend John Hughes, D.D. On spine: Life of Archbishop John Hughes. Includes bibliographical references. [BX4705.H79H3 1969] 74-83423
1. Hughes, John, Abp., 1797-1864.

HEMESATH, Caroline. 282'.092'4 B
From slave to priest: a biography of the Rev. Augustine Tolton (1854-1897), first Afro-American priest of the United States. Chicago, Franciscan Herald Press [1973] xiii, 174 p. illus. 21 cm. Bibliography: p. [167]-169. [BX4705.T6813H4] 73-11113 ISBN 0-8199-0468-6 5.95
1. Tolton, Augustine, 1854-1897. I. Title.

HINDMAN, Jane F. 282'.092'4 B
An ordinary saint : the life of John Neumann / by Jane F. Hindman. New York : Arena Lettres, c1977. ix, 146 p. ; 18 cm. A biography of the bishop renowned for his good deeds who was proclaimed a saint in 1977. [BX4700.N4H56] 92 77-75429 ISBN 0-88479-004-5 : 1.95
1. Neumann, John Nepomucene, Saint, 1811-1860—Juvenile literature. 2. Christian saints—United States—Biography—Juvenile literature. I. Title.

HOGAN, John Joseph, 282'.0924 B
Bp., 1829-1913.
On the mission in Missouri, 1857-1868 / by John Joseph Hogan Glorieta, N.M. : Rio Grande Press, 1976. p. cm. (A Rio Grande classic) Reprint of the 1892 ed. published by J. A. Heilmann, Kansas City, Mo. [BX1415.M8H6 1976] 76-29732 ISBN 0-87380-111-3 lib.bdg. : 10.00
1. Catholic Church in Missouri. 2. Hogan, John Joseph, Bp., 1829-1913. 3. Catholic Church—Clergy—Biography. 4. Clergy—Missouri—Biography. 5. Missouri—Biography. I. Title.

HORGAN, Paul, 1903- 282'.092'4 B
Lamy of Santa Fe, his life and times / Paul Horgan. New York : Farrar, Straus and Giroux, 1975. 523 p., [8] leaves of plates : ill. ; 24 cm. Includes bibliographical references and index. [BX4705.L265H67 1975] 75-5870 ISBN 0-374-18300-7 : 15.00
1. Lamy, John Baptist, Abp., 1814-1888. I. Title.

JAN, Father, C.S.C. 282'.0924 B
When dreams come true, by Father Jan (Sigmund A. Jankowski). Notre Dame, Ind., 1970. 189 p. illus., ports. 19 cm. [BX4705.J333A3] 77-105320
I. Title.

JANET, Paul Alexandre 282'.0924 B
Rene, 1823-1899.
Fenelon, his life and works. Translated and edited with introd., notes, and index by Victor Leuliette. Port Washington, N.Y., Kennikat Press [1970] xx, 307 p. port. 21 cm. Reprint of the 1914 ed. Bibliography: p. 294-301. [PQ1796.J313 1970] 78-113315
1. Fenelon, Francois de Salignac de La Mothe-, Abp., 1651-1715. I. Leuliette, Victor, ed.

JEZERNIK, 282'.0924 B
Maksimilijan.
Frederick Baraga; a portrait of the first bishop of Marquette, based on the archives of the Congregatio de Propaganda Fide. New York, Studia Slovenica, 1968. 155 p. maps, port. 23 cm. (Studia Slovenica, 7) [BX4705.B18J4] 68-16856
1. Baraga, Frederick, Bp., 1797-1868. I. Title. II. Series.

JOANNES XXIII, Pope, 282'.0924 B
1881-1963.
My bishop; a portrait of Mgr. Giacomo Maria Radini Tedeschi. With a foreword by H. E. Cardinale, and an introd. by Loris Capovilla. Translated by Dorothy White. New York, McGraw-Hill [1969] 143 p. illus., ports. 25 cm. Translation of Mons. Giacomo Maria Radini Tedeschi. [BX4705.R286J63] 69-13212 6.95
1. Radini Tedeschi, Giacomo Maria, 1857-1914. I. Title.

JONES, Christopher 282'.0924
William.
Listen, pilgrim. With a foreword by Daniel Berrigan. Milwaukee, Bruce Pub. Co. [1967, c1968] xiii, 134 p. 22 cm. In prose and verse. [BX4705.J673A3] 68-16811
I. Title.

JONES, Christopher 282'.0924
William.
Listen, pilgrim. With a foreword by Daniel Berrigan. Milwaukee, Bruce Pub. Co. [1967, c1968] xiii, 134 p. 22 cm. In prose and verse. [BX4705.J673A3] 68-16811
I. Title.

KELLY, Frederic 282'.092'4 B
Joseph, 1922-
Man before God; Thomas Merton on social responsibility. [1st ed.] Garden City, N.Y., Doubleday, 1974. xxiv, 287 p. 22 cm. Includes bibliographical references. [BX4705.M542K44] 73-10970 ISBN 0-385-09399-3 7.95
1. Merton, Thomas, 1915-1968.

KELLY, Josephine. 282'.0924 B
Dark shepherd. Paterson, N.J., St. Anthony Guild Press [1967] v, 169 p. illus. 20 cm. Biography of the first Negro bishop in the United States. [BX4705.H37K4] 92 67-19690
1. Healy, James Augustine, Bp., 1830-1900. I. Title.

LAMBERT, Bernard J 282'.0924
Shepherd of the wilderness; a biography of Bishop Frederic Baraga [by] Bernard J. Lambert. L'Anse, Mich., 1967. xiv, 255 p. maps (on lining papers), port. 24 cm. Bibliography: p. 253-255. [BX4705.B18L3] 67-29795
1. Baraga, Friedrich, Bp., 1797-1868. I. Title.

LANGAN, Tom. 282'.092'4 B
John Neumann : harvester of souls / Tom Langan. Huntington, IN : Our Sunday Visitor, c1976. 155 p. ; 21 cm. [BX4700.N4L35] 76-21416 ISBN 0-87973-758-1 pbk. : 2.95
1. Neumann, John Nepomucene, Bp., 1811-

1860. 2. Catholic Church—Bishops—Biography. 3. Bishops—Pennsylvania—Philadelphia—Biography. 4. Philadelphia—Biography.

LAPATI, Americo D. 282.0924
Orestes A. Brownson. New Haven, Conn., Coll. & Univ. Pr. [1966, c.1965] 159p. 21cm. (Twayne's U.S. authors ser. 88) Bibl. [B908.B64L3] 1.95 pap.,
1. Brownson, Orestes Augustus, 1803-1876. I. Title.

LAPATI, Americo D. 282.0924 B
Orestes A. Brownson, by Americo D. Lapati. New York, Twayne Publishers [1965] 159 p. 21 cm. (Twayne's United States authors series, 88) Bibliography: p. 148-152. [B908.B64L3] 65-18907
1. Brownson, Orestes Augustus, 1803-1876.

LAURO, Joseph, 1912- 282'.0924 B
Action priest; the story of Father Joe Lauro. By Joseph Lauro and Arthur Orrmont. With a foreword by Richard Cardinal Cushing. New York, Morrow, 1971 [c1970] 357 p. port. 22 cm. [BX4705.L3684A3] 75-118269 8.95
I. Orrmont, Arthur, joint author. II. Title.

LEGERE, J. Roy, 1922- 282'.092'4 B
Be my son / J. Roy Legere. Notre Dame, Ind. : Ave Maria Press, c1976. 191 p. : ill. ; 21 cm. Autobiographical. [BX4705.L515A33] 76-41592 ISBN 0-87793-121-6 pbk. : 2.95
1. Legere, J. Roy, 1922- 2. Catholics in New Brunswick—Biography. 3. Catholics in Connecticut—Biography. I. Title.

LEO, Franciscan, 13th cent. 282'.092'4 B
Scripta Leonis, Rufini et Angeli, Sociorum S. Francisci. The writings of Leo, Rufino and Angelo, companions of St. Francis; edited and translated by Rosalind B. Brooke. Oxford, Clarendon Press, 1970. xviii, 357 p., plate. 1 illus. 23 cm. (Oxford medieval texts) Includes Latin texts and English translations. Includes index. Bibliography: p. [xiii]-xviii. [BX4700.F6L455] 74-163267 £4.00
1. Francesco d'Assisi, Saint, 1182-1226. I. Rufinus, Frater. II. Angelus, frater, d. 1258? III. Brooke, Rosalind B., ed. IV. Francesco d'Assisi, Saint. Legend. Speculum perfectionis. V. Title. VI. Series.

LIBERSAT, Henry. 282'.092'4 B
Ragin' Cajun. Liguori, Mo., Liguori Publications [1974] 192 p. 18 cm. Autobiography. [BX4705.L622A37] 74-77996 1.95 (pbk.).
1. Libersat, Henry. I. Title.

LIEVSAY, John Leon. 282'.092'4 B
Venetian Phoenix: Paolo Sarpi and some of his English friends (1606-1700) Lawrence, University Press of Kansas [1973] 262 p. 23 cm. Bibliography: p. 235-250. [BX4705.S36L53] 73-6818 ISBN 0-7006-0108-2 11.00
1. Sarpi, Paolo, 1552-1623. I. Title.

LO Gatto-Perry, Joseph J. T. 282'.0924 B
An Italian pioneer in America [by Joseph J. T. Lo Gatto-Perry. Netcong, N.J., 1969] 110 p. illus. 23 cm. [BX4705.G484L6] 75-81350
1. Gianci, Carlo, 1881-1968. I. Title.

LOISY, Alfred Firmin, 1857-1940. 282'.0924 B
My duel with the Vatican; the autobiography of a Catholic modernist. Authorized translation by Richard Wilson Boynton. With a new introd. by E. Harold Smith. New York, Greenwood Press, 1968 [c1924] xiii, 357 p. 22 cm. Translation of Choses passees. Includes bibliographical references. [BX4705.L7A3 1968] 68-19290
1. Modernism—Catholic Church. I. Title.

LOUIS-LEFEBVRE, Marie Therese. 282'.0924 B
Abbe Huvelin, Apostle of Paris, 1839-1910, by M.-Th.-Louis-Lefebvre. Translated from the French by the Earl of Wicklow. Enl. ed. with unpublished documents. Dublin, Clonmore and Reynolds [1967] 237 p. port. 22 cm. Imprint covered by label: Christian Classics, Westminster, Md. Translation of Un pretre l'abbe Huvelin. Bibliographical footnotes. [BX4705.H94L63 1967] 79-2545 25/-
1. Huvelin, Henri, 1838-1910. I. Title.

LOUISE de Marillac, Saint, 1591-1660. 282'.092'4 B
Letters of St. Louise de Marillac. Translated from the French by Sister Helen Marie Law [and] Daughters of Charity. [Emmitsburg, Md., Saint Joseph's Provincial House Press] 1972. 629 p. 26 cm. [BX4700.L66A413 1972] 72-97031
1. Louise de Marillac, Saint, 1591-1660.

LOW, Anthony, 1935- 282'.0924 B
Augustine Baker. New York, Twayne Publishers [1970] 170 p. 21 cm. (Twayne's English authors series, 104) Bibliography: p. 155-165. [BX4705.B12L68] 74-99527
1. Baker, Augustine, 1575-1641.

LOYOLA, Ignacio de, Saint, 1491-1556. 282'.092'4 B
The autobiography of St. Ignatius Loyola, with related documents. Edited with introd. and notes by John C. Olin. Translated by Joseph F. O'Callaghan. New York, Harper & Row [1974] vii, 112 p. illus. 21 cm. (Harper torchbooks) Bibliography: p. 111-112. [BX4700.L7A313 1974] 73-7468 ISBN 0-06-139170-0 2.95 (pbk.)
1. Loyola, Ignacio de, Saint, 1491-1556. I. Title.

MCCALLUM, John Dennis, 1924- 282'.092'4 B
The story of Dan Lyons, S.J., by John D. McCallum. New York, Guild Books [1973] xviii, 443 p. illus. 22 cm. [BX4705.L97M3] 72-94967 7.95
1. Lyons, Daniel. I. Title.

MARITAIN, Raissa. 282'.092'4 B
Raissa's Journal / presented by Jacques Maritain ; pref. by Rene Voillaume. Enl. with new matter for this translation. Albany : Magi Books, [1975] c1974. xxii, 404 p., [4] leaves of plates : ports. ; 19 cm. [BX4705.M3994A3313 1975] 72-95648 ISBN 0-87343-041-7 : 12.95
1. Maritain, Raissa. I. Title.

MARSHALL, Hugh, 1926- 282'.0924 B
Orestes Brownson and the American Republic; an historical perspective. Washington, Catholic University of America Press, 1971. vii, 308 p. 23 cm. Bibliography: p. 293-302. [B908.B64M28] 74-142187 ISBN 0-8132-0508-5
1. Brownson, Orestes Augustus, 1803-1876. I. Title.

MATEJIC, Mateja. 282'.092'4 B
Biography of Saint Sava / Mateja Matejic. Columbus, Ohio : Kosovo Pub. Co., 1976. 128 p. : ill. ; 23 cm. Bibliography: p. 127-128. [BX719.S35M37] 77-366931
1. Sava, Saint, Abp. of Serbia, 1169-1237. 2. Christian saints—Serbia—Biography. I. Title.

MATEJIC, Mateja. 282'.092'4 B
Biography of Saint Sava / Mateja Matejic. Columbus, Ohio : Kosovo Pub. Co., 1976. 128 p. : ill. ; 23 cm. Bibliography: p. 127-128. [BX719.S35M37] 77-366931
1. Sava, Saint, Abp. of Serbia, 1169-1237. 2. Christian saints—Serbia—Biography. I. Title.

MAYNARD, Theodore, 1890-1956. 282'.0924 B
Orestes Brownson: Yankee, radical, Catholic. New York, Hafner Pub. Co., 1971 [c1943] xvi, 456 p. port. 21 cm. "Facsimile of the 1943 edition." Bibliography: p. 433-443. [B908.B64M3 1943a] 70-152267
1. Brownson, Orestes Augustus, 1803-1876.

MOCKUS, Tony, 1929- 282'.092'4 B
"I'm learning from Protestants how to be a better Catholic" / Tony Mockus, with Ken Anderson. Waco, Tex. : Word Books, c1975. 142 p. : ill. ; 23 cm. [BX4705.M587A34] 74-27485 4.95
1. Mockus, Tony, 1929- I. Anderson, Kenneth, 1917- II. Title.

MONCHANIN, Jules. 282'.092'4 B
In quest of the absolute : the life and work of Jules Monchanin / edited and translated by Joseph Weber. Kalamazoo, Mich. : Cistercian Publications, 1977. p. cm. (Cistercian studies series ; no. 51) Bibliography: p. [BX4705.M6312A34] 77-3596 ISBN 0-87907-851-0 : 10.95
1. Monchanin, Jules. 2. Catholics in India—Biography. 3. Theology—Addresses, essays, lectures. I. Weber, Joseph, 1931- II. Title. III. Series.

MOREAU, Roland, abbe. 282'.092'4 B
Francois Dardan d'Isturitz, martyr des Carmes (1733-1792) [Bayonne, Impr. des Cordeliers, 1966] 30 p. illus. 24 cm. Cover and half title: Un Basque martyr de la Revolution: Francois Dardan, 1733-1792. [BX4705.D2735M67] 74-156638
1. Dardan, Francois, 1733-1792. I. Title: Un Basque martyr de la Revolution: Francois Dardan

MOREY, Adrian, 1904- ed. 282.0924
Gilbert Foliot and his letters [by] Adrian Morey, C. N. L. Brooke [New York] Cambridge [c.]1965. xv, 312p. 23cm. (Cambridge studies in medieval life and thought, new ser., v.11) Bibl. [BR754.F55M6] 65-17204 12.00
1. Foliot, Gilbert, Bp. of London, 1107 (ca.)-1187. I. Brooke, Christopher Nugent Lawrence, joint ed. (Series) II. Title.

†MOYNIHAN, James H. 282'.092'4 B
The life of Archbishop John Ireland / James H. Moynihan. New York : Arno Press, 1976, c1953. xii, 441 p. : port. ; 24 cm. (The Irish-Americans) Reprint of the ed. published by Harper, New York. Includes index. Bibliography: p. 419-425. [BX4705.I7M67 1976] 76-6358 ISBN 0-405-09351-9 : 27.00
1. Ireland, John, Abp., 1838-1918. I. Title. II. Series.

MURPHY, Frank. 282'.092'4 B
Daniel Mannix: Archbishop of Melbourne 1917-1963. [New, i.e., 2d ed.] Melbourne, Polding Press, 1972. 288 p. illus. 19 cm. Includes bibliographical references. [BX4705.M314M87 1972] 73-154985 ISBN 0-85884-001-4 2.95
1. Mannix, Daniel, Abp., 1864-1963.

NECHELES, Ruth F., 1936- 282.0924 B
The Abbe Gregoire, 1787-1831; the odyssey of an egalitarian [by Ruth F. Necheles Westport, Conn., Greenwood Pub. Corp. [1971] xviii, 333 p. port. 22 cm. (Contributions in Afro-American and African studies, no. 9) "A Negro Universities Press publication." Bibliography: p. [291]-317. [DC146.G84N4] 75-105987 ISBN 0-8371-3312-2
1. Gregoire, Henri, Constitutional Bp. of Blois, 1750-1831. I. Title. II. Series.

NOONAN, Daniel P. 282'.0924
Missionary with a mike: the Bishop Sheen story, by D. P. Noonan. [1st ed.] New York, Pageant Press [1968] 213 p. 21 cm. [BX4705.S612N6] 68-17834
1. Sheen, Fulton John, Bp., 1895- I. Title.

NOONAN, Daniel P. 282'.0924 [B]
The passion of Fulton Sheen, by D. P. Noonan. New York, Pyramid Books [1975, c1972] 156 p. illus. 18 cm. [BX4705.S612N63] 70-173885 ISBN 0-515-03658-7 1.25 (pbk.)
1. Sheen, Fulton John, Bp., 1895- I. Title.

O'DONOGHUE, Richard. 282'.092'4 B
Like a tree planted. Dublin, Gill [1968] vii, 269 p. 21 cm. [BX4705.O39O36 1968] 75-300737 30/-
1. O'Flynn, James Christopher, 1881-1962. I. Title.

ORAISON, Marc. 282'.0924 B
Strange voyage; the autobiography of a non-conformist. Translated by J. F. Bernard. [1st ed.] Garden City, N.Y., Doubleday, 1970 [c1969] 236 p. 22 cm. Translation of Tete dure. [BX4705.O498A33] 77-116243 5.95
I. Title.

ORSINI, Joseph E. 282'.092'4 B
The anvil / by Joseph E. Orsini. Plainfield, N.J. : Logos International, [1974] 111 p. ; 18 cm. [BX4705.O715A28] 73-93895 ISBN 0-88270-089-8 : 1.25
1. Orsini, Joseph E. 2. Pentecostalism. I. Title.

ORSINI, Joseph E. 282'.092'4 B
Hear my confession / Joseph Orsini. New and updated ed. Plainfield, N.J. : Logos International, c1977. 144 p. ; 21 cm. [BX4705.O715A3 1977] 77-73151 ISBN 0-88270-231-9 pbk. : 2.95
1. Orsini, Joseph E. 2. Catholic Church—Clergy—Biography. 3. Clergy—New Jersey—Biography. 4. Pentecostalism—Catholic Church. I. Title.

PALLOTTI, Vincenzo, Saint, 1795-1850. 282'.0924
Pious Society of the Catholic Apostolate. Translated and edited under the supervision of Louis J. Lulli, from the Italian critical ed. published in Rome, Italy, by Francesco Moccia. Baltimore, Pallottine Fathers & Brothers Press, 1968. xviii, 177 p. 24 cm. (His Complete writings, v. 1) Bibliographical footnotes. [BX890.P25 vol. 1] 67-31436
1. Pallottines. I. Title. II. Series.

PALMER, Christopher Harold. 282'.092'4 B
The prince bishop; a life of St. Francis de Sales [by] C. H. Palmer. IlFracombe; Stockwell, [1975 c1974] 204 p. port. 22 cm. [BX4700.F85Q3] 75-321845 ISBN 0-7223-0409-9
1. Francoes de Sales, Saint, 8p. of Geneva, 1567-1622. I. Title.
Distributed by Christian Classics for 7.95.

PERRELLA, Robert. 282'.092'4 B
They call me the showbiz priest, by Robert Perrella ("Father Bob"). New York, Trident Press [1973] 287 p. ports. 22 cm. [BX4705.P4325A33] 73-82874 ISBN 0-671-27112-1 7.95
1. Perrella, Robert. I. Title.

PEYTON, Patrick J. 282.0924
All for her; the autobiography of Father Patrick Peyton, C.S.C. Garden City, N.Y., Doubleday [1967] 286 p. illus., ports. 22 cm. [BX4705.P4458A3] 67-22441
I. Title.

PEYTON, Patrick J. 282'.092'4 B
All for her; the autobiography of Father Patrick Peyton. [Rev. ed.] Hollywood, Calif., Family Theater Publications [1973] viii, 241 p. illus. 18 cm. [BX4705.P4458A3 1973] 73-181329 1.50
1. Peyton, Patrick J. I. Title.

PIERRE le Venerable, 1092(ca.)-1156. 282'.0924
The letters of Peter the Venerable. Edited, with an introd. and notes, by Giles Constable. Cambridge, Harvard University Press, 1967. 2 v. facsim., map. 25 cm. (Harvard historical studies, 78) Bibliography: p. 349-361. [BX4705.P473A4] 67-10086
1. Constable, Giles, ed. I. Title. II. Series.

PIERRE le Venerable, 1092(ca.)-1156. 282'.0924
The letters of Peter the Venerable. Edited, with an introd. and notes, by Giles Constable. Cambridge, Harvard University Press, 1967. 2 v. facsim., map. 25 cm. (Harvard historical studies 78) Bibliography: p. 349-361. [BX4705.P473A4] 67-10086
I. Constable, Giles, ed. II. Title. III. Series.

POAGE, Godfrey Robert, 1920- 282'.092'4 B
In garments all red : the life story of St. Maria Goretti / by Godfrey Poage. Boston : St. Paul Editions, c1977. 118 p. : ill. ; 18 cm. [BX4700.M368P6 1977] 77-4485 pbk. : 1.50
1. Maria Goretti, Saint, 1890-1902. 2. Christian saints—Italy—Biography. I. Title.

POWERS, John R. 282'.092'4 B
Do black patent-leather shoes really reflect up? / John Powers. Chicago : Regnery, [1975] p. cm. [BX4705.P664A32 1975] 75-13247 ISBN 0-8092-8177-5 : 7.95
1. Powers, John R. I. Title.

PURCELL, Mary, 1906- 282'.092'4 B
Matt Talbot and his times / by Mary Purcell ; with a foreword by Dermot Ryan. Rev. ed. Chicago : Franciscan Herald Press, [1977] p. cm. [BX4705.T27P8 1977] 77-3556 ISBN 0-8199-0657-3 : 4.95
1. Talbot, Matthew, 1856-1925. 2. Catholics in Dublin—Biography. 3. Dublin—Biography. I. Title.

QUITSLUND, Sonya A. 282'.092'4 B
Beauduin, a prophet vindicated [by] Sonya A. Quitslund. New York, Newman Press [1973] xvii, 366 p. illus. 24 cm. Bibliography: p. 338-358. [BX4705.B2595Q5] 72-86594 ISBN 0-8091-0168-8 10.00
1. Beauduin, Lambert, 1873-1960. I. Title.

REINHOLD, Hans Ansgar, 1897- 282'.0924 B
H.A.R.; the autobiography of Father Reinhold. [New York] Herder and Herder [1968] x, 150 p. 21 cm. [BX4705.R433A3] 67-29678
I. Title.

RENNER, R Richard, 1896- 282.0924
Savonarola, the first great Protestant, by R. Richard Renner. [1st ed.] New York, Greenwich Book Publishers [c1965] 153 p. 21 cm. Bibliography: p. 153. [DG737.97.R4] 65-24258
1. Savonarola, Girolamo Maria Francesco Matteo, 1452-1498. I. Title.

RENNER, Richard, M.D., 1896- 282.0924
Savonarola, the first great Protestant, by R. Richard Renner, M.D. New York, Greenwich Bk. Pubs., [282 7th Ave., 1966, c.1965] 153p. 21cm. Bibl. [DG737.97.R4] 65-24258 2.95
1. Savonarola, Girolamo Maria Francesco Matteo, 1452-1498. I. Title.

RHYGYFARCH, 1056-1099 282'.0924
Life of St. David: the basic mid twelfthcentury Latin text with introduction, critical apparatus and translation by J. W. James. Cardiff, pub. on behalf of the Bd. of Celtic Studies by Wales Univ. Pr., 1967 xliv, 49p. plate (diagr.) 26cm. Tr. of Vita Davidis. [BX4700.D3R5 1967] 67-88094 6.00
1. David, Saint, 6th cent. I. James, John Williams. ed. II. Wales. University. Board of Celtic Studies. III. Title.
Distributor: Verry, Mystic, Conn.

ROCKWELL, Anne F. 282'.0924 B
Glass, stones & crown; the Abbe Suger and the building of St. Denis [by] Anne Rockwell. [1st ed.] New York, Atheneum, 1968. 80 p. illus. 25 cm. The life and accomplishments of the religious leader who used his power to unite nobles and peasants under the King of the Franks, and helped begin the powerful

French empire of the twelfth century. His rebuilding of St. Denis established the Gothic design in church architecture. [DC89.7.S8R6] 92 AC 68
1. Suger, Abbot of Saint Denis, 1081-1151. 2. Saint-Denis, France (Benedictine abbey) I. Title.

RYAN, Thomas 282'.092'4 B
Richard, 1898-
Orestes A. Brownson : a definitive biography / Thomas R. Ryan. Huntington, Ind. : Our Sunday Visitor, c1976. 872p. ; 27 cm. Includes index. Biography:p. 851-763. [B908.B64R78] 76-29141 ISBN 087973-884-7 : 29.95
1. Brownson, Orestes Augustus, 1803-1876. 2. Philosophers-United States-Biography.

ST. Cyres, Stafford 282'.0924 B
Harry Northcote, Viscount, 1869-
Francois de Fenelon. Port Washington, N.Y., Kennikat Press [1970] viii, 311 p. illus., ports. 22 cm. Reprint of the 1901 ed. Includes bibliographical references. [PQ1796.S3 1970] 72-113319
1. Fenelon, Francois de Salignac de La Mothe-, Abp., 1651-1715.

SALTMAN, Avrom. 282'.0924 B
Theobald, Archbishop of Canterbury. New York, Greenwood Press, 1969. xvi, 594 p. illus. 23 cm. (University of London historical studies, 2) Reprint of the 1956 ed. Part 2 (p. [179]-556): Introduction to the charters.—Texts of the charters.—Supplementary documents.—Manuscripts. [BX4705.T482S3 1969] 69-14068
1. Theobald, Abp. of Canterbury, d. 1161. 2. Gt. Brit.—Church history—Sources. I. Series: London. University. Historical studies, 2

SCHEETZ, Leo A., 282'.0924 B
1896-
Going her way; the joy of fifty years in the priesthood [by] Leo A. Scheetz. [1st ed.] New York, Exposition Press [1971] 220 p. 22 cm. (An Exposition-testament book) [BX4705.S487A3] 70-171715 ISBN 0-682-47347-2 4.00
I. Title.

SCHLESINGER, Arthur 282.0924
Meier, 1917-
A pilgrim's progress: Orestes A. Brownson, by Arthur M. Schlesinger, Jr. Boston, Little, Brown [1966] xii, 320 p. 21 cm. Previous editions published under title: Orestes A. Brownson; a pilgrim's progress. Bibliography: p. [299]-305. [B908.B64S35] 66-29050
1. Brownson, Orestes Augustus, 1803-1876. I. Title.

SCHURHAMMER, Georg, 282'.092'4 B
1882-1971.
Francis Xavier; his life, his times. Translated by M. Joseph Costelloe. Rome, Jesuit Historical Institute, 1973- v. illus. 25 cm. Translation of Franz Xaver, sein Leben und seine Zeit. Contents.Contents.—v. 1. Europe, 1506-1541. Bibliography: v. 1, p. [744]-758. [BX4700.F8S2313] 72-88247 20.00 (U.S.) (v. 1)
1. Francisco Xavier, Saint, 1506-1552.
Publisher's address: Creighton University, Omaha, Neb. 60131.

SCHUTZ, Roger. 282'.092'4 B
Festival / Brother Roger ; translated by Brethren of the Taize community. New York : Seabury Press, [1974] c1973. 174 p. ; 18 cm. Translation of Ta fete soit sans fin. "A Crossroad book." [BR1725.S39A313 1974] 73-17913 ISBN 0-8164-2583-3 : 2.95
1. Schutz, Roger. I. Title.

SCHUTZ, Roger. 282'.092'4 B
Struggle and contemplation; journal, 1970-2 [by] Brother Roger. New York, Seabury Press [1974] p. cm. "A Crossroad book." Translation of Lutte et contemplation. [BR1725.S39A2813] 74-13954 ISBN 0-8164-2106-4 2.95 (pbk.)
1. Schutz, Roger. 2. Contemplation. I. Title.

SCOTT, A. Brian. 282'.092'4 B
Malachy / A. Brian Scott. Dublin : Veritas Publications, 1976. 119 p. ; 19 cm. Bibliography: p. 118-119. [BX4700.M23S28] 77-463451 ISBN 0-905092-10-4 : £1.00
1. Malachy O'Morgair, Saint, 1094?-1148. 2. Bernard de Clairvaux, Saint, 1091?-1153. Vita Sancti Malachiae. 3. Christian saints—Ireland—Biography.

SHAW, Richard, 282'.092'4 B
1941(Oct.9)-
Dagger John : the unquiet life and times of Archbishop John Hughes of New York / Richard Shaw. New York : Paulist Press, c1977. vi, 403 p., [2] leaves of plates : ill. ; 24 cm. Includes bibliographical references and index. [BX4705.H79S5] 77-80799 ISBN 0-8091-0224-2 : 10.95
1. Hughes, John, Abp., 1797-1864. 2. Catholic Church—Bishops—Biography. 3. Bishops—New York (City)—Biography. I. Title.

SHEED, Francis 282'.092'4 B
Joseph, 1897-
The church and I [by] Frank Sheed. [1st ed.] Garden City, N.Y., Doubleday, 1974. 383 p. 22 cm. [BX4705.S587A33] 73-83670 ISBN 0-385-08440-4 7.95
1. Sheed, Francis Joseph, 1897- 2. Catholic Church—Doctrinal and controversial works—Catholic authors. I. Title.

SHEEN, Fulton John, 282'.0924
Bp., 1895-
The quotable Fulton J. Sheen. Comp., ed. by Frederick Gushurst and the staff of Quote. [1st ed.] Anderson, S.C., Droke House; dist. by Grosset, New York [1967] ix, 313p. 20cm. [BL29.S45] 4.95
1. Religion—Quotations, maxims, etc. I. Title.

SHEERIN, John B. 282'.092'4 B
Never look back : the career and concerns of John J. Burke / John B. Sheerin. New York : Paulist Press, c1975. 254 p. ; 24 cm. Bibliography: p. 253-254. [BX4705.B898S5] 75-19689 ISBN 0-8091-0200-5 : 7.95
1. Burke, John Joseph, 1875-1936. I. Title.

SILENT pilgrimage to 282'.092'4 B
God : the spirituality of Charles de Foucauld / by a Little Brother of Jesus ; translated by Jeremy Moiser ; pref. by Rene Voillaume. Maryknoll, N.Y. : Orbis Books, 1975. 99 p. ; 20 cm. Translation of Ce que croyait Charles de Foucauld. Bibliography: p. 94-95. [BX4705.F65C3713] 74-32516 ISBN 0-88344-459-3 : 4.95
1. Foucauld, Charles Eugene, vicomte de, 1858-1916. I. Little Brother of Jesus.

SPALDING, Martin 282'.0924 B
John, Abp., 1810-1872.
Life, times, and character of the Right Reverend Benedict Joseph Flaget. New York, Arno Press, 1969. xvi, 406 p. 23 cm. (Religion in America) 1852 ed. published under title: Sketches of the life, times, and character of the Rt. Rev. Benedict Joseph Flaget, first Bishop of Louisville. Includes bibliographical references. [BX4705.F6S6 1969] 71-83441
1. Flaget, Benedict Joseph, Bp., 1763-1850. I. Title.

SPALDING, Thomas W. 282'.092'4 B
Martin John Spalding: American churchman [by] Thomas W. Spalding. Washington, Catholic University of America Press [1973] xi, 373 p. 23 cm. Bibliography: p. 353-364. [BX4705.S73S64] 74-171040 12.00
1. Spalding, Martin John, Abp., 1810-1872.

STEARNS, Peter N. 282'.0924
Priest and revolutionary; Lamennais and the dilemma of French Catholicism [by] Peter N. Stearns. [1st ed.] New York, Harper & Row [1967] x, 209 p. 22 cm. (Character in crisis) Bibliographical references included in "Notes" (p. 197-200) "Bibliographical essay": p. 201-203. [BX4705.L26S7] 66-20760
1. Lamennais, Hugues Felicite Robert de, 1782-1854. 2. Catholic Church in France. I. Title.

STEINER, Johannes, 282'.0924
1902-
Therese Neumann; a portrait based on authentic accounts, journals, and documents. Staten Island, N.Y., Alba House [1967] 278 p. illus., facsims., map, ports. 22 cm. Translation of Theres Neumann von Konnersreuth. Includes bibliographical references. [BX4705.N47S73] 66-27536
1. Neumann, Therese, 1898-1962.

STINGER, Charles L., 282'.092'4 B
1944-
Humanism and the church fathers : Ambrogio Traversari (1386-1439) and Christian antiquity in the Italian Renaissance / Charles L. Stinger. Albany : State University of New York Press, 1977. xvii, 328 p., [4] leaves of plates : ill. ; 22 cm. Bibliography: p. 301-314. [BX4705.T737S85] 76-21699 ISBN 0-87395-304-5 : 20.00
1. Traversarius, Ambrosius, Camaldulensis, 1386-1439. 2. Fathers of the church. 3. Renaissance—Italy. I. Title.

STROUSSE, Flora, 282'.0924 B
1897-
John La Farge, gentle Jesuit. Illustrated by Salem Tamer. New York, P. J. Kenedy [1968, c1967] 188 p. illus., ports. 22 cm. (American background books, 33) A biography of the American Jesuit who devoted himself to fighting prejudice of all sorts, especially during his term as editor of a major journal of Catholic opinion. [BX4705.L237S7] 92 AC 68
1. La Farge, John, 1880-1963. I. Tamer, Salem, illus. II. Title. III. Series.

SULLIVAN, Marion F. 282'.0924 B
Westward the bells [by] Marion F. Sullivan. [Staten Island, N.Y., Alba House, 1971] xvi, 220 p. illus. 22 cm. Bibliography: p. 211-215. [F864.S5425] 75-169139 ISBN 0-8189-0218-3 6.95
1. Serra, Junipero, 1713-1784. 2. Indians of North America—California—Missions. I. Title.

SULLIVAN, William 282.0924
Laurence, 1872-1935
Under orders; the autobiography of William Laurence Sullivan. Boston, Beacon [1966, c1944] 200p. port. 21cm. Bibl. [BX9869.S8A3 1966] 66-23781 4.50 bds.,
I. Title.

SWEENEY, David Francis 282.0924
The life of John Lancaster Spalding, First Bishop of Peoria, 1840-1916. [New York] Herder & Herder [1966, c.1965] 384p. port. 22cm. (Makers of Amer. Catholicism, v.1) Bibl. [BX4705.S7S39] 65-13480 7.50
1. Spalding, John Lancaster, Abp., 1840-1916. I. Title.

†SWEENEY, Francis 282'.092'4 B
W., 1916-
Every man my brother / Francis Sweeney. [Boston] : St. Paul Editions, c1976. 172 p. ; 22 cm. Includes index. Bibliography: p. 165-167. [BX4700.R36S83] 77-370075 4.00
1. Realino, Bernardino, Saint, 1530-1616. 2. Christian saints—Italy—Biography. I. Title.

TIERNEY, Mark. 282'.092'4 B
Croke of Cashel : the life of Archbishop Thomas William Croke, 1823-1902 / Mark Tierney. Dublin : Gill and Macmillan, 1976. xvi, 293 p. : ill. ; 23 cm. Includes bibliographical references and index. [BX4705.C7829T54 1976] 77-359491 ISBN 0-7171-0804-X : £8.50
1. Croke, Thomas William, 1823-1902. 2. Catholic Church—Bishops—Biography. 3. Bishops—Ireland—Cashel—Biography. 4. Cashel, Ire.—Biography. I. Title.

TREVINO, Jose 282'.0924 B
Guadalupe, 1889-
The spiritual life of Archbishop Martinez [by] Joseph G. Trevino. Translated by Sister Mary St. Daniel Tarrant. St. Louis, B. Herder Book Co. [1966] xiii, 219 p. 21 cm. (Cross and crown series of spirituality, no. 33) Translation of Monsenor Martinez, semblanza de su vida interior. [BX4705.M41256T73] 66-29272
1. Martinez, Luis Maria, Abp., 1881-1956. I. Title.

UMINSKI, Sigmund H. 282'.0924 B
No greater love; a story of Saint Stanislaus Kostka, by Sigmund H. Uminski. With a foreword by John Cardinal Krol. New York, Polish Publication Society of America [1969] xv, 57 p. illus. 23 cm. (Saints who made history) [BX4700.S7U4] 70-97138 3.00
1. StanisOaw Kostka, Saint, 1550-1568. I. Title.

UMINSKI, Sigmund H. 282'.0924 B
The royal prince; the story of Saint Casimir, by Sigmund H. Uminski. With a foreword by Alfred L. Abramowicz. New York, Polish Publication Society of America [1971] xiii, 146 p. illus., ports. 22 cm. Bibliography: p. 136-141. [BX4700.K3U55] 76-147844 4.00
1. Kazimierz, Saint, 1458-1484. I. Title.

VAN ZELLER, Hubert, 282.0924
1905-
One foot in the cradle; an autobiography. NewYork, Holt [1966, c.1965] xi, 282p. illus., ports. 22cm. [BX4705.V33A3 1966] 66-22064 5.95
I. Title.

VANZILLOTTA, Gino, 282'.092'4 B
1929-
A royal adventure, St. Francis of Paola / by Gino Vanzillotta 1st ed. New York : Vantage Press, c1975. 107 p. ; 22 cm. Bibliography: p. 107. [BX4700.F83V35] 75-321708 4.50
1. Franciscus de Paula, Saint, 1416-1507. I. Title.

VITA del clarissimo 282'.092'4 B
signor Girolamo Miani gentil huomo venetiano.English.
Life of Jerome Emiliani, most distinguished Venetian nobleman. Author anonymous of the XVIth century. [Translation by the Somascan Publishers] Introd. by Carlo Pellegrini. Manchester, N.H., Somascan Publishers [1973] xix, 20 p. illus. 23 cm. Previously attributed to A. Lippomano; possibly by P. Contarini; cf. introd. [BX4700.J47V5713] 73-78492
1. Jerome Emiliani, Saint, 1486-1537. I. Pellegrini, Carlo. II. Lippomano, Andrea. Vita del clarissimo signor Girolamo Miani gentil huomo venetiano. 1973. III. Contarini, Pietro, ca. 1490-1563. Vita del clarissimo signor Girolamo Miani gentil huomo venetiano. 1973. IV. Title.

WALSH, John C. 282'.092'4 B
The day after Christmas / J. C. Walsh. [s.l. : s.n., c1976] 186 leaves ; 28 cm. "Number 9 of an edition limited to twenty copies." [BX4705.W2574A33] 77-152057
1. Walsh, John C. 2. Catholic Church—Clergy—Biography. 3. Clergy—United States—Biography. I. Title.

WEBER, Francis J. 282'.092'4 B
Francisco Garcia Diego, California's transition bishop, by Francis J. Weber. Los Angeles, Dawson's Book Shop, 1972 [c1971] x, 63 p. illus. 22 cm. "Limited to a press run of 250 copies." Includes bibliographical references. [BX4705.G244W42] 78-167849
1. Garcia Diego y Moreno, Francisco, Bp., 1785-1846.

WEBER, Francis J. 282'.092'4 B
Joseph Sadoc Alemany; harbinger of a new era, by Francis J. Weber. Los Angeles, Dawson's Book Shop, 1973. viii, 70 p. illus. 21 cm. "Limited to ... 250 copies." Includes bibliographical references. [BX4705.A487W42] 72-77295
1. Alemany, Joseph Sadoc, Abp., 1814-1888.

*WEDGE, Florence 282'.0924 (B)
The thirst of Matt Talbot. Pulaski, Wis., Franciscan Pubs. [1967] 48p. 18cm. .25 pap.,
I. Title.

WHEELER, William 282'.092'4 B
Gordon.
Saint William of York / by William G. Wheeler. London : Catholic Truth Society, 1976. [12] p. : ill. ; 19 cm. [BX4705.F567W47] 76-373767 ISBN 0-85183-168-0 : £0.12
1. Fitzherbert, William, Saint, d. 1154. 2. Christian saints—York, Eng.—Biography. 3. York, Eng.—Biography.

WILSON, Robert H. 282'.092'4 B
St. John Neumann, 1811-1860, fourth Bishop of Philadelphia / Robert H. Wilson. Philadelphia : Institutional Services, Archdiocese of Philadelphia, c1977. 39 p. : ill. (some col.) ; 24 cm. [BX4705.N45W54] 77-70313
1. Neumann, John Nepomucene, Bp., 1811-1860. 2. Catholic Church—Bishops—Biography. 3. Bishops—Pennsylvania—Philadelphia—Biography. 4. Philadelphia—Biography. I. Title.

WOODGATE, Mildred 282.0924
Violet, 1904-
Junipera Serra, apostle of California, 1713-1784 by M. V. Woodgate. Westminster, Md., Newman [1966] 162p. illus. 27cm. Bibl. [F8.64.S546] 66-8807 3.95
1. Serra, Juniper, 1713-1784. I. Title.

YORK, Raymond. 282'.0924 B
Pentecost comes to Central Park. [New York] Herder and Herder [1969] 160 p. 22 cm. Autobiographical. [BX4705.Y56A3] 69-11391 4.95
I. Title.

ZAHN, Gordon Charles, 282'.0924
1918-
In solitary witness: the life and death of Franz Jagerstatter, [by] Gordon C. Zahn. London, G. Chapman, 1966. [9], 278 p. 4 plates (incl. ports.) 22 1/2 cm. 30/- (B66-18552) Facsim. on endpapers. Bibliography: p. 274-277. [BX4705.J265Z3] 67-81115
1. Jagerstatter, Franz, 1907-1943. I. Title.

FITZSIMONS, Matthew A., 282'.094
1912-
The Catholic Church today: Western Europe, edited by M. A. Fitzsimons. Contributors: Jean Becarud [and others] Notre Dame [Ind.] University of Notre Dame Press [1969] xx, 350 p. 24 cm. (International Studies of the Committee on International Relations, University of Notre Dame) Bibliographical footnotes. [BX1490.A2F5] 68-58334 10.00
1. Catholic Church in Europe. 2. Europe—Religion. I. Becarud, Jean. II. Title. III. Series: Notre Dame, Ind. University. Committee on International Relations. International studies

MOREY, Adrian, 1904- 282'.0942
The Catholic subjects of Elizabeth I / Adrian Morey. Totowa, N.J. : Rowman and Littlefield, 1977. p. cm. Includes index. Bibliography: p. [BX1492.M57] 77-2231 ISBN 0-87471-970-4 : 15.00
1. Elizabeth, Queen of England, 1533-1603. 2. Catholics in England—History. 3. Persecution—England. I. Title.

CLARK, James Alan, 282'.097293
1929-
The church and the crisis in the Dominican Republic, by James A. Clark. Westminster, Md., Newman Press, 1967 [c1966] xxvii, 265 p. illus., ports. 22 cm. Bibliography: p. 255-259. [BX1459.D6C53] 66-28930
1. Catholic Church in the Dominican Republic. 2. Dominican Republic—History—1961- I. Title.

MURRAY, Andrew E. 282'.1788
The skyline synod; Presbyterianism in Colorado and Utah [by] Andrew E. Murrav [sic] Denver, Golden Bell Press [1971] 151 p. illus. 23 cm. (Presbyterian Historical Society. Publications, v. 10) Bibliography: p. 129-133. [BX8947.C6M87] 72-180975 2.95
1. Presbyterian Church in Colorado. 2. Presbyterian Church in Utah. 3. United Presbyterian Church in the U.S.A. Synods. Colorado-Utah. I. Title. II. Series.

POWELL, James M., ed. 282.4
Innocent I I I Vicar of Christ or lord of the world? Boston, Heath [1963] 74 p. 24 cm. (Problems in European civilization) [BX1236.P6] 63-12804
I. Innocentius III, Pope, 1160 or 61-1216.

SCHAEFERS, William Henry, 282.4
1891-
Catholic highlights of Europe; Kansans abroad. Boston, Christopher Pub. House [1956] 205p. illus. 21cm. [BX1490.S35] 56-42850
1. Catholic Church in Europe. 2. Shrines—Europe. I. Title.

SCHAEFERS, Willian Henry, 282.4
1891-
Catholic highlights of Europe; Kansans abroad. Boston, Christopher Pub. House [1956] 205p. illus. 21cm. [BX1490.S35] 56-42850
1. Catholic Church in Europe. 2. Shrines—Europe. I. Title.

ANSON, Peter Frederick, 282.41
1889-
Underground Catholicism in Scotland, by Peter F. Anson; illustrations by the author. Montrose, Standard Press, 1970. xi, 344 p. illus. 23 cm. Includes bibliographical references. [BX1498.A8] 78-582429 ISBN 0-900871-01-6 £2.25
1. Catholic Church in Scotland. I. Title.

MACKENZIE, Compton, Sir, 282.41
1883-
Catholicism and Scotland. Port Washington, N.Y., Kennikat Press [1971] 187 p. 21 cm. Reprint of the 1936 ed. Includes bibliographical references. [BX1497.M3 1971] 75-118486
1. Catholic Church in Scotland. 2. Scotland—Church history. I. Title.

SCOTT, Moncrieff, George, 282.41
1910-
The mirror and the cross: Scotland and the Catholic faith. Baltimore, Helicon Press [1961, c1960] 168p. illus. 23cm. [BX1497.S35 1961] 61-19226
1. Catholic Church in Scotland—Hist. 2. Scotland—Church history. I. Title.

SCOTT-MONCRIEFF, George 282.41
Irving, 1910-
The mirror and the cross: Scotland and the Catholic faith. Baltimore, Helicon [1961, c.1960] 168p. illus. 61-19226 3.95
1. Catholic Church in Scotland—Hist. 2. Scotland—Church history. I. Title.

BIELER, Ludwig. 282.415 s
St. Patrick and the coming of Christianity. Dublin, Gill [1967] [8], 100 p. 22 cm. (A History of Irish Catholicism, v. 1, 1) Bibliography: 7th-8th prelim. pages. [BX1503.H55 vol. 1, no. 1] 74-17605 7/6
1. Patrick, Saint, 373?-463? I. Title. II. Series.

BIEVER, Bruce Francis. 282'.415
Religion, culture, and values : a cross-cultural analysis of motivational factors in native Irish and American Irish Catholicism / Bruce Francis Biever. New York : Arno Press, 1976, c1965. xxxiii, 836 p. ; 24 cm. (The Irish-Americans) Originally presented as the author's thesis, University of Pennsylvania, 1965. Includes index. Bibliography: p. [xxi]-xxxiii. [BX1503.B5 1976] 76-6322 ISBN 0-405-09319-5 : 47.00
1. Catholic Church in Ireland. 2. Catholic Church in the United States. 3. Sociology, Christian (Catholic) 4. Religion. I. Title. II. Series.

BLANSHARD, Paul, 1892- 282.415
The Irish and Catholic power; an American interpretation. With the suppl. and an introd. to the reprint ed. Westport, Conn., Greenwood Press [1972, c1953] xvi, 380 p. 22 cm. Original ed. issued in series: Beacon studies in church and state. Bibliography: p. 364-367. [BX1505.B55 1972] 70-112321 ISBN 0-8371-4708-5
1. Catholic Church in Ireland. 2. Catholic Church—Doctrinal and controversial works—Protestant authors. 3. Ireland—Social conditions. 4. Irish in the United States. I. Title.

CZARNOWSKI, Stefan. 282'.415
Le culte des heros et ses conditions sociales / Stefan Czarnowski. New York : Arno Press, 1975, c1919. p. cm. (European sociology) Reprint of the ed. published by F. Alcan, Paris, in series Travaux de l'Annee sociologique and Bibliotheque de philosophie contemporaine. Includes index. [BX4700.P3C9 1975] 74-25745 ISBN 0-405-06500-0
1. Patrick, Saint, 373?-463? 2. Heroes. I. Title. II. Series. III. Series: L'Annee sociologique. Travaux.

DANIEL-ROPS, Henry [Real 282.415
name: Henry Jules Charles Petiot], ed.
The miracle of Ireland. Translated from the French by the Earl of Wicklow. Baltimore, Helicon Press [1959] 166p. illus. 22cm. 59-6615 4.50
1. Catholic Church in Ireland. I. Title.

FENNELL, Desmond, comp. 282.415
The changing face of Catholic Ireland. Foreword by Karl Rahner. Washington, Corpus Books [1968] 223 p. 23 cm. [BX1505.2.F4] 68-8981 5.95
1. Catholic Church in Ireland—History. 2. National characteristics, Irish. I. Title.

GWYNN, Aubrey Osborn, 282.415 s
1892-
The twelfth-century reform [by] Aubrey Gwynn. Dublin, Gill [1968] 68 p. 28 cm. (A History of Irish Catholicism, v. 2, 1) Includes bibliographical references. [BX1503.H55 vol. 2, no. 1] 70-17601 7/6
1. Catholic Church in Ireland—History. I. Title. II. Series.

GWYNN, Denis Rolleston, 282.415 s
1893-
Great Britain: England and Wales [by] Denis Gwynn. Dublin, Gill [1968] 54, 28, [1] p. 21 cm. (A History of Irish Catholicism, v. 6, 1) Bibliography: p. [29] at end. [BX1503.H55 vol. 6, no. 1] 78-259364 7/6
1. Catholic Church in Great Britain. 2. Irish in Great Britain. I. Handley, James Edmund. Scotland. 1968. II. Title. III. Series.

HAND, Geoffrey Joseph 282.415 s
Philip.
The Church in the English lordship, 1216-1307 [by] Geoffrey Hand. Anglo-Irish church life: fourteenth centuries [by] Aubrey Gwynn. Dublin, Gill [1968] [4], 43, 76 p. 21 cm. (A History of Irish Catholicism, v. 2, 3/4) Bibliography: 3d-4th prelim. pages. [BX1503.H55 vol. 2, no. 3/4] 76-17600
1. Catholic Church in Ireland—History. I. Gwynn, Aubrey Osborn, 1892- Anglo-Irish church life: fourteenth and fifteenth centuries. 1968. II. Title. III. Series.

A History of Irish 282.415
Catholicism. [General editor: Patrick J. Corish] Dublin, Gill [1967- v. 22 cm. Includes bibliographies. [BX1503.H55] 73-17590 7/6 ea.
1. Catholic Church in Ireland—History. I. Corish, Patrick J., 1921- ed.

LARKIN, Emmet J., 1927- 282'.415
The historical dimensions of Irish Catholicism / Emmet Larkin ; with a new introd. New York : Arno Press, 1976. p. cm. (The Irish-Americans) The essays were previously published in the American historical review, 1967-1975. Contents.Contents.—Economic growth, capital investment, and the Roman Catholic Church in nineteenth-century Ireland.—The devotional revolution in Ireland, 1850-1875.—Church, state, and nation in modern Ireland. [BX1503.L37 1976] 76-6350 ISBN 0-405-09344-6 : 15.00
1. Catholic Church in Ireland—Addresses, essays, lectures. I. Title. II. Series.

MCAVOY, Thomas 282'.415 s
Timothy, 1903-1969.
The United States of America: The Irish clergyman [by] Thomas T. McAvoy. The Irish layman [by] Thomas N. Brown. [Dublin] Gill and Macmillan [1970] 100 p. 21 cm. (A History of Irish Catholicism, v. 6, 2) Bibliography: p. [98]-100. [BX1503.H55 vol. 6, no. 2] 70-18739 14/-
1. Catholics in the United States. 2. Irish in the United States. I. Brown, Thomas N., 1920- The Irish layman. 1970. II. Title. III. Series.

MCGLADE, Joseph. 282.415 s
The missions: Africa and the Orient. Dublin, Gill [1967] 94 p. 22 cm. (A History of Irish Catholicism, v. 6, 8) Bibliography: p. [93]-94. [BX1503.H55 vol. 6, no. 8] 73-259360 7/6
1. Catholic Church—Missions. 2. Missions, Irish. I. Title. II. Series.

MILLETT, Benignus, 282.415 s
1922-
Survival and reorganization, 1650-1695 [by] Benignus Millett. The origins of Catholic nationalism [by] Patrick J. Corish. Dublin, Gill [1968] [4], 63, 64 p. 21 cm. (A History of Irish Catholicism, v. 3, 7/8) Bibliography: 3d-4th prelim. pages. [BX1503.H55 vol. 3, no. 7/8] 71-17595 7/6
1. Catholic Church in Ireland—History. 2. Nationalism and religion—Ireland. I. Corish, Patrick J., 1921- The origins of Catholic nationalism. 1968. II. Title. III. Series.

MOONEY, Canice, 1911- 282.415 s
1963.
The Church in Gaelic Ireland: thirteenth to fifteenth centuries. Dublin, Gill and Macmillan [1969] [4], 62 p. 21 cm. (A History of Irish Catholicism, v. 2, 5) Bibliography: p. 3d-4th prelim. pages. [BX1503.H55 vol. 2, no. 5] 78-25046 ISBN 0-7171-0263-7 10/-
1. Catholic Church in Ireland. I. Title. II. Series.

MOONEY, Canice, 1911- 282.415 s
1963.
The first impact of the Reformation [by] Canice Mooney. The counter-reformation [by] Frederick M. Jones. Dublin, Gill [1967] [4], 40, 53 p. 21 cm. (A History of Irish Catholicism, v. 3, 2/3) Bibliography: 3d-4th prelim. pages. [BX1503.H55 vol. 3, no. 2/3] 78-17594 7/6
1. Reformation—Ireland. 2. Counter-Reformation—Ireland. I. Jones, Frederick M. The counter-reformation. 1967. II. Title. III. Series.

MOULD, Daphne Desiree 282.415
Charlotte Pochin.
Irish pilgrimage. New York, Devin-Adair Co., 1957. 153p. illus. 21cm. Includes bibliography. [BX1503.M6 1957] 57-8867
1. Catholic Church in Ireland. 2. Celtic Church. 3. Pilgrims and pilgrimages—Ireland. I. Title.

MURPHY, Ignatius, 1938- 282.415 s
Catholic education: Primary education [by] Ignatius Murphy. Secondary education [by] Seamus V. O Suilleabhain. The university question [by] Fergal McGrath. [Dublin] Gill and Macmillan [1971] 142 p. 21 cm. (A History of Irish Catholicism, v. 5, 6) At head of title: The Church since emancipation. Includes bibliographical references. [BX1503.H55 vol. 5, no. 6] 71-277414 ISBN 0-7171-0272-6 16/-
1. Catholic Church in Ireland—Education—History. I. O Suilleabhain, Seamus V., 1921- Secondary education. 1971. II. McGrath, Fergal, 1895- The university question. 1971. III. Title. IV. Title: The Church since emancipation. V. Series.

WHYTE, John Henry, 282.415 s
1928-
Political problems, 1850-60 [by] John H. Whyte. Political problems, 1860-78 [by] Patrick J. Corish Dublin, Gill [1967] [4], 39, 59 p. 22 cm. (A History of Irish Catholicism, v. 5, 2/3) Bibliography: 3d-4th prelim. pages. [BX1503.H55 vol. 5, no. 2/3] 70-18506
1. Catholic Church in Ireland—History. 2. Ireland—Politics and government—1837-1901. I. Corish, Patrick J., 1921- Political problems, 1860-78. 1967. II. Title. III. Series.

[BEDELL, William] d. 282.41509
1670
A true relation of the life and death of the Right Reverend father in God William Bedell, lord bishop of Kilmore in Ireland. Ed. from a ms. in the Bodleian Lib., Oxford. Amplified with genealogical and historical chapters, comp. from orig. sources, by the representative of the bishop's mother's family of Elliston, Thomas Wharton Jones, F.R.S. [Westminster] Printed for the Camden Society, 1872. New York, Johnson Reprint, 1965. [2],xvii, 268p. 22cm. [Camden soc. Pubns., new ser., 4) [DA20.C17 new ser., vol. 4] A17 13.50
1. Bedell, William, bp. of Kilmore, 1571-1642. I. Jones, Thomas Wharton, 1808-1891, ed. II. Title.

DURHAM, Eng. (Diocese) 282.41509
Bishop, 1284-1311 (Antony Bek)
Records of Antony Bek, bishop and patriarch, 1283-1311. Edited and calendared by C. M. Fraser. Durham, Andrews, 1953. xix, 252p. 23cm. (The publications of the Surtees Society, v.162) Most of the records are in Latin, some are in English. [DA20.S9 vol.162] 54-4254
1. Gt. Brit.—Church history—Sources. I. Fraser, C. M., ed. II. Title. III. Series: Surtees Society, Durham, Eng. Publications, v. 162

HUDLESTON, Christophe 282.41509
Roy, 1905- ed.
Durham recusants' estates, 1717-1778. Durham, Published for the Society by Andrews, 1962. v. 22 cm. (The Publications of the Surtees Society, v. 173 for the year 1958. Transcribed from certificates in the archives of the clerk of the peace of Durham and the County Record Office and from a microfilm of the registers made in 1717, preserved at the Public Record Office in London. [DA20.S9] 63-3785
1. Durham, Eng. (County)—Hist.—Sources. 2. Durham, Eng. (County)—General. 3. Catholics in Durham, Eng. (County) I. Title. II. Series: Surtees Society, Durham, Eng. Publications, v. 173, etc.

HUDLESTON, Christophe 282.41509
Roy, 1905- ed.
Durham recusants' estates, 1717-1778. Durham, Published for the Society by Andrews, 1962. v. 22 cm. (The Publications of the Surtees Society, v. 173 for the year 1958. Transcribed from certificates in the archives of the clerk of the peace of Durham and the County Record Office and from a microfilm of the registers made in 1717, preserved at the Public Record Office in London. [DA20.S9] 63-3785
1. Durham, Eng. (County) — Hist. — Sources. 2. Durham, Eng. (County) — General. 3. Catholics in Durham, Eng. (County) I. Title. II. Series: Surtees Society, Durham, Eng. Publications, v. 173, etc.

LOSH, James, 1763-1833. 282.41509
Diaries and correspondence. Edited by Edward Hughes. Durham, Published for the Society by Andrews, 1962-63. 2 v. 23 cm. to Charles, 2nd Earl Grey, and Henry Brougham. [DA20.S9 vol. 171, etc.] 62-52267
1. Gt. Brit. — Hist. — 1800-1837 — Sources. I. Hughes, Edward, 1890- ed. II. Title. III. Series: Surtees Society, Durham, Eng. Publications, v. 171, 174

LOSH, James, 1763-1833. 282.41509
Diaries and correspondence. Edited by Edward Hughes. Durham, Published for the Society by Andrews, 1962- v. 23cm. (The publications of the Surtees Society, v. 171) Contents.v. 1. Diary, 1811-1823. [DA20.S9 vol. 171, etc.] 62-52267
1. Gt. Brit.—Hist.—1800-1837— Sources. I. Hughes, Edward. 1899- ed. II. Title. III. Series: Surtees Society, Durham, Eng. Publications, v. 171

LOSH, James, 1763-1833. 282.41509
Diaries and correspondence. Edited by Edward Hughes. Durham, Published for the Society by Andrews, 1962-63. 2 v. 23 cm. The publications of the Surtees Society, v. 171, 174) Contents.Contents. -- v. Diary, 1811-1823. -- v. Diary, 1824-1833. Letters to Charles, 2nd Earl Grey, and Henry Brougham. [DA20.S9 vol. 171, etc.] 62-52267
1. Gt. Brit. — Hist. — 1800-1837 — Sources. I. Hughes, Edward, 1890- ed. II. Title. III. Series. IV. Series: Surtees Society, Durham, Eng. Publications, v. 171, 174

GWYNN, Aubrey Osborn, 282.416
rev. 1892-
The medieval province of Armagh, 1470-1545. Dundalk, W. Tempest Dundalgan Pr. [Chester Springs, Pa., Dufour, 1966] xi, 287p. 23cm. Bibl. [BX1506.A7G9] 47-23345 6.00 bds.,
1. Armagh, Ire. (Ecclesiastical province) I. Title.

MACNAMEE, James Joseph, 282.418
Bp., 1876-
History of the Diocese of Ardagh. Dublin, Browne and Nolan, 1954. 858p. illus. 23cm. [BX1507.A64M2] 55-32975
1. Ardagh, Ire. (Diocese)—Hist. 2. Parishee—Ardagh, Ire. (Diocese) I. Title.

GWYNN, Aubrey Osborn, 282.419
1892-
A history of the Diocese of Killaloe, by Aubrey Gwynn [and] Dermot F. Gleeson. Dublin, M. H. Gill [1962- v. facsims., fold. map, plates. 26 cm. Includes bibliographies. [BX1507.K53G9] 79-274891
1. Catholic Church. Diocese of Killaloe, Ire. I. Gleeson, Dermot F. II. Title.

BOLSTER, Evelyn. 282'.419'5
A history of the Diocese of Cork from the earliest times to the Reformation. Shannon, Ire., Irish University Press [1972] xlviii, 548 p. illus. 25 cm. Bibliography: p. 505-528. [BX1507.C67B65] 72-171170 ISBN 0-7165-0995-4 Price not set
1. Catholic Church. Diocese of Cork, Ire. I. Title.
Order from Irish University Press, White Plains, N.Y.

AVELING, Hugh. 282'.42
The handle and the axe : the Catholic recusants in England from Reformation to emancipation / [by] J. C. H. Aveling. London : Blond and Briggs, 1976. 384 p. ; 23 cm. Includes index. Bibliography: p. [361]-375. [BX1492.A85] 77-367707 ISBN 0-85634-047-2 : £9.50
1. Catholics—England—History. I. Title.

BRETT, M. 282'.42
The English Church under Henry I / by M. Brett. London : Oxford University Press, 1975. xii, 282 p. ; 23 cm. (Oxford historical monographs) A revision of the author's thesis. Includes index. Bibliography: p. [247]-266. [BR750.B757 1975] 76-350376 ISBN 0-19-821861-3 : 19.50 (U.S.)

1. Catholic Church in England—Government—History. 2. Henry I, King of England, 1068-1135. 3. England—Church history—Medieval period, 1066-1485. I. Title.

BRETT, M. 282'.42
The English Church under Henry I / by M. Brett London : Oxford University Press, 1975. xii, 282 p. ; 23 cm. (Oxford historical monographs) A revision of the author's thesis. Includes index. Bibliography: p. [247]-266. [BR750.B757 1975] 76-350376 ISBN 0-19-821861-3 : 19.50
1. Catholic Church in England—Government—History. 2. Henry I, King of England, 1068-1135. 3. England—Church history—Medieval period, 1066-1485. I. Title.
Distributed by Oxford University Press, N.Y.

CARAMAN, Philip, 1911- ed. 282.42
The other face; Catholic life under Elizabeth I. New York, Sheed & Ward [1961, c.1960] 3344p. illus. Bibl. 61-11798 4.95
1. Catholic Church in Great Britain—Hist.—Sources. 2. Gt. Brit.—Church history—16th cent. I. Title.

CARTHY, Mary Peter. 282.42
Catholicism in English-speaking lands. [1st ed.] New York, Hawthorne Books [1964] 141 p. 21 cm. (The Twentieth century encyclopdeia of Catholicism, v. 92. Section 9: The Church and the modern world) Bibliography: p. [139]-141. [BX1401.A1C37] 64-14162
1. Catholic Church in Great Britain. 2. Catholic Church in the U.S. 3. Catholic Church — Hist. I. Title. II. Series: The Twentieth century encyclopedia of Catholicism, v. 92

CARTHY, Mary Peter 282.42
Catholicism in English-speaking lands. New York, Hawthorn [c.1964] 141p. 21cm. (Twentieth cent. ency. of Catholicism, v.92. Sect. 9: The church and the mod. world) Bibl. 64-14162 3.50 bds.,
1. Catholic Church in Great Britain. 2. Catholic Church in the U.S. 3. Catholic Church—Hist. I. Title. II. Series: The Twentieth century encyclopedia of Catholicism, v.92

CATHOLIC emancipation, 282.42
1829 to 1929; essays by various writers. Freeport, N.Y., Books for Libraries Press [1966] ix, 280 p. 21 cm. (Essay index reprint series) "First published 1929." Contents.Contents.—Introduction, by Cardinal Bourne.—Joy in harvest: a sequel to the Second spring, by W. Barry.—The Catholic Church and the spiritual life, by Archbishop Goodier.—The Catholic Church and education, by Sir J. Gilbert.—The Catholic Church and literature, by Algernon Cecil.—The Catholic Church and science, by Sir B. C. A. Windle.—The Catholic Church and music, by E. Oldmeadow.—Catholics in public life, by Viscount Fitzalan.—Catholics and philanthropy, by the Bishop of Brentwood.—Religious orders of men, by Abbot Butler.—Religious communities of women, by M. Monahan.—The influence of Catholic laywomen, by M. Fletcher.—Statistical progress of the Catholic Church, by H. Thurston.—The outlook, by G. K. Chesterton. Includes bibliographical references. [BX1493.C3 1966] 67-22084
1. Catholic Church in England.

CLANCY, Thomas H 282.42
Papist pamphleteers; the Allen-Persons party and the political throught of the Counter-Reformation in England, 1572-1615. Chicago, Loyola University Press, 1964. xi, 256 p. 24 cm. (Jesuit studies; contributions to the arts and sciences by members of the Society of Jesus) Bibliographical references included in "Notes" (p. 201-229) [BX1492.C55] 64-14078
1. Counter-Reformation — England. 2. Catholics in England. I. Title.

CLANCY, Thomas H. 282.42
Papist pamphleteers; the Allen-Persons party and the political thought of the Coonter-Reformation in England, 1572-1615. Chicago, Loyola Univ. Pr. [c.]1964. xi, 256p. 24cm. (Jesuit studies; contributions to the arts and scis. by members of the Soc. of Jesus) Bibl. 64-14078 6.00
1. Counter-Reformation—England. 2. Catholics in England. I. Title.

COURTENAY, William, Abp. 282.42
of Canterbury, 1342?-1396.
The metropolitan visitations of William Courtency, Archbishop of Canterbury, 1381-1396; documents transcribed from the original manuscripts of Courteney's register, with an introd. describing the Archbishop's investigations by Joseph Henry Dahmus. Urbana, University of Illinois Press, 1950. 209 p. 27 cm. (Illinois studies in the social sciences, v. 31, no. 2) Text in Latin. [H31.I 4 vol. 31, no. 2] 50-8868
1. Visitations, Ecclesiastical—England. 2. Gt. Brit.—Church history—Sources. I. Title. II. Series: Illinois. University. Illinois studies in the social sciences, v. 31, no. 2

CUTTS, Edward Lewes, 1824- 282.42
1901.
Parish priests and their people in the Middle Ages in England. New York, AMS Press [1970] xvii, 579 p. illus., maps, plan, ports. 23 cm. Reprint of the 1898 ed. Includes bibliographical references. [BR747.C9 1970] 74-107457 ISBN 0-404-01898-X
1. Great Britain—Church history—Medieval period, 1066-1485. 2. Clergy—England. 3. Great Britain—Social life and customs—Medieval period, 1066-1485. I. Title.

DEVLIN, Christopher 282.42
Hamlet's divinity, and other essays. Introd. by C. V. Wedgwood. Carbondale, Ill., Southern Ill. Univ. Pr. [1964, c.1963] 157p. geneal. table. 20cm. 64-13635 5.00 bds.,
1. Catholics in England. 2. Gt. Brit.—Hist.—Elizabeth, 1558-1603. I. Title.

HAVRAN, Martin J 282.42
The Catholics in Caroline England. Standord, Calif., Stanford University Press, 1962. 208p. 23cm. Includes bibliography. [BX1492.H3] 62-9561
1. Catholics in England. 2. Gt. Brit.—Church history—17th cent. I. Title.

LAWRENCE, Clifford Hugh, 282.42
ed.
The English church and the papacy in the Middle Ages, edited by C. H. Lawrence. With a foreword by David Knowles. New York, Fordham University Press [1965] vii, 265 p. 23 cm. Bibliography: p. [243]-252. [BR750.L35] 65-12529
1. Gt. Brit. — Church history — Medieval period. 2. Catholic Church in England — Hist. I. Title.

LAWRENCE, Clifford Hugh, 282.42
ed.
The English church and the papacy in the Middle Ages. Foreword by David Knowles. New York, Fordham [c.1965] vii. 265p. 23cm. Bibl. [BR750.L35] 65-12529 6.00
1. Gt. Brit.—Church history—Medieval period. 2. Catholic Church in England—Hist. I. Title.

LEYS, Mary Dorothy Rose. 282.42
Catholics in England, 1559-1829, a social history. New York, Sheed and Ward [1962, c1961] 220 p. 22 cm. [BX1492.L48] 62-15277
1. Catholics in England.

MACDOUGALL, Hugh A. 282.42
The Acton-Newman relations; the dilemma of Christian liberalism. New York, Fordham [c.] 1962. 199p. 23cm. 62-22014 5.00
1. Acton, John Emerich Edward Dalberg Acton, baron, 1834-1902. 2. Newman, John Henry, Cardinal, 1801-1890. 3. Liberalism (Religion)—Catholic Church. I. Title.

MEYER, Arnold Oskar, 1877- 282.42
1944.
England and the Catholic Church under Queen Elizabeth. Translated by J. R. McKee. Introd. to the 1967 ed., by John Bossy. New York, Barnes & Noble [1967] xxxiv, 555 p. 23 cm. "Chronological list of unpublished documents": p. [533]-543. [DA356.M413 1967a] 67-3420
1. Catholic Church in England. 2. Great Britain—History—Elizabeth, 1558-1603. I. Title.

POLLEN, John Hungerford, 282.42
1858-1925.
The English Catholics in the reign of Queen Elizabeth; a study of their politics, civil life, and government, 1558-1580, from the fall of the old church to the advent of the Counter-Reformation. New York, B. Franklin [1971] xi, 387 p. facsims., ports. 22 cm. (Burt Franklin research & source works series, 582. Selected essays in history, economics, and social science, 242) Reprint of the 1920 ed. [BX1492.P5 1971] 71-153897 ISBN 0-8337-2798-2
1. Catholic Church in Great Britain. 2. Gt. Brit.—History—Elizabeth, 1558-1603. 3. Gt. Brit.—Church history—16th century. I. Title.

SOUTHWELL, Robert, 1561?- 282.42
1595.
An humble supplication to Her Maiestie, Edited by R. C. Bald. Cambridge [Eng.] University Press, 1953. xxii, 79, [I] p. 23cm. 'Reprint ... based on Ms. Petyt 538.36 in the Library in the Inner Temple.' Includes a reproduction of the title page of the octavo ed. of 1600. falsely dated 1595. Appendices (p. 59-[80]): 1. The proclamation of 1591.--2. The proceedings in Rome in 1602--3. Donne and Southwell. Bibliographical footnotes. [BX1780.S644] 53-12826
1. Gt. Brit. Sovereigns, etc., 1558-1606 (Elizabeth) Declaration of great troubles pretended against the realme. 2. Penal laws (against nonconformists)—England. 3. Catholic Church—Doctrinal and controversial works—Catholic author. I. Title.

STONOR, Robert Julian, 282.42
1909-
Stonor, a Catholic sanctuary in the Chilterns from the fifth century til to-day. Newport, Mon., R. H. Johns, 1951. 400 p. illus. 23 cm. [BX1494.C5S8] 51-38718
1. Stonor family. 2. Catholics in England. 3. Persecution. I. Title.

TRIMBLE, William Raleigh 282.42
The Catholic laity in Elizabethan England, 1558-1603. Cambridge, Mass., Belknap Pr. of Harvard [c.]1964. vii, 290p. 25cm. Bibl. 63-20773 6.25
1. Catholics in England. 2. Gt. Brit.—Church history—16th cent. I. Title.

WATKIN, Edward Ingram, 282.42
1888-
Roman Catholicism in England, from the Reformation to 1950. London, New York, Oxford University Press, 1957. 244p. 17cm. (The Home university library of modern knowledge, 231) Includes bibliography. [BX1491.W3] 57-59238
1. Catholic Church in England—Hist. I. Title.

WATKIN, Edward Ingram, 282.42
1888-
Roman Catholicism in England, from the Reformation to 1950. London, New York, Oxford University Press, 1957. 244 p. 17 cm. (The Home university library of modern knowledge, 231) Includes bibliography. [BX1491.W3] 57-59238
1. Catholic Church in England — Hist. I. Title.

WILKIE, William E. 282'.42
The cardinal protectors of England; Rome and the Tudors before the reformation [by] William E. Wilkie. [Cambridge, Eng., New York] Cambridge University Press [1974] viii, 262 p. 23 cm. Bibliography: p. [240]-246. [BR750.W54] 73-82462 ISBN 0-521-20332-5 14.50
1. Catholic Church—Relations (diplomatic) with Great Britain. 2. Great Britain—Foreign relations—Catholic Church. I. Title.

HALE, William Hale, 282.4209
1795-1870, ed.
Account of the executors of Richard, Bishop of London, 1303, and of the executors of Thomas Bishop of Exeter, 1310; edited, from the original mss. in the possession of the Dean and Chapter of S. Paul's, and from the archives oe [sic] the city of Exeter, by W. H. Hale, H. T. Ellacombe. [Westminster, Eng.] Printed for the Camden Soc., 1874. New York. Johnson Reprint, 1965 xxix, 148, 4p. illus. geneal. table. 22cm. In Latin [DA20.C17 new ser., no. 10] A17 13.50
1. Gravesend, Richard de, Bp. of London, d. 1303. 2. Button, Thomas de. Bp. of Exeter, d. 1307. I. Ellacombe, Henry Thomas, 1790-1885, joint ed. II. Title. III. Series: Camden Soc. Pubns. new series, 10

LAW, Thomas Graves, 282.4209
1836-1904, ed.
The archpriest controversy. Documents relating to the dissensions of the Roman Catholic clergy, 1597-1602; 2v. Ed. from the Petyt mss. of the Inner Temple by Thomas Graves Law [Westminster] Printed for the Camden Soc., 1896-1898. New York, Johnson Reprint, 1965. 2v. (various p.) 22cm. (Camden Soc. Pubns., new ser., no.56, 58) Vol.2. has imprint: London [etc.] Longmans, Green, and co., 1898. [DA20.C17 new ser., no. 56, 58] A17 27.00 set,
1. Catholic church—Clergy. 2. Jesuits in England. 3. Catholic church in England. I. Title.

AVELING, Hugh 282.4274
Northern Catholics: the Catholic recusants of the North Riding of Yorkshire. 1558-1790. London, Dublin [etc] G. Chapman, 1966. 477p. 4 plates (incl. facsim.) 23cm. (Studies in theol. & church hist. ser.) Maps on end-papers. Bibl. [BX1494.Y6A9] 66-68727 12.50
1. Yorkshire, Eng. North Riding—Church history. 2. Catholics in Yorkshire, Eng. I. Title.
American distributor: Hillary House, New York.

ATTHILL, William 282'.427'48
Lombe, 1807-1884.
Documents relating to the foundation and antiquities of the Collegiate Church of Middleham, in the County of York. With an historical introd. and incidental notices of the castle, town, and neighbourhood. [1st AMS ed.] Printed for the Camden Society, 1847. New York, AMS Press [1968] xxix, 112 p. illus. 24 cm. English or Latin. Originally issued as Publication no. 38 of the Camden Society. Includes bibliographical references. [BX5370.M5C64 1968] 70-161702
1. Collegiate Church of Middleham. I. Title. II. Series: Camden Society, London. [Publications] 38.

OUR Lady & St. 282'.427'87
Michael, Workington : centenary, 1876-1976. [Workington] : [The Priory], [1976] [2], 20, [1] p. : ill., ports. ; 25 cm. Cover title. [BX4631.W64O946] 77-359587 ISBN 0-9505428-0-6 : £0.30
1. Our Lady & St. Michael Catholic Church, Workington, Eng.

DOBSON, Richard 282'.428'1
Barrie.
Durham Priory, 1400-1450 [by] R. B. Dobson. Cambridge [Eng.] University Press, 1973. xiii, 428 p. illus. 23 cm. (Cambridge studies in medieval Life and thought, 3d ser., v. 6) Bibliography: p. 392-408. [BX2596.D8D6] 72-89809 ISBN 0-521-20140-3
1. Durham Priory. I. Title. II. Series.
Distributed by Cambridge University Press, N.Y; 22.50.

YORK, Eng. (Diocese) 282'.428'43
Archbishop, 1480-1500 (Thomas Rotherham)
The register of Thomas Rotherham, Archbishop of York, 1480-1500 / edited by Eric E. Barker. [York, Eng.] : Canterbury and York Society, 1976- v. ; 25 cm. ([Canterbury and York series] ; v. 69) Cover title: Diocesis Eboracensis, registrum Thome Rotherham. [BX1495.Y67Y67 1976] 77-353537
1. York, Eng. (Diocese)—History—Sources. I. Barker, Eric Ernest. II. Title. III. Series: Canterbury and York Society. Canterbury and York series ; v. 69.

BAUER, Clemens, 1899- 282.43
Deutscher Katholizismus; Entwicklungslinien und Profile. [1. Aufl.] Frankfurt am Main, J. Knecht [1964] 135 [1] p. 20 cm. Bibliography: p. [136] [BX1536.2.B3] 67-108858
1. Catholic Church in Germany. I. Title.

LEWY, Guenter, 1923- 282.43
The Catholic Church and Nazi Germany. [1st ed.] New York, McGraw-Hill [1964] xv, 416 p. map. 22 cm. Bibliographical references included in "Notes" (p. 345-404) [BX1536.L4] 64-21072
1. Catholic Church in Germany—History—1933-1945. I. Title.

ZAHN, Gordon Charles, 282.43
1918-
German Catholics and Hitler's wars; a study in social control. New York, Sheed & Ward [c.1962] 232p. Bibl. 62-9102 4.75
1. Catholic Church in Germany—Hist.—20th cent. 2. Church and state in Germany—1933-1945. I. Title.

ZUBEK, Theodoric J 282.437
The church of silence in Slovakia. [Whiting, Ind.] J. J. Lach [1956] 310p. 23cm. [BX1520.S67Z8] 56-29675
1. Catholic Church in Slovakia. 2. Church and state in Slovakia. I. Title.

ZUBEK, Theodoric J 282.437
The church of silence in Slovakia. [Whiting, Ind.] J. J. Lach [1956] 310 p. 23 cm. [BX1520.S67Z8] 56-29675
1. Catholic Church in Slovakia. 2. Church and state: in Slovakia. I. Title.

MINDSZENTY, Jozsef, 282.4391
Cardinal, 1892-
'... the world's most orphaned nation.' New York, J. Tarlo [1962] 111p. 22cm. [BX4705.M5565A34] 62-5932
1. Hungary—Pol. & govt.—1945- I. Title.

MINDSZENTY, Jozsef, 282.4391
Cardinal, 1892-
' . . . the world's most orphaned nation.' [Tr.] New York, J. Tarlo [dist. Bkmailer., c.1962] 111p. 22cm. 62-5932 3.00 pap.,
1. Hungary—Pol. & govt.—1945- I. Title.

BOSWORTH, William Arthur 282.44
Catholicism and crisis in modern France; French Catholic groups at thethreshold of the Fifth Republic. Princeton, N. J., Princeton [c.] 1962. xv, 407p. illus., maps. Bibl. 61-7414 8.50
1. Catholic Church in France. I. Title.

DOMENACH, Jean Marie, 282.44
comp.
The Catholic avant-garde; French Catholicism since World War II [compiled by] Jean-Marie Domenach and Robert de Montvalon. [1st ed. Translated from the French by Brigid Elson and others] New York, Holt, Rinehart and Winston [1967] x, 245 p. 22 cm. Bibliographical references included in "Notes" (p. 241-245) [BX1530.2.D613] 67-10093
1. Catholic Church in France. 2. Sociology,

Christian (Catholic) I. Montvalon, Robert de, joint comp. II. Title.

FOLLIET, Joseph. 282.44
La Maladie infantile des catholiques francais Lyon, Chronique sociale de France, 1966. 192 p. 18 cm. (Le Fond du probleme) 13 f. [BX1530.2.F6] 67-83046
1. Catholic Church in France. I. Title.

HUXLEY, Aldous Leonard, 1894-1963 282.44
Grey eminence; a study in religion and politics. New York, Harper [1966, c.1941] 278p. port. 21cm. (Colophon bk., CN82K) [DC123.9 L5H8] 66-15224 1.75 pap.,
1. Le Clerc du Temblay,Francois, 1577-1638. I. Title.

*LESNE, Emile 282.44
Histoire de la propriete ecclesiastique en France; v4 New York, Johnson Reprint, 1964. 848p. 26cm. First pub. in Lille, France, 1938, as Fascicule XLVI of Memoires et Travaux publies par des professeurs des Facultes Catholiques de Lille. Contents.v.4, Les livres 'Scriptoria' et Bibliotheques du commencement du VIIIe a la fin du XIe siecle. First pub. in Lille, France, 1938, as Fascicule XLVI of Memoires et Travaux publies par des professeurs des Facultes Catholiques de Lille. 25.00 pap.,
I. Title.

PHILLIPS, Charles Stanley, 1883- 282.44
The church in France, 1789-1848; a study in revival, by C. S. Phillips. New York, Russell & Russell, 1966. viii, 315 p. 23 cm. First published in 1929. Bibliography: p. 305-307. [BX1530.P5 1966] 66-24748
1. Catholic Church in France. 2. France—Church history. 3. Church and state in France. 4. Ultramontanism. I. Title.

PHILLIPS, Charles Stanley, 1883- 282.44
The church in France, 1848-1907, by C. S. Phillips. New York, Russell & Russell [1967] 341 p. 23 cm. Reprint of the 1936 ed. A continuation of the author's The church in France, 1789-1848. [BX1530.P52 1967] 66-24749
1. Catholic Church in France. 2. France—Church history. 3. Church and state in France. I. Title.

RIGALDUS, Odo, Abp. of Roven, d.1275 282.44
The register of Eudes of Rouen. Tr. [from Latin] by Sidney M. Brown. Ed., introd., notes. appendix by Jeremiah F. O'Sullivan. New York, Columbia [c.]1964. xxxvi, 779p. 24cm. (Records of civilization: sources and studies, no. 72) Bibl. 63-17613 15.00
1. France—Church history—Middle Ages—Sources. 2. Catholic Church in France—Hist.—Sources. I. Brown, Sydney MacGillvary, 1895-1952. tr. II. O'Sullivan, Jeremiah Francis, 1903- ed. III. Title. IV. Series.

ROSIER, Irenaeus, 1918- 282.44
I looked for God's absence: France. [Translated from the Dutch by Hona Ricardo] New York, Sheed and Ward [1960] 231p. 22cm. [BX1530.2.R613] 60-12877
1. Catholic Church in France. 2. Miners—France. I. Title.

ROSIER, Irenaeus [Secular name: Gerardus Ant. Serv. Rosier.] 282.44
I looked for God's absence: France. [Translated from the Dutch by Ilona Ricardo] New York, Sheed and Ward [c.1960] 231p. 22cm. 60-12877 3.95
1. Catholic Church in France. 2. Miners—France. I. Title.

SMITH, Katharine Lawrence, 1874- 282.44
People, pomp & circumstance in Saint Denis and Notre Dame, Paris. [1st ed.] New York, Blackmore Press [1955] 117p. 21cm. [BX4629.P3S55] 55-30111
1. Saint-Denis, France. Eglise abbatiale de Saint-Denis. 2. Paris. Notre-Dame (Cathedral) I. Title.

SPENCER, Philip Herbert, 1924- 282'.44
Politics of belief in nineteenth-century France: Lacordaire, Michon, Veuillot, by Philip Spencer. New York, H. Fertig, 1973. 284 p. 23 cm. Reprint of the 1954 ed. published by Faber and Faber, London. Bibliography: p. 267-275. [BX1530.S6 1973] 77-80592 10.50
1. Catholic Church in France. 2. Lacordaire, Jean Baptiste Henri Dominique de, 1802-1861. 3. Michon, Jean Hippolyte, 1806-1881. 4. Veuillot, Louis Francois, 1813-1883. I. Title.

VAN KLEY, Dale. 282'.44
The Jansenists and the expulsion of the Jesuits from France, 1757-1765 / Dale Van Kley. New Haven : Yale University Press, 1975. x, 270 p. ; 25 cm. (Yale historical publications : Miscellany ; 107) Includes index. Bibliography: p. 239-257. [BX4722.V27] 74-26390 ISBN 0-300-01748-0 : 15.00
1. Jansenists. 2. Jesuits in France. I. Title. II. Series.

-AUGE, Thomas E. 282.440924
Frederic Ozanam and his world [by] Thomas E Auge. Milwaukee, Bruce Pub. Co.[c1966) xi, 148 p. 21 cm. [BX4705.O8A83] 66-15088
1. Oznam, Antoine Frederic, 1813-1853. I. Title.

AUGE, Thomas E. 282.440924
Frederic Ozanam and his world. Milwaukee, Bruce [c.1966] xi, 148p. 21cm. [BX4705.O8A83] 66-15088 3.75
1. Ozanam, Antoine Frederic, 1813-1853. I. Title.

TACKETT, Timothy, 1945- 282'.44'97
Priest & parish in eighteenth-century France : a social and political study of the cures in a diocese of Dauphine, 1750-1791 / by Timothy Tackett. Princeton, N.J. : Princeton University Press, c1977. xiii, 350 p. : ill. ; 23 cm. Includes index. Bibliography: p. 307-331. [BX1532.G3T3] 76-29801 ISBN 0-691-05243-3 : 19.50
1. Catholic Church—Clergy—Biography. 2. Clergy—France—Gap (Diocese)—Biography. 3. Parishes—France—Gap (Diocese) I. Title.

BLANSHARD, Paul, 1892- 282.46
Freedom and Catholic power in Spain and Portugal, an American interpretation. Boston, Beacon Press [1962] 300p. 21cm. Includes bibliography. [BX1775.S6B5] 62-9368
1. Catholic Church—Doctrinal and controversial works—Protestant authors. 2. Catholic Church in Spain. 3. Catholic Church in Portugal. 4. Church and State in Spain. 5. Church and state in Portugal. I. Title.

BLANSHARD, Paul Bleecher, 1892- 282.46
Freedom and Catholic power in Spain and Portugal, an American interpretation. Boston, Beacon [c.1962] 300p. Bibl. 62-9368 3.95 bds.,
1. Catholic Church—Doctrinal and controversial works—Protestant authors. 2. Catholic Church in Spain. 3. Catholic Church in Portugal. 4. Church and state in Spain. 5. Church and state in Portugal. I. Title.

COOPER, Norman B. 282'.46
Catholicism and the Franco regime / Norman B. Cooper. Beverly Hills, Calif. : Sage Publications, 1975. 48 p. ; 22 cm. (Sage research papers in the social sciences ; ser. no. 90-019 : Contemporary European studies) Bibliography: p. 47-48. [BX1585.2.C68] 75-322983 ISBN 0-8039-9938-0 pbk. : 2.50
1. Catholic Church in Spain—History. 2. Church and state in Spain. 3. Spain—Politics and government—1939- I. Title. II. Series: Sage research papers in the social sciences : Contemporary European studies.

LINEHAN, Peter. 282.46
The Spanish church and the Papacy in the thirteenth century. Cambridge [Eng.] University Press, 1971. xvii, 389 p. 23 cm. (Cambridge studies in medieval life and thought, third series, no. 4) Bibliography: p. 335-365. [BR1024.L55] 75-154505 ISBN 0-521-08039-8
1. Spain—Church history. 2. Papacy—History. I. Title. II. Series.

TELEPUN, L. M., pseud. 282.47
The bloody footprints. New York, Vantage Press [1954] 145p. illus. 23cm. [BR936.T4] 53-12143
1. Russia—Church history—1917- I. Title.

TOLSTOI, Dmitrii Andreevich, graf, 1823-1889. 282.47
Romanism in Russia: an historical study, by the Count Dmitry Tolstoy. Translated [from the French] by Mrs. M'Kibbin. With pref. by Robert Eden. [New York, AMS Press, 1971] 2 v. 19 cm. Reprint of the 1874 ed. Translation of Le catholicisme romain en Russie. Includes bibliographical references. [BX1558.T613 1971] 76-131026 ISBN 0-404-06495-7 (v. 1)
1. Catholic church in Russia. I. Title.

ZATKO, James J. 282.47
Descent into darkness; the destruction of the Roman Catholic Church in Russia, 1917-1923 [Notre Dame, Ind.] Univ. of Notre Dame Pr., 1965. ix, 232p. 24cm. Bibl. [BX1558.3Z3] 65-10976 6.95
1. Catholic Church in Russia. 2. Russia—Church history—1917- I. Title.

BRIZGYS, Vincentas, Bp., 1903- 282'.47'5
Religious conditions in Lithuania under Soviet Russian occupation, by Vincent Brizgys. [Chicago, Lithuanian Catholic Press, 1968] 40 p. illus., ports. 23 cm. [BX1559.L5B74] 75-304129
1. Catholic Church in Lithuania. 2. Lithuania—Church history. I. Title.

VAITKUS, Mykolas, 1883- 282'.47'5
Keturi ganytojai; stsiminimai. [Chicago, Lietuviskos knygos klubas c1960] 180 p. 20 cm. [BX1559.L5V27] 61-22732
1. Catholic Church in Lithuania. I. Title.

GARSTEIN, Oskar 282.48
Rome and the Counter-Reformation in Scandinavia, until the establishment of the S. Congregatio de Propaganda Fide in 1622. v.1. Based on source material in the Kolsrud collection. [Oslo] Universites-forlaget [dist. New York, Oxford, 1964, c.1963] v. 24cm. (Scandinavian Univ. bks.) Contents.v.1. 1539-1583. Bibl. 64-1040 7.20
1. Counter-Reformation—Scandinavia. 2. Scandinavia—Church history. 3. Catholic Church in Scandinavia. I. Title.

BRINKEL, B. G. F., 1927- 282.492
Those Dutch Catholics [by] Jan C. Groot [and others] Edited by Michel van der Plas and Henk Suer. Pref. by Desmond Fisher. New York, Macmillan [1968, c1967] 164 p. 22 cm. [BX1551.2.B713 1968] 68-14330
1. Catholic Church in the Netherlands. I. Suer, Henk, joint author. II. Groot, Jan C., 1908- III. Title.

FRANCK, Frederick, 1909- 282.492
Exploding church; from Catholicism to catholicism. New York, Delacorte Press [1968] x, 309 p. 22 cm. [BX1551.2.F7] 68-14965
1. Catholic Church in the Netherlands. 2. Theology, Catholic—Netherlands. I. Title.

ZWINGLI, Ulrich, 1484-1531. 282'.494
Selected works. Edited by Samuel Macauley Jackson. Introd. by Edward Peters. [Translations from the German by Lawrence A. McLouth; translations from the Latin by Henry Preble and George W. Gilmore] Philadelphia, University of Pennsylvania Press [1972, c1901] xxx, 258 p. 21 cm. (Pennsylvania paperback, 49) Original ed. issued as v. 1 of Translations and reprints from the original sources of European history, new ser. Includes bibliographical references. [BR410.Z87 1972] 72-80383 ISBN 0-8122-7670-1 3.95
1. Reformation—Switzerland—History—Sources. I. Series: Pennsylvania. University. Dept. of History. Translations and reprints from the original sources of history, ser. 2, v. 1.

BAUER, Thomas J 282.51
The systematic destruction of the Catholic Church in China. [New York, World Horizons Reports, 1954] 42p. illus., map. diagrs. 25cm. (World horizons report no. 11) Bibliographical footnotes. [BX1665.B3] 57-25419
1. Catholic Church in China. 2. Persecution—China. I. Title. II. Series.

PALMER, Gretta. 282.51
God's underground in Asia. New York, Appleton-Century-Crofts [c1953] 376p. 22cm. [BX1665.P25] 52-13762
1. Catholic Church in China. 2. China—Hist.—1945- 3. Persecution. I. Title.

BIERNATZKI, William E. 282'.519'5
Korean Catholicism in the 1970s : a Christian community comes of age / William E. Biernatzki, Luke Jin-chang Im, and Anselm K. Min ; pref. by Francois Houtart. Maryknoll, N.Y. : Orbis Books, [1975] xv, 172, [66] p. ; 22 cm. Includes bibliographical references. [BX1670.5.B53] 74-78451 ISBN 0-88344-265-5 : 12.95
1. Catholic Church in Korea. I. Im, Luke Jin-chang, joint author. II. Min, Anselm K., joint author. III. Title.

LAURES, John, 1891- 282.52
The Catholic Church in Japan; a short history, by Johannes Laures. Westport, Conn., Greenwood Press [1970, c1954] xi, 252 p. front. 23 cm. [BX1668.L3 1970] 73-100165 ISBN 8-371-29744-
1. Catholic Church in Japan—History. 2. Missions—Japan. I. Title.

SPAE, Joseph John, 1913- 282.52
Catholicism in Japan, a sociological study, by Joseph J. Spae. [2d rev. ed.] Tokyo, I.S.R. Press [1964] xi, 111 p. illus., ports. 22 cm. "First appeared in the March 1963 issue of Contemporary religions in Japan." Bibliography: p. 88. [BX1668.S65 1964] 65-22928
1. Catholic Church in Japan. I. Title.

TAMBIMUTTU, Francis O. 282.5489
A profile of Ceylon's Catholic heritage. Maryknoll, N.Y., Maryknoll Pubns. [c.1961] 103p. illus. (World horizon reports, report no. 28) 61-18504 1.00 pap.,
1. Catholic Church in Ceylon. I. Title.

CATHOLIC Students' Mission Crusade, U S A 282.59
Southeast Asia in five hours. 2d ed. [Cincinnati] 1961. 70p. illus. 22cm. (CSMC five-hour series) [BX1649.C3 1961] 61-65650
1. Catholic Church in Southeastern Asia. I. Title.

CATHOLIC Students' Mission Crusade, u.S.A. 282.59
Southeast Asia in five hours. 2d ed. [Cincinnati, Author, c.1955, 1961] 70p. illus. (CSMC five-hr. ser.) 61-65650 .60 pap.,
1. Catholic Church in Southeastern Asia. I. Title.

STAFFORD, Ann, pseud 282.59
Saigon journey. New York, Taplinger Pub. Co., 1960. 188 p. 21 cm. [BX1643.S75] 60-13079
1. Catholics in Asia. 2. Women in Asia. I. Title.

STAFFORD, Ann 282.59
Saigon journey. New York, Taplinger Pub. Co. [c.]1960. vii, 188p. 21cm. 3.50 half cloth,
1. Catholics in Asia. 2. Women in Asia. I. Title.

PERRIN-JASSY, Marie France. 282'.6
Basic community in the African churches. Translated by Jeanne Marie Lyons. Maryknoll, N.Y., Orbis Books [1973] xvi, 257 p. illus. 21 cm. Translation of La communaute de base dans les Eglises africaines. Bibliography: p. 253-257. [BR1440.P4713] 72-93342 ISBN 0-88344-025-3 4.95
1. Africa, East—Religion. 2. Luo (Nilotic tribe) I. Title.

PERRIN-JASSY, Marie France. 282'.6
Basic community in the African churches. Translated by Jeanne Marie Lyons. Maryknoll, N.Y., Orbis Books [1973] xvi, 257 p. illus. 21 cm. Translation of La communaute de base dans les Eglises africaines. Bibliography: p. 253-257. [BR1440.P4713] 72-93342 ISBN 0-88344-025-3 4.95
1. Africa, East—Religion. 2. Luo (Nilotic tribe) I. Title.

CHURCH in Africa (The); 282.67
Christian mission in a context of change, a seminar. Ed. by William J. Wilson. Maryknoll, N.Y., Maryknoll 1967. xii, 177p. 19cm. (World horizon bks.) Seminar was held in Washington, D.C., Sept. 22, 1965 under the auspices of AFRIC & the Mission Secretariat. [BX1675.C5] 67-29405 2.75 pap.,
1. Catholic Church in Sub-Saharan Africa. I. Wilson, William Joseph, 1936- ed.

WILSON, William Joseph, 1936- ed. 282.67
The Church in Africa; Christian mission in a context of change, a seminar. Edited by William J. Wilson. Maryknoll, N. Y., Maryknoll Publications, 1967. xii, 177 p. 19 cm. (World horizon books) The seminar was held in Washington D. C., Sept. 22, 1965 under the auspices of AFRIC and the Mission Secretariat. [BX1675.C5] 67-29405
1. Catholic Church Sub-Saharan Africa. I. Title.

BROWN, William Eric, 1893-1957. 282.68
The Catholic Church in South Africa: from its origins to the present day. Edited by Michael Derrick. New York, P. J. Kenedy [1960] 384p. illus., map. Bibl. notes: p.360-372. 60-13569 7.50
1. Catholic Church in South Africa—Hist. I. Title.

EBERHARDT, Newman C. 282.7
A survey of American church history. St. Louis, B. Herder [c.1964] ix, 308p. 21cm. Adaptation and augmentation of sects. pertaining to N. and S. Amer. of the author's A summary of Catholic history. Bibl. [BX1401.E3] 64-7636 2.95 pap.,
1. Catholic Church in America—Hist. 2. Catholic Church in the U.S.—Hist. 3. America—Church history. I. Title.

THORNTON, Francis Beauchesne, 1898- 282.7
Catholic shrines in the United States and Canada. New York, W. Funk [1954] xii, 340p. illus., maps. 24cm. [BX2320.T4] 53-10386
1. Shrines—U. S. 2. Shrines— Canada. I. Title.

JAENEN, Cornelius J. 282'.71
The role of the church in New France / Cornelius J. Jaenen. Toronto ; New York : McGraw-Hill Ryerson, c1976. x, 182 p. ; 23 cm. (The Frontenac library ; 7) Includes index. Bibliography: p. 171-175. [BX1421.2.J34] 76-376080 ISBN 0-07-082258-1 : 6.95

1. Catholic Church in Canada. 2. Indians of North America—Canada—Missions. I. Title.

DEDERICK, Colin. 282'.7127'4
The Church of the Visitation. Hamilton, Ont., Slovak Pub. Co., 1970. 58 p. illus., ports. 23 cm. Bibliography: p. 15. [BX4605.W56C483] 73-162730
1. Church of the Visitation, Winnipeg.

FLYNN, L. J. 282'.713'72
Built on a rock : the story of the Roman Catholic Church in Kingston, 1826-1976 / L. J. Flynn. [Kingston, Ont.] : Archdiocese of Kingston, c1976. xviii, 409 p. : ill. ; 24 cm. "Published ... to commemorate the 150th anniversary of the founding of the Diocese, January 27, 1976." Includes index. Bibliography: p. 385-386. [BX1423.K56F55] 76-358875
1. Catholic Church. Archdiocese of Kingston, Ont. 2. Catholic Church in Ontario. I. Title.

RICARD, Robert 282.72
The spiritual conquest of Mexico; an essay on the apostolate and the evangelizing methods of the mendicant orders in New Spain, 1523-1572. Tr. by Lesley Byrd Simpson. Berkeley, Univ. of Calif. Pr., 1966. xii, 423p. illus. 24cm. Bibl. [BX1428.R53] 66-16286 10.00
1. Mexico—Church history. 2. Catholic Church in Mexico. 3. Indians of Mexico—Missions. 4. Mexico—Hist.—Conquest, 1519-1540. 5. Indians of Mexico—Languages—Bibl. I. Title.

RICARD, Robert. 282'.72
The spiritual conquest of Mexico : an essay on the apostolate and the evangelizing methods of the mendicant orders in New Spain, 1523-1572 / by Robert Ricard ; translated by Lesley Byrd Simpson. Berkeley : University of California Press, 1974, c1966. xii, 423 p., [4] leaves of plates : ill. ; 24 cm. (California library reprint series) Translation of La conquete spirituelle du Mexique. Includes index. Bibliography: p. 381-414. [BX1428.R513 1974] 74-193364 ISBN 0-520-02760-4 : 13.75
1. Catholic Church in Mexico. 2. Mexico—Church history. 3. Indians of Mexico—Missions. 4. Mexico—History—Conquest, 1519-1540. 5. Indians of Mexico—Languages—Bibliography. I. Title. II. Series.

BARRY, Colman James, 282'.729'6
1921-
Upon these rocks; Catholics in the Bahamas [by] Colman J. Barry. Collegeville, Minn., St. John's Abbey Press [1973] ix, 582 p. illus. 24 cm. [BX1449.2.B37] 73-85273 ISBN 0-8146-0812-4 5.00 (Pbk.)
1. Catholic Church in the Bahamas. I. Title.

ACADEMY of American 282.73
Franciscan History.
United States documents in the Propaganda Fide archives; a calendar, by Finbar Kenneally. Washington, 1966- v. 26 cm. (Publications of the Academy of American Franciscan History. Propaganda Fide calendar: 1st ser., v. 1-3.) On spine: Propaganda Fide calendar. [BX1405.A63] 66-8979
1. Catholic Church in the United States—History—Sources. I. Kenneally, Finbar, comp. II. Catholic Church. Congregatio de Propaganda Fide. III. Title. IV. Title: Propaganda fide calendar.

AMERICA'S Catholic 282'.73
heritage : some bicentennial reflections, 1776-1976 / by Francis J. Weber. [Boston] : St. Paul Editions, 1976. ix, 146 p. ; 23 cm. [BX1406.2.A65] 75-10171 4.50
1. Catholic Church in the United States—Addresses, essays, lectures. I. Weber, Francis J.

[BABO, Bede] 1900- 282.73
Our Catholic heritage, by a Benedictine monk. New York, Benziger, 1950. 344 p. 21 cm. [BX1406.B26] 51-336
1. Catholic Church in the United States—History. I. Title.

BARRY, Colman James, 1921- 282.73
The Catholic Church and German Americans. Milwaukee, Bruce [1953] xii, 348p. ports., facsim. 24cm. 'In its original form ... submitted as a doctoral dissertation at the Catholic University of America.' 'The sources': p. 329-337. [BX1407.G4B3] 53-9930
1. Catholic Church in the U. S. 2. Germans in the U. S. I. Title.

*BILLINGTON, Ray Allen 282.73
The Protestant crusade, 1800-1860; a study of the origins of American nativism. Chicago, Quadrangle [1964, c.1938] 514p. illus. 21cm. (QP12) Bibl. 2.65 pap.,
I. Title.

BILLINGTON, Ray Allen, 282.73
1903-
The Protestant Crusade, 1800-1860; a study of the origins of American nativism. New York, Rinehart [1952, '1938] viii, 514p. illus., maps. 21cm. Bibliography: p. 445-504. [BX1406.B5 1952] 52-14020
1. Catholics in the U. S. 2. Protestants in the U. S. 3. U. S.—Hist.—1783-1865. 4. U. S.—Pol. & govt.—1815-1861. 5. American Party. 6. Persecution. 7. Nativism. I. Title.

BILLINGTON, Ray Allen, 282.73
1903-
The Protestant Crusade, 1800-1860; a study of the origins of American nativism. Gloucester, Mass., Peter Smith, 1963 [c.1938] viii, 514p. illus., maps. 21cm. Bibl. 6.50
1. Catholics in the U.S. 2. Protestants in the U.S. 3. U.S.—Hist.—1783-1865. 4. U.S.—Pol. & govt.—1815-1861. 5. American Party. 6. Persecution. 7. Nativism. I. Title.

BLANSHARD, Paul, 1892- 282.73
American freedom and Catholic power. 2d ed., rev. and enl. Boston, Beacon Press [1958] 402p. 21cm. [BX1770.B55 1958] 58-6240
1. Catholic Church—Doctrinal and controversial works—Protestantauthors. 2. Catholic Church in the U. S. 3. Church and state in the U. S. I. Title.

BOHR, David. 282'.73
Evangelization in America : proclamation, way of life, and the Catholic Church in the United States / David Bohr. New York : Paulist Press, c1977. xii, 289 p. ; 23 cm. Bibliography: p. 282-289. [BV601.2.B63] 77-80806 ISBN 0-8091-2039-9 pbk. : 6.95
1. Catholic Church in the United States. 2. Apostolate (Theology) 3. Christian ethics—Catholic authors. I. Title.

CATHOLIC Church in the U. 282.73
S. Bishops.
The national pastorals of the American hierarchy, 1792-1919; with a forward, notes, and index by Peter Guilday. Westminster, Md., Newman Press, 1954. xi, 358p. 22cm. [BX1405.A56 1954] 54-11373
1. Catholic Church—Pastoral letters and charges. I. Guilday, Peter Keenan, 1884-1947, ed. II. Title.

CATHOLIC Church in the U. 282.73
S. Bishops.
Our bishops speak: national pastorals and annual statements of the hierarchy of the United States; resolutions of episcopal committees and communications of the Administrative Board of the National Catholic Welfare Conference. 1919-1951. With a foreword, notes, and index by Raphael M. Huber. Milwaukee, Bruce [1952] xxxiii, 402 p. 24 cm. "Companion to ... The national pastorais of the American hierarchy: 1791-1919." [BX1405.A57] 52-6477
1. Catholic Church—Pastoral letters and charges. I. National Catholic Welfare Conference. Administrative Board. II. Huber, Raphael M., Father, 1883- III. Title.

THE Catholic directory, 282.73
Byzantine rite Apostolic Exarchate of Philadelphia, U. S. A. (Ukrainian Greek Catholic) 1952- Philadelphia. v. illus., ports., maps. 25cm. [BX1407.U6C3] 53-16272
1. Catholic Church. Byzantine rite (Ukrainian Exarchate in the U. S.

CHRIST, Frank L. ed. 282.73
American Catholicism and the intellectual ideal, edited by Frank L. Christ and Gerard E. Sherry. New York, Appleton-Century-Crofts [c.1961] 318p. tables. Bibl.: p.301-313 60-15028 2.35 pap.,
1. Catholics in the U. S. 2. U. S.—Intellectual life. I. Sherry, Gerard E., joint ed. II. Title.

COGLEY, John. 282'.73
Catholic America. New York, Dial Press, 1973. 304 p. 22 cm. (Two centuries of American life) Bibliography: p. 291-293. [BX1406.2.C57] 72-10241 9.95
1. Catholic Church in the United States. 2. Catholics in the United States. I. Title.

COGLEY, John. 282'.73
Catholic America. Garden City, N.Y., Doubleday, 1974 [c1973] 237 p. 18 cm. (Image books, D332) Bibliography: p. [228]-230. [BX1406.2.C57] ISBN 0-385-08916-3 1.75 (pbk.)
1. Catholic Church in the United States. 2. Catholics in the United States. I. Title.
L.C. card no. for the hardbound edition: 72-10241.

COLAIANNI, James F., 1922- 282.73
The Catholic left: the crisis of radicalism within the church. Introd. by Donald J. Thorman. [1st ed.] Philadelphia, Chilton [1968] xx, 232 p. 21 cm. Bibliographical footnotes. [BX1406.2.C6] 68-29313
1. Catholic Church in the United States. 2. Church renewal—Catholic Church. I. Title.

THE Commonweal. 282.73
Catholicism in America, a series of articles from the Commonweal. [1st ed.] New York, Harcourt, Brace [1954] 242p. 22cm. [BX1406.C53] 54-5256
1. Catholic Church in the U. S. I. Title.

CONTEMPORARY Catholicism 282.73
in the United States, edited by Philip Gleason. Contributors: Jay J. Coakley [and others] Notre Dame [Ind.] University of Notre Dame [1969] xviii, 385 p. 24 cm. (International studies of the Committee on International Relations, University of Notre Dame) Bibliographical footnotes. [BX1406.2.C63] 68-58335 10.00
1. Catholic Church in the United States. I. Gleason, Philip, ed. II. Coakley, Jay J. III. Series: Notre Dame, Ind. University. Committee on International Relations International studies)

CROSS, Robert D. 282.73
The emergence of liberal Catholicism in America. Chicago, Quadrangle [1968,c.1958] 326p. 21cm. (QP44) Bibl. [BX1407.A5C7] 2.65 pap.,
1. Americanism (Catholic controversy) I. Title.

CURRAN, Francis Xavier, 282.73
1914-
Catholics in colonial law. Chicago, Loyola [c.1963] vii, 129p. 24cm. Bibl. 63-24861 3.95
1. Catholic Church in the U.S.—Hist.—Sources. 2. Church and state in the U.S. I. Title.

CURRAN, Francis Zacier, 282.73
1914-
Catholics in colonial law. Chicago, Loyola University Press [1963] vii, 129 p. 24 cm. "Collections of documents": p. 127-129. 63-24861
1. Catholic Church in the U.S. — Sources. I. Title.

DOHEN, Dorothy 282.73
Nationalism and American catholicism. Introd. by Joseph P. Fitzpatrick. New York, Sheed & Ward [1967] xiv, 210p. 22cm. Bibl. [BX1406.2.d6] 67-13762 6.00
1. Catholic Church in the U. S. 2. Nationalism and religion—U. S. I. Title.

DOHEN, Dorothy. 282.73
Nationalism and Americn catholicism. With an introd. by Joseph P. Fitzpatrick. New York, Sheed and Ward [1967] xiv, 210 p. 22 cm. Bibliography: p. 193-205. [BX1406.2.D6] 67-13762
1. Catholic Church in the U.S. 2. Nationalism and religion — U.S. I. Title.

DOLAN, Jay P., 1936- 282'.73
Catholic revivalism in the United States, 1830-1900 / Jay P. Dolan. Notre Dame, Ind. : University of Notre Dame Press, c1977. p. cm. Includes index. Bibliography: p. [BX1406.2.D64] 77-89755 ISBN 0-268-00722-5 : 10.00
1. Catholic Church in the United States—History. 2. Parish missions—United States. 3. Revivals—United States. I. Title.

DOLAN, Jay P., 1936- 282'.73
Catholic revivalism in the United States, 1830-1900 / Jay P. Dolan. Notre Dame, Ind. : University of Notre Dame Press, c1977. p. cm. Includes index. Bibliography: p. [BX1406.2.D64] 77-89755 ISBN 0-268-00722-5 : 10.00
1. Catholic Church in the United States—History. 2. Parish missions—United States. 3. Revivals—United States. I. Title.

DOTY, William Lodewick, 282.73
1919-
Trends and counter-trends among American Catholics. St. Louis, B. Herder [c.1962] 247p. 21cm. 62-15403 4.75
1. Catholic Church in the U.S. I. Title.

DUHAMEL, Pierre Albert, 282.73
1920- ed.
Essays in the American Catholic tradition. New York, [Holt] Rinehart [and Winston, c.1960] 271p. 60-7933 1.75 pap.,
1. Catholic Church in the U. S.—Addresses, essays, lectures. I. Title.

EGAN, Patrick Kevin. 282.73
The influence of the Irish on the Catholic Church in America in the nineteenth century: O'Donnell lecture delivered at University College, Galway, on 14th June 1968, by Patrick K. Egan. Dublin, National University of Ireland [1969] 22 p. 22 cm. (O'Donnell lecture, 12th) [BX1407.I7E33] 75-466215 2/-
1. Irish in the United States. 2. Catholic Church in the United States—History. I. Title. II. Series.

ELLIS, John Tracy, 1905- 282.73
American Catholicism. Garden City, N.Y., Doubleday [1965, c.1956] 196p. 18cm. (Image bk., D190) Bibl. Bibl. [BX1406.E4] .85 pap.,
1. Catholic Church in the U.S.—Hist. I. Title.

ELLIS, John Tracy, 1905- 282.73
American Catholicism. 2d ed., rev. Chicago, University of Chicago Press [1969] xviii, 322 p. 21 cm. (The Chicago history of American civilization) Includes bibliographical references. [BX1406.2.E37 1969] 69-19274
1. Catholic Church in the United States—History. I. Title. II. Series.

ELLIS, John Tracy, 1905- 282.73
American Catholicism. [Chicago] University of Chicago Press [1956] xiii, 207 p. 21 cm. (Charles R. Walgreen Foundation. Lectures) (The Chicago history of American civilization) Bibliographical references included in "Notes" (p. 160-180) "Suggested reading": p. 188-197. [BX1406.E4] 56-11002
1. Catholic Church in the United States—History. I. Title. II. Series. III. Series: Chicago. University. Charles R. Walgreen Foundation for the Study of American Institutions. Lectures.

ELLIS, John Tracy, 1905- 282.73
American Catholics and the intellectual life. [1st ed.] Chicago, Heritage Foundation [1956] 63p. 22cm. [BX1407.I5E4] 56-9934
1. Catholics in the U. S. 2. U. S.—Intellectual life. I. Title.

ELLIS, John Tracy, 1905- 282.73
Catholics in Colonial America. Baltimore, Helicon [1965] 486 p. 24 cm. (Benedictine studies, v. 8) Bibliographical footnotes. [BX1406.2.E39] 64-10920
1. Catholic Church in the U.S—History—Colonial period. I. Title. II. Series.

ELLIS, John Tracy, 1905- 282.73
ed.
Documents of American Catholic history. Milwaukee, Bruce Pub. Co. [1956] xxiv, 677p. 25cm. Includes bibliographical references. [BX1405.E4] 56-13199
1. Catholic Church in the U. S.-Hist.-Sources. I. Title.

ELLIS, John Tracy, 1905- 282.73
ed.
Documents of American Catholic history. [2d ed.] Milwaukee, Bruce [c.1962] xxii, 667p. 23cm. Bibl. 62-12432 8.50
1. Catholic Church in the U.S.—Hist.—Sources. I. Title.

ELLIS, John Tracy, 1905- 282'.73
comp.
Documents of American Catholic history. [Rev. ed.] Chicago, H. Regnery Co. [1967] 2 v. (xii, 702 p.) 17 cm. (Logos) Contents.Contents.—v. 1. The church in the Spanish colonies to the Second Plenary Council at Baltimore in 1866.—v. 2. From the Second Plenary Council at Baltimore in 1866 to the present. [BX1405.E42] 67-5312
1. Catholic Church in the United States—Sources. I. Title.

FICHTER, Joseph Henry, 282.73
1908-
Priest and people, by Joseph H. Fichter. New York, Sheed and Ward [1965] xiv, 203 p. 22 cm. Includes bibliographical references. [BX1406.2.F5] 65-12195
1. Catholic Church in the U.S. — Addresses, essays, lectures. I. Title.

FICHTER, Joseph Henry, 282.73
1908-
Priest and people. New York, Sheed [c.1965] xiv, 203p. 22cm. Bibl. [BX1406.2.F5] 65-12195 4.50
1. Catholic Church in the U.S.—Addresses, essays, lectures. I. Title.

FLYNN, George Q. 282'73
Roosevelt and romanism : Catholics and American diplomacy, 1937-1945 / George Q. Flynn. Westport, Conn. : Greenwood Press, 1976. p. cm. (Contributions in American history ; no. 47) Includes bibliographical references and index. [BX1406.2.F58] 75-35343 ISBN 0-8371-8581-5 : 13.95
1. Roosevelt, Franklin Delano, Pres. U.S., 1882-1945. 2. Catholics in the United States—History. 3. United States—Foreign relations—1933-1945. I. Title.

FLYNN, George Q. 282'73
Roosevelt and romanism : Catholics and American diplomacy, 1937-1945 / George Q. Flynn. Westport, Conn. : Greenwood Press, 1976. xx, 268 p. ; 22 cm. (Contributions in American history ; no. 47) Includes bibliographical references and index. [E806.F55] 75-35343 ISBN 0-8371-8581-5 lib.bdg. : 13.95
1. Roosevelt, Franklin Delano, Pres. U.S., 1882-1945. 2. United States—Foreign relations—1933-1945. 3. Catholics in the United States—History. I. Title.

GLEASON, Philip, comp. 282.73
Catholicism in America. New York, Harper & Row Pub. [1970] 159 p. 21 cm. (Interpretations of American history) Contents.Contents.—The formation of the Catholic minority, by T. T. McAvoy.—The distinctive tradition of American Catholicism, by J. Hennesey.—Catholics, Protestants, and public education, by V. P. Lannie.—Irish Catholic life in Yankee City, by S. Thernstrom.—German Catholics and the national controversy, by C. J. Berry.—Catholicism and woman suffrage, by J. J. Kenneally.—Pro-Germanism and American Catholicism, 1914-1917, by E. Cuddy.—Catholicism and Americanism in the 1930s, by D. J. O'Brien.—American Catholics and the intellectual life, by J. T. Ellis.—The crisis of Americanization, by P. Gleason. Includes bibliographical references. [BX1406.2.G57] 74-121629
1. Catholics in the United States—Addresses, essays, lectures. I. Title.

GREELEY, Andrew M 1928- 282.73
The Catholic experience; an interpretation of the history of American Catholicism [by] Andrew M. Greeley. [1st ed.] Garden City, N.Y., Doubleday, 1967. 307 p. 22 cm. [BX1406.2.G6S] 67-22445
1. Catholic Church in the U S.—Hist. I. Title.

GREELEY, Andrew M., 1928- 282.73
The Catholic experience; an interpretation of the history of American Catholicism [by] Andrew M. Greeley. [1st ed.] Garden City, N.Y., Doubleday, 1967. 307 p. 22 cm. [BX1406.2.G68] 67-22445
1. Catholic Church in the U.S.—History. I. Title.

GREELEY, Andrew M., 1928- 282.73
Come blow your mind with me [by] Andrew M. Greeley. Garden City, N.Y., Doubleday, 1971. 236 p. 22 cm. Contents.Contents.—Come blow your mind with me.—A new chance for the sacred?—The bread of faith.—New gods—or old?—The psychedelic and the sacred.—The risks of community.—Leadership in the church of the future.—American Catholicism 1950 to 1980.—The adolescent church.—After secularity: a post-Christian postscript.—Religion on the Catholic campus.—Sense and sensitivity in the Catholic Church.—The first papal press conference: a dream.—Conclusion. [BX1406.2.G69] 73-139026 5.95
1. Catholic Church—History—1965- 2. Catholic Church in the United States. 3. U.S.—Religion. 4. Youth—Religious life. I. Title.

GREELEY, Andrew M., 1928- 282'.73
The communal Catholic : a personal manifesto / Andrew M. Greeley. New York : Seabury Press, c1976. x, 198 p. ; 22 cm. "A Crossroad book." [BX1406.2.G694] 75-43844 ISBN 0-8164-0299-X : 8.95
1. Catholics in the United States. 2. Sociology, Christian (Catholic) I. Title.

GREELEY, Andrew M., 1928- 282.73
The hesitant pilgrim; American Catholicism after the Council, by Andrew M. Greeley. New York, Sheed & Ward [1966] xxi, 276 p. 22 cm. [BX1406.2.G7] 66-22013
1. Catholic Church in the United States—Addresses, essays, lectures. I. Title.

GRIFFIN, Joseph Aloysius, 1901- 282'.73
The contribution of Belgium to the Catholic Church in America (1523-1857), by Joseph A. Griffin. Washington, Catholic University of America, 1932. [New York, AMS Press, 1974] xvi, 235 p. geneal. table 23 cm. Reprint of the author's thesis, Catholic University of America, 1932, which was issued as v. 13 of the Catholic University of America. Studies in American church history. Bibliography: p. 223-230. [BV2240.B4G7 1974] 73-3568 ISBN 0-404-57763-6 10.00
1. Catholic Church in North America. 2. Catholic Church in the United States—History. 3. Belgians in the United States. 4. Missions—United States. 5. Indians of North America—Missions. 6. Missionaries, Belgian. 7. Missions, Belgian. I. Title. II. Series: Catholic University of America. Studies in American church history, v. 13.

HABIG, Marion Alphonse, 1901- 282.73
Heralds of the King; the Franciscans of the St. Louis-Chicago Province, 1858-1958. Chicago, Franciscan Herald Press [1958] 856p. illus. 27cm. Includes bibliography. [BX3650.S26H3] 58-10525
1. Franciscans. Province of the Sacred Heart. I. Title.

HALLINAN, Paul J. 282'.73
Days of hope and promise. The writings and speeches of Paul J. Hallinan. Edited by Vicent A. Yzermans. A memoir by Joseph L. Bernardin. A tribute by John Tracy Ellis. Collegeville, Minn., Liturgical Press [1973] xviii, 228 p. illus. 24 cm. [BX891.H3] 73-75293 ISBN 0-8146-0424-2 6.95
1. Catholic Church—Collected works. 2. Theology—Collected works—20th century. I. Title.
Publisher's Address: St. John's Abbey Collegeville, Minn. 56521.

HERNAEZ, Francisco Javier, 1816-1876 282.73
Coleccion de bulas, breves y otros documentos relativos a la iglesia de America y Filipinas; 2v. New York, Kraus Reprint, 1963. 2v. 2072p. 26cm. 41-89648 85.50 set,
1. Catholic church in America. 2. Catholic church in the Philippine islands. 3. Spain—Colonies. 4. Portugal—Colonies. I. Title.

HERR, Dan, ed. 282.73
Through other eyes; some impressions of American Catholicism by foreign visitors from 1777 to the present, ed. by Dan Herr, Joel Wells. Westminster, Md., Newman 1965 [c.1964] xi, 261p. 22cm. [BX1406.2.H4] 64-66036 4.95
1. Catholic Church in the U. S.—Foreign opinion. I. Wells, Joel, joint ed. II. Title.

HITCHCOCK, James. 282.73
The decline and fall of radical Catholicism. [New York] Herder and Herder [1971] 228 p. 21 cm. Includes bibliographical references. [BX1406.2.H5] 73-146297 6.50
1. Catholic Church—History—1965- 2. Catholic Church in the United States. I. Title.

KANE, John Joseph, 1909- 282.73
Catholic- Protestant conflicts in America. Chicago, Regnery, 1955. 244p. 22cm. [BX1780.K3] 55-10870
1. Catholic Church—Doctrinal and controversial works—Catholic authors. 2. Catholic Church in the U. S. I. Title.

KEATING, Edward M., 1925- 282.73
The scandal of silence, by Edward M. Keating. New York, Random House [1965] 214 p. 22 cm. [BX1406.2.K38] 65-11264
1. Catholic Church in the U.S.—Addresses, essays, lectures. I. Title.

KERWIN, Jerome Gregory, 1896- 282.73
Politics, government. Catholics. New York, Paulist Pr. [c.1961] 128p. (Deus bks.) 61-16661 .75 pap.,
1. Catholic Church in the U.S. 2. Church and state in the U.S. I. Title.

KOTRE, John N. 282.73
The view from the border; a social-psychological study of current Catholicism [by] John N. Kotre. Chicago, Aldine [1971] x, 268 p. illus., forms. 22 cm. (Aldine treatises in social psychology) Bibliography: p. 261-264. [BT738.K68] 73-131044 ISBN 0-202-25040-7
1. Sociology, Christian (Catholic)—Statistics. 2. Christianity—Psychology—Statistics. I. Title.

LALLY, Francis J. 282.73
The Catholic Church in a changing America. [1st ed.] Boston, Little, Brown [1962] 143p. 20cm. [BX1406.L33] 62-17950
1. Catholic Church in the U.S. I. Title.

LALLY, Francis J. 282.73
The Catholic Church in a changing America. Boston, Little [c.1962] 143p. 20cm. 62-17950 3.75 bds.,
1. Catholic Church in the U.S. I. Title.

LANDIS, Benson Young, 1897- 282.73
The Roman Catholic Church in the United States; a guide to recent developments, by Benson Y. Landis. [1st ed.] New York, Dutton, 1966. 192 p. 21 cm. Bibliography: p. 182-186. [BX1406.2.L3] 65-19963
1. Catholic Church in the U.S. I. Title.

LECKIE, Robert. 282'.73
American and Catholic. [1st ed.] Garden City, N.Y., Doubleday, 1970. xix, 388 p. 24 cm. (Religion in America series) [BX1406.2.L4] 70-111174 7.95
1. Catholics in the United States. I. Title.

LONGO, Gabriel Anthony, 1926- 282.73
Spoiled priest; the authobiography of an expriest, by Gabriel Longo. New York, Bantam [1967, c.1966] 283p. 18cm. (N3512) [BX4705.L717A3] .95 pap.,
I. Title.

LONGO, Gabriel Anthony, 1926- 282.73
Spoiled priest; the autobiography of an ex-priest[by] Gabriel Longo. [1st ed.] New Hyde Park, N. Y., University Bks. [1966] 252p. illus., ports. 24cm. [BX4705.L717A3] 66-15077 5.95 bds.,
I. Title.

MCAVOY, Thomas Timothy, ed. 282.73
Roman Catholicism and the American way of life. [Notre Dame. Ind.] University of Notre Dame, [c.]1960. viii, 248p. 24cm. Bibliographical footnotes. 59-14100 4.50
1. Catholics in the U.S. I. Title.

MCAVOY, Thomas Timothy, 1903- 282.73
The great crisis in American Catholic history, 1895-1900. Chicago, H. Regnery Co., 1957. 402p. 22cm. [BX1407.A5M18] 57-11728
1. Americanism (Catholic controversy) I. Title.

MCAVOY, Thomas Timothy, 1903- 282.73
The great crisis in American Catholic history, 1895-1900. [Ind.] Univ. of Notre Dame Pr. [c.]1963. 327p. 21cm. (Ndp 29) 1.95 pap.,
1. Americanism (Catholic controversy) I. Title.

MCAVOY, Thomas Timothy, 1903- 282.73
The great crisis in American Catholic history, 1895-1900. Chicago, H. regnery Co., 1957. 402p. 22cm. [BX1407.A5M18] 57-11728
1. Americanism (Catholic controversy) I. Title.

MCAVOY, Thomas Timothy, 1903- ed. 282.73
Roman Catholicism and the American way of life. [Notre Dame, Ind.] University of Notre Dame, 1960. viii, 248p. 24cm. Bibliographical footnotes. [BX1406.M2] 59-14100
1. Catholics in the U. S. I. Title.

MCAVOY, Thomas Timothy, 1903-1969. 282.73
The formation of the American Catholic minority, 1820-1860, by Thomas T. McAvoy. Philadelphia, Fortress Press [1967] viii, 37 p. 19 cm. (Facet books. Historical series, 6) First published in The Review of politics, v. 10, Jan. 1948, p. 13-34. Includes bibliographical references. [BX1406.2.M2] 67-22985
1. Catholics in the United States. 2. Catholic Church in the United States. I. Title.

MCAVOY, Thomas Timothy, 1903-1969. 282.73
A history of the Catholic Church in the United States. Notre Dame [Ind.] University of Notre Dame Press [1969] v, 504 p. 25 cm. Bibliography: p. 469-483. [BX1406.2.M23] 68-27580
1. Catholic Church in the United States—History. I. Title.

MCAVOY, Thomas Timothy, 1903-1969. 282'.73
Roman Catholicism and the American way of life. Edited by Thomas T. McAvoy. Freeport, N.Y., Books for Libraries Press [1973] p. (Essay index reprint series) Reprint of the 1960 ed. [BX1406.2.M24 1973] 72-13177 ISBN 0-8369-8167-7
1. Catholics in the United States. I. Title.

MCCARTHY, Thomas Patrick, 1920- 282.73
Guide to the diocesan priesthood in the United States. Washington, Catholic University of America Press, 1956. 167p. ports., maps (1 fold) 24cm. [BX1406.M22] 57-935
1. Catholic Church in the U. S.— Dioceses. 2. Bishops—U. S.—Portraits. I. Title. II. Title: The diocesan priesthood in the United States.

MCDONALD, Donald, 1920- 282.73
Catholics in conversation; seventeen interviews with leading American Catholics. [1st ed.] Philadelphia, Lippincott [1960] 288p. 21cm. [BX1406.M24] 60-14212
1. Catholic Church in the U. S. I. Title.

MACEOIN, Gary, 1909- 282.73
New challenges to American Catholics. New York, Kenedy [c.1965] 187p. 22cm. Bibl. [BX1406.2.M3] 65-15454 4.50
1. Catholic Church in the U.S.—Addresses, essays, lectures. I. Title.

MCGURN, Barrett 282'.73
A reporter looks at American Catholicism. [1st ed.] New York, Hawthorn [1967] 256p. 22cm. (Catholic perspectives) Bibl. [BX1406.2.M33] 66-15345 5.95 bds.,
1. Catholic Church in the U.S. I. Title.

MARINO, Anthony I 282.73
The Catholics in America. [1st ed.] New York, Vantage Press [1960] 300p. 21cm. Includes bibliography. [BX1406.M315] 60-15583
1. Catholics in the U. S. I. Title.

MARTIN. BERNARD H ed. 282.73
An understanding of our time: Catholic responsibility in a pluralistic society. [Washington?] National Federation of Catholic College Students [1960] 92p. 22cm. (Contemporary issues: examination and evaluation, phase 2) Includes bibliography. [BX1406.M316] 61-592
1. Catholics in the U. S. 2. Students—U. S. I. Title.

MAYNARD, Theodore, 1890-1956. 282.73
The Catholic Church and the American idea. New York, Appleton-Century-Crofts [1953] 309 p. 21 cm. [BX1406.M326] 53-10016
1. Catholic Church in the United States. 2. Catholics in the United States.

MAZZUCHELLI, Samuel Charles, 1806-1864 282.73
Memoirs. Forword by James P. Shannon. Chicago, Priory Pr. [1967] xxi, 329p. maps. 24cm. Folded map mounted on back cover. Reprint of the first English tr. by Sister Mary Benedicta Kennedy pub. in 1915. [BX1406.M35 1967] 67-14014 10.00
1. Catholic Church in the U. S. 2. Indians of North America—Missions. 3. Catholic Church—Missions. I. Title.

MINNOR of 150-year progress, 1810 to 1960, of the Catholic Church in the United States of America; useful handbook for information, study, and reference. [Donald J. Hutter, editor] Cleveland, Mirror Pub. Co., 1964] 71 p. illus. 18 cm. "[Contains] 1962 Catholic statistics of the United States, Canada, and 100 foreign countries, miscellaneous information [and] highlights." [BX1406.M56] 74-11120 282.73
1. Catholic Church in the United States—Statistics. 2. Catholic Church in Canada—Statistics. I. Hutter, Donald J., ed.

MORSE, Samuel Finley Breese, 1791-1872. 282'.73
Foreign conspiracy against the liberties of the United States : the numbers of Brutus / Samuel Finley Breese Morse. New York : Arno Press, 1977. 188 p. ; 21 cm. (Anti-movements in America) Reprint of the 1835 ed. published by Leavitt, Lord, New York. [BX1770.M55 1977] 76-46090 ISBN 0-405-09963-0 : 13.00
1. Catholic Church in the United States. 2. United States—Politics and government—1815-1861. I. Title. II. Series.

NATIONAL Catholic Welfare Conference 282.73
National Catholic Welfare Conference; an agency of the archbishops and bishops of the United States to organize, unify and coordinate Catholic activities for the general welfare of the Church. Washington [1961] 51p. illus. 22cm. [BX1404.N25 1961] 61-65382
1. Catholic Church in the U. S. I. Title.

NEW Rochelle, N. Y. College of New Rochelle. 282.73
Catholicism in American culture; semicentenary lecture series, 1953-54. New Rochelle [c1955] 70p. 28cm. Cover title. 'In celebration of the fiftieth anniversary of the founding of the College of New Rochelle. [BX1406.N44] 57-4028
1. Catholic Church in the U. S. 2. U. S.—Civilization. I. Title.
Contents omitted.

NOVAK, Michael 282.73
A new generation, American and Catholic. [New York] Herder & Herder [c.1964] 250p. 21cm. 64-13688 4.50
1. Catholics in the U.S. I. Title.

O'BRIEN, David J. 282'.73
The renewal of American Catholicism [by] David J. O'Brien. New York, Oxford University Press, 1972. xiii, 302 p. 22 cm. Includes bibliographical references. [BX1406.2.O23] 72-85825 ISBN 0-19-501601-7 7.95
1. Catholic Church in the United States. I. Title.

O'CONNOR, John, 1921- 282.73
American Catholic exodus [by] Philip Berrigan [and others] Edited by John O'Connor. Washington, Corpus Books [1968] 224 p. 23 cm. [BX880.O25 1968b] 68-8980 5.95
1. Catholic Church—Addresses, essays, lectures. 2. Catholic Church in the United States.—Addresses, essays, lectures. I. Berrigan, Philip. II. Title.

O'DEA, Thomas F 282.73
American Catholic dilemma: an inquiry into the intellectual life. Introd. by Gustave Weigel. New York, Sheed and Ward [1958] 173p. 22cm. Includes bibliography. [BX1407.I5O3] 58-5887
1. Catholics in the U. S. 2. U. S.—Intellectual life. I. Title.

O'DEA, Thomas F. 282.73
American Catholic dilemma: an inquiry into the intellectual life. Introd. by Gustave Weigel. [New York] New Amer. Lib. [1962, c.1958]

144p. (Mentor Omega bk., MP404) Bibl. .60 pap.,
1. Catholics in the U. S. 2. U. S.—Intellectual life. I. Title.

O'NEILL, James Milton, 1881- 282.73
Catholicism and American freedom. [1st ed.] New York, Harper [1952] 287 p. 22 cm. [BX1406.O5] 51-11945
1. Catholic Church in the U.S. 2. Church and state in the U.S. 3. Church and state—Catholic Church. 4. Blanshard, Paul, 1892- Communism, democracy, and Catholic power. I. Title.

ONG, Walter J. 282.73
American Catholic crossroads; religious-secular encounters in the modern world. New York, Collier [1962, c.1959] 158p. 18cm. (AS251) .95 pap.,
1. Catholic Church—Addresses, essays, lectures. 2. Catholic Church in the U.S. I. Title.

ONG, Walter J 282.73
American Catholic crossroads; religious-secular encounters in the modern world. New York, Macmillan, 1959. 160p. 22cm. [BX1395.O5] 59-7973
1. Catholic Church—Addresses, essays, lectures. 2. Catholic Church in the U. S. I. Title.

ONG, Walter J 282.73
Frontiers in American Catholicism; essays on ideology and culture. New York, Macmillan, 1957. 125p. 22cm. [BX1406.O53] 57-5730
1. Catholic Church in the U. S. 2. Religious thought—U. S. I. Title.

ONG WALTER J. 282.73
Frontiers in American Catholicism; essays on ideology and culture. New York, Macmillan, 1961 [c.1957] 125p. (Macmillan paperback, 78) Bibl. 1.25 pap.,
1. Catholic Church in the U.S. 2. Religious thought—U.S. I. Title.

PUTZ, Louis J ed. 282.73
Chicago, Fides Publishers Association [1956] xxiii, 415p. 22cm. Bibliographical footnotes. [BX1406.P84] 56-11629
1. Catholic Church in the U. S. I. Title.

PUTZ, Louis J ed. 282.73
The Catholic Church, U. S. A. Contributors: John J. Wright [and others] Chicago, Fides Publishers Association [1956] xxiii, 415p. 22cm. Bibliographical footnotes. [BX1406.P84] 56-11629
1. Catholic Church in the U. S. I. Title.

QUINN, Bernard, 1928- 282'.73
Distribution of Catholic priests in the United States, 1971 / Bernard Quinn. Washington : Glenmary Research Center, 1975. v, 31, [1] fold. leaf of plates p. : map ; 28 cm. "GRC A-52/P-119." "Produced for the United States Catholic Conference by the Glenmary Research Center." [BX1407.C6Q56] 75-326803 ISBN 0-914422-04-9 : 3.50
1. Catholic Church in the United States—Clergy—Statistics. 2. Catholic Church in the United States—Statistics. I. United States Catholic Conference. II. Glenmary Research Center. III. Title.

RAHILL, Peter James, 1910- 282.73
The Catholic in America; from colonial times to the present day. Chicago, Franciscan Herald Press [1961] 156p. illus. 21cm. [BX1406.2.R3] 61-8953
1. Catholics in the U. S. I. Title.

ROEMER, Theodore, Father, 1889- 282.73
The Catholic Church in the United States. St. Louis, Herder, 1950. viii, 444 p. port., fold. maps. 25 cm. Bibliography: p. 415-425. [BX1406.R58] 50-1839
1. Catholic Church in the U.S. — Hist. 2. Secular name: Edward Henry Roemer. I. Title.

RUSKOWSKI, Leo Francis, 1907- 282'.73
French emigre priests in the United States (1791-1815), by Leo F. Ruskowski. Washington, Catholic University of America Press, 1940. [New York, AMS Press, 1974] ix, 150 p. 23 cm. Reprint of the author's thesis, Catholic University of America, 1940, which was issued as v. 32 of the Catholic University of America. Studies in American church history. Bibliography: p. 133-144. [BX1407.F7R87 1974] 73-3586 ISBN 0-404-57782-2 7.00
1. Catholics in the United States. 2. French in the United States. 3. Missionaries, French. 4. Emigres. I. Title. II. Series: Catholic University of America. Studies in American church history, v. 32.

SARGENT, Daniel, 1890- 282.73
Our land and Our Lady. Notre Dame, Ind., University of Notre Dame [1955, c1939] 263p. 21cm. [BX1406.S3 1955] 55-9560
1. Catholics in the U. S. I. Title.

SCHARPER, Philip J. 282.73
Meet the American Catholic [by] Philip J. Scharper. Nashville, Broadman Press [1969] 151 p. 20 cm. [BX1389.S33] 69-19957
1. Catholic Church—History—20th century. 2. Church renewal—Catholic Church. I. Title.

SCHARPER, Phillip, ed. 282.73
American Catholics: a Protestant-Jewish view [by] Stringfellow Barr [and others] With an afterword by Gustave Weigel. New York, Sheed & Ward [1959] 235p. 21cm. Includes bibliography. [BX1406.S36] 59-12093
1. Catholics in the U. S. 2. Catholic Church—Relations. 3. Protestant churches—Relations. 4. Judaism—Relations. I. Barr, Stringfellow, 1897- II. Title.

SCHAUINGER, Joseph Herman, 1912- 282.73
Profiles in action; American Catholics in public life, by J. Herman Schauinger. Milwaukee, Bruce [1966] x, 251p. 24cm. Bibl. [E184.C3S3] 66-25044 4.95
1. Catholics in the U. S.—Biog. I. Title.

SHAUGHNESSY, Gerald, Bp., 1887-1950. 282.73
Has the immigrant kept the faith? New York, Arno Press, 1969. 289 p. 24 cm. (Religion in America) Reprint of the 1925 ed. Bibliography: p. 17-25. [BX1406.S4 1969] 76-83437
1. Catholic church in the United States. 2. Catholics in the United States. 3. U.S.—Emigration and immigration. I. Title.

SHIELDS, Currin V. 282.73
Democracy and Catholicism in America. New York, McGraw-Hill, 1958. 310 p. 21 cm. Includes bibliography. [BX1406.S56] 57-13341
1. Church and state in the U.S. 2. Catholic Church in the U.S. 3. Church and state—Catholic Church. I. Title.

SHUSTER, George, 1939- 282'.73
Statistical profile of Black Catholics / by George Shuster, Robert M. Kearns ; foreword by Bernard Quinn. Washington : Josephite Pastoral Center, c1976. vii, 42 p. ; 28 cm. Chiefly tables. Errata slip inserted. "Data sources": p. 37-38. [BX1407.N4S58] 76-363302
1. Afro-American Catholics—Statistics. I. Kearns, Robert M., joint author. II. Title.

SUGRUE, Thomas, 1907- 282.73
A Catholic speaks his mind on America's religious conflict. [1st ed.] New York, Harper [1952] 64 p. 20 cm. Full name: Thomas Joseph Sugrue. [BX1406.S8] 52-6283
1. Catholic Church in the U.S. 2. Church and state — Catholic Church. I. Title.

TAVARD, Georges Henri, 1922- 282.7'3
Catholicism U.S.A., by George H. Tavard. Translated by Theodore DuBois. New York, Newman Press [1969] ix, 130 p. 22 cm. Translation of Les Catholiques americains. Includes bibliographical references. [BX1406.2.T313] 70-78921 4.95
1. Catholics in the United States. I. Title.

THORMAN, Donald J. 282.73
American Catholics face the future, by Donald J. Thorman. [1st American ed.] Wilkes-Barre, Pa., Dimension Books [1968] 299 p. 21 cm. [BX1751.2.T5 1968] 68-31386
1. Catholic Church—Doctrinal and controversial works—Catholic authors. 2. Catholic Church in the United States. I. Title.

WAKIN, Edward. 282.73
The de-Romanization of the American Catholic Church [by] Edward Wakin and Joseph F. Scheuer. New York, Macmillan [1966] 318 p. 21 cm. Bibliographical references included in "Notes" (p. 296-308) [BX1406.2.W3] 66-15661
1. Catholic Church in the U.S.—Addresses, essays, lectures. 2. Catholics in the U.S. I. Scheuer, Joseph F., joint author. II. Title.

WAKIN, Edward 282.73
The de-Romanization of the American Catholic Church [by] Edward Wakin, Joseph F. Scheuer, New York, Macmillan [c.1966] 318p. 22cm. Bibl. [BX1406.2.W3] 66-15661 6.95
1. Catholic Church in the U. S.—Addresses, essays, lectures. 2. Catholics in the U. S. I. Scheuer, Joseph F., joint author. II. Title.

WARD, Leo Richard, 1893- ed. 282.73
The American apostolate; American Catholics in the twentieth century. Westminster, Md., Newman Press, 1952. 298 p. 24 cm. [BX1406.W3] 52-8006
1. Catholic Church in the U.S. I. Title.

WARD, Leo Richard, 1893- 282.73
Catholic life, U.S.A.; contemporary lay movements. St. Louise, Herder [1959] 263 p. 21 cm. Includes bibliography. [BX1406.W32] 59-13388
1. Catholic Church in the U.S. I. Title.

WEAD, Doug. 282'.73
Catholic charismatics: are they for real? Carol Stream, Ill., Creation House [1973] 120 p. 22 cm. First published in 1972 under title: Father McCarthy smokes a pipe and speaks in tongues. [BX2350.57.W42 1973] 73-82862 ISBN 0-88419-044-7 3.95
1. Pentecostalism. I. Title.

WEIGEL, Gustave, 1906- 282.73
Faith and understanding in America. New York, Macmillan, 1959. 170 p. 22 cm. "Essays and lectures." [BX4817.W4] 59-5989
1. Catholic Church — Relations — Protestant churches. 2. Protestant churches — Relations — Catholic Church. 3. U.S. — Religion. I. Title.

WEIGEL, Gustave, 1906- 282.73
Faith and understanding in America. New York, Macmillan [1962, c.1950-1959] 191p. 18cm. (123) 1.45 pap.,
1. Catholic Church—Relations—Protestant churches. 2. Protestant churches—Relations—Catholic Church. 3. U.S.—Religion. I. Title.

ELLIS, John Tracy, 1905- 282.73081
Perspectives in American Catholicism. Baltimore, Helicon [1963] 313 p. 24 cm. (Benedictine studies, 5) "Articles, addresses and sermons": p. 301-305. [BX1406.2.E4] 63-12093
1. Catholic Church in the U.S. — Hist. — Addresses, essays, lectures. I. Title. II. Series.

ELLIS, John Tracy, 1905- 282.73081
Perspectives in American Catholicism. New York, Helicon dist. Taplinger, c.1963 313p. 24cm. (Benedictine studies, 5) 63-12093 6.00
1. Catholic Church in the U.S.—Hist.—Addresses, essays, lectures. I. Title. II. Series.

LUCEY, William Leo, 1903- 282.741
The Catholic Church in Maine. Francestown, N. H., M. Jones Co. [c1957] 372p. illus. 23cm. Includes bibliography. [BX1415.M2L8] 58-1592
1. Catholic Church in Maine.—Hist. I. Title.

ANNUAL Catholic 282.7419
information guide and business directory, complete; listing clergy, parishes, missions, schools and hospitals, Diocese of Portland, Maine. [Portland. Church World Pub. Co.] v. 28cm. [BX1417.P63A5] 59-47667
1. Portland. Me. (Diocese)—Direct.

BURLINGTON, Vt. (Diocese) 282.743
1853-1953: one hundred years of achievement by the Catholic Church in the Diocese of Burlington, Vermont...Centenary memorial book.... Lowell, Mass., Sullivan Bros., printers [1953] 223p. illus. 30cm. [BX1417.B85A5] 53-33410
1. Burlington, Vt. (Diocese)-Hist. I. Title.

FROST, John Edward. 282.744
Channels of grace; a souvenir of the Catholic Archdiocese of Boston. Edited by Warren Carberg. Boston, Hawthorne Press [1954] 1v. (unpaged) illus., ports. 27cm. On cover: A 'Fancy this' sketch book. [BX1417.B6F7] 55-18764
1. Boston (Archdiocese) I. Title.

DWYER, Margaret Clifford. 282.744'23
Centennial history of St. Mary of the Assumption Church, Northampton, Massachusetts, 1866-1966. South Hackensack, N.J., Custombook, c1966. 1 v. (unpaged) illus. (part col.) ports. (part col.) 28 cm. Includes bibliography. [BX4603.N7S3] 66-30710
1. Northampton, Mass. St. Mary of the Assumption Church. I. Title.

SPRINGFIELD, Mass. 282.74426
Saint Paul The Apostle Church. Saint Paul the Apostle Church.
Commemorating the dedication of Saint Paul the Apostle Church. Springfield, Massachusetts. [Springfield] 1964. 1 v. (unpaged) illus. (part col.) ports. (part col.) 28 cm. [BX4603.S75S32] 63-22184
I. Title.

WALTHAM, Mass. Sacred Heart Church. 282.7444
Sacred Heart Church, Waltham, Massachusetts. Founded 1922, new church dedicated 1964. South Hackensack, N.J., Custombook, c1963. 1 v. (unpaged) illus. (part col.) ports. (part col.) 28 cm. [BX4603.W27S2] 63-21631
I. Title.

MERWICK, Donna. 282'.744'61
Boston priests, 1848-1910; a study of social and intellectual change. Cambridge, Mass., Harvard University Press, 1973. xiii, 276 p. 22 cm. Bibliography: p. 249-259. [BX1418.B7M43] 72-79309 ISBN 0-674-07975-2 12.00
1. Catholic Church—Clergy. 2. Catholic Church in Boston. 3. Clergy—Massachusetts—Boston. I. Title.

BRAINTREE, Mass. St. Thomas More Church. 282.7447
Commemorating the 25th anniversary of St. Thomas More Church, Braintree, Massachusetts [Braintree? c1963] 1 v. (unpaged) illus. (part col.) ports. 29 cm. Cover title. [BX4603.B76S3] 63-21629
I. Title.

CONLEY, Patrick T. 282'.745
Catholicism in Rhode Island : the formative era / Patrick T. Conley, Matthew J. Smith. [Providence] : Diocese of Providence, 1976. xiv, 173 p. : ill. ; 30 cm. Includes index. Bibliography: p. 153-162. [BX1415.R5C6] 76-62863
1. Catholic Church in Rhode Island—History. 2. Rhode Island—Church history. I. Smith, Matthew J., joint author. II. Title.

PROVIDENCE (Diocese) 282.745
The synod of the Diocese of Providence. Providence. v. 24cm. [BX1417.P7A25] 54-19221
I. Title.

WALSH, Richard A. 282'.745'2
The centennial history of Saint Edward Church, Providence, Rhode Island, 1874-1974, by Richard A. Walsh. With an introd. by Louis E. Gelineau. [Providence? R.I., 1974] 242 p. illus. 24 cm. Bibliography: p. [240]-242. [BX4603.P7S258] 74-163508
1. Saint Edward Church, Providence. 2. Providence—Biography. I. Title.

HARTFORD (Archdiochese) Synod. 1st, 1959. 282.7463
First Synod of the Archidocese of Hartford, celebrated April 15, 1959, by by His Excellency, the Most Reverend Henry J. O'Brien, DD., Archbishop of Hartford [at] Church of Saint Lawrence O'Toole, Hartford, Connecticut. [Hartford, Hartford Roman Catholic Diocesan Corp., c1959] xxvii, 111p. 24cm. [BX1417.H3A28] 60-43103
I. Title.

BROWNE, Henry Joseph, 1919- 282.747
St. Ann's on East Twelfth Street, New York City, 1852-1952. New York, Roman Catholic Church of St. Ann, 1952. 65 p. illus. 21 cm. [BX4603.N6S25] 52-64995
1. New York, St. Ann's Church (Catholle) I. Title.

HOGUE, Roswell A 1890- 282.747
Centennial, 1853-1953: St.Peter's Roman Catholic Church Plattsburgh, N. Y. [Plattsburg? 1953] 182p. illus. 22cm. [BX4603.P6H6] 54-20985
1. Plattsburg, N. Y. St. Peter's Church. I. Title.

MAKULEC, Louis L 1907- 282.747
Church of St. Stanislaus Bishop and Martyr. on East Seventh Street in New York City, 1874-1954. New York, Roman Catholic Church of St. Stanislaus, B. M., 1954. 240p. illus. 27cm. [BX4603.N6S72] 54-11904
1. New York. St. Stanislaus' Church. I. Title.

TAYLOR, Mary Christine. 282'.747
A history of the foundations of Catholicism in Northern New York / by Mary Christine Taylor. New York : United States Catholic Historical Society, 1976. xi, 440 p., [1] leaf of plates : ill. ; 23 cm. (Monograph series - United States Catholic Historical Society ; 32) Bibliography: p. 404-438. [BX1415.N7T39] 77-359034
1. Catholic Church in New York (State)—History. 2. New York (State)—Church history. I. Title. II. Series: United States Catholic Historical Society. Monograph series ; 32.

BURTON, Katherine (Kurz) 282.7471
The dream lives forever; the story of St. Patrick's Cathedral. Foreword by Francis Cardinal Spellman. New York, Longmans, Green, [c.]1960. xiii, 238p. col. front. 22cm. (2p. bibl.) 60-10210 4.50
1. New York, St. Patrick's Cathedral. I. Title.

BURTON, Katherine (Kurz) 1890- 282.7471
The dream lives forever; the story of St. Patrick's Cathedral. Foreword by Francis Cardinal Spellman. [1st ed.] New York, Longmans, Green, 1960. 238p. illus. 21cm. [BX4603.N6A33] 60-10210
1. New York. St. Patrick's Cathedral. I. Title.

DOLAN, Jay P., 1936- 282'.747'1
The immigrant church : New York's Irish and German Catholics, 1815-1865 / Jay P. Dolan ; foreword by Martin E. Marty. Baltimore : Johns Hopkins University Press, [1975] xiv, 221 p. : ill. ; 21 cm. Includes bibliographical references and index. [BX1418.N5D64] 75-12552 ISBN 0-8018-1708-0 : 10.00
1. Catholics in New York (City) 2. Catholics, Irish. 3. Catholics, German. I. Title.

KELLY, George Anthony, 282'.747'1
1916-
Catholics and the practice of the faith, 1967 and 1971, by George A. Kelly. New York, St. John's University Press [1972] 2 v. illus. 23 cm. Contents.Contents.—pt. 1. Catholic youth.—pt. 2. Catholic parents. Includes bibliographical references. [BX1418.N5K44] 75-187342
1. Catholics in New York (City) 2. Family—Religious life. I. Title.

KELLY, George Anthony, 282'.747'1
1916-
The parish, as seen from the Church of St. John the Evangelist, New York City, 1840-1973, by George A. Kelly. New York, St. John's University [1973] xii, 163 p. illus. 26 cm. Bibliography: p. 157-160. [BX4603.N6S374] 73-4567 ISBN 0-87075-067-4 10.00
1. St. John the Evangelist Catholic Church, New York. I. Title.

NEW York, Church of Our 282.7471
Lady of Esperanza.
Our Lady of Esperanza, New York: fiftieth anniversary. [New York, 624 W. 156 St., Author, 1963] unpaged. illus. 28cm. 63-17841 apply
I. Title.

DEER Park, N.Y.St. 282.74721
Cyril and St. Methodius Church
Saint Cyril and Saint Methodius Church, Deer Park, Long Island, New York, [Deer Park, 1963] 1 v. (unpaged) illus. (part col.) 28 cm. Cover title. 63-22183
I. Title.

NEW York, St. Nicholas 282.747275
of Tolentine Church
St. Nicholas of Tolentine Church, Bronx, New York, founded 1906. New York, Custombook, c.1963. [72]p. illus. (pt. col.) ports. (pt. col.) 28cm. 63-21630 5.00
I. Title.

NEW York. St. Nicholas 282.747275
of Tolentine Church.
St. Nicholas of Tolentine Church Bronx, New York, founded 1906. New York, Custombook, c1963. [72] p. illus. (part col.) ports. (part col.) 28 cm. [BX4603.N6S55] 63-21630
I. Title.

OUR Lady of Angels 282'.747'275
Parish, Bronx, New York.
Our Lady of Angels Parish, Bronx, New York. White Plains, N.Y. : Monarch Pub., c1974. [76] p. : ill. ; 28 cm. [BX1418.B78O9 1974] 74-14423
1. Our Lady of Angels Parish, Bronx, New York.

THE Beacon 282'.747'43
(Washington D.C.)
Twenty-fifth anniversary [1926-1951] St. Francis Xavier Parish, Washington, D.C. [Washington, 1951?] unpaged. illus. 28cm. 'Special silver jubilee edition sWashington, D.C. St. Francis Xavier Church. [BX4603.W32S324] 54-34430
I. Title.

BONTA, Robert Eugene. 282'.747'43
The cross in the valley; the history of the establishment of the Catholic Church in the northern San Josquin Valley of California up to 1863. [Fresno, Calif.] Academy of California Church History [1963] xxi, 308 p. illus., ports., mpas. 22 cm. Bibliography: p. 265-278. [BX4603.S8S2] 63-23225
1. Stockton, Calif. St. Mary of the Assumption. 2. Catholic Church in San Josquin Valley, Calif. I. Title.

BRENNAN, Philip 282'.747'43
Vincent, 1926-
St. Mary of the Immaculate Conception, Fredericksburg, Virginia; the story of a church, 1858-1958. Centennial celebration, December 10, 1958. [Fredericksburg? Va., 1958 or 9] 55p. illus. 24cm. [BX4603.F74S3] 61-21755
1. Fredericksburg, Va. St. Mary of the Immaculate Conception (Church) I. Title.

BROWNE, Henry Joseph, 282'.747'43
1919-
The parish of St. Michael, 1857-1957; a century of grace on the West Side. New York, Church of St. Michael, 1957. 72p. 26cm. [BX4603.N6S4] 58-34895
1. New York, Church of St. Michael. I. Title.

KOWRACH, Edward J 282'.747'43
How silently; a history of the Catholic Church of the Big Bend missions and St. Anne Church, Medical Lake. [Medical Lake? Wash., 1963] 94 p. illus. 20 cm. Includes bibliography. [BX4603.M4S3] 64-32521
1. Medical Lake, Wash. St. Anne Church. 2. Spokane (Diocese) I. Title.

KUCAS, Antanas, 1900- 282'.747'43
Sv. Petro lietuviu parapija South Bostone. The history of St. Peter's Lituanian parish, South Boston. Adapted from the Lithuanian text by Albert J. Contons. Boston, 1956. 303 p. illus., ports. 23 cm. Lithuanian and English. "Auksiniam parapijos jubillejui pamineti, 1904-1954." Bibliography: p. 299. [BX4603.B7S53] 64-40740
1. South Boston. St. Peter's Church. I. Title.

MCNAMARA, Robert 282'.747'43
Francis, 1910-
Historic St. Mary's Church, Albany, New York; being the annals of the second Roman Catholic parish established in New York State and the original cathedral church of the Catholic Diocese of Albany. First church dedicated Anno Domini 1798. By Robert F. McNamara, with decorations and sketches by John C. Meninhan. [Albany, St. Mary's] Parish, 1973. 62 p. illus. 23 cm. [BX4603.A62S25] 72-97108
1. Albany. St. Mary's Church. I. Title.

NEW York. Queen of 282'.747'43
Angels Church.
Queen of Angels Church, Sunnyside, New York; dedication May 23, 1964. [South Hackensack, N.J., Custombook, 1964] 1 v. (unpaged) illus (part col.) ports. 15 x 22 cm. [BX4603.N6Q45] 64-21002
I. Title.

NIES, Frederick C 282'.747'43
The story of St. Boniface Church, 1857-1957, on the occasion of its 100th anniversary. [Erie Pa., 1957] 213p. illus. 29cm. [BX4603.E6S3] 57-44917
1. Eire, Pa. St. Boniface Church. I. Title.

REILLY, George. 282'.747'43
Commemorating St. Andrew's 75th anniversary and dedication of our new church. Westwood, New Jersey. History compiled and prepared by George Reilly (Westwood] c1964. 1 v. (unpaged) illus. (part col.) ports. (part col.) 28 cm. [BX4603.W54S2] 64-19837
1. Westwood, N.J. St. Andrew's Church. I. Title.

SPRINGFIELD, Mass. 282'.747'43
St. Patrick's Church.
Commemorating the dedication of St. Patrick's Church, Springfield, Massachusetts. [Springfield] 1964. 1 v. (unpaged) illus. (part col.) ports. 28 cm. [BX4603.S75S3] 64-36024
I. Title.

TAYLOR, Mary 282'.747'5
Christine.
A history of Catholicism in the north country. [Camden, N.Y., Printed by A. M. Farnsworth Sons, 1972] xii, 282 p. illus. 28 cm. On cover: Diocese of Ogdensburg centennial, 1872-1972. Includes bibliographical references. [BX1417.O3T38] 72-188926
1. Ogdensburg, N.Y. (Diocese) I. Title. II. Title: Diocese of Ogdensburg centennial, 1872-1972.

GAUTHIER, Jeffrey A. 282'.747'54
The heritage of Saint Matthew's Parish of Black Brook, New York, 1832-1876-1976 / by Jeffrey A. Gauthier. [Black Brook? N.Y. : Gauthier?, c1977] 44 p. : ill. ; 27 cm. Cover title. Bibliography: p. 43. [BX4603.B52S243] 77-150937
1. Saint Matthew's Parish, Black Brook, N.Y. I. Title.

MCNAMARA, Robert 282.747'8
Francis, 1910-
The Diocese of Rochester, 1868-1968, by Robert F McNamara. with a foreword by Fulton J. Sheen [Rochester, N.Y.] Diocese of Rochester, 1968. xx, 618 p. illus., maps (on lining papers), ports. 24 cm. Bibliographical references included in "Notes" (p. 539-603) [BX1417.R6M3] 68-19638
1. Rochester, N.Y. (Diocese)—History. I. Title.

MI-CHA-EL : 282'.747'89
a history of St. Michael's Parish, the Diocese of Rochester, from 1874 to 1974. [Rochester, N.Y. : s.n., 1974] 48 p. : ill. ; 28 cm. Cover title: Michael, who is like God? [BX4603.R58S245] 75-329964
1. St. Michael's Parish, Rochester, N.Y. 2. Rochester, N.Y.—Biography. I. Title: Michael, who is like God?

CATHOLIC telephone guide and directory, central and western Pennsylvania. 282.748
Loretto, Pa. v. 23 cm. [BX1415.P4C3] 52-43123
1. Catholic Church in Pennsylvania—Direct.

GALLAGHER, John P., 1924- 282.748
A century of history; the Diocese of Scranton, 1868-1968, by John P. Gallagher. Foreword by J. Carroll McCormick. [Scranton] Diocese of Scranton [1968] xiv, 615 p. illus., map (on lining paper), ports. 23 cm. Bibliographical references included in "Notes" (p. 463-524) [BX1417.S4G3] 68-56284 9.50
1. Scranton (Diocese)—History. I. Title.

HAMMILL, Martina. 282.748
The expansion of the Catholic Church in Pennsylvania; a brief sketch of the organization and expansion of the church from the colonial period to the present. [Pittsburgh? 1960] 205p. 24cm. Includes bibliography. [BX1415.P4H3] 61-21871
1. Catholic Church in Pennsylvania—Hist. I. Title.

BARRETT, Joseph P. 282'.748'11
The sesquicentennial history of Saint Denis Parish, 1825-1975 : an Augustinian suburban parish with roots deep in the past / by Joseph P. Barrett, in cooperation with Edwin T. Grimes. Devon, Pa. : W. T. Cooke Pub. Co., [1975] xii, 212 p. : ill. ; 32 cm. Cover title: Saint Denis sesquicentennial, 1825-1975. Includes index. Bibliography: p. 209-210. [BX4603.H35S242] 74-29440
1. Saint Denis Church, Havertown, Pa. I. Grimes, Edwin T., joint author. II. Title. III. Title: Saint Denis sesquicentennial, 1825-1975.

CAMPBELL, William 282.74811
Edward, 1898-
... *how unsearchable His ways;* one hundred twenty-fifth anniversary, Saint Patrick's Church [by] William E. Campbell. [Lebanon? Pa., 1965] xxxii, 208 p. illus. (part col.) plans, ports. 26 cm. [BX4603.P52S49] 64-66418
1. Philadelphia. St. Patrick's Church. I. Title.

PHILADELPHIA. St. 282.74811
Agatha's Church.
Saint Agatha's Church, Philadelphia, Pennsylvania. South Hackensack, N.J., Custombook [1966] 1v. (unpaged) illus. (part col.) ports. 28 cm. Addenda slip inserted. [BX4603.P52S24] 66-6777
1. Philadelphia. St. Agatha's Church. I. Title.

FOSTER, John J., 282'.748'19
1912-
The story of Assumption of B.V.M. Church, Lebanon, Pennsylvania, compiled by John J. Foster. Lebanon, Pa., 1951. 118 p. illus. 22 cm. [BX4603.L35S243] 75-303539
1. Lebanon, Pa. St. Mary's Catholic Church. I. Title.

25TH anniversary of the Queen of the Most Holy Rosary Church, October, 1975, Elysburg, Pennsylvania. 282'.748'31
New York : Park Pub. Co., c1975. [32] p. : ill. ; 26 cm. [BX4603.E47O437] 75-41695
1. Queen of the Most Holy Rosary Church, Elysburg, Pa.

PITTSTON, Pa. St. 282.74832
Mary's Assumption Church.
St. Mary's Assumption Church, Pittston, Pennsylvania; 1863-1963 one hundred years. New York, Custombook, 1963. 1 v. (unpaged) illus. (part col.) 28 cm. [BX4603.P56S2] 63-21628
I. Title.

CATOIR, John T 282.749
A brief history of the Catholic Church in New Jersey, by John T. Catoir. [Clifton, N.J., c1965] iii, 74 p. Bibliography: p. 66-71. [BX1415.N5C3] 66-40655
1. Catholic Church in New Jersey — Hist. I. Title.

OUR Lady of Mount 282'.749'26
Carmel Church, Bayonne, N.J. Diamond Jubilee Book Committee.
Our Lady of Mount Carmel Church, Bayonne, New Jersey, U.S.A. : seventy-five years, 1898-1973. [Bayonne, N.J. : Our Lady of Mt. Carmel Church Diamond Jubilee Book Committee], c1974. 623 p., [2] fold. leaves of plates : ill. ; 32 cm. English or Polish. [BX1418.B3O9 1974] 75-309828
1. Our Lady of Mount Carmel Church, Bayonne, N.J.

FICHTER, Joseph Henry, 282.75
1908-
Southern parish. Chicago, University of Chicago Press [1951- v. illus. 24 cm. Contents.v. 1. Dynamics of a city church. [BX1407.S6F5] 51-6359
1. City churches. 2. Parishes—Southern States. 3. Social surveys—Southern States. 4. Catholics in the Southern States. I. Title.

O'CONNELL, Jeremiah 282.75
Joseph, 1821-1894
Catholicity in the Carolinas and Georgia: leaves of its history. Westminister, Md., 73 W. Main St., Ars Sacra, 1964. 647p. port. 19cm. Bibl. 40-20196 15.00
1. Catholic church in North Carolina—Hist. 2. Catholic church in South Carolina—Hist. 3. Catholic church in Georgia—Hist. I. Title.

BALTIMORE. St. John the 282.752
Evangelist Church.
St. John the Evangelist Church, Baltimore, Maryland, 1853-1953. [Baltimore] 1953. 110 p. illus. 29 cm. [BX4603.B3S42] 54-925
I. Title.

CANN, Joseph C. 282'.752'38
History of Saint Francis Xavier Church and Bohemia Plantation, now known as Old Bohemia, Warwick, Maryland / researched by the Old Bohemia Historical Society's History Committee, Joseph C. Cann, chairman ... [et al.] ; compiled and edited by Joseph C. Cann. [s.l.] : The Society, c1976. xxii, 271 p., [1] leaf of plates : ill. (some col.) ; 24 cm. Bibliography: p. 263. [BX4603.W3S342] 76-151886
1. Saint Francis Xavier Church, Warwick, Md. 2. Bohemia Plantation, Md. 3. Church records and registers—Maryland—Warwick. I. Old Bohemia Historical Society. History Committee. II. Title.

ST. Ignatius Church, 282'.752'51
Oxon Hill, Md.
St. Ignatius Church, Oxon Hill, Maryland. [White Plains, N.Y.] : Monarch Pub., c1974. [32] p. : ill. ; 28 cm. [BX4603.O93S344 1974] 74-17834
1. St. Ignatius Church, Oxon Hill, Md.

JOERNDT, Clarence V., 282'.752'74
1898-
St. Ignatius, Hickory, and its missions, by Clarence V. Joerndt. [Baltimore, Printed by Publication Press, 1972] xii, 536 p. illus. 24 cm. Includes bibliographical references. [BX4603.H52S344] 72-92408 11.00
1. St. Ignatius Church, Hickory, Md. 2. Hickory, Md.—Biography. I. Title.

HUTZELL, Rita Clark. 282'.752'92
Mother of churches : a history of St. Mary's Church, Hagerstown, Maryland / by Rita Clark Hutzell. [Hagerstown, Md.] : Saint Mary's Parish, 1976. 84 p. : ill. ; 27 cm. Includes bibliographical references. [BX4603.H26S344] 76-24141
1. Saint Mary's Parish, Hagerstown, Md. I. Title.

GATTI, Lawrence P, 1914- 282.753
Historic St. Stephen's; an account of its eighty-five years, 1867-1952, on the occasion of the silver jubilee of the present pastor, Reverend Joseph F. Denges. Washington [1952] 144 p. illus. 23 cm. [BX4603.W32S36] 52-64453
1. Washington, D. C. St. Stephen's Church (Catholic) I. Title.

LANGLEY, Harold D. 282.753
St. Stephen Martyr Church and the community, 1867-1967 [by] Harold D. Langley. Washington [1968] vi, 131 p. illus. (part col.), facsims., ports. 29 cm. "Sponsored by the St. Stephen's Centennial Committee." Bibliography: p. 131. [BX4603.W32S4] 68-57029
1. Washington, D.C. St. Stephen's Church (Catholic) I. Washington, D.C. St. Stephen's Church (Catholic) Centennial Committee. II. Title.

MCKENNA, Bernard 282.753
Aloysius.
A song in stone to Mary, as told by Bernard A. McKenna to the author Victor F. O Daniel. Philadelphia [1953] ixxxvi, 509p. illus. ports. facsims. 24cm. [BX4603.W32N32] 53-20857
1. Washington, D. C. National Shrine of the Immaculate Conception. I. O'Daniel, Victor Francis, 1868- II. Title.

RODRIGUES, Jeanne. 282'.755'291
St. Mary's, Fairfax Station, Virginia : the beginnings and growth of a community / by Jeanne Rodrigues with William Hammond. Fairfax Station, Va. : St. Mary's Church, [1975] 48 p. : ill. ; 21 cm. Bibliography: p. 44-48. [BX4603.F26S247] 75-13488 2.00
1. St. Mary's Church, Fairfax Station, Va. I. Hammond, William, joint author.

BAILEY, James Henry 282.755451
History of St. Peter's Church, Richmond, Virginia: 125 years, 1834-1959. [Richmond, Va., 1107 E. Cary St. Lewis Printing Co., 1959] 81p. illus. 21cm. (3p. bibl.) 59-3861 pap., gratis
1. Richmond, St. Peter's Church. I. Title.

O'CONNELL, Jeremiah 282'.756
Joseph, 1821-1894.
Catholicity in the Carolinas and Georgia: leaves of its history ... A.D. 1820 - A.D. 1878. New York, D. & J. Sadlier. [Spartanburg, S.C., Reprint Co., 1972, c1879] 647 p. ports. 23 cm. Includes bibliographical references. [BX1410.O3 1972] 73-187371 ISBN 0-87152-099-0
1. Catholic Church in North Carolina—History. 2. Catholic Church in South Carolina—History. 3. Catholic Church in Georgia—History. I. Title.

GANNON, Michael V 282.759
The cross in the sand; the early Catholic Church in Florida, 1513-1870 [by] Michael V. Gannon. Gainesville, University of Florida Press, 1965. xv, 210 p. illus. facsims., maps, plans, ports. 27 cm. "Sources": p. 191-198. [BX1415.F55G3] 65-27283
1. Catholic Church in Florida — Hist. 2. Missions — Florida — Hist. I. Title.

GANNON, Michael V. 282.759
The cross in the sand; the early Catholic Church in Florida, 1513-1870. Gainesville, Univ. of Fla. Pr. [c]1965. xv, 210p. illus., facsims., maps, plans, ports. 27cm. Bibl. [BX1415.F55G3] 65-27283 6.00
1. Catholic Church in Florida—Hist. 2. Missions—Florida—Hist. I. Title.

ST. Martha's Catholic 282'.759'61
Parish, Sarasota, Fla. History Committee.
The story of St. Martha's Catholic Parish : Sarasota, Florida, 1912-1977 / compiled by the Parish History Committee. [Sarasota, Fla.] : St. Martha's Catholic Parish, 1977. vii, 325 p. : ill. ; 22 cm. Bibliography: p. 291. [BX4603.S59S157] 78-100726
1. St. Martha's Catholic Parish, Sarasota, Fla. I. Title.

CARROLL, Mary Teresa 282'.76
Austin, Mother, d.1909.
A Catholic history of Alabama and the Floridas. Freeport, N.Y., Books for Libraries Press [1970] 373 p. 23 cm. "First published 1908." Includes bibliographical references. [BX1410.C3 1970] 70-124228
1. Catholic Church in the Southern States—History. I. Title. II. Title: Alabama and the Floridas.

PILLAR, James L. 282.762
The Catholic Church in Mississippi, 1837-65. New Orleans, Hauser [c.1964] xviii, 380p. illus., ports., maps. 24cm. Bibl. 63-23197 8.00
1. Natchez-Jackson (Diocese) 2. Catholic Church in Mississippi. I. Title.

PILLAR, James L. 282.762
The Catholic Church in Mississippi, 1837-65 New Orleans. Hauser Press, [1964] xviii, 380 p. illus. ports., maps. 24 cm. Bibliography: p. [349]-359. [BX1415.M7P5] 63-23197
1. Natchez-Jackson (Diocese) 2. Catholic Church in Mississippi. I. Title.

BEZOU, Henry C., comp. 282.763
New Orleans (Archdiocese) The necrology of the Archdiocese of New Orleans, 1702-1964, compiled by Henry C. Bezou. Foreword by John P. Cody. [New Orleans, 1964] [77] p. 14 x 16 cm. [BX1417.N35A5] 64-66219
1. Clergy — New Orleans (Archdiocese) 2. Registers of births, etc. — Louisiana. I. Title.

NEW Orleans. St. 282.763
Patrick's Church.
St. Patrick's of New Orleans, 1833-1958; commemorative essays for the 125th anniversary, by Roger Baudier [and others] Edited by Charles L. Dufour. [1st ed.] New Orleans [1958] 137p. illus. 27cm. [BX4603.N46S6] 58-11207
I. Baudier, Roger, 1893- II. Dufour, Charles L., ed. III. Title.

HUBER, Leonard Victor, 282.763355
1903-
The Basilica on Jackson Square and predecessors, dedicated to St. Louis King of France, 1727-1965, by Leonard V. Huber and Samuel Wilson, Jr. [1st ed. New Orleans? 1965] 80 p. illus., facsims., ports. 24 cm. Bibliography: p. 77-78. [BX4603.N46B33] 65-26657
1. New Orleans. Basilica of St. Louis King of France. I. Wilson, Samuel, 1911- joint author. II. Title.

ANCONA, Angelo 282.763'42
Anthony.
The church at Franklin, Louisiana, before 1940. Lafayette, La., U.S.L. Press, 1968. vi, 132 l. illus., map, ports. 28 cm. Thesis (M.A.)—Notre Dame Seminary. Bibliography: leaves [128]-132. [BX4603.F67A82] 79-12156
1. Franklin La. Assumption of the Blessed Virgin Mary Church. I. Title.

MARY Xavier, Sister, 282'.764'113
1890-
A century of sacrifice; the history of the cathedral parish, Corpus Christi, Texas, 1853-1953, by Mary Xavier. [Corpus Christi? Tex.] 1953. vii, 64, [2] p. illus. 22 cm. Bibliography: p. [65]-[66] [BX4603.C77C67] 73-155549
1. Corpus Christi Cathedral. I. Title.

ST. James Catholic 282'.764'34
Church, Seguin, Tex.
The centennial story, 1873-1973. Seguin, Tex. : St. James Catholic Church, [1973?] 64 p. : ill. ; 28 cm. Cover title. [BX4603.S63S347 1970z] 75-331288
1. St. James Catholic Church, Seguin, Tex. 2. Seguin, Tex.—Biography. I. Title.

ST. Louis Church, 282'.764'42
Castroville; a history of the Catholic Church in Castroville, Texas. Written and compiled by Ted Gittinger [and others. Castroville, Tex., St. Louis Catholic Church, 1973] 137 p. illus. 24 cm. Bibliography: p. [123]-[124] [BX4603.C37S276] 74-155414
1. St. Louis Church, Castroville, Tex. I. Gittinger, Ted.

KENNEDY, Edward. 282'.764'492
A parish remembers; fifty years of Oblate endeavour in the valley of the Rio Grande (1909-1959) [Mercedes, Tex., Mercedes Enterprise, 1959] 64 p. illus. 19 cm. Includes bibliographical references. [BX1418.M4K46] 74-153839
1. Catholic Church in Mercedes, Tex. 2. Missions—Mercedes, Tex. I. Title.

MATTINGLY, Mary Ramona, 282'.769
Sister.
The Catholic Church on the Kentucky frontier (1785-1812). Washington, Catholic University of America, 1936. [New York, AMS Press, 1974] viii, 235 p. map. 23 cm. Reprint of the author's thesis, Catholic University of America, 1936, which was issued as v. 25 of the Catholic University of America. Studies in American church history. Bibliography: p. 219-232. [BX1415.K4M3 1974] 73-3579 ISBN 0-404-57775-X 10.00
1. Catholic Church in Kentucky—History. I. Title. II. Series: Catholic University of America. Studies in American church history, v. 25.

SPALDING, Martin John, 282.769
Abp., 1810-1872.
Sketches of the early Catholic missions of Kentucky; from their commencement in 1787 to the jubilee of 1826-7. New York, Arno Press, 1972. xvi, 308 p. 22 cm. (Religion in America, series II) Reprint of the 1844 ed. [BX1415.K4S6 1972] 70-38548 ISBN 0-405-04087-3
1. Catholic Church in Kentucky. 2. Catholic Church in Kentucky—Biography. 3. Kentucky—Church history. I. Title.

CREWS, Clyde F. 282'.769'44
Presence and possibility: Louisville Catholicism and its cathedral; an historical sketch of the Louisville Catholic experience as seen through the Cathedral of the Assumption [by] Clyde F. Crews. [Louisville? Ky., 1973] 97 p. illus. 23 cm. Bibliography: p. 92-94. [BX4603.L64C373] 73-170163
1. Cathedral of the Assumption, Louisville, Ky. I. Title.

HAMILTON, Albert, 1940- 282'.771
The Catholic journey through Ohio / by Albert Hamilton. Columbus : Catholic Conference of Ohio, 1976. 86 p. : ill. ; 26 cm. [BX1415.O3H34] 76-7828 1.95
1. Catholic Church in Ohio—History. I. Catholic Conference of Ohio. II. Title.

HYNES, Michael J 282.771
History of the Diocese of Cleveland; origin and growth, 1847-1952. [1st ed.] Cleveland, Diocese of Cleveland, 1953. 520p. illus. 25cm. [BX1417.C6H9] 53-34341
1. Cleveland (Diocese)—Hist. I. Title.

A People: 100 282'.771'32
years. [Editor in chief: Jean Jagelewski. Cambridge, Md., Western Pub. Co., c1973] 300 p. illus. 29 cm. Cover title. On spine: St. Stanislaus, 1873-1973. English or Polish. [BX4603.C65S336] 73-90634
1. St. Stanislaus Church, Cleveland. I. Jagelewski, Jean, ed.

MCAVOY, Thomas Timothy, 282.772
1903-1969.
The Catholic Church in Indiana, 1789-1834. New York, AMS Press, 1967 [c1940] 226 p. 23 cm. (Studies in history, economics, and public law, no. 471) Originally presented as the author's thesis, Columbia University. Bibliography: p. 209-219. [BX1415.I6M2 1967] 75-29193
1. Catholic Church in Indiana—History. 2. Catholics in Indiana. 3. French in Indiana. I. Title. II. Series: Columbia studies in the social sciences, no. 471.

MCNAMARA, William, 1895- 282'.772
The Catholic Church on the northern Indiana frontier, 1789-1844. Washington, Catholic University of America, 1931. [New York, AMS Press, 1974] vii, 84 p. 23 cm. Reprint of the author's thesis, Catholic University of America, 1931, which was issued as v. 12 of the Catholic University of America. Studies in American church history. Bibliography: p. 82-84. [BX1415.I6M3 1974] 73-3567 ISBN 0-404-57762-8 6.00
1. Catholic Church in Indiana—History. 2. Catholic Church—Missions. 3. Indians of North America—Missions. 4. Indians of North America—Indiana. I. Title. II. Series: Catholic University of America. Studies in American church history, v. 12.

SCHULTHEIS, Rose May 282.772
Dawson, 1890-
Pioneer bishops of Indiana; sketches of the first four bishops whose combined work was the foundation, organization and establishment of the Catholic Church in Indiana, 1834-1877: Simon Brute de Remur, 1834-1839, Celestine de la Hailandiere, 1839-1847. John Stephen Bazin, 1847-1848 [and] Maurice de St. Palais, 1848-1877. [Vincennes? Ind.] 1950. [47] p. illus., ports. 24 cm. Bibliography: p. [6] [BX1415.I6S4] 50-12530
1. Bishops — Indiana. 2. Catholic Church in Indiana. I. Title.

FRANCISCANS, Province of 282.773
the Saored Heart.
History of St. Peter's Church, Chicago, Illinois. Chicago, c1953. 158p. illus. 21cm. [BX4603.C5S32] 53-39540
1. Chicago. St. Peter's Church (Catholic) I. Title.

MCMAHON, John Joseph, 282.773
1913-
Catholic map directory of the Chicago metropolitan area. [1st ed. Chicago, D. F. Keller Co., 1955] 112p. maps (1 fold.) 23cm. [BX1415.I3M25] 55-33816
1. Catholic Church in Illinois—Direct. I. Title.

MOORE, Stephen N 1886- 282.773
History of Holy Trinity Parish, Bloomington, Illinois. [Streator? Ill., 1952] 280 p. illus. 22 cm. [BX4603.B6H6] 52-38627
1. Bloomington, Ill. Holy Trinity Church. I. Title.

TELEPHONE directory and 282.773
Catholic guide of Chicago Archdiocese. Chicago, Catholic Service Co. v. illus. 24cm. annual. [BX1417.C46T4] 53-31155
1. Chicago (Archdiocese)—Direct.

MERTZ, James J., 282'.773'11
1882-
Madonna della Strada Chapel, Loyola University : an apostolate of love / James J. Mertz. [Chicago] : Loyola University Press, c1975. 62 p. : ill. ; 23 cm. [BX4603.C5M35] 75-325365 ISBN 0-8294-0246-2
1. Loyola University, Chicago. Madonna della Strada Chapel. I. Title.

SWEETSER, Thomas P. 282'.773'11
The Catholic parish : shifting membership in a changing church / by Thomas P. Sweetser. Chicago : Center for the Scientific Study of Religion, [1974] x, 134 p. : ill. ; 23 cm. (Studies in religion and society) Includes index. Bibliography: p. 98-100. [BX1418.C4S93] 74-84543 ISBN 0-913348-06-6 : 3.95
1. Catholic Church in Chicago metropolitan area—Case studies. 2. Parishes—Chicago metropolitan area—Case studies. I. Title. II. Series: Studies in religion and society series.

MILLER, Robert R. 282'.773'31
That all may be one : a history of the Rockford Diocese / by Robert R. Miller. Rockford, Ill. : Diocese of Rockford, c1976. xvi, 368 p. : ill. ; 29 cm. Includes index. Bibliography: p. 355-356. [BX1417.R63M54] 76-43531
1. Catholic Church. Diocese of Rockford, Ill. I. Title.

WALKER, Fintan Glenn, 282'.773'9
1896-
The Catholic Church in the meeting of two frontiers: the southern Illinois country (1763-1793). Washington, Catholic University of America, 1935. [New York, AMS Press, 1974] xiv, 170 p. 23 cm. Reprint of the author's thesis, Catholic University of America, 1935, which was issued as v. 19 of the Catholic University of America. Studies in American church history. Bibliography: p. 148-163. [BX1415.I3W3 1974] 73-3574 ISBN 0-404-57769-5 7.50
1. Catholic Church in Illinois—History. 2. Catholic Church in Indiana—History. 3. Catholic Church—Missions. I. Title. II. Series: Catholic University of America. Studies in American church history, v. 19.

WITTENAUER, Josephine 282'.773'91
Carole.
History of Saint Augustine of Canterbury Parish, 1824-1974. Hecker, Ill. : St. Augustine of Canterbury Church, [1974] xxii, 194 p. : ill. ; 23 cm. Bibliography: p. 188-189. [BX4603.H4S248] 75-304583
1. Saint Augustine of Canterbury Parish, Hecker, Ill. 2. Hecker, Ill.—Biography. I. Title.

PARE, George. 282.774
The Catholic Church in Detroit, 1701-1888 Detroit, Gabriel Richard Press, 1951. xv, 717 p. illus., ports., maps (on lining papers) 24 cm. Bibliographical footnotes. [BX1418.D6P3] 51-32288
1. Catholic Church in Detroit. I. Title.

MECKE, Theodore H. 282'.774'33
A brief history of St. Paul's Parish, Grosse Pointe Farms, Michigan [by Theodore H. Mecke. 1st ed. Grosse Pointe Farms, Mich., 1973] 34, [1] p. 19 cm. Bibliography: p. [35] [BX4603.G76S345] 73-80650
1. St. Paul's Church, Grosse Pointe Farms, Mich. I. Title.

MADISON, Wis. (Diocese) 282.775
Synod. 1st, 1956.
First synod of the diocese of Madison, celebrated February 22, 1956, by William P. O'Connor, Bishop of Madison. [Madison, 1956] 158p. 24cm. [BX1417.M3A5 1956] 56-35685
I. O Connor, William Patrick, Bp., 1886- II. Title.

MADISON, Wis. (Doocese) 282.775
Synod. 1st, 1956.
First synod of the diocese of Madison, celebrated February 22, 1956, by William P. O'Connor, Bishop of Madison. [Madison, 1956] 158p. 24cm. [BX1417.M3A5 1956] 56-35685
I. O'Connor, William Patrick, Bp., 1886- II. Title.

RUMMEL, Leo. 282'.775
History of the Catholic Church in Wisconsin / Leo Rummel. Madison : Wisconsin State Council, Knights of Columbus, 1976. viii, 261 p., [8] leaves of plates : ill. ; 25 cm. Includes bibliographical references. [BX1415.W6R85] 75-32625
1. Catholic Church in Wisconsin. I. Knights of Columbus. Wisconsin State Council. II. Title.

ANDERL, Stephen, 1910- 282.77547
Parish of the Assumption; the life and times of the Mystical Christ in Durand, Wisconsin, 1860-1960. Park Falls, Wis., Weber Pub. Co., 1960. 360p. illus. 21cm. Includes bibliography. [BX4603.D8A8] 61-2602
1. Durand. Wis. Congregation of the Assumption of the Blessed Virgin Mary. I. Title.

REARDON, James Michael. 282.776
The Catholic Church in the Diocese of St. Paul, from earliest origin to centennial achievement; a factual narrative. St. Paul, North Central Pub. Co., 1952. xv. 726p. illus. ports. 25cm. Bibilographical references: p. 691-707. [BX1417.S3R4] 53-82
1. St. Paul (Archdiocese)—Hist. I. Title.

VOIGT, Robert J 282.77669
Pierzana: 1865-1965; the religious and secular history of the community at Pierz, Minnesota by Robert T. Voight [Saint Cloud, Minn., Mills Creative Printing, 1965] 197 p. illus., map. ports. 24 cm. [BX4603.P53S4] 65-6684
1. Pierz, Minn. St. Joseph's Church. I. Title.

SCHUMACHER, Claire W. 282'.776'77
This is our St. Rose Church in Proctor, Minnesota : a Catholic's viewpoint of history / researched, written, and designed by Claire W. Schumacher. 1st ed. Proctor : The Church, c1976. 84 p. : ill. ; 27 cm. [BX4603.P65S347] 76-22312 ISBN 0-917378-01-6
1. St. Rose Church, Proctor, Minn. I. Title.

STORCH, Neil T. 282'.776'771
Guide to the archives and manuscripts of the Diocese of Duluth / Neil T. Storch. [Duluth : University of Minnesota, Duluth, 1977] iii, 16 p. ; 22 cm. (Social science research publications) Cover title. Includes index. [CD3319.D84S76] 77-152995
1. Catholic Church. Diocese of Duluth—Archives. I. Catholic Church. Diocese of Duluth. II. Title. III. Series.

SCHUILING, Walter 282'.776'82
John, 1953-
History of St. Philip's Parish, 1897-1975 / Walter John Schuiling. [Bemidji, Minn. : s.n.], c1977. vii, 283 p., [5] leaves of plates : ill. ; 28 cm. Thesis (M.A.)—Bemidji State University. Vita. Bibliography: p. 211-217. [BX4603.B48S247] 77-151715

1. St. Philip's Church, Bemidji, Minn. I. Title.

GREER, Edward C 282.777
Cork Hill Cathedra; the chronicle of St. Margaret's and Sacred Heart Parish, Davenport, Iowa, 1856-1956. Davenport, Idwa, Printed by Gordon Print. Co., 1956. 248p. illus. 23cm. [BX4603.D29S2] 57-4313
1. Davenport, Iowa. Sacred Heart Cathedral. 2. Davenport, Iowa (Diocese) I. Title.

GREER, Edward C 282.777
Cork Hill Cathedral; the chronicle of St. Margaret's and Sacred Heart Parish, Davenport, Iowa, 1856-1956. Davenport, Iowa, Printed by Gordon Print. Co., 1956. 248p. illus. 23cm. [BX4603.D29S2] 57-43132
1. Davenport, Iowa. Sacred Heart Cathedral. 2. Davenport, Iowa (Diocese) I. Title.

ST. Louis (Archdiocese) 282.778'6
The necrology of the Archdiocese of Saint Louis, 1705-1967. Compiled by Peter J. Rahill. Foreword by George J. Gottwald. [3d ed. St. Louis, 1968] 1 v. (unpaged) 16 cm. [BX1417.S2A42 1968] 68-20573
1. Clergy—St. Louis (Archdiocese) 2. Registers of births, etc.—Missouri. I. Rahill, Peter James, 1910- comp. II. Title.

ST. Louis (Archdiocese) 282.7786
The necrology of the Archdiocese of Saint Louis, 1705-1963. Compiled by Peter J. Rahill. Foreword by Joseph Cardinal Ritter. [St. Louis, 1964] [88] p. 14 x 16 cm. [BX1417.S2A12] 64-15628
1. Clergy—St. Louis (Archdiocese) 2. Registers of births, etc.—Missouri. I. Rahill, Peter James, 1910- comp. II. Title.

ST. Louis (Archdiocese) 282.778'6
The necrology of the Archdiocese of Saint Louis, 1705-1967. Compiled by Peter J. Rahill. Foreword by George J. Gottwald. [3d ed. St. Louis, 1968] 1 v. (unpaged) 16 cm. [BX1417.S2A42 1968] 68-20573
1. Clergy—St. Louis (Archdiocese) 2. Registers of births, etc.—Missouri. I. Rahill, Peter James, 1910- comp. II. Title.

BARRY, R. K. 282'.778'66
The history of Our Lady of Mount Carmel Parish, Baden, Missouri. Compiled by R. K. Barry. [Baden? Mo., 1972?] 48 p. illus. 28 cm. Cover title: Our Lady of Mt. Carmel centennial celebration, 1872-1972. [BX4603.B28O862] 74-152668
1. Our Lady of Mount Carmel Church, Baden, Mo. 2. Baden, Mo.—Biography. I. Title. II. Title: Our Lady of Mt. Carmel centennial celebration, 1872-1972.

FAHERTY, William 282'.778'86
Barnaby.
Dream by the river; two centuries of Saint Louis Catholicism, 1766-1967. Saint Louis, Piraeus [1973] ix, 246 p. illus. 32 cm. Includes bibliographical references. [BX1417.S2F35] 73-77204 ISBN 0-88273-213-7 12.95
1. St. Louis (Archdiocese) I. Title.

FAHERTY, William 282'.778'86
Barnaby.
Dream by the river; two centuries of Saint Louis Catholicism, 1766-1967. Saint Louis, Piraeus [1973] ix, 246 p. illus. 32 cm. Includes bibliographical references. [BX1417.S2F35] 73-77204 ISBN 0-88273-213-7 12.95
1. St. Louis (Archdiocese) I. Title.
Available from Forum House.

SALPOINTE, Jean Baptiste, 282.78
Abp., 1825-1898.
Soldiers of the cross; notes on the ecclesiastical history of New Mexico, Arizona, and Colorado. [1st ed.] Albuquerque, N.M., C. Horn [1967] xiv, 299 p. illus., facsims., ports. 24 cm. Reprint of the 1898 ed. [BX1412.S3 1967] 67-29317
1. Catholic Church in New Mexico—History. 2. Catholic Church in Arizona—History. 3. Catholic Church in Colorado—History. 4. Missions—Southwest, Old. 5. Indians of North America—Southwest, Old. I. Title.

SALPOINTE, Jean Baptiste 282.78
Abp. 1825-1898.
Soldiers of the cross; notes on the ecclesiastical history of New Mexico, Arizona, and Colorado. [1st ed.] Albuquerque, N.M., C. Horn [1967] xiv, 299 p. illus., facsims., ports. 24 cm. Reprint of the 1898 ed. [BX1412.S3] 67-29317
1. Catholic Church in New Mexico—Hist. 2. Catholic Church in Arizona—Hist. 3. Catholic Church in Colorado—Hist. 4. Missions—Southwest, Old. 5. Indians of North America—Southwest, Old. I. Title.

TOWERS of faith and 282'.781'19
courage : a pictorial history of Saint Fidelis Parish, Victoria, Kansas, Saint Ann's Parish, Walker, Kansas, Sacred Heart Parish, Emmeram, Kansas, published on the occasion of the Centennial Celebration marking the arrival of the first Volga-German immigrants in Ellis County, Kansas. Dallas : Taylor Pub. Co., c1976. 272 p. : ill. ; 29 cm. [BX1415.K3T68] 76-374435
1. Catholic Church in Ellis, Co., Kan. 2. Ellis, Co., Kan.—Church history.

CASPER, Henry Weber, 282.782
1909-
History of the Catholic Church in Nebraska. Milwaukee, Catholic Life Publications, 1960- v. illus. 23cm. Includes bibliography. [BX1415.N2C3] 60-51663
1. Catholic Church in Nebraska—Hist. I. Title.

A Bicentennial 282'.782'335
centennial history, Sacred Heart Church, Hebron, Nebraska, 1876-1976. Hebron, Neb. : Sacred Heart Church, c1976. vi, 205 p. : ill. ; 28 cm. Cover title: The bell of Sacred Heart Church. Includes index. [BX4603.H38S22] 76-24301
1. Sacred Heart Church, Hebron, Neb. 2. Hebron, Neb.—Biography. I. Title: The bell of Sacred Heart Church.

MURRAY, Robert J. 282'.783'144
A church grows on a tree claim; a history of Sacred Heart Parish, Aberdeen, South Dakota, by Robert J. Murray. [Aberdeen, S.D., Sacred Heart Parish, 1974] 112 p. illus. 29 cm. On spine: A history of Sacred Heart Parish. Bibliography: p. 110. [BX4603.A24S265] 74-8499
1. Church of the Sacred Heart of Jesus of Aberdeen. I. Title.

KAROLEVITZ, Robert F. 282.783'394
Pioneer church in a pioneer city; the story of Sacred Heart Parish, Yankton, South Dakota, 1871-1971, by Robert F. Karolevitz. [1st ed. Aberdeen, S.D., North Plains Press, 1971] 96 p. illus., facsims., map, ports. 31 cm. Bibliography: p. 93. [BX4603.Y3K3] 74-164645
1. Yankton, S.D. Sacred Heart Church. I. Title.

CARTER, Carrol Joe. 282'.788'36
Rocky Mountain religion : a history of Sacred Heart Parish, Alamosa, Colorado / by Carrol Joe Carter. Alamosa, Colo. : Sangre de Cristo Print., c1976. 106 p. : ill. ; 25 cm. [BX4603.A58S222] 76-375228 6.00
1. Sacred Heart Church, Alamosa, Colo. I. Title.

BUCHANAN, Rosemary. 282.78966
The first 100 years: St. Genievieves Parish, 1859-1959 [Las Cruces? N. M., 1961] 96p. illus. 20cm. [BX4603.L26S3] 61-25568
1. Las Cruces, N. M. St. Genevieve's Church. I. Title.

BOESCH, Mark. 282.79
The cross in the West. Illustrated by H. Lawrence Hoffman. New York, Vision Books [1956] 186p. illus. 22cm. (Vision books, 12) [BX1412.B6] 56-7281
1. Catholic Church in the West. 2. Missions—The West. I. Title.

BOESCH, Mark J. 1917- 282.79
The cross in the West. Illustrated by H. Lawrence Hoffman. New York Vision Books [1956] 186 p. illus. 22 cm (Vision books, 12) [BX1412.B6] 56-7281
1. Catholic Church in the West. 2. Missions—The West. I. Title.

MCSWEENEY, Thomas Denis. 282.794
Cathedral on California Street; the story of St. Mary's Cathedral, San Francisco, 1854-1891, and of Old St. Mary's, a Paulist church, 1894-1951. Fresno, Academy of California Church History, 1952. 94p. illus. 23cm. (Academy of California Church History. Publication no.4) [BX4603.S5S33] 56-38596
1. San Francisco. St. Mary's Cathedral. California Street. 2. San Francisco. St. Mary's Church. I. Title.

QUEEN, William M 1893- 282.794
Sanctuary lights on the Monterey Peninsula. Fresno, Calif., Academy Library Guild, 1954. 55p. illus. 22cm. Includes bibliography. [BX1415.C2Q4] 54-37089
1. Catholic Church in California. 2. Shrines—California. 3. Spanish missions of California. I. Title.

SOME California Catholic 282'.794
reminiscences for the United States Bicentennial / edited by Francis J. Weber. [New Haven?] : Published for the California Catholic Conference by the Knights of Columbus, c1976. ix, 166 p. ; 21 cm. [BX1415.C2S58] 75-27946
1. Catholics in California—Addresses, essays, lectures. I. Weber, Francis J. II. California Catholic Conference.

WEBER, Francis J. 282'.794
California Catholicism : a Holy Year tribute / Francis J. Weber. Los Angeles : [s.n.], 1975. xii, 208 p. ; 23 cm. Includes index. [BX1415.C2W37] 74-21932 12.00
1. Catholic Church in California. 2. Catholic Church in California—Biography. 3. California—Biography. I. Title.

WEBER, Francis J. 282'.794
California's Catholic heritage / Francis J. Weber. Los Angeles : Dawson's Book Shop, 1974. xv, 218 p. ; 23 cm. A collection of articles from the author's newspaper series by the same title. Includes index. [BX1415.C2W38] 73-82443 12.00
1. Catholic Church in California—Addresses, essays, lectures. I. Title.

WEBER, Francis J. 282.794
California's reluctant prelate; the life and times of Right Reverend Thaddeus Amat, C.M. (1811-1878) Los Angeles, Dawson Book Shop, 1964. xv, 234 p. illus., ports. 22 cm. Bibliography: p. [223]-229. [BX4705.A5675W4] 63-21211
1. Amat, Thaddeus, Bp., 1811-1878. 2. Catholic Church in California. I. Title.

WEBER, Francis J. 282.794
Catholic footprints in California [by] Francis J. Weber. [Newhall, Calif.] Hogarth Press, 1970. xx, 235 p. illus. 22 cm. A collection of 125 essays previously published as newspaper articles. [BX1415.C2W39] 70-122247 10.00
1. Catholic Church in California. I. Title.

WEBER, Francis J. 282'.794
The pilgrim church in California [by] Francis J. Weber. Los Angeles, Dawson's Book Shop, 1973. xx, 252 p. illus. 22 cm. Select group of essays, rev. and augmented, which were prepared originally for a column that appeared weekly in The Tidings, and sporadically in other religious and secular newspapers, since April 15, 1963. [BX1415.C2W42] 72-77294 12.00
1. Catholic Church in California. 2. Catholic Church—Missions. 3. Missions—California. 4. California—History. I. Title.

WEBER, Francis J., ed. 282.794082
Documents of California Catholic history, 1784-1963. Los Angeles, Dawson's [c.]1965. xiv, 364p. coat of arms, mounted col. port. 22cm. Bibl. [BX1415.C2W4] 65-13157 12.50
1. Catholic Church—California—Hist.—Sources. I. Title.

WEBER, Francis J ed. 282.794082
Documents of California Catholic history, 1784-1963, by Francis J. Weber. Los Angeles, Dawson's Book Shop, 1965. xiv, 364 p. coat of arms, mounted col. port. 22 cm. "Sixty-five selections ... prefaced with a short descriptive introduction along with an identification of the holding or publishing agency and the date of issuance. Explanatory notes are added only where essential to a proper understanding of particular documents." Includes bibliographical references. [BX1415.C2W4] 65-13157
1. Catholic Church — California — Hist. — Sources. I. Title.

**OFFICIAL Catholic* 282.7949058
directory, 1964. Diocese of San Diego, Calif. San Diego, San Bernardino, Riverside and Imperial Counties [Ed. by Msgr. James P. O'Shea] San Diego, Calif., Southern Cross [1963] 68p. illus. 23cm. pap., 5.00; after June 1964, 1.00

WEBER, Francis J. 282'.794'94
Saint Vibiana's Cathedral : a centennial history / by Francis J. Weber. Los Angeles : Weber, 1976. 73 p. : ill. ; 25 cm. Includes bibliographical references. [BX4603.L27S258] 74-21935
1. Saint Vibiana's Cathedral, Los Angeles.

OFFICIAL Catholic 282.79498
Directory, 1963. Diocese of San Diego, California: San Diego, San Bernardino, Riverside and Imperial Counties. Ed.: Rt. Rev. Msgr. James P. O'Shea. San Diego, Calif., Alcala Pk., Southern Cross Pr., 1962. 72p. illus. 23cm. pap., 5.00; after June, 1.00

SCHOENBERG, Wilfred P. 282.795
A chronicle of the Catholic history of the Pacific Northwest, 1743-1960. Arr. after the manner of certain medieval chronicles and annotated with copious notes for further reference. [Spokane, Wash., 1224 E. Euclid, Gonzaga Preparatory Sch., c.1962. 570p. 24cm. Bibl. 62-13279 12.50
1. Catholic Church in the Pacific Northwest—Hist. I. Title.

BRADLEY, Cyprian, 1884- 282.796
History of the diocese of Boise, 1863-1952 [i. e. 1953] by Cyprian Bradley and Edward J. Kelly. Boise, Idaho, 1953 [i.e. 1954]- v. illus. 24cm. [BX1417.B57B7] 54-32014
1. Boise, Idaho (Diocese)—Hist. I. Kelly, Edward J., Bp., 1800- joint author. II. Title.

BALCOM, Mary Gilmore. 282.798
The Catholic Church in Alaska, by Mary G. Balcom. Chicago, Adams Press [1970] 150 p. illus., map, ports. 22 cm. Bibliography: p. 143. [BX1415.A4B3] 78-97897
1. Catholic Church in Alaska. I. Title.

BASIC ecclesiastical 282.8
statistics for Latin America, 1954- Maryknoll, N. Y., [Maryknoll Publications, etc.] v. tables. 24-29cm. Vols. for issued as World horizon report no. Editors: 1951- W. J. Gibbons with F. B. Avesing and A. Adamek, 1960- [BX1426.B3] 59-17230
1. Catholic Church in Spanish America—Stat. I. Gibbons, William, Joseph, 1912- ed. II. Series: World horizon reports, report no

BETWEEN honesty and hope; 282.8
documents from and about the Church in Latin America. Issued at Lima by the Peruvian Bishops' Commission for Social Action. Translated by John Drury. Maryknoll, N.Y., Maryknoll Publications [1970] xxiv, 247 p. 23 cm. (Maryknoll documentation series) "Originally published in 1969 as the second edition of Signos de renovacion: recopilacion de documentos post-conciliares de la Iglesia en America Latina." [BX1426.2.S5213] 78-143185 2.95
1. Catholic Church in Latin America—Addresses, essays, lectures. I. Catholic Church. Conferencia Episcopal Peruana. Comision Episcopal de Accion Social.

BURCH, Thomas Kirby, 1934- 282.8
Basic ecclesiastical statistics for Latin America, 1954; compiled by Thomas K. Burch and Donald J. Burton. William J. Gibbons, editor. Maryknoll, N. Y., World Horizons Reports [1955] 54p. 29cm. [BX1426.B8] 55-39162
1. Catholic Church in Spanish America—Stat. I. Burton, Donald Joseph, 1934- joint author. II. Title.

THE Church and social 282'.8
change in Latin America. Henry A. Landsberger, editor. Contributors Emanuel de Kadt [and others] Notre Dame, University of Notre Dame Press [1970] xiii, 240 p. 24 cm. (International studies of the Committee on International Relations, University of Notre Dame) Includes bibliographical references. [BX1426.2.C47] 77-85355 9.50
1. Catholic Church in Latin America—Addresses, essays, lectures. 2. Latin America—Social conditions—Addresses, essays, lectures. I. Landsberger, Henry A., ed. II. De Kadt, Emanuel Jehuda. III. Series: Notre Dame, Ind. University. Committee on International Relations. International studies

CONSIDINE, John Joseph, 282'.8
1897- ed.
The religious dimension in the new Latin America, edited by John J. Considine. Notre Dame, Ind., Fides Publishers [1967, c1966] xviii, 238 p. 22 cm. (A Fides paperback textbook) "Under the sponsorship of the Catholic Inter-American Cooperation Program." Bibliographical footnotes. [BX1426.2.C6] 66-30591
1. Catholic Church in Latin America—Addresses, essays, lectures. 2. Latin America—Religion—Addresses, essays, lectures. I. Catholic Inter-American Cooperation Program. II. Title.

GHEERBRANT, Alain. 282'.8
The rebel Church in Latin America / Alain Gheerbrant ; translated [from the French] by Rosemary Sheed ; with an introduction by Richard Gott. Harmondsworth ; Baltimore : Penguin, 1974. 357 p. ; 19 cm. (The Pelican Latin American library) Translation of L'Eglise rebelle d'Amerique latine. [BX1425.A2G513] 75-323350 ISBN 0-14-021801-7 : £0.75 ($3.25 U.S.)
1. Catholic Church in Latin America—Collected works. I. Title.

GREENLEAF, Richard E., 282.8
comp.
The Roman Catholic Church in colonial Latin America, edited with an introduction by Richard E. Greenleaf. [1st ed.] New York, Knopf [1971] xi, 272 p. 19 cm. (Borzoi books on Latin America) [BX1426.2.G73 1971] 71-130774 ISBN 0-394-30290-7 4.50
1. Catholic Church in Latin America—History—Addresses, essays, lectures. I. Title.

HUFF, Russell J., 1936- 282.8
On wings of adventure; some personal experiences with the Catholic Church in Latin America, by Russell J. Huff. Notre Dame [Inl.] Dujarie [c.1967] 86p. illus. 22cm. [BX1426.2.H8] 67-28934 2.75
1. Catholic Church in Latin America. 2. Latin America—Descr. & trav. I. Title.

LATIN American 282.8
institutional development: the changing Catholic Church [by] Luigi Einaudi [and

others] Santa Monica, Calif., Rand Corp., 1969. xi, 81 p. illus. 28 cm. ([Rand Corporation] Memorandum RM-6136-DOS) Prepared for Office of External Research, Dept. of State under contract SCC-1006-03987-69. Includes bibliographical references. [Q180.A1R36 no. 6136] 72-14754
1. Catholic Church in Latin America. I. Einaudi, Luigi R., 1936- II. Series: Rand Corporation. Research memorandum RM-6136-DOS

LATORRE Cabal, Hugo. 282'.8
The revolution of the Latin American church / by Hugo Latorre Cabal ; translated from the Spanish by Frances K. Hendricks and Beatrice Berler. Norman : University of Oklahoma Press, c1977. p. cm. Translation of La revolucion de la iglesia latinoamericana. [BX1426.2.L33513] 77-9117 ISBN 0-8061-1449-5 : 9.95
1. Catholic Church in Latin America—History. I. Title.

SCHMITT, Karl Michael, 1922- comp. 282'.8
The Roman Catholic Church in modern Latin America. Edited with an introd. by Karl M. Schmitt. [1st ed.] New York, Knopf [1972] x, 225 p. 19 cm. (Borzoi books on Latin America) Bibliography: p. [217]-225. [BX1461.2.S34] 73-165753 ISBN 0-394-47389-2
1. Catholic Church in Latin America—Addresses, essays, lectures. I. Title.

CATHOLIC Students' Mission Crusade, U.S.A. 282.81
Brazil in five hours [by] Bishop Agnello Rossi [and others]. Cincinnati 36, 5100 Shattuc Ave. Catholic Students' Mission Crusade, U.S.A., National Center, 66p. illus. 22cm. (CSMC fivehour series) Includes bibl. 60-51233 .60 pap.,
1. Catholic Church in Brazil. I. Rossi, Angello, Bp. II. Title.

KENNEDY, John Joseph. 282.82
Catholicism, nationalism, and democracy in Argentina. [Notre Dame, Ind.] University of Notre Dame Press, 1958. 219p. 21cm. (International studies of the Committee on International Relations, University of Notre Dame) [BX1462.K4] 57-14970
1. Catholic Church in the Argentine Republic. 2. Nationalism and religion—Argentine Republic. I. Title.

ARRIAGA, Pablo Jose de, 1564-1622. 282.85
The extirpation of idolatry in Peru. Translated and edited by L. Clark Keating. [Lexington] University of Kentucky Press [1968] xxiv, 192 p. 23 cm. Includes bibliographical references. [F3444.A7673] 68-12964
1. Indians of South America—Peru. 2. Missions—Peru. 3. Jesuits in Peru. I. Keating, Louis Clark, 1907- ed. II. Title.

WATTERS, Mary, 1896- 282.87
A history of the church in Venezuela, 1810-1930. [1st AMS ed.] New York, AMS Press [1971] ix, 260 p. 23 cm. Reprint of the 1933 ed. Bibliography: p. 238-252. [BR730.W3 1971] 70-137303 ISBN 0-404-06877-4
1. Venezuela—Church history. 2. Catholic Church in Venezuela. I. Title.

CATHOLIC Students' Mission Crusade, U.S.A. 282.914
Philippines in five hours: Braganza, Bustos. Camara, Constantino, Floresca [and] Mempin. Cincinnati, Catholic Students' Mission Crusade. U.S.A. [1959] 93p. illus. 22cm. (CSMC five hour series) (3p. bibl.) 59-30490 .50 pap.,
1. Catholic Church in the Philippine Islands. I. Title.

MANILA (Ecclesiastical province) Council, 1771. 282.914
The Provincial Council of Manila of 1771 (its text followed by a commentary on Actio II, De episcopis) By Pedro N. Bantigue, priest of the archdiocese of Manila, Philippines Washington, Catholic University of America Press, 1957. xiv, 261p. 23cm. (Catholic University of America. Canon law studies, no. 376) Part of text in Latin. The editor's thesis--Catholic University of America. Vita. Bibliography: p. 245-252. [BX1660.M3A53] 58-2437
1. Bishops—Philippine Islands. I. Bantigue, Pedro Natividad, 1920- ed. II. Title. III. Series.

PIONEERING days of 282'.9315'7
the Church in North Otago, 1840-1900; a diocesan centennial project. [Dunedin, N.Z., Printed by the N.Z. Tablet Co. 1973?] 39 p. illus. 18 x 25 cm. Cover title. [BX1686.O85P56] 73-178205
1. Catholic Church in Otago, N.Z.

O'FARRELL, Patrick James. 282.94
The Catholic Church in Australia; a short history; 1788-1967 [by] Patrick O'Farrell. [Melbourne] Nelson [(Australia) 1968] x, 294 p. illus., map. 19 cm. (Nelson's Australasian paperbacks) Bibliography: p. 281-288. [BX1685.O34] 78-385803 1.75
1. Catholic Church in Australia—History.

SUTTOR, T. L. 282.94
Hierarchy and democracy in Australia. 1788-1870: the formation of Australian Catholicism [by] T. L. Suttor. Melbourne, Melbourne Univ. Pr.: London, Cambridge 1965. xi, 344p. 8 plates (incl. ports.) 23cm. Bibl. [BX1685.S9] 65-23584 12.50
1. Catholic Church in Australia. 2. Australia—Church history—19th. cent. I. Title.
Available from Cambridge in New York.

TRUMAN, Tom [Thomas Charles Truman] 282.94
Catholic action and politics. [Rev. and enl. 2d ed. dist. New York, Hillary, 1962. c.1960] 283p. 22cm. Bibl. 61-65435 6.00
1. Catholic Church in Australia. 2. Church and state in Australia. 3. Catholic action—Australia. I. Title.

EBSWORTH, Walter A. 282'.945
Pioneer Catholic Victoria, by Walter Ebsworth. Melbourne, Polding Press, 1973. ix, 531 p. maps (on lining papers), plates. 23 cm. [BX1686.V5E27] 73-164720 ISBN 0-85884-096-0 8.95
1. Catholic Church in Victoria, Australia. I. Title.

283 Anglican Churches

BAYNE, Stephen Fielding, Jr. Bp., 1908- ed. 283
Mutual responsibility and interdependence in the body of Christ, with related background documents. Ed., introd., concluding chapter by Stephen F. Bayne. Jr. Foreword by the Archbishop of Canterbury. New York, Seabury, 1963. 79p. 21cm. Outcome of the meeting of two bodies in London, Ontario, during the week before the Anglican Congress at Toronto in August, 1963: the Advisory Council on Missionary Strategy and the Consultative Body of the Lambeth Conference. 63-25471 .75 pap.,
1. Anglican Communion. I. Advisory Council on Missionary Strategy. II. Lambeth Conference. III. Title.

CLEAVELAND, George Julius. 283
Reformation and reunion; Protestant-Catholic tensions and suggested solutions. New York, Carlton Press [1963] 126 p. 21 cm. (A Reflection book) Bibliography: p. 125-126. [BR375.C57] 63-2665
1. Reformation — England. 2. Church of England — Relations — Catholic Church. 3. Catholic Church — Relations — Anglican Communion. 4. Anglican orders. 5. Christian union. I. Title.

CLEVELAND, George Julius 283
Reformation and reunion; Protestant-Catholic tensions and suggested solutions. New York, Carlton [c.1963] 126p. 21cm. (Reflection bk.) Bibl. 63-2665 2.50
1. Reformation—England. 2. Church of England—Relations—Catholic Church. 3. Catholic Church—Relations—Anglican Communion. 4. Anglican orders. 5. Christian union. I. Title.

DE CANDOLE, Henry. ed. 283
The people of God, edited by Henry De Candole and Patrick Cowley. London, Faith Press; New York, Morehouse-Gorham Co. [1951] 151 p. 19 cm. [BX5131.D44] 52-10174
1. Church of England. 2. Christian life. I. Title.

ELLISON, Gerald [Alexander] 283
The Anglican Communion, past and future. [Lectures] Greenwich, Conn., Seabury Press, [c.]1960. 92p. 21cm. (bibl.) 60-5887 pap., apply
1. Anglican Communion. I. Title.

FAIRWEATHER, Eugene Rathbone, ed. 283
The Oxford movement. Edited by Eugene R. Fairweather. New York, Oxford University Press, 1964. xvi, 400 p. 24 cm. (A Library of Protestant thought) Bibliography: p. 385-392. [BX5099.F3] 64-19451
1. Theology — Collections. 2. Oxford movement. I. Title. II. Series.

FAIRWEATHER, Eugene Rathbone, ed. 283
The Oxford movement, Ed. by Eugene R. Fairweather. New York, Oxford [c.]1964. xvi, 400p. 24cm. (Lib. of Protestant thought) Bibl. 64-19451 7.00
1. Theology—Collections. 2. Oxford movement. I. Title. II. Series.

FERRIS, Paul, 1929- 283
The Church of England. With a comment to the American reader by James A. Pike. New York, Macmillan [1963] 224 p. 22 cm. [BX5131.2.F4 1963] 63-13194
1. Church of England. I. Title.

FERRIS, Paul, 1929- 283
The Church of England. Comment to the American reader by James A. Pike. New York, Macmillan [c.1962, 1963] 224p. 22cm. Bibl. 63-13194 4.95
1. Church of England. I. Title.

FLETCHER, Harris Francis, 1892- 283
The use of the Bible in Milton's prose; with an index of the Biblical quotations and citations arranged in the chronological order of the prose works; another index of all quotations and citations in the order of the books of the Bible; and an index of the quotations and citations in the De doctrina. New York, Gordon Press, 1972. 176 p. 21 cm. Reprint of the 1929 ed., which was issued as v. 14, no. 3 of the University of Illinois studies in language and literature. Bibliography: p. 172-173. [PR3592.B5F55 1972] 72-87899 ISBN 0-87968-014-8 8.00
1. Milton, John, 1608-1674—Knowledge—Bible. 2. Milton, John, 1608-1674. De doctrina Christiana. I. Title. II. Series: Illinois. University. Illinois studies in language and literature, v. 14, no. 3.

HERKLOTS, Hugh Gerard Gibson, 1903- 283
The Church of England and the American Episcopal Church, from the first voyages of discovery to the first Lambeth Conferency [by] H. G. G. Herklots. London, Mowbray; New York, Morehouse-Barlow, 1966. xiii, 183 p. illus. 22 cm. (B66-5892) Bibliographical footnotes. [BX5927.8.H4] 66-70108
1. Protestant Episcopal Church in the U.S.A. — Relations — Church of England. 2. Church of England — Relations — protestant Episcopal Church in the U.S.A. I. Title.

HERKLOTS, Hugh Gerard Gibson, 1903- 283
The Church of England and the American Episcopal Church, from the first voyages of discovery to the first Lambeth Conference. London. Mowbray; New York, Morehouse [c.] 1966. xiii, 183p. illus. 22cm. Bibl [BX5927.8.H4] 66-70108 6.00 bds.,
1. Protestant Episcopal Church in the U.S.A.—Relations—Church of England. 2. Church of England—Relations—Protestant Episcopal Church in the U.S.A. I. Title.

HIGGINS, John Seville, Bp., 1904- 283
One faith and fellowship; the missionary story of the Anglican Communion. Foreword by the Archbishop of Canterbury. Greenwich, Conn., Seabury Press, 1958. 226p. illus. 22cm. Includes bibliography. [BX5005.H53] 58-7174
1. Anglican Communion. I. Title.

JEFFERSON, Philip Clarke, ed. 283
The Church in the 60's. The Anglican Congress 1963. Foreword by Archbishop of Canterbury. [Dist.] Greenwich, Conn., Seabury [1962] 153p. illus. 19cm. 1.50 pap.,
1. Anglican Communism. I. Anglican Congress, Toronto, 1963. II. Title.

JOHNSON, Howard Albert, 1915- 283
Global odyssey; an Episcopalian's encounter with the Anglican Communion in eighty countries. Photos. by the author. [1st ed.] New York, Harper & Row [1963] 448 p. illus. 24 cm. [BX5005.J6] 63-7606
1. Anglican Communion. I. Title.

KNAPP-FISHER, E G 283
The churchman's heritage; a study in the ethos of the English Church. Greenwich, Conn., Seabury Press [1954] 96p. 21cm. [BX5131.K64] 54-14529
1. Church of England. I. Title.

LEIDT, William E., ed. 283
Anglican mosaic. Foreword by the Metropolitan of India. The Anglican Congress, [dist. Greenwich. Conn., Seabury, 1962] 185p. illus. maps. (pt. col.) 21cm. Bibl. 63-1451 2.25 pap.,
1. Anglican Communion—Addresses, essays, lectures. I. Title.

LEIDT, William E ed. 283
Anglican mosiac. Foreword by the Metropolitan of India. The Anglican Congress, 1963. [Toronto? Distributed in U.S. by the Seabury Press, Greenwich, Conn., 1962] 185 p. illus. 21 cm. [BX5006.L4] 63-1451
1. Anglican Communion — Addresses, essays, lectures. I. Title.

MORGAN, Dewi. 283
Agenda for Anglicans. With a pref. by Stephen Bayne. New York, Morehouse-Barlow [1963] 167 p. 19 cm. [BX5005.M6 1963] 63-4039
1. Anglican Communion. I. Title.

MORGAN, Dewi 283
Agenda for Anglicans. Pref. by Stephen Bayne. New York, Morehouse-Barlow [c.1963] 167p. 19cm. 63-4039 1.75 pap.,
1. Anglican Communion. I. Title.

NEILL, Stephen Charles, Bp. 283
Anglicanism [by] Stephen Neill. 3d ed.] Baltimore, Penguin Books [1965] 468 p. 18 cm. (Pelican books, A421) Bibliography: p. [445]-460. [BX5005.N4 1965] 65-2941
1. Anglican Communion. I. Title.

NEILL, Stephen Charles, Bp. 283
Anglicanism [3d ed.] Baltimore, Penguin [c.1958-1965] 468p. 18cm. (Pelican bks., A421) Bibl. [BX5005.N4] 65-2941 1.95 pap.,
1. Anglican Communion. I. Title.

OLLARD, Sidney Leslie, 1875-1949 283
A short history of the Oxford movement London, Faith Pr. Reprints. [dist. New York, Morehouse, 1964, c.1963] 194p. port. 19cm. (Faith pr. reprints, 1) Bibl. 64-1276 1.50 pap.,
1. Oxford movement. I. Title.

PAGE, Robert Jeffress, 1922- 283
New directions in Anglican theology; a survey from Temple to Robinson New York, Seabury [1965] viii, 208p. 22cm. Bibl. [BT28.P3] 65-21312 4.95
1. Theology—20th cent. 2. Theology, Doctrinal—Hist.—Gt. Brit. I. Title. II. Title: Anglican theology.

SMITH, Harry Robert, 1894- 283
The church for you; an introduction to the Episcopal Church. Foreword by Norman B. Nash. Greenwich, Conn., Seabury Press, 1956. 93p. 19cm. Includes bibliography. [BX5935.S676] 56-1893
1. Protestant Episcopal Church in the U. S. A. I. Title.

SMITH, Harry Robert, 1894- 283
The church for you; an introduction to the Episcopal Church. Foreword by Norman B. Nash. Greenwich, Conn., Seabury Press, 1956. 93 p. 19 cm. Includes bibliography. [BX5935.S676] 56-1893
1. Protestant Episcopal Church in the U.S.A. I. Title.

TAVARD, Georges Henri, 1922- 283
The quest for catholicity, a study in Anglicanism. [New York] Herder & Herder [1964] ix, 227p. 23cm. Bibl. 63-18162 5.95
1. Church of England—Relations—Catholic Church. 2. Anglo-Catholicism. 3. Catholicity. 4. Catholic Church—Relations—Church of England. I. Title.

VIDLER, Alexander Roper, 1899- ed. 283
Soundings; essays concerning Christian understanding. Cambridge [Eng.] University Press, 1962. 267 p. 23 cm. [BX5131.2.V5] 62-51532
1. Church of England — Doctrinal and controversial works. I. Title.

VIDLER, Alexander Roper, 1899- ed. 283
Soundings; essays concerning Christian understanding. [New York] Cambridge [c.] 1962. 267p. 23cm. 62-51532 3.95
1. Church of England—Doctrinal and controversial works. I. Title.

WAND, John William Charles, Bp. of London, 1885- 283
Anglicanism in history and today. [1st American ed.] New York, T. Nelson, 1962 [c1961] 265 p. 24 cm. (History of religion) Includes bibliography. [BX5005.W3] 62-3773
1. Anglican Communion. I. Title.

WAND, John William Charles, Bp. of London, 1885- 283
What the Church of England stands for; a guide to its authority in the twentieth century. London, A. R. Morbray; New York, Morehouse-Gorham Co. [1951] 131 p. 20 cm. [BX5131.W3] 52-7355
1. Church of England. I. Title.

WAND, John William Charles, Bp. of London, 1885- 283
What the Church of England stands for; a guide to its authority in the twentieth century, by J. W. C. Wand. Westport, Conn., Greenwood Press [1972, c1959] 131 p. 22 cm. [BX5131.2.W35 1972] 76-106700
1. Church of England. I. Title.

WHITE, James F. 283
The Cambridge movement; the ecclesiologists and the Gothic revival. [New York] Cambridge, 1962. xii, 272p. 8 plates. 23cm. Bibl. 62-52258 6.00

1. Ecclesiological Society. 2. Churches, Anglican. 3. Church architecture—Gt. Brit. I. Title.

WHITELEY, Peter. 283
Frontier mission; an account of the Toronto Congress, 1963 [a personal impression] Toronto, Anglican Book Centre; New York, Seabury Press, 1963. vii, 94 p. 19 cm. [BX5021.A65] 63-25476
1. Anglican Congress, Toronto, 1963. I. Title.

WHITELEY, Peter 283
Frontier mission; an account of the Toronto Congress, 1963 [a personal impression] Toronto, Anglican Bk. Centre; New York, Seabury, 1963. vii, 94p. 19cm. 63-25476 .65 pap.,
1. Anglican Congress, Toronto, 1963. I. Title.

[WHITTINGHAM, William] 283
d.1579.
A brieff discours off the troubles begonne at Franckford in Germany, Anno Domini 1554. Abowte the Booke off off [sic] common prayer and ceremonies and contienued by the Englishe men theyre to thende off Q. Maries raigne ... [Amsterdam, Theatrum Orbis Terrarum; Da Capo Press, 1972] ccxv p. 21 cm. (The English experience, its record in early printed books published in facsimile, no. 492) "S.T.C. no. 25442." Reprint of the 1574 ed. Cover title: Troubles abowte the Booke of common prayer. Title on spine: Booke of Common prayer, 1574. [BX5653.F8W6 1574a] 71-38228 ISBN 9-02-210492-3 9.00
1. Frankfurt am Main. English Church. 2. Church of England—Doctrinal and controversial works. 3. Puritans—Frankfurt am Main. 4. British in Frankfurt am Main. I. Title. II. Title: Troubles abowte the Booke of common prayer. III. Title: Booke of common prayer, 1574. IV. Series.

BENTON, Angelo Ames, 283'.03
1837-1912, ed.
The church cyclopaedia : a dictionary of church doctrine, history, organization, and ritual ... designed especially for the use of the laity of the Protestant Episcopal Church in the United States of America / edited by A. A. Benton. Detroit : Gale Research Co., 1975, c1883. 810 p. ; 23 cm. Reprint of the ed. published by M. H. Mallory, New York. [BR95.B5 1975] 74-31499 ISBN 0-8103-4204-9 : 28.00
1. Protestant Episcopal Church in the U.S.A.—Dictionaries. 2. Theology—Dictionaries. I. Title.

CRUM, Rolfe Pomeroy, 1889- 283.03
A dictionary of the Episcopal Church, compiled from various authentic sources; with a foreword by Henry St. George Tucker. 11th ed., with pronunciations according to Webster's and Thorndike-Barnhart's dictionaries. Baltimore, Trefoil Pub. Society, c1954. 98p. illus. 20cm. [BX5007.C7 1954] 55-15394
1. Protestant Episcopal Church in the U. S. A.—Dictionaries. I. Title.

CRUM, Rolfe Pomeroy, 1889- 283.03
A dictionary of the Episcopal Church, compiled from various authentic sources; with a foreword by Henry St. George Tucker. 10th ed., rev. and enl. Baltimore, Trefoil Pub. Society, c1953. 96p. illus. 19cm. [BX5007.C7 1953] 53-38199
1. Protestant Episcopal Church in the U. S. A.—Dictionaries. I. Title.

CRUM, Rolfe Pomeroy, 1889- 283.03
A dictionary of the Episcopal Church, compiled from various authentic sources; with a foreword by Frederick Deane Goodwin. 8th ed., rev. and enl., including an addendum (page 94) Baltimore, Trefoil Pub. Society, '1951. 96 p. illus. 19 cm. [BX5007.C7 1951] 52-17002
1. Protestant Episcopal Church in the U. S. A.—Dictionaries. I. Title.

ECKEL, Frederick L., Jr. 283.03
A concise dictionary of ecclesiastical terms. Drawings by William Duncan. Boston 8, 16 Ashburton Place Whittemore Associates, [c.1960] 64p. illus. 19cm. 60-50385 .60 pap.,
1. Protestant Episcopal Church in the U. S. A.—Dictionaries. 2. Liturgics—Dictionaries. I. Title.

KIRK, Kenneth Escott, Bp. 283.04
of Oxford, 1886-1954.
Beauty and bands, and other papers. Prepared by E. W. Kemp. Greenwich, Conn., Seabury Press, 1957. 288p. illus. 19cm. [BX5133.K55B4] 57-3596
1. Church of England—Addresses, essays, lectures. I. Title.

EPISCOPAL Church annual 283.058
(The) 1961. [ed. Clifford P. Morehouse] New York, Morehouse-Barlow Co. [c.1961] 567, a-115 p. illus., ports. Title varies 46-33254 5.75
1. Protestant Episcopal Church in the U.S.A.—Yearbooks.

EPISCOPAL Church annual 283.058
(The) 1967. New York, Morehouse [1967] illus. 22cm. Ed.: 1964- C. P. Morehouse. Title varies. 46-33254 7.50
1. Protestant Episcopal Church in the U.S.A.—Yearbooks. I. Morehouse, Clifford P., ed.

EPISCOPAL Church annual 283.058
(The) 1964 [Ed.: Clifford P. Morehouse. Assist. ed.: Rev. Rodney F. Cobb] New York, Morehouse [1964, c.1963] various p. illus. 22cm. title varies. 46-33254 6.25
1. Protestant Episcopal Church in the U.S.A.—Yearbooks. I. Morehouse, Clifford P., ed. II. Cobb, Rodney F., ed.

EPISCOPAL Church annual 283.058
(The) 1964. [Ed.: Clifford P. Morehouse. Asst. ed. William V. Albert] New York, Morehouse [1965, c.1964] 1v. (various p.) illus. 22cm Title varies. 46-33254 6.25
1. Protestant Episcopal Church in the U.S.A.—Year-books. I. Morehouse, Clifford P., ed. II. Albert, William V., assistant ed.

EPISCOPAL Church annual 283.058
(The) 1963. New York, Morehouse [c.1962] 573p. illus. 22cm. Ed: C. P. Morehouse; asst. ed.: R. F. Cobb. Title varies. 46-33254 6.25
1. Protestant Episcopal Church in the U.S.A.—Yearbooks. I. Morehouse, Clifford P., ed. II. Cobb, Rodney F., ed.

EPISCOPAL Church annual 283.058
(The) 1968. New York, Morehouse Barlow [1968] v. illus., ports., maps (pt. fold.) 22cm. The 5th-21st years, 1886-1902 (called v. 1-17) issued quarterly, one number each year retaining the features of the annual, the other numbers being clergy lists. Title varies: 1882-85, 1903-08, 1922-52, The Living church annual; the yearbook of the Episcopal Church (subtitle varies)--1886-89, Living church and clergy list quarterly, containing an almanac and calendar.--1890-1902, The Living Church quarterly, containing an almanac and calendar (varies slightly)--1909-14, The Living church annual and Whittaker's churchman's almanac.--1915-21, The Living church annual and churchman's almanac. Vols. for 1882-85 edited by C. W. Leffingwell and A. Seymour. Imprint varies: 1882-85. Chicago, S. A. Maxwell [etc.]--1886-1938, Milwaukee, Morehouse Pub. Co. [etc.] Absorbed Whittaker's churchman's almanacin 1909, and the Churchman's year book and American church almanac in 1922. [BX5830.L5] 46-33254 7.50
1. Protestant Episcopal Church in the U.S.A.—Yearbooks. I. Leffingwell, Charles Wesley, 1840-1928, ed. II. Seymour, Arthur. ed.

LE NEVE, John 283.05842
Fasti ecclesiae anglicanae, 1300-1541. II. Hereford diocese, comp. by Joyce M. Horn. [dist. New York, Oxford, c.]1962. 61p. 6.00 pap.,
I. Title.

LE NEVE, John, 1679- 283.05842
1741
Fasti ecclesiae Anglicanae, 1300-1541 [v.]8 [London] Univ. of London, Inst. of Hist. Res., Athlone Pr. [dist. New York, Oxford [c.]1964. 97p. 26cm. Contents.[v.]8. Bath and Wells diocese, comp. by B. Jones. 62-53072 4.80
1. Clergy—England. I. Title.

LENEVE, John, 1679-1741 283.05842
Fasti ecclesiae Anglicanae, 1300-1541; v.4 [London] Univ. of London, Inst. of Historical Res., Athlone Pr [dist. New York, Oxford, c.] 1963. 70p. 26cm. Contents.1 Monastic cathedrals (Southern proviince) comp. by B. Jones. Bibl. 63-53072 2.80
1. Clergy—England. I. Title.

LE NEVE, John, 1697- 283.05842
1741
Fasti ecclesiae Anglicanae, 1300-1541, vs. 5 & 6 [rev., expanded ed.] [London] Univ. of London, Inst. of Hist. Res., Athlone Pr.[dist. New York, Oxford, 1964, c.1963] 2 v. (86; 128 p.) 26 cm. Contents.v. 5. St. Pauls, London, comp. by J. M. Horn.--v.6. Northern province (York, Carlisle and Durham) Comp. by B. Jones. 62-53072 v.5, 4.00; v.6, 5.60
1. Clergy—England. I. Title.

AMERICAN Church Union. 283.0631
The 1954 Chicago international Catholic congress ... August 1-3, 1954; [official report] New York, American Church Publications [1955?] 99p. illus., ports. 23cm. Bibliographical footnotes. [BX5021.A6 1954] 55-3598
1. Anglican Communion—Congresses. I. Title. II. Title: International Catholic congress.

LAMBETH Conference 283.06342
1958.
The encyclical letter from the bishops, together with the resolutions and reports. [London] S. P. C. K.; [Greenwich, Conn.] Seabury Press, 1958. 66. 171p. 21cm. [BX5021.L6 1958] 61-2323
I. Title.

MORGAN, Dewi. 283.06342
The bishops come to Lambeth. London,-A.R. Mowbray; New York, Morehouse-Gorham Co. [1957] 142p. 19cm. Includes bibliography. [BX5021.L5M6] 57-59336
1. Lambeth Conference. I. Title.

MOSS, Claude Beaufort, 283.076
1888-
Answer me this. [1st ed.] New York, Longmans, Green, 1959. 212p. 21cm: [BX5930.2.M66] 59-13546
1. Questions and answers—Theology. 2. Protestant Episcopal Church in the U. S. A.—Doctrinal and controversial works. I. Title.

CHURCH and the twentieth 283'.08
century (The), by Norman Sykes [others] G. L. H. Harvey ed. Freeport, N.Y., Bks. for Libs. Pr. [1967] xviii, 448p. 22cm. (Essay index reprint ser.) Reprint of the 1936 ed. Bibl. [BX5035.C48 1967] 67-26747 12.50
1. Church of England—Addresses, essays, lectures. I. Sykes, Norman, 1897-1961. II. Harvey, George Leonard Hunton. ed.
Contents Omitted.

SYKES, Norman, 1897-1961. 283'.08
The Church and the twentieth century, by Norman Sykes [and others] G. L. H. Harvey, editor. Freeport, N. Y., Books for Libraries Press [1967] xviii, 448 p. 22 cm. (Essay index reprint series) Reprint of the 1936 ed. Bibliographical footnotes. [BX5035.C48] 67-26747
1. Church of England—Addresses, essays, lectures. I. Harvey, George Leonard Hunton, ed. II. Title.
-Contents omitted

ANGLICAN Congress, 283.082
Toronto, 1963
Report of proceedings. Ed. by E. R. Fairweather, Edit. Comm. Anglican Congress [dist. New York, Seabury, 1964] xv, 312p. 22cm. 64-1038 2.00 pap.,
1. Anglican Communion—Congresses. I. Fairweather, Eugene Rathbone, ed. II. Title.

BAYNE, Stephen Fielding, 283.082
Bp., 1908-
An Anglican turning point: documents and interpretations. Austin, Tex., Church Historical Society, 1964. ix. 317 p. 24 cm. (Church Historical Society. (U.S.) Publications new series; sources, no. 2) [BX5003.B3] 65-2510
1. Anglican Communion — Addresses, essays, lectures. 2. Anglican Communion — Hist. — Sources. I. Title. II. Series.

THE Holy Cross magazine. 283.082
All for the love of God, a Holy Cross omnibus. [1st ed.] New York, Holy Cross Press [1957] 250p. 24cm. [BX5840.H6] 57-7735
1. Protestant Episcopal Church in the U. S. A.—Addresses, essays, lectures. I. Milligan, Ralph T., ed. II. Title.

CHIDSEY, Alan Lake. 283.09
The bishop; a portrait of the Right Reverend Clinton S. Quin. Houston, Tex., Gulf Pub. Co. [1966] 239 p. 22 cm. [BX5995.15C5] 65-29026
1. 1. Quinn, Clinton Simon, Bp. I. Title.

HAUGAARD, William P. 283'.09
Elizabeth and the English Reformation: the struggle for a stable settlement of religion, by William P. Haugaard. London, Cambridge University P., 1968. xv, 392 p. 23 cm. Bibliography: p. 360-372. [BX5071.H3] 68-23179 ISBN 0-521-07245-X 80/- ($12.50)
1. Church of England—History. 2. Elizabeth, Queen of England, 1533-1603. 3. Great Britain—Church history—16th century. I. Title.

MAKOWER, Felix. 283.09
The constitutional history and constitution of the Church of England. New York, B. Franklin [1960?] x, 543p. 24cm. (Burt Franklin research & source works series # 9) Translation of Die Verfassung der Kirche von England. 'Conspectus of literature': p.504-534. [BX5150.M32 1960] 61-2869
1. Church of England—Government. 2. Church of England—Hist. I. Title.

SIMCOX, Carroll Eugene, 283'.09
1912-
The historical road of Anglicanism, by Carroll E. Simcox. Chicago, Regnery [1968] xiii, 235p. 22cm. Bibl. [BX5005.S5] 67-28496 6.25
1. Anglican Communion—Hist I. Title.

WAKEMAN, Henry Offley, 283'.09
1852-1899.
An introduction to the history of the Church of England, from the earliest times to the present day. New York, AMS Press [1972] xx, 505 p. 19 cm. Reprint of the 1908 ed. [BX5055.W3 1972] 77-137302 ISBN 0-404-06802-2
1. Church of England—History. I. Title.

WAKEMAN, Henry Offley, 283'.09
1852-1899.
An introduction to the history of the Church of England, from the earliest times to the present day. [9th ed.] Rev., with an additional chapter, by S. L. Ollard. London, Rivingtons. St. Clair Shores, Mich., Scholarly Press, 1970. xxii, 519 p. 22 cm. Date in original imprint on t.p. not legible (1949 or 1919?) [BX5055.W3 1970] 72-115285 ISBN 0-403-00256-7
1. Church of England—History. I. Ollard, Sidney Leslie, 1875-1949, ed. II. Title.

WAND, John William 283.09
Charles, Bp. of London, 1885-
The Second Reform. London, Faith Press; New York, Morehouse-Gorham Co. [1953] 67p. 19cm. [BX5093.W3] 53-9068
1. Church of England—Hist. 2. Gt. Brit.—Church history—19th cent. I. Title.

HUGHES, John Jay. 283'.09'034
Absolutely null and utterly void; the papal condemnation of Anglican orders, 1896. Washington, Corpus Books [1968] xviii, 347 p. illus. 22 cm. Bibliography: p. 309-342. [BX5178.H8] 68-30988 7.95
1. Catholic Church. Pope, 1878-1903 (Leo XIII). Apostolicae curae (13 Sept. 1896) 2. Anglican orders. I. Title.

PROTESTANT Episcopal 283'.09'046
Church in the U.S.A. Advisory Committee on Theological Liberty and Social Responsibility.
Theological freedom and social responsibility; report of the Advisory Committee of the Episcopal Church. Stephen F. Bayne, Jr., chairman. New York, Seabury Press [1967] xi, 180 p. 21 cm. Contents.Contents.—Introduction: the charge to the Advisory Committee.—The report.—The advisory papers: Some thoughts on heresy, by J. Macquarrie. Detecting error and seeking truth, by J. V. L. Casserley. The identifiability of the church, by J. Knox.—Orthodoxy, heresy, and freedom, by E. L. Mascall. Modern heresy: posture, not doctrine, by P. Moore, Jr. A will to community, by J. C. Murray. Doctrine, data, and due process by J. A. Pike. Prophetic ministry to the world, by J. A. T. Robinson. The willingness to live in tension, by T. Sorg. Mission for freedom: a bishop's reflections, by A. R. Stuart. F.B.I.—faith, bureaucracy, and inquiry in the church, by A. A. Vogel.—Select bibliography (p. 178-180) Bibliographical references included in "Notes." [BT1317.P76] 67-30698
1. Heresy. 2. Liberty of speech in the church. I. Bayne, Stephen Fielding, Bp., 1908- II. Title.

ERIC Graham. 1888- 283'.09214
1964: Dean of Oriel, Principal of Cuddeson, Bishop of Brechin [by] Robert T. Holtby London, New York Oxford Univ. Pr., 1967. xi, 160p. 4 plates (ports.) 22cm. Bibl [BX5199.G69H6] (B) 67-114881 2.90 pap.,
1. Graham, Eric, Bp. of Brechin, 1888-1964. I. Holtby, Robert Tinsley.

HOLTBY, Robert 283'.09214(B)
Tinsley.
Eric Graham, 1888-1964: Dean of Oriel, Principal of Cuddesdon, Bishop of Brechin [by] Robert T. Holtby. London, New York [etc.] Oxford U. P., 1967. xii, 160 p. 4 plates (ports.) 22 cm. Bibliographical footnotes. [BX5199.G69H6] 67-114881
1. Graham, Eric, Bp. of Brechin, 1888-1964. I. Title.

DARK, Sidney, 1874- 283'.0922
1947.
Five Deans: John Colet, John Donne, Jonathan Swift, Arthur Penrhyn Stanley, William Ralph Inge. Freeport, N.Y., Books for Libraries Press [1969] 255 p. 23 cm. (Essay index reprint series) Reprint of the 1928 ed. [BX5197.D25 1969b] 71-93332
1. Colet, John, 1467?-1519. 2. Donne, John, 1573-1631. 3. Swift, Jonathan, 1667-1745. 4. Stanley, Arthur Penrhyn, 1815-1881. 5. Inge, William Ralph, 1860-1954. I. Title.

DARK, Sidney, 1874- 283'.0922
1947.
Five Deans: John Colet, John Donne, Jonathan Swift, Arthur Penrhyn Stanley, William Ralph Inge. Port Washington, N.Y., Kennikat Press [1969] 255 p. 21 cm. (Essay and general literature index reprint series) Reprint of the 1928 ed. [BX5197.D25 1969] 70-86011
1. Colet, John, 1467?-1519. 2. Donne, John, 1573-1631. 3. Swift, Jonathan, 1667-1745. 4. Stanley, Arthur Penrhyn, 1815-1881. 5. Inge, William Ralph, 1860-1954. I. Title.

DURHAM, Eng. 283'.092'2 B
University. Durham Colleges. Dept. of Palaeography and Diplomatic.
Lists of deans and major canons of Durham, 1541-1900 / [compiled by P. Mussett]. Durham : [University of Durham, Department of Palaeography and Diplomatic], 1974. [1], xi, 105 p. ; 21 cm. Includes index. Bibliography: p. x-xi. [BX5197.D8 1974] 76-353655 ISBN 0-902193-42-2 : free
1. Church of England—Biography. 2. Deans, Cathedral and collegiate—Durham, Eng. 3. Durham, Eng.—Biography. I. Mussett, P. II. Title.

EDWARDS, David 283'.0922 B
Lawrence.
Leaders of the Church of England, 1828-1944, [by] David L. Edwards. London, New York, Oxford University Press, 1971. viii, 358 p. 8 plates, illus., ports. 23 cm. Includes bibliographical references. [BX5197.E3] 71-883686 ISBN 0-19-213110-9 £3.90
1. Church of England—Biography. I. Title.

THE lives of Philip 283'.092'2 B
and Matthew Henry / J. B. Williams. Edinburgh ; Carlisle, Pa. : Banner of Truth Trust, 1974. 2 v. in 1 : ports. ; 23 cm. Includes The life of the Rev. Philip Henry, A.M. with funeral sermons for Mr. and Mrs. Henry, by Matthew Henry, corrected and enlarged by J. B. Williams, 1825, and Memoirs of the life, character and writings of the Rev. Matthew Henry, by J. B. Williams, 1828. Includes indexes. [BX5207.H38L58] 75-327558 ISBN 0-85151-178-3 : £2.95
1. Henry, Philip, 1631-1696. 2. Henry, Matthew, 1662-1714. 3. Henry, Katharine, 1629-1707. I. Williams, John Bickerton, Sir, 1792-1855. II. Henry, Matthew, 1662-1714. The life of the Rev. Philip Henry. 1974. III. Williams, John Bickerton, Sir, 1792-1855. Memoirs of the life, character and writings of the Rev. Matthew Henry. 1974.

MORSE-BOYCOTT, 283'.0922 B
Desmond Lionel, 1892-
Lead, kindly light; studies of the saints and heros of the Oxford movement. Freeport, N.Y., Books for Libraries Press [1970] 240 p. 23 cm. (Essay index reprint series) Reprint of the 1933 ed. Contents.Contents.—Introduction. The romance of the century.—John Henry Newman.—Hugh James Rose.—Richard Hurrell Froude.—Isaac Williams.—John Keble.—Edward Bouverie Pusey.—Charles Marriott.—Frederick William Faber.—Henry Edward Manning.—Christina Rossetti.—Charles Fuge Lowder.—Robert Radclyffe Dolling.—Henry Parry Liddon.—Father Ignatius.—Arthur Henry Stanton.—Mary Scharlieb.—Frank Weston.—Arthur Tooth.—Thomas Alexander Lacey.—Mother Kate. [BX5100.M6 1970] 70-107728 ISBN 8-369-15291-
1. Church of England—Biography. 2. Oxford movement. 3. Anglo-Catholicism. I. Title.

RIDOUT, Lionel 283'.092'2 B
Utley.
Renegade, outcast, and maverick: three Episcopal clergymen in the California gold rush, by Lionel U. Ridout. San Diego, University Press, San Diego State University, c1973. iii, 127 p. 24 cm. On spine: Pioneer clergy. Includes bibliographical references. [BX5990.R52] 74-180275
1. Leavenworth, Thaddeus, 1802-1893. 2. Ver Mehr, John Leonard, ca. 1809-1886. 3. Ewer, Ferdinand Cartwright, 1826-1883. I. Title. II. Title: Pioneer clergy.

TEALE, William 283'.092'2 B
Henry, 1810-1878.
Lives of English laymen, Lord Falkland, Izaak Walton, Robert Nelson. Freeport, N.Y., Books for Libraries Press [1972] p. (Essay index reprint series) Reprint of the 1842 ed. Includes bibliographical references. [CT781.T4 1972] 72-3363 ISBN 0-8369-2930-6
1. Falkland, Lucius Cary, 2d Viscount, 1610?-1643. 2. Walton, Izaak, 1593-1683. 3. Nelson, Robert, 1656-1715. I. Title.

ADDISON, William. 283'.0924 B
Worthy Dr. Fuller. Westport, Conn., Greenwood Press [1971] xxi, 298 p. illus. 23 cm. Reprint of the 1951 ed. Bibliography: p. 290-294. [BX5199.F8A6 1971] 71-106707 ISBN 0-8371-3437-4
1. Fuller, Thomas, 1608-1661. I. Title.

ALLEN, Michael, 1927- 283'.0924
This time, this place. Indianapolis, Bobbs-Merrill [1971] viii, 170 p. 22 cm. Autobiographical. [BX5995.A54A3] 74-123221 4.95
I. Title.

ARNOTT, Anne. 283'.092'4 B
Wife to the archbishop / by Anne Arnott. London : Mowbrays, 1976. x, 161 p., [12] p. of plates : ill., ports. ; 23 cm. [BX5199.C5673A8] 77-355087 ISBN 0-264-66266-0 : £3.60
1. Coggan, Jean, 1908- 2. Clergymen's wives—England—Biography. I. Title.

ASHMUN, Jehudi, 1794- 283'.0924 B
1828.
Memoir of the life and character of the Rev. Samuel Bacon. Freeport, N.Y. Books for Libraries Press, 1971. viii, 288 p. 23 cm. (The Black heritage library collection) On spine: Life of the Rev. Samuel Bacon. Reprint of the 1822 ed. [BX5995.B3A8 1971] 77-154070 ISBN 0-8369-8781-0
1. Bacon, Samuel, 1781-1820. I. Title. II. Title: Life of the Rev. Samuel Bacon. III. Series.

ASTON, Margaret. 283'.0924 B
Thomas Arundel: a study of church life in the reign of Richard II. Oxford, Clarendon P., 1967. xiv, 456 p. front., 17 plates (incl. 2 maps, diagr.), tables. 22 1/2 cm. Based on thesis, Oxford University. Bibliography: p. [424]-436. [BR754.A7A8] 67-89463
1. Arundel, Thomas, 1353-1414. 2. Great Britain—Church history—Medieval period, 1066-1485. I. Title.

BAILEY, Hugh C. 283'.0924 B
Edgar Gardner Murphy, gentle progressive, by Hugh C. Bailey. Coral Gables, Fla., University of Miami Press [1968] xii, 274 p. illus., ports. 21 cm. Bibliography: p. [247]-258. [BX5995.M85B3] 68-29705 8.50
1. Murphy, Edgar Gardner, 1869-1913. 2. Southern States—History—1865- I. Title.

BARRETT, Thomas van 283'.092'4 B
Braam.
Great morning of the world / Thomas van Braam Barrett. Nashville : Abingdon Press, [1975] 189 p. ; 20 cm. [BX5995.B374B37] 75-16416 ISBN 0-687-15725-0 : 6.95
1. Barrett, Harry. I. Title.

BELLOC, Hilaire, 283'.092'4 B
1870-1953.
Cranmer, Archbishop of Canterbury 1533-1556 New York, Haskell House Publishers, 1973 [c1931] 333 p. illus. 23 cm. [DA317.8.C8B4 1973] 72-4495 ISBN 0-8383-1610-7 13.95 (lib. bdg.)
1. Cranmer, Thomas, Abp. of Canterbury, 1489-1556.

BENNETT, Gareth 283'.092'4 B
Vaughan.
The Tory crisis in church and state 1688-1730 : the career of Francis Atterbury Bishop of Rochester / G. V. Bennett. Oxford : Clarendon Press, 1975. xvii, 335 p., [5] leaves of plates : ill. ; 23 cm. Includes index. Bibliography: p. [311]-324. [DA501.A8B46] 76-358312 ISBN 0-19-822444-3 : £10.00 ($26.00 U.S.)
1. Atterbury, Francis, Bp. of Rochester, 1662-1732. 2. Church of England—History. 3. Church and state in England. 4. Jacobites. I. Title.

BOWIE, Walter 283'.0924 B
Russell, 1882-1969.
Learning to live. Nashville, Abingdon Press [1969] 288 p. 22 cm. Autobiography. Bibliographical footnotes. [BX5995.B63A3] 69-18450 4.95
I. Title.

BOYD, Malcolm, 1923- 283'.0924 B
As I live and breathe; stages of an autobiography. New York, Random House [1970, c1969] xi, 276 p. 22 cm. [BX5995.B66A3] 76-85608 6.95
I. Title.

BRAY, Thomas, 1658- 283'.0924
1730.
Rev. Thomas Bray: his life and selected works relating to Maryland. Edited by Bernard C. Steiner. New York, Arno Press, 1972. 252 p. 23 cm. (Religion in America, series II) Reprint of the 1901 ed., which was issued as no. 37 of Fund publication of Maryland Historical Society. Contents.Contents.—A short historical account of the life and designs of Thomas Bray, D.D., R. Rawlinson.—An essay towards promoting all necessary and useful knowledge, by T. Bray.—Apostolick charity, its nature and excellence considered.—The necessity of an early religion.—Several circular letters to the clergy of Maryland.—A memorial representing the present state of religion on the continent of North America.—The present state of the Protestant religion in Maryland.—A letter from Dr. Bray to such as have contributed towards propagating Christian knowledge in the plantations.—A memorial representing the present case of the Church in Maryland with relation to its establishment by law.—Bibliotheca parochialis.—An answer to a letter from Dr. Bray, by J. Wyeth.—A list of His Majesty's Council of Maryland and the Burgesses of the General Assembly of the said province.—"Notes" (p. 235-252) [F184.B83 1972] 79-39862
1. Maryland—History—Colonial period, ca. 1600-1775. 2. Maryland—Religion. I. Series: Maryland Historical Society. Fund publication, no. 37.

BROSE, Olive J. 283'.0924 B
Frederick Denison Maurice, rebellious conformist [by] Olive J. Brose. [Athens] Ohio University Press [1972, c1971] xxiii, 308 p. illus. 22 cm. Bibliography: p. 294-301. [BX5199.M3B76] 74-141380 ISBN 0-8214-0092-4 12.50
1. Maurice, Frederick Denison, 1805-1872.

BURGGRAAFF, 283'.092'4 B
Winfield.
Walter Edmund Bentley: actor, priest, missioner, 1864-1962, founder of the Actors' Church Alliance. [Staten Island? N.Y., 1970?] 31 p. illus. 23 cm. [PN2287.B4327B8] 72-178356
1. Bentley, Walter Edmund, 1864-1962. 2. Actors' Church Alliance of America.

CAMERON, Kenneth 283'.092'4 B
Walter, 1908- comp.
Ammi Rogers and the Episcopal Church in Connecticut, 1790-1832; his Memoirs and documents illuminating historical, religious, and personal backgrounds. Hartford, Transcendental Books [1974] 138 l. illus. 29 cm. "Memoirs of the Rev. Ammi Rogers, A.M.": leaves 15-91. [BX5995.R6C35] 74-173629
1. Rogers, Ammi, 1770-1852. 2. Protestant Episcopal Church in the U.S.A.—Connecticut—History—Sources. I. Rogers, Ammi, 1770-1852. Memoirs of the Rev. Ammi Rogers, A.M. 1974. II. Title.

CARVILL, H. C., 1928- 283'.0924 B
Royal servants: an Episcopal family heritage, by H. C. Carvill. Little Rock, 1968. 20 l. geneal. table. 30 cm. Bibliography: leaves 19-20. [BX5995.B825C3] 70-13585
1. Bruce, Caleb Alexander, 1818-1895. I. Title. II. Title: An Episcopal family heritage.

CHADWICK, Owen. 283'.092'4 B
Edward King: Bishop of Lincoln, 1885-1910. [Lincoln, Eng.] Friends of Lincoln Cathedral, 1968. 31 p. port. 22 cm. (Lincoln Minster pamphlets. Second series, no. 4) Includes bibliographical references. [BX5199.K5C4] 75-303738
1. King, Edward, Bp. of Lincoln, 1829-1910.

CHILLINGWORTH, 283'.092'4 B
William, 1602-1644.
The works of William Chillingworth. New York, AMS Press [1972] 3 v. 23 cm. Reprint of the 1938 ed. [BX5037.C48 1972] 72-946 ISBN 0-404-01570-0 21.00 ea.
1. Church of England—Collected works. 2. Catholic Church—Doctrinal and controversial works. 3. Theology—Collected works—17th century.
62.50 a set.

CLARKE, Martin 283'.092'4 B
Lowther.
Paley; evidences for the man [by] M. L. Clarke. [Toronto, Buffalo] University of Toronto Press [1974] viii, 161 p. 22 cm. Includes bibliographical references. [BX5199.P26C55 1974] 73-86991 ISBN 0-8020-2112-3 10.00
1. Paley, William, 1743-1805.

CLEOBURY, F. H. 283'.092'4 B
From clerk to cleric / [by] F. H. Cleobury ; with a foreword by Edward Carpenter. Cambridge : J. Clarke, 1976. [4], 44 p. ; 20 cm. [BX5199.C564A34] 77-359492 ISBN 0-227-67825-7 : £1.50
1. Cleobury, F. H. 2. Church of England—Clergy—Biography. 3. Clergy—England—Biography. I. Title.

CRANAGE, David Herbert 283'.092'4
Somerset, 1866-
Not only a dean, being the reminiscences of the Very Reverend D. H. S. Cranage. London, Faith Press; New York, Morehouse-Gorham [1952] 234p. illus. 23cm. [BX5199.C73A3] 55-18133
1. Church of England—Clergy—Correspondence, reminiscences, etc. I. Title.

DAWLEY, Powel Mills, 283'.092'4
1907-
John Whitgift and the English Reformation. New York, Scribner, 1954. xii, 254p. 21cm. (The Hale lectures, 1953) Bibliography: p. 231-242. [BX5199.W535D3] 54-11017
1. Whitgift, John, Abp. of Canterbury, 1530?-1604. I. Title. II. Series: Seabury-Western Theological Seminary, Evanston, Ill. The Hale lectures, 1953

DAWSON, Edwin Collas, 283'.0924 B
1849-1925.
James Hannington, D.D., F.L.S., E.R.G.S., first bishop of eastern equatorial Africa; a history of his life and work, 1847-1885. New York, Negro Universities Press [1969] x, 451 p. illus., map, port. 23 cm. Reprint of the 1887 ed. [BV3522.H3D3 1969] 69-19355
1. Hannington, James, Bp., 1847-1885.

DEAL, Williams 283'.092'4 B
John Newton, author of the song "Amazing grace," by William Deal. Westchester, Ill., Good News Publishers [1974] 80 p. 18 cm. (One evening book OE140) [BX5199.N55D35] 74-76011 0.95 (pbk.).
1. Newton, John, 1725-1807.

EDWARDS, Brian H. 283'.092'4 B
God's outlaw / [by] Brian H. Edwards. Welwyn ; Grand Rapids, Mich. : Evangelical Press, 1976. 180 p. : ill., facsims., port. ; 22 cm. Includes index. Bibliography: p. 171-174. [BR350.T8E25] 77-363319 ISBN 0-85234-067-2 : £2.70. ISBN 0-85234-066-4 pbk.
1. Tyndale, William, d. 1536. 2. Christian biography—England. I. Title.

EDWARDS, David 283'.092'4 B
Lawrence.
Ian Ramsey, Bishop of Durham; a memoir [by] David L. Edwards. London, New York, Oxford University Press, 1973. 101 p. illus., port. 23 cm. [BX5199.R22E38] 73-179441 ISBN 0-19-213111-7 £2.00
1. Ramsey, Ian T. I. Title.

ELLIS, Joseph J. 283'.092'4 B
The New England mind in transition; Samuel Johnson of Connecticut, 1696-1772 [by] Joseph J. Ellis. New Haven, Yale University Press, 1973. xii, 292 p. illus. 23 cm. (Yale historical publications. Miscellany, 98) Bibliography: p. 271-286. [LD1245 1754.E44] 73-77149 ISBN 0-300-01615-8 10.00
1. Johnson, Samuel, 1696-1772. I. Title. II. Series.

FFRENCH-BEYTAGH, 283'.092'4 B
Gonville Aubie.
Encountering darkness [by] Gonville Ffrench-Beytagh. New York, Seabury Press [1974, c1973] 283 p. 22 cm. "A Crossroad book." Autobiographical. [BX5700.6.Z8F473] 73-17895 ISBN 0-8164-1149-2 6.95
1. Ffrench-Beytagh, Gonville Aubie. 2. Church and race problems—Africa, South. I. Title.

GOOSE, Edmund William, 283'.0924
Sir, 1849-1928.
Jeremy Taylor. New York, Greenwood Press, 1968 [c1904] xi, 234 p. 19 cm. [BX5199.T3G6 1968] (B) 68-28590
1. Taylor, Jeremy, Bp. of Down and Connor, 1613-1667.

GOSSE, Edmund 283'.0924 B
William, Sir, 1849-1928.
Jeremy Taylor. New York, Macmillan, 1904. Grosse Pointe, Mich., Scholarly Press, 1968. xi, 234 p. 20 cm. (English men of letters) [BX5199.T3G6 1968b] 71-5151
1. Taylor, Jeremy, Bp. of Down and Connor, 1613-1667.

GROVES, Reginald, 1908- 283'.0924
Conrad Noel and the Thaxted Movement; an adventure in Christian socialism, by Reg Groves. New York, A. M. Kelley [1968] 334 p. port. 23 cm. Bibliographical references included in "Sources and acknowledgements" (p. 327-328) [BX5199.N65G7 1968] 68-3219
1. Noel, Conrad, 1869-1942. I. Title.

†GUNSTONE, John 283'.092'4 B
Thomas Arthur.
Living together : the warm and candid story of one man's experience in a Christian community / John Gunstone ; drawings by Sylvia Lawton. 1st American ed. Minneapolis : Bethany Fellowship, 1976. 125 p. : ill. ; 18 cm. (Dimension books) [BX5186.B37G86 1976] 76-57794 ISBN 0-87123-325-8 pbk. : 1.95
1. Barnabas Fellowship. 2. Gunstone, John Thomas Arthur. 3. Church of England—Clergy—Biography. 4. Pentecostalism—Church of England. 5. Clergy—England—Biography. I. Title.

HARPER, John C. 283'.092'4 B
Sunday: a minister's story [by] John C. Harper. [1st ed.] Boston, Little, Brown [1974] xi, 238 p. 21 cm. Autobiographical. [BX5995.H33A35] 74-4401 ISBN 0-316-34709-4 6.95
1. Harper, John C. I. Title.

HARRIS, Gordon L. 283'.092'4 B
A new command : the life of Bruce Medaris, Major General, USA, retired / Gordon Harris. Plainfield, N.J. : Logos International, c1976. v, 313 p., [7] leaves of plates : ill. ; 21 cm. [BX5995.M43H37] 76-10533 ISBN 0-88270-181-9 : 3.50
1. Medaris, John B., 1902- 2. Protestant Episcopal Church in the U.S.A.—Clergy—Biography. 3. Clergy—United States—Biography. 4. Generals—United States—Biography. I. Title.

HENDERSON, John L. H. 283'.0924 B
John Strachan, 1778-1867 [by] J. L. H. Henderson. [Toronto] University of Toronto Press [1969] 112 p. 21 cm. (Canadian biographical studies) Includes bibliographical references. [BX5620.S75H4] 70-408188 4.50
1. Strachan, John, Bp., 1778-1867.

HEYWARD, Carter. 283'.092'4 B
A priest forever / Carter Heyward. 1st ed. New York : Harper & Row, c1976. 146 p. : ill. ; 21 cm. Includes bibliographical references. [BX5995.H46A34 1976] 75-36736 ISBN 0-06-063893-1 : 6.95
1. Heyward, Carter. 2. Ordination of women—Protestant Episcopal Church in the U.S.A. I. Title.

HOBHOUSE, Stephen 283'.092'4
Henry, 1881-1961.
William Law and eighteenth century Quakerism; including some unpublished letters and fragments of William Law and John Byrom. New York, B. Blom, 1972. 342 p. illus. 21 cm. Reprint of the 1927 ed. published by G. Allen & Unwin, London. Includes bibliographical references. [BX5199.L3H62 1972] 77-175870 14.50
1. Law, William, 1686-1761. 2. Byrom, John, 1692-1763. 3. Dodshon, Frances (Henshaw) Paxton, 1714-1793. 4. Friends, Society of. I. Title.

HOPKINS, Hugh 283'.092'4 B
Alexander Evan.
Charles Simeon of Cambridge / Hugh Evan Hopkins. [Grand Rapids, Mich.] : W. B. Eerdmans Pub. Co., 1977. 236 p. : ill. (on lining paper) ; 25 cm. Includes bibliographical references and index. [BX5199.S55H66 1977] 77-153375 ISBN 0-8028-3498-1 : 7.95
1. Simeon, Charles, 1759-1836. 2. Church of England—Clergy—Biography. 3. Clergy—England—Cambridge—Biography. 4. Cambridge, Eng.—Biography. I. Title.

HOWELL, Robert Lee. 283'.092'4 B
Lost Mountain days, by Robert L. Howell. [1st ed.] Boston, Jarrow Press, 1973. 122 p. 18 cm. [BX5995.H72H34] 73-75351 ISBN 0-912190-12-4 2.50 (pbk.)
1. Howell, Robert Lee. 2. Mason Parish. I. Title.

HUFFMAN, Carolyn. 283'.092'4 B
Bloom where you are / Carolyn Huffman. Santa Ana, Calif. : Vision House Publishers, 1976. 152 p. ; 21 cm. Includes bibliographical references. [BX5995.H74A33] 75-42853 ISBN 0-88449-024-6 pbk. : 2.95
1. Huffman, Carolyn. 2. Protestant Episcopal Church in the U.S.A.—Biography. 3. Clergymen's wives—Pennsylvania—Pittsburgh—Biography. 4. Pittsburgh—Biography. I. Title.

HUNTLEY, Frank 283'.0924
Livingstone, 1902-
Jeremy Taylor and the Great Rebellion; a study of his mind and temper in controversy. Ann Arbor, University of Michigan Press [1970] ix, 131 p. 22 cm. Bibliography: p. 113-125. [BX5199.T3H82] 72-107975 ISBN 0-472-08470-4 7.50
1. Taylor, Jeremy, Bp. of Down and Connor, 1613-1667. I. Title.

IREMONGER, Frederick 283'.092'4
Athelwold, 1878-
William Temple, Archbishop of Canterbury; his life and letters Abridged ed. by D. C. Somervell. London, New York, Oxford University Press, 1963. 292 p. 20 cm. (Oxford AErbacks, no 59) [BX5199.T42I72] 64-1859
1. 1. Temple, William, Abp. of Canterbury, 1881-1944. I. Title.

JACKSON, Thomas, 283'.092'4 B
1942-
Go back, you didn't say "May I"; the diary of a young priest. New York, Seabury Press [1974] vi, 238 p. 22 cm. "A Crossroad book." [BX5995.J23A33] 74-11382 ISBN 0-8164-1170-0 7.95
1. Jackson, Thomas, 1942- I. Title.

JARRATT, Devereux, 283'.0924 B
1733-1801.
The life of the Reverend Devereux Jarratt. New York, Arno Press, 1969. 223 p. 23 cm. (Religion in America) "A series of letters addressed to the Rev. John Coleman." Reprint of the 1806 ed. [BX5995.J27A3 1969] 79-83427
I. Coleman, John, 1758?-1816. II. Title.

JASPER, Ronald Claud 283/0924
Dudley.
George Bell. Bishop of Chichester [by] Ronald C D. Jasper. London, New York Oxford Univ. Pr., 1967. xi, 401p. front., 13 plates (incl. ports.). 23cm. Bibl. [BX5199.B355J3] (B) 67-10893 11.20
1. Bell, George Kennedy Allen, Bp. of Chichester 1883-1958. I. Title.

KEARNEY, Flora 283'.0924
McLaughlin, 1920-
James Hervey and eighteenth-century taste. Muncie, Ind., Ball State University, 1969. v, 50 p. 23 cm. (Publications in English, no. 9) (Ball State monograph no. 14.) Bibliography: p. 48-50. [BX5199.H5K4] 79-625280
1. Hervey, James, 1714-1758. I. Title. II. Series: Indiana. Ball State University, Muncie. Publications in English, no. 9. III. Series: Indiana. Ball State University, Muncie. Ball State monograph no. 14

KELLOCK, Harold, 283'.0924 B
1879-
Parson Weems of the cherry-tree; being a short account of the eventful life of the Reverend M. L. Weems. Ann Arbor, Mich., Gryphon Books, 1971. ix, 212 p. illus. 22 cm. "Facsimile reprint of the 1928 edition." [E302.6.W4K4 1928a] 75-107137
1. Weems, Mason Locke, 1759-1825. I. Title.

KIVENGERE, Festo. 283'.092'4 B
I love Idi Amin : the story of triumph under fire in the midst of suffering and persecution in Uganda / Festo Kivengere, with Dorothy Smoker. Old Tappan, N.J. : F. H. Revell Co., c1977. 63 p. : ill. ; 18 cm. (New Life ventures) [BX5700.8.Z8K58] 77-79929 ISBN 0-8007-9004-9 : 0.95
1. Kivengere, Festo. 2. Church of Uganda, Rwanda, Burundi, and Boga—Zaire—Bishops—Biography. 3. Amin, Idi, 1925- 4. Bishops—Uganda—Biography. I. Smoker, Dorothy, joint author. II. Title.

KNOX, John, 1900- 283'.092'4 B
Never far from home : the story of my life / John Knox. Waco, Tex. : Word Books, [1975] 170 p. ; 23 cm. [BX5995.K57A33] 74-82657 5.95
1. Knox, John, 1900- I. Title.

KNOX, R Buick. 283'.0924 (B)
James Ussher, Archbishop of Armagh, b R Buick Knox. Cardiff, University of Wales P., 1967. [7], 205 p. plate, port. 23 cm. 35/- (B 68-00565) Bibliography: p. 194-201. [BX5595.U8K5] 68-75114
1. Ussher, James, Abp. of Armagh, 1581-1656. I. Title.

KNOX, R. Buick. 283'.0924
James Ussher, Archbishop of Armagh, by R. Buick Knox. Cardiff, Univ. of Wales Pr., 1967. [7], 205p. plate, port. 23cm. Bibl. [BX5595.U8K5] (B) 68-75114 10.00
1. Ussher, James, Abp. of Armagh, 1581-1656. I. Title.
Distributed by Verry, Mystic, Conn.

LANGSTAFF, John 283'.0924 B
Brett, 1889-
Likable people who changed a world, 1917-1922. [1st ed.] New York, Vantage Press [1970] xxv, 576 p. illus., ports. 22 cm. [BX5995.L28A3] 77-13856 7.50
I. Title.

LEMMON, Sarah 283'.0924 B
McCulloh.
Parson Pettigrew of the "Old Church", 1744-1807. Chapel Hill, University of North Carolina Press, 1970. 168 p. 23 cm. (The James Sprunt studies in history and political science, v. 52) Bibliography: p. [149]-155. [F251.J28 vol. 52] 76-132259 ISBN 0-8078-5052-7
1. Pettigrew, Charles, 1744-1807. I. Title. II. Series.

LEWIS, Clive Staples, 283'.0924
1898-1963.
Letters to an American lady. Edited by Clyde S. Kilby. Grand Rapids, Mich., W. B. Eerdmans Pub. Co. [1967] 121 p. facsims. (on lining papers) 23 cm. [BX5199.L53A42] 67-30853
I. Title.

LEWIS, James, 1935- 283'.092'4 B
West Virginia pilgrim / James Lewis. New York : Seabury Press, c1976. 211 p. ; 22 cm. "A Crossroad book." [BX5995.L38A37] 75-37790 ISBN 0-8164-0297-3 : 7.95
1. Lewis, James, 1935- I. Title.

LOWE, Bob. 283'.0924 B
Letters to John / Bob Lowe. Christchurch : Whitcoulls, 1976. 121 p. ; 21 cm. [BX5720.5.Z8L67] 77-369163 ISBN 0-7233-0472-6 : 4.50
1. Lowe, Bob. 2. Church of the Province of New Zealand—Clergy—Biography. 3. Clergy—New Zealand—Biography. I. Title.

MACFARLANE, Alan. 283'.092'4 B
The family life of Ralph Josselin, a seventeenth-century clergyman : an essay in historical anthropology / by Alan Macfarlane. New York : Norton, [1977] c1970. p. cm. (The Norton library) Reprint of the ed. published by the University Press, Cambridge, Eng. Includes index. Bibliography: p. [BX5199.J66M3 1977] 77-440 ISBN 0-393-00849-5 pbk. : 3.95
1. Josselin, Ralph, 1617-1683. 2. Church of England—Clergy—Biography. 3. Clergy—England—Biography. I. Title.

MCKINSTRY, Arthur R 283'.092'4 B
All I have seen : the McKinstry memoirs / by the fifth bishop of Delaware, 1939-1954 [A. R. McKinstry]. Wilmington, Del. : Serendipity Press, c1975. 266 p. : ill. ; 24 cm. [BX5995.M32A34] 75-24664 ISBN 0-914988-02-6 : 10.00
1. McKinstry, Arthur R. I. Title.

MANUEL, Frank Edward. 283'.092'4
The religion of Isaac Newton / Frank E. Manuel. Oxford : Clarendon Press, 1974. vi, 141 p. ; 23 cm. (Fremantle lectures ; 1973) Includes bibliographical references and index. [QC16.N7M32] 75-302605 ISBN 0-19-826640-5 : 11.25
1. Newton, Isaac, Sir, 1642-1727—Religion and ethics. I. Title. II. Series.

MARSH, Peter T. 283'.0924
The Victorian church in decline; Archbishop Tait and the Church of England, 1868-1882 [by] P. T. Marsh. [Pittsburgh] University of Pittsburgh Press [1969] x, 344 p. illus., port. 23 cm. Bibliography: p. 328-335. [BX5199.T278M3 1969b] 72-80032 8.95
1. Tate, Archibald Campbell, Abp. of Canterbury, 1881-1882. 2. Church of England—History. I. Title.

MARSHALL, William M. 283'.092'4 B
George Hooper, 1640-1727, Bishop of Bath and Wells / [by] William M. Marshall. Sherborne : Dorset Publishing Co., 1976. [8], 221 p. : ill., facsims., ports. ; 22 cm. Includes index. Bibliography: p. 204-212. [BX5199.H814M37 1976] 76-377651 ISBN 0-902129-27-9 : £4.50
1. Hooper, George, Bp. of Bath and Wells, 1640-1727. 2. Church of England—Bishops—Biography. 3. Bishops—England—Biography. I. Title.

MEACHAM, Standish. 283'.0924 B
Lord Bishop; the life of Samuel Wilberforce, 1805-1873. Cambridge, Mass., Harvard University Press, 1970. x, 328 p. port. 25 cm. Bibliography: p. [ix]-x. [BX5199.W6M4] 70-102669 13.50
1. Wilberforce, Samuel, Bp. of Winchester, 1805-1873. I. Title.

MELCOMBE, George Bubb 283'.092'4
Dodington, baron 1691-1762.
The political journal of George Bubb Dodington, Edited by John Carswell and Lewis Arnold Dralle. Oxford, Clarendon Press, 1965. xxv, 476 p. facsim. 23 cm. [DA501.M5A3] 65-9274
1. Gt. Brit. — Hist. — George II, 1727-1760 — Sources. 2. Gt. Brit. — Hist. — George III, 1760-1820 — Sources. I. Carswell, John, ed. II. Dralle, Lewis Arnold, ed. III. Title.

MIDGLEY, Graham. 283'.092'4 B
The life of Orator Henley. Oxford, Clarendon Press, 1973. ix, 297 p. illus. 22 cm. "A list of Henley's writings" (p. [288]-291) [BX5199.H444M53 1973] 73-162280 ISBN 0-19-812032-X
1. Henley, John, 1692-1756. I. Title.
Distributed by Oxford University Press N.Y. 19.25.

MOSSNER, Ernest 283'.0924 B
Campbell, 1907-
Bishop Butler and the age of reason; a study in the history of thought. New York, B. Blom, 1971. xv, 271 p. 21 cm. Reprint of the 1936 ed. Bibliography: p. 241-261. [BX5199.B9M6 1971] 69-13247
1. Butler, Joseph, Bp. of Durham, 1692-1752. 2. Religious thought—Gt. Brit. I. Title.

MOZLEY, James 283'.0924 B
Frederic, 1887-
William Tyndale, by J. F. Mozley. Westport, Conn., Greenwood Press [1971] ix, 364 p. illus., ports. 23 cm. Reprint of the 1937 ed. Bibliography: p. vii. [BR350.T8M6 1971] 70-109801 ISBN 0-8371-4292-X
1. Tyndale, William, d. 1536.

NEVE, Rosemary, 283'.092'4 B
1923-
At the name of Jesus / by Rosemary Neve. Evesham : James, 1976. 110 p. ; 19 cm. [BX5199.N53A34] 77-363320 ISBN 0-85305-189-5 : £2.25
1. Neve, Rosemary, 1923- 2. Anglicans—Biography. I. Title.

ORR, Robert R. 283'.0924
Reason and authority: the thought of William Chillingworth, by Robert R. Orr. London, Oxford U.P., 1967. xi, 217 p. 22 1/2 cm. Rewritten and shortened verson of author's thesis, University of London. Bibliography: p. [206]-213. [BX5199.C47O7] 67-99857
1. Chillingworth, William, 1602-1644. 2. Authority (Religion) I. Title.

PATON, Alan. 283'.092'4 B
Apartheid and the archbishop: the life and times of Geoffrey Clayton, Archbishop of Cape Town. New York, Scribner [1974, c1973] xiii, 311 p. ports. 23 cm. Bibliography: p. xi-xii. [BX5700.6.Z8C556 1974] 73-17998 ISBN 0-684-13713-5 10.00
1. Clayton, Geoffrey Hare, Abp., 1884-1957. I. Title.

PIKE, Diane Kennedy. 283'.0924 B
Search: the personal story of a wilderness journey. [1st ed.] Garden City, N.Y., Doubleday, 1970, [c1969] xii, 198 p. col. map (on lining papers) 22 cm. [BX5995.P54P5] 74-108620 4.95
1. Pike, James Albert, Bp., 1913-1969. I. Title.

POLLARD, Albert 283.0924
Frederick, 1869-1948
Thomas Cranmer and the English reformation, 1489-1556. [Unaltered, unabridged ed.] Hamden, Conn., Archon [dist. Shoe String] 1965[c.1905] xv, 399p. illus., ports. 19cm. Bibl. [DA317.8.C8P8] 65-24503 8.50
1. Cranmer, Thomas, Abp. of Canterbury, 1489-1556. I. Title.

PORTER, Anthony 283'.0924 B
Toomer, 1828-1902.
Led on! Step by step, scenes from clerical, military, educational, and plantation life in the South, 1828-1898; an autobiography. New York, Putnam, 1898. Miami, Fla., Mnemosyne Pub. Co. [1969] xv, 462 p. illus., ports. 23 cm. [BX5995.P6A3 1969] 75-89383
I. Title.

PULKINGHAM, W. 283'.092'4 B
Graham.
Gathered for power, by Graham Pulkingham. Illus. by Cathleen. New York, Morehouse-Barlow Co. [1972] 138, [5] p. illus. 22 cm. Bibliography: p. [141]-143] [BX5995.P767A33] 72-80885 ISBN 0-8192-1130-3 2.50
1. Pulkingham, W. Graham. 2. Church of the Redeemer, Houston, Tex. I. Title.

RAINSFORD, William 283'.0924 B
Stephen, 1850-1933.
The story of a varied life; an autobiography. Freeport, N.Y., Books for Libraries Press [1970] 481 p. illus., ports. 23 cm. Reprint of the 1922 ed. [BX5995.R3A35 1970] 70-126249
I. Title.

ROBIN, Arthur de 283'.092'4 B
Quetteville.
Mathew Blagden Hale : the life of an Australian pioneer bishop / [by] A. de Q. Robin. Melbourne : Hawthorn Press, 1976. iv, 227 p., 2 leaves of plates, (ports.) ; 22 cm. Includes index. Bibliography: p. 216-221. [BX5199.H215R6] 77-362808 ISBN 0-7256-0167-1 : 14.95
1. Hale, Matthew Blagdon. 2. Church of England—Bishops—Biography. 3. Bishops—Australia—Biography.

ROBIN, Arthur de 283'.0924
Quettevillef.
Charles Perry, Bishop of Melbourne; the challenges of a colonal episcopate, 1847-76 [by] A. de Q. Robin. [Nedlands, Perth] Univ. of Western Australia Pr. [1967] x, 229p. illus., facsim, maps (on lining-papers) ports. 25cm. Bibl. [BX5720.P4R6] (B) 67-27319 8.50 bds.,
1. Perry, Charies, 1807-1891. I. Title.
Distributed by Verry, Mystic, Conn.

ROE, Gordon. 283'.092'4 B
J. B. Dykes (1823-1876), priest & musician : essays / by Gordon Roe & Arthur Hutchings. [Durham] : [St Oswald's Parochial Church Council], [1976]. [5], 25, [3] p. : ill., port. ; 22 cm. Cover title. Bibliography: p. [2]. [BX5199.D94R63] 77-356903 ISBN 0-9505339-0-4 : £0.45
1. Dykes, John Bacchus, 1823-1876. 2. Church of England—Clergy—Biography. 3. Clergy—England—Biography. 4. Musicians—England—Biography. I. Hutchings, Arthur, 1906- joint author.

ROSS Williamson, 283'.092'4 B
Hugh, 1901-
Jeremy Taylor. [Folcroft, Pa.] Folcroft Library Editions, 1973. p. Reprint of the 1952 ed. published by Dobson, London, in series: A Pegasus biography. [BX5199.T3R65 1973] 73-15705 20.00
1. Taylor, Jeremy, Bp. of Down and Connor, 1613-1667.

ROSS Williamson, 283'.092'4 B
Hugh, 1901-
Jeremy Taylor / Hugh Ross Williamson. Norwood, Pa. : Norwood Editions, 1975. 179 p., [5] leaves of plates : ill. ; 24 cm. Reprint of the 1952 ed. published by D. Dobson, London, in series: A Pegasus biography.

Includes index. Bibliography: p. 176. [BX5199.T3R65 1975] 75-31842 ISBN 0-88305-778-6 : 25.00
1. Taylor, Jeremy, Bp. of Down and Connor, 1613-1667.

SHAPIRO, Barbara J. 283'.0924 B
John Wilkins, 1614-1672; an intellectual biography [by] Barbara J. Shapiro. Berkeley, University of California Press, 1969. 333 p. port. 24 cm. Bibliographical references included in "Notes" (p. 251-320) [LF724.W5S5] 73-84042 9.50
1. Wilkins, John, Bp. of Chester, 1614-1672. 2. Religion and science—History of controversy.

SHOEMAKER, Helen 283'.0924 B
(Smith)
I stand by the door; the life of Sam Shoemaker [by] Helen Smith Shoemaker. [1st ed.] New York, Harper & Row [1967] xviii, 220, [2] p. 22 cm. "Books written by Dr. Samuel Moor Shoemaker": p. [222] [BX5995.S347S5] 66-20784
1. Shoemaker, Samuel Moor, 1893-1963. I. Title.

SKARDON, Alvin 283'.0924 B
Wilson, 1912-
Church leader in the cities: William Augustus Muhlenberg [by] Alvin W. Skardon. Philadelphia, University of Pennsylvania Press [1971] 343 p. illus., geneal. tables, ports. 24 cm. Originally presented as the author's thesis, University of Chicago, 1960, under the title: William Augustus Muhlenberg: pioneer urban church leader. Bibliography: p. 312-334. [BX5995.M8S54 1971] 70-92853 ISBN 0-8122-7596-9 15.00
1. Muhlenberg, William Augustus, 1796-1877. I. Title.

SMITH, Audley 283'.092'4
Lawrence, 1899-1954.
Richard Hurd's Letters on chivalry and romance. [Folcroft, Pa.] Folcroft Library Editions, 1973. 25 p. 26 cm. Reprint of the 1939 ed., originally presented as the author's thesis, Johns Hopkins University, 1936. Includes bibliographical references. [PR3517.H78Z8 1973] 73-5558 4.50
1. Hurd, Richard, Bp. of Worcester, 1720-1808. Letters on chivalry and romance. I. Title.

STEINER, Bruce E. 283'.092'4 B
Samuel Seabury, 1729-1796; a study in the High Church tradition [by bruce E. Steiner] [Athens] Ohio University Press [1972, c1971] xiii, 508 p. illus. 22 cm. Bibliography: p. 464-482. [BX5995.S3S73] 78-181686 ISBN 0-8214-0098-3 13.50
1. Seabury, Samuel, Bp., 1729-1796.

STEPHENSON, Colin. 283'.092'4 B
Merrily on high. [1st American ed.] New York, Morehouse-Barlow Co. [1973, c1972] 192 p. 22 cm. [BX5199.S819A33 1973] 73-166415 ISBN 0-8192-1152-4 4.95
1. Stephenson, Colin. I. Title.

STERLING, Chandler 283'.092'4 B
W., Bp., 1911-
Beyond this land of whoa, by Chandler W. Sterling. Philadelphia, United Church Press [1973] 141 p. 22 cm. "A Pilgrim Press book." [BX5995.S786A32] 73-5904 ISBN 0-8298-0261-4 4.95
1. Sterling, Chandler W., Bp., 1911- I. Title.

STRANKS, Charles 283'.092'4 B
James.
The life and writings of Jeremy Taylor, by C. J. Stranks. [Folcroft, Pa.] Folcroft Library Editions, 1973. p. Reprint of the 1952 ed. published by S.P.C.K., London, for the Church Historical Society. [BX5199.T3S8 1973] 73-11259 25.00
1. Taylor, Jeremy, Bp. of Down and Connor, 1613-1667. I. Church Historical Society (Gt. Brit.) II. Title.

STRINGFELLOW, 283'.092'4 B
William.
The death and life of Bishop Pike / William Stringfellow and Anthony Towne. 1st ed. Garden City, N.Y. : Doubleday, 1976. xxxii, 446 p., [8] leaves of plates : ill. ; 22 cm. "Books by James A. Pike": [445]-446. [BX5995.P54S83] 75-32721 ISBN 0-385-07455-7 : 10.00
1. Pike, James Albert, Bp., 1913-1969. I. Towne, Anthony, joint author. II. Title.

STRYPE, John, 1643- 283'.092'4 B
1737.
Historical collections of the life and acts of the Right Reverend Father in God, John Aylmer ... A new ed. New York, B. Franklin Reprints [1974] xviii, 219, [3] p. 23 cm. (Burt Franklin research & source works series. Philosophy & religious history monographs, 147) Reprint of the 1821 ed. published by the Clarendon Press, Oxford, Eng. Bibliography: p. [221]-[222] [BX5199.A9S8 1974] 74-979 ISBN 0-8337-4427-5 20.00
1. Aylmer, John, Bp. of London, 1521-1594. I. Title.

STRYPE, John, 1643- 283'.092'4
1737.
The history of the life and acts of the Most Reverend Father in God, Edmund Grindal ... To which is added an appendix of original mss. ... New York, B. Franklin [1974] xxi, 607 p. port. 23 cm. (Burt Franklin research and source work series. Philosophy and religious history monographs, 145) Reprint of the ed. published in 1821 by Clarendon Press, Oxford, Eng. [BX5199.G74S8 1974] 78-183700 ISBN 0-8337-3445-8 50.00 (2 volumes)
1. Grindal, Edmund, Abp. of Canterbury, 1519?-1583. I. Title. II. Series.

SWEET, Charles 283'.0924 B
Filkins, 1854or5-1927.
A champion of the cross. New York, AMS Press [1971] ix, 374 p. illus., port. 23 cm. Reprint of the 1894 ed. [BX5995.H67S8 1971] 76-144692 ISBN 0-404-07202-X
1. Hopkins, John Henry, 1820-1891. I. Title.

TOON, Peter, 1939- 283'.092'4 B
John Charles Ryle : evangelical bishop / by Peter Toon and Michael Smout. Cambridge : J. Clarke, 1976. 123 p., plate : port. ; 24 cm. "Selected list of tracts and books by J. C. Ryle": p. 121. [BX5199.R9T66 1976b] 77-358597 ISBN 0-227-67826-5 : £3.75
1. Ryle, John Charles, Bp. of Liverpool, 1816-1900. 2. Church of England—Bishops—Biography. 3. Bishops—England—Biography. I. Smout, Michael, 1937- joint author.

WARD, Wilfrid 283'.092'4 B
Philip, 1856-1916.
William George Ward and the Oxford movement / by Wilfrid Ward. New York : AMS Press, 1977. xxix, 462 p. : ill. ; 23 cm. Reprint of the 1889 ed. published by Macmillan, London, New York. [BX4705.W3W35 1977] 75-29625 ISBN 0-404-14043-2 : 31.50
1. Ward, William George, 1812-1882. 2. Catholics in England—Biography. 3. Oxford movement. I. Title.

WARNER, Abraham 283'.092'4 B
Joseph, b.1821.
The private journal of Abraham Joseph Warner; extracts from volumes I, III, and IV (4 November 1838 to 25 December 1864). Extracted by Herbert B. Enderton. [San Diego? Calif., 1973] ix, 319 p. illus. 23 cm. "Limited edition of two hundred copies." [BX5995.W346A33] 73-78433
1. Warner, Abraham Joseph, b. 1821. I. Enderton, Herbert B. II. Title.

WATTS, Isaac, 1674- 283'.0924
1748.
Reliquiae juveniles; miscellaneous thoughts in prose and verse, 1734. A facsimile reproduction with an introd. by Samuel J. Rogal. Gainesville, Fla., Scholars' Facsimiles & Reprints, 1968. ix, xx, 350 p. 23 cm. Original t.p. has imprint: London, Printed for R. Ford and R. Hett, 1734. "Reproduced from a copy owned by Samuel J. Rogal." [BX5200.W36 1968] 68-17018
I. Title.

WATTS, Isaac, 1674- 283'.092'4
1748.
The works of the reverend and learned Isaac Watts, containing, besides his sermons and essays on miscellaneous subjects, several additional pieces, selected from his manuscripts by the Rev. Dr. Jennings and the Rev. Dr. Dodridge, in 1753: to which are prefixed Memoirs of the life of the author, compiled by George Burder. London, J. Garfield, 1810-1811. [New York, AMS Press, 1971] 6 v. 28 cm. [PR3763.W2A6 1971] 70-131027 ISBN 0-404-06890-1

WEEKS, Philip E. 283'.092'4 B
After you receive power / Philip E. Weeks. New York : Morehouse-Barlow Co., c1974. 106 p. ; 20 cm. [BT123.W4] 74-80380 ISBN 0-8192-1185-0 pbk. : 2.95
1. Weeks, Philip E. 2. Baptism in the Holy Spirit. I. Title.

WOOD, Christine. 283'.092'4 B
Exclusive by-path : the autobiography of a pilgrim / by Christine Wood. Evesham : James, 1976. 141 p. ; 19 cm. [BX5179.W74A33] 76-373348 ISBN 0-85305-183-6 : £2.80
1. Wood, Christine. 2. Church of England—Biography. 3. Plymouth Brethren—Biography. I. Title.

WOODFORDE, James, 283'.0924 B
1740-1803.
Woodforde at Oxford, 1759-1776: [extracts from his diary] edited by W. N. Hargreaves-Mawdsley Oxford, Clarendon P. for the Oxford Historical Society, 1969. [1], xviii, 351 p. plate, port. 23 cm. (Oxford Historical Society. [Publications] new ser., v. 21) [LF517.W6 1969] 76-565426 ISBN 0-901775-01-0 4/4/-
1. Oxford. University—Students. I. Hargreaves-Mawdsley, W. N., ed. II. Title. III. Series.

YOUNG, Charles R. 283'.0924
Hubert Walter, Lord of Canterbury and Lord of England [by] Charles R. Young. Durham, N. C., Duke University Press, 1968. viii, 196 p. 25 cm. (Duke historical publications) Includes bibliographical references. [BR754.H8Y6] 68-24438
1. Hubert Walter, Abp. of Canterbury, d. 1205. I. Series.

YOUNG, Mary Blamir. 283'.0924
Richard Wilton: a forgotten Victorian. London, Allen & Unwin, 1967. 3-225p. 8 plates, illus., geneal. table, ports. 23cm. [BX5199.W69Y6] (B) 68-98929 5.25 bds.,
1. Wilton, Richard, 1827-1903. I. Title.
Distributed by Fernhill House, 162 E. 23 St., New York, N.Y. 10010.

LOCHHEAD, Marion. 283.41
Episcopal Scotland in the nineteenth century. London, Murray [1966] xii, 278p. illus., 8 plates (incl. ports.) 23cm. Bibl. [BX5300.L6] 66-66628 8.50
1. Episcopal Church in Scotland—Hist. I. Title.
American distributor: Hillary House, New York.

PHILLIPS, John, 1940- 283'.41
The reformation of images : destruction of art in England, 1535-1660 / by John Phillips. Berkeley : University of California Press, c1973. xiii, 228 p., [14] leaves of plates : ill. ; 24 cm. Includes index. Bibliography: p. 211-220. [BR757.P5] 72-97739 ISBN 0-520-02424-9 : 10.00
1. Iconoclasm. 2. England—Church history. 3. Art—England—Mutilation, defacement, etc. I. Title.

ROW, John, 1568-1646. 283'.41
The historie of the Kirk of Scotland. [Edinburgh] Printed for the Maitland Club, 1842. [New York, AMS Press, 1973] 2 v. (lxiii, 544 p.) 24 cm. Original ed. issued as no. 55 of the Publications of the Maitland Club. Contents.Contents.—Pt. 1. Row, J. The historie of the kirk, 1558-1637. Row, W. The Coronis; being a continuation of the Historie.—Pt. 2. Row, J. A supplement of the Historie of the kirk, 1637-1639. Row, W. Additional illustrations of the Historie. Includes bibliographical references. [BX9071.R68 1973] 70-174969 ISBN 0-404-53039-7 37.00
1. Church of Scotland—History. I. Row, William, 1614?-1698. II. Row, John, 1598?-1672? III. Title. IV. Series: The Maitland Club, Glasgow. Publications, no. 55.

GOLDIE, Frederick. 283'.411
A short history of the Episcopal Church in Scotland : from the Restoration to the present time / [by] Frederick Goldie. 2nd ed. Edinburgh : St Andrew Press, 1976. viii, 181 p. ; 19 cm. On spine: The Epsicopal Church in Scotland. Includes index. Bibliography: p. 173-176. [BX5300.G6 1976] 76-381842 ISBN 0-7152-0315-0 : 1.40
1. Episcopal Church in Scotland—History. I. Title. II. Title: The Episcopal Church in Scotland.

IRISH Anglicanism, 1869-1969; 283'.415
essays on the role of Anglicanism in Irish life, presented to the Church of Ireland on the occasion of the centenary of its disestablishment, by a group of Methodist, Presbyterian, Quaker, and Roman Catholic scholars. Edited by Michael Hurley. Dublin, A. Figgis, 1970. xi, 236 p. 25 cm. Contents.Contents.—Disestablishment: 1800-1869, by K. B. Nowlan.—Church renewal: 1869-1877, by G. C. Daly.—Early Irish ecclesiastical studies, by F. Grannell.—Education, by T. F. Kelly.—Anglican-Presbyterian relations, by J. M. Barkley.—Anglican-Methodist relations, by F. Jeffrey.—The Church overseas, by T. McDonald.—Political life: 1870-1921, by T. O'Neill.—The Irish language movement, by D. Greene.—Anglo-Irish literature, by A. Martin.—Economic life, by J. F. Meenan.—Political life in the South, by J. H. Whyte.—Aspects of the Northern situation, by D. Kennedy.—Demographic trends, by T. Keane.—Recent liturgical reform, by V. Ryan.—Papal primacy then and now, by P. O'Connell.—The future, by M. Hurley. Includes bibliographical references. [BX5550.I75] 74-263766
1. Church of Ireland—Establishment and disestablishment—Addresses, essays, lectures. I. Hurley, Michael, 1923- ed.

JOHNSTON, Thomas J 283.415
A history of the Church of Ireland, by Thomas J. Johnston, John L. Robinson [and] Robert Wyse Jackson. Dublin, A. P. C. K. [1953] 313p. illus. 23cm. [BR792.J6] 55-16482
1. Ireland-Church history. 2. Church of Ireland-Hist. I. Title.

MCDOWELL ROBERT BRENDAN 283'.415
The Church of Ireland, 1869-1969 / by R.B. McDowell London ; Boston : Routledge and Kegan Paul, 1975. x, 157 p. ; 23 cm. (Studies in Irish history : Second series ; v. 10) Includes index. Bibliography: p. 147-142. [BX5500.M26] 76-350085 ISBN 0-7100-8072-7 : £3.75
1. Church of Ireland—History. 2. Church and state in Ireland. I. Title. II. Series: Studies in Irish history ; v. 10.

WILSON, William Gilbert. 283'.415
The Church of Ireland—why conservative? A brief review of Disestablishment and some of its effects, by W. G. Wilson. Dublin, A.P.C.K., 1970. 44 p. 18 cm. [BX5520.W53] 72-184525 ISBN 0-900010-01-0 4/-
1. Church of Ireland. I. Title.

POYNTZ, S. G. 283'.418'35
St. Ann's : the church in the heart of the city / S. G. Poyntz. [Dublin : Representative Church Body Library, 1976] 105 p. : ill. ; 23 cm. Author's note, 1976. Includes bibliographical references. [BX5570.D8S246] 77-358422
1. St. Ann's Church, Dublin. I. Title.

ABBEY, Charles John, 283'.42
1833-
The English Church and its bishops, 1700-1800, by Charles J. Abbey. London, Longmans, Green, 1887. [New York, AMS Press, 1971] 2 v. 23 cm. Bibliography: v. 2, p. [361]-369. [BX5088.A6 1971] 77-130230 ISBN 0-404-00290-0
1. Church of England—History. 2. Bishops—England. I. Title.

BARLOW, Frank. 283.42
Durham jurisdictional peculiars. London, Oxford University Press, 1950. xviii, 164 p. maps. 23 cm. (Oxford historical series. British series) Bibliographical footnotes. [BX5195.D9A25] 53-36464
1. Durham Cathedral. 2. Church—Gt. Brit. 3. Exemption (Canon law) I. Title.

BEST, Geoffrey Francis 283.42
Andrew.
Temporal pillars: Queen Anne's Bounty, the Ecclesiastical Commissioners, and the Church of England. Cambridge [Eng.] University Press, 1964. xiv, 582 p. 2 fold. maps. 24 cm. Bibliography: p. 558-569. [BX5165.B39] 64-2873
1. Queen Anne's Bounty 2. Gt. Brit. Ecclesiastical Commissioners for England I. Title.

BEST, Geoffrey Francis 283.42
Andrew
Temporal pillars: Queen Anne's Bounty, the Ecclesiastical Commissioners, and the Church of England. [New York] Cambridge [c.]1964. xiv, 582p. fold. maps. 24cm. Bibl. 64-2873 12.50
1. Queen Anne's Bounty. 2. Gt. Brit. Ecclesiastical Commissioners for England. I. Title.

BOSHER, Robert S 283.42
The making of the Restoration settlement; the influence of the Laudians, 1649-1662. New York, Oxford University Press, 1951. xvi, 309p. 22cm. Bibloography: p. 297-299. [BX5085.B] A53
1. Church of England—Hist. 2. Gt. Brit.—Church history—17th cent. 3. Gt. Brit.—Hist.—Restoration, 1660-1688. I. Title.

BROSE, Olive J 283.42
Church and Parliament; the reshaping of the Church of England, 1828-1860. Stanford, Calif., Stanford University Press, 1959. vi, 239p. 23cm. Issued also with variations in microfilm form as thesis, Columbia University, under title: The survival of the Church of England as by law established, 1828-1860. Bibliography: p.[221]-233. [BX5093.B84] 59-7423
1. Church and state. 2. Church and state in Great Britain. 3. Church of England—Hist. I. Title.

BROWN, Ford K 283.42
Fathers of the Victorians; the age of Wilberforce. Cambridge [Eng.] University Press, 1961. 568p. 24cm. Bibliography: p. 534-546. [BX5125.B74 1961] 61-65439
1. Evangelicalism—Church of England. 2. Wilberforce, William, 1759-1833. I. Title.

CASSERLEY, Julian Victor Langmead, 1909- 283.42
The Church to-day and to-morrow; the prospect for post-Christianity. London. S. P. C. K. [New York, Morehouse, c.1965] xi, 114p. 19cm. (Here and now) [BR123.C42] 65-3203 1.50 pap.,
1. Christianity—20th cent. I. Title.

CHADWICK, Owen, ed. 283.42
The mind of the Oxford movement. Stanford, Calif., Stanford University Press [c1960] 239p. 23cm. (A Library of modern religious thought) [BX5099.C45] 60-15256
1. Oxford movement. I. Title.

CHURCH, Richard William, 1815-1890 283.42
The Oxford movement; twelve years. 1833-1845. [Hamden, Conn.] Archon, 1966. xv, 416p. 18cm. Reprint of the 3d ed., 1892. [BX5100.C5 1966] 66-18647 11.00
1. Oxford movement. I. Title.

CHURCH, Richard William, 1815-1890. 283'.42
The Oxford movement; twelve years, 1833-1845. Edited and with an introd. by Geoffrey Best. Chicago, University of Chicago Press [1970] xxxi, 280 p. map. 23 cm. (Classics of British historical literature) [BX5100.C5 1970] 77-115873 ISBN 0-226-10618-7
1. Oxford movement.

CRAGG, G R. 283.42
From Puritanism to the age of reason; a study of changes in religious thought within the Church of England, 1660 to 1700. Cambridge, University Press, 1950. vi, 247 p. 20 cm. Bibliography: p. [231]-242. [BX5085.C7] 51-9405
1. Church of England—Hist.—17th cent. 2. Religious thought—England. I. Title.

CRAGG, Gerald Robertson 283.42
From Puritanism to the age of reason; a study of changes in religious thought within the Church of England, 1660 to 1700. Cambridge [Eng.] Univ. Pr., 1966. vi, 247p. 19cm. [BX50585.C7] 51-9405 4.50; 1.75 pap.,
1. Church of England—Hist.—17th cent. 2. Religious thought—England. I. Title.
Available from the publisher's New York office.

DAWSON, Christopher Henry, 1889-1970. 283'.42
The spirit of the Oxford movement / by Christopher Dawson. New York : AMS Press, [1976] p. cm. Reprint of the 1934 ed. published by Sheed & Ward, London. [BX5100.D3 1976] 75-30020 ISBN 0-404-14025-4 : 9.50
1. Oxford movement. I. Title.

DILWORTH-HARRISON, Talbot, 1886- 283.42
John Bull considers his church. With a foreword by the Bishop of London. London, New York, Longmans, Green [1952] 110 p. 17 cm. (The Bishop of London's Lent book) [BX5055.D46] 52-7385
1. Church of England—Hist. 2. Gt. Brit.—Church history. 3. Church of England—Doctrinal and controversial works. I. Title.

DURHAM, Eng. (Diocese) Bishop, 1406-1437 (Thomas Langley) 283.42
The register of Thomas Langley, Bishop of Durham, 1406-1437. Edited by R. L. Storey. Durham, Published for the society by Andrews, 1956- v. 22cm. (The Publications of the Surtees Society, v. 164 [DA20.S9 vol. 164,etc.] 56-4109
1. Gt. Brit.—Church history— Medieval period—Sources. I. Storey, R. L., ed. II. Title. III. Series: Surtees Society, Durham, Eng. Publications, v.164

EARLE, Nick, 1926- 283.42
What's wrong with the church. New York, Penguin dist. Atheneum, c.1961 156p. (Penguin special, S199) Bibl. 61-66623 .85 pap.,
1. Church of England. I. Title.

HUNTER, Leslie Stannard, Bp. of Sheffield, 1890- ed. 283.42
The English Church a new look; ed. by Leslie S. Hunter, with contributions by Edward F. Carpenter [others] Baltimore. Penguin [c.1966] 176p. 18cm. (Pelican bks. A795) Contributors: Edward F. Carpenter. Alfred Jowett, T. R. Milford, Max Warren, Edward R. Wickham, Leslie S. Hunter. Bibl. [BX5157.H8] 66-71602 .95 pap.,
1. Church and state—Church of England. I. Title.

HUNTER, Leslie Stannard, Bp. of Sheffield, 1890- ed. 283.42
The English Church: a new look; edited by Leslie S. Hunter, with contributions by Edward F. Carpenter [and others] Harmondsworth, Penguin, 1966. 176 p. 18 1/2 cm. (Pelican books, A795) 4/6 (B 66-5891) Contributors: Edward F. Carpenter, Alfred Jowett, T. R. Milford, Max Warren, Edward R. Wickham, Leslie S. Hunter. Includes bibliographical references. [BX5157.H8] 66-71602
1. Church and state — Church of England. I. Title.

INSIGHT, James 283.42
Country parson. New York, Fell [1964, c.1961] 186p. 21cm. 63-23063 3.95 bds.,
I. Title.

O'CONNELL, Marvin Richard. 283'.42
The Oxford conspirators; a history of the Oxford movement 1833-45, by Marvin R. O'Connell. [New York] Macmillan [1969] x, 468 p. 24 cm. Bibliographical references included in "Notes" (p. 427-456) [BX5098.O25] 68-31279
1. Oxford movement. I. Title.

OXFORD (Diocese) Bishop, 1845-1869 (Samuel Wilberforce) 283.42
Bishop Wilberforce's visitation returns for the Archdeaconry of Oxford in the year 1854. Transcribed and edited by E. P. Baker. [Oxford, 1954] vi, 171p. 24cm. (Oxfordshire Record Society. [Oxfordshire record series] v.35) [DA670.O9A3 vol. 35] 57-59016
1. Visitations, Ecclesiastical—England. I. Title. II. Series.

PAUL, Leslie Allen, 1905- 283'.42
A church by daylight; a reappraisement of the Church of England and its future [by] Leslie Paul. New York, Seabury Press [1974] p. cm. "A Crossroad book." [BX5055.2.P36] 73-21566 ISBN 0-8164-1158-1 9.75
1. Church of England—History. I. Title.

SHAW, William Arthur, 1865-1943. 283'.42
A history of the English church during the civil wars and under the Commonwealth, 1640-1660. New York, B. Franklin Reprints [1974] 2 v. 23 cm. (Burt Franklin research & source works series. Philosophy and religious history monographs, 138) Reprint of the 1900 ed. published by Longmans, Green, New York. Includes bibliographical references. [BX5073.S5 1974] 78-184708 ISBN 0-8337-4389-9
1. Church of England—Government. 2. Church of England—History. I. Title.

SIMON, Walter G 283.42
The Restoration episcopate, by Walter G. Simon. New York, Bookman Associates [1965] 238 p. 22 cm. Bibliography: p. 216-229. [BX5176.S5] 64-25059
1. Church of England — Bishops. 2. Gt. Brit. — Church history — 17th cent. I. Title.

WALSH, Walter, 1847-1912. 283'.42
The secret history of the Oxford Movement. 4th ed. London, S. Sonnenschein, 1898. [New York, AMS Press, 1973] xv, 424 p. 23 cm. Includes bibliographical references. [BX5098.W3 1973] 73-101915 ISBN 0-404-06819-7 25.00
1. Oxford movement. I. Title.

WIGMORE-BEDDOES, Dennis George. 283'.42
Yesterday's radicals: a study of the affinity between Unitarianism and Broad Church Anglicanism in the nineteenth century, by Dennis G. Wigmore-Beddoes; foreword by Alec Vidler. Cambridge, J. Clarke, 1971. 182 p. 23 cm. Based on the author's thesis (M.A.), Birmingham University. Bibliography: p. 166-177. [BX5117.W53] 73 162379 £2.10
1. Broad Church Movement. 2. Unitarianism. I. Title.

NUTTALL, Geoffrey Fillingham, 1911- 283.420924
Howel Harris, 1714-1773; the last enthusiast. Cardiff, Univ. of Wales Pr. [Mystic, Conn., Verry, 1965] x, 87p. 22cm. Bibl. [BX5207.H3N8] 65-29739 3.00
1. Harris, Howel, 1714-1773. I. Title.

MATTHEWS, Walter Robert, 1881- ed. 283.421
A history of St. Paul's Cathedral and the men associated with it, ed. by W. R. Matthews, W. M. Atkins. Foreword by Sir Ernest Barker [New ed.] London, J. Baker, New York, Hillary House [1966, c.1964] xxiii, 380p. 58 illus. (incl. plans, ports.) 24cm. Bibl. [BX5195.L7A28] 65-9501 6.50
1. London. St. Paul's Cathedral. I. Atkins, William Maynard, joint ed. II. Title.

BROWN, Howard Miles. 283'.423'78
A century for Cornwall : the diocese of Truro, 1877-1977 / by H. Miles Brown. Truro : Oscar Blackford Ltd, 1976. x, 141 p., leaf of plate, [8] p. of plates : ill., ports. ; 23 cm. Errata slip inserted. Includes index. [BX5105.C65B76] 77-353776 ISBN 0-9505314-0-5 : £3.50
1. Church of England in Cornwall, Eng.—History. 2. Truro, Eng. (Diocese) 3. Cornwall, Eng.—Church history. I. Title.

BLOOM, James Harvey, 1860- 283'.42'48
Shakespeare's church, otherwise the collegiate Church of the Holy Trinity of Stratford-upon-Avon; an architectural and ecclesiastical history of the fabric and its ornaments, by J. Harvey Bloom. Illustrated by L. C. Keighley-Peach. New York, Haskell House, 1971. xiv, 292 p. illus. 23 cm. Reprint of the 1902 ed. [DA690.S92B6 1971] 73-116790 ISBN 0-8383-1032-X
1. Church of the Holy Trinity, Stratford-upon-Avon. I. Title.

CHURCH of the Holy Trinity, Stratford-upon-Avon. 283'.424'8
The vestry minute-book of the Parish of Stratford-on-Avon from 1617 to 1699 A.D. New York, AMS Press [1971] 158 p. 23 cm. Reprint of the 1899 ed. [DA690.S92C46 1971] 72-142244 ISBN 0-404-00366-4
1. Stratford-upon-Avon—History—Sources. I. Title.

VERNEY, Stephen 283.4248
Fire in Coventry. Westwood, N. J., Revell [1965, c.1964] 95p. 19cm. [BX5107.C7V4] 65-1931 1.95 bds.,
1. Coventry. Eng. (Diocese) 2. Coventry Cathedral. I. Title.

WARWICK, Eng. St. Mary's Church. 283'.424'8
Ministers' accounts of the collegiate church of St. Mary, Warwick 1432-85. Transcribed and edited by Dorothy Styles, with a memoir of Philip Boughton Chatwin by Philip Styles. Oxford, Printed for the Dugdale Society at the University Press, 1969. Lv, 198 p. illus. 26 cm. (Publications of the Dugdale Society, v. 26) Includes bibliographical references. [DA670.W3D9 vol. 26] 76-531616
1. Warwick, Eng.—Church history—Sources. I. Styles, Dorothy, ed. II. Title. III. Series: Dugdale Society. Publications, v. 26

HARNAN, J. W. 283'.425'1
A history of All Saints' Church, Ockbrook: including a brief account of the early origins of the village and parish, by J. W. Harnan. Darby, J. W. Harnan, 1971. (4), 34 p. map, plans. 22 cm. [BX5370.O3A45] 72-183821 ISBN 0-9502209-0-6 £0.25
1. All Saints Church, Ockbrook, Eng. 2. Ockbrook, Eng. I. Title.

LLOYD, Philip. 283'.425'42
Fifty years, thirteen centuries : a history of the Church and some churchmen in Leicestershire to mark the golden jubilee of the refounding of the Diocese of Leicester, 1926-1976 / ... historical notes Philip Lloyd, historical biographies Terence Y. Cocks. [Leicester] : [The Diocese of Leicester], [1976] 88 p. : ill., ports. ; 21 cm. Bibliography: p. 88. [BX5107.L3L58] 77-368642 ISBN 0-901046-07-8 : £0.80
1. Leicester, Eng. (Diocese)—History. 2. Leicestershire, Eng.—Church history. I. Cocks, Terence Y., joint author. II. Title.

JONES, Alan David. 283'.426'712
A short history of the Parish and Church of Bush End, Hatfield Broad Oak in the county of Essex. [Hatfield Broad Oak] : [The Author], [1976] [8] p. ; 21 cm. [BX5195.H34H375] 76-382469 ISBN 0-905534-01-8 : £0.10
1. Hatfield Broad Oak Church. 2. Hatfield Broad Oak, Eng.—History. I. Title: A short history of the Parish and Church of Bush End, Hatfield Broad Oak ...

OPENSHAW, Eunice M. 283'.427'34
The story of S. Paul's Church, Heaton Moor / written by Eunice M. Openshaw. [Stockport] : [The author], 1976. 55 p., [8] p. of plates : ill., facsim., ports. ; 21 cm. Cover title: S. Paul's Church Heaton Moor, 1877-1976. [BX5195.H38S366] 77-364636 ISBN 0-9505582-0-6 : £0.90
1. St. Paul's Church, Heaton Moor, Eng. I. Title.

EELES, Francis Carolus. 283'.427'53
The parish church of St. Kentigern, Crosthwaite, With an account of its literary associations by H. D. Rawnsley, and an introd. by H. H. Williams. Carlisle, C. Thurnam and Sons, printers, 1953. 79p. illus. 20cm. [BX5195.C7E35] 54-42456
1. Crosthwaite Church, Keswick, Eng. (Cumberland) I. Title.

THE Parish of All Hallows, Allerton, 1876-1976 / [editor Alec Ellis]. [Allerton] : [Parish of All Hallows], [1976] 57 p. : ill., maps, ports. ; 25 cm. Bibliography: p. 57. [BX5195.A5A447] 77-350971 ISBN 0-9505256-0-X : £1.20 283'.427'53
1. All Hallows Parish Church, Allerton, Eng. (Lancashire) I. Ellis, Alec, 1932-

SPEAK, Harold. 283'.428'15
St Paul's Church, Alverthorpe : parish and people, 1825[-]1975 : an outline history / by Harold Speak and Jean Forrester. Ossett : The authors [for] the Parochial Church Council, Alverthorpe St Paul's Church, 1976. [1], 26 p. : ill., ports. ; 21 cm. Cover title. [BX5195.A55S367] 76-382450 ISBN 0-902829-04-1 : £0.35
1. St. Paul's Church, Alverthorpe, Eng. 2. Alverthorpe, Eng.—History. I. Forrester, Jean F., joint author. II. Title.

PENRY, John, 1563-1593 283.429
Three treatises concerning Wales. Introd. by David Williams. Cardiff, Univ. of Wales Pr. [Mystic, Conn., Verry. 1966] xxix, 168p. 23cm. Bibl. [BX5103.P47] 61-25778 5.00
1. Church of England in Wales. I. Title.
Contents omitted.

DONALD, Gertrude. 283'.43
Men who left the movement: John Henry Newman, Thomas W. Allies, Henry Edward Manning, Basil William Maturin. Freeport, N.Y., Books for Libraries Press [1967] viii, 422 p. 21 cm. (Essay index reprint series) Reprint of the 1933 ed. [BX5100.D6 1967] 67-23207
1. Newman, John Henry, Cardinal, 1801-1890. 2. Allies, Thomas William, 1813-1903. 3. Manning, Henry Edward, Cardinal, 1808-1892. 4. Maturin, Basil William, 1847-1915. 5. Oxford movement. I. Title.

COLE, Edmund Keith, 1919- 283'.676'24
The cross over Mount Kenya; a short history of the Anglican Church in the Diocese of Mount Kenya (1900-1970) [by] Keith Cole. [Melbourne? Church Missionary Historical Publications Trust (Victoria), 1970] 75 p. illus. 21 cm. [BX5700.55.A44M683] 73-170347
1. Church of the Province of Kenya. Diocese of Mount Kenya. I. Title.

BELLWOOD, W A 283'.68
Whither the Transkei [by] W. A. Bellwood. Cape Town, H. Timmins, 1964. 124 p. illus., map (on lining papers) ports. 20 cm. [DT846.K2B4] 64-55125
1. Kaffraria I. Title.

WIRGMAN, Augustus Theodore, 1846-1917. 283'.68
The history of the English church and people in South Africa. New York, Negro Universities Press [1969] 276 p. 18 cm. Reprint of the 1895 ed. [BR1450.W5 1969] 74-77219
1. Africa, South—History. 2. Africa, South—Church history. I. Title.

VOS, K. 283'.68'2
The church on the hill; St. John's Parish, Wynberg [by] K. Vos. Cape Town, Struik, 1972. 174 p. illus. 22 cm. [BX5700.6.Z7W8678] 73-162705 ISBN 0-86977-022-5
1. St. John's Parish, Wynberg, South Africa. I. Title.
Distributed by Verry; 6.25

LANGHAM-CARTER, R. R. 283'.68'7
Under the mountain; the story of St. Saviour's, Claremont [by] R. R. Langham-Carter. [Claremont, S.A., Southern Press, 1973] 31 p. illus. 23 cm. [BX5983.C55S34] 73-178981
1. St. Saviour's, Claremont, South Africa. I. Title.

CARRINGTON, Philip, Abp., 1892- 283.71
The Anglican Church in Canada. a history. Toronto [New York, Collins, c.]1963. 320p. illus., ports., maps. 22cm. Bibl. 63-5057 5.50
1. Anglican Church of Canada—Hist. I. Title.

ERVIN, Spencer, 1886- 283'.71
The political and ecclesiastical history of the Anglican Church of Canada. Ambler, Pa., Trinity Pr. [c1967] xvi, 286p. 21cm. Vol. 5 of a ser. on the govt. of the churches of the Anglican Communion. Bibl. [BX5610.E7] 68-2424 6.00
1. Anglican Church of Canada—Hist. I. Title.

JONES, Elwood H. 283'.713'67
St. John's, Peterborough : the sesquicentennial history of an Anglican parish, 1826-1976 / by Elwood H. Jones. Peterborough, [Ont.] : Maxwell Review, 1976. 110 p. : ill. ; 23 cm. [BX5617.P47S244] 77-361693
1. Saint John's Church, Peterborough, Ont. I. Title.

ADDISON, James Thayer, 1887- 283'.73
The Episcopal Church in the United States, 1789-1931. [Hamden, Conn.] Archon Books,

1969 [c1951] xii, 400 p. 23 cm. Bibliography: p. 382-385. [BX5880.A33 1969] 69-15786
1. Protestant Episcopal Church in the U.S.A.—History. I. Title.

ADDISON, James Thayer, 1887- 283.73
The Episcopal Church in the United States, 1789-1931 New York, Scribner, 1951. xii, 400 p. 24 cm. Bibliography: p. 382-385. [BX5880.A33] 51-10050
1. Protestant Episcopal Church in the U. S. A.—Hist. I. Title.

ALBRIGHT, Raymond Wolf, 1901- 283.73
A history of the Protestant Episcopal Church [by] Raymond W. Albright. New York, Macmillan [c1964] x. 406 p. 24 cm. Bibliography: p. 382-397. [BX5880.A4] 64-21168
1. Protestant Episcopal Church in the U.S.A.—Hist. I. Title.

ALBRIGHT, Raymond Wolf, 1901- 283.73
A history of the Protestant Episcopal Church. New York, Macmillan [c.1964] x, 406p. 24cm. Bibl. 64-21168 12.50
1. Protestant Episcopal Church in the U.S.A.—Hist. I. Title.

ATWATER, George Parkin, 1874-1932. 283.73
The Episcopal Church: its message for men of today. Rev. ed. New York, Morehouse-Gorham Co., 1953. 190p. 21cm. [BX5930.A8 1953] 54-483
1. Protestant Episcopal Church in the U. S. A. I. Title.

BERNARDIN, Joseph Buchanan, 1899- 283.73
An introduction to the Episcopal Church. [3d ed.] New York, Morehouse-Gorham Co. [1957] 116p. 19cm. [BX5930.B4 1957] 57-20940
1. Protestant Episcopal Church in the U. ,s. A. I. Title.

BRIDENBAUGH, Carl. 283'.73
Mitre and sceptre: transatlantic faiths, ideas, personalities. and politics. 1689-1775. London, New York Oxford Univ. Pr., 1967. xx, 354p. front., 2 plates (incl. facsims.). 21 cm. (Galaxy bk., GB197) Bibl. footnotes. [BX5881.B77 1967] 68-114035 1.95 pap.,
1. Church of England in America. 2. Episcopacy. I. Title.

BRIDENBAUGH, Carl. 283.73
Mitre and sceptre; transatlantic faiths, ideas, personalities, and politics, 1689-1775. New York, Oxford University Press, 1962. xiv, 354 p. illus. 24 cm. "Short-title list of manuscripts": p. 341. Bibliographical footnotes. [BX5881.B77] 62-16574
1. Church of England in America. 2. Episcopacy. I. Title.

CASWALL, Henry, 1810-1870. 283'.73
America and the American church. New York, Arno Press, 1969. xviii, 368 p. illus., map. 22 cm. (Religion in America) Reprint of the 1839 ed. [BX5880.C3 1969] 77-83413
1. Protestant Episcopal Church in the U.S.A.—History. 2. Kenyon College, Gambier, Ohio. 3. U.S.—Description and travel—1848-1865. I. Title.

CHANDLER, Thomas Bradbury, 1726-1790. 283.73
An appeal to the public, in behalf of the Church of England in America. New York, Printed by J. Parker, 1767. xi, 127p. 20cm. [BX5881.C56] 62-55944
1. Church of England in America—Government. 2. Church of England —Bishops. I. Title.

CHORLEY, Edward Clowes, 1865-1949 283.73
Men and movements in the American Episcopal Church. Hamden, Conn., Archon Books, 1961 [c.1946] ix, 501p. (Hale lectures) Bibl. 61-4971 10.00
1. Protestant Episcopal Church in the U.S.A.—Parties and movements. 2. Protestant Episcopal Church in the U. S. A.—Hist. I. Title. II. Series: Seabury-Western Theological Seminary, Evanston, Ill. The Hale lectures

THE Convention militant : 57th General Convention, Protestant Episcopal Church, Boston, 1952. [Boston : The Church militant, 1952] 48 p. : ill. ; 28 cm. Cover title. [BX5820.C6 1952] 75-317099 283'.73
1. Protestant Episcopal Church in the U.S.A.—Congresses. I. Protestant Episcopal Church in the U.S.A. General Convention, Boston, 1952. II. The Church militant.

COUBURN, John B ed. 283.73
Viewpoints; some aspects of Anglican thinking, edited by John B. Coburn and W. Norman Pittenger. Foreword by Robert F. Gibson. Greenwich, Conn., Seabury Press, 1959. 267p. 22cm. Includes bibliography. [BX5930.2.C6] 59-9804
1. Protestant Episcopal Church in the U. S. A.—Doctrinal and controversial works. 2. Theology—Addresses, essays, lectures. I. Pittenger, William Norman, 1905- joint ed. II. Title.

CROSS, Arthur Lyon, 1873-1940. 283.73
The Anglican episcopate and the American Colonies. Hamden, Conn., Archon Books, 1964. ix, 368 p. 22 cm. Revised and enlarged version of thesis, Harvard University. Bibliography: p. [350]-357. [BX5881.C8 1964] 64-7768
1. "Originally Published 1902 [as] Harvard Historical studies ix: reprinted 1964 in an unabridged and unaltered edition." 2. Church of England in America. 3. Episcopacy. I. Title.

CROSS, Arthur Lyon, 1873-1940 283.73
The Anglican episcopate and the American Colonies. Hamden, Conn., Archon [dist. Shoe String] 1964. ix, 368p. 22cm. (Orig. pub. 1902 [as] Harvard hist. studies IX; reprinted 1964 in an unabridged and unaltered ed.) Bibl. [BX5881.C8] 64-7768 9.00
1. Church of England in America. 2. Episcopacy. I. Title.

DE MILLE, George Edmed, 1898- 283.73
The Episcopal Church since 1900; a brief history New York, Morehouse-Gorham, 1955. 223p. 22cm. [BX5882.D45] 55-7433
1. Protestant Episcopal Church in the U. S. A.—Hist. I. Title.

ELGIN, Kathleen, 1923- 283'.73
The Episcopalians; the Protestant Episcopal Church. Written and illustrated by Kathleen Elgin. With a foreword by Charles L. R. Pedersen. New York, D. McKay Co. [1970] 112 p. illus. 26 cm. (The Freedom to worship series) Bibliography: p. [110] [BX5930.2.E4 1970] 75-97805 4.95
1. Protestant Episcopal Church in the U.S.A. 2. Polk, Leonidas, Bp., 1806-1864. I. Title.

ERVIN, Spencer, 1886- ed. 283.73
The Episcopal Church in the United States and the National Council of Churches. Bala-Cynwyd, Pa., 1954. 69p. 24cm. [BX6.N2E7] 55-3566
1. National Council of the Churches of Christ in the United States of America. 2. Protestant Episcopal Church in the U. S .A. 3. Protestantism. I. Title.

FACSIMILES of early Episcopal Church documents (1759-1789) 283'.73 Edited by Kenneth Walter Cameron. Hartford, Transcendental Books [1970] 68 l. port. 29 cm. Cover title: Early Episcopal Church documents, 1759-1789. Facsim. reproduction of the New York? 1880? ed. Documents 29-33 omitted. Original t.p. reads: Fac-similes of church documents; papers issued by the Historical Club of the American Church, 1874-79. Privately printed. [BX5881.F3 1970] 74-268868
1. Protestant Episcopal Church in the U.S.A.—History—Sources. I. Cameron, Kenneth Walter, 1908- ed. II. Historical Club of the American Church. III. Title: Early Episcopal Church documents, 1759-1789.

GRAY, William, 1927- 283'.73
The Episcopal Church welcomes you: an introduction to its history, worship, and mission [by] William and Betty Gray. Introd. by John Maury Allin. New York, Seabury Press [1974] xiv, 110 p. illus. 21 cm. "A Crossroad book." Bibliography: p. [109]-110. [BX5930.2.G7] 73-17898 ISBN 0-8164-0253-1 5.95
1. Protestant Episcopal Church in the U.S.A. I. Gray, Betty, joint author. II. Title.

JOHNSON, Howard Albert, 1915- ed. 283.73
This church of ours; the Episcopal Church: what it is and what it teaches about living, by Stephen F. Bayne, Jr. [and others] Foreword by the Bishop of New York. Greenwich, Conn., Seabury Press, 1958. 129p. 20cm. [BX5930.J6] 58-10841
1. Protestant Episcopal Church in the U. S. A. I. Bayne, Stephen Fielding, Bp., 1908- II. Title.

KRUMM, John McGill, 1913- 283.73
Why I am an Episcopalian. New York, Nelson [1957] 192 p. 21 cm. [BX5930.K8] 57-11897
1. Protestant Episcopal Church in the U.S.A. I. Title.

LOVELAND, Clara O 283.73
The critical years; the reconstitution of the Anglican Church in the United States of America: 1780-1789. Greenwich, Conn., Seabury Press, 1956. vi, 311p. 22cm. 'Catalogue of correspondence': p. (289)-293. Bibliography: p. [294]-306. [BX5881.L6] 56-10567
1. Protestant Episcopal Church in the U.S.A.—Hist. I. Title.

MCGOWEN, Drusilla 283.73
The church grows. Illus. by Richard W. Lewis. New York, Seabury [c.1956-1964] vii, 242p. illus. 21cm. (Church's teaching R-5C) 64-13709 2.00 pap.,
1. Church history—Primitive and early church—Juvenile fiction. I. Protestant Episcopal Church in the U. S. A. National Council. Dept. of Christian Education. II. Title. III. Series.
Contents omitted.

MANROSS, William Wilson, 1905- comp. 283.73
The Fulham papers in the Lambeth Palace Library; American colonial section calendar and indexes. Oxford, Clarendon Pr. [New York, Oxfoed, c.]1965. xxii, 524p. 25cm. [BX5881.M26] 65-8687 20.20
1. Church of England in America—Hist.—Sources—Abstracts. I. Lambeth Palace. Library. II. Title.

MANROSS, William Wilson, 1905- 283.73
A history of the American Episcopal Church. [2d ed., rev. and enl.] New York, Morehouse-Gorham, 1950. xiv. 415 p. 24 cm. Bibliography: p. 373-386. [BX5880.M35 1950] 50-8326
1. Protestant Episcopal Church in the U. S. A.—Hist. I. Title.

MANROSS, William Wilson, 1905- 283.73
A history of the American Episcopal Church. [3d ed., rev.] New York, Morehouse-Gorham, 1959. 420p. 21cm. Includes bibliography. [BX5880.M35 1959] 59-1356
1. Protestant Episcopal Church in the U. S. A.—Hist. I. Title. II. Title: American Episcopal Church.

MURPHY, Du Bose, 1893- 283.73
Life in the church. With a foreword by Henry W. Hobson. [Rev. ed.] Chicago, Wilcox & Follett [1950] 122 p. 20 cm. "A Cloister Press book." [BX5935.M8] 50-12071
1. Protestant Episcopal Church in the U.S.A. I. Title.

PERRY, William Stevens, Bp., 1832-1893, ed. 283'.73
Historical collections relating to the American colonial church. New York, AMS Press [1969] 5 v. in 4. 26 cm. Reprint of the 1870-78 ed. Contents.Contents.—v. 1. Virginia.—v. 2. Pennsylvania.—v. 3. Massachusetts.—v. 4. Maryland.—v. 5. Delaware. Includes bibliographical references. [BX5881.P42] 75-99948
1. Church of England in America—History—Sources. I. Title.

PIKE, James Albert, 1913- ed. 283.73
Modern Canterbury pilgrims and why they chose the Episcopal Church John H. Hallowell [and others] New York, Morehouse-Gorham, 1956. 317p. 21cm. [BX5990.P5] 56-6116
1. Protestant Episcopal Church in the U. S. A. 2. Converts, Anglican. I. Hallowell, John Hamilton, 1913- II. Title.

PIKE, James Albert, Bp., 1913- 283.73
Modern Canterbury pilgrims and why they chose the Episcopal Church: John H. Hallowell [and others] New York, Morehouse-Gorham, 1956. 317p. 21cm. [BX5990.P5] 56-6116
1. Protestant Episcopal Church in the U. S. A. 2. Converts, Anglican. I. Hallowell, John Hamilton, 1913- II. Title.

PITTENGER, William Norman, 1905- 283.73
The Episcopalian way of life. Englewood Cliffs, N. J., Prentice-Hall [1957] 188 p. illus. 22 cm. [BX5930.P34] 57-5230
1. Protestant Episcopal church in the U.S.A. I. Title.

PROTESTANT Episcopal Church in the U. S. A. 283.73
Annotated constitution and canons for the government of the Protestant Episcopal Church in the United States of America, adopted in general conventions, 1789-1952. By Edwin Augustine White. 2d ed., rev., 1954, by Jackson A. Dykman. Published after review by a joint committee of General Convention. Greenwich, Conn., Seabury Press [1954] 2v. 24cm. [BX5955.A5 1954] 54-1136
I. White, Edwin Augustine, 1856-1925. II. Dykman, Jackson Annan, 1887- III. Title. IV. Title: Constitution and canons.

SHOEMAKER, Robert W., 1924- 283.73
The origin and meaning of the name "Protestant Episcopal." [New York, American Church Publications, 1959] 338 p. 24 cm. Includes bibliography. [BX5935.S62] 59-16467
1. Protestant Episcopal Church in the U.S.A. — Name. I. Title.

SIMCOX, Carroll Eugene, 1912- 283.73
An approach to the Episcopal Church. New York, Morehouse-Barlow, 1961 181 p. 21 cm. [BX5930.2.S54] 61-5469
1. Protestant Episcopal Church in the U.S.A. I. Title.

SIMCOX, Carroll Eugene, 1912- 283.73
An approach to the Episcopal Church. New York, 17, 14 E. 41 St., Morehouse-Barlow c.] 1961. 184p. 61-5469 3.00
1. Protestant Episcopal Church in the U. S. A. I. Title.

STOWE, Walter Herbert, 1895- 283.73
The Episcopal Church; a miniature history. [2d ed., rev. and enl.] Philadelphia, Church Historical Society [1952, c1944] 64p. 19cm. (Church Historical Society publications, no. 15) [BX5880.S8 1952] 53-6879
1. Protestant Episcopal Church in the U. S. A.—Hist. I. Title.

WHITE, William, Bp., 1748-1836. 283.73
The case of the Episcopal churches in the United States considered; edited by Richard G. Salomon. [Philadelphia, 1954] 78p. facsim. 23cm. (Church Historical Society [Philadelphia] Publication no. 39) 'The present edition...[was] originally printed in Historical magazine of the Protestant Episcopal Church, volume XXII (1953) pages 433-506.' Bibliographical footnotes. [BX5881.W47C3 1954] 54-13248
1. Protestant Episcopal Church in the U. S. A.— Hist. I. Salomon, Richard Georg, 1884- ed. II. Title. III. Series.
Contents omitted.

WILLIAMSON, William B. 283.73
A handbook for Episcopalians. New York, Morehouse-Barlow Co. [1961] 223 p. 21 cm. (Handbooks for churchmen series) Includes bibliography. [BX5930.2.W5] 61-14387
1. Protestant Episcopal Church in the U.S.A. I. Title.

CAMERON, Kenneth Walter, 1908- 283'.74
Letter-book of the Rev. Henry Caner, S.P.G. missionary in colonial Connecticut and Massachusetts until the Revolution; a review of his correspondence from 1728 through 1778. Hartford, Transcendental Books [1972] 224 p. illus. 29 cm. [BX5885.C34] 72-186099
1. Church of England in New England—History—Sources. I. Caner, Henry, 1700-1792.

NEESON, Margaret Graham. 283'.741'53
On solid granite; the story of St. George's Church, its village, priests, and people. Modern photos. by Jack Neeson. Old photos. reproduced by Charles Gifford. Long Cove, Me., St. George's Episcopal Chapel [1974] 154 p. illus. 22 cm. Bibliography: p. 144-148. [BX5980.L7S246] 74-77660
1. St. George's Episcopal Chapel, Long Cove, Me. I. Title.

BRINKLER, Alfred, 1880- 283'.741'9
The Cathedral Church of Saint Luke, Portland, Maine; a history of its first century. Portland, Me., House of Falmouth [1967] 86 p. illus. 22 cm. [BX5980.P7C3] 67-9452
1. Portland, Me. Cathedral Church of Saint Luke — Hist. I. Title.

BRINKLER, Alfred, 1880- 283'.741'9
The Cathedral Church of Saint Luke, Portland, Maine; a history of its first century. Portland, Me., House of Falmouth [1967] 86p. illus. 22cm. [BX5980.P7C3] 67-9452 4.50
1. Portland, Me. Cathedral Church of Saint Luke—Hist. I. Title.

ROTHWELL, Kenneth S. 283'.743
A goodly heritage; the Episcopal Church in Vermont. Edited by Kenneth S. Rothwell. Photography by Edward P. Lyman, Jr., with Samuel J. Hatfield and William W. Stone. Burlington, Vt., Document Committee, Cathedral Church of Saint Paul [1973] 56 p. illus. 28 cm. Includes bibliographical references. [BX5917.V5R67] 73-88188
1. Protestant Episcopal Church in the U.S.A. Vermont (Diocese) 2. Protestant Episcopal Church in the U.S.A.—Vermont. I. Title.

DAY, Gardiner Mumford, 1900- 283.744
The biography of a church; a brief history of Christ Church, Cambridge, Massachusetts. Cambridge, Mass, Priv. print. at the Riverside Press, 1951. 186 p. illus. 24 cm. [BX5980.C2C46] 51-14147
1. Cambridge, Mass. Christ Church. I. Title.

CHAPMAN, Gerard, 1913- 283.7441
St. James' Parish. Great Barrington, Massachusetts, 1762-1962. [Great Barrington] Protestant Episcopal Soc. of Great Barrington [1963, c.1962] 92p. illus. 24cm. Bibl. 63-6518 3.00
1. Great Barrington, Mass. St. James' Parish. I. Title.

CHAPMAN, Gerard, 1913- 283.7441
St. James' Parish, Great Barrington, Massachusetts, 1762-1962. [Great Barrington] Protestant Episcopal Society of Great Barrington, 1962. 92 p. illus. 24 cm. Bibliography: p. 91. [BX5980.G64S3] 63-6518
1. Great Barrington, Mass. St. James' Parish. I. Title.

LOVELL, Daisy Washburn. 283'.744'82
Glad tidings; centennial history of Saint Gabriel's Episcopal Church, Marion, Massachusetts, 1871-1971. Marion, Mass., Saint Gabriel's Episcopal Church [1973] 288 p. illus. 26 cm. [BX5980.M313S344] 73-82234
1. Saint Gabriel's Episcopal Church, Marion, Mass. I. Title.

WHITE, Hunter C. 283.745
Old St. Paul's in Narragansett. [Wakefield? R.I., 1957. 56 p. illus. 24 cm. [BX5980.W6W5] 58-16283
1. Wickford, R.I. St. Paul's Church. I. Title.

CATIR, Norman Joseph. 283.7452
Saint Stephen's Church in Providence; the history of a New England Tractarian parish, 1839-1964. Providence, St. Stephen's Church, 1964. xvi, 222 p. illus., ports. 22 cm. Bibliography: p. [211]-214. [BX5980.P9S3] 64-20900
1. Providence. Saint Stephen's Church. I. Title.

BREWSTER, Mary B 1889- 283.746
St. Michael's Parish, Litchfield, Connecticut, 1745-1954; a biography of a parish and of many who have served it. [Litchfield 1954] 186p. illus. 24cm. [BX5980.L5S3] 54-40757
1. Litchfield, Conn. St. Michael's Church. I. Title.

BURR, Nelson Rollin, 1904- 283'.746
First American diocese: Connecticut, its origin, its growth, its work, by Nelson R. Burr. Hartford, Church Missions Pub. Co. [1970] 48 p. map. 21 cm. [BX5918.C7B79] 72-169342
1. Protestant Episcopal Church in the U.S.A. Connecticut Diocese. I. Title.

BURR, Nelson Rollin, 1904- 283.746
The story of the diocese of Connecticut, a new branch of the vine. [Hartford, Church Missions Pub. Co., c1962] 568 p. illus 24 cm. [BX5918.C7B8] 63-35497
1. Protestant Episcopal Church in the U.S.A. Connecticut Diocese. I. Title.

CAMERON, Kenneth Walter, 1908- comp. 283'.746
Anglican climate in Connecticut; historical perspectives from imprints of the late colonial and early national years. Hartford, Transcendental Books [1974] 237 l. illus. 29 cm. [BX5917.C8C27] 74-173630
1. Protestant Episcopal Church in the U.S.A.—Connecticut—History—Sources. 2. Protestant Episcopal Church in the U.S.A.—Doctrinal and controversial works. I. Title.

CAMERON, Kenneth Walter, 1908- comp. 283'.746
The Anglican Episcopate in Connecticut (1784-1899); a sheaf of biographical and institutional studies for churchmen and historians with early ecclesiastical documents. Hartford, Transcendental Books [1970] 252 l. illus., ports. 29 cm. Bibliography: leaves 250-251. [BX5917.C8C28] 71-13537
1. Protestant Episcopal Church in the U.S.A.—Connecticut. I. Title.

CAMERON, Kenneth Walter, 1908- comp. 283'.746
Connecticut churchmanship; records and historical papers concerning the Anglican Church in Connecticut in the eighteenth and early nineteenth centuries. Hartford, Transcendental Books [1969] 1 v. (various pagings) illus., facsims., ports. 29 cm. [BX5917.C8C34] 70-10390
1. Protestant Episcopal Church in the U.S.A.—Connecticut—History—Sources. I. Title.

CAMERON, Kenneth Walter, 1908- comp. 283'.746
Historical resources of the Episcopal Diocese of Connecticut. Index by Carolyn Hutchens. Hartford, Transcendental Books [1966] iv, 315 l. illus., maps (part col.), ports. 29 cm. Based on the Inventory of the church archives of Connecticut. Protestant Episcopal, by the Historical Records survey. Connecticut. [BX5918.C7C3] 76-218714
1. Protestant Episcopal Church in the U.S.A. Connecticut (Diocese) 2. Churches—Connecticut. 3. Archives—Connecticut. I. Historical Records Survey. Connecticut. Inventory of the church archives of Connecticut. Protestant Episcopal. II. Title.

THE Church of England in 283'.746
pre-Revolutionary Connecticut : new documents and letters concerning the loyalist clergy and the plight of their surviving church / edited by Kenneth Walter Cameron. Hartford : Transcendental Books, c1976. 350 leaves, [3] leaves of plates : ill. ; 29 cm. Includes index. Bibliography: leaf [2] [BX5917.C8C49] 76-374761
1. Church of England in Connecticut—History—Sources. 2. Protestant Episcopal Church in the U.S.A.—Connecticut—History—Sources. I. Cameron, Kenneth Walter, 1908-

COCKE, Charles Francis. 283'.746
Parish lines, Diocese of Virginia. Richmond, Virginia State Library, 1967. xv, 321 p. col. maps. 23 cm. (Virginia State Library publications, no. 28) "Parish changes of 1967": p. 275-276. Bibliography: p. 271-274. [BX5918.V8C6] A 67
1. Protestant Episcopal Church in the U.S.A. Virginia (Diocese) 2. Parishes—Virginia. I. Title. II. Series: Virginia. State Library, Richmond. Publications, no. 28

HANCOCK, Henry Nicholas. 283.746
Transatlantic exchange; a look at the church in New England. London, A. R. Mowbray; New York, Morehouse-Gorham Co. [1951] 75 p. 19 cm. [BX5885.H3] 52-7472
1. Protestant Episcopal Church in the U. S. A.—New England. I. Title.

PROTESTANT Episcopal Church in the U. S. A. Washington (Diocese) 283'.746
Opportunity for tomorrow; a survey of the Diocese of Washington. Washington, 1954. 111 l. illus. 28cm. [BX5918.W3A53] 55-23529
I. Title.

PROTESTANT Episcopal Church in the U. S. A. Western North Carolina (Diocese) 283'.746
Journal of the annual convention. [Hendersonville, Flanagan Print. Co.] v. 23cm. First convention held 1923. [BX5918.W53A3] 54-27703
I. Title.

HEWES, Philip. 283'.746'2
St. James Parish, Farmington, Connecticut: centennial history, 1873/1973. [Farmington, Conn., 1973] viii, 66 p. illus. 24 cm. Bibliography: p. 58-59. [BX5980.F35S344] 73-178391
1. Saint James Episcopal Church, Farmington, Conn. I. Title.

BURR, Nelson Rollin, 1904- 283'.746'3
A history of Grace Episcopal Church, Hartford, Connecticut; in commemoration of the one hundredth anniversary of the consecration of the church, 1868-1968. 2d ed. [Hartford, 1968] xvi, 199 p. illus., plan, ports. 23 cm. [BX5980.H37G7 1968] 74-262001
1. Hartford. Grace Episcopal Church. I. Title.

MYERS, Minor, 1942- 283'.746'5
History of Calvary Church, Stonington. Stonington, Conn., Calvary Churchwomen, 1973. ix, 122 p. illus. 23 cm. [BX5980.S86C345] 73-90269
1. Calvary Church, Stonington, Conn.

LITCHFIELD, Norman. 283.7467
History of St. Peter's Church in Oxford, Connecticut. [Ann Arbor Mich., 1958] 119p. illus. 23cm. [BX5980.O85S3] 59-29213
1. Oxford, Conn. St. Peter's Church. I. Title.

STILES, H Nelson, comp. 283.7467
A chronicle of two hundred years of St. John's Church. North Haven, Conn., St. John's Episcopal Church, 1959. 103 p. illus. 23 cm. Includes bibliography. [BX5980.N77S3] 59-35889
1. North Haven, Conn. St. John's Church. I. Title.

CAMERON, Kenneth Walter, 1908- 283'.746'9
The genesis of Christ Church, Stratford, Connecticut, pre-Revolutionary Church of England; background and earliest annals, commemoration of the two hundred fiftieth anniversary. With a detailed index. An appendix by Carolyn Hutchens. Hartford, Transcendental Books [1972] 64 l. illus., facsims. 29 cm. Includes bibliographical references. [BX5980.S88C5 1972] 72-195488
1. Stratford, Conn. Christ Church. I. Title.

JOHNSON, John Howard, 1897- 283.747
A place of adventure, and other articles and sermons. New York, 1954. 128p. 19cm. [BX5980.N5M34] 54-27861
1. New York. St. Martin's Church. 2. Protestant Episcopal Church in the U.S.A.—Sermons. 3. Sermons, American. I. Title.

JOHNSON, John Howard, 1897- 283.747
A place of adventure; essays and sermons. Foreword by Hughell E. W. Fosbroke. [Rev. ed.] Greenwich, Conn., Seabury Press, 1955. 130p. 19cm. [BX5980.N5M34 1955] 55-13760
1. New York. St. Martin's Church. 2. Protestant Episcopal Church in the U.S.A.—Sermons. 3. Sermons, American. I. Title.

NEW York. Trinity Church. 283.747
Book of commemoration of the one hundreth anniversary of the consecration of the present church edifice and the two hundred and fiftieth anniversary of the founding of the parish of Trinity Church in the City of New York, 1946-1947. [New York? 1950] 80 p. mounted illus., plan. 23 cm. [BX5980.N5T76] 50-4952
I. Title.

NEW York. Trinity Church. 283.747
A guide book to Trinity Church and the Parish of Trinity Church in the city of New York, founded 1697. [rev. ed. New York, 1950] 59 p. illus. 22 cm. [BX5980.N5T675] 50-30969
I. Title.

RAY, Randolph, 1886- 283.747
My Little Church Around the Corner. In collaboration with Villa Stiles. New York, Simon and Schuster, 1957. 365p. illus. 22cm. [BX5995.R37A3] 57-12396
1. Protestant Episcopal Church in the U. S. A.—Clergy—Correspondence, reminiscences, etc. 2. New York. Church of the Transfiguration. I. Title.

RUSSELL, Charles Howland, 1891- 283.747
The Church of the Epiphany, 1833-1958. New York, Published for the Church of the Epiphany by Morehouse-Gorham Co. [1956] 71p. illus. 24cm. [BX5980.N5E63] 56-14234
1. New York. Church of the Epiphany. I. Title.

EHLE, John 283.7471
Shepherd of the streets; the story of the Reverend James A. Gusweller and his crusade on the New York West Side. Foreword by Harry Golden. New York, Sloane, [c.]1960. xi, 239p. illus. 22cm. 60-8997 4.00
1. Gusweller, James Alfred, 1923- 2. New York, Church of St. Matthew and St. Timothy. 3. Puerto Ricans in New York (City) 4. Building laws—New York (City) I. Title.

KENNEDY, James William, 1905- 283.7471
The unknown worshipper. New York, Morehouse-Barlow for the Church of the Ascension [1964] 202p. 46 illus. (incl. facsim., plan, ports.) 22cm. 64-20210 4.00
1. New York, Church of the Ascension. I. Title.

MOREHOUSE, Clifford Phelps, 1904- 283'.747'1
Trinity: Mother of churches; an informal history of Trinity Parish in the city of New York [by] Clifford P. Morehouse. New York, Seabury Press [1973] xi, 338 p. illus. 22 cm. Bibliography: p. 325-327. [BX5980.N5T74] 72-94206 ISBN 0-8164-0246-9 8.95
1. New York (City). Trinity Church. I. Title.

BEDFORD, N. Y. St. Matthew's Church. 283.74727
A sesquicentennial history of St. Matthew's Protestant Episcopal Church, Bedford, New York. By Members of the parish family. [Bedford, 1960] 70p. illus. 24cm. [BX5980.B42S3] 61-21189
I. Title.

CROFUT, Doris. 283'.747'31
St. Mary's-in-Tuxedo, 1888-1975 / by Doris Crofut. Tuxedo Park, N.Y. : Printed by Library Research Associates for St. Mary's-in-Tuxedo, 1975. 58 p. : ill., ports. ; 23 cm. [BX5980.T89S243] 76-350022
1. St. Mary's-in-Tuxedo. 2. Tuxedo, N.Y.—Biography. I. Title.

WEIR, Leona R. 283'.747'73
History of Christ Church, Guilford, New York, 1830-1955, in commemoration of its 125th anniversary. Compiled by Leona R. Weir. [Guilford?] 1955. xiv, 56 p. illus. 23 cm. [BX5980.N5C358] 283'.755'32 76-218347
1. Guilford, N.Y. Christ Church. I. Title.

HALL, Lewis R. M. 283'.747'74
Zion Church, 1818-1968; historical notes, prepared for the sesquicentennial celebration, by Lewis R. M. Hall. [Gilbertsville, N.Y., V. Buday, 1968?] [15] p. illus. 24 cm. Bibliography: p. [15] [BX5980.M63Z563] 73-171824
1. Zion Church, Morris, N.Y. I. Title.

ALLING, Roger. 283.74783
Beside the house, a short history of Christ Church Corning New York. Williamsport, Pa., Grit Pub. Co., 1965. xvi, 87 p. illus., ports. 23 cm. [BX5980.C76C5] 65-6842
1. Corning, N.Y. Christ Church. I. Title.

GARLAND, Merwin A., 1899- 283'.747'95
The history of Trinity Episcopal Church, Fredonia, New York, 1822-1967, by Merwin A. Garland. With a foreward by Lauriston L. Scaife and Henry P. Krusen. Including a history of Trinity Parish, Fredonia, Chautauque Co., W.N.Y., by Thomas P. Tyler. Dunkirk, N.Y., McClenathan Printery, 1968. 329 p. illus., ports. 22 cm. Includes bibliographical references. [BX5980.F87T75] 70-633
1. Fredonia, N.Y. Trinity Episcopal Church—History. I. Tyler, Thomas Pickman, 1817-1892. II. Title.

DEMILLE, George Edmed, 1898- 283'.74797
St. Paul's Cathedral, Buffalo, 1817-1967; a brief history, by George E. DeMille. [Buffalo? 1967, c1966] x, 214 p. illus., map, ports. 23 cm. Bibliography: p. 212. [BX5980.B9S28] 67-3448
1. Buffalo. St. Paul's Cathedral—History.

ASPINWALL, Marguerite. 283.748
A hundred years in His house; the story of the Church of the Holy Trinity on Rittenhouse Square, Philadelphia, 1857-1957. Decorated by Jack Bowling. [Philadelphia? 1956] 72p. illus. 24cm. [BX5980.P5H6] 57-21737
1. Philadelphia. Church of the Holy Trinity (Protestant Episcopal) I. Title.

ASPINWALL, Marguerite. 283.748
A hundred years •in house; the story of the Church of the Holy Trinity on Rittenhouse Square. Philadelphia, 1857-1957. Decorated by Jack Bowling. [Philadelphia? 1956] 72p. illus. 24cm. [BX5980.P5H6] 57-21737
1. Philadelphia. Church of the Holy Trinity (Protestant Episcopal) I. Title.

BIRDSBORO, Pa. St. Michael's Church. 283.748
The history of St. Michael's Protestant Episcopal Church, Birdsboro, Pennsylvania, in celebration of the one hundredth anniversary, 1851-1951. [Birdsboro? Pa., 1951] 109 p. illus., ports. 24 cm. "[Prepared by] a book committee composed of Daniel K. Miller. chairman. Mrs. John S. Herbein [and others]" [BX5980.B45S3] 51-26524
I. Miller, Daniel K. II. Title.

TWELVES, J. Wesley, 1890- 283'.748
A history of the Diocese of Pennsylvania of the Protestant Episcopal Church in the U.S.A., 1784-1968, by J. Wesley Twelves. [Philadelphia, Diocese of Pennsylvania, 1969] vii, 270 p. illus., ports. 24 cm. Bibliography: p. 265. [BX5918.P4T9] 79-78366
1. Protestant Episcopal Church in the U.S.A. Pennsylvania (Diocese) I. Title.

WELTY, Hugh Brady. 283.748
Christ Church, Greensburg; an early Episcopal parish in western Pennsylvania. Ann Arbor, Edwards Bros., 1955. 93p. illus. 23cm. [BX5980.G7W4] 55-42632
1. Greensburg, Pa. Christ Church. I. Title.

WOLFGANG, Ralph T 283.748
History of the Diocese of Harrisburg Protestant Episcopal Church, 1904-1954. With foreword by John Thomas Hiestand, Bishop of Harrisburg. [Harrisburg, Pa.] Diocese of Harrisburg, 1954. 135p. illus. 23cm. [BX5918.H3W6] 55-15390
1. Protestant Episcopal Church in the U.S.A. Harrisburg (Diocese)—Hist. I. Title.

DILLER, William F. 283'.748'15
St. James' Church (Protestant Episcopal) at mid-century, by William F. Diller. Lancaster, Pa., Vestry, St. James' Church, 1971. v, 163 p. illus., ports. 24 cm. Bibliography: p. 155. [BX5980.L24S34] 79-26945
1. Lancaster, Pa. St. James' Church.

GANTZ, Charlotte Orr. 283'.748'21
The first hundred years, Trinity Church,

Solebury, Pennsylvania / by Charlotte Orr Gantz ; ill. by Barbara McArthur & Joanne McNaught. [Solebury, Pa.] : Centennial Committee of Trinity Episcopal Church, 1976, c1975. 51 p. : ill. ; 23 cm. [BX5980.S57T743] 76-352204
1. Trinity Episcopal Church, Solebury, Pa. I. Title.

GANTZ, Charlotte Orr. 283'.748'21
The first hundred years, Trinity Church, Solebury, Pennsylvania / by Charlotte Orr Gantz ; ill. by Barbara McArthur & Joanne McNaught. [Solebury, Pa.] : Centennial Committee of Trinity Episcopal Church, 1976, c1975. 51 p. : ill. ; 23 cm. [BX5980.S57T743] 76-352204
1. Trinity Episcopal Church, Solebury, Pa. I. Title.

GANTZ, Charlotte Orr. 283'.748'21
The first hundred years, Trinity Church, Solebury, Pennsylvania / by Charlotte Orr Gantz ; ill. by Barbara McArthur & Joanne McNaught. [Solebury, Pa.] : Centennial Committee of Trinity Episcopal Church, 1976, c1975. 51 p. : ill. ; 23 cm. [BX5980.S57T743] 76-352204
1. Trinity Episcopal Church, Solebury, Pa. I. Title.

RADDIN, George Gates, 283'.748'32
1906-
The wilderness and the city; the story of a parish, 1817-1967. Wilkes-Barre, Pa., St. Stephen's Episcopal Church [1968] xviii, 777 p. illus., ports. 23 cm. [BX5980.W69S3] 68-27845
1. Wilkes-Barre, Pa. St. Stephen's Church—History. I. Title.

MANTLE, Eric. 283'.748'86
Trinity and Pittsburgh. [Pittsburgh, 1969] 32 p. illus. (part col.), ports. 24 cm. Cover title. Bibliography: p. 31-32. [BX5980.P6T755] 79-279390
1. Pittsburgh. Trinity Cathedral. I. Title.

BURR, Nelson Rollin, 283.749
1904-
The Anglican Church in New Jersey. Philadelphia, Church Historical Society [1954] xvi, 768p. maps, tables. 24cm. (Church Historical Society [Philadelphia] Publication no. 40) [BX5917.N55B8] 54-12793
1. Protestant Episcopal Church in the U. S. A.—New Jersey. I. Title. II. Series.

VAUGHAN, Samuel S. 283'.749'21
The little church; one hundred years at the Church of the atonement, 1868-1968, Tenafly, New Jersey, by Samuel S. Vaughan. [1st ed. Tenafly, N.J., 1969] 123 p. illus., ports. 22 cm. [BX6081.T4C488] 72-11393
1. Tenafly, N.J. Church of the Atonement. I. Title.

MCGINNIS, William 283.74941
Carroll, 1884-
History of St. Peter's Church in Perth Amboy, New Jersey, 1685-1956. [Perth Amboy, N. J., 1956] 99p. illus. 24cm. Includes bibliography. [BX5980.P4P53] 59-41581
1. Perth Amboy, N. J., St. Peter's Episcopal Church. I. Title.

MATHER, Edith B. D. 283'.749'98
The gingerbread church; St. Peter's by the Sea, Cape May Point, New Jersey, 1880-1970, by Edith B. D. Mather. [Wynnewood, Pa., Produced by Livingston Pub. Co., 1970] xiii, 79 p. illus., map (on lining papers), ports. 24 cm. On spine: St. Peter's-by-the-Sea. [BX5980.C23S395] 72-113824
1. Cape May Point, N.J. St. Peter's by the Sea (Church) I. Title.

SILLIMAN, Charles A 283.7511
The story of Christ Church Christiana Hundred and its people. Wilmington, Del., 1960. 211 p. illus. 24 cm. [BX5980.N36C5] 60-10269
1. Christ Church Christiana Hundred, New Castle Co., Del. I. Title.

HARPER, Anna Ellis. 283.752
History of St. Michael's Parish. [St. Michaels? Md., 1956] 62p. illus. 20cm. [BX5980.S27H3] 56-44832
1. St. Michael's Parish, Talbot Co., Md. I. Title.

JONES, Nellie W. 283.752
A school for bishops; a history of the Church of St. Michael and All Angels, Baltimore, Maryland, 1876-1951. [Baltimore? 1952] 150 p. illus. 24 cm. [BX5980.B2C53] 52-27706
1. Baltimore. Church of St. Michael and All Angels. I. Title.

FLEMING, John R. 283'.752'44
The story of old Christ Church, 1672-1972, Port Republic, Maryland; an informal history, by John R. Fleming. With drawings by Kenneth W. Webb. [Port Republic, Md.] Vestry of Christ Church, 1972. viii, 52 p. illus. 25 cm. "In celebration of the 300th anniversary of the founding of Christ Church." [BX5980.P67C484] 72-188359
1. Christ Church, Port Republic, Md. I. Title.

DORSEY, Noah Ernest, 283'.752'56
1873-
All Saints' Chapel in Centralia, Anne Arundel County, Maryland, being a short history of the first quarter-century (1875-1901) of the work of the Protestant Episcopal Church at Annapolis Junction, Maryland / prepared by N. Ernest Dorsey. [Washington, D.C. : N. E. Dorsey], 1952. 57 leaves : ill. ; 28 cm. [BX5980.A47A433] 75-316966
1. All Saints' Chapel, Annapolis Junction, Md. 2. Protestant Episcopal Church in the U.S.A.—Annapolis Junction, Md.

BALTIMORE. Church of the 283.7526
Redeemer.
This parish under God, 1855-1955; a record of the people, the moments, and especially the high purposes that have, in its first century, made this parish a home for Christian worship and fellowship. Baltimore [1955] 123p. illus. 24cm. [BX5980.B2C52] 59-20261
I. Title.

BEIRNE, Francis F 283'.752'6
1890-
St. Paul's Parish , Baltimore; a chronicle of the mother church, by Francis F. Beirne. [Baltimore, Horn-Shafer Co., c1967] iv, 288 p. plan. plates, port. 24 cm. [BX5980.B2S28] 67-31296
1. Baltimore. St. Paul's Parish. I. Title.

BRIX, Marie Louise. 283'.752'74
Emmanuel Episcopal Church, 1868-1968. [Bel Air? Md., 1968] 28 p. illus. 23 cm. Cover title. "Commemorating the one-hundredth anniversary of the founding of Emmanuel Episcopal Church." [BX5980.B43E4] 68-4612
1. Bel Air, Md. Emmanuel Episcopal Church—History.

WEIGHTMAN, Richard 283'.752'84
Hanson, 1882-
History of St. John's Episcopal Church, Norwood Parish, 1874-1965. Bethesda-Chevy Chase, Md., St. John's Episcopal Church, Norwood Parish, 1968. xi, 124 p. illus., ports. 23 cm. On cover: St. John's Norwood, 1874-1965. [BX5980.C4N67] 68-23555
1. Chevy Chase, Md. Norwood Parish—History. I. Title. II. Title: St. John's Norwood, 1874-1965.

GREEN, Constance 283'.753
(McLaughlin) 1897-
The church on Lafayette Square; a history of St. John's Church, Washington, D.C., 1815-1970. Washington, Potomac Books [1970] ix, 116 p. illus., plans, ports. 24 cm. [BX5980.W3J62] 78-141034
1. Washington, D.C. St. John's Church, Lafayette Square. I. Title.

SPAULDING, Dorothy W. 283'.753
Saint Paul's Parish, Washington, one hundred years [by] Dorothy W. Spaulding, with contributions and assistance from the rector and members of St. Paul's. Washington, 1967. vii, 101 p. illus., ports. 24 cm. Bibliography: p. 97-98. [BX5980.W3P33] 72-9547
1. Washington, D.C. St Paul's Parish. I. Title.

HAMILTON, Eleanor Meyer. 283'.754
The flair & the fire : the story of the Episcopal Church in West Virginia, 1877-1977 / by Eleanor Meyer Hamilton. Charleston : Diocese of West Virginia, Protestant Episcopal Church, 1977. 395 p., [24] leaves of plates : ill., maps (on lining papers) ; 24 cm. Includes index. [BX5917.W4H35] 77-151356
1. Protestant Episcopal Church in the U.S.A.—West Virginia—History. I. Title.

BRYDON, George MacLaren, 283.755
1875-
Highlights along the road of the Anglican Church; the Church of England in England and her oldest daughter, the Protestant Episcopal Church of Virginia. Richmond, Virginia Diocesan Library, 1957. 58p. illus. 23cm. [BX5917.V8B725] 58-2675
1. Protestant Episcopal Church in the U. S. A.—Virginia. 2. Church of England in Virginia. I. Title.

BRYDON, George MacLaren, 283.755
1875-
Virginia's mother church and the political conditions under which it grew. Richmond, Virginia Historical Society, 1947-52. 2v. port. 24cm. Vol. 2 has imprint: Philadelphia, Church Historical Society. Contents.[v. 1] An interpretation of the records of the Coloby of Virginia and of the Anglican Church of that colony, 1607-1727.--v.2. The story of the Anglican Church and the development of religion in Virginia, 1727-1814. Includes bibliographies. [BX5917.V8B77] 48-1123
1. Church of England in Virginia. 2. Virginia—Church history. I. Title.

COCKE, Charles Francis 283.755
Parish lines, Diocese of Southern Virginia. Richmond, Va. State Lib., 1964. 287p. col. maps. 24cm. Bibl. A64 5.00 pap.,
1. Protestant Episcopal Church in the U.S.A. Southern Virginia (Diocese) 2. Parishes—Virginia. I. Title.

PROTESTANT Episcopal 283.755
Church in the U. S. A. Southwestern Virginia (Diocese)
Journal of the annual council. [Roanoke?] v. 23cm. [BX5918.S922A3] 53-16396
I. Title.

QUENZEL, Carrol Hunter, 283.755
1906-
The history and background of St. George's Episcopal Church, Fredericksburg, Virginia. Richmond, 1951. viii, 124 p. illus., port. 24 cm. Bibliography: p. [75]-81. [BX5980.F85S34] 51-11242
1. Fredericksburg, Va. St. George's Episcopal Church. I. Title.

QUENZEL, Carrol Hunter, 283.755
1906-
The history and background of St. George's Episcopal Church. Fredericksburg, Virginia. Richmond, 1951. viii, 124p. illus., port. 24cm. Bibliography: p. [75]-81. [BX5980.F85S34] 51-11242
1. Fredericksburg. Va. St. George's Episcopal Church. I. Title.

UP from independence : 283'.755
the Episcopal Church in Virginia : articles / by George J. Cleaveland ... [et al.]. [s.l.] : Interdiocesan Bicentennial Committee of the Virginias, 1976. iii, 125 p. : ill. ; 23 cm. Includes bibliographical references. [BX5917.V8U6] 76-380758
1. Protestant Episcopal Church in the U.S.A.—Virginia—Addresses, essays, lectures. 2. Virginia—Church history—Addresses, essays, lectures. I. Cleaveland, George Julius.

GALPIN, William 283'.755'32
Freeman, 1890-1963.
Grace Church; one hundred twenty-five years of downtown ministry. [Utica? N. Y., 1963] ix, 134 p. illus. (part col.) ports. 26 cm. [BX5980.U8G7] 63-19025
1. Utica, N. Y. Grace Church I. Title.

HALL, Edward Hagaman, 283'.755'32
1858-1936.
A guide to the Cathedral Church of Saint John the Divine in the City of New York, 16th ed. [New York] The Dean and Chapter of the Cathedral Church, 1955. 191 p. illus., port., plan. 18 cm. [BX5980.N5J65] 64-36624
1. New York. Cathedral of St. John the Divine. I. Title.

HALL, Kathryn 283'.755'32
Evangeline, 1924-
History of the Episcopal Church of Bethesda-by-the-Sea, documented from authentic and contemporary sources. By Kathryn E. Hall. [Palm Beach Fla.] 1964. 31-88 p. illus., ports. 30 cm. Caption title. [BX5980.P25B44] 64-56658
1. Palm Beach, Fla. Church of Bethesda-by-the-Sea. I. Title.

KANSAS City, Mo. St. 283'.755'32
Andrew's Episcopal Church.
The spirit of St. Andrew's, 1913-1963. Kansas City [1963?] 112 p. illus., ports. 29 cm. [BX5980.K3S3] 64-56060
I. Title.

KIRK, Rudolf, 1898- 283'.755'32
The Church of St. John the Evangelist; a parish history, by Rudolf Kirk and Clara Marburg Kirk. New Brunswick, N. J., 1961. 97p. illus: 24cm. Includes bibliography. [BX5980.N35C53] 62-1938
1. New Brunswick, N. J. Church of St. John the Evangelist. I. Kirk, Clara (Marburg) 1903- joint author. II. Title.

LINDSLEY, James 283'.755'32
Elliott.
A history of St. Stephen's Church, Millburn, New Jersey, 1851-1963. Millburn? N.J., 1963 68 p. illus. 23 cm. [BX5980.M54S3] 66-58398
1. Millburn, N.J. St. Stephen's Church. I. Title.

LYON, Josephine A 283'.755'32
1862-1939.
The chronicle of Christ Church. With an introd. by Chauncey Brewster Tinker. [New Haven? introd. 1941] 166 p. illus. 24 cm. [BX5980.N37C5] 63-56481
1. New Haven. Christ Church. I. Title.

MENTLEY, Gertrude B 283'.755'32
A church and a village grow up. Middletown, N.Y., 1963. 119, xviii p. illus., ports. 23 cm. Errata slip inserted. [BX5980.M53G7] 64-28497
1. Middletown, N.Y. Grace Church. 2. Middletown, N.Y. — Hist. I. Title.

MINGHINI, Lorraine. 283'.755'32
History of Trinity Episcopal Church and Norborne Parish, Martinsburg, Berkeley County, West Virginia, Diocese of West Virginia. 185th anniversary, 1771-1956. By Lorraine Minghini and Thomas E. VanMetre. [Martinsburg? W. Va., 1956?] 204p. illus. 24cm. [BX5980.M32T7] 57-41149
1. Martinsburg, W. Va. Trinity Episcopal Church. 2. Norborne Parish, Berkeley Co., W. Va. 3. Protestant Episcopal Church in the U. S. A.—West Virginia. I. VanMetre, Thomas Earle, joint author. II. Title.

NELSON, Lucy (Green) 283'.755'32
1895- ed.
St. John's Church, Mobile, a history. Compiled from the Minutes of the vestries and the Church registers, 1853-1963. [Mobile, Ala., c1963] 234 p. illus., ports., facsims. 23 cm. [BX5980.M55S3] 64-26092
1. Mobile, Ala. St. John's Church I. Title.

NEW York. Trinity 283'.755'32
Church.
Year-book and register of the Parish of Trinity Church in the City of New York. [New York] v. in 19-22cm. [BX5980.N5T6] 59-57766
I. Title.

PALM Beach, Fla. 283'.755'32
Church of Bethesda-by-the-Sea.
Chronicles, the Church of Bethesda-by-the-sea, Palm Beach, Florida. 1889-1964. [West Palm Beach, Fla., Distinctive Print., 1964] 216 p. illus. (part col.) ports. (part col.) 29 cm. [BX5980.P25B4] 64-15437
I. Title.

SINCLAIR, Caroline 283'.755'32
Baytop.
Abingdon Church: a chronology of its history, 1650-1970, Gloucester County, Virginia, 1972. [White Marsh, Va., Abingdon Church, 1972] xiii, 62 p. illus. 24 cm. Bibliography: p. 61-62. [BX5980.G5A6] 72-89434
1. Abingdon Church, Gloucester County, Va.

SMITH, Charles 283'.755'32
William Frederick, 1905-
The story of Christ Church, Exeter, New Hampshire, 1865-1965, by Charles W. F. Smith and Edith P. Leonard. [Exeter? N.H., 1965] 52 p. illus., ports. 23 cm. [BX5980.E93C5] 65-66444
1. Exeter, N. H. Christ Church. I. Leonard, Edith P., joint author. II. Title.

WATERFORD, N.Y. Grace 283'.755'32
Church.
The commemoration of the one hundred fiftieth anniversary of the founding of Grace Church, Waterford, New York; 1810-1960. [Waterford? 1960] 119 p. illus.23 cm. "The history of Grace Church ... by William H. Law": p. 41-88. [BX5980.W33G7] 62-2977
I. Law, William Holden. II. Title.

HATCH, Charles E. 283.755'42
Grace Church; general study, by Charles E. Hatch, Jr. Washington, Office of History and Historic Architecture, Eastern Service Center, 1970. v, 92 p. 23 plates. 26 cm. At head of title: Colonial National Historical Park, Yorktown, Virginia. Includes bibliographical references. [BX5980.Y6G7] 78-612222
1. Yorktown, Va. Grace Church. I. Title. II. Title: Colonial National Historical Park, Yorktown, Virginia.

HUGHES, Jennie. 283.755451
All Saints Episcopal Church, Richmond, Virginia, 1888-1958. Richmond, 1960. 69p. illus. 26cm. [BX5980.R5A45] 60-16745
1. Richmond. All Saints Episcopal Church. I. Title.

KYLE, Louisa Venable. 283'.755'51
The history of Eastern Shore Chapel and Lynnhaven Parish, 1642-1969. Designed by Morris L. McKinney. 1st ed. Norfolk, Va., Printed by Teagle & Little, 1969. 121 p. illus., map, ports. 24 cm. "This book is ... designed by Morris L. McKinney." Bibliography: p. [115] [BX5980.P83L95] 78-104011 5.95
1. Lynnhaven Parish, Princess Anne Co., Va. I. Title.

NORFOLK, Va. St. 283'.755'52
Paul's Church (Protestant Episcopal)
Vestry book of Elizabeth River Parish, 1749-1761. Edited by Alice Granbery Walter. [New York?] 1967 [c1969] 43 p. facsims. 25 cm. [F234.N8N88] 71-254097
1. Norfolk, Va.—History—Colonial period, ca. 1600-1775—Sources. 2. Church records and registers—Norfolk, Va. I. Title.

COCKE, Charles Francis 283.7557
Parish lines, Diocese of Southwestern Virginia.

Richmond, Virginia State Library, 1960. 196p. col. maps, diagrs. (Virginia. State Library [Richmond] Publications, no. 14) Bibl.: p.179-180. 60-14622 4.00 pap.,
1. Protestant Episcopal Church in the U. S. A. Southwestern Virginia (Diocese) 2. Parishes—Virginia. I. Title. II. Series.

RUFFIN, Beverley, 1893- 283'.755'91
Augusta Parish, Virginia, 1738-1780. Verona, Va., McClure Press [1970] vii, 71 p. 23 cm. Bibliography: p. 56-58. [BX5917.V8R8] 73-133388
1. Church of England in Virginia. 2. Augusta County, Va.—History. I. Title.

DUNCAN, Norvin C 283.756
Pictorial history of the Episcopal Church in North Carolina, 1701-1964, by Norvin C. Duncan. Asheville, N.C. [1965] xxviii, 154 p. illus., facsim., ports. 29 cm. [BX5917.N8D8] 65-3103
1. Protestant Episcopal Church in the U.S.A. — North Carolina. I. Title. II. Title: History of the Episcopal Church in North Carolina, 1701-1964.

LEWIS, Henry Wilkins, 1916- 283.756
Northampton parishes. Jackson, N. C., 1951. ix, 120 p. illus., ports., map. 27 cm. Bibliographical footnotes. [BX5917.N8L4] 52-20939
1. Protestant Episcopal Church in the U. S. A.—Northampton Co.,N. C. 2. Churches—Northampton Co., N. C. I. Title.

POWELL, William Stevens, 1919- 283.756
St. Luke's Episcopal Church, 1753-1953. Salisbury, N.C., St. Luke's Episcopal Church, 1753. 76p. illus. 23cm. [BX5980.S23S3] 53-39479
1. Salisbury, N.C. St. Luke's Episcopal Church. I. Title.

SMITH, Stuart Hall. 283.756
The history of Trinity Parish, Scotland Neck [and] Edgecombe Parish, Halifax County [by] Stuart Hall Smith [and] Claiborne T. Smith, Jr. Scotland Neck, N. C., 1955. 115p. illus. 24cm. [BX5980.S4T7] 55-25504
1. Scotland Neck, N. C. Trinity Church. 2. Edgecomb Parish, Halifax Co., N. C. 3. Smith, Claiborne T. I. Title.

WINSLOW, Raymond A. 283'.756'144
History of the Church of the Holy Trinity, Hertford, North Carolina [by] Raymond A. Winslow, Jr. [Hertford?] 1969. 60 p. 23 cm. Bibliography: p. 59-60. [BX5980.H47C5] 70-18467
1. Hertford, N.C. Church of the Holy Trinity. I. Title.

†CLARKE, Philip G. 283'.757
Anglicanism in South Carolina, 1660-1976 : a chronological history of dates and events in the Church of England and the Episcopal Church in South Carolina / compiled by Philip G. Clarke, Jr. Easley, S.C. : Southern Historical Press, c1976. 156 p. ; 24 cm. Bibliography: p. 154-155. [BX5917.5.S6C56] 76-23346 ISBN 0-89308-042-X : 10.00
1. Protestant Episcopal Church in the U.S.A.—South Carolina—History—Chronology. 2. Church of England in South Carolina—History—Chronology. I. Title.

DALCHO, Frederick, 1770?-1836. 283'.757
An historical account of the Protestant Episcopal Church in South Carolina. New York, Arno Press, 1972. vii, 613 p. 23 cm. (Religion in America, series II) Reprint of the 1820 ed. [BX5917.S6D2 1972] 71-38445 ISBN 0-405-04064-4
1. Protestant Episcopal Church in the U.S.A.—South Carolina. 2. South Carolina—History—Colonial period, ca. 1600-1775. I. Title.

WILLIAMS, George Walton, 1922- 283.757
St. Michaels, Charleston 1751-1951. Columbia, University of South Carolina Press, 1951. ix, 375 p. illus., map (on lining papers) 24 cm. Bibliography: p. 362-370. [BX5980.C3S36] 52-132
1. Charleston, S.C. St. Michael's Church. I. Title.

MALONE, Henry Thompson 283.758
The Episcopal Church in Georgia, 1733-1957. Atlanta, Protestant Episcopal Church in the Diocese of Atlanta [c.1960] 334p. illus. end paper map 25cm. 60-53599 2.95
1. Protestant Episcopal Church in the U.S.A.—Georgia. I. Title.

MALONE, Henry Thompson. 283.758
The Episcopal Church in Georgia, 1733-1957. Atlanta, Protestant Episcopal Church in the Diocese of Atlanta [1960] 334p. illus. 25cm. [BX5917.G4M3] 60-53599
1. Protestant Episcopal Church in the U. S. A.—Georgia. I. Title.

BALFOUR, Robert C. 283'.758'98
The history of St. Thomas Episcopal Church, by R. C. Balfour, Jr. Tallahassee, Printed by Rose Print Co. [1968] 229 p. illus., ports. 24 cm. [BX5980.T4S3] 68-4292
1. Thomasville, Ga. St. Thomas Episcopal Church—Hist. I. Title.

BALFOUR, Robert C. 283'.758'98
The history of St. Thomas Episcopal Church, by R. C. Balfour, Jr. Tallahassee, Printed by Rose Print. Co. [1968] 229 p. illus., ports. 24 cm. [BX5980.T4S3] 68-4292
1. Thomasville, Ga. St. Thomas Episcopal Church—History. I. Title.

CUSHMAN, Joseph D 283.759
A goodly heritage; the Episcopal Church in Florida, 1821-1892 [by] Joseph D. Cushman, Jr. Gainesville, University of Florida Press, 1965. xiii, 219 p. illus., ports. 24 cm. Bibliography: p. [207]-212. [BX5917.F55C8] 65-28693
1. Protestant Episcopal Church in the U.S.A. — Florida. 2. Protestant Episcopal Church in the U.S.A. South. Florida (Diocese). I. Title.

CUSHMAN, Joseph D. 283.759
A goodly heritage; the Episcopal Church in Florida, 1821-1892. Gainesville, Univ. of Fla., Pr. [c.]1965. xiii, 219p. illus., ports. 24cm. Bibl. [BX5917.F55C8] 65-28693 6.50 bds.,
1. Protestant Episcopal Church in the U.S.A.—Florida. 2. Protestant Episcopal Church in the U.S.A. South. Florida (Diocese). I. Title.

HOAG, Amey R 283.759
Thy lighted lamp; a history of Holy Trinity Episcopal Church, Melbourne, Florida. [Eau Gallie? Fla., 1958] 105p. illus. 22cm. Includes bibliography. [BX5980.M38H6] 58-44986
1. Melbourne, Fla. Holy Trinity Episcopal Church. I. Title.

CUSHMAN, Joseph D. 283'.759'3
The sound of bells : the Episcopal Church in South Florida, 1892-1969 / Joseph D. Cushman, Jr. Gainesville : University Presses of Florida, 1976. xiv, 378 p., [10] leaves of plates : ill. ; 24 cm. Continues A goodly heritage: The Episcopal Church in Florida, 1821-1892. "A University of Florida book." Includes index. Bibliography: p. 359-367. [BX5918.S65C87] 75-30946 ISBN 0-8130-0518-3 : 15.00
1. Protestant Episcopal Church in the U.S.A. South Florida (Diocese) 2. Protestant Episcopal Church in the U.S.A.—Florida. 3. Florida—Church history. I. Title.

WOOD, Mattie Pegues. 283.761
The life of St. John's Parish; a history of St. John's Episcopal Church from 1834 to 1955. [Montgomery? Ala., 1955] 193p. illus. 24cm. [BX5980.M58S37] 56-18086
1. Montgomery, Ala. St. Johns Church (Protestant Episcopal) I. Title.

CARTER, Hodding. 283.763
So great a good; a history of the Episcopal Church in Louisiana and of Christ Church Cathedral, 1805-1955, by Hodding Carter and Betty Werlein Carter. Sewanee, Tenn., University Press, 1955. 447p. illus. 24cm. [BX5918.L8C3] 56-28135
1. Protestant Episcopal Church in the U. S. A. Louisiana (Diocese)—Hist. 2. New Orleans. Christ Church Episcopal Cathedral. I. Carter, Betty Werlein, joint author. II. Title.

BATTLE, William James, 1870- 283.764
The story of All Saints Chapel, Austin, Texas, 1900-1950. Austin, 1951. 117 p. illus. 25 cm. [BX5980.A95A4] 52-16999
1. Austin, Tex. All Saints Chapel. I. Title.

BESSLEY, Claude A 283.764
The Episcopal Church in northern Texas, until 1895. Wichita Falls, 1952. 65p. 23cm. [BX5918.D25B4] 54-27708
1. Protestant Episcopal Church in the U. S. A. Dallas (Diocese) 2. Protestant Episcopal Church in the U. S. A. Northern Texas (Missionary district) I. Title.

BROWN, Lawrence L 283.764
The Episcopal Church in Texas, 1838-1874; from its foundation to the division of the diocese Austin, Tex., Church Historical Society, 1963. 271 p. illus., ports., maps, facsim, 24 cm. [BX5917.T4B7] 63-19457
1. Protestant Episcopal Church in the U.S.A. — Texas. I. Title.

WARD, Hortense (Warner) 1902- 283.764113
A century of missionary effort; the Church of Good Shepherd, 1860-1960. [Austin? Tex, 1960] 211 p. illus. 24 cm. Includes bibliography. [BX5980.C77G65] 60-51251
1. Corpus Christi, Tex. Church of the Good Shepherd. I. Title.

HARPER, Michael. 283'.764'1411
A new way of living; how the Church of the Redeemer, Houston, found a new life-style. Plainfield, N.J., Logos International [1973] 144 p. 21 cm. Includes bibliographical references. [BX5980.H66C53] 73-180328 ISBN 0-88270-066-9 4.95
1. Church of the Redeemer, Houston, Tex. I. Title.

PULKINGHAM, W. Graham. 283'.764'1411
They left their nets; a vision for community ministry [by] W. Graham Pulkingham. New York, Morehouse-Barlow Co. [1973] xiii, 102 p. 22 cm. [BX5980.H66C56] 73-84091 ISBN 0-8192-1156-7 2.95 (pbk.)
1. Church of the Redeemer, Houston, Tex. I. Title.

PROTESTANT Episcopal Church in the U.S.A. Oklahoma (Diocese) 283.766
Journal of the annual meeting of the convention together with reports. [n.p.] v. 22 cm. [BX5918.O4A3] 52-29974
I. Title.

DAVIES-RODGERS, Ellen 283.768
The romance of the Episcopal Church in west Tennessee, 1832-1964. Photos., reproductions by Nadia Price. Brunswick, Tenn., Plantation Pr. [1964] 232p. illus., facsims., ports. 24cm. Bibl. 64-20656 8.00
1. Protestant Episcopal Church in the U. S. A.—Tennessee. 2. Protestant Episcopal Church in the U. S. A.—Tennessee (Diocese) I. Title.

JONES, George William, 1888-1952. 283.768
Candles in the dark boreen; writings. [Sherwood? Tenn., 1954] 321p. illus. 24cm. [BX5980.S5J6] 55-57973
1. Sherwood, Tenn. Epiphany Mission. I. Title.

LINDSEY, Edwin Samuel, 1897- 283.768
Centennial history of St. Paul's Episcopal Church, Chattanooga, Tennessee, 1853-1953. [Chattanooga] Vestry of St. Paul's Parish, 1953. 199p. illus. 25cm. [BX5980.C33S3] 53-19894
1. Chattanooga, Tenn. St. Paul's Episcopal Church. I. Title.

RODGERS, Ellen (Davies) 283.768
The romance of the Episcopal Church in west Tennessee, 1832-1964 by Ellen Davies-Rodgers. With illus., photos. and reproductions by Nadia Price. Brunswick, Tenn., Plantation Press [1964] 232 p. illus., facsims., ports. 24 cm. Bibliographical footnotes. [BX5918.T2R6] 64-20656
1. Protestant Episcopal Church in the U. S. A.—Tennessee. 2. Protestant Episcopal Church in the U. S. A. Tennessee (Diocese) I. Title.

RODGERS, Ellen (Davies) 283.768
The romance of the Episcopal Church in west Tennessee, 1832-1964. Photos, and reproductions by Nadia Price. Brunswick, Tenn., Plantation Press [1964] 232 p. illus., facsims., ports. 24 cm. Bibliographical footnotes. [BX5917.T2D3] 64-20656
1. Protestant Episcopal Church in the U.S.A.—Tennessee. 2. Protestant Episcopal Church in the U.S.A.—Tennessee (Diocese) I. Title.

DAVIES-RODGERS, Ellen 283.76819
The Holy Innocents: the story of a historic church and country parish (Haysville, Wythe Depot) Arlington. Shelby County, Tennessee, including the unpublished diaries of Capt. Kenneth Garrett, churchman and Civil War soldier. Photos., reprod. by Nadia Price. (Brunswick) Memphis, Tenn., 38128 Plantation Pr. [1966] 460p. illus., facsims., fold, plan, ports. 24cm. Bibl. [BX5980.A64C55] 66-16254 8.00
1. Arlington, Tenn. Church of the Holy Innocents. I. Garrett, Kenneth, 1831-1919. II. Title.

DAVIES-RODGERS, Ellen, 1903- 283'.768'19
The great book: Calvary Protestant Episcopal Church, 1832-1972, Memphis, Shelby County, Tennessee. Photography by Nadia. Memphis, Plantation Press [1973] 994 p. illus. 24 cm. Bibliography: p. 973. [BX5980.M4C343] 72-84829 20.00
1. Memphis. Calvary Episcopal Church. 2. Memphis—Biography. I. Title.
Publisher's Address: Brunswich, Memphis, Tenn. 38128.

RODGERS, Ellen (Davies) 283.76819
The Holy Innocents; the story of a historic church and country parish (Haysville, Wythe Depot) Arlington, Shelby County, Tennessee, including the unpublished diaries of Capt. Kenneth Garrett, churchman and Civil War soldier. Photos, and reproductions by Nadia Price. Brunswick, Tenn., Plantation Press [1965] 400 p. illus., facisms., fold. plan. ports. 24 cm. Bibliographical footnotes. [BX5980.A64C55] 66-16254
1. Arlington, Tenn. Church of the Holy Innocents. I. Garrett, Kenneth, 1831-1919. II. Title.

ST. John's Bicentennial Committee. 283'.768'85
St. John's Episcopal Church in Knoxville, Tennessee, 1946-1976 / prepared and edited by St. John's Bicentennial Committee. Knoxville : Vestry of St. John's Parish, 1977. x, 100 p. : ill. ; 25 cm. Cover title: St. John's Church, Knoxville, 1946-1976. Includes index. [BX5980.K64S347] 77-155375
1. St. John's Episcopal Church, Knoxville, Tenn.—History. I. Title. II. Title: St. John's Church, Knoxville, 1946-1976.

SWINFORD, Frances Keller. 283'.769
The great elm tree; heritage of the Episcopal Diocese of Lexington, by Frances Keller Swinford & Rebecca Smith Lee. With an epilogue by William R. Moody. Lexington, Ky., Faith House Press, 1969. xii, 456 p. illus., ports. 24 cm. Bibliographical footnotes. [BX5918.L5S9] 78-8747 9.50
1. Protestant Episcopal Church in the U.S.A. Lexington (Diocese) I. Lee, Rebecca Washington (Smith) 1894- joint author. II. Title.

DORR, William Meriwether. 283'.769'44
A centennial of Grace, 1868-1968; being a history of Grace Church from its beginnings in 1853 to the present day. Louisville, Ky., 1968] [72] p. illus. 24 cm. Cover title. [BX5980.G62D67] 75-304266
1. Grace Church, Louisville, Ky. I. Title.

MORRIS, J. Wesley. 283'.771'78
Christ Church, Cincinnati, 1817-1967. This history recorded by J. Wesley Morris. [Cincinnati, Printed by Cincinnati Lithographing Ohio Press, 1967] v, 196 p. illus., ports. 25 cm. [BX5980.C5C55] 67-5898
1. Cincinnati. Christ Church. I. Title.

STRANGE, Georgianne. 283'.772'52
Trinity Episcopal Church, 1919-1969; a chronicle of the church on the corner of Thirty-third and Meridian Streets in Indianapolis, first called the Church of the Advent and, presently, Trinity Episcopal Church. Indianapolis, Published by the Rector, Wardens, and Vestrymen of Trinity Episcopal Church, 1969. 113 p. illus., ports. 24 cm. [BX5980.I5T75] 283'.755'32 77-17804
1. Indianapolis. Trinity Episcopal Church. I. Title.

LILLY, Eli, 1885- 283.772521
History of the Little Church on the Circle; Christ Church Parish, Indianapolis, 1837-1955. Indianapolis, The rector, wardens, and vestrymen of Christ Protestant Episcopal Church, 1957. 376p. illus. 26cm. [BX5980.I5C5] 59-2357
1. Indianapolis. Christ Church. I. Title.

FORBES, John Van Gelder. 283'.773
The Springfield mitre; a history of the politics and consequences of an Episcopal election in Illinois, 1962-1967 [by] John Forbes. Pelham, N.Y., American Church Publications [1971] xii, 263 p. 22 cm. Bibliography: p. 249-263. [BX5918.S93F67] 72-27489 2.50
1. Protestant Episcopal Church in the U.S.A. Springfield (Diocese) I. Title.

SWARTZBAUGH, Constance H 283.77348
The Episcopal Church in Fulton County, Illinois, 1835-1959; with some early history of the Episcopal Church in Illinois and the English settlement at Albion. [Canton? Ill., 1959] 187 p. illus. 24 cm. Includes bibliography. [BX5917.I3S9] 61-22285
1. Protestant Episcopal Church in the U.S.A. — Illinois — Fulton Co. I. Title.

COLEMAN, Robert J. 283'.774'27
To a goodly heritage; a history of St. Paul's Episcopal Church [by] Robert J. Coleman. Lansing, Mich., 1970. xvi, 140 p. illus. (part col.), facsim., ports. 24 cm. [BX5980.L33P38] 70-105329
1. Lansing, Mich. St. Paul's Episcopal Church. I. Title.

SWAN, Isabella E. 283'.774'33
The ark of God; a history of the Episcopal Church, Grosse Ile, Michigan, by Isabella E. Swan. [1st ed.] Grosse Ile, 1968] xii, 95p. illus., ports. 23cm. Sponsored by the wardens

and vestrvmen, St. James Church of Grosse Ile. [BX5980.G74S2] 67-25016 5.00 pap.,
1. Grosse Ile, Mich. St. James Episcopal Church. I. Title.
Order from the author, 27740 Southpointe, Grosse Ile, Mich. 48138.

WYANDOTTE, Mich. St. Stephen's Episcopal Church. 283.77433
A centennial record; 1860-1960. Wyandotte, Mich., St. Stephen's Episcopal Parish,[1960] 96 p. illus. 29 cm. [BX5980.W94S3] 61-28809
I. Title.

JOHNSON, Irwin C 283.77434
St. John's centennial book, 1858-1958, by Irwin C. Johnson and George W. Stark in collaboration with Charles E. Grinyer and Ralph J. Burton. Detroit, St. John's Church, c1958. 113p. illus. 24cm. [BX5980.D45S3] 58-59568
1. Detroit. St. John's Church. I. Stark, George Washington, 1884- joint author. II. Title.

MADISON, Wis. Grace Episcopal Church. 283.77584
Grace Episcopal Church, Madison, Wisconsin; a history of the parish, commemorating the centennial anniversary of the first service held in Grace Church, Feburary 14, 1858. Madison, 1958. 75p. illus. 23cm. [BX5980.M22G7] 59-32736
I. Title.

TALBOT, William L. 283'.777'99
Saint John's Church in Keokuk : a history, 1850-1975 / by William L. Talbot ; with The stained glass of Saint John's by Alice Bowers. Keokuk, Iowa : The Church, 1975. 202 p., [29] leaves of plates : ill. ; 24 cm. Includes bibliographical references and index. [BX5980.K36S247] 75-38945
1. Saint John's Church, Keokuk, Iowa. 2. Keokuk, Iowa—Biography. I. Title.

KLEINE, Glen. 283'.778'66
St. Paul's Episcopal Church, 1866-1966, [by G. Kleine. St. Louis? 1967] 22 p. illus., ports. 22 x 28 cm. Cover title. [BX5980.S2S25] 71-13703
1. St. Louis. St. Paul's Episcopal Church. I. Title.

RODGERS, Eugene L. 283'.778'66
And then a cathedral; a history of Christ Church Cathedral, St. Louis, Missouri, by Eugene L. Rodgers. [St. Louis, Christ Church Cathedral, 1970] 93 p. illus., ports. 23 cm. Bibliography: p. 92-93. [BX5980.S2C48] 70-19302
1. St. Louis. Christ Church Cathedral. I. Title.

MARTIN, Aquinata, Sister, 1896- 283'.782
The Catholic Church on the Nebraska frontier (1854-1885), by M. Aquinata Martin. Washington, Catholic University of America, 1937. [New York, AMS Press, 1974] ix, 202 p. 23 cm. Reprint of the author's thesis, Catholic University of America, 1937, which was issued as v. 26 of the Catholic University of America. Studies in America church history. Bibliography: p. 183-198. [BX1415.N2M3 1974] 73-3580 ISBN 0-404-57776-8 8.50
1. Catholic Church in Nebraska. 2. Catholics in Nebraska. I. Title. II. Series: Catholic University of America. Studies in American church history, v. 26.

SNEVE, Virginia Driving Hawk. 283'.783
That they may have life : the Episcopal Church in South Dakota, 1859-1976 / Virginia Driving Hawk Sneve. New York : Seabury Press, c1977. xiv, 224 p. : ill. ; 23 cm. Includes index. Bibliography: p. 218-220. [BX5917.5.S8S65] 76-55342 ISBN 0-8164-2141-2 : 5.95
1. Protestant Episcopal Church in the U.S.A.—South Dakota. 2. South Dakota—Church history. I. Title.

WILKINS, Robert p. 283.784
God giveth the increase; the history of the Episcopal Church in North Dakota by Robert P. Wilkins and Wynona H. Wilkins. Fargo, North Dakota Institute for Regional Studies, 1959. xiv, 206 p. illus., ports., map (on lining paper) 24 cm. Biliography: p. 194-199. [BX5917;N9W5] 59-62934
1. Protestant Episcopal Church in the U.S.A. — North Dakota. I. Wilkins, Wynona H., joint author. II. Title.

BRECK, Allen duPont. 283.788
The Episcopal Church in Colorado, 1860-1963. [1st ed.] Denver, Big Mountain Press [c1963] ix, 450 p. plates (part col.) ports. (part col.) 27 cm. (The West in American history, no. 2) Bibliography: p. 419-431. [BX5918.C6B7] 63-23029
1. Protestant Episcopal Church in the U.S.A. Colorado (Diocese) I. Title. II. Series.

BRECK, Allen duPont 283.788
The Episcopal Church in Colorado, 1860-1963. Denver, Big Mountain Pr. [dist. Swallow, c.1963] ix, 450p. plates (pt. col.) ports. (pt. col.) 27cm. (West in Amer. hist., no. 2) Bibl. 63-23029 10.00
1. Protestant Episcopal Church in the U.S.A. Colorado (Diocese) I. Title.

DANEY, Isabel Stevenson. 283.78855
Pueblo's first cross; Episcopal church history. Dever, Big Moutain Press [1966] 246 p. illus., group ports. 23 cm. Bibliography: p. 246. [BX5919.P8D3] 66-4044
1. Protestant Episcopal Church in the U.S.A. — Pueblo, Colo. 2. Pueblo, Colo. — Church history. I. Title.

DANEY, Isabel Stevenson 283.78855
Pueblo's first cross: Episcopal church history. Denver, Big Mountain dist. Swallow c.1966 246p. illus., group ports. 23cm. Bibl. [BX5919.P8D3] 66-4044 4.50
1. Protestant Episcopal Church in the U.S.A.—Pueblo, Colo. 2. Pueblo, Colo.—Church history. I. Title.

PERKINS, Mary Louise. 283'.788'56
An house not made with hands; a century of the Episcopal faith in Colorado Springs, Colorado, 1872-1972. [Colorado Springs] Episcopal Centennial Committee of Colorado Springs [1972] xii, 84 p. illus. 28 cm. Includes the history of Grace Church and St. Stephen's, Church of the Holy Spirit, Church of St. Michael the Archangel, and Chapel of Our Saviour. [BX5919.C6P47] 74-152285
1. Protestant Episcopal Church in the U.S.A.—Colorado Springs. I. Title.

JESSETT, Thomas Edwin 1902 1902- 283.79
Pioneering God's country; the history of the Diocese of Olympia, 1853- 1953. Tacoma, Wash., Church Lantern Press, 1953. 54p. illus. 23cm. [BX5918.O5J3] 54-30473
1. Protestant Episcopal Church in the U.S. Olympia (Diocese)—Hist. I. Title.

WALLACE, Jerry, 1894- 283'.791'77
The Episcopal Church comes to Arizona; the century-old trek of Grace Church, 1874-1974. Tucson, Ariz., Grace Episcopal Church, 1974. ix, 49 p. illus. 24 cm. [BX5980.T83G728] 74-180334
1. Grace Episcopal Church, Tucson, Ariz. I. Title.

PARSONS, Edward Lambe, Bp., 1868- 283.794
The diocese of California; a quarter century, 1915-1940. Austin, Tex., Church Historical Society [1958] 165p. illus. 24cm. (Church Historical Society. Publication no. 46) [BX5918.C2P3] 58-4045
1. Protestant Episcopal Church in the U. S. A. California (Diocese)—Hist. I. Title.

BARNES, Calvin Rankin, 1891- 283'.794'98
The Parish of Saint Paul, San Diego, California: its first hundred years, by C. Rankin Barnes. [San Diego] Published by the Parish, 1969. 62 p. illus., ports. 23 cm. [BX5980.S34S32] 72-182743
1. San Diego, Calif. St. Paul's Church. I. Title.

MORRELL, William Parker, 1899- 283'.931
The Anglican Church in New Zealand; a history [by] W. P. Morrell. Dunedin, Anglican Church of the Province of New Zealand; [distributed by J. McIndoe] 1973. 277 p. illus. 22 cm. Bibliography: p. [254]-265. [BX5720.5.A4M67] 73-177145
1. Church of the Province of New Zealand—History. I. Title.

CARTER, Harry Garlin. 283'.9312'2
Parish of Saint Andrew Cambridge; centennial chronicle, 1871-1971, based on the text of Harry G. Carter, edited and arranged by Lilian M. Hanton and George N. Marshall. [Cambridge, N.Z.] Printed by the Cambridge Independent, 1971. 55 p. illus. ports. 22 cm. [BX5720.5.Z7C35] 74-162574
1. St. Andrew's Parish, Cambridge, N.Z. I. Hanton, Lilian May, ed. II. Marshall, George Nairn, ed. III. Title.

EVANS, John H. 283.931'57
Southern see; the Anglican Diocese of Dunedin, New Zealand [by] John H. Evans. [Dunedin, J. McIndoe for] the Standing Committee of the Diocese of Duendin [1968] xvi, 325 p. illus., map, ports. 23 cm. Bibliography: p. [299]-306. [BX5720.5.A44D8] 78-455672 5.75
1. Church of the Province of New Zealand. Diocese of Dunedin—History. I. Title.

SHEVILL, Ian W. A., Bp. 283.94
Half time. [by] Ian Shevill. Brisbane, Sydney, Jacaranda; San Francisco, Tri-Ocean [1966] 143p. illus., ports. 22cm. [BX5720.S4A3] 67-76636 5.95 bds.,
I. Title.

284 Protestants Of Continental Origin

ADAM, Karl, 1876- 284
One and holy; translated by Cecily Hastings. New York, Sheed & Ward, 1951. 130 p. 20 cm. [BX4817.A3] 51-7382
1. Luther, Martin, 1483-1546. 2. Catholic Church—Relations—Lutheran Church. 3. Lutheran Church—Relations—Catholic Church. 4. Church. I. Title.

ADAM, Karl, 1876- 284
One and holy. Translated by Cecily Hastings. New York, Greenwood Press [1969, c1951] vii, 130 p. 23 cm. Translation of Una Sancta in katholischer Sicht. [BX4818.3.A313 1969] 79-95111
1. Catholic Church—Relations—Protestant churches. 2. Luther, Martin, 1483-1546. 3. Protestant churches—Relations—Catholic Church. 4. Reformation—Germany. I. Title.

ANDERSON, William Ketcham, 1888-1947. 284
Protestantism, a symposium. Edited by William K. Anderson. Freeport, N.Y., Books for Libraries Press [1969, c1944] vi, 282 p. 24 cm. (Essay index reprint series) Contents.Contents.—Introduction, by S. M. Cavert.—Was the Reformation needed? By J. T. McNeill.—Protestantism and the primitive church, by M. Rist.—Protestantism before Luther, by E. P. Booth.—Luther and his tradition, by A. R. Wentz.—Zwingli and the reformed tradition, by G. W. Richards.—Calvin and his tradition, by G. Harkness.—The Anglican tradition, by A. C. Zabriskie.—The independent tradition, by J. M. Batten.—Protestantism in American history, by W. W. Sweet.—Sectarianism run wild, by C. S. Braden.—Cardinal principles of Protestantism, by A. C. Knudson.—Protestantism and the Bible, by W. G. Chanter.—Christian theology, by H. F. Rall.—Worship and the sacraments, by O. T. Olson.—Protestantism and music, by C. and H. A. Dickinson.—The Protestant emphasis on preaching, by H. E. Luccock.—The mystical spirit, by W. E. Hocking.—Ethics, by F. J. McConnell.—The open mind, by R. W. Sockman.—In the Far East, by K. S. Latourette.—In Europe, by H. S. Leiper.—In Latin America, by G. Baez-Camargo.—In American education, by E. C. Colwell.—Our responsibility for a new world, by P. B. Kern.—A growing ecumenicity, by H. P. Van Dusen. Bibliographical footnotes. [BX4810.A53 1969] 69-18918
1. Protestantism. 2. Protestant churches.

ARNOLD, Eberhard, 1883-1935. 284
History of the Baptizers movement. [Edited and translated from the German by the Society of Brothers. Rifton, N.Y., Plough Pub. House of the Woodcrest Service Committee, 1970] 213-233 p. 26 cm. "First published in the Mennonite quarterly review, July 1969." "The original German manuscript is based on shorthand notes taken on November 10, 1935 ... when Eberhard Arnold spoke to the household of the Rhon-Bruderhof." Bibliographical footnotes. [BX4931.2.A73 1970] 76-98462
1. Dissenters, Religious. 2. Anabaptists. I. Title.

*BOUYER, Louis 284
The spirit and forms of Protestantism. Tr. by A. V. Littledale. Cleveland, World [1964] 234p. 21cm. (Meridian bks., M180) 1.95 pap.,
I. Title.

BOUYER, Louis, 1913- 284
The spirit and forms of Protestantism. Translated by A. V. Littledale. Westminster, Md., Newman Press, 1956. 234 p. 22 cm. [BX4668.B67] 56-10001
1. Converts, Catholic. 2. Protestantism. I. Title.

BROWN, Robert McAfee, 1920- 284
The spirit of Protestantism. New York, Oxford University Press, 1961. 264 p. 21 cm. Includes bibliographies. [BX4811.B74] 61-8367
1. Protestantism. I. Title.

COBB, John B. 284
Varieties of Protestantism. Philadelphia, Westminister Press [1960] 271 p. 21 cm. Includes bibliography. [BX4810.C54] 60-5082
1. Protestantism. 2. Sects. I. Title.

DILLENBERGER, John. 284
Protestant Christianity interpreted through its development [by] John Dillenberger [and] Claude Welch. New York, Scribner, 1954. 340 p. 22 cm. [BX4807.D5] 54-10367
1. Protestantism—History. I. Welch, Claude, joint author.

DILLENBERGER, John 284
Protestant Christianity interpreted through its development [by] John Dillenberger [and] Claude Welch. New York, Scribner [c.1958] xii, 340p. 21cm. (Scribner library SL17) 1.45 pap.,
1. Protestantism—Hist. I. Welch, Claude, joint author. II. Title.

DRUMMOND, Andrew Landale. 284
Story of American Protestantism. Boston, Beacon Press, 1950. xii, 418 p. 23 cm. Bibliography: p. 407-413. [BR515.D8 1950] 50-12382
1. U.S.—Church history. 2. Protestant churches—U.S.

DUNSTAN, John Leslie, 1901- ed. 284
Protestantism. New York, Washington Sq. [1962, c.1961] 257p. 17cm. (Great religions of modern man) Bibl. .60 pap.,
1. Protestantism. I. Title.

FERM, Vergilius Ture Anselm, 1896- ed. 284
The Protestant credo. New York, Philosophical Library [1953] 241p. 22cm. [BX4815.F4] 53-7907
1. Protestantism—Addresses, essays, lectures. I. Title.

FIELDHOUSE, Marvin L 284
The modern menace of Protestantism, by Marvin L. Fieldhouse. [1st hard cover ed.,] New York, Vantage Press [1964] 62 p. 21 cm. [BX4815.F5] 64-56576
1. Protestantism. I. Title.

FIELDHOUSE, Marvin L. 284
The modern menace of Protestantism. New York, Vantage [c.1964] 62p. 21cm. 64-56576 2.00 bds.,
1. Protestantism. I. Title.

FLEW, Robert Newton, 1886- ed. 284
The catholicity of Protestantism; being a report presented to His Grace the Archbishop of Canterbury by a group of Free Churchmen. Edited by R. Newton Flew and Rupert E. Davies. With a foreword by the Archbishop of Canterbury. Philadelphia, Muhlenberg Press [1954] 159p. 21cm. Bibliographical footnotes. [BX4817] 54-3942
1. Protestantism. 2. Catholicity. I. Fisher, Geoffrey Francis, Abp. of Canterbury, 1887- II. Davies, Rupert Eric, 1909- joint ed. III. Title.

GARRISON, R. Benjamin. 284
Portrait of the church: warts and all [by] R. Benjamin Garrison. New York, Abingdon Press [1964] 160 p. 20 cm. Bibliographical footnotes. [BX4811.G3] 64-20771
1. Protestants — 20th cent. 2. Church — Addresses, essays, lectures. I. Title.

GARRISON, R. Benjamin 284
Portrait of the church: warts and all. Nashville, Abingdon [c.1964] 160p. 20cm. Bibl. 64-20771 3.00 bds.,
1. Protestantism—20th cent. 2. Church—Addresses, essays, lectures. I. Title.

GARRISON, Winfred Ernest, 1874- 284
A Protestant manifesto. New York, Abingdon-Cokesbury Press [1952] 207 p. 24 cm. [BX4810.G28] 52-5377
1. Protestantism. I. Title.

HALL, Clarence Wilbur, 1902- 284
Protestant panorama; a story of the faith that made America free, by Clarence W. Hall and Desider Holisher. With an introd. by Charles P. Taft. New York, Farrar, Straus and Young [1951] 180 p. illus. 26 cm. Bibliography: p. 179-180. [BR525.H26] 51-13261
1. Protestant churches—U.S. 2. U.S.—Religion. I. Holisher, Desider, 1901- joint author. II. Title.

HAMILTON, Kenneth. 284
The Protestant way. Fair Lawn, N. J., Essential Books, 1956. 264p. 22cm. [BX4810.H23] 56-4967
1. Protestantism. I. Title.

HAMILTON, Kenneth Gardiner, 1893- 284
The Protestant way. Fair Lawn, N. J., Essential Books, 1956. 264p. 22cm. [BX4810.H23] 56-4967
1. Protestantism. I. Title.

HARDON, John A 284
Christianity in conflict; a Catholic view of Protestantism. Westminster, Md., Newman Press, 1959. 300p. 23cm. Sequel to The Protestant churches of America. [BX4811.H3] 59-14802
1. Protestantism. 2. Catholic Church—Doctrinal and controversial works—Catholic authors. I. Title.

HARDON, John A 284
The Protestant churches of America. Westminster, Md., Newman Press, 1956. 365p. 22cm. [BR516.H25] 56-13249
1. Sects—U. S. 2. Protestant churches—U. S. 3. U. S.—Religion. I. Title.

HARTSHORNE, Marion Holmes. 284
The faith to doubt; a Protestant response to criticisms of religion. Englewood Cliffs, N.J. Prentice-Hall [1963] 111 p. 21 cm. (A Spectrum book) [BX4817.H3] 63-9947
1. Protestantism. 2. Faith I. Title.

HARTSHORNE, Marion Holmes 284
The faith to doubt; a Protestant response to criticisms of religion. Englewood Cliffs, N.J., Prentice [c.1963] 111p. 21cm. (Spectrum bk.) 63-9947 3.95; 1.75 pap.,
1. Protestantism. 2. Faith. I. Title.

HEIM, Karl, 1874- 284
The nature of Protestantism. Translated and with a foreword by John Schmidt. Philadelphia, Fortress Press [1963] 164 p. 18 cm. "Transalation from the fourth and fifth revised and expanded edition of Das Wesen des evangelischen Christentums." Includes bibliography. [BX4810.H42] 63-12534
1. Protestantism. I. Title.

HEIM, Karl, 1874- 284
The nature of Protestantism. Tr. [from German] by Schmidt. Philadelphia, Fortress [c.1963] 164p. 18cm. Bibl. 63-12534 1.75 pap.,
1. Protestantism. I. Title.

*HUNT, George L., ed. 284
Where we are in church union; a report on the present accomplishments of the Consultation on Church Union. Ed. by George L. Hunt, Paul A. Crow, Jr. New York, Association Pr. [c.1965] 126p. 16cm. (Reflection bk.) .50 pap.,
I. Title.

JENNEY, Ray Freeman, 1891- 284
I am a Protestant. [1st ed.] Indianapolis, Bobbs-Merrill [1951] 239 p. 21 cm. [BX4810.J43] 51-12229
1. Protestantism. I. Title.

KERR, High Thomson, 1909- 284
What divides Protestants today. New York, Association Press [1958] 127p. 16cm. (An Association Press reflection book) Includes bibliography. [BR516.5.K4] 58-11532
1. Sects—U. S. 2. Protestant churches—U. S. I. Title.

KERR, Hugh Thomson, 1909- 284
Positive Protestantism, a return to first principles. Englewood Cliffs, N. J., Prentice-Hall [1963] 108 p. 21 cm. (A Spectrum book) [BX4811.K4] 63-7989
1. Protestantism — 20th cent. I. Title.

KERR, Hugh Thomson, 1909- 284
Positive Protestantism; an interpretation of the gospel. Philadelphia, Westminster Press [1950] 147 p. 21 cm. [BX4810.K4] 50-10304
1. Protestantism. 2. Christianity—Essence, genius, nature. I. Title.

KERR, Hugh Thomson, 1909- 284
Positive Protestantism, a return to first principles. Englewood Cliffs, N.J., Prentice [c.1950, 1963] 108p. 21cm. (Spectrum bk.) 63-7989 1.75 pap.,
1. Protestantism—20th cent. I. Title.

LITTEL, Franklin Hamlin. 284
The free church. Boston, Starr King Press [1957] 171p. 22cm. [BX4817.L55] 57-10927
1. Protestantism. 2. Dissenters. 3. Anabaptists. I. Title.

LITTELL, Franklin Hamlin. 284
The free church. Boston, Starr King Press [1957] 171p. 22cm. [BX4817.L55] 57-10927
1. Protestantism. 2. Dissenters. 3. Anabaptists. I. Title.

MACGREGOR, Geddes. 284
The coming reformation. Philadelphia, Westminster Press [1960] 160p. 22cm. [BX4811.M25] 60-11071
1. Protestantism. 2. Lord's Supper (Liturgy) I. Title.

MACGREGOR, Geddes [John Geddes MacGregor] 284
The coming reformation. Philadelphia, Westminister Press [c.1960] 160p. 22cm. 60-11071 3.50
1. Protestantism. 2. Lord's Supper (Liturgy) I. Title.

MANISCALCO, Joseph 284
The Waldenses. Text, illus. by Joe Maniscalco. Nashville Southern Pub. Assn. [c.1966] 1 v. (unpaged) illus. 25cm. [BX4881.2.M3] 66-4839 2.50
1. Waldenses—Juvenile literature. I. Title.

MANSCHRECK, Clyde Leonard 284
The Reformation and Protestantism today. New York, Association Press [c.1960] 128p. 16cm. (An Association Press reflection book) (bibl. and bibl. notes) 60-6570 .50 pap.,
1. Protestantism. 2. Reformation. I. Title.

MANSCHRECK, Clyde Leonard, 1917- 284
The Reformation and Protestantism today. New York, Association Press [1960] 128p. 16cm. (An Association Press reflection book) Includes bibliography. [BX4811.M3] 60-6570
1. Protestantism. 2. Reformation. I. Title.

MIELKE, Arthur W 284
This is Protestantism. [Westwood, N. J.] F. H. Revell Co. [1961] 127p. 24cm. [BX4811.M5] 61-9243
1. Protestantism. I. Title.

NEW York. Missionary Research Library. 284
Protestant churches of Asia, the Middle East, Africa, Latin America, and the Pacific area. New York, 1959. 75p. 28cm. 'Revision of The younger churches--Some facts and observations.' [BX4805.2.N45 1959] 59-44072
1. Protestant churches. 2. Sects. 3. Missions. I. Title.

PATTEE, Richard, 1906- 284
The regilious question in Spain. Washington, National Council of Catholic Men [1950] 56 p. map. 22 cm. [BX4851.P3] 50-4304
1. Protestant churches — Spain. 2. Religious liberty — Spain. I. Title.

PAUCK, Wilhelm, 1901- 284
The heritage of the Reformation. Rev. and enl. ed. Glencoe [Ill.] Free Press [1961] 399p. 22cm. Includes bibliography. [BX4810.P3 1961] 60-7096
1. Protestantism. I. Title.

PAUCK, Wilhelm, 1901- 284
The heritage of the Reformation. Boston, Beacon Press, 1950. 312 p. 23 cm. (The Phoenix series, 2) Bibliographical references included in "Notes" (p. 295-306) [BX4810.P3] 50-7345
1. Protestantism. I. Title.

PIPER, Otto A 1891- 284
Protestantism in an ecumenical age: its root, its right, its task, by Otto A. Piper. Philadelphia, Fortress Press [1965] ix, 254 p. 22 cm. Bibliographical footnotes. [BX8.2.P5] 65-13408
1. Ecumenical movement. 2. Protestantism—20th cent. I. Title.

PIPER. OTTO A., 1891- 284
Protestantism in an ecumenical age: its root, its right, its task. Philadelphia, Fortress [c.1965] ix, 254p. 22cm. Bibl. [BX8.2.P5] 65-13408 4.50
1. Ecumenical movement. 2. Protestantism—20th cent. I. Title.

POL, Willem Hendrik van de, 1897- 284
World Protestantism. Rev. ed., translated by T. Zuydwijk. New York] Herder and Herder [1964] xii, 316 p. 22 cm. [BX4811.P613] 64-19733
1. Protestantism. I. Title.

POL, Willem Hendrik van de, 1897- 284
World Protestantism [Rev. ed., tr. from Dutch by T. Zuydwijk. New York] Herder & Herder [c.1964] xii, 346p. 22cm. 64-19733 6.50
1. Protestantism. I. Title.

POLAND, Burdette C 284
French Protestantism and the French Revolution; a study in church and state, thought and religion, 1685-1815. Princeton, Princeton University Press, 1957. ix, 315p. maps. 25cm. Bibliography: p. 301-309. [BX4843.P6] 57-5846
1. Protestant churches— France. 2. France—Hist.—Revolution—Religious history. I. Title.

POLAND, Burdette C 284
French Protestantism and the French Revolution; a study in church and state, thought and religion, 1685-1815. Princeton, Princeton University Press, 1957. ix, 315p. maps. 25cm. Bibliography: p. 301-309. [BX4843.P6] 57-5846
1. Protestant churches—France. 2. France—Hist.—Revolution—Religious history. I. Title.

SCHAFF, Philip, 1819-1893. 284
The principle of Protestantism. Translated from the German by John W. Nevin, 1845. Philadelphia, United Church Press [1964] 268 p. facsim. 23 cm. (Lancaster series on the Mercersburg theology, v. 1) "Bibliographic notes": p. 19-20. Bibliography: p. 255-268. [BX4810.S263] 64-14141
1. Protestantism. 2. Mercersburg theology. I. Title. II. Series.

SCHAFF, Philip, 1819-1893 284
The principle of Protestantism. Tr. from German by John W. Nevin, 1845. Philadelphia, United Church [c.1964] 268p. facsim. 23cm. (Lancaster ser. on the Mercersburg theology, v.1) Bibl. 64-14141 4.50 pap.,
1. Protestantism. 2. Mercersburg theology. I. Title. II. Series.

SOPER, David Wesley, 1910- ed. 284
Room for improvement; next steps for Protestants. with chapters by Chad Walsh [and others] Chicago, Wilcox and Follett Co. [1951] 126 p. 22 cm. [BX4817.S6] 51-14846
1. Protestantism. 2. U.S. — Religion. 3. Theology — 20th cent. I. Title.

THOMSON, John A F. 284
The later Lollards, 1414-1520. New York, Oxford [c.]1965. 272p. 23cm. (Oxford hist. ser., 2d ser.) Bibl. [BX4901.2.T5] 66-452 6.75
1. Lollards. I. Title.

THOMSON, John A. F 284
The later Lollards, 1414-1520, by John A. F. Thomson. [London, Oxford University Press, 1965. 272 p. 23 cm. (Oxford historical series, 2d ser.) Bibliography: p. [254]-232. [BX4901.2.T5] 66-452
1. Lollards. I. Title.

TILLICH, Paul, 1886- 284
The Protestant era. Translated by James Luther Adams. Abridged ed. [Chicago] University of Chicago Press [1957] 242p. 21cm. (Phoenix books, P19) [BX4817] 57-14060
1. Protestantism. 2. Theology. Doctrinal—Addresses, essays, lectures. 3. Christianity—Philosophy. I. Title.

TILLICH, Paul, 1886- 284
The Protestant era. Translated by James Luther Adams. Abridged ed. [Chicago, University of Chicago Press [1957] 242 p. 21 cm. (Phoenix books, P19) [BX4817] 57-14060
1. Protestantism. 2. Theology, Doctrinal—Addresses, essays, lectures. 3. Christianity—Philosophy. I. Title.

WHALE, John Seldon, 1896- 284
The Protestant tradition; an essay in interpretation. Cambridge [Eng.] University Press, 1955. 359 p. 20 cm. [BX4810.W5] 55-4857
1. Protestantism. 2. Theology, Doctrinal—History—Modern period. I. Title.

WILBURN, Ralph Glenn, 1909- 284
The prophetic voice in Protestant Christianity. St. Louis, Bethany Press [1956] 298p. 23cm. [Bethany history series] [BX4817.W5] 56-10171
1. Protestantism. 2. Revelation. 3. Ecumenical movement. I. Title.

WILBURN, Ralph Glenn, 1909- 284
The prophetic voice in Protestant Christianity. St. Louis, Bethany Press [1956] 298 p. 23 cm. [Bethany history series] [BX4817.W5] 56-10171
1. Protestantism. 2. Revelation. 3. Ecumenical movement. I. Title.

WOLF, Richard C 284
Our Protestant heritage; a cooperative weekday church school text, grades 7-8. W. Kent Gilbert, editor. Illustrated by Paul Remmey maps and charts by John Geiszel. [Philadelphia] Published for the Cooperative Publication Association by Muhlenbert Press [1956] 112. 160p. illus. 23cm. (The Cooperative series: texts for weekday religious education classes and released-time religious education instruction) The main work is preceded by the 'Teacher's guide,' by Lucile Desjardins (112p.) with special t.p. [BX4807.W6] 56-3914
1. Week-day church schools—Teachers manuals. 2. Protestantism—Hist. I. Desjardins, Lucile, 1892- II. Title.

HUNT, George Laird, ed. 284.04
Ten makers of modern Protestant thought: Schweitzer, Rauschenbusch, Temple, Kirkegaard, Barth, Brunner, Niebuhr, Tillich, Bultmann, Buber. New York, Association Press [1958] 126 p. 18 cm. (An Association Press reflection book) [BX4825.H8] 58-6478
1. Theologians. I. Title.

FERM, Vergilius Ture Anselm, 1896- 284.09
Pictorial history of Protestantism; a panoramic view of western Europe and the United States. New York, Philosophical Library [1957] xi, 368 p. illus., ports., maps, facsims., music. 29 cm. [BX4805.F4] 57-14163
1. Protestantism—History. 2. Protestantism—History—Pictures, illustrations, etc. I. Title.

BRAATEN, Carl E., 1929- ed. and tr. 284.0943
Kerygma and history; a symposium on the theology of Rudolf Bultmann. Selected tr., ed. by Carl E. Braaten, Roy A. Harrisville. Nashville, Abingdon [c.1962] 235p. 23cm. Bibl. 62-9383 5.00
1. Bultmann, Rudolf Karl, 1884- I. Harrisville, Roy A., joint ed. and tr. II. Title.

POLLOCK, John Charles. 284'.0947
The faith of the Russian Evangelicals, by J. C. Pollock. Grand Rapids, Zondervan Pub. House [1969, c1964] 190 p. 21 cm. Bibliography: p. 187-190. [BX4849.P6 1969] 71-81037
1. Protestants in Russia. 2. Baptists—Russia. 3. Persecution—Russia. I. Title.

IGLEHART, Charles W. 284.0952
A century of Protestant Christianity in Japan. [Published in cooperation with the Japan Committee. Division of Foreign Missions, National Council of the Churches of Christ in the U.S.A.] Rutland, Vt., C. E. Tuttle Co. [1959] 384p. 22cm. 59-11758 3.00
1. Protestant churches—Japan. 2. Japan—Church history. I. Title.

THOMAS, Winburn T 284.0952
Protestant beginnings in Japan, the first three decades, 1859-1889 [1st ed.] Tokyo, Rutland, Vt., C. E. Tuttle Co. [1959] 258 p. group port. 22 cm. "Originally presented as a dissertation to the faculty of the Graduate School of Yale University ... for the degree of doctor of philosophy." Bibliographical references included in "Notes" (p. 213-233) "A bibliography concerning the post-restoration development of Christianity in Japan" (p. 241-247) [BR1305.T5 1959] 59-6489
1. Protestant churches — Japan. 2. Missions — Japan. I. Title.

MCGAVRAN, Donald Anderson, 1897- 284.0972
Church growth in Mexico, by Donald McGavran, John Huegel, Jack Taylor. Grand Rapids, Mich., Eerdmans [c.1963] 136p. map, diagrs. 21cm. Bibl. 63-17788 1.95 pap.,
1. Protestant churches—Mexico. I. Title.

HARDON, John A. 284.0973
The Protestant churches of America. [Rev. ed.] Westminster, Md., Newman Press, 1958. 365 p. 21 cm. [BR516.5.H3 1958] 62-51063
1. Sects—United States. 2. Protestant churches—United States. 3. United States—Religion—1945- I. Title.

MARTY, Martin E. 284.0973
Second chance for American Protestants. New York, Harper [c.1963] 175p. 22cm. 63-10962 3.50 bds.,
1. Protestantism—20th cent. I. Title.

PARKER, Thomas Valentine, 1878- 284.0973
American Protestantism, an appraisal. New York, Philosophical Library [1956] 219p. 22cm. [BR525.P27] 56-13948
1. Protestant churches—U. S. I. Title.

STRINGFELLOW, William. 284.0973
A private and public faith. Grand Rapids, Eerdmans [c1962] 93 p. 22 cm. [BX4817.S8] 62-21368
1. Protestantism — 20th cent. 2. U.S. — Religion. I. Title.

STRINGFELLOW, William 284.0973
A private and public faith. Grand Rapids, Mich., Eerdmans [c.1962] 93p. 22cm. 62-21368 3.00
1. Protestantism—20th cent. 2. U. S.—Religion. I. Title.

BAILEY, Kenneth Kyle, 1923- 284.0975
Southern white Protestantism in the twentieth century [by] Kenneth K. Bailey. [1st ed.] New York, Harper & Row [1964] x, 180 p. 22 cm. "A bibliographical essay": p. 169-172. [BR535.B3] 64-19493
1. Southern States—Church history. 2. Protestantism—Southern States. I. Title.

BARBIERI, Sante Uberto, Bp. 284.098
Land of Eldorado. New York, Friendship Press [1961] 161p. illus. 20cm. Includes bibliography. [BR600.B26] 61-6628
1. Protestant churches— Spanish America. 2. Spanish America—Religion. 3. Spanish America—Civilization. I. Title.

ARDEN, Gothard Everett, 1905- 284.1
Augustana heritage; a history of the Augustana Lutheran Church. Rock Island, Ill., Augustana Press [1963] 424 p. illus. 24 cm. [BX8049.A85] 62-22405
1. Augustana Evangelical Lutheran Church. I. Title.

ARDEN, Gothard Everett, 1905- 284.1
Augustana heritage; a history of the Augustana Lutheran Church. Rock Island, Ill., Augustana [c.1963] 424p. illus. 24cm. 62-22405 4.95
1. Augustana Evangelical Lutheran Church. I. Title.

AUGUSTANA Evangelical Lutheran Church. 284.1
Protokoll, arsmote. Red Wing, Minn. v. 20 cm. Issued 18 by the church under its earlier name: Skandinaviska ev. lutherska Augustana-synoden. [BX8049.A29] 50-46481
I. Title.

AUGUSTANA Evangelical Lutheran Church. Centennial Publication Committee. 284.1
This is my church. Robert Mortvedt, chairman [and others] Editor: John R. Nyberg; art director: William T. Schaeffer; photography: Paul Wychor, Bruce Sifford. [Chicago] Augustana Book Concern, c1960. 100p. illus. 32cm. [BX8049.A63] 60-1376
1. Augustana Evangelical Lutheran Church—Hist. I. Nyberg, John R., ed. II. Title.

AUGUSTANA Evangelical Lutheran Church. Columbia Conference. 284.1
Minutes of the annual convention. Rock Island, Ill., Augustana Book Concern, printers. v. 23 cm. Issued by the conference under the church's variant name: AugustanaSynod. [BX8049.1.C6A3] 50-46480
I. Title.

AUGUSTANA Evangelical Lutheran Church. Iowa Conference. 284.1
Official minutes of the annual convention. Rock Island, Ill., Augustana Book Concern, Printers. v. illus. 23 cm. Issued by the conference under the church's variant name: AugustanaSynod. [BX8049.1.I8A3] 50-46483
I. Title.

AUGUSTANA Evangelical Lutheran Church. Kansas Conference. 284.1
Minutes of the annual convention. Rock Island, Ill., Augustana Book Concern, printers. v. illus. 23 cm. Issued by the conference under the church's earlier name: Evangelical Lutheran Augustana Synod. [BX8049.1.K2A3] 50-46477
I. Title.

AUGUSTANA Evangelical Lutheran Church. Minnesota Conference. 284.1
Minutes of the annual convention. Rock Island, Ill., Augustana Book Concern, printers. v. 23 cm. Issued by the conference under the church's variant name: AugustanaSynod. [BX8049.1.M6A3] 50-46478
I. Title.

AUGUSTANA Evangelical Lutheran Church. Synodical Council. 284.1
Synodical Council resolutions, annual convention. [Des Moines?] v. 22 cm. Issued by the council under the church's variant name: Augustana Synod. [BX8049.A65] 50-46479
I. Title.

BECK, Victor Emanuel, 1894- 284.1
Why I am a Lutheran. New York, Nelson [c1956] 100p. 21cm. Includes bibliography. [BX8065.B3] 56-7113
1. Lutheran Church. I. Title.

ELERT, Werner, 1885-1954. 284.1
The structure of Lutheranism. Translated by Walter A. Hansen. Foreword by Jaroslav Pelikan. Werner Elert, professor of theology, by Robert C. Schultz. Saint Louis, Concordia Pub. House, 1962- v. port. 25 cm. Contents.The theology and philosophy of life of Lutheranism, especially in the sixteenth and seventeenth centuries. Includes bibliographical references. [BX8065.E543] 62-19955
1. Lutheran Church—Doctrinal and controversial works. I. Title.

ELERT, Werner, 1885-1955. 284.1
The structure of Lutheranism. Translated by Walter A. Hansen. Foreword by Jaroslav Pelikan. Werner Elert, professor of theology, by Robert C. Schultz. Saint Louis, Concordia Pub. House, 1962- v. 25 cm. Includes bibliography. [BX8065.E543] 62-19955
1. Lutheran Church — Doctrinal and controversial works. 2. Church and social problems — Lutheran Church. I. Title.

ELERT, Werner, 1885-1955 284.1
The structure of Lutheranism: v.1. Tr. by Walter A. Hansen. Foreword by Jaroslav Pelikan. Werner Elert, professor of theology, by Robert C. Schultz. Saint Louis, Concordia [c.]1962. 547p. 25cm. Bibl. 62-19955 10.95
1. Lutheran Church—Doctrinal and controversial works. 2. Church and social problems—Lutheran Church. I. Title.

EVANGELICAL and Reformed Church. Synods. Southwest Ohio. 284.1
Abstract of the minutes of the annual meeting. Cincinnati. v. 23 cm. Caption title, 1950: Minutes. Issues for some years included in Minutes of the Northeast Ohio Synod. [BX7470.S65A5] 52-26678
I. Title.

HEINECKEN, Martin J 284.1
Christ frees and unites. Philadelphia, Muhlenberg Press [1957] 111p. 21cm. (The Kunbel-Miller lectures, 1957) Includes bibliography. [BX8065.H383] 57-11301
1. Lutheran Church. 2. Lutheran World Federation. 3. Church—Unity. I. Title.

LUTHERAN churches of the world. 284.1
Foreword by Carl E. Lund-Quist. Minneapolis, Augsburg Pub. House [1957] x, 333p. ports. 23cm. 'Successor to the Lutheran world almanacs published from 1921 to 1937 and The Lutheran churches of the world published in 1952.' [BX8018.L78] 57-9727
1. Lutheran Church—Hist.

LUTHERAN churches of the world. 284.1
Foreword by Carl E. Lund-Quist. Minneapolis, Augsburg Pub. House [1957] x, 333p. ports. 23cm. 'Successor to the Lutheran world almanacs published from 1921 to 1937 and The Lutheran churches of the world published in 1952.' [BX8018.L78] 57-9727
1. Lutheran Church—Hist. I. Title.

LUTHERAN World Federation. Assembly. 5th, Evian-les-Bains, France, 1970. 284'.1
Sent into the world; the proceedings of the Fifth Assembly of the Lutheran World Federation. Edited by LaVern K. Grosc. Minneapolis, Augsburg Pub. House [1971] 165 p. 23 cm. [BX8004.L9 1970] 79-135216 ISBN 0-8066-1103-0
1. Lutheran Church—Congresses. I. Grosc, LaVern K., ed. II. Title.

SAYRES, Alfred N 284.1
March on with strength, by Alfred N. Sayres and Robert S. Stanger: illustrated by George Malick. Philadelphia, Christian Education Press [1953] 95p. illus. 24cm. [BX7465.S3] 53-9920
1. Evangelical and Reformed Church—Hist. I. Stanger, Robert C., joint author. II. Title.

SAYRES, Alfred Nevin. 284.1
March on with strength, by Alfred N. Sayres and Robert S. Stanger; illustrated by George Malick. Philadelphia, Christian Education Press [1953] 95 p. illus. 24 cm. [BX7465.S3] 53-9920
1. Evangelical and Reformed Church—Hist. I. Stanger, Robert C., joint author. II. Title.

SOLBERG, Richard W 1917- 284.1
As between brothers; the story of Lutheran response to world need. Auspices, dept. of World Service, Lutheran World Federation. Minncapolis, Augsburg Pub. House [1957] 224p. illus. 22cm. [BX8074.B4S6] 57-12882
1. Lutheran Church—Charities. I. Lutheran World Federation. Dept. of World Service. II. Title.

SOLBERG, Richard W 1917- 284.1
As between brothers; the story of Lutheran response to world need. Auspices, Dept. of World Service, Lutheran World Federation. Minneapolis, Augsburg Pub. House [1957] 224 p. illus. 22 cm. [BX8074.B4S6] 57-128823
1. Lutheran Church — Charities. I. Lutheran World Federation. Dept. of World Service. II. Title.

SWIHART, Altman K., 1903- 284.1
Luther and the Lutheran Church 1483-1960. New York, Philosophical Library [c.1960] 703p. illus. 22cm. Bibl.: p.662-689 60-13641 7.50
1. Luther, Martin, 1483-1546. 2. Lutheran Church—Hist. 3. Lutheran Church in the U. S.—Hist. I. Title.

SWIHART, Altman K 1903- 284.1
Luther and the Lutheran Church 1483-1960. New York, Philosophical Library [1960] 703 p. illus. 22 cm. Includes bibliography. [BR325.S84] 60-13641
1. Luther, Martin, 1483-1546. 2. Lutheran Church — Hist. 3. Lutheran Church in the U.S. — Hist. I. Title.

SYMPOSIUM on Seventeenth Century Lutheranism. 284'.1
Selected papers. Saint Louis [Executive Subcommittee of the Continuation Committee of] the Symposium of Seventeenth Century Lutheranism, 1962- v. 22 cm. Includes bibliographical references. [BX8004.S93] 62-17680
1. Lutheran Church — Hist. — 17th cent. 2. Theology, Doctrinal — Hist. — 17th cent. I. Title.

TRAVER, Amos John, 1889- 284.1
A Lutheran handbook. Rev. ed. Philadelphia, Muhlenberg Press [1957, c1956] 104 p. 21 cm. [BX8065.T7] 56-11947
1. Lutheran Church. I. Title.

TRAVER, Amos John, 1889- 284.1
A Lutheran handbook. [2d rev. ed.] Philadelphia, Fortress Press [1964] x, 98 p. 29 cm. Bibliography: p. 97-98. [BX8065.T7] 63-12993
1. Lutheran Church. I. Title.

TRAVER, Amos John, 1889- 284.1
A Lutheran handbook [2d rev. ed.] Philadelphia, Fortress [c.1964] x, 98p. 20cm. Bibl. 64-12993 1.50 pap.,
1. Lutheran Church. I. Title.

*WALKER, Brooke 284.1
A Lutheran parish handbook. Ed., layout, art work by T. E. Mails [Hayfield, Minn. Box 11, Hayfield Pub. Co., 1964, c.1963] 63p. illus. 15cm. .50 pap.,
I. Title.

WALTHER, Carl Ferdinand Wilhelm, 284.1
The form of a Christian congregation. Presented-pub. by resolution of the Ev. Luth. Pastoral Conference of St. Louis, Mo. 2d unchanged ed. St. Louis, Mo., 1864. Tr. [from German] by John Theodore Mueller. St. Louis, Concordia [c.1963] xiv, 200p. 24cm. 63-21160 5.00
1. Lutheran Church—Government. I. Title.

WALTHER, Carl Ferdinand Wilhelm, 1811-1887. 284.1
The form of a Christian congregation. Presented and published by resolution of the Ev. Luth. Pastoral Conference of St. Louis, Mo. 2d unchanged ed. St. Louis, Mo., 1864. Translated by John Theodore Mueller. Saint Louis, Concordia Pub. House [1963] xiv, 200 p. 24 cm. Translation of Die rechte Gestalt einer vom Staate unabhangigen evangelisch-lutherischen Ortsgemeinde. [BX8065.W34 1963] 63-21160
1. Lutheran Church — Government. I. Title.

*WEAVER, J. Bruce 284.1
Belonging to the people of God; a handbook for church members. Frank W. Klos, ed. Philadelphia, Lutheran Church Pr. [1966] 191p. illus. (pt. col.) (LCA Sch. of religion ser.) price unreported pap.,
1. Worship—Lutheran church. I. Title.

BODENSIECK, Julius, 1894- ed. 284.103
The encyclopedia of the Lutheran Church, edited by Julius Bodensieck for the Lutheran World Federation. Minneapolis, Augsburg Pub. House [1965] 3 v. (xxii, 2575 p.) illus., ports. 27 cm. Includes bibliographies. [BX8007.B6] 64-21500
1. Lutheran Church — Dictionaries. 2. Theology — Dictionaries. I. Lutheran World Federation. II. Title.

BODENSIECK, Julius, 1894- ed. 284.103
The encyclopedia of the Lutheran Church, 3v., ed. by Julius Bodensieck for the Lutheran World Federation. Minneapolis, Augsburg [c.1965] 3v. (xxii, 2575p.) illus., ports. 27cm. Bibl. [BX8007.B6] 64-21500 37.50 set,
1. Lutheran Church—Dictionaries. 2. Theology—Dictionaries. I. Lutheran World Federation. II. Title.

LUTHERAN cyclopedia. 284.103
Erwin L. Lueker, editor in chief. Saint Louis, Concordia Pub. House [1954] xii, 1160p. 24cm. Includes bibliographies. [BX8007.L8] 54-14349
1. Lutheran Church—Dictionaries. 2. Theology—Dictionaries I. Lueker, Erwin Louis, 1914- ed.

LUTHERAN cyclopedia / 284'.1'03
Erwin L. Lueker, editor. Rev. ed. St. Louis : Concordia Pub. House, [1975] xiv, 845 p. ; 26 cm. [BX8007.L8 1975] 75-2096 ISBN 0-570-03255-5 : 24.95
1. Lutheran Church—Dictionaries. 2. Theology—Dictionaries. I. Lueker, Erwin Louis, 1914- ed.

GIERTZ, Bo Harold, Bp., 1905- 284.104
The message of the church in a time of crisis, and other essays; translated from the Swedish by Clifford Ansgar Nelson. Rock Island, Ill., Augustan Book Concern [1953] 64p. illus. 23cm. [BX8011.G5] 53-25509
1. Lutheran Church—Addresses, essays, lectures. I. Title.

LUTHERAN World Federation. Assembly. 3d, Minneapolis, 1957. 284.104
Messages of the Third Assembly; the opening worship sermon, keynote address, sub-theme lectures, and the resulting theses. Minneapolis, Augsburg Pub. House, 1957. 119 p. 22 cm. Bibliographical footnotes. [BX8004.L9 1957] 57-14826
1. Lutheran Church — Congresses. I. Title.

MESSAGES of the Third Assembly; 284.104
the opening worship sermon, keynote address, sub-theme lectures, and the resulting theses. Minneapolis, Augsburg Pub. House, 1957. 119 p. 22 cm. Bibliographical footnotes. [BX8004.L9 1957] 57-14826
1. Lutheran Church — Congresses.

EVANGELICAL and Reformed Church. 284.1058
Year book. 19-61. [St. Louis?] Board of Business Management. v. 23 cm. "Combining the Year book and almanac published ... from 1935 to 1944 and the book of Statistical tables of the congregation issued periodically from 1935 to 1942." United with the Year book of the Congregational Christian churches to form the Year book of the United Church of Christ. Vols. called contain statistics of two years back (e.g. 1953 has 1951 statistics); beginning with 1958 (which covers 1956 and 1957 statistics) each vol. contains statistics for the previous year. [BX7457.A43] 54-19222
1. Evangelical and Reformed Church — Yearbooks. I. Evangelical and Reformed Church. Board of Business Management. II. Title.

EVANGELICAL and Reformed Church. 284.1058
Year book and almanac. [St. Louis] Board of Business Management of the Evangelical and Reformed Church. v. illus. 23 cm. Published 1935-44. Cf. Evangelical and Reformed Church. Year book, 1953. "Combining the Almanac and year book published since 1864 by the Reformed Church in the United States, and the Evangelical year book published since 1911 by the Evangelical Synod of North America." Superseded by the Year book of the Evangelical and Reformed Church. [BX7457.A42] 66-51918
1. Evangelical and Reformed Church — Yearbooks. I. Evangelical and Reformed Church. Board of Business Management. II. Title.

SUELFLOW, August Robert, 1922- 284.10778
The heart of Missouri; a history of the Western District of the Lutheran Church, Missouri Synod, 1854-1954. Saint Louis, Concordia Pub. House [1954] 226p. illus. 23cm. [BX8061.M73S8] 54-33307
1. Lutheran Church—Missouri Synod. Districts. Western—Hist. I. Title.

HAMEL, Johannes 284.1081
A Christian in East Germany; [writings gathered from several different sources. Translated from the German by Ruth and Charles C. West.] New York, Association Press [c.1960] 126p. 20cm. 60-12716 3.00 bds.,
1. Lutheran Church—Addresses, essays, lectures. I. Title.

THIELICKE, Helmut, 1908- . 284.1081
Out of the depths. Translation by G. W. Bromiley. Grand Rapids, Eerdmans [1962] 89 p. 21 cm. "Essays ... selected and translated from Die Lebensangst und ihre Ueberwindung." [BX8011.T473] 62-22385
1. Lutheran Church — Addresses, essays, lectures. I. Title.

THIELICKE, Helmut, 1908- 284.1081
Out of the depths. Tr. [from German] by G. W. Bromiley. Grand Rapids, Mich., Eerdmans [c.1954, 1962] 89p. 21cm. 62-22385 2.50
1. Lutheran Church—Addresses, essays, lectures. I. Title.

LUTHERAN World Federation. Assembly. 4th, Helsinki, 1963. 284.1082
Messages of the Helsinki Assembly, the Lutheran World Federation; Christ today. Minneapolis, Augsburg [1963] 122p. illus., groups port. (on covers) 22cm. 63-23599 1.95 pap.,
1. Lutheran Church—Congresses. I. Title. II. Title: Christ today.

BERGENDOFF, Conrad John Immanuel, 1895- 284'.109
The church of the Lutheran Reformation; a historical survey of Lutheranism [by] Conrad Bergendoff. St. Louis, Concordia 1967. xv, 339p. 24cm. Bibl. [BX8018.B45] 67-16893 9.00
1. Lutheran Church—Hist. I. Title.

BERGENDOFF, Conrad John Immanuel, 1895- 284'.109
The church of the Lutheran Reformation; a historical survey of Lutheranism [by] Conrad Bergendoff. Saint Louis, Concordia Pub.

House, 1967. xv, 339 p. 24 cm. Bibliography: p. 319-325. [BX8018.B45] 67-16893
1. Lutheran Church — Hist. I. Title.

LOEW, Ralph W. 284'.1'09
The Lutheran way of life, by Ralph W. Loew. Englewood Cliffs, N.J., Prentice-Hall [1966] 192 p. 21 cm. "Notes and bibliography": p. 178-188. [BX8065.2.L6] 66-24980
1. Lutheran Church. I. Title.

THE Lutheran Church, 284'.1'09
past and present / edited by Vilmos Vajta. Minneapolis : Augsburg Pub. House, c1977. vii, 392 p. ; 22 cm. Translation of Die Evangelisch-Lutherische Kirche, Vergangenheit und Gegenwart. Bibliography: p. 371-380. [BX8018.L7613] 76-46120 ISBN 0-8066-1573-7 : 9.50
1. Lutheran Church—History—Addresses, essays, lectures. 2. Theology, Lutheran—Addresses, essays, lectures. I. Vajta, Vilmos.

WEBER, Erwin, 1921- 284'.1'09
From Luther to 1580 : a pictorial account : places, persons, and events leading to the Book of Concord / by Erwin Weber ; text by Ingetraut Ludolphy ; pref. by Conrad Bergendoff. St. Louis : Concordia Pub. House, c1977. 224 p. : ill. ; 29 cm. Includes bibliographical references. [BX8018.W42] 76-58401 ISBN 0-570-03264-4 : 14.95
1. Lutheran Church—History—Pictorial works. 2. Luther, Martin, 1483-1546—Portraits, etc. 3. Lutherans in Germany—Portraits. I. Title.

ADAMS, James 284'.1'0924 B
Edward, 1941-
Preus of Missouri and the great Lutheran civil war / James E. Adams. 1st ed. New York : Harper & Row, c1977. x, 242 p. ; 21 cm. Includes index. [BX8080.P73A65 1977] 76-62931 ISBN 0-06-060071-3 : 10.00
1. Preus, Jacob Aall Ottesen, 1920- 2. Lutheran Church—Clergy—Biography. 3. Lutheran Church—Missouri Synod—Doctrinal and controversial works. 4. Clergy—United States—Biography. I. Title.

ATKINSON, James, 284'.1'0924 B
1914-
Martin Luther and the birth of Protestantism. Baltimore, Penguin Books [1968] 352 p. maps. 19 cm. "Select bibliography of books in English": p. [337]-340. [BR325.A8 1968b] 75-2378 1.95
1. Luther, Martin, 1483-1546. I. Title.

BAILEY, James Martin, 284'.1'0924
1929-
The steps of Bonhoeffer; a pictorial album [by] J. Martin Bailey [and] Douglas Gilbert. Philadelphia, Pilgrim Press [1969] 128 p. illus., ports. 30 cm. [BX4827.B57B3] 79-93527 6.95
1. Bonhoeffer, Dietrich, 1906-1945. I. Gilbert, Douglas, joint author. II. Title.

BETHGE, Eberhard, 284'.1'0924 B
1909-
Dietrich Bonhoeffer; man of vision, man of courage. Translated from the German by Eric Mosbacher [and others] under the editorship of Edwin Robertson. New York, Harper & Row, 1970. xxiv, 867 p. illus., facsims., ports. 25 cm. [BX4827.B57B43] 70-109075 17.95
1. Bonhoeffer, Dietrich, 1906-1945. I. Title.

BONHOEFFER, Dietrich, 284'.10924
1906-1945.
Letters and papers from prison. Edited by Eberhard Bethge. Rev. ed. New York, Macmillan [1967] 240 p. illus., ports. 22 cm. Translation of Widerstand und Ergebung. [BX4827.B57A43] 67-19951
I. Title.

BOSANQUET, Mary. 284'.1'0924 B
The life and death of Dietrich Bonhoeffer. [1st ed.] New York, Harper & Row [1969, c1968] 287 p. illus., ports. 22 cm. Bibliographical footnotes. [BX4827.B57B6] 69-17003 5.95
1. Bonhoeffer, Dietrich, 1906-1945. I. Title.

BOSANQUET, Mary. 284'.1'0924 [B]
The life and death of Dietrich Bonhoffer. New York, Harper [1973, c.1968] 287 p. illus., ports. 21 cm. (Colophon Books, CN294) Bibliographical footnotes. [BX4827.B57B6] 68-17003 ISBN 0-06-090294-9 2.95 (pbk.)
1. Bonhoeffer, Dietrich, 1906-1945. I. Title.

CHRISTIANSON, 284'.1'0924 B
Christopher J.
God did not ordain silence, by Christopher J. Christiason. Plainfield, N.J., Logos International [1974] 120 p. 21 cm. [BX8080.C5A33] 73-84157 ISBN 0-88270-069-3 4.95
1. Christianson, Christopher J. I. Title.
Pbk., 2.50, ISBN 0-88270-054-5.

COWIE, Leonard W. 284'.1'0924 B
Martin Luther, leader of the Reformation [by] Leonard W. Cowie. New York, Praeger [1969] vi, 122 p. illus., maps, ports. 23 cm. (Praeger pathfinder biographies) Bibliography: p. 120. [BR325.C68] 69-12703 4.25
1. Luther, Martin, 1483-1546.

CURTIS, Charles J. 284'.10924
Soderblom, ecumenical pioneer, by Charles J. Curtis. Minneapolis, Augsburg Pub. House [1967] viii, 149 p. illus., ports. 22 cm. Includes bibliographies. [BX8080.S6C8] 67-11719
1. Soderblom, Nathan, Abp., 1866-1931. I. Title.

EELLS, Hastings, 284'.1'0924 B
1895-
Martin Bucer. New York, Russell & Russell [1971] 539 p. port. 23 cm. "First published in 1931." Bibliography: p. [424]-432. [BR350.B93E4 1971] 79-151547
1. Butzer, Martin, 1491-1551. 2. Reformation—Germany.

ELDER, Michael 284.10924
The young Martin Luther [by] Michael Elder. Illus. by Lewis Davies. New York, Roy [1966] 126p. illus. 21cm. [BR325.E4 1966a] 66-22228 3.25 bds.,
1. Luther, Martin, 1483-1546—Juvenile literature. I. Title.

ELMEN, Paul. 284'.1'0924 B
Wheat flour messiah : Eric Jansson of Bishop Hill / Paul Elmen. Carbondale : Published for the Swedish Pioneer Historical Society by Southern Illinois University Press, c1976. p. cm. Includes index. Bibliography: p. [BX7990.J3E45] 76-28380 ISBN 0-8093-0787-1 : 7.95
1. Jansson, Erik, 1808-1850. 2. Jansonists. 3. Bishop Hill, Ill.—History. 4. Jansonists—Biography. I. Title.

FERM, Vergilius 284'.1'0924 B
Ture Anselm, 1896-
Cross-currents in the personality of Martin Luther; a study in the psychology of religious genius, by Vergilius Ferm. North Quincy, Mass., Christopher Pub. House [1972] 186 p. 21 cm. Bibliography: p. 181-186. [BR334.2.F4] 71-189362 6.50
1. Luther, Martin, 1483-1546—Psychology. I. Title.

FISCHER, Robert H. 284'.1'0924
Franklin Clark Fry: a palette for a portrait. Edited by Robert H. Fischer. [Springfield, Ohio, Lutheran quarterly, Wittenberg University] 1972. xiii, 369 p. port. 23 cm. "Supplementary number of the Lutheran quarterly, v. 24." 92 "memos" by churchmen about their experiences with Franklin Clark Fry. Bibliography of Fry's works: p. 339-361. [BX8080.F74F57] 72-78582
1. Fry, Franklin Clark, 1900-1968—Addresses, essays, lectures. 2. Fry, Franklin Clark, 1900-1968—Bibliography. I. Lutheran quarterly.

FISCHER, Robert H 284'.1'0924
Luther, by Robert H. Fischer. Frank W. Klos, editor. Gustav Rehberger, illustrator. Philadelphia, Lutheran church Press [c1966] 192 p. illus. 21 cm. (LCA School of religion series) Includes 5 German chorales with English translations in close score. Bibliography: p. 191-192. [BR325.F58] 67-1178
1. Luther, Martin, 1483-1546. I. Title.

FORKER, Cora, 1918- 284'.1'0924 B
Daystar : the story of the Rev. James Edward Morecraft, the God to whom he belonged, and the people he loved and served / by Cora Forker and Lois Wiley. Harrisburg, Pa. : Stackpole Books, [1975] p. cm. [BX8080.M567F67] 75-23241
1. Morecraft, James Edward. I. Wiley, Lois, 1931- joint author. II. Title.

INTERPRETING Luther's 284'.1'0924
legacy; essays in honor of Edward C. Fendt. Edited by Fred W. Meuser and Stanley D. Schneider. Minneapolis, Augsburg Pub. House [1969] ix, 189 p. port. 23 cm. Originally given as lectures at the Evangelical Lutheran Theological Seminary, Columbus, Ohio, 1967-68, in commemoration of the 450th anniversary of the Reformation. Contents.—Luther and the First commandment, by R. M. Hals.—Luther's principles of Biblical interpretation, by R. W. Doermann.—Scripture and tradition in Luther and in our day, by T. S. Liefeld.—The changing Catholic view of Luther, by F. W. Meuser.—A positive response to Erik Erikson's Young man Luther, by L. Elhard.—The Smalcald Articles and their significance, by J. S. Schaaf.—Luther's understanding of heaven and the hell, by H. Schwarz.—Concern for the person in the Reformation. by H. H. Zietlow.—Luther's liturgical surgery, by E. L. Brand.—Luther, preaching, and the Reformation, by S. D. Schneider.—Luther as Seelsorger, by A. H. Becker.—Martin Luther, parish educator, by G. H. Doermann.—Luther, man of prayer, by L. Ludwig.—Notes (p. 177-189) [BR326.I5] 69-14189 3.50
1. Luther, Martin, 1483-1546—Addresses, essays, lectures. I. Fendt, Edward Charles, 1904- II. Meuser, Fred W., ed. III. Schneider, Stanley D., ed. IV. Evangelical Lutheran Theological Seminary, Columbus, Ohio.

JACOBS, Henry 284'.1'0924 B
Eyster, 1844-1932.
Martin Luther, the hero of the Reformation, 1483-1546. New York, Putnam. [New York, AMS Press, 1973] xv, 454 p. illus. 19 cm. Reprint of the 1898 ed. which was issued as v. 1 of Heroes of the Reformation. Includes bibliographical references. [BR325.J2 1973] 72-170838 ISBN 0-404-03544-2 18.00
1. Luther, Martin, 1483-1546. I. Title.

KUHNS, William. 284'.1'0924
In pursuit of Dietrich Bonhoeffer. With a foreword by Eberhard Bethge. Dayton, Ohio, Pflaum Press, 1967. xiii, 314 p. port. 22 cm. Bibliography: p. [287]-297. [BX4827.B59K8] 67-29763
1. Bonhoeffer, Dietrich, 1906-1945. I. Title.

KURTZ, John W. 284'.1'0924 B
John Frederic Oberlin / by John W. Kurtz. Boulder, Colo. : Westview Press, [1976] p. cm. Includes index. Bibliography: p. [BX4827.O3K87] 76-25211 ISBN 0-89158-118-9 : 15.00
1. Oberlin, Johann Friedrich, 1740-1826-

LEE, Robert E. A. 284'1'0924
Martin Luther: the Reformation years. Based on the film 'Martin Luther.' Ed. by Robert E. A. Lee. Minneapolis, Augsburg [1967] 96p. illus. 28cm. [BR325.L46] 67-25369 2.50 pap.,
1. Luther, Martin, 1483-1546. I. Martin, Luther (Motion picture) II. Title.

LILJE, Hanns, Bp., 284'.1'0924 B
1899-
The valley of the shadow / Hanns Lilje ; translated and with an introd. by Olive Wyon. Philadelphia : Fortress Press, 1966, 1977 printing. 128 p. ; 18 cm. Translation of Im finstern Tal. [BX8080.L49A313 1977] 76-55522 ISBN 0-8006-1699-5 : 2.95
1. Lilje, Hanns, Bp., 1899- 2. Lutheran Church—Bishops—Biography. 3. Bishops—Germany—Biography. 4. Anti-Nazi movement—Biography. I. Title.

LUTHER for an 284'.1'0924
ecumenical age; essays in commemoration of the 450th anniversary of the Reformation. Carl S. Meyer, ed., St. Louis, Concordia [1967] 311p. 24cm. Bibl. [BR326.L83] 67-30472 9.00
1. Luther, Martin, 1483-1546—Addresses, essays, lectures. I. Meyer, Carl Stamm, 1907- ed.

LUTHER, Martin, 284'.1'0924 B
1483-1546.
Luther. Edited by Ian D. Kingston Siggins. New York, Barnes & Noble Books [1972] x, 209 p. 23 cm. (Evidence and commentary) Bibliography: p. 190-203. [BR331.E5S53 1972b] 73-166414 ISBN 0-06-496246-6 10.50
1. Luther, Martin, 1483-1546. I. Siggins, Ian D. Kingston, ed.
Pbk. 5.50; ISBN 0-06-496247-4.

LUTHER, Martin, 1483- 284'.1'0924
1546.
95 theses, with the pertinent documents from the history of the Reformation. Kurt Aland, editor. Saint Louis, Concordia Pub. House [1967] 116 p. 21 cm. Contents.—The prehistory of the ninety-five theses and their connection with the history of the Reformation.—The ninety-five theses and A sermon on indulgence and grace.—The letters of Luther in connection with the ninety-five theses.—Luther's words on the theses in his table talk.—Luther's recollections. Bibliographical references included in "Notes" (p. 97-116) [BR332.D6A45] 67-27726
1. Luther, Martin, 1483-1546. Disputatio pro declaratione virtutis indulgentiarum. I. Aland, Kurt, ed. II. Title.

LUTHER, Martin, 1483- 284'.1'0924
1546.
95 theses, with the pertinent documents from the history of the Reformation. Kurt Aland, editor Saint Louis, Concordia Pub. House [1967] 116 p. 21 cm. Contents.—The prehistory of the ninety-five theses and their connection with the history of the Reformation.—The ninety-five theses and A sermon on indulgence and grace.—The letters of Luther in connection with the ninety-five theses.—Luther's words on the theses in his table talk.—Luther's recollections. Bibliographical references included in "Notes" (p. 97-116) [BR332.D6A45] 67-27726
I. Luther, Martin, 1483-1546. Disputatio pro declaration virtutis indulgentiarum. I. Aland, Kurt, ed. II. Title.

LUTHER, Martin, 1483- 284'.1'0924
1546.
95 theses, with the pertinent documents from the history of the Reformation. Kurt Aland, editor Saint Louis, Concordia Pub. House [1967] 116 p. 21 cm. Contents.CONTENTS.--The prehistory of the ninety-five theses and their connection with the history of the Reformation.--The ninety-five theses and A sermon on indulgence and grace.--The letters of Luther in connection with the ninety-five theses.--Luther's words on the theses in his table talk.--Luther's recollections. Bibliographical references included in "Notes" (p. 97-116) [BR332.D6A45] 67-27726
1. Luther, Martin, 1483-1546. Disputatio pro declaratione virtutis indulgentiarum. I. Aland, Kurt, ed. II. Title.

MUHLENBERG, Henry 284'.1'0924 B
Melchior, 1711-1787.
The notebook of a colonial clergyman : condensed from The journals of Henry Melchior Muhlenberg / translated and edited by Theodore G. Tappert and John W. Doberstein. Philadelphia : Fortress Press, 1975, c1959. vi, 249 p. ; 20 cm. Includes index. [BX8080.M9A43 1975] 75-24119 ISBN 0-8006-1804-1 pbk. : 3.50
1. Muhlenberg, Henry Melchoir, 1711-1787. I. Title.

NORELIUS, Eric, 1833- 284'.1'0924
1916
The journals of Eric Norelius, a Swedish missionary on the American frontier. Tr., ed., introd. by G. Everett Arden. Philadelphia, Fortress [1967] vii, 207p. 21cm. (Seminar eds) [BX8080.N6A 333] 67-11909 2.75 pap.,
I. Arden, Gothard Everett, 1905- ed. and tr. II. Title.

NORELIUS, Eric, 1833- 284'.1'0924
1916.
The journals of Eric Norelius, a Swedish missionary on the American frontier. Translated, edited, and with an introd. by G. Everett Arden. Philadelphia, Fortress Press [1967] vii, 207 p. 21 cm. (Siminar editions) [BX8080.N6A333] 67-11909
I. Arden, Gothard Everett, 1905- ed. and tr. II. Title.

QUAM, John Elliott. 284'.1'0924
Jorgen Eriksson; a study in the Norwegian reformation, 1571-1604. [New Haven, Conn.] 1968. xii, 272 l. port. 28 cm. Thesis—Yale University. Bibliography: leaves 259-272. [BR403.Q3] 77-2688
1. Jorgen Eriksson, 1535-1604. 2. Reformation—Norway.

ROGNESS, Michael. 284'.1'0924
Philip Melanchthon; reformer without honor. Minneapolis, Augsburg Pub. House [1969] ix, 165 p. 23 cm. Bibliographical references included in "Notes" (p. 141-165) [BR335.R63] 78-84815 4.95
1. Melanchthon, Philipp, 1497-1560.

ROSENBLUM, Arthur. 284'.1'0924 B
Johann Christoph Blumhardt; a summarized translation of the biography by Friedrich Zundel, with parts added. [Rifton? N.Y., 1967] 125 p. 30 cm. 200 copies. No. Translated by Art Rosenblum. [BX8080.B615R67] 71-12276 3.00
1. Blumhardt,Johann Christoph, 1805-1880. I. Zundel, Friedrich. Johann Christoph Blumhardt. II. Title.

SKATTEBoL, Olaf, 284'.1'0924 B
1847-1930.
Translation of extracts of biographical notes, memories from childhood, youth, etc. / written by Olaf Skattebol ; [translated by Enevold F. Schroder]. Oslo : Enevold F. Schroder, 1976] 25 leaves ; 30 cm. Cover title. [BX8080.S396A3513] 76-381853
1. Skattebol, Olaf, 1847-1930. 2. Lutheran Church—Clergy—Biography. 3. Clergy—Norway—Biography. I. Title.

SPAETH, Adolph, 284'.1'0924 B
1839-1910.
Charles Porterfield Krauth. New York, Arno Press, 1969. 2 v. in l. port. 23 cm. (Religion in America) Reprint of the 1898-1909 ed. Contents.Contents.—v. 1. 1823-1859.—v. 2. 1859-1883. Includes bibliographical references. [BX8080.K68S62] 78-83440
1. Krauth, Charles Porterfield, 1823-1883.

SPITZ, Lewis 284'.1'0924 B
William, 1922-
Life in two worlds; biography of William Sihler, by Lewis W. Spitz. Saint Louis, Concordia Pub. House [1968] 199 p. 21 cm. Bibliographical references included in "Notes" (p. 178-191) [BX8080.S38S6] 68-13364
1. Sihler, Wilhelm, 1801-1885. I. Title.

STAUFFER, Richard 284'.1.'0924
Luther as seen by Catholics. [Tr. by Mary Parker, T. H. L. Parker] Richmond, Knox [1967] 83p. 22cm. (Ecumenical studies in hist., no. 7) Tr. of Luther vu par les catholiques. Bibl. [BR333. 2. S713] 67-21482 1.95 pap.,

1. Luther, Martin, 1483-1546—Criticism and interpretation—Hist. 2. Theology, Doctrinal—Hist.—20th cent. I. Title. II. Series.

STAUFFER, Richard, 1921- 284'.1'0924
Luther as seen by Catholics. [Translated by Mary Parker and T. H. L. Parker] Richmond, John Knox Press [1967] 83 p. 22 cm. (Ecumenical studies in history, no. 7) Translation of Luther vu par les catholiques. Includes bibliographies. [BR333.2.S713] 67-21482
1. Luther, Martin, 1483-1546—Criticism and interpretation—Hist. 2. Theology, Doctrinal—Hist.—20th cent. I. Title. II. Series.

STEFFENS, Helmut 284.10924
In the footsteps of Martin Luther, by M. A. Kleeberg, Gerhard Lemme. Illus., jacket, cover design by Alexander Alfs. Tr. [from German] by Erich Hopka. [Licensed Eng. ed.] St. Louis, Concordia [1966] 223p. illus., facsims., plates, ports. 25cm. [BR327.S8413] 65-26709 3.95
1. Luther, Martin, 1483-1546—Portraits, etc. I. Lemme, Gerhard, joint author. II. Title.

STRAND, Kenneth Albert, 1927- comp. 284'.1'0924
Essays on Luther. Edited by Kenneth A. Strand. [Ann Arbor, Mich] Ann Arbor Publishers, 1969. 122 p. 22 cm. Contents.Contents.—Introduction: new light on Luther, by A. Hyma.—Luther and the peasants' war: a brief summary, by R. N. Crossley.—Martin Luther and the devotio moderna in Herford, by W. M. Landeen.—Luther's condemnation of the Rostock New Testament, by K. A. Strand.—Luther's dilemma: restitution or reformation? By L. Verduin.—The peasants' war in Germany: some observations on recent historiography, by R. N. Crossley.—Luther's schooling in Magdeburg: a note on recent views, by K. A. Strand. Includes bibliographies. [BR326.S74] 73-76590 2.75
1. Luther, Martin, 1483-1546. I. Title.

STUPPERICH, Robert, 1904- 284.10924 (B)
Melanchthon, Translated by Robert H. Fischer. Philadelphia, Westminster Press [1965] 175 p. 21 cm. Bibliography: p. 160-166. [BR335.S733] 65-20620
1. Melanchthon, Phillipp, 1497-1500. I. Title.

STUPPERICH, Robert, 1904- 284.10924
Melanchthon. Translated by Robert H. Fisher. Philadelphia, Westminster Press [1965] 175 p. 21 cm. Bibliography: p. 160-166. [BR335.S733] [B] 65-20620
1. Melanchthon, Philipp, 1497-1560.

STUPPERICH, Robert, 1904- 284.10924
Melanchtnon. [from German] by Robert H. Fischer. Philadelphia, Westminster [c1965] 175p. 21cm. Bibl. [BR335.S733] 65-20620 3.95
1. Melanchtnon, Philipp, 1497-1560. I. Title.

THULIN, Oskar, ed. 284.10924
A life of Luther, told in pictures and narrative by the reformer and his contemporaries. Translated by Martin O. Dietrich. Philadelphia, Fortress Press [1966] 210 p. illus., facisims., ports. (part pcol.) 26 cm. Translation of Martin Luther. "Reference":p. 206-209. [BR325.T4713] 66-24281
1. Luther, Martin, I. Title.

THULIN, Oskar, ed. 284.10924
A life of Luther, told in pictures and narrative by the reformer and his contemporaries. Tr. by Martin O. Dietrich. Philadelphia, Fortress [1966] 210p. illus., facsims., ports. (pt. col.) 26cm. Tr. of Martin Luther. Bibl. [BR325.T4713] 66-24281 9.00
1. Luther, Martin, 1483-1546. I. Title.

THULIN, Oskar, ed. 284.10924
A life of Luther, told in pictures and narrative by the reformer and his contemporaries. Translated by Marten O. Dietrick. Philadelphia, Fortress Press [1966] 210 p. illus., facsims., ports. (part col.) 26 cm. Translation of Martin Luther. "References": p. 206-209. [BR325.T4713] [B] 66-24281
1. Luther, Martin, 1483-1546. I. Title.

TOWNSEND, Allan W. 284'.1'0924 B
A short life of Luther [by] Allan W. Townsend. Philadelphia, Fortress Press [1967] iv, 76 p. illus. 18 cm. Bibliographical references included in "Notes" (p. 76) [BR325.T67] 67-21532
1. Luther, Martin, 1483-1546. I. Title.

ULRICH, Betty Garton. 284'.1'0924
A way we go. Saint Louis, Concordia Pub. House [1970] 164 p. 21 cm. [BX8080.U4A3] 75-114180
I. Title.

VORKINK, Peter, comp. 284'.1'0924
Bonhoeffer in a world come of age; essays by Paul M. van Buren [and others] With a foreword by John C. Bennett. Philadelphia, Fortress Press [1968] xv, 141 p. 18 cm. (A Fortress paperback original) "These articles ... originally appeared in the fall 1967 issue of the Union Seminary quarterly review (vol. XXIII, no. 1)." Contents.—Bonhoeffer's paradox: living with God without God, by P. M. van Buren.—Faith and worldliness in Bonhoeffer's thought, by P. L. Lehmann.—Bonhoeffer's Christology and his "Religionless Christianity," by E. Bethge.—Turning points in Bonhoeffer's life and thought, by E. Bethge.—The other letters from prison, by M. von Wedemeyer-Weller.—Reading Bonhoeffer in English translation: some difficulties, by J. D. Godsey.—Bibliography, compiled by P. Vorkink, II (p. 133-140) [BX4827.B57V6] 68-14355
1. Bonhoeffer, Dietrich, 1906-1945. I. Van Buren, Paul Matthews, 1924- II. Union Seminary quarterly review. III. Title.

WEISHEIT, Eldon. 284'.1'0924 B
The preacher's yellow pants. Art by Michael Norman. St. Louis, Concordia Pub. House [1973] [48] p. col. illus. 27 cm. Aggravated by the preacher's yellow pants, the parishoners endeavor to get him dressed in black. [BX8080.W95W44] 74-159833 ISBN 0-570-03420-5 3.25
1. Wyneken, Friedrich Konrad Dietrich, 1810-1876—Juvenile literature. I. Norman, Michael, illus. II. Title.

WOGEN, Norris L. 284'.1'0924 B
The shadow of His hand : the dramatic account of one man's quest for fulness of life in the Spirit / Norris L. Wogen. Minneapolis : Bethany Fellowship, [1974] 127 p. ; 21 cm. [BX8080.W65A37] 74-21059 ISBN 0-87123-533-1 pbk. : 2.25
1. Wogen, Norris L. 2. Pentecostalism. I. Title.

WURMBRAND, Richard. 284'.1'0924
The Wurmbrand letters. Pomona, Calif., Cross Publications [1967] 169 p. illus., port. 26 cm. [BX8080.W86A3] 72-612
1. Communism and religion. I. Title.

ZIMMERMANN, Wolf Dieter, 1911- ed. 284'.10924
I knew Dietrich Bonhoeffer. Edited by Wolf-Dieter Zimmermann and Ronald Gregor Smith. Translated from the German by Kathe Gregor Smith. [1st ed.] New York, Harper & Row [1967, c1966] 238 p. illus., ports. 22 cm. Translation of Begegnungen mit Dietrich Bonhoeffer. [BX4827.B59Z513 1967] 67-11502
1. Bonhoeffer, Dietrich, 1906-1945. I. Smith, Ronald Gregor, joint ed. II. Title.

YONKERS, N.Y. 284'.1'09747277
Saint John's Evangelical Lutheran Church.
Built on the rock, 1869-1969; a history of Saint John's Evangelical Lutheran Church, Yonkers, New York. [Yonkers, 1970] 90 p. illus., facsims., ports. 29 cm. 500 copies printed. No. 486. Bibliography: p. 50. [BX8076.Y6S25] 72-119757
1. Yonkers, N.Y. Saint John's Evangelical Lutheran Church. I. Title.

HEISSENBUTTEL, Ernest G 284.10974886
Pittsburgh Synod history; its auxiliaries and institutions, 1845-1962 by Ernest G. Heissenbuttel and Roy H. Johnson. Warren, Ohio, Published by the Pittsburgh Synod of the United Lutheran Church at Studio of Printcraft,inc. [1963] 483 p. illus. 24 cm. The 2d of a two-volume synodical history, the 1st appeared in 1959 under title: Pittsburgh Synod congregational histories. Includes bibliography. [BX8061.P6H42] 63-5777
1. Pittsburgh Synod of the Evangelical Lutheran Church — Hist. 2. Pittsburgh Synod of the United Lutheran Church in America — Hist. I. Johnson, Roy H., joint author. II. Title.

AABERG, Theodore A. 284'.13
A city set on a hill; a history of the Evangelical Lutheran Synod (Norwegian Synod) 1918-1968 [by] Theodore A. Aaberg. [Mankato, Minn., Board of Publications, Evangelical Lutheran Synod, 1968] xiv, 289 p. col. illus., col. ports. 24 cm. Includes bibliographical references. [BX8055.E9A6] 68-8593 5.95
1. Evangelical Lutheran Synod—History. I. Title.

WENTZ, Abdel Ross, 1883- 284'.13
Pioneer in Christian unity: Samuel Simon Schmucker. Philadelphia, Fortress Press [1967] xi, 372 p. port. 24 cm. Bibliographical footnotes. "Published writings of Samuel Simon Schmucker, 1799-1873": p. 355-364. [BX8080.S3W4] 67-10596
1. Schmucker, Samuel Simon, 1799-1873. I. Title.

A Biographical 284'.131'0922 B
directory of clergymen of The American Lutheran Church. Arnold R. Mickelson, editor; Robert C. Wiederaenders, associate editor. Minneapolis, Augsburg Pub. House, 1972. ix, 1054 p. ports. 24 cm. Published in 1962 under title: A biographical directory of pastors of The American Lutheran Church, compiled by J. M. Jensen, C. E. Linder, and G. Giving. [BX8047.7.B56] 72-80314 ISBN 0-8066-9293-6 15.00
1. American Lutheran Church (1961-)—Clergy—Directories. I. Mickelson, Arnold R., 1922- ed. II. Jensen, John Martin, 1893- comp. A biographical directory of pastors of the American Lutheran Church.

HOLAND, Hjalmar Rued, 1872-1963. 284'.1312'0977573
Coon Prairie : an historical report of the Norwegian Evangelical Lutheran Congregation at Coon Prairie, written on the occasion of its 75th anniversary in 1927 / by Hjalmar R. Holand ; translated by Oivind M. Hovde. Decorah, Iowa : [s.n.], 1977. 305 p. : ill. ; 24 cm. Includes index. [BX8076.N64H6413 1977] 77-361704
1. Norwegian Evangelical Lutheran Congregation at Coon Prairie. I. Title.

DANKER, Frederick W. 284'.1322
No room in the brotherhood : the Preus-Otten purge of Missouri / by Frederick W. Danker ; assisted by Jan Schambach. St. Louis : Clayton Pub. House, c1977. 373 p. : ill. ; 24 cm. Includes bibliographical references. [BX8061.M7B36] 77-74386 ISBN 0-915644-10-X : 11.25
1. Lutheran Church—Missouri Synod—History. 2. Association of Evangelical Lutheran Churches—History. I. Schambach, Jan, joint author. II. Title.

A Tree grows in 284'.1322
Missouri / edited by John H. Baumgaertner. Milwaukee : Agape Publishers, 1975. xxix, 151 p. ; 22 cm. "An English District centennial publication." Bibliography: p. 139-143. [BX8061.M75T7] 75-9245 ISBN 0-914618-01-6 pbk. : 2.95
1. Lutheran Church-Missouri Synod. Districts. English. I. Baumgaertner, John H.

WEISHEIT, Eldon. 284'.1322
The zeal of His house; five generations of Lutheran Church-Missouri Synod history (1847-1972). St. Louis, Concordia Pub. House [1973] 126 p. illus. 22 cm. Bibliography: p. 125-126. [BX8061.M7W44] 73-76988 ISBN 0-570-03516-3 1.75 (pbk.)
1. Lutheran Church-Missouri Synod—History. I. Title.

HEINTZEN, Erich H. 284'.1322'0924 B
Love leaves home; Wilhelm Loehe and the Missouri Synod [by] Erich H. Heintzen. Condensed by Frank Starr. St. Louis, Concordia Pub. House [1973] 80 p. illus. 22 cm. Condensation and simplification of the author's thesis, University of Illinois, 1964. [BX8080.L57H442] 72-94586 ISBN 0-570-03513-9 1.50 (pbk.)
1. Lohe, Wilhelm, 1808-1872. 2. Lutheran Church—Missouri Synod. I. Starr, Frank. II. Title.

VEHSE, Eduard, 1802-1870. 284'.1322'09
The Stephanite emigration to America : with documentation / by Carl Eduard Vehse ; translated by Rudolph Fiehler. Tucson : M. R. Winkler, c1975. 136 p. ; 29 cm. Translation of Die Stephan'sche Auswanderung nach Amerika. [BX8061.M7V4313] 75-323063
1. Lutheran Church—Missouri Synod—History. 2. Stephan, Martin, 1777-1846. 3. Lutheran Church—Doctrinal and controversial works. 4. Lutherans in Missouri. 5. Germans in Missouri. 6. Missouri—History. I. Title.

DIBELIUS, Otto, Bp., 1880- 284.143
In the service of the Lord: the autobiography of Otto Dibelius. Translated from the German by Mary Ilford. [1st ed.] New York, Holt, Rinehart and Winston [1964] 280 p. illus., ports. 22 cm. Translation of Ein Christ ist immer im Dienst. [BX8080.D47A323] 63-22051
I. Title.

SPENER, Philipp Jakob, 1635-1705 284.143
Pia desideria, by Philip Jacob Spener. Tr. [from German] introd. by Theodore G. Tappert. Philadelphia, Fortress [c.1964] vii, 131p. 21cm. (Seminar eds.) Bibl. 64-12995 1.75 pap.,
1. Pietism. 2. Germany—Religion—17th cent. I. Title.

DUIN, Edgar Charles. 284'.147
Lutheranism under the tsars and the Soviets. Ann Arbor : Xerox University Microfilms, 1975c1976. p. cm. (Monograph publishing on demand, sponsor series) "Published under aegis of the Luthern Theological Seminary". Bibliography: p. [BX8063.R9D84] 75-37478 ISBN 0-8357-0155-7(v.1) ISBN 0-8357-0156-5(v.2) : 43.00(set)
1. Lutheran Church in Russia. 2. Lutherans in Russia. I. Title.

NODTVEDT, Magnus, 1893- 284.14810924
Rebirth of Norway's peasantry; folk leader Hans Nielsen Hauge. Tacoma, Wash., Pacific Lutheran Univ. Pr. [1965] xi, 305p. illus., ports. 24cm. Bibl. [BX8080.H3N6] 65-9429 5.95
1. Hauge, Hans Nielsen, 1771-1824. 2. Peasantry—Norway. I. Title.

FLORIN, Hans W 284'.168
Lutherans in South Africa, by Hans W. Florin. (Durban, Lutheran Publishing House), [1967]. 180 p. 22 cm. R3.00 So. Afr. Bibliography: p. 176-180. [BX8063.S7F5 1967] 68-71411
1. Lutheran Church in South Africa. I. Title.

ARDEN, Gothard Everett, 1905- 284.17
Meet the Lutherans; introducing the Lutheran Church in North America. Rock Island, Ill., Augustana [c.1962] 74p. 20cm. Bibl. 62-18194 1.45 pap.,
1. Lutherans in the U.S. 2. Lutherans in Canada. I. Title.

ARDEN, Gothard Everett, 1905- 284.17
Meet the Lutherans; introducing the Lutheran Church in North America. Rock Island, Ill., Augustana Press [1962] 74p. 20cm. Includes bibliographies. [BX8041.A82] 62-18194
1. Lutherans in the U. S. 2. Lutherans in Canada. I. Title.

NELSON, E. Clifford, 1911- 284'.17
Lutheranism in North America, 1914-1970, by E. Clifford Nelson. Foreword by Kent S. Knutson. Minneapolis, Augsburg Pub. House [1972] xvi, 315 p. illus. 23 cm. Bibliography: p. 302-304. [BX8041.N37] 70-159016 ISBN 0-8066-1138-3 7.50
1. Lutheran Church in the United States. I. Title.

*WOLF, Richard 284.17
Lutherans in North America. Frank W. Klos, ed. John Gretzer, artist. Philadelphia, Lutheran Church Pr. [c.1965] 150p. illus. 21cm. (LCA sch. of religion ser.) A short-term study course for adults. With Teacher's guide, by Ruth Lister. pap., 1.50; teacher's guide pap., 1.25
I. Title.

LARSEN, Jens Peter Mouritz 284.172972
Virgin Islands story, by Jens Larsen. Philadelphia, Fortress [c.1950] vii, 256p. illus. 18cm. Bibl. [F2136.L3 1950b] 68-10292 2.50 pap.,
1. Virgin Islands of the United States—Hist. 2. Lutheran Church in the Virgin Islands. I. Title.

ALMANAC. 284.173
Minneapolis, Augsburg Pub. House. v. 16 cm. Includes a directory of the Evangelical Lutheran Church. [BX8009.A48] 50-55679
1. Lutheran Church—Yearbooks. I. Evangelical Lutheran Church.

AMERICAN Lutheran Church 284.173
1965 yearbook. William Larsen, ed. Shirley A. Ledin, assoc. ed. Minneapolis, Augsburg, c.1964. 408p. ports. 22cm. 54-16304 1.25 pap.,
1. Lutheran Church—Yearbooks. I. Title.

AMERICAN Lutheran Church. 284.173
Yearbook. Columbus, Wartburg Press. v. 23cm. Issue for edited by the Dept. of Stewardship and Finance. [BX8009.A54] 54-16304
1. Lutheran Church—Yearbooks. I. Title.

AMERICAN Lutheran Church (1930-1960) 284.173
Statistical tables. Columbus, Ohio. v. diagrs. 28cm. Compiled by the church's Statistician. [BX8061.A5A35] 58-29847
1. American Lutheran Church (1930-1960)—Stat. I. Title.

AMERICAN Lutheran Church 284.173
1964 Year- book. William Larsen, ed., Shirley A. Ledin, assoc. ed. Minneapolis, Augsberg, c.1963. 400p. illus., map. 22cm. 54-16304 1.25 pap.,
1. Lutheran Church—Yearbooks.

AMERICAN LUTHERAN CHURCH 284.173
(1930-1960)
Yearbook. Columbus, Wartburg Press. v. 23cm. Issue for edited by the Dept. of Stewardship and Finance. [BX8009.A54] 54-16304

1. Lutheran Church— Yearbooks. I. Title.

BERGENDOFF, Conrad John Immanuel, 1895- 284.173
The doctrine of the church in American Lutheranism. Philadelphia, Muhlenberg Press [1956] 93p. 21cm. [BX8041.B43] 56-11946
1. Lutheran Church in the U. S.—Government. 2. Church. I. Title.

DOLAK, George. 284.173
A history of the Slovak Evangelical Lutheran Church in the United States of America, 1902-1927. Saint Louis, Mo., Concordia Pub. House [c1955] 207p. illus. 24cm. [BX8060.S55D6] 55-11458
1. Slovak Evangelical Lutheran Synod of the United States of America—Hist. I. Title.

EVANGELICAL Lutheran Synod in the Midwest of the United Lutheran Church in America. 284.173
Synodal-Bericht. Verhandlungen. [Hastings? Neb.] v. 23 cm. Reports for issued by the synod under an earlier name: Deutsche Evangelisch-lutherische Synode von Nebraska. [BX8061.M65A3] 51-20682
I. Title.

FEVOLD, Eugene L. 284'.173
The Lutheran Free Church; a fellowship of American Lutheran congregations, 1897-1963, by Eugene L. Fevold. Minneapolis, Augsburg Pub. House [1969] vii, 342 p. illus., ports. 22 cm. Bibliographical footnotes. [BX8055.L8F4] 69-14188 5.00
1. Lutheran Free Church.

GRASTY, Sue Watkins, ed. 284'.173
Our God is marching on; a centennial history of Bethlehem Lutheran Church, Round Top, Texas, by Martin H. Obst, John G. Banik, and other contributors. Austin, Tex., Printed by Von Boeckmann-Jones [1966] 120 p. illus., map (on lining papers) music, ports. 24 cm. Bibliographical footnotes. [BX8076.R65B4] 67-7368
1. Round Top, Tex. Bethlehem Lutheran Church. I. Obst, Martin H. II. Banik, John G. III. Title.

HARKINS, George F 284.173
The church and her work. Arthur H. Getz, editor. Philadelphia, Muhlenberg Press [1960] 144p. illus. 20cm. Includes bibliography. [BX8048.H35] 60-3594
1. United Lutheran Church in America. I. Title.

JENSEN, John Martin, 1893- 284.173
A biographical directory of pastors of The American Lutheran Church. Compiled by John M. Jensen, Carl E. Linder [and] Gerald Giving. Minneapolis, Augsburg Pub. House [1962] 857p. ports. 24cm. [BX8047.7.J4] 62-3457
1. The American Lutheran Church (1961-)—Direct. I. Title.

KOEHLER, John Philipp, 1859-1951. 284'.173
The history of the Wisconsin Synod. Edited and with an introd. by Leigh D. Jordahl. [Mosinee, Wis.] Protes'tant Conference; [order agent, John Springer, Two Rivers, Wis.] 1970. xxix, 260 p. ports. 28 cm. Originally published in monthly installments in the Faith-life magazine, Feb. 1938-Jan. 1944. [BX8061.W6K6] 75-117375 8.50
1. Evangelical Lutheran Joint Synod of Wisconsin and Other States. I. Jordahl, Leigh D., 1926- ed. II. Title.

LUFFBERRY, Henry Benner. 284.173
Thy mission high fulfilling; a study of faith and life. Arthur H. Getz, editor. Prepared and published by action of the United Lutheran Church in America in convention assembled. Philadelphia, Muhlenberg Press [1954] 129p. illus. 21cm. [BX8048.L8] 54-2977
1. United Lutheran Church in America. 2. Stewardship, Christian. I. Title.

LUTHERAN Church in America. 284.173
Yearbook. 1963- Philadelphia, Board of Publication of the Lutheran Church in America. v. illus., ports. 22 cm. [BX8048.2.A35] 63-25562
1. Lutheran Church in America — Yearbooks. I. Title.

LUTHERAN Church inAmerica 284.173
Yearbook. 1963- Philadelphia, Board of Publication of the Lutheran Church in America. v. illus., ports. 22 cm. [BX8048.2.A35] 63-25562
1. Lutheran Church in America — Yearbooks. I. Title.

THE Lutherans in North America / edited by E. Clifford Nelson, in collaboration with Theodore G. Tappert ... [et al.]. Philadelphia : Fortress Press, c1975. xi, 541 p. : ill. ; 26 cm. Includes bibliographical references and index. [BX8041.L87] 74-26337 ISBN 0-8006-0409-1 : 22.50 ISBN 0-8006-1409-7 pbk. : 12.95 284'.173
1. Lutheran Church in North America. 2. Lutherans in North America. I. Nelson, E. Clifford, 1911-

MAILS, Thomas E. 284.173
The nature of heresy in our time, written, illus. by T. E. Mails. Hayfield, Minn., Hayfield Pub. Co. [1964, c.1963] 259p. illus. 24cm. 64-5676 4.95
1. Pastoral theology—Lutheran Church. I. Title.

MARTIN Luther Colloquium, 2d, Lutheran Theological Seminary, 1971. 284'.173
Luther in America : Martin Luther Colloquium, 1971. [Gettysburg, Pa. : Lutheran Theological Seminary], 1972. 52 p. ; 23 cm. (Bulletin - Lutheran Theological Seminary ; v. 52, no. 1) "On October 27, 1971, the Institute for Luther Studies conducted its second annual 'Martin Luther Colloquium.'" [BX8041.A38 1971] 75-317096
1. Luther, Martin, 1483-1546—Congresses. 2. Lutheran Church in the United States—Congresses. I. Gettysburg. Theological Seminary of the United Lutheran Church in America. Institute for Luther Studies. II. Title.

THE Maturing of American Lutheranism; essays in honor of Willard Dow Allbeck upon the completion of thirty years as Wittenberg Synod Professor of Historical Theology at Hamma School of Theology, Wittenberg University, Springfield, Ohio. Edited by Herbert T. Neve and Benjamin A. Johnson. Minneapolis, Augsburg Pub. House [1968] vii, 272 p. port. 22 cm. Contents.Contents.—Introduction: The theology of the next step, by H. T. Neve.—The long-range logic of Reformation thought, by A. R. Wentz.—Some suggestions for a sociology of American Protestantism, by K. H. Hertz.—The Word of God according to the Lutheran Confessions, by T. G. Tappert.—Justification by faith in the twentieth century, by H. T. Neve.—The Lutheran Reformation in American historiography, by L. W. Spitz.—Introduction: Samuel Simon Schmucker and the ecumenical age, by B. A. Johnson.—This unassuming servant of the Master: Michael Schweigert, by R. H. Fischer.—Frederick H. Knubel: pioneer in American Lutheran participation in the modern ecumenical movement, by D. A. Flesner.—Ohio's accord with Missouri, 1868-1880, by C. S. Meyer.—A case study in Lutheran unity efforts: ULCA conversations with Missouri and the ALC, 1936-1940, by E. C. Nelson.—En route to unity, by G. E. Arden.—Bibliography of Willard Dow Allbeck publications (p. 269-272) Bibliographical references included in "Notes" (p. 237-268) [BX8011.A1M3] 68-13427 284'.173
1. Lutheran Church—Addresses, essays, lectures. 2. Allbeck, Willard Dow, 1898- —Bibliography. I. Allbeck, Willard Dow, 1898- II. Neve, Herbert T., ed. III. Johnson, Benjamin A., ed.

MEUSER, Fred W 284.173
The formation of the American Lutheran Church; a case study in Lutheran unity. Columbus, Ohio, Wartburg Press, 1958. xiv, 327p. ports., maps. 22cm. 'In its original form, this book was submitted as a dissertation to the faculty of the Graduate School of Yale University in candidacy for the degree of doctor of philosophy.' Bibliography: p. 302-317. [BX8061.A5M4] 58-11791
1. American Lutheran Church—Hist. I. Title.

MORTENSEN, Enok, 1902- 284'.173
The Danish Luteran Church in America; the history and heritage of the American Evangelical Lutheran Church. Philadelphia, Board of Publication, Lutheran Church in America [1967] xiv, 320 p. illus., ports. 24 cm. (Studies in church history, ser. 2 no. 25) Includes bibliographical references. [BX8057.M63] 67-16469
1. Danish Evangelical Lutheran Church of America. 2. American Evangelical Lutheran Church. 3. Lutherans, Danish, in the U.S. I. Title. II. Series: Kirkehistoriske studier, ser. 2, no. 25

MORTENSEN, Enok, 1902- 284'.173
The Danish Lutheran Church in America; the history and heritage of the American Evangelical Lutheran Church. Philadelphia, Board of Pubn., Lutheran Church in Amer. [1967] xiv, 320p. illus., ports. 24cm. (Studies in church hist., ser. 2, no. 25) Bibl. [BX8057.M63] 67-16469 6.50
1. Danish Evangelical Lutheran Church of America. 2. American Evangelical Lutheran Church. 3. Lutherans, Danish, in the U. S. I. Title. II. Series: Kirkehistoriske studier, ser. 2, no. 25
Distributed by Fortress.

NATIONAL Lutheran Council. 284.173
Christ for the moving millions, a conference on mobility ... held at the Sheraton- Cadillac Hotel, Detroit, Michigan, December 14-15-16, 1954. Sponsored by National Lutheran Council; arr. by Division of American Missions. Chicago [1955] viii, 116p. illus., maps. 23cm. Bibliographical footnotes. [BV2784.N3 1954] 56-525
1. Migration, Internal—U. S. 2. Missions—U. S. 3. Social surveys—U. S. I. Title.

NATIONAL Lutheran Council. 284.173
Lutheran church directory for the United States and Canada. New York, National Lutheran Council. v. 23 cm. Title varies: Lutheran directory and statistical handbook. [BX8009.L84] 68-6062
1. Lutheran Church in the U. S.—Direct. 2. Lutheran Church in Canada—Direct. I. Title. II. Title: Lutheran directory and statistical handbook.

NATIONAL Lutheran Council. Division of American Missions. 284'.173
County-by-county; population and Lutheran Church membership study [1950 1960. Chicago, 1962] 1 v.(unpaged) maps, tables. 29 cm. Caption title. [BX8041.A42] 63-5558
1. Lutheran Church in the U.S. — Membership — Stat. I. Title.

ODMAN, Charlotte. 284.173
Know your synod. Rock Island, Ill., Augustana Press [1962] 110p. illus. 23cm. [BX8048.2.O3] 62-18195
1. Lutheran Church in America. I. Title.

ODMAN, Charlotte 284.173
Know your synod. Rock Island, Ill., Augustana [c.1962] 110p. maps (pt. col.) 23cm. 62-18195 1.00 pap.,
1. Lutheran Church in America. I. Title.

ONE (Minneapolis) 284.173
America's Lutherans, edited by Omar Bonderud and Charles Lutz. Reprinted from One magazine. Columbus, Ohio, Wartburg Press, 1955. 63p. illus. 22cm. [BX8041.O55] 56-2524
1. Lutheran Church in the U. S. I. Bonderud, Omar, ed. II. Title.

PACIFIC Synod of the United Lutheran Church in America. 284.173
The first fifty years of the Pacific Synod, 1901- 1951, by Edwin Bracher, historian. Seattle, 1951. 99p. illus. 25cm. Includes bibliography. [BX8061.P2A35] 62-2436
I. Bracher, Edwin. II. Title.

POOLE, Donald R 284.173
History of the Georgia-Alabama Synod of the United Lutheran Church in America, 1860-1960 [by] Donald R. Poole. [Birmingham, Ala., 1959] 82 p. illus., ports. 23 cm. Bibliographical footnotes. [BX8061.G4P6] 67-37417
1. Georgia-Alabama Synod of the United Lutheran Church in America—Hist. I. Title.

SCHMUCKER, Samuel Simon, 1799-1873. 284'.173
The American Lutheran Church. New York, Arno Press, 1969. x, 280 p. port. 22 cm. (Religion in America) Reprint of the 1851 ed. "List of publications by Lutheran ministers in the United States": p. 74-84. [BX8041.S4 1969] 72-83436
1. Lutheran Church—History. 2. Lutheran Church in the United States. I. Title.

SCHWARTZKOPF, Louis J 284.173
The Lutheran trail; a history of the Synodical Conference Lutheran churches in northern Illinois. Saint Louis, Concordia Pub. House [1950] xix, 698 p. illus., maps. 21 cm. Bibliography: p. 681-693. [BX8042.I6S3] 51-619
1. Lutheran Church in Illinois. 2. Churches — Illinois. 3. Evangelical Lutheran Synodical Conference of North America — Illinois. I. Title.

STAUDERMAN, Albert P 284.173
Our new church. Philadelphia, Lutheran Church Press [1962]. 64 p. illus. 21 cm. (Leadership education series) [BX8048.2.S75] 62-2393
1. Lutheran Church in America. I. Title.

STAUDERMAN, Albert P. 284.173
Our new church. Philadelphia 29 2900 Queen Lane Lutheran Church Pr., [c.1962] 64p. illus. 21cm. (Leadership educ. ser.) 62-2393 1.00
1. Lutheran Church in America. I. Title.

A study of generations; report of a two-year study of 5,000 Lutherans between the ages of 15-65, their beliefs, values, attitudes, behavior [by] Merton P. Strommen [and others] Minneapolis, Augsburg Pub. House [1972] 411 p. illus. 24 cm. Bibliography: p. 396-400. [BX8041.S78] 74-176478 ISBN 0-8066-1207-X 12.50 284'.173
1. Lutherans in the United States—Statistics. 2. Lutheran Church—Doctrinal and controversial works—Statistics. I. Strommen, Merton P.

SVERDRUP, Georg, 1848-1907. 284'.173
The heritage of faith; selections from the writings of Georg Sverdrup. Translated by Melvin A. Helland. Minneapolis, Augsburg Pub. House [1969] 136 p. 23 cm. Contents.Contents.—The Norwegian matrix.—Church and congregation.—The struggle for unity.—The church and social problems.—Theological education.—Exposition of Scripture. [BX8011.S92] 70-84805 5.00
1. Lutheran Church—Collected works. I. Title.

SYNOD of Ohio of the United Lutheran Church in America. 284.173
Minutes of the annual convention. [Columbus? Ohio] v. 24cm. [BX8061.O62A3] 54-16303
I. Title.

THORKELSON, Willmar. 284'.173
Lutherans in the U.S.A. Minneapolis, Augsburg Pub. House [1969] 42 p. 20 cm. "A revision of articles published in The Lutheran." [BX8041.T48] 77-84812 1.00
1. Lutheran Church in the United States. I. Title.

WEIDERAENDERS, Robert C. 284'.173
The synods of American Lutheranism [by] Robert C. Wiederaenders and Walter G. Tillmanns. [St. Louis] Lutheran Historical Conference [1968] xiii, 209 p. maps. 23 cm. (Lutheran Historical Conference. Publication no. 1) Includes bibliographies. [BX8041.W5] 68-25502
1. Lutheran Church in the United States. 2. Lutheran Church in the United States—Bibliography. I. Tillmanns, Walter G., joint author. II. Title. III. Series.

WENTZ, Abdel Ross, 1883- 284.173
A basic history of Lutheranism in America. Rev. ed. Philadelphia, Fortress Press [1964] viii, 439 p. 24 cm. Bibliography: p. 398-421. [BX8041.W38] 64-12996
1. Lutheran Church in the U.S. — Hist. I. Title.

WENTZ, Abdel Ross, 1883- 284.173
A basic history of Lutheranism in America. Rev. ed. Philadelphia, Fortress [c.1955, 1964] viii, 439p. 24cm. Bibl. 64-12996 6.95
1. Lutheran Church in the U.S.—Hist. I. Title.

WENTZ, Frederick K. 284'.173
Lutherans in concert; the story of the National Lutheran Council, 1918-1966 [by] Frederick K. Wentz. Minneapolis, Augsburg Pub. House [1968] ix, 221 p. illus., ports. 22 cm. Bibliography: p. 199-200. [BX8041.A44] 68-13727
1. National Lutheran Council. 2. Lutheran Church in the U.S. I. Title.

WOLF, Richard C 284.173
Lutherans in North America, By Richard C. Wolf. Frank W. Klos, editor. John Gretzer, artist. Philadelphia, Lutheran Church Press [1965] v, 150 p. illus., map. 21 cm. (LCA school of religion series) -- Teacher's guide; a short-term study course for adults, by Ruth Lister. Frank W. Klos, editor. Philadelphia, Lutheran Church Press [1965] 63 p. illus. 21 cm. (LCA school of religion series) BX1403.2.W6 Guide [BX1403.2.W6] 65-6903
1. Lutheran Church in North America — Hist. 2. Lutheran Church in the U.S. — Hist. I. Lister, Ruth. II. Title.

WOLF, Richard C ed. 284.17308
Documents of Lutheran unity in America [edited] by Richard C. Wolf. Philadelphia, Fortress Press [1966] xxvii, 672 p. 23 cm. "Sources": p. 641-659. [BX8041.A485] 65-26439
1. Lutheran Church in the U.S. — Collections. 2. Christian union — Collections. 3. Lutheran Church in the U.S. — Hist. — Sources. I. Title.

WOLF, Richard C., ed. 284.17308
Documents of Lutheran unity in America. Philadelphia, Fortress [c.1966] xxvii, 672p. 23cm. Bibl. [BX8041.A485] 65-26439 2.50
1. Lutheran Church in the U.S.—Collections. 2. Christian union—Collections. 3. Lutheran Church in the U. S.—Hist.—Sources. I. Title.

LUTHERAN Historical Conference. 284'.17309
Proceedings: program - minutes - papers. [St. Louis? 1964?] 1 v. (various pagings) 29 cm. Cover title. "Second biennial meeting, Concordia Historical Institute and Concordia Seminary ... October 29-30, 1964." [BX8018.L79] 73-172255
1. Lutheran Church—History—Congresses. I.

Concordia Historical Institute. II. Concordia Theological Seminary, St. Louis.

WALTHER, Carl 284.173'0924
Ferdinand Wilhelm, 1811-1887.
Letters of C. F. W. Walther; a selection. Translated, edited, and with an introd. by Carl S. Meyer. Philadelphia, Fortress Press [1969] xii, 155 p. 21 cm. (Seminar editions) Bibliographical footnotes. [BX8080.W3A413] 72-84539 2.25
I. Title.

KREIDER, Harry Julius, 284.174
1896-
History of the United Lutheran Synod of New York and New England. Written at the request of the synod. Philadelphia, Muhlenberg Press, 1954- v. port., map (on lining papers) diagr. 24cm. Bibliographical footnotes. [BX8061.N78K7] 54-9180
1. United Lutheran Synod of New York and New England—Hist. I. Title.

BERKENMEYER, Wilhelm 284'.1747
Christoph, 1686-1751.
The Albany protocol; Wilhelm Christoph Berkenmeyer's chronicle of Lutheran affairs in New York Colony, 1731-1750. Translated by Simon Hart and Sibrandina Geertruid Hart-Runeman. Translation initiated by Harry J. Kreider. Edited by John P. Dern. Ann Arbor, Mich., 1971. lx, 643 p. illus., facsims., geneal. tables, maps. 23 cm. Translated from a photostatic copy of the Dutch MS. in the library of the Lutheran Theological Seminary at Gettysburg. The bound photostatic copy has title on spine: Berkenmeyer chronicle. Bibliography: p. 592-600. [BX8080.B447A313] 74-27484
1. Lutheran Church in New York (Colony)—History—Sources. I. Title. II. Title: Berkenmeyer chronicle.

KREIDER, Harry Julius, 284'.1'747
1896-
Lutheranism in colonial New York. New York, Arno Press, 1972, [c1942] xviii, 158 p. 24 cm. (Religion in America, series II) Originally presented as the author's thesis, Columbia University, 1942. Bibliography: p. 149-158. [BX8042.N7K7 1972] 78-38452 ISBN 0-405-04072-5
1. Lutheran Church in New York (State) 2. Lutheran Church in New Jersey. 3. New York (State)—Church history. 4. New Jersey—Church history. I. Title.

NEW York. Evangelical 284.1747
Lutheran Church of St. Matthew.
Protocol of the Lutheran Church in New York City, 1702-1750. Translated by Simon Hart and Harry J. Kreider. New York, The Synod [i. e. United United Lutheran Synod of New York and New England] 1958. xxi, 523p. map, facsims. 28cm. Bibliography: p. xx. [BX8076.N4S27] 58-2867
1. New York (City)—Church history. 2. Lutheran Church in New York (City) I. Hart, Simon, tr. II. Kreider, Harry Julius, 1896- tr. III. United Lutheran Synod of New York and New England. IV. Title.

GROTTKE, Theodore L 284.174728
A history of Christ Evangelical Lutheran Church, Airmont, Suffern, New York, formerly Ramapo Lutheran Church, organized June 14, 1715, Mahwah, New Jersey. Prepared by Theodore L. and Erna H. Grottke. [Suffern, N.Y., 1965] 69 p. illus., maps, port 23 cm. "Presented on the occasion of the 250th anniversary of the congregation, June 14, 1965." Includes bibliographies. [BX8076.S85C5] 66-31561
1. Suffern, N.Y. Christ Evangelical Lutheran Church. I. Grottke, Erna H., joint author. II. Title.

BARREN Hill, Pa. St. 284'.1747'43
Peter's Lutheran Church.
St. Peter's Lutheran Church, Barren Hill, Pa.; two hundred years of Christian service, 1752-1952. Harold F. Doebler, pastor George A. Ludwig, church historian. [Philadelphia] United Lutheran PublicationHouse [c1952] 192p. illus. 24cm. [BX8076.B3S3] 58-47770
I. Doebler, Harold F. II. Ludwig, George A. III. Title.

HEINS, Henry Hardy, 284'.1747'43
1923-
Swan of Albany : a history of the oldest congrgation of the Lutheran Church in America / by Henry H. Heins. Albany : First Lutheran Church, 1976. xii, 241 p. : ill. ; 27 cm. Includes index. [BX8076.A3F54] 76-22221
1. Albany. First Lutheran Church. I. Title.

STUBBE, Ray William. 284'.1747'43
The heritage of those that fear Thy name; a history written in commemoration of the seventy-fifth anniversary of the Evangelical Lutheran Church of the Redeemer, Milwaukee, Wisconsin. [Milwaukee, 1965] 123, xvii p. illus., ports. 28 cm. Bibliographical references included in "Footnotes" (p. i-ix) [BX8076.M53E93] 66-3665
1. Milwaukee. Evangelical Lutheran Church of the Redeemer. I. Title.

HEISSENBUTTEL, Ernest G 284.1748
Pittsburgh Synod congregational histories. Warren, Ohio, Studio of Printcraft, 1959. 434p. illus. 24cm. The first of a two-volume synodical history, prepared under authorization of the Executive Committee of the Pittsburgh Synod of the Evangelical Lutheran Church. [BX8061.P6H4] 59-2372
1. Pittsburgh Synod of the Evangelical Lutheran Church. 2. Churches—Pennsylvania. I. Title.

FISHER, Wallace E 284.174815
From tradition to mission [by] Wallace E. Fisher. New York, Abingdon Press [1965] 208 p. 21 cm. Bibliography: p. 180-198. [BX8076.L3T74] 65-15971
1. Lancaster, Pa. Trinity Lutheran Church. 2. City churches. I. Title.

FISHER, Wallace E. 284.174815
From tradition to mission. Nashville, Abingdon [c.1965] 208p. 21cm. Bibl. [BX8076.L3T74] 65-15971 3.50
1. Lancaster, Pa. Trinity Lutheran Church. 2. City churches. I. Title.

WEISER, Frederick 284*.1748*15
Sheely, 1935-
A congregation named Saint John's; two hundred years of parish life in Saint John's Evangelical Lutheran Church, Maytown, Pennsylvania, 1767-1967, by Frederick S. Weiser. With an intro. by Ronald E. Peirson. Maytown, Pa., Church Council, 1967. 103 p. illus., ports. 24 cm. Bibliographical references included in "Notes." [BX8076.M4S35] 68-71
1. Maytown, Pa. St. John's Evangelical Lutheran Church. I. Title.

WEISER, Frederick 284'.1748'15
Sheely, 1935-
A congregation named Saint John's; two hundred years of parish life in Saint John's Evangelical Lutheran Church, Maytown, Pennsylvania, 1767-1967, by Frederick S. Weiser. With an introd. by Ronald E. Peirson. Maytown, Pa., Church Council, 1967. 103 p. illus., ports. 24 cm. Bibliographical references included in "Notes." [BX8076.M4S35] 68-71
1. Maytown, Pa. St. John's Evangelical Lutheran Church. I. Title.

DIEFFENBACH, Ray J. 284'.1748'16
An historical account of the building of Altalaha Lutheran Church, Rehrersburg, Pa. in 1808 and the bell tower of 1849. Compiled by Ray J. Dieffenbach and Schuyler C. Brossman. Edited by Larry R. Hassler. Rehrersburg, Pa., Church Council of Altalaha Lutheran Church, 1973. 27 p. 22 cm. [BX8076.R34A63] 73-299016
1. Rehrersburg, Pa. Altalaha Evangelical Lutheran Church. 2. Rehrersburg, Pa.—Biography. I. Brossman, Schuyler C. II. Title.

TREXLER, Mark K ed. 284.174816
The Lutheran Church in Berks County, 1723-1958. Kutztown, Pa., Kutztown Pub. Co. [1959] 348 p. illus. 24 cm. "Published by authorization of the Reading Conference of the Lutheran Ministerium of Pennsylvania in convention assembled, May 8, 1958." Includes bibliography. [BX8061.P409T7] 59-14104
1. Evangelical Lutheran Ministerium of Pennsylvania. Conferences. Reading. 2. Lutheran Church in Pennsylvania. 3. Churches — Pennsylvania — Berks Co. 4. Clergy — Pennsylvania — Berks Co. I. Title.

KEMP, Franklin W. 284'.1'749'85
St. Andrew's by-the-Sea; the history of St. Andrew's Evangelical Lutheran Church, Atlantic City, New Jersey 1889-1969, by Franklin W. Kemp. [Atlantic City, St. Andrew's Evangelical Lutheran Church] 1970. 148 p. illus., ports. 24 cm. [BX8076.A75S34] 74-19224
1. Atlantic City. St. Andrew's by-the-Sea.

EHINGER, Aline Noren. 284'.1751'5
Bridge across the years : a history of the Presbyterian Church of Dover, including chapters on the life of the community and denomination / by Aline Noren Ehinger. [Dover? Del. : s.n.], 1975. xi, 419 p., [4] leaves of plates : ill. ; 24 cm. Includes index. Bibliography: p. 406-415. [BX9211.D64P73] 76-359392
1. Presbyterian Church of Dover. I. Title.

AURORA, W. Va. Saint 284.1754
Paul's Lutheran Church.
The Aurora documents: a accurate and complete translation and transcription of books i and ii of the original records of Saint Paul's Lutheran Church, Aurora, Preston Country, West Virgina, founded March 24, 1787, by Karl K. Gower. 1st ed. Oakland, Md., Sincell Pub. Co. [1957] 124p. illus. port. 23cm. [BX8076.A8S37] 57-8699
I. Gower, Karl K., ed. and tr. II. Title.

EISENBERG, William 284.1755
Edward.
This heritage; the story of Lutheran beginnings in the lower Shenandoah Valley, and of Grace Church, Winchester. Winchester, Va., Trustees of Grace Evangelical Lutheran Church, 1954. 395p. illus. 24cm. [BX8076.W52G7] 54-29668
1. Winchester, Va. Grace Evangelical Lutheran Church. I. Title.

LUTHERAN Church in 284'.1757
America. South Carolina Synod. History of the Synod Committee.
A history of the Lutheran Church in South Carolina. [Columbia, S.C.] South Carolina Synod of the Lutheran Church in America, 1971. xiii, 966 p. illus. 24 cm. Bibliography: p. 917-931. [BX8061.S6A5] 73-185448
1. Lutheran Church in America. South Carolina Synod. 2. Lutheran Church in South Carolina.

KENTUCKY-TENNESSEE Synod 284.176
of the United Lutheran Church in America.
Minutes of the annual convention. [Nashville?] v. illus. 23 cm. [BX8061.K4A3] 52-65851
I. Title.

MISSISSIPPI Synod of the 284.1762
United Lutheran Church in America.
Proceedings of the convention. [Louisville, Miss.] v. 23cm. annual. Cover title.: Minutes of the convention. Vols. for include the Minutes of the annual convention of the Women's Missionary Society of the Mississippi Synod and also minutes of other synodical auxiillary societies. [BX8061.M68A3] 53-16394
I. Title.

HISTORY and 284'.1764
rededication of Saint John Evangelical Lutheran Church of 1867 on October 26th, 1958, Meyersville, Texas. [Meyersville? Tex., 196-?] 24 p. illus. 22 cm. [BX8076.M43S255] 74-151150
1. Saint John Evangelical Lutheran Church, Meyersville, Tex.

ZIEHE, Heinz Carl, 1900- 284.1764
A centennial story of the Lutheran Church in Texas. [1851-1951. Seguin? Tex., 1954; v. 1, c1951] 2 v. illus. 23cm. [BX8032.T4Z5] 54-34235
1. Lutheran Church in Texas. I. Title.

NEW Ulm, Tex. St. 284'.1764'25
John Lutheran Church.
Hundredth anniversary 1867-1968 New Ulm, Tex. [1968] 1 v. (unpaged) illus., facsims., ports. 22 cm. [BX8076.N37S3V] 75-2682
1. New Ulm, Tex. St. John Lutheran Church. I. Title.

WALTMANN, Henry G. 284'.1769
History of the Indiana-Kentucky Synod of the Lutheran Church in America: its development, congregations, and institutions. Edited by Henry G. Waltmann. Indianapolis, Central Pub. Co., 1971. xiii, 445 p. illus. 24 cm. Includes bibliographical references. [BX8061.I67W34] 74-184076
1. Indiana-Kentucky Synod of the Lutheran Church in America.

ACKER, Julius William. 284.177
Strange alitars; a scriptural appraisal of the lodge. Saint Louis, Concordia Pub. House [1959] 94p. 19cm. Includes bibliography. [HS164.A3] 59-2478
1. Secret societies— U. S. I. Title.

HERRMANN, J E ed. 284.177
You, your congregation, your synod. Design and layout [by] Egon W. Gebauer. St. Louis, Lutheran Church, Missouri Synod, Dept. of Stewardship, Missionary Education, and Promotion [1952] 125p. illus. 23cm. [BX8061.M7H4] 52-44596
1. Lutheran Church—Missouri Synod. I. Title.

MEYER, Carl Stamm, 1907- 284.177
. ed.
Moving frontiers; readings in the history of the Lutheran Church -- Missouri Synod. Edited by Carl S. Meyer. St. Louis, Concordia Pub. House [1964] xii, 500 p. maps (part fold.) 25 cm. Bibliography: p. [443]-449. [BX8061.M7M42] 63-21161
1. Lutheran Church — Missouri Synod — Hist. — Collections. I. Title.

MEYER, Carl Stamm, 1907- 284.177
ed.
Moving frontiers; readings in the history of the Lutheran Church--Missouri Synod. St. Louis, Concordia [1964] xii, 500p. maps (pt. fold.) 25cm. Bibl. 63-21161 8.50
1. Lutheran Church—Missouri Synod—Hist.—Collections. I. Title.

WARTBURG SYNOD, United 284.177
Lutheran Church in America.
Minutes of the annual convention. [Milwaukee?] v. 23 cm. [BX8061.W25A3] 52-65850
I. Title.

ALLBECK, Willard Dow, 284.1771
1898-
A century of Lutherans in Ohio, by Willard D. Allbeck. [Yellow Springs, Ohio] Antioch Press, 1966. viii, 309 p. 22 cm. Bibliography: p. [299] -304. [BX8042.O3A65] 66-13389
1. Lutheran Church in Ohio. I. Title.

INDIANA Synod of the 284.1772
United Lutheran Church in America.
Minutes of the annual convention. [v. p.] v. 24cm. Conventions held 19 -47 called -100th. Title varies: 19 -53, Proceedings (cover title, 1935-53, Minutes) Proceedings of the 19 convention include also the proceedings of the conventions of the Women's Missionary Society, the Lutheran Brotherhood and the Luther League. [BX806.I68A3] 56-26870
I. Title.

BETHLEHEM Evangelical 284'.17'731
Lutheran Church.
A living heritage, 1871-1971, to honor the centennial observance of Bethlehem Evangelical Lutheran Church. Clifton H. Kittelson, pastor. [Elgin, Ill., Brethren Press, 1971] 160 p. illus. 25 cm. [BX8076.E43B483] 72-192076
1. Bethlehem Evangelical Lutheran Church. I. Kittelson, Clifton H. II. Title.

CENTURY; Salem 284'.1773'11
Lutheran Church. [Chicago, c1968] 142 p. illus. ports. 27 cm. Title on spine: Salem Lutheran Church, 1868-1968. [BX8076.C5S34] 70-263746
1. Chicago. Salem Lutheran Church. I. Title: Salem Lutheran Church, 1868-1968.

MICHIGAN Synod of the 284.1774
United Lutheran Church in America.
Minutes of the convention. [Detroit, etc.] v. 23cm. annual. Title varies: Proceedings of the convention. Vols. for include the Proceedings of the conventions of the Women's Missionary Society and the Lutheran Brotherhood. [BX8061.M6A3] 53-20706
I. Title.

SUELFLOW, Roy Arthur, 284'.1775
1918-
Walking with wise men; a history of the South Wisconsin District of the Lutheran Church--Missouri Synod, by Roy A. Suelflow. Milwaukee, South Wisconsin District of the Lutheran Church--Missouri Synod [1967] 221 p. 23 cm. Bibliographical references included in "Footnotes" (p. 186-216) [BX8061.M79S9] 67-29002
1. Lutheran Church—Missouri Synod. Districts. South Wisconsin—Hist. I. Title.

SUELFLOW, Roy Arthur, 284.177594
1918-
A plan for survival, by Roy A. Suelflow. New York, Greenwich Book Publishers [c1965] 204 p. 21 cm. [BX8043.M5S8] 65-17086
1. Lutherans in Milwaukee. I. Title.

SUELFLOW, Roy Arthur, 284.177594
1918-
A plan for survival, by Roy A. Suelflow New York, Greenwich Bk. Pubs. [1966, c.1965] 204p. 21cm. [BX8043.M5S8] 65-17036 4.50
1. Lutherans in Milwaukee. I. Title.

DOLVEN, Oswald Earl 284.1776
Famous firsts in Minnesota Lutheranism. [Horace, N.D., Lutheran Parsonage, 1960] 47p. illus. 30cm. Includes bibliography. 60-1522 1.25 pap.,
1. Lutheran Church in Minnesota. 2. Churches—Minnesota. I. Title.

GOLDEN jubilee history 284'.1776
of the Minnesota District of the Wisconsin Evangelical Lutheran Synod and its member congregations, 1918-1968. [Minneapolis, Ad Art Advertising Co., c1969] 367 p. illus. 24 cm. "Authorized by the Golden Jubilee Convention of the Minnesota District at Dr. Martin Luther College, New Ulm, Minnesota, July 29-August 1, 1968." [BX8061.W6G66] 74-158379
1. Wisconsin Evangelical Lutheran Synod. Minnesota District.

FORSTER, Walter Otto. 284.1778
Zion on the Mississippi; the settlement of the Saxon Lutherans in Missouri, 1839-1841. Saint Louis, Concordia Pub. House, 1953. xiv, 606p. illus., ports., maps (part fold.) facsims. 24cm. An expansion and revision of 'the study ... originally prepared as a doctoral dissertation at Washington University in Saint Louis.' Bibliography: p. 584-594. [BX8061.M7F6] 53-9271
1. Stephan, Martin, 1777-1846. 2. Lutheran

Church—Missouri Synod—Hist. 3. Lutherans in Missouri. 4. Germans in Missouri. I. Title. II. Title: Saxon Lutherans in Missouri.

RUDNICK, Milton L. 284.1778
Fundamentalism & the Missouri Synod; a historical study of their interaction and mutual influence [by] Milton L. Rudnick. Saint Louis, Concordia Pub. House [1966] xii, 152 p. 24 cm. Bibliography: p. [139]-144. [BX8061.M7R8] 66-28229
1. Lutheran Church—Missouri Synod. 2. Fundamentalism. I. Title.

SCHAEFER, Lyle L. 284'.1788
Faith to move mountains; a history of the Colorado District of the Lutheran Church-Missouri Synod from the earliest mission work, 1872-1968 [by] Lyle L. Schaefer. Denver, Colorado District, Lutheran Church-Missouri Synod, 1969. xii, 233 p. illus., maps, ports. 23 cm. Bibliography: p. 212-221. [BX8061.M745S3] 79-83171
1. Lutheran Church-Missouri Synod. Districts. Colorado. I. Title.

BRADFIELD, Irene. 284'.1795'49
Trinity Lutheran Church, 1899-1974 / [writer, Irene Bradfield]. Gresham, Or. : Trinity Lutheran Church, [1974] 61 p. : ill. ; 22 cm. [BX8076.G76T743] 75-308824
1. Trinity Lutheran Church, Gresham, Or. 2. Gresham, Or.—Biography. I. Trinity Lutheran Church, Gresham, Or.

BACHMANN, Ernest Theodore. 284'.181
Lutherans in Brazil; a story of emerging ecumenism, by E. Theodore Bachmann. Foreword by Fredrik A. Schiotz. Minneapolis, Augsburg Pub. House [1970] 79 p. maps (on lining papers) 20 cm. "A note on readings": p. 77-79. [BX8063.B77B3] 70-121959
1. Lutheran Church in Brazil. I. Title.

CALVIN, Jean, 1509-1564. 284'.2
Letters of John Calvin. Compiled from the original manuscripts and edited with historical notes by Jules Bonnet. New York, B. Franklin [1973] 4 v. facsims. 22 cm. (Burt Franklin research & source works series. Philosophy & religious history monographs, 116) Reprint of the ed. published in Edinburgh by T. Constable (v. 1-2) and in Philadelphia by the Presbyterian Board of Publication (v. 3-4), 1855-58. Translated from the original Latin or French mss. by D. Constable (v. 1-2) and M. R. Gilchrist (v. 3-4) Includes bibliographical references. [BX9418.A4E5 1973] 70-185936 ISBN 0-8337-4021-0 75.00 (4 vols.)
I. Bonnet, Jules, 1820-1892, ed. II. Title.

CALVIN, Jean, 1509-1564. 284.2
Theological threatises. Translated with introductions and notes by J. K. S. Reid. Philadelphia, Westminster Press [1954] 355p. 24cm. (The Library of Christian classics, v. 22) Bibliography: p. 344-346. [BX9420.T68] 54-9956
1. Reformed Church— Collected works. 2. Theology—Collected works—16th cent. I. Title. II. Series: The Library of Christian classics (Philadelphia) v. 22

CALVIN, Jean, 1509-1564. 284.2
Tracts and treatises. With a short life of Calvin by Theodore Bezu. Translation from the original Latin by Henry Beveridge. Historical notes and intord. added to the present ed. by Thomas F. Torrance. [Grand Rapids, Eerdmans [c1958] 3v. 23cm. Vols. 2-3 translated from the original Latin and French. Contents.v. 1. On the Reformation of the church.--v. 2. On the doctrine and worship of the church.--v.3. In defense of the Reformed faith. [BX9420.A3 1958] 58-9546
1. Reformed Church—Collected works. 2. Theology—Collected works—16th cent. I. Title.

CALVINISTIC Action Committee. 284.2
God-centered living; or, Calvinism in action, a symposium. Grand Rapids, Baker Book House, 1951. 270 p. 24 cm. "Books on Calvinism and Calvinistic action, by H. Henry Meeter": p. 257-270. [BX9422.C28] 52-40063
1. Calvinism. 2. Christian life. I. Title. II. Title: Calvinism in action.

DAKIN, Arthur, 1884- 284'.2
Calvinism, by A. Dakin. Port Washington, N.Y., Kennikat Press [1972] 252 p. 21 cm. Reprint of the 1940 ed. Includes bibliographical references. [BX9422.D3 1972] 72-153211 ISBN 0-8046-1521-7
1. Calvinism.

DURHAM, Eng. (Diocese) 284.2
Bishop, 1530-1559 (Cuthbert Tunstall)
The registers of Cuthbert Tunstall, Bishop of Durham, 1530-59, and James Pilkington, Bishop of Durham, 1561-76; edited and calendared by Gladys Hinde. Durham, Andrews, 1952. xxxvi, 198p. 23cm. (The publications of the Surtees Society, v. 161) [DA20.S9 vol.161] 54-18830
1. Gt. Brit.—Church history—Sources. I. Durham, Eng. (Diocese) Bishop, 1561-1576 (James Pilkington) II. Hinde, Gladys, ed. III. Title. IV. Series: Surtees Society, Durham, Eng. Publications, v. 161

HOOGSTRA, Jacob Tunis, 1900- ed. 284.2
American Calvinism; a survey, edited for the Calvinistic Action Committee. Grand Rapids, Baker Book House, 1957. 137p. group port. 21cm. Papers read at the Calvinistic conference held in Grand Rapids, June 20-21, 1956, sponsored by the Calvinistic Action Committee, with more relevant discussions. [BX9422.H63] 57-2540
1. Calvinism—U. S. 2. Theology, Doctrinal—Hist.—U. S. I. Calvinistic Action Committee. II. Title.

HOOGSTRA, Jacob Tunis, 1900- ed. 284.2
American Calvinism;a survey, edited for the Calvinistic Action Committee. Grand Rapids, Baker Book House, 1957. 137p. group port. 21cm. Papers read at the Calvinistic conference held in Grand Rapids, June 20-21, 1956, sponsored by the Calvinistic Action Committee, with more relevant discussions. [BX9422.H63] 57-2540
1. Calvinism—U. S. 2. Theology, Doctrinal—Hist. —U. S. I. Calvinistic Action Committee. II. Title.

MCNEILL, John Thomas, 1885- 284.2
The history and character of Calvinism. New York, Oxford University Press, 1954. x, 466 p. 22 cm. Bibliography: p. 441-450. [BX9422.M32] 54-6911
1. Calvinsim.

OLSON, Arnold Theodore 284.2
Believers only; an outline of the history and principles of the Free Evangelical movement in Europe and North America affiliated with the Intl. Fed. of Free Evangelical Churches. Minneapolis, Free Church Pubns. [c.1964] 367p. group port. 22cm. Bibl. 64-22145 4.95
1. Internationaler Bund Freier Evangelischer Gemeinden. I. Title.

O'MALLEY, John Steven. 284'.2
Pilgrimage of faith: the legacy of the Otterbeins, by J. Steven O'Malley. Metuchen, N.J., Scarecrow Press, 1973. xiii, 212 p. 22 cm. (ATLA monograph series, no. 4) Thesis—Drew University, 1970. Bibliography: p. 197-207. [BX9422.2.O4 1973] 73-5684 ISBN 0-8108-0626-6 6.50
1. Reformed Church—Doctrinal and controversial works. 2. Otterbein, Georg Gottfried, 1731-1800. 3. Otterbein, Johann Daniel, 1736-1804. 4. Otterbein, Philip William, Bp., 1726-1813. 5. Pietism—History. I. Title. II. Series: American Theological Library Association. ATLA monograph series, no. 4.

WARBURTON, Ben A 284.2
Calvinism: its history and basic principles, its fruits and its future, and its practical application to life. [1st ed.] Grand Rapids, Eerdmans. 1955. 249p. 23cm. [BX9422.W29] 54-12337
1. Calvinism. I. Title.

FLETCHER, Elaine J. 284'.2'0924 B
Farel the firebrand [by] Elaine Jessie Fletcher. Washington, Review and Herald Pub. Association [1972] 128 p. illus. 22 cm. [BR350.F3F43] 75-164936 2.95
1. Farel, Guillaume, 1489-1565. I. Title.

BRATT, John H., ed. 284.24
The rise and development of Calvinism; a concise history. Grand Rapids, Eerdmans [1959] 134 p. 22 cm. Includes bibliographies. [BX9422.2.B7] 59-8747
1. Calvin, Jean, 1509-1564. 2. Calvinism—History. I. Title.

ARMSTRONG, Brian G. 284'.244
Calvinism and the Amyraut heresy; Protestant scholasticism and humanism in seventeenth-century France [by] Brian G. Armstrong. Madison, University of Wisconsin Press, 1969. xx, 330 p. facsims., ports. 25 cm. Bibliography: p. 288-317. [BX9424.5.F8A7] 72-84949
1. Calvin, Jean, 1509-1564—Theology. 2. Amyraut, Moise, 1596-1664. 3. Calvinism—France—History. I. Title.

PALM, Franklin Charles, 1890- 284'.244
Calvinism and the religious wars. New York, H. Fertig, 1971 [c1932] ix, 117 p. 21 cm. Includes bibliographical references. [BX9422.P3 1971] 78-80579
1. Calvin, Jean, 1509-1564. 2. Calvinism. 3. France—History—Wars of the Huguenots. I. Title.

WETZEL, Daniel Jacob, 1888- 284.2748
Two hundredth anniversary history of First Reformed Church, Reed and Washington Streets, Reading, Pennsylvania. [Reading] The Consistory, 1953. 119p. illus. 24cm. [BX7481.R4F5] 54-30219
1. Reading, Pa. First Reformed Church. I. Title.

ANABAPTIST beginnings (1523-1533) : a source book / edited by William R. Estep. Nieuwkoop : B. de Graaf, 1976. vii, 172 p. ; 25 cm. (Bibliotheca humanistica et reformatorica ; v. 16) Includes bibliographical references. [BX4930.A48] 77-352561 ISBN 9-06-004337-5 : fl 75.00 284'.3
1. Anabaptists—History—Sources. I. Estep, William Roscoe, 1920- II. Title. III. Series.

BAX, Ernest Belfort, 1854-1926. 284'.3
Rise and fall of the Anabaptists. New York, A. M. Kelley, 1970. vi, 407 p. 22 cm. (Reprints of economic classics) Reprint of the 1903 ed. [BX4931.B3 1970] 75-101125
1. Anabaptists. I. Title.

BAX, Ernest Belfort, 1854-1926 284.3
Rise and fall of the Anabaptists. New York, Amer Scholar Pubns., 1966. vi, 407p. 24cm. Reprint of 1903 ed. [BX4931.B3 1966] 65-24235 10.00
1. Anabaptists. I. Title.
Publishers address: 80 E. 11th St., New York, N. Y., 10003

BLANKE, Fritz, 1900- 284.3
Brothers in Christ; the history of the oldest Anabaptist congregation, Zollikon, near Zurich, Switzerland. Translated by Joseph Nordenhaug. Scottdale, Pa., Herald Press [1961] 78p. 20cm. Includes bibliography. [BX4933.S9B53] 61-6723
1. Anabaptists —Zollikon, Swtzerland. I. Title.

BLANKE, Fritz, 1900- 284.3
Brothers in Christ; the history of the oldest Anabaptist congregation, Zollikon, near Zurich, Switzerland. Tr. [from German] by Joseph Nordenhaug. Herald Press [c.1961] Scottdale, Pa., Herald Press [c.1961] 78p. Bibl. 61-6723 1.25 pap.,
1. Anabaptists—Zollikon, Switzerland. I. Title.

BURRAGE, Henry Sweetser, 1837-1926. 284'.3
A history of the Anabaptists in Switzerland. New York, B. Franklin [1973] 231 p. 21 cm. (Burt Franklin research and source works series. Philosophy & religious history monographs, 124) Reprint of the 1882 ed. published by American Baptist Publication Society, Philadelphia. Includes bibliographical references. [BX4933.S9B8 1973] 76-183240 ISBN 0-8337-4015-6 13.50
1. Anabaptists—Switzerland. I. Title.

CLASEN, Claus Peter. 284'.3
Anabaptism; a social history, 1525-1618: Switzerland, Austria, Moravia, South and Central Germany. Ithaca, Cornell University Press [1972] xviii, 523 p. maps. 24 cm. Bibliography: p. 493-508. [BX4931.2.C57] 78-37751 ISBN 0-8014-0696-X 17.50
1. Anabaptists—History. I. Title.

DAVIS, Kenneth Ronald, 1929- 284'.3
Anabaptism and asceticism; a study in intellectual origins. Scottdale, Pa., Herald Press, 1974. 365 p. port. 23 cm. (Studies in Anabaptist and Mennonite history, no. 16) Originally presented as the author's thesis, University of Michigan, under the title: Evangelical Anabaptism and the medieval ascetic tradition. Bibliography: p. [349]-360. [BX4931.2.D37 1974] 73-19593 ISBN 0-8361-1195-8
1. Anabaptists. 2. Asceticism. 3. Devotio moderna. I. Title. II. Series.

DYCK, Cornelius J., ed. 284.3
A legacy of faith; the heritage of Menno Simons. A sixtieth anniversary tribute to Cornelius Krahn. Newton, Kan., Faith & Life [c.1962] 260p. illus. 24cm. (Mennonite historical ser., 8) 62-19863 5.50
1. Krahn, Cornelius. 2. Mennon Simons, 1496-1561. 3. Anabaptists—Netherlands—Addresses, essays, lectures. I. Title.

ESTEP, William Roscoe, 1920- 284.3
The Anabaptist story. Nashville, Broadman Press [1963] 238 p. 22 cm. Includes bibliography. [BX4931.E8] 63-11164
1. Anabaptists—History. I. Title.

ESTEP, William Roscoe, 1920- 284'.3
The Anabaptist story / William R. Estep. Grand Rapids : Eerdmans, [1975] viii, 250 p. : maps ; 22 cm. Reprint of the ed. published by Broadman Press, Nashville; with new pref. Includes index. Bibliography: p. 236-244. [BX4931.2.E83 1975] 74-26736 ISBN 0-8028-1594-4 pbk. : 3.95
1. Anabaptists—History. I. Title.

GREBEL, Konrad, 1498?-1526. 284'.3
Conrad Grebel's programmatic letters of 1524, with facsimiles of the original German script of Grebel's letters. Transcribed and translated by J. C. Wenger. Scottdale, Pa., Herald Press [1970] 71 p. facsims., port. 19 x 27 cm. Two letters addressed to Thomas Munzer. [BX4946.G7A43 1970] 70-101708
1. Anabaptists—History—Sources. I. Munzer, Thomas, 1490 (ca.)-1525. II. Title.

GRITSCH, Eric W. 284'.3 B
Reformer without a church; the life and thought of Thomas Muentzer, 1488?-1525, by Eric W. Gritsch. Philadelphia, Fortress Press [1967] xiv, 214 p. map, port. 24 cm. Bibliography: p. 199-208. [BX4946.M8G7] 67-20144
1. Munzer, Thomas, 1490 (ca.)-1525. I. Title.

HERSHBERGER, Gly Franklin, 1896- ed. 284.3
The recovery of the Anabaptist vision; a sixtieth anniversary tribute to Harold S. Bender. Scottdale, Pa., Herald Press [1957] viii, 360p. port. 23cm. Bibliographical footnotes. [BX4929.B4H4] 57-10214
1. Bender, Harold Stauffer, 1897- 2. Anabaptists—Addresses, essays, lectures. 3. Mennonites—Addresses, essays, lectures. I. Title.

HERSHBERGER, Guy Franklin, 1896- ed. 284.3
The recovery of the Anabaptist vision; a sixtieth anniversary tribute to Harold S. Bender. Scottdale, Pa., Herald Press [1957] viii, 360p. port. 23cm. Bibliographical footnotes. [BX4929.B4H4] 57-10214
1. Bender, Harold Stauffer, 1897- 2. Anabaptists—Addresses, essays, lectures. 3. Mennonites—Addresses, essays, lectures. I. Title.

LITTEL, Franklin Hamlin. 284.3
The Anabaptist view of the church; a study in the origins of sectarian Protestantism. 2d ed., rev. and enl. Boston, Starr King Press [1958] 229p. 21cm. Includes bibliography. [BX4931.L5 1958] 58-6338
1. Anabaptists. 2. Church. I. Title.

LITTELL, Franklin Hamlin. 284.3
The Anabaptist view of the church: an introduction to sectarian Protestantism. [Hartford?] American Society of Church History, 1952. xii, 148 p. 25 cm (Studies in church history, v. 8) "In original form this study was submitted to ... Yale University ... for the degree of doctor of philosophy." Bibliography: p. 113-145. [BX4931.L5] 52-3597
1. Anabaptists. 2. Church. I. Title. II. Series: Studies in church history (Hartford) v.8

LITTELL, Franklin Hamlin 284.3
The origins of sectarian Protestantism; a study of the Anabaptist view of the church (Orig. title: The Anabaptist view of the church) New York, Macmillan [c.1952-1964] 231p. 21cm. (08708) Bibl. 1.45 pap.,
1. Anabaptists. 2. Church. I. Title.

LITTELL, Franklin Hamlin. 284.3
The origins of sectarian Protestantism; a study of the Anabaptist view of the church. New York, Macmillan [1964] xviii, 231 p. 21 cm. (Macmillan paperback edition) "MP 146." "Submitted in its original form to the faculty of the Graduate School of Yale University in partial fulfillment of the requirements for the degree of doctor of philosophy." Published in 1952 under title: The Anabaptist view of the church. Bibliography: p. 215-222. [BX4931.L5 1964] 64-20302
1. Anabaptists. 2. Church. I. Title.

OYER, John Stanley, 1925- 284.3
Lutheran reformers against Anabaptists: Luther. Melanchthon, and Menius, and the Anabaptists of central Germany. The Hague. M. Nijhoff. [New York, Heinman. 1966, c.] 1964 269p. fold. map. 24cm. Bibl. [BX4931.2.O9] 66-3408 11.00
1. Anabaptists. 2. Lutheran Church—Relations—Anabaptists. 3. Anabaptists—Relations—Lutheran Church. 4. Reformation. I. Title.

PETR Z MLADENOVIC d.1451 284.3
John Hus at the Council of Constance [by] Peter of Mladonovice] Tr. from Latin and the Czech with notes, introd. by Matthew Spinka. New York, Columbia [1966, c.1965] 327p. 24cm. (Records of civilization: sources and studies, no. 73) Bibl. [BX4917.P413] 65-11019 8.75
1. Hus, Jan. 1369-1415. 2. Constance, Council

of, 1414-1418. I. Spinka, Matthew, 1890- II. Title. III. Series.
Contents omitted.

RUTH, John L. 284'.3 B
Conrad Grebel, son of Zurich : commissioned by Conrad Grebel College, Waterloo, Ontario, in observance of the 450th anniversary of the Mennonites / John L. Ruth. Scottdale, Pa. : Herald Press, 1975. 160 p. : ill. ; 26 cm. [BX4946.G7R87] 75-8829 ISBN 0-8361-1767-0 : 6.95
1. Grebel, Konrad, 1498-1526. I. Title.

SPINKA, Matthew, 1890- 284.3
John Hus; a biography. Princeton, N.J., Princeton University Press, 1968. v, 344 p. illus., maps. 23 cm. Bibliography: p. 323-330. [BX4917.S69] 68-20880 10.00
1. Hus, Jan, 1369-1415.

SPINKA, Matthew, 1890- 284.3
John Hus and the Czech reform. Hamden, Conn., Archon [dist. Shoe String] 1966[c.1941] vii, 81p. 22cm. First pub. in 1941 by Univ. of Chic. Pr. Bibl. [BX4917.S7 1966] 66-18645 3.00
1. Hus, Jan, 1369-1415. I. Title.

SPINKA, Matthew, 1890- 284.3
John Hus' concept of the church. Princeton, N.J., Princeton [c.]1966. ix, 432p. 22cm. Bibl. [BX4917.S73] 66-10928 12.00
1. Hus, Jan, 1369-1415. 2. Church—History of doctrines—Middle Ages. I. Title.

SPINKA, Matthews, 1890- 284.3
John Hus' concept of the church. Princeton, N.J., Princeton University Press, 1966. ix, 432 p. 22 cm. Bibliography: p. 411-417. [BX4917.S73] 66-10928
1. Hus, Jan, 1369-1415. 2. Church — History of doctrines — Middle Ages. I. Title.

VEDDER, Henry Clay, 1853-1935. 284'.3 B
Balthasar Hubmaier; the leader of the Anabaptists. New York, AMS Press [1971] xxiv, 333 p. illus., facsim., map, ports. 19 cm. (Heroes of the Reformation) Reprint of the 1905 ed. [BX4946.H8V4 1971] 79-149670 ISBN 0-404-06755-7
1. Hubmaier, Balthasar, d. 1528. 2. Anabaptists.

WENGER, John Christian, 1910- 284.3
Even unto death; the heroic witness of the sixteenth-century Anabaptists. Richmond, John Knox Press [1961] 127 p. 21 cm. Includes bibliography. [BX4931.2.W4] 61-15763
1. Anabaptists. I. Title.

WENGER, John Christian, 1910- 284.3
Even unto death; the heroic witness of the sixteenth-century Anabaptists. Richmond, Va., John Knox [c.1961] 127p. Bibl. 61-15763 2.50
1. Anabaptists. I. Title.

YODER, John Howard, comp. 284'.3
The legacy of Michael Sattler. Trnaslated and edited by John H. Yoder. Scottdale, Pa., Herlad Press, 1973. 183 p. illus. 23 cm. (Classics of the Radical Reformation, 1) Bibliography: p. 178-182. [BX4929.Y6 1973] 72-6333 ISBN 0-8361-1187-7 9.95
1. Theology—Collected works 16th century. 2. Anabaptists—Collected works. I. Sattler, Michael, 1527. II. Title. III. Series.

VERHEYDEN, A. L. E. 284.3493
Anabaptism in Flanders, 1530-1650; a century of struggle. [Manuscript tr. from the Flemish by Meintje Kuitse, Jan Matthijssen, John Howard Yoder] Scottdale, Pa., Herald Pr. [c.1961] xvi, 136p. maps. (Studies in Anabaptist and Mennonite hist., 9) Bibl. 61-13872 3.75
1. Anabaptists—Flanders. I. Title. II. Series.

VERHEYDEN, A L E 284.3493
Anabaptism in Flanders, 1530-1650; a century of struggle. [Manuscript translation from the Flemish by Meintje Kuitse, Jan Matthijssen, and John Howard Yoder Scottdale, Pa., Herald Press [1961] xvi, 136 p. maps. 24 cm. (Studies in Anabaptist and Mennonite history, 9) Bibliographical footnotes. [BX4933.B4V4] 61-13872
1. Anabaptists — Flanders. I. Title. II. Series.

ADELBERG, Roy P 284.4
The way in the world [by] Roy P. Adelberg. New York, Friendship Press [1965] 127 p. illus. 21 cm. [BV4515.2.A3] 65-11427
1. Christian life — Stories I. Title.

BAUMAN, Edward W. 284.4
Beyond belief. Philadelphia, Westminster [c.1964] 127p. 21cm. 64-14088 2.95
1. Christianity—20th cent. I. Title.

IREDALE, Edith (Brubaker) 284.4
A promise fulfilled. Elgin, Ill., Brethren Pr. [c.1962] 208p. 62-16018 3.00
1. Church of the Brethren—Indiana. I. Title.

MORLAND, Samuel bart., Sir 1625-1695. 284.4
The history of the Evangelical churches of the valleys of Piemont; containing a most exact geographical description of the place, and a faithfull account of the doctrine, life and persecutions of the ancient inhabitants. Together with a most naked and punctual relation of the late bloudy massacre, 1655, and a narrative of all the following transactions to the year of Our Lord, 1658. London, Printed by H. Hills for A. Byfield, 1658. [Fort Smith? Ark., 1955] [1]p., reprint: [68], 709p. illus., port., fold. map. 24cm. [BX4880.M8 1658a] 59-18661
1. Waldenses. 2. Pledmont—Hist. I. Title. II. Title: The Evangelical churches of the valleys of Plemont.

MYERS, T Cecil. 284.4
Faith for a time of storm. New York, Abingdon Press [1963] 155 p. 21 cm. Includes bibliography. [BV4832.2.M9] 63-15710
1. Devotional literature. I. Title.

ROBINSON, Virgil E. 284'.4
Brave men to the battle; the story of the Waldenses, by Virgil E. Robinson. Cover and illus. by James Converse. Mountain View, Calif., Pacific Press Publishing Association [1967] 116 p. illus. 22 cm. (Panda book P-105) [BX4881.2.R6] 66-29350
1. Waldenses. I. Title.

*SALSTRAND, George A. E. 284.4
A good steward. Grand Rapids, Mich., Baker Bk. [c.]1965. 76p. 22cm. 1.00 pap.,
I. Title.

UTT, Walter C. 284'.4
Home to our valleys! : True story of the incredible Glorious Return of the Waldenses to their native land / by Walter C. Utt. Mountain View, Calif. : Pacific Press Pub. Association, c1977. 160 p. : map ; 22 cm. (A Destiny book ; D-161) [BX4881.2.U87] 75-30138 pbk. : 3.50
1. Waldenses. I. Title.

WARNER, Henry James. 284'.4
The Albigensian heresy. New York, Russell & Russell [1967] 2 v. in 1. 20 cm. Reprint of the 1922-1928 ed. Vol. 2 has subtitle: Its suppression by Crusade and Inquisition. [BX4891.W32] 66-27174
1. Albigenses. I. Title.

WARNER, Henry James. 284'.4
The Albigensian heresy. New York, Russell & Russell [1967] 2 v. in 1. 20 cm. Reprint of the 1922-1928 ed. Vol. 2 has subtitle: Its suppression by Crusade and Inquisition. [BX4891.W32] 66-27174
1. Albigenses. I. Title.

WHITTIER, Isabel Mary Skolfield. 284'.4
The Waldensians. [Brunswick? Me., 1957] unpaged. illus. 23 cm. [BX4881.5.U5W5] 61-40200
1. Waldenses in the U.S. 2. Waldenses in Italy. I. Title.

THE Primittive Baptist church meeting directory. 284.405873 2d ed., rev. Elon College, N. C., Primitive Baptist Pub. House, 1959. 96p. 16cm. [BX6380.P67 1959] 59-39193
1. Primitive Baptists—Direct.

REU, Johann Michael, 1869-1943. 284'.4'0924
Thirty-five years of Luther research. New York, AMS Press [1970] 155 p. facsims. (part fold.), ports. 18 cm. Reprint of the 1917 ed. Includes bibliographical references. [BR325.R52 1970] 79-131505 ISBN 0-404-05284-3
1. Luther, Martin, 1483-1546—Criticism and interpretation—History. I. Title.

*CLEMENT, Mary, comp. 284.429
Correspondence and records of the S.P.G. relating to Wales, 1701-1750, edited by Mary Clement Cardiff, University of Wales [1973] vii, 102 p. 23 cm. [BR470] ISBN 0-7083-0519-9
1. Church history—18th century. I. Title.
Distributed by Verry, for 6.50.

HANKS, Marion D. 284'.48'933
Now and forever [by] Marion D. Hanks. Illus. by Bill Kuhre. Salt Lake City, Bookcraft [1974] 166 p. col. illus. 24 cm. A collection of essays offering spiritual guidance to Mormon youth concerning everyday situations. [BV4531.2.H32] 74-75165 ISBN 0-88494-212-0 2.95 (pbk.)
1. Youth—Religious life. I. Kuhre, William, illus. II. Title.

BAIRD, Charles Washington, 1828-1887. 284'.5
History of the Huguenot emigration to America. Baltimore, Regional Pub. Co., 1966. 2 v. illus., fold. facsim., maps, plan. 23 cm. First published in 1885. Bibliographical footnotes. [E29.H9B16 1966] 66-29569
1. Huguenots in America. 2. Huguenots in the United States. 3. Huguenots—History. I. Title.

KINGDON, Robert McCune, 1927- 284'.5
Geneva and the consolidation of the French Protestant movement, 1564-1572; a contribution to the history of Congregationalism, Presbyterianism, and Calvinist resistance theory [by] Robert M. Kingdon. Madison, University of Wisconsin Press, 1967. 241 p. facsims. 25 cm. Bibliography: p. 220-234. [BX9454.2.K5] 67-24373
1. Beze, Theodore de, 1519-1605. 2. Huguenots in France. 3. France—Church history—16th century. I. Title.

LEE, Hannah Farnham (Sawyer) 1780-1865. 284'.5
The Huguenots in France and America. Baltimore, Genealogical Pub. Co., 1973. 2 v. in 1 19 cm. Reprint of the 1843 ed. [BX9454.L4 1973] 72-10564 ISBN 0-8063-0531-2
1. Huguenots in France. 2. Huguenots in the United States. I. Title.

ROCHE, Owen I. A. 284.5
The days of the upright; the story of the Huguenots, by O. I. A. Roche. [1st ed.] New York, C. N. Potter [1965] xi, 340 p. plan, ports. 24 cm. Bibliography: p. 329-333. [DC111.R49] 65-17790
1. Huguenots in France. 2. Huguenots—History. I. Title.

SMILES, Samuel, 1812-1904. 284'.5
The Huguenots: their settlements, churches, and industries in England and Ireland. With an appendix relating to the Huguenots in America. Baltimore, Genealogical Pub. Co., 1972. 448 p. 22 cm. Reprint of the 1868 ed. Includes bibliographical references. [BX9458.G7S5 1972] 72-39366 ISBN 0-8063-0497-9
1. Huguenots in England. 2. Huguenots in Ireland. 3. Huguenots in the United States. I. Title.

REAMAN, George Elmore, 1889- 284.509
The trail of the Huguenots in Europe, the United States. South Africa, and Canada. Baltimore, Genealogical [c.1963] 318p. fold. map. 23cm. [BX9454.2.R4] 65-21923 6.50
1. Huguenots—Hist. I. Title.

KELLEY, Donald R. 284'.5'0924 B
Francois Hotman; a revolutionary's ordeal, by Donald R. Kelley. [Princeton, N.J.] Princeton University Press [1973] xvi, 370 p. illus. 23 cm. Bibliography: p. 347-359. [DC112.H67K44] 72-735 13.50
1. Hotman, Francois, sieur de Villiers Saint Paul, 1524-1590. 2. France—Politics and government—16th century.

BAIRD, Henry Martyn, 1832-1906. 284'.5'0944
The Huguenots and the revocation of the Edict of Nantes. New York, Scribner, 1895. [New York, AMS Press, 1972] 2 v. front., 2 fold. maps. 23 cm. Conclusion of the narrative begun in the author's Rise of the Huguenots and continued in his Huguenots and Henry of Navarre. [DC111.B265 1972] 76-161752 ISBN 0-404-08003-0
1. Huguenots in France. 2. Edict of Nantes. 3. France—History—Bourbons, 1589-1789. I. Title.

GRANT, Arthur James, 1862-1948. 284'.5'0944
The Huguenots. [Hamden, Conn.] Archon Books, 1969. 255 p. map. 19 cm. Reprint of the 1934 ed. Bibliography: p. 250-252. [BX9454.G7 1969] 69-11552
1. Hugenots—History. 2. Hugenots in France.

DOUGLAS, Donald. 284.573
The Huguenot; the story of the Huguenot emigrations, particularly to New England, in which is included the early life of Apollos Rivoire, the father of Paul Revere. With an introd. by C. C. Little. [1st ed.] New York, Dutton, 1954. 384 p. 22 cm. Includes bibliography. [BX9459.R4D6] 54-5035
1. Revere, Paul, 1702-1754. 2. Huguenots. I. Title.

GREENFIELD, John, 1865- 284.6
Power from on high; or, The two hundredth anniversary of the great Moravian revival, 1727-1927. [Warsaw, Ind.] 1928. 94 p. 20 cm. Published in 1967 under title: When the spirit came. [BX8565.G8] 28-14268
1. Moravian Church — Hist. I. Title.

GREENFIELD, John, 1865- 284.6
Power from on high; or, The two hundredth anniversary of the great Moravian revival, 1727-1927. Atlantic City, N.J., World Wide Revival Prayer Movement [1931] 93 p. 19 cm. Published in 1967 under title: When the spirit came. [BX8565.G8 1931] 33-22249
1. Moravian Church — Hist. I. Title.

GREENFIELD, John, 1865- 284'.6
When the spirit came; the story of the Moravian revival of 1727. Minneapolis, Bethany Fellowship [1967] 94 p. 19 cm. First published in 1928 under title: Power from on high. [BX8565.G8 1967] 67-6387
1. Moravian Church—History. I. Title.

HAMILTON, John Taylor, 1859- 284'.6
A history of the church known as the Moravian Church, or the Unitas Fratrum, or the Unity of the Brethren, during the eighteenth and nineteenth centuries. Bethlehem, Pa., Times Pub. Co., Printers, 1900. [New York, AMS Press, 1971] xi, 631 p. illus. 22 cm. Title on spine: A history of the Moravian church. Bibliography: p. [v]-viii. [BX8565.H3 1971] 70-134379 ISBN 0-404-08427-3 25.50
1. Moravian Church—History. I. Title. II. Title: A history of the Moravian Church.

HAMILTON, John Taylor, 1859- 284'.609
History of the Moravian Church; the renewed Unitas Fratrum, 1722-1957, by J. Taylor Hamilton and Kenneth G. Hamilton. Maps drawn by Fred Bees. [Bethlehem, Pa., Interprovincial Board of Christian Education, Moravian Church in America, 1967] 723 p. illus., maps, ports. 24 cm. First ed. published in 1900 under title: A history of the church known as the Moravian church. Bibliographical references included in "Notes" (p. 654-675) Bibliography: p. 676-679. [BX8565.H3 1967] 67-24086
1. Moravians—Church history. I. Hamilton, Kenneth Gardiner, 1893- joint author. II. Title.

LANGTON, Edward [Frederick Edward Palmer Langton] 1886- 284.609
History of the Moravian Church; the story of the first international Protestant church. London, Allen & Unwin. [dist. Mystic, Conn., Verry, 1964] 173p. ports. 23cm. Bibl. 56-2587 3.00
1. Moravian Church—Hist. I. Title.

HARDING, Barbara. 284'.6'0924 B
The boy, the man, and the Bishop; a biography of the Everyday Counselor, Bishop Herbert Spaugh. [Charlotte, N.C., Barnhardt Brothers, 1970] 178 p. illus., ports. 22 cm. [BX8593.S63H3] 79-20294
1. Spaugh, Herbert, 1896- I. Title.

FRIES, Adelaide Lisetta, 1871-1949. 284'.6'09758
The Moravians in Georgia, 1735-1940 Baltimore, Genealogical Pub. Co., 1967. 252 p. maps, ports. 24 cm. First published in 1905. [BX8567.G4F8 1967] 67-30756
1. Moravians in Georgia. I. Title.

FRIES, Adelaide Lisetta, 1871-1949. 284'.6'09758
The Moravians in Georgia, 1735-1740. Baltimore, Genealogical Pub. Co., 1967. 252 p. maps, ports. 24 cm. First published in 1905. [BX8567.G4F8] 67-30756
1. Moravians in Georgia. I. Title.

SESSLER, Jacob John, 1899- 284'.673
Communal pietism among early American Moravians. New York, H. Holt. [New York, AMS Press, 1971] 265 p. illus. 22 cm. Reprint of the 1933 ed. Thesis—Columbia University. Originally published as no. 8 of Studies in religion and culture. American religion series. Vita. Bibliography: p. 239-260. [BX8566.S4 1971] 70-134387 ISBN 0-404-08430-3 12.00
1. Moravian Church—History. 2. Congregation of God in the spirit. 3. Moravians in the United States. 4. Moravians in Pennsylvania. I. Title. II. Series: Studies in religion and culture. American religion series, 8

GOLLIN, Gillian Lindt. 284'.6748'22
Moravians in two worlds; a study of changing communities. New York, Columbia University Press, 1967. viii, 302 p. 24 cm. Bibliography: p. [273]-288. [BX8568.B4G6] 67-19653
1. Moravians in Pennsylvania. 2. Bethlehem, Pa.—History. 3. Herrnhut, Ger.—History. I. Title.

BETHLEHEM, Pa. Moravian Church. 284'.6'74827
The Bethlehem diary. Translated and edited by Kenneth G. Hamilton. Bethlehem, Pa.,

Archives of the Moravian Church, 1971- v. 24 cm. Begun in 1742 and written by successive members of the clergy, vols. 1-50 were originally written in German, vol. 51- are in English. The MS. is in the Archives of the Moravian Church in Bethlehem, Pa. [BX8566.B48] 70-179417
1. Moravian Church—U.S.—History—Sources. I. Hamilton, Kenneth Gardiner, 1893- ed. II. Title.

FRIES, Adelaide Lisetta, 1871-1949, ed 284.6756
Records of the Moravians in North Carolina, v.9, ed. by Minnie J. Smith. Raleigh, N.C., State Dept. of Archives and Hist., 1964. xii, 4372-5056p. illus., ports. facsims. 24cm. (Pubns. of the N.C. State Dept. of Archives) Contents.v.9. 1838-1847 23-27045 3.00
1. Moravians in North Carolina. I. Title. II. Series: North Carolina, State Dept. of Archives and History. Publications.

JAMES, Hunter. 284'.6756
The quiet people of the land : a story of the North Carolina Moravians in Revolutionary times / by Hunter James ; ill. by Jim Stanley. Chapel Hill : Published for Old Salem, inc., by the University of North Carolina Press, c1976. xvi, 156 p. : ill. ; 24 cm. (The Old Salem series) Includes index. Bibliography: p. 145-147. [BX8567.N8J35] 75-44042 ISBN 0-8078-1282-X : 7.95
1. Moravians in North Carolina. 2. North Carolina—Church history. I. Old Salem, inc., Winston-Salem, N.C. II. Title. III. Series.

REICHEL, Levin Theodore, 1812-1878. 284'.6756
The Moravians in North Carolina; an authentic history. Baltimore, Genealogical Pub. Co., 1968. iv, 206 p. 24 cm. Reprint of the 1857 ed. [F265.M8R3 1968] 68-19907
1. Moravians in North Carolina. 2. Wachovia, N.C.—History.

WARE, Charles Crossfield, 1886- 284.675667
Star in Wachovia; centennial history of the Christian Church Disciples of Christ, Pfafftown, N. C. Wilson, N. C., 1965. 151 p. illus., ports. 24 cm. [BX7331.P4C75] 66-2172
1. Pfafftown, N. C. Christian Church. I. Title.

OLSSON, Karl A 284.7
By one spirit. [1st ed.] Chicago, Covenant Press [c1962] 811 p. illus. 24 cm. [BX7547.A4O4] 63-1196
1. Evangelical Covenant Church of America — Hist. I. Title.

OLSSON, Karl A ed. 284.7
The Evangelical Convenant Church. Pt. 1: Swedish Convenanters, by David Nyvall. Pt. 2: The Convenant comes of age, by Karl A. Olsson. Chicago, Convenant Press [1954] 191p. 22cm. [BX7549.A4O4] 54-4772
1. Evangelical Mission Convenant Church of America—Hist. I. Nyvall, David, 1863- The Swedish Convenanters. II. Title.

PREUS, Johan Carl Keyser, 1881- ed. 284.7
Norsemen found a church; an old heritage in a new land. J. C. K. Preus, editor; T. F. Gullixson [and] E. C. Reinertson, associate editor [s] Minneapolis, Augsburg Pub. House [1953] x, 427p. maps (on lining papers) facsims. 22cm. 'Prepared on the occasion of the centennial of the founding of the Synod for the Norwegian Evangelical Lutheran Church in America. 1853-1953.' Bibliography: p. 419-427. [BX8052.P7] 53-3690
1. Synod for the Norwegian Evangelical Lutheran Church in America. I. Title.

AUGUSTANA annual. 284.773
Rock Island, Ill., Augustana Book Concern. v. illus., ports. 22 cm. Began publication with 1948 issue. "Yearbook of the Augustana Evangelical Lutheran Church." [BX8009.A8] 51-15936
1. Lutheran Church—Yearbooks. I. Augustana Evangelical Lutheran Church.

AUGUSTANA Evangelical Lutheran Church. 284.773
Report of the annual convention. [Rock Island, Ill.] v. illus., ports. 23 cm. Issued by the church under its earlier name: Evangelical Lutheran Augustana Synod of North America. Includes Minutes of Augustana Brotherhood coavention and Minutes of Woman's Missionary Society convention. [BX8049.A33] 50-27608
I. Title.

BJORKLUND, Clifford W 1921- 284.773
According to Thy Word; a confirmation study of Bible history, church history, and the Christian faith, by Clifford W. Bjorklund [and others] Issued under the auspices of the Board of Youth Work of the Vangelical Mission Covenant Church of America. Chicago, Covenant Press [1954] 439p. illus. 24cm. [BX7549.B5] 55-36415
1. Evangelical Mission Covenant Church of America. I. Title.

BRUCE, Gustav Marius, 1879- 284.773
Ten studies on the Lutheran Church. [Rev. ed.] Minneapolis, Augsburg Pub. House [1952] 104 p. 20 cm. (Ten-week teacher-training course books) [BX8065.B88 1952] 52-2277
1. Evangelical Lutheran Church. 2. Lutheran Church. I. Title.

JENSEN, John Martin, 1893- 284.773
The United Evangelical Lutheran Church, an interpretation, by John M. Jensen. Minneapolis, Augsburg Pub. House [1964] viii, 311 p. illus., ports. 23 cm. Bibliography: p. 296-300. [BX8058.J4] 64-21508
1. United Evangelical Lutheran Church. 2. Lutherans, Danish, in the U.S. I. Title.

JENSEN, John Martin, 1893- 284.773
The United Evangelical Lutheran Church, an interpretation. Minneapolis, Augsburg [c.1964] viii, 311p. illus., ports. 23cm. Bibl. 64-21508 6.50
1. United Evangelical Lutheran Church. 2. Lutherans, Danish, in the U.S. I. Title.

NELSON, E. Clifford 284.773
The Lutheran Church among Norwegian-Americans; a history of the Evangelical Lutheran Church by E. Clifford Nelson and Eugene L. Fevold. Minneapolis, Augsburg Pub. House [c.1960] 2 v. xix, 357p; xix, 379p. illus. 23cm. Includes bibliography. 60-6438 12.50, bxd.
1. Norwegians, Lutheran. 2. Norwegians in the U.S. 3. Evangelical Lutheran Church—Hist. I. Fevold, Eugene L., joint author. II. Title.

NELSON, E Clifford, 1911- 284.773
The Lutheran Church among Norwegian-Americans; a history of the Evangelical Lutheran Church by E. Clifford Nelson and Eugene L. Fevold. Minneapolis. Augsburg Pub. House [1960] 2v. illus. 23cm. Based on E. C. Nelson's 'doctoral dissertation. 'The union movement among Norwegian-American Lutherans, 1880-1917' (Yale University, 1952) ... and Eugene L. Fevold's Norwegian-American Lutheranism, 1870-1890' (Ph. D. dissertation, University of Chicago, 1951) Includes bibliography. [BX8050.N4] 60-6438
1. Norwegians, Lutheran. 2. Norwegians in the U. S. 3. Evangelical Lutheran Church—Hist. I. Fevold, Eugene L., joint author. II. Title.

NYHOLM, Paul C 1895- 284.773
The Americanization of the Danish Lutheran churches in America, a study in immigrant history. Copenhagen, Institute for Danish Church History, distributed by Augsburg Pub. House. Minneapolis [1963] 480 p. illus., ports., maps. 24 cm. (Studies in church history. ser. 2, no. 16) An abridgement of the author's dissertation. University of Chicago, 1952. Includes bibliographical references. [BX8056.N83] 62-19928
1. Lutherans, Danish, in the U.S. 2. Lutheran Church in the U.S. I. Title. II. Series: Copenhagen. Universitet. Institut for dansk kirkehistorie. Kirkehistoriske studier, ser. 2, no. 16

NYSTROM, Daniel, 1886- ed. 284.773
A family of God; echoes from the saga of the Augustana Lutheran Church—glimpses of its life and character as an immigrant church with a specific early task and as an American church sharing responsibility in the Christian mission to America and the world. Rock Island, Ill., Augustana [c.1962] 262p. illus. 62-12910 3.95
1. Augustana Evangelical Lutheran Church—Hist. I. Title.

OLSON, Oscar Nils, 1876- 284.773
The Augustana Lutheran Church in America. Rock Island, Ill., Augustana Book Concern [1950- v. illus. ports., facsims. 20 cm. "Published under the auspices of the Executive Council of the Augustana Lutheran Church." Contents.[1] Pioneer period, 1846-1860. Bibliography: v. 1, p. 382-391 [BX8049.O5] 50-11464
1. Augustana Evangelical Lutheran Church—Hist. I. Title.

PETERSON, John, 1870- 284.773
A biographical directory of pastors of the Evangelical Lutheran Church, compiled by John Peterson, Olaf Lysnes [and] Gerald Giving. Minneapolis, Augsburg Pub. House [1952] 651 p. ports. 24 cm. [BX8054.P4] 52-33803
1. Evangelical Lutheran Church — Clergy. 2. Lutheran Church — Biog. I. Title.

REIMERT, W. D 284.773
The first century, 1855-1955: St. John's Lutheran Church. Allentown, Pa. [1955] 86p. illus. 20cm. [BX8076.A35S35] 56-41918
1. Allentown, Pa. St. John's Evangelical Lutheran Church. I. Title.

WEST New York, N. J. St. John's Evangelical Lutheran Church. 284.773
Eighty years of history of St. John's Evangelical Lutheran Church of West New York, New Jersey, 1871-1951. [Compiled by Erwin Miller. West New York, 1951] unpaged. illus. 23cm. [BX8076.W38S3] 53-26462
I. Miller, Erwin, 1908- comp. II. Title.

BIEBER, Edmund Ellis, 1906- 284.7748
Springfield Church; a brief history of Trinity Evangelical Lutheran Church of Springfield Township, Bucks County, Pa., from 1751 to 1953. [Pleasant Valley, Pa.] Springfield Church Council [1953] 207p. illus. 22cm. [BX8076.S77B5] 53-29747
1. Trinity Evangelical Lutheran Church, Springfield Township, Bucks Co., Pa. I. Title.

ROCKFORD, Ill. First Lutheran Church. 284.776
Centennial, the First Evangelical Lutheran Church, 1854-1954. [Linden J. Lundstrom, author and editor] Rockford [1954] 182, [95]p. illus., ports. 28cm. [BX8076.R62F5] 54-30232
I. Lundstrom, Linden J. II. Title.

AUGUSTANA Evangelical Lutheran Church. Minnesota Conference. 284.7776
Protokoll, 1869-1878 [i. e. 1868-1879. Rock Island, Ill., 1951] 193 p. 28 cm. Cover title. Erratum slip mounted on p. [2] of cover. "Protokoll hallet vid Minnesota-konferensens extra sammantrade St. Paul, Minn. d. 30. maj-1. junl 1882": p. 187-193. [BX8049.1.M6A28] 51-39976
I. Title.

JOHNSON, Emeroy. 284.7776
God gave the growth; the story of the Lutheran Minnesota Conference, 1876-1958. Minneapolis, T. S. Denison [1958] 266p. illus. 24cm. [BX8049.IM6T6] 58-10162
1. Augustana Evangelical Lutheran Church. Minnesota Conference—Hist. I. Title.

LARSON, J Edor, 1885- 284.7776
History of the Red River Valley Conference of the Augustana Lutheran Church. [Warren? Minn.] Red River Valley Conference, 1953. 173p. illus. 23cm. [BX8049.1.R4L3] 54-17453
1. Augustana Evangelical Lutheran Church. Red River Valley Conference. I. Title.

DIRECTORY of independent Catholic churches : a unique collection of various clergy, churches, convents, monasteries, and other religious groups serving God and man through the media of the Holy Catholic & Orthodox churches throughout the world. 1st ed. San Francisco : Distributed by St. Procopius Orthodox Catholic Church, 1974. 54 p. ; 29 cm. Cover title: Official Catholic directory of independent Catholic churches. [BX4716.4.D57] 75-322015 284'.8
1. Independent Catholic churches—Directories. I. Title: Official Catholic directory of independent Catholic churches.

PIETRKIEWICZ, Jerzy. 284'.8 B
The third Adam / Jerzy Peterkiewicz. London : Oxford University Press, 1975. x, 243 p., [8] leaves of plates : ill. ; 24 cm. Includes index. Bibliography: p. [233]-234. [BX4795.M28K686] 76-350380 ISBN 0-19-212198-7 : 19.00
1. Kowalski, Jan Maria Michal, 1871-1942. 2. Mariavites. I. Title.
Distributed by Oxford University Press, N.Y.

ESCHOLIER, Marc, 1906- 284'.84
Port-Royal; the drama of the Jansenists. [1st American ed.] New York, Hawthorn Books [1968] 343 p. illus. 24 cm. Bibliography: p. 323-332. [BX4730.E67 1968] 68-19111
1. Port-Royal.

NEALE, John Mason, 1818-1866. 284'.84
A history of the so-called Jansenist Church of Holland; with a sketch of its earlier annals, and some account of the Brothers of the Common Life. Oxford, J. Henry and J. Parker, 1858. [New York, AMS Press, 1970] xii, 411 p. 24 cm. Includes bibliographical references. [BX4733.N4 1970] 71-133820 ISBN 0-404-04656-8
1. Kerkgenootschap der Oud-Bisschoppelijke Clerezie. 2. Brothers of the Common Life. I. Title.

CLARK, Ruth. 284'.84'0942
Strangers & sojourners at Port Royal; being an account of the connections between the British Isles and the Jansenists of France and Holland. New York, Octagon Books, 1972. xviii, 360 p. illus. 23 cm. Reprint of the 1932 ed. Bibliography: p. 278-304. [BX4730.C55 1972] 72-6953 ISBN 0-374-91664-0
1. Port Royal. 2. Jansenists. 3. Great Britain—Church history—Modern period, 1485- 4. Jansenists—Bibliography. I. Title.

APOSTOLIC Faith Mission. 284.9
A historical account of the Apostolic Faith, a Trinitarian-fundamental evangelistic organization: its origin, functions, doctrinal heritage, and departmental activities of evangelism. Portland, Or. [Apostolic Faith Pub. House, 1965] 315 p. illus., ports. 23 cm. Includes hymns with music. "Memoir album" (p. [305]-315) blank for historical notations, etc. [BX6194.A7A17] 66-45475
1. Apostolic Faith Mission. I. Title.

MCCULLOH, Gerald O., ed. 284.9
Man's faith and freedom; the theological influence of Jacobus Arminius. Nashville, Abingdon [c.1962] 128p. 20cm. Contains the addresses delivered in the Arminius symposium held at Amsterdam, Leiden, and Utrecht, in Holland, August 4-7, 1960. Bibl. 62-10414 2.50
1. Arminius, Jacobus, 1560-1609. 2. Arminianism. I. Title.

BANGS, Carl Oliver, 1922- 284'.9'0924 B
Arminius; a study in the Dutch Reformation [by] Carl Bangs. Nashville, Abingdon Press [1971] 382 p. illus. 24 cm. Bibliography: p. 361-368. [BX6196.B28] 78-148078 ISBN 0-687-01744-0 9.95
1. Arminius, Jacobus, 1560-1609. I. Title.

285 Presbyterian & Related Churches

DAVIES, Alfred Mervyn 285
Presbyterian heritage. Richmond, Va., Knox [c.1965] 141p. 21cm. [BX8931.2.D3] 65-10136 1.95 pap.,
1. Presbyterian Church—Hist. I. Title.

HANKO, Charles William, 1920- 285
The Evangelical Protestant movement. Brooklyn, Educators Pub. Co., 1955. 84p. 23cm. [BX7850.H3] 55-43026
1. Evangelical Protestant Church of North America. 2. Lutheran Church—Relations—Reformed Church. 3. Reformed Church—Relations—Lutheran Church. I. Title.

HOUGH, H D 1922- 285
Churchmanship, a primer for Presbyterian churchmen. Charleroi, Pa., Courier and digest [1955] 105p. illus. 21cm. [BX9190.H66] 56-19292
1. Presbyterian Church—Government. I. Title.

LINGLE, Walter Lee, 1868- 285
Presbyterians, their history and beliefs. [Rev. ed.] Rev. by T. Watson Street. Richmond, John Knox Press [c1960] 128p. 24 cm. [BX8931.L5 1960] 60-16432
1. Presbyterianism. 2. Presbyterianism—Hist. I. Title.

MACKAY, John Alexander, 1889- 285
The Presbyterian way of life. Englewood Cliffs, N. J., Prentice-Hall [1960] 238p. 21cm. [BX9175.2.M3] 60-14198
1. Presbyterianism. I. Title.

MCNEILL, John Thomas, 1885- 285
Ecumenical testimony; the concern for Christian unity within the Reformed and Presbyterian churches, by John T. McNeill and James Hastings Nichols. Philadelphia, Westminster Press [1974] 320 p. 24 cm. Includes bibliographical references. [BX8.2.M323] 74-977 ISBN 0-664-20998-X 10.00
1. Christian union—Reformed Church. 2. Christian union—Presbyterian Church. I. Nichols, James Hastings, 1915- II. Title.

SLOSSER, Galus Jackson, 1887- ed. 285
They seek a country; the American Presbyterians, some aspects. Contributors: Frank H. Caldwell [and others] New York, Macmillan, 1955. xvi, 330 p. illus., ports. 22 cm. Bibliography: p. 322-324. [BX8935.S55] 55-14554
1. Presbyterian Church in the U.S. (General)—History. I. Title.

*MILLER, Basil 285.00924 (B)
Charles G. Finney; official biography for the Finney Sesquicentennial Conference Chicago 1942. Minneapolis, Bethany Fellowship [1966, c.1941] 137p. 19cm. (BF 150) 1.50 pap.,
I. Title.

HENDERSON, George David, 1888- 285.09
Presbyterianism. Aberdeen, University Press [1955] 179p. 23cm. (Chalmers lectures) [BX8931.H4] 55-4298
1. Presbyterian Church—Hist. 2. Presbyterianism. I. Title.

LOETSCHER, Lefferts 285.09
Augustine, 1904-
A brief history of the Presbyterians. Rev. and enl. Philadelphia, Westminster Press [1958] 125p. 20cm. [BX8932.L6 1958] 58-5963
1. Presbyterian Church— Hist. I. Title.

*BALDWIN, Ethel May 285.0924
Henrietta Mears and how she did it. Glendale, Calif., 91205. 725 E. Colorado, Box 1591 Gospel Lights Pubns. c.1966 91205, Gospel Light Pubns. [725 E. Colorado, Box 1591, c.1966] 190p. photogs. 18cm. (Regal bks., G195-9) .95 pap.,
I. Title.

SPALDING, Samuel 285'.092'4
Charles, 1878-
I've had me a time! With autobiographical sketch, selected poems, and sermons. Great Barrington, Mass., Friends of Gould Farm, 1961. 72 p. port. 21 cm. "Limited edition of not more than one thousand copies, the first two hundred and fifty of which, at least, are to be numbered and autographed ... no. [C30]" [BX9225.S63A3] 285'.2'0924 78-230256
I. Title.

TROSSE, George, 285'.092'4 B
1631-1713.
The life of the Reverend Mr. George Trosse, written by himself, and published posthumously according to his Order in 1714. Edited by A. W. Brink. Montreal, McGill-Queen's University Press, 1974. xi, 140 p. port. 23 cm. Includes bibliographical references. [BX5207.T75A33 1974] 73-79097 ISBN 0-7735-0153-3 9.75
1. Trosse, George, 1631-1713. I. Brink, A. W., ed. II. Title.
Distributed by McGill Queens University Press, New York.

PRESBYTERIAN Church 285'.09713'52
in Canada. Presbyteries. Hamilton, Ont.
The Presbytery of Hamilton, 1836-1967. Hamilton, Ont., 1967. 148 p. illus., map, plates, ports. 28 cm. Cover title. [BX9003.H3P7] 71-460079 1.00
1. Presbyterian Church in Canada. Presbyteries. Hamilton, Ont. I. Title.

MURRAY, Andrew E. 285.0973
Presbyterians and the Negro; a history, by Andrew E. Murray. Philadelphia, Presbyterian Hist. Soc. 1966. xiv, 270p. 24cm. (Presbyterian Hist. Soc. pubns., 7) Bibl. [BX8946. N4M8] 67-20 6.00
1. Prsbyterians. Negro. 2. Church and race problems—U. S. I. Title. II. Series: Presbyterian Historical Scoiety. Publications, 7
Publisher's address: 520 Withrspoon Bldg., Phila., Pa., 19107.

GARRISON, Pinkney J 1906- 285.1
Presyterian policy and procedures: the Presbyterian Church, U. S. Richmond, John Knox Press [1953] 190p. 25cm. [BX8966.G37] 53-11602
1. Presbyterian Church in the U.S.—Government. I. Title.

KING, Ray A. 285.1
A history of the Associate Reformed Presbyterian Church [by] Ray A. King. Charlotte, N.C., Board of Christian Education of the Associate Reformed Presbyterian Church [1966] viii, 132 p. 22 cm. (The Covenant life curriculum) Bibliography: p. 126-130. [BX8999.A82K5] 67-996
1. Associate Reformed Presbyterian Church—History. I. Title.

MILLER, Park Hays, 1879- 285.1
Why I am a Presbyterian. New York, T. Nelson [1956] 200 p. 21 cm. [BX9175.M5] 56-12396
1. Presbyterian Church. I. Title.

UNITED Presbyterian Church 285.1
in the U.S.A.
Presbyterian law for the local church; a handbook for church officers and members. Edited by Eugene Carson Blake. Rev. Philadelphia, 1963. 141 p. 22 cm. [BX8956.A6 1963] 262.05'132 68-2705
1. United Presbyterian Church in the U.S.A.—Government. I. Blake, Eugene Carson, 1906- ed. II. Title.

BATES, Lucille M. 285'.1'0924 B
Walter McGill; preacher and penman, by Lucille M. Bates. San Antonio, Tex., Naylor Co. [1971] xv, 110 p. illus., maps, ports. 22 cm. [BX9225.M217B38] 70-152303 ISBN 0-8111-0402-8 5.95
1. McGill, Walter Marshall.

CAMPBELL, Olive 285'.1'0924 B
Arnold (Dame) 1882-1954.
The life and work of John Charles Campbell, September 15, 1868-May 2, 1919. [Madison, Wis., Printed by College Printing & Typing Co., 1968] viii, 657 p. map. 28 cm. [BX9225.C28C3] 68-6039
1. Campbell, John Charles, 1867-1919. I. Title.

DAVIDS, Richard C. 285'.1'0924 B
The man who moved a mountain, by Richard C. Davids. Philadelphia, Fortress Press [1970] xii, 253 p. illus., ports. 23 cm. [BX9225.C526D36] 75-99609 5.95
1. Childress, Robert W., 1890-1956. 2. Missions—Blue Ridge Mountains, Virginia. I. Title.

DIEHL, George West. 285'.1'0924 B
The Rev. Samuel Houston, V.D.M. [Verona, Va., McClure Press, 1970.] 123 p. illus., map, port. 24 cm. Includes bibliographical references. [BX9225.H75D5] 70-133502 5.95
1. Houston, Samuel, 1758-1839.

DRURY, Clifford 285'.10924 (B)
Merrill, 1897-
William Anderson Scott, "no ordinary man." Glendale, Calif., A. H. Clark Co., 1967. 352 p. illus., ports. 25 cm. Bibliography: p. [344]-345. [BX9225.S34D7] 67-22431
1. Scott, William Anderson, 1813-1885. I. Title.

DRURY, Clifford 285'.10924 B
Merrill, 1897-
William Anderson Scott, "no ordinary man." Glendale, Calif., H. Clark Co. 1967. 352 p. illus. ports. 25 cm. Bibliography: p. [344]-345. [BX9225.S34D7] 67-22431
1. Scott, William Anderson, 1813-1885.

HATCH, Carl E. 285'.1'0924 B
The Charles A. Briggs heresy trial; prologue to twentieth-century liberal protestantism [by] Carl E. Hatch. [1st ed.] New York, Exposition Press [1969] 139 p. 22 cm. (An Exposition-university book) Bibliography: p. [133]-139. [BX9193.B7H37] 70-98955 6.00
1. Briggs, Charles Augustine, 1841-1913. 2. Trials (Heresy)—U.S. I. Title.

HODGE, Archibald 285'.1'0924 B
Alexander, 1823-1886.
The life of Charles Hodge [by] Alexander A. Hodge. New York, Arno Press, 1969. viii, 620 p. port. 23 cm. (Religion in America) Reprint of the 1881 ed. With selections from the reminiscences, letters, and writings of Charles Hodge. [BX9225.H6H6 1969] 71-83425
1. Hodge, Charles, 1797-1878. I. Hodge, Charles, 1797-1878.

PALMER, Benjamin 285'.1'0924 B
Morgan, 1818-1902.
The life and letters of James Henley Thornwell. New York, Arno Press, 1969. xi, 614 p. port. 23 cm. (Religion in America) Reprint of the 1875 ed. [BX9225.T64P3 1969] 78-83432
1. Thornwell, James Henley, 1812-1862. I. Thornwell, James Henley, 1812-1862. II. Title.

PILCHER, George 285'.1'0924 B
William.
Samuel Davies; apostle of dissent in colonial Virginia. [1st ed.] Knoxville, University of Tennessee Press [1971] xi, 229 p. map, port. 24 cm. Bibliography: p. 196-214. [BX9225.D33P55] 77-134737 ISBN 0-87049-121-0 9.75
1. Davies, Samuel, 1723-1761.

POWELL, Robert 285'.1'0924 B
Charles.
Anton T. Boisen, 1876-1965 : breaking an opening in the wall between religion and medicine / by Robert Charles Powell. [Buffalo?] : Association of Mental Health Clergy, c1976. 47 p. : ports. ; 23 cm. "A special supplement to the AMHC forum, vol. 29, no. 1, October 1976." Bibliography: p. 38-46. [BX9225.B568P68] 76-151903
1. Boisen, Anton Theophilus, 1876-1975. 2. Presbyterian Church—Clergy—Biography. 3. Chaplains, Hospital—United States—Biography. 4. Clergy—United States—Biography. I. Association of Mental Health Clergy. AMHC forum. II. Title.

STREET, T Watson. 285.10973
The story of southern Presbyterians. Richmond, John Knox Press [1960] 134 p. illus. 21 cm. Includes bibliography. [BX8962.S75] 60-11623
1. Presbyterian Church in the U.S. — Hist. I. Title.

STREET, T. Watson 285.10973
The story of southern Presbyterians. Richmond, Va., John Knox Press [c.1960] 134p. illus. 21cm. Bibl. and bibl. notes: p.128-134. 60-11623 1.50 pap.,
1. Presbyterian Church in the U.S.—Hist. I. Title.

BELFOUR, Stanton. 285.10974886
Centennial history of the Shadyside Presbyterian Church. Pittsburgh [1966] xii, 154 p. illus., ports. 24 cm. Bibliography: p. 153. [BX9211.P6S53] 66-9034
1. Pittsburgh. Shadyside Presbyterian Church. I. Title.

BROCKMANN, Charles 285.10975676
Raven, 1888-
Mecklenburg Presbytery, a history. Photos. by Bruce Roberts. Charlotte, N.C., Office of the Executive Secretary. Mecklenburg Presbytery, 1962. 148 p. illus. 32 cm. [BX8968.M4B7] 63-990
1. Presbyterian Church in the U.S. Presbyteries. Mecklenburg. I. Title.

BROCKMANN, Charles 285.10975676
Raven, 1888-
Mecklenburg Presbytery, a history Photos. by Bruce Roberts. Mecklenburg Presbytery [dist. Charlotte, N.C., McNally, & Loftin, c.]1962. 148p. 32cm. Bibl. 63-900 5.00
1. Presbyterian Church in the U.S. Presbyteries. Mecklenburg. I. Title.

WHITE, William 285'.1'0975743
Boyce, 1929-
History of the First Presbyterian Church of Rock Hill, South Carolina, 1869-1969, by William Boyce White, Jr. [Richmond] Printed by order of the Session in commemoration of the centenary of the church [by Whittet & Shepperson] 1969. 134 p. illus., ports. 24 cm. Bibliographical references included in "Notes" (p. 131-134) [BX9211.R64F57] 73-96802
1. Rock Hill, S.C. First Presbyterian Church. I. Title.

FRY, John R. 285'.131
The trivialization of the United Presbyterian Church / John R. Fry. 1st ed. New York : Harper & Row, [1975] x, 85 p. ; 21 cm. Includes bibliographical references. [BX8955.F79 1975] 75-9319 ISBN 0-06-063074-4 : 5.95
1. United Presbyterian Church—Doctrinal and controversial works. I. Title.

HOW in the world. 285'.131
[Edited by Earl K. Larson, Jr. Philadelphia, 1966?] 283 p. illus., ports. 26 cm. "Compiled under the 177th General Assembly's call to Renewal and Extension of the Church's Ministry in the World for the study and understanding of the whole work of the United Presbyterian Church in the United States of America for 1965-1966." [BX8955.H68] 70-19337
1. United Presbyterian Church in the U.S.A. I. Larson, Earl K., ed.

MCINTIRE, Carl, 1906- 285'.131
The death of a church. Collingswood, N.J., Christian Beacon Press [1967] viii, 215 p. 18 cm. "The Confession of 1967": p. 179-195. [BX8955.M3] 78-14671
1. United Presbyterian Church in the U.S.A. Confession of 1967. 2. United Presbyterian Church in the U.S.A.—Doctrinal and controversial works. I. United Presbyterian Church in the U.S.A. Confession of 1967. 1967. II. Title.

PRESBYTERIAN Church in 285'.131
the U. S. A. Board of Christian Education.
Report. Philadelphia. v. 24cm. annual. sPresbyterian Church in the U. S. A.--Education. [BX8950.A28] 57-52819
I. Title.

PRESBYTERIAN Church in 285'.131
the U. S. A. Board of Christian Education.
Report. Philadelphia. v. 24cm. annual. [BX8950.A28] 57-52819
1. Presbyterian Church in the U. S. A.—Education. I. Title.

SHANNON, Foster H., 285'.131
1930-
The growth crisis in the American church : a Presbyterian case study / Foster H. Shannon. South Pasadena, Calif. : William Carey Library, c1977. xv, 159 p. : ill. ; 22 cm. Includes index. Bibliography: p. [151]-155. [BR517.S38] 76-51359 ISBN 0-87808-152-6 pbk. : 4.95
1. United Presbyterian Church in the U.S.A. 2. Church growth—United States—Case studies. I. Title.

UNITED Presbyterian 285'.131
Church in the U.S.A. General Assembly. Special Committee on Church Membership Trends.
Membership trends in the United Presbyterian Church in the U.S.A. ; research report / prepared by Special Committee of the General Assembly Mission Council to Study Church Membership Trends ; chairperson, C. Edward Brubaker .... [New York?] : The Assembly, c1976. xiv, 315 p. : ill. ; 28 cm. [BX8950.U56 1976] 76-370965 5.00
1. United Presbyterian Church in the U.S.A.—Membership—Statistics. I. Brubaker, Charles Edward, 1917- II. Title.

SMITH, Wilbur 285'.131'0924 B
Moorehead, 1894-
Before I forget, by Wilbur M. Smith. Chicago, Moody Press [1971] 304 p. 24 cm. Autobiographical. [BR1725.S552A3] 79-155684 5.95
I. Title.

BRACKENRIDGE, R. 285'.131'09764
Douglas.
Voice in the wilderness; a history of the Cumberland Presbyterian Church in Texas, by R. Douglas Brackenridge. With introd. by Thomas H. Campbell. San Antonio, Trinity University Press [1968] xi, 192 p. illus. 24 cm. Bibliography: p. [178]-182. [BX8973.T4B7] 68-20136
1. Cumberland Presbyterian Church in Texas. I. Title.

PRESBYTERIAN Church in 285'.132
the U.S.A.
Records of the Presbyterian Church in the United States of America, 1706-1788. New York, Arno Press, 1969. 582 p. 24 cm. (Religion in America) Reprint of the 1904 ed. [BX8952.P73 1969] 75-83434
1. Presbyterian Church in the U.S.A.—History.

SPRINKLE, Patricia 285'.132
Houck.
The birthday book; first fifty years. Atlanta, Board of Women's Work, Presbyterian Church in the United States, 1972. xii, 296 p. illus. 23 cm. Includes bibliographical references. [BX8960.S67] 72-191652
1. Presbyterian Church in the U.S. Woman's Auxiliary. 2. Presbyterian Church in the U.S. Board of Women's Work. I. Title.

PRESBYTERIAN 285'.133'02573
Church in the U. S.
Ministerial directory of the Presbyterian Church, U. S., 1861-1967. Compiled by E. D. Witherspoon, Jr. Published by order of the General Assembly. Doraville, Ga., Foote & Davies, 1967. vii, 648 p. 24 cm. Supplements Ministerial directory of 1941 and of 1951. Bibliography: p. 648. [BX9220.P7] 68-3645
1. Presbyterian Church—Biog. 2. Presbyterian Church in the U.S.—Biog. I. Witherspoon, Eugene Daniel, 1932- II. Title.

PRESBYTERIAN 285'.133'02573
Church in the U.S.
Ministerial directory of the Presbyterian Church, U.S., 1861-1967. Compiled by E. D. Witherspoon, Jr. Published by order of the General Assembly. Doraville, Ga., Foote & Davies, 1967. vii, 648 p. 24 cm. Supplements Ministerial directory of 1941 and of 1951. Bibliography: p. 648. [BX9220.P7 1967] 68-3645
1. Presbyterian Church—Biography. 2. Presbyterian Church in the U.S.—Biography. I. Witherspoon, Eugene Daniel, 1932- II. Title.

CAMPBELL, Thomas H. 285.13509
Good news on the frontier; a history of the Cumberland Presbyterian Church. Memphis, Frontier Pr. [1965] 172p. 21cm. (Convent life curriculum) Bibl. [BX8972.C29] 65-6577 1.25
1. Cumberland Presbyterian Church. I. Title.

BARRUS, Ben M. 285'.135'0973
A people called Cumberland Presbyterians [by] Ben M. Barrus, Milton L. Baughn [and] Thomas H. Campbell. Foreword by C. Ray Dobbins. Introd. and chapter 16 by Hubert W. Morrow. [1st ed.] Memphis, Tenn., Frontier Press [1972] xiii, 625 p. illus. 24 cm. Bibliography: p. 573-600. [BX8972.B37] 72-78012 10.00
1. Cumberland Presbyterian Church—History. I. Baughn, Milton L., joint author. II. Campbell, Thomas H., joint author. III. Title.

HATLEY, Roy O. 285'.14764'351
A ninety-year record of Madison Square Presbyterian Church: 1882-1972. Compiled by Mr. and Mrs. Roy O. Hatley. Church Editing Committee: Marg-Riette Hamlett [and others. Special ed. San Antonio, Tex., Printed by Munguia Printers, 1972] 248 p. illus. 24 cm. [BX9211.S37M334] 72-181179
1. San Antonio. Madison Square Presbyterian Church. I. Hatley, Roy O., Mrs., joint author. II. Title.

ARMSTRONG, Maurice 285.173
Whitman, 1905- ed.
The Presbyterian enterprise; sources of American Presbyterian history, edited by Maurice W. Armstrong, Lefferts A. Loetscher [and] Charles A. Anderson. Philadelphia, Westminster Press [1956] 336p. 24cm. Bibliography: p. 323-328. [BX8935.A7] 56-7368
1. Presbyterian Church in the U. S. (General)—Hist. I. Title.

ARMSTRONG, Maurice 285.173
Whitman, 1905- ed.
The Presbyterian enterprise; sources of American Presbyterian history, edited by

Maurice W. Armstrong, Lefferts A. Loetscher [and] Charles A. Anderson. Philadelphia, Westminster Press [1956] 336p. 24cm. Bibliography: p. 323-328. [BX8935.A7] 56-7368
1. Presbyterian Church in the U. S. (General)—Hist. I. Title.

DAYTON, Charles Henry, 1892- 285.173
A brief history of the Presbytery of Geneva and a tribute to some early ministers, by Charles H. Dayton and John Garth Coleman. Sesquicentennial of the Presbytery of Geneva, 1805-1955. [Shortsville? N. Y.] Geneva-Lyons c67p. illus. 28cm. On cover: Growth of the church on the 'Northwestern Frontier.' [BX8958.G4D3] 55-32281
1. Presbyterian Church in the U. S. A. Presbyteries. Geneva-lyons. I. Coleman, John Garth, joint author. II. Title. III. Title: Growth of the church on the 'Northwestern Frontier.'

LAKE, Benjamin J 285.173
The story of the Presbyterian Church in the U. S. A. Philadelphia, Westminster Press [1956] 126p. 19cm. [BX8952.L3] 56-7367
1. Presbyterian Church in the U. S. A.—Hist. I. Title.

LAKE, Benjamin J 285.173
The story of the Presbyterian Church in the U.S.A. Philadelphia, Westminster Press [1956] 126p. 19cm. Presbyterian Church in the U.S.A.--Hist. [BX8952.L3] 56-7367
I. Title.

LEXINGTON, Va. Lexington Presbyterian Church. 285.173
A handbook for Presbyterians, prepared by the officers of the Lexington Presbyterian Church, Lexington, Va., Edwin G. Adair [and others] Richmond, John Knox Press [1951] 100 p. illus. 21 cm. [BX8962.L4] 51-7680
1. Presbyterian Church in the U. S. 2. Presbyterianism. I. Title.

LEXINGTON, Va. Lexington Presbyterian Church. 285.173
A handbook for Presbyterians, Prepared by the officers of the Lexington Presbyterian Church, Lexington, Virginia. Ed in G. Adair and other. 11th print. rev. Richmond, Va., John Knox Press [1963, c1951] 109 p. illus., maps. 21 cm. [BX8965.L4] 63-22504
1. Presbyterian Church in the U.S. 2. Presbyterianism. I. Title.

LOETSCHER, Lefferts Augustine, 1904- 285.173
The broadening Church; a study of theological issues in the Presbyterian Church since 1869. Philadelphia, University of Pennsylvania Press, 1954. 195p. 24cm. Includes bibliographical references. [BX8952.L6] 54-7110
1. Presbyterian Church in the U. S. A.—Hist. I. Title. II. Title: Theological issues in the Presbyterian Church since 1869.

MARSDEN, George M., 1939- 285'.173
The evangelical mind and the new school Presbyterian experience; a case study of thought and theology in nineteenth-century America [by] George M. Marsden. New Haven, Yale University Press, 1970. xiii, 278 p. 23 cm. (Yale publications in American studies, 20) Bibliography: p. [256]-264. [BX8937.M37] 75-118731 ISBN 0-300-01343-4 10.00
1. Presbyterian Church in the U.S.A. (New school) 2. Evangelicalism—United States. I. Title. II. Series.

PRESBYTERIAN Church in the U. S. A. 285.173
The Constitution of the Presbyterian Church in the United States of America, being its standards subordinate to the Word of God; viz., the Confession of faith, the Larger and Shorter catechisms, the Form of government, the Book of discipline, and the Directory for the worship of God, as ratified and adopted by the Synod of New York and philadelphia in the year of Our Lord 1788 and as amended, together with the general rules for judicatories. [Rev. ed.] Philadelphia, Published for the Office of the General Assembly by the Board of Christian Education of the Presbyterian Church in the U. S. A. [1956] ix, 457p. 26cm. [BX8955.A3 1956a] 56-10495
1. Presbyterian Church in the U. S. A.—Doctrinal and controversial works. 2. Presbyterian Church in the U. S. A.—Discipline. 3. Presbyterian Church in the U. S. A.—Catechisms and creeds. I. Title.

PRESBYTERIAN Church in the U. S. A. 285.173
Presbyterian law for the local church; a handbook for church officers and members, edited by Eugene Carson Blake. 4th ed. rev. [Philadelphia] Published for the Office of the General Assembly by the Division of Publication of the Board of Christian Education of the Presbyterian Church in the United States of America, 1957. 129p. 20cm. [BX8956.A6 1957] 57-11181
1. Presbyterian Church in the U. S. A.—Government. I. Blake, Eugene Carson, 1906- ed. II. Title.

PRESBYTERIAN Church in the U. S. A. 285.173
Presbyterian law for the local church; a handbook for church officers and members. Edited by Eugene Carson Blake. 3d ed., rev. [Philadelphia] Published for the Office of the General Assembly by the Division of Publication of the Board of Christian Education of the Presbyterian Church in the United States of America, 1956. 129p. 20cm. [BX8956.A6 1956] 56-10494
1. Presbyterian Church in the U. S. A.—Government. I. Blake, Eugene Carson, 1906- ed. II. Title.

PRESBYTERIAN Church in the U. S. Board of Church Extension. 285.173
Building the church. Edited by Patrick D. Miller, executive secretary. Atlanta, Dickson [1958] 93p. illus. 21cm. Includes bibliography. [BX8962.A4] 58-44411
1. Presbyterian Church in the U. S.—Hist. I. Title.

SPENCE, Thomas Hugh, 1889- 285.173
The Historical Foundation and its treasures. Rev. ed. Montrent, N.C., Historical Foundations Publications, 1960. 171 p. illus. 24 cm. Includes bibliography. [BX8905.H5S63 1960] 60-15691
1. Historical Foundation of the Presbyterian and Reformed Churches. I. Title.

SWEET, Willia, Warren, 1881-1959, ed. 285.173
The Presbyterians, a collection of source materials. New York, Cooper Square Publishers, 1964 [c1936] xii, 939 p. maps. 22 cm. (His Religions on the American frontier, 1783-1840, v. 2) Bibliography: p. 888-917. [BX8935.S75 1964] 65-1622
1. Presbyterian Church in the U.S. (General) — Hist. — Sources. 2. Presbyterian Church in the U.S. (General) — Hist. 3. Frontier and pioneer life — U.S. I. Title.

THOMPSON, Ernest Trice, 1894- 285.173
Tomorrow's church; tomorrow's world. Richmond, John Knox Press [1960] 128 p. 21 cm. Includes bibliography. [BX8965.T5] 60-15825
1. Presbyterian Church in the United States. I. Title.

THOMPSON, Ernest Trice, 1894- 285.173
Tomorrow's church; tomorrow's world. Richmond, Va. John Knox Press [c.1960] 128p. 21cm. Bibl.: p.[125]-128. 60-15825 1.50 pap.,
1. Presbyterian Church in the United States. I. Title.

TRINTERUD, Leonard J., 1904- 285'.173
The forming of an American tradition; a re-examination of colonial Presbyterianism [by] Leonard J. Trinterud. Freeport, N.Y., Books for Libraries Press [1970, c1949] 352 p. 24 cm. Bibliography: p. [309]-320. [BX8936.T7 1970] 78-124262
1. Presbyterian Church in the U.S. (General)—History I. Title.

UNITED Presbyterian Church in the U.S.A. 285.173
Presbyterian law for the local church; a handbook for church officers and members, edited by Eugene Carson Blake. 6th ed., rev. [Philadelphia] Published for the Office of the General Assembly by the General Division of Publication of the Board of Christian Education of the United Presbyterian Church in the U. S. A. [dist. Westminster Press] 1960 [c.1953-1960] 144p. 20cm. 60-3669 1.50 bds.,
1. United Presbyterian Church in the U. S. A.—Government. I. Blake, Eugene Carson. II. Title.

UNITED Presbyterian Church in the U.S.A. 285.173
Presbyterian law for the local church; a handbook for church officers and members, edited by Eugene Carson Blake. 6th ed., rev. [Philadelphia] Published for the Office of the General Assembly by the General Divison of Publication of the Board of Christian Education of the United Presbyterian Church in the U.S.A., 1960. 144 p. 20 cm. [BX8956.A6 1960] 60-3669
1. United Presbyterian Church in the U.S.A. — Government. I. Blake, Eugene Carson, 1906- ed. II. Title.

UNITED Presbyterian Church of North America. 285.173
The confessional statement and The book of government and worship. [Pittsburgh, Board of Christian Education of the United Presbyterian Church of North America, 1951] 195 p. 16 cm. Cover title. In 2 pts., each with special t.p. [BX8985.A3] 51-26517
1. United Presbyterian Church of North America — Catechisms and creeds. 2. United Presbyterian Church of North America — Government. I. Title.

BOYD, George Adams. 285.1747
Centennial history of the Webb Horton Memorial Presbyterian Church. Middletwn, N. Y., Session of the Church, 1954. 170p. illus. 24cm. [BX9211.M53W4] 54-37269
1. Middletown, N. Y. Webb Horton Memorial Presbyterian Church. I. Title.

MCKAY, Ellen Cotton. 285.1747
A history of the Rye Presbyterian Church; a documentary story of Presbyterianism in Rye. New York, from the date of its settlement in 1660 until the present time. Rye, N. Y., Presbyterian Church [1957] 260p. illus. 24cm. Includes bibliography. [BX9211.R9R9] 57-45930
1. Rye. N. Y. Rye Presbyterian Church. I. Title.

MCKAY, Ellen Cotton. 285.1747
A history of the Rye Presbyterian Church; a documentary story of presbyterianism in. rye, new york, from the date of its settlement in 1660 until the present time. Rye, N. Y., Presbyterian Church [1957] 260p. illus: 24cm. Includes bibliography. [BX9211.R9R9] 57-45930
1. Rye, N. Y. Rye Presbyterian Church. I. Title.

NICHOLS, Robert Hastings, 1873-1955. 285.1747
Presbyterianism in New York State; a history of the Synod and its predecessors. Edited and completed by James Hastings Nichols. Philadelphia, Published for the Presbyterian Historical Society by Westminister Press [1963] 288 p. 21 cm. (Presbyterian Historical Society. Studies in Presbyterian history) Includes bibliography. [BX8957.N7N5] 63-8820
1. Presbyterian Church in the U.S.A. Synods. New York. 2. United Presbyterian Church in the U.S.A. Synods. New York. 3. Presbyterian Church in New York. I. Nichols, James Hastings, 1915- II. Title.

NICHOLS, Robert Hastings, 1873-1955. 285.1747
Presbyterianism in New York State; a history of the Synod and its predecessors. Ed., completed by James Hastings Nichols. Philadelphia, Pub. for Presbyterian Historical Soc. by Westminster [c.1963] 288p. 21cm. (Presbyterian Historical Soc. Studies in Presbyterian hist.) Bibl. 63-8820 4.00
1. Presbyterian Church in the U.S.A. Synods. New York. 2. United Presbyterian Church in the U.S.A. Synods. New York. 3. Presbyterian Church in New York. I. Nichols, James Hastings, 1915- II. Title.

HALL, Basil Douglas. 285.17471
The life of Charles Cuthbert Hall: "One among a thousand." With tributes by Harry Emerson and Henry Sloane Coffin. New York, Carlton Press [1965] 280 p. port. 21 cm. (A Reflection book) "Books written by Charles Cuthbert Hall": p. 263-264. [BX9225.H25H3] 66-7159
1. Hall, Charles Cuthbert, 1852-1908. I. Title.

NEW York. Fifth Avenue Presbyterian Church. 285.17471
A noble landmark of New York; the Fifth Avenue Presbyterian Church. 1808-1958. New York, 1960. 174p. illus. 23cm. [BX9211.N5FIS] 60-9133
I. Title.

MEHALICK, J. Richard. 285'.1747'25
Church and community, 1675-1975 : the story of the First Presbyterian Church of Smithtown, New York / J. Richard Mehalick. 1st ed. Hicksville, N.Y. : Exposition Press, c1976. 151 p. : ill. ; 24 cm. Bibliography: p. 149-150. [BX9211.S67F575] 76-355016
1. Smithtown Branch, N.Y. First Presbyterian Church of Smithtown. I. Title.

LEE, Arthur C. 285'.1747'277
History of the First Presbyterian Church of Yorktown from 1906 to 1975 / by Arthur C. Lee. [s.l. : s.n.], c1976 ([Yorktown Heights, N.Y. : Mohansic Press]) 75 p. : ill. ; 22 cm. [BX9211.Y66F574] 76-368308
1. First Presbyterian Church of Yorktown. 2. Yorktown, N.Y.—Biography.

SMITH, Catherine Ruth, 1906- 285.1747277
These years of grace; the history of Westminster Presbyterian Church, Yonkers, New York, 1858-1964. Yonkers, N.Y., First Westminster Presbyterian Church, 1965. xix, 582 p. illus., ports. 24 cm. Bibliography: p. 557-560. [BX9211.Y6F55] 65-26440
1. Yonkders, N.Y. First Westminster Presbyterian Church. 2. Yonkers, N.Y. Westminster Presbyterian Church. 3. Yonkers, N.Y. First Presbyterian Church. I. Title.

PREDMORE, Helen R., 1893- 285'.1747'31
The Chester (N.Y.) Presbyterian Church : a history, 1799-1965 / Helen R. Predmore. Monroe, N.Y. : Library Research Associates, [1975] xii, 377 p. : ill. ; 24 cm. Includes index. Bibliography: p. 377. [BX9211.C36F576] 73-89297 ISBN 0-912526-11-4 : 9.45
1. First Presbyterian Church of Chester, New York. 2. Chester, N.Y.—Biography. I. Title.

COLLIER, Robert H. 285'.1747'42
A history of the Jermain Memorial Church Congregation of Watervliet, New York, 1814-1974 / Robert H. Collier. Albany : Argus-Greenwood, 1976. ix, 77 p. : ill. ; 22 cm. [BX9211.W36J473] 77-374017
1. Jermain Memorial Church Congregation, Watervliet, N.Y. I. Title: A history of the Jermain Memorial Church Congregation ...

BRISTOL, V. Irene. 285'.1747'56
The history of the First Presbyterian Church of Heuvelton / by V. Irene Bristol. [Heuvelton, N.Y. : First Presbyterian Church of Heuvelton], c1975. 79 p. : ill. ; 22 cm. Includes bibliographical references. [BX9211.H45F573] 75-329552
1. First Presbyterian Church of Heuvelton. 2. Heuvelton, N.Y.—Biography. I. Title.

TRUMP, Clara K. 285'.1747'95
First Presbyterian Church of Westfield, New York, 1808-1968; a history, by Clara K. Trump. [Westfield? N.Y., 1968] 148 p. illus., ports. 28 cm. [BX9211.W52F57] 70-1035
1. Westfield, N.Y. First Presbyterian Church.

MCELWAIN, Madison E 285.1748
Faith and works at Middle Octorara since 1727; a history of Middle Octorara Presbyterian Church, R. D. 3, Quarryvill, Pennsylvania. Edited by Sanders P. McComsey. [Manheim? Pa., 1956] 582p. illus. 23cm. [BX9211.M54M3] 56-38606
1. Middle Octorara Presbyterian Church, Lancaster Co., Pa. I. Title.

MORRIS, A Wayne. 285.1748
The Octorara family of churches. Sketches by the author. Honey Brook, Pa., Herald Pub. Co. [c1960] unpaged. illus. 21x24cm. [BX8947.P4M6] 61-2322
1. Presbyterian Church in Pennsylvania. 2. Churches—Pennsylvania. I. Title.

CATTO, William T. 285.1'748'11
A semi-centenary discourse, delivered in the First African Presbyterian Church, Philadelphia, May, 1857, by William T. Catto. Freeport, N.Y., Books for Libraries Press, 1971. 111 p. 23 cm. (The Black heritage library collection) Reprint of the 1857 ed. [BX9211.P5F53 1971] 78-154073 ISBN 0-8369-8784-5
1. Philadelphia. First African Presbyterian Church. 2. Gloucester, John, 1776 or 7-1822. I. Title. II. Series.

PHILADELPHIA. Overbrook Presbyterian Church. 285.174811
The place where Thy glory dwells; the story of Overbrook Presbyterian Church, 1890-1958. [Philadelphia, 1958] 139p. illus. 24cm. [BX9211.P5O8] 59-33739
I. Title.

ALBERT, Alphaeus Homer, 1891- 285.1749
History of the First Presbyterian Church, Hightstown, New Jersey, 1857-1957, by Alphaeus H. and Lillian S. Albert, assisted by Ann Ruth Taylor. Hightstown, N. J., First Presbyterian Church, 1957. 144p. illus. 22cm. [BX9211.H5F5] 58-15400
1. Hightstown, N. J. First Presbyterian Church. I. Albert, Lillian Smith, joint author. II. Title.

LOCKWARD, Lynn Grover, 1878- 285.1749
A Puritan heritage; the First Presbyterian Church in Horse-Neck (Caldwell, N. J.) Illus. by the author. [Caldwell? N. J., 1955] 488p. illus. 24cm. [BX9211.C146L6] 56-19293
1. Caldwell, N. J. First Presbyterian Church. I. Title.

WIGHT, Edward Van Dyke, 1869- 285.1749
History of the Kingston Presbyterian Church, Kingston, New Jersey. Rev. and brought up to date for the hundredth anniversary of the church building, 1852-1952. [Kingston? N. J.,

1953, c1952] 59p. illus. 23cm. [BX9211.K5K5] 53-20855
1. Kingston, N. J. Kingston Presbyterian Church. I. Title.

ELLISON, Harry C 285.174937
Church of the Founding Fathers of New Jersey; a history, First Presbyterian Church. Elizabeth, New Jersey, 1664-1964. Prepared under the authority of the Session by Harry C. Ellison. Cornish, Me., Carbrook Press [1964] 196, [19] p. illus., ports. 24 cm. Bibliography: p. [210]-[215] [BX9211.E4F54] 65-2845
1. Elizabeth, N.J. First Presbyterian Church. I. Title.

THE Presbyterian 285'.1749'65
Church of Lawrenceville. [2d ed.]. [Lawrenceville, N.J. : Presbyterian Church, 1974, c1948] xiii, 156 p., [6] leaves of plates : ill. ; 25 cm. Cover title. Consists of a reproduction of the 1st ed. (1948) edited by H. J. Podmore, covering the period 1698-1948, and of a new section (p. 136-156) written by M. Adams, covering the period 1948-1973 and commemorating the 275th anniversary of the church in 1973. Includes indexes. Bibliography: p. 123-125. [BX9211.L38P736 1974] 75-316588
1. Lawrenceville, N.J. Presbyterian Church. I. Podmore, Harry J. II. Adams, Margaret, 1910-

MAKAR, Janos. 285'.1749'76
The story of an immigrant group in Franklin, New Jersey, including a collection of Hungarian folk songs sung in America. Translated by August J. Molnar. [Franklin, N.J., 1969] 170 p. illus., ports. 25 cm. Rev. translation of A franklini magyar egyhaz tortenete, neprajza. Includes unacc. melodies with words. Bibliographical footnotes. [BX8949.F7M33 1969] 70-92155
1. Franklin Hungarian Presbyterian Church. 2. Hungarians in Franklin, N.J. 3. Folk-songs, Hungarian—U.S. I. Title.

NELSEN, Hart M. 285'.175
The Appalachian Presbyterian: some rural-urban differences; a preliminary report, by Hart M. Nelsen. Bowling Green, Western Kentucky University, Office of Research and Services, 1968. iv, 59 l. 29 cm. ([Western Kentucky University. Office of Research and Services] Research bulletin no. 5) "[A report of a] two-year research project ... being carried out by Western Kentucky University for the Boards of Christian Education of the United Presbyterian Church in the United States of America and the Presbyterian Church in the United States." [BX8941.N44] 78-253230
1. Presbyterians in the Appalachian region—Statistics. I. Presbyterian Church in the U.S. Board of Christian Education. II. United Presbyterian Church in the U.S.A. Board of Christian Education. III. Title. IV. Series: Western Kentucky University. College of Commerce. Office of Research and Services. Research bulletin no. 5.

THOMPSON, Ernest Trice, 285.175
1894-
The changing South and the Presbyterian Church in the United States. Richmond, John Knox Press [1950] 221 p. map. 21 cm. Bibliographical references included in "Notes and acknowledgements" (p. [215]-221) [BX8962.T5] 50-8262
1. Presbyterian Church in the U.S. 2. Southern States. I. Title.

THOMPSON, Ernest Trice, 285.175
1894-.
Presbyterians in the South. Richmond, John Knox Press [c1963-] v. map (on lining papers) 24 cm. Contents.CONTENTS. -- v. 1. 1607-1861. Bibliography: v. 1, p. [597]-608. [BX8941.T5] 63-19121
1. Presbyterian Church in the U.S. — Hist. 2. Presbyterian Church in the Southern States. I. Title.

THOMPSON, Ernest Trice, 285.175
1894-
Presbyterians in the South; v.1. Richmond, Va., Knox [c.1963] 629p. map (on lining papers) 24cm. Contents.v.1. 1607-1861. Bibl. 63-19121 9.75
1. Presbyterian Church in the U. S.—Hist. 2. Presbyterian Church in the Southern States. I. Title.

SMITH, Anna Lee 285'.1752'74
Kirkwood.
Bethel Presbyterian Church at Madonna, Maryland, 1769-1969: two hundredth anniversary. [Bel Air? Md., 1969?] 56 p. illus. 23 cm. Cover title. [BX9211.M34S6] 75-313334
1. Bethel Presbyterian Church, Madonna, Md. 2. Madonna, Md.—Biography.

GEORGETOWN Presbyterian 285'.1753
Church. Washington, D.C.
The Presbyterian Congregation in George Town, 1780-1970. [Prepared by Dorothy Schaffter] Washington, Session of Presbyterian Congregation in George Town, 1971. 115 p. illus. 23 cm. Bibliography: p. 114-115. [BX9211.W3G463 1971] 75-304498
1. Georgetown Presbyterian Church. Washington, D.C. I. Schaffter, Dorothy.

NANNES, Caspar Harold, 285'.1753
1903-
The National Presbyterian Church & Center, by Caspar Nannes. [Washington, Printing: Vinmar Lithographing Co., 1970] 51 p. illus. (part col.), ports. 29 cm. Bibliography: p. 51. [BX9211.W3N37] 75-17178
1. Washington, D.C. National Presbyterian Church. I. Title.

BRIMM, Henry M., comp. 285'.1755
Yesterday and tomorrow in the Synod of Virginia. Henry M. Brimm [and] William M. E. Rachal, editors. Richmond, Synod of Virginia, Presbyterian Church in the United States, 1962. 131 p. 21 cm. "The six addresses which make up this book were presented as the major feature of the Synod of Virginia's observance of the centennial of the Presbyterian Church in the United States." [BX8957.V57B74] 74-172641
1. Presbyterian Church in the U.S.A. Synods. Virginia. I. Rachal, William M. E., joint comp. II. Presbyterian Church in the U.S.A. Synods. Virginia. III. Title.

PRESBYTERIAN Church in 285.1755
the U. S. Presbyteries. Honover.
Minutes. [n. p.] v. 23cm. Issued [BX8968.H3A3] 52-16064
I. Title.

WILSON, Howard 285'.1755
McKnight.
The Lexington Presbytery heritage; the Presbytery of Lexington and its churches in the Synod of Virginia, Presbyterian Church in the United States. [Verona, Va.] McClure Press [1971] xiii, 510 p. illus., facsim., maps, ports. 24 cm. Bibliography: p. 399-412. [BX8947.V8W53] 72-156142 8.50
1. Presbyterian Church in the U.S. Presbyteries. Lexington. I. Title.

WILSON, Howard McKnight. 285.1755
The Tinkling Spring, headwater of freedom; a study of the church and her people, 1732-1952. Fisherville, Va., Tinkling Spring and Hermitage Presbyterian Churches, 1954. xviii, 542p. illus., ports., maps (1 fold.) facsims. 24cm. Bibliography: p. [393]-409. [BX9211.T5W5] 54-11987
1. Tinkling Spring Church, Augusta Co., Va. I. Title.

WOODWORTH, Robert Bell, 285.1755
1868-
A history of the Presbyterian Church in Winchester, Virginia, 1780-1949, based on official documents; by Robert Bell Woodworth, with the collaboration of Clifford Duval Grim and Ronald S. Wilson. Winchester, Printed for the Church by Pifer Print. Co., 1950. 152 p. illus., ports., map. 24 cm. [BX9211.W64W6] 50-21591
1. Winchester, Va. Presbyterian Church. I. Title.

VIENNA Presbyterian 285'.1755'291
Church, Vienna, Va. Centennial Committee.
Centennial 1974 / [The Centennial Committee, Vienna Presbyterian Church ; Dave LeRoy, editor ; Hal Bowman, picture editor]. Vienna, Va. : Vienna Presbyterian Church, 1974. v, 81 p. : ill. ; 23 cm. [BX9211.V5V538 1974] 75-317114
1. Vienna Presbyterian Church, Vienna, Va. I. LeRoy, Dave, 1920-

WATTERS, Frank. 285'.1755'293
A history: the Idylwood Presbyterian Church. Falls Church, Va., 1974. 103, [28] p. illus. 23 cm. [BX9211.F28I388] 75-301775
1. Idylwood Presbyterian Church, Falls Church, Va. I. Title.

COLE, Lucy (Cole) 285.175546
History of woman's work in East Hanover Presbytery, by Mrs. Charles F. Cole; introd. by Edward Mack. Richmond, Richmond Press, 1938. 151 p. ports. 19 cm. [BX8968.H3C6] 38-18517
1. Presbyterian Church in the U.S. Presbyteries. Hanover. 2. Presbyterian Church in the U.S. Woman's Auxiliary. 3. Women in church work — Virginia. I. Title.

STAHL, Thomas K. 285'.1755'665
A history of the First Presbyterian Church, Danville, Virginia, 1826-1976 / Thomas K. Stahl. Danville : The Church, 1976. xii, 69 p. : ill. ; 24 cm. Bibliography: p. 55. [BX9211.D23F577] 77-150932
1. First Presbyterian Church, Danville, Va. I. Title.

BALES, Tipton C 1884- 285.1755811
Landmarks of faith, a history of the Clifton Forge Presbyterian Church, 1881-1957; organization, background, growth. Clifton Forge, Va. [1959] 107p. illus. 24cm. [BX9211.C63B3] 59-49515
1. Clifton Forge, Va. Presbyterian Church. I. Title.

DIEHL, George West. 285'.1755'852
Old Oxford and her families. [Verona, Va.] McClure Press [1971] ix, 217 p. illus. 24 cm. Includes bibliographical references. [BX9211.V38O433] 79-160702 7.50
1. Old Oxford Presbyterian Church. 2. Rockbridge Co., Va.—Genealogy. I. Title.

SECOND Presbyterian 285'.1755'911
Church, Staunton, Va.
A history of the Second Presbyterian Church, Staunton, Virginia, 1875-1975. Staunton, Va. : The Church, c1975. 76 p. : ill. ; 24 cm. Includes index. [BX9211.S8S4 1975] 75-332489
1. Second Presbyterian Church, Staunton, Va. 2. Staunton, Va.—Biography. I. Title.

TURNER, Herbert 285'.1755'916
Snipes, 1891-
Bethel and her ministers, 1746-1946 / Herbert S. Turner ; 1946-1974 [by] Herbert S. Turner and James Sprunt. 2d ed. Verona, Va. : McClure Print. Co., 1974. 271 p. : ill. ; 24 cm. Includes index. Bibliography: p. 255-256. [BX9211.A94B47 1974] 74-15372 8.50
1. Bethel Presbyterian Church, Augusta Co., Va. I. Sprunt, James, 1901- joint author. II. Title.

MCGEACHY, Neill 285.1756
Roderick, 1909-
A history of the Sugaw Creek Presbyterian Church, Mecklenburg Presbytery, Charlotte, North Carolina. Rock Hill, S. C., Printed by Record Print Co., 1954. 195p. illus. 23cm. [BX9211.C28S8] 55-16848
1. Charlotte, N. C. Sugaw Creek Presbyterian Church. I. Title.

RUMPLE, Jethro. 285'.1756
The history of Presbyterianism in North Carolina. Richmond, Library of Union Theological Seminary in Virginia, 1966. xvii, 349 p. 28 cm. (Library of Union Theological Seminary in Virginia. Historical transcripts, no. 3) "Reprinted from the North Carolina Presbyterian, 1878-1887." [BX8947.N8R8] 71-3331
1. Presbyterian Church in North Carolina—History. I. Title. II. Series: Richmond. Union Theological Seminary. Library. Historical transcripts, no. 3

SPENCE, Thomas Hugh, 285.1756
1899-
The Presbyterian congregation on Rocky River. Concord, N. C., Rocky River Presbyterian Church, 1954. 238p. illus. 25cm. [BX9211.C14R6] 55-19724
1. Rocky River Church, Cabarrus Co., N. C. I. Title.

TURNER, Herbert 285.175658
Snipes, 1891-
Church in the old fields: Hawfields Presbyterian Church and community in North Carolina. Chaper Hill, University of North Carolina Press -(1962] 207 p. illus. 24 cm. Includes bibliography. [BX9211.A28H3] 62-6806
1. Hawfields Presbyterian Church, Alamance Co., N.C. I. Title.

TURNER, Herbert 285.175658
Snipes, 1891-
Church in the old fields: Hawfields Presbyterian Church and community in North Carolina. Chapel Hill, Univ. of N. C. Pr. [c.1962] 297p. illus. 24cm. Bibl. 62-6806 6.00
1. Hawfields Presbyterian Church, Alamance Co., N.C. I. Title.

PERRY, Octavia 285'.1756'62
(Jordan)
History of the First Presbyterian Church, High Point, North Carolina, 1859-1959. [High Point, N.C., Hall Print. Co., 1959] xxiii, 325 p. illus. (part col.), ports. 24 cm. [BX9211.H48F54] 68-4551
1. High Point, N.C. First Presbyterian Church. I. Whipple, Mildred. II. Title.

MATTHEWS, Louise 285'.1756'76
Barber.
A history of Providence Presbyterian Church, Mecklenburg County, North Carolina. Illus. by Al Fincher. [Charlotte, N.C., Brooks Litho] 1967. xvi, 338 p. illus., ports. 24 cm. Bibliography: p. 311-320. [BX9211.M38P75] 67-9139
1. Providence Presbyterian Church, Mecklenburg Co., N.C. I. Title.

BLACKMUN, Ora. 285'.1756'88
A spire in the mountains; the story of 176 years of a church and a town growing together, 1794-1969. Asheville, N.C., First Presbyterian Church, 1970. viii, 387 p. illus., facsims., map, port. 24 cm. Bibliography: p. 379-383. [BX9211.A72F572] 72-24381
1. Asheville, N.C. First Presbyterian Church. I. Title.

QUATTLEBAUM; PAUL, 1886- 285.1757
The Kingston Presbyterian Church, Pee Dee Presbytery, Conway, South Carolina, 1858-1958. Conway, S. C., Kingston Presbyterian Church [1958] 126p. illus. 24cm. [BX9211.C687Q8] 58-37263
1. Conway, S. C. Kingston Presbyterian Church. I. Title.

TOWNSEND, Leah, 1889- 285'.1757
South Carolina Baptists, 1670-1805. Baltimore, Genealogical Pub. Co., 1974. 391 p. 22 cm. Reprint of the 1935 ed. published by Florence Print. Co., Florence, S.C. Originally presented as the author's thesis, University of South Carolina, 1926. Bibliography: p. 306-325. [BX6248.S6T6 1974] 74-6312 ISBN 0-8063-0621-1 15.00
1. Baptists—South Carolina. I. Title.

BOGGS, Annie Lee. 285'.1757'25
Pendleton Presbyterian Church, 1789-1966; church history. [Pendleton? S.C., 1966] 117 p. illus., facsims., ports. 23 cm. Cover title. Bibliography: p. 117. [BX9211.P28P4] 77-261778 3.00
1. Pendleton, S.C. Presbyterian Church. I. Title.

LILLY, Edward G. 285'.1757'915
Beyond the burning bush : First (Scots) Presbyterian Church, Charleston, S.C. : historical viewpoints with brief sketches of the history, buildings, and lives of the ministers / Edward Guerrant Lilly. Charleston, S.C. : Garnier, 1971. 73 p., [4] leaves of plates : ill. ; 24 cm. Bibliography: p. 73. [BX9211.C26F574] 74-184896
1. First Scots Presbyterian Church, Charleston, S.C. 2. Charleston, S.C.—Biography. I. Title.

CARTLEDGE, Groves 285.175811
Harrison, 1820-1899.
Historical sketches; Presbyterian Churches and early settlers in northeast Georgia. Compiled by Jessie Julia Mize and Virginia Louise Newton. Athens, Ga., 1960. 208p. illus. 24cm. [BX8947.G4C3] 60-15929
1. Presbyterian Church in Georgia. 2. Madison Co., Ga.—Hist. 3. Cartledge family. I. Mize, Jessie Julia, 1910- II. Title. III. Title: Presbyterian Churches and early settlers in northeast Georgia.

PRESBYTERIAN Church in 285.1759
the U.S. Synods. Florida.
Minutes of the annual meeting. [Orlando, etc.] v. 21-23 cm. [BX8967.F5A3] 52-36171
I. Title.

POSEY, Walter Brownlow, 285.176
1900-
The Presbyterian Church in the Old Southwest, 1778-1838. Richmond, John Knox Press, 1952. 192 p. map (on lining papers) 25 cm. Bibliographical references included in "Notes" (p. [139]-185) [BX8941.P65] 52-14324
1. Presbyterian Church in the Old Southwest — Hist. I. Title.

PRESBYTERIAN Church in 285.1761
the U.S. Presbyteries. Mobile.
Minutes. [Mobile?] v. 22 cm. [BX8968.M6A3] 52-16066
I. Title.

MAHONEY, William 285'.1761'47
James.
One hundred and fifty years : a sesquicentennial history of Montgomery's First Presbyterian Church / by William James Mahoney, Jr. ; introd. by Harry N. Miller, Jr. MOntgomery, Ala. : First Presbyterian Church of Montgomery, [1974] xiv, 146 p. : ill. ; 23 cm. Includes index. Bibliography: p. 137. [BX9211.M75F575] 75-304560
1. Montgomery, Ala. First Presbyterian Church. 2. Montgomery, Ala.—Biography. I. Title.

CHISOLM, J. Julian. 285'.1762'26
History of the First Presbyterian Church of Natchez, Mississippi. Natchez, McDonald's Printers & Publishers, 1972. 171 p. illus. 25 cm. Includes bibliographical references. [BX9211.N32F573] 72-169256
1. First Presbyterian Church, Natchez, Miss. I. Title.

ST. AMANT, Penrose, 285.1763
1915-
A history of the Presbyterian Church in Louisiana. [New Orleans] Synod of Louisiana [1961] 303p. illus. 22cm. Includes bibliography. [BX8947.L8S23] 60-16815
1. Presbyterian Church in Louisiana. 2. Presbyterian Church in the U. S. Synods. Louisiana. I. Title.

PASCHAL, George H. 285'.1764
One hundred years of challenge and change; a history of the Synod of Texas of the United Presbyterian Church in the U.S.A., by George H. Paschal, Jr. and Judith A. Benner. San Antonio, Trinity University Press [1968] x, 259 p. 24 cm. Bibliography: p. [244]-249. [BX8941.P35] 68-20488 6.00
1. United Presbyterian Church in the U.S.A. Synods. Texas—History. I. Benner, Judith A., joint author. II. Title.

CLARK, Margaret Lasater. 285'.1764'113
On this bluff ... Centennial history, 1867-1967, First Presbyterian Church, Corpus Christi, Texas, by Margaret Lasater Clark and Historical Committee. Illustrated by Jerry Seagle. [Corpus Christi, Tex., Renfrow, c1967] 190 p. illus. (part col.), maps, ports. 28 cm. Bibliography: p. 186. [BX9211.C77F5] 79-8652
1. Corpus Christi, Tex. First Presbyterian Church. I. Corpus Christi, Tex. First Presbyterian Church. Historical Committee. II. Title.

DAVIS, John Henry, 1899- 285'.1768'19
The William W. Goodman gift; documents pertaining to the Second Presbyterian Church of Memphis after it had been seized during the Civil War, including a handwritten and signed endorsement of Abraham Lincoln directing the return of the church to its trustees. [Memphis] Southwestern at Memphis, 1970. 19 p. illus. 23 cm. (Burrow Library monograph no. 7) Cover title. [BX9211.M396S43] 77-277382
1. Memphis. Second Presbyterian Church. I. Goodman, William W., 1900- II. Title. III. Series: Memphis. Southwestern at Memphis. Burrow Library. Monograph no. 7

PARTLOW, Thomas E. 285'.1768'54
Sugg's Creek Cumberland Presbyterian Church : an early history / by Thomas E. Partlow. Lebanon, Tenn : Partlow, 1974. 52 p. : ill. ; 27 cm. Includes index. Bibliography: p. 44-45. [BX9211.W634S936] 75-305491
1. Sugg's Creek Cumberland Presbyterian Church, Wilson Co., Tenn. 2. Wilson Co., Tenn.—Biography. I. Title.

BOYER, Reba Bayless. 285'.1768'865
A history of Mars Hill Presbyterian Church, by Reba B. Boyer and Budd L. Duncan. [Athens, Tenn., 1973] 126 p. 24 cm. [BX9211.A77M373] 73-92011
1. Mars Hill Presbyterian Church, Athens, Tenn. 2. Athens, Tenn.—Biography. I. Duncan, Budd L., joint author. II. Title.

SANDERS, Robert Stuart. 285.1769
History of Walnut Hill Presbyterian Church, Fayette County, Kentucky. Introd. by J. Winston Coleman. Frankfort, Kentucky Historical Society, 1956. 88p. illus. 23cm. [BX9211.W28S3] 57-17932
1. Walnut Hill Presbyterian Church, Fayette Co., Ky. I. Title.

SANDERS, Robert Stuart. 285.176947
Annals of the First Presbyterian Church, Lexington, Kentucky, 1784-1959. Louisville, Ky., Dunne Press, 1959. 192p. illus. 24cm. [BX9211.L47F5] 59-1240
1. Lexington, Ky. First Presbyterian Church. I. Title.

SANDERS, Robert Stuart. 285.176947
History of the Second Presbyterian Church, Lexington, Kentucky, of the United Presbyterian Church in the U S A 1815-1965. Lexington, Second Presbyterian Church, 1965. 242 p. illus., plan, ports. 24 cm. [BX9211.L47S47] 66-3075
1. Lexington, Ky. Second Presbyterian Church. I. Title.

MCKINNEY, William Wilson, 1893- ed. 285.177
The Pre-byterian Valley. Foreword by Eugene Carson Blake. Pittsburgh, Davis & Warde, 1958. 639p. illus. 22cm. 'Published as a religious feature of the Pittsburgh Bicentennial Year 1958-1959 in recognition of the continued influence of Presbyterianism throughout the two hundred years of Pittsburgh's growth and expansion.' Includes bibliography. [BX8935.M2] 58-14156
1. Presbyterian Church in the Ohio Valley. I. Title.

MITCHELL, Osborne. 285'.1771'6
The Synod of Wheeling, an old Scotch-Irish synod. [Wheeling? W. Va., 1971] 16 p. 23 cm. [BX8957.W45M57] 74-153607
1. Presbyterian Church in the U.S.A. (Old School). Synods. Wheeling. I. Title.

PRESBYTERIAN Church in the U.S.A. (Old School) Synods. South Carolina and Georgia. 285'.1771'6
Minutes of ... sessions 1845- Charleston. v. 22 cm. [BX8957.S6A3] 50-44682
I. Title.

RUDOLPH, L. 285.1772
Hoosier Zion; the Presbyterians in early Indiana. New Haven, Yale University Press, 1963. 218 p. illus. 23 cm. (Yale publications in religion) Presbyterian Historical Society publications, 4. [BX8947.I6R8] 62-8261
1. Presbyterian Church in Indiana. I. Title.

RUDOLPH, L. C. 285.1772
Hoosier Zion; the Presbyterians in early Indiana. New Haven, Conn., Yale, 1963. 218p. illus. 23cm. (Yale pubns. in religion, Presbyterian Historical Soc. pubns., 4) Bibl. 62-8261 5.00
1. Presbyterian Church in Indiana. I. Title.

GRIFFIN, Frederick Porter. 285'.1772'21
The Corydon Presbyterian Church through 150 years (oldest continuous church in Corydon) 1819-1969, the church of the Governor. Mentone, Ind., Superior Print. Co., 1969. 56 p. illus., ports. 21 cm. On cover: History of the United Presbyterian Church. [BX9211.C78C6] 75-279373
1. Corydon Presbyterian Church. I. Title.

COMIN, John, 1869-1947. 285.1774
History of the Presbyterian Church in Michigan, by John Comin and Harold F. Fredsell. Ann Arbor, Ann Arbor Press, 1950. x, 215 p. ports. 24 cm. "Summer camp edition."--Dust jacket. Bibliography: p. 198-202. [BX8947.M5C6] 51-5324
1. Presbyterian Church in Michigan. I. Fredsell, Harold F. II. Title.

DETROIT. Jefferson Avenue Presbyterian Church. 285.1774
One hundred years of service, 1854--1954; a review of the historical background and development of the Jefferson Avenue Presbyterian Church. Detroit, 1954. 116p. illus. 24cm. [BX9211.D4J4] 56-47873
I. Title.

GROSSE, Pointe, Mich. Grosse Pointe Memorial Church. 1965 Centennial Committee. 285.177433
The Grosse Pointe Memorial Church (the United Presbyterian Church in the U.S.A.) history 1865-1965. [Grosse Pointe? Mich., 1965] ix, 110 p. illus., facsims., maps (on lining papers) port. 26 cm. [BX9211.G87G7] 65-26426
I. Title.

FREDSELL, Harold F. 285.1774'34
John Monteith and Detroit Presbyterianism, by Harold F. Fredsell. Ann Arbor, Mich., Ann Arbor Press, 1966. 285 p. illus. 24 cm. Bibliography: p. 262-266. [BX9225.M53F7] 66-27862
1. Monteith, John, 1788-1868. 2. Presbyterian Church in the U.S.A. Presbyteries. Detroit. 3. Presbyterian Church in Detroit. I. Title.

PRESBYTERIAN Church in the U.S.A. Synods. Wisconsin. 285.1775
Early Presbyterianism in Wisconsin. Centennial ed. [Waukesha? Wis., 1951] 116 p. illus. 22 cm. [BX8947.W6A3] 51-33042
1. Presbyterian Church in Wisconsin. I. Title.

WICKLEIN, Edward C. 285'.1775
Badger kirk; an historical study in the bounds of the former Synod of Wisconsin United Presbyterian Church in the U.S.A., by Edward C. Wicklein. [Waukesha, 1974- v. illus. 28 cm. Contents.Contents.—v. 1. A Wisconsin history of the Associate Presbyterian Church of North America, Associate Reformed Presbyterian Church of the West (later of America) Reformed Presbyterian Church of North America, Reformed Presbyterian Church, General Synod, United Presbyterian Church of North America. Bibliography: v. 1, leaves 28-29. [BX8947.W6W53] 74-166461
1. Presbyterian Church in Wisconsin—Collected works. I. Title.

WICKLEIN, Edward C. 285'.1775 s
A Wisconsin history of the Associate Presbyterian Church of North America, Associate Reformed Presbyterian Church of the West (later of America) Reformed Presbyterian Church of North America, Reformed Presbyterian Church, General Synod, United Presbyterian Church of North America, with historical sketches of each congregation, 1840-1958, by Edward C. Wicklein. [Waukesha, 1974] 29 l. illus. 28 cm. (His Badger kirk, v. 1) Bibliography: leaves 28-29. [BX8947.W6W53 vol. 1] 285'.1775 74-166460
1. Presbyterian Church in Wisconsin. I. Title.

OSWALD, Anthony Lewis, 1898- 285.1781
40+, 3--; forty years with benefits of clergy, three without! By A. Lewis O. Hutchinson, Kan., Rotherwood Press, 1952. 320 p. 22 cm. [BR1725.O75A3] 52-270501
1. Hutchinson, Kan. First Presbyterian Church. I. Title.

CREIGH, Dorothy (Weyer) 285'.17'82398
The first hundred years: the First Presbyterian Church, Hastings, Nebraska, 1873-1973. [Hastings, Neb., 1973] 164 p. illus. 27 cm. Bibliography: p. 151. [BX9211.H225F572] 73-86370
1. Hastings, Neb. First Presbyterian Church. 2. Hastings, Neb.—Biography. I. Title.

REUSSER, Walter Christian, 1892- 285'.1787'95
The United Presbyterian Church of Laramie, Wyoming, 1869-1969; an historical sketch of the church for the first 100 year [by] Walter C. Reusser. Laramie, Wyo., 1969. 150 p. illus., col. plates, ports. 23 cm. [BX9211.L37U56] 72-262459
1. Laramie, Wyo. United Presbyterian Church. I. Title.

SCHOOLLAND, John Bernard, 1894- 285'.1788'63
A pioneer church: being a reverently realistic account of the First Presbyterian Church of Boulder, Colorado in it's total pioneer origin, 1872-1972, by John B. Schoolland. [Boulder, Colo., First Presbyterian Church of Boulder, c1972] xvi, 182 p. illus. 27 cm. Bibliography: p. 175. [BX9211.B67F577] 72-92858
1. First Presbyterian Church, Boulder, Colo. I. Title.

BRACKENRIDGE, R. Douglas. 285'.179
Iglesia Presbiteriana : a history of Presbyterians and Mexican Americans in the Southwest / by R. Douglas Brackenridge and Francisco O. Garcia-Treto. San Antonio : Trinity University Press, [1974] xiv, 262 p : ill. ; 25 cm. (Presbyterian Historical Society publication series ; 15) Includes index. Bibliography: p. [249]-255. [BV2788.M4B7 1974] 74-76777 ISBN 0-911536-53-1 : 8.00
1. Presbyterian Church in the New Southwest. 2. Missions to Mexican Americans—Southwest, New. 3. Mexican Americans—Southwest, New. I. Garcia-Treto, Francisco O., joint author. II. Title. III. Series: Presbyterian Historical Society. Publications ; no. 15.

SMITH, Richard Knox. 285'.1791
Datelines and by-lines; a sketchbook of Presbyterian beginnings and growth in Arizona. Line drawings by Caroline Lansing. [Phoenix, Synod of Arizona, United Presbyterian Church in the U.S.A., 1969] 90 p. illus., ports. 23 cm. Prepared on the occasion of the centennial year of the Presbyterian Church in Arizona. Contents.Contents.—Dateline: Arizona Territory, by R. K. Smith.—By-lines: a synod grows, by J. M. Nelson. Includes bibliographical references. [BX8947.A7S6] 78-259829
1. Presbyterian Church in Arizona. I. Nelson, James Melvin. II. United Presbyterian Church in the U.S.A. Synods. Arizona. III. Title.

EDWARDS, Ben F 1873- 285.1794
100 years of achievement and challenge; a brief history of the First Presbyterian Church of Oakland, California. Oakland, Centennial Committee of the First Presbyterian Church, 1953. 72p. illus. 24cm. [BX9211.O2E3] 53-23622
1. Oakland, Calif. First Presbyterian Church. I. Title.

FILLMORE, Lowell. 285'.2
Things to be remembered. Lee's Summit, Mo., Unity School of Christianity, 1952. 186p. 17cm. [BX9890.U5F547] 55-44649
I. Unity School of Christianity—Doctrinal and controversial works. II. Title.

HENDERSON, George David, 1888- 285.2
Why we are Presbyterians. [Edinburgh?] Church of Scotland Publications [1953?] 86p. 19cm. [BX9175.H4] 53-40457
1. Presbyterianism. I. Title.

PILGRIM, Geneva R Hanna. 28.52
Books, young people, and reading guidance [by] Geneva R. Hanna [and] Mariana K. McAllister. New York, Harper [c1960] 219 p. 21 cm. (Exploration series in education) [Z1037.P54] 59.12674
1. Children's literature—Bibl. I. McAllister, Mariana Kennedy, joint author. II. Title.

WHITNEY, Frank B 285'.2
Be of good courage. Lee's Summit, Mo., Unity School of Christianity, 1953. 153p. illus. 17cm. Verse and prose. [BX9890.U5W44] 54-32721
1. Unity School of Christianity—Doctrinal and controversial works. I. Title.

YONGE, Stanley. 285'.2
Carmarthen Road United Reformed Church, Swansea, 1876-1976 / [by Stanley Yonge]. [Swansea] : [Carmarthen Road United Reformed Church], 1976. [1], 33 p. : ill., ports. ; 21 cm. [BX9890.U25Y66] 76-366903 ISBN 0-9504930-0-7 : £0.25
1. Carmarthen Road United Reformed Church.

ALLEN, Robert, 1904- 285'.2'0924
James Seaton Reid, a centenary biography. With a foreword by John Foster. Belfast, W. Mullan, 1951. 207p. illus. 22cm. [BX9225.R38A65] 55-17401
1. Reid, James Seaton, 1793-1851. I. Title.

BADGER, Colin Robert, 1906- 285'.2'0924 B
The Reverend Charles Strong and the Australian Church [by] C. R. Badger. Melbourne, Abacada Press [on behalf of the Charles Strong Memorial Trust, 1971] 335 p. illus., ports. 23 cm. Includes bibliographical references. [BR1725.S84B3] 72-883252 ISBN 0-909505-00-4 8.50
1. Strong, Charles, 1844-1942. 2. Australian Church. I. Title.

BARCLAY, William, lecturer in the University of Glasgow. 285'.2'0924 B
William Barclay : a spiritual autobiography. [Grand Rapids] : Eerdmans, [1975] 122 p. ; 22 cm. Bibliography: p. 122. [BS2351.B28A37 1975] 73-76528 ISBN 0-8028-3464-7 5.95
1. Barclay, William, lecturer in the University of Glasgow. I. Title. II. Title: A spiritual autobiography.

CALHOUN, William Gunn, 1910- 285'.2'0924 B
Samuel Doak, 1749-1830: his life, his children, Washington College [Washington College, Tenn., Pioneer Printers] 1966. vii, 51 p. illus. 21 cm. Includes bibliographical references. [LD5731.W513D62] 73-157719
1. Doak, Samuel, 1749-1830. 2. Washington College, Washington Co., Tenn.

COWAN, Henry, 1844-1932. 285'.2'0924 B
John Knox, the hero of the Scottish Reformation. New York, AMS Press [1970] xxxiii, 404 p. illus., port. 19 cm. Reprint of the 1905 ed. Bibliography: p. xxiii-xxxiii. [BX9223.C68 1970] 70-133817
1. Knox, John, 1505-1572.

GOREHAM, Norman J. 285'.2'0924 B
Isaac Ambrose, Lancashire nonconformist / by Norman J. Goreham. Preston : Henry L. Kirby, 1977. [1], 9 p. ; 21 cm. Bibliography: p. [9] [BX5207.A47G67] 77-371584 ISBN 0-9505653-0-X : £0.15
1. Ambrose, Isaac, 1604-1664. 2. Dissenters, Religious—England—Lancashire—Biography. 3. Lancashire, Eng.—Biography. I. Title.

GRIEVE, Christopher Murray, 1892- 285'.2'0924 B
John Knox / [by] Hugh MacDiarmid [i.e., C. M. Grieve], Campbell Maclean, Anthony Ross. Edinburgh : Ramsay Head Press, 1976. 96 p. ; 19 cm. (New assessments) Contents.Contents.—Maclean, C. The paradox of Knox.—Ross, A. Man or myth.—MacDiarmid. H. Knox, Calvinism and the arts. [BX9223.G74] 76-377409 ISBN 0-902859-31-5 : £2.50
1. Knox, John, 1505-1572—Addresses, essays, lectures. I. Maclean, Campbell. II. Ross, Anthony.

HAMILTON, James, 1814-1867. 285'.2'0924 B
Life of Lady Colquhoun. Inverness, Free Presbyterian Church of Scotland, 1969. [8], 210 p. 19 cm. [BX9225.C637H34] 71-529178 ISBN 0-902506-02-1 7/6
1. Colquhoun, Janet (Sinclair) Lady, 1781-1846. I. Title.

KISSINGER, Dorothy May (Vale) 1916- 285'.2'0924
Say a good word; a biography of the Reverend Roy Ewing Vale, D. D., LL. D., moderator of the 156th General Assembly of the Presbyterian Church, U.S.A. [Mesa? Ariz., 1963] 243 p. port. 24 cm. [BX9225.V28K5] 63-25797
1. Vale, Roy Ewing, 1885-1959. I. Title.

LANG, John Dunmore, 1799-1878. 285'.2'0924 B
Reminiscences of my life and times both in church and state in Australia for upwards of fifty years. Edited with an introduction and notes by D. W. A. Baker. Melbourne, Heinemann, 1972. viii, 240 p. port. 22 cm. [BX9225.L26A3 1972] 72-165750 ISBN 0-85561-015-8 8.75
1. Lang, John Dunmore, 1799-1878. I. Baker, David William Archdall, ed. II. Title.

MCCOY, F. N. 285'.2'0924 B
Robert Baillie and the second Scots Reformation [by] F. N. McCoy. Berkeley, University of California Press [1974] xi, 244 p. 24 cm. Bibliography: p. [220]-228. [BX9225.B333M3] 72-93527 ISBN 0-520-02447-8 10.00
1. Baillie, Robert, 1602-1662. 2. Covenanters. I. Title.

MACMILLAN, David S. 285'.2'0924 B
John Dunmore Lang, [by] David S. Macmillan. Melbourne, New York Oxford University Press [1962] 30 p. illus., ports. 19 cm. (Great Australians) Bibliography: p. 30. [BX9225.L26M3 1962] 79-17546
1. Lang, John Dunmore, 1799-1878.

MAKEMIE, Francis, 285'.2'0924 B
1658-1708.
The life and writings of Francis Makemie. Edited with an introd. by Boyd S. Schlenther. Philadelphia, Presbyterian Historical Society, 1971. 287 p. 24 cm. (Presbyterian Historical Society publications, 11) Includes bibliographical references. [BX9225.M34A3 1971] 76-30771 6.00
I. Schlenter, Boyd S., 1936- ed. II. Series: Presbyterian Historical Society. Publications, 11.

MUIR, Edwin, 1887- 285'.2'0924 B
1959.
John Knox: portrait of a Calvinist. Port Washington, N.Y., Kennikat Press [1972] 316 p. ports. 22 cm. Reprint of the 1929 ed. [BX9223.M8 1972] 78-159096 ISBN 0-8046-1639-6
1. Knox, John, 1505-1572.

MUIR, Edwin, 1887- 285'.2'0924 B
1959.
John Knox: portrait of a Calvinist. Freeport, N.Y., Books for Libraries Press [1971] 316 p. ports. 23 cm. Reprint of the 1929 ed. [BX9223.M8 1971] 76-148892 ISBN 0-8369-5656-7
1. Knox, John, 1505-1572.

REID, William 285'.2'0924 B
Stanford, 1913-
Trumpeter of God; a biography of John Knox [by] W. Stanford Reid. New York, Scribner [1974] xvi, 353 p. illus. 24 cm. Bibliography: p. [328]-340. [BX9223.R4] 73-1356 ISBN 0-684-13782-8 12.50
1. Knox, John, 1505-1572. I. Title.

RIDLEY, Jasper 285'.2'0924 B
Godwin.
John Knox [by] Jasper Ridley. New York, Oxford University Press [1968] vi, 596 p. ports. 22 cm. Bibliography: p. [552]-574. [BX9223.R5] 68-55648 9.50
1. Knox, John, 1505-1572.

SANDERS, Robert 285'.2'0924
Stuart.
The Reverend Robert Stuart, D. D., 1772-1856, a pioneer in Kentucky Presbyterianism, and his descendants. Louisville, Ky., Dunne Press, 1962. 167p. illus. 24cm. [BX9225.S788S3] 62-6330
1. Stuart, Robert, 1772-1856. 2. Stuart family. I. Title.

SEGESVARY, Lewis. 285'.2'0924
I give you a new land. [Minneapolis, Osterhus Pub. House, 1953 or 4] 143p. 20cm. [BX9225.S36.A3] 56-26565
1. Presbyterian Church—Clergy—Correspondence, reminiscences, etc. I. Title.

TURELL, Ebenezer, 285'.2'0924 B
1702-1778.
The life and character of the Reverend Benjamin Colman, D.D. A facsim. reproduction with an introd. by Christopher R. Reaske. Delmar, N.Y., Scholars' Facsimiles & Reprints, 1972. xxiii, 18, 238 p. port. 23 cm. Original ed. has imprint: Boston, New-England, Printed and sold by Rogers and Fowle in Queen-street, and by J. Edwards in Cornhill, MDCCXLIX. "A catalogue of Dr. Colman's works": p. 233-236. [BX7260.C683T8 1749ab] 72-4539 ISBN 0-8201-1104-X
1. Colman, Benjamin, 1673-1747.

WHITEFIELD, George, 285'.2'0924 B
1714-1770.
Journals, 1737-1741, to which is prefixed his Short account (1746) and Futher account (1747) Gainesville, Fla., Scholars' Facsimiles & Reprints, 1969. viii, 515 p. port. 24 cm. Reprint of the 1905 ed., with a new introd. by W. V. Davis. [BX9225.W4A216 1969] 73-81363 17.50
1. Great Awakening.

SMITH, Noel. 285'.2'09667
The Presbyterian Church of Ghana, 1835-1960: a younger Church in a changing society; maps by Brian Watson. Accra, Ghana Universities P.; London, Oxford U. P., 1966. [8], 304 p. 4 plates (incl. ports.), 9 maps, tables, 22 1/2 cm. 45/- (B 67-14562) Maps on endpapers. Bibliography: p. 281-285. [BX9162.G5S6] 68-100261
1. Presbyterian Church in Ghana. I. Title.

DOUGLAS, James Dixon. 285.241
Light in the north; the story of the Scottish Covenanters, by J. D. Douglas. [American ed.] Grand Rapids, W. B. Eerdmans Pub. Co. [1964] Bibliography: p. 211-213. [BX9081.D6 1964] 64-22025
1. Covenanters. I. Title.

DOUGLAS, James Dixon 285.241
Light in the north; the story of the Scottish Convenanters [Amer. ed.] Grand Rapids, Mich., Eerdmans [c.1964] 220p. 23cm. (Advance of Christianity through the centuries, v.6) Bibl. [BX9081.D6] 64-22025 3.75
1. Convenanters. I. Title. II. Series.

LANG, Andrew, 1844-1912. 285.241
John Knox and the Reformation. Port Washington, N.Y., Kennikat Press [1967] xiv, 281 p. illus., ports. 22 cm. Reprint of 1905 ed. Bibliographical footnotes. [BX9223.L2 1967] 66-25923
1. Knox, John, 1505-1572. I. Title.

LOUDEN, R. Stuart 285.241
The true face of the Kirk; an examination of the ethos and traditions of the Church of Scotland. New York, Oxford [c.]1963. 148p. 23cm. Bibl. 63-2495 3.40
1. Church of Scotland. I. Title.

MACINNES, Rev. John. 285.241
The Evangelical movement in the Highlands of Scotland, 1688 to 1800. Aberdeen, University Press, 1951. xii, 299p. 22cm. Bibliographical footnotes. [BR787.H6M32] 54-16105
1. Evangelical revival. 2. Highlands of Scotland—Church history. I. Title.

SMELLIE, Alexander, 1857- 285.241
1923.
Men of the Covenant. [10th ed. (facsim. of 7th ed.) London] Banner of Truth Trust, 1960 (stamped: distributed by Bible Truth Depot, Swengel, Pa. facsim.: 534 p. illus. 13 cm. [BX9081.S65 1909a] 60-50627
1. Covenanters. I. Title.

UNITED Free Church of 285.241
Scotland.
Fasti, 1900-1929, edited by John Alexander Lamb. Edinburgh, Oliver and Boyd [1956] xi, 639p. 26cm. [BX9089.A53] 57-17600
1. United Free Church of Scotland— Clergy. 2. Churches—Scotland. 3. Scotland—Biog. I. Lamb, John Alexander, ed. II. Title.

SMELLIE, Alexander, 285'.2411
1857-1923.
Men of the Covenant : the story of the Scottish Church in the years of the Persecution / Alexander Smellie. Edinburgh ; Carlisle, Pa. : Banner of Truth Trust, 1975. xxii, 535 p., [49] leaves of plates : ill. ; 22 cm. Reprint of the 1924 edition. Includes index. [BX9081.S65 1975] 75-322828 ISBN 0-85151-212-7 : £2.75
1. Covenanters. I. Title.

SMELLIE, Alexander, 285'.2411
1857-1923.
Men of the Covenant : the story of the Scottish Church in the years of the Persecution / Alexander Smellie. Edinburgh ; Carlisle, Pa. : Banner of Truth Trust, 1975. xxii, 535 p., [49] leaves of plates : ill. ; 22 cm. Reprint of the 1924 edition. Includes index. [BX9081.S65 1975] 75-322828 ISBN 0-85151-212-7 : 10.95
1. Covenanters. I. Title.

WATSON, John, 1850- 285'.2'411
1807.
The Scot of the eighteenth century : his religion and his life / by John Watson. Folcroft, Pa. : Folcroft Library Editions, 1976. vi, 345 p. ; 23 cm. Reprint of the 1907 ed. published by Hodder and Stoughton, London. [BR785.W37 1976] 76-47571 ISBN 0-8414-9459-2 lib. bdg. : 35.00
1. Christianity—Scotland. I. Title.

LATHAM, S. R. 285'.2412'5
Greyfriars Parish Church, Aberdeen, 1471-1971: a commemoration of five hundred years; editor S. R. Latham. Aberdeen, Aberdeen University Press, 1971. 36, [4] p. illus., maps, ports. 25 cm. [BX9215.A23G734] 72-170570 ISBN 0-900015-10-1 £0.30
1. Greyfriars Parish Church.

THE English 285'.242
Presbyterians, from Elizabeth Puritanism to modern Unitarianism, by C. Gordon Bolam [and others] Boston, Beacon Press [1968] 297 p. 23 cm. Bibliographical footnotes. [BX9055.E5 1968b] 67-22137 10.00
1. Presbyterian Church in England. I. Bolam, Charles Gordon.

BAILEY, Thomas Melville, 285'.271
1912-
The covenant in Canada / by T. M. Bailey. Hamilton, Ont. : Macnab, 1975. 160 p. : ill. ; 19 x 24 cm. Cover title. [BX9001.B34] 76-357174 ISBN 0-919874-02-9
1. Presbyterian Church in Canada. 2. Presbyterian Church in Canada—Biography. I. Title.

MOIR, John S. 285'.271
Enduring witness : a history of the Presbyterian Church in Canada / by John S. Moir. Hamilton, Ont. : Presbyterian Church in Canada, [1974?] xiii, 311 p., [16] leaves of plates : ill. ; 24 cm. Includes bibliographical references and index. [BX9002.C2M64] 75-312621
1. Presbyterian Church in Canada—History. I. Title.

HISTORY of Deer 285'.2752'71
Creek Harmony Presbyterian Church, 1837-1972. [Darlington, Md. : Deer Creek Harmony Presbyterian Church, 1976?] 19, 40, 39 p. : ill. ; 23 cm. Cover title. Reprint of 3 works: the 1905 ed. of A. P. Silver's History of the Deer Creek Harmony Church of Glenville, Harford Co., Maryland; the 1937 ed. of W. E. Silver & E. L. Shelling's Deer Creek Harmony Presbyterian Church centennial celebration, 1837-1937; and the 1972 ed. of B. S. Silver & Mrs. Leonard C. Culpepper's Deer Creek Harmony Presbyterian Church, 1938-1972. [BX9211.G66D433 1976] 77-357001
1. Deer Creek Harmony Presbyterian Church, Glenville, Md. I. Silver, Albert Peter, 1852-1905. History of the Deer Creek Harmony Church of Glenville, Harford Co., Maryland. 1976? II. Silver, William Easter. Deer Creek Harmony Presbyterian Church centennial celebration, 1837-1937. 1976? III. Silver, Benjamin Stump, 1922- Deer Creek Harmony Presbyterian Church, 1938-1972. 1976?

PINNELL, Lois M. 285'.2754'62
French Creek Presbyterian Church; a memorial to the 150 years of service of the French Creek Presbyterian Church, by Lois M. Pinnell. Parsons, W. Va., McClain Print. Co., 1971. v, 249 p. illus. 23 cm. [BX9211.F88F76] 72-174565 ISBN 0-87012-110-3
1. French Creek Presbyterian Church.

BELZ, Ella C. 285'.2755'293
Falls Church Presbyterian Church, 1873-1973 / by Ella C. Belz. [Falls Church, Va.] : Belz, c1976. ix, 242 p. : ill. ; 23 cm. [BX9211.F28F343] 76-20365
1. Falls Church Presbyterian Church. I. Title.

ALVEY, Edward. 285'.2'755366
History of the Presbyterian Church of Fredericksburg, Virginia, 1808-1976 / Edward Alvey, Jr. Fredericksburg, Va. : Session of The Presbyterian Church, 1976. xiv, 204 p., [8] leaves of plates : ill. ; 24 cm. Includes bibliographical references and index. [BX9211.F84P733] 76-45001 7.50
1. Presbyterian Church, Fredericksburg, Va. I. Title.

PARRY, Gordon. 285'.29315'7
Spire on the hill / by Gordon Parry. [Dunedin] : [Centenary Committee, First Church of Otago], [1973] [34] p. : ill., facsim., ports. ; 15 x 21 cm. Caption title. On cover: First Church of Otago, 1873-1973. [BX9215.O85F576] 75-320925 1.50
1. First Church of Otago. I. Title.

WALLSEND. St. Andrew's 285'.294'4
Presbyterian Church.
St. Andrew's Presbyterian Church Wallsend centenary. [Newcastle, N.S.W., 1967] [14] p. illus. 27 cm. Cover title. [BX9215.W3S28] 75-488897
1. Wallsend. St. Andrew's Presbyterian Church.

HANZSCHE, William Thomson, 285.4
1891-
Know your Church; the United Presbyterian Church in the U.S.A. Rev., rewritten by Earl F. Zeigler. Philadelphia, Board of Christian Educ. of the United Presbyterian Church in the United States of America [dist. Westminister Pr., 1962, c.1961] 63p. Rev. of the author's 'Know your church! The Presbyterian Church: its history, organization, and program,' pub. in 1946, orig. pub. in 1933 under title, 'Our Presbyterian Church.' 61-14520 .85 pap.,
1. United Presbyterian Church in the U. S. A. I. Zeigler, Earl Frederick, 1889- II. Title.

JAMISON, Wallace N 285.473
The United Presbyterian story; a centennial study, 1858-1958. Pittsburgh, Geneva Press [1958] 253p. illus. 21cm. Includes bibliography. [BX8982.J3] 58-1931
1. United Presbyterian Church of North America—Hist. I. Title.

SANDERS, Robert Stuart. 285.4769
An historical sketch of Ebenezer Reformed Presbyterian Church, Jessamine County, Kentucky. [1st ed.] Frankfort, Ky., Roberts Print. Co., 1954. 71p. illus. 23cm. [BX9211.J53E2] 54-36563
1. Ebenezer Associate Reformed Presbyterian Church, Jessamine Co., Ky. I. Title.

COLE, Maurice F 285.477438
The First Presbyterian Church of Royal Oak, Michigan: the first fifty years [by] Maurice F. Cole. [Royal Oak? Mich., 1964] 115 p. illus., ports. 23 cm. [BX9211.R76F5] 65-1542
1. Royal Oak, Mich. First Presbyterian Church. I. Title.

ARNDT, Elmer J F 285.7
The faith we proclaim; the doctrinal viewpoint generally prevailing in the Evangelical and Reformed Church, by Elmer J. F. Arndt, under the guidance and with the counsal of the Theological Committee. Philadelphia, Christian Education Press [1960] 135p. 22cm. [BX7471.A75] 60-6934
1. Evangelical and Reformed Church—Doctrinal and contreversial works. I. Title.

ARNDT, Elmer J. F. 285.7
The faith we proclaim; the doctrinal viewpoint generally prevailing in the Evangelical and Reformed Church, by Elmer J. F. Arndt, under the guidance and with the counsel of the Theological Committee. Philadelphia, Christian Education Press [c.1960] xiii, 135p. 22cm. 60-6934 2.50
1. Evangelical and Reformed Church—Doctrinal and controversial works. I. Title.

CHRISTIAN Reformed Church. 285.7
Centennial Committee.
One hundred years in the New World; the story of the Christian Reformed Church from 1857 to 1957: its origin growth, and institutional activities, together with an account of the celebration of its anniversary in its centennial year. [Grand Rapids, c1957] 218p. illus. 28cm. [BX6815.A47] 58-30379
1. Christian Reformed Church—Hist. I. Title.

DAVIS, Charles Moler, 1900- 285.7
ed.
Readings in the geography of Michigan. Selected and edited by Charles M. Davis. Ann Arbor, Mich., Ann Arbor Publishers, 1964. ix, 321 p. illus., maps. 28 cm. [F566.D24] 65-26800
1. Michigan. I. Title.

DUNN, David, 1887- 285.7
A history of the Evangelical and Reformed Church [by] David Dunn, [others] Philadelphia, Christian Education Press [c.1961] 369p. illus. Companion volume to The faith we proclaim, by Elmer J. F. Arndt. Bibl. 61-6039 5.95
1. Evangelical and Reformed Church—Hist. I. Title.

GOD'S covenant 285'.7
faithfulness : the 50th anniversary of the Protestant Reformed Churches in America / Gertrude Hoeksema, editor. Grand Rapids : Reformed Free Pub. Association ; distributed by Kregel Publications, [1975] 117, 64 p. : ill. ; 23 cm. [BX9250.G6] 75-990 ISBN 0-8254-2824-6 : 5.95
1. Protestant Reformed Churches of America. I. Hoeksema, Gertrude.

HALL, George Lyman, 1913- 285.7
Our Michigan, by George L. Hall and Kenneth C. Ray. [St. Louis, State Pub. Co., c1962] 139 p. illus. 26 cm. (Our state series) Includes bibliography. [F566.H19] 62-58070
1. Michigan. I. Ray, Kenneth C., joint author. II. Title.

HORTON, Douglas, 1891- 285.7
The United Church of Christ: its origins, organization, and role in the world today. New York, T. Nelson [1962] 287 p. 22 cm. Includes bibliography. [BX9885.H6] 62-10371
1. United churches of Christ.

KUIPER, Rienk Bouke, 1886- 285.7
To be or not to be reformed. Whither the Christian Reformed Church? Grand Rapids, Zondervan Pub. House [1959] 194p. 21cm. [BX6821.K8] 59-38171
1. Christian Reformed Church. I. Title.

MICHIGAN. Tourist Council. 285.7
Canoe trails of Michigan. [2d ed. Lansing, 195--] 52p. 18cm. Cover title. Fold col. map inserted. [F566.M6717] 56-42539
1. Canoes and canceing—Michigan. 2. Michigan—Descr. & trav. 3. Rivers—Michigan. I. Title.

NEWCOMB, Delphine. 285.7
Exploring Michigan. Editorial consultant:

Nicholas P. Georgiady. [Rev. ed.] Chicago, Follett Pub. Co. [c1963] 96 p. illus. (part col.) 26 cm. Includes bibliographies. [F566.N5] 63-23934
1. Michigan — Descr. & trav. — 1951- I. Title.

SCHOOLLAND, Marian M 1902- 285.7
Children of the Reformation; the story of the Christian Reformed Church, its origin and growth. Grand Rapids, Eerdmans [1958] 112p. illus. 23cm. [BX6815.S35] 58-13060
1. Christain Reformed church—hist. I. Title.

VAN HALSEMA, Thea (Bouma) 285.7
I will build by church. Illustrated by Dirk Gringhuia. Centennial ed.; the Christian Reformed Church centennial, 1857-1957. Grand Rapids, Mich., International Publications; distrisbuted by Kregel's [1956] 190 p. illus. 24 cm. [BX6816.V3] 56-12763
1. Christian Reformed Church — Hist. I. Title.

VAN HALSEMA THEA(BOUMA) 285.7
I will build my church. Illustrated by Dirk Gringhuis. Centennial ed.; the Christian Refromed Chruch centennial, 1857-1957. Grand Rapids, Mich., International Publications distributed by Kregel's [1956] 190p. illus. 24cm. [BX6816.V3] 56-12763
1. Christian Reformed Church—Hist. I. Title.

PIETY and patriotism : 285'.709
Bicentennial studies of the Reformed Church in America, 1776-1976 / edited by James W. Van Hoeven. Grand Rapids : Eerdmans, c1976. 191 p. ; 21 cm. (The Historical series of the Reformed Church in America ; no. 4) Includes bibliographical references. [BX9515.P5] 76-369401 ISBN 0-8028-1663-0 : 3.95
1. Reformed Church in America—History—Addresses, essays, lectures. 2. Reformed Church in America—Doctrinal and controversial works—Addresses, essays, lectures. I. Van Hoeven, James w. II. Series: Reformed Church in America. The historical series ; no. 4.

ADAIR, James R., 1923- 285'.7'0924 B
M. R. De Haan: the man and his ministry [by] James R. Adair. Grand Rapids, Zondervan Pub. House [1969] 160 p. illus., ports. 21 cm. [BR1725.D38A6] 79-81039
1. De Haan, Martin Ralph, 1891-1964.

APPEL, Theodore, 1823-1907. 285'.7'0924 B
The life and work of John Williamson Nevin. New York, Arno Press, 1969. 776 p. facsim., port. 24 cm. (Religion in America) Reprint of the 1889 ed. [BX9593.N4A6 1969] 71-83409
1. Nevin, John Williamson, 1803-1886. I. Title.

BOEHM, John Philip, 1683-1749. 285'.7'0924 B
Life and letters of the Rev. John Philip Boehm, founder of the Reformed Church in Pennsylvania, 1683-1749. Edited by the Rev. William J. Hinke. New York, Arno Press, 1972 [c1916] xxiv, 501 p. illus., map (1 fold.) 24 cm. (Religion in America, series II) [BX9593.B6A3 1972] 71-38784 ISBN 0-405-04069-5
1. Reformed Church in the United States—Pennsylvania. I. Hinke, William John, 1871-1947, ed.

GROENHOFF, Edwin L. 285'.7'0924 B
The quiet prince; a biography of Dr. Melvin G. Larson, Christian journalist [by] Edwin L. Groenhoff. Minneapolis, His International Service [1974] 127 p. illus. 22 cm. [BX7548.Z8L373] 74-79531 ISBN 0-911802-36-3 5.95
1. Larson, Melvin Gunnard, 1916-1972. I. Title.

SYMON, Benjamin Goodall, 1935-1957. 285'.7'0924
Benjamin Goodall Symon, Jr., his biography and letters, by Lowell Russell Ditzen in collaboration with Elizabeth Carter Symon. Amherst, Mass., Amherst College Press, 1963. xiii, 91 p. port. 24 cm. [BX9593.S9A4] 63-23346
1. Ditzen, Lowell Russell. I. Title.

*DE JONG, Peter Y. 285'.731
The Christian Reformed church: a study manual. 3d rev. Grand Rapids, Mich., Baker Bk. [1967] 114p. 22cm. 1.00 pap.,
I. Title.

DE RIDDER, Richard. 285'.731
My church, written by Richard De Ridder and Thea B. Van Halsema. Grand Rapids, Produced by the Committee on Education of the Christian Reformed Church [1967] 259 p. illus., maps, ports. 24 cm. [BX6814.D4] 67-7957
1. Christian Reformed Church — Study and teaching. I. Van Halsema, Thea (Bouma) joint author. II. Title.

DE RIDDER, Richard. 285'.731
My church, written by Richard De Ridder and Thea B. Van Halsema. Grand Rapids, Produced by the Committee of Education of the Christian Reformed Church [1967] 259 p. illus., maps, ports. 24 cm. [BX6814.D4] 67-7957
1. Christian Reformed Church—Study and teaching. I. Van Halsema, Thea (Bouma) joint author. II. Title.

SCHOOLLAND, Marian M., 1902- 285'.731
De kolonie : the church that God transplanted / by Marian M. Schoolland. Grand Rapids, Mich. : [Board of Publications of the Christian Reformed Church, 1974] c1973-1974. 266 p. : ill. ; 18 cm. "Appeared as a serial story in the Banner in 1973-74." [BX6815.S36] 74-27175
1. Christian Reformed Church—History. I. Title.

REFORMED Church in America. Commission on History. 285.73205
Historical directory of the Reformed Church in America, 1628-1965. Peter N. VandenBerge, ed. New Brunswick, N.J. [1966] xix, 348p. 23cm. Successor to C. E. Corwin's A manual of the Reformed Church in America (formerly Reformed Protesant Dutch Church) 1628-1922, 5th ed., 1922 [BX9507.A55] 66-21948 5.00
1. Reformed Church in America—Direct. I. VandenBerge. Peter N., ed. II. Corwin, Charles Edward, 1868-1958. A manual of the Reformed Church in America. III. Title.

HARMELINK, Herman. 285'.732'09
Ecumenism and the Reformed Church. Grand Rapids, Eerdmans [1968] 112 p. 21 cm. (The Historical series of the Reformed Church in America, no. 1) Bibliography: p. 95-98. Bibliographical references included in "Notes" (p. 99-106) [BX9515.H3] 68-57154 2.45
1. Reformed Church in America—History. 2. Christian union—Reformed Church in America—History. I. Title. II. Series: Reformed Church in America. The historical series, no. 1

SHIELD, Frederic K. 285'.732'0922 B
Lillie Helena Kull and Friedrich Kienholz Schild: a tribute [by Frederic K. Shield] Winter Park [Fla.] 1967. 47 l. 2 ports. 29 cm. [BX9543.S33S47] 72-299114
1. Schild, Friedrich Kienholz, 1868-1933. 2. Schild, Lillie Helena Kull, 1869-1957. I. Title.

RINGER, Francis E. 285.7'34'0974811
Church in travail; story of Philadelphia Synod, Evangelical and Reformed Church, 1939-1962 [by] Francis E. Ringer. [Philadelphia, Printed by Graphic Print. Associates, c1964] vi, 224 p. 24 cm. Bibliographical footnotes. [BX7470.P4R5] 285'.771'9 77-49489
1. Evangelical and Reformed Church. Synods. Philadelphia. 2. United Church of Christ. Conferences. Pennsylvania Southeast. I. Title.

THE Old North 285'.749'21
Reformed Church of Dumont, New Jersey, 1724-1974. Dumont, N.J. : The Church, [1976] c1974. p. cm. "This book is number of a limited edition of five hundred." Bibliography: p. [BX9531.D85O46 1976] 76-6085 7.95
1. Old North Reformed Church, Dumont, N.J.

PEELER, Banks J., 1897- 285'.75
A story of the Southern Synod of the Evangelical and Reformed Church, 1740-1968, by Banks J. Peeler. Published under the supervision of the Board of Editors, and authorized by the Synod. [Salisbury, N.C., c1968] xiii, 505 p. illus., ports. 25 cm. Includes bibliographies. [BX7470.S6P4] 71-12189
1. Evangelical and Reformed Church. Synods. Southern. I. Title.

KELLERMEYER, Josephine M. 285'.771'9
A short history of the Southeast Ohio Synod of the Evangelical and Reformed Church, together with historical sketches of the local churches which were a part of it, 1939-1963. Compiled by Josephine M. Kellermeyer (Mrs. Hugo C.) for the Southeast Ohio Synod's History Committee. Canton, Ohio, Distributed from Trinity Church [1971?] 220 p. illus., maps. 21 cm. [BX7470.S63K44] 73-170779
1. Evangelical and Reformed Church. Synods. Southeast Ohio. I. Evangelical and Reformed Church. Synods. Southeast Ohio. History Committee. II. Title.

BIRCH, John Joseph, 1894- 285.7747
The pioneering church of the Mohawk Valley; de banbreckende kerk van de Mohawk Vallei. Schenctady, N. Y., The Consistory, First Reformed Church, 1955. 204p. illus. 24cm. [BX9531.S48F53] 56-21480
1. Schenectady, N. Y. First Reformed Church. I. Title.

NEW York. Collegiate Church. Marble Collegiate Church. Marble Club. 285.7747
The Marble Collegiate Church. [Blanche Tessaro Cleaver, editor] New York, 1954. unpaged. illus. 20cm. [BX9531.N5C715] 55-24617
1. New York. Collegiate Church. Marble Collegiate Church. I. Cleaver, Blanche Tessaro, 1904- ed. II. Title.

TAPPAN, N.Y. Reformed Church. 285'.77'4728
Tappan Reformed Church, 1694-1969: two and three quarter centuries of service. [Tappan? N.Y., 1969?] 1 v. (unpaged) illus., ports. 29 cm. On cover: Church at the crossroads for 275 years. [BX9531.T3A48] 70-14137
I. Title.

PRICE, Charles Henry, 1899- ed. 285.77'48'12
A history of Christ Reformed Church at Indian Creek (Indianfield). Compiled, edited, and published, by Charles H. Price. Telford, Pa., 1966. xix, 499 p. port. 24 cm. Bibliography: p. xvii-xix. [BX9581.C48P7] 67-2018
1. Christ Reformed Church at Indian Creek, Franconia Township, Montgomery Co., Pa. I. Title.

HENRIE, Rodney Arden. 285'.7748'38
A history of the Orangeville Evangelical and Reformed Church, Orangeville, Pennsylvania. Lancaster[?] Pa., [1957?] 48 p. illus., port. 23 cm. Thesis (B.D.)—Theological Seminary of the Evangelical and Reformed Church. Bibliography: p. 47. [BX7481.O7O75] 74-8206
1. Orangeville Evangelical and Reformed Church. I. Title.

HARMELINK, Herman. 285'.7749
The Reformed Church in New Jersey [1660-1969] by Herman Harmelink, III, William W. Coventry [and] Sharon Thoms Scholten. [n.p.] Synod of New Jersey, 1969. 110 p. illus. 23 cm. Bibliography: p. 108-110. [BX9516.N5H37] 78-91396
1. Reformed Church in America—New Jersey—History. I. Coventry, William W., 1930- joint author. II. Scholten, Sharon Thoms, 1933- joint author. III. Title.

LEIBY, Adrian Coulter. 285'.7749
The United Churches of Hackensack and Schraalenburgh, New Jersey, 1686-1822 / Adrian C. Leiby ; drawings by Richard G. Belcher. River Edge, N.J. : Bergen County Historical Society, 1976. 336 p. : ill. ; 24 cm. Includes index. Bibliography: p. 315-322. [BX9516.N5L44] 76-12114
1. Reformed Church in America—New Jersey—History. 2. Dutch in New Jersey. I. Title: The United Churches of Hackensack ...

OLD Paramus Reformed Church, Ridgewood, N.J. Historical Committee. 285'.7749'21
Old Paramus Reformed Church in Ridgewood, New Jersey, the years 1725-1975 / [prepared for the 250th anniversary of Old Paramus Reformed Church by the Historical Committee]. Ridgewood, N.J. : Old Paramus Reformed Church, c1975. 64 p. : ill., facsims. ; 29 cm. Cover title. [BX9531.R55O4 1975] 75-322483
1. Old Paramus Reformed Church, Ridgewood, N.J. 2. Ridgewood, N.J.—History.

CANTON, Ohio. First Evangelical and Reformed Church. 285.7772
History of the First Evangelical and Reformed Church Canton [1960?] 116p. illus. 24cm. [BX7481.C3F5] 61-40201
I. Title.

LANG, Elfrieda Wilhelmina Henrietta, 1904- 285.7772
The history of Trinity Evangelical and Reformed Church, 1853-1953, Mount Vernon, Indiana. St. Louis, Eden Pub. House, 1953. 206p. illus. 24cm. [BX7481.M6L3] 53-39549
1. Mount Vernon, Ind. Trinity Evangelical and Reformed Church. I. Title.

BRUINS, Elton J., 1927- 285'.77'7415
The Americanization of a congregation; a history of the Third Reformed Church of Holland, Michigan, by Elton J. Bruins. Grand Rapids, Eerdmans [1970] 122 p. illus., ports. 21 cm. (The Historical series of the Reformed Church in America, no. 2) Includes bibliographical references. [BX9531.H6T5] 77-112950 2.95
1. Holland, Mich. Third Reformed Church. I. Title. II. Series: Reformed Church in America. The historical series, no. 2

COTTON, John, 1584-1652. 285'.8
John Cotton on the churches of New England. Edited by Larzer Ziff. Cambridge, Mass., Belknap Press of Harvard University Press, 1968. 401 p. 22 cm. (The John Harvard library) Contents.Contents.—A sermon delivered at Salem, 1636.—The keys to the kingdom of heaven, 1644.—The way of the Congregational churches cleared, 1648.—Glossary of names. Bibliographical footnotes. [BX7230.C748] 68-17636
1. Congregational churches—Discipline. 2. Congregational churches—Doctrinal and controversial works. I. Ziff, Larzer, 1927- ed. II. Title. III. Series.

EDWARDS, Jonathan, 1703-1758. 285'.8 s
Apocalyptic writings / Jonathan Edwards ; edited by Stephen J. Stein. New Haven : Yale University Press, 1977. x, 501 p. ; 24 cm. (The works of Jonathan Edwards ; v. 5) Contents.Contents.—Notes on the apocalypse.—An humble attempt. Includes bibliographical references and indexes. [BX7117.E3 1957 vol. 5] [BS2825.A2] 228'.06 76-30845 ISBN 0-300-01945-9 : 28.50
1. Bible. N.T. Revelation—Commentaries. I. Edwards, Jonathan, 1703-1758. An humble attempt to promote explicit agreement and visible union of God's people ... 1977. II. Title. Contents omitted

EDWARDS, Jonathan, 1703-1758. 285'.8 s
The great-awakening: A faithful narrative. The distinguishing marks. Some thoughts concerning The revival, letters relating to The revival. Preface to True religion by Joseph Bellamy. Edited by C. C. Goen. New Haven, Yale University Press, 1972. ix, 595 p. 24 cm. (His Works, v. 4) Includes bibliographical references. [BX7117.E3 1957 vol. 4] [BR520] 277.3 75-179472 ISBN 0-300-01437-6 18.50
1. Great Awakening. I. Goen, C. C., ed. II. Title.

EDWARDS, Jonathan, 1703-1758. 285'.8 s
Original sin. Edited by Clyde A. Holbrook. New Haven, Yale University, 1970. xi, 448 p. 24 cm. (His Works, v. 3) Includes bibliographical references. [BX7117.E3 1957 vol. 3] [BT720] 233'.14 72-179794 ISBN 0-300-01198-9
1. Sin, Original. I. Holbrook, Clyde A., ed.

JENKINS, Daniel Thomas, 1914- 285.8
Congregationalism: a restatement. New York, Harper [1954] 152p. 20cm. [BX7231] 54-14932
1. Congregationalism. I. Title.

SHEPARD, Thomas, 1605-1649. 285'.8
The works. Edited by John Adams Albro. Hildesheim, New York, G. Olms, 1971. 3 v. 22 cm. (Anglistica & Americana, 96) Reprint of the ed. published in Boston in 1853. Includes bibliographical references. [BX7117.S5 1971] 73-870571
1. Congregational churches—Collected works. 2. Theology—Collected works—17th century. I. Albro, John Adams, 1799-1866, ed. II. Title. III. Series.

MATHER, Cotton, 1663-1728 285.8081
Selections. Ed., with introd. and notes, by Kenneth B. Murdock. New York, Hafner Pub. Co. [1961, c.1926] 377p. (Hafner library of classics no. 20; American authors series.) 60-11056 2.45 pap.,
1. Congregational churches—Collected works. 2. Theology—Collected works—18th cent. I. Title.

DEXTER, Henry Martyn, 1821-1890. 285'.8'09
The Congregationalism of the last three hundred years as seen in its literature; with special reference to certain recondite, neglected, or disputed passages. In twelve lectures, delivered on the Southworth Foundation in the Theological Seminary at Andover, Mass., 1876-1879. New York, B. Franklin [1970] 2 v. 24 cm. (Burt Franklin research & source works series, 519) (Selected essays in history, economics & social science, 157.) Reprint of the 1880 ed. Bibliography: v. 2, p. [5]-286. [BX7131.D4 1970] 68-58213
1. Congregationalism—History. 2. Congregationalism—Bibliography. 3. Autographs—Facsimiles. I. Andover Theological Seminary. II. Title.

ALLEN, Gwenfread Elaine, 1904- 285'.8'0922 B
Bridge builders; the story of Theodore and Mary Atherton Richards, by Gwenfread E. Allen. [Honolulu] Hawaii Conference

Foundation, 1970. 260 p. illus. 24 cm. [BV3680.H4R4762] 75-131598
1. Richards, Theodore, 1867-1948. 2. Richards, Mary (Atherton) I. Title.

DODDS, Elisabeth D. 285'.8'0922 B
Marriage to a difficult man; the "uncommon union" of Jonathan and Sarah Edwards, by Elisabeth D. Dodds. Philadelphia, Westminster Press [1971] 224 p. 21 cm. Includes bibliographical references. [BX7260.E3D6] 73-141195 ISBN 0-664-20900-9 5.95
1. Edwards, Jonathan, 1703-1758. 2. Edwards, Sarah, 1710-1758. I. Title.

HURLBURT, Mabel S. 285'.8'0922
Farmington; church & town. Stonington, Conn., Pequot Pr. [1967] xiii, 110p. illus., ports. 24cm. [BX7255.F43F54] 67-16951 7.50
1. Farmington, Conn. First Church of Christ Congregational. I. Title.

WALKER, Williston, 285'.8'0922
1860-1922.
Ten New England leaders. New York, Arno Press, 1969. v, 471 p. 23 cm. (Religion in America) "Lectures ... delivered on the 'Southworth Foundation' in Andover Theological Seminary in 1898-1899." Reprint of the 1901 ed. Contents.Contents.—William Bradford.—John Cotton.—Richard Mather.—John Eliot.—Increase Mather.—Jonathan Edwards.—Charles Chauncy.—Samuel Hopkins.—Leonard Woods.—Leonard Bacon. Includes bibliographical references. [BX7259.W3 1969] 76-83445
1. Congregational churches—Biography. 2. New England—Church history. I. Title.

ABBOTT, Lyman, 1835- 285.8'0924 B
1922.
Henry Ward Beecher. Cambridge, Riverside Press, 1904. Miami, Fla., Mnemosyne Pub. Co. [1969] xxxviii, 457 p. ports. 23 cm. Bibliography: p. [xvii]-xxxviii. [BX7260.B3A65 1969] 78-89428
1. Beecher, Henry Ward, 1813-1887.

ALLEN, Alexander 285'.8'0924 B
Viets Griswold, 1841-1908.
Jonathan Edwards. New York, B. Franklin [1974, c1889] Reprint of the ed. published by Houghton, Mifflin, Boston, in series: American religious leaders. Bibliography: p. [BX7260.E3A6 1974] 72-81931 ISBN 0-8337-3926-3
1. Edwards, Jonathan, 1703-1758.

BERK, Stephen E. 285'.8'0924 B
Calvinism versus democracy; Timothy Dwight and the origins of American evangelical orthodoxy, by Stephen E. Berk. [Hamden, Conn.] Archon Books, 1974. xiv, 252 p. 22 cm. Bibliography: p. [229]-245. [BX7260.D84B47] 73-20053 ISBN 0-208-01419-5 14.50
1. Dwight, Timothy, 1752-1817. 2. Calvinism—United States. 3. Evangelicalism—United States. I. Title.

BOYLSTON, Ruth 285'.8'0924 (B)
Harrington.
Before many witnesses; the life of Howard James Chidley. [Winchester, Mass., University Press, 1967] [BX7260.C56B6] 67-9765
I. Chidley, Howard James, 1878-1966. II. vii, 155 p. illus. ports. 23 cm. III. Title.

BROWN, Ira Vernon. 285'.8'0924
Lyman Abbott, Christian evolutionist; a study in religious liberalism, by Ira V. Brown. Westport, Conn., Greenwood Press [1970, c1953] ix, 303 p. port. 23 cm. Bibliography: p. [243]-255. [BX7260.A2B7 1970] 79-97325
1. Abbott, Lyman, 1835-1922.

BURG, Barry 285',8'0924 B
Richard, 1938-
Richard Mather of Dorchester / B. R. Burg. [Lexington, Ky.] : University Press of Kentucky, c1976. xiii, 207 p. ; 23 cm. Includes index. Bibliography: p. [191]-200. [BX7260.M368B87] 75-41987 ISBN 0-8131-1343-1 : 15.95
1. Mather, Richard, 1596-1669. 2. Congregational churches—Clergy—Biography. 3. Clergy—Massachusetts—Biography. I. Title.

CARSE, James. 285'.8'0924
Jonathan Edwards & the visibility of God. New York, Scribnr [1967] 191 p. 22 cm. Bibliographical footnotes. [BX7260.E3C3] 67-24040
1. Edwards, Jonathan, I. Title.

CARSE, James. 285'.8'0924
Jonathan Edwards & the visibility of God. New York, Scribner [1967] 191 p. 22 cm. Bibliographical footnotes. [BX7260.E3C3] 67-24040
1. Edwards, Jonathan, 1703-1758. I. Title.

CHENEY, Mary A. 285'.8'0924 B
(Bushnell) ed.
Life and letters of Horace Bushnell [by] Mary Bushnell Cheney. New York, Arno Press, 1969. x, 579 p. ports. 23 cm. (Religion in America) Reprint of the 1880 ed. [BX7260.B9C5 1969] 74-83415
1. Bushnell, Horace, 1802-1876.

CLAPP, Theodore, 285'.8'0924 B
1792-1866.
Autobiographical sketches and recollections, during a thirty-five years' residence in New Orleans. Freeport, N.Y., Books for Libraries Press [1972] viii, 419 p. port. 23 cm. Reprint of the 1857 ed. [BX9225.C547A3 1972] 77-38346 ISBN 0-8369-6763-1
1. New Orleans—History. I. Title.

COOK, George Allan 285'.80924(B)
John Wise, early American democrat. New York, Octagon, 1966. ix, 246p. 21cm. Bibl. [BX7260.W565C6 1966] 66-28373 7.50
1. Wise, John, 1652-1725. I. Title.

COOLEY, Timothy 285'.8'0924 B
Mather, 1772-1859.
Sketches of the life and character of the Rev. Lemuel Haynes, A.M., for many years pastor of a church in Rutland, Vt., and late in Granville, New York. With some introductory remarks by William B. Sprague. New York, Negro Universities Press [1969] 345 p. port. 23 cm. "Originally published in 1837." [BX7260.H315C6 1969] 70-88426
1. Haynes, Lemuel, 1753-1833. I. Title.

DAVIS, Jerome, 285'.80924 (B)
1891-
A life adventure for peace; an autobiography. Foreword by James A. Pike. [1st ed.] New York, Citadel Press [1967] xiii, 208 p. 21 cm. 67-18083
I. Title.

DAVIS, Jerome, 285'.80924(B)
1891-
A life adventure for peace: an autobiography: Foreword by Mames A. Pike. [1st ed.] New York, Citadel [1967] xiii, 208p. 21cm. [BX7260.D34A3] 67-18083 2.45 pap.,
I. Title.

DORN, Jacob 285'.8'0924 (B)
Henry.
Washington Gladden; prophet of the social gospel. [Columbus] Ohio State University Press [1968, c1967] x, 489 p. port. 23 cm. Bibliography: p.[449]-469. [BX7260.G45D6] 67-17173
1. Gladden, Washington, 1836-1918. I. Title.

EATON, Arthur 285'.8'0924 B
Wentworth Hamilton, 1849-1937.
The famous Mather Byles; the noted Boston Tory preacher, poet, and wit, 1707-1788. With a new introd. and a pref. by George Athan Billias. Boston, Gregg Press, 1972 [c1914] x, x, 258 p. illus. 23 cm. (The American Revolutionary series. The Loyalist library) Reprint of the ed. published by W. A. Butterfield, Boston. "Doctor Byles's chief published writings": p. 240-246. [BX7260.B95E3 1972] 72-8697 ISBN 0-8398-0458-X 13.00 (Lib. ed.)
1. Byles, Mather, 1707-1788. I. Series: The Loyalist library.

ELSMERE, Jane 285'.8'0924 B
Shaffer.
Henry Ward Beecher; the Indiana years, 1837-1847. Indianapolis, Indiana Historical Society, 1973. xiii, 317 p. illus. 24 cm. Bibliography: p. 303-306. [BX7260.B3E47] 74-156947
1. Beecher, Henry Ward, 1813-1887.

FINNEY, Charles 285'.8'0924 B
Grandison, 1792-1875.
The autobiography of Charles G. Finney / condensed & edited by Helen Wessel. Minneapolis : Bethany Fellowship, c1977. 230 p. ; 21 cm. Condensed version of Memoirs of Rev. Charles G. Finney, originally published in 1876. [BX7260.F47A352 1977] 77-2813 ISBN 0-87123-010-0 pbk. : 3.50
1. Finney, Charles Grandison, 1792-1875. 2. Congregational churches—Clergy—Biography. 3. Clergy—United States—Biography. 4. Evangelists—United States—Biography. I. Wessel, Helen Strain, 1924- II. Title.

FINNEY, Charles 285'.8'0924 B
Grandison, 1792-1875.
Memoirs of Rev. Charles G. Finney. New York, A. S. Barnes, 1876. [New York, AMS Press, 1973] p. [BX7260.F47A4 1973] 74-168025 ISBN 0-404-00047-9

GRIFFIN, Edward M., 285'.8'0924
1937-
Jonathan Edwards, by Edward M. Griffin. Minneapolis, University of Minnesota Press [1971] 46 p. 21 cm. (University of Minnesota pamphlets on American writers, no. 97) Bibliography: p. 41-46. [BX7260.E3G73] 75-633326 ISBN 0-8166-0601-3 0.95
1. Edwards, Jonathan, 1703-1758. I. Series: Minnesota. University. Pamphlets on American writers, no. 97

GROSS, Fred W., 285'.8'0924 B
1895-
The pastor; the life of an immigrant [by] Fred W. Gross. Philadelphia, Dorrance [1973] 182 p. illus. 21 cm. Bibliography: p. 181-182. [BX7260.G785A3] 73-76214 ISBN 0-8059-1843-4 4.95
1. Gross, Fred W., 1895- I. Title.

HIBBEN, Paxton, 285'.8'0924 B
1880-1928.
Henry Ward Beecher: an American portrait. Foreword by Sinclair Lewis. New York, Beekman Publishers, 1974. xiv, 361 p. 23 cm. (American newspapermen, 1790-1933) Reprint of the 1942 ed. published by the Press of the Readers Club, New York. Bibliography: p. 317-329. [BX7260.B3H5 1974] 73-23116 ISBN 0-8464-0019-7 17.50
1. Beecher, Henry Ward, 1813-1887.

HOLBROOK, Clyde A. 285'.8'0924
The ethics of Jonathan Edwards; morality and aesthetics [by] Clyde A. Holbrook. Ann Arbor, University of Michigan Press [1973] ix, 227 p. 22 cm. A revision of the author's thesis, Yale University. Bibliography: p. 223-227. [BX7260.E3H57 1973] 72-91506 ISBN 0-472-44800-5 10.00
1. Edwards, Jonathan, 1703-1758—Ethics. I. Title.

JONATHAN Edwards; 285'.8'0924 B
his life and influence. Papers and discussions by Conrad Cherry [and others] Edited by Charles Angoff. Rutherford [N.J.] Fairleigh Dickinson University Press [1974, c1975] 65 p. 21 cm. (The Leverton lecture series) Includes bibliographical references. [BX7260.E3J66] 74-4516 ISBN 0-8386-1571-6 4.50
1. Edwards, Jonathan, 1703-1758. I. Cherry, C. Conrad. II. Angoff, Charles, 1902- ed. III. Title. IV. Series.

JONATHAN Edwards; 285'.8'0924 B
his life and influence. Papers and discussions by Conrad Cherry [and others] Edited by Charles Angoff. Rutherford [N.J.] Fairleigh Dickinson University Press [1974, c1975] 65 p. 21 cm. (The Leverton lecture series) Includes bibliographical references. [BX7260.E3J66] 74-4516 ISBN 0-8386-1571-6 4.50
1. Edwards, Jonathan, 1703-1758. I. Cherry, C. Conrad. II. Angoff, Charles, 1902- ed. III. Title. IV. Series.

KEMPER, Robert G. 285'.8'0924 B
An elephant's ballet / Robert G. Kemper. New York : Seabury Press, c1977. p. cm. "A Crossroad book." [BX7260.K38A34 1977] 77-22165 ISBN 0-8164-0373-2 : 6.95
1. Kemper, Robert G. 2. Congregationalists—United States—Biography. 3. Clergy—United States—Biography. 4. Blind—United States—Biography. I. Title.

KEMPER, Robert G. 285'.8'0924 B
An elephant's ballet / Robert G. Kemper. New York : Seabury Press, c1977. p. cm. "A Crossroad book." [BX7260.K38A34 1977] 77-22165 ISBN 0-8164-0373-2 : 6.95
1. Kemper, Robert G. 2. Congregationalists—United States—Biography. 3. Clergy—United States—Biography. 4. Blind—United States—Biography. I. Title.

KENT, Harold 285'.8'0924 B
Winfield.
Dr. Hyde and Mr. Stevenson; the life of the Rev. Dr. Charles McEwen Hyde, including a discussion of the open letter of Robert Louis Stevenson. [1st ed.] Rutland, Vt., C. E. Tuttle [1973] 390 p. illus. 22 cm. "Father Damien, an open letter": p. 344-356. Includes bibliographical references. [BX7260.H9K46] 72-83673 ISBN 0-8048-1062-1 10.00
1. Hyde, Charles McEwen, 1832-1899. I. Stevenson, Robert Louis, 1850-1894. Father Damien. 1973. II. Title.

KENT, Harold 285'.8'0924 B
Winfield.
Dr. Hyde and Mr. Stevenson; the life of the Rev. Dr. Charles McEwen Hyde, including a discussion of the open letter of Robert Louis Stevenson. [1st ed.] Rutland, Vt., C. E. Tuttle [1973] 390 p. illus. 22 cm. "Father Damien, an open letter": p. 344-356. Includes bibliographical references. [BX7260.H9K46] 72-83673 ISBN 0-8048-1062-1 10.00
1. Hyde, Charles McEwen, 1832-1899. I. Stevenson, Robert Louis, 1850-1894. Father Damien. 1973. II. Title.

KNUDTEN, Richard D. 285'.8'0924 B
The systematic thought of Washington Gladden, by Richard D. Knudten. New York, Humanities Press, 1968. ix, 301 p. geneal. table. 24 cm. Bibliography: p. 265-294. [BX7260.G45K58] 68-27098 6.50
1. Gladden, Washington, 1836-1918. 2. Social gospel. I. Title.

LEVIN, David, 1924- 285'.8'0924 B
comp.
Jonathan Edwards; a profile. [1st ed.] New York, Hill and Wang [1969] xxi, 263 p. 21 cm. (American profiles) Bibliography: p. 257-259. [BX7260.E3L4] 68-30760 5.95
1. Edwards, Jonathan, 1703-1758.

MATHER, Increase, 285'.8'0924 B
1639-1723.
The life and death of that reverend man of God, Mr. Richard Mather / by Increase Mather. Facsim. reproduction with an introd. and notes / by William J. Scheick. Bainbridge, N.Y. : York Mail-Print, 1974. 93 p. ; 20 cm. Photoreprint of the 1874 ed. published by D. Clapp, Boston. Includes bibliographical references. [BX7260.M368M3 1974] 75-323580 ISBN 0-913126-06-3
1. Mather, Richard, 1596-1669. I. Title.

MEAD, Sidney Earl, 285'8'0924
1904-
Nathaniel William Taylor, 1786-1858; a Conneticut liberal [Hamden, Conn.] Archon, 1967 [c.1942] xi, 259p. 23cm. Bibl. [BX260.T32M35 1967] 67-15932 7.00
1. Taylor, Nathaniel William, 1786-1858. I. Title.

MERIDETH, Robert. 285.8'0924
The politics of the universe; Edward Beecher, abolition, and orthodoxy. Nashville, Vanderbilt University Press [1968] xi, 274 p. 23 cm. "Bibliographic essay": p. 245-255. [BX7260.B28M4] 68-21869 ISBN 0-8265-1123-6 5.95
1. Beecher, Edward, 1803-1895. I. Title.

MILLER, Perry, 285'.8'0924 B
1905-1963.
Jonathan Edwards. Westport, Conn., Greenwood Press [1973, c1949] xv, 348 p. port. 22 cm. Original ed. issued in the American men of letters series. Bibliography: p. 331-333. [BX7260.E3M5 1973] 72-7877 ISBN 0-8371-6551-2 14.25
1. Edwards, Jonathan, 1703-1758. I. Series: The American men of letters series.

MORGAN, Jill. 285'.8'0924
A man of the word; life of G. Campbell Morgan. New York, F. H. Revell [1951] 404p. plates. 22cm. [BX7260.M] A53
1. Morgan, George Campbell, 1863-1945. I. Title.

PROCTOR, Henry 285'.8'0924 B
Hugh, 1868-1933.
Between Black and white; autobiographical sketches. Freeport, N.Y., Books for Libraries Press, 1971. xi, 189 p. illus. 23 cm. (The Black heritage library collection) Reprint of the 1925 ed. [E185.97.P95 1971] 79-173611 ISBN 0-8369-8903-1
I. Title. II. Series.

RANKIN, Alexander 285.80924
Taylor, 1803-1885.
Alexander Taylor Rankin, 1803-1885, his diary and letters: a pioneer minister who fought lawlessness with religion on the prairies of eastern Kansas and the frontier settlements of Denver, where life was harsh and brutal. [Edited] by Nolie Mumey Boulder, Colo., Johnson Pub. Co., 1966. 188 p. illus., ports. 29 cm. The diary and letters date from 1859 to 1861. "A limited edition of four hundred signed and numbered copies." No. 44. [BX9225.R33A3] 66-9515
1. Presbyterian Church in the U.S. (General) — Clergy — Correspondence, reminiscences, etc. 2. Frontier and pioneer life — Kansas. 3. Frontier and pioneer life — Colorado. I. Mumey, Nolie, 1891- ed. II. Title.

SCHEICK, William J. 285.8'092'4
The writings of Jonathan Edwards : theme, motif, and style / by William J. Scheick. 1st ed. College Station : Texas A & M University Press, [1975] xiv, 162 p. ; 24 cm. Includes index. Bibliography: p. [151]-154. [PS742.S3] 75-18689 ISBN 0-89096-004-6 : 8.50
1. Edwards, Jonathan, 1703-1758—Criticism and interpretation. I. Title.

SHEPARD, Thomas, 285'.8'0924
1605-1649.
The works of Thomas Shepard, first pastor of the First Church, Cambridge, Mass., with a memoir of his life and character. New York, Ams Press, 1967. 3 v. 23 cm. Title page includes original imprint: Boston, Doctrinal Tract and Book Society, 1853. [BX7117] 67-31836
1. Congregational churches—Collected works. 2. Theology—Collected works—17th cent. I. Title.

SHEPARD, Thomas, 285'.8'0924
1605-1649.
The works of Thomas Shepard, first pastor of

the First Church, Cambridge, Mass., with a memoir of his life and character. New York, Ams Press, 1967. 3 v. 23 cm. Title page includes original imprint: Boston, Doctrinal Tract and Book Society, 1853. [BX7117] 67-31836
1. Congregational churches—Collected works. 2. Theology—Collected works—17th century.

SHUFFELTON, Frank, 1940- 285'.8'0924 B
Thomas Hooker, 1586-1647 / Frank Shuffelton. Princeton, N.J. : Princeton University Press, c1977. xii, 324 p. ; 23 cm. Includes index. Bibliography: p. 309-317. [BX7260.H596S55] 76-45912 ISBN 0-691-05249-2 : 17.50
1. Hooker, Thomas, 1586-1647. 2. Congregationalists—Connecticut—Hartford—Biography. 3. Clergy—Connecticut—Hartford—Biography. 4. Hartford—Biography.

SIMONSON, Harold Peter, 1926- 285'.8'0924 B
Jonathan Edwards, theologian of the heart, by Harold P. Simonson. Grand Rapids, W. B. Eerdmans Pub. Co. [1974] 174 p. 23 cm. Includes bibliographical references. [BX7260.E3S56] 74-4494 ISBN 0-8028-3448-5
1. Edwards, Jonathan, 1703-1758. I. Title.

SOMMER, Daniel, 1850-1940. 285'.8'0924 B
Daniel Sommer, 1850-1940; a biography. [Edited and] compiled by William E. Wallace. [Lufkin? Tex., 1969] 307 p. illus., ports. 22 cm. Based on The record of my life, by Daniel Sommer. [BX7077.Z8A3] 76-10389
I. Wallace, William Edwin, 1928- ed.

SPONSELLER, Edwin H. 285'.8'0924
Northampton and Jonathan Edwards [by] Edwin Sponseller. Shippensburg, Pa., Shippensburg State College, 1966. 32 p. 23 cm. (Shippensburg State College, Shippensburg, Pa. Faculty monograph series, v. 1, no. 1) "A note on the sources": p. 32. [BX7260.E3S66] 66-64511
1. Edwards, Jonathan, 1703-1758. 2. Northampton, Mass.—Church history. I. Title. II. Series: Pennsylvania. State College, Shippensburg. Faculty monograph series, v. 1, no. 1.

WALKER, George Leon, 1830-1900. 285'.8'0924 B
Thomas Hooker, preacher, founder, democrat. New York, MSS Information Corp. [1972] p. Reprint of the 1891 ed., issued in Makers of America series. "Published works": p. 184-195. [F97.H78 1972] 72-8338 ISBN 0-8422-8120-7
1. Hooker, Thomas, 1586-1647. 2. Connecticut—History—Colonial period. I. Title. II. Series: Makers of America.

WEEKS, Genevieve C. 285'.8'0924 B
Oscar Carleton McCulloch, 1843-1891 : preacher and practitioner of applied Christianity / Genevieve C. Weeks. Indianapolis : Indiana Historical Society, 1976. xvii, 248 p. : ill. ; 24 cm. Includes index. Bibliography: p. 223-235. [BX7260.M216W43] 77-150445
1. McCulloch, Oscar C., 1843-1891. 2. Congregational churches—Clergy—Biography. 3. Clergy—Indiana—Indianapolis—Biography. 4. Indianapolis—Biography.

WEIGLE, Luther Allan, 1880- 285'.8'0924 B
The glory days : from the life of Luther Allan Weigle / Luther Allan Weigle. New York : Friendship Press, [1976] p. cm. Bibliography: p. [BX7260.W444A33] 76-21779 ISBN 0-377-00058-2 pbk. : 5.95
1. Weigle, Luther Allan, 1880- 2. Weigle, Luther Allan, 1880- —Bibliography. 3. Congregational churches—Sermons. 4. Sermons, American. I. Title.

WINSLOW, Ola Elizabeth. 285'.8'0924
John Eliot, apostle to the Indians. Boston, Houghton Mifflin, 1968. 225 p. illus., facsims. 22 cm. Bibliography: p. [213]-218. [E78.M4E595] 68-19633 5.95
1. Eliot, John, 1604-1690.

WINSLOW, Ola Elizabeth. 285'.8'0924 B
Jonathan Edwards, 1703-1758; a biography. New York, Octagon Books, 1973 [c1940] xii, 406 p. illus. 24 cm. Reprint of the ed. published by Macmillan. Bibliography: p. 373-393. [BX7260.E3W5 1973] 73-9771 14.00
1. Edwards, Jonathan, 1703-1758.

WOOD, James Playsted, 1905- 285'.8'0924 B
Mr. Jonathan Edwards. New York, Seabury Press [1968] 166 p. 22 cm. Bibliography: p. [159]-160. A biography of the eighteenth-century Congregational minister who, as a philosopher, theologian, and scholar, affected the religious life of colonial America. [BX7260.E3W6] 92 AC 68
1. Edwards, Jonathan, 1703-1758. I. Title.

EDWARDS, Jonathan, 1703-1758. 285.8'32
Works. Perry Miller, general editor. [New Haven, Yale University Press, 1957- v. port., facsim. 24 cm. Half title; each vol. has also special t.p. Contents.Contents.—v. 1. Freedom of the will.—v. 2. Religious affections. [BX7117.E3 1957] 57-2336
1. Congregational churches—Collected works. 2. Theology—Collected works—18th century. I. Miller, Perry, 1905- ed.

ADAMSON, William R 285.8320924
Bushnell rediscovered [by] William R. Adamson. Philadelphia, United Church Press [1966] 144 p. 21 cm. Bibliographical references included in "Notes" (p. 129-144) [BX7260.B9A6] 66-23990
1. Bushnell, Horace, 1802-1876. I. Title.

ADAMSON, William R. 285.8320924
Bushnell rediscovered [by] William R. Adamson. Philadelphia, United Church Press [1966] 144 p. 21 cm. Bibliographical references included in "Notes" (p. 129-144) [BX7260.B9A6] 66-23990
1. Bushnell, Horace, 1802-1876. I. Title.

EATON, Arthur Wentworth Hamilton, 1849-1937. 285'.832'0924 B
The famous Mather Byles; the noted Boston Tory preacher, poet, and wit, 1707-1788. Freeport, N.Y., Books for Libraries Press [1971] x, 258 p. illus. 23 cm. Reprint of the 1914 ed. Includes bibliographical references. [BX7260.B95E3 1971] 74-165626 ISBN 0-8369-5933-7
1. Byles, Mather, 1707-1788. I. Title.

GENERAL Council of the Congregational and Christian Churches of the United States. 285'.833'06273
Digest of minutes of meetings 1931-1965. New York, Published under direction of the Executive Committee of the General Council, 1971. x, 307 p. 24 cm. [BX7107.G38] 72-194144
I. Title.

LOBINGIER, John Leslie, 1884- 285.8330922
Pilgrims and pioneers in the Congregational Christian tradition. Philadelphia, United Church Pr. [c.1965] 191p. 21cm. Bibl. [BX7259.L6] 65-17465 2.95 pap.,
1. Congregational churches—Biog. I. Title.

LOBINGIER, John Leslie, 1884- 285.8330922 (B)
Pilgrims and pioneers in the Congregational Christian tradition. Philadelphia, United Church Press [1965] 191 p. 21 cm. Includes bibliographical references. [BX7259.L6] 65-17465
1. Congregational churches — Biog. I. Title.

HORTON, Douglas, 1891- 285.834
Reform & renewal; exploring the United Church of Christ [by] Douglas Horton [and others] Philadelphia, United Church Press [1966] 119 p. 19 cm. "Based on the Lancaster convocation lectures delivered at Lancaster Theological Seminary on April 20-21, 1965." [BX9885.A4] 66-15480
1. United Church of Christ — Addresses, essays, lectures. I. Title.

OBENHAUS, Victor. 285'.834
And see the people, a study of the United Church of Christ [by] Victor Obenhaus with Ross Blount. [Chicago] Chicago Theological Seminary [1968] 123 p. forms. 28 cm. [BX9886.O2] 71-250
1. United Church of Christ. I. Blount, Ross, C. II. Chicago Theological Seminary. III. Title.

REFORM & renewal; 285.834
exploring the United Church of Christ [by] Douglas Horton [others] Philadelphia, United Church Pr. [c1966] 119p. 19 cm. Based on the Lancaster convocation lects. delivered at Lancaster Theological Seminary, April 20-21, 1965. [BX9885.A4] 66-15480 1.45 pap.
1. United Church of Christ—Addresses, essays, lectures. I. Horton, Douglas, 1891-

UNITED Church Board for Homeland Ministries. Division of Publication. 285.834
The church in our world; a study of the nature and mission of the United Church of Christ. Illinois ed. New York, Produced by Division of Publication, United Church Board for Homeland Ministries [1965] 199 p. map. 29 cm. Includes bibliographies. [BX9885.A45] 66-6155
1. United Church of Christ — Addresses, essays, lectures. I. Title.

MEYERS, Robert Rex, 1923- ed. 285.83408
Voices of concern; critical studies in Church of Christism. Edited by Robert Meyers. Saint Louis, Mission Messenger [1966] 263 p. 21 cm. [BX7321.2.M4] 66-7992
1. Churches of Christ — Addresses, essays, lectures. I. Title.

GUNNEMANN, Louis H. 285'.834'09
The shaping of the United Church of Christ : an essay in the history of American Christianity / Louis H. Gunnemann. New York : United Church Press, c1977. 257 p. ; 22 cm. (A Pilgrim book) Includes bibliographical references and index. [BX9884.G86] 77-4900 ISBN 0-8298-0335-1 : 8.00
1. United Church of Christ—History. I. Title. II. Series.

ESCOTT, Harry. 285.841
A history of Scottish Congregationalism. Glasgow, Congregational union of scotland, 1960. 400p. 23 cm. Bibl. [BX7185.E8] 60-40206 6.00
1. Congregational churches in Scotland—Hist. 2. Congregational Union of Scotland—Hist. I. Title.
Available from Humanities in New York.

GOODWIN, Thomas, 1600-1680. 285.842
An apologeticall narration. [Editor:] Robert S. Paul. Philadelphia, United Church Press [c1963] v. 134 p. 21 cm. Facsim, of the original ed., with t.p. reading: An apologeticall narration, humbly submitted to the honourable Houses of Parliament, by The: Goodwin [and others] London, Printed for Robert Dawiman, m. D.C. XLIII. "Bibliographical note": p. 127-130. [BR757.G7 1643a] 63-21913
1. Congregationalism. I. Paul, Robert S., ed. II. Title.

STURNEY, Alfred Charles. 285.842
The story of Kingston Congregational Church. [Stourbridge? Worcestershire] 1955. 60p. illus. 22cm. [BX7256.K5C64] 57-38956
1. Kingston-upon-Thames, Eng. Congregational Church. I. Title.

KANGAS, Paul D 285.87
A history of the Finnish Congregational churches in North America. [n.p.] 1964. 76 p. 22 cm. Bibliography: p. 72. [BX7147.F5K3] 65-2297
1. Congregationalists, Finnish. I. Title. II. Title: The Finnish Congregational churches in North America.

HOSKINS, Fred. 285'.873
Congregationalism, betrayed or fulfilled? [Newton Centre? Mass, 1962] 54 p. 2 ports. 22 cm. (The Southworth lecture, 1962) Includes also other addresses and tributes delivered at the 10th anniversary meeting of the Congregational Christian Historical Society, Apr. 26-27, 1962. Contents.Contents.—Congregationalism, betrayed or fulfilled? By F. Hoskins.—What is past is prologue, by J. F. English.—A history of the society, by J. A. Harrer.—Frederick Louis Fagley, by D. Horton.—Some notes on the life of Frederick Louis Fagley, 1879-1958, by R. M. Fagley. Bibliographical footnotes. [BX7232.H64] 78-3558
1. Congregationalism. I. Congregational Christian Historical Society. II. Title. III. Series: The Southworth lectures, Andover Theological Seminary, 1962

ROUNER, Arthur Acy. 285.873
The Congregational way of life. Englewood Cliffs, N. J., Prentice-Hall [1960] 182p. 22cm. Includes bibliography. [BX6331.2.R65] 60-13800
1. Congregationalism. I. Title.

STARKEY, Marion Lena. 285.873
The Congregational way; the role of the Pilgrims and their heirs in shaping America. Garden City, N.Y., Doubleday [c.] 1966. xiii, 324p. map (on lining papers) 24 cm. (Religion in Amer. ser.) Bibl. [BX7135.S7] 66-12199 5.95
1. Congregational churches in the U.S.—Hist. I. Title.

SWEET, William Warren, 1881-1959, ed. 285.873
The Congregationalists, a collection of source materials. New York, Cooper Square Publishers, 1964 [c1939] xi, 435 p. maps. 22 cm. (His Religion on the American frontier, 1783-1840, v. 3) Bibliography: p. 407-418. [BX7131.S9 1964] 65-1621
1. Congregational churches in the U.S. — Hist. — Sources. 2. Congregational churches in the U.S. — Hist. 3. Frontier and pioneer life — U.S. I. Title.

FOSTER, Frank Hugh, 1851-1935 285.874
A genetic history of the New England theology. New York, Russell, 1963. 568p. 22cm. Bibl. 63-12564 10.00
1. New England theology. I. Title.

HAROUTUNIAN, Joseph, 1904- 285.874
Piety versus moralism; the passing of the New England theology. Hamden, Conn., Archon [dist. Shoe String] 1964[c.1932] xxv, 329p. 22cm. Bibl. 64-24715 8.00
1. New England theology. I. Title.

WISE, John, 1652-1725 285.874
The churches quarrel espoused (1713). A facsimile repro. with introd. by George A. Cook. Gainesville, Fla., Scholars' Facsimiles, 1966. viii, 152p. 23cm. Reproduced from a copy in the Hist. Soc. of Pa. Orig. t. p. reads: The churches quarrel espoused; or, A reply in satyre, to certain proposals made . . . N. York, Printed and sold by William Bradford, 1713. [BX7136.W61713a] 66-10006 6.00
1. Congregational churches in New England. I. Title.

WISE, John, 1652-1725. 285.874
The churches quarrel espoused (1713). A facsimile reproduction with an introd. By George A. Cook. Gainesville, Fla., Scholars' Facsimiles & Reprints, 1966. viii, 152 p. 23 cm. "Reproduced from a copy in . . . [the] Historical Society of Pennsylvania." Original t. p. reads: The churches quarrel espoused; or, A reply in satyre, to certain proposals made . . . N. York, Printed and sold by William Bradford, 1733. [BX7136.W6 1713a] 66-10006
1. Congregational churches in New England. I. Title.

BEEBE, Richard W. 285'.8741'75
The first 200 years : the history of the First Congregational Church, Fryeburg, Maine / by Richard W. Beebe. [s.l. : s.n.], c1975 (Center Conway, N.H. : Walker's Pond Press) 118, [4] p. : ill. ; 23 cm. Bibliography: p. [119] [BX7255.F75F573] 75-15182
1. First Congregational Church, Fryeburg, Me. 2. Fryeburg, Me.—Biography. I. Title.

ASHBY, Thompson Eldridge, 1883-1953. 285'.8'7419
A history of the First Parish Church in Brunswick, Maine. Edited by Louise R. Helmreich. Brunswick, Me., Printed by J. H. French, 1969. xv, 414 p. illus., ports. 24 cm. [BX7255.B83F5] 73-18835
1. Brunswick, Me. First Parish Church. I. Helmreich, Louise R., ed. II. Title.

PROPER, David R. 285'.8742'9
History of the First Congregational Church, Keene, New Hampshire, by David R. Proper. Keene, N.H., 1973. xvi, 232 p. illus. 24 cm. [BX7255.K43F576] 73-172822
1. Keene, N.H. First Congregational Church. 2. Keene, N.H.—Biography.

SHUSTER, Ruth W 285.8744
Gathered in 1707; a history of the First Congretional Church, Braintree, Massachusetts, 1707-1957 [Braintree? Mass., 1957] 138 p. illus. 24 cm. [BX7255.B74F5] 58-17608
1. Braintree, Mass. First Congretional Church. I. Title.

WORTHLEY, Harold Field. 285'.8744
An inventory of the records of the particular (Congregational) churches of Massachusetts gathered 1620-1805. Cambridge, Harvard University Press, 1970. xiv, 716 p. 24 cm. (Harvard theological studies, 25) Issued also as v. XVI, pts. 1 and 2, of the Proceedings of the Unitarian Historical Society. Includes bibliographical references. [BX7148.M4W65] 76-16086
1. Congregational churches in Massachusetts—Directories. I. Title. II. Series.

SOUTHWICK Congregational Church. Church History Committee. 285'.87'4426
Southwick Congregational Church history, 1773-1973. [Southwick, Mass., 1973] 68 p. illus. 19 cm. Cover title. Bibliography: p. 66. [BX7255.S73S687 1973] 73-175211
1. Southwick Congregational Church. I. Title.

CANFIELD, Alyce. 285'.8744'4
God in Hollywood. New York, Wisdom House [1961] 160p. 19cm. [BR560.H64C3] 62-1133
1. Hollywood, Calif.—Religion. 2. Actors—Religious life. I. Title.

FRAY, Harold R. 285'.8744'4
Conflict and change in the church, by Harold R. Fray, Jr. Boston, Pilgrim Press [1969] xiv, 113 p. 21 cm. [BV637.7.F7] 73-76085 2.95
1. Newton, Mass. Eliot Church. 2. Suburban churches—Case studies. I. Title.

GUSTAFSON, Cloyd V 285'.8744'4
A doctrinal survey of selected Protestant groups in Portland. [Portland? 1956] unpaged.

28cm. regon, and vicinity. [BR560.P82G8] 56-40844
1. Portland, Or.—Religion. 2. Sects—Oregon—Portland. I. Title.

GUSTAFSON, Cloyd V 285'.8744'4
A doctrinal survey of selected Protestant groups in Portland. Oreg n, and vicinity. [Portland 1956] unpaced. 28cm. [BR560.P82G8] 56-40844
1. Portland, Or.—Religion. 2. Sects—Oregon—Portland. I. Title.

MANSUR, Ina G. 285'.8744'4
A New England church, 1730-1834 / Ina Mansur. Freeport, Me. : Bond Wheelwright Co., 1974. xvii, 238 p. : ill. ; 23 cm. Includes indexes. Bibliography: p. 217-223. [BR560.B36M36] 74-76868 ISBN 0-87027-139-3 : 8.95 ISBN 0-87027-140-7 pbk. : 5.95
1. First Congregational Society, Bedford, Mass. 2. Bedford, Mass.—Church history. 3. Bedford, Mass.—Biography. I. Title.

MANSUR, Ina G. 285'.8744'4
A New England church, 1730-1834 / Ina Mansur. Freeport, Me. : Bond Wheelwright Co., 1974. xvii, 238 p. : ill. ; 23 cm. Includes indexes. Bibliography: p. 217-223. [BR560.B36M36] 74-76868 ISBN 0-87027-139-3. ISBN 0-87027-140-7 pbk. : 5.95
1. First Congregational Society, Bedford, Mass. 2. Bedford, Mass.—Church history. 3. Bedford, Mass.—Biography. I. Title.

RANDALL, Ruth (Kimball) 285.87446
History of the First Church in Malden, Malden, Massachusetts, 1649-1959. [Malden? Mass., 1959] 60p. illus. 23cm. Includes bibliography. [BX7255.M17F5] 59-52131
1. Malden, Mass. First Church of Christ (Congregational) I. Title.

ENGLIZIAN, H. 285'.8744'61
Crosby.
Brimstone Corner; Park Street Church, Boston, by H. Crosby Englizian. Foreword by Harold John Ockenga. Chicago, Moody Press [1968] 286 p. illus., ports. 22 cm. Bibliography: p. 260-270. [BX7255.B7P33] 68-18882
1. Boston. Park Street Church. I. Title.

POTWIN, George Stephen, 285.8746
1893-1952.
East Windsor heritage; two hundred years of church and community history, 1752-1952. East Windsor, Con., First Congregational Church [1952] 63 p. illus. 24 cm. [BX7255.E26F5] 52-13798
1. East Windsor, Conn. First Congregational Church. I. Title.

GRAY, Henry David, 285'.8746'3
1908-
Old South Congregational Church, a brief history and guide book, 1670-1970. [Hartford] Conn., Old South Congregational Church in Hartford, 1970. 80 p. illus. 24 cm. [BX7255.H4S68] 76-19368
1. Hartford. South Congregational Church. I. Title.

HARTFORD, Asylum Hill 285.87463
Congregational Church.
The history of Asylum Hill Congregational Church, Hartford, CT centennial, 1865-1965 [Hartford, 1965] 167 p. illus., ports. 23 cm. Bibliography: p. 158-159. [BX7255.H4A78] 65-6578
1. Hartford. Asylum Hill Congregational Church. I. Mansfield, Lillian M. II. Title.

STRONG, Leah A 285.87463 (B)
Joseph Hopkins Twichell, Mark Twain's friend and pastor, by Leah A. Strong. Athens, University of Georgia Press [1966] x, 182 p. port. 25 cm. Bibliography: p. 172-179. [BX7260.T99S8] 66-23072
1. Twichell, Joseph Hopkins, 1838-1918. 2. Clemens, Samuel Langhorne, 1835-1910. I. Title.

STRONG, Leah A. 285.87463
Joseph Hopkins Twichell, Mark Twain's friend and pastor. Athens, Univ. of Ga. Pr. [c.1966] x, 182p. port. 25cm. Bibl. [BX7260.T99S8] 66-23072 5.00
1. Twichell, Joseph Hopkins, 1838-1918. 2. Clemens, Samuel Langhorne, 1835-1910. I. Title.

WELD, Stanley B. 285'.8746'3
The history of Immanuel Church, 1824-1967 [by] Stanley B. Weld. [Hartford, Printed by Connecticut Printers, 1968] 115 p. illus. 24 cm. Bibliography: p. 115. [BX7255.H4I43] 68-5929
1. Hartford. Immanuel Church—History. I. Title.

CLARKE, Elizabeth W. 285'.8746'9
The first three hundred years: the history of the First Congregational Church of Greenwich Connecticut, 1665-1965. Edited by Elizabeth W. Clarke. (Greenwich ? Conn., 1967) 300 p. illus. (part col.) ports. 24 cm. Includes bibliographical footnotes. [BX7255.G77F5] 67-5060
1. Greenwich, Conn. First Congregational Church — Hist. I. Title.

NEW York. Broadway 285.8747
Tabernacle Church.
Year book. New York. v. 19 cm. [BX7255.N5B78] 50-41893
I. Title.

SEIBERT, Earl W. 285'.8748'19
Tulpehocken Trinity United Church of Christ, 1727-1977 / Earl W. Seibert. Richland, Pa. : Tulpehocken Trinity United Church of Christ, c1977. 100 p. : ill. ; 23 cm. On cover: Recall. Prepared under the auspices of the Tulpehocken Trinity United Church of Christ, Historical Committee. Bibliography: p. 52-53. [BX9886.Z7T847] 77-151540 4.00
1. Tulpehocken Trinity United Church of Christ. I. Tulpehocken Trinity United Church of Christ. Historical Committee.

HUFFMAN, Charles 285.875592
Herbert.
The St. Michaels story, 1764-1964: the United Church of Christ; two centuries of church history. [Staunton Va, 1964] 66 p. illus., facsims., ports. 23 cm. Bibliography: p. 64. [BX9886.Z7S34] 65-1161
1. St. Michael's United Church of Christ, Rockingham Co., Va. I. Title.

BURLINGTON-ALAMANCE 285'.8756'58
County Chamber of Commerce.
Histories of United Church of Christ in Burlington and Alamance County, North Carolina. Prepared and compiled by the Burlington-Alamance County Chamber of Commerce in cooperation with the participating churches. [Burlington? N.C.] 1963. 1 v. (various pagings) 28 cm. Cover title. [BX9884.Z5N63 1963] 75-303578
1. United Church of Christ in Alamance Co., N.C. 2. United Church of Christ in Burlington, N.C. I. Title.

SHEPHERD, Banks D. 285'.8756'72
New Gilead Church; a history of the German Reformed people on Coldwater, by Banks D. Shepherd. [Concord? N.C., 1966] 63 p. illus., facsims., ports. 29 cm. Bibliography: p. 59. [BX9567.C6S5] 74-6086
1. New Gilead United Church of Christ. I. Title.

HANSON, Muriel R 285'.8758'231
A history of the First Congregational Church of Ridgefield 1712-1962 [Ridgefield, Conn., First Congregational Church, 1962] 53 p. illus. 26 cm. [BX7255.R49F5] 63-412
1. Ridgefield, Conn. First Congregational Church. I. Title.

MIDDLETON, 285'.8758'231
Merlissie Ross.
The Black church vs. the system / Merlissie Ross Middleton. 1st ed. New York : Vantage Press, c1976. 71 p. : maps ; 21 cm. Bibliography: p. 69-71. [BX7255.A75F575] 76-382765 ISBN 0-533-02289-4 : 4.95
1. First Congregational Church, Atlanta. 2. Afro-American churches—Case studies. I. Title.

SPINKA, Matthew, 285'.8758'231
1890-
A history of the First Church of Christ, Congregational, West Hartford, Conn. [West Hartford, Conn., First Church of Christ, 1963?] 174 p. illus., ports. 24 cm. Includes bibliographies. [BX7255.W47F56] 68-4553
1. West Hartford, Conn. First Church of Christ—Hist. I. Title.

SPINKA, Matthew, 285'.8758'231
1890-
A history of the First Church of Christ, Congregational, West Hartford, Conn. [West Hartford, Conn., First Church of Christ, 1963?] 174 p. illus., ports. 24 cm. Includes bibliographies. [BX7255.W47F56] 68-4553
1. West Hartford, Conn. First Church of Christ—History.

SPRINGFIELD, Mass. 285'.8758'231
St. John's Congregational Church. St. John's Congregational Church.
The history of St. John's Congregational Church, Springfield, Massachusetts, 1844-1962. [Springfield, History Committee, St. John's Congregational Church, 1962] 138 p. illus. 29 cm. [BX7255.S75S3] 63-35505
I. Title.

HOLM, Sarah E. 285'.8771'37
The stately mansion; a history of the United Church of Christ of Kent, by Sarah E. Holm, Dorothy Parsons [and] Loris Troyer. James N. Holm, editor. Kent, Ohio [1969] vii, 131 p. illus., facsims., maps, ports. 28 cm. "Published in Kent, Ohio, on the occasion of the 150th anniversary of the Church." Bibliography: p. 51-53. [BX9886.Z7K4] 75-261957
1. Kent, Ohio. United Church of Christ of Kent. I. Parsons, Dorothy, joint author. II. Troyer, Loris, joint author. III. Holm, James N., ed. IV. Title.

DES Plaines, Ill. 285'.8773'1
First Congregational Church.
Congregational centennial, 1869-1969; a one hundred year history of the First Congregational Church of Des Plaines, Illinois. [Des Plaines? Ill.] 1969. xv, 151 p. (p. 148-151 blank for notes) illus., ports. 27 cm. Bibliography: p. 147. [BX7255.D55F53] 77-19344
1. Des Plaines, Ill. First Congregational Church. I. Title.

LADD, Percy C., 285'.8773'39
1883-1962.
The First Congregational Church of Moline; a one hundred and twenty-five year history, 1844/1969. Edited by W. Clifford Lant & Benedict K. Zobrist. With concluding chapter by William S. Mellish. Moline, Ill., First Congregational Church of Moline, 1969. vi, 69 p. illus., facsims., maps, ports. 29 cm. [BX7255.M69F5] 79-83112
1. Moline, Ill. First Congregational Church.

SEXTON, Jessie Ethelyn. 285'.8774
Congregationalism, slavery, and the Civil War. [Lansing] Michigan Civil War Centennial Observance Commission [1966] 23 p. 23 cm. Bibliography: p. 23. [BX7148.M5S48] 66-65601
1. Congregational churches in Michigan—Hist. 2. Michigan—Hist.—Civil War. 3. Slavery and the church—Congregational churches. I. Michigan. Civil War Centennial Observance Commission. II. Title.

DILLMAN, Daisy Ellen, 285.8776
1880-
100 years in Excelsior. Minneapolis, Holden Print. Co., 1953. 72p. illus. 26cm. [BX7255.E9D5] 53-33069
1. Excelsior, Minn. Congregational Church. I. Title.

KENNEDY, Theodore. 285'.8781'65
Plymouth Congregational Church, 1854-1954 [by Ted and Grace Kennedy] Lawrence [1954?] 21 p. illus., ports. 23 cm. Cover title. [BX7255.L38K4] 73-11195
1. Lawrence, Kan. Plymouth Congregational Church. I. Kennedy, Grace, joint author. II. Title.

UNITED Church of Christ. 285.8788
Conferences. Colorado.
The Bible and the gold rush; a century of Congregationalism in Colorado, by [the committee] Virginia Greene Millikin [and others] Artist: Oz Black. Denver, Published for the Congregational Churches of Colorado by the Big Mountain Press, 1962. 316 p. illus. 24 cm. [BX7148.C6U5] 62-53004
1. Congregational Churches in Colorado. I. Millikin, Virginia Greene. II. Title.

UNITED Church of Christ, 285.8788
Conferences Colorado.
The Bible and the gold rush; a century of Congregationalism in Colorado, by [the committee] Virginia Greene Millikin [others] Artist: Oz Black, Denver, Pub. for the Congregational Churches of Colorado by the Big Mountain Pr. [dist. Swallow, c.]1962. 316p. illus., map. 24cm. 62-53004 5.00
1. Congregational Churches in Colorado. I. Millikin, Virginia Greene. II. Title.

MCSTAY, Esther 285.879465
A century in Eden; a short history of Eden Congregational Church of Hayward, California. Consultant: Amey Jensen. [San Leandro, Calif. 94577] San Leandro Print. Serv.,2500 Alvarado, 1965. 52p. illus., ports. 22cm. [BX7255.H48E4] 66-1563 2.00 pap.,
1. Hayward, Calif. Eden Congregational Church. I. Title.

ZENTMYER, George 285'.8794'97
Aubrey, 1913-
The lighted cross; the first 100 years of Riverside's first church, 1872-1972. [G. A. Zentmyer, editor] Riverside, Calif., First Congregational Church [1972] 214 p. illus. 29 cm. Includes bibliographical references. [BX7255.R55F579] 72-86093
1. First Congregational Church, Riverside, Calif. I. Title.

BACHELDER, Horace 285'.8795'41
Lyman.
The liberal church at the end of the Oregon Trail; a history of the First Congregational Society of Oregon City and of the Atkinson Memorial Congregational Church, from the first meeting in 1844 to the 125th anniversary in 1969. [Portland, Or., Watson Print. Co., 1969] 137 p. illus., ports. 23 cm. Bibliography: p. 136-137. [BX7255.O76F5] 75-98940
1. Oregon City, Or. First Congregational Society. 2. Oregon City, Or. Atkinson Memorial Congregational Church. I. Title.

STARE, Frederick 285'.8797'46
Arthur, 1877-
A history of Olivet Congregational Church, Columbus, Wisconsin, by Fred A. Stare. [Columbus, Wis., Printed by Columbus Journal Republican, 1963?] vii, 367 p. illus., ports. 24 cm. On spine: History of Olivet Congregational United Church of Christ, Columbus, Wisconsin, 1850-1961. [BX7255.C68O5] 71-10220
1. Columbus, Wis. Olivet Congregational Church. I. Title.

BANCROFT, Richard Abp. of 285.9
Canterbury. 1544-1610, supposed author.
Tracts ascribed to Richard Bancroft, edited from a manuscript in the Library of St. John's College, Cambridge, by Albert Peel. Cambridge, University Press, 1953. xxix, 168p. 21cm. Bibliographical footnotes. [BX9320.B3] 53-7565
1. Puritans—Controversial literature. 2. Brownists. 3. Presbyterians in England. I. Peel, Albert, 1887-1949, ed. II. Title.
Contents omitted.

BYINGTON, Ezra Hoyt, 1825- 285'.9
1901.
The Puritan in England and New England. 4th ed., with a chapter on witchcraft in New England. New York, B. Franklin [1972] xlii, 457 p. illus. 22 cm. (Burt Franklin research & source works series. American classics in history and social science, 233) Reprint of the 1900 ed. Bibliography: p. [xxvii]-xxxi. [BX9321.B8 1972] 70-183241 ISBN 0-8337-4017-2
1. Puritans. 2. Witchcraft—New England. I. Title.

EMERSON, Everett H., 1925- 285.9
John Cotton. New Haven, Conn., Coll. & Univ. Pr. [c.1965] 176p. 21cm. (Twayne's U.S. authors ser., T-80) [BX7260.C79E5] 1.95 pap.,
1. Cotton, John, 1584-1652. I. Title.

EMERSON, Everett H., 1925- 285.9
John Cotton, by Everett H. Emerson. New York, Twayne Publishers [1965] 176 p. 21 cm. (Twayne's United States authors series, 80) [BX7260.C79E5] 65-13000
1. Cotton, John, 1584-1652.

HALLER, William, 1885- 285.9
Elizabeth I and the Puritans Ithaca, N. Y., Pub. for the Folger Shakespeare Lib. [by] Cornell [1965, c.1964] 40p. facsims., ports. 22cm. (Folger bklets. on Tudor and Stuart civilization) Bibl. [BX9334.2.H3] 64-7542 1.00 pap.,
1. Elizabeth, Queen of England, 1533-1603. 2. Puritans—England. I. Title. II. Series.

KNAPPEN, Marshall Mason, 285'.9
1901-
Two Elizabethan Puritan diaries, by Richard Rogers and Samuel Ward. Edited, with an introd., by M. M. Knappen. Gloucester, Mass., P. Smith, 1966 [c1933] xiii, 148 p. facsims., map. ports. 21 cm. (Studies in church history, v. 21. Reprint of the 1933 edition. Contents.Contents.--The diary of Richard Rogers.--The diary of Samuel Ward.--Historical notes from Ward's ms. "Adversarian."--Selected Bibliography: (p. 137-140) [BX9339.R6K6 1966] 67-3219
1. Puritans. Rogers, Richard, 1550?-1618. Diary. Ward, Samuel, d. 1643. Diary. 2. Studies in church history (Hartford) v. 2) I. Title.

KNOX, Samuel James 285.9
Walter Travers: paragon of Elizabethan Puritanism. London, Methuen [dist. New York, Humanities, 1963, c.1962 172p. illus. 23cm. Bibl. 63-1754 6.00
1. Travers, Walter, 1548?-1635. I. Title.

MARCHANT, Ronald Albert 285.9
The Puritans and the church courts in the Diocese of York, 1560-1642 [London] Longmans [Mystic, Conn., Verry, 1965, c.1960] xii, 330p. maps. 23cm. Bibl. [BX9335.Y6M3] 61-237 12.50
1. Puritans. 2. York, Eng. (Diocese) I. Title.

MORGAN, Edmund Sears 285.9
Visible saints; the history of a Puritan idea. [New York] N. Y. Univ. Pr. [c.]1963. 159p. 22cm. Bibl. 63-9999 4.50
1. Puritans. 2. Church—History of doctrines. I. Title.

THE New Puritanism. 285'.9
Papers by Lyman Abbott [and others] during the semi-centennial celebration of Plymouth Church, Brooklyn, N.Y., 1847-1897. With introd. by Rossiter W. Raymond. Freeport, N.Y., Books for Libraries Press [1972] 275 p. 23 cm. (Essay index reprint series) "First

published in 1897." [BX9327.N46 1972] 70-39672 ISBN 0-8369-2732-X
1. Puritans—Addresses, essays, lectures. 2. Theology—Addresses, essays, lectures. I. Abbott, Lyman, 1835-1922. II. Brooklyn. Plymouth Church.

*PERRY, Ralph Barton, 1876- 285.9
Puritanism and democracy. New York, Harper [1964, c.1944] xvi, 688p. 21cm. (Acad. Lib.; Torchbk. TB-1138) 3.95 pap.,
I. Title.

SCHNEIDER, Herbert Wallace, 1892- 285.9
The Puritan mind. [Ann Arbor] University of Michigan Press [1958] 267 p. 21 cm. (Ann Arbor paperbacks, AA21) Bibliographical footnotes. [BX9321.S4 1958] 58-14941
1. Puritans. 2. New England—Church history. I. Title.

SIMPSON, Alan 285.9
Puritanism in old and New England. [Chicago] Univ. of Chic. Pr. [1961, c.1955] 125p. (Charles R. Walgreen Found. lectures; Phoenix bk. P66) Bibl. 1.35 pap.,
1. Puritans. I. Title.

STECK, James S. 285'.9
The intellectual pleasures of the Puritans [by] James S. Steck. [Shippensburg, Pa.] Shippensburg Collegiate Press, 1967. 16 p. 23 cm. (Shippensburg State College, Shippensburg, Pa. Faculty monograph series, v. 2, no. 1) Bibliography: p. 16. [BX9327.S68] 67-65700
1. Puritans. I. Title. II. Series: Pennsylvania. State College, Shippensburg. Faculty monograph series, v. 2, no. 1.

STOUGHTON, John, 1807-1897. 285'.9
Spiritual heroes; or, Sketches of the Puritans, their character and times. With and introductory letter, by Joel Hawes. Freeport, N.Y., Books for Libraries Press [1973] p. (Essay index reprint series) "First published 1848." [BX9334.S7 1973] 73-1194 ISBN 0-518-10066-9
1. Puritans. I. Title.

TOON, Peter, 1939- 285'.9
Puritans and Calvinism. Swengel, Pa., Reiner Publications, 1973. 110 p. 23 cm. "First five chapters ... originally appeared as nine separate articles in the monthly magazine, The Gospel magazine." Includes bibliographical references. [BX9322.T66] 73-166984 3.25
1. Puritans. 2. Calvinism. I. Title.

WATKINS, Owen C. 285'.9
The Puritan experience; studies in spiritual autobiography [by] Owen C. Watkins. New York, Schocken Books [1972, c1971] x, 270 p. 23 cm. Bibliography: p. 241-260. [BX9322.W36 1972b] 70-150987 ISBN 0-8052-3425-X
1. Friends, Society of. 2. Puritans. 3. Witness bearing (Christianity) I. Title.

WHITE, Eugene Edmond, 1919- 285'.9
Puritan rhetoric: the issue of emotion in religion, by Eugene E. White. Foreword by David Potter. Carbondale, Southern Illinois University Press [1972] xiv, 215 p. 23 cm. (Landmarks in rhetoric and public address) Bibliography: p. 213-215. [BR112.W46] 76-181987 ISBN 0-8093-0563-1 7.95
1. Enthusiasm. 2. Puritans. I. Title. II. Series.

EMERSON, Everett H., 1925- 285'.9'08
English Puritanism from John Hooper to John Milton [by] Everett H. Emerson. Durham, N.C., Duke University Press, 1968. xii, 313 p. ports. (on lining paper) 25 cm. Bibliography: p. [295]-306. [BX9313.E4] 68-29664 10.00
1. Theology—Collections—Puritan authors. 2. Puritans—Collections. I. Title.

TRINTERUD, Leonard J., 1904- comp. 285'.9'08
Elizabethan Puritanism, edited by Leonard J. Trinterud. New York, Oxford University Press, 1971. xv, 454 p. 24 cm. (A Library of Protestant thought) Bibliography: p. 441-444. [BX9334.2.T75] 74-141652 11.50
1. Puritans—England. 2. Gt. Brit.—Church history—16th century—Sources. I. Title. II. Series.

MIDDLEKAUFF, Robert. 285'.9'0922
The Mathers : three generations of Puritan intellectuals, 1596-1728 / [by] Robert Middlekauff. New York : Oxford University Press, 1976,c1971. 440p. ; 21 cm. Includes index. Includes bibliographical notes. [F67.M4865] 79-140912 ISBN 0-19-502115-0 pbk. : 4.50
1. Mather, Richard, 1596-1669. 2. Mather, Increase, 1639-1723. 3. Mather, Cotton, 1663-1728. 4. Puritans-Massachusetts. I. Title.
The 1971hardcover ed.is available for 13.95

BUNYAN, John, 1628-1688 285'.9'0924
God's knotty log; selected writings of john Bunyan. Ed., introd. by Henri A. Talon [Magnolia, Mass., P. Smith, 1967, c.1961] 313p. 19cm. (Living age bk.; Meridian bk. rebound) Bibl. [BR75.B73 1961] 208 3.75
I. Title.

BUNYAN, John, 1628-1688. 285'.9'0924
The pilgrim's progress. Edited and introduced by Henri A. Talon. Cleveland, World Pub. Co. [1965, c1961] xxx, 255 p. 22 cm. Published in 1961 in God's knotty log; selected writings of John Bunyan. [PR3330.A1] 66-2800
I. Talon, Henri Antoine, 1909- ed. II. Title.

BUNYAN, John, 1628-1688. 285'.9'0924
The pilgrim's progress. Including an introd. to the book and a note on the William Blake designs by A. K. Adams, together with an essay on John Bunyan by Thomas Babington Macaulay. 16 pages of illus. including reproductions of the front. and 8 designs for the 1st part, by William Blake. New York, Dodd, Mead [1968] xxiii, 303 p. illus. 22 cm. (Great illustrated classics [Titan editions]) [PR3330.A2B5 1968] 68-16180
I. Blake, William, 1757-1827, illus. II. Title.

BUNYAN, John, 1628-1688. 285'.9'0924
Pilgrim's progress in modern English. Retold by James H. Thomas. Illustrated by John M. Cadel. Chicago, Moody Press [1964] 256 p. illus. 23 cm. [PR3330.A33T5] 64-25255
I. Thomas, James Henderson, 1800- II. Title.

BUNYAN, John, 1628-1688. 285'.9'0924 B
The works of John Bunyan. With an introd. to each treatise, notes, and a sketch of his life, times, and contemporaries. Edited by George Offor. Glasgow, Blackie and Son, 1856. [New York, AMS Press, 1973] 3 v. illus. 27 cm. Contents.Contents.—v. 1-2. Experimental, doctrinal, and practical.—v. 3. Allegorical, figurative, and symbolical. [BR75.B7 1973] 78-154136 ISBN 0-404-09250-0 49.50 per vol.
1. Bunyan, John, 1628-1688. I. Offor, George, 1787-1864, ed.
Three volumes 145.00.

HENRY, Stuart Clark. 285'.9'0924 B
Unvanquished Puritan; a portrait of Lyman Beecher, by Stuart C. Henry. Grand Rapids, Mich., W. B. Eerdmans Pub. Co. [1973] 299 p. illus. 23 cm. Includes bibliographical references. [BX7260.B33H4] 72-94608 ISBN 0-8028-3426-4 7.95
1. Beecher, Lyman, 1775-1863. I. Title.

PEARSON, Andrew Forret Scott, 1886- 285.90924(B)
Tomas Cartwright and Elizabethan Puritanism, 1535-1603, by A. F. Scott Pearson. Gloucester, Mass., P. Smith, 1966. xvi. 511p. port. 21cm. First pub. in 1925. Bibl. [BX9339.C35P4 1966] 67-869 8.50
1. Cartwright, Thomas, 135-1603. 2. Puritans. I. Title.

SHEPARD, Thomas, 1605-1649. 285'.9'0924 B
God's plot; the paradoxes of Puritan piety; being The autobiography & journal of Thomas Shepard. Edited with an introd. by Michael McGiffert. [Amherst] University of Massachusetts Press, 1972. vii, 252 p. 24 cm. (The Commonwealth series [v. 1]) Bibliography: p. [239]-241. [BX7260.S53A32] 71-181364 ISBN 0-87023-100-6 12.00
I. Shepard, Thomas, 1605-1649. The autobiography. 1972. II. Shepard, Thomas, 1605-1649. The journal. 1972. III. Title. IV. Series: The Commonwealth series (Amherst, Mass.) v. 1.

SPRUNGER, Keith L. 285'.9'0924 B
The learned doctor William Ames; Dutch backgrounds of English and American Puritanism [by] Keith L. Sprunger. Urbana, University of Illinois Press [1972] xi, 289 p. illus. 24 cm. Bibliography: p. [263]-[276] [BX9339.A65S6] 77-175172 ISBN 0-252-00233-4 10.00
1. Ames, William, 1576-1633. I. Title.

TOON, Peter, 1939- 285'.9'0924 B
God's statesman: the life and work of John Owen, pastor, educator, theologian. Grand Rapids, Mich., Zondervan Pub. House [1973, c1971] viii, 200 p. 23 cm. Bibliography: p. [188]-195. [BX5207.O88T66 1973] 72-95518 ISBN 0-85364-133-1 5.95
1. Owen, John, 1616-1683. I. Title.

VAN DYKEN, Seymour. 285'.9'0924 B
Samuel Willard, 1640-1707; preacher of orthodoxy in an era of change Grand Rapids, Eerdmans [1972] 224 p. 23 cm. Bibliography: p. 195-211. [BX7260.W5V3] 75-168438 ISBN 0-8028-3408-6 5.95
1. Willard, Samuel, 1640-1707.

WALKER, Eric Charles, 1903- 285'.9'0924 B
William Dell: master Puritan, by Eric C. Walker. Cambridge, Heffer, 1970. x, 238 p., 2 plates. illus., map, ports. 22 cm. Bibliography: p. 228-231. [BX9339.D37W3] 79-552862 ISBN 0-85270-018-0 £3.00
1. Dell, William, d. 1664. I. Title.

WHEELWRIGHT, John, 1592?-1679. 285'.9'0924
John Wheelwright: his writings, including his Fast-day sermon, 1637; and his Mercurius americanus, 1645; with a paper upon the genuineness of the Indian deed of 1629, and a memoir, by Charles H. Bell. Freeport, N.Y., Books for Libraries Press [1970] viii, 251 p. facsims. 23 cm. "First published 1876." Bibliography: p. [149]-151. [F67.W547 1970] 70-128897 ISBN 0-8369-5517-X
1. Winthrop, John, 1588-1649, supposed author. A short story. 2. Massachusetts—History—Colonial period, ca. 1600-1775—Sources. 3. New Hampshire—History—Colonial period, ca. 1600-1775—Sources. 4. Antinomianism.

SEYMOUR, St. John Drelincourt. 285'.9'09415
The puritans in Ireland 1647-1661, by St. John D. Seymour. Oxford, Clarendon P., 1969. xii, 240 p. 23cm. "First published in 1912." Bibliography: p. [xi]-xii. [BR795.S48 1969] 70-471426 65/-
1. Ireland—Church history. 2. Puritans—Ireland. 3. Gt. Brit.—History—Puritan Revolution, 1642-1660. I. Title.

BROWN, John, 1830-1922. 285'.9'0942
The English Puritans. [Folcroft, Pa.] Folcroft Library Editions, 1973. p. Reprint of the 1910 ed. published at the University Press, Cambridge, in series: The Cambridge manuals of science and literature. Bibliography: p. [BX9334.B7 1973] 73-12821 15.00
1. Puritans—England. I. Title.

COOLIDGE, John S. 285'.9'0942
The Pauline Renaissance in England: Puritanism and the Bible, by John S. Coolidge. Oxford, Clarendon, 1970. xiv, 162 p. 23 cm. Bibliography: p. [152]-158. [BX9322.C6 1970] 73-17854 42/-
1. Puritans. I. Title.

CRAGG, Gerald Robertson. 285'.9'0942
Puritanism in the period of the great persecution, 1660-1688, by Gerald R. Cragg. New York, Russell & Russell [1971] 325 p. 23 cm. Reprint of the 1957 ed. with new pref. Bibliography: p. 303-320. [BX9334.C7 1971] 76-143557
1. Puritans. 2. Gt. Brit.—Church history—17th century. I. Title.

FRERE, Walter Howard, Bp. of Truro, 1863-1938, ed. 285'.9'0942
Puritan manifestoes; a study of the origin of the Puritan revolt with a reprint of the Admonition to the Parliament and kindred documents, 1572. Edited by W. H. Frere and C. E. Douglas. New York, B. Franklin [1972] xxxi, 155 p. 22 cm. (Burt Franklin research and source works series. Philosophy & religious history monographs, 107) Reprint of the 1907 ed. published as no. 72 of the Church Historical Society's publications. Contents.Contents.—Puritan manifestoes.—An admonition to the Parliament.—The letters of Gualter and Beza.—An exhortation to the byshops to deale brotherly with theyr brethren.—An exhortation to the bishops and their clergie to aunswer a little booke, etc.—A second admonition. Includes bibliographical references. [BX9331.F7 1972] 79-183703 ISBN 0-8337-4119-5 15.00
1. Puritans—Great Britain. I. Douglas, Charles Edward, joint author. II. Title. III. Series: Church Historical Society (Gt. Brit.) Publications, 52.

HENSON, Herbert Hensley, Bp. of Durham, 1863-1947. 285'.9'0942
Puritanism in England. New York, B. Franklin [1972] viii, 294 p. 22 cm. (Burt Franklin research and source works series. Selected studies in history, economics, and social science, n.s. 19. (c) Modern European studies) Reprint of the 1912 ed. [BX9334.H37 1972] 70-185944 ISBN 0-8337-4177-2 15.00
1. Puritans—England. I. Title.

PORTER, Harry Culverwell, comp. 285'.9'0942
Puritanism in Tudor England. [Edited by] H. C. Porter. Columbia, University of South Carolina Press [1970] xv, 311 p. 23 cm. (History in depth) Bibliography: p. 301-304. [BX9334.2.P67 1970b] 75-145532 ISBN 0-87249-222-2 9.95
1. Puritans—England. I. Title.

EMERSON, Everett H., 1925- 285'.9'0973
Puritanism in America, 1620-1750 / by Everett Emerson. Boston : Twayne Publishers, c1977. p. cm. (Twayne's world leaders series ; TWLS 71) Includes index. Bibliography: p. [BX9354.2.E47] 77-4354 ISBN 0-8057-7692-3 lib.bdg. : 8.50
1. Puritans—United States. I. Title.

MCGIFFERT, Michael, comp. 285'.9'0973
Puritanism and the American experience. Edited by Michael McGiffert. Reading, Mass., Addison-Wesley [1969] viii, 280 p. 22 cm. (Themes and forces in American history series) Essays. Bibliography: p. 275-280. Bibliographical footnotes. [BX9354.2.M3] 69-18403
1. Puritans—U.S.—Addresses, essays, lectures. 2. U.S.—Civilization—Addresses, essays, lectures. I. Title.

REINITZ, Richard, comp. 285'.9'0973
Tensions in American Puritanism. New York, Wiley [1970] xiii, 192 p. 22 cm. (Problems in American history) Bibliography: p. 188-192. [BX9313.R4] 70-100325
1. Puritans—Collections. I. Title.

BACON, Leonard, 1802-1881. 285'.9'0974
The genesis of the New England churches. New York, Arno Press, 1972. 485 p. illus. 23 cm. (Religion in America, series II) Reprint of the 1874 ed. [F68.B12 1972] 74-38435 ISBN 0-405-04056-3
1. Puritans—New England. 2. Pilgrim Fathers. 3. New England—Church history. 4. Massachusetts—History—Colonial period, ca. 1600-1775. 5. Massachusetts—History—New Plymouth, 1620-1691. I. Title.

BLISS, William Root, 1825-1906. 285'.9'0974
Side glimpses from the colonial meeting-house. Detroit, Gale Research Co., 1970. 256 p. 22 cm. Reprint of the 1894 ed. [F7.B64 1970] 70-140410
1. New England—Social life and customs. 2. Puritans—New England. 3. Witchcraft—New England. I. Title.

ELLIOTT, Emory, 1942- 285'.9'0974
Power and the pulpit in Puritan New England / Emory Elliott. Princeton, N.J. : Princeton University Press, [1975] xi, 240 p. ; 23 cm. Includes index. Bibliography: p. 205-234. [BV4208.U6E43] 74-29093 ISBN 0-691-07206-X : 10.00
1. Preaching—History—New England. 2. Puritans—New England. I. Title.

JAMES, Sydney V., comp. 285'.9'0974
The New England Puritans, edited by Sydney V. James. New York, Harper & Row [1968] vi, 169 p. 21 cm. (Interpretations of American history) Includes bibliographical references. [BX9354.2.J3] 69-11114
1. Puritans—New England—Addresses, essays, lectures. I. Title.

PURITAN New England 285'.9'0974
: essays on religion, society, and culture / Alden T. Vaughan and Francis J. Bremer, editors. New York : St. Martin's Press, c1977. vii, 395 p. ; 24 cm. Includes bibliographical references. [BX9355.N35P87] 76-52589 ISBN 0-312-65695-5 : 5.95
1. Puritans—New England—Addresses, essays, lectures. 2. New England—Civilization—Addresses, essays, lectures. I. Vaughan, Alden T., 1929- II. Bremer, Francis J.

RUTMAN, Darrett Bruce. 285'.9'0974
American Puritanism; faith and practice, by Darrett B. Rutman. Philadelphia, Lippincott [1970] xii, 139 p. 21 cm. (Pilotbooks) (The Lippincott history series.) Includes bibliographical references. [F7.R8] 79-100370
1. Puritans—New England. I. Title.

RUTMAN, Darrett Bruce. 285'.9'0974
American Puritanism / by Darrett B. Rutman. New York : Norton, c1977. p. cm. Reprint of the 1970 ed. published by Lippincott, Philadelphia, in series: Pilotbooks and The Lippincott history series. Includes bibliographical references and index. [F7.R8 1977] 76-49541 ISBN 0-393-00842-8 pbk. : 2.95
1. Puritans—New England. 2. New England—Religious life and customs. I. Title.

VAUGHAN, Alden T., 1929- comp. 285'.9'0974
The Puritan tradition in America, 1620-1730.

Edited by Alden T. Vaughan. New York, Harper & Row [1972] xxviii, 348 p. 21 cm. (Documentary history of the United States) Includes bibliographical references. [F7.V32 1972] 78-174703 ISBN 0-06-139641-9
1. Puritans—New England—History—Sources. I. Title.

GARRETT, Christina Hallowell 285.942
The Marian exiles, a study in the origins of Elizabethan Puritanism, by Christina Hallowell Garrett, M.A. Cambridge [Eng.] Univ. Pr., 1938. ix, 388p. front. 22cm. Bibl. [BX9338.G3] 38-25099 8.50
1. Puritans. 2. Gt. Brit.—Pol. & govt.—1553-1558. 3. Gt. Brit.—Biog. 4. Gt. Brit.—Church history—16th cent. I. Title.
Available from Cambridge in New York.

GT. Brit. Army. 285.942
Puritanism and liberty, being the Army debates (1647-9) from the Clarke manuscripts with supplementary documents selected, ed., introd. by A. S. P. Woodhouse. Foreword by A. D. Lindsay. [2d ed. Chicago] Univ. of Chic. Pr. [1965] 100, 506p. 22cm. [BX9331.A55] A51 price unreported
1. Puritans. 2. Gt. Brit.—Pol. & govt.—1642-1649. 3. Religious liberty—Gt. Brit. I. Woodhouse, Arthur Sutherland Pigott, ed. II. Clarke, Sir William, 1623-1666. III. Title.

GT. Brit. Army Council. 285.942
Puritanism and liberty, being the Army debates (1647-9) from the Clarke manuscripts with supplementary documents selected and edited with an introd. by A. S. P. Woodhouse. Foreword by A. D. Lindsay. [2d ed. Chicago] University of Chicago Press [1951] 100, 506 p 22 cm. Includes the debates in the General Council of the Army at Putney, Oct. 28-29 and Nov. 1. 1647, and in the Council of Officers at Whitehall, Jan. 13 and Dec. 14, 1648 and Jan. 8-11, 1649. [BX9331.A55] A51
1. Puritans. 2. Gt. Brit.—Pol. & govt.—1642-1649. 3. Religious liberty—Gt. Brit. I. Gt. Brit. Army. Council of Officers. II. Woodhouse. Arthur Sutherland Pigott. ed. III. Clarke, William, Sir 1623-1666. IV. Title.

HALLER, William, 1885- 285.942
The rise of Puritanism; or, The way to the New Jerusalem as set forth in pulpit and press from Thomas Cartwright to John Lilburne and John Milton, 1570-1643. [Gloucester, Mass., P. Smith, 1965, c.1938] 464p. illus. 21cm. (Harper torchbks., TB22 rebound) Bibl. [BX9334.H3] 4.25
1. Puritans. 2. Religious literature, English. 3. English literature—Early modern (to 1700)—Hist. & crit. I. Title.

HALLER, William, 1885- 285.942
The rise of Puritanism; or, The way to the New Jerusalem as set forth in pulpit and press from Thomas Cartwright to John Lilburne and John Milton, 1570-1643. New York, Harper [1957, c1938] 464 p. illus. 21 cm. (Harper torchbooks, TB22) [BX9334.H3 1957] 57-10117
1. Puritans—Great Britain. 2. Christian literature, English. 3. English literature—Early modern, 1500-1700—History and criticism. I. Title.

KNAPPEN, Marshall Mason, 1901- 285.942
Tudor puritanism, a chapter in the history of idealism, by M. M. Knappen. Gloucester, Mass., P. Smith [1964, c.1938] xii, 555p. 21cm. Bibl. 7.50
1. Puritans. 2. Idealism. I. Title.

KNAPPEN, Marshall Mason, 1901- 285.942
Tudor puritanism, a chapter in the history of idealism [New preface by the author] Chicago, Univ. of Chic. [1965, c.1939] xvi, 555p. 21cm. (Phoenix bk. P194) [BX9334.K5] 39-10082 3.45 pap.,
1. Puritans. 2. Idealism. I. Title.

NUTTALL, Geoffrey Fillingham, D.D. 1911- 285.9429
The Welsh saints, 1640-1660: Walter Cradock, Vavasor Powell, Morgan Llwyd. Cardiff, Univ. of Wales Pr. [dist. Mystic. Conn., Verry, 1964] x, 93p. 23cm. Delivered as a course of lects. at the Univ. Coll. of N. Wales March 1957. Bibl. A59 2.75
1. Cradock, Walter, 1606?-1659. 2. Powell, Vavasor, 1617-1670. 3. Llwyd, Morgan, 1619-1659. I. Title.

286 Baptist, Disciples, Adventist

BACKUS, Isaac, 1724-1806. 286
Isaac Backus on church, state, and Calvinism; pamphlets, 1754-1789. Edited by William G. McLoughlin. Cambridge, Mass., Belknap Press of Harvard University Press, 1968. vi, 525 p. 24 cm. (The John Harvard library) On spine: Isaac Backus Pamphlets, 1754-1789. Includes bibliographical references. [BX6217.B25] 68-14268
1. Baptists—Collected works. 2. Theology—Collected works—18th century. I. McLoughlin, William Gerald, ed. II. Title. III. Series.

BAPTIST General Conference of America. 286
Fifteen eventful years: a survey of the Baptist General Conference. 1945-1960. edited by David Guston and Martin Erikson. Chicago, Harvest [Publications, 1961] 231p. 22cm. [BX6247.S8B36] 61-14300
I. Title.

CHILDERS, James Saxon, 1899- ed. 286
A way home; the Baptists tell their story. [1st ed.] Atlanta, Tupper and Love [1964] vii, 235 p. 22 cm. "Some books about Baptists": p. 232-235. [BX6331.2.C5] 64-15304
1. Baptists—History. 2. Baptists—U.S. I. Title. II. Title: The Baptists tell their story.

FARMER, Foy (Johnson), 1887- 286
Hitherto; history of North Carolina Woman's Missionary Union. Raleigh, Woman's Missionary Union of North Carolina, 1952. 171 p. illus. 21 cm. [BV2766.B4893F3] 52-40065
1. Baptists. North Carolina. State Convention. Woman's Missionary Union. I. Title.

FICKETT, Harold L 286
A layman's guide to Baptist beliefs, by Harold L. Fickett, Jr. Introd. by W. A. Criswell. Grand Rapids, Zondervan Pub. House [1965] 184 p. 21 cm. [BX6331.2.F5] 64-8846
1. Baptists — Doctrinal and controversial works. I. Title.

FICKETT, Harold L., Jr. 286
A laymen's guide to Baptist beliefs. Introd. by W. A. Criswell. Grand Rapids, Mich., Zondervan [c.]1965. 184p. 21cm. [BX6331.2.F5] 64-8846 3.50 bds.,
1. Baptists—Doctrinal and controversial works. I. Title.

GARRETT, James Leo. 286
Baptist relations with other Christians. Edited by James Leo Garrett. Valley Forge [Pa.] Judson Press [1974] 224 p. 23 cm. Includes bibliographical references. [BX6329.A1G37] 73-16788 ISBN 0-8170-0602-8 12.00
1. Baptists—Relations. I. Title.

*HINKLE, J. Herbert. 286
Soul winning in black churches, [by] J. Herbert Hinkle. Grand Rapids, Mich, Baker Book House [1973] 105 p. 18 cm. [BX6440] ISBN 0-8010-4072-8 0.95 (pbk.)
1. Church attendance—U.S.—1960- 2. Baptists, Negro—U.S.—1960- I. Title.

HISCOX, Edward Thurston, 1814-1901. 286
The Hiscox guide for Baptist churches. Valley Forge, Judson Press [1964] 253 p. 21 cm. A revision of the author's The new directory for Baptist churches, which was first published under title: The Baptist church directory. [BX6331.H6] 64-15797
1. Baptists — Doctrinal and controversial works. 2. Baptists — Government. I. Title. II. Title: Guide for Baptist churches.

HISCOX, Edward Thurston, 1814-1901 286
The Hiscox guide for Baptist churches. Valley Forge, Pa., Judson [c.1964] 253p. 21cm. Rev. of the author's The new directory for Baptist churches, which was first pub. under title: The Baptist church directory. 64-15797 2.95
1. Baptists—Doctrinal and controversial works. 2. Baptists—Government. I. Title. II. Title: Guide for Baptist churches.

LUMPKIN, William Latane. 286
Baptist foundations in the South; tracing through the Separates the influence of the Great Awakening, 1754-1787. Nashville, Broadman Press [1961] 166 p. 21 cm. [BX6389.63.L8] 61-12413
1. Separate Baptists—History. 2. Baptists—Southern States—History. I. Title.

MARING, Norman Hill, 1914- 286
A Baptist manual of polity and practice [by] Norman H. Maring, Withrop S. Hudson. Valley Forge [Pa.] Judson [c.1963] 237p. 21cm. 62-18079 4.50
1. Baptists—Government. I. Hudson, Withrop Still, 1911- joint author. II. Title.

MEAD, Frank Spencer, 1898- 286
The Baptists. Nashville, Broadman Press [1954] 55p. illus. 19cm. 'From [the author's] See these banners go.' [BX6332.M37] 54-12661
1. Baptists. I. Title.

MESHACK, B. A. 286
Is the Baptist Church relevant to the Black community / by B. A. Meshack. San Francisco : R and E Research Associates, 1976. v, 98 p. ; 28 cm. Bibliography: p. 98. [BX6443.M45] 75-38304 ISBN 0-88247-385-9 pbk. : 8.00
1. Afro-American Baptists. 2. Afro-American churches. I. Title.

*MONROE, Doris 286
When Marcia goes to church. Illus. by Maggie Dugan. Nashville, Broadman [1966] 48p. illus. (pt. col.) 23cm. 1.35 bds.,
1. Baptist church—Juvenile literature. I. Title.

NEWTON, Louie De Votie 286
Why I am a Baptist [Gloucester, Mass., P. Smith, 1965, c.1957] ix, 306p. 21cm. (Beacon paperback, BP203 rebound) [BX6495.N48A3] 3.25
1. Baptists—Clergy—Correspondence, reminiscences, etc. I. Title.

NEWTON, Louie De Votie, 1892- 286
Why I am a Baptist. Boston, Beacon [1965, c.1957] 306p. 21cm. (BP 203) [BX6495.N48A3] 1.25 pap.,
1. Baptists—Clergy—Correspondence, reminiscences, etc. I. Title.

ODLE, Joe T. 286
Why I am a Baptist. Compiled by Joe T. Odle. Nashville, Broadman Press [1972] 128 p. 20 cm. [BX6331.2.O35] 71-189504 ISBN 0-8054-5517-5 3.50
1. Baptists—Doctrinal and controversial works. I. Title.

PENDLETON, James Madison, 1811-1891. 286
Baptist Church manual, by J. M. Pendleton. [Rev. ed.] Nashville, Broadman Press [1966] 182 p. 16 cm. Published in 1912 under title: Church manual, designed for the use of Baptist Churches. [BX6340.P4 1966] 67-1767
1. Baptists—Government. I. Title. II. Title: Church manual.

REID, Frances W. 286
Mars Hill Baptist Church (constituted 1799) Clarke-Oconee Co., Georgia [by] Frances W. Reid and Mary B. Warren. Athens, Ga., Heritage Papers, 1966. 71 p. 28 cm. Cover title. [F292.O3R4] 70-15343
1. Mars Hill Baptist Church. 2. Registers of births, etc.—Oconee County, Ga. I. Warren, Mary Bondurant, joint author.

WOOLLEY, Davis C., 1908- ed. 286
Baptist advance; the achievements of the Baptist of North America for a century and a half [Editorial committee: Robert Andrew Baker and others. Managing editor: Davis Collier Wooley] Nashville, Tenn., Broadman Press [1964] xvi, 512 p. illus., maps, ports. 23 cm. Bibliography: p. 501-506. [BX6233.B3] 64-14046
1. Baptists — North America. I. Title.

HAYS, Brooks. 286.03
The Baptist way of life [by] Brooks Hays [and] John E. Steely. Englewood Cliffs, N.J., Prentice-Hall [1963] xvii, 205 p. 21 cm. [The Way of life series] Bibliographical footnotes. [BX6331.2.H3] 63-16742
1. Baptists — Handbooks, manuals, etc. I. Steely, John E., joint author. II. Title.

HAYS, Brooks 286.03
The Baptist way of life [by] Brooks Hays, John E. Steely. Englewood Cliffs, N. J., Prentice [c.1963] xvii, 205p. 21cm. [Way of life ser.] Bibl. 63-16742 3.95 bds.,
1. Baptists—Handbooks, manuals, etc. I. Steely, John E., joint author. II. Title.

PATTERSON, W. Morgan. 286'.072'2
Baptist successionism; a critical view [by] W. Morgan Patterson. Valley Forge, Pa., Judson Press [1969] 80 p. 20 cm. Bibliographical footnotes. [BX6331.2.P33] 69-16389
1. Baptists—History—Historiography. I. Title.

BAKER, Robert Andrew. 286.09
The Baptist march in history. Nashville, Convention Press [1958] 136p. 19cm. Includes bibliography. [BX6231.B2] 58-8649
1. Baptists—Hist. I. Title.

BURGESS, W. J 1897- 286.09
Baptist faith and martyrs' fires, by W.J.Burgess. Little Rock, Arklk Baptist Publications Committee [1964] 609 p. 23 cm. Bibliography: p. 608-609. [BX6231.B78] 64-18767
1. Baptists — Hist. 2. Baptists — Doctrinal and controversial works. I. Title.

BURGESS, W. J., 1897- 286.09
Baptist faith and martyrs' fires. Little Rock, Ark., 716 Main St. Baptist Pubns. Comm., [c.1964] 609p. 23cm. Bibl. 64-18767 5.95
1. Baptists.—Hist. 2. Baptists—Doctrinal and controversial works. I. Title.

COX, Norman Wade, 1888- 286.09
Dreams, dungeons, diadems: in England, in New England, in Virginia, today and tomorrow. [Nashville? c1954] 50p. 23cm. [BX6232.C65] 55-42359
1. Baptists—Hist. I. Title.

DAVIS, Alton Arthur, 1900- 286.09
The Baptist story; sermons on the trail of blood. A series of sermons on Baptist doctrines and church history. 2d ed. Shawnee, Okla., Printed by Oklahoma Baptist University Press [1952] 170 p. illus. 24 cm. Previously published under title: Sermons on the trail of blood. [BX6232.D3 1952] 52-39269
1. Baptists—Hist. I. Title.

FORD, Samuel Howard, 1819-1905. 286.09
The origin of the Baptists, traced back by milestones on the track of time. [New ed.] Texarkana, Ark., Baptist Sunday School Committee [1950] xiii, 105 p. 20 cm. On cover: S. F. [i. e. H.] Ford. Bibliographical footnotes. [BX6231.F6 1950] 50-2158
1. Baptists—Hist. I. Title.

OVERBEY, Edward H 286.09
A brief history of the Baptist. Niles, Ill., Independent Baptist Publications, c1962. 148p. illus: 19cm. Includes bibliography. [BX6232.O9] 62-43479
1. Baptists—Hist. I. Title.

ROWE, Henry Kalloch, 1869-1941. 286.09
The Baptist witness. Revised by Robert G. Torbet. Philadelphia, Judson Press [1953] 127p. illus. 20cm. [BX6231.R6 1953] 53-67779
1. Baptists—Hist. I. Torbet, Robert George, 1912- II. Title.

TORBET, Robert George, 1912- 286.09
The Baptist story. Philadelphia, Judson Press [1957] 136p. 19cm. (American Baptist training series: advanced course) [BX6231.T59] 57-9584
1. Baptists—Hist. I. Title.

TORBET, Robert George, 1912- 286.09
The Baptist story. Philadelphia, Judson Press [1957] 136 p. 19 cm. (American Baptist training series: advanced course) [BX6231.T59] 57-9584
1. Baptists — Hist. I. Title.

TORBET, Robert George, 1912- 286.09
A history of the Baptists. With a foreword by Kenneth Scott Latourett. Rev. Valley Forge, Judson Press [1963] 553 p. 22 cm. [BX6231.T6] 63-8225
1. Baptists — Hist. I. Title.

TORBET, Robert George, 1912- 286.09
A history of the Baptists. With a foreword by Kenneth Scott Latourette. [1st ed.] Philadelphia, Judson Press [1950] 538 p. 22 cm. Bibliography: p. 509-526. [BX6231.T6] 50-9198
1. Baptists — Hist. I. Title.

TORBET, Robert George, 1912- 286'.09
A history of the Baptists, by Robert G. Torbet. Valley Forge, Judson Press [1973, c.1963] 585 p. 21 cm. First publsihed in 1950. Reissued. [BX6231.T6] 63-8225 ISBN 0-8170-0074-7 7.95
1. Baptists—History. I. Title.

ADAMS, Theodore Floyd, 1898- 286.'0922
Baptists around the world [by] Theodore F. Adams. Nashville, Broadman Press [1967] 128 p. 20 cm. [BX6493.A3] 67-10306
1. Baptists—Biography. I. Title.

CARTER, Edward R. 286'.0922 B
Biographical sketches of our pulpit, written and collated by E. R. Carter. Chicago, Afro-Am Press, 1969. ix [i.e. xix], 216 p. illus., ports. 22 cm. Reprint of the 1888 ed. [BX6453.C33 1969] 72-99355
1. Baptists, Negro. 2. Baptists—Georgia. I. Title.

PEGUES, A. W., 1859- 286'.0922 B
Our Baptist ministers and schools. With an introd. C. L. Purce. Springfield, Mass., Willey, 1892. New York, Johnson Reprint Corp., 1970. 622, 18 p. illus. 23 cm. (The Basic Afro-American reprint library) [BX6453.P4] 78-31017
1. Baptists, Negro—Biography. 2. Theological seminaries, Baptist. 3. Baptists—Education—Directories. I. Title. II. Series.

TULL, James E. 286'.092'2 B
Shapers of Baptist thought [by] James E. Tull. Valley Forge [Pa.], Judson Press [1972] 255 p.

24 cm. Includes bibliographical references. [BX6331.2.T84] 72-75359 ISBN 0-8170-0503-X 10.00
1. Baptists—Doctrinal and controversial works. 2. Baptists—Biography. I. Title.

WOOD, Presnall H. 286'.0922
Prophets with pens [by] Presnall H. Wood and Floyd W. Thatcher. Dallas, Baptist Standard Pub. Co. [1969] 158 p. ports. 23 cm. Outgrowth of the author's thesis, Southwestern Baptist Seminary. [BX6201.B72W6] 71-103137 4.25
1. Baptist standard. 2. Baptists—Biography. I. Thatcher, Floyd W., joint author. II. Title.

FORD, Zerno 286'.0924 (B)
Matthew.
Phoeba Granny Ford [by Z. M. Ford] Owensboro, Ky., Messenger Job Print. Co. [1967] 105 p. illus., ports. 23 cm. [CT275.F6815F6] 67-9511
1. Ford, Phoeba Louvicy Swink, 1859-1945. I. Title.

HARRISON, George 286'.0924
Bagshawe, 1894-
John Bunyan; a study in personality, by G. B. Harrison. [Hamden, Conn.] Archon, 1967. 191p. 19cm. Reprint of the 1928 London ed. [PR3331.H3 1967] 67-14501 5.00
1. Bunyan, John, 1628-1688. I. Title.

HATCHER, William 286'.0924 B
Eldridge, 1834-1912.
John Jasper; the unmatched Negro philosopher and preacher. New York, Negro Universities Press [1969] 183 p. illus., port. 23 cm. Reprint of the 1908 ed. [E185.97.J36] 71-88413
1. Jasper, John, 1812-1901.

HUSS, John Ervin, 286'.0924 B
1910-
Robert G. Lee; the authorized biography, by John E. Huss. Grand Rapids, Zondervan Pub. House [1967] 252 p. illus., ports. 23 cm. Bibliography: p. 245. [BX6495.L39H8] 67-24828
1. Lee, Robert Greene, 1886-

LATOURETTE, Kenneth 286'.0924 (B)
Scott, 1884-
Beyond the ranges; an autobiography. Grand Rapids, Eerdmans [1967] 161 p. 23 cm. [BR139.L3A3] 67-13980
1. Yale University. Divinity School. I. Title.

LATOURETTE, Kenneth 286/.0924
Scott, 1884-
Beyond the ranges; an autobiography. Grand Rapids, Eerdmans [1967] 161p. 23 cm. [BR139.L3A3] (B) 67-13980 3.95
1. Yale University. Divinity School. I. Title.

MCLOUGHLIN, William 286'.0924 B
Gerald.
Isaac Backus and the American pietistic tradition [by] William G. McLoughlin. Edited by Oscar Handlin. Boston, Little, Brown [1967] xii, 252 p. 20 cm. (The Library of American biography) "A note on the sources": p. [234]-238. [BX6495.B32M28] 67-19143
1. Backus, Isaac, 1724-1806. I. Title. II. Series.

MAGEE, James H., 286'.0924 B
1839-
The night of affliction and morning of recovery; an autobiography, by J. H. Magee. Cincinnati, 1873. Miami, Fla., Mnemosyne Pub. Co. [1969] 173 p. port. 23 cm. [E185.97.M2 1969] 77-89397
I. Title.

MIMS, Lambert C. 286'.0924
For Christ and country [by] Lambert C. Mims. Old Tappan, N.J., F. H. Revell Co. [1969] 128 p. 21 cm. [BX6495.M5A3] 70-85310 3.50
I. Title.

SCANLON, A. Clark. 286'.0924
Witch doctor's son [by] A. Clark Scanlon. Nashville, Convention Press [1968] 88 p. illus., map, ports. 21 cm. (1968 Foreign mission graded series) "Church study course [of the Sunday School Board of the Southern Baptist Convention] This book is number 1094 in category 10, section for juniors." [BX6495.B4S3] 68-20685
1. Batz, Manuel, 1928-1963. 2. Baptists—Guatemala. I. Southern Baptist Convention. Sunday School Board. II. Title.

TARR, Leslie K. 286'.0924 B
Shields of Canada; T. T. Shields, 1873-1955, by Leslie K. Tarr. Grand Rapids, Baker Book House [1967] 218 p. illus., facsim., ports. 23 cm. [BX6495.S49T3] 67-29222
1. Shields, Thomas Todhunter, 1873-1955. I. Title.

TARR, Leslie K 286'.0924 (B)
Shields of Canada; T. T. Shields, 1873-1955, by Leslie K. Tarr. Grand Rapids, Baker Book House [1967] 218 p. illus., facsim., ports. 23 cm. [BX6495.S49T3] 67-29222
1. Shields, Thomas Todhunter, 1873-1955. I. Title.

THOMPSON, Evelyn 286.0924 (B)
Wingo.
Luther Rice: believer in tomorrow. Nashville, Broadman Press [c1967] 234 p. 22 cm. Bibliography: p. 226-228. [BX6495.R55T5] 67-10034
I. Rice, Luther, 1783-1836. II. Title.

THOMPSON, Evelyn 286.0924 (B)
Wingo
Luther Rice: believer in tomorrow. Nashville, Broadman [c.1967] 234p. 22cm. Bibl. [BX6495.R55T5] 67-10034
1. Rice, Luther, 1783-1836. I. Title.

WHITE, Charley C. 286'.0924 B
No quittin' sense, by C. C. White and Ada Morehead Holland. Austin, University of Texas Press [1969] xi, 216 p. illus., ports. 24 cm. The author's life story, based on tape recordings of his own narrative, and written down in book form by A. M. Holland. [BX6455.W47A3] 70-100645 5.45
I. Holland, Ada Morehead. II. Title.

BOURDEAUX, Michael. 286'.0947
Religious ferment in Russia: Protestant opposition to Soviet religious policy. London, Melbourne, Macmillan; New York, St. Martin's, 1968. xi, 255p. 23cm. Bibl. [BX6310.R9B6 1968] 68-15656 8.95
1. Baptists—Russia. 2. Russia—Church history—1917- 3. Church and state in Russia—1917- I. Title.

ARMSTRONG, O. K. 286'.0973
Baptists who shaped a nation / O. K. and Marjorie Armstrong. Nashville : Broadman Press, [1975] 123 p. ; 18 cm. Excerpts from the authors' The indomitable Baptists, published in 1967 by Doubleday, Garden City, N.Y. Includes bibliographical references. [BX6235.A752 1975] 74-27925 ISBN 0-8054-6517-0 pbk. : 1.95
1. Baptists—United States. 2. Baptists—Bigraphy. I. Armstrong, Marjorie Moore, joint author. II. Title.

ARMSTRONG, O. K. 286'.0973
The indomitable Baptists: a narrative of their role in shaping American history [by] O. K. Armstrong and Marjorie M. Armstrong. [1st ed.] Garden City, N.Y., Doubleday, 1967. xiv, 392 p. 25 cm. (Religion in America series) Bibliography: p. 375-384. [BX6235.A75] 66-20926
1. Baptists—United States. I. Armstrong, Marjorie Moore, joint author. II. Title.

BAKER, Robert Andrew. 286.0973
A Baptist source book, with particular reference to Southern Baptists [by] Robert A. Baker. Nashville, Tenn. [1966] vii, 246 p. 24 cm. [BX6235.B28] 66-22076
1. Baptists—Hist.—Sources. I. Title.

BAKER, Robert Andrew 286.0973
A Baptist source book, with particular reference to Southern Baptists [by] Robert A. Baker. Nashville, Tenn., Broadman [1966] viii 216p. 24cm. [BX6235.B28] 66-22076 6.50
1. Baptists—Hist.—Sources. I. Title.

BAPTISTS and the 286'.0973
American experience / James E. Wood, Jr., editor. Valley Forge, Pa. : Judson Press, c1976. 384 p. ; 23 cm. Includes index. Bibliography: p. 361-376. [BX6235.B36] 76-22689 ISBN 0-8170-0721-0 : 15.00
1. Baptists—United States—Addresses, essays, lectures. I. Wood, James Edward.

JUDY, Marvin T. 286'.0973
Serve to survive. [Dallas?] c1957. 122 l. illus. 28cm. [BV638.4.J8] 57-41485
1. Larger parishes. 2. Sociology, Rural. I. Title.

JUDY, Marvin T 286'.0973
Serve to survive. [Dallas?] c1957. 122 l. illus. 28cm. [BV638.4.J8] 57-41485
1. Larger parishes. 2. Sociology, Rural. I. Title.

MARING, Norman Hill, 286'.0973
1914-
American Baptists; whence and whither [by] Norman H. Maring. Valley Forge [Pa.] Judson Press [1968] 127 p. 22 cm. On cover: American Baptist Convention; the history, the witness, the challenge. Includes bibliographies. [BX6235.M3] 68-22755
1. American Baptist Convention. 2. Baptists—United States. I. Title.

NEWMAN, Robert C. 286'.0973
Baptists and the American tradition / Robert C. Newman. Des Plaines, Ill. : Regular Baptist Press, c1976. xiii, 76 p. ; 21 cm. Bibliography: p. [73]-76. [BX6235.N53] 76-7166 pbk. : 1.95
1. Baptists—United States—History. I. Title.

RAY, Jefferson Davis, 286'.0973
1860-1951.
The country preacher. Nashville, Tenn., Sunday School Board of the Southern Baptist Convention [1925] 132 p. 20 cm. Bibliography: p. 128-132. [BV638.7.R35] 26-23224
1. Pastoral theology. 2. Rural clergy — Southern States. I. Title.

SHAW, Bynum. 286'.0973
Divided we stand; the Baptists in American life; a history. Durham, N.C., Moore Pub. Co. [1974] 250 p. 24 cm. Bibliography: p. 231-239. [BX6235.S48] 73-86777 ISBN 0-87716-044-9 8.95
1. Baptists—United States. I. Title.

GEORGIA Tax Institute, 286'.09755
University of Georgia.
Georgia Tax Institute. [Proceedings] [3d]- 1953- [Athens] v. 23 cm. Vols. for 1953- issued as the Bulletin of the University of Georgia. Proceedings of the 1st-2d (1951-52) institutes issued jointly with the Proceedings of the 5th-6th Accounting Institute, University of Georgia. Vol. for 1953 includes proceedings of the 7th and is called 7th in continuation of the numbering of those meetings. Vols. for 1953- prepared by the university's Division of General Extension. Institutes for 1953- sponsored by the Georgia Society of Certified Public Accountants, and similar bodies. [HJ2360.G4] 57-46261
1. Taxation—U.S.—Congresses. I. Georgia. University. Division of General Extension. II. Title.

SEMPLE, Robert Baylor, 286'.09755
1769-1831.
History of the Baptists in Virginia. Rev. and extended by G. W. Beale. With a pref. by Joe M. King. Cottonport [La.] Polyanthos, 1972. ix, 536 p. 23 cm. Reprint of the 1894 ed., published under title: A history of the rise and progress of the Baptists in Virginia, with a new pref. [BX6248.V8S4 1972] 74-175210
1. Baptists—Virginia. I. Beale, George William, 1842- ed. II. Title.

TAX Executives 286'.09755
Institute.
Membership list. New York. v. 23cm. [HJ2360.T248] 55-22247
I. Title.

PARKER, LoRetta C. 286'.09758'21
This is our song; the centennial history of Center Hill Baptist Church, Campton, (Gratis), Walton County, Georgia. Compiled and written by LoRetta C. Parker. Editorial assistance by Perce W. Jackson. [Orlando, Fla., Printed by E. J. Daniels Publishers, 1968, c1967] 228 p. 21 cm. Includes bibliographies. [BX6480.C67P3] 68-7941
1. Campton, Ga. Center Hill Baptist Church. I. Title.

BEE, Fanna K. 286'.09761'781
Sesquicentennial history: Ruhama Baptist Church, 1819-1969 [by] Fanna K. Bee and Lee N. Allen. Birmingham, Ala., Ruhama Baptist Church, 1969. xiii, 299 p. illus., ports. 24 cm. Includes bibliographical references. [BX6480.B54R78] 74-81236 4.95
1. Birmingham, Ala. Ruhama Baptist Church. I. Allen, Lee N. II. Title.

MASON, Zane Allen, 286'.09764
1919-
Frontiersmen of the faith; a history of Baptist pioneer work in Texas, 1865-1885. San Antonio, Tex., Naylor Co. [1970] ix, 219 p. 22 cm. Bibliography: p. 195-212. [BX6248.T4M34] 75-106148 7.95
1. Baptists—Texas. I. Title.

MCBETH, Leon. 286'.09764'28
The First Baptist Church of Dallas; centennial history, 1868-1968. Grand Rapids, Zondervan Pub. House [1968] 358 p. illus. 23 cm. Includes bibliographical references. [BX6480.D26F56] 68-4749
1. Dallas. First Baptist Church—History.

DAVIS Creek Church. 286'.09768'94
Minutes of Davis Creek Church, 1797-1907. Edited by Lawrence Edwards. [Montevallo, Ala., Times Print. Co., c1968] 244 p. illus., map (on lining papers), ports. 24 cm. [BX6480.D33A5] 79-1426
I. Edwards, Lawrence, 1907- ed.

LEININGER, Louis 286'.09773'89
Lee, 1899-
Heritage and history of the East St. Louis Baptist Association, 1787-1917-1967. Foreword by Carvin C. Bryant. Introd. by A. E. Prince. [Collinsville? Ill.] Collinsville Herald, inc., 1968. 196 p. illus., ports. 21 cm. Bibliography: p. 193-196. [BX6209.E28L4] 68-7966
1. East St. Louis Baptist Association. I. Title.

MILLER, Clifford R. 286'.09795
Baptists and the Oregon frontier, by Clifford R. Miller. Ashland, Southern Oregon College; [available from Oregon Baptist Convention, Portland, 1967] 225 p. illus., maps, ports. 23 cm. Bibliography: p. 212-216. [BX6248.O7M5] 67-8398
1. Baptists — Oregon. I. Title.

MILLER, Clifford R. 286/.09795
Baptists and the Oregon frontier, by Clifford R. Miller. Ashland, Southern Oregon College; [available from Oregon Baptist Convention, Portland, 1967] 225p. illus., maps, ports. 23cm. Bibl. [BX6248.O7M5] 67-8398 4.95; 2.95 pap.,
1. Baptists—Oregon. I. Title.
Publisher's addresses: 0245 S.W. Bancroft St., Portland, Ore. 97201.

WARDIN, Albert W. 286'.09795
Baptists in Oregon, by Albert W. Wardin, Jr. Portland, Ore., Judson Baptist College, 1969. 635 p. maps. 24 cm. Bibliography: p. 577-599. [BX6248.O7W3] 74-9751
1. Baptists—Oregon. I. Title.

ACKLAND, Donald F. 286.1
Joy in church membership. Nashville, Convention Press [1955] 136p. 20cm. [BX6340.A25] 56-889
1. Baptists—Membership. I. Title.

HISCOX, Edward Thurston, 286'.1
1814-1901.
The new directory for Baptist churches. Grand Rapids, Kregel Publications [1970, c1894] 608 p. 19 cm. First published under title: The Baptist church directory. Includes bibliographical references. [BX6331.H6 1970] 71-125114 5.95
1. Baptists—Doctrinal and controversial works. 2. Baptists—Government. I. Title.

JOHNSON, Gordon G 286.1
My church; a manual of Baptist faith and action. Chicago, Baptist Conference Press [1957] 158p. illus. 20cm. Includes bibliography. [BX6332.J6] 57-7705
1. Baptists. I. Title.

JOHNSON, Gordon G. 286'.1
My church, by Gordon G. Johnson. Evanston, Il[l.] Harvest Publications [1973] 187 p. 19 cm. On cover: A manual of Baptist faith and action. Bibliography: p. 185-187. [BX6331.2.J58 1973] 73-87817
1. Baptists. I. Title.

JOHNSON, Gordon G. 286'.1
My church, by Gordon G. Johnson. Evanston, Il[l.] Harvest Publications [1973] 187 p. 19 cm. On cover: A manual of Baptist faith and action. Bibliography: p. 185-187. [BX6331.2.J58 1973] 73-87817 2.50 (pbk.)
1. Baptists. I. Title.

STEALEY, Sydnor Lorenzo, 286.1
ed.
A Baptist treasury. New York, Crowell [1958] 323 p. 21 cm. [BX6215.S76] 58-12291
1. Baptists. I. Title.

TATUM, E Ray. 286.100924(B)
Conquest or failure? Biography of J. Frank Norris by E. Ray Tatum. Dallas, Baptist Historical Foundation.[1966] 295 p. illus., ports. 21 cm. Bibliographical footnotes. [BX6495.N59T3] 66-8241
1. Norris, John Franklyn, 1877-1952. I. Title.

WATSON, Ellen 286'.1'062757
Batson.
A history of the Bethel Baptist Association. Art work by Williams and Swanson. Spartanburg, S.C., Spartan Baptist Association [1968?] 38 p. fold. map. 23 cm. Bibliography: p. 30-31. [BX6248.S6W37] 75-303750
1. Baptists. South Carolina. Bethel Association. I. Title.

BENEDICT, David, 1779- 286'.1'09
1874.
A general history of the Baptist denomination in America, and other parts of the world. Freeport, N.Y., Books for Libraries Press [1971] 2 v. 23 cm. Reprint of the 1813 ed. On spine: History of the Baptist denomination. Includes bibliographical references. [BX6231.B4 1971] 73-152974 ISBN 0-8369-5726-1
1. Baptists—History. I. Title.

COLE, Edward B. 286'.1'09
The Baptist heritage / Edward B. Cole. Elgin, Ill. : D. C. Cook Pub. Co., 1977, c1976. 205 p. ; 18 cm. (Church heritage series) Includes bibliographies. [BX6331.2.C66] 76-11915 ISBN 0-89191-055-7 : 2.50
1. Baptists—Doctrinal and controversial works. 2. Baptists—History. I. Title.

*POSEY, A. R. 286.109
The New Testament baptizing ones. New York, Exposition [1966] 110p. 21cm. (EP 44129) 4.00
I. Title.

AKINS, Wade, 1944- 286'.1'0924 B
Streets aflame / Wade Akins ; [foreword by Arthur Blessitt]. Newtown, PA : Timothy Books, c1975. iii, 86 p., [2] leaves of plates : ill. ; 18 cm. [BV3785.A37A37] 75-18908 ISBN 0-914964-08-9 : 1.75
1. Akins, Wade, 1944- 2. Evangelistic work. I. Title.

BINNS, Walter Pope. 286'.1'0924 B
My life story. [Wolfe City, Tex., Southern Baptist Press, 1968] 81 p. facsim., ports. 23 cm. Cover title. [BX6495.B49A3] 68-57708
I. Title.

BROACH, Claude U. 286'.1'0924 B
Before it slips my mind [by] Claude Upshaw Broach. Charlotte, N.C., Delmar Print. Co. [1974] 121 p. 24 cm. [BX6495.B696A32] 74-83798 4.95
1. Broach, Claude U. I. Title.
Publisher's address: 9601 Monroe Rd. Charlotte, N.C. 28212

CARRAWAY, W. B. 286'.1'0924 B
Mr. Benevolence of Association Baptists; a biography of Clarence Ballard Stanley, by W. B. Carraway. [Texarkana, Ark., 1974] 100 p. illus. 23 cm. [BX6495.S755C37] 74-80033
1. Stanley, Clarence Ballard, 1889-1969. I. Title.

CLARK, John Kenneth. 286'.1'0924 B
Telling it like it was : a country preacher tells his story / by J. Kenneth Clark. Halifax, Va. : Clark, 1974. ix, 200 p. ; 24 cm. [BX6495.C552A37] 74-194714 4.95
1. Clark, John Kenneth. I. Title.

CROWLEY, Dale. 286'.1'0924 B
My life, a miracle. Washington, National Bible Knowledge Association [1971] xi, 211 p. illus., facsims., ports. 23 cm. [BV3785.C86A3] 73-155933 5.00
I. Title.

DANIELS, Velma Seawell. 286'.1'0924 B
Patches of joy / Velma Seawell Daniels ; foreword by Frank G. Slaughter. Gretna, La. : Pelican Pub. Co., 1976. p. cm. Includes index. [BX6495.D3A35] 76-4773 ISBN 0-88289-101-4 : 4.95
1. Daniels, Velma Seawell. 2. Christian life—Baptist authors. I. Title.

DAVIS, Noah, 1803or4- 286'.1'0924 B
A narrative of the life of Rev. Noah Davis, a colored man, written by himself. [Philadelphia, Rhistoric Publications, 1969] 86 p. illus., port. 21 cm. (Afro-American history series) (Rhistoric publications, no. 213.) Cover title. Reprint of the 1859 ed., with "Noah Davis and the Narrative of restraint; a bibliographical note, by Maxwell Whiteman" added. [E444.D37 1969] 74-77050
1. Davis, Noah, 1803 or 4- 2. Slavery in the United States—Personal narratives. 3. Freedmen in Maryland. I. Title.

DAY, Owen T. 286'.1'0924 B
The hallelujah hole : the story of a frontier preacher / Owen T. Day with Nancy C. Thomas. Valley Forge, Pa. : Judson Press, c1976. 174 p. : map ; 23 cm. [BX6495.D42D39] 76-18149 ISBN 0-8170-0709-1 : 6.95
1. Day, Frank, 1862- I. Thomas, Nancy C., joint author. II. Title.

DIBACCO, Thomas V. 286'.1'0924 B
Moorefield; home of early Baptist preacher Jeremiah Moore, by Thomas V. DiBacco. Fairfax,Va., Fairfax County Division of Planning, 1971. vi, 52 p. 23 cm. Bibliography: p. 49-52. [BX6495.M57D5] 72-183057 1.50
1. Moore, Jeremiah, 1746-1815. 2. Moorefield, Va. 3. Baptists—Virginia. I. Title.

FORD, Marolyn. 286'.1'0924 B
These blind eyes now see / Marolyn Ford with Phyllis Boykin. Wheaton, Ill. : Victor Books, c1977. 126 p. ; 18 cm. [BX6495.F665A37] 76-62742 ISBN 0-88207-657-4 pbk. : 1.75
1. Ford, Marolyn. 2. Baptists—United States—Biography. 3. Blind—United States—Biography. I. Boykin, Phyllis, joint author. II. Title.

FORD, Marolyn. 286'.1'0924 B
These blind eyes now see / Marolyn Ford with Phyllis Boykin. Wheaton, Ill. : Victor Books, c1977. 126 p. ; 18 cm. [BX6495.F665A37] 76-62742 ISBN 0-88207-657-4 pbk. : 1.75
1. Ford, Marolyn. 2. Baptists—United States—Biography. 3. Blind—United States—Biography. I. Boykin, Phyllis, joint author. II. Title.

FURMAN, James Clement. 286'.1'0924 B
From movies to ministry (and victory over alcohol) / by James Clement Furman. Raleigh : Christian Action League of N.C., c1977. 121 p., [8] leaves of plates : ill. ; 22 cm. Autobiographical. [BX6495.F84A34] 77-70572 ISBN 0-918648-01-7 pbk. : 2.95
1. Furman, James Clement. 2. Baptists—Clergy—Biography. 3. Clergy—South Carolina—Biography. I. Title.

FURMAN, James Clement. 286'.1'0924 B
From movies to ministry (and victory over alcohol) / by James Clement Furman. Raleigh : Christian Action League of N.C., c1977. 121 p., [8] leaves of plates : ill. ; 22 cm. Autobiographical. [BX6495.F84A34] 77-70572 ISBN 0-918648-01-7 pbk. : 2.95
1. Furman, James Clement. 2. Baptists—Clergy—Biography. 3. Clergy—South Carolina—Biography. I. Title.

GEORGE Washington University, Washington, D.C. Office of the University Historian. 286'.1'0924
Luther Rice, founder of Columbian College [by Elmer Louis Kayser] Washington, 1966. 32 p. 22 cm. "Bibliographical note": p. 31-32. [BX6495.R55G4] 67-6661
1. Rice, Luther, 1783-1836. I. Kayser, Elmer Louis, 1896-

GRANT, Myrna. 286.1'092'4 B
Vanya. Carol Stream, Ill., Creation House [1974] 222 p. ports. 22 cm. Map on lining-paper. [BX6495.M53G72] 73-89729 ISBN 0-88419-071-4 4.95
1. Moiseev, Ivan Vasil'evich, 1952-1972. 2. Persecution—Russia. I. Title.

HALL, William Preston, 1918- 286'.1'0924 B
Admired and condemned / by William Preston Hall, Jr. 1st ed. Honea Path, S.C. : Hall, 1974. 300 p. : ill. ; 21 cm. [BX6495.H263A32] 74-75519
1. Hall, William Preston, 1918- I. Title.

HARRINGTON, Bob, 1927- 286'.1'0924 B
The chaplain of Bourbon Street. With Walter Wagner. [1st ed.] Garden City, N.Y., Doubleday, 1969. 214 p. 22 cm. Autobiography. [BX6495.H267A3] 69-10969 4.95
I. Wagner, Walter, 1927- II. Title.

HAVNER, Vance, 1901- 286'.1'0924 B
Three-score & ten. Old Tappan, N.J., F. H. Revell Co. [1973] 127 p. front. 21 cm. Autobiographical. [BX6495.H288A33] 72-10390 ISBN 0-8007-0578-5 4.95
I. Title.

HERNDON, Bob. 286'.1'0924 B
Eight days with Bob Harrington; "chaplain of Bourbon Street" hits sawdust trail. Written and photographed by Bob Herndon. Produced by Bill Faulkner. New Orleans, B. Harrington [1972] 273 p. illus. 23 cm. [BV3785.H346H47] 72-195221 5.00
1. Harrington, Bob, 1927- 2. Revivals—Huntington, W. Va. I. Title.

HOVEY, Alvah, 1820-1903. 286'.1'0924 B
A memoir of the life and times of the Rev. Isaac Backus. New York, Da Capo Press, 1972. 369 p. 23 cm. (The Era of the American Revolution) Reprint of the 1858 ed. [BX6495.B32H6 1972] 73-148598 ISBN 0-306-70415-3 15.00
1. Backus, Isaac, 1724-1806.

KEITH, Billy. 286'.1'0924 B
W. A. Criswell: the authorized biography; the story of a courageous and uncompromising Christian leader. Old Tappan, N.J., Revell [1973] 224 p. illus. 21 cm. [BX6495.C74K4] 73-14830 ISBN 0-8007-0615-3 5.95
1. Criswell, Wallie A.

LEE, Robert Greene, 1886- 286'.1'0924 B
Payday everyday / Robert G. Lee. Nashville : Broadman Press, [1975] c1974. 146 p. : ill. ; 21 cm. [BX6495.L39A36 1975] 74-80721 ISBN 0-8054-5548-5 : 3.95
1. Lee, Robert Greene, 1886- I. Title.

LUDEMAN, Annette Martin. 286'.1'0924 B
Pioneering in the faith; James Floyd Kimball, Baptist minister and missionary, 1853-1918. [Quanah, Tex., Nortex Offset Publications, c1973] 84 p. illus. 28 cm. [BX6495.K49L82] 73-80111
1. Kimball, James Floyd, 1853-1918. I. Title.

MCGEE, Sarah H. 286'.1'0924 B
God called the play / by Sarah H. McGee. [Charlotte, N.C.] : Charlotte Pub., 1975. 72 p. : ill. ; 20 cm. [BX6495.M229M3] 75-7841 ISBN 0-914998-04-8
1. McGee, Alan. I. Title.

MASON, Gwen. 286'.1'0924 B
Service from sea to sea: depicting the ministries of Frederic William Patterson, minister, denominational executive, and college president, in Canada, both west and east, 1895-1948. Compiled and written by Gwen and Merle H. Mason. [Ontario, Calif., Duplicated at the First Baptist Church, 1970- v. illus. 27 cm. Contents.Contents.—v. 1. A man of the cloth in the West. [BX6495.P28M3] 74-180514
1. Patterson, Frederic William, 1877- I. Mason, Merle H., joint author. II. Title.

†MATTIX, Velva. 286'.1'0924 B
I cried ... and He answered / Velva Mattix. Denver : Accent Books, c1976. 160 p. : ill. ; 21 cm. [BX6495.M363A35] 76-42815 ISBN 0-916406-59-8 pbk. : 2.95
1. Mattix, Velva. 2. Baptists—Wyoming—Midwest—Biography. 3. Midwest, Wyo.—Biography. 4. Friedreich's ataxia—Biography. I. Title.

O'BRIEN, Bonnie Ball. 286'.1'0924 B
Harry P. Stagg : Christian statesman / Bonnie Ball O'Brien. Nashville : Broadman Press, c1976. 190 p. : ill. ; 21 cm. Bibliography: p. 190. [BX6495.S744O25] 76-18622 ISBN 0-8054-7215-0 pbk. : 3.00
1. Stagg, Harry P., 1898- 2. Baptists—Clergy—Biography. 3. Clergy—New Mexico—Biography.

OWENS, Loulie (Latimer) 286'.1'0924 B
Oliver Hart, 1723-1795; a biography. Art work by Leonard Cave. Greenville, S.C., Printed and distributed by the South Carolina Baptist Historical Society, 1966. 41 p. illus. 23 cm. Bibliography: p. 36-41. [BX6495.H275O9] 73-172381
1. Hart, Oliver, 1723-1795.

PECK, John Mason, 1789-1855. 286.10924
Forty years of pioneer life; memoir of John Mason Peck, D. D. Edited from his journals and correspondence by Rufus Babcock. Introd. by Paul M. Harrison. Foreword by Herman R. Lantz. Carbondale, Southern Illinois University Press, [1965] ixxviii, 360 p. port. 22 cm. (Perspectives in sociology) [F353.P35] 65-12394
1. Mississippi Valley. 2. Baptists—U. S. I. Babcock, Rufus, 1798-1875 ed. II. Title. III. Series.

PECK, John Mason, 1789-1855 286.10924
Forty years of pioneer life; memoir of John Mason Peck, D.D. Ed. from his journals and correspondence by Rufus Babcock. Introd. by Paul H. Harrison. Foreword by Herman R. Lantz. Carbondale, Southern Ill. Univ. Pr. [c.1965] lxxviii, 360p. port. 22cm. (Perspectives in sociol.) [F353.P35] 65-12394 10.00
1. Mississippi Valley. 2. Baptists—U. S. I. Babcock, Rufus, 1798-1875, ed. II. Title. III. Series.

PHILLIPS, Bertha Wilson. 286'.1'0924 B
A time for everything. [North Newton, Kan., Mennonite Press, 1974] 218 p. 24 cm. [BX6495.P47A36] 73-93113
1. Phillips, Bertha Wilson. 2. Christian life—Baptist authors. I. Title.

PROCTER, Marjorie. 286'.1'0924 B
The world my country : the story of Daw Nyein Tha of Burma / by Marjorie Procter. London : Grosvenor Books, 1976. 142 p., [8] p. of plates : ill., ports. ; 19 cm. (A Grosvenor biography) [BX6495.N88P76] 77-364619 ISBN 0-901269-22-0 : £1.25
1. Nyein Tha, Daw. 2. Baptists—Burma—Biography. I. Title.

PRUDEN, Edward Hughes. 286'.1'0924 B
A window on Washington / Edward Hughes Pruden. 1st ed. New York : Vantage Press, c1976. 136 p. ; 21 cm. Includes bibliographical references. [BX6495.P78A38] 77-353145 ISBN 0-533-02086-7 : 5.95
1. Pruden, Edward Hughes. 2. Baptists—Clergy—Biography. 3. Clergy—Washington, D.C.—Biography. 4. Washington, D.C.—Biography. 5. Statesmen—United States—Biography. I. Title.

ROBERTS, Cecil A. 286'.1'0924 B
Bob Harrington: God's happy hero, by C. A. Roberts. Nashville, T. Nelson [1974] 188 p. illus. 22 cm. [BX6495.H267R6] 74-4354 ISBN 0-8407-5078-1
1. Harrington, Bob, 1927-

ROBIN, 1944-1975. 286'.1'0924 B
Don't bury me 'til I'm dead / Robin. Denver : Accent Books, c1977. 128 p. ; 21 cm. [BX6495.R655A32] 76-50299 ISBN 0-916406-61-X : 2.95
1. Robin, 1944-1975. 2. Baptists—Georgia—Biography. 3. Cancer—Biography. 4. Death. I. Title.

ROGERS, Truett. 286'.1'0924 B
Bibles & battle drums / Truett Rogers. Valley Forge, PA : Judson Press, c1976. 158 p. : ill. ; 22 cm. Bibliography: p. 157-158. [BX6495.J54R63] 75-38193 ISBN 0-8170-0699-0 : 7.95
1. Jones, David, 1736-1820. I. Title.

ROSS, John Simpson. 286'.1'0924 B
Footprints on the Mendocino coast; a biography of Rev. John Simpson Ross. Editor: Julia L. Moungovan. 1st ed. Fort Bragg, Calif., Mendocino County Historical Society [1970] 34 l. port. 28 cm. (Mendocino County Historical Society. Monograph no. 3) Principally a memoir written by J. S. Ross in 1909. [BX6495.R674A3] 79-25826
I. Moungovan, Julia L., ed. II. Title. III. Series.

THOMPSON, Lorne F. 286'.1'0924 B
The raw edge of courage [by] Lorne F. Thompson. Grand Rapids, Baker Book House [1970] 199 p. 21 cm. Autobiographical. [BX6495.T44A3] 70-141553 3.95
I. Title.

WALSTON, Marie. 286'.1'0924 B
These were my hills. Valley Forge [Pa.] Judson Press [1972] 128 p. 24 cm. [BX6495.W3A3] 72-189436 ISBN 0-8170-0563-3
I. Title.

WALSTON, Marie. 286'.10924 [B]
These were my hills. New Canaan, Conn., Keats [1974, c1972] 134 p. 18 cm. (A Pivot family reader) [BX6495.W3A3] 1.50 (pbk.)
I. Title.
L.C. card number for original ed.: 72-189436.

WHITE, Douglas Malcolm, 1909- 286'.1'0924 B
Vance Havner, journey from Jugtown : a biography / by Douglas M. White. Old Tappan, N.J. : F. H. Revell Co., c1977. 192 p. ; ill. ; 21 cm. [BV3785.H392W48] 77-9458 ISBN 0-8007-0893-8 : 6.95
1. Havner, Vance, 1901- 2. Evangelists—United States—Biography. I. Title.

WORTHINGTON, Anne, 1943- 286'.1'0924 B
Pop. Bowie, Md., Golden Triangle Pub. Co., 1972. 245 p. illus. 19 cm. [BX6495.R75W67] 76-188929 8.98
1. Ruffin, Charles Edward. I. Title.

GUNN, Jack Winton. 286.109762635
A Christian heritage; the history of First Baptist Church, Grenada, Mississippi. Grenada, Baptist Press [1959] 291p. illus. 22cm. Includes bibliography. [BX6480.G73G8] 59-15625
1. Grenada, Miss. First Baptist Church. I. Title.

BAYLESS, O. L., 1912- 286'.1'0978
A history of the Colorado Baptist General Convention, compiled by O. L. Bayless. [Denver] Rocky Mountain Baptist [1966] xii, 219 p. illus., ports. 22 cm. Cover title: Southern Baptist witness in the Rocky Mountain empire. [BX6248.C57B38] 70-13523
1. Baptists. Colorado. General Convention. I. Title. II. Title: Southern Baptist witness in the Rocky Mountain empire.

CAMPOLO, Anthony. 286'.131
A denomination looks at itself [by] Anthony Campolo, Jr. Valley Forge [Pa.] Judson Press [1971] 125 p. 22 cm. Includes bibliographical references. [BX6207.A35C35] 70-144085 ISBN 0-8170-0518-8 3.50
1. American Baptist Convention—Statistics. I. Title.

MIDDLETON, Robert G. 286'.131
Training for discipleship : manual for church membership preparation / Robert G. Middleton. Valley Forge, Pa. : Judson Press, c1976. 64 p. ; 22 cm. Bibliography: p. 62-64. [BV820.M48] 75-33239 ISBN 0-8170-0659-1 : 1.95
1. Church membership—Handbooks, manuals, etc. I. Title.

SHELLEY, Bruce Leon, 1927- 286'.131
A history of conservative Baptists, by Bruce L. Shelley. [Wheaton, Ill., Conservative Baptist Press, 1971] 140 p. 20 cm. Includes bibliographical references. [BX6359.58.S5] 72-178333
1. Conservative Baptist Association of America—History. I. Title.

A Voice in the Village 286'.131 B : Howard Moody, twenty years on Washington Square / edited by Annette Kuhn. New York : Judson Memorial Church, [1977] p. cm. Bibliography: p. [BX6495.M548V64] 77-4288 5.50
1. Moody, Howard—Addresses, essays, lectures. 2. Judson Memorial Church—Addresses, essays, lectures. 3. Baptists—Clergy—Biography—Addresses, essays, lectures. 4. Clergy—New York (City)—Biography—Addresses, essays, lectures. 5. New York (City)—Biography—Addresses, essays, lectures. I. Kuhn, Annette, 1945-
Publisher's address: 55 Washington Square, New York, NY 10012

*FUNDAMENTAL BAPTIST 286.13105 CONGRESS OF NORTH AMERICA, Grand Rapids, 1966.
The biblical faith of Baptists; bk. 2. Messages presented at the Congress, Oct. 3-6, 1966. Des Plaines, Ill., 60018, Regular Baptist Pr., 1800 Oakton Blvd. [1966] 212p. 23cm. 3.95
1. Baptist Church—Congresses. I. Title.

BRUSH, John 286'.131'09744 Woolman.
Baptists in Massachusetts. Valley Forge [Pa.] Judson Press [1970] 78 p. illus., ports. 22 cm. [BX6248.M4B7] 72-107652
1. Baptists—Massachusetts. I. Title.

KELSEY, George D. 286'.132
Social ethics among Southern Baptists, 1917-1969, by George D. Kelsey. Metuchen, N.J., Scarecrow Press, 1973 [c1972] ix, 274 p. 22 cm. (ATLA monograph series, no. 2) A revision of the author's thesis, Yale. [BX6207.A48K44 1973] 72-6332 ISBN 0-8108-0538-3
1. Southern Baptist Convention. 2. Church and social problems—Baptists. 3. Social ethics. I. Title. II. Series: American Theological Library Association. ATLA monograph series, no. 2.

KELSEY, George D. 286'.132
Social ethics among Southern Baptists, 1917-1969, by George D. Kelsey. Metuchen, N.J., Scarecrow Press, 1973 [c1972] ix, 274 p. 22 cm. (ATLA monograph series, no. 2) A revision of the author's thesis, Yale. [BX6207.A48K44 1972] 72-6332 ISBN 0-8108-0538-3 7.50
1. Southern Baptist Convention. 2. Church and social problems—Baptists. 3. Social ethics. I. Title. II. Series: American Theological Library Association. ATLA monograph series, no. 2.

BAKER, Robert Andrew. 286'.132'09
The Southern Baptist Convention and its people, 1607-1972 [by] Robert A. Baker. Nashville, Tenn., Broadman Press [1974] 477 p. 24 cm. Bibliography: p. 465-469. [BX6207.S68B34] 73-91614 ISBN 0-8054-6516-2 11.95
1. Southern Baptist Convention—History. I. Title.

BAKER, Robert 286.1320924 (B) Andrew.
The first Southern Baptists [by] Robert A. Baker. Nashville, Broadman Press [c1966] 80 p. 21 cm. (A Broadman historical monograph) Bibliographical references included in "Notes" (p. 69-80) [BX6495.S4B3] 66-10663
1. Screven, William, 1629?-1713. 2. Charleston, S.C. First Baptist Church. I. Title.

BAKER, Robert Andrew 286.1320924
The first Southern Baptists. Nashville, Broadman [c.1966] 80p. 21cm. (Broadman hist. monograph) Bibl. [BX6495.S4B3] 66-10663 1.25 pap.,
1. Screven, William, 1629?-1713. 2. Charleston, S. C. First Baptist Church. I. Title.

BRYANT, James C. 286'.132'0924 B
The Morningside man : a biography of James Pickett Wesberry / by James C. Bryant. Atlanta : Morningside Baptist Church, [1975] xiv, 263 p., [4] leaves of plates : ill. ; 24 cm. [BX6495.W38B78] 75-309844 6.95
1. Wesberry, James Pickett. I. Morningside Baptist Church, Atlanta. II. Title.

BURTON, Joe 286'.132'0924 B Wright, 1907-
Road to Augusta : R. B. C. Howell and the formation of the Southern Baptist Convention / Joe W. Burton. Nashville : Broadman Press, c1976. 186 p. : ill. ; 20 cm. Bibliography: p. 184-186. [BX6495.H68B87] 75-16581 ISBN 0-8054-6520-0 : 6.95
1. Howell, Robert Boyte Crawford, 1801-1868. 2. Southern Baptist Convention—History. 3. Baptists—Southern States—Biography. 4. Southern States—Biography. I. Title.

COLE, James, 1920- 286'.132'0924
Saint J. D., by James Cole and Robert Lee. Waco, Tex., Word Books [1969] 163, [2] p. 23 cm. Bibliographical references included in "Notes" (p. [164]-165]) [BX6495.G78C6] 70-85829 3.95
1. Grey, J. D., 1906- I. Lee, Robert, 1915- joint author. II. Title.

GOODWIN, Bennie. 286'.132'0924 B
Martin Luther King, Jr. : God's messenger of love, justice and hope / by Bennie Goodwin. Jersey City : Goodpatrick, c1976. 89 p. ; 22 cm. [BX6455.K56G66] 76-382764 2.00
1. King, Martin Luther. 2. Baptists—Clergy—Biography. 3. Clergy—United States—Biography.

REID, Jim. 286'.132'0924 B
Praising God on the Las Vegas Strip / Jim Reid ; foreword by Creath Davis. Grand Rapids : Zondervan Pub. House, [1975] 183 p. ; 21 cm. [BV3775.L3R44] 74-25335 5.95
1. Reid, Jim. 2. Evangelistic work—Las Vegas, Nev. I. Title.

ROUTH, Porter, 286'.132'0922 B 1911-
Chosen for leadership : sketches of 39 presidents of the Southern Baptist Convention / Porter Routh. Nashville : Broadman Press, c1976. 110 p. : ports. ; 19 cm. Published in 1953 under title: Meet the presidents. [BX6493.R68 1976] 76-14632 ISBN 0-8054-6529-4 pbk. : 2.50
1. Southern Baptist Convention—Biography. 2. Baptists—Biography. I. Title.

SULLIVAN, James 286'.132'0924 B L.
God is my record / James L. Sullivan. Nashville : Broadman Press, [1974] 145 p. : ill. ; 21 cm. [BX6495.S799A33] 74-78609 ISBN 0-8054-5134-X : 3.95
1. Sullivan, James L. 2. Southern Baptist Convention. Sunday School Board. I. Title.

ARTER, Jared 286'.133'0924 B Maurice.
Echoes from a pioneer life. Freeport, N.Y., Books for Libraries Press, 1971. 126 p. illus. 23 cm. (The Black heritage library collection) Reprint of the 1922 ed. [E185.97.A7A33 1971] 72-170688 ISBN 0-8369-8877-9
I. Title. II. Series.

ASHER, Jeremiah, 286'.133'0924 B b.1812.
Incidents in the life of the Rev. J. Asher. With an introd. by Wilson Armistead. Freeport, N.Y., Books for Libraries Press, 1971. 80 p. 23 cm. (The Black heritage library collection) Reprint of the 1850 ed. On spine: Life of Rev. J. Asher. [E185.97.A82 1971] 74-168506 ISBN 0-8369-8860-4
I. Title. II. Title: Life of Rev. J. Asher. III. Series.

ENGLISH, James W. 286'.133'0924
Handyman of the Lord: the life and ministry of the Rev. William Holmes Borders, by James W. English. [1st ed.] New York, Meredith Press [1967] ix, 177 p. 21 cm. Published in 1973 under title: The prophet of Wheat Street. [BX6455.B63E5] 67-12637
1. Borders, William Holmes, 1905- 2. Negroes—Atlanta. I. Title.

ENGLISH, James W. 286'.133'0924 B
The prophet of Wheat Street; the story of William Holmes Borders, a man who refused to fail, by James W. English. Elgin, Ill., D. C. Cook Pub. Co. [1973] 205 p. 18 cm. First ed. published in 1967 under title: Handyman of the Lord. [BX6455.B63E5 1973] 73-78715 ISBN 0-912692-19-7 1.25
1. Borders, William Holmes, 1905- 2. Negroes—Atlanta. I. Title.

FLOYD, Silas 286'.133'0924 B Xavier, 1869-
Life of Charles T. Walker ... With an introd. by Robert Stuart MacArthur. New York, Negro Universities Press [1969] 193 p. illus., ports. 23 cm. Reprint of the 1902 ed. [BX6455.W3F5 1969] 70-97423
1. Walker, Charles Thomas, 1858-1921. I. Title.

MILLER, Harriet 286'.133'0975 Parks.
Pioneer colored Christians. Freeport, N.Y., Books for Libraries Press, 1971. 103 p. illus. 23 cm. (The Black heritage library collection) Reprint of the 1911 ed. [E185.7.M5 1971] 73-37313 ISBN 0-8369-8950-3
1. Carr family. 2. Negroes—Religion. 3. Negroes—Southern States. I. Title. II. Series.

BARKER, Rosalind Allen. 286.14
Your guide to Europe. Nashville, Convention Press [1961] 130p. illus. 19cm. (1961 foreign mission graded series, young people) 'A publication of the Foreign Mission Board, Richmond, Virginia.' [BX6275.B28] 61-7554
1. Europe—Descr. & trav.—Guide-books. 2. Baptists—Europe. I. Title.

HENDRICKS, Virginia 286.14 (Harris)
Teen traveler abroad. Nashville, Convention Press [1961] 90p. illus. 21cm. (1961 foreign mission graded series: intermediate) [BX6275.H4] 61-7556
1. Baptists—Europe. 2. Europe—Descr. & trav.—1945- I. Title.

JEREMY, David J. 286'.1426'795
A century of grace / by David J. Jeremy, John Barfield, Kenneth S. Newman. [Southend-on-Sea] : Avenue Baptist Church, 1976. [5], 50 p., [8] p. of plates : ill., facsim., map, ports. ; 25 cm. Bibliography: p. [47]-[48]. [BX6490.S68A934 1976] 77-369093 ISBN 0-9505620-0-9
1. Avenue Baptist Church, Southend-on-Sea, Eng. I. Barfield, John, B.A., joint author. II. Newman, Kenneth S., joint author. III. Title.

OLIVER, Reginald 286'.1429'54 Campbell Burn.
100 years Baptist witness in Llandrindod Wells, 1876[-]1976 / [by R. C. B Oliver. [Llandrindod Wells] : [The author], [1976] 40 p., [4] p. of plates : ill., ports. ; 22 cm. Cover title. [BX6293.L59O43] 76-377416 ISBN 0-9505075-0-4 : £0.60
1. Baptists—Llandrindod Wells, Wales. 2. Llandrindod Wells, Wales—Church history. I. Title.

TEGENFELDT, Herman G., 286'.1591 1913-
A century of growth: the Kachin Baptist Church of Burma [by] Herman G. Tegenfeldt. South Pasadena, Calif., William Carey Library [1974] xxv, 512 p. illus. 24 cm. Bibliography: p. [485]-502. [BX6316.B9T43] 74-4415 ISBN 0-87808-416-9
1. Baptists—Burma. 2. Missions to Kachin tribes. I. Title.

FRIDELL, Elmer A 286.1593
Baptists in Thailand and the Philippines. [1st ed.] Philadelphia, Judson Press [1956] 80p. 21cm. [BV3315.F7] 56-7571
1. Baptists—Thailand. 2. Baptists—Philippine Islands. 3. Missions—Thailand. 4. Missions—Phillippine Islands. I. Title.

PROVIDENCE Baptist 286'.1666'2 Church, Monrovia, Liberia.
Providence Baptist Church official souvenir program dedicatorial ceremonies. Monrovia, Liberia : The Church, [1976] 43 p., [5] leaves of plates : ill. ; 28 cm. Cover title. [BX6490.M6P766] 77-372079
1. Providence Baptist Church, Monrovia, Liberia.

IVISON, Stuart, 1906- 286.171
The Baptists in Upper and Lower Canada before 1820 [by] Stuart Ivison [and] Fred Rosser. [Toronto] University of Toronto Press [c1956] vi, 193p. plates, ports., maps. 24cm. Bibliographical references included in 'Notes' (p. [169]-178) [BX6251.I85] A57
1. Baptists—Canada. I. Rosser, Fred, 1902- joint author. II. Title.

MCKERROW, Peter 286'.1716 Evander, 1841-1906.
McKerrow : a brief history of the coloured baptists of Nova Scotia, 1783-1895 / introduced, edited, footnoted, and annotated by Frank Stanley Boyd; assisted by Mary I. Allen Boyd; with a foreword by Elliott P. Skinner. Halifax, N.S. : Afro Nova Scotian Enterprises, 1976. xxv, 124 p., [22] leaves of plates : ill. ; 23 cm. Includes index. Bibliography: p. 109-117. [BX6446.C2M3 1976] 77-356193
1. Baptists, Black—Nova Scotia—History. I. Boyd, Frank Stanley. II. Boyd, Mary I. Allen.

HAVERFIELD, William M 286.172
Buenos dias. Nashville, Convention Press [1960] 94p. illus. 20cm. (Foreign mission graded series, intermediate, 1960) [BX6255.H3] 60-9538
1. Baptists—Mexico. I. Title.

BAPTIST-CATHOLIC 286'.173 Regional Conference, Daytona Beach, Fla., 1971.
Issues and answers; [speeches] Sponsored by Home Mission Board, Dept. of Interfaith Witness and Bishops' Committee for Ecumenical and Interreligious Affairs for National Conference of Catholic Bishops. [Prepared by the Dept. of Interfaith Witness, Home Mission Board of the Southern Baptist Convention. Atlanta, Ga., 1971] 114 l. 28 cm. Cover title. [BX6329.R6B35 1971] 75-24067
1. Southern Baptist Convention—Relations—Catholic Church—Congresses. 2. Catholic Church—Relations—Southern Baptist Convention—Congresses. I. Southern Baptist Convention. Dept. of Interfaith Witness. II. Catholic Church. National Conference of Catholic Bishops. Bishops' Committee for Ecumenical and Interreligious Affairs. III. Title.

BAPTIST General 286.173 *Conference of America.* Annual [of the] Swedish Baptist churches of America. Chicago. v. 22-26cm. Title varies: -1930 [BX6247.S8B35] 56-51010

BAPTISTS. South Carolina. 286.173 Charleston Association.
Baptist Church discipline; a historical introduction to the practices of Baptist churches, with particular attention to the Summary of church discipline adopted in 1773 by the Charleston Association [by] James Leo Garrett, Jr. Nashville, Broadman [c.1962] vii, 52p. 21cm. (Broadman historical monograph) First pub. in 1774 under title: A summary of church-discipline. 62-11391 .85 pap.,
1. Baptists—Government. I. Garrett, James Leo. II. Title.

BOYD, Jesse Laney, 1881- 286.173
A history of Baptists in America, prior to 1845. [1st ed.] New York, American Press [c1957] 205p. illus. 21cm. [BX6235.B6] 57-14902
1. Baptists—U. S.—Hist. I. Title. II. Title: Baptists in America.

DAVIS, Lawrence B. 286'.173
Immigrants, Baptists, and the Protestant mind in America [by] Lawrence B. Davis. Urbana, University of Illinois Press [1973] 230 p. 24 cm. Bibliography: p. [204]-220. [BX6237.D38] 72-81264 ISBN 0-252-00247-4 8.95
1. Baptists—United States. 2. Church work with foreigners. 3. United States—Emigration and immigration. 4. Protestant churches—United States. I. Title.

DAWSON, Joseph Martin, 286.173 1879-
Baptists and the American Republic. Nashville, Broadman Press [1956] 228p. 21cm. [BX6235.D37] 56-13845
1. Baptists—U. S. 2. Baptists—Influence. I. Title.

HERRING, Reuben. 286'.173
The Baptist almanac and repository of indispensable knowledge : being a compendium of events both amazing and amusing of that great host known far and wide as Baptists ... / Reuben Herring. Nashville : Broadman Press, c1976. 159 p. : ill. ; 24 cm. Includes index. Bibliography: p. 153-155. [BX6235.H47] 75-35397 ISBN 0-8054-6521-9 pbk. : 5.95
1. Southern Baptist Convention—History—Anecdotes, facetiae, satire, etc. 2. Baptists—United States—History—Anecdotes, facetiae, satire, etc. I. Title.

HILL, Samuel S., Jr. 286.173
Baptists North and South, by Samuel S. Hill, Jr., Robert G. Torbet. Valley Forge, Pa., Judson [c.1964] 143p. 22cm. Bibl. 64-13128 2.00 pap.,
1. Baptists—U.S. 2. Southern Baptist Convention. 3. American Baptist Convention. I. Torbet, Robert George, 1912- joint author. II. Title.

THE Lord's free people 286'.173 *in a free land* : essays in Baptist history in honor of Robert A. Baker / edited by William R. Estep. A bicentennial ed. Fort Worth, Tex. : [School of Theology, Southwestern Baptist Theological Seminary], 1976. xiii, 198 p. ; 24 cm. Contents.Contents.—Drumwright, H. Preface.—Estep, W. R. Introduction.—Fletcher, J. A pen portrait.—Diemer, C. J., Jr. Roger Williams.—Neely, H. K. Baptist beginnings in the middle colonies.—D'Amico, D. F. Piet, and intellect.—Carter, J. E. American Baptist confessions of faith.—Baker, R. A. Baptist and religious liberty in the Revolutionary era.—Oliveira, Z. M. de. Richard Furman, father of the Southern Baptist Convention.—Fish, R. The effect of revivals on Baptist growth in the South.—McBeth, L. Southern Baptist higher education.—Morgan, D. H. Changing concepts of ministry among Baptists.—Estep, W. R. Southern Baptists in search of an identity.—Anderson, J. C. Episodic North American influence on certain Baptist beginnings in Latin America. "Bibliography of published writings of Robert Andrew Baker, compiled by Keith C. Wills": p. 195-198. [BX6235.L67] 76-12702 6.50
1. Baptists—United States—Addresses, essays, lectures. 2. Baker, Robert Andrew. I. Baker, Robert Andrew. II. Estep, William Roscoe, 1920- III. Fort Worth, Tex. Southwestern Baptist Theological Seminary. School of Theology.

OLSON, Adolf, 1886- 286.173
A centenary history, as related to the Baptist General Conference of America. Chicago, Baptist Conference Press [1952] xiii, 635 p. ports., diagr. 24 cm. (Centenary series) Bibliography: p. 611-626. [BX6247.S8O4] 52-10815
1. Baptist General Conference of America—Hist. I. Title. II. Series: Baptist General Conference of America. Centenary series

PANKEY, William 286'.1'73
Russell.
Edge of paradise; fifty years in the pulpit. Parsons, W. Va., McClain Print. Co., 1972. x, 245 p. coat of arms. 23 cm. [BX6495.P26A3] 79-174564 ISBN 0-87012-111-1
1. Pankey family. I. Title.

PELT, Owen D 286.173
The story of the National Baptists, by Owen D. Pelt and Ralph Lee Smith. [1st ed.] New York, Vantage Press [1960] 272p. illus. 22cm. Includes bibliography. [BX6443.P4] 60-15470
1. National Baptist Convention of the United States of America—Hist. I. Smith, Ralph Lee, joint author. II. Title.

PELT, Owen D. 286.173
The story of the National Baptists, by Owen D. Pelt and Ralph Lee Smith. New York, Vantage Press [c.1960] 272p. illus. 22cm. Bibl.: p.264-267 60-15470 3.75 bds.,
1. National Baptist Convention of the United States of America—Hist. I. Smith, Ralph Lee, joint author. II. Title.

PEPPER, Clayton. 286'.173
Streams of influence; an historical evaluation of the Town and Country Church Movement within the American Baptist Convention [by] Clayton A. Pepper. Illustrated by Betty B. Janssen. Valley Forge, Pa., Division of Parish Development and Missions, American Baptist Churches in the U.S.A. [1973] 160 p. illus. 22 cm. Includes bibliographical references. [BV638.P4] 73-1463
1. American Baptist Convention. 2. Rural churches—United States. I. Title.

ROUTH, Porter, 1911- 286.173
77,000 churches. Nashville, Broadman Press [1964] 128 p. 20 cm. [BX6235.R68] 64-15099
1. Baptists — U.S. I. Title.

ROUTH, Porter, 1911- 286.173
77,000 churches. Nashville, Broadman [c.1964] 128p. 20cm. 64-15099 1.50
1. Baptists—U.S. I. Title.

SMITH, W Earle. 286.173
Foundations for freedom; a consideration of Baptists, their heritage and contribution to American life. With a foreword by Benjamin F. Browne. [1st ed.] Philadelphia, Judson Press [1952] 112 p. illus. 20 cm. [BX6331.S6] 52-9488
1. Baptists—Doctrinal and controversial works. 2. Baptists—U.S. I. Title.

SWEET, Willia, Warren, 286.173
1881-1959, ed.
The Baptists, a collection of source material. General introd. by Shirley Jackson Case. New York, Cooper Square Publishers, 1964. vii, 652 p. 22 cm. (His Religion on the American frontier, 1783-1830, v. 1) Bibliography: p. 629-637. [BX6235.S8 1964] 63-21092
1. Baptists — Hist. — Sources. 2. Baptists — U.S. 3. Frontier and pioneer life — U.S. I. Title.

SWEET, William Warren, 286.173
1881-1959, ed.
The Baptists, a collection of source material. General introd. by Shirley Jackson Case. New York, Cooper Square Publishers, 1964. vii, 652 p. 22 cm. (His Religion on the American frontier, 1783-1830, v. 1) Bibliography: p. 629-637. [BX6235.S8 1964] 63-21092
1. Baptists—History—Sources. 2. Baptists—United States. 3. Frontier and pioneer life—United States. I. Title.

WAMBLE, G. Hugh, 1923- 286.173
Through trial to triumph. Nashville, Convention Press [1958] 142 p. 19 cm. Includes bibliography. [BX6207.A4089] 58-2884
1. Southern Baptist Convention — Hist. I. Title.

BULLOCK, Samuel Howard. 286.1744
They loved him; a dialogue thesis written in diary form, setting forth the dramatic story of the Pleasant Hill Baptist Church. [Roxbury ? Mass., 1951] 244 p. 21 cm. Includes the author's thesis, Staley College of Spoken Word, "Radio preaching today": p. 143-190. [BX6445.B6P55] 51-30703
1. Boston. Pleasant Hill Baptist Church. I. Title.

JOHNSON, Katharine W. 286'.1745
Rhode Island Baptists : their zeal, their times / Katharine W. Johnson. Valley Forge, Pa. : Judson Press, [1975] 128 p. : ill. ; 23 cm. Bibliography: p. 127-128. [BX6248.R4J64] 75-310769
1. Baptists—Rhode Island. I. Title.

ANDERSON, Margaret Jobe. 286.1747
The widening way. [Olean? N. Y., 1950?] 65 p. illus., ports. 24 cm. [BX6480.O5F5] 51-21951
1. Olean. N. Y. First Baptist Church. I. Title.

BAPTIST Church Extension 286.1747
Society of Brooklyn and Queens.
Report. [New York] v. illus. 23 cm. annual. Report year ends Apr. 30. Reports for include report of the Woman's Auxiliary covering the same period. [BV2766.B444] 52-20668
1. Baptists—Missions. 2. Missions—New York (City) I. Title.

NEW York Baptist City 286.1747
Society.
Report. [New York] v. 23 cm. annual. Report year ends Apr. 30. Reports for ... include report of the Baptist Fresh Air Home Society for the same period of time. [BX6205.N4A3] 52-25699
1. Baptists — New York (City) I. Title.

DE PLATA, William R. 286'.1747'1
Tell it from Calvary; the record of a sustained Gospel witness from Calvary Baptist Church of New York City since 1847, by William R. De Plata. New York, Calvary Baptist Church [1973 c1972] xii, 189 p. illus. 24 cm. [BX6480.N5C33] 72-92842 4.95
1. New York (City). Calvary Baptist Church. 2. Baptists—Biography. 3. Baptists—Sermons. 4. Sermons, American. I. Title.
pap. 3.50.

FIRST Baptist 286'.1748'225
Church, Chamblee, Ga.
A Century in North DeKalb : the story of the First Baptist Church of Chamblee, 1875-1975. Chamblee, Ga. : The Church, c1975. vii, 204 p. : ill. ; 23 cm. Includes bibliographies. [BX6480.C29F573 1975] 75-324690 8.95
1. First Baptist Church, Chamblee, Ga. 2. Chamblee, Ga.—Biography. I. Title.

FULLINGTON, Walbridge B. 286.1749
comp.
The history of the Bordentown Baptist Church (The First Baptist Church of Bordentown) Bordentown, N. J., organized 1751. Bordentown, Two Hundredth Anniversary Committee of the First Baptist Church, 1951. 155 p. illus. 23 cm. [BX6480.B6B3] 52-44048
1. Bordentown, N. J. Baptist Church. I. Title.

MARING, Norman Hill, 286.1749
1914-
Baptists in New Jersey; a study in transition. Valley Forge, Pa., Judson [c.1964] 379p. illus., map, ports. 23cm. Bibl. 64-24074 3.50
1. Baptists—New Jersey. I. Title.

ZDEPSKI, Stephen. 286'.1749'71
Baptists in Kingwood, New Jersey : a history of the Kingwood Baptist Church at Baptistown and Locktown and the present Baptistown Baptist Church / by Stephen Zdepski. [s.l. : s.n.], 1974 (Phillipsburg, N.J. : Harmony Print. Co.) 37 p. : ill. ; 22 cm. Bibliography: p. 37. [BX6248.N5Z37] 74-193279
1. Baptists—Hunterdon Co., N.J. I. Title.

BARNES, William Wright, 286.175
1883-
The Southern Baptist Convention, 1845-1953. Nashville, Broadman Press [1954] x, 330 p. 24 cm. Bibliography: p. 314-323. [BX6207.A4083] 53-13534
1. Southern Baptist Convention—Hist. I. Title.

CROUCH, Austin. 286.175
How Southern Baptists do their work. Nashville, Broadman Press ['1951] 99 p. 20 cm. [BX6241.C7] 52-21508
1. Southern Baptist Convention—Government. I. Title.

[FALLIS, William J]ed. 286.175
The Ridgecrest story. Nashville, Broadman Press [1933] 64p. illus. 23cm. [BX6476.R5F3] 56-33679
1. Ridgecrest. N. C. Southern Baptist Assembly. I. Title.

MIDDLETON, Robert Lee, 286.175
1894-
A drama come true; a history, Ridgecrest Baptist Assembly, 50th anniversary, 1907-1957. Nashville, Convention Press [1957] 72p. illus. 23cm. [BX6476.R5M5] 57-10107
1. Ridgecrest, N. C. Southern Baptist Assembly. I. Title.

MIDDLETON, Robert Lee, 286.175
1894-
A dream come true; a history, Ridgecrest Baptist Assembly, 50th anniversary, 1907-1957. Nashville, Convention Press [1957] 72p. illus. 23cm. [BX6476.R5M5] 57-10107
1. Ridgecrest, N. C. Southern Baptist Assembly. I. Title.

POSEY, Walter Brownlow, 286.175
1900-
The Baptist Church in the lower Mississippi Valley seventeen seventy-six--eighteen forty-five. [Lexington] University of Kentucky Press [1957] viii, 166p. 24cm. Bibliographical footnotes. [BX6241.P6] 57-11382
1. Baptists—Southern States. I. Title.

DAVIS, Margaret 286.175251
Alexander
All the cloudy days were made bright; a history of the First Baptist Church, Hyattsville, Marvland. Hyattsville, Md., First Baptist Church [1965] xiv. 108p. illus., ports. 24cm. [BX6480.H9F53] 65-17871 price unreported
1. Hyattsville, Md. First Baptist Church. I. Title.

HANEY, David. 286'.1'75256
Breakthrough into renewal; how a traditional church caught a sense of mission. Nashville, Broadman Press [1974] 128 p. 21 cm. Bibliography: p. 8. [BX6480.A5H473] 73-93905 ISBN 0-8054-5545-0 3.95
1. Heritage Baptist Church, Annapolis. 2. Church renewal—Case studies. I. Title.

CLARK, Ecward Oliver, 286.1753
1893-
Faith fulfilled the story of Chevy Chase Baptist Church of Washington, D.C., 1923-1956. [Washington, 1957] 129p. illus. 22cm. [BX6480.W3C5] 58-16287
1. Washington, D.C. Chevy Chase Baptist Church. I. Title.

WANN, John L. 286'.1753
A compilation and history of National Baptist Memorial Church (formerly Immanuel Baptist Church), Washington, D.C., 1906 to about 1976 / by John L. Wann. [Washington : s.n.], c1976. ix, 459 p. : ill. ; 24 cm. [BX6480.W3N378] 76-150944
1. National Baptist Memorial Church, Washington, D.C. I. Title: A compilation and history of National Baptist Memorial Church (formerly Immanuel Baptist Church) ...

MORRIS, Byron T. 286'.1754'47
A charge to keep; history of the First Baptist Church of Kenova, West Virginia, by Byron T. Morris. Parsons, W. Va., McClain Print. Co., 1971. 140 p. illus. 23 cm. [BX6480.K44F575] 76-141386 ISBN 0-87012-092-1
1. Kenova, W. Va. First Baptist Church. I. Title.

BONNER, J. William, 286'.1754'57
1905-
History of the Clarksburg Baptist Church, Clarksburg, West Virginia / by J. William Bonner. [s.l. : s.n.], c1977 (Morgantown, W. Va. : Morgantown Printing and Binding Co.) 226 p. : ill. ; 24 cm. [BX6480.C449C582] 77-362604
1. Clarksburg Baptist Church. I. Title.

BIRKITT, James N. 286.1'755
Carving out a kingdom; Carmel Baptist Church, 1773-1965, her history, relation to Baptist beginnings, religious persecutions, and influence. Compiled by James N. Birkitt. [Richmond, Christian Enterprises] 1965. vi, 148 p. illus., ports. 20 cm. Bibliography: p. 147-148. [BX6480.C27B5] 286'.1755'496 68-2391
1. Carmel Baptist Church, Caroline County, Va. 2. Baptists—Virginia. I. Title.

JAMES, William 286.1'755'23
Carey, 1867-1958.
Leigh Street Baptist Church, 1854-1954 : a brief history of its first one hundred years in the service of Christ / [W. C. James]. Richmond, Va. : [s.n.], 1954. xiii, 129 p., [10] leaves of plates : ill. ; 27 cm. [BX6480.R5L444] 286'.1755'496 75-310743
1. Leigh Street Baptist Church, Richmond. I. Title.

GOTT, John Kenneth. 286.1755'275
History of Long Branch Baptist Church, Fauquier County, Virginia. From centennial history (1786-1886) by Wayland F. Dunaway, and sesquicentennial history (1886 [i.e. 1786]-1936) by C. Wirt Trainham. Revised and extended by John K. Gott. Richmond, Williams Print. Co., 1967. 84 p. illus., ports. 23 cm. [BX6480.L66G6] 68-2238
1. Long Branch Baptist Church. I. Dunaway, Wayland Fuller, 1841-1916. II. Trainham, C. Wirt. III. Title.

HEFLIN, Cecil C. 286'.1755'275
The history of the Broad Run Baptist Church : bicentennial, 1762-1962 / [Cecil C. Heflin]. [Broad Run, Va. : s.n., 1962] 23 l. : ill. ; 27 cm. Caption title. [BX6480.N48B764] 75-317115
1. Broad Run Baptist Church, New Baltimore, Va. I. Title.

HOLMES, Winnibel F. 286'.1755'273
Centennial history of the First Baptist Church, Woodbridge, Virginia, 1876-1976 / by Winnibel F. Holmes. Woodbridge, Va. : The Church, c1976. 52 p., [3] leaves of plates : ill. ; 22 cm. Bibliography: p. 52. [BX6480.W87F53] 76-151799
1. First Baptist Church of Woodbridge. I. Title: Centennial history of the First Baptist Church, Woodbridge ...

BOLLS, Kate 286'.1755'296
(McChesney)
Cooks Creek Presbyterians: a heritage of faith. Compiled and written by Kate McChesney Bolls and Bennett Harman Powell. [Harrisonburg, Va., Park View Press, 1965] xi. 132 p. illus., maps, ports. 24 cm. Bibliography: p. 131-132. [BX9211.C75B6] 67-50296
1. Cooks Creek Presbyterian Church, Rockingham Co., Va. I. Powell, Bennett (Harman) II. Title.

EATON, James 286'.1755'296
Waterbury.
History of the First Presbyterian Church of Babylon, Long Island, from 1730 to 1912. Babylon, Printed by the Babylon Pub. Co. [c1912] 64p. illus. 24cm. [BX9211.B12F5] 57-55738
1. Babylon, N. Y. First Presbyterian Church. I. Title.

LUBBOCK, Tex. First 286'.1755'296
Presbyterian Church.
The first fifty years, First Presbyterian Church, Lubboc, Texas, September 4, 1903-September 3, 1953. Bi-centennial Committee: Ben White, chairman [and others. Lubbock, 1954] 52p. illus. 23cm. [BX9211.L83F5] 55-36413
I. Title.

MCKOY, Henry Bacon, 286'.1755'296
1893-
A history of the First Presleytenian Church in Greenville, South Carolina. Greenville, 1962. 373p. illus. 24cm. [BX9211.G85F5] 62-52802
1. Greenville, S. C. First Presbyterian Church. I. Title.

PIERCE, Doris 286'.1755'296
(Whittier)
History of the Berling [sic] Presbyterian Church, founded 1829. Berlin Township, Delaware County, Ohio. Galena, Ohio, Women's Association of the Berlin Presbyterian Church [1964] 51 l. illus., map. 28 cm. Bibliography: leaf 51. [BX9211.B37P5] 66-1619
1. Berlin Presbyterian Church, Berlin Township, Delaware Co., Ohio. I. Title.

ROBB, Mary Cooper. 286'.1755'296
The Presbyterian Church of Sewickley, Pennsylvania, 1838-1963. Prepared under the auspices of the church's General Committee on its 125th anniversary. [Sewickley? 1963] 104 p. illus. 22 cm. [BX9211.S6R6] 63-13781
1. Sewickley, Pa. Presbyterian Church. I. Title.

SANDERS, Robert 286'.1755'296
Stuart.
Presbyterianism in Versailles and Woodford County, Kentucky. Louisville, Ky., Dunne Press, 1963. 220 p. illus. 24 cm. [BX9211.V4P7] 63-2045
1. Versailles, Ky. Presbyterian Church. 2. Presbyterians in Woodford Co., Ky. I. Title.

SENGEL, William 286'.1755'296
Randolph.
Can these bones live? Pastoral reflections on the Old Presbyterian Meeting House of Alexandria, Virginia through its first two hundred years. Alexandria? Va. [1973] x, 98 p. illus. 23 cm. Bibliography: p. 97-98. [BX9211.A32F577] 73-180228
1. Alexandria, Va. First Presbyterian Church. I. Title.

STERLING, Alice M 286'.1755'296
Central Presbyterian Church; a history, 1851-1953. New Castle, Pa. [1953] unpaged. illus. 23cm. [BX9211.N45C4] 54-38487
1. New Castle, Pa. Central Presbyterian Church. I. Title.

TULSA, Okla. First 286'.1755'296
Presbyterian Church.
A history of the First Presbyterian Church of Tulsa, Oklahoma, 1885-1960. [Tulsa, 1960] 60 p. illus. 20 x 28 cm. [BX9211.T8A3] 63-2728
I. Title.

WESTFIELD, N.J. 286'.1755'296
Presbyterian Church.
Commemorative history of the Presbyterian Church in Westfield, New Jersey, 1728-1962. Rev. ed. [Westfield, 1963] 253 p. illus., ports., map. 24 cm. Revised ed. of McKinney's Commemorative history of the Presbyterian Church in Westfield, New Jersey, 1728-1928, with continuations by Shelby G. Fell. [BX9211.W5W4 1963] 64-36015
1. Westfield, N.J. Presbyterian Church. I. McKinney, William Kerr. Commemorative history of the Presbyterian Church in Westfield, New Jersey, 1728-1928. II. Fell, Shelby G., ed. III. Title.

WINANS, George 286'.1755'296
Woodruff.
Three hundred years of worship and service: the First Presbyterian Church in Jamaica, New York, 1662-1962. Jamaica, N. Y., Published by

the Church, 1962. 84 p. illus. 24 cm. [BX9211.J3F5] 62-14517
1. Jamaica, N. Y. First Presbyterian Church. I. Title.

THOMPSON, Archie Paul, 1921- 286'.1755'47
Lyles Baptist Church, 1774-1974, Fluvanna County, Virginia / A. Paul Thompson. 1st ed. [s.l. : s.n., 1974] (Charlottesville, Va. : King Lindsay Print. Corp.) v, 124 p. : ill. ; 23 cm. [BX6480.L9T47] 74-193283
1. Lyles Baptist Church, Fluvanna Co., Va. 2. Fluvanna Co., Va.—Biography.

BOLES, John B. 286'.1755'482
A bicentennial history of Chestnut Grove Baptist Church, 1773-1973, by John B. Boles. [Baltimore? 1973] 27 p. 23 cm. Includes bibliographical references. [BX6480.C38B64] 74-153559
1. Chestnut Grove Baptist Church. I. Title.

ALEXANDRIA, Va. First Baptist Church. 286'.1755'496
Thine is the power; the story of the First Baptist Church, Alexandria, Virginia, 1803-1953. [Alexandria, 1953] unpaged. illus. 28cm. [BX6480.A34F5] 54-30250
I. Title.

BIRKITT, James N 286'.1755'496
Carving out a kingdom; Carmel Baptist Church, 1773-1965, her history, relation to Baptist beginnings, religious persecutions, and influence. Compiled by James N. Birkitt. [Richmond, Christian Enterprises] 1965. vi, 148 p. illus., ports. 20 cm. Bibliography: p. 147-148. [BX6480.C27B5] 68-2391
1. Carmel Baptist Church, Caroline County, Va. 2. Baptists—Virginia. I. Title.

BOWMAN, Jesse E 286'.1755'496
A history of the James City and the James River Baptist Churches. Williamsburg, Va., Trumpet Pub. Co. [1954?] 93p. illus. 22cm. [BX6480.J26J33] 55-41739
1. James City Baptist Church, James City Co., Va. 2. James River Baptist Church, James City Co., Va. I. Title.

PETTIGREW, George R 286'.1755'496
Annals of Ebenezer, 1778-1950; a record of achievement. [n. p., 1951?] 150p. illus. 24cm. [BX6480.F62E2] 54-32587
1. Ebenezer Baptist Church, Florence Co., S. C. I. Title.

PIERCE, Adelaide Hall, comp. 286'.1755'496
Deming's Bridge Cemetery, Trespalacios Baptist Church, 1852-1898. and Hawley Cemetery. 1898-1960, Matagorda County, Texas. Palacios, Tex., Printed by the Palacios beacon, 1960. 75p. illus. 20cm. Consists mainly of minutes of the Trespalacios Baptist Church, 1852-91. An addendum, 'Hawley Cemetery, 1898 to April 1960 Deming's Bridge Cemetery, 1850 to1898 ([8]p., inserted) lists Hawley Cemetery graves, 1852-1960. [BX6480.M28T7] 61-40202
1. Registers of births, etc.—Blessing, Tex. I. Trespalacios Baptist Church, Matagorda Co., Tex., II. Title.

SAN Antonio. First Baptist Church. 286'.1755'496
In the shadow of His hand; the first century of the First Baptist Church of San Antonio, Texas, 1861-1961. [San Antonio, 1961] 160p. illus. 28cm. [BX6480.S365F5] 61-24799
I. Title.

SUGAR Grove Baptist Church, Davies Co., Ky. 286'.1755'496
A history of Sugar Grove Baptist Church, 1861-1961 Compiled by Lawrence C. Lashbrook [and] Annas B. Westerfield. [n. p., 1961] 80 p. illus. 24 cm. Bibliography: p. 4. [BX6480.S895] 64-39518
1. Lashbrook, Lawrence C., comp. I. Westerfield, Annas B., joint comp. II. Title.

WARE, R. M., Mrs. 286'.1755'496
The history of Emmanuel Baptist Church, Amherst County, Virginia, by Mrs. R. M. Ware. [Washington, Printed by Franklin] 1965. 10 l. 28 cm. Cover title. [BX6480.A4E4] 74-10446
1. Amherst Co., Va. Emmanuel Baptist Church. I. Title.

WARREN, Ohio. First Baptist Church. 286'.1755'496
One hundred fifty years; history, First Baptist Church, Warren, Ohio 1803-1953, by Twila Coe Dilley, church historian. [Warren, 1953] 59p. illus. 23cm. [BX6480.W28F5] 55-24542
1. Dilley, Twila Coe. I. Title.

PANKEY, William Russell. 286'.1'75559
The history of Salem Baptist Church; organized 1794, Chesterfield, Virginia. Richmond, Va. [1965?] 72 p. port. 22 cm. Cover title. "These historical addresses were given in connection with the 170th anniversary of Salem Baptist Church in 1964." [BX6480.C37S2] 70-256412
1. Chesterfield, Va. Salem Baptist Church. I. Title.

TOWNS, Elmer L. 286'.1755'671
Capturing a town for Christ [by] Elmer Towns. Old Tappan, N.J., Revell [1973] 191 p. illus. 21 cm. At head of title: Jerry Falwell. Includes 6 sermons by T. Falwell and a message by the author (p. 111-191) [BX6480.L94T488] 73-1869 ISBN 0-8007-0598-X 5.95
1. Thomas Road Baptist Church. 2. Evangelistic work—Lynchburg, Va. I. Falwell, Jerry. II. Title.
Pbk. 2.95

SEXTON, Mark S., 1952- 286'.1755'7
The chalice and the covenant : a history of the New Covenant Baptist Association, 1868-1975 / by Mark S. Sexton. Winston-Salem, N.C. : Hunter Pub. Co., 1976. xvi, 319 p. : ill. ; 24 cm. Includes indexes. [BX6444.N8S49] 76-150888 15.00
1. New Covenant Baptist Association. 2. Afro-American Baptists—North Carolina. 3. Afro-American Baptists—Virginia. I. Title.

HENDRICKS, Garland A. 286.1756
Biography of a country church. Nashville, Broadman Press [1950] xiv, 137 p. illus., ports. 20 cm. [BX6480.W27O5] 50-58193
1. Olive Chapel Baptist Church, Wake Co., N. C. I. Title.

NASH, Bessie Hursey, 1904- 286'.1756'34
From a mustard seed; a history of the First Baptist Church, Hamlet, North Carolina. [Raleigh, N.C., Printed by Sparks Press, 1973] xii, 153 p. illus. 24 cm. [BX6480.H315F576] 74-156960
1. First Baptist Church, Hamlet, N.C. 2. Hamlet, N.C.—Biography. I. Title.

HISTORY of the Wake Baptist Association, its auxiliaries and churches, 1866-1966. 286'.1756'54 Raleigh, N.C. : [C. R. Trotter], c1976. [118] p. : ill. ; 29 cm. Written by C. R. Trotter and others. Includes bibliographical references. [BX6444.N8H57] 76-17376
1. Wake Baptist Association. I. Trotter, Claude Russell.

BURLINGTON-ALAMANCE County Chamber of Commerce. 286'.1756'58
Histories of Baptist churches in Burlington and Alamance County, North Carolina. Prepared and compiled by the Burlington-Alamance County Chamber of Commerce in cooperation with the participating churches. [Burlington, N.C.] 1963. 1 v. (various pagings) 28 cm. Cover title. [BX6249.B87B87 1963] 75-303392
1. Baptists—Burlington, N.C. 2. Baptists—Alamance Co., N.C. I. Title.

HENDRICKS, Garland A. 286.175668
Saints and sinners at Jersey Settlement; the life story of Jersey Baptist Church. [Thomasville, N. C., Charity Children] 1964. iii, 203p. illus., port. 22cm. 64-6370 price unreported
1. Jersey Baptist Church, Davidson Co., N. C. I. Title.

ALLRED, Hoyle T. 286'.1756'773
Without trumpets / Hoyle T. Allred. Durham, N.C. : Moore Pub. Co., c1977. 104 p. ; 23 cm. Bibliography: p. 79-82. [BX6209.G3A43] 76-57851 ISBN 0-87716-079-1 : 10.95
1. Gaston Baptist Association. I. Title.

BRYSON, Jeter Lawrence, 1930- 286'.1756'785
The Lovely Lady of Catawba County; a history of the First Baptist Church, Newton, North Carolina, 1882-1967, by J. L. Bryson, Jr. [Newton, N.C., Printed by Epps Print. Co., 1967] 207 p. illus., ports. 22 cm. [BX6480.N58F5] 67-6601
1. Newton, N.C. First Baptist Church. I. Title.

EGGERS, Herman R. 286'.1756'843
The First Baptist Church at Boone, North Carolina; a history [by] Herman R. Eggers. [Boone? N.C.] 1969. 86 p. illus. 24 cm. [BX6480.B59F573] 73-172513
1. First Baptist Church, Boone, N.C. 2. Boone, N.C.—History.

YOUNG, James Oliver, 1910-1967. 286'.1756'865
A Baptist looks back; the origin and early history of Roan Mountain Baptist Association, now Mitchell Baptist Association. Boone, N.C., 1968. viii, 117 p. ports. 24 cm. Bibliography: p. 115. [BX6209.M66Y65] 72-261967
1. Mitchell Baptist Association. I. Title.

KING, Joe Madison, 1923- 286.1757
A history of South Carolina Baptists, by Joe M. King. Incorporating in part works by Leah Townsend and W. J. McGlothlin. [Columbia] General Board of the South Carolina Baptist Convention [1964] xxii, 494 p. illus., maps (on lining papers) ports. 24 cm. Bibliography: p. 452-461. [BX6428.S6K5] 64-19485
1. Baptists — South Carolina. 2. Baptists. South Carolina. State convention. I. Title.

KING, Joe Madison, 1923- 286.1757
A history of South Carolina Baptists. Incorporating in part works by Leah Townsend, W. J. McGlothlin [Columbia] Gen. Bd. of the S. C. Baptist Convention [dist. R. L. Brian Co., 1440 Main St., c.1964] xxii, 494p. illus., maps (on lining papers) ports. 24cm. Bibl. [BX6428.S6K5] 64-19485 5.95
1. Baptists—South Carolina. 2. Baptists. South Carolina. State convention. I. Title.

OWENS, Loulie (Latimer) 286'.1757
Saints of clay; the shaping of South Carolina Baptists. Illus. by Michael Gaffney. [Columbia, S.C., R. L. Bryan Co., 1971] xii, 146 p. illus. 24 cm. Bibliography: p. [137]-139. [BX6248.S6O87] 79-31166
1. Baptists—South Carolina. I. Title.

FLYNN, Jean Martin, 1917- 286'.1757'27
History of the First Baptist Church of Taylors, South Carolina. [Clinton, S. C.] Jacobs Bros., 1964. vii, 133 p. illus., ports. 24 cm. Bibliographical references included in "Footnotes" (p. 118-130) [BX6480.T38F54] 68-67
1. Taylors. First Baptist Church—Hist. I. Title.

FLYNN, Jean Martin, 1917- 286'.1757'27
History of the First Baptist Church of Taylors, South Carolina. [Clinton, S.C.] Jacobs Bros., 1964. vii, 133 p. illus., ports. 24 cm. Bibliographical references included in "Footnotes" (p. 118-130) [BX6480.T38F54] 68-67
1. Taylors. First Baptist Church—History. I. Title.

SPARKS, Claude Ezell. 286'.1757'41
A history of Padgett's Creek Baptist Church. [Union, S. C., Counts Print. Co., 1967] v, 172 [27] p. illus., map, ports. 22 cm. [BX6480.P26P34] 68-1836
1. Padgett's Creek Baptist Church. I. Title.

SPARKS, Claude Ezell. 286'.1757'41
A history of Padgett's Creek Baptist Church. [Union, S.C., Counts Print. Co., 1967] v, 172, [27] p. illus., map, ports. 22 cm. [BX6480.P26P34] 68-1836
1. Padgett's Creek Baptist Church. I. Title.

ALLEN, William Cox. 286.175771
A history of the First Baptist Church, Columbia, South Carolina. In commemoration of a record of one hundred and fifty years. 1809-1959 and a building of one hundred years, 1859-1959. [Columbia, 1959] 240p. illus. 24cm. [BX6480.C66F5] 60-17171
1. Columbia, S. C. First Baptist Church. I. Title.

BEESON, Leola (Selman) 286.1758
Historical sketch of the First Presbyterian Church of Milledgeville, Georgia, by Mrs. J. L. Beeson. [Milledgeville Ga., 1955] 151p. illus. 24cm. [BX9211.M553D4] 55-42627
1. Milledgeville. Ga. First Presbyterian Church. I. Title.

FAULK, Lanette (O'Neal). comp. 286.1758
Historical collections of Richland Baptist Church. Macon, Ga., Printed by J. W. Burke Co. [1950] xi, 92 p. illus., group port. 24 cm. [BX6480.R49F3] 50-3244
1. Richland Baptist Church, Twiggs Co., Ga. I. Title.

HARWELL, Jack U. 286'.1758
An old friend with new credentials; a history of the Christian index, by Jack U. Harwell. Atlanta, The Christian Index, Executive Committee of the Baptist Convention of the State of Georgia [1972] vii, 204 p. ports. 24 cm. Bibliography: p. 193. [BX6201.C463H37] 72-81129 4.95
1. The Christian index. I. Title.

LESTER, James Adams. 286'.1758
A history of the Georgia Baptist Convention, 1822-1972. [Atlanta? Executive Committee, Baptist Convention of the State of Georgia, 1972] xvii, 846 p. illus. 24 cm. Bibliography: p. 827-834. [BX6248.G4L47] 72-81133
1. Baptists. Georgia. Convention. 2. Baptists—Georgia. I. Title.

NEWTON, Louie De Votie, 1892- 286.1758
Fifty golden years; the Atlanta Association of Baptist Churches, 1909- 1958. Research by Jack U. Harwell. [Hapeville? Ga., 1958] 92p. illus. 22cm. [BX6209.A77N4] 58-14050
1. Baptists. Georgia. Atlanta Association. I. Title.

CHURCH, Mary L 286.1758125
Seventy years in Clarkesville Baptist Church. [n.p., c1958] 51p. illus. 24cm. [BX6480.C45C6] 59-20258
1. Clarkesville, Ga. Clarkesville Baptist Church. I. Title.

KNIGHT, Walker L., 1924- 286'.1758'225
Struggle for integrity, by Walker L. Knight. Waco, Tex., Word Books [1969] 182 p. illus. 23 cm. Bibliography: p. 181-182. [BX6480.D37O2] 72-85832 4.95
1. Decatur, Ga. Oakhurst Baptist Church. I. Title.

ATLANTA. Sconed-Ponce de Leon Baptist Church. 286.1758231
A history of the Second-Ponce de Leon Baptist Church, Atlanta, Georigia, centennial year, 1854-1954. [Atlanta] Darby Print. Co., 1954. 149p. illus. 28cm. [BX6480.A74S42] 59-32739
I. Title.

PRICE, Nelson L. 286'.1758'245
I've got to play on their court / Nelson L. Price. Nashville, Tenn. : Broadman Press, c1975. 140 p. : ill. ; 20 cm. [BX6480.M25R676] 75-8326 ISBN 0-8054-5554-X : 4.95
1. Roswell Street Baptist Church, Marietta, Ga. I. Title.

GOOCH, Betty. 286'.1758'272
To the glory of God : the history of Pleasant Union Baptist Church, 1942-1976 / compiled and written by Betty Gooch and Shelby Dorsey. [s.l. : s.n., 1977], 1977. 181 p. : ill. ; 23 cm. Cover title: To God be the glory. Bibliography: p. 181. [BX6476.G34P583] 77-151701
1. Pleasant Union Baptist Church, Gainesville, Ga. I. Dorsey, Shelby, joint author. II. Title. III. Title: To God be the glory.

GREEN, Harold Frederic, 1932- 286'.1758'272
Not made for defeat ... : the history of the Central Baptist Church from 1890-1974 / by Harold Frederic Green. 1st ed. Gainesville, GA : Green Books, [1974] 336 p. : ill. ; 23 cm. [BX6480.G34C463] 74-78911 7.95
1. Central Baptist Church, Gainesville, Ga. I. Title.

GARDNER, Robert Grosvenor. 286'.1758'35
The Rome Baptist Church, 1835-1865 / Robert G. Gardner Rome, Ga. : First Baptist Church, 1975. 75 p. : ill. ; 23 cm. Bibliography: p. 75. [BX6480.R65R654] 75-318794
1. Rome Baptist Church.

BARKLEY, H. E. 286'.1'758463
Links of gold; history of the First Baptist Church, West Point, Georgia, organized 1849, by H. E. Barkley. [West Point, Ga., Printed by Hester Print. Co., 1971] 190 p. illus., ports. 24 cm. Bibliography: p. 183-184. [BX6480.W42B37] 72-24925
1. West Point, Ga. First Baptist Church. I. Title.

JONES, Billy Walker. 286.17585
History of Ebenezer Missionary Baptist Assocation (of Georgia) 1814-1964 [by Billy Walker Jones, with Esther Pool Adkins and others. Dry Branch? Ga., 1965] iii, 256 p. illus., map, ports. 25 cm. [BX6248.G4J6] 65-5230
1. Baptists. Georgia. Ebenezer Missionary Baptist Association. I. Adkins, Esther Pool, joint author. II. Title.

SMITH, Travis Edwin, 1898- 286'.1758'573
History of the First Baptist Church of Milledgeville, Georgia, 1811-1975 / by T.E. Smith Atlanta : Cherokee Pub. Co., 1976. xvi, 279 p. : ill. ; 24 cm. Includes bibliographical references and index. [BX6480.M54F577] 75-46192 ISBN 0-87797-035-1 : 10.00
1. First Baptist Church, Milledgeville, Ga. 2. Milledgeville, Ga.—Biography. I. Title.

SIMMS, James Meriles. 286'.1758'724
The first Colored Baptist church in North America. Constituted at Savannah, Georgia, January 20, A.D. 1788. With biographical sketches of the pastors. Written for the church by James M. Simms. New York, Negro Universities Press [1969] 264 p. illus. 23 cm.

Reprint of the 1888 ed. [BX6480.S45F55 1969] 70-82074 ISBN 0-8371-1561-2
1. Savannah. First Bryan Baptist Church. I. Title.

JOINER, Edward Earl. 286'.1759
A history of Florida Baptists. [Jacksonville, Fla., Printed by Convention Press, [1972] 326 p. illus. 25 cm. Bibliography: p. 314-318. [BX6248.F6J64] 78-185685
1. Baptists. Florida. Convention. 2. Baptists—Florida. I. Title.

FIRST Baptist 286'.1759'381
Church, Miami, Fla.
First Baptist Church, Miami, Florida, 1896-1961; 65 years of service. Miami [1961?] 76 p. illus. 23 cm. Cover title. [BX6480.M43F573] 73-172524
1. First Baptist Church, Miami, Fla. 2. Miami, Fla.—Biography. I. Title.

LASTINGER, Eula 286'.1759'62
Tucker.
The first one hundred years in the life of Friendship Baptist Church, 1875-1975 / by Eula Tucker Lastinger [s.l. : s.n., 1975] (Atlanta : Print Shop) iv, 119 p. : ill. ; 22 cm. Includes bibliographical references. [BX6480.F77F744] 75-316073
1. Friendship Baptist Church, Fruitville, Fla. 2. Fruitville, Fla.—Biography. I. Title.

SNELL, Marvis R. 286'.1759'62
Testimony to pioneer Baptists : the origin and development of the Gillette First Baptist Church / by Marvis R. Snell. [s.l. : s.n.], c1974 (Deleon Springs, Fla. : Printed by E. O. Painter Print. Co.) xi, 355 p., [17] leaves of plates : ill., map ; 24 cm. Includes index. Bibliography: p. 299. [BX6480.G54F577] 74-21156
1. Gillette First Baptist Church. 2. Manatee Co., Fla.—Biography. I. Title.

BRATCHER, Alfred Lewis, 286.1761
1905-
Eighty-three years; the moving story of church growth, including significant sermons and addresses. Montgomery, Ala., Paragon Press [1950] viii, 113 p. illus., ports. 22 cm. [BX6480.M6F62] 50-57830
1. Montgomery, Ala. First Baptist Church (Negro) I. Title.

CRISMON, Leo T 286.1761
Kentucky Baptist atlas; descriptive comments on historical Baptist sites in Kentucky, by Leo T. Crismon and George Raleigh Jewell. [Middletown, Ky., Kentucky Baptist Historical Society 1964] 1 v. (unpaged) illus., col. map, ports. 31 cm. [BX6248.K4C7] 65-9260
1. Baptists—Kentucky. I. Jewell, George Raleigh, joint author. II. Title.

RILEY, Benjamin 286.1761
Franklin, 1849-1925.
History of the Baptists of Alabama: from the time of their first occupation of Alabama in 1808, until 1894: being a detailed record of denominational events in the State during... eighty-six years, and furnishing biographical sketches of those who have been conspicuous in the annals of the denomination, besides much other incidental matter relative to the secular history of Alabama. Issued under the auspices of the Alabama Baptist Historical Society. Birmingham, Roberts, 1895. 481 p. illus., ports. 23 cm. Index, by William R. Snell. [Birmingham? Ala., 1962] [26] 1. 18 cm. [BX6248.A2R48] 40-22693
1. Baptists, Alabama. I. Snell, William R. II. Alabama Baptist Historical Society. III. Title.

BROWN, Bessie 286'.1761'49
Conner.
A history of the First Baptist Church, Tuskegee, Alabama, 1839-1971. [Tuskegee? Ala., 1972] iii 1., 89 p. illus. 24 cm. [BX6480.T88F5] 73-188683
1. Tuskegee, Ala. First Baptist Church.

BAXTER, Duncan 286.176166
Annals and growth of the First Baptist Church of Fort Payne, Alabama, 1885-1963. Birmingham, Ala., Banner Pr. [c.1964] 107p. illus., port. 21cm. (Banner bk.) Bibl. 64-7038 4.00
1. Fort Payne, Ala. First Baptist Church. I. Title.

BAXTER, Duncan. 286.176166
Annals and growth of the First Baptist Churct of Fort Payne, Alabama, 1885-1963. Birmingham, Ala., Banner Press [1964] 107 p. ullus., port. 21 cm. (A Banner book) Includes bibliographical references. [BX6480.F66F5] 64-7038
1. Fort Payne, Ala. First Baptist Church. I. Title.

GILMORE, J. 286'.1761'781
Herbert.
They chose to live; the racial agony of an American church [by] J. Herbert Gilmore, Jr. Grand Rapids, Eerdmans [1972] 206 p. 22 cm. [BT734.2.G527] 72-75577 ISBN 0-8028-3415-9 2.95
1. First Baptist Church, Birmingham, Ala. 2. Church and race problems—Birmingham, Ala.—Case studies. I. Title.

HANLIN, Katherine 286'.1761'78
Hale.
The steeple beckons; a narrative history of the First Baptist Church, Trussville, Alabama, 1821-1971. [Trussville, Ala., First Baptist Church, 1973] xiii, 252 p. illus. 24 cm. Bibliography: p. 207-211. [BX6480.T78F57] 72-92280
1. First Baptist Church, Trussville, Ala. 2. Trussville, Ala.—Biography. I. Title.

ATCHISON, Ray M 1921- 286.176179
Baptists of Shelby County; history of the Shelby Baptist Association of Alabama [by] Ray M. Atchison. Birmingham, Ala., Banner Press [1964] 192 p. illus., fold. map. 24 cm. Bibliography: p. [165[-166. [BX6209.S63A8] 64-24926
1. Baptists. Alabama. Shelby Baptist Association. I. Title.

MCKINLEY, Sybil. 286'.1761'82
A tiny speck in God's scheme of things; history of Brent Baptist Church, Brent, Alabama. [1st ed. Birmingham, Ala., Printed by Oxmoor Press, 1972] xii, 126 p. illus. 24 cm. On spine: History of Brent Baptist Church. [BX6480.B54B734] 72-77524
1. Brent Baptist Church. I. Title. II. Title: History of Brent Baptist Church.

BLACKMAN, Nancy 286'.1761'84
Dean.
Brow of the hill above the Warrior : history of the Holt First Baptist Church, Holt, Alabama, 1904-1974 / by Nancy Dean Blackman. Holt, Ala. : Holt First Baptist Church, c1976. xiv, 250 p. : ill. ; 24 cm. [BX6480.H64H643] 76-150833
1. Holt First Baptist Church. I. Title.

MCLEMORE, Richard 286'.1762
Aubrey, 1903-
A history of Mississippi Baptists, 1780-1970. [Jackson, Miss.] Mississippi Baptist Convention Board [1971] xiii, 386 p. 24 cm. Bibliography: p. 368-370. [BX6248.M7M25] 77-29590 7.00
1. Baptists. Mississippi. Convention. 2. Baptists—Mississippi. I. Title.

FARR, Eugene Ijams. 286'.1762'59
A history of Richland Baptist Church, Richland, Mississippi / by Eugene Ijams Farr. [s.l. : s.n.], c1976 (Florence, MS. : Messenger Press) xv, 358 p. : ill. ; 22 cm. [BX6480.R493R523] 77-358468
1. Richland Baptist Church, Richland, Miss. I. Title.

FARR, Eugene Ijams. 286'.1762'59
A history of Richland Baptist Church, Richland, Mississippi / by Eugene Ijams Farr. [s.l. : s.n.], c1976 (Florence, MS. : Messenger Press) xv, 358 p. : ill. ; 22 cm. [BX6480.R493R523] 77-358468
1. Richland Baptist Church, Richland, Miss. I. Title.

GREENE, Glen Lee, 1915- 286'.1763
House upon a rock: about Southern Baptists in Louisiana. 1st ed. Alexandria, Executive Board of the Louisiana Baptist Convention, 1973. 363 p. illus. 24 cm. Bibliography: p. 340-344. [BX6248.L6G7] 73-86696 5.95
1. Baptists. Louisiana. Louisiana Baptist Convention. I. Title.

GREENE, Glen Lee, 1915- 286.1'763
Louisiana Baptist historical atlas / by Glen Lee Greene. 1st ed. Alexandria : Executive Board of the Louisiana Baptist Convention, 1975. 32 p. : ill. ; 28 cm. [BX6248.L6G73] 76-350557
1. Baptists—Louisiana. 2. Churches—Louisiana. 3. Louisiana—Church history. I. Baptists. Louisiana. Louisiana Baptist Convention. II. Title.

ST. AMANT, Penrose, 286.1763
1915-
A short history of Louisiana Baptists, by C. Penrose St. Amant. Nashville, Broadman Press [1948] 142 p. 20 cm. Prepared at the request of the program committee for the centennial session of the Louisiana Baptist convention, Nov. 29-Dec. 2, 1948. "Selected bibliography": p. 141-142. [BX6248.L6S3] 49-13236
1. Baptists—Louisiana. I. Baptists. Louisiana. Louisiana Baptist Convention. II. Title.

GREENE, Glen Lee, 286.176384
1915-
A history of the Baptists of Oak Ridge, Louisiana, 1797-1960. Nashville, Tenn., Parthenon Press, 1960. 183p. illus. 22cm. Includes bibliography. [BX6249.O3G7] 60-14853
1. Baptists—Oak Ridge, La. 2. Oak Ridge, La. Baptist Church. I. Title.

HEMPHILL, Annie Mae 286'.1763'94
Tooke.
A brief history of Rocky Springs Baptist Church, organized 1845. Rev. Lisbon, La., 1968. 16 p. 22 cm. Cover title. Bibliography: p. 16. [BX6480.C448R63 1968] 74-165053
1. Rocky Springs Baptist Church, Claiborne Parish, La. I. Title.

BAKER, Robert Andrew. 286'.1'764
The blossoming desert; a concise history of Texas Baptists [by] Robert A. Baker. Waco, Tex., Word Books [1970] 282 p. 22 cm. Includes bibliographical references. [BX6248.T4B3] 73-127035 5.95
1. Baptists—Texas. I. Title.

BERGER, Tom. 286'.1'764
Baptist journalism in nineteenth-century Texas. [Austin] Dept. of Journalism Development Program, University of Texas at Austin [1969?] iv, 73 p. illus. 24 cm. Bibliography: p. 71-72. [PN4897.T44B4] 75-633594 4.00
1. Press, Baptist—Texas—History. 2. Baptists—Texas. I. Title.

JONES, Eva 286'.1'764175
McDaniel.
From darkness to light; the story of the First Baptist Church of San Augustine, Texas. Researched by the Business Women's Missionary Society. Illus. by Raye McGilbery Wise. San Antonio, Tex., Naylor [1970] xxii, 106 p. illus., facsims., ports. 22 cm. [BX6480.S366F55] 78-131482 6.95
1. San Augustine, Tex. First Baptist Church. I. San Augustine, Tex. First Baptist Church. Business Women's Missionary Society. II. Title.

BRYAN, Tex. First 286.176424
Baptist Church.
A better day is dawning; history of the first one hundred years of the First Baptist Church of Bryan, Texas, November 18, 1866-November 18, 1966. Austin, Tex., Printed by Von-Boeckmann-Jones [1966] xi, 107 p. illus., ports. 24 cm. Bibliography: p. 99. [BX6480.B8F5] 67-23
I. Title.

CHUMBLEY, Joe W. 286'.1764'265
Kentucky Town and its Baptist church : or, Ann Eliza and Pleasant Hill / by Joe W. Chumbley. Houston, Tex. : D. Armstrong Co., c1975. 263 p. : ill. ; 23 cm. Bibliography: p. 263. [BX6480.K46K473] 75-332946
1. Kentuckytown Baptist Church. 2. Kentuckytown, Tex.—History. I. Title.

TIDWELL, Donavon 286'.1764'518
Duncan.
A history of the Baptists at Iredell, Texas. Irving, Tex., Griffin Graphic Arts [1968] 66, [8] p. 18 cm. Bibliography: p. [67]-[69] [BX6249.I35T5] 73-272
1. Baptists—Iredell—History. I. Title.

RIKE, Charles 286'.1764'556
Jesse.
First Baptist Church, Farmersville, Texas, centennial story, 1865-1965. [Tyler, Tex., Printed by Tyler Print Shop, 1965] 40 p. illus., ports. 22 cm. Cover title. [BX6480.F3F5] 72-217330
1. Farmersville, Tex. First Baptist Church.

GASKIN, Jesse Marvin, 286.1766
1917-
Trail blazers of Sooner Baptists. Shawnee, Oklahoma Baptist University Press [1953] 200 p. illus. 20 cm. [BX6248.O5G3] 53-33153
1. Baptists— Oklahoma—Hist. I. Title.

SAPP, Phyllis 286.1766381
Woodruff, 1908- ed.
Lighthouse on the corner; a history of the First Baptist Church, Oklahoma City, Oklahoma. Malinda Brown, director of research. Oklahoma City, Century Press, 1964. xiv, 135, vii p. illus., ports. 24 cm. [BX6480.O4F5] 64-57876
1. Oklahoma City. First Baptist Church. I. Title.

SAPP, Phyllis 286.1766381
Woodruff, 1908- ed.
Lighthouse on the corner; a history of theFirst Baptist Church, Oklahoma City, Oklahoma. Malinda Brown, director of research. Oklahoma City, Century Pr., 412 N. Hudson, [c.]1964. xiv, 135, vii p. illus., ports. 24cm. [BX6480.O4F5] 64-57876 3.00
1. Oklahoma City, First Baptist Church. I. Title.

FOREMAN, Lawton Durant, 286.1767
1913-
The life and works of Benjamin Marcus Bogard by L. D. Foreman, Alta Payne. Little Rock. Ark. [1966] 2 v. illus., ports. 23cm. [BX6495.B63F6] 66-6965 15.00 set
1. Bogard, Ben Marquis, 1868- I. Payne, Alta, joint author II. Title.
Available from Rev. L. D. Foreman, 2520 S. Oak, Little Rock, Ark. 72204

KENDALL, William 286'.1768
Frederick.
A history of the Tennessee Baptist Convention / W. Fred Kendall. Brentwood : Executive Board of the Tennessee Baptist Convention, 1974. 384 p. : ill. ; 24 cm. Includes index. Bibliography: p. 368-372. [BX6248.T2K46 1974] 74-84554
1. Baptists. Tennessee. Convention. 2. Baptists—Tennessee. I. Title.

NIXON, W Hubert. 286.176853
History of the Indian Creek Baptist Church and related events [by] W. H. Nixon. [Dowelltown? Tenn.] c1965. xiv, 271 p. illus., ports. 21 cm. [BX6480.I 5N5] 66-86895
1. Indian Creek Baptist Church, De Kalb Co., Tenn. I. Title.

MAY, Lynn E. 286'.1'76855
The First Baptist Church of Nashville, Tennessee, 1820-1970 [by Lynn E. May, Jr. [Nashville, First Baptist Church, 1970] 331 p. illus., ports. 24 cm. Includes bibliographical references. [BX6480.N3F55] 72-136021
1. Nashville. First Baptist Church. I. Title.

HOOD, John O., 1894- 286'.1768'8
History of the Chilhowee Baptist Association, by John O. Hood for Chilhowee Baptist Association. [Nashville, Curley Printing Company, c1970] xiv, 370 p. illus., ports. 24 cm. Bibliography: p. 369-370. [BX6209.C52H6] 79-127476
1. Chilhowee Baptist Association. I. Chilhowee Baptist Association. II. Title.

BAPTISTS in Kentucky, 286'.1769
1776-1976 : a bicentennial volume / edited by Leo Taylor Crismon. Middletown : Kentucky Baptist Convention, 1975. vi, 330 p. ; 24 cm. Includes bibliographical references. [BX6248.K4B36] 76-356672
1. Baptists—Kentucky. 2. Kentucky—Church history. I. Crismon, Leo T.

CROSS, Irvie Keil, 1917- 286.1769
The truth about conventionism. Little Rock, Ark., Printed by Seminary Press [1955] 80 p. illus. 24 cm. [BX6207.A4084] 55-42019
1. Southern Baptist Convention. 2. United Baptists. Kentucky. Cumberland River Association. I. Title.

CROSS, Irvie Keil, 1917- 286.1769
The truth about conventionism; the Southern Baptist Convention, a new denomination. 2d ed., rev. and enl. Little Rock, Ark., Printed by Seminary Press [1956] 93 p. illus. 23 cm. [BX6207.A4084 1956] 56-38686
1. Southern Baptist Convention. 2. United Baptists. Kentucky. Cumberland River Association. I. Title.

KIMBROUGH, Bradley 286.1769
Thomas, 1880-
Jubilee in '53; the seequicentennial history of the Long Run Association of Baptists. Louisville, Ky., Long Rup Association of Baptists, 1953. 124p. 23cm. [BX6209.L7K5] 54-19253
1. Baptists. Kentucky. Long Run Association. I. Title.

SINGER, J. W., 286'.1'769425
1905-
A history of the Baptist Church at the Stamping Ground, Ky., 1795- by J. W. Singer. Rev. and enl. [Stamping Ground, Ky.] 1970. 278 p. illus., ports. 24 cm. [BX6480.S84S5] 71-118990
1. Stamping Ground Baptist Church. I. Title.

BETHEL Baptist 286'.1769'493
Church, Washington Co., Ky.
Records of Bethel Baptist Church, Washington County, Kentucky, 1817-1875. Copied and published by Alma Ray Sanders Ison [and] Evelyn Prewitt Sanders, with church history by Vernice B. Pinkston. Harrodsburg, Ky., Mercer Print. Co., 1970. 152 l. 28 cm. [BX6480.W32A5] 73-150024 5.00
1. Bethel Baptist Church, Washington Co., Ky. I. Ison, Alma Ray Sanders. II. Sanders, Evelyn Prewitt.

MARCUM, Elvis. 286'.1772'19
Outreach, God's miracle business / Elvis Marcum ; [foreword by Kenneth L. Chafin]. Nashville : Broadman Press, c1975. 151 p. : ill. ; 19 cm. Bibliography: p. 139-140. [BX6480.N46G75] 75-10507 ISBN 0-8054-5556-6 pbk. : 2.95
1. Graceland Baptist Church, New Albany, Ind. I. Title.

HOFFMAN, Harold 286'.1772'52
Richard.
A light in the forest; a history of the First Baptist Church of Indianapolis, Indiana, 1822-

1966. Indianapolis, J. C. Collins, 1966. iv, 121 p. illus., ports. 23 cm. Bibliography: p. 119-121. [BX6480.I53H6] 74-6697
1. Indianapolis. First Baptist Church. I. Title.

ERICSON, Carl George, 1890- 286.1773
Harvest on the prairies centennial history of the Baptist Conference of Illinois, 1856-1956. Chicago, Published by Baptist Conference Press for Baptist Conference of Illinois [1956] 157p. illus. 20cm. [BX6248.I3E7] 56-11837
1. Baptists. Illinois. Baptist Conference of Illinois. I. Title.

WE were there : 286'.1773
an oral history of the Illinois Baptist State Association, 1907-1976 / [edited by] Robert J. Hastings. Springfield : The Association, 1976. xvi, 270 p. : ill. ; 24 cm. Includes index. Bibliography: p. 255-261. [BX6248.I3W4] 75-23435 ISBN 0-9600896-1-6 : 4.99
1. Illinois Baptist State Association. 2. Baptists—Illinois. I. Hastings, Robert J.

NYGAARD, Normal Eugene, 1897- 286.1778
Where cross the crowded ways; the story of the Third Baptist Church of St. Louis, Missouri, and its minister, Dr. C. Oscar Johnson. New York, Greenberg [1950] viii, 240 p. illus., ports. 21 cm. "Where cross the crowded ways of life" (words and music): verse of frontispiece. [BX6480.S27T47] 50-4729
1. Johnosn, Charles Oscar, 1886- 2. St. Louis. Third Baptist Church. I. Title.

ST. Stephen Baptist Church, Kansas City, Mo. History Committee. 286'.1778'411
Symbols of God's grace; seventy years history. St. Stephen Baptist Church, Kansas City, Missouri. [Thelma M. Dumas, chairman. 2d ed. Kansas City, St. Stephen Baptist Church, 1974, c1973] 538 p. illus. 26 cm. Edition for 1963 published under title: Meeting the challenge of change. [BX6480.K3S3 1973] 74-176286
1. St. Stephen Baptist Church, Kansas City, Mo. 2. Kansas City, Mo.—Biography. I. Dumas, Thelma M. II. Title.

UNITED Baptists. Missouri. Central Missouri Association. 286.17788
Minutes, 1859-1957, inclusive. [Salem? Mo., 1957?] 362 p. 23 cm. Cover title. [BX6434.M52C4] 59-31714
I. Title.

FREDRIKSON, Roger. 286'.1783'371
God loves the dandelions / Roger Fredrikson. Waco, Tex. : Word Books, [1975] 168 p. : ill. ; 23 cm. Includes bibliographical references. [BX6480.S73F573] 74-27481 5.95
1. First Baptist Church, Sioux Falls, S.D. I. Title.

FREDRIKSON, Roger. 286'.1783'371
God loves the dandelions / Roger Fredrikson. Waco, Tex. : Word Books, [1975] 168 p. : ill. ; 23 cm. Includes bibliographical references. [BX6480.S73F573] 74-27481 5.95
1. First Baptist Church, Sioux Falls, S.D. I. Title.

TINGLEY, Ralph. 286'.1783'371
Mission in Sioux Falls : the First Baptist Church, 1875-1975 / Ralph & Kathleen Tingley. Sioux Falls, S.D. : First Baptist Church, c1975. 222 p. : ill. ; 24 cm. Includes bibliographical references. [BX6480.S73F577] 75-29740
1. First Baptist Church, Sioux Falls, S.D. 2. Sioux Falls, S.D.—Biography. I. Tingley, Kathleen, joint author. II. Title.

TUCKER, Michael R. 286'.1788'56
The church that dared to change / Michael R. Tucker. Wheaton, Ill. : Tyndale House Publishers, 1975. x, 129, [2] p. ; 21 cm. Bibliography: p. [131] [BX6480.C65T456] 74-21971 ISBN 0-8423-0280-8 : 2.95
1. Temple Baptist Church, Colorado Springs. 2. Church renewal—Case studies. I. Title.

STRATTON, David Hodges, 1927- 286.1789
The first century of Baptists in New Mexico, 1849-1950. Albuquerque Women's Missionary Union of New Mexico, 1954 121p. 22cm. [BX6248.N6S8] 54-30702
1. Baptists—New Mexico. I. Title.

RUHLMAN, John J. 286'.179
A history of Northwest Regular Baptists : the General Association of Regular Baptist Churches in Washington, Oregon, and Idaho, 1939-1975 / by John J. Ruhlman, Jr. Schaumburg, Ill. : Regular Baptist Press, 1977,c1976 xiii, 334 p. : ill. ; 24 cm. Includes index. Bibliography: p. 319-325. [BX6389.34.W2R83] 76-12767 ISBN 0-87227-000-9 : 12.50
1. Northwest Regular Baptist Fellowship—Directories. I. Title.

LOONEY, Floyd, 1906- 286.1794
History of California Southern Baptists. Fresno, Calif., Board of Directors of the Southern Baptist General Convention of California, 1954. 494p. illus. 24cm. [BX6248.C2L6] 54-28235
1. Baptists. California. South Baptist General Convention of California. 2. Churches—California. I. Title.

HINE, Leland D. 286.17949
Baptists in southern California [by] Leland D. Hine. Valley Forge [Pa.] Judson [1966] 192p. illus., map, ports. 23cm. Pub. in coop. with the Southern Calif. Baptist Convention. Bibl. [BX6248.C2H5] 66-25622 3.00
1. Baptists—California. I. Baptists. California. Southern California Baptist Convention. II. Title.

FICKETT, Harold L. 286'.1794'93
Hope for your church; ten principles of church growth, by Harold L. Fickett, Jr. [2d ed.] Glendale, Calif., G/L Regal Books [1972] 159 p. illus. 20 cm. [BX6480.V33F53 1972] 72-94164 ISBN 0-8307-0207-5 1.95
1. First Baptist Church, Van Nuys, Calif. I. Title.

CARLSON, Gordon, 1895- 286'.1795
Seventy-five years history of Columbia Baptist Conference, 1889-1964 Seattle, Columbia Baptist Conference, c1964. xvi, 288 p. illus., ports. 24 cm. Bibliography: p. 278-279. [BX6359.33.C37] 73-264535
1. Columbia Baptist Conference. I. Title.

JOHNSON, Roy Lee, 1901- 286'.1795
Northwest Southern Baptists; a history of Southern Baptists who migrated to the Pacific Northwest from 1844 onward ... Edited by Roy L. Johnson. [Portland, Baptist General Convention of Oregon-Washington, 1968] 868 p. illus., ports. 23 cm. An official publication of the Baptist General Convention of Oregon-Washington, commemorating its 20th anniversary. Includes bibliographies. [BX6245.J6] 74-4014
1. Baptist General Convention of Oregon-Washington. I. Title.

SHELLEY, Bruce Leon, 1927- 286'.1795
Conservative Baptists, a story of twentieth-century dissent. Denver, Conservative Baptist Theological Seminary, 1960. 164 p. 21 cm. [BX6359.53.S5] 63-881
1. Conservative Baptist Association of America. I. Title.

COLLINS Street Baptist Church, Melbourne, 1843-1968; 286'.194'5
125th anniversary. Edited by Wallace Landells [Melbourne?, 1968?] 23 p. illus., ports., facsims. 24 cm. Cover title. Bibliography: p. [24] [BX6326.M4C6] 76-427706 unpriced
1. Melbourne. Collins Street Baptist Church. I. Landells, Wallace, ed.

BAXTER, Norman Allen. 286.209
History of the Freewill Baptists a study in New England separatism. Rochester, N. Y., American Baptist Historical Society [1957] 212p. illus. 21cm. Includes bibliography. [BX6373.B35 1957] 57-59389
1. Free Will Baptists (Founded in N. H.)—Hist. I. Title.

DAVIDSON, William Franklin. 286'.2'09
An early history of Free Will Baptists; the original Free Will Baptists in America, a continuing witness from infancy to identity (1727-1830). Nashville, Randall House Publications [1974- v. 22 cm. Thesis—New Orleans Baptist Theological Seminary. Bibliography: v. 1, p. 225-238. [BX6373.D38] 74-181581 3.95 (v. 1)
1. Free Will Baptist (Founded in N.C.)—History. I. Title.

MORGAN, James Logan. 286'.2'0976797
History of the East Black River Association of Free Will Baptists, 1891-1896 / by James Logan Morgan. Newport, Ark. : Jackson County Historical Society, 1977. 16 p. ; 22 cm. Cover title. [BX6374.A8M67] 78-301872
1. East Black River Association of Free Will Baptists. I. Title.

ZERFASS, Samuel Grant, 1866- 286.3
Souvenir book of the Ephrata Cloister : complete history from its settlement in 1728 to the present time : included is the organization of Ephrata Borough and other information of Ephrata connected with the cloister / by S. G. Zerfass. New York : AMS Press, 1975. 84 p., [1] leaves of plates : ill. ; 23 cm. (Communal societies in America) Reprint of the 1921 ed. published by J. G. Zook, Lititz, Pa. [F159.E6Z58 1975] 72-2960 ISBN 0-404-10724-9 : 12.50
1. Seventh-day Baptists in Pennsylvania—History. 2. Ephrata Community—History. 3. Ephrata, Pa.—History. I. Title.

SAMMONS, Wiley W., 1907- 286'.4
Identity of the true Baptist Church; doctrine, precept & practice from 1701-1971 in west Tennessee, North Carolina and Alabama, by Wiley W. Sammons. [Collierville, Tenn., 1971] xx, 299 p. illus. 23 cm. [BX6387.S24] 77-31641
1. Primitive Baptists—Doctrinal and controversial works. I. Title.

THE Primitive Baptist church meeting directory. 286.4058
Elon College, N. C., Primitive Baptist Pub. House [1958] 96p. 16cm. [BX6380.P67] 58-28869
1. Primitive Baptists—Direct.

*NORQUIST, N. Leroy. 286.433
The church in the New Testament and today. Philip R. Hoh, ed., Mae Gerhard, illus. Philadelphia, Lutheran Church Pr. [c1966] 112p. illus. 21 cm. (LCA Sunday church sch. ser.) 1.00 pap., teacher's guide, pap., 1.25
1. Religious education (young adults) Lutheran. I. Title.

*PRINZ, Harvey L. 286.433
They knew Jesus. Mariorie Garhart, ed. William Plummer, ed. Philadelphia, Lutheran Church Pr. [1966] 48p. illus. (pt. col.) 21x28cm. (LCA vacation church sch. ser.) .50 pap.,
1. Religious education (Elementary)—Lutheran. I. Title.

ASHBURN, Jesse Anderson, 1861- 286.4756
History of the Fisher s River Primitive Baptist Association from its organization in 1832, to 1904, by Jesse A. Ashburn; reprinted with a second volume, from 1905 to 1953, by Francis Preston Stone. [Elon College, N. C., Primitive Baptist Pub. House, [1953] 350p. illus. 23cm. [BX6384.N62F5 1953] 54-22114
1. Primitive Baptists. North Carolina. Fisher's River Primitive Baptist Association. I. Stone, Francis Pieston, 1872- II. Title.

ANKAUM, Freeman, 1890- 286.5
Sidelights on Brethren history. Elgin, Ill., Brethren [c.1962] 174p. illus. 21cm. 62-3730 2.75
1. Church of the Brethren—Hist. I. Title.

BOWMAN, Earl McKinley, 1896- 286'.5 B
An unknown parson / Earl McKinley Bowman. [s.l. : s.n., c1976] ([Verona, Va. : McClure Print. Co.]) viii, 240 p., [2] leaves of plates : ill. ; 23 cm. [BX7843.B67A36] 76-19707
1. Bowman, Earl McKinley, 1896- 2. Church of the Brethren—Clergy—Biography. 3. Church of the Brethren—Sermons. 4. Clergy—United States—Biography. 5. Sermons, American. I. Title.

BOWMAN, Paul Haynes, ed. 286.5
The adventurous future; a compilation of addresses, papers, statements, and messages associated with the clebration of the two-hundred-fiftieth anniversary of the Church of the Bretiten. An anniversary volume, 1708-1958. Elgin, Ill., Brethren Press [1959] 296p. 23cm. [BX7809.B6] 59-39708
1. Church of the Brethren—Addresses, essays, lectures. I. Title.

BRUMBAUGH, Martin Grove, 1862-1930. 286'.5
A history of the German Baptist Brethren in Europe and America. Mount Morris, Ill., Brethren Pub. House, 1899. [New York, AMS Press, 1971] xxii, 559 p. illus. 22 cm. Includes bibliographical references. [BX7815.B8 1971] 73-134377 ISBN 0-404-08425-7 24.00
1. Church of the Brethren—History. I. Title. II. Title: German Baptist Brethren in Europe and America.

BRUMBAUGH, Martin Grove, 1862-1930. 286.5
A history of the German Bptist Brethren in Europe and America. Mount Morris, Ill., Brethren Pub. House, 1899. North Manchester, Ind., L. W. Shultz, 1961] 559 p. illus. 23 cm. [BX7815.B8 1961] 63-32877
1. Church of the Brethren — Hist. I. Title.

CARPER, Frank S. 286'.5
History of the Palmyra Church of the Brethren 1892-1967 Palmyra, Pa., Palmyra Church of the Brethren, 1967. xv, 340 p. illus., ports. (part col.) 24 cm. [BX7831.P3C3] 68-2375
1. Palmyra Church of the Brethren. I. Title.

CARPER, Frank S. 286'.5
History of the Palmyra Church of the Brethren, 1892-1967, by Frank S. Carper. Palmyra, Pa., Palmyra Church of the Brethren, 1967. xv, 340 p. illus., ports. (part col.) 24 cm. [BX7831.P3C3] 68-2375
1. Palmyra Church of the Brethren. I. Title.

THE Church of the Brethren: 286'.5
past and present. Edited by Donald F. Durnbaugh. Contributors: Desmond W. Bittinger [and others] Woodcuts by I. J. Sanger. Elgin, Ill., Brethren Press [1971] 182 p. illus. 26 cm. Bibliography: p. 170-175. [BX7821.2.C48] 70-24517 3.95
1. Church of the Brethren—Addresses, essays, lectures. I. Durnbaugh, Donald F., ed. II. Bittinger, Desmond Wright, 1905-

CHURCH of the Brethren. Brethren Service Commission. 286.5
Report, Brethren service project, Castaner, Puerto Rico. [Elgin, Ill.] v. 29 cm. annual. [BX7827.3.A3] 51-24097
1. Church of the Brethren—Charities. I. Title.

CHURCH of the Brethren. Districts. Eastern Pennsylvania. 286'.5
History of the Church of the Brethren, Eastern Pennsylvania, 1915-1965. [Lancaster, Pa., 1965] xii, 357 p. illus., ports. 24 cm. Continues the narrative begun in History of the Church of the Brethren of the Eastern District of Pennsylvania published in 1915. [BX7820.P42A52] 67-7135
1. Church of the Brethren — Pennsylvania. I. Title.

CHURCH of the Brethren. Districts. Western Pennsylvania. 286.5
Two centuries of the Church of the Brethren in Western Pennsylvania, 1751-1950. Authorized by the District Conference of Western Pennsylvania, published by the Historical Committee. Elgin, Ill., Brethren Pub. House, 1953. 656 p. illus., ports. 23cm. Bibliography: p. [653]-656. [BX7817.P4A5] 53-31316
1. Church of the Brethren— Pennsylvania. 2. Churches—Pennsylvania. 3. Clergy—Pennsylvania. I. Title.

CHURCH of the Brethren. Ministry and Home Mission Commission. 286.5
Book of worship. Elgin, Ill., Brethren Press [1964] 397 p. 17 cm. Rewritten by a committee of five, appointed by the Ministry and Home Mission Commission under authorization of the General Brotherhood Board. [BX7825.A47] 64-4927
1. Church of the Brethren. Liturgy and ritual. I. Title.

CHURCH of the Brethren. Ministry and Home Mission Commission. 286.5
Book of worship. Elgin, Ill., Brethren Pr. [c.1964] 397p. 17cm. Rewritten by a comm. of 5, appointed by the Ministry and Home Mission Commn. under authorization of the General Brotherhood Bd. 64-4927 4.25; 4.75 deluxe ed.,
1. Church of the Brethren, Liturgy and ritual. I. Title.

DURNBAUGH, Donald F., comp. 286'.5
The Brethren in colonial America; a source book on the transplantation and development of the Church of the Brethren in the eighteenth century. Edited by Donald F. Durnbaugh. Elgin, Ill., Brethren Press [1967] 659 p. illus., facsims. 23 cm. Bibliographical references included in "Notes" (p. [609]-633) [BX7816.D8] 67-9253
1. Church of the Brethren—History. I. Title.

GARBER, Mary Crumpacker. 286.5
The Brethren story caravan; illustrated by Ruth Weimer. Elgin, Ill., House of the Church of the Brethren [1950] 79 p. illus. 21 cm. [BX7815.G3] 50-8152
1. Church of the Brethren—Hist. I. Title.

GILLIN, John Lewis, 1871-1958. 286'.5
The Dunkers; a sociological interpretation. New York, 1906. [New York, AMS Press, 1974] 238 p. 23 cm. (Communal societies in America) Thesis, Columbia University, 1906. Vita. Bibliography: p. [233]-238. [BX7815.G5 1974] 72-8248 ISBN 0-404-11002-9
1. Church of the Brethren—History. I. Title.

GOULD, William L., 1917- 286'.5
A light in the valley : a history of the Codorus Church of the Brethren / by William L. Gould. Loganville, Pa. : The Church, 1976. 189 p., [20] leaves of plates : ill., map (on lining papers) ; 24 cm. Includes bibliographical references. [BX7831.L633G68] 77-153075
1. Codorus Church of the Brethren, Loganville, Pa. 2. Codorus Church of the Brethren, Loganville, Pa.—Biography. 3. Loganville, Pa.—Biography. I. Title.

GOULD, William L., 1917- 286'.5
A light in the valley : a history of the Codorus Church of the Brethren / by William L. Gould. Loganville, Pa. : The Church, 1976.

189 p., [20] leaves of plates : ill., map (on lining papers) ; 24 cm. Includes bibliographical references. [BX7831.L633G68] 77-153075
1. Codorus Church of the Brethren, Loganville, Pa. 2. Codorus Church of the Brethren, Loganville, Pa.—Biography. 3. Loganville, Pa.—Biography. I. Title.

KENT, Homer Austin, 1898- 286'.5
Conquering frontiers; a history of the Brethren Church (the National Fellowship of Brethren Churches) by Homer A. Kent, Sr. [Rev. ed.] Winona Lake, Ind., BMH Books [1972] 245 p. illus. 24 cm. 1958 ed. published under title: 250 years conquering frontiers. Bibliography: p. 228-230. [BX7829.N33K4 1972] 72-187886
1. National Fellowship of Brethren Churches—History. I. Title.

KENT, Homer Austin, 1898- 286.5
250 years conquering frontiers; a history of the Brethren Church by Homer A. Kent Sr. Winona Lake, Ind., Brethren Missionary Herald Co. [1958] 233 p. illus. 23 cm. [BX7829.N33K4] 58-38245
1. National Fellowship of Brethren Churches — Hist. I. Title.

LEHMAN, James H. 286'.5
The old Brethren / James H. Lehman. Elgin, Ill. : Brethren Press, 1976. 384 p. : ill. ; 18 cm. Includes bibliographical references and index. [BX7815.L44] 76-20274 ISBN 0-87178-650-8 pbk. : 2.45
1. Church of the Brethren—History. I. Title.

MILLER, Dessie Rebecca, 1913- 286.5
Learning the Brethren way with Jim and Jane; illustrated by Harry Durkee. Elgin, Ill., Brethren Pub. House [1951] 80 p. illus. 23 cm. [BX7822.M5] 51-12235
1. Church of the Brethren. I. Title.

RONK, Albert T. 286'.5
History of the Brethren Church; its life, thought, mission, by Albert T. Ronk. [Ashland, Ohio, Printed by Brethren Pub. Co., 1968] 524 p. port. 23 cm. Bibliographical footnotes. [BX7829.B53R6] 68-23554
1. Brethren Church (Ashland, Ohio)—History. I. Title.

SACHSE, Julius Friedrich, 1842-1919. 286'.5
The German sectarians of Pennsylvania; a critical and legendary history of the Ephrata cloister and the Dunkers. Philadelphia, Printed for the author, 1899. [New York, AMS Press, 1971] 2 v. illus. 22 cm. Contents.Contents.—v. 1. 1708-1742.—v. 2. 1742-1800. [BX7817.P4S3 1971] 73-134385 ISBN 0-404-08340-4 45.00
1. Ephrata Community. 2. Church of the Brethren. 3. Ephrata, Pa. 4. Pennsylvania Germans. 5. Printing—History—Pennsylvania. I. Title.

SAPPINGTON, Roger Edwin, 1929- 286.5
The Brethren along the Snake River; a history of the Church of the Brethren in Idaho and western Montana. Elkin, Ill., Brethren Pr. [1966] 158p. illus., ports. 23cm. Bibl. [BX7820.I3S3] 66-3302 5.00
1. Church of the Brethren. Districts. Idaho and Western Montana. I. Title.

KLEIN, Walter Conrad, Bp., 1904- 286'.5'0924 B
Johann Conrad Beissel, mystic and martinet, 1690-1768, by Walter C. Klein. Philadelphia, Porcupine Press, 1972. ix, 218 p. 22 cm. (The American utopian adventure) Reprint of the 1942 ed., issued in series: Pennsylvania lives. Bibliography: p. 207-211. [F159.E6K55 1972] 74-187453 ISBN 0-87991-012-7
1. Beissel, Johann Conrad, 1690-1768. 2. Ephrata Community. I. Series: Pennsylvania lives.

SAPPINGTON, Roger Edwin, 1929- 286'.5'09755
The Brethren in Virginia: the history of the Church of the Brethren in Virginia [by] Roger E. Sappington. Harrisonburg, Committee for Brethren History in Virginia, 1973. xiii, 520 p. illus. 23 cm. Includes bibliographical references. [BX7817.V8S26] 74-165140
1. Church of the Brethren in Virginia. I. Title.

WINE, Joseph Floyd, 1917- 286'.5'09755992
A history of Calvary Church of the Brethren, Front Royal Road, Winchester, Virginia, 22601. Boyce, Va., Printed by Carr Pub. Co., 1972. 72 p. illus. 23 cm. [BX7831.C25W55] 72-95960
1. Calvary Church of the Brethren. I. Title.

ABBOTT, Byrdine Akers, 1866-1936 286.6
The Disciples; an interpretation. St. Louis, Pub. for Abbott Bks. by Bethany [1964, c.1924] 271p. 20cm. 64-392 1.50 pap.,
1. Disciples of Christ. I. Title.

ADAMS, Hampton, 1897- 286.6
Why I am a Disciple of Christ. New York, Nelson [1957] 144 p. 22 cm. [BX7321.A2] 57-11894
1. Disciples of Christ. I. Title.

BLAKEMORE, William Barnett, 1912- 286.6
The discovery of the church: a history of Disciple ecclesiology. by Wm. Barnett Blakemore. Nashville, Reed [1966] 104 p. 23 cm. (The Reed lecureres for 1965 Bibliographical references included in "Notes" (p. 101-104) [BN7323.4.B55] 66-9839
1. Disciples of Christ — Relations — Addresses, essays, lectures. I. Title. II. Series.

BLAKEMORE, William Barnett, 1912- 286.6
The discovery of the church: a history of Disciple ecclesiology, by Wm. Barnett Blakemore. Nashville, Reed [1966] 104p. 23cm. (Reed lects. for 1965) Bibl. [BX7323.4.B55] 66-9839 2.95 bds.,
1. Disciples of Christ—Relations—Addresses, essays, lectures. I. Title. II. Series.
Publisher's address is: Wilson Bates Blvd., Nashville.

DE GROOT, Alfred Thomas, 1903- 286.6
New possibilities for Disciples and Independents, with a history of the Independents, Church of Christ Number Two. St. Louis, Bethany Press [1963] 112 p. 22 cm. First published as Church of Christ Number Two. Bibliographical footnotes. [BX7323.4.D4 1963] 63-21760
1. Disciples of Christ — Relations. I. Title. II. Title: Church of Christ Number Two.

DE GROOT, Alfred Thomas, 1903- 286.6
New possibilities for Disciples and Independents, with a history of the Independents, Church of Christ Number Two. St. Louis, Bethany [c.1963] 112p. 22cm. First pub. as Church of Christ Number Two. Bibl. 63-21760 1.25 pap.,
1. Disciples of Christ—Relations. I. Title. II. Title: Church of Christ Number Two.

FORD, Harold W 286.6
A history of the restoration plea; being a history of the statements of the plea of the churches of Christ for Christian unity upon the basis of a restoration of the church of the New Testament. Oklahoma City, Okla., Semco Color Press, 1952. 230p. 22cm. [BX7315.F57] 53-21571
1. Disciples of Christ—Hist. I. Title. II. Title: Restoration ples.

GARRISON, Wilfred Ernest, 1874 286.6
Heritage and destiny; an American religious movement looks ahead. St. Louis, Bethany [c.] 1961. 159p. 61-15530 3.50
1. Disciples of Christ—Hist. I. Title.

LAIR, Loren E 286.6
The Christian churches and their work. St. Louis, Bethany Press [1963] 196 p. 23 cm. (A Bethany basic book) [BX7321.2.L3] 63-8821
1. Disciples of Christ. I. Title.

LAIR, Loren E. 286.6
The Christian churches and their work. St. Louis, Bethany [c.1963] 296p. 23cm. (Bethany basic bk.) 63-8821 3.95
1. Disciples of Christ. I. Title.

MATTOX, Fount William, 1909- 286.6
The eternal kingdom; a history of the Church of Christ. Rev. and with additional chapters by John McRay. Delight, Ark., Gospel Light Pub. Co. [1961] 351p. 23cm. [BR146.M37 1961] 61-37766
1. Church history. 2. Churches of Christ—Hist. I. Title.

MURCH, James DeForest, 1892- 286.6
Christians only, a history of the restoration movement. Cincinnati, Standard Pub. [1962] 392p. 24cm. Includes bibliography. [BX7315.M9] 61-18657
1. Disciples of Christ—Hist. 2. Churches of Christ—Hist. I. Title.

PUGH, Samuel F. ed. 286.6
Primer for new Disciples; a guide book for new members of the Christian Churches (Disciples of Christ) [Prepared under the auspices of the Local Church Life Committee, Home and State Missions Planning Council, Christian Churches (Disciples of Christ) Indianapolis, Dept. of Church Development, United Christian Missionary Society, 1963] 176 p. illus. 23 cm. [BX7321.2.P8] 63-16372
1. Disciples of Christ—Handbooks, manuals, etc. I. Disciples of Christ. Home and State Missions Planning Council. Local Church Life Committee. II. Title.

PUGH, Samuel F., ed. 286.6
Primer for new Disciples; a guide book for new members of the Christian Churches (Disciples of Christ) [Prepared under the auspices of the Local Church Life Committee. Home and State Missions Planning Council, Christian Churches (Disciples of Christ) Indianapolis, Dept. of Church Development, United Christian Missionary Soc., Dist. St. Louis, Bethany, c.1963] 176p. illus. 23cm. 63-16372 2.75
1. Disciples of Christ—Handbooks, manuals, etc. I. Disciples of Christ, Home and State Missions Planning Council. Local Church Life Committee. II. Title.

STONE, Barton Warren, 1772-1844. 286.6
History of the Christian Church in the West. With illus. by Riley B. Montgomery and William Clayton Bower, and a foreword by Roscoe M. Pierson. Lexington, Ky., College of the Bible, 1956. 53p. illus. 23cm. [BX7315.S76] 56-2294
1. Disciples of Christ—Hist. 2. Churches of Christ—Hist. I. Title.

STONE, Barton Warren, 1772-1844. 286.6
History of the Christian Church in the West. With illus. by Riley B. Montgomery and William Clayton Bower, and a foreword by Roscoe M. Pierson. Lexington, Ky., College of the Bible, 1956. 53 p. illus. 23 cm. [BX7315.S76] 56-2294
1. Disciples of Christ — Hist. 2. Churches of Christ — Hist. I. Title.

TEEGARDEN, Kenneth L. 286'.6
We call ourselves Disciples / [by Kenneth L. Teegarden]. Saint Louis : Bethany Press, [1975] 116 p. ; 22 cm. [BX7321.2.T43] 75-22119 ISBN 0-8272-4209-3 pbk. : 3.25
1. Christian Church (Disciples of Christ) I. Title.

THOMAS, James David, 1910- 286.6
"We be brethren"; a study in Biblical interpretation. [1st ed.] Abilene, Tex., Biblical Research Press, 1958. 262 p. illus. 23 cm. [BX7094.C95T48] 58-48844
1. Churches of Christ — Doctrinal and controversial works. 2. Bible — Hermeneutics. I. Title.

TUCKER, William Edward, 1932- 286'.6
Journey in faith : a history of the Christian Church (Disciples of Christ) / by William E. Tucker and Lester G. McAllister. Saint Louis : Bethany Press, [1975] 505 p. : ill. ; 24 cm. Includes index. Bibliography: p. [463]-488. [BX7315.T8] 75-11738 ISBN 0-8272-1703-X : 12.95
1. Christian Church (Disciples of Christ)—History. I. McAllister, Lester G., joint author. II. Title.

FOGARTY, John Patrick, 1912- comp. 286.6058
Yearbook of Churches of Christ. 1946/47- Abilene, Tex., Hicks Print. Co. v. illus., ports. 19 cm. Compilers: 1946/47- J. P. Fogarty and O. L. Hicks. [BX7075.A1Y4] 48-19443
1. Churches of Christ — Direct. I. Hicks, Olan L. comp II. Title.

PANEL of Scholars. 286.6082
The renewal of church; the panel reports. W. B. Blakemore, editor. St. Louis, Bethany Press, 1963. 3 v. 23 cm. Contents.-- v. 1. The reformation of tradition, edited by Ronald E. Osborn. -- v. 2. The reconstruction of theology, edited by R. G. Wilburn. -- v. 3. The revival of the churches, edited by W. B. Blakemore. Includes bibliographies. [BX7309.P3] 62-21959
1. Disciples of Christ — Addresses, essays, lectures. I. Blakemore, William Barnett, 1912- ed. II. Title.

PANEL of Scholars 286.6082
The renewal of church; the panel reports; v. 1 & 2 W. B. Balkemore, ed. St. Louis, Bethany [c.]1963. 356, 347p. 23cm. Contents.v.1. The reformation of tradition, edited by Ronald E. Osborn. v. 2. Reconstruction of theology. Bibl. 62-21959 6.00 bds., ea.,
1. Disciples of Christ—Addresses, essays, lectures. I. Blakemore, William Barnett, 1912- II. Title.

COCHRAN, Louis, 1899- 286'.6'09
Captives of the Word [by] Louis Cochran and Bess White Cochran. [1st ed.] Garden City, N.Y., Doubleday [1969] xi, 274 p. 25 cm. ([Religion in America series]) Bibliography: p. [255]-263. [BX7315.C57] 73-84365 5.95
1. Disciples of Christ—History. 2. Churches of Christ—History. I. Cochran, Bess (White) 1899- joint author. II. Title.

COREY, Stephen Jared, 1873- 286.609
Fifty years of attack and controversy; the consequences among disciples of Christ. [Des Moines] Committee on Publication of the Corey Manuscript [1953] 306p. illus. 22cm. Includes bibliography. [BX7315.C6] 54-19247
1. Disciples of Christ—Hist. 2. Christian standard. I. Title.

DISCIPLES of Christ Historical Society. 286'.6'09 s
Hampton Adams; a register of his papers in the Disciples of Christ Historical Society. Nashville, 1969. 26 l. 28 cm. (Its Register no. 3) [CD3529.N37D57 no. 3] 216.286'6'0924 B 72-31727
1. Adams, Hampton, 1897-1965—Archives.

*BASHAM, Don. 286/.6/0924
Face up with a miracle. Northridge, Calif., Voice Christian Pubns [1967] 169p. 21cm. 3.95
I. Title.

CASTLEMAN, William J., 1908- 286.60924
On this foundation; a historical literary biography of the early life of Samuel Guy Inman . . . covering the period, 1877-1904, by Wm. J. Castleman. St. Louis, Printed as a private ed. by Bethany Pr. [1966] 176p. 23cm. Bibl. [BX7343.I54C3] 66-8316 3.95
1. Inman, Samuel Guy, 1877-1965. I. Title.

EAMES, Samuel Morris, 1916- 286.60924
The philosophy of Alexander Campbell, by S. Morris Eames. Foreword by Perry E. Gresham. A comprehensive bibliography of Alexander Campbell's writings, by Claude E. Spencer. Bethany, W. Va., Bethany College [1966] 110 p. 24 cm. "A Bethany College Benedum Foundation regional American studies publication." [BX7343.C2E32] 66-28349
1. Campbell, Alexander, 1788-1866. I. Title.

FITCH, Alger Morton. 286'.6'0924 B
Alexander Campbell, preacher of reform and reformer of preaching [by] Alger Morton Fitch, Jr. Austin, Tex., Sweet Pub. Co. [1970] 134 p. illus., facsims., port. 21 cm. Bibliography: p. 119-134. [BX7343.C2F5] 70-113160 ISBN 0-8344-0060-X
1. Campbell, Alexander, 1788-1866. I. Title.

FRASER, Donald, 1870-1933. 286'.6'0924 B
The autobiography of an African; retold in biographical form & in the wild African setting of the life of Daniel Mtusu. Westport, Conn., Negro Universities Press [1970] 209 p. illus., port. 23 cm. Reprint of the 1925 ed. [BV3625.N82F7 1970] 78-138006 ISBN 0-8371-5653-X
1. Mtusu, Daniel, d. 1917. 2. Missions to Angoni. I. Title.

GRESHAM, Perry Epler. 286'.6'0924 B
Campbell and the colleges. Nashville, Disciples of Christ Historical Society, 1973. 114 p. 22 cm. (The Forrest F. Reed lectures for 1971) Includes bibliographical references. [LB695.C352G73] 73-161134
1. Campbell, Alexander, 1788-1866. 2. Universities and colleges—United States—History. I. Title. II. Series: The Reed lectures, 1971.

HOLDER, Ray. 286'.6'0924 B
William Winans : Methodist leader in antebellum Mississippi / by Ray Holder. Jackson : University Press of Mississippi, 1976. p. cm. Includes index. Bibliography: p. [BX8495.W657H64] 76-26967 ISBN 0-87805-027-2 :7.95
1. Winans, William, 1788-1857. 2. Methodist Church—Clergy—Biography. 3. Clergy—Mississippi—Biography. 4. Mississippi—Biography.

HUNTER, Joseph Boone. 286'.6'0924 B
Along the way. Fort Worth, Tex., Branch-Smith, 1972. xiii, 171 p. port. 22 cm. Autobiographical. [BX7343.H83A3] 71-188574 ISBN 0-87706-020-7
I. Title.

MCALLISTER, Lester G. 286'.6'0924(B)
Z. T. Sweeney: preacher and peacemaker, by Lester G. McAllister. St. Louis, Christian Board of Publication [1968] 128 p. port. 23 cm. Bibliography: p. 123-124. [BX7343.S94M3] 68-5649
1. Sweeney, Zachary Taylor, 1849-1926.

MURCH, James DeForest, 1892- 286'.6'0924 B
B. D. Phillips; life and letters. Memorial ed. [Louisville, Ky., Printed by Standard Print.

Co., 1969] x, 256 p. illus., ports. 24 cm. [BX6793.P47M8] 70-110433
1. Phillips, Benjamin Dwight, 1885-1968.

SANDLIN, James Lee. 286'.6'0924 B
Musings of a parson. San Antonio, Tex., Naylor Co. [1971] xvii, 202 p. port. 22 cm. [BX7343.S23A3] 73-138865 ISBN 0-8111-0387-0 5.95
1. Disciples of Christ—Sermons. 2. Sermons, American. I. Title.

STONE, Barton 286'.6'0924 B
Warren, 1772-1844.
The biography of Eld. Barton Warren Stone, written by himself; with additions and reflections, by John Rogers. New York, Arno Press, 1972. ix, 404, 4 p. port. 23 cm. (Religion in America, series II) Reprint of the 1847 ed. [BX7343.S8A3 1972] 79-38463 ISBN 0-405-04089-X
1. Disciples of Christ. I. Rogers, John, 1800-1867, ed. II. Title.

WILBURN, James R. 286'.6'0924 B
The hazard of the die; Tolbert Fanning and the restoration movement [by] James R. Wilburn. Austin, Tex., Sweet Pub. Co. [1969] 288 p. 22 cm. Bibliographical references included in "Footnotes" (p. [261]-279) [BX7077.Z8F37] 74-77235 4.95
1. Fanning, Tolbert, 1810-1874. I. Title.

WRATHER, Eva Jean. 286'.6'0924
Creative freedom in action; Alexander Campbell on the structure of the church. St. Louis, Bethany Press [1968] 32 p. 21 cm. Bibliographical references included in "Notes" (p. 31-32) [BX7343.C2W7] 68-7826
1. Campbell, Alexander, 1788-1866. 2. Disciples of Christ—History. I. Title.

BANOWSKY, William Slater. 286.63
The mirror of a movement; Churches of Christ as seen through the Abilene Christian College lectureship [by] William S. Banowsky. Dallas, Christian Pub. Co. [1965] xiv, 444 p. illus., ports. 23 cm. Includes bibliographical references. [BX7075.A1A232] 65-14993
1. Abilene Christian College. Abilene Christian College Bible lectures. 2. Churches of Christ. I. Title.

CLARK, Mavis Thorpe 286.63
Pastor Doug: the story of an Aboriginal leader. Melbourne, Landsdowne; London, Newnes, 1966. [7] 245p. 12 plates (incl. ports.) 23cm. [BV3667.N5C55 1966] 66-72165 5.50 bds.,
1. Nicholls, Douglas Ralph, 1906- 2. Missions—Australia. I. Title.
Available from Ginn in Boston.

CLARK, Mavis Thorpe. 286'.63 B
Pastor Doug: the story of Sir Douglas Nicholls, Aboriginal leader [by] Mavis Thorpe Clark. Rev. ed. Melbourne, Lansdowne Press, 1972. 259 p., 6 plates. 23 cm. [BV3667.N5C55 1972] 73-176912 ISBN 0-7018-0017-8 6.95
1. Nicholls, Douglas Ralph, Sir, 1906- 2. Missions—Australia. I. Title.

ECKSTEIN, Stephen Daniel. 286.63
History of the Churches of Christ in Texas, 1824-1950. Austin, Tex., Firm Foundation Pub. House, 1963. xvi, 378 p. 20 cm. Bibliography: p. 331-345. [BX7075.Z5T4] 64-28484
1. Churches of Christ — Texas. I. Title.

WHAT lack we yet? : 286'.63
an evaluation / J. D. Thomas, editor. Abilene, Tex. : Biblical Research Press, c1974. 319 p. : ports. ; 23 cm. [BX7076.W45] 75-30691
1. Churches of Christ—Doctrinal and controversial works—Addresses, essays, lectures. I. Thomas, James David, 1910-

WILSON, Ealon V. 286'.63 B
The colorful and eventful life of St. Clair W. Smith, nineteenth century trail-blazer, western frontier missionary, Christian college founder-president, preacher and educator, by Ealon V. Wilson. With accounts of ancestors, contemporaries and descendants across the land, from Kentucky and Tennessee to Texas, New Mexico, California, etc. [Limited 1st ed.] Memphis, 1967. 46 p. illus. 21 cm. [BX6793.S63W55] 74-166166
1. Smith, St. Clair W., 1844-1909. 2. Smith family. I. Title.

BIDDLE, Conley J., 286'.63'0924 B
1907-
Trails, trials, triumphs, by Conley J. Biddle. [1st ed.] West Des Moines, Iowa, R. L. Hill Pub. Co., 1972. 536 p. illus. 23 cm. [BX6793.B5A3] 72-89783 10.00
1. Biddle, Conley J. I. Title.

THOMPSON, Wilson, 286'.63'0924
1788-1866.
The autobiography of Elder Wilson Thompson; his life, travels, and ministerial labors. Springfield, Ohio, E. T. Aleshire, 1962. 363 p. illus. 23 cm. [BX6793.T54A3] 63-1325
I. Title.

MERWIN, Wallace C. 286'.651
Adventure in unity; the Church of Christ in China, by Wallace C. Merwin. Grand Rapids, Mich., Eerdmans [1974] 232 p. 23 cm. Bibliography: p. 226-228. [BX7014.M47] 73-22119 ISBN 0-8028-3441-8 6.95
1. Church of Christ in China. I. Title.

HARRELL, David Edwin 286.673
A social history of the Disciples of Christ; v.1. Nashville, Disciples of Christ Hist. Soc. 1966. v, 25cm. Rev. of the author's doctoral dissertation written at Vanderbilt Univ. in 1962. Contents.v.1. Quest for a Christian America: The Disciples of Christ and American society to 1866. Bibl. [BX7316.H27] 66-8396 5.95
1. Disciples of Christ.—Hist. I. Title.
101-19th Ave. So., Nashville, Tenn. 37212

METROPOLITAN 286'.673
Nicolai—agent in Soviet Secret Police; how the Communists are using the National Council of the Churches of Christ in the United States of America. [Compiled by Carl McIntire. Collingswood, N.J., 20th Century Reformation Hour, 1959] 70 p. illus. 31 cm. [BX6.N2M46] 73-172526
1. National Council of the Churches of Christ in the United States of America. 2. Nikolai, Metropolitan of Krututsy and Kolomna, 1892-1961. 3. Communism and Christianity. I. McIntire, Carl, 1906- comp.

PRATT, Henry J., 1934- 286'.6'73
The liberalization of American Protestantism; a case study in complex organizations [by] Henry J. Pratt. Detroit, Wayne State University Press, 1972. 303 p. 24 cm. Bibliography: p. [293]-299. [BX6.N2P7] 74-38837 ISBN 0-8143-1475-9 15.95
1. National Council of the Churches of Christ in the United States of America. 2. Christianity and politics. I. Title.

WHITLEY, Oliver Read. 286.673
Trumpet call of Reformation. St. Louis, Mo., Bethany Press [1959] 252 p. 23 cm. Includes bibliography. [BX7315.W49] 59-13169
1. Disciples of Christ — Hist. 2. Religion and sociology. I. Title.

CRAMBLET, Wilbur H., 286'.6754
1892-
The Christian Church (Disciples of Christ) in West Virginia; a history of its cooperative work, by Wilbur H. Cramblet. St. Louis, Bethany Press [1971] 562 p. illus., facsims., map, ports. 24 cm. Bibliography: p. 531-536. [BX7317.W48C7] 76-24252 ISBN 0-8272-0432-9 7.95
1. Disciples of Christ—West Virginia. I. Title.

HOLDER, Naomi Dail. 286'.6756'355
History of Wheat Swamp Christian Church, including the conditions in Europe and the colonies / by Naomi Dail Holder. [La Grange? N.C. : s.n.], c1977. 121 p. : ill. ; 22 cm. Includes bibliographical references. [BX7331.W47H64] 77-150024
1. Wheat Swamp Christian Church. I. Title.

WARE, Charles 286'.6757
Crossfield, 1886-
South Carolina Disciples of Christ; a history. Charleston, Christian Churches of South Carolina, 1967. 216 p. illus., facsims., ports. 24 cm. [BX7317.S6W3] 67-19866
1. Disciples of Christ—South Carolina. I. Title.

BARBER, William Joseph, 286.6758
1927-
The Disciple assemblies of eastern North Carolina, by Wm. Joseph Barber. St. Louis, Mo., Printed as a private edition by the Bethany Press [1966] xxii, 289 p. illus., geneal. ports. 22 cm. Based on a thesis, Butler University, 1959. Bibliography: p. 274-277. [BX7317.N8B3] 68-935
1. Disciples of Christ—North Carolina. 2. Disciples of Christ, Negro. I. Title.

MOSELEY, Joseph Edward, 286.6758
1910-
Disciples of Christ in Georgia. St. Louis, Bethany Press [1954] 400p. 23cm. [BX7317.G4M6] 55-14026
1. Disciples of Christ—Georgia. I. Title.

WARE, Charles 286.6758
Crossfield, 1886-
Hookerton history. [New Bern? N.C.] 1960. 74 p. 23 cm. [BX7317.N8W27] 62-32250
1. Disciples of Christ — North Carolina. 2. Disciples of Christ. North Carolina. Hookerton Union. 3. Churches — North Carolina. 4. Clergy — North Carolina. I. Title.

WARE, Charles 286.6758
Crossfield, 1886-
Pamlico profile. [New Bern? N.C.] 1961. 63 p. 23 cm. [BX7317.N8W32] 62-30429
1. Disciples of Christ — North Carolina. 2. Disciples of Christ. North Carolina. Pamlico Union. 3. Churches — North Carolina. 4. Clergy — North Carolina. I. Title.

ALLEY, Joe Kenneth, 286.6762
1926-
Churches of Christ in Mississippi, 1836-1954. Booneville, Miss [1953] 79p. illus. 20cm. [BX7094.C95A7] 54-15473
1. Churches of Christ—Mississippi. I. Title.

BOREN, Carter E., 1912- 286'.6764
Religion on the Texas frontier, by Carter E. Boren. San Antonio, Tex., Naylor Co. [1968] xv, 375 p. 22 cm. Bibliography: p. 343-365. [BX7317.T4B6] 68-9294 10.00
1. Disciples of Christ—Texas. I. Title.

HALL, Colby Dixon, 1875- 286.6764
Texas Disciples; a story of the rise and progress of that Protestant movement known as Disciples of Christ or Christian Churches, as it developed in Texas; including, through the nineteenth century decades, a story of the kindred movement, the Churches of Christ. Fort Worth, Texas Christian Universty Press [1953] 436p. illus. 22cm. [BX7317.T4H3] 54-33265
1. Disciples of Christ—Texas. 2. Churches of Christ—Texas. I. Title.

NORTON, Herman Albert. 286'.6'768
Tennessee Christians; a history of the Christian Church (Disciples of Christ) in Tennessee, by Herman A. Norton. Nashville, Reed [1971] v, 309 p. map (on lining papers) 24 cm. Bibliography: p. 296-300. [BX7317.T37N67] 71-25012 7.95
1. Disciples of Christ—Tennessee. I. Title.

BOWER, William Clayton, 286.6769
1878-
Central Christian Church, Lexington, Kentucky, a history. St. Louis, Priv. print. by Bethany Press, 1962. 192 p. illus. 23 cm. [BX7331.L48C43] 63-1088
1. Lexington, Ky. Central Christian Church. I. Title.

BURLESON, Lolo Eaheart. 286.6769
Our heritage; a history of the First Christian Church, Albany, Texas. [Diamond anniversary, 1886-1961. Albany?Tex. c1961. 99 l. illus. 28cm. [BX7331.A4F53] 62-1543
1. Albany, Tex. First Christian Church. I. Title.

PIERSON, Roscoe Mitchell 286.6769
The Disciples of Christ in Kentucky: a finding list of the histories of local congregations of Christian churches. Compiled by Roscoe M. Pierson. Lexington. Ky., College of the Bible Library, 1962. ii, 63 l. 28 cm. [BX7317.K4P5] 66-15012
1. Disciples of Christ—Kentucky. I. Title.

SAN Diego, Calif. 286.6769
Central Christian Church.
Our book of jubilee, 1886-1961, Central Christian Church, San Diego, California; the life story of a downtown church, with its historic setting in a Spanish background, the Protestant advent, and the coming of the Disciples. Compiled by the Seventy-fifth Anniversary Diamond Jubilee Committee. Ben F. Dixon, editor. San Diego, Official Board, Central Christian Church, 1961. 135p. illus. 23cm. Includes bibliography. [BX7331.S3A3] 62-32248
I. Dixon, Benjamin Franklin, 1892- ed. II. Title.

WARE, Charles 286.6769
Crossfield, 1886-
Kentucky's Fox Creek; vignettes of the village church and of the R. H. Crossfield heritage. Wilson, N.C., 1957. 70 p. illus. 23 cm. Includes bibliography. [BX7331.F6W3] 57-14407
1. Fox Creek Church, Anderson Co., Ky. 2. Crossfield, Richard Henry, 1868-1951. I. Title.

WILLIAMS, Irene 286'.6769'883
Aldridge, 1904-
A record of Poole Church of Christ, Poole, Webster County, Kentucky. Evansville, Ind., 1969. v, 97 l. 28 cm. Cover title: Poole Church of Christ. Typescript. [F459.P65W5] 74-275312
1. Poole Church of Christ. 2. Registers of births, etc.—Poole, Ky. I. Title.

SHAW, Henry K 286.677
Buckeye Disciples; a history of the Disciples of Christ in Ohio. St. Louis, Christian Board of Publication [1952] 504 p. maps. 22 cm. "A centennial publication of the Ohio Christian Missionary Society, 1851-1952." Bibliography: p. 468-472. [BX7317.O3S45] 52-14332
1. Disciples of Christ—Ohio—Hist. I. Disciples of Christ. Ohio. Ohio Christian Missionary Society. II. Title.

HAYDEN, Amos Sutton, 286'.6771
1813-1880.
Early history of the Disciples in the Western Reserve, Ohio; with biographical sketches of the principal agents in their religious movement. Cincinnati, Chase & Hall. [New York, Arno Press, 1972, c1875] 476 p. 22 cm. (Religion in America, series II) [BX7317.O3H3 1972] 76-38449 ISBN 0-405-04068-7
1. Disciples of Christ—Ohio. I. Title.

OWENS, Harvey W., 286'.6'77249
1895-1968.
The history of First Christian Church, Greencastle, Indiana, 1830-1972, by Harvey W. Owens and associates. [Greencastle? Ind., 1973] 142 p. illus. 29 cm. [BX6781.G73F576] 73-174249
1. First Christian Church, Greencastle, Ind. 2. Greencastle, Ind.—Biography. I. Title.

FORSTER, Ada L 286.6776
A history of the Christian Church and Church of Christ in Minnesota. St. Louis, Christian Board of Publication, 1953. 136p. illus. 23cm. [BX7317.M7F65] 53-19916
1. Disciples of Christ—Minnesota. 2. Churches—Minnesota. I. Title.

SMITH, Elsie Higdon. 286'.6'78188
Potwin Christian Church. [North Newton, Kan., Printed by the Mennonite Press] 1969. 163 p. map, plates, ports. 24 cm. [BX6781.P6C5] 78-99962
1. Potwin Christian Church.

PORTLAND, Or. First 286.6795
Christian Church.
Seventy-five rewarding years; a history of First Christian Church, Portland, Oregon. Portland, 1955. 105p. illus. 23cm. [BX7331.P64A3] 55-43881
I. Title.

MONTGOMERY, J Dexter. 286.682
Disciples of Christ in Argentina, 1906-1956; a history of the first fifty years of mission work. St. Louis, Bethany Press [1956] 180p. illus. 21cm. [BX7319.A7M6] 56-6253
1. Disciples of Christ—Argentine Republic. I. Title.

ASOCIACION General de la 286.7
Iglesia Adventista del Septimo Dia.
Manual de la iglesia. Mountain View, Calif., Publicaciones Interamericanas, Pacific Pr. [c.] 1963. 317p. 17cm. 3.00
I. Title.

CAMPBELL, George A 286.7
Mary Kennedy's victory. Mountain View, Calif., Pacific Press Pub. Association [1953] 95p. illus. 19cm. [BX6154.C25 1953] 53-11217
1. Seventh-Day Adventists. I. Title.

**COMMUNION With God;* 286.7
a devotional guide for the School of Prayer, comprised of materials drawn from the Bible and the writings of Ellen G. White, issued under the auspices of the Ministerial Assoc. Mountain View, Calif., Pacific Pr. Pub. [c.1964] 107p. 22cm. 1.25 pap.,

COMPREHENSIVE index to the 286.7
writings of Ellen G. White, v.1. Prepared under the direction of the Board of Trustees of the Ellen G. White Estate. Omaha, Nebr., Pac. Pr. Pub. [c.1962] 1064p. 22cm. Contents.v.1. Scripture index. 62-14313 12.50
1. White, Ellen Gould (Harmon) 1827-1915—Dictionaries, indexes, etc.

COMPREHENSIVE index to the 286.7
writings of Ellen G. White, v.2, G-Q. In three pts.: scripture index, topical index, quotation index. With appendix containing glossaries, tables, supplementary statements. Prepared under the direction of the Bd. of Trustees of the Ellen G. White Estate. Omaha, Neb., Pacific Pr. Pub. [c.1962] 1070-2205p. 22cm. 12.50
1. White, Ellen Gould (Harmon) 1827-1915—Dictionaries, indexes, etc.

COMPREHENSIVE index to the 286.7
writings of Ellen G. White.
Prepared under the direction of the Board of Trustees of the Ellen G. White Estate. Omaha, Pacific Press Pub. Association [1962-63] 3 v. 22 cm. [BX6111.W9C6] 62-14313
1. White, Ellen Gould (Harmon) 1827-1915 — Dictionaries, indexes, etc. I. Title.

DOUTY, Norman Franklin, 286.7
1899-
Another look at Seventh-Day Adventism, with special reference, Questions on doctrine. Grand Rapids, Mich., Baker Bk., 1962. 224p. 23cm. Bibl. 62-17678 3.50
1. Seventh-day Adventists—Doctrinal and controversial works. I. Title.

*DOWARD, Jan S. 286.7
Battleground, by Jan S. Doward. [Rev. ed.]

Nashville, Southern Pub. [c.1968] 95p. 21cm. Orig. pub. in 1954 under title Out of the Storm. 1.50 pap.,
1. Seventh-Day Adventists—Doctrinal and controversial works. I. Title.

*EDWARDS, Josephine 286.7
Cunnington
Reuben's portion. Illus. by Joseph W. Malmede. Nashville Southern Pub. Assn. [1967, c.1957] 208p. illus. 21cm. (Summit bk.) 1.50 pap.,
1. Seventh-Day Adventists—Doctrinal and controversial works. I. Title.

*FAGEL, William A. 286.7
Trois heures a vivre [Mountain View, Calif., Pacific Pr. Pub., 1968] 63p. 18cm. (Eds. Inter-Americaines) French language ed. of Three hours to live, tr. by Louise Wyns. .30 pap.,
1. Seventh Day Adventists—Doctrinal and Controversial works. I. Title.

FROOM, Le Roy Edwin, 1890- 286'.7
Movement of destiny. Washington, Review and Herald Pub. Association [1971] 700 p. 24 cm. Includes bibliographical references. [BX6121.F76] 70-136291
1. Adventists. I. Title.

HERNDON, Booton. 286.7
The seventh day; the story of the Seventh-Day Adventists. [1st ed.] New York, McGraw- Hill [1960] 267p. 21cm. [BX6153.H4] 60-14998
1. Seventh-Day Adventists—Hist. I. Title.

*LIBBY, Raymond H. 286.7
Quoi! Plus de Dieu? Et autres messages bibliques. [Mountain View, Calif., Pacific Pr. Pub., 1968] 65p. 18cm. (Eds. Inter-Americaines) French language tr. of What! No God? tr. by Danielle Volf-Ducret. .30 pap.,
1. Seventh Day Adventist—Doctrinal and controversial works. I. Title.

*LOEWEN, M. E. 286.7
Religious liberty and the seventh-day adventist. Nashville, Tenn., Southern Pub. [c.1964] 62p. 18cm. 1.35 pap.,
I. Title.

LOUGHBOROUGH, John Norton, 286'.7
1832-1924.
The great Second Advent movement, its rise and progress. New York, Arno Press, 1972. 480 p. illus. 23 cm. (Religion in America, series II) Reprint of the 1905 ed. [BX6121.L6 1972] 71-38453 ISBN 0-405-04073-3
1. Seventh-Day Adventists. 2. Adventists. I. Title.

MAXWELL, Arthur S. 286.7
C'est la fin! [Mountain View, Calif., Pacific Pr. Pub., [1968] 94p. 18cm. (Eds. Inter-Americaines) French language ed. of This is the end! tr. by Louise Wyns. .30 pap.,
1. Seventh Day Adventists—Doctrinal and controversial works. I. Title.

MAXWELL, Arthur Stanley, 286.7
1896-
Your friends, the Adventists. Mountain View, Calif., Pacific Press Pub. Association [1960] 95p. illus. 29cm. [BX6154.M35] 61-679
1. Seventh-Day Adventists. I. Title.

MITCHELL, David, 286.7
Jan.1,1914-
Seventh-Day Adventists, faith in action. [1st ed.] New York, Vantage Press [1958] 334 p. illus. 21 cm. [BX6154.M5] 58-10668
1. Seventh-Day Adventists. I. Title. II. Title: Faith in action.

MITCHELL, David, 1914- 286.7
Seventh-Day Adventists, faith in action. [1st ed.] New York, ,vantage Press [1958] 334p. illus. 21cm. [BX6154.M5] 58-10668
1. Seventh-Day Adventists. I. Title. II. Title: Faith in action.

OLIPHANT, Bill, ed. 286.7
Seventh-Day Adventists today: a report in depth. Homer Norris, art. Contributors: Dorothy Aitken [and others] Nashville, Southern Pub. Association [1966] 159 p. illus., ports. 28 cm. [BX6154.O4] 66-5923
1. Seventh-day Adventists — Addresses, essays, lectures. I. Aitken, Dorothy Lockwood. II. Title.

PEREZ MARCIO, Braulio 286.7
Libertad del temor [por] Braulio Perez Marcio, Hector Pereyra Suarez, Fernando Chaij. Mexico, Ediciones Interamericanas [dist. Mountain View, Calif., Pacific Pr., c.1964] 510p. illus. (pt. col.) 23cm. Bibl. 64-4099 9.25
1. Seventh-Day Adventists—Doctrinal and controversial works. I. Pereyra Suarez, Hector. II. Chaij, Fernando. III. Title.

RITCHIE, Cyril J. 286.7
While it is day. Mountain View, Calif., Pacific Press Pub. Association [1951] xii, 179 p. 20 cm. [BX6154.R5] 51-21257
1. Seventh-Day Adventists — Doctrinal and controversial works. 2. Second Advent. I. Title.

ROBINSON, Dores Eugene. 286.7
The story of our health message; the origin, character, and development of health education in the Seventh-Day Adventist Church. Nashville, Southern Pub. Association [1955] 431p. 18cm. (Christian home library) [BR115.H4R62 1955] 55-3318
1. Seventh-Day Adventists. 2. Hygiene. 3. Medicine and religion. I. Title. II. Title: Our health message.

SEVENTH-DAY Adventist Bible 286.7
student's sourcebook. Ed. by Don F. Neufeld, Julia Neuffer. Washington, D.C., 6856 Eastern Ave., N.W., Review and Herald Pub. Assn., 1962. 1189p. 25cm. (Commentary reference ser., v.3) Successor to the Source book for Bible students pub. in 1919. 62-9139 13.75
1. Seventh-Day Adventists—Dictionaries. 2. Theology—Dictionaries. I. Neufeld, Don F., ed. II. Neuffer, Julia, ed. III. Source book for Bible students. IV. Title: Bible student's source book.

SIGNS of the times. 286.7
The living witness; significant articles from the Signs of the times, 1874 -- 1959. Edited by Richard Lewis. Mountain View, Calif., Pacific Press Pub. Association [1959] 264 p. 23 cm. [BX6111.S5] 59-12526
1. Seventy-day Adventists — Addresses, essays, lectures. I. Title.

*SPARKS, Enid 286.7
Dana's date with trouble, and other true stories. Illus. by Vance Locke. Nashville, Southern Pub. Assn. [1967, c.1960] 204p. illus. 21cm. (Summit bk.) 1.50 pap.,
1. Seventh-Day Adventists—Doctrinal and Controversial works—Juvenile literature. I. Title.

UTT, Richard H 286.7
A century of miracles. Mountain View, Calif., Pacific Press Pub. Association [1963] 190 p. illus. 28 cm. [BX6154.U7] 63-16042
1. Seventh Day Adventists — Pictures, illustrations, etc. I. Title.

UTT, Richard H. 286.7
A century of miracles. Mountain View, Calif., Pac. Pr. Pub. [c.1963] 190p. illus. (pt. col.) 28cm. 63-16042 4.95
1. Seventh Day Adventists—Pictures, illustrations, etc. I. Title.

*VANDEMAN, George E. 286.7
Un jour memorable [Mountain View, Calif., Pacific Pr. Pub., 1968] 93p. 18cm. (Eds. Inter-Americaines) French language ed. of A day to remember, tr. by Danielle Volf-Ducret. .30 pap.,
1. Seventh Day Adventists—Doctrinal and controversial works. I. Title.

*WALDO, Charlotte E. 286.7
It's a great life. Nashville, Southern Pub. Assn. [1967, c.1959] 182p. 20cm. (Summit bk.) 1.50 pap.,
1. Seventh-Day Adventists—Doctrinal and Controversial works. I. Title.

*WHITE, Elena G. de. 286.7
Mensajes selectos de los ecritos de Elena G. de White; v.1. Mountain View, Calif., Pacific Pr. [1967] 520p. 18cm. Titulo de este libro en ingles: Selected messages. 3.75
1. Seventh-day Adventists—Doctrinal and controversial works. I. Title.

WHITE, Ellen Gould 286.7
(Harmon), 1827-1915
The great controversy between Christ and Satan. New York, Pyramid [1967,c.1950] 576p. 18cm. Pub. 1870-78, under title: The spirit of prophecy. (N-1719) [BX6111.W57 1950] .95 pap.,
1. Seventh-Day Adventists—Doctrinal and controversial works. I. Title.

WHITE, Ellen Gould (Harmon) 286.7
1827-1915.
The great controversy between Christ and Satan; the conflict of the ages in the Christian dispensation. Mountain View, Calif., Pacific Press Pub. Association [c1950] xiii, 709 p. illus. (part col.) ports. 23 cm. Published, 1870-78, under title: The spirit of prophecy. Bibliography: p. 681-683. [BX6111.W57] 51-21254
1. Seventy-Day Adventists—Doctrinal and controversial works. I. Title.

WHITE, Ellen Gould (Harmon) 286.7
1827-1915
[He epikeimene pale] Mountain View, Calif., Pacific Pr. Pub. [c.1964] 144p. illus. 20cm. Selections in Greek from the author's The great controversy between Christ and Satan pub. 1870-78, under the title: The spirit of prophecy. Pub. in English in 1936 under the title: Impending conflict. [BX6111.W5715] 65-362 1.00 pap.,
1. Seventh-Day Adventists—Doctrinal and controversial works. I. Title.

WHITE, Ellen Gould (Harmon) 286.7
1827-1915
Premiers ecrits. Mountain View, Calif., Pac. Pr. Pub. [1963, c.1962] 328p. 18cm. (Pubns. inter-americaines) 62-21828 3.50
1. Seventh-day Adventists—Doctrinal and controversial works. I. Title.

WHITE, Ellen Gould (Harmon) 286.7
1827-1915.
Selected messages from the writings of Ellen G. White; significant and ever-timely counsels gathered from periodical articles, manuscript statements, and certain valuable pamphlets and tracts long out of print. Washington, Review and Herald Pub. Association [1958] 2 v. 18 cm. (Christian home library) [BX6111.W515] 58-2733
1. Seventh-Day Adventists — Collected works. 2. Theology — Collected works — 19th cent. I. Title.

WHITE, Ellen Gould (Harmon) 286.7
1827-1915.
The triumph of God's love; the story of the vindication of the character of God and the salvation of mankind. Nashville, Southern Pub. Association [1957] 429p. illus. 26cm. Published, 1870-78, under title: The spirit of prophecy. [BX6111.W57 1957] 57-3640
1. Seventh-Day Adventists—Doctrinal and controversial works. I. Title.

WHITE, Ellen Gould (Harmon) 286.7
1827-1915.
The triumph of God's love; the story of the vindication of the character of God and the salvation of mankind. Nashville, Southern Pub. Association [1957] 429 p. illus. 26 cm. Published, 1870-78, under title: The spirit of prophecy. [BX6111.W57 1957] 57-3640
1. Seventh-Day Adventists — Doctrinal and controversial works. I. Title.

WILSON, James Orville 286.7
Cheer up, world, it's better ahead. Washington, D.C., Review & Herald [1963, c.1962] 128p. illus. (pt. col.) 21cm. 1.00 pap.,
I. Title.

NOORBERGEN, Rene 286.709
Ellen G. White, prophet of destiny. New Canaan, Conn. Keats [1974] 260 p. 18 cm. [BX6193.W5N66] 1.75 (pbk.)
1. White, Ellen Gould (Harmon) 1827-1915. I. Title.
L.C. card number for original edition: 70-190456.

SEVENTH-DAY Adventists. 286.709
General Conference. Dept. of Education.
The story of our church. Mountain View, Calif., Pacific Press Pub. Association [c1956] 580p. illus. 24cm. [BX6153.A57] 56-13326
1. Seventh-Day Adventists—Hist. I. Title.

SEVENTH-DAY ADVENTISTS. 286.709
GENERAL CONFERENCE. DEPT. OF EDUCATION.
The story of our church. Mountain View, Calif., Pacific Press Pub. Association [c1956] 580 p. illus. 24 cm. [BX6153.A57] 56-13326
1. Seventh-Day Adventists — Hist. I. Title.

OCHS, Daniel A., 286'.7'0922 B
1890-
The past and the presidents : biographies of the General Conference presidents / by Daniel A. Ochs and Grace Lillian Ochs. Nashville : Southern Pub. Association, [1974] 231 p. : ports. ; 21 cm. [BX6191.O26] 73-92699 ISBN 0-8127-0084-8 pbk. : 4.95
1. Seventh-Day Adventists—Biography. I. Ochs, Grace Lillian, joint author. II. Title.

WALL, Frank E., 286'.7'0922 B
1894-1972.
Uncertain journey : Adventist workers with a Mennonite heritage / Frank E. Wall and Ava C. Wall. Washington : Review and Herald Pub. Association, [1974] 160 p. ; 21 cm. Bibliography: p. 159-160. [BX6189.A1W34 1974] 74-196956 3.50
1. Seventh-Day Adventists—Biography. 2. Converts, Seventh-Day Adventist. 3. Mennonites—History. I. Wall, Ava C., joint author. II. Title.

WHY I joined ... 286'.7'0922 B
moving stories of changed lives, as told to Herbert E. Douglass. [Editor: Thomas A. Davis] Washington, Review and Herald Pub. Association [1974] 63 p. ports. 19 cm. [BX6191.W45] 74-78174
1. Seventh-Day Adventists—Biography. I. Douglass, Herbert E.

ANDERSON, Godfrey 286'.7'0924 B
Tryggve, 1909-
Outrider of the apocalypse: life and times of Joseph Bates, by Godfrey T. Anderson. Mountain View, Calif., Pacific Press Pub. Association [1972] 143 p. illus. 22 cm. (Dimension 112) Bibliography: p. 130-137. [BX6193.B3A83] 76-182495
1. Bates, Joseph, 1792-1872. I. Title.

BATES, Joseph, 286'.7'0924 B
1792-1872.
The autobiography of Elder Joseph Bates; embracing a long life on shipboard, with sketches of voyages on the Atlantic and Pacific Oceans, the Baltic and Mediterranean Seas; also impressment and service on board British war ships, long confinement in Dartmoor Prison, early experience in reformatory movements; travels in various parts of the world and a brief account of the great Advent movement of 1840-44. Battle Creek, Mich., Steam Press of the Seventh-day Adventist Pub. Association, 1868. [Nashville, Southern Pub. Association, 1970] 306 p. port. 21 cm. (Heritage library) [BX6193.B3A3 1970] 73-20192

ECONOMOU, Elly. 286'.7'0924
Beloved enemy. Mountain View, Calif., Pacific Pr. Pub. Assn. [c.1968] 136p. 22cm. (Destiny bk.) [BX61913.E25A3] 68-25796 pap., price unreported
I. Title.

HIRSCHMANN, Maria 286'.7'0924
Anne.
I changed gods. Mountain View, Calif., Pacific Press Pub. Association [1968] 128 p. illus. 22 cm. (A Destiny book D-118) [BX6193.H54A3] 68-29918
I. Title.

HOLMES, C. Raymond, 286'.7'0924 B
1929-
Stranger in my home [by] C. Raymond Holmes. Nashville, Southern Pub. Association [1974] 128 p. 21 cm. (A Crown book) [BX6193.H64A37] 73-92530 ISBN 0-8127-0075-9 2.50 (pbk.).
1. Holmes, C. Raymond, 1929- 2. Converts, Seventh-Day Adventist. I. Title.

LOEWEN, Gertrude. 286'.7'0924 B
Crusader for freedom; the story of Jean Nussbaum. Nashville, Southern Pub. Association [1969] 227 p. ports. 22 cm. [BX6193.N8L6] 77-86336
1. Nussbaum, Jean, 1888-1967. I. Title.

ROBINSON, Ella May 286'.7'0924
(White) 1882-
S. N. Haskell, man of action. Washington, Review and Herald Pub. Association [1967] 256 p. illus., ports. 22 cm. Bibliographical footnotes. [BX6193.H32R6] 67-21869
1. Haskell, Stephen Nelson. I. Title.

ROMANO, Juanita 286'.7'0924 B
Napoles.
The wind blows free on Cupcake Hill. Mountain View, Calif., Pacific Press Pub. Association [1973] 112 p. 22 cm. (A Destiny book, D-141) The author recalls her childhood in Hawaii, her growing-up years in the Philippines as the daughter of Seventh Day Adventist missionaries, and her marriage and battle with disease in the United States. [BX6193.R65A37] 73-85875
1. Romano, Juanita Napoles. I. Title.

ROTH, Don A., 1927- 286'.7'0924 B
The individualist; a biography of Bert Rhoads, by Don A. Roth. Nashville, Southern Pub. Association [1968] 126 p. port. 22 cm. A biography of the man who overcame poverty and ill health to serve most of his ninety-six years as an educator and writer for the Seventh-Day Adventist Church. [BX6193.R45R6] 92 AC 68
1. Rhoads, Bert. I. Title.

ROTH, Don A., 1927- 286.7'0924 B
The individualist; a biography of Bert Rhoads, by Don A. Roth. Nashville, Southern Pub. Association [1968] 126 p. port. 22 cm. [BX6193.R45R6] 68-20844
1. Rhoads, Bert. I. Title.

WHITE, Ellen Gould 286.70924
(Harmon) 1827-1915
I'd like to ask Sister White . . .'; the questions you might ask, answered from statements selected from the writings of Ellen G. White. Illus. by Thomas Dunbebin. Washington, D.C. Review & Herald [1965] 160p. illus. 22cm. Companion volume to His messenger. [BX6193.W5A3] 65-27860 3.95
I. Title.

WOOD, Miriam. 286'.7'0924 B
When Lena moved the cemetery. Washington, Review and Herald Pub. Association [1974] 124 p. illus. 21 cm. [BX6193.J66W66] 74-78022 3.50
1. Jones, Lena Cady. I. Title.

BEACH, John G. 286'.73' B
Notable women of spirit : the historical role of women in the Seventh-day Adventist Church / by John G. Beach. Nashville, Tenn. : Southern Pub. Association, c1976. 125 p. ; 21 cm. Bibliography: p. 123-125. [BV4415.B42] 76-6620 ISBN 0-8127-0115-1
1. Women in church work—Seventh-Day Adventists. I. Title.

BLISS, Sylvester, 286'.73 B
d.1863.
Memoirs of William Miller, generally known as a lecturer on the prophecies, and the second coming of Christ. Boston, J. V. Himes, 1853. [New York, AMS Press, 1971] vi, 426 p. port. 22 cm. Includes bibliographical references. [BX6193.M5B6 1971] 72-134374 ISBN 0-404-08422-2 17.50
1. Miller, William, 1782-1849.

CASON, Virginia. 286'.73 B
H. M. S. Richards, man alive / [Virginia Cason]. [Sacramento, Calif.] : Freedom House, [1974] ca. 200 p. : ill. (some col.), ports. (some col.) ; 29 cm. [BX6193.R5C37] 74-81143
1. Richards, Harold Marshall Sylvester, 1894- I. Title.

CRISS, Lillian M. 286'.73 B
That tent by the sawdust pile / Lillian Criss. Mountain View, Calif. : Pacific Press Pub. Association, 1976c1977 144 p. ; 22 cm. (A Destiny book ; D-155) [BX6193.B87C74] 76-41462 pbk. : 3.50
1. Burton, Annamae. 2. Seventh-Day Adventists—United States—Biography. I. Title.

DAVIDSON, Charles 286'.73
Theodore, Bp., 1905-
Upon this rock, by C. T. Davidson. Cleveland, Tenn., White Wing Pub. House and Press [1973- v. illus. 24 cm. Vol. 2: 1923-1943. Bibliography: v. 1, p. 651-655. [BX7020.A4D38] 73-173411 11.95 (v. 1)
1. Church of God—History. I. Title.

DECENZO, John. 286'.73 B
The seekers : a young couple's desperate search for God / by John DeCenzo, with Jeanise M. DeCenzo. Mountain View, Calif. : Pacific Press Pub. Association, c1977. 112 p. ; 22 cm. (A Destiny book ; D159) [BX6189.D425A37] 76-20904 pbk. 3.50
1. DeCenzo, John. 2. DeCenzo, Jeanise M. 3. Converts, Seventh-Day Adventist—United States—Biography. I. DeCenzo, Jeanise M., joint author. II. Title.

DELAFIELD, D. A., 1913- 286'.73 B
Ellen G. White in Europe, 1885-1887 : prepared from Ellen G. White papers and European historical sources / D. A. Delafield. Washington : Review and Herald Pub. Association, [1975] 320 p. : ill. ; 22 cm. [BX6193.W5D43] 74-24318
1. White, Ellen Gould Harmon, 1827-1915. I. Title.

FREIWIRTH, Paul K., 286'.73 B
1927-
Why I left the Seventh-Day Adventists, by Paul K. Freiwirth. [1st ed.] New York, Vantage Press [1970] 120 p. 21 cm. Bibliography: p. 107-120. [BX6154.F68] 72-194741 3.50
1. Seventh-Day Adventists—Doctrinal and controversial works. I. Title.

GALE, Robert, 1915- 286'.73 B
The urgent voice : the story of William Miller / Robert Gale. Washington : Review and Herald Pub. Association, [1975] 158 p. ; 21 cm. Includes bibliographical references. [BX6193.M5G34] 74-83677 3.50
1. Miller, William, 1782-1849. 2. Adventists—History. I. Title.

HARE, Eric B 286.73 (B)
An Irish boy and God; The biography of Robert Hare [by] Eric B. Hare. Washington, Review and Herald Pub. Association [1965] 192 p. illus., ports. 22 cm. [BX6193.H3H3] 65-18677
1. Hare, Robert, 1850-1953. I. Title.

LARSON, Jeanne R. 286'.73 B
Valao of the South Seas / by Jeanne Larson. Nashville : Southern Pub. Association, [1975] 125 p. : ill. ; 21 cm. (A Crown book) [BX6189.V34L37] 75-1934 ISBN 0-8127-0096-1 pbk. : 2.95
1. Converts, Seventh-Day Adventist. I. Title.

MAXSON, Eva. 286'.73 B
A mountain to climb / by Eva Maxson. Mountain View, Calif. : Pacific Press Pub. Association, c1976. 122 p. : ill. ; 22 cm. (A destiny book ; D-158) [BX6193.L56M38] 775 pbk. : 2.95
1. Lindsay, Pearl. 2. Seventh-Day Adventists—Caribbean area—Biography. I. Title.

*MAXWELL, Arthur S. 286'.73
Your friends the Adventists. Mountain View, Calif., Pacific Pr. Pub. [1968] 95p. illus. 18cm. .30 pap.
1. Seventh-Day Adventists. I. Title.

MITTLEIDER, Kenneth J. 286'.73
Your church and you, by Kenneth J. Mittleider. Nashville, Southern Pub. Association [1972] 61 p. 21 cm. [BX6154.M53] 72-81260
1. Seventh-Day Adventists—Doctrinal and controversial works. I. Title.

NOORBERGEN, Rene. 286'.73 B
Ellen G. White, prophet of destiny. New Canaan, Conn., Keats Pub. [1972] xiv, 241 p. illus. 22 cm. Bibliography: p. 229-231. [BX6193.W5N66] 70-190456 ISBN 0-87983-014-X 6.95
1. White, Ellen Gould (Harmon) 1827-1915. I. Title.

NUMBERS, Ronald L. 286'.73 B
Prophetess of health : a study of Ellen G. White / Ronald L. Numbers. 1st ed. New York : Harper & Row, c1976. xiv, 271 p. : ill. ; 21 cm. Includes bibliographical references and index. [BX6193.W5N85 1976] 75-36752 ISBN 0-06-066325-1 : 10.00
1. White, Ellen Gould Harmon, 1827-1915. I. Title.

OLIPHANT, Bill 286.73
Seventh-Day Adventists today: a report in depth. Art, Homer Norris Nashville, Southern Pub. Assn. [c.1966] 159p. illus. 28cm. 2.95 pap.,
I. Title.

OLSEN, Mahlon Ellsworth, 286'.73
1873-1952.
A history of the origin and progress of Seventh-Day Adventists. Washington, Review and Herald Pub. Association. [New York, AMS Press, 1972] 768 p. illus. 22 cm. Reprint of the 1925 ed. Bibliography: p. 746. [BX6153.O6 1972] 76-134375 ISBN 0-404-08423-0 30.00
1. Seventh-Day Adventists. I. Title.

OLSON, Albert Victor, 286.73
1884-1963
Through crisis to victory, 1888-1901; from the Minneapolis meeting to the reorganization of the General Conference, by A. V. Olson. Washington. D. C., Review & Herald [1966] 320p. 22cm. Bibl. [BX6153.O63] 66-20839 4.95
1. Seventh-Day Adventists—Hist. I. Title.

OSMUNSON, Robert Lee. 286'.73 B
Hannah : true story of a spirited Oklahoma girl's struggle for life, love, and peace with God / by Robert L. Osmunson. Mountain View, Calif. : Pacific Press Pub. Association, c1976. 112 p. ; 22 cm. (A Destiny book) [BX6193.H26O8] 76-22295 pbk. : 3.50
1. Hagstotz, Hannah Yanke, 1908- 2. Seventh-Day Adventists—Oklahoma—Biography.

RICCHIUTI, Paul B. 286'.73 B
Ellen : [trial and triumph on the American frontier] / Paul B. Ricchiuti. Mountain View, Calif. : Pacific Press Pub. Association, 1976c1977 159 p. ; 22 cm. (Destiny book ; D-160) Includes bibliographical references. [BX6193.W5R5] 76-44051 pbk. : 3.50
1. White, Ellen Gould Harmon, 1827-1915. 2. Adventists—United States—Biography. I. Title.

†ROBINSON, Virgil E. 286'.73 B
James White / Virgil Robinson. Washington : Review and Herald Pub. Association, c1976. 316 p. : ill. ; 22 cm. Includes bibliographical references. [BX6193.W54R6] 75-16921 7.50
1. White, James, 1821-1881. 2. Seventh-Day Adventists—United States—Biography.

ROBINSON, Virgil E. 286'.73 B
John Nevins Andrews, flame for the Lord / Virgil Robinson ; [ill., Kurt Reichenbach]. Washington : Review and Herald Pub. Association, c1975. 122 p. : ill. ; 21 cm. (Penguin series) "Previously printed under the title J. N. Andrews, prince of scholars" in Review and herald, 1975. [BX6193.A5R6] 75-18077
1. Andrews, John Nevins, 1829-1883. I. Title. II. Title: Flame for the Lord.

SEVENTH-DAY Adventist 286.73
encyclopedia; v.10 Washington, Review & Herald 1966. xviii, 1452p. maps. 25cm. (Commentary ref. ser. v.10) [BX6154.S39] 66-17322 14.75
1. Seventh-Day Adventists—Dictionaries.

SEVENTH-DAY Adventist 286'.73
encyclopedia. Rev. ed. Washington : Review and Herald Pub. Association, 1976. xx, 1640 p. : map ; 25 cm. (Commentary reference series ; v. 10) [BX6154.S39 1976] 75-43265
1. Seventh-Day Adventists—Dictionaries.

SEVENTH-DAY Adventists. 286'.73
General Conference. Bureau of Public Relations.
Seventh-Day Adventist fact book; a reference notebook. Nashville, Southern Pub. Association [1967] 94 p. 19 cm. Pages 87-90 blank for "Local directory"; p. 91-94 blank for "Memo." [BX6154.S395] 67-19918
1. Seventh-Day Adventists. I. Title.

SEVENTH-DAY Adventists. 286'.73
General Conference. Bureau of Public Relations.
Seventh-Day Adventist fact book; a reference notebook. Nashville, Southern Pub. Association [1967] 94 p. 19 cm. Pages 87-90 blank for "Local directory"; p. 91-94 blank for "Memo." [BX6154.S395] 67-19918
1. Seventh-Day Adventists. I. Title.

UTT, Richard H. 286'.73
The builders; a photo story of Seventh-Day Adventists at work around the world, by Richard H. Utt. Mountain View, Calif., Pacific Press Pub. Association [1970] 128 p. illus. (part col.), ports. 26 cm. [BX6154.U69] 74-125991
1. Seventh-Day Adventists—Pictorial works. I. Title.

UTT, Richard H 286'.73
A century of miracles, by Richard H. Utt. Mountain View, Calif., Pacific Press Pub. Association [c1966] 160 p. illus. (part col.), ports. (part col.) 27 cm. [BX6154.U7] 66-15534
1. Seventh-Day Adventists — Pictures, illustrations, etc. I. Title.

VANDEMAN, George E. 286.73
Destination life. Mountain View, Calif., Pacific Pr. Pub. [c.1966] 92p. 18cm. [BX6154.V254] 66-21954 .30 pap.,
1. Seventh-Day Adventists—Doctrinal and controversial works. I. Title.

WHITE, James, 1821- 286'.73 B
1881.
Sketches of the Christian life and public labors of William Miller, gathered from his memoir by the late Sylvester Bliss, and from other sources. Battle Creek, Mich., Steam Press of the Seventh-Day Adventist Publishing Association, 1875. [New York, AMS Press, 1972] 413 p. port. 22 cm. [BX6193.M5W5 1972] 70-134376 ISBN 0-404-08424-9 16.50
1. Miller, William, 1782-1849. I. Bliss, Sylvester, d. 1863. Memoirs of William Miller. II. Title.

WOOD, Miriam. 286'.73
His initials were F. D. N.; a life story of elder F. D. Nichol, for twenty-one years editor of the Review and herald, by Miriam and Kenneth Wood. [Washington] Review and Herald Publishing Association, 1967. 256 p. illus., ports. 22 cm. [BX6193.N5W6] 67-21872
1. Nichol, Francis David, 1897-1966. I. Wood, Kenneth H., joint author. II. Title.

WOOD, Miriam. 286'.73 B
Reluctant saint, reluctant sinner / Miriam Wood. Washington : Review and Herald Pub. Association, c1975. 127 p. ; 21 cm. [BX6193.W64A29] 74-25818 2.95
1. Wood, Miriam. I. Title.

COFFEY, Cecil Reeves, 286'.771
1925-
Seventh-Day Adventists in Canada, by Cecil Coffey. Nashville, Southern Pub. Association [1968] 79 p. illus. (part col.), col. map. 28 cm. [BX6154.C57] 68 2360
1. Seventh-Day Adventists—Canada. I. Title.

COOPER, Charles S. 286.7711
Wilderness parish. Mountain View, Calif., Pacific Press [c.1961] 136p. illus. 61-10881 4.00
1. Seventh-Day Adventists—British Columbia. I. Title.

THE Rise of Adventism; 286'.773
religion and society in mid-nineteenth-century America. Edwin S. Gaustad, editor. [1st ed.] New York, Harper & Row [1974] xx, 329 p. 24 cm. Lectures delivered during 1972-73 at the University Church, Loma Linda University, Loma Linda, Calif. Contents.Contents.—Hudson, W. S. A time of religious ferment.—Smith, T. L. Social reform.—Blake, J. B. Health reform.—Greene, J. C. Science and religion.—Hine, R. V. Communitarianism.—Moore, R. L. Spiritualism.—Sandeen, E. R. Millennialism.—McLoughlin, W. G. Revivalism.—Arthur, D. T. Millerism.—Butler, J. M. Adventism and the American experience.—Carner, V., Kubo, S., and Rice, C. Bibliographical essay (p. 207-317) [BR525.R57 1974] 74-4637 ISBN 0-06-063094-9
1. United States—Religion—19th century. 2. Adventists. I. Gaustad, Edwin Scott, ed.

HANSEN, Louis A. 286'.775
From so small a dream, by Louis A. Hansen. Nashville, Southern Pub. Association [1968] 288 p. 21 cm. [BX6153.H33] 68-29501
1. Seventh-Day Adventists—Southern States. I. Title.

MCCUMBER, Harold 286'.7794
Oliver, 1895-
The Advent message in the Golden West, by Harold O. McCumber. Rev. Mountain View, Calif., Pacific Press Pub. Association [1968] 184 p. illus., map, ports. 22 cm. (Dimension, 106) First ed. published in 1946 under title: Pioneering the message in the Golden West. [BX6153.M2 1968] 68-5957
1. Seventh-Day Adventists—California. I. Title.

287 Methodist Churches

BETTS, Albert Deems, 1882- 287
History of South Carolina Methodism. Columbia, S. C., Advocate Press, 1952. 544p. illus. 24cm. [BX8248.S6B4] 52-41238
1. Methodist Church in South Carolina. I. Title.

CHILCOTE, Thomas F. 287
The articles of religion of the Methodist Church. Nashville, Methodist Evangelistic Materials, [1969] 80 p. 19 cm. [BX8335.C48] 62-17342
1. Methodist Church — Catechisms and creeds — English. I. Title.

HARMON, Nolan Bailey, 1892- 287
Understanding the Methodist Church. Nashville, Methodist Pub. House [1955] 191p. 20cm. [BX8331.H27] 55-5738
1. Methodist Church. I. Title.

HARMON, Nolan, Bailey, 1892- 287
Understanding the Methodist Church. Rev. ed. Nashville, Methodist Pub. House [1961] 191p. 20cm. [BX8331.2.H3 1961] 61-16939
1. Methodist Church. I. Title.

HAZZARD, Lowell Brestel. 287
A pocket book of Methodist beliefs, by Lovell B. Hazzard. Nashville, Methodist Evangelistic Materials [1962] 149 p. 14 cm. [BX8332.H35] 62-14883
1. Methodist Church — Doctrinal and controversial works. I. Title.

HOLT, Ivan Lee, Bp., 1886- 287
The World Methodist movement, by Ivan Lee Holt and Elmer T. Clark. [Nashville, The Upper Room, 1956] 148p. illus. 19cm. [BX2807.W6H6] 56-58198
1. World Methodist Council. 2. Ecumenical movement. 3. Methodist Church—Stat. I. Clark, Elmer Talmage, 1886- II. Title.

JACKMAN, Everett E 1899- 287
The Nebraska Methodist story; authorized centennial history of Nebraska Methodism, 1854-1954. [Wymore, Neb.] Nebraska Conference, Methodist Historical Society [1954] 238p. illus. 23cm. [BX8248.N2J3] 54-32012
1. Methodist Church in Nebraska. I. Title.

KEARNS, Francis E 287
The church is mine. Nashville, Graded Press [1962] 122p. 20cm. (Basic Christian books) Includes bibliography. [BX8331.2.K4] 62-4863
1. Methodist Church. I. Title.

KENNEDY, Gerald Hamilton, 287
Bp., 1907-
The Methodist way of life. Englewood Cliffs, N.J., Prentice-Hall [1958] 216 p. illus. 21 cm. Includes bibliography. [BX8331.K36] 58-6214
1. Methodism. I. Title.

LEE, Umphrey, 1893-1958. 287
Our fathers and us; the heritage of the Methodists. Dallas, Southern Methodist University Press, 1958. 123p. 23cm. Includes bibliography. [BX8331.L43] 58-14109
1. Methodism. I. Title.

LEHMBERG, Ben F 287
A new awakening for Methodism. Nashville, Methodist Evangelistic Materials [c1963] 71 p. 19 cm. [BX8332.L4] 63-22398
1. Methodism. I. Title.

METHODIST Church (United 287
States). Ad Hoc Committee on E.U.B. Union.
The constitution for the United Methodist Church, with enabling legislation and other historic documents. Recommended for adoption by 1967 annual conferences of: the Methodist Church [and] the Evangelical United Brethren Church. [n.p., 1967] viii, 59 p. 23 cm. Submitted by the Ad Hoc Committee on E.U.B. Union, the Methodist Church and the Commission on Church Union, the Evangelical United Brethren Church. [BX8329.E9M38] 68-6599

1. Methodist Church (United States)—Relations—Evangelical United Brethren Church. 2. Evangelical United Brethren Church—Relations—Methodist Church (United States) 3. United Methodist Church (United States) I. Evangelical United Brethren Church. Commission on Church Union. II. Title.

MIDDLETON, William Vernon, 1902- 287
Methodism in Alaska and Hawaii; new patterns for living together. Introd. by Bishop A. Frank Smith. [1st ed.] New York, Editorial Dept., Joint Section of Education and Cultivation, Board of Missions of the Methodist Church [1958] 144 p. illus. 19 cm. Includes bibliography. [BX8248.A23M5] 58-9904
1. Methodist Church in Alaska. 2. Methodist Church in the Hawaiian Islands. I. Title.

PALMER, Louis De Forest, 1871- 287
Herosim and romance; early Methodism in northeastern Pennsylvania. [Stroudsburg, Pa., 1950. 248 p. illus., ports., map. 24 cm. "References and notes": p. 232-243. [BX8248.P4P25] 50-11235
1. Methodist Church in Pennsylvania. I. Title.

SELECMAN, Charles Claude, Bp., 1874- 287
The Methodist first reader, 'On being a Christian,' by Charles C. Selecman and George H. Jones. Nashville, Tidings [1956] 95p. illus. 19cm. Includes bibliography. [BX8332.S45] 56-8196
1. Methodism. I. Jones, George Hawkins, 1905- joint author. II. Title. III. Title: On being a Christian.

SEMMEL, Bernard. 287
The Methodist revolution. New York, Basic Books [1973] viii, 273 p. 25 cm. Bibliography: p. 243-262. [BX8276.S45] 72-89282 ISBN 0-465-04570-7 10.95
1. Methodism. 2. Great Britain—Religion. I. Title.

SHORT, Roy Hunter, Bp., 1902- 287
Methodism and Christian experience. Nashville, Methodist Evangelistic Materials [c1962] 64 p. 19 cm. [BV4501.2.S45] 62-20478
1. Christian life—Methodist authors. I. Title.

SLAGER, Albert L. 287
Early Methodism in the Miami Valley 1798-1920 : including a history of the Central Methodist Episcopal Church, Springfield, Ohio, with sketches of the other Methodist churches in the city / by Albert L. Slager. [Springfield, Ohio] : Central Methodist Episcopal Church, [1955?] 79 p. : ill. ; 20 cm. Bibliography: p. 79. [BX8248.O3S55] 75-314853
1. Methodist Church in the Miami Valley, Ohio. 2. Central Methodist Episcopal Church, Springfield, Ohio. I. Title.

SMITH, Roy Lemon, 1887- 287
Why I am a Methodist. New York, Hermitage House, 1955. 223 p. 22 cm. [BX8331.S56] 55-8728
1. Methodism. I. Title.

SMITH, Roy Lemon, 1887- 287
Why I am a Methodist. Boston, Beacon [1965, c.1965] 223p. 21cm. (BP199) [BX8331.S56] 1.25 pap.,
1. Methodism. I. Title.

STUART, Reginald Ray, 1882- 287
How firm a foundation; a centennial history of the First Methodist Church, San Leandro, California, by Reginald R. Stuart & Grace D. Stuart. [San Leandro] FirstMethodist Church, 1953. 112p. illus. 28cm. [BX8481.S42F5] 53-30050
1. San Leandro, Calif. First Methodist Church. I. Stuart, Grace Dell, 1889- joint author. II. Title.

SWEET, William Warren, 1881- 287
Methodism in American history. Revision of 1953. Nashville, Abingdon Press [1954] 472p. illus. 23cm. [BX8235.S9 1953] 54-5943
1. Methodism—Hist. 2. Methodists in the U. S. I. Title.

TENNEY, Mary Alice, 1889- 287
Blueprint for a Christian world; an analysis of the Wesleyan way. Winona Lake, Ind., Light and Life Press, 1953. 292p. 22cm. [BX8331.T42] 53-33414
1. Methodism. I. Title.

WORLD Methodist Council. 287.0621
Handbook of information. [n. p., 1959?] 78 p. 18 cm. [BX8207.W6A68] 59-18049
I. Title.

IRONMONGER, Elizabeth (Hogg) 1891- 287.075542
Methodism in York County, Virginia. [Richmond? c1959] 91p. illus. 23cm. Includes bibliography. [BX8248.V817] 61-33994
1. Methodist Church in York Co., Va. I. Title.

WATSON, Philip Saville, 1909- comp. 287.082
The message of the Wesleys; a reader of instruction and devotion, compiled and with an introd. by Philip S. Watson. New York, Macmillan [1964] xx, 263 p. 18 cm. "Mp 169." Includes bibliographies. [BX8215.W3] 64-18268
1. Methodism — Collections. I. Wesley, John, 1703-1791. II. Wesley, Charles, 1707-1788. III. Title.

CLARK, Elmer Talmage, 1886- 287.09
An album of Methodist history. New York, Abingdon-Cokesbury Press [1952] 336 p. (chiefly illus., ports., maps, facsims.) 31 cm. [BX8232.C6] 52-5733
1. Methodism—Hist.—Pictorial works. I. Title.

CAMERON, Richard Morgan, 1898- 287.09
The rise of Methodism, a source book. New York, Philosophical Library [1954] xv, 397p. diagr., geneal. table. 23cm. Bibliographical references included in 'Notes' (p. [363]-385) [BX8231.C3] 54-8668
1. Methodism—Hist. I. Title.

DAVIES, Rupert E., 1909- 287.09
Methodism. [Baltimore] Penguin [c.1963] 224p. 18cm. (Pelican orig., A591) Bibl. 63-4019 .85 pap.,
1. Methodism—Hist. I. Title.

DAVIES, Rupert Eric, 1909- 287.09
Methodism. [Baltimore] Penguin Books [1963] 224 p. 18 cm. (A Pelican original, A591) [BX8331.2.D3] 63-4019
1. Methodism — Hist. I. Title.

DAVIES, Rupert Eric, 1909- 287'.09
Methodism / [by] Rupert E. Davies. New and revised ed. London : Epworth Press, 1976. 196 p. ; 22 cm. Includes index. Bibliography: p. [187]-188. [BX8331.2.D3 1976] 77-360471 ISBN 0-7162-0280-8 : £1.75
1. Methodism—History. I. Title.

LEE, Umphrey, 1893- 287.09
A short history of Methodism, by Umphrey Lee and William Warren Sweet. Henry M. Bullock, general editor. Nashville, Abingdon Press [1956] 160p. illus. 20cm. [BX8231.L43] 56-7763
1. Methodism—Hist. I. Sweet, William Warren 1881- joint author. II. Title.

LUCCOCK, Halford Edward, 1885- 287.09
Endless line of splendor. Illus. by Lynd Ward. Chicago, The Advance for Christ and His Church [1951] 96 p. illus. 24 cm. [BX8232.L8] 51-2777
1. Methodism—Hist. I. Title.

LUCCOCK, Halford Edward, 1885-1960. 287'.09
Endless line of splendor / by Halford E. Luccock and Webb Garrison ; ill. by Lynd Ward. 2d rev. ed. Evanston, Ill. : United Methodist Communications, 1975. 112 p. : ill. ; 24 cm. [BX8232.L8 1975] 75-320003
1. Methodism—History. I. Garrison, Webb B., joint author. II. Title.

WHO'S who in the Methodist Church. 287.0922
Compiled by the editors of Who's who in America and the A. N. Marquis Co., inc. with the cooperation of the Council of Secretaries of the Methodist Church. Nashville, Abingdon Press [1966] vii, 1489 p. 27 cm. Second ed. of Who's who in Methodism. [BX8213.W52 1966] 66-26876
1. Methodist Church—Biography—Dictionaries. I. Who's who in America.

BAKER, Frank, 1910- 287'.0924 B
John Wesley and the Church of England. Nashville, Abingdon Press [1970] viii, 422 p. 26 cm. Bibliography: p. 407-412. [BX8495.W5B33 1970b] 73-23809 ISBN 0-687-20445-3 14.50
1. Wesley, John, 1703-1791. 2. Church of England. I. Title.

DOBREE, Bonamy, 1891- 287'.092'4 B
John Wesley. [Folcroft, Pa.] Folcroft Library Editions, 1974. p. cm. Reprint of the 1933 ed. published by Duckworth, London, which was issued as no. 4 of Great lives. Bibliography: p. [BX8495.W5D57 1974] 74-7428 10.00 (lib. bdg.).
1. Wesley, John, 1703-1791.

ETHRIDGE, Willie (Snow) 287'.0924 B
Strange fires; the true story of John Wesley's love affair in Georgia. New York, Vanguard Press [1971] 254 p. 24 cm. Bibliography: p. 249-254. [BX8495.W5E84 1971] 77-170902 ISBN 0-8149-0693-1 6.95
1. Wesley, John, 1703-1791. 2. Hopkey, Sophy. I. Title.

LIPSKY, Abram, 1872-1946. 287'.0924 B
John Wesley; a portrait. New York, AMS Press [1971, c1928] ix, 305 p. facsim., ports. 19 cm. Bibliography: p. 297-300. [BX8495.W5L47 1971] 76-155619 ISBN 0-404-03994-4
1. Wesley, John, 1703-1791.

LUNDY, Clyde Enoch. 287'.092'4 B
A lot o' livin' / Clyde Enoch Lundy ; with introd. by Roy H. Short. [Knoxville? Tenn.] : Holston Conference Archives and History, c1974. ix, 347 p. : ill. ; 23 cm. [BX8495.L75A34] 74-79443
1. Lundy, Clyde Enoch. I. Title.

*MILLER, Basil 287.0924(B)
John Wesley; 'I look upon the world as my parish.' Introd. by Stephen W. Paine. Minneapolis, Bethany Fellowship [1966, c.1943] 140p. 19cm. (BF150) 1.50 pap.,
1. Wesley, John, 1703-1791. I. Title.

MONK, Robert C. 287.0924
John Wesley; his puritan heritage; a study of the Christian life [by] Robert C. Monk. Nashville, Abingdon [1966] 286p. 24cm. Based on thesis. Priceton Univ. Bibl. [BX8495.W5M6] 66-15494 5.50
1. Wesley, John, 1703-1791. 2. Puritans. I. Title.

MYERS, Elisabeth P 287.0924
Singer of six thousand songs; a life of Charles Wesley, by Elisabeth P. Myers. Drawings by Leonard Vosburgh. London, New York, T. Nelson [1965] 160 p. illus. 21 cm. Bibliography: p. 159. [BX8495.W4M9] 65-20772
1. Wesley, Charles, 1707-1788. I. Title.

MYERS, Elisabeth P. 287.0924
Singer of six thousand songs; a life of Charles Wesley, Drawings by Leonard Vosburgh. New York, Nelson [c.1965] 160p. illus. 21cm. Bibl. [BX8495.W4M9] 65-20772 2.95; 2.92 lib. ed.
1. Wesley, Charles, 1707-1788. I. Title.

PILMORE, Joseph, 1734?-1825. 287'.0924
The journal of Joseph Pilmore, Methodist itinerant, for the years August 1, 1769, to January 2, 1774. With a biographical sketch of Joseph Pilmore by Frank B. Stanger. Editors: Frederick E. Maser [and] Howard T. Maag. Philadelphia, Printed by Message Pub. Co. for the Historical Society of the Philadelphia Annual Conference of the United Methodist Church, 1969. 262 p. illus., facsim., ports. 24 cm. [BX8495.P548A3] 79-11727 5.00
I. Title.

THE Place of Wesley in the Christian tradition / 287'.092'4
edited by Kenneth E. Rowe. Metuchen, N.J. : Scarecrow Press, 1976. iii, 165 p. ; 23 cm. "Essays delivered at Drew University in celebration of the commencement of the publication of the Oxford edition of the works of John Wesley." Includes index. "A selected bibliography [by] Lawrence D. McIntosh": p. 134-159. [BX8495.W5P53] 76-27659 ISBN 0-8108-0981-8 : 6.00
1. Wesley, John, 1703-1791. I. Rowe, Kenneth E.

SCOTT, Orange, 1800-1847. 287'.0924 B
The life of Rev. Orange Scott: In two parts. By Lucius C. Matlack. Freeport, N.Y., Books for Libraries Press, 1971. 307 p. port. 23 cm. (The Black heritage library collection) Reprint of the 1847-48 ed. Each part has special t.p. [BX8495.S37A3 1971] 70-138343 ISBN 0-8369-8735-7
I. Matlack, Lucius C., ed. II. Title. III. Series.

TYERMAN, Luke, 1819or20-1889. 287'.092'4 B
The life and times of the Rev. John Wesley, M.A., founder of the Methodists. New York, B. Franklin [1973] 3 v. ports. 23 cm. (Burt Franklin research & source works series. Philosophy & religious history monographs 132) Reprint of the 1872 ed. published by Harper & Brothers, New York. Includes bibliographical references. [BX8495.W5T8 1973] 73-14910 ISBN 0-8337-4710-X 72.50
1. Wesley, John, 1703-1791.

VICKERS, John Ashley. 287'.092'4 B
Thomas Coke and World Methodism / [by] John A. Vickers. Bognor Regis : World Methodist Historical Society (British Section), 1976. 20 p. ; 21 cm. A Wesley Historical Society lecture delivered at the Methodist Conference in Sheffield, 1964. [BX8495.C6V49] 77-366326 ISBN 0-9505559-0-8 : £0.40
1. Coke, Thomas, Bp., 1747-1814—Addresses, essays, lectures. 2. Methodist Church—Bishops—Biography—Addresses, essays, lectures. 3. Bishops—England—Biography—Addresses, essays, lectures. 4. Bishops—United States—Biography—Addresses, essays, lectures. I. Title.

WILDER, Franklin. 287'.0924 B
Immortal mother. [1st ed.] New York, Vantage Press [1967, c1966] 230 p. port. 21 cm. [BX8495.W55W5] 67-1127
1. Wesley, Susanna (Annesley) 1670-1742. I. Title.

WOOD, Arthur Skevington. 287'.0924
The burning heart; John Wesley, evangelist, by A. Skevington Wood. Grand Rapids, Eerdmans [c.1967] 302p. 23cm. Bibl. [BX8495.W5W7 1967b] 68-20489 4.95
1. Wesley, John, 1703-1791. I. Title.

GILL, Frederick Cyril, 1898- 287'.0942
The romantic movement and Methodism; a study of English romanticism and the evangelical revival, by Frederick C. Gill. New York, Haskell House, 1966. 189 p. 24 cm. Reprint of the 1937 ed. Bibliography: 179-184. [BX8276.G5 1966] 68-1308
1. Evangelical revival. 2. Methodism. 3. Romanticism—England. I. Title.

GILL, Frederick Cyril, 1898- 287'.0942
The romantic movement and Methodism; a study of English romanticism and the evangelical revival, by Frederick C. Gill. New York, Haskell House, 1966. 189 p. 24 cm. Reprint of the 1937 ed. Bibliography: 179-184. [BX8276.G5 1966] 68-1308
1. Evangelical revival. 2. Methodism. 3. Romanticism—England. I. Title.

BAKER, Frank, 1910- 287'.0973
From Wesley to Asbury : studies in early American Methodism / by Frank Baker. Durham, N.C. : Duke University Press, 1976. xiv, 223 p. ; 25 cm. Includes index. Bibliography: p. [207]-216. [BX8236.B34] 75-39454 ISBN 0-8223-0359-0 : 9.75
1. Methodist Church in the United States. 2. Wesley, John, 1703-1791. 3. Asbury, Francis, Bp. 1745-1816. I. Title.

LEE, Jesse, 1758-1816. 287'.0973
A short history of the Methodists / by Jesse Lee. Rutland, Vt. : Academy Books, 1974. 394 p., [2] leaves of plates : ill. ; 18 cm. Reprint of the 1810 ed. printed by Magill and Clime, Baltimore, with additional indexes. "Limited facsimile edition of 600 copies." [BX8235.L4 1974] 74-84416 ISBN 0-914960-04-0 : 6.95
1. Methodist Church in the United States. I. Title.

METHODIST Church (United States) Ad Hoc Committee on E. U. B. Union. 287'.0973
The United Methodist Church: the plan of union as adopted by the general conferences, November, 1966 and the annual conferences, 1967 of the Methodist Church and the Evangelical United Brethren Church. [n. p.] Ad Hoc Committee on E. U. B. Union, the Methodist Church [and] the Commission on Union, the Evangelical United Brethren Church [1967] v, 376 p. 28 cm. Contents.Message from the Joint Commissions.--Historical statement.--pt. 1. The constitution. Index to part 1.--pt. 2. Doctrinal statements and the general rules.--pt. 3. Social principles.--pt. 4. Organization and administration. Index to part 4.--Enabling legislation. Index to Enabling legislation. [BX8329.E9M48] 68-4886
1. Methodist Church (United States)—Relations—Evangelical United Brethren Church. 2. Evangelical United Brethren Church—Relations—Methodist Church (United States) 3. United Methodist Church (United States) I. Evangelical United Brethren Church. Commission on Church Union. II. Title. III. Title: The plan of union.

CHREITZBERG, Abel McKee, 1820-1908. 287'.09757
Early Methodism in the Carolinas. Prepared at the request of the South Carolina Conference. Nashville, Pub. House of the Methodist Episcopal Church, South, 1897. [Spartanburg, S.C., Reprint Co., 1972] xiv, 364 p. illus. 23 cm. Bibliography: p. [vii] [BX8248.S6C5 1972] 70-187362 ISBN 0-87152-090-7
1. Methodist Church in South Carolina. I. Title.

SHIPP, Albert Micajah, 1819-1887. 287'.09757
The history of Methodism in South Carolina. Nashville, Southern Methodist Pub. House, 1884. [Spartanburg, S.C., Reprint Co., 1972] 652 p. 23 cm. [BX8248.S6S5 1972] 70-187373 ISBN 0-87152-101-6
1. Methodist Church in South Carolina. I. Title.

BROOKS, William Erle, 1931- 287'.09759
From saddlebags to satellites; a history of Florida Methodism. William E. Brooks, editor. [Nashville, Printed by the Parthenon Press, 1969] 268 p. illus., maps, ports. 24 cm. Bibliographical references included in "Notes" (p. 267-268) [BX8248.F6B7] 73-78753
1. Methodist Church in Florida. I. Title.

LAZENBY, Marion Elias, 1885-1957. 287.09761
History of Methodism in Alabama and West Florida; being an account of the amazing march of Methodism through Alabama and West Florida. [Nashville? 1960] 1256p. illus. 24cm. [BX8248.A2L3] 61-25779
1. Methodist Church in Alabama. 2. Methodist Church in Florida. I. Title.

CLEGG, Leland, 1898- 287'.09766
Oklahoma Methodism in the twentieth century, by Leland Clegg and William B. Oden. [Nashville, Printed by Parthenon Press 1968] 488 p. illus., ports. 24 cm. Bibliographical footnotes. [BX8248.O4C5] 68-3869
1. Methodist Church in Oklahoma. I. Oden, William B., 1935- joint author. II. Title.

VERNON, Walter N. 287'.09767
Methodism in Arkansas, 1816-1976 / Walter N. Vernon. Little Rock : Joint Committee for the History of Arkansas Methodism, c1976. 490 p. : ill. ; 24 cm. Includes bibliographical references and index. [BX8248.A8V47] 76-368309
1. Methodist Church in Arkansas. I. United Methodist Church (United States). Joint Committee for the History of Arkansas Methodism. II. Title.

WEST, Roberta B. 287'.09786
How they brought the good news of Methodism to north Montana / by Roberta B. West. [Chinook? Mont.] : West, [1974] 537 p. : ill. ; 29 cm. Includes index. Bibliography: p. 113-116. [BX8248.M9W47] 75-303211
1. Methodist Church in Montana. 2. Montana—Biography. I. Title.

STOKES, Mack B 287.1
Our Methodist heritage. Nashville, Graded Press [1963] 128 p. 20 cm. (Basic Christian books) Bibliographical footnotes. [BX8495.W5S7] 63-5864
1. Wesley, John. 1703-1791. 2. Methodism. I. Title.

TENNEY, Mary Alice, 1889- 287.1
Living in two worlds; how a Christian does it! Winona Lake, Ind., Light and Life Press [1958] 118 p. 20 cm. [BX8332.T4] 58-26314
1. Methodism I. Title.

WESLEYAN Church. Office of the General Secretary. 287'.1'025
Church location directory for the Wesleyan Church—United States, Canada, & British Isles / prepared by the General Secretary's directory service. Marion, Ind. : Wesley Press, c1975. 95 p. : ill. ; 22 cm. Pages 88-95, blank for notes. [BX9995.W4W47 1975] 75-327421
1. Wesleyan Church—Directories. I. Title: Church location directory for the Wesleyan Church ...

SEMMENS, Bernard L. 287'.1'09
The Conferences after Wesley, an attempt to keep the record straight; a study of the basic documents of early Methodism, by Bernard L. Semmens. Melbourne, National Press [1971] 106 p. tables. 22 cm. ANL [BX8207.A1S45] 70-882982 ISBN 0-909470-01-4
1. Methodist Church—Congresses—History. 2. Wesley, John, 1703-1791. I. Title.

MORROW, Thomas Manser. 287'1'0922
Early Methodist women [by] Thomas M. Morrow, London, Epworth Pr., 1967. 119p. 20cm. [BX8493.M6] 68-96621 3.00 bds.,
1. Methodist Church—Biog. 2. Woman—Biog. I. Title.
American distributor: Verry, Mystic, Conn.

STEVENSON, Arthur Linwood, 1891- 287'.1'0922 B
Natives of Petersburg, Virginia, and vicinity in the Methodist ministry, by Arthur L. Stevenson. Brevard, N.C., 1973. 44 p. 22 cm. (His Native Methodist minister series, 4th) [BX8491.S7] 74-150410
1. Methodist Church—Biography. 2. Petersburg, Va.—Biography. I. Title.

STEVENSON, Arthur Linwood, 1891- 287'.1'0922 B
Natives of the Northern Neck of Virginia in the Methodist ministry, by Arthur L. Stevenson. Brevard, N.C., 1973. 44 p. 22 cm. (His Native Methodist minister series, 5th) [BX8491.S72] 73-181605
1. Methodist Church—Biography. 2. Virginia—Biography. I. Title.

BRUNSON, Alfred, 1793-1882. 287'.1'0924 B
A western pioneer / Alfred Brunson. New York : Arno Press, 1975. 418, 413 p. ; 21 cm. (The Mid-American frontier) Reprint of the 1872-1879 ed. published by Hitchcock and Walden, Cincinnati. [BX8495.B78A3 1975] 75-89 ISBN 0-405-06856-5 : 46.00
1. Brunson, Alfred, 1793-1882. I. Title. II. Series.

BUNTING, Jabez, 1779-1858. 287'.1'0924 B
Early Victorian Methodism : the correspondence of Jabez Bunting, 1830-1858 / W. R. Ward. Oxford ; New York : Oxford University Press, 1976. xxiii, 440 p. ; 25 cm. (Publications - University of Durham) Includes bibliographical references and index. [BX8495.B884A4 1976] 76-366431 ISBN 0-19-713140-9 : 5.95
1. Bunting, Jabez, 1779-1858. I. Ward, William Reginald. II. Title. III. Series: Durham, Eng. University. Publications.

COLLINS, John Smiley, 1924- 287'.1'0924 B
Man of devotion, Francis Asbury, by J. Smiley Collins. [Nashville] Upper Room [1971] 86 p. 21 cm. Includes bibliographical references. [BX8495.A8C64] 70-155494
1. Asbury, Francis, Bp., 1745-1816. I. Title.

FRANK, William P. 287'.1'0924 B
God's impatient builder; the story of the Reverend James R. Hughes, by William P. Frank. [Wynnewood, Pa., Livingston Pub. Co., c1972] 136 p. illus. 24 cm. [BX8495.H82F7] 72-9310
1. Hughes, James Richard, 1922-1969. I. Title.

GORDON, Arthur. 287'.1'0924 B
One man's way; the story and message of Norman Vincent Peale, a biography. Rev. and enl. ed. of Minister to millions. Englewood Cliffs, N.J., Prentice-Hall [1972] 324 p. illus. 21 cm. Published in 1958 under title: Norman Vincent Peale; minister to millions. [BX9543.P4G6 1972] 72-3311 ISBN 0-13-636084-X 5.95
1. Peale, Norman Vincent, 1898- I. Title.

HARMON, Rebecca Lamar. 287'.1'0924
Susanna, mother of the Wesleys. Nashville, Abingdon Press [1968] 175 p. illus., ports. 22 cm. Bibliography: p. 170-172. [BX8495.W55H3] 68-11463
1. Wesley, Susanna (Annesley) 1670-1742. I. Title.

JONES, Eli Stanley, 1884- 287'.1'0924
A song of ascents; a spiritual autobiography [by] E. Stanley Jones. Nashville, Abingdon Press [1968] 400 p. 23 cm. [BX8495.J58A3] 68-17451
I. Title.

MILLER, Robert Moats. 287'.1'0924 B
How shall they hear without a preacher? The life of Ernest Fremont Tittle. Chapel Hill, University of North Carolina Press [1971] xii, 524 p. illus. 24 cm. Bibliography: p. [515]-518. [BX8495.T67M5] 74-149031 ISBN 0-8078-1173-4 12.50
1. Tittle, Ernest Fremont, 1885-1949. I. Title.

POLLOCK, John Charles. 287'.1'0924 B
George Whitefield and the Great Awakening [by] John Pollock. [1st ed.] Garden City, N.Y., Doubleday, 1972. x, 272 p. 22 cm. [BX9225.W4P65] 72-76198 ISBN 0-385-03466-0 6.95
1. Whitefield, George, 1714-1770. I. Title.

QUIMBY, Chester Warren, 1891- 287.1'0924
Sojourner in two worlds; a memoir of Dr. Rollin Hough Walker, professor of English Bible at Ohio Wesleyan University, 1900-1936. Assembled, arranged, and edited by Chester Warren Quimby. [Long Beach? Miss.] 1967. 55 p. 28 cm. [BX8495.W2426Q5] 74-5874
1. Walker, Rollin Hough, 1865-1955. I. Title.

RUDOLPH, L. 287.10924(B)
Francis Asbury [by] L. C. Rudolph. Nashville, Abingdon Press [1966] 240 p. ports. 23 cm. Bibliography: p. 227-234. [BX8495.A8R8] 66-21970
1. Asbury, Francis, Bp., 1745-1816. I. Title.

RUDOLPH, L. C. 287.10924
Francis Asbury [by] L. C. Rudolph. Nashville, Abingdon [1966] 240p. ports 23cm. Bibl. [BX8495.A8R8] 66-21970 5.00
1. Asbury, Francis, Bp., 1745-1816. I. Title.

WEATHERHEAD, Andrew Kingsley, 1923- 287'.1'0924 B
Leslie Weatherhead : a personal portrait / A. Kingsley Weatherhead. Nashville : Abingdon, [1975] 269 p. : port. ; 23 cm. [BX8495.W329W4] 75-17574 ISBN 0-687-21375-4 : 7.95
1. Weatherhead, Leslie Dixon, 1893-

WILDER, Franklin. 287'.1'0924 B
Father of the Wesleys; a biography. [1st ed.] New York, Exposition Press [1971] 220 p. port. 22 cm. Bibliography: p. 219-220. [BX5199.W396W5] 72-146917 ISBN 0-682-47238-7 6.00
1. Wesley, Samuel, 1662-1735. I. Title.

WILDER, Franklin. 287'.1'0924 B
Martha Wesley / by Franklin Wilder. 1st ed. Hicksville, N.Y. : Exposition Press, c1976. 136 p. ; 21 cm. Bibliography: p. 135-136. [BX8495.W53W54] 76-360632 ISBN 0-682-48488-1 : 6.50
1. Wesley, Martha, 1707-1791.

HALEVY, Elie, 1870-1937. 287'.142
The birth of Methodism in England. Translated and edited by Bernard Semmel. Chicago, University of Chicago Press [1971] ix, 81 p. 21 cm. Translation of 2 articles entitled La naissance du Methodisme en Angleterre which appeared in the Revue de Paris Aug. 1 and 15, 1906, p. 519-539 and 841-867, respectively. Includes bibliographical references. [BX8276.H27 1971] 72-131959 ISBN 0-226-31309-3
1. Methodism—History. 2. Methodist Church in Great Britain. I. Semmel, Bernard, ed.

LEE, Umphrey, 1893-1958. 287'.142
The historical backgrounds of early Methodist enthusiasm. New York, AMS Press, 1967. 176 p. 23 cm. (Studies in history, economics and public law, no. 339) Reprint of the 1931 ed., originally presented as the author's thesis, Columbia University. Bibliography: p. 149-172. [BR112.L4 1967] 74-29899
1. Wesley, John, 1703-1791. 2. Enthusiasm. 3. Great Britain—Church history—Modern period, 1485- 4. Methodism—History. I. Title. II. Series: Columbia studies in the social sciences, no. 339.

METHODIST Church (United States) Ad hoc Committee on E.U.B. Union. 287.142
The plan of union; report to the General Conferences, November, 1966, of the Methodist Church and the Evangelical United Brethren Church, submitted by the Ad Hoc Committee on E.U.B. Union, the Methodist Church [and] the Commission on Union, the Evangelical United Brethren Church. [n. p., 1966] v. 361 p. 28 cm. Cover title. [BX8329.E9M4] 66-7385
1. Methodist Church (United States) — Relations — Evangelical United Brethren Church. 2. Evangelical United Brethren Church — Relations — Methodist Church (United States) I. Evangelical United Brethren Church. Commission on Church Union. II. Methodist Church (United States) General Conference. III. Evangelical United Brethren Church. General Conference. IV. Title.

RACK, Henry D 287.142
The future of John Wesley's Methodism, by Henry D. Rack. Richmond, John Knox Press [1965] 80 p. 22 cm. (Ecumenical studies in history, no. 2) Bibliographical footnotes. [BX8329.A1R3] 65-15426
1. Methodist Church—Relations. I. Title. II. Series.

RACK, Henry D. 287.142
The future of John Wesley's Methodism. Richmond, John Knox [c.1965] 80p. 22cm. (Ecumenical studies in hist., no. 2) Bibl. [BX8329.A1R3] 65-15426 1.75 pap.,
1. Methodist Church—Relations. I. Title. II. Series.

FULCHER, Ernest A. 287'.1421'73
The Methodist Chapel, Derby Road, Woodford, 1876-1976 / by Ernest A. Fulcher. London : Woodford Methodist Church, 1976. [4], 55 p., [4] p. of plates : ill., 2 facsims., port. ; 23 cm. [BX8483.W65F84] 77-371975 ISBN 0-9504893-0-1 : £1.00
1. Woodford Methodist Church. I. Title.

KINDER, Arthur Gordon. 287'.1427'31
One hundred years of Trinity / [by A. Gordon Kinder]. [Sale] : [The author], [1976] 15 p. : ill. ; 22 cm. Cover title: Trinity Methodist Chapel, Sale, centenary, 1875-1975. [BX8483.S3K56] 77-353216 ISBN 0-9505228-0-5 : £0.40
1. Trinity Methodist Chapel, Sale, Eng. 2. Methodist Church in Sale, Eng. I. Title. II. Title: Trinity Methodist Chapel, Sale, centenary, 1875-1975.

BENJAMIN, Frederick Albert. 287'.1427'87
A facet of life in Keswick, 1757-1975 : Methodism / by Frederick A. Benjamin and O. M. Mathews. [Keswick] : Keswick Southey Street Methodist Church Council, 1975. [2], 33 p. : ill., facsims., map, plans, ports. ; 21 cm. [BX8278.K47B46] 75-327969 ISBN 0-904358-03-8 : £0.50
1. Methodist Church in Keswick, Eng. 2. Keswick, Eng.—Church history. I. Mathews, O. M., joint author. II. Title. III. Title: Methodism.

JONES, George Hawkins, 1905- 287.173
The Methodist tourist guidebook through the 50 States. Prepd. by George H. Jones. Nashville, Pub. in cooperation with the Assn. of Methodist Hist. Socs. by Tidings [1966] 300p. 19cm. Resource Persons--and materials: p. 286-295. [BX8235.J6] 66-22153 2.00
1. Methodist Church in the U. S.—Buildings. 2. Methodist Church in the U. S.—Direct. I. Association of Methodist Historical Societies. II. Title.

MCLEISTER, Ira Fofd. 287.173
History of the Wesleyan Methodist Church of America. Rev. [i. e. 3d] by Roy Stephen Nicholson. Marion, Ind., Wesley Press, 1959. 558p. illus. 24cm. [BX8431.W4M3 1959] 59-2268
1. Wesleyan Methodist Connection (or Church) of America. I. Nicholson, Roy Stephen. II. Title.

MCLEISTER, Ira Ford. 287'.173
Conscience and commitment : the history of the Wesleyan Methodist Church of America / by Ira Ford McLeister, Roy Stephen Nicholson. 4th rev. ed. / edited by Lee M. Haines, Jr., Melvin E. Dieter. Marion, Ind. : Wesley Press, 1976. xviii, 693 p. : ill. ; 22 cm. (Wesleyan history series ; 1) First-3d ed. published under title: History of the Wesleyan Methodist Church of America. Includes index. Bibliography: p. 653-659. [BX8431.W4M3 1976] 76-374759
1. Wesleyan Methodist Connection (or Church) of America—History. I. Nicholson, Roy Stephen, joint author. II. Title. III. Series.

MCLEISTER, Ira Ford. 287'.173
Conscience and commitment : the history of the Wesleyan Methodist Church of America / by Ira Ford McLeister, Roy Stephen Nicholson. 4th rev. ed. / edited by Lee M. Haines, Jr., Melvin E. Dieter. Marion, Ind. : Wesley Press, 1976. xviii, 693 p. : ill. ; 22 cm. (Wesleyan history series ; 1) First-3d ed. published under title: History of the Wesleyan Methodist Church of America. Includes index. Bibliography: p. 653-659. [BX8431.W4M3 1976] 76-374759
1. Wesleyan Methodist Connection (or Church) of America—History. I. Nicholson, Roy Stephen, joint author. II. Title. III. Series.

THOMAS, Paul Westphal. 287'.173
The days of our pilgrimage : the history of the Pilgrim Holiness Church / by Paul Westphal Thomas, Paul William Thomas ; edited by Melvin E. Dieter, Lee M. Haines, Jr. Marion, Ind. : Wesley Press, 1976. xviii, 382 p. : ill. ; 23 cm. (Wesleyan history series ; 2) Includes index. Bibliography: p. 357-361. [BX8795.P453T47] 76-374750
1. Pilgrim Holiness Church—History. I. Thomas, Paul William, joint author. II. Title. III. Series.

HILSON, James Benjamin, 1908- 287.1757
History of the South Carolina Conference of the Wesleyan Methodist Church of America; fifty-five years of Wesleyan Methodism in South Carolina. Introd. by Oliver G. Wilson. [Greenville? Ill., 1950] 308 p. illus., ports. 20 cm. [BX8431.W4H5] 50-2107
1. Wesleyan Methodist Connection (or Church) of America. Conferences. South Carolina. I. Title.

METHODISM'S Aldersgate 287.1942
heritage, by four Wesleyan scholars. Nashville, [1908 Grand Ave., Methodist Evangelistic Materials c.1964] 62p. 19cm. Bibl. 64-17883 .60 pap.,
1. Wesley, John, 1703-1791. 2. Methodism—Addresses, essays, lectures.

BOSSENCE, William Henry, 1935- 287'.1945
Kyabram Methodism / by William Henry Bossence. Melbourne : Hawthorn Press, 1974. ii, 190 p. : plates ; 22 cm. Includes bibliographical references and index. [BX8326.K92B67] 75-315028 ISBN 0-7256-0098-5 : 6.50

1. Methodist Church in Kyabram, Australia. 2. Kyabram, Australia—Church history. I. Title.

PROBERT, John Charles Cripps. 287.44237
Primitive Methodism in Cornwall (a history and sociology) [by] J. C. C. Probert. Redruth (Corn.) [Cornish Methodist Historical Assn., 1966] [4] 128 p. illus. 25 1/2 cm. 7/6 (B 66-17609) Bibliography: p. [4] [BX8277.C6P7] 66-76554
1. Methodist Church in Cornwall, Eng. I. Cornish Methodist Historical Association. II. Title.

HARMON, Nolan Bailey, 1892- 287'.6
Understanding the United Methodist Church, by Nolan B. Harmon. 2d rev. ed. Nashville, Abingdon Press [1974] 176 p. 22 cm. Published in 1955 and 1961 under title: Understanding the Methodist Church. [BX8382.2.H35 1974] 73-20001 ISBN 0-687-43005-4 2.95
1. United Methodist Church (United States) I. Title.

JONES, Charles Edwin, 1932- 287'.6
Perfectionist persuasion: the holiness movement and American Methodism, 1867-1936. Metuchen, N.J., Scarecrow Press, 1974. xx, 242 p. illus. 22 cm. (ATLA monograph series, no. 5) Includes bibliographical references. [BX7990.H6J66] 74-13766 ISBN 0-8108-0747-5
1. Holiness churches—United States. I. Title. II. Series: American Theological Library Association. ATLA monograph series, no. 5.

JONES, Charles Edwin, 1932- 287'.6
Perfectionist persuasion: the holiness movement and American Methodism, 1867-1936. Metuchen, N.J., Scarecrow Press, 1974. xx, 242 p. illus. 22 cm. (ATLA monograph series, no. 5) Includes bibliographical references. [BX7990.H6J66] 74-13766 ISBN 0-8108-0747-5 8.00
1. Holiness churches—United States. I. Title. II. Series: American Theological Library Association. ATLA monograph series, no. 5.

MCGRAW, James, comp. 287'.6
The holiness pulpit. Kansas City, Mo., Beacon Hill Press [1957] 128p. 20cm. [BX7990.H6M2] 57-40549
1. Holiness-Sermons. 2. Sermons, American. I. Title.

MILLER, Raymond Wiley, 1895- 287.6
We funny Methodists; a public relations audit for Methodist laymen, by Raymond W. Miller. Atlanta, Spiritual Life Publishers [1965] xii, 87 p. 20 cm. Bibliographical footnotes. [BX8331.2.M5] 65-24822
1. Methodism. I. Title.

NATIONAL United Methodist Convocation on the Black Church, Atlanta, 1973. 287'.6
Experiences, struggles, and hopes of the Black church / edited by James S. Gadsden. Nashville : Tidings, c1975. x, 149 p. ; 18 cm. Includes bibliographical references. [BR563.N4N37 1973] 75-3633
1. Negro churches—United States—Congresses. I. Gadsden, James S. II. United Methodist Church (United States) III. Title.

RUMBOUGH, Constance Hickey. 287.6
The story and work of the Methodist Church a vacation church school unit for junior boys and girls pupil's book, John Wesley, by McNeer and Ward. Nashville, Methodist Pub. House [c1959] 63p. 23cm. [BX8332] 60-1418
1. Methodist Church. I. Title.

STOKES, Mack B. 287'.6
Major United Methodist beliefs [by] Mack B. Stokes. Rev. and enl. Nashville, Abingdon Press [1971] 128 p. 19 cm. 1956 ed. published under title: Major Methodist beliefs. [BX8332.S685 1971] 77-173955 ISBN 0-687-22923-5
1. Methodist Church—Doctrinal and controversial works. I. Title.

STRAUGHN, James Henry, Bp. 1877- 287.6
Inside Methodist union. Nashville, Methodist Pub. House [1958] 192 p. illus. 24 cm. [BX8383.S77] 58-0519
1. Methodist Church (United States) — Hist. I. Title.

WASHBURN, Paul, 1911- 287'.6
United Methodist primer. Nashville, Tidings [1969] 108 p. illus. 19 cm. Bibliographical references included in "Notes" (p. 75-77) [BX8387.W3] 68-59146
1. United Methodist Church (United States) I. Title.

HISTORY of American Methodism (The) 287.609
3v. Edit. Bd.: Emory Stevens Bucke, gen. ed. [others] Nashville, Abingdon [c.1964] 3v. (various p.) illus., ports., facsims. 24cm. Bibl. 64-10013 27.50 set, bxd.
1. Methodism—Hist. 2. Methodist Church in the U.S.—Hist. 3. Methodist Church (United States)—Hist. I. Bucke, Emory Stevens, ed. II. Title: American Methodism.

ADAMS, John P., 1923- 287'.6'0924 B
At the heart of the whirlwind / John P. Adams. 1st ed. New York : Harper & Row, c1976. xi, 146 p. ; 21 cm. Includes bibliographical references. [BX8495.A414A34 1976] 75-9343 ISBN 0-06-060080-2 : 6.95
1. Adams, John P., 1923- 2. Radicalism—United States. I. Title.

ALLEN, Charles Livingstone, 1913- 287'.6'0924 B
What I have lived by : an autobiography / Charles L. Allen. Old Tappan, N.J. : F. H. Revell Co., c1976. p. cm. [BX8495.A518A33] 76-40914 ISBN 0-8007-0805-9 : 5.95. ISBN 0-8007-0806-7 gift ed. : 9.95
1. Allen, Charles Livingstone, 1913- 2. Methodist Church—Clergy—Biography. 3. Clergy—United States—Biography. I. Title.

CAROTHERS, Merlin R. 287'.6'0924 B
Walking & leaping [by] Merlin R. Carothers. Edited by David Manuel, Jr. Plainfield, N.J., Logos International [1974] ix, 129 p. illus. 21 cm. [BX8495.C29A33] 74-79173 ISBN 0-88270-102-9 2.50 (pbk.).
1. Carothers, Merlin R. I. Title.

CONNOR, Elizabeth, 1884- 287'.6'0924 B
Methodist trail blazer, Philip Gatch, 1751-1834, his life in Maryland, Virginia and Ohio. Cincinnati, Creative Publishers, 1970. xii, 244 p. illus., maps, port. 25 cm. Includes bibliographical references. [BX8495.G35C6] 76-101704 7.00
1. Gatch, Philip, 1751-1834. I. Title.

COVINGTON, Jim. 287'.6'0924 B
Jim, I need you : miracles in the life of a minister / Jim Covington. Philadelphia : Dorrance, [1975] 75 p. ; 22 cm. [BX8495.C64A33] 75-314501 ISBN 0-8059-2134-6 : 4.00
1. Covington, Jim. I. Title.

DABNEY, Virginius, 1901- 287'.6'0924 B
Dry messiah; the life of Bishop Cannon. Westport, Conn., Greenwood Press [1970, c1949] vii, 353, ix p. illus., ports. 23 cm. Bibliography: p. 349-353. [BX8495.C245D2 1970] 73-110825 ISBN 0-8371-3225-8
1. Cannon, James, Bp., 1864-1944. I. Title.

EARLY, Sarah J. W. 287'.6'0924 B
Life and labors of Rev. Jordan W. Early, one of the pioneers of African Methodism in the West and South, by Sarah J. W. Early. Freeport, N.Y., Books for Libraries Press, 1971. 161 p. port. 23 cm. (The Black heritage library collection) "First published 1894." On spine: Rev. Jordan W. Early. [BX8473.E27E27] 72-164386 ISBN 0-8369-8845-0
1. Early, Jordan W., b. 1814. I. Title. II. Series.

EDWARDS, Hal L. 287'.6'0924 B
The gift of wholeness / Hal L. Edwards ; foreword by Keith Miller. Waco, Tex. : Word Books, [1975] 172 p. : ill. ; 23 cm. [BX8495.E32A33] 74-27479 5.95
1. Edwards, Hal L. 2. Christian life—Methodist authors. I. Title.

FISHER, Lee. 287'.6'0924 B
Fire in the hills; the story of Parson Frakes and the Henderson Settlement. Introd. by Billy Graham. Nashville, Abingdon Press [1971] 158 p. illus., ports. 21 cm. [BX8495.F75F54] 73-134247 ISBN 0-687-13080-8 4.95
1. Frakes, Hiram, 1888- 2. Henderson Settlement. I. Title.

FOX, Isadore (Hurlbut) 287.60924 (B)
The immortal chaplain; the story of Rev. George L. Fox, 1900-1943, by Isadore H. Fox. Introd. by Arthur Wentworth Hewitt. [1st ed.] New York, Exposition Press [1965] 84 p. port. 21 cm. [UH23.F68] 65-4883
1. Fox, George Lansing, 1900-1943. I. Title.

FOX, Isadore (Hurlbut) 287.60924
The immortal chaplain; the story of Rev. George L. Fox, 1900-1943, by Isadore H. Fox. Introd. by Arthur Wentworth Hewitt. New York, Exposition [c.1965] 84p. port. 21cm. [UH23.F68] 65-4883 4.00
1. Fox, George Lansing, 1900-1943. I. Title.

HENRY, John Robertson, 1868-1949. 287'.6'0924 (B)
Fifty years on the lower East Side of New York. [n.p.] c1966. 231 p. col. ports. 24 cm. [BX8495.H415A3] 67-8756
I. Title.

LAW, Virginia W. 287.6'0924
As far as I can step [by] Virginia Law. Waco, Tex., Word Books [1970] 157 p. 23 cm. Autobiographical. [BX8495.L36A3 1970] 74-111963 3.95
I. Title.

LEE, Jesse, 1758-1816. 287'.6'0924 B
Memoir of the Rev. Jesse Lee. With extracts from his journals. New York, Arno Press, 1969. viii, 360 p. 23 cm. (Religion in America) Reprint of the 1823 ed. [BX8495.L4A3 1969] 72-83428

MCCLAIN, Dayton E. 287'.6'0924 B
The miracle of two cents; the story of a truly remarkable life, by Dayton E. McClain. With a foreword by Samuel Engle Burr, Jr. Edited by Henry d'Arcy. Linden, Va., Burr Publications, 1968. xii, 48 p. 23 cm. [BX8495.M15A3] 68-58719 2.45
1. Success. I. Title.

MOORE, Arthur James, Bp., 1888- 287'.6'0924 B
Bishop to all peoples [by] Arthur J. Moore. Nashville, Abingdon Press [1973] 144 p. 23 cm. Autobiography. [BX8495.M567A3] 73-6701 ISBN 0-687-03571-6 5.95
1. Moore, Arthur James, Bp., 1888- I. Title.

PONTON, Mungo Melanchthon, 1860- 287'.6'0924 B
Life and times of Henry M. Turner; the antecedent and preliminary history of the life and times of Bishop H. M. Turner, his boyhood, education and public career, and his relation to his associates, colleagues and contemporaries, by M. M. Ponton. New York, Negro Universities Press [1970] 173 p. port. 23 cm. "Originally published in 1917." [E185.97.T94 1970] 70-109363
1. Turner, Henry McNeal, Bp., 1834-1915.

POPE, William Kenneth, 1901- 287'.6'0924 B
A Pope at roam : the confessions of a bishop / by W. Kenneth Pope. [s.l. : s.n.], c1976 (Nashville : Parthenon Press) 176 p. : port. ; 23 cm. [BX8495.P58A35] 76-354196
1. Pope, William Kenneth, 1901- I. Title.

SMITH, Asbury 287.60924
Love abounds; a profile of Harry Denman, a modern disciple, by Asbury Smith, J. Manning Potts. Nashville, Upper Room [1965] 112p. port. 20cm. [BX8495.D44S5] 65-26133 price unreported
1. Denman, Harry, 1893- I. Potts, James Manning, 1895- joint author. II. Title.

SMITH, Charles Merrill. 287'.6'0924 B
Different drums : how a father and son bridged generations with love and understanding / by Charles Merrill Smith ; with a foreword and an afterword by Terrence Lore Smith. 1st ed. New York : Saturday Review Press, [1975] 166 p. ; 22 cm. [BX8495.S575A33 1975] 75-15539 7.95
1. Smith, Charles Merrill. 2. Conflict of generations. I. Smith, Terrence Lore. II. Title.

STANLEY, Walter Edgar, 1894- 287'.6'0924 B
Reaching for the stars. Philadelphia, Dorrance [1972] vii, 95 p. 22 cm. [BX8382.2.Z8S8] 72-75579 ISBN 0-8059-1694-6 3.95
1. Methodist Church—Sermons. 2. Meditations. 3. Sermons, American. I. Title.

TAYLOR, William, Bp., 1821-1902. 287'.6'0924 B
Story of my life. Edited by John Clark Ridpath. Illustrated by Frank Beard. Freeport, N.Y., Books for Libraries Press, 1972 [c1895] 2 v. (770 p.) illus. 28 cm. (The Black heritage library collection) [BX8495.T3A3 1972] 72-3999 ISBN 0-8369-9107-9 59.50
I. Title. II. Series.

URBANTKE, Carl, 1831-1912. 287'.6'0924 B
Texas is the place for me; the autobiography of a German immigrant youth: Carl Urbantke. Translated from the German by Ella Urbantke Fischer. Introd. and index: Robert C. Cotner. Austin, Pemberton Press, 1970. x, 99 p. illus., map, ports. 24 cm. Translation of Aus meinen Lebensfuhrungen. [BX8495.U7A313] 71-28609 5.95
I. Title.

VEGLAHN, Nancy. 287'.6'0924
Peter Cartwright, pioneer circuit rider. New York, Scribner [1968] 192 p. port. 22 cm. Bibliography: p. 189-190. [BX8495.C36V4] 68-28357 3.95
1. Cartwright, Peter, 1785-1872—Juvenile literature.

VERNON, Walter N. 287'.6'0924 B
Forever building; the life and ministry of Paul E. Martin [by] Walter N. Vernon. Foreword by Joseph D. Quillian, Jr. Dallas, Southern Methodist University Press [1973] x, 146 p. illus. 24 cm. Includes bibliographical references. [BX8495.M324V47] 73-88016 ISBN 0-87074-142-X 6.95
1. Martin, Paul Elliott, 1897- I. Title.

VICKERS, John Ashley. 287'.6'0924 B
Thomas Coke: apostle of Methodism [by] John Vickers. Nashville, Abingdon Press [1969] xiv, 394 p. illus., maps (on lining papers), port. 26 cm. (The Wesley Historical Society lecture, no. 30) "A list of Coke's publications": p. 375-382. Bibliography: p. 383-387. [BX8495.C6V5 1969b] 70-14555 14.50
1. Coke, Thomas, Bp., 1747-1814. I. Title. II. Series: Wesley Historical Society. The Wesley Historical Society lectures, no. 30

VINCENT, Leon Henry, 1859-1941. 287'.6'0924 B
John Heyl Vincent; a biographical sketch. Freeport, N.Y., Books for Libraries Press [1970] 319 p. port. 23 cm. Reprint of the 1925 ed. [BX8495.V5V5 1970] 71-124263 ISBN 8-369-54513-
I. Vincent, John Heyl, Bp., 1832-1920.

WRIGHT, Robert Lake. 287'.6'0924 B
The days of our years / Robert Lake Wright. Chattanooga : Wright, [1974] 158 p. : ill. ; 20 cm. [BX8495.W77A33] 74-83937 3.50
1. Wright, Robert Lake. I. Title.

MASER, Frederick E. 287.60973
The dramatic story of early American Methodism. Ed. by the Assn. of Methodist Hist. Socs. Nashville, Abingdon [c.1965] 109p. illus. 19cm. Bibl. [BX8236.M3] 65-29544 .70 pap.,
1. Methodist Church in the U.S.—Hist. I. Association of Methodist Historical Societies. II. Title.

WILSON, Robert Leroy, 1925- 287'.6'0973
Trends on ministerial membership of annual conferences of the United Methodist Church, 1960-1970, by Robert L. Wilson. Dayton, Ohio, Program Council, United Methodist Church [1971] 11 p. 28 cm. (United Methodist Church. Research information bulletin, 71-3) Caption title. [BX8382.2.Z5W55] 72-184854
1. United Methodist Church (United States)—Clergy—Statistics. I. Title. II. Series: United Methodist Church (United States). Program Council. Research information bulletin 71-3

MARTIN, Tenn. First Methodist Church. 287.60976824
A history of First Methodist Church, Martin, Tennessee, 1874-1960. Martin, c1960. 86p. illus. 23cm. [BX8481.M25F5] 61-20100
I. Title.

TUCKER, Frank C. 287.609778
The Methodist Church in Missouri, 1798-1939; a brief history, by Frank C. Tucker. Produced for the Joint Comm. of the Hist. Soc. of the Missouri East & the Missouri West Annual Conf. [Nashville Parthenonory] 1966. 354p. illus. 23cm. Bibl. [BX8248.M8T8] 66-6304 4.50
1. Methodist Church in Missouri—Hist. I. Joint Com-East and the Missouri West Annual Conferences. II. Title.

HILLIARD, Frances McAnally Blackburn. 287'.631'0924 B
Stepping stones to glory : from circuit rider to editor and the years in between : life of David Rice McAnally, 1810-1895 / by Frances McAnally Blackburn Hilliard. Baltimore : Gateway Press, 1975. 139 p. : ill. ; 23 cm. [BX8495.M14H54] 75-18536 10.00
1. McAnally, David Rice, 1810-1895. I. Title.

BARKER, Esther T. 287'.632'0922 B
Shooting Creek was our parish / by Esther T. Barker. Chicago : Adams Press ; Maryville, TN : may be ordered from Barker, c1977. 209 p. : ill. ; 22 cm. [BX6081.S53B37] 77-353941 3.95
1. Shooting Creek-Murphy Parish. 2. Barker, Paul A. 3. Barker, Esther T. I. Title.

CARTWRIGHT, Peter, 1785-1872. 287'.632'0924 B
Autobiography of Peter Cartwright, the backwoods preacher. Edited by W. P. Strickland. Freeport, N.Y., Books for Libraries Press [1972] 525 p. port. 23 cm. Reprint of the 1856 ed. [BX8495.C36A3 1972] 70-38344 ISBN 0-8369-6761-5

GRAVELY, William, 1939- 287'.632'0924 B
Gilbert Haven, Methodist abolitionist; a study in race, religion, and reform, 1850-1880. Edited by the Commission on Archives and History of the United Methodist Church. Nashville, Abingdon Press [1973] 272 p. illus. 24 cm. Bibliography: p. 258-263. [BX8495.H28G7] 72-14179 ISBN 0-687-14702-6 8.95
1. Haven, Gilbert, Bp., 1821-1880. 2. Slavery in the United States. 3. Church and race problems—United States. I. United Methodist Church (United States). Commission on Archives and History.

LACY, Creighton. 287'.632'0924
Frank Mason North: his social and ecumenical mission. Nashville, Abingdon Press [1967] 300 p. port. 24 cm. Bibliographical footnotes. [BX8495.N6L3] 67-14983
1. North, Frank Mason, 1850-1935. I. Title.

MILLER, J. Wesley, 1869-1934. 287'.632'0924 B
"All my days for Jesus"; the diary of the Rev. J. Wesley Miller of Bethel, Vermont. Edited by J. W. Miller, III. Springfield, Mass., 1959. [50] l. 28 cm. [BX8495.M525A3] 75-304150
1. Miller, J. Wesley, 1869-1934. 2. Registers of births, etc.—Bethel, Vt. 3. Bethel, Vt.—History. I. Title.

MORGAN, Clarita Hutchison, 1908- 287'.632'0924 B
Reverend Edward Morgan, 1751?-1844; pioneer local preacher of the Methodist Episcopal Church in southwest Virginia. Ordained by Bishop Francis Asbury, 1801. [Radford? Va.] 1973. iv, 121, 14 p. illus. 29 cm. "One hundred copies ... printed." Includes bibliographical references. [BX8495.M617M67] 74-158969
1. Morgan, Edward, 1751?-1844. 2. Morgan family.

PECK, John Mason, 1789-1858. 287'.632'0924 B
Father Clark. Upper Saddle River, N.J., Literature House [1970] 287 p. 23 cm. Reprint of the 1855 ed. [BX6495.C55P4 1970] 72-104539 ISBN 0-8398-1560-3
1. Clark, John, 1758-1833. I. Title.

WILLIAMS, John Paul, 1900- 287'.632'097442
Social adjustment in Methodism; the adjustment of the Methodist Episcopal Church to the changing needs of its constituency, as illustrated by a survey of the opinions of Methodists living in and near Springfield, Massachusetts. With an introd. by Lewis O. Hartman. New York, Bureau of Publications, Teachers College, Columbia University, 1938. [New York, AMS Press, 1972, i.e. 1973] ix, 131 p. 22 cm. Reprint of the 1938 ed., issued in series: Teachers College, Columbia University. Contributions to education, no. 765. Originally presented as the author's thesis, Columbia. Includes bibliographical references. [BX8331.W52 1972] 76-177639 ISBN 0-404-55765-1 10.00
1. Methodist Episcopal Church. 2. Methodism. I. Title. II. Series: Columbia University. Teachers College. Contributions to education, no. 765.

MILLER, Gene Ramsey 287.633
A history of North Mississippi Methodism, 1820-1900. Nashville, Parthenon Pr. [1966] 158p. illus., maps. 24cm. Study first appeared as a doctoral dissertation in hist. at Miss. State Univ. Bibl. [BX8381.M755M5 1966] 66-6772 3.95
1. Methodist Episcopal Church, South. Conferences. North Mississippi. I. Title.

PALMER'S directory of the Methodist Episcopal Church for [the] Dakota Conference. 287.633
[Highmore, Dakota] v. 20cm. [BX8381.D22P3] 56-30565
1. Methodist Episcopal Church. Conferences. Dakota—Direct. 2. Churches—Dakota. I. Palmer, John G.

PALMER'S directory of the Methodist Episcopal Church for [the] Dakota Conference. 287.633
[Highmore, Dakota] v. 20cm. [BX8381.D22P3] 56-30565
1. Methodist Episcopal Church. Conferences. Dakota—Direct. 2. Churches—Dakota. I. Palmer, John G.

LEARY, William. 287'.6425'3
Methodism in the city of Lincoln from its origin in the eighteenth century to the present day. Lincoln, William Leary, Woodlands, Riseholme, 1969. 79 p. illus., facsim. 23 cm. "First edition limited to 500 copies." Bibliography: p. 79. [BX8278.L48L4] 76-438085 unpriced
1. Lincoln, Eng. 2. Methodism—History. I. Title.

WUNDERLICH, Friedrich, Bp. 287.643
Methodists linking two continents. Nashville, Methodist Pub. House [1959] 143 p. 20 cm. Includes bibliography. [BX8301.W8] 60-5239
1. Methodist Church in Germany — Hist. 2. Methodist Church in Germany — Biog. I. Title.

WUNDERLICH, Friedrich, Bp. 287.643
Methodists linking two continents. Nashville, Methodist Pub. House [dist. by Abingdon Press] [c.1960] 143 p. 20 cm. Bibl. 60-5239 3.00 bds.,
1. Methodist Church in Germany—Hist. 2. Methodist Church in Germany—Biog. I. Title.

TAYLOR, Key W 287.656
Roots, religion, and revival, in the interest of an enterprise of spiritual and organic development of the rural churches, and of rural church extension, and of rural evangelism by the North Carolina Annual Conference, Se. J., the Methodist Church. By Key W. Taylor. [Raleigh, N.C.] Commission on Town and Country Work, North Carolina Annual Conference, Southeastern Jurisdiction, Methodist Church, 1965. 117 p. illus., map, group port. 23 cm. Bibliography: p. 115-116. [BX8248.N8T3] 65-29071
1. Rural churches. 2. Methodist Church (United States) Conferences. North Carolina. I. Title.

METHODIST Church (United States) Provisional Conferences. Southeast Africa. 287.66
Official journal. Cleveland, Transvaal. v. illus. 21 cm. annual. Journals for 1942 are issued by the Southeast Africa Provisional Conference of the Methodist Episcopal Church. [BX8321.M4] 50-48759
I. Title.

BARTELS, Francis Lodowic, 1910- 287.6667
The roots of Ghana Methodism, by F. L. Bartels. Cambridge [Eng.] University Press, 1965. xiii, 368 p. 24 cm. Bibliographical citations included in "References" (p. [324]-349) [BX8322.G5B3] 64-21525
1. Methodist Church in Ghana. I. Title.

BARTELS, Franis Lodowic, 1910- 287.6667
The roots of Ghana Methodism [New York]. Cambridge [c.]1965. xiii, 368p. 24cm. Bibl. [BX8322.G5B3] 64-21525 9.50
1. Methodist Church in Ghana. I. Title.

REID, Alexander James. 287.6667
Congo drumbeat; history of the first half century in the establishment of the Methodist Church among the Atetela of central Congo, by Alexander J. Reid. [1st ed.] New York, World Outlook Press [1964] 158 p. 20 cm. Bibliographical footnotes. [BX8322.C6R4] 64-8145
1. Methodist Church in the Congo. 2. Missions — Congo. I. Title.

ANDERSEN, Arlow William. 287.673
The salt of the earth; a history of Norwegian-Danish Methodism in America. [Evanston, Ill., 1013 Wash. St., Norwegian-Danish Methodist. Hist. Soc., 1963, c.1962] 338p. illus. 23cm. 63-1933 5.00
1. Methodist Church in the U. S. 2. Norwegians in the U. S. 3. Danes in the U. S. 4. Methodist Episcopal Church. Conferences. Norwegian and Danish—Hist. I. Title.

ASSOCIATION of Methodist Historical Societies. 287'.673
Forever beginning, 1766-1966; historical papers presented at American Methodism's bicentennial celebration, Baltimore, Maryland,April 21-24, 1966 Lake Junaluska, N.C., Association of Methodist Historical Societies, 1967. vii, 254 p. 28 cm. Bibliographical footnotes. [BX8235.F6] 67-7706
1. Methodist Church in the U.S.—Hist.—Societies, etc. I. Title.

FELTON, Ralph Almon, 1882- 287'.673
The ministry of the Central Jurisdiction of the Methodist Church / by Ralph A. Felton. Atlanta, Ga. : Gammon Theological Seminary, [1954?] 61 p. ; 23 cm. [BX8435.F44] 75-303641
1. Methodist Church (United States) I. Title.

FERGUSON, Charles Wright, 1901- 287'.6'73
Organizing to beat the Devil; Methodists and the making of America [by] Charles W. Ferguson. [1st ed.] Garden City, N.Y., Doubleday, 1971. x, 466 p. 24 cm. Includes bibliographical references. [BX8235.F44] 73-139018 7.95
1. Methodists in the United States. I. Title.

FINLEY, James Bradley, 1781-1856. 287'.673
Sketches of Western Methodism. New York, Arno Press, 1969. 551 p. port. 23 cm. (Religion in America) Reprint of the 1854 ed. [BX8245.F5 1969] 79-83419
1. Methodist Episcopal Church—History. I. Title.

FOREVER beginning, 1766-1966; 287'.673
historical papers presented at American Methodism's bicentennial celebration, Baltimore, Maryland, April 21-24, 1966. Lake Junaluska, N.C., Assn. of Methodist Hist. Socs., 1967. viii, 254p. 28cm. Bibl. [BX8235.F6] 67-7706 2.50
1. Methodist Church in the U.S.—Hist.—Societies, etc. I. Association of Methodist Historical Societies.

GARRISON, Webb B. 287'.673
Giving wings to a warm heart; the story of benevolence giving in the Methodist Church, 1939-1968, by Webb Garrison. [Evanston, Ill.] Commission on Promotion and Cultivation of the Methodist Church [1968] 118 p. illus. 21 cm. [BX8347.G3] 68-21254
1. Methodist Church—Charities. 2. Methodist Church—Finance. I. Methodist Church (United States). Commission on Promotion and Cultivation. II. Title.

GROSS, John Owen, 1894- 287.673
The beginnings of American Methodism. Nashville, Abingdon Press [c.1961] 142p. Bibl. 61-5193 2.50
1. Methodist Church in the U.S.—Hist. I. Title.

HELLER, Herbert L 1908- 287.673
Indiana Conference of the Methodist Church, 1832-1956. Under the auspices of the Historical Society of the Indiana Conference. [n. p., 1956] 452p. illus., ports., maps. 23cm. [BX8382.I52] 57-3404
1. Methodist Church (United States) Conferences. Indiana. I. Title.

JONES, Kenneth S. 287'.673
Twelve came riding. Kenneth S. Jones, editor. Prepared for the Association of Methodist Historical Societies. Nashville, Abingdon Press [1967] 173 p. maps, ports. 20 cm. Reports of "Saddlebags East", the horseback rides made by twelve Methodist ministers from their pastorates to Baltimore to participate in the celebration of the Bicentennial of American Methodism, April 21-24, 1966. Contents.Contents.—John R. Allan: fifteen years of preparation.—Daniel T. Benedict, Sr.: to both questions "yes".—John L. Camp: pax ecumenicus.—Charles E. Covington: Saddlebags West.—Sidney C. Dillinger: Missouri to Baltimore, 1966.—Tommy Faggart: doctor's orders; go somewhere on a horse.—Woodrow W. Hayzlett: three and a half days, seven horses.—R. Kenneth Keiper: a tale of two preachers, horse and rider.—Sumner L. Martin: "forever beginning".—William W. Richardson: incredible Iowan.—Lester Spencer: take an idea, wrap it in a person.—Dan W. Tohline: two centuries later it's the witness that counts.—Epilogue. [BX8235.J63] 67-11713
1. Methodist Church—Anniversaries, etc. I. Association of Methodist Historical Societies. II. Title.

MATLACK, Lucius C. 287'.6'73
The history of American slavery and Methodism from 1780 to 1849, and History of the Wesleyan Methodist Connection of America. Freeport, N.Y., Books for Libraries Press, 1971. 2 pts. (368, 15 p.) in 1. 23 cm. (The Black heritage library collection) Reprint of the 1849 ed. [E441.M43 1971] 77-138342 ISBN 0-8369-8734-9
1. Wesleyan Methodist Connection (or Church) of America. 2. Slavery and the church—Methodist Episcopal Church. I. Title. II. Title: History of the Wesleyan Methodist Connection of America. III. Series.

METHODIST Church (United States) Dept. of Research and Survey. 287.673
The Methodist Church in urban America, a fact book, by Robert L Wilson, associate director [and] Alan K. Waltz, assistant director. Philadelphia [1962] 94 p. illus. 23 cm. [BX8342.A33] 63-5730
1. Methodist Church (United States) — Membership — Stat. 2. City churches. I. Wilson, Robert Leroy, 1925- . II. Title.

MIDDLETON, William Vernon, 1902- 287'.673
The arm of compassion; Methodism's ministry to the handicapped. [1st ed.] New York, Editorial Dept., Joint Section of Education and Cultivation, Board of Missions of the Methodist Church [1962] 111p. 19cm. Includes bibliography. [BX8347.M5] 62-15059
1. Methodist Church—Charities. 2. Church work with the handicapped. I. Title.

NATIONAL Methodist Student Conference. 287.673
Report. [Nashville] v. illus., ports 22 cm. [BX8207.N43] 51-30984
I. Title.

THE New Christian advocate. 287.673
v.1- Oct. 1956- [Chicago, Methodist Pub. House] v. illus., ports. 20cm. monthly. Supersedes in part the Christian advocate. An official organ of the Methodist Church. [BX8201.N38] 59-31717
1. Methodist Church—Period. 2. Practical theology —Period. I. Methodist Church (United States)

NORWOOD, Frederick Abbott. 287'.673
The story of American Methodism; a history of the United Methodists and their relations [by] Frederick A. Norwood. Nashville, Abingdon Press [1974] 448 p. 23 cm. Includes bibliographical references. [BX8235.N65] 74-10621 ISBN 0-687-39640-9
1. Methodist Church in the United States. I. Title.

NORWOOD, John Nelson, 1879- 287'.673
The schism in the Methodist Episcopal Church, 1844 : a study of slavery and ecclesiastical politics / by John Nelson Norwood Philadelphia : Porcupine Press, 1976. 225 p. : map (on lining papers) ; 22 cm. (Perspectives in American history ; no. 33) Originally presented as the author's thesis, Cornell University. Reprint of the 1923 ed. published by Alfred University, Alfred, N.Y., which was issued as v. 1. of Alfred University studies. Includes index. Bibliography: p. [195]-217. [BX8237.N6 1976] 76-10284 ISBN 0-87991-357-6 lib.bdg. : 12.50
1. Methodist Episcopal Church—History. 2. Methodist Episcopal Church, South—History. 3. Slavery and the church—Methodist Episcopal Church. I. Title. II. Series: Perspectives in American history (Philadelphia) ; no.33. III. Series: Alfred University studies ; v. 1.

ROSE, Delbert R 287.673
A theology of Christian experience; interpreting the historic Wesleyan message, by Delbert R. Rose. [2d ed.] Minneapolis, Bethany Fellowship [1965] 314 p. ports. 22 cm. Revision of thesis, State University of Iowa. Bibliography: p. 307-314. [BX6.N42R6] 65-20789
1. Smith, Joseph H. 2. National Holiness Association. I. Title.

ROSE, Delbert R. 287.673
A theology of Christian experience; interpreting the historic Wesleyan message. Minneapolis, Bethany [c.1965] 314p. ports. 22cm. Bibl. [BX6.N42R6] 65-20789 4.95
1. Smith, Joseph H. 2. National Holiness Association. I. Title.

SHIPPEY, Frederick Alexander, 1908- 287.673
Selected work documents; six research studies. Prepared for the Commission for Study and Action on the Jurisdictional System, the Methodist Church. [Madison? N.J.] c1960. 212 p. illus. 28 cm. [BX8388.S42] 60-29865
1. Methodist Church (United States) — Government. 2. Methodist Church (United States) Jurisdictional Conferences. I. Title.

SWEET, William Warren, 1881-1959, ed. 287.673
The Methodists, a collection of source materials. New York, Cooper Square Publishers, 1964. ix, 800 p. illus., facsims., maps. 22 cm. (His Religion on the American frontier, 1783-1840, v. 4) Bibliography: p. 733-770. [BX8235.S92 1964] 65-1623
1. Methodists in the U.S. — Hist. — Sources. 2. Methodists in the U.S. — Hist. 3. Frontier and pioneer life — U.S. I. Title.

VERNON, Walter N. 287'.673
One in the Lord : a history of ethnic minorities in the South Central Jurisdiction, the United Methodist Church / authors, Walter N. Vernon, Alfredo Nanez, John H. Graham ; editor, Walter N. Vernon. Oklahoma City : Commission on Archives and History, South Central Jurisdiction, United Methodist Church, c1977. vi, 146 p. : ill. ; 23 cm. Includes bibliographical references and index. [BV4468.V47] 77-150215
1. United Methodist Church (United States). South Central Jurisdiction. 2. Church work with minorities—Methodist Church. I. Nanez, Alfredo, joint author. II. Graham, John H., joint author. III. United Methodist Church (United States). South Central Jurisdiction. Commission on Archives and History. IV. Title.

BAKER, George Claude, 1904- 287'.6'74
An introduction to the history of early New

England Methodism 1789-1839, by George Claude Baker, Jr. New York, AMS Press [1969] vii, 145 p. 23 cm. Title on spine: Early New England Methodism. Reprint of the 1941 ed. Issued also as thesis, Columbia University. Bibliography: p. [83]-138. [BX8239.B3 1969] 70-95393
1. Methodist Church in New England. 2. Methodism—Bibliography. I. Title. II. Title: Early New England Methodism.

DORION, Eustache 287'.6'74
Charles Edouard, 1872- ed.
New England Methodism: the story of the New England Convention of Methodist Men, held in Tremont Temple, Boston, Mass., November 11-13, 1914. New York, Methodist Book Concern [1915] 158 p. illus. 21 cm. [BX8239.D6] 15-7265
1. Methodist Church in New England. I. Title.

DORION, Eustache 287'.6'74
Charles Edouard, 1872- ed.
New England Methodism: the story of the New England Convention of Methodist Men, held in Tremont Temple, Boston, Mass., November 11-13, 1914. New York, Methodist Book Concern [1915] 158 p. illus. 21 cm. [BX8239.D6] 15-7265
1. New England Convention of Methodist Men, Boston, 1914. 2. Methodism — Addresses, essays, lectures. 3. Methodist Church in New England. I. Title.

BELL, Raymond Martin, 287.6748
1907-
Early Methodist Church buildings in the Pittsburgh Conference. Washington, Pa., 1950. 7 l. 28 cm. Bibliography: leaf 7. [BX8248.P4B4] 51-34079
1. Methodist Episcopal Church. Conferences. Pittsburgh. 2. Churches—Pennsylvania. I. Title.

SMELTZER, Wallace Guy, 287'.6748
1900-
The history of United Methodism in Western Pennsylvania : the 150th anniversary volume of the Western Pennsylvania Annual Conference of the United Methodist Church / by Wallace Guy Smeltzer. [Pittsburgh? : United Methodist Church] : copies available from Cokesbury Book Store, 1975. 436 p. ; 24 cm. Includes bibliographical references and index. [BX8248.P4S59] 76-351564 9.00
1. Methodist Church in Pennsylvania. I. United Methodist Church (United States) II. Title.

SMELTZER, Wallace Guy, 287.6748
1900-
The Leopold von Ranke manuscripts of Syracuse Conference of the Methodist Church. Nashville, Printed by the Parthenon Press, 1951. 448 p. maps, diagrs. 24 cm. Bibliographical footnotes. [BX8382.S6] 51-3574
1. Methodist Church (United States) Conferences. Pittsburgh. I. Title.

SMELTZER, Wallace Guy, 287'.6748
1900-
Methodism in Western Pennsylvania, 1784-1968. Wallace Guy Smeltzer, editor. [Pittsburgh?, Western Pennsylvania Conference of the Methodist Church; distributed by the Cokesbury Book Store, Pittsburgh] 1969. 923 p. maps. 24 cm. At head of title: An historical records volume. "Norman Carlysle Young, editor of Methodist Protestant ministerial records." "Sources of Methodist history in western Pennsylvania": p. 917-923. [BX8248.P4S6] 70-9601 10.00
1. Methodist Church in Pennsylvania. I. Young, Norman Carlysle, 1928- II. Title.

BELL, Raymond 287'.6748'82
Martin, 1907-
A history of United Methodism in Greene and Washington Counties, Pennsylvania (mainly the Washington District of the Western Pennsylvania Conference) / by Raymond Martin Bell. Washington, Pa. : Bell, 1977. 34 leaves ; 29 cm. [BX8382.2.A42W473] 77-378345
1. United Methodist Church. Western Pennsylvania Conference. Washington District. I. Title: A history of United Methodism in Greene and Washington Counties ...

METHODIST Church (United 287.6749
States) Conferences. New Jersey.
The Methodist trail in New Jersey; one hundred and twenty-five years of Methodism in the New Jersey annual conference, 1836-1961. Frank Bateman Stanger, ed. [Camden, N.J.] 115 N. 5th St., N. J. Annual Conf. of the Methodist Church [dist. N.J. Methodist Conf., c.]1961. 295p. illus. 61-17685 3.00
1. Methodist Church in New Jersey. I. Stanger, Frank Bateman, ed. II. Title.

JACKSON, Charles S. 287'.6749'23
The United Methodist Church in Wayne, New Jersey, 1853-1973, by Charles S. Jackson and F. J. Yetter. [Wayne, N.J., United Methodist Women of the United Methodist Church in Wayne, 1974] 66 p. illus. 22 cm. Cover title: Growing with a community: the story of a Christian congregation. [BX8481.W36U54] 73-93077
1. United Methodist Church in Wayne, New Jersey. I. Yetter, F. J., joint author. II. Title: Growing with a community; the story of a Christioan congregation.

MORROW, Ralph Ernest. 287.675
Northern Methodism and reconstruction. [East Lansing] Michigan State University Press, 1956. ix, 269p. 24cm. Bibliography: p. 251-261. [BX8383.M6] 56-6113
1. Methodist Episcopal Church in the Southern States. 2. Reconstruction. I. Title.

METHODIST Church 287'.6752
(United States). Conferences. Baltimore. American Methodist Historical Society.
American Methodist bicentennial, 1766-1966; an official souvenir book. Souvenir book committee: Edison M. Amos [and others] Baltimore [1966] viii, 128 p. illus., ports. 28 cm. "Officially celebrated in Baltimore, April twenty-first to April twenty-fourth, nineteen hundred sixty-six." [BX8248.M3M4 1966] 76-4726
1. Methodist Church in Maryland. 2. Methodist Church—Anniversaries, etc. I. Amos, Edison M., ed. II. Title.

METHODIST Church 287.67521
(United States) Dept. of Research and Survey.
Let's get acquainted; a survey of Methodism in Delaware and the Eastern Shores of Maryland [by] James H. Davis, director. Philadelphia. National Division of the Board of Missions of the Methodist Church [1965] 61 p. illus., maps. 28 cm. Cover title. [BN8382.P37] 65-8475
1. Methodist Church (United States) Conferences. Peninsula. I. Davis, James Hill, 1931- . II. Title.

LOESCHKE, Naomi. 287'.6752'71
History of Taylor's Chapel, 1770-1968. [History collected and edited by Naomi (Mrs. Donald) Loeschke. Baltimore? 1968] [40] l. illus. 29 cm. Cover title. Includes bibliographical references. [BX8481.B2T38] 77-17019
1. Baltimore. Taylor's Chapel. I. Title.

THOSE incredible 287'.6'75271
Methodists; a history of the Baltimore Conference of the United Methodist Church. Edited by Gordon Pratt Baker. Baltimore, Commission on Archives and History, The Baltimore Conference, 1972. ix, 597 p. maps (on lining papers) 24 cm. Bibliography: p. 512-526. [BX8382.2.A42B357] 72-185862
1. United Methodist Church (United States). Baltimore Conference. I. Baker, Gordon Pratt, ed. II. United Methodist Church (United States). Baltimore Conference. Commission on Archives and History.

BROWN, Lillian Brooks. 287'.6753
A living centennial, commemorating the one hundredth anniversary of Metropolitan Memorial United Methodist Church. Washington [Printed by Judd & Detweiler] 1969. 88 p. illus., facsims., ports. 32 cm. [BX8481.W3M463] 78-76377
1. Washington, D.C. Metropolitan Memorial United Methodist Church. I. Title.

CALKIN, Homer L. 287'.6753
Castings from the Foundry mold; a history of Foundry Church, Washington, D.C., 1814-1964, by Homer L. Calkin. [Nashville, Parthenon Press, 1968] 377 p. illus. 24 cm. Includes bibliographical references. [BX8481.W3F66] 68-2953
1. Washington, D.C. ?Foundry Methodist Church. I. Title.

CALKIN, Homer L 287.6753
Chronology and historical narratives of Foundry's 150 years, 1814-1964, by Homer L. Calkin. [Washington, 1965] 1 v. (unpaged) 24 cm. "Issued as supplements to the church bulletin during the twenty-two weeks of Foundry's sesquicentennial celebration [Nov. 22, 1964-Apr. 15, 1965]" [BX8481.W3F67] 66=86335
1. Washington, D.C. Foundry Methodist Church. I. Title.

HISTORY, Mount Vernon 287'.6753
Place United Methodist Church, 1850-1976 / Royce L. Thompson, editor. Washington : The Church, 1977. 136 p. : ill. ; 23 cm. Bibliography: p. 127-136. [BX8481.W325H57] 77-74710
1. Mount Vernon Place United Methodist Church. I. Thompson, Royce L.

WHITE, Frank 287.675454
Stonewall, 1877-1961.
Three score and ten, a history of the Highland Avenue Methodist Church [by] Frank S. White. Fairmont, W. Va. [1964] ix, 64 p. illus., facsim., ports. 28 cm. [BX8481.F3H5] 64-63632
1. Fairmont, W. Va. Highland Avenue Methodist Church. I. Title.

WASHBURN, Charles 287.675457
Henry, 1875-1956.
History of the New Bethel Methodist Church, Good Hope, W. Va.; June 1, 1956. [Lost Creek, W. Va., New Bethel Methodist Church, 1960] 109 p. illus. 24 cm. [BX8481.N34W3] 60-10794
1. New Bethel Methodist Church, Harrison Co., W. Va. I. Title.

SWEET, William Warren, 287.6755
1881-
Virginia Methodism, a history. Illus. by Erle Prior. Richmond, Whittet & Shepperson [1955] 427p. illus. 21cm. [BX8248.V8S9] 55-3600
1. Methodist Church in Virginia. I. Title.

GEORGE, Lawrence W 287.675516
This is Tangier Island and its church [by] L. W. George. [Martinsville, Va.] Radio Fellowship [1965] 51 p. illus., port. 22 cm. 66-5536
1. Tangier, Va. Swain Memorial Methodist Church. I. Title.

CHATTANOOGA. 287'.6755'296
Centenary Methodist Church.
Centenary ... the story of a church [by] the Historical Committee: E. E. Wiley, Jr. [and others], Mary Thomas Peacock, Chairman. Chattanooga, Tenn., 1962. 100p. illus. 24cm. Includes bibliography. [BX8481.C42C4] 62-13034
I. Title.

HEDMAN, Kathryn 287'.6755'296
Pierpoint, 1916-
Washington Street United Methodist Church, Alexandria, Virginia : reflections, 1849-1974 / researcher and editor, Kathryn Pierpoint Hedman. [Alexandria? Va. : Washington Street United Methodist Church?, 1974] 348 p. : ill. ; 23 cm. [BX8481.A53W373] 75-301769
1. Washington Street United Methodist Church. 2. Alexandria, Va.—Biography.

JEWELL, Marianne H. 287'.6755'293
Dulin from saddlebags to satellites, a story of faith and service [by] Marianne H. Jewell. Falls Church, Va., Dulin United Methodist Church, 1969. viii, 180 p. illus., ports. 24 cm. Bibliography: p. 179-180. [BX8481.F33D83] 79-94689
1. Falls Church, Va. Dulin United Methodist Church. I. Title.

MICHIGAN City, Ind. 287'.6755'296
First Methodist Church.
One hundred twenty-fifth anniversary, First Methodist Church, Michigan City, Indiana, 1835-1960. [Michigan City, 1960] 57p. illus. 22cm. [BX8481.M5F5] 61-39207
I. Title.

PORTER, Elizabeth 287'.6755'296
Gamble.
History of the Wetumpka Methodist Church, prepared for the celebration of the centennial of the erection of the church building, 1854-1954. [By] Elizabeth Gamble Porter [and] Madora Lancaster Smith. Wetumpka, Ala., 1954. 56p. 23cm. [BX8481.W48P6] 55-18973
1. Wetumpka. Ala. Methodist Church. I. Smith, Madora Lancaster, joint author. II. Title.

STUKENBROEKER, Fern 287'.6755'296
C.
A watermelon for God : a history of Trinity United Methodist Church, Alexandria, Virginia, 1774-1974 / by Fern C. Stukenbroeker. Alexandria, Va. : Stukenbroeker, 1974. xiii, 268 p. : ill. ; 24 cm. Bibliography: p. 261-268. [BX8481.A53T747] 74-195119
1. Trinity United Methodist Church, Alexandria, Va. I. Title.

WHITE, Edith Denny. 287.6755451
The elect ladies of Centenary; the story of the organization and development of the woman's work in Centenary Methodist Church, Richmond, Virginia, through one hundred and fifty years, 1810-1960, by Edith Denny White (Mrs. Roscoe M. White) [Richmond? 1964] ix, 154 p. 23 cm. [BX8481.R45C385] 64-24099
1. Richmond. Centenary Methodist Church. 2. Women in church work — Richmond. I. Title.

STEVENSON, Arthur 287'.6755'51
Linwood, 1891-
Native Methodist preachers of Norfolk and Princess Anne Counties, Virginia / by Arthur L. Stevenson. Brevard, N.C. : Stevenson, 1975. 49 p. ; 22 cm. (His Native Methodist preacher series ; 6th) [BX8491.S69] 76-351183
1. Methodist Church in Norfolk Co., Va.—Clergy. 2. Methodist Church in Princess Anne Co., Va.—Clergy. 3. Norfolk Co., Va.—Biography. 4. Princess Anne Co., Va.—Biography. I. Title: Native Methodist preachers of Norfolk and Princess Anne Counties ...

BLUNT, Ruth H. 287'.6755'671
A history of Memorial United Methodist Church, founded 1884, Lynchburg, Virginia / written for our Nation's Bicentennial celebration, 1976, by Ruth H. Blunt, Dorothy Hughes, Mary Hight Creasy. Appomattox, Va. : Times Virginian Print. Corp., 1975. 82 p. : ill. ; 27 cm. Cover title: Memorial Methodist Church, 1884-1975, Lynchburg, Virginia. Includes bibliographies. [BX8481.L88M453] 75-330976
1. Memorial United Methodist Church, Lynchburg, Va. 2. Lynchburg, Va.—Biography. I. Hughes, Dorothy, 1895- joint author. II. Creasy, Mary Hight, joint author. III. Title.

ARRINGTON, Mary 287'.6755'922
Marie Koontz.
A white church on a high hill; a historical sketch of Mountain Valley Evangelical United Brethren Church, 1833-1970. [Harrisonburg, Va., Printed at Park View Press, 1970] xxi, 307 p. illus., ports. 23 cm. [BX8481.M78A9] 73-21638
1. Mountain Valley United Methodist Church. I. Title.

MACALLISTER, Dale 287'.6755'922
E., 1947-
Donovan Memorial Church in the Singers Glen community : an historical sketch, 1875-1975, the Donovan Memorial United Methodist Church, Singers Glen, Virginia / Dale E. MacAllister. [s.l. : s.n.], c1976 (Timberville, Va. : Coffman Print. and Photography) xi, 287 p. : ill. ; 23 cm. Includes bibliographical references and index. [BX8481.S573M3] 76-374926
1. Donovan Memorial United Methodist Church, Singers Glen, Va. I. Title.

FITTS, William 287'.6756'88
Thrower, 1897-
A history of Central Methodist Church, Asheville, North Carolina, 1837-1967 [by] William T. Fitts, Jr. Asheville, N.C. [1968] viii, 95 p. illus., ports. 24 cm. [BX8481.A8F5] 68-7608
1. Asheville, N.C. Central Methodist Church. I. Title.

OWEN, Fred Colley. 287'.6757'33
St. Paul United Methodist Church, Ninety Six, South Carolina: church history, 1875-1972. Greenwood, S.C., Drinkard Print. Co. [1974] 61 p. illus. 24 cm. Cover title: History of St. Paul United Methodist Church, 1875-1972. [BX8481.N55S35] 74-172782
1. St. Paul United Methodist Church, Ninety Six, S.C.

HUFF, Archie Vernon, 287'.6757'71
1937-
Tried by fire : Washington Street United Methodist Church, Columbia, South Carolina / Archie Vernon Huff, Jr. [Greenville? S.C.] : Huff, [1975] xii, 163 p. : ill. ; 24 cm. Includes index. Bibliography: p. 133-136. [BX8481.C72W373] 75-314986
1. Washington Street United Methodist Church, Columbia, S.C. I. Title.

A Time to keep; 287'.6759'23
history of the First United Methodist Church of Oviedo, Florida, 1873-1973. [Union Park, Fla., University Print., 1973] 72 p. illus. 23 cm. [BX8481.O9T55] 74-155316
1. First United Methodist Church of Oviedo.

ALDRICH, Guy V 287.675963
Seven miles out; the story of Pasadena Community Church, St. Petersburg, Florida, 1924-1960 [by] Guy V. Aldrich. [Tampa, Fla. [1965?] [BX8481.S315P32] 66-6973
1. St. Petersburg, Fla. Pasadena Community Church. I. Title.

AGNEW, Theodore L. 287'.676
The South Central Jurisdiction, 1939-1972; a brief history and an interpretation, by Theodore L. Agnew. Oklahoma City, Commission on Archives and History, South Central Jurisdiction, United Methodist Church [1973] 96 p. 23 cm. [BX8382.2.A42S682] 73-180924
1. United Methodist Church (United States). South Central Jurisdiction. I. Title.

POSEY, Walter Brownlow, 287'.676
1900-
The development of Methodism in the old Southwest, 1783-1824. Philadelphia, Porcupine Press, 1974. 151 p. illus. 22 cm. (Perspectives in American history, no. 19) Reprint of the 1933 ed. published by Weatherford Print. Co., Tuscaloosa, Ala., which was also issued as the author's thesis, Vanderbilt University.

Bibliography: p. [130]-144. [BX8241.P67 1974] 73-18408 ISBN 0-87991-339-8 10.00
1. Methodist Church in the Old Southwest—History. I. Title. II. Series: Perspectives in American history (Philadelphia), no. 19.

FIRST United 287'.6761'781
Methodist Church, Birmingham, Ala.
Century of worship, 1872-1972; the story of a century of service to God and man. [Birmingham, Ala., 1972] 126 p. illus. 21 cm. [BX8481.B62F56] 72-92910
1. First United Methodist Church, Birmingham, Ala. I. Title.

HAMILTON, Alfred P 287.6762
Galloway Memorial Methodist Church, 1836-1956; a history compiled from very scanty records of private individuals, archives from the Methodist Room, Milisaps College, general minutes of the church at large and Mississippi conference journals, minutes of the Woman's Society of Christian Service, and of the official board of the church. [Nashville, Parthenon, 1956] 240p. illus. 23cm. [BX8481.J32G33] 56-34887
1. Jackson, Miss. Galloway Memorial Methodist Church. I. Title.

JONES, William Burwell. 287.6762
Methodism in the Missipi Conference 1870-1894 Jackson, Hawkins Foundation, Mississippi Conference Historical Society [1951] 508 p. 20 cm. "Written at the request of the Conference, and continuing the history of the Mississippi Conference as written by John G. Jones and J. B. Cain." [BX8248.M7J64] 51-6650
1. Methodist Episcopal Church, South, in Mississippi. 2. Methodism—Biog. I. Title.

BAILEY, Pearle 287'.6762'82
Provine, 1881-1970.
The history of the Coffeeville Methodist Church, 1824-1970; the community and people who contributed to our start and growth and the beginning of Methodism in the United States and the South, with connecting links of state and local history, compiled by Pearle Provine Bailey. [Coffeeville? Miss., 1970] xiii, 190 p. illus., ports. 24 cm. Bibliography: p. 190. [BX8481.C64B3] 70-24079
1. Coffeeville United Methodist Church. I. Title.

GRIMES, Lewis Howard, 287.6764
1915-
Cloud of witnesses; a history of First Methodist Church, Houston, Texas, by Lewis Howard Grimes assisted by the First Methodist Historical Committee: L. E. Brazelton, Sr., chairman [and others] Foreword by A. Frank Smith. Houston, First Methodist Church, 1951. 206 p. 21 cm. [BX8481.H8F5] 52-17000
1. Houston, Tex. First Methodist Church. I. Title.

NAIL, Olin Webster, 287.6764
1890- ed.
History of Texas Methodism, 1900-1960. Austin, Tex., Capital Print. Co., c1961. 526p. illus. 24cm. [BX8248.T4N28] 61-45728
1. Methodist Church in Texas. I. Title. II. Title: Texas Methodism, 1900-1960.

WEINERT, Willie Mae. 287.6764
Methodism in Seguin, 1841-1951. [Seguin, Tex.] First Methodist Church of Seguin, 1951. 67p. illus. 23cm. [BX8481.S45W4] 56-26549
1. Seguin, Tex. First Methodist Church. 2. Methodist Church in Texas. I. Title.

CRENSHAW, Rosa 287'.6764'145
Dieu.
Cornerstone; a history of Beaumont and Methodism, 1840-1968, by Rosa Dieu Crenshaw and W. W. Ward. [Special limited ed.] Beaumont, Tex., First Methodist Church Historical Committee [1968] xv, 269 p. illus., facsims., plan, ports. 24 cm. "First written history of the First Methodist Church, prepared for the 1968 cornerstone." Bibliographical references included in "Authors' notes" (p. 250-253) [BX8481.B35F53] 68-59594 5.85
1. Beaumont, Tex. First Methodist Church. I. Ward, Wendell Whittier, 1894- joint author. II. Title.

CLOUSE, Joe V. 287'.6764'197
The history of Maud United Methodist Church, 1874-1974. Written by Joe V. Clouse and F. E. Cooley. [Maud, Tex., 1974] 1 v. (unpaged) illus. 28 cm. [BX8481.M3M38] 74-83517
1. Maud United Methodist Church. 2. Maud, Tex.—Biography. I. Cooley, Floyd E., joint author. II. Title.

CLOUSE, Joe V. 287'.6764'276
The history of Cheatham Memorial United Methodist Church, Edgewood, Texas, by Joe V. Clouse. Grand Saline, Tex., A. Roberson, Printer, 1972. 71 p. illus. 28 cm. Includes bibliographical references. [BX8481.E3C58] 72-78521
1. Cheatham Memorial United Methodist Church. I. Title.

JOHNSON, Doris Miller. 287.676428
Golden prologue to the future; a history of the Highland Park Methodist Church. [Dallas? 1966] 143 p. illus., ports. 24 cm. Bibliography: p. 136-139. [BX8481.D23H54] 66-80435
1. Dallas. Highland Park Methodist Church. I. Title.

MISCH, Fannie B. 287.676686
Methodist trails to First Methodist Church, Tulsa, Oklahoma [by] Mrs. J. O. Misch. [Tulsa, Okla., 546 N. Santa Fe. Author c.1961] 141 p. illus. Bibl. 61-59842 3.00 pap.,
1. Tulsa, Okla, First Methodist Church. I. Title.

CARTER, Deane G., 287'.6767'14
1894-
Methodists in Fayetteville, 1832-1968, by Deane G. Carter. Fayetteville, Ark., Central United Methodist Church [1968] iv, 127 p. illus. 28 cm. "The Central United Methodist Church through one hundred thirty-six years; Wiggins, Trinity, Sequoyah; and notes on St. James Church, Western Methodist Assembly, and Wesley Foundation." Bibliography: p. 119. [BX8249.F3C3] 68-7971
1. Methodist Church in Fayetteville, Ark. I. Title.

CARTER, Cullen Tuller, 287.6768
1880- ed.
History of Methodist churches and institutions in middle Tennessee, 1787-1956. Nashville, Parthenon Press [1956] 443p. illus. 24cm. [BX8248.T2C3] 56-28137
1. Methodist Church in Tennessee. 2. Churches—Tennessee. 3. Methodist Church (United States) Conferences. Tennessee. 4. Methodist Episcopal Church, South. Conferences. Tennessee. I. Title. II. Title: Methodist churches and institutions in middle Tennessee, 1787-1956.

WHITTINGTON, Earle 287.676819
Ligon.
St. John's Methodist Church: centennial history, 1859-1959. Memphis [1960] 95 p. illus. 24 cm. [BX8481.M35S3] 60-13840
1. Memphis. St. John's Methodist Church. I. Title.

SPRAKER, Nettie L. 287'.6768'885
The story of First Methodist Church, Maryville, Tennessee; from the saddle-bag trail to the runway of today, 1815-1966, by Nettie L. Spraker. [Maryville? Tenn.] 1967. 54 p. illus., ports. 23 cm. Bibliography: p. 54. [BX8481.M28F5] 73-21366
1. Maryville, Tenn. First Methodist Church. I. Title.

DORRIS, Jonathan Truman, 287.6769
1883-
Methodism and the home church; the First Methodist Church, Richmond, Kentucky. An anniversary publication by Jonathan Truman Dorris and Maud Weaver Dorris. Nashville, Printed for the authors by the Methodist Pub. House, 1952. 128 p. illus. 20 cm. [BX8481.R46D6] 52-30633
1. Richmond, Ky. first Methodist Church. I. Title.

HUNSCHER, Helen Alvina, 287.6771
1904-
Gates Mills and a history of its village church. Gates Mills, Ohio, Priv. published for St. Christopher's-by-the-River [1955] 123p. illus. 23cm. [BX5980.G37S34] 55-11300
1. Gates Mills, Ohio. St. Christopher's-by-the-River (Church) 2. Gates Mills, Ohio. Gates Mills Methodist Episcopal Church. I. Title.

CUYAHOGA Falls, 287'.6771'36
Ohio. First United Methodist Church. History and Records Committee.
The history of the First United Methodist Church of Cuyahoga Falls, Ohio, 1830-1969. [Cuyahoga Falls, Ohio, F. W. Orth Co., 1968] 265 p. illus., facsims., ports. 23 cm. On spine: First United Methodist Church history. [BX8481.C9F5] 68-59189 4.80
1. Cuyahoga Falls, Ohio. First United Methodist Church. I. Title.

SMITH, Jean Herron. 287'.6771'72
Four churches, one church / by Jean Herron Smith. [s.l. : s.n.], c1975 (Miamisburg, Ohio : Miamisburg News) 72, ix p. : ill. ; 22 cm. [BX8481.M48S63] 75-32342
1. St. James United Methodist Church, Miamisburg, Ohio. I. Title.

STOUT, Percy Ray, 287'.677175
1890-
The first one hundred and fifty years of the First United Methodist Church, Hamilton, Ohio, 1819-1969. Compiled and illustrated by Percy Ray Stout. Edited by Paul F. Erwin. [Cincinnati, Lithographed by Brinker, inc.] 1969 [c1970] 146 p. illus., maps, ports. 24 cm. Bibliography: p. 146. [BX8481.H28F5] 74-107745
1. Hamilton, Ohio. First United Methodist Church. I. Title.

GILMORE, G. Don 287.677178
In the midst; how the power of Christ transformed the life of a church. Grand Rapids, Mich., Eerdmans [c.1962] 100p. 21cm. 62-21365 2.50
1. Cincinnati, Groesbeck Methodist Church. 2. Christian life. I. Title.

HERRICK, Horace N 1847- 287.6772
1915.
A history of the North Indiana Conference of the Methodist Episcopal Church, from its organization in 1844 to the present, by H. N. Herrick and William Warren Sweet. Indianapolis, W. K. Stewart Co., 1917-[57] 2v. illus., ports., maps. 24cm. Vol. 2 by F. A. Norwood has title: History of the North Indiana Conference, 1917-1956. Vol. 2 published by the Conference Historical Society, Muncie, Ind. Bibliographical footnotes. [BX8382.N62] 17-11449
1. Methodist Church (United States) Conferences. North Indiana. 2. Methodist Episcopal Church. Conferences. North Indiana. I. Sweet, William Warren, 1881- joint author. II. Norwood, Frederick Abbott. III. Title.

MELTON, J. Gordon. 287'.6'773
Log cabins to steeples; the complete story of the United Methodist way in Illinois, including all constituent elements of the United Methodist Church, by J. Gordon Melton. [Chicago] Commissions on Archives and History, Northern, Central, and Southern Illinois Conferences [1974] xxvii, 417 p. illus. 24 cm. Bibliography: p. 372-384. [BX8248.I3M37] 74-173644 6.95
1. Methodist Church in Illinois. I. Title.

SCOTT, Margaret 287'.6775'75
Helen.
Glory to Thy name; a story of a church. Richland Center, Wis., Richland County Publishers, 1973. 110, xiv p. illus. 26 cm. Bibliography: p. 107-110. [BX8481.R43T747] 73-76879
1. Trinity United Methodist Church, Richland Center, Wis. 2. Richland Center, Wis.—Biography. I. Title.

MUELLER, Erhart. 287'.6775'76
The history of the Salem Church of Honey Creek; 1844-1946, Salem Evangelical Church, 1946-1969, Salem Evangelical United Brethren Church, 1969, Salem United Methodist Church. [Honey Creek? Wis., 1969?] 153 p. illus. 22 cm. On cover: Salem Church, 1844-1969. [BX8481.H77S35] 74-152494
1. Salem United Methodist Church, Honey Creek, Wis. 2. Honey Creek, Wis.—Biography. I. Title.

STEPHENS, Frank 287.677829
Fletcher.
History of the Missouri Methodist Church of Columbia, Missouri, and its Columbia predecessors [by] Frank F. Stephens. Nashville, Parthenon Press [1965] 237 p. illus., ports. 23 cm. Bibliographical footnotes. [BX8481.C715M5] 65-63217
1. Columbia, Mo. Missouri Methodist Church. I. Title.

HAIR, Mary Scott. 287.6778'794
O happy day; a history of the Methodist Church at Hurley, Missouri. [Hurley ? Mo., 1966] 64 p. illus. 24 cm. [BX8481.H87H3] 67-1235
1. Hurley, Mo. Methodist Church. I. Title.

TUCKER, Frank C 287.677896
Old McKendree Chapel. Cape Girardeau, Mo., Missourian Litho and Print. Co. [1959] 54 p. illus. 23 cm. [BX8481.C21M3] 59-3098
1. McKendree Chapel, Cape Girardeau Co., Mo. I. Title.

HOLTER, Don W., 1905- 287'.6781
Fire on the prairie; Methodism in the history of Kansas [by] Don W. Holter. Designed and illustrated by Dolores Gwinn. [Kansas City, Mo., Editorial Board of the Kansas Methodist History, 1969] xi, 298 p. illus., ports. 16 x 24 cm. Bibliography: p. 281-290. [BX8248.K2H6] 77-77521
1. Methodist Church in Kansas. 2. Kansas—History. I. Title.

HOWARD, Edith V. 287'.6781'65
The German Methodist Episcopal Church of Lawrence, Kansas; a history of the church, 1859-1918, and biographical sketches of many who served as ministers and layman [sic] Also an account of the ladies organization, the Frauenverein, and of the Old Friends Club, by Edith V. Howard. Topeka, Kan. [1974] iii, 35 l. illus. 28 cm. [BX8481.L28G474] 74-171916
1. German Methodist Episcopal Church, Lawrence, Kan. 2. Lawrence, Kan.—Biography.

HOWELL, Erle 287.679
Methodism in the Northwest. Ed. by Chapin D. Foster. Nashville, Parthenon Pr., Printers, 1966. 468p. illus., ports. 24cm. Bibl. [BX8245.H6] 66-6619 5.50
1. Methodist Church in the Pacific Northwest. I. Foster, Chapin D., ed. II. Title.
Available from the Methodist Historical Society, Wesley Gardens, Des Moines, Washington 98016.

LOOFBOUROW, Leonidas 287.6794
Latimer, 1877-
Cross in the sunset, the development of Methodism in the California-Nevada Annual Conference of the Methodist Church and of its predecessors, with roster of all members of the conference. San Francisco, Historical Society of the California-Nevada Annual Conference of the Methodist Church [1961-66, v. 1, 1966] 2 v. illus., maps, ports. 24 cm. Bibliographical footnotes. [BX8382.C3L6] 61-41337
1. Methodist Church (United States) Conferences. California-Nevada — Hist. I. Title.

LOOFBOUROW, Leonidas 287.6794
Latimer, 1877-
In search of God's gold; a story of continued Christian pioneering in California. San Francisco, Published under the auspices of the Historical Society of the California Nevada Annual Conference of the Methodist Church, and cooperation with the College of the Pacific, Stockton, Calif., 1950. 313 p. illus., ports. 23 cm. [BX8248.C2L6] 50-3472
1. Methodist Church in California. I. Title.

NORMAN, Albert E 287.679466
A steeple among the oaks, a centennial history of the First Methodist Church, Oakland, California, 1862-1962, by Albert E. Norman. Oakland, Calif., 1962. 73 p. illus., ports. 27 cm. Errata slip mounted on first leaf. [BX8481.O3F5] 64-5422
1. Oakland, Calif. First Methodist Church. I. Title.

JERVEY, Edward Drewry, 287.67949
1929-
The history of Methodism in Southern California and Arizona. Nashville, Printed by the Parthenon Press for the Historical Society of the Southern California-Arizona Conference [1960] 247p. illus. 24cm. Includes bibliography. [BX8248.C2J4 1960] 60-33247
1. Issued in 1958 in microfilm form, as thesis, Boston University. 2. Methodist Church in California, Southern. 3. Methodist Church in Arizona. I. Title. II. Title: Methodism in southern California and Arizona.

PIERCE, Alfred Mann, 287.67949
1874-
A history of Methodism in Georgia, February 5, 1736-June 24, 1955. [Atlanta] North Georgia Conference Historical Society [1956] 345p. illus. 24cm. [BX8248.G4P5] 56-46848
1. Methodist Church in Georgia. I. Title.

PIERCE, Alfred Mann, 287.67949
1874-
A history of Methodism in Georgia, February 5, 1736-June 24, 1955 [Atlanta] North Georgia Conference Historical Society [1956] 345p. illus. 24cm. [BX8248.G4P5] 56-46848
1. Methodist Church in Georgia. I. Title.

VERSTEEG, John Marinus, 287.67949
1888- ed.
Methodism: Ohio Area (1812-1962) John D. Green, research associate. [Cincinnati!] Ohio Area Sesquicentennial Committee [1962] 372 p. illus. 24 cm. [BX8248.O3V4] 62-51530
1. Methodist Church in Ohio. I. Title.

YARNES, Thomas David, 287.67949
1883-1957.
A history of Oregon Methodism. Edited by Harvey E. Tobie. [n.p.] Printed by the Parthenon Press for the Oregon Methodist Conference Historical Society [196-?] 352 p. 24 cm. [BX8248.O7Y3] 62-50602
1. Methodist Church in Oregon. I. Title.

OLIPHANT, James 287'.6795'37
Orin, 1894-
The First United Methodist Church of Salem, Oregon : a story of the growth and transition of the oldest Methodist church west of the Rocky Mountains / by J. Orin Oliphant and May C. Oliphant. Salem, Or. : [s.n.], 1974. 152 p. : ill. ; 22 cm. Includes bibliographical references. [BX8481.S34F576] 74-30923
1. First United Methodist Church, Salem, Or. I. Oliphant, May C., joint author. II. Title.

STEPHENSON, Frank W. 287'.7'0924
For such a time: Bishop James H. Straughn,

A.B., B.S.T., D.D., LL.D.; a brief account of Bishop Straughn's life and his part in bringing the Methodist Protestant Church into the Methodist Church, by Frank W. Stephenson. [Grand Rapids? 1967] 64 p. illus., ports. 21 cm. [BX8495.S79S7] 67-8469
1. Straughn, James Henry, Bp., 1877- 2. Methodist Church (United States)—History. I. Title.

AFRICAN Methodist Episcopal Church. 287.8
Doctrine and discipline of the African Methodist Episcopal Church, published by order of the General Conference held in Chicago, Illinois, May 1952. Edited and approved by the Compilation Committee: D. Ormonde Walker, chairman [and others. 35th rev. ed. Nashville? 1953, c1952] viii, 581p. 16cm. [BX8448.A3 1953] 53-30052
1. African Methodist Episcopal Church—Doctrinal and controversial works. 2. African Methodist Episcopal Church—Discipline. I. Title.

AFRICAN Methodist Episcopal Zion Church. Christian Education Dept. 287.8
Report. Chicago. v. 23 cm. quadrennial. [LC576.A43] 50-55500
1. African Methodist Episcopal Zion Church—Education. I. Title.

ALLEN, Richard, Bp. 287.8
The life experience and Gospel labors of the Rt. Rev. Richard Allen, to which is annexed the rise and progress of the African Methodist Episcopal Church in the United States of America. Containing a narrative of the yellow fever in the year of Our Lord 1793. With an address to the people of color in the United States. Written by himself and published by his request. With an introd. by George A. Singleton. Nashville, Abingdon Press [c.1960] 93p. front. 20cm. 60-6927 1.50 bds.,
1. African Methodist Episcopal Church—Hist. I. Title.

ALLEN, Richard, Bp., 1760-1831. 287.8
The life experience and Gospel labors of the Rt. Rev. Richard Allen, to which is annexed the rise and progress of the African Methodist Edpiscopal Church in the United States of America. Containing a narrative of the yellow fever in the year of Our Lord 1793. With an address to the people of color of the United States. Written by himself and published by his request. With an introd. by George A. Singleton. New York, Abingdon Press [1960] 93p. illus. 20cm. Republished in honor of the biocentennial of the author's birth. [BX8449.A6A3 1960] 60-6927
1. African Methodist Episcopal Church—Hist. I. Title.

BRADLEY, David Henry. 287.8
A history of the A. M. E. Zion Church. Nashville, Parthenon Press [1956- v. 24cm. [BX8453.B7] 56-26188
1. African Methodist Episcopal Zion Church—Hist. I. Title.

SINGLETON, George A 287.8
The romance of African Methodism; a study of the African Methodist Episcopal Church. New York, Exposition Press [1952] 251 p. illus. 22 cm. [BX8443.S45] 51-13284
1. African Methodist Episcopal Church—Hist. I. Title.

TOWNSEND, Vince M 1869- 287.8
Fifty-four years of African Methodism; reflections of a presiding elder on the law and doctrine of the African Methodist Episcopal Church. [1st ed.] New York, Exposition Press [1953] 158p. 21cm. [BX8447.T68] 53-11271
1. African Methodist Episcopal Church—Government. 2. African Methodist Episcopal Church—Doctrinal and controversial works. I. Title.

AFRICAN Methodist Episcopal Zion Church. 287.806273
Message of the bishops... to the General Conference. Chicago. v. 23 cm. quadrennial. [BX8451.A35] 51-17500
I. Title.

RICHARDSON, Harry Van Buren. 287'.8'09
Dark salvation : the story of Methodism as it developed among Blacks in America / Harry V. Richardson. 1st ed. Garden City, N.Y. : Anchor Press, 1976. viii, 324 p. ; 22 cm. (C. Eric Lincoln series on Black religion) Includes bibliographical references and index. [BX8435.R5] 76-3009 ISBN 0-385-00245-9 : 10.00
1. Methodist Church in the United States. 2. Afro-American Methodists. I. Title. II. Series.

COPPIN, Levi Jenkins, Bp., 1848-1923. 287'.8'0924 B
Unwritten history. New York, Negro Universities Press [1968, c1919] 375 p. ports. 18 cm. [BX8495.C62A3 1968] 68-55878
I. Title.

HEARD, William Henry, Bp., 1850-1937. 287'.8'0924 B
From slavery to the bishopric in the A.M.E. Church. New York, Arno Press, 1969. vii, 104 p. illus., port. 18 cm. (The American Negro, his history and literature) Reprint of the 1924 ed. Bibliographical references included in "Notes" (p. vii) [BX8449.H4A3] 69-18564
1. African Methodist Episcopal Church. I. Title. II. Series.

PAYNE, Daniel Alexander, Bp., 1811-1893. 287'.8'0924 B
Recollections of seventy years. New York, Arno Press, 1968. 335 p. illus., ports. 21 cm. (The American Negro, his history and literature) Reprint of the 1888 ed. [BX8449.P3A3 1968] 68-29015
1. African Methodist Episcopal Church. I. Title. II. Series.

TURNER, Henry McNeal, Bp., 1834-1915. 287'.8'0924 B
Respect Black; the writings and speeches of Henry McNeal Turner. Compiled and edited by Edwin S. Redkey. New York, Arno Press, 1971. ix, 199 p. port. 24 cm. (The American Negro, his history and literature) [E185.T87 1971] 79-138695 ISBN 0-405-01984-X
1. Negroes—Addresses, essays, lectures. I. Title. II. Series.

BROOKS, George Alexander. 287'.83 B
Peerless laymen in the African Methodist Episcopal Zion Church / by George Alexander Brooks, Sr. State College, Pa. : Himes Print. Co., 1974- v. : ports. ; 23 cm. [BX8473.A1B76] 75-324341
1. African Methodist Episcopal Zion Church—Biography. I. Title.

GEORGE, Carol V. R. 287'.83 B
Segregated Sabbaths; Richard Allen and the emergence of independent Black churches 1760-1840 [by] Carol V. R. George. New York, Oxford University Press, 1973. x, 205 p. front. 21 cm. Bibliography: p. 184-198. [BX8449.A6G46] 73-76908 7.95
1. Allen, Richard, Bp., 1760-1831. 2. African Methodist Episcopal Church. 3. Negro churches—United States. I. Title.

HOOVER, Dorothy E. 287'.83
A layman looks with love at her church [by] Dorothy E. Hoover. Philadelphia, Dorrance [1970] xiv, 183 p. illus., ports. 22 cm. Bibliography: p. 165-166. [BX8443.H65] 77-85966 4.95
1. African Methodist Episcopal Church. I. Title.

LAKEY, Othal Hawthorne. 287'.83
The rise of "Colored Methodism"; a study of the background and the beginnings of the Christian Methodist Episcopal Church. Dallas, Crescendo Book Publications, c1972. iv, 128 p. 22 cm. Bibliography: p. 126-128. [BX8463.L34] 73-81153
1. Christian Methodist Episcopal Church. I. Title.

PAYNE, Daniel Alexander, Bp., 1811-1893. 287'.83
History of the African Methodist Episcopal Church. New York, Arno Press, 1969. xvi, 502 p. ports. 25 cm. (The American Negro, his history and literature) "Volume 1." No more published? Reprint of the 1891 ed., with a new pref. by H. L. Moon. [BX8443.P28 1969] 69-18573
1. African Methodist Episcopal Church—History. I. Title. II. Series.

PAYNE, Daniel Alexander, Bp., 1811-1893. 287'.83
The semi-centenary and the retrospection of the African Methodist Episcopal Church. Semicentenary and the retrospection of the African Methodist Episcopal Church Freeport, N.Y., Books for Libraries Press, 1972. 189 p. 23 cm. (The Black heritage library collection) Reprint of the 1866 ed. [BX8447.P36 1972] 76-37598 ISBN 0-8369-8974-0
1. African Methodist Episcopal Church. I. Title. II. Series.

TURNER, Henry McNeal, Bp., 1834-1915. 287'.83
The genius and theory of Methodist polity; or, The machinery of Methodism, practically illustrated through a series of questions and answers. New foreword by Archibald J. Carey, Jr. Northbrook, Ill., Metro Books, 1972. xii, 318 p. 23 cm. Reprint of the 1885 ed. [BX8448.T87 1972] 75-99416 ISBN 0-8411-0089-6
1. African Methodist Episcopal Church—Government. I. Title. II. Title: The machinery of Methodism.

WALKER, Clarence Earl. 287'.83
A rock in a weary land : a history of the African Methodist Episcopal Church during the Civil War and Reconstruction / by Clarence Earl Walker. [s.l.] : Walker, c1976. i, 268 leaves ; 28 cm. Bibliography: leaves 257-268. [BX8443.W27] 76-363303
1. African Methodist Episcopal Church—History. I. Title.

WALLS, William Jacob, Bp., 1885- 287'.83
The African Methodist Episcopal Zion Church; reality of the Black church, by William J. Walls. Charlotte, N.C., A.M.E. Zion Pub. House [1974] 669 p. illus. 24 cm. Bibliography: p. 629-644. [BX8457.W34] 74-3536 10.00
1. African Methodist Episcopal Zion Church. Publisher's address: 401 E 2nd. Street, Charlotte, N.C. 28202.

WRIGHT, Richard Robert, 1878- 287.83 (B)
87 years behind the black curtain; an autobiography, by Richard R. Wright, Jr. Philadelphia, Rare Book Co., 1965. 354 p. 24 cm. [BX8449.W7A3] 66-8242
1. African Methodist Episcopal Church — Clergy — Correspondence, reminiscences, etc. 2. Negro clergy — Correspondence, reminiscences, etc. I. Title.

SMITH, David, 1784- 287'.83'0924 B
Biography of Rev. David Smith of the A.M.E. Church. Freeport, N.Y., Books for Libraries Press, 1971. vii, 135 p. illus. 23 cm. (The Black heritage library collection) Reprint of the 1881 ed. Includes The history of the origin and development of Wilberforce University, by Bishop D. A. Payne (p. [99]-132). [BX8449.S6A3 1971] 77-168520 ISBN 0-8369-8872-8
1. Wilberforce University, Wilberforce, Ohio. I. Payne, Daniel Alexander, Bp., 1811-1893. II. Title. III. Series.

PHILLIPS, Charles Henry, Bp., 1858-1951. 287'.873
The history of the Colored Methodist Episcopal Church in America. New York, Arno Press, 1972. 247 p. port. 22 cm. (Religion in America, series II) Reprint of the 1898 ed. [BX8463.P5 1972] 73-38459 ISBN 0-405-04080-6
1. Christian Methodist Episcopal Church. I. Title.

SHAW, James Beverly Ford. 287.873
The Negro in the history of Methodism. [Nashville] Parthenon Press [1954] 234p. 21cm. Includes bibliography. [BX8435.S53] 54-28241
1. Methodists, Negro. I. Title.

RAY, Emma J., 1859- 287'.873'0922 B
Twice sold, twice ransomed; autobiography of Mr. and Mrs. L. P. Ray. Introd. by C. E. McReynolds. Freeport, N.Y., Books for Libraries Press, 1971. 320 p. illus. 23 cm. (The Black heritage library collection) Reprint of the 1926 ed. [BX8473.R3A3 1971] 76-173613 ISBN 0-8369-8905-8
I. Ray, Lloyd P., 1860- II. Title. III. Series.

SCHOONOVER, Melvin E. 287'.87471
Making all things human; a church in East Harlem [by] Melvin E. Schoonover. Foreword by William Stringfellow. [1st ed.] New York, Holt, Rinehart and Winston, 1969] ix, 188 p. 22 cm. [BX6480.N577C45] 74-84680 4.95
1. New York (City). Chambers Memorial Baptist Church. I. Title.

AFRICAN Methodist Episcopal Church. 287'.8748'11
Articles of association of the African Methodist Episcopal Church of the city of Philadelphia in the Commonwealth of Pennsylvania. [Philadelphia, Rhistoric Publications, 1969] 21 p. 21 cm. (Afro-American history series) (Rhistoric publication no. 201.) Cover title. Reprint of the 1799 ed., with "The founding of Mother Bethel and the African Methodist Episcopal Church, 1799; a bibliographical note, by Maxwell Whiteman" added. [BX8448.A28 1969] 79-77038
I. Title.

GREENE, Carroll, comp. 287'.8752'56
The Mount Moriah A.M.E. Church; a documentary report—background and potential. Compiled by Carroll Greene, Jr. Baltimore, Commission on Negro History and Culture [1972] 1 v. (various pagings) 28 cm. Includes bibliographical references. [BX8481.A56M683] 73-622655
1. Mount Moriah African Methodist Episcopal Church, Annapolis, Md. I. Title.

TISE, Larry E. 287'.8756'67
A house not made with hands: Love's Methodist Church, 1791-1966, by Larry E. Tise. [Greensboro, N.C.] Piedmont Press, 1966. x, 116 p. illus., ports. 24 cm. Bibliography: p. 107-111. [BX8481.W25L68] 74-15907
1. Walkertown, N.C. Love's Methodist Church. I. Title.

GAINES, Wesley John, Bp., 1840-1912. 287'.8758
African Methodism in the South; or, Twenty-five years of freedom. With an introd. by W. S. Scarborough. Chicago, Afro-Am Press, 1969. xxii, 305 p. port. 22 cm. Reprint of the 1890 ed. Includes bibliographical references. [BX8444.G4G3 1969] 71-99379
1. African Methodist Episcopal Church—Georgia. I. Title.

GLYNN, Robert L. 287'.8761'84
"How firm a foundation" : a history of the first Black church in Tuscaloosa County, Alabama / by Robert L. Glynn ; edited by Harold L. Bishop. [Tuscaloosa] : Friends of the Hunter's Chapel African Methodist Episcopal Zion Church, c1976. xiv, 135 p. : ill. ; 23 cm. Bibliography: p. 133. [BX8481.T874G59] 76-150255 5.00
1. Hunter's Chapel African Methodist Episcopal Zion Church, Tuscaloosa, Ala. I. Title.

GRAHAM, John H 287'.8762
Mississippi circuit riders, 1865-1965, by John H. Graham. Nashville, Parthenon Press,[1967] 229 p. group port. 22 cm. Bibliography: p. 223-229. [BX8436.M7G7] 67-9583
1. Itinerancy (Church polity)—Methodist Church—Hist. 2. Methodists, Negro. I. Title.

GRAHAM, John H. 287'.8762
Mississippi circuit riders, 1865-1965, by John H. Graham. Nashville, Parthenon Press [1967] 229 p. group port. 22 cm. Bibliography: p. 223-229. [BX8436.M7G7] 67-9583
1. Itinerancy (Church polity)—Methodist Church—History. 2. Methodists, Negro. I. Title.

UNIVERSAL House of Justice. 287'.89
Wellspring of guidance : messages, 1963-1968 / Universal House of Justice. 1st rev. ed. Wilmette, Ill. : Baha'i Pub. Trust, 1976. viii, 150 p. ; 23 cm. Includes index. [BP380.U5 1976] 76-129996 ISBN 0-87743-032-2 : 6.75 pbk. : 3.75
1. Bahaism—Doctrinal and controversial works. I. Title.

CONGREGATIONAL Methodist Church. 287.9
Constitution and government of the Congregational Methodist Churches of the United States of America. 12th ed. [J. A. Cook, editor] Decatur, Miss., The Watchman [1953] 118p. 16cm. [BX8431.C7A5 1953] 53-39546
1. Congregational Methodist Church—Discipline. 2. Congregational Methodist Church—Doctrinal and controversial works. I. Title.

EVANGELICAL Methodist Church. 287.9
Discipline of the Evangelical Methodist Church, 1953 [on cover: 1954] General superintendents: J. H. Hamblen [and] Lucian D. Smith. Editors: Ronald D. Driggers [and] Ralph Lucian D. Smith. Editors: Ronald D. Driggers [and] Ralph A. Vanderwood. Chicago, Good News Press [1954] 224p. 16cm. [BX8431.E88A3 1954] 54-36565
1. Evangelical Methodist Church—Doctrinal and controversial works. 2. Evangelical Methodist Church—Discipline. I. Title.

FOWLER, Wilton R 287.9
A history of the Congregational Methodist Church. [n.p.] c1957. 109 l. illus. 28cm. Includes bibliography. [BX8431.C7F7] 57-44558
1. Congregational Methodist Church—Hist. I. Title.

GRANT, John Webster. 287'.92
The Canadian experience of church union. Richmond, John Knox Press [1967] 106 p. 22 cm. (Ecumenical studies in history no. 8) [BX9881.G7] 67-21481
1. United Church of Canada. 2. Christian union—Canada. I. Title. II. Series.

MOYER, Kenneth Allan, 1913- 287'.92'0924 B
Preacher on the roof / by Kenneth A. Moyer ; illustrated by Joanne Jackson. [s.l. : s.n.], c1976. 74 p. : ill. ; 28 cm. Cover title. [BX9883.M65A35] 77-366089
1. Moyer, Kenneth Allan, 1913- 2. United Church of Canada—Clergy—Biography. 3. Clergy—Canada—Biography. I. Title.

EDWARDS, Josephine 287'.97 B
Cunnington.
A light shining in Cornwall. Nashville, Southern Pub. Association [1969] 96 p. 22 cm. [BV3785.B7E3] 74-79875
1. Bray, William, 1794-1868. I. Title.

LEEDY, Roy B 287.97
The Evangelical Church in Ohio; being a history of the Ohio Conference and merged conferences of the Evangelical Church in Ohio, now the Evangelical United Brethren Church, 1816-1951. [Cleveland] Ohio Conference of the Evangelical United Brethren Church, 1959. 850p. illus. 24cm. Includes bibliography. [BX7520.O4L4] 59-18589
1. Evangelical Church. Conferences. Ohio—Hist. 2. Churches—Ohio. 3. Clergy—Ohio. I. Title.

MARSTON, Leslie Ray, Bp., 287.97
1894-
From age to age a living witness; a historical interpretation of Free Methodism's first century. Winona Lake, Ind., Light and Life Press [1960] 608p. illus., maps (part col.) 23cm. Bibliography: p.591-596. [BX8413.M35] 60-10621
1. Free Methodist Church—Hist. I. Title.

TAYLOR, Jesse Paul, Bp., 287.97
1895-
Goodly heritage. Winona Lake, Ind., Light and Life Press [1960] 138 p. 20 cm. "Originally delivered, for the most part, as addresses at ministers and superintendents conferences." [BX8413.T36] 60-10622
1. Free Methodist Church — Hist. — Addresses, essays, lectures. I. Title.

WALKER, Alan. 287'.97
Heritage without end; a story to tell to the nation. Illus. by Frank Whitmore. [5th ed. Melbourne] General Conference Literature and Publications Committee of the Methodist Church of Australasia; wholesale distributor: E. K. Ditterich, Benalla, Victoria [1953] 95 p. illus. 22 cm. [BX8325.W3 1953] 77-234287
1. Methodist Church in Australia. I. Title.

JONES, John Griffing, 287.9762
1804-1888.
A complete history of Methodism as connected with the Mississippi Conference of the Methodist Episcopal Church, South, 1799-1845. Written at the unanimous request of the conference, by John G. Jones, Rev. ed. by E. Russ Williams, Jr. Baton Rouge, Claitor's Book Store, 1966. 2 v. in 1. port. 23 cm. A re-issue of the original 2 vol. work first published 1887-1908 with introductory matter and a name index added. [BX8248.M7J6 1966] 66-17805
1. Methodist Episcopal Church, South, in Mississippi. I. Williams, E. Russ, ed. II. Methodist Episcopal Church, South. Conferences. Mississippi III. Title.

288 Unitarianism

BARLETT, Laile E. 288
Bright galaxy; ten years of Unitarian fellowships. Boston, Beacon Press [1960] 255p. 21cm. [BV2595.U5B3] 60-5816
1. Unitarian churches—Missions. I. Title. II. Title: Unitarian fellowships.

BARTLETT, Laile E. 288
Bright galaxy; ten years of Unitarian fellowships. Boston, Beacon Press [c.1960] xv, 255p. 21cm. (bibl. footnotes) 60-5816 3.50
1. Unitarian churches—Missions. I. Title. II. Title: Unitarian fellowships.

BARTOL, Cyrus Augustus, 1813- 288
1900.
Discourses on the Christian spirit and life. New York, Arno Press, 1972 [c1850] vi, 408 p. 22 cm. (The Romantic tradition in American literature) [BX9843.B29D5 1972] 72-4951 ISBN 0-405-04622-7 20.00
1. Unitarianism. I. Title. II. Series.

CARNES, Paul Nathaniel, 1921- 288
For freedom and belief; a manual for Unitarians. Boston, Beacon Press [1952] 71p. illus. 20cm. (Beacon reference series) [BX9842.C27] 53-6423
1. Unitarian churches —Doctrinal and controversial works. I. Title.

CHANNING, William Ellery, 288
1780-1842.
Unitarian Christianity and other essays. Edited, with an introd. by Irving H. Bartlett. New York, Liberal Arts Press [1957] xxxii, 121 p. 21 cm. (The American heritage series, no. 21) Bibliography: p. xxxi. [BX9843.C5U5] 57-14626
1. Unitarianism. I. Title.

CHEETHAM, Henry H. 288
Unitarianism and Universalism, an illustrated history. Drawings by Roger Martin. Boston, Beacon [c.1962] 124p. 21cm. 62-10818 3.95
1. Unitarianism—Hist. 2. Universalism—Hist. I. Title.

ELGIN, Kathleen, 1923- 288
The Unitarians; the Unitarian Universalist Association. Written and illustrated by Kathleen Elgin. With a foreword by Constance H. Burgess. New York, McKay [1971] 95 p. illus. 26 cm. (The Freedom to worship series) Bibliography: p. 94. Introduces the principles of Unitarian beliefs and traces the career of Dorothea Dix, who was guided by these principles in her efforts to improve the condition of the mentally ill. [BX9841.2.E4] 75-165085 4.95
1. Unitarian churches—Juvenile literature. I. Title.

FRITCHMAN, Stephen Hole, 288
1902-
Unitarianism today; an eloquent protest against the forces of authority that demand blind conformity, an eloquent defense of free men who deviate from orthodoxies. Boston, American Unitarian Association, 1950. 58 p. 22 cm. "A 125th anniversary publication." "Represents, with minor editorial changes, the substance of thirteen radio talks on Unitarianism dellvered by the author over station KGFJ. Hollywood, California, from December, 1949, to February, 1950." [BX9841.F75] 50-13986
1. Unitarianism. I. Title.

HOPKINS, Jeannette. 288
Fourteen journeys to Unitarianism; statements of religious belief prepared from personal interviews. Boston, Beacon Press [1955, c1954] 77p. 19cm. [BX9842.H78] 54-12456
1. Unitarianism. I. Title.

KOT, Stanislaw, 1885- 288
Socinianism in Poland; the social and political ideas of the Polish Antitrinitarians in the sixteenth and seventeenth centuries. Translated from the Polish by Earl Morse Wilbur. Boston,Starr King Press [1957] xxvii, 226p. 22cm. Translation of Idelogja polityczna 1 spoleczna Braci Polskich zwanych Arjanaml. Bibliographical footnotes. [BT1480.K63] 57-12746
1. Socinianism. I. Title.

LYTTLE, Charles Harold, 1884- 288
Freedom moves west; a history of the Western Unitarian Conference, 1852-1952. Boston, Beacon Press [1952] xx298 p. illus. ports. 22 cm. "Bibilographical guide": p. [276]-284. [BX9807.W4L8] 52-5960
1. Western Unitarian Conference. I. Title.

MACLEAN, Angus Hector, 1892- 288
The wind in both ears. Boston, Beacon [c.1965] viii, 144p. 22cm. [BX9841.2.M25] 65-12242 4.95
1. Unitarianism—Addresses, essays, lectures. I. Title.

MENDELSOHN, Jack, 1918- 288
Why I am a Unitarian Universalist. Boston, Beacon [1966, c.1964] 213p. 21cm. (BP209) First. pub. in 1960 under title: Why I am a Unitarian. 1.25 pap.,
1. Unitarian Churches—Doctrinal and controversial works. I. Title.

MENDELSOHN, Jack, 1918- 288
Why I am a Unitarian Universalist. New York, Nelson [1964] 213 p. 22 cm. First published in 1960 under title: Why I am a Unitarian. [BX9841.M55 1964] 64-25286
1. Unitarian Churches—Doctrinal and controversial works. I. Title.

PARKE, David B ed. 288
The epic of Unitarianism; original writings from the history of liberal religion. Boston, Starr King Press [1957] 164p. 22cm. [BX9813.P3] 57-7797
1. Unitarianism. I. Title.

PARKE, David B., ed. 288
The epic of Unitarianism; original writings from the history of liberal religion. Boston, Beacon Press [1960, c.1957] xii, 164p. 21cm. (Beacon ser. in liberal religion, LR 6) (Bibl.: p.155-157) 1.45 pap.,
1. Unitarianism. I. Title.

SHUTE, John Raymond. 288
His honor the heretic; [papers] Monroe, N. C., Nocalore Press, 1950. 76p. 24cm. [BX9815.S6] 56-47838
1. Unitarianism—Addresses, essays, lectures. I. Title.

SCHOLEFIELD, Harry Barron, 288.02
ed.
The Unitarian Universalist pocket guide. Boston Beacon [1963] 69p. 19cm. 63-18180 .50
1. Unitarian Universalist Association—Handbooks, manuals, etc. I. Title.

ELIOT, Frederick May 288.081
Frederick May Eliot; an anthology; selected and edited by Alfred P. Stiernotte. With a memorial address by Wallace W. Robbins. Boston, Beacon Press [c.1959] xxxi, 300p. illus. (front.) 22cm. (bibl.: p.267-300) 59-13477 5.00
1. Unitarian churches—Addresses, essays, lectures. I. Title.

PARKER, Theodore, 1810- 288.082
1860.
An anthology. Edited, with an introd. and notes, by Henry Steele Commager. Boston, Beacon Press [c.1960] viii, 391p. 22cm. 60-14677 6.00
1. Unitarian churches—Collected works. 2. Theology—Collected works—19th cent. I. Title.

THREE prophets of 288.082
religious liberalism: Channing, Emerson, Parker. Introd. by Conrad Wright. Boston, Beacon Press [1961] 152p. (Beacon paperbacks in liberal religion, LR12) 61-3679 1.25 pap.,
1. Unitarianism—Addresses, essays, lectures. 2. Liberalism (Religion) I. Wright, Conrad.
Contents omitted.

WRIGHT, Conrad. 288.082
Three prophets of religious liberalism: Channing, Emerson, Parker. Introduced by Conrad Wright. Boston, Beacon Press [1961] 152 p. 21 cm. (Beacon paperbacks in liberal religion, LR12) Bibliographical footnotes. [BX9843.A1T5] 61-3679
1. Unitarianism—Addresses, essays, lectures. 2. Liberalism (Religion) I. Title.

WILBUR, Earl Morse, 1866- 288.09
A history of Unitarianism. Cambridge, Harvard University Press, 1945-52. 2v. 22cm. Contents.[1] Socinianism and its antecedents.--[2] In Transylvania, England, and America. Bibliographical footnotes. [BX9831.W49] A45
1. Unitarian churches—Hist. 2. Socinianism. I. Title.

WILBUR, Earl Morse, 1866- 288.09
A history of Unitarianism. Boston, Beacon Press [1965? c1945] 2 v. 22 cm. Reprint of work first published 1945-1952. Contents.Contents. -- [1] Socinianism and its antecedents. -- [2] In Transylvania, England, and America. Bibliographical footnotes. [BX9831.W492] 65-29746
1. Unitarian churches — Hist. 2. Socinianism. I. Title.

WRIGHT, Conrad. 288'.09
The liberal Christians; essays on American Unitarian history. Boston, Beacon Press [1970] x, 147 p. 21 cm. Contents.Contents.—Rational religion in eighteenth century America.—The rediscovery of Channing.—Emerson, Barzillai Frost, and the Divinity School address.—The minister as reformer.—Henry W. Bellows and the organization of the National Conference.—From standing order to secularism. Includes bibliographical references. [BX9843.W78L5 1970] 76-84801 7.50
1. Unitarianism—Addresses, essays, lectures. I. Title.

ELIOT, Samuel Atkins, 288'.0922
1862-1950, ed.
Heralds of a liberal faith. Boston, American Unitarian Association, 1910-[52] 4 v. 23 cm. Vol. 4 has imprint: Boston, Beacon Press. Contents.1. The prophets.--2. The pioneers.--3. The preachers.--4.The pilots. [BX9867.E4] A 11
1. Unitarianism. I. Title.

FRITCHMAN, Stephen 288'.0922
Hole, 1902-
Men of liberty; ten Unitarian pioneers. With illus. by Hendrik Willem Van Loon. Port Washington, N.Y., Kennikat Press [1968, c1944] xi, 180 p. illus. 21 cm. (Essay and general literature index reprint series) Contents.Contents.—Michael Servetus.—Faustus Socinus.—Francis David.—John Biddle.—Joseph Priestley.—Thomas Jefferson.—William Ellery Channing.—Ralph Waldo Emerson.—Theodore Parker.—Magnus Eiriksson. [BX9867.F7 1968] 68-15826
1. Unitarian churches—Biography. I. Title.

ALBRECHT, Robert C. 288'.0924 B
Theodore Parker by Robert C. Albrecht. New York, Twayne Publishers [1971] 160 p. 21 cm. (Twayne's United States authors series, 179) Bibliography: p. 150-155. [BX9869.P3A43] 76-120521
1. Parker, Theodore, 1810-1860.

BALLOU, Adin, 1803- 288'.092'4 B
1890.
Autobiography of Adin Ballou, 1803-1890, containing an elaborate record and narrative of his life from infancy to old age : with appendixes / completed and edited by William S. Heywood. Philadelphia : Porcupine Press, 1975. xviii, 586 p. : ports. ; 22 cm. (The American utopian adventure : series two) Reprint of the 1896 ed. published by Vox Populi Press, Lowell, Mass. Includes index. "Published works of Adin Ballou": p. [573]-574. [BX9969.B27A3 1975] 74-26603 ISBN 0-87991-033-X lib.bdg. : 22.50
1. Ballou, Adin, 1803-1890. I. Heywood, William Sweetzer, 1824-1903.

CARUTHERS, J. Wade. 288'.092'4 B
Octavius Brooks Frothingham, gentle radical / J. Wade Caruthers. University : University of Alabama Press, c1977. ix, 279 p., [3] leaves of plates : ill. ; 25 cm. Includes index. Bibliography: p. [262]-268. [BX9869.F83C37] 76-18079 ISBN 0-8173-5166-3 12.50
1. Frothingham, Octavius Brooks, 1822-1895. I. Title.

CHADWICK, John White, 288'.0924 B
1840-1904.
Theodore Parker, preacher and reformer. Boston, Houghton, Mifflin, 1900. St. Clair Shores, Mich., Scholarly Press, 1971. xx, 422 p., ports. 22 cm. Bibliography: p. [xi]-xx. [BX9869.P3C5 1971] 72-144939 ISBN 0-403-00925-1
1. Parker, Theodore, 1810-1860.

CLARKE, James 288'.0924 B
Freeman, 1810-1888.
Autobiography, diary, and correspondence. Edited by Edward Everett Hale. New York, Negro Universities Press [1968, c1891] 430 p. port. 23 cm. "Writings of James Freeman Clarke": p. [416]-419. [BX9869.C6A3 1968] 68-55876
I. Title.

CONWAY, Moncure 288'.0924 B
Daniel, 1832-1907.
Autobiography; memories and experiences of Moncure Daniel Conway. New York, Da Capo Press, 1970 [c1904] 2 v. illus., facsims., ports. 24 cm. [BX9869.C8A3 1970] 76-87495
1. Slavery in the United States—Anti-slavery movements.

CONWAY, Moncure 288'.0924 B
Daniel, 1832-1907.
Autobiography: memories and experiences of Moncure Daniel Conway. New York, Negro Universities Press [1969] 2 v. illus., facsims., ports. 22 cm. Reprint of the 1904 ed. [BX9869.C8A3 1969] 71-88405
1. Slavery in the United States—Anti-slavery movements.

CROTHERS, Louise 288.0924
(Bronson) 1861-1939.
A family chronicle. [Concord N.H., 1966] ix, 253 p. illus., ports. 20 cm. [BX9869.C87C7 1966] 66-5808
1. Crothers, Samuel McChord, 1857-1927. I. Title.

DIXON, Madeline Cutler. 288.0924
With halo atilt [by] Madeline C. Dixon. Boston, Beacon Press [1965] 236 p. 21 cm. [BX9869.C94D5] 65-23470
1. Cutler, Julian Stearns, b. 1854. I. Title.

GANNETT, William 288'.0924 B
Channing, 1840-1923.
Ezra Stiles Gannett, Unitarian minister in Boston, 1824-1871; a memoir, by his son William C. Gannett. Port Washington, N.Y., Kennikat Press [1971] xv, 572 p. illus., ports. 22 cm. (Kennikat Press scholarly reprints. Series on literary America in the nineteenth century) Reprint of the 1875 ed. Bibliography: p. [565]-572. [BX9869.G3G3 1971] 79-122654
1. Gannett, Ezra Stiles, 1801-1871.

GREELEY, Dana McLean, 288'.0924 B
1908-
25 Beacon Street, and other recollection. Boston, Beacon Press [1971] viii, 232 p. port. 21 cm. [BX9841.2.G73 1971] 78-136229 ISBN 0-8070-1666-7 10.00
1. Unitarian churches—Doctrinal and controversial works. I. Title.

MENDELSOHN, Jack, 288'.0924 B
1918-
Channing, the reluctant radical; a biography. [1st ed.] Boston, Little, Brown [1971] 308 p. illus. 22 cm. Includes bibliographical references. [BX9869.C4M45 1971] 75-161863 8.95
1. Channing, William Ellery, 1780-1842.

PARKER, Theodore, 288'.092'4 B
1810-1860.
Theodore Parker: American transcendentalist; a critical essay and a collection of his writings, by Robert E. Collins. Metuchen, N.J., Scarecrow Press, 1973. v, 271 p. illus. 22 cm. Contents.Contents.—Essay: A forgotten American.—Selections from Theodore Parker: Transcendentalism. A discourse of the transient and permanent in Christianity. The position and duties of the American scholar. The political destination of America and the signs of the times. The writings of Ralph

Waldo Emerson. A sermon of war.—Selected bibliography (p. 261-264) [BX9869.P3A25 1973] 73-9593 ISBN 0-8108-0641-X 7.50
1. Parker, Theodore, 1810-1860. 2. Emerson, Ralph Waldo, 1803-1882. 3. Transcendentalism—Collected works. I. Collins, Robert E., ed.

STANDLEY, Fred L. 288'.092'4 B
Stopford Brooke, by Fred L. Standley. New York, Twayne Publishers [1972] 158 p. 21 cm. (Twayne's English authors series, TEAS 135) Bibliography: p. 149-154. [BX9869.B8S72] 77-152017
1. Brooke, Stopford Augustus, 1832-1916.

WARE, Henry, 1794-1843. 288'.092'4 B
Memoirs of the Rev. Noah Worcester, D.D., by Henry Ware, Jr. With a pref., notes, and a concluding chapter, by Samuel Worcester. Boston, J. Munroe, 1844. [New York, J. S. Ozer, 1972] xii, 155 p. front. 22 cm. (The Peace movement in America) A facsim. reprint. [BX9869.W8W3 1844a] 78-137557 8.95
1. Worcester, Noah, 1758-1837. I. Worcester, Samuel, 1793-1844, ed. II. Title. III. Series.

WEAVER, George Sumner, 1818-1908. 288'.092'4
Autobiography; a sketch of a busy life, 1914. [Schenectady, N.Y., E. L. Robinson, 1965] 121 p. facsim., port. 23 cm. 125 copies printed. [BX9969.W4A3] 64-41427
I. Title.

WEISS, John, 1818-1879. 288'.0924 B
Life and correspondence of Theodore Parker. New York, Bergman Publishers [1969] 2 v. illus., ports. 24 cm. Reprint of the 1864 ed. [BX9869.P3W4 1969b] 68-28772
1. Parker, Theodore, 1810-1860. I. Parker, Theodore, 1810-1860. Correspondence. II. Title.

WEISS, John, 1818-1879. 288'.0924 B
Life and correspondence of Theodore Parker. New York, Da Capo Press, 1970. 2 v. illus., ports. 24 cm. Reprint of the 1864 ed. [BX9869.P3W4 1970] 76-106987
1. Parker, Theodore, 1810-1860. I. Parker, Theodore, 1810-1860. Correspondence. 1970. II. Title.

WEISS, John, 1818-1879. 288'.0924 B
Life and correspondence of Theodore Parker. New York, Arno Press, 1969. 2 v. in 1 illus., facsim., ports. 24 cm. (Religion in American) Reprint of the 1864 ed. [BX9869.P3W4 1969d] 70-83446
1. Parker, Theodore, 1810-1860. I. Parker, Theodore, 1810-1860. Correspondence. 1969. II. Title.

WEISS, John, 1818-1879. 288'.0924 B
Life and correspondence of Theodore Parker, minister of the Twenty-eighth Congregational Society, Boston. New York, D. Appleton, 1864. Freeport, N.Y., Books for Libraries Press [1969] 2 v. illus., facsim., ports. 23 cm. (Select bibliographies reprint series) [BX9869.P3W4 1969] 69-16854
1. Parker, Theodore, 1810-1860. I. Title.

WEISS, John, 1818-1879. 288'.0924
Life and correspondence of Theodore Parker, minister of the Twenty-eighth Congregational Society, Boston. New York, Negro Universities Press [1969] 2 v. 23 cm. Reprint of the 1864 ed. [BX9869.P3W4 1969c] 74-97443
1. Parker, Theodore, 1810-1860. I. Parker, Theodore, 1810-1860. Correspondence. 1969. II. Title.

*UNITARIAN Church, Bloomington, Illinois. 288.0977359
One hundred fifteen years of churchmanship (a history of Unitarianism in Bloomington-Normal) by members of the parish. Bloomington, Ill., Unitarian Church [1975] iv, 147 p. ill. 22 cm. Includes index. [BX9833.5] 6.00.
1. Unitarian churches. I. Title.
Available from publisher: 1613 E. Emerson St. 61701.

FOOD and Agriculture Organization of the United Nations. 288.14058
Trade yearbook. Annuaire du commerce. Anuario de comercio. v.15, 1961. [New York, Columbia, c.1962] 365p. 28cm. annual. 59-35986 3.50 bds.,
1. Produce trade—Stat. I. Title.

REECE, Colleen L. 288.3'092'2 B
The unknown witnesses, by Colleen L. Reece. [Independence, Mo., Herald Pub. House, 1974] 159 p. 18 cm. [BX8693.R43] 73-87642 ISBN 0-8309-0107-8 5.00

1. Bible—Biography. 2. Mormons and Mormonism—Biography. I. Title.

BARTLETT, Josiah R 288'.32
Moment of truth: our next four hundred years; an analysis of Unitarian Universalism [by] Josiah R. and Laile E. Bartlett. Berkeley, Calif. [1968] xv, 179 p. illus. 22 cm. Bibliography: p. 175-179. [BX9941.2.B3] 68-26626
1. Unitarian Universalist Association. I. Bartlett, Laile E., joint author. II. Title.

HUNTER, Edith Fisher, 1919- 288.320924
Sophia Lyon Fahs; a biography, by Edith F. Hunter. Boston, Beacon [1966] xi, 276p. 21cm. Bibl. [BX9869.F3H8] 66-23784 5.95 bds.,
1. Fahs, Sophia Blache (Lyon) 1876- I. Title.

ARRINGTON, Leonard J. 288.3'3 B
From Quaker to Latter-Day Saint : Bishop Edwin D. Woolley / Leonard J. Arrington. Salt Lake City : Deseret Book Co., 1976. xiii, 592 p. ; 24 cm. Includes index. Bibliography: p. 497-500. [BX8695.W57A77] 76-43171 ISBN 0-87747-591-1 : 6.95
1. Woolley, Edwin Dilworth, 1897-1881. 2. Mormons and Mormonism—Biography. I. Title.

BICKERSTAFF, George. 288.3'3
The church story / by George Bickerstaff ; ill. by Douglas Jordan. Salt Lake City, Utah : Bookcraft, 1974- v. : col. ill. ; 29 cm. Contents.Contents.—book 1. From Sacred Grove to Land of Zion. [BX8611.B4] 74-21758 ISBN 0-88494-274-0 (v. 1)
1. Church of Jesus Christ of Latter-Day Saints—History—Juvenile literature. I. Jordan, Douglas, ill. II. Title.

FRITCHMAN, Stephen Hole, 1902- 288'.33'0924 B
Heretic : a partisan autobiography / by Stephen H. Fritchman. [Boston] : Beacon Press, c1977. 362 p., [4] leaves of plates : ports. ; 22 cm. "A Skinner House book." Includes bibliographical references. [BX9869.F815A34] 77-70244 pbk. : 3.95
1. Fritchman, Stephen Hole, 1902- 2. Unitarian churches—Clergy—Biography. 3. Clergy—United States—Biography. I. Title.

FRITCHMAN, Stephen Hole, 1902- 288'.33'0924 B
Heretic : a partisan autobiography / by Stephen H. Fritchman. [Boston] : Beacon Press, c1977. 362 p., [4] leaves of plates : ports. ; 22 cm. "A Skinner House book." Includes bibliographical references. [BX9869.F815A34] 77-70244 pbk. : 3.95
1. Fritchman, Stephen Hole, 1902- 2. Unitarian churches—Clergy—Biography. 3. Clergy—United States—Biography. I. Title.

HOWLETT, Duncan 288.330924
No greater love: the James Reeb Story. New York, Harper [c.1966] xii, 242p. illus., ports. 22cm. [BX9869.R4H6] 66-11489 4.95
1. Reeb, James Joseph, 1927-1965. I. Title.

MCGIFFERT, Arthur Cushman, 1892- 288'.33'0924 B
Pilot of a liberal faith, Samuel Atkins Eliot, 1862-1950 / Arthur Cushman McGiffert, Jr. [Boston] : Beacon Press, 1976. 321 p. : ill. ; 23 cm. "A Skinner House book." Includes index. [BX9869.E37M28] 76-373984 12.95
1. Eliot, Samuel Atkins, 1862-1950. 2. Unitarian churches in the United States—Biography. I. Title.

HEYMEN, Ralph. 288.4
The art of Christian living; Christian faith and mental health. Grand Rapids, Mich., Baker Book House [1973 c1963] 171 p. 18 cm [BV4501.2] ISBN 0-8010-4076-0 1.25 (pbk)
1. Christian life I. Title.
LC card no. for orig. ed. 63-15079

LAVAN, Spencer. 288'.54
Unitarians and India : a study in encounter and response / by Spencer Lavan. [Boston] : Beacon Press, c1977. vi, 217 p. ; 22 cm. "A Skinner House book." Includes bibliographical references and index. [BX9835.I8L38] 77-75488 3.95
1. Unitarians in India—History. I. Title.

COOKE, George Willis, 1848-1923. 288'.73
Unitarianism in America. [1st AMS ed.] Boston, American Unitarian Association, 1902. [New York, AMS Press, 1971] xi, 463 p. illus., ports. 22 cm. Includes bibliographical references. [BX9833.C7 1971] 72-155153 ISBN 0-404-01699-5
1. Unitarianism. I. Title.

COOKE, George Willis, 1848-1923. 288'.73
Unitarianism in America; a history of its origin and development. Boston, American Unitarian Association, 1902. St. Clair Shores, Mich., Scholarly Press [1969?] xi, 463 p. illus., ports. 22 cm. Bibliographical footnotes. [BX9833.C7 1969] 77-8815
1. Unitarianism. I. Title.

A Stream of light : 288'.73
a sesquicentennial history of American Unitarianism / Conrad Wright, editor. 1st ed. Boston : Unitarian Universalist Association, 1975. xiv, 178 p. : ill. ; 23 cm. Includes bibliographical references and index. [BX9833.S74] 75-3875 6.00
1. Unitarian churches in the United States—Addresses, essays, lectures. 2. Unitarianism—History—Addresses, essays, lectures. I. Wright, Conrad.

WRIGHT, Conrad. 288.73
The beginnings of Unitarianism in America. Boston, Starr King Press; distributed by Beacon Press [1955] 305p. maps. 22cm. 'Bibliographical appendix p.[281]-291. 'Bibliographical note': p.[292]-294. [BX9833.W7] 55-8138
1. Unitarianism in the U. S. I. Title.

WRIGHT, Conrad. 288'.73
The beginnings of Unitarianism in America / Conrad Wright. Hamden, Conn. : Archon Books, 1976, c1955. 305 p. : maps ; 23 cm. Reprint of the 1966 ed. published by Beacon Press, Boston. A revision of the author's thesis, Harvard University. Includes index. Bibliography: p. [292]-294. [BX9833.W7 1976] 76-20681 ISBN 0-208-01612-0 : 15.00
1. Unitarian churches in the United States. 2. Unitarianism—History. I. Title.

UNITARIAN Universalist Association. 288.73058
Directory. 1962-1963. Boston, 25 Beacon St. Author, [1963] 283p. 23cm. 62-5422 4.00; 3.00 pap., lib. ed.,
I. Title.

ALLEN, Joseph Henry, 1820-1898. 288'.74
Our liberal movement in theology, chiefly as shown in recollections of the history of Unitarianism in New England. New York, Arno Press, 1972 [c1882] iv, 220 p. 23 cm. (Religion in America, series II) [BX9833.4.A43 1972] 73-38432 ISBN 0-405-04053-9
1. Unitarianism—History. I. Title.

MARSHALL, George N ed. 288.744
The church of the Pilgrim Fathers, selected and edited by George N. Marshall from the writings of John Cuckson [and others] Boston, Beacon Press, 1950. xx, 143 p. illus. 21 cm. Contents.--Foreword: "Old First."--Genesis of the Pilgrim church, by J. Cuckson.--John Robinson; two modern studies: Seventeenth-century liberal, by F. J. Taylor. The man who taught the Pilgrims, by J. E. Kalas.--The Pilgrims and early Plymouth, by H. W. Royal.--The Pilgrim's church in Plymouth, by A. Lord.--The historical Pilgrim church and the modern witness, by G. N. Marshall.--The National Memorial Pilgrim Church, by A. B. Whitney and G. N. Marshall.--Why a Unitarian church? by A. R. Hussey.--Appendix: Some historical notes on the First Church, by F. A. Jenks.--Suggested reading list. [BX9861.P65F55] 50-58120
1. Plymouth, Mass. First Church 2. Congregationalism—Hist. 3. Unitarianism—Hist. I. Title.

MANSUR, Ina G. 288'.744'4
The story of the First Parish in Bedford Unitarian Universalist. Compiled for the 150th anniversary of the second meetinghouse, 1817-1967, by Ina G.Mansur. [Bedford, Mass., 1967] [62] p. illus., ports. 27 cm. On cover: The story of the First Parish of Bedford, Unitarian Universalist. [BX9833.6.B4M3] 78-5832
1. Bedford, Mass. First Parish in Bedford Unitarian Universalist. I. Title.

MOFFORD, Juliet Haines. 288'.744'5
The history of North Parish Church of North Andover, 1645-1974 : and firm thine ancient vow / by Juliet Haines Mofford. North Andover, Mass. : Mafford, 1975. xxvi, 326 p. : ill. ; 25 cm. Includes index. Bibliography: p. [291]-301. [BX9861.N65N675] 75-39493
1. North Parish Church, North Andover, Mass. 2. North Andover, Mass.—Biography. I. Title. II. Title: And firm thine ancient vow.

KRING, Donald Walter. 288'.747'1
Liberals among the orthodox: Unitarian beginnings in New York City, 1819-1839. Boston, Beacon Press [1974] ix, 278 p. illus. 24 cm. Includes bibliographical references. [BX9833.6.N49K74] 73-21275 ISBN 0-8070-1662-4 12.50
1. Unitarian Church of All Souls, New York. 2. New York (City). Community Church. 3. Unitarian churches in New York (City) I. Title.

GEFFEN, Elizabeth M. 288.74811
Philadelphia Unitarianism, 1796-1861. Philadelphia, Univ. of Pennsylvania Press [c.1961] 323p. illus. Bibl. 60-11411 6.00
1. Unitarians in Philadelphia. I. Title.

BALTIMORE. FIRST UNITARIAN CHURCH OF BALTIMORE (UNIVERSALIST AND UNITARIAN) 288.75271
A heritage to hold in fee, 1817-1917, by Rebecca Funk, church historian, with the Historical Committee of the church. Baltimore, Garamond Press, 1962. 121 p. illus. 24 cm. Includes bibliography. [BX9861.B3F5] 62-22301
1. Baltimore. First Unitarian Church. I. Funk, Rebecca. II. Title.

PITTSBURGH'S First 288.75271
Unitarian Church, by George Swetnam [and others] Pittsburgh, Boxwood Press [1961] 125p. 22cm. Includes bibliography. [BX9861.P55F5] 61-19849
1. Pittsburgh. First Unitarian Church. I. Swetnam, George.

STAPLES, Laurence Carlton, 1891- 288'.753
Washington Unitarianism; a rich heritage, by Laurence C. Staples. Washington, 1970. 175 p. illus., ports. 24 cm. Bibliography: p. 174-175. [BX9861.W3S7] 74-22094
1. Washington, D.C. All Souls Church. I. Title.

BULL, Elias B. 288'.757'915
Founders and pew renters of the Unitarian Church in Charleston, S.C., 1817-1874, by Elias B. Bull. [Charleston] Unitarian Church in Charleston, S.C., Press [1970] iii, 47 p. 22 cm. [F279.C445B8] 76-268863
1. Charleston, S.C. Unitarian Church. 2. Registers of births, etc.—Charleston, S.C. I. Title.

THORNTON, Jerry. 288'.774'27
Ideas have consequences : 125 years of the liberal tradition in the Lansing area / by Jerry Thornton. [East Lansing, Mich. : Unitarian Universalist Church, 1973] 99 p. : ill. ; 28 cm. Imprint stamped on t.p. Bibliography: p. 96-97. [BX9861.E37U546] 75-303731
1. Unitarian Universalist Church, East Lansing, Mich. I. Title.

OTTO, Elinor Sommers. 288'.776'58
The story of Unity Church, 1872-1972. St. Paul, Unity Church of St. Paul, 1972. viii, 130 p. illus., ports. 26 cm. Bibliography: p. 125. [BX9861.S29O8] 72-179644
1. St. Paul. Unity Church. I. Title.

CROMPTON, Arnold. 288.79
Unitarianism on the Pacific coast: the first sixty years. Boston, Beacon Press [1957] 182 p. 22 cm.sUnitarian churches in the Pacific States. [BX9833.46.C7] 57-6638
I. Title.

289 Other Denominations & Sects

BACH, Marcus, 1906- 289
Faith and my friends. [1st ed.] Indianapolis, Bobbs-Merrill [1951] 302 p. 22 cm. [BL98.B2] 51-9823
1. Religions, Modern. I. Title.

BACH, Marcus, 1906- 289
They have found a faith. Freeport, N.Y., Books for Libraries Press [1971, c1946] 300 p. 23 cm. (Essay index reprint series) [BR516.5.B3 1971] 74-134049 ISBN 0-8369-2481-9
1. Sects—United States. I. Title.

BREESE, Dave W. 289
Know the marks of cults / Dave Breese. Wheaton, Ill. : Victor Books, [1975] 128 p. ; 18 cm. (An Input book) [BR157.B73] 75-21907 ISBN 0-88207-704-X pbk. : 1.50
1. Sects—Controversial literature. I. Title.

BURRELL, Maurice Claude. 289
Whom then can we believe? / by J. Stafford Wright and Maurice C. Burrell. Chicago : Moody Press, 1976. p. cm. London ed., with authors' names in reverse order, published in 1973 under title: Some modern faiths. Includes bibliographical references. [BR157.B84 1976] 75-34304 ISBN 0-8024-9502-8 : 0.95
1. Sects. I. Wright, John Stafford, joint author. II. Title.

CHRISTIANITY today. Symposium 289
The challenge of the cults; a Christianity Today symposium, by Harold Lindsell [others] Grand Rapids, Zondervan [c.1961] 80p. Bibl. 61-42475 1.00 pap.,
1. Sects—U. S. I. Lindsell, Harold, 1913-

DAVIES, Horton. 289
Christian deviations: the challenge of the new

spiritual movements. Philadelphia, Westminster Press [1965] 144 p. 19 cm. "A revised edition of The challenge of the sects [first published in 1954 under title Christian deviations]" Includes bibliographies. [BL98.D3 1965] 65-21054
1. Religions, Modern. I. Title.

DAVIES, Horton 289
Christian deviations: the challenge of the new spiritual movements. Philadelphia, Westminster [c.1954-1965] 144p. 19cm. Rev. ed. of The challenge of the sects first pub. in 1954 under title Christian deviations. Bibl. [BL98.D3] 65-21054 1.45 pap.,
1. Religion, Modern. I. Title.

ORRMONT, Arthur. 289
Love cults & faith healers. New York, Ballantine Books [1961] 192p. 18cm. (Ballantine books, F456K) Includes bibliography. [BR516.5.O75] 61-2029
1. Sects—U. S. I. Title.

ROBERTSON, Irvine. 289
What the cults believe. Chicago, Moody Press [1966] 128 p. 22 cm. Bibliography: p. 124-128. [BR157.R58] 66-16223
1. Sects. I. Title.

ROBERTSON, Irvine 289
What the cults believe. Chicago, Moody [c.1966] 128p. 22cm. Bibl. [BR157.R58] 66-16223 2.95
1. Sects. I. Title.

WILSON, Bryan R. 289
Sects and society; a sociological study of the Elim Tabernacle, Christian Science, and Christadelphians. Berkeley, University of California Press, 1961. 397 p. 22 cm. Bibliography: p. 374-388. [BX7435.E54W5] 61-65000
1. Elim Foursquare Gospel Alliance. 2. Christian Science — Gt. Brit. 3. Christadelphians — Gt. Brit. 4. Church and social problems — Gt. Brit. I. Title.

WILSON, Bryan R. 289
Sects and society; a sociological study of the Elim Tabernacle, Christian Science, and Christadelphians. Berkeley, Univ. of Calif. Pr. [c.]1961. 397p. Bibl. 61-65000 5.75
1. Elim Foursquare Gospel Alliance. 2. Christian Science—Gt. Brit. 3. Christadelphians—Gt. Brit. 4. Church and social problems—Gt. Brit. I. Title.

STERNER, R Eugene. 289.0
We reach our hands in fellowship; an introduction to the Church of God. Anderson. Ind., Warner Press [1960] 64 p. 19 cm. [BX7026.S75] 60-10187
1. Church of God (Anderson, Ind.) — Doctrinal and controversial works. I. Title.

HOEKEMA, Anthony A., 1913- 289.0973
The four major cults: Christian Science, Jehovah's Witnesses, Mormonism, Seventh-Day Adventism. Grand Rapids, Eerdmans [1963] xiv, 447 p. 24 cm. Bibliography: p. 417-435. [BR516.5.H6] 63-17783
1. Sects—U.S. 2. Christian Science. 3. Jehovah's Witnesses. 4. Mormons and Mormonism. 5. Seventh-Day Adventists. I. Title.

THE Christian 289.105
intelligencer and eastern chronicle. v. 1-16; Sept. 1821-Dec. 30, 1836. Portland [etc.] Me., Printed by Todd & Smith [etc.] 16 v. 21-31 cm. Vol. 1, no. 1-3 in Miscellaneous pamphlets, v. 839 (AC901.M5)Frequency varies. Title varies. Sept. 1821-Jan. 13, 1827, The Christian intelligencer. Edited by R. Streeter. L. C. set incomplete: v. 6, 13-16 and scattered issues wanting. [BX9901.C5] 57-52360
1. Universalism—Period. I. Streeter, Russell, ed.

THE Christian leader; 289.105
a journal of the Universalist fellowship. Boston [Universalist Pub. House] v. in illus., ports. 26-40 cm. Frequency varies. Began publication in 18?8. Cf. Union list of serials. Vols. 3-40. no. 7 also called 82d-119th year (v. 3, no. 17-v. 40, no. 7 also called new ser.) "Continuing the Christian leader and its predecessors (1819 to 1897) the Universalist and its predecessors (1827 to 1897) the Gospelbanner (1835 to 1897)" Title varies: 189 -Dec. 26, 1925. The Universalist leader. Subtitle varies (some issues without subtitle) [BX9901.U55] 52-31755
1. Universalist Church—Period.

BROOKS, Seth R. 289.1'092'4 B
Recollections and reflections of Seth R. Brooks and Corinne H. Brooks / edited by William Lloyd Fox. Washington : Universalist National Memorial Church, 1977. 106 p. ; 23 cm. [BX9969.B75A35] 77-84948
1. Brooks, Seth R. 2. Brooks, Corinne H. 3. Universalists—Washington, D.C.—Biography. 4. Washington, D.C.—Biography. I. Brooks, Corinne H., joint author. II. Fox, William Lloyd.

REVEREND Elhanan 289.1'0924 B
Winchester: biography and letters. New York, Arno Press, 1972. 252, 100 p. port. 23 cm. (Religion in America, series II) Reprint of Biography of Rev. Elhanan Winchester, by E. M. Stone, first published 1836; and of Ten letters addressed to Mr. Paine, in answer to his pamphlet, entitled The age of reason, by E. Winchester, first published 1795. [BX9969.W7R48] 72-38464 ISBN 0-405-04090-3
1. Winchester, Elhanan, 1751-1797. 2. Paine, Thomas, 1737-1809. The age of reason. I. Stone, Edwin Martin, 1805-1883. Biography of Rev. Elhanan Winchester. 1972. II. Winchester, Elhanan, 1751-1797. Ten letters addressed to Mr. Paine, in answer to his pamphlet, entitled The age of reason. 1972.

CASSARA, Ernest, 1925- comp. 289.1'73
Universalism in America; a documentary history. Boston, Beacon Press [1971] xi, 290 p. 21 cm. Includes bibliographical references. [BX9941.2.C38] 77-136226 ISBN 0-8070-1664-0 10.00
1. Universalism. I. Title.

ROBINSON, Elmo Arnold, 1887- 289.1'73
American Universalism; its origins, organization, and heritage. [1st ed.] New York, Exposition Press [1970] 266 p. 22 cm. (An Exposition-testament book) Bibliography: p. [239]-245. [BX9933.R59] 76-126375 7.50
1. Universalist Church—U.S. I. Title.

SCOTT, Clinton Lee. 289.173
The Universalist Church of America, a short history. Boston, Universalist Historical Society [c1957] 124p. 22cm. Includes bibliography. [BX9933.S3] 58-20928
1. Universalist Church of America—Hist. I. Title.

WILLIAMS, George Huntston, 1914- 289.1'73
American universalism; a bicentennial historical essay. [Boston] Universalist Historical Society [1971] v, 94 p. 23 cm. (The Journal of the Universalist Historical Society, v. 9) Includes bibliographical references. [BX9903.U524 vol. 9] [BX9933] 76-27471
1. Universalist Church—U.S. I. Title. II. Series: Universalist Historical Society. Journal, v. 9.

WATT, Donald. 289.1'746
From heresy toward truth; the story of Universalism in Greater Hartford and Connecticut, 1821-1971. [West Hartford] Universalist Church of West Hartford, Conn. [1971] x, 177 p. illus. 23 cm. [BX9933.5.C8W38] 76-177978 3.75
1. Universalist Church—Connecticut. I. Title.

STANDER, Thomas F. 289.1'771'75
The universalist saga of Bunker Hill / by Thomas F. Stander. Baltimore : Gateway Press, 1974. 35 p. : ill. ; 22 cm. Bibliography: p. 35. [BX9961.B85S73] 74-80998 pbk. : 5.00
1. Bunker Hill Universalist Church. I. Title.

ALWARD, Benjamin B comp. 289.3
Handy Scripture guide. 1st ed. Salt Lake City, Deseret Book Co., 1957. 225p. 18cm. [BX8631.A7] 57-47818
1. Mormons and Mormonism—Doctrinal and controversial works. 2. Bible—Indexes, Topical. I. Title.

ALWARD, Benjamin B comp. 289.3
Know the Latter-Day Scriptures. Salt Lake City, Deseret Book Co., 1958. 571p. 23cm. 'Thirty-eight basic subjects of the Gospel supported by more than one thousand scriptural passages taken from the Book of Mormon, Doctrine and covenants, and Pearl of great price.' [BX8631.A72] 58-30624
1. Mormons and Mormonism—Doctrinal and controversial works. I. Book of Mormon. II. Smith, Joseph. 1805-1844. The pearl of great price. III. Smith, Joseph, 1805-1844. Doctrine and covenants. IV. Title.

ALWARD, Benjamin B comp. 289.3
A look at Mormonism: pictorial highlights of the church and its people. 1st ed. Salt Lake City, Deseret Book Co., 1956. 202p. illus. 28cm. [BX8638.A6] 57-32594
1. Mormons and Mormonism—Pictures, illustrations, etc. I. Title.

ANDERSON, Einar. 289.3
I was a Mormon. Grand Rapids, Zondervan Pub. House [1964] 186 p. illus., ports. 23 cm. Bibliography: p. 183-186. [BX8645.A65] 64-15556
1. Mormons and Mormonism — Doctrinal and controvesial works. I. Title.

ANDERSON, Einar 289.3
I was a Mormon. Grand Rapids, Mich., Zondervan [c.1964] 186p. illus., ports. 23cm Bibl. [BX8645.A65] 64-15556 2.95 bds.,
1. Mormons and Mormonism—Doctrinal and controversial works. I. Title.

ANDERSON, Nels, 1889- 289.3
Desert saints: the Mormon frontier in Utah. Chicago, University of Chicago Press [1966] xxxvi, 459 p. illus., ports. 21 cm. First published 1942. Bibliography: p. 447-452. [BX8611.A49 1966] 66-19134
1. Mormons and Mormonism—History. I. Title.

ANDRUS, Hyrum Leslie, 1924- 289.3
Joseph Smith and world government. Salt Lake City, Deseret Book Co. 1958. 127p. illus. 20cm. [BX8695.S6A7] 58-2284
1. Smith, Joseph, 1805-1844. I. Title.

ANDRUS, Hyrum Leslie, 1924- 289.3
Liberalism, conservatism, Mormonism, by Hyrum L. Andrus. Salt Lake City, Deseret Book Co., 1965. xi, 100 p. 24 cm. Bibliographical footnotes. [BX8638.A76] 65-27489
1. Church and state — Mormonism. 2. Sociology, Christian (Mormon) I. Title.

ARBAUGH, George Bartholomew, 1905- 289.3
Gods, sex, and saints; the Mormon story. Rock Island, Ill., Augustana Press [1957] 61p. 20cm. [BX8645.A7] 57-8570
1. Mormons and Mormonism. I. Title.

ATKINSON, Mabel Sanford. 289.3
The land shadowing with wings. Independence, Mo., Herald House [1952] 270 p. 21 cm. "The language and content of the Book of Mormon in slmplified and abbrevialed form."--Dust jacket. [BX8627.A2A8] 52-9297
1. Book of Mormon stories. I. Book of Mormon. II. Title.

BACH, Marcus, 1906- 289.3
The Mormon. [Salt Lake City] Deseret Book Co., by special arrangement with the Bobbs-Merrill Co. [1951] 63 p. 20 cm. "From [the author's] Faith and my friends." [BX8611.B3] 51-8642
1. Mormons and Mormonism—Hist. I. Title.

BAILEY, Paul Dayton 289.3
Grandpa was a polygamist; a candid remembrance. Los Angeles, Westernlore Press, c.1960. 181p. illus. 21cm. 60-13175 5.50
1. Mormons and Mormonism. I. Title.

BAILEY, Paul Dayton, 1906- 289.3
The armies of God [by] Paul Bailey. Garden City, N.Y., Doubleday, 1968. ix, 300 p. illus. 22 cm. Bibliography: p. [285]-291. [BX8611.B317] 68-29282 5.95
1. Mormons and mormonism—History, Military. I. Title.

BAILEY, Paul Dayton, 1906- 289.3
Grandpa was a polugamist; a candid remembrance. Los Angeles, Westernlore Press, 1960. 181p. illus. 21cm. [BX8638.B3] 60-13175
1. Mormons and Mormonlsm. I. Title.

BARKER, James Louis, 1880-1958. 289.3
Restoration of the divine church. Salt Lake City, K. M. Barker [c1960] 140p. 24cm. Includes bibliography. [BX8611.B32] 61-37758
1. Mormons and Mormonism—Hist. I. Title.

BENNETT, Archibald F 1896- 289.3
Searching with success; a genealogical text. Salt Lake City, Deseret Book Co., 1962. 262p. illus. 24cm. [CS16.B42] 62-4379
1. Genealogy. 2. Mormons and Mormonism—Geneal. I. Title.

BENNETT, Archibald F. 1896- 289.3
Searching with success; a genealogical text. Salt Lake City, Utah, Deseret Bk. Co. [c.] 1962. 262p. illus. 24cm. 62-4379 2.95
1. Genealogy. 2. Mormons and Mormonism—Geneal. I. Title.

BENNETT, Wallace Foster. 289.3
Why I am a Mormon. New York, T. Nelson [1958] 256p. 21cm. [BX8635.B39] 58-8020
1. Mormons and Mormonism. I. Title.

BENNION, Howard S 289.3
Genealogical research; a practical mission, by Howard S. Bennion. Salt Lake City, Descret Sunday School Union [1964] viii, 226 p. facsims., forms, plans. 23 cm. vii. 126 p. facsims., forms. 23 cm. CS16.B44 Suppl. "For the Sunday Schools of the Church of Jesus Christ of Latter-Day Saints." Teacher's supplement, by Donna D. Sorensen. Salt Lake City, Descret Sunday School Union [1964] [CS16.B44] 65-2968
1. Sorensen, Donna D. 2. Genealogy — Research. 3. Mormons and Mormonism — Geneal, I. Church of Jesus Christ of Latter-Day Saints. II. Title.

BENNION, Lowell Lindsay, 1908- 289.3
An introduction to the Gospel. Course no. 28 for the Sunday schools of the Church of Jesus Christ of Latter-Day Saints. Salt Lake City, Deseret Sunday School Union Board [1955] 319p. illus. 24cm. [BX8G10.B4] 56-16954
1. Mormons and Mormonism—Doctrinal and controversial works. 2. Church of Jesus Christ of Latter-Day Saints. Deseret Sunday School Union. I. Title.

BENNION, Lowell Lindsay, 1908- 289.3
Religion and the pursuit of truth. Salt Lake City, Deseret Book Co., 1959. 180p. 24cm. [BX8635.2.B4] 59-33737
1. Mormons and Mormonism—Doctrinal and controversial works. 2. Religion and science—1900- I. Title.

BERRETT, William Edwin. 289.3
The restored church; a brief history of the growth and doctrines of the Church of Jesus Christ of Latter-Day Saints. 10th ed. [Salt Lake City] Deseret Book Co., 1961. 490p. illus. 27cm. Includes bibliography. [BX8611.B35 1961] 61-65165
1. Mormons and Mormonism. I. Title.

BERRETT, William Edwin. 289.3
Teachings of the Book of Mormon. [Salt Lake City] Printed by the Desert News Press [1952] 239 p. 20 cm. [BX9627.B4] 52-44397
1. Book of Mormon. I. Title.

BIBLE. English. 1959. Authorized. 289.3
Holy Scriptures of the Church of Jesus Christ of Latter-Day Saints: Holy Bible. Book of Mormon. Doctrine and covenants. Pearl of great price. Including indexes, concordances, and the combination reference to the four standard works, masterpieces of religious art, a pictorial history of the church, family genealogical records, Bible maps, and other inspirational and informative features. [1st ed.] Salt Lake City, Published by Deseret Book Co., for Wheelwright Publications [1960] 1v. (various pagings) col. illus., col. maps, col. ports. 30cm. Each work has special t. p. [BX8621.D4 1960] 60-2641
1. Mormons and Mormonism. I. Book of Mormon. II. Smith, Joseph, 1805-1844. The doctrine and covenants of the Church of Jesus Christ of Latter—Day Saints. III. Smith, Joseph, 1805-1844. Pearl of great price. IV. Church of Jesus Christ of Latter-Day Saints. V. Title.

BOOK of Mormon. 289.3
The Book of Mormon; an account written by the hand of Mormon, upon plates taken from the plates of Nephi. By Joseph Smith, Junior. Palmyra [N. Y.] Printed by E. B. Grandin for the author, 1830. [Salt Lake City; W. C. Wood, 1958] [33] p., facsim. (588 p.), [27] p. illus., ports., map. facsims. 24cm. (Joseph Smith begins his work; [edited by] Wilford C. Wood, v. 1) Reproduced from uncut sheets of the 1st ed. in the possession of Wilford C. Wood. [BX8621.W6 vol. 1] 58-2405
I. Smith, Joseph, 1805- 1844. II. Title. III. Series: Wood, Wilford C., ed. Joseph Smith begins his work, v. 1

BOOK of Mormon. 289.3
Book of Mormon commentary, by Eldin Ricks. [1st ed. Salt Lake City] Deseret News Press, 1951- v. 19cm. Contents.v.1. The first book of Nephl. Includes bibliographies. [BX8623 1951] 55-42346
I. Ricks, Eldin, ed. II. Title.

BOOK of Mormon. 289.3
Christ in the Book of Mormon, compiled by Ezra L. Marler. Salt Lake City, Deseret Book Co., 1956. 156p. 16cm. [BX8623 1956] 56-42692
1. Jesus Christ—Mormon interpretations. I. Marler, Ezra L., ed. II. Title.

BOOK of Mormon. 289.3
Commentary on the Book of Mormon, by George Reynolds and Janne M. Sjodahl. Edited and arranged by Philip C. Reynolds. [1st ed.] Salt Lake City, 1955 [i. e. 1956]- v. 24cm. [BX8627.R39] 60-20122
1. Book of Mormon. I. Reynolds, George, 1842-1909. II. Sjodahl, Janne Mattson, 1853-1939. III. Title.

BOOK of Mormon. 289.3
Gospel teachings in the Book of Mormon, compiled by Ezra L. Marler. Salt Lake City, Deseret Book Co., 1956. 155p. 16cm. [BX8623 1956a] 56-45154
I. Marler, Ezra L., comp. II. Title.

BOOK of Mormon. 289.3
Gospel teachings the Book of Mormon, compiled by Ezra L. Marler. Salt Lake City,

DeSeret Book Co., 1956. 155p. 16cm. [BX8623 1956a] 56-45154
I. Marler, Ezra L. comp. II. Title.

BOOK of Mormon. 289.3
History and stories in the Book of Mormon. Compiled by Ezra L. Marler. Salt Lake City, Deseret Book Co., 1956. 180p. 16cm. [BX8627.A2A3] 57-19525
1. Book of Mormon stories. I. Marler, Ezra L. comp. II. Title.

BOOK of Mormon. 289.3
"Is that in the Book of Mormon?" A classified collection of the unusual, and perhaps surprising items of general human interest contained in the Book of Mormon ... By D. Clyde Lloyd. [1st ed. Salt Lake City, 1962] 152 p. 21 cm. [BX8627.A1A4] 63-1934
1. Book of Mormon — Indexes, Topical. I. Lloyd, D. Clyde. II. Title.

BOOK of Mormon. 289.3
The New Testament of ancient America; adapted from the third book of Nephi of the Book of Mormon. Independence, Mo., Herald House [c1955] 216p. 12cm. [BX8623 1955] 56-7615
I. Title.

BOOK of Mormon. Spanish 289.3
Libro de Mormon. Traducido de las laminas originales al ingles por Jose Smith, hijo. [Traducido del ingles al espanol por Carlos R. Hield] Independence, Mo., Junta de Publicaciones, Iglesia Reorganizada de Jesucristo de los Santos de los Ultimos Dias [dist. Herald House] [c.]1960. 839p. 19cm. 60-3097 3.50; 2.00 pap.,
1. Smith, Joseph, 1805-1844. I. Title.

BOUCHER, Theophiel. 289.3
Mormonism -- faith or fallacy. [1st ed.] New York, Pageant Press [1960, c1959] 432p. 21cm. [BX8645.B64] 59-14473
1. Mormons and Mormonism—Doctrinal and controversial works. I. Title.

BRIGHAM Young University, 289.3
Provo, Utah. University Archaeological Society. U.A.S. newsletter.
Progress in archaeology; an anthology. Compiled and edited by Ross T. Christensen. Provo, Utah, Brigham Young University, 1963. xiii, 219 p. illus., maps. 23 cm. ([Brigham Young University, Provo, Utah] University Archaeological Society. Special publications, no. 4) "Selections from the first 85 issues of the U.A.S. newsletter, 1951-1963, presenting views and discoveries of special interest to students of the Scriptures." Bibliographical footnotes. [BX8627.B67] 230.93 68-2299
1. Book of Mormon—Antiquities. 2. Bible—Antiquities. I. Christensen, Ross Taylor, 1918- ed. II. Title. III. Series.

BROWN, Hugh B 289.3
Eternal quest. Selected, arr. and edited by Charles Manley Brown. Salt Lake City, Bookcraft [c1956] 448p. 24cm. [BX8609.B7] 58-48849
1. Mormons and Mormonism— Addresses, essays, lectures. I. Title.

BROWN, Hugh B. 289.3
Mormonism . . . address . . . delivered on Monday, Feb. 26, 1962, to the students at the Pittsburgh Theological Seminary, Pittsburgh, Pa. Salt Lake City, Utah, Deseret [c.1962] 62p. illus. 20cm. 62-3768 .50 pap.,
1. Mormons and Mormonism. I. Title.

BROWN, Hugh B. 289.3
Vision and valor [by] Hugh B. Brown. Salt Lake City, Bookcraft, 1971. x, 262 p. port. 24 cm. [BX8609.B73] 70-154210
1. Mormons and Mormonism—Addresses, essays, lectures. I. Title.

BRYANT, Verda Evelyn 289.3
(Bilger)
Between the covers of the Doctrine and covenants. Independence, Mo., Herald House, 1958. 272p. illus. 21cm. [BX8673.B7] 58-8199
1. Reorganized Church of Jesus Christ of Latter-Day Saints—Hist. 2. Smith, Joseph, 1805-1844. Doctrine and covenants. I. Title.

BURTON, Alma P 1913- comp. 289.3
Stories from Mormon history, by Alma P. Burton and Clea M. Burton. 1st ed. Salt Lake City, Deseret Book Co. [1960] 310p. 24cm. [BX8611.B79] 60-33251
1. Mormons and Mormonism—Hist. I. Burton, Clea M., joint comp. II. Title.

CACHE Genealogical Library, 289.3
Logan, Utah.
Handbook for genealogical correspondence. John F. Valentine, editor. Salt Lake City, Bookcraft, 1963. 273 p. illus. 24 cm. [CS16.C3] 63-23732
1. Genalogy. I. Vallentine, John F., ed. II. Title.

CANNON, George Quayle, 289.3
1827-1901.
The life of Nephi, the son of Lehi, who emigrated from Jerusalem, in Judea, to the land which is now known as South America, about six centuries before the coming of our Savior. Salt Lake City, Deseret Book Co., 1957. 167p. 16cm. [BX8629.C3 1957] 57-59396
1. Book of Mormon. I. Title.

CARMER, Carl Lamson, 1893- 289.3
The farm boy and the angel [by] Carl Carmer. [1st ed.] Garden City, N.Y., Doubleday, 1970. 237 p. 22 cm. Bibliography: p. 220-229. [BX8635.2.C36] 76-105616 5.95
1. Mormons and Mormonism. I. Title.

CHEVILLE, Roy Arthur, 1897- 289.3
Scriptures from ancient America; a study of the Book of Mormon. [Independence, Mo.] Dept. of Religious Education, Reorganized Church of Jesus Christ of Latter Day Saints [1964] 368 p. 21 cm. [BX8628.C5] 64-12944
1. Book of Mormon — Introductions. I. Title.

CHEVILLE, Roy Arthur, 1897- 289.3
Scriptures from ancient America; a study of the Book of Mormon [Independence, Mo.] Dept. of Religious Education, Reorganized Church of Jesus Christ of Latter Day Saints [dist. Herald Pub Co., c.1964] 368p. 21cm. 64-12944 3.75; 2.50 pap.,
1. Book of Mormon—Introductions. I. Title.

CLARK, James Ratcliffe, 289.3
1910-
The story of the Pearl of great price. [1st ed.] Salt Lake City, Bookcraft [1955] 253p. illus. 24cm. [BX8629.P6C55] 56-16603
1. Smith, Joseph, 1805-1844. Pearl of great price. I. Title. II. Title: Pearl of great price.

CLARK, Joshua Reuben, 1871- 289.3
1961.
Behold the Lamb of God; selections from the sermons and writings published and unpublished by J. Reuben Clark, Jr., on the life of the Savior. Salt Lake City, Deseret Book Co., 1962. 382 p. illus. 24 cm. [BX8639.C5B4] 63-1083
1. Mormons and Mormonism — Doctrinal and controversial works. I. Title.

CLINEFELTER, William R 289.3
The covenant and the kingdom by William R. Clinefelter and the Dept. of Religious Education. [Independence, Mo.,] Dept. of Religious Education, Reorganized Church of Jesus Christ of Latter Day Saints [1964] 138 p. 21 cm. [BT155.C54] 64-23133
1. Covenants (Theology) I. Reorganized Church of Jesus Christ of Latter-Day Saints. Dept of Religious Education. II. Title.

CLINEFELTER, William R. 289.3
The covenant and the kingdom, by William R. Clinefelter and the Dept. of Religious Educ. [Independence, Mo.] Dept. of Religious Educ., Reorganized Church of Jesus Christ of Latter Day Saints [c.1964] 138p. 21cm. 64-23133 2.00; 1.25 pap.,
1. Covenants (Theology) I. Reorganized Church of Jesus Christ of Latter-Day Saints. Dept. of Religious Education. II. Title.

COOK, Alonzo Laker. 289.3
A study of the gospel of Our Savior. [Independence, Mo., Zion's Print. and Pub. Co., 1946-50. 2v. port. 19cm. Vol. 2 has imprint: Tremonton, Utah. [BX8635.C6] 47-17025
1. Mormons and Mormonism—Doctrinal and controversial works. I. Title.

COWAN, Richard O., 1934- 289.3
The Doctrine and covenants, our modern scripture [by] Richard O. Cowan. 2d ed. rev. Provo, Utah, Brigham Young University Press [1969] xix, 151 p. illus. 28 cm. Bibliography: p. 145-146. [BS8628.C69 1969] 76-243194
1. Smith, Joseph, 1805-1844. Doctrine and covenants. 2. Mormons and Mormonism—Doctrinal and controversial works. I. Title.

CROWTHER, Jean Decker. 289.3
Growing up in the church. Illustrated by Carol Niederhauser [and] Roger Matkin. Salt Lake City, Deseret Book Co., 1965. ix. 76 p. illus. 24 cm. [BX8610.C7] 65-28861
1. Religious education — Text-books for children — Mormon. I. Title.

A Decade of the best; 289.3
the Elbert A. Smith award winning articles of 1961-1970. [Independence, Mo., Herald Pub. House, 1972] 239 p. front. 21 cm. Collection of articles published in the Saints' herald. [BX8637.D4] 72-182435 ISBN 0-8309-0058-6
1. Mormons and Mormonism—Addresses, essays, lectures. 2. Theology—Addresses, essays, lectures. I. Saints' herald.

DE JONG, Gerrit, 1892- 289.3
The Gospel today [by] Gerrit de Jong, Jr. Salt Lake City, Deseret Book Co., 1966. viii, 387 p. col. illus. 24 cm. "Recommended readings": p. [379]-383. Bibliographical footnotes. [BX8635.2.D4] 66-29995
1. Mormons and Mormonism. I. Title.

THE Doctrine and covenants 289.3
speaks, by Roy W. Doxey. Salt Lake City, Deseret Book Co. [1964- v. 24 cm. Bibliography: v. 1, p. [563]-564. [BX8628.D685] 64-57862
1. Smith, Joseph, 1805-1844. Doctrine and covenants.

DOXEY, Roy Watkins, 1908- 289.3
The Doctrine and covenants speaks, by Roy W. Doxey. Salt Lake City, Deseret Book Co. [1964- v. 24 cm. Bibliography: v. 1, p. [563]-564. [BX8628.D685] 64-57862
1. Smith, Joseph, 1805-1844. Doctrine and covenants. I. Title.

DOXEY, Roy Watkins, 1908- 289.3
ed.
The Latter-day prophets and the Doctrine and covenants. Salt Lake City, Deseret Book Co., 1963-65. 4 v. 24 cm. [BX8628.D69] 64-2097
1. Smith, Joseph, 1805-1844. Doctrine and covenants. I. Smith, Joseph, 1805-1844. Doctrine and covenants. II. Title.

DOXEY, Roy Watkins, 1908- 289.3
ed.
The Latter-day prophets and the Doctrine and covenants. Salt Lake City, Deseret Book Co., 1963-65. 4 v. 24 cm. [BX8628.D69] 64-2097
1. Smith, Joseph, 1805-1844. Doctrine and covenants. I. Smith, Joseph, 1805-1844. Doctrine and covenants. II. Title.

DYER, Alvin R. 289.3
The fallacy, Salt Lake City, Utah, Deseret [c.] 1964. xi, 153p. col. illus. col. ports. 24cm. Bibl. 64-30375 price unreported
1. Mormons and Mormonism—Doctrinal and controversial works. 2. Reorganized Church of Jesus Christ of Latter-Day Saints—Doctrinal and controversial works. I. Title.

DYER, Alvin R. 289.3
The Lord speaketh, the true significance of the Sacred Grove interview with the Prophet, Joseph Smith. Salt Lake City, Deseret [c.] 1964. xxiii, 337p. 24cm. Bibl. 64-3444 3.58 bds.,
1. Mormons and Mormonism. I. Title.

EDWARDS, Francis Henry, 289.3
1897-
Authority and spiritual power: Reorganized Church of Jesus Christ of Latter Day Saints. Independence, Mo., Herald House [1956] 125p. 21cm. [BX8674.E3] 56-11958
1. Reorganized Church of Jesus Christ of Latter-Day Saints— Doctrinal and controversial works. I. Title.

EDWARDS, Francis Henry, 289.3
1897-
For such a time. Independence, Mo., Herald Pub. House, 1963. 351 p. 21 cm. Chiefly selections from the author's editorials, articles, sermons, etc. [BX8674.E32] 62-22193
1. Reorganized Church of Jesus Christ of Latter-Day Saints—Collected works. I. Title.

EDWARDS, Francis Henry, 289.3
1897-
For such a time. Independence, Mo., Herald Pub. [c.]1963. 351p. 21cm. 62-22193 3.75
1. Reorganized Church of Jesus Christ of Latter-Day Saints—Collected works. I. Title.

ELLEDGE, Helen 289.3
Book of Mormon stories for children. Illus. by Edith Brockway. Independence, Mo., Herald House [c.]1962. 125p. 24cm. 62-20014 1.75 bds.,
1. Book of Mormon stories. I. Title.

FARNSWORTH, Dewey. 289.3
Book of Mormon evidences in ancient America, compiled by Dewey Farnsworth [and] Edith Wood Farnsworth. Salt Lake City, Deseret Book Co., c1953. 176p. illus., maps. 31cm. Bibliography: p.175-176. [BX8627.F3] 54-27103
1. Book of Mormon. I. Farnsworth, Edith Wood, joint author. II. Title.

FETTING, Otto, 1871-1933. 289.3
The Word of the Lord. Independence, Mo., Church of Christ, 1951. 228 p. 21 cm. "Revelations on the building of the temple and instruction to the Church of Christ" made to Otto Fetting and W. A. Draves from February 4, 1927 to June 11, 1945. [BX8680.F4W6 1951] 52-16063
1. Independence, Mo. Church of Christ. I. Draves, Wilhelm A. II. Title.

FRASER, Gordon Holmes. 289.3
What does the Book of Mormon teach? An examination of the historical and scientific statements of the Book of Mormon, by Gordon H. Fraser. Chicago, Moody Press [1964] 128 p. 18 cm. (M. P. colportage library, 501) Includes bibliographies. [BX8627.F7] 64-4647
1. Book of Mormon. I. Title.

FRASER, Gordon Holmes 289.3
What does the Book of Mormon teach? An examination of the historical and scientific statements of the book of Mormon. Chicago, Moody [c.1964] 128p. 18cm. (M. P. colportage lib., 501) Bibl. 64-4647 .39 pap.,
1. Book of Mormon. I. Title.

FREE, Jack 289.3
Mormonism and inspiration; a study. Concord, Calif. Pacific Pub. Co. [1963, c.1962] 381p. 21cm. 63-2729 4.50
1. Mormons and Mormonism—Sacred books—Inspiration. I. Title.

GENEALOGICAL Associates. 289.3
Genealogy and local history; an archival and bibliographical guide. 2d rev. ed. Evanston, Ill., c1962. 125 l. 28 cm. [CS16.G37 1962] 63-2316
1. Genealogy. I. Title.

GENEALOGICAL Society of the 289.3
Church of Jesus Christ of Latter-Day Saints.
Handbook of genealogy and temple work. Salt Lake City, Genealogical Society of Utah, 1924. 336 p. illus., coats of arms. 20 cm. [CS16.G4] 25-16249
1. Genealogy. 2. Mormons and Mormonism—Geneal. I. Title.

GLANZ, Rudolf 289.3
Jew and Mormon: historic group relations and religious outlook. New York, 620 W. 711 St., Author, 1963. 379p. 24cm. Bibl. 63-16229 6.00
1. Mormons and Mormonism—Relations—Judaism. 2. Judaism—Relations—Mormonism. I. Title.

GOD'S final message to the 289.3
nations of the world: The fullness of the everlasting gospel and 'The World of the Lord' (as delivered to the nations of the earth) Presented by the Remnant Group of the Church of Christ. [1st ed.] New York, Exposition Press [1955] 192p. 21cm. [BX8680.R34G6] 55-11131
1. Church of Christ (Remnant Group) I. The Word of the Lord. II. Title: The fullness of the everlasting gospel.

GREEN, Forace, comp. 289.3
Cowley & Whitney on doctrine. Salt Lake City, Bookcraft [1963] 517 p. illus. 24 cm. "Originally published as Cowley's Talks on doctrine and [Whitney's] Saturday night thoughts." [BX8635.G74] 63-4149
1. Mormons and Mormonism—Doctrinal and controversial works. I. Cowley, Matthias Foss, 1858- Talks on doctrine. II. Whitney, Orson Ferguson, 1855-1931. Saturday night thoughts. III. Title.

GREEN, Forace, comp. 289.3
Cowley & Whitney on doctrine. Salt Lake City, Bkcraft [c.1963] 517p. illus. 24cm. Orig. pub. as Cowley's Talks on doctrine and [Whitney's] Saturday night thoughts. 63-4149 4.00
1. Mormons and Mormonism—Doctrinal and controversial works. I. Cowley, Matthias Foss, 1858-Talks on doctrine. II. Whitney, Orson Ferguson, 1855-1931. Saturday night thoughts. III. Title.

HAMMOND, Fletcher B 289.3
Geography of the Book of Mormon. [Salt Lake City? 1959] 157p. illus. 24cm. [BX8627.H32] 60-19259
1. Book of Mormon. I. Title.

HANSON, Paul M 1878- 289.3
Jesus Christ among the ancient Americans. [Completely rev. ed.] Independence, Mo., Herald Pub. House, 1959. 204p. illus. 21cm. Includes bibliography. [BX8638.H3 1959] 59-8363
1. Mormons and Mormonism. I. Title.

HARMER, Lewis J 289.3
Revelation. Salt Lake City, Bookcraft [1957] 297p. 24cm. [BX8643.R4H3] 58-15187
1. Revelation (Mormonism) I. Title.

HARTSHORN, Chris Benson. 289.3
A commentary on the Book of Mormon [by] Chris B. Hartshorn. Independence, Mo., Herald Pub. House [1964] 504 p. maps. 28 cm. [BX8627.H35] 63-19791
1. Book of Mormon I. Title.

HARTSHORN, Chris Benson 289.3
A commentary on the Book of Mormon. Independence, Mo., Herald [c.1964] 504p. maps. 23cm. 63-19791 6.50
1. Book of Mormon. I. Title.

HARTSHORN, Chris Benson. 289.3
A survey of the doctrine and covenants. Independence, Mo., Herald House, 1961. 168p. 21cm. Includes bibliography. [BX8628.H3] 61-17863
1. Reorganized Church of Jesus Christ of Latter-Day Saints. Book of doctrine and covenants. I. Title.

HARTSHORN, Chris Benson 289.3
A survey of the doctrine and covenants. Independence, Mo., Herald House [c.]1961. 168p. Bibl. 61-17863 2.00
1. Reorganized Church of Jesus Christ of Latter-Day Saints. Book of doctrine and covenants. I. Title.

HOWELLS, Rulon Stanley, 1902- 289.3
The Mormon story; a pictorial account of Mormonism. [1st ed.] Salt Lake City, Bookcraft [1957] 179p. illus. 28cm. [BX8638.H64] 57-14509
1. Mormons and Mormonism—Pictures, illustrations, etc. I. Title.

HOWELLS, Rulon Stanley, 1902- 289.3
The Mormon story; a pictorial account of Mormonism. 11th ed. Salt Lake City, Bookcraft, 1963. 179p. illus. 32cm. 63-3998 3.95
1. Mormons and Mormonism—Pictures, illustrations, etc. I. Title.

HOWELLS, Rulon Stanley, 1902- 289.3
The Mormon story; a pictorial account of Mormonism. 21st ed. Salt Lake City, Bookcraft, 1964. 100p. illus. (pt. col.) maps (pt. col.) ports. (pt. col.) 32cm. 64-6467 price unreported
1. Mormons and Mormonism—Pictures illustrations, etc. I. Title.

HUNTER, Milton Reed, 1902- 289.3
Archaeology and the Book of Mormon. [1st ed.] Salt Lake City, Deseret Book Co. [c1956- v. illus. 25cm. [BX8627.H82] 57-17933
1. Book of Mormon. I. Title.

HUNTER, Rodello. 289.3
A daughter of Zion. Drawings by Allan P. Nielson. [1st ed.] New York, Knopf, 1972. xiv, 285 p. illus. 22 cm. [BX8695.H83A3] 74-171116 ISBN 0-394-47032-X 6.95
1. Mormons and Mormonism. I. Title.

JENSEN, Margie Calhoun, comp. 289.3
When faith writes the story. Salt Lake City, Bookcraft [1973] xvi, 280 p. 24 cm. Includes bibliographical references. [BX8608.J46] 73-88615
1. Church of Jesus Christ of Latter-Day Saints—Collected works. I. Title.

JONES, Vincent L 289.3
The jurisdictional approach to genealogical research; a manual of systematic procedures [by] Vincent L. Jones, Arlene H. Eakle [and] Mildred H. Christensen. Woods Cross, Utah 1965- v. 28 cm. [CS9.J6] 65-3343
1. Genealogy—Research. 2. Mormons and Mormonism—Geneal. I. Eakle, Arlene H., joint author. II. Christensen, Mildren H., joint author. III. Title.

JONES, Wesley M. 289.3
A critical study of Book of Mormon sources. Detroit, Harlo Pr. [1965, c.]1964. 99p. 21cm. [BX8627J6] 65-1851 4.50
1. Book of Mormon. I. Title.

KIRKHAM, Francis Washington, 1877- 289.3
A new witness for Christ in America, the Book of Mormon. [Enl. 3d ed. Independence, Mo., Press of Zion's Print. and Pub. Co., 1951] 2v. 20cm. First published in 1937 under title: Source material concerning the origin of the Book of Mormon. [BX8627.K5 1951] 56-29311
1. Book of Mormon. 2. Mormons and Mormonism. I. Title.

KIRKHAM, Oscar A 1880- 289.3
Say the good word. Salt Lake City, Deseret Book Co.. 1958. 273p. illus. 24cm. [BX8609.K5] 58-35735
1. Mormons and Mormonism—Addresses, essays, lectures. I. Title.

KJELGAARD, James Arthur, 1910- 289.3
The coming of the Mormons; illustrated by Stephen J. Voorhies. New York, Random House [1953] 183 p. illus. 22 cm. (Landmark books, 37) [BX8611.K55] 53-6257
1. Mormons and Mormonism—History. I. Title.

KJELGAARD, James Arthur, 1910-1959. 289.3
The coming of the Mormons; illustrated by Stephen J. Voorhies. New York, Random House [1953] 183 p. illus. 22 cm. (Landmark books, 37) A brief history of the Mormons in America: their journey westward, their founding of Salt Lake City, and their influence on and development of the West. [BX8611.K55] AC 68
1. Mormons and Mormonism—History. I. Voorhies, Stephen J., illus. II. Title.

KOURY, Aleah G. 289.3
The truth and the evidence; a comparison between doctrines of the Reorganized Church of Jesus Christ of Latter Day Saints and the Church of Jesus Christ of Latter-Day Saints, by Aleah G. Koury. [Independence, Mo., Herald Pub. House. 1965] 112 p. 18 cm. Bibliographical footnotes. [BX8674.K6] 65-26287
1. Reorganized Church of Jesus Christ of Latter-Day Saints—Doctrinal and controversial works. 2. Church of Jesus Christ of Latter-Day Saints—Doctrinal and controversial works. I. Title.

LEE, Hector Haight, 1908- 289.3
The three Nephites; the substance and significance of the legend in folklore. Albuquerque, University of New Mexico Press, 1949. 162 p. map. 23 cm. (University of New Mexico publications in language and literature, no. 2) Bibliography: p. 127-134. [BX8627.L44] 49-47373
1. Nephites. I. Title. II. Series: New Mexico. University. University of New Mexico publications in language and literature, no. 2

LINFORD, Marilynne Todd. 289.3
ABC's for young LDS. Illustrated by Joyce Bigelow Mann. Salt Lake City, Bookcraft, 1971. 60 p. col. illus. 29 cm. Brief alphabetically arranged entries, from Adam to Zion, define basic concepts of Mormon theology. [BX8635.2.L55] 70-175138
1. Mormons and Mormonism—Juvenile literature. I. Mann, Joyce Bigelow, illus. II. Title.

LINN, William Alexander, 1846-1917 289.3
The story of the Mormons: from the date of their origin to the year 1901. New York, Russell, 1963. 637p. illus. 23cm. 63-12565 10.00
1. Mormons and Mormonism. 2. Utah—Hist. I. Title.

LINN, William Alexander, 1846-1917. 289.3
The story of the Mormons; from the date of their origin to the year 1901. from the date of their origin to the year 1901. New York, Russell & Russell, 1963. 637 p. illus. 23 cm. [BX8611.L5 1963] 63-12565
1. Mormons and Mormonism. 2. Utah — Hist. I. Title.

LOUTENSOCK, Sarah. 289.3
The plan of salvation; a Christian's defense of the economic system of Jesus Christ. Boston, Forum Pub. Co. [1963] 504 p. illus. 24 cm. [BX8628.L6] 63-599
1. Smith, Joseph, 1805-1844; The doctrine and covenants of the Church of Jesus Christ of Latter-Day Saints. 2. Mormons and Mormonism — Doctrinal and controversial works. I. Title.

LOUTENSOCK, Sarah 289.3
The plan of salvation; a Christian's defense of the economic system of Jesus Christ. Boston, Forum [c.1963] 504p. illus. 24cm. 63-599 3.50
1. Smith, Joseph, 1805-1844. The doctrine and covenants of the Church of Jesus Christ of Latter-Day Saints. 2. Mormons and Mormonism—Doctrinal and controversial works. I. Title.

MCGAVIN, Elmer Cecil 289.3
How we got the Book of Mormon. Salt Lake City, Utah, Deseret Book Co. [c.1960] 128p. illus. Bibl. 60-51359 1.50
1. Book of Mormon. I. Title.

MCKAY, David Oman, 1873-1970. 289.3
Stepping stones to an abundant life. Compiled by Llewelyn R. McKay. Salt Lake City, Utah, Deseret Book Co., 1971. x, 445 p. port. 24 cm. [BX8609.M27] 77-158727 ISBN 0-87747-442-7 5.95
1. Mormons and Mormonism—Addresses, essays, lectures. I. Title.

MCKINLAY, Lynn A 289.3
For behold ye are free; a series of lectures. Salt Lake City, Deseret Book Co., 1956. 158p. illus. 24cm. [BX8635.M326] 57-17934
1. Mormons and Mormonism—Doctrinal and controversial works. 2. Free will and determinism. I. Title.

MCKINLAY, Lynn A 289.3
The spirit giveth life; a series of five lectures. Salt Lake City, Deseret Book Co., 1955. 144p. illus. 24cm. [BX8635.M328] 55-35833
1. Mormons and Mormonism—Doctrinal and controversial works. I. Title.

MCNIFF, William John 289.3
Heaven on earth; a planned Mormon society, by William J. McNiff. Philadelphia, Porcupine Press, [1973 c.1972] 262, 134-174 p. 22 cm. (The American utopian adventure) Reprint of the 1940 ed. published by the Mississippi Valley Press, Oxford, Ohio, which was issued as v. 1 of Annals of America; together with H. Gardner's Communism among the Mormons, reprinted from the Quarterly journal of economics, v. 37 (1922) Bibliography: p. [239] -247. [BX8635.M332] 72-187474 ISBN 0-87991-001-1 12.50
1. Mormons and Mormonism. I. Gardner, Hamilton, 1859- Communism among the Mormons. 1972. II. Title.

MCNIFF, William John. 289.3
Heaven on earth; a planned Mormon society, by William J. McNiff. Oxford, Ohio, Mississippi Valley Press, 1940. [New York, AMS Press, 1974] 261 p. 23 cm. (Communal societies in America) Bibliography: p. [239]-247. [BX8635.M332 1974] 72-8632 ISBN 0-404-11007-X 14.00
1. Mormons and Mormonism. I. Title.

MARTIN, Walter Ralston, 1928- 289.3
The maze of Mormonism. Grand Rapids, Zondervan Pub. House [1962] 186p. 21cm. (The Modern cult library) Includes bibliography. [BX8645.M39] 62-7372
1. Mormons and Mormonism—Dictrinal and controversial works. I. Title.

MINER, Caroline Eyring. 289.3
Building a home to last forever. [Salt Lake City] Deseret Book Co., 1962. 104p. 20cm. [BX8643.F3M5] 62-52928
1. Home. I. Title.

MONSON, Leland H 289.3
Ancient America speaks. Salt Lake City, Deseret Book Co., 1958. 190p. 24cm. [BX8627.M58] 59-339
1. Book of Mormon. I. Title.

NEELEY, Deta Petersen. 289.3
A child's story of the Pearl of great price. Salt Lake City, Printed by the Deseret News Press, 1954. 143p. illus. 20cm. [BX8629.P58N4] 54-42578
1. Smith, Joseph, 1805-1844. Pearl of great price. I. Title.

NIBLEY, Hugh, 1910- 289.3
An approach to the Book of Mormon: course of study for the Melchizedek Priesthood quorums of the Church of Jesus Christ of Latter-Day Saints. [Salt Lake City] Council of the Twelve Apostles of the Church of Jesus Christ of Latter- Day Saints, 1957. 416p. 24cm. [BX8627.N46] 57-29431
1. Book of Mormon. I. Title.

NIBLEY, Hugh, 1910- 289.3
Lehi in the desert, & The world of the Jaredites. Salt Lake City, Bookcraft Pub. Co. [c1952] 272p. 22cm. [B8627.N48] 53-28737
1. Book of Mormon. I. Title. II. Title: The world of the Jaredites.

NIBLEY, Hugh, 1910- 289.3
Sounding brass; informal studies of the lucrative art of telling stories about Brigham Young and the Mormons. Salt Lake City, Bookcraft [1964] 286[8]p. illus. 24cm. Bibl. 64-5722 price unreported
1. Mormons and Mormonism—Doctrinal and controversial works—Hist. & crit. I. Title.

NIBLEY, Hugh, 1910- 289.3
The world and the prophets. Salt Lake City, Deseret Book Co. [1954] 250p. 24cm. [BX8635.N5] 55-20567
1. Mormons and Mormonism. I. Title.

NIBLEY, Hugh Winder, 1910- 289.3
The world and the prophets. Enl. ed. Salt Lake City, Deseret, 1962[c.1954] 281p. 14cm. 62-52146 3.95
1. Mormons and Mormonism. I. Title.

NIBLEY, Preston, comp. 289.3
The witnesses of the Book of Mormon. Salt Lake City, Deseret Book Co., 1953. 200p. 24cm. [BX8627.N49] 54-17455
1. Book of Mormon. I. Title.

OAKMAN, Arthur A. 289.3
The call of Christ in an age of dilemma; six studies based upon the Apostolic epistle of 1964, by Arthur A. Oakman. Independence, Mo., Herald Pub. House [1964] 64 p. 22 cm. Includes bibliographies. [BX8675.O2] 64-9183
1. Reorganized Church of Jesus Christ of Latter-Day Saints. I. Title.

OAKS. LEWIS WESTON, 1892- 289.3
The Word of wisdom and you. Salt Lake City, Bookcraft [1958] 273p. 24cm. [BX8629.W6O23] 58-10838
1. Word of wisdom. I. Title.

O'DEA, Thomas F. 289.3
The Mormons. Chicago, Univ. of Chic. Pr. [1964, c.1957] 288p. 21cm. (Phoenix bk., P 162) 1.95 pap.,
1. Mormons and Mormonism. I. Title.

PACKER, Athol B 289.3
An open door; a study of the basic teachings of Christ and His church. Independence, Mo., Herald House [1959] 191p. 21cm. [BX8674.P2] 58-14400
1. Reorganized Church of Jesus Christ of Latter-Day Saints—Doctrinal and controversial works. I. Title.

PETERSEN, Emma Marr. 289.3
Book of Mormon stories for young Latter-Day Saints: illustrated by Milton E. Swensen. Salt Lake City, Bookcraft Pub. Co., 1951. 293 p. illus. 24 cm. [BX8627.A2P4] 52-255860
1. Book of Mormon stories. I. Title.

PETERSEN, Mark E 289.3
One Lord, one faith! Salt Lake City, Deseret Book Co., 228p. 24cm. [BX8639.P4O4] 62-52926
1. Mormons and Mormonism—Doctrinal and controversial works. I. Title.

PETERSEN, Mark E 289.3
Toward a better. life. Salt Lake City, Deseret Book Co., 1960. 345p. 24cm. [BX8609.P45] 60-34861
1. Mormons and Mormonism—Addresses, essays, lectures. I. Title.

PRATT, Parley Parker, 1807-1857 289.3
Key to the science of theology, designed as an introduction to the first principles of spiritual philosophy, religion, law and government, as delivered by the ancients, and as restored in this age, for the final development of universal peace. truth, and knowledge. 9th ed. Salt Lake City, Deseret, 1965. 170p. 20cm. [BX8635.P85] 65-25454 price unreported
1. Mormons and Mormonism—Doctrinal and controversial works. I. Title.

PRATT, Parley Parker, 1807-1857. 289.3
Writings of Parley Parker Pratt, one of the first missionaries and a member of the First Quorum of the Twelve Apostles of the Church of Jesus Christ of Latter-Day Saints, edited and published by his grandson Parker Pratt Robinson. 1st ed. Salt Lake City, 1952. 385p. illus. 24cm. [BX8609.P75] 53-15574
1. Mormons and Mormonism—Collected works. 2. Theology— Collected works—19th cent. I. Title.

REORGANIZED Church of Jesus Christ of Latter-Day Saints. 289.3
Church directory; locations of branch and missions in all countries. Independence, Mo. v. 16 cm. [BX8606.A35] 52-29973
1. Reorganized Church of Jesus Christ of Latter-Day Saints — Direct. I. Title.

REORGANIZED Church of Jesus Christ of Latter-Day Saints. 289.3
Church member's manual; duties and privileges of members. [2d revision] Independence, Mo., Herald House, 1957. 128p. 16cm. [BX8675.A4 1957] 57-8433
1. Reorganized Church of Jesus Christ of Latter-Day Saints— Membership. I. Title.

REORGANIZED Church of Jesus Christ of Latter-Day Saints. 289.3
Parliamentary procedure in the church, by Fred L. Young [general church secretary] Independence, Mo., Herald House, 1960. 101p. 18cm. (Pastors' reference library) 'Based on Roberts Rules of order.' [BX8671.A542] 60-9002
1. Reorganized Church of Jesus Christ of Latter-Day Saints— Parliamentary practice. I. Young, Fred L. II. Title.

REORGANIZED Church of Jesus Christ of Latter-Day Saints. 289.3
Priesthood orientation studies. Prepared by the director of priesthood and leadership education. [Independence, Mo., Herald Pub. House, 1964] 212 p. 18 cm. Bibliography: p. 212. [BX8674.R4] 64-14810
1. Church officers. 2. Reorganized Church of Jesus Christ of Latter-Day Saints — Handbooks, manuals, etc. I. Title.

REORGANIZED Church of Jesus Christ of Latter-Day Saints 289.3
Priesthood orientation studies. Prepared by the director of priesthood and leadership education [Independence, Mo., Herald Pub. House, c.1964] 212p. 18cm. Bibl. 64-14810 2.50

1. Church officers. 2. Reorganized Church of Jesus Christ of Latter-Day Saints—Handbooks, manuals, etc. I. Title.

REORGANIZED Church of Jesus Christ of Latter Day Saints. 289.3
Rules and resolutions. Independence, Mo., Herald House, 1952. 215 p. 18 cm. [BX8671.A5445] 52-43441
1. Reorganized Church of Jesus Christ of Latter Day Saints — Government. I. Title.

REORGANIZED Church of Jesus Christ of Latter-Day Saints. 289.3
Zionic problems, a close-up view; lectures and discussions at the Business and Professional Men's Institute, February, 1953. [Independence, Mo., 1953] 162p. illus. 28cm. [BX8671.A547] 54-28239
1. Reorganized Church of Jesus Christ of Latter-Day Saints. I. Title.

REORGANIZED Church of Jesus Christ of Latter-Day Saints. Children's Division. 289.3
Learning God's way; a book for children who want to become church members. Illustrated by Beverly Logan. [Independence, Mo., Herald Pub. House, 1964] 85 p. col. illus. 22 cm. [BX8610.A49] 64-18779
1. Religious education — Text-books for children — Mormon. I. Title.

REORGANIZED Church of Jesus Christ of Latter-Day Saints. Committee on Ministry to College People. 289.3
A quest for meaning; handbook for college students. Prepared under the direction of the Committee on Ministry to College People, Reorganized Church of Jesus Christ of Latter Day Saints. [Independence, Mo., Herald Pub. House, 1965] 175 p. illus. (part col.) 18 cm. Includes bibliographies. [BX8674.A45] 65-18297
1. Reorganized Church of Jesus Christ of Latter-Day Saints — Handbooks, manuals, etc. 2. Religious education — Text-books for young people — Mormon. I. Title.

REORGANIZED Church of Jesus Christ of Latter-Day Saints. Committee on Ministry to College People. 289.3
A quest for meaning; handbook for college students. Prep. under the direction of the Comm. on Ministry to College People, Reorganized Church of Jesus Christ of Latter Day Saints [Independence, Mo., Herald Pub., c.1965] 175p. illus. (pt. col.) 18cm. Bibl. Includes bibliographies. [BX8674.A45] 65-18297 2.00 pap.,
1. Reorganized Church of Jesus Christ of Latter-Day Saints—Handbook, manuals, etc. 2. Religious education—Text-books for young people—Mormon. I. Title.

REYNOLDS, George, 1842-1909. 289.3
A complete concordance of the Book of Mormon. Edited and arr. by Philip C. Reynolds. Salt Lake City, Distributed by Deseret Book Co. [1957] iv, 852p. 27cm. [BX8627.A1R4 1957] 57-59334
1. Book of Mormon—Concordances. I. Title.

REYNOLDS, George, 1842-1909. 289.3
The story of the Book of Mormon. Salt Lake City, Distributed by Deseret Book Co., 1957. 364p. illus. 24cm. [BX8627.R4 1957] 57-59114
1. Mormons and Mormonism. I. Book of Mormon. II. Title.

RICH, Wendell O 289.3
Distinctive teachings of the restoration. 1st ed. [Salt Lake City] Printed by Deseret News Press [1962] 216 p. 24 cm. "Originally presented to ... Utah State University ... as a doctoral thesis." Includes bibliography. [BX8635.2.R5] 63-4804
1. Mormons and mormonism — Doctrinal and controversial works. 2. Mormons and Mormoniam — Education. I. Title.

RICHARDS, Le Grand, Bp., 1886- 289.3
A marvelous work and a wonder. Salt Lake City, Deseret Book Co., 1950. xvi, 376 p. 23 cm. An expansion of the author's mimeographed outline, The message of Mormonism. [BX8635.R45] 51-18844
1. Mormons and Mormonism—Doctrinal and controversial works. I. Title.

ROBERTS, Brigham Henry, 1857-1933 289.3
The Gospel; an exposition of its first principles, and man's relationship to deity, 10th ed. Salt Lake City, Deseret, 1965 ix, 292p. 24cm. Cover title: The Gospel and man's relationship to deity. [BX8631.R6] 65-25455 price unreported
1. Mormons and Mormonism—Doctrinal and controversial works. I. Title. II. Title: The Gospel and man's relationship to deity.

RONA, Herbert, 1906- 289.3
Peace to a Jew. [1st ed.] New York, Pageant Press [1952] 118p. 21cm. [BX8695.R64A3] 53-19918
1. Converts. Mormon. I. Title.

SAINT'S herald. 289.3
Question time. Independence, Mo., Herald House, 1955-67. 2 v. 21 cm. A collection of questions and answers from the Saints' herald, official organ of the Reorganized Church of Jesus Christ of Latter Day Saints. [BX8671.Q4] 55-12245
1. Questions and answers—Theology. 2. Reorganized Church of Jesus Christ of Latter Day Saints—Doctrinal and controversial works. I. Title.

SAINT'S herald Question time 289.3
[answers to 457 often-asked questions from the Saint's herald, well indexed for ready use; questions about the church, the scriptures, and problems of life, Reorganized Church of Jesus Christ of Latter-Day Saints. Independence, Mo.] Herald House [1967] v. 21cm. has as subtitle: A collection of often-asked questions and answers from the Saint's herald. Well indexed for ready use [BX6871.S23] 55-12245 5.95
1. Questions and answers—Theology. 2. Reorganized Church of Jesus Christ of Latter-Day Saints

SKOUSEN, Willard Cleon, 1913- 289.3
The challenge of our times. [1st ed.] Salt Lake City, Bookcraft Publishers [1953] 167p. 23cm. [BX8635.S55] 53-37091
1. Mormons and Mormonism—Doctrinal and controversial works. I. Title.

SKOUSEN, Willard Cleon, 1913- 289.3
The first 2000 years Salt Lake City, Bookcraft [1953] 401 p.24 cm. [BX8627.S57] 58-48865
1. Book of Mormon. I. Title.

SMITH, Joseph Fielding, 1876- 289.3
Man, his origin and destiny. Salt Lake City, Deseret Book Co., 1954. 563p. 24cm. [BX8635.S65] 54-1762
1. Mormons and Mormonism—Doctrinal and controversial works. 2. Man (Theology) 3. Religion and science—1900- I. Title.

SPERRY, Sidney Branton, 1895- 289.3
Book of Mormon testifies. [1st ed.] Salt Lake City, Bookcraft [1952] 416p. 24cm. [BX8627.S75] 53-026249
1. Book of Mormon. I. Title.

SPERRY, Sidney Branton, 1895- 289.3
Problems of the Book of Mormon. Salt Lake City 4, Utah, 1186 S. Main St. Bookcraft, [c.1964] 253p. 24cm. Bibl. 64-3036 3.25
1. Book of Mormon. I. Title.

STARKS, Arthur E 1911- 289.3
A complete concordance to the Book of Mormon. Independence, Mo., Herald Pub. House, 1950. 501 p. 23 cm. [BX8627.A1S75] 50-3396
1. Book of Mormon — Concordances. I. Title.

STEWART, Georgia Metcalf. 289.3
How the church grew; Reorganized Church of Jesus Christ of Latter Day Saints. Independence, Mo., Herald House [1959] 342 p. 21 cm. [BX8673.S8] 59-11404
1. Reorganized Church of Jesus Christ of Latter-Day Saints — Hist. I. Title.

STEWART, Ora (Pate) 1910- 289.3
Treasures unearthed; little known facts about the Book of Mormon. [1st ed.] Salt Lake City, Bookcraft [1953] 154p. 16cm. [BX8627.S78] 53-39870
1. Book of Mormon. I. Title.

STEWART, Ora (Pate) 1910- 289.3
We believe a simplified treatment of the Articles of faith. [1st ed.] Salt Lake City, Bookcraft [1954] 112p. 16cm. [BX8629.P6S8] 55-23528
1. Smith, Joseph, 1805-1844. The pearl of great price. I. Title.

STOWELL, Earl. 289.3
The magic of Mormonism. Salt Lake City, Bookcraft [c1965] 264 p. 24 cm. Bibliography: p. 245-246. [BX8635.2.S75] 66-6717
1. Mormons and Mormonism. I. Title.

TAYLOR, Samuel Woolley, 1907- 289.3
I have six wives; a true story of present-day plural marriage. New York, Greenberg [1956] 275p. 22cm. [BX8641.T3] 56-7978
1. Polygamy. 2. Mormons and Mormonism. I. Title.

TAYLOR, Samuel Woolley, 1907- 289.3
I have six wives; a true story of present-day plural marriage. New York, Greenberg [1956] 275 p. 22 cm. [BX8641.T3] 56-7978
1. Polygamy. 2. Mormons and Mormonism. I. Title.

TERRY, Keith. 289.3
From the dust of decades; a saga of the papyri and mummies [by] Keith Terry and Walter Whipple. Salt Lake City, Bookcraft, 1968. 118 p. illus., facsims. 24 cm. Includes bibliographical references. [BX8622.T44] 68-29490
1. Smith, Joseph, 1805-1844. 2. Mormons and Mormonism—History—Sources. I. Whipple, Walter, joint author. II. Title.

UTAH Academy of Sciences, Arts and Letters. 289.3
Symposium on Mormon culture; papers presented at the fall meetings of the Jtah Academy of Sciences, Arts, and Letters, held at Utah State Agricultural College, Logan, Utah, November 14, 1952. [Logan 1952] 1v. (various pagings) 28cm. [BX8638.U8 1952a] 54-24165
1. Mormons and Mormonism. I. Title.

WHALEN, William Joseph. 289.3
The Latter-Day Saints in the modern day world; an account of contemporary Mormonism. New York, John Day Co. [1964] 319 p. illus., ports. 21 cm. Bibliography: p. 309-314. [BX8635.2.W5] 64-10944
1. Mormons and Mormonism. I. Title.

WIDTSOE, John Andreas, 1872-1952. 289.3
The message of the Doctrine and convenants. Edited and arranged with a foreword by G. Homer Durham. Salt Lake City, Bookcraft, 1969. xii, 179 p. 24 cm. The transcript of lectures delivered by the author at the University of Southern California, April-June, 1936. [BX8628.W53 1969] 74-77460 3.50
1. Reorganized Church of Jesus Christ of Latter Day Saints. Book of doctrine and convenants. I. Title.

YARRINGTON, Roger 289.3
The auditorium; world headquarters building of the Reorganized Church of Jesus Christ of Latter Day Saints. Independence, Mo., Herald House [c.1962] 90p. illus. (pt. col.) 26cm. 62-9963 2.95
1. Reorganized Church of Jesus Christ of Latter-Day Saints. 2. Independence, Mo. Auditorium. I. Title.

YOUNG, Kimball, 1893- 289.3
Isn't one wife enough? Illustrated with photos. [1st ed.] New York, Holt [1954] 476 p. illus. 22 cm. [BX8641.Y8] 54-5461
1. Polygamy. 2. Mormons and Mormonism. I. Title.

ZOBELL, Albert L., Jr., comp. 289.3
The glorious purpose; more moments with the prophets. [Salt Lake City, Utah] Deseret [1963, c.]1962. 104p. 16cm. 63-1321 1.00
1. Mormons and Mormonism—Quotations, maxims, etc. I. Title. II. Title: Moments with the prophets.

ZOBELL, Albert L., comp. 289.3
Moments with the prophets. Salt Lake City, Utah, Deseret Book Co. [c.1960] 218p. 16cm. 61-596 1.00
1. Mormons and Mormonism. 2. Aphorisms and apothegms. I. Title.

REORGANIZED Church of Jesus Christ of Latter-Day Saints. 289.3'02'02
Church member's manual; duties and privileges of members. [3d revision] Independence, Mo., Herald House, 1969. 120 p. 16 cm. [BX8675.A4 1969] 77-80872
1. Reorganized Church of Jesus Christ of Latter-Day Saints—Membership. I. Title.

BROOKS, Melvin R 289.303
L. D. S. reference encyclopedia. Salt Lake City, Bookcraft, 1960. 540p. 24cm. [BX8605.5.B7] 60-44463
1. Mormons and Mormonism—Dictionaries. I. Title.

BROOKS, Melvin R 289.303
L.D.S. Reference encyclopedia. Salt Lake City, Bookcraft, 1960-65. 2 v. 24 cm. [BX8605.5.B7] 60-44463
1. Mormons and Mormonism — Dictionaries. I. Title.

BRIGHAM Young University, Provo, Utah. Adult Education and Extension Services. 289.304
Our leaders speak; eternal truths spoken at Brigham Young University. Compiled by the Brigham Young University, Adult Education and Extension Services, Extension Publications. Selected and arranged by Soren F. Cox. Salt Lake City, Deseret Book Co., 1957. 206p. illus. 24cm. [BX8639.A1B7] 58-27399
1. Mormons and Mormonism—Addresses, essays, lectures. I. Cox, Soren F., ed. II. Title.

CHURCH of Jesus Christ of Latter-Day Saints. 289.304
Messages of inspiration; selected addresses of the general authorities of the Church of Jesus Christ of Latter-Day Saints. Salt Lake City, Deseret Book Co., 1957. 356 p. illus. 24 cm. [BX8608.A4] 57-2587
1. Mormons and Mormonism—Addresses, essays, lectures. I. Title.

CHURCH of Jesus Christ of Latter-Day Saints. 289.304
Messages of inspiration; selected addresses of the general authorities of the Church of Jesus Christ of Latter-Day Saints. Salt Lake City, Deseret Book Co., 1957. 356p. illus. 24cm. [BX8608.A4] 57-2587
1. Mormons and Mormonism—Addresses, essays, lectures. I. Title.

MCKAY, David Oman, 1873- 289.304
Cherished experiences, from the writings of David O. McKay. Compiled by Clare Middlemiss. Salt Lake City, Deseret co. [1955] 209p. illus. 24cm. [BX8609.M25] 55-30116
1. Mormons and Mormonism—Addresses, essays, lectures. I. Title.

RICHARDS, Stephen L 1879- 289.304
Where is wisdom? Addresses. Salt Lake City, Deseret Book Co. [1955] 432p. illus. 24cm. [BX8609.R53] 56-17872
1. Mormons and Mormonism—Addresses, essays, lectures. I. Title.

CANNON, George Quayle, 1827-1901. 289.3'08
Writings from the Western standard. New York, Paladin Press [1969] xv, 512 p. 22 cm. Reprint of the 1864 ed. [BX8609.C3 1969] 69-19547 25.00
1. Mormons and Mormonism. I. Title.

CRACROFT, Richard H., 1936- comp. 289.3'08
A believing people; literature of the Latter-Day Saints [by] Richard H. Cracroft [and] Neal E. Lambert. [Provo, Utah] Brigham Young University Press [1974] xvi, 495 p. 26 cm. Includes bibliographical references. [BX8608.C7] 74-6038 ISBN 0-8425-0929-1
1. Church of Jesus Christ of Latter-Day Saints—Collected works. I. Lambert, Neal E., 1934- joint comp. II. Title.

CRACROFT, Richard H., 1936- comp. 289.3'08
A believing people; literature of the Latter-Day Saints [by] Richard H. Cracroft [and] Neal E. Lambert. [Provo, Utah] Brigham Young University Press [1974] xvi, 495 p. 26 cm. Includes bibliographical references. [BX8608.C7] 74-6038 ISBN 0-8425-0930-5 7.95 (pbk.)
1. Church of Jesus Christ of Latter-Day Saints—Collected works. I. Lambert, Neal E., 1934- joint comp. II. Title.
Hardbound 10.95; ISBN: 0-8425-0929-1.

BENSON, Ezra Taft. 289.3081
... so shall ye reap; [selected addresses. Compiled by Reed A. Benson. Salt Lake City. Deseret Book Co., 1960 351p. illus. 24cm. [BX8609.B43] 60-51164
1. Mormons and Mormonism—Addresses, essays, lectures. I. Title.

OAKMAN, Arthur A 289.3081
Resurrection and eternal life; a series of lectures delivered to the Melchisedec priesthood of Independence, Missouri. January 5-12, 1958. [Independence. Mo.] Herald House. Reorganized Church of Jesus Christ of Latter Day Saints [1959] 256p. 21cm. [BX8674.O2] 59-8361
1. Reorganized Church of Jesus Christ of Latter-Day Saints—Doctrinal and controversial works. 2. Resurrection. 3. Future life. I. Title.

PRATT, Orson, 1811-1881 289.3081
Masterful discourses and writings [N. B. Lundwall, comp.] Salt Lake City, Bookcraft [1963, c.1962] 656p. ports. 24cm. 63-5908 price unreported
1. Mormons and Mormonism—Collected works. I. Title.

CHURCH of Jesus Christ of Latter-Day Saints. 289.3082
Life's directions; a series of fireside addresses, by the general authorities of the Church of Jesus Christ of Latter-Day Saints. Salt Lake City, Deseret Book Co., 1962. 191p. illus. 24cm. [BX8639.A1A3] 62-38083
1. Mormons and Mormonism—Addresses, essays, lectures. I. Title.

ZOBELL, Albert L., comp. 289.3082
The joy that endures. Salt Lake City, Deseret [c.]1963. 96p. 16cm. 63-4967 1.00
1. Mormons and Mormonism—Quotations, maxims, etc. I. Title.

BARRETT, Ivan J., 1910- 289.3'09
Joseph Smith and the restoration; a history of the Church to 1846 [by] Ivan J. Barrett. [2d ed.] [Provo, Utah] Young House, Brigham Young University Press [1973] ix, 674 p. illus. 24 cm. Bibliography: p. 651-666. [BX8611.B325 1973] 70-167990
1. Church of Jesus Christ of Latter-Day Saints—History. 2. Smith, Joseph, 1805-1844. I. Title.

BERRETT, William Edwin, ed. 289.309
Readings in L. D. S. Church history from original manuscripts, by William E. Berrett and Alma P. Burton. 1st ed. Salt Lake City, Deseret Book Co., 1953- v. facsims. 24cm. Bibliography: v.1, p.537-539. [BX8611.B346] 53-23418
1. Mormons and Mormonism—Hist. I. Burton, Alma P., 1913- joint ed. II. Title.

BERRETT, William Edwin, ed. 289.309
Readings in L. D. S. Church history from original manuscripts, by William E. Berrett and Alma P. Burton. 1st ed. Salt Lake City, Deseret Book Co., 1953-58. 3v. facsims. 24cm. Includes bibliographies. [BX8611.B346] 53-23418
1. Mormons and Mormonism—Hist. I. Burton, Alma P., 1913- joint ed. II. Title.

BURTON, Alma P 1913- 289.309
Mormon trail from Vermont to Utah; a guide to historic places of the Church of Jesus Christ of Latter-Day Saints. [2d ed. Salt Lake City, Deseret Book Co., 1953] 84p. illus. 23cm. [BX8611.B78] 53-36467
1. Mormons and Mormonism— Hist. I. Title.

BURTON, Alma P 1913- 289.309
Mormon trail from Vermont to Utah; a guide to historic places of the Church of Jesus Christ of Latter-Day Saints. [Rev. ed.] Salt Lake City, Deseret Book Co., 1960. 103p. illus. 23cm. Includes bibliography. [BX8611.B78 1960] 60-50906
1. Mormons and Mormonism—Hist. I. Title.

BURTON, Alma P 1913- 289.309
Mormon trail: Vermont to Utah; a guide to historic places of the Church of Jesus Christ of Latter-Day Saints, by Alma P. Burton. Rev. and enl. Salt Lake City, Deseret Book Co., 1966. 103 p. (p. 100-103, blank for "Notes") illus., maps (part fold.) port. 23 cm. Cover title: Mormon trail from Vermont to Utah. Earlier editions published with title: Mormon trail from Vermont to Utah. Bibliography: p. 99. [BX8611.B78] 66-8721
1. Mormons and Mormonism in the U.S. — Historic buildings, monuments, etc. I. Title.

DAY, Robert B. 289.3'09
They made Mormon history [by] Robert B. Day. Salt Lake City, Deseret Book Co., 1968. viii, 364 p. illus., ports. 24 cm. Bibliography: p. [345]-354. [BX8611.D34] 68-58285 4.95
1. Mormons and Mormonism—History. I. Title.

ELGIN, Kathleen, 1923- 289.3'09
The Mormons: the Church of Jesus Christ of Latter-Day Saints, written and illustrated by Kathleen Elgin. With a foreword by Ray Knell. New York, D. McKay Co. [1969] 96 p. illus., maps. 26 cm. (The Freedom to worship series) Bibliography: p. 94. An introduction to the history, organization, theology, and present-day position of the Mormon Church. Includes a biography of one early Mormon pioneer and lawmaker, Charles Coulson Rich. [BX8635.2.E4] 74-81898 3.95
1. Mormons and Mormonism—Juvenile literature. I. Title.

FIFE, Austin E 289.309
Saints of sage & saddle; folklore among the Mormons, by Austin and Alta Fife. Bloomington, Indiana University Press, 1956. 367 p. illus. 22 cm. [BX8611.F5] 56-11997
1. Mormons and Mormonism — Hist. 2. Folklore — U.S. I. Fife, Alta (Stephens) II. Title.

FIFE, Austin E 289.309
Saints of sage & saddle; folklore among the Mormons, by Austin and Alta Fife. Gloucester, Mass., P. Smith, 1966 [c1956] xiv, 367 p. illus., map (on lining papers) 21 cm. Includes unacc. melodies. Bibliography: p. 339-342. [BX8611.F5 1966] 66-31847
1. Mormons and Mormonism — Hist. 2. Folklore — U.S. I. Fife, Alta (Stephens) joint author. II. Title.

FIFE, Austin E. 289.309
Saints of sage & saddle; folklore among the Mormons, by Austin and Alta Fife. Bloomington, Indiana University Press, 1956. 367 p. illus. 22 cm. [BX8611.F5] 56-11997
1. Mormons and Mormonism—History. 2. Folk-lore—U.S. I. Fife, Alta (Stephens). II. Title.

GRANT, Carter Eldredge. 289.309
The kingdom of God restored. Salt Lake City, Deseret Book Co., 1955. 602p. illus. 24cm. [BX8611.G7] 55-12598
1. Mormons and Mormonism—Hist. I. Title.

MAYHEW, Henry, 1812-1887. 289.3'09
The Mormons; or Latter-day Saints: a contemporary history. New York, AMS Press [1971] 326 p. illus. 22 cm. Reprint of the 1852 ed. [BX8611.M3 1971] 71-134398 ISBN 0-404-08440-0 12.50
1. Smith, Joseph, 1805-1844. 2. Mormons and Mormonism. I. Title.

MULLEN, Robert Rodolf, 1908- 289.309
The Latter-Day Saints; the Mormons yesterday and today [by] Robert Mullen. [1st ed.] Garden City, N.Y., Doubleday, 1966. xvi, 316 p. illus., map (on lining papers) ports. 24 cm. "Bibliography and notes": p. [289]-303. [BX8635.2.M8] 66-20920
1. Mormons and Mormonism. I. Title.

PETERSEN, Emma Marr. 289.309
The story of our church for young Latter-Day Saints; illustrated by Milton E. Swensen. [1st ed.] Salt Lake City, Bookcraft Pub. Co. [1952] 311p. illus. 24cm. [BX8611.P4] 53-28738
1. Mormons and Mormonism—Hist. I. Title.

PETERSEN, Emma Marr. 289.309
The story of our church for young Latter-Day Saints; illustrated by Milton E. Swensen. [4th ed.] Salt Lake City, Bookcraft Pub. Co. [1958] 311p. illus. 24cm. [BX8611.P4 1958] 58-48853
1. Mormons and Mormonism—Hist. I. Title.

SLETTEN, Nettie. 289.309
God and mankind versus Satan; tracts on divine judgment and salvation. [1st ed.] New York, Exposition Press [1957] 192p. 21cm. [BX8611.S56] 57-9225
1. Mormons and Mormonism—Hist. I. Title.

SLETTEN, Nettie. 289.309
God and mankind versus Satan; tracts on divine judgment and salvation. [1st ed.] New York, Exposition Press [1957] 192 p. 21 cm. [BX8611.S56] 57-9225
1. Mormons and Mormonism — Hist. I. Title.

SMITH, Joseph Fielding, 1876- 289.309
Church history and modern revelation, covering the first period: Joseph Smith, the prophet. Alphabetical index and digest of the above study course, by Andrew K. Smith. [Salt Lake City] Council of the Twelve Apostles of the Church of Jesus Christ of Latter-Day Saints [1953] 2v. 24cm. [BX8611.S66] 54-22110
1. Smith, Joseph, 1805-1844. 2. Mormons and Mormonism— Hist. I. Title.

WEST, Ray Benedict, 1908- 289.309
Kingdom of the saints; the story of Brigham Young and the Mormons. New York, Viking Press, 1957. 389 p. illus. 22 cm. [BX8611.W4] 57-6437
1. Young, Brigham, 1801-1877. 2. Mormons and Mormonism — Hist. I. Title.

WEST, Ray Benedict, 1908- 289.309
Kingdom of the saints; the story of Brigham Young and the Mormons. New York, Viking Press, 1957. 389 p. illus. 22 cm. [BX8611.W4] 57-6437
1. Young, Brigham, 1801-1877. 2. Mormons and Mormonism—History. I. Title.

ANDERSON, Joseph, 1889- 289.3'092'2 B
Prophets I have known; Joseph Anderson shares life's experiences. [Salt Lake City] Deseret Book Co., 1973. xii, 248 p. illus. 24 cm. [BX8693.A5] 73-88327 ISBN 0-87747-508-3 4.95
1. Church of Jesus Christ of Latter-Day Saints—Biography. I. Title.

ASHTON, Wendell J. 289.3'0922 B
Theirs is the kingdom [by] Wendell J. Ashton. Pen sketches by Nelson White. [2d ed.] Salt Lake City, Bookcraft, 1970. x, 300 p. ports. 24 cm. Bibliography: p. [291]-295. [BX8693.A8 1970] 74-126081
1. Mormons and Mormonism—Biography. I. Title.

BENNETT, Frances Grant. 289.3'0922
Glimpses of a Mormon family. Salt Lake City, Deseret Book Co., 1968. xi, 308 p. illus. 24 cm. [CT275.B56223A3] 68-25349
I. Title.

CHEVILLE, Roy Arthur, 1897- 289.3'0922 B
They made a difference, by Roy Cheville. [Independence, Mo., Herald Pub. House, 1970] 350 p. ports. 21 cm. "A roster of thirty persons whose participation made significant impact upon the Latter Day Saint Movement: The Early Church, 1820-1844; the Reorganized Church, 1853-1970." [BX8678.A2] 78-101568 6.95
1. Reorganized Church of Jesus Christ of Latter-Day Saints—Biography. I. Title.

CUMMING, John, 1915- 289.3'0922
The pilgrimage of Temperance Mack, by John & Audrey Cumming. Mount Pleasant, Mich. [1967] 72 p. 19 cm. [BX8695.M26C8] 68-2070
1. Mack, Temperance, d. 1850. 2. Covey, Almira Mack, 1804 or 5-1886. I. Cumming, Audrey, 1916- joint author. II. Title.

ELLSWORTH, Samuel George, 1916- 289.3'092'2 B
Dear Ellen; two Mormon women and their letters, by S. George Ellsworth. Salt Lake City, Tanner Trust Fund, University of Utah Library [1974] x, 92 p. 26 cm. (Utah, the Mormons, and the West, no. 3) Includes correspondence between Ellen Pratt McGary and Ellen Spencer Clawson, May 1856-Aug. 1857. Includes bibliographical references. [BX8695.C29E44] 73-91999 12.00
1. Clawson, Ellen Spencer, 1832-1896. 2. McGary, Ellen Pratt, 1832-1895. I. Clawson, Ellen Spencer, 1832-1896. II. McGary, Ellen Pratt, 1832-1895. III. Title. IV. Series.

FRIEND to friend 289.3'092'2 B
: general authorities speak to children. Salt Lake City : Deseret Book Co., 1977. 63 p. : ill. ; 29 cm. A compilation of stories and experiences from the lives of leading authorities of the Church of Jesus Christ of Latter-Day Saints that stress Mormon values and beliefs. [BX8693.F74] 77-2974 ISBN 0-87747-629-2 : 3.95
1. Church of Jesus Christ of Latter-Day Saints—Biography—Juvenile literature. 2. Children—Religious life. I. Friend.

FRIEND to friend 289.3'092'2 B
: general authorities speak to children. Salt Lake City : Deseret Book Co., 1977. 63 p. : ill. ; 29 cm. A compilation of stories and experiences from the lives of leading authorities of the Church of Jesus Christ of Latter-Day Saints that stress Mormon values and beliefs. [BX8693.F74] 77-2974 ISBN 0-87747-629-2 : 3.95
1. Church of Jesus Christ of Latter-Day Saints—Biography—Juvenile literature. 2. Children—Religious life. I. Friend.

HARTSHORN, Leon R., comp. 289.3'0922 B
Classic stories from the lives of our prophets. Compiled by Leon R. Hartshorn. Salt Lake City, Utah, Deseret Book Co., 1971. ix, 334 p. ports. 24 cm. Contents.Contents.—Joseph Smith.—Brigham Young.—John Taylor.—Wilford Woodruff.—Lorenzo Snow.—Joseph F. Smith.—Heber J. Grant.—George Albert Smith.—David O. McKay.—Joseph Fielding Smith. Includes bibliographical references. [BX8693.H29] 73-155235 ISBN 0-87747-438-9 4.95
1. Church of Jesus Christ of Latter-Day Saints—Collections. I. Title.

HARTSHORN, Leon R., comp. 289.3'092'2 B
Exceptional stories from the lives of our apostles. Compiled by Leon R. Hartshorn. Salt Lake City, Deseret Book Co., 1972. x, 307 p. ports. 24 cm. Includes bibliographical references. [BX8693.H293] 72-90346 ISBN 0-87747-486-9 4.95
1. Church of Jesus Christ of Latter-Day Saints—Biography. I. Title.

HARTSHORN, Leon R., comp. 289.3'092'2 B
Powerful stories from the lives of Latter-day Saint men, compiled by Leon R. Hartshorn. Salt Lake City, Deseret Book Co., 1974. ix, 298 p. ports. 24 cm. [BX8693.H32] 74-75033 ISBN 0-87747-504-0 4.95
1. Church of Jesus Christ of Latter-Day Saints—Biography. I. Title.

HARTSHORN, Leon R., comp. 289.3'092'2 B
Remarkable stories from the lives of Latter-Day Saint women. Compiled by Leon R. Hartshorn. Salt Lake City, Utah, Deseret Book Co., 1973. xi, 274 p. illus. 24 cm. Includes bibliographical references. [BX8693.H33] 73-87239 ISBN 0-87747-504-0 4.95
1. Church of Jesus Christ of Latter-Day Saints—Biography. 2. Woman—Biography. I. Title.

NIBLEY, Preston. 289.3'092'2 B
The presidents of the Church. [13th ed., rev. and enl.] Salt Lake City, Deseret Book, 1974. 488 p. ports. 24 cm. [BX8693.N5 1974] 74-170278 6.95
1. Church of Jesus Christ of Latter-Day Saints—Biography. I. Title.

RUOFF, Norman D. comp. 289.3/0922
Witness to the world; a collection of testimonies and inspirational writings from the pages of the Resforation witness, ed., comp. by Norman D. Ruoff. [Independence, Mo., Herald Pub., 1967] 216p. 20cm. [BX8678.A46] 67-30460 3.50
1. Reorganized Church of Jesus Christ of Latter-Day Saints—Biog. 2. Restoration witness. I. Title.

SMITH, Lucy (Mack) 1776-1855. 289.3'0922 B
Biographical sketches of Joseph Smith, the prophet. New York, Arno Press, 1969. 282 p. 23 cm. (Religion in America) Reprint of the 1908 ed. [BX8695.S6S6 1969] 73-83439
1. Smith, Joseph, 1805-1844—Family. 2. Mack family. I. Title.

STEWART, John J. 289.3'0922 B
Remembering the McKays; a biographical sketch with pictures of David O. and Emma Ray McKay, by John J. Stewart. Salt Lake City, Deseret Book Co., 1970. 48 p. ports. 23 cm. [BX8695.M27S8] 70-136243
1. McKay, David Oman, 1873-1970. 2. McKay, Emma Ray, 1877- I. Title.

WEST, Emerson Roy. 289.3'092'2 B
Profiles of the presidents. Salt Lake City, Desert Book Co., 1974. viii, 418 p. illus. 24 cm. Bibliography: p. [403]-405. [BX8693.W47 1974] 74-167281 ISBN 0-87747-489-3 5.95
1. Church of Jesus Christ of Latter-Day Saints—Biography. 2. Church of Jesus Christ of Latter-Day Saints—Government. I. Title.

ANDERSON, Richard Lloyd. 289.3'092'4 B
Joseph Smith's New England heritage; influences of grandfathers Solomon Mack and Asael Smith. Salt Lake City, Desert Book Co., 1971. xix, 230 p. illus. 24 cm. Bibliography: p. [225]-227. [BX8695.S6A68] 74-186263 ISBN 0-87747-460-5 4.95
1. Smith, Joseph, 1805-1844. 2. Smith family. I. Title.

ANDRUS, Hyrum Leslie, 1924- comp. 289.3'092'4 B
They knew the prophet. Compiled by Hyrum L. Andrus and Helen Mae Andrus. Salt Lake City, Bookcraft [1974] xii, 207 p. 24 cm. [BX8695.S6A73] 74-75538 ISBN 0-88494-210-4
1. Smith, Joseph, 1805-1844—Collected works. I. Andrus, Helen Mae, joint comp. II. Title.

ARRINGTON, Leonard J. 289.3'092'4 B
Charles C. Rich, Mormon general and Western frontiersman [by] Leonard J. Arrington. Provo, Utah, Brigham Young University Press [1974] xvii, 386 p. illus. 24 cm. (Studies in Mormon history, v. 1) Includes bibliographical references. [BX8695.R46A77] 74-13624 ISBN 0-8425-1051-6 7.50
1. Rich, Charles Coulson, 1809-1883. I. Title. II. Series.

BACKMAN, Milton Vaughn. 289.3'0924
Joseph Smith's first vision; the first vision in its historical context [by] Milton V. Backman, Jr. Salt Lake City, Bookcraft, 1971. xiv, 209 p. illus., maps, ports. 24 cm. Bibliography: p. [193]-204. [BX8695.S6B3] 72-149592
1. Smith, Joseph, 1805-1844. 2. Visions. 3. New York (State)—Religion. I. Title.

BLAKE, Reed. 289.3'092'4 B
24 hours to martyrdom. Salt Lake City, Bookcraft [1973] xiii, 157 p. illus. 19 cm. Bibliography: p. [151]-157. [BX8695.S6B5] 73-77238 1.95
1. Smith, Joseph, 1805-1844. I. Title.

BLAKE, Reed. 289.3'092'4 B
24 hours to martyrdom Salt Lake City, Bookcraft [1973] xiii, 157 p. illus. 19 cm. Bibliography: p. [151]-157. [BX8695.S6B5] 73-77238
1. Smith, Joseph, 1805-1844. I. Title.

BRODIE, Fawn (McKay) 1915- 289.3'0924 B
No man knows my history; the life of Joseph Smith, the Mormon prophet, by Fawn M. Brodie. 2d ed., rev. and enl. New York, Knopf, 1971. xiii, 499, xx p. illus., map, ports. 22 cm. Bibliography: p. 490-499. [BX8695.S6B7 1971] 71-136333 ISBN 0-394-46967-4 10.00
1. Smith, Joseph, 1805-1844. I. Title.

BROWN, James Stephens, b.1828. 289.3'0924 B
Life of a pioneer; being the autobiography of James S. Brown. Salt Lake City, G. Q.

Cannon, 1900. [New York, AMS Press, 1971] xix, 520 p. illus. 22 cm. [BX8695.B7A3 1971] 78-134389 ISBN 0-404-08432-X 21.00
I. Title.

BURT, Olive 289.3'0924 B
(Woolley) 1894-
Brigham Young [by] Olive Burt. New York, J. Messner [1956] 192 p. 22 cm. Bibliography p. 188. A biography of the Mormon convert who later became the President of his church and led his people to the Great Salt Lake Valley to establish a large Mormon colony. [BX8695.Y7B8] 92 AC 68
1. Young, Brigham, 1801-1877. I. Title.

CHENEY, Thomas E. 289.3'092'4 B
The golden legacy; a folk history of J. Golden Kimball [by] Thomas E. Cheney. Provo, Utah, Brigham Young University Press [1973] xii, 155 p. port. 23 cm. Bibliography: p. 145-146. [BX8695.K52C5] 73-77684 ISBN 0-8425-0084-7 6.95
1. Kimball, Jonathan Golden, 1853-1938. I. Title.

CULMSEE, Carlton 289.3'0924 B
Fordis, 1904-
A modern Moses at West Tintic; essay, by Carlton Culmsee. Logan, Utah State University Press, 1967. 40 p. 24 cm. (Utah State University. Monograph series, v. 14, no. 1) [BX8680.S88G8] 67-65621
1. Gudmundson, Moses S. 2. Church of Jesus Christ of Latter-Day Saints. I. Title. II. Series: Utah. State University of Agriculture and Applied Science, Logan. Monograph series, v. 14, no. 1

DE JONG, Gerrit, 289.30924 (B)
1892-
The testimony of President Heber J. Grant, by Gerrit De Jong, Jr. Salt Lake City, Deseret Book Co., 1965. vi, 54 p. col. port. 20 cm. Bibliographical footnotes. [BX8695.G7D4] 65-28867
1. Grant, Heber Jeddy, 1856-1945. I. Title.

EVANS, Richard L. 289.3'092'4 B
Richard L. Evans—the man and the message, by Richards [sic] L. Evans, Jr. Salt Lake City, Bookcraft [1973] xii, 324 p. illus. 24 cm. [BX8695.E9E9] 73-84591
1. Evans, Richard Louis, 1906-1971. I. Evans, Richard Louis, 1906-1971. II. Title.

EVANS, Richard L. 289.3'092'4 B
Richard L. Evans—the man and the message, by Richards [sic] L. Evans, Jr. Salt Lake City, Bookcraft [1973] xii, 324 p. illus. 24 cm. [BX8695.E9E9] 73-84591 4.95
1. Evans, Richard Louis, 1906-1971. I. Evans, Richard Louis, 1906-1971. II. Title.

FISH, Joseph, 1840- 289.3'0924 B
1926.
The life and times of Joseph Fish, Mormon pioneer. Edited by John H. Krenkel. Danville, Ill., Interstate Printers & Publishers [1970] 543 p. 3 maps (2 on lining papers), port. 24 cm. Includes bibliographical references. [BX8695.F57A3 1970] 70-110886
1. Mormons and Mormonism. I. Title.

FITZPATRICK, Doyle 289.3'0924 B
C.
The King Strang story; a vindication of James J. Strang, the Beaver Island Mormon King, by Doyle C. Fitzpatrick. [1st ed.] Lansing, Mich., National Heritage, 1970. xxviii, 289 p. illus., facsims., geneal. table, map (on lining papers), ports. 24 cm. [BX8680.S88S84] 70-140603 7.95
1. Strang, James Jesse, 1813-1856. 2. Beaver Island, Mich.—History. I. Title.

FLETCHER, Rupert J. 289.3'092'4 B
Alpheus Cutler and the Church of Jesus Christ, by Rupert J. Fletcher and Daisy Whiting Fletcher. [Independence, Mo., Church of Jesus Christ, 1973] 350 p. 21 cm. [BX8680.C84F55] 73-92999
1. Church of Jesus Christ (Cutlerites) 2. Cutler, Alpheus, 1784-1864. I. Fletcher, Daisy Whiting, joint author. II. Title.

FLINT, Bert C 289.3'0924
An outline history of the Church of Christ (Temple Lot) [1st ed.] Rev. and prepared for publication by the revising committee. Independence, Mo., Board of Publications, Church of Christ (Temple Lot), 1953. 160p. illus. 22 cm. [BX8680.T43F5] 55-44142
1. Church of Christ (Temple Lot)—Hist. I. Title.

GATES, Susa (Young) 289.3'0924 B
1856-1933.
The life story of Brigham Young: Mormon leader, founder of Salt Lake City, and builder of an empire in the uncharted wastes of Western America, by Susa Young Gates, in collaboration with Leah D. Widtsoe. Freeport, N.Y., Books for Libraries Press [1971] 287 p. illus., map, ports. 24 cm. Reprint of the 1930 ed. [BX8695.Y7G3 1971] 74-164602 ISBN 0-8369-5886-1
1. Young, Brigham, 1801-1877. 2. Mormons and Mormonism. I. Widtsoe, Leah Eudora (Dunford) 1874- joint author. II. Title.

GIBBONS, Francis 289.3'092'4 B
M., 1921-
Joseph Smith, martyr, prophet of God / Francis M. Gibbons. Salt Lake City : Deseret Book Co., 1977. ix, 377 p. ; 23 cm. Includes index. Bibliography: p. 366-368. [BX8695.S6G52] 77-2019 ISBN 0-87747-637-3 : 6.95
1. Smith, Joseph, 1805-1844. 2. Mormons and Mormonism in the United States—Biography. 3. Mormons and Mormonism—History. I. Title.

GIBBONS, Francis 289.3'092'4 B
M., 1921-
Joseph Smith, martyr, prophet of God / Francis M. Gibbons. Salt Lake City : Deseret Book Co., 1977. ix, 377 p. ; 23 cm. Includes index. Bibliography: p. 366-368. [BX8695.S6G52] 77-2019 ISBN 0-87747-637-3 : 6.95
1. Smith, Joseph, 1805-1844. 2. Mormons and Mormonism in the United States—Biography. 3. Mormons and Mormonisın—History. I. Title.

HARTSHORN, Leon R. 289.3'0924 B
Joseph Smith: prophet of the restoration, by Leon R. Hartshorn. Salt Lake City, Deseret Book Co., 1970. 124 p. 24 cm. Includes bibliographic references. [BX8695.S6H32] 71-130321 ISBN 0-87747-372-2 3.95
1. Smith, Joseph, 1805-1844.

HICKMAN, William A., 289.3'0924 B
1815-1877or8.
Brigham's destroying angel: being the life, confession, and startling disclosures of the notorious Bill Hickman, the Danite chief of Utah. Written by himself, with explanatory notes by J. H. Beadle. Freeport, N.Y., Books for Libraries Press [1971] vii, 221 p. illus. 23 cm. Reprint of the 1904 ed. [F826.H63 1971] 74-165642 ISBN 0-8369-5951-5
1. Utah—History. 2. Mormons and Mormonism. I. Title.

HILL, Donna. 289.3'092'4 B
Joseph Smith, the first Mormon / by Donna Hill. 1st ed. Garden City, N.Y. : Doubleday, 1977. xviii, 527 p., [8] leaves of plates : ill. ; 25 cm. Includes index. Bibliography: p. [495]-513. [BX8695.S6H54] 73-15345 ISBN 0-385-00804-X : 12.50
1. Smith, Joseph, 1805-1844. 2. Mormons and Mormonism—Biography. I. Title.

HILTON, Eugene, 289.3'0924 B
1889-
My second estate; the life of a Mormon. [Oakland, Calif., Hilton Family, 1968] 245 p. illus., facsims., ports. 28 cm. Cover title. "Volume of family lore and pictures ... prepared especially for the families descended from Eugene Hilton and Ruth Naomi Savage." Bibliographical footnotes. [BX8695.H5A3] 70-11040
I. Title.

HIRSHSON, Stanley 289.3'0924 B
P., 1928-
The lion of the Lord; a biography of Brigham Young [by] Stanley P. Hirshson. [1st ed.] New York, Knopf, 1969. xx, 391, xxvi p. illus. 25 cm. Bibliography: p. 377-391. [BX8695.Y7H55] 70-79334 8.95
1. Young, Brigham, 1801-1877. I. Title.

HUNTER, Milton 289.3'092'4 B
Reed, 1902-
Brigham Young the colonizer, by Milton R. Hunter. [4th ed., rev.] Santa Barbara, Calif., Peregrine Smith, 1973. xviii, 399 p. illus. 23 cm. A revision of the author's thesis, University of California, Berkeley, 1935. Bibliography: p. [384]-389. [BX8695.Y7H8 1973] 73-85421 ISBN 0-87905-017-9 8.95
1. Young, Brigham, 1801-1877. 2. Mormons and Mormonism. I. Title.

LARSON, Andrew Karl. 289.3'0924 B
Erastus Snow; the life of a missionary and pioneer for the early Mormon Church. Salt Lake City, University of Utah Press [1971] 814 p. illus., facsims., ports. 27 cm. (University of Utah publications in the American West, v. 5) Bibliography: p. [775]-787. [BX8695.S747L37] 75-634390 ISBN 0-87480-031-5
1. Snow, Erastus, 1818-1888. I. Series: Utah. University. Publications in the American West, v. 5.

MILLER, Jacob, 289.3'0924 (B)
1835-1911.
Journal. Prepared for publication by Joseph Royal Miller and Elna Miller. [Salt Lake City] Mercury Pub. Co., 1967, c1968. 199 p. illus., port. 26 cm. [CT275.M52527A3] 68-5134
I. Miller, Joseph Royal, ed. II. Miller, Elna, joint ed. III. Title.

MILLER, Jacob, 1835- 289.3'0924 B
1911.
Journal. Prepared for publication by Joseph Royal Miller and Elna Miller. [Salt Lake City] Mercury Pub. Co., 1967, c1968. 199 p. illus., port. 26 cm. [CT275.M52527A3] 68-5134
I. Miller, Joseph Royal, ed. II. Miller, Elna, joint ed.

NEELEY, Deta 289.3'0924 B
Petersen.
A child's story of the prophet Lorenzo Snow, by Deta Peterson [i.e. Petersen] Neeley, Nathan Glen Neeley, and Melba Jensen Priday. Salt Lake City, Deseret Book Co., 1968. 100 p. 20 cm. A biography of a convert to the Church of Jesus Christ of Latter-day Saints who served his Church as a missionary, as a state prisoner, and eventually as its President. [BX8695.S75N4] 92 70-4178 2.25
1. Snow, Lorenzo. 1814-1901—Juvenile literature. I. Neeley, Nathan Glen, joint author. II. Priday, Melba Jensen, joint author. III. Title.

PETERSEN, Emma 289.3'092'4 B
Marr.
The Prophet's story for young people. Salt Lake City, Bookcraft, 1973. v, 121 p. illus. 24 cm. [BX8695.S6P38] 73-90804
1. Smith, Joseph, 1805-1844—Juvenile literature. I. Title.

PETERSEN, LaMar, 289.3'092'4 B
1910-
Hearts made glad : the charges of intemperance against Joseph Smith the Mormon prophet / LaMar Petersen ; drawings by Linda Marion. [Salt Lake City : Petersen], c1975. iv, 258 p. : ill. ; 23 cm. Includes index. Bibliography: p. 245-253. [BX8695.S6P39] 75-21678
1. Smith, Joseph, 1805-1844. 2. Temperance. I. Title.

REDD, Amasa Jay, 1895- 289.3'0924
Lemuel Hardison Redd, Jr., 1856-1923, pioneer, leader, builder. compiled and edited by Amasa Jay Redd. Biography written by Albert R. Lyman. Biographical contributions by family members. Photos. arr. by Amasa Mason Redd. Salt Lake City, 1967. 229 p. illus. 29 cm. Includes bibliographical references. [BX8695.R4R4] 68-4357
1. Redd, Lemuel Hardison, 1856-1923. I. Lyman, Albert R., 1880- II. Title.

REDD, Amasa Jay, 1895- 289.3'0924
Lemuel Hardison Redd, Jr., 1856-1923, pioneer, leader, builder, compiled and edited by Amasa Jay Redd. Biography written by Albert R. Lyman. Biographical contributions by family members. Photos arr. by Amasa Mason Redd Salt Lake City, 1967. 229 p. illus. 29 cm. Includes bibliographical references. [BX8695.R4R4] 68-4357
1. Redd, Lemuel Hardison, 1856-1923. I. Lyman, Albert R., 1880- II. Title.

SCHINDLER, Harold, 289.3'0924
1929-
Orrin Porter Rockwell: man of God, son of thunder. Illustrated by Dale Bryner. Salt Lake City, University of Utah Press, 1966. 399 p. illus., maps, ports. 26 cm. Bibliography: p. 366-385. [BX8695.R6S32] 66-29846
1. Rockwell, Orrin Porter, 1813-1878.

TANNER, Annie 289.3'092'4 B
Clark, 1864-1941.
A mormon mother; an autobiography. [1st rev. ed.] [Salt Lake City] Tanner Trust Fund, University of Utah Library [1973] xxix, 346 p. 23 cm. (Utah, the Mormons, and the West) [BX8695.T27A33 1973] 73-86679 10.00
1. Tanner, Annie Clark, 1864-1941. I. Title. II. Series.

WEEKS, Robert Percy, 289.3'0924 B
1915-
King Strang; a biography of James Jesse Strang, by Robert P. Weeks. Ann Arbor [Mich.] Five Wives Press, 1971. vi, 82 p. facsim. 22 cm. Bibliography: p. 80-82. [BX8680.S88S88] 73-25917
1. Strang, James Jesse, 1813-1856. I. Title.

WERNER, Morris 289.3'092'4 B
Robert, 1897-
Brigham Young / by M. R. Werner. Westport, Conn. : Hyperion Press, 1975, c1925. p. cm. Reprint of the ed. published by Harcourt, Brace, New York. Includes index. Bibliography: p. [BX8695.Y7W4 1975] 75-351 ISBN 0-88355-254-X : 26.50
1. Young, Brigham, 1801-1877. 2. Mormons and Mormonism.

WIDTSOE, John 289.3'0924 B
Andreas, 1872-1952.
In the gospel net; the story of Anna Karine Gaarden Widtsoe, by John A. Widtsoe. [3d ed.] Salt Lake City, Bookcraft [1966] 140 p. illus., maps, ports. 24 cm. [BX8695.W54W5 1966] 67-2680
1. Widtsoe, Anna Karine (Gaarden) 1849-1919. I. Title.

WIGHT, Levi Lamoni, 289.3'0924 B
1836-1918.
The reminiscences and Civil War letters of Levi Lamoni Wight; life in a Mormon splinter colony on the Texas frontier. Davis Bitton, editor. Salt Lake City, University of Utah Press [1970] 191 p. facsim., geneal. table, map, ports. 24 cm. (University of Utah publications in the American West, v. 4) Includes bibliographical references. [BX8678.W5A3 1970] 74-120412 ISBN 0-87480-060-9
I. Title. II. Series: Utah. University. Publications in the American West, v. 4

YOUNG, Brigham, 289.3'092'4 B
1801-1877.
Letters of Brigham Young to his sons / edited and introduced by Dean C. Jessee ; with a foreword by J. H. Adamson. Salt Lake City : Deseret Book Co., 1974. xliv, 375 p. : ports. ; 25 cm. (The Mormon heritage series ; v. 1) Includes bibliographical references and index. [BX8695.Y7A4 1974] 74-80041 ISBN 0-87747-522-9 : 9.95
1. Young, Brigham, 1801-1877. 2. Mormons and Mormonism—Biography. I. Jessee, Dean C., ed. II. Title.

YOUNG, Brigham, 1801- 289.3'0924
1877.
Manuscript history of Brigham Young, 1801-1844. Elden Jay Watson. [Salt Lake City, Smith Secretarial Service, c1968] xxxv, 274 p. illus., facsims., port. 26 cm. "From volumes 25 and 26 of Millennial Star." [BX8695.Y7A3] 75-15709
I. Watson, Elden Jay. II. Title.

YOUNG, Brigham, 1801- 289.3'0924
1877.
Manuscript history of Brigham Young, 1846-1847. [Edited by] Elden J. Watson. [Salt Lake City, Utah, J. Watson, 1971] 672 p. illus. 23 cm. [BX8695.Y7A3 1971] 77-27431
I. Watson, Elden Jay. II. Title.

CROSSFIELD, R. C. 289.3'2
Book of Onias, by R. C. Crossfield. New York, Philosophical Library [1969] vii, 62 p. 23 cm. [BX8638.C7] 70-86503 3.50
1. Mormons and Mormonism—Doctrinal and controversial works. I. Title.

CURTIS, Thomas Arnold, 289.3'2
1953-
The pearl of great price comprehensive concordance, by Thomas A. Curtis and Jeffery Hill. Salt Lake City, Hawkes Publications [1973] 190 p. 21 cm. [BX8629.P5C87] 73-78980 2.95
1. Smith, Joseph, 1805-1844. The pearl of great price—Concordances. I. Hill, Jeffery, joint author. II. Smith, Joseph, 1805-1844. The pearl of great price. III. Title.

CURTIS, Thomas Arnold, 289.3'2
1953-
The pearl of great price comprehensive concordance, by Thomas A. Curtis and Jeffery Hill. Salt Lake City, Hawkes Publications [1973] 190 p. 21 cm. [BX8629.P5C87] 73-78980 2.95
1. Smith, Joseph, 1805-1844. The pearl of great price—Concordances. I. Hill, Jeffery, joint author. II. Smith, Joseph, 1805-1844. The pearl of great price. III. Title.

DOXEY, Roy Watkins, 1908- 289.3'2
Prophecies and prophetic promises, from the Doctrine and covenants [by] Roy W. Doxey. Salt Lake City, Utah, Deseret Book Co., 1969. xiii, 349 p. 24 cm. Bibliography: p. [330]-333. [BX8628.D694] 74-101993 4.95
1. Mormons and Mormonism—Doctrinal and controversial works. I. Smith, Joseph, 1805-1844. Doctrine and covenants. 1969. II. Title.

DOXEY, Roy Watkins, 1908- 289.3'2
Walk with the Lord; teachings of the Pearl of great price [by] Roy W. Doxey. Salt Lake City, Deseret Book Co., 1973. xiii, 208 p. 23 cm. Bibliography: p. [199]-201. [BX8635.2.D68] 73-86166 ISBN 0-87747-502-4 4.95
1. Church of Jesus Christ of Latter-Day Saints—Doctrinal and controversial works. I. The Pearl of great price. II. Title.

DOXEY, Roy Watkins, 1908- 289.3'2
Walk with the Lord; teachings of the Pearl of great price [by] Roy W. Doxey. Salt Lake City, Deseret Book Co., 1973. xiii, 208 p. 23 cm. Bibliography: p. [199]-201. [BX8635.2.D68] 73-86166 ISBN 0-87747-502-4 4.95
1. Church of Jesus Christ of Latter-Day Saints—Doctrinal and controversial works. I. The Pearl of great price. II. Title.

HILTON, Lynn M. 289.3'2
A concordance of the Pearl of great price [by] Lynn M. Hilton. Provo, Utah, Brigham Young University Press [1968] iv, 91 p. 28 cm. [BX8629.P6H5 1968] 68-3571
1. Smith, Joseph, 1805-1844. Pearl of great price—Concordances. I. Title.

HOWARD, Richard P. 289.3'2
Restoration scriptures; a study of their textual development, by Richard P. Howard. [Independence, Mo.] Dept. of Religious Education, Reorganized Church of Jesus Christ of Latter Day Saints [1969] 278 p. facsims. 23 cm. Includes bibliographical references [BX8627.H67] 73-85800
1. Reorganized Church of Jesus Christ of Latter Day Saints. Book of doctrine and covenants. 2. Book of mormon. 3. Bible—Criticism, Textual. I. Reorganized Church of Jesus Christ of Latter Day Saints. Dept. of Religious Education. II. Title.

NIBLEY, Hugh, 1910- 289.3'2
The message of the Joseph Smith papyri : an Egyptian endowment / Hugh Nibley. Salt Lake City : Deseret Book Co., 1975. xiii, 305 p. : ill. ; 29 cm. Includes an edition of the late Egyptian mortuary work known as the Book of breathings, comprising text and translation of Joseph Smith papyri no. 10 and 11, and of Louvre papyrus no. 3284. Includes index. Bibliography: p. [287]-298. [PJ1559.B43N5] 75-18734 ISBN 0-87747-485-0 : 14.95
1. Book of breathings. 2. Funeral rites and ceremonies—Egypt. 3. Cultus, Egyptian. I. Smith, Joseph, 1805-1844. II. Book of breathings. English & Egyptian. 1975. III. Title.

REORGANIZED Church of 289.3'2
Jesus Christ of Latter-Day Saints.
Book of doctrine and covenants. Carefully selected from the revelations of God, and given in the order of their dates. Enl. and improved ed. Independence, Mo., Herald Pub. House, 1970. 419, 39 p. 21 cm. "Contains a historical preface for each revelation or section." [BX8628.A4 1970] 78-134922 ISBN 0-8309-0035-7
I. Title. II. Title: Doctrine and covenants.

SMITH, Joseph, 1805-1844. 289.3'2
The doctrine and covenants, of the Church of Jesus Christ of Latter-Day Saints, containing the revelations given to Joseph Smith, Jun., the prophet, for the building up of the Kingdom of God in the last days. Divided into verses, with references, by Orson Pratt, Sen. Westport, Conn., Greenwood Press [1971] 503 p. 23 cm. Reprint of the 1880 ed. [BX8628.A3 1971b] 69-14082 ISBN 0-8371-4101-X
1. Mormons and Mormonism—Doctrinal and controversial works. I. Pratt, Orson, 1811-1881. II. Church of Jesus Christ of Latter-Day Saints.

TODD, Jay M. 289.3'2
The saga of the Book of Abraham [by] Jay M. Todd. Salt Lake City, Deseret Book Co., 1969. ix, 404 p. illus., facsims., maps, ports. 24 cm. [BX8629.P6T6] 71-82121 4.95
1. Smith, Joseph, 1805-1844. The pearl of great price. Book of Abraham. I. Title. II. Title: Book of Abraham.

BANKHEAD, Reid E. 289.3'22
The word and the witness; the unique mission of the Book of Mormon [by] Reid E. Bankhead [and] Glenn L. Pearson. Salt Lake City, Bookcraft, 1970. ix, 246 p. 24 cm. [BX8627.B3] 74-127953
1. Book of Mormon. 2. Mormons and Mormonism—Doctrinal and controversial works. I. Pearson, Glenn Laurentz, joint author. II. Title.

BICKERSTAFF, George. 289.3'22
Book of Mormon stories for children. Illus. by Allen Reinhold. Salt Lake City, Utah, Bookcraft, 1971- v. col. illus. 30 cm. Contents.Contents.—book 1. The Jaredite nation. Lehi's trek to the seashore.—book 2. The promised land. Nephites and Mulekites combine.—book 3. Exiles return to Zarahemla Reign of Judges begins.—book 4. Mission to Lamanites. General Moroni. [BX8627.A2B52] 73-175139
1. Book of Mormon stories. I. Reinhold, Allen, illus. II. Book of Mormon. III. Title.

BOOK of Mormon. 289.322
The Book of Mormon. Translated by Joseph Smith, Jr. Compared with the original manuscript and the Kirtland edition of 1837, which was carefully re-examined and compared with the original manuscript by Joseph Smith and Oliver Cowdery. Authorized ed. Independence, Mo., Board of Publication of the Reorganized Church of Jesus Christ of Latter Day Saints, 1966. xi, 414 p. 20 cm. [BX8623] 66-15423
I. Smith, Joseph, 1805-1844. II. Cowdery, Oliver. III. Reorganized Church of Jesus Christ of Latter-Day Saints. Board of Publication. IV. Title.

BOOK of Mormon. 289.3'22
The Book of Mormon; an account written by the hand of Mormon upon plates taken from the plates of Nephi. Translated by Joseph Smith, Jr. Salt Lake City, Church of Jesus Christ of Latter-Day Saints, 1964 [c1963] 558 p. 18 cm. [BX8623 1964] 72-8846
I. Smith, Joseph, 1805-1844. II. Church of Jesus Christ of Latter-Day Saints.

BOOK of Mormon 289.322
The Book of Mormon. Tr. by Joseph Smith. Jr. Compared with the original ms. and the Kirtland ed. of 1837. which was carefully re-examined and compared with the orig. ms. by Joseph Smith, Oliver Cowdery. Authorized ed. Independence, Mo., Bd. of Pubn. of the Reorganized Church of Jesus Christ of Latter Day Saints [dist. Herald Pub., c]1966 xi, 414p. 20cm. [BX8623 1966] 66-15423 3.95
I. Smith. Joseph, 1805-1844. II. Cowdery, Oliver. III. Reorganized Church of Jesus Christ of Latter Day Saints. Board of Publication. IV. Title.

BOOK of Mormon. 289.3'22
The Book of Mormon story. An adaptation by Mary Pratt Parrish, with illus. by Ronald Crosby. Salt Lake City, Deseret Book Co., 1966. xii, 221 p. illus. (part col.) 27 cm. [BX8627.A2P27] 67-2814
1. Book of Mormon stories. I. Parrish, Mary Pratt. II. Title.

BUTTERWORTH, F. Edward. 289.3'22
The sword of Laban, by F. Edward Butterworth. Illustrated by Don Wagler. Independence, Mo.] Reorganized Church of Jesus Christ of Latter Day Saints [1969- v. illus., map. 21 cm. Paraphrased from the Book of Mormon. Bibliography: p. 120. [BX8627.A2B87] 70-101571
I. Reorganized Church of Jesus Christ of Latter Day Saints. II. Book of Mormon. III. Title.

CHEESMAN, Paul R. 289.3'22
The keystone of Mormonism; little known truths about the Book of Mormon [by] Paul R. Cheesman. Salt Lake City, Deseret Book Co., 1973. vi, 176 p. illus. 24 cm. Bibliography: p. [165]-167. [BX8627.C473] 73-77366 ISBN 0-87747-494-X 3.95
1. Book of Mormon. I. Title.

CHEESMAN, Paul R. 289.3'22
These early Americans; external evidences of the Book of Mormon, by Paul R. Cheesman. Salt Lake City, Deseret Book Co., 1974. 298 p. illus. 24 cm. Bibliography: p. 275-288. [BX8627.C476] 73-93662 ISBN 0-87747-517-2 5.95
1. Book of Mormon. 2. Indians—Antiquities. 3. America—Antiquities. I. Title.

CHEVILLE, Roy Arthur, 289.3'22
1897-
The Book of Mormon speaks for itself, by Roy A. Cheville. [Independence, Mo., Published for] the Dept. of Christian Education, Reorganized Church of Jesus Christ of Latter Day Saints [by Herald Pub. House, 1971] 203 p. 21 cm. [BX8627.C49] 76-167492 ISBN 0-8309-0046-2 4.25
1. Book of Mormon. I. Title.

CROWTHER, Duane S. 289.3'22
Reading guide to the book of Mormon : a simplified program featuring brief outlines and doctrinal summaries / Duane S. Crowther. Bountiful, Utah : Horizon Publishers, c1975. 169 p. : ill. ; 23 cm. [BX8627.C76] 75-5322 ISBN 0-88290-045-5 : 4.95
1. Book of Mormon. I. Book of Mormon. II. Title.

ETZENHOUSER, Rudolph, 289.3'22
1856-
From Palmyra, New York, 1830, to Independence, Missouri, 1894. Independence, Mo., Ensign Pub. House, 1894. [New York, AMS Press, 1971] 444 p. 22 cm. The Book unsealed, rev. and enl., which was first published in 1892, forms part one of this work. [BX8627.E78 1971] 73-134393 ISBN 0-404-08435-4 17.50
1. Smith, Joseph, 1805-1844. 2. Book of Mormon. 3. Mormons and Mormonism—Doctrinal and controversial works. I. Title.

HILTON, Lynn M. 289.3'22
In search of Lehi's trail / Lynn M. Hilton, Hope Hilton ; photography by Gerald W. Silver. Salt Lake City : Deseret Book Co., 1977 148 p. : col. ill. ; 29 cm. Includes bibliographical references and index. [BX8627.H53] 76-54478 ISBN 0-87747-620-9 : 9.95
1. Lehi (Book of Mormon character) 2. Book of Mormon—Biography. I. Hilton, Hope A., joint author. II. Title.

LUDLOW, Daniel H. 289.3'22
A companion to your study of the Book of Mormon / Daniel H. Ludlow. Salt Lake City : Deseret Book Co., 1976. 396 p. : ill. ; 24 cm. Includes index. [BX8627.L83] 76-27139 ISBN 0-87747-610-1 : 6.95
1. Book of Mormon. I. Title.

NIBLEY, Hugh, 1910- 289.3'22
Since Cumorah; the Book of Mormon in the modern world. Salt Lake City, Deseret, 1967. xviii, 451p. illus. 24cm. Bibl. [BX8627.N485] 67-21349 4.95
1. Book of Mormon. I. Title.

NIBLEY, Hugh, 1910- 289.3'22
Since Cumorah; the Book of Mormon in the modern world. Salt Lake City,Deseret Book Co., 1967. xviii, 451 p. illus. 24 cm. Bibliographical footnotes. [BN8627.N485] 67-21349
1. Book of Mormon. I. Title.

PEARSON, Glenn Laurentz. 289.3'22
Teaching with the Book of Mormon / Glenn L. Pearson and Reid E. Bankhead. Rev. and enl. ed. of the book formerly published under title Doctrinal approach to the Book of Mormon. Salt Lake City : Bookcraft, 1976. xi, 100 p. ; 24 cm. Includes index. [BX8627.P37 1976] 76-23688 ISBN 0-88494-305-4 pbk. : 3.50
1. Book of Mormon. I. Bankhead, Reid E., joint author. II. Title.

PRIDDIS, Venice. 289.3'22
The Book and the map : new insights into Book of Mormon geography / Venice Priddis ; ill. by Christopher Priddis, maps by Annette Priddis. Salt Lake City : Bookcraft, 1975. 169 p. : ill., maps ; 24 cm. Includes index. Bibliography: p. [159]-161. [BX8627.P74] 75-4326 ISBN 0-88494-277-5
1. Book of Mormon—Geography. I. Title.

SMITH, Joseph, 1805-1844. 289.322
The Book of Mormon. Translated by Joseph Smith, Jr. Compared with the original manuscript and the Kirkland Edition of 1837, which was carefully re-examined and compared with the original manuscript by Joseph Smith and Oliver Cowdery. Foreword by Marcus Bach. New York, Family Library [1973, c.1966] xxvii, 414 p. 18 cm. (Family Library, FY3034) [BX8623 1966] ISBN 0-515-03034-1 1.75 (pbk)
I. Cowdery, Oliver. II. Reorganized Church of Jesus Christ of Latter-Day Saints. III. Book of Mormon. IV. Title.
L.C. card no. for the hardbound edition: 66-15423.

SPERRY, Sidney Branton, 289.3'22
1895-
Answers to Book of Mormon questions, by Sidney B. Sperry. Salt Lake City, Bookcraft [1967] 261 p. 24 cm. 1964 ed. has title: Problems of the Book of Mormon. Includes bibliographical references. [BX8627.S77 1967] 67-3C255
1. Book of Mormon. I. Title.

SPERRY, Sidney Branton, 289.3'22
1895-
Book of Mormon compendium, by Sidney B. Sperry. Salt Lake City, Bookcraft, 1968. 588 p. 24 cm. Bibliographical footnotes. [BX8627.S74] 68-56892 6.95
1. Book of Mormon. I. Title.

SPERRY, Sidney Bronton, 289.3'22
1895-
Answers to Book of Mormon questions, by Sidney B. Sperry. Salt Lake City, Bookcraft [1967] 261 p. 24 cm. 1964 ed. has title: Problems of the Book of Mormon. Includes bibliographical references. [BX8627.S77 1967] 67-30255
1. Book of Mormon. I. Title.

STOUT, Walter Milton, 289.3'22
1886-
The Book of Mormon practical geography, by Walter M. Stout. [Upland? Calif.] 1970. 64 p. col. maps. 22 cm. [BX8627.S795] 78-284625 1.50
1. Book of Mormon—Geography. I. Book of Mormon. II. Title.

WASHBURN, Jesse Nile, 289.3'22
1901-
Book of Mormon: lands and times [by] J. Nile Washburn. [Bountiful, Utah, Horizon Publishers, 1974] 304 p. illus. 24 cm. Includes bibliographical references. [BX8627.W33] 74-166329 ISBN 0-88290-020-X 4.95
1. Book of Mormon.

CHEESMAN, Paul R. 289.3'22'0922 B
Great leaders of the Book of Mormon [by] Paul R. Cheesman. Poetry: Millie Foster Cheesman. Ports.: Stuart Heimdal. Salt Lake City, Utah, Promised Land Publications [1970] 96 p. col. illus. 31 cm. A full-page, color portrait accompanies a brief biographical sketch and poem about each of nineteen leaders of the Book of Mormon. [BX8627.C47] 76-18884
1. Book of Mormon—Biography—Juvenile literature. I. Cheesman, Millie Foster. II. Heimdal, Stuart, illus. III. Title.

GABBOTT, Mabel 289.3'22'0922 B
Jones.
Heroes of the Book of Mormon / Mabel Jones Gabbott ; illustrated by Howard Post. Salt Lake City : Deseret Book Co., 1975. 45 p. : ill. ; 29 cm. [BX8627.G27] 75-22770 ISBN 0-87747-570-9
1. Book of Mormon—Biography—Juvenile literature. I. Title.

LUNDSTROM, 289.3'22'0922 B
Joseph.
Book of Mormon personalities. [Salt Lake City] Deseret Book Co., 1969. 111 p. illus. (part col.) 24 cm. "Book of Mormon personalities first appeared in the Deseret news as ... a series on the editorial page of the Church news." [BX8627.L85] 76-102890 3.95
1. Book of Mormon—Biography. I. Title.

MATTHEWS, Robert J. 289.3'22'0922
Who's who in the Book of Mormon / Robert J. Matthews. [Salt Lake City] : Deseret Book Co., c1976. vii, 75 p. ; 23 cm. Includes bibliographical references and index. [BX8622.M37] 76-377261 ISBN 0-87747-613-6 pbk. : 1.95
1. Book of Mormon—Biography. 2. Book of Mormon—Concordances. I. Title.

ALLEN, Edward Jones, 289.3'3
1898-
The second United Order among the Mormons, by Edward J. Allen. New York, AMS Press, 1967 [c1936] 148 p. 23 cm. (Studies in history, economics and public law, no. 419) Originally presented as the author's thesis, Columbia University. Bibliography: p. 144-145. [BX8611.A47 1967] 71-29858
1. Mormons and Mormonism. I. Title. II. Series: Columbia studies in the social sciences, 419.

BAILEY, Paul Dayton, 289.3'3 B
1906-
Polygamy was better than monotony. With some home-town primitives by Don Louis Perceval. Los Angeles, Westernlore Press, 1972. 200 p. illus. 22 cm. [BX8638.B32] 72-83538 7.95
1. Mormons and Mormonism. I. Title.

BROOKS, Juanita, 1898- 289.3'3 B
Emma Lee / Juanita Brooks. Logan : Utah State University Press, 1975. 113 p., [2] leaves of plates : ill. ; 24 cm. (Western Text Society series) [BX8695.F7B76] 75-4629 ISBN 0-87421-080-1 : 4.50
1. French, Emma Bachellor, 1836-1897. I. Series: Western Text Society. Western Text Society series.

BURTON, Alma P., 1913- 289.3'3
comp.
Doctrines from the prophets; choice selections from the Latter-Day leaders, compiled and arranged by Alma P. Burton. Salt Lake City, Bookcraft, 1970. x, 476 p. 24 cm. [BX8608.B85] 76-115487
1. Mormons and Mormonism—Collections. I. Title.

CAMPBELL, Eugene E., 289.3'3
1915-
Hugh B. Brown, his life and thought / Eugene E. Campbell and Richard D. Poll. Salt Lake City : Bookcraft, 1975. xii, 331 p. : ill. ; 24 cm. Includes index. [BX8695.B69C35] 75-34834 ISBN 0-88494-293-7
1. Brown, Hugh B. I. Poll, Richard Douglas, 1918- II. Title.

CHRISTENSEN, Leon N., 289.3'3
1907-
The little book : why I am a Mormon / by Leon N. Christensen. Boston : Branden Press, c1976. 185 p., [3] leaves of plates ; 23 cm. Bibliography: p. 184-185. [BX8635.2.C46] 74-31827 ISBN 0-8283-1606-6 : 12.50
1. Church of Jesus Christ of Latter-day Saints—Doctrinal and controversial works. I. Title.

DURHAM, Reed C. 289.3'3
Succession in the church [by] Reed C. Durham, Jr. [and] Steven H. Heath. Salt Lake City, Bookcraft, 1970. viii, 207 p. 24 cm. [BX8657.D8] 72-119915
1. Mormons and Mormonism—Government. I. Heath, Steven H., joint author. II. Title.

FLAKE, Lawrence R. 289.3'3 B
Mighty men of Zion : General Authorities of the last dispensation / Lawrence R. Flake. Salt Lake City : K. D. Butler, 1974. xx, 536 p. : ports. ; 24 cm. Includes indexes. Bibliography: p. [521]-[525] [BX8693.F57] 75-308408 7.95

1. Church of Jesus Christ of Latter-Day Saints—Biography. I. Title.

GUNNISON, John Williams, 1812-1853. 289.3'3
The Mormons, or, Latter-day Saints, in the valley of the Great Salt Lake: a history of their rise and progress, peculiar doctrines, present condition, and prospects, derived from personal observation, during a residence among them. Freeport, N.Y., Books for Libraries Press [1972] ix, 13-168 p. front. 23 cm. Reprint of the 1852 ed. [BX8611.G8 1972] 70-38355 ISBN 0-8369-6772-0
1. Mormons and Mormonism. I. Title.

HAM, Wayne, comp. 289.3'3
Publish glad tidings; readings in early Latter Day Saint sources. Selected and edited by Wayne Ham. [Independence, Mo.] Herald Pub. House [1970] 444 p. illus., ports. 21 cm. Selected from The Evening and the morning star, and other publications. [BX8608.H33] 78-125306 8.95
1. Church of Jesus Christ of Latter-Day Saints—History—Sources. I. Evening and morning star. II. Title.

HANSEN, Klaus J. 289.3'3
Quest for empire; the political kingdom of God and the Council of Fifty in Mormon history, by Klaus J. Hansen. [East Lansing] Mich. State Univ. Pr., 1967. 237p. 22cm. Bibl. [BX8611.H295] 66-26957 6.50
1. Church of Jesus Christ of Latter-Day Saints: Council of Fifty. 2. Kingdom of God (Mormonism) I. Title.

HANSEN, Klaus J. 289.3'3
Quest for empire; the political kingdom of God and the Council of Fifty in Mormon history, by Klaus J. Hansen. Lincoln, University of Nebraska Press [1974, c1967] xvi, 237 p. 21 cm. "A Bison book." Reprint of the 1970 ed. published by Michigan State University Press, East Lansing; with new pref. by the author. Bibliography: p. 214-220. [BX8611.H295 1974] 74-8002 ISBN 0-8032-5769-4 3.95 (pbk.)
1. Church of Jesus Christ of Latter-Day Saints. Council of Fifty. 2. Kingdom of God (Mormonism) I. Church of Jesus Christ of Latter-Day Saints. Council of Fifty. II. Title.

HARTSHORN, Leon R., comp. 289.3'3 B
Outstanding stories by general authorities. Compiled by Leon R. Hartshorn. Salt Lake City, Deseret Book Co., 1970-73. 3 v. ports. 24 cm. [BX8693.H3] 73-136241 ISBN 0-87747-369-2 (v. 1) 4.95 per vol.
1. Church of Jesus Christ of Latter-Day Saints—Biography. I. Title.

HETTRICK, Ric. 289.3'3 B
From among men : biographies of 26 Latter-Day apostles / Ric and Marcia Hettrick. Independence, Mo. : Herald Pub. House, c1976. 220 p. : ports. ; 21 cm. [BX8693.H44] 76-27242 ISBN 0-8309-0170-1
1. Mormons and Mormonism—Biography. I. Hettrick, Marcia, joint author. II. Title.

HILL, Marvin S., comp. 289.3'3
Mormonism and American culture. Edited by Marvin S. Hill and James B. Allen. New York, Harper & Row [1972] vii, 189 p. 21 cm. (Interpretations of American history) Bibliography: p. 185-189. [BX8611.H55] 72-82900 ISBN 0-06-042819-8 Pap. $2.95
1. Mormons and Mormonism—History. I. Allen, James B., joint comp. II. Title.

THE History of the Reorganized Church of Jesus Christ of Latter Day Saints. 289.3'3 Independence, Mo. : Herald House, 1967- , c1896- v. : ill. ; 23 cm. Authors' name in publisher's pref. of v. 1: Joseph Smith and Heman C. Smith; v. 2: Heman Smith; v. 5-7: pref. signed: F. Henry Edwards. Includes indexes. Contents.Contents.—v. 1. 1805-1835.—v. 2. 1836-1844.—v. 3. 1844-1872.—v. 4. 1873-1890.—v. 5. 1890-1902.—v. 6. 1903-1915.—v. 7. 1915-1925. [BX8673.H57] 75-302471 ISBN 0-8309-0075-6 (v. 7)
1. Reorganized Church of Jesus Christ of Latter Day Saints—History. I. Smith, Joseph, 1832-1914. II. Smith, Heman Conoman, 1850- III. Edwards, Francis Henry, 1897-

HOLM, Francis W., 1898- 289.3'3
The Mormon Churches; a comparison from within [by] Francis W. Holm, Sr. [Kansas City, Mo., Midwest Press, 1970] 238 p. 21 cm. [BX8635.2.H63] 71-114837
1. Church of Jesus Christ of Latter-Day Saints. 2. Reorganized Church of Jesus Christ of Latter-Day Saints. I. Title.

HOWE, Eber D., b.1798. 289.3'3
Mormonism unvailed : or, A faithful account of that singular imposition and delusion, from its rise to the present time : with sketches of the characters of its propagators, and a full detail of the manner in which the famous Golden Bible was brought before the world ... / by E. D. Howe. New York : AMS Press, [1976] p. cm. (Communal societies in America) Reprint of the 1834 ed. printed and published by the author, Painesville, Ohio. [BX8635.H64 1976] 72-2967 ISBN 0-404-10730-3 : 15.00
1. Mormons and Mormonism—Doctrinal and controversial works. I. Title.

JONES, York F., 1925- 289.3'3 B
Lehi Willard Jones; biography, by York and Evelyn Jones. [Salt Lake City, Woodruff Print. Co., 1972] xiii, 258 p. illus. 24 cm. [F834.C4J6] 72-181634
1. Jones, Lehi Willard, 1854-1947. 2. Cedar City, Utah—History. 3. Mormons and Mormonism in Utah. I. Jones, Evelyn, joint author.

KAPP, Ardeth Greene, 1931- 289.3'3 B
Miracles in pinafores & bluejeans / Ardeth Greene Kapp. Salt Lake City : Deseret Book Co., 1977. 81 p. ; 24 cm. A woman shares the experiences of herself and others which exemplify the principles of living a spiritually enriched life. [BX8695.K35A35] 92 77-4268 ISBN 0-87747-644-6 : 3.95
1. Kapp, Ardeth Greene, 1931- 2. Mormons and Mormonism in Utah—Biography. I. Title.

KAPP, Ardeth Greene, 1931- 289.3'3 B
Miracles in pinafores & bluejeans / Ardeth Greene Kapp. Salt Lake City : Deseret Book Co., 1977. 81 p. ; 24 cm. A woman shares the experiences of herself and others which exemplify the principles of living a spiritually enriched life. [BX8695.K35A35] 92 77-4268 ISBN 0-87747-644-6 : 3.95
1. Kapp, Ardeth Greene, 1931- 2. Mormons and Mormonism in Utah—Biography. I. Title.

KIMBALL, Spencer W., 1895- 289.3'3 B
One silent sleepless night / Spencer W. Kimball ; ill. by Sherry Thompson. Salt Lake City : Bookcraft, 1975. 62 p. : ill. ; 24 cm. [BX8695.K53A34] 75-34832 ISBN 0-88494-291-0
1. Kimball, Spencer W., 1895- I. Title.

LEE, Harold B., 1899-1973. 289.3'3
Ye are the light of the world : selected sermons and writings of president Harold B. Lee. Salt Lake City : Deseret Book Co., 1974. x, 364 p. ; 24 cm. Companion volume to the author's Stand ye in holy places. Includes bibliographical references and index. [BX8609.L44 1974] 74-28800 ISBN 0-87747-542-3 : 5.95
1. Mormons and Mormonism—Collected works. I. Title.

LIVING saints witness at work 289.3'3 B / compiled by T. Ed Barlow. Independence, Mo. : Herald Pub. House, c1976. 126 p. : ill. ; 21 cm. [BX8678.A28] 76-27227 ISBN 0-8309-0153-1
1. Reorganized Church of Jesus Christ of Latter-Day Saints—Biography. 2. Christian life—Mormon authors. I. Barlow, T. Ed, 1931-

MCCONKIE, Joseph F. 289.3'3 B
True and faithful; the life story of Joseph Fielding Smith [by] Joseph F. McConkie. Salt Lake City, Utah, Bookcraft, 1971. 102 p. illus. 24 cm. Includes bibliographical references. [BX8695.S64M25] 76-175137
1. Smith, Joseph Fielding, 1876- I. Title.

MCKAY, David Oman, 1873-1970. 289.3'3 B
Cherished experiences, from the writings of President David O. McKay / compiled by Clare Middlemiss. Rev. and enl. Salt Lake City : Deseret Book Co., 1976. xii, 204 p. : ill. ; 24 cm. Includes index. [BX8609.M25 1976] 76-5178 ISBN 0-87747-030-8 5.95
1. McKay, David Oman, 1873-1970. 2. Mormons and Mormonism—Addresses, essays, lectures. I. Title.

MAPLES, Evelyn. 289.3'3
Norman learns about the Scriptures. Illus. by Garry R. Hood. [Independence, Mo., Herald Pub. House, 1972] 36 p. illus. 21 cm. A brother and sister learn about the Scriptures and the teachings of the Reorganized Church of Jesus Christ of Latter-Day Saints. [BX8674.M36] 72-189295 ISBN 0-8309-0060-8
1. Reorganized Church of Jesus Christ of Latter-Day Saints—Juvenile literature. 2. Bible—Juvenile literature. I. Hood, Garry R., illus. II. Title.

MERKLEY, Christopher, 1808- 289.3'3 B
Biography of Christopher Merkley. Written by himself. Freeport, N.Y., Books for Libraries Press [1972] 46 p. 23 cm. Reprint of the 1887 ed. [BX8695.M35A3 1972] 70-38363 ISBN 0-8369-6780-1
1. Mormons and Mormonism.

MERRILL Library. Special Collections Dept. 289.3'3
Name index to the Library of Congress collection of Mormon diaries. Logan, Utah State University Press, 1971. 391 p. 28 cm. (Western Text Society series, v. 1, no. 2) [BX8693.M47 1971] 75-636249
1. Mormons and Mormonism—Biography—Indexes. I. Title. II. Title: Library of Congress collection of Mormon diaries. III. Series: Western Text Society. Western Text Society series, v. 1, no. 2.

MERRILL, Melissa. 289.3'3 B
Polygamist's wife / by Melissa Merrill. Salt Lake City : Olympus Pub. Co., c1975. 167 p. : ill. ; 24 cm. [BX8695.M37A36] 74-29659 ISBN 0-913420-52-2 : 7.95
1. Merrill, Melissa. 2. Polygamy. I. Title.

MERRILL, Melissa. 289.3'3
Polygamist's wife / by Melissa Merrill. New York : Pocket Books, 1977c1975. 176p. ; 18 cm. (A Kangaroo Book) [BX8695.M37A36] ISBN 0-671-81053-7 pbk. : 1.75
1. Merrill, Melissa. 2. Polygamy. I. Title.
L.C. card no. for c1975 Olympus Pub. Co., ed.: 74-29659.

MORRELL, Jeanette (McKay)
Highlights in the life of President David O. McKay. Salt Lake City, Deseret Book Co., 1966. xi, 318 p. illus., coat-of-arms, ports. 24 cm. [BX8695.M27M6] 66-30512
1. McKay, David Oman, 1873- I. Title.

MOURITSEN, Dale C. 289.3'3
A defense and a refuge; priesthood correlation and the establishment of Zion [by] Dale C. Mouritsen. [Provo, Utah] Brigham Young University Publications [1972] v, 85 p. 23 cm. Bibliography: p. 75-79. [BX8635.2.M65] 70-190287 ISBN 0-8425-1461-9
1. Church of Jesus Christ of Latter-Day Saints—Doctrinal and controversial works. I. Title.

MULDER, William. 289.33
Among the Mormons; historic accounts by contemporary observers. Edited by William Mulder & A. Russell Mortensen. Lincoln, Univ. of Nebraska Pr. [1973, c.1958] xiv, 482, xiv p. 20 cm. (Bison Book, BB568) [BX8611.M79] ISBN 0-8032-5778-3 pap., 2.45
1. Mormons and Mormonism—History—Sources. 2. Reorganized Church of Jesus Christ of Latter Day Saints—History—Sources. I. Mortensen, Arlington Russell, 1911- joint ed. II. Title.

PEARSON, Carol Lynn. 289.3'3 B
The flight and the nest / Carol Lynn Pearson. Salt Lake City : Bookcraft, 1975. xiii, 121 p. : ill. ; 24 cm. Includes bibliographical references and index. [BX8693.P4] 75-31079 ISBN 0-88494-288-0 : 3.50
1. Mormons and Mormonism—Biography. 2. Women—Biography. 3. Women. I. Title.

PORTER, Larry C. 289.3'3
Illustrated stories from church history / Larry C. Porter, narrative ; Vernon Murdock, artist .... 1st ed. Provo, Utah : Promised Land Publications, 1974- c1973- v. : col. ill. ; 32 cm. Relates events in the history of the Mormon movement. [BX8611.P65] 75-310031
1. Church of Jesus Christ of Latter-Day Saints—History—Juvenile literature. I. Murdock, Vernon, ill. II. Title.

PRATT, Orson, 1811-1881. 289.3'3 B
The Orson Pratt journals / compiled and arranged by Elden J. Watson. Salt Lake City : E. J. Watson, 1975. xii, 583 p. : port. ; 24 cm. Includes index. Bibliography: p. 563-567. [BX8695.P69A36 1975] 76-354771
1. Pratt, Orson, 1811-1881. I. Watson, Elden Jay. II. Title.

REORGANIZED Church of Jesus Christ of Latter-Day Saints. 289.3'3
Highlights of the 968 World Conference. [Independence, Mo., Herald Pub. House? 1968] 124 p. illus. 23 cm. [BX8605.A5] 68-6769
1. Reorganized Church of Jesus Christ of Latter-Day Saints—Congresses. I. Title.

RICHARDS, Le Grand, Bp., 1886- 289.3'3
Le Grand Richards speaks. Compiled by G. LaMont Richards. Salt Lake City, Deseret Book Co., 1972. xvi, 292 p. ports. 24 cm. [BX8609.R52] 72-76068 ISBN 0-87747-469-9 4.95
1. Mormons and Mormonism—Collected works. I. Title.

SESSIONS, Gene Allred. 289.3'3 B
Latter-day patriots : nine Mormon families and their Revolutionary War heritage / Gene Allred Sessions. Salt Lake City : Deseret Book Co., 1975. xiv, 219 p., [1] leaf of plates : ill. ; 24 cm. Includes bibliographical references and index. [BX8693.S47] 75-37276 ISBN 0-87747-600-4
1. Mormons and Mormonism—Biography. 2. United States—History—Revolution, 1775-1783. I. Title.

SMITH, Joseph, 1805-1844. 289.3'3
A book of commandments for the government of the Church of Christ, organized according to law on the 6th of April 1830. Zion [Mo.] W. W. Phelps, 1833. [Independence, Mo., Herald House, 1972] [8], 160 p. facsim. 12 cm. Half title: Herald heritage reprint of the Book of commandments. Facsim. reproduction, with a pref., of a part of a 1st ed. of the Book of doctrine and covenants, printed at Independence, Mo., but never published. Cf. Pref. [BX8628.A3 1833a] 72-181703 ISBN 0-8309-0066-7 3.50
1. Mormons and Mormonism—Doctrinal and controversial works. I. Church of Jesus Christ of Latter-Day Saints. II. Reorganized Church of Jesus Christ of Latter Day Saints. III. Title.

SMITH, Joseph Fielding, 1913- 289.3'3 B
The life of Joseph Fielding Smith, tenth President of the Church of Jesus Christ of the Latter-day Saints [by] Joseph Fielding Smith, Jr. and John J. Stewart. Salt Lake City, Deseret Book Co., 1972. xvi, 404 p. illus. 24 cm. Bibliography: p. [389]-392. [BX8695.S64S6] 72-90344 ISBN 0-87747-484-2 4.95
1. Smith, Joseph Fielding, 1876- I. Stewart, John J., joint author. II. Title.

STEPHENS, Kenneth D., 1919- comp. 289.3'3
So great a cause! A surprising new look at the Latter Day Saints, selected from sacred scriptures, including those of the Latter-day Saints, by Kenneth D. Stephens. [Healdsburg, Calif., Naturegraph Publishers, 1973] 215 p. illus. (part col.) 22 cm. Bibliography: p. [212]-215. [BX8635.2.S67 1973] 72-13406 ISBN 0-87961-007-7 6.50
1. Church of Jesus Christ of Latter-Day Saints—Doctrinal and controversial works. 2. Prophecies. I. Title.
pap. 3.50; ISBN 0-87961-006-9.

TALMAGE, John R., 1911- 289.3'3 B
The Talmage story; life of James E. Talmage - educator, scientist, apostle [by] John R. Talmage. Salt Lake City, Bookcraft, 1972. 246 p. illus. 24 cm. [BX8695.T25T34] 77-189831
1. Talmage, James Edward, 1862-1933. I. Title.

TANNER, Annie Clark, 1864-1941. 289.3'3 B
A biography of Ezra Thompson Clark / by Annie Clark Tanner ; introd. by Obert C. Tanner. Salt Lake City : Tanner Trust Fund, University of Utah Library, c1975. xi, 82 p. : ill. ; 23 cm. (Utah, the Mormons, and the West ; no. 5) Includes index. [BX8695.C286T36 1975] 74-82361 8.50
1. Clark, Ezra Thompson, 1823-1901. I. Title. II. Series.

TANNER, Nathan Eldon, 1898- 289.3'3
Seek ye first the Kingdom of God, by N. Eldon Tanner. Compiled by LaRue Sneff. Salt Lake City, Deseret Book Co., 1973. ix, 303 p. port. 24 cm. [BX8609.T28] 73-91712 ISBN 0-87747-510-5 4.95
1. Mormons and Mormonism—Collected works. I. Title.

TAYLOR, Samuel Woolley, 1907- 289.3'3 B
The Kingdom or nothing : the life of John Taylor, militant Mormon / by Samuel W. Taylor. New York : Macmillan, c1976. x, 406 p. ; 24 cm. Includes index. Bibliography: p. 386-396. [BX8695.T3T39] 75-38962 ISBN 0-02-616600-3 : 8.95
1. Taylor, John, 1808-1887. 2. Mormons and Mormonism—History. I. Title.

WAR, conscription, conscience, and mormonism. 289.3'3 Santa Barbara, Calif., Mormon Heritage, 1971. 116, viii columns. 22 x 28 cm. Includes bibliographical references. [BX8643.W3W37] 72-180689 1.25
1. Church of Jesus Christ of Latter-Day Saints—Doctrinal and controversial works. 2. Conscientious objectors. 3. War and religion.

WARNER, James A. 289.3'3
The Mormon way / photos./text by James A. Warner and Styne M. Slade. Englewood Cliffs, N.J. : Prentice-Hall, c1976. 173 p. : ill. ; 24 cm. [BX8638.W37] 76-7624 ISBN 0-13-601088-1 : 25.00
1. Mormons and Mormonism—Pictorial works. I. Slade, Styne M., joint author. II. Title.

WEBB, Robert C. 289.3'3
The real Mormonism : a candid analysis of an interesting but much misunderstood subject in history, life, and thought / by Robert C. Webb. New York : AMS Press, 1975. xii, 463 p. ; 23 cm. (Communal societies in America) Reprint of the 1916 ed. published by Sturgis & Walton Co., New York. Includes index. [BX8635.W44 1975] 72-2971 ISBN 0-404-10736-2 : 29.00
1. Mormons and Mormonism. I. Title.

WHO'S who in service—a 289.3'3 B
look at areas of service participation by members of the Reorganizaed Church of Jesus Christ of Latter Day Saints. Independence, Mo. : Herald Pub. House, c1977. 164 p. ; 26 cm. [BX8678.A48] 76-29064 ISBN 0-8309-0173-6 : 12.00
1. Reorganized Church of Jesus Christ of Latter Day Saints—Biography. I. Herald Publishing House.

YORGASON, Blaine M., 289.3'3 B
1942-
Tall timber : the struggles of James Yorgason, a Mormon polygamist / by Blaine M. Yorgason. [Rexburg, Idaho] : Ricks College Press, 1976. xx, 315 p. : ill. ; 29 cm. Includes index. Bibliography: p. 224-228. [BX8695.Y67Y67] 76-28588 25.00
1. Yorgason, James, 1847-1917. 2. Mormons and Mormonism—Biography. I. Title.

YOUNG, Ann Eliza (Webb) 289.3'3
b.1844.
Wife no. 19. New York, Arno Press, 1972 [c1875] 605 p. illus. 23 cm. (American women: images and realities) [BX8641.Y7 1972] 72-2634 ISBN 0-405-04488-7 27.00
1. Mormons and Mormonism. 2. Polygamy. I. Title. II. Series.

RICH, Russell R., 289.3'3'09
1912-
Ensign to the nations; a history of the church from 1846 to the present [by] Russell R. Rich. [Provo, Utah] Brigham Young University Publications [1972] xviii, 663 p. illus. 24 cm. Bibliography: p. 645-654. [BX8611.R47] 72-91730 ISBN 0-8425-1540-2 7.95
1. Church of Jesus Christ of Latter-Day Saints—History. I. Title.

WEST, Emerson Roy. 289.3'3'0922 B
Profiles of the Presidents. Salt Lake City, Deseret Book Co., 1972. 375 p. illus. 24 cm. Bibliography: p. [361]-363. [BX8693.W47] 72-90347 ISBN 0-87747-489-3 5.95
1. Church of Jesus Christ of Latter-Day Saints—Biography. 2. Church of Jesus Christ of Latter-Day Saints—Government. I. Title.

GREEN, Nelson 289.3'3'0924 B
Winch.
Mormonism: its rise, progress, and present condition. Embracing the narrative of Mrs. Mary Ettie V. Smith, of her residence and experience of fifteen years with the Mormons; containing a full and authentic account of their social condition—their religious doctrines, and political government ... By N. W. Green. Hartford, Belknap & Bliss, 1870. [New York, AMS Press, 1972] 472 p. illus. 22 cm. [BX8695.S7G74 1972] 79-134401 ISBN 0-404-08445-1 19.50
1. Smith, Mary Ettie V. (Coray) 2. Mormons and Mormonism. I. Title.

HESLOP, J. M. 289.3'3'0924 B
Joseph Fielding Smith; a prophet among the people [by] J. M. Heslop and Dell R. Van Orden. Salt Lake City, Deseret Book Co., 1971. xi, 171 p. ports. 24 cm. [BX8695.S63H48] 77-175121 ISBN 0-87747-454-0 3.95
1. Smith, Joseph Fielding, 1876- I. Van Orden, Dell R., joint author.

CLAYTON, William, 289.3'427'2
1814-1879.
Manchester Mormons; the journal of William Clayton, 1840 to 1842. Edited by James B. Allen and Thomas G. Alexander. Santa Barbara [Calif.] Peregrine Smith, 1974. 248 p. illus. 23 cm. (Classic Mormon diary series, v. 1) Includes bibliographical references. [BX8617.G7C55 1974] 73-89749 ISBN 0-87905-024-1 8.95
1. Clayton, William, 1814-1879. 2. Mormons and Mormonism in Manchester, Eng. 3. Manchester, Eng.—Religion. I. Title.

SCHARFFS, Gilbert W. 289.3'43
Mormonism in Germany; a history of the Church of Jesus Christ of Latter-Day Saints in Germany between 1840 and 1970, by Gilbert W. Scharffs. Salt Lake City, Deseret Book Co., 1970. xiv, 256 p. illus., maps. 24 cm. Based on the author's thesis, Brigham Young University. Bibliography: p. [227]-231. [BX8617.G4S3 1970] 70-136240 ISBN 0-87747-368-4 5.50
1. Mormons and Mormonism in Germany. I. Title.

YOUNG, Karl E., 1903- 289.3'72'1
The long hot summer of 1912 episodes in the flight of the Mormon colonists from Mexico by Karl E. Young [Provo, Utah, Brigham Young University, 1967] vii, 67 p. 23 cm. (Charles E. Merrill monograph series in the humanities and social sciences, [v. 1] no. 1) Bibliography: p. 67. [F1392.M6Y59] 72-188006 1.00
1. Mormons and Mormonism in Mexico. I. Title. II. Series.

ARRINGTON, Leonard J. 289.3'73
Building of the city of God : community & cooperation among the Mormons / Leonard J. Arrington, Feramorz Y. Fox, Dean L. May. Salt Lake City : Deseret Book Co., 1976. xiii, 497 p. : ill. ; 24 cm. Includes bibliographical references and index. [BX8611.A77] 76-27141 ISBN 0-87747-590-3 : 7.95
1. Mormons and Mormonism—History. 2. Collective settlements—History. I. Fox, Feramorz Y., 1881-1957, joint author. II. May, Dean L., joint author. III. Title.

HUNTRESS, Keith Gibson, 289.373
1913- ed.
Murder of an American prophet: events and prejudices surrounding the killing of Joseph and Hyrum Smith, Carthage, Illinois, June 27, 1844; materials for analysis. San Francisco, Chandler [1963, c.1960] 232p. illus. 23cm. 63-9886 2.25 pap.,
1. Mormons and Mormonism—Hist. I. Title.

MULDER, William, ed. 289.373
Among the Mormons; historic accounts by contemporary observers, edited by William Mulder and A. Russell Mortensen. [1st ed.] New York, Knopf, 1958. 482p. illus. 25cm. [BX8611.M79] 58-5825
1. Mormons and Mormonism—Hist.—Sources. I. Mortensen, Arlington Russell, 1911- joint ed. II. Title.

OSCARSON, R Don. 289.373
The travelers' guide to historic Mormon America, by R. Don Oscarson, with Stanley B. Kimball, research and text and Leslie F. Medley, art and layout. Salt Lake City, Bookcraft, 1965. 84 p. illus., facsims., col. maps, plans, ports. 16 x 24 cm. Bibliography: p. 84. [BX8611.O8] 66-6608
1. Mormons and Mormonism in the U.S. — Historic houses, etc. I. Kimball, Stanley Buchholz. II. Medley, Leslie F., illus. III. Title.

TAYLOR, Philip A. M. 289.373
Expectations westward; the Mormons and the emigration of their British converts in the nineteenth century [by] P. A. M. Taylor. Ithaca, N. Y., Cornell University Press, 1966. xvi, 277 p. illus., maps (part fold.) 23 cm. Bibliography: p. [250]-266. [BX8611.T36 1966] 66-13812
1. Mormons and Mormonism—History. 2. U.S.—Emigration and immigration. I. Title.

TURNER, Wallace, 1921- 289.373
The Mormon establishment. Boston, Houghton, 1966. 343p. illus. 22cm. [BX8635.2.T8] 66-19476 6.00
1. Mormons and Mormonism. I. Title.

WYATT, Clair L. 289.3'73
"... some that trouble you ..."; subcultures in Mormonism [by] Clair L. Wyatt. Salt Lake City, Bookcraft [1974] x, 92 p. 24 cm. Includes bibliographical references. [BX8635.5.W9] 74-75167 ISBN 0-88494-209-0 2.95
1. Church of Jesus Christ of Latter-Day Saints—Apologetic works. 2. Sects. I. Title.

LAYTON, 289.373'0924 (B)
Christopher, 1821-1898.
Christopher Layton. Edited by Myron W. McIntyre and Noel R. Barton. [2d ed. Kaysville, Utah] Christopher Layton Family Organization [c1966] vii, 438 p. illus., ports. 24 cm. First ed. published in 1911 under title: Autobiography of Christopher Layton. "Genealogical appendix": p. [253]-408. Bibliographical references included in "Notes" (p. 221-252) [F826.L43 1966] 67-7931
1. Layton family. 2. Mormons and Mormonism. I. McIntyre, Myron W., 1923- ed. II. Barton, Noel R., 1942- ed. III. Title.

DRAUGHON, Wallace R. 289.3'756
History of the Church of Jesus Christ of Latter-Day Saints in North Carolina : with a detailed record of the church in Durham / by Wallace R. Draughon. Durham, N.C. : Durham Ward of the Church of Jesus Christ of Latter-Day Saints, 1974. vii, 310 p. : ill. ; 24 cm. Includes indexes. [BX8615.N67D7] 75-301355 10.00
1. Church of Jesus Christ of Latter-Day Saints—North Carolina. 2. Church of Jesus Christ of Latter-Day Saints. North Carolina Mission. I. Title.

MCGAVIN, Elmer Cecil 289.3773
The Nauvoo Temple. Salt Lake City, Deseret [1963, c.1962] 185p. illus. 24cm. 63-1780 2.50
1. Nauvoo, Ill. Temple. I. Title.

FLANDERS, Robert 289.377343
Bruce.
Nauvoo; kingdom on the Mississippi. Urbana, University of Illinois Press, 1965. vii, 304 p. illus., map (on lining papers) ports. 24 cm. Bibliography: p. 342-350. [F549.N37F55] 65-19110
1. Nauvoo, Ill. — Hist. 2. Church of Jesus Christ of Latter-Day Saints. 3. Mormons and Mormonism in Illinois. I. Title.

FLANDERS, Robert Bruce 289.377343
Nauvoo; kingdom on the Mississippi. Urbana, Univ. of Ill. Pr. [c]1965. vii, 364p. illus., map (on lining papers) ports. 24cm. Bibl., [F549.N37F55] 65-19110 6.50
1. Nauvoo, Ill.—Hist. 2. Church of Jesus Christ of Latter-Day Saints. 3. Mormons and Mormonism in Illinois. I. Title.

FLANDERS, Robert 289.377343
Bruce.
Nauvoo; Kingdom on the Missippi. Urbana, University of Illinois Press [1975] c1965 vii., 364 p. illus., 23 cm. Bibliography: p. 342-350. [F549.N37F55] 65-19110 ISBN 0-252-00561-9 3.95 (pbk.)
1. Nauvoo, Ill.—History. 2. Church of Jesus Christ of Latter-Day Saints. 3. Mormons and Mormonism in Illinois. I. Title.

HAWTHORNE, Paul. 289.3'773'43
Nauvoo / by Paul Hawthorne. Decatur : House of Illinois, [1974] 54 p. : ill. ; 21 cm. [BX8615.I3H38] 74-18145
1. Mormons and Mormonism in Nauvoo, Ill. I. Title.

TAYLOR, Samuel 289.3'773'43
Woolley, 1907-
Nightfall at Nauvoo [by] Samuel W. Taylor. New York, Macmillan [1971] x, 403 p. 21 cm. Bibliography: p. [375]-391. [BX8615.I3T39] 72-139965 7.95
1. Mormons and Mormonism in Nauvoo, Ill. I. Title.

DYER, Alvin Rulon. 289.3778
The refiner's fire; historical highlights of Missouri. Salt Lake City, Deseret Book Co., c1960] 141 p. illus. 24 cm. Includes bibliography. [BX8615.M8D9] 61-22324
1. Mormons and Mormonism in Missouri. I. Title.

DYER, Alvin Rulon. 289.3'778
The refiner's fire; the significance of events transpiring in Missouri, by Alvin R. Dyer. [2d ed. rev. and enl.] Salt Lake City, Deseret Book Co., 1968. 334, [3] p. illus. (part col.), facsims., maps, plans. 24 cm. Includes music. Bibliography: p. [335]-[337] [BX8615.M8D9 1968] 68-29075
1. Mormons and Mormonism in Missouri. I. Title.

GEDDES, Joseph Arch, 289.3'778
1884-
The United Order among the Mormons (Missouri phase) : an unfinished experiment in economic organization / by Joseph A. Geddes. New York : AMS Press, 1975, c1924. 172 p. ; 23 cm. (Communal societies in America) Reprint of the ed. published by the Desert News Press, Salt Lake City. Originally presented as the author's thesis, Columbia University, 1924. Includes bibliographical references and index. [BX8615.M8G4 1975] 72-8247 ISBN 0-404-11001-0 : 10.00
1. Mormons and Mormonism in Missouri. I. Title.

WILCOX, Pearl. 289.3'778
The Latter Day Saints on the Missouri frontier. [Independence? Mo., 1972] 367 p. illus. 21 cm. Bibliography: p. 351-355. [BX8615.M8W5] 72-83317
1. Reorganized Church of Jesus Christ of Latter-Day Saints—History. 2. Mormons and Mormonism in Missouri. I. Title.

PARTRIDGE, Mark N., 289.3*787
1894-
With book and plow; history of a Mormon settlement, by Mark N. Partridge. [Lovell, Wyo, Mountain States Printing Co., 1967] x, 275 p. illus., ports. 24 cm. Bibliography: p. 273-275. [F769.C6P3] 67-7168
1. Cowley 2. Mormons and Mormonism in Wyoming I. Title.

PARTRIDGE, Mark N., 289.3'787'33
1894-
With book and plow : history of a Mormon settlement / by Mark N. Partridge. Rev. ed. [s.l.] : Partridge, 1976, c1967. x, 291 p. : ill. ; 24 cm. Includes bibliographical references and index. [F769.C68P37 1976] 76-368321
1. Cowley—History. 2. Cowley—Biography. 3. Mormons and Mormonism in Cowley. I. Title.

MCCLINTOCK, James H., 289.3'791
1864-1934.
Mormon settlement in Arizona; a record of peaceful conquest of the desert. Phoenix, Ariz., 1921. [New York, AMS Press, 1971] xi, 307 p. illus. 22 cm. Bibliography: p. 279-[280] [F811.M124 1971] 78-134397 ISBN 0-404-08439-7 14.00
1. Mormons and Mormonism in Arizona. 2. Arizona—History—To 1950. I. Title.

PETERSON, Charles S. 289.3'791'33
Take up your mission; Mormon colonizing along the Little Colorado River, 1870-1900 [by] Charles S. Peterson. Tucson, University of Arizona Press [1973] xii, 309 p. illus. 24 cm. Bibliography: p. 273-295. [F817.L5P47] 72-89621 ISBN 0-8165-0397-4 9.50
1. Mormons and Mormonism in Arizona. 2. Little Colorado Valley, Ariz.—History. I. Title.

FERRIS, Benjamin G. 289.3'792
Utah and the Mormons. The history, government, doctrines, customs, and prospects of the Latter-day Saints. From personal observation during a six months' residence at Great Salt Lake City. New York, AMS Press [1971] 377 p. illus. 22 cm. Reprint of the 1854 ed. [BX8635.F47 1971] 77-134394 ISBN 0-404-08436-2 15.00
1. Mormons and Mormonism. I. Title.

GROW, Stewart L 289.3792
A tabernacle in the desert. Salt Lake City, Deseret Book Co., 1958. 101p. illus. 23cm. [BX8685.S35G7] 58-35742
1. Salt Lake City. Tabernacle. I. Title.

REMY, Jules, 1826-1893. 289.3'792
A journey to Great-Salt-Lake City by Jules Remy and Julius Brenchley; with a sketch of the history, religion, and customs of the Mormons, and an introduction on the religious movement in the United States. By Jules Remy. With 10 steel engravings and a map. London, W. Jeffs, 1861. [New York, AMS Press, 1972] 2 v. illus. 22 cm. Translation of Voyage au pays des Mormons. Bibliography: v. 2, p. 561-569. [F826.R3913 1972] 75-134399 ISBN 0-404-08441-9 (set) 42.00
1. Mormons and Mormonism. 2. Utah—Description and travel. 3. California—Description and travel—1848-1869. 4. Nevada—Description and travel. 5. Overland journeys to the Pacific. I. Title.

HILTON, Lynn M. 289.3'792'25
The story of Salt Lake Stake of the Church of Jesus Christ of Latter-Day Saints; 125 year history, 1847-1972. Lynn M. Hilton, editor. Salt Lake City, Utah, Salt Lake Stake [1972] x, 336 p. illus. 24 cm. Includes bibliographical references. [BX8611.H57] 72-89166
1. Salt Lake Stake. I. Title.

STENHOUSE, Fanny, 289.3'792'25
1829-
Tell it all; the tyranny of Mormonism; or, An Englishwoman in Utah, by Mrs. T. B. H. Stenhouse. New York, Praeger [1971] xii, 404 p. illus. 23 cm. (Travellers' classics) 1888 ed. published under title: The tyranny of Mormonism. [BX8645.S67 1971] 73-148137 29.50
1. Mormons and Mormonism—Doctrinal and controversial works. I. Title.

PARR, Lucy. 289.3'792'51
Not of the world : a living account of the United Order / Lucy Parr. Bountiful, Utah : Horizon Publishers, [1975] 231 p. : ill. ; 24 cm. Pages 128-141 printed in incorrect order. Includes index. Bibliography: p. 225-228. [BX8611.P34] 75-5320 ISBN 0-88290-047-1 : 5.95
1. Mormons and Mormonism in Orderville, Utah. 2. Orderville, Utah—History. I. Title.

HEMPEL, Charles Julius, 289.4
1811-1879.
The true organization of the new church, as indicated in the writings of Emanuel Swedenborg, and demonstrated by Charles Fourier. New York, W. Radde, 1848. [New York, AMS Press, 1972] 454 p. 22 cm. [BX8711.H45 1972] 74-134424 ISBN 0-404-08464-8 18.00
1. Swedenborg, Emanuel, 1688-1772. 2. Fourier, Francois Marie Charles, 1772-1837. I. Swedenborg, Emanuel, 1688-1772. II. Fourier, Francois Marie Charles, 1772-1837. III. Title.

SIGSTEDT, Cyriel Sigrid 289.4
(Ljungberg Odhner)
Wonder footprints, stories about heaven for children, by Sigrid Odhner Sigstedt. Illustrated by Claire E. Berninger. [(Philadelphia, Printed by Blaetz brothers, inc., 1937] 2p. 1., 7-46, [2] p. illus. 26cm. 'For the six memorable relations on which these stories are based, see the work on Conjugial love, by Emanuel Swedenborg, nos. 74-82 and the True Christian religion, no. 791. --p. [48] [BX8729.H4S5] 38-13101
1. Swedenborg, Emmanuel, 1688-1772. I. Title.

SWEDENBORG, Emanuel, 1688- 289.4
1772
Arcana coelestia. The heavenly arcana, contained in the Holy Scripture or Word of the Lord unfolded, beginning with the book of Genesis. Together with wonderful things seen in the world of spirits and in the heaven of angels; v.1. Tr. from Latin. Thoroughly rev. ed. by John Faulkner Potts. Standard ed. New York, Swedenborg Found., 1963. 585p. 21cm. 63-1828 3.50; 2.50 text ed.,
1. New Jerusalem Church—Doctrinal and controversial works. 2. Bible. O. T. Genesis—Commentaries. 3. Bible. O. T. Exodus—Commentaries. I. Title.

BEAMAN, Edmund 289.4'0924 B
Addison, b.1811.
Swedenborg and the new age; or, "The Holy City New Jerusalem," ... New York, AMS Press [1971] 225 p. 22 cm. Reprint of the 1881 ed. [BX8748.B36 1971] 77-134422 ISBN 0-404-08458-3 10.00
1. Swedenborg, Emanuel, 1688-1772. I. Title. II. Title: The Holy City New Jerusalem.

JONSSON, Inge. 289.4'0924
Emanuel Swedenborg. Translated from the Swedish by Catherine Djurklou. New York, Twayne Publishers [1971] 224 p. 21 cm. (Twayne's world authors series. Sweden, TWAS 127) Bibliography: 213-220. [BX8748.J64] 72-120397
1. Swedenborg, Emanuel, 1688-1772.

SIGSTEDT, Cyriel 289.4'0924 B
Sigrid (Ljungberg Odhner)
The Swedenborg epic; the life and works of Emanuel Swedenborg, by Cyriel Odhner Sigstedt. New York, Bookman Associates, 1952. New York, AMS Press, 1971] xvii, 517 p. illus. 23 cm. (Communal societies in America) Includes bibliographical references. [BX8748.S53 1971] 78-137269 ISBN 0-404-05999-6
1. Swedenborg, Emanuel, 1688-1772. I. Title.

SPOERL, Howard Davis, 289.4'092'4
1903-
There was a man; the letters, papers and poems of Howard Davis Spoerl. Edited by Paul B. Zacharias. North Quincy, Mass., Christopher Pub. House [1972] 193 p. port. 21 cm. [BF109.S69A25 1972] 72-78904 4.95
1. Psychologists—United States—Correspondence, reminiscences, etc. I. Zacharias, Paul B., ed. II. Title.

FIELD, George, 289.4'7
1809or10-1883.
Memoirs, incidents & reminiscences of the early history of the New Church in Michigan, Indiana, Illinois, and adjacent States; and Canada. New York, AMS Press [1971] vii, 368 p. 22 cm. Reprint of the 1879 ed. [BX8715.F5 1971] 70-134423 ISBN 0-404-08463-X
1. New Jerusalem Church in the United States. 2. New Jerusalem Church in Canada.

BLOCK, Marguerite (Beck) 289.4'73
1889-
The New Church in the New World; a study of Swedenborgianism in America. With a new introd. by Robert H. Kirven. New York, Octagon Books, 1968 [c1932] xxiii, 464 p. port. 24 cm. (Studies in religion and culture. American religion series, 5) Bibliography: p. 437-449. [BX8716.B6 1968] 67-18752
1. New Jerusalem Church. I. Title. II. Series.

BRADEN, Charles Samuel, 289.5
1887-
Christian Science today; power, policy, practice. Dallas, Southern Methodist University Press, 1958. xvi, 432p. facsims. 23cm. Bibliography: p. 403-417. [BX6943.B7] 58-11399
1. Christian Science. I. Title.

BRADEN, Charles Samuel, 289.5
1887-
Christian Science today; power, policy, practice. With a new foreword [by] Charles S. Braden. Dallas, Southern Methodist University Press [1969] xxii, 432 p. facsims. 23 cm. Bibliography: p. 403-417. [BX6943.B7 1969] 78-10211
1. Christian Science. I. Title.

CHRISTIAN Science 289.5
Publishing Society.
A century of Christian Science healing. Boston [1966] x, 256 p. 25 cm. Bibliographical footnotes. [BX6950.C5] 66-15060
1. Christian science. 2. Faith-cure. I. Title.

CLEMENS, Clara. 289.5
Awake to a perfect day; my experience with Christian Science. [1st ed.] New York, Citadel Press [1956] 159p. 21cm. [BX6996.C56A3] 56-7673
1. Christian Science. I. Title.

COREY, Arthur. 289.5
Behind the scenes with the metaphysicians. Los Angeles, DeVorss [1968] xix, 261 p. port. 22 cm. [BX6997.C64] 68-56357
1. Christian Science. 2. Eddy, Mary (Baker) 1821-1910. I. Title.

COREY, Arthur. 289.5
Christian Science class instruction. [3d rev. ed.] Los Gatos, Calif., Farrallon Press [1950] xviii, 301 p. facsims. 21 cm. [BX6943.C6 1950] 50-54979
1. Eddy, Mary (Baker) 1821-1910. 2. Christian Science. I. Title.

DAVIS, Alice Pitman, 1893- 289.5
From a boundless basis; the spirit of truth leads to all truth. Seymour, Iowa, Herald Pub. Co. [1952] 100 p. 23 cm. [BX6943.D27] 52-41522
1. Christian Science. I. Title.

EDDY, Mary (Baker), 1821- 289.5
1910.
Retrospection and introspection, Christian healing, Rudimental divine science. [Boston, Published by the Trustees under the Will of Mary Baker G. Eddy, 1968] 145 p. 18 cm. Each work has also special t.p. [BX6941.R4 1968] 68-6955 0.95
1. Christian science. I. Eddy, Mary (Baker), 1821-1910. Christian healing. 1968. II. Eddy, Mary (Baker), 1821-1910. Rudimental divine science. 1968. III. Title. IV. Title: Christian healing. V. Title: Rudimental divine science.

EDDY, Mary (Baker), 1821- 289.5
1910.
Rudimental divine science. No and yes. Rudimenti della scienza divina. No e si. [Boston, Trustees under the will of Mary Baker G. Eddy, 1952] 2 v. in 1. 20 cm. English and Italian. "Authorized Literature of the First Church of Christ, Scientist, in Boston, Massachusetts." "Rudimental divine science" previously issued in English under title: Rudiments and rules of divine science. "No and yes" previouslyissued under title: Christian science: no and yes. [BX6941.R876] 52-32716
1. Christian Science. I. Title. II. Title: No and yes.

EDDY, Mary (Baker) 1821- 289.5
1910.
Science and health with key to the Scriptures. [Authorized ed.] Boston, Pub. by the Trustees under the will of Mary Baker G. Eddy dist. New York, Harper [1963, c.1890-1906] 700p. 21cm. 1.95 pap.,
1. Christian science. I. Title.

EDDY, Mary (Baker) 1821- 289.5
1910.
Watches, prayers, arguments given to students. With a foreword by Gilbert C. Carpenter, Jr. [n. p.] 1950 [i. e. 1952?] xvi, 113p. 19cm. [BX6941.W3] 56-41434
1. Christian Science. I. Title.

ELLIS, James G. 289.5
The key to Christian Science and the Bible; research by Mediratas [pseud.] Annotated on the writings of the original unextirpated first edition of "Science and health" by Mary Baker Eddy, published in 1875; as well as Bible quotations applicable to this work. [Bell, Calif.] Golden Rulers ['1951] 106 p. 22 cm. [BX6943.E4] 51-14438
1. Eddy, Mary (Baker) 1821-1910. Science and health. 1875. 2. Christian Science. I. Title.

EUSTACE, Herbert 289.5
Willoughby.
Christian Science: its clear, correct teaching, and complete writings Berkeley, Calif., Lederer, Street Zeus Co. [1953] 1v. 18cm. [BX6943.E8 1953] 53-28735
1. Christian Science. I. Title.

EUSTACE, Herbert 289.5
Willoughby.
Christian Science: its clear, correct teaching, and complete writings, by Herbert W. Eustace. Berkeley, Calif. Lederer Street & Zeus Co. [1964] 1037 p. 19 cm. [BX6943.E8] 65-1964
1. Christian Science. I. Title.

GAUMER, Irwin C 289.5
Lest we forget: things we would like to remember, a memory and reference book and a complete dictionary of Science and health with key to the Scriptures by Mary Baker Eddy. [1st ed.] New York, Vantage Press [c1963] 222 p. 21 cm. [BX6941.S525] 63-23646
1. Eddy, Mary (Baker) 1821-1910 — Dictionaries, indexes, etc. I. Eddy, Mary (Baker) 1821-1910. Science and health with key to the Scriptures. II. Title.

GAUMER, Irwin C. 289.5
Lest we forget: things we would like to remember, a memory and reference book and a complete dictionary of Science and health with key to the Scriptures by Mary Baker Eddy. New York, Vantage [c.1963] 222p. 21cm. 63-23646 3.75
1. Eddy, Mary (Baker) 1821-1910—Dictionaries, indexes, etc. I. Eddy, Mary (Baker) 1821-1910. Science and health with key to the Scriptures. II. Title.

HOPKINS, Emma Curtis. 289.5
Class lessons, 1888 / by Emma Curtis Hopkins ; compiled and edited by Elizabeth C. Bogart. Marina del Rey, Calif. : DeVorss, c1977. xiv, 284 p., [1] leaf of plates : port. ; 24 cm. [BX6997.H65] 76-40852 ISBN 0-87516-219-3 : 9.50
1. Christian Science. I. Title.

JOHN, DeWitt. 289.5
The Christian Science way of life, by DeWitt John. With A Christian Scientist's life, by Erwin D. Canham. Englewood Cliffs, N. J., Prentice-Hall [1962] 246 p. 21 cm. Includes bibliography. [BX6943.J6] 62-10651
1. Christian Science. I. Canham, Erwin D. II. Title. III. Title: A Christian Scientist's life.

JOHN, DeWitt, 1915- 289.5
The Christian Science way of life / by DeWitt John. Boston : Christian Science Pub. Society, [1971] c1962. viii, 205 p. ; 21 cm. Reprint fo the ed. published by Prentice-Hall, Englewood Cliffs, N.J., omitting A Christian Scientist's life, by E. D. Canham. Includes index. Bibliography: p. 195-197. [BX6943.J6 1971] 75-24128
1. Christian Science. I. Title.

JOHNSON, Charles Croxton. 289.5
'Meat of the word' in Christian Science; [Mary Baker Eddy's unexpurgated version of Christian Science as taken from her 'Precious volume,' and correlated with the current authorized textbook. New York, C.C. Johnson Publications, 1953] 31v. 22cm. [BX6941.S532] 56-42690
1. Christian Science. I. Eddy, Mary (Baker) 1821-1910. Science and health. II. Title.

KENNEDY, Hugh Anketell 289.5
Studdert, 1877-1943.
Christian Science and)organized religion; a plea for an impartial consideration and the examination of a new point of view. [Rev. ed.] Los Gatos, Calif., Farallon Foundation [1961] 170p. 21cm. 170p. 21cm. [BX6958.K4 1961] 61-34295
1. Church of Christ, Scientist—Government. 2. Boston. First Church of Christ. 3. Christian Science Publishing Society. I. Title.

LEISHMAN, Thomas Linton, 289.5
1900-
Why I am a Christian Scientist. New York, Nelson [1958] 245 p. 21 cm. Includes bibliography. [BX6943.L4] 58-13651
1. Christian Science. I. Title.

LEISHMAN, Thomas Linton, 289.5
1900-
Why I am a Christian Scientist. Boston, Beacon [1966, c.1958] 245p. 21cm. (BP208) Bibl. [BX6943.L4] 58-13651 1.25 pap.,
1. Christian Science. I. Title.

LUND, Harold Woodhull 289.5
Clarity of the science of Christian Science. Bridgeport, Conn., Author, 1963. 217p. 24cm. 63-4425 apply
1. Christian Science. I. Title.

MARTIN, Walter Ralston, 289.5
1928-
The Christian Science myth, by Walter R. Martin and Norman H. Klann. Paterson, N. J., Biblical Truth Pub. Society [c1954] 184p. 20cm. Includes bibliography. [BX6955.M35] 55-28234
1. Christian Science. I. Klann, Norman H., joint author. II. Title.

MOEHLMAN, Conrad Henry, 289.5
1879-
Ordeal by concordance; an historical study of a recent literary invention. [1st ed.] New York, Longmans, Green, 1955. 171p. 24cm. [BX6941.S528] 55-11448
1. Hegel, Georg Wilheim Friedrich, 1770-1831. 2. Haushalter, Walter Milton, 1889- Mrs. Eddy purloins from Hegel. 3. Lieber, Francis, 1800-1872, supposed author. The metaphysical relation of Hegel. 4. Eddy, Mary (Baker) 1821-1910. Science and health. I. Title.

MOORE, Irene S. 289.5
The bridge: a book for Christian Scientists, by Irene S. Moore. Santa Monica, Calif., DeVorss [1971] xxxvi, 380 p. illus. 25 cm. Bibliography: p. 378-380. [BX6943.M66] 75-122775 10.00
1. Christian Science. I. Title.

PEEL, Robert, 1909- 289.5
Christian Science: its encounter with American culture. [1st ed.] New York, Holt [1958] 239p. 22cm. Includes bibliography. [BX6943.P4] 58-8542
1. Christian Science. 2. Transcendentalism (New England) I. Title.

PEEL, Robert Arthur, 1909- 289.5
Christian Science: its encounter with American culture. Garden City, N.Y., Doubleday [1965, c.1958] xii, 224p. 18cm. (Anchor bk., A446) Bibl. [BX6943.P4] 1.25 pap.,
1. Christian Science. 2. Transcendentalism (New England) I. Title.

SWAN, Alexander. 289.5
God on Main Street, a Christian Scientist speaks to the doctor, the clergy of all faiths, and you. New York, Greenberg [1951] xii, 234 p. 21 cm. [BX6950.S9] 51-9549
1. Christian Science. 2. Faith-cure. I. Title.

TAYLOR, John Howard. 289.5
The way is strait and narrow. [1st ed.] New York, Vantage Press [1956] 399p. 21cm. [BX6943.T3] 56-6836
1. Christian Science. I. Title.

TAYLOR, John Howard. 289.5
The way is strait and narrow. [1st ed.] New York, Vantage Press [1956] 399 p. 21 cm. [BX6943.T3] 56-6836
1. Christian Science. I. Title.

BEASLEY, Norman. 289.509
The continuing spirit. New York, Duell, Sloan and Pearce [1956] 403 p. 22 cm. [BX6931.B38] 56-5050
1. Christian Science—History. I. Title.

BEASLEY, Norman. 289.509
The cross and the crown; the history of Christian Science. [1st ed.] New York, Duell, Sloan and Pearce [1952] xi, 664 p. col. port. 22 cm. [BX6931.B4] 52-9086
1. Christian Science—History. I. Title.

BABBITT, Marcy. 289.5'092'2 B
Living Christian Science : fourteen lives / by Marcy Babbitt. Englewood Cliffs, N.J. : Prentice-Hall, [1975] x, 255 p. : ports. ; 22 cm. Includes bibliographical references. [BX6990.B3] 74-20673 ISBN 0-13-538884-8 : 7.95
1. Christian Science—Biography. I. Title.

THE Christian Science 289.5'0924
journal.
Mary Baker Eddy; a centennial appreciation. Boston, Christian Science Pub. Society [1967] 115 p. 24 cm. Articles reprinted from the Christian Science journal, Jan. to Dec. 1966. Includes bibliographical references. [BX6995.C48] 67-16977
I. Eddy, Mary (Baker) 1821-1910. II. Title.

DAKIN, Edwin 289.5'0924 B
Franden, 1898-
Mrs. Eddy. Gloucester, Mass., P. Smith, 1968 [c1929] 553 p. 21 cm. On spine: Mrs. Eddy: the biography of a virginal mind. Bibliography: p. [525]-537. [BX6995.D3 1968] 72-107
1. Eddy, Mary (Baker) 1821-1910. I. Title.

DAKIN, Edwin 289.5'0924 B
Franden, 1898-
Mrs. Eddy; the biography of a virginal mind. New York, Scribner [1970] xx, 563 p. 21 cm. (The Scribner library. Emblem editions) First published in 1930. [BX6995.D3 1970] 79-99571 2.95
1. Eddy, Mary (Baker) 1821-1910. I. Title.

HOUPT, Charles 289.5'092'4 B
Theodore, 1912-
Bliss Knapp, Christian Scientist / Charles Theodore Houpt. [s.l.] : Houpt, 1976. iv, 619, [2] p., [6] leaves of plates : ill. ; 28 cm. "References to and articles by Bliss Knapp in the Christian Science periodicals": p. [621]. [BX6996.K49H68] 76-369136
1. Knapp, Bliss, 1877- 2. Christian Science—Biography. I. Title.

KING, Marian. 289.5'0924 B
Mary Baker Eddy: child of promise. Illustrated by David Hodges. Englewood Cliffs, N.J., Prentice-Hall [1968] vi, 184 p. illus. 22 cm. [BX6995.K5] 68-11942
1. Eddy, Mary (Baker) 1821-1910.

MILMINE, Georgine. 289.5'0924 B
The life of Mary Baker G. Eddy and the history of Christian Science. Grand Rapids, Baker Book House [1971, c1909] xxxiv, 495 p. illus., facsims., ports. 22 cm. "Willa Sibert Cather, editor."—dust jacket. "It will probably never be possible to determine exactly which passages are primarily the work of Miss Cather, those which remain substantially the work of Mrs. Milmine, or even those portions which are the work of other editiorial writers in the New York Offices of McClure's." [BX6995.M5 1971] 76-155860 5.95
1. Eddy, Mary (Baker), 1821-1910. 2. Christian Science. I. Cather, Willa Sibert, 1873-1947, ed. II. Title.

PEEL, Robert, 1909- 289.5'0924 B
Mary Baker Eddy; the years of discovery. New York, Holt, Rinehart and Winston [1972, c1966] xi, 370 p. 21 cm. Includes bibliographical references. [BX6995.P4 1972] 72-200871 ISBN 0-03-086648-0 3.45
1. Eddy, Mary (Baker) 1821-1910.

PEEL, Robert, 1909- 289.50924 B
Mary Baker Eddy; the years of discovery. [1st ed.] New York, Holt, Rinehart and Winston [1966] xi, 372 p. port. 25 cm. Bibliographical references included in "Notes" (p. 309-359) [BX6995.P4] 66-14855
1. Eddy, Mary (Baker) 1821-1910.

PEEL, Robert, 1909- 289.5'0924 B
Mary Baker Eddy; the years of trial. [1st ed.] New York, Holt, Rinehart and Winston [1971] vii, 391 p. port. 25 cm. Includes bibliographical references. [BX6995.P42] 73-31119 ISBN 0-03-086700-2 8.95
1. Eddy, Mary (Baker) 1821-1910.

PEEL, Robert, 1909- 289.5'092'4
Mary Baker Eddy : the years of discovery / Robert Peel. Boston : Christian Science Pub. Society, [1973] c1966. xi, 372 p., [1] leaf of plates : port. ; 25 cm. Originally published by Holt, Rinehart and Winston, New York. Includes bibliographical references and index. [BX6995.P4 1973] 75-322478
1. Eddy, Mary Baker, 1821-1910.

PEEL, Robert, 1909- 289.5'092'4 B
Mary Baker Eddy : the years of authority / Robert Peel. 1st ed. New York : Holt, Rinehart and Winston, c1977. p. cm. Third vol. in the author's 3-vol. biography, the 1st and 2d of which are Mary Baker Eddy: the years of discovery, and Mary Baker Eddy: the years of trial. Includes bibliographical references and index. [BX6995.P38] 77-6275 ISBN 0-03-021081-X : 14.95
1. Eddy, Mary Baker, 1821-1910. 2. Christian Scientists—United States—Biography. I. Title.

SMAUS, Jewel 289.5'0924 B
(Spangler)
Mary Baker Eddy: the golden days. Illustrated with photos. by Gordon Noble Converse. Boston, Christian Science Pub. Society, 1966. 193 p. illus., port. 25 cm. Bibliography: p. 186-188. [BX6995.S52] 66-30537
1. Eddy, Mary (Baker) 1821-1910. I. Title.

TOMLINSON, Homer 289'.5'0924
Aubrey, Bp., 1892-1968.
"It came to pass in those days": the shout of a king. Queens Village, N.Y., Church of God, U.S.A. Headquarters, 1968. [4], 219 p. illus. 19 cm. On spine: The shout of a king. Bibliography: 2d prelim. page. [BX7060.Z8T63] 73-172331
1. Tomlinson, Homer Aubrey, Bp., 1892-1968. 2. Church of God of Prophecy. I. Title. II. Title: The shout of a king.

TOMLINSON, Irving 289.5'0924
Clinton, 1860-
Twelve years with Mary Baker Eddy; recollections and experiences [by] Irving C. Tomlinson. Boston, Christian Science Pub. Society [c1966] 229 p. illus. ports. 23 cm. First published in 1945. [BX6995.T6] 67-9117
I. Eddy, Mary (Baker) 1821-1910. II. Title.

WE knew Mary Baker 289.5'0924
Eddy. [- ser.] Boston, Christian Science Pub. Society [1967- v. col. port. 21 cm. [BX6995.W42] 68-128
1. Eddy, Mary (Baker) 1821-1910. I. Christian Science Publishing Society.

WILBUR, Sibyl, 289.5'092'4 B
1871-1946.
The life of Mary Baker Eddy / Sibyl Wilbur. Boston : Christian Science Pub. Society, 1976. xvi, 406 p., [17] leaves of plates : ill. ; 23 cm. Includes bibliographical references and index. [BX6995.W5 1976] 76-368305 ISBN 0-87510-006-6 : 7.50
1. Eddy, Mary Baker, 1821-1910. I. Title.

LAIRD, Margaret. 289.5'2
Christian Science re-explored; a challenge to original thinking. Rev. ed. Los Angeles, Margaret Laird Foundation [1971] xliii, 276 p. 22 cm. [BX6943.L25 1971] 70-140599 8.00
1. Christian Science. I. Title.

NOWELL, Ames. 289.522
Mary Baker Eddy, her revelation of divine egoism. New York, Veritas Institute [c1965] xviii, 264 p. facsims. 24 cm. [BX6995.N6] 65-15383
1. Eddy, Mary (Baker) 1821-1910. I. Title.

RIZZOTTO, Mary. 289.5'415
The beginnings of Christian Science in Ireland / by Mary Rizzotto. [s.l. : Rizzotto], 1976. 8, v, 63 leaves ; 30 cm. Includes index. [BX6935.I73R59] 77-356493
1. Christian Science—Ireland—History. I. Title.

GOTTSCHALK, Stephen. 289.5'73
The emergence of Christian Science in American religious life. Berkeley, University of California Press [1973] xxix, 305 p. 25 cm. Includes bibliographical references. [BX6943.G66] 72-85530 ISBN 0-520-02308-0 10.00
1. Church of Christ, Scientist. I. Title.

MERRITT, Robert E. 289.5'73
Christian Science and liberty; from orthodoxy to heresy in one year, my story, by Robert E. Merritt, as told in collaboration with Arthur Corey. Los Angeles, De Vorss [1970] 224 p. illus., ports. 22 cm. [BX6943.M4] 70-132847 5.50
1. Christian Science. I. Corey, Arthur. II. Title.

WILLIAMSON, Margaret, 289.5'744'6
1886-
The Mother Church extension. Boston, Christian Science Pub. Society [1968] 85, xxiv p. illus. 21 cm. [BX6980.B7W5 1968] 75-1851
1. Boston. First Church of Christ, Scientist. I. Title.

ARMSTRONG, Joseph, 289.5'774'6
1848-1907.
The Mother Church; a history of the building of the original edifice of the First Church of Christ, Scientist, in Boston, Massachusetts. Boston, Christian Science Pub. Society [1968] 100, xvii p. illus. (part col.) 21 cm. [BX6980.B7A7 1968] 74-1142
1. Boston. First Church of Christ, Scientist. I. Title.

BRADSHAW, Angela. 289.6
World costumes. With 16 c1952] plates in colour and 142 p. of drawings. New York, Macmillan [1961, c191p. illus. 29cm. [GT596.B] A62
1. Costume—History—20th cent. I. Title.

BRAYSHAW, Alfred Neave, 289.6
1861-1940
The Quakers, their story and message, 3d ed. rev. London, Allem & Unwin [dist. Mystic, Conn., Verry, 1964, c.1938] 369p. 19cm. 3.00 bds.,
1. Friends, Society of, England. 2. Friends, Society of—Hist. I. Title.

BRINTON, Anna (Cox) ed. 289.6
Then and now; Quaker essays: historical and contemporary, by friends of Henry Joel Cadbury on his completion of twenty-two years as chairman of the American Friends Service Committee. Freeport, N.Y., Books for Libraries Press [1970, c1960] 352 p. port. 23 cm. (Essay index reprint series) Includes bibliographical references. [BX7615.B7 1970] 72-128214 ISBN 0-8369-1905-X
1. Friends, Society of—Addresses, essays, lectures. 2. Cadbury, Henry Joel, 1883- I. Title.

BRINTON, Howard Haines, 289.6
1884-
Friends for 300 years; the history and beliefs of the Society of Friends since George Fox started the Quaker movement. [1st ed.] New York, Harper [1952] 239 p. 22 cm. [BX7631.B7] 52-5424
1. Friends, Society of—History. I. Title.

BRINTON, Howard Haines, 289.6
1884-
Guide to Quaker practice. Wallingford, Pa., Pendle Hill [1955] 64p. 20cm. (Pendle Hill pamphlets, no. 20) [BX7740.B7 1955] 55-11311
1. Friends, Society of— Government. I. Title.

BRINTON, Howard Haines, 289.6
1884-
Light and life in the Fourth Gospel, by Howard H. Brinton. [Wallingford, Pa., Pendle Hill Publications, 1971] 32 p. 20 cm. (Pendle Hill pamphlet 179) [BS2615.2.B75] 76-178679 0.70
1. Friends, Society of—Doctrinal and controversial works. 2. Bible. N.T. John—Criticism, interpretation, etc. I. Title.

BRINTON, Howard Haines, 289.6
1884-
Meeting house & farm house, by Howard H. Brinton. [Wallingford, Pa., Pendle Hill Publications, 1972] 34 p. 20 cm. (Pendle Hill pamphlet 185) Includes bibliographical references. [BX7732.B7228] 72-80096 ISBN 0-87574-185-1 0.70
1. Friends, Society of. I. Title.

BRINTON, Howard Haines, 289.6
1884-
Quakerism and other religions. Wallingford, Pa., Pendle Hill [1957] 40p. 19cm. (A Pendle Hill pamphlet, no. 93) [BX7732.B7237] 57-10748
1. Friends, Society of. 2. Friends, Society of—Relations. I. Title.

BRONNER, Edwin B., 1920- 289.6
Quakerism and Christianity, by Edwin B. Bronner. [Wallingford, Pa., Pendle Hill Publications, 1967] 21 p. 19 cm. (Pendle Hill pamphlet 152) [BX7732.B74] 67-18689
1. Friends, Society of. I. Title.

BYRD, Robert Oakes 289.6
Quaker ways in foreign policy. [Toronto] University of Toronto Press [1960] 230p. 24cm. bibl. and bibl. footnotes 60-2161 5.00
1. Friends, Society of. 2. International relations. I. Title.

CARROLL, Kenneth Lane. 289.6
The creative centre of Quakerism. Kenneth L. Carroll, editor. Birmingham, Eng., Philadelphia, Friends World Committee for Consultation, 1965. iii, 111 p. 20 cm. [BX7732.C28 1965] 72-234291
1. Friends, Society of—Doctrinal and controversial works. I. Title.

COMFORT, William Wistar, 289.6
1874-1955.
The Quaker persuasion: yesterday, today, tomorrow; a handbook for Friends and friends of the Friends. With an introd. by Richmond Pearson Miller. [1st ed.] Philadelphia, F. H. Gloeckner, c1956. 72p. illus. 21cm. [BX7731.C654] 56-12944
1. Friends, Society of. I. Title.

ELGIN, Kathleen, 1923- 289.6
The Quakers; the Religious Society of Friends, written and illustrated by Kathleen Elgin. With a foreword by Richmond P. Miller. New York, D. McKay [1968] 96 p. illus., map. 26 cm. (Freedom to worship series) Bibliography: p. 94-95. A history of the Quakers—their founding, leaders, and development and growth in America, and an explanation of current functions of the organizations. [BX7731.2.E4] AC 68
1. Friends, Society of. I. Title.

FOX, George, 1624-1691. 289.6
Narrative papers of George Fox, unpublished or uncollected. Edited from the mss. with introductions and notes by Henry J. Cadbury. Richmond, Ind., Friends United Press [1972] xii, 249 p. facsims. 22 cm. Includes bibliographical references. [BX7617.F74] 72-10114 ISBN 0-913408-06-9
1. Friends, Society of—Collected works. I. Cadbury, Henry Joel, 1883- ed. II. Title.

FOX, George, 1624-1691. 289.6
Narrative papers of George Fox, unpublished or uncollected. Edited from the mss. with introductions and notes by Henry J. Cadbury. Richmond, Ind., Friends United Press [1972] xii, 249 p. facsims. 22 cm. Includes bibliographical references. [BX7617.F74] 72-10114 ISBN 0-913408-06-9 6.95
1. Friends, Society of—Collected works. I. Cadbury, Henry Joel, 1883- ed. II. Title.

FRIENDS, Society of. 289.6
Epistles. [Philadelphia?] v. 18 cm. [BX7615.A45] 51-38128
1. Friends, Society of—Epistles. I. Title.

GUMMERE, Amelia (Mott) 289.6
1859-1937.
The Quaker; a study in costume. New York, B. Blom, 1968. vi, 232 p. illus., ports. 25 cm. Reprint of the 1901 ed. [BX7748.C7G8 1968] 68-56494
1. Friends, Society of. 2. Costume. I. Title.

HIRST, Margaret Esther. 289.6
The Quakers in peace and war; an account of their peace principles and practice, by Margaret E. Hirst. With an introd. by Rufus M. Jones. With a new introd. for the Garland ed. by Edwin B. Bronner. New York, Garland Pub., 1972. 560 p. 22 cm. (The Garland library of war and peace) Reprint of the 1923 ed. [BX7748.W2H5 1972] 70-147671 ISBN 0-8240-0429-9
1. Friends, Society of—History. 2. Pacifism—History. I. Title. II. Series.

HOBART, John Henry, 1902- 289.6
Can Quakerism speak to the times? Wallingford, Pa., Pendle Hill, c1954. 32p. 20cm. (A Pendle Hill pamphlet, #78) [BX7732.H62] 54-8844
1. Friends, Society of —Doctrinal and controversial works. I. Title.

HOMAN, Walter Joseph. 289.6
Children & Quakerism; a study of the place of children in the theory and practice of the Society of Friends, commonly called Quakers. New York, Arno Press, 1972. 162 p. 24 cm. (Family in America) Reprint of the 1939 ed. Originally presented as the author's thesis, Yale, 1934. Bibliography: p. 145-160. [BX7748.C45H6 1972] 70-169387 ISBN 0-405-03864-X
1. Friends, Society of—Education. 2. Children—Religious life. I. Title. II. Series.

HUBBARD, Geoffrey. 289.6
Quaker by convincement. Harmondsworth, Penguin, 1974. 254 p. 18 cm. (Pelican books, A1663) Includes index. Bibliography: p. [245]-246. [BX7731.2.H82] 74-165322 ISBN 0-14-021663-4 £0.45 ($1.95 U.S.)
1. Friends, Society of. I. Title.

JORNS, Auguste. 289.6
The Quakers as pioneers in social work. Translated by Thomas Kite Brown, Jr. Port Washington, N.Y., Kennikat Press [1969] 269 p. 21 cm. Reprint of the 1931 ed. Translation of Studien uber die Sozialpolitik der Quaker. [BX7747.J65 1969] 68-8232
1. Friends. I. Title.

JORNS, Auguste. 289.6
The Quakers as pioneers in social work. Translated by Thomas Kite Brown, Jr. Montclair, N.J., Patterson Smith, 1969. 269 p. 22 cm. (Patterson Smith reprint series in criminology, law enforcement, and social problems. Publication no. 27) Translation of Studien uber die Sozialpolitik der Quaker. Reprint of the 1931 edition. Bibliography: p. 241-247. [BX7747.J65 1969b] 69-14934
1. Friends, Society of. I. Title.

KENWORTHY, Leonard Stout, 289.6
1912- ed.
Quaker leaders speak, by Leonard S. Kenworthy in collaboration with Therese Herzog [and others] Philadelphia, Available from Friends Book Store [1952] 111 p. 21 cm. A collection of articles which were previously published separately in the "Speaks series." [BX7791.K43] 52-9418
1. Friends, Society of—Blog. I. Title.

KENWORTHY, Leonard Stout, 289.6
1912-
Toward a fourth century of Quakerism; a collection of essays. [Brooklyn? 1952] 116 p. 24 cm. [BX7617.K4] 52-9419
1. Friends, Society of—Addresses, essays, lectures. I. Title.

LAUGHLIN, Sceva Bright, 289.6
1881- ed.
Beyond dilemmas; Quakers look at life. Edited by S. B. Laughlin. Port Washington, N.Y., Kennikat Press [1969, c1937] 305 p. 23 cm. (Essay and general literature index reprint series) Contents.Contents.—Preface, by S. B. Laughlin.—Introduction, by D. V. Steere.—The Quaker's conception of God, by R. M. Jones.—The basis of authority in religion, by E. Russell.—The theory of worship by H. H. Brinton.—The Quaker method of reaching decisions, by D. E. Trueblood.—Friends and social thinking, by C. M. Case.—Marriage, the family, and the community, by R. H. Dann.—The economic life, by D. E. Henley.—The individual and the state, by W. C. Woodward.—The control and use of natural resources, by J. R. Smith.—The problem of crime, by S. B. Laughlin.—The problem of peace, by F. J. Libby.—Quakerism through oriental eyes, by T. Iwahashi. [BX7615.L3 1969] 79-86035 ISBN 0-8046-0567-X
1. Friends, Society of—Addresses, essays, lectures. 2. Church and social problems—Friends, Society of. I. Title.

LIPPINCOTT, Horace Mather, 289.6
1877-
Quaker meeting houses, and a little humor. Jenkintown, Pa., Old York Road Pub. Co., 1952. 136 p. illus. 23 cm. [BX7635.L5] 52-34440
1. Churches, Friend. I. Title.

LOUKES, Harold 289.6
The Quaker contribution. New York, Macmillan [1965] 127p. 19cm. Bibl. [BX7731.2.L6] 65-18468 2.95
1. Friends, Society of. I. Title.

MAURER, Herrymon, 1914- ed. 289.6
The Pendle Hill reader; introd. by Elton Trueblood [1st ed.] New York, Published in association with Pendle Hill by Harper [1950] xii. 208 p. 22 cm. "The various parts ... have appeared separately as Pendle Hill pamphlets over a ten-year period." Contents.--The reality of the spiritual world, by T. R. Kelly.--Christ in catastrophe, by E. Fuchs.--Our hearts are restless, by G. Kilpack.--The Quaker doctrine of inward peace, by H. H. Briston.--The self to the self, by D. Willson.--Community and worship, by D. D. Steere.--Rethinking Quaker Principles, by R. M. Jones.--Christianity and civilization, by A. J. Toynbee. [BX7615.M3] 51-9036
1. Friends, Society of—Addresses, essays, lectures. I. Title.

MAURER, Herrymon, 1914- ed. 289.6
The Pendle Hill reader. Introd. by Elton Trueblood. Freeport, N.Y., Books for Libraries Press [1971? c1950] xii, 208 p. 23 cm. (Essay index reprint series) "The various parts ... have appeared separately as Pendle Hill pamphlets over a ten year period ... specially edited and

revised." Contents.Contents.—The reality of the spiritual world, by T. R. Kelly.—Christ in catastrophe, by E. Fuchs.—Our hearts are restless, by G. Kilpack.—The Quaker doctrine of inward peace, by H. H. Brinton.—The self to the self, by D. Willson.—Community and worship, by D. V. Steere.—Rethinking Quaker principles, by R. M. Jones.—Christianity and civilisation, by A. J. Toynbee. [BX7615.M3 1971] 74-142668 ISBN 0-8369-2415-0
1. Friends, Society of—Addresses, essays, lectures. I. Title.

MICHAEL, Brother S.S.F. 289.6
A concern for unity : the Quakers / [by] Brother Michael SSF. Oxford : S.L.G. Press, 1976. [2], 17 p. ; 21 cm. (Fairacres publications ; no. 56 ISSN 0307-1405s) [BX7732.M5]t77-350997 ISBN 0-7283-0058-3 : £0.30
1. Friends, Society of—Doctrinal and controversial works. I. Title. II. Series: Fairacres publications ; no. 56.

PENN, William, 1644-1718. 289.6
The rise and progress of the people called Quakers / by William Penn ; [with an introd. by James Newby]. Richmond, Ind. : Friends United Press, [1976] 86 p. ; 18 cm. Reprint of the ed. published in Philadelphia. [BX7617.P5B7 1976] 76-57832 ISBN 0-913408-32-8 1.95
1. Friends, Society of—History. I. Title.

PENN, William, 1644-1718. 289.6
The select works of William Penn. 4th ed. London, Printed and sold by W. Phillips, G. Yard, 1825. New York, Kraus Reprint Co., 1971. 3 v. 24 cm. [BX7617.P5A1 1971] 73-154550
1. Friends, Society of—Collected works. 2. Penn, William, 1644-1718. 3. Theology—Collected works—18th century. I. Title.

PENN, William, 1644-1718. 289.6
The witness of William Penn Edited with an introd. [by] Frederick B. Tolles and E. Gordon Alderfer. New York, Macmillan, 1957. xxx, 205p. 22cm. Selected passages from the author's works. Bibliography: p. 203-205. [BX7617.P5A1 1957] 57-10894
1. Friends, Society of—Collected works. 2. Theology—Collected works—18th cent. I. Tolles, Frederick Barnes, 1915- ed. II. Alderfer, Everett Gordon, 1915- ed. III. Title.

PENN, William, 1644-1718. 289.6
The witness of William Penn. Edited with an introd. [by] Frederick B. Tolles and E. Gordon Alderfer. New York, Macmillan, 1957. xxx, 205 p. 22 cm. Selected passages from the author's works. Bibliography: p. 203-205. [BX7317.P5A1 1957] 57-10894
1. Friends, Society of—Collected works. 2. Theology—Collected works—18th century. I. Tolles, Frederick Barnes, 1915- ed. II. Alderfer, Everett Gordon, 1915- ed. III. Title.

SCHROEDER, Janet E. 289.6
Dialogue with the other; Martin Buber and the Quaker experience, by Janet E. Schroeder. [Wallingford, Pa., Pendle Hill Publications, 1973] 32 p. 19 cm. (Pendle Hill pamphlet 192) Includes bibliographical references. [BX7737.S37] 73-92486 ISBN 0-87574-192-4
1. Friends, Society of. 2. Buber, Martin, 1878-1965. I. Title.

STEERE, Douglas Van, 1901- 289.6
On listening to another. New York, Harper [1955] 71p. 20cm. London ed. (Allen & unwin) has title: Where words come from. [BX7737.S8 1955a] 55-11482
1. Friends, Society of. I. Title.

SYKES, John. 289.6
The Quakers; a new look at their society. [1st American ed.] Philadelphia, Lippincott, 1959 [c1958] 287 p. 22 cm. Includes bibliography. [BX7731.2.S9 1959] 59-11144
1. Friends, Society of. I. Title.

SYKES, John. 289.6
The Quakers; a new look at their society. [1st American ed.] Philadelphia, Lippincott, 1959 [c1958] 287 p. 22 cm. Includes bibliography. [BX7731.2.S9 1959] 59-11144
1. Friends, Society of.

TOLLES, Frederick Barnes 289.6
Quakers and the Atlantic culture. New York, Macmillan [c.]1960. xiii, 160p. 22cm. (bibl. notes: p.135-156) 60-7085 3.95
1. Friends, Society of—Hist. 2. Friends, Society of—Influence. 3. U. S.—Civilization. I. Title.

TOLLES, Frederick Barnes, 1915- 289.6
Quakers and the Atlantic culture. New York, Macmillan, 1960. 160 p. 22 cm. Includes bibliography. [BX7631.2.T6] 60-7085
1. Friends, Society of — Hist. 2. Friends, Society of — Influence. 3. U.S. — Civilization. I. Title.

TRUEBLOOD, David Elton, 1900- 289.6
The people called Quakers, by D. Elton Trueblood. [1st ed.] New York, Harper & Row [1966] xi, 298 p. 22 cm. Bibliography: p. 289-291. [BX7731.2.T7] 66-15046
1. Friends, Society of. I. Title.

WEISBORD, Marvin Ross. 289.6
Some form of peace; true stories of the American Friends Service Committee at home and abroad [by] Marvin R. Weisbord. New York, Viking Press [1968] xix, 168 p. 22 cm. [BX7747.W4 1968] 68-23996
1. Friends, Society of. American Friends Service Committee. I. Title.

WHAT future for Friends? 289.6
Report of the St. Louis Conference, a gathering of concerned Friends, October 5-7, 1970, St. Louis, Missouri. [Philadelphia, Pa.] Published at the request of the Conference by Friends World Committee for Consultation (American Section) [1971?] vi, 58 p. 22 cm. [BX7607.A28] 73-171491 1.00
1. Friends, Society of—Congresses. I. Friends, Society of.

WOODMAN, Charles Mellen, 1875- 289.6
Quakers find a way; their discoveries in practical living. [1st ed.] Indianapolis, Bobbs-Merrill [1950] 280 p. 22 cm. Bibliography: p. 273-274. [BX7731.W76] 50-8879
1. Friends, Society of. 2. Christian life—Friend authors. I. Title.

YOUNG, Mildred Binns 289.6
Another will gird you: a message to the Society of Friends. [Wallingford, Pa., Pendle Hill, 1960] 23p. 20cm. (Pendle Hill pamphlet 109) 60-11608 .35 pap.,
1. Friends, Society of. I. Title.

BARBOUR, Hugh, comp. 289.6'08
Early Quaker writings, 1650-1700. Edited by Hugh Barbour and Arthur O. Roberts. Grand Rapids, Eerdmans [1973] 622 p. 24 cm. Includes bibliographical references. [BX7615.B34] 72-93617 ISBN 0-8028-3423-X 9.95
1. Friends, Society of—Collected works. I. Roberts, Arthur O., joint comp. II. Title.

CADBURY, Henry Joel, 1883- 289.6'08
Friendly heritage; letters from the Quaker past, by Henry J. Cadbury. Norwalk, Conn., Silvermine Publishers [1972] x, 342 p. illus. 25 cm. "A Friends journal book." Originally published in the Friends intelligencer and the Friends journal. Includes bibliographical references. [BX7617.C33] 79-153813 9.95
1. Friends, Society of—Collected works. I. Title.

POINTING, Horace Bertram, 1891- 289.6'08
Man on a moving stairway, and other Quakerly essays, by Horace Pointing. Annandale, Va., Turnpike Press, 1966. viii, 120 p. 23 cm. [BX7632.P63] 66-24035
1. Friends, Society of—Addresses, essays, lectures. I. Title.

WOOLMAN, John, 1720-1772. 289.6'08
The works of John Woolman. New York, Garrett Press, 1970. xiii, xiv, 436 p. 22 cm. Reprint of the 1774 ed., with a new foreword by William A. Beardslee. [BX7617.W6 1970] 75-93672
1. Friends, Society of—Collected works. 2. Slavery in the United States—Controversial literature—1753-1770. I. Title.

WOOLMAN, John, 1720-1772. 289.6'08
The works of John Woolman. With a new foreword by William A. Beardslee. New York, MSS Information Corp. [1972] p. "Reprint of the first edition published ... in 1774." [BX7617.W6 1972] 72-8107 ISBN 0-8422-8135-5
1. Friends, Society of—Collected works. 2. Slavery in the United States—Controversial literature—1753-1770.

BRINTON, Howard Haines, 1884- 289.6081
Creative worship, and other essays, Wallingford, Pa., PendleHill [1964, c.1957] vii, 153p. 23cm. Bibl. 63-23448 3.00
1. Friends, Society of . I. Title. II. Title: Divine-human society. III. Title: Quakerism and other religions.
Contents omitted.

BRINTON, Anna (Cox) ed. 289.6082
Then and now; Quaker essays, historical and contemporary, by friends of Henry Joel Cadbury, on his completion of twenty-two years as chairman of the American Friends Service Committee. Philadelphia, University of Pennsylvania Press. [1960] 352p. illus., port. 22cm. Includes bibliography. [BX7615.B7] 60-14095
1. Cadbury, Henry Joel, 1883- 2. Friends, Society of—Addresses, essays, lectures. I. Title.

BRINTON, Anna [Shipley] (Cox) ed. 289.6082
Then and now; Quaker essays, historical and contemporary, by friends of Henry Joel Cadbury, on his completion of twenty-Two years as chairman of the American Friends Service Committee. Philadelphia, University of Pennsylvania Press [c.1960] 352p. illus., port. 22cm. Bibl. footnotes 60-14095 5.00
1. Cadbury, Henry Joel, 1883- 2. Friends, Society of—Addresses, essays, lectures. I. Title.

LIPPINCOTT, Horace Mather, 1877- ed. 289.6082
Through a Quaker archway. New York, T. Yoseloff [1959] 200 p. 22 cm. [BX7615.L5] 59-11338
1. Friends, Society of—Addresses, essays, lectures. I. Title.

WEST, Jessamyn, ed. 289.6082
The Quaker reader. Selected and introduced by Jessamyn West. New York, Viking Press [1962] 522 p. 22 cm. Includes bibliography. [BX7615.W4] 62-9147
1. Friends, Society of—Collected works. I. Title.

DOHERTY, Robert W. 289.6'09
The Hicksite separation; a sociological analysis of religious schism in early nineteenth century America, by Robert W. Doherty. New Brunswick, N.J., Rutgers University Press [1967] vii, 157 p. map. 22 cm. Includes bibliographical references. [BX7637.D6] 67-13077
1. Friends, Society of.—History. I. Title.

FOULDS, Elfrida Vipont Brown, 1902- 289.6'09
The story of Quakerism : through three centuries / by Elfrida Vipont. 3d ed. rev. Richmond, Ind. : Friends United Press, 1977. 324 p., [8] leaves of plates : ill. ; 21 cm. Includes index. Bibliography: p. 309-313. [BX7631.2.F65 1977] 77-152525 pbk. : 5.95
1. Friends, Society of—History. I. Title.

FOULDS, Elfrida Vipont Brown, 1902- 289.6'09
The story of Quakerism : through three centuries / by Elfrida Vipont. 3d ed. rev. Richmond, Ind. : Friends United Press, 1977. 324 p., [8] leaves of plates : ill. ; 21 cm. Includes index. Bibliography: p. 309-313. [BX7631.2.F65 1977] 77-152525 pbk. : 5.95
1. Friends, Society of—History. I. Title.

FRIENDS, Society of (Hicksite). General Conference. Religious Education Committee. 289.6*09
Quaker reflections to light the future. Foreword by Henry J. Cadbury. Notes by Frederick B. Tolles. Philadelphia, [1967] 60 p. (chiefly illus.) 28 cm. [BX7752.A45] 74-9140
1. Friends, Society of (Hicksite)—History—Pictorial works. I. Tolles, Frederick Barnes. II. Title.

JONES, Rufus Matthew, 1863-1948. 289.6'09
The later periods of Quakerism. Westport, Conn., Greenwood Press [1970] 2 v (xxxvi, 1020 p.) 23 cm. Reprint of the 1921 ed. Includes bibliographical references. [BX7631.J6 1970] 74-109758 ISBN 0-8371-4248-2
1. Friends, Society of—History. I. Title.

ROBSON, Walter, 1842-1929. 289.6'09
An English view of American Quakerism; the journal of Walter Robson (1842-1929) written during the fall of 1877, while traveling among American Friends. Edited by Edwin B. Bronner. Philadelphia, American Philosophical Society, 1970. xviii, 162 p. illus., port. 24 cm. (Memoirs of the American Philosophical Society, v. 79) Bibliographical footnotes. [BX7637.R6] 71-107345
1. Friends, Society of—History. I. Bronner, Edwin B., 1920- ed. II. Title. III. Series: American Philosophical Society, Philadelphia. Memoirs, v. 79

BEST, Mary Agnes, d.1942. 289.6'0922
Rebel saints. Freeport, N.Y., Books for Libraries Press [1968] 333 p. illus. ports. 23 cm. (Essay index reprint series) Reprint of the 1925 ed. Bibliography: p. 333. [BX7791.B4 1968] 68-55839
1. Friends, Society of—Biography. 2. Friends, Society of—History. I. Title.

DALGLISH, Doris N. 289.6'0922
People called Quakers, by Doris N. Dalglish. Freeport, N.Y., Books for Libraries Press [1969] 169 p. 23 cm. (Essay index reprint series) Reprint of the 1938 ed. Contents.Contents.—The first Quaker poet.—An American saint.—A digression on women and the eighteenth century.—A neighbour of Wordsworth.—A friend from France.—Convert and critic. [BX7791.D3 1969] 78-90628
1. Story, Thomas, 1662-1742. 2. Woolman, John, 1720-1772. 3. Wilkinson, Thomas, 1751-1836. 4. Grellet, Stephen, 1773-1855. 5. Stephen, Caroline Emelia, 1834-1909. 6. Friends, Society of—Biography. I. Title.

FOGELKLOU, Emilia, 1878- 289.6'0922
The atonement of George Fox [by] Emilia Fogelklou Norlind. Edited by Eleanore Price Mather. [Wallingford, Pa., Pendle Hill Publications, 1969] 31 p. 20 cm. (Pendle Hill pamphlet 166) Bibliography: p. 30-31. [BX7676.2.F6] 75-84675 0.55
1. Friends, Society of—History. 2. Fox, George, 1624-1691. 3. Nayler, James, 1617?-1660. I. Title.

HAINES, Marie. 289.6'092'2 B
Brave rebels. Newberg, Or., Barclay Press [1972] xiii, 160 p. illus. 21 cm. Bibliography: p. 159-160. [BX7791.H25] 72-88677 ISBN 0-913342-02-5 4.50
1. Friends, Society of—Biography. I. Title.

BARBOUR, Hugh. 289.6'092'4 B
Margaret Fell speaking / Hugh Barbour. [Wallingford, Pa. : Pendle Hill Publications], 1976. 32 p. ; 20 cm. (Pendle Hill pamphlet ; 206 ISSN 0031-4250s) Includes bibliographical references. [BX7795.F75B37] 76-4224 ISBN 0-87574-206-8 : 0.95
1. Fox, Margaret Askew Fell, 1614-1702. I. Fox, Margaret Askew Fell, 1614-1702. Margaret Fell speaking. 1976. II. Title.

BENTON, Josephine Moffett. 289.6'0924
John woolman, most modern of ancient Friends. Philadelphia, Friends Central Bureau [195-?] 62p. 21cm. 'Publication of Religious Education Committee of Friends GeneralConference.' [BX7795.W7B4] 62-1975
1. Woolman, John, 1720-1772. I. Title.

BOULDING, Elise. 289.6'092'4 B
Born remembering / by Elise Boulding. [Wallingford, Pa. : Pendle Hill Publications], 1975. 30 p. ; 19 cm. (Pendle Hill pamphlet ; 200 ISSN 0031-4250) Bibliography: p. 30. [BX7795.B56A33] 74-30805 ISBN 0-87574-200-9 : 0.95
1. Boulding, Elise. I. Title.

BRINTON, Anna (Cox) 289.60924
The wit and wisdom of William Bacon Evans. [Wallingford, Pa., Pendle Hill Publications, 1966] 47 p. port. 20 cm. (Pendle Hill pamphlet 146) [BX7795.E86B7] 66-24443
1. Evans, William Bacon. I. Title.

BRINTON, Howard Haines, 1884- 289.6'0924
The religion of George Fox, 1624-1691, as revealed by his epistles [by] Howard H. Brinton [Wallingford, Pa., Pendle Hill Publications, 1968] 32 p. 20 cm. (Pendle Hill pamphlet 161) Bibliographical footnotes. [BX7795.F7B75] 68-57978 0.55
1. Fox, George, 1624-1691. I. Title.

EDMUNDSON, William, 1627-1712. 289.6'0924 B
The journal (abridged) of Wm. Edmondson, Quaker apostle to Ireland & the Americas, 1627-1712. Edited by Caroline N. Jacob. Foreword by Henry J. Cadbury. [Philadelphia] Philadelphia Yearly Meeting [of the] Religious Society of Friends; [distributed by Friends Books Store, 1968] xii, 124 p. 18 cm. Bibliography: p. 124. [BX7795.E4A32] 68-54861 1.50
1. Edmundson, William, 1627-1712. I. Jacob, Caroline Nicholson, ed. II. Cadbury, Henry Joel, 1883-

EDMUNDSON, William, 1627-1712. 289.6'092'4 B
The journal of William Edmundson, 1627-1712 (abridged and designed for daily devotional reading) Edited by Alfred D. Deutsch. [Richmond, Ind., Friends United Press, 1974] iv, 65 p. 22 cm. [BX7795.E4A33] 74-6439 ISBN 0-913408-11-5 1.50 (pbk.).
1. Edmundson, William, 1627-1712. I. Deutsch, Alfred D., 1931- ed.

EDMUNDSON, William, 1627-1712. 289.6'092'4 B
The journal of William Edmundson, 1627-1712 (abridged and designed for daily devotional reading) Edited by Alfred D. Deutsch. Richmond, Ind., Friends United Press [1974] p. cm. Includes bibliographical references. [BX7795.E4A33] 74-6439 ISBN 0-913408-11-5

1. Edmundson, William, 1627-1712. I. Deutsch, Alfred D., 1931- ed.

ELLIOTT, Errol T. 289.6'092'4 B
Life unfolding : the spiritual pilgrimage of a Quaker plainsman / by Errol T. Elliott. Richmond, Ind. : Friends United Press, [1975] xviii, 162 p. ; 21 cm. Autobiographical. [BX7795.E54A33] 75-9806 ISBN 0-913408-15-8. ISBN 0-913408-17-4 pbk.
1. Elliott, Errol T. I. Title.

ELLIOTT, Errol T. 289.6'092'4 B
Life unfolding : the spiritual pilgrimage of a Quaker plainsman / by Errol T. Elliott. Richmond, Ind. : Friends United Press, [1975] xviii, 162 p. ; 21 cm. Autobiographical. [BX7795.E54A33] 75-9806 ISBN 0-913408-15-8 : 5.95 ISBN 0-913408-17-4 pbk. : 4.95
1. Elliott, Errol T. I. Title.

ELLIOTT, Errol T. 289.6'092'4 B
Quaker profiles from the American West, by Errol T. Elliott. Richmond, Ind., Friends United Press [1972] xxii, 172 p. illus. 22 cm. [BX7791.E47] 72-5126
1. Friends, Society of—Biography. I. Title.

ELLIOTT, Errol T. 289.6'092'4 B
R. Ernest Lamb, Irish-American Quaker : the life, work, and wit of a world Friend / by Errol T. Elliott. Richmond, IN : Friends United Press, c1977. xiv, 140 p. : ill. ; 22 cm. [BX7795.L28E44] 77-70184 ISBN 0-913408-29-8 : 4.95
1. Lamb, Richard Ernest, 1887-1973. 2. Friends, Society of—United States—Biography. 3. Friends, Society of—Clergy—Biography. I. Title.

ELLIOTT, Errol T. 289.6'092'4 B
R. Ernest Lamb, Irish-American Quaker : the life, work, and wit of a world Friend / by Errol T. Elliott. Richmond, IN : Friends United Press, c1977. xiv, 140 p. : ill. ; 22 cm. [BX7795.L28E44] 77-70184 ISBN 0-913408-29-8 : 4.95
1. Lamb, Richard Ernest, 1887-1973. 2. Friends, Society of—United States—Biography. 3. Friends, Society of—Clergy—Biography. I. Title.

ENDY, Melvin B. 289.6'092'4 B
William Penn and early Quakerism [by] Melvin B. Endy, Jr. [Princeton, N.J.] Princeton University Press [1973] viii, 410 p. 24 cm. Based on the author's thesis. Bibliography: p. 378-395. [F152.2.E52] 72-7798 ISBN 0-691-07190-X 17.50
1. Penn, William, 1644-1718. 2. Friends, Society of—History. I. Title.

FOX, George, 1624-1691. 289.6'092'4 s
A collection of many select and Christian epistles, letters and testimonies / written on sundry occasions by that ancient, eminent, faithful Friend, and minister of Christ Jesus, George Fox. New York : AMS Press, 1975. 2 v. ; 23 cm. (The works of George Fox ; v. 7-8) On spine: Epistles. Reprint of the 1831 ed. published by M. T. C. Gould, Philadelphia. [BX7617.F54 1975 vol. 7-8] 230'.9'6 75-16207 ISBN 0-404-09357-4 : 30.00
1. Friends, Society of—Collected works. 2. Fox, George, 1624-1691. I. Title.

FOX, George, 1624-1691. 289.6'092'4 s
Gospel truth demonstrated, in a collection of doctrinal books, given forth by that faithful minister of Jesus Christ, George Fox : containing principles essential to Christianity and salvation, held among the people called Quakers. New York : AMS Press, [1975] p. cm. (The works of George Fox ; v. 4-6) Reprint of the 1831 ed. published by M. T. C. Gould, Philadelphia. [BX7617.F54 1975 vol. 4-6] [BX7730] 230'.9'6 75-16199 ISBN 0-404-09354-X(v.4) : 30.00
1. Friends, Society of—Doctrinal and controversial works. I. Title: Gospel truth demonstrated ...

FOX, George, 1624-1691. 289.6'092'4 s
The great mystery of the great whore unfolded : and Antichrist's kingdom revealed unto destruction / by George Fox. New York : AMS Press, 1975. 616 p. ; 23 cm. (The works of George Fox ; v. 3) Reprint of the 1831 ed. published by M. T. C. Gould, Philadelphia. Includes index. [BX7617.F54 1975 vol. 3] [BX7730] 230'.9'6 75-16195 ISBN 0-404-09353-1 : 30.00
1. Friends, Society of—Doctrinal and controversial works. I. Title.

FOX, George, 1624-1691. 289.6'092'4 B
The journal of George Fox. Edited from the mss. by Norman Penney. With an introd. by T. Edmund Harvey. New York, Octagon Books, 1973. 2 v. ports. 24 cm. Reprint of the 1911 ed. published by the University Press, Cambridge. [BX7795.F7A2 1973] 73-8978 ISBN 0-374-92826-6 40.00 (2 vol. set)
1. Fox, George, 1624-1691. I. Penney, Norman, 1858-1933, ed. II. Title.

FOX, George, 1624-1691. 289.6'092'4
A journal or historical account of the life, travels, sufferings, Christian experiences, and labour of love in the work of the ministry, of that ancient, eminent, and faithful servant of Jesus Christ, George Fox. New York : AMS Press, 1975. 2 v. ; 22 cm. (The works of George Fox ; v. 1-2) Reprint of the 1831 ed. published by M. T. C. Gould, Philadelphia. Includes index. [BX7617.F54 1975 vol. 1-2] [BX7795.F7] 289.6'092'4 B 75-16194 ISBN 0-404-09351-5 : 30.00
1. Fox, George, 1624-1691. I. Title: A journal or historical account of the life, travels, sufferings, Christian experiences ...

FOX, George, 1624-1691. 289.6'092'4
The works of George Fox. New York : AMS Press, [1975] p. cm. Reprint of the 1831 ed. published by M. T. C. Gould, Philadelphia. Contents.Contents.—v. 1-2. A journal or historical account of the life, travels, sufferings, Christian experiences, and labour of love in the work of the ministry of that ancient, eminent, and faithful servant of Jesus Christ, George Fox.—v. 3. The great mystery of the great whore unfolded; and Antichrist's kingdom revealed unto destruction.—v. 4-6. Gospel truth demonstrated, in a collection of doctrinal books, given forth by that faithful minister of Jesus Christ, George Fox: containing principles essential to Christianity and salvation, held among the people called Quakers.—v. 7-8. A collection of many select and Christian epistles, letters and testimonies, written on sundry occasions, by that ancient, eminent, faithful Friend and minister of Christ Jesus, George Fox. [BX7617.F54 1975] 72-154113 ISBN 0-404-09350-7 : 30.00
1. Friends, Society of—Collected works. 2. Theology—Collected works—17th century.

FRIENDS, Society of. Literature Committee. 289.6'0924
New appreciations of George Fox; a tercentenary collection of studies. Foreword by J. Rendel Harris. Port Washington, N.Y., Kennikat Press [1971] 181, [1] p. 22 cm. First published in 1925 for the Literature Committee of the Society of Friends. Contents.Contents.—The life of George Fox in outline, by T. E. Harvey.—George Fox, by J. W. Graham.—George Fox and his religious background, by H. G. Wood.—The psychology of George Fox, by R. M. Jones.—George Fox as a pioneer, by E. Russell.—The stand for peace, by M. E. Hirst.—The missionary spirit of Fox, by R. Davis.—George Fox as a social reformer, by E. Grubb.—The "Journal" of George Fox, by J. St. Loe Strachey.—Shorter articles and extracts.—Chronology. Bibliography: p. 181-[182] [BX7795.F7A7 1971] 78-118539
1. Fox, George, 1624-1691—Addresses, essays, lectures. I. Title.

GARRETT, Alfred Cope, 1867-1946. 289.6'0924
A short life of Stephen Grellet (1773-1855) [Pocket ed.] Philadelphia, Friends' Book Store [19--] 128 p. port. 17 cm. "Reprinted from vol. iv of Quaker biographies." [BX7795.G7G3] 51-31299
1. Grellet, Stephen, 1773-1855. I. Title.

HAYNES, George Emerson. 289.6'092'4 B
Edward Hicks, Friends' minister / by George Emerson Haynes. Doylestown, Pa. : C. Ingerman at the Quixott Press, 1974. xi, 60 p. : ill. ; 23 cm. [BX7795.H48H38] 74-189464
1. Hicks, Edward, 1780-1849.

HICKS, Elias, 1748-1830. 289.6'0924 B
Journal of the life and religious labours of Elias Hicks. New York, Arno Press, 1969. 451 p. 23 cm. (Religion in America) Reprint of the 1832 ed. [BX7795.H5A3 1969] 78-83424
I. Title.

HINSHAW, David, 1882- 289.6'0924 B
Rufus Jones, master Quaker. Freeport, N.Y., Books for Libraries Press [1970, c1951] xi, 306 p. illus., ports. 23 cm. Bibliography: p. 295-298. [BX7795.J55H5 1970] 74-133522
1. Jones, Rufus Matthew, 1863-1948.

JONES, Thomas Elsa, 1888- 289.6'092'4 B
Light on the horizon; the Quaker pilgrimage of Tom Jones, by Thomas E. Jones. Richmond, Ind., Friends United Press [1973] vii, 225 p. illus. 22 cm. [BX7795.J58A34] 73-12707 ISBN 0-913408-08-5 4.95
1. Jones, Thomas Elsa, 1888- 2. Fisk University, Nashville. 3. Earlham College, Richmond, Ind. I. Title.

JONES, Thomas Elsa, 1888- 289.6'092'4 B
Light on the horizon; the Quaker pilgrimage of Tom Jones, by Thomas E. Jones. Richmond, Ind., Friends United Press [1973] vii, 225 p. illus. 22 cm. [BX7795.J58A34] 73-12707 ISBN 0-913408-08-5 4.95
1. Jones, Thomas Elsa, 1888- 2. Fisk University, Nashville. 3. Earlham College, Richmond, Ind. I. Title.

KAHOE, Walter, ed. 289.60924(B)
Clarence Pickett, a memoir, [Moylan? Penn.] 1966. v, 52p. mounted ports. 23cm. Bibl. [BX7795.P55K3] 66-21720 2.00 bds.,
1. Pickett, Clarence Evan, 1884-1965. I. Title.
Available from the editor at the Rose Valley Pr., Moylan, Pa., 19065.

KELLY, Richard M. 289.60924 (B)
Thomas Kelly, a biography [by] Richard M. Kelly. [st ed.] New York, Harper & Row [1966] 125 p. illus., ports. 20 cm. Bibliographical footnotes. [BX7795.K4K4] 66-11486
1. Kelly, Thomas Raymond, 1896-1941. I. Title.

KELLY, Richard M. 289.60924
Thomas Kelly, a biography New York, Harper [c.1966] 125p. illus., ports. 20cm. Bibl. [BX7795.K4K4] 66-11486 3.75
1. Kelly, Thomas Raymond, 1893-1941. I. Title.

MATHER, Eleanore Price, 1910- 289.6'0924 B
Anna Brinton; a study in Quaker character. [Wallingford, Pa., Pendle Hill Publications, 1971] 39 p. ports. 20 cm. (Pendle Hill pamphlet 176) Includes bibliographical references. [BX7795.B76M38] 74-152086 0.70
1. Brinton, Anna (Cox)

MOULTON, Phillips P., 1909- 289.6'092'4 B
The living witness of John Woolman [by] Phillips P. Moulton. [Wallingford, Pa., Pendle Hill Publications, 1973] 32 p. 19 cm. (Pendle Hill pamphlet 187) "Pendle Hill clusters": p. 29-32. [BX7795.W7M68] 72-94969 ISBN 0-87574-187-8 0.70
1. Woolman, John, 1720-1772. I. Title.

NEWPORT, David, 1822-1911. 289.6'0924
Eudemon, spiritual & rational; the apology of a preacher for preaching. Philadelphia, Lippincott, 1901. 527 p. port. 23 cm. [BX7795.N45A3] 1-30362
I. Title.

PENNINGTON, Levi Talbott, 1875- 289.6'0924 B
Rambling recollections of ninety happy years, by Levi T. Pennington. [1st ed.] Portland, Or., Metropolitan Press, 1967. xvi, 187 p. illus., ports. 23 cm. 500 copies printed. [BX7795.P43A3] 67-3486
I. Title.

ROSENBLATT, Paul. 289.6'0924
John Woolman. New York, Twayne Publishers [1969] 163 p. 22 cm. (Twayne's United States authors series, TUSAS 147) Bibliography: p. 153-158. [PS892.R6] 68-24307
1. Woolman, John, 1720-1772. I. Title.

TRUEBLOOD, David Elton, 1900- 289.6'0924
Robert Barclay [by] D. Elton Trueblood. [1st ed.] New York, Harper & Row [1967, c1968] xi, 274 p. illus., coat of arms, facsims., port. 22 cm. Bibliography: p. 252-257. Bibliographical footnotes. [BX7795.B343T7] 68-11731
1. Barclay, Robert, 1648-1690. I. Title.

TRUEBLOOD, David Elton, 1900- 289.6'0924
Robert Barclay [by] D. Elton Trueblood. [1st ed.] New York, Harper & Row [1967, c1968] xi, 274 p. illus., coat of arms, facsims., port. 22 cm. Bibliography: p. 252-257. Bibliographical footnotes. [BX7795.B343T7] 68-11731
1. Barclay, Robert, 1648-1690.

TRUEBLOOD, David Elton, 1900- 289.6'092'4 B
While it is day; an autobiography [by] Elton Trueblood. [1st ed.] New York, Harper & Row [1974] xi, 170 p. 22 cm. [BX7795.T75A37] 73-18680 ISBN 0-06-068741-X 5.95
1. Trueblood, David Elton, 1900- I. Title.

WOOLMAN, John, 1720-1772. 289.6'0924 B
The journal and major essays of John Woolman. Edited by Phillips P. Moulton. New York, Oxford University Press, 1971. xviii, 336 p. 24 cm. (A Library of Protestant thought) Contents.Contents.—The journal of John Woolman.—Major essays of John Woolman: Introduction to the essays. Some considerations on the keeping of Negroes. Considerations on keeping Negroes, part second. A plea for the poor. Bibliography: p. 315-318. [BX7795.W7A3 1971b] 71-171970 10.50
1. Slavery in the United States—Controversial literature. 2. Poor. I. Title. II. Series.

WOOLMAN, John, 1720-1772. 289.6'0924 B
The journal of John Woolman, and A plea for the poor. The John Greenleaf Whittier ed. text. Introd. by Frederick B. Tolles. Gloucester, Mass., P. Smith, 1971 [c1961] xii, 249 p. 21 cm. Reprint of two works published in 1774 and 1793 respectively; the first work originally had title: A journal of the life, gospel labours, and Christian experiences of that faithful minister of Jesus Christ, John Woolman. Includes bibliographical references. [BX7795.W7A3 1971] 72-27383
I. Woolman, John, 1720-1772. A plea for the poor. 1971.

WOOLMAN, John, 1720-1772. 289.6'0924 B
The works of John Woolman. 2d ed. Philadelphia, Printed by J. Crukshank, 1775. Miami, Fla., Mnemosyne Pub. Co. [1969] 2 v. in 1 (xiv, 432 p.) 23 cm. [BX7617.W6 1969] 78-83893
1. Friends, Society of—Collected works.

YOLEN, Jane H. 289.6'092'4 B
Friend: the story of George Fox and the Quakers, by Jane Yolen. New York, Seabury Press [1972] x, 179 p. map. 24 cm. Bibliography: p. [173]-175. A biography of the English pacifist who founded the Quaker movement in the seventeenth century. [BX7795.F7Y65] 92 74-171865 5.95
1. Fox, George, 1624-1691—Juvenile literature. 2. Friends, Society of—Juvenile literature. I. Title.

YOUNG, Mildred (Binns) 289.6'0924
Woolman and Blake: prophets for today. [Wallingford, Pa., Pendle Hill Publications, 1971] 32 p. 19 cm. (Pendle Hill pamphlet 177) "First presented as the annual John Woolman Memorial Lecture in September, 1963, at Mount Holly, New Jersey." [BX7795.W7Y65 1971] 72-170018 0.70
1. Woolman, John, 1720-1772. 2. Blake, William, 1757-1827. I. Title.

SESQUICENTENNIAL 289.6*0975284
Sandy Spring Friends Meeting House, 1817-1967. [Sandy Spring? Md., 1967?] 88 p. illus. 24 cm. Organized by the Sandy Spring Friends Monthly Meeting. [BX7780.S25S47] 72-260115
1. Sandy Spring, Md. Friends Meeting House. I. Sandy Spring, Md. Friends Meeting House. II. Friends, Society of. Sandy Spring Monthly Meeting.

HANCOCK, Thomas, 1783-1849. 289.6'415
The principles of peace, exemplified in the conduct of the Society of Friends in Ireland, during the rebellion of the year 1798. With a new introd. for the Garland ed. by Naomi Churgin Miller. New York, Garland Pub. Co., 1974. 13, 213 p. 22 cm. (The Garland Library of war and peace) Reprint of the 1829 ed. published by T. Kite, Philadelphia. [BX7681.H3 1974] 70-147620 ISBN 0-8240-0377-2 9.00
1. Friends, Society of. Ireland. I. Title. II. Series.

BARBOUR, Hugh. 289.642
The Quakers in Puritan England. With a foreword by Roland H. Bainton. New Haven, Yale University Press, 1964. xviii, 272 p. illus., facsims., map. 24 cm. (Yale publications in religion, 7 [i.e. 8]) Based on thesis, Yale University. "Bibliographical note": p. 258-262. [BX7676.B28] 63-13957
1. Friends, Society of. Gt. Brit. 2. Friends, Society of — Hist. I. Title. II. Series.

BARBOUR, Hugh 289.642
The Quakers in Puritan England. Foreword by Roland H. Bainton. New Haven, Conn., Yale [c.]1964. xviii, 272p. illus., facsims., map. 24cm. (Yale pubns. in religion, 7, i.e. 8) Bibl. 63-13957 6.00
1. Friends, Society of. Gt. Brit. 2. Friends, Society of—Hist. I. Title. II. Series.

BRAITHWAITE, William Charles, 1862-1922. 289.642
The second period of Quakerism. 2d ed. prepared by Henry J. Cadbury. [New York] Cambridge Univ. Press [c.]1961[ ] xxxvi, 735p. Bibl. 61-3449 5.50
1. Friends, Society of—Gt. Brit. 2. Friends, Society of—Hist. I. Title.

ISICHEI, Elizabeth Allo. 289.6'42
Victorian Quakers, by Elizabeth Isichei. London, Oxford U.P., 1970. xxvi, 326 p. 23

cm. (Oxford historical monographs) "Based on a thesis submitted for the Oxford Doctorate of Philosophy." Bibliography: p. [292]-319. [BX7676.I83] 78-485692 65/-
1. Friends, Society of. Gt. Brit.—History. I. Title.

LLOYD, Arnold. 289.642
Quaker social history, 1669-1738. With an introd. by Herbert G. Wood. London, New York, Longmans, Green [1950] xv, 207 p. illus., facsims. 23 cm. Bibliography: p. 185-194. [BX7676.L6] 50-7502
1. Friends, Society of—Hist. 2. Friends, Society of—Charities. 3. Friends, Society of. England. I. Title.

RAISTRICK, Arthur. 289.6'42
Quakers in science and industry; being an account of the Quaker contributions to science and industry during the 17th and 18th centuries. New York, Kelley, 1968. 361 p. illus., geneal. tables, ports. 23 cm. Reprint of the 1950 edition with a new introd. [BX7676.R3 1968] 68-18641
1. Friends, Society of. Gt. Brit. 2. Friends, Society of—Biography. 3. Scientists, British. 4. Great Britain—Industries—History. I. Title.

VANN, Richard T. 289.6'42
The social development of English Quakerism, 1655-1755, by Richard T. Vann. Cambridge, Mass., Harvard University Press, 1969. xiv, 259 p. front. 22 cm. Bibliography: p. [217]-250. Bibliographical footnotes. [BX7676.2.V34] 79-78524 7.00
1. Friends, Society of—History. 2. Friends, Society of. England. I. Title.

GODBER, Joyce. 289.6'425'6
Friends in Bedfordshire and West Hertfordshire / by Joyce Godber. Bedford : The author, 1975. 100 p., leaf of plate, 8 p. of plates : ill., facsims., map, port. ; 22 cm. Includes index. Bibliography: p. 94. [BX7677.B4G6] 76-357175 £2.00
1. Friends, Society of. Bedfordshire, Eng. 2. Friends, Society of. Hertfordshire, Eng. 3. Bedfordshire, Eng.—Church history. 4. Hertfordshire, Eng.—Church history. I. Title.

DURHAM, Harriet Frorer. 289.6'729
Caribbean Quakers. [Hollywood, Fla., Printed by Dukane Press, 1972] viii, 133, xxxviii p. illus. 24 cm. Bibliography: p. xxv-xxviii. [BX7665.D87] 72-83494
1. Friends, Society of. Caribbean area. I. Title.

BACON, Margaret H. 289.6'73
The quiet rebels; the story of the Quakers in America [by] Margaret H. Bacon. New York, Basic Books [1969] viii, 229 p. illus. 22 cm. ([Culture & discovery books]) Bibliography: p. 211-214. [BX7635.B3] 69-16954 5.95
1. Friends, Society of—History. 2. Friends, Society of—Influence. I. Title.

BOWDEN, James, b.1811. 289.6'73
The history of the Society of Friends in America. New York, Arno Press, 1972. 2 v. in 1. illus., facsims., maps. (3 fold. maps) 23 cm. (Religion in America, series II) Reprint of the 1850-54 ed. [BX7635.B6 1972] 73-38440 ISBN 0-405-04061-X
1. Friends, Society of—History. I. Title.

BROCK, Peter, 1920- 289.6'73
Pioneers of the peaceable kingdom. Princeton, N.J., Princeton University Press [1970, c1968] xvi, 382 p. 22 cm. "The chapters of the present volume are reprinted from a more extensive book: Pacifism in the United States: from the Colonial era to the First World War (Princeton University Press, 1968)." Bibliography: p. 359-373. [BX7635.B76] 70-123078 ISBN 0-691-00573-7 3.45
1. Friends, Society of—History. 2. Pacifism—History. I. Title.

BRONNER, Edwin B., 1920- ed. 289.673
American Quakers today. Philadelphia, Pa., 19102 Friends World Comm. Amer. Sect. 152-A North 15th St. [c.]1966 111p. illus., fold. map. 20cm. Bibl. [BX7637.B7] 66-15823 1.00 pap.,
1. Friends, Society of. I. Title.

ELLIOTT, Errol T. 289.6'73
Quakers on the American frontier; a history of the westward migrations, settlements, and developments of Friends on the American Continent [by] Errol T. Elliott. Richmond, Ind., Friends United Press [1969] 434 p. illus., ports. 23 cm. Bibliography: p. 364-375. [BX7635.E44] 78-123884 6.50
1. Friends, Society of—History. I. Title.

FROST, Jerry William. 289.6'73
The Quaker family in colonial America; a portrait of the Society of Friends [by] J. William Frost. New York, St. Martin's Press [1973] vi, 248 p. 25 cm. Bibliography: p. 228-245. [BX7636.F76] 72-95835 12.95
1. Friends, Society of. 2. Friends in the United States. 3. United States—Church history—Colonial period. I. Title.

JAMES, Sydney V. 289.673
A people among peoples; Quaker benevolence in eighteenth-century America. Cambridge, Mass., Harvard [c.]1963. xv, 405p. 25cm. Bibl. 62-20248 8.00
1. Friends, Society of—Charities. I. Title. II. Title: Quaker benevolence in eighteenth-century America.

JAMES, Sydney V 289.673
A people amont peoples: Quaker benevolence in eighteenth-century America. Cambridge, Harvard University Press, 1963. xv, 405 p. 25 cm. Bibliographical references included in "Sources" and "Notes" (p. 337-397) [BX7747.J3] 62-20248
1. Friends, Society of—Charities. I. Title. II. Title: Quaker benevolence in eighteenth-century America.

JONES, Rufus Matthew, 1863-1948. 289.673
The Quakers in the American Colonies, by Rufus M. Jones, assisted by Isaac Sharpless and Amelia M. Gummere. New York, Russell & Russell, 1962. 603 p. 22 cm. [E184.F89J7 1962] 62-10687
1. Friends, Society of—History. 2. U.S.—History—Colonial period. I. Title.

JONES, Rufus Matthew, 1863-1948 289.673
The Quakers in the American colonies by Rufus M. Jones assisted by Isaac Sharpless, Amelia M. Gummere. New introd. by Frederick B. Tolles New York Norton [1966] xxxii, 603p. maps. 20cm. (Norton lib., N356) Bibl. [E184.F89J7] 66-6939 3.25 pap.,
1. Friends. Society of—Hist. 2. U.S.—Hist.—colonial period. I. Sharpless Isaac. 1848-1920. II. Gummere, Amelia (Mott) 1859-1937. III. Title.

NEWMAN, Daisy. 289.6'73
A procession of Friends; Quakers in America. [1st ed.] Garden City, N.Y., Doubleday, 1972. xvii, 460 p. 25 cm. (Religion in America series) Bibliography: p. [430]-443. [BX7635.N48] 79-160875 10.00
1. Friends, Society of. 2. Friends in the United States. I. Title.

HALLOWELL, Richard Price, 1835-1904. 289.6'744
The Quaker invasion of Massachusetts. Freeport, N.Y., Books for Libraries Press [1973] p. Reprint of the 1883 ed. [F67.H18 1973] 72-12800 ISBN 0-8369-7139-6
1. Friends, Society of. Massachusetts. 2. Massachusetts—History—Colonial period. I. Title.

SELLECK, George A. 289.6'744'61
Quakers in Boston, 1656-1964 : three centuries of Friends in Boston and Cambridge / George A. Selleck. Cambridge, Mass. : Friends Meeting at Cambridge, 1976. xii, 349 p. : ill. ; 23 cm. Includes index. Bibliography: p. 320-334. [BX7649.B6S44] 77-357562
1. Friends, Society of. Boston—History. 2. Friends, Society of. Cambridge, Mass.—History. 3. Boston—Church history. 4. Cambridge, Mass.—Church history. I. Title.

ATKINSON, D. Watson. 289.6'748'21
The Friendly invaders, by D. Watson Atkinson. Doylestown, Pa., C. Ingerman at the Quixott Press, 1969. 86 p. illus. 23 cm. 500 copies. [F157.B8A86] 72-249907
1. Friends, Society of. Bucks Co., Pa. 2. Bucks Co., Pa.—History. I. Title.

IRWIN, Richard T. 289.6'749'74
The Religious Society of Friends in Randolph Township; a history, by Richard T. Irwin. [Ironia, N.J.] A.R.B.O.R., American Revolution Bicenntial Observance Randolph Township [1973] 2, 55 l. map. 30 cm. Bibliography: leaves [1]-2 (1st group) [BX7649.R36178] 75-303637
1. Friends, Society of. Randolph Township, N.J. 2. Registers of births, etc.—Randolph Township, N.J. I. Title.

WEEKS, Stephen Beauregard, 1865-1918. 289.6'75
Southern Quakers and slavery; a study in institutional history. New York, Bergman Publishers [1968] xiv, 400 p. map. 24 cm. (Johns Hopkins University studies in historical and political science, extra volume 15) Reprint of the 1896 ed. Bibliography: p. [345]-362. [H31.J62 vol. 15, 1968] 66-28477
1. Friends, Society of—History. 2. Slavery in the United States—History. I. Title. II. Series: Johns Hopkins University. Studies in historical and political science. Extra volumes, 15.

FORBUSH, Bliss, 1896- 289.6'752
A history of Baltimore Yearly Meeting of Friends; three hundred years of Quakerism in Maryland, Virginia, the District of Columbia, and central Pennsylvania. [Sandy Spring, Md., Baltimore Yearly Meeting of Friends, 1972] v, 174 p. illus., map (on lining papers) 23 cm. Bibliography: p. 162-163. [BX7607.B2F67] 72-85807 3.00
1. Friends, Society of. Baltimore Yearly Meeting. I. Title.

FORBUSH, Bliss, 1896- 289.6'752
A history of Baltimore Yearly Meeting of Friends; three hundred years of Quakerism in Maryland, Virginia, the District of Columbia, and central Pennsylvania. [Sandy Spring, Md., Baltimore Yearly Meeting of Friends, 1972] v, 174 p. illus., map (on lining papers) 23 cm. Bibliography: p. 162-163. [BX7607.B2F67] 72-85807 3.00
1. Friends, Society of. Baltimore Yearly Meeting. I. Title.

FRIENDS, Society of. 289.6'752
Proceedings of the conference of Friends of America. Philadelphia[etc.] American Friend [etc.] v. 20cm. Title varies slightly. [BX7607.A32] 56-51001
I. Title.

FRIENDS, Society of (Hicksite) General Conference. 289.6'752
Proceedings of the Friends' General Conference. [Philadelphia] v. 23-31 cm. Title varies slightly. Proceedings for 1906- issued as Supplement to Friends' intelligencer. [BX7607.A43] 52-24490
1. Friends' intelligencer. Supplement. I. Title.

FRIENDS, Society of. Nebraska Yearly Meeting. 289.6'752
Minutes of the annual assembly. Central City, Neb., Fitch Bros. v. 22 cm. [BX7607.N37A2] 51-36154
I. Title.

CARROLL, Kenneth Lane. 289.6'752'1
Quakerism on the Eastern Shore [by] Kenneth Carroll. [Baltimore] Maryland Historical Society [1970] xi, 328 p. illus. 24 cm. Bibliography: p. 287-292. [BX7649.E3C3] 70-112986
1. Friends, Society of. Eastern Shore, Md. I. Title.

ANSCOMBE, Francis Charles. 289.6756
I have called you Friends; the story of Quakerism in North Carolina. Boston, Christopher Pub. House [1959] 407p. illus. 24cm. Includes bibliography. [BX7648.N8A6] 59-7080
1. Friends, Society of. North Carolina. 2. Friends, Society of. North Carolina Yearly Meeting. I. Title.

FRIENDS, Society of. North Carolina Yearly Meeting. 289.6'756
Carolina Quakers; our heritage, our hope. Tercentenary 1672-1972. Edited by Seth B. Hinshaw [and] Mary Edith Hinshaw. [Greensboro, N.C., 1972] iv, 160 p. illus. 28 cm. Bibliography: p. 158. [BX7648.N8A48] 72-187233
1. Friends, Society of. North Carolina. I. Hinshaw, Seth B., ed. II. Hinshaw, Mary Edith, ed. III. Title.

BURKE, James Lee, 1935- 289.6'771'69
Mount Pleasant and the early Quakers of Ohio / James L. Burke, Donald E. Bensch. [Columbus] : Ohio Historical Society, [1975] vi, 45 p. : ill. ; 25 cm. "Text previously appeared in Ohio history, volume 83, number 4, autumn 1974, in a somewhat different format." Bibliography: p. 43-44. [BX7649.M68B87] 75-315472
1. Friends, Society of—Mount Pleasant, Ohio. 2. Friends, Society of. Ohio Yearly Meeting. 3. Mount Pleasant, Ohio—History. I. Bensch, Donald E., joint author. II. Title.

HADLEY, Lucile F 289.6771765
Quaker historical collections: Springfield Friends Meeting, 1809-1959, near Wilmington, Clinton County, Ohio. Compiled by Committee: Lucile F. Hadley [and others. Wilmington? Ohio, 1959] 108p. illus., ports. 23cm. Bibliography: p. 104-105. [BX7780.S6H3] 59-44077
1. Friends, Society of. Springfield Monthly Meeting, Clinton Co., Ohio. I. Title.

RATCLIFF, Richard P. 289.6'772'64
The Quakers of Spiceland, Henry County, Indiana; a history of Spiceland Friends Meeting, 1828-1968, by Richard P. Ratcliff. [New Castle, Ind., Community Print. Co., 1968] 78 p. illus., ports. 23 cm. Bibliography: p. 75-78. [BX7649.S65R3] 73-3081 2.00
1. Friends, Society of. Spiceland Monthly Meeting. I. Title.

LE SHANA, David C. 289.6'794
Quakers in California; the effects of 19th century revivalism on western Quakerism [by] David C. Le Shana. With a foreword by D. Elton Trueblood. Newberg, Or., Barclay Press [1969] xi, 186 p. 24 cm. Bibliographical references included in "Notes" (p. 161-181) [BX7648.C2L4] 70-92470 4.95
1. Friends, Society of—History. 2. Friends, Society of. California Yearly Meeting. 3. Friends, Society of. Pacific Yearly Meeting. I. Title.

BEEBE, Ralph K., 1932- 289.6'795
A garden of the Lord; a history of Oregon Yearly Meeting of Friends church, by Ralph K. Beebe. Chapter illus. by Stan Putman. Newberg, Or., Barclay Press [1968] vii, 288 p. illus., facsim., ports. 23 cm. Bibliographical references included in "Notes" (p. 203-222) [BX7607.O7B4] 68-56609 5.95
1. Friends, Society of. Oregon Yearly Meeting—History. I. Title.

BENDER, Harold Stauffer, 1897- 289.7
Mennonites and their heritage; a handbook of Mennonite history and beliefs. [Rev. ed.] Scottdale, Pa., Herald Press 1964. 148 p. 20 cm. Consists of first two of "a series of six booklets, each by a different writer" originally published by the Mennonite Central Committee, 1942-1945. Contents.CONTENTS. -- Mennonite origins and the Mennonites of Europe, by H. S. Bender. -- Mennonites in America, by C. H. Smith. [BX8115.M43] 64-11287
1. Mennonites — Hist. I. Smith, Charles Henry, 1875-1948. II. Title.

BENDER, Ross Thomas, 1929- 289.7
The people of God, by Ross Bender. Report of the study project to develop a model for theological education in the Free Church tradition. Scottdale, Pa., Herald Press [1971] 208 p. 22 cm. "Sponsored by the Associated Mennonite Biblical Seminaries." Includes bibliographical references. [BX8121.2.B45] 70-141828 ISBN 0-8361-1632-1 6.95
1. Mennonites. 2. Church. 3. Theology—Study and teaching. I. Associated Mennonite Biblical Seminaries. II. Title.

BRUNK, George Reuben, 1871-1938. 289.7
Ready Scriptural reasons, by George R. Brunk. Rev. by George R. Brunk, Jr. Scottdale, Pa., Herald Press [1954] 158p. 21cm. [BX8121.B7 1954] 53-9048
1. Mennonite Church—Doctrinal and controversial works. 2. Questions and answers—Theology. I. Title.

DETWEILER, Richard C. 289.7
Mennonite statements on peace, 1915-1966; a historical and theological review of Anabaptist-Mennonite concepts of peace witness and church-state relations, by Richard C. Detweiler. Scottdale, Pa., Herald Press [1968] 71 p. 18 cm. Bibliography: p. 64-69. [BX8128.P4D4] 76-613
1. Mennonites—Doctrinal and controversial works. 2. Church and state—Mennonites. 3. Peace (Theology) I. Title.

EATON, Joseph W 1919- 289.7
Man's capacity to reproduce; the demography of a unique population, by Joseph W. Eaton and Albert J. Mayer. Glencoe, Ill., Free Press [1954] 59p. map, diagrs., tables. 24cm. 'Reprinted . . . from Human biology, vol. 25, no. 3 . . . 1954.' Bibliography: p. 58-59. [BX8129] 54-11586
1. Hutterite Brethren—Stat. 2. Demography—Case studies. 3. Population—Case studies. I. Mayer, Albert J., joint author. II. Title.

*FAIRFIELD, James, ed. 289.7
The touch of God;; the personal story of eleven broadcasters and how they became 'new creatures in Christ,' as told to James Fairfield. Scottdale, Pa., Herald [c.1965] 64p. 20cm. .50 pap.,
I. Title.

GIBBONS, Phebe Earle 289.7
The Plain people; essays. Illus. from Olden times, by H. L. Fisher. Witmer, Pa., Applied Arts Assocs., c.1963. 50p. illus. 28cm. (Pennsylvania Dutch dollar bklets.) 63-22941 1.00 pap.,
1. Amish—Sect. 2. Pennsylvania Dutch. I. Title.

HERSHBERGER, Guy Franklin, 1896- 289.7
The Mennonite Church in the Second World War. Scottdale, Pa., Mennonite Pub. House, 1951. 308 p. 24 cm. [BX8129.M5H4] 52-17629
1. Mennonite Church—Hist. 2. World War, 1939-1945—Mennonites. I. Title.

HOSTETLER, John Andrew, 1918- 289.7
Amish life. Scottdale, Pa., Herald Press, 1952. 32 p. illus. 23 cm. [E184.M45H6] 53-16572

1. Mennonites in the U.S. 2. Mennonites—Social life and customs. I. Title.

KAPLAN, Bert, 1919- 289.7
Personality in a communal society; an analysis of the mental health of the Hutterites by Bert Kaplan and Thomas F. A. Plaut. Lawrence, 1956. xi, 116p. map, tables. 23cm. (University of Kansas Publications. Social science studies) Bibliography: p. 106. [BX8129.H8K3] 56-63000
1. Hutterite Brethren. 2. Mental hygiene. 3. Personality. I. Plaut, Thomas F. A., joint author. II. Title. III. Series: Kansas. University. Social science studies

KINGDOM, cross, and 289.7
community : essays on Mennonite themes in honor of Guy F. Hershberger / edited by John Richard Burkholder and Calvin Redekop. Scottdale, Pa. : Herald Press, 1976. 323 p. ; 23 cm. Includes indexes. Contents.Contents.—Schlabach, T. F. To focus a Mennonite vision.—Gross, L. History and community in the thought of Guy F. Hershberger.—Kreider, R. S. Discerning the times.—Lind, M. C. Reflections on Biblical hermeneutics.—Kraus, C. N. Toward a theology for the disciple community.—Bauman, H. E. Forms of covenant community.—Burkholder, J. L. Nonresistance, nonviolent resistance, and power.—Burkholder, L. J. Nonresistance, nonviolent resistance, and power.—Burkholder, J. R. A perspective on Mennonite ethics.—Juhnke, J. C. Mennonites in militarist America.—Redekop, J. H. The state and the free church.—Lapp, J. A. Civil religion is but Old Establishment writ large.—LaRocque, E. The ethnic church and the minority.—Smucker, D. E. Gelassenheit, entrepreneurs, and remnants.—Peachen, P. The peace churches as ecumenical witness.—Brown, D. W. The free church of the future.—Hershberger, G. F. Our citizenship is in heaven. "A bibliography of the writings of Guy F. Hershberger, 1922-1976, Elizabeth H. Bauman": p. [286]-300. [BX8109.K56] 76-29663 ISBN 0-8361-1139-7 : 12.95
1. Mennonite Church—Doctrinal and controversial works—Addresses, essays, lectures. 2. Hershberger, Guy Franklin, 1896- 3. Christianity and culture—Addresses, essays, lectures. I. Hershberger, Guy Franklin, 1896- II. Burkholder, John Richard, 1928- III. Redekop, Calvin Wall, 1925-
COntents omitted

KRAHN, Cornelius, ed. 289.7
A century of witness; the General Conference Mennonite Church. Edited by Cornelius Krahn and John F. Schmidt. Newton, Kan., Mennonite Publication Office, 1959. 93p. illus. 23cm. (Mennonite historical series, no. 5) Includes bibliography. [BX8129.G4M4 vol.5] 60-33248
1. General Conference Mennonite Church—Hist. I. Schmidt, John F., joint ed. II. Title.

LIND, Millard, 1918- 289.7
Answer to war; illustrated by Allan Eitzen. Scottdale, Pa., Mennonite Pub. House, 1952. 143 p. 20 cm. [BR115.P4L5] 52-30259
1. Pacifism. I. Title.

MAST, John B. ed. and tr. 289.7
The letters of the Amish division of 1693-1711. [Oregon City, Or.] C. J. Schlabach [*1950] 120 p. map. 16 cm. [BX8129.A5M3] 51-19431
1. Mennonites—Hist.—Sources. I. Title.

MENNONITES and their 289.7
heritage; a handbook of Mennonite history and beliefs [Rev. ed.] Scottdale, Pa., Herald [c.1964] 148p. 20cm. Consists of first two of 'a series of six booklets, each by a different writer' originally published by the Mennonite Central Committee, 1942-1945. 64-11287 1.50 pap.,
1. Mennonites—Hist. I. Bender, Harold Stauffer, 1897- II. Smith, Charles Henry, 1875-1948.
Contents omitted.

RICE, Charles Scott, 1910- 289.7
The Amish year [by] Charles S. Rice [and] Rollin C. Steinmetz. New Brunswick, N. J., Rutgers University Press [1956] 224p. illus. 24cm. [BX8117.P4R45] 56-10989
1. Mennonites in Pennsylvania. 2. Mennonites—Soc. life & cust. I. Steinmetz, Rollin C. II. Title.

SCHROETER, Elizabeth 289.7
Arlene.
From here to the pinnacles; memories of Mennonite life in the Ukraine and in America. [1st ed.] New York, Exposition Press [1956] 320p. 21cm. Autobiography. [BX8143.S35A3] 56-9566
1. Mennonites in the Ukraine. 2. Mennonites in the U. S. I. Title.

SCHROETER, Elizabeth 289.7
Arlene.
From here to the pinnacles memories of Mennonite life in the Ukraine and in America. [1st ed.] New York, Exposition Press [1956] 320p. 21cm. Autobiography. [BX8143.S35A3] 56-9566
1. Mennonites in the Ukraine. 2. Mennonites in the U. S. I. Title.

STORMS, Everck Richard. 289.7
History of the United Missionary Church. Elkhart, Ind., Bethel Pub. Co. [1958] 309 p. illus. 24 cm. [BX9889.A4S8] 58-43134
1. United Missionary Church — Hist. I. Title.

WENGER, John Christian, 289.7
1910-
Separated unto God; a plea for Christian simplicity of life and for a Scriptural nonconformity to the world. Scottdale, Pa., Mennonite Pub. House, 1951. xv, 350 p. front. 24 cm. "Written at the request of the General Problems Committee of Mennonite General Conference and of the Publishing Committee of Mennonite Publication Board." Includes bibliographies. [BV4501.W474] 52-17421
1. Christian life. 2. Mennonite Church — Doctrinal and controversial works. I. Title.

WINGERT. NORMAN AMBROSE, 289.7
1898-
A relief worker's notebook. Illus. by Irene Margul. Nappanee, Ind., E. V. Pub. House [c1952] 128p. illus. 20cm. [BX8128.W4W54] 53-17041
1. Mennonites—Charities. I. Title.

ZOOK, Noah. 289.7
Seeking a better country, a history. [1st ed.] Gordonville, Pa., Printed for and distributed by Old Order Book Society, [1963] 124 p. illus. 20 cm. [BX8115.Z6] 63-33067
1. Bible — History of Biblical events. 2. Church hsitory. 3. Mennonites — Hist. I. Title.

DYCK, Cornelius J., ed. 289.7'02
An introduction to Mennonite history; a popular history of the Anabaptists and the Mennonites. Cornelius J. Dyck, editor. Scottdale, Pa., Herald Press [1967] 324 p. illus., maps. 23 cm. "Prepared under the direction of the Institute of Mennonite Studies." Includes bibliographies. [BX8115.D9] 67-10557
1. Mennonites—History. 2. Anabaptists—History. I. Institute of Mennonite Studies, Elkhart, Ind. II. Title.

THE Mennonite 289.703
encyclopedia; a comprehensive reference work on the Anabaptist-Mennonite movement. Hillsboro, Kan., Mennonite Brethren Pub. House, 1955- v. 26cm. [BX8106.M37] 55-4563
1. Mennonites—Dictionaries. 2. Anabaptists—Dictionaries.

SMITH, Charles Henry, 289.709
1875-1948.
The story of the Mennonites. 4th ed., rev. and enl. by Cornelius Krahn. Newton, Kan., Mennonite Publication Office, 1957. 856 p. illus. 21 cm. First published in 1920 under title: The Mennonites. Includes bibliography. [BX8115.S65 1957] 58-40286
1. Mennonites—History.

SMITH, Charles Henry, 289.709
1875-1948.
The story of the Mennonites. 3d ed., rev. and enl. by Cornelius Krahn. Newton, Kan., Mennonite Publication Office, 1950. x, 856 p. illus., ports. 21 cm. First published in 1920 under title: The Mennonites. Bibliography: p. 821-833. [BX8115.S65 1950] 51-3348
1. Mennonites—History. I. Krahn, Cornelius. II. Title.

WENGER, John Christian, 289.709
1910-
Glimpses of Mennonite history and doctrine. [3d ed.] Scottdale, Pa., Herald Press [1959] 258 p. illus. 23 cm. Includes bibliography. [BX8115.W48 1959] 59-65068
1. Mennonites — Hist. I. Title.

WENGER, John Christian, 289.7'09
1910-
How Mennonites came to be / J. C. Wenger. Scottdale, Pa. : Herald Press, c1977. 71 p. : port. ; 18 cm. (Mennonite faith series ; 1) Bibliography: p. 71. [BX8122.W46] 77-86332 ISBN 0-8361-1832-4 pbk. : 0.75
1. Mennonites—History. 2. Church history. I. Title.

ARNOLD, Eberhard, 289.7'092'2 B
1883-1935.
Seeking for the Kingdom of God; origins of the Bruderhof Communities, by Eberhard and Emmy Arnold. Selected and edited from earlier sources and memories by Heini and Annemarie Arnold. Rifton, N.Y., Plough Pub. House, 1974. xxi, 284 p. front. 21 cm. [BX8129.B68A684 1974] 74-6317 7.50
1. Arnold, Eberhard, 1883-1935. 2. Arnold, Emmy. 3. Bruderhof Communities. I. Arnold, Emmy. II. Title.

DYCK, Cornelius J. 289.7'092'2 B
Twelve becoming; biographies of Mennonite disciples from the sixteenth to the twentieth century [by] Cornelius J. Dyck. Illustrated by Richard Loehle. Newton, Kan., Faith and Life Press [1973] 126 p. illus. 28 cm. [BX8141.D9] 73-75174 ISBN 0-87303-865-7 4.50 (pbk.)
1. Mennonites—Biography. I. Title.

ERB, Paul, 1894- 289.7'0924 B
Orie O. Miller; the story of a man and an era. Scottdale, Pa., Herald Press [1969] 304 p. illus., ports. 23 cm. Includes bibliographies. [BX8143.M54E7] 75-76624 7.95
1. Miller, Orie O., 1892-

HARDER, Geraldine 289.7'092'4 B
Gross.
When apples are ripe; the story of Clayton Kratz. Drawings by Allan Eitzen. Scottdale, Pa., Herald Press [1972, c1971] 223 p. illus. 21 cm. Chronicles the life of a young American Mennonite who vanished into a Russian prison in the early 1920's. [BX8128.W4H37] 92 73-160722 ISBN 0-8361-1656-9 4.95
1. Kratz, Clayton, b. 1896—Juvenile literature. 2. Mennonites in Russia—Juvenile literature. 3. Russia—History—Revolution, 1917-1921—Civilian relief. I. Title.

KOEHN, Lloyd, 1914- 289.7'092'4 B
Reminiscences and concerns. [Lehigh? Kan., Printed by Lee Print., 1974] 142 p. illus. 22 cm. [BX8143.K6A37] 73-93620
1. Koehn, Lloyd, 1914- I. Title.

KROEKER, Nettie, 289.7'092'4 B
1900-
Far above rubies : the story of Helena Wiens / by Nettie Kroeker. Winnipeg : Christian Press, c1976. 368 p. : ill., facsims., maps, ports. ; 24 cm. Bibliography: p. 368. [BX8143.W45K76] 77-368212 10.00
1. Wiens, Helena. 2. Mennonites—Manitoba—Biography. I. Title.

MATSON, Louise 289.7'092'4 B
Klassen.
Louise : Louise Klassen Matson's flight to freedom as told to Margaret J. Anderson. Wheaton, Ill. : H. Shaw Publishers, c1977. 134 p. : map ; 18 cm. [BX8143.M37A35] 77-71626 ISBN 0-87788-517-6 pbk. : 1.95
1. Matson, Louise Klassen. 2. Mennonites—Russia—Biography. 3. Mennonites—United States—Biography. I. Anderson, Margaret J.

ARNOLD, Eberhard, 1883- 289.7'3
1935.
Foundation and orders of Sannerz and the Rhon Bruderhof / by Eberhard Arnold ; [translated from the German by the Society of Brothers]. Rifton, N.Y. : Plough Pub. House, c1976- p. cm. Contents.—v. 1. Introductory history: the basis for our orders, 1920-1929. [BX8129.B65A72 1976] 76-5856 ISBN 0-87486-162-4 pbk. : 1.25 (v. 1)
1. Bruderhof Communities. 2. Hutterite Brethren. I. Title.

ARNOLD, Eberhard, 1883- 289.7'3
1935.
Why we live in community / by Eberhard Arnold. English ed. Rifton, NY : Plough Pub. House, 1976. p. cm. Translation of Warum wir in Gemeinschaft leben, which was published in Die Wegwarte, III:8-9, May-June 1927. [BV4405.A76 1976] 76-16185 ISBN 0-87486-168-3 pbk. : 1.00
1. Bruderhof Communities. 2. Christian communities. I. Title.

CHURCH of God in Christ. 289.7'3
Official manual with the doctrines and discipline of the Church of God in Christ, 1973. Written by the authorization and approval of the General Assembly. Memphis, Church of God in Christ Pub. House [1973] xl, 256 p. 16 cm. [BX7056.Z5C45 1973] 74-158966
1. Church of God in Christ—Handbooks, manuals, etc. I. Title.

DEETS, Lee Emerson, 1898- 289.7'3
The Hutterites : a study in social cohesion: with a new epilog by the author and an appendix, The origins of conflict in the Hutterische communities / Lee Emerson Deets. Philadelphia : Porcupine Press, 1975. ix, 64 p. ; 22 cm. (The American utopian adventure, series two) Reprint of the ed. published at Gettysburg, Pa., which was issued as the author's thesis, Columbia, 1939. Includes bibliographical references. [BX8129.H8D4 1975] 74-26737 ISBN 0-87991-029-1 lib.bdg. : 8.50
1. Hutterite Brethren. I. Title.

FLINT, David. 289.7'3
The Hutterites : a study in prejudice / David Flint. Toronto : Oxford University Press, 1975. viii, 193 p. : ill. ; 21 cm. Includes index. Bibliography: p. [184]-189. [BX8129.H8F55] 76-353828 ISBN 0-19-540230-8 pbk. : 5.95
1. Hutterite Brethren. I. Title.
Distributed by Oxford University Press, New York

HIEBERT, Clarence. 289.7'3
The Holdeman people: the Church of God in Christ, Mennonite, 1859-1969. South Pasadena, Calif., William Carey Library [1973] xxii, 663 p. illus. 24 cm. Bibliography: p. 621-641. [BX8129.C4H5] 72-94133 ISBN 0-87808-411-8
1. Church of God in Christ, Mennonite. 2. Holdeman, John, 1832-1900. I. Title.

HORSCH, John, 1867-1941. 289.7'3
The Hutterian Brethren, 1528-1931, and The principle of nonresistance as held by the Mennonite Church. With a new introd. for the Garland ed. by Peter Brock. New York, Garland Pub., 1971 [i.e. 1972, c1931] 9, xxi, 168, 60 p. 22 cm. (The Garland library of war and peace) Reprint of no. 2 of Studies in Anabaptist and Mennonite history, 1931, and the 1927 ed. of The principle of nonresistance as held by the Mennonite Church. Bibliography: p. 151-156. [BX8129.H8H6 1972] 74-147672 ISBN 0-8240-0430-2
1. Hutterite Brethren—History. 2. Evil, Non-resistance to. 3. Mennonites. I. Horsch, John, 1867-1941. The principle of nonresistance as held by the Mennonite Church. 1972. II. Title. III. Title: The principle of nonresistance as held by the Mennonite Church. IV. Series.

KAUFMAN, Edmund George. 289.7'3 B
General Conference Mennonite pioneers. Compiled by Edmund G. Kaufman. North Newton, Kan., Bethel College, 1973. xii, 438 p. illus. 24 cm. Includes bibliographical references. [BX8141.K38] 72-97979 6.75
1. General Conference Mennonite Church—Biography. I. Title.

KAUFMAN, Edmund George. 289.7'3 B
General Conference Mennonite pioneers. Compiled by Edmund G. Kaufman. North Newton, Kan., Bethel College, 1973. xii, 438 p. illus. 24 cm. Includes bibliographical references. [BX8141.K38] 72-97979 6.75
1. General Conference Mennonite Church—Biography. I. Title.

KREIDER, Robert S. 289.7'3
Where are we going? By Robert S. Kreider. Newton, Kan., Faith and Life Press [1971] 34 p. 18 cm. (The Schowalter memorial lecture series) [BX8129.G4K84] 70-171943 ISBN 0-87303-915-7
1. General Conference Mennonite Church. I. Title. II. Series.

PANNABECKER, Samuel 289.7'3
Floyd, 1896-
Open doors : the history of the General Conference Mennonite Church / Samuel Floyd Pannabecker. Newton, Kan. : Faith and Life Press, c1975. xv, 462 p., [3] leaves of plates : ill. ; 24 cm. (Mennonite historical series) Partly a revision and updating of the author's thesis, 1943. Includes index. Bibliography: p. 439-452. [BX8129.G4P33] 75-9417 18.50
1. General Conference Mennonite Church—History. I. Title.

REDEKOP, Calvin Wall, 289.7'3
1925-
The Old Colony Mennonites; dilemmas of ethnic minority life. Foreword by Everett C. Hughes. Baltimore, Johns Hopkins Press [1969] xiv, 302 p. illus., map. 23 cm. Bibliography: p. [287]-288. [BX8129.O4R4] 69-13192 10.00
1. Old Colony Mennonites.

*STOLL, Joseph 289.73
The Lord is my shepherd. LaGrange, Ind., Pathway Pub. [1966, c.1965] 186p. 23cm. 2.75
I. Title.

TOEWS, John A. 289.7'3
A history of the Mennonite Brethren Church : pilgrims and pioneers / by John A. Toews ; edited by A. J. Klassen. Fresno, Calif. : Board of Christian Literature, General Conference of Mennonite Brethren Churches, [1975] xxi, 513 p. : ill. ; 23 cm. Includes index. Bibliography: p. 484-490. [BX8129.B7T63] 74-33718
1. Mennonite Brethren Church of North America—History. I. Title.

WINDOWS : 289'.73
selected readings in Seventh-Day Adventist church history, 1844-1922 / compiled by Emmett K. Vande Vere. Nashville : Southern Pub. Association, c1975. 319 p. ; 22 cm. Includes bibliographies and index. [BX6153.W56] 75-27641 ISBN 0-8127-0104-6

1. Seventh-Day Adventists—History—Sources. I. Vande Vere, Emmett K.

ARNOLD, Eberhard, 1883-1935. 289.7'3'0924 B
Else von Hollander, January 1932, by Eberhard Arnold, and others. [Translated from the German and edited by the Society of Brothers]. Rifton, N.Y., Plough Pub. House [1972, c1973] xii, 111 p. illus. 20 cm. [BX8143.H64A83] 72-96191 ISBN 0-87486-111-X 3.00
1. Hollander, Else von, 1885-1932. I. Title.

HOFER, Jesse W., 1910- 289.7'3'0924 B
An Amish boy remembers: from behind those fences, by Jesse W. Hofer. San Antonio, Naylor Co. [1973] xiii, 225 p. illus. 22 cm. [CT275.H6285A33] 73-10014 ISBN 0-8111-0500-8
1. Hofer, Jesse W., 1910- I. Title.

SCHRAG, Martin H. 289.7'4
The European history (1525-1874) of the Swiss Mennonites from Volhynia, by Martin H. Schrag. Edited by Harley J. Stuckey. North Newton, Kan., Swiss Mennonite Cultural & Historical Association [1974] 128 p. illus. 23 cm. (Swiss Mennonite Cultural and Historical Association. A centennial series) A revision of the author's thesis (M.A.), Eastern Theological Seminary, 1956. Bibliography: p. 115-126. [BX8119.E9S37 1974] 74-75708
1. Mennonites, Swiss, in Europe. I. Stucky, Harley J., ed. II. Title. III. Series.

ROOSEN, B. C. 289.7'43'515
History of the Mennonite Community of Hamburg and Altona / by Berend Carl Roosen ; translated and edited by Dorothy Jenson Schimmelpfennig. Salt Lake City : [s.n., 1974] x, 86 p. ; 22 cm. Includes bibliographical references. [BX8119.G3R6613] 74-186465
1. Mennonites in Hamburg. 2. Mennonites in Altona, Ger. I. Schimmelpfennig, Dorothy Jenson, tr. II. Title.

BELK, Fred Richard, 1937- 289.7'47
The great trek of the Russian Mennonites to Central Asia, 1880-1884 / Fred Richard Belk. Scottdale, Pa. : Herald Press, 1976. 251 p. : ill. ; 23 cm. (Studies in Anabaptist and Mennonite history ; 18) Originally presented as the author's thesis, Oklahoma State University. Includes index. Bibliography: p. [230]-241. [BX8119.R8B44 1976] 75-28340 ISBN 0-8361-1103-6 : 9.95
1. Mennonites in Russia. I. Title. II. Series.

TOEWS, John B 289.7'47
Lost fatherland; the story of the Mennonite emigration from Soviet Russia, 1921-1927, by John B. Toews. Scottdale, Pa., Herald Press [1967] 262 p. illus., maps. ports. 23 cm. (Studies in Anabaptist and Mennonite history, no. 12) Bibliography: p. 244-256. [BX8119R8T6] 67-23294
1. Mennonites in Russia. 2. Mennonites, Russian. I. Title. II. Series.

TOEWS, John B. 289.7'47
Lost fatherland; the story of the Mennonite emigration from Soviet Russia, 1921-1927, by John B. Toews. Scottdale, Pa., Herald Press [1967] 262 p. illus., maps, ports. 23 cm. (Studies in Anabaptist and Mennonite history no. 12) Bibliography: p. 244-256. [BX8119.R8T6] 67-23294
1. Mennonites in Russia. 2. Mennonites, Russian. I. Title. II. Series.

GENERAL Conference Mennonite Church. 289.77
Mennonitisches Jahrbuch. Newton, Kan., Mennonite Publication Office. v. illus. 23 cm. "Herausgegeben von der Publikationsbehorde der Allgemeinen Konferenz der Mennonitengemeinden von Nord Amerika," 19 issued also in English. [BX8107.G37] 51-36182
1. Mennonites—Yearbooks. I. General Conference Mennonite Church. Publication Board. II. Title.

GENERAL Conference Mennonite Church. 289.77
Year book. Berne, Ind., Mennonite Book Concern. v. illus., ports. 24 cm. Issued 19 by the General Conference Publication Board. [BX8107.G4] 52-41379
1. Mennonites—Yearbooks. I. General Conference Mennonite Church. Publication Board. II. Title.

HOSTETLER, John Andrew, 1918- 289.77
The Hutterites in North America, by John A. Hostetler and Gertrude Enders Huntington. Photos. by Kryn Taconis. New York, Holt, Rinehart and Winston [1967] viii, 119 p. illus., map. 24 cm. (Case studies in cultural anthropology) Bibliography: p. 117-119. [BX8129.H8H64] 67-21647
1. Hutterite Brethren—North America. I. Huntington, Gertrude Enders, joint author. II. Title. III. Series.

DAVIES, Blodwen. 289.7'713
A string of amber; the heritage of the Mennonites. Vancouver [B.C.] Mitchell Press [1974, c1973] 228 p. illus. 24 cm. Label mounted on t.p.: W. S. Heinman, New York. [BX8117.O57D38] 74-172746 10.00
1. Mennonites in Ontario. I. Title.

HOSTETLER, John Andrew, 1918- 289.7'73
Amish society, by John A. Hostetler. Rev. ed. [Baltimore] Johns Hopkins Press [1968] xviii, 369 p. illus., maps. 22 cm. Bibliography: p. 344-357. [BX8129.A6H6 1968] 68-15450
1. Mennonites—Social life and customs. 2. Mennonites in the United States. I. Title.

HOSTETLER, John Andrew, 1918- 289.7'73
Hutterite society [by] John A. Hostetler. Baltimore, Johns Hopkins University Press [1974] xvi, 403 p. illus. 24 cm. Bibliography: p. [373]-392. [BX8129.H8H63] 74-6827 ISBN 0-8018-1584-3 12.50
1. Hutterite Brethren. 2. Collective settlements. I. Title.

KAUFFMAN, J. Howard, 1919- 289.7'73
Anabaptists four centuries later : a profile of five Mennonite and Brethren in Christ denominations / J. Howard Kauffman and Leland Harder. Scottdale, Pa. : Herald Press, 1975. 399 p. : ill. ; 23 cm. Includes bibliographical references and index. [BX8121.2.K36] 74-30347 ISBN 0-8361-1136-2 : 9.95. ISBN 0-8361-1137-0 pbk. : 6.95
1. Mennonite Church—Statistics. 2. General Conference Mennonite Church—Statistics. 3. Mennonite Brethren Church of North America—Statistics. 4. Brethren in Christ—Statistics. 5. Evangelical Mennonite Church—Statistics. 6. Mennonites—Statistics. I. Harder, Leland, 1926- joint author. II. Title.

KAUFFMAN, J. Howard, 1919- 289.7'73
Anabaptists four centuries later : a profile of five Mennonite and Brethren in Christ denominations / J. Howard Kauffman and Leland Harder. Scottdale, Pa. : Herald Press, 1975. 399 p. : ill. ; 23 cm. Includes bibliographical references and index. [BX8121.2.K36] 74-30347 ISBN 0-8361-1136-2 : 9.95. ISBN 0-8361-1137-0 pbk. : 6.95
1. Mennonite Church—Statistics. 2. General Conference Mennonite Church—Statistics. 3. Mennonite Brethren Church of North America—Statistics. 4. Brethren in Christ—Statistics. 5. Evangelical Mennonite Church—Statistics. 6. Mennonites—Statistics. I. Harder, Leland, 1926- joint author. II. Title.

MILLER, Elizabeth M 289.773
From the fiery stakes of Europe to the Federal courts of America. [1st ed.] New York, Vantage Press [1963] 125 p. 21 cm. [BX8129.A6M5] 63-2167
1. Mennonites in the U.S. I. Title.

MILLER, Elizabeth M. 289.773
From the fiery stakes of Europe to the Federal courts of America. New York, Vantage [c.1963] 125p. 21cm. 63-2167 2.75 bds.,
1. Mennonites in the U.S. I. Title.

MULLEN, Pearson A 289.7'73
The plain people, a pictorial essay. Photos. by Pearson A. Mullen; text by Patricia Fulford Mullen. [Bethpage? N. Y., 1958] 72p. 28cm. [BX8117.P4M8] 58-46463
1. Mennonites in Pennsylvania. 2. Mennonites—Soc. life & cust. I. Mullen, Patricia (Fulford) II. Title.

SMITH, Charles Henry, 1875-1948. 289.7'73
The coming of the Russian Mennonites; an episode in the settling of the last frontier, 1874-1884. Freeport, N.Y., Books for Libraries Press [1973] p. Reprint of the 1927 ed. [BX8115.S64 1973] 72-10789 ISBN 0-8369-7123-X
1. Mennonites—History. 2. Mennonites, Russian, in North America. I. Title.

STOLTZFUS, Grant M., 1916- 289.7'73
Mennonites of the Ohio and Eastern Conference; from the colonial period in Pennsylvania to 1968, by Grant M. Stoltzfus. Scottdale, Pa., Herald Press [1969] 459 p. illus., ports. 23 cm. (Studies in Anabaptist and Mennonite history, no. 13) Includes bibliographical references. [BX8117.O34S7] 68-20541 7.95
1. Mennonite Church. Ohio and Eastern Conference. I. Title. II. Series.

WENGER, John Christian, 1910- 289.7'73
The Mennonite Church in America, sometimes called old Mennonites, by J. C. Wenger. Scottdale, Pa., Herald Pr., [c.1966] 384p. illus., ports. 23cm. (Mennonite hist., v. 2) Written at the request of the Hist. & Research Comm. of Mennonite Gen. Conf. Introd., and chapters 1, 4, 5 and 10 by H. S. Bender. cf. Pref. Bibl. [BX8116.W4] 66-23903 7.95
1. Mennonite Church—Hist. 2. Mennonites in the U.S. I. Bender, Harold Stauffer, 1897-1962. II. Mennonite Church. Historical and Research Committee. III. Title. IV. Series.

WENGER, John Christian, 1910- 289.7'73
The Mennonite Church in America, sometimes called Old Mennonites, by J. C. Wenger. Scottsdale, Pa., Herald Press [c1966] 384 p. illus., ports. 23 cm. (Mennonite history, v. 2) "Written at the request of the Historical and Research Committee of Mennonite General Conference." Introd. and chapters 1, 4, 5, and 10 by H. S. Bender. Cf. Pref. Bibliography: p. 369-377. [BX8116.W4] 66-23903
1. Mennonite Church — Hist. 2. Mennonites in the U.S. I. Bender, Harold Stauffer, 1897-1962. II. Mennonite Church. Historical and Research Committee. III. Title. IV. Series.

SMITH, Elmer Lewis. 289.7748
The Amish people: seventeenth-century tradition in modern America; a complete, illustrated story of the "Old Order" sect of southeastern Pennsylvania. Photos. by Melvin J. Horst [1st ed.] New York, Exposition Press [1958] 285 p. illus. 21 cm. (An Exposition-university book) [BX8117.P4S6 1958] 58-2329
1. Mennonites in Pennsylvania. I. Title.

TORTORA, Vincent R. 289.7748
The Amish folk of Pennsylvania Dutch country. Amish drawings by Valerie Seward and Kiehl and Christian Newswanger. Lancaster, Pa., P.O. Box 1274, Photo Arts Press, c.1960. 34p. illus. 28cm. 60-4576 1.00 pap.,
1. Mennonites in Pennsylvania. I. Title.

WARNER, James A. 289.7'748
The gentle people; a portrait of the Amish [by] James A. Warner [and] Donald M. Denlinger. [Soudersburg, Pa., Mill Bridge Museum in cooperation with Grossman, New York, 1969] 184 p. illus. (part col.) 29 cm. [BX8129.A6W3 1969] 74-80831 20.00
1. Mennonites in Pennsylvania. I. Denlinger, Donald M., joint author. II. Title.

DENLINGER, A. Martha. 289.7'748'15
Real people : Amish and Mennonites in Lancaster County, Pennsylvania / A. Martha Denlinger. Scottdale, Pa. : Herald Press, [1975] 96 p. : ill. ; 22 cm. Includes index. Bibliography: p. 92-93. [BX8117.P4D46] 74-16966 ISBN 0-8361-1756-5
1. Mennonites in Lancaster Co., Pa. 2. Amish in Lancaster Co., Pa. I. Title.

DENLINGER, A. Martha. 289.7'748'15
Real people : Amish and Mennonites in Lancaster County, Pennsylvania / A. Martha Denlinger. Scottdale, Pa. : Herald Press, [1975] 96 p. : ill. ; 22 cm. Includes index. Bibliography: p. 92-93. [BX8117.P4D46] 74-16966 ISBN 0-8361-1756-5 pbk. : 1.95
1. Mennonites in Lancaster Co., Pa. 2. Amish in Lancaster Co., Pa. I. Title.

WENGER, Eli D. 289.7'748'15
The Weaverland Mennonites, 1766-1968, including a biography of Bishop Benjamin W. Weaver with excerpts from his diary, by Eli D. Wenger. Transcript of the Weaverland Mennonite cemeteries, by George G. Sauder. [Adamstown, Pa., Printed by Ensinger Print. Service] 1968. 363 p. illus., plan, ports. 24 cm. [BX8143.W3W35] 78-261963
1. Weaver, Benjamin Witwer, 1853-1928. 2. Mennonite Church. Lancaster County Conference. I. Sauder, George G. Transcript of the Weaverland Mennonite cemeteries. 1968. II. Title. III. Title: Transcript of the Weaverland Mennonite cemeteries.

ERB, Paul, 1894- 289.7'75
South central frontiers; a history of the South Central Mennonite Conference. Scottdale, Pa., Herald Press, 1974. 519 p. illus. 23 cm. (Studies in Anabaptist and Mennonite history, 17) Bibliography: p. [491]-495. [BX8129.M5E7] 74-12108 ISBN 0-8361-1196-6 14.95
1. Mennonite Church. South Central Conference—History. I. Title. II. Series.

ERB, Paul, 1894- 289.7'75
South central frontiers; a history of the South Central Mennonite Conference. Scottdale, Pa., Herald Press, 1974. 519 p. illus. 23 cm. (Studies in Anabaptist and Mennonite history, 17) Bibliography: p. [491]-495. [BX8129.M5E7] 74-12108 ISBN 0-8361-1196-6 14.95
1. Mennonite Church. South Central Conference—History. I. Title. II. Series.

HUBER, Harold E., 1939- 289.7'751'7
With eyes of faith; a history of Greenwood Mennonite Church, Greenwood, Delaware, 1914-1974, by Harold E. Huber. Greenwood, Del., Country Rest Home, 1974. 344 p. illus. 24 cm. Bibliography: p. 328-337. [BX8131.G733H8] 74-83345
1. Greenwood Mennonite Church, Greenwood, Del. 2. Greenwood, Del.—Biography. I. Title.

BRUNK, Harry Anthony. 289.7755
History of Mennonites in Virginia. [Harrisonburg, Va., 1959- v. illus. 24cm. Contents.v. 1. 1727-1900. Includes bibliography. [BX8117.V5B7] 59-3747
1. Mennonites in Virginia. I. Title.

PANNABECKER, Samuel Floyd, 1896- 289.7'77
Faith in ferment; a history of the Central District Conference. Newton, Kan., Faith and Life Press [1968] 385 p. illus., ports. 24 cm. (Mennonite historical series) Bibliography: p. [371]-376. [BX8129.G4P3] 68-16258
1. General Conference Mennonite Church. Central District Conference. I. Title. II. Series.

LEHMAN, James O. 289.7'771'61
Crosswinds : from Switzerland to Crown Hill / James O. Lehman. Rittman, Ohio : Crown Hill Mennonite Church, 1975. 112 p. : ill. ; 22 cm. Includes bibliographical references and index. [BX8131.R573L43] 75-323612
1. Crown Hill Mennonite Church, Rittman, Ohio. 2. Rittman, Ohio—Biography. I. Crown Hill Mennonite Church, Rittman, Ohio. II. Title.

LEHMAN, James O. 289.7'771'61
Sonnenberg, a haven and a heritage; a sesquicentennial history of the Swiss Mennonite community of southeastern Wayne County, Ohio [by] James O. Lehman. Kidron, Ohio, Kidron Community Council, 1969. 384 p. illus., maps, ports. 23 cm. "150th anniversary, Sonnenberg/Kidron, 1819 to 1969." Bibliography: p. 362-373. [BX8117.O34L4] 70-91796
1. Mennonites in Ohio. I. Title.

WENGER, John Christian, 1910- 289.7772
The Mennonites in Indiana and Michigan. Scottdale, Pa., Herald Press [1961] xv, 470 p. illus., ports. 24 cm. (Studies in Anabaptist and Mennonite history, no. 10) Bibliography: p. 452-458. [BX8117.I5W4] 61-14723
1. Mennonites in Indiana. 2. Mennonites in Michigan. I. Title. II. Series.

WENGER, John Christian, 1910- 289.7772
The Mennonites in Indiana and Michigan. Scottdale, Pa., Herald Pr. [c.1961] xv, 470p. illus. (Studies in Anabaptist and Mennonite hist., no. 10) Bibl. 61-14723 7.95
1. Mennonites in Indiana. 2. Mennonites in Michigan. I. Title. II. Series.

YODER, Thomas. 289.7'773'61
The Cullom Mennonite Church / by Thomas Yoder. Normal : Illinois Mennonite Historical and Genealogical Society, 1975. iiii, 71, [1] p. : ill. ; 22 cm. Bibliography: p. 70-[72] [BX8131.C843Y6] 76-353729
1. Cullom Mennonite Church. 2. Cullom, Ill.—History. I. Title.

A Centennial history of the Lower Deer Creek Mennonite Church, 1877-1977. 289.7'777'655 Kalona, Iowa : [Centennial Historical Committee of the Lower Deer Creek Mennonite Church], c1977. 79 p. : ill. ; 23 cm. [BX8131.K344C46] 78-302321
1. Lower Deer Creek Mennonite Church. I. Lower Deer Creek Mennonite Church. Centennial Historical Committee.

PARISH, Arlyn John. 289.7'781
Kansas Mennonites during World War I. [Hays, Fort Hays Kansas State College] 1968. vii, 62 p. 23 cm. (Fort Hays studies. New series. History series, no. 4) Includes bibliographical references. [D6.F6 no. 4] 68-64152
1. Mennonites in Kansas. 2. European War, 1914-1918—Religious aspects. I. Title. II. Series.

WEDEL, David C. 289.7'781'5
The story of Alexanderwohl, by David C. Wedel. [Goessel, Kan.] Goessel Centennial Committee [1974] 194 p. illus. 24 cm. Includes bibliographical references. [BX8131.G632W4] 74-79022
1. Alexanderwohl Mennonite Church. I. Title.

RILEY, Marvin P. 289.7'783
South Dakota's Hutterite colonies, 1874-1969, by Marvin P. Riley [and] Darryll R. Johnson. Brookings, Rural Sociology Dept., South Dakota State University [1970] 39 p. illus., map. 23 cm. (Agricultural Experiment Station, South Dakota State University. Bulletin 565) Pages 38-39 blank. "Revises and replaces Bulletin 530, 'The Hutterites: South Dakota's communal farmers.'" Includes bibliographical references. [BX8129.H8R55] 72-631366
1. Hutterite Brethren—South Dakota. I. Johnson, Darryll R., joint author. II. Title. III. Series: South Dakota. Agricultural Experiment Station, Brookings. Bulletin 565

ANDREWS, Edward Deming, 1894- 289.8
The people called Shakers; a search for the perfect society. New enl. ed. New York, Dover Publications [1963] xvi, 351 p. illus., facsims. 22 cm. "T1081." Bibliography: p. 293-297. [BX9765.A6 1963] 63-17896
1. Shakers — Hist. I. Title.

ANDREWS, Edward Deming, 1894- 289.8
The people called Shakers; a search for the perfect society. New enl. ed. New York, Dover [c.1953, 1963] xvi, 351p. illus., facsims. 22cm. (T1081) Bibl. 63-17896 2.00 pap.,
1. Shakers—Hist. I. Title.

ANDREWS, Edward Deming, 1894- 289.8
The people called Shakers; a search for the perfect society. New enl. ed. [Gloucester, Mass., P. Smith, 1964, c.1963] xvi, 351p. illus., facsims. 22cm. (Dover bk., T1081 rebound) Bibl. 4.00
1. Shakers—Hist. I. Title.

ANDREWS, Edward Deming, 1894- 289.8
The Shaker order of Christmas, by Edward and Faith Andrews. New York, Oxford University Press, 1954. unpaged. illus. 16cm. [BX9781.A5] 54-12701
1. Shakers. 2. Christmas. I. Andrews, Faith, joint author. II. Title.

ANDREWS, Edward Deming, 1894-1964. 289.8
The community industries of the Shakers. Introd. by Cynthia Elyce Rubin. [Charlestown, Mass.] Emporium Publications [1971?, c1932] 322 p. illus. 20 cm. Original ed. issued as New York State Museum handbook 15. Bibliography: p. 294-307. [BX9784.A6 1932a] 72-88941 ISBN 0-88278-005-0 3.95
1. Shakers—Industries. I. Title. II. Series: New York (State). State Museum, Albany. Handbook 15.

ANDREWS, Edward Deming, 1894-1964. 289.8
The community industries of the Shakers. Philadelphia, Porcupine Press, [1972 i.e.1973] 322 p. illus. 22 cm. (The American utopian adventure) Reprint of the 1932 ed., issued as Handbook 15 of the New York State Museum. Bibliography: p. 294-307. [BX9784.A6 1972] 77-187478 ISBN 0-87991-010-0 13.50
1. Shakers—Industries. I. Title. II. Series: New York (State). State Museum, Albany. Handbook, 15.

ANDREWS, Edward Deming, 1894-1964. 289.8
Fruits of the Shaker tree of life : memoirs of fifty years of collecting and research / Edward Deming Andrews, Faith Andrews. Stockbridge, Mass. : Berkshire Traveller Press, c1975. 222 p. : ill. ; 28 cm. [BX9771.A64 1975] 75-33901 ISBN 0-912944-31-5 : 17.50. ISBN 0-912944-32-3 pbk. : 8.95
1. Shakers. I. Andrews, Faith, joint author. II. Title.

ANDREWS, Edward Deming, 1894-1964. 289.8
The people called Shakers; a search for the perfect society. New York, Oxford University Press, 1953. xvi, 309 p. illus. 24 cm. Bibliography: p. 293-297. [BX9765.A6] 53-9181
1. Shakers—History. I. Title.

ARBAUGH, George Bartholomew, 1905- 289.8
Gods, sex, and saints; the Mormon story. Rock Island, Ill., Augustana Press [1957] 61p. 20cm. [BX8645.A7] 57-857
1. Mormons and Mormonism I. Title.

BROWN, Thomas, b.1766. 289.8
An account of the people called Shakers: their faith, doctrines, and practice, exemplified in the life, conversations, and experience of the author during the time he belonged to the society. To which is affixed a history of their rise and progress to the present day. Troy, Printed by Parker and Bliss, 1812 [New York, AMS Press, 1972] 372 p. 22 cm. [BX9771.B8 1972] 70-134415 ISBN 0-404-08459-1 14.50
1. Shakers. I. Title.

ELKINS, Hervey. 289.8
Fifteen years in the senior order of Shakers: a narration of facts concerning that singular people. Hanover [N.H.] Dartmouth Press, 1853. [New York, AMS Press, 1973] 136 p. 23 cm. [BX9771.E4 1973] 72-2984 ISBN 0-404-10746-X 7.50
1. Shakers. I. Title.

EVANS, Frederick William, 1808-1893. 289.8
Shakers : compendium of the origin, history, principles, rules and regulations, government, and doctrines of the United Society of Believers in Christ's Second Appearing ... / by F. W. Evans. 4th ed. New York : AMS Press, 1975. 190 p. ; 19 cm. (Communal societies in America) Reprint of the 1867 ed. published in New Lebanon, N.Y. Bibliography: p. [188]-190. [BX9771.E85 1975] 72-2985 ISBN 0-404-10747-8
1. Shakers. 2. Shakers—Biography. 3. Lee, Ann, 1736-1784. 4. Lee, William, 1740-1784. 5. Whittaker, James, 1751-1787. 6. Hocknell, John, 1723?-1799. 7. Meacham, Joseph, 1742-1796. 8. Wright, Lucy, 1760-1821. I. Title: Compendium of the origin, history, principles, rules and regulations, government, and doctrines of the United Society of Believers in Christ's Second Appearing.

EVANS, Frederick William, 1808-1893. 289.8
Shakers; compendium of the origin, history, principles, rules and regulations, government, and doctrines of the United Society of Believers in Christ's Second Appearing. With biographies of Ann Lee, William Lee, Jas. Whittaker, J. Hocknell, J. Meacham, and Lucy Wright. New York, B. Franklin [1972] 184 p. 19 cm. (Burt Franklin research and source work series. Philosophy & religious history monographs, 101) [BX9771.E85 1972] 72-75873 ISBN 0-8337-4091-1
1. Shakers. 2. Shakers—Biography.

LAMSON, David Rich, 1806-1886. 289.8
Two years' experience among the Shakers. New York, AMS Press [1972] 212 p. illus. 22 cm. Reprint of the 1848 ed. [BX9773.L3 1972] 71-134418 ISBN 0-404-08477-X 8.50
1. Shakers. I. Title.

MACE, Aurelia Gay, 1835-1910. 289.8
The aletheia: spirit of truth; a series of letters in which the principles of the United Society known as Shakers are set forth and illustrated. 2d ed. Farmington, Me., Press of the Knowlton & McLeary Co., 1907. [New York, AMS Press, 1974] 146 p. illus. 19 cm. (Communal societies in America) [BX9771.M18 1974] 72-2989 ISBN 0-404-10751-6 12.50
1. Shakers. I. Title.

MARSHALL, Mary, b.1780. 289.8
A portraiture of Shakerism. New York, AMS Press [1972] xvi, 446 p. 22 cm. Reprint of the 1822 ed. [BX9773.M3A3 1972] 70-134420 ISBN 0-404-08461-3 17.50
1. Lee, Ann, 1736-1784. 2. Shakers. I. Title.

MELCHER, Marguerite (Fellows) 289.8
The Shaker adventure. Cleveland, Chio Western Reserve University Press 1960[c.1941, 1957] ix, 319p. 22cm. (bibl. note: p. 294-301) 41-51750 3.00 pap.,
1. Shakers—Hist. I. Title.

MELCHER, Marguerite (Fellows) 289.8
The Shaker adventure. [Gloucester, Mass., P. Smith, 1965, c.1941] ix, 319p. (Princeton bk. rebound) Bibl. (Princeton bk. rebound) Bibl. [BX9765.M4] 5.00
1. Shakers—Hist. I. Title.

MILLER, Amy Bess Williams. 289.8
Shaker herbs : a history and a compendium / Amy Bess Miller. 1st ed. New York : C. N. Potter : distributed by Crown Publishers, c1976. xiv, 272 p. : ill. ; 26 cm. Includes index. Bibliography: p. 260-263. [BX9785.M4M54 1976] 76-40485 ISBN 0-517-52494-5 : 12.95
1. Shakers. 2. Herbs—Therapeutic use. 3. Botany, Medical. I. Title.

SHAKERS. 289.8
The constitution of the United Societies, of Believers (called Shakers). New York : AMS Press, 1976. p. cm. (Communal societies in America) Reprint of the 1833 ed. published in Watervliet, Ohio. [BX9776.S48 1976] 72-2992 ISBN 0-404-10754-0
1. Shakers. I. Title.

SHAKERS. 289.8
A summary view of the Millennial Church, or United Society of Believers, commonly called Shakers. Comprising the rise, progress, and practical order of the society. Together with the general principles of their faith and testimony. 2d ed., rev. and improved. Republished by the society with the approbation of the ministry. Albany, Printed by C. Van Benthuysen, 1848. [New York, AMS Press, 1973] vii, 384 p. 23 cm. Pref. signed: Calvin Green, Seth Y. Wells. Includes bibliographical references. [BX9771.A3 1973] 72-2993 ISBN 0-404-10755-9 20.00
1. Shakers. I. Green, Calvin. II. Wells, Seth Youngs. III. Title.

SPRIGG, June. 289.8
By Shaker hands / June Sprigg. 1st ed. New York : Knopf, 1975. xi, 212, vii p. : ill. ; 31 cm. Includes index. Bibliography: p. [209]-212. [BX9771.S67 1975] 75-8214 ISBN 0-394-49144-0 : 15.00
1. Shakers. I. Title.

WHITE, Anna, 1831-1910. 289.8
Shakerism; its meaning and message, by Anna White and Leila S. Taylor. New York, AMS Press [1972] 417 p. illus. 22 cm. Reprint of the 1904 ed. [BX9771.W5 1972] 73-134421 ISBN 0-404-08462-1 21.00
1. Shakers. I. Taylor, Leila Sarah, joint author. II. Title.

YOLEN, Jane H. 289.8
Simple gifts : the story of the Shakers / by Jane Yolen ; illustrated by Betty Fraser. New York : Viking Press, [1976] p. cm. Includes index. Bibliography: p. Traces the rise and decline of the Shakers who immigrated to the United States from England in 1774, settling throughout New England. [BX9771.Y67] 76-14420 ISBN 0-670-64584-2 : 6.95
1. Shakers Juvenile literature. I. Fraser, Betty. II. Title.

SHAKERS. 289.8'092'2 B
Testimonies of the life, character, revelations, and doctrines of Mother Ann Lee, and the elders with her, through whom the word of eternal life was opened in this day, of Christ's second appearing, collected from living witnesses, in union with the church. 2d ed. New York : AMS Press, 1975. 302 p. ; 19 cm. (Communal societies in America) Reprint of the 1888 ed. printed by Weed, Parsons, Albany, N.Y. [BX9793.L4S5 1975] 72-2994 ISBN 0-404-10756-7 : 16.00
1. Lee, Ann, 1736-1784. 2. Lee, William, 1740-1784. 3. Whittaker, James, 1751-1787. 4. Shakers. I. Title: Testimonies of the life, character, revelations, and doctrines of Mother Ann Lee ...

CAMPION, Nardi Reeder. 289.8'092'4 B
Ann the Word : the life of Mother Ann Lee, founder of the Shakers / Nardi Reeder Campion. 1st ed. Boston : Little, Brown, c1976. xiv, 208 p. : ill. ; 21 cm. Includes index. Bibliography: p. 197-200. [BX9793.L4C35] 76-6568 ISBN 0-316-12767-1 lib.bdg. : 6.95
1. Lee, Ann, 1736-1784. 2. Shakers—History. I. Title.

[EVANS, Frederick William] 1808-1893. 289.8'092'4 B
Autobiography of a Shaker, and Revelation of the Apocalypse. With an appendix. New and enl. ed., with port. Glasgow, United Pub. Co.; New York, American News Co., 1888. [New York, AMS Press, 1973] xvi, 271 p. port. 19 cm. Appendix to new ed. (p. 120-271) includes essays on Shakers and Shakerism by the author and others. [BX9793.E8A3 1973] 72-2986 ISBN 0-404-10748-6 12.50
1. Evans, Frederick William, 1808-1893. 2. Shakers. 3. Bible. N.T. Revelation—Prophecies. I. Title. II. Title: Revelation of the Apocalypse.

[EVANS, Frederick William] 1808-1893. 289.8'092'4 B
Autobiography of a Shaker, and Revelation of the Apocalypse. With an appendix. New and enl. ed., with port. Philadelphia, Porcupine Press, 1972. xvi, 271 p. port. 22 cm. (The American Utopian adventure) Reprint of the 1888 ed. [BX9793.E8A3 1972] 79-187481 ISBN 0-87991-002-X
1. Evans, Frederick William, 1808-1893. 2. Bible. N.T. Revelation—Prophecies. 3. Shakers. I. Title. II. Title: Revelation of the Apocalypse.

DESROCHE, Henri. 289.8'0973
The American Shakers; from neo-Christianity to presocialism. Translated from the French and edited by John K. Savacool. Amherst, University of Massachusetts Press, 1971. 357 p. illus., maps. 25 cm. Translation of Les Shakers americains d'un neo-christianisme a un pre-socialisme? Includes bibliographical references. [BX9766.D413] 78-123537 9.50
1. Shakers. I. Title.

EVANS, Frederick William, 1808-1893. 289.8'0973
Shaker communism; or, Tests of divine inspiration. The second Christian or gentile Pentecostal Church, as exemplified by seventy communities of Shakers in America. London, J. Burns, 1871. [New York, AMS Press, 1974] vii, 120 p. 19 cm. (Communal societies in America) Published in New Lebanon, N.Y., in 1853 under title: Tests of divine inspiration. [BX9771.E9 1974] 72-2987 ISBN 0-404-10749-4
1. Shakers. I. Title.

FABER, Doris, 1924- 289.8'0973
The perfect life: the Shakers in America. New York, Farrar, Straus and Giroux [1974] vii, 215 p. illus. 21 cm. Bibliography: p. 207-208. Traces the history of the Shakers in America, from their founding in England to their few surviving colonies in New England. [BX9766.F3] 73-90968 ISBN 0-374-35819-2 6.95
1. Shakers—United States—Juvenile literature. I. Title.

ROBINSON, Charles Edson, 1836-1925. 289.8'0973
A concise history of the United Society of Believers called Shakers / by Charles Edson Robinson. Westport, Conn. : Hyperion Press, 1975, c1893. p. cm. (The Radical tradition in America) Reprint of the ed. printed at East Canterbury, N.H. [BX9766.R6 1975] 75-342 ISBN 0-88355-245-0 : 13.50
1. Shakers—United States. I. Title.

THE Shaker image / 289.8'0974
Elmer R. Pearson, picture editor ; [text by] Julia Neal ... ; with a pref. by Walter Muir Whitehill ; and captions by Amy Bess Miller and John H. Ott. Boston : New York Graphic Society, 1974. 190 p. : ill. ; 29 cm. "The Shakers as they saw themselves and as others saw them [by] Julia Neal": p. 23-60. Published in collaboration with the Shaker Community, Inc., Hancock, Mass. Bibliography: p. 189-190. [BX9766.S5] 73-89954 ISBN 0-8212-0539-0 : 17.50
1. Shakers—United States—Pictorial works. I. Pearson, Elmer R. II. Neal, Julia. III. Shaker Community, inc.

SEARS, Clara Endicott, 1863- comp. 289.8'09744'3
Gleanings from old Shaker journals / compiled by Clara Endicott Sears. Westport, Conn. : Hyperion Press, 1975, c1916. p. cm. (The Radical tradition in America) Reprint of the ed. published by Houghton Mifflin, Boston. [BX9768.H3S4 1975] 75-344 ISBN 0-88355-247-7 : 26.00
1. Shakers—Harvard, Mass. 2. Harvard, Mass.—History. I. Title.

FILLEY, Dorothy M. 289.8'09747'42
Recapturing Wisdom's Valley : the Watervliet Shaker heritage, 1775-1975 / by Dorothy M. Filley ; edited by Mary L. Richmond. Colonie, N.Y. : Town of Colonie, c1975. p. cm. Published on the occasion of an exhibition celebrating the bicentennial of Shaker settlement. [BX9768.W2F53] 75-27133 ISBN 0-89062-010-5
1. Shakers—Watervliet, N.Y.—Exhibitions. 2. Watervliet, N.Y.—History—Exhibitions. I. Title.

SHAKER Museum, Old Chatham. 289.8'09747'39
The Shaker Museum, Old Chatham, N.Y. [Old Chatham, Shaker Museum Foundation, 1968] [47] p. illus. 24 cm. Cover title. Text by J. S. Williams and R. W. Meader. [BX9772.S5] 68-30329
1. Shakers. I. Williams, John Stanton, 1901- II. Meader, Robert W.

MCNEMAR, Richard, 1770-1839. 289.8'09769
The Kentucky revival; or, A short history of the late extraordinary outpouring of the spirit of God in the western states of America, agreeably to Scripture promises and prophecies concerning the latter day, with a brief account of the entrance and progress of what the world call Shakerism among the subjects of the late revival in Ohio and Kentucky. Presented to the true Zion traveler as a memorial of the wilderness journey. New York, E. O. Jenkins, 1846. [New York, AMS Press, 1974] 156 p. 19 cm. (Communal societies in America) "Observations on church government, by the Presbytery of Springfield" (p. [133]-156) has special t.p. [BX9767.K4M3 1974] 72-2990 ISBN 0-404-10752-4 9.00
1. Shakers. 2. Revivals—Kentucky. 3. Church polity. I. Springfield (Ohio). Presbytery. Observations on church government. 1974. II. Title.

NEAL, Julia. 289.8'09769
By their fruits : the story of Shakerism in South Union, Kentucky / by Julia Neal. Philadelphia : Porcupine Press, 1975, c1947.

279 p., [4] leaves of plates : ill. ; 22 cm. (The American utopian adventure : series two) Reprint of the ed. published by the University of North Carolina Press, Chapel Hill. Includes index. Bibliography: p. 271-273. [BX9768.S8N4 1975] 74-26579 ISBN 0-87991-003-8
1. Shakers—South Union, Ky. I. Title.

NEAL, Julia. 289.8'09769
The Kentucky Shakers / Julia Neal. [Lexington] : University Press of Kentucky, c1977. 97, [1] p., [4] leaves of plates : ill. ; 22 cm. (The Kentucky Bicentennial bookshelf) Bibliography: p. 95-[98] [BX9767.K4N42] 76-46029 ISBN 0-8131-0236-7 : 4.95
1. Shakers—Kentucky—History. I. Title. II. Series.

THOMAS, Samuel 289.8'09769'485
W., 1938- comp.
The simple spirit; a pictorial study of the Shaker community at Pleasant Hill, Kentucky [compiled by] Samuel W. Thomas [and] James C. Thomas. [Harrodsburg, Ky.] Pleasant Hill Press, 1973. 128 p. illus. 25 cm. Part of illustrative matter in pocket. [BX9768.P6T47] 73-83223
1. Shakers—Pictorial works. 2. Pleasanthill, Ky.—Pictorial works. I. Thomas, James Cheston, 1939- joint comp. II. Title.

MACLEAN, John 289.8'09771
Patterson, 1848-1939.
Shakers of Ohio : fugitive papers concerning the Shakers of Ohio, with unpublished manuscripts / by J. P. MacLean. Philadelphia : Porcupine Press, 1975. 415 p., [7] leaves of plates : ill. ; 22 cm. (The American utopian adventure : Series two) Reprint of the 1907 ed. published by F. J. Heer Print. Co., Columbus, Ohio. Includes bibliographical references. [BX9767.O3M3 1975] 74-32001 ISBN 0-87991-020-8 lib.bdg. : 17.50
1. Shakers—Ohio. I. Title.

SHAKER HISTORICAL 289.873
SOCIETY.
Selected papers. Cleveland, 1957. 111 p. 24 cm. [BX9759.S5] 57-13233
1. Shakers. — Addresses, essays, lectures. 2. Warrensville, O. — Hist. I. Title.
Shakerism for today, by M.C. Andorn. -- Shaker medicines, by H.D. Piercy. -- Early Warrensville: The forest primeval, 1807-1817, by C.B. Piercy.

PIERCE, Caroline Behlen, 289.8771
1886-
The Valley of God's Pleasure; a saga of the North Union Shaker community, [1st ed.] New York, Stratford House, 1951. 247 p. illus. 24 cm. [BX9768.N7P5] 51-13140
1. Shakers — North Union, Ohio. I. Title.

ADAMS, Norman, fl.1972- 289.9
Goodbye, beloved Brethren. Aberdeen, Impulse Publications Ltd, 1972. 162, [5] p. illus., facsim., ports. 20 cm. Bibliography: p. [162] [BX8809.T39A63] 73-162292 ISBN 0-901311-13-8 £2.50
1. Taylor, Jim. 2. Plymouth Brethren. I. Title.

ALLEN, James, 1864-1912. 289.9
As a man thinketh. Edited for contemporary readers by William R. Webb. Illustrated by James Hamil. [Kansas City, Mo.] Hallmark Editions [1968] 61 p. illus. 20 cm. [BF639.A48 1968] 68-19597 2.50
1. New Thought. I. Title.

ALLEN, James, 1864-1912. 289.9
As a man thinketh; James Allen's greatest inspirational essays. Edited by William B. Franklin and William R. Webb. Illustrated by Bruce Baker. [Kansas City, Mo., Hallmark, 1971] 68 p. col. illus. 27 cm. (Hallmark crown editions) [BF639.A48 1971] 75-127755 ISBN 0-87529-155-4 5.00
1. New Thought. I. Morgan, James, 1944- ed. II. Webb, William R., ed. III. Title.

ANCIENT faith in 289.9
conflict. [Tampa, Fla., Temple Publishers, 1955] 269p. illus. 24cm. (Florida Christian College lecture series, 1955) [BX7094.C95C6] [BX7094.C95C6] 286.6 55-57265 55-57265
1. Churches of Christ—Addresses, essays, lectures. I. Cope, James Rogers, 1917- ed. II. Series: Florida Christian College, Temple Terrace, Fla. Lecture series, 1955

ANDERSON, Stanley Edwin. 289.9
Armstrongism's 300 errors exposed by 1300 Bible verses [by] Stanley E. Anderson. Nashville, Church Growth Publications [1973] 215 p. 22 cm. Bibliography: p. 210-211. [BR1725.A77A83] 77-185796 2.45
1. Armstrong, Herbert W. 2. Armstrong, Garner Ted. 3. Worldwide Church of God. I. Title.
Publisher's address: 5110 Delaware Ave., Nashville, Tenn. 37209

APOSTOLIC FAITH MISSION. 289.9
Minister's manual. Portland, Or. [1950] 400 p. 18 cm. [BX6194.A7A2 1950] 50-26164
1. Apostolic Faith Mission—Doctrinal and controversial works. I. Title.

ARMSTRONG, Ken S 289.9
Face to face with the Church of the Nazarene. Boulder, Colo., 1958. 87p. illus. 24cm. Based on 'a doctoral dissertation ... available at the Iliff School of Theology.' [BX8699.N3A8] 58-49555
1. Church of the Nazarene—Stat. I. Title.

ASSEMBLIES of God, General 289.9
Council.
Like a river...; 50th anniversary. [Springfield? Mo., 1964?] 75 p. illus. (part col.), ports. 28 cm. [BX6198.A7A45] 70-291563
1. Assemblies of God, General Council I. Title.

ASSOCIATION for Research 289.9
and Enlightenment, Virginia Beach, Va.
A search for God; compiled by the study groups of the Association for Research and Enlightenment. 4th ed. Virginia Beach, Va., 1952. 131 p. 21 cm. [BX9999.V5A72] 52-42680
I. Title.

*AZRAEL 289.9
Third book of Azrael; teachings of the Great White Brotherhood. Los Angeles, DeVorss [c.1964] 210p. 23cm. 3.00 pap.,
I. Title.

BACH, Marcus 289.9
The challenge of change. Lee's Summit, Mo., Unity Bks. [1967] 143p. 20cm. [BX9890.U5B29] 67-14509 3.95
1. Unity School of Christianity. I. Title.

BACH, Marcus, 1906- 289.9
The challenge of change. Lee's Summit, Mo., Unity Books [1967] 143 p. 20 cm. Unity School of Christianity. [BX9890.U5B29] 67-14509
I. Title.

BACH, Marcus, 1906- 289.9
The unity way of life. [1st ed.] Englewood Cliffs, N. J., Prentice-Hall [1962] 182 p. 21 cm. [BX9890.U5B3] 62-18246
1. Unity School of Christianity. I. Title.

BECKFORD, James A. 289.9
The trumpet of prophecy : a sociological study of Jehovah's Witnesses / James A. Beckford. New York : Wiley, [1975] xii, 244 p. ; 25 cm. "A Halsted Press book." Includes indexes. Bibliography: p. 224-234. [BX8526.B4] 75-14432 ISBN 0-470-06138-3 : 17.95
1. Jehovah's Witnesses. 2. Religion and sociology. I. Title.

BEEBE, Tom. 289.9 B
Who's who in New Thought : biographical dictionary of New Thought : personnel, centers, and authors' publications / by Tom Beebe. Lakemont, Ga. : CSA Press, c1977. 318 p. : maps ; 24 cm. Bibliography: p. 286-311. [BF648.A1B43] 77-152019 ISBN 0-87707-189-6 : 6.95
1. New Thought—United States—Directories. I. Title.

BENNER, Hugh C 289.9
Rendezvous with abundance. Kansas City, Mo., Beacon Hill Press [1958] 126p. 20cm. [BX8699.N3B38] 58-14768
1. Church of the Nazarene. I. Title.

BISHOP, Tania Kroitor 289.9
Record of the spirit. San Gabriel, Calif., P. O. Box 51 Willing Pub. Co. [c.1959] 89p. 21cm. 60-1042 3.00
1. New Thought. 2. Lord's prayer. I. Title.

BITTINGER, Emmert F., 1925- 289.9
Heritage and promise; perspectives on the Church of the Brethren [by] Emmert F. Bittinger. [Elgin, Ill., Brethren Press, 1970] 158 p. illus. 21 cm. Bibliography: p. 148-150. [BX7821.2.B54] 70-19266 1.95
1. Church of the Brethren. I. Title.

BLOCH-HOELL, Nils 289.9
The Pentecostal movement; its origin, development, and distinctive character [Oslo] Universite forlaget [dist. New York, Humanities, 1965, c.1964] 255p. 24cm. (Scandinavian univ. bks.) Bibl. [BX8795.P25B553] 65-3204 6.00 bds.,
1. Pentecostal churches—Norway. I. Title.

BRADEN, Charles Samuel, 289.9
1887-
Spirits in rebellion; the rise and development of new thought. Dallas, Southern Methodist University Press, 1963. 571 p. 23 cm. Includes bibliography. [BF639.B576] 63-13245
1. New Thought — Hist. 2. International New Thought Alliance. I. Title.

BRADEN, Charles Samuel, 289.9
1887-
Spirits in rebellion; the rise and development of new thought. Dallas, Southern Methodist Univ. Pr. [c.]1963. 571p. 23cm. Bibl. 63-13245 7.50
1. New Thought—Hist. 2. International New Thought Alliance. I. Title.

BROOKS, Henry Chauncey, 289.9
Bp., 1896-
The way of the cross leads to the crown; doctrine, life [and] sermons of Bishop Henry C. Brooks. Compiled and edited by L. Frances Hill-Watkins. [Washington? 1950] 207 p. illus., port. 20 cm. [BX9999.W3W3] 51-31771
1. Washington, D. C, Way of the Cross Church of Christ. I. Title.

BROWN, Charles Ewing, 1883- 289.9
When the trumpet sounded; a history of the Church of God reformation movement. Anderson, Ind., Warner Press [1951] 402 p. ports. (on lining papers) 21 cm. [BX7094.C673B7] 51-5411
1. Warner, Daniel Sidney, 1842-1895. 2. Church of God (Anderson, Ind.)—Hist. I. Title.

BRUMBACK, Carl, 1917- 289.9
Suddenly. . . from heaven; a history of the Assemblies of God. Springfield, Mo., Gospel Pub. House [1961] 380p. illus. 23cm. Includes bibliography. [BX6198.A7B7] 61-18607
1. Assemblies of God, General Council—Hist. I. Title.

BUTTERWORTH, Eric. 289.9
Unity: a quest for truth. [1st ed.] New York, R. Speller [1965] 89 p. 19 cm. [BX9890.U5B8] 65-20535
1. Unity school of Christianity—Addresses, essays, lectures. 2. Christian life. I. Title.

CALLEY, Malcolm J C 289.9
God's people; West Indian Pentecostal sects in England [by] Malcolm J. C. Calley. London, New York, Oxford University Press, 1965. xiv, 182 p. illus. 23 cm. "Issued under the auspices of the Institute of Race Relations, London." Bibliography: p. [170]-173. [BX8762.Z7G73] 66-536
1. Pentecostal churches—Gt. Brit. 2. West Indians in Gt. Brit. I. Title.

CALLEY, Malcolm J. C. 289.9
God's people: West Indian Pentecostal sects in England New York, Oxford [c.]1965. xiv, 182p. illus. 23cm. Issued under the auspices of the Inst. of Race Relations, London. Bibl. [BX8762.Z7G73] 66-536 5.60
1. Pentecostal churches—Gt. Brit. 2. West Indians in Gt. Brit. I. Title.

CAMPBELL, Faith, 1913- 289.9 B
Stanley Frodsham, prophet with a pen. Springfield, Mo., Gospel Pub. House [1974] 146, [1] p. 18 cm. (Radiant books) "Books by Stanley H. Frodsham": p. [147] [BX6198.A7F763] 74-77406 1.25
1. Frodsham, Stanley Howard, 1882-1969. I. Title.

CARAKER, Andrew 289.9
The adventure into the reality of you. New York, Speller [1966, c.1965] x, 167p. 19cm. Bibl. [BF639.C24] 65-25568 3.95 bds.,
1. New Thought. I. Title.

CARDEN, Karen W. 289.9
The persecuted prophets / Karen W. Carden and Robert W. Pelton. South Brunswick : A. S. Barnes, [1975] p. cm. [BX7990.H6C28 1975] 74-10322 ISBN 0-498-01511-4 : 9.95
1. Snake cults (Holiness churches) 2. Holiness churches—Appalachian Mountains, Southern. I. Pelton, Robert W., 1934- joint author. II. Title.

CHAMBERS, Roger R. 289.9
The plain truth about Armstrongism [by] Roger R. Chambers. Grand Rapids, Baker Book House [1972] 146 p. 18 cm. (Direction books) Includes bibliographical references. [BR1725.A77C47] 72-185905 ISBN 0-8010-2337-8 1.25
1. Armstrong, Herbert W. 2. Worldwide Church of God. I. Title.

CHRISTENSEN, William E 289.9
In such harmony; a history of the Federated Church of Columbus, Nebraska. Columbus, Neb., Telegraph Print. Co. [1964] xiii, 82 p. illus., ports. 23 cm. Bibliographical references included in "Sources" (p. 63-78) [BX9999.C6F4] 64-36022
1. Columbus, Neb. Federated Church. I. Title.

THE Church annual; 289.9
year book of the United Brethren in Christ. 1889- Dayton, Ohio. no. illus., ports. 23 cm. Title varies: 1889-1934, The Year-book of the United Brethren inChrist. [BX9875.A17] 52-33200
1. United Brethren in Christ—Yearbooks. I. Church of the United Brethren in Christ (New constitution)

CHURCH of Christ (Holiness) 289.9
U.S.A.
Manual of the history, doctrine, government, and ritual of the Church of Christ (Holiness) U.S.A., 1926. True holiness. 1st ed. Norfolk, Va., Guide Pub. Co. [1928] 83 p. 16 cm. "Published by orders of the National Convention of the Church of Christ (Holiness) U.S.A., held in Jackson, Miss., August 22-29, 1926." [BX7012.Z5A4] 67-43288
1. Church of Christ (Holiness) U.S.A. Liturgy and ritual. I. Title.

CHURCH of God evangel. 289.9
The evangel reader; selections from the Church of God evangel, 1910-1958, compiled and edited with introd. and notes by Charles W. Conn. [1st ed.] Cleveland, Tenn., Pathway Press [1958,54 256p. illus. 22cm. [BX7094.C73A4] 57-7457
1. Church of God (General Assembly) I. Conn, Charles W., ed. II. Title.

CHURCH of God of Prophecy. 289.9
Bible Training Camp.
Lessons in Bible training, prepared especially for first term students of Bible Training Camp, the official institution of Bible training in the Church of God of Prophecy. Written and compiled by the faculty. [Cleveland, Tenn.] Printed by the White Wing Pub. House & Press [1954- v. illus. 24cm. [BX7059.A23] 59-35654
1. Church of God of Prophecy—Doctrinal and controversial works. I. Title. II. Title: Bible training.

CHURCH of Illumination. 289.9
Manual, order of service and ritual; prepared especially for the priests and ministers consecrated and ordained to the service of God, in the priesthood of Melchizedek and Church of Illumination, by R. Swinburne Clymer. Limited ed. Quakertown, Pa. Priv. print. by Philosophical Pub. Co. [1952] 100p. 23cm. [BX7063.Z5A4] 59-37880
I. Clymer, Reuben Swinburne, 1878- II. Title.

CHURCH of the United 289.9
Brethren in Christ (New constitution)
Partners in the conquering cause. Dayton, Ohio [1924] 114 p. illus. 17 cm. Published by the board under the denomination's earlier name: United Brethren in Christ. [BX9875.A65 1924] 62-56748
I. Title.

COAD, Frederick Roy. 289.9
A history of the Brethren movement; its origins, its worldwide development, and its significance for the present day, by F. Roy Coad. Grand Rapids, Eerdmans [1968] 327 p. 23 cm. Bibliography: p. 307-316. [BX8800.C6 1968b] 76-1653 6.95
1. Plymouth Brethren. I. Title.

COBBINS, Otho Beale, Bp., 289.9
ed.
History of Church of Christ (Holiness) U.S.A., 1895-1965. Otho B. Cobbins, editor-in-chief. [1st ed.] Chicago, National Pub. Board Church of Christ (Holiness) U.S.A. [1966] 446 p. illus., ports. 23 cm. Includes hymns, in part in shape-note notation. [BX7012.A4C6] 66-22333
1. Church of Christ (Holiness) U.S.A.—History. I. Church of Christ (Holiness) U.S.A. II. Title.

COLE, Marley. 289.9
Jehovah's Witnesses; the new world society. [1st ed.] New York, Vantage Press [1955] 229 p. illus. 21 cm. [BX8526.C58] 54-12653
1. Jehovah's Witnesses.

COLE, Marley. 289.9
Triumphant kingdom. New York, Criterion Books [1957] 256p. 22cm. [BX8526.C583] 57-8262
1. Jehovah's Witnesses. I. Title.

CONN, Charles W 289.9
Like a mighty army, moves the Church of God, 1886-1955. [1st ed.] Cleveland, Tenn., Church of God Pub. House, 1955. 380p. illus. 25cm. [BX7094.C73C57] 55-9666
1. Church of God (General Assembly) I. Title.

CONN, Charles W 289.9
Pillars of Pentecost. [1st ed.] Cleveland, Tenn., Pathway Press, 1956. 141p. 21cm. [BX8795.P25C6] 56-6820
1. Pentecostal churches. I. Title.

CORE, Arthur C. 289.9 B
Philip William Otterbein; pastor ecumenist ... By Arthur C. Core. Dayton, Ohio, Board of Publication, Evangelical United Brethren Church [1968] 127 p. illus., facsims., port. 22 cm. Includes bibliographical references. [BX9877.O8C6] 68-22446
1. Otterbein, Philip William, Bp., 1726-1813. I. Title.

CROSS, James A. 1911- ed. 289.9
Healing in the church. Cleveland, Tenn., Pathway [c.1962] 141p. 21cm. 62-4471 2.50
1. Church of God (Cleveland, Tenn.)—Doctrinal and controversial works. 2. Church of God (Cleveland, Tenn.)—Sermons. 3. Faithcure. I. Title.

CURTIS, Donald. 289.9
The golden bridge; science of mind in daily living. West Nyack, N.Y., Parker Pub. Co. [1969] xii, 211 p. 24 cm. [BF639.C884] 69-11732 6.95
1. New Thought. 2. Self-realization. 3. Success. I. Title. II. Title: Science of mind in daily living.

CURTIS, Donald. 289.9
New age understanding. Unity Village, Mo., Unity Books [1972, c1973] 142 p. 20 cm. [BX9890.U5C87] 72-92276
1. Unity School of Christianity. I. Title.

CURTIS, Donald. 289.9
New age understanding. Unity Village, Mo., Unity Books [1972, c1973] 142 p. 20 cm. [BX9890.U5C87] 72-92276
1. Unity School of Christianity. I. Title.

CUSTER, Dan 289.9
The miracle of mind power. Englewood Cliffs, N. J., Prentice-Hall [c.1960] xix, 263p. 24cm. 60-14196 4.95
1. New Thought. I. Title.

CUTHBERT, Arthur A. 289.9 B
The Life and world-work of Thomas Lake Harris, written from direct personal knowledge / by Arthur A. Cuthbert. New York : AMS Press, 1975. 413, xix p. ; 18 cm. (Communal societies in America) Reprint of the 1909 ed. published by C. W. Pearce, Glasgow, Scot. Includes index. [PS1819.H6Z6 1975] 72-2954 ISBN 0-404-10719-2 : 27.50
1. Harris, Thomas Lake, 1823-1906. I. Title.

D'ANDRADE, Hugh. 289.9 B
Charles Fillmore: herald of the new age. [1st ed.] New York, Harper & Row [1974] xiv, 145 p. 21 cm. Bibliography: p. [144]-145. [BX9890.U5D36] 73-6337 ISBN 0-06-061682-2 5.95
1. Fillmore, Charles, 1854-1948. 2. Unity School of Christianity.

DAYTON, Donald W. 289.9
The American Holiness movement; a bibliographic introduction, by Donald W. Dayton. Wilmore, Ky., B. L. Fisher Library, Asbury Theological Seminary, 1971. 59 p. 22 cm. (Occasional bibliographic papers of the B. L. Fisher Library) "Originally published in the 1971 'Proceedings' of the American Theological Library Association." [Z7845.H6D37] 73-31588 2.00
1. Holiness churches—Bibliography. I. Title. II. Series: Fisher (B. L.) Library. Occasional bibliographic papers.

DELOACH, Charles F. 289.9
The Armstrong error, by C. F. DeLoach. Plainfield, N.J., Logos International [1971] 117 p. 18 cm. On cover: The plain truth on Herbert W. Armstrong. Includes bibliographical references. [BR1725.A77D4] 73-129817 ISBN 0-912106-13-1 0.95
1. Armstrong, Herbert W. I. Title.

DOUKHOBOR Research Committee. 289.9
The Doukhobors of British Columbia. Harry B. Hawthorn, editor. Vancouver, University of British Columbia, 1955. xii, 288p. illus. maps (on lining papers) 25cm. 'Based on the Report of the Doukhobor Research Committee ... presented to the Government of British Cocumbia in 1962.' [BX7433.D65] 55-3479
1. Dukhobors. I. Hawthorn, Harry Bertram, 1910- ed. II. Title.

DOUKHOBOR Research Committee. 289.9
Report. Harry B. Hawthorn, editor. [Vancouver] University of British Columbia, 1952. ix, 342 p. 30 cm. Errata slip inserted. [BX7433.D68] 52-66045
1. Dukhobors. I. Hawthorn, Harry Bertram, 1910- ed. II. Title.

DRAKEFORD, John W. 289.9
Children of doom; a sobering look at the commune movement [by] John W. Drakeford. Nashville, Broadman Press [1972] 143 p. illus. 21 cm. Includes bibliographical references. [BV4487.C5D7] 72-79166 ISBN 0-8054-5522-1 4.95
1. Children of God (Movement) I. Title.

DUBB, Allie A. 289.9
Community of the saved : an African revivalist church in the East Cape / Allie A. Dubb. Johannesburg : Witwatersrand University Press for African Studies Institute, 1976. xvii, 175 p., [10] p. of plates : ill. ; 22 cm. Bibliography: p. 173-175. [BX8762.Z6E173] 76-375918 ISBN 0-85494-292-0 : R7.00
1. Bhengu, Nicholas B. H., 1909- 2. Pentecostal churches—South Africa—East London—Case studies. 3. East London—Church history. I. Title.

DURASOFF, Steve. 289.9
Bright wind of the spirit: Pentecostalism today. Englewood Cliffs, N.J., Prentice-Hall [1972] 277 p. 22 cm. Bibliography: p. 271-272. [BX8763.D87] 72-6536 ISBN 0-13-083089-5 6.95
1. Pentecostalism. I. Title.

ELLER, Paul Himmel, 1905- 289.9
These Evangelical United Brethren. Dayton, Ohio, Otterbein Press, 1950. 128 p. illus., ports. 22 cm. Bibliography: p. 126-127. [BX7556.A4E5] 51-100
1. Evangelical United Brethren Church—Hist. I. Title.

EVANGELICAL United Brethren Church. 289.9
The book of ritual. Authorized by the General Conference. Harrisburg, Pa., Evangelical Press [1952] 127 p. 18 cm. [BX7556.Z5A38] 52-27191
I. Title.

EVANGELICAL United Brethren Church. 289.9
The discipline of the Evangelical United Brethren Church, by order of the thirty-seventh session of the General Conference of the Evangelical United Brethren Church (second in the United Church) 1951 ed. Dayton, Ohio, Otterbein Press [1952, '1951] iv, 702 p. 18 cm. [BX7556.Z5A4 1952] 52-21510
1. Evangelical United Brethren Church—Government. I. Title.

FORD, Jack, 1908- 289.9
In the steps of John Wesley; the Church of Nazarene in Britain. Kansas City, Mo., Nazarene Pub. House [1968] 300 p. 23 cm. Thesis—University of London. Bibliography: p. 284-300. [BX8699.N335G74] 68-5844
1. Church of the Nazarene—Great Britain. 2. Holiness churches—Great Britain. I. Title.

FREEMAN, James Dillet. 289.9
Happiness can be a habit. Drawings by Robert Kipniss. Garden city, New York, Doubleday [1968,c.1966] 90p. 21cm. (W15) [BX9890.U5F68] 66-17396 1.95 pap.,
1. Unity School of Christianity. 2. Happiness. I. Title.

FREEMAN, James Dillet. 289.9
Happiness can be a habit. Drawings by Robert Kipniss. [1st ed.] Garden City, N.Y., Doubleday, 1966. 190 p. illus. 22 cm. [BX9890.U5F68] 66-17396
1. Unity School of Christianity. 2. Happiness. I. Title.

GIBBLE, Phares Brubaker, 1888- 289.9
History of the East Pennsylvania Conference of the Church of the United Brethren in Christ. Dayton, Ohio, Otterbein Press, '1951. xiii, 593 p. illus., ports., map. 24 cm. Bibliography: p. 584-586. [BX9875.A4E2] 51-3636
1. Church of the United Brethren in Christ (New constitution) Conferences. East Pennsylvania. I. Title.

GILLUM, Perry. 289.9
These stones speak / by Perry Gillum. Cleveland, Tenn. : White Wing Pub. House and Press, [1974] 121 p. : ill. ; 23 cm. [BX7058.G54] 74-194734
1. Church of God of Prophecy—History. 2. Church of Prophecy Marker Association. I. Title.

GLOVIER, David Franklin, 1889- 289.9
Pictorial history of the Virginia Conference; the Church of the United Brethren in Christ from 1800 to 1946, and the Evangelical United Brethren Church from 1946, at which time the Church of the United Brethren in Christ and the Evangelical Church united to form the Evangelical United Brethren Church, 1800-1964. [Staunton, Va., 1965] 350 p. illus., fold. col. map, ports. 24 cm. [BX7556.A43V53] 65-8486
1. Evangelical United Brethren Church. Conferences. Virginia — Hist. I. Title.

GOLDSMITH, Joel S., 1892- 289.9
Beyond words and thoughts; from the metaphysical consciousness to the mystical [by] Joel S. Goldsmith. Edited by Lorraine Sinkler. New York, Julian Press, 1968. x, 180 p. 22 cm. [BF639.G5574] 68-19018
1. New Thought. I. Sinkler, Lorraine, ed. II. Title.

GOLDSMITH, Joel S., 1892- 289.9
Consciousness unfolding. New York, Julian [c.]1962. 269p. 21cm. 62-19299 3.95
1. New Thought. I. Title.

GOLDSMITH, Joel S., 1892- 289.9
God, the substance of all form. New York, Julian [c.]1962. 174p. 21cm. 62-19301 3.50
1. New Thought. I. Title.

GOLDSMITH, Joel S., 1892- 289.9
Leave your nets. Ed. by Lorraine Sinkler. New York, Julian [c.]1964. 150p. 22cm. [BF639.G563] 64-24789 3.50
1. New Thought. I. Title.

GOLDSMITH, Joel S 1892- 289.9
Leave your pets [by] Joel S. Goldsmith. Edited by Lorraine Sinkler. New York, Julian Press, 1964. 150 p. 22 cm. [BF639.G563] 64-24789
1. New Thought I. Title.

GOLDSMITH, Joel S 1892- 289.9
Living now [by] Joel S. Goldsmith. Edited by Lorraine Sinkler. New York, Julian Press, 1965. x. 212 p. 22 cm. "First appeared in 1963 in the form of letters." [BF639.G5657] 65-26943
1. New Thought. I. Sinkler, Lorraine, ed. II. Title.

GOLDSMITH, Joel S. 1892- 289.9
Living now. Ed. by Lorraine Sinkler. New York, Julian [c.]1965. x, 212p. 22cm First appeared in 1963 in the form of letters. [BF639.G5657] 65-26943 4.50
1. New Thought. I. Sinkler, Lorraine, ed. II. Title.

GOLDSMITH, Joel S. 1892- 289.9
Living the infinite way. Rev. ed. New York, Harper [c.1961] 128p. 61-9646 2.50 bds.,
1. New Thought. I. Title.

GOLDSMITH, Joel S., 1892- 289.9
The Master speaks. New York, Julian [c.] 1962. 333p. 21cm. 62-19300 3.95
1. New thought. I. Title.

GOLDSMITH, Joel S., 1892- 289.9
Realization of oneness; the practice of spiritual healing, by Joel S Goldsmith, Ed. by Larraine Sinkler. New York, Julian, 1967. 209p. 22cm. [BF639.G5688] 67-17570 5.00
1. New thought. I. Title.

GOLDSMITH, Joel S., 1892- 289.9
Realization of oneness; the practice of spiritual healing, by Joel S. Goldsmith. Edited by Lorraine Sinkler. New York, Julian Press, 1967. 209 p. 22 cm. [BF639.G5688] 67-17570
1. New Thought. I. Title.

GOLDSMITH, Joel S., 1892- 289.9
The world is new. New York, Harper [c.1962] 209p. 62-7953 3.50 bds.,
1. New Thought. I. Title.

GOLDSMITH, Joel S., 1892-1964. 289.9
A parenthesis in eternity. Edited by Lorraine Sinkler. [1st ed.] New York, Harper & Row [1964, c1963] viii, 366 p. 22 cm. [BF639.G5695] 64-10368
1. New thought. 2. Mysticism. I. Title.

GOLDSMITH, Joel S., 1892-1964. 289.9
The thunder of silence. [1st ed.] New York, Harper [1961] 192 p. 20 cm. [BF639.G58] 61-7340
1. New Thought. I. Title.

GROMACKI, Robert Glenn. 289.9
The modern tongues movement. Philadelphia, Presbyterian and Reformed Pub. Co., 1967. 165 p. 22 cm. Bibliography: p. [153]-161. [BL54.G7] 66-30705
1. Glossalalia. I. Title.

HANSON, Muriel. 289.9
Fifty years and seventy places, by Muriel Hanson. Minneapolis, Free Church Publications [1967] 111 p. illus., map, ports. 19 cm. [BX7548.A45C34] 75-8111
1. Evangelical Free Church of America—History. 2. Canada—Church history. I. Title.

HARRIS, Sara. 289.9 B
Father Divine, by Sara Harris, with the assistance of Harriet Crittendon [i.e.] Crittenden. Newly rev. and expanded, and with an introd. by John Henrik Clarke. New York, Collier Books [1971] xxxiv, 377 p. 19 cm. [BX7350.H37 1971] 78-146617
1. Baker, George, self-named Father Divine. I. Crittenden, Harriet, joint author.

HARRIS, Thomas Lake, 1823-1906. 289.9
A lyric of the morning land. New York, Patridge and Brittan, 1854. 256 p. 10 cm. [PS1819.H6L9] 65-59679
I. Title.

HARRIS, Thomas Lake, 1823-1906. 289.9
The wisdom of the adepts : esoteric science in human history / by Thomas Lake Harris. New York : AMS Press, 1975. xxxvi, 527 p. ; 23 cm. (Communal societies in America) Reprint of the 1884 ed. privately printed at Fountain Grove, Santa Rosa, Calif. [BX9998.H44 1975] 72-2957 ISBN 0-404-10721-4 : 34.50
1. Brotherhood of the New Life. I. Title.

HEFLEY, James C. 289.9
The church that takes on trouble / James and Marti Hefley. Elgin, Ill. : D. C. Cook Pub. Co., c1976. 242 p., [6] leaves of plates : ill. ; 22 cm. [BX9999.C45H43] 76-6579 ISBN 0-912692-95-2 : 5.95
1. LaSalle Street Church, Chicago. I. Hefley, Marti, joint author. II. Title.

HERBSTREITH, Ann. 289.9
The book of life. San Antonio, Naylor Co. [1971] viii, 67 p. 22 cm. [BF1999.H567] 77-165553 ISBN 0-8111-0415-X 3.95
I. Title.

HISTORICAL waymarks of the Church of God, (headquarters, Oregon, Illinois). 289.9
Oregon, Ill. : Church of God General Conference, c1976. 120 p. : ill. ; 22 cm. Includes index. [BX6183.H57] 76-365612
1. Church of God (Abrahamic Faith)—History.

HOLLENWEGER, Walter J., 1927- 289.9
The Pentecostals; the charismatic movement in the churches [by] W. J. Hollenweger. [Translated by R. A. Wilson with revisions by the author. 1st U.S. ed.] Minneapolis, Augsburg Pub. House [1972] xx, 572 p. illus. 25 cm. Translation of Enthusiastisches Christentum. Bibliography: p. [523]-557. [BX8763.H613] 70-176103 ISBN 0-8066-1210-X
1. Pentecostalism. I. Title.

HOLLIDAY, Robert Kelvin, 1933- 289.9
Tests of faith. Oak Ill, W. Va, Fayette Tribune, 1966. 104p. illus., ports. 23cm. Bibl. [BX7990.H6H59] 66-25996 5.00
1. Snake cults (Holiness churches) 2. Holiness churches I. Title.

HOLMES, Fenwicke Lindsay, 1883- 289.9 B
Ernest Holmes: his life and times [by] Fenwicke L. Holmes. New York, Dodd, Mead [1970] x, 308 p. illus., ports. 22 cm. [BF648.H6H58] 70-96765 6.95
1. Holmes, Ernest Shurtleff. I. Title.

HOLT, Simma. 289.9
Terror in the name of God; the story of the Sons of Freedom Doukhobors. New York, Crown Publishers [1965] xxiv, 312 p. illus., map (on lining papers) ports. 24 cm. Bibliography: p. [301]-306. [BX7433.H6 1965] 65-24316
1. Dukhobors. 2. Sons of Freedom. I. Title.

HOOVER, Mario G. 289.9
Origin and structural development of the Assemblies of God, by Mario G. Hoover. [Springfield, Mo.] 1968 [c1970] 214 p. 27 cm. Thesis (M.A.)—Southwest Missouri State College. Bibliography: p. [189]-196. [BX6198.A7H6] 75-299802
1. Assemblies of God, General Council. I. Title.

HOPKINS, Joseph Martin, 1919- 289.9
The Armstrong empire; a look at the Worldwide Church of God. [Grand Rapids] Eerdmans [1974] 304 p. map. 21 cm. Bibliography: p. 286-291. [BR1725.A77H66] 74-8255 3.95
1. Worldwide Church of God. 2. Armstrong, Herbert W. 3. Armstrong, Garner Ted. I. Title.

HORNADAY, William H. D. 289.9
The inner light, an informal portrait of a philosopher, by William H. D. Hornaday and Harlan Ware. New York, Dodd, Mead [1964] viii, 274, [1] p. 21 cm. Bibliography: p. [275] [BF648.H6H6] 64-22708
1. Holmes, Ernest Shurtleff. I. Ware, Harlan, joint author. II. Title.

HORNSHUH, Fred, 1884- 289.9
Historical sketches of the Bible Standard Churches Inc. in 1919 before merging with the Open Bible Churches Inc. in 1935 / by Fred Hornshuh, Sr. Eugene, Or. : Eugene Bible College, 1976. vi, 125 p. : ill. ; 22 cm. [BX6510.B665H67] 76-377265
1. Bible Standard Churches. I. Title: Historical sketches of the Bible Standard Churches ...

HOSHOR, John. 289.9 B
God in a Rolls Royce; the rise of Father Divine: madman, menace, or messiah. Freeport, N.Y., Books for Libraries Press,

1971. 272 p. illus., ports. 23 cm. (The Black heritage library collection) Reprint of the 1936 ed. [BX7350.H6 1971] 70-170698 ISBN 0-8369-8888-4
1. Baker, George, self-named Father Divine. I. Title. II. Series.

HUDSON, David. 289.9 B
Memoir of Jemima Wilkinson. New York, AMS Press [1972] 288 p. port. 22 cm. First published in 1821 under title: History of Jemima Wilkinson. Reprint of the 1844 ed. [BR1719.W5H8 1972] 78-134417 ISBN 0-404-08475-3 12.50
1. Wilkinson, Jemima, 1752-1819. I. Title.

IUPPENLATZ, William L 1879- 289.9
Regeneration and the superman. Boston, Christopher Pub. House [1959] 118p. 21cm. [BX9890.U5 I84] 59-7082
1. Unity School of Christianity. I. Title.

*JOLLEY, Jennie A. 289.9
As an angel of light or Bible tongues and holiness and their counterfeits. New York, Vantage [c.1964] 112p. 21cm. 2.75 bds.,
I. Title.

KASSARJIAN, Kevork, 1912- 289.9
Behind the iron altar. Philadelphia, Olivier, Maney [1950] 208 p. illus., port. 21 cm. [BX9999.L65R4] 50-6364
1. Los Angeles. Saint James Armenian Apostolic Church. I. Title.

KEMP, Russell A. 289.9
Live youthfully now, by Russell A. Kemp. Unity Village, Mo., Unity Books [1969] 223 p. 20 cm. [BX9890.U5K45] 79-93890
1. Unity School of Christianity—Doctrinal and controversial works. I. Title.

KENDRCK, Klaude. 289.9
The promise fulfilled; a history of the modern Pentecostal movement. Springfield, Mo., Gospel Pub. House [1961] 237p. 23cm. 'Outgrowth of a dissertation presented ... [at] the University of Texas ...for the degree of doctor of philosophy in history.' Includes bibliography. [BX8762.K4] 61-28191
1. Pentecostal churches—Hist. I. Title.

KERN, Richard, 1932- 289.9 B
John Winebrenner: nineteenth century reformer. Harrisburg, Pa., Central Pub. House, 1974. xi, 226 p. illus. 23 cm. Bibliography: p. 215-226. [BX7096.W5K47] 74-84501
1. Winebrenner, John, 1797-1860.

LA BARRE, Weston, 1911- 289.9
They shall take up serpents; psychology of the southern snake-handling cult. New York, Schocken Books [1969] ix, 208 p. illus. 21 cm. Reprint of the 1962 ed., with a new introd. by the author. Bibliographical references included in "Notes" (p. 183-198) [BL441.L3 1969] 71-91547 2.45
1. Serpents (in religion, folk-lore, etc.) 2. Serpent worship—Southern States. 3. Psychology, Religious. I. Title.

LAMBERT, J Cameron. 289.9
Thoughts are things: attract what you want by thinking; a study in applied psychology. [New York? c1957] 144p. 23cm. [BF639.L12] 57-14864
1. New Thought. I. Title.

LANDERS, Lucille 289.9
Walking in obedience [the nutritional aspects of the Word of wisdom] Illus. by John Brlej. Salt Lake City, Bookcraft. [1963] 128p. illus. 24cm. 63-25377 price unreported
1. Nutrition. 2. Word of wisdom. I. Title.

LAUSTER, Bobbie. 289.9 B
Herman Lauster; one man and God. Cleveland, Tenn., Pathway Press [1967] 208 p. 21 cm. (Missionary series) [BX7034.Z8L3] 67-21742
1. Lauster, Herman, 1901-1964.

LEVITT, Zola. 289.9
The spirit of Sun Myung Moon / Zola Levitt. Irvine, Calif. : Harvest House Publishers, c1976. 127 p. ; 18 cm. Includes bibliographical references. [BX9750.S4L48] 76-40677 ISBN 0-89081-028-1 pbk. : 1.75
1. Moon, Sun Myung. I. Title.

LOISGLOVER 289.9
Loisglover revealed, by her first disciples. Boston, Christopher Pub. House [c.1960] 166p. illus. 21cm. 'Compilation of talks, lessons and revelations.' 60-12734 3.75
I. Title.

LOISGLOVER, 1895- 289.9
Loisglover revealed, by her first disciples. Boston, Christopher Pub. House [1960] 166p. illus. 21cm. 'Compilation of talks, lessons and revelations.' [BX9998.L62] 60-12734
I. Title.

LOWE, Harry William. 289.9
Radio Church of God; how its teachings differ from these of Seventh-day Adventists, by Harry W. Lowe. Mountain View, Calif., Pacific Press Pub. Association [1970] 143 p. 19 cm. Includes bibliographical references. [BR1725.A77L68] 77-101250
1. Armstrong, Herbert W. 2. Radio Church of God. 3. Seventh-Day Adventists—Doctrinal and controversial works.

LUGIBIHL, Walter H 1883- 289.9
The Missionary Church Association; historical account of its origin and development, by Walter H. Lugibihl and Jared F. Gerig. Berne, Ind., Economy Print. Concern, 1950 [c1951] 164 p. illus., ports. 20 cm. [BX8530.M5L8] 51-25526
1. Missionary Church Association—Hist. I. Gerig, Jared F. 1907- joint author. II. Title.

LUNDE, Norman S. 289.9
You unlimited, through the secret power within you. New York, Dodd [c.1965] xiii, 173p. 21cm. [BF639.L883] 65-23608 3.50
1. New Thought. I. Title.

LUNDE, Norman S 289.9
You unlimited, through the secret power within you, by Norman S. Lunde. New York, Dodd, Mead [1965] xiii, 173 p. 21 cm. [BF639.L883] 65-23608
1. New Thought. I. Title.

MCCORMICK, Donald, 1911- 289.9
Temple of love [1st Amer. ed.] New York, Citadel [1965, c.1962] 221p. illus., ports. 21cm. Bibl. [HQ967.G7M3] 65-15487 4.50
1. Free love. I. Title.

MCDANIEL, Harold W., 1920- 289.9
History of Forestdale Evangelical United Brethren Church, by Harold W. McDaniel. Foreword by Fred L. Dennis. Knoxville, Tenn., Forestdale E.U.B. Church, 1956. 138 p. illus. 21 cm. [BX7556.Z7K55] 75-303350
1. Forestdale Evangelical United Brethren Church, Knoxville, Tenn. 2. Knoxville, Tenn.—Biography. I. Title.

MACDONALD, Elinor 289.9
Your greatest power. Lee's Summit, Mo., Unity Bks. [1966] 317p. 20cm. [BX9890.U5M24] 66-6467 2.95
1. Unity School of Christianity. I. Title.

MCFADDEN, Michael 289.9
The Jesus revolution. New York, Harper & Row [1972] vi, 212 p. 18 cm. (Harrow books) [BV4531.2.M24] 72-6315 ISBN 0-06-087018-4 pap. 1.25
1. Jesus People—United States. I. Title.

MCKINNEY, George Dallas, 289.9
1932-
The theology of the Jehovah's Witnesses. Grand Rapids, Zondervan Pub. House [1962] 130p. 21cm. [BX8526.M25] 62-6242
1. Jehovah's Witnesses—Doctrinal and controversial works. I. Title.

MACMILLAN, A. H., 1877- 289.9
Faith on the march. Englewood Cliffs, N.J., Prentice-Hall [1957] 245 p. illus. 21 cm. [BX8525.7.M3] 57-8528
1. Jehovah's Witnesses—History. I. Title.

MCPHERSON, Aimee Semple, 289.9 B
1890-1944.
The story of my life. Waco, Tex., Word Books [1973] 255 p. illus. 23 cm. [BX7990.I68M285] 72-96350 5.95
1. McPherson, Aimee Semple, 1890-1944. I. Title.

MCPHERSON, Aimee Semple, 289.9 B
The story of my life. Waco, Tex., Word Books [1973] 255 p. illus. 23 cm. [BX7990.I68M285] 72-96350 5.95
1. McPherson, Aimee Semple, 1890-1944. I. Title.

MARDIROSSIAN, Haig M 289.9
The forgotten faith of the true worshipers. [1st ed.] New York, Vantage Press [1958] 499p. 21cm. [BX9998.M3] 57-9689
I. Title.

MARSHALL, June Glover. 289.9 B
A biographical sketch of Richard G. Spurling, Jr. / by June Glover Marshall. Cleveland, Tenn. : Pathway Press, [1974] 29 p. : port. ; 16 cm. [BX7020.Z8S685] 74-27630
1. Spurling, Richard G., 1858-1935. I. Title.

MARTIN, Marie-Louise. 289.9 B
Kimbangu : an African prophet and his church / Marie-Louise Martin ; with a foreword by Bryan R. Wilson ; translated by D. M. Moore. 1st American ed. Grand Rapids : Eerdmans, 1976. xxiv, 198 p. ; 23 cm. Translation of Kirche ohne Weisse. Includes indexes. Bibliography: p. 185-188. [BX7435.E44M3713 1976] 75-45371 ISBN 0-8028-3483-3 : 8.95
1. Kimbangu, Simon, 1889?-1951. 2. Eglise de Jesus-Christ sur la terre par le prophete Simon Kimbangu.

MARTIN, Walter Ralston, 289.9
1928-
The rise of the cults. Grand Rapids, Division of Cult Apologetics, Zondervan Pub. House [1955] 117p. 20cm. [BR516.M28] 56-1128
1. Sects—U. S. 2. Religions. I. Title.

MASSEY, James Earl. 289.9 B
Raymond S. Jackson: a portrait. With a foreword by Charles E. Brown. [Anderson, Ind., Warner Press, 1967] 96 p. ports. 22 cm. Bibliographical footnotes. [BX7027.Z8M3] 76-3552
1. Jackson, Raymond Samuel, 1892- I. Title.

MAUDE, Aylmer, 1858-1938. 289.9
A peculiar people: the Doukhobors. New York, AMS Press, 1970. xi, 338 p. illus., maps, ports. 19 cm. Reprint of the 1904 ed. [BX7433.M3 1970] 72-131033 ISBN 0-404-04275-9
1. Dukhobors. I. Title.

MELOON, Marion. 289.9 B
Ivan Spencer, willow in the wind / by Marion Meloon. Plainfield, N.J. : Logos International, c1974. xv, 234 p., [4] leaves of plates : ill. ; 21 cm. Errata slip inserted. [BX8764.Z8S75] 74-82565 ISBN 0-88270-091-X : 5.95 ISBN 0-88270-092-8 pbk. : 2.95.
1. Spencer, Ivan, 1888-1970. 2. Elim Bible Institute.

MENZIES, William W. 289.9
Anointed to serve; the story of the Assemblies of God, by William W. Menzies. Springfield, Mo., Gospel Pub. House [1971] 436 p. illus., port. 23 cm. Bibliography: p. 406-424. [BX6198.A7M43] 79-146707
1. Assemblies of God, General Council—History. I. Title.

MILHOUSE, Paul William, 289.9 B
1910-
Nineteen bishops of the Evangelical United Brethren Church / by Paul W. Milhouse. [s.l.] : Milhouse, [1974] 118 p. : ports. ; 24 cm. Includes bibliographical references. [BX7556.Z8A28] 74-195206
1. Evangelical United Brethren Church—Clergy. 2. Evangelical United Brethren Church—Biography. I. Title.

MILHOUSE, Paul William, 289.9 B
1910-
Philip William Otterbein; pioneer pastor to Germans in America, by Paul W. Milhouse. Nashville, Upper Room [1968] 71 p. illus. 16 cm. Includes bibliographical references. [BX9877.O8M5] 68-19994
1. Otterbein, Philip William, Bp., 1726-1813.

*MITCHELL, Hazel Robertson 289.9
Gift from my mother. New York, Pageant [c.1965] 257p. 24cm. 4.50
I. Title.

MOORE, Mark Reynolds, 1916- 289.9
Fifty years ... and beyond; a history of the Chicago Central District, Church of the Nazarene. [Kankakee? Ill., 1954] 149p. illus. 29cm. [BX8699.N3M6] 55-16552
1. Church of the Nazarene. Districts. Chicago Central District—Hist. I. Title.

MOORE, Willard Burgess. 289.9
Molokan oral tradition; legends and memorates of an ethnic sect. Berkeley, University of California Press, 1973. vii, 82 p. 27 cm. (University of California publications. Folklore studies, 28) Bibliography: p. 81-82. [BX8530.M6M66] 72-619685 ISBN 0-520-09483-2
1. Molckans in Los Angeles. I. Title. II. Series: California. University. University of California publications. Folklore studies, 28.

MULLER, Albert. 289.9
Meet Jehovah's Witnesses: their confusion, doubts and contradictions. Pulaski, Wis., Franciscan Publishers [1964] 116 p. 19 cm. Bibliographical references included in "Footnotes" (p. 97-108) [BX8526.M8] 64-5292
1. Jehovah's Witnesses — Doctrinal and controversial works. I. Title.

MULLER, Albert 289.9
Meet Jehovah's Witnesses: their confusion, doubts and contradictions. Pulaski, Wisc., Franciscan Pubs. [c.1964] 116p. 19cm. Bibl. 64-5292 .50 pap.,
1. Jehovah's Witnesses—Doctrinal and controversial works. I. Title.

MURPHY, Joseph, 1898- 289.9
You can change your whole life. San Gabriel, Calif:, Willing public co [1961] 185p. 21cm. [BF639.M843] 62-737
1. New Thought. I. Title.

NICHOL, John Thomas. 289.9
Pentecostalism. [1st ed.] New York, Harper & Row [1966] xv, 264 p. 22 cm. "Much of this material was originally submitted to satisfy the doctoral requirements at the Boston University Graduate School." Bibliography: p. 247-255 [BX8763.N5] 66-20782
1. Pentecostal churches. 2. Pentecostalism. I. Title.

NICHOLS, R. Eugene. 289.9
Esoteric keys to personal power / by R. Eugene Nichols. Lakemont, Ga. : CSA Press, c1977. 141 p. ; 21 cm. Includes bibliographical references. [BL624.N5] 76-56593 ISBN 0-87707-186-1 : 2.95
1. Spiritual life. 2. New Thought. I. Title.

NOYES, George 289.9 B
Wallingford, ed.
Religious experience of John Humphrey Noyes, founder of the Oneida Community. Freeport, N.Y., Books for Libraries Press [1971] xiii, 416 p. illus., ports. 23 cm. Reprint of the 1923 ed. [BX8795.P4N8 1971] 72-152998 ISBN 0-8369-5750-4
1. Noyes, John Humphrey, 1811-1886.

O'CONNOR, Elizabeth. 289.9
Call to commitment; the story of the Church of the Saviour, Washington, D.C. [1st ed.] New York, Harper & Row [1963] 205 p. illus. 22 cm. [BX9999.W3C5] 63-10963
1. Washington, D.C. Church of the Saviour. I. Title.

O'CONNOR, Elizabeth. 289.9
Call to commitment; the story of the Church of the Saviour, Washington, D.C. New York, San Francisco, Harper and Row [1975 c1963] xiv, 205 p. 20 cm. Includes bubliographical references. [BX9999.W3C5] ISBN 0-06-066329-4 2.95 (pbk.)
1. Washington, D.C.—Church of the Saviour. I. Title.
L.C. card no. for original edition: 63-10963.

O'CONNOR, Elizabeth. 289.9
Journey inward, journey outward. [1st ed.] New York, Harper & Row [1968] x, 175 p. illus. 22 cm. [BX9999.W3C52] 68-11728
1. Washington, D.C. Church of the Saviour. I. Title.

O'CONNOR, Elizabeth. 289.9
Journey inward, journey outward / Elizabeth O'Connor. New York : Harper & Row, 1975, c1968. x, 175 p., [2] leaves of plates : ill. ; 21 cm. Includes bibliographical references. [BX9999.W3C52 1975] 75-310905 ISBN 0-06-066332-4 pbk. : 3.95
1. Washington, D.C. Church of the Saviour. I. Title.

OWENS, Claire Myers. 289.9
Discovery of the self. Introd. by Anthony Sutich. Boston, Christopher Pub. House [c1963] 334 p. 21 cm. [CT275.O87A33] 63-22782
I. Title.

OWENS, Claire Myers. 289.9
Discovery of the self. Introd. by Anthony Sutich. Boston, Christopher Pub. [c.1963] 334p. 21cm. 63-22782 3.95
I. Title.

PALMER, Alma Kennedy. 289.9
The beautiful eternal now. Boston, Christopher Pub. House [1963] 61 p. 21 cm. [BF639.P12] 63-11505
1. New Thought. I. Title.

PALMER, Alma Kennedy. 289.9
The beautiful eternal now. Boston, Christopher [c.1963] 61p. 21cm. 63-11505 2.00
1. New Thought. I. Title.

PALMER, Bernard Alvin, 289.9
1914-
Peoples : church on the go / Bernard Palmer. Wheaton, Ill. : Victor Books, c1976. 111 p. : ill. ; 21 cm. [BX9999.T666P34] 76-18626 ISBN 0-88207-656-6 pbk. : 2.50
1. Toronto. Peoples Church. I. Title.

PALMER, Donald C. 289.9
Explosion of people evangelism, by Donald C. Palmer. Chicago, Moody Press [1974] 191 p. illus. 22 cm. Bibliography: p. 186-191. [BX8762.Z7C646] 73-15087 ISBN 0-8024-2413-9 2.95 (pbk.)
1. Pentecostal churches—Colombia. 2. Church growth. I. Title.

PATTERSON, William Archie, 289.9
1898-
From the pen of Bishop W. A. Patterson. 1st ed. Memphis, Deakins Typesetting Service [1970] xx, 122 p. facsim., ports. 23 cm. [BX7056.P35] 71-141820
1. Church of God in Christ—Doctrinal and controversial works. I. Title.

PELTON, Robert W., 1934- 289.9
Snake handlers: God-fearers? Or, fanatics? [By] Robert W. Pelton and Karen W. Carden.

Nashville, T. Nelson [1974] 110, [49] p. illus. 21 cm. [BX7990.H6P38] 74-3046 2.95 (pbk)
1. Snake cults (Holiness churches) I. Carden, Karen W., joint author. II. Title.

PENTON, M. James, 1932- 289.9
Jehovah's Witnesses in Canada : champions of freedom of speech and worship / M. James Penton. Toronto : Macmillan of Canada, c1976. xi, 388 p. ; 24 cm. Includes index. Bibliography: p. [370]-373. [BX8525.8.C2P46] 77-356230 ISBN 0-7705-1340-9
1. Jehovah's Witnesses—Canada. 2. Religious liberty—Canada. I. Title.

**PERSPECTIVES on the new* 289.9
Pentecostalism / Russell P. Spittler, Editor. Grand Rapids : Baker Book House, c1976. 268p. ; 23 cm. Includes bibliographical references. [BX8762] ISBN 0-8010-8076-2 : 7.95
1. Pentecostal churches. I. Spittler, Russell P., ed.

PIKE, Edgar Royston, 1896- 289.9
Jehovah's Witnesses: who they are, what they teach, what they do. New York, Philosophical Library [1954] 140p. 20cm. [BX8526] 54-4399
1. Jehovah's Witnesses. I. Title.

POPOFF, Eli Alex, 1921- 289.9
An historical exposition on the origin and evolvement of the basic tenets of the Doukhobor life-conception, by Eli A. Popoff. [Grand Forks, B.C.? 1966] 58 p. 22 cm. Cover title: Historical exposition on Doukhobor beliefs. [BX7433.P67] 68-92665 1.00 Can.
1. Dukhobors. I. Title. II. Title: Historical exposition on Doukhobor beliefs.

POPOFF, Haralan, 1907- 289.9
I was a Communist prisoner. Grand Rapids, Mich., Zondervan [c.1966] 287p. illus.,maps, ports. 23cm. [BX8764.Z8P6] 66-13695 4.95 bds.,
I. Title.

POPOFF, Haralan, 1907- 289.9 B
Tortured for his faith; an epic of Christian courage and heroism in our day, by Haralan Popov. Grand Rapids, Zondervan Pub. House [1970] 156 p. 18 cm. [BR1608.B8P6] 77-102834 0.75
1. Persecution—Bulgaria. 2. Prisoners—Bulgaria—Personal narratives. I. Title.

POPOFF, Haralan, 1907- 289.9 B
Tortured for his faith : an epic of Christian courage and heroism in our day / by Haralan Popov. Rev. ed. Grand Rapids, Mich. : Zondervan Pub. House, 1975. 140 p. ; 18 cm. [BX8764.Z8P62 1975] 76-360631 1.50
1. Popoff, Haralan, 1907- 2. Persecution—Bulgaria. 3. Prisoners—Bulgaria—Personal narratives. I. Title.

PRICE, Ernest Bruce, 1932- 289.9
God's channel of truth, is it the Watchtower? By E. B. Price. Mountain View, Calif., Pacific Press Pub. Association [c1967] 112 p. illus. 19 cm. [BX6154.P68] 67-30889
1. Seventh-Day Adventists—Doctrinal and controversial works. 2. Jehovah's Witnesses—Doctrinal and controversial works. I. Title.

RAMSEY, Arthur Michael, 289.9
Abp. of Canterbury, 1904-
The charismatic Christ, by Michael Ramsey, Robert E. Terwilliger [and] A. M. Allchin. New York, Morehouse-Barlow Co. [1973] 108 p. 19 cm. Addresses and sermons presented at the 3d national conference of Trinity Institute in January 1972. Includes bibliographical references. [BT202.R33] 73-160621 ISBN 0-8192-1141-9 2.50
1. Jesus Christ—Person and offices—Addresses, essays, lectures. 2. Holy Spirit—Addresses, essays, lectures. I. Terwilliger, Robert E. II. Allchin, A. M. III. Trinity Institute. IV. Title.

RASNAKE, J. Samuel, 1932- 289.9
Pentecost fully come: a history of the Appalachian District of the Assemblies of God [by] J. Samuel Rasnake. Bristol, Tenn., Westhighlands Church [1971] viii, 156 p. illus., ports. 23 cm. Includes bibliographical references. [BX6198.A7R38] 70-26302 5.95
1. Assemblies of God, General Council. Appalachian District. I. Title.

RASNAKE, J. Samuel, 1932- 289.9
Stones by the river : a history of the Tennessee District of the Assemblies of God / J. Samuel Rasnake. Bristol, Tenn. : Westhighlands Church, [1975] vi, 195 p., [6] leaves of plates : ill. ; 23 cm. Includes bibliographical references and index. [BX6198.A7R39] 75-308771 6.95
1. Assemblies of God, General Council. Tennessee District. I. Title.

RAYMOND, Walter W. 289.9
Thoughts of a spiritual vagabond, by Walter W. Raymond. Dallas, Book Craft, 1969. 120 p. 22 cm. [BF639.R3315] 79-7541 4.95
1. New Thought. I. Title.

REMINISCENCES: talks with 289.9
the master; a book for those who wish to get acquainted with Beinsa Douno, the master sent to promote brotherhood. Written by M. P., a pupil. Translated from the original. [Los Angeles, Sunrise Press & Books, 1968] 85 p. 21 cm. [BF648.D8R4] 70-4005
1. Dunov, Petur. I. P., M. II. P. M.

ROGERS, Philip George 289.9
The sixth trumpeter; the story of Jezreel and his tower. London, New York, Oxford [c.] 1963. 154p. illus. 23cm. 63-2166 6.00
1. Jezreel, James Jershom, 1840-1885. I. Title.

ROSARY Band (The) 289.9
Seven steps to heaven. New York, Vantage Press [c.1960] 138p. 2.95
I. Title.

ROWLAND, May. 289.9
The magic of the word. Unity Village, Mo., Unity Books [1972] 182 p. 20 cm. [BX9890.U5R68] 73-180756 ISBN 0-87159-095-6
1. Unity School of Christianity. I. Title.

SAVOY, Gene. 289.9
The prophecies of Jamil / by Gene Savoy. Reno, Nev. : International Community of Christ, c1976- v. ; 29 cm. (The Sacred teaching of light ; codex 4, v. 1) Contents.Contents.—[book 1] First prophecy to the Americas.—book 2. Second prophecy to the Americans. [BP605.I45S3] 76-12710
1. International Community of Christ. I. Title. II. Series.

SAVOY, Gene. 289.9
Symposium VII, vision analysis / by Gene Savoy. Reno, Nev. : International Community of Chirst, c1977. 41 p. ; 29 cm. [BP605.I45S33] 78-100691
1. Internationl Community of Christ. I. International Community of Chirst. II. Title.

SCHNELL, William J., 1905- 289.9
Christians: awake! . . . Restoring the art of Witnessing, evangelizing and soul-winning. Grand Rapids, Mich., Baker Bk., 1962[c.1961] 157p. 19cm. 62-3985 1.50 pap.,
1. Jehovah's Witnesses—Doctrinal and controversial works. 2. Evangelistic work. I. Title.

SCHNELL, William J., 1905- 289.9
Thirty years a Watch Tower slave; the confessions of a converted Jehovah's Witness. Grand Rapids, Baker Book House, 1956. 207 p. illus. 23 cm. [BX8526.S35] 56-13037
1. Watch Tower Bible and Tract Society. 2. Jehovah's Witnesses—Doctrinal and controversial works. I. Title.

SEDER, A. R., Mrs. 289.9
Index to the subjects of obituaries (Sterbfalle, Todesanzeigen) abstracted from Der Christliche Botschafter of the Evangelical Church, 1836-1866. Compiler: Mrs. A. R. Seder. [Naperville? Ill., 1967] iv, 295 p. 27 cm. Cover title. [BX7541.S4] 68-5168
1. Evangelical Association of North America—Biography. 2. Obituaries—Indexes. I. Der Christliche Botschafter. II. Title.

SHAKARIAN, Demos, 1913- 289.9 B
The happiest people on earth : the long-awaited personal story of Demos Shakarian / as told to John and Elizabeth Sherrill. Old Tappan, N.J. : Chosen Books : distributed by F. H. Revell Co., c1975. 187 p. ; 22 cm. [BX8764.Z8S474] 75-33902 ISBN 0-912376-14-7 : 6.95
1. Shakarian, Demos, 1913- 2. Full Gospel Business Men's Fellowship International. I. Sherrill, John. II. Sherrill, Elizabeth. III. Title.

SHAW, Plato Ernest, 1883- 289.9
1947.
The Catholic Apostolic Church, sometimes called Irvingite; a historical study. Freeport, N.Y., Books for Libraries Press [1972, c1946] viii, 264 p. illus. 24 cm. (Biography index reprint series) Bibliography: p. 258-260. [BX6571.S47 1972] 75-38332 ISBN 0-8369-8129-4
1. Catholic Apostolic Church.

SHERMAN, Harold Morrow, 289.9
1898-
How to solve mysteries of your mind and soul; a way to find a philosophy of life that meets the needs of today and tomorrow [by] Harold Sherman. Los Angeles. DeVorss [1965] 212 p. 24 cm. [BF639.S549] 65-18958
1. New Thought. I. Title.

SHERRILL, John L. 289.9
They speak with other tongues, by John L. Sherrill. [1st ed.] New York, McGraw Hill [1964] vii, 165 p. 21 cm. Bibliography: p. 163-165. [BX8763.S5] 64-25003
1. Pentecostal churches. 2. Glossolalia. I. Title.

SIKKING, Robert P. 289.9
Light for our age / by Robert P. Sikking. Unity Village, Mo. : Unity Books, c1976. 124 p. ; 20 cm. [BX9890.U5S53] 76-366864 3.95
1. Unity School of Christianity—Doctrinal and controversial works. I. Title.

SIKKING, Sue. 289.9
Seed of the new age. [1st ed.] Garden City, N.Y., Doubleday, 1970. 117 p. 22 cm. [BX9890.U5S54] 79-99216 3.95
1. Unity School of Christianity. I. Title.

SINKLER, Lorraine. 289.9 B
The spiritual journey of Joel S. Goldsmith, modern mystic. [1st ed.] New York, Harper & Row [1973] xii, 194 p. 22 cm. Includes bibliographical references. [BF648.G64S57 1973] 72-13190 ISBN 0-06-067386-9 5.95
1. Goldsmith, Joel S., 1892-1964. 2. New Thought. I. Title.

SKARIN, Annalee. 289.9
The temple of God. Los Angeles, De Vorss [1958] 224 p. 22 cm. [BF639.S62] 59-24411
1. New thought I. Title.

SMITH, Chuck, 1927- 289.9
The reproducers; new life for thousands [by] Chuck Smith with Hugh Steven. Glendale, Calif., G/L Regal Books [1972] 146 p. illus. 20 cm. [BV4447.S58] 72-77115 ISBN 0-8307-0159-1 1.95
1. Smith, Chuck, 1927- 2. Costa Mesa, Calif. Calvary Chapel. 3. Church work with youth—Costa Mesa, Calif. I. Steven, Hugh. II. Title.

SMITH, John W. V., 1914- 289.9
A brief history of the Church of God reformation movement / by John W. V. Smith. Rev. ed. Anderson, Ind. : Warner Press, c1976. 157 p. ; 21 cm. Previous ed. published under title: Truth marches on. [BX7025.S55 1976] 76-363569 ISBN 0-87162-188-6
1. Church of God (Anderson, Ind.)—History. I. Title.

SMITH, Timothy Lawrence, 289.9
1924-
Called unto holiness; the story of the Nazarenes: the formative years. Kansas City, Mo., Nazarene Pub. House [1962] 413 p. 23 cm. Includes bibliography. [BX8699.N33S4] 62-11409
1. Church of the Nazarene — Hist. I. Title.

SMITH, Timothy Lawrence, 289.9
1924-
Called unto holiness; the story of the Nazarenes: the formative years. Kansas City, Mo., Nazarene Pub. House [dist.] Beacon Hill Pr. [c.1962] 413p. 23cm. 62-11409 4.95
1. Church of the Nazarene—Hist. I. Title.

SONTAG, Frederick. 289.9 B
Sun Myung Moon and the Unification Church / Frederick Sontag. Nashville, Tenn. : Abingdon Press, c1977. 224 p. : ill. ; 23 cm. Bibliography: p. 217-224. [BX9750.S4S66] 77-9075 ISBN 0-687-40622-6 : 8.95
1. Segye Kidokkyo T'ongil Sillyong Hyophoe. 2. Moon, Sun Myung. I. Title.

STEELE, Robert V. P. 289.9 B
Storming heaven; the lives and turmoils of Minnie Kennedy and Aimee Semple McPherson [by] Lately Thomas. New York, Morrow, 1970. 364 p. illus. 25 cm. Includes bibliographical references. [BX7990.I68M33] 74-118057 10.00
1. McPherson, Aimee Semple, 1890-1944. 2. Kennedy, Minnie, 1871-1947. I. Title.

STEELE, Robert V P 289.9
The vanishing evangelist; the Aimee Semple McPherson kidnaping affair, by Lately Thomas. New York, Viking Press, 1959. xiv, 334 p. illus., ports. 23 cm. [BX7990.I 68M35] 59-8351
1. McPherson, Aimee Semple, 1890-1944. I. Title.

STERLING, Chandler W., 289.9
Bp., 1911-
The Witnesses : one God, one victory / Chandler W. Sterling. Chicago : Regnery, [1975] x, 198 p. ; 22 cm. [BX8526.S73 1975] 74-26874 ISBN 0-8092-8368-9 : 8.95
1. Jehovah's Witnesses. I. Title.

STERNER, R. Eugene 289.9
We reach our hands in fellowship; an introduction to the Church of God. Anderson, Ind., Warner Press [dist. Gospel Trumpet Press, c.1960] 64p. 19cm. 60-10187 pap., apply, plastic binding
1. Church of God (Anderson, Ind.)—Doctrinal and controversial works. I. Title.

STEVENSON, William Charles, 289.9
1936-
The inside story of Jehovah's Witnesses [by] W. C. Stevenson. [1st American ed.] New York, Hart Pub. Co. [1968, c1967] 211 p. 21 cm. First published under title: Year of doom, 1975. Bibliography: p. [210]-211. [BX8526.S76 1968] 68-29531 5.95
1. Jehovah's Witnesses—Doctrinal and controversial works. I. Title.

STILSON, Max 289.9
How to deal with Jehovah's witnesses. Grand Rapids, Mich., Zondervan [1964, c.1962] 61p. 21cm. Bibl. 63-5948 .60 pap.,
1. Jehovah's Witnesses—Doctrinal and controversial works. I. Title.

STOLEE, Haakon Jacobs, 289.9
1882-
Speaking in tongues. Minneapolis, Augsburg Pub. House [1963] 142 p. 20 cm. First published in 1936 under title: Pentercostalism. [BL54.S7] 63-16604
1. Glossolalia. 2. Pentecostal churches — Hist. I. Title.

STOLEE, Haakon Jacobs, 289.9
1882-
Speaking in tongues. Minneapolis, Augsburg [c.1963] 142p. First pub. in 1936 under title: Pentecostalism. 63-16604 1.95 pap.,
1. Glossolalia. 2. Pentecostal churches—Hist. I. Title.

STROUP, Herbert Hewitt, 289.9
1916-
The Jehovah's Witnesses. New York, Russell & Russell [1967, c.1945] vii, 180p. 22cm. Bibl. [BX8525.7.S8 1967] 66-27157 7.50
1. Jehovah's Witnesses—Hist. I. Title.

STROUP, Herbert Hewitt, 289.9
1916-
The Jehovah's Witnesses. New York, Russell & Russell [1967, c1945] vii, 180 p. 22 cm. Bibliography: p. [169]-173. [BX8525.7.S8] 66-27157
1. Jehovah's Witnesses — Hist. I. Title.

SUNDKLER, Bengt Gustaf 289.9
Malcolm, 1909-
Zulu Zion and some Swazi Zionists / Bengt Sundkler. London ; New York : Oxford University Press, 1976. 337 p., [6] leaves of plates : ill. ; 22 cm. (Oxford studies in African affairs) Includes index. Bibliography: p. 329-332. [BR1450.S9] 76-378094 ISBN 0-19-822707-8 : 17.50
1. Zionist churches (Africa)—South Africa. 2. Sects—South Africa. 3. Pentecostal churches—South Africa. I. Title. II. Series.

SWALM, E. J., 1897- 289.9 B
"My beloved brethren ...": personal memoirs and recollections of the Canadian Brethren in Christ Church, by E. J. Swalm. Nappanee, Ind., Evangel Press [1969] 156 p. illus. 21 cm. [BX9675.Z8S9] 73-172782
1. Swalm, E. J., 1897- 2. Brethren in Christ—Canada. I. Title.

SYNAN, Vinson. 289.9
The Holiness-Pentecostal movement in the United States. Grand Rapids, Mich., Eerdmans [1971] 248 p. 23 cm. Bibliography: p. 225-239. [BX8763.S96] 79-162033 5.95
1. Pentecostalism. I. Title.

TANEYHILL, Richard Henry, 289.9
1822-1898
The Leatherwood god. 1869-70 a source ofWilliam Dean Howells's novel of the same name, in two versions. Facsimile reporductions with an introd. by George Kummer. Gainesville, Fla., Scholars' Facsimiles 1966. xvi, 86p. 23cm. Reproduced from copies in Western Reserve Hist. Soc. [F499.S16T16 1870a] 66-11025 5.00
1. Dylks, Joseph C. 2. Dylksites. 3. Salesville, O.—Hist. I. Title.
Contents omitted.

THOMPSON, Roy A. 289.9
Toward new horizons [by] Roy A. Thompson. Minneapolis, Free Church Publications [1969] 142 p. port. 21 cm. "Developments in the Evangelical Free Church of America in the decade following the Diamond Jubilee, 1959-1969." [BX7548.A4T45] 73-86579
1. Evangelical Free Church of America—History. I. Title.

THURMAN, Howard, 1899- 289.9
Footprints of a dream; the story of the Church for the Fellowship of All Peoples. New York, Harper [1959] 157 p. illus. 20 cm. [BN9999.S3C5] 59-11412
1. San Francisco. Church for the Fellowship of All Peoples. I. Title.

THURSTON, Mark A. 289.9
Experiments in a search for God : the Edgar Cayce path of application / Mark A. Thurston. Virginia Beach, Va. : A.R.E. Press, c1976. vi,

139 p. : ill. ; 22 cm. Bibliography: p. 139. [BX9999.V5T48] 76-373076 ISBN 0-87604-090-3 pbk. : 2.95
1. Association for Research and Enlightenment, Virginia Beach, Va. A search for God. 2. Cayce, Edgar, 1877-1945. 3. Psychical research. I. Title.

TODD, James J 289.9
Heal thyself through Christ-Messiah. New York, Institute of Healing Metaphysics [1958] 192 p. 20 cm. [BX9998.T6] 58-27493
I. Title.

THE Truth and facts of the 289.9
United House of Prayer for All People and the most honorable Bishop W. McCollough, leader. [1st ed. Washington, 1968] viii, 100 p. illus., ports. 23 cm. [BX9998.M27T7] 74-1351
1. McCollough, W., 1915- 2. United House of Prayer for All People.

TURNER, Harold W. 289.9
History of an African independent Church, by H. W. Turner. Oxford, Clarendon Pr., 1967. 2 v. plates. (incl. ports.). maps, tables, diagrs. 23cm. Vol. 2 has title: Africa independent Church. Contents.v. 1. The Church of the Lord (Aladura).--v. 2. The life and faith of the Church of the Lord (Aladura). Bibl. [BX7068.5.N5T8] 67-112230 7.30 v.1,; 11.20 v.2,
1. Church of the Lord (Aladura) 2. Nigeria—Church history. I. Title. II. Title: African independent Church.
Available from Oxford Univ. Pr., New York.

THE Unification Church ; as 289.9
others see us / [edited by W. Farley Jones]. [Washington] : Holy Spirit Association for the Unification of World Christianity, 1974. vii, 156 p. : ill. ; 28 cm. Letters received by the Holy Spirit Association for the Unification of World Christianity. [BP605.S25U53] 74-17902
1. Segye Kidokkyo T'ongil Sillyong Hyophoe. 2. Moon, Sun Myung. I. Jones, William Farley, 1943- comp. II. Segye Kidokkyo T'ongil Sillyong Hyophoe. III. Title: As others see us.

•VAN NUYS, Roscoe Golden. 289.9
Yesterday, today, and tomorrow. New York, Vantage [1968] 140p. 20 cm. 3.50
I. Title.

WAGNER, C. Peter. 289.9
Look out! The Pentecostals are coming [by] C. Peter Wagner. [1st ed.] Carol Stream, Ill., Creation House [1973] 196 p. 22 cm. Bibliography: p. 183-186. [BX8762.Z7L38] 73-77528 ISBN 0-88419-040-4 4.95
1. Pentecostal churches—Latin America. I. Title.

WAKEFORD, Oneta. 289.9
Change your thoughts and alter your life. Minneapolis, Denison [1960] 166 p. 22 cm. [BF639.W15] 60-14933
1. New Thought. I. Title.

WAKEFORD, Oneta 289.9
Change your thoughts and alter your life. Minneapoils, Denison [c.1960] 166p. 22cm. (Bibl. footnotes) 60-14933 3.50
1. New Thought. I. Title.

WALTER, Paul H 289.9
A small voice crying in the wilderness. Los Angeles, Great Western Book Pub. Co., 1962. 160 p. 23 cm. [BX8526.W22] 63-2732
1. Jehovah's Witnesses — Doctrinal and controversial works. I. Title.

WARD, Hiley H. 289.9 B
Prophet of the black nation [by] Hiley H. Ward. Philadelphia, Pilgrim Press [1969] xviii, 222 p. 22 cm. Bibliographical references included in "Notes" (p. 213-222) [BX9886.Z8C57] 71-94451 5.95
1. Cleage, Albert B. I. Title.

WATCH Tower Bible and Tract 289.9
Society
Babylon the Great has fallen! God's Kingdom rules [New York, Author, c.1963] 703p. illus., col. maps (lining papers) 19cm. 63-5913 .75
1. Jehovah's Witnesses—Doctrinal and controversial works. I. Title.

WATCH Tower Bible and Tract 289.9
Society.
Jehovah's Witnesses in the divine purpose. [1st ed.] New York, 1959] 311 p. illus. 24 cm. [BX8526.W25] 59-40392
1. Jehovah's Witnesses. I. Title.

WATCH Tower Bible and Tract 289.9
Society of Pennsylvania.
Life everlasting in freedom of the sons of God [1st ed. New York, Watchtower Bible and Tract Society of New York, 1966] 410 p. illus., maps (on lining paper) 19 cm. [BX8526.W364] 66-8655
1. Jehovah's Witness — Doctrinal and controversial works. I. Title.

WATCH Tower Bible and Tract 289.9
Society of Pennsylvania.
The truth that leads to eternal life. [1st ed. New York, Watch Tower Bible and Tract Society of New York, 1968] 190 p. illus. (part col.) 17 cm. On spine: Truth. [BX8526.W322] 68-5502
1. Jehovah's Witnesses—Doctrinal and controversial works. I. Title.

WATCH TOWER BIBLE AND TRACT 289.9
SOCIETY.
What has religion done for mankind? 1st ed. Brooklyn, 1951 350 p. illus. 19 cm. [BX8526.W33] 51-35356
1. Jehovah's Witnesses — Doctrinal and controversial works. I. Title.

WEAD, Doug. 289.9 B
The C. M. Ward story, with Doug Wead. Harrison, Ark. : New Leaf Press, c1976. 255 p. ; 23 cm. Includes index. [BX6198.A78W43] 76-22267 ISBN 0-89221-022-2 : 5.95
1. Ward, C. M. 2. Assemblies of God, General Council—Clergy—Biography. 3. Clergy—United States—Biography. I. Ward, C. M. II. Title.

WHALEN, William Joseph. 289.9
Armageddon around the corner; a report on Jehovah's Witnesses. New York, J. Day Co. [1962] 249 p. illus. 21 cm. Includes bibliography. [BX8526.W47] 62-10958
1. Jehovah's Witnesses. I. Title.

WHALEN, William Joseph 289.9
Armageddon around the corner; a report on Jehovah's Witnesses. New York, John Day [c.1962] 249p. illus. 21cm. Bibl. 62-10958 4.75
1. Jehovah's Witnesses. I. Title.

WHITE, Timothy. 289.9
A people for His name; a history of Jehovah's Witnesses and an evaluation. [1st ed.] New York, Vantage Press [1968] 418 p. 21 cm. Includes bibliographical references. [BX8525.7.W47] 68-2944
1. Jehovah's Witnesses—History. I. Title.

WILSON, Robert S., 1907- 289.9
History of the Evangelical Congregational Church / by Robert S. Wilson. Myerstown, Pa. : Wilson, 1976. vi, 77 p. : ill. ; 23 cm. A revision of the author's Brief history of the Evangelical Congregational Church. Includes index. [BX7545.E8W54 1976] 76-16339
1. Evangelical Congregational Church—History. I. Title.

WINEHOUSE, Irwin. 289.9
The Assemblies of God, a popular survey. With an introd. by J. Roswell Flower. [1st ed.] New York, Vantage Press [1959] 224 p. illus. 21 cm. [BX6198.A7W5] 59-11875
1. Assemblies of God, General Council. I. Title.

WOLFRAM, Gertrude (Metlen) 289.9
1888-
The widow of Zarephath, a church in the making. Zarephath, N.J., Pillar of Fire, 1954. 244p. illus. 24cm. [BX8795.P5W74] 55-16559
1. Pillar of Fire Church—Hist. I. Title.

WOMACK, David A. 289.9
The wellsprings of the Pentecostal movement, by David A. Womack. Written in cooperation with the Committee on Advance for the General Council of the Assemblies of God. Springfield, Mo., Gospel Pub. House [1968] 96 p. 21 cm. Bibliographical footnotes. [BX8763.W65] 68-7288
1. Pentecostal churches. 2. Church. I. Assemblies of God, General Council. Committee on Advance. II. Title.

WOOD, William W. 289.9
Culture and personality aspects of the Pentecostal Holiness religion. The Hague, Mouton, [New York, Humanities, 1966, c.1965] 125p. illus., maps. 24cm. Bibl. [BX8764.W6] 66-518 7.75
1. Pentecostal churches. 2. Psychology, Religious. I. Title.

WOODCOCK, George, 1912- 289.9
The doukhobors [by] George Woodcock and Ivan Avakumovic. Toronto, New York, Oxford University Press, 1968. 382 p. illus. 24 cm. Bibliography: p. [370]-375. [BX7433.W6] 79-351156 7.50 Can.
1. Dukhobors. I. Avakumovic, Ivan, joint author. II. Title.

WUST, Klaus German, 1925- 289.9 B
The saint-adventurers of the Virginia frontier : southern outposts of Ephrata / Klaus Wust. Edinburg, Va. : Shenandoah History Publishers, 1977. 125 p. : ill. ; 22 cm. "An exacted relation on the appearance of a disembodied spirit: translation of the Relation of 1761": p. 87-101. Includes index. Bibliography: p. 104-120. [BX9680.S3W87] 76-48566 ISBN 0-917968-04-2 : 8.00
1. Eckerlin, Samuel, 1703-1781. 2. Eskerlin, Israel, b. 1710 or 11. 3. Eckerlin, Gabriel. 4. Sabbatarians—Biography. 5. Sabbatarians—Virginia. 6. Ephrata Community. I. Abgeforderte Relation der Erscheinung eines entleibten Geists. English. 1977. II. Title.

YAMAMOTO, J. Isamu. 289.9
The puppet master : an inquiry into Sun Myung Moon and the Unification Church / J. Isamu Yamamoto. Downers Grove, Ill. : InterVarsity Press, c1977. 136 p. ; 21 cm. Includes bibliographical references. [BX9750.S4Y36] 76-55622 ISBN 0-87784-740-1 pbk. : 3.95
1. Segye Kidokkyo T'ongil Sillyong Hyophoe—Doctrinal and controversial works. 2. Moon, Sun Myung.

YOUNG, Pauline (Vislick), 289.9
1896-
The pilgrims of Russian-town. The community of spiritual Christian jumpers in America, by Pauline V. Young, with an introd. by Robert E. Park. New York, Russell & Russell [1967] 296p. port. 22cm. (Univ. of Chicago sociological ser.) The struggle of a primitive religious society to maintain itself in an urban environment. Text in English. First pub. in 1932. Bibl. [BX8530.M6Y6 1967] 66-27375 9.00
1. Molokans. I. Title.

THORWALL, LaReau. 289.9'0924 B
And light new fires; the story of Axel Johnson Thorwall, an immigrant blacksmith who exchanged his forge for a frock coat, by LaReau Thorwall as told to Mel Larson. Foreword by John B. Anderson. Minneapolis, Free Church Publications [1969] 186 p. illus. 22 cm. [BX7548.Z8T48] 70-103414 4.95
1. Thorwall, Axel Johnson, 1890-1960. I. Larson, Melvin Gunnard, 1916- II. Title.

KENT, Homer A 289.92
250 years conquering frontiers; a history of the Brethren Church. Winona Lake, Ind., Brethren Missionary Herald Co. [1958] 233p. illus. 23cm. [BX7829.N33K4] 286.5 58-38245
1. National Fellowship of Brethren Churches—Hist. I. Title.

MILLER, John Ezra, 1865- 289.92
1947.
The story of our church. Rev. and enl. ed. Elgin, Ill., Brethren Pub. House [1957] 214p. illus. 20cm. [BX7815.M5 1957] 286.5 57-58547
1. Church of the Brethren—Hist. I. Title.

PLEASANT Hill. 289.92
Elgin, Ill., Brethren Pub. House c[1956] 259p. illus. 21cm. [BX7831.P56W4] 286.5 57-20881
1. Pleasant Hill Church of the Brethren, Macoupin Co., Ill. I. Weddle, Ethel Harshbarger.

SHULTZ, Lawrence W 289.92
Schwarzenau yesterday and today, where the Brethren began in Europe. Told in picture and storyt Milford, Ind. [1954] 111p. illus. 22cm. [BX7819.G4S4] [BX7819.G4S4] 286.5 54-28242 54-28242
1. Schwarzenau, Ger. 2. Church of the Brethreu—Hist. I. Title.

WEDDLE, Ethel •289.92
Harshbarger.
Pleasant Hill. Elgin, Ill., Brethren Pub. House [c1956] 250 p. illus. 21 cm. [BX7831.P56W4] 286.5 57-20881
1. Pleasant Hill Church of the Brethren, Macoupia Co., Ill. I. Title.

290 OTHER RELIGIONS & COMPARATIVE

ADAMS, William Henry 290
Davenport, 1828-1891.
Curiosities of superstition, and sketches of some unrevealed religions. London, J. Masters, 1882. Detroit, Singing Tree Press, 1971. 328 p. 22 cm. Includes bibliographical references. [BL85.A3 1971] 76-155434
1. Religions. 2. Superstition. 3. Folk-lore. I. Title.

AFNAN. RUHI, Effendi. 290
The great prophets: Moses, Zoroaster, Jesus. New York, Philosophical Library [1960] 457p. 22cm. [BL85.A4] 60-16205
1. Religions. 2. Civilization—Hist. I. Title.

AFNAN, Ruhi, effendi 290
The great prophets: Moses, Zoroaster, Jesus. New York, Philosophical Library [c.1960] 457p. 22cm. 60-16205 5.00
1. Religions. 2. Civilization—Hist. I. Title.

ALLEN, Edgar Leonard 290
Christianity among the religions. Boston, Beacon Press [1961, c.1960] 159p. (LR 9) 1.45 pap.,
1. Christianity and other religions. I. Title.

ALLEN, Edgar Leonard 290
Christianity among the religious. London, G. Allen & Unwin [dist. Mystic, Conn.,] Verry, 1964, c.1960 159p. 23cm. Bibl. 60-3325 4.00
1. Christianity and other religions. I. Title.

ANDERSEN, William Niclaus. 290
What is new and old in religion; a book for the rationally minded. Philadelphia, Dorrance [1957] 168p. 20cm. [BL80.A63] 57-8484
1. Religions. I. Title.

ANDERSON, James Norman 290
Dalrymple, ed.
The world's religions. [2d ed.] Grand Rapids, Eerdmans [1953] 208p. 23cm. Bibliography (p. 197-203) [BL80] 54-1600
1. Religions. I. Title.
Contents omitted.

ANSLEY, Delight. 290
The good ways. New rev. ed. Decorations by Robert Hallock. New York, Crowell [c1959] 214p. illus. 21cm. [BL82.A5 1959] 59-14674
1. Religions. I. Title.

ANSLEY, Delight. 290
The good ways. Decorations by Robert Hallock. New York, Crowell [1950] ix, 214 p. illus. 21 cm. Bibliography: p. 211. [BL82.A5] 50-13198
1. Religions. I. Title.

ARCHER, John Clark, 1881- 290
Faiths men live by. Rev. by Carl E. Purinton. 2d ed. New York, Ronald Press [1958] 553p. 22cm. Includes bibliography. [BL80.A7 1958] 58-7375
1. Religions. I. Title.

ARMSTRONG, Arthur Hilary. 290
Christian faith and Greek philosophy [by] A. H. Armstrong and R. A. Markus. New York, Sheed and Ward [1964, c1960] ix, 162 p. 19 cm. Bibliographical footnotes. [BR128.G8A7 1964] 64-13564
1. Christianity and other religions—Greek. 2. Philosophy, Ancient. 3. Greece—Religion. I. Markus, Robert Austin, 1924- joint author. II. Title.

ASHBY, Philip H 290
The conflict of religions. New York, Scribner, 1955. 225p. 21cm. Includes bibliography. [BL85.A8] 55-9681
1. Religions. I. Title.

ASHBY, Philip H. 290
History and future of religious thought; Christianity, Hinduism, Buddhism, Islam. Englewood Cliffs, N.J. Prentice-Hall [1963] 171 p. 21 cm. (A Spectrum book) "S-64." [BL80.2.A8] 63-15411
1. Religions. I. Title.

ASHBY, Philip H. 290
History and future of religious thought: Christianity, Hinduism, Buddhism, Islam. Englewood Cliffs, N.J., Prentice [c.1963] 171p. 21cm. (Spectrum bks. S-64) Bibl. 63-15411 4.25; 1.95 pap.,
1. Religions. I. Title.

AYRES, Lew, 1908- 290
Altars of the East. [1st ed.] Garden City, N. Y., Doubleday, 1956. 284p. illus. 22cm. [BL1031.A9] 56-7530
1. Asia—Religion. 2. Religions. I. Title.

BACH, Marcus, 1906- 290
Had you been born in another faith; the story of religion as it is lived and loved by those who follow the path of their parental faith. Illustrated by Polly Bolian. Englewood Cliffs, N.J., Prentice-Hall [1961] 186 p. illus. 21 cm. [BL80.2.B28] 61-12979
1. Religions. I. Title.

BACH, Marcus, 1906- 290
Major religions of the world. New York, Abingdon Press [1959] 128p. 20cm. [BL80.2.B3] 59-4175
1. Religions. I. Title.

BACH, Marcus, 1906- 290
Major religions of the world. Henry M. Bullock, general editor. Nashville, Graded Press [1959] 128p. 20cm. (Basic Christian books) [BL80.2.B3 1959] 59-16799
1. Religions. I. Title.

BACH, Marcus, 1906- 290
Major religions of the world. New York, Abingdon Press [1959] 128 p. 20 cm. [BL80.2.B3] 59-41759
1. Religions. I. Title.

BADLEY, John Haden, 1865- 290
Form and spirit; a study in religion. Boston, Beacon Press [1952] 247 p. 22 cm. [BL48.B17 1952] 52-6215
1. Religion. I. Title.

BAHM, Archie J 290
The world's living religions, by Archie J. Bahm. [New York, Dell Pub. Co., 1964] 384 p. illus. 18 cm. (A Laurel original) Laurel edition 9704. Bibliography: p. [360]-369. [BL80.2.B35] 65-1136
1. Religions. I. Title.

BELL, Harold Idris, Sir 1879- 290
Cults and creeds in Graeco-Roman Egypt. New York, Philosophical Library [1953] x, 117p. 23cm. (Forwood lectures, 1952 bBibliography: p. 106-107. [BL2455.B4] 54-7929
1. Egypt—Religion—Greco-Roman period. 2. Jews in Egypt. 3. Egypt—Church history. I. Title. II. Series.

BENTWICH, Norman De Mattos 290
The religious foundations of internationalism; a study in international relations through the ages. [2d ed.] New York, Bloch Pub. Co. [1959. i.e., 1960] 303p. 23cm. (4p. bibl.) 60-685 5.00 bds.,
1. International relations—Hist. 2. Religions—Hist. 3. International cooperation 4. Religion and sociology. 5. War and religion. I. Title.

BERRY, Gerald L. 1915- 290
Religions of the world. New York, Barnes & Noble [1956] 136p. 21cm. (Everyday handbooks, 224) [BL80.B478 1956] 56-12163
1. Religions. I. Title.

BOAS, Maurits Ignatius, 1892- 290
God, Christ, and pagan. [Rev. ed. dist. New York, Humanities, 1962, c.1961] 187p. 23cm. Bibl. 61-2974 5.00
1. Cult. 2. Christianity and other religions. 3. Paganism. I. Title.

BOAS, Maurits Ignatius, M.D. 290
1892-
God, Christ, and pagan. New York, Fell [1964] 187p. 22cm. Bibl. 63-14283 5.00 bds.,
1. Cult. 2. Christianity and other religions. 3. Paganism. I. Title.

BONES, Ben Roland, 1885- 290
Ben Roland gospels. [1st ed.] New York, Pageant Press [1956] 116p. 21cm. [BL50.B65] 56-12554
1. Religion. I. Title.

BOUQUET, Alan Coates, 1884- 290
The Christian faith and non-Christian religions. [Welwyn, Herts.] J. Nisbet [1958] 430p. 23cm. (The Library of constructive theology) [BR127.B64 1958] 59-1261
1. Christianity and other religions. 2. Religions. I. Title.

BOUQUET, Alan Coates, 1884- 290
The Christian faith and non-Christian religions. New York, Harper [1959, c1958] 430 p. 22 cm. (The Library of constructive theology) Includes bibliography. [BR127.B64] 59-5152
1. Christianity and other religions. 2. Religions. I. Title.

BOUQUET, Alan Coates, 1884- 290
Comparative religion, a short outline [New, rev.] London. Cassell [New York, Barnes & Noble, 1964, c.1961] 324p. 21cm. (Belle Sauvage lib.) Bibl. 62-41983 4.50
1. Religions. I. Title.

BRADEN, Charles Samuel, 1887- 290
Jesus compared; a study of Jesus and other great founders of religions. Englewood Cliffs, N. J., Prentice-Hall, 1957. 230p. 23cm. [BR127.B67] 57-6088
1. Christinnanity and other religions. 2. Jesus Christ Biog. I. Title.

BRADEN, Charles Samuel, 1887- 290
The world's religions, a short history. Rev. Nashville, Abingdon Press [1954] 256 p. 21 cm. [BL80.B66 1954] 54-5510
1. Religions. I. Title.

BROWNE, Lewis, 1897- 290
This believing world; a simple account of the great religions of mankind, by Lewis Browne . . . with more than seventy illustrations and animated maps drawn by the author. New York, Macmillan, 1961 [c.1926, 1954] 347p. (Macmillan paperback, 83) 1.75
1. Religions. I. Title.

BULFINCH, Thomas, 1796-1867. 290
The age of fable; or, Stories of gods and heroes. Introductory essay by Dudley Fitts. Illustrated by Joe Mugnaini. New York, Heritage Press [1959, c1958] xix, 230p. illus. 29cm. [BL310.B82 1959] 59-16165
1. Mythology. I. Mugnaini, Joe, illus. II. Title.

BULFINCH, Thomas, 1796-1867 290
The age of fable. Garden City, N.Y., Doubleday [1961] 389p. (Dolphin bk. C132 .95 pap.,
I. Title.

BULFINCH, Thomas, 1796-1867 290
The age of fable, Introd. by Daniel B. Dodson. Greenwich, Conn., Fawcett [c.1961] 336p. (Premier bk., d144) .50 pap.,
1. Mythology. I. Title.

BULFINCH, Thomas, 1796-1867. 290
A book of myths; selections from Bulfinch's Age of fable, with illustrations by Helen Sewell. New York, Macmillan [1966, c1942] 126, [2] p. illus. (part col.) 26 cm. "Eleventh printing". [BL310.B85 1966]
1. Mythology. I. Sewell, Helen, 1896- illus. II. Title.

BULFINCH, Thomas, 1796-1867 290
Collier Mythology of Greece and Rome; v.1. New York, [1962] 380p. 18cm. (HS24) .65 pap.,
1. Mythology. I. Title.

BULFINCH, Thomas, 1796-1867. 290
Mythology, a modern abridgement, by Edmund Fuller. [New York, Dell Pub. Co., 1959] 448p. 17cm. (Laurel edition, LXIII) [BL310.B82 1959a] 59-4132
1. Mythology. 2. Chivalry. 3. Folk-lore—Europe. 4. Charlmagne (Romances, etc I. Fuller, Edmund, 1914- II. Title.

BULFINCH, Thomas, 1796-1867 290
Mythology: The age of fable, or beauties of mythology. Foreword by Palmer Bovie [New York] New Amer. Lib. [c.1962] 408p. 18cm. (Mentor classics, MP449) .60 pap.,
1. Mythology. I. Title.

BULFINCH, Thomas, 1796-1867. 290
The Trojan War, with introductory notes on the Grecian divinities. Adapted from The age of fable. [New York] Priv. print. by K. H. Volk, 1957. 54p. (on double leaves) mounted illus. 26cm. [BL310.B82 1957] 58-49556
1. Mythology, Greek. I. Title.

BULTMANN, Rudolf Karl, 1884- 290
Primitive Christianity in its contemporary setting. Translated by R. H. Fuller. New York, Meridian Books, 1956. 240 p. 18 cm. (Living age books, LA 4) Translation of Das Urchristentum im Rahmen der antiken Religionen. [BR128.A2B83] 56-9240
1. Christianity and other religions. I. Title.

BURTON, Ormond Edward, 1893- 290
A study in creative history; the interaction of the eastern and western peoples to 500 B.C., by O. E. Burton. Port Washington, N.Y., Kennikat Press [1971] 320 p. 22 cm. (Kennikat classics series) Reprint of the 1932 ed. [BL96.B8 1971] 71-105821
1. Religions—History. 2. Civilization, Ancient. 3. History, Ancient. I. Title.

BURTT, Edwin Arthur, 1892- 290
Man seeks the divine; a study in the history and comparison of religions. New York, Harper [1957] 561p. 22cm. Includes bibliography. [BL80.B8] 56-13264
1. Religions. I. Title.

BURTT, Edwin Arthur, 1892- 290
Man seeks the divine; a study in the history and comparison of religions. 2d ed. New York, Harper [c.1957, 1964] xii 514p. 22cm. Bibl. 64-12798 5.75
1. Religions. I. Title.

BURTT, Edwin Arthur, 1892- 290
Mann seeks the divine; a study in the history and comparison of religions [by] Edwin A. Burtt. 2d ed. New York, Harper & Row [1964] xii, 514 p. 22 cm. Bibliography: p. 495-498. [BL80.2.B8] 64-12798
1. Religions. I. Title.

CATHOLIC Students' Mission 290
Crusade, U S A
Perspective in religion and culture; a symposium on some leading systems of thought current in the 20th century [by] Paul Dent [and others] and quoting the American bishops pastoral on secularism. Symposium editor, J. Paul Spaeth. Cincinnati, Published for Catholic Students' Mission Crusade, U. S. A. [by] Paladin Press [1957] 1v. (various pagings) 26cm. Includes bibliography. [BL87.C3 1957] 58-33654
1. Catholic Church—Apologetic works. 2. Religions. I. Spaeth, J. Paul, ed. II. Title.

CHESTERTON, Gilbert Keith, 290
1874-1936.
The everlasting man. Garden City, N. Y., Image Books [1955, c1925] 274p. 19cm. (A Doubleday image book, D18) [BL48.C5 1955] 55-14903
1. Religion. 2. Christianity and other religions. 3. Catholic Church—Apologetic works. I. Title.

COOKE, Gerald 290
As Christians face rival religions; an interreligious strategy for community without compromise. New York, Association [c.1962] 190p. 20cm. (Haddam House bk.) Bibl. 62-9394 3.75 bds.,
1. Christianity and other religions. 2. Intercultural communication. I. Title.

DAS, Bhagavan, 1869-1958, 290
comp.
The essential unity of all religions. Wheaton, Ill., Theosophical Press [1966] liv, 683 p. 20 cm. Reprint of the "Second edition, greatly enlarged, 1939." [BL48] 66-6517
1. Religion. 2. Religions. 3. Sacred books. I. Title.

DAS BHAGVAN, 1869-1958, comp. 290
The essential unity of all religions. Wheaton, Ill., Theosophical Pr. [1966] liv. 683p. 20cm. Reprint of the Second ed, greatly enl., 1939. [BL48] 66-6517 2.25 pap.,
1. Religion. 2. Religions. 3. Sacred books (Selections: Extracts, etc.) I. Title.

DAVIES, Horton. 290
Christian deviations; essays in defence of the Christian faith. New York, Philosophical Library [1954] 126p. 20cm. [BL98] 54-12269
1. Religions, Modern. I. Title.
Contents omitted.

DE Waal Malefijt, Annemarie, 290
1914-
Religion and culture; an introduction to anthropology of religion. New York, Macmillan [1968] vii, 407 p. illus., map. 21 cm. Bibliography: p. 360-389. [GN470.D4] 68-12717
1. Religion, Primitive. I. Title.

DE WAAL MALEFIJT, Annemarie, 290
1914-
Religion and culture; an introduction to anthropology of religion. New York, Macmillan [1968] vii, 407 p. illus., map. 21 cm. Bibliography: p. 360-389. [GN470.D4] 68-12717
1. Religion. Primitive. I. Title.

ELIADE, Mircea 290
The sacred and the profane; the nature of religion. Tr. from French by Wilard R. Trask. New York, Harper [1961, c.1957-1959] 256p. (Harper torchbks. Cloister lib., TB81) Bibl. 1.45 pap.,
1. Religion. I. Title.

ELIADE, Mircea, 1907- 290
The sacred and the profane; the nature of religion. Translated from the French by Willard R. Trask. [1st American ed.] New York, Harcourt, Brace [1959] 256 p. 22 cm. Includes bibliography. [BL48.E413] 58-10904
1. Religion. I. Title.

ELLIOTT, Harvey Edwin, 1878- 290
The origin of religion as revealed by the chisel, the quill, and the spade. Cleveland, Herd Pub. Co. 1953] 309p. 22cm. Includes bibliography. [BL80.E55] 54-16317
1. Religions. I. Title.

EVERETT, John Rutherford, 290
1918-
Religion in human experience, an introduction. New York, Holt [1950] xvii, 556 p. illus. 22 cm. Bibliography: p. 531-538. [BL80.E9] 50-8225
1. Religions. I. Title.

FAIRCHILD, Johnson E., ed. 290
Basic beliefs; a simple presentation of the religious philosophies of mankind. New York, Hart [1965, c.1959] 192p. 21cm. [BL80.2.F26] 1.25 pap.,
1. Religions. I. Title.

FAIRCHILD, Johnson E., ed. 290
Basic beliefs; the religious philosophies of mankind. New York, Sheridan House [1959] 190 p. 22 cm. (A Cooper Union forum) [BL80.2.F26] 59-8331
1. Religions. I. Title. II. Series.

FARMER, Herbert Henry, 1892- 290
Revelation and religion; studies in the theological interpretation of religious types. New York, Harper [1954] 244p. 23cm. [The Gifford lectures, 1950] [BL48] 54-10941
1. Religion. I. Title.

FAUSSET, Hugh L'Anson, 1895- 290
Fruits of silence; studies in the art of being. London, New York, Abelard-Schuman [1963] 224 p. 23 cm. [BL51.F37] 63-10584
1. Religion — Philosophy. 2. Yoga. I. Title.

FAUSSET, Hugh L'Anson, 1895- 290
Fruits of silence; studies in the art of being. New York, Abelard [c.1963] 224p. 23cm. 63-10584 4.50
1. Religion—Philosophy. 2. Yoga. I. Title.

FERM, Vergilius Ture Anselm, 290
1896- ed.
Ancient religions (Orig. pub. as Forgotten religions; including some living primitive religions) New York, Citadel [1965, c.1950] xv, 392p. illus. 21cm. (C-209) Bibl. [BL80.F38] 2.25 pap.,
1. Religions. I. Title.

FERM, Vergilius Ture Anselm, 290
1896- ed.
Forgotten religions, including some living primitive religions. New York, Philosophical library [1950] xv, 392 p. illus. 24 cm. Includes bibliographies. [BL80.F38] 50-5099
1. Religions. I. Title.

FERM, Vergilius Ture Anselm, 290
1896- ed.
Forgotten religions, including some living primitive religions. Freeport, N.Y., Books for Libraries Press [1970, c1950] xv, 392 p. illus. 23 cm. (Essay index reprint series) Contents.Contents.—Editor's preface, by V. Ferm.—The dawn of religions, by P. Ackerman.—The religion of ancient Egypt, by S. A. B. Mercer.—Sumerian religion, by S. N. Kramer.—Assyro-Babylonian religion, by A. L. Oppenheim.—Hittite religion, by H. G. Guterbock.—The religion of the Canaanites, by T. H. Gaster.—Religion in prehistoric Greece, by G. E. Mylonas.—Mystery religions of Greece, by G. E. Mylonas.—The inhabited world, by C. A. Robinson, Jr.—Mithraism, by I. J. S. Taraporewala.—Manichaeism, by I. J. S. Taraporewala.—Mazdakism, by I. J. S. Taraporewala.—Old Norse religion, by M. Fowler.—Tibetan religion, by L. An-che.—The religion of the Australian aborigines, by A. P. Elkin.—South American Indian religions, by J. H. Steward.—Shamanism, by M. Eliade.—The religion of the Eskimos, by M. Lantis.—The religion of the Navaho Indians, by L. C. Wyman.—The religion of the Hopi Indians, by M. Titiev. Includes bibliographies. [BL87.F47 1970] 70-128240
1. Religions—Addresses, essays, lectures. I. Title.

FERM, Vergilius Ture Anselm, 290
1896- ed.
Living schools of religion (Religion in the twentieth century) Ames, Iowa, Littlefield, Adams, 1956 [c1948] 470p. 21cm. (Littlefield college outlines) New students outline series, 125. 'Originally published as Religion in the twentieth century ... 1948.' [BL98] 56-13734
1. Religions. I. Title.

FINGESTEN, Peter. 290
East is East: Hinduism, Buddhism, Christianity; a comparison. Philadelphia, Muhlenberg Press [1956] 181p. illus. 20cm. [BR128.H5F5] 56-5641
1. Christianity and other religions—Hinduism. 2. Christianity and other religions—Buddhims. 3. Hinduism. 4. Buddha and Buddhism. I. Title.

FORMAN, Henry James, 1879- 290
Truth is one; the story of the world's great living religions in pictures and text [by] Henry James Forman and Roland Gammon. New York, Harper [1954] 224 p. illus. 29 cm. [BL90.F6] 54-8950
1. Religions—Pictures, illustrations, etc. I. Gammon, Roland, joint author. II. Title.

FRIESS, Horace Leland, 1900- 290
Religion in various cultures, by Horace L. Friess. Herbert W. Schenider. New York, Johnson Reprint [1966, c.1932, 1960] xxii, 586p. incl. illus., plates. facsims. 24cm. (Half-title: Studies in religion and culture) Bibl. [BL85.F7] 12.50
1. Religions. I. Schneider, Herbert Wallace, 1892- joint author. II. Title.

GAER, Joseph, 1897- 290
How the great religions began. [New York] Apollo Eds. [1968c.1956] 424p. 20cm. (A195) [BL80.G23 1956] 2.50 pap.,
1. Religions. I. Title.

GAER, Joseph, 1897- 290
How the great religions began. Wood engravings by Frank W. Peers. [New York] New American Library [1954] 240p. illus. 19cm. (A Signet key book, K308) [BL80] 54-2130
1. Religions. I. Title.

GAER, Joseph, 1897- 290
How the great religions began. New and rev. ed. New York, Dodd, Mead, 1956. 424 p. 21 cm. [BL80.G23 1956] 56-5743
1. Religions. I. Title.

GAER, Joseph, 1897- 290
What the great religions believe. New York, Dodd, Mead [1963] 261 p. 21 cm. Includes bibliography. [BL80.2.G3] 63-16374
1. Religions. I. Title.

HAM, Wayne. 290
Man's living religions; a course for adult study. [Independence, Mo., Herald Pub. House, c1966] 327 p. illus. 21 cm. [BL80.2.H27] 66-29091

1. Religions. I. Title.

HARDON, John A. 290
Religions of the world. Westminster, Md., Newman Press, 1963. x, 539 p. 24 cm. "Quoted references": p. 475-485. Bibliography: p. 487-505. [BL80.2.H3] 63-12236
1. Religions. I. Title.

HAYDON, Albert Eustace, 1880- 290
Biography of the gods. Freeport, N.Y., Books for Libraries Press [1972] ix, 352 p. 23 cm. (Essay index reprint series) Reprint of the 1941 ed. [BL80.H33 1972] 74-37848 ISBN 0-8369-2595-5
1. Religions. 2. Gods. I. Title.

HAYDON, Albert Eustace, 1880- 290
ed.
Modern trends in world religions, edited by A. Eustace Haydon. Freeport, N.Y., Books for Libraries Press [1968] xiv, 255 p. 23 cm. (Essay index reprint series) Reprint of the 1934 ed. [BL80.H35 1968] 68-29214
1. Religions—Addresses, essays, lectures. I. Title.

HENDRICKS, Rhoda A 290
Mythology pocket crammer. New York, Ken Pub. Col,; distributed to the book trade by Doubleday, Garden City, N. Y. [1963] 160 p. 14 cm. (The Pocket crammer series) [BL303.H46] 63-5155
1. Mythology — Dictionaries. I. Title.

HENDRICKS, Rhoda A. 290
Mythology pocket grammer. Garden City, N.Y. Ken Pub. Co.; dist. Doubleday, [c.1963] 160p. 14cm. (Pocket grammer ser.) 63-5155 1.00 pap., plastic bds.
1. Mythology—Dictionaries. I. Title.

HERZBERG, Max John, 1886- 290
Myths and their meaning. Boston, Allyn and Bacon, 1962. 359 p. illus. 21 cm. (The Academy classics) [[BL310]] A 62
1. Mythology. I. Title.

HERZBERG, Max John, 1886- 290
Myths and their meaning. Boston, Allyn and Bacon, 1962. v, 359 p. illus. 21 cm. (The Academy classics) [BL310.H45 1962] 78-9413
1. Mythology. I. Title.

HIGGINS, Godfrey, 1773-1833. 290
Anacalypsis. An attempt to draw aside the veil of the Saitic Isis; or, An inquiry into the origin of languages, nations, and religions. New Hyde Park, N.Y., University Books [1965] 2 v. illus., port. 31 cm. Bibliography: v. 2, p. [463]-464. [BL430.H46] 64-241266
1. Religion — Hist. I. Title.

HILLARD, Frederick Hadaway. 290
The Buddha, the Prophet, and the Christ. London, G. Allen & Unwin; New York, Macmillan [1956] 169p. 19cm. (Ethical and religious classics of East and West. no. 16) [BL72.H5] 57-202
1. Religions—Biog. 2. Buddha and Buddhism. 3. Muhammad, the prophet. 4. Jesus Christ—Divinity. I. Title.

HILLIARD, Frederick Hadaway. 290
The Buddha, the Prophet, and the Christ. London, G. Allen & Unwin; New York, Macmillan [1956] 169p. 19cm. (Ethical and religious classics of East and West, no. 16) [BL72.H5] 57-202
1. Religions—Biog. 2. Buddha and Buddhism. 3. Muhammad, the prophet. 4. Jesus Christ—Divinity. I. Title.

HOPKINS, Pryns, 1885- 290
World invisible. Penobscot, Me., Traversity Press [c1963] i.e. c1964] 165 p. illus., ports., fold. map. 23 cm. [BL1035.H6] 62-20779
1. Asia — Religious life and customs. I. Title.

HOPKINS, Pryns, 1885- 290
World invisible. Penobscot, Me., Traversity Pr. [c. 1964] 165p. illus., ports., fold. map. 23cm. 62-20779 price unreported.
1. Asia—Religious life and customs. I. Title.

HOWELLS, William White, 1908- 290
The heathens, primitive man and his religions. Pub. in co-operation with the Amer. Mus. of Natural Hist. Garden City, N.Y., Doubleday [c.1948, 1962] 306p. illus., map. (Natural hist, lib.; Anchor bks., N19) Bibl. 1.45 pap.,
1. Religion, Primitive. I. Title.

HUME, Robert Ernest, 1877- 290
1948.
The world's living religions, with special reference to their sacred scriptures and in comparison with Christianity; an historical sketch. Completely rev. New York, Scribner [1959] 335 p. 20 cm. Includes bibliography. [BL98.H8 1959] 58-12515
1. Religions. 2. Christianity and other religions. I. Title.

HUTCHISON, John Alexander 290
Ways of faith; an introduction to religion [by] John A. Hutchison [and] James Alfred Martin, Jr. 2d ed. New York, Ronald Press Co. [c.1960] v, 597p. 22cm. Includes bibliography. 60-7770 5.75
1. Religions. I. Martin, James Alfred, joint author. II. Title.

HUTCHISON, John Alexander, 290
1912-
Ways of faith; an introduction to religion [by] John A. Hutchison [and] James Alfred Martin, Jr. 2d ed. New York, Ronald Press Co. [1960] 597p. 22cm. Includes bibliography. [BL80.2.H8 1960] 60-7770
1. Religions. I. Martin, James Alfred, 1917- joint author. II. Title.

JAMES, Edwin Oliver, 1886- 290
The ancient Gods; the history and diffusion of religion in the ancient Near East and the eastern Mediterranean. [1st Amerian ed.] New York, Putnam [1960] 359 p. illus., map. 24 cm. (The Putnam history of religion) Bibliography: p. 346-352. [BL96.J32 1960] 60-8472
1. Religions—History. 2. Near East—Religion. I. Title.

JAMES, Edwin Oliver, 1886- 290
Christianity and other religions, by E. O. James. Philadelphia, Lippincott [1968] 191 p. 21 cm. (Knowing Christianity) Includes bibliographical references. [BR127.J33 1968] 68-24602 2.95
1. Christianity and other religions.

JAMES, Edwin Oliver, 1886- 290
Comparative religion; an introductory and historical study. [Rev. ed.] London, Methuen; New York, Barnes & Noble [1962, c1961] 334p. 21cm. (University paperbacks, UP-37) Includes bibliography. [BL80.J3 1962] 62-855
1. Religions. 2. Religion, Primitive. I. Title.

JAMES, Edwin Oliver, 1886- 290
Comparative religions: an introductory and historical study. [Rev. ed.] London, Methuen; New York, Barnes & Noble [1963, c.1961] 334p. 21cm. (Univ. paperbacks, UP-37) Bibl. 62-855 4.50; 1.95 pap.,
1. Religions. 2. Religion, Primitive. I. Title.

JAMES, Edwin Oliver, 1886- 290
Myth and ritual in the ancient Near East; an archeological and documentary study. [New York, Barnes & Noble, 1961, c1958] 352p. map. Bibl. 6.50
1. Religions. 2. Mythology. 3. Ritual. I. Title.

JAMES, Edwin Oliver, 1886- 290
Myth and ritual in the ancient Near East; an archeological and Documentary study. New York, Praeger [1958] 352 p. illus. 23 cm. Includes bibliography. [BL96.J33 1958a] 58-11630
1. Religions. 2. Mythology. 3. Ritual. I. Title.

JAMES, Edwin Oliver, 1886- 290
Prehistoric religion; a study in prehistoric archaeology. New York, Barnes & Noble [1961, c.1957] 300 p. illus. Bibl. 61-3103 6.50
1. Religion, Primitive. 2. Religions—Hist. I. Title.

JAMES, Edwin Oliver, 1886- 290
Prehistoric religion a study in prehistoric archaeology. New York, Praeger [1957] 300p. illus. 23cm. (Books that matter) [BL480.J32] 57-11090
1. Religion, Primitive. 2. Religions—Hist. I. Title.

JOHNSON, Mary Parker. 290
The shortest path to heaven; a book dealing with the principal religions of the world and the chief religious cults and sects in the U. S. A. [1st ed.] New York, Exposition Press [1959] 203p. 21cm. Includes bibliography. [BL80.J58] 59-16016
1. Religions. 2. Sects—U. S. I. Title.

*JURJI, Edward J., ed. 290
The great religions of the modern world. Princeton. N.J., Princeton [1967, c.1946] 387p. 21cm. (Princeton paperbacks 81) Confucianism.--Taoism.--Hinduism.--Buddhism.--Shintoism.--Islam. --Judaism.--Eastern Orthodoxy.--Roman Catholicism.--Protestantism. Bibl. 2.95 pap.,
1. Religions. I. Title.

JURJI, Edward Jabra, 1907- 290
The Christian interpretation of religion; Christianity in its human and creative relationships with the world's cultures and faiths. New York, Macmillan, 1952. 318 p. 21 cm. [BL48.J8] 52-10200
1. Religion. 2. Religions. 3. Christianity and other religions. 4. Apologetics—20th cent. I. Title.

JURJI, Edward Jabra, 1907- 290
The phenomenology of religion. Philadelphia, Westminster Press [1963] ix, 308 p. 24 cm. Bibliographical footnotes. [BL80.2.J8] 63-12594
1. Religious. I. Title.

KEETON, Morris T. 290
Values men live by; an invitation to religious inquiry. Nashville, Abingdon Press [c.1960] 224 p. 23 cm. Bibl.: p. 213-218. 60-10909 3.50
1. Religion. I. Title.

KELLET, Ernest Edward, 1864- 290
1950
A short history of religions, by E. E. Kellett. [Baltimore] Penguin [1963] 605p. 18cm. (Pelican Bk. A576) Bibl. 1.65 pap.,
1. Religions—Hist. I. Title.

KIMPEL, Benjamin Franklin. 290
The symbols of religious faith; a preface to an understanding of the nature of religion. New York, Philosophical Library [1954] 198p. 22cm. [BL48.K47] 54-11306
1. Religion. I. Title.

KRAEMER, Hendrik, 1888- 290
Religion and the Christian faith. Philadelphia, Westminster Press [1957] 461p. 24cm. [BL48.K67 1957] 57-5016
1. Religion. 2. Christianity and other religions. I. Title.

KRAEMER, Hendrik, 1888- 290
World cultures and world religions; the coming dialogue. Philadelphia, Westminster Press [1960] 386 p. 24 cm. Includes bibliography. [BR127.K7] 60-12261
1. Christianity and other religions. 2. Philosophy, Comparative. I. Title.

KRITZECK, James. 290
Sons of Abraham: Jews, Christians, and Moslems. Baltimore, Helicon [1965] 126 p. 21 cm. Bibliographical references included in "Notes" (p. 97-116) Bibliography:p. 117-126. [BP171.K7] 65-15039
1. Islam — Relations — Christianity. 2. Islam — Relations — Judaism. 3. Christianity and other religious — Islam. 4. Judaism — Relations — Islam. I. Title.

KRITZECK, James 290
Sons of Abrahma: Jews, Christians, and Moslems. Helicon [dist. New York, Taplinger, c.1965] 126p. 21cm. [BP171.K7] 65-15039 3.50 bds.,
1. Islam—Relations—Christianity. 2. Islam—Relations—Judaism. 3. Christianity and other religions—Islam. 4. Judaism—Relations—Islam. I. Title.

LANDIS, Benson Young, 1897- 290
World religions. New York, Dutton, 1960 (Dutton Everyman paperback) .95 pap.,
1. Religions. I. Title.

LANDIS, Benson Young, 1897- 290
World religions; a brief guide to the principal beliefs and teachings of the religions of the world and to the statistics of organized religion. [1st ed.] New York, Dutton, 1957. 158 p. 21 cm. [BL80.L3] 57-5344
1. Religions. I. Title.

LANTERNARI, Vittorio. 290
The religions of the oppressed; a study of modern messianic cults. Translated from the Italian by Lisa Sergio. [1st American ed.] New York, Knopf, 1963. 343 p. 22 cm. Translation of Movimenti religiosi di liberta e di salvezza dei popoli oppressi. Includes bibliography. [BL85.L363 1963] 62-15568
1. Nativistic movements. I. Title.

LAROUSSE encyclopedia of 290
mythology. With an introd. by Robert Graves. [Translated by Richard Aldington and Delano Ames, and rev. by a panel of editorial advisers from the Larousse mythologie generale, edited by Felix Guirland] New York, Prometheus Press, 1959. viii, 500p. illus., col. plantes, maps. 30cm. Bibliography: p. [493]-494. [BL310.G853] 59-11019
1. ythologie generalle. 2. Mythology. 3. Folk-lore. I. Fuirand, Fellx ed.

LAZARON, Morris Samuel, 1888- 290
Bridges--not walls. [1st ed.] New York, Citadel Press [1959] 191p. 21cm. [BL85.L38] 59-14061
1. Religions. I. Title.

LEGGE, Francis 290
Forerunners and rivals of Christianity, from 330 B.C. to 330 A.D. New Hyde Park, N.Y., University Bks. [c.1964] 2 v. in 1. (202; 462p.) 24cm. Bibl. 64-24125 10.00
1. Christianity and other religions. 2. Religions. I. Title.

LEVI, Carlo, 1902- 290
Of fear and freedom. Translated from the Italian by Adolphe Gourevitch. New York, Farrar, Straus, 1950. xix, 135 p. 21 cm. Translation of Paura della liberta. [BL50.L413] 50-5061
1. Religion. I. Title.

LEVY, Gertrude Rachel, 1883- 290
Religious conceptions of the stone age, and their influence upon European thought. New York, Harper [1963] 349p. illus. 21cm. First pub. in England under title: The gate of horn. (Harper torchbk., cloister lib., TB106) Bibl. 1.95 pap.,
1. Religion, Primitive. I. Title.

LEVY, Gertrude Rachel, 1883- 290
Religious conceptions of the stone age, and their influence upon European thought [Gloucester, Mass., P. Smith, 1966] xxxii, 349p. illus., maps. 21cm. First pub. in England in 1948 by Faber & Faber under title: The gate of horn; a study of the religious conceptions of the stone age and their influence upon European thought (Harper torchbk., Cloister lib. rebound) Bibl. [GN470.L47] 4.00
1. Religion, Primitive. I. Title.

*LEWIS, H. D. 290
World religions: meeting points and major issues, by H. D. Lewis, Robert Lawson Slater. London. C. A. Watts, 1966. vii. 207p. 19cm. (New thinker's lib., 11) Bibl. 3.75 bds.
1. Religions. I. Slater, Robert Lawson. joint author. II. Title.
American distributor: Intl. Pubns. Serv., New York.

LEWIS, Hywel David. 290
The study of religions; meeting points and major issues [by] H. D. Lewis and Robert Lawson Slater. Baltimore, Penguin Books [1969, c1966] 221 p. 19 cm. (A Pelican book, A1011) First published in 1966 under title: World religions. Bibliography: p. 211-[213] [BL80.2.L47 1969] 72-3874 1.25
1. Religions. 2. East and West. I. Slater, Robert Henry Lawson, joint author. II. Title.

LEWIS, John, 1889- 290
The religions of the world made simple. New York, Made Simple Books; distributed to the book trade by Garden City Books, Garden City, N. Y. [1958] 191p. 27cm. (The Made simple series) [BL82.L4] 58-14937
1. Religion—Hist. I. Title.

LIFE (Chicago) 290
The world's great religions. New York, Time, inc., 1957. 310p. illus. (part col., part fold.) ports. 37cm. Expansion of the material which originally appeared in six issues, from Feb.-Dec. 1955. [BL80.L73] 57-13674
1. Religions. I. Title.

LIFE (Chicago) 290
The world's great religions, by the editorial staff of Life. Life special ed. for young readers. New York, Simon and Schuster [1958] 192 p. illus. 29 cm. [A Deluxe golden book] [BL80.L74] 58-4280
1. Religions. I. Title.

LIFE (Chicago) 290
The world's great religions. New York, Time, inc., 1957. 310 p. illus. (part col., part fold.) ports. 37 cm. Expansion of the material which originally appeared in six issues, from Feb-Dec. 1955. [BL80.L73] 57-13674
1. Religions. I. Title.

LIFE (Chicago) 290
The world's great religions [v.] by the edit. staff of Life. Special family ed. New York, Time [1963] 3v. (330p.) illus. (pt. col.) ports. (pt. col.) maps (pt. col.) 28cm. Contents.v.1. Religions of the East.--v.2. Religions of the West.--v.3. The glories of Christendom. 63-11285 1.39 ea.,
1. Religions. I. Title.

LOEW, Cornelius Richard 290
Myth,sacred history,and philosophy. the pre-Christian religious heritage of the West [by] Cornelius Loew. New York, Harcourt [1967] ix, 284p. 21cm. Bibl. [BL96.L6] 67-16822 2.95 pap.,
1. Religious thought—Ancient period. I. Title.

LOEW, Cornelius Richard. 290
Myth, sacred history, and philosophy; the pre-Christian religious heritage of the West [by] Cornelius Loew. New York, Harcourt, Brace & World [1967] ix, 284 p. 21 cm. Bibliography: p. [277]-282. [BL96.L6] 67-16822
1. Religious thought — Ancient period. I. Title.

LOMAX, Louis E., 1922- 290
When the word is given; a report on Elijah Muhammad, Malcolm X, and the Black Muslim world. [1st ed.] Cleveland, World Pub. Co. [1963] 223 p. illus., ports. 21 cm. "Suggested additional reading": p. 213-214. [BP222.L6] 63-21624
1. Black Muslims. I. Title.

LYON, Quinter Marcellus. 290
The great religions. [1st ed.] New York, Odyssey Press [1957] 732p. illus. 21cm. Includes bibliography. [BL80.L9] 57-1753
1. Religions. I. Title.

LYONE QUINTER MARCELLUS. 290
The great religions. [1st ed.] New York, Odyssey Press [1957] 732p. illus. 21cm. Includes bibliography. [BL80.L9] 57-1753
1. Religions. I. Title.

MCCROSSEN, Vincent A 290
The empty room. New York, Philosophical Library [1955] 156p. 23cm. [BL85.M185] 55-14870
1. Religions. 2. Catholic Church—Doctrinal and controversial works—Catholic authors. I. Title.

MEES, Gualtherus Hendrik, 290
1903-
The revelation in the wilderness dealing with the revelation of the meaning of the symbolism contained in the traditions of old in the wilderness of the mind and of the modern world); an exposition of traditional psychology. Deventer, N. Kluwer, 1951-54. 3v. illus. 25cm. Contents.v. 1. The book of signs [with Supplement]--v. 2. The book of battles [with Supplement]--v. 3. The book of stars [with Supplement] [BL313.M4] 53-33702
1. Mythology. 2. Symbolism. 3. Religion, Primitive. I. Title. II. Title: The book of signs.

MENCKEN, Henry Louis, 1880- 290
1956
Treatise on the gods. [Rev. ed.] New York, Random [1963, c.1930] 287p. 19cm. (Vintage Bk., V-232) Bibl. 1.95 pap.,
1. Religion. 2. Gods. I. Title.

MILLER, Milton C. 290
Our religion and our neighbors; a study of comparative religion emphasizing the religions of the Western World by Milton G. Miller, Sylvan D. Schwartzman. Illus. by William Steinel. New York, Union of Amer. Hebrew Cong. [c.1963] xiv, 297p. illus. (pt. col.) ports., maps (pt. col.) ports., maps (pt. col.) facsims. 27cm. Bibl. 63-14742 3.95
1. Religions. 2. Judaism—Relations. I. Schwartzman, Sylvan David, joint author. II. Title.

MILLER, Milton G 290
Our religion and our neighbors; a study of comparative religion emphasizing the religions of the Western World, by Milton G. Miller and Sylvan D. Schwartzman. [Experimental ed.] New York, Union of American Hebrew Congregations [1959] 357p. illus. 23cm. Includes bibliography. [BL82.M58] 59-2451
1. Religions. 2. Judaism—Relations. I. Schwartzman, Sylvan David, joint author. II. Title.

MILLER, Milton G 290
Our religion and our neighbors; a study of comparative religion emphasizing the religions of the Western World by Milton G. Miller and Sylvan D. Schwartzman. Illustrated by William Steinel. New York, Union of American Hebrew Congregations [1963] xiv, 297 p. illus. (part col.) ports., maps (part col.) facsims. 27 cm. Includes bibliographies. [BL82.M58] 63-14742
1. Religions. 2. Judaism — Relations. I. Schwartzman, Sylvan David, joint author. II. Title.

MONDALE, Robert Lester, 1904- 290
Values in world religions. Boston, Starr King Press [1958] 109p. 21cm. [BL80.M58] 58-6339
1. Religions. I. Title.

MORRIS, Charles William, 290
1901-
Paths of life; preface to a world religion. New York, G. Braziller, 1956. 257p. 22cm. [BD431.M885 1956] 56-58029
1. Life. I. Title.

MUNSTER, Ernest Greve. 290
A new Bible. [1st ed.] Brooklyn, G. J. Rickard [1958] 91p. 17cm. [BL50.M85] 58-10103
1. Religion. I. Title.

MURRELL, Ethel (Ernest) 1905- 290
The golden thread. [1st ed.] New York, Vantage Press [1956] 144p. 21cm. Includes bibliography. [BL80.M85] 56-6850
1. Religions. I. Title.

NEEDLEMAN, Jacob. 290
The new religions. [1st ed.] Garden City, N.Y., Doubleday, 1970. xii, 245 p. 22 cm. Includes bibliographical references. [BL2520.N4] 71-121951 5.95
1. Sects—United States. 2. Religions. I. Title.

NEILL, Stephen Charles, Bp. 290
Christian faith and other faiths; the Christian dialogue with other religions. London, New York, Oxford University Press, 1961. 241 p. 23 cm. (The Moorehouse lectures, Melbourne, 1960) Includes bibliography. [BR127.N37] 61-19234
1. Christianity and other religions. 2. Religions. I. Title.

NETTIS, Joseph 290
Man and his religions. Text, photos. by Joseph Nettis. Philadelphia, United Church Pr. [c.1963] 62p. 19cm. 1.00 pap.,
I. Title.

NIELSEN, Niels Christian, 290
1921-
The layman looks at world religions. St. Louis, Bethany Press [1962] 112p. 21cm. [BL80.2.N5] 62-179158
1. Religions. I. Title.

NOSS, John Boyer 290
Living religions [by] John B. Noss. Rev. ed. Philadelphia, United Church Pr. [1967] 121p. 19cm. Bibl. [BL95.N6 1967] 67-17925 1.95 pap.,
1. Religions. I. Title.

NOSS, John Boyer. 290
Living religions [by] John B. Noss. Rev. ed. Philadelphia, United Church Press [1967] 121 p. 19 cm. Bibliography: p. 119-121. [BL95.N6] 67-17925
1. Religions. I. Title.

NOSS, John Boyer. 290
Man's religions. Rev. ed. New York, Macmillan [1956] 784p. 25cm. Includes bibliographies. [BL80.N65 1956] 56-7326
1. Religions. I. Title.

NOSS, John Boyer. 290
Man's religions. 3d ed. New York, Macmillan [1963] 816 p. illus. 24 cm. [BL80.2.N6 1963] 63-8182
1. Religions. I. Title.

ODEBERG, Hugo, 1898- 290
Pharisaism and Christianity. Tr. [from Swedish] by J. M. Moe. St. Louis, Concordia [c.1943, 1964] 112). 21cm. 63-21162 1.75 pap.,
1. Christianity and other religions—Judaism. 2. Pharisees. I. Title.

OLSON, Bernhard Emmanuel. 290
Faith and prejudice; intergroup problems in Protestant curricula, New Haven, Yale University Press, 1963. 451 p. illus. 24 cm. (Yale publications in religion, 4) Bibliography: p. 423-435. [DS145.O4] 61-15000
1. Religious education—Text-books—Protestant. 2. Antisemitism. 3. Judaism—Relations—Christianity. 4. Christianity and other religions—Judaism. I. Title.

OSBORN, Arthur Walter, 1891- 290
The axis and the rim; the quest for reality in a modern setting. [1st American ed.] New York, T. Nelson [1963] 203 p. 23 cm. Includes bibliography. [BL80.2.O8] 63-2689
1. Religions. I. Title.

OSBORN, Arthur Walter, 1891- 290
The axis and the rim; the quest for reality in a modern setting. New York, Nelson [c.1963] 203p. 23cm. Bibl. 63-2689 5.00
1. Religions. I. Title.

PACAUT, Marcel 290
The churches of the West. Tr. [from French] by Bernard Denvir. New York, Walker [1963, c.1962] 160p. 21cm. (Sun bk., SB-9. Religion and mythology) Bibl. 62-12754 3.50
1. Catholic Church. 2. Protestant churches. 3. Judaism. I. Title.

PARKES, James William, 1896- 290
Common sense about religion, by John Hadham [pseud.] New York, Macmillan, 1961. 176p. 22cm. (The Common sense series) [BL80.2.P3 1961a] 61-16727
1. Religions. 2. Theology, Doctrinal—Popular works. 3. Christianity—20th cent. I. Title.

[PARKES JAMES WILLIAM] 1896- 290
Common sense about religion, by John Hadham [pseud.] New York, Macmillan [c.] 1961. 176p. (Common sense ser.) 61-16727 2.95
1. Religions. 2. Theology, Doctrinal—Popular works. 3. Christianity—20th cent. I. Title.

PERRY, Edmund. 290
The gospel in dispute; the relation of Christian faith to other missionary religions. [1st ed.] Garden City, N. Y., Doubleday, 1958. 230p. 22cm. (Christian faith series) Includes bibliography. [BR127.P4] 58-12053
1. Christianity and other religions. 2. Apologetics—20th cent. I. Title.

POTTER, Charles Francis, 290
1885-
The great religious leaders. New York, Washington Sq. Pr. [1962, c.1929, 1958] 496p. (W1077) Bibl. .90 pap.,
1. Religion—Hist. 2. Christian biography. 3. Religions—Hist. I. Title.

POTTER, Charles Francis, 290
1885-1962.
The great religious leaders. A revision and updating of "The story of religion" in the light of recent discovery and research including the Qumran scrolls. New York, Simon and Schuster, 1958. 493 p. 24 cm. [BL80.P6 1958] 58-13791
1. Religion—History. 2. Christian biography. 3. Religions—History. I. Title.

RADHAKRISHNAN. SARVEPALLI 290
Sir 1888-
East and west in religion. London, G. Allen & Unwin [dist. New York, Barnes & Noble 1964] 146p. 1 l. 20cm. First pub. in 1933. 34-11195 2.00 bds.,
1. Religions. 2. Religion—Philosophy. I. Title.
Previously distributed by Macmillan.

RADHAKRISHNAN, Sarvepalli, 290
Sir 1888-
Eastern religions and western thought. 2d ed. London, Oxford University Press [1951] xiii, 906p. 23cm. 'Lectures ... given in the years 1906-93 ... revised andslightly expanded.; [BL2003.R3 1951] 56-34044
1. Religions—Addresses, essays, lectures. 2. India—Religion. 3. Hinduism—Relations. 4. Philosophy, Comparative —Addresses, essays, lectures. I. Title.

RADHAKRISHNAN, Sarvepalli, 290
Pres. India, 1888-
Eastern religions and Western thought. New York, Oxford University Press, 1959. 396p. 21cm. (A Galaxy book, GB27) 'Lectures ... given in the years 1936-38 ... revised and silghtly expanded.; Includes bibliography. [BL2003 R3 1959] 59-3890
1. Religions—Addresses, essays, lectures. 2. India—Religion. 3. Hinduism—Relations. 4. Philosophy, Comparative—Addresses, essays, lectures. I. Title.

RANK, Otto, 1884-1939. 290
The myth of the birth of the hero; a psychological interpretation of mythology, translated by F. Robbins and Smith Ely Jelliffe. New York, R. Brunner, 1952. 100 p. 23 cm. Bibliographical footnotes. [BL313.R3 1952] 52-9509
1. Mythology. 2. Psychology, Pathological. 3. Heroes. I. Title.

RANK, Otto, 1884-1939. 290
The myth of the birth of the hero, and other writings. Edited by Philip Freund. New York, Vintage Books, 1959. xiv, 315, xv p. 19 cm. (A Vintage book, K-70) Bibliographical footnotes. [BL313.R263] 59-593
1. Mythology. 2. Psychology, Pathological. 3. Heroes. 4. Psychoanalysis—Addresses, essays, lectures. I. Title.

ROBERTS, Irene. 290
Let there be light. New York, Vantage Press [c1950] 119 p. 23 cm. [BL390.R52] 51-49
1. Religions (Proposed, universal, etc.) I. Title.

ROBINSON, Herbert Spencer. 290
Myths and legends of all nations, by Herbert Spencer Robinson and Knox Wilson. [1st ed.] Garden City, N.Y. Garden City Pub. Co. [1950] xii, 244 p. 22 cm. [BL310.R6] 50-6035
1. Mythology. 2. Legends. 3. Folk-Lore. I. Wilson, Knox, 1901- II. Title.

ROSS, Floyd H. 290
The great religions by which men live. (Orig. title: Questions that matter most asked by the world's religions.) By Floyd H. Ross, Tynette Hills. Greenwich, Conn., Fawcett [1963, c.1956] 192p. 18cm. (Premier bk., R199) .60 pap.,
I. Title.

ROSS, Floyd Hiatt. 290
Questions that matter most, asked by the world's religions, by Floyd H. Ross and Tynette W. Hills. With a foreword by Vergilius Ferm. Boston, Beacon Press [1954] Boston, Beacon Press [1954] 266p. illus. 22cm. 26p. 23cm. --A guide for teachers using Questions that matter most, asked by the world's religions, by Floyd H. Ross and Tynette Wilson Hills. [BL80.R65] 54-10685
1. Religions. I. Hills, Tynette Wilson, 1926 joint author. II. Title.

ROWLEY, Harold Henry, 1890- 290
Prophecy and religion in ancient China and Israel. New York, Harper [1956] 154p. 22cm. 'Lectures ... originally delivered at the School of Oriental and African Studies of the University of London as the Louis H. Jordan lectures in comparative religion for 1954.' [BL633.R6 1956a] 56-12074
1. Prophets. 2. China—Religion—Relations—Judaism. 3. Judaism—Relations— Chinese. I. Title.

SACRED books of the East (The). 290
Tr. by various Oriental scholars, Ed. by F. Max Muller [Delhi, Motilal Banarsidass, 1966] 50v. 23cm. (Sacred bks. of the East ser.) Unesco collection of representative works: Indian ser. First pub. in 1879 by the Clarendon Pr. Reprinted 1966. Contents.v. 1, 15. The Upanishads.--2, 14. The sacre laws of the Aryas.--3, 16, 27-28, 39-40. The sacred books of China.--4, 23. 31. The Zend-avesta.--5, 18, 24, 37, 47. Pahlavi texts.--6, 9. The Quar'an.--7. The Institutes of Visnu.--8. The Bhagavadgita.--10. The Dhammapada; Sutta-nipata.--11. Buddhist suttas.--12, 26, 41, 43-44. The Satapatha-Brahmana.--13, 17, 20. Vinaya texts.--19. The Fo-sho-hing-tsanking.--21. The Saddharma-pundarika.--22, 45. Jaina sutras.--25. Manu.--29, 30. The Grihya-sutras.--32, 46. Vedic hymns.--33. The minor law-books.--34, 38. The Vedanta-sutras. 35-36. The questions of King Milinda.--42. Hymns of the Atharva-veda.--48. The Vedanta-Sutras.--49. Buddhist Mahayana texts.--50. Bibl. 250.00 6.00 Index. set, ea.,
1. Religions, Eastern—Sacred Books. I. Muller, F. Max, ed.
American distributor: Verry, Mystic, Conn.

SCHNEIDER, Delwin Byron. 290
No God but God; a look at Hinduism, Buddhism, and Islam, by Del Byron Schneider. Minneapolis, Augsburg Pub. House [1969] vii, 136 p. illus., maps, ports. 20 cm. Bibliographical footnotes. [BL80.2.S33] 74-84806 2.95
1. Religions. I. Title.

SCHURE, Edouard, 1841-1929. 290
The great initiates; a study of the secret history of religions. Tr. from French by Gloria Rasberry. Introd. by Paul M. Allen. [Steiner, dist. Stamford, Conn., Herman Pub., 1962, c.1961] 526p. 22cm. (St. George bks.) 61-8623 8.50
1. Religions I. Title.

SEMAAN, Andrew Nicola, 1876- 290
Religion and brotherhood of man; a manifestation of the spiriti-god in man. [1st ed.] Brooklyn [1950] 640 p. illus., ports. 25 cm. [BL390.S4] 50-3841
1. Religions (Proposed, universal, etc.) 2. Religions. 3. Brotherliness. I. Title.

SLATER, Robert Henry Lawson. 290
Can Christians learn from other religions? New York, Seabury Press, 1963. 94 p. 21 cm. Includes bibliography. [BR127.S57] 63-16287
1. Christianity and other religions. I. Title.

SLATER, Robert Henry Lawson 290
Can Christians learn from other religions? New York, Seabury [c.]1963. 94p. 21cm. Bibl. 63-16287 1.95 pap.,
1. Christianity and other religions. I. Title.

SLATER, Robert Henry Lawson. 290
World religions and world community. New York, Columbia University Press, 1963. 299 p. 23 cm. (Lectures on the history of religions, new ser., no. 6) [BL25.L4 no. 6] 63-9805
1. Religions — Addresses, essays, lectures. I. Title.

SLATER, Robert Henry Lawson 290
World religions and world community. New York, Columbia [c.]1963. 299p. 23cm. (Lectures on the hist. of religions, new ser., no. 6) Bibl. 63-9805 6.00
1. Religions—Addresses, essays, lectures. I. Title.

*SMART. NINIAN 290
World religions: a dialogue. Baltimore, Penguin [1966] 154p. 19cm. (Pelican bk., A 786) 1.25 pap.,
I. Title.

SMART, Ninian, 1927- 290
World religions: a dialogue. Harmondsworth, Penguin, 1966. 154 p. 18 1/2 cm. (Pelican books, A786) (B 66-10255) Originally published as A dialogue of religions. London, S. C. M. Press, 1960. [BL425.S6 1966] 66-75270
1. Religions. I. Title.

SMITH, Homer William, 1895- 290
Man and his gods Foreword by Albert Einstein. [1st ed.] Boston, Little, Brown, 1952. 501 p. 22 cm. [BL80.S65] 52-5512
1. Religion—Hist. I. Title.

SMITH, Huston. 290
The religions of man. [1st ed.] New York, Harper [1958] 328 p. 22 cm. Includes bibliography. [BL80.S66] 56-11923
1. Religions. I. Title.

SMITH, Huston. 290
The religions of man. [1st ed.] New York, Harper [1958] 328 p. 22 cm. Includes bibliography. [BL80.S66] 56-11923
1. Religions.

*SMITH, Huston, 1919- 290
The religions of man. New York, Harper [1964, c.1958] 328p. 21cm. (CN/43) 1.95 pap.,
I. Title.

SMITH, Wilfred Cantwell, 1916- 290
The faith of other men. [New York] New American Library [1963] 140 p. 21 cm. [BL85.S5 1963] 63-21610
1. Religions. 2. Christianity and other religions. I. Title.

SOPER, Edmund Davison, 1876-1961. 290
The religions of mankind. 3d ed., rev. New York, Abingdon-Cokesbury Press [1951] 253 p. 24 cm. [BL80.S75 1951] 51-13635
1. Religions.

SPEER, Robert Elliott, 1867-1947. 290
The finality of Jesus Christ. Grand Rapids, Zondervan [1968, c1960] 386 p. 23 cm. (The L. P. Stone lectures at Princeton Theological Seminary, 1932-3) (The Gay lectures at Southern Baptist Theological Seminary, 1932-3.) Contents.Contents.—lecture 1. The Church's conception of Christ in the first two centuries.—lecture 2. The attitude of primitive Christianity toward non-Christian religions.—lecture 3. The view of Christ and of non-Christian religions which generated and sustained the expansion of Christianity.—lecture 4. Can we still hold the primitive view of Christ?—lecture 5. What view, then, shall we take today of non-Christian religions? Bibliographical footnotes. [BR85] 68-12957
1. Jesus Christ—Divinity. 2. Christianity and other religions. 3. Christianity—Addresses, essays, lectures. I. Title. II. Series: Princeton Theological Seminary. Stone lectures, 1932-3. III. Series: The Gay lectures, 1932-3

SPIEGELBERG, Frederic, 1897- 290
Living religions of the world. Englewood Cliffs, N. J., Prentice-Hall, 1956. xii, 511p. illus. 22cm. Bibliography: p. 487-408. [BL80.S76] 56-11009
1. Religions. 2. Religion—Philosophy. I. Title.

SPIEGELBERG, Frederic, 1897- 290
Living religions of the world. Englewood Cliffs, N.J., Prentice-Hall, 1956. xii, 511 p. illus. 22 cm. Bibliography: p. 487-498. [BL80.S76] 56-11009
1. Religions. 2. Religion — Philosophy. I. Title.

STILSON, Max 290
Major religions of the world. Grand Rapids, Mich., Zondervan [c.1964] 123p. 21cm. Bibl. 64-11951 1.95 bds.,
1. Religions. I. Title.

STOWE, David M 290
When faith meets faith. New York, Friendship Press [1963] 191 p. 20 cm. [BR127.S82] 63-8691
1. Christianity and other religions. I. Title.

STOWE, David M. 290
When faith meets faith, by David M. Stowe. Rev. ed. New York, Friendship [1967] 192p. 19cm. Bibl. [BR127.S82 1967] 67-10834 1.75 pap.,
1. Christianity and other religions. I. Title.

STOWE, David M. 290
When faith meets faith, by David M. Stowe. Rev. ed. New York, Friendship Press [1967] 192 p. 19 cm. Bibliography: p. 190-192. [BR127.S82] 67-10834
1. Christianity and other religions. I. Title.

THOMPSON, Laurence G. 290
Chinese religion; an introduction [by] Laurence G. Thompson. Belmont, Calif., Dickenson Pub. Co. [1969] 119 p. 23 cm. (The Religious life of man) Includes bibliographies. [BL1802.T5] 69-17301
1. China—Religion. I. Title.

TILLICH, Paul, 1886-1965. 290
Christianity and the encounter of the world religions. New York, Columbia University Press, 1963. viii, 97 p. 21 cm. (Bampton lectures in America, no. 14) [BR127.T56] 63-7508
1. Christianity and other religions. I. Title. II. Series.

TILLICH, Paul Johannes Oskar, 1886- 290
Christianity and the encounter of the world religions. New York, Columbia [1964, c.1963] 97p. 21cm. (55) 1.25 pap.,
1. Christianity and other religions. I. Title.

TOYNBEE, Arnold Joseph, 1889- 290
Christianity among the religions of the world. New York, Scribner [1957] 116p. 21cm. (Hewett lectures, 1956) [BR127.T6] 57-12066
1. Christianity and other religions. 2. Religions. I. Title.

TOYNBEE, Arnold Joseph, 1889- 290
Christianity among the religions of the world. New York, Scribner [1957] 116 p. 21 cm. (Hewett lectures, 1956) [BR127.T6] 57-12066
1. Christianity and other religions. 2. Religions. I. Title.

TOYNBEE, Arnold Joseph, 1889- 290
Christianity among the religions of the world. New York, Scribners [1963, c.1957] 116p. 21cm. (Scribner lib., SL89) 1.25 pap.,
1. Christianity and other religions. 2. Religions. I. Title.

TOYNBEE, Arnold Joseph, 1889- 290
An historian's approach to religion; based on Gifford lectures delivered in the University of Edinburgh in the years 1952 and 1953. New York, Oxford University Press, 1956. 318 p. 22 cm. [BL48.T68] 56-10187
1. Religion. 2. Civilization — Hist. I. Title.

TOYNBEE, Arnold Joseph, 1889- 290
An historian's approach to religion; based on Gifford lectures delivered in the University of Edinburgh in the years 1952 and 1953. London, New York, Oxford University Press, 1956. 316p. 23cm. [BL48.T68 1956a] 56-14616
1. Religion. 2. Civilization—Hist. I. Title.

TOYNBEE, Arnold Joseph, 1889- 290
An historian's approach to religion; based on Gifford lectures delivered in the University of Edinburgh in the years 1952 and 1953. New York, Oxford University Press, 1956. 318 p. 22 cm. [BL48.T68] 56-10187
1. Religion. 2. Civilization—History. I. Title.

VASSALL, William F 290
The origin of Christianity; a brief study of the world's early beliefs and their influence on the early Christian church, including an examination of the lost books of the Bible. [1st ed.] New York, Exposition Press [1952] 183 p. 21 cm. [BL80.V27] 52-10685
1. Religions...Hist. 2. Christianity — Origin. 3. Bible. N. T. Apocryphal books — Criticism, interpretation, etc. I. Title.

VICEDOM, Georg F 290
The challenge of the world religions. Translated by Barbara and Karl Hertz. Philadelphia, Fortress Press [1963] 161 p. 21 cm. Translation of Die Mission der Weltreligionen. [BL98.V513] 63-7907
1. Christianity and other religions. 2. Religious thought — 20th cent. I. Title.

VICEDOM, Georg F. 290
The challenge of the world religions. Tr. [from German] by Barbara & Karl Hertz. Philadelphia, Fortress Pr. [c.1963] 161p. 21cm. 63-7907 3.50
1. Christianity and other religions. 2. Religious thought—20th cent. I. Title.

VISSER 'T HOOFT, Willem Adolph, 1900- 290
No other name; the choice between syncretism and Christian universalism. Philadelphia, Westminister Press [1963] 128 p. 19 cm. Bibliographical footnotes. [BR127.V5] 64-10084
1. Christianity and other religions. I. Title.

VISSER 'T HOOFT, Willem Adolph, 1900- 290
No other name; the choice between syncretism and Christian universalism. Philadelphia, Westminster [c.1963] 128p. 19cm. Bibl. 64-10084 2.50
1. Christianity and other religions. I. Title.

VOSS, Carl Hermann. 290
In search of meaning; living religions of the world. Illustrated by Eric Carle. Cleveland, World Pub. Co. [1968] 191 p. illus. 24 cm. (Excalibur books) Bibliography: p. 173-182. [BL80.2.V66 1968] 67-23356
1. Religions. I. Title.

WACH, Joachim, 1898-1955. 290
The comparative study of religions. Edited with an introd. by Joseph M. Kitagawa. New York, Columbia University Press, 1958. 231 p. 23 cm. (Lectures on the history of religions, sponsored by the American Council of Learned Societies, new ser., no. 4) Includes bibliography. [BL25.L4 no. 4] 58-9237
1. Religions. I. Title.

WACH, Joachim, 1898-1955 290
The comparative study of religions. Ed., introd. by Joseph M. Kitagawa. New York, Columbia [1961, c.1958] 231p. Bibl. 1.75 pap.,
1. Religious. I. Title.

WATT, William Montgomery 290
Truth in the religions: a sociological and psychological approach. [dist. Chicago, Aldine, Edinburgh at the University Pr. 1963] 190p. 23cm. Bibl. 6.00
I. Title.

WATTS, Alan Wilson, 290
1915- Cleveland, World [1967, c.1964] xii, 236p. 21cm. (Meridian bks., M237) Bibl. 2.45 pap.,
1. Christianity and other religions. I. Title: Beyond theology;

WATTS, Alan Wilson, 1915- 290
Beyond theology; the art of Godmanship [by] Alan Watts. New York, Pantheon Books [1964] xii, 236 p. 21 cm. Bibliography: p. 231-232. [BR127.W28] 64-18352
1. Christianity and other religions. I. Title.

WATTS, Alan Wilson, 1915-1973. 290
Beyond theology; the art of Godmanship [by] Alan Watts. New York, Pantheon Books [1964] xii, 236 p. 21 cm. Bibliography: p. 231-232. [BR127.W28] 64-18352
1. Christianity and other religions. I. Title.

WATTS, Harold Holliday, 1906- 290
The modern reader's guide to religions. New York, Barnes & Noble [1964] xi, 620 p. 24 cm. Bibliography: p. 587-597. [BL80.2.W3] 64-17645
1. Religious. I. Title.

WATTS, Harold Holliday, 1906- 290
The modern reader's guide to religions. New York, Barnes & Noble [1964] xi, 620 p. 24 cm. Bibliography: p. 587-597. [BL80.2.W3] 64-17645
1. Religions. I. Title.

WATTS. HAROLD HOLLIDAY., 1906- 290
The modern reader's guide to religions. New York, Barnes & Noble [1968] xi, 620p. 22cm. Bibl. [BL80.2.W3] 64-17645 3.50 pap.,
1. Religions. I. Title.

WEBER, Max, 1864-1920. 290
The sociology of religion. Translated by Ephraim Fischoff. Introd. by Talcott Parsons. Boston, Beacon Press [1963] lxvii, 304 p. 22 cm. "First published in Germany, in 1922 ... under the title 'Religionssoziologie,' from Wirtschaft und Gesellschaft." [BL60.W433] 62-16644
1. Religion and sociology. I. Title.

WELLS, Charles Arthur, 1897- 290
Journey into light; a study of the long search for truth in a world darkened by dogma, and an examination of first century Christianity as the only solution for the moral dilemmas of the nuclear age. With illus. by the author. New York, Between the Lines Press [1958] 142 p. illus. 23 cm. [BL50.W36] 58-36372
1. Religion. 2. Dogma. I. Title.

WILLIAMS, David Rhys, 1890- 290
World religions and the hope for peace; with a pref. by John Haynes Holmes. Boston, Beacon Press 1951. 221 p. 22 cm. [BL80.W65] 51-14426
1. Religions. I. Title.

ZAEHNER, R. C. 290
The comparison of religions. New preface by the author. Boston, Beacon [1962, c.1958] 230p. (LR15) 1.65 pap.,
I. Title.

ZAEHNER, Robert Charles. 290
Christianity and other religions, by R. C. Zaehner. [1st ed.] New York, Hawthorn Books [1964] 148, [1] p. 21 cm. (The Twentieth century encyclopedia of Catholicism, v. 146. Section 15: Non-Christian beliefs) Bibliography: p. [149] [BR127.Z3] 64-14164
1. Christianity and other religions. 2. Religions. I. Title. II. Series.

ZAEHNER, Robert Charles 290
Christianity and other religions. New York. Hawthorn [c.1964] 148, [1] p. 21cm. (20th cent. ency. of Catholicism. v. 146. Section 15: Non-Christian beliefs) Bibl. 64-14164 3.50 bds.,
1. Christianity and other religions. 2. Religions. I. Title. II. Series.

ZAEHNER, Robert Charles. 290
The comparison of religions. With a new pref. by the author. Boston, Beacon Press [1962, c1958] 230 p. 21 cm. (Beacon paperback no. LR15) [BL80.2.Z28 1962] 62-51998
1. Religions. I. Title.

BRADLEY, David G. 290.2
A guide to the world's religions. Englewood Cliffs, N.J., Prentice [c.1963] 182p. 21cm. (Spectrum bk., S-51) Bibl. 63-191 3.95; 1.95 pap.,
1. Religions—Outlines, syllabi, etc. I. Title.

GASKELL, George Arthur 290.3
Dictionary of all scriptures and myths. New York, Julian Press [c.] 1960. 844p. 26cm. Published in 1923 under title: A dictionary of the sacred language of all scriptures and myths. 60-9923 15.00
1. Symbolism—Dictionaries. I. Title.

GAYNOR, Frank, 1911- ed. 290.3
Dictionary of mysticism. New York, Philosophical Library [1953] 208p. 24cm. [BL31.G32] 53-13354
1. Religion—Dictionaries. 2. Occult sciences —Dictionaries. 3. Mysticism—Dictionaries. I. Title.

GLASENAPP, Helmuth von [Otto Max Helmuth von Glasenapp] 1891- 290.3
Non-Christian religions A to Z. Based on the work of Helmuth von Glasenapp. Ed. under the supervision of Horace L. Friess. [Tr. from German by Eric Protter] New York, Grosset [1963, c.1957] 278p. illus., maps. 21cm. (Universal ref. lib.) Bibl. 63-3397 4.25
1. Religions—Dictionaries—English. I. Friess, Horace Leland, 1900- ed. II. Title.

KASTER, Joseph. 290.3
Putnam's concise mythological dictionary. Based upon Gods, by Bessie Redfield. New York, Putnam [1963] [9], 180 p. 20 cm. Bibliography: 7th-8th prelim. pages. [BL31.K3] 63-9663
1. Mythology—Dictionaries. 2. Religion—Dictionaries. I. Redfield, Bessie Gordon, 1868- comp. Gods. II. Title. III. Title: Mythological dictionary.

PARRINDER, Edward Geoffrey. 290'.3
A dictionary of non-Christian religions, by Geoffrey Parrinder. Philadelphia, Westminster Press [1973, c1971] 320 p. illus. 24 cm. Bibliography: p. 318-320. [BL31.P36 1973] 73-4781 ISBN 0-664-20981-5 10.75
1. Religions—Dictionaries. I. Title.

SYKES, Egerton. 290.3
Everyman's dictionary of non-classical mythology. London, Dent; New York, Dutton [1952] xviii, 262 p. plates. 20 cm. (Everyman's reference library) Bibliography: p. xvi-xviii. [BL303.S9] 52-3946
1. Mythology — Dictionaries. I. Title.

WEDECK, Harry Ezekiel, 1894- 290'.3
Dictionary of pagan religions, by H. E. Wedeck and Wade Baskin. [1st ed.] New York, Philosophical Library [1971] 363 p. 22 cm. [BL31.W4] 79-86508 10.00
1. Religions—Dictionaries. I. Baskin, Wade, joint author. II. Title.

WOODCOCK, Percival George. 290.3
Short dictionary of mythology. New York, Philosophical Library [1953] 156 p. 24 cm. [BL303.W6] 53-7910
1. Mythology—Dictionaries. I. Title.

ROWLEY, Harold Henry, 1890- 290.4
Submission in suffering, and other essays on Eastern thought. Cardiff, Univ. of Wales Pr. [dist. Mystic, Conn., Verry, 1964] ix, 170p. 22cm. Bibl. 64-7114 3.00
1. Mo, Ti, fl. 400 B.C. 2. Affliction—Comparative studies. 3. Golden rule. I. Title.

SODERBLOM, Nathan, [Lars Olaf Jonathan Soderblom.] abp. 1866-1931 290.4
The living God; basal forms of personal religion. The Gifford lectures, delivered in the Univ. of Edinburgh in the year 1931. [Gloucester, Mass., P. Smith, 1963] 398p. 21cm. (Beacon Pr. bk. rebound) Bibl. 4.50
1. Religions—Addresses, essays, lectures. 2. Religion—Hist. 3. Revelation. 4. Religion—Philosophy. 5. Christianity and other religions. I. Title.

SODERBLOM, Nathan [Lars Olof Jonathan Soderblom] abp., 1866-1931 290.4
The living God; basal forms of personal religion. The Gifford lectures, delivered in the Univ. of Edinburgh in the year 1931. Biographical introd. by Yngve Brilioth. Boston, Beacon [1962] 398p. 21cm. (LR 17) Bibl. 2.45 pap.,
1. Religions—Addresses, essays, lectures. 2. Religion—Hist. 3. Revelation. 4. Religion—Philosophy. 5. Christianity and other religions. I. Brilioth, Yngve Torgny, 1891. II. Title.

**RELIGION in human culture;* a guide. Iowa City, Sernoll, inc., 410 E. Market St. [c.1965] 134 1. 28cm. Prep. by the teachers and assistants of the course Religion in human culture, State Univ., Iowa City, Iowa. 5.75 pap., plastic bdg. 290.76

HERVEY, James W. 290.81
Patterns in church history; essays on comparative religion, the Reformation, and John Wesley. [1st ed.] New York, Exposition Press [1963] 113 p. 21 cm. (An Exposition -- testament book) Includes bibliography. [BL87.114] 63-4295

1. Religions — Addresses, essays, lectures. I. Title.

HERVEY, James W. 290.81
Patterns in church history; essays on comparative religion, the Reformation, and John Wesley. New York, Exposition [c.1963] 96p. 21cm. (Exposition. Testament bk.) Bibl. 63-4295 3.50
1. Religions—Addresses, essays, lectures. I. Title.

BACHELDER, Louise, comp. 290.82
Time for reflection. With illus. by Pat Stewart. Mount Vernon, N.Y., Peter Pauper Press [1968] 62 p. col. illus. 19 cm. [PN6081.B17] 68-3278
1. Quotations, English. I. Title.

BOUQUET, Alan Coates, 1884- ed. 290.82
Sacred books of the world. [An anthology with full commentary, illustrating the development from the formulas and invocations of primitive magic to the hymns and revelations of the twentieth century] London, Baltimore, Penguin Books [1954] 343p. 18cm. (Pelican books, A283) A companion source-book to Comparative religion. [BL70.B6] 54-3069
1. Sacred books (Selections: Extracts, etc.) I. Title.

BOUQUET, Alan Coates, 1884- ed. 290.82
Sacred books of the world. London, Cassell [dist. New York, Barnes & Noble, 1964, c.1954 342p. 21cm. (Belle sauvage lib.) Companion source-book to the author's Comparative religion. 63-22884 3.75
1. Sacred books (Selections: Extracts, etc.) I. Title.

DANIELOU, Jean 290.82
Introduction to the great religions [by] Jean Danielou [others] Tr. [from French] by Albert J. La Mothe. Jr. Notre Dame, Ind., Fides [1967, c.1964] 159p. 18cm. (Dome bk., D55) [BL80.2.D313] 64-16499 .95 pap.,
1. Religions. 2. Christionity and other religions. I. La Mothe, Albert' J., tr. II. Title. III. Title: The great religions.

DANIELOU, Jean. 290.82
Introduction to the great religions [by] Jean Danielou [and others] Translated by Albert J. LaMothe, Jr. Notre Dame, Ind., Fides Publishers, [1964] 142 p. 21 cm. [BL80.2.D313] 64-16499
1. Religions. 2. Christianity and other religions. I. LaMothe, Albert J., tr. II. Title. III. Title: Introduction to the great religions

ELIADE, Mircea, 1907- ed. 290.82
The history of religions; essays in methodology. Edited by Mircea Eliade and Joseph M. Kitagawa. With a pref. by Jerald C. Brauer. [Chicago] University of Chicago Press [1959] xi, 163 p. 23 cm. Bibliographical footnotes. [BL41.E5] 59-11621
1. Religion—Study and teaching. I. Kitagawa, Joseph Mitsuo, 1915- joint ed.

GAER, Joseph, 1897- 290.82
The wisdom of the living religions. New York, Apollo Eds. [1961, c.1956] Bibl. 1.95 pap.,
1. Quotations. 2. Religious literature (Selections: Extracts, etc.) I. Title.

GAER, Joseph, 1897- 290.82
The wisdom of the living religions. New York, Dodd, Mead, 1956. 338 p. 21 cm. [BL29.G27] 56-8362
1. Quotations. 2. Religious literature (Selections: Extracts, etc.) I. Title.

JONES, Jessie Mae (Orton). comp. 290.82
This is the way; prayers and precepts from world religions. Illustrated by Elizabeth Orton Jones. New York, Viking Press, 1951. 62 p. illus. 23 x 26 cm. [BL560.J6] 51-13305
1. Prayers. 2. Religious literature (Selections: Extracts, etc.) I. Title.

LESSA, William Armand, ed. 290.82
Reader in comparative religion, an anthropological approach; [edited by] William A. Lessa [and] Evon Z. Vogt. Evanston, Ill., Row, Peterson [1958] 508p. illus. 25cm. Includes bibliography. [BL80.L47] 58-13742
1. Religions—Collections. I. Vogt, Evon Zartman, 1918- joint ed. II. Title.

MCKAIN, David W. ed. 290.82
Christianity: some non-Christian appraisals, edited by David W. McKain. With an introd. by Robert Lawson Slater. New York, McGraw-Hill [1964] viii, 289 p. 21 cm. Bibliography: p. 289. [BR127.M3555] 64-16295
1. Christianity and other religions—Addresses, essays, lectures. I. Title.

PAUL Carus Memorial Symposium Peru, Ill., 1957 290.82
Modern trends in world religions. Edited by Joseph M. Kitagawa. La Salle, Ill., Open Court Pub. Co., [c.1959] 286p. 21cm. bibl. 60-1277 3.50
1. Religions—Addresses, essays, lectures. I. Kitagawa, Joseph Mitsuo, ed. II. Title.

VOS HOWARD FREDERIC, 1925- ed. 290.82
Religions in a changing world, a presentation of world religion, in the mid-twentieth century facing the ouslaughts of rising nationalism, communism, and increasing mass communication. Chicago, Moody Press [1959] 441 p. illus., ports. 24 cm. Includes bibliographies. [BL80.2.V6] 59-3137
1. Religions. I. Title.

ZAEHNER, Robert Charles, ed. 290.82
The concise encyclopedia of living faiths. Contributors: A. L. Basham [and others. 1st ed.] New York, Hawthorn Books [1959] 431 p. illus. (part col.) port. (1 col.) map. 26 cm. Includes bibliography. [BL80.2.Z3] 59-9601
1. Religions. I. Basham, Arthur Llewellyn. II. Title. III. Title: Living faiths.

YEAR. 290.84
A picture-history of the Bible and Christianity in 1000 pictures, with the inspiring stories of all the world's great religions. Introd. by Albert Schweitzer, forewords by leaders of the major faiths. [Wilton, Conn., 1957] 252 p. illus. 29 cm. [BL90.Y4 1956] 57-14504
1. Religions — lectures, illustrations, etc. I. Title. II. Title: Bible and Christianity.

YEAR. 290.84
A picture history of the Bible and Christianity in 1000 pictures, with the inspiring stories of all the world's great religions. Introd. by Albert Schweitzer, forewords by leaders of the major faiths. [Los Angeles] [1952] 192 p. illus. 37 cm. [BL90.Y4] 52-13502
1. Religions—Pictures, illustrations, etc. I. Title. II. Title: Bible and Christianity.

CONERLY, Porter W. 290.9
Genealogy of the gods. New York, Monograph Press [1957] 218 p. 22 cm. [BL80.C68] 57-7906
1. Religions—History. 2. Civilization—History. I. Title.

FINEGAN, Jack, 1908- 290.9
The archeology of world religions; the background of primitivism, Zoroastrianism, Hinduism, Jainism, Buddhism, Confucianism, Taoism, Shinto, Islam, and Sikhism. Princeton, Princeton University Press, 1952. xi, 599 p. illus., maps, facsims. 25 cm. Bibliographical footnotes. [BL80.F5] 52-5839
1. Religions—History. I. Title.

JAMES, Edwin Oliver, 1886- 290.9
History of religions. New York, Harper [1958, c1957] 237 p. illus. 19 cm. [BL80.J32 1958] 57-12934
1. Religions—History.

THE Great Asian religions; an anthology. Compiled by Wing-tsit Chan [and others. New York] Macmillan [1969] xvii, 412 p. 24 cm. Bibliography: p. 379-388. [BL1035.G7] 69-10182 290'.95
1. Asia—Religion. I. Chan, Wing-tsit, 1901- comp.

MANIKAM, Rajah Bhushanam, 1897- ed. 290.95
Christianity and the Asian revolution. Madras, Published for Friendship Press, New York, by Diocesan Press [1955] 293p. 23cm. [BL1055.M3] 56-2627
1. East (Far East)—Religion. 2. East (Far East)—Soc. condit. 3. East (Far East)—Church history. 4. Christians in the East (Far East) I. Title.

ORMOND, Ron, 1912- 290.95
Into the strange unknown, by the two men who lived every moment of it: Ron Ormond & Ormond McGill. Foreword by Ralph Willard. Photos. by Ron Ormond. Hollywood, Calif., Esoteric Foundation [1959] 204p. illus. 23cm. [BL1055.O7] 60-2147
1. Asia— Religion. I. McGill, Ormond. II. Title.

REICHELT, Karl Ludvig, 1877-1952. 290.95
Meditation and piety in the Far East; a religious-psychological study. Translated from the Norwegian [by] Sverre Holth. New York, Harper [c1954] 171p. 22cm. (Lutterworth library, v. 42. Missionary research series, no. 19) 'Originally appeared as volume 1 of Fromhetstyer of helligdommer 1 Ost-Asia. Bibliography: p.167-168. [BL1055] 55-782
1. East (Far East)—Religion. I. Title.

RELIGION and change in contemporary Asia. Edited by Robert F. Spencer. Minneapolis, University of Minnesota Press [1971] v, 172 p. map. 23 cm. Lectures presented at the University of Minnesota in the spring of 1968, and sponsored by the All-University Committee. Includes bibliographical references. [BL1035.R38] 76-139450 ISBN 0-8166-0610-2 6.50 290'.95
1. Asia—Religion—Addresses, essays, lectures. I. Spencer, Robert F., ed.

RING, George Cyril, 1890- 290.95
Religions of the Far East: their history to the present day. Milwaukee, Bruce [1950] x, 350 p. illus. 23 cm. (Science and culture series) Bibliography: p. 337-342. [BL1031.R5] 50-1813
1. Asia — Religion. 2. Religions. I. Title.

HUGHES, Ernest Richard, 1883- 290.951
Religion in China, by E. R. Hughes and K. Hughes. London, New York, Hutchinson's University Library, 1950. 151 p. 19 cm. (Hutchinson's university library: world religions, no. 39) [BL1801.H8] 50-8459
1. China—Religion. I. Hughes, K. joint author. II. Title.

JURJI, Edward Jabra, 1907- 290.956
The Middle East, its religion and culture. Philadelphia, Westminster Press [1956] 159p. 22cm. [BL1060.J8] 56-9553
1. Near East—Religion. 2. Near East—Civilization. I. Title.

PARRINDER, Edward Geoffrey. 290.9669
Religion in an African city. London, New York, Oxford University Press, 1953. 211p. illus. 19cm. [BL2465.P29] 53-1344
1. Ibadan, Nigeria—Religion. I. Title.

PARRINDER, Geoffrey. 290.9669
Religion in an African city. London, New York, Oxford University Press, 1953. 211p. illus. 19cm. [BL2465.P29] 53-1344
1. Ibadan, Nigeria—Religion. I. Title.

GARABEDIAN, John H. 290'.973
Eastern religions in the electric age [by] John H. Garabedian and Orde Coombs. New York, Grosset & Dunlap [1969] 160 p. 22 cm. [BJ1661.G28] 68-31347 4.50
1. Youth—Conduct of life. 2. Youth—Religious life. 3. Religions. I. Coombs, Orde, joint author. II. Title.

ROWLEY, Peter. 290'.973
New gods in America; an informal investigation into the new religions of American youth today. New York, D. McKay Co. [1971] xv, 208 p. illus., ports. 21 cm. Bibliography: p. 205-208. [BL80.2.R66] 72-165087 5.95
1. Sects—U.S. 2. Youth—Religious life. 3. Religions. I. Title.

291 Comparative Religion

ANDERSON, Gerald h ed. 291
Sermons to men of other faiths and traditions. Gerald H. Anderson, editor. Nashville, Abingdon Press [1966] 183 p. 21 cm. [BR127.A7] 66-10923
1. Christianity and other religious. 2. Christian union — Sermons. 3. Sermons, English. I. Title.

ANDERSON, Gerald H., ed. 291
Sermons to men of other faiths and traditions. Nashville, Abingdon [c.1966] 183p. 21cm. [BR127.A7] 66-10923 3.25
1. Christianity and other religions. 2. Christian union—Sermons. 3. Sermons, English. I. Title.

ANDERSON, James Norman Dalrymple. 291
Christianity and comparative religion [by] J. N. D. Anderson. Downers Grove, Ill., Inter-varsity Press [1971, c1970] 126 p. 20 cm. "Based on the Church of Ireland series of theological lectures for 1970, given at the Queen's University of Belfast, Northern Ireland." Bibliography: p. [113]-116. [BR127.A74 1971] 73-135847 ISBN 0-87784-477-1
1. Christianity and other religions. I. Title.

ANDERSON, James Norman Dalrymple, ed. 291
The world's religions / edited by Sir Norman Anderson. 4th ed., rev. Grand Rapids, Mich. : Eerdmans, 1976. 244 p. : ill. ; 21 cm. Includes bibliographies and index. [BL80.A64 1976] 75-26654 ISBN 0-8028-3001-3 pbk. : 3.95
1. Religions. 2. Christianity and other religions. I. Title.

ARCHER, John Clark, 1881-1957. 291
Faiths men live by. Freeport, N.Y., Books for Libraries Press [1971] ix, 497 p. 23 cm. (Essay index reprint series) Reprint of the 1934 ed. Includes bibliographical references. [BL80.A7 1971] 79-156606 ISBN 0-8369-2266-2
1. Religions. I. Title.

BADLEY, John Haden, 1865-1967. 291
Form and spirit; a study in religion. Port Washington, N.Y., Kennikat Press [1971] 247 p. 22 cm. (Essay and general literature index reprint series) Reprint of the 1951 ed. [BL48.B17 1971] 77-113347
1. Religion. I. Title.

BAKER, Liva. 291
World faiths; a story of religion. New York, Abelard [1966, c.1965] x, 237p. illus. 23cm. Bibl. [BL92.B3] 65-23653 4.95
1. Religions—Juvenile literature. I. Title.

BARON, Salo Wittmayer, 1895- 291
Modern nationalism and religion. New York, Meridian Books [1960, c1947] 363p. 21cm. (Jewish Publications Society series, JP18) [BL65.N3B3 1960] 60-14922
1. Nationalism and religion. I. Title.

BERGOUNIOUX, Frederic Marie 291
Primitive and prehistoric religions, by F.-M. Bergounioux, Joseph Goetz. Tr. from French by C. R. Busby. New York, Hawthorn [c.1966] 160p. 21cm. (20th century encyclopedia of Catholicism, v.140. Sect. 15: Non-Christian beliefs) Title. (Series: The Twentieth century encyclopedia of Catholicism, v.140) Bibl. [GN470.B3413] 64-14166 3.50 bds.,
1. Religion, Primitive. I. Goetz, Joseph. II. Title. III. Series.
Contents omitted.

BERGOUNIOUX, Frederic Marie. 291
Primitive and prehistoric religions, by F.-M. Bergounioux and Joseph Goetz. Translated from the French by C. R. Busby. [1st ed.] New York, Hawthorn Books [1966] 160 p. 21 cm. (The Twentieth century encyclopedia of Catholicism, v. 140. Section 15: Non-Christian beliefs) Translation of Les religions des prehistoriques et des primitifs. Contents.Contents.—Prehistoric religion, by F.-M. Bergounioux.—Primitive religion, by J. Goetz. Bibliography: p. 159-160. [GN470.B3413] 64-14166
1. Religion, Primitive. I. Goetz, Joseph. II. Title. III. Series: The Twentieth century encyclopedia of Catholicism, v. 140

*BIGELOW, Laura Gates. 291
Feed my sheep. New York, Vantage [1967] 241p. 21cm. Bibl. 3.95 bds.,
I. Title.

BODIN, Jean, 1530-1596. 291
Colloquium of the seven about secrets of the sublime = colloquium heptaplomeres de rerum sublimium arcanis abditis / by Jean Bodin ; translation with introd., annotations, and critical readings, by Marion Leathers Daniels Kuntz. Princeton, N.J. : Princeton University Press, [1975] lxxxi, 509 p. ; 25 cm. Includes index. Bibliography: p. lxxiii-lxxxi. [B781.B33C6413 1975] 73-2453 ISBN 0-691-07193-4 : 25.00
1. Catholic Church—Relations. 2. Religions. 3. Religion—Philosophy. I. Title.

BRADEN, Charles Samuel, 1887- 291
War, communism, and world religions. [1st ed.] New York, Harper [1953] 281 p. 22 cm. [BL65.W2B7] 53-8366
1. War and religion. 2. Communism and religion. I. Title.

BRADLEY, David G. 291
Circles of faith; a preface to the study of the world's religious [by-) David G. Bradley. Nashville, Abingdon Press [1966] 239 p. 23 cm. Bibliographical footnotes. [BL80.2B69] 66-15491
1. Religions. I. Title.

BRADLEY, David G. 291
Circles of faith; a preface to the study of the world's religions. Nashville, Abingdon [c.1966] 239p. 23cm. Bibl. [BL80.2.B69] 66-15491 4.50
1. Religions. I. Title.

BRANDON, Samuel George Frederick 291
History, time, and deity; a historical and comparative study of the conception of time in religious thought and practice. Manchester [Eng.] Univ. Pr., New York, Barnes & Noble [c.1965] xii, 240p. illus. 23cm. (Forwood lects. in the philosophy and hist. of religion, 1964) Bibl. Title. (Series: Forwood lectures, 1964) [BL65.H5B7] 65-8681 6.50
1. History (Theology)—Comparative studies. 2. Time (Theology)—Comparative studies. I. Title. II. Series.

BRANDON, Samuel George Frederick. 291
Religion in ancient history: studies in ideas, men, and events [by] S. G. F. Brandon. New York, Scribner [1969] xiv, 412 p. illus. 25 cm. Bibliography: p. 387-396. [BL27.B7] 73-82691 12.50
1. Religion—Addresses, essays, lectures. I. Title.

BULFINCH, Thomas, 1796-1867 291
Bulfinch's mythology: The age of chivalry and Legends of Charlemagne, or romance of the Middle Ages. Foreword by Palmer Bovie [New York] New Amer. Lib. [c.1962] 608p. 18cm. (Mentor classic, MT450) .75 pap.,
1. Mythology. 2. Chivalry. 3. Folk-lore—Europe. 4. Charlemagne (Romances, etc.) I. Title. II. Title: The age of fable. III. Title: The age of chivalry. IV. Title: Legends of Charlemagne.

CAILLOIS, Roger 291
Man and the sacred; translated [from the French] by Meyer Barash. [Glencoe] Ill., Free Press of Glencoe [1960, c.1959] 190p. 22cm. Includes bibliography. 59-6826 4.50 bds.,
1. Religion and sociology. 2. Religion. 3. Rites and ceremonies. I. Title.

CAIN, Arthur H. 291
Young people and religion [by] Arthur H. Cain. New York, John Day Co. [1970] 159 p. 21 cm. Bibliography: p. 156-159. Examines the philosophical principles of the world's major religions and discusses the nature of the religious experience and its importance to man. [BL48.C3] 73-124155 4.95
1. Religion—Juvenile literature. 2. Religions—Juvenile literature. I. Title.

CAMPBELL, Joseph, 1904- 291
The hero with a thousand faces. New York, Meridian Books, 1956 [c1949] 416 p. illus. 19 cm. (Meridian books, M22) [BL313] 56-6574
1. Mythology. 2. Psychoanalysis. I. Title.

CASSELS, Louis. 291
What's the difference? A comparison of the faiths men live by. Garden City, N.Y., Doubleday [1968,c.1965] 221p. 21cm. (Waymark bk., W10) Bibl. [BL425.C3] 65-17248 1.95 pap.,
1. Creeds—Comparative studies. 2. Religions. I. Title.

CASSELS, Louis. 291
What's the difference? A comparison of the faiths men live by. [1st ed.] Garden City, N.Y., Doubleday, 1965. xi, 221 p. 22 cm. [BL425.C3] 65-17248
1. Creeds—Comparative studies. 2. Religions. I. Title.

CATOIR, John T. 291
The way people pray; an introduction to the history of religions, by John T. Catoir. New York, Paulist Press [1974] v, 138 p. 18 cm. (Deus books) [BL80.2.C37] 73-91369 ISBN 0-8091-1805-X 1.45 (pbk.)
1. Religions. I. Title.

*CHARROUX, Robert. 291
Masters of the world. Translated by Lowell Blair. [New York] Berkley Pub. Co. [1974, c1967] xi, 252 p. illus. 18 cm. (A Berkley medallion book) [BT22] ISBN 0-425-02710-4 1.50 (pbk.)
1. Theology, Doctorinal—History. I. Title.

COLUM, Padraic, 1881-1972. 291
Myths of the world. 20 engravings by Boris Artzybasheff. New York, Grosset & Dunlap [1959? c1930] 327 p. illus. 21 cm. (The Universal library, UL-50) First published in 1930 under title: Orpheus: myths of the world. [BL310.C55 1959] 59-1389
1. Mythology. 2. Legends. I. Title.

CONFERENCE on New Approaches in Social Anthropology, Jeses College, Cambridge, Eng., 1963. 291
Anthropological approaches to the study of religion, edited by Michael Banton. New York, F. A. Praeger [1966] xiii, 176 p. illus. 23 cm. (A. S. A. Monographs, 3) Derived from material presented at a conference sponsored by the Association of Social Anthropologists of the Commonwealth. Includes bibliographies. [BL60.C58 1963c] 65-16223
1. Religion and Sociology. 2. Religion, Primitive. I. Banton, Michael P. ed. II. Association of Social Anthropologists of the Commonwealth. III. Cambridge. University. Jesus College. IV. Title. V. Series.

CONFERENCE on New Approaches in Social Anthropology, Jesus College, Cambridge, Eng., 1963 291
Anthropological approaches to the study of religion ed. by Michael Banton. New York, Praeger [c.1966] xlii, 176p. illus. 23cm. (A. S. A. monographs, 3) Derived from material presented at a conf. sponsored by the Assn. of Soc.Anthropologists of the Commonwealth. Bibl. [BL60.C58] 65-16223 6.50
1. Religion and sociology. 2. Religion, Primitive. I. Banton, Michael T., ed. II. Association of Social Anthropologists of the Commonwealth III. Cambridge. University. Jesus College. IV. Title. V. Series.

CONFERENCE on the Philosophy of Religion, University of Birmingham, 1970. 291
Truth and dialogue in world religions: conflicting truth-claims. Edited by John Hick. Philadelphia, The Westminster Press [1974] 164 p. 21 cm. Selected papers of the conference held in April, 1970. British ed. published under title: Truth and dialogue, the relationship between world religions. [BL51.C635 1970] 74-7244 ISBN 0-664-20713-8 5.95
1. Religion—Philosophy—Congresses. 2. Religions—Congresses. I. Hick, John, ed. II. Title.

CREIGHTON, David. 291
Deeds of gods and heroes [by] David Creighton. New York, St. Martin's Press [1967] 216 p. illus., map (on lining paper) 22 cm. Includes bibliographical references. Examines the mythologies of Greece, Rome, Egypt, Babylon, Troy, North America and Scandinavia. [PZ8.1.C873De] AC 67
1. Mythology. I. Title.

CUTTAT, Jacques Albert 291
The encounter of religions; a dialogue between the West and the Orient, with an essay on the prayer of Jesus. Translated [from the French] by Pierre de Fontnouvelle with Evis McGrew. Foreword by Dietrich von Hildebrand. New York, Desclee [1960] 159p., 22cm. (Bibl. notes) 60-10163 3.50
1. Religions. 2. Hesychasm. I. Title.

DAVIS, Charles, 1923- 291
Christ and the world religions. [New York] Herder and Herder [1971, c1970] 157 p. 22 cm. Originally given as the Sir D. Owens Evans Memorial Lectures at the University College of Wales, Aberystwyth, during the 1969-70 session. Bibliography: p. 143-149. [BR127.D37 1971] 73-168546 5.95
1. Christianity and other religions. I. Title.

*DEVADUTT, Vinjamuri E. 291
The Bible and the faiths of men. New York, Friendship [1967] 64p. 18cm. .85 pap.,
I. Title.

DICK, Kenneth C. 291
Man, father of the gods, by Kenneth C. Dick. [1st ed.] Brooklyn, T. Gaus' Sons, 1971. 550 p. 22 cm. (His Mighty pagan, v. 1) [BL80.2.D5] 76-148608 11.95
1. Religions. 2. Mysteries, Religious. 3. Sects. I. Title.

DUNLAP, Knight, 1875-1949. 291
Religion: its functions in human life; a study of religion from the point of view of psychology. Westport, Conn., Greenwood Press [1970, c1946] xi, 362 p. 23 cm. (McGraw-Hill publications in psychology) Reprint of the 1946 ed. Includes bibliographical references. [BL48.D8 1970] 77-100158
1. Religion. I. Title.

DYE, James W., comp. 291
Religions of the world; selected readings [compiled by] James W. Dye [and] William H. Forthman. New York, Appleton Century Crofts [1967] xi, 636 p. 24 cm. (The Century philosophy series) Includes bibliographies. [BL29.D9] 67-18207
1. Religious literature. I. Forthman, William H., joint comp. II. Title.

DYER, Alvin Rulon. 291
This age of confusion; presaging the need for the restoration of the truth concerning life's great questions: Who am I? Whence am I? Whither am I going? By Alvin R. Dyer. Salt Lake City, Deseret Book Co., 1965. xxvi, 344 p. maps. 24 cm. Bibliography: p. [333]-336] [BL85.D9] 65-27486
1. Religions. I. Title.

EDUCATIONAL Research Council of America. Social Science Staff. 291
The human adventure, four world views / prepared by the Social Science Staff of the Educational Research Council of America. Learner-verified ed. 2. Boston : Allyn and Bacon, c1975. v, 154 p. : ill. (some col.) ; 26 cm. (Concepts and inquiry, the Educational Research Council social science program) Includes index. Explains the fundamentals of four classical approaches to life: the traditional Chinese, Buddhist, Hebrew, and Greek. [BL92.E37 1975] 74-4923 pbk. : 3.80
1. Religions—Juvenile literature. I. Title. II. Title: Four world views. III. Series.

ELIADE, Mircea, 1907- 291
Occultism, witchcraft, and cultural fashions : essays in comparative religions / Mircea Eliade. Chicago : University of Chicago Press, 1976. 148 p. ; 21 cm. Includes bibliographical references and index. [BL80.2.E43] 75-12230 ISBN 0-226-20391-3 : 6.95
1. Religions—History. 2. Occult sciences. I. Title.

ELIADE, Mircea, 1907- 291
Patterns in comparative religion. Tr. [from French] by Rosemary Sheed. Cleveland, World [1963, c.1958] 484p. 21cm. (Meridian bk., M155) Bibl. 2.25 pap.,
1. Religions. I. Title.

ELIADE, Mircea, 1907- 291
Patterns in comparative religion. Translated by Rosemary Sheed. New York, Sheed & Ward [1958] xv, 484 p. 22 cm. Translation of Traite d'histoire des religions. Includes bibliographies. [BL80.E513] 58-5885
1. Religions. I. Title.

ELIADE, Mircea, 1907- 291
Zalmoxis, the vanishing God; comparative studies in the religions and folklore of Dacia and Eastern Europe. Translated by Willard R. Trask. Chicago, University of Chicago Press [1972] x, 260 p. 23 cm. Translation of De Zalmoxis a Gengis-Khan. Includes bibliographical references. [BL975.G5E414] 72-76487 ISBN 0-226-20398-0
1. Getae—Religion. 2. Zamoixis. 3. Folklore—Romania. 4. Dacia—Religion. I. Title.

ELLWOOD, Robert S., 1933- 291
Many peoples, many faiths : an introduction to the religious life of mankind / Robert S. Ellwood, Jr. Englewood Cliffs, N.J. : Prentice-Hall, c1976. xiii, 365 p. : ill. ; 24 cm. Includes index. Bibliography: p. 341-355. [BL80.2.E45] 75-37878 ISBN 0-13-555995-2 : 10.95
1. Religions. 2. Religion. I. Title.

EVANS-PRITCHARD, Edward Eban 1902- 291
Theories of primitive religion. Oxford, Clarendon Pr. [New York, Oxford, c.]1965. 132p. 23cm. (Sir D. Owen Evans lects., 1962) Bibl. [GN470.E9] 65-29790 4.00
1. Religion, Primitive. I. Title. II. Series.

EVANS-PRITCHARD, Edward Evan, 1902- 291
Theories of primitive religion. Oxford, Clarendon Pr., [1967, c.1965] 132p. 22cm. (Sir Owen Evans. lects., 1962) Bibl. [GN470.E9] 65-29790 2.00 pap.,
1. Religion, Primitive. I. Title. II. Series.
Available from Oxford Univ. Pr., New York.

FERM, Vergilius Ture Anselm, 1896- ed. 291
Religion in the twentieth century. Edited by Vergilius Ferm. New York, Greenwood Press [1969, c1948] xix, 470 p. 23 cm. Includes bibliographies. [BL98.F4 1969] 74-90706
1. Religions. I. Title.

FRAZER, James George Sir 291
The golden bough a study in magic and religion. 1 volume. Abriged ed. New York, Macmillan, [1960, c.1922, 1950] xvi, 864p. 22cm. (Macmillan paperbacks, 5) 2.50 pap.,
1. Mythology. 2. Religion, Primitive. 3. Magic. 4. Superstition. I. Title.

FRAZER, James George, Sir 1854-1941. 291
Adonis, Attis, Osiris; studies in the history of Oriental religion. 3d ed., rev., enl. New Hyde Park, N.Y., University Bks. [1962, c.1961] xxviii, 317, 321p. illus. 'Part IV of [the author's] The golden bough, a study in magic and religion.' Bibl. 61-15336 10.00
1. Adonis. 2. Attis. 3. Osiris. 4. Religions—Hist. I. Title.

FRAZER, James George, Sir, 1854-1941. 291
The golden bough; a study in magic and religion. Abridged ed. New York, Macmillan, 1951 [c1950] xvi, 864 p. 22 cm. [BL310.F72 1951] A 52
1. Mythology. 2. Religion, Primitive. 3. Magic. 4. Superstition. I. Title.

FRAZER, James George, Sir 1854-1941 291
The new Golden bough; a new abridgment of the classic work. Ed., notes, foreword. by Theodor H. Gaster [New York] New Amer. Lib. [1964, c.1959] 832p. 18cm. (Mentor bk., MY594) Bibl. 1.25 pap.,
1. Mythology. 2. Religion, Primitive. 3. Magic. 4. Superstition. I. Title.

FRAZER, James George, Sir 1854-1941 291
The new Golden bough; a new abridgment of the classic work. Ed., notes, foreword. by Theodor H. Gaster. Garden City, N.Y., Doubleday 1961 [c.1959] xx, 426p. (Doubleday anchor magnum A270) Bibl. 1.95 pap.,
1. Mythology. 2. Religion, Primitive. 3. Magic. 4. Superstition. I. Title.

FRAZER, James George, Sir, 1854-1941. 291
The new Golden bough: a new abridgment of the classic work. Edited, and with notes and foreword, by Theodor H. Gaster. New York, Criterion Books [1959] xxx, 738 p. 24 cm. Bibliographical references included in "Notes" and in "Additional notes." [BL310.F72 1959] 59-6125
1. Mythology. 2. Religion, Primitive. 3. Magic. 4. Superstition. I. Title.

FRIEDER, Emma. 291
Essays in religion. 2d rev. ed. New York, Hurst Pub. Co. [1971] 152 p. 22 cm. Bibliography: p. [147]-152. [BL50.F73 1971] 77-26292 5.00
1. Religion—Addresses, essays, lectures. I. Title.

FRIEDER, Emma. 291
Essays in religion. [1st ed.] New York, Exposition Press [1968] 152 p. 22 cm. (An Exposition-testament book) Bibliography: p. [147]-152. [BL50.F73] 68-24888 5.00
1. Religion—Addresses, essays, lectures. I. Title.

FRIEDMAN, Maurice S. 291
Touchstones of reality; existential trust and the community of peace [by] Maurice Friedman. [1st ed.] New York, Dutton, 1972. 341 p. 22 cm. Includes bibliographical references. [BL48.F75 1972] 74-165598 ISBN 0-525-22160-3 10.00
1. Religions. 2. Religion. I. Title.

FRIEDMAN, Maurice S. 1921- 291
Touchstones of reality; existential trust and the community of peace, [by] Maurice Friedman. New York, Dutton, 1974 341 p. 19 cm. [BL48.F75 1974] ISBN 0-525-47369-6 3.95 (pbk.)
1. Religious. 2. Religion. I. Title.
L.C. card no. for original ed.: 74-165598.

GASTER, Theodor Herzl, 1906- 291
Thespis; ritual, myth and drama in the ancient Near East. Foreword by Gilbert Murray. New York, Schuman [1950] xv, 498 p. 24 cm. "Translations of ancient Near Eastern dramatic texts": p. 111-443. Bibliography: p. 483-494. [BL1060.G3] 50-6864
1. Levant—Religion. 2. Rites and ceremonles. 3. Mythology. 4. Drama. 5. Seasons. I. Title.

GOLDBERG, Ben Zion, 1895- 291
The sacred fire; the story of sex in religion. Introd. by Charles Francis Potter. New York, Grove [1962, c.1930, 1958] 288p. illus. 18cm. (Black cat bk., BC-23) Bibl. .75 pap.,
1. Sex and religion. I. Title.

GOODE, William J. 291
Religion among the primitives; with an introd. by Kingsley Davis. Glencoe, Ill., Free Press ['1951] 321 p. 25 cm. Bibliography: p. 259-269. [BL60.G6] 51-11596
1. Religion and sociology. 2. Religion, Primitive. I. Title.

GOODE, William Josiah. 291
Religion among the primitives; with an introd. by Kingsley Davis. Glencoe, Ill., Free Press [1951] 321 p. 25 cm. Bibliography: p. 259-269. [BL60.G6] 51-11596
1. Religion and sociology. 2. Religion, Primitive. I. Title.

GOODE, William Josiah 291
Religion among the primitives. Introd. by Kingsley Davis. New York, Free Pr. [1964, c.1951] 321p. 21cm. Bibl. 1.95 pap.,
1. Religion and sociology 2. Religion, Primitive. I. Title.

GRAY, Louis Herbert, 1875-1955,ed. 291
The mythology of all races. Louis Herbert Gray, editor. George Foot Moore, consulting editor. New York, Cooper Square Publishers, 1964 [c1916-32] 13 v. illus., maps (part fold.) plates (part col.) 24 cm. Vols. 2, 4-5, 7-8, 13 are edited by J. A. Macculloch and G. F. Moore. Includes bibliographies. [BL25.M8] 65-3246
1. Mythology. I. Macculloch, John Arnott, 1868-1950 ed. II. Title.

GRIMAL, Pierre, ed. 291
Larousse world mythology [Tr. from French by Patricia Beardsworth] New York, Putnam [c.1965] 560p. illus., col. plates. 30cm. Bibl. [BL311.G683] 65-19763 25.00; until Jan. 1, 19.95
1. Mythology. I. Title.

GRIMAL, Pierre, 1912- ed. 291
Larousse world mythology. [Translated by Patricia Beardsworth] New York, Putnam [1965] 560 p. illus., col. plates. 30 cm. Translation "from Mythologies de la

Mediterranee au Gange and Mythologies des steppes, des iles et des forets." Bibliography: p. 546-547. [BL311.G683 1965] 65-19763
1. Mythology. I. Title.

HABEL, Norman C 291
Yahweh versus Baal: a conflict of religious cultures; a study in the relevance of Ugaritic materials for the early faith of Israel, by Norman C. Habel. New York, Published for the School for Graduate Studies, Concordia Seminary, St. Louis [by] Bookman Associates, 1964. 128 p. 21 cm. (Concordia Theological Seminary, St. Louis Graduate study no. 6) Revised and shortened ed. of the author's thesis, Concordia Theological Seminary. Bibliography: p. 119-121. [BL1670.H3] 64-14448
1. Res Shamra. 2. Palestine — Religion. 3. Bible. O.T. — Criticism, interpretation, etc. I. Title. II. Series: Concordia Theological Seminary, St. Louis. School for Graduate Studies. Graduate study no. 6

HASKINS, James, 1941- 291
Religions. [1st ed.] Philadelphia, Lippincott [1973] 157 p. 21 cm. Bibliography: p. 152-154. Discusses the history, practices, and beliefs of the five major religions in the world today: Hinduism, Buddhism, Judaism, Christianity, and Islam. [BL92.H37] 72-11768 ISBN 0-397-31212-1 4.95
1. Religions—Juvenile literature. I. Title.

HAWKRIDGE, Emma. 291
The wisdom tree. Illustrated with photos., line drawings by Theresa Garrett Eliot. Freeport, N.Y., Books for Libraries Press [1970, c1945] xvi, 504 p. illus. 23 cm. (Essay index reprint series) Bibliography: p. [487]-495. [BL80.H32 1970] 72-128257
1. Religions. I. Title.

HAYS, Hoffman Reynolds. 291
In the beginnings; early man and his gods. New York, Putnam [1963] 575 p. illus., maps. 24 cm. Bibliography: p. 539-558. [BL430.H39] 63-16173
1. Religion, Primitive. I. Title.

HOCKING, William Ernest, 1873-1966. 291
Living religions and a world faith / by William Ernest Hocking. New York : AMS Press, 1976. 291 p. ; 23 cm. (Philosophy in America) Reprint of the 1940 ed. published by Macmillan, New York, issued in series: Hibbert lectures, 1938. Includes bibliograhical references and index. [BL410.H6 1976] 75-3187 ISBN 0-404-59189-2 : 20.50
1. Religions (Proposed, universal, etc.) 2. Religion. 3. Christianity and other religions. I. Title. II. Series: Hibbert lectures (New York) ; 1938.

†HOPFE, Lewis M. 291
Religions of the world / Lewis M. Hopfe. Beverly Hills, Calif. : Glencoe Press, c1976. xii, 308 p. : ill. ; 23 cm. Includes bibliographical references and index. [BL80.2.H66] 75-8425 ISBN 0-02-474810-2 pbk. : 7.95
1. Religions. I. Title.

HOPKINS, Edward Washburn, 1857-1932. 291
Origin and evolution of religion. New York, Cooper Square Publishers, 1969. 370 p. 23 cm. Reprint of the 1923 ed. Bibliographical footnotes. [BL430.H6 1969] 76-79199 10.00
1. Religion, Primitive. 2. Folk-lore. 3. Religions. 4. Nature worship. 5. Trinities. I. Title.

HUME, Robert Ernest, 1877-1948. 291
The world's living religions, with special reference to their sacred scriptures and in comparison with Christianity; an historical sketch. Completely rev. New York, Scribner [1972, c1959] xii, 335 p. 21 cm. (The Scribner Library. Lyceum editions, SL 349) Bibliography: p. 291-311. [BL98.H8 1972] 72-175350 ISBN 0-684-31054-6 3.95
1. Religions. 2. Christianity and other religions. I. Title.

HUXLEY, Francis. 291
The way of the sacred / Francis Huxley. Garden City, N.Y. : Doubleday, 1974. 320 p. : ill. (some col.) ; 26 cm. Includes index. [BL600.H8 1974] 73-19368 ISBN 0-385-04618-9 : 14.95
1. Holy, The. 2. Symbolism. 3. Rites and ceremonies. I. Title.

IBN KAMMUNAH, Sa'd ibn Mansur, 13th cent. 291
Sa d b. Mansar Ibn Kammuna's examination of the inquiries into the three faiths; a thirteenth-century essay in comparative religion. Ed. by Moshe Perlmann. Berkeley, Univ. of Calif. Pr. 1967. xii, 119p. 26cm. (Univ. of Calif. pubns. Near Eastern studies, v. 6) Added t. p. in Arabic. [BL75.12] 67-65689 4.00 pap.,
1. Religions—Early works to 1800. I. Perlmann, Moshe, ed. II. Title Examination of the inquiris into the three faiths. III. Title. IV. Series: California. University. Universty of Calforna publications. Near Eastern studies, v.6

INTERNATIONAL Congress of Anthropological and Ethnological Sciences, 9th, Chicago, 1973. 291
The realm of the extra-human : ideas and actions / editor Agehananda Bharati The Hague : Mouton ; Chicago : distributed by Aldine, c1976. xi, 521 p., [5] leaves of plates : ill. ; 24 cm. (World anthropology) Includes bibliographies and indexes. [BL21.I64 1973] 77-353259 ISBN 0-202-90027-4 : 24.50
1. Religion—Congresses. 2. Rites and ceremonies—Congresses. I. Agehananda Bharati, Swami, 1923- II. Title. III. Series.

INTERNATIONAL Congress of Anthropological and Ethnological Sciences, 9th, Chicago, 1973. 291
The Realm of the extra-human : agents and audiences / ed. Agehananda Bharati The Hague : Mouton ; Chicago : distributed by Aldine, c1976. xii, 556 p., [6] leaves of plates : ill. ; 24 cm. (World anthropology) Includes bibliographies and index. [BL21.I64 1973a] 77-353256 ISBN 0-202-90026-6 : 27.50
1. Religion—Congresses. 2. Rites and ceremonies—Congresses. 3. Shamanism—Congresses. I. Agehananda Bharati, Swami, 1923- II. Title. III. Series.

JACK, Alex, 1945- 291
The new age dictionary / Alex Jack. Brookline, Mass. : Kanthaka Press, c1976. 224 p. ; 22 cm. [BP601.J3] 76-6217 ISBN 0-916926-03-6 : 10.00 ISBN 0-916926-02-8 pbk. : 5.00
1. Cults—Dictionaries. 2. Religions—Dictionaries. 3. Occult sciences—Dictionaries. 4. English language—Glossaries, vocabularies, etc. I. Title.

JAMES, Edwin Oliver, 1886- 291
The beginnings of religion; an introductory and scientific study. London, New York, Hutchinson's University Library [1950?] 159 p. 19 cm. (Hutchinson's university library: World religions, no. 8) Bibliography at end of each chapter. [BL430.J29] A 52
1. Religion, Primitive. I. Title.

JENSEN, Adolf Ellegard, 1899- 291
Myth and cult among primitive peoples. Translated by Marianna Tax Choldin and Wolfgang Weissleder. Chicago, University of Chicago Press [c1963] x, 349 p. 22 cm. [GN470.J413] 63-20909
1. Religion, Primitive. I. Title.

JENSEN, Adolf Ellegard, 1899- 291
Myth and cult among primitive peoples. Tr. [from German] by Marianna Tax Choldin, Wolfgang Weissleder. Chicago, Univ. of Chic. Pr. [c.1963] x, 349p. 22cm. 63-20909 8.75
1. Religion, Primitive. I. Title.

JEVONS, Frank Byron, 1858- 291
Comparative religion / by F. B. Jevons. Folcroft, Pa. : Folcroft Library Editions, 1976. vii, 154 p. ; 22 cm. Reprint of the 1913 ed. published at the University Press, Cambridge, Eng., in series: The Cambridge manuals of science and literature. Includes index. Bibliography: p. 145-146. [BL82.J48 1976] 76-57969 ISBN 0-8414-5326-8 lib. bdg. : 12.50
1. Religions. I. Title.

KELLETT, Arnold 291
Isms and ologies; a guide to unorthodox and non-Christian beliefs. New York, Philosophical [c.1965] 156p. 19cm. Bibl. [BR157] 65-28943 4.75 bds.,
1. Sects. I. Title.

KELLETT, Ernest Edward, 1864-1950. 291
A short history of religions. Freeport, N.Y., Books for Libraries Press [1971] 602 p. 23 cm. (Essay index reprint series) Reprint of the 1934 ed. Includes bibliographical references. [BL80.K43 1971] 71-156671 ISBN 0-8369-2281-6
1. Religions—History. I. Title.

KIM, Young Oon. 291
Living religions of the Middle East / Young Oon Kim. 1st ed. New York : Golden Gate Pub. Co., 1976. x, 275 p. ; 21 cm. (World religions ; v. 1) Includes bibliographies and index. [BM561.K5] 76-23739
1. Judaism. 2. Zoroastrianism. 3. Islam. I. Title.

KING, Winston Lee, 1907- 291
Buddhism and Christianity: some bridges of understanding. Philadelphia, Westminster [c.1962] 240p. 22cm. Bibl. 62-11075 5.00
1. Christianity and other religions—Buddhism. 2. Buddha and Buddhism—Relations—Christianity. I. Title.

KRAMER, Samuel Noah, 1897- ed. 291
Mythologies of the ancient world. Chicago, Quadrangle Books [c.1961] 480p. illus. Bibl. 7.50
1. Mythology. I. Title.

KRAMER, Samuel Noah, 1897- ed. 291
Mythologies of the ancient world. With contributions by Rudolf Anthes [and others. 1st ed.] Garden City, N.Y., Doubleday, 1961. 480 p. illus. 18 cm. (Anchor books, A229) Includes bibliography. [BL311.K7] 60-13538
1. Mythology. I. Title.

LEACH, Edmund Ronald. 291
Dialectic in practical religion; edited by E. R. Leach. London, published for the Department of Archaeology and Anthropology by Cambridge U.P., 1968. viii, 207 p. illus. 25 cm. (Cambridge papers in social anthropology, no. 5) Bibliography: p. 203-207. [GN470.L37] 67-21960 40/-
1. Religion, Primitive—Addresses, essays, lectures. I. Title. II. Series.

LOWIE, Robert Harry, 1883-1957. 291
Primitive religion. New York, Liveright [1970, c1948] xxii, 388 p. 21 cm. (Black and gold library) Bibliography: p. 367-381. [GN470.L6 1970] 75-114373 2.95
1. Religion, Primitive.

MCKAIN, David W. 291
Christianity : some non-Christian appraisals / edited by David W. McKain ; with an introd. by Robert Lawson Slater. Westport, Conn. : Greenwood Press, 1976, c1964. p. cm. Reprint of the ed. published by McGraw-Hill, New York. Bibliography: p. [BR127.M22 1976] 76-966 ISBN 0-8371-8144-5
1. Christianity and other religions—Addresses, essays, lectures. I. Title.

MCKAIN, David W. 291
Christianity : some non-Christian appraisals / edited by David W. McKain ; with an introd. by Robert Lawson Slater. Westport, Conn. : Greenwood Press, 1976, c1964. viii, 289 p. ; 23 cm. Reprint of the ed. published by McGraw-Hill, New York. Bibliography: p. 289. [BR127.M22 1976] 76-966 ISBN 0-8371-8144-5 lib.bdg. : 16.00
1. Christianity and other religions—Addresses, essays, lectures. I. Title.

MASSEY, Gerald, 1828-1907. 291
A book of the beginnings, containing an attempt to recover and reconstitute the lost origines of the myths and mysteries, types and symbols, religion and language, with Egypt for the mouthpiece and Africa as the birthplace / by Gerald Massey ; introd. by Leslie Shepard. Secaucus, N.J. : University Books, [1974] 2 v. ; 24 cm. Reprint of the 1881 ed. published by Williams and Norgate, London. Contents.Contents.—v. 1. Egyptian origines in the British Isles.—v. 2. Egyptain origines in the Hebrew, Akkado-Assyrian and Maori. Includes bibliographical references. [BL313.M37 1974] 74-75172 ISBN 0-8216-0211-X : 30.00
1. Mythology. 2. Religion, Primitive. 3. Folk-lore. 4. Language and languages—Etymology. 5. Egyptian language—Etymology—Names. I. Title: A book of the beginnings ...

MEHTA, Phirozshah Dorabji. 291
The heart of religion / P. D. Mehta. Tisbury [Eng.] : Compton Russell, 1976. vi, 436 p. ; 24 cm. Includes index. Bibliography: p. [391]-401. [BL48.M37 1976] 76-364994 ISBN 0-85955-029-X : £7.50
1. Religion. 2. Religions. I. Title.

MEYNELL, Hugo Anthony. 291
Sense, nonsense, and Christianity; an essay on the logical analysis of religious statements [by] Hugo A. Meynell. London, New York, Sheed and Ward [1964] 281 p. 18 cm. (Stagbooks) Bibliography: p. [271]-278. [BL65.L2M43] 67-66331
1. Religion and language. 2. Semantics (Philosophy) I. Title.

MIDDLETON, John, 1921- comp. 291
Gods and rituals; readings in religious beliefs and practices. [1st ed.] Garden City, N.Y., Published for the American Museum of Natural History [New York, by] the Natural History Press, 1967. x, 468 p. illus. 22 cm. (American Museum sourcebooks in anthropology) Bibliography: p. [437]-450. [GN470.M48] 67-12870
1. Religion, Primitive—Addresses, essays, lectures. I. American Museum of Natural History, New York. II. Title. III. Series.

MULLER, Friedrich Max, 1823-1900. 291
Anthropological religion / by F. Max Muller. New York : AMS Press, [1975] xxvii, 464 p. ; 18 cm. Reprint of the 1892 ed. published by Longmans, Green, London, New York, which was issued as Gifford lectures, 1891. Includes bibliographical references and index. [BL48.M76 1975] 73-18822 ISBN 0-404-11428-8 24.00
1. Religion. 2. Religions. 3. Soul. I. Title. II. Series: Gifford lectures ; 1891.

MULLER, Friedrich Max, 1823-1900. 291
Theosophy : or, Psychological religion / by F. Max Muller. New York : AMS Press, [1975] p. cm. Reprint of the 1903 ed. published by Longmans, Green, London, which had originally been issued in series, Gifford lectures, 1892, and was reissued as no. 4 of the author's collected works in 1898. Includes index. Bibliography: p. [BL87.M765 1975] 73-18830 34.50
1. Religions—Addresses, essays, lectures. 2. Religion—Philosophy—Addresses, essays, lectures. 3. Psychology, Religious—Addresses, essays, lectures. 4. Theism—Addresses, essays, lectures. I. Title. II. Series: Gifford lectures, 1892.

**MYTHOLOGY* 291
[notes] by Julia Wolfe Loomis Edit. bd. of consultants: Stanley Cooperman, Charles Leavitt. Unicio J. Violi. New York, Monarch Pr. [c.1965] 155p. 22cm. (Monarch notes and study guides 523-1) Cover title. Bibl. 1.00 pap.,

NATIONAL Geographic Society, Washington, D.C. Book Service. 291
Great religions of the world. Washington, National Geographic Society [1971] 420 p. illus. 27 cm. (The story of man library) Includes bibliographical references. [BL80.2.N347] 75-161575 ISBN 0-87044-103-5 11.95
1. Religions. I. Title.

NOCK, Arthur Darby, 1902- 291
Conversion; the old and the new in religion from Alexander the Great to Augustine of Hippo. [New York] Oxford [1961] xii, 309p. (Oxford paperbacks, 30) Bibl. 1.85 pap.,
1. Conversion. 2. Psychology, Religious. 3. Christianity and other religious. I. Donnellan lectures, 1931. II. Lowell institute lectures, 1933. III. Title.

NOTTINGHAM, Elizabeth Kristine, 1900- 291
Religion and society. Garden City, N.Y., Doubleday, 1954. 84 p. 24 cm. (Doubleday short studies in sociology, SSS5) [BL60.N6] 54-11418
1. Religion and sociology. I. Title.

O'DEA, Janet K. 291
Judaism, Christianity, and Islam [by] Janet K. O'Dea, Thomas F. O'Dea [and] Charles J. Adams. New York, Harper & Row [1972] 246 p. illus. 24 cm. (Religion and man) Bibliography: p. 221-223. [BL80.2.O32] 79-185897 ISBN 0-06-044893-8
1. Bible. O.T.—Theology. 2. Judaism—History—Medieval and early modern period, 425-1789. 3. Church history. 4. Islam—History. I. O'Dea, Thomas F., joint author. II. Adams, Charles J., joint author. III. Title. IV. Series.

PARKS, Mercer H. 291
The task worthy of travail / Mercer H. Parks. Houston, Tex. : Pacesetter Press, [1975] v, 522 p. ; 24 cm. Includes bibliographical references and index. [BL85.P34] 74-11835 ISBN 0-88415-784-9 : 15.00
1. Religions. 2. Creation (Literary, artistic, etc.) I. Title.

PARRINDER, Edward Geoffrey. 291
A book of world religions, by E. G. Parrinder. Chester Springs, Pa. Dufuor Editions, 1967. 176 p. illus., facsims., maps, ports. 26 cm. [BL80.2.P33] 67-15196
1. Religions. I. Title.

PARRINDER, Edward Geoffrey. 291
Comparative religion / by Geoffrey Parrinder. Westport, Conn. : Greenwood Press, 1975, c1962. 130 p. ; 22 cm. Reprint of the ed. published by Allen & Unwin, London. Includes bibliographical references and index. [BL80.2.P34 1975] 73-19116 ISBN 0-8371-7301-9
1. Religions. I. Title.

PARRINDER, Edward Geoffrey 291
What world religions teach. London, Harrap [Mystic, Conn., Verry, 1966, c.1963] 223p. 22cm. Bibl. [BL80.2.P35] 64-36019 3.50 bds.,
1. Religions. I. Title.

RADIN, Paul, 1883- 291
Primitive religion: its nature and origin. New

York, Dover Publications, 1957. 322p. 21cm. 'An unabridged republication of the first edition [published in 1937] with a new perface by the author.' [GN470.R3 1957] 57-4452
1. Religion, Primitive. I. Title.

RADIN, Paul, 1883- 291
Primitive religion: its nature and origin [Gloucester, Mass., P. Smith, 1964, c.1937, 1957] 322p. 21cm. (Dover bk. rebound) Bibl. 3.85
1. Religion, Primitive. I. Title.

RADIN, Paul, 1883-1959. 291
Primitive religion: its nature and origin. New York, Dover Publications, 1957. 322 p. 21 cm. "An unabridged republication of the first edition [published in 1937] with a new preface by the author." [GN470.R3 1957] 57-4452
1. Religion, Primitive. I. Title.

RAGLAN, FitzRoy Richard Somerset, baron, 1885- 291
The hero; a study in tradition, myth, and drama. [1st Vintage ed.] New York, Vintage Books, 1956. 296p. 19cm. (Vintage books, K32) [BL325.H46R3 1956] 56-13693
1. Heroes. 2. Mythology. 3. Folk-lore. 4. Drama. I. Title.

RAHNER, Hugo, 1900- 291
Greek myths and Christian mystery. With a foreword by E. O. James. [Translation by Brian Battershaw] New York, Harper & Row [1963] 399 p. illus. 23 cm. [BR128.G8R33] 63-16404
1. Christianity and other religions—Greek. 2. Mythology, Greek. 3. Mysteries, Religious. I. Title.

RAHNER, Hugo, 1900- 291
Greek myths and Christian mystery. Foreword by E. O. James. [Tr. by Brian Battershaw] New York, Harper [c.1963] 399p. illus. 23cm. 63-16404 10.00
1. Christianity and other religions—Greek. 2. Mythology, Greek. 3. Mysteries, Religious. I. Title.

RAHNER, Hugo, 1900-1968. 291
Greek myths and Christian mystery. With a foreword by E. O. James. [Translation by Brian Battershaw] New York, Biblo and Tannen, 1971 [c1963] xxii, 399 p. illus. 22 cm. Translation of Griechische Mythen in christlicher Deutung. Includes bibliographical references. [BR128.G8R33 1971] 79-156736 ISBN 0-8196-0270-1
1. Christianity and other religions—Greek. 2. Mythology, Greek. 3. Mysteries, Religious. 4. Greece—Religion. I. Title.

RASCHKE, Carl A. 291
Religion and the human image / Carl A. Raschke, James A. Kirk, Mark C. Taylor. Englewood Cliffs, N.J. : Prentice-Hall, c1977. xi, 274 p. ; 23 cm. Includes bibliographies and index. [BL48.R29] 76-43047 ISBN 0-13-773424-7 pbk. : 6.95
1. Religion. 2. Religions. I. Kirk, James A., joint author. II. Taylor, Mark C., 1945- joint author. III. Title.

RELIGION and man; 291
an introduction [by] Robert D. Baird [and others]. W. Richard Comstock, general editor. New York, Harper & Row [1971] viii, 676 p. illus. 24 cm. Includes bibliographies. [BL48.R4] 79-141175 ISBN 0-06-041337-9
1. Religion. 2. Religions. I. Baird, Robert D., 1933- II. Comstock, W. Richard, ed.

RELIGIOUS syncretism in 291
antiquity : essays in conversation with Geo Widengren / edited by Birger A. Pearson. Missoula, Mont. : Published by Scholars Press for the American Academy of Religion and the Institute of Religious Studies, University of California, Santa Barbara, 1975. p. cm. (Symposium series - American Academy of Religion and Institute of Religious Studies, University of California, Santa Barbara ; no. 1) Based on a symposium held in Santa Barbara, Calif., on April 21-22, 1972, sponsored by the Institute of Religious Studies of the University of California, Santa Barbara. Includes bibliographical references. [BL21.R45] 75-29421 ISBN 0-89130-037-6 : 4.90
1. Religion—Congresses. I. Widengren, Geo, 1907- II. Pearson, Birger Albert. III. California. University, Santa Barbara. Institute of Religious Studies. IV. Series: American Academy of Religion. Symposium series — American Academy of Religion and Institute of Religious Studies, University of California, Santa Barbara ; no. 1.

RICE, Edward. 291
The five great religions. Photos. by the author. New York, Four Winds Press [1973] 180 p. illus. 26 cm. [BL80.2.R49] 72-87074 7.46
1. Religions. I. Title.

SALIBA, John A. 291
"Homo religiosus" in Mircea Eliade : an anthropological evaluation / by John A. Saliba. Leiden : Brill, 1976. vi, 210 p. ; 25 cm. (Supplementa ad Numen : Altera series) (Dissertaiones ad historiam religionum pertinentes ; v. 5) Bibliography: p. [178]-209. [BL48.S26] 76-482577 ISBN 9-00-404550-3 : fl 48.00
1. Eliade, Mircea, 1907- 2. Religion—History. 3. Anthropology—History. I. Title. II. Series. III. Series: Numen : Supplementa : Altera series.

SALTUS, Edgar Everston, 1855-1921. 291
The lords of the ghostland; a history of the ideal. [1st AMS ed.] New York, AMS Press [1970] 215 p. 23 cm. Reprint of the 1907 ed. [BL85.S3 1970] 71-116003 ISBN 0-404-05539-7
1. Religions. I. Title.

SCHURE, Edouard, 1841-1929. 291
From Sphinx to Christ; an occult history. Blauvelt, N.Y., R. Steiner Publications, 1970. 284 p. 22 cm. Translation of L'evolution divine. Includes bibliographical references. [BL80.S28 1970] 70-130818 10.00
1. Religions. I. Title.

SCHURE, Edouard, 1841-1929. 291
The great initiates : a study of the secret history of religions / by Edouard Schure ; translated from the French by Gloria Rasberry ; introd. by Paul M. Allen. Blauvelt, N.Y. : Multimedia Pub. Corp., 1976, c1961. 526 p. : port. ; 21 cm. (Steinerbooks) Translation of Les grands inities. Includes bibliographical references and index. [BL80.S33 1976] 76-360634 6.95
1. Religions. I. Title.

SMART, Ninian, 1927- 291
The religious experience of mankind / by Ninian Smart. 2d ed. New York : Scribner, c1976. xii, 594 p. : ill. ; 24 cm. Includes index. Bibliography: p. [563]-568. [BL80.2.S6 1976] 76-1437 ISBN 0-684-14647-9 : 17.50. ISBN 0-684-14648-7 pbk. : 6.95.
1. Religions—History. 2. Religion. 3. Experience (Religion) I. Title.

SPARKS, Jack. 291
The mindbenders : a look at current cults / Jack Sparks. Nashville : T. Nelson, c1977. vii, 283 p. ; 21 cm. Bibliography: p. 281-283. [BP603.S65] 77-3564 ISBN 0-8407-5614-3 : 3.95
1. Cults. I. Title.

SPENCE, Lewis. 291
The outlines of mythology. Introd. by Daniel B. Dodson [Gloucester, Mass., Peter Smith, 1963, c.1944, 1961] 144p. 19cm. (Premier bk. rebound) Bibl. 2.50
1. Mythology. I. Title.

SPINK, Walter M. 291
The axis of Eros [by] Walter M. Spink. New York, Schocken Books [1973] 191 p. illus. 25 cm. [BL460.S67] 73-79055 ISBN 0-8052-3512-4 10.00
1. Phallicism—Miscellanea. 2. Sin—Miscellanea. I. Title.

SPINK, Walter M. 291
The axis of Eros [by] Walter M. Spink. Baltimore, Penguin Books [1975, c1973] 191 p. illus. 24 cm. [BL460.S67] ISBN 0-14-004017-X 3.95 (pbk.)
1. Phallicism—Miscellanea. 2. Sin—Miscellanea I. Title.
L.C. card number for original ed.: 73-79055

SPRINGER, Charles R 291
Christianity and rival religions, by Charles R. Springer. Philadelphia, Fortress Press [1966] vii, 53 p. 19 cm. (A Fortress book) Bibliographical footnotes. [BR127.S76] 66-10797
1. Christianity and other religions. I. Title.

SPRINGER, Charles R. 291
Christianity and rival religions. Philadelphia, Fortress [c.1966] vii. 53p. 19cm. (Fortress bk.) Bibl. [BR127.S76] 66-10797 1.00 bds.,
1. Christianity and other religions. I. Title.

SRIVASTAVA, Rama Shanker. 291
Comparative religion / by Rama Shanker Srivastava ; with a foreword by N. K. Devaraja. New Delhi : Munshiram Manoharlal Publishers, 1974, c1973. xv, 316 p. ; 23 cm. Includes index. Bibliography: p. [305]-311. [BL80.2.S67 1974] 74-904268 14.00
1. Religions. I. Title.
Distributed by South Asia Books.

STONER, Carroll. 291
All gods children : the cult experience—salvation or slavery? / Carroll Stoner and Jo Anne Parke. Radnor, Pa. : Chilton, c1977. xviii, 324 p. ; 22 cm. Includes index. Bibliography: p. [308]-309. [BP603.S8 1977] 77-3396 ISBN 0-8019-6620-5: 8.95
1. Cults. 2. Youth—Religious life. I. Parke, Jo Anne, joint author. II. Title.

SYLVIA MARY, Sister. 291
Nostalgia for paradise. New York, Desclee [1966, c1965] x, 230 p. 22 cm. Bibliographical footnotes. [BR127.S9] 65-15995
1. Christianity and other religions — Addresses, essays, lectures. I. Title.

SZUNYOGH, Bela, 1923- 291
Crisis in religion; an introduction to the science and philosophy of religion. [1st ed.] New York, Exposition Press [1955] 135p. illus. 21cm. [BL48.S965] 55-10306
1. Religion. 2. Religion—Philosophy. I. Title.

TANNER, Florice. 291
The mystery teachings in world religions. Wheaton, Ill., Theosophical Pub. House [1973] 192 p. 21 cm. (A Quest book original) Includes bibliographical references. [BL80.2.T29] 73-8887 ISBN 0-8356-0439-X 2.45 (pbk.)
1. Religions. I. Title.

TO Promote Good Will (Television program) 291
To promote good will [by] William Kailer Dunn, [others] Ed. by Lee Joyce Richmond, Mary E. Weller. Helicon [dist. New York, Taplinger, c.1965] 184p. 21cm. Transcribed from tape recordings of discussions between a rabbi, a Catholic priest, and a Protestant minister in the Baltimore interfaith program, sponsored by the American Legion. [BL410.T6] 65-24132 4.50 bds.,
1. Religions—Relations. I. Dunn, William Kailer. II. Richmond. Lee Joyce, ed. III. Weller, Mary Eileen, ed. IV. American Legion. V. Title.

VICKERY, John B. 291
The literary impact of The golden bough, by John B. Vickery. Princeton, Princeton University Press [1973] viii, 435 p. 25 cm. Includes bibliographical references. [BL310.F713V52] 72-4049 ISBN 0-691-06243-9 16.50
1. Frazer, James George, Sir, 1854-1941. The golden bough. I. Title.

VIGEVENO, H. S. 291
The listener, by H. S. Vigeveno. Glendale, Calif., G/L Regal Books [1971] 153 p. 18 cm. [BR157.V5] 73-123872 ISBN 0-8307-0084-6 0.95
1. Sects. 2. Religions. 3. Atheism. I. Title.

WATTS, Alan Wilson, 1915- 291
Behold the spirit; a study in the necessity of mystical religion [by] Alan Watts. [New ed.] New York, Pantheon Books [1971] xxviii, 257 p. 22 cm. Bibliography: p. 253-257. [BV5082.W37 1971] 79-162581 ISBN 0-394-47341-8 5.95
1. Mysticism. I. Title.

WHALEN, William Joseph. 291
Other religions in a world of change / William J. Whalen, Carl J. Pfeifer. Notre Dame, Ind. : Ave Maria Press, [1974] 127 p. : ill. ; 21 cm. Selected articles which appeared in the weekly NC News Service Know your faith columns in 1973. Includes index. Bibliography: p. 121-124. [BL80.2.W45] 74-81341 ISBN 0-87793-075-9 : 1.75
1. Religions. 2. Sects. I. Pfeifer, Carl J. II. Title.

WHITSON, Robley Edward. 291
The coming convergence of world religions. New York, Newman Press [1971] xiii, 209 p. 24 cm. Includes bibliographical references. [BL85.W47] 74-162344 6.50
1. Religions. 2. Theology. I. Title.

WHITTAKER, Thomas, 1856-1935. 291
Priests, philosophers and prophets; a dissertation on revealed religion. Port Washington, N.Y., Kennikat Press [1970] 251 p. 22 cm. Reprint of the 1911 ed. Bibliographical footnotes. [BL48.W4 1970] 77-102589
1. Religion. 2. Christianity and other religions. I. Title.

WORDS of the world's 291
religions : an anthology / Robert S. Ellwood, Jr. Englewood Cliffs, N.J. : Prentice-Hall, c1977. x, 421 p. ; 23 cm. Includes bibliographical references. Reading selections exploring the religious traditions of Judaism, Christianity, and Islam, in addition to Eastern religions and those of ancient Egypt and the Near East. [BL25.W67] 76-49545 ISBN 0-13-965004-0 pbk. : 7.95
1. Religions—Addresses, essays, lectures. 2. Religion—Addresses, essays, lectures. I. Ellwood, Robert S., 1933-

YAGER, Thomas C. 1918- 291
The best in life / by Thomas C. Yager. [Los Angeles? : Yager?, 1975] vii, 101 p. : ports. ; 25 cm. Includes bibliographies and index. [BL80.2.Y25] 75-15008
1. Religions. I. Title.

ZAEHNER, Robert Charles. 291
At sundry times : an essay in the comparison of religions / by R. C. Zaehner. Westport, Conn. : Greenwood Press, 1977, c1958. 230 p. ; 22 cm. Reprint of the ed. published by Faber and Faber, London. Includes bibliographical references and index. [BL80.2.Z27 1977] 76-49621 ISBN 0-8371-9354-0 lib. bdg. : 15.00
1. Religions. 2. Christianity and other religions. I. Title.

ZAEHNER, Robert Charles. 291
Concordant discord: the interdependence of faiths: being the Gifford lectures on natural religion delivered at St. Andrews in 1967-1969, by R. C. Zaehner. Oxford, Clarendon P., 1970. ix, 464 p. 24 cm. (Gifford lectures, 1967/69) Includes bibliographical references. [BL625.Z17] 76-540412 ISBN 0-19-826624-3 80/-
1. Mysticism—Comparative studies—Addresses, essays, lectures. I. Title. II. Series.

ZEHAVI, A. M. 291
Handbook of the world's religions. Edited by A. M. Zehavi. New York, Watts, 1973. vii, 203 p. illus. 27 cm. Includes bibliographical references. [BL80.2.Z43] 73-9283 ISBN 0-531-02644-2 8.95
1. Religions. I. Title.

LISTON, Robert A. 291'.02'4055
By these faiths : religions for today / Robert A. Liston. New York : J. Messner, c1977. 192 p. ; 22 cm. Includes index. Bibliography: p. 187. Discusses the attitudes, beliefs, and practices of the world's major religions and several minor sects and cults. [BL92.L57] 77-23324 ISBN 0-671-32836-0 lib. bdg. : 7.29
1. Religions—Juvenile literature. 2. Sects—Juvenile literature. I. Title.

*BRAY, Frank Chapin, 1866- 291.03
Bray's university dictionary of mythology. New York, Apollo [1964, c.1935] 323p. 20cm. (A-81) 1.95 pap.,
1. Mythology—Dictionaries. I. Title.

A Dictionary of 291'.03
comparative religion. General editor: S. G. F. Brandon. New York, Scribner [1970] 704 p. 27 cm. Includes bibliographies. [BL31.D54 1970] 76-111390 17.50
1. Religions—Dictionaries. I. Brandon, Samuel George Frederick, ed.

SEBEOK, Thomas Albert, 1920- ed. 291.04
Myth: a symposium. Philadelphia, American Folklore Society, 1955. 110p. diagrs. 26cm. (Bibliographical and special series of the American Folklore Society, v. 5) [BL310.S37] 56-1838
1. Mythology— Addresses, essays, lectures. I. Title. II. Series: American Folklore Society. Bibliographical and special series, v. 5

†DE RIOS, Marlene Dobkin. 291'.042
The wilderness of mind : sacred plants in crosscultural perspective / Marlene Dobkin De Rios. Beverly Hills : Sage Publications, c1976. 79 p. ; 22 cm. (Sage research papers in the social sciences ; ser. no. 90.039 : Cross-cultural studies series) Sponsored by the East-West Center. Bibliography: p. 73-78. [GN472.4.D47] 76-55088 ISBN 0-8039-0752-4 pbk. : 3.00
1. Religion, Primitive. 2. Hallucinogenic plants. 3. Hallucinogenic drugs and religious experience. I. East-West Center. II. Title. III. Series: Sage research papers in the social sciences : Cross-cultural studies series.

ERMAN, Adolf, 1854-1937. 291'.042
A handbook of Egyptian religion. Published in the original German ed. as a handbook, by the General Verwaltung of the Berlin Imperial Museums. Translated by A. S. Griffith. Boston, Milford House [1973] p. Translation of Die Agyptische Religion. Reprint of the 1907 ed. published by A. Constable, London. [BL2441.E653 1973] 73-13699 ISBN 0-87821-183-7 25.00 (lib. bdg.)
1. Egypt—Religion. 2. Mythology, Egyptian. I. Title.

JAMES, Edwin Oliver, 1886- 291'.042
The beginnings of religion; an introductory and scientific study, by E. O. James. Westport, Conn., Greenwood Press [1973] 159 p. 22 cm. Reprint of the 1950 ed., which was issued as no. 8 of Hutchinson's university library: World religions. Includes bibliographies. [BL430.J29 1973] 72-11737 ISBN 0-8371-6706-X
1. Religion, Primitive. I. Title.

JAMES, Edwin Oliver, 1886- 291'.042
The beginnings of religion; an introductory

and scientific study, by E. O. James. Westport, Conn., Greenwood Press [1973] 159 p. 22 cm. Reprint of the 1950 ed., which was issued as no. 8 of Hutchinson's university library: World religions. Includes bibliographies. [BL430.J29 1973] 72-11737 ISBN 0-8371-6706-X 8.50
1. Religion, Primitive. I. Title.

MALINOWSKI, Bronislaw, 1884-1942. 291'.042
The foundation of faith and morals : an anthropological analysis of primitive beliefs and conduct with special reference to the fundamental problems of religion and ethics : delivered before the University of Durham at Armstrong College, Newcastle-upon-Tyne, February 1935 / by Bronislaw Malinowski. [Folcroft, Pa.] : Folcroft Library Editions, 1974. p. cm. Reprint of the 1936 ed. published by Oxford University Press, H. Milford, London, which was issued as Riddell memorial lectures, 7th ser., 1934-35. [GN470.M2 1974] 74-20949 ISBN 0-8414-5965-7 lib. bdg. : 6.50
1. Religion, Primitive. 2. Trobriand Islands—Religion. 3. Religion. I. Title. II. Series: Riddell memorial lectures ; 7th ser., 1934-35.

MALINOWSKI, Bronislaw, 1884-1942. 291'.042
The foundations of faith and morals : an anthropological analysis of primitive beliefs and conduct with special reference to the fundamental problems of religion and ethics : delivered before the University of Durham at Armstrong College, Newcastle-upon-Tyne, February 1935 / by Bronislaw Malinowski. Folcroft, Pa. : Folcroft Library Editions, 1974. x, 62 p. ; 26 cm. Reprint of the 1936 ed. published by Oxford University Press, H. Milford, London, which was issued as Riddell memorial lectures, 7th ser., 1934-35. Includes bibliographical references. [GN470.M2 1974] 74-20949 ISBN 0-8414-5965-7 lib. bdg.
1. Religion, Primitive. 2. Trobriand Islands—Religion. 3. Religion. I. Title. II. Series: Riddell memorial lectures ; 7th ser., 1934-35.

MIDDLETON, John, 1921- comp. 291'.042
Gods and rituals : readings in religious beliefs and practices / edited by John Middleton. Austin : University of Texas Press, [1976] c1967. p. cm. (Texas Press sourcebooks in anthropology ; 6) Reprint of the ed. published by the Natural History Press, Garden City, N.Y., in series: American Museum sourcebooks in anthropology. Includes index. Bibliography: p. [GN470.M48 1976] 75-44032 ISBN 0-292-72708-9 pbk. : 6.95
1. Religion, Primitive—Addresses, essays, lectures. I. Title. II. Series. III. Series: American Museum sourcebooks in anthropology.

MULLER, Friedrich Max, 1823-1900. 291'.042
Physical religion / by F. Max Muller. New York : AMS Press, 1975. xii, 410 p. ; 19 cm. Reprint of the 1891 ed. published by Longmans, Green, London and New York, which was issued as Gifford lectures, 1890. Includes bibliographical references and index. [BL430.M83 1975] 73-18811 ISBN 0-404-11451-2 : 31.00
1. Vedas. 2. Religion, Primitive. 3. Natural theology. I. Title. II. Series: Gifford lectures ; 1890.

PERRY, William James. 291'.042
The origin of magic and religion, by W. J. Perry. Port Washington, N.Y., Kennikat Press [1971] ix, 212 p. front. 21 cm. Reprint of the 1923 ed. Includes bibliographical references. [BL430.P4 1971] 73-118543
1. Religion, Primitive. 2. Magic. I. Title.

KIRBAN, Salem. 291'.08 s
Armstrong's Church of God. Huntingdon Valley, Pa., S. Kirban Inc. [1970] 53 p. illus. (part col.), ports. 22 cm. (His Doctrines of devils, no. 1) [BL85.K56 no. 1] 70-21613 1.50
1. Radio Church of God. 2. Armstrong, Herbert W. I. Title.

KIRBAN, Salem. 291'.08 s
Christian Science. Huntingdon Valley, Pa., S. Kirban Inc. [1974] 59 p. 22 cm. (His Doctrines of devils, no. 4) Includes bibliographical references. [BL85.K56 no. 4] [BX6955] 289.5 74-163512 ISBN 0-912582-11-1 1.95 (pbk.)
1. Christian Science.

KIRBAN, Salem. 291'.08
Doctrines of devils; exposing the cults of our day. Huntingdon Valley, Pa., S. Kirban Inc. [1970- v. illus. (part col.), ports. 22 cm. Contents.Contents.—no. 1. Armstrong's Church of God.—no. 2. Mormonism. [BL85.K56] 75-124142
1. Religions—Controversial literature—Collected works. 2. Sects—Controversial literature—Collected works. I. Title.

KIRBAN, Salem. 291.08 s
Jehovah's Witnesses. Huntingdon Valley, Pa., S. Kirban Inc., c1972. 77 p. illus. 22 cm. (His Doctrine of devils, no. 3) Includes bibliographical references. [BL85.K56 no. 3] [BX8526] 289.9 73-174907 ISBN 0-912582-03-0 1.95
1. Jehovah's Witnesses—Doctrinal and controversial works.

KIRBAN, Salem. 291'.08 s
Mormonism. Huntingdon Valley, Pa., S. Kirban Inc. [1971] 61 p. illus. (part col.), ports. 22 cm. (His Doctrines of devils, no. 2) [BL85.K56 no. 2] [BX8645] 289'.3'3 72-196423 1.50
1. Mormons and Mormonism—Doctrinal and controversial works. I. Title.

WACH, Joachim, 1898-1955. 291'.08
Understanding and believing : essays / by Joachim Wach ; edited with an introd. by Joseph M. Kitagawa. Westport, Conn. : Greenwood Press, 1975, c1968. p. cm. Reprint of the 1st ed. published by Harper & Row, New York, which was issued as no. TB1399 of the Harper torchbooks. "Bibliography of Joachim Wach (1922-55)": p. [BL27.W26 1975] 75-31987 ISBN 0-8371-8488-6 : 12.75
1. Wach, Joachim, 1898-1955—Bibliography. 2. Religion—Addresses, essays, lectures. I. Title.
Contents omitted.

WACH, Joachim, 1898-1955. 291'.08
Understanding and believing; essays. Edited with an introd. by Joseph M. Kitagawa. [1st ed.] New York, Harper & Row [1968] xviii, 204 p. 21 cm. (Harper torchbooks, TB1399) Contents.Contents.—The self-understanding of modern man.—Stefan George; poet and priest of modern paganism.—The problem of death in modern philosophy.—General revelation and the religions of the world.—The paradox of the gospel.—Redeemer of man.—Seeing and believing.—Belief and witness.—The meaning and task of the history of religions.—Religious commitment and tolerance.—The problem of truth in religion.—The Christian professor.—The crisis in the university.—Hugo of St. Victor on virtues and vices.—To a rabbi friend.—On felicity.—A prayer.—Bibliography of Joachim Wach, 1922-55 (p. 188-196) Bibliographical footnotes. [BL27.W26] 68-29897 2.95
1. Wach, Joachim, 1898-1955—Bibliography. 2. Religion—Addresses, essays, lectures. I. Title.

LESSA, William Armand, ed. 291.082
Reader in comparative religion, an anthropological approach [ed. by] William A. Lessa, Evon Z. Vogt. 2d ed. New York, Harper [c.1958, 1965] xiii, 656p. illus. 27cm. Bibl. [BL80.2.L44] 65-12678 10.50
1. Religions—Collections. I. Vogt, Evon Zartman, 1918- joint ed. II. Title.

LESSA, William Armand, ed. 291.082
Reader in comparative religion, an anthropological approach [edited by] William A. Lessa [and] Evon Z. Vogt. 2d ed. New York, Harper & Row [1965] xiii, 656 p. illus. 27 cm. "Selected monographs on non-Western religious systems": p. 640-645. Bibliography: p. 646-653. [BL80.2.L44 1965] 65-12678
1. Religions—Collections. I. Vogt, Evon Zartman, 1918- joint ed. II. Title.

•ELIADE, Mircea. 291.09
Man and the sacred; a thematic source book of the history of religions New York, Harper & Row, [1974, c1967]. xiii, 173 p. 21 cm. Contains chapter 3 of From primatives to Zen. Bibliography: p. 171-172. [BL74.E4] 73-20950 ISBN 0-06-062137-0 2.25 (pbk.)
1. Religions—History—Sources. I. Title.

•ELIADE, Mircea, 1907- 291.09
Death, afterlife, and eschatology; a thematic source book of the history of religions. New York, Harper & Row [1974 c1967] xi., 109 p. 21 cm. Part 3 of From Primitives to Zen. Bibliography: 107-108. [BL74.E4] 73-20493 ISBN 0-06-062139-7 1.95 (pbk.)
1. Religions—History—Sources. I. Title.

ELIADE, Mircea, 1907- 291'.09
From primitives to Zen; a thematic sourcebook of the history of religions. [1st U.S. ed.] New York, Harper & Row [1967] xxv, 644 p. 24 cm. Bibliography: p. 635-643. [BL74.E4 1967] 66-20775
1. Religions—History—Sources. I. Title.

HINSHAW, Joseph Howard, 1890 291'.09
Elements of truth, by Joseph H. Hinshaw. New York, Philosophical Lib. [1967] xii, 144p. 22cm. Bibl. [BL80.2.H5] 67-13370 4.50
1. Religions—Hist. I. Title.

ALTIZER, Thomas J. J. 291'.092'4
Mircea Eliade and the dialectic of the sacred / by Thomas J. J. Altizer. Westport, Conn. : Greenwood Press, 1975, c1963. 219 p. ; 21 cm. Reprint of the ed. published by Westminster Press, Philadelphia. Includes bibliographical references and index. [BL43.E4A7 1975] 73-15398 ISBN 0-8371-7196-2 lib.bdg. : 12.25
1. Eliade, Mircea, 1907- I. Title.

ELIADE, Mircea, 1907- 291'.092'4 B
No souvenirs : journal, 1957-1969 / Mircea Eliade ; translated from the French by Fred H. Johnson, Jr. 1st ed. New York : Harper & Row, c1977. xiv, 343 p. ; 22 cm. Includes index. [BL43.E4A34 1977] 76-9969 ISBN 0-06-062141-9 : 15.00
1. Eliade, Mircea, 1907- 2. Religion historians—United States—Biography. I. Title.

GASTER, Theodor Herzl, 1906- 291.093
Thespis; ritual, myth.,and drama in the ancient Near East.Foreword by Gilbert Murray. New York, Harper [1966, c.1950] 512p. 21cm. (Torchbk.; Acad. Lib., TB1281) Bibl. [BL96.G3 1961] 2.95 pap.,
1. Near East—Religion. 2. Rites and ceremonies—Near East. 3. Mythology. 4. Religious drama—Hist. & crit. 5. Seasons. I. Title.

GREEN, Miranda J. 291'.09362
A corpus of religious material from the civilian areas of Roman Britain / Miranda J. Green. Oxford, Eng. : British Archaeological Reports, 1976. 320 p. : ill. ; 30 cm. (British archaeological reports ; 24) Cover title: The religions of civilian Roman Britain. Includes indexes. Bibliography: p. 143-155. [BL980.G7G73] 76-375606 £5.90 ($13.00 U.S.)
1. Great Britain—Religion. 2. Great Britain—Antiquities. I. Title. II. Title: The religions of civilian Roman Britain. III. Series.

MANUEL, Frank Edward 291.094
The eighteenth century confronts the gods. New York, Atheneum, 1966[c.1959] 336p. illus. 21cm. (97) Bibl. [BL41.M3] 59-10318 2.95 pap.,
1. Religions—Hist.—Study. 2. Religious thought—18th cent. 3. Enlightenment. I. Title.

MANUEL, Frank Edward. 291.094
The eighteenth century confronts the gods. Cambridge, Harvard University Press, 1959. 336p. illus. 25cm. Includes bibliography. [BL41.M3] 59-10318
1. Religious—Hist.—Study. 2. Religious thought—18th cent. 3. Enlightenment. I. Title.

ASIAN religions: 1971. 291'.095
Bardwell L. Smith, editor. Chambersburg, Pa., American Academy of Religion [1971] 239 p. 23 cm. Proceedings of the Asian Religions Section of the 1971 American Academy of Religion annual meeting. Includes bibliographical references. [BL1035.A72] 72-31029
1. Asia—Religion—Addresses, essays, lectures. I. Smith, Bardwell L., 1925- ed.

PARK, O'Hyun. 291'.095
Oriental ideas in recent religious thought. Lakemont, Ga., CSA Press [1974] 206 p. 23 cm. Bibliography: p. 195-206. [BL1055.P37] 73-83915 ISBN 0-87707-129-2 5.95
1. Asia—Religion. 2. Hinduism. 3. Buddha and Buddhism. 4. Confucius and Confucianism. 5. Taoism. I. Title.

SOOTHILL, William Edward, 1861-1935. 291'.0951
The three religions of China; lectures delivered at Oxford. 2d ed. Westport, Conn., Hyperion Press [1973] 271 p. 23 cm. Reprint of the 1923 ed. published by Oxford University Press, London. Includes bibliographical references. [BL1801.S6 1973b] 73-899 ISBN 0-88355-093-8 13.50
1. China—Religion. I. Title.

MCKENZIE, Peter Rutherford. 291'.0966
Inter-religious encounters in West Africa : Samuel Ajayi Crowther's attitude to African traditional religion and Islam / by P. R. McKenzie. [Leicester] : Study of Religion Sub-department, University of Leicester, 1976. 115 p., 4 p. of plates : ill., maps, ports. ; 24 cm. (Leicester studies in religion ; 1) Distributed by Leicester University Bookshop. Includes index. Bibliography: p. 107-110. [BV3625.N6C68] 77-367628 ISBN 0-905510-00-3 : £3.00
1. Crowther, Samuel Adjai, Bp., 1806?-1891. 2. Missionaries—Nigeria—Biography. 3. Missions—Nigeria. 4. Africa, West—Religion. I. Title. II. Series.

MCBETH, Leon. 291'.0973
Strange new religions / Leon McBeth. Nashville : Broadman Press, c1977. 154 p. ; 19 cm. Includes bibliographies. [BL2530.U6M3] 76-47780 ISBN 0-8054-1806-7 pbk. : 2.75
1. Cults—United States. 2. United States—Religion. 3. Occult sciences—United States. I. Title.

WHALEN, William Joseph. 291'.0973
Minority religions in America [by] William J. Whalen. Staten Island, N.Y., Alba House [1972] Includes bibliographies. [BR516.5.W438] 79-38979 ISBN 0-8189-0239-6
1. Sects—U.S. I. Title.

ANGUS, Samuel, 1881-1943. 291'.1
The religious quests of the Graeco-Roman world; a study in the historical background of early Christianity. New York, Biblo and Tannen, 1967. xx, 444 p. 24 cm. Reprint of the 1929 ed. Bibliographical footnotes. [BR165.A55 1967] 66-30791
1. Church history—Primitive and early church. 2. Christianity and other religions. I. Title.

BROWN, Anton U 291.1
Dignitarian way. Orange, Calif [1960] 118p. 23cm. Includes bibliography. [BL390.B75] 60-44564
1. Religions (Proposed, universal, etc.) I. Title.

DOBBS, John, D. D., 1894- 291.1
The ninth hour. New York, Greenwich [1961, c.1960] 270p. illus. 60-53188 3.50
I. Title.

LUONGO, Anthony M. 291'.1
Let there be unity of religions within diversity; the way to go, by Anthony M. Luongo. [Chicago, Adams Press; distributed by Trans World Publications, Brooklyn, 1967] vii, 143 p. 23 cm. [BL390.L85] 67-19576
1. Religions (Proposed, universal, etc.) I. Title.

MARTIN, Malachi. 291'.1
The encounter. New York, Farrar, Straus and Giroux [1970, c1969] xvi, 488 p. 22 cm. Bibliographical footnotes. [BM585.M365] 70-97135 10.00
1. Judaism—Controversial literature. 2. Christianity—Controversial literature. 3. Islam—Controversial literature. I. Title.

RADHAKRISHNAN, Sarvepalli, Pres. India, 1888- 291'.1
Recovery of faith. New York, Greenwood Press, 1968 [c1955] xvii, 205 p. 20 cm. (World perspectives, v. 4) Bibliographical footnotes. [BL48.R23 1968] 68-21329
1. Religion. 2. Belief and doubt. I. Title. II. Series.

SMART, Ninian, 1927- 291'.1
The yogi and the devotee: the inter play between the Upanishads and Catholic theology. London, Allen & Unwin, 1968. 174p. 23cm. Bibl. [BR128.H5S6] 68-105847 5.00
1. Natural theology. 2. Christianity and other religions—Hinduism. 3. Hinduism—Relations—Christianity. I. Title.
Distributed by Humanities, New York.

BEVAN, Edwyn Robert, 1870-1943 291/.1/08
Hellenism and Christianity. Freeport, N.Y., Bks. for Libs. Pr. [1967] 275p. 22cm. (Essay index reprint ser.) Essays. [BR128.G8B4 1967] 67-26714 8.50
1. Christianity and other religions—Greek. 2. Hellenism. I. Title.

MODERN religious movements in India, 291/.1/0954
by J. N. Farquhar. [1st Indian ed.] Delhi, Munshiram Manoharlal [1967] xv, [i], 471p. illus., ports., plans. 23cm. (Hartford-Lamson lects. on the religions of the world) The Hartford-Lamson lectures on the religions of of the world (Delhi) Bibl. [BL2001.F3 1967] [PL480:I-E-8770] SA67 7.50
1. India—Religion. I. Farouhar, John Nicol, 1861-1929 II. Series.
American distributor: Verry, Mystic, Conn.

SNELLGROVE, David L 291'.1'09591
Himalayan pilgrimage; a study of Tibetan religion, by a traveller through western Nepal. Oxford B. Cassirer [1961] 304 p. illus. 22 cm. Includes bibliography. [BL2030.N3S5] 61-42472
1. Nepal — Religion. 2. Nepal — Descr. & trav. I. Title.

SPIRO, Melford E. 291'.1'09591
Burmese supernaturalism; a study in the explanation and reduction of suffering. Englewood Cliffs, N.J., Prentice-Hall [1967] x, 300 p. 23 cm. (Prentice-Hall college anthropology series) Bibliography: p. 281-289. [BL2030.B8S67] 67-27956
1. Burma—Religion. 2. Animism. 3. Buddha and Buddhism—Influence. I. Title.

ROSENBERG, Stuart E. 291.12
More loves than one; the Bible confronts psychiatry. New York, T. Nelson [1963] 190 p. 22 cm. [BM652.5.R6] 63-10927
1. Psychiatry and religion. 2. Love (Judaism) I. Title.

ROSENBERG, Stuart E. 291.12
More loves than one; the Bible confronts psychiatry. New York, Ungar [1965, c.1963] 190p. 22cm. Bibl. [BM652.5.R6] 1.45 pap.,
1. Psychiatry and religion. 2. Love (Judaism) I. Title.

ASIATIC mythology; 291.13
a detailed description and explanation of the mythologies of all the great nations of Asia, by J. Hackin [others] Introd. by Paul-Louis Couchoud. Tr. by F. M. Atkinson. New York, Crowell [1963] 459p. illus., col. plates. 30cm. 63-20021 12.50
1. Mythology, Oriental. 2. Art, Oriental. 3. Asia—Religion. I. Hackin, Joseph, 1886-1941.

BARNARD, Mary. 291'.13
The mythmakers. Athens, Ohio University Press [1967, c1966] 213 p. 22 cm. Bibliography: p. [195]-203. [BL304.B3] 66-20061
1. Myth. I. Title.

BLACKWELL, Thomas, 1701-1759. 291.1'3
Letters concerning mythology, London, 1748 / Thomas Blackwell. New York : Garland Pub., 1976. p. cm. (The Renaissance and the gods ; 42) Reprint of the 1748 ed. printed in London. [BL305.B55 1976] 75-27887 ISBN 0-8240-2091-X lib.bdg. : 40.00
1. Mythology. I. Title. II. Series.

BOLLE, Kees W. 291'.13
The freedom of man in myth [by] Kees W. Bolle. [Nashville] Vanderbilt University Press, 1968. xiv, 199 p. 20 cm. Bibliographical footnotes. [BL304.B6] 68-8564 ISBN 0-8265-1125-2 5.00
1. Myth. 2. Mysticism. I. Title.

BULFINCH, Thomas, 1796-1867. 291.13
The age of fable. Afterword and bibliography by Martin Bucco. New York, Harper & Row [1966] 377 p. 19 cm. (A Harper perennial classic) Bibliography:p. 365. [BL310.B82] 66-2059
1. Mythology. I. Title.

*BULFINCH, Thomas, 1796-1867 291.13
The age of fable [Introd. by Earle Toppings] New York, Airmont [c.1965] 292p. illus. 18cm. (Classics ser., CL80) .60 pap.,
I. Title.

BULFINCH, Thomas, 1796-1867 291.13
The age of fable. Afterword, bibl. by Martin Bucco. New York, Harper [c.1966] 377p. 19cm. (Harper perennial classic) Bibl. [BL310.B82] 66-2059 1.75; .75 pap.,
1. Mythology. I. Title.

BULFINCH, Thomas, 1796-1867. 291'.13
Mythology: the age of fable. With a foreword by Robert Graves. Illustrated by Joseph Papin. Garden City, N.Y., International Collectors Library [1968] xvi, 383 p. illus. 22 cm. [BL310.B82 1968] 68-3624
1. Mythology. I. Graves, Robert, 1895-

BURLAND, Cottie Arthur, 1905- 291.1'3
Myths of life & death / C. A. Burland. New York : Crown Publishers, 1974. 256 p. : ill. ; 24 cm. Includes index. Bibliography: p. [252] [BL311.B88 1974] 74-79865 12.50
1. Mythology. I. Title.

CAMPBELL, Joseph, 1904- 291'.13
The flight of the wild gander; explorations in the mythological dimension. New York, Viking Press [1969] viii, 248 p. illus. 22 cm. Bibliographical references included in "Notes" (p. 227-240) [BL304.C35 1969] 69-18803 7.50
1. Myth—Addresses, essays, lectures. I. Title.

CAMPBELL, Joseph, 1904- 291.1'3
The flight of the wild gander; explorations in the mythological dimension. Chicago, Regnery [1972, c1969] viii, 248 p. illus. 21 cm. "A Gateway edition." Includes bibliographical references. [BL304.C35 1972] 70-183820 2.65
1. Myth—Addresses, essays, lectures. I. Title.

CAMPBELL, Joseph, 1904- 291'.13
The hero with a thousand faces. [2d ed. Princeton, N.J.] Princeton University Press [1968, c1949] xxiii, 416 p. illus. 24 cm. (Bollingen series, 17) Bibliographical footnotes. [BL313.C28 1968] 68-7394 6.00
1. Mythology. 2. Psychoanalysis. I. Title. II. Series.

CAMPBELL, Joseph, 1904- 291'.13
The masks of God. New York, Viking, 1959-[68] 4v. illus. 22cm. Contents.[4] Creative mythology. Bibl. [GN470.C32] 59-8354 10.00
1. Mythology. I. Title.

CAMPBELL, Joseph, 1904- 291'.13
The masks of God. New York, Viking Press [1969, c1959- v. illus. 22 cm. Contents.Contents.—[1] Primitive mythology. Includes bibliographical references. [BL311.C272] 71-9761 7.95 (v. 1)
1. Mythology. I. Title.

CAMPBELL, Joseph, 1904- 291'.13
Occidental mythology / Joseph Campbell. New York : Penguin Books, [1976] p. cm. (His The masks of God ; v. 3) Includes bibliographical references and index. [BL311.C276] 76-23179 8.95 ISBN 0-670-003-00-X pbk. : 3.95
1. Mythology. I. Title. II. Series.

CAMPBELL, Joseph, 1904- 291.1'3
Primitive mythology / Joseph Campbell. New York : Penguin Books, [1976] p. cm. (His The masks of God ; v. 1) Includes bibliographical references and index. [GN470.C33 1976] 76-25192 ISBN 0-670-00298-4 pbk. : 3.75
1. Religion, Primitive. 2. Mythology. I. Title. II. Series.

CONTI, Natale, 1520?-1580? 291'.1'3
Mythologiae : Venice, 1567 / Natalis Comes. New York : Garland Pub., 1976. p. cm. (The Renaissance and the gods ; no. 11) Reprint of the 1567 ed. published by Comin da Trino, Venice. [BL720.C6 1976] 75-27853 ISBN 0-8240-2060-X : 40.00
1. Mythology, Classical. I. Title. II. Series.

COX, George William, 1827-1902. 291'.13
An introduction to the science of comparative mythology and folklore. 2d ed. London, K. Paul, Trench, 1883. Detroit, Singing Tree Press, 1968. xvi, 380 p. 22 cm. Bibliographical footnotes. [BL310.C6 1968] 68-20124
1. Mythology. 2. Folklore. I. Title. II. Title: Comparative mythology and folklore.

COX, George William, 1827-1902. 291'.13
The mythology of the Aryan nations. Port Washington, N.Y., Kennikat Press [1969] 2 v. 23 cm. Half-title: Aryan mythology. Reprint of the 1870 ed. Bibliographical footnotes. [BL660.C6 1969] 68-8202
1. Mythology, Aryan. 2. Aryans. I. Title. II. Title: Aryan mythology.

DOANE, Thomas William, 1852-1885. 291'.13
Bible myths and their parallels in other religions, being a comparison of the Old and New Testament myths and miracles with those of heathen nations of antiquity, considering also their origin and meaning. New foreword by Leslie Shepard. 4th ed. New Hyde Park, N.Y., University Books [1971] xxxiii, 589 p. illus. 25 cm. Reprint of the 1908 ed. Bibliography: p. xxi-xxxiii. [BL2775.D5 1971] 70-120900 10.00
1. Bible—Criticism, interpretation, etc. 2. Mythology. I. Title.

ELIADE, Mircea, 1907- 291.13
Mephistopheles and the Androgyne: studies in religious myth and symbol. Tr. [from French] by J. M. Cohen. New York, Sheed [1965, c.1965] 223p. 22cm. Bibl. [BL87.E413] 66-12265 5.00
1. Experience (Religion) 2. Light and darkness (in religion, folklore, etc.) 3. Polarity (in religion, folklore, etc.) 4. Unity and plurality (in religion, folklore, etc.) 5. Regeneration (in religion, folk-lore. etc.) 6. Rape (in religion, folk-lore, etc.) 7. Symbolism—Study and teaching. I. Title.

ELIADE, Mircea, 1907- 291.13
Myth and reality. Tr. from French by Willard R. Trask. [1st Amer. ed.] New York. Harper [1968,c.1963] v. 212p. 20cm. (World perspectives, v. 31 Harper torchbks., TB 1369) Bibl. [BL304.E413] 63-16508 1.75 pap.,
1. Myth. 2. Mythology—Addresses, essays, lectures. I. Title. II. Series.

ELIADE, Mircea, 1907- 291.13
Myth and reality. Translated from the French by Willard R. Trask. [1st American ed.] New York, Harper & Row [1963] xiv, 204 p. 20 cm. (World perspectives, v. 31) "Basic bibliography": p. 203-204. Bibliographical footnotes. [BL304.E413] 63-16508
1. Myth. 2. Mythology—Addresses, essays, lectures. I. Title.

ELIADE, Mircea, 1907- 291.13
Myths, dreams, and mysteries; the encounter between contemporary faiths and archaic realities. Translated by Philip Mairet. New York, Harper [1961, c1960] 256 p. 22 cm. (The Library of religion and culture) Includes bibliography. [BL311.E413 1961] 60-15616
1. Mythology. 2. Dreams. 3. Mysteries, Religious. I. Title.

ELIADE, Mircea, 1907- 291.1'3
Myths, rites, symbols : a Mircea Eliade reader / edited by Wendell C. Beane and William G. Doty. New York : Harper & Row, 1976, c1975. 2 v. (xxviii, 465 p.) ; 21 cm. (Harper colophon books ; CN 510) Includes bibliographical references. [BL304.E43 1976] 75-7931 ISBN 0-06-090510-7(V.1) pbk. : 3.95
1. Myth. 2. Rites and ceremonies. 3. Symbolism. I. Title.

FAHS, Sophia Blanche Lyon, 1876- 291.13
Beginnings: earth, sky, life, death; stories, ancient and modern, by Sophia Lyon Fahs and Dorothy T. Spoerl. Boston, Starr King Press [1958] 217 p. illus. 24 cm. "A combination and revision of Beginnings of earth and sky, by Sophia L. Fahs...and Beginnings of life and death, by Sophia L. Fahs and Dorothy T. Spoerl." Includes bibliography. [BV1561.F2] 58-11973
1. Religious education—Text-books for children—Unitarian. 2. Mythology—Juvenile literature. I. Spoerl, Dorothy T., joint author. II. Title.

FONTENROSE, Joseph Eddy, 1903- 291.13
The ritual theory of myth [by] Joseph Fontenrose. Berkeley. Univ. of Calif. Pr. 1966. 77p. 23cm. (Univ. of Calif. pubns., Folklore studies. 18) Bibl. [BL304.F6] 66-8139 2.50 pap.,
1. Myth. I. Title. II. Series: California. University of California publications. Folklore studies, 18

FRAZER, James George, Sir, 1854-1941. 291.1'3
Aftermath : a supplement to The golden bough / by Sir James George Frazer. New York : AMS Press, [1976] p. cm. Reprint of the 1937 ed. published by Macmillan, New York. Includes index. [BL310.F715 1976] 75-41104 ISBN 0-404-14543-4 : 28.50
1. Mythology. 2. Religion, Primitive. 3. Magic. 4. Superstition. I. Frazer, James George, Sir, 1854-1941. The golden bough. II. Title.

FRAZER, James George, Sir, 1854-1941. 291'.13
The golden bough; a study in magic and religion. With an introd. by Stanley Edgar Hyman and illus. by James Lewicki. New York, Limited Editions Club, 1970. 2 v. (xxiii, 884 p.) illus. (part col.) 30 cm. Issued in case. [BL310.F72 1970] 75-13057
1. Mythology. 2. Religion, Primitive. 3. Magic. 4. Superstition. I. Title.

FRAZER, James George, Sir, 1854-1941. 291.13
The new golden bough; a new abridgement of the classic work. Edited, and with notes and foreword, by Theodor H. Gaster. [New York] New American Library [1964, c1959] 832 p. 19 cm. (A Mentor book) Includes bibliographical references. [BL310] 66-1736
1. Mythology. 2. Religion, Primitive. 3. Magic. 4. Superstitution. I. Gaster, Theodor Herzl, 1906- ed. II. Title.

FREUND, Philip, 1909- 291.13
Myths of creation. Illustrated by Milton Charles. New York, Washington Square Press, 1965 [i.e. 1966] vi, 304 p. 22 cm. [BL325.C7F7 1966] 65-19372
1. Creation—Comparative studies. 2. Cosmogony. I. Title.

GASTER, Theodor Herzl, 1906- 291.1'3
Thespis : ritual, myth, and drama in the ancient Near East / Theodor H. Gaster ; foreword by Gilbert Murray. New York : Norton, [1977] c1961. p. cm. (The Norton library) Originally published in 1966 by Harper & Row, New York. Includes index. Bibliography: p. [BL96.G3 1977] 77-14475 ISBN 0-393-00863-0 pbk. : 5.95
1. Near East—Religion. 2. Rites and ceremonies—Near East. 3. Mythology. 4. Religious drama—History and criticism. 5. Seasons. I. Title.

GASTER, Theodor Herzl, 1906- 291.1'3
Thespis : ritual, myth, and drama in the ancient Near East / Theodor H. Gaster ; foreword by Gilbert Murray. New York : Norton, [1977] c1961. p. cm. (The Norton library) Originally published in 1966 by Harper & Row, New York. Includes index. Bibliography: p. [BL96.G3 1977] 77-14475 ISBN 0-393-00863-0 pbk. : 5.95
1. Near East—Religion. 2. Rites and ceremonies—Near East. 3. Mythology. 4. Religious drama—History and criticism. 5. Seasons. I. Title.

GASTER, Theodor Herzl, 1906- 291.1'3
Thespis : ritual, myth, and drama in the ancient Near East / Theodor H. Gaster ; foreword by Gilbert Murray. New and rev. ed. New York : Gordian Press, 1975. p. cm. Reprint of the 1961 ed. published by Anchor Books, Garden City, N.Y. Includes indexes. Bibliography: p. [BL96.G3 1975] 75-15735 ISBN 0-87752-188-3 : 15.00
1. Near East—Religion. 2. Rites and ceremonies—Near East. 3. Mythology. 4. Religious drama—History and criticism. 5. Seasons. I. Title.

GASTER, Theodor Herzl, 1906- 291.1'3
Thespis; ritual, myth, and drama in the ancient Near East. Foreword by Gilbert Murray. New and rev. ed. Garden City, N.Y., Doubleday, 1961. 515 p. 19 cm. (Anchor books, A230) Includes bibliography. [BL96.G3 1961] 61-7650
1. Near East—Religion. 2. Rites and ceremonies—Near East. 3. Mythology. 4. Religious drama—History and criticism. 5. Seasons. I. Title.

GAUTRUCHE, Pierre, 1602-1681. 291.1'3
The poetical histories, London 1671 / Pierre Gautruche ; translated by Marius D'Assigny. Appendix de Diis et heroibus poeticis, Roven 1705 /Joseph de Jouvency. New York : Garland Pub., 1976. 540 p. in various pagings ; 23 cm. (The Renaissance and the gods) Reprint of The poetical histories, a translation of L'histoire poetique pour l'intelligence des poetes and De diis & heroibus poeticis, an appendix to the ed. of Ovid's Metamorphoseon published by R. Lallemant. Includes index. [BL720.G35 1976] 76-23078 ISBN 0-8240-2081-2 lib.bdg. : 40.00
1. Mythology, Classical. 2. Hieroglyphics. I. D'Assigny, Marius, 1643-1717. II. Jouvency, Joseph de, 1643-1719. Appendix de Diis et heroibus poeticis. 1976. III. Title. IV. Series.

GAYLEY, Charles Mills, 1858-1932. 291.1'3
The classic myths in English literature and in art. Accompanied by an interpretative and illustrative commentary. New ed. rev. and enl. New York, Blaisdell Pub. Co. [1963, c1911] xii, 597 p. illus. (part col.) geneal. tab., maps (part fold. col.) 20 cm. "Based originally on Bulfinch's Age of fable (1855)" Bibliographical references included in "Preface" (p. v-xi) (Selections: Extracts, etc.) [BL721.G3 1963] 65-6686
I. Bulfinch, Thomas, 1796-1867. Age of fable. II. Title.

GOODRICH, Norma Lorre 291.13
The ancient myths. [New York] New American Library [c.1960] 256p. illus. maps (A Mentor book, MD313) Bibl. 60-16972 .50 pap.,
1. Mythology. I. Title.

HOOKE, Samuel Henry, 1874- 291.13
Middle Eastern mythology. Baltimore, Penguin Books [1963] 198 p. illus. 18 cm. (Pelican books) [BL311.H6] 63-2044
1. Mythology, Semitic. 2. Mythology, Egyptian. I. Title.

HOOKE, Samuel Henry, 1874- 291.13
Middle Eastern mythology. Baltimore, Penguin [c.1963] 198p. illus. 18cm. (Pelican bks., A546) 63-2044 .95 pap.,
1. Mythology, Semitic. 2. Mythology, Egyptian. I. Title.

IONS, Veronica. 291.1'3
The world's mythology in colour / Veronica Ions ; introduction by Jacquetta Hawkes. London ; New York : Hamlyn, 1974. 350 p. : chiefly ill. (chiefly col.) ; 29 cm. Includes index. Bibliography: p. 340-341. [BL311.I54] 76-350372 ISBN 0-600-31301-8 : £4.95
1. Mythology. I. Title.

JUNG, Carl Gustav, 1875-1961. 291.1'3
Essays on a science of mythology; the myth of the divine child and the mysteries of Eleusis, by C. G. Jung and C. Kerenyi. Translated by R. F. C. Hull. [Rev. ed. Princeton, N.J.] Princeton University Press [1969, c1959] viii, 200 p. 21 cm. (Bollingen series, 22) Translation of Einfuhrung in das Wesen der Mythologie. Bibliography: p. 184-196. [BL313.J83 1969] 76-88547 ISBN 0-691-09851-4
1. Mythology. 2. Psychoanalysis. I. Kerenyi, Karoly, 1897-1973. II. Title. III. Series.

JUNG, Carl Gustav, 1875-1961. 291.13
Essays on a science of mythology; the myths of the divine child and the divine maiden, by

C. G. Jung and C. Kerenyi. Translated by R. F. C. Hull. Rev. ed. New York, Harper & Row [1963] viii, 200 p. 21 cm. (The Bollingen library, v. 22) Harper torchbooks, TB2014. Translation of Einfuhrung in das Wesen der Mythologie. Bibliography: p 184-196. [BL313.J83 1963] 63-3824
1. Mythology. 2. Psychoanalysis. I. Kerenyi, Karoly, 1897- joint author. II. Title. III. Series: Bollingen series, 22

KELSEY, Morton T. 291.1'3
Myth, history, and faith : the remythologizing of Christianity / by Morton T. Kelsey. New York : Paulist Press, [1974] v, 185 p. ; 21 cm. Includes bibliographical references. [BL304.K38] 73-94216 ISBN 0-8091-1827-0 pbk. : 4.50
1. Myth. 2. Theology. I. Title.

KEYSER, William R. 291.1'3
The days of the week / by William R. Keyser ; illustrated by Howard Simon. New York : Harvey House, c1976. 45 p. : ill. ; 29 cm. Retells the Greek, Roman, and Nordic myths from which the names of the days of the week are derived. [BL325.D33K49 1976] 75-27482 ISBN 0-8178-5442-8 lib.bdg. ; 5.59
1. Days—Juvenile literature. 2. Week—Juvenile literature. 3. Mythology—Juvenile literature. I. Simon, Howard, 1903- II. Title.

LANG, Andrew, 1844-1912. 291.1'3
Custom and myth / by Andrew Lang. 2nd ed., revised. Wakefield : EP Publishing, 1974 [i.e.1976] [7], 312 p. : ill. ; 19 cm. Reprint of the 2d, rev. ed. published in 1885 by Longmans, London. Includes index. [BL310.L3 1974] 74-189327 12.95
1. Mythology. I. Title.
Distributed by British Book Center, New York.

LANG, Andrew, 1844-1912. 291'.13
Magic and religion. [1st AMS ed.] London, New York, Longmans, Green, 1901. [New York, AMS Press, 1971] x, 316 p. 23 cm. [BL310.L34 1971] 76-137255 ISBN 0-404-03857-3
1. Mythology. 2. Religion, Primitive. I. Title.

LANG, Andrew, 1844-1912. 291'.13
Magic and religion. New York, Greenwood Press [1969] x, 316 p. 23 cm. Reprint of the 1901 ed. Contents.Contents.—Science and superstition.—The theory of loan-gods, or borrowed religion.—Magic and religion.—The origin of the Christian faith.—The approaches to Mr. Frazer's theory.—Attemps to prove the Sacaean criminal divine.—Zakmuk, Sacaea, and Purim.—Mordecai, Esther, Vashti, and Haman.—Why was the mock-king of the Sacaea whipped and hanged?—Calvary.—The ghastly priest.—South African religion.—"Cup and ring:" An old problem solved.—First-fruits and taboos.—Walking through fire.—Appendices. Mr. Tylor's theory of borrowing. The martyrdom of Dasius. The ride of the beardless one. Bibliographical footnotes. [BL310.L34 1969] 69-13964
1. Mythology. 2. Religion, Primitive. I. Title.

LANG, Andrew, 1844-1912. 291'.13
Modern mythology. London, Longmans, Green, 1897. New York, AMS Press [1968] xxiv, 212 p. 22 cm. Contents.Contents.—Introduction.—Recent mythology.—The story of Daphne.—The question of allies.—Mannhardt.—Philology and Demeter Erinnys.—Totemism.—The validity of anthropological evidence.—The philological method in anthropology.—Criticism of fetishism.—The riddle theory.—Artemis.—The fire-walk.—The origin of death.—Conclusion. Bibliographical footnotes. [BL310.L35 1968] 68-54279
1. Mythology. I. Title.

LANG, Andrew, 1844-1912. 291'.13
Myth, ritual, and religion. New York, AMS Press [1968] 2 v. in 1. 23 cm. Reprint of the 1906 ed. Bibliographical footnotes. [BL310.L4 1968] 68-54280
1. Mythology. 2. Myth. 3. Religion, Primitive. 4. Rites and ceremonies. I. Title.

LARSEN, Stephen. 291.1'3
The shaman's doorway : opening the mythic imagination to contemporary consciousness / Stephen Larsen. 1st ed. New York : Harper & Row, c1976. xii, 244 p. : ill. ; 22 cm. Includes bibliographical references. [BL304.L37 1976] 75-9337 ISBN 0-06-064929-1 : 10.00
1. Myth. 2. Mythology. 3. Consciousness. I. Title.

LARSEN, Stephen. 291.1'3
The shaman's doorway : opening the mythic imagination to contemporary consciousness / Stephen Larsen. New York : Harper & Row, 1977c1976. xii, 244p. : ill, ; 21 cm. (Harper Colophon Books) Includes bibliographical references. [BL304.L37] ISBN 0-06-090547-6 pbk. : 3.95

1. Myth. 2. Consciousness. 3. Mythology. I. Title.
L.C. card no. for original ed.:75-9337.

LEVI-STRAUSS, Claude. 291'.13
The raw and the cooked. Translated from the French by John and Doreen Weightman. [1st U.S. ed.] New York, Harper & Row [1969] xiii, 387 p. illus., chart, maps, 25 cm. (His Introduction to a science of mythology, 1) Translation of Le cru et le cuit. Bibliography: p. 361-370. [BL304.L4813 1969] 67-22501 10.00
1. Mythology. I. Title.

LITTLETON, C. Scott. 291.13
The new comparative mythology; an anthropological assessment of the theories of Georges Dumezil. Berkeley, University of California Press, 1966. xiii, 242 p. 25 cm. Bibliography: p. 215-233. [BL43.D8L5] 66-23181
1. Dumezil, Georges, 1898- 2. Mythology—Methodology. 3. Mythology, Aryan. I. Title.

LITTLETON, C. Scott. 291.1'3
The new comparative mythology: an anthropological assessment of the theories of Georges Dumezil [by] C. Scott Littleton. Rev. ed. Berkeley, University of California Press, 1973. xv, 271 p. 23 cm. Bibliography: p. 239-259. [BL43.D8L5 1973] 72-89243 ISBN 0-520-02404-4 11.95
1. Dumezil, Georges, 1898- 2. Mythology—Methodology. I. Title.
Pbk., 3.65, ISBN 0-520-02403-6.

LOOMIS, Julia Wolfe 291.13
Mythology. New York, Monarch Pr. [1966, c.1965] 155p. illus. 22cm. (Monarch notes and study guides, 523-1) Bibl. [BL311] 66-1768 2.50
1. Mythology—Outlines, syllabi, etc. I. Title.

MARY SYLVIA, Sister 291.13
Nostalgia for paradise, by Sister Mary Sylvia. New York, Desclee [1966, c.1965] 230p. 22cm. Bibl. 4.75
I. Title.

MASSEY, Gerald, 1828-1907. 291.1'3
The natural genesis : or, Second part of A book of the beginnings, containing an attempt to recover and reconstitute the lost origins of the myths and mysteries, types and symbols, religion and language, with Egypt from the mouthpiece and Africa as the birthplace / by Gerald Massey. New York : S. Weiser, 1974. 2 v. : ill. ; 27 cm. "Comparative vocabulary of Sanskrit and Egyptian": v. 2, p. [507]-519. Reprint of the 1883 ed. published by Williams and Norgate, London. Includes bibliographical references and index. [BL313.M38 1974] 73-92166 ISBN 0-87728-248-X : 50.00
1. Mythology. 2. Mythology, Egyptian. 3. Folk-lore. 4. Christianity and other religions. I. Title.

MIDDLETON, John, 1921- comp. 291'.13
Myth and cosmos; readings in mythology and symbolism. Garden City, N.Y., Published for the American Museum of Natural History [by] the Natural History Press, 1967. xi, 368 p. illus. 21 cm. (American Museum sourcebooks in anthropology) Bibliography: p. [349]-356. [BL313.M48] 67-12883
1. Mythology—Addresses, essays, lectures. 2. Symbolism—Addresses, essays, lectures. I. American Museum of Natural History, New York. II. Title. III. Series.

MIDDLETON, John, 1921- comp. 291.1'3
Myth and cosmos : readings in mythology and symbolism / edited by John Middleton. Austin : University of Texas Press, [1976] c1967. p. cm. (Texas Press sourcebooks in anthropology ; 5) Reprint of the ed. published for the American Museum of Natural History by the Natural History Press, Garden City, N.Y., issued in series: American sourcebooks in anthropology. Includes index. Bibliography: p. [BL313.M48 1976] 75-43817 ISBN 0-292-75030-7 pbk. : 5.95
1. Mythology—Addresses, essays, lectures. 2. Symbolism—Addresses, essays, lectures. I. Title. II. Series. III. Series: American Museum sourcebooks in anthropology.
Contents omitted.

MULLER, Friedrich Max, 1823-1900. 291.1'3
Comparative mythology / Friedrich Max Muller. New York : Arno Press, 1977. p. cm. (International folklore) Reprint of the 1909 ed. published by G. Routledge, London. Includes index. [BL311.M8 1977] 77-70612 ISBN 0-405-10111-2 : 14.00
1. Mythology. I. Title. II. Series.

MUNZ, Peter, 1921- 291.1'3
When the golden bough breaks; structuralism or typology? London, Boston, Routledge & K. Paul [1973] xii, 143 p. 23 cm. Bibliography: p. 131-138. [BL311.M83] 73-87315 ISBN 0-7100-7650-9 £2.25
1. Mythology. 2. Myth. 3. Symbolism. I. Title.

MUNZ, Peter, 1921- 291.1'3
When the golden bough breaks; structuralism or typology? London, Boston, Routledge & K. Paul [1973] xii, 143 p. 23 cm. Bibliography: p. 131-138. [BL311.M83] 73-87315 ISBN 0-7100-7650-9 7.50
1. Mythology. 2. Myth. 3. Symbolism. I. Title.

MURRAY, Henry Alexander, 1893- ed. 291.13
Myth and mythmaking. New York, G. Braziller, 1960. 381 p. 22 cm. [BL311.M85] 59-12232
1. Mythology—Addresses, essays, lectures. I. Title.

MYTH and law among the 291'.13
Indo-Europeans; studies in Indo-European comparative mythology. Edited by Jaan Puhvel. Berkeley, University of California Press, 1970. x, 276 p. 24 cm. (Publications of the UCLA Center for the Study of Comparative Folklore and Mythology, 1) "Most of the works ... were originally presented at a symposium held under the joint auspices of the Center [for the Study of Comparative Folklore and Mythology] and of the Section of Indo-European Studies [of the University of California, Los Angeles] on March 17-18, 1967." Bibliography: p. [247]-268. [BL660.M9] 75-627781 ISBN 0-520-01587-8 10.00
1. Mythology, Aryan—Addresses, essays, lectures. I. Puhvel, Jaan, ed. II. California. University. University at Los Angeles. Center for the Study of Comparative Folklore and Mythology. III. Series: California. University. University at Los Angeles. Center for the Study of Comparative Folklore and Mythology. Publications, 1

MYTH in Indo-European 291.1'3
antiquity. Edited by Gerald James Larson. Co-edited by C. Scott Littleton and Jaan Puhvel. Berkeley, University of California Press, 1974. vi, 197 p. 24 cm. (Publications of the UCSB Institute of Religious Studies) Essays resulting from a conference held in Mar. 1971 at the University of California, Santa Barbara. Bibliography: p. [191]-192. [BL660.M93] 72-93522 ISBN 0-520-02378-1 10.00
1. Dumezil, Georges, 1898- —Addresses, essays, lectures. 2. Mythology, Aryan—Addresses, essays, lectures. I. Larson, Gerald James, ed. II. Littleton, C. Scott, ed. III. Puhvel, Jaan, ed. IV. Series: California. University, Santa Barbara. Institute of Religious Studies. Publications.

MYTHS / 291.1'3
Alexander Eliot ... [et al.] New York : McGraw-Hill, c1976. 320 p. : ill. ; 33 cm. Includes index. Bibliography: p. 302-304. [BL315.M95] 76-20186 ISBN 0-07-019193-X : 39.95
1. Mythology—Addresses, essays, lectures. 2. Myth—Addresses, essays, lectures. I. Eliot, Alexander.

NEW Larousse encyclopedia 291'.13
of mythology. Introduction by Robert Graves [translated from the French by Richard Aldington & Delano Ames, & revised by a panel of editorial advisors from the Larousse mythologie generale edited by Felix Guirand] New ed. London, New York, Hamlyn, 1968. xi, 500 p. 32 plates, illus. (some col.) 30 cm. First ed. published in 1959 under title: Larousse encyclopedia of mythology. Bibliography: p. [486]-487. [BL311.L33 1968] 78-436741 84/-
1. Mythology. 2. Folk-lore. I. Guirand, Felix, ed. Mythologie generale.

OHMANN, Richard Malin, ed. 291.13
The making of myth. New York, Putnam [1963, c.] 1962. 179p. 21cm. (Controlled essay materials, v.1) Bibl. 62-12846 2.00 pap.,
1. Myth—Addresses, essays, lectures. I. Title.

PARKER, Derek. 291.1'3
The immortals / [by] Derek & Julia Parker. London : Barrie and Jenkins, 1976. 208 p. : ill. (some col.), facsim., port. ; 30 cm. "A Webb & Bower book" Ill. on lining papers. Includes index. Bibliography: p. 204-205. [BL311.P37 1976b] 77-357776 ISBN 0-214-20283-6 : £7.95
1. Mythology. 2. Folk-lore. I. Parker, Julia, joint author. II. Title.

REISS, Joseph 291.13
Language, myth, and man. New York, Philosophical [c.1963] 134p. 21cm. 63-15605 4.50 bds.,
1. Religion—Addresses, essays, lectures. I. Title.

ROBINSON, Herbert Spencer. 291.1'3
Myths and legends of all nations / by Herbert Spencer Robinson and Knox Wilson. Totowa, N.J. : Littlefield, Adams, 1976. xii, 244 p. ; 21 cm. (A Littlefield, Adams quality paperback ; no. 319) Includes indexes. [BL310.R6 1976] 75-35613 ISBN 0-8226-0319-5 : 2.95
1. Mythology. 2. Legends. 3. Folk-lore. I. Wilson, Knox, 1901- joint author. II. Title.

SEBEOK, Thomas Albert, 1920- ed. 291.13
Myth: a symposium. Bloomington, Ind. Univ. Pr. [c.1958, 1965] 180p. illus. 21cm. (Midland bk. MB83) Bibl. [BL310.S37] 65-29803 2.45 pap.,
1. Mythology—Addresses, essays, lectures. I. Title.

SEBEOK, Thomas Albert, 1920- ed. 291.13
Myth: a symposium. Edited by Thomas A. Sebeok. Bloomington, Indiana University Press [1965] 180 p. illus. 21 cm. (A Midland book, MB83) Contents.—Myth, symbolism, and truth, by D. Bidney.—The eclipse of solar mythology, by R. M. Dorson.—Myth, metaphor, and simile, by R. Th. Christiansen.—The structural study of myth, by C. Levi-Strauss.—The personal use of myth in dreams, by D. Eggan.—Myth and ritual, by Lord Ragian.—The ritual view of myth and the mythic, by S. E. Hyman.—The semantic approach to myth, by P. Wheelwright.—Myth and folktales, by S. Thompson. Includes bibliographies. [BL310.S37 1965] 65-29803
1. Mythology—Addresses, essays, lectures. I. Title.

SPENCE, Lewis, 1874- 291.13
The outlines of mythology. Introd. by Daniel B. Dodson. Greenwich, Conn., Fawcett [c.1944, 1961] 144p. (Premier bk., d143) Bibl. .50 pap.,
1. Mythology. I. Title.

SPENCE, Lewis, 1874-1955. 291.1'3
The outlines of mythology / by Lewis Spence. Folcroft, Pa. : Folcroft Library Editions, 1977. p. cm. Reprint of the 1944 ed. published by Watts, London, which was issued as no. 99 of Thinker's library. Includes index. Bibliography: p. [BL311.S68 1977] 77-3223 ISBN 0-8414-7803-1 lib. bdg. : 15.00
1. Mythology. I. Title. II. Series: The Thinker's library ; no. 99.

WARD, Donald. 291'.13
The divine twins; an Indo-European myth in Germanic tradition. Berkeley, University of California Press, 1968. x, 137 p. 26 cm. (University of California publications. Folklore studies, 19) Bibliography: p. 113-127. [BL325.T8W36] 78-626557 4.50
1. Twins (in religion, folk-lore, etc.) I. Title. II. Series: California. University. University of California publications. Folklore studies, 19

*WEIGEL, James. 291.13
Mythology; including Egyptian, Babylonian, Indian, Greek, Roman, and Norse mythologies, Arthurian legends, introduction to mythology, narratives and commentaries; biographical essay, recommended reading, genealogical tables ... by James Weigel, Jr. Lincoln, Neb., Cliff's Notes [1973] 210 p. 21 cm. Bibiography: p. 194-195. [BL310] ISBN 0-8220-1485-8 1.95 (pbk.)
1. Mythology. I. Title.

RUTHVEN, K. K. 291.1'301
Myth / [by] K. K. Ruthven. London : Methuen, 1976. [8], 104 p. ; 20 cm. (The Critical idiom ; 31) Distributed in the USA by Harper & Row, Barnes & Noble Import Division. Includes index. Bibliography: p. [84]-100. [PN56.M94R8 1976] 77-354267 5.75
1. Myth in literature. 2. Mythology in literature. I. Title.

BHATTACHARJI, Sukumari. 291'.13'0934
The Indian theogony; a comparative study of Indian mythology from the Vedas to the Puranas. [London] Cambridge University Press, 1970. xiii, 396 p. 24 cm. Bibliography: p. 364-374. [BL2001.2.B48] 79-96080 7/-/- ($22.00)
1. Mythology, Indic. I. Title.

MACKENZIE, Donald Alexander, 1873-1936. 291.1'3'0951
Myths of China and Japan / by Donald A. Mackenzie. Boston : Longwood Press, 1977. xvi, 404 p., [34] leaves of plates : ill. ; 22 cm. Reprint of the 1923 ed. published by Gresham Pub. Co., London, in series: Myth and legend in literature and art. Includes bibliographical references and index. [BL1802.M33 1977] 77-6878 ISBN 0-89341-149-3 lib.bdg. : 45.00
1. Mythology, Chinese. 2. Mythology, Japanese. 3. Folk-lore—China. 4. Folk-lore—Japan. 5. China—Civilization. 6. Japan—

Civilization. I. Title. II. Series: Myth and legend in literature and art.

ALBRIGHT, William Foxwell, 1891- 291.14
From the stone age to Christianity; monotheism and the historical process. 2d ed., with a new introd. Baltimore, Johns Hopkins Press, 1957. 432p. 21cm. [BL221.A47 1957a] 57-59184
1. Monotheism. 2. Religion, Primitive. 3. History—Philosophy. 4. History—Methodology. I. Title.

ALBRIGHT, William Foxwell, 1891- 291.14
From the stone age to Christianity; monotheism and the historical process. 2d ed. with a new introd. Garden City, N.Y., Doubleday, 1957. 432p. 19cm. (Doubleday anchor books, A100) [BL221.A47 1957] 57-5562
1. Monotheism. 2. Religion, Primitive. 3. History—Philosophy. 4. History—Methodology. I. Title.

ALBRIGHT, William Foxwell, 1891-1971. 291.14
From the stone age to Christianity; monotheism and the historical process. 2d ed. with a new introd. Garden City, N.Y., Doubleday, 1957. 432 p. 19 cm. (Doubleday anchor books, A100) [BL221.A47 1957] 57-5562
1. Monotheism. 2. Religion, Primitive. 3. History—Philosophy. 4. History—Methodology. I. Title.

ALTIZER, Thomas J. J. 291.14
Oriental mysticism and Biblical eschatology. Philadelphia, Westminster [c.1961] 218p. Bibl. 61-10990 4.95
1. Christianity and other religions—Buddhism. 2. Mysticism—Buddhism. 3. Eschatology—Biblical teaching. I. Title.

ALTIZER, Thomas J J 291.14
Oriental mysticism and Biblical eschatology. Philadelphia, Westminster Press [1961] 218p. 21cm. Includes bibliography. [BR128.B8A4] 61-10990
1. Christianity and other religions—Buddhism. 2. Mysticism—Buddhism. 3. Eschatology—Biblical teaching. I. Title.

KEITH, W Holman, 1900- 291.14
Divinity as the eternal feminine. [1st ed.] New York, Pageant Press [1960] 194p. 21cm. [BL390.K43] 60-53292
1. Religions (Proposed, universal, etc.) I. Title.

MUKERJEE, Radhakamal, 1889- 291.14
The theory and art of mysticism. Foreword by William Ernest Hocking. [dist. New York, Taplinger, 1961, c.1960] 352p. Bibl. 5.25
I. Title.

O'BRIEN, Elmer 291.14
Varieties of mystic experience, an anthology and interpretation. New York, New Amer. Lib. [1965, c.1964] 252p. 18cm. (Mentor-Omega bk. MT631) [BV5082.2025] .75 pap.,
1. Mysticism—Hist. 2. Mysticism—Collections. I. Title.

O'BRIEN, Elmer. 291.14
Varieties of mystic experience, an anthology and interpretation. [1st ed.] New York, Holt, Rinehart and Winston [1964] x, 321 p. 24 cm. [BV5082.2.O25] 64-21918
1. Mysticism—History. 2. Mysticism—Collections. I. Title.

SPENCER, Sidney, 1888- 291.14
Mysticism in world religion. Baltimore, Penguin [c.1963] 363p. 19cm. (Pelican bks. A594) Bibl. 63-3923 1.65 pap.,
1. Mysticism—Comparative studies. I. Title.

STACE, Walter Terence, 1886- ed. 291.14
The teachings of the mystics being selections from the great mystics and mystical writings of the world. New York New American Library [1972] 240 p. 18 cm. (A Mentor book, MJ1181) [BL625.S75] 60-15528 Pap. 1.95
1. Mysticism. I. Title.

ZAEHNER, Robert Charles 291.14
Hindu and Muslim mysticism. [dist. New York, Oxford Univ. Press, c.]1960[ ] 234p. (Jordan lectures in comparative religion, 5) Bibl. 61-1206 4.80
1. Mysticism—India. 2. Mysticism—Mohammedanism. I. Title.

ZAKATARIOUS. 291.1'4
The secret of the golden calf; towards the foundation of a polytheistic psychology and the reawakening of the polytheistic faith. Berkeley, Calif., House of Zwillingsbruder Press, 1974. 80 p. illus. 24 cm. [BL355.Z34] 74-177232 10.00
1. Polytheism. 2. Psychology, Religious. 3. Golden calf (Bible) I. Title.

CHURCHES and states: 291'.17
the religious institution and modernization, by Victor D. Du Bois [and others] Edited by Kalman H. Silvert. With a foreword by Kenneth W. Thompson. New York, American Universities Field Staff [1967] xiv, 224 p. 24 cm. "This vol. grew out of a conference on 'the religious institution and modernism', sponsored by the American Universities Field Staff and held at Indiana University in October 1966." [BL60.C47] 67-22384
1. Religion and sociology—Addresses, essays, lectures. I. Du Bois, Victor D. II. Silvert, Kalman H., ed. III. American Universities Field Staff. IV. Title: The religion institution and modernization.

SMITH, Donald Eugene, 1927- comp. 291'.17
Religion, politics, and social change in the Third World; a sourcebook. Edited with introductory notes by Donald Eugene Smith. New York, Free Press [1974, c1971] xv, 286 p. 21 cm. Bibliography: p. 267-271. [BL65.P7S635] 3.95 (pbk)
1. Religion and politics. 2. Religion and state. 3. Religion and sociology. 4. Socialism and religion. I. Title.
L.C. card number for original ed.: 73-143516.

*ALI SHAH, Ikbal The Sirdar 291.172
The spirit of The east: an anthology of the scriptures of The east. New York, E. P. Dutton, 1975 [c1973] vi, 276 p. 18 cm. Bibliography: p. 276 [BL410] ISBN 0-525-47395-5 2.95 (pbk.)
1. Comparative religion. I. Title.

BEN-JOCHANNAN, Yosef. 291'.172
African origins of the major "Western religions". [New York, Alkebu-lan Books, c1970] xxvi, 356 p. 25 cm. (African-American heritage series) Bibliography: p. 342-354. [BL2400.B43] 75-22630
1. Africa—Religion. 2. Religions—African influences. I. Title. II. Series.

FORTMANN, Henricus Martinus Maria, 1912-1970. 291'.172
Discovery of the East; reflections on a new culture [by] Han Fortman. [Translated from the Dutch by Patrick Gaffney] Notre Dame, Ind. Fides Publishers [1971] 100 p. 18 cm. (A Fides dome book, D-80) Translation of Oosterse renaissance. Includes bibliographical references. [AC19.F6713] 72-167956 ISBN 0-8190-0081-7 1.25
I. Title.

SMITH, Donald Eugene, 1927- ed. 291.1770954
South Asian politics and religion. Princeton, N. J., Princeton, 1966. xii, 563p. 25cm. Articles contributed to a seminar held in Colombo, Ceylon, in July 1964, which was sponsored by the Council on Religion and Intl. Affairs. Bibl. [BL65.S8S6] 66-8738 15.00
1. Religion and state—South Asia. I. Council on Religion and International Affairs. II. Title.

BLYDEN, Edward Wilmot, 1832-1912 291'.17'83
Christianity, Islam and the Negro race [by] Edward W. Blyden; Introd. by Christopher Fyfe. Edinburgh, University Pr., 1967. xviii, ix, 407p. 23cm. (African heritage bks., I) Bibl. [DT4.B54 1967] 67-105041 6.50
1. Negro race—Addresses, essays, lectures. 2. Christianity—Africa—Addresses, essays, lectures. 3. Islam—Africa—Addresses, essays, lectures. I. Title. II. Series.
American distributor: Aldine, Chicago.

ZUMBRO Valley Medical Society. Medicine and Religion Committee. 291.1'7832'1
Religious aspects of medical care : a handbook of religious practices of all faiths / compiled by Medicine and Religion Committee, Zumbro Valley Medical Society, Rochester, Minnesota. St. Louis : Catholic Hospital Association, [1975] viii, 64 p. ; 29 cm. [BL65.M4Z85 1975] 74-18147 ISBN 0-87125-019-5 pbk. : 4.00
1. Medicine and religion. I. Title.

COHEN, Chapman, 1868- 291.1'7834'1
Religion & sex : studies in the pathology of religious development / by Chapman Cohen. New York : AMS Press, 1975. xiii, 286 p. ; 18 cm. Reprint of the 1919 ed. published by T. N. Foulis, London, in series: The Open mind library. Includes bibliographical references and index. [BL65.S4C63 1975] 72-9631 ISBN 0-404-57430-0 : 14.50
1. Sex and religion. I. Title.

PARSONS, Elsie Worthington Clews, 1875-1941. 291.1'7834'12
Religious chastity : an ethnological study / by John Main [i.e. E. W. C. Parsons]. New York : AMS Press, [1975] xii, 365 p. ; 23 cm. Reprint of the 1913 ed. published by Macaulay Co., New York. Includes index. Bibliography: p. 325-354. [BL458.P37 1975] 72-9672 ISBN 0-404-57489-0 : 22.50
1. Women (in religion, folklore, etc.) 2. Sex and religion. 3. Chastity. I. Title.

PLASKOW, Judith, comp. 291.1'7834'12
Women and religion; papers of the Working Group on Women and Religion, 1972-73. Edited by Judith Plaskow [and] Joan Arnold Romero. Rev. ed. [Chambersburg, Pa.] American Academy of Religion; [distributed by Scholar's Press, Missoula, Mont., 1974] v, 210 p. 23 cm. Selected papers from two conferences, held in 1972 and 1973. Includes bibliographical references. [BL458.P55 1974] 74-83126 ISBN 0-88420-117-1 1.50 (pbk.)
1. Women and religion—Congresses. I. Romero, Joan Arnold, joint comp. II. Working Group on Women and Religion. III. Title.

SEXIST religion and women in the church; 291.1'7834'12 no more silence! Edited by Alice L. Hageman, in collaboration with the Women's Caucus of Harvard Divinity School. New York, Association Press [1974] 221 p. 22 cm. Chiefly lectures delivered at Harvard Divinity School, 1972-73. Includes bibliographical references. [BL458.S49] 73-21672 ISBN 0-8096-1840-0 6.25
1. Women and religion. I. Hageman, Alice L., ed. II. Harvard University. Divinity School. Women's Caucus.
Pbk. 3.95 Contents omitted.

STONE, Merlin. 291.1'7834'12
When god was a woman / by Merlin Stone. New York : Dial Press, 1976. p. cm. Includes index. Bibliography: p. [BL458.S76] 76-22544 ISBN 0-8037-6813-3 : 7.95
1. Women in religion. I. Title.

NEVASKAR, Balwant. 291'.1785
Capitalists without capitalism; the Jains of India and the Quakers of the West. Westport, Conn., Greenwood Pub. Co. [1971] xxviii, 252 p. 22 cm. (Contributions in sociology, no. 6) Includes bibliographical references. [BX7731.2.N48] 72-98709 ISBN 0-8371-3297-5 11.50
1. Friends, Society of. 2. Jainism. 3. Religion and economics. I. Title.

AMERICAN Association for the Advancement of Science. Section on Medical Sciences. 291.18082
Evolution nervous control from primitive organisms to man; a symposium organized by the Section on Medical Sciences of the American Association for the Advancement of Science and presented at the New York meeting on December 29-30, 1956. Arr. by Bernard B. Brodie and Allan D. Bass. Edited by Allan D. Bass. Washington, 1959. vii, 231 p. illus., ports., diagrs. 21cm. (Publication of the American Association for the Advancement of Science, no. 32) Includes bibliographies. [QP352.A5 1956] 59-10142
1. Nervous system—Collected works. I. Bass, Allan D., ed. II. Title. III. Series: American Association for the Advancement of Science. Publication no. 32

CHRISTIAN, William A., 1905- 291.2
Oppositions of religious doctrines; a study in the logic of dialogue among religions [by] William A. Christian. [New York] Herder and Herder [1972] ix, 129 p. 22 cm. (Philosophy of religion series) Bibliography: p. 128. [BL80.2.C527] 76-173830 6.95
1. Religions. I. Title.

COBB, John B. 291.2
The structure of Christian existence, by John B. Cobb, Jr. Philadelphia, Westminster Press [1967] 160 p. 21 cm. [BT60.C54] 67-21792
1. Christianity—Essence, genius, nature. I. Title.

DEFOE, Daniel, 1961?-1731, supposed author. 291.2
An abstract of the remarkable passages in the life of a private gentleman. Relating to trouble of mind, some violent temptations and a recovery ...4th ed. Boston, Printed by Rogers and Fowle for Edwards, 1744. 192 p. 15 cm. Caption title: An account of some remarkable passages in the life of a private gentleman. Ascribed both to D. Defoe and Dr. T. Woodcock. -- ef. D. Defoe. Works, edited by W. Hazlett; and W. T. Morgan. Bibliography of British history (1700-1715) [BJ1597.A25 1744] 65-58528
I. Woodcock, T., supposed author. II. Title.

ELIADE, Mircea, 1907- 291.2
Gods, goddesses, and myths of creation; a thematic source book of the history of religions. New York, Harper & Row [1974] xiii, 162 p. 21 cm. First part, consisting of chapters 1 and 2, of the author's From primitives to Zen. Bibliography: p. 158-161. [BL74.E42 1974] 73-20949 1.95 (pbk.).
1. Religions—History—Sources. I. Eliade, Mircea, 1907- From primitives to Zen. Chap. 2. Myths of creation and of origin. II. Title.

FRIEDLANDER, Ira, comp. 291.2
Wisdom stories for the planet Earth. [1st ed.] New York, Harper & Row [1973] xvi, 108 p. 22 cm. [BJ1597.F74 1973] 72-78333 ISBN 0-06-068511-5 4.95
1. Allegories. I. Title.

HANSON, Virginia, comp. 291.2
Karma : the universal law of harmony / edited by Virginia Hanson. Wheaton, Ill. : Theosophical Pub. House, [1975] ix, 137 p. ; 21 cm. (A Quest book) Includes bibliographical references. [BP573.K3H3 1975] 74-18957 ISBN 0-8356-0462-4 pbk. : 2.50
1. Karma. I. Title.

HEBBLETHWAITE, Brian. 291.2
Evil, suffering, and religion / Brian Hebblethwaite. New York : Hawthorn Books, 1976. vii, 115 p. ; 21 cm. (Issues in religious studies) Includes index. Bibliography: p. 111. [BJ1401.H4 1976] 76-15424 ISBN 0-8015-2438-5 pbk. : 3.50
1. Good and evil. 2. Suffering. 3. Theodicy. I. Title.

IBN Kammunah, Sa'd ibn Mansur, 13thcent. 291.2
Ibn Kammuna's Examination of the three faiths; a thirteenth-century essay in the comparative study of religion. Translated from the Arabic, with an introd. and notes by Moshe Perlmann. Berkeley, University of California Press, 1971. xi, 160 p. 23 cm. Translation of Tanqih al-abhath lil-milal al-thalath. Includes bibliographical references. [BL75.I213] 73-102659 ISBN 0-520-01658-0 8.50
1. Religions—Early works to 1800. I. Perlmann, Moshe, ed. II. Title: Examination of the three faiths.

LEACH, Maria. 291.2
The beginning: creation myths around the world. Illus. by Jan Bell Fairservis. New York, Funk & Wagnalls, 1956. 253 p. illus. 22 cm. [BL225.L4] 56-7775
1. Creation. I. Title.

LEE, Jung Young. 291.2
Cosmic religion. New York, Philosophical Library [1973] 109 p. 23 cm. [BL48.L33] 73-82163 ISBN 0-8022-2125-4 4.50
1. Religion. I. Title.

LINNIK, Philip S. 291.2
Brotherhood of men; a fact-finding report to Mr. and Mrs. America. New York, Vantage [c.1961] 143p. 3.50 bds.,
I. Title.

MCCAFFERTY, Lawrence M. 291.2
River of light; essays on Oriental wisdom and the meaning of Christ, by Lawrence M. McCafferty. New York, Philosophical Library [1969] 91 p. 22 cm. [BL80.2.M25] 69-14356 4.75
1. Religions. I. Title.

MACQUARRIE, John. 291.2
God-talk; an examination of the language and logic of theology. [1st Amer. ed.] New York, Harper [1967] 255p. 22cm. Bibl. [BR115.L25M3 1967] 67-14993 6.00
1. Religion and language. 2. Communication (Theology) I. Title.

*PARRINDER, Geoffrey. 291.2
Introduction to Asian religions / [by] Geoffrey Parrinder. New York Oxford Univ. Pr., 1976,c1957. 138p. ; 21 cm. Includes index. [BL85] 76-15098 ISBN 0-19-519858-1 pbk. : 2.50
1. Religions-Relations. 2. History-Theology. 3. Religion-History. I. Title.

POOR, Laura Elizabeth. 291.2
Sanskrit and its kindred literatures; studies in comparative mythology. Boston, Milford House [1973, c1880] p. Reprint of the ed. published by Roberts Bros., Boston. Bibliography: p. [BL313.P6 1973] 73-13748 ISBN 0-87821-179-9 30.00 (lib. bdg.)
1. Mythology. 2. Literature, Ancient. 3. Literature, Medieval. I. Title.

RICHMOND, Ian Archibald, 1902- 291.2
Archaeology and the after-life in pagan and Christian imagery. London, New York, Oxford University Press, 1950. 57 p. plates. 22 cm. (Riddell memorial lectures, 20th ser.) At head of title: University of Durham. Bibliographical footnotes. [BL735.R5] 51-2512
1. Eachatology, Greco-Roman. 2. Eachatology. I. Title. II. Series.

SANDMEL, Samuel. 291.2
The several Israels, and an essay: Religion and

modern man. New York, Ktav Pub. House, 1971. 160 p. 24 cm. (The James A. Gray lectures, 1968) "Lectures ... given at Duke University on October 28-30, 1968." [BM613.S24] 73-149607 ISBN 0-87068-160-5
1. Jews—Election, Doctrine of. 2. Christianity. 3. Zionism. 4. Liberalism (Religion) I. Title. II. Series: The James A. Gray lectures at Duke University, 1968.

SMITH, Robert D 291.2
Comparative miracles [by] Robert D. Smith. [St. Louis] B. Herder Book Co. [1965] vi, 184 p. 21 cm. Bibliography: p. 181-184. [BT97.2.S6] 65-25085
1. Miracles. I. Title.

SMITH, Robert D. 291.2
Comparative miracles. [St. Louis] B. Herder [c.1965] vi. 184p. 21cm. Bibl. [BT97.2.S6] 65-25085 2.75 pap.,
1. Miracles. I. Title.

SWANSON, Guy E 291.2
The birth of the gods; the origin of primitive beliefs. Ann Arbor, University of Michigan Press [1960] ix, 260 p. tables. 22 cm. Bibliography: p. [244]-255. [GN470.S9] 60-9974
1. Religion, Primitive. I. Title.

SWANSON, Guy E. 291.2
The birth of the gods; the origin of primitive beliefs. Ann Arbor, Univ. of Mich. Pr. [1964, c.1960] ix, 260p tables. 21cm. (Ann Arbor paperback, AA93) Bibl. 4.95; 1.95 pap.,
1. Religion, Primitive. I. Title.

GREAT men search for God 291.2'1
/ compiled by Harold Whaley ; with ill. by Stanley Clough. Mount Vernon, N.Y. : Peter Pauper Press, [1975] 62 p. : ill. ; 20 cm. [BT175.G73] 75-308054 1.95
1. God. I. Whaley, Harold. II. Clough, Stanley.

*HILLIS, Dick 291.21
Strange gods. Chicago, Moody [c.1966] 79p. 18cm. (Compact bks., no. 55) .29 pap.,
I. Title.

MAXIMUS TYRIUS 291.21
Maximus of Tyre on the dispute about images. Calligraphed, illus., introd. by Ben Shahn [New York] Pantheon [1964, c.1963. 32]p. illus. 18x24cm. 64-18325 4.95
1. Christian art and symbolism. I. Shahn, Ben 1898- ed. and illus. II. Title.

WENTZ, Walter Yeeling 291.2'1
Evans.
The fairy-faith in Celtic countries, by W. Y. Evans Wentz. New York, Lemma Pub. Corp., 1973. xxviii, 524 p. 22 cm. Reprint of the 1911 ed. published by H. Frowde, London. Includes bibliographical references. [GR137.W4 1973] 72-87990 ISBN 0-87696-057-3 22.50
1. Folk-lore, Celtic. I. Title.

BOWKER, John 291.2'11
Problems of suffering in religions of the world. [London] Cambridge University Press [1975, c1970] xii, 318 p. 22 cm. Bibliography: p. 293-297. [BL65.S85B68] 77-93706 ISBN 0-521-09903-X
1. Suffering. I. Title.
Distributed by Cambridge University Press, N.Y. for 15.95; 4.95 (pbk.)

BRUNS, J. Edgar, 1923- 291.2'11
God as woman, woman as God [by] J. Edgar Bruns. New York, Paulist Press [1973] v, 89 p. 18 cm. (Paulist Press/Deus books) Includes bibliographies. [BL458.B78] 73-75247 ISBN 0-8091-1771-1 1.25 (pbk.)
1. Women and religion. I. Title.

BURLAND, Cottie Arthur, 291.2'11
1905-
Gods and heroes of war / C. A. Burland ; with ill. by Honi Werner. New York : Putnam, [1974] 127 p. : ill. ; 22 cm. Includes index. [BL311.B87 1974] 73-88518 ISBN 0-399-20383-4. ISBN 0-399-60873-7 lib. bdg. : 4.49
1. Mythology. I. Title.

CHIBA, Reiko 291.211
The seven lucky gods of Japan. Rutland, Vt., Tuttle [1965, c.1966] 42p. (on double leaves) illus. 17cm. [BL2211.S36C5] 65-25467 2.95
1. Seven gods of fortune. I. Title.

DELORIA, Vine. 291.2'11
God is red. New York, Grosset & Dunlap [1973] 376 p. 22 cm. Includes bibliographical references. [BL2776.D44 1973] 72-90851 ISBN 0-448-02168-4 7.95
1. Christianity—Controversial literature. 2. Indians—Religion and mythology. I. Title.

DELORIA, Vine 291.2'11
God is red [by] Vine Deloria, Jr. [New York, Dell, 1975 c1973] 376 p. 21 cm. (A Delta book) Includes bibliographical references [BL2776.D44 1975] 2.95 (pbk.)
1. Christianity—Controversial literature. 2. Indians—Religion and mythology. I. Title.
L.C. card no. for original ed.: 72-90851

DUMEZIL, Georges, 1898- 291.2'11
The destiny of the warrior. Translated by Alf Hiltebeitel. Chicago, University of Chicago Press [1970] xv, 168 p. 24 cm. Translation of Heur et malheur du guerrier. Includes bibliographical references. [BL660.D79413] 75-113254 ISBN 0-226-16970-7
1. Heroes. 2. War (in religion, folk-lore, etc.) 3. Mythology, Aryan. I. Title.

FERGUSON, John, 1921- 291.2'11
The place of suffering. Cambridge, J. Clarke, 1972. 137 p. 23 cm. [BT732.7.F47] 73-157107 ISBN 0-227-67803-6 £1.75
1. Suffering. I. Title.

GAUSDAL, Johannes. 291.211
The Santal khuts; contribution to animistic research. Oslo, Aschehoug; Cambridge, Harvard University Press, 1960. 218 p. illus., facsims., tables. 24 cm. (Institutte for sammenlignende kulturforskning. Serie B: Skrifter, 50) [GN471.G3 1960] 63-4260
1. Santals. 2. Animism. I. Title. II. Series. III. Series: Instituttet for sammenlignende kulturforskning, Oslo. Serie B: Skrifter, 50

HALBWACHS, Maurice, 1877- 291.211
1945.
Sources of religious sentiment. Tr. [from French] by John A. Spaulding. [New York] Free Pr. of Glencoe [c.1962] 109p. Bibl. 62-10589 4.00
1. Durkheim, Emile, 1858-1917. 2. Religion, Primitive. I. Title.

HAYDON, Albert Eustace, 291.211
1880-
Biography of the gods [by] A. Eustace Haydon. New York, Ungar [1967] xiii, 352p. 21cm. Reprint of the 1941 ed. Bibl. [BL80.H33 1967] 67-13617 5.75; 1.95 pap.,
1. Religious. 2. Gods. I. Title.

JAMES, Edwin Oliver, 291.211
1886-
The cult of the mother-goddess; an archaeological and documentary study. New York, Barnes & Noble [1961, c.1959] 300p. Bibl. 61-3056 6.50
1. Mother-goddesses. I. Title.

JAMES, Edwin Oliver, 291.211
1886-
The cult of the mother goddess; an archaeological and documentary study. New York, Praeger [1959] 300 p. 23 cm. (Books that matter) Includes bibliography. [BL325.M6J3 1959] 59-8623
1. Mother-goddesses. I. Title.

JENNINGS, Gary. 291.2'11
March of the gods / Gary Jennings ; drawings by Dan Culhane. New York : Association Press, c1976. 189 p. : ill. ; 22 cm. Includes index. [BL473.J46] 76-8832 ISBN 0-8096-1912-1 : 7.95
1. Gods—Juvenile literature. 2. God—Comparative studies—Juvenile literature. 3. Religion—Juvenile literature. I. Title.

LANTERO, Erminie 291.2'11
Huntress.
Feminine aspects of divinity. [Wallingford, Pa.] Pendle Hill [1973] 32 p. 20 cm. (Pendle Hill pamphlet 191) Bibliography: p. 32. [BL458.L3] 73-84214 ISBN 0-87574-191-6 0.70 (pbk.)
1. Women and religion. 2. Sex (Theology) I. Title.

NIDA, Eugene Albert, 291.211
1914-
Introducing animism [by] Eugene A. Nida [and] William A. Smalley. New York, Friendship Press [1959] 64p. illus. 23cm. Includes bibliography. [GN471.N5] 59-6049
1. Animism. I. Smalley, William Allen, joint author. II. Title.

PARKER, Derek. 291.2'11
The immortals / Derek & Julia Parker. New York : McGraw-Hill, c1976. 207 p. : ill. (some col.) ; 30 cm. "A Webb & Bower book." Includes index. Bibliography: p. 204-205. [BL311.P37] 76-6940 ISBN 0-07-048493-7 : 19.95
1. Mythology. 2. Folk-lore. I. Parker, Julia. II. Title.

RACZ, Istvan, 1908- 291.2'11
The unknown god. Photos. by Istvan Racz. Text by Carl A. Keller [and others] With a foreword by Walter Nigg. Translated by Simon and Erika Young. New York, Sheed and Ward [1970] ix, 278 p. illus. 29 cm. [BL205.R33] 79-125830 19.50
1. God—Comparative studies—Addresses, essays, lectures. 2. Gods—Addresses, essays, lectures. I. Keller, Carl A., joint author. II. Title.

ROBERTS, Jimmy Jack 291.2'11
McBee.
The earliest semitic pantheon; a study of the Semitic deities attested in Mesopotamia before Ur III, by J. J. M. Roberts. Baltimore, Johns Hopkins University Press [1972] xvii, 174 p. 27 cm. Includes bibliographical references. [BL1600.R6] 70-186515 ISBN 0-8018-1388-3
1. Gods, Semitic. I. Title.

STONE, Merlin. 291.2'11
The Paradise papers : the suppression of women's rites / [by] Merlin Stone. London : Virago : Quartet Books, 1976. [15], 275, [9] p., 16 p. of plates : ill., maps ; 23 cm. American ed. published under title: When god was a woman. Includes index. Bibliography: p. 261-275. [BL458.S76 1976b] 76-374034 ISBN 0-7043-2805-4 : £4.95
1. Women in religion. I. Title.

TIEDE, David Lenz. 291.2'11
The charismatic figure as miracle worker. [Missoula? Mont.] Published by Society of Biblical Literature for the Seminar on the Gospels, 1972. vi, 324 p. 22 cm. (Society of Biblical Literature. Dissertation series, no. 1) Originally presented as the author's thesis, Harvard. Bibliography: p. 293-312. [BJ1521.T48 1972] 72-87359
1. Moses. 2. Jesus Christ—Person and offices. 3. Virtue. 4. Miracles. I. Title. II. Series.

BERGER, Charles G. 291.212
Our phallic heritage, by C. G. Berger. [1st ed.] New York, Greenwich Book Publishers [1966] 216 p. illus. 23 cm. Bibliographical footnotes. [BL460.B4] 66-12676
1. Phallicism. I. Title.

BROWN, Sanger, 1884- 291.2'12
Sex worship and symbolism / Sanger Brown II. New York : AMS Press, 1975. 149 p. : ill. ; 19 cm. Reprint of the 1922 ed. published by R. G. Badger, Boston. Includes index. Bibliography: p. 139-142. [BL460.B7 1975] 72-9624 ISBN 0-404-57419-X : 10.95
1. Phallicism. 2. Sex and religion. 3. Symbolism. I. Title.

CONRAD, Jack Randolph. 291.2'12
The horn and the sword; the history of the bull as symbol of power and fertility. With photographic illus. and drawings by James MacDonald. Westport, Conn., Greenwood Press [1973, c1957] 222 p. illus. 22 cm. [BL443.B8C6 1973] 72-9822 ISBN 0-8371-6604-7 12.25
1. Bull (in religion, folk-lore, etc.) I. Title.

DULAURE, Jacques- 291.2'12
Antoine, 1755-1835.
The gods of generation : a history of phallic cults among ancients & moderns / Jacques-Antoine Dulaure ; translated from the French by A. F. N. New York : AMS Press, 1975. 280 p. ; 19 cm. Translation of Des divinites generatrices. Reprint of the 1934 ed. priv. print. by Panurge Press, New York. Includes bibliographical references and index. [BL460.D82 1975] 72-9635 ISBN 0-404-57433-5 : 24.50
1. Phallicism. 2. Sex and religion. 3. Religion, Primitive. I. Title.

FRAZER, James George, 291.2'12
Sir, 1854-1941.
The workship of nature / by James George Frazer. Volume I. New York : AMS Press, [1974, i.e.1975] p. cm. No more published. Reprint of the 1926 ed. published by Macmillan, New York, which was issued as the Gifford lectures, 1924-1925. [BL435.F7 1974] 73-21271 ISBN 0-404-11427-X : 35.00
1. Nature worship. 2. Religion, Primitive. I. Title. II. Series: Gifford lectures ; 1924-1925.

GUBERNATIS, Angelo de, 291.2'12
conte, 1840-1913.
Zoological mythology; or, The legends of animals. London, Trubner, 1872. Detroit, Singing Tree Press, 1968. 2 v. 22 cm. Bibliographical footnotes. [BL325.A6G8 1968] 68-58904
1. Mythology, Aryan. 2. Animal lore. 3. Animals, Legends and stories of. 4. Folk-lore. I. Title. II. Title: Legends of animals.

HAWKES, Jacquetta 291.212
(Hopkins) 1910-
Man and the sun. New York, Random [c.1962] 277p. illus. 22cm. 62-8448 5.00 bds.,
1. Sun-worship. 2. Sun lore. I. Title.

JAMES, Edwin Oliver, 291.212
1886-
The worship of the Sky-god; a comparative study in Semitic and Indo-European religion. [London] Univ. of London, Athlone Pr. [dist. New York, Oxford, c.]1963. vi, 175p. 23cm. (Jordan lects. in comparative religion, 6) Bibl. 63-6471 4.00
1. Sky-gods. I. Title. II. Series.

JOBES, Gertrude. 291.212
Outer space: myths, name meanings, calendars from the emergence of history to the present day, by Gertrude and James Jobes. New York, Scarecrow Press, 1964. 479 p. charts. 22 cm. Bibliography: p. 411-417. [BL438.J6] 64-11783
1. Mythology. 2. Astronomy. 3. Stars (in religion, folk-lore, etc.) I. Jobes, James, joint author. II. Title.

KNIGHT, Richard Payne, 291.212
1750-1824
Sexual symbolism; a history of phallic workship, 2v. in 1 byRichard Payne Knight, Thomas Wright. Introd. by Ashley Montagu. [New York, N.Y., 10003, Matrix House, 119 Fifth Ave.] 1966[c.1957] 2v. in 1 (217; 196p.) illus. 21cm. (Agora softback, A-12) Contents.v.1. A discourse on the worship of Priapus and its connection with the mystic theology of the ancients, by R. P. Knight.--v.2. The worship of the generative powers during the Middle Ages of western Europe, by T. Wright. Bibl. [BL460.K6] 2.25 pap.,
1. Phallicism. 2. Priapus. I. Wright, Thomas, 1810-1877. II. Knight, Richard Payne, 1750-1824. A discourse on the worship of Priapus. III. Wright, Thomas, 1810-1877. The worship of the generative powers. IV. Title. V. Title: A discourse on the worship of Priapus. VI. Title: The worship of the generative power.

LA Barre, Weston, 1911- 291.212
They shall take up serpents; psychology of the southern snake-handling cult. Minneapolis, University of Minnesota Press [1962] 208 p. illus. 23 cm. Includes bibliography. [BL441.L3 1962] 61-18819
1. Barefoot, Beauregard. 2. Serpents (in religion, folk-lore, etc.) 3. Serpent-worship. I. Title.

MASANI, Rustom Pestonji, 291.2'12
Sir, 1876-1966.
Folklore of wells : being a study of water-worship in East and West / by R. P. Masani. Folcroft, Pa. : Folcroft Library Editions, 1977. p. cm. Reprint of the 1918 ed. published by D. B. Taraporevala Sons, Bombay. Includes bibliographical references. [GR690.M37 1977] 77-11936 ISBN 0-8414-6216-X : 20.00
1. Holy wells. 2. Water (in religion, folk-lore, etc.) I. Title.

OLCOTT, William Tyler, 291.2'12
1873-1936
Myths of the sun (Sun lore of all ages); a collection of myths and legends concerning the sun and its worship. [Magnolia, Mass., Peter Smith, 1968,c.1914] 337p. 19cm. (Capricorn bk. rebound) First pub. in 1914 under title: Sun lore of all ages. Bibl. [BL325.S8O5 1967] 68-2765 4.00
1. Sun (in religion folk-lore etc.) 2. Mythology. I. Title.

OLCOTT, William Tyler, 291.2'12
1873-1936.
Myths of the sun (Sun lore of all ages); a collection of myths and legends concerning the sun and its worship. New York, Capricorn Books [1967, c1914] 307 p. 19 cm. First published in 1914 under title: Sun lore of all ages. Bibliographical footnotes. [BL325.S8O5 1967] 68-2765
1. Sun (in religion folk-lore, etc.) 2. Mythology. I. Title.

OLCOTT, William Tyler, 291.2'12
1873-1936.
Sun lore of all ages; a collection of myths and legends concerning the sun and its worship. Boston, Milford House [1973] p. Reprint of the 1914 ed. published by Putnam, New York. Bibliography: [BL325.S8O5 1973] 73-13711 ISBN 0-87821-181-0 30.00 (lib. bdg.)
1. Sun (in religion, folk-lore, etc.) I. Title.

SENDER, Ramon. 291.2'12
Being of the sun, written by Ramon Sender & Alicia Bay Laurel. Drawn & lettered by Alicia with musical notation by Ramon. Songs: music by Ramon & words by Alicia except where otherwise noted. [1st ed.] New York, Harper & Row [1973] 202 p. illus. 28 cm. [BL435.S46] 73-4060 ISBN 0-06-012523-3 4.95
1. Nature-worship. I. Laurel, Alicia Bay, joint author. II. Title.

STONE, Lee Alexander, 291.2'12
1879-
The story of phallicism / by Lee Alexander Stone ; with other essays on related subjects by eminent authorities ; introd. by Frederick Starr. New York : Ams Press, 1976. xvi, 652 p. ; 19 cm. Reprint of the 1927 ed. published by P. Covici, Chicago. [BL460.S85 1976] 72-9682 34.50
1. Phallicism—Addresses, essays, lectures. 2. Prostitution—Addresses, essays, lectures. I. Title.
Contents omitted

TALBOT, Percy Amaury, 291.2'12
1877-1945.
Some Nigerian fertility cults. New York, Barnes & Noble [1967] xi, 140 p. illus. 22 cm. Reprint of the 1927 ed. Bibliographical footnotes. [BL2470.N5T3 1967a] 67-6629
1. Phallicism. 2. Nigeria—Religion. 3. Cultus—Nigeria. I. Title.

WALL, Otto Augustus, 291.2'12
1846-1922.
Sex and sex worship (phallic worship); a scientific treatise on sex, its nature and function, and its influence on art, science, architecture, and religion— with special reference to sex worship and symbolism. College Park, Md., McGrath Pub. Co., 1970 [c1922] xv, 608 p. illus. 24 cm. Bibliography: p. 599-603. [BL460.W2 1970] 73-119244 ISBN 0-8434-0091-9
1. Phallicism. I. Title.

CONRAD, Jack Randolph. 291.2124
The horn and the sword; the history of the bull as symbol of power and fertility. With photographic illus. and drawings by James MacDonald. [1st ed.] New York, Dutton, 1957. 222 p. illus. 22 cm. [BL443.B8C6] 57-8972
1. Bull (in religion, folk-lore, etc.) I. Title.

ANCESTORS / 291.2'13
editor William H. Newell. The Hague : Mouton ; Chicago : distributed in the USA and Canada by Aldine, 1976. xv, 403 p., [4] leaves of plates : ill. ; 24 cm. (World anthropology) Papers prepared for the 9th International Congress of Anthropological and Ethnological Sciences, Chicago, 1973. Includes bibliographical references and indexes. [BL467.A5] 76-382811 ISBN 0-202-90036-3 (Aldine) : 26.50
1. Ancestor worship—Congresses. 2. Ancestor worship—Japan—Congresses. I. Newell, William Hare. II. International Congress of Anthropological and Ethnological Sciences, 9th, Chicago, 1973. III. Title. IV. Series.

CLES-REDEN, Sibylle 291.213
Emilie (von Reden) Baronin von Cles, 1910-
The realm of the great goddess; the story of the megalith builders. [Tr. from German by Eric Mosbacher] Englewood Cliffs, N.J., Prentice, 1962 [c.1960, 1961] 328p. illus. 26cm. Bibl. 62-5936 10.00
1. Religion, Primitive. 2. Salvation—Comparative studies. I. Title.

FRAZER, James George, 291.213
Sir 1854-1941
The fear of the dead in primitive religion. New York, Biblo & Tannen, 1966. viii., 204p. 21cm. (Lects. delivered on the William Wyse Found. at Trinity Coll., Cambridge, 1932-33) Title. (Series: Cambridge. University. Trinity College. William Wyse Foundation. Lectures delivered on the William Wyse Foundation, 1932-33) Reprint of the work first pub. in 1933 as [v.1] of a 3-vol. set with the same title. Bibl. [BL470.F72] 66-15215 7.50
1. Dead in religion, folk-lore, etc.) 2. Ancestor worship. 3. Religion, Primitive. I. Title. II. Series.

HADAS, Moses, 1900- 291.213
Heroes and gods; spiritual biographies in antiquity, by Moses Hadas, Morton Smith. New York, Harper [c.1965] xiv, 266p. 21cm. (Religious perspectives, v. 13) [BL325.H46H3] 65-15397 5.00
1. Heroes. I. Smith, Morton, 1915- joint author. II. Title. III. Series.

HADAS, Moses, 1900-1966. 291.213
Heroes and gods; spiritual biographies in antiquity, by Moses Hadas and Morton Smith. [1st ed.] New York, Harper & Row [1965] xiv, 266 p. 21 cm. (Religious perspectives, v. 13) [BL325.H46H3] 65-15397
1. Heroes. I. Smith, Morton, 1915- joint author. II. Title. III. Series.

HADAS, Moses, 1900-1966. 291.2'13
Heroes and gods; spiritual biographies in antiquity, by Moses Hadas and Morton Smith. Freeport, N.Y., Books for Libraries Press [1970, c1965] xiv, 266 p. 23 cm. (Essay index reprint series) [BL325.H46H3 1970] 77-117800
1. Heroes. 2. Biography (as a literary form) I. Smith, Morton, 1915- II. Title.

HOOKE, Samuel Henry, 291.213
1874- ed.
Myth, ritual, and kingship; essays on the theory and practice of kingship in the ancient Near East and in Israel. Oxford, Clarendon Press, 1958. xi, 208p. 23cm. 'Lectures ... given at the University of Manchester in the autumn of 1955 and the spring of 1956 ... now published, with one addition.' Bibliographical footnotes. [BL325.K5H6] 58-3963
1. Kings and rulers (in religion, folk-lore, etc.) 2. Mythology. 3. Ritual. I. Title.

MURRAY, Margaret Alice 291.213
The genesis of religion. London, Routledge & Paul [dist. New York, Philosophical, c.1963] v, 88p. 23cm. Bibl. 63-5949 3.75
1. Women and religion. I. Title.

RAGLAN, Fitz Roy Richard 291.2'13
Somerset, Baron, 1885-
The hero : a study in tradition, myth, and drama / by Lord Raglan. Detroit : Gale Research Co., [1975] p. cm. Reprint of the 1937 ed. published by Oxford University Press, New York. Includes index. Bibliography: p. [BL325.H46R3 1975] 75-16397 ISBN 0-8103-4088-7
1. Heroes. 2. Mythology. 3. Folk-lore. 4. Drama. I. Title.

RAGLAN, FitzRoy Richard 291.2'13
Somerset, Baron, 1885-
The hero : a study in tradition, myth, and drama / Lord Raglan. Westport, Conn. : Greenwood Press, 1975, c1956. p. cm. Reprint of the ed. published by Vintage Books, New York. Includes index. Bibliography: p. [BL325.H46R3 1975b] 75-23424 ISBN 0-8371-8138-0 lib.bdg. : 15.00
1. Heroes. 2. Mythology. 3. Folk-lore. 4. Drama. I. Title.

JAYNE, Walter Addison, 291.214
1853-1929.
The healing gods of ancient civilizations. New Hyde Park, N. Y., University Books [1962] xxi, 569p. illus. 24cm. Bibliography: p. [523]-542. [BL325.H4J3 1962] 62-13503
1. Gods. 2. Mythology. 3. Medicine, Ancient. I. Title.

JUNG, Carl Gustav, 1875- 291.214
Essays on a science of mythology; the myths of the divine child and the divine maiden, by C. G. Jung, C. Kerenyi. Tr. [from German] by R. F. C. Hull. Rev. ed. New York, Harper [1963,c.1949, 1959] 200p. 21cm. (Harper torchbks.; Bollingen lib., TB2014) Bibl. 1.85 pap.,
1. Mythology. 2. Psychonalaysis. I. Kerenyi, Karoly, 1897. II. Title.

NEUMANN, Erich. 291.214
The great mother; an analysis of the archetype. Translated from th e German by Ralph Manheim. [New York] Pantheon Books [1955] xiiii, 380p. illus. 27cm. (Bollingen series, 47) Bibliography: p. 339-352. [BL85.N4] 55-10026
1. Mother-goddesses. 2. Religions. I. Title. II. Series.

CARUS, Paul, 1852-1919. 291.2'16
The history of the devil and the idea of evil, from the earliest times to the present day / by Paul Carus. La Salle, Ill. : Open Court Pub. Co., [1974]. 496 p. : ill. ; 25 cm. (Open Court paperback) [BF1505.C37 1974] 74-190618 ISBN 0-87548-307-0 : 5.95
1. Devil. 2. Demonology. 3. Good and evil. I. Title: The history of the devil and the idea of evil ...

CAVENDISH, Richard. 291.2'16
The powers of evil in Western religion, magic, and folk belief / Richard Cavendish. 1st American ed. New York : Putnam, 1975. ix, 299 p. ; 22 cm. Includes index. Bibliography: p. [275]-283. [BJ1401.C34 1975] 75-7933 ISBN 0-399-11484-X : 7.95
1. Good and evil. 2. Supernatural. I. Title.

JUNG, Leo, 1892- 291.2'16
Fallen angels in Jewish, Christian, and Mohammedan literature. New York, Ktav Publishing House, 1974. viii, 174 p. 24 cm. Reprint of the 1926 ed. published by the Dropsie College for Hebrew and Cognate Learning. Originally presented as the author's thesis, Univ. of London. Bibliography: p. 163-165. [BL480.J8 1974] 73-22476 ISBN 0-87068-236-9 12.50
1. Demonology. I. Title.

RUSSELL, Jeffrey Burton. 291.2'16
The Devil : perceptions of evil from antiquity to primitive Christianity / Jeffrey Burton Russell. Ithaca, N.Y. : Cornell University Press, c1977. 276 p. : ill. ; 24 cm. Includes index. Bibliography: p. [261]-270. [BL480.R86] 77-3126 ISBN 0-8014-0938-1 : 15.00
1. Devil—History of doctrines. 2. Good and evil. I. Title.

SCOTT, Walter, Sir, 291.2'16
bart., 1771-1832.
Letters on demonology and witchcraft / by Sir Walter Scott, bart. ; with an introd. by Henry Morley. New York : Gordon Press, 1974. 320 p. ; 24 cm. "First published 1884." [BF1531.S5 1974] 73-7435 ISBN 0-87968-180-2 : 29.95
1. Demonology. 2. Witchcraft. I. Title.

WOODS, William Howard, 291.2'16
1916-
A history of the devil / William Woods. 1st American ed. New York : Putnam, 1974, c1973. 251 p. : ill. ; 22 cm. Includes index. Bibliography: p. 235-237. [BL480.W66 1974] 73-93751 ISBN 0-399-11327-4 : 6.95
1. Devil. I. Title.

BRANDON, Samuel George 291.22
Frederick
Creation legends of the ancient Near East. [London] Hodder & Stoughton [Mystic, Conn., Verry, 1965, c.1963] xiv, 241p. illus. 23cm. Bibl. [BL325.C7B7] 64-55391 7.00
1. Creation—Comparative studies. I. Title.

CHALMERS, Randolph 291.22
Carleton, ed.
The meaning of life in five great religions. Edited by R. C. Chalmers and John A. Irving. Philadelphia, Westminister Press [1965] v. 165 p. 19 cm. Contents.Foreword, by R. C. Chalmers. -- Encounter, by W. S. Taylor. -- Hinduism, by P. Nagaraja Rao. -- Buddhism, by S. Hanayama. -- Judaism by E. L. Fackenhelm. -- Christianity, by R. C. Chalmers. -- Islam, by M. Rasjidi. -- From encounter to community, by C. D. Jay. Bibliographical footnotes. [BL50.C45 1965] 65-10961
1. Life — Addresses, essays, lectures. I. Iring, John A., joint ed. II. Title.

KENNY, John Peter, 1916- 291.2'2
Christ outside Christianity: the supernatural in non-Christian religions [by] J. P. Kenny. Melbourne, Spectrum, 1971. viii, 64 p. 18 cm. Bibliography: p. 62-64. [BT759.K45] 73-155503 ISBN 0-909837-09-0 1.50
1. Salvation outside the church. 2. Religions. I. Title.

KULANDRAN, Sabapathy 291.22
Grace; a comparative study of the doctrine in Christianity and Hinduism. Foreword by Hendrik Kraemer. London, Lutterworth Pr. [New York, Humanities, 1965, c.1964] 278p. 23cm. (Lutterworth lib.) Bibl. [BR128.H5K8] 66-1674 6.75
1. Grace (Theology)—Comparative studies. 2. Christianity and other religions—Hinduism. 3. Hindusism—Relations—Christianity. I. Title.

LIVING faiths and 291.2'2
ultimate goals : salvation and world religions / edited by S. J. Samartha. 1st U.S. ed. Maryknoll, N.Y. : Orbis Books, c1974. xvii, 119 p. ; 24 cm. Result of the world conference on mission and evangelism held at Bangkok from Dec. 29, 1972 to Jan. 8, 1973 on the theme: Salvation today. Includes bibliographical references. [BL476.L58] 75-7610 ISBN 0-88344-297-3 pbk. : 3.95
1. Salvation—Comparative studies—Addresses, essays, lectures. I. Samartha, Stanley J.

MADRIGAL, Jose A., 1945- 291.2'2
El salvaje y la mitologia, el arte y la religion / Jose A. Madrigal. Miami, Fla. : Ediciones Universal, 1975. 55 p. ; 21 cm. (Coleccion Polymita) "500 ejemplares." Bibliography: p. 51-54. [BL476.M3] 75-1692
1. Salvation. I. Title.

ORIGINS : 291.2'2
Creation texts from the ancient Mediterranean : a chrestomathy / co-edited and translated, with an introd. and notes, by Harris Lenowitz & Charles Doria ; pref. by Jerome Rothenberg. 1st ed. Garden City, N.Y. : Anchor Press, 1975. p. cm. Bibliography: p. [BL226.O74] 74-18844 ISBN 0-385-01922-X pbk. : 3.95
1. Creation—Collected works. 2. Cosmogony—Early works to 1800—Collected works. I. Lenowitz, Harris. II. Doria, Charles.

PADOVANO, Anthony T. 291.2'2
American culture and the quest for Christ, by Anthony T. Padovano. New York, Sheed & Ward [1970] x, 309 p. 22 cm. Includes bibliographical references. [BL85.P26] 77-82597 6.95
1. Salvation—Comparative studies. 2. U.S.—Civilization. I. Title.

BRANDON, Samuel George 291.22082
Frederick ed
The saviour god; comparative studies in the concept of salvation, presented to Edwin Oliver James, professor emeritus in the University of London, by colleagues and friends to commemorate his seventy-fifth birthday. New York, Barnes & Noble [1963] xxii, 242 p. port. 23 cm. English, Italian, or French. "A list of the principal published writings of E. O. James": p. xiii-xxi. Includes bibliographical references. [BL475.B7] 63-25478
I. Title.
Contents omitted

BRANDON, Samuel George 291.22082
Frederick, ed.
The saviour god; comparative studies in the concept of salvation, presented to Edwin Oliver James, professor emeritus in the Univ. of London, by colleagues and friends to commemorate his seventy-fifth birthday. New York, Barnes & Noble [c.1963] xxii, 242p. port. 23cm. Bibl. 63-25478 7.50
1. James, Edwin Oliver, 1886- 2. Salvation—Comparative studies. I. Title.

BRANDON, Samuel George 291.2'3
Frederick.
The judgment of the dead: the idea of life after death in the major religions [by] S. G. F. Brandon. New York, Scribner [1969, c1967] xii, 300 p. illus. 22 cm. Bibliography: p. 253-273. [BL547.B7 1969] 68-57077 6.95
1. Judgment Day—Comparative studies. I. Title.

CAYCE, Edgar, 1877-1945 291.2'3
Edgar Cayce on reincarnation, by Noel Langley; under editorship of Hugh Lynn Cayce. [1st hardbound ed.] New York, Hawthorn [1968,c.1967] 286p. 22cm. Presents data from 2500 readings given by Edgar Cayce from 1925 through 1944. Bibl. [BL515.C3 1968] 68-14394 4.95
1. Reincarnation. I. Langley, Noel, 1911- comp. II. Title.

CERMINARA, Gina. 291.23
Many lives, many loves. New York, W. Sloane Associates, 1963. 246 p. illus. 21 cm. [BL515.C38] 63-13710
1. Reincarnation. I. Title.

CERMINARA, Gina. 291.23
Many lives, many loves. [New York] New American Library [1974, c1963] 170 p. 18 cm. (A Signet book) [BL515.C38] 1.50 (pbk.)
1. Reincarnation. I. Title.
L.C. card no. for original: 63-13710.

COLTON, Ann Ree. 291.2'3
Draughts of remembrance. [1st ed.] Glendale, Calif., Arc Pub. Co. [1959] iv, 177 p. 20 cm. [BL515.C6] 67-9622
1. Reincarnation. I. Title.

DUNNE, John S., 1929- 291.23
The city of the gods; a study in myth & mortality, by John S. Dunne. New York, Macmillan [1965] xii, 243 p. 22 cm. Includes bibliographical references. [BL504.D8 1965] 65-11604
1. Death—Comparative studies. I. Title.

*DURANT, Richard 291.23
Spiritual evolution via cause and effect. New York, Vantage [c.1965] 127p. 21cm. 2.95 bds.,
I. Title.

FRAZER, James George, 291.2'3
Sir, 1854-1941.
The fear of the dead in primitive religion / James George Frazer. New York : Arno Press, 1977, c1933-1936. 706 p. in various pagings ; 27 cm. (The Literature of Death and dying) Reprint of the ed. published by Macmillan, London, which was issued as the 1932-1933 Lectures delivered on the William Wyse Foundation. Includes bibliographical references and indexes. [BL470.F7 1977] 76-19571 ISBN 0-405-09566-X : 43.00
1. Dead (in religion, folk-lore, etc.)—Addresses, essays, lectures. 2. Ancester worship—Addresses, essays, lectures. 3. Religion, Primitive—Addresses, essays, lectures. I. Title. II. Series. III. Series: Cambridge. University. Trinity College. William Wyse Foundation. Lectures delivered on the William Wyse Foundation ; 1932-1933.

FRAZER, James George, 291.2'3
Sir, 1854-1941.
The fear of the dead in primitive religion / James George Frazer. New York : Arno Press, 1977, c1933-1936. 706 p. in various pagings ; 27 cm. (The Literature of Death and dying) Reprint of the ed. published by Macmillan, London, which was issued as the 1932-1933 Lectures delivered on the William Wyse Foundation. Includes bibliographical references and indexes. [BL470.F7 1977] 76-19571 ISBN 0-405-09566-X : 43.00
1. Dead (in religion, folk-lore, etc.)—Addresses, essays, lectures. 2. Ancester worship—Addresses, essays, lectures. 3. Religion, Primitive—Addresses, essays, lectures. I. Title. II. Series. III. Series: Cambridge. University. Trinity College. William Wyse Foundation. Lectures delivered on the William Wyse Foundation ; 1932-1933.

THE Future as the 291.2'3
presence of shared hope, edited and with an introd. by Maryellen Muckenhirn. New York, Sheed and Ward [1968] 181 p. 22 cm. Essays presented at the John XXIII Institute theology symposium held at Saint Xavier College, Chicago, on Oct. 27-29, 1967. Includes bibliographies. [BT821.2.F8] 68-26038 4.95
1. Eschatology—Addresses, essays, lectures. 2. Hope—Addresses, essays, lectures. I. Muckenhirn, Maryellen, ed. II. John XXIII Institute, Chicago. III. Saint Xavier College, Chicago.

*HANLEY, Elizabeth. 291.2'3
Life after death / Elizabeth Hanley. New York : Nordon Publications, c1977. 206p. ; 18 cm. (Leisure Books) [BL535] ISBN 0-8439-0451-8 pbk. : 1.50
1. Future life. I. Title.

HEAD, Joseph, ed. 291.23
Reincarnation; an East-West anthology including quotations from the world's religions & from over 400 Western thinkers. Compiled and edited by Joseph Head and S. L. Cranston. New York, Julian Press, 1961. 341 p. 25 cm. [BL515.H38] 61-14420
1. Reincarnation. I. Cranston, S. L., joint ed. II. Title.

HEAD, Joseph, comp. 291.2'3
Reincarnation; an East-West anthology including quotations from the world's religions & from over 400 Western thinkers. Compiled and edited by Joseph Head and S. L. Cranston. Wheaton, Ill., Theosophical Pub. House [1968, c1961] x, 341 p. 21 cm. (A Quest book) [BL515.H38 1968] 68-146
1. Reincarnation. I. Cranston, S. L., joint comp.

HEAD, Joseph, comp. 291.2'3
Reincarnation in world thought; a living study of reincarnation in all ages; including selections from the world's religions, philosophies, and sciences, and great thinkers of the past and present, compiled and edited by Joseph Head [and] S. L. Cranston. New York, Causeway Books; published by arrangement with The Julian Press, New York, c1967. 461 p. illus. Based on the compiler's Reincarnation, an East-West anthology. [BL515.H39] 67-17571
1. Reincarnation. I. Cranston, S. L., joint comp. II. Title.

HENDERSON, Joseph L 291.23
The wisdom of the serpent; the myths of death, rebirth and resurrection by Joseph L. Henderson and Maud Oakes. New York, G. Braziller, 1963. xxiv, 262 p. illus. 22 cm. (Patterns of myth. I: Myth and experience) Bibliography: p. 247-253. [BL504.H4] 63-18189
1. Death — Comparative studies. I. Oakes, Maud van Cortiandt, 1903- joint author. II. Title. III. Series.

HENDERSON, Joseph L. 291.23
The wisdom of the serpent; the myths of death, rebirth and resurection by Joseph L. Henderson, Maud Oakes. New York, Braziller [c.]1963. xxiv, 262p. illus. 22cm. (Patterns of myth. I: Myth and experience) Bibl. 63-18189 6.00
1. Death—Comparative studies. I. Oakes, Maud van Cortlandt, 1903— joint author. II. Title. III. Series.

HICK, John. 291.2'3
Death and eternal life / John Hick. London : Collins, 1976. 495 p. ; 22 cm. Includes index. Bibliography: p. [467]-481. [BL535.H52] 76-383985 ISBN 0-00-215157-X : £5.95
1. Future life. 2. Death. I. Title.

HODSON, Geoffrey. 291.2'3
Reincarnation, fact or fallacy? An examination and exposition of the doctrine of rebirth. [Rev. ed.] Wheaton, Ill., Theosophical Pub. House [1967] 83 p. 18 cm. (A Quest book) [BP573.R5H6 1967] 67-4405
1. Theosophy. 2. Reincarnation. I. Title.

JONES, Gladys V. 291.23
The flowering tree. New York, W. Sloane Associates, 1965. 316 p. 22 cm. Bibliography: p. 315-316. [BL518.J6] 65-20504
1. Reincarnation. 2. Karma. I. Title.

KAPLEAU, Philip, 1912- 291.2'3
comp.
The wheel of death : a collection of writings from Zen Buddhist and other sources on death—rebirth—dying / edited by Philip Kapleau, assisted by Paterson Simons. New York : Harper & Row, 1974, c1971. xviii, 110 p. : ill. ; 21 cm. (Harper colophon books ; CN 377) Includes bibliographical references and index. [BD444.K33 1974] 74-188867 ISBN 0-06-090377-5 pbk. : 2.25
1. Death—Collected works. 2. Reincarnation—Collected works. I. Simons, Paterson, joint comp. II. Title.

KAPLEAU, Phillip- comp. 291.23
The Wheel of death A collection of writings from Zen Buddhist and other sources on death, rebirth, dying [comp. by] Philip Kapleau. Assisted by Paterson Simmons. New York Harper & Row 1974 [1971] xviii, 110 p. 20 cm. (Harper Colophon books.) Bibliography: p. 100-103. [BD444.K33] 74-149748 ISBN 0-06-064241-6 2.25 (pbk.)
1. Death—Collections. 2. Reincarnation—Collections. I. Title.

LASHMET, Edwin F 291.2'3
Think for yourself. [1st ed.] New York, Greenwich Book Publishers, [1962] 32 p. 22 cm. [BL518.L3] 69-15300
1. Reincarnation. I. Title.

LASHMET, Edwin F 291.2'3
Think for yourself. [1st ed.] New York, Greenwich Book Publishers, [1962] 32 p. 22 cm. [BL518.L3] 69-15300
1. Reincarnation. I. Title.

LEEK, Sybil. 291.2'3
Reincarnation: the second chance. New York, Stein and Day [1974] 262 p. 24 cm. Bibliography: p. 249-256. [BL515.L43] 73-93034 ISBN 0-8128-1693-5 7.95
1. Reincarnation.

LEEK, Sybil. 291.2'3
Reincarnation: the second chance. New York, Bantam Books [1975, c1974] 212 p. 18 cm. Bibliography: p. 199-205. [BL515.L43] 1.50 (pbk.)
1. Reincarnation. I. Title.
L.C. card number for original ed.: 73-93034.

LOPATIN, Ivan Alexis 291.23
The cult of the dead among the natives of the Amur Basin. The Hague, Mouton [dist. New York, Humanities Press, 1960] 211 p. p. [203]-206 fold. map. 24 cm. (Central Asiatic studies, 6) imprint covered by label: New york, Humanities Press. Bibl. 60-4182 pap., 9.00
1. Tunguses 2. Dead (in relig, folk-lore, etc.) 3. Indians of North America—Religion and mythology. I. Title. II. Series.

MARSELLA, Elena Maria 291.23
The quest for Eden. New York, Philosophical Lib. [c.1966] 275p. 22cm. Bibl. [BL540.M3] 66-16172 5.00
1. Paradise. I. Title.

MARTIN, Eva M., ed. 291.23
Reincarnation: the ring of return. Comp., introd. by Eva Martin. New Hyde Park, N.Y., University Bks. [1963] xi, 306p. 22cm. 63-18492 5.00
1. Reincarnation—Collections. I. Title.

MEW, James, b.1837. 291.2'3
Traditional aspects of hell (ancient and modern) Ann Arbor, Mich., Gryphon Books, 1971. xv, 448 p. illus. 22 cm. "This is a facsimile reprint of the 1903 edition published in London by S. Sonnenschein & Company, Limited." [BL545.M4 1971] 73-140321
1. Hell—Comparative studies. I. Title.

MOORE, Marcia. 291.2'3
Reincarnation, key to immortality [by] Marcia Moore [and] Mark Douglas. [1st ed.] York Cliffs, Me., Arcane Publications [1968] xv, 394 p. 23 cm. Bibliography: p. 349-352. [BL515.M63] 67-19603 5.95
1. Reincarnation. I. Douglas, Mark, joint author. II. Title.

PARRINDER, Edward 291.2'3
Geoffrey.
Avatar and incarnation, by Geoffrey Parrinder. New York, Barnes & Noble [1970] 296 p. 23 cm. (Wilde lectures in natural and comparative religion) Bibliography: p. 280-287. [BL510.P3 1970] 71-12730 ISBN 3-89013-587- 9.50
1. Incarnation—Comparative studies. 2. Avatars. 3. Christianity and other religions. I. Title. II. Series.

RELIGIOUS encounters with 291.2'3
death : essays in the history and anthropology of religion / edited by Frank E. Reynolds and Earle H. Waugh. University Park : Pennsylvania State University Press, c1976. p. cm. Based on papers prepared for the annual convention of the American Academy of Religion held in Chicago, 1973. Includes index. [BL504.R44 1976] 76-14981 ISBN 0-271-01229-3 : 12.50
1. Death—Addresses, essays, lectures. I. Reynolds, Frank, 1930- II. Waugh, Earle H. III. American Academy of Religion.

RELIGIOUS encounters with 291.2'3
death : essays in the history and anthropology of religion / edited by Frank E. Reynolds and Earle H. Waugh. University Park : Pennsylvania State University Press, 1977c1976 p. cm. Based on papers prepared for the annual convention of the American Academy of Religion held in Chicago, 1973. Includes index. [BL504.R44 1976] 76-14981 ISBN 0-271-01229-3 : 14.50
1. Death—Addresses, essays, lectures. I. Reynolds, Frank, 1930- II. Waugh, Earle H. III. American Academy of Religion.

RUTTER, Owen, 1889-1944. 291.2'3
The scales of Karma. New York, S. Weiser, 1971. 207 p. 20 cm. First published in London in 1940. [BL2015.K3R88 1971] 78-131206 ISBN 0-87728-027-4 2.95
1. Karma. I. Title.

SHARMA, Ishwar Chandra. 291.2'3
Cayce, Karma, and reincarnation / I. C. Sharma ; introd. by Hugh Lynn Cayce. 1st ed. New York : Harper & Row, [1975] xiii, 172 p. ; 20 cm. Includes bibliographical references. [BL515.S45 1975] 74-25707 ISBN 0-06-067328-1 pbk. : 3.95
1. Cayce, Edgar, 1877-1945. 2. Reincarnation. 3. Karma. 4. Religion. I. Title.

SMITH, Susy. 291.2'3
Reincarnation for the millions, by Suzy [i. e. Susy] Smith. Los Angeles, Sherbourne Press [c1967] 160 p. 21 cm. (For the millions series, FM-13) [BL515.S6] 67-21875 1.95
1. Reincarnation. I. Title.

STEARN, Jess. 291.2'3
The search for the girl with the blue eyes. [1st ed.] Garden City, N.Y., Doubleday, 1968. 304 p. 22 cm. [BL518.S7] 67-20920
1. MacIver, Joanne. 2. Reincarnation. 3. Hypnotism. I. Title.

STENDAHL, Krister, ed. 291.23
Immortality and resurrection; four essays, by Oscar Cullmann, Harry A. Wolfson, Werner Jaeger, Henry J. Cadbury. New York, Macmillan [c.1965] 149p. 18cm. Title. (Series: The Ingersoll lecture, Harvard University, 1955, etc.) Ingersoll lects. given at Harvard between 1955 and 1959. [BT923.S74] 65-17522 1.45 pap.,
1. Immortality—Addresses, essays, lectures. 2. Resurrection—Addresses, essays, lectures. I. Title. II. Series.

TOYNBEE, Arnold Joseph, 291.2'3
1889-1975.
Life after death / Arnold Toynbee, Arthur Koestler, and others. New York : McGraw-Hill, c1976. 272 p. ; 22 cm. Includes bibliographical references and index. [BL535.T69 1976] 76-16175 ISBN 0-07-065124-8 : 9.95
1. Future life—Addresses, essays, lectures. I. Koestler, Arthur, 1905- joint author. II. Title.

WALKER, Edward Dwight, 291.23
1859-1890
Reincarnation; a study of forgotten truth. Introd. by S. Digby Smith. New Hyde Park, N. Y. Univ. Bks. [c.1965] xix, 383p. 22cm. Bibl. [BP573.R5W3] 65-13657 5.00
1. Reincarnation. 2. Theosophy. I. Title.

WOODWARD, Mary Ann. 291.2'3
Edgar Cayce's story of karma; God's book of remembrance. Selections, arrangement and comments by Mary Ann Woodward. New York, Coward-McCann [1971] 283 p. 22 cm. [BL2015.K3W66] 70-135254 6.95
1. Karma. I. Cayce, Edgar, 1877-1945. II. Title. III. Title: Story of karma.

JOHNSON, Donald. 291.291
God and gods in Hinduism [by] Donald and Jean Johnson. New Delhi, Arnold-Heinemann India [1972] 88 p. illus. 22 cm. Label on t.p.: Dist. in the U.S.A. by Fernhill House [BL1216.J58] 71-928606 3.50
1. Gods, Hindu. I. Johnson, Jean, joint author. II. Title.

BISHOP, James Alonzo, ed. 291.3
Go with God [ed. by] Jim Bishop. A treasury of the great prayers of alltime and all faiths, plus a moving personal narrative of prayer by the author. Derby, Conn., Monarch Books [1960, c.1958] 349p. 19cm. (Monarch human behavior bk. MB504) .50 pap.,
1. Prayers. I. Title.

DE PIERREFEU, Elsa (tudor) 291.3
Unity in the spirit. Rindge, N. H., R. R. Smith, 1955. 167p. 23cm. [BL560.D4] 55-9047
1. Prayer. I. Title.

DROWER, Ethel Stepana 291.3
(Stevens) Lady
Water into wine; a study of ritual idiom in the Middle East. London, Murray [Mystic, Conn., Verry, 1965] 273p. illus. 23cm. [BL619.S3D7] 56-4507 6.00
1. Sacred meals. 2. Lord's Supper. I. Title.

ELIADE, Mircea, 1907- 291.3
Birth and rebirth; the religious meanings of initiation in human culture. Translated from the French by Willard R. Trask. [1st ed.] New York, Harper [1958] 175 p. 22 cm. (The Library of religion and culture) (Haskell lectures, 1956.) Translation of Naissances mystiques. Includes bibliography. [BL615.E4] 58-10374
1. Initiations (in religion, folk-lore, etc.) I. Title.

FLIADE, Mircea, 1907- 291.3
Rites and symbols of initiation; the mysteries of birth and rebirth. Tr. from French by Willard R. Trask [Gloucester, Mass., P. Smith, 1966, c.1958] xv, 175p. 21cm. (Harper torchbk.,TB1236H, Acad. lib. rebound) Bibl. [BL615.E4] 3.50
1. Initiations (in religion, folklore, etc.) I. Title.

HARRISON, Jane Ellen, 291'.3
1850-1928.
Ancient art and ritual. New York, Greenwood Press [1969, c1951] 256 p. illus. 23 cm. Bibliography: p. 253-254. [BH91.H32 1969] 69-13924
1. Art, Primitive. 2. Ritual. 3. Aesthetics. I. Title.

HILLIARD, Frederick 291.3
Hadaway.
How men worship, by F. H. Hilliard. New York, Roy Publishers [1965] ix, 184 p. illus., map. 20 cm. [BL550.H5] 66-10772
1. Worship—Comparative studies. I. Title.

JOHNSTON, William, 1925- 291.'3
Silent music : / William Johnston. William Johnston. New York : Harper & Row, 1976c1974. 188p. ; 18 cm. (Perennial library) Includes index. Bibliography: p [179]-180. [BL627.J63] ISBN 0-06-080386-X pbk. : 1.95
1. Meditation. I. Title.
L.C. card no. for 1974 edition: 73-18688

MANGOENDJAJA, K. 291.3
My inner guidance. New York, [P.O. Bx. 176, Old Chelsea Stat.] Dharma Bk. Co., 71p. 1.50 pap.,
I. Title.

NOLA, Alfonso Maria di, 291.3
comp.
The prayers of man, from primitive peoples to present times. Ed. by Patrick O'Connor. Tr. by Rex Benedict. New York, I. Obolensky [c.1961] 544p. 25cm. 60-13420 8.50
1. Prayers. 2. Cultus. I. O'Connor, Patrick, 1925- ed. II. Title.

NOLA, Alfonso Maria di, 291.3
comp.
The prayers of man, from primitive peoples to present times. Edited by Patrick O'Connor. Translations by Rex Benedict. New York, I. Obolensky [1961] 544p. 25cm. [BL560.N6] 60-13420
1. Prayers. 2. Cultus. I. O'Connor, Patrick, 1925- ed. II. Title.

PARRINDER, Edward Geoffrey 291.3
Worship in the world's religions. New York, Association [c.1961] 239p. Bibl. 61-14183 3.75 bds.,
1. Cultus. 2. Worship. I. Title.

PARRINDER, Edward Geoffrey. 291.3
Worship in the world's religions / by Geoffrey Parrinder. Totowa, N.J. : Littlefield, Adams, 1976, c1961. 239 p. ; 21 cm. (A Littlefield, Adams quality paperback ; no. 316) Reprint of the 1974 ed. published by Sheldon Press, London. Includes bibliographies and index. [BL550.P3 1975] 75-34031 ISBN 0-8226-0316-0 pbk. : 3.50
1. Cultus. 2. Worship—Comparative studies. I. Title.

STEINER, Rudolf 291.3
Christianity as mystical fact and The mysteries of antiquity tr. from German, rev., ed. by Andrew Lisovsky. Blauvelt, N.Y., Rudolf Steiner Pubns. [c.]1963 127p. 28cm. 3.50 pap.,
I. Title.

STEINER, Rudolf, 1861-1925. 291.3
Christianity as mystical fact and the mysteries of antiquity. Translated from the German and with notes by E. A. Frommer, Gabrielle Hess and Peter Kandler. Introd. by Alfred Heidenreich. [1st ed.] West Nyack, N.Y., R. Steiner Publications,[1961; label: distributed by Herman Pub. Service., Stamford, Conn.] 241 p. 22 cm. Includes bibliography. [BR127.S785] 61-18165
1. Christianity and other religions. 2. Mysteries, Religious. I. Title.

STEINER, Rudolf, 1861-1925 291.3
Christianity as mystical fact and the mysteries of antiquity. Tr. from German, notes by E.A. Fromer, Gabrielle Hess, Peter Kandler. Introd. by Alfred Heidenreich. R. Steiner Stamford, Conn., [dist. Herman Pub. Serv., 1962, c.1961] 241p. Bibl. 61-18165 5.00
1. Christianity and other religions. 2. Mysteries, Religious. I. Title.

WALSINGHAM, Thomas, 291.3
fl.1360-1420
De archana deorum. Ed. by Robert A. van Kluyve. Durham, N. C., Duke Univ. Pr., 1968. xxii, 227p. facsims. (on lining papers) 28cm. The Archana deorum . . . is an early fifteenth-century paraphrase and explication of Ovid's Metamorphoses, introd. by treatises on the natures and iconography of the pagan gods. The text. which apparently survives only in St. John's College (Oxford) MS 124, is here presented in its first ed. Bibl. [PA8595.W312D4 1968] 67-31120 14.75
I. Van Kluyve, Robert A. ed. II. Ovidius Naso, Publius. Metamorphoses. III. Oxford.

University. St. John's College. MSS. 124. IV. Title. V. Title: Archana deorum.

GEBAUER, Paul, 1900- 291.32
Spider divination in the Cameroons. [Milwaukee] Published by order of the Board of Trustees, 1964. 157 p. (p. 155-157 advertisements) illus., maps, port. 27 cm. (Milwaukee. Public Museum. Publications in anthropology, 10) Bibliography: p. 153. [BF1773.G4] 65-5376
1. Divination. 2. Spiders — Cameroons. I. Title. II. Series.

CHANG, Ch'eng-chi, ed. 291.322
Teachings of Tibetan yoga. Tr., annotated by Garma C. C. Chang. New Hyde Park, N.Y., University Bks. [c.1963] 128p. 24cm. 62-22082 5.00
1. Tantrism, Buddhist. 2. Yoga. I. Nadapada. II. Title. III. Title: Tibetan yoga.
Contents omitted.

CHANG, Ch'eng-chi, ed. 291.322
Teachings of Tibetan yoga. Translated and annotated by Garma C. C. Chang. New Hyde Park, N.y., University Books [1963] 128 p. 24 cm. Contents.The teaching of Mahamundra. -- The epitome of an introduction to the six yogas of Naropa. [BL1480.C513] 62-22082
1. Tantrism, Buddhist. 2. Yoga. I. Nadapada. II. Title. III. Title: Tibetan yoga.

MIDDLETON, John, 1921- ed. 291.33
Witchcraft and sorcery in East Africa [by] John Beattie [and others] Edited by John Middleton and E. H. Winter. Foreword by E. E. Evans-Pritchard. New York, Praeger [1963] viii, 302 p. diagrs. 23 cm. Full name: John Francis Marchment Middleton. Includes bibliographies. [GN475.8.M5] 63-18833
1. Witchcraft — Africa, East. I. Winter, Edward Henry, joint ed. II. Title.

MIDDLETON, John Francis 291.33
Marchment 1921- ed.
Witchcraft and sorcery in East Africa [by] John Beattie [others] Ed. by John Middleton, E. H. Winter. Foreword by E. E. Evans-Pritchard. New York, Praeger [c.1963] viii, 302p. diagrs. 23cm. Bibl. 63-18833 7.50
1. Witchcraft—Africa, East. I. Winter, Edward Henry, joint ed. II. Title.

MURRAY, Margaret Alice 291.33
The witch-cult in western Europe. Oxford, Clarendon Pr., [dist. New York, Oxford, 1963] 303, [1] p. 20cm. Bibl. 1.50 pap.,
1. Witchcraft—Gt. Brit. 2. Ethnology. I. Title.

REYNOLDS, Barrie. 291.33096894
Magic, divination, and witchcraft among the Barotse of Northern Rhodesia. Berkeley, University of California Press, 1963. xix, 181 p. illus., maps, tables. 25 cm. (Robins series, no. 3) Bibliography: p. 170-173. [BF1584.R5R4] 63-5737
1. Witchcraft—Rhodesia, Northern. 2. Lozi (African tribe) I. Title. II. Series.

CHYTRAEUS, David, 1531- 291.34
1600.
On sacrifice; a Reformation treatise in Biblical theology. De sacrificiis of 1569 tr. for the first time into a modern language and ed. in tr. by John Warwick Montgomery. St. Louis, Concordia [c.]1962. 151p. 21cm. Bibl. 61-18224 2.75 pap.,
1. Sacrifice. I. Montgomery, John Warwick, ed. and tr. II. Title.

GIRARD, Rene, 1923- 291.3'4
Violence and the sacred / Rene Girard ; translated by Patrick Gregory. Baltimore : Johns Hopkins University Press, c1977. vii, 333 p. ; 24 cm. Translation of La violence et le sacre. Includes index. Bibliography: p. 319-323. [BL600.G5413] 77-4539 ISBN 0-8018-1963-6 : 17.50
1. Rites and ceremonies. 2. Sacrifice. I. Title.

GIRARD, Rene, 1923- 291.3'4
Violence and the sacred / Rene Girard ; translated by Patrick Gregory. Baltimore : Johns Hopkins University Press, c1977. vii, 333 p. ; 24 cm. Translation of La violence et le sacre. Includes index. Bibliography: p. 319-323. [BL600.G5413] 77-4539 ISBN 0-8018-1963-6 : 17.50
1. Rites and ceremonies. 2. Sacrifice. I. Title.

HUBERT, Henri, 1872-1927. 291.34
Sacrifice: its nature and function [by] Henri Hubert and Marcel Mauss. Translated by W.D. Halls. Foreword by E.E. Evans-Pritchard. [Chicago] University of Chicago Press [1964] ix, 165 p. 23 cm. Translation of Essai sur la nature et le fonction du sacrifice. Bibliographical references included in "Notes" (p. 104-156) [BL570.H813] 64-12260
1. Sacrifice. I. Mauss, Marcel, 1872-1950, joint author. II. Title.

HUBERT, Henri, 1872-1927 291.34
Sacrifice: its nature and function [by] Henri Hubert, Marcel Mauss. Tr. [from French] by W. D. Halls. Foreword by E. E. Evans-Pritchard [Chicago] Univ. of Chic. Pr. [c.1964] iv, 165p. 23cm. Bibl. 64-12260 3.25
1. Sacrifice. I. Mauss, Marcel, 1872-1950, joint author. II. Title.

JAMES, Edwin Oliver, 291.3'4
1886-
Origins of sacrifice; a study in comparative religion, by E. O. James. Port Washington, N.Y., Kennikat Press [1971] xv, 313 p. 22 cm. Reprint of the 1933 ed. Bibliography: p. 291-309. [BL570.J3 1971] 299'.21 75-118530
1. Sacrifice—Comparative studies. 2. Christianity and other religions. I. Title.

JAMES, Edwin Oliver, 1886- 291.34
Sacrifice and sacrament. New York, Barnes & Noble [1962] 319p. 23cm. [BL570.J32] 62-6074
1. Sacrific —Hist. I. Title.

BYLES, Marie Beuzeville 291.344
Paths to inner calm. London, G. Allen & Unwin [New York, Hillary House. 1966, c.1965] 208p. 23cm. Bibl. [BL1478.6.B93] 65-6317 5.50 bds.,
1. Meditation (Buddhism) 2. Monasticism and religious orders, Buddhist. I. Title.

BACHOFEN, Johann Jakob, 291.35
1815-1887
Walls: Res sanctae, res sacrae; a passage from 'Versuch ueber die Graebersymbolik der Alten.' Tr. by B. Q. Morgan. Note on J. J. Bachofen by Lewis Mumford. Lexington, Ky., 220 Market St., Stamperia del Santuccio, 1962[c.]1961. [7]p. 29cm. (Stamperia del Santuccio. Broadside 3) 61-42168 7.00
1. Walls (in religion, folk-lore, etc.) I. Morgan, Bayard Quincy, 1883- tr. II. Title. III. Series.

INTERNATIONAL Congress on 291.3'5
Religion, Architecture, and the Arts, 3d, Jerusalem, 1973.
Sacred space, meaning and form : the Third International Congress on Religion, Architecture, and the Arts / Moshe Davidowitz, general chairman ; edited by David James Randolph. New York : United Church Board for Homeland Ministries, c1976. iii, 131 p. : ill. ; 23 cm. [NA4595.I57 1973] 76-21385
1. Architecture and religion—Congresses. 2. Space (Architecture)—Congresses. 3. Symbolism in architecture—Congresses. 4. Arts and religion—Congresses. I. Davidowitz, Moshe. II. Randolph, David James, 1934- III. United Church Board for Homeland Ministries. IV. Title.

JAMES, Edwin Oliver, 1886- 291.35
From cave to cathedral; temples and shrines of prehistoric, classical, and early Christian times [by] E. O. James. New York, F. A. Praeger [1965] 404 p. 200 illus., plans. 24 cm. Bibliography: p. [381]-388. [BL580.J3] 65-10910
1. Shrines. I. Title.

SOLTAU, Henry W., 1805- 291.3'5
1875.
The Tabernacle, the priesthood and the offerings. [Illustrated ed.] Grand Rapids, Mich., Kregel Publications [1972?] xii, 474 p. illus. 22 cm. Includes bibliographical references. [BM654.S56] 72-88590 ISBN 0-8254-3703-2 5.95
1. Tabernacle.

WILLIAMS, Colin Wilbur, 291.3'5
1921-
Jerusalem : a universal cultural and historical resource : prepared for a study committee of the Aspen Institute of Humanistic Studies / by Colin Williams. Palo Alto, Calif. : Aspen Program on Communications & Society, [1975] p. cm. Bibliography: p. [BM729.P3W54] 75-8707 ISBN 0-915436-03-5 : 2.00
1. Jerusalem in Judaism. 2. Jerusalem in the Bible. 3. Jerusalem in Islam. I. Aspen Institute of Humanistic Studies. II. Title.

GIBSON, George Miles, 291.36
1896-
The story of the Christian year. Illus. by the author. Nashville, Abingdon [1963, c.1945] 238p. illus. 21cm. (Apex bks., N3) Bibl. 1.50 pap.,
1. Church year. 2. Festivals. I. Title.

BACHOFEN, Johann Jakob, 291.3'7
1815-1887.
Myth, religion, and mother right; selected writings of J. J. Bachofen. Translated from the German by Ralph Manheim. With a pref. by George Boas and an introd. by Joseph Campbell. New Jersey, Princeton University Press , [1967] lvii, 309 p. illus. 24 cm. (Bollingen series, 84) Translation of Mutterrecht und Urreligion. Includes bibliographies. [D7.B2713] 67-22343
1. Religion, Primitive. 2. Symbolism. 3. Mythology, Classical. 4. Matriarchy. I. Title. II. Series.

BACHOFEN, Johann Jakob, 291.3'7
1815-1887.
Myth, religion, and mother right; selected writings of J. J. Bachofen. Translated from German by Ralph Manheim. With a preface by George Boas and an introd. by Joseph Campbell. [Princeton, N.J.] Princeton University Press [1973, c.1967] lvii, 309 p. 22 cm. (Princeton/Bollingen paperbacks) (Bollingen series, 84) Translated and adapted from Johann Jakob Bachofen: Mutterrecht and Urreligion. Bibliography: p. 257-270. [D7.B2713] 67-22343 ISBN 0-691-01797-2 3.45 (pbk.)
1. Religion, Primitive. 2. Symbolism. 3. Mythology, Classical. 4. Matriarchy. I. Title. II. Series.

BEVAN, Edwyn Robert, 291.3'7
1870-1943.
Symbolism and belief. Port Washington, N.Y., Kennikat Press [1968] 391 p. 23 cm. (Essay and general literature index reprint series.) (Gifford lectures, 1933-34) Reprint of the 1938 ed. Bibliographical footnotes. [BL603.B4 1968] 68-26211
1. Symbolism. 2. Belief and doubt. 3. God—Knowableness—Addresses, essays, lectures. 4. Religion—Philosophy. I. Title. II. Series.

BINDER, Pearl. 291.3'7
Magic symbols of the world. London, New York, Hamlyn, 1972. 127 p. chiefly illus. (some col.), facsims. 30 cm. Bibliography: p. 124. [GR600.B5] 73-154300 ISBN 0-600-02545-4 £1.95
1. Charms. 2. Talismans. 3. Signs and symbols. I. Title.

BORD, Janet, fl.1972- 291.3'7
Mazes and labyrinths of the world / [by] Janet Bord. London : Latimer New Dimensions, 1976. 2-181 p. : ill., facsims., plans ; 26 cm. Includes index. Bibliography: p. 173. [BL325.L3B67] 76-363034 ISBN 0-901539-35-X : £7.50
1. Labyrinths. I. Title.

DESMONDE, William Herbert, 291.37
1921-
Magic, myth, and money; the origin of money in religious ritual. [New York] Free Pr. [c.1962] 208p. Bibl. 62-10584 5.00
1. Money (in religion, folklore, etc.) I. Title.

ELIADE, Mircea, 1907- 291.37
Images and symbols; studies in religious symbolism. Translated by Philip Mairet. New York, Sheed & Ward [1961] 189 p. 22 cm. Includes bibliography. [BL600.E413] 61-7290
1. Symbolism. I. Title.

THE golden well; [291.37]
an anatomy of symbols. New York, Sheed and Ward, 1950. xiv, 191 p. 21 cm. Bibliographical footnotes. [BF1623.S9D6 1950a] 704.946 50-10712
1. Symbolism. I. Donnelly, Dorothy (Boillotat), 1903-

GOLDSMITH, Elizabeth 291.3'7
Edwards, 1860-
Ancient pagan symbols, by Elisabeth Goldsmith. New York, Putnam, 1929. [New York, AMS Press, 1973] xxxvii, 220 p. illus. 19 cm. [BL600.G6 1973] 77-168153 ISBN 0-404-02861-6 8.75
1. Symbolism. 2. Mythology. 3. Art and mythology. I. Title.

GOLDSMITH, Elizabeth 291.3'7
Edwards, 1860-
Ancient pagan symbols / by Elisabeth Goldsmith. Detroit : Gale Research Co., 1976, c1929. xxxvii, 220 p., [12] leaves of plates : ill. ; 23 cm. Reprint of the ed. published by Putnam, New York. Includes index. [BL600.G6 1976] 68-18025 ISBN 0-8103-4140-9 : 8.00
1. Symbolism. 2. Mythology. 3. Art and mythology. I. Title.

HANNAY, James Ballantyne, 291.3'7
1855-
Symbolism in relation to religion; or, Christianity: the sources of its teaching and symbolism. Port Washington, N.Y., Kennikat Press [1971] xv, 394 p. illus., port. 23 cm. "First published circa 1915." Includes bibliographical references. [BL48.H355 1971] 79-118523
1. Religion. 2. Christianity—Origin. I. Title.

HOWEY, M. Oldfield. 291.3'7
The encircled serpent; a study of serpent symbolism in all countries and ages, by M. Oldfield Howey. London, Rider. Detroit, Gale Research Co., 1975. p. cm. Reprint of the 1926 ed. Includes bibliographies. [BL441.H6 1975] 74-19166 ISBN 0-8103-4133-6 20.00
1. Serpent worship. 2. Symbolism. I. Title.

INSTITUTE for Religious 291.37
and Social Studies, Jewish Theological Seminary of America.
Religious symbolism. Edited by F. Ernest Johnson. New York, Institute for Religious and Social Studies; distributed by Harper [c1955] ix, 263p. 21cm. (Religion and civilization series) Includes bibliographies. [BL600.I5] 54-7119
1. Symbolism. 2. Christian art and symbolism. 3. Rites and ceremonies. I. Johnson, Frederick Ernest, 1884- ed. II. Title. III. Series.

INSTITUTE for Religious 291.3'7
and Social Studies. Jewish Theological Seminary of America.
Religious symbolism. Edited by F. Ernest Johnson. Port Washington, N.Y., Kennikat Press [1969, c1955] ix, 263 p. 23 cm. (Essay and general literature index reprint series.) (Religion and civilization series) "Based on lectures given at the Institute for Religious and Social Studies of the Jewish Theological Seminary of America during the winter of 1952-1953." Contents.Contents.—The foundations of Christian symbolism, by C. C. Richardson.—The liturgical revival in Protestantism, by M. P. Halverson.—Symbolism in Catholic worship, by D. J. Sullivan.—Symbolism and Jewish faith, by A. J. Heschel.—Religious symbols crossing cultural boundaries, by D. J. Fleming.—Theology and symbolism, by P. J. Tillich.—A psychologist's view of religious symbols, by G. Watson.—Symbolism in contemporary church architecture, by A. A. Dirlam.—Religious use of the dance, by T. Shawn.—Religious symbolism in contemporary literature, by N. A. Scott, Jr.—Developments in religious drama, by M. Wefer.—The future of religious symbolism, a Jewish view, by M. M. Kaplan.—The future of religious symbolism, a Catholic view, by J. LaFarge.—The future of religious symbolism, a Protestant view, by S. R. Hopper. Includes bibliographical references. [BL600.I5 1969] 68-26191
1. Symbolism. 2. Christian art and symbolism. 3. Rites and ceremonies. I. Johnson, Frederick Ernest, 1884- ed. II. Title. III. Series.

MACKENZIE, Donald 291.3'7
Alexander, 1873-1936.
The migration of symbols and their relations to beliefs and customs. New York, Knopf, 1926. Detroit, Gale Research Co., 1968. xvi, 219 p. illus. 22 cm. Bibliographical footnotes. [BL603.M3 1968] 68-18029
1. Symbolism. I. Title.

MACKENZIE, Donald 291.3'7
Alexander, 1873-1936.
The migration of symbols and their relations to beliefs and customs. New York, AMS Press [1970] xvi, 219 p. illus. 23 cm. Reprint of the 1926 ed. Includes bibliographical references. [BL603.M3 1970] 73-121283 ISBN 0-404-04136-1
1. Symbolism. I. Title.

MUKERJEE, Radhakamal, 291.37
1889-
The symbolic life of man. Bombay, Hind Kitabs [dist. New York, W. S. Heinman, 1959, i.e.1961] 294p. 25cm. Bibl. footnotes. 60-52160 8.00
1. Symbolism. I. Title.

MURRAY-AYNSLEY, Harriet 291.3'7
Georgiana Maria (Manners-Sutton) 1827?-1898.
Symbolism of the East and West. With introd. by Sir George C. M. Birdwood. Port Washington, N.Y., Kennikat Press [1971] xxiv, 212 p. illus. 23 cm. "First published in 1900." Includes bibliographical references. [CB475.M8 1971] 74-118538 ISBN 0-8046-1162-9
1. Symbolism. 2. Folk-lore. I. Title.

MURRAY-AYNSLEY, Harriet 291.3'7
Georgiana Maria (Manners-Sutton) 1827?-1898.
Symbolism of the East and West. With introd. by Sir George C. M. Birdwood. London, G. Redway, 1900. Detroit, Gale Research Co., 1971. xxiv, 212 p. illus. 24 cm. "A facsimile reprint." Includes bibliographical references. [GR67.M8 1900a] 77-141748
1. Symbolism. 2. Folk-lore. 3. Man—Migrations. I. Title.

SNYDER, William Richard. 291.37
The sun, the cross, and the soul of man; fact and faith find harmony. [1st ed.] New York, Exposition Press [1965] 302 p. illus. 22 cm. Bibliography: p. [301]-302. [BL603.S66] 65-4090
1. Symbolism. I. Title.

SNYDER, William Richard 291.37
The sun, the cross, and the soul of man; fact and faith find harmony. New York, Exposition [c.1965] 302p. illus. 22cm. Bibl. [BL603.S66] 65-4090 5.00
1. Symbolism. I. Title.

BRIGHAM, Amariah, 1798-1849. 291.3'8
Observations on the influence of religion upon the health and physical welfare of mankind. New York, Arno Press, 1973 [c1835] 331 p. 22 cm. (Mental illness and social policy: the American experience) Reprint of the ed. published by Marsh, Capen & Lyon, Boston. Includes bibliographical references. [BL65.M4B7 1973] 73-2389 ISBN 0-405-05197-2 15.00
1. Rites and ceremonies. 2. Nervous system—Hygiene. 3. Revivals. I. Title. II. Series.

COME, let us celebrate 291.3'8
: meeting God in Christian and non-Christian feasts / edited by I. Puthiadam. Bangalore : Asian Trading Corp., 1976. 233, xxix p. ; 23 cm. [BL2015.F3C65] 76-911320 Rs15.00
1. Fasts and feasts—India. I. Puthiadam, I.

GAVIN, Frank Stanton Burns, 1890-1938. 291.3'8
The Jewish antecedents of the Christian sacraments. New York, Ktav Pub. House, 1969. viii, 120 p. 24 cm. Reprint of the 1928 ed. Bibliographical footnotes. [BV800.G35 1969] 68-56890 6.95
1. Jews. Liturgy and ritual. Benedictions. 2. Sacraments. 3. Proselytes and proselyting, Jewish. 4. Conversion—Comparative studies. 5. Lord's Supper. I. Title.

OESTERLEY, William Oscar Emil, 1866-1950. 291.3'8
The sacred dance; a study in comparative folklore. Brooklyn, Dance Horizons [1968?] x, 234 p. 21 cm. (Series of republications by Dance Horizons, no. 13) Reprint of the 1923 ed. Bibliographical footnotes. [BL605.O4] 68-28047 3.95
1. Dancing (in religion, folk-lore, etc.) 2. Religion, Primitive. I. Title.

OESTERLEY, William Oscar Emil, 1866-1950. 291.3'8
The sacred dance; a study in comparative folklore. Brooklyn, Dance Horizons [1968?] x, 234 p. 21 cm. (Series in republications by Dance Horizons, no. 13) Reprint of the 1923 ed. Bibliographical footnotes. [BL605.O4 1968] 68-28047 3.95
1. Dancing (in religion, folk-lore, etc.) 2. Religion, Primitive. I. Title.

BOZKA, Honora. 291.4
Tell me, talented teen, who are you? [1st ed.] New York, Vantage Press [1963] 87 p. 21 cm. [BJ1661] 64-57322
1. Youth — Conduct of life. I. Title.

CHAUDHURI, Haridas. 291.4
Philosophy of meditation. New York, Philosophical Library [1965] viii, 55 p. 23 cm. [BL627.C5] 65-11635
1. Meditation. I. Title.

CHAUDHURY, Haridas 291.4
Philosophy of meditation. New York, Philosophical [c.1965] viii, 55p. 23cm. [BL627.C5] 65-11635 3.75 bds.,
1. Meditation. I. Title.

HENDERSON, C. William. 291.4
Awakening : ways to psychospiritual growth / C. William Henderson. Englewood Cliffs, N.J. : Prentice-Hall, [1975] xi, 244 p. ; 21 cm. (A Spectrum book) (Transpersonal books) [BP603.H46] 75-11596 ISBN 0-13-055467-7 : 8.95 ISBN 0-13-055459-6 pbk. : 3.95
1. Self-realization—Societies, etc. 2. Sects. 3. Religions. I. Title.

KRAFT, William F., 1938- 291.4
The search for the holy, by William F. Kraft. Philadelphia, Westminster Press [1971] 185 p. 19 cm. Bibliography: p. [181]-185. [BL53.K7] 72-152336 ISBN 0-664-24923-X 3.25
1. Holy, The. I. Title.

MARECHAL, Joseph, 1878-1944 291.4
Studies in the psychology of the mystics. Tr. [from French] introductory foreword, by Algar Thorold. Albany, Magi Bks., 33 Buckingham Dr. [1965] v, 344p. 21cm. First pub. in Eng. by Burns, Oates and Washbourne, 1927. Bibl. [BL625.M3] 65-1694 3.75 pap.,
1. Mysticism—Psychology. 2. Psychology, Religious. I. Title.

MOHLER, James A. 291.4
Dimensions of love, East and West / James A. Mohler. 1st ed. Garden City, N.Y. : Doubleday, 1975. xvi, 392 p. ; 22 cm. Includes index. Bibliography: p. [364]-374. [BD436.M58] 74-9458 ISBN 0-385-02473-8 : 9.95
1. Love—History. 2. Love (Theology)—History. I. Title.

STRENG, Frederick J. 291.4
Understanding religious man [by] Frederick J. Streng. Belmont, Calif., Dickenson Pub. Co. [1969] 132 p. 23 cm. (The Religious life of man) Includes bibliographies. [BL48.S77] 70-76372
1. Religion. I. Title.

WALKER, Kenneth Macfarlane, 1882- 291.4
The mystic mind. New York, Emerson [c.1962, 1965] 176p. 22cm. First ed. pub. in London in 1962 under title: The conscious mind, a commentary on the mystics. Bibl. [BL625.W28] 65-16758 3.95
1. Mysticism—Comparative studies. I. Title.

WINSKI, Norman. 291.4
Mysticism for the millions; a primer on mysticism. With an introd. by Gerald Heard. [1st ed.] Los Angeles, Sherbourne Press [1965] xiv, 98 p. 22 cm. Bibliography: p. [97]-98. [BL625.W54] 65-15791
1. Mysticism — Comparative studies. I. Title.

WINSKI, Norman 291.4
Mysticism for the millions; a primer on mysticism. Introd. by Gerald Heard. Los Angeles, Sherbourne [c.1965] xiv, 98p. 22cm. Bibl. [BL625.W54] 65-15791 2.98 bds.,
1. Mysticism—Comparative studies. I. Title.

BACH, Marcus, 1906- 291.42
Miracles do happen. Garden City, New York, Doubleday [1968, c. 1965] vi, 162p. 21cm. (W13) Orig. pub. as Spiritual breakthroughs for our time [BL53.D6] 65-15309 1.95 pap.,
I. Title.

BACH, Marcus, 1906- 291.42
Spiritual breakthroughs for our time. [1st ed.] Garden City, N.Y., Doubleday, 1965. vi, 162 p. 22 cm. [BF1999.B2] 65-22578
I. Title.

*CHENEY, Sheldon. 291.42.
Men who have walked with God; being the story of mysticism through the ages told in the biographies of representative seers and saints with experts from their writings and saying. [New York, Dell, 1974, c1945]. xiv, 395 p. illus. 21 cm. (A Delta book) [BL625] 3.45 (pbk.)
1. Mysticism—Comparative studies. 2. Mysticism (comparative religion). I. Title.

DODDS, Eric Robertson, 1893- 291.42
Pagan and Christian in an age of anxiety; some aspects of religious experience from Marcus Aurelius to Constantine, by E. R. Dodds. Cambridge [Eng.] University Press, 1965. xii, 144 p. 23 cm. (The Wiles lectures, 1963) Includes bibliographical references. [BL53.D6] 65-15309
1. Experience (Religion) — Addresses, essays, lectures. I. Title. II. Series.

DODDS, Eric Robertson, 1893- 291.42
Pagan and Christian in an age of anxiety: some aspects of religious experience from Marcus Aurelius to Constantine [New York] Cambridge [c.]1965. xii, 144p. 23cm. (Wiles lects., 1963) Bibl. [BL53.D6] 65-15309 5.50
1. Experience (Religion)—Addresses, essays, lectures. I. Title. II. Series.

EDWARDS, Ethel. 291.4'2
Psychedelics and inner space. Cincinnati, Psyche Press [1969] 253 p. 22 cm. Bibliographical footnotes. [BL624.E35] 70-6653
1. Spiritual life. 2. Hallucinogenic drugs and religious experience. I. Title.

FERGUSON, John, 1921- 291.4'2
An illustrated encyclopaedia of mysticism and the mystery religions / [by] John Ferguson. London : Thames and Hudson, 1976. 228 p. : ill., ports. ; 25 cm. American ed. published under title: An illustrated encyclopedia of mysticism and the mystery religions. Bibliography: p. 217-227. [BL625.F44 1976] 77-352543 ISBN 0-500-01140-0 : £6.50
1. Mysticism—Dictionaries. 2. Religions—Dictionaries. I. Title.

FOX, Matthew, 1940- 291.4'2
Whee! We, wee, all the way home : a guide to the new sensual spirituality / by Matthew Fox. [Wilmington, N.C.] : Consortium, c1976. xiv, 226 p. : ill. ; 23 cm. Bibliography: p. 216-217. [BV4501.2.F67] 76-19775 ISBN 0-8434-0606-2 : 10.00
1. Spirituality. 2. Ecstasy. I. Title.

FURSE, Margaret Lewis. 291.4'2
Mysticism, window on a world view / Margaret Lewis Furse. Nashville : Abingdon Press, c1977. 220 p. ; 22 cm. Includes bibliographical references and indexes. [BL625.F87] 76-56816 ISBN 0-687-27674-8 pbk. : 5.95
1. Mysticism. I. Title.

FURSE, Margaret Lewis. 291.4'2
Mysticism, window on a world view / Margaret Lewis Furse. Nashville : Abingdon Press, c1977. 220 p. ; 22 cm. Includes bibliographical references and indexes. [BL625.F87] 76-56816 ISBN 0-687-27674-8 pbk. : 5.95
1. Mysticism. I. Title.

GHOSE, Sisirkumar. 291.4'2
Mystics and society; a point of view. Foreword by Aldous Huxley. New York, Asia Pub. [c.1968] xv, 116p. 23cm. Bibl. refs. included in Notes [BL625.G47 1968] 68-7335 3.75
1. Mysticism. I. Title.
Available from Taplinger.

*GROVE, Nadina K. 291.4/2
A personal exploration of expansion of consciousness, paranormal injunctions and the illumined Bible [Henderson, Nev., 1967] 117p. 22cm. 2.50 pap.
I. Title.
Order from the author, Box 464, Henderson, Nev. 89015.

HAPPOLD, Frederick Crossfield, 1893- 291.4'2
Mysticism: a study and an anthology, [by] F. C. Happold. Revised ed. Harmondsworth, Penguin, 1970. 407 p. 18 cm. (Pelican books) [BL625.H25 1970] 73-159216 ISBN 0-14-020568-3 £0.45
1. Mysticism. I. Title.

JAE Jah Noh. 291.4'2
Do you see what I see : a message from a mystic / by Jae Jah Noh. Wheaton, Ill. : Theosophical Pub. House, 1977. 159 p. ; 21 cm. (A Quest book) [BL624.J33] 77-5255 ISBN 0-8356-0499-3 pbk. : 3.95
1. Spiritual life. 2. Mysticism. I. Title.

JAE Jah Noh. 291.4'2
Do you see what I see : a message from a mystic / by Jae Jah Noh. Wheaton, Ill. : Theosophical Pub. House, 1977. 159 p. ; 21 cm. (A Quest book) [BL624.J33] 77-5255 ISBN 0-8356-0499-3 pbk. : 3.95
1. Spiritual life. 2. Mysticism. I. Title.

JONES, Rufus Matthew, 1863-1948. 291.4'2
New studies in mystical religion; the Ely lectures delivered at Union Theological Seminary, New York. New York, Krishna Press, 1974. 205 p. 24 cm. Reprint of the 1927 ed. published by Macmillan, New York, and issued in series: Elias P. Ely lectures on the evidence of Christianity, 1927. Includes bibliographical references. [BV5082.J6 1974] 73-15412 ISBN 0-87968-102-0 35.00 (lib. bdg.).
1. Mysticism. I. Title. II. Series: Elias P. Ely lectures on the evidence of Christianity, 1927.

KATSAROS, Thomas. 291.4'2
The Western mystical tradition; an intellectual history of Western civilization, by Thomas Katsaros and Nathaniel Kaplan. New Haven, College & University Press [1969- v. 21 cm. Includes bibliographical references. [BV5075.K33] 71-92544 7.50
1. Mysticism—History. I. Kaplan, Nathaniel, joint author. II. Title.

KOLLEK, Teddy, 1911- 291.4'2
Pilgrims to the Holy Land; the story of pilgrimage through the ages [by] Teddy Kollek and Moshe Pearlman. [1st U.S. ed.] New York, Harper and Row [1970] 204 p. illus. 29 cm. [DS108.9.K63 1970b] 74-123946 15.00
1. Pilgrims and pilgrimages—Palestine—History. I. Pearlman, Moshe, 1911- joint author. II. Title.

KUTHUMI, 19thcent. 291.4'2
Studies of the human aura / Kuthumi. Colorado Springs : Summit University Press, c1975. 118 p., [1] leaf of plates : ill. ; 21 cm. "A Summit Lighthouse publication." [BF1389.A8K87] 74-24022 2.95
1. Aura. I. Title.

MERTON, Thomas, 1915-1968. 291.4'2
Mystics and Zen masters. New York, Farrar, Strauss and Giroux [1967] x, 303 p. 22 cm. Bibliographical references included in "Notes" (p. 289-303) [BL625.M38] 66-20167
1. Mysticism. 2. Zen Buddhism. I. Title.

NORDBERG, Robert B. 291.4'2
The teenager and the new mysticism [by] Robert B. Nordberg. [1st ed.] New York, R. Rosen Press [1973] xii, 126 p. port. 22 cm. Includes bibliographies. Discusses the many different methods, old and new, currently being used by those in search of mystical experience. [BL625.N67] 72-92837 ISBN 0-8239-0278-1 3.99
1. Mysticism—Juvenile literature. I. Title.

PARRINDER, Edward Geoffrey. 291.4'2
Mysticism in the world's religions / [by] Geoffrey Parrinder. London : Sheldon Press, 1976. viii, 210 p. ; 21 cm. Includes index. Bibliography: p. 199-203. [BL625.P37 1976] 76-369829 ISBN 0-85969-085-7 : £4.95. ISBN 0-85969-086-5 pbk.
1. Mysticism—Comparative studies. I. Title.

RILEY, Isaac Woodbridge, 1869-1933. 291.4'2
The meaning of mysticism / by Woodbridge Riley. Folcroft, Pa. : Folcroft Library Editions, 1975, c1930. p. cm. Reprint of the ed. published by R. R. Smith, New York. [BV5082.R5 1975] 75-26512 ISBN 0-8414-7227-0 lib. bdg. : 15.00
1. Mysticism. I. Title.

RUSSELL, George William, 1867-1935. 291.42
The candle of vision, by AE. Introd. by Leslie Shepard. New Hyde Park, N.Y., University Books [1965] xiv, 175 p. 22 cm. "A bibliography of 'AE'": p. [xii] [PR6035.U7C3] 65-22696
I. Title.

RUSSELL, George William, 1867-1935 291.42
The candle of vision, by AE. Introd. by Leslie Shepard. New Hyde Park, N. Y., University Bks. [c.1965] xiv, 175p. 22cm. Bibl. [PR6035.U7C3] 65-22696 5.00
I. Title.

RUSSELL, George William, 1867-1935. 291.4'2
The candle of vision, by AE (George William Russell). Introd. by Leslie Shepard. Wheaton, Ill., Theosophical Pub. House [1974, c1965] xiv, 175 p. 21 cm. (A Quest book) Autobiographical. "A bibliography of 'AE'": p. [xii] [PR6035.U7Z52 1974] 73-17195 ISBN 0-8356-0445-4 2.25 (pbk.)
1. Russell, George William, 1867-1935. I. Title.

SARAYDARIAN, H. 291.4'2
The hidden glory of the inner man / by H. Saraydarian. Agoura, Calif. : Aquarian Educational Group, c1968, 1975 printing. 95 p. ; 27 cm. "1st revised impression." Original ed. has title: Magnet of life. Includes bibliographical references. [BF1999.S336 1975] 74-33110
1. Soul. I. Title.

SARGANT, William Walters. 291.4'2
The mind possessed; a physiology of possession, mysticism and faith healing. Baltimore, Penguin Books [1975, c1974] xii, 212 p. illus. 20 cm. Bibliography: p. [200]-203. [BL53.S27 1975] ISBN 0-14-004034-X 2.50 (pbk.)
1. Psychology, Religious. 2. Spirit possession. 3. Demoniac possession. I. Title.
L.C. card number for original ed.: 73-15627

SARGANT, William Walters. 291.4'2
The mind possessed; a physiology of possession, mysticism, and faith healing [by] William Sargant. Philadelphia, Lippincott, 1974 [c1973] xii, 212 p. illus. 22 cm. Bibliography: p. [200]-203. [BL53.S27 1974] 73-15627 ISBN 0-397-01011-7 7.95
1. Psychology, Religious. 2. Spirit possession. 3. Demoniac possession. I. Title.

SOLOMON, Victor, 1928- 291.42
A handbook on conversions to the religions of the world. [New York] Stravon Educational Press [1965] xviii, 416 p. illus., ports. 22 cm. Includes bibliographical references. [BL639.S6] 65-22701
1. Conversion—Comparative studies. I. Title. II. Title: Conversions to the religions of the world.

SPENCER, Sidney, 1888- 291.4'2
Mysticism in world religion. Gloucester, Mass., P. Smith, 1971 [c1963] 363 p. 21 cm. (Pelican books, A594) Bibliography: p. [341]-354. [BL625.S65 1971] 70-22894
1. Mysticism—Comparative studies. I. Title.

STAAL, Frits. 291.4'2
Exploring mysticism / Frits Staal. Harmondsworth : Penguin, 1975. [1], 224 p. : 1 ill. ; 18 cm. (A Pelican book) Includes index. Bibliography: p. 209-218. [BL625.S73 1975] 75-328922 ISBN 0-14-021847-5 : £0.70
1. Mysticism—Study and teaching. I. Title.

STAAL, Frits. 291.4'2
Exploring mysticism : a methodological essay / Frits Staal. Berkeley : University of California Press, [1975] xix, 230 p., [9] leaves of plates : ill. ; 25 cm. Includes index. Bibliography: p. 215-224. [BL625.S73] 74-76391 ISBN 0-520-02726-4 : 15.00 pbk. : 4.95
1. Mysticism—Study and teaching. I. Title.

STEIGER, Brad. 291.4'2
Revelation: the divine fire. Englewood Cliffs, N.J., Prentice-Hall [1973] 316 p. 24 cm. Bibliography: p. 311-312. [BL53.S675 1973] 72-10243 ISBN 0-13-779322-7 7.95

1. Revelation. 2. Religion, Psychology. I. Title.

*SUBRAMUNIYA, Master. 291.42
The clear white light by Master Subramuniya. San Francisco, Calif., Comstock House, [1973, c1972] 70 p., 14 cm. "A Western Mystic's transcendental experience." Published in 1968 by Wailua University of Contemplative Arts and in 1971 by Gilmore and Co. [BL1228] 2.00 (pbk.)
1. Experience—Innerlight. I. Title.

SUZUKI, Daisetz Teitaro, 1870-1966. 291.4'2
Mysticism: Christian and Buddhist; the Eastern and Western way. [New York] Macmillan [1969, c1957] 160 p. 18 cm. Bibliographical footnotes. [BL625.S85 1969] 77-82562 1.45
1. Mysticism. I. Title.

SUZUKI, Daisetz Teitaro, 1870-1966. 291.4'2
Mysticism, Christian and Buddhist / by Daisetz Teitaro Suzuki. Westport, Conn. : Greenwood Press, 1975, c1957. xix, 214 p. ; 23 cm. Reprint of the ed. published by Harper, New York, which was issued as v. 12 of World perspectives. Includes bibliographical references. [BL625.S85 1975] 75-31442 ISBN 0-8371-8516-5 lib. bdg. : 13.50
1. Mysticism. I. Title.

THORNTON, Edward, 1907- 291.4'2
The diary of a mystic; foreword by C. A. Meier. London, Allen & Unwin, 1967 3-180p. 23cm. [BL625.T47] 67-114174 4.00 bds.,
1. Mysticism. I. Title.
Distributed by Hillary House, New York

TRANCE, healing, and hallucination; 291.4'2
three field studies in religious experience [by] Felicitas D. Goodman, Jeanette H. Henney [and] Esther Pressel. New York, Wiley [1974] xxiii, 388 p. illus. 23 cm. (Contemporary religious movements) "A Wiley-Interscience publication." Each field study was originally presented as a thesis, Ohio State University. Contents.Contents.—Henney, J. H. Spirit-possession belief and trance behavior in two fundamentalist groups in St. Vincent.—Pressel, E. Umbanda trance and possession in Sao Paulo, Brazil.—Goodman, F. D. Disturbances in the Apostolic Church: a trance-based upheaval in Yucatan.—Bibliography (p. 365-380) [BV5090.T7] 74-4159 ISBN 0-471-31390-4 12.50
1. Trance. 2. Spirit possession. 3. Umbanda (Cultus) 4. Pentecostalism. I. Henney, Jeanette H. Spirit-possession belief and trance behavior in two fundamentalist groups in St. Vincent. 1974. II. Pressel, Esther. Umbanda trance and possession in Sao Paulo, Brazil. 1974. III. Goodman, Felicitas D. Disturbances in the Apostolic Church. 1974.
Contents omitted.

TRANSPERSONAL psychologies / 291.4'2
edited by Charles T. Tart. London : Routledge and Kegan Paul, 1975. [7] , 502 p. : ill. ; 24 cm. Includes indexes. Bibliography: p. [475]-485. [BL53.T67 1975b] 76-373802 ISBN 0-7100-8298-3 : 23.50
1. Psychology, Religious. I. Tart, Charles T., 1937-
Distributed by Routledge and Kegan Paul,Boston.

VAN OVER, Raymond, comp. 291.4'2
Chinese mystics. Edited and with an introd. by Raymond Van Over. [1st ed.] New York, Harper & Row [1973] xxx, 183 p. 21 cm. [BL1802.V3 1973] 72-78072 pap 2.45
1. Mysticism—China—Collections. 2. Religious literature, Chinese. I. Title.

WHITSON, Robley Edward 291.42
Mysticism and ecumenism. New York, Sheed [1966] xv, 209p. 22cm. Bibl. [BL625.W53] 66-12260 4.95
1. Mysticism—Comparative studies. I. Title.

EASTERN mysticism / 291.4'2'095
edited with an introd. and commentary by Raymond Van Over. New York : New American Library, 1977- v. ; 18 cm. (A Mentor book) Contents.Contents.—v. 1. The Near East and India. Includes bibliographical references. [BL625.E28] 77-73988 pbk. : 2.50
1. Mysticism—Asia—Collected works. 2. Mysticism—Near East—Collected works. I. Van Over, Raymond.

ABERNETHY, George L ed. 291.43
Living wisdom from the world's religions; 365 daily readings of insight and inspiration, edited by George L. Abernethy. [1st ed.] New York, Holt, Rinehart and Winston [1965] ix, 237 p. 22 cm. "Sources and bibliography": p. 227-237. [BL29.A2] 65-22447
1. Religious literature (Selections: Extracts, etc.) 2. Devotional calendars. I. Title.

ABERNETHY, George L. ed. 291.43
Living wisdom from the world's religions; 365 daily readings of insight and inspiration. New York, Holt [c.1965] ix, 237p. 22cm. Bibl. [BL29.A2] 65-22447 4.95 bds.,
1. Religious literature (Selections: Extracts, etc.) 2. Devotional calendars. I. Title.

ALLEN, James, 1864-1912. 291.4'3
The gift of inner peace; inspirational writings. Edited by Marianne Wilson. [Kansas City, Mo.] Hallmark Editions [1971] 61 p. illus. 20 cm. [BF637.P3A43 1971] 73-127741 ISBN 0-87529-168-6 3.00
1. Peace of mind. I. Title.

APPROACHES to meditation. 291.4'3
Edited by Virginia Hanson. Wheaton, Ill., Theosophical Pub. House [1973] x, 147 p. 21 cm. (A Quest book) "First published as a special issue of the journal the American theosophist." Includes bibliographical references. [BL627.M37] 73-80 ISBN 0-8356-0436-5 1.75
1. Meditation. I. Hanson, Virginia, ed. II. The American theosophist (Wheaton, Ill.)

BENARES, Camden. 291.4'3
Zen without Zen masters / Camden Benares ; with commentary by Robert Anton Wilson ; illustrated by Deborah M. Cotter. Berkeley, Calif. : And/Or Press, c1977. 127 p. : ill. ; 23 cm. Bibliography: p. 125. [BL627.B45] 77-151928 ISBN 0-915904-24-1 pbk. : 4.95
1. Meditation—Anecdotes facetiae, satire, etc. 2. Spiritual life—Anecdotes, facetiae, satire, etc.

GARDNER, Adelaide. 291.4'3
Meditation; a practical study with exercises. [Rev. ed.] Wheaton, Ill., Theosophical Pub. House [1968] 116 p. 18 cm. (A Quest book) Bibliography: p. 113. [BP573.C7G37 1968] 68-5856 1.25
1. Meditation. 2. Attention.

GOLEMAN, Daniel. 291.4'3
The varieties of the meditative experience / Daniel Goleman. 1st ed. New York : Dutton, c1977. p. cm. Includes bibliography and index. [BL627.G66 1977] 76-46306 ISBN 0-525-47448-X pbk. : 3.50
1. Meditation. I. Title.

GOLEMAN, Daniel. 291.4'3
The varieties of the meditative experience / Daniel Goleman. 1st ed. New York : Dutton, c1977. p. cm. Includes bibliography and index. [BL627.G66 1977] 76-46306 ISBN 0-525-47448-X pbk. : 3.50
1. Meditation. I. Title.

GROUP for the Advancement of Psychiatry. Committee on Psychiatry and Religion. 291.4'3
Mysticism : spiritual quest or psychic disorder? / Formulated by the Committee on Psychiatry and Religion. New York : Group for the Advancement of Psychiatry, 1976. p. 705-825 ; 23 cm. (Publication - Group for the Advancement of Psychiatry ; v. 9, no. 97) Includes bibliographical references. [RC321.G7 no. 97] [BL625] 76-45931 ISBN 0-87318-134-4 : 4.00
1. Mysticism. I. Title. II. Series: Group for the Advancement of Psychiatry. Report ; no. 97.

JOHNSTON, William, 1925- 291.4'3
Silent music : the science of meditation / William Johnston. 1st U.S. ed. New York : Harper & Row, [1974] 190 p., [2] leaves of plates : ill. ; 22 cm. Includes index. Bibliography: p. [179]-180. [BL627.J63 1974] 73-18688 ISBN 0-06-064193-2 : 7.95
1. Meditation. I. Title.

LYMAN, Frederick C. 291.4'3
The posture of contemplation [by] Frederick C. Lyman, Jr. New York, Philosophical Library [1969] 123 p. 22 cm. [BL627.L9] 68-54973 3.95
1. Meditation. 2. Contemplation. I. Title.

LYON, Quinter Marcellus. 291.43
Meditations from world religious [by] Quinter M. Lyon. New York, Abingdon Press [1966, c1960] xi, 234 p. 20 cm. (Apex books) First published in 1960 under title: Quiet strength from world religions. "Acknowledgments and bibilography of sources": p. 229-232. [BL29.L93 1966] 66-210
1. Religious literature (Selections:Extracts, etc) 2. Meditations. I. Title.

MACHOVEC, Frank J. 291.4'3
OM : a guide to meditation and inner tranquility / by Frank J. MacHovec. Mount Vernon, N.Y. : Peter Pauper Press, c1973. 64 p. ; 20 cm. [BL627.M3] 75-305040 1.95
1. Meditation. I. Title.

MEDITATIONS of the masters : 291.4'3
selections / adapted by Ellen Kei Hua ; drawings by Maky. Ventura, Calif. : Thor Pub. Co., [1977] p. cm. "A Farout Press book." [BL624.M4] 76-47649 ISBN 0-87407-203-4 pbk. : 2.25
1. Spiritual life—Addresses, essays, lectures. I. Hua, Ellen Kei, 1945-

MIDDAUGH, Karen, comp. 291.4'3
Pathways to happiness; inspiration from the world's great religions. Illustrated by Norman LaLiberte. [Kansas City, Mo., Hallmark Cards, inc., 1972] 60 p. illus. 20 cm. (Hallmark editions) [BL627.M5] 76-171966 ISBN 0-87529-242-9 2.50
1. Meditation—Collections. I. Title.

MURPHY, Carol R. 291.4'3
The available mind [by] Carol R. Murphy. [Wallingford, Pa., Pendle Hill Publications, 1974] 30 p. 20 cm. (Pendle Hill pamphlet 193) Bibliography: p. 27. [BL627.M87] 73-94186 ISBN 0-87574-193-2 0.70
1. Meditation. I. Title.

NARANJO, Claudio. 291.4'3
On the psychology of meditation [by] Claudio Naranjo and Robert E. Ornstein. New York, Viking Press [1971] 248 p. 23 cm. (An Esalen book) Bibliography: p. [247]-248. [BL627.N37 1971] 76-149270 ISBN 0-670-52506-5 7.95
1. Meditation—Psychology. I. Ornstein, Robert Evans. II. Title.

NARANJO, Claudio. 291.4'3
On the psychology of meditation / Claudio Naranjo and Robert E. Ornstein. New York : Penguin Books, 1976. 248 p. : ill. ; 20 cm. (An Esalem book) Bibliography: p. [247]-248. [BL627.N37 1976] 77-2052 ISBN 0-14-004420-5 pbk. : 2.50
1. Meditation—Psychology. I. Ornstein, Robert Evans, joint author. II. Title.

SEED. 291.4'3
[New York, Harmony Books, 1973] A-G, AH, 210, 120 p. illus. 22 cm. Cover title. Illustrative matter includes 120 p. of playing-cards. [BL624.S43] 72-89362 ISBN 0-517-50409-X 6.39
1. Meditations.

STEERE, Douglas Van, 1901- 291.4'3
Contemplation and leisure / Douglas V. Steere. Wallingford, Pa. : Pendle Hill Publications, 1975. 31 p. ; 19 cm. (Pendle Hill pamphlet ; 199) Includes bibliographical references. [BV5091.C7S73] 74-30803 ISBN 0-87574-199-1 : 0.95
1. Contemplation. 2. Leisure. I. Title.

STONE, Justin. 291.4'3
The joys of meditation : a do-it-yourself book of instruction in varied meditation techniques / by Justin F. Stone. Albuquerque, N.M. : Far West Pub. Co., 1973. 95 p. ; ill. ; 23 cm. "Sun books." [BL627.S75] 73-88725
1. Meditation. I. Title.

*SUBRAMUNIYA, Master. 291.43
Beginning to meditate, by Master Subramuniya. Kapaa, Hawai, Wailua University of Contemplative Arts, [1973, c.1972] 18 p., illus., 14 cm. [BV4800] 1.00 (pbk.)
1. Meditations. I. Title.

WHITMAN, Evelyn Ardis, 1905- 291.4'3
Meditation : journey to the self / by Ardis Whitman. New York : Simon and Schuster, c1976. 189 p. ; 21 cm. [BL627.W49] 75-44316 ISBN 0-671-22211-2 : 7.95
1. Meditation. 2. Introspection. I. Title.

WOOD, Ernest, 1883- 291.4'3
Concentration; an approach to meditaion. Wheaton, Ill., Theosophical Pub. House [1967] 154p. 18cm. (Quest bk.) [BP573.C7W62 1967] 67-2874 .95 pap.,
1. Attention. 2. Meditation. I. Title.

FRANCK, Frederick, 1909- 291.4'4
Pilgrimage to now/here. With 19 drawings by the author. [Maryknoll, N.Y., Orbis Books, 1974] 156 p. illus. 24 cm. [BL624.F72] 73-78933 ISBN 0-88344-386-4 3.95 (pbk.)
1. Franck, Frederick, 1909- 2. Spiritual life. I. Title.

FRANCK, Frederick, 1909- 291.4'4
Pilgrimage to now/here. With 19 drawings by the author. [Maryknoll, N.Y., Orbis Books, 1974] 156 p. illus. 24 cm. [BL624.F72] 73-78933 ISBN 0-88344-386-4 6.95
1. Franck, Frederick, 1909- 2. Spiritual life. I. Title.
Pbk. 3.95; ISBN 0-88344-387-2.

ORIENTAL meditation / 291.4'4
edited by Harold Whalen ; ill. by Jeannee Wong. Mount Vernon, N.Y. : Peter Pauper Press, c1976. 62 p. : col. ill. ; 20 cm. [BL29.O73] 76-354802 1.95
1. Religion—Quotations, maxims, etc. I. Whalen, Harold.

PHILLIPS, Bernard, 1915- 1974. 291.4'4
Religion and the life of man / by Bernard Phillips ; edited by O'Hyun Park. Lakemont, Ga. : CSA Press, c1977. 186 p. ; 21 cm. Includes bibliographical references. [BL50.P49 1977] 77-74731 ISBN 0-87707-181-0 pbk. 3.75
1. Religion—Addresses, essays, lectures. 2. Logical positivism—Addresses, essays, lectures. I. Title.

INMAN, Thomas, 1820-1876. 291.5
Ancient pagan and modern Christian symbolism. Rev. and enl. With an essay on Baal worship, on the Assyrian sacred "grove," and other allied symbols, by John Newton. 4th ed. Kennebunkport, Me., Milford House, 1970. xxxix, 147 p. 200 illus. 23 cm. Reprint of the 1922 ed. [BL603.I54 1970] 70-88627
1. Symbolism. 2. Christian art and symbolism. I. Newton, John, M.R.C.S.E. II. Title.

LEVER, A. W. 291.5
The moral law of world truth, freedom and friendship for a lasting world peace. New York, Vantage [c.1963] 85p. 21cm. 2.75
I. Title.

SMURL, James F., 1934- 291.5
Religious ethics; a systems approach [by] James F. Smurl. Englewood Cliffs, N.J., Prentice-Hall [1971, c1972] x, 160 p. 24 cm. Includes bibliographies. [BJ1012.S54 1972] 78-159447 ISBN 0-13-773051-9
1. Ethics. I. Title.

KRISHNAMURTI, Jiddu, 1895- 291.5'44
Life ahead, by J. Krishnamurti. Edited by D. Rajagopal. Wheaton, Ill., Theosophical Pub. House [1967] 191 p. 21 cm. (A Quest book) [BJ1581.2.K75] 67-8629
1. Conduct of life. 2. Society, Hindu. 3. Hinduism. I. Title.

KRISHNAMURTI, Jiddu, 1895- 291.5'44
Life ahead, by J. Krishnamurti. Edited by D. Rajagopal. Wheaton, Ill., Theosophical Pub. House [1967] 191 p. 21 cm. (A Quest book) [BJ1581.2.K75 1967] 67-8629
1. Conduct of life. 2. Sociology. I. Title.

CHAPMAN, Rick. 291.6
How to choose a guru. New York, Harper & Row [1973] ix, 146 p. 18 cm. (Perennial library, P 285) [BL624.C44 1973] 72-13950 ISBN 0-06-080285-5 1.25
1. Gurus. I. Title.

SCHURE. EDOUARD, 1841- 1929. 291.6
The ancient mysteries of the East: Rama/Krishna. Introd. by Paul M. Allen. Blauvelt, N.Y., Rudolf Steiner Publications [1971] 11-134 p. 18 cm. (Steinerbooks) Published also in 1961 as the 1st and 2d chapters of the author's The great initiates which was G. Rasberry's translation of Les grands inities. Includes bibliographical references. [BL1225.R3S3813] 70-125797 1.45
1. Krishna. 2. Rama (Hindu deity) I. Schure, Edouard, 1841-1929. Les grands inities. Krishna. English. 1971. II. Title. III. Title: Rama/Krishna.

SCHURE, Edouard, 1841- 1929. 291.6
The light of the mysteries: Jesus. Blauvelt, N.Y., Rudolf Steiner Publications, 1971. 126 p. illus. 18 cm. (Steinerbooks) Originally published as the last chapter of the author's Les grands inities. [BT308.S35 1971] 77-150528 1.45
1. Jesus Christ—Miscellanea. I. Title.

SCHURE, Edouard, 1841- 1929. 291.6
The mysteries of ancient Egypt: Hermes/Moses. Introd. by Paul M. Allen. Blauvelt, N.Y., Rudolf Steiner Publications [1971] 11-134 p. 18 cm. (Steinerbooks) Published also in 1961 as the 3d and 4th chapters of the author's The great initiates which was G. Rasberry's translation of Les grands inities. Includes bibliographical references. [BL2441.S3513] 72-150260 1.45
1. Moses. 2. Egypt—Religion. I. Schure, Edouard, 1841-1929. Les grands inities. Moses. English. 1971. II. Title. III. Title: Hermes/Moses.

SCHURE, Edouard, 1841- 1929. 291.6
The mysteries of ancient Greece: Orpheus/Plato. Blauvelt, N.Y., Rudolf Steiner Publications, 1971. 11-134 p. illus. 18 cm. (Steinerbooks) Published also in 1961 as the 5th and 7th chapters of the author's The great initiates which was G. Rasberry's translation of Les grands inities. Includes bibliographical references. [BL795.O7S3813] 76-150261 1.45
1. Orpheus. 2. Plato. 3. Mysteries, Religious. I. Schure, Edouard, 1841-1929. Les grands

inities. Plato. English. 1971. II. Title. III. Title: Orpheus/Plato.

JAMES, Edwin Oliver, 1886- 291.61
The nature and function of priesthood; a comparative and anthropological study. [New York, Barnes & Noble, 1961, c.1955] 336p. Bibl. 61-45011 6.00
1. Priests. I. Title.

SEMINAR on the Nature of 291.6'1
Guruship, Christian Institute of Sikh Studies, 1974.
The nature of guruship / edited by Clarence O. McMullen. Delhi : Published for the Christian Institute of Sikh Studies, Batala, by I.S.P.C.K., 1976. 217 p., [3] leaves of plates : ill. ; 23 cm. Organized by Christian Institute of Sikh Studies. Includes bibliographical references and index. [BL624.S46 1974] 76-903150 Rs30.00
1. Gurus—Congresses. I. Christian Institute of Sikh Studies. II. Title.

CASE, Shirley Jackson, 291.6'2
1872-1947.
Experience with the supernatural in early Christian times. New York, B. Blom, 1971. vii, 341 p. 22 cm. Reprint of the 1929 ed. Includes bibliographical references. [BR128.A2C27 1971] 75-174851
1. Supernatural. 2. Christianity and other religions. I. Title.

ELIADE, Mircea, 1907- 291.6'2
Shamanism: archaic techniques of ecstasy. Translated from the French by Willard R. Trask. [Princeton, N.J.] Princeton University Press [1972, c1964] xxiii, 610 p. 22 cm. (Princeton/Bollingen paperbacks) (Bollingen series, 76) Translation of Le chamanisme et les techniques archaïques de l'extase. Bibliography: p. 518-569. [BL2370.S5E413 1972] 74-171056 ISBN 0-691-09827-1 3.95
1. Shamanism. I. Title. II. Series.

ELIADE MIRCEA, 1907- 291.62
Shamanism: archaic techniques of ecstasy. Tr. from French by Willard R. Trask [Rev., enl. New York, Bollingen Found.; dist.] Pantheon [c.1964] xxii, 610p. 25cm. (Bollingen ser., 76) Bibl. 63-10339 6.00
1. Shamanism. I. Title. II. Series.

EPSTEIN, Perle S. 291.6'2
Oriental mystics & magicians / Perle Epstein. 1st ed. Garden City, N.Y. : Doubleday, [1975] 151, [2] p. : ill. ; 25 cm. Bibliography: p. [153] [BL1035.E65] 74-22407 ISBN 0-385-02338-3 : 5.95 ISBN 0-385-08343-2 lib.bdg. : 6.70
1. East—Religion. 2. Magic—East. 3. Religions—Biography. I. Title.

LOMMEL, Andreas. 291.6'2
Shamanism; the beginnings of art. New York, McGraw [1966,c.1967] 175p. illus. (pt. col.) 27cm. Tr. of Die Welt der fruhen Jager, Medizinmanner, Schamanen, Kunstler. Bibl. [GN477.L613] 66-24886 12.00
1. Medicine-man. I. Title.

CAMPBELL, Myrtle. 291.63
The continuity of the prohpets. [1st ed.] New York, Pageant Press [1952] 169p. 21cm. Includes bibliography. [BP370.C25] 52-14507
1. Bahaism. 2. Religions—Biog. I. Title.

CHADWICK, Nora Kershaw, 291.6'3
1891-
Poetry & prophecy / by N. Kershaw Chadwick. Norwood, Pa. : Norwood Editions, 1976. xvi, 110 p., [8] leaves of plates : ill. ; 23 cm. Reprint of the 1942 ed. published by the University Press, Cambridge, Eng. Includes bibliographical references and index. [BL633.C45 1976] 76-8245 ISBN 0-8482-0350-X lib bdg. : 15.00
1. Prophecy. 2. Inspiration. 3. Religion and poetry. I. Title.

CHADWICK, Nora Kershaw, 291.6'3
1891-
Poetry & prophecy / by N. Kershaw Chadwick. Folcroft, Pa. : Folcroft Library Editions, 1975. xvi, 110 p., [7] leaves of plates : ill. ; 23 cm. Reprint of the 1942 ed. published by the University Press, Cambridge, Eng. Includes bibliographical references and index. [BL633.C45 1975] 75-44139 ISBN 0-8414-3381-X lib.bdg. : 22.50
1. Prophecy. 2. Inspiration. 3. Religion and poetry. I. Title.

GRATUS, Jack. 291.6'3
The false messiahs / by Jack Gratus. New York : Taplinger Pub. Co., 1976, c1975. 285 p. ; 23 cm. Includes index. Bibliography: p. [272]-279. [BL475.G67 1976] 75-29890 ISBN 0-8008-2588-8 : 10.95
1. Messiah. 2. Messianism. I. Title.

GRAVES, Kersey, 1813- 291.6'3
1883.
The world's sixteen crucified saviors; or, Christianity before Christ, containing new, startling, and extraordinary revelations in religious history, which disclose the oriental origin of all the doctrines, principles, precepts, and miracles of the Christian New Testament, and furnishing a key for unlocking many of its sacred mysteries, besides comprising the history of 16 heathen crucified gods. New foreword by Leslie Shepard. 6th ed., rev. and enl. New Hyde Park, N.Y., University Books [1971] x, 436 p. port. 22 cm. "First published in 1875." [BL2775.G73 1971] 72-118611 10.00
1. Christianity—Controversial literature. I. Title. II. Title: Christianity before Christ.

ROBERTSON, John 291.6'3
Mackinnon, 1856-1933.
Pagan Christs. [Introd. by Hector Hawton] New Hyde Park, N.Y., University Books [1967] 171 p. 22 cm. [BL85.R6 1967] 66-23914
1. Religions. 2. Messiah—Comparative studies. I. Title.

VAN BUSKIRK, William 291.6'3 B
Riley.
The saviors of mankind. Freeport, N.Y., Books for Libraries Press [1969] xiv, 537 p. 23 cm. (Essay index reprint series) Reprint of the 1929 ed. Contents.Contents.—Lao-Tze.—Confucius.—Guatama.—Zoroaster.—Aakhnaton.—Moses.—Isaiah of Babylon.—Socrates.—Jesus of Nazareth.—Saul of Tarsus.—Mahomet. [BL72.V3 1969] 71-86790
1. Religions—Biography. 2. Prophets. I. Title.

CHANLER, Julie 291.6'3'0922 B
(Olin) 1882-1961.
His messengers went forth. Illustrated by Olin Dows. Freeport, N.Y., Books for Libraries Press [1971, c1948] 64 p. illus. 23 cm. (Biography index reprint series) [BL72.C45 1971] 77-148209 ISBN 0-8369-8056-5
1. Religions—Biography. I. Title.

BRADEN, Charles Samuel, 291.8
1887-
The scriptures of mankind, an introduction. New York, Macmillan, 1952. 496 p. 22 cm. Includes bibliography. [BL71.B7] 52-10590
1. Sacred books—Hist. & crit. I. Title.

HOLY Book and holy 291.8
tradition. Edited by F. F. Bruce and E. G. Rupp. Grand Rapids, Eerdmans [1968] viii, 244 p. illus. 23 cm. Papers presented at an international colloquium held in November 1966 in the Faculty of Theology of Manchester University. Bibliographical footnotes. [BL71.H6 1968b] 70-3048 5.95
1. Sacred books—Addresses, essays, lectures. 2. Tradition (Theology)—Addresses, essays, lectures. I. Bruce, Frederick Fyvie, 1910- ed. II. Rupp, Ernest Gordon, ed. III. Victoria University of Manchester. Faculty of Theology.

WHITNEY, John Raymond, 291.8
1920-
Religious literature of the West [by] John R. Whitney and Susan W. Howe. Minneapolis, Augsburg Pub. House [1971] 315 p. illus., maps. 24 cm. Originally published under title: Student's guide to religious literature of the West. Bibliography: p. 308-310. [BL71.W5 1971] 70-158996 ISBN 0-8066-1118-9
1. Bible—Study—Outlines, syllabi, etc. 2. Mishnah—Study—Outlines, syllabi, etc. 3. Koran—Study—Outlines, syllabi, etc. I. Howe, Susan W., joint author. II. Title.

WHITNEY, John Raymond, 291.8
1920-
Student's guide to religious literature of the West. Prepared by John R. Whitney and Susan W. Howe. Harrisburg, Dept. of Public Instruction, 1968. ix, 367 p. illus., maps. 28 cm. Bibliography: p. 365-367. [BL71.W5] 77-10306
1. Bible—Study—Outlines, syllabi, etc. 2. Mishnah—Study—Outlines, syllabi, etc. 3. Koran—Study—Outlines, syllabi, etc. I. Howe, Susan W., joint author. II. Pennsylvania. Dept. of Public Instruction. III. Title. IV. Title: Religious literature of the West.

BOUQUET, Alan Coates, 291.8'2
1884-
Sacred books of the world: a companion source-book to comparative religion, by A. C. Bouquet. Harmondsworth, Penguin, 1967. 345 p. 18 cm. (Pelican books, A253) 8/6 (B67-24457) [BL70.B6] 68-112466
1. Sacred books (Selections: Extracts, etc.) I. Title.

BOUQUET, Alan Coates, 291.8'2
1884-
Sacred books of the world: a companion source-book to comparative religion, by A. C. Bouquet. Harmondsworth, Penguin, 1967. 345 p. 18 cm. (Pelican books, A253) [BL70.B6 1967] 68-112466 8/6
1. Sacred books. I. Title.

BROWNE, Lewis, 1897- ed. 291.82
The world's great scriptures; an anthology of the sacred books of the ten principal religions, comp. and annotated with historical introductions and interpretative comments by Lewis Browne. With decorations and maps by the ed. New York, Macmillan [1961, c.1946] 559p. (Macmillan paperback, MP54) 2.95 pap.,
1. Sacred books (Selections: Extracts, etc.) I. Title.

FROST, S. E., 1899- ed. 291.8'2
The sacred writings of the world's great religions. Selected and edited by S. E. Frost, Jr. New York, McGraw-Hill [1972, c1943] vi, 410 p. 21 cm. [BL70.F7 1972] 72-192672 ISBN 0-07-022520-6
1. Sacred books. I. Title.

LANCZKOWSKI, Gunter 291.82
Sacred writings; a guide to the literature of religions. Tr. [from German] by Stanley Godman. New York, Harper [1966, c.1956, 1961] 147p. illus. 21cm. (Harper chapel bk., CB21H) Bibl. [BL71.L313] 66-2996 1.45 pap.,
1. Sacred books—Introductions. I. Title.

MARTIN, Alfred Wilhelm, 291.8'2
1862-1933.
Seven great Bibles; the sacred Scriptures of Hinduism, Buddhism, Zoroastrianism, Confucianism (Taoism), Mohammedanism, Judaism, and Christianity. New York, Cooper Square Publishers, 1975. xx, 277 p. 23 cm. Reprint of the 1930 ed. published by F. A. Stokes Co., New York, in series: World unity library. [BL71.M3 1975] 74-11849 ISBN 0-8154-0495-6 7.50
1. Sacred books—History and criticism. I. Title. II. Series: World unity library.

ORIENTAL treasures. 291.8/2
[Ed. by Edward Lewis, Robert Myers] With reprods. from the oriental collection of the William Rockhill Nelson Gallery of Art-Atkins Museum. [Kansas City, Mo.] Hallmark Eds. [1967] 62p. col. illus. 20cm. [BL1010.O7] 67-17882 2.50 bds.,
1. Sacred literature (Selections: Extracts, etc.) I. Lewis, Edward W. ed. II. Myers, Robert J. ed. III. William Rockhill Nelson Gallery of Art and Mary Atkins Museum of Fine Arts, Kansas City. Mo.
Contents Omitted.

PARRINDER, Edward 291.82
Geoffrey.
Upanishads, Gita and Bible; a comparative study of Hindu and Christian Scriptures. [New York] Association Press [1963, c1962] 136 p. 23 cm. Bibliographical footnotes. [BR128.H5P37 1963] 63-8884
1. Sacred books—Comparative studies. 2. Christianity and other religions—Hinduism. I. Title.

PARRINDER, Edward 291.8'2
Geoffrey.
Upanishads, Gita, and Bible; a comparative study of Hindu and Christian scriptures, by Geoffrey Parrinder. New York, Harper & Row [1972, c1962] 136 p. 21 cm. (Harper torchbooks, TB 1660) Includes bibliographical references. [BR128.H5P37 1972] 72-188029 ISBN 0-06-131660-1 2.25
1. Sacred books—Comparative studies. 2. Christianity and other religions—Hinduism. I. Title.

PREBISH, Charles S. 291.8'2
Introduction to religions of the East : reader / edited by Charles S. Prebish and Jane I. Smith. Dubuque, Iowa : Kendall/Hunt Pub. Co., [1974]. xiii, 182 p. : ill. ; 23 cm. [BL70.P73] 74-82806 ISBN 0-8403-0985-6 : 7.50
1. Sacred books—Collected works. I. Smith, Jane I., joint comp. II. Title. III. Title: Religions of the East.

SCHMIDT, Paul Frederic, 291.82
1925-
Religious knowledge ... Free Press of Glencoe [1961] 147p. 24cm. [BL51.S4573] 60-10901
1. Knowledge, Theory of (Religion) I. Title.

SCHMIDT, Paul Frederic, 291.82
1925-
Religious knowledge. [Glencoe, Ill.] Free Press [c.1961] 147p. 60-10901 4.00
I. Title.

BEAM, Maurice. 291.9
Cults of America. [New York, Macfadden-Bartell Corp., 1964] 127 p. 18 cm. [BR516.5B4] 64-5760
1. Sects — U.S. I. "A Macfadden original." II. Title.

BEAM, Maurice 291.9
Cults of America [New York, Macfadden c.1964] 127p. 18cm. (MB60-183) 64-5760 .60 pap.,
1. Sects—U. S. I. Title.

MARTIN, Walter Ralston, 291.9
1928-
The kingdom of the cults; an analysis of the major cult systems in the present Christian era. Grand Rapids, Mich., Zondervan [c.1965] 443p. 25cm. Bibl. [BR516.5.M283] 64-22840 5.95
1. Sects—U.S. I. Title.

292 Classical (Greek & Roman) Religion

ADAM, James, 1860-1907. 292
The religious teachers of Greece. Clifton, N. J., Reference Books Publishers, 1965. xix, 407 p. 23 cm. (Gifford lectures, 1904-1900) Library of religious and philosophical thought. First published in 1908. Bibliographical footnotes. [BL785.A3 1965] 65-22086
1. Greece — Religion. 2. Greek literature — Hist. & crit. 3. Philosophy, Ancient. I. Title. II. Series.

AULAIRE, Ingri (Mortenson) 292
d', 1904--
Ingri and Edgar Parin d'Aulaire's Book of Greek myths. Garden City, N.Y., Doubleday [c.1962] 192p. illus. (pt. col.) 32cm. 62-15877 4.95
1. Mythology, Greek—Juvenile literature. I. Aulaire, Edgar Parin d', 1898- joint author. II. Title. III. Title: Book of Greek myths.

CAMPBELL, Joseph, 1904- 292
The masks of God: Occidental mythology. New York, Viking, 1964. x, 564p. illus. 22cm. 64-2011 7.95
1. Mythology. I. Title.

COLUM, Padraic, 1881- 292
The Golden Fleece and the heroes who lived before Achilles. Illus. by Willy Pogany. New York, Macmillan, 1962[c.1921, 1949] 317p. 22cm. 62-16104 3.95
1. Argonauts—Juvenile literature. I. Title.

CUMONT, Franz Valery Marie, 292
1868-1947.
Astrology and religion among the Greeks and Romans. New York, Dover Publications [1960] 115p. (T581) Bibl. footnotes 60-50835 1.35 pap.,
1. Religion. 2. Greece—Religion. 3. Rome—Religion. 4. Astrology. I. Title.

CUMONT, Franz Valery Marie, 292
1868-1947
Astrology and religion among the Greeks and Romans [Tr. from French. Gloucester, Mass., Peter Smith, 1962] 115p. 21cm. (Dover bk., rebound) 3.35
1. Religion. 2. Greece—Religion. 3. Rome—Religion. 4. Astrology. I. Title.

CUMONT, Franz Valery Marie, 292
1868-1947.
The Oriental religions in Roman paganism. Introductory essay by Grant Showerman. Authorized tr. [from French. Gloucester, Mass., Peter Smith, 1962] 298p. (Dover bk. rebound) Bibl. 3.75
1. Rome—Religion. 2. Religions. I. Title.

CUMONT, Franz Valery Marie, 292
1868-1947.
The Oriental religions in Roman paganism. With an introductory essay by Grant Showerman. Authorized translation. New York, Dover Publications [1956] 298 p. 21 cm. "An unabridged and unaltered republication of the first English translation published in 1911." [BL805.C8 1956] 58-259
1. Rome—Religion. 2. Religions. I. Title.

DIETRICH, B. C. 292
The origins of Greek religion [by] B. C. Dietrich. Berlin, New York, de Gruyter, 1974. xvii, 345 p. 24 cm. Bibliography: p. [315]-321. [BL782.D5] 74-164201 ISBN 3-11-003982-6 53.40
1. Crete—Religion. 2. Mycenae—Religion. 3. Greece—Religion. I. Title.

DUTHIE, Alexander 292
The Greek mythology, a reader's handbook. Philadelphia, Dufour, 1961[ ] 168p. illus. 61-14085 2.95 bds.,
1. Mythology, Greek. I. Title.

ELGIN, Kathleen, 1923- 292
The first book of mythology, Greek-Roman written and illustrated by Kathleen Elgin. New York, F. Watts, c1955. 61p. illus. 23cm. (The First books, 67) [BL725.E4] 55-9600
1. Mythology, Classical- juvenile literature. I. Title.

EVSLIN, Bernard. 292
Heroes, gods and monsters of the Greek myths. Illustrated by William Hofmann. New York, Four Winds Press [1967] 223 p. illus. 22 cm. Bibliography: p. 223. Retellings of the ancient Greek myths, arranged in four sections: the Gods, Nature Myths, Demigods,

and Fables. Includes a brief section on words from the Greek myths which are part of the English language. [BL782.E9] AC 68
1. Mythology, Greek. I. Hofmann, William, illus. II. Title.

FESTUGIERE, Andre Marie Jean 292
Personal religion among the Greeks, Berkeley, University of California Press, 1960[c.1954] 186p. 19cm. (Sather classical lectures, v. 26) Bibl. notes p.143-176 1.50 pap.,
1. Greece—Religion. I. Title. II. Series.

FESTUGIERE, Andre Marie Jean, 292
1898-
Personal religion among the Greeks. Berkeley, University of California Press, 1954. viii, 186p. front. 24cm. (Sather classical lectures, v. 26) Bibliographical references included in 'Notes' (p.[141]-176) [BL785.F4] 53-11234
1. Greece—Religion. I. Title. II. Series.

FOX, William Sherwood, 1878- 292
Greek and Roman [mythology] New York, Cooper Square Publishers, 1964 [c1916] lxii, 354 p. illus., 63 plates (part col.) 24 cm. (The Mythology of all races, v. 1) Bibliography: p. [333]-354. [BL25.M8 1964 vol. 1] 63-19086
1. Mythology, Classical. I. Title. II. Series.

FREEHOF, Solomon Bennett, 292
1892-
Reform Jewish practice and its rabbinic background. [v. 1 & 2. combined ed.] New York, Union of Amer. Hebrew Congregations [1963, c.1944] 196; 138p. 20cm. Bibl. 5.95
1. Reform Judaism. I. Title.

THE Golden treasury of myths 292
and legends; adapted from the world's great classics, by Anne Terry White. Illustrated by Alice and Martin Provensen. De luxe ed. New York, Golden Press [1959] 164 p. col. illus. 29 cm. (A Giant golden book) [BL310.G6] 59-1560
1. Mythology. 2. Legends. I. White, Anne Terry.

GRANT, Frederick Clifton, 292
1891- ed.
Hellenistic religions; the age of syncretism. New York, Liberal Arts Press [1953] 196p. 21cm. (The Library of religion, v. 2) [BL96.G7] 54-779
1. Religions. 2. Greece—Religion. I. Title.

GRANT, Frederick Clifton, 292
1891-
Roman Hellenism and the New Testament. New York, Scribners [c.1962] Bibl. 62-9639 3.95
1. Christianity and other religions—Greek. I. Title.

GRANT, Michael, 1914- 292
Myths of the Greeks and Romans. [1st ed.] Cleveland, World Pub. Co. [1962] 487 p. illus. 23 cm. [BL722.G7] 62-15713
1. Mythology, Classical. I. Title.

GRANT, Michael, 1914- 292
Myths of the Greeks and Romans [New York] New Amer. Lib. [1964, c.1962] 432p. illus. 18cm. (Mentor bk., MQ562) Bibl. .95 pap.,
1. Mythology, Classical. I. Title.

GRAVES, Robert, 1895- 292
The Greek myths [2.v.] Baltimore, Penguin [dist. New York, Atheneum, 1961, c.1955] 370; 412p maps (1 fold-out) (Pelican bk., A508; A509) 1.45 pap., ea.,
1. Mythology, Greek. I. Title.

GRAVES, Robert, 1895- 292
The Greek myths. [London] Penguin Books [1955] 2 v. 2 maps (1 fold. col.) 18 cm. (Penguin books, 1026-1027) Bibliographical footnotes. [BL781.G65] 55-28237
1. Mythology, Greek. I. Title.

GRAVES, Robert, 1895- 292
The Greek myths. Baltimore, Penguin Books [1955] 2 v. 2 maps (1 fold. col.) 19 cm. (Penguin books, 1026-1027) Bibliographical footnotes. [BL781.G65 1955a] 55-8278
1. Mythology, Greek. I. Title.

GUTHRIE, W. K. C. 292
The religion and mythology of the Greeks. v.2, chap. 40. [New York] Cambridge [c.]1961[ ] 55p. Bibl. 1.25 pap.,
I. Title.

GUTHRIE, William Keith 292
Chambers, 1906-
The Greeks and their gods. Boston, Beacon Press, 1956. xiv, 388 p. 22 cm. Bibliographical footnotes. [BL781.G8 1951] 51-218
1. Greece—Religion.

GUTHRIE, William Keith 292
Chambers, 1906-
The Greeks and their gods. Boston, Beacon Press, 1951. xvi, 388 p. 22 cm. Bibliographical footnotes. [BL781.G8 1951] 51-2187
1. Greece—Religion. I. Title.

GUTHRIE, William Keith 292
Chambers, 1906-
Orpheus and Greek religion; a study of the Orphic Movement [by] W. K. C. Guthrie. [Rev. ed.] New York, Norton [1966, i.e. 1967] x, 291p. illus. 21cm. Bibl. [BL820.O7G8 1967] 67-250 6.50
1. Orpheus. 2. Dionysia. 3. Mysteries, Religious. 4. Cultus, Greek. I. Title.

GUTHRIE, William Keith 292
Chambers, 1906-
Orpheus and Greek religion; a study of the Orphic movement. [2d ed. rev.] New York, Norton [1966] xix, 291p. illus. 20cm. (Methuen's handbks. of archaeology;Norton lib. N377) [BL820.O7G8 1952] 1.95 pap.,
1. Orpheus. 2. Dionysia. 3. Mysteries, Religious. 4. Cultus, Greek. I. Title.

*HAMILTON, Edith. 292
Mythology. Illus. by Steele Savage. Large type ed. New York, Watts [1966,c1942] xiv, 497p. illus. 29 cm. (Keith Jennison bk.) 8.95
1. Mythology. I. Title.

*HAMILTON, Edith 292
Mythology [Reissue] Illus. by Steele Savage [New York] New Amer. Lib. [1964, c.1940, 1942] 335p. illus. 18cm. (Mentor bk. MP520) .60 pap.,
I. Title.

HAMILTON, Edith, 1867- 292
Mythology. Illustrated by Steele Savage. [New York] New American Library [1953, c1942] 335p. illus. 18cm. (A Mentor book, Ma 86) [BL310] 53-2244
1. Mythology. I. Title.

HAMILTON, Edith, 1867- 292
Mythology. Illus. by Steele Savage. [New York] Grosset [1961, c.1940, 1942] 497p. (Little, Brown & Co. ed.; Universal Library, UL933) 1.95 pap.,
1. Mythology. I. Title.

HAMILTON, Edith, 1867-1963. 292
Mythology. Illustrated by Steele Savage. [New York] Grosset & Dunlap [1963, c1942] xiv. 497 p. illus., geneal. tables. 21 cm. (The Universal library. UL93) "A Little, Brown & Company edition." [BL310.H3] 64-5048
1. Mythology. I. Title.

HARRISON, Jane Ellen, 1850- 292
1928.
Epilegomena to the study of Greek religion, and Themis; a study of the social origins of Greek religion. [1st American ed.] New Hyde Park, N. Y., University Books [1962] lvi, 600 p. illus. 24 cm. Bibliographical footnotes. [BL785.H38 1962] 62-16379
1. Cultus, Greek. I. Title. II. Themis.

HARRISON, Jane Ellen, 1850- 292
1928.
Mythology. [Illustrated ed.] New York, Harcourt, Brace & World [1963, c1924] 111 p. illus. 21 cm. (A Harbinger book, Ho24) [BL781.H28] 63-3642
1. Mythology, Greek. I. Title.

HARRISON, Jane Ellen, 1850- 292
1928.
Mythology. New York, Cooper Square Publishers, 1963. xviii, 155 p. illus. 19 cm. (Our debt to Greece and Rome) Bibliographical references included in "Notes" (p. 151-153) Bibliography: p. 154-155. [BL781.H28 1963a] 63-10305
1. Mythology, Greek. I. Title. II. Series.

HARRISON, Jane Ellen, 1850- 292
1928.
Prolegomena to the study of Greek religion. [3d ed.] New York, Meridian Books, 1955. xxii, 682p. 21cm. (Meridian books, MG3) [BL785.H4 1955] 55-9705
1. Greece—Religion. 2. Mythology, Greek. 3. Cultus, Greek. 4. Mysteries, Religious. I. Title.

HARRISON, Jane Ellen, 1850- 292
1928
Themis; a study of the social origins of Greek religion. With an excursus on the ritual forms preserved in Greek tragedy by Gilbert Murray. Chapter on the origin of the Olympic games by F. M. Cornford. Cleveland, World [1962, c.1912, 1927] xxxvi, 559p. illus., map. plans. 21cm. (Meridian bks., M145) Bibl. 62-18676 2.45 pap.,
1. Cultus, Greek. 2. Olympic games. I. Title.

HAWTHORNE, Nathaniel, 1804- 292
1864
Pegasus, the winged horse; a Greek myth retold by Nathaniel Hawthorne. Introd. by Robert Lowell. Illus. by Herschel Levit. New York, Macmillan, 1963. 39p. col. illus. 34cm. Orig. pub. in the author's A wonder book, under title: The Chimaera. 63-24867 1.95 bds.,
1. Pegasus—Juvenile literature. I. Title.

HAWTHORNE, Nathaniel, 1804- 292
1864.
A wonder book, and Tanglewood tales. [Fredson Bowers, textual editor. Columbus] Ohio State University Press [1972] xi, 463 p. illus. 25 cm. (The centenary edition of the works of Nathaniel Hawthorne, v. 7. Writings for children, 2) A collection of Greek myths retold as fairy tales. [PS1850.F63 vol. 7] [PZ8.1] 77-150221 ISBN 0-8142-0158-X
1. Mythology, Classical—Juvenile literature. I. Bowers, Fredson Thayer, ed. II. Hawthorne, Nathaniel, 1804-1864. III. Title. IV. Title: Tanglewood tales.

HUS, Alain. 292
Greek and Roman religion. Translated from the French by S. J. Tester. [1st ed.] New York, Hawthorn Books [1962] 155p. 21cm. (The Twentieth century encyclopedia of Catholicism, v. 142. Section 15: Non-Christian beliefs) [BL722.H813] 62-20916
1. Greece—Religion. 2. Rome—Religion. I. Title.

HYDE, Walter Woodburn, 1871- 292
1966.
Greek religion and its survivals. New York, Cooper Square Publishers, 1963. ix, 230 p. 19 cm. (Our debt to Greece and Rome) Bibliography: p. 228-230. [BL785.H8 1963] 63-10268
1. Greece—Religion. 2. Folk-lore, Greek (Modern) I. Title. II. Series.

KERENYI, Karoly 292
The heroes of the Greeks. Translated by H. J. Rose. New York, Grove Press [1960, c1959] xxiv, 439p. illus. 23cm. (Myth and man) (Bibl. notes: p.381-412) 60-8387 6.50
1. Mythology, Greek. 2. Heroes. I. Title.

KERENYI, Karoly, 1897- 292
The gods of the Greeks. [German text has been rendered into English by Norman Cameron] London, New York, Thames, and Hudson [1951] xvi, 304 p. illus. 23 cm. (Myth and man) [BL781.K363] 51-14117
1. Mythology, Greek. I. Title. II. Series.

KERENYI, Karoly, 1897- 292
The religion of the Greeks and Romans. [Tr. by Christopher Holme] New York, Dutton [c.1962] 303p. illus. 24cm. 62-5328 10.00
1. Greece—Religion. 2. Rome—Religion. I. Title.

KERENYI, Karoly, 1897- 292
The religion of the Greeks and Romans [by] C. Kerenyi. Westport, Conn., Greenwood Press [1973, c1962] p. Includes bibliographical references. [BL722.K4 1973] 72-9823 ISBN 0-8371-6605-5
1. Greece—Religion. 2. Rome—Religion. I. Title.

KERENYI, Karoly, 1897- 292
The religion of the Greeks and Romans [by] C. Kerenyi. [Translated by Christopher Holme] With 124 monochrome plates. Westport, Conn., Greenwood Press [1973, c1962] 303 p. illus. 23 cm. Reprint of the ed. published by Dutton, New York. Includes bibliographical references. [BL722.K4 1973] 72-9823 ISBN 0-8371-6605-5 17.00
1. Greece—Religion. 2. Rome—Religion. I. Title.

KINGSLEY, Charles, 1819-1875 292
The heroes. Illus. with 4 colour plates & line drawings by Joan Kiddell-Monroe. New York, Dutton [1963] 210p. illus. (pt. col.) 22cm. (Children's illus. classics, 58) 63-4140 3.25
1. Mythology, Greek—Juvenile literature. I. Title.

KINGSLEY, Charles, 1819-1875. 292
The heroes. Illustrated by Ron King. Santa Rosa, Calif., Classic Press [1968] 215 p. illus., map. 29 cm. (Educator classic library, 10) Stories based on the Greek myths about Perseus, Jason and the Argonauts, Theseus, and the twelve labors of Heracles. [PZ8.1.K614H42] 74-2316
1. Mythology, Greek—Juvenile literature. I. King, Ron, illus. II. Title.

KOMROFF, Manuel, 1890- 292
Gods and demons. New York, Lion Books [1954] 189p. 18cm. (Lion library edition, LL 8) [BL310.K63] 55-21995
1. Mythology. I. Title.

LAING, Gordon Jennings, 1869- 292
1945.
Survivals of Roman religion. New York, Cooper Square Publishers, 1963. xiii, 257 p. 19 cm. (Our debt to Greece and Rome) Bibliography: p. 253-257. [BL805.L3 1963] 63-10280
1. Rome—Religion. 2. Christianity and other religions. I. Title. II. Series.

LANG, Andrew, 1844-1912 292
Tales of Troy and Greece. Illus. by Edward Bawden. New York, Roy [1963] 299p. illus. 21cm. 63-10578 3.95
1. Mythology, Greek—Juvenile literature. I. Title.

LATTIMORE, Richmond 292
Alexander, 1906-
Themes in Greek and Latin epitaphs. Urbana, Univ. of Ill. Pr., 1962. 354p. 21cm. (IB5/81) Bibl. 1.95 pap.,
1. Epitaphs. 2. Death. I. Title. II. Title: Greek and Latin epitaphs. III. Title: Latin epitaphs.

*LINDSAY, Jack, 1900- 292
Helen of Troy woman and goddess. Totowa, N.J., Rowman and Littlefield, [1974] 448 p. 23 cm. [PN57.H4L5] ISBN 0-87471-581-4 16.00
1. Helen of Troy 2. Helen of Troy in Literature. 3. Greek Literature—History and criticism. 4. Mythology, Greek. I. Title.

MCLEAN, Mollie 292
Adventures of the Greek heroes [by] Mollie McLean, Anne Wiseman. Illus. by Witold T. Mars. Boston, Houghton [c.]1961. 174p. col. illus. 61-10628 1.32 pap.,
1. Mythology, Greek—Juvenile literature. I. Wiseman, Anne, joint author. II. Title.

MEAD, George Robert Stow, 292
1863-1933
Orpheus. New York, Barnes & Noble [1965] 208p. 21cm. Bibl. [BL795.Q7M4] 65-3755 6.50
1. Orpheus. I. Title.

MOFFITT, Frederick James, 292
1896-
Diary of a warrior king; adventures from the Odyssey, by Frederick J. Moffitt. Consultant: M. A. Jagendorf [and] Carolyn W. Field. Illustrated by Bill Shields. Morristown, N.J., Silver Burdett Co. [1967] 90 p. col. illus., col. map. 25 cm. (Folk literature around the world) A diary of Odysseus which begins seven days after leaving Troy and records the many misfortunes that stripped him of crew and ship on the long journey home. [PZ8.1.M698Di] AC 68
1. Mythology, Greek. I. Shields, Bill, illus. II. Homerus. Odyssea. III. Title.

MORFORD, M. P. O. 292
Classical mythology, by Mark P. O. Morford and Robert J. Lenardon. New York, McKay [1971] x, 498 p. illus., maps. 22 cm. Bibliography: p. 461-462. [BL722.M67] 78-124550 4.95
1. Mythology, Classical. I. Lenardon, Robert J., 1928- joint author.

MORFORD, M. P. O. 292
Classical mythology / Mark P. O. Morford, Robert J. Lenardon. 2d ed. New York : McKay, 1977. xvi, 524 p. : ill. ; 24 cm. Includes indexes. Bibliography: p. 493-494. [BL722.M67 1977] 77-2230 ISBN 0-679-30336-7 : 14.95. ISBN 0-679-30344-8 pbk. : 7.95
1. Mythology, Classical. I. Lenardon, Robert J., 1928- joint author. II. Title.

MURRAY, Gilbert, 1866- 292
Five stages of Greek religion. [3d ed.] Boston, Beacon Press [1951] 235 p. 17 cm. [BL781.M8] 52-9869
1. Greece — Religion. I. Title.

MURRAY, Gilbert, 1866- 292
Five stages of Greek religion. Garden City, N. Y., Doubleday, 1955. 221p. 18cm. (Doubleday anchor books, A51) [BL781.M8 1955] 55-2467
1. Greece—Religion. I. Title.

NILSSON, Martin P. [Nils 292
Martin Persson Nilsson]
Greek folk religion. With a foreword to the Torchbook edition by Arthur Darby Nock. New York, Harper [1961, c.1940] 166p. illus., (Harper Torchbooks, the Cloister Library, TB 78) Bibl. footnotes 1.25 pap.,
1. Greece—Religion. 2. Mythology, Greek. I. Title.

NILSSON, Martin Persson, 292
1874-
Greek folk religion. With a foreword to the Torchbook ed. by Arthur Darby Nock. New York, Harper [1961] 166p. illus. 21cm. (Harper torchbooks, TB78. The Cloister library) First published in 1940 under title: Greek popular religion. Includes bibliography. [BL781.N5 1961] 61-594
1. Greece—Religion. 2. Mythology, Greek. I. Title.

NILSSON, Martin Persson, 292
1874-
A history of Greek religion. 2d ed. [Tr. from Swedish by F. J. Fielden. New York, Norton [1964] 316p. 20cm. (Norton lib., N287) Bibl. 64-57031 1.75 pap.,
1. Greece—Religion. 2. Mythology, Greek. 3. Crete—Antiq. I. Title.

NILSSON, Martin Persson, 1874- 292
The Mycenaean origin of Greek mythology. New York, Norton [1963, c1932] 258 p. 20 cm. (The Norton library, N234) Bibliographical footnotes. [BL793.M8N53] 63-23840
1. Mythology, Greek. 2. Civilization, Mycenaean. I. Title.

NILSSON, Martin Persson [Nils Martin Persson Nilsson] 1874- 292
The Mycenaean origin of Greek mythology. New York, Norton [1963, c.1932] 258p. 18cm. (N234) 1.55 pap.,
1. Mythology, Greek. 2. Civilization, Mycenaean. I. Title.

NILSSON, Martin Persson [Nils Martin Persson Nilsson] 1874- 292
Greek folk religion. Foreword to the Torchbook ed. by Arthur Darby Nock. [Gloucester, Mass., Peter Smith. 1961, c.1940] 166p. illus. (Harper torchbooks, TB 78. Cloister library rebound in cloth) First published in 1940 under title: Greek popular religion. Bibl. 3.25
1. Greece—Religion. 2. Mythology, Greek. I. Title.

NORTON, Daniel Silas, 1908-1951. 292
Classical myths in English literature [by] Dan S. Norton and Peters Rushton, with an introd. by Charles Grosvenor Osgood. New York, Rinehart [1952] 444 p. illus. 21 cm. [BL313.N6] 52-5597
1. Mythology, Classical. 2. Mythology in literature.

NORTON, Daniel Silas, 1908-1951. 292
Classical myths in English literature [by] Dan S. Norton and Peters Rushton. With an introd. by Charles Grosvenor Osgood. New York, Greenwood Press [1969, c1952] xvi, 444 p. 22 cm. [BL727.N67 1969] 70-92305 ISBN 0-8371-2440-9
1. Mythology, Classical. 2. Mythology in literature. I. Rushton, Peters, 1915-1949. II. Title.

OTTO, Walter Friedrich, 1874- 292
The Homeric gods; the spiritual significance of Greek religion. Translated by Moses Hadas. [New York] Pantheon [1954] 310p. illus. 22cm. Translation of Die Gotter Griechenlands. [BL781.O712] 54-7070
1. Greece—Religion. 2. Mythology, Greek. 3. Civilization, Greek. I. Title.

OTTO, Walter Friedrich, 1874- 292
The Homeric gods; the spiritual significance of Greek religion. Tr. [from German] by Moses Hadas. Boston, Beacon [1964, c.1954] 310p. illus. 21cm. (BP178) Bibl. 1.95 pap.,
1. Greece—Religion. 2. Mythology, Greek. 3. Civilization, Greek. I. Title.

PFISTER, Friedrich, 1883- 292
Greek gods and heroes. Tr. from German by Mervyn Savil. London, Macgibbon & Kee [dist. Chester Spring, Pa., Dufour, 1962, c.1961] 272p. illus. 22cm. 61-65881 8.50 bds.,
1. Mythology, Greek. I. Title.

PRICE, Margaret (Evans) 1888- 292
Myths and enchantment tales, adapted from the original text. Illustrated by Evelyn Urbanowich. New York, Rand McNally [1960] 192 p. illus. 23 cm. Twenty-six myths which encompass most of the rich folk heritage left by the ancient Greeks. [PZ8.1.P933My4] AC 68
1. Mythology, Greek. I. Urbanowich, Evelyn, illus. II. Title.

ROSE, Herbert Jennings, 1883- 292
Gods and heroes of the Greeks; an introduction to Greek mythology [Gloucester, Mass., Peter Smith, 1963, c.1958] 202p. 19cm. (Meridian bks., M59 rebound) Bibl. 3.50
1. Mythology, Greek. I. Title.

ROSE, Herbert Jennings, 1883- 292
Religion in Greece and Rome, with a new introd. by the author. New York, Harper [1959] 312 p. 21 cm. (Harper torchbooks, TB55) "Originally published as Ancient Greek religion (1946) and Ancient Roman religion (1948)" Includes bibliography. [BL722.R66] 59-11124
1. Greece—Religion. 2. Rome—Religion. I. Title.

ROSE, Herbert Jennings, 1883-1961. 292
Gods and heroes of the Greeks; an introduction to Greek mythology. New York, Meridian Books [1958] 202 p. 19 cm. (Meridian books, M59) [BL785.R7 1958] 58-11926
1. Mythology, Greek. I. Title.

ROUSE, William Henry Denham, 1863-1950. 292
Gods, heroes and men of ancient Greece. [New York New American Library [1957] 189p. 18cm. (A Signet key book, KD357) [BL781] 57-3981
1. Mythology, Greek. I. Title.

SABIN, Frances Ellis, 1870- 292
Classical myths that live today. Ralph V. D. Magoffin, classical editor. Chicago, S. Burdett Co. [1958] 347, lxii p. illus. 20 cm. Includes bibliography. [BL725.S15 1958] 58-4572
1. Mythology, Classical. 2. English poetry (Selections: Extracts, etc.) I. Magoffin, Ralph Van Deman, 1874-1942, ed.

SCHREIBER, Morris 292
Stories of gods and heroes; famous myths and legends of the world, adapted by Morris Schreiber. Illus. by Art Seiden. New York, Grosset [1964]c. 1960 101p. col. illus. 33cm. 60-52135 3.95; 4.05 bds., lib. ed.,
1. Mythology—Juvenile literature. 2. Legends—Juvenile literature. I. Title.

*SCHWAB, Gustav 292
Gods and heroes; myths and epics of ancient Greece. Greenwich. Conn., Fawcett [1965, c.1946] xiii, 736p. illus. 18cm. (Premier bk., p289) 1.25 pap.,
1. Mythology, Classical. 2. Mythology—Greece. I. Title.

SEZNEC, Jean 292
The survival of the pagan gods; the mythological tradition and its place in Renaissance humanism and art. Tr. from French by Barbara F. Sessions. New York, Harper [1961, c.1953] xvi, 376p. illus. (Harper torchbks., Bollingen lib., TB 2004) Bibl. 2.25 pap.,
1. Humanism. 2. Art. Renaissance. 3. Mythology. Classical. 4. Gods in art. I. Title.

SISSONS, Nicola Ann, comp. 292
Myths and legends of the Greeks. Illus. by Rafaello Busoni. New York, Hart [1962, c.1960] 189p. illus. Pub. in 1960 under the title: World-famous myths and legends of the Greeks. 62-12233 2.95
1. Mythology, Greek—Juvenile literature. I. Title.

WARNER, Rex, 1905- 292
Men and gods. Illustrated by Elizabeth Corsellis. New York, Farrar, Straus and Young, 1951. 223 p. illus. 21 cm. [BL781.W3] 51-10289
1. Mythology, Greek. I. Title.

WARNER, Rex, 1905- 292
Men and gods. Illustrated by Edward Gorey. New York, Looking Glass Library; distributed by Random House [1959] 287 p. illus. 19 cm. (Looking glass library, 4) [BL782.W35] 59-13336
1. Mythology, Greek. I. Title.

WARNER, Rex, 1905- 292
The vengeance of the gods. Illustrated by Susan Einzing. [East Lansing] Michigan State College Press, 1955. 192p. illus. 20cm. [BL781] 55-7698
1. Mythology, Greek. I. Title.

WECHSLER, Herman Joel, 1904- 292
Gods and goddesses in art and legend; great myths as pictured by great masters. New York, Washington Sq. Pr. [1961.c.1950] 111, [1]p. 64 plates (part col.) (W-732) Bibl. .60 pap.,
1. Gods in art. 2. Mythology, Classical. I. Title.

WECHSLER, Herman Joel, 1904- 292
Gods and goddesses in art and legend; great myths as pictured by great masters. New York, Pocket Books [1950] 111, [1] p. 64 plates. 17 cm. (Pocket book 661) Bibliography: p. 111-[112] [N7760.W45] 50-3895
1. Gods in art. 2. Mythology, Classical. I. Title.

WILLOUGHBY, Harold Rideout, 1890- 292
Pagan regeneration; a study of mystery initiations in the Graeco-Roman world. [Chicago] University of Chicago Press [1960, c1929] 307 p. 22 cm. (Chicago reprint series) Includes bibliography. [BL727.W5 1960] 60-51202
1. Mysteries, Religious. 2. Initiations (in religion, folk-lore, etc.) 3. Greece — Religion. 4. Rome — Religion. I. Title.

WITTING, Alisoun 292
A treasury of Greek mythology. Illus. by James Barry. Irvington-on-Hudson, N.Y., Harvey House [1966, c.1965] 125p. col. illus. 27cm. [BL782.W57] 65-24973 3.50; 3.36 lib. ed.,
1. Mythology, Greek—Juvenile literature. I. Barry James E., illus. II. Title.

YOUNG, Arthur Milton, 1900- 292
Legend builders of the West. [Pittsburgh] University of Pittsburgh Press [1958] 255 p. illus. 25 cm. [BL785.Y6] 58-9160
1. Mythology, Greek. 2. Art and mythology. 3. Literature, Comparative — Themes, motives. I. Title.

GRANT, Michael, 1914- 292'.003
Gods and mortals in classical mythology [by] Michael Grant and John Hazel. Springfield, Mass., G. & C. Merriam Co. [1973] 447 p. illus. (part col.) 26 cm. "A Merriam-Webster." Bibliography: p. 444-446. [BL715.G67 1973] 73-5650 ISBN 0-87779-087-6 15.00
1. Mythology—Dictionaries. I. Hazel, John, joint author. II. Title.

GRANT, Michael, 1914- 292'.003
Gods and mortals in classical mythology [by] Michael Grant and John Hazel. Springfield, Mass., G. & C. Merriam Co. [1973] 447 p. illus. (part col.) 26 cm. "A Merriam-Webster." Bibliography: p. 444-446. [BL715.G67 1973] 73-5650 ISBN 0-87779-087-6 15.00
1. Mythology—Dictionaries. I. Hazel, John, joint author. II. Title.

KRAVITZ, David, 1939- 292'.003
Who's who in Greek and Roman mythology / David Kravitz ; illustrations by Lynne S. Mayo. 1st American ed. New York : C. N. Potter : distributed by Crown Publishers, [1976] c1975. 246 p. : ill. ; 24 cm. Published in 1975 by New English Library, London, under title: The dictionary of Greek & Roman mythology. [BL715.K7 1976] 76-29730 ISBN 0-517-52746-4 : 10.00 ISBN 0-517-52747-2 pbk. : 3.95
1. Mythology—Dictionaries. I. Title.

WOLVERTON, Robert E. 292.0202
An outline of classical mythology [by] Robert E. Wolverton. Totowa, N.J., Littlefield, Adams, 1966. xviii, 127p. geneal. tables. 21cm. (Littlefield, Adams quality paperback, no. 97) [BL722.W6] 66-18149 1.50 pap.,
1. Mythology, Classical—Outlines, syllabi, etc. I. Title. II. Title: Classical mythology.

AKEN, Andreas Rudolphus Antonius van. 292.03
The encyclopedia of classical mythology [by A. R. A. van Aken. Translated from the Dutch by D. R. Welsh] Englewood Cliffs, N.J., Prentice-Hall [1965] 155 p. illus., maps. 22 cm. (A Spectrum book) "Originally entitled: Elseviers mythologische encyclopedie." [BL715.A413] 64-23566
1. Mythology—Dictionaries. I. Title.

KIRKWOOD, Gordon MacDonald, 1916- 292.03
A short guide to classical mythology. New York [Holt] Rinehart [and Winston, 1960, c.1959] 109p. (Rinehart English pamphlets) Includes bibl. 60-1973 1.00 pap.,
1. Mythology—Dictionaries. I. Title.

ZIMMERMAN, John Edward, 1901- 292.03
Dictionary of classical mythology. [1st ed.] New York, Harper & Row [1964] xx, 300 p. 21 cm. Bibliography: p. 295-300. [BL715.Z5] 63-20319
1. Mythology—Dictionaries. I. Title.

BAILEY, Cyril, 1871-1957. 292'.07
Phases in the religion of ancient Rome. Westport, Conn., Greenwood Press [1972] ix, 340 p. 22 cm. Original ed. issued 1932 as v. 10 of Sather classical lectures. Includes bibliographical references. [BL801.B25 1972] 75-114460 ISBN 0-8371-4759-X
1. Rome—Religion. 2. Cultus, Roman. I. Title. II. Series: Sather classical lectures, v. 10.

BURRISS, Eli Edward. 292'.07
Taboo, magic, spirits; a study of primitive elements in Roman religion. Westport, Conn., Greenwood Press [1972] x, 250 p. 22 cm. Reprint of the 1931 ed. Includes bibliographical references. [BL805.B8 1972] 72-114489 ISBN 0-8371-4724-7 11.25
1. Rome—Religion. 2. Cultus, Roman. 3. Religion, Primitive. 4. Taboo. 5. Magic, Roman. I. Title.

DOMASZEWSKI, Alfred von, 1856-1927. 292'.07
Abhandlungen zur romischen Religion / Alfred von Domaszewski. New York : Arno Press, 1975. vii, 240 p. [1] fold. leaf of plates : ill. ; 23 cm. (Ancient religion and mythology) Reprint of the 1909 ed. published by B. C. Teubner, Leipzig. Includes bibliographical references and index. [BL810.D65 1975] 75-10633 ISBN 0-405-07008-X
1. Rome—Religion—Addresses, essays, lectures. I. Title. II. Series.

DOMASZEWSKI, Alfred von, 1856-1927. 292'.07
Die Religion des romischen Heeres / Alfred von Domaszewski. New York : Arno Press, 1975. 121 p., [3] leaves of plates : ill. ; 24 cm. (Ancient religion anc mythology) Reprint of the 1895 ed. published by F. Lintz, Trier, which was also issued as v. 14 of Westdeutsche Zeitschrift fur Geschichte und Kunst. Includes bibliographical references. [DG135.D65 1975] 75-10634 ISBN 0-405-07012-8
1. Rome—Religious life and customs. 2. Soldiers—Rome—Religious life. I. Title. II. Series.

DU CHOUL, Guillaume, 16th cent. 292'.07
Discours de la religion des anciens Romains illustre : Lyon, 1556 / Guillaume du Choul. New York : Garland, 1976. p. cm. (The Renaissance and the gods : no. 9) Reprint of the 1556 ed. published by G. Rouille, Lyon. [BL800.D8 1976] 75-27851 ISBN 0-8240-2058-8 : 40.00
1. Rome—Religion. I. Title. II. Series.

DUMEZIL, Georges, 1898- 292'.07
Archaic Roman religion, with an appendix on the religion of the Etruscans. Translated by Philip Krapp. Foreword by Mircea Eliade. Chicago, University of Chicago Press [1970] 2 v. (xxx, 715 p.) 24 cm. Translation of La religion romaine archaique. Includes bibliographies. [BL802.D813] 76-116981 ISBN 0-226-16968-5 25.00
1. Rome—Religion. I. Title.

FOWLER, William Warde, 1847-1921. 292'.07
The religious experience of the Roman people, from the earliest times to the age of Augustus. New York, Cooper Square Publishers, 1971. xviii, 504 p. 22 cm. (Gifford lectures, 1909-10) Reprint of the 1911 ed. Includes bibliographical references. [BL801.F7 1971] 71-145870 ISBN 0-8154-0372-0
1. Rome—Religion. 2. Cultus, Roman. I. Title. II. Series.

GRANT, Frederick Clifton, 1891- 292'.07
Ancient Roman religion. New York, Liberal Arts Press [1957] 252p. 21cm. (The Library of religion, no. 8) [BL801.G7] 57-3661
1. Rome—Religion. I. Title.

GRANT, Michael, 1914- 292'.07
Roman myths. New York, Scribners [1973, c.1971] xvi, 293 p. illus. 20 cm. (Lyceum editions) [BL802.G7 1972] 75-162749 ISBN 0-684-13237-0 pap., 3.50
1. Mythology, Roman. I. Title.

MARCHI, Attilio de, 1855-1915. 292'.07
Il culto privato di Roma antica / Attilio de-Marchi. New York : Arno Press, 1975. 420 p. in various pagings : ill. ; 24 cm. (Ancient religion and mythology) Reprint of the 1896-1903 ed. published by U. Hoepli, Milan. Includes bibliographical references and index. [BL801.M3 1975] 75-10641 ISBN 0-405-07011-X
1. Cultus, Roman. 2. Inscriptions—Rome. I. Title. II. Series.

OGILVIE, Robert Maxwell. 292'.07
The Romans and their gods in the age of Augustus [by] R. M. Ogilvie. New York, Norton [1970, c1969] 135 p. illus., facsim., map, plan. 21 cm. (Ancient culture and society) Bibliography: p. 129-130. [BL802.O36 1970] 75-95886 5.00
1. Rome—Religion. I. Title.

PALMER, Robert E. A. 292'.07
Roman religion and Roman Empire ; five essays / Robert E. A. Palmer. Philadelphia : University of Pennsylvania Press, [1974] xii, 291 p. : ill. ; 24 cm. (The Haney Foundation series ; 15) Includes index. Bibliography: p. [277]-280. [BL802.P34] 73-89289 ISBN 0-8122-7676-0 : 25.00
1. Rome—Religion. I. Title.

PLUTARCHUS. 292'.07
The Roman questions of Plutarch : a new translation with introductory essays & a running commentary / by H. J. Rose. New York : Arno Press, 1975. p. cm. (Ancient religion and mythology) Reprint of the 1924 ed. published by the Clarendon Press, Oxford. Includes bibliographies. [DG121.P5 1975] 75-14267 ISBN 0-405-07272-4 : 12.00
1. Rome—Religion. 2. Rome—Social life and customs. I. Rose, Herbert Jennings, 1883-1961. II. Title. III. Series.

SMITH, John Holland. 292'.07
The death of classical paganism / John Holland Smith. New York : Scribner, c1976. vii, 280 p. ; 24 cm. Includes index. Bibliography: p. [269]-274. [BL802.S6] 76-28906 ISBN 0-684-14449-2 : 12.95
1. Rome—Religion. 2. Paganism. 3. Church and state in Rome—History. 4. Rome—History—Empire, 30 B.C.-476 A.D. I. Title.

TAYLOR, Lily Ross, 1886- 292'.07
The divinity of the Roman emperor / by Lily Ross Taylor. Philadelphia : Porcupine Press, 1975. p. cm. Reprint of the 1931 ed. published by the American Philological Association, Middletown, Conn., which was issued as no. 1 of Philological monographs. [DG124.T3 1975b] 75-31647 ISBN 0-87991-606-0
1. Cultus, Roman. 2. Emperor worship, Roman. I. Title. II. Series: Philological monographs ; no. 1.

VARRO, Marcus Terentius. 292'.07
M. Terenti Varronis Antiquitatum rerum divinarum libri I, XIV, XV, XVI / edited by Reinholdo Agahd. New York : Arno Press, 1975. 381 p. ; 23 cm. (Ancient religion and mythology) Reprint of the 1898 ed. (Lipsiae, In aedibus B. G. Teubneri) which was issued as an offprint from Jahrbucher fur classische Philologie, supplement 24. "Quaestionse Varronianae": p. [7]-136. Includes bibliographical references and indexes. [BL800.V372 1975] 75-10661 ISBN 0-405-07268-6
1. Rome—Religion. I. Agahd, Reinhold. II. Title. III. Title: Antiquitates rerum divinarum. IV. Series.

WISSOWA, Georg, 1859- 292'.07
1931.
Gesammelte Abhandlungen zur romischen Religions- und Stadtgeschichte / Georg Wissowa. New York : Arno Press, 1975. vi, 329 p. : ill. ; 23 cm. (Ancient religion and mythology) Reprint of the 1904 ed. published by C. H. Beck, Munchen. Includes bibliographical references and indexes. [BL810.W57 1975] 75-10663 ISBN 0-405-07279-1
1. Rome—Religious life and customs—Addresses, essays, lectures. 2. Rome—Civilization—Addresses, essays, lectures. I. Title. II. Series.

ADAM, James, 1860-1907. 292'.08
The religious teachers of Greece. Edited with a memoir, by his wife, Adela Marion Adam. Freeport, N.Y., Books for Libraries Press [1972] xix, lv, 467 p. 22 cm. Reprint of the 1909 ed., which was issued as the 1904-1906 Gifford lectures. Includes bibliographical references. [BL785.A3 1972] 72-2565 ISBN 0-8369-6843-3
1. Greece—Religion. 2. Greek literature—History and criticism. 3. Philosophy, Ancient. I. Title. II. Series: Gifford lectures, 1904-1906.

BEVAN, Edwyn Robert, 292'.08
1870-1943, comp.
Later Greek religion. London, J. M. Dent, New York, E. P. Dutton, 1927. [New York, AMS Press, 1973] xl, 234 p. 23 cm. (The Library of Greek thought, LGT 9) A compilation of extracts in English from Greek authors. Contents.Contents.—The early Stoics: Zeno of Citium. Persaeus of Citium. Cleanthes of Assos. Chrysippus of Soli. Aratus of Soli. Antipater of Tarsus. Boethus of Sidon.—Epicurus.—The school of Aristotle: the Peripatetics (Theophrastus).—The Sceptics.—Deification of kings and emperors.—Sarapis.—The historians: Polybius. Diodorus of Sicily.—Posidonius.—Popular religion.—Philo of Alexandria.—The Stoics of the Roman Empire: Musonius Rufus. Cornutus. Epictetus. Dio (Chrysostom) of Prusa. Marcus Aurelius.—Second-century Platonists: Plutarch. Maximus of Tyre. Numenius.—Second-century believers: Pausanias. Aelius Aristides.—Second-century scepticism (Lucian of Samosata).—The hermetic writings.—Gnosticism (Valentinus).—Neoplatonism: Plotinus. Porphyry. Iamblichus. Christian criticism.—The last word. [BL781.B4 1973] 76-179282 ISBN 0-404-07807-9 12.50
1. Greece—Religion. 2. Philosophy, Ancient. 3. Religious thought—Greece. 4. Greek literature—Translations into English. 5. English literature—Translations from Greek. I. Title. II. Series.
Contents Omitted.

CAMPBELL, Lewis, 1830- 292'.08
1908.
Religion in Greek literature; a sketch in outline. Freeport, N.Y., Books for Libraries Press [1971] x, 423 p. 23 cm. Reprint of the 1898 ed. Based on the Gifford lectures, 1894 and 1895, given by the author at the University of St. Andrews. [BL785.C3 1971] 79-148874 ISBN 0-8369-5645-1
1. Greece—Religion. 2. Greek literature—History and criticism. I. Title.

CORNFORD, Francis 292'.08
Macdonald, 1874-1943, comp.
Greek religious thought, from Homer to the age of Alexander. New York, AMS Press [1969] xxxv, 252 p. 23 cm. Reprint of the 1923 ed. [BL781.C55 1969] 79-98637
1. Greece—Religion. 2. Philosophy, Ancient. 3. Religious thought—To 600. 4. Greek literature—Translations into English. 5. English literature—Translations from Greek. 6. Religious thought—Greece. I. Title.

DOWRICK, Stephanie. 292'.08
Land of Zeus : the Greek myths retold by geographical place of origin / Stephanie Dowrick. 1st ed. in the U.S.A. Garden City, N.Y. : Doubleday, 1976, c1974. xiv, 223 p. : maps ; 22 cm. "A consolidation of ... Greek Island mythology and Land of Zeus: myths of the Greek gods and heroes." Includes index. Bibliography: p. [213] [BL782.D7 1976] 74-25102 ISBN 0-385-05629-X : 7.95
1. Mythology, Greek. I. Title.

FARNELL, Lewis Richard, 292'.08
1856-1934.
Outline-history of Greek religion / by Lewis Richard Farnell. Chicago : Ares Publishers, 1974. 160 p. ; 24 cm. Reprint of the 1921 ed. published by Duckworth, London, which was issued as v. 1 of Duckworth's student series. Bibliography: p. 158-160. [BL781.F43 1974] 74-77882 ISBN 0-89005-025-2 : 7.50
1. Greece—Religion. I. Title. II. Series: Duckworth's student series ; v. 1.

FOUCART, Paul Francois, 292'.08
1836-1926.
Des associations religieuses chez les Grecs, thiases, eranes, orgeons / Paul Frah cois Foucart. New York : Arno Press, 1975. xv, 243 p., [2] leaves of plates (1fold.) : ill. ; 23 cm. (Ancient religion and mythology) Reprint of the 1873 ed. published by Klincksieck, Paris. [BL785.F7 1975] 75-10637 ISBN 0-405-07014-4
1. Greece—Religion. 2. Cultus, Greek. 3. Mysteries, Religious. 4. Inscriptions, Greek. I. Title. II. Series.

GARDNER, Ernest Arthur, 292'.08
1862-1939.
Religion and art in ancient Greece. Port Washington, N.Y., Kennikat Press [1969] ix, 120 p. 18 cm. (Kennikat classics series) First published in 1910. [BL785.G3 1969] 77-101041 ISBN 0-8046-0707-9
1. Greece—Religion. 2. Art, Greek. 3. Art and religion—Greece. 4. Mythology, Classical, in art. I. Title.

GRUPPE, Otto, 1851-1921. 292'.08
Griechische Mythologie und Religionsgeschichte / Otto Gruppe. New York : Arno Press, 1975. 2 v. (xiv, 1923 p.) ; 24 cm. (Ancient religion and mythology) Reprint of the 1906 ed. published by C. H. Beck, Munich, which was issued as v. 5, pt. 2 of Handbuch der klassischen Altertums-Wissenschaft. Includes bibliographical references and index. [BL781.G7 1975] 75-10638 ISBN 0-405-07015-2
1. Greece—Religion. 2. Mythology, Greek. I. Title. II. Series. III. Series: Handbuch der klassischen Altertums-Wissenschaft ; Bd. 5, T. 2.

HARRISON, Jane Ellen, 292'.08
1850-1928.
Prolegomena to the study of Greek religion / Jane Ellen Harrison. New York : Arno Press, 1975. p. cm. (Ancient religion and mythology) Reprint of the 3d ed., 1922, published by University Press, Cambridge. First published in 1903. [BL785.H4 1975] 75-10639 ISBN 0-405-07018-7 : 39.00
1. Greece—Religion. 2. Mythology, Greek. 3. Cultus, Greek. 4. Mysteries, Religious. I. Title. II. Series.

HENDRICKS, Rhoda A., 292'.08
comp.
Classical gods and heroes; myths as told by the ancient authors. Translated and introduced by Rhoda A. Hendricks. New York, Morrow, 1974 [c1972] xi, 322 p. 22 cm. "Morrow paperback editions." Bibliography: p. 294. [BL722.H45 1974] 74-2014 ISBN 0-688-05279-7 3.95 (pbk.).
1. Mythology, Classical. I. Title.

HERBERGER, Charles F. 292'.08
The thread of Ariadne; the labyrinth of the calendar of Minos [by] Charles F. Herberger. New York, Philosophical Library [1972] xi, 158 p. illus. 22 cm. Bibliography: p. 156-158. [BL793.C7H47] 72-78167 ISBN 0-8022-2089-4 12.00
1. Mythology, Minoan. 2. Calendar, Minoan. 3. Cnossus, Crete. Palace of Minos. Toreador Fresco. I. Title.

LLOYD-JONES, Hugh. 292'.08
The justice of Zeus. Berkeley, Univ. of California Pr. [1973, c.1971] xiv, 230 p. 21 cm. (Campus, 92) (Sather classical lectures, v. 41) Includes bibliographical references. [BL782.L57] 71-121190 2.85 (pbk.)
1. Greece—Religion. 2. Dike (The word) I. Title. II. Series.

NILSSON, Martin Persson, 292'.08
1874-1967.
The Minoan-Mycenaean religion and its survival in Greek religion. 2d., rev. ed. New York, Biblo and Tannen, 1971. xxiv, 656 p. illus. 24 cm. Reprint of the 1950 ed., which was issued as no. 9 of Skrifter utgivna av Kungl. Humanistiska vetenskapssamfundet i Lund. Includes bibliographical references. [BL793.M8N5 1971] 70-162300 ISBN 0-8196-0273-6
1. Greece—Religion. 2. Crete—Antiquities. 3. Civilization, Mycenaean. I. Title. II. Series: Humanistiska vetenskapssamfundet i Lund. Skrifter, 9.

NILSSON, Martin Persson, 292'.08
1874-1967.
The Mycenaean origin of Greek mythology. A new introd. and bibliography by Emily Vermeule. Berkeley, University of California Press [1972, c1932] xv, 258 p. 22 cm. Original ed. issued as v. 8 of Sather classical lectures. Bibliography: p. xiv-xv. [BL793.M8N53 1972] 70-181440 ISBN 0-520-01951-2 3.65
1. Mythology, Greek. 2. Civilization, Mycenaen. I. Vermeule, Emily. II. Title. III. Series: Sather classical lectures, v. 8.

OTTO, Walter Friedrich, 292.08
1874-1958
Dionysus myth and cult. Tr. [from German] introd. by Robert B. Palmer. Bloomington, Ind. Univ. Pr. [c.1965] xxi, 243p. illus. 22cm. Bibl. [BL820.B20813] 65-11792 6.50
1. Dionysus. 2. Mythology, Greek. 3. Cultus, Greek. I. Title.

OTTO, Walter Friedrich, 292.08
1874-1958
Dionysus, myth and cult. Tr., introd. by Robert B. Palmer. Bloomington, Indiana Univ. Pr. [1967, c.1965] xxi, 243p. illus. 20cm. (Midland bk., MB95) Bibl. [BL820.B20813] 2.65 pap.,
1. Dioysus. 2. Mythology, Greek. 3. Cultus, Greek. I. Title.

OTTO, Walter Friedrich, 292.08
1874-1958.
Dionysus, myth and cult. Translated with an introd. by Robert B. Palmer. Bloomington, Indiana University Press [1965] xxi, 243 p. illus. 22 cm. Bibliographical references included in "Notes" (p. 211-236) [BL820.B2O813] 65-11792
1. Dionysus. 2. Mythology, Greek. 3. Cultus, Greek. I. Title.

PINSENT, John, 1922- 292'.08
Greek mythology. London, New York, Hamlyn, 1969. 5-141 p. illus. (some col.) 29 cm. Illus. on lining papers. Bibliography: p. 136. [BL782.P53] 78-449216 25/-
1. Mythology, Greek. I. Title.

POLLARD, John Richard 292'.08
Thornhill, 1914-
Seers, shrines, and sirens; the Greek religious revolution in the sixth century B. C. South Brunswick [N. J.] A. S. Barnes [1967, c1965] 164 p. 22 cm. Bibliography: p. 155-158. [BL782.P6 1967] 66-24658
1. Greece—Religion. I. Title.

ROHDE, Erwin, 1845-1898 292.08
Psyche; the cult of souls and belief in immortality among the Greeks. Introd. to the Torchbk. ed. by W. K. C. Guthrie. Tr. from the 8th ed. by W. B. Hills. New York, Harper [1966] 2v. (xxii, 626p.) 21cm. (Lib. of religion and culture) Harper torchbks. Cloister lib TB140. [BL785.R64 1966] 66-7958 1.95; 2.45 pap., v.1, v.2,
1. Greece—Religion. I. Title.

ROHDE, Erwin, 1845-1898. 292'.08
Psyche; the cult of souls and belief in immortality among the Greeks. Freeport, N.Y., Books for Libraries Press [1972] xvi, 626 p. 22 cm. "First published 1920." Translated by W. B. Hillis from the 8th ed. of Psyche; Seelencult und Unsterblichkeitsglaube der Griechen. Issued in 1925 in series: International library of psychology, philosophy, and scientific method. Includes bibliographical references. [BL785.R64 1972] 75-37911 ISBN 0-8369-6749-6
1. Greece—Religion. I. Title. II. Series: International library of psychology, philosophy, and scientific method.

*SCHWAB, Gustav. 292'.08
Gods and heroes : myths and epics of ancient Greece / Gustav Schwab ; introd. by Werner Jaeger. New York : Pantheon Books [1977]. 764p. : ill. ; 24 cm. Translated from the German text and it's Greek sources by Olga Marx and Ernst Morwitz. [BL780.S37] 47-873 12.95 ISBN 0-394-73402-5 pbk. : 5.95
1. Mythology, Greek. 2. Mythology, Classical. I. Marx, Olga, tr. II. Morwitz, Ernst, tr. III. Title.

STENGEL, Paul. 292'.08
Die griechischen Kultusaltertumer / Paul Stengel. New York : Arno Press, 1975. ix, 268 p., [3] fold. leaves of plates ; 23 cm. (Ancient religion and mythology) Reprint of the 3d ed. published in 1920 by C. H. Beck, Munich, which was issued as v. 5, pt. 3 of Handbuch der klassischen Altertumswissenschaft. Includes bibliographical references and index. [BL781.S7 1975] 75-10656 ISBN 0-405-07264-3
1. Cultus, Greek. 2. Greece—Religion. I. Title. II. Series. III. Series: Handbuch der klassischen Altertums-Wissenschaft ; Bd. 5, Abt. 3.

WARNER, Rex, 1905- 292'.08
The stories of the Greeks. New York, Farrar, Straus & Giroux [1967] x, 405 p. illus. 24 cm. Contents.Contents.—Introduction.—Men and gods.—Greeks and Trojans.—The vengeance of the gods. [BL782.W36] 67-18535
1. Mythology, Greek. I. Title.

ZIELINSKI, Tadeusz, 292'.08
1859-1944.
The religion of ancient Greece, an outline by Thaddeus Zielinski. Translated from the Polish with the author's co-operation by George Rapall Noyes. Freeport, N.Y., Books for Libraries Press [1970] x, 235 p. 23 cm. Translation of Religja Grecji starozytnej. Reprint of the 1926 ed. [BL781.Z53 1970] 76-107838 ISBN 8-369-52227-
1. Greece—Religion. 2. Civilization, Greek. I. Title.

ZUNTZ, Gunther, 1902- 292'.08
Persephone: three essays on religion and thought in Magna Graecia. Oxford, Clarendon Press, 1971. xiii, 427 p., 31 plates; illus., plans. 25 cm. Bibliography: p. 414-417. [BL793.S5Z85] 72-300059 ISBN 0-19-814286-2 £9.00
1. Empodocles. Katharmoi. 2. Sicily—Religion. 3. Persephone. 4. Greece—Religion. I. Title.

THE New Century 292'.08'03
handbook of Greek mythology and legend. Edited by Catherine B. Avery. New York, Appleton-Century-Crofts [1972] viii, 565 p. 21 cm. "Selected from the New Century classical handbook." [BL782.N45] 75-183796 ISBN 0-390-66946-6 7.95
1. Mythology, Greek—Dictionaries. I. Avery, Catherine B., ed. II. The New Century classical handbook.

BANIER, Antoine, 1673- 292'.1'3
1741.
The mythology and fables of the ancients explain'd from history : London, 1739-40 / Antoine Danier. New York : Garland Pub., 1976. 4 v. ; 23 cm. (The Renaissance and the gods ; 40) Translation of La mythologie et les fables expliquees par l'histoire. Reprint of the 1739-1740 ed. printed for A. Millar, London. Includes bibliographical references and index. [BL305.B3 1976] 77-140 ISBN 0-8240-2089-8 : 40.00 per vol.
1. Mythology. 2. Folk-lore. I. Title. II. Series.

BATMAN, Stephen, 292'.1'3
d.1584.
The golden booke of the leaden gods : London 1577 / Stephen Batman. The third part of ... Yvychurch : London 1592 / Abraham Fraunce. The fountaine of ancient fiction : London 1599 / [translated by] Richard Lynche. New York : Garland Pub., 1976. p. cm. (The Renaissance and the gods ; 13) The third work, by V. Cartari, is a translation of Le imagini de i dei gli antichi. [BL720.B37] 75-27856 ISBN 0-8240-2062-6 lib.bdg. : 40.00
1. Mythology, Classical. 2. Heresies and heretics. I. Fraunce, Abraham, fl. 1582-1633. The third part of the Countesse of Pembrokes Yuychurch. 1976. II. Cartari, Vincenzo, b. ca. 1500. Le imagini de i dei gli antichi. English. 1976. III. Title. IV. Series.

BROWN, Robert, 1844- 292'.13
Semitic influence in Hellenic mythology, with special reference to the recent mythological works of the Rt. Hon. Prof. F. Max Muller and Mr. Andrew Lang. Clifton, N.J., Reference Book Publishers, 1966. xv, 228 p. 23 cm. (Library of religious and philosophical thought) On cover: Library of religious and philosophic thought. Reprint of the 1898 ed. [BL785.B7] 65-27053
1. Mythology, Greek. 2. Mythology, Semitic. 3. Muller, Friedrich Max, 1823-1900. Contributions to the science of mythology. 4. Lang, Andrew, 1844-1912. Modern mythology. I. Title.

CARTARI, Vincenzo, 292'.1'3
b.ca.1500.
Le imagini ... degli dei / Vincenzo Cartari. New York : Garland Pub., 1976. p. cm. (The Renaissance and the gods ; 12) Reprint of the 1571 ed. published by V. Valgrisi, Venice, under title: Le imagini de i dei de gli antichi. [BL720.C2 1976] 75-27855 ISBN 0-8240-2061-8 : 40.00
1. Mythology, Classical. I. Title. II. Series.

DETIENNE, Marcel. 292'.1'3
The gardens of Adonis : spices in Greek mythology / Marcel Detienne ; translated by Janet Lloyd. Atlantic Highlands, N.J. : Humanities Press, c1976. p. cm. (European philosophy and the human sciences) Translation of Les jardins d'Adonis. Includes index. Bibliography: p. [BL795.A7D4713 1976] 76-10538 ISBN 0-391-00611-8
1. Aromatic plants (in religion, folk-lore, etc.) 2. Adonis. I. Title.

HARRISON, Jane Ellen, 1850-1928. 292'.1'3
Myths of Greece and Rome / by Jane Harrison. Folcroft, Pa. : Folcroft Library Editions, 1976. 79 p. ; 23 cm. Reprint of the 1927 ed. published by E. Benn, London, in series: Benn's sixpenny library. Bibliography: p. 79. [BL721.H35 1976] 76-46570 ISBN 0-8414-4907-4 lib. bdg. : 10.00
1. Mythology, Classical. I. Title.

KIRK, Geoffrey Stephan. 292'.1'3
The nature of Greek myths / G. S. Kirk. Woodstock, N.Y. : Overlook Press, 1975, c1974. 332 p. ; 24 cm. Includes index. Bibliography: p. [305]-[306] [BL782.K57 1975] 74-21683 15.00
1. Mythology, Greek. I. Title.

KIRK, Geoffrey Stephen. 292'.1'3
The nature of Greek myths / [by] G. S. Kirk. Harmondsworth : Penguin, 1974. 332 p. ; 19 cm. (A Pelican book) Includes index. Bibliography: p. [305]-306. [BL782.K57] 74-196296 ISBN 0-14-042175-0 pbk. : 3.75
1. Mythology, Greek. I. Title.
Distributed by Penguin, Baltimore, Md.

LEMMI, Charles William, 1882- 292'.13
The classic deities in Bacon; a study in mythological symbolism, by Charles W. Lemmi. New York, Octagon Books, 1971 [c1933] ix, 224 p. 24 cm. Bibliography: p. 215-221. [B1199.M8L4 1971] 70-120639
1. Bacon, Francis, Viscount, St. Albans, 1561-1626. 2. Bacon, Francis, Viscount St. Albans, 1561-1626. De sapientia veterum. 3. Mythology, Classical. 4. Mythology in literature. 5. Symbolism in literature. 6. Literature, Comparative—Classical and English. 7. Literature, Comparative—English and classical. I. Title.

LEMMI, Charles William, 1882- 292'.1'3
The classic deities in Bacon; a study in mythological symbolism, by Charles W. Lemmi. Folcroft, Pa., Folcroft Press [1969, c1933] ix, 224 p. 26 cm. Originally presented as the author's thesis, Johns Hopkins, 1935. Bibliography: p. 215-221. [B1199.M8L4 1969] 72-193482
1. Bacon, Francis, Viscount St. Albans, 1561-1626. 2. Bacon, Francis, Viscount St. Albans, 1561-1626. De sapientia veterum. 3. Mythology, Classical. 4. Mythology in literature. 5. Symbolism in literature. 6. Literature, Comparative—Classical and English. 7. Literature, Comparative—English and classical. I. Title.

LOVERDO, Costa de, 1921- 292'.13
Gods with bronze swords. Translated by Nancy Amphoux. [1st ed.] Garden City, N.Y., Doubleday, 1970. x, 273 p. illus., maps. 22 cm. Translation of Les dieux aux epees de bronze. Bibliography: p. [258]-260. [BL722.L613] 70-114752 6.95
1. Mythology, Classical. I. Title.

MOORE, Patrick. 292'.1'3
Legends of the planets / Patrick Moore. Sandton [South Africa] : Valiant Publishers, 1976. 115 p. : ill. (some col.) ; 27 cm. [BL722.M66 1976b] 77-373989 ISBN 0-86884-017-3 : R7.50
1. Mythology, Classical—Juvenile literature. 2. Planets (in religion, folklore, etc.)—Juvenile literature. I. Title.

MURRAY, Gilbert, 1866-1957. 292'.1'3
Five stages of Greek religion / by Gilbert Murray. Westport, Conn. : Greenwood Press, 1976. p. cm. Reprint of the 1925 2d ed. published by Columbia University Press, New York. Includes index. Contents.Contents.—Saturnia Regna.—The Olympian conquest.—The great schools.—The failure of nerve.—The last protest.—Appendix: Translation of the treatise of Sallustius. [BL781.M8 1976] 76-27675 ISBN 0-8371-9080-0 lib.bdg. : 16.25
1. Greece—Religion. I. Sallustius, Neoplatonius. De diis et mundo. English. 1976. II. Title.

PEROWNE, Stewart, 1901- 292'.1'3
Roman mythology. London, New York, Hamlyn, 1969. 141 p. illus. (some col.), maps, ports. 29 cm. Illus. on lining papers. Bibliography: p. 138. [BL802.P46] 79-499664 ISBN 0-600-03347-3 25/-
1. Mythology, Roman. I. Title.

POMEY, Francois Antoine, 1618-1673. 292'.1'3
The Pantheon : London, 1694 / Antoine Pomey ; translated by J. A. B. New York : Garland Pub., 1976. p. cm. (The Renaissance and the gods ; 34) Translation of Pantheum mythicum. Reprint of the 1694 ed. printed by B. Motte for R. Clavel and C. Harper, London. [BL720.P65 1976b] 75-27879 ISBN 0-8240-2083-9 lib.bdg. : 40.00
1. Mythology, Classical. I. Title. II. Series.

ROSS, Alexander, 1590-1654. 292'.1'3
Mystagogus poeticus : or, The muses interpreter / Alexander Ross. New York : Garland Pub., 1976. p. cm. (The Renaissance and the gods ; 30) Reprint of the 1648 ed. printed by T. W. for T. Whitaker, London. [BL720.R7 1976] 75-27875 ISBN 0-8240-2079-0 lib.bdg. : 40.00
1. Mythology, Classical. I. Title. II. Series.

SEZNEC, Jean. 292.1'3
The survival of the pagan gods : the mythological tradition and its place in Renaissance humanism and art / by Jean Seznec ; translated from the French by Barbara F. Sessions. Princeton, N.J. : Princeton University Press, 1972, c1953. xiv, 376 p. : 108 ill. ; 21 cm. (Bollingen series ; 38) "Originally published in French as La survivance des dieux antiques, Studies of the Warburg Institute, vol. XI, London, 1940." Reprint of the ed. published by Pantheon Books, New York. Includes index. Bibliography: p. 327-345. [BR135.S483 1972] 76-350683 ISBN 0-691-09829-8. ISBN 0-691-01783-2 pbk.
1. Humanism. 2. Art, Renaissance. 3. Mythology, Classical. 4. Gods in art. I. Title. II. Series.

THRACIAN legends / 292'.1'3
Alexander Fol ... [et al.] ; tranl. [from the Bulgarian by] Y. Pencheva. Sofia : Sofia-Press, 1976. 144 p., 30 leaves of plates : ill. ; 22 cm. Bibliography: p. 139-143. [BL975.T5T48] 77-550819
1. Mythology, Thracian. 2. Thracians—Religion. I. Fol, Aleksandur.

TOOKE, Andrew, 1673-1732. 292'.1'3
The Pantheon : London, 1713 / [written by Fra. Pomey] ; [translated and adapted by] Andrew Tooke. New York : Garland Pub., 1976. p. cm. (The Renaissance and the gods ; 35) Adaptation of F. A. Pomey's Pantheum mythicum. Reprint of the 1713 ed. printed for C. Harper, London. Includes index. [BL720.T8 1976] 75-27880 ISBN 0-8240-2084-7 : 40.00
1. Mythology, Classical. I. Title. II. Series.

SMITH, William Robertson, 1846-1894. 292.2
The religion of the Semites; the fundamental institutions. New York, Meridian Books, 1956. xiv, 507 p. 21 cm. (The Meridian library, ML4) First published in 1889 as the first series of the author's "Lectures on the religion of the Semites" (Burnett lectures, Aberdeen University, 1888-89) Bibliographical footnotes. [BL1600.S6 1956] 56-11577
1. Semites — Religion. 2. Sacrifice. 3. Cultus, Semitic. I. Title.

ELIOT, Alexander. 292'.2'1
Creatures of Arcadia, and creatures of a day. Illustrated by Eugene Berman. Indianapolis, Bobbs-Merrill [1967] xl, 157 p. illus. 22 cm. Based chiefly on Greek myths. [BL782.E55] 67-25174
1. Mythology, Greek. I. Title.
Contents omitted

ELIOT, Alexander. 292'.2'1
Creatures of Arcadia, and creatures of a day. Illustrated by Eugene Berman. Indianapolis, Bobbs-Merrill [1967] xl, 157 p. illus. 22 cm. Based chiefly on Greek myths. Contents.Contents.—The sense of myth.—The white heifer.—The children of Nemesis.—The gorgon.—The bull blood.—The beggar by the fire.—The fox and the grapes.—The full glory.—The wisdom of Cheiron.—The eagle and the tortoise.—The incredible crayfish.—The asp and the file.—The fond companions.—The trials of Psyche. [BL782.E55] 67-25174
1. Mythology, Greek. I. Title.

GREEN, Roger Lancelyn. 292.21
Heroes of Greece and Troy, retold from the ancient authors. With drawings by Heather Copley and Christopher Chamberlain. New York, H. Z. Walck, 1961. 337 p. illus. 24 cm. "First published in 1958 ... in two volumes entitled Tales of the Greek heroes and The tale of Troy." [BL782.G7 1961] 61-14925
1. Mythology, Greek. 2. Troy—Romances, legends, etc. I. Title.

GREEN, Roger Lancelyn. 292.21
Tales of the Greek heroes, retold from the ancient authors. Illustrated by Betty Middleton-Sandford. [Harmonds-worth, Middlesex] Penguin Books [1958] 205p. illus. 18cm. (Puffin books, PS119) [BL781.G66] 59-17233
1. Mythology, Greek. I. Title.

KING, William, 1663-1712 292.21
An historical account of the heathen gods and heroes, necessary for the understanding of the ancient poets. Introd. by Hugh Ross Williamson. Carbondale, Southern Ill. Univ. Pr. [c.1965] 256p. 6 plates. 23cm. (Centaur classics) [BL720.K5] 64-18550 12.00
1. Mythology. Classical. I. Title. II. Title: The heathen gods and heroes.

MOELLERING, Howard Armin. 292.21
Plutarch on superstition: Plutarch's De superstitione, its place in the changing meaning of deisidaimonia and in the context of his theological writings. [Rev. ed.] Boston, Christopher Pub. House [1963] 188 p. 21 cm. Bibliography: p. 158-164. [B601.D44M6 1963] 63-14334
1. Plutarchus. De superstitione. 2. Fear of God. 3. Superstition. I. Title.

MOELLERING, Howard Armin 292.21
Plutarch on superstition; Plutarch's De superstitione, its place in the changing meaning of deisidaimonia and in the context of his theological writings [Rev. ed.] Boston, Christopher Pub. [c.1963] 188p. 21cm. Bibl. 63-14334 4.00
1. Plutarchus. De superstitione. 2. Fear of God. 3. Superstition. I. Title.

RUSKIN, John, 1819-1900. 292'.21
The queen of the air; being a study of the Greek myths of cloud and storm. With an introd. by Charles Eliot Norton. Brantwood ed. New York, Maynard, Merrill, 1893. St. Clair Shores, Mich., Scholarly Press, 1972 [c1891] p. (The works of John Ruskin) [PR5259.A1 1972] 72-8405 ISBN 0-403-02054-9
I. Title.

ALEXANDER, William Hardy, 1878- 292.211
The Tacitean "non liquet" on Seneca. Berkeley, University of California Press, 1952. 269-386 p. 24 cm. (University of California publications in classical philology, v. 14, no. 8) Bibliographical footnotes. [PA25.C3 vol. 14, no. 8] A 52
1. Tacitus, Cornelius. Annales. 2. Seneca, Lucius Annaeus. I. Title. II. Series: California. University. University of California publications in classical philology, v. 14, no. 8

APOLLODORUS. 292'.2'11
Gods and heroes of the Greeks : The library of Appolodorus / translated with introd. and notes by Michael Simpson ; drawings by Leonard Baskin. Amherst : University of Massachusetts Press, 1976. vi, 311 p. : ill. ; 24 cm. Translation of Viviotheke, often formerly believed to be the work of Apollodorus, the Athenian grammarian, but now generally ascribed to a later Apollodorus. Includes index. Bibliography: p. [305]-306. [PA3870.A55A28] 75-32489 ISBN 0-87023-205-3 : 12.00. ISBN 0-87023-206-1 pbk. : 5.95
1. Mythology, Greek. I. Apollodorus, of Athens. Vivliotheke. II. Simpson, Michael, 1934- III. Baskin, Leonard, 1922- IV. Title.

BACON, Francis, Viscount St. Albans, 1561-1626. 292'.2'11
De sapientia veterum : London, 1609, and The wisedome of the ancients : translated by Arthur Gorges : London, 1619 / Francis Bacon. New York : Garland, 1976. p. cm. (The Renaissance and the gods ; no. 20) Reprints of the 1609 ed. of De sapientia veterum published by R. Barker, London, and the 1619 ed. of The wisedome of the ancients published by J. Bill, London. [B1180.D6 1976] 75-27863 ISBN 0-8240-2068-5 : 40.00
1. Mythology, Greek. I. Gorges, Arthur, Sir, 1557 (ca.)-1625. II. Title. III. Title: The wisedome of the ancients. IV. Series.

BACON, Francis, Viscount St. Albans, 1561-1626. 292'.2'11
The wisedome of the ancients. London, 1619. New York, Da Capo Press, 1968. 175 p. 16 cm. (The English experience, no. 1) Translation of De sapientia veterum. [B1180.D62E5 1968] 68-54614
1. Mythology, Greek. I. Title.

BARNES, Hazel Estella. 292'.2'11
The meddling gods; four essays on classical themes [by] Hazel E. Barnes. Lincoln, University of Nebraska Press [1974] 141 p. 21 cm. Contents.Contents.—The look of the Gorgon.—Death and cocktails: The Alcestis theme in Euripides and T. S. Eliot.—Homer and the meddling gods.—The case of Sosia versus Sosia. Includes bibliographical references. [BL785.B3] 73-92003 ISBN 0-8032-0838-3 25.00 (lib. bdg.)
1. Mythology, Greek. I. Title.
Contents omitted.

BARTHELL, Edward E. 292'.2'11
Gods and goddesses of ancient Greece, by Edward E. Barthell, Jr. Coral Gables, Fla., University of Miami Press [1971] xi, 416 p. 28 cm. Bibliography: p. [397]-398. [BL782.B36] 72-129664 ISBN 0-87024-165-6 25.00
1. Mythology, Greek. I. Title.

BENNETT, Curtis, 1921- 292'2'11
God as form : essays in Greek theology, with special reference to Christianity and the contemporary theological predicament / by Curtis Bennett. 1st ed. Albany : State University of New York Press, 1976. p. cm. [BL795.G6B46] 75-43851 ISBN 0-87395-325-8 : 20.00
1. Gods, Greek. 2. God. I. Title.

BROWN, Robert F., 1941- 292'.2'11
Schelling's treatise on "The deities of Samothrace" : a translation and an interpretation / by Robert F. Brown. Missoula, Mont. : Published by Scholars Press for American Academy of Religion, c1977. viii, 65 p. ; 24 cm. (Studies in religion ; no. 12) Bibliography: p. 64-65. [BL793.S3S332 1977] 76-42239 ISBN 0-89130-087-2 : 4.20
1. Schelling, Friedrich Wilhelm Joseph von, 1775-1854. Ueber die Gottheiten von Samothrace. 2. Mythology, Greek. 3. Samothrace—Religion. I. Schelling, Friedrich Wilhelm Joseph von, 1775-1854. Ueber die Gottheiten von Samothrace. English. 1976. II. Title. III. Series: American Academy of Religion. AAR studies in religion ; no. 12.

CONFERENCE on Classics, University College, 1958. 292.211
Nigeria and the classics; papers, edited by John Ferguson. [Ibadan? 1959?] 74 p. 25 cm. Cover title. "Organise of Extra-Mural Studies in collaboration with the of Classics and the Classical Association of Nigeria." Bibliographical footnotes. [PA25.C624 1958] 68-32706
1. Classical philology—Addresses, essays, lectures. I. Ferguson, John, 1921- ed. II. Ibadan, Nigeria. University. Dept. of Extra-Mural Studies. III. Title.
-Contents omitted.

COOK, Arthur Bernard, 1868-1952 292.211
Zeus; a study in ancient religion [v.1; v.2,pts.1&2] New York, Biblo & Tannen, 1965. 3v. (885; 1397p.) illus. (pt. fold. in pocket) plans, col. plates. 24cm. Reprint of the work first pub. 1914-40. Contents.v.1. Zeus, god of the bright sky. -- v.2. Zeus, god of the dark sky. Bibl. [BL820.J8C62] 64-25839 v.1, 37.50; v.2, pts.1&2, set, 75.00
1. Zeus. 2. Cultus, Greek. 3. Sun-worship. 4. Classical antiquities. 5. Folk literature—Themes, moties. I. Title.

DEUTSCH, Helene, 1884- 292'.2'11
A psychoanalytic study of the myth of Dionysus and Apollo: two variants of the son-mother relationship. New York, International Universities Press [1969] 101 p. 21 cm. (The Freud anniversary lecture series, 1967) "Part I is an expanded version of the lecture entitled Bisexuality and immortality in the Dionysus myth, ... presented at the New York Academy of Medicine on April 11, 1967." "Publications by Dr. Deutsch": p. 92-101. Bibliography: p. 85-88. [BL820.B2D48] 70-85198 3.50
1. Dionysus. 2. Apollo. I. Title. II. Series.

EVSLIN, BERNARD. 292'.2'11
Heroes, gods and monsters of the Greek myths. Illustrated by William Hofmann. New York, Four Winds Press [1967] 223 p. illus. 22 cm. Bibliography: p. 223. [BL782.E9] 67-23541
1. Mythology, Greek. I. Title.

EVSLIN, Bernard. 292'.2'11
Heroes, gods and monsters of the Greek myths. Illustrated by William Hofmann. New York, Four Winds Press [1967] 223 p. illus. 22 cm. Bibliography: p. 223. [BL782.E9] 67-23541
1. Mythology, Greek. I. Title.

FISCHER, Carl John, 1936- 292'.2'11
The myth and legend of Greece [by] Carl Fischer. Dayton, Ohio, G. A. Pflaum [1968] v, 202 p. 19 cm. [BL782.F57] 68-54898 0.95
1. Mythology, Greek. I. Title.

FOWLER, William Warde, 1847-1921. 292'.2'11
Roman ideas of Deity in the last century before the Christian era; lectures delivered in Oxford for the common university fund. Freeport, N.Y., Books for Libraries Press [1969] vii, 167 p. 22 cm. (Select bibliographies reprint series) Reprint of the 1914 ed.

Bibliographical footnotes. [BL805.F75 1969] 75-102236
1. Rome—Religion. 2. Monotheism. I. Title.

GATES, Doris, 1901- 292'.2'11
The golden god, Apollo. Illustrated by Constantinos CoConis. [1st ed.] New York, Viking Press [1973] 110 p. illus. 25 cm. Retells the Greek myths in which Apollo plays a major role, including that of his birth and the tales of Daphne and Phaethon. [PZ8.1.G1684Go] 72-91397 ISBN 0-670-34412-5 5.95 (lib. bdg.)
1. Apollo—Juvenile literature. I. Coconis, Constantinos, illus. II. Title.

GATES, Doris, 1901- 292'.2'11
Lord of the sky: Zeus. Illustrated by Robert Handville. [1st ed.] New York, Viking Press [1972] 126 p. illus. 25 cm. A retelling of the Greek myths centered around Zeus including the tales of Europa, King Minos, and others. [PZ8.1.G1684Lo] 72-80514 ISBN 0-670-44051-5 4.95
1. Zeus—Juvenile literature. I. Handville, Robert, illus. II. Title.

GATES, Doris, 1901- 292'.2'11
The warrior goddess: Athena. Illustrated by Don Bolognese. [1st ed.] New York, Viking Press [1972] 121 p. illus. 25 cm. Retells the Greek myths in which Athena plays a major role, including those of Perseus, the Golden Fleece, and Arachne. [PZ8.1.G1684War] 72-80515 ISBN 0-670-74996-6 4.95
1. Athena—Juvenile literature. I. Bolognese, Don, illus. II. Title.

GAYLEY, Charles Mills, 292'.2'11
1858-1932, ed.
The classic myths in English literature and in art, based originally on Bulfinch's "Age of fable" (1855), accompanied by an interpretative and illustrative commentary. New ed., rev. and enl. Boston, Milford House [1973] p. Reprint of the 1911 ed. published by Ginn, Boston. [BL721.G3 1973] 73-13946 ISBN 0-87821-186-1 50.00 (lib. bdg.)
1. Mythology, Classical. 2. Mythology, Norse. 3. English poetry (Selections: Extracts, etc.) 4. Mythology, Classical, in art. I. Bulfinch, Thomas, 1796-1867. Age of fable. II. Title.

GIRALDI, Lilio 292'.2'11
Gregorio, 1479-1552.
De deis gentium : Basel, 1548 / Lilio Gregorio Giraldi. New York : Giraldi, 1976. p. cm. (The Renaissance and the gods ; no. 8) Reprint of the 1548 ed. [PA8520.G58D4 1976] 75-27850 ISBN 0-8240-2057-X : 40.00
I. Title. II. Series.

*GRAVES, Robert 292.211
Greeks, gods and heroes [New York, Dell, 1965, c.1960] 127p. 17cm. (Laurel leaf lib., 3221) .45 pap.,
I. Title.

GRIGSON, Geoffrey, 292'.2'11
1905-
The goddess of love : the birth, triumph, death and return of Aphrodite / Geoffrey Grigson. New York : Stein and Day, 1977, c1976. 256 p. : ill. ; 24 cm. Includes index. Bibliography : p. 243-246. [BL820.V5G74 1977] 76-6845 12.95
1. Aphrodite. I. Title.

GRIGSON, Geoffrey, 292'.2'11
1905-
The goddess of love : the birth, triumph, death and return of Aphrodite / Geoffrey Grigson. London : Constable, 1976. 256 p. : ill. ; 24 cm. Includes index. Bibliography: p. 243-246. [BL820.V5G74 1976b] 77-356747 ISBN 0-09-460170-4 : £6.50
1. Aphrodite. I. Title.

HAARHOFF, Theodroe 292.211
Johannes. 1802-.
Roman life and letters; studies presented to H. J. Haarhoff, professor of classics at the University of the Witwatersrand, 1922-1957. Cape Town, A. A. Balkeman, 1959. 178 p. port. 24 cm. Latin literature--Addresses, essays, lectures. (Acta classica, v. 1) Contents.Professor T. J. Haarhoff, an appreciation. by A. Petrie.--De praepositionis apud poetas Latinos loco scripalt H. Wagenvoort.--A lost manuscript of Lucretius, by G. P. Goold.--Vergil's Latin, by W. F. Jackson Knight.--Vergil and Lucretius, by B. Farrington.--Vergil's debt to Catullus, by R. E. H. Westendorp Boerina.--Boerma.--Humanitas Horatiana, a.p. 1-37, von K, Bilchner.--Lo Hercules Octacus e di Seneca ed e anteriore al Furens, dl E. Paratore.--The dream of Pompey, by H. J. Rose.--A propos d'Apulee, par P. J. Enk.--Battles and sieges in Ammianus Marcellinus, by C. P. T. Naude.--Stoisynse invioed op Tiberius Gracchus, deur F. Smuts.--The death of Marius, by T.F. Carney,--The policy of Augustus in Greece, by J. A. O. Larsen.--The frontier policy of the Roman emperors down to a.p. 200, by M. Cary.--Writing and the epic, by S. Davis.--Die probleem van de oorsprong van die groot Alexandrynse bibiloteek, deur C. A. van Rooy.--A list of publications by T. J. Haarhoff. [PA25.A2] 64-41695
I. Title. II. Series.

KERENYI, Karoly, 1897- 292.211
Asklepios; archetypal image of the physician's existence. Translated from the German by Ralph Manheim. [New York] Pantheon Books [1959] xxvii, 151 p. illus. 26 cm. (Bollingen series, 65. Archetypal images in Greek religion, v. 3) "Originally published in German as Der gottliche Arzt." Bibliography: p. 127-139. [BL820.A4K413] 59-13516
1. Aesculapius. I. Title. II. Series. III. Series: Archetypal images in Greek religion, v. 3

KERENYI, Karoly, 1897- 292.211
Prometheus: archetypal image of human existence. Tr. from German by Ralph Manheim. Bollingen Found. [dist. New York, Pantheon, c.1963] xxvi, 152p. 16 plates. 27cm. (Bollingen ser., 65. Archetypal images in Greek religion, v.1) Bibl. 63-1080 5.00
1. Prometheus. I. Title. II. Series: Bollingen series, 65 III. Series: Archetypal images in Greek religion, v.1)

KERENYI, Karoly, 1897- 292.211
Prometheus: archetypal image of human existence. Translated from the German by Ralph Manheim. [New York, Bollingen Foundation; distributed by] Pantheon Books [1963] xxvi, 152 p. 16 plates. 27 cm. (Bollingen series, 65. Archetypal images in Greek religion, v. 1) "Translated from Prometheus: die menschliche Existenz in griechischer Deutung ... 1959 ... Earlier version: Prometheus: das griechische Mythologem von der menschlichen Existenz, copyright 1946." Bibliography: p. 135-143. [BL820.P68K43] 63-1080
1. Prometheus. Bollingen series, 65. Archetypal images in Greek religion, v. 1) I. Title. II. Series.

KERENYI, Karoly, 292'.2'11
1897-1973.
Dionysos; archetypal image of the indestructable life [by] C. Kerenyi. Translated from the German by Ralph Manheim. [Princeton, N.J.] Princeton University Press [1975] p. cm. (Bollingen series, 65. Archetypal images in Greek religion, v. 2) "Translated from the original manuscript of the author." Bibliography: p. [BL820.B2K4713] 78-166395 ISBN 0-691-09863-8 27.50
1. Dionysus. I. Title. II. Series: Bollingen series, 65. III. Series: Archetypal images in Greek religion, v. 2.

KERENYI, Karoly, 292'.2'11
1897-1973.
Zeus and Hera : archetypal image of father, husband, and wife / C. Kerenyi ; translated from the German by Christopher Holme. Princeton, N.J. : Princeton University Press, [1975] xvii, 211 p. ; 26 cm. (Archetypal images in Greek religion ; v. 5) "Translated from the original manuscript of the author. Subsequently published in German: Zeus und Hera: Urbild des Vaters, des Gatten und der Frau." Includes index. Bibliography: p. 183-195. [BL820.J8K4713] 74-23858 ISBN 0-691-09864-6 : 13.50
1. Zeus. 2. Hera. I. Title. II. Series. III. Bollingen series ; 65

LINFORTH, Ivan Mortimer, 292'2'11
1879-
The arts of Orpheus, by Ivan M. Linforth. New York, Arno Press, 1973 [c1941] xviii, 370 p. 23 cm. (Philosophy of Plato and Aristotle) Reprint of the ed. published by University of California Press, Berkeley. [BL820.07L5 1973] 72-9296 ISBN 0-405-04847-5 18.00
1. Orpheus. 2. Dionysus. 3. Mysteries, Religions. I. Title. II. Series.

LINFORTH, Ivan Mortimer, 292.211
1879-
The pyre on Mount Oeta in Sophocles' "Trachiniae." Berkeley, University of California Press, 1952. 255-267 p. 24 cm. (University of California publications in classical philology, v. 14, no. 7) Bibliographical footnotes. [PA25.C3 vol. 14, no. 7] A52
1. Sophocles. Trachiniae. I. Title. II. Series: California. University. University of California publications in classical philology, v. 14, no. 7

MACKAY, Louis Alexander, 292.211
1901-
Notes on Lucretius. Berkeley, University of California Press, 1950. 433-445 p. 24 cm. (University of California publications in classical philology, v. 13, no. 14) [PA25.C3 vol. 13, no. 14] A50
1. Lucretius Carus, Titus. I. Title. II. Series: California. University. University of California publications in classical philology, v. 13, no. 14

NEUDLING, Chester Louis, 292.211
1916-
A prosopography to Catullus. Oxford [Eng.] 1955. 290p. 15cm. (Iowa studies in classical philology, no. 12) Based on thesis, University of Iowa. Bibliography: p. 190. [PA25.I6 no. 12] A61
1. Catullus. C. Valerius. I. Title. II. Series.

NITZSCHE, Jane Chance, 292'.2'11
1945-
The genius figure in antiquity and the Middle Ages. New York, Columbia University Press, 1975. xi, 201 p. 23 cm. Bibliography: p. [171]-184. [BL477.N57] 74-17206 ISBN 0-231-03852-6 12.00
1. Genius (Companion spirit) I. Title.

O'BRIEN, Michael John. 292.211
The unity of the Laches. (In Yale classical studies. New Haven. 24 cm. v. 18 (1963) p. [131]-147) Bibliographical footnotes. [[PA25.Y3 vol. 18]] 63-5847
1. Plato. Laches. I. Title.

PARKE, Herbert William, 292'.2'11
1903-
The oracles of Zeus: Dodona, Olympia, Ammon, by H. W. Parke. Cambridge, Harvard University Press, 1967. x, 294 p. illus. 23 cm. Includes bibliographical references. [BL820.J8] 68-1424
1. Zeus. 2. Oracles, Greek. 3. Cultus, Greek. I. Title.

PARKE, Herbert William, 292'.2'11
1903-
The oracles of Zeus: Dodona, Olympia, Ammon, by H. W. Parke. Cambridge, Harvard University Press, 1967. x, 294 p. illus. 23 cm. Includes bibliographical references. [BL820.J8] 68-1424
1. Zeus. 2. Oracles, Greek. 3. Cultus, Greek. I. Title.

PATCH, Howard Rollin, 292'.2'11
1889-1963.
The tradition of the goddess Fortuna in Roman literature and in the transitional period / by Howard Rollin Patch. Folcroft, Pa. : Folcroft Library Editions, 1976. Reprint of the 1922 ed. published by Smith College, Northampton, Mass., which was issued as v. 3, no. 3 of the Smith College studies in modern languages. A portion of the author's thesis, Harvard, 1915, presented under the title: The goddess Fortuna in medieval literature. Bibliography: p. [BL820.F7P37 1976] 76-41188 ISBN 0-8414-6753-6 lib. bdg. : 10.00
1. Fortuna (Goddess) I. Title. II. Series: Smith College studies in modern languages ; v. 3, no. 3.

PATRICK, Richard. 292'.211
All colour book of Greek mythology, by Richard Patrick; introduction by Barbara Leonie Picard. London, New York, Octopus Books Ltd, 1972. 103 p., chiefly col. illus. 30 cm. [BL782.P3 1972] 73-152184 ISBN 0-7064-0071-2 £0.99
1. Mythology, Greek. I. Title.

SCHOO, Jan, 1897- 292'.2'11
Hercules' labors: fact or fiction? [1st American ed.] Chicago, Argonaut, 1969. xvi, 131 p. maps. 23 cm. Bibliography: p. 119-124. [BL820.H5S28 1969] 67-17574
1. Hercules. I. Title.

SCOTT, Kenneth. 292'.2'11
The imperial cult under the Flavians / Kenneth Scott. New York : Arno Press, 1975. p. cm. (Ancient religion and mythology) Reprint of the 1936 ed. published by W. Kohlhammer, Stuttgart. Includes bibliographical references. [DG124.S35 1975] 75-10655 ISBN 0-405-07263-5 : 12.00
1. Cultus, Roman. 2. Emperor worship, Roman. I. Title. II. Series.

SELTMAN, Charles Theodore 292.211
The twelve Olympians. New York, Crowell [c.1960] 208p. illus., map, 22cm. (Bibl.: p.[11] and bibl. footnotes) 60-9164 4.50
1. Mythology, Greek. I. Title.

SELTMAN, Charles 292.211
Theodore, 1886-
The twelve Olympians. New York. [Apollo Eds., 1962, c.1960] 208p. illus., map (A33) 1.95 pap.,
1. Mythology, Greek. I. Title.

SHOWERMAN, Grant, 1870- 292'.2'11
1935.
The great mother of the gods. Chicago, Argonaut, 1969. 113 p. illus. 24 cm. (The Argonaut library of antiquities) "An unchanged reprint of the 1901 edition." Bibliographical footnotes. [BL820.C8S5 1969] 67-29110
1. Cybele. 2. Mythology, Classical. I. Title.

SMUTNY, Robert Jaroslav, 292.211
1919-
The text history of the Epigrams of Theocritus. Berkeley, University of California Press, 1955. [6], 29-94p. 24cm. (University of California publications in classical philology, v. 15, no. 2) Based on thesis, University of California. Bibliographical references included in 'Notes' (p. 87-94) Bibliography: 6th prelim. page. [PA25.C3 vol. 15, no.2] A55
1. Theocritus. Epigrammata. I. Title. II. Series: California, University. University of California publications in classical philology. v. 15, no. 2

SOBOL, Donald J., 1924- 292'.2'11
The Amazons of Greek mythology [by] Donald J. Sobol. South Brunswick, A. S. Barnes [1972] 174 p. 22 cm. Bibliography: p. 163-165. [BL820.A6S62] 70-168371 ISBN 0-498-07902-3 6.95
1. Amazons. I. Title.

SUHR, Elmer George, 292'.2'11
1902-
Before Olympos; a study of the aniconic origins of Poseidon, Hermes, and Eros, by Elmer G. Suhr. [1st ed.] New York, Helios [1967] 175p. illus. 21cm. First v. of the author's trilogy, The column of the cosmos. Bibl. [BL781.S75] 67-19630 5.95 bds.,
1. Greece—Religion. 2. Cupid. 3. Mercurius. 4. Neptunus. I. Title.

SUHR, Elmer George, 292'.2'11
1902-
Before Olympos; a study of the aniconic origins of Poseidon, Hermes, and Eros, by Elmer G. Suhr.[1st ed.] New York, Helios Books [1967] 175 p. illus. 21 cm. The first vol. of the author's trilogy, The column of the cosmos. Bibliographical references included in "Notes to the text" (p. [143]-175) [BL781.S75] 67-19630
1. Cupid. 2. Mercurius. 3. Neptunus. 4. Greece — Religion. I. Title.

SUHR, Elmer George, 292'.2'11
1902-
The spinning Aphrodite; the evolution of the goddess from earliest pre-Hellenic symbolism through late classical times, by Elmer G. Suhr. [1st ed.] New York, Helios Books [1969] 218 p. illus., plates. 22 cm. Second vol. of the author's trilogy, The Column of the cosmos. Includes bibliographical references. [BL820.V5S9] 68-21940 6.95
1. Venus (Goddess) I. Title.

TABELING, Ernst. 292'.2'11
Mater larum : zum Wesen der Larenreligion / von Ernst Tabeling. New York : Arno Press, 1975. 103 p. ; 23 cm. (Ancient religion and mythology) Reprint of the 1932 ed. published by V. Klostermann, Frankfurt am Main, which was issued as Bd. 1 of Frankfurter Studien zur Religion und Kultur der Antike. Originally presented as the author's thesis, Frankfurt am Main. Includes bibliographical references and index. [BL820.L3T3 1975] 75-10657 ISBN 0-405-07265-1
1. Lares. I. Title. II. Series. III. Series: Frankfurter Studien zur Religion and Kultur der Antike ; Bd. 1.

TOMAINO, Sarah F. 292'.2'11
Persephone, bringer of spring [by] Sarah F. Tomaino. Pictures by Ati Forberg. New York, Crowell [1971] [40] p. illus. (part col.) 26 cm. A retelling of the Greek myth in which Persephone returns from the underworld each year to bring spring to the earth. [PZ8.1.T58Pe] 71-87160 ISBN 0-690-61448-9 4.50
1. Persephone—Juvenile literature. I. Forberg, Ati, illus. II. Title.

WEINSTOCK, Stefan. 292'.2'11
Divus Julius. Oxford, Clarendon Press, 1971. xix, 469 p., [28] leaves. illus., plan. 25 cm. Bibliography: p. xix. [DG262.W4] 72-177850 ISBN 0-19-814287-0 £9.00
1. Caesar, C. Julius—Cult. 2. Emperor worship, Roman. 3. Cultus, Roman. I. Title.

CENTER for 292'.2'13
Hermeneutical Studies in Hellenistic and Modern Culture.
The deification of Alexander the Great : protocol of the twenty-first colloquy, 7 March 1976 / The Center for Hermeneutical Studies in Hellenistic and Modern Culture; Ernst Badian. Berkeley, Calif. : The Center, [1976] p. cm. (Protocol series of the colloquies of the Center for Hermeneutical Studies in Hellenistic and Modern Culture ; no. 22) Bibliography: p. [DF234.2.C4 1976] 76-29614 ISBN 0-89242-020-0 : 2.50
1. Alexander the Great, 356-323 B.C.—Cult—Addresses, essays, lectures. 2. Apotheosis—Addresses, essays, lectures. I. Badian, E. II. Title. III. Series: Center for Hermeneutical Studies in Hellenistic and Modern Culture. Protocol series of the colloquies ; no. 21.

FONTENROSE, Joseph Eddy, 1903- 292.213
The cult and myth of Pyrros at Delphi. Berkeley, University of California Press, 1960. iv, 191-266p. illus., map. 26cm. (University of California publications in classical archaeology, v. 4, no. 3) Bibl. 61-62773 2.50 pap.,
1. Pyrros (Greek mythology) I. Title. II. Series: California. University. University of California publications in classical archaeology, v. 4, no. 3

GATES, Doris, 1901- 292'.2'13
Mightiest of mortals, Heracles / by Doris Gates ; ill. by Richard Cuffari. New York : Viking Press, [1975] p. cm. Retells the exploits of the Greek demi-god Heracles, including the tales of his twelve labors. [PZ8.1.G1684Mi] 398.2 75-16374 ISBN 0-670-47556-4 : 6.95
1. Heracles—Juvenile literature. I. Cuffari, Richard, 1925- II. Title.

TAYLOR, Lily Ross, 1886- 292'.2'13
The divinity of the Roman emperor / Lily Ross Taylor. New York : Arno Press, 1975. p. cm. (Roman history) Reprint of the 1931 ed. published by the American Philological Association, Middletown, Conn., which was issued as no. 1 of Philological monographs. [DG124.T3 1975] 75-7348 ISBN 0-405-07068-3 : 17.00
1. Caesar, C. Julius—Cult. 2. Augustus, Emperor of Rome, 63 B.C.-14 A.D.—Cult. 3. Cultus, Roman. 4. Emperor worship, Roman. I. Title. II. Series. III. Series: Philological monographs ; no. 1.

MALLE, Quentin Froebel. 292.218
Votive religion at Caere: prolegomena, by Quentin F. Maule and H. R. W. Smith. Berkeley, University of California Press, 1959. x, 128p. illus., plates. 26cm. (University of California publications in classical archaeology, v. 4, no. 1) Includes bibliographies. [DE1.C3 vol. 4, no. 1] A59
1. Terra-cottas, Etruscan. 2. Cerveteri, Italy—Antiq. 3. Votive offerings. 4. Etrurians—Religion. I. Smith, Henry Roy William, 1891- joint author. II. Title. III. Series: California. University. University of California publications in classical archaeology, v. 4, no. 1

IRESON, Robert 29.2222
The Penguin car handbook. [Harmondsworth. Middlesex; Baltimore] Penguin Books [1960] 320p. illus., diagrs. 18cm. (Penguin handbooks, PH55) 60-36334 1.45 pap.,
1. Automobiles—Handbooks, manuals, etc. I. Title.

CUMONT, Franz [Valery Marie] 292.23
After life in Roman paganism; lectures delivered at Yale University on the Silliman Foundation. New York, Dover Publications [1959 i.e., 1960] xv, 224p. 21cm. (Yale University. Mrs. Hepsa Ely Silliman memorial lectures, T573) 'An unabridged and unaltered republication of the first edition published by Yale University Press in 1922.' (Bibl. Footnotes) 59-65210 1.35 pap.,
1. Rome—Religion. 2. Future life. I. Title.

CUMONT, Franz Valery Marie, 1868-1947 292.23
After life in Roman paganism; lectures delivered at Yale University on the Silliman Foundation. [Gloucester, Mass., Peter Smith, 1962] 224p. (Yale Univ. Mrs. Hepsa Ely Silliman memorial lectures. Dover bk. rebound) Bibl. 3.35
1. Rome—Religion. 2. Future life. I. Title.

BISHOP, James Alonzo, 1907- ed. 292.3
Go with God. [1st ed.] New York, McGraw-Hill [1958] 410 p. 22 cm. [BL560.B5] 58-13856
1. Prayers. I. Title.

FOUCART, Paul Francois, 1836-1926. 292.3
Les mysteres d'Eleusis / Paul Francois Foucart. New York : Arno Press, 1975. 508 p. ; 23 cm. (Ancient religion and mythology) Reprint of the 1914 ed. published by A. Picard, Paris. Includes bibliographical references. [BL795.E5F63 1975] 75-10636 ISBN 0-405-07013-6
1. Eleusinian mysteries. I. Title. II. Series.

MOULINIER, Louis. 292'.3
Le pur et l'impur dans la pensee des Grecs d'Homere a Aristote / Louis Moulinier. New York : Arno Press, 1975. 449 p. ; 24 cm. (Ancient religion and mythology) Reprint of the 1952 ed. published by C. Klincksieck, Paris, which was issued as no. 11 of Etudes et commentaires. Includes bibliographical references and index. [PA427.M6 1975] 75-10642 ISBN 0-405-07260-0
1. Greek language—Semantics. 2. Rites and ceremonies—Greece. 3. Greek literature—History and criticism. 4. Purity, Ritual (Greek religion) I. Title. II. Series.

TRESP, Alois, ed. 292'.3
Die Fragmente der griechischen Kultschriftsteller / Alois Tresp. New York : Arno Press, 1975. vii, 235 p. ; 23 cm. (Ancient religion and mythology) German or Greek. Reprint of the 1914 ed. published by A. Topelmann, Giessen, which was issued as Bd. 15, Heft 1 of Religionsgeschichtliche Versuche und Vorarbeiten. Includes bibliographical references and indexes. [BL781.T74 1975] 75-10660 ISBN 0-405-07267-8
1. Cultus, Greek—History—Sources. 2. Greece—Religion—History—Sources. I. Title. II. Series. III. Series: Religionsgeschichtliche Versuche und Vorarbeiten ; Bd. 15, Heft 1.

WILLETTS, R. 1915- 292.3
Cretan cults and festivals. New York, Barnes & Noble [1962] xii, 362 p. 23 cm. Bibliography: p. 325-337. [BL793.C7W5] 62-4945
1. Crete — Religion. 2. Fasts and feasts — Crete. I. Title. II. Series.

WILLETTS, R. F., 1915- 292.3
Cretan cults and festivals. New York, Barnes & Noble [c.1962] xii, 362p. 23cm. Bibl. 62-4945 8.75
1. Crete—Religion. 2. Fasts and feasts—Crete. I. Title.

WILLOUGHBY, Harold Rideout 292.3
Pagan regeneration; a study of mystery initiations in the Graeco-Roman world, by Harold R. Willoughby. Chicago, University of Chicago Press [1960, c.1929] xi, 307p. 22cm. (Chicago reprint series) (Bibls.) 4.50
1. Mysteries, Religious. 2. Greece—Religion. 3. Rome—Religion. I. Title. II. Title: Regeneration, Pagan.
Contents omitted.

AMANDRY, Pierre, 1912- 292'.3'2
La mantique appollinienne a Delphes : essai sur le fonctionnement de l'Oracle / Pierre Amandry. New York : Arno Press, 1975. 290 p., 6 leaves of plates : ill. ; 23 cm. (Ancient religion and mythology) Reprint of the 1950 ed. published by E. de Boccard, Paris, which was issued as fasc. 170 of Bibliotheque des Ecoles francaises d'Athenes et de Rome. Includes index. Bibliography: p. [241]-260. [DF261.D35A4 1975] 75-10627 ISBN 0-405-07003-9
1. Delphian oracle. I. Title. II. Series. III. Series: Bibliotheque des Ecoles francaises d'Athenes et de Rome ; fasc. 170.

DEMPSEY, T. 292'.3'2
The Delphic oracle; its early history, influence, and fall, by T. Dempsey. With a prefatory note, by R. S. Conway. New York, B. Blom, 1972. xxiii, 199 p. 21 cm. Reprint of the 1918 ed. Bibliography: p. xiii-xvi. [DF261.D35D4 1972] 69-13234
1. Delphian oracle. I. Title.

FLACELIERE, Robert, 1904- 292.32
Greek oracles. Tr. [from French] by Douglas Garman. New York, Norton [1966, c.1965] ix, 92p. plan, 16 plates. 23cm. [BF1765.F5513] 65-25935 4.50 bds.,
1. Oracles, Greek. I. Title.

ROUSE, William Henry Denham, 1863-1950. 292'.3'4
Greek votive offerings / William Henry Denham Rouse. New York : Arno Press, 1975. p. cm. (Ancient religion and mythology) Reprint of the 1902 ed. published by the University Press, Cambridge, Eng. [BL795.V6R6 1975] 75-10654 ISBN 0-405-07262-7 : 27.00
1. Votive offerings—Greece. 2. Greece—Religion. 3. Greece—Antiquities. I. Title. II. Series.

DOW, Sterling, 1903- 292.36
A sacred calendar of Eleusis [by] Sterling Dow, Robert F. Healey. Cambridge, Mass., Harvard [1966, c.1965] 58p. 2 plates 24cm. (Harvard theol. studies, 21) Bibl. [BL795.E5D6] 66-2146 2.00 pap.,
1. Eleusinian mysteries. 2. Religious calendars—Greek religion. I. Healey, Robert F., joint author. II. Title.

ORPHEUS. Hymni. 292'.3'8
The Orphic hymns : text, translation, and notes / by Apostolos N. Athanassakis. Missoula, Mont. : Published by Scholars Press for the Society of Biblical Literature, c1977. p. cm. (Texts and translations ; 12) (Graeco-Roman religion series ; 3) Bibliography: p. [BL820.B2O76 1977] 76-54179 ISBN 0-89130-119-4 : 4.50
1. Hymns, English—Translations from Greek. 2. Hymns, Greek—Translations into English. 3. Dionysia. I. Title. II. Series. III. Series: Society of Biblical Literature. Texts and translations ; 12.

KERENYI, Karoly, 1897- 292'.4'2
Eleusis;archetypal image of mother and daughter [by] C. Kerenyi. Translated from the German by Ralph Manheim. [New York, Bollingen Foundation; distributed by] Pantheon Books [1967] xxxvii, 257 p. illus., plans. 26 cm. (Bollingen series, 65. Archetypal images in Greek religion, v. 4) Translated from the original MS. of the author. Bibliography: p. 217-233. [BL795.E5K413 1967b] 68-7597
1. Eleusinian mysteries. 2. Eleusis. I. Title. II. Series: Bollingen series, 65. III. Series: Archetypal images in Greek religion, v. 4

KERENYI, Karoly, 1897-1973. 292'.4'2
Eleusis : archetypal image of mother and daughter / C. Kerenyi ; translated from the German by Ralph Manheim. New York : Schocken Books, 1976, c1967. p. cm. (Women's studies) (Reprint of the d. published by Bollingen Foundation, New York, and distributed by Pantheon Books, which was issued as v. 4 of Archetypal images in Greek religion and as v. 65 of Bollingen series.) Reprint of the ed. published by Bollingen Foundation, New York, and distributed by Pantheon Books, which was issued as v. 4 of Archetypal images in Greek religion and as v. 65 of Bollingen series. Includes index. Bibliography: p. [BL795.E5K413 1976] 76-9148 ISBN 0-8052-0548-9 pbk. : 6.95
1. Eleusinian mysteries. 2. Eleusis. I. Title. II. Series: Archetypal images in Greek religion ; v. 4. III. Series: Bollingen series ; 65.

SCHWARTZ, Eduard, 1858-1940. 292'.5
Ethik der Griechen / Eduard Schwartz. New York : Arno Press, 1976, c1951. 269 p. : port. ; 24 cm. (History of ideas in ancient Greece) Reprint of the ed. published by K. F. Koehler, Stuttgart. Includes bibliographical references and index. [BJ161.S427 1975] 75-13293 ISBN 0-405-07337-2
1. Ethics, Greek. I. Title. II. Series.

BOUCHE-LECLERCQ, Auguste, 1842-1923. 292'.6'1
Les pontifes de l'ancienne Rome / Auguste Bouche-Leclercq. New York : Arno Press, 1975. vii, 439 p. ; 23 cm. (Ancient religion and mythology) Reprint of the 1871 ed. published by Librairie A. Franck, Paris. Originally presented as the author's thesis, Paris, 1871. Bibliography: p. [viii]. [BL815.P7B68 1975] 75-10630 ISBN 0-405-07006-3
1. Priests, Roman. I. Title. II. Series.

PREIBISCH, Paul, 1851- 292'.6'1
Two studies on the Roman pontifices. New York : Arno Press, 1975. 48, 47 p. ; 24 cm. (Ancient religion and mythology) Reprint of Fragmenta librorum pontificiorum, first published 1878 by J. Reylander, Tilsit, in Programm des koniglichen Gymnasiums zu Tilsit; and of Quaestiones de libris pontificiis, first published in 1874 by W. Friedrich, Bratislava. Latin or German. [DG135.9.P73 1975] 75-10647 ISBN 0-405-07271-6
1. Rome—Libri pontificum. 2. Cultus, Roman. 3. Rome—Religious life and customs. I. Preibisch, Paul, 1851- Quaestiones de libris pontifciis. 1975. II. Title. III. Series.

MYLONAS, George Emmanuel, 1898- 292.65
Eleusis and the Eleusinian mysteries. Princeton, N. J., Princeton University Press, 1961. xx, 346p. illus., map. 25cm. Bibliography: p. 321-324. Bibliographical footnotes. [DF261.E4M88] 61-7421
1. Eleusis. 2. Eleusinian mysteries. I. Title.

EDELSTEIN, Emma Jeannette Levy, 1904- 292'.9
Asclepius : a collection and interpretation of the testimonies / Emma Jeannette Edelstein and Ludwig Edelstein. New York : Arno Press, 1975. 774 p. in various pagings : 24 cm. (Ancient religion and mythology) Reprint of the 1945 ed. published by Johns Hopkins Press, Baltimore as v. 2 of the second series, Texts and documents, of the Publications of the Institute of the History of Medicine, the Johns Hopkins University. Includes indexes. Bibliography: p. 259-260. [BL820.A4E37 1975] 75-10635 ISBN 0-405-07009-8
1. Aesculapius. 2. Cultus, Greek. I. Edelstein, Ludwig, 1902-1965. II. Title. III. Series. IV. Series: Johns Hopkins University. Institute of the History of Medicine. Publications : 2d ser., Texts and documents ; v. 2.

NILSSON, Martin Persson, 1874-1967. 292'.9
The Dionysiac mysteries of the Hellenistic and Roman age / Martin P. Nilsson. New York : Arno Press, 1975. p. cm. (Ancient religion and mythology) Reprint of the 1957 ed. published by C. W. K. Gleerup, Lund, Sweden, as no. 5 of Skrifter utg. av Svenska institutet i Athen, 8. [BL820.B2N5 1975] 75-10643 ISBN 0-405-07261-9 : 9.00
1. Dionysia. I. Title. II. Series. III. Series: Svenska institutet i Athen. Skrifter : Acta, Series altera ; 5.

293 Germanic Religion

AULAIRE, Ingri (Mortenson) d', 1904- 293
Norse gods and giants [by] Ingri and Edgar Parin d'Aulaire. [1st ed.] Garden City, N.Y., Doubleday [1967] 154 p. illus. (part col.) 32 cm. A collection of the myths of the Norsemen, containing stories of the gods Odin, Thor, Loki, Njord, Frey, and the others of the Aesir. [PZ8.1.A86No] AC 67
1. Mythology, Norse. I. Aulaire, Edgar Parin d', 1898- joint author. II. Title.

BRANSTON, Brian, 1914- 293
Gods of the North. New York, Vanguard Press [1955] 318 p. illus. 23 cm. (Myth and man) A Thames and Hudson book. [BL860.B67] 55-7888
1. Mythology, Norse. I. Title.

BRANSTON, Brian, 1914- 293
The lost gods of England / Brian Branston. New York : Oxford University Press, 1974. 216 p. : ill. (some col.) ; 25 cm. Includes index. [BL980.G7B7 1974b] 74-78753 ISBN 0-19-519796-8 : 10.00
1. Mythology, English. 2. Mythology, Anglo-Saxon. I. Title.

BRANSTON, Brian, 1914- 293
The lost gods of England. [2d ed.] London, Thames and Hudson [1974] 216 p. illus. (part col.) 25 cm. [BL980.G7B7 1974] 74-179873 ISBN 0-500-11013-1
1. Mythology, English. 2. Mythology, Anglo-Saxon. I. Title.
Distributed by Oxford University Press, New York, 10.00.

CHANTEPIE de la Saussaye, Pierre Daniel, 1848-1920. 293
The religion of the Teutons. Translated from the Dutch by Bert J. Vos. [Boston] Milford House [1973] p. Translation of Geschiedenis van den Godsdienst der Germanen. Reprint of the 1902 ed. published by Ginn, Boston, which was issued as v. 3 of Handbooks on the history of religions. Bibliography: p. [BL860.C45 1973] 73-186792 ISBN 0-87821-097-0 50.00 (lib. bdg.)
1. Mythology, Germanic. 2. Mythology, Norse. 3. Germanic tribes—Religion. I. Title. II. Series: Handbooks on the history of religions, v. 3.

CHANTEPIE de la Saussaye, Pierre Daniel, 1848-1920. 293
The religion of the Teutons / by P. D. Chantepie de la Saussaye ; translated from the Dutch by Bert J. Vos. Portland, Me. : Longwood Press, 1977. vii, 504 p., [2] leaves of plates : maps ; 22 cm. Translation of Geschiedenis van den godsdienst ger Germanen. Reprint of the 1902 ed. published by Ginn, Boston, which was issued as v. 3 of Handbooks on the history of religions. Includes bibliographical references and index. [BL860.C413 1977] 76-27519 ISBN 0-89341-030-6 : 50.00
1. Mythology, Germanic. 2. Mythology, Norse. 3. Germanic tribes—Religion. I. Title. II. Series: Handbooks on the history of religions ; v. 3.

COOLIDGE, Olivia E. 293
Legends of the North; illustrated by Edouard Sandoz. Boston, Houghton Mifflin, 1951. x, 260 p. illus. 24 cm. [BL860.C65] 51-9247
1. Mythology. I. Title.

CRAIGIE, William Alexander, Sir, 1867-1957. 293
The religion of ancient Scandinavia. Freeport, N.Y., Books for Libraries Press [1969] xi, 71, [1] p. 23 cm. (Select bibliographies reprint series) Reprint of the 1906 ed. Bibliography: p. 71-[72] [BL860.C7 1969] 74-99657
1. Mythology, Norse. I. Title.

DAVIDSON, Hilda Roderick (Ellis) 293
Pagan Scandinavia [by] H. R. Ellis Davidson. New York, F.A. Praeger [1967] 214 p. illus. 21 cm. (Ancient peoples and places, v. 58) Bibliography: p. 149-159. [BL860.D38] 67-24530
1. Scandinavia—Religion. 2. Scandinavia—Antiq. I. Title.

DAVIDSON, Hilda Roderick (Ellis) 293
Pagan Scandinavia [by] H. R. Ellis Davidson. New York, F. A. Praeger [1967] 214 p. illus. 21 cm. (Ancient peoples and places, v. 58) Bibliography: p. 149-159. [BL860.D38 1967b] 67-24530

1. *Scandinavia—Religion. 2. Scandinavia—Antiquities. I. Title.*

GREEN, Roger Lancelyn 293
Myths of the Norsemen; retold from the old Norse poems and tales by Roger Lancelyn Green. Drawings by Brian Wildsmith [Chester Springs, Pa.] Dufour [1964, c.1960] 190p. illus. 22cm. Pub. in Harmondsworth, Eng., in 1960 under title: The saga of Asgard. 64-12718 3.50 bds.,
1. Mythology, Norse. I. Title.

GRIMM, Jakob Ludwig Karl, 1785-1863. 293
Teutonic mythology. Translated from the fourth ed. with notes and appendix by James Steven Stallybrass. New York, Dover Publications [1966] 4 v. (viii, 1887 p.) 22 cm. "Unabridged and unaltered republication of the work first published ... in 1883 ... [to] 1888." [BL860.G753] 66-15933
1. Mythology, Germanic. 2. Mythology, Norse. 3. Germanic tribes—Religion. 4. Magic, Germanic. 5. Superstition. 6. Names, Germanic. I. Stallybrass, James Steven, 1826-1888, ed. and tr. II. Title.

GRIMM. JAKOB LUDWIG KARL, 1785-1863 293
Teutonic mythology. Tr. from the 4th ed. with notes. appendix by James Steven Stalllybrass [Magnolia, Mass., P. Smith. 1967] 4v. (viii, 1887p.) 22cm. (Dover bks. rebound) Unabridged, unaltered repubn. of the work first pub. 1883-1888 by George Bell [BL860.G753] 4.75 ea.,
1. Mythology, Germanic. 2. Mythology, Norse. 3. Germanic tribes—Religion. 4. Magic, Germanic. 5. Superstition. 6. Names. Germanic. I. Stallybrass, JamesSteven, 1826-1888, ed. and tr. II. Title.

HOSFORD, Dorothy G. 293
Thunder of the gods; illustrated by Claire & George Louden. [1st ed.] New York, Holt [1952] 115 p. illus. 21 cm. [BL865.H64] 52-9038
1. Mythology, Germanic—Juvenile literature. I. Title.

KAVANAGH, Peter. 293
Irish mythology, a dictionary. New York, P. Kavanagh Hand-Press [1958-59] 3v. 23cm. 'Limited to 100 numbered copies of which this is number 50.' Slip inserted in v. 1: There are also 17 extra series copies numbered 101-116. The 17th is unnumbered. [BL980.I7K3] 58-48141
1. Mythology, Irish—Dictionaries. I. Title.

MUNCH, Peter Andreas, 1810-1863. 293
Norse mythology; legends of gods and heroes. In the revision of Magnus Olsen. Translated from the Norwegian by Sigurd Bernhard Hustvedt. New York, American-Scandinavian Foundation, 1926 [c1927] Detroit, Singing Tree Press 1968. xvii, 392 p. 20 cm. Translation of Norrone gude- og heltesagn. Bibliography: p. 279-280. [BL860.M86 1968] 68-31092
1. Mythology, Norse. 2. Legends, Norse. I. Olsen, Magnus Bernhard, 1878-1963.

TURVILLE-PETRE, Edward Oswald Gabriel. 293
Myth and religion of the North; the religion of ancient Scandinavia. [1st ed.] New York, Holt, Rinehart and Winston [1964] ix, 340 p. illus. 25 cm. Bibliography: p. 321-329. [BL860.T8] 64-11276
1. Scandinavia—Religion. 2. Mythology, Norse. I. Title.

WALSH, John Herbert. 293
Norse legends and myths. Illustrated by Tom Taylor. London, New York, Longmans, Green [1957] 182 p. 17 cm. (The Heritage of literature series. Section A, no. 68) [BL860.W33] 58-1468
1. Mythology, Norse. I. Title.

TURVILLE-PETRE, Edward Oswald Gabriel. 293'.0948
Myth and religion of the North : the religion of ancient Scandinavia / E. O. G. Turville-Petre. Westport, Conn. : Greenwood Press, 1975, c1964. ix, 340 p., [12] leaves of plates : ill. ; 23 cm. Reprint of the ed. published by Holt, Rinehart and Winston, New York. Includes index. Bibliography: p. 321-329. [BL860.T8 1975] 75-5003 ISBN 0-8371-7420-1 lib.bdg. : 19.75
1. Mythology, Norse. 2. Scandinavia—Religion. I. Title.

MUNCH, Peter Andreas, 1810-1863. 293'.11
Norse mythology; legends of gods and heroes, by Peter Andreas Munch, in the revision of Magnus Olsen. Translated from the Norwegian by Sigurd Bernhard Hustvedt. New York, AMS Press [1970] xvii, 392 p. 23 cm. Translation of Norrone gude- og heltesagn. Reprint of the 1926 ed., which was issued as no. 27 of Scandinavian classics. Bibliography: p. 279-280. [BL860.M86 1970] 74-112002 ISBN 0-404-04538-3
1. Mythology, Norse. 2. Legends, Norse. I. Olsen, Magnus Bernhard, 1878-1963. II. Title. III. Series: Scandinavian classics, no. 27.

DAVIDSON, Hilda Roderick (Ellis) 293'.13
Scandinavian mythology [by] H. R. Ellis Davidson. London, New York, Hamlyn, 1969. 2-143 p. illus. (some col.), map. 29 cm. Bibliography: p. 138. [BL860.D384] 76-497286 25/-
1. Mythology, Norse. I. Title.

GELLING, Peter. 293'.13
The chariot of the sun, and other rites and symbols of the northern bronze age, by Peter Gelling and Hilda Ellis Davidson. Foreword by Christopher Hawkes. New York, Praeger [1969] ix, 200 p. illus. (part col.), map. 26 cm. Bibliography: p. 185-189. [BL863.G4 1969] 68-54466 7.50
1. Mythology, Norse. 2. Sun (in religion, folk-lore, etc.) I. Davidson, Hilda Roderick (Ellis) joint author. II. Title.

KAUFFMANN, Friedrich, 1863-1941. 293'.1'3
Northern mythology / by Friedrich Kauffmann ; [translated by M. Steele Smith] Folcroft, Pa. : Folcroft Library Editions, 1976. xii, 106 p. ; 23 cm. Translation of Deutsche Mythologie. Reprint of the 1903 ed. published by Dent, London, in series: The Temple primers. Includes index. Bibliography: p. 99-100. [BL860.K33 1976] 76-5464 ISBN 0-8414-5524-4 lib. bdg. : 12.50
1. Mythology, Norse. 2. Mythology, Germanic. I. Title.

KAUFFMANN, Friedrich, 1863-1941. 293'.1'3
Northern mythology / by Friedrich Kauffmann ; [translated by M. Steele Smith] Folcroft, Pa. : Folcroft Library Editions, 1976. xii, 106 p. ; 23 cm. Translation of Deutsche Mythologie. Reprint of the 1903 ed. published by Dent, London, in series: The Temple primers. Includes index. Bibliography: p. 99-100. [BL860.K33 1976] 76-5464 ISBN 0-8414-5524-4 lib. bdg. : 12.50
1. Mythology, Norse. 2. Mythology, Germanic. I. Title.

VANDERCOOK, John W. 293.17294
Black majesty, the life of Christophe, King of Haiti. New York, Scholastic [1963, c.1928, 1956] 156p. 17cm. (T463) Bibl. .35 pap.,
I. Title.

ANDERSON, Rasmus Bjorn, 1846-1936. 293'.2'11
Norse mythology; or, The religion of our forefathers, containing all the myths of the Eddas, systematized and interpreted. With an introd., vocabulary and index. 5th ed. [Boston] Milford House [1974] p. cm. Reprint of the 1891 ed. published by S. C. Griggs, Chicago. Bibliography: p. [BL860.A6 1974] 76-186790 ISBN 0-87821-086-5 45.00
1. Mythology, Norse. 2. Icelandic and Old Norse literature. 3. Northmen—Religion. I. Title.

ANDERSON, Rasmus Bjorn, 1846-1936. 293'.2'11
Norse mythology : or, The religion of our forefathers, containing all the myths of the Eddas / systematized and interpretated, with an introd., vocabulary and index, by R. B. Anderson. Boston : Longwood Press, 1977. p. cm. Reprint of the 2d ed. published in 1891 by S. C. Griggs, Chicago. Bibliography: p. [BL860.A6 1977] 77-6879 ISBN 0-89341-147-7 lib.bdg. : 25.00
1. Mythology, Norse. 2. Icelandic and Old Norse literature. 3. Northmen—Religion. I. Title. II. Title: The religion of our forefathers.

DAVIDSON, Hilda Roderick (Ellis) 293.211
Gods and myths of northern Europe. Baltimore, Penguin [c.1964] 251p. 19cm. (Pelican bk. A670) Bibl. 64-56969 1.25 pap.,
1. Mythology, Germanic. 2. Mythology, Norse. 3. Europe, Northern—Religion—Hist. I. Title.

DUMEZIL, Georges, 1898- 293'.2'11
Gods of the ancient Northmen. Edited by Einar Haugen; introd. by C. Scott Littleton and Udo Strutynski. Berkeley, University of California Press, 1973. xlvi, 157 p. 24 cm. (UCLA Center for the Study of Comparative Folklore and Mythology. Publications, 3) Translation of Les dieux des Germains and 4 articles written between 1952 and 1959. Includes bibliographical references. [BL860.D7813] 74-157819 ISBN 0-520-02044-8 9.00
1. Mythology, Norse. 2. Germanic tribes—Religion. I. Title. II. Series: California. University. University at Los Angeles. Center for the Study of Comparative Folklore and Mythology. Publications, 3.

GREEN, Roger Lancelyn. 293'.2'11
Myths of the Norsemen, retold from the old Norse poems and tales. Illustrated by Brian Wildsmith. [Harmondsworth, Eng.] Penguin Books [1970, c1960] 208 p. illus. 18 cm. (Puffin books, 464) First puboished in 1960 under title: The saga of Asgard. [BL860.G68 1970] 72-24349 0.95 (U.S.)
1. Mythology, Norse. I. Title.

KERENYI, Karoly, 1897- 293'.2'11
Hermes guide of souls : the mythologem of the masculine source of life / Karl Kerenyi ; translated from German by Murray Stein. Zurich : Spring Publications, 1976. vi, 104 p. ; 21 cm. Translation of Hermes der seelenfuhrer. Includes bibliographical references. [BL820.M5K413] 77-353912 ISBN 0-88214-207-0
1. Hermes. I. Title.

GUERBER, Helene Adeline, d.1929. 293'.8
Myths of northern lands; narrated with special reference to literature and art. Detroit, Singing Tree Press, 1970. 319 p. illus., ports. 23 cm. Reprint of the 1895 ed. [BL860.G8 1970] 70-124583
1. Mythology, Norse. 2. Mythology, Germanic. 3. Legends, Germanic. I. Title.

294 Religions Of Indic Origin

AGEHANANDA BHARATI, Swami 294
The Tantric tradition. London, Rider [New York, Hillary House, 1966. c.]1965. 350p. tables. 22cm. Bibl. [BL1495.T3A35] 66-2336 8.50
1. Tantrism. I. Title.

ALEXANDER, Mithrapuram K. 294
The Yoga system, by Mithrapuram K. Alexander. [Rev. ed.] North Quincy, Mass., Christopher Pub. House [1971, c1968] 87 p. illus. 21 cm. [B132.Y6A48 1971] 77-140373 ISBN 0-8158-0257-9 3.95
1. Yoga. I. Title.

ANANDAMURTI. 294
Baba's grace; discourses of Shrii Shrii Anandamurti. [Los Altos Hills, Calif., Ananda Marga Publications, 1973] 197 p. illus. 19 cm. [BP610.A513] 74-75331 ISBN 0-88476-001-4 2.95
1. Spiritual life. I. Title.

ANANDAMURTI. 294
The great universe; discourses on society. [Los Altos Hills, Calif., Ananda Marga Publications, c1973] 271 p. illus. 19 cm. [BP610.A514] 74-75332 ISBN 0-88476-002-2 3.25
I. Title.

ARVON, Henri, 1914- 294
Buddhism. Tr. [from French] by Douglas Scott. New York, Walker [1963, c.1962] 136p. 21cm. (Sun bk. SB-4. Religion and mythology) 62-12753 3.50
1. Buddha and Buddhism. I. Title.

BANCROFT, Anne, 1923- 294
Religions of the East. New York, St. Martin's Press [1974] 256 p. illus. 26 cm. Bibliography: p. 250-252. [BL80.2.B36 1974] 72-97352 12.95
1. Religions. I. Title.

BHATTACHARYYA, Narendra Nath. 294
Ancient Indian rituals and their social contents / Narendra Nath Bhattacharyya. Delhi : Manohar Book Service, 1975. xvi, 184 p. ; 23 cm. Includes index. Bibliography: p. [165]-176. [BL2003.B4] 75-903622 12.75
1. Rites and ceremonies—India. 2. Cultus—India. 3. India—Religion. I. Title.
Dist. by Rowman & Littlefield

*BJORNSTAD, James. 294
The transcendental mirage / by James Bjornstad. Minneapolis : Bethany Fellowship, 1976. 93p. : ill. ; 18 cm. (Dimension books) Bibliography: p. [91]-93. [BL627] 76-6614 ISBN 0-87123-556-0 pbk. : 1.50
1. Transcendental meditation. I. Title.

BLOOMFIELD, Harold H., 1944- 294
Happiness : the TM program, psychiatry, and enlightenment / Harold H. Bloomfield, Robert Kory. New York : Dawn Press : distributed by Simon and Schuster, [1976] p. cm. Includes index. [BL627.B55] 76-3754 ISBN 0-671-22269-4 : 8.95
1. Transcendental Meditation. 2. Happiness. I. Kory, Robert, joint author. II. Title.

BLOOMFIELD, Harold H., 1944- 294
Happiness : the TM program, psychiatry, and enlightenment / [by] Harold H. Bloomfield and] Robert B. Kory. New York : Pocket Books, 1977,c1976. 304p. ; 18cm. (A Kangaroo Book) Includes index. [BL627.B55] ISBN 0-671-81294-7 pbk. : 1.95
1. Transcendental Meditation. 2. Happiness. I. Kory, Robert B., joint author. II. Title.
L.C. card no. for 1976 Simon and Schuster ed.:76-3754.

BLOOMFIELD, Harold H., 1944- 294
TM :* discovering inner energy and overcoming stress / Harold H. Bloomfield, Michael Peter Cain, Dennis T. Jaffe, and Robert B. Kory ; foreword by Hans Selye ; introd. by R. Buckminster Fuller. Boston : G. K. Hall, 1976, c1975. p. cm. "*Transcendental meditation." "Published in large print." Includes index. Bibliography: p. [BL627.B56 1976] 76-4910 ISBN 0-8161-6366-9
1. Transcendental Meditation. 2. Sight-saving books. I. Cain, Michael Peter, 1941- joint author. II. Jaffe, Dennis T., joint author. III. Title.

BLOOMFIELD, Maurice, 1855-1928. 294
The religion of the Veda; the ancient religion of India (from Rig-Veda to Upanishads). New York, AMS Press [1969] xv, 300 p. 23 cm. Reprint of the 1908 ed., published by J. P. Putnam's sons, London, in series: American lectures on the history of religions, 7th series, 1906-1907. Includes bibliographical references. [BL1115.B6 1969] 70-94310
1. Vedas—Criticism, interpretation, etc. 2. Brahmanism. I. Title. II. Series: American lectures on the history of religions, 7th series, 1906-1907.

COOMARASWAMY, Ananda Kentish, 1877-1947. 294
Hinduism and Buddhism. Westport, Conn., Greenwood Press [1971] 86 p. 23 cm. Reprint of the 1943 ed. Includes bibliographical references. [BL1201.C6 1971] 78-138215 ISBN 0-8371-5570-3
1. Hinduism. 2. Buddha and Buddhism. I. Title.

EBON, Martin, comp. 294 B
Maharishi : the founder of Transcendental Meditation / edited by Martin Ebon. New York : New American Library, 1968, 1975 printing. xvii, 149 p. ; 18 cm. (A Signet book) Contents.Contents.—Ebon, M. Twentieth century guru.—Newhouse, J. C. New York is ready!—Ballantine, M. The road to bliss consciousness.—Singh, K. How does meditation work?—Lefferts, B. Chief guru of the western world.—Butterworth, C. The Beatles without mask.—The Beatles talk about Maharishi.—White, P. The case of Mia Farrow.—Read, E. Why Efrem Zimbalist is silent.—Crenshaw, J. Maharishi's man in L.A.—McNeill, D. He turned us on!—Crenshaw, J. The hippies: beyond pot and LSD.—Crenshaw, J. His global man Friday.—Zielinski, L. Yoga, meditation, mantras.—Winters, R. America's love affair with yoga.—Maynard, A. From Gurdjieff to Maharishi.—Fleming, G. The house on 78th Street.—Otani, J.-P. Springtime on the Ganges.—Mahesh Yogi, M. Toward world peace.—Ebon, M. What next for the TM movement? [BL1175.M29E2 1975] 75-353100 1.50
1. Mahesh Yogi, Maharishi—Addresses, essays, lectures. I. Title.

*EBON, Martin, comp. 294
TM; how to find peace of mind through meditation, edited by Martin Ebon. [New York] New American Library [1976 c1975] 246 p. 18 cm. (A Signet Book) [BL627] 1.50 (pbk.)
1. Transcendental Meditation. I. Title.

EDENS, David, 1926- 294
Making the most of family worship [by] David and Virginia Edens. Nashville, Broadman [1968] 128p. 20cm. Bibl. [BV200.E3] 68-15851 1.50 bds.,
1. Family—Religious life. 2. Family—Prayer-books and devotions. I. Edens, Virginia. joint author. II. Title.

ELIOT, Charles Norton Edgecumbe, Sir 1862-1931. 294
Hinduism and Buddhism; an historical sketch. New York, Barnes & Noble, 1954. 3v. 22cm. Bibliographical footnotes. [BL1031.E6 1954] 34-14201
1. Hinduism. 2. Buddha and Buddhism. 3. Asia—Religion. I. Title.

GARGI, Balwant, 1916- 294
Nirankari Baba. [Delhi] Thomson Press (India), Publication Division, 1973,[i.e.1974] 172 p. illus. 23 cm. [BP605.S12G37] 73-906699
1. Sant Nirankari Mandal. 2. Singh, Gurbachan, 1930- I. Title.
Distributed by International Publications Service; 9.00.

GHURYE, Govind Sadashiv, 1893- 294
Gods and men. Bombay, Popular Book Depot [dist. New York, Heinman, 1963] 300p. 22cm. Bibl. SA63 7.50
1. India—Religion—Hist. I. Title.

GOLDHABER, Nat. 294
TM : an alphabetical guide to the transcendental meditation program / by Nat Goldhaber and Denise Denniston ; with special sections by Peter McWilliams. 1st ed. New York : Ballantine Books, 1976. p. cm. [BL627.G64] 76-8830 ISBN 0-345-24096-0 : 3.95
1. Transcendental Meditation. I. Denniston, Denise, joint author. II. McWilliams, Peter. III. Title.

GURU Bawa, Shaikh Muhaiyaddeen. 294
The divine luminous wisdom that dispels the darkness; God-man, man-God, by M. R. Shaikh Muhaiyaddeen Guru Bawa. Philadelphia, Delaware Valley Printers [1972] viii, 276 p. illus. 22 cm. [BL624.G87] 72-188357
1. Spiritual life. I. Title.

HARPER, Marvin Henry, 1901- 294
Gurus, swamis, and avataras: spiritual masters and their American disciples. Philadelphia, Westminster Press [1972] 271 p. 22 cm. Bibliography: p. [251]-266. [BP603.H37] 76-175547 ISBN 0-664-20927-0 7.50
1. Sects. 2. Religions. I. Title.

HEMINGWAY, Patricia Drake. 294
The transcendental meditation primer : now stop tension & start living / Patricia Drake Hemingway. New York : D. McKay Co., [1975] xviii, 264 p. ; 22 cm. Includes index. Bibliography: p. 252-254. [BL627.H43] 75-6918 ISBN 0-679-50554-7 : 8.95
1. Transcendental meditation. I. Title.

HUBBARD, La Fayette Ronald, 1911- 294
The Phoenix lectures / by L. Ron Hubbard. 3d ed. Los Angeles : American Saint Hill Organization, 1974, c1969. x, 320 p. ; 21 cm. "Lecture series given by L. Ron Hubbard to the professional course, Phoenix, Arizona, in July 1954, compiled into book form by the editorial staff of the Publications Organization World Wide." [BP605.S2H83 1974] 74-195931 ISBN 0-88404-006-2 : 7.00
1. Scientology. I. Publications Organization World Wide. II. Title.

HUMPHREYS, Christmas, 1901- 294
Buddhism. Harmondsworth, Middlesex, Penguin Books [1951] 256 p. 19 cm. (Pelican books, A 228) Includes bibliography. [BL1420.H8] 52-41242
1. Buddha and Buddhism—Hist. I. Title.

*JEFFERSON, William. 294
The story of the Maharishi. New York, Pocket Books [1976] 128 p. 18 cm. Bibliography: p. 125-128. [BL627] ISBN 0-671-80526-6 1.50 (pbk.)
1. Mahesh Yogi, Maharishi. 2. Transcendental meditation. I. Title.

JOHNSON, Samuel, 1822-1882. 294
Oriental religions and their relation to universal religion. Freeport, N.Y., Books for Libraries Press [1973] p. (Essay index reprint series) Reprint of the 1873, 1878, and 1885 ed. published by J. R. Osgood, Houghton, Osgood, and Houghton, Mifflin, Boston, respectively. Contents.Contents.—v. 1. India.—v. 2. China.—v. 3. Persia. Includes bibliographical references. [BL1020.J64 1973] 73-4714 ISBN 0-518-10086-3
1. India—Religion. 2. China—Religion. 3. Philosophy, Chinese. 4. China—Civilization. 5. Iran—Religion. I. Title.

KEITH, Arthur Berriedale, 1879-1944. 294
Indian [mythology] by A. Berriedale Keith. Iranian [mythology] by Albert J. Carnoy. New York, Cooper Square Publishers, 1964 [c1917] ix, 404 p. illus., 44 plates (part col.) 24 cm. (The Mythology of all races, v. 6) Bibliography: p. [369]-404. [BL25.M8 1964 vol. 6] [BL1031.K4036] 63-19091
1. Mythology, Indic. 2. Mythology, Aryan. I. Carnoy, Albert Joseph, 1878- II. Title. III. Series.

KIM, Young Oon. 294
India's religious quest / Young Oon Kim. 1st ed. New York : Golden Gate Pub. Co., 1976. x, 191 p. ; 21 cm. (World religions ; v. 2) Includes bibliographies and index. [BL1202.K47] 76-151925
1. Hinduism. 2. Jainism. 3. Sikhism. 4. Buddhism. I. Title.

KORY, Robert B. 294
The transcendental meditation program for business people / Robert B. Kory. New York : AMACOM, c1976. 91 p. : graphs ; 22 cm. (An AMA management briefing) Bibliography: p. 89-91. [BL627.K67] 76-3696 ISBN 0-8144-2189-X pbk. : 7.50
1. Transcendental Meditation. 2. Executive ability. I. Title. II. Series: American Management Associations. An AMA management briefing.

*LAWRENCE, Bruce B. 294
Shahrastani on the Indian religion / Bruce B. Lawrence ; preface by Franz Rosenthal. The Hague : Mouton, c1976. 297p. ; 24 cm. (Religion and society ; 4) Includes index. Label on t.p.: Distributed in the U.S.A. by Humanities Press Atlantic Highlands, N.J. Bibliography: pp. [279]-292. [BL2015] 23.25
1. India-Religion and mythology. I. Ash-Shahrastani, Abd al-Karim. II. Title.

*LEVINE, Faye. 294
The strange world of the Hare Krishnas. Greenwich, Conn., Fawcett [1974] 189 p. 18 cm. (Fawcett world library) [BP603] 0.95 (pbk.)
1. Hare Krishna sect. I. Title.

LEWIS, Gordon Russell, 1926- 294
What everyone should know about transcendental meditation / Gordon R. Lewis. Glendale, Calif. : G/L Regal Books, [1975] 92 p. ; 18 cm. Bibliography: p. 77-79. [BL627.L49] 74-32326 ISBN 0-8307-0353-5 pbk. : 1.45
1. Transcendental meditation. I. Title.

LOKA : 294
a journal from Naropa Institute / edited by Rick Fields. 1st ed. Garden City, N.Y. : Anchor Press, 1975. 142 p. : ill. ; 28 cm. [BP605.N3L64] 74-31515 ISBN 0-385-02312-X : 4.00
1. Naropa Institute. I. Fields, Rick. II. Naropa Institute.

MEHTA, Phirozshah Dorabji 294
Early Indian religious thought; an introduction and essay. London, Luzac [dist. Mystic, Conn., Verry, 1965] 532p. 23cm. Bibl. [BL2003.M4] 58-2912 8.50
1. Religious thought—India. 2. India—Religion. I. Title.

MULLER, Friedrich Max, 1823-1900. 294
Lectures on the origin and growth of religion, as illustrated by the religions of India : delivered in the Chapter-House, Westminster Abbey in April, May, and June 1878 / by F. Max Muller. New ed. New York : AMS Press, 1976. xvi, 408 p. ; 18 cm. Reprint of the 1882 ed. published by Longmans, Green, London, which was issued as the Hibbert lectures, 1878. Includes bibliographical references and index. [BL2001.M8 1976] 73-18816 ISBN 0-404-11440-7 : 20.00
1. India—Religion. 2. Religion—History. I. Title. II. Series: The Hibbert lectures (London) ; 1878.

THE Nectar of chanting : 294
transliteration and English rendition of sacred texts and mantras. Oakland, Ca. : S.Y.D.A. Foundation, California, c1975. 151 p. : ports. ; 18 cm. Errata slip inserted. [BL560.N4] 76-352138 pbk. : 3.50
1. Mantras. 2. Incantations. I. Syda Foundation, California.
Contents omitted.

OATES, Bob. 294 B
Celebrating the dawn : Maharishi Mahesh Yogi and the TM technique / epilogue by Maharishi Mahesh Yogi ; written by Robert Oates, Jr. New York : Putnam, c1976. 227 p. : ill. ; 24 cm. [BF637.T68017 1976] 76-14884 ISBN 0-399-11815-2 : 12.95
1. Mahesh Yogi, Maharishi. 2. Transcendental Meditation. 3. Yogis—Biography. I. Title.

PAGAL Baba. 294
Temple of the Phallic King; the mind of India: Yogis, Swamis, Sufis, and Avataras, by Pagal Baba. Edited and with photos. by Edward Rice. New York, Simon and Schuster [1973] 282 p. illus. 24 cm. [BL2001.2.P24] 72-90386 ISBN 0-671-21479-9 9.95
1. India—Religion. I. Title.

PARRINDER, Edward Geoffrey. 294
The Christian debate: light from the East, by Geoffrey Parrinder. [1st ed. in the U. S. A.] Garden City, N. Y., Doubleday, 1966 [c1964] 159, [1] p. 22 cm. "For further reading": p. [160] [BR128.H5P36 1966] 66-10516
1. Robinson, John Arthur Thomas, Bp., 1919- Honest to God. 2. Christianity and other religions—Hinduism. 3. Hinduism—Relations—Christianity. I. Title.

PELLEY, William Dudley, 1890- 294
Know your karma; design for destiny. [1st ed. Noblesville, Ind., Soulcraft Chapels, c1954] 318p. 22cm. [BL2015.K3P4] 55-19990
1. Karma. I. Title.

PURUSOTTAMA PANDITA. 294
The early Brahmanical system of gotra and pravara; a translation of the Gotra-pravara-manjari, with an introd. by John Brough. Cambridge [Eng.] University Press, 1953. xvii, 227p. 24cm. Includes bibliographies. [BL1215.E5P82] A58
1. Brahmanism. 2. Endogamy and exogamy. I. Brough, John, 1917- ed. and tr. II. Title. III. Title: Gotra-pravara-mañjari.

RAJANEESH, Acharya, 1931- 294
The book of the secrets : discourses on "Vigyana Bhairava Tantra" / Bhagwan Shree Rajneesh ; compilation, Ma Yoga Astha ; editors, Ma Ananda Prem, Swami Ananda Teerth. London : Thames and Hudson, 1976- v. ; 21 cm. [BL1245.T3R33 1976] 77-356775 ISBN 0-500-27076-7 (v. 1) : £3.95 (v. 1)
1. Tantrism—Addresses, essays, lectures. 2. Meditation—Addresses, essays, lectures. I. Title.

RAM Dass. 294
Grist for the mill / by Ram Dass, in collaboration with Stephen Levine. Santa Cruz, Calif. : Unity Press, 1977. 173 p. : ill. ; 22 cm. (The Mindfulness series) [BP610.R3514] 76-40447 ISBN 0-913300-17-9 : 7.95. ISBN 0-913300-16-0 pbk. : 3.95
1. Ram Dass. 2. Spiritual life. I. Levine, Stephen, joint author. II. Title.

ROOF, Simons Lucas, 1920- 294
Journeys on the razor-edged path. Illus. by Frank Kramer. New York, Crowell [1959] 204 p. illus. 22 cm. [BL2003.R65] 59-12504
1. India—Religion. I. Title.

ROSS, Floyd Hiatt. 294
The meaning of life in Hinduism and Buddhism. Boston, Beacon Press [1953] 167p. 22cm. [BL2603.R65 1953] 53-7041
1. Life. 2. Hinduism. 3. Buddha and Buddhism. I. Title.

SCHWEITZER, Albert, 1875- 294
Indian thought and its development. Translated by Mrs. Charles E. B. Russell. Boston, Beacon Press [1957] 272p. 21cm. (Beacon paperback no. 37) Translation of Die Weltanschauung der indischen Denker. [BL2003] 57-3911
1. India—Religion. 2. Hinduism. 3. Buddha and Buddhism 4. Jainism. I. Title.

SCIENTOLOGY: a world religion emerges in the space age. 294
[Hollywood, Calif.] Church of Scientology Information Service, Dept. of Archives [1974] xvi, 109, 63 p. illus. 32 cm. (Church of Scientology Information Service. Dept. of Archives. Archival series, 1) [BP605.S2S3] 74-171028 10.00
1. Scientology. I. Church of Scientology Information Service. Dept. of Archives. II. Series: Church of Scientology Information Service. Dept. of Archives. Archival series — Church of Scientology Information Service, Dept. of Archives, 1.

SEEGER, Elizabeth. 294
Eastern religions. Illustrated with photos. New York, Crowell [1973] 213 p. illus. 24 cm. Bibliography: p. 201-204. Introduces the history, philosophies, and rituals of such Eastern religions as Hinduism, Buddhism, Shintoism, Confucianism, and Taoism. [BL92.S43] 73-10206 ISBN 0-690-25342-7 4.95
1. Asia—Religion—Juvenile literature. 2. Religions—Juvenile literature. I. Title.

SHAH, Douglas. 294
The meditators / by Douglas Shah. Plainfield, N.J. : Logos International, c1975. x, 147 p. : ill. ; 21 cm. [BL627.S53 1975] 75-7478 ISBN 0-88270-125-8 : 5.95 ISBN 0-88270-126-6 pbk. : 3.50
1. Transcendental Meditation. 2. Meditation. 3. Sects. 4. Religions. I. Title.

TANTRAS. Kularnavatantra. 294
Kularnava tantra / John Woodroffe and M. P. Pandit ; [introd. by Arthur Avalon]. [Madras : Ganesh, 1974 128 p. ; 22 cm. Label on t.p.: Distributed by Vedanta Press, Hollywood. Includes bibliographical references. [BL1135.T47A38] 75-554059 4.00
I. Woodroffe, John George, Sir, 1865-1966. II. Pandit, Madhav Pundalik, 1918- III. Title.

VIDYARTHI, Pandeya Brahmeshwar. 294
Early Indian religious thought : a study in the sources of Indian theism with special reference to Ramanuja / P. B. Vidyarthi. 1st ed. New Delhi : Oriental Publishers & Distributors, 1976. xv, 239 p. ; 22 cm. (World's wisdom series ; no. 1) Includes indexes. Bibliography: p. [228]-233. [BL2001.2.V5] 76-904388 Rs55.00
1. Ramanuja, founder of sect. 2. India—Religion. 3. Religious thought—India. 4. Theism. I. Title. II. Series.

WEBER, Max, 1864-1920. 294
The religion of India; the sociology of Hinduism and Buddhism. Translated and directed by Hans H. Gerth and Don Martindale. Glencoe, Ill., Free Press [1958] 392 p. 21 cm. Translation of Hinduismus und Buddhismus, published as v. 2 of the author's Gesammelte Aufsatze zur Religionssoziologie. Includes bibliography. [BL2001.W443] 58-6491
1. India—Religion. 2. India—Social conditions. I. Title.

WHITE, John Warren, 1939- 294
Everything you want to know about TM, including to do it : a look at higher consciousness and the enlightenment industry / John White. New York : Pocket Books, 1976. 191 p. ; 18 cm. Bibliography: p. 189-190. [BL627.W45] 76-351823 1.95
1. Transcendental Meditation. I. Title.

WINTERNITZ, Moriz, 1863-1937. 294
A history of Indian literature. Translated from the original German by S. Ketkar, and rev. by the author. New York, Russell & Russell [1971] 2 v. 25 cm. Reprint of the 1927-33 ed. Vol. 2 translated by S. Ketkar and H. Kohn. Translation of Geschichte der indischen litteratur. Includes bibliographical references. [PK2903.W63 1971] 73-151559
1. Sanskrit literature—History and criticism. 2. Indic literature—History and criticism. 3. Pali literature—History and criticism. 4. Jaina literature—History and criticism. I. Title.

YOUNGER, Paul. 294
Introduction to Indian religious thought. Philadelphia, Westminster Press [1972] 142 p. 20 cm. [BL2001.2.Y63] 70-172155 ISBN 0-664-20926-2 4.95
1. India—Religion. 2. Religious thought—India. I. Title.

*ATKINSON, Edwin T. 294'.09
Religion in the Himalayas. Delhi, Cosmo Publications 1974 vi, 699-934 p., 22 cm. The present book is an Off-print from The Himalyan Gazetteer, Vol. II, forming Chapters VIII, IX, X and is complete in itself. [BL2001]
1. India—Religion. I. Title.
Distributed by International Scholarly Book Service, 15.00.

BANERJEE, P. 294'.09
Early Indian religions [by] P. Banerjee. New York, Wiley [1973] xii, 241 p. illus. 23 cm. "A Halsted Press book." Bibliography: p. [225]-234. [BL2001.2.B3 1973] 73-5869 ISBN 0-470-04670-8 8.75
1. India—Religion—History. I. Title.

MONIER-WILLIAMS, Monier, Sir, 1819-1899 294'.0954
Religious thought and life in India : Vedism, Brahmanism, and Hinduism : an account of the religions of the Indian peoples, based on a life's study of their literature and on personal investigations in their own country / by Monier Williams. 1st Indian ed. New Delhi : Oriental Books Reprint Corp. : distributed by Munshiram Manoharlal Publishers, 1974. xii, 520 p. ; 23 cm. Reprint of the 1883 ed. published by John Murray, London. [BL2001.M6 1974] 75-901785 ISBN 0-88386-636-6 : 18.00
1. India—Religion. 2. Hinduism. 3. Brahmanism. 4. Cultus, Hindu. I. Title.
Distributed by South Asia Books.

RENOU, Louis, 1896-1966. 294'.0954
Religions of ancient India. New York, Schocken Books [1968, c1953] viii, 139 p. 21 cm. (Jordan lectures in comparative religion, 1) Bibliographical footnotes. [BL2001.2.R4 1968] 68-16660
1. India—Religion. I. Title. II. Series.

BADARAYANA 294.1
The Vedanta Sutras. [2v.] Commentary by Sankara. Tr. by George Thibaut. New York, Dover [1962] 2v. (448;503p.) 22cm. (Sacred bks. of the East v. 34, 38; T994; T995) Contents.pt. 1. Adhyaya I-IIPada I-II)--pt. 2. Adhyaya II (Pada III-IV)-IV. 62-53242 2.00 pap., ea.,
1. Brahmanism. I. Sankaracarya. II. Thibaut, George Frederick William, 1848-1914, ed. and tr. III. Title. IV. Series: The Sacred books of the East, v. 34, 38

BADARAYANA 294.1
The Vedanta Sutras; 2 pts. Commentary by Sankara. Tr. by George Thibaut [Gloucester, Mass., P. Smith, 1963] 2v. (448; 503p.) 22cm. (Sacred bks. of the East, v.34, 38.) (Dover bks. rebound) Contents.Pt. 1 [Adhyaya I-II. (Pada I-II]--Pt. 2. [Adhyaya II-IV (Pada I-IV] 4.00 ea.,
1. Brahmanism. I. Sankaracarya. II. Thibault, George Frederick William, 1848-1914, ed. & tr. III. Title. IV. Series: The Sacred books of the East, v.34, 38

CHATTERJI, Jagadish 294'.1
Chandra.
The wisdom of the Vedas. With an introd. by John Dewey. Wheaton, Ill., Theosophical Pub. House [1973] p. (A Quest book) Published in 1931 under title: India's outlook on life. [BL1115.C45 1973b] 73-8888 ISBN 0-8356-0440-3(pbk.)
1. Vedas. 2. Philosophy, Hindu. I. Title.

CHATTERJI, Jagadish 294'.1
Chandre.
The wisdom of the Vedas. With an introd. by John Dewey. Wheaton, Ill., Theosophical Pub. House [1973] 99 p. 23 cm. Published in 1931 under title: India's outlook on life. [BL1115.C45 1973] 73-8889 ISBN 0-8356-0214-1 3.95
1. Vedas. 2. Philosophy, Hindu.

CHATTOPADHYAYA, Kshetresh 294'.1
Chandra, 1896-1974.
Studies in Vedic and Indo-Iranian religion and literature / by Kshetresh Chandra Chattopadhyaya ; edited by Vidya Niwas Misra. 1st ed. Varanasi : Bharatiya Vidya Prakasana, 1976- v. : ill. ; 22 cm. Includes bibliographical references. [BL1115.C455 1976] 76-905840 Rs45.00 (v. 1.)
1. Vedas—Criticism, interpretation, etc.—Addresses, essays, lectures. I. Misra, Vidyaniwas, 1926- II. Title.

GOSVAMI, Satsvarupa 294'.1
Dasa, 1939-
Readings in Vedic literature : the tradition speaks for itself / by Satsvarupa dasa Gosvami. New York : Bhaktivedanta Book Trust, [1977] p. cm. Includes indexes. Bibliography: p. [BL1107.G67] 76-24941 ISBN 0-912776-88-9 pbk. : 1.95
1. Vedic literature—Addresses, essays, lectures. 2. Hinduism—Addresses, essays, lectures. I. Title.

GOSVAMI, Satsvarupa 294'.1
Dasa, 1939-
Readings in Vedic literature : the tradition speaks for itself / by Satsvarupa dasa Gosvami. New York : Bhaktivedanta Book Trust, [1977] p. cm. Includes indexes. Bibliography: p. [BL1107.G67] 76-24941 ISBN 0-912776-88-9 pbk. : 1.95
1. Vedic literature—Addresses, essays, lectures. 2. Hinduism—Addresses, essays, lectures. I. Title.

KEITH, Arthur Berriedale, 294'.1
1879-1944.
The religion and philosophy of the Veda and Upanishads. Westport, Conn., Greenwood Press [1971] 2 v. (xviii, 683 p.) 27 cm. Reprint of the 1925 ed. Includes bibliographical references. [BL1150.K43 1971] 71-109969 ISBN 0-8371-4475-2
1. Vedas. 2. Upanishads. 3. Philosophy, Hindu. 4. India—Religion. I. Title.

MACDONELL, Arthur Anthony, 294'.1
1854-1930.
Vedic mythology. New York, Gordon Press, 1974. 174 p. 24 cm. (Series: Buhler, Georg, 1837-1898, ed. Grundriss der indo-arischen Philologie und Altertumskunde, Bd. 3, Hft. 1 A.) Reprint of the 1897 ed. published by K. J. Trubner, Strassburg, which was issued as Bd. 3, Hft. 1 A, of Grundriss der indo-arischen Philologie und Altertumskunde, hrsg. von G. Buhler. [BL2001.M23 1974] 74-8799 ISBN 0-87968-153-5 29.95 (lib. bdg.)
1. Mythology, Hindu. I. Title. II. Series.

MALKANI, Ghanshamdas 294.1
Rattanmal
Philosophy of the self; or, A system of idealism based upon Advait Vedanta. New York, Johnson Reprint [1966] vi, 218, iv p. 18cm. Twelve lectures delivered at the Indian Inst. of Phil. between July 1938 & March 1939. [B132.A3M33] 4.00 pap.,
1. Advaita. I. Title.

PANDIT, Madhav Pundalik, 294'.1
1918-
Gems from the Veda / M. P. Pandit. Madras : Ganesh, 1973. x, 102 p. ; 22 cm. Label mounted on t.p.: Distributed by Vedanta Press, Hollywood, Calif. English and Sanskrit. [BL1146.P23G43] 75-300714 2.50
1. Hindu meditations. I. Title.

SANTUCCI, James A. 294'.1
An outline of Vedic literature / by James A. Santucci. Missoula, Mont. : Published by Scholars Press for the American Academy of Religion, c1976. ix, 69 p. ; 24 cm. (Aids for the study of religion series; no. 5) Bibliography: p. ix. [BL1110.S35] 76-27859 ISBN 0-89130-085-6 pbk. : 3.00
1. Vedic literature—History and criticism. 2. Vedic literature—Bibliography. I. Title. II. Series.

STEIN, William Bysshe, 294.1
1915- ed.
Two Brahman sources of Emerson and Thoreau: Rajah Rammohun Roy, Translation of several principal books, passages, and texts of the Veds (1832). William Ward, A. view of the history, literature, and mythology of the Hindoos. part III, section XIII Of the six Darshanas (1822). Facsimile repro. ed., introd., by William Bysshe Stein. Gainesville, Fla., Scholars' Facsimiles, 1967. xx, viii, 118, 113-292p. 22cm. Orig. t. ps. have imprints: London Parbuty, Allen, &. Co., 1832, and London, Printed for Kingsbury, Parbury, and Allen, 1822, respectively. [BL1107.S7] 67-10340 9.00
1. Hinduism—Collections. I. Rammohun Roy, raja, 1772?-1833. Translation of several principal books, passages, and texts of the Veds. II. Ward, William, 1769-1823. A view of the history, literature, and mythology of the Hindoos. III. Title.

UPANISHADS, English. 294.1
The Upanishads [Tr., ed.] by Swami Nikhilananda. Abridged ed. New York, Harper [1964, c.1963] 392p. 21cm. (Harper torchbks. The Cloister lib., TB 114) 1.95 pap.,
I. Nikhilananda, Swami, ed. and tr. II. Title.
Contents omitted.

VEDAS. Selections. 294.1
Hymns from the Vedas. Original text and English translation with introd. and notes [by] Abinash Chandra Bose. With a foreword by Sarvepalli Radhakrishnan. Bombay, New York, Asia Pub. House [1966] xv, 387 p. 25 cm. [BL1115.A22B6 1966] SA 66
I. Bose, Abinash Chandra, ed. and tr. II. Title.

THE Vedic experience : 294'.1
Mantramanjari : an anthology of the Vedas for modern man and contemporary celebration / edited and translated with introductions and notes by Raimundo Panikkar, with the collaboration of N. Shanta ... [et al.]. Berkeley : University of California Press, c1977. xxxvii, 937 p. : ill. ; 24 cm. Includes bibliographical references and indexes. [BL1110.V42] 74-16714 ISBN 0-520-02854-6 : 30.00
1. Hinduism—Sacred books—Collected works. I. Panikkar, Raymond, 1918-

ARNOLD, Edward Vernon, 294'.12
1857-1926.
The Rigveda. New York, AMS Press [1972] 56 p. 19 cm. Reprint of the 1900 ed., which was issued as no. 9 of the Popular studies in mythology, romance and folklore. Bibliography: p. 39-42. [PK3017.A7 1972] 73-139172 ISBN 0-404-53509-7 5.50
1. Vedas. Rigveda—Criticism, interpretation, etc. I. Title. II. Series: Popular studies in mythology, romance and folklore, no. 9.

VEDAS. Rgveda. English. 294'.12
Selections.
Hymns from the Rig-Veda / translated by Jean Marie Alexandre Le Mee. 1st ed. New York : Knopf, 1975. p. cm. [PK3016.A2E5 1975] 75-9541 ISBN 0-394-49354-0 : 12.50 ISBN 0-394-73055-0 pbk. : 5.95
I. Le Mee, Jean Marie Alexandre, 1931- II. Title.

DESAI, Gandabhai 294'.14
Girijashanker, 1896-
Thinking with the Yajurveda [by] Gandabhai G. Desai. Bombay, New York, Asia Pub. House [1967] xxv, 184 p. 22 cm. Bibliography: p. [173]-178. [BL1115.D38] SA 68 20.00
1. Vedas. Yajurveda—Criticism, interpretation, etc. I. Title.

VEDAS. Atharvaveda. 294'.15
English.
Hymns of the Atharva-Veda, together with extracts from the ritual books and the commentaries. Translated by Maurice Bloomfield. New York, Greenwood Press [1969] lxxiv, 716 p. 23 cm. (The Sacred books of the East [v. 42]) Bibliographical footnotes. [PK3406.E5 1969] 69-14131 ISBN 0-8371-1879-4
I. Bloomfield, Maurice, 1855-1928, ed. II. Title. III. Series.

BRAHMANAS. 294'.2
Aitareyabrahmana. English.
The Aitareya Brahmanam of the Rigveda, containing the earliest speculations of the Brahmans on the meaning of the sacrificial prayers, and on the origin, performance and sense of the rites of the Vedic religion. Edited, translated and explained, with pref., introductory essay, and a map of the sacrificial compound at the Soma sacrifice, by Martin Haug. Allahabad, Panini Office, 1922. [New York, AMS Press, 1974] lv, 368 p. illus. 23 cm. Original ed., a reprint of Haug's translation of 1863, minus the Sanskrit text, issued as extra v. 4 of The Sacred books of the Hindus. Includes Sayana's commentary, the Madhaviyavedarthaprakasa. [BL1119.5.A36E54 1974] 73-3830 ISBN 0-404-57848-9 27.50
I. Haug, Martin, 1827-1876, tr. II. Sayana, son of Mayana, d. 1387. Madhaviyavedarthaprakasa. English. 1974. III. Title. IV. Series: The Sacred books of the Hindus, extra

ASOKA, King of Magadha, 294.3
fl.259B.C.
Edicts; edited and translated by N. A. Nikam and Richard McKeon. [Chicago] University of Chicago Press [1958] xxvii, 68 p. map. 19 cm. (Philosophy and world community; an international collection of texts, v. 2) Bibliography: p. xxii. [BL1450.A813] 59-5748
1. Buddhism. I. Nikam, Narayanrao Appurao, ed. and tr. II. McKeon, Richard Peter, 1900- ed. and tr. III. Series.

ASVAGHOSA. Buddhacarita. 294.3
English.
Buddhist Mahayana texts. Delhi, Motilal Banarsidass [1965] xiii, 207 xxvi, 208 p. 23 cm. (The sacred books of the East, v. 49) UNESCO collection of representative works: Indian series. Contents.CONTENTS OMITTED. Bibliographical footnotes. [BL1410.B87] S A
1. Buddha and Buddhism — Sacred books. I. Sukhavativyuha. II. Vajracchedika. III. Prajnaparmitas. IV. Amitayurdhyanasutra. V. Cowell, Edward Byles, 1826-1903, ed. and tr. VI. Miller, Friedrick Max, 1823-1900, ed. and tr. VII. Takakusu, Junjirao, tr. VIII. Title. IX. Title: Mahayana texts. X. Series: The sacred books of the East (Delhi) v. 49. Series: UNESCO collection of representative works: Indian series

BAHM, Archie J 294.3
Philosophy of the Buddha. New York, Harper [1959, c1958] 175p. 22cm. Includes bibliography. [BL1451.2.B2 1959] 58-12935
1. Buddha and Buddhism. I. Title.

BAHM, Archie J. 294.3
Philosophy of the Buddha. New York, Collier [1962, c.1958] 157p. (AS195V) Bibl. .95 pap.,
1. Buddha and Buddhism. I. Title.

BENZ, Ernst, 1907- 294.3
Buddhism or communism; which holds the future of Asia? Tr. from German by Richard and Clara Winston. Garden City, N.Y. Doubleday [1966, c.1963, 1965] 185p. 18cm. [BL1459.S7B43] 65-13094 .95 pap.,
1. Buddhism and state. 2. Communism and Buddhism. I. Title.

BENZ, Ernst, 1907- 294.3
Buddhism or communism: which holds the future of Asia?Tr. from German by Richard and Clara Winston [1st ed. in the U. S. A.] Garden City, N. Y., Doubleday, 1965 [c.1963, 1965] 234p. 22cm. [BL1459.S7B43] 65-13094 4.50
1. Buddhism and state. 2. Communism and Buddhism. I. Title.

BERRY, Thomas Mary, 1914- 294.3
Buddhism, by Thomas Berry. [1st ed.] New York, Hawthorn Books [1967] 187 p. 21 cm. (Twentieth century encyclopedia of Catholicism, v. 145. Section 15: Non-Christian beliefs) Includes bibliographies. [BL1451.2.B39] 66-15226
1. Buddha and Buddhism. I. Title. II. Series: The Twentieth century encyclopedia of Catholicism, v. 145

BERRY, Thomas Mary, 1914- 294.3
Buddhism / by Thomas Berry. New York : Crowell Co., 1975, c1967. 187, [2] p. ; 21 cm. Reprint of the ed. published by Hawthorn Books, New York, which was issued as v. 145 of Twentieth century encyclopedia of Catholicism. Bibliography: p. [185]-[189] [BQ4022.B47 1975] 75-10518 ISBN 0-8152-0384-5 pbk. : 2.95
1. Buddhism. I. Title. II. Series: The Twentieth century encyclopedia of Catholicism ; v. 145.

BEYER, Stephan, comp. 294.3
The Buddhist experience; sources and interpretations. Encino, Calif., Dickenson Pub. Co. [1974] vii, 274 p. illus. 23 cm. (The Religious life of man series) [BQ4012.B49] 73-93289 ISBN 0-8221-0127-0 4.95 pbk.
1. Buddha and Buddhism. 2. Buddhist literature. I. Title.

BUDDHIST studies in honour 294.3
of I. B. Horner / edited by L. Cousins, A. Kunst, and K. R. Norman. Dordrecht ; Boston : D. Reidel Pub. Co., c1974. xi, 239 p. ; 23 cm. "Selected bibliography of publications by I. B. Horner": p. ix-xi. [BQ4055.B853] 74-77963 ISBN 90-277-0473-2 lib.bdg. : 33.00
1. Horner, Isaline Blew, 1896- 2. Buddha and Buddhism—Addresses, essays, lectures. I. Horner, Isaline Blew, 1896- II. Cousins, L. III. Kunst, Arnold. IV. Norman, K. R.

BUDDHIST thought and Asian 294.3
civilization : essays in honor of Herbert V. Guenther on his sixtieth birthday / edited by Leslie S. Kawamura and Keith Scott. Emeryville, Calif. : Dharma Pub., c1977. xviii, 307 p. : ill. ; 23 cm. "Herbert V. Guenther's publications": p. [xiii]-xviii. Includes bibliographical references. [BQ120.B824] 77-71194 ISBN 0-913546-51-8 : 19.95
1. Guenther, Hervert V.—Addresses, essays, lectures. 2. Buddhism—Addresses, essays, lectures. I. Guenther, Herbert V. II. Kawamura, Leslie S. III. Scott, Keith, 1937-

BURTT, Edwin Arthur, 1892- 294.3
ed.
The teachings of the compassionate Buddha; edited with introd. and notes. [New York] New American Library [1955] 217 p. 18 cm. (A Mentor religious classic) Includes bibliography. [BL1410.B94] 55-5474
1. Buddha and Buddhism—Sacred books. I. Title.

CH'EN, Kenneth Kuan Sh'eng, 294.3
1907-
Buddhism; the light of Asia, by Kenneth K.S. Ch'en. Woodbury, N. Y., Barron's Educational Series, Inc. [1968] viii, 297 p. 21 cm. (Barron's compact studies of world religions, 272) Bibliography: p. 289-292. [BL1451.2.C5] 67-30496
1. Buddhism. I. Title.

CH'EN, Kenneth Kuan 294.3
Sheng, 1907-
Buddhism; the light of Asia, by Kenneth K. S. Ch'en. Woodbury, N.Y., Barron's Educational Series, inc. [1968] viii, 297 p. 21 cm. (Barron's compact studies of world religions, 272) Bibliography: p. 289-292. [BL1451.2.C5] 67-30496
1. Buddha and Buddhism. I. Title.

CONZE, Edward, 1904- 294.3
Buddhism; its essence and development. With a pref. by Arthur Waley. New York, Philosophical Library [1951] 212, [12] p. 22 cm. Bibliography: p. [11]-[12] at end. [BL1451.C58 1951a] 51-14081
1. Buddha and Buddhism. I. Title.

CONZE, Edward, 1904- 294.3
Buddhism; its essence and development. With a pref. by Arthur Waley. New York, Harper [1959] 212 p. illus. 21 cm. (Harper torchbooks, TB58) Includes bibliography. [BL1451.2.C6 1959] 59-10345
1. Buddha and Buddhism.

CONZE, Edward, 1904- 294.3
Buddhist texts through the ages. Newly translated from the original Pali, Sanskrit, Chinese, Tibetan, Japanese, and Apabhramsa. Edited in collaboration with I. B. Horner, D. Snellgrove [and] A. Waley. New York, Philosophical Library [1954] 322 p. 23 cm. "Designed as a sequel to Dr. Conze's book, Buddhism." [BL1410.C6 1954a] 54-10622
1. Buddha and Buddhism—Sacred books. I. Title.

CONZE, Edward, 1904- 294.3
Buddhist thought in India; three phases of Buddhist philosophy [Ann Arbor] Univ. of Mich. Pr. [1967, c.1962] 302p. 20cm. (Ann Arbor paperbacks, AA129) Orig. pub. in Britain by Allen & Unwin. Continuation of Buddhist meditation. Bibl. [BL1453] 2.45 pap.,
1. Buddha and Buddhism. 2. Philosophy, Buddhist. 3. Mahayana Buddhism. I. Title.

COOMARASWAMY, Ananda 294.3
Kentish, 1877-1947
Buddha and the gospel of Buddhism. New Hyde Park, N.Y., Univ. Bks. [c.1964] ix, 369p. illus. 24cm. Bibl. 64-16160 10.00
1. Buddha and Buddhism. I. Title.

COOMARASWAMY, Ananda 294.3
Kentish, 1877-1947.
Buddha and the gospel of Buddhism [by] Ananda K. Coomaraswamy. Rev. by Dona Luisa Coomaraswamy. New York, Harper & Row [1964] vii, 369 p. illus. 21 cm. (Harper torchbooks. The Cloister library, TB119) Bibliography: p. 347-349. [BL1451.C6 1964a] 64-56434
1. Buddha and Buddhism. I. Title.

DAHLKE, Paul, 1865-1928. 294.3
Buddhist stories. Translated by the Bhikkhu Silacara. Freeport, N.Y., Books for Libraries Press [1970] 330 p. 21 cm. (Short story index reprint series) Reprint of the 1913 ed. Translation of Buddhistische Erzahlungen. Contents.Contents.—Death and life.—Architect of his fate.—The love of humanity.—Nala the silent.—Renunciation. [BL1455.D3 1970] 71-106285
1. Buddha and Buddhism. I. Title.

*DAVIDS, T. W. Rhys. 294.3
Lectures on the origin and growth of religion, as illustrated by some points in the history of Indian Buddhism. by T. W. Rhys Davids. Allahabad, India, Rachna Prakashan, [1972] 267 p., 22 cm. [BL1420] ISBN 0-8426-0402-2

1. Buddha and Buddhism—India—History. I. Title.
Distributed by Verry, 11.50.

DE BARY, William Theodore, comp. 294.3
The Buddhist tradition in India, China & Japan. Edited by Wm. Theodore De Bary. With the collaboration of Yoshito Hakeda and Philip Yampolsky and with contributions by A. L. Basham, Leon Hurvitz, and Ryusaku Tsunoda. New York, Modern Library [1969] xxii, 417 p. 20 cm. (Readings in Oriental thought) (The Modern library of the world's best books [205]) Bibliography: p. [399]-401. Bibliographical footnotes. [BL1405.D4] 68-29391 2.45
1. Buddha and Buddhism—Collections. I. Title.

DHAMMAPADA. English. 294.3
The wayfarer, an interpretation of the Dhammapada [by] Wesley La Violette. Los Angeles, De Vorss, 1956. 125p. 24cm. [BL1411.D5E6] 56-59217
I. La Violette, Wesley, 1894- II. Title.

DHIRAVAMSA. 294.3
A new approach to Buddhism. Lower Lake, Calif., Dawn Horse Press [1974, c1972] 67 p. port. 22 cm. [BQ4022.D45 1974] 74-81623 ISBN 0-913922-08-0 1.95 (pbk.)
1. Buddha and Buddhism—Addresses, essays, lectures. I. Title.

DICKHOFF, Robert Ernst. 294.3
Agharta, by Robert Ernst Dickhoff, Sungma Red Lama, the messenger of Buddha. Boston, Bruce Humphries [c1951] 106p. illus. 21cm. [BL1455.D49] 52-11789
1. Buddha and Buddhism. I. Title.

**A Dictionary of Buddhism.* 294.3 Introd. by T. O. Ling. New York, Scribner's [1972] x, 277 p. 20 cm. (Lyceum eds.) "The text of this book is taken from A dictionary of comparative religion, ed. by S. G. F. Brandon." [BL1451] ISBN 0-684-13133-1 pap., 2.95
1. Buddhism—Dictionaries. I. Brandon, Samuel George Frederick. A dictionary of comparative religion. II. Title.

DRUMMOND, Richard Henry. 294.3
Gautama the Buddha; an essay in religious understanding. Grand Rapids, Eerdmans [1974] 239 p. 22 cm. Bibliography: p. 219-228. [BQ4132.D78] 73-22281
1. Gautama Buddha—Teachings. 2. Christianity and other religions—Buddhism.

DUMOULIN, Heinrich. 294.3
Buddhism in the modern world / Heinrich Dumoulin, editor, John C. Maraldo, associate editor. New York : Macmillan, c1976. xii, 368 p. ; 24 cm. Newly rev. English translation of the work originally published in German in 1970 under title: Buddhismus der Gegenwart. Includes index. Bibliography: p. 323-349. [BQ4015.D8513] 75-42342 ISBN 0-02-533790-4 : 12.95
1. Buddhism. I. Maraldo, John C., joint author. II. Title.

DUTT, Nalinaksha. 294.3
Early monastic Buddhism. [2d ed.] Calcutta, Firma K. L. Mukhopadhyay, 1971. ii, 311 p. 22 cm. Includes bibliographical references. [BQ4115.D87 1971] 79-924755
1. Gautama Buddha—Teachings. 2. Gautama Buddha. I. Title.
Distributed by Verry pap. 6.00

DUTT, Sukumar, 1891- 294.3
The Buddha and five after-centuries. London, Luzac [dist. Mystic, Conn., Verry, 1965] xxiv, 259p. illus. 22cm. Bibl. [BL1421.1.D8] 65-6660 10.00
1. Buddha and Buddhism—Hist.—To 100 A.D. I. Title.

DUTT, Sukumar, 1891- 294.3
Early Buddhist monachism. [rev.] [dist. New York, Taplinger, 1961] x, 172p. Bibl. 61-2737 5.25
1. Monasticism and religious orders, Buddhist. I. Title.

FACTER, Dolly. 294.3
The doctrine of the Buddha. New York, Philosophical Library [1965] xv, 132 p. 22 cm. [BL1451.2.F3] 65-11949
1. Buddha and Buddhism. I. Title.

FACTER, Dolly 294.3
The doctrine of the Buddha. New York, Philosophical [c.1965] xv, 132p. 22cm. [BL1541.2.F3] 65-11949 4.75
1. Buddha and Buddhism. I. Title.

FAUCETT, Lawrence William. 294.3
Seeking Gotama Buddha in his teachings; an analytical arrangement of passages from the earliest scriptures of Buddhism. [Radnor? Pa., 1962] 73 p. illus. 29 cm. (Selections: Extracts, etc.) "A source book of selections especially from the Dialogues of the Buddha, The kindred sayings, book 1, The Sutta Nipata, The Prakrit Dhammapada, The Vinaya with passages favored by the Emperor Asoka." Bound with the Author's spiritual evolution in India. [Radnor? Pa., 1962] [BL1410.F3] 63-45293
1. Buddha and Buddhism — Sacred books. I. Title.

FLOETHE, Louise Lee. 294.3
A thousand and one Buddhas. Illustrated by Richard Floethe. New York, Farrar, Straus & Giroux [1967] [50] p. col. illus. 21 x 26 cm. "An Ariel book." Tells of the building of the Temple of a Thousand and One Buddhas in Kyoto, conceived and executed by a twelfth century Emperor as an inspiration to peace. [BL1478.5.K9S23] AC 67
1. Kyoto. Renge-o-in Hondo. 2. Buddhist shrines. I. Floethe, Richard, illus. II. Title.

FOUCHER, Alfred Charles Auguste, 1865-1952. 294.3
The life of the Buddha, according to the ancient texts and monuments of India. Abridged translation by Simone Brangier Boas. [1st ed.] Middletown, Conn., Wesleyan University Press [1963] xiv, 272 p. illus. 25 cm. Bibliography: p. [269]-272. [BL1470.F623] 63-17795
1. Gautama Buddha. I. Title.

GARD, Richard Abbott, 1914- ed. 294.3
Buddhism. New York, Washington Sq. [1963, c.1961] 252p. 16cm. (Great religions of modern man. W800) Bibl. .60 pap.,
1. Buddha and Buddhism. I. Title.

GARD, Richard Abbott, 1914- ed. 294.3
Buddhism. New York, G. Braziller, 1961. 256 p. 21 cm. (Great religions of modern man) Includes bibliography. [BL1405.G3] 61-15499
1. Buddha and Buddhism.

[GRAY, Terence James Stannus] 294.3
Open secret [by] Wei Wu Wei [pseud.] [Hong Kong] Hong Kong Univ. Pr. [New York, Oxford, c.1965] xi, 194p. 24cm. [BL1493.G7] 65-8876 3.00 pap.,
1. Zen Buddhism. I. Title.

GRIMM, George, 1868-1945. 294.3
The doctrine of the Buddha; the religion of reason and meditation, by George Grimm. Edited by M. Keller-Grimm & Max Hoppe. [Translated by Bhikkhu Silacara.] Delhi, Motilal Banarsidass [1973] vi, 413 p. 25 cm. Reprint of the first English edition published in Berlin in 1958. Translation of Die Lehre des Buddho, due Religion der Vernuft und der Meditation. [BL1451.2.G713 1973]
1. Buddha and Buddhism. 2. Philosophy, Hindu. I. Title.
Available from Verry, Mystic, Conn., for 10.50. L.C. card no. for the 1958 (German) edition: 59-2071. ISBN 0-8426-0489-8.

HALL, Manly Palmer, 1901- 294.3
Buddhism and psychotherapy, by Manly P. Hall. 1st ed. Los Angeles, Philosophical Research Society [1967] 324 p. illus. 24 cm. [BL1475.P7H3] 67-1347
1. Buddha and Buddhism—Psychology. I. Title.

HUMPHREYS, Christmas, 1901- 294.3
Exploring Buddhism. Wheaton, Ill., Theosophical Pub. House [1975, c1974] 191 p. 21 cm. (A Quest book) [BQ4022.H85 1975] 74-12206 ISBN 0-8356-0454-3 2.50 (pbk.).
1. Buddha and Buddhism. I. Title.

HUMPHREYS, Christmas, 1901- 294.3
An invitation to the Buddhist way of life for Western readers. New York, Schocken Books [1969] 223 p. 23 cm. Title on spine: The Buddhist way of life. Bibliographical footnotes. [BL1451.2.H79] 74-75222 7.95
1. Buddha and Buddhism. I. Title. II. Title: The Buddhist way of life.

HUMPHREYS, Christmas, 1901- 294.3
Studies in the middle way; being thoughts on Buddhism applied. 3d ed. London, Pub. for the Buddhist Soc. by Allen & Unwin [dist. Mystic, Conn., Verry, 1964, c.1959] 169p. 23cm. 64-57303 3.00 bds.,
1. Buddha and Buddhism. I. Title.

HUMPHREYS, Christmas [Travers Christmas Humphreys] 1901- ed. 294.3
The wisdom of Buddhism. NewYork, Random House [1961, c.1960] 280p. Bibl. 61-12139 4.95
1. Buddha and Buddhism. I. Title.

HUNG, Ying-ming, fl. 1596. 294.3
A Chinese garden of serenity [reflections of a Zen Buddhist] Epigrams from the Ming dynasty 'Discourses on vegetable roots.' Tr. by Chao Tze-chiang. Mount Vernon, N.Y., Peter Pauper [1963, c.1959] 60p. 19cm. 63-6506 1.00
1. Buddhist meditations. I. Title.

HUNT, Ernest, 1876- 294.3
Buddhist sermons. Honolulu, T. Ichinose [1955- v. illus. 21cm. [BL1453.H8] 55-32271
1. Buddha and and Buddhism. I. Title.

HUNT, Ernest, 1876- 294.3
Buddhist stories for children, by E. K. Shinkaku Hunt. Illus. by Eli R. Marozzi. [Honolulu] T. Ichinose, c1959. 73p. illus. 24cm. [BL1455.H85] 59-51375
1. Buddha and Buddhism—Juvenile literature. I. Title.

JACOBSON, Nolan Pliny 294.3
Buddhism: the religion of analysis. New York, Humanities [1966] 202p. 19cm. Bibl. [BL1451.2.J3] 65-22665 5.00 bds.,
1. Buddha and Buddhism. I. Title.

JACOBSON, Nolan Pliny. 294.3
Buddhism: the religion of analysis. New York, Humanities Press, 1965 [i.e. 1966] 202 p. 19 cm. Bibliography: p. [178]-186. [BL1451.2.J3] 65-22665
1. Buddhism. I. Title.

LATOURETTE, Kenneth Scott, 1884- 294.3
Introducing Buddhism. New York, Friendship Press [1956] 64p. illus. 23cm. [BL1451.L247] 56-10152
1. Buddha and Buddhism. 2. Buddha and Buddhism—Relations— Christianity. 3. Christianity and other religions—Buddhism. I. Title.

LAW, Bimala Churn, 1892- 294.3
The Buddhist conception of spirits. 2d ed., rev. and enl. London, Luzac [dist. Mystic, Conn., Verry, 1965] xi, 114p. 21cm. (Law's res. ser., pub. no.3) First ed., 1923. [BL1475.S65L3] 40-14176 2.50
1. Spirits. 2. Buddha and Buddhism. I. Title.

LEVY, Paul, 1909- 294.3
Buddhism: a "mystery religion"? New York, Schocken Books [1968, c1957] 111 p. 21 cm. (Jordan lectures in comparative religion, 3) Bibliographical footnotes. [BL1453.L4 1968] 68-17561
1. Buddha and Buddhism. I. Title. II. Series.

LING, Trevor Oswald. 294.3
The Buddha : Buddhist civilization in India and Ceylon / Trevor Ling. Harmondsworth ; Baltimore [etc.] : Penguin, 1976. 347 p. : map ; 19 cm. (A Pelican book) Includes index. Bibliography: p. [326]-329. [BQ286.L56 1976] 77-365180 ISBN 0-14-021894-7 : £0.90 ($2.95 U.S.)
1. Buddhism—India. 2. Buddhism—Sri Lanka. 3. Civilization, Buddhist. I. Title.

LING, Trevor Oswald. 294.3
The Buddha : Buddhist civilization in India and Ceylon / Trevor Ling. Baltimore : Penguin [1976c1973] 347p. ; 18 cm. (Pelican books) Includes index. Bibliography: p. 326-329. [BL1420.L56] ISBN 0-14-021894-7 pbk. : 2.95
1. Buddha and Buddhism-India. 2. Buddha and Buddhism-Ceylon. 3. Civilization, Buddhist. I. Title.
L. C. card no. for original edition: 73-165906.

LING, Trevor Oswald. 294.3
The Buddha; Buddhist civilization in India and Ceylon [by] Trevor Ling. New York, Scribner [1973] 287 p. 25 cm. (Makers of new worlds) Bibliography: p. [270]-273. [BQ286.L56 1973b] 73-1353 ISBN 0-684-13401-2 10.00
1. Buddha and Buddhism—India. 2. Buddha and Buddhism—Ceylon. 3. Civilization, Buddhist. I. Title.

LUBAC, Henri de, 1896- 294.3
Aspects of Buddhism; translated by George Lamb. New York, Sheed and Ward, 1954. 192p. 21cm. [BL1453.L8] 54-6142
1. Buddha and Buddhism—Addresses, essays, lectures. I. Title.

MATSUNAMI, Kodo, 1933- 294.3
Introducing Buddhism. [4th] rev. ed. [Honolulu] Jodo Mission of Hawaii [1973] 304 p. illus. 19 cm. "What to read on Buddhism": p. [273]-287. [BQ4022.M37 1973] 73-80081 5.00
1. Jodoshu. 2. Buddha and Buddhism. I. Title.

MATSUNAMI, Kodo, 1933- 294.3
Introducing Buddhism / by Kodo Matsunami. Rev. ed. Rutland, Vt. : C. E. Tuttle Co., 1976. 304 p., [4] leaves of plates : ill. ; 19 cm. Includes indexes. Bibliography: p. [273]-287. [BQ4022.M37 1976] 75-28970 ISBN 0-8048-1192-X : 3.95
1. Buddhism. 2. Jodoshu. I. Title.

MILINDAPANHA. 294.3
The questions of King Milinda [2v.] Tr. from Pali by T. W. Rhys Davids. New York, Dover [1963] 2v. (various p.) 22cm. (Sacred bks. of the East, v. 35-6) 63-19514 2.25 pap., ea.,
I. Davids, Thomas William Rhys, 1843-1922, ed. and tr. II. Title. III. Series: The Sacred books of the East (New York)

MILINDAPANHA 294.3
The questions of King Milinda; 2 pts. Tr. from Pali by T. W. Rhys Davids [Gloucester, Mass., P. Smith, 1964] 2v. 22cm. (Sacred bks. of the East, v.35-36) (Dover bks. rebound) 4.25 ea.,
I. Davids, Thomas William Rhys, 1843-1922; ed., and tr. II. Title. III. Series: The Sacred books of the East (New York) v.35-36

MORGAN, Kenneth William, ed. 294.3
The path of the Buddha; Buddhism interpreted by Buddhists. New York, Ronald Press Co. [1956] x, 432p. maps (on lining papers) 22cm. Bibliography: p. 401-405. [BL1420.M6] 56-9981
1. Buddha and Buddhism—Hist. I. Title.

NAYLOR, David, 1935- 294.3
Thinking about Buddhism / [by] David Naylor. Guildford (Luke House, Farnham Rd, Guildford, Surrey) : Lutterworth Educational, 1976. 56 p. : ill., map, ports. ; 21 cm. (World religions) Bibliography: p. 10. [BQ4022.N38] 76-372774 ISBN 0-7188-2158-0 : £1.50
1. Buddhism. I. Title.

OBEYESEKERE, Gananath. 294.3
The two wheels of Dhamma; essays on the Theravada tvadition in India and Ceylon, by Gananath Obeyesekere [and] Frank Reynolds. Bardwell L. Smith, editor. Chambersburg, Pa., American Academy of Religion, 1972] 121 p. 24 cm. (AAR studies in religion, no. 3) Includes bibliographical references. [BQ356.O2] 70-188906 2.50 (pbk.)
1. Buddha and Buddhism—Ceylon—Addresses, essays, lectures. 2. Buddha and Buddhism—Early Buddhism—Addresses, essays, lectures. I. Reynolds, Frank, 1930- II. Smith, Bardwell L., 1925- III. Title. IV. Series.
Contents omitted.

PARDUE, Peter A. 294.3
Buddhism; a historical introduction to Buddhist values and the social and political forms they have assumed in Asia [by] Peter A. Pardue. New York, Macmillan [1971] xii, 203 p. 22 cm. Bibliography: p. [181]-195. [BL1420.P37] 79-158931 5.95
1. Buddha and Buddhism—History. I. Title.

PEIRIS, William. 294.3
The Western contribution to Buddhism. With a foreword by H. Saddhatissa Maha Thera. [1st ed.] Delhi, Motilal Banarsidass [1973] xxviii, 287 p. 48 ports. 23 cm. Includes bibliographical references. [BQ164.P44] 73-91127 ISBN 0-842-60537-1
1. Scholars, Buddhist. 2. Buddha and Buddhism—Study and teaching. I. Title.
Distributed by Verry, 15.00

PERCHERON, Maurice, 1891- 294.3
Buddha and Buddhism. Translated by Edmund Stapleton. New York, Harper [c1957] 191p. illus. 18cm. (Men of wisdom, 3) [BL1451.P413] 58-5221
1. Buddha and Buddhism. I. Title.

POLITELLA, Joseph, 1910- 294.3
Buddhism, a philosophy of the spirit and a way to the eternal. Iowa City, Sernoll [c.1966] viii, 144p. 22cm. (Crucible bks.) Bibl. [BL1451.2.P6] 67-850 2.25 pap.,
1. Buddha and Buddhism. I. Title.

POLITELLA, Joseph, 1910- 294.3
Buddhism, a philosophy of the spirit and a way to the eternal. Iowa City, Sernoll [c1966] viii, 144 p. 22 cm. (Crucible books) Bibliography: p. 133. [BL1451.2.P6] 67-850
1. Buddha and Buddhism. I. Title.

PREBISH, Charles S. 294.3
Buddhism—a modern perspective / edited by Charles S. Prebish. University Park : Pennsylvania State University Press, [1975] xv, 330 p. ; 23 cm. Includes index. Bibliography: p. [311]-318. [BQ4012.P73] 74-26706 ISBN 0-271-01185-8 : 14.50 ISBN 0-271-01195-5 pbk. : 7.95
1. Buddha and Buddhism. I. Title.

[RAS-CHUN] 294.3
Tibet's great yogi, Milarepa. A biography from the Tibetan, being the Jetsun-kahbum, or biographical history of Jetsun-Milarepa, according to the late Lama Kazi Dawa Samdup's English rendering, edited with introd. and annotations by W. Y. Evans-Wentz. 2d ed. London, New York, Oxford University Press, 1951. xxviii, 315p. illus. (1 col.) 23cm. [BL1411.R3E] A54
1. Mi-la Ras-pa, 1068-1122. I. Lamaism. II.

Zia-ba-Beamgrub, Kaxi, 1868-1922, tr. III. Wentx, Walter Yeeling Evans, ed. IV. Title.

RNAM-PAR-GROL-BAHI lam-las 294.3
sByans-pahi yon-tan bsTan-pa.
Vimuktimarga dhutaguna-nirdesa; a Tibetan text critically edited and translated into English by P. V. Bapat. Bombay, New York, Asia Pub. House [1964] xxx, 123 p. 25 cm. (Delhi University Buddhist studies, no. 1) added t. p. in Tibetan. Attributed by the editor to Upatissa. Another issue, published in New York, BL1478.N313 1964a [BL1478.N313] SA64
1. Monasticism and religious orders, Buddhist — Rules. I. Upatissa, supposed author. II. Bapat, Purushottam Vishvanath, ed. III. Title. IV. Series: Delhi. University. Buddhist studies, no.1

ROBINSON, Richard H., 1926- 294.3
The Buddhist religion; a historical introduction [by] Richard H. Robinson. Belmont, Calif., Dickenson Pub. Co. [1970] vi, 136 p. 23 cm. (The Religious life of man) Bibliography: p. 117-128. [BL1451.2.R6] 79-103033
1. Buddha and Buddhism. I. Title.

ROBINSON, Richard H., 1926- 294.3
The Buddhist religion : a historical introduction / Richard H. Robinson, Willard L. Johnson. 2d ed. Encino, Calif. : Dickenson Pub. Co., c1977. xi, 243 p. : ill. ; 23 cm. (The Religious life of man series) Includes index. Bibliography: p. 226-237. [BQ4012.R6 1977] 76-49233 ISBN 0-8221-0193-9 : 6.50
1. Buddhism. I. Johnson, Willard L., joint author. II. Title.

SADDHATISSA, H. 294.3
The Buddha's way [by] H. Saddhatissa. [1st American ed.] New York, G. Braziller [1972, c1971] 139 p. illus. 22 cm. Bibliography: p. 132-133. [BL1456.21.S23 1972] 71-183184 ISBN 0-8076-0635-9 5.95
1. Buddha and Buddhism—Early Buddhism, ca. 486 B.C.-ca. 100 A.D.—Introductions. I. Title.

SAYINGS of Buddha. 294.3
Illustrated with wood-engravings by Boyd Hanna for the Peter Pauper Press. Mt. Vernon, N. Y. [1957] 61 p. illus. 19 cm. [BL1451.S33] 57-4255
1. Buddha and Buddhism. I. Peter Pauper Press, Mt. Vernon, N. Y. Peter Pauper Press Mount Vernon New York

SCHUON, Frithjof., 1907- 294.3
In the tracks of Buddhism; tr. from French by Marco Pallis. London, Allen & Unwin, 1968. 3-168p. 23cm. Tr. of various works. Bibl. [BL1451.2.S313] 68-85847 4.25 bds.,
1. Buddha and Buddhism. 2. Buddha and Buddhism—Relations—Shinto. 3. Shinto—Relations—Buddhism. I. Title.
Distributed by Humanities, New York.

SHAFTEL, Oscar. 294.3
An understanding of the Buddha. New York, Schocken Books [1974] viii, 247 p. 21 cm. Bibliography: p. [236]-244. [BQ4012.S5] 72-80041 ISBN 0-8052-3544-2 8.50
1. Buddha and Buddhism. I. Title.

SHCHERBATSKOI, Fedor 294.3
Ippolitovich, 1866-1942
The central conception of Buddhism, and the meaning of the word 'dharma,' by Th. Stcherbatsky. [3d ed., dist. S. Pasadena, Calif., Hutchins Oriental Bks., 1961] 99p. Bibl. 61-59841 3.50
1. Buddha and Buddhism. I. Title.

SMITH, Frederick Harold. 294.3
The Buddhist way of life, its philosophy and history. London, New York. Hutchinson's University Library, 1951. 189 p. 19 cm. (Hutchinson's university library, World religions) [BL1451.S55] 51-7707
1. Buddha and Buddhism. I. Title.

STRAUSS, C. T. 294.3
The Buddha and his doctrine, by C. T. Strauss. Port Washington, N.Y., Kennikat Press [1970] vii, 116 p. illus. 19 cm. Reprint of the 1923 ed. [BL1451.S7 1970] 79-102584
1. Buddha and Buddhism. I. Title.

STRYK, Lucien, comp. 294.3
World of the Buddha; a reader, edited with introd. and commentaries by Lucien Stryk. [1st ed.] Garden City, N.Y., Doubleday, 1968. lvi, 423 p. 22 cm. Includes selections from the Tripitaka and other Buddhist works. [BL1415.5.S8] 68-11766
1. Buddhist literature. I. Tripitaka. English. Selections. II. Title.

SUZUKI, Daisetz Teitaro, 294.3
1870-
Essays in Zen Buddhism (second series) With 25 collotype reproductions of old masters. [Edited by Christmas Humphreys] Boston, Beacon Press, 1952. 348p. plates. 19cm. (His Complete works) Bibliographical footnotes. [BL1430.S] A54
1. Zen (Sect) 2. Buddha and Buddhism—China. I. Title.

SUZUKI, Daisetz Teitaro, 294.3
1870-
Living by Zen. London, New York, Rider [1950] 187 p. 19 cm. (His Complete works) [BL1430.S785] A51
1. Zen (Sect) 2. Buddha and Buddhism — China. I. Title.

SZEKELY, Edmond Bordeaux. 294.3
The living Buddha. [Mil Robles, Calif.] Mille Meditations, 1968. 71 p. illus. 31 cm. [BL1455.S9] 68-7932
1. Buddha and Buddhism—Addresses, essays, lectures. I. Title.

TAKADA, Koin, 1924- 294.3
The spirit of Buddhism today. [Adapted by Philip Yampolsky. Tokyo] Tokuma Shoten Pub. Co. [1973] xv, 110 p. 22 cm. "Translated ... selections from three of the author's recent collections of popular essays." Contents.Contents.—As man relates to man.—The heart that respects.—White flowers.—The spirit of almsgiving.—The story of a Buddhist statue in stone.—The ovation that moved me most.—This very form is itself emptiness. [BQ126.T34213] 73-85864 9.95 (U.S.)
1. Buddha and Buddhism—Addresses, essays, lectures. I. Title.
Distributed by Japan Publications Trading Co., San Francisco, for 9.95.

THOMAS, Edward Joseph, 1869- 294.3

The history of Buddhist thought. [2d ed.] New York, Barnes & Noble [1951] xvi, 316 p. illus. 25 cm. (The History of civilization. [Pre-history and antiquity)) Bibliography: p. 293-301. [BL1420IT5] 52-7826
1. Buddha and Buddhism — Hist. I. Title. II. Series: The History of civilization (New York

WALEY, Arthur. 294.3
The real Tripitaka, and other pieces. New York, Macmillan [1952] 291 p. 22 cm. [BL1473.H8W3] 52-8884
1. Hsiian-tsang, 596 (ea.)-664. 2. Tales, Chinese. I. Title.

WALSHE, Maurice O'Connell 294.3
Buddhism for today. New York, Philosophical [1963, c.1962] 143p. 19cm. 64-9518 3.75
1. Buddha and Buddhism. I. Title.

WELCH, Holmes. 294.3
The practice of Chinese Buddhism. Cambridge, Harvard, 1967- v. illus., maps, ports. 25cm. (Harvard East Asian studies. 26) Contents.[1] 1900-1950 Bibl. [BL1430.W4] 67-13256 12.50
1. Buddha and Buddhism—China. I. Title. II. Series: Harvard East Asian series, 26

WELCH, Holmes. 294.3
The practice of Chinese Buddhism. Cambridge, Harvard University Press, 1967- v. illus., maps, ports. 25 cm. (Harvard East Asian studies, 26) Contents.--[1] 1900-1950. Bibliography: v. [1], p. [527]-530. [BL1430.W4] 67-13256
1. Buddha and Buddhism—China. I. Title. II. Series: Harvard East Asian series, 26

ZURCHER, Erik. 294.3
Buddhism: Its origin and spread in words, maps, and pictures. New York, St. Martin's Press [1962] 96 p. illus. 22 cm. Concise histories of world religions] Includes bibliography. [BL1420.Z8] 62-9944
1. Buddha and Buddhism—Hist. I. Title.

ZURCHER, Erik. 294.3
Buddhism: its origin and spread in words, maps. and pictures. New York, St. Martin's [c.1962] 96p. illus. (pt. col.) maps 22cm. (Concise histories of world religions) Bibl. 62-9944 4.00
1. Buddha and Buddhism.—Hist. I. Title.

APPLETON, George 294.3002
On the eightfold path; Christian presence amid Buddhism. New York, Oxford Univ. Press [c.] 1961. 156p. (Christian presence series) Bibl. 61-3398 2.50 bds.,
1. Buddha and Buddhism—Relations—Christianity. 2. Christianity and other religions—Buddhism. I. Title.

APPLETON, George. 294.3002
On the eightfold path; Christian presence amid Buddhism. New York, Oxford University Press, 1961. 156p. 19cm. (Christian presence series) Includes bibliography. [BR128.B8A6 1961] 61-3398
1. Buddha and Buddhism—Relations—Christianity. 2. Christianity and other religions—Buddhism. I. Title.

ARNOLD, Edwin, Sir 1832- 294.3002
1904
The light of Asia; or, The great renunciation (Mahabhinishkramana). Being the life and teaching of Gautama, prince of India and founder of Buddhism (as told in verse by an Indian Buddhist). Garden City, N. Y., Doubleday [1961] 150p. (Dolphin bk. C289) .95 pap.,
1. Buddha and Buddhism—Poetry. I. Title.

RAHULA, Walpola 294.3002
What the Buddha taught. Foreword by Paul Demieville. New York, Grove [1962, c.1959] 103p. illus. 21cm. (Evergreen orig., E-330) Bibl. 62-16338 1.75 pap.,
1. Buddha and Buddhism. I. Title.

RAHULA, Walpola 294.3002
What the Buddha taught. Foreword by Paul Demieville [Gloucester, Mass., Peter Smith, 1963.c.1959] 103p. illus. 21cm. (Evergreen orig. E-330 rebound) Bibl. 3.75
1. Buddha and Buddhism. I. Title.

RAHULA, Walpola. 294.3002
What the Buddha taught, by Walpola Sri Rahula. Foreward by Paul Demieville Revised edition New York, Grove Press [1974, c1959] xvi, 151 p. illus. 21 cm. (Evergreen) [BL1451.2R3 1974] 73-21017 ISBN 0-394-17827-0
1. Buddha and Buddhism. I. Title.
Distributed by Random House for 2.95 (pbk.).

BUDDHIST temples in 294.30035
Japan: Nara. [Photogs. by Ken Domon, others. Dist. New York, Perkins Oriental, 1962, c.1961] 315p. illus. (pt. col.) 36cm. Japanese text. English title on box. 4-page leaflet inserted 'An English language supplement to Buddhist temples of Japan: Nara.' J62 18.00, bxd.
1. Temples—Japan—Nara (City) 2. Temples, Buddhist. I. Domon, Ken, 1909- II. Fukuyama, Toshio, 1905-

BUDDIST temples in 294.30035
Japan: Kroto. [Photgs. by Yoshio Watanabe, Yukio Futagawa. Dist. New York, Perkins Oriental, 1962, c.1961] 311 p. illus. (pt. col.) 36 cm. Japanese text. English title on box. 4-page leaflet inserted "An English language supplement to Buddist temples of Japan: Kroto. J62 18.00, bxd.
1. Temples—Japan—Kroto. 2. Temples—Buddhist. I. Watanabe, Yoshio, 1907- II. Fukuyama, Toshio, 1905-

HAGA, Koshiro, 1908- 294.30035
Zen temples in Kyoto; the thought and history [Dist. New York 1, 255 Seventh Ave., Perkins Oriental Bks., 1962] 283p. illus. 22cm. Japanese text, with summary in English. J62 3.50 bds.,
1. Kuzunishi, Sosei. I. Title.

NIKKO; 294.30035
the fine art and history, by Y. Okada [other. New York 1, 255 Seventh Ave., Perkins Oriental Bks., 1962] 256p. illus. (pt. col.) 22cm. Japanese text, with summary in English. Added t.p. J62 3.50 bds.,
1. Nikko, Japan (Tochigi Prefecture) I. Okada, Jo, 1911- II. Kuzunishi, Sosei.

DUTT, Sukumar, 1891- 294.3004
Buddhist monks and monasteries of India; their history and their contribution to Indian culture. London, G. Allen and Unwin [dist. New York, Hillary House, 1963. c.1962] 397p. illus., maps. 24cm. Bibl. 63-24879 10.00
1. Monasticism and religious orders, Buddhist. I. Title.

THE way of action; 294.3005
a working philosophy for Western life. New York, Macmillan, 1960[ ] 195p. illus. 23cm. (Bibl.: p.193-195 and Bibl. footnotes) 60-3965
1. Buddha and Buddhism. I. umphreys, Christmas, [Travers Christmas Humphreys]

CONZE, Edward [Name 294.30082
orig.: Eberhard Julius Dietrich Conze 1904- ed.
Buddhist texts through the ages. Tr. from Pali, Sanskrit, Chinese, Tibetan, Japanese, and Apabhramsa. Ed. with I. B. Horner, D. Snellgrove, A. Waley. New York, Harper [1964] 322p. 21cm. (Cloister lib., TB113) Bibl. 1.85 pap.,
1. Buddha and Buddhism—Sacred books (Selections: Extracts, etc.) I. Title.

FEER, Leon [Henri Leon 294.30082
Feer] 1830-1902
A study of the Jatakas, analytical and critical. Tr. by G. M. Foulkes from the French article in the Journal asiatique. Calcutta, Susil Gupta [dist. Pasadena, Calif., Hutchins, 1963] 126p. 22cm. Verbatim English version of the author's orig. French article, which first appeared in the two issues of the Journal asiatique, May-June and August-September 1875. SA 63 4.50
1. Jatakas. I. Title.

JATA KAS 294.30082
Ten Jatakas stories, each illustrating one of the ten paramita with Pali text. Introd., English tr. by I. B. Horner. London, Luzac [dist. Mystic, Conn., Verry, 1965] 93p. illus. 22cm. [BL1411.J3E65] 59-44935 5.00
I. Horner, Isaline Blew, 1896- ed. and tr. II. Title.

WARREN, Henry Clarke, 294.30082
1854-1899, ed. and tr.
Buddhism in translations passages selected from the Buddhist sacred books and translated from the original Pali into English. New York, Atheneum, 1963 [1896] xx, 496 p. 19 cm. [BL1410.W3] 63-879
1. Buddha and Buddhism — Sacred books (Selections: Extracts, etc.) I. Title.

WARREN, Henry Clarke, 294.30082
1854-1899, ed. and tr.
Buddhism in translations; passages selected from the Buddhist sacred books and translated from the original Pali into English. New York, Atheneum, 1963 [c1896] xx, 496 p. 19 cm. [BL1410.W3 1963] 63-879
1. Buddha and Buddhism—Sacred books.

STRENG, Frederick J 294.3'01
Emptiness; a study in religious meaning [by] Frederick J. Streng. Nashville, Abingdon Press [1967] 252 p. 24 cm. (Leadership education series) Bibliography: p. 229-247. [BL1416.N33S7] 67-11010
1. Sunyata. I. Title.

STRENG, Frederick J. 294.3'01
Emptiness; a study in religious meaning [by] Frederick J. Streng. Nashville, Abingdon Press [1967] 252 p. 24 cm. Bibliography: p. 229-247. [BL1416.N33S7] 67-11010
1. Nagarjuna, Siddha. 2. Sunyata. I. Title.

HUMPHREYS, Christmas, 294.3'02'02
1901- comp.
A Buddhist students' manual / edited by Christmas Humphreys. Detroit : Gale Research Co., 1975. p. cm. Reprint of the 1956 ed. published by the Buddhist Society, London. Includes bibliographies. [BQ4020.H85 1975] 76-164352 ISBN 0-8103-4188-3 : 14.00
1. Buddhism—Handbooks, manuals, etc. 2. Buddhism—England—History. I. Title.
Contents omitted.

MACQUITTY, William. 294.3'022'2
Buddha. New York, Viking Press [1969] 128 p. illus. (part col.), col. ports. 26 cm. (A Studio book) Bibliography: p. 128. [BL1455.M33 1969] 77-87246 10.00
1. Buddha and Buddhism—Pictures, illustrations, etc. I. Title.

A Dictionary of 294.3'03
Buddhism. Introd. by T. O. Ling. New York, Scribner [1972] x, 277 p. 22 cm. Extracted from A Dictionary of comparative religion. Includes bibliographical references. [BQ130.D5] 72-37231 ISBN 0-684-12763-6 7.95
1. Buddha and Buddhism—Dictionaries. I. Ling, Trevor Oswald. II. A Dictionary of comparative religion.

HUMPHREYS, Christmas, 294.303
1901-
A popular dictionary of Buddhism. [1st American ed.] New York, Citadel Press [1963] 223 p. 20 cm. Based on A brief glossary of Buddhist terms, by A. C. March. Full name: Travers Christmas Humphreys. [BL1403.H8 1963] 63-16729
1. Buddha and Buddhism — Dictionaries. I. March, Arthur Charles, 1880- A brief glossary of Buddhist terms. II. Title.

HUMPHREYS, Christmas 294.303
[Travers Christmas Humphreys] 1901-
A popular dictionary of Buddhism. New York, Citadel [c.1962, 1963] 223p. 20cm. Based on A brief glossary of Buddhist terms, by A. C. March. 63-16729 4.00
1. Buddha and Buddhism—Dictionaries. I. March, Arthur Charles, 1880- A brief glossary of Buddhist terms. II. Title.

CONZE, Edward, 1904- 294.3'08
Thirty years of Buddhist studies; selected essays. Columbia, University of South Carolina Press [1968] xii, 274 p. 23 cm. Bibliographical footnotes. [BL1451.2.C63 1968] 68-17432
1. Buddha and Buddhism—Addresses, essays, lectures. I. Title.

SHAKU, Soyen. 294.3'08
Sermons of a Buddhist abbot; addresses on religious subjects, including the Sutra of forty-two chapters. Translated from the Japanese MS. by Daisetz Teitaro Suzuki. New York, S. Weiser, 1971. 7, 220 p. port. 21 cm. Reprint of the 1906 ed. Includes bibliographical references. [BL1477.5.S47 1971] 73-166411 ISBN 0-87728-160-2 2.50
1. Buddhist sermons. I. Suzuki, Daisetz Teitaro, 1870-1966, tr. II. Title.

SHAKU, Soyen. 294.3'08
Zen for Americans. Translated by Daisetz Teitaro Suzuki. La Salle, Ill., Open Court [1974, c1906] 7, 220 p. illus. 21 cm. (Open court paperback) Reprint of the 1913 ed. published by Open Court Pub. Co. under title: Sermons of a Buddhist abbot. Includes bibliographical references. [BQ4055.S5 1974] 74-176035 ISBN 0-87548-273-2 2.95 (pbk.)
1. Buddha and Buddhism—Addresses, essays, lectures. I. Title.

HUNT, Ernest, 1876- ed. 294.3082
Short talks on Buddhism, edited by Shinkaku. [Honolulu, T. Ichinose, 1959] 85p. 21cm. [BL1405.H85] 59-51376
1. Buddha and Buddhism—Addresses, essays, lectures. I. Title.

EDWARDES, Michael. 294.3'09
In the blowing out of a flame : the world of the Buddha and the world of man / [by] Michael Edwardes. London : Allen and Unwin, 1976. 208 p. : map ; 23 cm. Includes index. Bibliography: p. [180]-204. [BQ266.E38] 76-362275 ISBN 0-04-294092-3 : £5.50
1. Buddhism—History. I. Title.

SWEARER, Donald K., 294.3'09'04
1934-
Buddhism in transition, by Donald K. Swearer. Philadelphia, Westminster Press [1970] 160 p. 20 cm. Includes bibliographical references. [BL1451.2.S95] 77-120122 5.50
1. Buddha and Buddhism—20th century. I. Title.

SNELLGROVE, David L. 294.3'0922
Four lamas of Dolpo; Tibetan biographies, ed. & tr. by David L. Snellgrove. Cambridge, Harvard, 1967- v. illus., 2 fold. maps, ports. 23cm. Contents.v.1. Introduction & translations. Bibl. [BL1490.A1S62] 67-7913 14.50
1. Lamas. I. Title.

BEAL, Samuel, 1825- 294.3'0951
1889.
Buddhism in China. Freeport, N.Y., Books for Libraries Press [1973] p. Reprint of the 1884 ed., issued in series: Non-christian religious systems. [BQ624.B4 1973] 72-12785 ISBN 0-8369-7129-9
1. Buddha and Buddhism—China. I. Title. II. Series: Non-christian religious systems.

BLOFELD, John Eaton 294.3'0951
Calthorpe, 1913-
The jewel in the lotus : an outline of present day Buddhism in China / by John Blofeld. Westport, Conn. : Hyperion Press, 1975. 193 p., [8] leaves of plates : ill. ; 23 cm. Reprint of the 1948 ed. published for the Buddhist Society by Sidgwick & Jackson, London. [BQ624.B55 1975] 74-10096 ISBN 0-88355-161-6 lib.bdg. : 13.00
1. Buddha and Buddhism—China. I. Title.

CH'EN, Kenneth Kuan 294.3'0951
Sheng, 1907-
The Chinese transformation of Buddhism [by] Kenneth K. S. Ch'en. Princeton, N.J., Princeton University Press [1973] ix, 345 p. 23 cm. Bibliography: p. 305-313. [BQ626.C52] 75-39782 ISBN 0-691-07187-X 15.00
1. Buddha and Buddhism—China. I. Title.

EDKINS, Joseph, 1823- 294.3'0951
1905.
Chinese Buddhism: a volume of sketches, historical, descriptive, and critical. 2d ed., rev. London, K. Paul, Trench, Trubner, 1893. New York, Paragon Book Reprint Corp., 1968. xxxiii, 453 p. 23 cm. [BL1430.E3 1968] 68-28810
1. Buddha and Buddhism—China. I. Title.

OVERMYER, Daniel L., 294.3'0951
1935-
Folk Buddhist religion : dissenting sects in late traditional China / Daniel L. Overmyer. Cambridge, Mass. : Harvard University Press, 1976. xi, 295 p. ; 24 cm. (Harvard East Asian series ; 83) Includes index. Bibliography: p. 261-280. [BQ628.O9 1976] 75-23467 ISBN 0-674-30705-4 : 12.50
1. Buddhism—China—History. 2. China—Religion—History. I. Title. II. Series.

WELCH, Holmes. 294.3'0951
Buddhism under Mao. Cambridge, Mass., Harvard University Press, 1972. xviii, 666 p. illus., maps (on lining papers) 25 cm. (Harvard East Asian series, 69) Bibliography: p. [647]-652. [BQ647.W44] 72-78428 ISBN 0-674-08565-5 15.00
1. Buddha and Buddhism—China (People's Republic of China, 1949-) I. Title. II. Series.

WELCH, Holmes. 294.3'0951
The Buddhist revival in China. With a section of photos. by Henri Cartier-Bresson. Cambridge, Harvard University Press, 1968. vi, 385 p. illus. col. maps (on lining papers) 25 cm. (Harvard East Asian series, 33) Bibliography: p. [355]-360. [BL1431.6.W4] 68-15645 11.95
1. Buddha and Buddhism—China—History. I. Title. II. Series.

WELCH, Holmes. 294.3'0951
The practice of Chinese Buddhism. Cambridge, Harvard University Press, 1967- v. illus., maps, ports. 25 cm. (Harvard East Asian studies, 26) Contents.Contents.—[1] 1900-1950. Bibliography: v. [1], p. [527]-530. [BL1430.W4] 67-13256
1. Buddha and Buddhism—China. I. Title. II. Series: Harvard East Asian series, 26

*ZURCHER, E. 294.30951
The Buddhist conquest of China; the spread and adaptation of Buddhism in early medieval China by E. Zurcher New York Humanities Press, [1973, c1972] 2 v. maps Contents.Contents—Text—Notes, Bibliography, indexes [BL1456] 45.00 set.
1. Buddha and Buddhism—China. I. Title.

ZURCHER, Erik 294.30951
The Buddhist conquest of China; the spread and adaptation of Buddhism in early medieval China, [2v.] Leiden, E. J. Brill, [1959] [New York dist. by The Humanities Press] 2 v. (xii, 468p.) maps. 25cm. (Sinica Leidensia, v. 11) Contents.1. Text.--2. Notes. Bibliography. Indexes Bibliography: p. [441]-447. 59-16762 18.00
1. Buddha and Buddhism—China. I. Title. II. Series.

MATSUNAGA, Daigan. 294.3'0952
Foundation of Japanese Buddhism / by Daigan Matsunaga, Alicia Matsunaga. Los Angeles : Buddhist Books International, [1974- v. ; 23 cm. Includes index. Contents.Contents.—v. 1. The aristocratic age. Bibliography: v. 1. p. [271]-275. [BQ676.M39] 74-83654 12.75
1. Buddha and Buddhism—Japan—History. I. Matsunaga, Alicia, joint author. II. Title.

SAUNDERS, Ernest Dale, 294.3'0952
1919-
Buddhism in Japan, with an outline of its origins in India / by E. Dale Saunders. Westport, Conn. : Greenwood Press, 1977. p. cm. Reprint of the 1964 ed. published by the University of Pennsylvania Press, Philadelphia. Bibliography: p. [BQ676.S28 1977] 77-24539 ISBN 0-8371-9746-5 lib.bdg. : 21.00
1. Buddhism—Japan—History. I. Title.

JOSHI, Lal, Mani. 294.3'0954
Studies in the Buddhistic culture of India during the 7th and 8th centuries A. D. by Lalmani Joshi. [1st ed.] Delhi, Motilal Banarsidass [1967] xli, 538p. 23cm. Revision of the author's thesis, Univ. of Gorakhpur, 1964. Bibl.: p. [459]-495. [BL1424.J6] SA68 9.00
1. Buddha and Buddhism—India. I. Title.
Distributed by Verry, Mystic, Conn.

WARDER, Anthony 294.3'0954
Kennedy.
Indian Buddhism, by A. K. Warder. [1st ed.] Delhi, Motilal Banarsidass [1970] ix, 622 p. maps. 22 cm. Bibliography: p. [519]-562. [BQ270.W37] 75-917116
1. Buddhist doctrines—India—History. I. Title.
Distributed by Verry 18.50

KHOSLA, Sarla. 294.3'0954'6
History of Buddhism in Kashmir. With a foreword by Karan Singh. New Delhi, Sagar Publications, 1972. xv, 188 p. illus. 22 cm. Originally presented as the authoress's thesis, Agra University, 1970. Bibliography: p. [162]-181. [BQ349.K37K54 1972] 72-905677
1. Buddha and Buddhism—Kashmir—History. I. Title.
Distributed by International Scholarly Book Service; ISBN 0-336-00370-6.

MALALGODA, Kitsiri. 294.3'09549'3
Buddhism in Sinhalese society, 1750-1900 : a study of religious revival and change / Kitsiri Malalgoda. Berkeley : University of California Press, c1976. xiii, 300 p. : map ; 25 cm. A revision and expansion of the author's thesis, Oxford, 1970. Includes index. Bibliography: p. 269-284. [BQ372.M34 1976] 74-22966 ISBN 0-520-02873-2 : 15.00
1. Buddhism—Ceylon—History. I. Title.

TAMBIAH, S. J. 294.3'09593
Buddhism and the spirit cults in north-east Thailand, [by] S. J. Tambiah. New York: Cambridge University Press, [1975 c1970] xi., 388 p.: illus., maps; 23 cm. (Cambridge studies in social anthropology; no. 2) [BL2075.T3] 73-108112 ISBN 0-521-09958-7 6.95 (pbk.)
1. Thailand—Religion. 2. Buddha and Buddhism—Relations. I. Title.

LECLERE, Adhemard, 294.3'09596
1853-1917.
Le buddhisme au Cambodge / Adhemard Leclere. New York : AMS Press, [1975] p. cm. Reprint of the 1899 ed. published by E. Leroux, Paris. [BQ452.L4 1975] 76-179215 ISBN 0-404-54843-1
1. Buddha and Buddhism—Cambodia. I. Title.

THIEN An, Thich, 294.3'09597
1926-
Buddhism and Zen in Vietnam in relation to the development of Buddhism in Asia / by Thich Thien-An ; edited, annotated, and developed by Carol Smith. Los Angeles : College of Oriental Studies, Graduate School, 1975. 301 p. : ill. ; 19 cm. Includes index. Bibliography: p. 281-289. [BQ9262.9.V5T45] 74-83391 ISBN 0-8048-1144-X : 12.50
1. Zen Buddhism—Vietnam—History. 2. Buddhism—Vietnam—History. I. Title: Buddhism and Zen in Vietnam ...

THIEN An, Thich, 294.3'09597
1926-
Buddhism and Zen in Vietnam in relation to the development of Buddhism in Asia / by Thich Thien-An ; edited, annotated, and developed by Carol Smith. Los Angeles : College of Oriental Studies, Graduate School, 1975. 301 p. : ill. ; 19 cm. Includes index. Bibliography: p. 281-289. [BQ9262.9.V5T45] 74-83391 ISBN 0-8048-1144-X : 12.50
1. Zen Buddhism—Vietnam—History. 2. Buddhism—Vietnam—History. I. Title: Buddhism and Zen in Vietnam ...

KASHIMA, Tetsuden. 294.3'0973
Buddhism in America : by Tetsuden Kashima. Tetsuden Kashima. Westport, Conn. : Greenwood Press, 1977. xvii, 272 p., [1] leaf of plates : ill. ; 22 cm. (Contributions in sociology ; no. 26) Includes index. Bibliography: p. 257-264. [BQ8712.9.U6K37] 76-57837 ISBN 0-8371-9534-9 lib.bdg. : 17.50
1. Buddhist Churches of America. 2. Sociology, Buddhist—United States. 3. Japanese in the United States. I. Title.

KASHIMA, Tetsuden. 294.3'0973
Buddhism in America : by Tetsuden Kashima. Tetsuden Kashima. Westport, Conn. : Greenwood Press, 1977. xvii, 272 p., [1] leaf of plates : ill. ; 22 cm. (Contributions in sociology ; no. 26) Includes index. Bibliography: p. 257-264. [BQ8712.9.U6K37] 76-57837 ISBN 0-8371-9534-9 lib.bdg. : 17.50
1. Buddhist Churches of America. 2. Sociology, Buddhist—United States. 3. Japanese in the United States. I. Title.

LAYMAN, Emma McCloy, 294.3'0973
1910-
Buddhism in America / Emma McClory Layman. Chicago : Nelson-Hall Publishers, c1976. xvii, 342 p., [4] leaves of plates : ill. ; 24 cm. Includes index. Bibliography: p. 323-329. [BQ732.L39] 76-4566 ISBN 0-88229-166-1 : 17.50
1. Buddhism—United States. I. Title.

ALLEN, George Francis, 294.31
ed. and tr.
The Buddha's philosophy; selections from the Pali canon and an introductory essay [by] G. F. Allen [Y. Siri Nyana) Foreword by A. L. Basham. New York, Macmillan [1959] 194p. illus. 23cm. (bibl.) 59-16992 5.75
1. Buddha and Buddhism. I. Title.

GARBE, Richard von 294.31
India and Christendom; the historical connections between their religions. Translated [from the German] by Lydia Gillingham Robinson. La Salle, Ill., Open Court Pub. Co., [c.]1959. x, 310p. 21cm. Bibl. 60-19257 283-298 3.50
1. Christianity and cther religions—Buddhism. 2. Buddhism—Relations—Christianity. 3. Christianity and other religions—Hinduism. 4. Hinduism—Relations—Christianity. I. Title.

HTIN AUNG, U. 294.31
Folk elements in Burmese Buddhism. London, New York, Oxford University Press, 1962. 140 p. 22 cm. [BL1453.H75] 63-301
1. Buddha and Buddhism. 2. Folk-lore—Burma. I. Title.

HTIN AUNG, U. Maung 294.31
Folk elements in Burmese Buddhism. New York, Oxford [c.]1962. 140p.22cm. Bibl. 63-301 2.90
1. Buddha and Buddhism. 2. Folk-lore—Burma. I. Title.

KING, Winston Lee, 1907- 294.31
A thousand lives away; Buddhism in contemporary Burma. Cambridge, Mass., Harvard, 1964[1965, c.1964] 238p. illus. 23cm. Bibl. [BL1443.K5] 65-2184 5.25
1. Buddha and Buddhism—Burma. I. Title.

RIEKER, Hans Ulrich, 1920- 294.31
Beggar among the dead. Tr. from German by Edward Fitzgerald. [New York, International Publication Service, c.1960, i.e., 1961] 224p. 61-869 6.25
I. Title.

WALTERS, John Beauchamp, 294.31
1903-
The essence of Buddhism. New York [Apollo, 1964, c.1961] 164p. 20cm. (A-93) Bibl. 1.25 pap.,
1. Hinayana Buddhism. I. Title.

WALTERS, John Beauchamp, 294.31
1903-
The essence of Buddhism. New York, Crowell [1962, c.1961] 164p. 20cm. Bibl. 62-12809 2.95 bds.,
1. Hinayana Buddhism. I. Title.

WALTERS, John Beauchamp, 294.31
1903-
Mind unshaken; a modern approach to Buddhism. New Rochelle, N.Y. dist. SportShelf, [1961] 127p. Bibl. 61-19911 4.50 bds.,
1. Hinayana Buddhism. I. Title.

SHATTOCK, E. H. 294.314
An experiment in mindfulness; an English admiral's experiences in a Buddhist monastery. [1st American ed.] New York, Dutton, 1960 [c1958] 158 p. 20 cm. [BL1478.6.S5 1960] 60-6073
1. Meditation (Buddhism] I. Title.

DHAMMAPADA English. 294.315
The Dhammapada, Tr. from the Pali, with an essay on Buddha and the Occident, by Irving Babbitt [New Directions, dist. Philadelphia, Lippincott, 1965, c.1936] x, 122p. 21cm. (NDP188) The present tr. is a rev. of the one first pub. by Max Muller in 1870 and later included in the Sacred books of the East. [BL1411.D5E52] 64-23655 1.45 pap.,
1. Buddha and Buddhism—Addresses, essays, lectures. I. Babbitt, Irving, 1865-1933, tr. II. Muller, Friedrich Max, 1823-1900, tr. III. Buddha and the Occident. IV. Title.

DHAMMAPADA. English. 294.315
The Dhammapada. Translated from the Pali, with an essay on Buddha and the Occident, by Irving Babbitt. [New York] [New Directions Pub. Corp.] [1965, c1936] x, 122 p. 21 cm. (A New Directions paperbook, NDP188) "The present translation is a revision of the one first published by Max Muller in 1870 and later included in ... the Sacred books of the East." [BL1411.D5E52 1965] 64-23655
1. Buddha and Buddhism—Addresses, essays, lectures. I. Babbitt, Irving, 1865-1933, tr. II. Muller, Friedrich Max, 1823-1900, tr. III. Buddha and the Occident.

DHAMMAPADA 294.318
The Gandhari Dharmapada. Ed., introd., commentary by John Brough. New York, Oxford [c.]1962. xxv, 319p. illus. 28cm. (London oriental ser., v. 7) In Prakrit (in Kharosthi script) Bibl. 62-5083 16.80
I. Brough, John, 1917- ed. II. Title. III. Series.

ARYASURA. 294.32
The Gatakamala; or, Garland of birth-stories, by Arya Sura. Translated from the Sanskrit by J. S. Speyer. London, H. Frowde, Oxford university Press Warehouse, 1895. xix, 350 p. 23 cm. (Sacred books of the Buddhists, v. 1) Edited by F. Max Muller. [BL1410.S2 vol. 1] 32-13982
I. Speyer, Jacob Samuel, 1849-1913, tr. II. Muller, Fredrich Max, 1823-1900, ed. III. Title. IV. Series.

BARDO THODOL. 294.32
The Tibetan book of the dead: or, The after-death experiences on the Bardo plane, according to Lama Kazi Dawa-Samdup's English rendering, by W. Y. Evans-Wentz. With a psychological commentary by C. G. Jung, introducing foreword by Lama Anagarika Govinda, and foreword by John Woodruffe [i. e. Woodroffe] 3d ed. London, New York, Oxford University Press, 1957. 1xxxiv, 249p. illus., plates., group port. 23cm. [BL1411.B3E6 1957] 57-3183
I. Zla-ba-Bsam- grub, Kazi, 1868-1922, tr. II. Wentz, Walter Yeeling Evans, ed. III. Title.

BENOIT, Hubert. 294.32
The supreme doctrine; psychological studies in Zen thought. Foreword by Aldous Huxley. New York, Pantheon Books [1955] 248p. illus. 22cm. [BL1432.Z4B42] 55-10286
1. Zen (Sect) I. Title.

DUMOULIN, Heinrich. 294.32
The development of Chinese Zen after the Sixth Patriarch in the light of Mumonkan. Translated from the German with additional notes and appendices by Ruth Fuller Sasaki. New York, First Zen Institute of America, 1953. xxii, 146p. col. front., tables. 26cm. Translation of Die Entwicklung deschinesischen Ch'an nach Huineng im Lichte des Wu-men-kuan. Errata slip inserted. Bibliography: p. 79-86. [BL1432.Z4Ds] 53-44660

1. Hui-k'al, fl. 13th cent. Wu-men-kuan. 2. Zen (Sect) I. Title.

ELIOT, Charles Norton Edgecumbe Sir 294.32
Japanese Buddhism. With a memoir of the author by Harold Parlett. New York, Barnes &Noble, 1959 [i.e.1960] xxxiv, 449p. 23cm. (bibl. footnotes) 60-341 7.00
1. Nichiren, 1222-1282. 2. Buddha and Buddhism—Japan. I. Title.

GETTY, Alice. 294.32
The gods of Northern Buddhism; their history, iconography and progressive evolution through the Northern Buddhist countries. With a general introd. on Buddhism translated from the French of J. Deniker. Illus. from the collection of Henry H. Getty. Rutland, Vt., C. E. Tuttle Co. [1962] 220 p. illus. (part. col.) diagr. 28 cm. Bibliography: p. [203]-207. [BL1483.G4 1962] 62-15617
1. Mahayana Buddhism. 2. Gods, Buddhist. I. Title.

GODDARD, Dwight, 1861-1939, ed. 294.32
A Buddhist bible. Rev. and enl. New York, Dutton, 1952. viii, 677 p. 21 cm. (Selections: Extracts, etc.) [BL1410.G6 1952] 52-7805
1. Buddha and Buddhism—Sacred books I. Title.

GUENTHER, Herbert V 294.32
The life and teaching of Naropa. Translated from the original Tibetan with a philosophical commentary based on the oral transmission. Oxford, Clarendon Press, 1963. xvi, 292 p. 23 cm. (UNESCO collection of representative works; Tibetan series) "This first English translation of the life and teachings of Naropa is based on an old Tibetan edition" of the work by lHa'i btsun-pa Rin-chen rnamrgyal of Brad-dkar. Appendix contains the complete text of the twelve instructions of Nadapada in Tibetan (transliterated) Bibliography: p. [281]-285. [BL1473.N3G83] 63-23887
1. Nadapada. I. lHa'I btsun-pa Rin-chen rNamrgyal, 12th cent. Nadapada. II. Title. III. Series.

GUENTHER, Herbert V. 294.32
The life and teaching of Naropa. Tr. from Tibetan with a philosophical commentary based on the Oral transmission. [New York] Oxford [c.]1963. xvi, 292p. 23cm. (UNESCO collection of representative works; Titbetan ser.) This first English tr. of the life and teachings of Naropa is based on an old Tibetan ed. of the work by lHa'i btsun-pa Rin-chen rnamrgyal of Brad-dkar. Appendix contains the complete text of the twelve instructions of Nadapada in Tibetan (transliterated) Bibl. 63-23887 10.00
1. Nadapada. I. lHa'I btsun-pa Rin-chen rNamrgyal,12th cent. II. Nadapada. III. Title. IV. Series.

HERRIGEL, Eugen, 1884- 294.32
Zen in the art of archery. With an introd. by D. T. Suzuki. Translated by R. F. C. Hull. [New York] Pantheon Books [1953] 109 p. 21 cm. [BL1442.Z4H43] 53-9945
1. Zen Buddhism. 2. Archery. I. Title.

HUMPHREYS, Christmas [Travers Christmas Humphreys 1910- 294.32
Zen Buddhism. New York, Macmillan [1962] 175p. Bibl. 1.25 pap.,
1. Zen (Sect.) I. Title.

THE platform sutra of the sixth patriarch. 294.32
The text of the Tun-huang manuscript with tr. introd., notes, by Philip B. Yampolsky. New York, Columbia 1967. xii, 216, [30] p. 24cm. (Records of civilization: sources and studies. no. 76) Tr. of (romanized); Liu-tsu ta shih fa pao t'an ching) Includes ed. Chinese text based on the MS. in the Stein Collection of Chinese MSS. in the British Mus. (S5475) Prepd. for the Columbia College Program of trs. from the oriental classics. Wm. Theodore de Bary, ed. Bibliography: p. [191]-204. [BL1432.] 8.50
1. Zen Buddhism. 2. 4H8428 294.3'927 I. Hui-Neng, 638-713 II. Yampolsky, Philip B. ed. III. Series.

REPS, Paul, 1895- comp. 294.32
Zen flesh, Zen bones: a collection of Zen & pre-Zen writings. Garden City, N.Y., Doubleday [1961] 174p. illus. (Anchor bk., A233) .95 pap.,
1. Zen (Sect) I. Title.

REPS, Paul, 1895- comp. 294.32
Zen flesh, Zen bones; a collection of Zen & pre-Zen writings. Tokyo, Rutland, Vt., C. E. Tuttle Co. [1957] 211 p. illus. 20 cm. [BL1432.Z4R4] 57-10199
1. Zen Buddhism. I. Title.

SADDHARMAPUNDARIKA 294.32
Saddharma-Pundarika; or, The lotus of the true law. Tr. by H. Kern [Gloucester, Mass., P. Smith, 1964] xlii, 454p. 22cm. (Sacred bks. of the East, v.21) Tr. based on a Sanskrit ms. on palm leaves, in the D. Wright collection, Univ. of Cambridge Lib. (Dover bk. rebound) 4.50
I. Kern, Hendrik, 1833-1917, tr. II. Cambridge. University. Library. Mss. (Add. 1682) III. Title. IV. Title: The lotus of the true law. V. Series: The Sacred books of the East (New York) v.21

SADDHARMAPUNDARIKA 294.32
Saddharma--Pundarika; or, The lotus of the true law. Tr. by H. Kern. New York, Dover [1963] xlii, 454p. 22cm. (Sacred bks. of the East, v.21) Unaltered republication of the work first pub., Oxford, 1884. Tr. based on a Sanskrit ms. on palm leaves, in the D. Wright Collection, Univ. of Cambridge Lib. 63-19509 2.45 pap.,
I. Kern, Hendrik, 1833-1917, tr. II. Cambridge. University. Library. Mss. (Add.

SAUNDERS, Ernest Dale, 1919- 294.32
Buddhism in Japan, with an outline of its origins in India, by E. Dale Saunders. Philadelphia, University of Pennsylvania Press [1964] 328 p. illus., ports. 22 cm. Bibliography: p. 289-295. [BL1440.S32 1964] 64-10900
1. Buddha and Buddhism—Japan—Hist. I. Title.

SAUNDERS, Ernest Dale, 1919- 294.32
Buddhism in Japan, with an outline of its origins in India. Philadelphia, Univ. of Pa. Pr. [c.1964] 328p. illus., ports. 22cm. Bibl. 64-10900 6.50
1. Buddha and Buddhism—Japan—Hist. I. Title.

SENZAKI, Nyogen, ed. and tr. 294.32
Buddhism and Zen, compiled, edited, and translated by Nyogen Senzaki and Ruth Strout McCandless. New York, Philosophical Library [1953] 91p. 22cm. 'Sho-do-ka, by Yoka-daishi': p. 31-72. Bibliography: p. 88. [BL1442.Z4S4] 53-7898
1. Zen (Sect) I. Hauan-chileh, d, 713 Sho-do-ka. II. McCandless, Ruth Strout, joint ed. and tr. III. Title.

SNELLGROVE, David L 294.32
Buddhist Himalaya; travels and studies in quest of the origins and nature of Tibetan religion. [New York] Philosophical Library [1957] 324 p. illus. 23 cm. Includes bibliography. [BL1485.S6] 57-59474
1. Lamaism. 2. Buddha and Buddhism. I. Title.

SNELLGROVE, David L. 294.32
Buddhist Himalaya; travels and studies in quest of the origins and nature of Tibetan religion. Oxford, Bruno Cassirer [Mystic, Conn., Verry, 1966] xii, 324p. illus. map. 22cm. Bibl. [BL1485.S6] 57-59474 7.50 bds.,
1. Lamaism. 2. Buddha and Buddhism. I. Title.

SUZUKI, Daisetz Teitaro, 1870- 294.32
Essays in Zen Buddhism (third series) London, New York, Published for the Buddhist Society by Rider [1953] 367p. illus. 19cm. (His Complete works) [BL1430.S8 3d series 1953] 54-2080
1. Zen (Sect) 2. Buddha and Buddhism—China. I. Title.

SUZUKI, Daisetz Teitaro, 1870- 294.32
Manual of Zen Buddhism. London, New York, Published for the Buddhist Society, by Rider [1950] 192p. illus. 19cm (His Complete works) [BL1430.S84 1950] 54-25783
1. Zen (Sect) 2. Buddha and Buddhism—China. 3. Buddha and Buddhism— Sacred books (Selections: Extracts, etc.) 4. Buddha and Buddhism. 5. Monasticism and religious orders, Buddhist. I. Title. II. Title: Zen Buddhism.

SUZUKI, Daisetz Teitaro, 1870- 294.32
Manual of Zen Buddhism. London, New York, Published for the Buddhist Society, by Rider [1950] 192 p. illus. 19 cm. (His Complete works) [BL1430.S84 1950] 54-25783
1. Zen (Sect) 2. Buddha and Buddhism—China. 3. Buddha and Buddhism—Sacred books (Selection: Extractions, etc.) 4. Buddha and Buddhism. 5. Monasticism and religious orders, Buddhist. I. Title. II. Title: Zen Buddhism.

SUZUKI, Daisetz Teitaro, 1870- 294.32
Studies in Zen. Edited by Christmas Humphreys. New York, Philosophical Library [1955] 212p. illus. 19cm. [BL1442.Z4S78] 55-14253
1. Zen (Sect) I. Title.

SUZUKI, Daisetz Teitaro, 1870- 294.32
Studies in Zen. London, New York, Published for the Buddhist Society by Rider [1955] 212p. port. 19cm. (His Complete works) [BL1442.Z4S78 1955a] 56-3476
1. Zen (Sect) I. Title.

*SUZUKI, Daisetz Teitaro, 1870- 294.32
Studies in Zen. Ed. by Christmas Humphreys [New York, Dell, 1964, c.1955] 210p. 20cm. (Delta bk. 8371) 1.85 pap.,
1. Zen (Sect) I. Title.

SUZUKI, Daisetz Teitaro, 1870- 294.32
Zen Buddhism, selected writings. Edited by William Barret. [1st ed.] Garden City, N.Y.,
1. Zen Buddhism

SUZUKI, Daisetz Teitaro, 1870-1966. 294.32
Outlines of Mahayana Buddhism. Prefatory essay by Alan Watts. New York, Schocken Books [1963] xxix, 383 p. 21 cm. (Schocken paperbacks) "SB59." [BL1483.S82 1963] 63-18394
1. Mahayana Buddhism.

SUZUKI, Daisetz Teitaro, 1870-1966. 294.32
Zen and Japanese Buddhism. [1st ed.] Tokyo, Japan Travel Bureau; C. E. Tuttle Co., distributors, Tokyo & Rutland, Vt. [1958] 150 p. illus. 19 cm. [BL1440.S85] 58-10641
1. Zen Buddhism. 2. Buddhism—Japan. I. Title.

SUZUKI, Daisetz Teitaro, 1870-1966. 294.32
Zen Buddhism, selected writings. Edited by William Barrett. [1st ed.] Garden City, N.Y., Doubleday, 1956. 294 p. 18 cm. (Doubleday anchor books, A90) [BL1430.S848] 56-9406
1. Zen Buddhism—China.

WATTS, Alan Wilson, 1915- 294.32
The way of Zen. [New York] Pantheon [1957] 236 p. illus. 22 cm. [BL1432.Z4W33] 57-7318
1. Zen (Sect) I. Title.

WATTS, Alan Wilson, 1915- 294.32
The way of Zen. [New York] Pantheon [1957] 236 p. illus. 22 cm. [BL1432.Z4W33] 57-7318
1. Zen Buddhism. I. Title.

WATTS, Alan Wilson, 1915- 294.32
The way of Zen. New York, Random [1965, c.1957] xvii, 236p. illus. 21cm. (Vintage Giant, v-298) [BL1432.Z4W33] 1.95 pap.,
*1. Zen. *Sect) I. Title.*

WENTZ, Walter Yeeling Evans, ed. 294.32
The Tibetan book of the great liberation; or, The method of realizing nirvana through knowing the mind, preceded by an epitome of Padma-Sambhava's biography and followed by Guru Phadampa Sangay's teachings. According to English renderings by Sardar Bahadur S. W. Laden La and by the Lamas Karma Sumdhon Paul, Lobzang Mingyur Dorje, and Kazi Dawa-Samdup. Introductions, annotations, and editing by W. Y. Evans-Wentz. With psychological commentary by C. G. Jung. London, New York, Oxford University Press, 1954. lxiv, 261 p. 9 plates. 23 cm. Contents.Contents.—Psychological commentary, by C. G. Jung.—General introduction, by W. Y. Evans-Wentz—An epitome of the life and teachings of Tibet's great guru Padma-Sambhava, according to the biography by his chief desciple Yeshey Tahogyal, based upon excerpts rendered into English by the late Sardar Bahadur S. W. Laden La, assisted by Lama Sonam Senge.—Here follows the [yogo of] knowing the mind, the seeing of reality, called self-liberation, from "The profound doctrine of self-liberation by meditation upon the peaceful and wrathful deties," by Padma-Sambhava, according to Lama Karma Sumdhon Paul's and Lama Lobzang Mingyur Dorje's English rendering.—The last testamentary teachings of the Guru Phadampa Sangay, according to the late LAMA Kazi Dawa-Sandup's English rendering. [BL1405.W45] 56-58518
1. Buddhism. 2. Nirvana. 3. Yoga. I. Padma Sambhava, ca. 717-ca. 762. II. Yshey Tahogyal. III. Phadampa Sangay, fl. 1100. IV. Jung, Carl Gustav, 1875-1961. V. Title.

GORDON, Antoinette K. 294.3221
The iconography of Tibetan Lamaism. (Rev. ed.) New York, Paragon, 1967. xxxi, 131p. illus., plates (pt. col.) 31cm. Bibl. [NB1046.T5G6] 25.00
1. Lamaism. 2. Idols and images. 3. Art, Buddhist. 4. Art—Tibet. I. Title.

BARDO thodol. 294.3223
The Tibetan book of the dead; or, The after-death experiences on the Bardo plane, according to Lama Kazi Da,a-Samdup's English rendering. Compiled and edited by W. Y. Evans-Wentz. [3d ed.] New York. Oxford University Press, 1960. lxxxiv, 249 p. illus., group port. 21 cm. (A Galaxy book BB39) Includes bibliography. [BL1411.B3E6 1960] 60-13909
I. Zla-ba-Basam-'grub, Kazi, 1868-1922, tr. II. Wentz, Walter Yeeling Evans, ed. III. Title.

HUI-NENG, 638-713. 294.3282
The sutra of the sixth patriarch on the pristine orthodox dharma. Translated from the Chinese by Paul F. Fung [and] George D. Fung. San Francisco, Buddha's Universal Church [1964] 187 p. 23 cm. [BL1432.Z4H843] 65-1175
1. Zen (Sect) I. Fung, Paul F., tr. II. Fung, George D., tr. III. Title.

ZIA-BA-BSAM-'GRUB, Kazi, 1868-1922, tr. 294.32
The Tibetan book of the dead; or, The after-death experiences on the Bardo plane, according to Lama Kazi Dawa-Samdup's English rendering, by W. Y. Evans-Wentz. With a psychological commentary by C. G. Jung, introducing foreword by Lama Anagarika Govinda, and foreword by John Woodruffe [i.e. Woodroffe] 3d ed. London, New York, Oxford University Press, 1957. lxxxiv, 249 p. illus., plates., group port. 23 cm. [BL1411.B3E6 1957] 57-3183
I. Wentz, Walter Yeeling Evans, ed. II. Bardo thodol. III. Title.

CH'EN, Kenneth Kuan Sh'eng, 1907- 294.320951
Buddhism in China, a historical survey, by Kenneth K. S. Ch'en. Princeton, N.J., Princeton University Press, 1964. xii, 560 p. map. 25 cm. (The Virginia and Richard Stewart memorial lectures) Princeton studies in the history of religion. Bibliography: p. 505-548. [BL1430.C486] 63-23402
1. Buddhism—China—History. I. Title. II. Series. III. Series: Princeton studies in the history of religions

TANTRAS. Hevajratantrarajanama. 294.3282
The Hevajra Tantra; a critical study, by D. L. Snellgrove. London, New York, Oxford University Press, 1959. 2 v. illus. 26 cm. (London oriental series, v. 6) Contents.-- v. 1. Introduction and translation. -- v. 2. Sanskrit and Tibetan texts (including commentary, the Yogaratnamaia, by Krisnacaryapada) Bibliography: v. 1, p. xiii-xv. [BL1411.T3E57] 60-282
I. Snellgrove, David L. ed. and tr. II. Krisnacaryapada. Yogaratnamaia. III. Title. IV. Series.

WAYMAN, Alex 294.3282
Analysis of the Sravakabhumi manuscript. Berkeley, Univ. of Calif. Pr., 1961. 185p. facsim. (Univ. of Calif. pubns. in classical philology, v. 17) Bibl 61-64259 5.00 pap.,
I. Asanga. Sravakabhumi. II. Title. III. Series: California. University. University of California publications in classical philology, v. 17

AITKEN, Robert 294.329
Zen training, a personal account. Honolulu 16, Hawaii, P. O. Box 7025 Old Island Books, [c.1960] 26p. 23cm. 60-4133 1.00 pap.,
1. Zen. (Sect) I. Title.

AMES, Van Meter, 1898- 294.329
Zen and American thought. Honolulu, Univ. of Hawaii Pr. [c.]1962. 293p. 24cm. Bibl. 62-12672 4.50
1. Zen (Sect) 2. Philosophy, American. I. Title.

BECKER, Ernest. 294.329
Zen: a rational critique. [1st ed.] New York, Norton [1961] 192p. 22cm. Includes bibliography. [BL1442.Z4B4] 61-7474
1. Zen (Sect) I. Title.

BECKER, Ernest 294.329
Zen: a rational critique. New York, Norton [c.1961] 192p. Bibl. 61-7474 4.00
1. Zen (Sect) I. Title.

BLYTH, Reginald Horace 294.329
Zen and Zen classics. [Dist. New York, Perkins, 1962, c.1960] 225p. illus. 19cm. Contents.v. 7. Zen essays, Christianity, Sex, Society, etc. Bibl. 62-51117 2.75
1. Zen (Sect) I. Title.

BRIGGS, William A. 1873- ed 294.329
Anthology of Zen. Foreword by William Barrett. New York, Grove [c.1961] 301p. (Evergreen original, E-289) 61-6714 2.95 pap.,
1. Zen (Sect) I. Title.

CHANG, Ch'eng-chi. 294.329
The practice of Zen [by] Chang Chen-chi. [1st ed.] New York, Harper [1959] 199 p. 22 cm. In English. Includes bibliography. [BL1432.Z4C5] 59-10330
1. Zen Buddhism. I. Title.

DUMOULIN, Heinrich. 294.329
A history of Zen Buddhism. Translated from the German by Paul Peachey. New York, Pantheon Books [1963] 335 p. illus. 21 cm. Translation of Zen. [BL1442.Z4D83] 62-17386
1. Zen (Sect) — Hist. I. Title.

DUMOULIN, Heinrich 294.329
A history of Zen Buddhism. Tr. from German by Paul Peachey. New York, Pantheon [c.1959, 1963] 325p. illus. 21cm. Bibl. 62-17386 7.50
1. Zen (Sect)—Hist. I. Title.

DUMOULIN, Heinrich. 294.329
A history of Zen Buddhism. Translated from the German by Paul Peachey. New York, Pantheon Books [1963] 335 p. illus. 21 cm. Translation of Zen. [BL1442.Z4D83] 62-17386
1. Zen Buddhism—History.

EKVALL, Robert Brainerd, 1898- 294.329
Religious observances in Tibet: patterns and function [by] Robert B. Ekvall. Chicago, University of Chicago Press [1964] xiii, 313 p. 24 cm. Bibliography: p. [297]-306. [BL1485.E38] 64-23423
1. Lamaism. 2. Tibet — Religious life and customs. I. Title.

EKVALL, Robert Brainerd, 1898- 294.329
Religious observances in Tibet: patterns and function. Chicago, Univ. of Chic. Pr. [c.1964] xiii, 313p. 24cm. Bibl. 64-23423 8.50
1. Lamaism. 2. Tibet—Religious life and customs. I. Title.

FROMM, Erich, ed. 294.329
Zen Buddhism & psychoanalysis [by] D. T. Suzuki, Erich Fromm, and Richard De Martino. New York, Harper [c.1960] viii, 180p. 22cm. (bibl. footnotes) 60-5293 4.00 bds.,
1. Zen (Sect). 2. Psychoanalysis. I. Suzuki, Daisetz Teitaro, 1870— II. Title.

GRAHAM, Aelred, 1907- 294.329
Zen Catholicism; a suggestion. [1st ed.] New York, Harcourt, Brace & World [1963] 228 p. 21 cm. [BL1442.Z4G7] 63-10596
1. Zen (Sect) 2. Catholic Church — Relations — Buddhism. I. Title.

GRAHAM, Aelred, 1907- 294.329
Zen Catholicism: a suggestion. New York, Harcourt [1967, c.1963] xxv, 228p. 21cm. (Harvest bk., HB118) Bibl. 1.95 pap.,
1. Zen (Sect) 2. Catholic Church—Relations—Buddhism. I. Title.

GRAHAM, Aelred, 1907- 294.329
Zen Catholicism; a suggestion. New York, Harcourt [c.1963] 228p. 21cm. Bibl. 63-10596 4.95
1. Zen (Sect) 2. Catholic Church—Relations—Buddhism. I. Title.

HAYAKAWA, Sessue Kintaro 294.329
Zen showed me the way . . . to peace, happiness, and tranquility [tr. from te Japanese] Edited by Croswell Bowen. Indianapolis, Bobbs-Merill [c.1960] 256p. illus. 22cm. 60-13600 3.95 bds.,
1. Zen (Sect) I. Title.

HAYAKAWA, Sessue Kintaro, 1889- 294.329
Zen showed me the way ... to peace, happiness, and tranquility. Edited by Croswell Bowen. [1st ed.] Indianapolis, Bobbs-Merrill [1960] 256p. illus. 22cm. [BL1442Z4H3] 60-13600
1. Zen (Sect) I. Title.

HERRIGEL, Eugen, 1884-1955. 294.329
The method of Zen. Edited by Hermann Tausend. Translated by R. F. C. Hull. [New York] Pantheon Books [1960] 124 p. 21 cm. Translation of Der Zen-Weg. [BL1442.Z4H443] 59-11957
1. Zen Buddhism.

HERRIGEL, Eugen, 1884-1955 294.329
Zen. Tr. [from German] by R. F. C. Hull. Including Zen in the art of archery, introd. by D. T. Suzuki; The method of Zen, ed. by Hermann Tausend. New York, McGraw [1964, c.1953, 1960] 109, 124p. 21cm. 64-56163 1.95 pap.,
1. Zen Buddhism. 2. Archery. I. Herrigel, Eugen, 1884-1955. The method of Zen. II. Title.

HOFFMANN, Helmut, 1912- 294.329
The religions of Tibet. Translated by Edward Fitzgerald. New York, MacMillan, 1961. 199 p. illus. 23 cm. Includes bibliography. [BL1485.H613] 61-4236
1. Lamaism. 2. Bon (Tibetan religion) I. Title.

HUANG-PO, fl.842-850. 294.329
The Zen teaching of Huang Po on the transmission of mind; being the teaching of the Zen Master Huang Po as recorded by the scholar P'ei Hsiu of the T'ang dynasty. Rendered into English by John Blofeld (Chu Ch'an) New York, Grove Press [1959, c1958] 135 p. 22 cm. "A complete translation of the Huang Po chu'an [i.e. Ch'uan] hsiu [i.e. hsin] fa yao, including the previously unpublished Wan Ling record containing dialogues, sermons and anecdotes." [BL1432.Z4H723 1959] 59-12215
1. Zen Buddhism. I. P'ei, Hsiu, fl. 842-859. II. Title.

HUI NENG 638-713 294.329
The Platform Scripture. [Tr., introd., notes by Wingtsit Chan] New York, St. John's, 1963. ix, 193p. 24cm. (Asian Inst. trs., no. 3) Bibl. 63-13727 3.50
I. Chan, Wing-tsit, 1901- ed. and tr. II. Title. III. Title: 'anching. IV. Series.

HUMPHREYS, Christmas, 1901- 294.329
Zen: a way of life. New York, Emerson Books [1965, c1962] vii, 199 p. 20 cm. Bibliography: p. 173-177. [BL1451.2.H82] 65-17332
1. Buddhism. 2. Zen Buddhism.

HUMPHREYS, Christmas, [Travers Christmas Humphreys] 294.329
Zen comes West; the present and future of Zen Buddhism in Britain. New York, Macmillan, 1960[ ] 207p. illus. 23cm. 60-3885 4.75
1. Zen (Sect) I. Title.

LEGGETT, Trevor, ed. and tr. 294.329
A first Zen reader. Rutland, Vt., C. E. Tuttle Co. [1960] 236p. illus. (part col.) 60-12739 3.75 bds.,
1. Zen (Sect) I. Title.

LINSSEN, Robert 294.329
Living Zen. Pref. by Christmas Humphreys. Foreword by R. Godel. Tr. [from French] by Diana Abrahams-Curiel. London, Allen & Unwin [dist. Mystic, Conn., Verry, 1964, c.1958] 348p. illus. 23cm. Bibl. A59 6.00
1. Zen (Sect) 2. Buddha and Buddhism. I. Title.

LINSSEN, Robert 294.329
Living Zen. Pref. by Christmas Humphreys. Foreword by R. Godel. Translated [from the French] by Diana Abrahams-Curiel. New York, Grove Press [1960, c.1958] 348p. illus. 21cm. (An Evergreen book, E-203) (Includes bibliography.) 60-198 2.25 pap.,
1. Zen (Sect) 2. Buddha and Buddhism. I. Title.

NEWARK Museum Association, Newark, N. J. 294.329
Catalogue of the Tibetan collection and other Lamaist articles in the Newark Museum. Newark, 1950- v. illus. 24cm. [BL1485.N45] 60-30105
1. Lamaism—Antiq. 2. Art, Buddhist. 3. Tibet—Antiq. I. Title.

OGATA, Sohaku, 1901- 294.329
Zen for the West. For the Buddhist Society of London. New York, Dial Press, 1959. 182p. illus., port. 22cm. Appendices (p. [79]- [176]): 1. A new translation of the Mu mon kwan.--2. A Zen interpretation of the Tao te ching.--3. List of Chinese characters with Japanese and Chinese transliterations and dates of people, places, and technical terms in Zen for the West and in the Mu mon kwan. [BL1442.Z4O37] 59-13401
1. Lao-tzu. Tao te ching. 2. Zen (Sect) I. Hui-k'ai. fl. 13th cent. my mon kwan II. Buddhist Society, London. III. Title.

OGATA, Sohaku, 1901- 294.329
Zen for the West [Pub.] for the Buddhist Soc. of London. New York [Apollo Eds., 1962, c.1959] 182p. 20cm. (A60) 1.65 pap.,
1. Lau-tzu. Tao te ching. 2. Zen (Sect) I. Hui-Kiai, fl. 13th cent. II. Buddhist Society, London. III. Title.

ORYU, 1720-1813 294.329
The iron flute; 100 Zen koan. With commentary by Genro Fugai, and Nyogen. Tr. and ed. by Nyogen Senzaki, Ruth Strout McCandless. Illus. by Toriichi Murashima. Rutland, Vt., Charles E. Tuttle Co. [1961] 175p. illus. Bibl. 60-11512 3.95
1. Zen (Sect.) I. Senzaki, Nyogen, ed. and tr. II. Title.

PETER Pauper Press, Mount Vernon, N. Y. 294.329
Zen Buddhism; an introduction to Zen, with stories, parables and koan riddles of the Zen masters. Decorated with figures from old Chinese ink- paintings. Mount Vernon, N. Y. [1959] 61p. col. illus. 19cm. [BL1432.Z4P4] 59-33730
1. Zen (Sect) I. Title.

POWELL, Robert 294.329
Zen and reality; an approach to sanity and happiness on a non-sectarian basis. [Dist. New York, Taplinger, 1962, c.1961] 140p. 23cm. Bibl. 61-65668 3.95 bds.,
1. Krishnamurti, Jiddu, 1895- 2. Zen (Sect) I. Title.

ROSS, Nancy Wilson, 1905- ed. 294.329
The world of Zen; an East-West anthology. New York, Random [1965, c.1960] 362p. illus. 21cm. Bibl. [BL1442.Z4R6] 3.95 pap.,
1. Zen (Sect) I. Title.

ROSS, Nancy Wilson, 1905- ed. 294.329
The world of Zen; an East-West anthology. New York, Random House [1960] 362 p. illus. 24 cm. Includes bibliography. [BL1442.Z4R6] 60-12155
1. Zen Buddhism. I. Title.

SUZUKI, D. T. 294.329
Zen Buddhism & psychoanalysis. [By] D. T. Suzuki, Erich Fromm, Richard De Martino. New York, Grove [1963, c.1960] 180p. 21cm. (Evergreen E-360) Bibl. 1.95 pap.,
I. Title.

SUZUKI, Daisetz Teitaro, 1870- 294.329
Essays in Zen Buddhism, first series. New York, Grove Press [1961] 387 p. 21 cm. (Evergreen original, E-309) [BL1432.Z4S8 1961] 61-11477
1. Zen (Sect) 2. Buddha and Buddhism—China. I. Title.

SUZUKI, Daisetz Teitaro, 1870- 294.329
Essays in Zen Buddhism, first series. New York, Grove Press [1961] 387p. (Evergreen original, E-309) 61-11477 2.95 pap.,
1. Zen (Sect) 2. Buddha and Buddhism—China. I. Title.

SUZUKI, Daisetz Teitaro, 1870- 294.329
The essentials of Zen Buddhism, selected from the writings of daisetz T. New York, Dutton, 1962. 544 p. 22 cm. Includes bibliography. [BL1442.Z4S76] 61-5041
1. Zen (Sect) I. Title. II. Title: Suzuki.

SUZUKI, Daisetz Teitaro, 1870- 294.329
Manual of Zen Buddhism. New York, Grove Press [1960] 192 p. illus. 21 cm. (Evergreen original, E-231) [BL1432.Z4S82 1960] 60-7637
1. Zen (Sect) 2. Buddha and Buddhism—China. 3. Buddha and Buddhism—Sacred books (Selections: Extracts, etc.) 4. Buddha and Buddhism. 5. Monasticism and religious orders, Buddhist. I. Title. II. Title: Zen Buddhism.

SUZUKI, Daisetz Teitaro, 1870- 294.329
The training of the Zen Buddhist monk. Illustrated by Zechu Sato. [1st American ed.] New York, University Books [1959] 161 p. illus. 22 cm. [BL1478.S85 1959] 59-14575
1. Monasticism and religious orders, Buddhist. 2. Buddha and Buddhism—Japan. 3. Zen (Sect) I. Title.

SUZUKI, Daisetz Teitaro, 1870- 294.329
Zen and Japanese culture. [Rev. and enl. 2d ed. New York] Pantheon Books [1959] xxiii, 478 p. 68 plates (incl. ports.) 24 cm. (Bollingen series, 64) First ed. published in 1938 under title: Zen Buddhism and its influence on Japanese culture. Bibliography: p. [443]-447. [BL1442.A4S8 1959] 58-12174
1. Zen (Sect) 2. Japan—Civilization. 3. Philosophy, Japanese. I. Title. II. Series.

SUZUKI, Daisetz Teitaro, 1870-1966. 294.329
Essays in Zen Buddhism, first series. New York, Grove Press [1961] 387 p. 21 cm. (Evergreen original,E-309) [BL1432.Z4S8 1961] 61-11477
1. Zen Buddhism—Addresses, essays, lectures.

SUZUKI, Daisetz Teitaro, 1870-1966. 294.329
The essentials of Zen Buddhism, selected from the writings of Daisetz T. Suzuki. Edited, and with an introd., by Bernard Phillips. [1st ed.] New York, Dutton, 1962. 544 p. 22 cm. Includes bibliography. [BL1442.Z4S76] 61-5041
1. Zen Buddhism.

SUZUKI, Daisetz Teitaro, 1870-1966. 294.329
Manual of Zen Buddhism. New York, Grove Press [1960] 192 p. illus. 21 cm. (Evergreen original, E-231) [BL1432.Z4S82 1960] 60-7637
1. Zen. 2. Buddha and buddhism—Sacred books. 3. Gods, Buddhist. I. Title: Zen Buddhism.

SUZUKI, Daisetz Teitaro, 1870-1966. 294.329
Zen and Japanese culture. [Rev. and enl. 2d ed. New York] Pantheon Books [1959] xxiii, 478 p. 68 plates (incl. ports.) 24 cm. (Bollingen series, 64) First ed. published in 1938 under title: Zen Buddhism and its influence on Japanese culture. Bibliography: p. [443]-447. [BL1442.Z4S8 1959] 58-12174
1. Zen Buddhism—Japan. 2. Japan—Civilization—Zen influences. 3. Philosophy, Japanese. I. Title. II. Series.

SWANN, Jeffrey. 294.329
Toehold on Zen. Illustrated by Ekon. [1st ed.] Cleveland, World Pub. Co. [1963, c1962] 122 p. illus. 21 cm. [BL1442.Z4S9] 63-14784
1. Zen Buddhism. I. Title.

*WATTS, Alan W. 294.329
The way of Zen (Reissue. New York] New Amer. Lib. [1964, c.1957] 224p. illus. 18cm. (Mentor bk., MP476) Bibl. .60 pap.,
I. Title.

WATTS, Alan Wilson, 1915- 294.329
The spirit of Zen; a way of life, work, and art in the Far East. New York, Grove Press [1960, c1958] 128 p. illus. 21 cm. (The Wisdom of the East) (An Evergreen book, E-219.) Includes bibliography. [BL1432.Z4W28 1960] 60-7347
1. Zen Buddhism—China. 2. Zen Buddhism—Japan. I. Title.

WATTS, Alan Wilson, 1915- 294.329
This is it, and other essays on Zen and spiritual experience. [New York] Pantheon Books [1960, c.1958, 1960] 158p. 22cm. Bibl.: p.155-158. 60-11758 3.50
1. Mysticism. 2. Zen (Sect) I. Title.

WIENPAHL, Paul. 294.329
The matter of Zen; a brief account of zazen. [New York] New York University Press, 1964. xi, 162 p. illus. 21 cm. Bibliographical references included in "Notes" (p. 147-162) [BL1478.6.W5] 64-10525
1. Meditation (Buddhism) 2. Zen Buddhism. I. Title. II. Title: Zazen, a brief account of.

WIENPAHL, Paul 294.329
The matter of Zen: a brief account of zazen [New York] N.Y.U. Pr. [c.]1964. xi, 162p. illus. 21cm. Bibl. 64-10525 3.95
1. Meditation (Buddhism) 2. Zen Buddhism. I. Title. II. Title: Zazen, a brief account of.

WOOD, Ernest, 1883- 294.329
Zen dictionary. New York, Philosophical Library [1962] 165 p. 22 cm. Bibliography: p. 163-165. [BL1403.W6] 62-12828
1. Zen (Sect) — Dictionaries. I. Title.

WOOD, Ernest Egerton, 1883- 294.329
Zen dictionary. New York, Philosophical [c.1962] 165p. 22cm. Bibl. 62-12828 4.75
1. Zen (Sect)—Dictionaries. I. Title.

DUMOULIN, Heinrich. 294.3'3'72
Christianity meets Buddhism. Translated by John C. Maraldo. La Salle, Ill., Open Court Pub. Co., 1974. 206 p. 22 cm. (Religious encounter: East and West) Includes bibliographical references. [BR128.B8D82] 73-82783 ISBN 0-87548-121-3 7.95
1. Christianity and other religions—Buddhism. 2. Buddha and Buddhism—Relations—Christianity. I. Title.

DUMOULIN, Heinrich. 294.3'3'72
Christianity meets Buddhism. Translated by John C. Maraldo. La Salle, Ill., Open Court

Pub. Co., 1974. 206 p. 22 cm. (Religious encounter: East and West) Includes bibliographical references. [BR128.B8D82] 73-82783 ISBN 0-87548-121-3 7.95
1. Christianity and other religions—Buddhism. 2. Buddha and Buddhism—Relations—Christianity. I. Title.

FAUSSET, Hugh I'Anson, 1895- 294.3'3'72
The flame and the light : meanings in Vedanta and Buddhism / Hugh I'Anson Fausset. Wheaton, Ill. : Theosophical Pub. House, 1976, c1958. 232 p. ; 21 cm. (A Quest book) Reprint of the 1969 ed. published by Greenwood Press, New York. Bibliography: p. 229-232. [B132.V3F35 1976] 76-2081 ISBN 0-8356-0478-0 pbk. : 3.75
1. Vedanta—Comparative studies. 2. Buddhism—Relations—Hinduism. 3. Hinduism—Relations—Buddhism. I. Title.

FAUSSET, Hugh I'Anson, 1895- 294.3'3'72
The flame and the light : meanings in Vedanta and Buddhism / by Hugh I'Anson Fausset. Wheaton, Ill. : Theosophical Pub. House, [1976] c1958. p. cm. (A Quest book) Reprint of the 1969 ed. published by Greenwood Press, New York. Includes bibliographical references. [B132.V3F35 1976] 76-2081 ISBN 0-8356-0478-0
1. Vedanta—Comparative studies. 2. Buddhism—Relations—Hinduism. 3. Hinduism—Relations—Buddhism. I. Title.

FOZDAR, Jamshed. 294.3'3'72
Buddha Maitrya-Amithaba has appeared / Jamshed K. Fozdar. New Delhi, India : Baha'i Publ. Trust, c1976. 591 p. ; 22 cm. Includes index. Bibliography: p. [532]-533. [BP365.F65] 75-6131
1. Bahaism—Relations—Buddhism. 2. Buddhism—Relations—Bahaism. 3. Buddhism. I. Title.

HUNTER, Louise H. 294.3'3'72
Buddhism in Hawaii; its impact on a yankee community [by] Louise H. Hunter. Honolulu, University of Hawaii Press, 1971. x, 266 p. illus. 25 cm. Bibliography: p. 251-255. [BL1448.U5H85] 76-116878 ISBN 0-87022-355-0 9.00
1. Buddha and Buddhism—Hawaii—History. I. Title.

WAKEFIELD, Donam Hahn. 294.3'3'72
Journey into the void; meeting of Buddhist and Christian. Huntington, Ind., Our Sunday Visitor, inc. [1971] 63 p. 21 cm. Bibliography: p. 63. [BR128.B8W3] 79-172038 1.25
1. Christianity and other religions—Buddhism. 2. Buddha and Buddhism—Relations—Christianity. I. Title.

SCHECTER, Jerrold. 294.3'3'77
The new face of Buddha; Buddhism and political power in southeast Asia. New York, Coward-McCann [1967] xix, 300 p. illus., map (on lining papers) ports. 22 cm. Bibliography: p. 279-286. [BL1459.S7S3] 67-10560
1. Buddhism and state. I. Title.

TAMBIAH, S. J. 294.3'3'77
World conqueror and world renouncer : a study of Buddhism and polity in Thailand against a historical background / S. J. Tambiah. Cambridge [Eng.] ; New York : Cambridge University Press, 1976. viii, 557p. : ill. ; 23 cm. (Cambridge Studies in social anthropology ; 15) Includes index. Bibliography: p. 531-540. [BQ554.T35] 76-8290 ISBN 0-521-21140-9 : 37.50
1. Buddhism and state—Thailand. 2. Buddhism—Thailand—History. I. Title.

MULDER, J. A. Niels. 294.3'3'78309593
Monks, merit, and motivation: Buddhism and national development in Thailand [by] J. A. Niels Mulder. 2d rev. ed. [De Kalb] Northern Illinois University, Center for Southeast Asian Studies; [distribution by Cellar Book Shop, Detroit] 1973. viii, 58 l. 28 cm. (Northern Illinois University. Center for Southeast Asian Studies. Special report no. 1) Bibliography: leaves 54-57. [BQ5160.T4M84 1973] 73-169368
1. Buddhist monks—Thailand. 2. Buddhism and social problems—Thailand. 3. Community development—Thailand. I. Title. II. Series: Illinois. Northern Illinois University, De Kalb. Center for Southeast Asian Studies. Special report no. 1.

BUDDHADASA, Bhikkhu, 1906- 294.3'4
Toward the truth. Edited by Donald K. Swearer. Philadelphia, Westminster Press [1971] 189 p. 19 cm. Includes bibliographical references. [BL1416.B8A33 1971] 72-135627 ISBN 0-664-24906-X 2.95
I. Title.

EKAKU, 1686-1769. 294.3'4
The Zen Master Hakuin: selected writings. Translated by Philip B. Yampolsky. New York, Columbia University Press, 1971. xii, 253 p. 24 cm. (Records of civilization: sources and studies, no. 86) Translation of Orategama, Yabukoji, and Hebilichigo (romanized form) Bibliography: p. [235]-238. [BL1442.Z4E3613] 75-145390 ISBN 0-231-03463-6 10.00
1. Zen Buddhism—Early works to 1800. I. Title. II. Series.

HERRIGEL, Eugen, 1884-1955. 294.3'4
The method of Zen [by] Eugen Herrigel. Ed. by Hermann Toausend. Tr. by R. F. C. Hull. New York, Vintage Books [1974] 124 p. 18 cm. Translation of Der Zen-Weg. Reprint of the ed. published by Pantheon Books, New York. [[BQ9266.H4713 1974]] 74-5120 ISBN 0-394-71244-7 1.95 (pbk.)
1. Zen Buddhism—Addresses, essays, lectures. I. Title.

IKEDA, Daisaku. 294.3'4
Guidance memo / Daisaku Ikeda ; translated by George M. Williams. Santa Monica, Calif. : World Tribune Press, [1975] 288 p. ; 19 cm. Includes index. [BQ8418.7.I3816] 75-13664 ISBN 0-915678-00-4
1. Soka Gakkai—Doctrines—Addresses, essays, lectures. I. Title.

NAGARJUNA, Siddha. 294.3'4
The precious garland and The song of the four mindfulnesses / Nagarjuna and Kaysang Gyatso, Seventh Dalai Lama ; translated and edited by Jeffrey Hopkins and Lati Rimpoche, with Anne Klein ; foreword by Tenzin Gyatso, Fourteenth Dalai Lama. 1st U.S. ed. New York : Harper & Row, [1975] 119 p. ; 21 cm. (The Wisdom of Tibet series ; 2) Translation of Rajaparikatharatnamala by Nagarjuna and a poem by the Seventh Dalai Lama. [BQ2872.E5 1975] 74-25688 ISBN 0-06-063541-X : 5.95
I. Bskal-bzan-rgya-mtsho, Dalai Lama VII, 1708-1757. The song of the four mindfulnesses causing the rain of achievements to fall. English. 1975. II. Title.

PRATT, Jane Abbott. 294.3'4
Consciousness and sacrifice; an interpretation of two episodes in the Indian myth of Manu. [New York] Analytical Psychology Club of New York [c1967] 70 p. 23 cm. (Contributions to Jungian thought) Bibliographical references included in "Notes"--(p. 65-70) [BL1215.S2P7] 68-7762
1. Manu. 2. Sacrifice. 3. Deluge. I. Title.

PULLEY, Sande. 294.3'4
A Yankee in the Yellow Robe; an American Buddhist monk's role in East-West cultural exchange [by] Sande Pulley (Bhikkhu Anuruddha) [1st ed.] New York, Exposition Press [1967] 130 p. illus., ports. 21 cm. [BL1478.95.P8A3] 67-9011
1. Buddhist converts. I. Title.

RAHULA, Walpola. 294.3'4
What the Buddha taught [by] Walpola Sri Rahula; with a foreword by Paul Demieville and a collection of illustrative texts translated from the original Pali. 2nd and enlarged ed. Bedford, Gordon Fraser Gallery, 1967. xvi, 151 p. front., 16 plates. 21 1/2 cm. (Gordon Fraser gift books) 16/6 Bibliography: p. 140-141. [BL1451.2.R3] 67-106375
1. Buddha and Buddhism. I. Title.

WATTS, Alan Wilson, 1915- 294.3'4
This is it, and other essays on Zen and spiritual experience [by] Alan Watts. New York, Vintage Books [1973] 158 p. 19 cm. Reprint of the 1960 ed. [BL625.W35 1973] 72-8394 ISBN 0-394-71904-2 1.65 (pbk)
1. Mysticism. 2. Zen Buddhism. I. Title.

THE Wisdom of the early Buddhists / compiled by Geoffrey Parrinder. New York : Directions Pub. Corp., 1977. 86 p. ; 21 cm. Includes bibliographical references. [BQ915.W57] 77-7945 ISBN 0-8112-0666-1 : 7.50 ISBN 0-8112-0667-X pbk. : 2.95 294.3'4
1. Gautama Buddha—Teachings. I. Parrinder, Edward Geoffrey.

YAMAGAMI, Sogen, 1878-1957. 294.3'4
Systems of Buddhistic thought / by Yamakami Sogen. San Francisco : Chinese Materials Center, 1976. xx, 315, lvi p. ; 26 cm. (Reprint series - Chinese Materials Center ; no. 55) Reprint of the 1912 ed. published by the University of Calcutta, Calcutta. Includes index. [BQ4145.Y35 1976] 77-373708 9.95
1. Buddhist doctrines. I. Title. II. Series: Chinese Materials Center. Reprint series — Chinese Materials Center ; no. 55.

BSTAN-'DZIN-RGYA-MTSHO, Dalai Lama XIV, 1935- 294.3'4'09515
The opening of the wisdom-eye and the history of the advancement of Buddhadharma in Tibet, by Tenzin Gyatsho the XIVth Dalai Lama of Tibet. [U.S.A. ed.] Wheaton, Ill., Theosophical Pub. House [1972, c1966] xv, 178 p. illus. 23 cm. (A Quest book) Translated from Tibetan by Thubten Kalzang Rinpoche, Bhikkhu Nagasena, and Bhikkhu Khantipalo. [BQ7935.B774O63 1972] 70-152732 ISBN 0-8356-0202-8 6.95
1. Buddhist doctrines. 2. Buddha and Buddhism—Tibet—History. I. Title.

GETTY, Alice. 294.3'4'11
The gods of Northern Buddhism. New York, Arno Press, 1974. p. cm. Reprint of the 1914 ed. published by Clarendon Press, Oxford, Eng. [BQ4630.G47 1974] 74-6872 ISBN 0-405-06188-9 30.00
1. Gods, Buddhist. 2. Mahayana Buddhism I. Title.

ARGUELLES, Jose, 1939- 294.3'4'2
Mandala [by] Jose and Miriam Arguelles. Foreword by Chogyam Trungpa. Berkeley, [Calif.] Shambala, 1972. 140 p. illus. (part col.) 28 cm. Bibliography: p. 130-134. [BL2015.M3A73] 70-189856 ISBN 0-87773-033-4 5.95
1. Mandala. I. Arguelles, Miriam, 1943- joint author. II. Title.

DONATH, Dorothy C. 294.3'4'2
Buddhism for the West: Theravada, Mahayana and Vajrayana; a comprehensive review of Buddhist history, philosophy, and teachings from the time of the Buddha to the present day [by] Dorothy C. Donath. New York, Julian Press [1971] xiii, 146 p. 21 cm. Bibliography: p. 143-146. [BL1456.D65] 78-170948 6.00
1. Buddhist doctrines—Introductions. I. Title.

DONATH, Dorothy C. 294.3'4'2
Buddhism for the West: Theravada; Mahayana and Vajrayana; a comprehensive review of Buddhist history, philosophy, and teachings from the time of the Buddha to the present day. New York, McGraw-Hill [1974, c1971] 146 p. 21 cm. Bibliography: p. 143-146. [BL1456.D65] ISBN 0-07-017533-0 2.45 (pbk.)
1. Buddhist doctrines—Introductions. I. Title.
L.C. card number for hardbound ed.: 78-170948

FOX, Douglas A., 1927- 294.3'4'2
The vagrant lotus: an introduction to Buddhist philosophy, by Douglas A. Fox. Philadelphia, Westminster Press [1973] 223 p. 22 cm. Bibliography: p. 213-215. [BQ4132.F69] 73-8692 ISBN 0-664-20975-0
1. Buddhist doctrines—Introductions. 2. Philosophy, Buddhist. I. Title.

GLASENAPP, Helmuth von, 1891-1963. 294.3'4'2
Buddhism—a non-theistic religion. With a selection from Buddhist scriptures, edited by Heinz Bechert. Translated from the German by Irmgard Schloegl. New York, G. Braziller [1970, c1966] 208 p. 23 cm. Translation of Buddhismus und Gottesidee. Includes bibliographical references. [BL1456.G5513] 71-78530 7.50
1. Buddhist doctrines. 2. Buddha and Buddhism—Sacred books. I. Bechert, Heinz, 1932- ed. II. Title.

HOLMES, Edmond Gore Alexander, 1850-1936. 294.3'4'2
The creed of Buddha [by] Edmond Holmes. Westport, Conn., Greenwood Press [1973] viii, 260 p. 20 cm. Reprint of the 1957 ed. [BQ872.H65 1973] 72-9918 ISBN 0-8371-6606-3
1. Gautama Buddha. 2. Buddha and Buddhism—Philosophy. I. Title.

MAITREYANATHA. 294.3'4'2
Madhyanta-vibhanga; discourse on discrimination between middle and extremes, ascribed to Bodhisattva Maitreya. Commented by Vasubandhu and Sthiramati. Translated from the Sanskrit by Th. Stcherbatsky. Reprint. [Calcutta, Indian Studies: Past & Present, 1971] 223 p. 23 cm. (Soviet indology series, no. 5) (Bibliotheca Buddhica. Reprint, 30) Imprint covered by label: Sole distributors: Firma K. L. Mukhopadhyay, Calcutta. Label mounted on t.p.: Distributed by Lawrence Verry, Mystic, Conn. Includes bibliographical references. [BQ2962.E5S53 1971] 78-920098 14.00
1. Yogacara (Buddhism) I. Vasubandhu. Madhyantavibhagasutrabhasya. II. Sthiramati. Madhyantavibhagasutrabhasyatika. III. Shcherbatskoi, Fedor Ippolitovich, 1866-1942, tr. IV. Title. V. Series: Bibliotheca Buddhica, 30.

NHAT Hanh, Thich. 294.3'4'2
Zen keys. Translated from the French by Albert and Jean Low, with an introd. by Philip Kapleau. [1st ed.] Garden City, N.Y., Anchor Press [1974] p. cm. Translation of Clefs pour le Zen. [BQ9265.9.N4513] 74-3556 ISBN 0-385-08066-2 1.95 (pbk.)
1. Zen Buddhism—Essence, genius, nature. I. Title.

SANTIDEVA, 7thcent. 294.3'4'2
Entering the path of enlightenment; the Bodhicaryavatara of the Buddhist poet Santideva. Translation with guide by Marion L. Matics. [New York] Macmillan [1970] 318 p. 22 cm. Published also under title: The path of light. Bibliography: p. 288-303. [BL1416.S33B613 1970] 73-110466
1. Buddhist doctrines. I. Matics, Marion L., tr. II. Title.

SCHUMANN, Hans Wolfgang. 294.3'4'2
Buddhism; an outline of its teachings and schools [by] H. Wolfgang Schumann. Translated by Georg Feuerstein. [1st U.S.A. ed.] Wheaton, Ill., Theosophical Pub. House [1974, c1973] 200 p. illus. 21 cm. (A Quest book) "Published under a grant from the Kern Foundation." Bibliography: p. [184]-188. [BQ4132.S38 1974] 74-6302 ISBN 0-8356-0452-7 2.45 (pbk.)
1. Buddhist doctrines—Introductions. I. Title.

SGAM-PO-PA, 1079-1153. 294.3'4'2
Jewel ornament of liberation [by] Sgam.Po.Pa. [Translated and annotated by Herbert V. Guenther] Berkeley, Shambala, 1971. xiv, 333 p. 22 cm. (Clear light series) Translation of Dam chos yid bzin gyi nor bu. "Index of book titles": p. 283-294. [BQ4330.S513 1971] 72-146507 ISBN 0-87773-026-1 4.50
1. Bodhisattva stages (Mahayana Buddhism) 2. Religious life (Mahayana Buddhism) I. Guenther, Herbert V., ed. II. Title.

STREETER, Burnett Hillman, 1874-1937. 294.3'4'2
The Buddha and the Christ; an exploration of the meaning of the universe and of the purpose of human life. Port Washington, N.Y., Kennikat Press [1970] xiii, 336 p. 23 cm. (The Bampton lectures for 1932) "First published in 1932." Bibliography: p. 111. [BR128.B8S84 1970] 72-102585
1. Christianity and other religions—Buddhism. 2. Buddha and Buddhism—Relations—Christianity. 3. Buddha and Buddhism—Japan. 4. Religion—Philosophy. I. Title. II. Series: Bampton lectures, 1932

*VERDU, Alfonso 294.342
Dialectical aspects in Buddhist thought studies in Sino-Japanese mahayana idealism n. p. University of Kansas, Center for East Asian studies, [1974] v., 273 p. illus., 23 cm. (International studies, East Asian Series,#8) [BQ4132] 74-78238 15.00 (pbk.)
1. Buddha and Buddhism. I. Title.
Distributed by Paragon Book Gallery, 14 East 38th St., New York, N.Y. 10016.

GORDON, Antoinette K. 294.3'4'21
The iconography of Tibetan Lamaism, by Antoinette K. Gordon, Rev. (i.e. 2d. ed.) New York, Paragon Book Reprint Corp. 1967 [c.1959] xxxi, 131 p. illus. plates (part col.) 31 cm. Bibliography: p. 111-118. [NB1046.T5G6 1967] 67-7111
1. Lamaism. 2. Idols and images. 3. Art, Buddist. 4. Art. Tibetan. I. Title.

†MOOR, Edward, 1771-1848. 294.3'4'211
The Hindu pantheon / by Edward Moor ; introductory preface by Manly P. Hall. Los Angeles : Philosophical Research Society, 1976. xiv, 467 p., 105 leaves of plates : ill. ; 32 cm. On spine: Moor's Hindu pantheon. At head of title: Sri Sarvva Deva Sabha. Reprint of the 1810 ed. printed for J. Johnson by T. Bensley, London. [BL1201.M63 1976] 76-26759 ISBN 0-89314-409-6 : 40.00
1. Mythology, Hindu. 2. Gods, Hindu. 3. Art, Hindu. I. Title.

WOODROFFE, John George, Sir, 1865-1936. 294.3'4'211
Hymns to the goddess. [Madras] Ganesh; distributed by Vedanta Press, Holywood, Calif., 1973. xii, 335 p. 23 cm. Includes bibliographical references. [BL1245.S4W58 1973] 74-152777 ISBN 0-87481-306-9 6.00
1. Shaktism. 2. Hymns, Sanskrit. 3. Sanskrit poetry—Translations into English. 4. English poetry—Translations from Sanskrit. I. Title.

NEBESKY-WOJKOWITZ, Rene de 294.3'4'21109515
Oracles and demons of Tibet : the cult and iconography of the Tibetan protective deities / by Rene de Nebesky-Wojkowitz. New York : Gordon Press, 1976, c1956. p. cm. English or Tibetan. Reprint of the ed. published by Mouton, 's-Gravenhage. "Tibetan sources": p. "Tibetan texts": p. [BL1945.T5N4 1976] 76-19106 ISBN 0-87968-463-1 lib.bdg. : 75.00
1. Tibet—Religion. 2. Gods, Lamaist. 3. Bon (Tibetan religion) I. Title.

CARUS, Paul, 1852-1919. 294.3'4'22
Karma/Nirvana. Illus. by Kwasong Suzuki. La Salle, Ill., Open Court Pub. Co., 1973. 135 p. illus. 22 cm. [BQ4435.C37 1973] 73-82781 ISBN 0-87548-249-X 5.95
1. Karma. 2. Nirvana. I. Carus, Paul, 1852-1919. Nirvana. 1973. II. Title.

JOHANSSON, Rune Edvin Andrews, 1918- 294.3'4'23
The psychology of nirvana; a comparative study of the natural goal of Buddhism and the aims of modern western psychology, by Rune E. A. Johansson. Garden City, Anchor Books [1970] 142 p. 19 cm. Bibliography: p. [137] [BL1456.66.J6 1970] 74-103789 1.45
1. Nirvana. 2. Buddha and Buddhism—Psychology. I. Title.

MATSUNAGA, Daigan. 294.3'4'23
The Buddhist concept of hell, by Daigan and Alicia Matsunaga. New York, Philosophical Library [1971, c1972] 152 p. illus. 22 cm. Bibliography: p. 145-147. [BL1456.68.M38] 73-145466 ISBN 0-8022-2048-7 4.95
1. Saddharmasmrtiupasthanasutra. 2. Hell (Buddhism) I. Matsunaga, Alicia, joint author. II. Title.

SHCHERBATSKOI, Fedor Ippolitovich, 1866-1942. 294.3'4'23
The conception of Buddhist nirvana (along with Sanskrta text of Madhayamaka-karika) by Th. Stcherbatsky. With comprehensive analysis & introd. [by Jaideva Singh] New York, Gordon Press, 1973. 1 v. (various pagings) 24 cm. Includes English translation and appended Sanskrit text of chapters 1 and 25 of Nagarjuna's Madhyamakakarika and of Candrakirti's commentary, Prasannapada. Includes bibliographical references. [BQ4263.S5 1973] 73-8277 ISBN 0-87968-058-X
1. Nirvana. 2. Madhyamika (Buddhism) I. Singh, Jaideva, ed. II. Nagarjuna, Siddha. Madhyamikasastra. 1973. III. Candrakirti. Prasannapada. 1973. IV. Title.

TATZ, Mark. 294.3'4'23
Rebirth : the Tibetan game of liberation / by Mark Tatz and Jody Kent. 1st ed. Garden City, N.Y. : Anchor Press, 1977. 231 p. : ill. ; 26 cm. Includes bibliographical references. [BQ7566.5.T37] 76-2845 ISBN 0-385-11421-4 : 6.95
1. Rebirth (Game) 2. Eschatology, Buddist. 3. Spiritual life (Lamaism) 4. Cosmology, Buddhist. I. Kent, Jody, joint author. II. Title.

WELBON, Guy Richard. 294.3'4'23
The Buddhist nirvana and its Western interpreters. Chicago, University of Chicago Press [1968] xi, 320 p. 23 cm. Bibliography: p. 305-310. [BL1456.66.W42] 67-25535
1. Nirvana. I. Title.

KORNFIELD, Jack, 1945- 294.3'4'3
Living Buddhist masters / by Jack Kornfield. Santa Cruz, Calif. : Unity Press, 1977. p. cm. (The Mindfulness series) Includes index. [BQ5612.K67] 76-48279 ISBN 0-913300-03-9 : 9.95. ISBN 0-913300-04-7 pbk. : 4.95
1. Meditation (Buddhism) I. Title.

LASSALLE, Hugo, 1898- 294.3'4'3
Zen meditation for Christians [by] H. M. Enomiya Lassalle. Translated by John C. Maraldo. La Salle, Ill., Open Court, 1974. 175 p. 21 cm. (Religious encounters: East and West) Includes bibliographical references. [BQ9288.L3713] 73-23024 ISBN 0-87548-151-5 7.95
1. Meditation (Zen Buddhism) 2. Mysticism—Comparative studies. I. Title.

LERNER, Eric. 294.3'4'3
Journey of insight meditation : a personal experience of the Buddha's way / Eric Lerner. New York : Schocken Books, 1977. 185 p. ; 21 cm. [BQ970.E777A34] 76-49726 ISBN 0-8052-3648-1 : 8.95
1. Lerner, Eric. 2. Buddhists—United States—Biography. 3. Meditation (Buddhism) I. Title.

SHIBAYAMA, Zenkei, 1894- 294.3'4'3
Zen comments on the Mumonkan. Translated into English by Sumiko Kudo. [1st ed.] New York, Harper & Row [1974] xvi, 361 p. illus. 24 cm. [BQ9289.H843S513] 73-18692 ISBN 0-06-067279-X 10.95
1. Hui-k'ai, Shih, 1183-1260. Wu men kuan. 2. Koan. I. Hui-k'ai, Shih, 1183-1260. Wu men kuan. English. 1974. II. Title.

WATTS, Alan Wilson, 1915- 294.3'4'3
The art of contemplation; a facsimile manuscript with doodles, by Alan Watts. Sausalito, Calif., Society for Comparative Philosophy [1972] 16 l. illus. 33 cm. [BQ5612.W38 1972] 72-194725
1. Meditation (Buddhism) I. Title.

WATTS, Alan Wilson, 1915- 294.3'4'3
The art of contemplation; a facsimile manuscript with doodles by Alan Watts. [1st ed.] New York, Pantheon Books [1972] 16 p. illus. 28 cm. Reprint of the 1972 limited ed. [BQ5612.W38 1972b] 72-10174 ISBN 0-394-70963-2 2.95
1. Meditation (Buddhism) I. Title.

SIMPSON, William, 1823-1899. 294.3'4'37
The Buddhist praying-wheel; a collection of material bearing upon the symbolism of the wheel and circular movements in custom and religious ritual. New introd. by Omar V. Garrison. New Hyde Park, N.Y., University Books [1970] ix, 303 p. illus. 24 cm. Includes bibliographical references. [BL604.W4S56 1970] 74-118597 7.95
1. Wheels (in religion, folk-lore, etc.) I. Title.

ANDERSON, Benedict R O'G 294.3'4'38
Mythology and the tolerance of the Javanese [by] Benedict R. O'G Anderson. Ithaca, N.Y., Modern Indonesia Project, Southeast Asia Program, Dept. of Asian Studies, Cornell University, 1965. x, 77 p. illus. 28 cm. (Cornell University. Modern Indonesia Project. Monograph series) [BL2120.J3A7] 67-2748
1. Mythology, Javanese. 2. National charicteristics, Javanese. 3. Toleration. I. Title. II. Series.

BEYER, Stephan. 294.3'4'38
The cult of Tara; magic and ritual in Tibet. Berkeley, University of California Press [1974, c1973] xxi, 542 p. 25 cm. (Hermeneutics: studies in the history of religions, 1) Bibliography: p. 503-519. [BQ4710.T34T53] 74-186109 ISBN 0-520-02192-4 20.00
1. Tara (goddess)—Cult—Tibet. 2. Buddha and Buddhism—Rituals. I. Title. II. Series.

KLEEN, Tyra af, 1874- 294.3'4'38
Mudras: the ritual hand-poses of the Buddha priests and the Shiva priests of Bali, by Tyra de Kleen. With an introd. by A. J. D. Campbell. New foreword by Omar V. Garrison. New Hyde Park, N.Y., University Books [1970] vi, 62 p. illus. 26 cm. [BL2120.B2K4 1970] 76-118604 5.00
1. Buddha and Buddhism—Bali (Island) 2. Sivaism. 3. Bali (Island)—Religion. I. Campbell, A. J. D. II. Title. III. Title: Ritual hand-poses. IV. Title: Hand-poses, Ritual.

KIMURA, Gibun, 1906- 294.3'4'4
Why pursue the Buddha? / By Gibun Kimura ; edited by Sosuke Nishimoto. Los Angeles : Nembutsu Press, c1976. 160 p. ; 23 cm. [BQ968.I487A35] 75-14981 ISBN 0-912624-00-0 5.95
1. Kimura, Gibun, 1906- 2. Religious life (Pure Land Buddhism)—Shin authors. I. Title.

NAGARJUNA, Siddha. 294.3'4'4
Golden zephyr / translated from the Tibetan and annotated by Leslie Kawamura. Emeryville, Calif. : Dharma Pub., c1975. xx, 165 p. : ill. ; 21 cm. (Tibetan translation series) Translation of Suhrllekha, by S. Nagarjuna, and of Bse sprin gi mchan 'grel Padma-dkar-po'i phren ba, by 'Jam-mgon 'Ju Mi-pham-rgya-mtsho. Includes indexes. Contents.Contents.—Nagarjuna, S. A letter to a friend.—Mi-pham-rgya-mtsho, 'Jam-mgon 'Ju. The garland of white lotus flowers, a commentary on Nagarjuna's A letter to a friend. Bibliography: p. [154]-157. [BQ5385.N3313] 75-5259 ISBN 0-913546-22-4 : 7.95. ISBN 0-913546-21-6 pbk. : 4.75
1. Religious life (Mahayana Buddhism) I. Mi-pham-rgya-mtsho, 'Jam-mgon 'Ju, 1846-1912. Bse sprin gi mchan 'grel Padma-dkar-po'i phren ba. English. 1975. II. Title. III. Series.
Contents omitted.

*NYANAPONIKA, ed. 294.344
Pathways of Buddhist thought; essays from The Wheel, edited by the Venerable Nyanaponika Mahathera and selected by M. O'C. Walshe. New York, Barnes & Noble [1972 c.1971] 255 p. 23 cm. The essays in this book are from the Wheel series of publications which have been issued during the past ten years by the Buddhist Publication Society, Kandy, Ceylon. [BL1478] ISBN 0-06-4952215 9.50
1. Buddhism—addresses, essays, lectures. I. Title.

REFLECTIONS of mind : 294.3'4'4
Western psychology meets Tibetan Buddhism / Tarthang Tulku, editor. Emeryville, Ca. : Dharma Pub., [1975] xii, 198 p. : ill. ; 22 cm. (Nyingma psychology series) Includes bibliographical references. [BQ4570.P76R43] 75-5254 ISBN 0-913546-14-3 pbk. : 3.95
1. Buddhism—Psychology—Addresses, essays, lectures. I. Tarthang Tulku.

COLEMAN, John E, 1930- 294.3'4'40924
The quiet mind [by] John E. Coleman. [1st ed.] New York, Harper & Row [1971] 239 p. maps. 22 cm. [BL627.C65 1971b] 71-148446 5.95
1. Meditation. 2. Peace of mind. 3. Buddha and Buddhism. 4. Psychical research. I. Title.

ELIOT, Alexander. 294.3'4'40924 B
Zen edge / Alexander Eliot. London : Thames and Hudson, c1976. 136 p. ; 23 cm. [BQ9288.E43] 76-382477 ISBN 0-500-01171-0 : £4.00
1. Eliot, Alexander. 2. Spiritual life (Zen Buddhism) I. Title.

BLOFELD, John Eaton Calthorpe, 1913- 294.3'4'42
The Tantric mysticism of Tibet; a practical guide, by John Blofeld. [1st ed.] New York, Dutton, 1970. 257 p. illus. 22 cm. Bibliography: p. 253. [BL1433.3.T3B55 1970b] 76-119478 ISBN 0-525-21423-2 6.95
1. Tantric Buddhism—Tibet. I. Title.

HUGHES, Catharine, 1935- comp. 294.3'4'42
The solitary journey: Buddhist mystical reflections. Edited and with photos. by Catharine Hughes. New York, Seabury Press [1974] 1 v. (unpaged) illus. 21 cm. "A Crossroad book." [BQ135.H83] 74-13780 ISBN 0-8164-2103-X
1. Buddha and Buddhism—Quotations, maxims, etc. I. Title.

JOHNSTON, William, 1925- 294.3'4'42
The still point: reflections on Zen and Christian mysticism. New York, Fordham University Press, 1970. xiii, 193 p. 21 cm. Includes bibliographical references. [BL625.J63] 75-95713 ISBN 0-8232-0860-5 7.50
1. Mysticism—Comparative studies. 2. Zen Buddhism—Relations—Christianity. 3. Christianity and other religions—Zen Buddhism. I. Title.

CHOGYAM Trungpa, Trungpa Tulku, 1939- 294.3'4'43
Meditation in action. Berkeley Shambala, 1970 [c1969] 74 p. 22 cm. (The Clear light series) [BJ1289.C48 1970] 78-11846 2.25
1. Ethics, Buddhist. I. Title.

DHIRAVAMSA. 294.3'4'43
The way of non-attachment : the practive of insight meditation / by Dhiravamsa. New York : Schocken Books, 1977, c1975. 160 p. ; 21 cm. [BQ5630.V5D48 1977] 76-48761 ISBN 0-8052-3644-9 : 6.95
1. Vipasyana (Buddhism) 2. Meditation (Buddhism) I. Title.

EASWARAN, Eknath. 294.3'4'43
The mantram handbook / Eknath Easwaran ; introd. by Richard B. Applegate. Berkeley, Calif. : Nilgiri Press, c1977. 260 p. ; 19 cm. Includes index. Bibliography: p. 249-250. [BL624.E17] 77-3222 ISBN 0-915132-10-9 pbk. : 5.00
1. Mantras. 2. Spiritual life. I. Title.

GOLDSTEIN, Joseph, 1944- 294.3'4'43
Emptying ... / Joseph Goldstein. Santa Cruz : Unity Press, [1975] p. cm. (Mindfulness series) [BQ5612.G64] 75-20304 ISBN 0-913300-05-5 pbk. : 3.95
1. Meditation (Buddishm) I. Title.

GOVINDA, Anagarika Brahmacari. 294.3'4'43
Creative meditation and multi-dimensional consciousness / by Anagarika Govinda. 1st ed. Wheaton, Ill. : Theosophical Pub. House, 1976. p. cm. (A Quest book) Includes index. [BQ8938.G68] 75-31616 ISBN 0-8356-0475-6. ISBN 0-8356-0472-1 pbk.
1. Meditation (Tantric Buddhism) 2. Meditation (Buddhism) 3. Buddhist meditations. I. Title.

GOVINDA, Anagarika Brahmacari. 294.3'4'43
Creative meditation and multi-dimensional consciousness / by Anagarika Govinda. 1st ed. Wheaton, Ill. : Theosophical Pub. House, 1976. p. cm. (A Quest book) Includes index. [BQ8938.G68] 75-31616 ISBN 0-8356-0475-6 : 11.00 ISBN 0-8356-0472-1 pbk. :
1. Meditation (Tantric Buddhism) 2. Meditation (Buddhism) 3. Buddhist meditations. I. Title.

THE Grace of Zen : 294.3'4'43
Zen texts for meditation / by Ito Tenzaa Chuya ... [et al.] ; introduced by Karlfried Durckheim ; with a pref. by Dom Aelred Graham ; [translation by John Maxwell]. New York : Seabury Press, 1977,c1976. 107 p. : ill. ; 21 cm. "A Crossroad book." [BQ9289.5.G7] 76-52584 ISBN 0-8164-2151-X pbk. : 3.95
1. Zen meditations. I. Ito, Chuya.

THE Grace of Zen : 294.3'4'43
Zen texts for meditation / by Ito Tenzaa Chuya ... [et al.] ; introduced by Karlfried Durckheim ; with a pref. by Dom Aelred Graham ; [translation by John Maxwell]. New York : Seabury Press, 1977,c1976. 107 p. : ill. ; 21 cm. "A Crossroad book." [BQ9289.5.G7] 76-52584 ISBN 0-8164-2151-X pbk. : 3.95
1. Zen meditations. I. Ito, Chuya.

HAMILTON-MERRITT, Jane. 294.3'4'43
A meditator's diary : a western woman's unique experiences in Thailand temples / Jane Hamilton-Merritt. 1st U.S. ed. New York : Harper & Row, c1976. 157 p. : ill. ; 21 cm. Bibliography: p. 149. [BQ5612.H35 1976] 76-10001 ISBN 0-06-065563-1 : 6.95
1. Hamilton-Merritt, Jane. 2. Meditation (Buddhism) 3. Buddhist meditations. I. Title.

HAMILTON-MERRITT, Jane 294.3'4'43
A meditator's diary : a western woman's unique experiences in Thailand temples / Jane Hamilton-Merritt. New York : Pocket Books, 1977,c1976. 189p. : ill. ; 18 cm. (A Kangaroo Book) Bibliography: p.189. [BQ5612.H35 1976] ISBN 0-671-81467-2 pbk. : 1.75
1. Hamilton-Merritt, Jane. 2. Meditation (Buddhism). 3. Buddhist meditations. I. Title.
L.C. card no. for 1976 Harpe & Row ed.: 76-10001.

HUBER, Jack T. 294.3443
Through an Eastern window [by] Jack Huber. Boston, Houghton Mifflin, 1967 [c1965] 121 p. 21 cm. [BL1478.6.H79] 67-17999
1. Meditation (Buddhism) 2. Zen Buddhism—Discipline. I. Title.

HUBER, Jack T. 294.3443
Through an Eastern window / Jack Huber. New York : St. Martin's Press [1976c1965] 121p. ; 21 cm. (Griffin books) [BL1478.6H79] 75-29928 pbk. : 2.95
1. Meditation(Buddhism) 2. Zen Buddhism-Discipline. I. Title.

HUMPHREYS, Christmas, 1901- 294.3'4'43
Concentration and meditation: a manual of mind development. Baltimore, Md., Penguin Books [1970, c1968] xi, 254 p. 18 cm. (A Pelican book, A1236) [BL1478.6.H85 1970] 78-16101 1.45
1. Meditation (Buddhism) I. Title.

LORRANCE, Arleen, 1939- 294.3'4'43
Musings for meditation / by a Buddha from Brooklyn, Arleen Lorrance. San Diego, Ca. : LP Publications, 1976. 174 p. : ill. ; 13 cm. [BL624.L67] 76-14783 ISBN 0-916192-03-2 pbk. : 2.50
1. Meditations. I. Title.

LOUNSBERY, Grace Constant. 294.3'4'43
Buddhist meditation in the southern school; theory and practice for westerners, by G. Constant Lounsbery. With a foreword by W. Y. Evans-Wentz. Tucson, Ariz., Omen Press, 1973 [c1935] xvii, 177 p. 21 cm. Bibliography: p. 171-172. [BQ5602.L68 1973] 73-76994 ISBN 0-912358-43-2 2.45
1. Meditation (Buddhism) I. Title.

NHAT Hanh, Thich. 294.3'4'43
The miracle of mindfulness! : A manual of meditation / Thich Nhat Hanh ; translated by Mobi Warren ; with ill. by Vo Dinh. Boston : Beacon Press, [1976] p. cm. [BQ5612.N48] 76-7747 ISBN 0-8070-1118-5 : 7.95 ISBN 0-8070-1119-3 pbk. :
1. Meditation (Buddhism) 2. Buddhist meditations. I. Title.

NYANAPONIKA. 294.3'4'43
The heart of Buddhist meditation (Satipattana); a handbook of mental training based on the Buddha's way of mindfulness, with an anthology of relevant texts translated from the Pali and Sanskrit. [1st American ed.] New York, Citadel Press [1969] 223 p. 22 cm. Includes bibliographical references. [BL1478.6.N88 1969b] 69-19724 6.00
1. Meditation (Buddhism) I. Title. II. Title: Satipatthana.

SEKIDA, Katsuki, 1893- 294.3'4'43
Zen training : methods and philosophy / Katsuki Sekida ; edited, with an introd., by A. V. Grimstone. 1st ed. New York : Weatherhill, 1975. 258 p. : ill. ; 22 cm. An expanded English version of An introduction to Zen for beginners, originally written in Japanese. Includes bibliographical references and index. [BQ9288.S4313] 75-17573 ISBN 0-8348-0111-6 : 8.95. ISBN 0-8348-0114-0 pbk. : 4.95
1. Meditation (Zen Buddhism) 2. Zen Buddhism—Discipline. I. Title.

SUJATA, A., 1948- 294.3'4'43
Beginning to see; a collection of epigrams about the problem of living and the freedom to be gained through the Buddha's insight meditation, by A. Sujata. Pen-art by Julie Wester. [Rev. ed.] Santa Cruz, [Calif.] Unity Press [1975] [96] p. illus. 21 cm. (Mindfulness series) [BQ5612.S9 1974] 74-8207 ISBN 0-913300-35-7 : 2.50
1. Buddhist meditations. 2. Epigrams, English. I. Title.

SUNNO Bhikku, 1945- 294.3'4'43
Living Buddhist masters / Sunno Bhikku. Santa Cruz, Calif. : Unity Press, 1975. p. cm. (Mindfulness series) Includes index. Bibliography: p. [BQ5612.S93] 75-20291 ISBN 0-913300-03-9 : 9.95. ISBN 0-913300-04-7 : 4.95
1. Meditation (Buddhism) 2. Buddhist monks—Burma—Biography. 3. Buddhist monks—Thailand—Biography. I. Title.

SUZUKI, Shunryu. 294.3'4'43
Zen mind, beginner's mind. Edited by Trudy Dixon. With an introd. by Richard Baker. [1st ed.] New York, Walker/Weatherhill [1970] 134 p. illus. 22 cm. [BL1478.6.S9 1970] 70-123326 4.50
1. Meditation (Zen Buddhism)—Addresses, essays, lectures. I. Dixon, Trudy, ed. II. Title.

SWEARER, Donald K., 1934- comp. 294.3'4'43
Secrets of the lotus; studies in Buddhist meditation. Edited by Donald K. Swearer. New York, Macmillan [1971] xii, 242 p. 21 cm. Bibliography: p. 236-237. [BL1478.6.S93] 75-150068 5.95
1. Meditation (Buddhism) 2. Meditation (Zen Buddhism) I. Title.

TARTHANG Tulku. 294.3'4'43
Gesture of balance : a guide to awareness, selfhealing, and meditation / Tarthang Tulku. Emeryville, Calif. : Dharma Pub., c1977. xii, 170 p., [3] leaves of plates : ill. ; 22 cm. (Nyingma psychology series) [BF637.M4T37] 75-5255 ISBN 0-913546-17-8. pbk. : 4.95
1. Meditation. 2. Awareness. 3. Budda and Buddism—Psychology. I. Title.

*TRUNGPA, Chogyam. 294.3'4'43
The myth of freedom and the way of meditation / by Choglyam Trungpa ; edited by John Baker and Marvin Casper ; illustrated by Glen Eddy. Berkeley, Calif. : Shambhala, c1976. xiii, 176 p. : ill. ; 21 cm. Includes index. [BQ 5625] 75-40264 ISBN 0-87773-084-9 pbk. : 3.95
1. Meditation (Buddhism) I. Title.
Distributed by Random House.

UCHIYAMA, Kosho, 1912- 294.3'4'43
Approach to Zen; the reality of Zazen/Modern civilization and Zen. [Tokyo] Japan Publications [1973] 122 p. illus. 21 cm. Translation of Seimei no jitsubutsu. [BQ9288.U2413] 73-83957 ISBN 0-87040-252-8 3.50 (pbk.)
1. Meditation (Zen Buddhism) I. Title.
Available from publisher's San Francisco office.

WILLIS, Janice Dean. 294.3'4'43
The diamond light; an introduction to Tibetan Buddhist meditations, comp. by Janice Dean Willis. [New York] S. & S. [1973, c.1972] 124 p. illus. 24 cm. (Touchstone Book) [BL1478.7.W55] 78-189747 ISBN 0-671-21526-4 pap., 2.45
1. Lamaist meditations. 2. Meditation (Lamaism) I. Title.

CHOGYAM Trungpa, Trungpa Tulku, 1939- 294.3'4'44
Cutting through spiritual materialism, by Chogyam Trungpa. Edited by John Baker and Marvin Casper. Illustrated by Glen Eddy. Berkeley, Shambhala, 1973. 250 p. illus. 22 cm. (The Clear light series) [BQ4302.C47] 73-86145 ISBN 0-87773-049-0 3.95
1. Spiritual life (Buddhism) I. Title.

GRAY, Terence James Stannus. 294.3'4'44
Ask the awakened; the negative way [by] Wei Wu Wei. [1st American ed.] Boston, Little, Brown [1973, c1963] xx, 282 p. port. 20 cm. [BQ5572.G7 1973] 73-5598 ISBN 0-316-92810-0 3.45
1. Buddhist devotional literature. I. Title.

NAGARJUNA, Siddha. 294.3'4'44
Nagarjuna's letter : Nagarjuna's "Letter to a friend" with a commentary by the venerable Rendawa, Zhonnu . Lo-dro / translated by Geshe Lobsang Tharchin and Artemus B. Engle. Howell, N.J. : Rashi Gempil Ling, First Kalmuk Buddhist Temple, c1977. xi, 262 p. ; 28 cm. Includes index. [BQ5385.N3313 1977] 77-156251
1. Religious life (Buddhism) 2. Priests, Buddhist—Correspondence. I. Red-mda'-ba Gzon-nu-blo-gros, 1349-1412. II. Title.

NEWTON, Frank. 294.3'4'44
The path of virtue (The Dhammapada) [Translated and paraphrased from the Sanscrit. Clarksville, Ark., Harmony Buddhist Mission, 1971] 40 p. illus., forms. 28 cm. Cover title: The Dhammapada from Sanscrit. [BL1411.D52N48] 78-173024
1. Buddhist sermons, English. 2. Family records. I. Dhammapada. II. Title.

RICHARDS, Harriet M. 294.3'4'44
Light your own lamp, by Harriet M. Richards. New York, Philosophical Lib. [1967] xi, 158p. 22cm. [BL1478.54.R5] 66-26971 4.00
1. Religious life (Buddhism) I. Title.

SADDHATISSA, H. 294.3'5
Buddhist ethics; essence of Buddhism, by H. Saddhatissa. Foreword by M. O'C. Walshe. [1st American ed.] New York, G. Braziller [1971, c1970] 202 p. 22 cm. Bibliography: p. 195-197. [BJ1289.S23 1971] 75-141044 ISBN 0-8076-0598-0 6.50
1. Buddhist ethics.

SHAN o yin kuo ching. English & Sogdian. 294.3'5
The 'Sutra of the causes and effects of actions' in Sogdian; edited by D. N. MacKenzie. London, New York, Oxford U.P., 1970. xiii, 77 p. 23 cm. (London oriental series, 22) English and/or Sogdian; Sogdian text is a translation of the Chinese original. Includes bibliographical references. [BQ2102.E5M3] 73-160456 ISBN 0-19-713560-9 65/-
I. MacKenzie, D. N., ed. II. Title. III. Series.

BARTHELEMY-SAINT-HILAIRE, Jules 1805-1895 294.361
Hiouen-thsang in India, by J. Barthelemy Saint-Hilaire. Tr. from French by Laura Ensor. [2d ed.] Calcutta, Anil Gupta, 1965. 107p. 19cm. An extract from the author's larger work Buddhism in India [BL1473.H8B33] SA66 3.00
1. Hsuan-tsang, 596 (ca.)-664. I. Title.
Available from Hutchins Oriental, Pasadena, Calif.

GTSAN-SMYON He-ru-ka, 1452-1507. 294.3'61 B
The life of Milarepa / a new translation from the Tibetan by Lobsang P. Lhalungpa, in collaboration with Far West Translats. 1st ed. New York : Dutton, c1977. xxix, 221 p. ; 21 cm. Translation of Mi-la-ras-pa'i rnam thar. Includes bibliographical references. [BQ7950.M557G813 1977] 76-46374 pbk. : 5.95
1. Mi-la-ras-pa, 1040-1123. 2. Lamas—Tibet—Biography. I. Lhalungpa, Lobsang Phuntshok, 1926- II. Title.

HSU-YUN, 1839-1959. 294.3'6'1 B
Empty Cloud : the autobiography of the Chinese Zen Master, Hsu Yun / translated by Upasaka Lu K'uan Yu (Charles Luk). Rochester, N.Y. : Empty Cloud Press, c1974. 120 p. ; 21 cm. Abridged translation of Hsu-yun ho shang nien p'u. [BQ962.S87A33213] 75-313534
1. Hsu-yun, 1839-1959. I. Title.

HUI-LI. 294.3'61 B
The life of Hiuen-Tsiang, by the shaman Hwui Li. With an introd. containing an account of the works of I-tsing, by Samuel Beal. With a pref. by L. Cranmer-Byng. New ed. Westport, Conn., Hyperion Press [1973] xlvii, 218 p. 23 cm. Reprint of the 1911 translation of Ta T'ang ta tz'u en ssu San Tsang fa shih chuan published by K. Paul, Trench, Trubner, London in series: Trubner's oriental series. Includes bibliographical references. [BQ8149.H787H813 1973] 73-880 ISBN 0-88355-074-1
1. Hsuan-tsang, 596 (ca.)-664. 2. I-ching, 635-713. I. Beal, Samuel, 1825-1889, tr. II. Title.

KUZUNISHI, Sosei. 294.3'61
The Zen life. Photos. by Sosei Kuzunishi. Text by Koji Sato. Translated by Ryojun Victoria. [1st English ed.] New York, Weatherhill [1972] 190 p. illus. 18 x 19 cm. Translation of Zen no seikatsu. [BQ9294.4.J3K8913] 79-185602 ISBN 0-8348-1508-7 6.50
1. Monastic and religious life (Zen Buddhism)—Japan. I. Sato, Koji, 1905- II. Title.

RAS-CHUN. 294.3'61 B
Tibet's great yogi, Milarepa: a biography from the Tibetan, being the Jetsun-kahbum, or biographical history of Jetsun-Milarepa, according to the late Lama Kazi Dawa-Samdup's English rendering; edited with introduction and annotations by W. Y. Evans-Wentz. 2nd ed. London, New York, Oxford U.P., 1969. xxviii, 315 p., 6 plates. illus. 21 cm. (A Galaxy book, GB294) Translation of Mi-la-ras-pa'i rNam-thar. [BL1473.M54R313 1969] 71-514047 20/-
1. Mi-la-ras-pa, 1038-1122. 2. Lamaism. I. Zla-ba-Bsam-'grub, Kazi, 1868-1922, tr. II. Wentz, Walter Yeeling Evans, ed. III. Title.

HUI-LI. 294.3'61'0924 B
The life of Hiuen-Tsiang, by the shaman Hwui Li. With an introd. containing an account of the works of I-tsing, by Samuel Beal. With a pref. by L. Cranmer-Byng. New ed. Westport, Conn., Hyperion Press [1973] xlvii, 218 p. 23 cm. Reprint of the 1911 translation of Ta T'ang ta tz'u en ssu San Tsang fa shih chuan published by K. Paul, Trench, Trubner, London in series: Trubner's oriental series. Includes bibliographical references. [BQ8149.H787H813 1973] 73-880 ISBN 0-88355-074-1 12.75
1. Hsuan-tsang, 596 (ca.)-664. 2. I-ching, 635-713. I. Beal, Samuel, 1825-1889, tr. II. Title.

RATO Khyongla Nawang Losang. 294.3'61'0924 B
My life and lives : the story of a Tibetan incarnation / Rato Khyongla Nawang Losang ; edited with an introd. by Joseph Campbell. 1st ed. New York : Dutton, c1977. p. cm. [BQ982.A767A35] 77-8399 ISBN 0-525-47480-3 pbk. : 3.50
1. Rato Khyongla Nawang Losang. 2. Lamas—Tibet—Biography. I. Campbell, Joseph, 1904- II. Title.

BARLAAM and Joasaph. English & Ethiopic. 294.3'63 B
Barlam and Yewaseef, being the Ethiopic version of a Christianized rescension of the Buddhist legend of the Buddha and the Bodhisattva / the Ethiopic text edited for the first time with an English translation and introd., etc., by E. A. Wallis Budge. New York : AMS Press, 1976. 2 v. : ill. ; 23 cm. Reprint of the 1923 ed. published at the University Press, Cambridge, Eng. Contents.Contents.—v. 1. Ethiopic text.—v. 2. The introduction, English translation, etc.: Introduction. The Book of Baralam and Yewasef, English translation. The preaching of St. Thomas in India (p. [279]-297) The acts of St. Thomas in India (p. [298]-338) Includes bibliographical references and index. [PJ9098.B313 1976] 73-18832 ISBN 0-404-11300-1 : 49.50 (2 vol set)
I. Budge, Ernest Alfred Thompson Wallis, Sir, 1857-1934. II. Bible. N.T. Apocryphal books. Acts of Thomas. English. 1976. III. Title. IV. Title: Buddha and the Bodhisattva.

BLOFELD, John Eaton Calthorpe, 1913- 294.3'63 B
The wheel of life; the autobiography of a Western Buddhist [by] John Blofeld. 2d ed. Berkeley [Calif.] Shambala, 1972. 291 p. illus. 22 cm. [BQ942.L64A3 1972] 72-189854 3.95
I. Title.

BYLES, Marie Beuzeville. 294.3'6'3
Footprints of Gautama the Buddha; being the story of the Buddha his disciples knew, describing portions of his ministerial life. Wheaton, Ill., Theosophical Pub. House [1967, c1957] 227 p. illus., map. 20 cm. (A Quest book) Includes bibliographical references. [BL1470.B9 1967] 68-5855 1.50
1. Gautama Buddha—Footprints. I. Title.

*CARUS, Paul. 294.363
The Gospel of Buddha, compiled from ancient records by Paul Carus, illus by O. Kopetzky. Chicago, Open Court Publishing Co. [1973] 311 p. illus., 21 cm. [B2915] ISBN 0-87548-228-7 2.95 (pbk.)
1. Gautama Buddha. 2. Gautama Buddha—Teachings. I. Title.

CARUS, Paul, 1852-1919. 294.3'6'3
The gospel of Buddha, according to old records. Told by Paul Carus. Tucson, Omen Press, 1972. xiv, 275 p. 21 cm. Includes bibliographical references. [BQ915.C37 1972] 72-90290 ISBN 0-912358-33-5 2.45
1. Gautama Buddha—Teachings. 2. Gautama Buddha. I. Title.

COHEN, Joan Lebold. 294.3'63 B
Buddha. Illustrated by Mary Frank. [New York] Delacorte Press [1969] 86 p. illus. 24 cm. "A Seymour Lawrence book." Relates Buddha's birth, boyhood, and search for enlightenment and the findings of this quest which became the bases of one of the world's great religions. [BL1470.C6] 92 69-10761 3.95
1. Gautama Buddha—Juvenile literature. I. Frank, Mary, 1933- illus. II. Title.

FOUCHER, Alfred Charles Auguste, 1865-1952. 294.3'63 B
The life of the Buddha, according to the ancient texts and monuments of India. Abridged translation by Simone Brangier Boas. Westport, Conn., Greenwood Press [1972, c1963] xiv, 272 p. 24 cm. Bibliography: p. [269]-272. [BQ884.F6813 1972] 72-6195 ISBN 0-8371-6476-1
1. Gautama Buddha. I. Title.

FOZDAR, Jamshed. 294.3'63 B
The god of Buddha [by] Jamshed K. Fozdar. New York, Asia Pub. House [1973] xii, 184 p. 24 cm. Bibliography: p. 178-179. [BQ918.G6F68 1973] 72-87303 ISBN 0-210-22395-2 8.00
1. Gautama Buddha. 2. God. 3. Buddha and Buddhism—Relations—Hinduism. 4. Hinduism—Relations—Buddhism. I. Title.

HARI Dass, Baba. 294.3'63 B
Hariakhan Baba, known, unknown / Baba Hari Dass. 1st ed. Davis, Calif. : Sri Rama Foundation, 1975. 93 p. : ill. ; 17 cm. [BL1175.H336H37] 75-3838
1. Hariakhan, Baba. I. Title.

†IKEDA, Daisaku. 294.3'63 B
The living Buddha : an interpretive biography / by Daisaku Ikeda ; translated by Burton Watson. 1st English ed. New York : Weatherhill, 1976. x, 148 p., [4] leaves of plates : ill. ; 24 cm. Translation of Watakushi no Shakuson kan. [BQ886.I3813] 75-40446 ISBN 0-8348-0117-5 : 7.95
1. Gautama Buddha. I. Title.

KELEN, Betty. 294.3'63 B
Gautama Buddha in life and legend. New York, Lothrop, Lee & Shepard Co. [1967] xiv, 192 p. ports. 22 cm. Bibliography: p. [187]-188. [BL1470.K4] 67-22598
1. Gautama Buddha. I. Title.

KIKUMURA, Norihiko. 294.3'63 B
Shinran: his life and thought. Los Angeles, Nembutsu Press [1972] 192 p. 23 cm. Translation of Shinran. [BQ8749.S557K513] 70-172538 4.95
1. Shinran, 1173-1263.

ROERICH, Elena Ivanovna. 294.3'6'3
Foundations of Buddhism, by Helena Roerich. [2d ed.] New York, Agni Yoga Society [1971] 157 p. 20 cm. Bibliography: p. [147] [BQ893.R63 1971] 73-151810
1. Gautama Buddha. I. Title.

SUGANA, Gabriele Mandel. 294.3'63
The life and times of Buddha; translated [from the Italian] by Vivian Hart. London, New York, Hamlyn, 1968. [1], 77 p. (chiefly illus. (chiefly col.)) 30 cm. (Portraits of greatness) Col. illus. on lining papers. [BL1455.S84] 70-434856 17/6
1. Buddha and Buddhism—Pictures, illustrations, etc. I. Title.

SWEARER, Donald K., 1934- 294.3'63
Wat Haripunjaya : a study of the Royal Temple of the Buddha's Relic, Lamphun, Thailand / by Donald K. Swearer. Missoula, Mont. : Published by Scholars Press for the American Academy of Religion, c1976. x, 94 p. : ill. ; 24 cm. (Studies in religion ; no. 10) Includes bibliographical references. [BQ6337.L352W378] 75-33802 ISBN 0-89130-052-X : 4.50
1. Wat Haripunjaya. 2. Gautama Buddha—Relics. I. Title. II. Series: American Academy of Religion. AAR studies in religion ; no. 10.

FOUCHER, Alfred Charles Auguste, 1865-1952. 294.3'63'0924 B
The life of the Buddha, according to the ancient texts and monuments of India. Abridged translation by Simone Brangier Boas. Westport, Conn., Greenwood Press [1972, c1963] xiv, 272 p. 24 cm. Bibliography: p. [269]-272. [BQ884.F68 1972] 72-6195 ISBN 0-8371-6476-1 14.75
1. Gautama Buddha. I. Title.

KELEN, Betty. 294.3'63'0924 B
Gautama Buddha in life and legend. New York, Lothrop, Lee & Shepard Co. [1967] xiv, 192 p. ports. 22 cm. Bibliography: p. [187]-188. Combines archeological fact and Buddhist theological legend to recount the life of Gautama Buddha, from the traditional story of his birth, through his quest for wisdom, the years as a sage and teacher, and his death. [BL1470.K4] 92 AC 68
1. Gautama Buddha. 2. Buddha and Buddhism. I. Title.

BLOOM, Alfred. 294.364
Shinran's gospel of pure grace. Tucson, Published for the Association for Asian Studies by the University of Arizona Press, 1965. xiv, 97 p. 24 cm. (Association for Asian Studies. Monographs and papers, no. 20) Bibliography: p. 89-93. [BL1442.S53B55] 64-8757
1. Shinran, 1173-1263. I. Association for Asian Studies. II. Title. III. Series.

BLOOM, Alfred 294.364
Shinran's gospel of pure grace. Tuscon, Pub. for the Assn. for Asian Studies by the Univ. of Ariz. Pr. [c.]1965. xiv, 97p. 24cm. (Assn. for Asian Studies. Monographs and papers. no. 20) Bibl. [BL1442.S53B55] 64-8757 5.00 bds.,

1. Shinran, 1173-1263. I. Association for Asian Studies. II. Title. III. Series.

KIM, Hee-Jin. 294.3'64 B
Dogen Kigen, mystical realist / Hee-Jin Kim. Tucson : Published for the Association for Asian Studies by the University of Arizona Press, c1975. xiv, 384 p. ; 23 cm. (Monographs of the Association for Asian Studies ; no. 29) Includes index. Bibliography: p. 359-370. [BQ9449.D657K56] 74-33725 ISBN 0-8165-0544-6 : 8.95. ISBN 0-8165-0513-6 pbk. : 4.95
1. Dogen, 1200-1253. I. Association for Asian Studies. II. Title. III. Series: Association for Asian Studies. Monographs of the Association for Asian Studies ; no. 29.

DATOR, James Allen. 294.3'65
Soka Gakkai, builders of the third civilization: American and Japanese members. Seattle, University of Washington Press [1969] xiii, 171 p. 23 cm. Bibliography: p. 151-171. [BL1442.S6D3] 68-8509 7.95
1. Soka Gakkai.

MURATA, Kiyoaki, 1922- 294.3'65
Japan's new Buddhism; an objective account of Soka Gakkai, by Kiyoaki Murata. Foreword by Daisaku Ikeda. [1st ed.] New York, Walker/Weatherhill [i.e. J. Weatherhill; distributed by Walker, 1969] xii, 194 p. illus., ports. 24 cm. Bibliography: p. 183-186. [BL1442.S6M87] 74-83640 5.95
1. Soka Gakkai. I. Title.

HORNER, Isaline Blew, 294.3'657
1896-
Women under primitive Buddhism : laywomen and almswomen / by I. B. Horner. Delhi : Motilal Banarsidass, 1975. xxiv 391 p., 6 leaves of plates : ill. ; 22 cm. Reprint of the 1930 ed. published by G. Routledge, London. Includes bibliographical references and index. [HQ1742.H6 1975] 76-911012 ISBN 0-8426-0955-5 : 13.50
1. Women—India. 2. Women in Buddhism. I. Title.
Distributed by Verry.

SATO, Giei, 1921-1967. 294.3'657
Unsui: a diary of Zen monastic life. Drawings by Giei Sato. Text by Eshin Nishimura. Edited and with introd. by Bardwell L. Smith. Honolulu, University Press of Hawaii [1973] xxviii, 114 p. col. illus. 26 cm. "An East-West Center book." Includes bibliographical references. [BQ9294.4.J3S25 1973] 73-78112 ISBN 0-8248-0277-2 8.95
1. Monastic and religious life (Zen Buddhism)—Japan. I. Nishimura, Eshin. II. Title.
Pbk. 4.95, ISBN 0-8248-0272-1.

SUZUKI, Daisetz Teitaro, 294.3657
1870-1966.
The training of the Zen Buddhist monk. Illustrated by Zenchu Sato. New York, University Books [1965] xxviii, 161 p. group ports., 43 plates. 24 cm. [BL1478.S85 1965] 65-23523
1. Monasticism and religious orders, Buddhist. 2. Zen Buddhism—Japan. I. Sato, Zenchu, illus. II. Title.

BUNNAG, Jane. 294.3'657'09593
Buddhist monk, Buddhist layman; a study of urban monastic organization in central Thailand. Cambridge [Eng.] University Press, 1973. xii, 219 p. illus. 24 cm. (Cambridge studies in social anthropology, no. 6) Bibliography: p. 210-212. [BQ6160.T42P462] 72-86420 ISBN 0-521-08591-8 16.50
1. Monastic and religious life (Buddhism)—Thailand—Phra Nakhon Si Ayutthaya. 2. Sociology, Buddhist. 3. Phra Nakhon Si Ayutthaya, Thailand—Social conditions. I. Title.
Distributed by Cambridge University Press N.Y.

KAKHUN, Sok, 294.3'657'0922 B
13thcent., comp.
Lives of eminent Korean monks; the Haedong kosung chon. Translated with an introd. by Peter H. Lee. Cambridge, Harvard University Press, 1969. xiii, 116 p. 26 cm. (Harvard-Yenching Institute studies, 25) Bibliography: p. [99]-110. [BL1460.K2613] 69-18037 7.00
1. Buddha and Buddhism—Korea—Biography. I. Title. II. Series.

MENDELSON, E. 294.3'657'09591
Michael, 1928-
Sangha and state in Burma : a study of monastic sectarianism and leadership / E. Michael Mendelson ; edited by John P. Ferguson. Ithaca, N.Y. : Cornell University Press, 1975. 400 p. ; 24 cm. Includes index. Bibliography: p. [377]-385. [BQ6160.B93M46] 75-13398 ISBN 0-8014-0875-X : 19.50
1. Monasticism and religious orders, Buddhist—Burma. 2. Buddhism and state—Burma. I. Title.

RAHULA, Walpola. 294.3'657'095493
The heritage of the bhikkhu : a short history of the bhikkhu in educational, cultural, social, and political life / Walpola Rahula ; foreword by Edmund F. Perry ; translated by K. P. G. Wijayasurendra, and revised by the author. New York : Grove Press : distributed by Random House, [1974] xxxii, 176 p. ; 22 cm. Translation of Bhiksuvage Urumaya. Includes index. Bibliography: p. 165-167. [BQ356.R3313] 73-19215 ISBN 0-8021-0012-0 pbk. : 3.95
1. Buddha and Buddhism—Ceylon—History. 2. Buddhist monks—Ceylon. 3. Buddhism and state—Ceylon. 4. Buddhism and social problems—Ceylon. I. Title.

WETERING, 294.3'657'0924 B
Janwillem van de, 1931-
The empty mirror; experiences in a Japanese Zen monastery. [1st American ed.] Boston, Houghton Mifflin, 1974 [c1973] 145 p. 22 cm. Translation of De lege spiegel. [BQ9294.4.J3W4713 1974] 73-12235 5.95
1. Monastic and religious life (Zen Buddhism)—Japan. I. Title.

WETERING, 294.3'657'0924 B
Janwillem van de, 1931-
A glimpse of nothingness : experiences in an American Zen community / Janwillem van de Wetering. 1st American ed. Boston : Houghton-Mifflin, 1975. 184 p. ; 22 cm. Translation of Het dagende niets. [BQ9289.5.W4713 1975] 74-31078 ISBN 0-395-20442-9 : 6.95
1. Meditation (Zen Buddhism) 2. Monastic and religious life (Zen Buddhism)—United States. I. Title.

HASEGAWA, Seikan, 1945- 294.3'8
The cave of poison grass : essays on the Hannya sutra / by Seikan Hasegawa. Arlington, Va. : Great Ocean Publishers, [1975] 182 p. : ill. ; 21 cm. (Companions of Zen training) Includes the Hannya sutra in Chinese romanization and an English translation. Includes bibliographical references and indexes. [BQ1887.H37] 75-6600 ISBN 0-915556-00-6 10.00 ISBN 0-915556-01-4 pbk. : 3.95
1. Prajnaparamitas. Hrdaya—Addresses, essays, lectures. I. Prajnaparamitas. Hrdaya. English & Chinese. 1975. II. Title. III. Series.

KEIKAI, comp. 294.3'8
Miraculous stories from the Japanese Buddhist tradition; the Nihon ryoiki of the monk Kyokai. Translated and annotated with an introd. by Kyoko Motomochi Nakamura. Cambridge, Harvard University Press, 1973. xii, 322 p. 25 cm. (Harvard-Yenching Institute. Monograph series, v. 20) Translation of Nihon-koku gempo zen'aku ryoiki. Bibliography: p. 301-317. [BQ5775.J3K4313] 72-87773 ISBN 0-674-57635-7 12.50
1. Legends, Buddhist. I. Nakamura, Kyoko, 1932- tr. II. Title. III. Series.

THE Lotus Sutra : 294.3'8
its history and practice today. Santa Monica, Calif. : World Tribune Press, c1977. 78 p. : ill., [1] leaf of plates ; 18 cm. [BQ2057.L67] 77-152891
1. Soka Gakkai—Prayer-books and devotion—English. 2. Saddharmapundarika—Criticism, interpretation, etc.

MULLER, Friedrich Max, 294.3'8
1823-1900, ed.
Buddhist texts from Japan / edited by F. Max Muller. New York : AMS Press, 1976. 265 p. in various pagings : facsims. ; 24 cm. Reprint of the 1881-84 ed. published by Clarendon Press, Oxford, which was issued as v. 1, pts. 1-3 of Anecdota oxoniensia. Aryan series. Includes bibliographical references. [BQ1138.M83 1976] 73-18824 ISBN 0-404-11430-X : 27.50
1. Buddhism—Sacred books. I. Title. II. Series: Anecdota oxoniensia. Aryan series ; v. 1, pts. 1-3.

PANCAVIMSATISAHASRIKA. 294.3'8
The large sutra on perfect wisdom, with the divisions of the Abhisamayalnkara / translated by Edward Conze. Berkeley : University of California Press, [1975] xxviii, 679 p. ; 24 cm. Includes index. [BQ1952.E5C66] 71-189224 ISBN 0-520-02240-8 : 25.00
I. Conze, Edward, 1904- II. Maitreyanatha. Abhisamayalankara. 1975. III. Title.

PRAJNAPARAMITAS. 294.3'8
Astasahasrika. English.
The perfection of wisdom in eight thousand lines & its verse summary. Translated by Edward Conze. Bolinas, Four Seasons Foundation; distributed by Book People, Berkeley, 1973. xxii, 325 p. 23 cm. (Wheel series, 1) Contains some sections of the Ratnagunasancayagatha. Includes bibliographical references. [BQ1912.E5C66 1973] 72-76540 ISBN 0-87704-048-6 5.00
I. Conze, Edward, 1904- tr. II. Prajnaparamitas. Ratnagunasancayagatha. English. Selections. 1973. III. Title. IV. Series.

PRAJNAPARAMITAS. 294.3'8
Ratnagunasancayagatha.
Prajna-paramita-ratna-guna-samcaya-gatha : Sanskrit recension A / edited with an introd., bibliographical notes, and a Tibetan version from Tunhuang by Akira Yuyama. Cambridge ; New York : Cambridge University Press, 1976. lxxii, 214 p. ; 23 cm. Revision of the author's Australian National University at Canberra, 1970, with title: A study of the Prajna-paramita-ratna-guna-samcaya-gatha. Bibliography: p. [199]-214. [BQ1920.Y86 1976] 75-32910 ISBN 0-521-21081-X : 25.00
I. Yuyama, Akira.

SURANGAMASUTRA 294.38
The Surangama Sutra (Leng Yen Ching); Chinese rendering by Master Paramiti of Central North India at Chih Chih Monastery, Canton, China, A. D. 705; commentary (abridged) by Ch'an Master Han Shan (1546-1623); translated by Upasaka Ly K'uan Yu (Charles Luk) London, Rider [New York, Hillary House, c.1966] xxiii, 262p. 22cm. [BL1411.S77E55] 66-70040 7.50
I. Pramiti, fl. 705, tr. II. Han-shan, 1546-1623. III. Lu, K'uan Yu, 1898- tr. IV. Title.

TANTRAS. 294.3'8
Candamaharosanatantra. English & Sanskrit.
The Candamaharosana Tantra, chapters I-VIII. A critical edition and English translation [by] Christopher S. George. New Haven, Conn., American Oriental Society, 1974. x, 135 p. 26 cm. (American Oriental series, 56) Introductory matter in English. Includes the Tibetan text of the Candamaharosanatantra. Bibliography: p. 126-129. [BQ3340.C352E53] 74-182286 14.50
1. Candamaharosana—Cult. 2. Tantric Buddhism—Rituals. I. George, Christopher S., ed. II. Tantras. Candamaharosanatantra. Tibetan. 1974. III. Title. IV. Series.

THREE unknown Buddhist 294.3'8
stories in an Arabic version. Introd., text & translation by S. M. Stern & Sofie Walzer. Columbia, University of South Carolina Press [1971] 38 p. 23 cm. Arabic text reproduced from ms. copy. Stories incorporated in Ibn Babawayh's Kamal al-din wa-tamam al-ni'mah (romanized form), from which the editors have extracted them. [GR265.T5 1971] 72-189034 ISBN 0-87249-211-7 4.95
1. Tales, Oriental. 2. Legends, Buddhist. I. Stern, Samuel Miklos, 1920-1969, tr. II. Walzer, Sophie, tr. III. Ibn Babwayh, Muhammad ibn 'Ali, d. 991 or 2. Kamal al-din wa-tamam al-ni'mah. English & Arabic. 1971.

TU-LUN, Shih, 1908- 294.3'8
The essentials of the Dharma blossom sutra [by] Tripitaka Master Tu Lun. Translated by Bhikshu Heng Ch'ien. San Francisco, Buddhist Text Translation Society; distributed in the United States by the Sino-American Buddhist Association, 1974- v. illus. 22 cm. The commentary was originally delivered as a series of lectures. The text of the sutra is a translation of Kumarajiva's version entitled Miao fa lien hua ching. [BQ2057.T84] 74-171025
1. Saddharmapundarika—Commentaries. I. Heng Ch'ien, Bhikshu, tr. II. Saddharmapundarika. English. 1974- III. Title.

TWO Zen classics : 294.3'8
Mumonkan and Hekiganroku / translation and commentaries by Katsuki Sekida ; edited with an introd. A. V. Grimstone. 1st ed. New York : Weatherhill, 1977. p. cm. Includes index. [BQ9289.H843T94] 77-2398 ISBN 0-8348-0131-0 : 12.50 pbk. : 7.95
1. Hui-k'ai, Shih, 1183-1260. Wu-men kuan. 2. Hsueh-tou, 980-1052. Pi yen lu. 3. Koan. I. Hui-k'ai, Shih, 1183-1260. Wu-men kuan. English. 1977. II. Hsueh-tou, 980-1052. Pi yen lu. English. 1977.

VIMALAKIRTINIRDESA. 294.3'8
English.
The holy teaching of Vimalakirti : a Mahayana scripture / translated by Robert A. F. Thurman. University Park : Pennsylvania State University Press, c1976. p. cm. Includes bibliographical references. [BQ2212.E5T47] 75-27196
I. Thurman, Robert A. F. II. Title.

VIMALAKIRTINIRDESA. 294.3'8
English.
The holy teaching of Vimalakirti : a Mahayana scripture / translated by Robert A. F. Thurman. University Park : Pennsylvania State University Press, c1976. ix, 166 p. ; 24 cm. Includes bibliographical references. [BQ2212.E5T47] 75-27196 ISBN 0-271-01209-9 : 14.50
I. Thurman, Robert A. F. II. Title.

WAYMAN, Alex. 294.3'8
The Buddhist Tantras; light on Indo-Tibetan esotericism. New York, S. Weiser, 1973. xiii, 247 p. illus. 24 cm. Includes bibliographical references. [BQ8915.4.W39] 73-79801 ISBN 0-87728-223-4 12.50
1. Tantric Buddhism. I. Title.

GODDARD, Dwight, 1861- 294.3'8'08
1939, ed.
A Buddhist Bible. Introd. by Huston Smith. Boston, Beacon Press [1970, c1938] xvi, 677 p. 21 cm. (Beacon paperback 357—Religion) [BL1410.G6 1970] 72-105327 3.95
1. Buddha and Buddhism—Sacred books. I. Title.

**THE Tibetan Book of* 294.3809515
the Dead; the great liberation through hearing in the Bardo, by Guru Rinpoche according to Karma Lingpa; a new translation from the Tibetan with commentary by Francesca Fremantle and Chogyam Trungpa. Berkeley, London, Shambhala, 1975 xx, 119 p. 23 cm. (Clear light series) Includes index. Bibliography: p. 111-112. [BL1411.B3] 74-29615 12.50.
1. Tibetan literature. 2. Buddhist literature.
Pbk. 3.95; ISBN: 0-87773-74-1 Distributed by Random House.

ASVAGHOSA. 294.3'82
The awakening of faith, attributed to Asvaghosha. Translated, with commentary, by Yoshito S. Hakeda. New York, Columbia University Press, 1967. xi, 128 p. 24 cm. "Prepared for the Columbia College program of translations from the oriental classics." Translation of the Chinese version of the Sanskrit manuscript: Mahayanasraddhotpadasastra. Bibliography: p. 119-122. [BL1416.A7M33] 67-13778
I. Hakeda, Yoshito S., tr. II. Title.

BUDDHAGHOSA. 294.3'82
The path of purification : Visuddhimagga / Bhadantacariya Buddhaghosa ; translated from the Pali by Bhikkhu Nyanamoli. Berkeley, Calif. : Shambhala Publications : distributed in the United States by Random House, 1976. 2 v. ; 22 cm. Includes index. [BQ2632.E5N36 1976] 75-40258 ISBN 0-87773-079-2(vol.1) pbk. : 4.95 ISBN 0-87773-080-6 (v. 2)
I. Nanamoli, Bhikkhu, d. 1960. II. Title.

DHAMMAPADA. ENGLISH. 294.3'82
The Dhammapada. Tr. from Pali by P. Lal. New York, Farrar [1967] 184p. illus. 21cm. Bibl. [BL1411.D5E59] 67-13413 4.50
1. Lal, P., tr. I. Title.

DHAMMAPADA. ENGLISH. 294.3'82
The Dhammapada. Translated from the Pali by P. Lal. New York, Farrar, Straus & Giroux [1967] 184 p. illus. 21 cm. Bibliography: p. [178]-184. 67-13413
I. Lal, P., tr. II. Title.

DHAMMAPADA. English. 294.3'82
The Dhammapada : the sayings of the Buddha / a new rendering by Thomas Byrom ; photography by Sandra Weiner ; with a pref. by Ram Dass. 1st ed. New York : Knopf : distributed by Random House, 1976. xiii, 165 p. : ill. ; 29 cm. [BQ1372.E54B97 1976] 76-10572 ISBN 0-394-40181-6 : 10.00
I. Byrom, Thomas. II. Title.

HUI-NENG, 638-713. 294.3'82
The sutra of Wei Lang (or Hui Neng). Translated from the Chinese by Wong Mou-lam. New ed. by Christmas Humphreys. Westport, Conn., Hyperion Press [1973] 128 p. 21 cm. Reprint of the 1944 ed. published for the Buddhist Society by Luzac & Co., London. [BQ9299.H854L613 1973] 73-879 ISBN 0-88355-073-3 8.50
1. Zen Buddhism—Early works to 1800. I. Wong, Mou-lam, tr. II. Humphreys, Christmas, 1901- ed. III. Buddhist Society of Great Britain and Ireland. IV. Title.

JATAKAS. English. 294.3'82
Selections. 1975.
Jataka tales / edited by Nancy DeRoin ; with original drawings by Ellen Lanyon. Boston : Houghton Mifflin, 1975. x, 82 p. : ill. ; 23 cm. Retells thirty of the five hundred tales told by the Buddha some five hundred years before the Christian era. [BQ1462.E5D47] 74-20981 ISBN 0-395-20281-7 : 5.95
1. Jatakas. I. DeRoin, Nancy. II. Lanyon, Ellen, ill. III. Title.

KU tsun su yu lu. 294.3'82
English.
The transmission of the mind outside the teaching / [translated and edited by] Upasaka Lu K'uan Yu (Charles Luk). New York : Grove Press : distributed by Random House, 1975- v. ; 21 cm. (An Evergreen book) "A translation of the Chinese collection of Ch'an texts called Ku tsun su yu lu." Includes bibliographical references. [BQ9267.K8713

1975] 75-15055 ISBN 0-8021-0104-6 pbk. : 2.95 (v. 1)
1. Zen Buddhism—Quotations, maxims, etc. I. Lu, K'uan Yu, 1898- II. Title.

NARIMAN, Gushtaspshah 294.3'82
Kaikhushro, d.1933.
Literary history of Sanskrit Buddhism (from Winternitz, Sylvain Levi, Huber) [by] J. [i.e. G.] K. Nariman. [2d ed. rep.] Delhi, Motilal Banarsidass [1972] xiv, 393 p. 23 cm. [BQ1105.N3 1972] 73-900542
1. Tripitaka—Criticism, interpretation, etc. 2. Sanskrit literature—History and criticism. I. Winternitz, Moriz, 1863-1937. II. Levi, Sylvain, 1863-1935. III. Huber, Eduard, 1879-1914. IV. Title.
Distributed by Verry, 15.00.

SADDHARMAPUNDARIKA. 294.3'82
English.
Scripture of the lotus blossom of the fine dharma : The lotus sutra / translated by Leon Hurvitz. New York : Columbia University Press, 1976. p. cm. (Buddhist studies and translations) Includes index. [BQ2052.E5H87] 75-45381 ISBN 0-231-03789-9 : 15.00 ISBN 0-231-03920-4 pbk. :
I. Hurvitz, Leon Nahum, 1923- II. Title. III. Title: The lotus sutra. IV. Series. V. Translations from oriental classics VI. Records of civilization—sources and studies ; no. 94

SRIMALASUTRA. 294.3'82
English.
The lion's roar of Queen Srimala; a Buddhist scripture on the Tathagatagarbha theory. Translated, with introd. and notes by Alex Wayman and Hideko Wayman. New York, Columbia University Press, 1974. xv, 142 p. port. 23 cm. Translation of the lost Sanskrit work made from a collation of the Chinese, Japanese, and Tibetan versions. Bibliography: p. [133]-138. [BQ1792.E5W394] 73-9673 ISBN 0-231-03726-0 10.00
I. Wayman, Alex, tr. II. Wayman, Hideko, tr. III. Title.

THE Threefold lotus 294.3'82
sutra / translated by Bunno Kato, Yoshiro Tamura, and Kojiro Miyasaka ; with revisions by W. E. Soothill, Wilhelm Schiffer, and Pier P. Del Campana. 1st ed. New York : Weatherhill, 1975. xviii, 383 p. ; 23 cm. Contents.Contents.—Innumerable meanings.—The Lotus flower of the wonderful law.—Meditation on the Bodhisattva universal virtue. [BQ2052.E5K37 1975] 74-23158 ISBN 0-8348-0105-1 : 19.00. ISBN 0-8348-0106-X pbk. : 10.00
1. Saddharmapundarika. 2. Mahayana Buddhism—Sacred books. I. Kato, Bunno, tr. II. Soothill, William Edward, 1861-1935. III. Wu liang i ching. English. 1975. IV. Saddharmapundarika. English. 1975. V. Kuan p'u hsien P'u-sa hsing fa ching. English. 1975.
Contents omitted.

TRIPITAKA. English. 294.3'82
Selections
The lion's roar; an anthology of the Buddha's teachings selected from the Pali canon [by] David Maurice. [1st Amer. ed.] New York, Citadel [1967,c.1962] 255p. 21cm. "The texts herein are largely from trs. which appeared in the Light of the Dhamma. [BL1411.T82M33 1967] 67-25651 4.95
I. Maurice, David. comp. II. The Light of the Dhamma. III. Title.

TRIPITAKA. English. 294.382
Selections.
The lion's roar; an anthology of the Buddha's teachings selected from the Pali canon [by] David Maurice. New York, Citadel Press [1967, c1962] 255 p. 21 cm. "The texts herein are largely from translations which appeared...in the Light of the Dhamma." [BL1411.T82M33 1967] 67-25651
I. Maurice, David, comp. II. The Light of the Dhamma. III. Title.

TRIPITAKA. English. 294.3'82
Selections.
The wisdom of Buddha. New York, Philosophical Library [1968] 117 p. 19 cm. [BL1411.T8E47] 68-5188
I. Title.

VIMALAKIRTINIRDESA. 294.3'82
English
The Vimalakirti nirdesa sutra (Wei mo chieh so shuo ching) Translated by Lu K'uan Yu (Charles Luk) Berkeley, Shambala [1972] xviii, 157 p. 23 cm. (The Clear light series) [BQ2212.E5L8 1972] 71-189851 ISBN 0-87773-035-0 7.50
I. Lu, K'uan Yu, 1898- tr. II. Title.

WRAY, Elizabeth. 294.3'82
Ten lives of the Buddha; Siamese temple paintings and Jataka tales, by Elizabeth Wray, Clare Rosenfield, and Dorothy Bailey, with photos. by Joe D. Wray. [1st ed.] New York, Weatherhill [1972] 154 p. illus. (part col.) 27 cm. Bibliography: p. 151-154. The ten most popular Jataka tales, stories of Buddha's previous incarnations, accompanied by photographs of Siamese temple paintings depicting them. Includes background essays on the Jatakas and Siamese temple painting. [BL1411.J32W7] 73-179982 ISBN 0-8348-0067-5 12.95
1. Jatakas—Illustrations—Juvenile literature. 2. Mural painting and decoration, Thai. I. Rosenfield, Clare, joint author. II. Bailey, Dorothy, joint author. III. Wray, Joe D., illus. IV. Jatakas. English. Selections. Wray. V. Title.

MISRA, Girija Shankar 294.3'822
Prasad, 1944-
The age of vinaya, by G. S. P. Misra. With a foreword by Govinda Chandra Pande. New Delhi, Munshiram Manoharlal [1972] xvi, 298 p. 22 cm. A revision of the author's thesis, University of Rajasthan. Bibliography: p. [279]-294. [BQ1157.M57 1972] 72-906003
1. Vinayapitaka—Criticism, interpretation, etc. 2. Buddha and Buddhism—Discipline. 3. India—Social life and customs—Sources. I. Title.
Distributed by Verry; 11.50.

PATIMOKKHA. English. 294.3'822
Buddhist monastic discipline: the Sanskrit Pratimoksa sutras of the Mahasamghikas and Mulasarvastivadins. [Edited by] Charles S. Prebish. University Park, Pennsylvania State University Press [1975] 156 p. 24 cm. "The Mahasamghika and Mulasarvastivadin Pratimoksa sutras presented face to face for easy comparison." Bibliography: p. [151]-156. [BQ2272.E5P73] 74-10743 ISBN 0-271-01171-8
1. Sarvastivadins. 2. Mahasanghikas. 3. Monasticism and religious orders, Buddhist—Rules. I. Prebish, Charles S., ed. II. Title.

UPASAK, Chandrika 294.3'822'03
Singh.
Dictionary of early Buddhist monastic terms based on Pali literature / C. S. Upasak. 1st ed. Varanasi : Bharati Prakashan, 1975. iii, 245 p. ; 26 cm. [BQ2319.U6] 75-902701 18.00
1. Vinayapitaka—Dictionaries. I. Title.
Distributed by South Asia Books.

DHAMMAPADA. English. 294.3'823
The Dhammapada : the sayings of the Buddha / a new rendering by Thomas Byrom ; photography by Sandra Weiner ; with a preface by Ram Dass. New York : Vintage Books, 1976. xiii, 165 p. : ill. ; 28 cm. [BQ1372.E54B97 1976b] 76-10573 ISBN 0-394-72198-5 : 5.95
I. Byrom, Thomas. II. Title.

DHAMMAPADA. English. 294.3'823
The Dhammapada; the path of perfection, translated from the Pali with an introduction by Juan Mascaro. [Harmondsworth] Penguin [1973] 93 p. 18 cm. (Penguin Classics) [BQ1372.E54M37] 73-165966 ISBN 0-14-044-284-7
I. Mascaro, Juan, tr.
Distributed by Penguin, Baltimore for 1.25 (pbk)

JATAKAS. English. 294.3'823
Selections.
Buddhist birth stories : or, Jataka tales / edited by V. Fausboll ; translated by Thomas William Rhys Davids. New York : Arno Press, 1977. p. cm. (International folklore) Reprint of the 1880 ed. published by Trubner, London, in series: Trubner's oriental series. "The Ceylon compiler's introduction, called the Nidana katha": p. Includes index. [BQ1462.E5F377 1977] 77-70620 ISBN 0-405-10090-6 : 27.00
I. Fausboll, Michael Viggo, 1821-1908. II. Davids, Thomas William Rhys, 1843-1922. III. Jatakas. Nidanakatha. English. 1977. IV. Title. V. Series.

JATAKAS. English. 294.3'823
Selections.
Buddhist birth stories : or, Jataka tales / edited by V. Fausboll ; translated by Thomas William Rhys Davids. New York : Arno Press, 1977. p. cm. (International folklore) Reprint of the 1880 ed. published by Trubner, London, in series: Trubner's oriental series. "The Ceylon compiler's introduction, called the Nidana katha": p. Includes index. [BQ1462.E5F377 1977] 77-70620 ISBN 0-405-10090-6 : 27.00
I. Fausboll, Michael Viggo, 1821-1908. II. Davids, Thomas William Rhys, 1843-1922. III. Jatakas. Nidanakatha. English. 1977. IV. Title. V. Series.

SUTTAPITAKA. English. 294.3'823
Selections.
Buddhist suttas. Translated from Pali by T. W. Rhys Davids. New York, Dover Publications [1969] xlviii, 320 p. 22 cm. (The Sacred books of the East, v. 11) Contents.Contents.—The Maha-parinibbana suttanta.—The Dhamma-kakka-ppavattana sutta.—The Tevigga suttanta.—The Akankheyya sutta.—The Ketokhila sutta.—The Maha-sudassana suttanta.—The Sabbasava sutta. [BL1411.S83E4 1969] 68-8043 2.75
I. Davids, Thomas William Rhys, 1843-1922. tr. II. Title. III. Series: The Sacred books of the East (New York) v. 11

SUTTAPITAKA. English. 294.3'823
Selections.
Some sayings of the Buddha, according to the Pali canon. Translated by F. L. Woodward, with an introd. by Christmas Humphreys. London, New York, Oxford University Press, 1973. xxii, 249 p. 21 cm. (A Galaxy book) A collection of passages from the Suttapitaka with a few selections from the Vinayapitaka. [BQ1192.E53W66 1973] 73-77921 ISBN 0-19-519737-2 1.95 (pbk.)
I. Woodward, Frank Lee, 1870 or 71-1952, tr. II. Humphreys, Christmas, 1901- III. Vinayapitaka. English. Selections. 1973. IV. Title.

CAUDHURI, Sukomal, 294.3'824
1939-
Analytical study of the Abhidharmakosa / by Sukomal Chaudhuri. Calcutta : Sanskrit College, 1976. xiv, 249 p., [1] leaf of plates : ill. ; 26 cm. (Calcutta Sanskrit College research series ; no. 114 : Studies ; no. 77) Title on spine: Abhidharmakosa. Originally published serially in our heritage, v. 21-23. Includes index. Bibliography: p. [233]-244. [BQ2687.C38] 76-904521 Rs35.00
1. Vasubandhu. Abhidharmakosa. 2. Abhidharma. I. Title. II. Title: Abhidharmakosa. III. Series: Calcutta. University. Sanskrit College. Dept. of Post-graduate Training and Research. Research series ; 114. IV. Series: Calcutta. University. Sanskrit College. Dept. of Post-graduate Training and Research. Research series. Studies ; 77.

BRANNEN, Noah S. 294.3'9
Soka Gakkai; Japan's militant Buddhists, by Noah S. Brannen. With photos. by Hideo Fujimori. Richmond, John Knox Press [1968] 181 p. illus. ports. 21 cm. Bibliographical references included in "Notes and acknowledgments" (p. [171]-177) "A selected bibliography of works in English": p. [179]-181. [BL1442.S6B7] 68-25017 5.50
1. Soka Gakkai.

KUKAI, 774-835. 294.3'9
Kukai: major works. Translated, with an account of his life and a study of his thought, by Yoshito S. Hakeda. New York, Columbia University Press, 1972. xiv, 303 p. 23 cm. (Records of civilization: sources and studies, no. 87) (UNESCO collection of representative works: Japanese series) "Prepared for the Columbia College program of translations from the oriental classics." Bibliography: p. [281]-287. [BQ8999.K8313 1972] 72-3124 ISBN 0-231-03627-2 12.50
1. Shingon (Sect)—Collected works. I. Hakeda, Yoshito S., tr. II. Title. III. Series. IV. Series: Records of civilization: sources and records, no. 87.

LU, K'uan Yu, 1898- 294.3'9
Practical Buddhism [by] Lu K'uan Yu (Charles Luk) [1st U.S. ed.] Wheaton, Ill., Theosophical Pub. House [1973, c1971] x, 167 p. 23 cm. [BQ9288.L83 1973] 72-91124 ISBN 0-8356-0212-5 5.95
1. Han-shan, 1546-1623. 2. Spiritual life (Zen Buddhism) 3. Enlightenment (Zen Buddhism) 4. Zen Buddhism—China. I. Title.

WILLIAMS, George M. 294.3'9
NSA seminar report, 1968-71. Compiled and edited from lectures delivered by George M. Williams. Santa Monica, Calif., World Tribune Press, 1972. iii, 120 p. illus. 23 cm. [BL1442.S6W54] 72-75438
1. Soka Gakkai—Doctrines. 2. Soka Gakkai—United States. I. Nichiren Shoshu Academy. II. Title.

STEINILBER-OBERLIN, 294.3'9'0952
Emile, 1878-
The Buddhist sects of Japan, their history, philosophical doctrines and sanctuarites, by E. Steinilber-Oberlin, with the collaboration of Kuni Matsuo. Translated from the French by Marc Loge. Westport, Conn., Greenwood Press [1970] 303 p. illus. 23 cm. Reprint of the 1938 ed. Translation of Les sects bouddhiques japonaises. Includes bibliographical references. [BL1440.S72 1970] 78-109854 ISBN 0-8371-4349-7
1. Buddhist sects—Japan. I. Matsuo, Kuninosuke, 1899- joint author. II. Title.

BERKELEY bussei. 294.391
[Berkeley, Calif.] v. illus. 28cm. 'Annual publications of the Berkeley Young Buddhist Association.' [BL1400.B43] 57-22215
1. Buddha and Buddhism—Yearbooks. I. Berkeley Young Buddhist Association, Berkeley, Calif.

CONFERENCE on Theravada 294.391
Buddhism. University of Chicago 1962
Anthropological studies in Theravada Buddhism [papers, by] Manning Nash [and others. New Haven] Yale [dist. Cellar Bk. Shop. Detroit. 1966] xii, 223p. illus., map. 23cm. (Yale Univ. Southeast Asia studies) Title. (Series: Yale University. Graduate School. Southeast Asia Studies. Cultural report series, no. 13) Cultural report series no. 13. Held under the auspices of the Comm. on Southern Asian Studies of the Univ. of Chic. Bibl. [BL1400.C6 1962a] 66-19029 5.50
1. Religion. Primitive—Congresses. 2. Buddha and Buddhism—Asia, Southeastern—Congresses. 3. Hinavana Buddhism—Congresses. I. Nash. Manning. II. Chicago. University. Committee on Southern Asian Studies. III. Title. IV. Series.

LESTER, Robert C. 294.3'91
Theravada Buddhism in Southeast Asia [by] Robert C. Lester. Ann Arbor, University of Michigan Press [1973] vii, 201 p. illus. 22 cm. Bibliography: p. 187-198. [BQ408.L47 1973] 71-185154 ISBN 0-472-57000-5 8.50
1. Buddha and Buddhism—Asia, Southeastern. 2. Hinayana Buddhism. I. Title.

SADDHATISSA, H. 294.3'91
The Buddha's way [by] H. Saddhatissa. London, Allen and Unwin, 1971. 3-139 p., 7 plates. illus. 23 cm. Bibliography: p. 132-133. [BQ4115.S2] 72-195619 ISBN 0-04-294070-2
1. Buddha and Buddhism—Early Buddhism—Introductions. I. Title.
Paperback ed., 2.95, 0-8076-0598-0. Available from Braziller, 5.95, 0-8076-0635-9.

GOMBRICH, Richard 294.3'91'095493
Francis.
Precept and practice: traditional Buddhism in the rural highlands of Ceylon, by Richard F. Gombrich. Oxford, Clarendon Press, 1971. xiv, 366 p. 23 cm. Bibliography: p. [349]-355. [BQ356.G65] 73-156617 ISBN 0-19-826525-5 £4.00
1. Buddha and Buddhism—Ceylon. 2. Ceylon—Religious life and customs. 3. Buddha and Buddhism—Early Buddhism. I. Title.

GOMBRICH, Richard 294.3'91'095493
Francis.
Precept and practice: traditional Buddhism in the rural highlands of Ceylon, by Richard F. Gombrich. Oxford, Clarendon Press, 1971. xiv, 366 p. 23 cm. Bibliography: p. [349]-355. [BQ356.G65] 73-156617 ISBN 0-19-826525-5
1. Buddha and Buddhism—Ceylon. 2. Ceylon—Religious life and customs. 3. Buddha and Buddhism—Early Buddhism. I. Title.
Distributed by Oxford University Press N.Y.; 13.00.

COOK, Francis H. 294.3'92
Hua-yen Buddhism : the jewel net of Indra / Francis H. Cook. University Park : Pennsylvania State University Press, c1977. xiv, 146 p. ; 24 cm. "Published in cooperation with the Institute for Advanced Studies of World Religions New York, N.Y." Includes bibliographical references and index. [BQ8218.C66] 76-43288 ISBN 0-271-01245-5 : 14.50
1. Avatamsakasutra—Criticism, interpretation, etc. 2. Kegon (Sect)—Doctrines. I. Institute for Advanced Studies of World Religions. II. Title.

COOK, Francis H. 294.3'92
Hua-yen Buddhism : the jewel net of Indra / Francis H. Cook. University Park : Pennsylvania State University Press, c1977. xiv, 146 p. ; 24 cm. "Published in cooperation with the Institute for Advanced Studies of World Religions New York, N.Y." Includes bibliographical references and index. [BQ8218.C66] 76-43288 ISBN 0-271-01245-5 : 14.50
1. Avatamsakasutra—Criticism, interpretation, etc. 2. Kegon (Sect)—Doctrines. I. Institute for Advanced Studies of World Religions. II. Title.

DASGUPTA, Shashibhusan. 294.3'92
An introduction to Tantric Buddhism / Shashi Bhushan Dasgupta ; foreword by Herbert V. Guenther. Berkeley, Calif. : Shambhala, 1974. xi, 211 p. ; 22 cm. Reprint of the 1958 ed. published by Calcutta University Press, Calcutta. Includes index. Bibliography: p. [199]-204. [BQ8915.4.D37 1974] 74-75094 ISBN 0-87773-052-0 : 3.95
1. Tantric Buddhism. I. Title.

DASGUPTA, Shashibhusan. 294.3'92
An introduction to Tantric Buddhism / Shashi Bhushan Dasgupta ; foreword by Herbert V. Guenther. Berkeley, Calif. : Shambhala, 1974. xi, 211 p. ; 22 cm. Reprint of the 1958 ed. published by Calcutta University Press, Calcutta. Includes index. Bibliography: p. [199]

-204. [BQ8915.4.D37 1974] 74-75094 ISBN 0-87773-052-0 pbk. : 3.95
1. Tantric Buddhism. I. Title.

GUENTHER, Herbert V. 294.392
Treasures on the Tebetan middle way / Herbert V. Guenther 2nd edition. Berkeley : Shambhala [1976] x, 156p. ; 21 cm. (Clear light) Includes bibliographical references and index. [BL1495.T3G78] 75-40260 ISBN 0-87773-002-4 pbk. : 4.50
1. Tantrism, Buddhist-Essence, genius, nature. I. Title.

MC GOVERN, William Montgomery, 1897-1964. 294.3'92
An introduction to Mahayana Buddhism, with especial reference to Chinese and Japanese phases. New York, AMS Press [1971] iv, 233 p. illus. 19 cm. Reprint of the 1922 ed. [BL1483.M3 1971] 70-149665 ISBN 0-404-04129-9
1. Mahayana Buddhism. I. Title.

NAGARJUNA, Siddha 294.392
Nagarjuna's philosophy as presented in the Mahaprajnaparamita-sastra, by K. Venkata Ramanan, [1st ed.] Rutland, Vt. Pub. for the Harvard-Yenching Inst. [by] Tuttle [1966] 409p. 22cm. Thesis--Visva-Bharati. Bibl. [BL1411.P66N33] 656 10.00 lim. ed.,
1. Prajnaparamitas I. Venkata, Ramanan, Krishniah, ed. II. Title. III. Title: Mahaprajnaparamita-sastra.

NISHIDA, Tenko, 1872-1968. 294.3'92
A new road to ancient truth, by Ittoen Tenko-san: being extracts from his writings translated by Makoto Ohashi in collaboration with Marie Beuzeville Byles; with an introduction by Marie Beuzeville Byles. New York, Horizon Press [1972, c1969] 183 p. illus. 21 cm. Selections from the author's Sange no seikatsu (Life of sange) published in 1950. [BP605.I8N53 1972] 75-151014 ISBN 0-8180-1310-9 5.95
1. Ittoen. I. Title.

SURANGAMASUTRA. English & Khotanese. 294.3'92
The Khotanese Surangamasamadhisutra; [edited] by R. E. Emmerick. London, New York, Oxford U. P., 1970. xxv, 134 p., 20 plates. facsims. 23 cm. (London oriental series, v. 23) Khotanese translation from the original Buddhist Sanskrit text. Khotanese text with English translation on facing pages. Includes partial text of the Tibetan version. Includes bibliographical references. [BL1411.S77E53] 72-185897 ISBN 0-19-713562-5 £5.00 ($14.00 U.S.)
I. Emmerick, R. E., ed. II. Title. III. Series.

SUZUKI, Daisetz Teitaro, 1870-1966. 294.3'92
On Indian Mahayana Buddhism. Edited with an introd. by Edward Conze. [1st ed.] New York, Harper & Row [1968] 284 p. 21 cm. (Harper torchbooks, TB1403) Includes bibliographical references. [BL1483.S818] 68-26896 2.45
1. Prajnaparamitas. 2. Gandavyuha. 3. Mahayana Buddhism. I. Conze, Edward, 1904- ed. II. Title.

SUZUKI, Daisetz Teitaro, 1870-1966. 294.3'92
Shin Buddhism. [1st ed.] New York, Harper & Row [1970] 93 p. 22 cm. [BL1442.S5S9 1970] 71-86908 3.95
1. Shin (Sect) I. Title.

WENTZ, Walter Yeeling Evans. 294.3'92
The Tibetan book of the great liberation; or, The method of realizing Nirvana through knowing the mind; preceded by an epitome of Padma-Sambhava's biography [by Yeshey Tshogyal] and followed by Guru Phadampa Sangay's teachings, according to English renderings by Sardar Bahadur S. W. Laden La and by the Lamas Karma Sumdhon Paul, Lobzang Mingyur Dorje, and Kazi Dawa-Samdup; introductions, annotations and editing by W. Y. Evans-Wentz, with psychological commentary by C. G. Jung. London, New York [etc.] Oxford U.P., 1968. lxiv, 261 p. 10 plates, illus., ports. 21 cm. [BL1495.T3W4 1968] 71-464839 ISBN 0-19-680696-8 19/6
1. Tantrism, Buddhist—Tibet. 2. Nirvana. 3. Yoga (Buddhist tantrism) I. Padma Sambhava, ca.717-ca.762. II. Ye-ses-mtsho-rgyal, 8th cent. III. Phadampa Sangay, fl. 1100. IV. Jung, Carl Gustav, 1875-1961. V. Title.

WILLIAMS, George M. 294.3'92
NSA seminars : an introduction to true Buddhism / by George M. Williams. Santa Monica, Calif. : World Tribune Press, 1974. 101 p. : ill. ; 22 cm. [BQ8418.5.W54] 74-77643
1. Soka Gakkai—Doctrines. 2. Nichiren Shoshu Academy. I. Title.

YAMAMOTO, Kosho 294.392
The other-power; the final answer arrived at in Shin Buddhism Oyama, Japan Karinbunko [Austin. Tex., Perkins Oriental, c.1965] viii, 146p. front. 19cm. Bibl. [BL1442.S5Y3] 66-3014 3.00
1. Shin (Sect)—Doctrines. I. Title.

ANESAKI, Masaharu, 1873-1949. 294.3'92'0924 B
Nichiren, the Buddhist prophet. Gloucester, Mass., P. Smith, 1966 [c1916] viii, 160 p. 21 cm. Bibliographical footnotes. [BL1442.N53A5 1966] 67-2824
1. Nichiren, 1222-1282. 2. Buddha and Buddhism—Japan. I. Title.

REICHELT, Karl Ludvig, 1877-1952. 294.3'92'0951
Truth and tradition in Chinese Buddhism; a study of Chinese Mahayana Buddhism. Translated from the Norwegian by Kathrina Van Wagenen Bugge. 2d ed. New York, Paragon Book Reprint Corp., 1968. x, 330 p. illus. 22 cm. Translation of Fra Ostens religiose liv. Reprint of the 1928 ed. Bibliographical footnotes. [BL1430.R42 1968] 68-59117
1. Buddha and Buddhism—China. 2. China—Religion. I. Title.

REISCHAUER, August Karl, 1879- 294.3'92'0952
Studies in Japanese Buddhism. New York, AMS Press [1970] xviii, 361 p. port. 23 cm. Reprint of the 1917 ed. "Selected bibliography of works in Japanese": p. 349-351. [BL1440.R5 1970] 73-107769
1. Buddha and Buddhism—Japan. I. Title.

ANNALS of the Nyingma lineage in America. 294.3'923 [Berkeley, Calif.] : Dharma Pub., 1975- v. : ill. ; 28 cm. Contents.Contents.—v. 1. 1969-1975. [BQ7662.2.A56] 75-323606 ISBN 0-913546-23-2
1. Tarthang Tulku. 2. Rnin-ma-pa (Sect)—United States—History.

BSTAN-'DZIN-RGYA-MTSHO, Dalai Lama XIV, 1935- 294.3'923
The Buddhism of Tibet and The key to the middle way / Tenzin Gyatso, the Fourteenth Dalai Lama ; translated in the main by Jeffrey Hopkins and Lati Rimpoche. 1st U.S. ed. New York : Harper & Row, [1975] 104 p. ; 21 cm. (The Wisdom of Tibet series ; 1) Includes index. Bibliography: p. 91-93. [BQ4022.B75 1975] 74-25686 ISBN 0-06-064831-7 : 5.95
1. Buddhism. 2. Lamaism. I. Bstan-'dzin-rgya-mtsho, Dalai Lama XIV, 1935- The key to the middle way. 1975. II. Title: The Buddhism of Tibet.

CLARK, Walter Eugene, 1881-1960, ed. 294.3923
Two Lamaistic pantheons. Ed., introd. indexes by Walter Eugene Clark from materials collected by the late Baron A. von Stael-Holstein. New York, Paragon, 1965. 2 v. in 1 (169; 314p.) illus., facsims. 27cm. Orig. pub. in 1937 in 2 v. by Harvard. Bibl. [BL1475.5.A1C55] 65-28578 25.00
1. Gods, Buddhist. 2. Gods, Lamaist. I. Peking. Paohsiang lou (Temple) II. Chu fo p'u-sa sheng hsiang tsan. III. Stael-Holstein, Alexander, Freiherr von, 1877-1937. IV. Title. V. Title: Lamaistic pantheons.

DAVID-NEEL, Alexandra, 1868-1969. 294.3'923
The secret oral teachings in Tibetan Buddhist sects [by] Alexandra David-Neel and lama Yongden. Foreword by Alan Watts. Translated by H. N. M. Hardy. [San Francisco] City Lights Books, 1967. 128 p. ports. 19 cm. Translation of Les enseignements secrets dans les sectes bouddhistes tibetaines. [BL1485.D2813] 68-737
1. Lamaism. I. Yongden, Albert Arthur. II. Title.

DAVID-NEEL, Alexandra, 1874- 294.3'923
The secret oral teachings in Tibetan Buddhist sects [by] Alexandra David-Neel and lama Yongden. Foreword by Alan Watts. Translated by H. N. M. Hardy. [San Francisco] City Lights Books, 1967. 128 p. ports. 19 cm. Translation of Les enseignements secrets dans les sectes bouddhistes tibetaines. [BL1485.D2813] 68-737
1. Lamaism. I. Yongden, Albert Arthur. II. Title.

GUENTHER, Herbert V. 294.3'923
Tibetan Buddhism in Western perspective : collected articles of Herbert V. Gunther. Emeryville, Calif. : Dharma Pub., c1977. xi, 261 p. : ill. ; 22 cm. Includes bibliographical references and indexes. [BQ7612.G83] 76-47758 ISBN 0-913546-49-6 : 8.95 ISBN 0-913546-50-X pbk. : 4.95
1. Lamaism—Addresses, essays, lectures. I. Title.

SIERKSMA, Fokke, 1917- 294.3'923
Tibet's terrifying deities; sex and aggression in religious acculturation [by] F. Sierksma. [Translated from the Dutch by Mrs. G. E. van Baaren-Pape] Rutland, Vt., G. E. Tuttle Co., [1966] 283 p. illus. (part col.) 27 cm. Bibliographical references included in "Notes" (p. 237-266) [BL1945.T5S53 1966a] 67-1211
1. Tibet—Religion. 2. Demonology, Lamaist. 3. Gods, Lamaist. 4. Art, Tibetan. 5. Demonology, Tibetan. I. Title.

LOBSANG RAMPA, Tuesday. 294.3'923'0924
The saffron robe, by T. Lobsang Rampa. [1st ed. New York] Pageant Press [c1966] 209 p. 21 cm. [BL1490.L6A35 1966] 66-26918
I. Title.

WADDELL, Laurence Austine, 1854-1938. 294.3'923'09515
Tibetan Buddhism, with its mystic cults, symbolism and mythology, and in its relation to Indian Buddhism. New York, Dover Publications [1972] xxiii, 598 p. illus. 22 cm. Reprint of the 1895 ed., which was published under title: The Buddhism of Tibet. Bibliography: p. 578-583. [BQ7602.W3 1972] 78-188810 ISBN 0-486-20130-9 4.50
1. Lamaism. I. Title.

WADDELL, Lawrence Austine, 1854-1938. 294.3'923'09515
The Buddhism of Tibet, or Lamaism. [2d ed.] Cambridge [Eng.] W. Heffer [1971] 1, 598 p. illus. 23 cm. Reprint of 1934 ed. Bibliography: p. 578-583. [BQ7602.W28 1971] 73-168233 ISBN 0-85270-062-8 13.50 (U.S.)
1. Lamaism. I. Title.

BLYTH, Reginald Horace. 294.3'927
Games Zen masters play : writings of R. H. Blyth / selected, edited, and with an introd. by Robert Sohl and Audrey Carr. New York : New American Library, 1976. 169 p. ; 18 cm. (A Mentor book) "Classic Zen texts with ... commentaries." [BQ9265.4.B55] 75-24786 pbk. : 1.50
1. Zen Buddhism. I. Title.

CHANG, Lit-sen, 1904- 294.3'927
Zen-existentialism: the spiritual decline of the West; a positive answer to the hippies. [Nutley, N.J., Presbyterian and Rejormed Pub. Co., 1969] xi, 254 p. 24 cm. Bibliography: p. [241]-254. [BQ9269.C47] 73-156862 5.95
1. Zen Buddhism—Controversial literature. I. Title.

DOGEN, 1200-1253. 294.3'927
A primer of Soto Zen; a translation of Dogen's Shobogenzo zuimonki. By Reiho Masunaga. [1st ed.] Honolulu, East-West Center Press [1971] 119 p. 23 cm. The present translation is based on the standard version by Menzan Zuiho as edited by Watsuji Tetsuro. [BL1442.S66S513] 76-126044 ISBN 0-8248-0094-X 6.00
I. Title.

DUMOULIN, Heinrich 294.3927
A history of Zen Buddhism. Tr. from German by Paul Peachey. New York, McGraw [1965, c.1963] viii, 335p. illus. 22cm. (McGraw paperbacks in religion and philosophy Bibl. [BL1493.D813] 65-8129 2.95 pap.,
1. Zen Buddhism—Hist. I. Title.

FUJIMOTO, Rindo, 1894- 294.3'927
The way of zazen. Translated by Tetsuya Inoue and Yoshihiko Tanigawa. With an introd. by Elsie P. Mitchell. Cambridge, Mass., Cambridge Buddhist Association, 1961. xiv, 26 p. 21 cm. [BL1478.6.F8] 79-221042
1. Meditation (Zen Buddhism) I. Title.

HAU Hoo. 294.3'927
The sound of the one hand : 281 Zen koans with answers / translated, with a commentary by Yoel Hoffmann ; foreword by Zen Master Hirano Sojo ; introd. by Ben-Ami Scharfstein. New York : Basic Books, c1975. p. cm. Translation of Gendai soji Zen hyoron. Bibliography: p. [BQ9369.H3813] 75-7274 ISBN 0-465-08078-2 : 10.00 ISBN 0-465-08079-0 pbk. : 4.95
1. Rinzai (Sect)—Controversial literature. I. Hoffmann, Yoel. II. Title.

HOOVER, Thomas, 1941- 294.3'927
Zen culture / Thomas Hoover. 1st ed. New York : Random House, c1977. xx, 262 p. : ill. ; 22 cm. Includes index. Bibliography: p. [235]-244. [DS821.H8126] 76-50559 ISBN 0-394-41072-6 : 8.95
1. Japan—Civilization—Zen influences. I. Title.

HSUEH-TOU, 980-1052. 294.3'927
The blue cliff record / translated from the Chinese Pi yen lu by Thomas and J. C. Cleary ; foreword by Taizan Maezumi Roshi. Boulder, Colo. : Shambhala ; [New York] : distributed by Random House, 1977- v. ; 22 cm. Bibliography: v. 1, p. 267-268 [BQ9289.H783A3513] 77-360597 ISBN 0-87773-094-6 : 5.95 (v. 1)
1. Koan. I. Title.

HYERS, M. Conrad. 294.3'927
Zen and the comic spirit [by] Conrad Hyers. Philadelphia, Westminster Press [1974, c1973] 192 p. illus. 21 cm. Includes bibliographical references. [BQ4570.H85H9 1974] 74-628 ISBN 0-664-20705-7 6.95
1. Zen Buddhism and humor. I. Title.
Pbk. 3.95, ISBN 0-664-24989-2.

I-HSUAN, Shih, d.867. 294.3'927
The Zen teaching of Rinzai : the record of Rinzai / translated from the Chinese Lin-chi lu by Irmgard Schloegl. Berkeley, Calif. : Shambhala, 1976, c1975. 96 p. ; 23 cm. (The Clear light series) Bibliography: p. 96. [BQ9399.I554L5513 1976] 75-40262 ISBN 0-87773-087-3 pbk. : 3.50
1. Zen Buddhism—Early works to 1800. I. Title.

IINO, Norimoto, 1908- 294.3'927
Zeal for Zen. New York, Philosophical Library [1967] 94 p. 22 cm. [BL1493.I4] 66-26968
1. Zen Buddhism. I. Title.

KAPLEAU, Philip, 1912- ed. 294.3927
The three pillars of Zen; teaching, practice, and enlightenment.Comp., ed., with trs., introds., notes by Philip Kapleau. Boston, Beacon [1967, c.1965] xix, 362p. 21cm. (BP 242) [BL1493.K3] 2.45 pap.,
1. Zen literature. I. Title.

KENNETT, Jiyu, 1924- 294.3'927
Selling water by the river: a manual of Zen training. New York, Vintage Books [1972] xxv, 317 p. 21 cm. [BL1442.S65K45 1972b] 72-1063 ISBN 0-394-71804-6 2.45
1. Soto (Sect) I. Title.

KENNETT, Jiyu, 1924- 294.3'927
Selling water by the river: a manual of Zen training. New York, Pantheon Books [1972] xxv, 317 p. 25 cm. Includes bibliographical references. [BQ9415.4.K45] 70-38836 ISBN 0-394-46743-4 10.00
1. Sotoshu. I. Title.

KENNETT, Jiyu, 1924- 294.3'927
Zen is eternal life / Jiyu Kennett. Emeryville, Calif. : Dharma Pub., c1976. xxxi, 452 p. : ill. ; 20 cm. First published in 1972 under title: Selling water by the river. Includes index. [BQ9415.4.K45 1976] 76-9387 ISBN 0-913546-37-2 : 12.95 ISBN 0-913546-38-0 pbk. : 5.95
1. Sotoshu. I. Title.

KUBOSE, Gyomay M., 1905- 294.3'927
Zen Koans [by] Gyomay M. Kubose. Original sumie illus. by Ryozo Ogura. Chicago, Regnery [1973] xiii, 274 p. illus. 22 cm. [BQ9289.K8] 72-11183 7.95; 2.95 (pbk.)
1. Koan. I. Title.

LASSALLE, Hugo, 1898- 294.3'927
Zen—way to enlightenment, by H. M. Enomiya-Lassalle. New York, Taplinger Pub. Co. [1968, c1966] 126 p. 21 cm. Bibliographical footnotes. [BL1493.L2813 1968] 68-17642
1. Zen Buddhism. I. Title.

LU, K'uan Yu, 1898- comp. 294.3'927
Ch'an and Zen teaching. Edited, translated, and explained by Lu K'uan Yu (Charles Luk). [1st American ed.] Berkeley [Calif.] Shambala Publications, 1970- [c1960] v. 22 cm. (The Clear light series) Contents.Contents.—ser. 1. Master Hsu Yun's discourses and Dharma words. Stories of six Ch'an masters. The diamond cutter of doubts. A straight talk on the heart Sutra. [BL1493.L813] 74-146510 ISBN 0-87773-009-1 2.75
1. Zen Buddhism. I. Title.

*LU, K'uan Y, 1898- 294.3'927
Ch'an and Zen teaching, edited, translated and explained by Lu K'uan Yu (Charles Luk) [1st Amer. ed.] Berkeley [Calif.] Shambala Pubns., 1973. v. illus. 22 cm. Contents.Contents.—series 3. The Altar Sutra of the Sixth Patriarch. Yung Chia's Song of Enlightenment. The Sutra of Complete Enlightenment. [BL1493.L813] ISBN 0-87773-044-X (v. 3) 3.95 (pbk.)
1. Zen Buddhism. I. Title.
Publisher's address: 1409 Fifth St., Berkeley, CA 94710.

MERTON, Thomas, 1915-1968. 294.3'927
Zen and the birds of appetite. [New York, New Directions, 1968] ix, 141 p. 21 cm. (A New Directions book) Bibliographical footnotes. [BL1442.Z4M4] 68-25546 5.25
1. Zen Buddhism—Addresses, essays, lectures. I. Title.

MITCHELL, Elsie P., 1926- 294.3'927
Sun Buddhas, moon Buddhas: a Zen quest by Elsie P. Mitchell. With a foreword by Aelred Graham. [1st ed.] New York, Weatherhill [1973] 214 p. 22 cm. Includes bibliographical references. [BQ972.I87A37 1973] 73-4037 ISBN 0-8348-0083-7 7.50
1. Mitchell, Elsie P., 1926- 2. Religious life (Zen Buddhism) I. Title.

MIURA, Isshu, 1903- 294.3927
The Zen Koan; its history and use in Rinzai Aen [by] Isshu Miura [and] Ruth Fuller Saski. With reproductions of ten drawings by Hakuin Ekaku. [1st ed.] New York, Harcourt, Brace & World [1965] xviii, 156 p. illus. 27 cm. "A Helen and Kurt Wolff book." [BL1493.M5 1965a] 65-19104
1. Koan. I. Sasaki, Ruth (Fuller) 1892 or 4- joint author. II. Title.

MIURA, Isshu, 1903- 294.3'927
Zen dust; the history of the koan and koan study in Rinzai (Lin-chi) Zen [by] Isshu Miura [and] Ruth Fuller Sasaki. With background notes, descriptive bibliography, genealogical charts, maps, indexes, and reproductions of drawings by Hakuin. [1st ed.] New York, Harcourt, Brace & World [1967, c1966] xxii, 574 p. illus., geneal. tables, maps. 27 cm. "A Helen and Kurt Wolff book." An expanded version of the authors' The Zen koan. Bibliography: p. 335-479. [BL1493.M49 1967] 66-10044
1. Koan. I. Sasaki, Ruth (Fuller) 1893 or 4- joint author. II. Title.

MIURA ISSHU, 1903- 294.3927
The Zen Koan; its history and use in Rinzai Zen [by] Isshu Miura, Ruth Fuller Sasaki. Reproductions of ten drawings by Hakuin Ekaku. New York, Harcourt [c.1965] xviii, 156p. illus. 27cm. (Helen and Kurt Wolff bk.) [BL1493.M5] 65-19104 4.50
1. Koan. I. Sasaki, Ruth (Fuller) 1893 or 4- joint author. II. Title.

OGATA, Sohaku, 1901- 294.3'927
Zen for the West. For the Buddhist Society of London. Westport, Conn., Greenwood Press [1973, c1959] 182 p. illus. 22 cm. Appendices (p. [79]-[176]): 1. A new translation of the Mu mon kwan.—2. A Zen interpretation of the Tao te ching.—3. List of Chinese characters with Japanese and Chinese transliterations and dates of people, places, and technical terms in Zen for the West and in the Mu mon kwan. Includes bibliographical references. [BQ9265.4.O36 1973] 72-9543 ISBN 0-8371-6583-0 9.50
1. Zen Buddhism. I. Buddhist Society, London. II. Hui-k'ai, Shih, 1183-1260. Wu-men kuan. English. 1959. III. Lao-tzu. Tao te ching. English. 1959. IV. Title.

P'ANG, Yun, ca.740-808. 294.3'927
The recorded sayings of Layman P'ang; a ninth-century Zen classic [compiled by Yu Ti] Translated from the Chinese by Ruth Fuller Sasaki, Yoshitaka Iriya [and] Dana R. Fraser. [1st ed.] New York, Weatherhill [1971] 109 p. illus. (part col.) 22 cm. Translation of P'ang chu shih yu lu. Bibliography: p. 99-103. [BL1432.Z3P313 1971] 77-157273 ISBN 0-8348-0057-8 5.00
1. Zen Buddhism—Early works to 1800. I. Yu, Ti, d. 818, comp. II. Title.

POWELL, Robert. 294.3'927
Zen and reality; an approach to sanity and happiness on a non-sectarian basis. New York, Viking [1975, c1961] 140, [2] p. 20 cm. Reprint of the ed. published by Allen and Unwin, London. Bibliography: p. [141]-[142] [BQ9265.6.P68 1975] 74-5808 ISBN 0-670-00588-6
1. Zen Buddhism. I. Title.

POWELL, Robert. 294.3'927
Zen and reality : an approach to sanity and happiness on a non-sectarian basis / Robert Powell. New York : Penguin Books, [1977, c1961] p. cm. Originally published by Allen and Unwin, London. Bibliography: p. [BQ9265.6.P68 1977] 77-4379 ISBN 0-14-004532-5 pbk. : 2.95
1. Zen Buddhism. I. Title.

SHIBAYAMA, Zenkei, 1894- 294.3'927
A flower does not talk; Zen essays. Translated by Sumiko Kudo. [1st ed.] Rutland, Vt., C. E. Tuttle Co. [1970] 264 p. illus. 19 cm. [BL1493.S48 1970] 79-109404 ISBN 0-8048-0884-8 2.75
1. Zen Buddhism—Addresses, essays, lectures. I. Title.

*STONE, Justin F. 294.3927
The joys of meditation; a do-it-yourself book of instruction in varied meditation techniques, by Justin F. Stone. Albuquerque, New Mexico, Far West Publishing Co [1973] 94 p. illus., 23 cm. (Sun books) [BL1493] 2.95 (pbk.)
1. Zen Buddhism. I. Title.

SUZUKI, Daisetz Teitaro, 1870-1966. 294.3'927
The essentials of Zen Buddhism; Selected from the writings of Daisetz T. Suzuki Edited, and with an introd., by Bernard Phillips. Westport, Conn., Greenwood Press [1973, c1962] xl, 544 p. 22 cm. Includes bibliographies. [BQ9265.4.S94 1973] 72-11306 ISBN 0-8371-6649-7 20.00
1. Zen Buddhism. I. Title.

SUZUKI, Daisetz Teitaro, 1870-1966. 294.3'927
Introduction to Zen Buddhism, including "A manual of Zen Buddhism / Daisetz Teitaro Suzuki ; foreword by C. G. Jung ; introd. to the Causeway ed. by Charles San. New York : Causeway Books, [1974] 136, 192, [7] leaves of plates : ill. ; 24 cm. Second work has separate t.p. Includes bibliographical references and indexes. [BQ9265.2.S89] 73-85123 ISBN 0-88356-022-4 : 10.00
1. Zen Buddhism. I. Suzuki, Daisetz Teitaro, 1870-1966. A manual of Zen Buddhism. 1974. II. Title.

SUZUKI, Daisetz Teitaro, 1870-1966. 294.3'927
What is Zen? Two unpublished essays and a reprint of the 1st ed. of The essence of Buddhism. New York, Harper & Row [1972] xii, 116 p. 18 cm. (Perennial Library) Contents.Contents.—Foreword by L. P. Yandell to the unpublished mss.—What is Zen?—Self and the unattainable.—The essence of Buddhism, 1st ed., 1946. [BQ9265.9.S96 1972] 72-169304 ISBN 0-06-080263-4 1.25 (pbk.)
1. Zen Buddhism—Essence, genius, nature. 2. Mahayana Buddhism—Essence, genius, nature. I. Suzuki, Daisetz Teitaro, 1870-1966. The essence of Buddhism. lst ed. 1972. II. Title.

SUZUKI, Daisetz Teitaro, 1870-1966. 294.3'927
Zen and Japanese culture / Daisetz T. Suzuki. Princeton, N.J. : Princeton University Press, 1970, c1959. xxiii, 478 p., [37] leaves of plates (3 fold.) : ill. ; 23 cm. (Princeton/Bollingen paperbacks ; 221) (Bollingen series ; 64) First ed. published in 1938 under title: Zen Buddhism and its influence on Japanese culture. Includes index. Bibliography: p. [443]-447. [BQ9262.9.J3S9 1970] 75-323168 ISBN 0-691-09849-2. ISBN 0-691-01770-0 pbk.
1. Zen Buddhism—Japan. 2. Japan—Civilization—Zen influences. I. Title. II. Series.

WIENPAHL, Paul. 294.3'927
Zen diary. New York, Harper & Row [1970] xi, 244 p. 22 cm. [BL1493.W5] 70-109059 6.95
1. Zen Buddhism—Essence, genius, nature. I. Title.

THE Wisdom of the Zen masters 294.3'927
/ translated by Irmgard Schloegl. New York : New Directions Pub. Corp., 1976. p. cm. (A New Directions book ; 415) Companion volume to Thomas Merton's The wisdom of the desert and Geoffrey Parriner's The wisdom of the forest. [BQ9267.W57] 75-42115 ISBN 0-8112-0609-2. ISBN 0-8112-0610-6 pbk.
1. Zen Buddhism—Quotations, Maxims, etc. 2. Zen Buddhism—Japan. I. Schloegl, Irmgard.

WOODWORTH, Hugh M. 294.3'927
Zen; the turn towards life, by Hugh Woodworth. Boston, Branden Press [1969] 31 p. 22 cm. [BL1493.W6] 68-28824 1.00
1. Zen Buddhism. I. Title.

YOKOI, Yuho, 1918- 294.3'927
Zen Master Dogen : an introduction with selected writings / by Yuho Yokoi, with the assistance of Daizen Victoria ; and with a foreword by Minoru Kiyota. 1st ed. New York : Weatherhill, 1976. 217 p. ; 23 cm. [BQ9449.D652Y63] 75-33200 ISBN 0-8348-0112-4 : 10.00 pbk. : 4.50
1. Dogen, 1200-1253. 2. Sotoshu—Collected works. I. Victoria, Daizen, 1939- joint author. II. Dogen, 1200-1253. Selected works. 1976. III. Title.

SEUNG Sahn. 294.3'927'08
Dropping ashes on the Buddha : the teaching of Zen master Seung Sahn / compiled and edited by Stephen Mitchell. 1st Evergreen ed. New York : Grove Press : distributed by Random House, 1976. xii, 232 p. ; 21 cm. (An Evergreen book) [BQ9266.S48] 75-37236 ISBN 0-8021-4015-7 : 4.95
1. Seung Sahn. 2. Zen Buddhism—Addresses, essays, lectures. I. Title.

SOHL, Robert, comp. 294.3'927'08
The gospel according to Zen; beyond the death of God. Robert Sohl [and] Audrey Carr, editors. New York, New American Library [1970] 133 p. illus. 18 cm. (A Mentor book) [BL1493.S64 1970] 72-20165 0.95
1. Zen Buddhism. I. Carr, Audrey, joint comp. II. Title.

STRYK, Lucien, ed. and tr. 294.392708
Zen: poems, prayers, sermons, anecdotes, interviews, selected and translated by Lucien Stryk and Takashi Ikemoto. [1st ed.] Garden City, N.Y., Anchor Books, 1965. xxxvii, 160 p. illus. 19 cm. "A485." [BL1493.S8] 65-20059
1. Zen Buddhism. I. Ikemoto, Takashi, 1906- joint ed. and tr. II. Title.

STRYK, Lucien, ed. and tr. 294.392708
Zen: poems, prayers, sermons, anecdotes, interviews, selected and translated by Lucien Stryk and Takashi Ikemoto. [1st ed.] Garden City, N. Y., Anchor Books, 1965. xxxvii, 160 p. illus. 19 cm. "A485." [BL1493.S8] 65-20059
1. Zen Buddhism. I. Ikemoto, Takashi, 1906- joint ed. and tr. II. Title.

SUZUKI, Daisetz Teitaro, 1870-1966. 294.3'927'08
The field of Zen; contributions to the Middle way, the journal of the Buddhist Society. Edited, with foreword, by Christmas Humphreys. [1st Perennial library ed.] New York, Harper & Row [1970] xvii, 105 p. ports. 18 cm. (Perennial Library, P 193) [BL1493.S88 1970] 76-17773 0.95
1. Zen Buddhism—Addresses, essays, lectures. I. The Middle way. II. Title.

HUMPHREYS, Christmas, 1901- 294.3'927'0942
A Western approach to Zen; an enquiry. [1st U.S.A. ed.] Wheaton, Ill., Theosophical Pub. House [1972, c1971] 212 p. 23 cm. Bibliography: p. 197. [BL1493.H8 1972] 72-76428 ISBN 0-8356-0211-7 5.95
1. Zen Buddhism—Essence, genius, nature. I. Title.

WATTS, Alan Wilson, 1915- 294.3'927'0924 B
In my own way; an autobiography, 1915-1965 [by] Alan Watts. New York, Vintage Books [1973, c1972] xi, 466 p. 18 cm. [BQ995.T8A33 1973] 73-5592 2.45
1. Watts, Alan Wilson, 1915- I. Title.

WATTS, Alan Wilson, 1915- 294.3'927'0924 B
In my own way; an autobiography, 1915-1965 [by] Alan Watts. [1st ed.] New York, Pantheon Books [1972] xii, 400 p. illus. 22 cm. [BL1473.W3A34] 72-3409 ISBN 0-394-46911-9 7.95
I. Title.

DR. A. N. Upadhye Memorial Seminar on Jaina Philosophy, Literature and Culture, University of Mysore, 1976. 294.4
Jainism : a study : [proceedings of the seminar held in memory of Dr. A. N. Upadhye] / editor, T. G. Kalghatgi. 1st ed. Mysore : Dept. of Jainology & Prakrits, University of Mysore : for copies, Prasaranga, 1976. xvii, 173 p., [1] leaf of plates : ill. ; 23 cm. (Department of Jainology & Prakrits publication ; no. 2) English or Kannada. Includes bibliographical references. [BL1301.D6 1976] 77-900575 Rs8.00
1. Jainism—Congresses. I. Upadhye, Adinath Neminath, 1906-1975. II. Kalghatgi, T. G. III. Title. IV. Series: Mysore. Univeristy. Jainasastra mattu Prakrta Vibhagada. Jainasastra mattu Prakrta Vibhagada prakatane ; no. 2.

GOPALAN, Subramania, 1935- 294.4
Outlines of Jainism [by] S. Gopalan. New York, Halsted Press [1973] viii, 205 p. 22 cm. Bibliography: p. [197]-199. [BL1351.2.G6] 73-13196 ISBN 0-85226-324-4 4.95 (pbk.)
1. Jainism. I. Title.

JAIN, Jyoti Prasad. 294.4
Religion and culture of the Jains / by Jyotiprasad Jain. 1st ed. New Delhi : Bharatiya Jnanpith Publication, 1976 xi, 196, [12] p. : ill. ; 22 cm. (Jnanapitha Murtidevi granthamala : English series ; 6) "Published on the occasion of the celebration of the 2500th Nirvana of Bhagavan Mahavira." Bibliography: p. [190]-196. [BL1351.2.J28] 75-905855 ISBN 0-13-771949-3 8.95
1. Mahavira. 2. Jainism. I. Mahavira. II. Title.
Distributed by South Asia Bks.

JAIN directory : 294.4'025'5482
who is who & Jain contribution in Tamil Nadu / compiled by C. L. Metha. 1st ed. Madras : Dhanraj Baid Jain College, 1976. xxx, 568 p., [2] leaves of plates : ill. ; 26 cm. "Bhagwan Mahaveera 2500th Nirvana Mahotsava." Advertising matter included in paging. Includes index. [BL1324.T35J34] 76-904866 Rs50.00
1. Jainism—India—Tamil Nadu—Directories. I. Metha, C. L. II. Title.

SINGH, Ram Bhushan Prasad, 1940- 294.4'0954'87
Jainism in early medieval Karnataka, c. A.D. 500-1200 / Ram Bhushan Prasad Singh ; with a foreword by A. L. Basham. 1st ed. Delhi : Motilal Banarsidass, 1975. xv, 175 p., [1] leaf of plates : fold. map ; 22 cm. A revision of the author's thesis, Patna University, 1972. Includes index. Bibliography: p. [140]-148. [BL1324.K37S55 1975] 76-900025 ISBN 0-8426-0981-4 10.50
1. Jainism—Karnataka, India. I. Title.
Distributed by Verry.

BHAGWAN Mahavira and his relevance in modern times 294.4'6'3
/ editors, Narendra Bhanawat, Prem Suman Jain, associate editor, V. P. Bhatt. 1st ed. Bikaner : Akhil Bharatavarshiya Sadhumargi Jain Sangha, 1976. xvi, 222 p. : ill. ; 23 cm. Includes bibliographical references. [BL1371.B46] 76-902510 Rs25.00
1. Mahavira—Addresses, essays, lectures. 2. Jainism—Addresses, essays, lectures. I. Bhanawat, Narendra, 1934- II. Jain, Prem Suman, 1942- III. Bhatt, V. P.

GUNABHADRA, 9thcentury. 294.4'8
Atmanushasana (Discourse to the soul). Edited, with translation & commentaries, by J. L. Jaini, assisted by Brahmachari Sital Prasada. Lucknow, Central Jaina Pub. House, 1928. [New York, AMS Press, 1974] 75 p. 23 cm. English and Sanskrit. Original ed. issued as v. 7 of the Sacred books of the Jainas and in series: Bibliotheca Jainica. [BL1311.A8G8613 1974] 73-3841 ISBN 0-404-57707-5
1. Jainism. I. Jaini, Jagmandar Lal, d. 1927, ed. II. Sital Prasad, Brahmachari, ed. III. Title. IV. Series: The Sacred books of the Jainas, v. 7. V. Series: Bibliotheca Jainica.

KUNDAKUNDA. 294.4'8
Samayasara (The soul-essence). The original text in Prakrit, with its Samskrit renderings, and a translation, exhaustive commentaries, and an introd. by J. L. Jaini, assisted by Brahmachari Sital Prasada. Lucknow, Central Jaina Pub. House, 1930. [New York, AMS Press, 1974] 8, 214 p. port. 23 cm. English and Prakrit, with each sloka of the original text rendered into Sanskrit. Original ed. issued as v. 8 of the Sacred books of the Jainas and as v. 3 of Jagmandarlal Jaini memorial series, and in series: Bibliotheca Jainica. [BL1311.S2K8613 1974] 73-3843 ISBN 0-404-57708-3
1. Jainism. I. Jaini, Jagmandar Lal, d. 1927, ed. II. Sital Prasad, Brahmachari. III. Title. IV. Series: The Sacred books of the Jainas, v. 8. V. Series: Jagmandarlal Jaini memorial series, v. 3. VI. Series: Bibliotheca Jainica.

NEMICANDRA Siddhantacakravartin. 294.4'8
Gommatsara jiva-kanda (The soul), by Nemichandra Siddhanta Chakravarti. Edited with introd., translation, and commentary by J. L. Jaini, assisted by Brahmachari Sital Prasadaji. Lucknow, Central Jaina Pub. House, 1927. [New York, AMS Press, 1974] p. cm. English, Sanskrit, and Prakrit. Original ed. issued as v. 5 of the Sacred books of the Jainas. [BL1311.G6N4513 1974b] 73-3839 ISBN 0-404-57705-9 37.50
1. Jainism. I. Jaini, Jagmandar Lal, d. 1927, ed. II. Sital Prasad, Brahmachari, ed. III. Title. IV. Series: The Sacred books of the Jainas, v. 5.

NEMICANDRA Siddhantacakravartin. 294.4'8
Gommatsara karma-kanda, by Nemichandra Siddhanta Chakravarti. Edited with introd., translation, and commentary by J. L. Jaini, assisted by Brahmachari Sital Prasada. Lucknow, Central Jaina Pub. House, 1927-37. [New York, AMS Press, 1974] 2 v. 23 cm. Vol. 2 edited with an introd., translation, and commentaries by Brahmachari Sital Prasada, assisted by Pandit Ajit Prasada. English, Sanskrit, and Prakrit. Original ed. issued as v. 6 and 10 of the Sacred books of the Jainas and in series: Bibliotheca Jainica; v. 2 also issued as v. 7 of the J. L. Jaina memorial series. [BL1311.G6N4513 1974] 73-3840 ISBN 0-404-57712-1
1. Jainism. I. Jaini, Jagmandar Lal, d. 1927, ed. II. Sital Prasad, Brahmachari, ed. III. Prasada, Ajit, 1874- ed. IV. Title. V. Series: The Sacred books of the Jainas, v. 6, [etc.] VI. Series: Bibliotheca Jainica. VII. Series: Jagmandarlal Jaini memorial series, v. 7.

AMRTACANDRA, fl.905. 294.4'8'2
Purushartha-siddhyupaya (Jaina-pravachana-rahasya-kosha). Edited, with an introd., translation, and original commentaries in English, by Ajit Prasada. Lucknow, Central Jaina Pub. House, 1933. [New York, AMS Press, 1974] 49, 85, 4, iii p. illus. 23 cm. English and Prakrit. Original ed. issued as v. 4 of the Sacred books of the Jainas, as no. 6 of J. L. Jaini memorial series, and in series:

Bibliotheca Jainica. [BL1311.P8A4513 1974] 73-3838 ISBN 0-404-57704-0
1. Jainism. I. Prasada, Ajit, 1874- ed. II. Title. III. Series: The Sacred books of the Jainas, v. 4. IV. Series: Jagmandarlal Jaini memorial series, no. 6. V. Series: Bibliotheca Jainica.

BHADRABAHU. 294.4'8'2
The Kalpa sutra and Nava tatva; two works illustrative of the Jain religion and philosophy. Translated from the Magadhi, with an appendix containing remarks on the language of the original, by J. Stevenson. Varanasi, Bharat-Bharati, 1972. xxviii, 144 p. 22 cm. First published in 1848. [BL1351.B4713 1972] 72-904882
1. Mahavira. 2. Jainism. I. Stevenson, John, 1798-1858, tr. II. Bhadrabahu. Navatattva. 1972. III. Title. IV. Title: Nava tatva.
Distributed by South Asia Books; 7.00, ISBN 0-88386-145-3.

KUNDAKUNDA. 294.4'8'2
The building of the cosmos; or, Panchastikayasara (The five cosmic constituents), by Kundakundacharya. Edited with philosophical and historical introd., translation, notes and an original commentary in English by A. Chakravartinayanar. Arrah, Central Jaina Pub. House, 1920. [New York, AMS Press, 1974] lxxxvi, 174 p. port. 23 cm. English and Prakrit, with each sloka of the original text rendered into Sanskrit; title also in Sanskrit. Original ed. issued as v. 3 of the Sacred books of the Jainas and in series: Bibliotheca Jainica. [BL1311.P3K8613 1974] 73-3837 ISBN 0-404-57703-2
1. Jainism. 2. Philosophy, Jaina. I. Chakravarti, Appaswami, ed. II. Title. III. Series: The Sacred books of the Jainas, v. 3. IV. Series: Bibliotheca Jainica.

KUNDAKUNDA. 294.4'8'2
Niyamsara (The perfect law). The original text in Prakrit, with its Samskrit renderings, translation, exhaustive commentaries, and an introd. in English, by Uggar Sain, assisted by Brahmachari Sital Prasada. Lucknow, Central Jaina Pub. House, 1931. [New York, AMS Press, 1974] 9, 78 p. 23 cm. English and Prakrit, with each sloka of the original text rendered into Sanskrit. Original ed. issued as v. 9 of the Sacred books of the Jainas and as v. 5 of Jagmandarlal Jaini memorial series and in series: Bibliotheca Jainica. [BL1311.N5K8613 1974] 73-3844 ISBN 0-404-57709-1
1. Jainism. I. Sain, Uggar, ed. II. Sital Prasad, Brahmachari, ed. III. Title. IV. Series: The Sacred books of the Jainas, v. 9. V. Series: Jagmandarlal Jaini memorial series, v. 5. VI. Series: Bibliotheca Jainica.

MANIKYANANDI. 294.4'8'2
Pariksamukham, by Manikyanandi (with Prameya-ratnamala, by Anantavirya). Edited with translation, introd., notes, and an original commentary in English, by Sarat Chandra Ghoshal. Lucknow, Central Jaina Pub. House, 1940. [New York, AMS Press, 1974] li, 206, 10, x p. 23 cm. English and Prakrit, with each sloka of the original text rendered into Sanskrit. Original ed. issued as v. 11 of the Sacred books of the Jainas and in series: Bibliotheca Jainica. Bibliography: p. [6]-10 (2d group) [BL1311.P34M3613 1974] 73-3845 ISBN 0-404-57711-3
1. Jainism. I. Ghoshal, Sarat Chandra, ed. II. Anantavirya. Prameyaratnamala. 1974. III. Title. IV. Series: The Sacred books of the Jainas, v. 11. V. Series: Bibliotheca Jainica.

NEMICANDRA 294.4'8'2
Siddhantacakravartin.
Davva-samgaha (Dravya-samgraha), by Nemichandra Siddhanta-chakravarti, with a commentary by Brahma-deva. Edited, with introd., translation, notes, and an original commentary in English, by Sarat Chandra Ghoshal. Arrah, Central Jaina Pub. House. [New York, AMS Press, 1974, c1917] p. cm. English and Prakrit, with each sloka of the original text rendered into Sanskrit. The commentary by Brahmadeva is in Sanskrit. Original ed. issued as v. 1 of the Sacred books of the Jainas, and in series: Bibliotheca Jainica. Bibliography: p. [BL1311.D3N4513 1974] 73-3835 ISBN 0-404-57701-6 21.50
1. Jainism. I. Brahmadeva, 17th cent. II. Ghoshal, Sarat Chandra, ed. III. Title. IV. Series: The Sacred books of the Jainas, v. 1. V. Series: Bibliotheca Jainica.

SIDDHANTA. Mulasutta. 294.4'8'2
Dasavealiya. English, Sanskrit & Prakrit.
Arya Sayyambhava's Dasavaikalika sutra (Dasaveyalia sutta). Translation and notes by Kastur Chand Lalwani. [1st ed.] Delhi, Motilal Banarsidass [1973] xx, 268 p. 22 cm. Title on spine: Dasavaikalika sutra. Introductory matter, notes, and glossary in English. Authorship uncertain. Has been attributed to Sayyambhava. [BL1311.S55E5 1973] 73-901561
I. Sayyambhava. II. Lalwani, Kasturchand, tr. III. Title: Dasavaikalika sutra.
Distributed by Verry, 10.00

SIDDHARTA. Selections. 294.4'8'2
English.
Jaina Sutras. Translated from Prakrit by Hermann Jacobi. New York, Dover Publications [1968] 2 v. 22 cm. (The Sacred books of the East, v. 22, 45) Contents.Contents.—pt. 1. The Akaranga sutra. The Kalpa sutra.—pt. 2. The Uttaradhyayana sutra. The Sutrakritanga sutra. Bibliographical footnotes. [BL1311.S5E5 1968] 68-9452 3.50 per vol.
I. Jacobi, Hermann Georg, 1850-1937, tr. II. Title. III. Series: The Sacred books of the East (New York) v. 22 [etc.]

UMASVATI, ca.135- 294.4'8'2
ca.219.
Tattvarthadhigama sutra (A treatise on the essential principles of Jainism), by Umasvami. Edited with introd., translation, notes, and commentary in English, by J. L. Jaini, assisted by Brahmchari Sri Sital Prasad. Arrah, Central Jaina Pub. House. [New York, AMS Press, 1974] 210, xxviii p. 23 cm. English and Sanskrit; title also in Sanskrit. Reprint of the 1920 ed. issued as v. 2 of the Sacred books of the Jainas and in series: Bibliotheca Jainica. [BL1311.T3U4513 1974] 73-3836 ISBN 0-404-57702-4
1. Jainism. I. Jaini, Jagmandar Lal, d. 1927, ed. II. Sital Prasad, Brahmachari, ed. III. Title. IV. Series: The Sacred books of the Jainas, v. 2. V. Series: Bibliotheca Jainica.

CHENNAKESAVAN, Sarasvati, 294.5
1918-
A critical study of Hinduism. New York, Asia Pub. House [1974] xiv, 159 p. 22 cm. Includes bibliographical references. [BL1202.C48] 74-174429 ISBN 0-210-22352-9 10.95
1. Hinduism. I. Title.

FARQUHAR, John Nicol, 1861- 294.5
1929
An outline of the religious literature of India, by J. N. Farquhar. Delhi, Motilal Banatsidass [1967] xviii, 451, [1]p. 22cm. (Orig. pub. by Oxford Univ. Pr. in The religious quest of India ser. in 1920) Bibl. [BL2001.F32] 8.50
1. India—Religion. 2. Christianity and other religious. 3. Religious literature, India. I. Title.
American distributor: Verry, Mystic, Conn.

HALL, Manly Palmer, 1901- 294.5
The guru, by his disciple; the way of the East as told to Manly Palmer Hall. New York, Philosophical Library [1958, c1944] 142p. illus. 22cm. [BF1999.H3247 1958] 59-41
I. Title.

HINDUISM : 294.5
new essays in the history of religions / edited by Bardwell L. Smith. Leiden : E. J. Brill, 1976. 231 p., [2] leaves of plates : ill ; 25 cm. (Studies in the history of religions, supplements to Numen ; 33) Includes bibliographies and index. [BL1210.H49] 76-369439 ISBN 9-00-404495-7 : 20.00
1. Hinduism—Addresses, essays, lectures. I. Smith, Bardwell L., 1925- II. Series.
Distributed by South Asia Books

HINDUISM; 294.5
edited by John R. Hinnells and Eric J. Sharpe. Newcastle upon Tyne, Oriel Press, 1972. x, 224 p. maps, plan. 23 cm. (World religions in education) Grown out of material delivered at the 1970 Shap course on Hinduism organized by the Department of Education, University of Newcastle upon Tyne. Bibliography: p. 201-211. [BL1202.H55] 72-127067 ISBN 0-85362-116-0 £4.00
1. Hinduism. I. Hinnells, John R., ed. II. Sharpe, Eric J., 1933- ed.

HISTORICAL studies in the 294.5
cult of the goddess Manasa; a socio-cultural study. Foreword by A. L. Basham. Calcutta, Punthi Pustak, 1966. xvi, iv, 377, xi p. llus., map. 23cm. Thesis--Univ. of London. Bibl. [BL1225.M3M3] [PL480:I-E-6397] SA 66 12.50
1. Manasa (Hindu deity) I. Maity, Pradyot Kumar, 1936-
American distributor: Verry, Mystic, Conn.

KIRK, James A., comp. 294.5
Stories of the Hindus; an introduction through texts and interpretation, by James A. Kirk. New York, Macmillan [1972] xviii, 269 p. 22 cm. Bibliography: p. 256-259. [BL1145.5.K57] 72-77651
1. Mythology, Hindu. 2. Hindu literature. I. Title.

*KRIYANANDA, Swami. 294.5
Letters to truth seekers. [by] Swami Kriyananda. Nevada City, Calif., Ananda Publications, [1973] 104 p., 21 cm. [BX382] 1.50 (pbk.)
1. Spiritual direction. 2. Address, essays, lectures. I. Title.

KUMARAPPA, Bharatan [Name 294.5
orig.: Benjamin Ebenezer Cornelius] 1896-
The Hindu conception of the deity as culminating in Ramanuja. Foreword by L. D. Barnett. London, Luzac [Mystic, Conn., Verry, 1965] 356p. 22cm. 4.50
1. God (Hinduism) 2. Absolute, The. 3. Upanishads. 4. Bhagavatas. 5. Ramanuja, founder of the sect. I. Title. II. Title: Ramanuja's conception of the deity.

LEMAITRE, Solange. 294.5
Hinduism. Translated from the French by John Francis Brown. [1st ed.] New York, Hawthorn Books [1959] 126p. 21cm. (The Twentieth century encyclopedia of Catholicism, v. 144. Section xiv: Non-Christian beliefs) Includes bibliography. [BL1202.L413] 59-12165
1. Hinduism. I. Title.

MORGAN, Kenneth William, 294.5
ed.
The religion of the Hindus. Contributors: D. S. Sarma [and others] New York, Ronald Press Co. [1953] 434 p. 22 cm. [BL1201.M65] 53-10466
1. Hinduism. 2. Hinduism—Sacred books (Selection: Extracts, etc.) I. Title.

NIKHILANANDA, Swami. 294.5
Hinduism: its meaning for the liberation of the spirit. [1st ed.] New York, Harper [1958] 196 p. 20 cm. (World perspectives, v. 17) [BL2010.N5] 58-6155
1. Hinduism. 2. Yoga. I. Title.

O'MALLEY, Lewis Sydney 294.5
Steward, 1874-1941.
Popular Hinduism; the religion of the masses. Cambridge, University Press, 1935. New York, Johnson Reprint Corp., 1970. viii, 246 p. 23 cm. (Landmarks in anthropology) Includes bibliographical references. [BL1201.O6 1970] 70-142072
1. Hinduism. 2. India—Religion. I. Title.

ORGAN, Troy Wilson. 294.5
The Hindu quest for the perfection of man. Athens, Ohio University [1970] x, 439 p. 25 cm. Bibliography: p. 348-419. [BL1202.O7] 73-81450 11.50
1. Hinduism. I. Title.

PITT, Malcolm. 294.5
Introducing Hinduism. New York, Friendship Press [1955] 60p. illus. 23cm. (Popular introductions to living religions) Includes bibliography. [BL1201P5] 54-10130
1. Hinduism. 2. Christianity and other religions—Hinduism. I. Title.

POLITELLA, Joseph, 1910- 294.5
Hinduism: its scriptures, philosophy, and mysticism. Iowa City, Sernoll [1966] viii, 122 p. 22 cm. (Crucible books) Bibliographical references included in "Notes" (p. 111-122) [BL1202.P64] 66-4457
1. Hinduism. I. Title.

POLITELLA, Joseph, 1910- 294.5
Hinduism: its scriptures, philosophy, and mysticism. Iowa City, Sernoll [1966] viii, 122p. 22cm. (Crucible bks.) Bibl. [BL1202.P64] 66-4457 1.95 pap.,
1. Hinduism. I. Title.
Publisher's address: 410 E Market St., Iowa City, Iowa.

PREMANANDA, Swami, 1861- 294.5
1918.
Swami Premananda; teachings and reminiscences. Edited and translated by Swami Prabhavananda. Biographical introd. by Clive Johnson. Hollywood, Calif., Vedanta Press [1968] 157 p. port. 17 cm. Originally published in Vedanta and the West. [BL1226.85.P7 1968] 77-5592
1. Hinduism. I. Prabhavananda, Swami, 1893- ed.

RADHAKRISHNAN, Sarvepalli 294.5
Sir
The Hindu view of life. New York, Macmillan [1962] 92p. 19cm. 1.00 pap.,
1. Hinduism. I. Title.

RADHAKRISHNAN, Sarvepalli, 294.5
Pres. India, 1888-
Religion and society. [2d ed.] London, Allen & Unwin. [dist. New York, Barnes & Noble, 1962] 248p. illus. 22cm. (Kamala lectures) Based on notes of lectures delivered in the Univ. of Calcutta and Benares in the winter of 1942. 62-53406 3.75
1. Religion and sociology. 2. Sociology, Hindu. I. Title.

RENOU, Louis, 1896- 294.5
The nature of Hinduism. Translated by Patrick Evans. New York, Walker [1963, c1962] 155 p. 21 cm. (A Sun book, SB-5. Religion and mythology) Translation of L'hindouisme. [BL1202.R413 1963] 62-12745
1. Hinduism.

RENOU, Louis, 1896-1966, 294.5
ed.
Hinduism. New York, G. Braziller, 1961. 255 p. 21 cm. (Great religions of modern man) Includes bibliography. [BL1107.R4] 61-15496
1. Hinduism.

RUTLEDGE, Denys 294.5
In search of a yogi. New York, Farrar [1963, c.1962] 321p. maps. 22cm. 63-9921 4.95 bds.,
1. Christianity and other religions—Hinduism. 2. India—Religion. 3. India—Descr. & trav.—1947- I. Title.

SEN, Kshitimohan 294.5
Hinduism. Penquin [dist. Boston, Houghton, 1962, c.1961 160p. (Pelican bk., A515) Bibl. 62-784 .95 pap.,
1. Hinduism. I. Title.

SINGER, Milton B., ed. 294.5
Krishna; myths, rites, and attitudes, edited by Milton Singer. With a foreword by Daniel H. H. Ingalls. Honolulu, East-West Center Press [1966] xvii, 277 p. 24 cm. Bibliography: p. [233]-237. [BL1220.S5] 65-20585
1. Krishna. I. Title.

SRINIVASACHARI, P. N., 294.5
1880-
The ethical philosophy of the Gita [3d ed.] Madras. Sri Ramakrishna [1966] xi, 163p. 19cm. [BL1130.S65 1966] 67-6620 1.75 bds.,
1. Mahabharata, Bhagavadgita—Ethics. I. Title.
American distributor: Vedanta Pr., Hollywood, Calif.

STONE, Justin. 294.5
Abandon hope! The way to fulfillment, by Justin F. Stone. Albuquerque, N.M., Sun Pub. Co. [1974] 128 p. illus. 23 cm. [BL1035.S8] 74-80481 3.50 (pbk.).
1. Asia—Religion—Addresses, essays, lectures. 2. Gurus—Addresses, essays, lectures. I. Title.

STROUP, Herbert Hewitt, 294.5
1916-
Like a great river; an introduction to Hinduism [by] Herbert Stroup. [1st ed.] New York, Harper & Row [1972] viii, 200 p. 22 cm. Bibliography: p. [185]-187. [BL1202.S77] 72-78049 ISBN 0-06-067757-0 5.95
1. Hinduism. I. Title.

THIEME, Paul, 1905- 294.5
Mitra and Aryaman. New Haven, 1957. 96 p. 25 cm. (Transactions of the Connecticut Academy of Arts and Sciences, v. 41) [Q11.C9 vol.41] A58
1. Mitra (Hindu deity) 2. Aryaman (Hindu deity) 3. Mythology, Aryan. I. Title. II. Series: Connecticut Academy of Arts and Sciences, New Haven. Transactions, v. 41

ZAEHNER, Robert Charles. 294.5
Hinduism [by] R. C. Zaehner. 2nd ed. London, Oxford U.P., 1966. [7], 210 p. 20 cm. (Oxford paperbacks, university series, opus 12) 7/6 (B66-18074) Bibliography: p. [193]-199. [BL1202.Z3] 67-72043
1. Hinduism. I. Title.

ZAEHNER, Robert Charles 294.5
Hinduism. New York, Oxford [c.]1962. 272p. 17cm. (Home univ. lib. of modern knowledge, 247) Bibl. 63-347 1.70
1. Hinduism. I. Title.

ZIMMER, Heinrich Robert, 294.5
1890-1943
Myths and symbols in Indian art and civilization. Ed. by Joseph Campbell. New York, Harper [1962, c.1946] 248p. illus. (Bollingen lib.; Harper torckbk., TB2005) 2.25 pap.,
1. Mythology, Hindu. 2. Symbolism. 3. Art, Hindu. 4. India—Civilization. I. Campbell, Joseph, 1904- ed. II. Title.

DOWSON, John, 1820-1881. 294.5'03
A classical dictionary of Hindu mythology and religion, geography, history, and literature. Boston, Milford House [1973] p. Reprint of the 1879 ed. published by Trubner, London, which was issued as no. 6 of Trubner's oriental series. [BL1105.D6 1973] 73-13680 ISBN 0-87821-185-3 35.00
1. Mythology, Hindu—Dictionaries. 2. Sanskrit literature—Dictionaries. I. Title.

WALKER, George Benjamin, 294.5'03
1913-
The Hindu world; an encyclopedic survey of Hinduism [by] Benjamin Walker. New York, Praeger [1968] 2 v. 24 cm. Includes bibliographies. [BL1105.W34 1968] 68-26182 35.00
1. Hinduism—Dictionaries. I. Title.

EMBREE, Ainslie Thomas, comp. 294.508
The Hindu tradition, edited by Ainslie T. Embree. New York, Modern Library [1966] xv, 363 p. 19 cm. (Readings in oriental thought) (The Modern library of the world's best books.) "Sources of English translations and selections": p. [349]-351. [BL1145.5.E5] 66-13011
1. Hindu literature. I. Title.

MARSHALL, Peter James, comp. 294.5'08
The British discovery of Hinduism in the eighteenth century, edited by P. J. Marshall. Cambridge [Eng.] University Press, 1970. viii, 310 p. 23 cm. (European understanding of India) Reprints of either essays or chapters from books originally published between 1767 and 1790. Contents.Contents.—Chapters on The religious tenets of the Gentoos, by J. Z. Holwell.—A dissertation concerning Hindoos, by A. Dow.—The translator's preface to A code of Gentoo laws, by N. B. Halhed.—Letter to Nathaniel Smith, from the Bhagvat-Geeta, by W. Hastings.—The translator's preface, from the Bhagvat-Geeta, by C. Wilkins.—On the Gods of Greece, Italy and India, by W. Jones.—On the Hindus, by W. Jones.—On the chronology of the Hindus, by W. Jones. [BL1210.M36] 73-111132 5/12/- ($17.50 U.S.)
1. Hinduism—Addresses, essays, lectures. I. Title.

ASHBY, Philip H. 294.5'09
Modern trends in Hinduism [by] Philip H. Ashby. New York, Columbia University Press, 1974. ix, 143 p. 24 cm. (Lectures on the history of religions, new ser., no. 10) Includes bibliographical references. [BL1150.A83] 73-20262 ISBN 0-231-03768-6 8.00
1. Hinduism—History. I. Title. II. Series.

ORGAN, Troy Wilson. 294.5'09
Hinduism; its historical development. Woodbury, N.Y., Barron's Educational Series [1974] iv, 425 p. 21 cm. (Barron's compact studies of world religions) Bibliography: p. 396-406. [BL1150.O73] 73-10676 ISBN 0-8120-0500-7 2.95 (pbk.).
1. Hinduism—History. I. Title.

OMAN, John Campbell, 1841-1911. 294.5'0954
The Brahmans, theists, and Muslims of India : studies of goddess-worship in Bengal, caste, Brahmaism, and social reform, with descriptive sketches of curious festivals, ceremonies, and faquirs / by John Campbell Oman. New York : AMS Press, [1975] xv, 341 p., [8] leaves of plates : ill. ; 23 cm. Reprint of the 1907 ed. published by G. W. Jacobs, Philadelphia. Includes bibliographical references and index. [BL2001.O45 1975] 76-179231 ISBN 0-404-54858-X : 22.50
1. India—Religion. 2. India—Social life and customs. I. Title.

OMAN, John Campbell, 1841-1911. 294.5'0954
The Brahmans, theists, and Muslims of India; studies of Goddess-worship in Bengal, caste, Brahmaism, and social reform, with descriptive sketches of curious festivals, ceremonies, and faquirs. With illus. from photographs and from drawings by William Campbell Oman. Delhi, Indological Book House [1973, i.e. 1974] xiv, 341 p. illus. 22 cm. Reprint of the 1907 ed. published by G. W. Jacobs, Philadelphia. Includes bibliographical references. [BL2001.O45 1973] 73-905235
1. India—Religion. 2. India—Social life and customs. I. Title.
Distributed by International Publications Service, 18.75

BABB, Lawrence A. 294.5'0954'3
The divine hierarchy popular Hinduism in central India / Lawrence A. Babb. New York : Columbia University Press, 1975. p. cm. Bibliography: p. [BL1150.B29] 75-16193 ISBN 0-231-03882-8 : 10.00
1. Hinduism—Chhattisgarh, India. 2. Chhattisgarh, India—Religious life and customs. I. Title.

JONES, Kenneth W. 294.5'0954'552
Arya dharm : Hindu consciousness in 19th-century Punjab / Kenneth W. Jones. Berkeley : University of California Press, c1976. xvi, 343 p., [1] leaf of plates : maps ; 25 cm. Includes bibliographical references and index. [BL1254.5.P86J66] 74-27290 ISBN 0-520-02920-8 : 12.95
1. Arya-samaj. 2. Hindus in the Punjab. 3. Punjab—History. I. Title.

SRINIVAS, Mysore Narasimhachar. 294.5095487
Religion and society among the Coorgs of South India [by] M. N. Srinivas. New York, Asia Pub. House [1965] xiv, 269 p. illus., maps, plan. 23 cm. Bibliography: p. [252] [BL2030.C6S7 1965] 66-145
1. Coorg, India — Religion. 2. Coorg, India — Soc. life & cust. I. Title.

SRINIVAS, Mysore Narasimhachar 294.5095487
Religion and society among the Coorgs of South India New York, Asia [dist. Taplinger, c.1952, 1965] ixv, 269p. illus., maps, plan. 23cm. Bibl. [BL2030.C6S7] 66-145 11.00
1. Coorg.India—Religion. 2. Coorg. India—Soc. life & cust. I. Title.

MOOKERJI, Radha Kumud, 1884- 294.51
Nationalism in Hindu culture. 2d ed. Delhi, S. Chand [1957] ii, 104p. 19cm. [DS423.M55 1957] SA66 2.50 bds.,
1. Nationalism—India. 2. Civilization, Hindu. I. Title.
Available from Verry in Mystic, Conn.

NOBLE, Margaret Elizabeth, 1867-1911 294.5'1'13
Myths of the Hindus & Buddhists, by Anda K. Coomaraswamy, and the Sister Nivedita (Margaret E. Noble) With 32 illus. by Indian artists under the supervision of Abanindro Nath Tagore i[Magnolia, Mass., P. Smith 1967] xii, 399p. illus. 22cm. (Dover bk. rebound) Authors' names in reverse order in other eds. Unabridged repubn. of the work orig. pub. in 1913 [BL2001.N6 1967] 5.00
1. Mythology, Hindu. 2. Buddha and Buddhism. I. Coomaraswamy, Ananda Kentish, 1877-1947, joint author. II. Title.

DUMEZIL, Georges, 1898- 294.5'1'3
The destiny of a king. Translated by Alf Hiltebeitel. Chicago, University of Chicago Press [1973] 155 p. 24 cm. Translation of part three of Mythe et epopee, vol. 2: Types epiques indo-europeens: un heros, un sorcier, un roi. Includes bibliographical references. [BL2003.D8513 1973] 73-75311 ISBN 0-226-16975-8 10.00
1. Mythology, Indic. I. Title.

NOBLE, Margaret Elizabeth, 1867-1911. 294.5'1'3
Myths of the Hindus & Buddhists, by Ananda K. Coomaraswamy and Sister Nivedita (Margaret E. Noble) With 32 illus. by Indian artists under the supervision of Abanindro Nath Tagore. New York, Dover Publicatons [1967] xii, 399 p. illus. 22 cm. Author's names in reverse order in other editions. "An unabridged republication of the work originally published ... in 1913." [BL2001.N6 1967] 67-14131
1. Mythology, Hindu. 2. Buddha and Buddhism. I. Coomaraswamy, Ananda Kentish, 1877-1947, joint author. II. Title.

ZIMMER, Heinrich Robert, 1890-1943. 294.5'1'3
Myths and symbols in Indian art and civilization. Edited by Joseph Campbell. New York, Harper [1962, c1946] xiii, 248 p. plates. 21 cm. (Harper torchbooks, TB 2005. The Bollingen library, 6) Reprint of the ed. published by Pantheon Books, New York. [BL2003.Z5 1962] 74-163423
1. Mythology, Hindu. 2. Symbolism. 3. Art, Hindu. 4. India—Civilization. I. Campbell, Joseph, 1904- ed. II. Title.

ZIMMER, Heinrich Robert, 1890-1943. 294.5'1'3
Myths and symbols in Indian art and civilization. Edited by Joseph Campbell. [Princeton, N.J.] Princeton University Press [1972, c1946] xiii, 248 p. plates. 22 cm. (Bolingen series, 6) Reprint of the ed. published by Pantheon Books, New York. [BL2003.Z5 1972] 74-163422 ISBN 0-691-09800-X
1. Mythology, Hindu. 2. Symbolism. 3. Art, Hindu. 4. India—Civilization. I. Campbell, Joseph, 1904- ed. II. Title. III. Series.

HINDU myths : 294.5'1'308
a sourcebook / translated from the Sanskrit with an introduction by Wendy Doniger O'Flaherty. Harmondsworth ; Baltimore : Penguin, 1975. 358 p. ; 19 cm. (The Penguin classics) Includes index. Bibliography: p. 302-309. [BL2001.2.H56] 75-323936 ISBN 0-14-044306-1 : £0.80 ($3.50 U.S.)
1. Mythology, Hindu. I. O'Flaherty, Wendy Doniger.

GRIFFITHS, Bede, 1906- 294.5'1'72
Vedanta & Christian faith. Los Angeles, Dawn Horse Press [1973] x, 89 p. illus. 21 cm. Includes bibliographical references. [BR128.H5G75 1973] 73-88179 1.95
1. Hinduism—Relations—Christianity. 2. Christianity and other religions—Hinduism. I. Title.

KLOSTERMAIER, Klaus. 294.5'1'72
In the paradise of Krishna; Hindu and Christian seekers. [Translated by Antonia Fonseca from the German] Philadelphia, Westminster Press [1971, c1969] ix, 118 p. 21 cm. Translation of Christ und Hindu in Vrindaban. [BR128.H5K573 1971] 76-128022 ISBN 0-664-24904-3 1.95
1. Christianity and other religions—Hinduism. 2. Hinduism—Relations—Christianity. I. Title.

SVARUPA Damodara Dasa, Brahmacari, 1941- 294.5'1'75
The scientific basis of Krsna consciousness, by Svarupa Damodara dasa. New York, Bhaktivedanta Book Trust [1974] 62 p. illus. 18 cm. Includes bibliographical references. [BL1220.S93] 74-18269 ISBN 0-912776-45-5 0.95 (pbk.)
1. Krishna (Cult) I. Title.

HINDU theology : 294.5'2
a reader / edited with an introd. and notes by Jose Pereira. 1st ed. Garden City, N.Y. : Image Books, 1976. 558 p. : ill. ; 18 cm. (An Image original) Includes bibliographical references and indexes. [BL1210.H47] 76-2842 ISBN 0-385-09552-X pbk. : 2.95
1. Hinduism—Addresses, essays, lectures. 2. Philosophy, Hindu—Addresses, essays, lectures. I. Pereira, Jose.

MEHER Baba, 1894-1969. 294.5'2
God speaks; the theme of creation and its purpose. 2d ed. rev. and enl. New York, Dodd, Mead, 1973. xxxv, 334 p. illus. (1 fold. in pocket) 23 cm. Includes bibliographical references. [BL1270.M377 1973] 72-13984 15.00
I. Title.

O'FLAHERTY, Wendy Doniger. 294.5'2
The origins of evil in Hindu mythology / Wendy Doniger O'Flaherty. Berkeley : University of California Press, c1976. xi, 411 p. ; 25 cm. (Hermeneutics, studies in the history of religions ; 6) Includes index. Bibliography: p. 381-396. [BJ1401.O35] 75-40664 ISBN 0-520-03163-6 : 15.00
1. Good and evil (Hinduism) I. Title. II. Series.

RAMACHANDRA AIYAR, G. 294.52
The Hindu ideal, by Sri Ramananda Saraswati Swaminah. Madras, Ganesh, 1959 [i.e.1960] dist. Hollywood, California, Vedanta Press 406p. illus. 25cm. Includes reproduction of the t.p. of the 1933 ed. published under the author's real name: G. Ramachandra Aiyar. 'Revised and enlarged edition of Atma Vidya.' 60-2997 5.00
1. Hinduism. I. Title.

RAY, Ajit Kumar. 294.5'2
The religious ideas of Rammohun Roy : a survey of his writings on religion particularly in Persian, Sanskrit, and Bengali / Ajit Kumar Ray ; with pref. by A. L. Basham. 1st ed. New Delhi : Kanak Publications (Books India Project), 1976. xii, 112 p. ; 22 cm. "Appendix A: Jawab tuhfatu'l muwahhidin; an anonymous defence of Rammohun Roy's "Tuhfatu'l muwahhidin' against the attacks of the Zoroastrians; translated with text, introduction, and notes": p. [66]-91. Bibliography: p. [99]-112. [BL1265.R3R39] 77-900843 Rs30.00 ($6.00 U.S.)
1. Rammohun Roy, Raja, 1772?-1833. I. Rammohun Roy, Raja, 1772?-1833. Tuhfatu'l muwahhidin. 1976. II. Title.

VASU, Srisa Chandra, rai bahadur, 1861-1918? 294.5'2
A catechism of Hindu dharma, by Srisa Chandra Vidyarnava. 2d ed., rev. and enl. Allahabad, Panini Office, 1919. [New York, AMS Press, 1974] 79 p. 23 cm. Original ed. issued as extra v. 3 of The Sacred books of the Hindus. Consists of questions and answers, some of which are supported by appropriate slokas in Sanskrit excerpted from the sacred literature of the Hindus. [BL1201.V34 1974] 73-3829 ISBN 0-404-57847-0
1. Hinduism. I. Title. II. Series: The Sacred books of the Hindua, extra v. 3.

NARAYAN, R. K., 1906- 294.521
God, demons, and others. Decorations by R. K. Laxman. New York, Viking [c.1964] 241p. illus. 24cm. 64-12225 6.50
1. Mvthology. Hindu. I. Title.

NARAYAN, R K 1906- 294.521
Gods, demons, and others. Decorations by R. K. Laxman. New York, Viking [1967, c.1964] 241p. illus. 20cm. (Compass bks., C202) 1.45 pap.,
1. Mythology, Hindu. I. Title.

ATHAVALE, Pandurang Vaijnath, 1920- 294.5'2'11
Glimpses of life of Lord Krishna, from the discourses of Rev. His Holiness Shastri Shri Pandurang V. Athavale. [1st ed.] [s.l. ; s.n., 1976] (Bombay : Associated Advertisers & Printers) xv, 315 p., [2] leaves of plates : ill. ; 23 cm. Includes scattered Sanskrit verses mainly from the Bhagavadgita. [BL1220.A78] 76-902179 Rs15.00
1. Krishna. I. Title.

BHOOTHALINGAM. MATHURAM 294.5211
The story of Rama. New York, Asia Pub. [dist. Taplinger, c.1964] 94p. plates. 26cm. 64-56070 6.50 bds.,
I. Valmiki. Ramayana. II. Title.

DANIELOU, Alain. 294.5211
Hindu polytheism. [New York, Bollingen Foundation; distributed by] Pantheon Books [1964] xxxi, 537 p. illus., plates. 26 cm. (Bollingen series, 73) Appendix (p. [387]-480): Sanskrit texts. Bibliography:p. [483]-491. [BL1216.D313] 62-18191
1. Gods, Hindu. I. Title.

DEVATA, 294.5'2'11
by a recluse of Vindhyachala. Allahabad, Panini Office, 1917. [New York, AMS Press, 1974] 274 p. 23 cm. Original ed. issued as v. 19 of The Sacred books of the Hindus. English or Sanskrit, with some explanations in Bengali and Hindi; foreword in English. [BL1216.D46 1974] 73-3811 ISBN 0-404-57819-5
1. Gods, Hindu. I. A recluse of Vindhyachala. II. Series: The Sacred books of the Hindus, v. 19.

DHAVAMONY, Mariasusai. 294.5'2'11
Love of God according to Saiva Siddhanta: a study in the mysticism and theology of Saivism. Oxford, Clarendon Press, 1971. xvii, 402 p. 23 cm. Bibliography: p. 379-386. [BL1215.B5D39] 72-562135 ISBN 0-19-826523-9 £4.20
1. Bhakti. 2. Sivaism. I. Title.

FRITH, Nigel. 294.5'2'11
The legend of Krishna / Nigel Frith. New York : Schocken Books, 1976, c1975. 237 p. ; 21 cm. [BL1220.F74 1976] 75-35449 ISBN 0-8052-3611-2 7.95
1. Krishna. I. Title.

HILTEBEITEL, Alf. 294.5'2'11
The ritual of battle : Krishna in the Mahabharata / Alf Hiltebeitel. Ithaca, N.Y. : Cornell University Press, 1976. 368 p. ; 22 cm. (Symbol, myth, and ritual series) Includes bibliographical references and index. [BL1220.H47] 75-18496 ISBN 0-8014-0970-5 : 19.50
1. Mahabharata. 2. Krishna. I. Title.

KINSLEY, David R. 294.5'2'11
The sword and the flute : Kali and Krsna, dark visions of the terrible and the sublime in Hindu mythology / David R. Kinsley. Berkeley : University of California Press, c1975. viii, 167, [1] p. ; 24 cm. (Hermeneutics, studies in the history of religions ; 3) Based in part on the author's thesis. Bibliography: p. 161-[168] [BL1220.K54] 73-91669 ISBN 0-520-02675-6 : 12.00
1. Krishna. 2. Kali (Hindu deity) I. Title. II. Series.

MARTIN, E. Osborn. 294.5'2'11
The gods of India: their history, character, & worship, by E. Osborn Martin. Delhi, Indological Book House, 1972. xiv, 330 p. illus., map. 22 cm. First published in 1914. Includes bibliographical references. [BL1216.M35 1972] 73-900085
1. Gods, Hindu. I. Title.
Distributed by South Asia Books, 10.00.

O'FLAHERTY, Wendy Doniger. 294.5'2'11
Asceticism and eroticism in the mythology of Siva. London, New York, Oxford University Press, 1973. xii, 386 p. illus. 24 cm. Bibliography: p. [326]-340. [BL1218.O34] 73-180569 ISBN 0-19-713573-0 £8.00
1. Siva (Hindu deity) 2. Mythology, Hindu. I. Title.

O'FLAHERTY, Wendy Doniger. 294.5'2'11
Asceticism and eroticism in the mythology of Siva. London, New York, Oxford University Press, 1973. xii, 386 p. illus. 24 cm. Bibliography: p. [326]-340. [BL1218.O34] 73-180569 ISBN 0-19-713573-0 25.75
1. Siva (Hindu deity) 2. Mythology, Hindu. I. Title.

SMITH, William L., 1942- 294.5'2'11
The myth of Manasa : a study in the popular Hinduism of medieval Bengal / by W. L. Smith. [Stockholm : Stockholms universitet, 1976] 201 p. ; 21 cm. Thesis—Stockholm. Added t. p. with thesis statement inserted. Bibliography: p. [194]-201. [BL1225.M3S64] 77-357193
1. Manasa (Hindu deity) I. Title.

SRIVASTAVA, A. K. 294.5'2'11
God and its relation with the finite self in Tagore's philosophy / by A. K. Srivastava. 1st

ed. Delhi : Oriental Publishers, 1976. 11, 166 p. ; 23 cm. Includes index. Bibliography: p. 159-162. [BL1205.S7] 76-902831 Rs40.00
1. Tagore, Rabindranath, Sir, 1861-1941. 2. God (Hinduism)—History of doctrines. 3. Self (Philosophy)—History. I. Title.

VIRAJANANDA, Swami, 294.5'2'11
1874or5-1951.
Toward the goal supreme. Introd. by Christopher Isherwood. Hollywood, Calif., Vedanta Press [1973, c1950] 155 p. 19 cm. [B5134.V57T6 1973] 73-87782 ISBN 0-87481-029-9 2.95 (pbk.)
1. God (Hinduism) I. Title.

CARMAN, John B. 294.5'2'110924
The theology of Ramanuja; an essay in interreligious understanding [by] John Braisted Carman. New Haven, Yale University Press, 1974. xii, 333 p. illus. 24 cm. (Yale publications in religion, 18) Revision of the author's thesis, Yale University, 1962, issued under title: The ideas of divine supremacy and accessibility in the theology of Ramanuja. Bibliography: p. 317-323. [BL1245.V33C37 1974] 73-77146 ISBN 0-300-01521-6 17.50
1. Ramanuja, founder of sect. I. Title. II. Series.

WASSON, Robert Gordon, 294.5'2'12
1898-
Soma and the fly-agaric; Mr. Wasson's rejoinder to Professor Brough. Cambridge, Mass., Botanical Museum of Harvard University, 1972. 57 p. illus. 25 cm. (Ethno-mycological studies, no. 2) Bibliography: p. 50-51. [BL1215.S6W36] 73-159656 3.00
1. Brough, John, 1917- 2. Soma. 3. Amanita muscaria. 4. Mushrooms (in religion, folk-lore, etc.) I. Title. II. Series.

WASSON, Robert Gordon, 294.5'21'2
1898-
Soma: divine mushroom of immortality, by R. Gordon Wasson. [New York] Harcourt Brace Jovanovich [1971] xiii, 380 p. illus., maps, col. plates. 26 cm. (Ethno-mycological studies, no. 1) Reprint of the 1968 ed. Includes bibliographical references. [BL1215.S6W37 1971] 74-25987 15.00
1. Soma. 2. Mushrooms (in religion, folk-lore, etc.) I. Title. II. Series.

GOPINATHA Rao, T. A., 294.5'21'8
1872-
Elements of Hindu iconography, by T. A. Gopinatha Rao. 2d ed. New York, Paragon Book Reprint Corp., 1968. 2 v. in 4. illus., plates. 25 cm. "An unaltered and unabridged reprint of the Madras 1914 edition." "Published under the patronage of the government of His Highness the Maharaja of Travancore." Selections from relevant texts in Sanskrit and Tamil: v. 1, pt. 2, p. 33-[160] (at end); v. 2, pt. 2, p. [1]-279 (at end) "List of the important works consulted": v. 1, pt. 1, p. xxix-[xxx]; v. 2, pt. 1, p. xxvii. [BL1201.G7 1968] 68-29408
1. Mythology, Hindu. 2. Art, Hindu. 3. Idols and images. I. Title. II. Title: Hindu iconography.

BHAKTIVEDANTA, A. C., 294.5'2'2
Swami, 1896-
Raja-vidya, the king of knowledge [by] A. C. Bhaktivedanta Swami Prabhupada. New York, Bhaktivedanta Book Trust [1973] 117 p. illus. 19 cm. [B132.K6B4 1973] 72-84845 ISBN 0-912776-40-4
1. Krishna. 2. Knowledge, Theory of (Hinduism) I. Title.

CHINMOY. 294.5'2'3
Death and reincarnation: eternity's voyage [by] Sri Chinmoy. [Jamaica, N.Y., Agni Press, 1974] 142 p. illus. 18 cm. [BL1215.D4C45] 74-81308 ISBN 0-88497-038-8 2.00 (pbk.)
1. Death (Hinduism) 2. Future life (Hinduism) 3. Reincarnation. I. Title.

GLASENAPP, Helmuth von 294.523
[Otto Max Helmuth von Glasenapp] 1891-
Immortality and salvation in Indian religions. Tr. from German by E. F. J. Payne. Calcutta, Susil Gupta India [dist. South Pasadena, Calif., Hutchins, 1963 112p. 22cm. Bibl. SA63 5.00
1. Immortality. 2. Salvation—Comparative studies. 3. India—Religion. I. Title.

ABBOTT, John, 1884- 294.5'3
The keys of power : a study of Indian ritual and belief / by J. Abbott ; new forward [sic] to 1974 ed. by Leslie Shepard. Secaucus, N.J. : University Books, 1974. xi, 560 p. : ill. ; 24 cm. Reprint of the 1932 ed. published by Methuen, London. Includes bibliographical references and index. [BL2003.A2 1974] 74-195207 ISBN 0-8216-0219-5 : 10.00
1. India—Religion. 2. Folk-lore—India. 3. Superstition. 4. India—Social life and customs. 5. Charms. 6. Rites and ceremonies—India. I. Title.

SANDILYA. 294.5'3
The one hundred aphorisms of Sandilya, with the commentary of Svapnesvara. Translated by Manmathanath Paul. Allahabad, Panini Office, 1911. [New York, AMS Press, 1974] 78, iii p. 23 cm. Original ed. issued as v. 7, pt. 2 of The Sacred books of the Hindus. English and Sanskrit; introd. in English. [BL1215.B5S253 1974] 73-3793 ISBN 0-404-57834-9 12.50
1. Bhakti. I. Paul, Manmathanath, ed. II. Svapnesvara. Sandilyasutrabhasya. English & Sanskrit. 1974. III. Title. IV. Series: The Sacred books of the Hindus, v. 7, pt 2.

VASU, Srisa Chandra, rai 294.5'3
bahadur, 1861-1918?
The daily practice of the Hindus, containing the morning and midday duties, by Srisa Chandra Vidyarnava. 3d ed., rev. and enl. Allahabad, Panini Office, 1918. [New York, AMS Press, 1974] viii, 198 p. 23 cm. Original ed. issued as v. 20 of The Sacred books of the Hindua. English and Sanskrit, with one quotation in Persian; foreword and explanatory matter in English. [BL1215.C8V37 1974] 73-3812 ISBN 0-404-57820-9
1. Cultus, Hindu. I. Title. II. Series: The Sacred books of the Hindus, v. 20.

VIDYARTHI, Lalita Prasad 294.53
The sacred complex in Hindu Gaya. New York, Asia Pub. House [dist. Taplinger, c.1961] xxiv 232p. illus. map. Bibl. 61-4851 4.50
1. Priests, Hindu. 2. Hinduism—Rituals. 3. Gaya-Ksetra. I. Title.

VIDYARTHI, Lalita Prasad. 294.53
The sacred complex in Hindu Gays. New York, Asia Pub. House [1961] xxiv. 232 p. illus. port., map. tables. 23 cm. Errata slip inserted. Bibliography: p. [219]-224. [BL1215.P75V5] 61-4851
1. Priests, Hindu. 2. Hinduism-Rituals. 3. Gaya-Ksetra. I. Title.

AGUILAR, H. 294.5'3'4
The sacrifice in the Rgveda : doctrinal aspects / H. Aguilar ; with a pref. by R. Panikkar. Delhi : Bharatiya Vidya Prakashan, 1976. ix, 222 p. ; 23 cm. Includes bibliographical references and index. [BL1215.S2A34] 76-902122 Rs50.00
1. Vedas. Rgveda—Criticism, interpretation, etc. 2. Sacrifice (Hinduism)—History. I. Title.

ACYUTANANDA 294.5'3'8
Sarasvati, Swami, comp.
Songs of the Vaisnava Acaryas / compiled by Adyutananda Svami. New York : Bhaktivedanta Book Trust, 1974. xv, 90 p. : ill. ; 18 x 26 cm. Songs in Sanskrit (romanized) and English. [BL1220.A27] 75-2031 ISBN 0-912776-56-0 : 2.95
1. Krishna (Cult) 2. Hindu hymns, English. 3. Hindu hymns, Sanskrit. I. Title.

ASVALAYANAGRHYASUTRA. 294.5'3.8
English & Sanskrit.
Asvalayana grhyasutram, with Sanskrit commentary of Narayana / English translation, introduction and index Narendra Nath Sharma ; with a foreword by Satya Vrat Shastri. 1st ed. Delhi : Eastern Book Linkers, 1976. xvi, 225 p. ; 22 cm. Sometimes attributed to Asvalayana. Introductory matter in English. Includes index. [BL1226.2.A7713] 76-905429 Rs50.00
1. Hinduism—Rituals. I. Sharma, Narendra Nath, 1940- II. Asvalayana. Asvalayanagrhyasutra. English and Sanskrit. 1976. III. Narayana, Naidhruva. Narayaniya. 1976.

BHARDWAJ, Surinder 294.5'3'8
Mohan.
Hindu places of pilgrimage in India; a study in cultural geography. Berkeley, University of California Press [1973] xviii, 258 p. illus. 24 cm. Bibliography: p. 233-247. [BL1227.A1B495] 73-174454 ISBN 0-520-02135-5 12.00
1. Pilgrims and pilgrimages—India. 2. Hindu shrines—India. I. Title.

BODEWITZ, H. W. 294.5'3'8
The daily evening and morning offering (Agnihotra) according to the Brahmanas / by H. W. Bodewitz. Leiden : Brill, 1976. xii, 211 p. ; 25 cm. (Orientalia Rheno-Traiectina ; v. 21) Includes indexes. Bibliography: p. [205]. [BL1226.82.A35B63] 76-380164 ISBN 9-00-404532-5 : fl 52.00
1. Agnihotra (Hindu rite) 2. Brahmanas. I. Title. II. Series.

MERSHON, 294.5'38'095986
Katharane Edson.
Seven plus seven; mysterious life-rituals in Bali. [1st ed.] Illustrated with photos. New York, Vantage Press [1971] 368 p. illus. 21 cm. [GN473.M4] 79-32163 7.50
1. Rites and ceremonies—Indonesia—Bali (Island) 2. Bali (Island)—Social life and customs. I. Title.

ANIRVAN, 1896- 294.5'4
To live within [comp. by] Lizelle Reymond. Foreword by Jacob Needleman. Translated from French by Nancy Pearson & Stanley Spiegelberg. Baltimore, Penguin [1973, c.1971] x 245, [27] p. 18 cm. (Penguin metaphysical library) Translation of La vie dans la vie. [B132.S3A713] 0-14 pap., 1.75
1. Sankhya. I. Reymond, Lizelle, comp. II. Title.
Contents omitted.

ANIRVAN, 1896- 294.5'4
To live within. [Compiled by] Lizelle Reymond. Foreword by Jacob Neddleman. Translated from the French by Nancy Pearson and Stanley Spiegelberg. [1st ed.] Garden City, N.Y., Doubleday, 1971. x, 245 p. illus., port. 22 cm. Translation of La vie dans la vie. Contents.Contents.—Life in a Himalayan hermitage, by L. Reymond.—Talks on samkhya, by Shri Anirvan.—The Bauls of Bengal, by Shri Anirvan.—Mystic songs. [B132.S3A713] 79-147361 6.95
1. Sankhya. I. Reymond, Lizelle, comp. II. Title.

DAVIS, Roy Eugene. 294.5'4
Darshan: the vision of light. Lakemont, Ga., CSA Press [1971] 206 p. illus. 23 cm. [BF1997.D38A3] 72-185617 ISBN 0-87707-075-X 5.95
1. Spiritual life. I. Title.

ELIADE, Mircea, 1907- 294.5'4
Yoga: immortality and freedom. Translated from the French by Willard R. Trask. [2d ed. with corrections and additional bibliographical notes. Princeton, N.J., Published by] Princeton University Press [for Bollingen Foundation, New York, 1969] xxii, 536 p. 25 cm. (Bollingen series, 56) Translation of Le yoga: immortalite et liberte. Bibliography: p. [433]-480. [B132.Y6E523 1969] 74-168024 7.50
1. Yoga. I. Title. II. Series.

FAUSSET, Hugh I'Anson, 294.5'4
1895-
The flame and the light; meanings in Vedanta and Buddhism. New York, Greenwood Press [1969, c1958] 232 p. 23 cm. Includes bibliographical references. [B132.V3F35 1969] 69-10089
1. Vedanta—Comparative studies. 2. Buddha and Buddhism—Relations—Hinduism. 3. Hinduism—Relations—Buddhism. I. Title.

GAYATRI Devi, 1906- 294.5'4
One life's pilgrimage : addresses, letters, and articles by the first Indian woman to teach Vedanta in the west / Srimata Gayatri Devi. Cohasset, Mass. : Vedanta Centre, c1977. ix, 341 p. : ill. ; 21 cm. [BL1228.G39] 77-150793 4.95
1. Spiritual life (Hinduism)—Addresses, essays, lectures. I. Title.

GAYATRI Devi, 1906- 294.5'4
One life's pilgrimage : addresses, letters, and articles by the first Indian woman to teach Vedanta in the west / Srimata Gayatri Devi. Cohasset, Mass. : Vedanta Centre, c1977. ix, 341 p. : ill. ; 21 cm. [BL1228.G39] 77-150793 4.95
1. Spiritual life (Hinduism)—Addresses, essays, lectures. I. Title.

GOPI Krishna, 1903- 294.5'4
Higher consciousness : the evolutionary thrust of kundalini / Gopi Krishna. New York : Julian Press, [1974] x, 198 p. : 22 cm. [BL263.G64] 74-75418 ISBN 0-87097-061-5 : 7.95
1. Evolution. 2. Yoga, Hatha. I. Title.

GURU Bawa, Shaikh 294.54
Muhaiyaddeen.
Truth & light: brief explanations [by] M. R. Guru Bawa [narrators Lee Hixon, Will Noffke] . Philadelphia Guru Bawa Fellowship of Philadelphia 1974. 144 p. illus. 18 cm. Radio interviews with Guru Bawa. [BL624.G884] 74-76219 ISBN 0-914390-03-1 4.95
1. Spiritual life. I. Hixon, Lex. II. Noffke, Will. III. Title.
Pbk. 1.95; ISBN 0-914390-04-X.

HAICH, Elisabeth. 294.5'4
Sexual energy and yoga / by Elisabeth Haich ; translated by D. Q. Stephenson. 1st American ed. New York : ASI Publishers, 1975, c1972. 158 p., [6] leaves of plates : ill. ; 21 cm. Translation of Sexuelle Kraft und Yoga. [BF692.H313 1975] 74-83158 ISBN 0-88231-009-7 pbk. : 5.00
1. Sex (Psychology) 2. Yoga, Hatha. I. Title.

KESHAVADAS, Swami, 1934- 294.5'4
Sadguru speaks : spiritual disciplines and mystical teachings / Sant Keshavadas. Washington : Temple of Cosmic Religion, c1975. 95 p. : ports ; 23 cm. [BL624.K47] 76-354610 3.50
1. Spiritual life. I. Title.

MATA, Daya. 294.5'4
Only love = formerly Qualities of a devotee / by Daya Mata. Los Angeles : Self-Realization Fellowship, 1976. xvi, 277 p., [12] leaves of plates : ill. ; 20 cm. [BP605.S36M37 1976] 75-44633 ISBN 0-87612-215-2 : 6.50
1. Spiritual life. I. Title. II. Title: Qualities of a devotee.

†MEHER Baba, 1894-1969. 294.5'4
The path of love / Meher Baba. New York : S. Weiser, 1976. 102 p. ; 23 cm. [BL1228.M4 1976] 76-15540 ISBN 0-87728-309-5 : 3.95
1. Spiritual life (Hinduism) I. Title.

MISHRA, Rammurti S., M.D. 294.54
*Kena Upanishad.*Ed.by Ann Adman. Orientala [dist.] N. Syracuse 12, N.Y., 102 David Dr. Yoga Soc. of Syracuse, [c.1963] 75p. 22cm. 1.75 pap.,
I. Title.

MOFFITT, John. 294.5'4
Journey to Gorakhpur; an encounter with Christ beyond Christianity. [1st ed.] New York, Holt, Rinehart and Winston [1972] xiv, 304 p. 22 cm. Includes bibliographical references. [BR127.M6] 70-155525 ISBN 0-03-086577-8 7.95
1. Christianity and other religions. I. Title.

†MUKTANANDA Paramhamsa, 294.5'4
Swami.
Selected essays / Muktananda ; edited by Paul Zweig. 1st ed. New York : Harper & Row, c1976. xiv, 173 p. : ports. ; 20 cm. [BL1228.M825 1976] 76-9994 ISBN 0-06-069860-8 : 3.95
1. Spiritual life (Hinduism)—Addresses, essays, lectures. I. Title.

NARADA. 294.5'4
The bhakti sutras of Narada, with explanatory notes and an introd. by the translator. Translated by Nandlal Sinha. Allahabad, Panini Office, 1911. [New York, AMS Press, 1974] xv, 32, iii p. 23 cm. Original ed. issued as v. 7, pt. 1 of The Sacred books of the Hindus. English and Sanskrit; introd. and commentary in English. [BL1215.B5N3313 1974] 73-3792 ISBN 0-404-57807-1
1. Bhakti. I. Sinha, Nandalal, ed. II. Title. III. Series: The Sacred books of the Hindus, v. 7, pt. 1.

NARADA. 294.5'4
Narada's Way of divine love: the bhakti sutras. Translated with a commentary by Swami Prabhavananda. Introd. by Christopher Isherwood. Hollywood, Calif., Vedanta Press [1971] xiv, 176 p. 19 cm. Bibliography: p. 176. [BL1215.B5N3313 1971] 75-161488 ISBN 0-87481-027-2 4.95
1. Bhakti. I. Prabhavananda, Swami, 1893- tr. II. Title.

RAM Dass. 294.5'4
The only dance there is; talks given at the Menninger Foundation, Topeka, Kansas, 1970, and at Spring Grove Hospital, Spring Grove, Maryland, 1972. [1st ed.] Garden City, N.Y., Anchor Press, 1974 [c1973] 180 p. 21 cm. [BF311.R29 1974] 73-14054 ISBN 0-385-08413-7 2.95 (pbk.)
1. Consciousness. 2. Yoga. I. Title.

RAM Dass. 294.5'4
The only dance there is / Ram Dass ; with an introd. by Stephen A. Appelbaum. New York : J. Aronson, 1976, c1973. 180 p. ; 25 cm. Lectures given in Topeka, Kansas, in 1970, and at Spring Grove State Hospital, Baltimore, in 1972. Includes index. [BF311.R291976] 76-372142 ISBN 0-87668-237-9 : 10.00
1. Consciousness—Addresses, essays, lectures. 2. Yoga—Addresses, essays, lectures. I. Title.

RAMANA, Maharshi. 294.5'4
The collected works of Ramana Maharshi. Edited and annotated by Arthur Osborne. New York, S. Weiser [1970, c1959] 192 p. 21 cm. [BL1146.R35A1 1970] 75-18518 2.75
I. Osborne, Arthur, 1906-

RICHMOND, Sonya. 294.5'4
Common sense about yoga. New York, St. Martin's Press [1972, c1971] 171 p. 23 cm. [B132.Y6R457 1972] 70-184556 ISBN 0-261-63235-3 4.95
1. Yoga. I. Title.

SIVARAM, Mysore, 1905- 294.5'4
Ananda and the three great acharyas / M. Sivaram. New Delhi : Vikas Pub. House, c1976. [10], 165 p. ; 22 cm. Bibliography: p. [7] (1st group) [BL1228.S588] 76-901494 Rs35.00
1. Sankaracarya. 2. Ramanuja, founder of sect. 3. Madhva, 13th cent. 4. Spiritual life (Hinduism)—History. I. Title.

*SUBRAMUNIYA, Master. 294.54
The search is within, by Master Subramuniya. San Francisco, Calif., Comstock House, [1973, c1972] 70 p., 14 cm. "A western mystic's

simple guidelines for spiritual living." [BL1228] 2.00 (pbk.)
1. Spiritual life. 2. Direction, spiritual. I. Title.

BHAGAT, M. G., 1922- 294.5'42
Ancient Indian asceticism / by M. G. Bhagat. New Delhi : Munshiram Manoharlal Publishers, 1976. xv, 367 p., [1] leaf of plates : ill. ; 23 cm. Revision of the author's thesis, University of Bombay, 1967. Includes index. Bibliography: p. [335]-356. [BL2015.A8B48 1976] 76-904001 18.50
1. Asceticism. 2. India—Religion. I. Title.
Distributed by South Asia Bks. Distributed by South Asia Bks.

MEHER Baba, 1894-1969. 294.5'42
The mastery of consciousness : an introduction and guide to practical mysticism and methods of spiritual development / as given by Meher Baba ; compiled and edited by Allan Y. Cohen. 1st ed. New York : Harper & Row, 1977. xx, 202 p. ; 21 cm. (Harper colophon books ; CN 371) Bibliography: p. [175]-183. [BL624.M43 1977] 76-55500 ISBN 0-06-090371-6 : 3.95
1. Meher Baba, 1894-1969. 2. Spiritual life—History of doctrines. 3. Mysticism—History. I. Cohen, Allen Y., 1939- II. Title.

MENEN, Aubrey. 294.5'42
The mystics. Photos. by Graham Hall. New York, Dial Press, 1974. 239 p. illus. 26 cm. Bibliography: p. 233. [BL1215.M9M46] 74-5258 ISBN 0-8037-6204-6
1. Mysticism—Hinduism. I. Title.

REYMOND, Lizelle. 294.5'42
Shakti; a spiritual experience. Introd. by Shri Anirvan. [1st ed.] New York, Knopf; [distributed by Random House] 1974. viii, 51 p. illus. 19 cm. "A Far West Press book." [BL1245.S4R43 1974] 74-7725 ISBN 0-394-49339-7
1. Shaktism. I. Title.

*SUBRAMUNIYA. Master. 294.542
The lotus of the heart, by Master Subramuniya. San Francisco, Calif., Comstock House, [1973, c1972] 72 p., illus., 14 cm. "A western mystic's three essays on awareness." [BL1228] 2.00 (pbk.)
1. Awareness. 2. Enlightment. I. Title.

ZAEHNER, Robert Charles. 294.5'42
Hindu and Muslim mysticism [by] R. C. Zaehner. New York, Schocken Books [1969, c1960] viii, 234 p. 21 cm. "Consists of eight lectures delivered (in a slightly abridged form) in May 1959 at the School of Oriental and African Studies in the University of London." Bibliographical footnotes. [BL2015.M9Z3 1969] 74-83675 2.45
1. Mysticism—India. 2. Mysticism—Islam. I. Title.

AJAYA, Swami, 1940- 294.5'43
Yoga psychology : a practical guide to meditation / by Swami Ajaya. Completely rev. ed. Glenview, Ill. : Himalayan International Institute of Yoga Science and Philosophy, 1976. 115 p. ; 22 cm. [BL627.A34 1976] 76-374539 pbk. : 2.95
1. Meditation. I. Title.

ARYA, Usharbudh. 294.5'43
Superconscious meditation / by Usharbudh Arya. Prospect Heights, Ill. : Himalayan International Institute of Yoga Science & Philosophy of USA, [1974- v. ; 22 cm. Bibliography: v. 1, p. 137-138. [BL627.A78] 74-187862
1. Meditation. I. Title.

BHAKTIVEDANTA, A.C., 294.5'43
Swami 1896-
Krsna consciousness: the topmost yoga system, by A. C. Bhaktivedanta Swami. Boston, Mass., Iskcon Press [1970] 57 p. 20 cm. [B132.Y6B5314] 77-127182 0.50
1. Yoga. I. Title.

BHAKTIVEDANTA Swami, A. 294.5'43
C., 1896-
Easy journey to other planets, by practice of supreme yoga [by] A. C. Bhaktivedanta Swami Prabhupada. Rev. ed. New York, Macmillan [1972] 96 p. 18 cm. [B132.Y6B5313 1972] 72-80068 1.25 (pbk.)
1. Yoga, Bhakti. 2. God (Hinduism) 3. Matter. I. Title.

BHAKTIVEDANTA Swami, A. 294.5'43
C., 1896-
Krsna consciousness; the topmost yoga system [by] A. C. Bhaktivedanta Swami Prabhupada. New York, Macmillan [1972] 110 p. 18 cm. [B132.Y6B5314 1972] 72-80069 1.25 (pbk)
1. Yoga. I. Title.

BHAKTIVEDANTA A.C Swami 294.5'43
1896-
Easy journey to other planets (by practice of supreme yoga), by A. C. Bhaktivedanta Swami. 2d ed. Boston, Iskon Press [1970] 49 p. 19 cm. [B132.Y6B5313 1970] 70-118080 0.50
1. Yoga, Bhakti. 2. God (Hinduism) 3. Matter. I. Title.

BHAKTIVEDENTA, A.C., 294.5'43
Swami 1896-
The first step in God realization [by] A. C. Bhaktivedanta Swami. Boston, Mass., Iskcon Press [1970] 60 p. 24 cm. Running title: Srimad-Bhagavatam. "Continuation of A. C. Bhaktivedanta Swami's ... project of translating and commentating upon the twelve cantos of the Srimad-Bhagavatam." English and Sanskrit; commentary in English. [BL627.B5] 70-127183 1.00
1. Meditation. 2. God (Hinduism) 3. Self-realization. I. Puranas. Bhagavatapurana. Selections. 1970. II. Title.

BHAKTIVEDNTA, A.C., 294.5'43
Swami 1896-
Krsna consciousness, the matchless gift / by A. C. Bhaktivedanta Swami Prabhupada. New York : Bhaktivedanta Book Trust, 1974. 118 p. ; 18 cm. At head of title: All glory to Sri Guru and Gauranga. Includes index. [B132.Y6B53136] 73-76634 ISBN 0-912776-61-7
1. Yoga. I. Title. II. Title: The matchless gift.

BLOOMFIELD, Harold H., 294.5'43
1944-
TM discovering inner energy and overcoming stress [by] Harold H. Bloomfield, Michael Peter Cain and Dennis T. Jaffe, in collaboration with Robert Bruce Kory. Foreward by Hans Selye; introd. by R. Buckminster Fuller. [New York] Dell [1975] 317 p. illus. 18 cm. Includes index. Bibliography: p. 285-305. [BL627.B56] 1.95 (pbk.)
1. Transcendental meditation. I. Cain, Michael Peter, 1941-, joint author. II. Jaffe, Dennis T., joint author. III. Title.
L.C. no. of original edition: 74-19289

BLOOMFIELD, Harold H., 294.5'43
1944-
TM: discovering inner energy and overcoming stress* [by] Harold H. Bloomfield, Michael Peter Cain [and] Dennis T. Jaffe, in collaboration with Robert Bruce Kory. Foreword by Hans Selye; introd. by R. Buckminster Fuller. New York, Delacorte Press [1975] xxvii, 290 p. illus. 22 cm. "*Transcendental meditation." Bibliography: p. [261]-280. [BL627.B56] 74-19289 ISBN 0-440-06048-6 8.95
1. Transcendental meditation. I. Cain, Michael Peter, 1941- joint author. II. Jaffe, Dennis T., joint author. III. Title.

BUKSBAZEN, John Daishin, 294.5'43
1939-
To forget the self : an illustrated introduction to Zen practice / text by John Daishin Buksbazen ; ill. by John Daido Loori ; foreword by Peter Matthiessen ; pref. by Chotan Aitken Roshi and Taizen Maezumi Roshi. Los Angeles : Zen Center of Los Angeles, 1977c1976. p. cm. (The Zen writings series ; 3) [BQ9288.B84] 76-9463 ISBN 0-916820-03-3 pbk. : 7.95
1. Meditation (Zen Buddhism) I. Title. II. Series.

CHINMOY. 294.5'43
My Lord's secrets revealed [by] Sri Chinmoy. [New York] Herder and Herder [1971] 107 p. 22 cm. [BL624.C47] 73-150298 3.95
1. Meditations. I. Title.

FAST, Howard Melvin, 294.5'43
1914-
The art of Zen meditation / Howard Fast. Culver City, Calif. : Peace Press, 1977. [45] p. : ill. ; 21 cm. [BQ9288.F37] 77-6222 ISBN 0-915238-15-2 pbk. : 3.00
1. Meditation (Zen Buddhism) I. Title.

FAST, Howard Melvin, 294.5'43
1914-
The art of Zen meditation / Howard Fast. Culver City, Calif. : Peace Press, 1977. [45] p. : ill. ; 21 cm. [BQ9288.F37] 77-6222 ISBN 0-915238-15-2 pbk. : 3.00
1. Meditation (Zen Buddhism) I. Title.

GOPI Krishna, 1903- 294.5'4'3
The awakening of Kundalini / Gopi Krishna. 1st ed. New York : Dutton, 1975. xii, 129 p. ; 21 cm. [BL1215.K8G66 1975] 74-28323 ISBN 0-525-47398-X pbk. : 3.25
1. Kundalini. 2. Meditation. 3. Yoga. I. Title.

HUGHES, Catharine, 294.5'4'3
1935- comp.
The smokeless fire : Hindu mystical reflections / edited and with photos. by Catharine Hughes. New York : Seabury Press, [1974] ca. 150 p. : ill. ; 20 cm. [BL1010.H83] 74-194692 ISBN 0-8164-2102-1 pbk. : 2.95
1. Hinduism—Collected works. I. Title.

KROLL, Una. 294.5'43
The healing potential of transcendental meditation / Una Kroll. Atlanta : John Knox Press, 1974. 176 p. ; 21 cm. First published in 1974 under title: TM. Includes bibliographical references. [BL627.K76 1974b] 74-7615 ISBN 0-8042-0598-1
1. Transcendental meditation. I. Title.

MUKTANANDA Paramhamsa, 294.5'43
Swami.
The spiritual instructions of Swami Muktananda. Edited, with introd. and epilogue, by Bubba Free John (Franklin Jones) [1st ed.] Lower Lake, Calif., Dawn Horse Press [1974] xv, 15 p. ports. 22 cm. Includes bibliographical references. [BL1228.M83] 73-86295 ISBN 0-913922-02-1 1.50
1. Spiritual life (Hinduism) I. Jones, Franklin, ed. II. Title.

PARAMPANTHI, Puragra, 294.5'43
Swami, 1928-
Creative self-transformation through meditation : a six week course / by Swami Parampanthi ; forewords by Earlyne and Robert Chaney. [Los Angeles] : Phoenix House, [1974] 159 p. (p. 157-159 advertisements) : ill. ; 23 cm. (Astara's library of mystical classics) [BL627.P37] 74-21803 ISBN 0-89031-019-X : 3.95
1. Meditation. I. Title.

PRABHAVANADA, Swami, 294.5'4'3
1893- comp.
Prayers and meditations compiled from the scriptures of India, edited by Swami Prabhavananda and Clive Johnson. Hollywood, Calif., Vedanta Press [1967] 136 p. illus. 18 cm. [BL1226.8.P7] 67-3515
1. Hinduism—Prayer-books and devotions—English. I. Johnson, Clive, 1930- joint comp. II. Title.

RAJANEESH, Acharya, 294.5'43
1931-
Meditation : the art of ecstasy / Bhagwan Shree Rajneesh ; edited by Ma Satya Bharti. 1st ed. New York : Harper & Row, 1976. xxi, 248 p. : port. ; 21 cm. (Harper colophon books ; CN 529) Most of this material originally appeared in the author's Dynamics of meditation. [BL627.R332 1976] 76-465 ISBN 0-06-090529-8 pbk. : 3.95
1. Meditation. 2. Kundalini. 3. Yoga. I. Title.

SATPRAKASHANANDA, Swami. 294.5'43
Meditation : its process, practice, and culmination / by Swami Satprakashananda. St. Louis : Vedanta Society of St. Louis, 1976. 264 p. ; 20 cm. Includes bibliographical references and index. [BL2015.M4S26] 76-15722 ISBN 0-916356-55-8 : 8.50
1. Meditation (Hinduism) 2. Meditations. I. Title.

SATSANG / 294.5'4'3
editor Vasant V. Paranjpe. 1st ed. Madison, Va. : Fivefold Path, c1976- v. ; 28 cm. Includes index. [BL624.S27] 75-39508 12.00 (v. 1)
1. Spiritual life. I. Paranjpe, Vasant Vithal, 1921-

SUBRAMUNIYA, Master. 294.5'43
Reflections. [2d ed.] San Francisco, T. R. Gilmore [1971] 67 p. illus. 16 cm. (On the path series) [BL624.S92 1971] 73-175221 2.95
1. Meditations. I. Title.

VIVEKANANDA, Swami, 1863- 294.5'43
1902.
Meditation and its methods according to Swami Vivekananda / compiled and edited by Swami Chetanananda ; foreword by Christopher Isherwood. 1st ed. Hollywood, Calif. : Vedanta Press, 1976. 127 p. ; 17 cm. Includes bibliographical references. [BL2015.M4V582 1976] 294.5'43 75-36392 75-36392 ISBN 0-87481-030-2 pbk. : 3.50 ISBN 0-87481-030-2 pbk. : pbk. : 3.50
1. Meditation (Hinduism) I. Chetanananda, Swami. II. Title.

AKHILANANDA, Swami. 294.5'44
Spiritual practices. Introd. by Walter G. Muelder. Boston, Branden Press [1972] 125 p. 23 cm. Includes bibliographical references. [BL1228.A34] 78-175140 ISBN 0-8283-1350-4 7.50
1. Spiritual life—Hindu authors. I. Title.

AKHILANANDA, Swami. 294.5'44
Spiritual practices, by Swami Akhilananda. Memorial ed. with reminiscences by his friends. Edited by Alice Mary Stark and Claude Alan Stark. Cape Cod, Mass., C. Stark [1974] 225 p. port. 23 cm. "Writings of Swami Akhilananda": p. 221. Includes bibliographical references. [BL1228.A34 1974] 74-76003 ISBN 0-89007-001-6 8.50
1. Akhilananda, Swami—Addresses, essays, lectures. 2. Spiritual life—Hindu authors. I. Title.

BHAHTIVEDANTA, A. C., 294.5'4'4
Swami 1896-
Elevation to Krsna consciousness [by] A. C. Bhaktivedanta Swami Prabhupada. New York, Bhaktivedanta Book Trust [1973] 99 p. 18 cm. [BL1220.B43] 73-76635 ISBN 0-912776-43-9 0.95 (pbk.)
1. Krishna (Cult) 2. Spiritual life (Hinduism) I. Title.
Publisher's address: 32 Tiffany Place, Brooklyn, N.Y. 11231

JONES, Franklin. 294.5'4'4
The knee of listening. [Los Angeles] Ashram [1972] 271 p. port. 23 cm. [BL1228.J65] 72-83720 ISBN 0-87707-093-8 7.95
1. Spiritual life—Hindu authors. I. Title.

JONES, Franklin. 294.5'4'4
The knee of listening. [Los Angeles] Ashram [1972] 271 p. port. 23 cm. [BL1228.J65] 72-83720 ISBN 0-87707-093-8 6.95
1. Spiritual life—Hindu authors. I. Title.

JONES, Franklin. 294.5'44
The method of the Siddhas. [1st ed.] Los Angeles, Dawn Horse Press [1973] xvii, 364 p. illus., ports. 22 cm. [BL624.J67] 73-85299 ISBN 0-913922-01-3
1. Spiritual life. I. Title.

JONES, Franklin. 294.5'44
The method of the Siddhas. [1st ed.] Los Angeles, Dawn Horse Press [1973] xvii, 364 p. illus., ports. 22 cm. [BL624.J67] 73-85299 ISBN 0-913922-01-3 3.95
1. Spiritual life. I. Title.

KRISHNAMURTI, Jiddy, 294.544
1895-
Life ahead, by J. Krishnamurti, edited by D. Rajagopal. New York, Harper and Row [1975 c1963] 191 p. 20 cm. [BJ1581.2K75] 74-25296 ISBN 0-06-064792-2. 2.50 (pbk.)
1. Conduct of life. 2. Sociology, Hindu. 3. Hinduism. I. Title.

*KRIYANANDA Swami 294.544
Eastern thoughts Western thoughts. [by] Swami Kriyananda. Nevada City, Calif., Ananda Publications, [1973] 121, [9] p., 21 cm. [B133] 1.50 (pbk.)
I. Title.
Publishers Address: Ananda Publications. Alleghany Star Route, Nevada City, Calif. 95959 '

MAHESH Yogi, Maharishi. 294.5'4'4
The science of being and art of living. [New York] New American Library [1968, c1963] 320 p. 22 cm. [BL627.M335 1968] 68-25334
1. Transcendental meditation. 2. Ontology. 3. Conduct of life. I. Title.

MAHESH YOGI, Maharishi. 294.5'4'4
The science of being and art of living. [New York] New Amer. Lib. [1968,c.1963] 320p. 22cm. [LB1146.M3S35 1968] 68-25334 5.95; bds., .95 pap.,
1. Religious life (Hinduism) I. Title.

RUPAGOSVAMI, 294.5'44
16thcent.
The nectar of instruction ; an authorized English presentation of Srila Rupa Gosvami's Sri Upadesamrta / with the original Sanskrit text, roman transliterations, synonyms, translations and elaborate purports by A. C. Bhaktivedanta Swami Prabhupada. New York : Bhaktivedanta Book Trust, 1976c1975 ix, 130 p., [2] leaves of plates : ill. ; 18 cm. Includes bibliographical references and indexes. [BL1228.R8613] 75-39755 ISBN 0-912776-85-4 pbk. : 1.95
1. Spiritual life (Hinduism) 2. Krishna—Cult. I. Bhaktivedanta Swami, A. C., 1896- II. Title.

SATCHIDANANDA, Swami. 294.5'44
Beyond words / Swami Satchidananda ; edited by Lester Alexander ; drawings by Peter Max. 1st ed. New York : Holt, Rinehart and Winston, c1977. 182 p. : ill. ; 24 cm. [BL1228.S27] 76-29896 ISBN 0-03-020871-8 : 7.95 ISBN 0-03-016911-9 pbk. : 4.95
1. Spiritual life (Hinduism)—Addresses, essays, lectures. 2. Conduct of life—Addresses, essays, lectures. I. Title.

VASUDEVADAS. 294.5'44
A time for eternity / Vasudevadas. 1st ed. Bedford, Va. : Prema Dharmasala and Fellowship Assn. Pub., 1976. 85 p. : port. ; 22 cm. [BL624.V36] 76-45579
1. Spiritual life. I. Title.

YUKTESWAR, Swami, 1855- 294.5'44
1936.
The holy science. Kaivalya darsanam. 7th ed. Los Angeles, Self-Realization Fellowship, 1972 [c1949] xxiv, 77 p. illus. 19 cm. [BP605.S4Y8 1972] 77-88199 ISBN 0-87612-051-6 2.50
1. Self-realization. I. Title.

HOPKINS, Edward Washburn, 1857-1932. 294.5'48
Ethics of India. Port Washington, N.Y., Kennikat Press [1968, c1924] xiv, 265 p. 20 cm. [BJ122.H6 1968] 68-15828
1. Hindu ethics. I. Title.

MANU. 294.5'48
The laws of Manu. Translated with extracts from seven commentaries by Georg Buhler. New York, Dover Publications [1969] cxxxviii, 620 p. 22 cm. (The Sacred books of the East, v. 25) Reprint of the 1886 ed. Bibliographical footnotes. [BL1125.A2B8] 68-9451 4.00
1. Hindu law. I. Buhler, Georg, 1837-1898, ed. II. Title. III. Series: The Sacred books of the East (New York) v. 25

*SUBRAMUNIYA, Master. 294.548
Reflections, by Master Subramuniya. San Francisco, Calif., Comstock House, [1973, c1972] 70 p., illus. 14 cm. "A Western Mystic's inspired thoughts on the path." Published by Wailua University of Contemplative Arts in 1969 and by Gilmore and Co. in 1971. [BL1228] 2.00 (pbk.)
1. Inspiration. I. Title.

*SUBRAMUNIYA, Master. 294.548
The self god, by Master Subramuniya. San Francisco, Calif., Comstock house, [1973, c1972] 70 p., 14 cm. "A Western Mystic's insight into Self-Realization." Previously published in 1959 by Wailua University of Contemplative Arts and in 1971 by Gilmore and Co. [BL1228] 2.00 (pbk.)
1. Self-realization. 2. Satisfaction. I. Title.

DIMOCK, Edward C 294.55
The place of the hidden moon; erotic mysticism in the Vaisnavasahajiya cult of Bengal [by] Edward C. Dimock, Jr. Chicago, University of Chicago Press [1966] xix, 299 p. 22 cm. Much of the material in this book was presented as part of the author's thesis, Harvard University, 1959. Bibliography: p. 271-283. [BL1245.S2D5] 66-13865
1. Sahajiya. 2. Sex and religion. I. Title.

DIMOCK, Edward C. 294.55
The place of the hidden moon; erotic mysticism in the Vaisnavasahajiya cult of Bengal. Chicago, Univ of Chicago Pr. [c.1966] xix, 299p. 22cm. Bibl. [BL1245.S2D5] 66-13865 7.50
1. Sahajiya. 2. Sex and religion. I. Title.

EZEKIEL, Isaac A 294.5'5
Kabir, the great mystic, by Isaac A. Ezekiel. [1st ed.] [Beas, India] Radha Soami Satsang Beas [1966] xviii, 440 p. port. 23 cm. Rs13 Bibliography: p. [439]-440. [BL2020.K3A37] SA67
1. Kabir, 15th cent. I. Title.

JUDAH, J. Stillson. 294.5'5
Hare Krishna and the counterculture [by] J. Stillson Judah. New York, Wiley [1974] xviii, 301 p. illus. 23 cm. (Contemporary religious movements) "A Wiley-Interscience publication." Bibliography: p. 199-213. [BL1220.J8 1974] 74-8209 ISBN 0-471-45200-9 12.95
1. Krishna (Cult)—United States. 2. Vaishnavism. 3. Youth—Religious life. I. Title.

*LORENZEN, David N. 294.55
The kapalikas and kalamukhas; two lost saivite sects, by David N. Lorenzen. Berkeley and Los Angeles, Univ. of California Pr. [1972] xiv, 214 p. 23 cm. Bibliography: p. [193]-202. [BL1245.A1] 70-138509 ISBN 0-520-01842-7 7.95
1. Hindu sects. I. Title.

MEHER, Baba, 1894- 294.55
Beams from Meher Baba on the spiritual panorama. [Mt. Vernon? N. Y., 1958] 88p. illus., port. 19cm. [BL1270.M365] 58-59805
I. Title.

MEHER BABA, 1894- 294.55
God speaks; the theme of creation and its purpose. New York, Dodd, Mead, 1955. 255p. illus. 22cm. [BL1270.M377] 55-9727
I. Title.

MEHER BABA, 1894- 294.55
Ways to attain the supreme reality. With interpretations in verse by Malcolm Schloss. Hollywood, Calif., M. Schloss, 1952. 75p. 22cm. [BL1270.M417] 53-17040
1. Hinduism. I. Schloss, Malcolm. II. Title.

MOOKERJEE, Ajitcoomar. 294.5'5
Tantra asana; a way to self-realization [by] Ajit Mookerjee. New York, George Wittenborn, Inc. [1971] 161 p. illus. (part col.) 32 cm. Bibliography: p. [141]-174. [BL1245.T3M6] 79-153698
1. Tantrism—Pictorial works. I. Title.

PURANAS. Brahmandapurana. Lalitasaharanama. 294.55
Sri Lalita Sahasranamam. Introd., commentary by Chaganty Suryanarayanamurthy. Madras, India, Ganesh [dist. Hollywood, Calif., Vedanta 1963 166+ various p. 26cm. 3.00 bds.,
I. Title.

SANDILYA 294.551
The aphorisms of Sandilva, with the commentary of Swapneswara; or, The Hindu doctrine of faith. Tr. by E. B. Cowell. [2d ed.] Calcutta. Anil Gupta, [So. Pasedena. Calif., Hutchins Oriental. 1965] xii, 132p. 22cm. [BL1215.B5S253] SA 66 5.00
1. Bhakti. I. Svapnesvara. II. Cowell. Edward Byles, 1826- 1903, tr. III. Title. IV. Title: The Hindu doctrine of faith.

RAYCHAUDHURI, Hemchandra, 1892-1957. 294.5'512
Materials for the study of the early history of the Vaishnava sect / by Hemchandra Raychaudhuri. 2d ed. New Delhi : Oriental Books Reprint Corp. : distributed by Munshiram Manoharlal Publishers, 1975. viii, 146 p. ; 22 cm. "Summary of a course of lectures on the early history of the Bhagavata Vaishnava sect which ... [the author] delivered ... during the last session (1918-19)." Reprint of the 1920 ed. published by the University of Calcutta, Calcutta. Includes index. "Bibliographic index": p. [119]-124. [BL1245.V3R33 1975] 75-908076 8.50
1. Vaishnavism. I. Title.
Distributed by South Asia Books.

SINHA, Jadunath, 1894- 294.5'512
The philosophy & religion of Chaitanya and his followers / by Jadunath Sinha. 1st ed. Calcutta : Sinha Pub. House, 1976. ii, ii, 151, ix p. ; 22 cm. Includes bibliographical references and index. [BL1245.V3S56] 77-901352 Rs25.00
1. Chaitanya, 1486-1534. 2. Vaishnavism. I. Title.

SREENIVASA Murthy, H. V. 294.5'512
Vaisnavism of Samkaradeva and Ramanuja; a comparative study [by] H. V. Sreenivasa Murthy. [1st ed.] Delhi, Motilal Banarsidass [1973] viii, 254 p. 23 cm. A revision of the author's thesis, Gauhati University. Bibliography: p. [236]-244. [BL1245.V3S64 1973] 73-900571
1. Sankaradeva, 1449-1569. 2. Ramanuja, founder of sect. 3. Vaishnavism. I. Title.
Distributed by Verry, 7.50

BHAKTIVEDANTA Swami, A. C., 1896- 294.5'513
Teachings of Lord Caitanya : the Golden Avatara / A. C. Bhaktivedanta Swami. New York : Bombay ; Bhaktivedanta Book Trust, c1974. xxv, 440 p., [10] leaves of plates : ill. ; 21 cm. Includes bibliographical references and index. [BL1245.V36B48 1974] 75-2060 ISBN 0-912776-07-2. ISBN 0-912776-08-0 (pbk.)
1. Chaitanya, 1486-1534. I. Title.

SIDDHANTASHASTREE, Rabindra Kumar, 1918- 294.5'513
Saivism through the ages / by Rabindra Kumar Siddhantashastree. New Delhi : Munshiram Manoharlal Publishers, c1974, 1975. viii, 188 p. ; 23 cm. Includes index. Bibliography: p. [171]-173. [BL1218.S5 1975] 75-902111 9.00
1. Siva (Hindu deity) 2. Sivaism. I. Title.
Distributed by South Asia Books, Columbia, Mo.

TAIMNI, I. K., 1898- 294.5'513
The ultimate reality and realization : Sivasutra, with text in Sanskrit, transliteration in roman, translation in English, and commentary / by I. K. Taimni. 1st ed. Madras ; Wheaton, Ill. : Theosophical Pub. House, 1976. xiv, 215 p. ; 22 cm. [BL1146.V326S527] 76-903636 Rs21.00
1. Vasugupta. Sivasutra. 2. Sivaism. I. Vasugupta. Sivasutra. 1976. II. Title.

BHATTACHARYYA, Narendra Nath. 294.5'514
History of the Sakta religion / by Narendra Nath Bhattacharyya ; edited by Mrs. Nirmal Jain. New Delhi : Munshiram Manoharlal Publishers, 1974, 1973. xiii, 188 p. ; 23 cm. Includes index. Bibliography: p. [167]-171. [BL1245.S4B49] 75-900273 12.00
1. Shaktism—History. I. Title.
Distributed by South Asia Books, Columbia, Miss.

KESHAVADAS, Swami, 1934- 294.5'514
Cosmic Shakti Kundalini (the universal mother) : a devotional approach / Sadguru Sant Keshavadas. Washington : Temple of Cosmic Religion, c1976. 112 p. : ill. ; 22 cm. [BL1245.S4K47] 76-11347 3.50
1. Shaktism. 2. Kundalini. I. Title.

PUSHPENDRA Kumar, 1936- 294.5'514
Sakti cult in ancient India, with special reference to the Puranic literature / Pushpendra Kumar. Varanasi : Bhartiya Pub. House, 1974 [i.e.,1975] xviii, 317 p., [4] leaves of plates : ill. ; 23 cm. Essentially a revision of the author's thesis, University of Delhi, 1967, with title: Sakti cult in the Puranas. Includes index. Bibliography: p. [279]-290. [BL1245.S4P85] 74-904146 16.00
1. Shaktism. I. Title.
Distributed by South Asia Books.

*WOODROFFE, Sir John George, 1865-1936. 294.5'5'14
The serpent power: being the Sat-cakra-nirupana and Paduka-pancaka, two works on Laya-Yoga, translated from the Sanskrit, with introduction and commentary by Sir John Woodroffe. [8th ed.] Madras, Ganesh & Co. [1972] xii, 569 p. 9 col. plates, front port. 23 cm.
1. Yoga. 2. Shaktism. I. Avalon, Arthur, 1865-1936. II. Title.
Distributed by Vedanta Pr., Hollywood, Calif., for 12.00. ISBN 0-87481-303-4.

WADLEY, Susan Snow, 1943- 294.5'514'095414
Shakti : power in the conceptual structure of Karimpur religion / Susan Snow Wadley. Chicago : Dept. of Anthropology, University of Chicago, 1975. x, 222 p. : ill. ; 23 cm. (The University of Chicago studies in anthropology) (Series in social, cultural, and linguistic anthropology ; no. 2) Bibliography: p. 217-222. [BL1226.2.W3] 76-37612 ISBN 0-916256-01-4
1. Hinduism—Rituals. 2. Hinduism—Karimpur, India. 3. Karimpur, India—Religious life and customs. 4. Religion and language. I. Title. II. Series. III. Series: Chicago. University. Dept. of Anthropology. The University of Chicago studies in anthropology.

ADI-GRANTH, English 294.553
Sri Guru-Granth Sahib. English version. Tr. annotated by Gopal Singh. New York, Taplinger [1965, c.1962] 4v. 29cm. [BL2017.4] 65-22279 80.00 set,
I. Singh, Gopal, 1917- ed. and tr. II. Title.

ADI-GRANTH. 294.553
Selections from the sacred writings of the Sikhs. Translated by Trilochan Singh [and others] Revised by George S. Fraser. Introd. by S. Radhakrishman. Foreword by Arnold Toynbee. New York, Macmillan, 1960. 288 p. 23 cm. (UNESCO collection of representative works: Indian series) "Might be described as an authorized English version of some of the sacred hymns of the Sikh scriptures." Contents.Contents.—Selections from the Adi Guru Granth.—Selections from the Dasm Granth. [BL2020.S5A54 1960] 60-4217
I. Daswen Padshah ka Granth. II. Singh, Trilochan, tr. III. Title. IV. Series.

ARJUN, 5th guru of the Sikhs, 1563-1606. 294.553
The psalm of peace; an English translation of Guru Arjun's Sukhmani, by Teja Singh. With a foreword by Nicholas Roerich. [Bombay, New York] Indian Branch, Oxford University Press [1950] xvii, 122 p. 19 cm. "Sukhmanl ... [is included] in the Holy Granth." [BL2020.S5A723] 52-4900
1. Sikhs. I. Singh, Teja. tr. II. Title.

ARNSBY-JONES, George. 294.553 (B)
The harvest is rich; the mission of Kirpal Singh. [1st ed.] New York, Pageant Press [1965] 179 p. port. 21 cm. [BL2017.9.S53A7] 64-66433
1. Singh, Kirpat. I. Title.

MACAULIFFE, Max Arthur, 1842 1913 294.553
The Sikh religion, its gurus. sacred writings, and authors Delhi, S. Chand [1963] 6v. in 3 (various p.) illus. 23cm. Includes tr. of the Adi-Granth. The rags of the Granth Sahib (vol. 5. p. [333]-351) are unaccompanied melodies. [BL2018.M313 1963] SA 66 set of 3v., 21.00
1. Sikhism. 2. India—Religion. I. Adi-Granth. II. Title.

PHILOSOPHY of Sikhism. 294.5'53
[2d ed.] Delhi, Sterling Pubs., 1966. 316p. 23cm. Bibl. [BL2018.S534 1966] [PL480:I-E7866] SA67 7.50
1. Sikhism. 2. Philosophy, Sikh. I. Singh, Sher, Gyani
American distributor: Verry, Mystic, Conn.

SINGH, Harbans, 1907- 294.55309
The heritage of the Sikh. New York, Asia Pub. [dist. Taplinger, 1965, c.1964] 219p. 25cm. [BL2017.6.S52] 65-16114 13.00
1. Sikhism—Hist. I. Title.

GURU Gobind 294.5'53'0924(B)
Singh, a biography [by] Srinder Singh Johar. [1st ed.] Delhi, Sterling [1967] 266p. 23cm. Bibl. [BL2017.9.G6J6] [PL480: I-E- 7867] SA 67 7.50
1. Govinda Simha, 10th guru of the Sikhs, 1666-1708. I. Johar, Surinder Sigh
American distributor: Verry, Mystic, Conn.

MCLEOD, W. H. 294.5'53'0924 B
Guru Nanak and the Sikh religion [by] W. H. McLeod. Oxford, Clarendon P., 1968. xii, 259 p. 24 cm. Bibliography: p. 233-240. [BL2017.9.N3M27] 74-373992 50/-
1. Nanak, 1st guru of the Sikhs, 1469-1538. 2. Sikhism. I. Title.

AKHILANANDA, Swami. 294.555
Modern problems and religion. Boston, Branden Pr. [1972? c.1964] 154 p. port. 22 cm. Bibl. refs. included in "Notes": p. 151-154. [BL1270.R3A5] 63-21752 ISBN 0-8283-1146-3 pap., 3.75
1. Ramakrishna. I. Title.

FRENCH, Harold W. 294.5'55
The swan's wide waters : Ramakrishna and Western culture / Harold W. French. Port Washington, N.Y. : Kennikat Press, 1974. viii, 220 p. ; 24 cm. (National university publications) Includes bibliographical references and index. [BL1270.R3F73] 74-77657 ISBN 0-8046-9055-3 : 11.95
1. Ramakrishna, 1836-1886. 2. Vivekananda, Swami, 1863-1902. I. Title.

PRABHAVANADA, Swami, 1893- 294.5'55
Religion in practice. With an introd. by Christopher Isherwood. Hollywood, Calif., Vedanta Press [1968] 260 p. 23 cm. Bibliography: p. 252-253. [B132.V3P53] 75-4009 4.95
1. Vedanta—Addresses, essays, lectures. I. Title.

VIDYATMANANDA, Swami. 294.555
Ramakrishna's teachings illustrated. Hollywood, Calif., Vedanta [c.1965] 63p. illus. 18cm. [BL1270.R3V5] 65-1620 1.00 pap.,
1. Ramakrishna, 1836-1886. I. Title.

YALE, John. 294.555
A Yankee and the swamis. Hollywood, Calif., Verdanta Press [1961] 224 p. illus. 22 cm. [B132.V3Y26] 61-65046
1. Vedanta. 2. Pilgrims and pilgrimages — India. I. Title.

YALE, John 294.555
A Yankee and the swamis. Hollywood 28, 1946 Vedanta Place Calif., Vedanta Pr., [c.1961] 224p. illus., map. 61-65046 3.95
1. Vedanta. 2. Pilgrims and pilgrimages—India. I. Title.

GAMBHIRANANDA, Swami 294.5'55'0922
The apostles of Shri Ramakrishna, comp., ed. by Swami Gambhirananda. [1st. ed.] Calcutta, Advaita Ashrama [1967] 401p. ports. 19cm. Partially replaces The disciples of Ramakrishna . . . [BL1270.R3G3] SA67 3.50 bds.,
1. Ramakrishna, 1836-1886- Friends and associates. I. Title.
American distributor: Vedanta Pr., Hollywood, Calif.

LEMAITRE, Solange. 294.5'55'0924 B
Ramakrishna and the vitality of Hinduism. Translated by Charles Lam Markmann. New York, Funk & Wagnalls [1969] xviii, 244 p. illus. 21 cm. Bibliography: p. 232-234. [BL1270.R3L43] 68-54059 4.95
1. Ramakrishna, 1836-1886. 2. Hinduism. I. Title.

MULLER, Friedrich Max, 1823-1900. 294.5'55'0924 B
Ramakrishna, his life and sayings / by F. Max Muller. New York : AMS Press, [1975] p. cm. Reprint of the 1899 ed. published by Scribner, New York. [B5134.R38M83 1975] 73-18812 ISBN 0-404-11452-0 : 14.50
1. Ramakrishna, 1836-1886. I. Ramakrishna, 1836-1886. Ramakrishna, his life and sayings. 1975. II. Title.

SATPRAKASHANANDA, Swami. 294.5'55'0924 B
The significance of Sri Ramakrishna's life and message in the present age : with the author's reminiscences of Holy Mother and some direct disciples / by Swami Satprakashananda. St. Louis : Vedanta Society of St. Louis, 1976. 208 p. ; 20 cm. On spine: Sri Ramakrishna's life and message in the present age. Includes bibliographical references and index. [BL1175.R26S26] 75-46386 ISBN 0-916356-54-X : 6.00
1. Ramakrishna, 1836-1886. 2. Hinduism—Biography. I. Title. II. Title: Sri Ramakrishna's life and message in the present age.

SRI Ramakrishna, in 294.5'55'0924
the eyes of Brahma and Christian admirers / edited by Nanda Mookerjee. 1st ed. Calcutta : Firma KLM, 1976. xiv, 141, [9] p., [2] leaves of plates : ill. ; 22 cm. Includes bibliographical

references and index. [BL1175.R26S693] 76-904430 Rs22.00 ($4.00 U.S.)
1. Ramakrishna, 1836-1886—Addresses, essays, lectures. I. Mookerjee, Nanda.

STARK, Claude Alan. 294.5'55'0924 B
God of all: Sri Ramakrishna's approach to religious plurality. Cape Cod, Mass. [1974] xvii, 236 p. port. 23 cm. Bibliography: p. 216-233. [BL1175.R26S8] 74-76001 ISBN 0-89007-000-8 12.00
1. Ramakrishna, 1836-1886. I. Title.

RAMMOHUN Roy, Raja, 1772?-1833. 294.5'562
The English works of Raja Rammohun Roy : with an English translation of "Tuhfatul Muwahhiddin." New York : AMS Press, [1977] p. cm. Reprint of the 1906 ed. published by the Panini Office, Bahadurganj Allahabad. Includes index. [BL1264.R35 1977] 75-41220 ISBN 0-404-14738-0 : 46.00
1. Brahma-samaj—Addresses, essays, lectures. 2. Hinduism—Addresses, essays, lectures. I. Title.

CARPENTER, Mary, 1807-1877. 294.5'562'0924 B
The last days in England of the Rajah Rammohun Roy / by Mary Carpenter. Riddhi ed. / edited by Swapan Majumdar. Calcutta : Riddhi, 1976. xii, 159 p., [1] leaf of plates : ill. ; 22 cm. Running title: Rammohun Roy. First published in 1866 by Trubner, London. Includes bibliographical references. [BL1265.R3C3 1976] 76-903877 Rs25.00
1. Rammohun Roy, Raja, 1772?-1833. 2. Brahma-samaj—Biography. 3. Hindus—Biography. I. Majumdar, Swapan, 1946- II. Title.

MULLER, Friedrich Max, 1823-1900. 294.5'562'0924 B
Keshub Chunder Sen / F. Max Mueller ; edited by Nanda Mookerjee. Calcutta : S. Gupta, 1976. ii, xvii, 117 p. ; 23 cm. Includes bibliographical references. [BL1265.S4M84 1976] 76-904243 Rs10.00 ($2.00 U.S.)
1. Sen, Keshab Chandra, 1838-1884. 2. Brahma-samaj—Biography. I. Mookerjee, Nanda. II. Title.

MUKTANANDA Paramhamsa, Swami. 294.5'6 B
Guru: Chitshaktivilas; the play of consciousness. [1st ed.] New York, Harper & Row [1971] xxx, 175 p. illus. 22 cm. [BL1175.M77A313 1971] 77-148442 ISBN 0-06-066045-7 5.95
1. Muktananda Paramhamsa, Swami. 2. Spiritual life (Hinduism) I. Title.

BRENT, Peter Ludwig. 294.5'6'1
Godmen of India [by] Peter Brent. [1st American ed.] Chicago, Quadrangle Books [1972, i.e. 1973] 346 p. 23 cm. [BL2003.B66 1972b] 73-190123 ISBN 0-8129-0258-0 10.00
1. Gurus—India. I. Title.

BUBBA Free John. 294.5'6'1 B
Garbage and the goddess : the last miracles and final spiritual instructions of Bubba Free John / compiled and edited by Sandy Bonder and Terry Patten, in collaboration with Bubba Free John. 1st ed. Lower Lake, Calif. : Dawn Horse Press, [1974] xxi, 393 p. : ill. ; 22 cm. [BP610.B814] 74-19796 ISBN 0-913922-10-2 : 4.95
1. Bubba Free John. I. Bonder, Sandy. II. Patten, Terry. III. Title.

BUBBA Free John. 294.5'6'1
The paradox of instruction : an introduction to the esoteric spiritual teaching of Bubba Free John / by Bubba Free John. 1st ed. Honolulu : The Dawn Horse Press, 1977. xv, 89 p. : ports. ; 22 cm. Bibliography: p. 79-86. [BP610.B816] 77-71191 ISBN 0-913922-27-7 : 3.50
1. Spiritual life. I. Title.

THE Divine descent : the life and mission of Her Holiness Sadguru Swami Sri Gnanananda Sarasvathi. 294.5'6'1 B
Madras : Sri Gnana Advaitha Peetam, 1976. 73 p., [13] leaves of plates : ill. ; 24 cm. [BL1175.G587D58] 76-904735 Rs7.00
1. Gnanananda Sarasvathi, Swami, 1929- 2. Hindus—Biography.

EBON, Martin, comp. 294.5'6'1
Maharishi, the guru; an international symposium. [New York] New American Library [1968] 144 p. 18 cm. (A Signet book) [BL1175.M29E2] 68-4493
1. Mahesh Yogi, Maharishi—Addresses, essays, lectures. I. Title.

EIDLITZ, Walther, 1892- 294.5'6'1
Unknown India; a pilgrimage into a forgotten world. New York, Roy [1952] 192 p. illus. 22 cm. [BL2003.E] A 54
1. India—Religion. I. Title.

MAHADEVAN, Telliyavaram Mahadevan Ponnambalam, 1911- 294.5'6'1 B
Ramana Maharshi : the sage of Arunacala / T. M. P. Mahadevan. London : Allen & Unwin, 1977. 186 p. ; 21 cm. Includes bibliographical references and index. [BL1175.R342M33] 77-354800 ISBN 0-04-149040-1 : 9.95 ISBN 0-04-149041-X pbk. : 4.50
1. Ramana, Maharshi. 2. Hindus—Biography.

NIZAMI, Khaliq Ahmad. 294.5'6'1
Some aspects of religion and politics in India during the thirteenth century. With a foreword by C. Collin Davies, & an introd. by Mohd. Habib. Bombay, New York, Asia Pub. House [c1961] xxii, iv, 421 p. illus. 25 cm. Label mounted on t.p.: Published for the Dept. of History, Allgarh Muslim University. Bibliography: p. 381-402. [BL2003.N5] S A
1. Religion and state — India — Hist. 2. Islam and state — India — Hist. 3. Islam — India — Hist. I. Agigarh, India. Muslim University. Dept. of History. II. Title.

RAMA, Swami, 1925- 294.5'6'1 B
Swami Rama of the Himalayas : photographs & quotations / edited by L. K. Misra. Glenview, Ill. : Himalayan Institute, c1976. [80] p. : ill. ; 23 cm. [BL1175.R253A55] 77-150898
1. Rama, Swami, 1925- —Quotations. 2. Rama, Swami, 1925- —Portraits, etc. 3. Gurus—India—Portraits. I. Title.

THE Sage of Kanchi / edited by T. M. P. Mahadevan. 294.5'6'1 B
New Delhi : Arnold-Heinemann Publishers (India), 1975. 93 p., [2] leaves of plates : ill. ; 22 cm. [BL1175.C56S24] 75-904253 ISBN 0-89253-018-9 lib.bdg. : 6.25
1. Chandrasekharendra Saraswati, Jagatguru Sankaracharya of Kamakoti, 1893- — Addresses, essays, lectures. I. Mahadevan, Telliyavaram Mahadevan Ponnambalam, 1911-
Distributed by Interculture

SRI Swami Satchidananda : a decade of service : commemorative volume. 294.5'6'1 B
[Pomfret Center, Ct. : Satchidananda Ashram-Yogaville], c1976. vii, 96 p. : ill. ; 22 x 29 cm. Issued as a special issue to v. 7, no. 3 and 4, of the Integral yoga magazine. [BL1175.S38S67] 76-376786
1. Satchidananda, Swami. 2. Hindus—Biography. I. Integral yoga.

SUBRAMANIAM, K. 294.5'6'1
Brahmin priest of Tamil Nadu [by]K. Subramaniam. New York, Wiley [1974] 183 p. illus. 22 cm. "A Halsted Press book." Based on the author's thesis, University of Saugar, 1969. Bibliography: p. [161]-167. [BL1215.P75S9] 74-13072 ISBN 0-470-83535-4
1. Priests, Hindu. I. Title.

KATJU, Shiva Nath. 294.5'6'10924 B
Review on the biography of Bhagawan Gopinath Ji of Kashmir : and ... letters expounding Shiva-Sakhti [sic] philosophy / by S. N. Katju. Srinagar : Bhagawan Gopinath Ji Trust, 1976. 39 p., [2] leaves of plates : ports. ; 23 cm. Cover title. [BL1175.G625F6734] 77-901796 Re1.00
1. Fotedar, S. N. Bhagawan Gopinath Ji of Kashmir. 2. Gopinath, 1898-1968. I. Title.

OSBORNE, Arthur, 1906- 294.5'6'10924 B
Ramana Maharshi and the path of self-knowledge. Foreword by S. Radhakrishnan. New York, S. Weiser [1970] 207 p. port. 21 cm. Reprint of the 1954 ed. [BL1146.R352O8 1970b] 76-18194 3.00 (pbk)
1. Ramana, Maharsi.

ROY, Dilip Kumar, 1897- 294.5'61'0922 B
Pilgrims of the stars [by] Dilip Kumar Roy and Indira Devi. New York, Macmillan [1973] xiii, 362 p. 21 cm. [BL1175.R6A3] 72-93632 7.95
1. Roy, Dilip Kumar, 1897- 2. Indira Devi, 1920- I. Indira Devi, 1920- II. Title.

ROY, Dilip Kumar, 1897- 294.5.61.0922 B
Pilgrims of the stars [by] Dilip Kuman Roy and Indira Devi. [New York Dell Books 1974, c1973] 362 p. 20 cm. (A Delta Book.) [BL1175.R6A3] 3.25 (pbk.)
1. Roy, Dilipkumar, 1897 2. Indira Devi, 1920- I. Indira Devi, 1920- II. Title.
L.C. card number for original ed.: 72-93632.

WIENER, Sita. 294.5'61'0924 B
Swami Satchidananda; his biography. [1st ed.] San Francisco, Straight Arrow Books; [distributed by the World, New York, 1970] 194 p. illus., ports. 22 cm. [BL1175.S38W5] 70-141477 7.95
1. Satchidananda, Swami.

SAI Baba and his message : a challenge to behavioural sciences / 294.5'6'2
edited by Satya Pal Ruhela, Duane Robinson. 1st. Bell Books ed. Delhi : Vikas Pub. House, 1976. xx, 330 p., [5] leaves of plates : ill., map ; 20 cm. Bibliography: p. [323]-325. [BL1175.S385S24] 76-900490 Rs9.70
1. Sathya Sai Baba, 1926- Addresses, essays, lectures. I. Ruhela, Satya Pal, 1935- II. Robinson, Duane.

SANDWEISS, Samuel H. 294.5'6'2
Sai Baba, the holy man ... and the psychiatrist / Samuel H. Sandweiss. San Diego, Calif. : Birth Day Pub. Co., c1975. 240 p. : ill. ; 23 cm. Includes bibliographical references. [BL1175.S385S26] 75-28784 4.25
1. Sathya Sai Baba, 1926- 2. Psychology, Religious. I. Title.

*TAPASYANANDA, Swami. 294.5'6'2
Swami Ramakrishnananda; the apostle of Sri Ramakrishna to the South, by Swami Tapasyananda. Madras, India, Shri Ramakrishna math, 1972. 270 p., 18 cm. [BL1175.]
1. Chakravarti, Sashi Bhushan. I. Title.
Distributed by Vedanta Press, Hollywood, Calif. 90068

SCHULMAN, Arnold. 294.5'6'20924
Baba. New York, Pocket Bks. [1973, c.1971] 174 p. illus., maps. 18 cm. [BL1175.S385S38 1971] ISBN 0-671-78260-6 pap., 1.25
1. Sathya Sai Baba, I. Title.

SCHULMAN, Arnold. 294.5'6'20924
Baba. New York, Viking Press [1971] 177 p. illus., map, ports. 22 cm. [BL1175.S385S38 1971] 77-151261 ISBN 0-670-14343-X 5.95
1. Sathya Sai Baba, 1926- I. Title.

ANZAR, Naosherwan. 294.5'6'3 B
The beloved : the life and work of Meher Baba / by Naosherwan Anzar. North Myrtle Beach, S.C. : Sheriar Press, [1974] xi, 146 p. : ill. ; 27 cm. [BL1175.M4A66] 75-301349 10.00
1. Meher Baba, 1894-1969. I. Title.

BHAKTIVEDANTA, A.C. Swami 1896- 294.5'6'3 B
Lord Caitanya in five features : chapter 7, Adi-lila of Krsnadasa Kaviraja Gosvami's Sri-Caitanya-caritamrta / A. C. Bhaktivedanta Swami. New York : Bhaktivedanta Book Trust, 1973. 156 p., [2] leaves of plates : ill. ; 21 cm. Bengali and English. [BL1245.V36K7733] 75-322016 ISBN 0-912776-52-8
1. Krshnadasa Kaviraja, b. 1518 or 19. Srisricaitanyacaritamrta. 2. Chaitanya, 1486-1534. I. Krshnadasa Kaviraja, b. 1518 or 19. Srisricaitanyacaritamrta. 1973. II. Title.

DUCE, Ivy Oneita. 294.5'6'3 B
How a master works / by Ivy Oneita Duce. Walnut Creek, CA : Sufism Reoriented, inc., 1975. xxiii, 768 p., [8] leaves of plates : ill. ; 25 cm. Bibliography: p. 767-768. [BL1175.M4D78] 75-17037 ISBN 0-915828-01-4 : 17.95
1. Meher Baba, 1894-1969. 2. Duce, Ivy Oneita. I. Title.

HOPKINSON, Henry Thomas, 1905- 294.5'6'3 B
Much silence : Meher Baba, his life and work / Tom and Dorothy Hopkinson. New York : Dodd, Mead, 1975, c1974. 191 p. : port. ; 22 cm. Includes bibliographical references. [BL1175.M4H66 1975] 74-26821 ISBN 0-396-07141-4 : 7.95
1. Meher Baba, 1894-1969. I. Hopkinson, Dorothy, joint author. II. Title.

IRANI, Manija Sheriar. 294.5'6'3 B
82 family letters to the western family of lovers and followers of Meher Baba / written by Mani (Manija Sheriar Irani) from December 1956 to August 1969 North Myrtle Beach, S.C. : Sheriar Press, c1976. vii, 366 p. : ports. ; 28 cm. Bibliography: p. 366. [BL1175.M4I7 1976] 76-151466
1. Meher Baba, 1894-1969. I. Title.

IRANI, Manija Sheriar. 294.5'6'3 B
82 family letters to the western family of lovers and followers of Meher Baba / written by Mani (Manija Sheriar Irani) from December 1956 to August 1969 North Myrtle Beach, S.C. : Sheriar Press, c1976. vii, 366 p. : ports. ; 28 cm. Bibliography: p. 366. [BL1175.M4I7 1976] 76-151466
1. Meher Baba, 1894-1969. I. Title.

KRSHNADASA Kaviraja, b.1518or19. 294.5'6'3 B
Sri Caitanya-caritamrta of Krsnadasa Kaviraja Gosvami : with the original Bengali text, Roman transliterations, synonyms, translation and elaborate purports / [by] A. C. Bhaktivedanta Swami. New York : Bhaktivedanta Book Trust, c1973- v. : col. ill., map ; 27 cm. Includes index. [BL1245.V36K7713 1973] 74-193363 ISBN 0-912776-51-X (v. 2)
1. Chaitanya, 1486-1534. I. Bhaktivendanta Swami, A. C., 1896- ed. II. Title.

PRABHAVANANDA, Swami, 1893- 294.5'6'3
The eternal companion: Brahmananda; teachings and reminiscences, with a biography. [3d ed., rev. and enl.] Hollywood, Calif., Vedanta Press [1970 c1960] viii, 301 p. port. 18 cm. [BL1175.B7P7 1970] 72-113256 ISBN 0-87481-023-X 4.50
1. Brahmananda, Swami, 1863-1922. I. Title.

DONKIN, William. 294.5'6'30924 B
The wayfarers; an account of the work of Meher Baba with the God-intoxicated, and also with advanced souls, sadhus, and the poor. Fully illustrated with many photos. and maps by William Donkin. With a foreword by Meher Baba. [San Francisco, Sufism Reoriented] 1969 [c1948] ix, 405, 15, 57 p. illus. (1 fold. map in pocket) 26 cm. Includes the Work of Meher Baba with advanced souls, sadhus, the mad and the poor, 15th March to 14th May 1948 (15 p.) and, 8th June 1948 to 1st August 1947 (57 p.) [BL1175.M4D6 1969] 74-84830 10.95
1. Meher Baba, 1894- I. Title.

IRANI, Manija Sheriar. 294.5'6'30924 B
Eighty-two family letters to the western family of lovers and followers of Meher Baba, written by Mani (Manija Sheriar Irani) from December 1956 to August 1969. New York, Society for Avatar Meher Baba, 1969. 1 v. (various pagings) port. 29 cm. On spine: Meher Baba family letters, 1956 to 1969. [BL1175.M4I7] 73-107028
1. Meher Baba, 1894- I. Title.

CHINMOY. 294.5'6'4
Mother India's lighthouse: India's spiritual leaders; flame-heights of the West, by Sri Chinmoy. Blauvelt, N.Y., R. Steiner Publications [1973] vii, 277 p. 18 cm. (Steinerbooks, 1732) [BL1170.C46] 74-189998 1.95 (pbk.)
1. Hinduism—Biography. 2. India—Biography. I. Title.

WILLIAMS, George Mason, 1940- 294.5'6'4 B
The quest for meaning of Swami Vivekananda; a study of religious change [by] George M. Williams. [Chico, Calif.] New Horizons Press [1974] x, 148 p. 22 cm. (The Religious quest, v. 1) Bibliography: p. 141-144. [BL1270.V5W54] 74-10906 ISBN 0-914914-00-6
1. Vivekananda, Swami, 1863-1902. I. Title. II. Series.

WILLIAMS, George Mason, 1940- 294.5'6'4 B
The quest for meaning of Svami Vivekananda; a study of religious change [by] George M. Williams. [Chico, Calif.] New Horizons Press [1974] x, 148 p. 22 cm. (The Religious quest, v. 1) Bibliography: p. 141-144. [BL1270.V5W54] 74-10906 ISBN 0-914914-01-4 3.95 (pbk.).
1. Vivekananda, Swami, 1863-1902. I. Title. II. Series.

BUBBA Free John. 294.5'6'5
No remedy : an introduction to the life and practice of the spiritual community of Bubba Free John / compiled and edited by Bonnie Beavan and Nina Jones in collaboration with Bubba Free John. 1st ed. Lower Lake, Calif. : Dawn Horse Press, 1976 xvi, 154 p. : ill. ; 14 x 21 cm. Includes bibliographical references. [BP605.D38B8 1975] 75-21551 ISBN 0-913922-20-X pbk. : 3.95
1. Dawn Horse Communion (Organization) I. Beavan, Bonnie. II. Jones, Nina. III. Title.

MILLER, David M., PhD. 294.5'6'5
Hindu monastic life : the monks and monasteries of Bhubaneswar / by David M. Miller and Dorothy C. Wertz. Montreal; Irvington, NY McGill-Queen's University Press 1976 xv, 228 p., [10] leaves of plates : ill. ; 25 cm. Includes index. Bibliography: p. [215]-218. [BL1226.85.M54] 76-373803 ISBN 0-7735-0190-8 : 22.00 ISBN 0-7735-0247-5 pbk. :
1. Monastic and religious life (Hinduism)—India—Bhubaneswar. 2. Monasteries, Hindu—India—Bhubaneswar. I. Wertz, Dorothy C., joint author. II. Title.

BESANT, Annie (Wood) 1847-1933. 294.58
Thought power, its control and culture. Wheaton, Ill., Theosophical Press, 1953. 128 p. 19 cm. [BF461.B5 1953] 54-965
1. Theosophy. 2. Thought and thinking. I. Title.

GREENWALT, Emmett A 294.58
The Point Loma community in California, 1897-1942: a theosophical experiment. Berkeley, University of California Press, 1955. 236p. illus., ports. 24cm. (University of California publications in history, v. 48) Bibliography: p. [203]-218. [E173.C15 vol. 48] 212 A55
1. Tingley, Katherine Augusta (Westcott) 1847-1926. 2. Lomaland Scholl, Point Loma, Calif. I. Title. II. Series: California. University of California publications in history, v. 48

SPINKS, F Pierce. *294.58 212
Theosophists: reunite! Boston, Christopher Pub. House [1958] 387 p. 21 cm. [BP510.T5S65] 58-8665
1. Theosophical Society. 2. Theosophy — Hist. I. Title.

GHERANDASAMHITA. 294.5'9
English and Sanskrit.
The Gheranda samhita / translated by Srisa Chandra Vasu. New York : AMS Press, [1974] ii, 59 p. ; 23 cm. Reprint of the 1914 ed. published by the Panini Office, Allahabad, which was issued as v. 15, pt. 2 of The Sacred books of the Hindus, under the general title: Yoga sastra. [B132.Y6G52413] 73-3804 ISBN 0-404-57836-5 : 14.50
1. Yoga, Hatha. I. Vasu, Srisa Chandra, rai bahadur, 1861-1918? ed. II. Title. III. Title: Yoga sastra. IV. Series: The Sacred books of the Hindus ; v. 15, pt. 2.

JOHNSON, Clive, 1930- 294.5'9
comp.
Vedanta; an anthology of Hindu scripture, commentary and poetry. Edited by Clive Johnson under the supervision of Swami Prabhavananda. [1st ed.] New York, Harper & Row [1971] xii, 243 p. 22 cm. Bibliography: p. 236-238. [PK2978.E5J6] 75-126033 6.95
1. Indic literature—Translations into English. 2. English literature—Translations from Indic literature. I. Title.

SIVARAHASYA. English. 294.5'9
Selections.
The heart of the Rihbu [i.e. Ribhu] gita. Edited, and with an introd., by Franklin Jones (Bubba Free John). Illustrated by Lydia Depole. [1st ed.] Los Angeles, Dawn Horse Press [1973] xi, 33 p. illus. 22 cm. Consists of chapter 26 of the Ribhu gita; and 6 verses selected from the whole text by Sri Ramana Maharshi. The Ribhu gita is pt. 6 of the Sivarahasya. [BL1146.S57213 1973] 73-88178 ISBN 0-913922-03-X 1.95
I. Ramana, Maharshi. II. Jones, Franklin, ed. III. Title.

SIVASAMHITA. English 294.5'9
and Sanskrit.
The Siva samhita / translated by Srisa Chandra Vasu. New York : AMS Press, [1974] 87 p. ; 23 cm. Reprint of the 1914 ed. published by the Panini Office, Allahabad, which was issued as v. 15, pt. 1 of The Sacred books of the Hindus, under the general title: Yoga sastra. [B132.Y6S56613 1974] 73-3803 ISBN 0-404-57815-2
1. Yoga, Hatha. 2. Shaktism. I. Vasu, Srisa Chandra, rai bahadur, 1861-1918? ed. II. Title. III. Title: Yoga sastra. IV. Series: The Sacred books of the Hindus ; v. 15, pt. 1.

VYASA. 294.5'9
The Siddhanta darsanam of Vyasa. Translated by Mohan Lal Sandal. Allahabad, Panini Office, 1925. [New York, AMS Press, 1974] vii, 112 p. 23 cm. Original ed. issued as v. 29 of The Sacred books of the Hindus. English and Sanskrit. [BL1135.V9E57] 73-3822 ISBN 0-404-57829-2
I. Sandal, Mohan Lal, ed. II. Title. III. Series: The Sacred books of the Hindus, v. 29.

AGEHANANDA Bharati, 294.5'92
Swami, 1923-
The Tantric tradition / Agehananda Bharati. Westport, Conn. : Greenwood Press, 1977. 349 p. ; 23 cm. Reprint of the 1965 ed. published by Rider, London. Includes index. Bibliography: p. 303-336. [BL1245.T3A64 1977] 77-7204 ISBN 0-8371-9660-4 lib.bdg. : 19.75
1. Tantrism. 2. Tantric Buddhism. I. Title.

BHAVE, Vinoba 294.592
Talks on the Gita. [Translators have retained some essential Sanskrit words] Introd. by Jayaprakash Narayan. New York, Macmillan. 1960[ ] 267p. 23cm. 60-4531 3.25
1. Mahabharata. Bhagavadgita. I. Title.

EDGERTON, Franklin, 1885- 294.592
The Bhagavad gita. Tr., interpreted by Franklin Edgerton. New York, Harper [1964] 202p. 21cm. (Torchbk.; Cloister lib., TB115) 1.45 pap.,
1. Mahabharata. Bhagavadgita. I. Title.

EDGERTON, Franklin, 1885- 294.592
1963, ed. and tr.
The beginnings of Indian philosophy; selections from the Rig Veda, Atharva Veda, Upanisads, and Mahabharata. Translated from the Sanskrit with an introd., notes and glossarial index. Cambridge, Harvard University Press, 1965. 362 p. 22 cm. (UNESCO collection of representative works Indian series) [BL1107.E2 1965a] 65-2314
1. Hinduism—Sacred books (Selections: extracts, etc.) I. Title. II. Series.

GUENTHER, Herbert V. 294.5'92
The Tantric view of life, by Herbert V. Guenther. Berkeley [Calif.] Shambala, 1972. x, 168 p. illus. 26 cm. (The Clear light series) Bibliography: p. 158-159. [BQ8918.3.G8 1972] 78-146511 ISBN 0-87773-028-8 8.50
1. Tantrism, Buddhist. I. Title.

MAHABHARATA 294.592
The Bhagavad-gita; a book of Hindu scriptures in the form of a dialogue between Prince Arjuna and the God Krishna. Mount Vernon, N. Y., Peter Pauper Press [1959] 61p. col. illus. 19cm. [PK3633.B5M2 1959] 59-16881
I. Peter Pauper Press, Mount Vernon, N. Y. II. Title.

MAHABHARATA 294.592
The Bhagavad gita; or, The Lord's lay with commentary and notes, as well as references to the Christian Seriptures. Translated from the Sanskrit by Mohini M. Chatterji. Pref. by Ainslie Embree. New York, Julian Press, 1960. xxi, 283p. 24cm. [BL1130.A4C5 1960] 60-3476
I. Chatterjee, Mohini Mohun, tr. II. Title.

MAHABHARATA 294.592
The Bhagavad gita; a sublime hymn of dialectics composed by the antique sage-bard Vyasa. With general and introductory essays, verse commentary, word notes, Samskrit text and English translation, by Nataraja Guru. New York, Asia Pub. House [1962] xv, 763p. 23cm. Text in Sanskrit (romanized) [PK3631.B5 1962] 62-6015
I. Nataraja Guru, 1895- ed. and tr. II. Title.

MAHABHARATA. 294.592
The Bhagvat-geeta, 1785. Translated, with notes, by Charles Wilkins. A facsimile reproduction, with an introd. by George Hendrick. Gainesville, Fla., Scholars' Facsimiles & Reprints, 1959. xiv p., facsim.: 156p. 21cm. (Scholars' facsimiles & reprints) 'Reproduced from a copy in the Library of Congress.; [PK3633.B5W5 1785a] 59-6527
I. Wilkins, Charles, Sir 1749 -1836, tr. II. Title.

MAHABHARATA. 294.592
Bhagavadgita. English.
The Bhagavad gita. Translated from the Sanskrit with an introd. by Juan Mascaro. Baltimore, Penguin Books 1962 121 p. 18 cm. (The Penguin classics, L121) [PK3633.B5M35 1962] 62-3433
I. Mascaro, Juan, ed. and tr.

MANU. 294.5'92
The laws of Manu. Translated with extracts from seven commentaries by G. Buhler. [1st AMS ed.] Delhi, Motilal Banarsidass. [New York, AMS Press, 1971] cxxxviii, 620 p. 23 cm. Reprint of the 1886 ed. Includes bibliographical references. [BL1125.A3B8 1971] 73-149682 ISBN 0-404-01148-9
1. Hindu law. I. Buhler, Georg, 1837-1898, ed. II. Title.

PANCARATRA. 294.5'92
Naradapancaratra. Jnanamrtasarasamhita. English
Sri Narada Pancharatnam: the Jnanamrita sara samhita. Translated into English by Swami Vijnanananda, alias Hari Prasanna Chatterji. Allahabad, Panini Office, 1921. [New York, AMS Press, 1974] p. cm. Original ed. issued as v. 23 of The Sacred books of the Hindus. [BL1135.P34A37 1974] 73-3816 ISBN 0-404-57823-3 25.00
I. Vijnanananda, Swami, 1868-1938, tr. II. Title. III. Series: The Sacred books of the Hindus, v. 23.

PANDIT, Madhav Pundalik, 294.592
1918-
The Upanishads, gateways of Knowledge [Hollywood, Calif., Vedanta Pr., 1961, c.]1960[ ] 174p. 25cm. 61-65699 3.00 bds.,
1. Upanishads—Criticism, interpretation, etc. I. Title.

UPANISHADS. English. 294.592
The Upanisads [2 pts.] Tr. by F. Max Miiller [Gloucester, Mass., P. Smith, 1963] 2 pts. (320; 350p.) 22cm. Contents.pt. 1. Chandogya Upanisad. Talavakara (Kena) Upanisad. Aitareya Upanisad. Kausitaki Upanisad. Vajasaneyi Upanisad.--Pt. 2. Katha Upanisad. Mundaka Upanisad. Taittiriya Upanisad. Brhadaranvaka Upanisad. Svetasvatara Upanisad. Prasna Upanisad. Maitrayani Upanisad. (Sacred bks. of the East, v.1, v.15. Dover bks. rebound) 4.00 ea.,
I. Miiller. Friedrich Max, 1823-1900, ed. and tr. II. Title. III. Series: The Sacred books of the East (New York) v.1, 15

UPANISHADS. English. 294.592
The Upanisads. Translated by F. Max Muller. New York, Dover Publications [1962] 2 v. 22 cm. (The Sacred books of the East, v. 1, 15) Contents.—pt. 1. Chandogya Upanisad. Talavakara (Kena) Upanisad. Aitareya Upanisad. Kausitaki Upanisad. Vajasaneyi (Isa) Upanisad.—pt. 2. Katha Upanisad. Mundaka Upanisad. Taittiriya Upanisad. Brhadaranyaka Upanisad. Svetasvatara Upanisad. Prasna Upanisad. Maitraayami Upanisad. [BL1120.A3M78 1962] 62-53180
I. Muller, Friedrich Max, 1823-1900, ed. and tr. II. Series: The Sacred books of the East (New York) v. 1, 15.

ZAEHNER, Robert Charles, 294.592
ed. and tr.
Hindu scriptures; selected, translated and introduced by R. C. Zaehner. London, Dent; New York, Dutton 1966. xxiii, 328 p. 18 1/2 cm. (B66-18670) (Everyman's library, no. 944) 18/- Original ed. edited by Nicol Macnicol. Includes the Bhagavadgita and selections from the Rgveda, Atharvaveda, and Upanishads. [BL1107.Z313] 67-70067
1. Hinduism — Sacred books (Selections: Extracts, etc.) 2. Vedas. Rgveda. English. Selections. I. Macnicol, Nicol, 1870-1952, ed. Hindu scriptures. II. Vedas, Atharvaveda. English. Selections. III. Upanishads. English. Selections. IV. Mahabharata. Bhagavadgita. V. Title. VI. Series.

BRAHMOPANISATSARASANGRAHA.
English & Sanskrit.
The Brahmopanisat-sara sangraha. Translated by Vidyatilaka. Allahabad, Panini Office, 1916. [New York, AMS Press, 1974] xi, ii, x, 80 p. 23 cm. Original ed. issued as v. 18, pt. 1 of The Sacred books of the Hindus. Includes the commentary, the Brahmopanisatsarasangrahadipika in English. [BL1120.A472 1974] 73-3809 ISBN 0-404-57818-7
I. Vidyatilaka, ed. II. Brahmopanisatsarasangrahadipika. English. 1974. III. Upanishads. English & Sanskrit. Selections. 1974. IV. Title. V. Series: The Sacred books of the Hindus, v. 18, pt. 1.

DEUSSEN, Paul, 1845-1919 294.5921
The philosophy of the Upanishads. Authorized English tr. by A. S. Geden [Magnolia, Mass., P. Smith, 1967] xiv, 429p. 22cm. (Dover bk. rebound) Unabridged, unaltered repubn. of the work orig. pub. in 1906 by T. & T. Clark [BL1120.D4 1966] 4.50
1. Upanishads—Criticism, interpretation, etc. I. Title.

DEUSSEN, Paul, 1845- 294.5921
1919.
The philosophy of the Upanishads. Authorized English translation by A. S. Geden. New York, Dover Publications [1966] xiv, 429 p. 22 cm. Translation first published in 1906. "The present work forms the second part of my General history of philosophy." [BL1120.D4 1966] 66-20325
1. Upanishads—Criticism, interpretation, etc. I. Title.

SANDAL, Mohan Lal. 294.5'921
Philosophical teachings in the Upanisads. [Allahabad, Panini office, 1926. New York, AMS Press, 1974] p. cm. Original ed. issued as extra v. 5 in The Sacred books of the Hindus. [BL1120.S18 1974] 73-3831 ISBN 0-404-57849-7 57.50
1. Upanishads—Criticism, interpretation, etc. I. Title. II. Series: The Sacred books of the Hindus, extra v. 5.

UPANISHADS. 294.5'921
Aitareyopanisad. English & Sanskrit.
Aitareya Upanisat. Translated by Srisa Chandra Vidyarnava and Mohan Lal Sandal. Allahabad, Panini Office, 1925. [New York, AMS Press, 1974] p. Original ed. issued as v. 30, pts. 1-2 of The Sacred books of the Hindus. English and Sanskrit; commentary in English. [BL1120.A432 1974] 73-3823 ISBN 0-404-57830-6 14.50
I. Vasu, Srisa Chandra, rai bahadur, 1861-1918?, ed. II. Sandal, Mohan Lal, ed. III. Title. IV. Series: The Sacred books of the Hindus, v. 30, pts. 1-2.

UPANISHADS. 294.5'921
Brhadaranyakopanisad. English & Sanskrit.
The Brihadaranyaka Upanisad, with the commentary of Sri Madhvacharya, called also Anandatirtha. Translated by Sris Chandra Vasu with the assistance of Ramaksya Bhattacharya. Allahabad, Panini Office, 1916. [New York, AMS Press, 1974] ii, 728 p. 23 cm. Original ed. issued as v. 14, pts. 1-9 of The Sacred books of the Hindus. English and Sanskrit; commentary in English. [BL1120.A4842 1974] 73-3802 ISBN 0-404-57814-4
I. Vasu, Srisa Chandra, rai bahadur, 1861-1918?, ed. II. Bhattacharya, Ramaksya, ed. III. Anandatirtha, surnamed Madhvacarya, 1197-1276. Bradaranyakopanisadbhasya. English. 1974. IV. Title. V. Series: The Sacred books of the Hindus,

UPANISHADS. 294.5'921
Chandogyopanisad. English & Sanskrit.
Chhandogya Upanisad, with the commentary of Sri Madhvacharya, called also Anandatirtha. Translated by Srisa Chandra Vasu. Allahabad, Panini Office, 1910. [New York, AMS Press, 1974] p. Original ed. issued as v. 3 of The Sacred books of the Hindus. Originally published as pt. 2 of The Upanisads, issued as v. 1 of the series. English and Sanskrit; commentary in English. [BL1120.A452 1974] 73-3788 ISBN 0-404-57803-9 44.50
I. Vasu, Srisa Chandra, rai bahadur, 1861-1918?, ed. II. Anandatirtha, surnamed Madhvacarya, 1197-1276. Chandogyopanisadbhasya. English. 1974. III. Title. IV. Series: The Sacred books of the Hindus

UPANISHADS. English 294.5'921
The ten principal Upanishads / put into English by Shree Purohit, swami, and W. B. Yeats. New York : Macmillan, 1975, c1937. 158 p. ; 21 cm. [BL1120.A3P8 1975] 75-15999 ISBN 0-02-071550-1 pbk. : 1.95
I. Purohit, swami, 1882- II. Yeats, William Butler, 1865-1939. III. Title.

UPANISHADS. English. 294.5'921
The thirteen principal Upanishads. Translated from the Sanskrit with an outline of the philosophy of the Upanishads. 2d ed., rev. London, New York, Oxford University Press [1971] xvi, 587 p. 21 cm. (A Galaxy book, GB365) Bibliography: p. 459-515. [BL1120.A3H8 1971] 71-30455 ISBN 0-19-501490-1 3.50 (U.S.)
1. Upanishads—Bibliography. 2. Philosophy, Hindu. I. Hume, Robert Ernest, 1877-1948, tr. II. Title.

UPANISHADS. English & 294.5'921
Sanskrit. Selections.
Isa, Kena, Katha, Prasna, Mundaka and Manduka Upanisads. Vol. 1. 2d ed. Allahabad, Panini Office, 1911. [New York, AMS Press, 1974] 320 p. 23 cm. Original ed. issued as v. 1 of The Sacred books of the Hindus. First ed., 1909-10, issued in two pts., pt. 1 with general title, The Upanisads, and pt. 2 with title, Chhandogya Upanisad. The remaining Upanishads appeared as independent vols. Includes Anandatirtha's commentary on each of the six Upanishads. Translated by Srisa Chandra Vasu. [BL1120.A3V37 1974] 73-4980 ISBN 0-404-57801-2
I. Anandatirtha, surnamed Madhvacarya, 1197-1276. II. Vasu, Srisa Chandra, rai bahadur, 1861-1918?, tr. III. Title. IV. Series: The Sacred books of the Hindus, v. 1.

UPANISHADS. ENGLISH. 294.5921
SELECTIONS.
The Upanishads. Translations from the Sanskrit with an introd. by Juan Mascaro. Baltimore, Penguin Books [1965] 142 p. 19 cm. (The Penguin classics, L163) [BL1120.A3M32] 65-29745
I. Mascaro, Juan, ed. and tr. II. Title.

UPANISHADS, English, 294.5921
Selections
The Upanishads. Tr. from Sanskrit, introd by Juan Mascaro. Baltimore, Penguin [c.1965] 142p. 19cm. (Penguin classics, L163) [BL1120.A3M32] 65-29745 .95 pap.,
I. Mascaro, Juan, ed. and tr. II. Title.

UPANISHADS. English. 294.5'921
Selections.
The wisdom of the forest : selections from the Hindu Upanishads / translated by Geoffrey Parrinder. New York : New Directions Pub. Corp., 1976. p. cm. (A New Directions book ; 414) "A companion volume to Thomas Merton's The wisdom of the desert (NDP 295) and Irmgard Schloegl's The wisdom of the Zen masters (NDP415)." [BL1120.A3P35 1976] 75-42114 ISBN 0-8112-0606-8 : 6.50 ISBN 0-8112-0607-6 pbk. :
I. Parrinder, Edward Geoffrey. II. Title.

UPANISHADS. 294.5'921
Isopanisad. English.
Sri Isopanisad / with introd., translation and authorized purports by A. C. Bhaktivedanta Swami. New York ; Bombay : The Bhaktivedanta Book Trust, 1974. xi, 139 p. : col. ill. ; 20 cm. Includes index. [BL1120.A522 1974] 75-500991 ISBN 0-912776-03-X pbk. : 1.95
I. Bhaktivedanta Swami, A. C., 1896- II. Title.

UPANISHADS. 294.5'921
Maitrayaniyopanisad. English & Sanskrit.
The Maitri Upanisat. Translated by Srisa Chandra Vidyarnava and Mohan Lal Sandal. Allahabad, Panini Office [1926. New York, AMS Press, 1974] p. cm. Original ed. issued as v. 31, pt. 2 of The Sacred books of the Hindus. [BL1120.A6252 1974] 73-3827 ISBN 0-404-57832-2 9.00
I. Vasu, Srisa Chandra, rai bahadur, 1861-1918?, ed. II. Sandal, Mohan Lal, ed. III. Title. IV. Series: The Sacred books of the Hindus, v. 31, pt. 2.

UPANISHADS. 294.5'921
Svetasvataropanisad. English & Sanskrit.
The Svetasvatara Upanisad. Translated by Siddhesvara Varma Shastri. Allahabad, Panini Office, 1916. [New York, AMS Press, 1974] p. Original ed. issued as v. 18, pts. 2-3 of The Sacred Books of the Hindus. English and Sanskrit; introductory matter and notes in English. [BL1120.A722 1974] 73-3810 ISBN 0-404-57840-3 14.50
I. Varma, Siddheshwar, 1887- ed. II. Title. III. Series: The Sacred books of the Hindus, v. 18, pts. 2-3.

UPANISHADS. 294.5'921
Taittiriyopanisad. English & Sanskrit.
The Tait[t]iriya Upanisat. Translated by Srisa Chandra Vidyarnava and Mohan Lal Sandal. Allahabad, Panini Press, 1925. [New York, AMS Press, 1974] p. cm. Original ed. issued as v. 30, pt. 3 of The Sacred books of the Hindus. English and Sanskrit; commentary in English. [BL1120.A732 1974] 73-3824 ISBN 0-404-57833-0 10.00
I. Vasu, Srisa Chandra, rai bahadur, 1861-1918?, ed. II. Sandal, Mohan Lal, ed. III. Title. IV. Series: The Sacred books of the Hindus, v. 30, pt. 3.

VASU, Srisa Chandra, 294.5'921
rai bahadur, 1861-1918?
Studies in the first six Upanisads; and the Isa and Kena Upanisads, with the commentary of Sankara. Translated by Srisa Chandra Vidyarnava. Allahabad. Panini Office, 1919. [New York, AMS Press, 1974] 152 p. 23 cm. Original ed. issued as v. 22, pt. 1 of The Sacred books of the Hindus. Includes translations in English of the Isopanisad and the Kenopanisad, with the respective commentaries of Sankaracarya, the Isopanisadbhasya and the Kenopanisadbhasya, and the commentary of Anantacarya on the Isopanisad, the Isavasyabhasya. Includes some slokas in Sanskrit. Intended to serve as an introd. to the author's translations of the Upanishads. [BL1120.V37 1974] 73-3814 ISBN 0-404-57822-5
1. Upanishads. I. Sankaracarya. Isopanisadbhasya. English. 1974. II. Sankaracarya. Kenopanisadbhasya. English. 1974. III. Anantacarya. Isavasyabhasya. English. 1974. IV. Upanishads. Isopanisad. English. 1974. V. Upanishads. Kenopanisad. English. 1974. VI. Title. VII. Series: The Sacred books of the Hindus, v. 22, pt. 1.

ATHAVALE, Pandurang 294.5'922
Vaijnath, 1920-
Valmiki Ramayana : a study / from the discourses of Pandurang V. Athavale. [s.l. : s.n., 1976] (Bombay : Associated Advertisers & Printers) vii, 209 p., [2] leaves of plates : ill. ; 22 cm. "Published on the occasion of the golden jubilee celebration, January 1976 of Shrimad Bhagvat Gita Pathashala." [PK3661.A8] 76-902310 Rs14.00
1. Valmiki. Ramayana. I. Title.

BAHADUR, Krishna 294.5'922
Prakash, 1924-
Ramacharitmanasa : a study in perspective / K. P. Bahadur. Delhi : Ess Ess Publications, 1976. 365 p., [8] leaves of plates : ill. ; 23 cm. Includes index. [PK1947.9.T83R3318] 76-904748 Rs80.00
1. Tulasidasa, 1532-1623. Ramacaritamanasa. I. Title.

HOPKINS, Edward 294.5'922
Washburn, 1857-1932.
Epic mythology. New York, Biblo and Tannen, 1969. 277 p. 26 cm. The mythology of the two epics of India, the Mahabharata and the Ramayana. Reprint of the 1915 ed. [BL1130.H6 1969] 76-75358
1. Mahabharata. 2. Valmiki. Ramayana. 3. Mythology, Hindu. I. Title.

*MAZUMDAR, Shudha 294.5922
Ramayana. Foreword by S. Radhakrishnan. Bombay, Orient Longmans [S. Pasadena, Calif., Hutchins Oriental, 1965, c.1958] xx, 540p. 19cm. 6.00 bds.,
I. Title.

WATSON, Jane (Werner) 294.5'922
1915-
Rama of the golden age; an epic of India. Retold by Jane Werner Watson. Illustrated by Paul Frame. Champaign, Ill., Garrard Pub. Co. [1971] 96 p. col. illus. 24 cm. ([A Readings shelf book]) A prose retelling of India's epic poem describing the good prince Rama's triumph over the evil demon king, Ravana. [PZ8.1.W34Ram] 70-126415 ISBN 0-8116-4206-2 2.59
I. Frame, Paul, 1913- illus. II. Valmiki. Ramayana. III. Title.

BARRACK, Howard J. 294.5'923
The thousand names of Visnu : Visnu Sahasranamam from the Mahabharata ; transliterated Sanskrit text, translation and commentary / by Howard J. Barrack ; foreword by Amritjit Singh. New York : Tara Publications, 1974. 120 p. ; 23 cm. Bibliography: p. 119-120. [BL1219.B3713] 74-194697
1. Mahabharata. Anusasanaparva. Visnusahasranama. 2. Vishnu. I. Mahabharata. Anusasanaparva. Visnusahasranama. English & Sanskrit. 1974. II. Title.

HOPKINS, Edward 294.5'923
Washburn, 1857-1932.
The great epic of India; its character and origin. Freeport, N.Y., Books for Libraries Press [1973] p. Reprint of the 1901 ed. published by Scribner, New York, in series: Yale bicentennial publications. [PK3641.H65 1973] 73-6582 ISBN 0-518-19049-8
1. Mahabharata. 2. Epic poetry, Sanskrit—History and criticism. I. Title. II. Series: Yale bicentennial publications.

MAHABHARATA. English. 294.5'923
The Mahabharata. Translated and edited by J. A. B. van Buitenen. Chicago, University of Chicago Press [1973- v. illus. 25 cm. Contents.Contents.—v. 1. The book of the beginning. Includes bibliographical references. [PK3633.A2B8] 72-97802 ISBN 0-226-84648-2
I. Buitenen, Johannes Adrianus Bernardus van, tr.

MAHABHARATA. 294.5'923
Harivamsa. English. Selections.
The transmigration of the seven Brahmans; a translation from the Harivansa of Langlois by Henry David Thoreau. Edited from manuscript with an introd. and notes by Arthur Christy. New York, Haskell House, 1972. xx p., 1 l., facsim. ([16] p.) 23 cm. The translation is from S. A. Langlois' French translation of the original Sanskrit, published in Paris, 1834, and entitled Harivansa; ou, Histoire de la famille de Hari, ouvrage formant un appendice du Mahabharata. The Thoreau translation is from v. 1, p. 100-110. Contents.Contents.—Introduction.—Thoreau's manuscript in facsimile.—The transcription.—The source. [PK3633.H3T5 1972] 72-3516 ISBN 0-8383-1563-1 7.95
I. Thoreau, Henry David, 1817-1862, tr. II. Langlois, Simon Alexandre, 1788-1854, tr. III. Christy, Arthur, 1899-1946, ed. IV. Title.

*RAO, Shanta Rameshwar. 294.5923
The Mahabharata. [New Delhi] Sangam Books [1974 c1968] xii, 219 p. 18 cm. [PK3633] ISBN 0-89253-041-3
1. Mahabharata. I. Title.
Distributed by Interculture Associates for 2.40 (pbk.)

SRI Visnu saharanamam 294.5'923
with the commentaries of Sri Sankaracarya and Sri Parasara Bhattar, by K. E. Parthasarathy. Madras; Ganesh, 1966. 363p. 24 cm. Sanskrit and English; introductory matter and notes in English. [BL1130.A35P3] [PL480:I-E-7745] SA67 3.95
I. Mahabharata. Anusasanaparva. Visnusahasranama. II. Sankaracarya. Visnusahasranamabhasya. III. Parasara Bhatta. Bhagavadgundrpn. IV. Parthasarathy, K. E., ed.
American distributor: Vedanata Pr., 1946 Vedanata Pl., Hollywood, Calif., 90028.

BARBORKA, Geoffrey A 294.5'924
The pearl of the Orient; the message of the Bhagavad-Gita for the Western World, by Geoffrey A. Barborka. Wheaton, Ill., Theosophical Pub. House [1968] iv, 191 p. 21 cm. (A Quest book) $1.75 [BL1130.B34] 68-7851
I. Mahabharata. Bhagavadgita. English. Selections. II. Title.

BARBORKA, Geoffrey A. 294.5'924
The pearl of the Orient; the message of the Bhagavad-Gita for the Western World, by Geoffrey A. Barborka. Wheaton, Ill., Theosophical Pub. House [1968] iv, 191 p. 21 cm. (A Quest book) [BL1130.B34] 68-7851 1.75
I. Mahabharata. Bhagavadgita. English. Selections. II. Title.

CHINMOY. 294.5'924
Commentary on the Bhagavad Gita; the song of the transcendental soul, by Sri Chinmoy. Blauvelt, N.Y., R. Steiner Publications [1973] xviii, 164 p. illus. 18 cm. (Steinerbooks, 1731) [BL1130.C54] 78-189999 1.95 (pbk.)
1. Mahabharata. Bhagavadgita. I. Title.

DE NICOLAS, Antonio T. 294.5'924
Avatara, the humanization of philosophy through the Bhagavad Gita : a philosophic journey through Greek philosophy, contemporary philosophy and the Bhagavad Gita on Ortega yGassett's intercultural theme, Man and circumstance: including a new translation with critical notes of the Bhagavad Gita / Antonio T. de Nicolas ; with prologue by Raimundo Panikkar. New York : N. Hayes, c1976. xv, 465 p. : ill. ; 24 cm. Includes bibliographical references and index. [BL1130.D46] 76-152 ISBN 0-89254-001-X : 18.00 ISBN 0-89254-002-8 pbk. :
1. Mahabharata. Bhagavadgita. 2. Philosophy—History. I. Mahabharata. Bhagavadgita. II. Title.

EASWARAN, Eknath. 294.5'924
The Bhagavad Gita for daily living : commentary, translation, and Sanskrit text / Eknath Easwaran. Berkeley, Calif. : Blue Mountain Center of Meditation, [1975- v. ; 24 cm. Includes indexes. Contents.Contents.—[1] Chapters 1 through 6. [BL1130.E2] 74-20130 ISBN 0-915132-03-6 : 12.95 (v. 1)
1. Mahabharata. Bhagavadgita. I. Mahabharata. Bhagavadgita. English & Sanskrit. 1975- II. Title.
Publisher's address: Box 381, Berkeley, Calif. 94701.

MAHABHARATA. 294.5'924
Bhagavadgia. English.
The Bhagavad Gita as it is. With introd., translation, and authorized purport by A. C. Bhaktivedanta Swami. New York, Macmillan [1968] 318 p. 21 cm. [BL1130.A4B47] 68-8322
1. Mahabharata. Bhagavadgita. I. Bhaktivedanta Swami, A.C.,

MAHABHARATA. 294.5'924
BHAGAVADGITA.
The Bhagavad-Gita, with a commentary based on the original sources by R. C. Zaehner. London, Oxford, Oxford Univ. Pr. [1973, c.1969] ix, 480 p. 21 cm. (Galaxy bk., GB389) Includes transliteration of original Sanskrit. Bibl footnotes. [PK3633.B5Z3] 73-381283 ISBN 0-19-501666-1 Pap., 3.95
1. Zaehner, Robert Charles. I. Title.

MAHABHARATA. 294.5924
Bhagavadgita
Bhagavad Gita; the song celestial The Sanskrit-text. tr. into English verse by Sir Edwin Arnold. Introd by Sri Prakasa. Illus. with paintings by Y. G. Snmati. New York, Heritage [dist. Dial, 1966, c.1965] xx, 128p. col. plates. 26cm. Sanskrit and English [PK3631.A2] 66-2759 6.50
I. Mahabharata. Bhagavadgita. English. II. Arnold. Edwin Sir 1832-1904, tr. III. Srimati, Y. G., illus. IV. Title.

MAHABHARATA. 294.5924
Bhagavadgita.
Bhagavad Gita; the song celestial. The Sanskrit-text, translated into English verse by Sir Edwin Arnold. With an introd. by Sri Prakasa. Illustrated with paintings by Y. G. Srimati. New York, Heritage Press [1965] xx, 128 p. col. plates. 26 cm. Sanskrit and English. [PK3631.A2 1965] 66-2759
I. Arnold, Edwin, Sir, 1832-1904, tr. II. Srimati, Y. G., illus. III. Mahabharata. Bhagavadgita. English.

MAHABHARATA. 294.5'924
Bhagavadgita. English
The Bhagavad Gita / translated by H. Saraydarian. Agoura, Calif. : Aquarian Educational Group, [1974?] 95 p. ; 27 cm. [PK3633.B5S2] 74-11759
I. Saraydarian, H.

MAHABHARATA. 294.5'924
Bhagavadgita. English.
Bhagavad-gita; recension by William Quan Judge, combined with his essays on the Gita. Pasadena, Calif., Theosophical University Press [1969] ix, 220 p. illus. 21 cm. [BL1130.A4J8] 79-92964 4.00
I. Judge, William Quan, 1851-1896. II. Title.

MAHABHARATA. 294.5'924
Bhagavadgita. English.
The Bhagavad-Gita, with a commentary based on the original sources, by R. C. Zaehner. Oxford, Clarendon P., 1969. xi, 480 p. 23 cm. Includes transliteration of original Sanskrit. Bibliographical footnotes. [PK3633.B5Z3] 73-381283 88/-
I. Zaehner, Robert Charles.

MAHABHARATA. 294.5'924
Bhagavadgita. English.
The Bhagavad Gita; a translation and critical commentary, by A. L. Herman. Springfield, Ill., C. C. Thomas [1973] xii, 188 p. illus. 24 cm. Bibliography: p. 172-174. [PK3633.B5H4] 73-8494 ISBN 0-398-02772-2 7.95
1. Mahabharata. Bhagavadgita. I. Herman, A. L.

MAHABHARATA. 294.5'924
Bhagavadgita. English
The Bhagavad Gita / translated by H. Saraydarian. Agoura, Calif. : Aquarian Educational Group, [1974?] 95 p. ; 27 cm. [PK3633.B5S2] 74-11759 6.00 pbk. : 5.00
I. Saraydarian, H.

MAHABHARATA. 294.5'924
Bhagavadgita. English.
The Bhagavad Gita. Translated, with introd. and critical essays, by Eliot Deutsch. [1st ed.] New York, Holt, Rinehart and Winston [1968] xi, 192 p. 22 cm. Bibliography: p. 191-192. [BL1130.A4D4] 68-10072 4.95
I. Deutsch, Eliot, ed.

MAHABHARATA. 294.5'924
Bhagavadgita. English.
The Bhagavad Gita. Translated and interpreted by Franklin Edgerton. Cambridge, Mass., Harvard University Press, 1972. xv, 202 p. 21 cm. "Originally published as volumes 38 and 39 of the Harvard Oriental series ... The Sanskrit text and Sir Edwin Arnold's translation have been omitted in this edition." Includes bibliographical references. [PK3633.B5E39 1972b] 73-154755 ISBN 0-674-06927-7
I. Edgerton, Franklin, 1885-1963, ed.

MAHABHARATA. 294.5'924
Bhagavadgita. English.
The Bhagavadgita; an English translation and commentary by W. Douglas P. Hill. 2d ed. [Madras, New York] Oxford University Press [1966] [10], 234 p. 22 cm. Rs 12.50 Reprint of the second abridged edition issued in 1953. First published, 1928. Bibliographical references included in "abbreviations": p. [10] (1st group) [PK3633.B5H5] S A
I. Hill, William Douglas Penneck, ed. and tr. II. Title.

MAHABHARATA. 294.5'924
Bhagavadgita. English.
The Bhagavadgita; an English translation and commentary by W. Douglas P. Hill. 2d ed. [Madras, New York] Oxford University Press [1966] [10], 234 p. 22 cm. Reprint of the second abridged edition issued in 1953. First published, 1928. Bibliographical references included in "abbreviations": p. [10] (1st group) [PK3633.B5H5 1966] SA 68 Rs12.50
I. Hill, William Douglas Penneck, ed. and tr.

MAHABHARATA. 294.5'924
Bhagavadgita. English & Sanskrit.
Bhagavad-gita as it is : with original Sanskrit text, Roman transliteration, English equivalents, translation, and elaborate purports / A. C. Bhaktivedanta Swami Prabhupada. Complete ed. New York : Collier Books, 1972, 1974 printing. xiii, 981 p., [24] leaves of plates : ill. ; 24 cm. Includes indexes. [BL1130.A4B47 1974] 75-312231 7.95
1. Mahabharata. Bhagavadgita. I. Bhaktivedanta Swami, A. C., 1896- II. Title.

MAHABHARATA. 294.5'924
Bhagavadgita. English & Sanskrit. 1972.
Bhagavad-gita as it is [by] A. C. Bhaktivedanta Swami Prabhupada. Complete ed., with original Sanskrit text, Roman transliteration, English equivalents, translation and elaborate purports. New York, Macmillan [1972] xiii, 981 p. illus. 25 cm. [BL1130.A365 1972] 72-79319 10.95
1. Mahabharata. Bhagavadgita. I. Bhaktivedanta Swami, A. C., 1896- tr. II. Title.
Paperback ed. 4.95

MAHABHARATA. 294.5'924
Bhagavadgita. English. Selections.
The Bhagavad Gita; a new verse translation [by] Ann Stanford. [1st ed. New York, Herder and Herder [1970] xxvii, 145 p. 21 cm. (An Azimuth book) [PK3633.B5S8] 77-110073 5.00
I. Stanford, Ann, tr. II. Title.

MAHABHARATA. 294.5'924
Bhagavadgita. English. Selections.
Bhagavad-gita as it is / with translations and elaborate purports by A. C. Bhaktivedanta Swami Prabhupada. Abridged ed. New York : Bhaktivedanta Book Trust, c1972, 1977 printing. p. cm. Includes bibliographical references and index. [BL1130.A4B472 1977] 75-34536 ISBN 0-912776-80-3 : 5.95
1. Mahabharata. Bhagavadgita. I. Bhaktivedanta Swami, A. C., 1896- II. Title.

MAHESH Yogi, Maharishi. 294.5'924
Maharishi Mahesh Yogi on the Bhagavad-gita: a new translation and commentary with Sanskrit text. Chapters 1 to 6. Harmondsworth, Penguin, 1969. 494 p. 1 illus. 18 cm. [PK3642.B5M25] 72-449366 10/-

1. Mahabharata. Bhagavadgita. I. Mahabharata. Bhagavadgita. II. Title.

*PARRINDER, Geoffrey 294.5'924
The bhagavadgita; a verse translation. New York, E. P. Dutton & Co. 1975 [c1974] x, 115 p. 21 cm. [PK3633] ISBN 0-525-47390-4 2.95 (pbk.)
I. Title.

PRANANANDA, Swami. 294.5'924
The wisdom of the Gita / by Swami Pranananda. Glenmont, N.Y. : Vedanta Vihar, c1977. 159 p. ; 18 cm. [BL1130.P68] 77-93925
1. Mahabharata. Bhagavadgita. I. Title.

*SRIMAD bhagavad-gita, 294.5924
translated by swami vireswarananda 1st edition. Madras, Sri Ranakrishna Math, 1974. xii, 369p. 9 cm. by 11 cm. [BL1130] ISBN 0-87481-421-9
1. Bhagavadgita.
Distributed by Vedanta Press for 4.25. Pbk., 1.25; ISBN 0-87481-464-2.

STEINER, Rudolf, 1861-1925. 294.5'924
The Bhagavad Gita and the Epistles of Paul; five lectures. Cologne, Dec. 28, 1912-Jan. 1, 1913. New York, Anthroposophic Press [1971] 102 p. 22 cm. "Translated from shorthand reports unrevised by the lecturer ... published with the title, Die Bhagavad Gita und die Paulusbriefe." [BL1130.S68813] 77-153704
1. Mahabharata. Bhagavadgita—Addresses, essays, lectures. 2. Bible. N.T. Epistles of Paul—Addresses, essays, lectures. I. Title.

STEINER, Rudolf, 1861-1925. 294.5'924
The occult significance of the Bhagavad Gita; nine lectures, Helsingfors, May 28-June 5, 1913. [Translated by George and Mary Adams] New York, Anthroposophic Press [1968] v, 142 p. 22 cm. Translation of Die okkulten Grundlagen der Bhagavad Gita. [BL1130.S713] 68-26703
1. Mahabharata. Bhagavadgita. 2. Anthroposophy. I. Title.

WADSWORTH, Cleome Carroll. 294.5924
Bhagavad Gita; a psychological recension. [1st ed. New York] Pageant Press [c1965] xxii, 95 p. 21 cm. Interpretative commentary on an English translation of the text. Bibliography: p. 93-95. [BL1130.W3] 65-27306
I. Mahabharata. Bhagavadgita. English. II. Title.

BHAKTIVEDANTA, A.C., Swami 1896- 294.5'925
Krsna : the supreme personality of Godhead : a summary study of Srila Vyasadeva's Srimad-Bhagavatam, tenth canto / A. C. Bhaktivedanta Swami. New York ; Bombay: Bhaktivedanta Book Trust, c1970, 1974 printing. 3 v. : col. ill. ; 28 cm. [BL1220.B44 1974] 75-304945 ISBN 0-912776-60-9
1. Krishna. 2. Puranas. Bhagavatapurana. I. Title.

*BROWN, Cheever Mackenzie. 294.5'925
God as mother: a feminine theology in India; an historical and theological study of the Brahmavaivarta Purana. Hartford, Vt. Claude Stark [1974] xiii, 264 p. 23 cm. Bibliography: p. 245-254. [BL1135] 74-76006 ISBN 0-89007-004-0 15.00
1. Puranas. Brahmavaivartapurana. I. Title.

NAUNIDHIRAMA. 294.5'925
The Garuda purana (Saroddhara), with English translation by Ernest Wood and S. V. Subrahmanyam, and an introd. from Sris Chandra Vasu. Allahabad, Panini Office, 1911. [New York, AMS Press, 1974] iv, 169 p. 23 cm. Original ed. issued as v. 9 of the Sacred books of the Hindus. English and Sanskrit; introd. in English. An adaptation and abridgement of the Garudapurana, "done for the helping of those who cannot understand the difficult earlier works." [BL1135.P73N3813] 73-3796 ISBN 0-404-57809-8
I. Wood, Ernest, 1883-1965, ed. II. Subrahmanyam, S. V., ed. III. Puranas. Garudapurana. IV. Title. V. Series: The Sacred books of the Hindus, v. 9.

PURANAS, Bhagavata purana 294.5925
Srimad Bhagwatam; pts. 1-3 With short life sketch of Lord Sri Chaitanya Mahaprabhu. the ideal preacher of Bhagwat dharma, original Sanskrit text, its Roman transliteration, English synonyms, English tr. and elaborate purport by A. C. Bhaktivedanta Swami. Delhi. League of Devotee [New York, Paragon, 1965] 3v. (various p.) 25cm. [BL1135.P7A22] SA64 18.00 set.,
1. Chaitanya, 1486-1534 I. Bhaktivedanta Swami, A. C., ed. II. Title.

PURANAS. 294.5'925
Bhagavatapurana. English & Sanskrit. Selections.
The Bhakti-ratnavali, with the commentary of Visnu Puri. Translated by a professor of Sanskrit (retired). Allahabad, Panini Office, 1912. [New York, AMS Press, 1974] x, viii, 153, vi, 4 p. 23 cm. Original ed. issued as v. 7, pt. 3 of The Sacred books of the Hindus. Includes the Bhaktiratnavali, a compilation of selections from the Bhagavatapurana, by Visnupuri, and his commentary, the Kantimala. Constitutes pt. 3 of the Bhakti sastra; the other treatise in the 2 v. set, the Naradasutra, appeared in 1911 as v. 7, pts. 1-2 of the series. [BL1135.P7A2 1974] 73-3794 ISBN 0-404-57835-7 20.00
I. A professor of Sanskrit (retired), ed. II. Visnupuri, fl. 1485. Bhaktiratnavali. English & Sanskrit. 1974. III. Visnupuri, fl. 1485. Kantimala. English & Sanskrit. 1974. IV. Title. V. Series: The Sacred books of the Hindus, v. 7, pt. 3.

PURANAS. 294.5'925
Brahmandapurana. Adhyatmaramayana. English.
The Adhyatma Ramayana / translated by Lala Baij Nath. New York : AMS Press, [1974] v, ii, 227 p. ; 23 cm. Reprint of the 1913 ed. published by the Panini Office, Allahabad, which was issued as extra v. 1 of The Sacred books of the Hindus. Includes some slokas in Sanskrit. [BL1135.P715A23 1974] 73-3828 ISBN 0-404-57846-2 : 20.00
I. Baij Nath, Lala, tr. II. Title. III. Series: The Sacred books of the Hindus ; extra v. 1.

PURANAS. 294.5'925
Brahmavaivartapurana. English.
The Brahma-vaivarta puranam. Translated into English by Rajendra Nath Sen. Allahabad, Panini Office, 1920-22. [New York, AMS Press, 1974] p. cm. Original ed. issued as v. 24, pts. 1-4 of The Sacred books of the Hindus. Contents.Contents.—pt. 1. Brahma and Prakriti khandas.—pt. 2. Ganesa and Krisna janma khandas. [BL1135.P717A36] 73-3817 ISBN 0-404-57824-1 57.50 (2 vol. set.)
I. Sen, Rajendra Nath, tr. II. Title. III. Series: The Sacred books of the Hindus, v. 24.

PURANAS. 294.5'925
Devibhagavatapurana. English
The Sri Mad Devi Bhagavatam. Translated by Swami Vijnanananda, alias Hari Prasanna Chatterji. Allahabad, Panini Office, 1921-23. [New York, AMS Press, 1974] p. cm. Original ed. issued as v. 26, pts. 1-4, of The Sacred books of the Hindus. Parts 2 and 4 have title: The Srimad Devi Bhagavatam; pt. 3 has title: The Devi Bhagavatam. [BL1135.P72A36 1974] 73-3819 ISBN 0-404-57826-8
I. Vijnanananda, Swami, 1868-1938, ed. II. Title. III. Title: The Srimad Devi Bhagavatam. IV. Title: The Devi Bhagavatam. V. Series: The Sacred books of the Hindus, v. 26, pts. 1-4.

PURANAS. 294.5'925
Matsyapurana. English.
The Matsya puranam. Translated by a taluqdar of Oudh. Allahabad, Panini Office, 1917. [New York, AMS Press, 1974] p. cm. Original ed. issued as v. 17, pts. 1-2, of The Sacred books of the Hindus. "Most of the appendices are from the pen of my brother, Rai Bahadur Srisa Chandra Vidyarnava." Includes some slokas in Sanskrit. [BL1135.P773E5 1974] 73-3808 ISBN 0-404-57817-9 57.50
I. A taluqdar of Oudh, tr. II. Vasu, Srisa Chandra, rai bahadur, 1861-1918? III. Title. IV. Series: The Sacred books of the Hindus, v. 17, pts. 1-2.

DERRETT, John Duncan Martin, 1922- 294.5'94
Essays in classical and modern Hindu law / by J. Duncan M. Derrett. Leiden : Brill, 1976- v. ; 25 cm. Contents.Contents.—v. 1. Dharmasastra and related ideas. Includes bibliographical references and indexes. [LAW] 76-372759 ISBN 9-00-404475-2 (v. 1) : fl 96.00 (v. 1)
1. Hindu law—Addresses, essays, lectures. I. Title.

LINGAT, Robert. 294.5'94
The classical law of India. Translated from the French with additions by J. Duncan M. Derrett. Berkeley, University of California Press [1973] xviii, 305 p. port. 24 cm. Translation of Les sources du droit dans le systeme traditionnel de l'Inde. "Sponsored by the Center for South and Southeast Asia Studies, University of California, Berkeley." Bibliography: p. 275-282. [LAW] 76-81798 ISBN 0-520-01898-2
1. Dharma. 2. Hindu law—Sources. I. California. University. Center for South and Southeast Asia Studies. II. Title.

VIDYASAGAR, Iswar Chandra, 1820-1891. 294.5'94
Marriage of Hindu widows / Isvarachandra Vidyasagara ; with an introd. by Arabinda Podder. Calcutta : K. P. Bagchi, 1976. xvi, ii, 144 p. ; 23 cm. Includes bibliographical references. [LAW] 76-900930 ISBN 0-88386-738-9 : 8.00
1. Remarriage (Hindu law) 2. Widows (Hindu law) I. Title.
Distributed by South Asia Books

YAJNAVALKYA. 294.5'94
Yajnavalkya Smriti, with the commentary of Vijnanesvara, called the Mitaksara and notes from the gloss of Balambhatta. Book I: The Achara adhyaya. Translated by Srisa Chandra Vidyarnava. Allahabad, Panini Office, 1918. [New York, AMS Press, 1974] xix, [1], 440 p. 23 cm. Original ed. issued as v. 21 of The Sacred books of the Hindus. The Sanskrit text and English translation of the first 50 slokas of the work appeared in 1909 as v. 2, pt. 1 of the series. "In the preparation of this translation I was greatly assisted by ... Sarayu Prasad Misra." Notes from the gloss of Vaidyanatha Payagunde omitted from chapters 5-9. Bibliography: p. [xx] [LAW] 73-3813 ISBN 0-404-57821-7
1. Hindu law. 2. Inheritance and succession—India. I. Vasu, Srisa Chandra, rai bahadur, 1861-1918?, ed. II. Misra, Sarayu Prasad, tr. III. Vijnanesvara, 11th cent. Mitaksara. English. 1974. IV. Vaidyanatha Payagunde. Balambhatti. English. 1974. V. Title: Smriti. VI. Series: The Sacred books of the Hindus, v. 21.

YAJNAVALKYA. 294.5'94
Yajnavalkya's Smriti, with the commentary of Vijnanesvara, called the Mitaksara, and the gloss of Balambhatta. Part I: The sources of Hindu law and the duties of a student. Translated by Srisa Chandra Vasu. Allahabad, Panini Office, 1909. [New York, AMS Press, 1974] vi, ii, 104, ii, ii p. 23 cm. Original ed. issued as v. 2, pt. 1 of The Sacred books of the Hindus. No more published. Includes the first 50 slokas of the Yajnavalkyasmrti. An English translation of one section of the work, the Acaradhyaya, appeared in 1918 as v. 21 of the series. English and Sanskrit; introductory matter in English. [LAW] 73-3787 ISBN 0-404-57802-0
1. Hindu law. I. Vasu, Srisa Chandra, rai bahadur, 1861-1918?, ed. II. Vijnanesvara, 11th cent. Mitaksara. English & Sanskrit. 1974. III. Vaidyanatha Payagunde. Balambhatti. English & Sanskrit. 1974. IV. Title: Smriti. V. Title: The sources of Hindu law and the duties of a student. VI. Series: The Sacred books of the Hindus, v. 2.

KRISHNAMURTI, Jiddu, 1895- 294.598
Life ahead. Edited by D. Rajagopal. New York, Harper & Row [1963] 191 p. 22 cm. [BJ1581.1.K75] 63-16403
1. Conduct of life. 2. Sociology, Hindu. 3. Hinduism. I. Title.

MCLEOD W H 294.6
The evolution of the Sikh community : five essays / W. H. McLeod. Delhi : Oxford University Press, 1975[i.e.1976] viii, 118 p. ; 22 cm. Includes index. Bibliography: p. [111]-114. [BL2018.M317] 76-900871 8.00
1. Sikhism—Addresses, essays, lectures. I. Title.
Distributed by Oxford, New York.

MCLEOD, W. H. 294.6'0954'552
The evolution of the Sikh community : five essays / W. H. McLeod. Oxford : Clarendon Press, 1976. viii, 119 p. ; 23 cm. Includes index. Bibliography: p. [111]-114. [DS432.S5M25] 76-369262 ISBN 0-19-826529-8 : 8.75
1. Sikhs—Addresses, essays, lectures. 2. Sikhism—Addresses, essays, lectures. I. Title.
Distributed by Oxford University Press N.Y. N.Y.

ARCHER, John Clark, 1881-1957. 294.6'172
The Sikhs in relation to Hindus, Moslems, Christians, and Ahmadiyyas; a study in comparative religion. New York, Russell & Russell [1971, c1946] xi, 353 p. illus. 23 cm. Includes bibliographical references. [BL2018.15.A72 1971] 76-139895
1. Sikhism. 2. India—Religion. I. Title.

JOHAR, Surinder Singh. 294.6'3'5
The Sikh gurus and their shrines / Surinder Singh Johar. Delhi : Vivek Pub. Co., 1976. viii, 328, p., [8] leaves of plates : ill. ; 23 cm. Includes index. Bibliography: p. [309]-313. [BL2018.36.A1J63] 76-905134 Rs65.00
1. Sikh shrines. 2. Sikhism. I. Title.

JANJUA, Harbhajan Singh. 294.6'3'502541
Sikh temples in the U.K. & the people behind their management / [by Harbhajan Singh Janjua]. London : Jan Publications, 1976. vi, 106 p. : ill., ports. ; 23 cm. [BL2018.36.G7J36] 76-373636 ISBN 0-905454-00-6 : £2.50
1. Temples, Sikh—Great Britain. I. Title.

YOGIJI, Harbhajan Singh Khalsa. 294.6'4'3
The teachings of Yogi Bhajan / Siri Singh Sahib Bhai Sahib Harbhajan Singh Khalsa Yogiji. New York : Hawthorn Books, c1977. ix, 193 p. ; 21 cm. [BL2018.42.Y63 1977] 76-56526 ISBN 0-8015-7461-7 pbk. : 5.95
1. Sikh devotional literature. I. Title.

KIRPAL Singh, 1894-1974. 294.6'4'4
The night is a jungle, and other discourses of Kirpal Singh. 1st ed. Tilton, N.H. : Sant Bani Press, 1975. xiii, 358 p. : ports. ; 21 cm. "The discourses, except the first four ... are translations from the Hindi." "Originally published in the monthly magazine Sat sandesh ... October 1969 ... April 1971." Contents.Contents.—Introduction.—God and man.—The higher values of life.—The kingdom of God.—The most natural way.—Guru, gurudev, and satguru.—Let us reform ourselves.—Oh mind! Listen for once.—Thief of your life's breath.—Chastity and forgiveness.—Change your habits now.—Gurubhakti: a lesson in love.—To gain His pleasure.—Protector and protection.—The night is a jungle. [BL2018.37.K6 1975] 75-9244
1. Religious life (Sikhism) I. Sat sandesh. II. Title.

GERU Tegh Bahadur : 294.6'61 B
background and the supreme sacrifice : a collection of research articles / edited by Gurbachan Singh Talib. Patiala : Punjabi University, 1976. xvi, 250 p. ; 25 cm. (Guru Tegh Bahadur's martyrdom tercentenary memorial series) Includes bibliographical references. [BL2017.9.T4G86] 77-900595 Rs30.00
1. Tegh Bahadur, 9th guru of the Sikhs, 1621-1675—Addresses, essays, lectures. 2. Sikh gurus—Biography—Addresses, Essays, lectures. 3. Sikhism—Addresses essays, lectures. I. Talib, Gurbachan Singh, 1911- II. Series: Guru Tegh Bahadara tiji shahidi shatabadi prakashana lari.

JOHAR, Surinder Singh. 294.6'61
Guru Tegh Bahadur : a biography / Surinder Singh Johar. New Delhi : Abhinav Publications, 1976 262 p., [1] leaf of plates : ill. ; 22 cm. Includes index. Bibliography: p. 245-249. [BL2017.9.T4J64] 75-908901 11.50
1. Tegh Bahadur, 9th guru of the Sikhs, 1621-1675. 2. Sikh gurus—Biography. I. Title.
Distributed by South Asia Books Columbia, Mo.

GUPTA, Hari Ram. 294.6'6'10922 B
History of Sikh gurus. New Delhi, U. C. Kapur [1973] xiv, 320 p. maps. 22 cm. Includes bibliographical references. [BL2017.8.G87] 73-906123
1. Sikh gurus—Biography. 2. Sikhism—History. I. Title.
Distributed by South Asia Books; 8.50

KIRPAL Singh, 1894-1974. 294.6'6'3 B
Kirpal Singh : a visual biography / compiled by Robert Leverant ; [photos., Malcolm Tillis et al.]. [Berkeley, Calif. : Images Press, c1974] 47 p. : ill. ; 17 cm. "Text from talks in San Jose, San Francisco & Dallas by Kirpal Singh in November 1972 & Morning talks." Bibliography: p. 47. [BL624.K57] 74-24723 ISBN 0-9600374-3-8 : 2.95
1. Kirpal Singh, 1894-1974. 2. Meditations.

KOHLI, Surindar Singh, 1920- 294.6'8'2
A critical study of Adi Granth, being a comprehensive and scientific study of Guru Granth Sahib, the scripture of the Sikhs / Surindar Singh Kohli. [2d ed.]. Delhi : Motilal Banarsidass, 1976. xxii, 391 p. ; 22 cm. Includes selections in Gurumukhi script. Originally presented as the author's thesis, University of Delhi. Includes index. Bibliography: p. 373-380. [BL2017.45.K63 1976] 76-901503 15.00
1. Adi-Granth—Criticism, interpretation, etc. I. Title.
Distributed by Verry

295 Zoroastrianism

CARTER, George William, 1867-1930. 295
Zoroastrianism and Judaism. With an introd. by Charles Gray Shaw. New York, AMS Press [1970] 116 p. 23 cm. Reprint of the 1918 ed. Bibliography: p. 107-114. [BL1566.J8C3 1970] 70-112489
1. Zoroastrianism—Relations—Judaism. 2. Judaism—Relations—Zoroastrianism.

CUMONT, Franz Valery Marie, 1868--1947. 295
The Mysteries of Mithra; translated from the 2d rev. French ed. by Thomas J. McCormack. New York, Dover Publications [1956] xiv, 239p. illus., fold. map. 21cm. Bibliographical footnotes. [BL1585.C83 1956] 57-3150
1. Mithraism. 2. Rome—Religion. I. Title.

CUMONT, Franz Valery Marie, 1868-1947 295
The mysteries of Mithra; tr. from the 2d rev. French ed. by Thomas J. McCormack [Gloucester, Mass., Peter Smith, 1962] 239p. illus. (Dover bk. rebound) 3.85
1. Mithraism. 2. Rome—Religion. I. Title.

DAWSON, Miles Menander, 1863-1942. 295
The ethical religion of Zoroaster; an account of what Zoroaster taught, as perhaps the very oldest and surely the most accurate code of ethics for man, accompanied by the essentials of his religion. New York, AMS Press [1969] xxvii, 271 p. 23 cm. Reprint of the 1931 ed. Bibliography: p. xvii-xix. [BL1570.D3 1969] 73-90100
1. Zoroastrianism. I. Avesta. Selections. English. 1969. II. Title.

DHALLA, Maneckji Nusservanji, 1875- 295
Zoroastrian theology from the earliest times to the present day. [New York, AMS Press, 1972] xxxii, 384 p. 23 cm. Bibliography: p. xxi-xxvi. [BL1571.D45 1972] 70-131038 ISBN 0-404-02123-9 17.50
1. Zoroastrianism. I. Title.

DHALLA, Maneckji Nusservanji, 1875-1956. 295
History of Zoroastrianism / by Maneckji Nusservanji Dhalla. New York : AMS Press, [1977, c1938] p. cm. Reprint of the ed. published by Oxford University Press, New York. Includes index. Bibliography: p. [BL1570.D5 1977] 74-21256 ISBN 0-404-12806-8 : 30.00
1. Zoroastrianism. I. Title.

DUCHESNE-GUILLEMIN, Jacques. 295
Symbols and values in Zoroastrianism, their survival and renewal. [1st ed.] New York, Harper and Row [1966] xvii, 167 p. plates. 22 cm. (Religious perspectives, v. 15) [BL1571.D8] 66-10234
1. Zoroastrianism. I. Title. II. Series.

DUCHESNE-GUILLEMIN, Jacques 295
Symbols and values in Zoroastrianism, their survival and renewal. New York, Harper [c.1966] xvii, 167p. plates. 22cm. (Religious perspectives, v.15) [BL1571.D8] 66-10234 5.00
1. Zoroastrianism. I. Title. II. Series.

DUCHESNE-GUILLEMIN, Jacques. 295
The Western response to Zoroaster, by J. Duchesne-Guillemin. Westport, Conn., Greenwood Press [1973, c1958] 112 p. 22 cm. Original ed. issued in series: Ratanbai Katrak lectures, 1956. Bibliography: p. [105]-112. [BL1571.D83 1973] 72-9593 ISBN 0-8371-6590-3
1. Zoroastrianism. I. Title. II. Series: Oxford. University. Ratanbai Katrak lectures, 1956.

DUCHESNE-GUILLEMIN, Jacques. 295
The Western response to Zoroaster, by J. Duchesne-Guillemin. Westport, Conn., Greenwood Press [1973, c1958] 112 p. 22 cm. Original ed. issued in series: Ratanbai Katrak lectures, 1956. Bibliography: p. [105]-112. [BL1571.D83 1973] 72-9593 ISBN 0-8371-6590-3 7.75
1. Zoroastrianism. I. Title. II. Series: Oxford. University. Ratanbai Katrak lectures, 1956.

INTERNATIONAL Congress on Mithraic Studies, 1st, Manchester University, 1971. 295
Mithraic studies; proceedings. John R. Hinnells, editor. [Manchester, Eng.] Manchester University Press. [Totowa, N.J.] Rowman and Littlefield [1974- p. cm. Includes bibliographical references. [BL1585.I57 1971] 74-7310 ISBN 0-87471-557-1 49.50 (2 v.).
1. Mithraism—Congresses. I. Hinnells, John R., ed. II. Title.

MASANI, Rustom Pestonji, Sir 1876- 295
Zoroastrianism: the religion of the good life. Foreword by John McKenzie. New York, Collier [1962] 126p. 18cm. First pub. in 1938 under title: The religion of the good life, Zoroastrianism. (AS 477v) 63-345 .95 pap.,
1. Zorastrianism. I. Title.

THE "Mithras liturgy" / 295
edited and translated by Marvin W. Meyer. Missoula, Mont. : Published by Scholars Press for the Society of Biblical Literature, c1976. x, 27 p. ; 24 cm. (Texts and translations - Society of Biblical Literature ; 10) (Graeco-Roman religion series ; 2) Text in English and Greek. "Part of the ... codex of Paris (Papyrus 574 of the Bibliotheque nationale) .... Lines 475-834." Bibliography: p. x. [BL1585.M47] 76-18288 ISBN 0-89130-113-5 : 2.80
1. Mithraism. I. Meyer, Marvin W. II. Title. III. Series. IV. Series: Society of Biblical Literature. Texts and translations ; 10.

MOULTON, James Hope, 1863-1917. 295
The treasure of the Magi; a study of Zoroastrianism. London, New York, H. Milford, 1917. [New York, AMS Press, 1972] xiii, 273 p. port. 23 cm. Original ed. issued in series: The Religious quest of India. [BL1570.M67 1972] 73-173004 ISBN 0-404-04508-1
1. Zoroastrianism. 2. Parsees. I. Title.

SZEKELY, Edmond Bordeaux. 295
The world picture of Zarathustra. Tecate, Calif., Essene School [1954, c1953] 6v. (in portfollo) illus. 34x36cm. Inside front cover of portfolio forms board for game of Asha. 32 markers in pocket. Contents.book 1. aAvesta. English. [BL1555.S9] 54-26092
I. Title.

WYNNE-TYSON, Esme, 1898- 295
Mithras; the fellow in the cap. New York, Barnes & Noble [1972, c1958] 227 p. 23 cm. Bibliography: p. 220. [BL1585.W94 1972] 72-190298 ISBN 0-389-04438-5
1. Mithraism. I. Title.

ZAEHNER, Robert Charles. 295
The dawn and twilight of Zoroastrianism. [1st American ed.] New York, Putnam [1961] 371 p. illus. 24 cm. (The Putnam history of religion) Includes bibliography. [BL571.Z3 1961] 61-8353
1. Zoroastrianism. I. Title.

ZAEHNER, Robert Charles. 295
The teachings of the magi; a compendium of Zoroastrian beliefs. London, Allen & Unwin; New York, Macmillan [1956] 156p. 19cm. (Ethical and religious classics of East and West, no. 14) [BL1570.Z3] 56-3626
1. Zoroastrianism. I. Title.

ZAEHNER, Robert Charles. 295
The teachings of the magi; a compendium of Zoroastrian beliefs. London, Allen & Unwin; New York, Macmillan [1956] 156 p. 19 cm. (Ethical and religious classics of East and West, no. 14) [BL1570.Z3] 56-3626
1. Zoroastrianism. I. Title.

ZAEHNER, Robert Charles. 295
Zurvan; a Zoroastrian dilemma, by R. C. Zaehner. With a new introd. by the author. New York, Biblo and Tannen, [1973 c.1972] xvi, 495 p. 24 cm. Reprint of the 1955 ed. Bibliography: p. [453]-458. [BL1571.Z33 1972] 72-7389 ISBN 0-8196-0280-9 17.50
1. Zoroastrianism. I. Title.

GEIGER, Wilhelm, 1856-1943. 295'.09
Zarathushtra in the Gathas, and in the Greek and Roman classics / translated from the German of Drs. Geiger and Windischmann, with notes on M. J. Darmester's theory regarding Tansar's letter to the King of Tabaristan, and the date of the Avesta, with an appendix on the alleged practice of consanguineous marriages in ancient Iran, by Darab Dastur Peshotan Sanjana. 2d ed. New York : AMS Press, 1977. 307 p. in various pagings ; 23 cm. Translation of Zarathushtra in den Gathas. Reprint of the 1899 ed. published by O. Harrassowitz, Leipzig. Includes bibliographical references. [BL1525.G4313 1977] 74-21260 ISBN 0-404-12810-6 : 24.50
1. Zoroastrianism—History. 2. Zoroaster. 3. Avesta—Criticism, interpretation, etc. I. Windischmann, Friedrich Heinrich Hugo, 1811-1861, joint author. II. Sanjana, Darab dastur Peshotan, 1857-1931. III. Title.

GEIGER, Wilhelm, 1856-1943. 295'.09
Zarathushtra in the Gathas, and in the Greek and Roman classics / translated from the German of Drs. Geiger and Windischmann, with notes on M. J. Darmester's theory regarding Tansar's letter to the King of Tabaristan, and the date of the Avesta, with an appendix on the alleged practice of consanguineous marriages in ancient Iran, by Darab Dastur Peshotan Sanjana. 2d ed. New York : AMS Press, 1977. 307 p. in various pagings ; 23 cm. Translation of Zarathushtra in den Gathas. Reprint of the 1899 ed. published by O. Harrassowitz, Leipzig. Includes bibliographical references. [BL1525.G4313 1977] 74-21260 ISBN 0-404-12810-6 : 24.50
1. Zoroastrianism—History. 2. Zoroaster. 3. Avesta—Criticism, interpretation, etc. I. Windischmann, Friedrich Heinrich Hugo, 1811-1861, joint author. II. Sanjana, Darab dastur Peshotan, 1857-1931. III. Title.

BIDEZ, Joseph, 1867-1945. 295'.1'3
Les mages hellenises, Zoroastre, Ostanes et Hystaspe d'apres la tradition grecque / Joseph Bidez and Franz Cumont. New York : Arno Press, 1975. xi, 297, 409 p. ; 23 cm. (Ancient religion and mythology) Reprint of the 1938 ed. published by Societe d'editions "Les Belles lettres," Paris. Includes bibliographical references and indexes. [BL1550.B58 1975] 75-10629 ISBN 0-405-07005-5
1. Hystaspes, King. 2. Zoroaster. 3. Osthanes. 4. Iran—Religion. 5. Greece—Civilization. I. Cumont, Franz Valery Marie, 1868-1947, joint author. II. Title. III. Series.

HINNELLS, John R. 295'.1'3
Persian mythology / [by] John R. Hinnells. London ; New York : Hamlyn, 1973. 2-143 p. : ill., (some col.), map, ports. ; 29 cm. Includes index. Bibliography: p. 138-139. [BL2270.H56] 74-193695 ISBN 0-600-03090-3 : £1.95
1. Mythology, Iranian. 2. Zoroastrianism. I. Title.

LAEUCHLI, Samuel 295'.2 11
Mithraism in Ostia; mystery religion and Christianity in the ancient port of Rome [by] Dennis Groh [others] Ed. by Samuel Laeuchli. Pref. by Giovanni Becatti. [Evanston, Ill.] Northwestern Univ. Pr. [1967] xii, 116p. illus., map. 24cm. (Garrett theol. studies, no. 1) Bibl. [BL1585.L28] 67-20690 5.00
1. Mithraism. 2. Ostia, Italy—Antiq. I. Groh, Dennis. II. Title. III. Series.

VERMASEREN, Maarten Jozef 295.211
**mithras,* the secret god. [Tr. by Therese and Vincent Megaw] New York, Barnes & Noble [c.1963] 200p. illus. 21cm. Bibl. 63-5861 4.50
1. Mithraism. I. Title.

MILLS, Lawrence Heyworth, 1837-1918. 295'.2'3
Avesta eschatology compared with the books of Daniel and Revelations : being supplementary to Zarathushtra, Philo, the Achaemenids, and Israel / by Lawrence H. Mills. [New York : AMS Press, 1977] c1908. vii, 85 p. : port. ; 22 cm. Reprint of the ed. published by Open Court Pub. Co., Chicago. Includes bibliographies references. [BL1515.4.M53 1977] 74-24644 ISBN 0-404-12816-5 : 9.00
1. Zoroastrianism. 2. Eschatology. 3. Judaism—Relations—Zoroastrianism. 4. Christianity and other religions—Zoroastrianism. 5. Christianity and other religions—Judaism. 6. Zoroastrianism—Relations—Christianity. I. Title.

AVESTA. Yasna. Gathas. English. 295'.63 B
The life of Zoroaster in the words of his own hymns, the Gathas, according to both documents, the priestly, and the personal, on parallel pages, (a new discovery in higher criticism) Translated by Kenneth Sylvan Guthrie. Brooklyn, Comparative Literature Press. [New York, AMS Press, 1972] 125 p. 19 cm. [BL1515.A35 1972] 73-131036 ISBN 0-404-02964-7 9.50
1. Zoroaster. I. Guthrie, Kenneth Sylvan, 1871-1940, tr. II. Title.

HERZFELD, Ernst Emil, 1879-1948. 295'.63 B
Zoroaster and his world. New York, Octagon Books, 1974 [c1947] 2 v. (xvii, 851 p.) 24 cm. Reprint of the ed. published by Princeton University Press, Princeton, N.J. Includes bibliographical references. [BL1555.H4 1974] 74-6219 ISBN 0-374-93877-6
1. Zoroaster. 2. Zoroastrianism. I. Title.

AVESTA. English. 295'.8
Avesta: the religious books of the Parsees; from Professor Spiegel's German translation of the original manuscripts. By Arthur Henry Bleeck. New York, Gordon Press, 1974. xx, 214 p. 24 cm. Reprint of the 1864 ed. printed for M. H. Cama by S. Austin, Hertford, Eng. Bibliography: p. [209]-211. [BL1515.A22 1974] 74-2843 ISBN 0-87968-133-0 29.95 (lib. bdg.)
I. Bleeck, Arthur Henry, 1827?-1877, tr. II. Spiegel, Friedrich von, 1820-1905, tr.

AVESTA. English. 1972. 295'.8'2
The Zend-Avesta. Translated by James Darmesteter. Westport, Conn., Greenwood Press [1972] 3 v. 23 cm. Reprint of the 1880-87 ed., which was issued as v. 4, 23, and 31 of The Sacred books of the East. Contents.Contents.—v. 1. The Vendidad.—v. 2. The Sirozahs, Yasts, and Nyayis.—v. 3. The Yasna, Visparad, Afrinagan, Gahs, and miscellaneous fragments, translated by L. H. Mills. [BL1515.A22 1972] 68-30997 ISBN 0-8371-3070-0
I. Darmesteter, James, 1849-1894, tr. II. Mills, Lawrence Heyworth, 1837-1918, tr. III. Title. IV. Series: The Sacred books of the East (New York) v. 4 [etc.]

AVESTA. YASHTS. 295.82
The Avestan hymn to Mithra; with an introd., translation, and commentary by Ilya Gershevitch. Cambridge [Eng.] University Press, 1959. xiv, 356p. 23cm. (University of Cambridge. Oriental publications, no. 4) Includes the Iranian text, transilterated, of Yast X. 'Karl F. Geldner's critical Apparatus to Yast X : p. 303-318. [PK6113.D 1959] 59-16271
I. Avesta. Yashts. English. II. Gershevitch, Ilya, ed. and tr. III. Geldner, Karl Friedrich, 1853-1929. IV. Title. V. Series: Cambridge. University. Oriental publications, no. 4

AVESTA. Yasna. English. 295'.8'2
Yashts in Roman script with translation / by Tehmurasp Rustamji Sethna. Karachi : Sethna, 1976. ii, 477 p. ; 22 cm. [BL1515.A22 1976] 76-930196 Rs20.00
I. Sethna, T. R. II. Title.

AVESTA. Yasna. Gathas. English & Avesta. 295'.8'2
The divine songs of Zarathushtra : a philological study of the Gathas of Zarathushtra, containing the text with literal translation into English, a free English rendering, and full critical and grammatical notes, metrical index, and glossary / Irach J. S. Taraporewala. New York : AMS Press, 1977. xlii, 1166 p. ; 23 cm. Reprint of the 1951 ed. published by D. B. Taraporevala Sons, Bombay. Includes index. Bibliography: p. 1160-1166. [BL1515.5.Y3A43 1977] 74-21251 ISBN 0-404-12802-5 : 125.00
I. Taraporewala, Irach Jehangir Sorabji, 1884-1956. II. Title.

AVESTA. Yasna. Gathas. English & Avesta. 295'.8'2
The gathas of Zarathushtra : text / with a free English translation by Irach J. S. Taraporewala. New York : AMS Press, [1977] xviii, 307 p. : port. ; 19 cm. Avesta text in romanized transcription. Reprint of the 1947 ed. published by the translator, Bombay. [BL1515.5.Y3A43 1977b] 74-21250 ISBN 0-404-12801-7 : 17.50
I. Taraporewala, Irach Jehangir Sorabji, 1884-1956. II. Title.

AVESTA. Yasna. Gathas. Polyglot. 295'.8'2
A study of the five Zarathushtrian (Zoroastrian) Gathas : with texts and translations, also with the Pahlavi translation for the first time edited with collation of manuscripts, and now prepared from all the known codices, also deciphered, and for the first time translated in its entirety into a European language, with Neryosangh's Sanskrit text edited with the collation of five MSS., and with a first translation, also with the Persian text contained in Codex 12b of the Munich collection edited in transliteration, together with a commentary, being the literary apparatus and argument to the translation of the Gathas in the XXXIst volume of the Sacred books of the East / by Lawrence H. Mills. New York : AMS Press, [1977] p. cm. Reprint of the 1894 ed. published by L. Mills, Oxford, available from F. A. Brockhaus, Leipsic, which was published with the assistance of the Secretary of State for India in Council and the Trustees of the Parsi Panchayet Translation Funa of Bombay. [BL1515.2.Y3A4 1977] 74-21252 ISBN 0-404-12803-3 : 57.50
I. Mills, Lawrence Heyworth, 1837-1918. II. Title.

DASATIR. English. 295'.82
The Desatir: or, The sacred writings of the ancient Persian prophets, together with the commentary of the fifth Sasan / translated by Mulla Firuz Bin Kaus ; edited and republished by Dhunjeebhoy Jamsetjee Medhora. Minneapolis : Wizards Bookshelf, 1975. ii, 13, 190 p. ; 23 cm. (Secret doctrine reference series) "Photographic copy of the 1888 edition." [BL2270.D3513 1888b] 73-84045 ISBN 0-913510-08-4 : 7.00
1. Iran—Religion—History—Sources. I. Firuz ibn Kavus, d. 1826 or 7. II. Medhora, Dhunjeebhoy Jamsetjee.

MILLS, Lawrence Heyworth, 1837-1918. 295.8'2
Our own religion in ancient Persia : being lectures delivered in Oxford presenting the Zend Avesta as collated with the pre-Christian exilic pharisaism, advancing the Persian question to the foremost position in our Biblical research / by Lawrence Mills. New York : AMS Press, 1977. xii, 193 p. ; 23 cm. Reprint of the 1913 ed. published by F. A. Brockhaus, Leipzig. [BL1515.5.M55 1977] 74-21262 ISBN 0-404-12811-4 : 45.00
1. Avesta—Addresses, essays, lectures. 2. Zoroastrianism—Relations—Christianity—Addresses, essays, lectures. 3. Christianity and other religions—Zoroastrianism—Addresses, essays, lectures. 4. Judaism—Relations—Zoroastrianism—Addresses, essays, lectures. 5.

Zoroastrianism—Relations—Judaism—Addresses, essays, lectures. I. Title.

MILLS, Lawrence 295'.8'2
Heyworth, 1837-1918.
Zara[theta]ustra, Philo, the Achaemenids, and Israel : being a treatise upon the antiquity and influence of the Avesta / for the most part delivered as university lectures by Lawrence H. Mills. New York : AMS Press, [1977] xiii, 460 p. ; 23 cm. Reprint of the 1903-1906 ed. published by F. A. Brockhaus, Leipzig. [BL1570.M5 1977] 74-21261 ISBN 0-404-12815-7 : 18.50
1. Avesta. 2. Zoroastrianism—Relations—Judaism. 3. Logos. 4. Judaism—Relations—Zoroastrianism. I. Title.
Contents omitted

296 Judaism

ABOTH. 1945. 296
Sayings of the Fathers; or, Pirke Aboth; the Hebrew text, with a new English translation and a commentary by Joseph H. Hertz. With a new collection of favourite moral sayings of the Jewish Fathers, and a foreword to this edition by Moses Schonfeld. New York, Behrman House [1945] 128 p. 21 cm. Vocalized. "Reprinted from the Chief Rabbi's edition of the Authorized daily prayer book." [BM506.A23H47] HE67
1. Aboth, English. I. Hertz, Joseph Herman, 1872-1946. II. Title. III. Title: Title romanized: Pirke avot.

ABOTH. 1962. 296
Ethics of the fathers. Translated and annotated by Hyman Goldin. New York, Hebrew Pub. Co. [1962] xiii, 144 p. 26 cm. "Bibliography and glossary": p. 108-113. [BM506.A23G59] 64-43262
1. Aboth — Commentaries. I. Aboth. English. 1962 II. Goldin, Hyman Elias, 1881- ed. and tr. III. Title.

ABOTH. 1962 296
Ethics of the fathers. Translated and arr. by Ben Zion Bokser. New York, Hebrew Pub. Co. [1962] 63 p. 22 cm. "The text and translation of this edition ... is reprinted from The prayer book, translated and arranged by Ben Zion Bokser ... The introductory essay ... is reprinted ... from the volume Great expressions of human rights, edited by R. M. MacIver, and published ... in 1950." [BM506.A2E5 1962] 64-33238
I. Aboth. English. 1962. II. Bokser, Ben Zion, 1907- ed. and tr. III. Title.

ABOTH. 1962. 296
Pirke Aboth. The ethics of the Talmud: Sayings of the Fathers. Edited with introd., translation and commentary by R. Travers Herford. Pref. by John J. Tepfer. New York, Schocken Books [1962] ix, 177 p. 21 cm. (Schocken paperbacks, SB23) Title on half-title and spine: Sayings of the Fathers. [BM506.A23H43 1962] 62-13138
1. Aboth—Commentaries. I. Aboth. English. 1962. II. Herford, Robert Travers, 1860-1950, ed. and tr. III. Title: Sayings of the Fathers.

ABRAHAMS, Israel. 1858-1925. 296
Jewish life in the Middle Ages. New York, Meridian Books and the Jewish Publication Society of America, Philadelphia [1958] xxvi, 452p. 21cm. (Jewish publication series, JP4) Bibliography: p. 431-436. [DS112.A15 1958] 58-11933
1. Jews Soc. life cust. 2. Judaism—Hist.—,medieval and early modern period. I. Title.

ACKERMAN, Nathan Ward, 1908- 296
Anti-Semitism and emotional disorder, a psychoanalytic interpretation by Nathan W. Ackerman and Marie Jahoda. [1st ed.] New York, Harper [1950] xiv, 135 p. 25 cm. (Studies in prejudice) Bibliography: p. 131-132. [DS145.A52] 50-5672
1. Antisemltism. I. Jahoda, Marie. joint author. II. Title. III. Series.

ADAM, Yehudi. 296
Mature Judaism; a programmatic outline. [1st ed.] Jericho, N.Y., Exposition Press [1974] ix, 73 p. 22 cm. [BM565.A36] 74-76018 ISBN 0-682-47965-9 5.00
1. Judaism. I. Title.

AGUS, Irving, Abraham, 1910- 296
Rabbi Meir of Rothenburg, his life and his works and sources for the religious, legal, and social history of the Jews of Germany in the thirteenth century, by Irving A. Agus. Philadelphia, Dropsie College for Hebrew and Cognate Learning, 1947. 2v.(xxxxiii, 749 p.) 24 cm. Bibliography: v 2. p. 703 719. [BM522.62.B34A4] 48-96
1. Meir ben Baruch, of Rothenburg, d 1298. 2. Responsa. 3. Jews in Germany. I. Title.

AGUS, Jacob Bernard 296
The evolution of Jewish thought: from Biblical times to the opening of the modern era. New York, Abelard-Schuman 1960[c.1959] 442p. Includes bibliography. 23cm. (Ram's horn books) 59-5612 7.50
1. Jews—Intellectual life. I. Title.

AGUS, Jacob Bernard, 1911- 296
The evolution of Jewish thought: from Biblical times to the opening of the modern era. London(New York, Abelard-Schuman [c1959] 442p. 23cm. (Ram's horn books) Includes bibliography. [DS113.A394] 59-5612
1. Jews Intellectual life. I. Title.

AGUS, Jacob Bernard, 1911- 296
The evolution of Jewish thought [by] Jacob B. Agus. New York, Arno Press, 1973 [c1959] 442 p. 23 cm. (The Jewish people: history, religion, literature) Reprint of the ed. published by Abelard-Schuman, London, in series: Ram's horn books. Includes bibliographical references. [BM155.2.A38 1973] 73-2185 ISBN 0-405-05251-0 22.00
1. Judaism—History. 2. Philosophy, Jewish. I. Title. II. Series.

ALBRIGHT, William Foxwell, 296
1891-
Yahweh and the gods of Canaan; a historical analysis of two contrasting faiths. Garden City, N.Y., Doubleday, 1968. xiv, 294 p. 22 cm. (The Jordan lectures, 1965) Bibliographical footnotes. [BM170.A4 1968] 68-22541 6.95
1. Judaism—History—To 70 A.D. 2. Canaanites—Religion. I. Title. II. Series: Jordan lectures in comparative religion, 1965

AMERICAN Committee of Jewish 296
Writers, Artists and Scientists.
New currents; a Jewish monthly, v. 1- Mar. 1943- [New York] v. illus. 27 cm. Issues for Mar.- published by Jewish Survey Corporation; 19 by the American Committee of Jewish Writers, Artists and Scientists. Ceased publications with v. 3, no. 3 (Mar. 1945)? [DS133.N48] 51-40451
1. Jews — Period. I. Title.

ARMSTRONG, George Washington, 296
1866-
The Zionists. [Fort Worth, Tex., Judge-Armstrong Foundation, 1950] 134 p. facsims. 22 cm. [DS141.A77] 50-3764
1. Jewish question. 2. Jews in the U. S. 3. Zionism. I. Title.

AUSUBEL, Nathan, 1899- 296
Pictorial history of the Jewish people, from Bible times to our own day throughout the world. New York, Crown Publishers [1953] 346 p. illus., ports., maps. 29 cm. Bibliography: p. 336-338. [DS118.A8] 52-10777
1. Jews—History—Pictorial works. I. Title.

BADI, Joseph. 296
Religion in Israel today; the relationship between state and religion. New York, Bookman Associates [1959] 140p. 23cm. Includes Israeli documents. Errata slip inserted. Bibliography: p. 132-134. [BM390.B3] 59-14626
1. Israel—Religion. 2. Religion and state—Israel. 3. Nationalism and religion—Israel. I. Title.

BAECK, Leo, 1873-1956. 296
The essence of Judaism. New York, Schocken Books [1961, c1948] 287 p. 21 cm. (Schocken paperbacks, SB6) "This rendition by Irving Howe is based on the translation from the German by Victor Grubenwieser [sic] and Leonard Pearl (Macmillan ... London, 1936) The text of the 1948 edition has been corrected." [BM560.B32 1961] 61-8992
1. Judaism. I. Howe, Irving. II. Grubwieser, Victor, tr. III. Title.

BAECK, Leo, 1873-1956. 296
Judaism and Christianity; essays, translated with an introd. by Walter Kaufmann. [1st ed.] Philadelphia, Jewish Publication Society of America, 1958. 292p. illus. 22cm. [BM535.B2] 58-8991
1. Judaism—Influence. 2. Judaism—Relations—Christianity. 3. Christinity and other religions—Judaism. I. Title.

BAECK, Leo, 1873-1956 296
Judaism and Christianity; essays. Tr. with introd. by Walter Kaufman. Jewish Pubn. Soc. of Amer. 292p. (Meridian bks. JP23) 1.55 pap.,
1. Judaism—Influence. 2. Judaism—Relations—Christianity. 3. Christianity and other religions—Judaism. I. Title.

BAECK, Leo, 1873-1956. 296
Judaism and Christianity; essays, tr. from German, introd. by Walter Kaufmann. New York, Harper [1966, c.1958] 292p. 21cm. (Torchbk., TB823N. Temple lib.) [BM535.B2] 2.45 pap.,
1. Judaism—Influence. 2. Judaism—Relations—Christianity. 3. Christianity and other religions—Judaism. I. Title.

BAECK, Leo, 1873-1956. 296
This people Israel: the meaning of Jewish existence. Translated and with an introductory essay by Albert H. Friedlander. [1st ed.] New York, Hold, Rinehart and Winston)[1965, c1964] 2 v. in 1 (xxii, 403 p.) 24 cm. Translation of dieses Volk: judische Existenz. Bibliographical footnotes. [BM613.B313] 64-14367
1. Jews—Election, Doctrine of. I. Title.

BALTHASAR, Hans Urs von, 296
1905-
Martin Buber & Christianity; a dialogue between Israel and the church. Tr. by Alenxander Dru. New York, Macmillan [1962, c.1958, 1961] 127p. 21cm. 62-5883 3.00
1. Buber, Martin, 1878- 2. Judaism—Relations—Christianity. 3. Christianity and other religions—Judaism. I. Title.

BAMBERGER, Bernard Jacob, 296
1904-
Proselytism in the Talmudic period, by Bernard J. Bamberger. With a foreword by Julian Morgenstern and a new introd. by the author. New York, KTAV Pub. House [1968, 1939] xxxiii, 310 p. 24 cm. Bibliography: p. 304-310. [BM729.P7B3 1968] 68-25720
1. Proselytes and proselyting, Jewish. I. Title.

BAMBERGER, Bernard Jacob, 296
1904-
Proselytism in the Talmudic period, by Bernard J. Bamberger. With a foreword by Julian Morgenstern and a new introd. by the author. New York, KTAV Pub. House [1968, c1939] xxxiii, 310 p. 24 cm. Bibliography: p. 304-310. [BM729.P7B3 1968] 68-25720
1. Proselytes and proselyting, Jewish.

BAMBERGER, Bernard Jacob, 296
1904-
The story of Judaism. New York, Schocken Books [1964] x, 471 p. 21 cm. (Schocken paperbacks) "SB77." Bibliography: p. 451-454. [BM561.B25 1964] 64-16463
1. Judaism. I. Title.

BAMBERGER, Bernard Jacob, 296
1904-
The story of Judaism. New York, Union of American Hebrew Congregations [1957] 477 p. 24 cm. (Commission on Jewish Education of the Union of American Hebrew Congregations and Central Conference of American Rabbis. Union adult series) Includes bibliography. [BM560.B323] 57-643
1. Judaism.

BARACK, Nathan A. 296
The Jewish way to life, by Nathan A. Barack. Middle Village, N.Y., Jonathan David Publishers [1974, i.e.1975] p. cm. Bibliography: p. [BM565.B29] 74-19272 7.95
1. Judaism. 2. Religious life (Judaism) I. Title.

BARON, Salo Wittmayer, 1895- 296
ed.
Judaism, postbiblical and Talmudic period, edited, with an introd. and notes by Salo W. Baron and Joseph L. Blau. New York, Liberal Arts Press [1954] 245 p. 21 cm. (The Library of religion, v. 3) [BM495.B3] 55-1342
1. Judaism—Collections. 2. Judaism—History—Post-exilic period, 586 B.C.-210 A.D. 3. Judaism—History—Talmudic period, 10-425. I. Blau, Joseph Leon, 1909- joint ed.

BARON, Salo Wittmayer, 1895- 296
A social and religious history of the Jews. 2d ed., rev. and enl. New York, Columbia University Press, 1952- v. 24cm. Contents.v. 1-2. Ancient times.--v. 3-5. High Middle Ages, 500-1200. Bibliography included in 'Notes,' at end of each vol. [DS112.B3152] 52-404
1. Jews—Hist. 2. Judaism. 3. Jews—Political and social conditions. I. Title.

BELFORD, Lee Archer, 1913- 296
Introduction to Judaism. New York, Association Press [1961] 128p. 15cm. (An Association Press reflection book, 545) [BM156.B4] 61-7114
1. Judaism—Hist. I. Title.

BERGER, Elmer, 1908- 296
A partisan history of Judaism. Foreword by Paul Hutchinson. New York, Devin-Adair Co., 1951. 142 p. 21 cm. Includes bibliography. [BM157.B4] 51-14830
1. Judaism. 2. Jewish sects. I. Title.

BERKOVITS, Eliezer, 1908- 296
Judaism: fossil or ferment? New York, Philosophical Library [1956] 176p. 23cm. [BM560.B363] 56-13997
1. Judaism. 2. Toynbee, Arnold Joseph, 1889- A study of history. I. Title.

BERKOVITS, Eliezer, 1908- 296
Judaism: fossil or ferment? New York, Philosophical Library [1956] 176p. 23cm. [BM560.B363] 56-13997
1. Toynbee, Arnold Joseph, 1889- A study of history. 2. Judaism. I. Title.

BERNSTEIN, Herman, 1876-1935. 296
The truth about "The protocols of Zion"; a complete exposure. Introd. by Norman Cohn. New York, Ktav Pub. House, 1971 [i.e. 1972] xxxii, 15-397 p. 24 cm. Reprint of the 1935 ed. with a new introd. Contains reprints of all the documents relating to the case, including Dialogues in hell between Machiavelli and Montesquieu (p. [75]-258.) and "Protocols of the wise men of Zion" (p. 295-359.) [DS145.P7B45 1972] 77-157884 ISBN 0-87068-176-1 19.95
1. "Protocols of the wise men of Zion." I. Joly, Maurice, 1831-1878. Dialogue aux enfers entre Machiavel et Montesquieu. English. 1972. II. "Protocols of the wise men of Zion." 1972. III. Title.

BERNSTEIN, Peretz, 1890- 296
Jew-hate as a sociological problem, by Peretz F. Bernstein. Translated by David Saraph. New York, Philosophical Library [1951] 300 p. 22 cm. Translation of Der Antisemitismus als Gruppenerscheinung. [DS145.B433] 51-1110
1. Antisemitism. I. Title.

BERNSTEIN, Peretz Friedrich, 296
1899-
Jew-hate as a sociological problem; translated by David Saraph. New York, Philosophical Library [1951] 300 p. 22 cm. Translation of Der Antisemitismus als Gruppenerscheiaung. [DS145.B433] 51-1110
1. Antisemitism. I. Title.

BERNSTEIN, Philip Sidney, 296
1901-
What the Jews believe; illustrated by Fritz Eichenberg. New York, Farrar, Straus and Young [1951, '1950] 100 p. illus. 21 cm. "An expansion of an article written for Life magazine [1950]" [BM560.B46] 51-2404
1. Judaism. I. Title.

BERNSTEIN, Philip Sidney, 296
1901-
What the Jews believe, by Philip S. Bernstein. Illustrated by Fritz Eichenberg. New York, Funk & Wagnalls [1968, c1950] 100 p. illus. 18 cm. (A Funk & Wagnalls paperbook F32) "An expansion of an article written for Life magazine [1950]" [BM560.B46 1968] 68-20970
1. Judaism. I. Title.

BIGMAN, Stanley K 296
The Jewish population of Greater Washington in 1956; report on an interview survey of size, social characteristics, residential mobility, community participation, and observance of some traditional Jewish practices. Washington, Jewish Community Council of Greater Washington, 1957. 173p. illus. 28cm. [F205.J5B5] 57-3905
1. Jews in Washington, D. C. 2. Jews—Stat. I. Jewish Community Council of Greater Washington. II. Title.

BLUE, Lionel. 296
To heaven with scribes and Pharises : the Jewish path to God. New York : Oxford University Press, 1976. 114p. ; 21 cm. [BM580.B59] ISBN 0-19-519831-X 5.95
1. Judaism. 2. Jewish way of life. I. Title.

B'NAI B'rith. Vocational 296
Service.
Small-town Jewry tell their story; a survey of B'nai B'rith membership in small communities in the United States and Canada, by Robert Shosteck, director of research. Washington, 1953. 57p. 23cm. Published by the service under its earlier name: B'nai B'rith Vocational Service Bureau. [E184.J5B559] 53-20700
1. Jews in the U. S. 2. Jews in Canada. 3. B'nai B'rith. I. Shosteck, Robert, 1910- II. Title.

BOBROW, Dorothy. 296
Tell me why, a primer for Judaism; illustrated by Edwin Herron. New York, Bookman Associates [1954] 90p. illus. 26cm. [BM580.B6] 54-9565
1. Judaism—Juvenile literature. I. Title.

BOKSER, Ben Zion, 1907- 296
The gift of life; a treasury of inspiration. London, New York, Abelard-Schuman [1958] 139p. 21cm. (Ram's horn books) [BM723.B6 1958] 58-6038
1. Devotional literature, Jewish. 2. Life. I. Title.

BOKSER, Ben Zion, 1907- 296
Judaism; profile of a faith. [1st ed.] New York, Knopf, 1963. viii, 293, viii p. 22 cm. Bibliographical footnotes. [BM561.B6] 63-20141
1. Judaism.

BOKSER, Ben Zion, 1907- 296
Judaism and modern man; essays in Jewish theology. New York, Philosophical Library [1957] 153p. 22cm. [BM560.B64] 58-77
1. Judaism. I. Title.

BOKSER, Ben Zion, 1907- 296
The wisdom of the Talmud; a thousand years of Jewish thought. New York, Philosophical Library [1951] 180 p. 21 cm. [BM504.B6] 51-14677
1. Talmud—Criticism, Interpretation, etc. I. Title.

BRASCH, Rudolph, 1912- 296
The Judaic heritage; its teachings, philosophy, and symbols, by R. Brasch. New York, D. McKay Co. [1969] x, 437 p. 22 cm. [BM561.B7] 69-20209 7.50
1. Judaism. I. Title.

THE Bridge; 296
a yearbook of Judaeo-Christian studies. v. 1- 1955- [New York] Pantheon Books. v. 24cm. 'Published for the Institute of Judaeo-Christian Studies, Seton Hall University.' Editor: 1955- [BM535.B7] 55-10281
1. Christianity and other religions—Judaism. 2. Judaism—Relations—Christianity. I. Desterrelcher, John M., 1904- ed. II. Seton Hall University, Institute of Judaeo-Christian Studies.

BRIDGE (The); 296
a yearbook of Judaeo-Christian studies; v.4. Ed. by John M. Oesterreicher. Pub. for the Inst. of Judaeo-Christian Studies, Seton Hall Univ. [New York] Pantheon [c.1962] 383p. 55-10281 4.50
1. Christianity and other religions—Judaism. 2. Judaism—Relations—Christianity. I. Oesterreicher, John M., 1904- ed. II. Seton Hall University. Institute of Judaeo-Christian Studies.

BRILLIANT, Nathan. 296
Activities in the religious school, by Nathan Brilliant and Libbie L. Braverman. New York, Union of American Hebrew Congregations [1951] 258 p. illus. 21 cm. [BM103.B7] 51-33035
1. Religious education, Jewish. I. Title.

BUBER, Martin 296
Tales of the Hasidim [Tr. by Olga Marx] New York, Schocken Books [1961, c.1947, 1948] 2v. 355p; 352p. Contents.v.1, Early masters. v.2, Later masters. (Schocken paperback SB1; SB2) Bibl. 1.65, pap., ea.
1. Tales, Hasidic. I. Marx, Olga, 1894- tr. II. Title.

BUBER, Martin, 1878- 296
Hasidism and modern man. Ed., tr. [from German] by Maurice Friedman. New York, Harper [1966, c.1958] 256p. 21cm. (Torchbk. TB839 Temple lib.) [BM198.B793] 1.75 pap.,
1. Hasidism. I. Title.

BUBER, Martin, 1878- 296
Two types of faith. Translated [from the German] by Norman P. Goldhawk. New York, Harper [1961] 177p. (Harper Torchbks. the Cloister lib. TB75) Bibl. footnotes 1.25 pap.,
1. Judaism—Relations—christianity. 2. Christianity and other religions—Judaism. 3. Jesus Christ—Jewish interpretations. 4. Belief and doubt. I. Title.

BUBER, Martin, 1878-1965. 296
Hasidism and modern man. Edited and translated by Maurice Friedman. New York, Horizon Press [1958] 256 p. 21 cm. "The first of a two-volume collection ... the second volume of which will appear as The origin and meaning of Hasidism, the two together to be called Hasidism and the way of man." [BM198.B793] 58-10225
1. Hasidism. I. Title.

BYRNES, Robert Francis. 296
Antisemitism in modern France. New Brunswick, N. J., Rutgers University Press [1950- v. 24 cm. Contents.v. 1. The prologue to the Dreyfus affair. Bibliographical footnotes. [DS135.F83B9] 50-10738
1. Dreyfus, Alfred, 1859-1935. 2. Antisemitism. 3. Jews in France—Hist. I. Title.

CARMEL, Abraham, 1911- 296
So strange my path; a spiritual pilgrimage [2d ed.] New York, Bloch [1964] 234p. 22cm. 64-17487 4.95
1. Proselytes and proselyting, Jewish—Converts from Christianity. I. Title.

CENTRAL Conference of American Rabbis. 296
Israel Bettan memorial volume. New York, 1961. 164p. port. 22cm. 'Some sermons of Israel Bettan : p. 63-62. 'Bibliography of Israel Bettan's writings, compiled by Theodore Wiener : p. 52-62. [BM730.A2C4] 61-14334
1. Bettan, Israel, 1889-1957. 2. Preaching, Jewish. I. Title.
Contents omitted.

CENTRAL Conference of American Rabbis. 296
Israel Bettan memorial volume. New York, Author [c.]1961. 164p. front. port. Bibl. 61-14334 5.00
1. Bettan, Israel, 1889-1957. 2. Preaching, Jewish. I. Title.

CHARRY, Elias. 296
The eternal people; the story of Judaism and Jewish thought through the ages [by] Elias Charry, Abraham Segal. New York, United Synagogue Comm., on Jewish Educ. [1967] xiv, 429p illus., facsims., maps, ports. 27cm. Bibl. [BM156.C42] 67-31848 5.95
1. Judaism—Juvenile literature. I. Segal, Abraham, 1910- joint author. II. Title.
Distributed by the United Synagogue Book Service.

THE Chicago pinkas. 296
v.1- Chicago, College of Jewish Studies, 1952- v. 24cm. Editor: v. 1- S. Rawidowicz. Vois 1- include section in Hebrew with added t. p.: sJews in Chicago. [F548.9.J5C4] 52-14663
I. Rawidowicz, Simon, 1897- ed. II. Chicago. College of Jewish Studies.

COHEN, Israel, 1879- 296
Travels in Jewry. [1st ed.] New York, Dutton, 1953. 372p. illus. 23cm. [DS143.C63] 53-6068
1. Jews—Hist.—1789- I. Title.

COHEN, Jack Joseph. 296
The case for religious naturalism; a philosophy for the modern Jew. New York, Reconstructionist Press [1958] 296p. 21cm. Includes bibliography. [BL48.C558] 57-14412
1. Religion. 2. Judaism. I. Title.

COHEN, Morris Raphael, 1880-1947. 296
Reflections of a wondering Jew. Boston, Beacon Press, 1950. viii, 168 p. 24 cm. Bibliographical footnotes. [BM45.C62] 50-7334
1. Jews—Addresses, essays, lectures. I. Title.

COHN, Arthur, 1862-1926. 296
Of Israel's teachings and destiny; sermons, studies, and essays. [Translated by Emile and Jenny Marmorstein. New York] Ahron Press, 1972. xxiv, 239 p. illus. 24 cm. Translation of selections from Von Israels Lehre und Leben. [BM45.C6313 1972] 72-170836
1. Festival-day sermons, Jewish. 2. Zionism—Addresses, essays, lectures. I. Title.

COHN, Haim Hermann, 1911- comp. 296
Jewish law in ancient and modern Israel; selected essays, with an introd. by Haim H. Cohn. [New York] Ktav Pub. House, 1971. xxxiv, 259 p. 24 cm. Contents.Contents.—Introduction, by H. Cohn.—The secularization of divine law, by H. H. Cohn.—The goring ox in Near Eastern law, by R. Yaron.—The penology of the Talmud, by H. H. Cohn.—Reflections on the trial and death of Jesus, by H. H. Cohn.—Jewish law and modern medicine, by M. Elon.—The problem of Jewish law in a Jewish state, by I. Englard.—The relationship between religion and state in Israel, by I. Englard.—Law and religion in Israel, by A. Rubinstein.—The rabbinical courts in the State of Israel, by M. Chigier. Includes bibliographical references. [LAW] 72-149604 ISBN 0-87068-137-0
1. Jewish law. I. Title.

COHON, Beryl David, 1898- 296
Introduction to Judaism, by Beryl D. Cohon. 3d rev. and enl. ed. New York, Bloch Pub. Co. [1964] xiii, 223 p. 21 cm. Bibliography: p. 222-223. [BM105.C6] 64-19144
1. Judaism — Study and teaching. I. Title.

COHON, Beryl David, 1898- 296
Introduction to Judaism. 3d rev. enl. ed. New York, Bloch [c.1964] xiii, 223p. 21cm. Bibl. 64-19144 3.00
1. Judaism—Study and teaching. I. Title.

COHON, Beryl David, 1898- 296
Judaism in theory and practice. Rev. New York, Bloch Pub. Co., 1954. 250 p. 24cm. [BM560.C595 1954] 54-14705
1. Judaism. 2. Jews—Rites and ceremonies. I. Title.

COHON, Beryl David, 1898- 296
Judaism in theory and practice, by Beryl D. Cohon. [3d rev. ed.] New York, Bloch Pub. Co. [1969, c1968] x, 276 p. 24 cm. Includes bibliographical references. [BM561.C6 1968] 68-57021 4.95
1. Jews—Rites and ceremonies. 2. Judaism. I. Title.

COHON, Samuel Solomon, 1888- 296
Judausm, a way of life. New York. Schocken [1962, c.1948] 411p. 21cm. (SB38) Bibl. 1.95 pap.,
1. Jews—Religion. I. Title.

COLODNER, Solomon, 1908- 296
Lessons in Jewish history;an outline of Jewish History from its early beginnings to modern times. New York, Bloch Pub. Co. [1954] 68p. illus. 23cm. [DS120.C6] 54-3756
1. Jews—Hist.—Outlines, syllabi, etc. I. Title.

COMMENTARY. 296
The new Red anti-Semitism; a symposium, edited by Elliot E. Cohen. Boston, Beacon Press [1953] 58p. 24cm. (A Beacon-Commentary study) 'Articles and essays from Commentary's pages.' [DS145.C58] 53-8385
1. Antisemitism. 2. Jews in Russia. I. Cohen, Ellot Ettelson, 1899- ed. II. Title.

A Course of lectures on the Jews / 296
ministers of the established church in Glasgow. New York : Arno Press, 1977. iv, 499 p. ; 23 cm. (Anti-movements in America) Reprint of the 1840 ed. published by Presbyterian Board of Publication, Philadelphia. [BM560.C65 1977] 76-46095 ISBN 0-405-09968-1 lib.bdg. : 28.00
1. Judaism—Works to 1900. 2. Judaism—Controversial literature. 3. Missions to Jews. I. Series.

CRONBACH, Abraham, 1882- 296
Judaism for today; Jewish thoughts for contemporary Jewish youth. Introd. by John Haynes Holmes. New York, Bookman Associates [c1954] 148p. 23cm. [BM560.C7] 54-515
1. Judaism. I. Title.

CROSS, Frank Moore, Jr. 296
The ancient library of Qumran and modern biblical studies. Garden City, N.Y., Doubleday, 1961[c.1958, 1961] 260.p. illus. (Anchor bk., A272) 1.25 pap.,
1. Qumran community. 2. Dead Sea scrolls. I. Title.

CROSS, Frank Moore. 296
The ancient library of Qumran and modern Biblical studies. [1st ed.] Garden City, N.Y., Doubleday, 1958. 196 p. illus. 22 cm. (The Haskell lectures, 1956-1957) Includes bibliography. [BM175.Q6C7] 58-5933
1. Dead Sea scrolls. 2. Qumran community. I. Title.

DAICHES, David, 1912-- 296
Two worlds; an Edinburgh Jewish childhood. [1st ed.] New York, Harcourt, Brace [c1956] 192p. illus. 21cm. [DS135.E55E3] 56-66564
1. Jews in Edinburgh. I. Title.

DANIELOU, Jean. 296
The Jews: views and counterviews; a dialogue between Jean Danielou and Andre Chouraqui. Westminster, Md., Newman Press [1967] 92 p. 21 cm. Translation of Les juifs. Bibliography: p. 87-89. "Supplementary reading": p. 91-92. [BM535.D3213] 67-23607
1. Catholic Church—Relations—Judaism. 2. Judaism—Addresses, essays, lectures. 3. Judaism—Relations—Catholic Church. I. Chouraqui, Andre, 1917- II. Title.

DAVIES, William David, 1911- 296
Torah in the Messianic age and/or the age to come. Philadelphia, Society of Biblical Literature, 1952. vii, 99 p. 23 cm. (Journal of Biblical literature. Monograph series, v. 7) Bibliographical footnotes. [BM535.D35] 52-40064
1. Christianity and other religions—Judaism. 2. Law (Theology) 3. Messiah. I. Title. II. Series.

DAVIS, George Thompson Brown, 1873- 296
Israel returns home according to prophecy. Philadelphia, Million Testaments Campaigns [1950] 114 p. illus. 19 cm. [BS649.J5D34] 51-35227
1. Jews—Restoration. I. Title.

THE Dead Sea manual of discipline. 296
Translation and notes by William Hugh Brownlee. New Haven, American Schools of Oriental Research, 1951. 60 p. 23 cm. (Bulletin of the American Schools of Oriental Research. Supplementary studies, nos. 10-12) [DS41.A55 no. 10/12] A51
1. Jewish sects. I. Browniee, William Hugh. ed. and tr. II. Series: American Schools of Oriental Research. Supplementary studies, no. 10-12

DEMANN, Paul, 1912 296
Judaism. Tr. from French by P. J. Hepburne-Scott. New York, Hawthorn [c.1961] 108p. (Twentieth century encyclopedia of Catholicism, v.73. Section 6: The word of God) Bibl. 61-15611 3.50
1. Judaism. 2. Catholic Church—Relations—Judaism. 3. Judaism—Relations— Catholic Church. I. Title.

DUCKAT, Walter B. 296
Opportunities in Jewish religious vocations. New York, Vocational Guidance Manuals [1952] 128 p. 20 cm. (Vocational guidance manuals) [BM652.D8] 52-12236
1. Rabbis. I. Title.

EISENSTEIN, Ira, 1906- 296
Creative Judaism. [Rev. ed.] New York, Jewish Reconstructionist Foundation, 1953. 179p. 24cm. [BM565.K32 1953] 53-1320
1. Judaism. 2. Jewish question. 3. Zionism. 4. Jews in the U. S. I. Title.

EISENSTEIN, Ira, 1906- 296
Judaism under freedom. With a foreword by Mordecai M. Kaplan. New York, Reconstructionist Press, 1956. 262p. 22cm. [BM197.7.E5] 56-12814
1. Reconstructionist Judaism. I. Title.

ELKINS, Dov Peretz. 296
Humanizing Jewish life / Dov Peretz Elkins. South Brunswick : A. S. Barnes, 1976. p. cm. Includes index. Bibliography: p. [BM723.E5] 75-38456 ISBN 0-498-01912-8 : 9.95
1. Temple Beth El, Rochester, N.Y. 2. Elkins, Dov Peretz. 3. Jewish way of life. 4. Fellowship (Judaism) I. Title.

ELKINS, Dov Peretz. 296
So young to be a rabbi; the education of an American clergyman. Pref. by Simon Greenberg. New York, T. Yoseloff [1969] 263 p. illus., ports. 22 cm. [BM45.E54] 68-27231 ISBN 0-498-06888-9 6.00
1. Judaism—Addresses, essays, lectures. I. Title.

ELMSLIE, William Alexander Leslie, 1885- 296
How came our faith; a study of the religion of Israel and its signifiance for the modern world. New York, Abingdon Press [1964, c1962] 477 p. maps. 21 cm. (Apex books) "P1-225." [BM605.E5 1964] 64-835
1. Judaism. 2. Bible. O. T.—Theology. I. Title.

ESSAYS in Greco-Roman and related Talmudic literature / 296
selected with a prolegomenon by Henry A. Fischel. New York : Ktav Pub. House, 1976. p. cm. (The Library of Biblical studies) Some of the essays are in German. Includes bibliographical references. [BM536.G7E87] 76-23256 ISBN 0-87068-260-1 : 29.50
1. Judaism—Relations—Greek—Addresses, essays, lectures. 2. Greece—Religion—Addresses, essays, lectures. 3. Rabbinical literature—History and criticism—Addresses, essays, lectures. 4. Hellenism—Addresses, essays, lectures. I. Fischel, Henry Albert, 1913- II. Title. III. Series.

EVANS, Robert Llewelyn. 296
The Jew in the plan of God. [1st ed.] New York, Loizeaux Bros. [1950] 196 p. 20 cm. [BS649.J5E8] 50-14802
1. Jews—Restoration. I. Title.

FACKENHEIM, Emil L. 296
Encounters between Judaism and modern philosophy; a preface to future Jewish thought, by Emil L. Fackenheim. New York, Basic Books [1973] xi, 275 p. 24 cm. Includes bibliographical references. [BM565.F32] 72-89177 ISBN 0-465-01969-2 10.00
1. Judaism and philosophy. 2. Judaism—20th century. I. Title.

FACKENHEIM, Emil L. 296
God's presence in history: Jewish affirmations and philosophical reflections, by Emil L. Fackenheim. New York, New York University Press, 1970. vii, 104 p. 22 cm. (The Deems lectures, 1968) Includes bibliographical references. [BM561.F2] 79-88135 5.00
1. Judaism. 2. Holocaust (Jewish theology) I. Title. II. Series.

FACKENHEIM, Emil L. 296
God's presence in history; Jewish affirmations and philosophical reflections. [New York] [Harper] [1973, c.1970] 104 p. 21 cm. (Torchbooks, TB1690) "Containing the Charles F. Deems Lectures delivered at New York University in 1968." Includes bibliographical references. [BM561.F2] ISBN 0-06-131690-3 2.25 (pbk)
1. Judaism. 2. Holocaust, Jewish (1939-1945) I. Title.
L.C. card no. for the hardbound ed.: 79-88135.

FARMER, William Reuben. 296
Maccabees, Zealots, and Josephus; an inquiry into Jewish nationalism in the Greco-Roman

period. New York, Columbia University Press, 1956. 239p. 23cm. Includes bibliography. [BM176.F37 1956] 56-7364
1. Josephus, Flavius. 2. Judaism—Hist.—Post-exilic period. 3. Bible. N. T.—History of contemporary events, etc. 4. Maccabees. 5. Jews—Nationality. I. Title.

FEIN, Harry H. 296
Light through the mist; quatrains based on maxims and apothegms found in Aboth (the Fathers) Boston, Humphries [1950] 66 p. 22 cm. [BM506.A2E65] 51-10903
I. Aboth. English. Paraphrases. II. Title.

FINKELSTEIN, Louis, 1895- ed. 296
The Jews: their history, culture, and religion. 2d ed. New York, Harper [1955] 2 v. (xxxiv, 1431 p.) illus., ports., maps (3 col. on fold. l.) music. 25 cm. Fourth ed. (1970-71) published as a 3 v. work. Vol 1 has title: The Jews: their history; v. 2: The Jews: their religion and culture; v. 3: The Jews: their role in civilization. Includes bibliographies. [DS102.4.F5 1955] 55-13891
1. Jews—History. 2. Judaism—History. 3. Jewish literature—History and criticism. 4. Civilization—Jewish influences.

FIRE, Esther. 296
Hte power of dynamic faith. Chicago, Rainbow Pub. Co. [1955] 191p.10cm. [BM723.F5] 55-42635
1. Faith. 2. Judaism. I. Title.

FLEG, Edmond, 1874-1963, ed. 296
The Jewish anthology. Translated by Maurice Samuel. Westport, Conn., Greenwood Press [1974, c1925] p. cm. Reprint of the ed. published by Harcourt, Brace, New York. Translation of Anthologie juive. [BM43.F5513 1974] 72-142934 ISBN 0-8371-5824-9
1. Jewish literature. 2. Judaism—Addresses, essays, lectures. I. Title.

FORSTER, Arnold. 296
A measure of freedom, an Anti-Defamation League report. [1st ed.] Garden City, N. Y., Doubleday, 1950. 256 p. 22 cm. Bibliographical references included in "Footnotes" (p. [213]-216) [E184.J5F613] 50-7254
1. Antisemitism. 2. Jews in the U.S. 3. Discrimination. I. Anti-Defamation League. II. Title.

FOWLER, C. 296
The amazing history of the Stone of Destiny. Redditch, Worcs., F. Donald, 1951. 59 p. 19 cm. [DS131.F7] 52-44040
1. Anglo-Israelism. I. Title.

FREDMAN, Joseph George, 1895- 296
Jews in American wars, by J. George Fredman and Louis A. Falk. [5th ed.] Washington, Jewish War Veterans of the United States of America [1954] 276p. illus. 24cm. [E184.J5F64 1954] 54-43956
1. Jews in the U. S. 2. Jews as soldiers. I. Folk, Louis Austin, 1895- joint author. II. Title.

FREEHOF, Lillian B (Simon), 296
1906-
Candle light stories; eight little tales for Chanuko. Drawings by Jane Bearman. New York, Block Pub. Co. [1951] viii, 83 p. col. illus. 28 cm. [BM695.H3F7] 51-10959
1. Hanukkah (Feast of lights) I. Title.

FREEMAN, Grace R. 296
Inside the synagogue, by Grace R. Freeman, Joan G. Sugarman. Photography by Justin E. Kerr, others. Illus. by Judith Oren. New York, Union of Amei. Hebrew Congregations [c.1963] unpaged. illus. 62-19996 2.50; 2.63 bds., lib. ed.,
1. Reform Judaism—Juvenile literature. I. Sugarman, Joan G., joint author. II. Title.

FRIEDMAN, Theodore, ed. 296
Jewish life in America, edited by Theodore Friedman and Robert Gordis. New York, Horizon Press, 1955. 352p. 22cm. [E184.J5F78] 55-11462
1. Jews in the U. S. I. Gordis, Robert, 1908- joint ed. II. Title.

FRISCH, Daniel, 1897-1950. 296
On the road to Zion, selected writings. [Edited by Trude Weiss-Rosmarin assisted by Carl Alpert, and others] New York, Zionist Organization of America, 1950. 240 p. port. 24 cm. [DS149.F92] 50-8880
1. Zionism—Addresses, essays, lectures. I. Title.

FULL, William Lovell, 1897- 296
The fall and rise of Israel; the story of the Jewish people during the time of their dispersal and regathering. Foreword by I. C. Rand. Grand Rapids, Zondervan Pub. Co. [1954] 424p. illus. 24cm. [DS123.H84] 55-433
1. Jews—Hist. 2. Zionism—Hist. 3. Palestine—Hist.—1917-1948. I. Title.

GAER, Joseph, 1897- 296
The lore of the Old Testament. [1st ed.] Boston, Little, Brown, 1951. xi, 388 p. 22 cm. "Notes on sources": p. [339]-300. "Reading list with notes": p. [361]-369. [BM530.G28] 51-12446
1. Folk-lore—Jews. I. Title.

GAER, Joseph, 1897- 296
Our Jewish heritage, by Joseph Gaer and Alfred Wolf. [1st ed.] New York, Holt [1957] 242p. illus. 22cm. Includes bibliography. [BM560.G18] 57-6188
1. Judaism. I. Wolf, Alfred, 1915- joint author. II. Title.

GAER, Joseph, 1897- 296
Our Jewish heritage, by Joseph Gaer, Alfred Wolf. 1967 ed. Hollywood, Calif., Wilshire [1967, c.1957] xiv, 242p. illus. 21cm. (Self-improvement lib.) Bibl. [BM560.G18] 2.00 pap.,
1. Judaism. I. Wolf, Alfred, 1915- joint author. II. Title.

GARTENHAUS, Jacob, 1896- 296
Winning Jews to Christ; a handbook to aid Christians in their approach to the Jews. Grand Rapids, Mich., Zondervan [c.1963] 182p. 21cm. 63-15736 3.50 bds.,
1. Judaism—Addresses, essays, lectures. 2. Jews—Conversion to Christianity. I. Title.

GARTENHAUS, Jacob, 1896- 296
Winning Jews to Christ; a handbook to aid Christians in their approach to the Jews. Grand Rapids, Zondervan Pub. House [1963] 182 p. 21 cm. [BV4922.G3] 63-15736
1. Judaism — Addresses, essays, lectures. 2. Jews — Conversion to Christianity. I. Title.

GASTER, Moses, 1856-1939, 296
comp.
The exempla of the rabbis; being a collection of exempla, apologues and tales culled from Hebrew manuscripts and rare Hebrew books. Prolegomenon by William G. Braude. New York, Ktav Pub. House [1968] lxv, 314, 208 p. 24 cm. Reprint of the 1924 ed. with additional preface. "The book of exempla, Hebrew text": p. 1-208 (3d group) Added t.p. in Hebrew. Bibliography: p. xlv-lxv. [BM530.G36 1968] 67-13416
1. Exempla. 2. Tales, Jewish. I. Title. II. Title: Sefer ha-ma'asiyot.

GASTER, Theodor Herzl, 1906- 296
The holy and the profane; evolution of Jewish folkways. New York, W. Sloane Associates, 1955. 256 p. 22 cm. [GR98.G3] 55-7551
1. Folk-lore—Jews. I. Title.

GASTER, Theodor Herzl, 1906- 296
Passover: its history and traditions. Boston, Beacon [1962, c.1949] 102p. illus., map. (LR16) Bibl. 1.45 pap.,
1. Passover. I. Title.

GASTER, Theodor Herzl, 1906- 296
Purim and Hanukkah, in custom and tradition; Feast of Lots, Feast of Lights. New York, Schuman [1950] xvi, 134 p. illus., map. 22 cm. (Great religious festivals series) Bibliography: p. [119]-126. [BM695.P8G3] 50-10632
1. Purim (Feast of Esther) I. Title.

GINSBERG, Louis, 1920- 296
History of the Jews of Petersburg, 1789-1950. Petersburg, Va., 1954. 118p. illus. 24cm. Includes bibliography. [F234.P4G5] 54-31054
1. Jews in Petersburg, Va. I. Title.

GINZBERG, Eli, 1911- 296
Agenda for American Jews, New York, King's Crown Press, 1950. x, 90 p. 23 cm. Bibliography: p. [89]-90. [BM560.G45] 50-10882
1. Jews—Civilization. 2. Jews in the U. S. I. Title.

GITTELSOHN, Roland Bertram, 296
1910-
Little lower than the angels; illustrated by Jacob Landau. New York, Union of American Hebrew Congregations [1955] 334p. illus. 24cm. (Comission on Jewish Education of the Union of American Hebrew Congregations and Contral Conference of American Rabbis. Union graded series) [BM570.G5] 56-203
1. Judaism. 2. Religion—Philosophy. I. Title.

GITTELSOHN, Roland Bertram, 296
1910-
The meaning of Judaism [by] Roland B. Gittelsohn. New York, World Pub. Co. [1970] 221 p. 24 cm. (Excalibur books) Bibliography: p. 213-216. [BM561.G55 1970] 75-101858 5.95
1. Judaism. I. Title.

GITTELSOHN, Roland Bertram, 296
1910-
Modern Jewish problems; a textbook for high school classes and Jewish youth groups. [Rev. ed.] New York, Union of American Hebrew Congregations [c1955] 277p. illus. 21cm. (Commission on Jewish Education of the Union of American Hebrew Congregations and Central Conference of American Rabbis. Union graded series) [DS141.G47 1955] 57-184
1. Jewish question. 2. Jews—Political and social conditions. I. Title.

GITTELSOHN, Roland Bertram, 296
1910-
Wings of the morning, by Roland B. Gittelsohn. Illustrated by Ismar David. New York, Union of American Hebrew Congregations [1969] xii, 387 p. illus. 25 cm. (Commission on Jewish Education of the Union of American Hebrew Congregation and Central Conference of American Rabbis. Union graded series) 1955 ed. published under title: Little lower than the angels. Bibliography: p. 381-387. [BM570.G5 1969] 73-96731
1. Judaism. I. Title. II. Series.

GLANZ, Rudolf. 296
The Jews in American Alaska, 1867-1880. [New York, H.H. Glanz, 1953] 46 p. 23 cm. [F915.J4G5] 54-38242
1. Jews in Alaska. I. Title.

GLATZER, Nahum Norbert, 1903- 296
ed.
Hammer on the rock; a short Midrash reader, edited by Nahum N. Glatzer. [Translated by Jacob Sloan] New York, Schocken Books [1948] 128 p. 20 cm. (Schocken library, 16) "Draws ... material from the nonlegal parts of the Talmud, the Haggadah ... and the midrashic writings." [BM512.G55] 49-257
1. Midrash—Translations into English. I. Talmud. English. Selections. II. Title.

GLAZER, Nathan. 296
American Judaism. [Chicago] University of Chicago Press [1957] 175 p. 21 cm. (The Chicago history of American civilization) [BM205.G5] 57-8574
1. Judaism—United States. 2. Jews in the United States. I. Title.

GLUSHKOW, Abraham Dave, 1892- 296
ed.
A pictorial history of Maryland Jewry. [Baltimore Jewish Voice Pub. Co., 1955] 192p. illus. 29cm. [F190.J5G52] 55-44913
1. Jews in Maryland. I. Title.

GODDARD, Alice L. 296
David, my Jewish friend, by Alice L. Goddard. Illus. by Siegmund Forst. New York, Friendship [1967] 62p. illus. (pt. col.) 23cm. To Thee we give ourselves [by] Guistav Gottheil and Malcolm H. Stern, based on [a] traditional melody (for voice and piano): p. 34. [BM573.G6] 67-5888 1.75 pap.,
1. Judaism—Juvenile literature. I. Title.

GODDARD, Alice L. j296
David, my Jewish friend, by Alice L. Goddard. Illustrated by Siegmund Forst. New York, Friendship Press [1967] 62 p. illus. (part col.) 23 cm. "To Thee we give ourselves [by] Gustav Gottheil and Malcolm H. Stern, based on [a] traditional melody" (for voice and piano): p. 34. [BM573.G6] 67-5888
1. Judaism — Juvenile literature. I. Title.

GODDARD, Alice L. 296
David, my Jewish friend, by Alice L. Goddard. Illustrated by Siegmund Forst. New York, Friendship Press [1967] 62 p. illus. (part col.) 23 cm. "To Thee we give ourselves [by] Gustav Gottheil and Malcolm H. Stern, based on [a] traditional melody" (for voice and piano): p. 34. The story of a friendship introduces young Christians to the customs and traditions of the Jewish faith. [BM573.G6] AC 67
1. Judaism. I. Forst, Sigmund, illus. II. Title.

GOLDBERG, David, 1886- 296
Stories about Judaism. Introductory notes and subjects for discussion by Samuel Halevi Baron. Illustrated by Edwin Herron [and Friedel Dzubas] New York, Bookman Associates [1954] 2v. illus. 22cm. [BM105.G56] 54-11991
1. Judaism—Study and teaching. 2. Reform Judaism. I. Title.

GOLDBERG, Israel, 1887- 296
Fulfillment: the epic story of Zionism, by Rufus Learsi [pseud. 1st ed.] Cleveland, World Pub. Co. [1951] x, 426 p. ports., maps. 25 cm. "Bibliographical note": p. 411. [DS149.G539] 51-14316
1. Zionism—Hist. I. Title.

[GOLDBERG, Israel] 1887- 296
Israel: a history of the Jewish people, by Rufus Learsi [pseud.] Cleveland, World [1966, c.1949] 715p. maps. 24cm. (Meridian bk. M199) Bibl. [DS118.G56] 49-8382 3.45 pap.,
1. Jews—Hist. I. Title.

GOLDBERG, Israel, 1887-1964. 296
The Jews in America, a history, by Rufus Learsi [pseud. 1st ed.] Cleveland, World Pub. Co. [1954] xiv, 382 p. illus., ports., maps. 25 cm. "Bibliographical note": p. [357] [E184.J5G613] 54-5347
1. Jews in the United States—History.

GOLDEN, Harry Lewis, 1902- 296
Jews in American history, their contribution to the United States of America, by Harry L. Golden and Martin Rywell. [Charlotte, N. C., H. L. Martin Co., 1950] xv, 498 p. 23 cm. On cover: 1492-1950. Bibliography: p. 463-468. [E184.J5G62] 50-7687
1. Jews in the U. S. 2. U. S.—Hist. I. Rywell, Martin, 1905- joint author. II. Title.

GOLDIN, Hyman Elias, 1881- 296
A treasury of Jewish holidays; history, legends, traditions: illustrated by Resko. New York, Twayne Publishers [1952] 308 p. illus. 24 cm. [BM690.G55] 52-6298
1. Fasts and feasts—Judaism. 2. Israel. I. Title.

GOLDSTEIN, Israel, 1896- 296
American Jewry comes of age; tercentenary addresses. New York, Bloch Pub. Co., 1955. 218p. illus. 21cm. [BM225.N5S457] 55-12321
1. New York. Congregation Shearith Israel. 2. Jews in the U. S. I. Title.

GOODMAN, Paul, 1875- 296
History of the Jews. Rev. and enl. by Israel Cohen. London, Dent; New York, Dutton [1951] xvi, 288 p, 19 cm. [DS118.G7 1951] 51-6128
1. Jews—Hist. I. Title.

GOODMAN, Paul, 1875-1949. 296
History of the Jews. Rev. and enl. by Israel Cohen. [8th ed.] London, Dent.; New York, Dutton [1951] xvi, 288p. 19cm. [DS118.G7 1951] 51-6128
1. Jews— Hist. I. Title.

GOPPELT, Leonhard, 1911- 296
Jesus, Paul and Judaism; an introduction to New Testament theology. English ed. translated and edited by Edward Schroeder. London, New York, T. Nelson [1964] 192 p. 21 cm. "This English translation represents the first half of ... Christentum und Judentum im ersten und zwelten Jahrhundert." Bibliographical footnotes. [BM535.G583] 64-25284
1. Bible. N.T. — Criticism, interpretation, etc. 2. Christianity and other religions — Judaism. 3. Judaism — Relations — Chrisiianity. I. Title.

GOPPELT, Leonhard, 1911- 296
Jesus, Paul and Judaism; an introduction to New Testament theology. Tr. [from German] ed. by Edward Schroeder. New York, Nelson [c.1964] 192p. 21cm. Bibl. 64-25284 3.95; 2.95 pap.,
1. Bible. N. T.—Criticism, interpretation, etc. 2. Christianity and other religions—Judaism. 3. Judaism—Relations—Christianity. I. Title.

GORDIS, Robert, 1908- 296
Judaism for the modern age. New York, Farrar, Straus, and Cudahy [1955] 368p. 22cm. Jews in the U. S. [BM560.G65] 55-7214
1. Judaism. I. Title. II. Series.

GRAVES, Robert, 1895- 296
Hebrew myths; the book of Genesis, by Robert Graves and Raphael Patai. [1st ed.] Garden City, N.Y., Doubleday, 1964. 311 p. maps. 25 cm. "Abbrevations, sources, and annotated bibliography": p. 281-294. [BS1236.G7] 63-19845
1. Bible. O.T. Genesis—Criticism, interpretation, etc. 2. Mythology, Jewish. 3. Mythology, Semitic. I. Patai, Raphael, 1910- joint author. II. Title.

GUTKIND, Eric, 1877- 296
Choose life, the Biblical call to revolt. New York, H. Schuman [1952] 312p. 22cm. [BM560.G94] 52-8676
1. Judaism. I. Title.

GUTKIND, Erich, 1877- 296
Choose life, the Biblical call to revolt. New York, H. Schuman [1952] 312 p. 22 cm. [BM560.G94] 52-8676
1. Judaism. I. Title.

GUTTMANN, Alexander. 296
Studies in Rabbinic Judaism / by Alexander Guttmann. New York : Ktav Pub. House, 1976. p. cm. Includes bibliographical references. [BM500.2.G87] 76-6553 17.50
1. Talmud—Criticism, interpretation, etc.—Addresses, essays, lectures. 2. Judaism—History—Talmudic period, 10-425—Addresses, essays, lectures. I. Title.

HACKER, Tina, comp. 296
Shalom; the heritage of Judaism in selected writings. Illustrated with photos. by Archie

Lieberman. [Kansas City, Mo., Hallmark Cards, inc., 1972] 61 p. col. illus. 20 cm. (Hallmark editions) [BM43.H22] 76-168970 ISBN 0-87529-230-5 2.50
1. Judaism—Quotations, maxims, etc. I. Title.

HADASSAH, the Women's Zionist Organization of America. 296
Report. [New York] v. 28 cm. annual. [DS149.A272] 51-40452
I. Title.

HALPERN, Ben. 296
The American Jew; a Zionist analysis. New York, Theodor Herzl Foundation, 1956. 174p. 28cm. Includes bibliography. [E184.J5H28] 56-8954
1. Jews in the U. S. 2. Zionism—U. S. I. Title.

HALPERN, Harry. 296
From where I stand. New York, Ktav Pub. House [1974] ix, 204 p. 24 cm. [BM45.H323] 74-6397 ISBN 0-87068-263-6 10.00
1. Judaism—Addresses, essays, lectures. 2. Jewish way of life—Addresses, essays, lectures. I. Title.

HALPERN, Salomon Alter. 296
Tales of faith. [Jerusalem] Boys Town Jerusalem Publishers; [sole dist.: P. Feldheim. New York] 1968. 216p. 22cm. Bibl. [BM530.H3] HE68 3.75
1. Tales, Jewish. 2. Legends, Jewish. I. Title.

HANDLIN, Oscar, 1915- 296
Adventure in freedom: three hundred years of Jewish life in America. New York, McGraw-Hill [1954] 282p. illus. 21cm. [E184.J5H29] 54-10634
1. Jews in the U. S.—Hist. I. Title.

HANNOVER, Nathan Nata, d.1683. 296
Abyss of despair (Yeven metzulah) The famous 17th century chronicle depicting Jewish life in Russia and Poland during the Chmielnicki massacres of 1648-49. Translated from the Hebrew by Abraham J. Mesch, with an introd., biographical sketch of the author, and explanatory notes by the translator. Pref. by Solomon Grayzel. New York, Bloch Pub. Co., 1950. xv, 128 p. illus., ports., map. 20 cm. [DS135.P6H32] 50-4456
1. Chmielnicki, Bohdan, hetman of the Cossacks, 1596-1657. 2. Jews in Poland—Hist. 3. Jews in the Ukraine—Hist. 4. Ukraine—Hist.—Sources. I. Title.

HARISTEIN, Jacob I ed. 296
The Jews in American history; a resource book for teachers of social studies and American history. Contributors: Morris Cohen [and others] Consultant, Gertrude Noar. [New York, Anti-Defamation League of B'nai B'rith, 1955?] 100p. 26cm. Includes bibliographies. [E184.J5H35] 56-4921
1. Jews in the U. S.—Hist.—Study and teaching. 2. Judaism—Study and teaching. 3. U. S.— Hist.—Study and teaching. I. Title.

HAY, Malcolm Vivian 296
Europe and the Jews; the pressure of Christendom on the people of Israel for 1900 years. Introd. by Thomas Sugrue. New preface by Walter Kaufmann. Boston, Beacon Press [c.1950, 1960] xxix, 352 p. 21 cm. (Beacon paperback no. 95) Bibl.: p. 317-325 1.95 pap.,
1. Jews—Persecutions. I. Title.

HAY, Malcolm Vivian, 1881- 296
The foot of pride; the pressure of Christendom on the people of Israel for 1900 years. With an introd. by Thomas Sugrue. Boston, Deacon Press, 1950. xxii, 352 p. 22 cm. Bibliography: p. [317]-325. [DS145.H39] 50-10545
1. Jews—Persecutions. I. Title.

HEBREW Union College jubilee volume, 1875-1925. 296 Board of editors: David Philipson [and others] New York, Ktav Pub. House, 1968. 521 p. illus., facsims., ports. 24 cm. Reprint of the 1925 ed. Contents.Contents.—The history of the Hebrew Union College, by D. Philipson.—The Hebrew Union College of yesterday and a great desideratum in its curriculum today, by K. Kohler.—Ezekiel 37:15-28, by W. Rosenau.—The importance of the tenses for the interpretation of the Psalms, by M. Buttenweiser.—Trial by ordeal among the Semites and in ancient Israel, by J. Morgenstern.—The men of the great synagogue, by H. Englander.—Palestine in Jewish theology, by S. S. Cohon.—The names of the rabbinical schools and assemblies in Babylon, by J. Z. Lauterbach.—Gaonic studies, by J. Mann.—The classification of science in medieval Jewish philosophy, by H. A. Wolfson.—Pico della Mirandola, by I. Abrahams.—Raphael Norzi, by H. G. Enelow.—Notes on sephardic Jewish history of the sixteenth century, by J. R. Marcus.—Songs and singers of the synagogue in the eighteenth century, by A. Z. Idelsohn.—Early reform in contemporaneous responses, by I. Bettan.—Negative tendancies in modern Hebrew literature, by J. Reider.—The social implications of prayer, by A. Cronbach.—The philosophy of Judaism and how it should be taught, by D. Neumark. Bibliographical footnotes. [BM42.H4 1968] 70-5822
1. Jews—History—Collections. 2. Judaism—History—Collections. I. Philipson, David, 1862-1949, ed. II. Hebrew Union College, Cincinnati.

HELLER, Abraham Mayer, 1896- 296
The Jew and his world. New York, Twayne Publishers [1965] 384 p. 22 cm. [BM561.H4] 65-14411
1. Judaism I. Title.

HELLER, Abraham Mayer, 1896- 296
The vocabulary of Jewish life. Rev. ed. New York, Hebrew Pub. Co. [1967] xiii, 353 p. 22 cm. [BM50.H4 1967] 66-23331
1. Judaism—Terminology. I. Title.

HERBERG, Will. 296
Judaism and modern man; an interpretation of Jewish religion. New York, Farrar, Straus and Young [1951] 313 p. 22 cm. [BM560.H44] 51-13107
1. Judaism. I. Title.

HERBERG, Will 296
Judaism and modern man an interpretation of Jewish religion. New York, Meridian Books and Jewish Publication Society of America [1959. c.1951] xi, 313p. 21cm. (J P 10) (bibl. notes) 1.45 pap.,
1. Judaism. I. Title.

HERBERG, Will. 296
Judaism and modern man; an interpretation of Jewish religion. New York, Meridian Books [1960, c1951] 313 p. 21 cm. ([Jewish Publication Society series] JP10) Includes bibliography. [BM561.H44 1960] 59-12913
1. Judaism.

HERTZ, Richard C 296
The American Jew in search of himself; a preface to Jewish commitment. New York, Bloch Pub. Co. [1962] 209p. 21cm. Includes bibliography. [BM197.H4] 62-14460
1. Reform Judaism. I. Title.

HERTZ, Richard C 296
Prescription for heartache. [1st ed.] New York, Pageant Press [1958] 138p. 21cm. [BM723.H4] 58-14132
1. Peace of mind. I. Title.

HESCHEL, Abraham, 1907- 296
The earth is the Lord's; the inner world of the Jew in East Europe. With wood engravings by Ilya Schor. New York, H. Schuman [1950] 109 p. illus. 26 cm. [BM337.H4] 50-7183
1. Jewish learning and scholarship. 2. Jews in Poland. I. Title.

HESCHEL, Abraham Joshua, 1907- 296
Between God and man; an interpretation of Judaism, from the writings of Abraham J. Heschel. Selected, edited, and introduced by Fritz A. Rothschild. [1st ed.] New York, Harper [1959] 279 p. 22 cm. Includes bibliography. [BM560.H45] 59-7161
1. Judaism. I. Title.

HESCHEL, Abraham Joshua, 1907- 296
The earth is the Lord's; the inner world of the Jew in East Europe. With wood engravings by Ilya Schor. New York, H. Schuman [1950] 109p. illus. 26cm. [BM337.H4] 50-7183
1. Jewish learning and scholarship. 2. Jews in Poland. I. Title.

HESCHEL, Abraham Joshua, 1907- 296
The earth is the Lord's; the inner world of the Jew in East Europe, and The Sabbath its meaning for modern man [expanded ed.] Wood engravings by Ilya Schor. Cleveland, World with the Jewish Pubn. Soc. of Amer. [1963, c.1950-1952] 109, 136p. illus. 21cm. (Meridian bks., JP28) Bibl. 62-19064 1.95 pap.,
1. Jewish learning and scholarship. 2. Jews in Poland. 3. Sabbath. I. Heschel. Abraham Joshua, 1907- The Sabbath. II. Title. III. Title: The Sabbath.

HESCHEL, Abraham Joshua, 1907- 296
The earth is the Lord's and The Sabbath. Wood engravings by Ilya Schor. New York, Harper [1966. c.1950-1952] 136p. illus. 21cm. (Harper Torchbk.; Temple lib., TB828) [BM337.H4 1964] 1.95 pap.,
1. Jewish learning and scholarship. 2. Jews in Poland. I. Title.

HESCHEL, Abraham Joshua, 1907- 296
God in search of man; a philosophy of Judaism. New York, Farrar, Straus Cudahy [1955] 437p. 22cm. [BM560.H46] 55-11188
1. Judaism. 2. Religion—Philosophy. I. Title.

HESCHEL, Abraham, Joshua, 1907- 296
The sabbath: its meaning for modern man. With wood engravings by Ilya Schor. New York, Farrar, Straus and Young [1951] 118p. illus. 24cm. [BM685.H4] 51-8400
1. Sabbath. I. Title.

HESCHEL, Abraham Joshua, 1907- 296
The Sabbath: its meaning for modern man. With wood engravings by Ilya Schor. New York, Farrar, Straus and Young [1951] 118 p. illus. 24 cm. [BM685.H4] 51-8400
1. Sabbath.

HESCHEL, Abraham Joshua, 1907-1972. 296
The earth is the Lord's; the inner world of the Jew in East Europe. With wood engravings by Ilya Schor. London, New York, Abelard-Schuman [1964] 109 p. illus. 25 cm. (Ram's horn books) [BM337.H4 1964] 64-18208
1. Jewish learning and scholarship. 2. Jews in Poland. I. Title.

HEYDT, Henry J. 296
Studies in Jewish evangelism. New York, American Board of Missions to the Jews ['1951] 237 p. 21 cm. [BM535.H48] 52-24899
1. Judaism. 2. Missions—Jews. 3. Christianity and other religions—Judaism. I. Title.

HIGGENS, Elford. 296
Hebrew idolatry and superstition: its place in folk-lore. Port Washington, N.Y., Kennikat Press [1971] x, 80 p. 21 cm. Reprint of the 1893 ed. [BL1650.H6 1971] 73-118527 ISBN 0-8046-1150-5
1. Palestine—Religion. 2. Superstition. 3. Judaism—History—To 70 A.D. 4. Folk-lore. I. Title.

HIRSCH, Samson Raphael. 1808-1888 296
The nineteen letters on Judaism, by Samson Raphael Hirsch (Ben Uziel) Prepared by Jacob Breuer in a new ed., based on the tr. by Bernard Drachman. New York. Feldheim [1964, c.1960] 144p. 22cm. 63-56496 3.50
1. Judaism—Works to 1900. I. Title. II. Title: The nineteen letters on Judaism.

HIRSCH, Samuel Abraham. 296
The cabbalists and other essays, by S. A. Hirsch. Port Washington, N.Y., Kennikat Press [1970] viii, 228 p. 20 cm. Reprint of the 1922 ed. Contents.Contents.—The cabbalists.—Prolegomena to a philosophy of the Jewish religion.—A universal religion.—Possibility or impossibility of a direct divine revelation.—The Mishnah.—Rashi as an exegete.—Public disputations in Spain.—Pfefferkorniana. [BM45.H5 1970] 74-102572
1. Judaism—Addresses, essays, lectures. I. Title.

HIRSHLER, Eric E ed. 296
Jews from Germany in the United States. Introd. by Max Gruenewald. New York, Farrar, Straus and Cudahy [1955] x, 182p. 22cm. Includes bibliographies. [E184.J5H58] 55-11442
1. Jews in the U. S. 2. Germans in the U. S. I. Title.

A history of the Jews. 296
4th ed., rev. and enl. New York, Knopf, 1953. xvi, 455, xvii p. maps. 25cm. Bibliography: p. 449-455. [DS117.S3 1953] 933 53-6860
1. Jews—Hist. I. Sachar, Abram Leon, 1899-

HOLTZ, Avraham. 296
The Holy City; Jews on Jerusalem. [1st ed.] New York, Norton [1970, c1971] 187 p. 22 cm. (B'nai B'rith Jewish heritage classics) Bibliography: p. 179-180. [BM729.P3H64 1971] 75-78069 6.00
1. Jerusalem in Judaism. 2. Jerusalem in literature. I. Title.

HOWLETT, Duncan. 296
The Essenes and Christianity; an interpretation of the Dead Sea scrolls. [1st ed.] New York, Harper [1957] 217p. 22cm. [BM175.E8H6] 56-12067
1. Essenes. 2. Dead Sea scrolls. I. Title.

HUGHES, Anselm, 1889- 296
Ars nova and the Renaissance, 1300-1540. Edited by Anselm Hughes and Gerlad Abraham London, New York, Oxford University Press, 1960. xiv, 565 p., illus., facsims., music. 26 cm. (New Oxford history of music, v. 3) Secular name: Humphrey Vaughan Hughes. Bibliography: p.[503]-529. [ML160.N44] 63-603
1. Music—Hist. & crit.—Medieval. I. Abraham, Gerald Ernest Heal, 1904- joint ed. II. Title. III. Series.

HUGHES, Anselm, 1889- ed. 296
Early medieval music. up to 1300. London, New York, Oxford University Press, 1954. 1955] xviii, 434p. map. facsims., music. 26cm. (New Oxford history of music, v. 2) Bibliography: p. [405]-417. [ML160.N44 vol.2] 54-14955
1. Music—Hist. & crit.—Medieval. I. Title. II. Title: —Another issue. III. Series.

HUGHES, Anselm, 1889- ed. 296
Early medieval music, up to 1300. London, New York, Oxford University Press, 1954. xviii, 434 p. map, facsims., music. 26 cm. (New Oxford history of music, v. 2) Another issue. [2d impression rev. 1955] Secular name: Humphrey Vaughan Hughes. Bibliography: p. [405]-417. [ML160.N44] 54-14955
1. Music—Hist. & crit.—Medieval. I. Title. II. Series.

HUGHES, Anselm Father 1899- ed. 296
Early medieval music, up to 1300. London, New York, Oxford University Press, 1954. xviii, 434p. map. facsims., music. 26cm. (New Oxford history of music, v. Bibliography: p.[405]-417. [ML160.N44 vol.2] 54-14955
1. Music—Hist.&crit.— Medieval. I. Title. II. Series.

HUISJEN, Albert. 296
A guide to church-centered Jewish evangelism; seeking Israel's lost sheep. Grand Rapids, Baker Book House [1966] 47 p. 22 cm. [BV2620.H75] 67-2672
1. Missions to Jews. I. Title.

IMAGE of the Jews; 296
[lectures by] Eugene Borowitz [and others] Teachers' guide to Jews and their religion. Foreword by Joseph Irwin. Teachers' guide by Ruth Seldin. [New York, Published for the] Anti-defamation League of B'nai B'rith [by Ktav Pub. House, 1970] viii, 151 p. 23 cm. Based on the full length scripts of the original closed-circuit TV programs on Jews and their religion, which was series 1 of the Image of the Jews; series 2 being The image of the Jew in literature. Contents.Contents.—Lectures: Who is the American Jew? By D. Schary. What is Judaism? By I. Greenberg. Jewish worship, by M. J. Routtenberg. Aspects of Jewish theology, by E. Borowitz. Judaism: orthodox, conservative, and reform, by M. Wyschogrod. The life cycle of the Jews, by J. Harlow.—Teachers' guide: Introduction by R. Seldin. The American Jew. What Jews believe. Jewish worship and the Jewish year. The life of the Jew.—Bibliography (p. 141-146).—Additional resources. [BM570.I45] 74-114981 2.95
1. Judaism—Study and teaching. I. Borowitz, Eugene B. II. Seldin, Ruth R. III. Anti-defamation League. IV. Jews and their religion.

INFELD, Herman Zvi, 1899- 296
Israel in The decline of the West, by Harry Infeld. New York, Block Pub. Co., 1940. xi, 257 p. 21 cm. "A scientific interpretation of Israel's fate in the light of Spengier's conception of history as expounded in the Untergang des Abendlandes." [DS113.I 5] 40-4804
1. Spengler, Oswald, 1880-1936. Der Untergang des Abendiandes. 2. Jews — Civilization. I. Title.

INSTITUTE of Jewish Affairs. 296
European Jewry ten years after the war; an account of the development and present status of the decimated Jewish communities of Europe. New York, 1956. 293p. 22cm. [DS135.E83 I47] 56-3051
1. Jews in Europe. I. Title.

INSTITUTE of Jewish Affairs. 296
European Jewry ten years after the war; an account of the development and present status of the decimated Jewish communities of Europe. New York, 1956. 293p. 22cm. [DS135.E83I47] 56-3051
1. Jews in Europe. I. Title.

INSTITUTE of Jewish Affairs. 296
The Institute annual. 1956- New York. v. 24cm. Supersedes its Survey of events in Jewish life. [DS101.I497] 57-2271
1. Jews—Societies, etc. I. Title.

INSTITUTE of Jewish Affairs. 296
Survey of events in Jewish life. 1953-54. New York. 2v. 28cm. Superseded by its The institute annual. [DS143.I57] 55-33197
1. Jews—Hist.—Yearbooks. I. Title.

JACOBS, Joseph, 1854-1916. 296
Jewish ideals, and other essays. Freeport, N.Y., Books for Libraries Press [1972] xviii, 242 p. illus. (fold. map) 23 cm. (Essay index reprint series) Reprint of the 1896 ed. Contents.Contents.—Jewish ideals.—The God of Israel: a history.—Mordecai: a protest against the critics.—Browning's theology.—

The true, the only, and the complete solution of the Jewish question.—Jehuda Halevi, poet and pilgrim.—Jewish diffusion of folk-tales.—The London Jewry, 1290.—Little St. Hugh of Lincoln.—"Aaron son of the devil".—Jewish history: its aims and methods. [DS102.5.J2 1972] 72-311 ISBN 0-8369-2795-8
1. Jews—History—Addresses, essays, lectures. 2. Hagin family. I. Title.

JACOBS (Joseph) Advertising and Merchandising, inc., New York. 296
Customs and traditions of Israel. [New York] Published by J. Jacobs for Dugan Bros. [1953] 64p. illus. 21cm. [BM650.J33] 54-42923
1. Jews—Rites and ceremonies. 2. Fasts and feasts—Judaism. I. Title.

JACOBS, Louis. 296
The Jewish festivals: New Year, the Day of Atonement, Tabernacles, Passover, Pentecost, Hanukkah, Purim. Worcester [Mass.] A. J. St. Onge, 1961. 63 p. illus. 67 mm. [BM690.J27] 64-36628
1. Fasts and feasts—Judaism. I. Title.

JESSUP, Gordon. 296
No strange God : an outline of Jewish life and faith / [by] Gordon Jessup. London : Olive Press, 1976. 125 p. : ill. ; 18 cm. Includes index. [BM580.J46] 77-373941 ISBN 0-904054-11-X : £0.90
1. Judaism. I. Title.

JEWISH Education Association of Essex County (New Jersey) 296
The Essex story; a history of the Jewish community in Essex County, New Jersey. Newark, N. J. [1955] 76p. illus. 23cm. [F142.E8J4] 56-19002
1. Jews in Essex Co., N. Y. I. Title.

†*THE Jewish expression /* 296
edited by Judah Goldin. New Haven : Yale University Press, 1976. xxiv, 470 p. ; 21 cm. (A Yale paperbound) Includes bibliographical references. [BM155.2.J48 1976] 77-352683 ISBN 0-300-01948-3 : 17.50 ISBN 0-300-01975-0 pbk. : 5.95
1. Judaism—History—Addresses, essays, lectures. I. Goldin, Judah, 1914-

JEWISH Statistical Bureau, New York. 296
Necrology of rabbis. New York, Jewish Statistical Bureau. no. in v. 28 cm. annual. Title varies slightly. no. 1-8, 1952/53-1959/60, in no. 9. [BM750.N4] 68-7052
1. Rabbis—U. S. 2. Rabbis—Canada. I. Title.

JEWISH Theological Seminary of America. 296
The Samuel Friedland lectures, 1960-1966. New York, 1966. viii, 95 p. 22 cm. "Essays ... brought together in honor of Mr. Friedland's seventieth birthday." Includes bibliographical references. [BM42.J4] 66-29526
1. Judaism—Addresses, essays, lectures. I. Friedland, Samuel. II. Title.
Contents omitted

JUDAH, ha-Levi, 12th cent. 296
The Kuzari (Kitab al Khazari); an argument for the faith of Israel. Introd. by Henry Slonimsky. (Translated from the Arabic by Hartwig Hirschfeld. 1st Schocken paperback ed.] New York, Schocken Books [1964] 321 p. 21 cm. (Schocken paperbacks, SB75) Bibliography: p. 311-313. [BM550.J813] 64-15222
1. Judaism — Apologetic works. I. Title.

JUDAH HA-LEVI, 12thcent. 296
The Kuzari (Kitab al Khazari); an argument for the faith of Israel. Introd. by Henry Slonimsky [Tr. from Arabic by Hartwig Hirschfeld] New York, Schocken [c.1964] 321p. 21cm. (SB75) Bibl. 64-15222 1.95 pap.,
1. Judaism—Apologetic works. I. Title.

JUSTICE, justice shalt thou 296
pursue ; papers on the occasion of the 175th birthday of the Reverend Dr. Julius Mark, as an expression of gratitude of the Jewish Conciliation Board with whose services and leadership Dr. Mark has long been identifies / edited by Ronald B. Sobel and Sidney Wallach. New York : Ktav Pub. House, 1975. p. cm. Includes bibliographical references. [BM42.J87] 75-17728 ISBN 0-87068-458-2 : 10.00
1. Mark, Julius, 1898- 2. Judaism—History—Addresses, essays, lectures. I. Mark, Julius, 1898- II. Sobel, Ronald B. III. Wallach, Sidney, 1905- IV. Jewish Conciliation Board.
Contents omitted

KAC, Arthur W 296
The spiritual dilemma of the Jewish people; its cause and cure. Chicago, Moody Press [1963] 128 p. 20 cm. [BM561.K3] 63-2919
1. Judaism. I. Title.

KAC, Arthur W., M.D. 296
The spiritual dilemma of the Jewish people: its cause and cure. Chicago, Moody [c.1963] 128p. 20cm. Bibl. 63-2919 2.25
1. Judaism. I. Title.

KADUSHIN, Max, 1895- 296
The rabbinic mind. New York, Jewish Theological Seminary of America, 1952. 394 p. 23 cm. Bibliographical footnotes. [BM560.K2] 52-44962
1. Judaism. I. Title.

KALLEN, Horace Meyer, 1882- 296
Judaism at bay; essays toward the adjustment of Judaism to modernity, by Horace M. Kallen. New York, Arno Press, 1972 [c1932] 256 p. 22 cm. (Religion in America, series II) [BM45.K35 1972] 74-38451 ISBN 0-405-04071-7
1. Judaism—Addresses, essays, lectures. I. Title.

KALLEN, Horace Meyer, 1882- 296
'Of them which say they are Jews,' and other essays on the Jewish struggle for survival. Edited by Judah Pilch. New York, Bloch Pub. Co., 1954. 242p. 24cm. [E184.J5K14] 54-10964
1. Jews in the U. S. I. Title.

KAPLAN, Mordecai Menahem, 1881- 296
Basic values in Jewish religion. [New York] Reconstructionist Press [1957] 111p. 25cm. 'Reprinted from The future of the American Jew, chapters 14 & 15.' [BM197.7.K24] 57-12333
1. Reconstructionist Judaism. I. Title.

KAPLAN, Mordecai Menahem, 1881- 296
Judaism as a civilization; toward a reconstruction of American-Jewish life. [Enl. ed.] New York, T. Yoseloff [1957] xvi, 601p. diagr. 25cm. Bibliographical references included in 'Notes' (p. 525-554) [BM197.7.K26 1957a] 57-2633
1. Reconstructionist Judaism. 2. Jews in the U. S. I. Title.

KAPLAN, Mordecai Menahem, 1881- 296
Judaism as a civilization: toward a reconstruction of American-Jewish life. [Enl. ed.] New York, Reconstructionist Press, 1957. xvi, 601p. 24cm. Bibliographical references included in 'Notes' (p. 525- 554) [BM197.7.K26 1957] 57-8533
1. Reconstructionist Judaism. 2. Jews in the U. S. I. Title.

KAPLAN, Mordecai Menahem, 1881- 296
Judaism without supernaturalism; the only alternative to orthodoxy and secularism. [1st ed.] New York, Reconstructionist Press, 1958. 254p. 21cm. [BM197.7.K28] 58-10056
1. Reconstructionist Judaism. 2. Supernatural. I. Title.

KAPLAN, Mordecai Menahem, 1881- 296
Judasim as a civilization; toward a reconstruction of American-Jewish life. [Enl. ed.] New York, Reconstructionist Press, 1957. xvi, 601p. 24cm. Bibliographical references included in 'Notes' (p.525-554) [BM197.7.K26 1957] 57-8533
1. Reconstructionlist Judaism. 2. News in the U. S. I. Title.

KAPLAN, Mordecai Menahem, 1881- 296
The purpose and meaning of Jewish existence; a people in the image of God. Philadelphia, Jewish Pub. Soc. of Amer. [c.]1964. x, 326p. 22cm. 64-15569 4.50
1. Judaism. I. Cohen, Hermann, 1842-1918. Religion der Vernunft. II. Title.

KAPLAN, Mordecai Menahem, 1881- 296
Questions Jews ask: reconstructionist answers. New York, Reconstructionist Press [1956] 532p. 23cm. [BM197.7.K3] 56-8577
1. Questions and answers—Jews. 2. Reconstructionist Judaism. I. Title.

KAPLAN, Mordecai Menahem, 1881- 296
Questions Jews ask: reconstructionist answers. New York, Reconstructionist Press [1956] 532p. 23cm. [BM197.7.K3] 56-8577
1. Questions and answers—Jews. 2. Reconstructionist Judaism. I. Title.

KAPLAN, Mordecal Menahem, 1881- 296
Judaism as a civilization; toward a Reconstructionist Press [1957] 111p. 25cm. 'Reprinted from The future of the American Jew, chapters 14 & 15.' [BM197.7.K26 1957] 57-8533
1. Reconstructionist Judaism. I. Title.

KATZ, Irving I 296
The Beth El story, with a history of the Jews in Michigan before 1850, by Irving I. Katz, and Three hundred years in America, by Jacob R. Marcus. Detroit, Wayne University Press, 1955. 238p. illus. 27cm. Includes bibliography. [BM225.D44*k3] 55-7560
1. Detroit. Temple Beth El. 2. Jews in Michigan. I. Marcus(Jacob Rader, 1896- Three hundred years in America. II. Title.

KATZ, Jacob, 1904- 296
Exclusiveness and tolerance; studies in Jewish-Gentile relations in medieval and modern times. New York, Schocken [1962, c.1961] 200p. 21cm. (Scripta Judaica: SB40) Bibl. 62-19396 1.75 pap.,
1. Judaism—Relations—Christianity. 2. Christianity and other religions—Judaism. 3. Jewish question—Hist. I. Title.

KATZ, Jacob, 1904- 296
Excusiveness and tolerance; studies in Jewish-Gentile relations in medieval and modern times. Oxford [c.]1961[ ] xv, 200p. (Scripta Judaica, 3) Bibl. 61-19429 3.40
1. Judaism—Relations—Christianity. 2. Christianity and other religions—Judaism. 3. Jewish question—Hist. I. Title. II. Series.

KERTZER, Morris Norman, 1910- 296
The art of being a Jew. [1st ed.] Cleveland, World Pub. Co. [1962] 247p. 21cm. [BM561.K43] 62-15714
1. Judaism. I. Title.

KERTZER, Morris Norman, 1910- 296
What is a Jew? Rev. ed. Cleveland, World Pub. Co. [1960] 217p. 21cm. Includes bibliography. [BM561.K45 1960-296] 60-14307
1. Judaism. 2. Jews—Rites and ceremonies. I. Title.

KERTZER, Morris Norman, 1910- 296
What is a Jew? [1st ed.] Cleveland, World Pub. Co. [1953] 214 p. 21 cm. [BM560.K45] 53-5526
1. Judaism. 2. Jews—Rites and ceremonies. I. Title.

KERTZER, Morris Norman, 1910- 296
What is a Jew? Rev. ed. New York, Macmillan [1966, c.1953, 1960] 189p. 18cm. Bibl. [BM561.K45] .95 pap.,
1. Judaism. 2. Jews—Rites and ceremonies. I. Title.

KERTZER, Morris Norman, 1910- 296
What is a Jew? [By] Morris N. Kertzer. Foreword by Leo Rosten. Newly rev. [3d] ed. New York, Bloch Pub. Co. [1973] xxii, 217 p. 22 cm. Includes bibliographical references. [BM561.K45 1973] 73-77280 ISBN 0-8197-0299-4 5.95
1. Jews—Rites and ceremonies. 2. Judaism. I. Title.

KLAPPHOLZ, Kurt, 1913- 296
Spiritual awakening; an interpretation of contemporary problems in the light of the eternal truths of religion. New York, Bloch Pub. Co., 1954. 100p. 21cm. [BM560.K55] 54-12273
1. Judaism. I. Title.

KLASS, Sholom. 296
Tales from our gaonim (sages). [Brooklyn] 1967- v. illus. 24 cm. Cover title: Tales of the gaonim (sages) "A compilation of stories, narratives, and legends about our gaonim (sages) from the 9th century, C.E. to the present as they appeared in the Jewish press. Short stories and anecdotes about wise men in Jewish history expressing the philosophy, ethics, and faith of the Jewish people. [BM750.K48] AC 67
1. Folklore—Jews. 2. Rabbis. I. Jewish press, Brooklyn. II. Title. III. Title: Tales of the gaonim (sages)

KLAUSNER, Joseph, 1874- 296
From Jesus to Paul. Tr. from Hebrew by William F. Stinespring. Boston, Beacon Press [1961, c.1943] 624p. (Beacon paperback BP 115) Bibl. 2.95 pap.,
1. Jews—Religion—Relations—Christianity. 2. Bible. N.T. Epistles of Paul—Theology—N.T. 3. Bible—Theology—N.T. Epistles of Paul. 4. Paul, Saint, apostle. I. Stinespring, William Franklin, 1901- tr. II. Title.

KOBLER, Franz, 1882- ed. 296
Her children call her blessed; a portrait of the Jewish mother. New York, Stephen Daye Press [1955] 392p. illus. 24cm. [BM729.W5K6] 55-6191
1. Women, Jewish. 2. Mothers in literature. I. Title.

KOBLER, Franz, 1882- ed. 296
A treasury of Jewish letters; letters from the famous and the humble. [New York] Publication of the East and West Library issued by Farrar, Straus, and Young [1953] 2v. (ixxix, 672p.) illus., ports. 22cm. Bibliography: v. 2, p. [613]-643. [DS119.K58] 53-8849
1. Jewish letters. I. Title.

KOFFLER, Jacob, 1889- 296
Exile to exile. Stamford, Conn., Kay Publishing [1955] 472p. 23cm. [DS118.K665] 55-33198
1. Jews—Hist. —586 B. C.—70 A. D. I. Title.

KOHN, Eugene, 1887- ed. 296
American Jewry; the tercentenary and after, 1694 [i. e. 1654]-1954. New York, Reconstructionist Press [1955] 159p. 22cm. [E184.J5K72] 55-7309
1. Jews in the U. S. I. Title.

KOHN, Eugene, 1887- 296
Good to be a Jew. New York, Reconstructionist Press [c1959] 180p. 22cm. Includes bibliography. [BM561.K6] 59-13350
1. Judaism. I. Title.

KOLITZ, Zvi, 1913- 296
Survival for what? New York, Philosophical Library [1969] xv, 219 p. 22 cm. [BM648.K6] 70-75761 6.50
1. Jews—Political and social conditions—1948- 2. Judaism—Apologetic works. I. Title.

KORN, Bertram Wallace. 296
Eventful years and experiences; studies in nineteenth century American Jewish history. Cincinnati, American Jewish Archives, 1954. xi, 249p. 24cm. (Publications of the American Jewish Archives, no. 1) Includes bibliographies. [E184.J5K78] 54-10965
1. Jews in the U. S.—Hist. I. Title. II. Series: Hebrew Union College-Jewish Institute of Religion. American Jewish Archives. Publications, no. 1

KRIPKE, Dorothy (Karp) 296
God and the story of Judaism [by] Dorothy K. Kripke [and] Meyer Levin. Stephen Kraft: art editor; Lorence F. Bjorklund: illustrations. New York, Behrman House [1962] 191 p. illus. 24 cm. (The Jewish heritage series) [BM573.K73] 62-17078
1. Judaism — Juvenile literature. I. Levin, Meyer, 1905- joint author. II. Title.

KRIPKE, Dorothy (Karp) 296
God and the story of Judaism [by] Dorothy K. Kripke, Meyer Levin. Stephen Kraft: art ed.; Lorence F. Bjorklund: illustrations. New York, Behrman [c.1962] 191p. illus. 24cm. (Jewish heritage ser.) 62-17078 2.95
1. Judaism—Juvenile literature. I. Levin, Meyer, 1905- joint author. II. Title.

KRIPKE, Dorothy (Karp) 296
Let's talk about Judaism. Pictures by Bobri [pseud.] New York, Behrman House, c1957. unpaged. illus. 25cm. [BM573.K75] 57-13094
1. Judaism—Juvenile literature. I. Title.

LAMM, Maurice 296
I shall glorify him, by Maurice Lamm a study guide to Herman Work's, This is My God an adult workbook on the vital religious problems of modern Jewry. New York, Bloch Pub. Co. [c.1960] vi, 89p. 26cm. 1.75 pap.,
1. Judaism. I. Title.

LAPID, Pinhas. 296
The prophet of San Nicandro. New York, Beechhurst Press [1953] 240p. illus. 25cm. [BM729.P7L32] 53-8027
1. Proselytes and proselyting, Jewish. I. Title.

LAPIDE, Phinn E 1922- 296
The prophet of San Nicandro. New York, Beechhurst Press [1953] 240p. illus. 25cm. [BM729.P7L32] 53-8027
1. Prosetytes and proselyting, Jewish. I. Title.

LAUTERBACH, Jacob Zallel, 1873-1942. 296
Rabbinic essays. New York, Ktav Pub. House, 1973 [c1951] xvi, 570 p. 24 cm. Original ed. published by Hebrew Union College Press, Cincinnati. Includes bibliographical references. [BM177.L38 1973] 73-2353 ISBN 0-87068-223-7 17.50
1. Jesus Christ—Jewish interpretations. 2. Lauterbach, Jacob Zallel, 1873-1942—Bibliography. 3. Judaism—History—Talmudic period—Addresses, essays, lectures. I. Title.
Contents omitted.

LAUTERBACH, Jacob Zallel, 1873-1942. 296
Studies in Jewish law, custom, and folklore. Selected, with an introd. by Bernard J. Bamberger. [New York] Ktav Pub. House [1970] xxi, 253 p. 24 cm. Contents.Contents.—The ceremony of breaking a glass at weddings.—The naming of children in Jewish folklore, ritual, and practice.—The origin and development of two Sabbath ceremonies.—The ritual for the Kapparot ceremony.—The belief in the power of the word.—The attitude of the Jew towards the non-Jew.—Talmudic-rabbinic view on birth

control.—Should one cover the head when participating in divine worship?—Responsum on question, "Shall women be ordained rabbis?"—The Jewish attitude toward autopsy.—Burial practices. Includes bibliographical references. [BM700.L3 1970] 71-78601 ISBN 0-87068-013-7
1. Jews—Rites and ceremonies—Addresses, essays, lectures. 2. Aliens (Jewish law) 3. Responsa—1800- I. Title.

LAZARUS, Josephine, 1846- 1910. 296
The spirit of Judaism. Freeport, N.Y., Books for Libraries Press [1972] 202 p. 23 cm. (Essay index reprint series) Reprint of the 1895 ed. [BM45.L34 1972] 77-38031 ISBN 0-8369-2602-1
1. Judaism—Addresses, essays, lectures. I. Title.

LEBESON, Anita (Libman), 1896- 296
Pilgrim people. [1st ed.] New York, Harper [1950] xiv, 624 p. ports., maps, facsims. 22 cm. Bibliography: p. 567-610. [E184.J5L568] 50-12859
1. Jews in the U. S.—Hist. I. Title.

LENCHITZ, Solomon, 1909- 296
Pictorial oddities from Hebraic literature. New York, Exposition Press [1950] 64 p. illus. 22 cm. [PN6268.J4L4] 51-422
1. Jews—Anecdotes. I. Title.

LESLAU, Wolf. 296
Falasha antrology, translated from Ethiopic sources with an introd. by Wolf Leslau. New Haven, Yale University Press, 1951. xiiii, 222 p. illus. 22 cm. (Yale Judaica series, v. 6) Includes bibliographies. [BM40.L37] 51-7505
1. Judaism—Collections. 2. Falashas. 3. Ethiopic literature—Translations into English. 4. English literature—Translations from Ethiopic. I. Title. II. Series.

LEVIN, Meyer, 1905- 296
Beginnings in Jewish philosophy. New York, Behrman House [1971] 192 p. illus. 25 cm. (The Jewish heritage series) Discusses the beliefs of Judaism and their application to life in today's world. [BM573.L48] 76-116677 ISBN 0-87441-063-0
1. Judaism—Juvenile literature. I. Title. II. Series.

LEVIN, Meyer, 1905- 296
In search, an autobiography. New York, Horizon Press, 1950. 524 p. 23 cm. [DS125.3.L4A3] 50-4306
1. Jews in Palestine. 2. Palestine—Pol. & govt. 3. Jews—Political and social conditions. I. Title.

LEVIN, Meyer, 1905- 296
In search; an autobiography, by Meyer Levin. New York, Pocket Books [1973 c.1950] 547 p. 18 cm. [DS125.3L4A3 1973] ISBN 0-671-78609-1 1.95 (pbk)
1. Jews in Palestine. 2. Palestine—Pol. & govt. 3. Jews—Political and social conditions. I. Title.
L.C. card no. for orig. ed.: 50-13325

LEVINE, Raphael H., 1901- 296
Holy mountain; two paths to one God. With an introd. by Stephen F.Bayne, Jr. Portland, Or., Binfords & Mort [1953] 248 p. illus. 22 cm. [BM535.L395] 53-4124
1. Judaism—Relations—Christianity. 2. Christianity and other religions—Judaism. I. Title.

LEVINE, Raphael H., 1901- 296
Two paths to one God: Judaism and Christianity. With an introd. by Stephen F. Bayne, Jr. [New, rev. ed.] New York, Collier Books [1962] 256 p. 18 cm. (Collier books, AS366) Published in 1953 under title: Holy mountain. [BM535.L395 1962] 62-18370
1. Judaism—Relations—Christianity. 2. Christianity and other religions—Judaism. I. Title.

LEVINGER, Elma (Ehrlich) 1887- 296
Jewish adventures in America; the story of 300 years of Jewish life in the United States. Designed by William Steinel. New York, Bloch Pub. Co., 1954 [i. e. 1955] 243p. illus. 24cm. [E184.J5L573] 54-11719
1. Jews in the U. S.—Hist. I. Title.

LEVINTHAL, Israel Herbert, 1888- 296
Point of view; an analysis of American Judaism. London, New York, Abelard-Schuman [1958] 112 p. 22 cm. (Ram's horn books) [BM196.L4] 58-10393
1. Jewish sects. 2. Judaism—U.S. I. Title.

LEVITAN, Tina Nellie, 1922- 296
The firsts of American Jewish history. [2d ed.] Brooklyn, Charuth Press [1957]c285p. illus. 22cm. Includes bibliography. [E184.J5L6644 1957] 57-9129
1. Jews in the U. S.—Hist. I. Title.

LEVITAN, Tina Nellie, 1922- 296
The firsts of American Jewish history, 1492-1951. Brooklyn, Charuth Press [1952] 172 p. illus. 22 cm. [E184.J5L6644] 52-28205
1. Jews in the U.S.—History. I. Title.

LEWIN, Issac, 1906- 296
In the struggle against discrimination; addresses before various organs of the United Nations and of the Congress of the United States. New York, Bloch Pub. Co., 1957. 148 p. 24 cm. [DS143.L39] 57-59295
1. Race discrimination. 2. Jews — Political and social conditions — 1948- I. Title.

LEWIN, Izak, 1906- 296
In the struggle against discrimination; addresses before various organs of the United Nations and of the Congress of the United States. New York, Bloch Pub. Co., 1957. 148p. 24cm. [DS143.L39] 57-59295
1. Race diserimination. 2. Jews—Political and social conditions. I. Title.

LEWISOHN, Ludwig, 1882- 296
The American Jew, character and destiny. New York, Farrar, Straus [1950] x, 175 p. 20 cm. Bibliographical footnotes. [E184.J5L665] 50-10552
1. Jews. 2. Jews in the U. S. I. Title.

LIEBERMAN, Herman, 1889- 296
Strangers to [BM21.L5] 55-11036
I. Title.

LIEBERMAN, Herman, 1889- 296
Strangers to Rainbow Press, 1955. 125p. 22cm. [BM21.L5] 55-11036
1. American Council for Judaism. I. Title.

LIPTZIN, Solomon, 1901- 296
Generation of decision; Jewish rejuvenation in America. New York, Bloch Pub. Co., 1958. 307p. 23cm. [E184.J5L75] 58-8503
1. Jews in the U. S.—Hist. 2. Jews in literature. I. Title.

LOEWENSTEIN, Rudolph M. 296
Christians and Jews, a psychoanalytic study. [Translated from the French by Vera Damman] New York, International Universities Press [1951] 224 p. 23 cm. Bibliography: p. 203-213. [DS145.L6442] 51-9717
1. Antisemitism. I. Title.

LOEWENSTEIN, Rudolph Maurice. 296
Christians and Jews, a psychoanalytic study. [Translated from the French by Vera Damman] New York, International Universities Press [1951] 224p. 23cm. Bibliography: p. 203-213. [DS145.L6442] 51-9717
1. Antisemitism. I. Title.

LOEWENSTEIN, Rudolph Maurice, M.D. 296
Christians and Jews, a psychoanalytic study. [Tr. from French by Vera Damman] New York, Dell [1963, c.1951] 226p. 21cm. (Delta bk. 1273) Bibl. 1.65 pap.,
1. Antisemitism. I. Title.

LONGHURST, John Edward, 1918- 296
The age of Torquemada. Illus. by Evelyn G. Byatt. Sandoval, N.M., Coronado Pr., Casa vieja [c.]1962. 170p. illus. 20cm. 62-4424 1.75 pap.,
1. Jews in Spain—Persecutions. 2. Inquisition. Spain. I. Torquemada, Tomas de, 1420-1498. II. Title.

MCCOWN, Chester Charlton, 1877-1958. 296
Man, morals, and history; today's legacy from ancient times and Biblical peoples. [1st ed.] New York, Harper [1958] 350p. illus. 22cm. Includes bibliography. [BM157.M2] 58-10366
1. History—Philosophy. 2. Civilization—Hist. 3. Judaism—Hist. I. Title.

MANDEL, Morris, 1911- 296
Thirteen, a teenage guide to Judaism. Illus. by Lil Goldstein. New York, Jonathan David [c.1961] 190p. col. illus. 29cm. 61-8452 7.95 bds.,
1. Judaism—Juvenile literature. I. Title.

MANDEL, Morris, 1911- 296
Thirteen, a teenage guide to Judaism. Illustrated by Lil Goldstein. New York, J. David [1961] 190p. illus. 29cm. [BM573.M3] 61-8452
1. Judaism—Juvenile literature. I. Title.

MANUAL of discipline, English. 296
The manual of discipline, translated and annotated with an introd. by P. Wernberg-Moller. Grand Rapids, Eerdmans, 1957. 180p. 24cm. (Studies on the texts of the desert of Judah, v. 1) Bibliography: p. [167]-178. [BM488.M3A3 1957] 58-14626
1. Qumran community. I. Wernberg-Moller, Preben, ed. and tr. II. Title. III. Series.

MARCUS, Jacob Rader, 1896- 296
Early American Jewry; the Jews of New York, New England, and Canada, 1649-1794. Philadelphia, Jewish Publication Society of America [1951- v. illus., ports., facsim. 22 cm. [F15.J5M3] 52-6307
1. Jews in New England. 2. Jews in New York (State) 3. Jews in Canada. I. Title.

MARCUS, Jacob Rader, 1896- 296
Three hundred years in America in Katz, Irving I The Beth El story ... Detroit, Wayne Univ. Press, 1955. [BM225.D44K3] 55-7560
I. Title.

MARENOF, Martha. 296
The builders of the Jewish people from ancient times to present times. Newton Centre, Mass., DOT Publications, 1956. 255p. illus. 23cm. (Her History through literature, v. 2) [DS120.M28] 56-13487
1. Jews—Hist. I. Title.

MARENOF, Martha. 296
The builders of the Jewish people from ancient times to present times. Newton Centre, Mass., DOT Publications, 1956. 255p. illus. 23cm. (Her History through literature, v. 2) [DS120.M28] 56-13487
1. Jews—Hist. I. Title.

MARKOWITZ, Samuel Harrison, 1892- 296
Leading a Jewish life in the modern world. Rev. ed. New York, Union of American Hebrew Congregations [1958] 327p. illus. 21cm. (Commission on Jewish Education of the Union of American Hebrew Congregations and Central Conference of American Rabbis. Union adult series) Includes bibliography. [BM650.M3 1958] 58-1928
1. Jews—Soc. life & cust. 2. Jews—Rites and ceremonies. 3. Jewish question. I. Title.

MARKOWITZ, Sidney L 1905- 296
What you should know about Jewish religion, history, ethics, and culture. New York, Citadel Press [c1955] 226p. 21cm. [BM560.M3] 55-11620
1. Judaism. I. Title.

MARKOWITZ, Sidney L., 1905- 296
What you should know about Jewish religion, history, ethics and culture. New York, Citadel [1962, c.1955] 226p. 1.75 pap.,
1. Judaism. I. Title.

MEYER, Peter, 1902- 296
The Jews in the Soviet satellites, by Peter Meyer [and others. Syracuse, N. Y.] Syracuse University Press [1953] viii, 637p. 24cm. Includes bibliographical references. [DS135.E83M4] 53-12364
1. Jews in Europe, Eastern. I. Title.
Contents omitted.

MILCH, Robert J. 296
How to be an American Jew, by Robert J. Milch. New York, T. Yoseloff [1969] 112 p. 22 cm. [BM205.M48 1969] 69-14874 3.95
1. Judaism—U.S. I. Title.

MINKIN, Jacob Samuel, 1885- 296
The romance of Hassidism. [New ed. New York] T. Yoseloff [1955, c1935] 398p. 22cm. [BM198.M5 1955] 56-13776
1. Hasidism. I. Title.

MODERN Jewish thought; 296
selected issues, 1889-1966. New introd. by Louis Jacobs. New York, Arno Press, 1973. 1 v. (various pagings) 24 cm. (The Jewish people: history, religion, literature) Collection of reprinted journal articles. Contents.Contents.—Agus, J. B. Mitzvot, yes; averot, no.—Brickner, B. R. Religious education: the God-idea in the light of modern thought and its pedagogic implications.—Cronbach, A. The psychoanalytic study of Judaism.—Graetz, H. The significance of Judaism for the present and the future.—Heller, B. J. The modernists revolt against God.—Kohn, J. The assault on reason.—Montefiore, C. G. The desire for immortality.—Roth, L. Moralization and demoralization in Jewish ethics.—Schechter S. The dogmas of Judaism.—Steinberg, M. Kierkegaard and Judaism.—Wilhelm, K. The idea of humanity in Judaism. Includes bibliographical references. [BM40.M58] 73-2221 ISBN 0-405-05283-9 20.00
1. Judaism—Addresses, essays, lectures. I. Arno Press. II. Title. III. Series.
Contents omitted.

MONTEFIORE, Claude Joseph Goldsmid, 1858-1938, ed. and tr. 296
A rabbinic anthology, selected and arr. with comments and introductions by C. G. Montefiore and H. Loewe. [New York] Meridian Books [1960] 853p. 22cm. (Greenwich editions) [BM40.M6 1960] 60-6770
1. Judaism— Collections. 2. Ethics, Jewish. 3. Jewish literature. I. Loewe, Herbert Martin James, 1882-1940, joint ed. and tr. II. Title.

MONTEFIORE CLAUDE JOSEPH GOLDSMID, 1858-1938, ed. and tr. 296
A rabbinic anthology, selected, arr., comments, introds. by C. G. Montefiore, H. Loewe. Jewish Pubn. Soc. [dist.] Cleveland, World [1963] 853p. 20cm. (Meridian bks. PP32) 3.25 pap.,
1. Judaism—Collections. 2. Ethics, Jewish. 3. Jewish literature. I. Loewe, Herbert Martin James, 1882-1940, joint ed. and tr. II. Title.

MOSES BEN, Mainion 1135-1204. 296
The code of Maimonides. New Haven. Yale University Press, 1949- v. 22cm. (Yale Judaica series, v. 2- Translation of Mishneh Torah. Contents.-book 9. The book of offerings.--book 10. The book of cleanness.--book 11. The book of torts.--book 12. The book of acquisition.--book 13. The book of civil laws.--book 14. The book of judges. [BM545.M54] 49-9495
1. Jewish law. I. Title. II. Series.

MOSES BEN MAIMON, 1135-1204. 296
The code of Maimonides. bk. 3, The book of seasons. Tr. from Hebrew by Solomon Gandz. Hyman Klein. Appendix by Ernest Wisenberg. New Haven, Conn., Yale Univ. Pr. [c.]1961. 633p. (Yale Judaic ser., v.14) 49-9495 10.00
1. Jewish law. I. Title. II. Series.

MURRAY, William Henry, 1869- 296
Adam and Cain; symposium of old Bible history, Sumerian Empire, importance of blood of race, juggling juggernaut of the leaders of the Jews, the Gothic civilization of Adam and the Ten commandments of his church. Tishomingo, Okla. [1951] 623 p. illus., ports. 21 cm. Bibliography: p. 623. [DS145.M83] 51-27694
1. Antisemitism. I. Title.

NAHMAN ben Simhah of Bratzlav 1770?-1810? 296
The tales of Rabbi Nachman [by] Martin Buber. Translated from the German by Maurice Friedman. New York, Horizon Press [1956] 214p. 22cm. [BM532.N33] 56-12329
1. Tales, Hasidic. I. Buber. Martin. 1878- II. Title.

NAHMAN BEN SIMHAH, of Bratzlav, 7702-1810? 296
The tales of Rabbi Nachman [by] Martin Buber. Tr. from German by Maurice Friedman [Gloucester. Mass., P. Smith, 1966, c.1956] 214p. 21cm. (Midland bk., MB33 rebound) [BM532.N33] 4.00
1. Tales. Hasidic. I. Buber, Martin, 1878. II. Title.

NATIONAL Jewish Youth Conference. 296
Proceedings. New York. v. illus. 28 cm. annual. [E184.J5N5965] 52-27198
1. Youth — Societies. 2. Jews in the U.S. I. Title.

NEMOY, Leon, 1901- ed. and tr. 296
Karaite anthology, excerpts from the early literature; translated from Arabic, Aramaic, and Hebrew sources, with notes by Leon Nemoy. New Haven, Yale University Press, 1952. xxvi, 412 p. 22 cm. (Yale Judaica series, v. 7) Bibliography: p. [394]-397. [BM175.K3N37] 52-5367
1. Karaites. 2. Jewish literature — Translations into English. I. Title. II. Series.

NEUSNER, Jacob, 1932- 296
Between time and eternity : the essentials of Judaism / Jacob Neusner ; [artwork by Tom Martin from drawings by Suzanne Richter Neusner]. Encino, Calif. : Dickenson Pub. Co., c1975. xi, 196 p. : ill. ; 21 cm. Includes bibliographical references and index. [BM155.2.N45] 75-8124 pbk. : 4.95
1. Judaism—History. I. Title.

NEUSNER, Jacob, 1932- 296
Judaism in the secular age; essays on fellowship, community, and freedom. New York, Ktav Pub. House, 1970. x, 181 p. 23 cm. Includes bibliographical references. [BM565.N48 1970] 78-92606 ISBN 0-87068-009-9 6.95
1. Judaism—20th century. I. Title.

NEUSNER, Jacob, 1932- comp. 296
Understanding rabbinic Judaism, from Talmudic to modern times. New York, Ktav Pub. House [1974] vii, 422 p. 23 cm. "Bibliography on Judaism from Talmudic to modern times, by David Goodblatt": p. 383-402. [BM155.2.N48] 73-22167 ISBN 0-87068-238-5 5.95 (pbk.)
1. Judaism—History—Addresses, essays,

lectures. 2. Rabbis. 3. Rabbinical literature—History and criticism. I. Title.

NEUSNER, Jacob, 1932- 296
The way of Torah: an introduction to Judaism. Belmont, Calif., Dickenson Pub. Co. [1970] xi, 116 p. 23 cm. (Religious life of man) Bibliography: p. 104-113. [BM580.N53] 79-113760
1. Judaism. I. Title.

NEUSNER, Jacob, 1932- 296
The way of Torah; an introduction to Judaism. 2d ed. Encino, Calif., Dickenson Pub. Co. [1974] xvii, 126 p. 23 cm. (The Religious life of man series) Bibliography: p. 113-123. [BM580.N53 1974] 73-88121 ISBN 0-8221-0120-3 3.50
1. Judaism. I. Title.

NEWMAN, Louis Israel, 1893- 296
The Jewish people, faith, and life; a manual and guidebook of inforamtion concerning Jewry and Judaism, by Louis I. Newman. New York, Bloch Pub. Co., 1965. x, 277 p. 22 cm. Bibliography: p. 257-277. [BM561.N4] 64-66308
1. Judaism — Handbooks, manuals, etc. I. Title.

NICHOLSON, Wallace B 1903- 296
The Hebrew sanctuary; a study in typology. Grand Rapids, Baker Book House, 1951. 67 p. 22 cm. [BM654.N5] 51-6813
1. Tabernacle. 2. Typology (Theology) I. Title.

PAGEL, Paul Homer. 296
The cross or the star? An honest appraisal of Judaism. Edited by Lois Marie Pagel. Inglewood, Calif., Alexandria House [1964] 223 p. 21 cm. [BM585.P3] 65-1332
1. Judaism — Controversial literature. I. Title.

PARKES, James William, 1896- 296
Prelude to dialogue; Jewish-Christian relationships [by] James Parkes. With a foreword by A. J. Heschel. [New York] Schocken Books [1969] xi, 227 p. 23 cm. Essays. Contents.Contents.—A reappraisal of the Christian attitude to Jewry.—The concept of a chosen people in Judaism and Christianity.—The meaning of Torah.—Judaism and Christian civilisation.—Verdict on Father Daniel.—Toynbee and the uniqueness of Jewry.—Jews, Christians, and Moslems in the history of Palestine.—The new face of Israel.—Israel and the Diaspora.—The theology of toleration.—A theology of the Jewish-Christian relationship.—The Bible, the world, and the Trinity. Bibliographical footnotes. [BM535.P238 1969b] 72-79758 5.95
1. Judaism—Relations—Christianity. 2. Christianity and other religions—Judaism. 3. Israel and the Diaspora. I. Title.

PATAI, Raphael, 1910- 296
Man and temple in ancient Jewish myth and ritual. 2d enl. ed., with a new introd. & postscript. New York, Ktay [1967] xiv, 247p. 24cm. Bibl. [BM530.P3 1967] 67-22754 5.95 bds.,
1. Mythology, Jewish. 2. Cultus, Jewish. 3. Jerusalem. Temple. I. Title.

PATERSON, Moira. 296
The bar mitzvah book / advisory editors, Eugene Borowitz, Nahum L. Rabinovitch, Louis Rabinowitz, edited by Moira Paterson ; contributions by Issac Babel ... [et al.]. New York : Praeger, 1975. 224 p., [16] leaves of plates : ill. ; 27 cm. [BM42.P34 1975] 74-20865 ISBN 0-275-33560-7 : 19.95
1. Judaism—Addresses, essays, lectures. I. Babel', Isaak Emmanuilovich, 1894-1941. II. Title.

PEARL, Chaim, 1919- 296
The guide to Jewish knowledge, by Chaim Pearl and Reuben S. Brookes. [1st American ed.] Bridgeport, Conn., Hartmore House [1972, c1958] 123 p. 23 cm. Bibliography: p. 115-116. [BM570.P4 1972] 75-187866 ISBN 0-87677-046-4
1. Judaism—Study and teaching. I. Brookes, Reuben Solomon, 1914- joint author. II. Title.

PESSIN, Deborah. 296
History of the Jews in America. Illus. by Ruth Gikow. New York, United Synagogue Comission on Jewish Education, 1957. 317p. illus. 25cm. Includes bibliographies. [E184.J5P38] 57-7421
1. Jews in the U. S.—Hist. I. Title.

PESSIN, Deborah. 296
History of the Jews in America. With an introd. by Moshe Davis. Illus. by Ruth Gikow. New York, Abelard-Schuman [1958, c1957] 287p. illus. 22cm. (A Ram's horn book) [E184.J5P38 1958] 58-2194
1. Jews in the U. S.—Hist. I. Title.

PFEIFFER, Robert Henry, 1892-1958. 296
History of New Testament times, with an introduction to the Apocrypha. Westport, Conn., Greenwood Press [1972, c1949] xii, 561 p. 24 cm. "The sequel and completion of ... [the author's] Introduction to the Old Testament." Bibliography: p. 531-541. [BM176.P4 1972] 77-138125 ISBN 0-8371-3559-1
1. Jews—History—586 B.C.-70 A.D. 2. Bible. O.T. Apocrypha—Introductions. 3. Judaism—History—Post-exilic period, 586 B.C.-210 A.D. 4. Hellenism. I. Title.

PHILADELPHIA. REFORM CONGREGATION KENESETH ISRAEL. 296
Reform Congregation Keneseth Israel; its first 100 years, 1847-1947. [Philadelphia, 1950] 64 p. illus., ports. 24 cm. [BM225.P5K455] 50-30349
I. Title.

PLAUT, W Gunther, 1912- 296
The case for the chosen people [by] W. Gunther Plaut. [1st ed.] Garden City, N.Y., Doubleday, 1965. viii, 205 p. 22 cm. Bibliographical references included in "Notes" (p. [197]-205) [BM561.P55] 65-19869
1. Judaism. I. Title.

PLAUT, W. Gunther, 1912- 296
Your neighbor is a Jew [by] W. Gunther Plaut. Philadelphia, Pilgrim Press [1968] 142 p. 21 cm. Consists chiefly of material originally published in the Toronto Globe and mail. [BM561.P56 1968] 68-28768 2.95
1. Judaism. I. Title.

PLAUT, W. Gunther, 1912- 296
Your neighbour is a Jew [by] W. Gunther Plaut. Toronto, Montreal, McClelland and Stewart [1967] 142 p. 23 cm. [BM561.P56] 68-92215 6.00 Can.
1. Judaism. I. Title.

PLOEG, J. P. M. van der, 1909- 296
The excavations at Qumran; a survey of the Judaean brotherhood and its ideas. Translated by Kevin Smyth. London, New York, Longmans, Green 1958 233 p. illus. 21 cm. Translation of Vondsten in de weestijn van Juda. Includes bibliography. [BM175.Q6P513] 58-4029
1. Dead Sea scrolls. 2. Qumran community. I. Title.

PLOEG, J. P. M. van der, 1909- 296
The excavations at Qumran; a survey of the Judaean brotherhood and its ideas. Translated by Kevin Smyth. London, New York, Longmans, Green [1958] 233 p. illus. 21 cm. Translation of Vondsten in de woestijn van Juda. Includes bibliography. [BM175.Q6P513] 58-4029
1. Qumran community. 2. Dead Sea scrolls. I. Title.

POLISH, David. 296
The higher freedom; a new turning point in Jewish history. Chicago, Quadrangle Books, 1965. 245 p. 22 cm. [BM561.P6] 65-10379
1. Judaism 2. Jews—Political and social condit.—1948- I. Title.

POOL, David de Sola, 1885- 296
An old faith in the New World; portrait of Shearith Israel, 1654-1954 [by] David and Tamar de Sola Pool. New York, Columbia University Press, 1955. xviii, 595p. illus., ports., maps, facsims., music 26cm. Bibliography: p. [555]-562. [BM225.N5S46] 55-6619
1. New York. Congregation Shearith Israel. 2. Judaism—U. S. I. Pool, Tamar (Hirschensohn) de Sola, 1893- joint author. II. Title.

POOL, David de Sola, 1885- 296
Portraits etched in stone; early Jewish settlers, 1682-1831. New York, Columbia University Press, 1952. xiv, 543 p. illus., ports. maps, geneal. tables. 26 cm. Bibliography: p. [513]-517. [F128.9.J5P6] 52-14151
1. New York (City) Chatham Square Cemetery. 2. Jews in New York (City) — Biog. 3. New York. Congregation Shearith Israel. I. Title.

POOL, David de Sola, 1885- 296
Why I am a Jew. New York, T. Nelson [1957] 207p. 21cm. [BM560.P6] 57-14829
1. Judaism. I. Title.

RABIN, Chaim. 296
Qumran studies. [London] Oxford University Press, 1957. 135p. 22cm. (Scripta Judalca, 2) Bibliographical footnotes. [BM175.Q6R3] 57-59398
1. Qumran community. 2. Judaism—Relations—Mohammedanism. 3. Mohammedanism—Relations—Judaism. I. Title.

RABINOWITZ, Shalom, 1859-1916. 296
Adventures of Mottel, the cantor's son, by Sholom Aleichem [pseud.] translated by Tamara Kahana. Illus. by Ilya Schor. New York, H. Schuman [1953] 342 p. illus. 22 cm. Translation of (Motel Peysi dem hazen's) Contents.Contents.—In Kasrilovka: Hoorah, I'm an orphan!—In America: Try not to love such a country. [E184.J5R213] 53-8054
1. Jews in the U.S. I. Title.

RAND, Howard B 1889- 296
Behold, He cometh! Haverhill, Mass, Destiny Publishers [1955] 100p. 22cm. [DS131.R25] 55-11580
1. Anglo-Israelism. I. Title.

RAPAPORT, Izaak. 296
Like a rose among the thorns; essays on the glorious union between Jewry and the moral and religious values of Judaism, by Rabbi Dr. I. Rapaport. Melbourne [E. H. Gibbs] 1968. xlix, 287 p. port. 22 cm. English or Yiddish. Added t.p. in Hebrew. [BM45.R293] 72-491482
1. Judaism—Addresses, essays, lectures. I. Title. II. Title: Azoy vi a royz tsvishn di derner.

REED, Walter E 296
Contract with God [by] Walter E. Reed and Fay Sand Reed. Foreword by Trude Weiss-Rosmarin. New York, Four Seasons Publishers [1965] xv, 144 p. 20 cm. Bibliography: p. [140]-144. [BM723.R4] 65-24038
1. Jewish way of life. 2. Bible. O.T. — Use. I. Reed, Fay Sand, joint author. II. Title.

REICHMANN, Eva G 296
Hostages of civilisation; the social sources of national socialist anti-semitism. Boston, Beacon Press [1951] 281 p. 22 cm. Bibliography: p. 268-277. [DS145.R45 1951] 51-5986
1. Antisemitism. 2. Jews in Germany — Hist. I. Title.

RESNER, Lawrence. 296
Eternal stranger; the plight of the modern Jew from Baghdad to Casablanca. Foreword by Bartley C. Crum. [1st ed.] Garden City, N. Y., Doubleday, 1951. 216 p. 21 cm. [DS135.A25R4] 51-13141
1. Jews in Africa, North. 2. Jews in the Near East. I. Title.

REZNIKOFF, Charles, 1894- 296
The Jews of Charleston; a history of an American Jewish community, by Charles Reznikoff with the collaboration of Uriah Z. Engelman. Philadelphia, Jewish Publication Society of America, 1950. xii, 343 p. illus., ports. 22 cm. Bibliographical references included in "Notes" (p. 267-325) [BM225.C4R4] 50-11674
1. Jews in Charleston, S.C. I. Title.

RIBALOW, Harold Uriel, 1919- ed. 296
Mid-century; an anthology of Jewish life and culture in our times. New York, Beechurst Press [1955] 598p. 24cm. sJews in the U. S. [E184.J5R5] 54-10691
1. Jews. I. Title.

RINGELBLUM, Emanuel, 1900-1944. 296
Notes from the Warsaw ghetto; the journal of Emmanuel Ringelblum. Edited and translated by Jacob Sloan. [1st ed.] New York, McGraw-Hill [1958] 369 p. illus. 22 cm. [DS135.P62W333] 58-8048
1. Jews in Warsaw. 2. World War, 1939-1945—Personal narratives, Jewish. I. Title.

ROBIN, Frederick Elliott, 1920- 296
The pursuit of equality; a half century with the American Jewish Committee. [Written by Frederick E. Robin and Selma G. Hirsh] New York, Crown Publishers [1957] 197p. illus., ports. 28cm. [E184.J5R6] 57-59291
1. American Jewish Committee. I. Hirsh, Selma G., joint author. II. Title.

ROBINSON, Nehemiah. 296
The United Nations and the World Jewish Congress. New York, Institute of Jewish Affairs, World Jewish Congress [1956?] vi, 285p. 23cm. [JX1977.3.W6R6] 58-2270
1. United Nations—Non-governmental advisory organizations. 2. World Jewish Congress. I. Title.

ROSE, Goodman Alikum, 1890- 296
Thoughts of a Jew and Jewish thoughts. New York, Bloch Pub. Co., 1950- v. 20cm. [BM560.R57] 53-1759
1. Judaism. I. Title.

ROSENBAUM, Samuel. 296
To live as a Jew, by Samuel Rosenbaum. Edited by Abraham J. Karp. [New York] Ktav Pub. House [1969] 216 p. illus. 24 cm. Includes traditional melodies. [BM105.R63] 70-91962 5.95
1. Judaism—Juvenile literature. I. Title.

ROSENBERG, Stuart E. 296
Bridge to brotherhood; Judaism's dialogue with Christianity. Foreword by James Parkes. New York, Abelard [c.1961] 178p. 61-5411 3.95
1. Judaism—Relations—Christianity. 2. Christianity and other religions—Judaism. I. Title.

ROSENBERG, Stuart E 296
Judaism, by Stuart E. Rosenberg. Glen Rock, N.J., Paulist Press [1966] 159 p. 18 cm. (Deus books) [BM561.R63] 66-22049
1. Judaism. I. Title.

ROSENBERG, Stuart E. 296
Judaism. Glen Rock. N.J. Paulist Pr. [c.1966] 159p. 18cm. (Deus bks.) [BM561.R63] 66-22049 .95 pap.,
1. Judaism. I. Title.

ROSENTHAL, Erich. 296
The Jewish population of Chicago, Illinois. [Chicago, College of Jewish Studies] 1952. 128p. illus. 23cm. 'Reprint from the Chicago Pinkas.' 'Originally presented as a doctroal dissertation ... University of Chicago.' Includes bibliography. [F548.9.J5R6] 53-18472
1. Jews in Chicago. 2. Chicago— Population. I. Title.

ROSENTHAL, Frank. 296
The Jews of Des Moines, the first century. Introd. by William D. Houlette. Des Moines, Jewish Welfare Federation [1957] 213p. illus. 22cm. [F629.D4R6] 57-4680
1. Jews in Des Moines. I. Title.

ROSSEL, Seymour. 296
Judaism / Seymour Rossel. New York : F. Watts, 1976. 61 p. : ill. ; 23 cm. (A First book) Includes index. Bibliography: p. [57]. An introduction to the many aspects of Judaism, including its historical development, beliefs, holidays, and branches. [BM105.R638] 75-31561 ISBN 0-531-00841-X : 3.90
1. Judaism—Juvenile literature. I. Title.

ROTENSTREICH, Nathan, 1914- 296
The recurring pattern; studies in anti-Judaism in modern thought. New York, Horizon [1964, c.1963] 135p. 23cm. Bibl. 64-15190 4.50
1. Judaism—Apologetic works. 2. Judaism—Historiography. 3. Judaism—Controversial literature—Hist. & crit. I. Title.

ROTH, Cecil, 1899- 296
A bird's-eye view of Jewish history. [Rev. ed.] New York, Union of American Hebrew Congregations, 1954. 466p. illus. 21cm. (Union adult series) [DS118.R6 1954] 55-31939
1. Jews—Hist. I. Title.

ROTH, Cecil, 1899- 296
The Jews of medieval Oxford. Oxford, Clarendon Press, 1951. 194 p. illus., fold. map. 23 cm. (Oxford Historical Society. [Publications] New ser., v. 9) Bibliographical footnotes. [DA690.O97O8 Ns., vol. 9] 52-864
1. Jews in Oxford. I. Title. II. Series.

ROTH, Cecil, 1899- 296
Personalities and events in Jewish history. Philadelphia, Jewish Publication Society of America, 1953 [i. e. 1954] 324p. 22cm. [DS119.R78] 53-7602
1. Jews—Hist.—Anecdotes. I. Title.

ROTH, Leon [Hyam Leon Roth] 1896- 296
Judaism: a portrait. New York, Viking Press, 1961 [c.1960] 240p. 61-5918 4.00
1. Judaism. I. Title.

ROTH, Leon [Hyam Leon Roth] 1896- 296
Judaism: a portrait. New York, Viking [1962, c.1960] 240p. (Compass bk. C104) 1.35 pap.,
1. Judaism. I. Title.

ROTH, Sol. 296
The Jewish idea of community / by Sol Roth. New York : Yeshiva University Press, Dept. of Special Publications, 1977. 164 p. ; 24 cm. Includes bibliographical references and index. [BM565.R65] 76-52376 ISBN 0-89362-005-X : 7.50
1. Judaism—Essence, genius, nature. I. Title.

RUBENOVITZ, Mignon (Levine) 296
Altars of my fathers Rev. 2d ed. New York, National Women's League of the United Synagogue of America [c1957] 92p. illus. 29cm. [BM657.A1R8 1957] 57-13467
1. Cultus, Jewish. 2. Jews—Antiq. I. Title.

RUDY, Esther, 1900- 296
Design for living; from Jewish life and lore. New York, Bloch Pub. Co., 1950. xiii, 224 p. 23 cm. [BM565.R8] 51-1392
1. Judaism. I. Title.

RUNES, Dagobert David, 1902- ed. 296
The Hebrew impact on western civilization. New York, Philosophical Library [1951] xiv,

922 p. 23 cm. Includes bibliographies. [DS113.R8] 51-102
1. Jews — Civilization. 2. Civilization, Occidental. I. Title.

RUSSELL, David Syme. 296
Between the Testaments. Philadelphis, Muhlenberg Press [1960] 176 p. 20 cm. Includes bibliography. [BM176.R8] 60-2960
1. Judaism—History—Post-exilic period. 2. Jews—History—586 B.C.-70 A.D. 3. Apocalyptic literature. I. Title.

THE Samuel Friedland lectures 296
1967-1974 New York : Jewish Theological Seminary of America, [1974] vii, 121 p. ; 22 cm. Contents.Contents.—Cohen, G. D. Foreword.—Finkelstein, L. Religion and ethics: rivals or partners.—Gordis, D. M. Towards a rabbinic philosophy of education.—Greenberg, S. Intellectual freedom in the Jewish tradition.—Holtz, A. Jerusalem—city of visions and prayers.—Lieber, D. Man in Jewish tradition.—Muffs, Y. God and the world: a Jewish view.—Siegel S. Judaism and the New Morality.—Silverman, D. W. Dreams, divination, and prophecy: Gersonides and the problem of precognition. Includes bibliographical references. [BM42.S22] 74-196811
1. Judaism—Addresses, essays, lectures. I. Friedland, Samuel. II. Jewish Theological Seminary of America.

SCHAUSS, Hayyim, 1884- 296
The lifetime of a Jew throughout the ages of Jewish history. Cincinnati, Union of American Hebrew Congregations, 1950. xiii, 332 p. illus., facsims. 24 cm. (Commission on Jewish Education of the Union of American Hebrew Congregations and [the] Central Conference of American Rabbis. Union adult series) Bibliographical references included in "Notes" (p. 305-322) [BM723.S3] 50-1758
1. Jews — Rites and ceremonies. 2. Jews — Soc. life & cust. I. Title. II. Series.

SCHECHTER, Solomon, 1847-1915. 296
Studies in Judaism. Freeport, N.Y., Books for Libraries Press [1972] xxv, 366 p. 23 cm. (Essay index reprint series) Reprint of the 1896 ed. Includes bibliographical references. [BM160.S3 1972] 78-38775 ISBN 0-8369-2670-6
1. Judaism—History—Addresses, essays, lectures. I. Title.

SCHOEPS, Hans Joachim. 296
The Jewish-Christian argument; a history of theologies in conflict. Translated by David E. Green [1st ed.] New York, Holt, Rinehart and Winston [1963] 208 p. 22 cm. Translation of Israel und Christenheit. [BM535.S2883] 63-10198
1. Judaism—Relations—Christianity. 2. Christianity and other religions—Judaism. I. Title.

SCHOLEM, Gershom Gerhard, 1897- 296
Major trends in Jewish mysticism. Based on the Hilda Stroock lectures delivered at the Jewish Institute of Religion, New York, 3d rev. ed. New York, Schocken Books [1954] 456p. 24cm. [BM723.S35 1954] 55-1150
1. Mysticism—Judaism. I. Title.

SCHOLEM, Gershom Gerhard, 1897- 296
The Messianic idea in Judaism and other essays on Jewish spirituality [by] Gershom Scholem. New York, Schocken Books [1971] viii, 376 p. 24 cm. Ten of the seventeen essays translated from German and one from Hebrew. Includes bibliographical references. [BM615.S33] 70-130212 15.00
1. Messiah. 2. Judaism—History—Addresses, essays, lectures. I. Title.

SCHOLES, Percy Alfred, 1877- 296
A miniature history of music for the general reader and the student. 4th ed. London, Oxford University Press, 1955. 53p. 19cm. 'First appeared as a series of seven articles in the Radio times.' [ML160.S37 1955] 56-28124
1. Music—Hist. & crit. 2. Music— Analysis, appreciation. I. Title.

SCHONFELD, Solomon, 1912- 296
Why Judaism. London, Shapiro Vallentine; New York, Bloch Pub. Co. [1963] 256 p. 19 cm. [BM561.S3] 63-25186
1. Judaism. 2. Jewish way of life. I. Title.

SCHONFELD, Solomon, 1912- 296
Why Judaism. London, Shapiro, Vallentine; 256p. 19cm. 63-25186 3.50 bds.,
1. Judaism. 2. Jewish way of life. I. Title.

SCHWARTZ, Charles. 296
Faith through reason; a modern interpretation of Judaism, by Charles Schwartz [and] Bertie G. Schwartz. New York, National Women's League of the United Synagogue of America, 1955 [c1946] 189p. 22cm. [BM565] 55-14594
1. Judaism. 2. Faith. I. Schwartz, Bertie G., joint author. II. Title.

SCHWARTZ, Charles, 1892-1969. 296
A modern interpretation of Judaism : faith through reason / Charles Schwartz, Bertie G. Schwartz. New York : Schocken Books, 1976, c1946. xii, 189 p. ; 21 cm. Reprint of the ed. published by the National Women's League of the United Synagogue of America, New York, under title: Faith through reason. [BM565.S37 1976] 75-35447 ISBN 0-8052-0526-8 pbk. : 4.95
1. Judaism. I. Schwartz, Bertie G., joint author. II. Title.

SCHWARTZMAN, Sylvan David. 296
Reform Judaism in the making. New York, Union of AmericanHebrew Congregations [1955] 194p. illus. 24cm. (Commission on Jewish Education of the Union of American Hebrew Congregations and Central Conference of American Rabbis. Union graded serie Includes bibliography. [BM197.S33] 56-204
1. Reform Judaism. I. Title.

SCHWARTZMAN, Sylvan David. 296
The story of Reform Judaism. New York, Union of American Hebrew Congregations [1953] 191p. illus. 24cm. (Commission on Jewish Education of the Union of American Hebrew Congregations and Central Conference of American Rabbis. Union graded series) [BM197.S34] 54-1803
1. Reform Judaism. I. Title.

SCHWARZ, Leo Walder, 1906- ed. 296
Great ages and ideas of the Jewish people, by Salo W. Baron [and others] New York, Random House [1956] xxvii, 515 p. 22 cm. "Suggestions for further reading": p. [485]-498. [DS113.S38] 56-9895
1. Judaism—History. I. Baron, Salo Wittmayer, 1895- II. Title.

SCHWARZ, Solomon M 296
The Jews in the Soviet Union. Foreword by Alvin Johnson. [Syracuse] Syracuse University Press [1951] xviii, 380 p. 24 cm. Includes bibliographical references. [DS135.R9S36] 51-5293
1. Jews in Russia. I. Title.

SCHWARZBART, Isaac I 296
25 years in the service of the Jewish people; a chronicle of activities of the World Jewish Congress. August 1932--February 1957. New York, World Jewish Congress, Organization Dept. [1957] 56p. 23cm. [DS101.W64S4] 57-2755
1. World Jewish Congress. I. Title.

SEGAL, Charles M 296
Fascinating facts about American Jewish history. New York, Twayne Publishers [1955] 159p. 23cm. [E184.J5S4] 55-872
1. Jews in the U. S.—Hist. I. Title.

THE Seventy-fifth anniversary 296
volume of the Jewish quarterly review. Edited by Abraham A. Neuman and Solomon Zeitlin. Philadelphia, Jewish quarterly review, 1967. xi, 592 p. 2 facsims. 25 cm. Bibliographical footnotes. [BM42.S47] 76-2626
1. Jews—History—Addresses, essays, lectures. 2. Judaism—History—Addresses, essays, lectures. 3. Jewish learning and scholarship. I. Neuman, Abraham Aaron, 1890- ed. II. Zeitlin, Solomon, 1892- ed. III. The Jewish quarterly review.

SHINEDLING, Abraham Isaac, 1897- 296
History of the Beckley Jewish community (Beckley, West Virginia) and of Congregation Beth El (the Beckley Hebrew Association) including Raleigh and Fayette Counties, West Virginia, 1895 to 1955, by Abraham L. Shinedling and Manuel Pickus. [Berkeley] 1955. xiii, 205p. illus., ports. 24cm. [F249.B39S5] 56-29864
1. Jews in Beckley, W. Va. 2. Beckley, W. Va. Congregation Beth El. I. Pickus, Manuel, 1931- joint author. II. Title.

SHOSTECK, Robert, 1910- 296
Small-town Jewry tell their story; a survey of B'nai B'rith membership in small communities in the United States and Canada. Washington, B'nai B'rith Vocational Service Bureau, 1953. 57p. 23cm. [E184.J5S48] 53-20700
1. Jews in the U. S. 2. Jews in Canada. 3. B'nai B'rith. I. Title.

SHULMAN, Albert M. 296
Gateway to Judaism: encyclopedia home reference, by Albert M. Shulman. South Brunswick, T. Yoseloff [1971] 2 v. (1056 p.) 24 cm. [BM570.S57] 69-15777 ISBN 0-498-06896-X 20.00
1. Jews—History—Study and teaching. 2. Judaism—Study and teaching. I. Title.

SILVER, Abba Hillel, 1893- 296
Where Judaism differed; an inquiry into the distinctiveness of Judaism. New York, Macmillan, 1956 318p. 22 cm. [BM560.S5] 56-9652
1. Judaism 2. Judaism—Relations—Christianity 3. Christianity and other religions—Judaism. I. Title.

SILVER, Abba Hillel, 1893- 296
Where Judaism differed; an inquiry into the distinctiveness of Judaism. New York, Macmillan, 1956. 318p. 22cm. [BM560.S5] 56-9652
1. Judaism. 2. Judaism— Relations—Christianity. 3. Christianity and other religions—Judaism. I. Title.

SILVER, Abba Hillel, 1893- 296
Where Judaism differed; an inquiry into the distintiveness of Judaism. New York, Macmillan, 1956. 318 p. 22 cm. [BX560.S5] 56-9652
1. Judaism. 2. Judaism — Relations — Christianity. 3. Christianity and other religions — Judaism. I. Title.

SILVER, Maxwell. 296
The way to God. New York, Philosophical Library [1950] x, 303 p. 23 cm. Bibliographical references included in "Notes" (p. 289-291) [BM648.S5] 50-6883
1. Jews—Religion—Apologetic works. I. Title.

SILVER, Samuel M. 296
Explaining Judaism to Jews & Christians, by Samuel M. Silver. Stamford, Conn. [1971?] 118 p. illus. 22 cm. [BM580.S45] 72-177247
1. Judaism. I. Title.

SILVER, Samuel M. 296
Explaining Judaism to Jews and Christians, by Samuel M. Silver. Artwork by Norman Manaly. New York, Arco [1973] 142 p. illus. 21 cm. [BM580.S45 1973] 72-96799 1.50 (pbk.).
1. Judaism. I. Title.

SILVERMAN, William B. 296
Judaism and Christianity: what we believe, by William B. Silverman. New York, Behrman House [1968] 246 p. illus., ports. 25 cm. Includes bibliographies. [BM105.S5] 68-27330
1. Judaism—Juvenile literature. 2. Christianity and other religions—Judaism. 3. Judaism—Relations—Christianity. I. Title.

SIMON, Solomon, 1895- 296
My Jewish roots; translated from the Yiddish by Shlomo Katz. [1st ed.] Philadelphia, Jewish Publication Society of America, 1956. 274p. 22cm. [DS135.R9S562] 56-7783
1. Jews in Russia. I. Title.

SIMON, Solomon, 1895- 296
My Jewish roots; translated from the Yiddish by Shlomo Katz. [1st ed.] Philadelphia, Jewish Publication Society of America, 1956. 274 p. 22 cm. [DS135.R9S562] 56-7783
1. Jews in Russia I. Title.

SIMONHOFF, Harry. 296
Jewish notables in America, 1776-1865; links of an endless chain. Foreword by David de Sola Pool. New York, Greenberg [1956] 402p. illus. 21cm. [E184.J5S53] 55-12359
1. Jews in the U. S.—Biog. I. Title.

SIMONHOFF, Harry. 296
Jewish notables in America, 1776-1865; links of an endless chain. Foreword by David de Sola Pool. New York, Greenberg [1956] 402 p. illus. 21 cm. [E184.J5S53] 55-12359
1. Jews in the U.S. — Biog. I. Title.

SIMONHOFF, Harry. 296
Under strange skies. New York, Philosophical Library [1953] 349p. 23cm. [DS135.A1S5] 53-11641
1. Jews—Diaspora. I. Title.

SINGER, Howard. 296
With mind and heart; an approach to Judaism for young people. New York, United Synagogue Commission on Jewish Education, 1961. 312 p. illus. 23 cm. [BM561.S5] 61-8307
1. Judaism. I. Title.

SKLARE, Marshall, 1921- 296
Conservative Judaism; an American religious movement. Glencoe, Ill., Free Press [1955] 298p. 22cm. Revision of thesis--Columbia University. [BM197.5.S45 1955] 55-7332
1. Conservative Judaism. I. Title.

SKLARE, Marshall, 1921- ed. 296
The Jews; social patterns of an American group. Glencoe, Ill., Free Press [1958] 669 p. 24 cm. Includes bibliography. [E184.J5S55] 57-9318
1. Jews in the United States.

SKLARE, Marshall, 1921- 296
The Riverton study; how Jews look at themselves and their neighbors, by Marshall Sklare and Marc Vosk. [New York, American Jewish Committee, 1957] 48 p. 23 cm. [BM560.S55] 58-1051
1. Judaism. I. Vosk, Marc, joint author. II. Title.

SLEEPER, James A., comp. 296
The new Jews, edited by James A. Sleeper and Alan L. Mintz. [1st ed.] New York, Vintage Books [1971] 246 p. 18 cm. [BM40.S45] 78-140727 ISBN 0-394-71669-8 2.45
1. Jews—Political and social conditions—1948-—Addresses, essays, lectures. 2. Judaism—Addresses, essays, lectures. I. Mintz, Alan L., joint comp. II. Title.

SMITH, Harold P 296
A treasure hunt in Judaism. Illus. by A. D. Bernstein. Rev. ed. New York, Hebrew Pub. Co. [1950] x, 211 p. illus. 21 cm. [BM650.S56] 50-14780
1. Jews—Rites and ceremonies. 2. Jews—Soc. life & cust. I. Title.

SOBEL, Samuel. 296
I love Thy house; a keepsake of the Commodore Levy Chapel, Norfolk. 2d ed. [Norfolk, Jewish Community Council] 1962. [90] p., music (31 p.) illus., ports. 20 cm. "Music of the Commodore Levy Chapel . . . [principally for the] Sabbath eve service": 31 p. (2d group) [BM225.N7C6 1962a] 63-13730
1. U.S. Naval Station, Norfolk, Va. Commodore Levy Chapel. 2. Levy, Uriah Phillips, 1792-1862. 3. Armed Forces — Prayer-books and devotions — English. I. Title.

SOBEL, Samuel 296
I love Thy house; a keepsake of the Commodore Levy Chapel, Norfolk, 2d ed. Norfolk, Va., 700 Spotswood Ave., Norfolk Jewish Community Council, 1963. 87p., music (31p.) illus., ports. 20cm. 62-17837 5.00: 1.50 pap.,
1. Levy Uriah Phillips, 1792-1862. 2. U.S. Naval Station, Norfolk, Va. Commodore Levy Chapel. 3. Armed Forces—Prayerbooks and devotions—English. I. Title.

SOLOFF, Mordecai Isaac. 296
Jewish life. Baltimore, Dept. of Reform Jewish Education of the Board of Jewish Education; distributed by Bloch Pub. Co., 1950. 79 p. illus. 24 cm. [BM700.S6 1950] 50-37396
1. Jews — Rites and ceremonies. 2. Hebrew language — Terms and phrases. I. Title.

SOMBART, Werner, 1863-1941. 296
The Jews and modern capitalism; translated by M. Epstein, with an introd. to the American ed. by Bart F. Hoselitz. Glencoe, Ill., Free Press [1951] xiii, 402 p. 22 cm. Translation of Die Juden und das Wirtschaftsleben. Bibliography: p. xxxii-xiii. "Notes and references": p.[353]-402. [DS141.S65 1951] 51-8461
1. Jews—Political and social conditions. 2. Economic conditions. I. Title.

SPECTER, Ruth Rachel. 296
The bud and the flower of Judaism. Springfield, Mo., Gospel Pub. House [1955] 310p. illus. 20cm. [BM560.S66] 56-17700
1. Judaism. I. Title.

SPIRO, Saul S. 296
Fundamentals of Judaism, by Saul Spiro. [New York] Ktav Pub. House [1969] x, 342 p. 24 cm. (An Essentials of Jewish learning book) Bibliography: p. 334-337. [BM561.S65] 77-91961 5.95
1. Judaism. I. Title.

STEIMAN, Sidney. 296
Custom and survival, a study of the life and work of Rabbi Jacob Molin (Moelin) known as the Maharil (c. 1360-1427) and his influence in establishing the ashkenazic minhag (customs of German Jewry) Foreword by Nahum N. Glatzer. New York, Bloch Pub. Co. [1963] xvii, 143 p. 24 cm. Bibliography: p. 137-140. [BM755.J22S8] 63-19988
1. Jacob ben Moses, ha-Levi, 1365 (ca.)-1427. 2. Jews in Germany. I. Title.

STEIMAN, Sidney 296
Custom and survival; a study of the life and work of Rabbi Jacob Molin (Moelln) known as the Maharil (c.1360-1427) and his influence in establishing the ashkenazic minhag (customs of German Jewry) Foreword by Nahum N. Glatzer. New York, Bloch [c. 1963] xvii, 143p. 24cm. Bibl. 63-19988 4.00
1. Jacob ben Moses, ha-Levi, 1365 (ca.)-1427. 2. Jews in Germany. I. Title.

STEINBERG, Milton, 1903- 296
A believing Jew; the selected writings of Milton Steinberg. [1st ed.] New York, Harcourt, Brace [1951] 318 p. 21 cm. [BM560.S82] 51-12040
1. Judaism. 2. Jews in the U.S. I. Title.

STEINBERG, Milton, 1903- 296
A partisan guide to the Jewish problem. Bobbs [dist. New York, Macfadden, 1963, c.1945] 308p. 21cm. (Charter bk., 134) Bibl. 1.75 pap.,
1. Jewish question. I. Title.

STEINBERG, Moses. 296
The greatest story never told. [Washington, 1952] 224 p. 24 cm. [BM580.S8] 52-3987
1. Judaism. I. Title.

STITSKIN, Leon D., comp. 296
Studies in Judaica. In honor of Dr. Samuel Belkin as scholar and educator. Edited by Leon D. Stitskin. New York, Ktav Pub. House [1974] 467 p. port. 24 cm. Contents.Contents.—Stitskin, L. D. Dr. Samuel Belkin as scholar and educator.—Belkin, S. Some obscure traditions mutually clarified in Philo and rabbinic literature.—Soloveitchick, J. B. Confrontation.—Soloveitchick, J. B. Lonely man of faith.—Stitskin, L. D. Maimonides' unbending opposition to astrology.—Stitskin, L. D. Ralbag's introduction to the Book of Job.—Rosenbloom, N. H. Luzzatto's ethico-psychological interpretation of Judaism.—Ury, Z. F. Salanter, the Musar movement.—Metzger, A. B. Z. Rabbi Kook's philosophy of repentance.—Hoening, S. B. Rabbinics and research: the scholarship of Dr. Bernard Revel. Includes bibliographical references. [BM42.S716] 74-7242 ISBN 0-87068-257-1 15.00
1. Belkin, Samuel. 2. Revel, Bernard, 1885-1940. 3. Judaism—Addresses, essays, lectures. 4. Musar movement. 5. Repentance (Judaism) I. Belkin, Samuel. II. Title.

SUGARMAN, Joan G 296
Joel finds out, by Joan G. Sugarman and Grace R. Freeman. Illustrated by Anita Rogoff. New York, Bookman Associates [1958] 273 p. illus. 23 cm. [BM573.S8] 58-2243
1. Judaism—Juvenile literature. 2. Jews—Biog.—Juvenile literature. I. Freeman, Grace R., joint author. II. Title.

SULMAN, Esther. 296
A goodly heritage; the story of the Jewish community in New London, 1860-1955, by Esther Sulman with the collaboration of Leonard J. Goldstein. New London, Conn., 1957. 81 p. illus. 23 cm. [BM225.N35S8] 57-31091
1. Jews in New London, Conn. 2. New London, Conn.—Synagogues. I. Title.

SWICHKOW, Louis J 296
Invocations. [Milwaukee] Bloch Pub. Co., 1951. 184 p. 18 cm. [BM675.O25S8 1951] 51-2743
I. Jews. Liturgy and ritual. Occasional prayers. II. Title.

SWIDLER, Leonard J. 296
Women in Judaism : the status of women in formative judaism / by Leonard Swidler. Metuchen, N.J. : Scarecrow Press, 1976. vi, 242 p. ; 22 cm. Includes bibliographical references and index. [BM729.W6S9] 75-46561 9.50
1. Women in Judaism. I. Title.

SZEKELY, Edmond Bordeaux. 296
The teachings of the Essenes, from Enoch to the Dead Sea scrolls. [San Diego, Calif., 1957] 94p. illus. 24cm. [BM175.E8S9] 57-39878
1. Essenes. I. Title.

SZEKELY, Edmond Bordeaux. 296
The teachings of the Essenes, from Enoch to the Dead Sea scrolls. [San Diego, Calif., 1957] 94 p. illus. 24 cm. [BM175.E8S9] 57-39878
1. Essenes. I. Title.

TABAK, Israel, 1904- 296
Treasury of holiday thoughts: High Holy Days and pilgrim festivals. New York, Twayne Publishers, [1958] 242 p. 23 cm. [BM690.T15] 58-2175
1. Fasts and feasts — Judaism. I. Title. II. Title: Holiday thoughts.

TELLER, Judd L 1912- 296
The Kremilin, the Jews, and the middle East. New York, T. Yoseloff [1957] 202p. 22cm. [DS135.R9T4] 57-7692
1. Jews in Russia. 2. Communism—Palestine. I. Title.

TELLER, Judd L 1912- 296
The Kremlin, the Jews, and the Middle East. New York, T. Yosoloff [1957] 202 p. 22 cm. [DS135.R9T4] 57-7692
1. Jews in Russia. 2. Communism — Palestine. I. Title.

TELLER, Judd L 1912- 296
Scapegoat of revolution. New York, Scribner, 1954. 352p. 22cm. [DS143.T39] 54-11019
1. Jews—Political and social conditions. 2. Communism—Jews. 3. Revolutionists. I. Title.

TENNEY, Jack Breckinridge, 1898- 296
Zion's fifth column; a Tenney report. Tujunga, Calif., Standard Publications, 1953. 92p. 22cm. [DS141.T44] 53-23413
1. Jewish question. 2. Zionism—Addresses, essays, lectures. I. Title.

TEPPER, Joseph L 296
A challenge to Jewry; a discussion on basic Jewish problems. New York, Vantage Press [1953] 135p. 23cm. [BM560.T45] 53-6482
1. Judaism. I. Title.

TREPP, Leo. 296
A history of the Jewish experience: eternal faith, eternal people. [Rev. ed.] New York, Behrman House [1973] xvi, 453 p. illus. 23 cm. Published in 1962 under title: Eternal faith, eternal people; a journey into Judaism. Bibliography: p. 420-429. [BM155.2.T7 1973] 73-3142 ISBN 0-87441-072-X 4.95 (pbk.)
1. Jews—Rites and ceremonies. 2. Judaism—History. I. Title.

TREPP, Leo. 296
Judaism; development and life. Belmont, Calif., Dickenson Pub. Co. [1966] vi, 216 p. 22 cm. Bibliography: p. 201-206. [BM561.T7] 66-23587
1. Judaism. I. Title.

TREPP, Leo. 296
Judaism: development and life. 2d ed. Encino, Calif., Dickenson Pub. Co. [1974] viii, 294 p. illus. 21 cm. Bibliography: p. 271-278. [BM561.T7 1974] 73-76614 ISBN 0-8221-0114-9 6.50 (pbk.)
1. Judaism. I. Title.

UMEN, Samuel. 296
Jewish concepts and reflections. New York, Philosophical Library [1962] 190 p. 23 cm. Includes bibliographies. [BM561.U4] 62-9774
1. Judaism. I. Title.

UMEN, Samuel 296
Jewish concepts and reflections. New York, Philosophical [c.1962] 190p. 23cm. Bibl. 62-9774 3.75
1. Judaism. I. Title.

UMEN, Samuel. 296
The nature of Judaism. New York, Philosophical Library [1960, c1961] 152 p. 22 cm. [BM45.U47] 60-15964
1. Judaism — Addresses, essays, lectures. I. Title.

UMEN, Samuel 296
The nature of Judaism. New York, Philosophical Library [1960, c.1961] 152p. 60-15964 3.75
1. Judaism—Addresses, essays, lectures. I. Title.

USSHER, Arland. 296
The magic people. New York, Devin-Adair Co., 1951. 177 p. 21 cm. [DS119.U8 1951] 51-6790
1. Jews—History. 2. Jewish question. I. Title.

VISHNIAC, Roman, 1897- 296
Polish Jews; a pictorial record, with an introd. essay by Abraham Joshua Heschel. New York. Schocken [1965, c.1947] 17p. 31 plates. 25cm. [DS135.P6V5] 2.45 pap.,
*1. Jews in Poland. I. *Heschel, Abraham, 1907- II. Title.*

WACHOLDER, Ben Zion. 296
Essays on Jewish chronology and chronography / by Ben Zion Wacholder. New York : Ktav Pub. House, 1976. p. cm. Includes bibliographical references. [BS637.2.W3] 75-45443 ISBN 0-87068-260-1 20.00
1. Abraham, the patriarch. 2. Jews. Liturgy and ritual. Haftaroth. 3. Bible. O.T.—Chronology—Addresses, essays, lectures. 4. Bible. O.T. Pentateuch—Liturgical use. 5. Mekilta. 6. Chronology, Jewish—Addresses, essays, lectures. I. Title.
Contents omitted.

WAR of the Sons of Light against the Sons of Darkness. 296
The scroll of the War of the Sons of Light against the Sons of Darkness. Edited with commentary and introd. by Yigael Yadin. Translated from the Hebrew by Batya and Chaim Rabin. [London] Oxford University Press, 1962. xix, 387 p. illus., diagrs., facsims. 24 cm. Text of scroll in Hebrew and English. [BM488.W3A233] 62-3327
I. Yadin, Yigael, 1917- ed. II. Title.

WAR of the Sons of Light against the Sons of Darkness. 296
The scroll of the war of the Sons of Light against the Sons of Darkness. Ed., commentary, introd. by Yigael Yadin. Tr. from Hebrew by Batya and Chaim Rabin. New York, Oxford, [c]1962[ ] xix 387p. illus. Text of scroll in Hebrew and English. 62-3327 10.10
1. Yadin, Yigael, 1917- ed. I. Title.

WAR of the Sons of Light against the Sons of Darkness. English. 296
The rules for the War of the Sons of Light with the Sons of Darkness. [Translated by Robert G. Jones from the Dea Sea scrolls in the Hebrew University. New Haven? 1956] [49] p. 21 cm. [BM488.W3A3 1956] 58-29041
1. Qumran community. I. Jones, Robert G., tr. II. Title.

WAXMAN, Meyer, 1884- 296
Blessed is the daughter [by] Meyer Waxman, Sulamith Ish-Kishor [and] Jacob Sloan. New York, Shengold Publishers [c1959] 157 p. illus. 29 cm. [BM729.W6W3] 59-11057
1. Women, Jewish. 2. Fasts anf feasts — Judaism. 3. Art, Jewish. I. Title.

WAXMAN, Meyer, 1884- 296
Judaism: religion and ethics. New York, T. Yoseloff [1958] 411 p. 24 cm. [BM560.W335] 58-9391
1. Judaism. 2. Ethics, Jewish.

WAXMAN, Mordecai, ed. 296
Tradition and change; the development of conservative Judaism. New York, Burning Bush Press, 1958. x, 477 p. 25 cm. [BM197.5.W3] 54-8409
1. Conservative Judaism — Addresses, essays, lectures. I. Title.

WEBER, Max, 1864-1920 296
Ancient Judaism; tr. ed. by Hans H. Gerth, Don Martindale. New York, Free Pr. [1967, c.1952] 484p. 21cm. (FP 93413) [BS1192.W413] 2.95 pap.,
1. Judaism—History of doctrines. 2. Sociology, Jewish. 3. Bible. O. T.—Theology. I. Title.

WEBER, Max, 1864-1920. 296
Ancient Judaism; translated and edited by Hans H. Gerth and Don Martindale. Glencoe, Ill., Free Press, 1952. 484 p. 21 cm. [BS1192.W413] 52-8156
1. Bible. O.T.—Theology. 2. Judaism—History of doctrines. 3. Sociology, Jewish. I. Title.

WEISBERG, Harold. 296
American Judaism: the next century. Rev. ed. Washington [B'nai B'rith Dept. of Adult Jewish Education, 1956. 61p. 23cm. (Dynamic discussions on the issues of the day) [BM205.W4 1956] 56-8890
1. Judaism—U.S. I. Title.

WEISS, Abraham 296
The Abraham Weiss jubilee volume; studies in his honor, presented by his colleagues and disciples on the occasion of his completing four decades of pioneering scholarship. New York [The Abraham Weiss Jubilee Comm., dist. Philipp Feldheim, c.] 1964. 1v. (various p.) illus., front. port. 24cm. Hebrew and English. Bibl. Added t.p. in Hebrew. HE64 12.50
I. Title.

WEITZ, Martin Mishli, 1907- 296
Life without strife. New York, Bloch Pub. Co., 1957. 200 p. illus. 24 cm. [BM560.W43] 58-2031
1. Judaism. I. Title.

WHEN yesterday becomes tomorrow; 296 125th anniversary celebration, Congregation Emanu-El of the City of New York, 1845-1970. [New York, Congregation Emanu-El of the City of New York, 1971] xiii, 205 p. illus., facsim. 22 cm. Consists chiefly of the anniversary lectures delivered Nov. 9, 1969, to March 29, 1970. Contents.Contents.—Foreword, by N. A. Perilman.—Address, by A. E. Coleman.—Will science destroy society? By E. Ubell.—When synagogues became temples, by M. Himmelfarb.—When yesterday becomes tomorrow, by B. Rustin.—Where are we—where are we going? By M. Sklare.—Creative piety and theology, by K. Stendahl.—The problems we face, by A. Kaplan.—An experiment in openness, by E. Flannery.—The living God and the dying religious style, by E. B. Borowitz.—Building new foundations, by E. Rivkin.—A reform of reform (the anniversary sermon) by D. J. Silver.—Proclamation, by J. V. Lindsay.—The anniversary program. [BM42.W48] 71-153637
1. Judaism—Addresses, essays, lectures. I. New York. Temple Emanu-El.

WHITLEY, Charles Francis. 296
The exilic age. Philadelphia, Westminster Press [1958] 160 p. 22 cm. [BM165.W5 1958] 58-5127
1. Judaism—History—Ancient period. I. Title.

WILLIAMS, Robert Henry. 296
Know your enemy; counter-intelligence information for governors, mayors, police personnel . . . [Santa Ana? Calif., c1950] 56 p. illus. 22 cm. [DS141.W447] 51-15775
1. Jewish question. 2. Jews in the U.S. I. Title.

WIRTH, Louis, 1897-1952. 296
The ghetto. Woodcut illus. by Todros Geller. [Chicago] University of Chicago Press [1956] 298 p. illus. 21 cm. (Phoenix books, P7) [DS123.W5 1956] 36-14116
1. Jews. 2. Jews — Political and social conditions. 3. Jews in Chicago. I. Title.

WIRTH, Louis, 1897-1952. 296
The ghetto. Woodcut illus. by Todros Geller. [Chicago] University of Chicago Press [1956] 298 p. illus. 21 cm. (Phoenix books, P7) [DS123.W5 1956] 56-14116
1. Jews. 2. Jews—Political and social conditions. 3. Jews in Chicago. I. Title.

WISE, Patrick. 296
Musical history and general knowledge of music; an outline for scholars and other music-lovers [by] Patrick Wise [and] Melville van der Spuy. [Cape Town] Nasou [pref. 1964] 184 p. illus., music, port. 23 cm. [ML160.W6] 66-45940 MN
1. Music — Hist. & crit. I. Spuy, Melville van der, joint author. II. Title.

WIZNITZER, Arnold. 296
The records of the earliest Jewish community in th New World; with a foreword by Salo W. Baron. New York, American Jewish Historical Society, 1954. xiii, 108p. illus., port., maps, facsims 24cm.*Translation of the Minute book of the Congregations Zur Israel of Recife and Magen Abraham of Mauricia, Brazil, 1648-1653;: p. 58-91. Bibliographical footnotes. [F2659.J5W5] 54-2217
1. Recife, Brazil, Kahal Kadosh Sur Israel. 2. Mauritia. Kahal Kadosh Maguen Abraham. 3. Jews in Brazil. I. Recife, Brazil Kahal Kadosh Sur Israel. Minute book. II. Mauritia. Kathal Kadosh Maguen Abraham. Minute book. III. Title.

WOLF, Edwin, 1911- 296
The history of the Jews of Philadelphia from colonial times to the age of Jackson [by] Edwin Wolf, 2d [and] Maxwell Whiteman. [1st ed.] Philadelphia, Jewish Publication Society of America, 1957 [c1956] 534p. illus. 24cm. (The Jacob R. Schiff library of Jewish contributions to American democracy) Originally written as a series of weekly articles which appeared in the Philadelphia Jewish exponent during 1954-1955.' Includes bibliographies. [F158.9.J5W86] 56-7780
1. Jews in Philadelphia—Hist. I. Whiteman, Maxwell, joint author. II. Title.

WOLSEY, Louis, 1877- 296
Sermons and addresses. Philadelphia, Congregation Rodeph Shalom, 1950. vi, 79 p. port. 24 cm. [BM740.W64] 50-35067
1. Sermons, Jewish — U.S. 2. Sermons, American — Jewish authors. I. Title.

WOOLDRIDGE, Harry Ellis, 1845-1917. 296
The polyphonic period; method of musical art. 2d ed., rev. by Percy C. Buck. London, Oxford University Press, 1929-32. 2v facsims., music. 23cm (The Oxford history of music, v. 1-2) Contents.pt. 1. 330-1400--pt. 2. 1400-c. 1600. Bibliographical footnotes. [ML160.O982 vol.1-2] 29-30280
1. Music—Hist. & crit.—Medieval. I. Buck, Percy Carter, Sir 1871-1947, ed. II. Title. III. Series.

WOUK, Herman, 1915- 296
This is my God. Garden City, N.Y., Doubleday, 1961 [c.1959] 353p. Bibl. 1.45 pap.,
1. Judaism. I. Title.

WOUK, Herman, 1915- 296
This is my God. [New York] Dell [1964, c.1959] 288p. 18cm. (8796) Bibl. .75 pap.,
1. Judaism. I. Lamm, Maurice. II. Title.

WOUK, Herman, 1915- 296
This is my God; the Jewish way of life. Garden City, N.Y., Doubleday, 1970. 356 p. 22 cm. Bibliography: p. [353]-356. [BM561.W65 1970] 79-78741
1. Judaism. I. Title.

WOUK, Herman, 1915- 296
This is my God; the Jewish way of life. New York, Pocket Books [1973, c.1970] xii, 305 p. 18 cm. First published in 1959. Includes bibliography. [BM561.W65] ISBN 0-671-78631-8 1.50 (pbk.)
1. Judaism. I. Title.
L.C. card no. for the hardbound edition: 59-11617.

ZADOKITE documents. 296
The Zadokite documents; I. The admonition. II. The laws. Edited with a translation and notes by Chaim Rabin, 2d rev. ed. Oxford, Clarendon Press, 1958. xvi, 103 p. 23 cm.

Hebrew and English. Includes bibliographical references. [BM175.Z3R3 1958] 58-2491
1. Rabin, Chaim, ed. and tr. II. Title.

ZARCHIN, Michael Moses, 1893- 296
Glimpses of Jewish life in San Francisco; history of San Francisco Jewry. San Francisco, Distributed by the author [1952] 221 p. 28 cm. Includes bibliography. [F869.S3Z27] 52-40169
1. Jews in San Francisco. 2. Jews — Biog. 3. San Francisco — Soc. life & cust. I. Title.

ZELIGS, Dorothy Freda. 296
A child's history of Jewish life; the first sixteen centuries of the Common Era. Illustrated by Jim Lee. [1st rev. ed.] New York, Bloch Pub. Co., 1956. 303p. illus. 25cm. [DS118.Z43 1956] 56-10733
1. Jews—Hist. I. Title.

ZERIN, Edward. 296
Our Jewish neighbors. New York, Abingdon Press [1959] 96 p. 19 cm. Includes bibliography. [BM573.Z4] 59-445
1. Judaism—Juvenile literature. I. Title.

ZIMMELS, Hirsch Jakob. 296
Ashkenazim and Sephardim: their relations, differences, and problems as reflected in the rabbinical reponsa. With a forword by Israel Brodie. London, Oxford University Press, 1958. xiv, 347 p. illus. 23 cm. (Jews' College publications, new ser., no. 2) Bibliographical footnotes. [BM182.Z5] 58-4526
1. Sephardim. 2. Jews—Rites and ceremonies. 3. Responsa. I. Title. II. Series: London, Jews' College. Publication, new ser., no. 2

ALTMANN, Alexander, 1906- 296'.01
Studies in religious philosophy and mysticism / by Alexander Altmann. Plainview, N.Y. : Books for Libraries Press, 1975, c1969. p. cm. (Essay index reprint series) Reprint of the ed. published by Cornell University Press, Ithaca. Includes bibliographical references and indexes. [B154.A4 1975] 75-14347 ISBN 0-518-10194-0 : 19.50
1. Philosophy, Jewish—Addresses, essays, lectures. 2. Mysticism—Judaism—Addresses, essays, lectures. I. Title.

HESCHEL, Abraham Joshua, 1907- 296.01
God in search of man; a philosophy of Judaism. New York, Meridian Books [1961, c1955] 437 p. 21 cm. Includes bibliography. [BM561.H46 1961] 59-7935
1. Judaism. I. Title.

HESCHEL, Abraham Joshua, 1907- 296.01
God in search of man; a philosophy of Judaism. New York, Harper [1966, c.1955] 437p. 21cm. (Torchbk., Temple lib., TB807) Bibl. [BM561.H46 1961] 2.95 pap.,
1. Judaism. 2. Religion—Philosophy. I. Title.

MELBER, Jehuda. 296'.01
Hermann Cohen's philosophy of Judaism. [New York] J. David [1968] xiv, 503 p. 23 cm. Bibliography: p. 469-475. [BM560.C573M4] 68-19960 7.95
1. Cohen, Hermann, 1842-1918. Religion der Vernunft. I. Title.

PEARL, Chaim, 1919- 296'.01
The medieval Jewish mind; the religious philosophy of Isaac Arama. Bridgeport, Conn., Hartmore House [1972, c1971] vii, 208 p. 23 cm. Bibliography: p. 198-201. [B759.A44P4 1972] 76-184221 ISBN 0-87677-043-X 7.95
1. Arama, Isaac, 1420 (ca.)-1494. I. Title.

LEONARD, Henry, pseud. 296'.02'07
Bagel power. New York, Crown Publishers [1969] [64] p. illus. 21 cm. On cover: A book of Dayenu cartoons. [NC1429.L45A43 1969] 78-93390 1.00
1. Jews—Caricatures and cartoons. I. Title.

BEN-ASHER, Naomi, ed. 296.03
The junior Jewish encyclopedia, edited by Naomi Ben-Asher[and] Hayim Leaf. Louis L. Ruffman, educational consultant; Jacob Sloan, editorial Consultant Alfred Werner, art consultant. New York, Shengold Publishers [1957] 350, [2]p. illus., ports., maps, facsims. 29cm. Bibliography: p.[351]-[352] [DS102.8.B4] 57-8450
1. Jews—Dictionaries and encyclopedias. I. Leaf, Hayim, joint ed. II. Title.

BEN-ASHER, Naomi, ed. 296.03
The junior Jewish encyclopedia, edited by Naomi Ben-Asher [and] Hayim Leaf. Louis L. Ruffman, educational consultant; Jacob Sloan, editorial consultant; Alfred Werner, art consultant. 2d rev. ed. New York, Shengold Publishers [1958] 350. [2]p. illus., ports., maps, facsims. 29cm. Bibliography: p.[351]-[352] [DS102.8.B4 1958] 58-8897
1. Jews—Dictionaries and encyclopedias. I. Leaf, Hayim, joint ed. II. Title.

BIRNBAUM, Philip 296.03
A book of Jewish concepts. New York, 79 Delancey St. Hebrew Pub. Co., [1964] x, 719p. 24cm. 64-16085 6.95
1. Judaism—Dictionaries. I. Title.

BIRNBAUM, Philip. 296'.03
A book of Jewish concepts / Philip Birnbaum. Rev. ed. New York : Hebrew Pub. Co., [1975] x, 722 p. ; 24 cm. Includes indexes. [BM50.B55 1975] 75-318521 ISBN 0-88482-876-X : 7.50
1. Judaism—Dictionaries. I. Title.

COHEN, Harry Alan, 1893- 296.03
A basic Jewish encyclopedia; Jewish teachings and practices listed and interpreted in the order of their importance today, by Harry A. Cohen. Foreword by Louis Finkelstein. Hartford, Conn., Hartmore House [1965] 205 p. 22 cm. [BM50.C6] 65-16998
1. Judaism — Dictionaries. I. Title.

COHEN, Harry Alan, 1893- 296.03
A basic Jewish encyclopedia; Jewish teachings and practices listed and interpreted in the order of their importance today. Foreword by Louis Finkelstein. Hartmore House [dist. New York, Taplinger, c.1965] 205p. 22cm. [BM50.C6] 65-16998 4.95
1. Judaism—Dictionaries. I. Title.

GLUSTROM, Simon. 296'.03
The language of Judaism. New York, J. David [1966] xiii, 331 p. 22 cm. [BM50.G55] 66-25121
1. Judaism—Dictionaries. I. Title.

GLUSTROM, Simon. 296'.03
The language of Judaism. 2d rev. ed. New York, Ktav Pub. House, 1973. xiii, 331 p. 21 cm. [BM50.G55 1973] 73-2352 ISBN 0-87068-224-5 3.95 (pbk.)
1. Judaism—Dictionaries. I. Title.

GOLDFARB, Solomon David. 296.03
Ready-reference Jewish encyclopedia. In collaboration with Rose Scharfstein. [New York] Shilo [1963] vi, 248 p. illus., maps, ports. 25 cm. [DS102.8.G6] 62-21343
1. Jews—Dictionaries and encyclopedias. I. Title.

THE New Jewish encyclopedia. 296.03
Edited by David Bridger in association with Samuel Wolk. With a foreword by Abba Eban. Art editor: Stephen Kayser. Consulting editors: Harold Hayes & Abraham Rothberg. With original photos. by Ann Zane Shanks & Marvin Koner. New York, Behrman House [1962] xvi, 541p. illus., ports. 28cm. [DS102.8.N4] 62-17079
1. Jews—Dict. & encyc. I. Bridger, David, 1907- ed. II. Title: Jewish encyclopedia.

NEW Jewish encyclopedia (The). 296.03
Ed. by David Bridger in assn. with Samuel wolk. Foreword by Abba Eban. Art ed.: Stephen Kayser. Consulting eds.: Harold Hayes, Abraham Rothberg. Orig. photos. by Ann Zane Shanks, Marvin Koner. New York, Behrman House [c.1962] xvi, 541p. illus., ports. 28cm. 62-17079 12.50, bxd.
1. Jews—Dict. & Ency. I. Bridger, David, 1907- ed. II. Title: Jewish encyclopedia.

RUBIN, Alvan D 296.03
A picture dictionary of of Jewish life. Pictures by Lili Cassel. New York, Behrman House, 1956. unpaged. illus. 25cm. [DS102.8.R8] 56-11294
1. Jews—Dict. & encyc. I. Title.

RUNES, Dagobert David, 1902- ed. 296.03
Concise dictionary of Judaism. New York, Philosophical Library [c1959] 237p. 64plates (incl. ports., facsims.) 22cm. [BM50.R8] 58-59474
1. Jews—Dictionaries and encyclopedias. I. Title.

RUNES, Dagobert David, 1902- 296'.03
Concise dictionary of Judaism. Edited by Dagobert D. Runes. New York, Greenwood Press [1969, c1966] 124 p. 23 cm. [BM50.R8 1969] 77-88933 ISBN 0-8371-2109-4
1. Jews—Dictionaries and encyclopedias. I. Title.

RUNES, Dagobert David, 1902- 296/.03
The war against the Jew, by Dagobert D. Runes. New York, Philosophical Lib. [1968] xxiv. 192p. 22cm. Bibl. [DS145.R86] 67-13371 6.00
1. Antisemitism—Dictionaries. I. Title.

SCHONFIELD, Hugh Joseph, 1901- 296.03
A popular dictionary of Judaism [by] Hugh Schonfield. [1st American ed.] New York, Citadel Press [1966, c1962] 153, [2] p. 19 cm. Bibliography: p. [155] [BM50.S3 1966] 66-24231
1. Judaism—Dictionaries. I. Title.

TARCOV, Edith. 296.03
The illustrated book of Jewish knowledge, by Edith and Oscar Tarcov. Illustrated by Adam Simone. [New York] Friendly House Publisher [1959] 127 p. illus. 27 cm. [DS102.8.T3] 59-9972
1. Jews — Dict. & encyc. I. Tarcov, Oscar joint author. II. Title.

TARCOV, Edith 296.03
The illustrated book of Jewish knowledge, by Edith and Oscar Tarcov. Illustrated by Adam Simone. [New York, 65 Suffolk St.] Friendly House Publishers [c.1959] 127p. illus. (col.), maps, diagrs. 27cm. 59-9972 2.95
1. Jews—Dict. & encyc. I. Tarcov, Oscar, joint author. II. Title.

WERBLOWSKY, Raphael Jehudah Zwi, 1924- ed. 296.03
The encyclopedia of the Jewish religion, edited by R. J. Zwi Werblowsky and Geoffrey Wigoder. [1st ed.] New York, Holt, Rinehart and Winston, 1966 [c1965] 415 p. plates (1 col.) 27 cm. [BM50.W45 1966] 66-10266
1. Judaism—Dictionaries. I. Wigoder, Geoffrey, 1922- joint ed. II. Title.

BELKIN, Samuel. 296.04
Essays in traditional Jewish thought. New York, Philosophical Library [c1956] 191p. 22cm. [BM45.B39] 57-1544
1. Judaism—Addresses, essays, lectures. I. Title.

BUBER, Martin, 1878- 296.04
At the turning; three addresses on Judaism. New York, Farrar, Straus and Young [1952] 62 p. 22 cm. [BM565.B87] 52-12304
1. Judaism. I. Title.

DUBNOV, Semen Markovich, 1860-1941. 296.04
Nationalism and history; essays on old and new Judaism. Ed. with an introd. essay by Koppel S. Pinson. Philadelphia, Jewish Publication Society of America [dist. World, 1961, c.1958] 385p. (Meridian bk. JP20) 1.65 pap.,
1. Jews—Addresses, essays, lectures. 2. Jewish question. 3. Jews—Hist. I. Title.

FEINBERG, Louis, 1887- 296.04
The spiritual foundations of Judaism, and other essays, selected addresses, and writings; with an appreciation by Emanuel Gamoran. Cincinnati, Congregation Adath Israel, 1951. xiv, 280 p. port. 24 cm. Includes one essay in Hebrew and one in Yiddish. [BM45.F37] 51-28418
1. Judaism—Addresses, essays, lectures. I. Title.

GINZBERG, Louis, 1873-1953. 296.04
On Jewish law and lore; [essays] Philadelphia, Jewish Publication Society of America, 1955. 262p. 22cm. [BM646.G55] 55-6707
1. Jewish law. 2. Folk-lore—Jews. I. Title.

GINZBERG, Louis, 1873-1953 296.04
On Jewish law and lore. Cleveland, World [1962, c.1955] 262p. 21cm. (Meridian bks., & the Jewish Pubn. Soc., JP26) Bibl. 1.75 pap.,
1. Jewish law. 2. Folk-lore—Jews. I. Title.

GREENBERG, Hayim, 1889-1953. 296.04
The inner eye; selected essays. New York, Jewish Frontier Association [1953] 393p. illus. 24cm. 'Most of the essays ... were translated from the Yiddish, Hebrew, or Russian; some were written directly in English.' [BM45.G7] 54-21458
1. Judaism—Addresses, essays, lectures. I. Title.

HERTZ, Ricard C 296.04
Wings of the morning. Detroit, Temple Beth El, 1956. 88p. 21cm. Addresses and essays. [BM45.H45] 57-24420
1. Judaism—Addresses, essays, lectures. I. Title.

JEWISH Theological Seminary of America. 296.04
Mordecai M. Kaplan; jubille volume on the occasion of his seventieth birthday. English section. New York, 1953. ix, 549p. illus., port. 24cm. Edited by Moshe Davis. Published simultaneously with the Hebrew section. Includes bibliographical references. [BM40.J56] 53-7712
1. Kaplan, Mordecai Menahem, 1881- 2. Judaism— Collections. I. Davis, Moshe, ed. II. Title.
Contents omitted.

SCHECHTER, Solomon, 1847-1915. 296.04
Studies in Judaism; a selection. New York, Meridian Books [1958] 372p. 21cm. [BM45.S31] 58-11934
1. Judaism—Addresses, essays, lectures. I. Title.

SCHNEIDERMAN, Harry, 1885- ed. 296.04
Two generations in perspective: notable events and trends, 1896-1956. With a foreword by Louis Finkelstein. New York, Monde Publishers [1957] 458p. illus. 22cm. [DS107.3.S256] 57-10890
1. Goldstein, Israel, 1896- 2. Jews—Hist.—1789-1945. 3. Jews—Hist.—1945- 4. Judaism—Addresses, essays, lectures. 5. Jews in the U. S.—Hist. I. Title.

SKOSS, Solomon Leon, 1884-1953. 296.04
Portrait of a Jewish scholar; essays and addresses. New York, Bloch Pub. Co., 1957. 150p. illus. 25cm. [BM45.S6] 57-9819
1. Judaism— Addresses, essays, lectures. I. Title.

SKOSS, Solomon Leon, 1884-1953. 296.04
Portrait of a Jewish scholar; essays and addresses. New York, Bloch Pub. Co., 1957. 150 p. illus. 25 cm. [BM45.S6] 57-9819
1. Judaism — Addresses, essays, lectures. I. Title.

STEINBACH, Alexander Alan, 1894- 296.04
Faith and love. New York, Philosophical Library [1959] 114 p. 22 cm. [BM45.S79] 59-13
1. Judaism — Addresses, essays, lectures. I. Title.

STERN, Harry Joshua, 1897- 296.04
Martyrdom and miracle, a collection of addresses. New York, Bloch Pub. Co., 1950. 246p. 21cm. [BM45.S84] 56-47453
1. Judaism—Addresses, essays, lectures. I. Title.

STERN, Horace, 1878- 296.04
The spiritual values of life; occasional addresses on Jewish themes. Philadelphia, Jewish Publication Society of America, 1953. 257p. 21cm. [BM45.S85] 53-2292
1. Judaism—Addresses, essays, lectures. I. Title.

JEWISH quarterly review. 296.05
(The) v.1-20. [New York] Ktav, 1966. 20v. (various p.) illus. 24 cm. Facsim. of a pubn. issued Oct. 1888-July 1908 in London & New York by Macmillan (1888-94 in London by D. Nutt), ed. by I. Abrahams, C.G. Montefiore, and superseded by a pubn. with the same title issued by Dropsie College for Hebrew, Philadelphia. Accompanied by 1v. index. [DS101.J482] 66-6352 40.00 set.
1. Judaism—Period. 2. Jews—Hist.—Period. I. Abrahams, Israel, 1858-1925, ed. II. Montefiore, Claude Joseph Goldsmid, 1858-1938, ed.

JEWISH social studies; 296.05
a quarterly journal devoted to contemporary and historical aspects of Jewish life. v. 1- Jan. 1939- New York, 1967. v. tables. 26cm. Ed. for the Conf. on Jewish relations. Cumulative index; vs. 1-25, 1939-1964. v. 26cm. [DS101.J555] 42-47218 10.00
1. Jews—Period. I. Conference on Jewish relations.
Order the index from Conf. on Jewish Social Studies, 1841 Broadway, N.Y., N.Y. 10023.

UNITED Synagogue of America. National Women's League. 296'.062'1
They dared to dream; a history of National Women's League, 1918-1968. New York [1967] 107 p. illus., facsims., ports. 23 cm. [BM21.U678] 67-7880
1. United Synagogue of America. National Women's League. I. Title.

EISENBERG, Azriel Louis, 1903- ed. 296.07
Readings in the teaching of Jewish history [by] Azriel Eisenberg and Abraham Segal. [New York] Jewish Education Committee of New York [1956] 226p. 25cm. (Jewish Education Committee of New York] Readings series) 'A companion volume to Teaching Jewish history by the same authors.' [DS115.95.E5] 56-3018
1. Jews—Hist.—Study and teaching. I. Segal, Abraham, 1910— joint ed. II. Title.

GOLDMAN, Israel M., 1904- 296'.07
Lifelong learning among Jews : adult education in Judaism from Biblical times to the twentieth century / by Israel M. Goldman ; introd. by Louis Finkelstein. New York : Ktav Pub. House, 1975. xxii, 364 p. : ill. ; 23 cm. Includes index. Bibliography: p. 351-357. [DS113.G75] 75-19216 ISBN 0-87068-291-1 : 15.00
1. Jews—Intellectual life—History. 2. Jewish

learning and scholarship—History. 3. Jewish religious education of adults—History. I. Title.

MACHTEI, Max, 1899- 296.07
This is my God; a primer for an abiding and sustaining faith. [1st ed.] New York, Pageant Press [1956] 94p. 21cm. [BM105.M3] 56-12549
1. Judaism—Study and teaching. I. Title.

NEUSNER, Jacob, 1932- 296'.07
The academic study of Judaism : essays and reflections / Jacob Neusner. New York : Ktav, 1975. 176 p. ; 23 cm. Includes bibliographical references and index. [DS113.N37] 75-5782 ISBN 0-87068-281-4 : 10.00
1. Jewish learning and scholarship—United States—Addresses, essays, lectures. 2. Jewish studies—United States—Addresses, essays, lectures. I. Title.

ROSENZWEIG, Franz, 1886-1929 296.07
On Jewish leariningn [Tr. from German] Ed. by N. N. Glatzer. New York, Schocken [1965, c.1955] 128p. 21cm. (SB111) Three treatises appeared orig. as individual pamphlets and were later included in Rosenzweig's Kleiner Schriften. [LC746.G4R62] 65-25411 3.50; 1.45 pap.,
1. Jews—Education. I. Glatzer, Nahum Norbet, 1903- ed. II. Buber, Martin, 1878-1965. III. Title.

ROSSEL, Seymour. 296'.07
When a Jew seeks wisdom : The sayings of the fathers / by Seymour Rossel with Hyman Chanover and Chaim Stern. New York : Behrman House, [1975] p. cm. (The Jewish values series) An examination of Jewish tradition and values, using as a basis Pirke Avot, the teachings of rabbis who lived from 300 B.C.E. to 200 C.E. [BM105.R64] 75-14119 4.95
1. Jewish religious education—Text-books for adolescents. 2. Ethics, Jewish—Juvenile literature. I. Chanover, Hyman, joint author. II. Stern, Chaim, joint author. III. Title.

CHICAGO. Hebrew Theological College. 296.0711
30th anniversary, 1922-1952. [Chicago, 1952] 196p. (chiefly advertisements) ports. 29cm. [BM90.C47] 53-29141
I. Title.

HEBREW Union College- 296'.07'11
Jewish Institute of Religion at one hundred years / edited by Samuel E. Karff. [Cincinnati] : Hebrew Union College Press, 1976. xviii, 501 p., [8] leaves of plates : ill. ; 24 cm. Includes bibliographical references and indexes. [BM90.H44H43] 75-17290 ISBN 0-87820-109-2 : 20.00
1. Hebrew Union College-Jewish Institute of Religion—Addresses, essays, lectures. I. Karff, Samuel E.

B'NAI B'rith Hillel Foundations. 296'.07'1173
Jewish studies in American colleges and universities; a catalogue. Washington, 1972. ix, 77 p. 23 cm. [BM75.B58 1972] 74-164126
1. Judaism—Study and teaching—United States—Directories. I. Title.

COLLOQUIUM on the Teaching of Judaica in American Universities, 1st, Brandeis University, 1969. 296'.071'173
The teaching of Judaica in American universities; the proceedings of a colloquium. Edited by Leon A. Jick. [Waltham? Mass.] Association for Jewish Studies [1970] 152 p. 24 cm. [BM75.C65 1969] 72-135521
1. Judaism—Study and teaching—U.S.—Congresses. 2. Jewish learning and scholarship—U.S.—Congresses. 3. Jews in the United States—Education—Congresses. I. Jick, Leon A., ed. II. Title.

GRATZ College, 296'.071'174811
anniversary volume; on the occasion of the seventy-fifth anniversary of the founding of the College, 1895-1970. Isidore David Passow [and] Samuel Tobias Lachs, editors. Philadelphia, 1971. 283, 26 p. geneal. table, music. 25 cm. Includes bibliographical references. [BM42.G7] 74-165031 12.50
1. Jews—History—Addresses, essays, lectures. 2. Judaism—History—Addresses, essays, lectures. I. Passow, Isidore David, ed. II. Lachs, Samuel Tobias, ed. III. Gratz College, Philadelphia.

REICHEL, O. Asher, 1921- 296'.072'024 B
Isaac Halevy, 1847-1914: spokesman and historian of Jewish tradition, by O. Asher Reichel. New York, Yeshiva University Press, 1969. 176 p. facsims., port. 24 cm. Includes, in Hebrew, "Facsimiles of Halevy's letters" (p. 129-158) Bibliography: p. 160-170. Bibliographical footnotes. [BM755.H225R4] 70-85704
1. Halevy, Isaak, 1847-1914. 2. Orthodox Judaism—Germany.

JICK, Leon A. 296'.073
The Americanization of the Synagogue, 1820-1870 / by Leon A. Jick Hanover, N.H. : Published for Brandeis University Press by the University Press of New England, 1976. xi, 247 p., [6] leaves of plates : ill. ; 23 cm. Includes index. Bibliography: p. [229]-239. [BM205.J52] 75-18213 ISBN 0-87451-119-4 : 12.50
1. Judaism—United States—History. 2. Jews in the United States—History. I. Title.

APPLEBAUM, Morton M 296.076
What everyone should know about Judaism; answers to the questions most frequently asked about Judaism. Foreword by John Haynes Holmes. New York, Philosophical Library [1959] 87p. 22cm. [BM51.A65] 59-4504
1. Questions and answers—Jews. I. Title.

BARISH, Louis. 296.076
Basic Jewish beliefs, by Louis and Rebecca Barish. New York, J. David [1961] 221p. 22cm. [BM51.B3] 61-8453
1. Questions and answers—Jews. I. Barish, Rebecca, joint author. II. Title.

GLUSTROM, Simon. 296.076
When your child asks; a handbook for Jewish parents. New York, Bloch Pub. Co., 1956. 164p. 21cm. [BM570.G55] 56-8039
1. Judaism—Study and teaching. I. Title.

BAECK, Leo, 1873-1956. 296.08
The Pharisees, and other essays. [Translated from the German] Introd. by Krister Stendahl. New York, Schocken Books [1966] xxv, 164 p. 21 cm. (Schocken paperbacks, SB122) Includes bibliographical references. [BM175.P4B33 1966] 66-15818
1. Pharisees. 2. Judaism—Addresses, essays, lectures. I. Title.

BUBER, Martin, 1878-1965. 296'.08
Mamre; essays in religion. Translated by Greta Hort. Westport, Conn., Greenwood Press [1970] xiii, 190 p. 23 cm. Reprint of the 1946 ed. Contents.—The faith of Judaism.—The two centres of the Jewish soul.—Imitatio Dei.—Biblical leadership.—Trust.—The interpretation of Chassidism.—The beginnings of Chassidism. [BM45.B8 1970] 72-97271 ISBN 0-8371-2591-X
1. Judaism—Addresses, essays, lectures. 2. Hasidism—Addresses, essays, lectures. I. Title.

BUBER, Martin, 1878-1965. 296'.08
On Judaism. Edited by Nahum N. Glatzer. New York, Schocken Books [1967] 242 p. 22 cm. Contents.—The early addresses (1909 918): Judaism and the Jews. Judaism and mankind. Renewal of Judaism. The spirit of the Orient and Judaism. Jewish religiosity. Myth in Judaism. The Holy way: a word to the Jews and to the nations. Herut: on youth and religion.—The later addresses (1939 951): The spirit of Israel and the world of today. Judaism and civilization. The silent question. The dialogue between heaven and earth.—Editor's postscript. Bibliographical references included in "Notes" (p. [227]-235) [BM45.B814] 67-28091
1. Judaism—Addresses, essays, lectures. I. Glatzer, Nahum Norbert, 1903- ed. II. Title.

CASPER, Bernard Moses, 1916- 296.08
Judaism today and yesterday [by] Bernard M. Casper. New York, T. Yoseloff [1965] 123 p. 22 cm. Bibliographical footnotes. [BM561.C3] 64-21347
1. Judaism — Addresses, essays, lectures. I. Title.

CASPER, Bernard Moses, 1916- 296.08
Judaism today and yesterday. New York. Yoseloff (c.1965) 128p. 22cm. Bibl. [BM561.C3] 64-21347 4.50
1. Judaism—Addresses, essays, lectures. I. Title.

COHEN, Arthur Allen, 1928- comp. 296'.08
Arguments and doctrines; a reader of Jewish thinking in the aftermath of the holocaust. Selected with introductory essays by Arthur A. Cohen. [1st ed.] New York, Harper & Row [1970] xviii, 541 p. 22 cm. Includes bibliographical references. [BM40.C54 1970] 78-83589 11.95
1. Judaism—20th century—Collections. I. Title.

COHEN, Hermann, 1842-1918. 296'.08
Reason and hope; selections from the Jewish writings of Hermann Cohen. Translated by Eva Jospe. New York, Norton [1971] 237 p. 22 cm. (B'nai B'rith Jewish heritage classics) [BM45.C613 1971] 70-133958 ISBN 0-393-04341-X 6.50
1. Judaism—Addresses, essays, lectures. I. Title.

CONE, Molly. 296'.08 s
About learning. Illustrated by Iris Schweitzer. [New York] Union of American Hebrew Congregations [1971] 62 p. col. illus. 21 cm. (Her Hear, O Israel, book 2) [BM107.C65 no. 2] [BS551.2] 296.3 68-9350
1. Bible stories, English—O.T. I. Schweitzer, Iris, illus. II. Title.

CONE, Molly. 296'.08
Hear, O Israel; the [shema' romanized form] story books. New York, Union of American Hebrew Congregations [1971- v. col. illus. 21 cm. Contents.Contents.—Book 1. First I say the [shema' romanized form]—Book 2. About learning. [BM107.C65] 72-197094
1. Judaism—Juvenile literature. I. Title.

EFRON, Benjamin, ed. 296.08
Currents and trends in contemporary Jewish thought. Contributing authors: Herbert M. Baumgard [and others] New York, Ktav Pub. House [1965] vii, 311 p. 24 cm. Includes bibliographies. [DS113.E36] 65-21741
1. Jewish learning and scholarship. I. Baumgard, Herbert M. II. Title.

EFRON, Benjamin, ed. 296.08
Currents and trends in contemporary Jewish thought. Contributing authors: Herbert M. Baumgard [and others] New York, Ktav Pub. House [1965] vii, 311 p. 24 cm. Includes bibliographies. [DS113.E36] 65-21741
1. Jewish learning and scholarship. I. Baumgard, Herbert M. II. Title.

ELFENBEIN, Israel, 1894- 296'.08
The American synagogue as a leavening force in Jewish life, and a collection of selected writings. Edited by Abraham Burstein. New York, Bloch Pub. Co. [1966] 203 p. port. 24 cm. Bibliographical footnotes. [BM45.E5] 67-1335
1. Judaism—Collected works. 2. Synagogues. I. Title.

FRIEDMAN, Theodore. 296.08
Letters to Jewish college students. New York, J. David [1965] 223 p. 24 cm. [BM727.F7] 65-17362
1. Students, Jewish — Religious life. I. Title.

FRIEDMAN, Theodore 296.08
Letters to Jewish college students. New York, J. David [c.1965] 223p. 24cm. [BM727.F7] 65-17362 4.95, 1.95 bds., pap.,
1. Students, Jewish—Religious life. I. Title.

GORDIS, Robert, 1908- comp. 296'.08
Faith and reason; essays in Judaism, edited by Robert Gordis and Ruth B. Waxman. New York, Ktav Pub. House, 1973. xxiii, 388 p. 27 cm. Includes bibliographical references. [BM40.G67] 72-429 ISBN 0-87068-188-5 15.00
1. Judaism—Addresses, essays, lectures. I. Waxman, Ruth B., joint comp. II. Judaism. III. Title.

HARPER & Row, inc. 296'.08
The eternal light; a heritage album mirroring four thousand years of Jewish inspiration and wisdom. Edited in consultation with the Jewish Publication Society of America. [1st ed.] New York [1966] viii, 247 p. illus. 30 cm. [BM40.H3] 66-20788
1. Judaism—Quotations, maxims, etc. I. Jewish Publication Society of America. II. Title.

HAUSDORFF, David Meyer, 1906- 296.08
The golden heritage; an inspirational treasury of Jewish thought for young adults of all ages, by David M. Hausdorff. New York, P. Feldheim [1966] 260 p. 23 cm. [BM43.H3] 66-26468
1. Judaism—Collections. I. Title.

HESCHEL, Abraham Joshua, 1907- 296.08
The insecurity of freedom; essays on human existence. New York, Farrar, Straus & Giroux [1956] xiv, 306 p. 21 cm. [BM45.H454] 66-16293
1. Judaism — Addresses, essays, lectures. I. Title.

HESCHEL, Abraham Joshua, 1907- 296.08
The insecurity of freedom; essays on human existence. New York, Farrar [c.1959-1966] xiv, 306p. 21cm. [BM45.H454] 66-16293 5.95
1. Judaism—Addresses, essays, lectures. I. Title.

HESCHEL, Abraham Joshua, 1907-1972. 296'.08
The wisdom of Heschel / Abraham Joshua Heschel ; selected by Ruth Marcus Goodhill. New York : Farrar, Straus and Giroux, 1975. xiv, 368 p. ; 22 cm. Includes bibliographical references. [BM45.H455 1975] 75-15945 ISBN 0-374-29124-1 : 8.95
1. Judaism—Quotations, maxims, etc. 2. Religion—Quotations, maxims, etc. I. Title.

JAKOBOVITS, Immanuel 296.08
Journal of a rabbi. New York, 10016. Living Bks., 207 E. 37th St. [c.1966] xiv, 503p. 23cm. [BM755.J28A3] 65-27066 6.95
1. Judaism. I. Title.

JOSPE, Alfred, 1909- comp. 296'.08
Tradition and contemporary experience; essays on Jewish thought and life. [New York] Published by Schocken Books for B'nai B'rith Hillel Foundations [1970] ix, 372 p. 21 cm. (Hillel library series) Includes bibliographical references. [BM565.J64] 77-110609 8.50
1. Judaism—20th century—Collections. I. Title. II. Series.

LOEWE, Raphael, ed. 296.08
Studies in rationalism, Judaism & universalism; in memory of Leon Roth. London, Routledge & K. Paul; New York, Humanities P., 1966. xiii, 357 p. front. (port.) 22 1/2 cm. 50/- Bibliography: p. 323-336. [BM42.L6] 67-70094
1. Roth, Leon, 1896-1963. 2. Judaism — Addresses, essays, lectures. I. Roth, Leon, 1896-1963. II. Title.

LOEWE, Rapheal, ed. 296.08
Studies in rationalism, Judaism & universalism; in memory of Leon Roth. London, Routledge & K. Paul: New York, Humanities 1966[i.e., 1967] xiii, 357p. front. (port.) 23cm. Bibl. [BM42.L6] 67-70094 8.50
1. Roth, Leon, 1896-1963. 2. Judaism—Addresses, essays, lectures. I. Roth, Leon, 1896-1963. II. Title.
Contents omitted.

MENDELSSOHN, Moses, 1729-1786. 296'.08
Jerusalem, and other Jewish writings. Translated and edited by Alfred Jospe. New York, Schocken Books [1969] viii, 179 p. 21 cm. Bibliography: p. 175-179. [BM565.M413] 69-17731 5.95
1. Judaism—Works to 1900. I. Jospe, Alfred, 1909- ed. II. Title.

NEUSNER, Jacob, 1932- 296.08
History and Torah; essays on Jewish learning. New York, Schocken Books [1965] 127 p. 23 cm. [BM45.N39] 65-21765
1. Judaism—Addresses, essays, lectures. 2. Jewish learning and scholarship. I. Title.

NEUSNER, Jacob, 1932- comp. 296'.08
The life of Torah; readings in the Jewish religious experience. Encino, Calif., Dickenson Pub. Co. [1974] xv, 237 p. illus. 23 cm. (The Religious life of man series) [BM561.N38] 73-91731 ISBN 0-8221-0124-6 3.50 (pbk.)
1. Judaism—Addresses, essays, lectures. 2. Judaism—United States—Addresses, essays, lectures. I. Title.

ROSENTHAL, Erwin Isak Jakob, 1904- 296'.08
Studia Semitica [by] Erwin I. J. Rosenthal. Cambridge, University Press, 1971. 2 v. 24 cm. (University of Cambridge. Oriental publications, no. 16-17) One essay in German. Contents.Contents.—v. 1. Jewish themes.—v. 2. Islamic themes. Includes bibliographical references. [BS1186.R68 1971] 70-116836 ISBN 0-521-07958-6 (v. 1) £6.20 ($22.00 U.S.)
1. Bible. O.T.—Criticism, interpretation, etc., Jewish—Addresses, essays, lectures. 2. Philosophy, Jewish—Addresses, essays, lectures. 3. Political science—History—Islamic Empire—Addresses, essays, lectures. 4. Islam and politics. I. Title. II. Series: Cambridge University. Oriental publications, no. 16-17

ROUTTENBERG, Max J., 1909- 296'.08
Seedtime and harvest [by] Max J. Routtenberg. New York, Bloch Pub. Co. [1969] xiii, 183 p. 22 cm. [BM45.R7] 70-84707 5.95
1. Judaism—Addresses, essays, lectures. I. Title.

SCHECHTER, Solomon, 1847-1915. 296'.08
Seminary addresses & other papers. New York, Arno Press, 1969. xiv, 253 p. 23 cm. (Religion in America) Reprint of the 1915 ed. Contents.Contents.—The emancipation of Jewish science.—The charter of the seminary.—Higher criticism - higher anti-Semitism.—The seminary as a witness.—Spiritual honeymoons.—Rebellion against being a problem.—The reconciliation of Israel.—Altar building in America.—Zionism: a statement.—The problem of religious education.—Moritz Steinschneider.—Rabbi as a personal example.—Lector Meir Friedmann.—Abraham Lincoln.—Benno

Badt.—The beginnings of Jewish Wissenschaft.—The test the rabbi should apply.—The Beth Hamidrash.—Humility and self-sacrifice as the qualifications of the rabbi.—The assistance of the public.—His Majesty's opposition.—"Lovingkindness and truth." [BM45.S25 1969] 79-83435
1. Judaism—Addresses, essays, lectures. I. Title.

SILVER, Abba Hillel, 1893-1963. 296'.08
Therefore choose life; selected sermons, addresses, and writings of Abba Hillel Silver. Edited by Herbert Weiner. With a memoir by Solomon B. Freehof. Cleveland, World Pub. Co. [1967- v. illus., ports. 25 cm. [BM45.S57] 66-25890
1. Judaism—Collected works. I. Title.

SLONIMSKY, Henry, 1884- 296'.08
Essays. Cincinnati, Hebrew Union College Press, 1967. 148 p. 22 cm. [BM514.S54] 67-25631
1. Midrash. 2. Judaism—Addresses, essays, lectures. I. Title.

SOLOVEITCHIK, Joseph Dov. 296'.08
Shiurei harav; a conspectus of the public lectures of Joseph D. Soloveitchik. Editor: Joseph Epstein. Consulting editors: Menachem Kasdan [and others] New York, Hamevaser [1974] v, 104 p. illus. 23 cm. [BM45.S67] 74-173599
1. Judaism—Addresses, essays, lectures. I. Title.

STITSKIN, Leon D., comp. 296'.08
Studies in Torah Judaism, edited by Leon D. Stitskin. [New York] Yeshiva University Press, 1969. xxi, 587 p. 24 cm. Originally published as separate monographs in the series Studies in Torah Judaism. Contents.Contents.—The philosophy of purpose, by S. Belkin.—Sabbath and festivals in the modern age, by E. Rackman.—Prayer, by E. Berkovits.—The Kaddish: man's reply to the problem of evil, by M. Luban.—The nature and history of Jewish law, by M. Lewittes.—Jewish law faces modern problems, by I. Jakobovits.—Knowledge and love in rabbinic lore, by L. Jung.—Science and religion, by S. Roth. Includes bibliographical references. [BM40.S72] 68-21858 12.50
1. Orthodox Judaism. 2. Jewish law—Addresses, essays, lectures. I. Title.

WISE, Isaac Mayer, 1819-1900. 296'.08
Selected writings of Isaac Mayer Wise. [Edited by] David Philipson and Louis Grossman[n] New York, Arno Press [1969] vi, 419 p. illus., ports. 23 cm. (Religion in America) Reprint of the 1900 ed. [BM45.W5 1969] 71-83433
1. Wise, Isaac Mayer, 1819-1900. 2. Judaism—Works to 1900.

WOLF, Arnold Jacob, ed. 296.08
Rediscovering Judaism; reflections on a new theology. Chicago, Quadrangle Books, 1965. 288 p. 22 cm. Bibliographical references included in "Notes" (p. 271-285) [BM42.W6] 65-18249
1. Judaism — Addresses, essays, lectures. 2. Jewish theology — Addresses, essays, lectures. I. Title.

WOLF, Arnold Jacob, ed. 296.08
Rediscovering Judaism; reflections on a new theology. Chicago, Quadrangle [c.]1965. 288p. 22cm. Bibl. [BM42.W6] 65-18249 6.50
1. Judaism—Addresses, essays, lectures. 2. Jewish theology—Addresses, essays, lectures. I. Title.

BUBER, Martin, 1878- 296.081
Israel and the world; essays in a time of crisis. [2d ed.] New York, Shocken Books, [1963] 266 p. 22 cm. (Schocken paperbacks) "SB66." [BM45.B78] 63-24512
1. Judaism — Addresses, essays, lectures. I. Title.

BUBER, Martin, 1878- 296.081
Israel and the world; essays in a time of crisis. [2d ed.] New York, Shocken [c.1948, 1963] 266p. 22cm. (Shocken paperbacks, SB66) Bibl. 63-24512 1.95 pap.,
1. Judaism—Addresses, essays, lectures. I. Title.

EISENDRATH, Maurice Nathan, 1902- 296.081
Can faith survive? The thoughts and afterthoughts of an American rabbi, by Maurice N. Eisendrath. [1st ed.] New York, McGraw-Hill [1964] 315 p. 22 cm. [BM561.E4] 64-25170
1. Judaism—Addresses, essays, lectures. 2. Judaism and social problems—Addresses, essays, lectures. I. Title.

HIRSCHBERG, Harris Hans, 1908- 296.081
Hebrew humanism [by] Harris H. Hirschberg. Los Angeles, California Writers [c1964] v, 230 p. 17 cm. Bibliography: p. 229-230. [BM561.H5] 65-3443
1. Judaism. I. Title.

LEVI, Leo. 296.081
Vistas from Mount Moria; a scientist views Judaism and the world. New York, Gur Pub. Co. [c1959] 154p. 24cm. [BM565.L4] 60-26132
1. Judaism. I. Title.

LEWIN, Isaac, 1906- 296.081
Late summer fruit; essays. New York, Bloch Pub. Co. [1960] 174 p. 24 cm. [BM45.L45] 60-16701
1. Judaism — Addresses, essays, lectures. I. Title.

LEWIN, Izak, 1906- 296.081
Late summer fruit essays. New York, Bloch Pub. Co. [c.1960] 174p. 24cm. 60-16701 3.00
1. Judaism—Addresses, essays, lectures. I. Title.

PEKARSKY, Maurice Bernard, 1905-1962 296.081
The legacy of Maurice Pekarsky. Ed., introd. by Alfred Jospe. Foreword by A. L. Sachar. Chicago, Quadrangle [c.]1965. 216p. 22cm. [BM45.P4] 65-12779 5.50
1. Judaism—Collected works. I. Title.

RAPPAPORT, Solomon, 1905- 296.081
Jewish horizons; aspects of Jewish life and thought. Johannesburg, B'nai B'rith; exclusive selling agents for the U. S. A., Bloch Pub. Co., New York, 1959. 264p.: 41p. 22cm. [BM45.R295] 59-43151
1. Judaism—Addresses, essays, lectures. 2. Jewish literature—Addresses, essays, lectures. I. Title.

SCHECHTER, Solomon 296.081
Seminary addresses, and other papers. With an introd. by Louis Finkelstein. [New York 28] [1109 Fifth Ave.] Burning Bush. Press [1960, c.1959] xxvi, 253p. front. 20cm. 60-308 4.00; 1.45 pap.,
1. Judaism—Addresses, essays, lectures. I. Title.

SCHECHTER, Solomon, 1847-1915 296.081
The wisdom of Solomon Schechter, by Bernard Mandelbaum. New York, Burning Bush Pr. [c.]1963. 136p. 28cm. (1913-1963) A United Synagogue jubilee pubn. 63-23895 1.75 pap.,
1. Judaism—Addresses, essays, lectures. I. Mandelbaum, Bernard, 1922- ed. II. Title.

ALTMANN, Alexander, 1906- ed. 296.082
Biblical and other studies. Cambridge, Mass., Harvard, 1963. viii, 266p. 25cm. (Philip W. Lown Inst. of Advanced Judaic Studies, Brandeis Univ. Studies and texts, v.1.) Bibl. 62-17214 apply
1. Judaism—Addresses, essays, lectures. 2. Bible. O. T.—Addresses, essays, lectures. I. Title. II. Series: Brandeis University, Waltham, Mass. Philip W. Lown Institute of Advanced Judaic Studies. Studies and texts, v.1

ALTMANN, Alexander, 1906- ed. 296.082
Studies in nineteenth-century Jewish intellectual history. Cambridge, Mass., Harvard [c.]1964. vi, 215p. 25cm. (Philip W. Lown Inst. of Advanced Judaic Studies, Brandeis Univ. Studies & texts, v.2) Bibl. 64-13418 5.75
1. Judaism-Addresses, essays, lectures. 2. Bible. O. T. Addresses, essays, lectures. I. Title. II. Series: Brandeis University, Waltham, Mass. Philip W. Lown Institute of Advanced Judaic Studies. Studies and texts, v.2

BERKOWITZ, William. 296.082
Ten vital Jewish issues. New York, T. Yoseloff [1964] 268 p. 22 cm. [BM42.B45] 64-13167
1. Judaism—Addresses, essays, lectures. I. Title.

CENTRAL Conference of American Rabbis. 296.082
Retrospect and prospect; essays in commemoration of the seventy-fifth anniversary of the founding of the Central Conference of American Rabbis, 1889-1964. Edited by Bertram Wallace Korn. New York, 1965. xvi, 272 p. 22 cm. Contents.Preface, by B. W. Korn. -- The history of the Conference, by S. L. Regner. -- Theological developments, by B. J. Bamberger. -- The Union prayer book: a study in liturgical development, by L. H. Silberman. -- The Conference stance on social justice and civil rights, by R. B. Gittelsohn. -- The Conference considers relations between religion and the state, by E. Lipman. -- The Conference view of the position of the Jew in the modern world, by A. J. Lelyveld. -- The Conference and Jewish religious education, by L. Fram. -- The Conference and the organized American Jewish community, by D. M. Eichhorn. -- The changing role of the rabbi, by J. K. Shankman. -- Summary and prospect, by L. I. Feuer. Includes bibliographical references. [BM42.C4] 65-20282
1. Judaism — Addresses, essays, lectures. I. Korn, Bertram Wallace, ed. II. Title.

EISENBERG, Azriel Louis, 1903- ed. 296.082
The Bar Mitzvah treasury. New York, Behrman House [1952] 316p. illus. 21cm. [BM40.E347] 53-1266
1. Judaism-Collections. I. Title.

HERTZBERG, Arthur, ed. 296.082
Judaism. New York, Washington Sq. [1963, c.1961] 261p. 16cm. (Great religions of modern man W. 802) Bibl. .60 pap.,
1. Judaism—Collections. I. Title.

HERTZBERG, Arthur, ed. 296.082
Judaism. New York, G. Braziller, 1961. 256 p. 21 cm. (Great religions of modern man) Includes bibliography. [BM43.H45] 61-15498
1. Judaism—Collections.

JUNG, Leo 296.082
Jewish leaders, 1750-1940 [Jerusalem] Boys Town, Jerusalem Pubs. [dist. New York 2, 96 E. Bdway., Philip Feldhiem, 1964, c.1963 564p. 22cm. Bibl. 6.00
1. Judaism—Biographical works. I. Title.

KASHER, Menachem Mendel, 1895- ed. 296.082
The Leo Jung jubilee volume; essays in his honor on the occasion of his seventieth birthday, 5722, 1962. Ed. by Menahem M. Kasher, Norman Lamm, Leonard Rosenfeld. New York [Block, c.1962] 242, 258p. illus. 24cm. Added t.p. in Hebrew. English or Hebrew. Bibl. 62-5935 7.50
1. Jung, Leo, 1892- 2. Judaism—Addreses, essays, lectures. I. Title.

LEWIS, Theodore N 296.082
My faith and people; convictions of a rabbi. New York, Behrman House [1961] 253 p. 22 cm. [BM45.L47] 60-88503
1. Judaism — Addresses, essays, lectures. I. Title.

MILLGRAM, Abraham Ezra, 1901- ed. 296.082
Great Jewish ideas. B'nai B'rith Dept. of Adult Jewish Educ. [dist. New York, Taplinger, c.1964] xi, 352p. 25cm. (B'nai B'rith great bks. ser., v.5) Bibl. 64-17292 4.95
1. Judaism—Collections. I. Title.

NATIONAL Hillel Summer Institute. 19th, Camp B'nai B'rith, 1964 296.082
Dimensions of Jewish existence today. Washington, D.C., B'nai B'rith Hillel Founds., 1640 Rhode Island Ave., N. W. [1965] vii, 135p. 22cm. Bibl. [BM30.N3] 65-4005 1.50
1. Judaism—Congresses. I. B'nai B'rith Hillel Foundations. II. Title.

NEW York. Public Library. 296.082
The Joshua Bloch memorial volume; studies in booklore and history. Edited by Abraham Beger, Lawrence Marwick [and] Isidore S. Meyer. New York, 1960. xix, 219p. port. 25cm. [BM42.N45] 60-5589
1. Bloch, Joshua, 1890-1957. 2. Judaism—Addresses, essays, lectures. 3. Jews—Hist.—Addresses, essays, lectures. 4. Printing—Hist.—Hebrew. I. Berger, Abraham, ed. II. Title.
Contents omitted.

NOVECK, Simon, ed. 296.082
Contemporary Jewish thought; a reader. Edited with introductory notes. [Washington] B'nai B'rith, Dept. of Adult Jewish Education [1963] 378 p. 25 cm. (B'nai B'rith great books series [v. 4]) [BM42.N6] 62-21933
1. Judaism—Collections. I. Title.

NOVECK, Simon, ed. 296.082
Great Jewish thinkers of the twentieth century. Edited with introductory essays. [Washington] B'nai B'rith, Dept. of Adult Jewish Education [1963] 326 p. 25 cm. (B'nai B'rith great books series [v. 3]) [BM42.N6] 62-21932
1. Judaism—Collections. I. Title.

PITTSBURGH. Rodef Shalom Congregation. 296.082
Essays in honor of Solomon B. Freehof, presented by the Rodef Shalom Congregation on the occasion of his seventieth birthday, August 8,1962. Editors: Walter Jacob, Frederick C. Schwartz [and] Vigor W. Kavaler. Pittsburgh, 1964. x, 333 p. port. 24 cm. Bibliographical footnotes. [BM755.F693P5] 64-16342
1. Freehof, Solomon Bennett, 2. Judaism—Addresses, essays, lectures. I. Freehof, Solomon Bennett, 1892- II. Jacob, Walter, 1930- ed. III. Schwartz, Fredrick C. ed. IV. Kavaler, Vigdor W. ed. V. Title.
contents omitted

SILVER, Daniel Jeremy, ed. 296.082
In the time of harvest, essays in honor of Abba Hillel Silver on the occasion of his 70th birthday. Board of eds.: Solomon B. Freehof [others] New York Macmillan [1963] viii, 459p. port. 26cm. Bibl. 62-21613 10.00
1. Silver, Abba Hillel, 1893- 2. Judaism—Addresses, essays, lectures. 3. Jews—Hist.—Addresses, essays, lectures. I. Title.

WEYNE, Arthur. 296.082
The less said; the view from a Jewish editor's head. New York, J. David [1964] 122 p. 22 cm. [E184.J5W48] 63-23293
1. Jews in the U.S — Addresses, essays, lectures. I. Title.

WEYNE, Arthur 296.082
The less said; the view from a Jewish editor's head. New York, J. David [c1964] 122p. 22cm. 63-23293 2.75: 1.45 pap.,
1. Jews in the U.S.—Addresses, essays, lectures. I. Title.

GREENBERG, Sidney, ed. 296.0822
A modern treasury of Jewish thoughts. Introd. by Charles Angoff. New York, T. Yoseloff [c.1960] 465p. 24cm. 59-7539 5.95
1. Jewish literature (Selections: Extracts, etc.). I. Title.

GREENBERG, Sidney, 1917- ed. 296.0822
A modern treasury of Jewish thoughts. Introd. by Charles Angoff. New York, T. Yoseloff [1960] 465p. 25cm. [BM43.G7] 59-7539
1. Jewish literature (Selections: Extracts, etc.) I. Title.

THE Jewish audio-visual review. 296.084
New York, National Council on Jewish Audio-Visual Materials. v. 28cm. annual. [BM103.J38] 57-46323
1. Judaism—Study and teaching—Audio-visual aids. I. National Council on Jewish Audio-Visual Materials.

APPROACHES to ancient 296'.09
Judaism : theory and practice / by William S. Green. Missoula, Mont. : Published by Scholars Press for Brown University, c1976. p. cm. (Brown Judaic studies ; no. 1) Includes bibliographical references and index. [BM173.A66] 76-57656 ISBN 0-89130-130-5
1. Judaism—History—Post-exilic period, 586 B.C.-210 A.D.—Addresses, essays, lectures. 2. Rabbinical literature—History and criticism—Addresses, essays, lectures. 3. Jewish studies—Addresses, essays, lectures. I. Green, William Scott. II. Title. III. Series.

BAMBERGER, Bernard Jacob, 1904- 296'.09
The story of Judaism [by] Bernard J. Bamberger. 3d, augm. ed. New York, Schocken Books [1970] viii, 484 p. 21 cm. (Schocken paperbacks on Jewish life and religion) Bibliography: p. 463-466. [BM155.2.B25 1970] 71-20600 ISBN 0-8052-0077-0 2.95
1. Judaism—History. I. Title.

BLUMENFELD, David. 296'.09
The story of Israel; the lives of Israel's prophets and kings, humanized and presented in a clear and comprehensive version. Dallas, Story Book Press [1950, '1949] 593 p. port. 24 cm. Published in part in 1927 under title: Modern Bible verses, book 1. [BM155.B6] 50-14801
1. Jews—Hist. I. Title.

BONSIRVEN, Joseph 296.09
Palestinian Judaism in the time of Jesus Christ. Tr. from French by William Wolf. New York, McGraw [1965, c.1950, 1964] xv, 271p. 21cm. [BM176.B573] 2.75 pap.,
1. Judaism—Hist.—Post-exilic period. 2. Religious thought—Ancient period. 3. Jewish theology—Hist. I. Title.

BONSIRVEN, Joseph. 296.09
Palestinian Judaism in the time of Jesus Christ. Translated from the French by William Wolf. [1st American ed.] New York, Holt, Rinehart and Winston [1964] xv, 271 p. 22 cm. Bibliography: p. [261]-271. [BM176.B573] 63-19466
1. Judaism—History—Post-exilic period, 586 B.C.-210 A.D. 2. Religious thought—To 600. 3. Jewish theology—History. I. Title.

CAHN, Ziv. 296.09
The philosophy of Judaism; the development of Jewish thought throughout the ages, the Bible, the Talmud, the Jewish philosophers, and the Cabala, until the present time. New York, Macmillan, 1962. 524p. 24cm. Includes bibliography. [BM157.C313] 61-14705
1. Judaism—Hist. 2. Philosophy, Jewish—Hist. I. Title.

CAHN, Zvi 296.09
The philosophy of Judaism; the development

of Jewish thought throughout the ages, the Bible, the Talmud, the Jewish philosophers, and the Cabala, until the present time. New York, Macmillan [c.]1962. 524p. Bibl. 61-14705 7.50
1. Judaism—Hist. 2. Philosophy, Jewish—Hist. I. Title.

CHARLES, Robert Henry, 1855-1931. 296'.09
Religious development between the Old and New Testaments / by R. H. Charles. Folcroft, Pa. : Folcroft Library Editions, 1977. p. cm. Reprint of the 1914 ed. published by Williams and Norgate, London, which was issued as no. 88 of the Home university library of modern knowledge. Includes index. [BM176.C5 1977] 77-23010 ISBN 0-8414-1813-6 lib. bdg. : 20.00
1. Judaism—History—Post-exile period, 586 B.C.-210 A. D.—Addresses, essays, lectures. I. Title.

CHOURAQUI, Andre Nathanael, 1917- 296.09
A history of Judaism. Tr. [from French] by Yvette Wiener. New York, Walker [1963, c.1962] 160p. 21cm. (Sun bk., SB-10. Religion & mythology) 62-12755 3.50
1. Judaism—Hist. I. Title.

EPSTEIN, Isidore, 1894- 296.09
Judaism; a historical presentation. [Gloucester, Mass., Peter Smith, 1963, c.1959] 348p. 19cm. (Pelican bks., A440 rebound) Bibl. 3.00
1. Judaism—Hist. I. Title.

FOHRER, Georg. 296'.09
History of Israelite religion. Translated by David E. Green. Nashville, Abingdon Press [1972] 416 p. 24 cm. Translation of Geschichte der israelitischen Religion. Bibliography: p. 11-13. [BM165.F6413] 72-2010 ISBN 0-687-17225-X 10.95
1. Bible. O.T.—Theology. 2. Judaism—History—To 70 A.D. I. Title.

THE Foundations of Jewish life: three studies. 296'.09 New York, Arno Press, 1973. 88, 68, xxx, 279, 77 p. port. 23 cm. (The Jewish people: history, religion, literature) Reprint of The glory of God, by I. Abrahams, first published in 1925 by Oxford University Press, London; of The economic conditions of Judaea after the destruction of the second temple, by A. Buchler, first published in 1912 by Oxford University Press, London; and of Studies in Jewish history, by A. Buchler, first published in 1956 by Oxford University Press, London. Includes bibliographical references. [BM40.F63] 73-2197 ISBN 0-405-05263-4 25.00
1. Jews—History—168 B.C.-135 A.D.—Addresses, essays, lectures. 2. Glory of God (Judaism) 3. Palestine—Economic conditions. 4. Tannaim—Addresses, essays, lectures. I. Abrahams, Israel, 1858-1925. The glory of God. 1973. II. Buchler, Adolf, 1867-1939. The economic conditions of Judaea after the destruction of the second Temple. 1973. III. Buchler, Adolf, 1867-1939. Studies in Jewish history. 1973. IV. Title. V. Series.

GLATZER, Nahum Norbert, 1903- ed. 296.09
Faith and knowledge; the Jew in the medieval world, edited and introduced by Nahum N. Glatzer. Boston, Beacon Press [1963] xx, 235 p. 21 cm. (His Beacon texts in the Judaic tradition, v. 2) Bibliography: p. 221-225. "Suggestions for further reading": p. 228-229. [PM180.G55] 63-17528
1. Judaism — Hist. — Medieval and early modern period. I. Title.

GLATZER, Nahum Norbert, 1903- ed. 296.09
Faith and knowledge; the Jew in the medival world, ed. introd. by Nahum N. Glatzer. Boston. Beacon [c.1963] xx, 235p. 21cm. (His Beacon texts in the Judaic tradition, v.2) Bibl. 63-17528 6.00 bds.,
1. Judaism—Hist.—Medieval and early modern period. I. Title.

GLATZER, Nahum Norbert, 1903- comp. 296'.09
The Judaic tradition; texts, edited and introduced by Nahum N. Glatzer. [Rev. ed. with a new introd.] Boston, Beacon Press [1969] xvi, 838 p. 21 cm. (Beacon paperback no. 316) "Consolidated edition of three volumes that appeared separately in 1961, 1963, and 1965." Contents.Contents.—The rest is commentary.—Faith and knowledge.—The dynamics of emancipation. Includes bibliographies. [BM40.G57 1969] 69-17798 3.95
1. Jews—Political and social conditions. 2. Judaism—History—Sources. 3. Judaism—Collections. I. Glatzer, Nahum Norbert, 1903- ed. The rest is commentary. II. Glatzer, Nahum Norbert, 1903- ed. Faith and knowledge. III. Glatzer, Nahum Norbert, 1903- ed. The dynamics of emancipation. IV. Title. V. Title: The rest is commentary. VI. Title: Faith and knowledge. VII. Title: The dynamics of emancipation.

GLATZER, Nahum Norbert, 1903- ed. 296.09
The rest is commentary; a source book of Judaic antiquity. Boston, Beacon [c.1961] xiv, 271p. (Beacon texts in the Judaic tradition, v.1) Bibl. 61-7250 6.00 bds.
1. Judaism—Hist.—Ancient period—Sources. 2. Jewish literature (Selections: Extracts, etc.) I. Title.

GOWAN, Donald E. 296'.09
Bridge between the Testaments : a reappraisal of Judaism from the Exile to the birth of Christianity / by Donald E. Gowan. Pittsburgh : Pickwick Press, 1976. xx, 514 p. : ill. ; 22 cm. (Pittsburgh theological monograph series ; 14) Includes bibliographies and index. [BM176.G65] 76-49996 ISBN 0-915138-19-0 : 9.95
1. Jews—History—586 B.C.-70 A.D. 2. Judaism—History—Post-exilic period, 586 B.C.-210 A.D. I. Title. II. Series.

*GRAYZEL, Solomon. 296'.09
A history of the Jews from the Babylonian exile to the present: 5728-1968. New York, New Amer. Lib. [1968] 768p. maps. 18cm. (Mentor bk., MW870) Bibl. 1.50 pap.,
1. Judaism—Hist. I. Title.

HEXTER, Jack H. 1910- 296.09
The Judaeo-Christian tradition [by] J. H. Hexter. New York, Harper & Row [1966] xiv, 114 p. maps. 21 cm. (Major traditions of world civilization) Bibliography: p. 101-112. [BM561.H48] 66-11264
1. Judaism. 2. Christianity. I. Title. II. Series.

A History of Judaism. 296'.09
New York : Basic Books, [1974] 2 v. : ill. ; 25 cm. Issued in a case. Contents.Contents.—v. 1. Silver, D. J. From Abraham to Maimonides. v. 2. Martin, B. Europe and the New World. Includes bibliographies and indexes. [BM155.2.H57] 73-90131 ISBN 0-465-03008-4 : 11.95 (vol. 1). 13.95 (vol. 2)
1. Judaism—History. I. Silver, Daniel Jeremy. From Abraham to Maimonides. 1974. II. Martin, Bernard, 1928- Europe and the New World. 1974.

HOWIE, Carl Gordon, 1920- 296.09
The creative era between the Testaments [by] Carl G. Howie. Richmond, John Knox Press [1965] 96 p. 21 cm. (Aletheia paperbacks) Bibliographical references included in "Notes and acknowledgements" (p. [93]-96) [BM176.H6] 65-10117
1. Judaism—Hist.—Post-exilic period. I. Title.

HOWIE, Carl Gordon, 1920- 296.09
The creative era between the Testaments. Richmond, Va., Knox [c.1965] 96p. 21cm. (Aletheia paperbacks) Bibl. [BM176.H6] 65-10117 1.45 pap.,
1. Judaism—Hist.—Post-exilic period. I. Title.

KAUFMANN, Yehezkel, 1889-1963. 296'.09
The Babylonian captivity and Deutero-Isaiah. [Translator: C. W. Efroymson. New York, Union of American Hebrew Congregations, 1970] xv, 236 p. 25 cm. (His History of the religion of Israel, v. 4, chapters 1, 2) Translation of v. 4, chapters 1-2 of Toldot ha-emunah ha-yisre'elit. Bibliography: p. 205-208. [BS1520.K3813 1970] 74-92167 7.50
1. Bible. O.T. Isaiah XL-LXVI—Criticism, interpretation, etc. 2. Judaism—History—Post-exilic period, 586 B.C.-210 A.D. I. Title.

KAUFMANN, Yehezkel, 1889-1963. 296'.09
History of the religion of Israel, from the Babylonian captivity to the end of prophecy / by Yehezkel Kaufmann ; translated by Clarence Efroymsen. New York : Ktav Pub. House, 1976. p. cm. Translation of v. 4 of Toldot ha-emunah ha-Yisre'elit. Includes index. Bibliography: p. [BM165.K33213 1976] 76-22497 25.00
1. Judaism—History—Post-exilic period, 586 B.C.-210 A.D. I. Title.

KAUFMANN, Yehezkel, 1889-1963. 296.09
The religion of Israel, from its beginnings to the Babylonian exile. Translated and abridged by Moshe Greenberg. Chicago, University of Chicago Press [1960] 486 p. 25 cm. [BM155.K3743] 60-5466
1. Judaism — Hist. I. Title.

KAUFMANN, Yehezkel, 1889-1963. 296.09
The religion of Israel, from its beginnings to the Babylonian exile. Translated and abridged by Moshe Greenberg. [Chicago] University of Chicago Press [1960] 486 p. 25 cm. Abridgement and translation of Toldot ha-emunah ha-yisre'elit (romanized form) [BM155.K3743] 60-5466
1. Judaism—History—To 70 A.D. I. Title.

KOHLER, Kaufmann, 1843-1926. 296'.09
The origins of the synagogue and the church. Edited by H. G. Enelow. New York, Arno Press, 1973 [c1929] xxxix, 297 p. port. 23 cm. (The Jewish people: history, religion, literature) Reprint of the ed. published by Macmillan, New York. Includes bibliographical references. [BM165.K65 1973] 73-2213 ISBN 0-405-05277-4 18.00
1. Jews. Liturgy and ritual—History. 2. Kohler, Kaufmann, 1843-1926. 3. Judaism—History—Post-exilic period. 4. Church history—Primitive and early church. I. Enelow, Hyman Gerson, 1876-1934, ed. II. Title. III. Series.

LODS, Adolphe, 1867-1948. 296'.09
The prophets and the rise of Judaism. Translated by S. H. Hooke. Westport, Conn., Greenwood Press [1971] xxiv, 378 p. illus. 23 cm. Translation of Les prophetes d'Israel et les debuts des judaisme. Reprint of the 1937 ed. Bibliography: p. 357-368. [BM165.L613 1971] 77-109772 ISBN 0-8371-4262-8 15.00
1. Judaism—History—To 70 A.D. 2. Prophets. I. Title.

MANN, Jacob, 1888-1940. 296'.09
The collected articles of Jacob Mann. New York, Behrman House [1973] p. Contents.Contents.—v. 1. Studies in ancient and medieval Jewish history.—v. 2. Gaonic studies.—v. 3. Karaitic and Genizah studies. [BM45.M32 1973] 73-6788 ISBN 0-87441-061-4 50.00
1. Judaism—History—Addresses, essays, lectures. 2. Geonic literature—History and criticism. 3. Karaitic literature. 4. Cairo Genizah. 5. Rabbinical literature.

MUILENBERG, James 296.09
The way of Israel: biblical faiths and ethics [Magnolia, Mass., P. Smith. 1966, c.1961] 165p. 21cm. (Torchbk., TB133G: Cloister lib. rebound) Bibl. [BM165.M8] 3.25
1. Judaism—Hist.—Ancient period. 2. Ethics, Jewish. 3. Bible. O.T.—Theology. I. Title.

MUILENBURG, James. 296.09
The way of Israel; Biblical faith and ethics. [1st ed.] New York, Harper [1961] 158 p. 22 cm. (Religious perspectives, v. 5) Includes bibliography. [BM165.M8] 61-12830
1. Bible. O.T.—Theology. 2. Judaism—History—Ancient period. 3. Ethics, Jewish. I. Title.

NEUSNER, Jacob, 1932- 296'.09
There we sat down: Talmudic Judaism in the making. Nashville, Abingdon Press [1971, c1972] 158 p. maps. 23 cm. Includes bibliographical references. [BM177.N48] 78-172812 ISBN 0-687-41631-0
1. Judaism—History—Tannaitic period, 10-220. I. Title.

PARKES, James William 296.09
The foundations of Judaism and Christianity. Chicago, Quadrangle Books, 1960[ ] xv, 344p. 23cm. (Bibl. footnotes) 60-13608 6.00
1. Christianity and other religions—Judaism. 2. Judaism—Relations—Christianity. 3. Judaism—Hist.—Post-exilic period. 4. Christianity—Origin. I. Title.

PARKES, James William, 1896- 296.09
A history of the Jewish people. Baltimore, Penguin [c.1962, 1964] 247p. 18cm. (Pelican bk. A662) 1.25 pap.,
1. Jews Hist. I. Title.

PFEIFFER, Charles F. 296.09
Between the Testaments. Grand Rapids, Baker Book House, 1959. 132 p. 22 cm. [BM176.P39] 59-8343
1. Jews—History—586 B.C.-70 A.D. I. Title.

PFEIFFER, Charles F. 296.09
Between the Testaments. Grand Rapids Baker Book House, [1974, c1959] 132 p. 22 cm. [BM176.P39] ISBN 0-8010-6873-8 3.95 (pbk.)
1. Jews—History-586 B.C.-70 A.D. I. Title.

PILCHIK, Ely Emanuel 296.09
Judaism outside the Holy Land; the early period. New York, Bloch [1964] 184p. 21cm. Bibl. 64-7539 3.75
1. Jews—Diaspora. I. Title.

PIPER, Otto, 1891- 296.09
The church meets Judaism, by Otto Piper, Jakob Jocz, and Harold Floreen. Foreword by H. Conrad Hoyer. Minneapolis, Augsburg Pub. House [c.1960] xiv, 98p. 20cm. 60-14167 1.75 pap.,
1. Christianity and other religions—Judaism. 2. Judaism—Relations—Christianity. 3. Missions—Jews. I. Title.

PIPER, Otto A 1891- 296.09
The church meets Judaism, by Otto Piper, Jakob Jocz, and Harold Floreen. Foreword by H. Conrad Hoyer. Minneapolis, Augsburg Pub. House [1960] 98p. 20cm. [BM535.P5] 60-14167
1. Christianity and other religions—Judaism. 2. Judaism—Relations —Christianity. 3. Missions—Jews. I. Title.

POLACK, Albert Isaac, 1892- 296'.09
Cup of life : a short history of post-biblical Judaism / Albert I. Polack and Joan Lawrence. London : SPCK, 1976. vii, 187 p. ; 22 cm. Bibliography: p. [183]-186. [BM155.2.P64] 76-375919 ISBN 0-281-02915-6 : £2.95
1. Jews—History—70- 2. Judaism—History. I. Lawrence, Joan, joint author. II. Title.

REIK, Theodor, 1888- 296.09
Mystery on the mountain; the drama of the Sinai revelation. New York, Harper [1959] 210p. 23cm. Includes bibliography. [BM170.R43] 59-10339
1. Jews—Hist.—To entrance into Canaan. 2. Commandments, Ten. 3. Initiations (in religion, folk-lore, etc.) 4. Psychoanalysis. I. Title.

RELIGION in a religious age. 296'.09 Edited by S. D. Goitein. Cambridge, Mass., Association for Jewish Studies, 1974. vii, 156 p. 23 cm. Papers from 2 regional conferences of the Association for Jewish Studies, held Apr. 8-9 at the University of California, Los Angeles and Apr. 29-30, 1973, at Brandeis University. Includes bibliographies. [BM180.R44] 74-7443 ISBN 0-87068-268-7
1. Cairo Genizah. 2. Judaism—History—Medieval and early modern period, 425-1789—Congresses. 3. Philosophy, Jewish. 4. Judaism—Relations—Islam. 5. Islam—Relations—Judaism. I. Goitein, Solomon Dob Fritz, 1900- ed. II. Association for Jewish Studies.

SACHAR, Howard Morley, 1928- 296.09
The course of modern Jewish history. New York, Dell, 1963 [c.1958] 630p. maps. 21cm. (Delta 1538) Bibl. 2.45
1. Jews—Hist.—1789-1945. 2. Jews—Hist.—1945- I. Title.

SACHAR, Howard Morley, 1928- 296.09
The course of modern Jewish history, Updated ad expanded ed. New York : Dell Pub. Co., 1977. 669p. : maps ; 21 cm. Bibliography:p.602-642. [DS125.S3] ISBN 0-440-51538-6 pbk. : 5.95
1. Jews-History-1789-1945. 2. Jews-History-1945. I. Title.

SLOAN, William Wilson. 296.09
A survey between the Testaments. Paterson, N.J., Littlefield, Adams, 1964. 231 p. 20 cm. (The New Littlefield college outlines, no. 40) On cover: Between the Testaments. Bibliography: p. 216-217. [BM176.S55] 63-22778
1. Jews — Hist. — 586 B. C.-70 A.D. 2. Judaism — Hist. — Post-Exilic period. I. Title. II. Title: Between the Testaments.

SLOAN, William Wilson 296.09
A survey between the Testaments. Paterson, N.J., Littlefield, Adams [c.]1964. 231p. 20cm. (New Littlefield coll. outlines, no. 40) On cover: Between the Testaments. Bibl. 63-22778 1.95 pap.,
1. Jews—Hist.—586 B.C.-70 A.D. 2. Judaism—Hist. Post-Exilic period. I. Title. II. Title: Between the Testaments.

TARSHISH, Allan, 1907- 296.09
Not by power; the story of the growth of Judaism. New York, Bookman Associates [1952] 277 p. 22 cm. [DS118.T3] 52-13777
1. Jews — Hist. I. Title.

TOOMBS, Lawrence E 296.09
The threshold of Christianity; between the Testaments. Philadelphia, Westminster Press [1960] 96 p. 20 cm. (Westminster guides to the Bible) [BM176.T6] 60-5226
1. Judaism — Hist. — Post-exille period. I. Title.

TOOMBS, Lawrence E. 296.09
The threshold of Christianity; between the Testaments. Philadelphia, Westminster Press [c.1960] 96p. 20cm. (Westminster guides to the Bible) 60-5226 1.50
1. Judaism—Hist.—Post-exilic period. I. Title.

TREPP, Leo. 296.09
Eternal faith, eternal people; a journey into Judaism. Englewood Cliffs, N.J., Prentice-Hall, 1962. 455 p. illus. 24 cm. Includes bibliography. [BM155.2.T7] 62-8304
1. Judaism — Hist. 2. Jews — Rites and ceremonies. I. Title.

TREPP, Leo. 296.09
Eternal faith, eternal people; a journey into Judaism. Englewood Cliffs, N. J., Prentice-Hall, 1962. 455 p. illus. 24 cm. Includes bibliography. [BM155.2.T7] 62-8304
1. Judaism—History. 2. Jews—Rites and ceremonies. I. Title.

WOLLMAN-TSAMIR, Pinchas, ed. 296.09
The graphic history of the Jewish heritage; an encyclopedic presentation [v.1. Eng. tr. by Sidney B. Hoenig Jacob Sloan, David Segal] New York, Shengold [c.1963] v. illus., tables (1 fold. in pocket) 29cm. Contents.[1] The Biblical period. 63-13318 15.00
1. Jews—Hist.—Outlines, syllabi, etc. I. Title.

FOERSTER, Werner, 1897- 296.0901
From the Exile to Christ; a historical introduction to Palestinian Judaism. Translated by Gordon E. Harris. [English ed.] Philadelphia, Fortress Press [1964] xiv, 247 p. 23 cm. Translation of Neutestamentliche Zeitgeschichte x: Das Judentum Palastinas zur Zeit Jesu und der Apostel. Bibliography: p. 230-234. [BM165.F613] 64-18151
1. Judaism — Hist. — Ancient period. I. Title.

FOERSTER, Werner, 1897- 296.0901
From the Exile to Christ; a historiecal introduction to Palestinian Judaism. Tr. [from German] by Gordon E. Harris [English ed.] Philadelphia, Fortress [c.1964] xiv, 247p. 23cm. Bibl. 64-18151 4.85
1. Judaism—Hist.—Ancient period. I. Title.

GUIGNEBERT, Charles Alfred Honore, 1867-1939. 296.0901
The Jewish world in the time of Jesus. With an introd. by Charles Francis Potter. [1st American ed.] New York, University Books [1959] xiii, 288 p. 22 cm. Bibliography: p. 263-277. [BM176.G82 1959] 59-14528
1. Jews—History—586 B.C.-70 A.D. 2. Bible, N.T.—History of contemporary events, etc. 3. Judaism—History—Post-exilic period, 586 B.C.-210 A.D. I. Title.

PFEIFFER, Robert Henry, 1892-1958. 296.0901
Religion in the Old Testament; the history of a spiritual triumph. Edited by Charles Conrad Forman. [1st ed.] New York, Harper [1961] xii, 276p. 24cm. Bibliography: p. 229-232. 'Bibliography of Robert H. Pfeiffer, compiled by Matilde V. Pfeiffer': p. 233-256. [BM165.P46] 61-5266
1. Judaism— Hist.—Ancient period. I. Title.

RENCKENS, Henricus 296.0901
The religion of Israel, by Henry Renckens. Tr. [from Dutch[by N. B. Smith. New York. Sheed [c.1966] xii, 370p. 22cm. Bibl. [BM165.R413] 66-12261 6.95
1. Judaism—Hist.—Ancient period. I. Title.

RENEKENS, Henricus. 296.0901
The religion of Israel, by Henry Renekens. Translated by N. B. Smith. New York, Sheed and Ward [1966] xii, 370 p. 22 cm. Bibliography: p. 334-355. [BM165.R413] 66-12261
1. Judaism — Hist. — Ancient period. I. Title.

RINGGREN, Helmer, 1917- 296.0901
Israelite religion. Translated by David E. Green. Philadelphia, Fortress Press [1966] xvi, 391 p. 23 cm. Bibliographical footnotes. [BM165.R513] 66-10757
1. Judaism — Hist. — Ancient period. I. Title.

RINGGREN, Helmer, 1917- 296.0901
Israelite religion. Tr. [from German] by David E. Green. Philadelphia, Fortress [c.1966] xvi, 391p. 23cm. Bibl. [BM165.R513] 66-10757 7.50
1. Judaism—Hist.—Ancient period. I. Title.

VRIEZEN, Theodorus Christiaan, 1899- 296.0901
The religion of ancient Israel, by Th. C. Vriezen. Philadelphia, Westminster Press [1967] 328 p. 23 cm. Translation of De Godsdienst van Israel. Bibliographical references included in "Notes" (p. 277-308) [BM165.V713] 67-22703
1. Judaism—History—Ancient period. I. Title.

WHITELOCKE, Lester T. 296'.09'01
The development of Jewish religious thought in the inter-testamental period / Lester T. Whitelocke. 1st ed. New York : Vantage Press, c1976. 143 p. ; 22 cm. Includes index. Bibliography: p. 129-139. [BM175.P4W47] 76-380362 ISBN 0-533-02215-0 : 7.50
1. Pharisees. 2. Judaism—History—Post-exilic period, 586 B.C.-210 A.D. I. Title.

ZEITLIN, Solomon, 1892- 296'.09'01
Solomon Zeitlin's Studies in the early history of Judaism. Selected with an introd. by the author. New York, Ktav Pub. House, 1973- v. 24 cm. Vol. 3 also has special title: Judaism and Christianity. Includes bibliographical references. [BM45.Z44] 72-5816 ISBN 0-87068-208-3 (v. 1)
1. Jews—Identity—Addresses, essays, lectures. 2. Jews Liturgy and ritual—Addresses, essays, lectures. 3. Jesus Christ—Passion—Role of Jews—Addresses, essays, lectures. 4. Judaism—History—Addresses, essays, lectures. 5. Jewish sects—Addresses, essays, lectures. I. Title: Studies in the early history of Judaism.

HENGEL, Martin. 296'.09'014
Judaism and Hellenism : studies in their encounter in Palestine during the early Hellenistic period / Martin Hengel ; [translated by John Bowden from the German] . 1st American ed. Philadelphia : Fortress Press, 1974. 2 v. ; 25 cm. Translation of Judentum und Hellenismus. A revision of the author's Habilitationschrift, Tubingen, 1966. Includes indexes. Bibliography: v. 2, p. [217]-266. [BM176.H413 1974b] 74-80427 34.00
1. Judaism—Relations—Greek. 2. Greece—Religion. 3. Hellenism. I. Title.

SURBURG, Raymond F., 1909- 296'.09'014
Introduction to the intertestamental period / Raymond F. Surburg. St. Louis : Concordia Pub. House, [1975] 197 p. ; 24 cm. Bibliography: p. 177-197. [BM176.S94] 75-1115 ISBN 0-570-03237-7 : 8.95
1. Bible. O.T. Aprocrypha—Introductions. 2. Judaism—History—Post-exilic period, 586 B.C.-210 A.D. 3. Apocryphal books (Old Testament)—Introductions. I. Title.

JEWS, Greeks and 296'.09'015
Christians : religious cultures in late antiquity : essays in honor of William David Davies / edited by Robert Hamerton-Kelly and Robin Scroggs. Leiden : Brill, 1976. xix, 320 p., [1] leaf of plates : port. ; 25 cm. (Studies in Judaism in late antiquity ; v. 21) Contents.Contents.—Sanders, E. P. The covenant as a soteriological category and the nature of salvation in Palestinian and Hellenistic Judaism.—Hamerton-Kelly, R. G. Some techniques of composition in Philo's Allegorical commentary with special reference to De agricultura.—Black, M. The throne-theophany prophetic commission and the "Son of man".—Caird, G. B. Homoeophony in the Septuagint.—Neusner, J. Method and substance in the history of Judaic ideas.—Urbach, E. E. Halakhah and history.—Gerhardsson, Birger. The hermeneutic program in Matthew 22:37-40.—Daube, D. A reform in acts and its models.—Moody Smith, D. The milieu of the Johannine miracle source.—Martyn, J. L. We have found Elijah.—Barrett, C. K. Jews and Judaizers in the epistles of Ignatius.—Schweizer, E. Christianity of the circumcised and Judaism of the uncircumcised.—Simon, M. A propos de l'ecole comparatiste.—Scroggs, R. Two homilies in Romans 1-11. Bibliography of the works by W. D. Davies: p. [1]-10. [BM176.J43] 77-353541
1. Davies, William David, 1911- 2. Bible. N.T.—Criticism, interpretation, etc.—Addresses, essays, lectures. 3. Judaism—History—Post-exilic period, 586 B.C.-210 A.D.—Addresses, essays, lectures. I. Davies, William David, 1911- II. Hamerton-Kelly, Robert. III. Scroggs, Robin. IV. Title. V. Series.

MOORE, George Foot, 1851-1931. 296'.09'015
Judaism in the first centuries of the Christian era, the age of the Tannaim. New York, Schocken Books [1971, c1927-30] 2 v. 21 cm. (Schocken paperbacks on Jewish life and religion) Includes bibliographical references. [BM177.M62] 72-146791 ISBN 0-8052-0294-3 (v. 1) 4.50 (each)
1. Tannaim. I. Title.

KAPLAN, Mordecai Menahem, 296.0903
The greater Judaism in the making; a study of the modern evolution of Judaism. New York, Reconstructionist Press [c.1960] xvi, 565p. 24cm. (Bibl. notes: p. 515-541) 59-15683 7.50 half cloth.,
1. Judaism—Hist.—Modern period. I. Title.

KAPLAN, Mordecai Menahem, 1881- 296.0903
The greater Judaism in the making; a study of the modern evolution of Judaism. New York, Reconstructionist Press [1960] 565p. 24cm. Includes bibliography. [BM190.K33] 59-15683
1. Judaism Hist.—Modern period. I. Title.

THE Role of religion 296'.09'03
in modern Jewish history / edited by Jacob Katz. New York : Ktav Pub. House, 1975. p. cm. Comprised of papers presented during two conferences arranged by the Association for Jewish Studies in Philadelphia, March 3-4, 1974, and in Toronto, April 28-29, 1974. Includes bibliographical references. [BM195.R57] 75-28081 ISBN 0-915938-00-6 : 10.00
1. Judaism—History—Modern period, 1750-—Congresses. I. Katz, Jacob, 1904- II. Association for Jewish Studies.

BOROWITZ, Eugene B. 296'.09'04
How can a Jew speak of faith today? By Eugene B. Borowitz. Philadelphia, Westminster Press [1969] 221 p. 21 cm. Includes bibliographical references. [BM601.B6] 69-10899 6.00
1. Judaism—Addresses, essays, lectures. I. Title.

GORDIS, Robert, 1908- 296.0904
Judaism in a Christian world. [1st ed.] New York, McGraw-Hill [1966] xxxiv, 253 p. 22 cm. Bibliographical references included in "Notes" (p. 235-245) [BM565.G66] 66-23275
1. Judaism—20th century. I. Title.

LEO Baeck Memorial Conference on Jewish Social Thought, New York, 1973. 296'.09'04
Leo Baeck Memorial Conference on Jewish Social Thought : papers delivered at the seventh Lerntag and the annual meeting of the American Federation of Jews from Central Europe, inc., 1973-1974 / Herbert A. Strauss, editor. New York : The Federation, [1974] 63 p. ; 22 cm. [BM30.L46 1973] 74-84607
1. Baeck, Leo, 1873-1956. 2. Buber, Martin, 1878-1965. 3. Judaism—20th century—Congresses. 4. Israel and the Diaspora—Addresses, essays, lectures. 5. Israel-Arab War, 1973—Addresses, essays, lectures. I. Strauss, Herbert Arthur, ed. II. American Federation of Jews from Central Europe.

B'NAI B'rith. Dept. of Adult Jewish Education. 296'.0922
Molders of the Jewish mind. Washington [1966] viii, 245 p. 22 cm. "A B'nai B'rith book." Bibliography: p. [239]-240. [BM750.B55] 66-27649
1. Jews—Biography. I. Title.

BUBER, Martin, 1878-1965. 296'.092'4 B
Meetings. Edited with an introd. and bibliography by Maurice Friedman. La Salle, Ill., Open Court Pub. Co., 1973. 115 p. 22 cm. Bibliography: p. 65-115. [B3213.B82E52 1973] 73-82780 ISBN 0-87548-085-3 5.95
I. Friedman, Maurice S., ed. II. Title.

BUBER, Martin, 1878-1965. 296'.092'4 B
To hallow this life; an anthology. Edited with an introd. by Jacob Trapp. Westport, Conn., Greenwood Press [1974, c1958] xiv, 174 p. 22 cm. Reprint of the ed. published by Harper, New York. [B3213.B82E57 1974] 73-11862 ISBN 0-8371-7096-6 10.00
I. Title.

CAUMAN, Samuel. 296'.0924
Jonah Bondi Wise; a biography, by Sam Cauman. New York, Crown Publishers [1966?] ix, 214 p. illus., ports. 23 cm. [BM755.W52C3] 66-29745
1. Wise, Jonah Bondi, 1881-1959.

GRATZ, Rebecca, 1781-1869. 296'.092'4 B
Letters of Rebecca Gratz / David Philipson, editor. New York : Arno Press, 1975, c1929. xxiv, 454 p. : port. ; 23 cm. (The Modern Jewish experience) Reprint of the ed. published by the Jewish Publication Society of America, Philadelphia. Includes index. [F158.9.J5G7 1975] 74-27987 ISBN 0-405-06714-3 : 29.00
1. Gratz, Rebecca, 1781-1869. I. Title. II. Series.

HODES, Aubrey. 296'.0924 B
Martin Buber; an intimate portrait. New York, Viking Press [1971] xii, 242 p. 23 cm. Revised ed. published in 1972 under title: Encounter with Martin Buber. Bibliography: p. 235-237. [B3213.B84H6 1971] 74-83249 ISBN 0-670-45904-6 7.95
1. Buber, Martin, 1878-1965.

HOENIG, Sidney Benjamin. 296'.0924
Rabbinics and research; the scholarship of Dr. Bernard Revel, by Sidney B. Hoenig. New York, Yeshiva University Press, 1968. 167 p. 24 cm. (Studies in Judaica, 2) Bibliography: p. 129-135. [BM755.R44H6] 71-19636
1. Revel, Bernard, 1885-1940. I. Title. II. Series.

KERTZER, Morris Norman, 1910- 296'.092'4 B
Tell me, rabbi / Morris N. Kertzer. New York : Bloch Pub. Co., 1977,c1976 xii, 196 p. ; 22 cm. [BM755.K37A35] 76-8324 ISBN 0-8197-0395-8 : 7.95
1. Kertzer, Morris Norman, 1910- 2. Rabbis—United States—Biography. 3. Jews in the United States—Anecdotes, facetiae, satire, etc. I. Title.

KERTZER, Morris Norman, 1910- 296'.092'4 B
Tell me, rabbi / Morris N. Kertzer. New York : Bloch Pub. Co., 1977,c1976 xii, 196 p. ; 22 cm. [BM755.K37A35] 76-8324 ISBN 0-8197-0395-8 : 7.95
1. Kertzer, Morris Norman, 1910- 2. Rabbis—United States—Biography. 3. Jews in the United States—Anecdotes, facetiae, satire, etc. I. Title.

KOHUT, Rebekah Bettelheim, 1864-1951. 296'.092'4 B
My portion : (an autobiography) / Rebekah Kohut. New York : Arno Press, 1975 [c1925] xvi, 301 p. ; 23 cm. (The Modern Jewish experience) Reprint of the ed. published by T. Seltzer, New York. Includes index. [HQ1413.K6A37 1975] 74-27995 ISBN 0-405-06722-4 : 19.00
1. Kohut, Rebekah Bettelheim, 1864-1951. I. Title. II. Series.

LANDAU, Sol, 1920- 296'.0924
Bridging two worlds; Rabbi Ezekiel Landau (1888-1965): his written and spoken legacy. Foreword by Helene Landau. New York, J. David [1968] xii, 123 p. group port. 23 cm. Bibliography: p. 122-123. [BM755.L32L3] 68-19961
1. Landau, Ezekiel, 1888-1965. 2. Sermons, American—Jewish authors. 3. Sermons, Jewish—United States. I. Title.

MIRSKY, Mark. 296'.092'4 B
My search for the Messiah : studies and wanderings in Israel and America / Mark Jay Mirsky. New York : Macmillan, c1977. x, 240 p. ; 22 cm. [BM205.M55] 76-54910 ISBN 0-02-585120-9 : 9.95
1. Mirsky, Mark—Religion and ethics. 2. Judaism—United States—Addresses, essays, lectures. 3. Israel—Social life and customs. I. Title.

NETANYAHU, Benzion. 296'.0924 B
Don Isaac Abravanel, statesman and philosopher, by B. Netanyahu. [2d ed.] Philadelphia, Jewish Publication Society of America [1968] xii, 350 p. 22 cm. Bibliography: p. 327-335. [BM755.A25N4 1968] 68-15789
1. Abravanel, Isaac, 1437-1508. I. Title.

NEW perspectives on 296'.092'4 B
Abraham Geiger : an HUC-JIR symposium / edited by Jakob J. Petuchowski. Cincinnati : Hebrew Union College - Jewish Institute of Religion, 1975. p. cm. Bibliography: p. [BM755.G4N48] 75-19131 ISBN 0-87820-201-3
1. Geiger, Abraham, 1810-1874. 2. Geiger, Abraham, 1810-1874—Bibliography. 3. Jewish studies—Germany—Addresses, essays, lectures. I. Petuchowski, Jakob Josef, 1925- II. Hebrew Union College — Jewish Institute of Religion.

NEW perspectives on 296'.092'4 B
Abraham Geiger : an HUC-JIR symposium / edited by Jakob J. Petuchowski. [Cincinnati] : Hebrew Union College-Jewish Institute of Religion ; New York : distributed by Ktav Pub. House, c1975. 58 p. : port. ; 23 cm. Bibliography: p. 55-58. [BM755.G4N48] 75-19131 ISBN 0-87820-201-3 pbk. : 2.50
1. Geiger, Abraham, 1810-1874. 2. Geiger, Abraham, 1810-1874—Bibliography. 3. Jewish studies—Germany—Addresses, essays, lectures. I. Petuchowski, Jakob Josef, 1925- II. Hebrew Union College-Jewish Institute of Religion.

SAMUEL, Maurice, 1895- 296'.092'4 B
The gentleman and the Jew. Westport, Conn., Greenwood Press [1972, c1950] viii, 325 p. 23 cm. Autobiographical. [BM755.S243A3 1972] 70-163541 ISBN 0-8371-6201-7 13.50
I. Title.

SCHAEDER, Grete. 296'.092'4 B
The Hebrew humanism of Martin Buber. Translated by Noah J. Jacobs. Detroit, Wayne State University Press, 1973. 503 p. 24 cm. Translation of Martin Buber; Hebraischer Humanismus. [B3213.B84S2713 1973] 70-39691 ISBN 0-8143-1483-X 17.50
1. Buber, Martin, 1878-1965. I. Title.

SIMON, Charlie May (Hogue) 1897- 296'.0924 B
Martin Buber: wisdom in our time; the story of an outstanding Jewish thinker and humanist, by Charlie May Simon. [1st ed.] New York, Dutton [1969] 191 p. illus., ports. 22 cm. Bibliography: p. 181-183. A biography of the Jewish philosopher and Zionist leader who became noted for his studies of Hasidism, a movement of Jewish mysticism. [B3213.B84S5] 92 74-81725 4.50

1. Buber, Martin, 1878-1965—Juvenile literature. I. Title.

TREACY, William, 1919- 296'.092'4 B
Wild branch on the olive tree / by William Treacy and Raphael Levine, in collaboration with Patricia Jacobsen. Portland, Or. : Binford & Mort, [1974] xix, 137 p., [20] leaves of plates : ill. ; 24 cm. [BM755.L447T73] 74-24492 ISBN 0-8323-0240-6 : 6.95
1. Levine, Raphael H., 1901- 2. Treacy, William, 1919- I. Levine, Raphael H., 1901- joint author. II. Jacobsen, Patricia, joint author. III. Title.

SCHOENBERNER, Gerhard. 296'.094
The yellow star; the persecution of the Jews in Europe, 1933-1945. Translated from German by Susan Sweet. New York, Bantam [1973, c.1969] 288 p. illus. 18 cm. (Bantam Book, Y7768) Translation of Der gelbe Stern. Bibliography: p. 283-286. [D810.J4S34] pap., 1.95
1. Jews in Europe—Persecution. 2. Holocaust, Jewish—1939-1945. I. Title.
L.C. card no. for the German language edition: 71-368263

CASTRO y Rossi, Adolfo de, 1823-1898. 296'.0946
The history of the Jews in Spain, from the time of their settlement in that country till the commencement of the present century. Written, and illustrated with divers extremely scarce documents, by Adolfo de Castro. Translated by Edward D. G. M. Kirwan. Westport, Conn., Greenwood Press [1972] vii, 276 p. front. 22 cm. Translation of Historia de los judíos en Espana. Reprint of the 1851 ed. [DS135.S7C3513 1972] 70-97273 ISBN 0-8371-2593-6
1. Jews in Spain—History. I. Title.

ABRAMOV, Shene'ur Zalman, 1908- 296'.095694
Perpetual dilemma : Jewish religion in the Jewish State / S. Zalman Abramov ; foreword by W. Gunther Plaut. Cranbury, N.J. : Associated University Presses, c1975. p. cm. Includes index. Bibliography: p. [BM390.A4] 74-5897 ISBN 0-8386-1687-9 : 15.00
1. Jews—Identity. 2. Judaism—Israel—History. 3. Judaism and state—Israel—History. 4. Israel—Politics and government—History. I. Title.

HESCHEL, Abraham Joshua, 1907- 296'.095694
Israel: an echo of eternity. Drawings by Abraham Rattner. New York, Farrar, Straus and Giroux [1969] 233 p. illus. 21 cm. Bibliographical footnotes. [BM729.P3H37 1969] 69-11573 5.50
1. Palestine in Judaism. 2. Israel. I. Title.

BELL, Harold Idris, Sir, 1879- 296'.0962
Jews and Christians in Egypt; the Jewish troubles in Alexandria and the Athanasian controversy. Illustrated by texts from Greek papyri in the British Museum. Edited by H. Idris Bell. With three Coptic texts, edited by W. E. Crum. Westport, Conn., Greenwood Press [1972] xii, 140 p. facsims. 26 cm. Reprint of the 1924 ed. Includes bibliographical references. [BR190.B4 1972] 79-97270 ISBN 0-8371-2587-1
1. Athanasius, Saint, Patriarch of Alexandria, d. 373. 2. Egypt—Church history—Sources. 3. Jews in Egypt—History—Sources. I. Crum, Walter Ewing, 1865-1944. II. Title.

BLAU, Joseph Leon, 1909- 296'.0973
Judaism in America : from curiosity to third faith / Joseph L. Blau. Chicago : University of Chicago Press, 1976. xiv, 156 p. ; 21 cm. (Chicago history of American religion) Includes bibliographical references and index. [BM205.B55] 75-5069 ISBN 0-226-05727-5 : 10.95
1. Judaism—United States—History. 2. Jews in the United States. 3. Zionism—United States. I. Title.

GLAZER, Nathan. 296'.0973
American Judaism. 2d ed. Chicago, University of Chicago Press, [1972] xi, 210 p. 21 cm. (The Chicago history of American civilization) Bibliography: p. 200-205. [BM205.G5 1972] 72-85433 ISBN 0-226-29839-6
1. Judaism—United States. 2. Jews in the United States. I. Title. II. Series.

HARDON, John A. 296'.0973
American Judaism [by] John A. Hardon. Chicago, Loyola University Press [1971] xii, 372 p. illus. 24 cm. Bibliography: p. 299-301. [BM205.H37] 72-148264 ISBN 0-8294-0199-7
1. Judaism—U.S.—History. I. Title.

LIEBMAN, Charles S. 296'.0973
Aspects of the religious behavior of American Jews by Charles S. Liebman. New York, Ktav Pub. House [1974] xvi, 284 p. 24 cm. Three essays originally published in the American Jewish year book, 1965, 1968, 1970. Includes bibliographical references. [BM205.L538] 74-546 ISBN 0-87068-242-3 12.50
1. Judaism—United States. 2. Rabbinical seminaries—United States. 3. Orthodox Judaism—United States. 4. Reconstructionist Judaism. I. Title.

MILLER, Alan W. 296'.0973
God of Daniel S.; in search of the American Jew, by Alan W. Miller. [New York] Macmillan [1969] 245 p. 22 cm. Bibliography: p. 241-245. [BM205.M5] 69-12652
1. Judaism—20th century. 2. Jews in the United States. I. Title.

NEUSNER, Jacob, 1932- 296'.0973
American Judaism: adventure in modernity. Englewood Cliffs, N.J., Prentice-Hall [1972] xv, 170 p. 23 cm. Bibliography: p. 155-156. [BM205.N48] 70-161677 ISBN 0-13-027870-X
1. Judaism—United States. I. Title.

ROSENTHAL, Gilbert S. 296'.0973
Four paths to one God; today's Jew and his religion [by] Gilbert S. Rosenthal. New York, Bloch Pub. Co. [1973] x, 323 p. 24 cm. Bibliography: p. 303-308. [BM205.R59] 73-77281 ISBN 0-8197-0286-2 8.95
1. Judaism—United States. I. Title.

SECTORS of American Judaism : Reform, Orthodoxy, Conservatism, and Reconstructionism / edited by Jacob Neusner. New York : Ktav Pub. House, [1975] xv, 326 p. ; 24 cm. (Understanding American Judaism ; v. 2) Includes bibliographical references. [BM205.S4] 75-8946 ISBN 0-87068-279-2 : 12.50 pbk. : 4.95 296'.0973
1. Judaism—United States—Addresses, essays, lectures. 2. Reform Judaism—United States—Addresses, essays, lectures. 3. Orthodox Judaism—United States—Addresses, essays, lectures. 4. Conservative Judaism—Addresses, essays, lectures. 5. Reconstructionist Judaism. I. Neusner, Jacob, 1932- II. Series.
Contents omitted.

ZEITLIN, Joseph, 1906- 296'.0973
Disciples of the wise; the religious and social opinions of American rabbis. Freeport, N.Y., Books for Libraries Press [1970, c1945] xiii, 233 p. 24 cm. (Teachers College, Columbia University. Contrbutions to education, no. 908) (Essay index reprint series.) Bibliography: p. 199-202. [BM205.Z4 1970] 71-121517
1. Judaism—U.S. 2. Rabbis—U.S. I. Title. II. Series: Columbia University. Teachers College. Contributions to education, no. 908

FESTSCHRIFT in honor of the 36th anniversary of Congregation Beth Hillel of Washington Heights, New York, New York, 1940-1976 / [edited by Eric Bloch, Martin Marx, Hugo Stransky]. New York : The Congregation, 1976. 71 p. : ill. ; 26 cm. On cover: Festschrift, Congregation Beth Hillel of Washington Heights, New York City. English or German. Contents.Contents.—Bloch, E. Congregation Beth Hillel, 1940-1975.—Neubauer, R. The education and activities of our youth.—Silbermann, K. Traditions of music at Congregation Beth Hillel.—Blank, W. B. Two decades of the rabbinate of Dr. Hugo Stransky at Congregation Beth Hillel.—Strauss, H. H. Ethnicity and the weight of history.—Simon, E. Der Kampf um den Alltag.—Serbu, M. Israel. Dies kleine Reich.—Stransky, H. Reflections on the Minhag Ashkenaz.—Bergmann, H. Der Segensspruch.—Hoenig, S. B. Filial succession in the rabbinate.—Bustan, A. In the land of visions and the burning bush. Includes bibliographical references. [BM225.N5B433] 76-373077 296'.09747'1
1. Congregation Beth Hillel of Washington Heights, New York. 2. Judaism—Addresses, essays, lectures. 3. Jews in New York (City)—History. I. Bloch, Eric. II. Marx, Martin. III. Stransky, Hugo. IV. Congregation Beth Hillel of Washington Heights, New York. V. Title: Festschrift, Congregation Beth Hillel of Washington Heights, New York City.

TEMPLE Beth El of Northern Westchester, Chappaqua, N.Y. 296'.09747'277
Temple Beth El, 1972. [Editor: Alice Wolff Ozaroff. Chappaqua, N.Y., 1974] 1 v. (unpaged) illus. 27 cm. Cover title. [BM225.C35T456 1974] 74-80959
1. Temple Beth El of Northern Westchester, Chappaqua, N.Y. 2. Jews in Chappaqua, N.Y. I. Ozaroff, Alice Wolff, ed.

TEBEAU, Charlton W. 296'.09759'381
Synagogue in the central city: Temple Israel of Greater Miami, 1922-1972 [by] Charlton W. Tebeau. Coral Gables, Fla., University of Miami Press [1972] 172 p. illus. 24 cm. [BM225.M5T4] 72-85107 ISBN 0-87024-239-3 7.95
1. Temple Israel of Greater Miami. 2. Jews in Miami, Fla. I. Title.

FRUCHTER, Nandor, Mrs. 296'.09772'52
Congregation B'nai Torah, the first 50 years / by Mrs. Nandor Fruchter. Indianapolis : Congregation B'nai Torah, 1973. 65 p. : ill. ; 23 cm. [BM225.I52C664] 75-511186
1. Congregation B'nai Torah, Indianapolis, Ind. 2. Jews in Indianapolis, Ind.—History.

BERMAN, Morton Mayer, 1899- 296'.09772'74
Our first century, 1852-1952: Temple Isaiah Israel, the united congregations of B'nai Sholom, Temple Israel and Isaiah Temple 5612-5712. Chicago [First Century Book Committee, Temple Isaiah Israel] 1952. 71p. illus. 29cm. [BM225.C5T4] 54-36209
1. Chicago. Temple Isaiah Israel. I. Title.

MONSKY, Jacob. 296'.09772'74
Within the gates; a religious, social, and cultural history, 1837-1962. New York, Congregation Shaare Zedek [c1964] 180 p. illus., ports. 24 cm. Erratum slip inserted. [BM225.N5S43] 64-7517
1. New York. Congregation Shaare Zedek. 2. Jews in New York (City) I. Title.

ZWEIG, Ruth G. 296'.09772'74
The first hundred and twenty-five years, by Ruth G. (Mrs. Elmer S.) Zweig. Fort Wayne, Indiana Jewish Historical Society, 1973. 30 p. 22 cm. (Indiana Jewish Historical Society. Publication no. 2) Based on research by I. L. Bronstein; report was presented in May 1973 at the 125th annual meeting of the congregation. [BM225.F67A259] 74-180975
1. Achduth Vesholom Congregation, Fort Wayne. 2. Jews in Fort Wayne. I. Title. II. Series: Indiana Jewish Historical Society. Publication — Indiana Jewish Historical Society, no. 2.

ADLER, Frank J., 1923- 296'.09778'411
Roots in a moving stream; the centennial history of Congregation B'nai Jehudah of Kansas City, 1870-1970 [by] Frank J. Adler. Kansas City, Mo., The Temple, Congregation B'nai Jehudah, 1972. xxiii, 466 p. illus., map (on lining paper) 26 cm. Includes bibliographical references. [BM225.K35A64] 72-80822
1. Congregation B'nai Jehudah. 2. Jews in Kansas City, Mo. I. Title.

NODEL, Julius J 1915- 296.0979549
The ties between; a century of Judaism on America's last frontier; the human story of Congregation Beth Israel, Portland, Oregon, the oldest Jewish congregation in the Pacific Northwest, by Julius J. Nodel in association with Alfred Apsler. Portland, Or., Temple Beth Israel, 1959. 194p. illus. 24cm. [BM225.P63B42] 59-65510
1. Portland, Or. Congregation Beth Israel. I. Title.

ABOTH de-rabbi Nathan. English. 296.1
The Fathers according to Rabbi Nathan. Translated from the Hebrew by Judah Goldin. New Haven, Yale University Press, 1955. xxvi, 277p. 23cm. (Yale Judaica series, v.10) Bibliographical references included in 'Notes' (p. (175)-221) [BM506.4.A2E5 1955] 55-6145
1. Ethics, Jewish. I. Goldin, Judah, 1914- tr. II. Title. III. Series.

ABOTH de-Rabbi Nathan. English. 296.1
The Fathers according to Rabbi Nathan. Translated from the Hebrew by Judah Goldin. New York, Schocken Books [1974, c1955] xxvi, 277 p. 20 cm. Reprint of the ed. published by Yale University Press, New Haven, which was issued as v. 10 of Yale Judaica series. Includes bibliographical references. [BJ1287.A22E5 1974] 74-9638 ISBN 0-8052-0465-2 4.95 (pbk.)
1. Ethics, Jewish. I. Goldin, Judah, 1914- tr. II. Title. III. Series: Yale Judaica series, v. 10.

ABOTH, English. 296.1
The living Talmud the wisdom of the Fathers and its classical commentaries, selected and translated with an essay by Judah Goldin. [New York] New American Library [1957] 247p. 18cm. (A Mentor religious classic, MD199) [BM506.A2E5 1957] 57-12142
I. Goldin, Judah, 1914- ed. and tr. II. Title.

ABOTH. English. 296.1
The living Talmud; the wisdom of the Fathers and its classical commentaries, selected and traslated with an essay by Judah Goldin. [Chicago] University of Chicago Press [1958, c1957] 244p. 23cm. Bibliographical references included in 'A note and acknowledgments' (p. 240-242) [BM506.A23G6] 58-5540
1. Aboth—Commentaries. I. Goldin, Judah, 1914- ed. and tr. II. Title.

ABOTH. English. 296.1
The living Talmud; the wisdom of the Fathers and its classical commentaries, selected and translated with an essay by Judah Goldin. [Chicago] University of Chicago Press [1958, c1957] 244 p. 23 cm. Bibliographical references included in "A note and acknowledgments" (p. 240-242) [BM506.A23G6] 58-5540
1. Aboth—Commentaries. I. Goldin, Judah, 1914- ed. and tr. II. Title.

ABOTH. English. 1958. *296.1
The living Talmud; the wisdom of the Fathers and its classical commentaries, selected and translated with an essay by Judah Goldin. [Chicago] University of Chicago Press [1958, c1957] 244 p. 23 cm. Bibliographical references included in "A note and acknowledgments" (p. 240-242) [BM506.A23G6 1958] 58-5540
1. Aboth — Commentaries. I. Goldin, Judah, 1914- ed. and tr. II. Title.

ADLER, Morris. 296.1
The world of the Talmud. Washington, B'nai B'rith Hillel Foundations, 1958. 148p. 19cm. (Hillel little books, v.4) [BM501.A3] 57-12179
1. Talmud—Hist. I. Title. II. Series.

CAPLAN, Samuel, ed. 296.1
The great Jewish books and their influence on history, ed. by Samuel Caplan, Harold U. Ribalow. Introd. by Ludwig Lewisohn. New York, Washington Sq. [1963, c.1962] 272p. 18cm. (W649) Bibl. .60 pap.,
1. Judaism—Collections. I. Title.

CAPLAN, Samuel, ed. 296.1*
The great Jewish books and their influence on history, edited by Samuel Caplan and Harold U.Ribalow; introd. by Ludwig Lewisohn. New York, Horizon Press [1952] 351 p. 22 cm. [BM40.C27] 52-9125
1. Judaism—Collections. I. Title.

CHAPMAN, Harry. comp. 296.1
Light, prayer, Zion-Jerusalem, and salvation in the book of Psalms; a collection of verses in the Psalms ... Appended to each section are quotations from the Jewish sages. [1st ed.] Los Angeles, 1952. 76 p. 18 cm. [BM495.C49] 52-44960
1. Hebrew literature—Translations into English. 2. English literature—Translations from Hebrew. I. Title.

CHAPMAN, Harry. comp. 296.1
Love of God, blessings, strength, and joy in the book of Psalms; a collection of verses in the Psalms ... Appended to each section are quotations from the Jewish sages. [1st ed.] Los Angeles, 1952. 61 p. 18 cm. [BM495.C5] 52-28966
1. Hebrew literature (Selections: Extracts, etc.) 2. Bible. O. T. Psalms—Indexes, Topical. I. Title.

COLLINS, John Joseph, 1946- 296.1
The Sibylline oracles of Egyptian Judaism / John J. Collins. Missoula, Mont. : Published by Society of Biblical Literature for the Pseudepigrapha Group, 1974, c1972. xiii, 238 p. ; 22 cm. (Dissertation series ; no. 13) Originally presented as the author's thesis, Harvard, 1972. Bibliography: p. 215-238. [BM485.C64 1974] 74-81099 ISBN 0-88414-039-3
1. Oracula sibyllina. 2. Judaism—Egypt. I. Title. II. Series: Society of Biblical Literature. Dissertation series ; no. 13.

*FREEHOF, Solomon B. 296.1
Our Biblical heritage; a course of study based upon Preface to scripture; pt. 1. New York, Dept. of Adult Jewish Education, Union of Amer. Hebrew Congregations, 838 Fifth Ave. [1965] vii, 101p. 28cm. Pt. 1 prep. by Walter Jacob. First pub. in 1950. cover title. 1.00 pap.,
I. Title.

FREEHOF, Solomon Bennett, 1892- 296.1
The responsa literature. Philadelphia, Jewish Publication Society of America, 1955. 304p. 22cm. [BM646.F68] 55-6706
1. Responsa. I. Title.

FREEHOF, Solomon Bennett, 1892- 296.1
A treasury of responsa. Philadelphia, Jewish Pubn. Soc. [1963, c.1962] 313p. 22cm. 62-12951 4.50
1. Responsa—Collections. 2. Judaism—Collections. I. Title.

GERSH, Harry. 296.1
The sacred books of the Jews. New York, Stein and Day [1968] 256 p. 25 cm. [BM496.5.G4 1968] 68-17320 8.95
1. Religious literature, Jewish—History and criticism. I. Title.

GINZBERG, Louis, 1873- 1953. 296.1*
Legends of the Bible. New York, Simon and Schuster, 1956. 646 p. 24 cm. "A shorter version of The legends of the Jews." [BM530.G512] 56-9915
1. Legends, Jewish.

GLATZER, Nahum Norbert, 1903- ed. 296.1
Hammer on the rock; a short Midrash reader, edited by Nahum N. Glatzer. [Translated by Jacob Sloan] New York, Schocken Books [1962] 128 p. 21 cm. (Schocken, SB32) "Draws ... material from the nonlegal parts of the Talmud, the Haggadah ... and the midrashic writings." [BM512.G55] 62-18155
1. Midrash—Translations into English. I. Talmud. English. Selections. II. Title.

GLATZER, Nahum Norbert, 1903- ed. 296.1
Hammer on the rock; a short Midrash reader, edited by Nahum N. Glatzer. [Translated by Jacob Sloan] New York, Schocken Books [1962] 128 p. 21 cm. (Schocken, SB32) "Draws ... material from the nonlegal parts of the Talmud, the Haggadah ... and the midrashic writings." [BM512.G55 1962] 62-18155
1. Midrash—Translations into English. I. Talmud. English. Selections. II. Title.

GOLDZIHER, Ignac, 1850- 1921. 296.1
Mythology among the Hebrews and its historical development. Translated from the German, with additions by the author, by Russell Martineau. New York, Cooper Square Publishers, 1967. xxxv, 457 p. 24 cm. "A Marandell book." Translation of Der Mythos bei den Hebraern und seine geschichtliche Entwickelung. Includes two essays by H. Steinthal. [BM530.G6 1967] 66-23969
1. Mythology, Jewish. 2. Judaism—History—To 70 A.D. I. Steinthal, Heymann, 1823-1889. II. Title.

GRAND, Ben Zion, 1879- 296.1
And I will make of thee a great nation; tales from Jewish history illuminating the spiritual and cultural heritage of Israel from the days of Abraham to the present, for students and laymen. New York, William-Frederick Press, 1952. 198 p. 24 cm. [PN6071.J5G7] 52-9946
1. Tales, Jewish. I. Title.

HERFORD, Robert Travers, 1860-1950. 296.1
Christianity in Talmud and Midrash, by R. Travers Herford. Clifton, N. J., Reference Book Publishers, 1966. xvi, 419 p. 23 cm. (Library of religious and philosophical thought) First published in London in 1903. Bibliography: p. xvi. [BM509.C5H4] 65-26183
1. Christianity in the Talmud. 2. Christianity in the Midrash. I. Title.

HERFORD, Robert Travers, 1860-1950. 296.1
Christianity in Talmud and Midrash / by R. Travers Herford. New York : Ktav Pub. House, [1975] xvi, 449 p. ; 23 cm. Reprint of the 1903 ed. published by Williams & Norgate, London. Includes index. Bibliography: p. xvi. [BM509.C5H4 1975] 75-33834 ISBN 0-87068-483-3 : 15.00
1. Christianity in the Talmud. 2. Christianity in the Midrash. 3. Rabbinical literature—Relation to the New Testament. I. Title.

ISAACS, Abram Samuel, 1852- 1920. 296.1
Stories from the rabbis. New York, B. Blom, 1972. 222 p. 18 cm. Reprint of the 1911 ed. Contents.Contents.—The Faust of the Talmud.—The wooing of the princess.—The Rip Van Winkle of the Talmud.—Rabbinical romance.—The shepherd's wife.—The repentant rabbi.—The inheritance.—Elijah in the legends.—When Solomon was King.—Rabbinical humor.—The Munchausen of the Talmud.—The rabbi's dream.—The gift that blessed.—In the sweat of thy brow.—A four-leaved clover.—The expiation.—A string of pearls.—The vanished bridegroom.—The lesson of the harvest. [BM530.I8 1972] 79-175868 12.50
1. Tales, Jewish. I. Title.

KADUSHIN, Max, 1895- 296.1j
The rabbinic mind. Appendix by Simon Greenberg. 2d ed. New York, Blaisdell [c.1952, 1965] xxv, 414p. 24cm. ibl. [BM561.K32] 65-14564 8.50
1. Judaism. I. Title.

LEWITTES, Mendell. 296.1
The nature and history of Jewish law / by Mendell Lewittes. New York : Yeshiva University, Dept. of Special Publications : selling agents, Bloch Pub. Co., 1966. 83 p. ; 23 cm. (Studies in Torah Judaism ; 9) Includes bibliographical references. [BM520.5.L43] 74-192042
1. Jewish law—History. I. Title. II. Series.

MIDRASH. English. Selections. 296.1
Hammer on the rock; a short Midrash reader. Edited by Nahum N. Glatzer. [Translated by Jacob Sloan] New York, Schocken Books [1962] 128p. 21cm. (Shocken SB32) 'Draws ... material from the nonlegal parts of the Talmud, the Haggadah ... and the midrashic writings.' [BM512.G55 1962] 62-18155
I. Taimud.English. Selections. II. Glatzer, Nahum Norbert, 1903- ed. III. Title.

MILLER, Avigdor. 296.1
Behold a people; a didactic history of scriptural times. New York, 5728 [1968] 371 p. 24 cm. Added t. p.: Sefer Hen 'am) [BM530.M453] 68-6944
1. Legends, Jewish. I. Title.

OESTERLEY, William Oscar Emil, 1866-1950. 296.1
A short survey of the literature of Rabbinical and mediaeval Judaism, by W. O. E. Oesterley and G. H. Box. New York, B. Franklin [1973] xi, 334 p. 22 cm. (Burt Franklin bibliography & reference series 490) Reprint of the 1920 ed. published by Macmillan, New York. Includes bibliographical references. [BM495.5.O35 1973] 72-82352 ISBN 0-8337-2602-1 18.50
1. Jews. Liturgy and ritual—History. 2. Rabbinical literature—History and criticism. 3. Hebrew literature, Medieval—History and criticism. I. Box, George Herbert, 1869-1933, joint author. II. Title.

PETUCHOWSKI, Jakob Josef, 1925- 296.1
Heirs of the Pharisees [by] Jakob J. Petuchowski. New York, Basic Books, [1970] vii, 199 p. 22 cm. Includes bibliographical references. [BM529.P363 1970] 75-110776 6.95
1. Tradition (Judaism) I. Title.

SCHWARTZ, Fanny Schneider. 296.1
The true mysteries of life; the psychology of the Bible, the Kabbalah, and the Dead Sea scrolls. [1st ed.] New York, Vantage Press [1957] 84p. illus. 21cm. [BM525.S38] 56-12313
1. Cabala. I. Title.

SEARCY, Harvey B., M.D. 296.1
We used what we had. Birmingham, Ala., Colonial Pr. [c.1961] 102p. 2.00
I. Title.

SILVERMAN, William B. 296.1
Rabbinic wisdom and Jewish values / William B. Silverman. Rev. ed. New York : Union of American Hebrew Congregations, c1971. 221 p. ; 22 cm. First ed. published in 1958 under title: Rabbinic stories for Christian ministers and teachers. Includes index. [BM530.S49 1971] 75-314804
1. Tales, Jewish. 2. Tales, Hasidic. I. Title.

TALMUD Yerushalmi. English. Selections. 296.1
The Talmud of Jerusalem; with a pref. by Dagobert D. Runes. New York, Wisdom Library [1956] 160p. 19cm. 'The text of these selections is based upon the translations from the original Hebrew and Aramaic by Professor H. Polano.' [BM502.P62 1956] 56-14440
I. Polano, Hymen tr. II. Title.

TALMUD Yerushalmi. English. Selections. *296.1
The Talmud of Jerusalem: with a pref. by Dagobert D. Runes. New York, Wisdom Library [1956] 160 p. 19 cm. "The text of these selections is based upon the translations from the original Hebrew and Aramaic by Professor H. Polano." [BM502.P62 1956] 56-14440
I. Polano, Hymen tr. II. Title.

TRATTNER, Ernest Robert, 1898- 296.1
Understanding the Talmud. New York, T. Nelson [1955] 211 p. 22 cm. [BM504.T7] 55-10608
1. Talmud—Introductions. I. Title.

UNTERMAN, Isaac, 1889- 296.1
The Talmud, origin and devedopment, methods and systems, causes and results, contents and significance, with commentaries, interpretations, glossary, and indices. [1st ed.] New York, Record Press, 1952. xv, 351 p. 24 cm. Bibliography: p. 320-328. [BM504.U5] 52-800
1. Talmud — Criticism, interpretation, etc. I. Title.

WAITE, Arthur Edward, 1857- 1942. 296.1
The secret doctrine in Israel: a study of the Zohar and its connections. New York, Occult Research Press [19--] 329p. illus. 23cm. [BM525.A59W3] 57-17485
1. Zohar. 2. Cabala. I. Title.

WAITE, Arthur Edward, 1857-1942. *296.1
The secret doctrine in Israel; a study of the Sohar and its connections. New York, Occult Research Press [19-] 329 p. illus. 23 cm. [BM525.A59W3] 57-17485
1. Zohar. 2. Cabala. I. Title.

ZOHAR. English. Selections. 296.1
The alphabet of creation, an ancient legend from the Zohar; with drawings by Ben Shahn. New York, Printed at the Spiral Press and published by Pantheon [1954] [45] p. illus. 28 cm. "Adapted by Ben Shahn from the English translation of Maurice Samuel and other sources." [BM525.A52S5] 54-11739
I. Shahn, Ben, 1898-1969, ed. and illus. II. Title.

LIEBERMAN, Saul, 1898- 296.1'08
Texts and studies. New York Ktav Pub. House [1974] viii, 318 p. 24 cm. Includes bibliographical references. [BM496.5.L5] 72-12046 ISBN 0-87068-210-5 20.00
1. Rabbinical literature—Addresses, essays, lectures. 2. Jews in Palestine—Addresses, essays, lectures. 3. Hellenism—Addresses, essays, lectures.

SILVER, Samuel M ed. 296.10822
A treasury of Jewish thoughts. Illuminations by Ezekiel Schloss. [New York] KTAV Pub. House [1964] 75 p. col. illus. 16 cm. [BM43.S5] 64-16660
1. Judaism—Quotations, maxims, etc. I. Title.

SILVER. SAMUEL M., ed. 296.10822
A treasury of Jewish thoughts Illuminations by Ezekiel Schloss [New York] KTAV [c.1964] 75p. col. illus. 16cm. 64-16660 1.00 bds.,
1. Judaism—Quotations. maxims. etc. I. Title.

ABOTH. 1960. 296.12
The living Talmud: the wisdom of the Fathers, and its classical commentaries. Selected and translated with an essay by Judah Goldin. With drawings by Ben-Zion. New York, Printed at the Spiral Press for the members of the Limited Editions Club, 1960. xxxi, 165 p. plates. 32 cm. Hebrew and English; commentaries in English. Bibliographical references included in "A note and acknowledgments" (p. 162-163) [BM506.A23G6 1960] 60-51859
1. Aboth—Commentaries. I. Goldin, Judah, 1914- ed. and tr. II. Aboth. English. 1960. III. Title.

ABOTH. 1964. 296.12
Ethics from Sinai; an eclectic, wide-ranging commentary on Pirke Avoth by Irving M. Bunim. New York, P. Feldheim [1964- v. 26 cm. Bibliographical footnotes. [BM506.A23B8] 64-4796
1. Aboth — Commentaries. I. Bunim, Irving M. II. Aboth. English. 1964. III. Title. IV. Title: Ethics from Sinai.

ABOTH. 1964. 296.12
Ethics from Sinai v.1, an electric, wide-ranging commentary on Pirke Avoth by Irving M. Bunim. New York, 96 East B'way. P. Feldheim, [c.1964] 360p. 26cm. Bibl. 64-4796 6.50
1. Aboth—Commentaries. I. Bunim, Irving M. II. Aboth. English. 1964. III. Title. IV. Title: Ethics from Sinai.

ABOTH. English. 1964. 296.12
Pirke Aboth. Sayings of the Fathers. Edited with translations and commentaries by Isaac Unterman. New York, Twayne Publishers, 1964. 408 p. 21 cm. Bibliography: p. 387-397. [BM506.A2E5 1964] 63-9782
I. Unterman, Isaac, 1889- ed. II. Title. III. Title: Title: Sayings of the Fathers.

ABOTH. ENGLISH. 1964. 296.12
Pirke Aboth . Sayings of the Fathers. Ed., tr., commentaries by Isaac Unterman. New York, Twayne [c.]1964. 408p. 21cm. Bibl. 63-9782 6.50
I. Unterman, Isaac, 1889- ed. II. Title. III. Title: Sayings of the Fathers.

ADLER, Morris. 296.12
The world of the Talmud. 2d ed. New York, Schocken Books [1963] 156 p. 21 cm. (Schocken paperbacks, SB58) Bibliography: p. 155-156. [BM501.A3 1963] 63-18390
1. Talmud—History. I. Title.

BOKSER, Ben Zion, 1907- 296.12
Wisdom of the Talmud. New York, Citadel Press [1962, c1951] 176 p. 21 cm. [[BM504]] 62-17830
1. Talmud—Criticism, interpretation, etc. I. Title.

BOKSER, Ben Zion, 1907- 296.12
Wisdom of the Talmud. New York, Citadel [1962, c.1951] 176p. 21cm. (C-103) 62-17830 1.50 pap.,
1. Talmud—Criticism, interpretation, etc. I. Title.

*BULKA, Reuven P., Rabbi. 296.12
The wit and wisdom of the Talmud, by Rabbi Dr. Reuven P. Bulka. Illustrations by Jeff Hill. Mount Vernon, N.Y., Peter Pauper Press, [1974] 62 p. illus. 19 cm. [BM504.5] 1.95
1. Talmud. I. Title.

COHEN, Abraham, 1887- 296.1'2
Everyman's Talmud / by A. Cohen ; with an introd. to the new American ed. by Boaz Cohen. New York : Schocken Books, 1975. p. cm. Reprint of the 1949 ed. published by E. P. Dutton, New York. "A summary of the teachings of the Talmud on religion, ethics, folk-lore, and jurisprudence." Bibliography: p. [BM504.3.C63 1975] 75-10750 ISBN 0-8052-0497-0 pbk. : 6.95
1. Talmud—Theology. 2. Jewish law. I. Title.

EXPLORING the Talmud / 296.1'2
edited by Haim Z. Dimitrovsky. New York : Ktav Pub. House, 1976- p. cm. Contents.Contents.—v. 1. Education. Includes bibliographical references. [BM500.2.E88] 76-7449 ISBN 0-87068-254-7 20.00 (v. 1)
1. Jews—Education—History—Addresses, essays, lectures. 2. Talmud—Addresses, essays, lectures. 3. Jewish learning and scholarship—History—Addresses, essays, lectures. I. Dimitrovsky, Hayim Zalman.

KOLATCH, Alfred J 1916- 296.12
Who's who in the Talmud, by Alfred J. Kolatch. New York, J. David [1964] 315 p. facsims. 23 cm. [BM501.15.K6] 64-24891
1. Talmud—Biog. 2. Talmud—Introductions. I. Title.

MEAD, George Robert Stow, 1863-1933. 296.1'2
Did Jesus live 100 B.C.? An enquiry into the Talmud Jesus stories, the Toldoth Jeschu, and some curious statements of Epiphanius, being a contribution to the study of Christian origins. New Hyde Park, N.Y., University Books [1968] xxxii, 442 p. 24 cm. Includes bibliographical references. [BM620.M4 1968] 68-18754
1. Jesus Christ—Jewish interpretations. 2. Jesus Christ—Chronology. 3. Epiphanius, Saint, Bp. of Constantia in Cyprus. 4. Toldot Yeshu. 5. Talmud—Legends. I. Title.

MISHNAH; 296.12
7v. [New York, 520 Fifth Ave., Judaica Pr., c.1963-1964] 7v. (various p. 23cm. Added t.p. Mishnayoth. Pointed Hebrew text. Eng. tr., introds., notes, supplements, appendix, indexes, addenda, corrigenda. 2d ed., rev., corr., enl. by Philip Blackman. Each tractate has special t.p. Vocalized. 64-3472 50.00 set,
1. Mishnah—Commentaries. I. Mishnah. English. II. Blackman, Philip, 1881- ed. and tr.

MOSES ben Maimon, 1135- 1204. 296.1'2
Maimonides' Introduction to the Talmud : a translation of the Rambam's introduction to his Commentary on the Mishna / translated and annotated by Zvi L. Lampel. New York : Judaica Press, 1975. 249, 37 p. ; 24 cm. Added t.p.: Hakdamat ha-Rambam le-ferusho la-Mishnayot. Selections from Kitab al-Siraj in English and Hebrew. Errata sheet inserted. Includes bibliographical references and indexes. [BM529.M672 1975] 74-25932 ISBN 0-910818-06-1 : 7.95
1. Mishnah—Introductions. 2. Talmud—Introductions. 3. Tradition (Judaism) I. Lampel, Zvi L. II. Title. III. Title: Introduction to the Talmud. IV. Title: Hakdamat ha-Rambam le-ferusho la-Mishnayot.

REDELHEIM, Abraham A., ed. and tr. 296.12
Mishnah. A modern guide to the Mishnah. Unabridged Hebrew text, completely vocalized and punctuated, modern English translation with copious notes, quotations, and source references by Abraham A. Redelheim. New York, Judaica Press [c1963- v. 23 cm. Contents.CONTENTS. -- 1. Pesahim (the Feast of the Passover) [BM497.2.R4] 63-23233
I. Title. II. Title: Meshnah. English.

SCHIMMEL, Harry C. 296.1'2
The oral law; a study of the rabbinic contribution to Torah she-be-al-peh, by Harry C. Schimmel. Association of Orthodox Jewish Scientists. Jerusalem, New York, Feldheim, 1971. 175 p. 23 cm. Rabbinic sources quoted in Hebrew. Includes bibliographical references. [BM520.5.S34] 74-156581
1. Jewish law—History. I. Title.

STEINSALZ, Adin. 296.1'2
The essential Talmud / Adin Steinsaltz : translated from the Hebrew [MS.] by Chaya Galai. London : Weidenfeld and Nicolson, 1976. vi, 296 p. ; 22 cm. Includes index.

[BM503.5.S8 1976] 77-365182 ISBN 0-297-77180-9 : £6.75
1. Talmud—Introductions. I. Title.

STRACK, Hermann Leberecht, 1848-1922. 296.12
Introduction to the Talmud and Midrash. New York, Meridian Books [1959, 1931] 372 p. 20 cm. (Jewish Publication Society series] JP8) Includes bibliography. [BM503.5.S73 1959] 59-7191
1. Talmud — Introductions. 2. Midrash. I. Title.

STRACK, Hermann Leberecht, 1848-1922. 296.12
Introduction to the Talmud and Midrash. New York, Meridian Books [1959, c1931] 371 p. 20 cm. ([Jewish Publication Society series] JP8) Includes bibliography. [BM503.5.S73 1959] 59-7191
1. Talmud—Introductions. 2. Midrash.

UNTERMAN, Isaac, 1889- 296.1'2
The Talmud; an analytical guide to its history and teachings. New York, Bloch Pub. Co. [1971, c1952] xv, 351 p. 21 cm. Bibliography: p. 320-328. [BM503.5.U57 1971] 73-148291 ISBN 0-8197-0189-0
1. Talmud—Introductions.

TALMUD. English. Selections. 296.1'205'21
The wit and wisdom of the Talmud / by Reuven P. Bulka : ill. by Jeff Hill. Mount Vernon, N.Y. : Peter Pauper Press, c1974. 62 p. : ill. ; 19 cm. [BM495.B84] 75-307215 1.95
1. Quotations, Talmudic. I. Bulka, Reuven P. II. Hill, Jeff. III. Title.

MIELZINER, Moses, 1828-1903. 296.1'206
Introduction to the Talmud. [4th ed.] New York, Bloch Pub. Co. [1969] xiv, 415 p. 22 cm. Reprint of the 3d ed., 1925, with a new bibliography, 1925-1967, by Alexander Guttmann. Includes bibliographical references. [BM503.5.M5 1969] 68-29908
1. Talmud—Introductions. I. Title.

DALMAN, Gustaf Hermann, 1855-1941, comp. 296.1'206'6
Jesus Christ in the Talmud, Midrash, Zohar, and the liturgy of the synagogue. New York, Arno Press, 1973. vi, 47, 108 p. 23 cm. (The Jewish people: history, religion, literature) Translation of Jesus Christus im Thalmud. English and Hebrew. Reprint of the 1893 ed. published by Deighton, Bell, Cambridge. "Jesus Christ in the Talmud, by Heinrich Laible. Translated by Rev. A. W. Streane": p. 1-108 (3d group) [BM620.D313 1973] 73-2190 ISBN 0-405-05256-1
1. Jesus Christ—Jewish interpretations. 2. Rabbinical literature—History and criticism. I. Title. II. Series.

NEUSNER, Jacob, 1932- 296.1'206'6
Invitation to the Talmud; a teaching book. [1st ed.] New York, Harper & Row [1973] xxii, 263 p. 22 cm. Bibliography: p. [247]-255. [BM503.5.N48] 73-6343 ISBN 0-06-066098-8 7.95
1. Talmud—Introductions. I. Title.

STEINSALZ, Adin. 296.1'206'6
The essential Talmud / Adin Steinsaltz ; translated from Hebrew by Chaya Galai. New York : Basic Books, c1976. vi, 296 p. ; 22 cm. Includes index. [BM503.5.S8] 75-36384 ISBN 0-465-02060-7 : 10.00
1. Talmud—Introductions. I. Title.

UNDERSTANDING the 296.1'206'6
Talmud / selected with introductions by Alan Corre. New York : Ktav Pub. House, 1975. xii, 468 p. ; 23 cm. Includes bibliographical references. [BM496.5.U52] 78-138459 ISBN 0-87068-140-0 : 15.00 pbk. : 5.95
1. Talmud—Theology—Addresses, essays, lectures. 2. Rabbinical literature—History and criticism—Addresses, essays, lectures. I. Corre, Alan D.

ABOTH. 1967. 296.1'23
Chapters of the Fathers. Translation and commentary by Samson Raphael Hirsch [rendered into English by Gertrude Hirschler] Jerusalem, New York. Published for the Samson Raphael Hirsch Publications Society by P. Feldheim. 1967. 117 p. 24 cm. Hebrew and English. [BM506.A23H5] HE67
I. Aboth. English. 1967. II. Hirsch, Samson Raphael, 1808-1888. III. Title. IV. Title: Chapters of the Fathers. V. Title: Title romanized: Pirke avot.

ABOTH. 1969 296.1'23
Pirke Aboth [Pirke avot] (romanized form) in etchings, by Saul Raskin. New York, Bloch [1969] 136 p. illus. 35 cm. Hebrew, Yiddish, and English. [BM506.A2 1969] 69-15987 12.50
I. Raskin, Saul, 1878-1966, illus. II. Aboth. III. Aboth. IV. Title.

FORCHHEIMER, Paul. 296.1'23
Living Judaism : the Mishna of Avoth with the commentary and selected other chapters of Maimonides translated into English and supplemented with annotations and a systematic outline for a modern Jewish philosophy / by Paul Forchheimer. Jerusalem ; New York : Feldheim Publishers, 1974. 240 p. ; 24 cm. Includes bibliographical references and index. [BM506.A23F66] 75-318520
1. Aboth—Commentaries. 2. Judaism and science. I. Moses ben Maimon, 1135-1204. Kitab al-Siraj. Aboth. English. 1974. II. Aboth. English. 1974. III. Title.

GUTTMANN, Alexander. 296.1'23
Rabbinic Judaism in the making; a chapter in the history of the Halakhah from Ezra to Judah I. Detroit, Wayne State University Press, 1970. xx, 323 p. 24 cm. Bibliography: p. 298-309. [BM501.2.G85 1970] 69-10525 ISBN 0-8143-1382-5 17.95
1. Tannaim. I. Title.

MISHNAH. English. Selections. 296.1'23
The mishnah; oral teachings of Judaism; selected and translated by Eugene J. Lipman. New York, Schocken Books [1974, c1970] 318 p. 21 cm. Includes bibliographical references. [BM947.5E5L55] 72-12621 ISBN 0-8052-0441-5. 3.95 (pbk.)
I. Lipman, Eugene J., ed. II. Title.

MISHNAH. English. Selections. 296.1'23
The Mishnah, oral teachings of Judaism. Selected and translated by Eugene J. Lipman. [1st ed.] New York, Norton [1970] 318 p. 22 cm. (The B'nai B'rith Jewish heritage classics) [BM497.5.E5L55] 73-78071 6.95
I. Lipman, Eugene J., ed. II. Title.

MISHNAH. Selections. 296.1'23
[Sh'ar la-Mishnah (romanized form)] Gateway to the Mishnah; a selection of pointed Hebrew texts, with translation, notes, and vocabulary [by] Isidore Fishman. [4th ed.] With a foreword by Philip Arian. Hartmore, Conn., Prayer Book Press [1970, c1956] xxviii, 213 p. 23 cm. [BM497.5.E5F5 1970] 79-103242
I. Fishman, Isidore, 1908- ed. II. Mishnah. English. Selections. III. Title: Gateway to the Mishnah.

MOSES ben Maimon, 1135-1204. 296.1'23
The commentary to Mishnah Aboth [by] Moses Maimonides. Translated, with an introd. and notes, and a translation of Mishnah Aboth by Arthur David. New York, Bloch Pub. Co. [1968] xxi, 166 p. 22 cm. The commentary is a translation of Samuel ibn Tibbon's Hebrew translation found in the Wilna ed. of the Babylonian Talmud of the Arabic Kitab al-siraj (romanized form) Bibliographical references included in "Notes" (p. 123-163) [BM506.A23M613] 68-27871
1. Aboth—Commentaries. I. David, Arthur, tr. II. Ibn Tibbon, Samuel ben Judah, ca. 1150-ca. 1230, tr. III. Aboth. English. 1968. IV. Title.

TALMUD Yerushalmi. Berakot. English. 296.1'24
The Talmud of Jerusalem. Translated for the first time by Moses Schwab. Vol. I. Berakhoth. New York, Hermon Press [1969] iv, 188 p. 25 cm. No more published. Reprint of the 1886 ed. Includes bibliographical references. [BM498.5.E52S3 1969] 77-76173 6.95
I. Schwab, Moise, 1839-1918, tr. II. Title.

TALMUD Yerushalmi. Selections. 296.1'24
Yerushalmi fragments from the Genizah. I. Text with various readings from the editio princeps, edited by Louis Ginzberg. Hildesheim, New York, G. Olms, 1970. ix, 372, vi p. 23 cm. (Texts and studies of the Jewish Theological Seminary of America, v. 3) Added t.p. in Hebrew. English pref., Hebrew text. Reprint of the New York ed., 1909. No more published. [BM498.2.G5 1970] 76-572165
1. Cairo Genizah. I. Ginzberg, Louis, 1873-1953, ed. II. Title. III. Title: Seride ha-Yerushalmi. IV. Series: Jewish Theological Seminary of America. Texts and studies, v. 3

GINZBERG, Louis, 1873-1953. 296.1'25
Geonica. [2d ed.] New York, Hermon Press [1968] 2 v. 24 cm. "Originally published [in 1909 under the same title] as volumes I and II of Texts and studies of the Jewish Theological Seminary of America." Vol. 2 has Hebrew texts with notes in English. Contents.Contents.—v. 1. The Geonim and their Halakic writings.—v. 2. Genizah studies: Geonic responsa. Sheeltot and Halakot gedolot. Includes bibliographical references. [BM501.5.G5 1968] 68-20901
1. Geonim. 2. Geonic literature. 3. Calvo genizah. I. Title.

TALMUD, Ta'anit. 296.1'25
The treatuse Ta'anit of the Babylonian Talmud. Critically ed. provided with a tr, notes by Henry Malter. Philadelphia, Jewish Pubn. Soc. [1967] xlii, 481p. 20cm. (JPS lib. of Jewish classics, 2) [BM506.T2E5 1967] HE67 4.50 bds.,
I. Talmud. Ta'anit. English. II. Malter, Henry, 1864-1925, ed. III. Title.

TOSEFTA. English. 296.1'262
The Tosefta / translated from the Hebrew by Jacob Neusner. New York : Ktav, 1977. p. cm. Contents.Contents.— —division 6. Tohorot. Includes bibliographical references and index. [BM508.13.E5 1977] 77-4277 ISBN 0-87068-430-2 (v. 6) : 29.50
I. Neusner, Jacob, 1932-

BARTH, Lewis M. 296'.14
An analysis of Vatican 30, by Lewis M. Barth. Cincinnati, Hebrew Union College-Jewish Institute of Religion, 1973. xvii, 342 p. 24 cm. (Monographs of the Hebrew Union College, no. 1) "Sample chapters from Vat. 30. [Bereshit rabba]": p. 121-225. Bibliography: p. 338-342. [BM517.M65B37] 72-8353 ISBN 0-87820-400-8
1. Midrash rabbah. Genesis—Criticism, Textual. I. Vatican. Biblioteca vaticana. MSS. (Vat. Ebr. 30) II. Midrash rabbah. Genesis. Selections. 1973. III. Title. IV. Series: Hebrew Union College-Jewish Institute of Religion. Monographs no. 1.

FELDMAN, Asher, 1873-1950. 296.1'4
The parables and similes of the rabbis, agricultural and pastoral / by A. Feldman. Philadelphia : R. West, 1976. ix, 290 p. ; 23 cm. Reprint of the 1927 ed. published by the University Press, Cambridge, Eng. Includes bibliographical references and indexes. [BM518.P3F4 1976] 76-44204 ISBN 0-8492-0800-9 : 30.00
1. Parables, Jewish. 2. Agriculture in the Midrash. I. Title.

FELDMAN, Asher, 1873-1950. 296.1'4
The parables and similes of the rabbis, agricultural and pastoral / by A. Feldman. Folcroft, Pa. : Folcroft Library Editions, 1975. p. cm. Reprint of the 2d ed., 1927, published by the University Press, Cambridge, England. Includes indexes. [BM518.P3F4 1975] 75-23127 ISBN 0-8414-4229-0 lib. bdg. : 27.50
1. Agriculture in the Midrash. 2. Parables, Jewish. I. Title.

FELDMAN, Asher, 1873-1950. 296.1'4
The parables and similes of the rabbis, agricultural and pastoral / by A. Feldman. Norwood, Pa. : Norwood Editions, 1975. p. cm. Reprint of the 2d ed. (1927) published by the University Press, Cambridge, England. Includes bibliographical references and indexes. [BM518.P3F4 1975b] 75-28380 ISBN 0-88305-201-6 : 27.50
1. Agriculture in the Midrash. 2. Parables, Jewish. I. Title.

FELDMAN, Asher, 1873-1950. 296.1'4
The parables and similes of the rabbis, agricultural and pastoral / by A. Feldman. Norwood, Pa. : Norwood Editions, 1975. p. cm. Reprint of the 2d ed. (1927) published by the University Press, Cambridge, England. Includes bibliographical references and indexes. [BM518.P3F4 1975b] 75-28380 ISBN 0-88305-201-6 lib.bdg. : 27.50
1. Agriculture in the Midrash. 2. Parables, Jewish. I. Title.

FELDMAN, Asher, 1873-1950. 296.1'4
The parables and similes of the rabbis, agricultural and pastoral / by A. Feldman. Folcroft, Pa. : Folcroft Library Editions, 1975. ix, 290 p. ; 24 cm. Reprint of the 2d ed., 1927, published by the University Press, Cambridge, England. Includes bibliographical references and indexes. [BM518.P3F4 1975] 75-23127 ISBN 0-8414-4229-0 lib. bdg. : 27.50
1. Agriculture in the Midrash. 2. Parables, Jewish. I. Title.

JEWS. Liturgy and ritual. Hagadah. Mss. 296.14
The Sarajevo Haggadah. Text [introd.] by Cecil Roth. New York, Harcourt [1963] 45p., facsim: 1v. (unpaged) col. plates. 23cm. Bibl. 63-2809 25.00
1. Illumination of books and manuscripts—Specimens, reproductions, etc. 2. Paintings, Jewish. 3. Manuscripts, Hebrew—Facsimiles. I. Roth, Cecil, 1899- II. Sarajevo, Semaluski muzej. III. Title.

JEWS. Liturgy and ritual. Hagadah. Selections. 1964. 296.14
A haggadah for the school, by Hyman Chanover. Illus. by Uri Shulevitz. New York, United Synagogue Commission on Jewish Education [218 E. 70 St., 1964, c. 1963] 78p. col. illus. 21cm. English and Hebrew. [BM675.P45C5] 64-18132 .95 pap.,
I. Chanover, Hyman, ed. II. Jews. Liturgy and ritual. Hagadah. English. Selections. 1964. III. Title.

JEWS. LITURGY AND RITUAL. HAGADAH. SELECTIONS. 1965. 296.14
A Haggadah for the school, by Hyman Chanover. Illustrated by Uri Shulevitz New York, United Synagogue Commission on Jewish Education, 1964 [c1963] 78 p. col. illus. 21 cm. English and Hebrew. [BM675.P45C5] 64-18132
I. Chanover, Hyman, ed. II. Jews. Liturgy and ritual. Hagadah. English. Selections, 1964. III. Title.

KADUSHIN, Max, 1895- 296.14
The rabbinic mind. With an appendix by Simon Greenberg. 2d ed. New York, Blaisdell Pub. Co. [1965] xxv, 414 p. 24 cm. Bibliographical reference included in "Notes" (p. 369-372) Bibliographical footnotes. [BM561.K32] 65-14564
1. Judaism. I. Title.

KADUSHIN, Max, 1895- 296.1'4
The rabbinic mind. With an appendix by Simon Greenberg. 3d ed. New York, Bloch Pub. Co. [1972] xxix, 414 p. 22 cm. Includes bibliographical references. [BM496.5.K3 1972] 75-189016 ISBN 0-8197-0007-X 9.95
1. Rabbinical literature—History and criticism. I. Title.
Pap. 4.95.

LEHRMAN, Simon Maurice. 1900- 296.14
The world of the Midrash. New York, Yoseloff [1962, c.1961] 163p. 22cm. (Popular Jewish lib.) Bibl. 62-14969 2.95
1. Midrash. I. Title.

MIDRASH. Pirke de Rabbi Eliezer. English 296.14
Pirke de Rabbi Eliezer (The chapters of Rabbi Eliezer the Great) according to the text of the manuscript belonging to Abraham Epstein of Vienna, tr. annotated,introd. indices by Gerald Friedlander. [2d ed.] New York, Hermon Pr. 10 E. 40th St., 1965. 1x, 490p. 24cm. [BM517.P7E5] 65-15088 9.75
I. Friedlander, Gerald, 1871- ed. and tr. II. Title.

MIDRASH.TEHILLIM. 296.14
The Midrash on Psalms. Translated from the Hebrew and Aramaic by William G. Braude. New Haven, Yale University Press, 1959. 2 v. 22cm. (Yale Judaica series, v. 13) [BM517.T52E5] 58-6535
I. Braude, William Gordon, 1907- tr. II. Title. III. Series.

MIDRASH Tehillim. English. 296.14
The Midrash on Psalms. Translated from the Hebrew and Aramaic by William G. Braude. New Haven, Yale University Press, 1959. 2 v. 22 cm. (Yale Judaica series, v. 13) [BM517.T52E5] 58-6535
I. Braude, William Gordon. 1907- tr. II. Title. III. Series.

PESIKTA rabbati. English. 296.1'4
Pesikta rabbati; discourses for feasts, fasts, and special Sabbaths. Translated from the Hebrew by William G. Braude. New Haven, Yale University Press, 1968. 2 v. (xi, 995 p.) 22 cm. (Yale Judaica series, v. 18) The translation is based on an eclectic text made up in the main of the 1st ed., Prague 1654, Codex Parma 1240, and Codex Casanata 3324. Bibliography: v. 2, p. 890-899. [BM517.P4E5] 68-27748 25.00
I. Braude, William Gordon, 1907- tr. II. Title. III. Series.

PIRKE, de-Rabbi Eliezer, 296.14
Pirke de Rabbi Eliezer (The chapters of Rabbi Eliezer the Great) according to the text of the manuscript belonging to Abraham Epstein of Vienna, translated and annotated, with intro. and indices, by Gerald Friedlander. [2d. American ed.] New York, Hermon Press, 1965. ix, 490 p. 24 cm. This translation was first published in London in 1916. [BM517.P7E5] 65-15088
I. Friedlander, Gerald, 1871- ed. and tr. II. Title. III. Title: The chapters of Rabbi Eliezer.

PIRKE de-Rabbi Eliezer. English. 296.1'4
Pirke de Rabbi Eliezer (The chapters of Rabbi Eliezer the Great) according to the text of the manuscript belonging to Abraham Epstein of Vienna. Translated and annotated with introd. and indices by Gerald Friedlander. New York, B. Blom, 1971. lx, 490 p. 21 cm. "First published London, 1916." [BM517.P7E5 1971] 70-174366
I. Friedlander, Gerald, 1871-1923, ed. II. Title: The chapters of Rabbi Eliezer the Great.

SCHATZ, Morris, 1890-1967. 296.1'4
Ethics of the Fathers in the light of Jewish history. New York, Bloch Pub. Co. [1971, c1970] 268 p. 24 cm. Includes text of Aboth in Hebrew and English. Includes bibliographical references. [BM506.A23S24 1971] 76-122680 6.50
1. Aboth—Commentaries. I. Aboth. 1971. II. Aboth. English. 1971. III. Title.

†SCHWARTZ, Howard, 1945- 296.1'4
Midrashim : collected Jewish parables / Howard Schwartz ; drawings by John Swanson ; foreword by Raphael Patai ; introd. by James S. Diamond. London : Menard Press ; Berkeley, Calif. : distributed by Serendipity Books, 1976. 63 p. : ill. ; 22 cm. [BM530.S47 1976] 77-365740 ISBN 0-903400-18-9 pbk. : 4.00
1. Legends, Jewish. 2. Parables, Jewish. I. Title.

SPIEGEL, Shalom, 1899- 296.1'4
The last trial; on the legends and lore of the command to Abraham to offer Isaac as a sacrifice: The akedah. Tr. from Hebrew, introd., by Judah Goldin. New York, Pantheon [1967] xxvi, 162p. front. 22cm. Tr. of (romanized: Me-agadot ha-'akedah) orig. pub. in Jewish Theological Seminary of America. The akedah by Ephraim ben Jacob of Bonn: p. [139]-152. Bibl. [BM518.I 8S653] 65-10213 6.00
1. Abraham, the patriarch—Legends. 2. Isaac, the patriarch—Legends. 3. Aggada. I. Ephraim ben Jacob, of Bonn, 1132-ca. 1200. The akedah. II. Title. III. Title: The akedah.

WRIGHT, Addison G. 296.1'4
The literary genre midrash [by] Addison G. Wright. Staten Island, N. Y., Alba [1967] 164p. 22cm. Bibl. [BM514.W7] 67-24920 2.95
1. Midrash—Hist. & crit. I. Title.

MILLER, Amos W., 1927- 296.1'405'2
Understanding the Midrash; interpretations of the Exodus for modern times, by Amos W. Miller. New York, J. David [1966] 185 p. 23 cm. [BM512.M5] 65-25507
1. Midrash — Translation into English. 2. Bible. O. T. Exodus I-VI — Commentaries. 3. Exodus, The. I. Title.

RAPAPORT, Samuel, 1837-1923, ed. and tr. 296.1'405'2
A treasury of the Midrash. New York, Ktav Pub. House, 1968. 264 p. 24 cm. First published in 1907 under title: Tales and maxims from the Midrash. [BM512.R3 1968] 68-9682 6.95
1. Midrash—Translations into English. I. Title.

RAPAPORT, Samuel, 1837-1923. 296.1'405'21
Tales and maxims from the Midrash. New York, B. Blom, 1971. vii, 264 p. 21 cm. Reprint of the 1907 ed. [BM512.R3 1971] 73-173177
1. Midrash—Translations into English. I. Title.

SIGAL, Phillip. 296.1'41'066
New dimensions in Judaism; a creative analysis of Rabbinic concepts. [1st ed.] New York, Exposition Press [1972] 260 p. 22 cm. (An Exposition-university book) Bibliography: p. [251]-252. [BM520.65.S54] 72-186485 ISBN 0-682-47429-0 10.00
1. Jewish law—Interpretation and construction. 2. Conservative Judaism. I. Title.

JEWS. Liturgy and ritual. Hagadah. 1965 296.142
Haggada. Jerusalem. Korea Pubs. [New York, The Jerusalem Tenach, 250 W. 57th St. [c.1965] iv. (unpaged) illus. (pt. col.) 24cm. Added t.p.: Haggada. Newly tr. throughout. Introd. by Harold Fisch. [BM675.P4F5] HE65 3.50 bds.,
I. Jews. Liturgy and ritual. Hagadah. English. 1965. II. Fisch, Harold, tr. III. Title.

*JEWS. Liturgy and ritual. Hagadah. Selections. 1974. 296.1'42
Haggadah"Me-ir Ay-ni-yim" Springfield, Mass. Jacob Freedman Liturgy Research Foundation, 1974. 134 p. illus. 28 cm. [BM675] 25.00
1. Jews. Liturgy and ritual. Hagadah. Selections. 1974. I. Freedman, Jacob. II. Title. Publisher's address: 68 Calhoun Street Springfield, Mass. 01107

MONTEFIORE, Claude Joseph Goldsmid, 1858-1938, ed. and tr. 296.1'42
A rabbinic anthology, selected and arranged with comments and introductions by C. G. Montefiore and H. Loewe, with a prolegomenon by Raphael Loewe. New York, Schocken Books [1974] cviii, 853 p. 24 cm. Reprint of the 1938 ed. published by Macmillan, London; with new prolegomenon. Includes bibliographical references. [BM516.M58 1974] 73-91340 ISBN 0-8052-3539-6 20.00
1. Aggada—Translations into English. 2. Midrash—Translations into English. 3. Ethics, Jewish. I. Loewe, Herbert Martin James, 1882-1940, joint ed. and tr. II. Title.

ALBERTSON, Edward. 296.1'6
Understanding the Kabbalah. Los Angeles, Sherbourne Press [1972, c1973] 135 p. illus. 21 cm. (For the millions series, FM 48) [BM525.A735] 70-182524 ISBN 0-8202-0114-6 2.50
1. Cabala. I. Title.

ASHLAG, Yehudah. 296.1'6
An entrance to the tree of life : a key to the portals of Jewish mysticism / Yehuda Ashlag ; compiled and edited by Philip S. Berg. Old City Jerusalem ; New York : Research Centre of Kabbalah, 1977. 205 p. ; 24 cm. Includes bibliographical references. [BM525.A82] 76-19855 11.00
1. Cabala. I. Title.

BLAU, Joseph Leon, 1909- 296.16
The Christian interpretation of the Cabala in the Renaissance. Port Washington, N.Y., Kennikat [1965, c.1944] viii, 167p. 22cm. Bibl. [BM525.B55] 65-27116 6.00
1. Cabala. 2. Christianity and other religions—Judaism. I. Thenaud, Jean, fl. 1511. La saincte et trescrestienne cabale. II. Title.

BLOOM, Harold. 296.1'6
Kabbalah and criticism / Harold Bloom. New York : Seabury Press, [1975] 126 p. ; 21 cm. (A Continuum book) [BM526.B55] 75-12820 ISBN 0-8164-9264-6 : 5.95
1. Cabala—History and criticism. 2. Criticism. I. Title.

FRANCK, Adolphe, 1809-1893. 296.1'6
The kabbalah; the religious philosophy of the Hebrews. Translated from the French. [New Hyde Park, N.Y.] University Books [1967] 224 p. 21 cm. Translation of La kabbale. [BM525.F73 1967] 67-19463
1. Cabala—History. I. Title.

FRANCK, Adolphe, 1809-1893. 296.1'6
The kabbalah; or, The religious philosophy of the Hebrews, by Adolph Franck. Rev. and enl. translation by I. Sossnitz. New York, Arno Press 1973 [c1926] 326 p. illus. 23 cm. (The Jewish people: history, religion, literature) Reprint of the ed. published by the Kabbalah Pub. Co., New York. Includes bibliographical references. [BM526.F713 1973] 73-2199 ISBN 0-405-05264-2 17.00
1. Cabala—History. I. Title. II. Series.

GONZALEZ-WIPPLER, Migene. 296.1'6
A Kabbalah for the modern world; how God created the universe. New York, Julian Press [1974] xiii, 171 p. illus. 22 cm. Bibliography: p. 169-171. [BM525.G58] 74-75419 ISBN 0-87097-062-3 7.95
1. Cabala. I. Title.

KENTON, Warren. 296.1'6
The way of Kabbalah / [by] Zev ben Halevi [i.e. W. Kenton]. London : Rider, 1976. 224 p. : ill. ; 22 cm. Includes index. [BM526.K46] 76-375923 ISBN 0-09-125410-8 : £4.75. ISBN 0-09-125411-6 pbk.
1. Cabala—History and criticism. I. Title.

LUZZATTO, Moses Hayyim, 1707-1747. 296.1'6
General principles of the Kabbalah, by Rabbi Moses C. Luzzatto. Translation by the Research Centre of Kabbalah. New York, Press of the Research Centre of Kabbalah; distributed by S. Weiser, 1970. xxxv, 232 p. 24 cm. Translation of Kelale hokhmat ha-emet. [BM525.L85613] 73-29163 12.95
1. Cabala. I. Title.

MATHERS, S. Liddell MacGregor, comp. 296.1'6
The Kabbalah unveiled, containing the following books of the Zohar: The book of concealed mystery, The greater Holy assembly [and] The lesser Holy assembly. Translated into English from the Latin version of Knorr von Rosenroth and collated with the original Chaldee and Hebrew text by S. L. MacGregor Mathers. [New ed.] New York, S. Weiser [1968] xiii, 360 p. illus. (part fold.) 23 cm. Reprint of the 1926 ed., which was published under title: Kabbala denudata. [BM525.A6S55 1970] 71-16504 8.50
1. Cabala. I. Sifra di-tseni'uta. English. 1968. II. Idra raba. English. 1968. III. Idra zuta. English. 1968. IV. Title.

MATHERS, S. Liddell MacGregor, comp. 296.1'6
The Kabbalah unveiled : containing the following books of the Zohar—The book of concealed mystery, The greater Holy assembly, The lesser Holy assembly / translated into English from the Latin version of Knorr von Rosenroth, and collated with the original Chaldee and Hebrew text by S. L. MacGregor Mathers. New York : Krishna Press, 1974 [i.e.1975] xiii, 360 p., [7] leaves of plates : ill. ; 24 cm. Reprint of the 1962 ed. published under title: Kabbala denudata. Includes index. [BM525.A6S55 1974] 73-8279 ISBN 0-87968-124-1 lib.bdg. : 34.95
1. Cabala. I. Sifra di-tseni'uta. English. 1974. II. Idra raba. English. 1974. III. Idra zuta. English. 1974. IV. Title.

PICK, Bernhard, 1842-1917. 296.1'6
The cabala: its influence on Judaism and Christianity. La Salle, Ill., Open Court [1974] 109, [2] p. 21 cm. (Open Court paperback) Reprint of the 1913 ed. published by the Open Court Pub. Co., Chicago. Bibliography: p. [110]-[111]. [BM526.P4 1974] 74-176088 ISBN 0-87548-199-X 1.45 (pbk.)
1. Cabala—History. I. Title.

PONCE, Charles. 296.1'6
Kabbalah; an introduction and illumination for the world today. [San Francisco, Straight Arrow Books; distributed by Quick Fox Inc., 1973] 297 p. illus. 23 cm. Bibliography: p. 280-285. [BM526.P57] 70-181712 ISBN 0-87932-045-1 5.95
1. Cabala—History and criticism. I. Title.

REGARDIE, Israel. 296.1'6
A garden of pomegranates; an outline of the Qabalah. 2d ed., rev. and enl. Saint Paul, Minn., Llewellyn Publications, 1970. 160 p. illus. 24 cm. [BM526.R4] 74-18984 ISBN 0-87542-663-8 5.00
1. Cabala—History and criticism. I. Title.

ROSENBERG, Roy A., 1930- comp. 296.1'6
The anatomy of God: the Book of concealment, the Great holy assembly and the Lesser holy assembly of the Zohar, with the Assembly of the tabernacle. Translation, introd., and annotations by Roy A. Rosenberg. New York, Ktav Pub. House, 1973. vii, 196 p. 24 cm. Bibliography: p. 189. [BM525.A6A27] 72-14428 ISBN 0-87068-220-2 8.50
1. Sifra di-tseni 'uta 2. Idra raba. 3. Idra zuta. 4. Idra de-mashkena. 5. Cabala. I. Title.

SCHOLEM, Gershom Gerhard, 1897- 296.1'6
Kabbalah [by] Gershom Scholem. [New York] Quadrangle/New York Times Book Co. [1974] 492 p. illus. 25 cm. (Library of Jewish knowledge) Includes bibliographical references. [BM526.S35 1974] 73-77035 ISBN 0-8129-0352-8 9.95
1. Cabala—History. I. Title.

SCHOLEM, Gershom Gerhard, 1897- 296.16
On the Kabbalah and its symbolism. Tr. from Gerby Ralph Manheim. New York, Schocken [c.1960, 1965] v, 216p. 24cm. ibl. [BM525.S3753] 65-11575 7.50
1. Cabala. I. Title.

THE Secret garden : 296.1'6
an anthology in the Kabbalah / edited by David Meltzer. New York : Seabury Press, c1976. p. cm. (A Continuum book) [BM525.A2S4] 76-6524 ISBN 0-8164-9287-5 : 15.00
1. Cabala—Translations into English. I. Meltzer, David.

SEFER Yezirah. English. 296.1'6
[Sefer Yetsirah (romanized form)] The Book of formation (Sepher Yetzirah) by Akiba ben Joseph. Translated from the Hebrew, with annotations, by Knut Stenring. Incl. the 32 paths of wisdom, their correspondence with the Hebrew alphabet and the Tarot symbols. With an introd. by Arthur Edward Waite. New York, Ktav Pub. House, 1970. 63 p. illus. 24 cm. "First published 1923." Bibliography: p. 63. [BM525.A412S8 1970] 71-119754 ISBN 0-87068-008-0
1. Labala. I. Akiba ben Joseph, ca. 50-ca. 132. II. Stenring, Knut, tr. III. Title: Book of formation.

SHARF, Andrew. 296.1'6
The universe of Shabbetai Donnolo / A. Sharf. New York : Ktav Pub. House, 1976. viii, 214 p. : ill. ; 23 cm. Includes index. Bibliography: p. 194-206. [BM525.A419D6637] 76-151524 ISBN 0-87068-485-X : 15.00
1. Donnolo, Shabbethai, 913-ca. 982. Sefer hakhmoni. 2. Sefer Yezirah. 3. Cabala. 4. Astrology, Jewish. 5. Cosmology, Jewish. I. Title.

[SOLOMON Shelemiel ben Hayyim] 296.1'6
Tales in praise of the ARI. Translated from the Hebrew by Aaron Klein and Jenny Machlowitz Klein. Drawings by Moshe Raviv. [1st ed.] Philadelphia, Pa., Jewish Publication Society of America, 1970. 62 p. illus. 34 cm. Translation of Shivhe ha-Ari (romanized form) [BM525.L835S623] 76-105064 7.50
1. Luria, Isaac ben Solomon, 1534-1572. I. Raviv, Mosheh, illus. II. Title.

STURZAKER, James. 296.1'6
Kabbalistic aphorisms. London, Wheaton, Ill., Theosophical Publishing House, 1971. x, 118 p. 1 illus. 20 cm. [BM525.S78 1971] 73-331216 ISBN 0-7229-5226-0 £1.50
1. Cabbala. I. Title.

SUARES, Carlo. 296.1'6
The Sepher Yetsira, including the original astrology according to the Qabala and its zodiac / Carlo Suares ; translated from the French by Micheline & Vincent Stuart. Boulder, Colo. : Shambhala ; New York : distributed in the U.S. by Random House, 1976. 173 p. ; 22 cm. [BM525.A419S913] 76-14206 ISBN 0-87773-093-8 : 5.95
1. Sefer Yezirah. 2. Cabala. 3. Astrology. I. Title: The Sepher Yetsira ...

WAITE, Arthur Edward, 1857-1942. 296.16
The holy Kabbalah; a study of the secret tradition in Israel as unfolded by sons of the doctrine for the benefit and consolation of the elect dispersed through the lands and ages of the greater exile. With an introd. by Kenneth Rexroth. New Hyde Park, N.Y., University Books [1960] 636 p. 24 cm. Includes bibliography. [BM525.W3 1960] 60-12164
1. Cabala. I. Title.

WAITE. ARTHUR EDWARD, 1857-1942 296.16
The holy Kabbalah; a study of the secret tradition in Israel as unfolded by sons of the doctrine for the benefit and consolation of the elect dispersed through the lands and ages of the greater exile. With and introd. by Kenneth Rexroth. New Hyde Park, N. Y., University Books [c.1960] xxxv, 636p. 24cm. (Bibl. footnotes) 60-12164 10.00
1. Cabala. I. Title.

WALLMAN, Joseph. 296.16
The Kabalah, from its inception to its evanescence. Brooklyn, Theological Research Pub. Co. [1958] 221 p. illus. 22 cm. Includes bibliography. [BM525.W33] 58-13717
1. Cabala. I. Title.

WERBLOWSKY, Raphael Jehudah Zwi, 1924- 296.16
Joseph Karo, lawyer and mystic. [London] Oxford University Press, 1962. xi, 315 p. 6 plates (incl. facsims.) 23 cm. (Scripta judaica, 4) "Manuscripts of the Maggid Mesharim": p. [297]-299. "Editions of the Maggid Mesharim": p. [304] "The works of R. Joseph Karo and the dates of their first editions": p. [305]-306. Bibliographical footnotes. [BM755.C28W4] 62-5933
1. Caro, Joseph, 1488-1575. I. Series.

THE Wisdom of the Jewish mystics / translated by Alan Unterman. New York : New Directions, 1976. 84 p. ; 24 cm. [BM525.A2W57 1976] 76-7933 ISBN 0-8112-0624-6. pbk. : 2.45 296.1'6
1. Cabala—Translations into English. 2. Hasidism. I. Unterman, Alan.

ZOHAR. English. Selections. 296.16
Zohar, the Book of splendor; selected and edited by Gershom G. Scholem. New York, Schocken Books [1963, c1949] 125 p. 21 cm. (Schocken paperbacks, SB45) [BM525.A52S35 1963] 63-11040
1. Cabala. 2. Bible. O.T. Pentateuch—Commentaries. I. Scholem, Gershom Gerhard, 1897- ed.

SAFRAN, Alexandre. 296.1'6'09
The kabbalah : law and mysticism in the Jewish tradition / Alexandre Safran ; [translated into English by Margaret A. Pater]. New York : Feldheim Publishers, 1975. 339 p. ; 24 cm. Translation of La cabale. Includes bibliographical references. [BM526.S2313] 74-80135 10.00
1. Cabala—History and criticism. I. Title.

SCHAYA, Leo, 1916- 296.1'6'09
The universal meaning of the Kabbalah, translated from the French by Nancy Pearson. Baltimore, Penguin [1973 c.1971] 180 p. 19 cm. (The Penguin Metaphysical Library) Translation of L'homme et 1'26 solu selon la Kabbale [BM526.S313] ISBN 0-14-003614-8 1.50 (pbk)
1. Cabala—History. I. Title.

PORTON, Gary G. 296.1'7
The traditions of Rabbi Ishamel / by G. Porton. Leiden : Brill, 1976- v. ; 25 cm. (Studies in Judaism in late antiquity ; v. 19) Contents.Contents.—The non-exegetical materials. Bibliography: v. 1, p. [226]-229. [BM502.3.I8P67] 76-381618 ISBN 9-00-404526-0 (v. 1) : fl 64.00 (v. 1)
1. Ishmael, tanna, fl. 2d cent. 2. Rabbinical literature—Translations into English. 3.

Rabbinical literature—History and criticism. I. Title. II. Series.

BRATTON, Fred Gladstone, 1896- 296.1'72
Maimonides, medieval modernist. Boston, Beacon Press [1967] ix, 159 p. 21 cm. Bibliography: p. 152-154. [BM755.M6B7] 67-24893
1. Moses ben Maimon, 1135-1204. I. Title.

MOSES ben Maimon, 1135-1204. 296.1'72
The reasons of the laws of Moses : from the "More nevochim" of Maimonides / [translated] by James Townley, with notes, dissertations, and a life of the author. Westport, Conn. : Greenwood Press, 1975. p. cm. Reprint of the 1827 ed. published by Longman, Rees, Orme, Brown, and Green, London. Includes bibliographical references and index. [BM520.7.M67213 1975] 78-97294 ISBN 0-8371-2618-5 : 16.75
1. Commandments (Judaism) 2. Commandments, Six hundred and thirteen. I. Townley, James, 1774-1883. II. Title.

MOSES BEN MAIMON, 1135-1204. 296.1'72
The commandments: Sefer Ha-Mitzvoth of Maimonides; translated from the Hebrew with foreword, notes, glossary, appendices and indices by Rabbi Dr. Charles B. Chavel. London, New York, Soncino P. [1967] 2 v. 26 1/2 cm. (B 67-25776) This English translation is based upon R. Joseph Kapach's Hebrew translation of the original Arabic text, Kitab Al-Fara' id. Contents.--v. 1. The positive commandments.--v. 2. The negative commandments. Bibliography: v. 2, p. [427]-431. [BM520.8.M6533] 68-100790 8/8/-
1. Commandments, Six hundred and thirteen. I. Chavel, Charles Ber, 1906- tr. II. Kafah, Joseph. III. Title.

SILVER, Daniel Jeremy 296.172
Maimonidean criticism and the Maimonidean controversy, 1180-1240. Leiden, E. J. Brill [dist. Cleveland, Temple Lib., Univ. Circle at Silver Park [c.]1965.
1. Moses ben Maimon, 1135-1204. I. Title.

FREEHOF, Solomon Bennett, 1892- 296.1'79
Reform responsa; and, Recent Reform responsa [by] Solomon B. Freehof. [New York] Ktav Pub. House, 1973 [c1963] 2 v. in 1. 23 cm. Bibliography: p. [219]-222 (2d group) [BM522.36.R383] 72-12300 ISBN 0-87068-203-2 15.00
1. Responsa—1800- 2. Reform Judaism. I. Freehof, Solomon Bennett, 1892- Recent Reform responsa. 1973. II. Title. III. Title: Recent Reform responsa.

FREEHOF, Solomon Bennett, 1892- 296.1'79
The responsa literature and A treasury of responsa [by] Solomon B. Freehof. [New York] KTAV Pub. House, 1973. 304, xiv, 313 p. 22 cm. Reprint of the 1955 ed. of The responsa literature and the 1963 ed. of A treasury of responsa, both published by the Jewish Publication Society, Philadelphia. Includes bibliographies. [BM523.F72] 72-12301 ISBN 0-87068-202-4 15.00
1. Responsa—History and criticism. 2. Responsa—Collections. I. Freehof, Solomon Bennett, 1892- A treasury of responsa. 1973. II. Title. III. Title: A treasury of responsa.

JACOBS, Louis. 296.1'79
Theology in the Responsa / [by] Louis Jacobs. London ; Boston : Routledge and Kegan Paul, 1975. xi, 378 p. ; 23 cm. (The Littman library of Jewish civilization) Includes index. Bibliography: p. 357-362. [BM523.J3] 75-315923 ISBN 0-7100-8010-7 : £6.00
1. Responsa—History and criticism. 2. Jewish theology—Addresses, essays, lectures. I. Title.

JACOBS, Louis. 296.1'79
Theology in the Responsa / [by] Louis Jacobs. London ; Boston : Routledge and Kegan Paul, 1975. xi, 378 p. ; 23 cm. (The Littman library of Jewish civilization) Includes index. Bibliography: p. 357-362. [BM523.J3] 75-315923 ISBN 0-7100-8010-7 : 18.75
1. Responsa—History and criticism. 2. Jewish theology—Addresses, essays, lectures. I. Title.

KLEIN, Isaac. 296.1'79
Responsa and halakhic studies / by Isaac Klein. New York : Ktav Pub. House, 1975. vii, 190 p. ; 24 cm. Includes bibliographical references and index. [BM52259.L37] 75-25634 ISBN 0-87068-288-1 : 10.00
1. Responsa—1800- 2. Jewish law—Addresses, essays, lectures. I. Title.

MANN, Jacob, 1888-1940. 296.1'79
The responsa of the Babylonian geonim as a source of Jewish history. New York, Arno Press, 1973. 1 v. (various pagings) 23 cm. (The Jewish people: history, religion, literature) Reprint of the 1917-21 ed. published by Dropsie College for Hebrew and Cognate Learning, Philadelphia, of articles originally published in the Jewish quarterly review. New series. [BM501.5.M36 1973] 73-2215 ISBN 0-405-05278-2 15.00
1. Responsa—To 1040. 2. Geonic literature—History and criticism. 3. Jews in Babylonia. I. Jewish quarterly review. New series. II. Title. III. Series.

NOVAK, David, 1941- 296.1'79
Law and theology in Judaism. Foreword by Louis Finkelstein. New York, Ktav Pub. House [1974] xvi, 176 p. 24 cm. Includes bibliographical references. [BM522.74.O9] 74-806 ISBN 0-87068-245-8 10.00
1. Responsa—1800- I. Title.

BLEICH, J. David. 296.1'8
Contemporary halakhic problems / by J. David Bleich. New York : Ktav, 1977. xviii, 403 p. ; 24 cm. (The Library of Jewish law and ethics ; v. 4) Includes bibliographical references and index. [BM520.3.B5] 77-3432 ISBN 0-87068-450-7 : 15.00
1. Jewish law—Addresses, essays, lectures. 2. Judaism—20th century—Addresses, essays, lectures. I. Title.

BROWN, Jonathan M. 296.1'8
Modern challenges to Halakhah, by Jonathan M. Brown. Chicago, Published for the Hebrew Union College-Jewish Institute of Religion by Whitehall Co. [1969] xv, 137 p. 24 cm. Originally presented as the author's thesis, Hebrew Union College-Jewish Institute of Religion. Bibliography: p. 129-137. [BM522.42.R6 1969] 78-83999
1. Hoffmann, David, 1843-1921. Melamed le-ho'il. 2. Orthodox Judaism. I. Hebrew Union College-Jewish Institute of Religion. II. Title.

CARO, Joseph, 1488-1575. 296.1'8
The kosher code of the orthodox Jew, being a literal translation of that portion of the sixteenth-century codification of the Babylonian Talmud which describes such deficiencies as render animals unfit for food (Hilkot Terefot, Shulhan 'aruk); to which is appended a discussion of Talmudic anatomy in the light of the science of its day and of the present time, by S. I. Levin and Edward A. Boyden. New York, Hermon Press [1969, c1940] xx, 243 p. illus., facsim. 24 cm. Bibliography: p. 233-234. [BM710.C2613 1969] 76-76170 7.50
1. Meat inspection (Jewish law) I. Levin, Solomon Isaac, 1886- tr. II. Boyden, Edward Allen, 1886- tr. III. Title.

COHEN, Boaz, 1899- 296.18
Jewish and Roman law, a comparative study. New York, Jewish Theological Seminary of America, 1966- v. 24 cm. Bibliographical footnotes. 66-6444
1. Jewish law. 2. Roman law. I. Title.

COHEN, Boaz, 1899- 296.18
Jewish and Roman law, a comparative study. [2v.] New York, Jewish Theological Seminary of America, [c.] 1966. 2v. (896+various p.) 24cm. Bibl. 66-6444 15.00 set,
1. Jewish law. 2. Roman law. I. Title.

DAUBE, David 296.18
Collaboration with tyranny in Rabbinic law; the Riddell memorial lectures, thirty-seventh series, delivered at the University of Newcastle upon Tyne on 9, 10, and 11 November 1965. New York, Oxford [1966, c.] 1965. [7], 104p. 20cm. (Riddell memorial lectes., 37th ser.; Newcastle upon Tyne. Univ. Pubns.) [JX4281.D3] 66-2413 2.40 bds.,
1. Asylum, Right of. 2. Jewish law. I. Title. II. Series.

DAUBE, David. 296.18
Studies in Biblical law. New York, Ktav Pub. House, 1969. viii, 328 p. 24 cm. Reprint of the 1947 ed. Includes bibliographies. [BS639.D3 1969] 70-78503
1. Jewish law. I. Title.

DOCUMENTS of the Jewish pious foundations from the Cairo Geniza / edited with translations, annotations and general introduction by Moshe Gil. Leiden : Brill, 1976. xviii, 611 p. ; 25 cm. (Publications of the Diaspora Research Institute ; v. 12) English and/or Arabic and Hebrew. Includes bibliographical references and indexes. [LAW] 77-361422 ISBN 9-00-404480-9 : fl 120.00 296.1'8
1. Cairo Genizah. 2. Charitable uses, trusts, and foundations (Jewish law)—Egypt. 3. Jews in Egypt—Charities—Sources. 4. Egypt—Social conditions. I. Gil, Moshe, 1921- II. Title. III. Series: ha-Makhon le-heker ha-tefutsot. Pirsume ha-Makhon ; sefer 12.

FREEHOF, Solomon Bennett, 1892- 296.1'8
Contemporary Reform responsa / by Solomon B. Freehof. [Cincinnati] : Hebrew Union College Press, 1974. ix, 309 p. ; 22 cm. Includes index. [BM522.36.R368] 74-23748 ISBN 0-87820-108-4 : 10.00
1. Responsa—1800- 2. Reform Judaism. I. Title.

JACOBS, Louis. 296.1'8
Jewish law. Illustrated by Irwin Rosenhouse. New York, Behrman House [1968] xii, 210 p. illus. 24 cm. (The Chain of tradition series, v. 1) [LAW] 68-27329
1. Jewish law.

JAKOBOVITS, Immanuel. 296.1'8
Jewish law faces modern problems : some questions and answers / compiled and reviewed by Immanuel Jakobovits. New York : Yeshiva University, Dept. of Special Publications : selling agents, Bloch Pub. Co., 1965. 153 p. ; 23 cm. (Studies in Torah Judaism ; 8) [BM520.3.J34] 74-191758
1. Jewish law—Addresses, essays, lectures. 2. Othodox Judaism—Addresses, essays, lectures. I. Title. II. Series.

KIRSCHENBAUM, Aaron. 296.1'8
Self-incrimination in Jewish law. Introd. by Arthur J. Goldberg. New York, Burning Bush Press [1970] xii, 212 p. 22 cm. Bibliography: p. 192-204. [LAW] 70-82311 6.95
1. Self-incrimination (Jewish law) I. Title.

PAN American Union. General Legal Division. 296.18
Inter-American treaties and conventions; signatures, ratifications, and deposits with explanatory notes. Washington, Pan American Union. 1954 v. 28 cm. (Its Treaty series no. 9) Vol. for 1954 issued by the Division of Law and Treaties, in the Union's Law and treaty series. [JX506] 61-45
1. Pan American treaties and conventions. 2. U.S. — For. rel. — Latin American. 3. Spanish America — For. rel. — U.S. I. Pan American Union. Division of Law and Treaties. Inter-American treaties and conventions. II. Title. III. Series. IV. Series: Pan American Union. Law and treaty series

PHILLIPS, Anthony. 296.1'8
Ancient Israel's criminal law; a new approach to the Decalogue. Oxford [Eng.] B. Blackwell, 1970. viii, 218 p. 23 cm. Based on the author's thesis, University of Cambridge, 1967. Bibliography: p. [193]-205. [BS1285.2.P48 1970] 74-95560 ISBN 0-631-12280-X £3.00
1. Commandments, Ten. 2. Criminal law (Jewish law) I. Title.

PHILLIPS, Anthony. 296.1'8
Ancient Israel's criminal law; a new approach to the Decalogue. New York, Schocken Books [1970] viii, 218 p. 24 cm. Based on the author's thesis entitled The religious background to Israel's criminal law, Cambridge University, 1967. Bibliography: p. [193]-205. [BV4655.P45 1970] 73-130213 ISBN 0-8052-3380-6 10.50
1. Commandments, Ten. 2. Criminal law (Jewish law) I. Title.

RABINOWITZ, Abraham Hirsch. 296.1'8
Taryag; a study of the origin and historical development, from the earliest times to the present day, of the tradition that the written Torah contains six hundred and thirteen mitzvoth. Jerusalem, Boys Town: [U. S. distributor: P. Feldheim, New York] 1967. 169 p. 22 cm. "In its original form the present work was presented as a thesis to the University of the Witwatersrand." Bibliography: p. [167]-169. Bibliographical footnotes. [BM520.8.R22] HE68
1. Commandments, Six hundred and thirteen. I. Title.

RABINOWITZ, Abraham Hirsch. 296.1'8
Taryag; a study of the origin and historical development, from the earliest times to the present day, of the tradition that the written Torah contains six hundred and thirteen mitzvoth. Jerusalem, Boys Town; [U.S. distributor: P. Feldheim, New York] 1967. 169 p. 22 cm. "In its original form the present work was presented as a thesis to the University of the Witwatersrand." Bibliography: p. [167]-169. Bibliographical footnotes. [BM520.8.R22] HE 68 IL12.00
1. Commandments, Six hundred and thirteen. I. Title.

SCHWARTZ, Helene E. 296.1'8
Justice by the book : aspects of Jewish and American criminal law / Helene E. Schwartz. New York : Women's League for Conservative Judaism, 1976. 107 p. ; 22 cm. Bibliography: p. 101-103. [K5015.S38] 76-41461
1. Criminal law (Jewish law) 2. Criminal law—United States. I. Title.

SHOHET, David Menahem, 1888- 296.1'8 s
The Jewish court in the Middle Ages : studies in Jewish jurisprudence according to the Talmud, Geonic, and Medieval German responsa / by David Menahem Shohet. New York : Hermon Press, 1974. xv, 224 p. ; 24 cm. (Studies in Jewish jurisprudence ; v. 3) Reprint of the 1931 ed. published in New York. Originally presented as the author's thesis, Columbia University, 1931. Includes index. Bibliography: p. 211-216. [LAW] 296.1'8 74-79442 ISBN 0-87203-049-0 11.50
1. Jews—History—70-1789. 2. Talmud. 3. Courts, Jewish. 4. Jewish law. 5. Responsa. I. Title. II. Series.

SILBERG, Moshe, 1900- 296.1'8
Talmudic law and the modern state. Translated by Ben Zion Bokser. Edited by Marvin S. Wiener. New York, Burning Bush Press [1973] xiii, 224 p. 22 cm. Translation of Kakh darko shel Talmud. Includes bibliographical references. [LAW] 73-76348 ISBN 0-8381-3112-3 7.95
1. Jewish law. I. Title.

STYLIANOPOULOS, Theodore. 296.1'8
Justin Martyr and the Mosaic law / by Theodore Stylianopoulos. Missoula, Mont. : Society of Biblical Literature : distributed by Scholars Press, University of Montana, 1975. p. cm. (Dissertation series ; no. 20) Originally presented as the author's thesis, Harvard Divinity School, 1974. Bibliography: p. [BR1720.J8S79 1975] 75-22445 ISBN 0-89130-018-X : 4.20
1. Justinus Martyr, Saint. 2. Christianity and other religions—Judaism. 3. Judaism—Relations—Christianity. 4. Jewish law. I. Title. II. Series: Society of Biblical Literature. Dissertation series ; no. 20.

WEISFELD, Israel Harold, 1906- 296.1'8
Labor legislation in the Bible and Talmud / by Israel H. Weisfeld. New York : Yeshiva University Press, Dept. of Special Publications, 1974. 108 p. ; 23 cm. (Studies in Judaica ; 5) Bibliography: p. 103-107. [LAW] 75-325882 7.50
1. Labor laws and legislation (Jewish law) I. Title. II. Series.

WHAT is the Halacha? : Encyclopedia of Halacha ; Otzar hat'shuvos : bibliography of responsa / by Abraham Scheinberg. New York : Shulsinger Bros., 1974- v. : port. ; 24 cm. Includes bibliographical references. [BM520.9.S33] 74-28756 15.00 296.1'8
1. Jewish law. 2. Responsa—Bibliography. I. Scheinberg, Abraham. Otzar hat'shuvos. 1974. II. Title. III. Title: Encyclopedia of Halacha. IV. Title: Bibliography of responsa.

ZIMMELS, Hirsch Jakob. 296.1'8
The echo of the Nazi holocaust in rabbinic literature / by H. J. Zimmels. [New York] : Ktav Pub. House, 1977, c1975. xxiii, 372 p. ; 24 cm. On spine: The Nazi holocaust. Includes bibliographical references and index. [D810.J4Z55 1977] 76-56778 ISBN 0-87068-427-2 : 17.50
1. Holocaust and Jewish law. 2. Holocaust, Jewish (1939-1945) 3. Responsa—1800- I. Title. II. Title: The Nazi holocaust.

GILMER, Harry Wesley. 296.1'8'014
The if-you form in Israelite law / by Harry Wesley Gilmer. Missoula, Mont. : Scholars Press, [1975] p. cm. An abstract of the author's thesis, Emory University, 1969. Bibliography: p. [LAW] 75-11644 ISBN 0-89130-002-3 : 4.20
1. Jewish law—Language. I. Title.

GILMER, Harry Wesley. 296.1'8'014
The if-you form in Israelite law / Harry W. Gilmer. Missoula, Mont. : Society of Biblical Literature : distributed by Scholars Press, 1975. p. cm. (Dissertation series ; no. 15) Bibliography: p. [LAW] 75-23136 ISBN 0-89130-004-X : 4.20
1. Jewish law—Language. I. Title. II. Series: Society of Biblical Literature. Dissertation series ; no. 15.

GILMER, Harry Wesley. 296.1'8'014
The if-you form in Israelite law / by Harry W. Gilmer. Missoula, Mont. : Published by Scholars Press for the Society of Biblical Literature, c1975. viii, 139 p. ; 22 cm. (Dissertation series ; no. 15) Bibliography: p. 117-121. [LAW] 75-23136 ISBN 0-89130-004-X : 4.20
1. Jewish law—Language. I. Title. II. Series: Society of Biblical Literature. Dissertation series ; no. 15.

COHEN, Boaz, 1899-1968. 296.18'08
Law and tradition in Judaism. New York, Ktav Pub. House, 1969 [c1959] xii, 243 p. 24 cm. Bibliographical footnotes. [LAW] 73-91960
1. Jewish law—Addresses, essays, lectures. 2. Jewish law—Philosophy. 3. Jewish law—Interpretation and construction. 4. Conservative Judaism. I. Title.

APPEL, Gersion. 296.3
A philosophy of mizvot : the religious-ethical concepts of Judaism, their roots in biblical law, and the oral tradition / by Gersion Appel. New York : Ktav Pub. House, [1975] xi, 288 p. ; 23 cm. Includes bibliographical references and indexes. [BM520.7.A65] 75-1226 ISBN 0-87068-250-4 : 12.50
1. Aaron, ha-Levi, of Barcelona, 13th cent. Sefer ha-hinukh. 2. Commandments (Judaism) 3. Ethics, Jewish. I. Title.

BARACK, Nathan A. 296.3
Faith for fallibles. New York, Bloch Pub. Co., 1952. 205 p. 21 cm. [BM560.B324] 52-3973
1. Judaism. I. Title.

BAZAK, Jacob. 296.3
Judaism and psychical phenomena; a study of extrasensory perception in Biblical, Talmudic, and Rabbinical literature in the light of contemporary parapsychological research. Translated from the Hebrew by S. M. Lehrman. New York, Garrett Pub. [1972] xv, 144 p. 24 cm. Translation of Le-ma'lah min ha-hushim. Bibliography: p. 140-144. [BM538.P2B3813] 71-184295 6.95
1. Judaism and parapsychology. I. Title.

BERGREN, Richard Victor. 296.3
The prophets and the law. Cincinnati, Hebrew Union College-Jewish Institute of Religion, 1974. p. cm. (Monographs of the Hebrew Union College, no. 4) Originally presented as the author's thesis, Hebrew Union College-Jewish Institute of Religion. Bibliography: p. [BS1198.B45 1974] 74-13370 ISBN 0-87820-403-2
1. Bible. O.T. Prophets—Theology. 2. Law (Theology)—Biblical teaching. I. Title. II. Series: Hebrew Union College-Jewish Institute of Religion. Monographs, no. 4.

BERKOVITS, Eliezer, 1908- 296.3
Crisis and faith / Eliezer Berkovits. New York : Sanhedrin Press, c1976. x, 180 p. ; 21 cm. Includes bibliographical references. [BM723.B44] 76-207 8.50
1. Jewish way of life. 2. Ethics, Jewish. 3. Jewish law. 4. Judaism—Israel. 5. Civilization, Modern—1950- I. Title.

BERKOVITS, Eliezer, 1908- 296.3
God, man, and history; a Jewish interpretation. New York, Jonathan David [1959] 202p. 23cm. Includes bibliography. [BM610.B44] 59-10541
1. God (Judaism) 2. Revelation (Jewish theology) I. Title.

BERKOVITS, Eliezer, 1908- 296.3
God, man, and history; a Jewish interpretation [Rev. ed.] New York, J. David [1965, c.1959] 192p. 22cm. Bibl. [BM610.B44] 4.95;2.45 pap.,
1. God (Judaism) 2. Revelation (Jewish theology) I. Title.

BINSTOCK, Louis. 296.3
The power of faith. New York, Prentice-Hall [1952] 240 p. 24 cm. [BM565.B5] 52-7633
1. Judaism. 2. Trust in God. I. Title.

BIRNBAUM, Philip, ed. 296.3
The new treasury of Judaism / compiled and edited by Philip Birnbaum. New York : Sanhedrin Press, c1977. p. cm. Published in 1962 under title: A treasury of Judaism. Includes selections from the Old Testament. [BM43.B5 1977] 77-9104 ISBN 0-88482-410-1 : 8.95
1. Judaism—Addresses, essays, lectures. 2. Ethics, Jewish—Addresses, essays, lectures. 3. Rabbinical literature—Translations into English. I. Bible. O.T. English. Selections. 1977. II. Title.

BOROWITZ, Eugene B. 296.3
A new Jewish theology in the making, by Eugene B. Borowitz. Philadelphia, Westminster Press [1968] 220 p. 22 cm. [BM195.B6] 68-25395 6.50
1. Jewish theology—History. I. Title.

BRAUDE, Morris, 1883- ed. and tr. 296.3
Conscience on trial; three public religious disputations between Christians and Jews in the thirteenth and fifteenth centuries, translated from several Hebrew and Latin sources, annotated and with commentary. New York, Exposition Press [1952] 147p. illus. 21cm. [BM590.B7] 52-11233
1. Christianity— Controversial literature. 2. Judaism—Apologetic works. I. Title.

CALL to America to build Zion. 296.3
New York : Arno Press, 1977. p. cm. (America and the Holy Land) Reprint of the 1814 ed. of Isaiah's message to the American nation, by J. McDonald, printed by E. & E. Hosford, Albany; the 1845 ed. of Discourse on the restoration of the Jews, by M. M. Noah, published by Harper, New York; and the 1936 ed. of Zionism in prophecy, distributed by Pro-Palestine Federation of America, New York. [BS649.J5C34] 77-70723 ISBN 0-405-10306-9 lib.bdg. : 15.00
1. Jews—Restoration—Addresses, essays, lectures. 2. Bible. O.T. Isaiah XVIII—Commentaries. 3. Grand Island, N.Y.—Addresses, essays, lectures. 4. Zionism—Addresses, essays, lectures. I. Noah, Mordecai Manuel, 1785-1851. Discourse on the restoration of the Jews. 1977. II. Bible. O.T. Isaiah XVIII. 1814. McDonald. 1977. III. Title: Zionism in prophecy. 1977. IV. Series.

CENTER for Hermeneutical Studies in Hellenistic and Modern Culture. 296.3
Jewish Gnostic Nag Hammadi texts : protocol of the third colloquy, 22 May 1972 / The Center for Hermeneutical Studies in Hellenistic and Modern Culture ; James M. Robinson. Berkeley, CA : The Center, c1975. p. cm. (Protocol series of the colloquies of the Center for Hermeneutical Studies in Hellenistic and Modern Culture ; no. 3) Includes bibliographical references. [BM536.G54C46 1975] 75-44331 ISBN 0-89242-002-2 : 2.00
1. Judaism—Relations—Gnosticism—Congresses. 2. Gnosticism—Relations—Judaism—Congresses. 3. Chenoboskion manuscripts—Congresses. I. Robinson, James McConkey, 1924- II. Title. III. Series: Center for Hermeneutical Studies in Hellenistic and Modern Culture. Protocol series of the colloquies ; no. 3.

COHEN, Hermann, 1842-1918. 296.3
Religion of reason; out of the sources of Judaism. Translated, with an introd., by Simon Kaplan. Introductory essay by Leo Strauss. New York, F. Ungar Pub. Co. [1972] xliii, 489 p. 25 cm. Translation of Religion der Vernunft aus den Quellen des Judentums. Includes bibliographical references. [BM560.C5713] 76-125962 ISBN 0-8044-5229-6 15.00
1. Judaism. I. Title.

COMMENTARY 296.3
The condition of Jewish belief; a symposium, comp. by the eds. of Commentary magazine. New York, Macmillan [c1966] 280p. 22cm. The material orig. appeared in Commentary magazine, Aug. 1966, no. 2, v. 42. [BM601.C63] 67-15049 5.95; 1.45 pap.,
1. Jewish Theology—Addresses, essays, lectures. 2. Judaism—Addresses, essays, lectures. I. Title.

COMMENTARY. 296.3
The condition or Jewish belief; a symposium, compiled by the editors of Commentary magazine. New York, Macmillan [c1966] 280 p. 21 cm. "The material ... originally appeared in Commentary magazine, August 1966, number 2, volume 42" [BM601.C63] 67-15049
1. Jewish theology — Addresses, essays, lectures. 2. Judalism — Addresses, essays, lectures. I. Title.

CONE, Molly. j 296.3
Who knows ten? Children's tales of the Ten commandments. Illustrated by Uri Shulevitz. [New York] Union of American Hebrew Congregations [1965] xii, 94 p. col. illus. 22 cm. (Union graded series) [BM520.75.C65] 65-24639
1. Commandments. Ten — Juvenile literature. I. Shulevitz., Uri, 1935- illus. II. Title. III. Series. IV. Series: Commission on Jewish Education of the Union of American Hebrew Congregations and Central Conference of American Rabbis. Union graded series

CONE, Molly 296.3
Who knows ten? Children's tales of the Ten commandments. Illus. by Uri Shulevitz. [New York] Union of Amer. Hebrew Cong. [c.1965] xii, 94p. col. illus. 22cm. (Union graded ser.) Title. (Series: Commission on Jewish Education of the Union of American Hebrew Congregations and Central Conference of American Rabbis. Union graded series) [BM520.75.C65] 65-24639 2.50
1. Commandments, Ten—Juvenile literature. I. Shulevitz, Uri, 1935- illus. II. Title. III. Series.

EISENSTEIN, Ira, 1906- ed. 296.3
Varieties of Jewish belief. [1st ed.] New York, Reconstructionist Press, 1966. vii, 270 p. 22 cm. [BM601.E5] 66-19674
1. Judaism—Addresses, essays, lectures. 2. Jewish theology—Addresses, essays, lectures. I. Title.

FACKENHEIM, Emil L. 296.3
Quest for past and future; essays in Jewish theology [by] Emil L. Fackenheim. Bloomington, Indiana University Press [1968] ix, 336 p. 22 cm. Bibliographical references included in "Notes" (p. 317-336) [BM601.F3 1968] 68-27346 8.50
1. Jewish theology—Addresses, essays, lectures. I. Title.

THE Faith of secular Jews / 296.3
edited and with an introd. by Saul L. Goodman. New York : Ktav Pub. House, 1976. xiii, 301 p. ; 23 cm. (The Library of Judaic learning) Includes bibliographical references and index. [BM565.F34] 76-39982 ISBN 0-87068-489-2 : 15.00
1. Judaism—20th century—Addresses, essays, lectures. 2. Judaism—United States—Addresses, essays, lectures. 3. Haskalah—United States—Addresses, essays, lectures. I. Goodman, Saul Lederman, 1901-

FEINSILVER, Alexander, 1910- 296.3
Aspects of Jewish belief. New York, Ktav Pub. House, [1973] x, 133 p. 21 cm. [BM580.F36] 73-2351 ISBN 0-87068-398-5 2.00 (pbk.)
1. Judaism. I. Title.

FLEG, Edmond, 1874-1963. 296.3
Why I am a Jew / by Emond Fleg. New York : Arno Press, 1975 [c1929] xvi, 84 p. ; 22 cm. (The Modern Jewish experience) Translation of Pourquoi je suis juif. Reprint of the 1945 ed. published by Bloch Pub. Co., New York. Includes bibliographical references. [BM560.F63 1975] 74-27984 ISBN 0-405-06711-9 : 9.00
1. Fleg, Edmond, 1874-1963. 2. Judaism. I. Title. II. Series.

FOX, Gresham George, 1883- 296.3
The Jews, Jesus and Christ. Chicago, Argus Books, 1953. 52p. 22cm. [BM535.F6] 53-12020
1. Jesus Christ—Jewish interpretations. 2. Judaism—Relations—Christianity. 3. Christianity and other religions—Judaism. I. Title.

FOX, Gresham George, 1888- 296.3
Jesus, Pilate, and Paul; an amazingly new interpretation of the trial of Jesus under Pontius Pilate, with a study of little known facts in the life of Paul before his conversion. Based upon the author's 'The Jews, Jesus, and Christ.' Chicago, Isaacs, 1955 [i. e. 1956] 159p. 20cm. [BM620.F6] 56-20605
1. Pilate, Pontius, 1st cent. 2. Jesus Christ—Jewish interpretations. 3. Jesus Christ— Trial. 4. Paul, Saint, apostle. I. Title.

FREEHOF, Solomon Bennett, 1892- 296.3
Spoken and heard; sermons and addresses, by Solomon B. Freehof. [Pittsburgh, Rodef Shalom Congregation, 1972] ix, 264 p. 24 cm. "Bibliography from Essays in honor of Solomon B. Freehof, by T. Wiener and L. Freehof: p. [229]-264. [BM740.2.F65] 73-161280
1. Freehof, Solomon Bennett, 1892-—Bibliography. 2. Sermons, American—Jewish authors. 3. Sermons, Jewish—United States. I. Title.

GEWIRTZ, Leonard B. 296.3
The authentic Jew and his Judaism; an analysis of the basic concepts of the Jewish religion. New York, Bloch [c.1961] 306p. 61-11414 4.75
1. Judaism. I. Title.

HASEL, Gerhard F. 296.3
The remnant : the history and theology of the remnant idea from Genesis to Isaiah / by Gerhard F. Hasel. 2d ed. Berrien Springs, Mich. : Andrews University Press, c1974. x, 478 p. ; 24 cm. (Andrews University monographs ; v. 5) (Studies in religion) Revised version of the author's thesis, Vanderbilt University, 1970, which was presented under title: The origin and early history of the remnant motif in ancient Israel. Includes index. Bibliography: p. 408-432. [BS1199.R37H37 1974] 76-351607
1. Bible. O.T.—Criticism, interpretation, etc. 2. Remnant (Theology)—Biblical teaching. 3. Remnant (Theology)—History of doctrines. I. Title. II. Series. III. Series: Andrews University. Monographs ; v. 5.

HELFGOTT, Benjamin Wolf. 296.3
The doctrine of election in tannaitic literature. New York, King's Crown Press, Columbia University, 1954 [c1952] xii, 209p. 21cm. Bibliography: p. [189]-197. [BM534.H4] 54-10154
1. Jews—Electrion, Doctrine of. 2. Tannaim. 3. Jews— Relations—Christianity. 4. Christianity and other religions—Judaism. I. Title.

HERTZ, Richard C. 296.3
What can a man believe? By Richard C. Hertz. New York, Bloch [1967] 95p. 21cm. Bibl. [BM601.H38] 66-29832 3.00
1. Jewish theology. I. Title.

HESCHEL, Abraham Joshua, 1907- 296.3
God in search of man; a philosophy of Judaism. New York, Octagon Books, 1972 [c1955] 437 p. 23 cm. [BM561.H46 1972] 78-169259 ISBN 0-374-93878-4
1. Judaism. I. Title.

HIRSCH, Emil Gustav, 1851-1923. 296.3
My religion, and The crucifixion viewed from a Jewish standpoint. New York, Arno Press, 1973. 382, 63 p. port. 23 cm. (The Jewish people: history, religion, literature) Reprint of the 1925 ed. of My Religion, published by Macmillan, New York; and of the 2d ed., 1908, of The crucifixion viewed from a Jewish standpoint, published by Bloch Pub. Co., New York. [BM45.H46 1973] 73-2207 ISBN 0-405-05271-5 23.00
1. Jesus Christ—Passion—Role of Jews. 2. Judaism—Addresses, essays, lectures. 3. Sermons, American—Jewish authors. 4. Sermons, Jewish—United States. I. Hirsch, Emil Gustav, 1851-1923. The crucifixion viewed from a Jewish standpoint. 1973. II. Title. III. Title: The crucifixion viewed from a Jewish standpoint. IV. Series.

HIRSCH, Emil Gustav, 1851-1923. 296.3
Theology of Emil G. Hirsch / David Einhorn Hirsch, editor. Wheeling, Ill. : Whitehall Co., c1977. 493 p. ; 26 cm. "All of these writings are from the Jewish encyclopedia." Includes bibliographical references and index. [BM600.H57 1977] 76-56964 ISBN 0-87655-539-3 pbk. : 12.50
1. Jewish theology—Addresses, essays, lectures. 2. Judaism—History of doctrines—Addresses, essays, lectures. I. Title.

JACOBS, Louis. 296.3
A Jewish theology. New York, Behrman House [1974, c1973] xi, 342 p. 23 cm. Bibliography: p. [323]-331. [BM601.J28 1974] 73-17442 ISBN 0-87441-248-X
1. Jewish theology. I. Title.

JACOBS, Louis. 296.3
Principles of the Jewish faith, an analytical study. New York, Basic Books [1964] xii, 473 p. 23 cm. Includes bibliographies. [BM601.J3 1964a] 64-23950
1. Jewish theology. I. Title.

JACOBS, Louis 296.3
Principles of the Jewish faith, an analytic study. New York, Basic [c.1964] xii, 473p. 23cm. Bibl. [BM601.J3] 64-23950 9.50
1. Jewish theology. I. Title.

KATZ, Steven T., 1944- 296.3
Jewish ideas and concepts / Steven T. Katz. New York : Schocken Books, 1977. p. cm. Includes index. Bibliography: p. [BM601.K37] 77-75285 ISBN 0-8052-3664-3 : 14.95
1. Jewish theology. 2. God (Judaism) 3. Ethics, Jewish. I. Title.

KATZ, Steven T., 1944- 296.3
Jewish ideas and concepts / Steven T. Katz. New York : Schocken Books, 1977. p. cm. Includes index. Bibliography: p. [BM601.K37] 77-75285 ISBN 0-8052-3664-3 : 14.95
1. Jewish theology. 2. God (Judaism) 3. Ethics, Jewish. I. Title.

KLAUSNER, Joseph, 1874- *296.3
The messianic idea in Israel, from its beginning to the completion of the Mishnah. Translated from the 3d Hebrew ed. by W. F. Stinespring. New York, Macmillan, 1955. 543p. 22cm. [BM615.K563] 55-14239
1. Messiah. I. Title.

KOHLER, Kaufmann, 1843-1926 296.3
Jewish theology, systematically and historically considered. Introd. by Joseph L. Blau. New York, KTAV [1968] xlvi, 505p. 24cm. Reprint of the 1918 ed. with introd. added. Bibl. footnotes. [BM600.K65 1968] 67-28641 12.50
1. Jewish theology. I. Title.

KOHN, Eugene, 1887- 296.3
Religion and humanity. New York, Reconstructionist Press, 1953. 154p. 21cm. [BM560.K6] 53-10661
1. Judaism. 2. Religion—Philosophy. I. Title.

LASKER, Daniel J. 296.3
Jewish philosophical polemics against Christianity in the Middle Ages / by Daniel J. Lasker. New York : Ktav Pub. House, 1977. xi, 286 p. ; 24 cm. Includes indexes. Bibliography: p. 257-273. [BM590.L37] 76-50657 ISBN 0-87068-498-1 : 17.50
1. Christianity—Controversial literature—History. 2. Judaism—Relations—Christianity. 3. Christianity and other religions—Judaism. I. Title.

LEVITT, Zola. 296.3
Jews and Jesus / by Zola Levitt. Chicago : Moody Press, c1977. p. cm. [BV2620.L46] 77-22370 ISBN 0-8024-4335-4 pbk. : 3.50
1. Levitt, Zola. 2. Missions to Jews. I. Title.

MCKENZIE, John L. 296.3
A theology of the Old Testament [by] John L. McKenzie. [1st ed.] Garden City, N.Y., Doubleday, 1974. 336 p. 22 cm. Includes

bibliographical references. [BS1192.5.M29] 72-76190 ISBN 0-385-08880-9 7.95
1. Bible. O.T.—Theology. I. Title.

MCKENZIE, John L. 296.3
A theology of the Old Testament John L. McKenzie. Garden City, N.Y. : Image Books, 1976 c1974. 355 p. ; 18 cm. Includes bibliographical references and index. [BS1192.5] ISBN 0-385-08880-9 pbk. : 1.95
1. Bible. O.T.—Theology. I. Title.
L.C. card no. for 1974 Doubleday ed.: 72-76190.

MARMORSTEIN, Arthur, 1882-1946. 296.3
The doctrine of merits in old rabbinical literature; and The old rabbinic doctrine of God: I. The names and attributes of God [and] II. Essays in anthropomorphism. New York, Ktay Pub. Co. [1968] 3 v. in 1. 24 cm. Vol. 1 first published, 1920; v. 2, 1927; v. 3, 1937. Bibliographical footnotes. [BM645.M4M33] 67-11904
1. Merit (Jewish theology) 2. God (Judaism)—Name. 3. God—Attributes. 4. Anthropomorphism. I. Title. II. Title: Rabbinical literature. III. The old rabbinic doctrine of God.

MARMORSTEIN, Arthur, 1882-1946. 296.3
Studies in Jewish theology; the Arthur Marmorstein memorial volume. Edited by J. Rabbinowitz and M. S. Lew. Freeport, N.Y., Books for Libraries Press [1972, c1950] xlvi, 228, 92 p. front. 23 cm. (Essay index reprint series) English and Hebrew. Contents.Contents.—The master, an appreciation, by the editors.—My father, a memoir, by E. Marmorstein.—Bibliography of the works of Arthur Marmorstein (p. [xxvi]-xlvi).—The background of the Haggadah.—The unity of God in rabbinic literature.—The imitation of God (Imitatio Dei) in the Haggadah.—The Holy Spirit in rabbinic legend.—The doctrine of the resurrection of the dead in rabbinic theology.—Participation in eternal life in rabbinic theology and in legend.—Judaism and Christianity in the middle of the third century.—ha-Emunah be-netsah Yisrael bi-derashot ha-Tana'im veha-Amora'im (romanized form)—Ra'ayon ha-ge'ulah be-agadat ha-Tana'im veha-Amora'im (romanized form)—Ma'amar 'al 'erkah ha-histori shel ha-agadah (romanized form) Bibliography: p. [xxvii]-xlvi. [BM177.M37 1972] 76-39174 ISBN 0-8369-2702-8
1. Talmud—Theology. 2. Aggada. I. Title.

MARX, Victor. 296.3
The greatness & the decadence of the Jews / Victor Marx. [1st ed.]. [Albuquerque, N.M.] : American Classical College Press, [1977] [16] leaves : ill. ; 28 cm. Cover title. [BM585.M375] 76-57996 ISBN 0-89266-038-4 : 49.50
1. Judaism—Controversial literature. 2. Jewish question. I. Title.

MILLER, Avigdor. 296.3S
Rejoice. O Youth; an integrated Jewish ideology. New York, 5722 [1961 62, c1962] 384 p. 21 cm. Added t. p. in Hebrew has title: (transliterated: Az nidberu) [BM723.M48] 63-1082
1. Jewish way of life. 2. Youth — Conduct of life. I. Title. II. Title: Az nidberu.

MODERN Jewish thought : 296.3
a source reader / edited by Nahum N. Glatzer. New York : Schocken Books, 1976. p. cm. Bibliography: p. [BM195.M6] 76-9139 ISBN 0-8052-3631-7 ISBN 0-8052-3631-7 12.00. ISBN 0-8052-0542-X pbk : 5.50
1. Judaism—History—Modern period, 1750-—Sources. I. Glatzer, Nahum Norbert, 1903-

MONTEFIORE, Claude Joseph Goldsmid, 1858-1938. 296.3
Judaism and St. Paul: two essays. New York, Arno Press, 1973. 240 p. 21 cm. (The Jewish people: history, religion, literature) Reprint of the 1914 ed. published by M. Goschen, London. Includes bibliographical references. [BS2652.M6 1973] 73-2222 ISBN 0-405-05284-7 15.00
1. Paul, Saint, apostle. 2. Bible. N.T. Epistles of Paul—Theology. 3. Rabbinical literature—Relation to the New Testament. 4. Reform Judaism. I. Title. II. Series.

MOSES ben Maimon, 1135-1204. 296.3
Maimonides; his wisdom for our time; selected from his twelfth-century classics. Edited, newly translated, and with an introd. by Gilbert S. Rosenthal. New York, Funk and Wagnalls [1969] 79 p. 23 cm. (A Sabra book) "Sources": p. [75]-79. [BM545.A45R6] 69-13466 2.95
1. Judaism—Works to 1900. I. Rosenthal, Gilbert S., ed. II. Title.

MOSES ben Maimon, 1135-1204. 296.3
A Maimonides reader, edited, with introductions and notes, by Isadore Twersky. New York, Behrman House [1972] xvii, 494 p. 24 cm. (Library of Jewish studies) Bibliography: p. 483-490. [BM545.A45T9 1972] 76-160818 ISBN 0-87441-200-5 12.50
1. Judaism—Works to 1900. I. Twersky, Isadore, ed. II. Title.

MOSES ben Maimon, 1135-1204. 296.3
The teachings of Maimonides. By A. Cohen. Prolegomenon by Marvin Fox. New York, Ktav Pub. House, 1968. xliv, 339 p. 24 cm. The text is a reprint of the 1927 ed. Includes bibliographical references. [BM545.A45C6 1968] 68-17310
I. Cohen, Abraham, 1887- ed. II. Title.

NEUSNER, Jacob, 1932- comp. 296.3
Understanding Jewish theology; classical issues and modern perspectives. New York, Ktav Pub. House [1973] x, 280 p. 23 cm. Includes bibliographical references. [BM43.N48] 72-13904 ISBN 0-87068-215-6 7.95
1. Jewish theology—Addresses, essays, lectures. 2. Judaism—Addresses, essays, lectures. I. Title.
Pbk. 3.95.

PETUCHOWSKI, Jakob Josef, 1925- 296.3
Ever since Sinai; a modern view of Torah. New York, Scribe Publications, 1961. 133p. 23cm. Includes bibliography. [BM561.P45] 61-10172
1. Judaism. I. Title.

PETUCHOWSKI, Jakob Josef, 1925- 296.3
Ever since Sinai; a modern view of Torah [by] Jakob J. Petuchowski. 2d ed., rev. New York, Scribe Publications, 1968. ix, 132 p. 22 cm. Includes bibliographical references. [BM529.P36 1968] 70-5270 1.95
1. Tradition (Judaism) I. Title.

PLOTKIN, Frederick. 296.3
Judaism & tragic theology [by] Frederick S. Plotkin. Foreword by Arthur A. Cohen. New York, Schocken Books [1973] xvi, 174 p. 21 cm. [BM601.P58] 73-81343 ISBN 0-8052-3519-1 7.95
1. Jewish theology. I. Title.

RANKIN, Oliver Shaw. 296.3
Jewish religious polemic of early and later centuries; a study of documents here rendered in English. [New York] Ktav Pub. House, 1970. viii, 256 p. illus. 24 cm. Reprint of the 1956 ed. Includes bibliographical references. [BM590.A1R3 1970] 68-25578 10.00
1. Judaism—Apologetic works. 2. Christianity—Controversial literature. I. Title.

RIVKIN, Ellis, 1918- 296.3
Leon da Modena and the Kol sakhal. Cincinnati, Hebrew Union College Press, 1952. xii, 144p. 24cm. 'First made its appearance, with but slight variations, in the Jewish quarterly review, new series,' v. 38 (1947/48)-v. 41 (1960/51) [BM590.L4R56] 52-67065
1. Leone da Modenn, 1571-1648, supposed author. Kol sakhal. 2. Judaism—Controversial literature. I. Title.

ROSENZWEIG, Franz, 1886-1929. 296.3
The star of redemption. Translated from the 2d ed. of 1930 by William W. Hallo. [1st ed.] New York, Holt, Rinehart and Winston [1971] xviii, 445 p. 24 cm. Translation of Der Stern der Erlosung. Includes bibliographical references. [BM565.R613] 71-118091 ISBN 0-03-085077-0 10.00
1. Judaism. 2. Cosmology. 3. Religion—Philosophy. I. Title.

ROSENZWEIG, Franz, 1886-1929. 296.3
The star of redemption. Translated from the 2d ed. of 1930 by William W. Hallo. Boston, Beacon Press [1972, c1971] xviii, 445 p. 21 cm. (Beacon Paperback, 441) Translation of Der Stern der Erlosung. Includes bibliographical references. [BM565.R613 1972] 72-1918 ISBN 0-8070-1129-0 3.95
1. Judaism. 2. Cosmology. 3. Religion—Philosophy. I. Title.

ROSNER, Fred. 296.3
Modern medicine and Jewish law. New York, Yeshiva University, Dept. of Special Publications, 1972. 216 p. 24 cm. (Studies in Torah Judaism, 13) Includes bibliographical references. [LAW] 72-172466 7.95
1. Medical laws and legislation (Jewish law) I. Title. II. Series.

RUBENSTEIN, Richard L. 296.3
After Auschwitz; radical theology and contemporary Judaism, by Richard L. Rubenstein. Indianapolis, Bobbs-Merrill [1966] xii, 287 p. 22 cm. Includes bibliographical references. [BM601.R8] 66-27886
1. Jewish theology. 2. Judaism—20th century. I. Title.

RUBENSTEIN, Richard L. 296.3
The religious imagination; a study in psychoanalysis and Jewish theology, by Richard L. Rubenstein. Indianapolis, Bobbs-Merrill [1968] xx, 246 p. 22 cm. Bibliography: p. 185-201. [BM601.R79] 67-24905
1. Jewish theology. I. Title.

SANDERS, E. P. 296.3
Paul and Palestinian Judaism : a comparison of patterns of religion / E. P. Sanders. 1st American ed. Philadelphia : Fortress Press, 1977. xviii, 627 p. ; 24 cm. Includes indexes. Bibliography: p. 557-582. [BM177.S2 1977] 76-62612 ISBN 0-8006-0499-7 : 25.00
1. Dead Sea scrolls—Criticism, interpretation, etc. 2. Bible. O.T. Apocrypha—Criticism, interpretation, etc. 3. Apocryphal books (Old Testament)—Criticism, interpretation, etc. 4. Bible. N.T. Epistles of Paul—Theology. 5. Tannaim. I. Title.

SAVIN, Jacob. 296.3
Judaism for non-Jews / by Jacob Savin. 1st ed. New York : Vantage Press, c1975. 170 p. ; 22 cm. Bibliography: p. 169-170. [BM565.S28] 74-81213 ISBN 0-533-01513-8 : 4.95
1. Judaism—Addresses, essays, lectures. 2. Proselytes and proselyting, Jewish—Addresses, essays, lectures. I. Title.

SAVOY, Gene. 296.3
The Essaei transcripts : a revolutionary new system with techniques based on the secret teachings of the Essaei colony and the Dead Sea scrolls / text by Gene Savoy and James C. Geoghegan. Reno, Nev. : International Community of Christ, c1975. xiii, 63, 171, 64 leaves : ill. ; 29 cm. [BP605.I45S28] 75-331081
1. International Community of Christ. I. Geoghegan, James C., 1922- joint author. II. Title.

SCHECHTER, Solomon, 1847-1915. 296.3
Aspects of rabbinic theology. [Introd. by Louis Finkelstein] New York, Schocken Books [1961] 384 p. 21 cm. First published in 1909 under title: Some aspects of rabbinic theology. Includes bibliography. [BM600.S3 1961] 61-14919
1. Jewish theology. I. Title.

SHAMIR, Yehuda, 1936- 296.3
Rabbi Moses ha-Kohen of Tordesillas and his book 'Ezer ha-emunah—a chapter in the history of the Judeo-Christian controversy. Coconut Grove, Fla., Field Research Projects, 1972. 2 v. map. 28 cm. Vol. 2 "includes the [Hebrew] text of Sefer 'Ezer ha-emunah and an appendix presenting Sefer 'Ezer ha-dat." Bibliography: v. 1, p. 223-236. [BM648.M673S52] 72-172722
1. Moses, ha-Kohen, of Tordesillas. 2. Abner of Burgos. 3. Judaism—Apologetic works. I. Moses, ha-Kohen, of Tordesillas. 'Ezer ha-emunah. 1972. II. Title: 'Ezer ha-emunah. III. Ti

SHAPIRO, David Solomon. 296.3
Studies in Jewish thought / by David S. Shapiro. New York : Yeshiva University Press, 1975- v. ; 24 cm. (Studies in Judaica ; 6) Includes bibliographical references. [BM45.S458] 75-329766 15.00
1. Bible. O.T.—Criticism, interpretation, etc.,—Addresses, essays, lectures. 2. Judaism—Addresses, essays, lectures. I. Title. II. Series.

TROKI, Isaac ben Abraham, 1533-1594. 296.3
[Hizuk emunah (romanized form)] or, Faith strengthened. Translated by Moses Mocatta. Introd. by Trude Weiss-Rosmarin. New York, Ktav Pub. House, 1970. xiv, 295, 13 p. 24 cm. In English. Originally published in 1851. Includes bibliographical references. [BM590.T72 1970] 74-126345 10.00
1. Jesus Christ—Jewish interpretations. 2. Christianity—Controversial literature. 3. Judaism—Apologetic works. I. Mocatta, Moses, 1768-1857, tr. II. Title. III. Title: Faith strengthened.

WOLF, Arnold Jacob. 296.3
Challenge to confirmands; an introduction to Jewish thinking. [1st ed.] New York, Scribe Publications [c1963] 161 p. 23 cm. Bibliographical references included in "Notes" (p. 152-160) [BM601.W6] 63-20184
1. Jewish theology. I. Title.

WOLF, Arnold Jacob 296.3
Challenge to confirmands; an introduction to Jewish thinking. New York, Scribe [c.1963] 161p. 23cm. Bibl. 63-20184 3.75
1. Jewish theology. I. Title.

WOLF, Arnold Jacob. 296.3
Challenge to confirmands; an introduction to Jewish thinking. [3d ed., rev. and enl.] New York, Scribe Publications [1967, c1963] xv, 165 p. 22 cm. Includes bibliographical references. [BM601.W6 1967] 70-10461 3.75
1. Jewish theology. 2. Confirmation (Jewish rite)—Instruction and study. I. Title.

ZERIN, Edward. 296.3
What Catholics should know about Jews, by Edward Zerin and Benedict Viviano. Edited by Augustine Rock. Chicago, Priory Press [1967] 121 p. 19 cm. "Most of the material is adapted from the [first] author's book Our Jewish neighbors." Includes bibliographies. An introduction to Jewish history, customs, worship, and way of life for Catholic youth at the junior high level. [BM580.Z45] AC 67
1. Judaism. 2. Christianity and other religions—Judaism. I. Viviano, Benedict. II. Title.

STEINBERG, Milton, 1903-1950. 296.3'08
A believing Jew; the selected writings of Milton Steinberg. Freeport, N.Y., Books for Libraries Press [1971, c1951] 318 p. 23 cm. (Essay index reprint series) Contents.Contents.—God and the world's end.—The social crisis and the retreat of God.—A protest against a new cult.—The future of Judaism in America.—A specimen Jew.—American Jewry's coming of age.—Indignation - a lost Jewish virtue.—The right not to be a Jew.—Commentary magazine.—The test of time.—When I think of Seraye.—Latter day miracles: Israel.—Our persistent failures.—A pity for the living.—The depth of Evil.—From the mountaintops.—Telling oneself the truth.—On being the victim of injustice.—The Sabbath of Sabbaths.—The fear of life.—Remember us unto life.—If man is God.—To hold with open arms. [BM740.S754 1971] 76-152215 ISBN 0-8369-2256-5
1. Sermons, American—Jewish authors. 2. Sermons, Jewish—U.S. 3. Judaism—U.S.—Addresses, essays, lectures. I. Title.

FRIEDMAN, Maurice S. 296.3'092'4
Martin Buber : the life of dialogue / Maurice S. Friedman. [3d ed.] Chicago : University of Chicago Press, 1976. xvii, 322 p. ; 21 cm. Includes index. Bibliography: p. 283-309. [B3213.B84F7 1976] 76-369402 ISBN 0-226-26356-8 : 12.50
1. Buber, Martin, 1878-1965.

MEYER, Michael A. 296.3'092'4
The origins of the modern Jew; Jewish identity and Europena culture in Germany, 1749-1824 [by] Michael A. Meyer. Detroit, Wayne State Univ. Pr., 1967. 249p. 24cm. Bibl. [BM316.M4] 910 67-12384 8.50
1. Judaism—Germany. 2. Jews in Germany—Intellectual life. I. Title.

MOORE, Donald J. 296.3'092'4
Martin Buber, prophet of religious secularism : the criticism of institutional religion in the writings of Martin Buber / by Donald J. Moore. 1st ed. Philadelphia : Jewish Publication Society of America, c1974. xxviii, 264 p. ; 22 cm. Bibliography: p. [261]-264. [B3213.B84M66] 74-12888 ISBN 0-8276-0055-0 : 6.00
1. Buber, Martin, 1878-1965.

PANKO, Stephen M. 296.3'092'4 B
Martin Buber / by Stephen M. Panko. Waco, Tex. : Word Books, c1976. 135 p. ; 23 cm. (Makers of the modern theological mind) Bibliography; p. 132-135. [BM755.B8P36] 76-2869 ISBN 0-87680-470-9 : 5.95
1. Buber, Martin, 1878-1965.

PETUCHOWSKI, Jakob Josef, 1925- 296 3'0924
The theology of Haham David Nieto; an eighteenth-century defense of the Jewish tradition. New and rev. ed. by Jakob J. Petuchowski. [New York] Ktav Pub. House [1970] xix, 166 p. 24 cm. Bibliography: p. 161-166. [BM755.N5P4 1970] 79-105752
1. Nieto, David, 1654-1728. I. Title.

ROSENBLOOM, Noah H. 296.3'092'4
Tradition in an age of reform : the religious philosophy of Samson Raphael Hirsch / Noah H. Rosenbloom. 1st ed. Philadelphia : Jewish Publication Society of America, c1976. xviii, 480 p. : port. ; 24 cm. Includes index. Bibliography: p. 455-470. [BM755.H48R63] 75-13438 ISBN 0-8276-0070-4 : 12.50
1. Hirsch, Samson Raphael, 1808-1888. 2. Judaism—Germany. I. Title.

RUBENSTEIN, Richard L. 296.3'092'4 B
Power struggle [by] Richard L. Rubenstein. New York, Scribner [1974] x, 193 p. 24 cm. Autobiographical. [BM755.R83A36] 73-1354 ISBN 0-684-13757-7 7.95
1. Rubenstein, Richard L. I. Title.

SHERMAN, Franklin. 296.3'0924
The promise of Heschel. [1st ed.] Philadelphia, Lippincott [1970] 103 p. 22 cm. (The Promise of theology) Bibliography: p. 101-103. [BM755.H37S47] 70-105549 3.95
1. Heschel, Abraham Joshua, 1907- I. Title.

BEGINNINGS, early 296.3'0973
American Judaica : a collection of ten publications, in facsimile, illustrative of the religious, communal, cultural & political life of American Jewry, 1761-1845 / introduced by Abraham J. Karp. Philadelphia : Jewish Publication Society of America, [1975] 1 case (11 v.) : ill. ; 25 cm. Title from case. English or Hebrew. Reprint of 10 publications published between 1761 and 1845 by various publishers. Includes bibliography. [BM205.B38] 75-23405 ISBN 0-8276-0076-3 : 20.00
1. Judaism—United States—History—Sources. 2. Jews in the United States—History—Sources. I. Karp, Abraham J.
Contents omitted

ABELSON, Joshua, 1873- 296.3'11
1940.
The immanence of God in rabbinical literature. New York, Hermon Press [1969] xii, 387 p. 24 cm. Reprint of the 1912 ed. Includes bibliographical references. [BM610.A28 1969] 68-9536 11.50
1. Immanence of God. 2. God (Judaism) 3. Rabbinical literature—History and criticism. I. Title.

CHRISTEN, Robert J., 296.3'11
comp.
Monotheism and Moses, edited with an introd. by Robert J. Christen and Harold E. Hazelton. Lexington, Mass., Heath [1969] xviii, 104 p. 24 cm. (Problems in European civilization) Bibliography: p. 103-104. [BL221.C48] 68-8047
1. Monotheism—Addresses, essays, lectures. 2. Jewish theology—Addresses, essays, lectures. I. Hazelton, Harold E., joint comp. II. Title. III. Series.

CLEMENTS, Ronald Ernest, 296.311
1929-
God and temple, by R. E. Clements. Philadelphia, Fortress Press, 1965. xi, 163 p. 23 cm. Rewritten from thesis (University of Sheffield, 1961) with title: The Divine dwelling-place in the Old Testament. Bibliography: p. 143-154. [BM655.C56] 65-6743
1. Jerusalem — Temple. 2. Presence of God. I. Title.

CLEMENTS, Ronald Ernest, 296.311
1929-
God and temple. Philadelphia, Fortress [c.] 1965. xi, 163p. 23cm. Bibl. [BM655.C56] 65-6473 3.75
1. Jerusalem—Temple. 2. Presence of God. I. Title.

DENTAN, Robert Claude, 296.3'11
1907-
The knowledge of God in ancient Israel [by] Robert C. Dentan. New York, Seabury Press [1968] xii, 278 p. 22 cm. Bibliographical references included in "Notes" (p. 245-264) [BM610.D4] 68-11593
1. God—Knowableness—Biblical teaching. I. Title.

JOHNSON, Aubrey Rodway 296.311
The one and the many in the Israelite conception of God. [2d ed.] Cardiff, Univ. of Wales Pr. [Mystic, Conn., Verry, 1966] iv. 44p. 22cm. 2d ed. First pub. in 1961. Bibl. [BT99.J57] 66-4138 2.00
1. God—Biblical teaching. I. Title.

JUNG, Leo, 1892- 296.3*11
Knowledge and love in rabbinic lore. New York, Yeshiva University, Dept. of Special Publications, 1963. 55 p. 23 cm. (Studies in Torah Judaism, 9) "Sixth in a series." Includes bibliographical references. [BM610.J85] 72-193219
1. God (Judaism)—Knowableness. 2. Love (Judaism) I. Title. II. Series.

KUSHNER, Harold S. 296.3'11
When children ask about God [by] Harold S. Kushner. New York, Reconstructionist Press, 1971. xii, 176 p. 23 cm. [BT102.K88] 76-155714 ISBN 0-910808-01-5
1. God. 2. Children—Religious life. I. Title.

KUSHNER, Harold S. 296.3'11
When children ask about God / Harold S. Kushner. New York : Schocken Books, 1976, c1971. xii, 176 p. ; 21 cm. [BM610.K85 1976] 76-9140 ISBN 0-8052-0549-7 pbk. : 2.95
1. God (Judaism)—Study and teaching. 2. Jewish religious education of children. 3. Jewish children—Religious life. I. Title.

LELYVELD, Arthur J. 296.3'11
Atheism is dead; a Jewish response to radical theology [by] Arthur J. Lelyveld. Cleveland, World Pub. Co. [1968] xii, 209 p. 21 cm. Bibliographical footnotes. [BM610.L42] 67-18031
1. God (Judaism) 2. Death of God theology. I. Title.

MANN, Thomas Wingate. 296.3'11
Divine presence and guidance in Israelite traditions : the typology of exaltation / Thomas W. Mann. Baltimore : Johns Hopkins University Press, c1977. x, 310 p. ; 26 cm. (The Johns Hopkins Near Eastern studies) Includes indexes. Bibliography: p. 272-285. [BS1192.6.M36] 76-49846 ISBN 0-8018-1919-9 : 14.00
1. Bible. O.T. Pentateuch—Criticism, interpretation, etc. 2. Presence of God. 3. Assyro-Babylonian religion—Relations—Judaism. 4. Judaism—Relations—Assyro-Babylonian. I. Title. II. Series: Johns Hopkins University. Near Eastern studies.

PATAI, Raphael, 1910- 296.3'11
The Hebrew goddess. [New York] Ktav Pub. House [1968, c1967] 349 p. illus. 24 cm. Bibliography: p. 329-336. [BM530.P28] 67-22753
1. Mother-goddesses. 2. Mythology, Jewish. I. Title.

WICKS, Henry J. 296.3'11
The doctrine of God in the Jewish apocryphal and apocalyptic literature, by Henry J. Wicks. With introd. by R. H. Charles. New York, Ktav Pub. House, 1971. xi, 371 p. 24 cm. Reprint of the 1915 ed. Originally presented as the author's thesis, University of London. Includes bibliographical references. [BS1700.W5 1971] 77-78502 ISBN 0-87068-149-4
1. Bible. O.T. Apocrypha—Theology. 2. Apocryphal books (Old Testament)—Theology. 3. God (Judaism) I. Title.

HIRSCH, W. 296.3'2
Rabbinic psychology; beliefs about the soul in Rabbinic literature of the Talmudic period, by W. Hirsch. New York, Arno Press, 1973. 291 p. port. 23 cm. (The Jewish people: history, religion, literature) Reprint of the 1947 ed. published by E. Goldston, London. Originally presented as the author's thesis, University of London. Bibliography: p. 281-286. [BM645.S6H5 1973] 73-2208 ISBN 0-405-05272-3 16.00
1. Soul (Judaism) 2. Immortality (Judaism) 3. Sin (Judaism) I. Title. II. Series.

KOOK, Abrahahm Isaac, 296.3'2
1865-1935.
Rabbi Kook's Philosophy of repentance a translation of Orot ha-teshuvah / by Alter B. Z. Metzger. New York : Yeshiva University Press, Dept. of Special Publications : selling agents, Bloch Pub. Co., 1968. 132 p. ; 23 cm. (Studies in Torah Judaism ; 11) Caption title: Orot ha-teshuvah. Lights of repentance. Includes bibliographical references. [BM645.R45K613] 74-192553
1. Repentance (Judaism) I. Title. II. Series.

SILVER, Abba Hillel, 1893- 296.32
A history of Messianie speculation in Isral, from the first through the seventeenth centuries. pwith a new pref. by the author. Boston, Beacon Press [1959] 268 p. 21 cm. (Beacon paperback no.80) Includes bibliography. [BM615.S5 1959] 59-6395
1. Messiah. I. Title.

WOLF, Arnold Jacob, comp. 296.3'2
What is man? [By] Arnold J. Wolf. [Washington, B'nai B'rith Adult Jewish Education, c1968] xv, 102 p. 21 cm. (A Jewish sources speak book) "A B'nai B'rith book." Bibliography: p. [97]-100. [BM627.W6] 68-31850 3.50
1. Man (Jewish theology) I. Title.

FELDMAN, Emanuel, 1927- 296.3'3
Biblical and post-Biblical defilement and mourning : law as theology / by Emanuel Feldman. New York : Yeshiva University Press, 1977. xx, 196 p. ; 24 cm. (The Library of Jewish law and ethics) Includes indexes. Bibliography: p. 181-188. [BM635.4.F44] 76-41187 ISBN 0-87068-287-3 : 12.50
1. Death (Judaism) 2. Death—Biblical teaching. 3. Purity, Ritual (Judaism) 4. Purity, Ritual—Biblical teaching. 5. Mourning (Jewish law) I. Title.

FELDMAN, Emanuel, 1927- 296.3'3
Biblical and post-Biblical defilement and mourning : law as theology / by Emanuel Feldman. New York : Yeshiva University Press, 1977. xx, 196 p. ; 24 cm. (The Library of Jewish law and ethics) Includes indexes. Bibliography: p. 181-188. [BM635.4.F44] 76-41187 ISBN 0-87068-287-3 : 12.50
1. Death (Judaism) 2. Death—Biblical teaching. 3. Purity, Ritual (Judaism) 4. Purity, Ritual—Biblical teaching. 5. Mourning (Jewish law) I. Title.

LEVEY, Samson H. 296.3'3
The Messiah: an Aramaic interpretation; the Messianic exegesis of the Targum, by Samson H. Levey. Cincinnati, Hebrew Union College-Jewish Institute of Religion, 1974. xxi, 180 p. 24 cm. (Monographs of the Hebrew Union College, no. 2) Based on the author's thesis, University of Southern California. Bibliography: p. 165-168. [BM625.L48] 74-6239
1. Bible. O.T. Aramaic—Criticism, interpretation, etc. 2. Messianic era (Judaism) I. Bible. O.T. English. Selections. 1974. II. Title. III. Title: The Messianic exegesis of the Targum. IV. Series: Hebrew Union College-Jewish Institute of Religion. Monographs, no. 2.

NICKELSBURG, George W. 296.3'3
E., 1934-
Resurrection, immortality, and eternal life in intertestamental Judaism [by] George W. E. Nickelsburg. Cambridge, Harvard University Press, 1972. 206 p. 24 cm. (Harvard theological studies, 26) A revision of the author's thesis, Harvard Divinity School, 1967. Bibliography: p. 181-191. [BS1199.E75N5 1972] 72-89143 pap. 3.00
1. Bible. O.T. Apocrypha—Theology. 2. Eschatology—Biblical teaching. 3. Apocryphal books (Old Testament)—Theology. I. Title. II. Series.

OLAN, Levi Arthur, 1903- 296.3'3
Judaism and immortality, by Levi A. Olan. New York, Union of American Hebrew Congregations [1971] x, 112 p. 20 cm. (Issues of faith) Bibliography: p. 105-106. [BM645.I5O4] 68-54571
1. Immortality (Judaism) I. Title. II. Series.

RIEMER, Jack, comp. 296.3'3
Jewish reflections on death. Edited by Jack Riemer. Foreword by Elizabeth Kubler-Ross. New York, Schocken Books [1975, c1974] viii, 184 p. 21 cm. [BM635.4.R53 1975] 74-18242 ISBN 0-8052-3560-4 7.95
1. Death (Judaism)—Addresses, essays, lectures. I. Title.

SARACHEK, Joseph, 1892- 296.3'3
The doctrine of the Messiah in medieval Jewish literature. [2d ed.] New York, Hermon Press [1968] xii, 339 p. 24 cm. Bibliography: p. 329-331. [BM615.S25 1968] 68-20900
1. Messiah. I. Title.

DRESNER, Samuel H. 296.333
The zaddik; the doctrine of the zaddik according to the writings of Rabbi Yaakov Yosef of Polnay. [Preface by Abraham J. Herschel] New York, Schocken Books [1974, c1960] 312 p. 21 cm. "Based upon a dessertation presented to the Jewish Theological Seminary of America in 1954 for the degree of doctor of Hebrew letters. Includes bibliographical references. [BM198.07] 60-7228 ISBN 0-8052-0437-7. 3.45 (pbk.)
1. Jacob Joseph, ha-Koren, of Polonnoye, d. ca 1782. 2. Hassidism—Philosophy. I. Title.

ARONSON, David, 1894- 296.38
The Jewish way of life. Rev. ed. [New York] National Academy for Adult Jewish Studies of the United Synagogue of America [c1957] 227p. 21cm. Includes bibliography. [BM723.A7 1957] 57-8370
1. Ethics, Jewish. I. Title.

BELKIN, Samuel. 296.38
In His image; the Jewish philosophy of man as expressed in rabbinic tradition. London, New York, Abelard-Schuman [1960] 290p. 22cm. (Ram's horn books) Includes bibliography. [BM645.M3B4] 60-7230
1. Man (Jewish theology) I. Title.

BIRNBAUM, Philip, ed. 296.38
A treasury of Judaism. New York, Hebrew Pub. Co. [1957] 431p. 24cm. [BM40.B46] 57-1073
1. Jewish literature. I. Title.

BIRNBAUM, Phillip ed. 296.38
A treasury of Judaism. New York, Hebrew Pub. Co. [1957] 431p. 24cm. [BM40.B46] 57-1073
1. Jewish literature. I. Title.

COHEN, Arthur A. 296.38
The natural and the supernatural Jew: an historical and theological introduction. New York, McGraw [1964, c.1962] 326p. 21cm. Bibl. 2.95 pap.,
1. Jewish theology. I. Title.

COHEN, Boaz, 1899- 296.38
Law and ethics in the light of the Jewish tradition. New York, 1957. 55p. 23cm. [BJ1280.C6] 59-47441
1. Ethics, Jewish. 2. Jewish law—Philosophy. I. Title.

CORDOVERO, Moses, 1522- 296.3'8
1570.
The palm tree of Deborah / Moses Cordovero ; translated from the Hebrew with an introd. and notes by Louis Jacobs. New York : Hermon Press, 1974, c1960. 133 p. ; 24 cm. Translation of Tomer Devorah. Reprint of the ed. published by Vallentine, Mitchell, London. Bibliography: p. 127-130. [BJ1287.C63T63 1974] 73-93366 ISBN 0-87203-039-3 : 6.95.
1. Ethics, Jewish. I. Title.

EISENBERG, Azriel Louis, 296.38
1903- ed.
Tzedakah; a way of life. Foreword by Philip Bernstein. Illus. by Janet and Alex D'Amato. New York Behrman House [1963] 127p. col. illus. 21cm. 63-15993 .65 pap.,
1. Jewish way of life—Stories. I. Title.

FINE, Helen 296.38
At Camp Kee Tov: ethics for Jewish juniors. Illus. by Seymour Fleishman. New York, Union of Amer. Hebrew Congregations [c.1961] 262p. illus. 25cm. (Union graded ser.) 61-9758 3.50
I. Title.

FRIEDMAN, Maurice S. 296.38
The covenant of peace; a personal witness. Wallingford, Pa., Pendle Hill. [c.1960] 32p. 19cm. (Pendle Hill pamphlet 110) (Bibl.) 60-9785 .35 pap.,
1. Pacifism. I. Title.

GLUSTROM, Simon 296.38
Living with your teenager; a guide for Jewish parents. New York, Bloch Pub. Co., [c.]1961. 175p. Bibl. 61-9085 3.50
1. Adolescence. 2. Questions and answers—Jews. I. Title.

GOLDSTEIN, Herbert Samuel, 296.38
1890-
Between the lines of the Bible; a modern commentary on the 613 commandments. New York, Crown Publishers [1959] 349 p. 24 cm. [BM520.8.G6] 59-14036
1. Commandments, Six hundred and thirteen. I. Title.

GOLDSTEIN, Sidney Emanuel, 296.38
1879-1955.
The synagogue and social welfare, a unique experiment (1907-1953) New York, Published for Stephen Wise Free Synagogue and Hebrew Union College- Jewish Institute of Religion by Bloch, 1955. 376p. illus. 24cm. [BM225.N5S8] 55-7541
1. New York. Stephen Wise Free Synagogue. 2. Synagogues. 3. Sociology, Jewish. I. Title.

GORDIS, Robert, 1908- 296.38
The root and the branch, Judaism and the free society. [Chicago] Univ. of Chic. Pr. [c.1962] 254p. 23cm. Bibl. 62-17133 3.95
1. Judaism. 2. Sociology, Jewish. I. Title.

HOROWITZ, George. 296.38
The spirit of Jewish law; a brief account of Biblical and rabbinical jurisprudence, with a special note on Jewish law and the State of Israel. Foreword by David de Sola Pool. New York, Central Book Co., 1953. xi, 812p. 24cm. Bibliography: p. xxxiv-xxxvii, 747-749. 53-7535
1. Jewish law. 2. Law—Israel. I. Title.

KAPLAN, Mordecai Menahem, 296.3'8
1881-
The religion of ethical nationhood; Judaism's contribution to world peace, by Mordecai M. Kaplan. [New York] Macmillan [1970] x, 205 p. 21 cm. [BM565.K28] 75-96745
1. Judaism—20th century. I. Title.

KLAPPHOLZ, Kurt, 1913- 296.38
The power within us. [1st ed.] Brooklyn, Torah Institute [1961] 93p. 22cm. [BM723.K55] 61-17349
1. Jewish way of life. I. Title.

KOHN, Jacob, 1881- 296.38
The moral life of man, its philosophical foundations. New York, Philosophical Library [c1956] 252p. 22cm. Includes bibliography. [BJ1011.K6] 170 57-1600
1. Ethics bibliography. 2. Ethics. 3. Ethics. Jewish. I. Title.

KUTZIK, Alfred J 296.38
Social work and Jewish values: basic areas of consonance and conflict. Washington, Public Affairs Press [1959] 01p. 24cm. [BM729.S7K8] 59-10230
1. Sociology, Jewish. 2. Social service. I. Title.

LAMM, Norman, comp. 296.3'8
The good society: Jewish ethics in action. New York, Viking Press [1974] xv, 240 p. 22 cm. (The B'nai B'rith Jewish heritage classics) (UNESCO collection of representative works, Israel series) Bibliography: p. 229-233. [BJ1279.L35 1974] 73-12852 ISBN 0-670-34653-5 8.95

1. Ethics, Jewish—Addresses, essays, lectures. I. Title. II. Series: United Nations Educational, Scientific and Cultural Organization. Unesco collection of representative works: Israel series.

LEIBOWITZ, Jacob, 1901- 296.38
Religious guidance. New York, Philosophical Library [1958] 100p. 23cm. [BM723.L43] 58-14759
1. Ethics, Jewish. I. Title.

LEVIN, Meyer, 1905- 296.3'8
The story of the Jewish way of life [by] Meyer Levin [and] Toby K. Kurzband. Stephen Kraft, art editor; Harry Lazarus, illus. New York, Behrman House [1959] 192 p. illus. 25 cm. (The Jewish heritage series) [BM723.L47] 59-13487
1. Jewish way of life. I. Kurzband, Toby K., joint author.

MENDENHALL, George E *296.38
Law and covenant in Israel and the ancient Near East. Pittsburgh, Biblical Colloquium, 1955. 50p. illus. 24cm. 'Reprinted from the Biblical archaeologist. Vol. xvii. no. 2 (May, 1954). pp. 26-46 and no. 3 (September, 1954), pp. 49-76.' 57-23356
1. Jewish law—Hist. 2. Law—Near East—Hist. & crit. 3. Covenants (Theology) I. Title.

ORENSTEIN, Walter. 296.38
Torah as our guide; laws and customs for Jewish youth, by Walter Orenstein and Hertz Frankel. New York, Hebrew Pub. Co. [1960] 270p. 21cm. [BM723.O7] 60-4879
1. Jewish way of life. 2. Fasts and feasts—Judaism. I. Frankel, Hertz., joint author. II. Title.

PLAUT, W Gunther, 1912- 296.38
Judaism and the scientific spirit. New York, Union of American Hebrew Congregations [1962] 82p. 20cm. (Issues of faith) Includes bibliography. [BM538.S3P5] 61-17139
1. Religion and science—1946- I. Title.

RABINOWITZ, Jacob J 1928- 296.38
Jewish law: its influence on the development of legal institutions. New York, Bloch Pub. Co., 1956. xiv, 386p. 24cm. Bibliographical footnotes. 56-58985
1. Jewish law. I. Title.

RABINOWITZ, Jacob J 1928- 296.38
Jewish law: its influence on the development of legal institutions. New York, Bloch Pub. Co., 1956. xiv, 386p. 24cm. Bibliographical footnotes. 56-58985
1. Jewish law. I. Title.

LEVINTHAL, Israel 296.38081
Herbert, 1888-
Judaism speaks to the modern world. London, New York, Abelard-Schuman [1963] 191 p. 23 cm. (Ram's horn books) [BM740.2.L4] 63-18670
1. Sermons, Jewish—U.S. 2. Sermons, American—Jewish authors. I. Title.

SILVERMAN, William B *296.38 170
The still small voice; the story of Jewish ethics. New York, Behrman House [1956-57] 2 v. illus. 24 cm. Includes bibliography. [BJ1280.S5] 55-11143
1. Ethics, Jewish. I. Title.

ABRAHAM bar Hiyya, ha- 296.3'85
Nasi, 12thcent.
The meditation of the sad soul [by] Abraham bar Hayya. Translated and with an introd. by Geoffrey Wigoder. New York, Schocken Books [1969, c1968] 148 p. 23 cm. (The Littman library of Jewish civilization) Translation of Hegyon ha-nefesh (romanized form) "Works of Abraham bar Hayya". p. 33. Bibliography: p. 31-33. [BJ1287.A25H43 1969b] 68-21682 5.95
1. Ethics, Jewish. I. Wigoder, Geoffrey, 1922- tr. II. Title.

AGUS, Jacob Bernard, 296.385
1911-
The vision and the way; an interpretation of Jewish ethics [by] Jacob B. Agus. New York, Ungar [1966] ix, 365 p. 21 cm. Bibliographical footnotes. [BJ1280.A45] 66-25104
1. Ethics, Jewish. I. Title.

BERECHIAH ben Natronai, 296.3'85
ha-Nakdan, 12thcent.
The ethical treatises of Berachya. Edited by Hermann Gollancz. New York, Arno Press, 1973. lv, 361, ix, 153 p. facsim. 23 cm. (The Jewish people: history, religion, literature) Reprint of the 1902 ed. published by D. Nutt, London. The "Compendium" (Sefer ha-hibur) is transcribed from the codex Parma (482), and the "Masref" (Sefer ha-matsref) from the codex Munich (65) Includes bibliographical references. [BJ1287.B4E5 1973] 73-2187 ISBN 0-405-05253-7 25.00
1. Ethics, Jewish. I. Gollancz, Hermann, Sir, 1852-1930, ed. II. Munich. Bayerische Staatsbibliothek. MSS. (Hebr. 65) III. Parma. Biblioteca palatina. MSS. (Hebr. 482) IV. Berechiah ben Natronai, ha-Nakdan, 12th cent. Sefer ha-matsref. English & Hebrew. 1973. V. Title. VI. Series.

BERNFELD, Simon, 1860- 296.3'85
1940.
The foundations of Jewish ethics, being volume one of The teachings of Judaism. Authorized translation from the 2d, rev. and enl. German ed., by Armin Hajman Koller. Introd. by Samuel E. Karff. New York, Ktav Pub. House [1968] xxxiii, 265 p. 24 cm. Reprint of the 1929 ed. with new introd., added. Compiled by the author for the Union of German Jews (Germany). Bibliography: p. 236-245. [BJ1279.B43 1968] 67-30441
1. Ethics, Jewish. I. Koller, Armin Hajman, 1878- tr. II. Verband der deutschen Juden. III. Bernfeld, Simon, 1860-1940. Die Lehren des Jundentums. English. 1968. IV. Title.

BLIDSTEIN, Gerald J. 296.3'85
Honor thy father and mother : filial responsibility in Jewish law and ethics / by Gerald Blidstein. New York : Ktav Pub. House, 1975, c1976. xiv, 234 p. ; 24 cm. (The Library of Jewish law and ethics) Includes bibliographical references and index. [BM523.5.R4B55] 75-38808 ISBN 0-87068-251-2 : 15.00
1. Commandments, Ten—Parents. 2. Ethics, Jewish. 3. Parent and child (Jewish law) I. Title.

BOROWITZ, Eugene B. 296.3'85
Choosing a sex ethic; a Jewish inquiry [by] Eugene B. Borowitz. [New York] Published by Schocken Books for B'nai B'rith Hillel Foundations [1969] ix, 182 p. 21 cm. (Hillel library series) Bibliography: p. 175-182. [HQ32.B65] 73-79123 5.00
1. Sexual ethics. 2. Ethics, Jewish. I. B'nai B'rith Hillel Foundations. II. Title. III. Series.

BUCHLER, Adolf, 1867- 296.3'85
1939.
Studies in sin and atonement in the Rabbinic literature of the first century. With prefatory note by the Chief Rabbi. Prolegomenon by Frederick C. Grant. New York, Ktav Pub. House [1967] xxxix, 461 p. 24 cm. (Library of Biblical studies) [BM630.B8] 67-11903
1. Judaism — Hist. — Talmudic period. 2. Sin — Jewish Interpretations. 3. Atonement (Judaism) I. Title. II. Series.

BUCHLER, Adolf, 1867- 296.3'85
1939.
Studies in sin and atonement in the Rabbinic literature of the first century. With prefatory note by the Chief Rabbi. Prolegomenon by Frederick C. Grant. New York, Ktav Pub. House [1967] xxxix, 461 p. 24 cm. (Library of Biblical studies) [BM630.B8 1967] 67-11903
1. Judaism—History—Talmudic period, 10-425 2. Sin (Judaism) 3. Atonement (Judaism) I. Title. II. Series.

EPSTEIN, Louis M., 1887- 296.3'85
1949.
Sex laws and customs in Judaism. Introd. by Ari Kiev. New York, Ktav Pub. House [1968, c1967] xxii, 251 p. 24 cm. "Companion to an earlier work: Marriage laws in the Bible and the Talmud." Bibliography: p. [235]-246. [BM720.S4E6 1968] 67-22751
1. Sexual ethics. 2. Ethics, Jewish. I. Title.

FALAQUERA, Shem-Tob ben 296.3'85
Joseph, ca. 1225-ca. 1295.
The book of the Seeker = Sefer ha-Mebaqqesh / by Shem Tob ben Joseph ibn Falaquera ; translated and edited by M. Herschel Levine. New York : Yeshiva University Press, Dept. of Special Publications, 1976. xlvi, 118 p. ; 23 cm. (Studies in Judaica ; 7) Cover title: Falaquera's Book of the Seeker. Bibliography: p. 116-118. [BJ1287.F33M413] 76-5653 pbk. : 4.95
1. Ethics, Jewish. I. Levine, Herschel, 1922- II. Title. III. Series.

GREENBERG, Simon, 1901- 296.3'85
The ethical in the Jewish and American heritage / by Simon Greenberg. New York : Jewish Theological Seminary of America : distributed by Ktav Pub. House, 1977. p. cm. (Moreshet series ; v. 4) Includes indexes. Bibliography: p. [BJ1280.G73] 77-8481 ISBN 0-87334-002-7 : 15.00
1. Ethics, Jewish. 2. Law and ethics. 3. Law—United States—History and criticism. 4. Jewish law—Philosophy. I. Title. II. Series: Moreshet (New York) ; v. 4.

GREENBERG, Simon, 1901- 296.3'85
The ethical in the Jewish and American heritage / by Simon Greenberg. New York : Jewish Theological Seminary of America : distributed by Ktav Pub. House, 1977. p. cm. (Moreshet series ; v. 4) Includes indexes. Bibliography: p. [BJ1280.G73] 77-8481 ISBN 0-87334-002-7 : 15.00
1. Ethics, Jewish. 2. Law and ethics. 3. Law—United States—History and criticism. 4. Jewish law—Philosophy. I. Title. II. Series: Moreshet (New York) ; v. 4.

HEBREW ethical wills / 296.3'85
selected and edited and with an introd. by Israel Abrahams. Facsim. of original 1926 ed., two v. in one / new foreword by Judah Goldin. Philadelphia : Jewish Publication Society of America, 1976, c1954. 19, xxvi, 348, 348 p. ; 22 cm. (The JPS library of Jewish classics) English and Hebrew. 1926 ed. issued under Hebrew title: Tsava'ot ge'one Yisrael. Photoreprint ed. Opposite pages numbered in duplicate. Includes bibliographical references. [BJ1286.W59T69 1976] 76-2898 ISBN 0-8276-0081-X : 14.50 ISBN 0-8276-0082-8 pbk. : 8.50
1. Wills, Ethical—Collected works. I. Abrahams, Israel, 1858-1925. II. Series: Jewish Publication Society of America. The JPS library of Jewish classics.

HERFORD, Robert Travers, 296.3'85
1860-1950.
Talmud and Apocrypha; a comparative study of the Jewish ethical teaching in the rabbinical and non-rabbinical sources in the early centuries. New York, Ktav Pub. House, 1971. 323 p. 24 cm. "First published 1933." [BJ1281.H4 1971] 72-150532 ISBN 0-87068-158-3 10.00
1. Bible. O.T.—Ethics. 2. Ethics, Jewish. 3. Talmud—Ethics. I. Title.

INSTITUTE for Judaism 296.3'85
and Contemporary Thought.
Modern Jewish ethics, theory and practice / edited by Marvin Fox. Columbus : Ohio State University Press, [1975] xii, 262 p. ; 24 cm. Primarily papers presented at the 1972 meeting of the Institute. Includes bibliographical references and index. [BJ1279.I57 1975] 74-28395 ISBN 0-8142-0192-X : 14.50
1. Ethics, Jewish—Congresses. 2. Jewish law—Congresses. 3. Philosophy, Jewish—Congresses. I. Fox, Marvin, ed. II. Title.

ISAACS, Abram Samuel, 296.3'85
1852-1920.
A modern Hebrew poet; the life and writings of Moses Chaim Luzzatto. New York, Office of the Jewish Messenger,; 1878. 53p. 18cm. [PJ5051.L8Z72] 57-53532
1. Luzzatto, Moses Hayyim, I. Title.

JACOBS, Louis. 296.3'85
Jewish values. [2d ed.] Hartford, Conn., Hartmore House [1969, c1960] 160 p. 22 cm. Includes bibliographical references. [BM723.J3 1969] 75-103241 3.95
1. Jewish way of life. I. Title.

KAHN, Robert I. 296.3'85
The letter and the spirit, by Robert I. Kahn. Waco, Tex., Word Books [1972] 93 p. 23 cm. (Contemporary Biblical ethics) Includes bibliographical references. [BJ1280.K3] 72-84164 2.95
1. Ethics, Jewish. I. Title.

KAHN, Robert I. 296.3'85
The letter and the spirit, by Robert I. Kahn. Waco, Tex., Word Books [1972] 93 p. 23 cm. (Contemporary Biblical ethics) Includes bibliographical references. [BJ1280.K3] 72-84164 2.95
1. Ethics, Jewish. I. Title.

KLING, Simcha, comp. 296.3'85
A sense of duty. [Washington, B'nai B'rith Adult Jewish Education, 1969, c1968] xii, 115 p. 21 cm. (Jewish sources speak books) "A B'nai B'rith book." Contents.Contents.—Developing character. Text: from The rule of the Rosh.—Going beyond the law. Text: If not higher, by Y. L. Peretz.—Using reason. Text: from The guide for the perplexed, by M. Maimonides.—Visiting the sick. Text: from Talmud (Tractate Nedarim).—Educating children. Text: from Kitzur Shulhan Arukh.—Preserving life. Text: from Talmud (Tractate Yoma).—Loving the land. Text: from The Kuzari, by Yehudah Halevi.—Being true to the Jewish people. Text: from Slavery amidst freedom, by Ahad Ha-Am.—Prayer. Text: from The duties of hearts, by Bahya ibn Pakuda.—Study. Text: The Talmud student, H. N. Bialik.—Observing the Sabbath. Text: from Hok Leyisrael, by H. Vital.—Loving God. Text: from The path of the upright, by M. H. Luzzatto.—Further reading (p. [107]-111) [BJ1279.K55] 68-31849 3.50
1. Ethics, Jewish—Collections. 2. Judaism—Collections. I. Title.

MONTEFIORE, Claude 296.3'85
Joseph Goldsmid, 1858-1938.
Ancient Jewish and Greek encouragement and consolation. Pref. by S. D. Temkin. Bridgeport, Conn., Hartmore House [1973, c1971] iv, 86 p. 23 cm. First published in 1917 under title: Ancient Jewish and Greek encouragement and consolation in sorrow and calamity. Expansion of address delivered on July 9, 1916 to the annual meeting of the West London Synagogue Association. Includes bibliographical references. [BM729.C6M66 1971] 75-184052 7.95
1. Consolation (Judaism) 2. Consolation (Greek religion) 3. Philosophy, Ancient. I. Title.

MOSES ben Maimon, 1135- 296.3'85
1204.
Ethical writings of Maimonides / [translated] by Raymond L. Weiss, with Charles E. Butterworth. New York : New York University Press, 1975. x, 182 p. ; 23 cm. Contents.Contents.—Laws concerning character traits.—Eight chapters.—On the management of health.—Letter to Joseph.—Guide of the perplexed.—Treatise on the art of logic.—The days of the Messiah. Includes bibliographical references. [BJ1287.M62E5 1975] 74-18951 ISBN 0-8147-0984-2 : 14.00
1. Ethics, Jewish—Addresses, essays, lectures. 2. Messianic era (Judaism)—Addresses, essays, lectures. I. Title.

MOSES BEN MAIMON, 1135- 296.3'85
1204.
The degrees of Jewish benevolence. [By] Moses Maimonides and [by] Israel Ibn al-Nakawa. Introd. by Abraham Cronbach. [Cincinnati?] Society of Jewish Bibliophiles, 1964. [54] p. 27 cm. Selections from Maimonides' Mishneh Torah, in Hebrew and English, and from Al Nakawa's Menorat ha-ma'or. [BJ1286.C5M63] 68-5540
1. Charity. 2. Ethics, Jewish. I. Ainakawa, Israel ben Joseph, d. 1391. Menorat ha-ma'or. II. Title.

MOSES BEN MAIMON, 1135- 296.3'85
1204.
The degrees of Jewish benevolence. [By] Moses Maimonides and [by] Israel Ibn al-Nakawa. Introd. by Abraham Cronbach. [Cincinnati?] Society of Jewish Bibliophiles, 1964. [54] p. 27 cm. Selections from Maimonides' Mishneh Torah, in Hebrew and English, and from Al Nakawa's Menorat ha-ma'or. [BJ1286.C5M63] 68-5540
1. Charity. 2. Ethics, Jewish. I. Alnakawa, Israel ben Joseph, d. 1391. Menorat ha ma'or. English. 1964. II. Title.

ROSENTHAL GILBERT S. 296.3'85
Generations in crisis; Judaism's answers to the dilemmas of our time [by] Gilbert S. Rosenthal. New York, Bloch Pub. Co. [1969] ix, 255 p. 22 cm. Includes bibliographical references. [BJ1285.R58] 79-76231 5.95
1. Ethics, Jewish. I. Title.

WEINFELD, Abraham Chaim. 296.3'85
Basic Jewish ethics and freedom of will, by Abraham C. Weinfeld. New York, Block Pub. Co. [1968] 26 p. 22 cm. Bibliography: p. 23-26. [BJ1461.W4] 68-25871
1. Freewill and determinism. 2. Ethics, Jewish. I. Title.

WIGDER, Shabsie. 296.3'85
The challenge of eternity; reflections on our times in light of the M'silas yeshorim, by Shabsie Wigder and Shmuel Elchonen Brog. New York, 1968. 106 p. 23 cm. [BJ1287.L83M528] 72-170352
1. Luzzatto, Moses Hayyim, 1707-1747. Me'silat yesharim. 2. Ethics, Jewish. I. Brog, Shmuel Elchonen, joint author. II. Title.

ZERAHIAH, ha-Yewani, 296.3'85
14th cent.
Sefer hayashar: the Book of the righteous. Edited and translated by Seymour J. Cohen. New York, Ktav Pub. House, 1973. xx, 298 p. 24 cm. Half title: in Hebrew. English and Hebrew. Includes bibliographical references. [BJ1287.Z4S42] 72-5818 ISBN 0-87068-197-4 12.50
1. Ethics, Jewish. I. Title. II. Title: The Book of the righteous.

SILVER, Daniel 296.3'85'08
Jeremy, comp.
Judaism and ethics. [New York] Ktav Pub. House [1970] 338 p. 24 cm. Collection of essays from the CCAR journal. Contents.Contents.—Introduction, by D. J. Silver.—The issues: Some current trends in ethical theory, by A. Edel. Contemporary problems in ethics from a Jewish perspective, by H. Jonas. What is the contemporary problematic of ethics in Christianity? By J. M. Gustafson. Modern images of man, by J. N. Hartt. Is there a common Judaeo-Christian ethical tradition? By I. M. Blank. Problematics of Jewish ethics, by M. A. Meyer. Revealed morality and modern thought, by N. Samuelson.—The Jewish background: Does Torah mean law? By J. Neusner. Confrontation of Greek and Jewish ethics: Philo: De Decalogo, by S. Sandmel. Reprobation, prohibition, invalidity: an examination of the Halakhic development concerning intermarriage, by L. Silberman.

Death and burial in the Jewish tradition, by S. B. Freehof. God and the ethical impulse, by W. G. Plaut.—Social action: Civil disobedience and the Jewish tradition, by S. G. Broude. Religious responsibility for the social order: A Jewish view, by E. L. Fackenheim. Toward a theology for social action, by R. G. Hirsch. The mission of Israel and social action, by E. Lipman. Some cautionary remarks, by J. Kravetz.—The mission of Israel: On the theology of Jewish survival, by S. S. Schwarzchild. Meaning and purpose of Jewish survival, by A. Gilbert. Beyond the apologetics of mission, by D. J. Silver. Includes bibliographical references. [BJ1279.S55] 78-105307 10.00
1. Ethics, Jewish—Collections. 2. Judaism and social problems—Collections. I. Title.

DE FER, Hugo 296.3'87
Jewish ethics & Catholic doctrine. [1st ed. Albuquerque, N.M.] American Classical College Press [1972] 16, 9 l. 29 cm. (A Science of man research book, 2) [BM585.D43] 78-167699 ISBN 0-913314-08-0 4.00
1. Judaism—Controversial literature. 2. Social problems. I. Title.

INTERNATIONAL Symposium 296.3'87 on the Holocaust, Cathedral of St. John the Divine, 1974.
Auschwitz, beginning of a new era? : Reflections on the holocaust : papers given at the International Symposium on the Holocaust, held at the Cathedral of Saint John the Divine, New York City, June 3 to 6, 1974 / edited by Eva Fleischner. [New York] : Ktav Pub. Co., c1977. xix, 469 p. ; 23 cm. Includes bibliographical references. [BM645.H6I57 1974] 76-53809 ISBN 0-87068-499-X : 17.50
1. Holocaust (Jewish theology)—Congresses. 2. Christianity and antisemitism—Congresses. 3. Judaism—Relations—Christianity—Congresses. 4. Christianity and other religions—Judaism—Congresses. I. Fleischner, Eva, 1925- II. New York (City). Cathedral of St. John the Divine. III. Title.

INTERNATIONAL Symposium 296.3'87 on the Holocaust, Cathedral of St. John the Divine, 1974.
Auschwitz, beginning of a new era? : Reflections on the holocaust : papers given at the International Symposium on the Holocaust, held at the Cathedral of Saint John the Divine, New York City, June 3 to 6, 1974 / edited by Eva Fleischner. [New York] : Ktav Pub. Co., c1977. xix, 469 p. ; 23 cm. Includes bibliographical references. [BM645.H6I57 1974] 76-53809 ISBN 0-87068-499-X : 17.50
1. Holocaust (Jewish theology)—Congresses. 2. Christianity and antisemitism—Congresses. 3. Judaism—Relations—Christianity—Congresses. 4. Christianity and other religions—Judaism—Congresses. I. Fleischner, Eva, 1925- II. New York (City). Cathedral of St. John the Divine. III. Title.

NEUSNER, Jacob, 1932- 296.3'87 comp.
Contemporary Judaic fellowship in theory and in practice. New York, Ktav Pub. House, 1972 [i.e. 1973] xxxii, 270 p. 24 cm. Includes bibliographical references. [BM720.F4N38] 72-431 ISBN 0-87068-187-7 12.50
1. Fellowship (Judaism)—Addresses, essays, lectures. 2. Judaism—United States—Addresses, essays, lectures. I. Title.

CONFERENCE on American- 296.3'87'1 Jewish Dilemmas, New York, 1971.
Conference on American-Jewish dilemmas; papers delivered at the fifth Lerntag of the American Federation of Jews from Central Europe. Herbert A. Strauss, editor. New York, American Federation of Jews from Central Europe, 1971. 54 p. 22 cm. Includes bibliographical references. [BM205.C65 1971] 79-179335
1. Judaism—U.S.—Congresses. I. Strauss, Herbert Arthur, ed. II. American Federation of Jews from Central Europe.

AGUS, Jacob Bernard, 296.3'87'2 1911-
Dialogue and tradition; the challenges of contemporary Judeo-Christian thought. London, New York, Abelard-Schuman [1971] xvi, 621 p. 22 cm. (Ram's horn books) Includes bibliographical references. [BM45.A34] 67-13460 ISBN 0-200-71549-6 12.95 (U.S.)
1. Jews—History—Philosophy. 2. Judaism—Relations—Christianity—Addresses, essays, lectures. 3. Christianity and other religions—Judaism—Addresses, essays, lectures. 4. Tradition (Judaism)—Addresses, essays, lectures. I. Title.

BARTH, Markus. 296.3'87'2
Israel and the church; contribution to a dialogue vital for peace. Richmond, John Knox Press [1969] 125 p. 21 cm. (Research in theology) Includes bibliographical references. [BM535.B28] 77-85426 ISBN 0-8042-0650-3 3.95
1. Judaism—Relations—Christianity. 2. Christianity and other religions—Judaism. I. Title.

COHEN, Arthur Allen, 296.3'87'2 1928-
The myth of the Judeo-Christian tradition [by] Arthur A. Cohen. [1st ed.] New York, Harper & Row [1969, c1970] xx, 223 p. 22 cm. Bibliographical footnotes. [BM535.C6] 70-88635 7.50
1. Judaism—Relations—Christianity. 2. Christianity and other religions—Judaism. I. Title.

COHEN, Arthur Allen, 296.3'87'2 1928-
The myth of the Judeo-Christian tradition, and other dissenting essays [by] Arthur A. Cohen. New York, Schocken Books [1971] xx, 223 p. 21 cm. Includes bibliographical references. [BM535.C6 1971] 77-152766 ISBN 0-8052-0293-5 2.75
1. Judaism—Relations—Christianity. 2. Christianity and other religions—Judaism. I. Title.

COHON, Beryl David, 296.3'87'2 1898-
Men at the crossroads; between Jerusalem and Rome, Synagogue and Church: the lives, times, and doctrines of the founders of Talmudic Judaism and New Testament Christianity, by Beryl D. Cohon. South Brunswick [N.J.] T. Yoseloff [1970] 270 p. 22 cm. Includes bibliographical references. [BM176.C62 1970] 71-88255 ISBN 0-498-07339-4 7.50
1. Jesus Christ—Jewish interpretations. 2. Paul, Saint, apostle. 3. Judaism—History—Post-exilic period, 586 B.C.-210 A.D. 4. Judaism—Relations—Christianity. 5. Christianity and other religions—Judaism. I. Title.

DE CORNEILLE, Roland. 296.3872
Christians and Jews; the tragic past and the hopeful future. Postscript by Balfour Brickner. [1st ed.] New York, Harper & Row [1966] viii, 181 p. 21 cm. (Harper chapelbooks, CB30) Bibliography: p. 178-181. [BM535.D4] 66-9045
1. Christianity and other religions—Judaism. 2. Judaism—Relations—Christianity. I. Title.

DISPUTATION and 296.3'87'2 *dialogue* : readings in the Jewish-Christian encounter / edited by Frank Ephraim Talmage. New York : Ktav Pub. House, 1975. p. cm. Bibliography: p. [BM535.D53] 75-25590 ISBN 0-87068-284-9 : 15.00 pbk. : 5.95
1. Judaism—Relations—Christianity. 2. Christianity and other religions—Judaism. I. Talmage, Frank.

ECKARDT, Arthur Roy, 296.3'87'2 1918-
Elder and younger brothers; the encounter of Jews and Christians [by] A. Roy Eckardt. New York, Scribner [1967] xx,188 p. illus. 24 cm. Bibliography: p. 179-184. [BM535.E26] 67-23687
1. Christianity and other religions—Judaism. 2. Judaism—Relations—Christianity. 3. Christianity and antisemitism I. Title.

ECKARDT, Arthur Roy, 296.3'87'2 1918-
Elder and younger brothers; the encounter of Jews and Christians [by] A. Roy Eckardt. New York, Scribner [1967] xx, 188 p. illus. 24 cm. Bibliography: p. 179-184. [BM535.E26] 67-23687
1. Christianity and other religions—Judaism. 2. Judaism—Relations—Christianity. 3. Christianity and anti semitism. I. Title.

ECKARDT, Arthur Roy, 296.3'87'2 1918-
Elder and younger brothers; the encounter of Jews and Christians [by] A. Roy Eckardt. New York, Schocken Books [1973, c.1967] xx, 172 p. illus. 21 cm. (Schocken paperbacks, SB379) Bibliography: p. 163-168. [BM535.E26] ISBN 0-8052-0379-6 pap., 3.45
1. Christianity and other religions—Judaism. 2. Judaism—Relations—Christianity. 3. Christianity and antisemitism. I. Title.

EDELMAN, Lily. 296.3/87/2
Face to face, a primer in dialogue, ed. by Lily Edelman. [Washington B'nai B'rith Adult Jewish Educ. [1967] vi, 122p. 22cm. Special enl. "spring 1967 issue (volume 9, number 4) of Jewish heritage. Bibl. [BM535.E35] 67-26132 3.00
1. Judaism—Relations—Christianity. 2. Christianity and other religions—Juadism. I. Jewish heritage. II. Title.
Available from Crown, New York.

HARSHBARGER, Luther H. 296.3'87'2
Judaism and Christianity; perspectives and traditions [by] Luther H. Harshbarger [and] John A. Mourant. With a foreword by Benjamin Kahn. Boston, Allyn and Bacon [1968] xiii, 480 p. 24 cm. Includes bibliographies. [BM535.H33] 68-19520
1. Christianity and other religions—Judaism. 2. Judaism—Relations—Christianity. I. Mourant, John Arthur, 1903- joint author. II. Title.

JACOB, Walter, 1930- 296.3'87'2
Christianity through Jewish eyes : the quest for common ground / Walter Jacob. [New York] : Hebrew Union College Press, [1974] x, 284 p. ; 24 cm. Includes index. Bibliography: p. 239-250. [BM535.J25] 74-23451 ISBN 0-87068-257-1 : 12.50
1. Judaism—Relations—Christianity—History. 2. Christianity and other religions—Judaism—History. 3. Reform Judaism—History—Addresses, essays, lectures. I. Title.

JEWISH expressions on 296.3'87'2 *Jesus* : an anthology / selected with an introd. by Trude Weiss-Rosmarin. New York : Ktav Pub. House, 1977. xix, 421 p. ; 23 cm. Reprint from various sources, 1943-1973. Includes bibliographical references. [BM620.J48] 76-45387 ISBN 0-87068-470-1 : 17.50
1. Jesus Christ—Jewish interpretations—Addresses, essays, lectures. I. Weiss-Rosmarin, Trude, 1908-

JUDAISM and 296.3'87'2 *Christianity;* selected accounts, 1892-1962. Pref. and introd. by Jacob B. Agus. New York, Arno Press, 1973. 1 v. (various pagings) 24 cm. (The Jewish people: history, religion, literature) Collection of reprinted journal articles. Contents.Contents.—Abrahams, I. Professor Schurer on life under the Jewish law.—Cohon, S. S. The place of Jesus in the religious life of his day.—Friedlander, M. The "Pauline" emancipation from the law: a product of the pre-Christian Jewish diaspora.—Ginzberg, L. Some observations on the attitude of the synagogue towards the apocalyptic-eschatological writings.—Gudemann, M. Spirit and letter in Judaism and Christianity.—Krauss, S. The Jews in the works of the church fathers.—Montefiore, C. G. Notes on the religious value of the fourth Gospel.—Montefiore, C. G. Rabbinic Judaism and the Epistles of St. Paul.—Moore, G. F. Christian writers on Judaism.—Schechter, S. The law and recent criticism—a discourse on C. H. Toy's Judaism and Christianity, London, 1890.—Schechter, S. Some Rabbinic parallels to the New Testament.—Wolfson, H. A. How the Jews will reclaim Jesus. Includes bibliographical references. [BM535.J824] 73-2212 ISBN 0-405-05276-6 20.00
1. Judaism—Relations—Christianity—Addresses, essays, lectures. 2. Christianity and other religions—Judaism—Addresses, essays, lectures. 3. Judaism—Apologetic works—Addresses, essays, lectures. I. Arno Press. II. Title. III. Series.
Contents Omitted.

ROSENSTOCK-HUESSY, 296.3'87'2 Eugen, 1888-
Judaism despite Christianity; the letters on Christianity and Judaism between Eugen Rosenstock-Huessy and Franz Rosenzweig, edited by Eugen Rosenstock-Huessy. University, Ala., University of Alabama Press [1969] v, 198 p. port. 25 cm. Contents.Contents.—Introduction, by H. Stahmer.—About the correspondence; essays, by A. Altmann and D. M. Emmet.—Prologue/epilogue to the letters; fifty years later, by E. Rosenstock-Huessy.—The dialogue on Christianity and Judaism; [letters] (p. 77-170)—The epilogue, by E. Rosenstock-Huessy.—Hitler and Israel; or, On prayer, by E. Rosenstock-Huessy. Bibliographical footnotes. [BM535.R635] 68-10993 ISBN 8-17-366067- 7.00
1. Judaism—Relations—Christianity. 2. Christianity and other religions—Judaism. I. Rosenzweig, Franz, 1886-1929. II. Title.

SANDMEL, Samuel. 296.3'87'2
We Jews and you Christians; an inquiry into attitudes. [1st ed.] Philadelphia, Lippincott [1967] x, 146 p. 21 cm. [BM535.S22] 67-28282
1. Judaism—Relations—Christianity. 2. Christianity and other religions—Judaism. I. Title.

SPEAKING of God 296.3'87'2 *today;* Jews and Lutherans in conversation. Edited by Paul D. Opsahl [and] Marc H. Tanenbaum. Philadelphia, Fortress Press [1974] xiii, 178 p. 24 cm. Papers presented at colloquia sponsored by the Division of Theological Studies of the Lutheran Council in the U.S.A., and the Interreligious Affairs Department of the American Jewish Committee. Bibliography: p. [175]-178. [BM535.S684] 73-89083 ISBN 0-8006-0275-7 6.95
1. Lutheran Church—Relations—Judaism—Addresses, essays, lectures. 2. Judaism—Relations—Lutheran Church—Addresses, essays, lectures. I. Opsahl, Paul D., ed. II. Tanenbaum, Marc H., ed. III. Lutheran Council in the United States of America. Division of Theological Studies. IV. American Jewish Committee. Interreligious Affairs Dept.

SYMPOSIUM on Jewish- 296.3'87'2 Christian Relations and Education, Baylor University, 1971.
Jewish-Christian relations in today's world. Edited by James E. Wood, Jr. Waco, Tex., Markham Press Fund of Baylor University Press, 1971. 164 p. 24 cm. Includes six papers presented at the Symposium sponsored by the J. M. Dawson Studies in Church and State of Baylor University and the Anti-Defamation League of B'nai B'rith. "A selected and annotated bibliography on Jewish-Christian relations," by J. E. Wood, Jr.: p. [139]-162. [BM535.S88 1971] 74-185826 4.50
1. Christianity and other religions—Judaism—Congresses. 2. Judaism—Relations—Christianity—Congresses. I. Wood, James Edward, ed. II. Baylor University, Waco, Tex. J. M. Dawson Studies in Church and State. III. Anti-defamation League. IV. Title.

*UNWIN, James O. 296'.3'87'2
The future of religion. [First ed.] New York, Exposition Press [1973] 126 p. 21 cm. Bibliography: p. 125-126. [BM535] ISBN 0-682-47605-6. 4.50
1. Christianity and other relations—Judaism. 2. Judaism—Relations—Christianity. I. Title.

ZERIN, Edward 296.3'87'2
What Catholics should know about Jews, by Edward Zerin, Benedict Viviano. Ed. by Augustine Rock. Chicago, Priory Pr. [1967] 121 p. 19cm. Most of the material is adapted from the [first] author's bk. Our Jewish neighbors. Bibl. [BM580.Z45] 67-14011 .95 pap.,
1. Judaism—Juvenile literature. 2. Christianity and other religions—Judaism. I. Viviano, Benedict. II. Title.

ROTH, Sol. 296.3'87'5
Science and religion / by Sol Roth. New York : Yeshiva University, Dept. of Special Publications : selling agents, Bloch Pub. Co., 1967. 61 p. ; 23 cm. (Studies in Torah Judaism ; 10) Includes bibliographical references. [BM538.S3R67] 74-192545
1. Judaism and science. I. Title. II. Series.

KONVITZ, Milton 296.3'87'7 Ridvas, 1908- comp.
Judaism and human rights. Edited by Milton R. Konvitz. New York, W. W. Norton [1972] 315 p. 22 cm. (The B'nai B'rith Jewish heritage classics) Contents.Contents.—Born free and equal: Man's dignity in God's world, by M. R. Konvitz. Judaism and equality, by E. Rackman. A common humanity under one God, by W. A. Irwin. Many are called and many are chosen, by M. R. Konvitz.—The rule of law: The Bible and the rule of law, by Lord Acton. Kingship under the judgment of God, by H. Frankfort. The rule of a higher law, by W. A. Irwin.—The democratic ideal: Judaism and the democratic ideal, by M. R. Konvitz. Foundations of democracy in the Scriptures and Talmud, by L. R. Finkelstein. Democratic aspirations in Talmudic Judaism, by B. Z. Bokser.—Freedom of conscience: Conscience and civil disobedience, by M. R. Konvitz. Freedom of religion—absolute and inalienable, by M. Mendelssohn. The right of dissent and intellectual liberty, by R. Gordis.—Life, liberty, and the pursuit of happiness: The good life, by M. R. Konvitz. The right of privacy, by N. Lamm. There shall be no poor, by R. G. Hirsch.—The earth is the Lord's: Man as temporary tenant, by S. Belkin. Do not destroy! By S. R. Hirsch. Ecology and the Jewish Tradition, by E. G. Freudenstein.—Pursuit of peace: The vision of Micah, by R. Gordis. Bibliography: p. 307. [BM40.K62 1972] 70-139400 ISBN 0-393-04357-6 7.50
1. Civil rights (Jewish law)—Addresses, essays, lectures. 2. Judaism—Addresses, essays, lectures. I. Title.

SCHWEID, 296.3'87'7095694 Eliezer.
Israel at the crossroads. Translated from the Hebrew by Alton Meyer Winters. Philadelphia, Jewish Publication Society of America, 1973. ix, 221 p. 22 cm. Translation of 'Ad mashber. [BM390.S3813] 72-87911 ISBN 0-8276-0001-1 5.95
1. Judaism—Israel. 2. Israel and the Diaspora. 3. Zionism. I. Title.

ZUCKER, Norman 296.3'87'7095694 L.
The coming crisis in Israel; private faith and public policy [by] Norman L. Zucker, with the assistance of Naomi Flink Zucker. Cambridge, Mass., MIT Press [1973] xii, 282 p. illus. 22 cm. Bibliography: p. 259-270. [BM390.Z8] 73-987 ISBN 0-262-24018-1 10.00

1. Israel—Religion. 2. Judaism—Israel. 3. Religion and state—Israel. I. Title.

HIRSCH, Rabbi Richard G. 296.3878
There shall be no poor. Foreword by Hubert H. Humphrey. [New York, Pub. by Union of Amer. Hebrew Congregations for the] Commn. on Social Action of Reform Judaism [c.1965] x, 109p. illus. 18cm. (Issues of conscience 6) Bibl. [HN40.J5H52] 65-28948 .75 pap.,
1. Judaism and social problems. 2. Poor—U.S. I. Commission on Social Action of Reform Judaism. II. Title.

HIRSCH, Richard G 296.3878
Judaism and cities in crisis; unless the Lord keep the city. [New York], Commission on Social Action of Reform Judaism [1961] 103p. 18cm. (Issues of conscience, 5) Includes bibliography. [HN40.J5H5] 61-39837
1. Judaism and social problems. 2. Cities and towns—Civic improvement. I. Title.

HIRSCH, Richard G 296.3878
There shall be no poor, by Richard G. Hirsch. Foreword by Hubert H. Humphrey. [New York, Published by Union of American Hebrew Congregations for the] Commission on Social Action of Reform Judaism [1965] x, 134 p. illus. 18 cm. (Issues of conscience [6]) Bibliography: p. 123-127. [HN40.J5H52] 65-28948
1. Judaism and social problems. 2. Poor — U.S. I. Commission on Social Action of Reform Judaism. II. Title.

JACOBS, Louis. 296.3'87'8
What does Judaism say about ...? [New York] Quadrangle [1973] vi, 346 p. illus. 25 cm. (The New York times library of Jewish knowledge) Includes bibliographical references. [BM50.J3] 73-77032 ISBN 0-8129-0349-8 7.95
1. Judaism—Dictionaries. I. Title.

†KIMBALL, Spencer W., 1895- 296.3'87'8342
Marriage & divorce : an address / given by Spencer W. Kimball in the Marriott Center at Brigham Young University on September 7, 1976. Salt Lake City : Deseret 1976. 31 p. : ill. ; 24 cm. [HQ734.K482] 76-49802 ISBN 0-87747-635-7 pbk. : 2.95
1. Marriage. 2. Divorce. 3. Mormons and mormonism. I. Title.

OTWELL, John H. 296.3'87'83412
And Sarah laughed : the status of woman in the Old Testament / John H. Otwell. Philadelphia : Westminster Press, c1977. p. cm. Includes index. Bibliography: p. [BS1199.W7O88] 76-54671 ISBN 0-664-24126-3 pbk. : 7.95
1. Bible. O.T.—Criticism, interpretation, etc. 2. Woman (Theology)—Biblical teaching. I. Title.

PRIESAND, Sally. 296.3'87'83412
Judaism and the new woman / by Sally Priesand ; introd. by Bess Myerson. New York : Behrman House, c1975. xvi, 144 p. ; 19 cm. (The Jewish concepts and issues series) Bibliography: p. 135-139. [BM729.W6P74] 75-21951 ISBN 0-87441-230-7 pbk. : 2.45
1. Women in Judaism. 2. Women, Jewish. I. Title.

RUNES, Dagobert David, 1902- 296.3'87'8345296
Let my people live! : An indictment / by Dagobert D. Runes. New York : Philosophical Library, [1974] 73 p. ; 22 cm. [DS145.R853] 74-75083 ISBN 0-8022-2141-6 : 5.00
1. Antisemitism—Addresses, essays, lectures. I. Title.

SILVER, Samuel M 296.3'87'8342
Mixed marriage between Jew and Christian / Samuel M. Silver. New York : Arco Pub. Co., c1977. 107 p. ; 21 cm. [BM713.S5] 76-13004 ISBN 0-668-04046-7 lib. bdg. : 5.95. ISBN 0-668-04047-5 pbk. : 2.95
1. Marriage—Jews. 2. Marriage, Mixed. I. Title.

RYLANDER, John V. 296.3'87'87
The Middle-East crisis in perspective / John V. Rylander. Broadview, Ill. : Gibbs Pub. Co., [1974] x, 134 p. : ill. ; 23 cm. [DS119.7.R93] 73-94088 4.95
1. Bible—Prophecies—Jews. 2. Jewish-Arab relations. I. Title.

MILLER, Patrick D. 296.3'87'873
The divine warrior in early Israel [by] Patrick D. Miller, Jr. Cambridge, Mass., Harvard University Press, 1973. 279 p. 22 cm. (Harvard Semitic monographs, v. 5) Includes bibliographical references. [BS1199.W2M54] 73-81264 ISBN 0-674-21296-7 5.95
1. War—Biblical teaching. I. Title. II. Series.

ABRAHAMS, Israel, 1858-1925. 296.4
A companion to the Authorised daily prayerbook; historical and explanatory notes. New rev. ed. New York, Hermon Press; [sole distributors: Bloch Pub. Co., New York] 1966. 234 p. 19 cm. [BM660.A15 1966] 66-19765
1. Jews. Liturgy and ritual. Authorised daily prayer book. I. Title.

ABRAHAMS, Israel, 1858-1925 296.4
A companion to the Authorised daily prayerbook; historical and explanatory notes New rev. ed. New York, Hermon Pr., [dist. Bloch, c.1966. 234p. 19cm. [BM660.A15 1966] 66-19765 3.50
1. Jews. Liturgy and ruual. Authorised daily prayer book. I. Title.

ABRAMSON, Lillan S 296.4
Join us for the hoildays. Illustrated by Jessie B. Robinson. [n. p., National Women's League of the United Synagogue of America ,531958] 63p. illus. 29cm. [BM690.A2] 58-12940
1. Fasts and feasts—Judaism—Juvenile literature. I. Title.

ABRAMSON, Lillian S 296.4
Jeremy's and Judy's Hanukah. Story by Lillian S. Abramson. Pictures by Laszlo Matulay. New York, Behrman House [c1956] unpaged, illus. 21cm. (The Play-and-learn library) [BM695.H3A6] 57-27798
1. Hanukkah (Feast of Lights)—Juvenile literature. I. Title.

BATES, Barbara S. 296.4
Bible festivals and holy days [by] Barbara Bates. Illustrated by Don Fields. Nashville, Broadman Press [1968] viii, 118 p. illus. 21 cm. Bibliography: p. 117-118. Explains the origins of Jewish holy days or festivals and describes the religious ceremonies and celebrations that are performed in synagogue and home. [BM690.B28] AC 68
1. Fasts and feasts—Judaism. I. Fields, Don, illus. II. Title.

BIAL, Morrison David, 1917- 296.4
The Hanukkah story. Pictures by Stephen Kraft. New York, Behrman House [1952] unpaged. illus. 23cm. [BM695.H3B5] 52-14825
1. Hanukkah (Feast of Lights) I. Title.

BIAL, Morrison David, 1917- 296.4
The Passover story. Pictures by Stephen Kraft. New York, Behrman House [1952] unpaged. illus. 23cm. [BM695.P3B5] 52-14826
1. Passover. I. Title.

BLOOMFIELD, Arthur Edward, 1895- 296.4
Where is the Ark of the Covenant? / by Arthur E. Bloomfield. 2d ed., rev. and enl. Minneapolis : Bethany Fellowship, c1976. 76 p. ; 18 cm. (Dimension books) First ed. published in 1965 under title: The Ark of the Covenant. Bibliography: p. [73]-76. [BM657.A8B55 1976] 76-2257 ISBN 0-87123-004-6 pbk. : 0.95
1. Ark of the Covenant. 2. Bible—Prophecies—Jews. I. Title.

BRIN, Ruth (Firestone) 296.4
Interpretations for the weekly Torah reading [by] Ruth F. Brin. Introd. by Jerome Lipnick. Drawings by Sharon Lerner. Minneapolis, Lerner Publications Co. [1965] 165 p. illus. 23 cm. Torah selections and commentary on opposite pages. [BS1225.3.B7] 65-17099
1. Bible. O. T. Pentateuch — Commentaries. I. Bible O. T. Pentateuch, English. Selections. 1965 II. Title.

BRIN, Ruth (Firestone) 296.4
Interpretations for the weekly Torah reading. Introd. by Jerome Lipnick. Drawings by Sharon Lerner. Minneapolis, Lerner [c.1965] 165p. illus. 23cm. Torah selections and commentary on opposite pages [BS1225.3.B7] 65-17099 3.95
1. Bibl. O. T. Pentateuch—Commentaries. I. Bible O. T. Pentateuch. English. Selections. 1965. II. Title.

CEDARBAUM, Sophia N. 296.4
Rosh ha-Shono, Yom Kippur; the High Holy Days. Pictures by Clare and John Ross. [New York] Union of Amer. Hebrew Congregations [c.1961] 30p. col. illus. 61-9694 .59 bds.,
1. High Holy Days—Juvenile literature. I. Title.

CEDARBAUM, Sophia N. 296.4
Shovuos, the birthday of the Torah. Pictures by Clare and John Ross. [New York] Union of Amer. Hebrew Congregations [c.1961] 30p. col. illus. 61-9697 .59 bds.,
1. Shovu'oth (Feast of Weeks)—Juvenile literature. I. Title.

CEDARBAUM, Sophia N. 296.4
Sukos and Simchas Torah. festivals of thanksgiving. Pictures by Clare and John Ross. [New York] Union of Amer. Hebrew Congregations [c.1961] 30p. col. illus. 61-9696 .59 bds.,
1. Sukkoth—Juvenile literature. I. Title.

CENTRAL Conference of American Rabbis. 296.4
Rabbi's manual. Rev. ed. New York, 1961. 156p. 18cm. [BM676.C4 1961] 61-10418
1. Rabbis—Handbooks, manuals, etc. I. Title.

CHAVEL, Charles Ber, 1907- 296.4
Holidays and festivals; a descriptive account of the annual cycle of Jewish days of joy, with a summary of the principles of faith. Illustrated by Sigmund Forst. New York, Press of Shulsinger Bros. [1956] unpaged. illus. 22x29cm. [BM690.C46] 56-3053
1. Fasts and feasts—Judaism. I. Title.

CHERNOFF, Robert. 296.4
Aspects of Judaism / by Robert Chernoff. 1st ed. New York : Vantage Press, [1975] 63 p. ; 21 cm. [BM700.C46] 75-318020 ISBN 0-533-01430-1 : 4.50
1. Jews—Rites and ceremonies. I. Title.

COHEN, Lenore 296.4
Came liberty beyond our hope; a story of Hanukkah. Illus. by Georges Gaal. Los Angeles, Ritchie [c.1963] 44p. col. illus. 26cm. 63-18332 3.50 bds.,
1. Hanukkah (Feast of Lights)—Juvenile literature. I. Title.

COHEN, Lenore 296.4
Passover to freedm. Illus. by Lucille Brown Greene. [Los Angeles] Ritchie [1967] 90p. col. illus., cl. map. 26cm. Bibl. [BS1245.5.C6] 67-15077 3.95 3.79 lib. ed.,
1. Bible stories, English—O.T. Exodus. 2. Passover—Juvenile literature. I. Title.
Distributed by Golden Gate.

COHEN, Lenore. j 296.4
Passover to freedom. Illustrated by Lucille Brown Greene. [Los Angeles] W. Ritchie Press [1967] 90 p. col. illus., col. map. 26 cm. Bibliography: p. 85. [BS1245.5.C6] 67-15077
1. Bible stories, English — O. T. Exodus. 2. Passover — Juvenile literature. I. Title.

COHEN, Lenore. 296.4
Passover to freedom. Illustrated by Lucille Brown Greene. [Los Angeles] Ritchie Press [1967] 90 p. col. illus., col. map. 26 cm. Bibliography: p. 85. A retelling of the story of the Exodus when the faith of Moses enabled the Jewish people to escape the tyranny of Egypt to receive the Law in the Wilderness at Sinai. Includes a section on the celebration of Passover, the festival of freedom. [BS1245.5.C6] AC 67
1. Bible stories—O.T. Exodus. 2. Passover. I. Greene, Lucille Brown, illus. II. Title.

CONE, Molly 296.4
The Jewish New Year. Illus. by Jerome Snvder New York, Crowell [1966] 1v. (unpaged) col. illus. 23cm. (Crowell holiday bk.) [BM695.N5C6] 66-7314 2.95 bds.,
1. Rosh ha-Shanah—Juvenile literature. 2. Rosh ha-Shanah—Juvenile literature I. Title.

CONE, Molly 296.4
The Jewish Sabbath. Illus. by Ellen Raskin. New York, Crowell [c.1966] 1v. (unpaged) col. illus. 22cm. (Crowell holiday bk.) [BM685.C66] 65-27292 2.95
1. Sabbath—Juvenile literature. I. Title.

CONE, Molly. 296.4
Purim. Illustrated by Helen Borten. New York, Crowell [1967] [40] p. illus. (part col.) 22 cm. (A Crowell holiday book) The story and customs of the gayest of Jewish holidays which celebrate how Queen Esther saved her people from the wicked Haman. [GT4995.P8C65] AC 67
1. Purim (Feast of Esther) 2. Fasts and feasts—Judaism. I. Borten, Helen, illus. II. Title.

CONE, Molly. j 296.4
Stories of Jewish symbols. Design and illus.: Siegmund Forst. New York, Bloch Pub. Co. [1963] 80 p. illus. 27 cm. Bibliography: p. 80. [BM657.A1C6] 63-22019
1. Cultus, Jewish — Juvenile literature. I. Title. II. Title: Jewish symbols.

CONE, Molly 296.4
Stories of Jewish symbols. Design, Illus.: Siegmund Forst. New York, Bloch [c.1963] 80p. illus. (pt. col.) 27cm. Bibl. 63-22019 3.50 bds.,
1. Cultus, Jewish—Juvenile literature. I. Title. II. Title: Jewish symbols.

DEMBITZ, Lewis Naphtali, 1833-1907. 296.4
Jewish services in synagogue and home / by Lewis N. Dembitz. New York : Arno Press, 1975, [c1898] 487 p. : ill. ; 22 cm. (The Modern Jewish experience) Reprint of the ed. published by the Jewish Publication Society of America, Philadelphia. Includes bibliographical references and indexes. [BM660.D45 1975] 74-27977 ISBN 0-405-06706-2 : 30.00
1. Jews. Liturgy and ritual. I. Title. II. Series.

DONIN, Hayim. 296.4
To be a Jew; a guide to Jewish observance in contemporary life. Selected and compiled from the Shulhan arukh and Responsa literature, and providing a rationale for the laws and the traditions [by] Hayim Halevy Donin. New York, Basic Books [1972] xv, 336 p. 25 cm. Includes bibliographical references. [BM700.D58] 72-89175 ISBN 0-465-08624-1 10.00
1. Jews—Rites and ceremonies. 2. Jewish way of life. I. Title.

DOPPELT, Frederic Aubrey. 296.4
A guide for Reform Jews, by Frederic A. Deppelt and David Polish. New York, Bloch Pub. Co., 1957. viii, 118p. 19cm. Bibliography: p. 118. [BM700.D6] 57-7766
1. Jews—Rites and ceremonies. 2. Reform Judaism. I. Polish, David, joint author. II. Title.

DOPPELT, Frederic Aubrey. 296.4
A guide for Reform Jews, by Frederic A. Doppelt and David Polish. Rev. ed., by David Polish. New York, Ktav Pub. House [1974, c1973] 124 p. 22 cm. Bibliography: p. 124. [BM700.D6 1974] 73-20243 ISBN 0-87068-237-7 2.50 (pbk.).
1. Reform Judaism—Ceremonies and practices. I. Polish, David, joint author. II. Title.

EFRON, Benjamin 296.4
Pathways through the prayerbook. Prayer translations by Samuel M. Silver. Illus. by Uri Shulevitz. [New York] KTAV [c.1962] 136p. illus. 27cm. Includes selections from the Jewish liturgy in Hebrew and English. 62-11407 2.50 bds.,
1. Jews. Liturgy and ritual. I. Title.

EISENBERG, Azriel Louis, 1903- ed. 296.4
The Confirmation reader. New York, Behrman House [c1953] 258p. 21cm. [BM570.E35] 53-11401
1. Confirmation (Jewish rite.)-Instruction and study. 2. Judaism-Study and teaching. I. Title.

EPSTEIN, Morris, 1922- 296.4
All about Jewish holidays and customs. Illustrated by Arnold Lobel. Rev. ed. [New York] Ktav Pub. House [1969, c1970] 142 p. illus. 26 cm. Bibliography: p. 134-135. Describes and gives the background of traditional Jewish holidays, customs, and symbols. [BM690.E64 1970] 71-106522 ISBN 0-87068-500-7
1. Jews—Rites and ceremonies—Juvenile literature. 2. Fasts and feasts—Judaism—Juvenile literature. I. Title.

EPSTEIN, Morris, 1922- 296.4
My holiday storybook; illustrated by Sigmund Forst. New York, KTAV Pub. House [1952] 54 p. illus. 26 cm. [BM690.E65] 53-15943
1. Fasts and feasts—Judaism—Juvenile literature. I. Title.

EPSTEIN, Morris, 1922- 296.4
A pictorial treasury of Jewish holidays and customs. New York, Ktav Pub. House [1959] 200 p. illus. 29 cm. [BM52.E65] 59-15662
1. Judaism—Pictures, illustrations, etc. 2. Jews—Rites and ceremonies. I. Title.

FISCHMAN, Joyce 296.4
Holiday work and play, written, illus. by Joyce Fischman. [New York Union of Amer. Hebrew Congregations [c.1961] 60p. illus. (pt. col.) 28cm. (Union graded ser.) 61-13968 .75 pap.,
1. Fasts and feasts—Judaism—Juvenile literature. I. Title.

FREEHOF, Solomon Bennett, 1892- 296.4
In the house of the Lord; our worship and our prayer book. New York, Union of American Hebrew Congregations ['1951] 162 p. illus. 21 cm. (Commission on Jewish Education of the Union of American Hebrew Congregations and Central Conference of American Rabbis. Union graded series) [BM669.F68 1951] 52-25580
1. Jews. Liturgy and ritual. I. Title.

GAMORAN, Mamie (Goldsmith) 296.4
Days and ways; the story of Jewish holidays and customs. Illustrated by Bernard Segal. Rev. ed. New York, Union of American Hebrew Congregations [1956, c1941] 205p. illus. 23cm. (Commission on Jewish Education of the Union of American Hebrew Congregations and Central Conference of American Rabbis. Union graded series) [BM690.G3 1956] 57-17477
1. Fasts and feasts—Judaism. 2. Jews —Soc. life & cust. I. Title.

GAMORAN, Mamie (Goldsmith) 296.4
Hillel's happy holidays. Illustrated by Temima N. Gezari. New ed. New York, Union of American Hebrew Congregations [1955] 219p. illus. 23cm. (Commission on Jewish Education

of the Union of American Hebrew Congregations and Central Conference of American Rabbis. Union graded series) [BM690.G313 1955] 57-20948
1. Fasts and feasts—Judaism—Juvenile literature. I. Title.

[GANZFRIED, Solomon] 1804- 296.4
1886.
The Jew and his duties: the essence of the Kitzur Shulhan arukh, ethically presented by Hyman E. Goldin. New York, Hebrew Pub. Co. [1953] 246p. 22cm. [BM560.G322 1953] 53-4104
1. Judaism. I. Goldin, Hyman Elias, 1881- ed. and tr. II. Title.

GARVEY, Robert. 296.4
The first book of Jewish holidays. Pictures by Sam Weiss; designed by Ezekiel Schloss. [New York] Ktav Pub. House [1954] unpaged. illus. 22x28cm. [BM690.G32] 54-12835
1. Fasts and feasts—Judalsm—Juvenile literature. I. Title.

GARVEY, Robert. 296.4
When it's Passover. Pictures by Laszlo Matulay. [New York] Ktav Pub. House [1954] unpaged. illus. 22cm. (A Two-in-one holiday book) Bound with the author's When it's Purim. [New York, 1954] [BM695.P3G33] 54-1800
1. Passover. I. Title.

GARVEY, Robert. 296.4
When it's Purim. Pictures by Laszlo Matulay. [New York] Ktav Pub. House [1954] unpaged. illus. 22cm. (A Two-in-one holiday book) Bound with the author's When it's Passover. [New York, 1954] [BM695.P3G33] 54-1853
1. Purim (Feast of Esther) I. Title.

GASTER, Theodor Herzl, 296.4
1906-
Festivals of the Jewish year; a modern interpretation and guide. New York, Sloane [1953] 308p. 22cm. Includes bibliography. [BM690.G33] 53-9341
1. Fasts and feasts—Judaism. I. Title.

GASTER, Theodor Herzl, 296.4
1906-
Festivals of the Jewish year a modern interpretation and guide. New York, Apollo Eds. [1961, c.1952, 1953] 308p. (A-28) Bibl. 1.95 pap.,
1. Fasts and feasts—Judaism. I. Title.

GASTER, Theodor Herzl, 296.4
1906-
Festivals of the Jewish year; a modern interpretation and guide. [Gloucester, Mass., Peter Smith, 1962, c.1952, 1953] 308 p. (Sloane bk. rebound) Bibl. 3.75
1. Fasts and feasts—Judaism. I. Title.

GILBERT, Arthur. 296.4
Your neighbor celebrates, by Arthur Gilbert and Oscar Tarcov. Foreword by James A. Pike. Book design by Ezekiel Schloss. New York, Friendly House Publishers [1957] 118 p. illus. 27 cm. [BM690.G5] 57-11732
1. Fasts and feasts—Judaism. I. Tarcov, Oscar, joint author. II. Title.

GLATZER, Nahum Norbert, 296.4
1903- comp.
Language of faith; a selection from the most expressive Jewish prayers. Gathered and edited by Nahum N. Glatzer. English-language ed. New York, Schocken Books [1975, c1974] 126 p. 21 cm. Includes bibliographical references. [BM724.G5 1975] 74-9142 ISBN 0-8052-3559-0 4.95
1. Jewish prayers. I. Title.

GLATZER, Nahum Norbert, 296.4
1903- comp.
Language of faith: a selection from the most expressive Jewish prayers. Original text & new English verse translations. Gathered and edited by Nahum N. Glatzer. New York, Schocken Books [1967] 335 p. 24 cm. English and Hebrew, Aramaic or Yiddish. Bibliographical references included in "Notes": (p. 321-332) [BM724.G5 1967] 65-14823
1. Jewish prayers. I. Title.

GOLDBERG, David, 1886- 296.4
Holidays for American Judaism. Explanatory notes by Samuel Halevi Baron. Illustrated by Patricia Passloff. New York, Bookman Associates [c1954] 182p. illus. 23cm. [BM690.G52] 55-486
1. Fasts and feasts—Judaism. I. Title.

GRAY, George Buchanan, 296.4
1865-1922.
Sacrifice in the Old Testament; its theory and practice. Prolegomenon by Baruch A. Levine. New York, Ktav Pub. House, 1971. liii, 434 p. 23 cm. (The Library of biblical studies) Reprint of the 1925 ed. [BS680.S2G7 1971] 72-105753 ISBN 0-87068-048-X
1. Sacrifice (Judaism) 2. Priests, Jewish. 3. Fasts and feasts—Judaism. I. Title. II. Series.

GREEN, Alan Singer, 1907- 296.4
Return to prayer: home and student devotions for Sabbath, every day, and special occasions; a complete starter set on the road back to prayer: interpretation, Hebrew, English, music. By Alan S. Green. New York, Union of American Hebrew Congregations [1971] x, 83 p. illus., music. 26 cm. [BM675.B4G74] 78-103980
1. Jews. Liturgy and ritual. Benedictions. 2. Jews—Prayer-books and devotions. I. Title.

HARRELSON, Walter J. 296.4
From fertility cult to worship [by] Walter Harrelson. [1st ed.] Garden City, N.Y., Doubleday, 1969. xv, 171 p. 22 cm. Six of the eight chapters included were presented as the Haskell lectures at the Graduate School of Theology, Oberlin College, in 1965. Bibliography: p. [157]-163. [BM656.H3] 66-14929 4.95
1. Worship (Judaism) I. Title.

HEINEMANN, Joseph. 296.4
Prayer in the Talmud : forms and patterns / by Joseph Heinemann. Berlin ; New York : de Gruyter, 1977. x, 320 p. : ill. ; 24 cm. (Studia judaica ; Bd. 9) A revision of the work originally published in Hebrew under title: ha-Tefilah bi-tekufat ha-Tana'im veha-Amora'im. Includes indexes. Bibliography: [302]-304. [BM660.H4613 1977] 77-1906 ISBN 3-11-004289-4 : 42.70
1. Jews. Liturgy and ritual—History. 2. Prayer (Judaism) 3. Rabbinical literature—History and criticism. I. Title. II. Series.

HERBERT, A S 296.4
Worship in ancient Israel. Richmond, John Knox Press [1959] 51p. 22cm. (Ecumenical studies in worship, no. 5) [BM658.H4] 59-8911
1. Worship. 2. Cultus, Jewish. I. Title.

HESCHEL, Abraham Joshua, 296.4
1907-
Man's quest for God; studies in prayer and symbolism. New York, Scribners [1966, c.1954] xiv, 151p. 21cm. (Scribner lib., SL127) Bibl. [BM669] 66-6070 ISBN CD 1.45 pap.,
1. Prayer (Judaism) 2. Jewish art and symbolism. I. Title.

ISH-KISHOR, Sulamith. j296.4
Pathways through the Jewish holidays. Edited by Benjamin Efron. [New York] Ktav Pub. House [1967] 144 p. illus. 26 cm. [BM690.I8] 67-18815
1. Fasts and feasts — Judaism — Juvenile literature. I. Title.

ISH-KISHOR, Sulamith. 296.4
Pathways through the Jewish holidays. Edited by Benjamin Efron. [New York] KTAV Pub. House [1967] 144 p. illus. 26 cm. An illustrated survey of the Jewish holidays, their history, practice, and celebration in the United States and Israel. [BM690.I8] AC 67
1. Fasts and feasts—Judaism. I. Title.

JEWISH life in art and 296.4
tradition : based on the collection of the Sir Isaac and Lady Edith Wolfson Museum, Hechal Shlomo, Jerusalem / Yehuda L. Bialer, Estelle Fink ; photos. by David Harris. 1st American ed. New York : Putnam, 1976. 189 p. : ill. (some col.) ; 26 cm. [BM657.A1J48 1976] 75-33424 ISBN 0-399-11695-8 : 16.95
1. Muze'on 'al shem Sir Aizik ve-Leidi Volfson be-Hekhal Shelomoh. 2. Liturgical objects—Judaism—Pictorial works. 3. Jews—Rites and ceremonies. I. Bialer, Judah Loeb. II. Fink, Estelle. III. Muze'on 'al shem Sir Aizik ve-Leidi Volfson be-Hekhal Shelomoh.

JEWISH life in art and 296.4
tradition : based on the collection of the Sir Isaac and Lady Edith Wolfson Museum, Hechal Shlomo, Jerusalem / Yehuda L. Bialer, Estelle Fink ; photos. by David Harris. London : Published for Hechal Shlomo by Weidenfeld and Nicolson, c1976. 189 p. : ill. (some col.) ; 26 cm. [BM657.A1J48] 76-365761 ISBN 0-297-77092-6 : £12.50
1. Liturgical objects—Judaism—Pictorial works. 2. Jews—Rites and ceremonies. 3. Muze'on 'al shem Sir Aizik ve-Leidi Volfson be-Hekhal Shelomoh. I. Bialer, Judah Loeb. II. Fink, Estelle. III. Muze'on 'al shem Sir Aizik ve-Leidi Volfson be-Hekhal Shelomoh.

JEWS. Liturgy and ritual. 296.4
High Holy Day prayers.
High Holy Day prayer book, for the Jewish personnel in the Armed Forces of the United States. [Prepared by the Commission of Jewish Chaplaincy of the National Jewish Welfare Board. New York, 1969] viii, 567 p. 13 cm. Hebrew and English. [BM667.S6A65 1969] 76-83977
1. Armed Forces—Prayer-books and devotions—Hebrew. 2. Armed Forces—Prayer-books and devotions—English. I. National Jewish Welfare Board. Commission on Jewish Chaplaincy. II. Jews. Liturgy and ritual. High Holy Day prayers. English.

JEWS. Liturgy and ritual. 296.4
Daily prayers.
[Sidur tefilot Yisrael (romanized form)] The Hirsch Siddur; the order of prayers for the whole year. Translation and commentary by Samson Raphael Hirsch. Jerusalem, New York, Feldheim, 1969. 752 p. 24 cm. Hirsch's German translation of and commentary on the prayers translated into English by the staff of the Samson Raphael Hirsch Publications Society. [BM675.D3H513] 69-20378
1. Jews. Liturgy and ritual. Daily prayers—Commentaries. I. Hirsch, Samson Raphael, 1808-1888. II. Jews. Liturgy and ritual. Daily prayers. English. 1969. III. Title: The Hirsch Siddur.

JEWS. Liturgy and ritual. 296.4
Benedictions.
Blessed art Thou, a treasury of prayers. Blessing and prayers for all occasions, with explanations and instructions. Hebrew, English translation and transliteration. Translated and arr. by Alex J. Goldman. New York, Hebrew Pub. Co. [1961] 68p. 26cm. [BM675.B4G613] 61-57614
I. Jews. Liturgy and ritual. Benedictions. English. II. Goldman, Alex J., ed. and tr. III. Title.

JEWS. Liturgy and ritual. 296.4
Children's services.
A prayer book for Jewish children. Text prepd. by Abraham Shusterman. Baltimore [1966] 87p. 21cm. [BM666.S46] 66-3129 3.95
I. Shusterman, Abraham, ed. II. Title.
Available from Har Sinai Congregation, 6300 Park Heights Ave., Baltimore, Md., 21215.

JEWS. Liturgy and ritual. 296.4
Daily prayers.
Prayer book for Jewish personnel in the Armed Forces of the United States. [New York? 1958] 470p. 13cm. 'Prepared by the Commission on Jewish Chaplaincy of the National Jewish Welfare Board.' Hebrew and English. [BM667.S6A6] 58-11572
1. Soldiers—Prayer-books and devotions—Hebrew. I. National Jewish Welfare board II. Title.

JEWS. Liturgy and ritual. 296.4
Haggadah. 1967.
The family Seder; a traditional Passover Haggadah for the modern home. Prepared by Alfred J. Kolatch. New York, J. David [1967] 124 p. illus. (part col.), port. 22 cm. English and Hebrew. [BM675.P4K64] 67-17778
1. Jews. Liturgy and ritual. Haggadah. English. 1967. I. Kolatch, Alfred J., 1916- ed. II. Title.

JEWS. Liturgy and ritual. 296.4
Mourners' prayers.
Not forgotten. New York, Hebrew Pub. Co. [1953] unpaged. 16cm. English and Hebrew. [BM675.M7H4] 53-39557
I. Jews. Liturgy and ritual. Mourners' prayers. English. II. Title.

JEWS. Liturgy and ritual. 296.4
Sabbath prayers.
The traditional prayer book for Sabbath and festivals. Edited and translated by David de Sola Pool. Authorized by the Rabbinical Council of America. New Hyde Park, N.Y., University Books by arrangement with Behrman House (New York) [c.1960] xvi, 879p. 27cm. 60-15311 until December 30, 12.50; afterwards, 17.50, bxd.
I. Jews. Liturgy and ritual. Sabbath prayers. English. II. Jews. Liturgy and ritual. Festival prayers. III. Jews. Liturgy and ritual. Festival prayers. English. IV. Pool, David de Sola, ed. and tr. V. Rabbinical Council of America. VI. Title.

JEWS. Liturgy and ritual 296.4
selections.
An introduction to prayers and holidays for the student. By Norman Schanin [designed by Ezekiel Schloss, New York] KTAV Pub. House [c.1960] 177p. col. illus. 27cm. Vocalized text. Hebrew and English. 1.95 bds.,
1. Children—Prayerbooks and Decorations—English. 2. Jews—Prayer-books and decorations—English. 3. Fasts and feasts—Judaism. I. Schanin, Norman. II. Title.

JOSPE, Alfred, 1909- comp. 296.4
Bridges to a holy time; new worship for the Sabbath and minor festivals. Edited by Alfred Jospe and Richard N. Levy. New York, Ktav Pub. House, 1973. 346 p. 22 cm. Includes some selections in Hebrew. Includes bibliographical references. [BM665.J67] 73-6095 ISBN 0-87068-226-1 4.00
I. Jews Liturgy and ritual. II. Levy, Richard N., joint comp. III. Title.

KADUSHIN, Max, 1895- 296.4
Worship and ethics, a study in rabbinic Judaism. [Evanston, Ill.] Northwestern University Press, 1964 [c1963] x, 329 p. 23 cm. Bibliographical references included in "Notes" (p. 239-305) [BM656.K3] 63-10586
1. Worship (Judaism) 2. Jewish way of life. I. Title.

KANOF, Abram, 1903- 296.4
Jewish ceremonial art and religious observance. New York, Abrams [1970] 253 p. 270 illus. (25 col.) 30 cm. Includes bibliographical references. [NK1672.K34] 69-12798
1. Jewish art and symbolism. I. Title.

KARP, Abraham J. 296.4
The Jewish way of life. Englewood Cliffs, N.J., Prentice [c.1962] 208p. 21cm. Bibl. 62-18281 3.95 bds.,
1. Jewish way of life. I. Title.

KATSH, Abraham Isaac, 1908- 296.4
ed.
Bar Mitzvah illustrated. New York City, Schengold Publishers [1955] 157p. illus. 29cm. [BM707.K28] 55-33815
1. Bar Mitzvah. 2. Judaism. I. Title.

KLAPERMAN, Libby M 296.4
Jeremy and the Torah. Story by Libby M. Klaperman. Pictures by Erika Weihs. New York, Behrman House [c1956] unpaged. illus. 21cm. (The Play-and-learn library) [BM573.K56] 57-31391
1. Judaism—Juvenile literature. I. Title.

KOLATCH, Mollie. 296.4
Sabbath is special. Story by Mollie Kolatch. Pictures by Evelyn Urbanowich. New York, Behrman House [c1956] unpaged. illus. 21cm. (The Play-and-learn library) [BM685.K6] 57-1543
1. Sabbath—Juvenile literature. I. Title.

KRAUS, Hans Joachim. 296.4
Worship in Israel; a cultic history of the Old Testament. Translated by Geoffrey Buswell. Richmond, John Knox Press [1966] xi, 246 p. 23 cm. Bibliographical footnotes. [BM656.K713] 65-16432
1. Worship (Judaism) I. Title.

KRAUS, Hans Joachim. 296.4
Worship in Israel: a cultic history of the Old Testament: translated [from the revised German ed.] by Geoffrey Buswell. Oxford, Blackwell, 1966. xi, 246 p. 23 cm. (B66-9307) Originally published as Gottesdienst in Israel. Munich, Kaiser Verlag, 1962. [BM656.K713] 66-72621
1. Worship (Judaism) I. Title.

KRAUS. HANS JOACHIM 296.4
Worship in Israel: a cultic history of the Old Testament Tr. [from German]4 by Geoffrey Buswell. Richmond. Va., Knox [c.1966] xi, 246p. 23cm. Bibl. [BM656.K713] 65-16432 6.00
1. Worship (Judaism) I. Title.

LEIDERMAN, Lillian T 296.4
Jewish holiday party book; a practical guide for mother and teacher, planned for children ages 5 to 12, by Lillian T. Leiderman and Lillian S. Abramson. New York, Bloch Pub. Co., 1954. 72 p. illus. 25 cm. [BM690.L35] 54-11436
1. Fasts and feasts—Judaism. I. Abramson, Lillian S., joint author. II. Title.

LEIDERMAN, Lillian T. 296.4
Jewish holiday party book; a practical guide to parties planned for children ages 5 to 12, by Lillian T. Leiderman, Lillian S. Abramson. [2nd rev. ed.] New York, Bloch 1966. 72p. illus. 25cm. In 2nd rev. ed. authors names are in reverse order. [BM690.L35] 54-11436 3.50 bds.,
1. Fasts and feasts—Judaism. I. Abramson, Lillian S., joint author. II. Title.

LEVI, Shonie B. 296.4
Across the threshold; a guide for the Jewish homemaker, by Shonie B. Levi & Sylvia R. Kaplan. New York, Farrar, Straus & Cudahy [1959] 258 p. illus. 22 cm. Includes bibliography. [BM726.L42] 59-12039
1. Women, Jewish—Religious life. 2. Jews—Social life and customs. 3. Jews—Rites and ceremonies. I. Kaplan, Sylvia R., joint author. II. Title.

*LEVI, Shonie B. 296.4
Guide for the Jewish homemaker [by] Shonie B. Levi, Sylvia R. Kaplan [2d rev. ed.] New York, Schocken [c.1959, 1964] 256p. illus. 21cm. First pub. in 1959 by Farrar under title: Across the threshold; a guide for the Jewish homemaker. (SB87) Bibl. 1.95 pap.,
1. Women, Jewish—Religious life. 2. Jews—Soc. life & cust. 3. Jews—Rites and ceremonies. I. Kaplan, Sylvia R., joint author. II. Title.

MANN, Jacob, 1888-1940. 296.4
The Bible as read and preached in the old synagogue; a study in the cycles of the readings from Torah and Prophets, as well as from Psalms, and in the structure of the Midrashic homilies. New York, Ktav Pub. House, 1971- v. 23 cm. (The Library of Biblical studies) English or Hebrew. Reprint of the 1940 ed. with a new prolegomenon by Ben Zion Wacholder. Contents.Contents.—v. 1. The Palestinian triennial cycle: Genesis and Exodus, with a Hebrew section containing manuscript material of Midrashim to these books. Includes bibliographical references. [BM663.M26] 70-105755 ISBN 0-87068-083-8
1. Jews. Liturgy and ritual. 2. Bible. O.T.—Liturgical use. 3. Midrash. 4. Preaching, Jewish. I. Title. II. Series.

MANSOOR, Menahem, ed. and tr. 296.4
Thanksgiving scroll. English. Grand Rapids, Eerdmans, 1961. xi, 227 p. 25 cm. (Studies on the texts of the desert of Judah, v. 3) Bibliography: p. [197]-208. [BM488.T5A3 1961] 61-1542
I. Title. II. Title: The Thanksgiving hymns.

MARTIN, Bernard, 1928- 296.4
Prayer in Judaism. New York, Basic Books [1968] xiii, 270 p. 25 cm. Translation of some fifty Jewish prayers. Each prayer is accompained by a commentary. Includes bibliographies. [BM669.M353] 68-54150 7.50
1. Jews. Liturgy and ritual. Sabbath prayers. 2. Jews. Liturgy and ritual. High Holy Day prayers. 3. Bible. O.T. Psalms—Liturgical use. I. Title.

MAXIMON, Saadyah. 296.4
The book of Hanukkah, the story of the Maccabees; a saga of heroism and dedication and a miracle, as retold by Saadyah Maximon. Incorporating an album of illus. in full color by Siegmund Forst. New York, Press of Shulsinger Bros. [1958] 127p. illus. 32cm. [BM695.H3M29] 58-47873
1. Hanukkah (Feast of Lights) I. Title.

MENDES, Henry Pereira, 1852-1937. 296.4
Bar-mitzvah for boyhood, youth, and manhood. Rev. [i. e. 3d] ed. New York, Bloch Pub. Co., 1956. 98p. 21cm. [BM707.M4 1956] 56-7149
1. Bar mitzvah. I. Title.

MENDES, Henry Pereira, 1852-1937. *296.4
Bar-mitzvah for boyhood, youth, and manhood. Rev. [i.e. 3d] ed. New York, Bloch Pub. Co., 1956. 98p. 21cm. [BM707.M4 1956] 56-7149
1. Bar mitzvah. I. Title.

MEYERS, Carol L. 296.4
The tabernacle menorah : a synthetic study of a symbol from the Biblical cult / by Carol L. Meyers. Missoula, Mont. : Published by Scholars Press for the American Schools of Oriental Research, c1976. xvii, 243 p. : ill. ; 22 cm. (American Schools of Oriental Research dissertation series ; no. 2) Originally presented as the author's thesis, Brandeis, 1974. Bibliography: p. 227-243. [BM657.M35M49 1976] 76-17105 ISBN 0-89130-107-0 : 4.00
1. Menorah. 2. Tabernacle. 3. Trees in the Bible. 4. Trees in art. 5. Neat East—Antiquities. I. Title. II. Series: Dissertation series ; no. 2.

MILGROM, Jacob, 1923- 296.4
Cult and conscience : the Asham and the priestly doctrine of repentance / by Jacob Milgrom. Leiden : Brill, 1976. xiii, 173 p. ; 25 cm. (Studies in Judaism in late antiquity ; v. 18) Includes indexes. Bibliography: p. [144]-150. [BS1199.S2M54] 76-375991 ISBN 9-00-404476-0 : fl 64.00
1. Sacrifice—Biblical teaching. 2. Repentance—Biblical teaching. 3. Asham (The Hebrew word) I. Title. II. Series.

MINDEL, Nissan. 296.4
The complete story of Tishrei. Brooklyn, Merkos L'Inyonei Chinuch, 1956. viii, 231p. illus. 23cm. (His Complete festival stories) [BM693.T6M5] 57-36874
1. Tishri. I. Title.

MORROW, Betty. 296.4 (j)
Jewish holidays, by Betty Morrow and Louis Hartman. Illustrated by Nathan Goldstein. Champaign, Ill., Garrard Pub. Co. [1967] 64 p. col. illus. 25 cm. (A Holiday book) [BM690.M68] 67-10707
1. Fasts and feasts—Judaism—Juvenile literature. I. Hartman, Louis, joint author. II. Title.

MUNK, Elie. 296.4
The world of prayer. New York, P. Feldheim, 1954-63. 2 v. 25 cm. [BM660.M813] A55
1. Jews. Liturgy and ritual. I. 'Olam ha-teflot. II. The world of prayer. III. Title.

PETUCHOWSKI, Jakob Josef, 1925- comp. 296.4
Contributions to the scientific study of Jewish liturgy, edited by Jakob J. Petuchowski. New York, Ktav Pub. House, 1970. xxviii, 502 p. 24 cm. Originally published in the Jewish quarterly review (Old and New series) and in the Hebrew Union College annual. Includes bibliographies. [BM660.P47] 72-132834 ISBN 0-87068-126-5
1. Jews. Liturgy and ritual—Addresses, essays, lectures. I. The Jewish quarterly review. II. Hebrew Union College annual. III. Title.

PETUCHOWSKI, Jakob Josef, 1925- comp. 296.4
Understanding Jewish prayer, by Jakob J. Petuchowski. New York, Ktav Pub. House, 1972. xiv, 175 p. 24 cm. Includes bibliographical references. [BM669.P47] 71-155169 ISBN 0-87068-186-9 6.95
1. Prayer (Judaism)—Addresses, essays, lectures. I. Title.
Contents Omitted.

POSY, Arnold, 1893- 296.4
Holiday night dreams. Drawings by Hella Arensen. New York, Bloch Pub. Co. [1953] 263p. illus. 23cm. [GR98.P65] 53-13382
1. Folk-lore—Jews. I. Title.

READINGS in Jewish worship 296.4
/ edited with introductions and notes by Joseph Heinemann, with Jakob J. Petuchowski. New York : Behrman House, [1975] p. cm. (Library of Jewish studies) Includes bibliographies and index. [BM665.R37] 75-25536 ISBN 0-87441-217-X : 12.50 ISBN 0-87441-237-4 pbk. : 4.95
1. Midrash—Translations into English. 2. Piyutim—Translations into English. 3. Jewish prayers. 4. Sermons, Hebrew—Translations into English. 5. Sermons, English—Translations from Hebrew. I. Heinemann, Joseph. II. Petuchowski, Jakob Josef, 1925- III. Jews. Liturgy and ritual. English. Selections. 1975.

REIK, Theodor, 1888-1970. 296.4
Pagan rites in Judaism: from sex initiation, magic, mooncult, tattooing, mutilation, and other primitive rituals to family loyalty and solidarity. New York, Farrar, Straus [1964] 206 p. 21 cm. Bibliographical references included in "Notes" (p. [183]-202) [BM534.R4] 64-12386
1. Judaism—Relations. 2. Cultus, Jewish. I. Title.

ROSENAU, William, 1865-1943. 296.4
Jewish ceremonial institutions and customs. 3d and rev. ed. Detroit, Singing Tree Press, 1971. 190 p. illus. 19 cm. "Facsimile reprint of the 1925 ed." [BM700.R58 1925a] 77-78222
1. Jews—Rites and ceremonies. I. Title.

ROSENBERG, Stuart E 296.4
A time to speak, of man, faith, and society. New York, Bloch Pub. Co., 1960. 181p. 22cm. [BM740.R669] 60-15795
1. Sermons, Jewish—Canada. 2. Sermons, English—Jewish authors—Canada. I. Title.

ROSENBERG STUART E. 296.4
A time to speak of man, faith, and society. New York, Bloch Pub. Co. [c.]1960. v, 181p. 22cm. 60-15795 3.50
1. Sermons, Jewish—Canada. 2. Sermons, English—Jewish authors—Canada. I. Title.

ROTH, Tobias. 296.4
A Jewish view of prayer and worship. [1st ed.] Washington, B'nai B'rith Youth Organization [1969] 61 p. col. illus. 18 cm. (Judaism pamphlet series) Cover title. Bibliography: p. 59-61. [BM669.R67] 75-19479
1. Prayer (Judaism) I. Title. II. Series.

ROWLEY, Harold Henry, 1890- 296.4
Worship in ancient Israel: its forms and meaning, by H. H. Rowley: Edward Cadbury Lectures delivered in the University of Birmingham. London, S. P. C. K., 1967. xv, 307 p. tables, 22 1/2 cm. (Edward Cadbury lectures, 1966) 42/- Bibliogrpahical footnotes. [BM656.R6] 67-93885
1. Worship (Judaism) 2. Cultus, Jewish — Hist. I. Title.

ROWLEY, Harold Henry, 1890- 296.4
Worship in ancient Israel; its forms and meaning, by H. H. Rowley. [American ed.] Philadelphia, Fortress Press [1967] xv, 307 p. 23 cm. (Edward Cadbury lectures 1965) Bibliographical footnotes. [BM656.R6 1967] 67-13036
1. Worship (Judaism) 2. Cultus, Jewish—History. I. Title. II. Series.

SCHARFSTEIN, Edythe, 1922- 296.4
The book of Passover, by Edythe and Sol Scharfstein. Pictures by Siegmond Forst. [New York] Ktav Pub. House, c1953. unpaged. illus. 26cm. [BM695.P3S33] 53-30194
1. Passover. I. Scharfastein, Sol, 1921- joint author. II. Title.

SCHARFSTEIN, Sol, 1921- 296.4
Chanukah is here, by Robert Sol [pseud.] Pictures by Gabe Josephson. [New York] Ktav Pub. House, c1953. unpaged. illus. 22cm. [BM695.H3S293] 54-22112
1. Hanukkah (Feast of Lights) I. Title.

SCHARFSTEIN, Sol, 1921- 296.4
The first book of Chanukah, by Robert Sol [pseud.] Pictures by Laszlo Matulay. New York, Ktav Pub. House [1956] unpaged. illus. 18x24cm. [BM695.H3S295] 57-15547
1. Hanukkah (Feast of lights) I. Title.

SCHARFSTEIN, Sol, 1921- 296.4
A wonderful Shabbos, story by Robert Sol [pseud.] Pictures by Lili Cassel. [New York] Ktav Pub. House [1954] unpaged. illus. 22cm. [BM685.S2] 54-28240
1. Sabbath—Juvenile literature. I. Title.

SEGAL, Samuel Michael, 1904- 296.4
The Sabbath book. [New ed.] New York, T. Yoseloff [1957] 238p. 25cm. [BM685.S4 1957] 57-13823
1. Sabbath. I. Title.

SELIG, Harris L 296.4
Links to eternity: Jewish holidays and festivals; homiletical essays. New York, Bloch Pub. Co., 1957. 389p. 24cm. [BM690.S43] 57-6790
1. Fasts and feasts-Judaism. I. Title.

SHEPHERD, Coulson 296.4
Jewish holy days; their prophetic and Christian significance. New York, Loizeaux [1961] 95p. 61-16660 1.50 pap.,
1. Typology (Theology) 2. Fasts and feasts—Judaism. 3. Jews—Conversion to Christianity. I. Title.

SIMON, Norma. 296.4
Hanukkah. Illus. by Symeon Shimin. New York, Crowell [1966] 1 v. (unpaged) illus. (part col.) 22 cm. (A Crowell holiday book) [BM695.H3S48] 66-7618
1. Hanukkah (Feast of lights)—Juvenile literature. I. Title.

SIMON, Norma 296.4
Passover, Illus. by Symeon Shimin. New York, Crowell [c.1965.40] p. illus. (pt. col.) 22cm. (Crowell holiday bk.) [BM695.P3S53] 65-11644 2.95 bds.,
1. Passover—Juvenile literature. I. Shimin, Symeon, 1902-illus. II. Title.

SIMPSON, William Wynn 296.4
Jewish prayer and worship, an introduction for Christians [by] William W. Simpson. New York, Seabury [1967, c.1965] 128p. 21cm. (Seabury paperback, SP 43) [BM660.S53] 67-21835 1.45 pap.,
1. Jews. Liturgy and ritual. I. Title.

SIMPSON, William Wynn. 296.4
Light and rejoicing : a Christian's understanding of Jewish worship / by W. W. Simpson. Belfast : Christian Journals Ltd., 1976. 138 p. ; 18 cm. Bibliography: p. 133-136. [BM700.S49] 76-375924 ISBN 0-904302-16-4 : £1.00
1. Jews—Rites and ceremonies. 2. Jews. Liturgy and ritual. I. Title.

SOLTAU, Henry W., 1805-1875. 296.4
The holy vessels and furniture of the Tabernacle. [1st American ed.] Grand Rapids, Mich., Kregel Publications [1969] 148 p. 10 col. illus. 24 cm. Reprinted from the 1851 ed., published under title: The holy vessels and furniture of the Tabernacle of Israel. [BM654.S55 1969] 74-85428 4.95
1. Tabernacle. I. Title.

SOLTES, Mordecai, 1893- 296.4
The Jewish holidays; a guide to their origin, significance and observance, including 250 questions and answers. [4th ed.] New York, Jewish Center Division, National Jewish Welfare Board [1952, c1943] 91p. 21cm. First ed. published in 1931 under title: Two hundred and fifty (250) questions and answers on the Jewish festivals. [BM690.S6 1952] 52-14440
1. Fasts and feasts—Judaism. 2. Jews—Rites and ceremonies. I. Title.

SPERLING, Abraham Isaac. 296.4
Reasons for Jewish customs and traditions. (Taamei haminhagim). Translated into English by Abraham Matts. New York, Bloch Pub. Co. [1968] 310 p. 24 cm. Translation of Ta'ame ha-minhagim (romanized form) [BM700.S653] 68-31711
1. Jews—Rites and ceremonies. 2. Fasts and feasts—Judaism. 3. Commandments (Judaism) I. Title.

SWICHKOW, Louis J. 296.4
Invocations and "D'var Torah" supplement. New York, Bloch [1964] xv, 231p. 18cm. [BM675.O25S8] 64-57861 3.50
I. Jews. Liturgy and ritual. Occasional prayers. II. Title.

THANKSGIVING hymns (The) 296.4
Tr., annotated with introd. by Menahem Mansoor. Grand Rapids, Mich., Eerdmans [c.1961] xi, 227p. 25cm. (Studies on the texts of the desert of Judah, v.3) Bibl. 61-4542 7.00
1. Mansoor, Menahem, ed. and tr. I. Series.

UNION of American Hebrew Congregations. 296.4
The theological foundations of prayer; a Reform Jewish perspective. Edited with introductions by Jack Bemporad. [New York] Commission on Worship, Union of American Hebrew Congregations [1967] 126 p. 23 cm. "Papers presented at the UAHC 48th Biennial." [BM669.U5] 68-1817
1. Prayer (Judaism) 2. Reform Judaism—Addresses, essays, lectures. I. Bemporad, Jack, ed. II. Title.

UNION of American Hebrew Congregations. 296.4
The theological foundations of prayer; a Reform Jewish perspective. Edited with introductions by Jack Bemporad. [New York] Commission on Worship, Union of American Hebrew Congregations [1967] 126 p. 23 cm. "Papers presented at the UAHC 48th Biennial." [BM669.U5] 68-1817
1. Prayer (Judaism) 2. Reform Judaism—Addresses, essays, lectures. I. Bemporad, Jack, ed. II. Title.

VAUGHAN, Patrick H. 296.4
The meaning of "bama" in the Old Testament : a study of etymological, textual and archaeological evidence / Patrick H. Vaughan. London ; New York : Cambridge University Press, 1974. xiv, 90 p. : ill. ; 23 cm. (Monograph series - Society for Old Testament Study ; 3) Includes index. Bibliography: p. 77-79. [BM656.V38] 73-89004 ISBN 0-521-20425-9 : 6.95
1. Bible. O.T.—Criticism, interpretation, etc. 2. Cultus, Jewish. 3. Bamah (The Hebrew word) 4. High places (Shrines) I. Title. II. Series: Society for Old Testament Study. Monograph series ; 3.

WEISENBERG, David H. 296.4
The Jewish way; a lucid exposition of Jewish observances and proper conduct, by David H. Weisenberg. North Quincy, Mass., Christopher Pub. House [1969] 181 p. illus. 21 cm. [BM700.W35] 69-16274 ISBN 0-8158-0026-6 4.95
1. Jews—Rites and ceremonies. I. Title.

WEITZMAN, Alan. 296.4
Living symbols, past and present. New York, Shengold Publishers [1969] 95 p. illus. (part col.) 24 cm. Provides a glimpse of Jewish history through brief explanations of the symbols of Judaism and the people who have followed this religion as a way of life. [BM657.A1W4] 75-83284 3.95
1. Liturgical objects—Judaism—Juvenile literature. I. Title.

WENGROV, Charles. j296.4
The book of the Sabbath; story and traditions, songs and music; being the heartwarming account of Friday evening and Saturday in the life of one Jewish family, interwoven with stories of adventure about the Sabbath in days long gone, written and illustrated especially for children, together with a full collection of beloved z'mirot and songs for the entire Sabbath, from beginning to end. Illustrated by Siegmund Forst. Music edited by Samuel Bugatch. New York. At the Press of Shulsinger Bros. [1962] 128 p. illus. 32 cm. [BM685.W39] 63-1968
1. Sabbath — Juvenile literature. I. Bugatch, Samuel, ed. II. Title.

YARDEN, Leon. 296.4
The tree of light; a study of the menorah, the seven-branched lampstand, by L. Yarden. Ithaca, N.Y., Cornell University Press [1971] vii, 162 p. illus. 26 cm. Includes bibliographical references. [BM657.M35Y37 1971] 79-127780 ISBN 0-8014-0596-3 11.50
1. Menorah. I. Title.

REIK, Theodor, 1888-1969. 296.4'01'9
Ritual : psycho-analytic studies / by Theodor Reik ; with a preface by Sigm. Freud ; translated from the 2d German ed. by Douglas Bryan. Westport, Conn. : Greenwood Press, 1975, c1946. 367 p. ; 22 cm. At head of title: The psychological problems of religion, I. Translation of Probleme der Religionspsychologie, v. 1. Reprint of the ed. published by Farrar, Straus, New York. Includes bibliographical references and index.

[GN473.R4 1975] 73-2645 ISBN 0-8371-6814-7 lib.bdg. : 18.25
1. Jews—Rites and ceremonies. 2. Rites and ceremonies. 3. Psychoanalysis. I. Title.

MAURICE Spertus 296.4'074'0177311
Museum of Judaica.
The Maurice Spertus Museum of Judaica; an illustrated catalog of selected objects. With introductory material by Arthur M. Feldman, Grace Cohen Grossman and Joseph Gutmann. Text by Grace Cohen Grossman. Chicago, Spertus College of Judaica Press, 1974. 98, [6] p. illus. (part col.) 26 cm. Bibliography: p. [104] [BM657.A1M35 1974] 74-178237
1. Liturgical objects—Judaism—Exhibitions. I. Grossman, Grace Cohen.

GARTENBERG, Leo, comp. 296.4082
Torah thoughts. New York, J. David [1964] xi, 236 p. 24 cm. [BM43.G3] 64-15745
1. Judaism — Addresses, essays, lectures. 2. Legends, Jewish. I. Title.

GARTENBERG, Leo, comp. 296.4082
Torah thoughts. New York, J. David [c.1964] xi, 236p. 24cm. 64-15745 5.95
1. Judaism—Addresses, essays, lectures. 2. Legends, Jewish. I. Title.

GARTENBERG, Leo, comp. 296.4082
Torah thoughts; v.2. New York, J. David [c.1965] xii, 217p. 24cm. [BM43.G3] 64-15745 5.95
1. Judaism—Addresses, essays, lectures. 2. Legends, Jewish. I. Title.

IDELSOHN, Abraham Zebi, 296.4'09
1882-1938
Jewish liturgy and its development. New York, Schocken [1967, c.1932] xix, 404p. 21cm. Bibl. [BM660.I4 1967] 67-14959 7.50; 2.95 pap.,
1. Jews. Liturgy and ritual—Hist. I. Title.

MILLGRAM, Abraham Ezra, 296.4'09
1901-
Jewish worship, by Abraham E. Millgram. [1st ed.] Philadelphia, Jewish Publication Society of America, 1971. xxiii, 673 p. 22 cm. Bibliography: p. 633-648. [BM660.M55] 77-151316 8.50
1. Jews. Liturgy and ritual—History. I. Title.

BARACK, Nathan A. 296.41
A history of the Sabbath, by Nathan A. Barrack. New York, J. David [1965] xvii, 202 p. 23 cm. Bibliography: p. 199-202. [BM685.B3] 64-8425
1. Sabbath—History. I. Title.

CENTRAL Conference of 296.4'1
American Rabbis.
[Tadrikh le-Shabat (romanized form)] a Shabbat manual. [New York] Published for the Central Conference of American Rabbis, by Ktav Pub. House, 1972. 104 p. 22 cm. Part of text in English and Hebrew. Includes unacc. melodies. [BM685.C44] 72-10299 ISBN 0-87068-199-0 2.50
1. Sabbath. I. Title. II. Title: A Shabbat manual.

CHIEL, Arthur A. 296.4'1
Guide to Sidrot and Haftarot, by Arthur A. Chiel. [New York] Ktav Pub. House [1971] 347 p. music. 24 cm. Includes selections from the Pentateuch and the Haftaroth in Hebrew with the English translation of the Jewish Publication Society of America. [BS1225.5.C48] 71-155840 ISBN 0-87068-573-2
1. Jews. Liturgy and ritual. Haftaroth—Study and teaching. 2. Bible. O.T. Pentateuch—Study—Outlines, syllabi, etc. I. Bible. O.T. Pentateuch. Hebrew. Selections. 1971. II. Bible. O.T. Pentateuch. English. Jewish Publication Society. Selections. 1971. III. Title.

FLINK, Eugene, comp. 296.4'1
Yavneh shiron. Editor: Eugene Flink. Associate editor: Tom Ackerman. [New York, Yavneh, 1969] 221, [1] p. illus. 22 cm. Added to t.p.: Shiron Yavneh (romanized form) Selections (p. 86-[222]) from Z'mirot, Tanach, Talmud, Liturgy, Songs of the land (In Hebrew and English) Contents.Contents.—Prologue: The Sabbath-faith through action, by C. Keller.—Around the Sabbath table, by Y. Vainstein.—Birkhat Hamazon, by Z. Schachter.—The Sabbath-meaning and spirit, by S. Spero.—Sabbath rest, by N. Lamm.—The Sabbath ritual, by E. Fromm.—Sabbath and creation, by W. Wurtzburger.—Work on the Sabbath.—Living the Sabbath, by Z. Schachter.—Sabbath in Moscow, by B. Poupko. [BM685.F55] 76-16847
1. Sabbath. I. Ackerman, Tom, joint comp. II. Jews. Liturgy and ritual. Zemirot. III. Jews. Liturgy and ritual. Zemirot. English. IV. Yavneh (Association) V. Title. VI. Title: Shiron Yavneh.

ADLER, Morris. 296.4'2
The voice still speaks; message of the Torah for contemporary man. Compiled by Jacob Chinitz. Foreword by Louis Finkelstein. New York, Bloch Pub. Co. [1969] xviii, 436 p. 25 cm. Transcriptions of sermons. [BM740.2.A3] 68-57433 10.00
1. Sermons, American—Jewish authors. 2. Sermons, Jewish—U.S. I. Title.

BAKER, Julius L. 296.4'2
Pri Yehudah, by Julius L. Baker. Columbus, Ohio, Printed by Pfeifer Print. Co. [1967] viii, 219 p. 24 cm. Text in English. [BM740.2.B27] 67-7523
1. Sermons, American—Jewish authors. 2. Sermons, Jewish—United States. I. Title.

BARACK, Nathan A 296.42
Mount Moriah view; sermons, essays, and editorials. New York, Bloch Pub. Co., 1956. 180p. 21cm. [BM45.B35] 56-3451
1. Judaism—Addresses, essays, lectures. I. Title.

BERZON, Bernard L 296.42
Good beginnings; [sermons] New York, J. David [1962] 2 1p. 23cm. [BM740.2.B4] 62-13695
1. Sermons, Jewish. I. Title.

BERZON, Bernard L. 296.42
Good beginnings; [sermons] New York, Jonathan David [c.1962] 201p. 23cm. 62-13695 6.75
1. Sermons, Jewish. I. Title.

BEST Jewish sermons. 296.42
New York, Jonathan David Co. v. 22cm. Editor: S. I. Teplitz. [BM740.B48] 58-3698
1. Sermons, Jewish —U.S. 2. Sermons, American—Jewish authors. I. Teplits, Saul I., ed.

BEST Jewish sermons 296.42
[of 5723-5724] New York, Jonathan David [c.1964] 211p. 22cm. Ed.: S. I. Teplitz. 58-3698 5.95
1. Sermons, Jewish—U.S. 2. Sermons, American—Jewish authors. I. Teplitz, Saul I., ed.

BEST Jewish sermons of 296.42
5721-5722. Ed. by Rabbi Saul I. Teplitz. New York, Jonathan David [c.1962] 238p. 21cm. 58-3698 5.95
1. Sermons, Jewish—U.S. 2. Sermons, American—Jewish authors. I. Teplitz, Saul I., ed.

COHEN, Beryl David, 1898- 296.42
My King and my God, intimate talks on the devotions of life. New York, Bloch Pub. Co. [1963] 239 p. 21 cm. [BM740.2.C6] 63-12428
1. Sermons, Jewish — U.S. 2. Sermons, American — Jewish authors. I. Title.

COHEN, Seymour J. 296.4'2
A time to speak, by Seymour J. Cohen. New York, J. David [1968] 314 p. 24 cm. Sermons. [BM740.2.C62] 68-19957
1. Sermons, American—Jewish authors. 2. Sermons, Jewish—United States. I. Title.

COHON, Beryl David, 1898- 296.42
From generation to generation; with a pref. by Samuel S. Cohon. Boston, B. Humphries ['1951] 133 p. 21 cm. [BM740.C63] 52-8905
1. Sermons, Jewish—U. S. 2. Sermons, American—Jewish authors. I. Title.

COHON, Beryl David, 1898- 296.42
My King and my God, intimate talks on the devotions of life. New York, Bloch [c.1963] 239p. 21cm. 63-12428 3.95
1. Sermons, Jewish—U.S. 2. Sermons, American—Jewish authors. I. Title.

COHON, Beryl David, 1898- 296.42
Out of the heart; intimate talks from a Jewish pulpit on the personal issues of life. [1st ed.] New York, Vantage Press [c1957] 120p. 21cm. [BM740.C64] 57-11258
1. Sermons, Jewish—U. S. 2. Sermons, American—Jewish authors. I. Title.

COHON, Beryl David, 1898- 296.4'2
Shielding the flame; a personal and spiritual inventory of a liberal rabbi, by Beryl D. Cohon. New York, Bloch Pub. Co. [1972] ix, 118 p. 22 cm. [BM740.2.C64] 72-4801 ISBN 0-8197-0293-5 4.95
1. Sermons, American—Jewish authors. 2. Sermons, Jewish—United States. I. Title.

COHON, Beryl David, 1898- 296.4'2
1976.
Come, let us reason together : sermons presented in days of crisis / by Beryl D. Cohon ; foreword by Abram L. Sachar. New York : Bloch Pub. Co., c1977. xii, 75 p. ; 22 cm. [BM740.2.C58 1977] 76-24330 ISBN 0-8197-0397-4 : 5.95
1. Sermons, American—Jewish authors. 2. Sermons, Jewish—United States. I. Title.

CRONBACH, Abraham, 1882- 296.42
Stories made of Bible stories. New York, Bkman. Assocs. [c.1961] 312p. 61-15675 4.50
1. Youth, Jewish—Religious life. 2. Sermons, American—Jewish authors. 3. Sermons, Jewish—U.S. I. Title.

DONIN, Hayim. 296.42
Beyond thyself: a collection of sermons. New York, Bloch Pub. Co. [1965] vii, 131 p. 21 cm. [BM740.2.D6] 65-19611
1. Sermons, American — Jewish authors. 2. Sermons, Jewish — U.S. I. Title.

DONIN, Hayim 296.42
Beyond thyself: a collection of sermons. New York, Bloch [c.1965] vii, 131p. 21cm. [BM740.2.D6] 65-19611 3.75
1. Sermons, American—Jewish authors. 2. Sermons, Jewish—U.S. I. Title.

FELDMAN, Abraham Jehiel, 296.4'2
1893-
Words of my mouth, being excerpts from a rabbi's messages to his congregation at annual meetings, 1926-1968 [by] Abraham J. Feldman. New York, Bloch Pub. Co. [1969, c1970] xvii, 194 p. 22 cm. [BM45.F385] 74-93294 5.95
1. Judaism—Addresses, essays, lectures. I. Title.

FREEHOF, Solomon Bennett, 296.4'2
1892-
J. Leonard Levy, prophetic voice, by Solomon B. Freehof and Vigdor W. Kavaler. [Pittsburgh, Rodef Shalom Congregation, 1970] xv, 233 p. port. 24 cm. Includes selected lectures by J. L. Levy. [BM740.F674] 75-263848
1. Sermons, American—Jewish authors. 2. Sermons, Jewish—U.S. I. Kavaler, Vigdor W., joint author. II. Levy, Joseph Leonard, 1865-1917.

FREEHOF, Solomon Bennett, 296.4'2
1892-
Preaching the Bible; sermons for Sabbaths and high holy days [by] Solomon B. Freehof. New York, Ktav Pub. House [1974] p. [BM740.2.F64] 74-889 ISBN 0-87068-244-X 12.50
1. Sermons, American—Jewish authors. 2. Sermons, Jewish—United States. 3. High Holy Day sermons. I. Title.

GITTELSOHN, Roland 296.4'2
Bertram, 1910-
Fire in my bones; essays on Judaism in a time of crisis [by] Roland B. Gittelsohn. New York, Bloch Pub. Co. [1969] xvi, 284 p. 22 cm. Includes bibliographical references. [BM740.2.G53] 78-93295 5.95
1. Sermons, American—Jewish authors. 2. Sermons, Jewish—U.S. I. Title.

GOLDFARB, Solomon David 296.42
Torah for our time; sermons and studies based on Biblical texts for Sabbaths and holidays. New York, Bloch [1965] 183p. 24cm. [BM740.2.G57] 65-27337 4.95
1. Sermons, Jewish—U.S. 2. Sermons, American—Jewish authors. 3. Sermons, Jewish—U.S. 4. Sermons, Jewish—U.S. 5. Sermons, Americans—Jewish authors I. Title.

GORDIS, Robert, 1908- 296.4'2
Leave a little to God; essays in Judaism. New York, Bloch Pub. Co. [1967] xii, 258 p. 24 cm. [BM746.G6] 67-22706
1. High Holy Day sermons. 2. Sermons, American—Jewish authors. I. Title.

GORDON, Solomon. 296.42
Voice of the heart. New York, Bloch Pub. Co. [1965] 147 p. 23 cm. [BM740.2G64] 64-66010
1. Sermons, American — Jewish authors. 2. Sermons, Jewish — u.s. I. Title.

GORDON, Solomon 296.42
Voice of the heart. New York, Bloch [c.1965] 147p. 23cm. [BM740.2G64] 64-66010 4.00
1. Sermons, American—Jewish authors. 2. Sermons, Jewish—U. S. I. Title.

GREENBERG, Sidney, 1917- 296.42
Adding life to our years. With a foreword by Morris Adler. New York, J. David [1959] 205p. 23cm. [BM740.2.G7] 59-10539
1. Sermons, Jewish—U. S. 2. Sermons, American —Jewish authors. I. Title.

GREENBERG, Sidney, 1917- 296.42
Finding ourselves; sermons on the art of living. New York, J. David [c.1964] xii, 258p. 22cm. [BM740.2.-G72] 64-19751 5.95
1. Sermons, Jewish—U.S. 2. Sermons, American—Jewish authors. I. Title.

HALPERN, Abraham E., 1891- 296.42
1962
A son of faith; from the sermons of Abraham E. Halpern, 1891-1962. Ed. by Bernard S. Raskas. New York, Bloch [c.1962] 320p. illus. 24cm. 62-20630 5.00
1. Sermons, Jewish. I. Title.

HERSHMAN, Abraham Moses, 296.42
1880-
Israel's fate and faith. Detroit, Congregation Shaarey Zedek, 1952. 352 p. 25 cm. [BM740.H37] 52-29314
1. Sermons. Jewish—U. S. 2. Sermons, American—Jewish authors. 3. Judaism—Addresses, essays, lectures. I. Title.

HERSHMAN, Abraham Moses, 296.42
1880-
Religion of the age and of the ages. New York, Bloch Pub. Co., 1953. 134p. 24cm. [BM740.H372] 53-10660
1. Sermons, Jewish—U. S. 2. Sermons, Jewish—American authors. I. Title.

HERTZ, Richard C 296.42
Faith in Jewish survival. Detroit, Temple Beth El, 1961. 56p. 22cm. [BM746.H4] 62-4893
1. High Holy Day sermons. I. Title.

HERTZ, Richard C. 296.4'2
Reflections for the modern Jew / by Richard C. Hertz and Dannel I. Schwartz. Birmingham, Mich. : Temple Beth El, 1974. 36 p. ; 24 cm. [BM746.H43] 75-313847
1. High Holy Day sermons. 2. Sermons, American—Jewish authors. 3. Sermons, Jewish—United States. I. Schwartz, Dannel I., joint author. II. Title.

JUNG, Leo, 1892- 296.42
Harvest: sermons, addresses, studies. New York, P. Feldheim, 1956. 324p. 24cm. [BM740.J83] 57-23159
1. Sermons, Jewish—U. S. 2. Sermons, Amerioan—Jewish authors. 3. Judaism—Addresses, essays, lectures. I. Title.

JUNG, Leo, 1892- 296.42
Harvest: sermons, addresses, studies. New York, P. Feldheilm, 1956. 324p. 24cm. [BM740.J83] 57-23159
1. Sermons, Jewish—U. S. 2. Sermons, American—Jewish authors. 3. Judaism—Addresses, essays, lectures. I. Title.

KANOTOPSKY, Harold B 296.42
Rays of Jewish splendor; selected sermons. [Brooklyn] Young Israel of Eastern Parkway [1956] 92p. 23cm. [BM740.K273] 56-23995
1. Sermons, Jewish—U. S. 2. Sermons, American —Jewish authors. I. Title.

KELLNER, Abraham A 296.42
My pulpit; sermons of times and seasons. [Long Branch, N. J.,] 1951. 207p. 23cm. [BM740.K39] 53-20373
1. Sermons, Jewish—U. S. 2. Sermons, American—Jewish authors. I. Title.

LOOKSTEIN, Joseph Hyman, 296.4'2
1902-
Faith and destiny of man; traditional Judaism in a new light, by Joseph H. Lookstein. New York, Bloch Pub. Co. [1967] x, 174 p. 24 cm. Bibliographical footnotes. [BM740.2.L6] 67-22918
1. Sermons, Jewish—United States. 2. Sermons, American—Jewish authors. I. Title.

MARK, Julius, 1898- 296.42
Reaching for the moon, and other addresses. New York, Farrar, Straus and Cudahy [1959] 177p. 22cm. [BM740.2.M3] 59-9171
1. Sermons, Jewish—U. S. 2. Sermons, American— Jewish authors. I. Title.

MASLIANSKY, Zebi Hirsch, 296.42
1856-1943.
Sermons. Translated by Edward Herbert. With a biographical sketch by Sulamith Schwartz Nardi. Rev. and edited by Abraham J. Feldman. New York, Hebrew Pub. Co. [1960] 345p. illus. 21cm. [BM740.M3 1960] 61-191
1. Sermons, Jewish— U. S. 2. Sermons, Yiddish—Translations into English. 3. Sermons, English— Translations from Yiddish. I. Title.

MASLIN, Simeon J. 296.4'2
As showers on tender grass; five K.A.M. sermons, 1968-1969, by Simeon J. Maslin. [Chicago, KAM, 1969] 38 p. 22 cm. [BM740.2.M32] 75-11411
1. American sermons—Jewish authors. 2. Sermons, Jewish—U.S. I. Title.

MOWSHOWITZ, Israel. 296.4'2
To serve in faithfulness / by Israel Mowshowitz. New York : Ktav Pub. House, [1975] xiii, 249 p. ; 24 cm. [BM740.2.M68] 74-32465 ISBN 0-87068-271-7 : 10.00
1. Sermons, American—Jewish authors. 2. Sermons, Jewish—United States. I. Title.

NAROT, Joseph R. 296.42
For whom the rabbi speaks; a collection of sermons and articles, by Joseph R. Narot. [1st ed.] Miami, Fla., Rostrum Bks. [1966] 134p. 22cm. [BM740.2.N3] 66-6312 1.65 pap.,

1. Sermons, Jewish—U.S. 2. Sermons, American—Jewish authors. I. Title.
Temple Israel of Greater Miami, 173 NE 19th, Miami, Fla. 33132

NEWMAN, Jacob. 296.42
The eternal quest; sermons for high holy days, festivals and special Sabbaths. New York, Bloch Pub. Co., 1965. xix, 203 p. 23 cm. [BM745.N4] 65-9665
1. Festival-day sermons, Jewish. 2. Sermons, English — Africa, South — Jewish authors. I. Title.

NEWMAN, Jacob 296.42
The eternal quest; sermons for high holy days, festivals and special Sabbaths. New York, Bloch [c.]1965. xix, 203p. 23cm. [BM745.N4] 65-9665 5.00
1. Festival-day sermons, Jewish. 2. Sermons, English—Africa, South—Jewish authors. I. Title.

NEWMAN, Julius, 1896- 296.42
Speak unto the children of Israel; sermons for every Sabbath and festival of the year for Jewish children. New York, Bloch Pub. Co. [c1960] 164 p. 22 cm. [BM743.N4] 60-7252
1. Children's sermons, Jewish. I. Title.

PESIKTA de-Rab Kahana. 296.4'2
English
Pesikta de-Rab Kahana / R. Kahana's compilation of discourses for Sabbaths and festal days ; translated from Hebrew and Aramaic by William G. (Gershon Zev) Braude and Israel J. Kapstein. 1st ed. Philadelphia : Jewish Publication Society of America, [1975] lvii, 593 p. ; 24 cm. Includes bibliographical references and indexes. [BM517.P34E53] 74-6563 ISBN 0-8276-0051-8 : 15.00
1. Bible. O.T.—Sermons. 2. Sermons, Jewish. I. Kahana. II. Braude, William Gordon, 1907- III. Kapstein, Israel James, 1904-

PILCHIK, Ely Emanuel. 296.42
Jeshurun sermons. New York, Bloch Pub. Co., 1957. 261p. 21cm. [BM740.P56] 57-8136
1. Sermons, Jewish—U. S. 2. Sermons, American —Jewish authors. I. Title.

PILCHIK, Ely Emanuel. 296.42
Jeshurun sermons New York, Bloch Pub. Co., 1957. 261p. 21cm. [BM740.P56] 5m-8136
1. Sermons, Jewish—U. S. 2. ermons, American—Jewish authors. I. Title.

RABINOWITZ, Louis Isaac, 296.42
1906-
Light and salvation; sermons for the high holy days. New York, Bloch [c.]1965. 349p. 22cm. [BM746.R3] 65-4075 5.50
1. High Holy Day sermons. 2. Sermons, American—Jewish authors. 3. Sermons, Jewish—U.S. I. Title.

RABINOWITZ, Louis Isaac, 296.42
1906-
Sabbath light; sermons on the Sabbath evening service. Johannesburg, Fieldhill Pub. Co.; selling agents: Bloch Pub. Co., New York, 1958. 1v. 23cm. Includes 'Evening service for Sabbath' (Hebrew and English) [BM740.R2876] 59-29225
1. Sermons, Jewish—Africa, South. 2. Sermons, English—Africa, South. I. Title.

RABINOWITZ, Louis Isaac, 296.42
1906-
Sparks from the anvil: sermons for Sabbaths, holy days and festivals. New York, Bloch Pub. Co., 1955. 347p. 22cm. [BM740.R288] 55-7543
1. Sermons, Jewish— Africa, South. 2. Sermons, English—Jewish authors. I. Title.

RABINOWITZ, Louis Issac, 296.42
1906-
Light and salvation; sermons for the high holy days, by Louis I. Rabinowitz. New York, Bloch Pub. Co., 1965. 349 p. 22 cm. [BM746.R3] 65-4075
1. High Holy Day sermons. 2. Sermons, American—Jewish authors. 3. Sermons, Jewish—U. S. I. Title.

RASKAS, Bernard S ed. 296.42
Beacons of light; thoughts for special days and occasions, compiled and edited by Bernard S. Raskas. New York, Bloch Pub. Co. [1965] viii, 263 p. 24 cm. [BM744.R3] 65-26712
1. Occasional sermons, Jewish. I. Title.

RASKAS, Bernard S., ed. 296.42
Beacons of light; thoughts for special days and occasions. New York, Bloch [c.1965] viii, 263p. 24cm. [BM744.R3] 65-26712 6.50 bds.,
1. Occasional sermons, Jewish. I. Title.

REICHERT, Irving 296.42
Frederick, 1895-
Judaism & the American Jew; selected sermons & addresses. San Francisco, Grabhorn Press, 1953. 245p. 29cm. [BM740.R385] 54-591

1. Sermons, Jewish—U. S. 2. Sermons, American—Jewish authors. I. Title.

ROODMAN, Solomon. 296.42
The suburbs of the Almighty; sermons and discourses. New York, J. David [c1962] 235 p. 23 cm. [BM740.2.R6] 62-15963
1. Sermons, Jewish — U.S. 2. Sermons, American — Jewish authors. I. Title.

RUDIN, Jacob Philip. 296.4'2
Very truly yours; a creative harvest of forty years in the pulpit. Introd. by Roland B. Gittelsohn. New York, Bloch Pub. Co. [1971] xiv, 299 p. 22 cm. [BM740.2.R8] 76-163016 ISBN 0-8197-0279-X 6.50
1. Sermons, American—Jewish authors. 2. Sermons, Jewish—U.S. I. Title.

SALIT, Norman, 1896-1960 296.42
The worlds of Norman Salit; sermons, papers, addresses. Posthumously chosen, ed. by Abraham Burstein. New York, Bloch [1966] 315p. port. 24cm. [BM740.2.S25] 66-8697 5.50
1. Sermons, Jewish—U.S. 2. Sermons, American—Jewish authors. I. Burstein, Abraham, 1893- ed. II. Title.

SILVERMAN, William B *296.42
Rabbinic stories for Christian ministers and teachers. New York, Abingdon Press [1958] 221 p. 22 cm. [PN6071.J5S49] 58-7436
1. Tales, Jewish. I. Title.

SILVERSTEIN, Baruch. 296.4'2
A Jew in love. New York, J. David [c1966] x, 188 p. 22 cm. [BM740.2.S5] 66-17799
1. Sermons, Jewish—U. S. 2. Sermons, American—Jewish authors. I. Title.

SINGER, Joseph I. 296.4'2
Margin for living, by Joseph I. Singer. New York, Shulsinger Brothers Press, 1970. 224 p. 24 cm. [BM745.S5] 78-18603 8.00
1. Festival-day sermons, Jewish. 2. Sermons, American—Jewish authors. I. Title.

STEINBACH, Alexander Alan, 296.42
1894-
Through storms we grow, and other sermons, lectures, and essays. Introd. by Robert Gordis. New York, Bloch Pub. Co. [1964] x, 260 p. 24 cm. [BM735.S7] 64-24231
1. Sermons, American—Jewish authors. 2. Sermons, Jewish. I. Title.

STEINBACH, Alexander Alan, 296.42
1894-
Through storms we grow, and other sermons, lectures, and essays. Introd. by Robert Gordis. New York, Bloch [c.1964] x, 260p. 24cm. 64-24231 4.95
1. Sermons, American—Jewish authors. 2. Sermons, Jewish. I. Title.

STEINBERG, Milton, 1903- 296.42
1950.
From the sermons of Rabbi Milton Steinberg; high holydays and major festivals, edited by Bernard Mandelbaum. New York, Bloch, 1954. 200p. 24cm. [BM740.S75] 54-12316
1. Festival-day sermons—Jewish authors. 2. Sermons, Jewish-U. S. 3. Sermons, American—Jewish authors. I. Title.

STEINBERG, Milton, 1903- *296.42
1950.
From the sermons of Rabbi Milton Steinberg. Edited by Bernard Mandelbaum. New York, Bloch, 1954- v. 24 cm. Contents.--[1] High holydays and major festivals.--[2] Only human--the eternal alibi; the weekly Sidrah and general themes. [BM740.2.S7] 54-12316
1. Sermons, Jewish—U.S. 2. Sermons, American—Jewish authors. I Mandelbaum, Bernard, 1922- ed. II. Title. III. Title: Only human—The eternal alibi.

TARSHISH, Jacob, 1892- 296.4'2
Prelude to happiness, by The Lamplighter [pseud.] 1st ed. Columbus, Ohio, F. J. Heer Print. Co., 1937. 108 p. port. 24 cm. "Third volume" [in a series of broadcasts] [BM740.T32] 64-58213
1. Sermons, Jewish—U.S. 2. Sermons, American—Jewish authors. I. Title.

WALLACK, Morton A., comp. 296.42
Eulogies, edited by Morton A. Wallack. New York, J. David [1965] xiii, 232 p. 22 cm. [BM744.3.W3] 65-17366
1. Funeral sermons, Jewish. 2. Sermons, American — Jewish authors. I. Title.

WEINSTEIN, Jacob Joseph, 296.42
1902-
The place of understanding; comments on the portions of the week and the holiday cycle. New York, Bloch Pub. Co., 1959. 181 p. 22 cm. [BM740.W38] 59-6855
1. Sermons, Jewish — U.S. 2. Bible. O.T. Pentateuch — Sermons. 3. Festival-day sermons — Jewish authors. 4. Sermons, American — Jewish authors. I. Title.

WISE, Judah L 1902- 296.42
On this day: brief bar mitzvah addresses based on the portions of the week (Sidrot) for each Sabbath of the year. New York, Bloch Pub. Co., 1954. 64p. 24cm. [BM707.3.W5] 54-7684
1. Bar Mitzvah sermons. I. Title.

KOLATCH, Alfred J., 296.4'2'08
1916-
Sermons for the sixties, by Alfred J. Kolatch. Introd. by Ben Zion Bokser. New York, J. David [c1965] 193 p. 24 cm. [BM740.2.K63] 65-26588
1. Sermons, American—Jewish authors. 2. Sermons, Jewish—U.S. I. Title.

BATES, Barbara S 296.4'3
Bible festivals and holy days [by] Barbara Bates. Illustrated by Don Fields. Nashville, Broadman Press [1968] viii, 118 p. illus. 21 cm. $3.25 Bibliography: p. 117-118. [BM690.B28] 68-22254
1. Fasts and feasts—Judaism—Juvenile literature. I. Title.

BATES, Barbara S. 296.4'3
Bible festivals and holy days [by] Barbara Bates. Illustrated by Don Fields. Nashville, Broadman Press [1968] viii, 118 p. illus. 21 cm. Bibliography: p. 117-118. [BM690.B28] 68-22254 3.25
1. Fasts and feasts—Judaism—Juvenile literature. I. Title.

BERKOVITS, Eliezer, 1908- 296.43
Prayer. New York, Yeshiva University, Dept. of Special Publications, 1962. 112 p. 23 cm. (Studies in Torah Judaism, 8) "Fifth in a series." Bibliographical references included in "Notes" (p. 105-110) [BM669.B44] 223.1 75-212123
1. Prayer (Judaism) I. Title. II. Series.

BRONSTEIN, Charlotte. 296.43
Tales of the Jewish holidays, as told by the light of the moon. With illus. by Art Seiden. New York, Behrman House [1960, c.1959] unpaged. illus. (col.) 25cm. 59-15811 2.95 bds.,
1. Fasts and feasts—Judaism—Juvenile literature. I. Title.

CEDARBAUM, David I 296.43
Teach me to pray, by David I. Cedarbaum and Libbie L. Braverman. Illus. by Victor M. Perlmutter. Music arrangements by Hyman Reznick. Chicago, Board of Jewish Education [1958, c1955-57] 2v. illus. 28cm. [BM666.C4] 55-10878
1. Jews—Prayer-books and devotions—Study and teaching. I. Braverman, Libble (Levin) 1900- joint author. II. Title. III. Title: Teach me to pray.

EPSTEIN, Morris, 1922- 296.43
Tell me about God and prayer; illustrated by Lawrence Dresser. New York, Ktav Pub. House [1953] 64 p. illus. 26 cm. [BM669.E6] 53-28740
1. Prayer (Judaism)—Juvenile literature. I. Title.

FARBER, Walter C. 296.4'3
Jewish holidays, by Walter C. Farber. [2d ed. Detroit] Jewish Heritage Pub. House [c 1967] iv, 83p. illus., map. 27cm. First ed. pub. in 1965 under title: Jewish holidays, cycle I. Text in English and Hebrew. [BM690.F38 1967] 68-1607 price unreported
1. Fasts and feasts—Judaism & Juvenile literature. I. Title.

GAMORAN, Mamie (Goldsmith) 296.43
Hillel's calendar. Illus. by Ida Libby Dengrove. New York, Union of American Hebrew Congregations [c.1960] 196p. illus. (part col.) (Commission on Jewish Education of the Union of American Hebrew Congregations and Central Conference of American Rabbis. Union graded series) 60-10180 2.75
1. Fasts and feasts—Judaism—Juvenile literature. I. Title.

GARVEY, Robert 296.43
Holidays are nice; around the year with the Jewish child. Illustrated by Ezekiel Scholss and Arnold Lobel. New York, Ktav Pub. House [c.1960] 52p. illus. (part col.) 34cm. 60-11068 1.95 bds.,
1. Fasts and feasts—Judaism—Juvenile literature. I. Title.

GERSH, Harry. 296.4'3
When a Jew celebrates. With Eugene B. Borowitz and Hyman Chanover. Illus. by Erika Weihs. New York, Behrman House [1971] 256 p. col. illus. 25 cm. (The Jewish values series) Describes the special days celebrated by a Jew and the Jewish community. [BM690.G45] 70-116678 ISBN 0-87441-091-6
1. Fasts and feasts—Judaism—Juvenile literature. I. Weihs, Erika, illus. II. Title.

GOLOMB, Morris. 296.4'3
Know your festivals and enjoy them; the how and why of the Jewish festivals. New York, Shengold Publishers [1973, c1972] 189 p. illus. 27 cm. Bibliography: p. 183. Traces the history of thirteen Jewish holidays explaining why and how they are celebrated. [BM690.G59] 72-90771 5.50
1. Fasts and feasts—Judaism—Juvenile literature. I. Title.

GREENBERG, Sidney, 1917- 296.4'3
comp.
High holiday Bible themes. New York, Hartmore House [1973- v. 25 cm. (Teaching and preaching) Contents.Contents.—v. 1. Rosh Hashana. [BM693.H5G73] 73-83990 ISBN 0-87677-152-5 12.50
1. High Holy Days—Addresses, essays, lectures. I. Title. II. Series.

HESCHEL, Abraham Joshua, 296.43
1907-1972.
Man's quest for God; studies in prayer and symbolism. New York, Scribner, 1954. 151 p. 22 cm. [BM669.H45] 54-10371
1. Prayer. 2. Symbolism. I. Title.

JACOBS, Louis 296.43
The Jewish festivals; New Year, the Day of Atonement, Tabernacles, Passover, Pentecost. Hanukkah Purim. Worcester, Mass., 7 Arden Rd., Achille J. St. Onge, 1961. 63p. illus. 7cm. 3.50 leather,
1. Fasts and Feasts—Judaism. 2. Bibliography—Microscopic and miniature editions—Specimens. I. Title.

JEWS. Liturgy and ritual. 296.4'3
High Holy Day prayers.
A contemporary High Holiday service for teenagers and ... [by] Sidney Greenberg and S. Allan Sugarman. Hartford, Conn., Prayer Book Press [1970] 1 v. (loose-leaf) illus. 30 cm. On cover: Mahazor le-Rosh ha-shanah ule-Yom ha-ki-purim (romanized form) Hebrew and English. [BM666.G658] 74-123891 ISBN 8-7677-0405-
I. Greenberg, Sidney, 1917- II. Sugarman, S. Allan. III. Jews. Liturgy and ritual. High Holy Day prayers. English. IV. Jews. Liturgy and ritual. Children's services. V. Title.

KARFF, Joan M. 296.4'3
The adventures of Adam, by Joan M. Karff. Illustrated by Patti Yale. Northbrook, Ill., Whitehall Co. [1970] 55 p. col. illus. 24 cm. An eight-year-old boy learns the meaning of six Jewish holidays: Sukos, Chanuko, Purim, Passover, Shavuos, and the Sabbath. [BM690.K33] 68-26395
1. Fasts and feasts—Judaism—Juvenile literature. I. Yale, Patti, illus. II. Title.

KIRSHENBAUM, David, 1902- 296.4'3
Feast days and fast days; Judaism seen through its festivals. New York, Bloch Pub. Co. [1969, c1968] 247 p. 24 cm. [BM745.K5] 68-58497 5.00
1. Festival-day sermons, Jewish. 2. Sermons, English—Canada—Jewish authors. I. Title.

KITOV, Eliyahu, 1912- 296.4'3
The book of our heritage; the Jewish year and its days of significance. Translated from the Hebrew 'Sefer hatoda'ah' by Nathan Bulman. Jerusalem, New York, "A" Publishers [1968] 3 v. 23 cm. Translation of Sefer ha-toda'ah (romanized form) Contents.Contents.—v. 1. Tishrey-Shevat.—v. 2. Adar Nisan.—v. 3. Iyar-Elul. [BM690.K5313] HE 68 52.50 ($15.00)
1. Fasts and feasts—Judaism. I. Title.

KLAPERMAN, Libby M 296.43
Jeremy and Judy say the Sh'ma. Story by Libby M. Klaperman. Pictures by Patricia Villemain. New York, Behrman House [cu956] unpaged. illus. 21cm. (The Play-and-learn library) [BM670.S15K56] 57-1654
1. Shema' (Jewish prayer)—Juvenile literature. I. Title.

KRIPKE, Dorothy (Karp) 296.43
Debbie in dreamland, her holiday adventures. Illus. by Bill Giacalone. Design of book and art supervision by Ezekiel Schloss. [New York27] [3080 Bway. National Women's League of the United Synagogue of America c.1960] 54p. col. illus. 25cm. 60-16588 2.95 bds.,
1. Fasts and feasts—Judaism—Juvenile literature. I. Title.

KRIPKE, Dorothy (Karp) 296.43
Debbie in dreamland, her holiday adventures. Illus. by Bill Glacolone. Design of book and art supervision by Ezekiel Schloss. [New York] National Women's League of the United Synagogue of America [1960] 54p. illus. 25cm. [BM690.K7] 60-16588
1. Fasts and feasts—Judaism—Juvenile literature. I. Title.

KUSHNER, Harold S. 296.4'3
Commanded to live / by Harold Kushner.

Bridgeport, Conn. : Hartmore House, c1973. 128 p. ; 21 cm. [BM745.K86] 73-91738 ISBN 0-87677-154-1 : 7.95
1. Festival-day sermons, Jewish. 2. Sermons, American—Jewish authors. 3. Sermons, Jewish—United States. I. Title.

LAZAR, Wendy. 296.4'3
The Jewish holiday book / by Wendy Lazar ; illustrated by Marion Behr. 1st ed. Garden City, N.Y. : Doubleday, c1977. 143 p. : col. ill. ; 22 cm. Includes index. Suggests easy handicraft and cooking projects for major Jewish holidays, the Sabbath celebration, and Israel Independence day. [BM690.5134] 76-42342 ISBN 0-385-11426-5 : 7.95.
1. Fasts and feasts—Judaism—Juvenile literature. 2. Hand craft—Juvenile literature. 3. Cookery, Jewish—Juvenile literature. I. Behr, Marion. II. Title.

MARGOLIS, Isidor. 296.43
Jewish holidays and festivals, by Isidor Margolis and Sidney L. Markowitz. Illus. by John Teppich. New York, Citadel Press [1962] 123p. illus. 21cm. [BM690.M3] 62-19769
1. Fasts and feasts—Judaism. I. Markowitz, Sidney L, 1906- joint author. II. Title.

RICHMOND, Harry R 1890- 296.43
God on trial. [Sermons] New York, B. Wheelwright Co., 1955. 156p. 21cm. [BM740.R47] 55-6261
1. Sermons, Jewish—U. S. 2. Sermons, American— Jewish authors. I. Title.

ROSENBERG, Stuart E 296.43
Man is free; sermons and addresses. New York, Bloch Pub. Co., 1957. 155p. 22cm. [BM740.R668] 57-13232
1. Sermons, Jewish—Canada. 2. Sermons, English—Jewish authors—Canada. I. Title.

SCHAUSS, Hayyim, 1884-1953 296.43
Guide to Jewish holy days: history and observance. Tr. [from Hebrew] by Samuel Jaffe. New York, Schocken [1962, c.1938] 316p. 21cm. (Schocken paperbacks, SB26) 62-13140 1.75 pap.,
1. Fasts and feasts—Judaism. I. Title.

SEIDMAN, Hillel. 296.4'3
The glory of the Jewish holidays. Edited by Moses Zalesky. [1st ed.] New York, Shengold Publishers [1969, c1968] 239 p. illus., facsims. 29 cm. [BM690.S42] 68-58504 10.00
1. Fasts and feasts—Judaism. I. Zalesky, Moses, 1905- ed. II. Title.

SHAPP, Martha. 296.4'3
Let's find out about Jewish holidays, by Martha and Charles Shapp. Pictures by Marvin Friedman. New York, F. Watts [1971] 48 p. col. illus. 23 cm. An easy-to-read introduction to the Jewish holidays explaining their origins in Jewish history. [BM690.S318] 74-131142 ISBN 0-531-00067-2
1. Fasts and feasts—Judaism—Juvenile literature. I. Shapp, Charles, joint author. II. Friedman, Marvin, illus. III. Title.

SPERO, Shubert, 296.4'3
God in all seasons. New York, Shengold [1967] 175 p. 23 cm. Includes bibliographical references. [BM745.S64] 67-30002
1. Festival-day sermons, Jewish. 2. Sermons, American—Jewish authors. I. Title.

SPERO, Shubert. 296.4'3
God in all seasons. New York, Shengold [1967] 175 p. 23 cm. Includes bibliographical references. [BM745.S64] 67-30002
1. Festival-day sermons, Jewish. 2. Sermons, American—Jewish authors. I. Title.

ZUCKERMANN, Benedict, 1818-1891. 296.4'3
A treatise of the Sabbatical cycle and the Jubilee : a contribution to the archaeology and chronology of the time anterior and subsequent to the captivity : accompanied by a table of Sabbatical years / translated from the German of B. Zuckermann by A. Lowy. New York : Hermon Press, 1974. 64 p. ; 24 cm. Translation of Uber Sabbathjahrcyclus und Jubelperiode. Reprint of the 1866 ed. printed for the Chronological Institute of London. Includes index. Bibliography: p. 4-6. [BM720.S2Z913 1974] 74-78326 ISBN 0-87203-044-X : 6.75
1. Sabbatical year (Judaism) 2. Jubilee (Judaism) I. Title.

SPIRO, Saul S. 296.4307
The joy of Jewish living; Jewish holidays and practices at home and in the synagogue, by Saul S. Spiro and Rena M. Spiro. Cleveland, Bureau of Jewish Education, 1965 [c1963] 208 p. illus. 24 cm. Bibliography: p. 204-205. [BM690.S67] 65-14982
1. Fasts and Feasts — Judaism. I. Spiro, Rena M., joint author. II. Title.

*AGNON, Samuel Joseph 296.431
Samuel [Joseph Czaczkes]
Days of awe; being a treasury of traditions, legends and learned commentaries concerning Rosh ha-Shan-ah, Yom Kippur and the days, between, culled from three hundred volumes, ancient and new. [Tr. from Hebrew by Maurice T. Galpert. Tr. rev. by Jacob Sloan. Ed., abridged by Nahum N. Glatzer] Introd. by Judah Goldin. New York, Schocken [1965, c.1948, 1965] xxxii, 297p. 21cm. (SB100) Bibl. [BM690.A433] 1.95 pap.,
1. Festivals—Jews. 2. Jews—Rites and ceremonies. 3. Legends, Jewish. I. Galpert, Maurice T., tr. II. Glatzer, Nahum Norbert, 1903- ed. III. Title.

ARZT, Max. 296.431
Justice and mercy: commentary on the liturgy of the new year and the day of Atonement. [1st ed.] New York, Holt, Rinehart and Winston [1963] 298 p. 21 cm. Bibliography: p. [297]-298. [BM695.N5A8] 63-11872
1. Rosh ha-Shanah. 2. Yom Kippur. I. Title.

BARISH, Louis. 296.431
High Holiday liturgy. New York, Jonathan David [c1959] 174p. 23cm. [BM675.H5B3] 59-10540
1. Jews. Liturgy and ritual. High Holy Day prayers. I. Title.

GINSBURG, Leo. 296.4'31
The comprehensive supplement to the Machzor for the Yamim noraim; Torah teaching, elucidation, meditation, and supplication, reflection, resolution, and regeneration. New York, Bloch [1972] vi, 181 p. illus. 22 cm. Added t.p. and text in Hebrew. Includes some selections in Hebrew. [BM675.H5G56] 72-85803 ISBN 0-8197-0294-3
1. Jews. Liturgy and ritual. High Holy Day prayers—Commentaries. I. Jews. Liturgy and ritual. High Holy Day prayers. 1972. II. Title. III. Title: Tosefet kolelet la-mahazor la-Yamin ha-nora'im.

KIEVAL, Herman 296.431
The High Holy Days; a commentary on the prayerbook of Rosh Hashanah and Yom Kippur. Book One: Rosh Hashanah. New York, Burning Bush Press [c.1959] ix, 234p. 24cm. (bibl. notes: p. 196-232) 59-14794 5.00
1. Jews. Liturgy and ritual. High Holy Day prayers. I. Title.

SIMON, Norma. 296.431
Rosh Hashanah. Illus. by Ayala Gordon. [New York] United Synagogue Commission on Jewish Education, c1959 unpaged. illus. 25 cm. [BM695.N5S5] 59-12528
1. Rosh ha-Shanah — Juvenile literature. I. Title.

SIMON, Norma. 296.431
Rosh Hashanah. Illus, by Ayala Gordon. [New York 27] United Synagogue Commission on Jewish Education, c.1959. unpaged. illus. (col.) 25 x 15cm. 59-12528 .95 bds.,
1. Rosh ha-Shanah—Juvenile literature. I. Title.

SIMON, Norma. 296.432
Yom Kippur. Illus. by Ayala Gordon. [New York] United Synagogue Commission on Jewish Education, c1959. unpaged. illus. 25 cm. [BM695.A8S5] 59-12529
1. Yom Kippur-Juvenile literature I. Title.

SIMON, Norma. 296.432
Yom Kippur. Illus. by Ayala Gordon. [New York 27] 3080 Bway. United Synagogue Commission on Jewish Education, c.1959. unpaged. illus. (col.) 25 x 15cm. 59-12529 .95 bds.,
1. Yom Kippur—Juvenile literature. I. Title.

GOODMAN, Philip, 1911- comp. 296.4'32'08
The Yom Kippur anthology. [1st ed.] Philadelphia, Jewish Publication Society of America, 1971. xxix, 399 p. illus., facsims., music. 22 cm. Companion volume to the compiler's The Rosh Hashanah anthology. Bibliography: p. 387-399. [BM695.A8G66] 72-151312 7.50
1. Yom Kippur. I. Title.

ADLER, David A. 296.4'33
The house on the roof : a Sukkot story / by David A. Adler ; pictures by Marilyn Hirsh. New York : Bonim Books, c1976. [32] p. : col. ill. ; 26 cm. [BM107.A34] 76-19014 ISBN 0-88482-905-7 : 5.95
1. Sukkoth—Juvenile literature. I. Hirsh, Marilyn. II. Title.

GOODMAN, Philip, 1911- comp. 296.4'33
The Sukkot and Simhat Torah anthology. [1st ed.] Philadelphia, Jewish Publication Society of America, 1973. xxxiii, 475 p. illus. 25 cm. Bibliography: p. [459]-475. [BM695.S8G66] 72-14058 ISBN 0-8276-0010-0 7.50
1. Sukkoth—Addresses, essays, lectures. 2. Simhat Torah—Addresses, essays, lectures. I. Title.

SIMON, Norma. 296.433
Our first Sukkah. Illus. by Ayala Gordon. [New York] United Synagogue Commission on Jewish Education, c1959. unpaged. illus. 25 cm. [BM695.S8S5] 59-12530
1. Sukkoth — Juvenile literature. I. Title.

SIMON, Norma 296.433
Our first Sukkah. Illus. by Ayala Gordon. [New York 27] 3080 Bway. United Synagogue Commission on Jewish Education, c.1959. unpaged. illus. (col.) 25x15cm. 59-12530 .95 bds.,
1. Sukkoth—Juvenile literature. I. Title.

ABRAMSON, Lillian S. 296.4'35
Hanukkah ABC, by Lillian Abramson. Illustrated by Gabe Josephson. New York, Shulsinger Bros. [1968] [55] p. col. illus. 26 cm. Each letter of the alphabet introduces a word or a name describing the customs and origins of Hanukkah. [BM695.H3A58] 70-3659
1. Hanukkah (Feast of Lights)—Juvenile literature. I. Josephson, Gabe, illus. II. Title.

AMERICAN Association for Medico-Physical Research. 296.435
Proceedings of the annual convention. [n. p.] v. illus. 23cm. Title varies slightly. Vols. for issued by the association under an earlier name: American Association for the Study of Spondylotherapy. [BM695.Al] 62-56658
1. Physical therapy—Societies, etc. I. Title.

CHIEL, Kinneret, ed. 296.435
The complete book of Hanukkah. Illustrated by Arnold Lobel. New York 2, 65 Suffolk St., Friendly House Publishers, [c.1959] xiii, 108p. illus. 26cm. (bibl.) 59-15661 2.50
1. Hanukkah (Feast of Lights)—Juvenile literature. I. Title.

CHIEL, Kinneret, ed. 296.4'35
The complete book of Hanukkah / by Kinneret Chiel ; illustrated by Arnold Lobel. New York : Ktav Pub. House, [1976] p. cm. Reprint of the 1959 ed. published by Friendly House Publishers, New York. Bibliography: p. [BM695.H3C5 1976] 75-40464 ISBN 0-87068-367-5 pbk. : 3.00
1. Hanukkah (Feast of Lights)—Juvenile literature. I. Title.

EDELMAN, Lily. 296.435
The sukkah and the big wind. With illus. by Leonard Kessler. [New York] United Synagogue Commission on Jewish Education, c1956. unpaged. illus. 28cm. [BM695.S8E3] 56-44770
1. Sukkoth—Juvenile literature. I. Title.

GREENFELD, Howard. 296.4'35
Chanukah / by Howard Greenfeld ; designed by Bea Feitler. 1st ed. New York : Holt, Rinehart and Winston, c1976. 39 p. : ill. ; 16 x 24 cm. [BM695.H3G67] 76-6527 ISBN 0-03-015566-5 : 4.95
1. Hanukkah (Feast of lights) I. Title.

MORROW, Betty. 296.4'35 (j)
A great miracle: the story of Hanukkah. Illustrated by Howard Simon. Irvington-on-Hudson, N.Y., Harvey House [1968] 40 p. illus. 26 cm. [BM695.H3M67] 68-22984 2.95
1. Hanukkah (Feast of Lights)—Juvenile literature. I. Simon, Howard, 1903- illus. II. Title.

ROSENBLUM, William F. 296.4'35
Eight lights; the story of Chanukah, by William F. and Robert J. Rosenblum. Illustrated by Shraga Weil. [1st ed.] Garden City, N. Y., Doubleday, 1967. 94 p. illus. 27 cm. [BM695.H3R6] 67-12543
1. Hanukkah (Feast of lights) I. Rosenblum, Robert J., joint author. II. Title.

SCHARFSTEIN, Edythe, 1922- 296.435
The book of Chanukah; poems, riddles, stories, songs, and things to do, by Edythe and Sol Scharfstein. Illustrated by Ezekiel Schloss and Arnold Lobel. 2d rev. ed. [New York] Ktav Pub. House, c1959. unpaged. illus. 25cm. [BM695.H3S3 1959] 59-9971
1. Hanukkah (Feast of Lights)—Juvenile literature. I. Scharfstein, Sol, 1921- joint author. II. Title.

SCHARFSTEIN, Edythe, 1922- 296.435
Chanukah treasure chest, by Edythe and Sol Scharfstein. Illus. by Ezekiel Schloss and Cyla London. [New York] Ktav Pub. House [1958] unpaged. illus. 32cm. [BM695.H3S2915] 59-17822
1. Hanukkah (feast of lights)—juvenile literature. I. Scharfstein, Sol, 1921- joint author. II. Title.

SIMON, Norma. 296.435
Hanukah in my house. Illus. by Ayala Gordon. [New York] United Synagogue Commission on Jewish Education, c1960. unpaged. illus. 25 cm. [BM695.H3S5] 60-3662
1. Hanukah (Feast of Lights) — Juvenile literature. I. Title.

WENGROV, Charles 296.435
Hanukkah in song and story; being the enthralling story of Hanukkah, in full, from the times of Alexander the Great to the victorious rebuilding of the Temple. Written and illustrated especially for children; together with a collection of beloved melodies for the eight nights of Hanukkah. Illustrated by Emanuel Schary. Music edited by Samuel Bugatch. New York [21 E. 4 St., [3] Shulsinger Bros. c.1960] 80p. illus. (part col.) map music. 32cm. 60-51055 1.50 bds.,
1. Hanukkah (Feast of Lights)—Juvenile literature. 2. Hanukkah (Feast of Lights)—Songs and music. I. Title.

THE Hanukkah anthology / Philip Goodman. 1st ed. Philadelphia : Jewish Publication Society of America, 1976. xxiii, 465 p. : ill. ; 25 cm. Bibliography: p. 440-465. [BM695.H3H37] 75-44637 ISBN 0-8276-0080-1 : 8.95 296.4'35'08
1. Hanukkah (Feast of lights)—Addresses, essays, lectures. 2. Hanukkah (Feast of lights)—Literary collections. I. Goodman, Philip, 1911-

SIMON, Norma. 296.436
Happy Purim night. Illus. by Ayala Gordon. [New York] United Synagogue Commission on Jewish Education, c1959 unpaged. illus. 25 cm. [BM695.P8S54] 59-12531
1. Purim (Feast of Esther) — Juvenie literature. I. Title.

SIMON, Norma 296.436
Happy Purim night. Illus. by Ayala Gordon. [New York 27] 3080 Bway.] United Synagogue Commission on Jewish Education, c.1959 unpaged. illus. (col.) 25x15cm. 59-12531 .95 bds.,
1. Purim (Feast of Esther)—Juvenile literature. I. Title.

SIMON, Norma. 296.436
The Purim party. Illus. by Ayala Gordon. [New York] United Synagogue Commission on Jewish Education, c1959. unpaged. illus. 25 cm. [BM695.P8S55] 59-12532
1. Purim (Feast of Esther) — Juvenile literature. I. Title.

SIMON, Norma. 296.436
The Purim party. Illus. by Ayala Gordon. [New York 27] 3080 Bway., United Synagogue Commission on Jesish Education, c.1959. unpaged. illus. (col.) 25 x 15cm. 59-12532 .95 bds.,
1. Purim (Feast of Esther)—Juvenile literature. I. Title.

FROM twilight to dawn; 296.437
the traditional Pessach Hagada, arranged by Rabbi Shlomo Kahn. New York 40, P.O. Box 62 Scribe Publications, [c.1960] 159p. Hebrew and English 60-10694 2.95
I. Kahn, Shlomo, ed. II. Jews. Liturgy and ritual. Hagadah. English. 1960. III. Title: From twilight to dawn.

GOODMAN, Philip, 1911- ed. 296.437
The Passover anthology. Philadelphia, Jewish Pubn. Soc. of America [1962, c.1961] 496p. illus. (JPS holiday ser.) Bibl. 61-11706 5.00
1. Passover. I. Title.

HYNES, Arleen. 296.4'37
The Passover meal; a ritual for Christian homes. New York, Paulist Press [1972] 63 p. illus. 17 cm. [BV199.P25H94] 76-187207 ISBN 0-8091-1653-7 0.75 (pbk.)
1. Jews. Liturgy and ritual. Hagadah. 2. Passover—Christian observance. 3. Family—Prayer-books and devotions—English. I. Title.

JEWS. Liturgy and ritual. Hagadah. 1969. 296.4'37
[Hagadah shel Pesah (romanized form)] From twilight to dawn; the traditional Passover Haggadah. Arr. by Shlomo Kahn. [2d ed. rev. and enl.] New York, Scribe Publications [1969] 177 p. illus. 24 cm. Hebrew and English. [BM675.P4K25 1969] 69-18887
I. Kahn, Shlomo. II. Jews. Liturgy and ritual. Hagadah. English. 1969. III. Title: From twilight to dawn.

JEWS. Liturgy and ritual. Hagadah. 1969. 296.4'37
The Passover Haggadah. With English translation, introd., and commentary based on the commentaries of E. D. Goldschmidt; edited by Nahum N. Glatzer. Rev. ed. New York, Schocken Books [1969] xxvii, 109 p. illus. 22 cm. Text in English and Hebrew on opposite pages. Translation of the Haggadah

text by Jacob Sloan. [BM675.P4G55 1969] 69-10846 4.50
I. Goldschmidt, Ernst Daniel. II. Glatzer, Nahum Norbert, 1903- ed. III. Jews. Liturgy and ritual. Hagadah. English. 1969. IV. Title.

JEWS. Liturgy and Ritual. Hagadah. 1974. 296.4'37
A Passover Haggadah; the New Union Haggadah edited by Herbert Bronstein for the Central Conference of American Rabbis. Drawings by Leonard Baskin. New York, Grossman Publishers, 1974 123 p. col. illus. 37 cm. Hebrew and English. Unaccompanied Melodies (Hebrew text Romanized): p. 97-122. [BM675.P4B76 1974] 73-16576 ISBN 0-670-54187-7 17.50
1. Jews. Liturgy and ritual. Hagadah. English. 1974. I. Bronstein, Herbert, ed. II. Baskin, Leonard, 1922- illus. III. Central Conference of American Rabbis. IV. Title.

JEWS. Liturgy and ritual. Hagadah. Selections. 1970. 296.4'37
The Passover Seder; pathways through the Haggadah, arranged by Arthur Gilbert. Illustrated by Ezekiel Schloss [and] Uri Shulevitz. Music arranged by Moshe Nathanson. [New York] Ktav Pub. House [1970] 64 p. col. illus. 26 cm. Partly in Hebrew. "Passover music" (melodies, part with words in English, part in Hebrew transliterated): p. 57-64. [BM675.P4G52 1970] 71-12643
I. Gilbert, Arthur, ed. II. Jews. Liturgy and ritual. Hagadah. English. Selections. 1970. III. Title.

JEWS. Liturgy and ritual. Benedictions. 296.4'37
The illustrated prayers, blessings and hymns; translated by Abraham Burstein. New York, Ktav Pub. House [1954] 198p. col. illus. 15cm. Hebrew and English. [BM675.B4B8] 55-46121
I. Burstein, Abraham, 1896- ed. and tr. II. Title.

JEWS. Liturgy and ritual. Festival prayers. 296.4'37
Festival prayer book, with supplementary prayers and readings and with a new English translation. New York, Jewish Reconstructionist Foundation, 1958. 546p. 19cm. [BM675.F45J37] 57-13301
I. Jews. Liturgy and ritual. Festival prayers. English. II. Jewish Reconstructionist Foundation. III. Title.

JEWS. Liturgy and ritual. Hagadah. 1953. 296.4'37
The Passover Haggadah; with English translation [by Jacob Sloan] Introd. and commentary based on the commentaries of E. D. Goldschmidt; edited by Nahum N. Glatzer. [New York] Schocken Books and Farrap, Straus and Young [1953] 113p. illus. 24cm. Half title: [BM675.P4G55] 53-1493
I. Jews, Liturgy and ritual. Hagadah. English. 1953. II. Glatzer, Nahum Norbert, 1903- ed. III. Title.

JEWS. Liturgy and ritual. Hagadah. 1965 296.437
Haggadah for Passover. Copied, illus. by Ben Shahn Tr., introd., hist. notes by Cecil Roth. Boston, Little [c.]1965. xix, 133p. illus., col. plates. 31cm. English and Hebrew [BM675.P4A3] 65-12443 20.00
I. Jews. Liturgy and ritual. Hagadah. English. 1965. II. Shahn, Ben, 1898- illus. III. Roth, Cecil, 1899- ed. IV. Title.

JEWS. Liturgy and ritual. Hagadah. Selections. 1965. 296.437
The Passover Seder; pathways through the Haggadah, arranged by Arthur Gilbert. Illus. by Ezekiel Schloss, Uri Shulevitz. Music arranged by Moshe Nathanson [New York] Ktav [c.1965] 64p. col. illus. 26cm. Partly in Hebrew. Passover music (unacc. melodies, pt. with words in English, part in Hebrew transliterated) [BM675.P4G52] 65-17003 .50 pap.,
I. Gilbert, Arthur, ed. II. Jews. Liturgy and ritual. Hagadah. English. Selections. 1965. III. Title.

JEWS. Liturgy and ritual. Haggadah. 1965. 296.437
Haggadah for Passover. Copied and illustrated by Ben Shahn. With a translation, introd., and historical notes by Cecil Roth. Boston, Little, Brown, 1965. xix, 133 p. illus., col. plates. 31 cm. Added t.p. in Hebrew. English and Hebrew. Based on Cecil Roth's ed. of 1934. [BM675.P4A3 1965] 65-12443
1. Jews. Liturgy and ritual. Hagadah. English. 1965. I. Shahn, Ben, 1898- illus. II. Roth, Cecil, 1899- ed. III. Title.

JEWS. LITURGY AND RITUAL. HAGADAH. 1966. 296.437
Hagadah for Pesach. [prepared by members and children of Congregation Solel, Highland Park, Ill. Highland Park? Ill., 1966] 72 p. illus. 24 cm. Partly in Hebrew. Unacc. melodies, most with words in Hebrew transliterated. [BM675.P4A3 1966] 66-5535
I. Jews. Liturgy and ritual. Hagadah. English. 1966. II. Highland Park, Ill. Congregation Solel. III. Title.

JEWS. LITURGY AND RITUAL. HAGADAH. SELECTIONS. 1965. 296.437
The Passover Seder; pathways through the Haggadah, arranged by Arthur Gilbert. Illustrated by Ezekiel Schloss [and] Uri Schulevitz Music arranged by Moshe Nathanson. [New York] Ktav Pub. House [1965] 64 p. col. illus. 26 cm. Partly in Hebrew. "Passover music" (unacc. melodies, part with words in English, part in Hebrew transliterated): p. 57-64. [BM675.P4G52] 65-17003
I. Gilbert, Arthur, ed. II. Jews. Liturgy and ritual. Hagadah. English. Selections. 1965. III. Title.

LEVITAN, Elsie. 296.4'37
Haggadah for a secular celebration of Pesach / [written and edited by Elsie Levitan, Max Rosenfeld, Bess Katz ; ill. and calligraphy by Ruthie Rosenfeld]. Philadelphia : Sholom Aleichem Club of Philadelphia, [1975] 63 p. : col. ill., music ; 25 cm. English, Hebrew, or Yiddish. Includes unacc. melodies. [BM675.P45L45] 75-311796
1. Haggadot, Secular. I. Rosenfeld, Max, 1913- joint author. II. Katz, Bess, joint author. III. Rosenfeld, Ruthie. IV. Jews. Liturgy and ritual. Hagadah. V. Sholom Aleichem Club of Philadelphia. VI. Title.

RAPHAEL, Chaim. 296.4'37
A feast of history; Passover through the ages as a key to Jewish experience. With a new translation of the Haggadah for use at the Seder. [Photos. by David Harris] New York, Simon and Schuster [1972] 250 p. illus. (part col.), facsims. (part col.), maps. 25 cm. Text of Hagadah (p. 158-250) in Hebrew and English. Bibliography: p. 157. [BM675.P4Z884] 72-176499 ISBN 0-671-21175-7 12.50
1. Jews. Liturgy and ritual. Hagadah. 2. Jews. Liturgy and ritual. Hagadah—Illustrations. 3. Illumination of books and manuscripts, Jewish. I. Harris, David, fl. 1967- illus. II. Jews. Liturgy and ritual. Hagadah. 1972. III. Jews. Liturgy and ritual. Hagadah. English. 1972. IV. Title.

SEGAL, Judah Benzion, 1912- 296.437
The Hebrew Passover, from the earliest times to A. D. 70. London. New York, Oxford University Press, 1963. xiv, 294 p. 26 cm. (London oriental series, v. 12) Bibliography: p. [270]-289. [BM695.P3S4] 63-3751
1. Passover. I. Title. II. Series.

SEGAL, Judas Benzion, 1912- 296.437
The Hebrew Passover, from the earliest times to A.D. 70. New York, Oxford [c.]1963. xiv, 294p. 26cm. (London oriental ser., v.12) Bibl. 63-3751 6.75
1. Passover. I. Title. II. Series.

WASKOW, Arthur I. 296.4'37
The freedom seder; a new Haggadah for Passover, by Arthur I. Waskow. [1st ed.] New York, Holt, Rinehart, Winston; [mail distribution by] Micah Press, Washington [1970] vii, 56 p. illus. 19 cm. [BM675.P45W3] 79-103557 3.95
I. Jews. Liturgy and ritual. Hagadah. English. 1970. II. Title.

WENGROV, Charles Rabbi 296.437
Passover in song and story; being a dramatic narrative account of the Hebrews in Egypt, from the days of Joseph to the great Exodus written and illustrated especially for children, together with a collection of best-loved melodies for the Passover seder. Illustrated by Emanuel Schary; music edited by Samuel Bugatch. New York3, 21 E. 4th St. Press of Shulsinger Bros., [c.1960] 64p. col. illus., map (on lining papers) 32cm. 'The songs of Passover' (unacc.): p.51-64. 60-1573 1.50 bds.,
1. Passover. I. Title.

YERUSHALMI, Yosef Hayim, 1932- 296.4'37
Haggadah and history : a panorama in facsimile of five centuries of the printed Haggadah from the collections of Harvard University and the Jewish Theological Seminary of America / by Yosef Hayim Yerushalmi. 1st ed. Philadelphia : Jewish Publication Society of America, [1974] 494 p. : facsims. ; 31 cm. Includes index. Bibliography: p. 489-492. [BM675.P4Z95] 73-21169 ISBN 0-8276-0046-1 : 27.50
1. Jews. Liturgy and ritual. Hagadah—Illustrations. 2. Harvard University. Library. 3. Jewish Theological Seminary of America. Library. I. Title.

*RANDOLPH, David. 296.438
Pentecost 1 [by] David Randolph and Jack Kingsbury. Philadelphia, Fortress Press, [1975] vii, 55 p. 22 cm. (Proclamation; aids for interpreting the lessons of the church year.) (Series B.) Includes bibliographical references. [BV4300.5] [[BV60]] 74-24959 ISBN 0-8006-40764 1.95 (pbk.)
1. Bible—Liturgical lessons. 2. Pentecost. I. Kingsbury, Jack. joint author. II. Title.

THE Shavuot anthology / Philip Goodman. 1st ed. Philadelphia : The Jewish Publication Society of America, 1975, c1974 xxv, 369 p. : ill. ; 24 cm. "Music for Shavuot, compiled and edited by Paul Kavon": p. [323]-337. Bibliography: p. 353-369. [BM695.S5S5] 74-25802 ISBN 0-8276-0057-7 : 7.95 296.4'38
1. Shavu'oth (Feast of Weeks)—Addresses, essays, lectures. 2. Shavu'oth (Feast of Weeks)—Literary collections. I. Goodman, Philip, 1911-

SIMON, Norma. 296.439
Simhat Torah. Illus. by Ayala Gordon. [New York] United Synagogue Commission on Jewish Education, c1960. unpaged. illus. 25 cm. [BM695.S6S5] 60-3736
1. Simhat Torah — Juvenile literature. I. Title.

COHON, Beryl David, 1898- 296.4'4
Vision and faith; confirmation services for Jewish congregations, by Beryl D. Cohon. New York, Bloch Pub. Co., 1968. ix, 62 p. 28 cm. [BM707.4.C6] 68-22888
1. Confirmation (Jewish rite) I. Title.

FRIEMAN, Donald G 296.44
Milestones in the life of the Jew; a basic guide to belief and ritual, by Donald G. Frieman. New York, Bloch Pub. Co. [1965] x, 116 p. 19 cm. [BM700.F75] 65-15710
1. Jews — Rites and ceremonies. I. Title.

FRIEMAN, Donald G. 296.44
Milestones in the life of the Jew; a basic guide to belief and ritual. New York, Bloch [c.1965] x, 116p. [BM700.F75] 65-15710 3.50
1. Jews—Rites and ceremonies. I. Title.

KITOV, Eliyahu, 1912- 296.44
The Jew and his home. Translated with an introd. by Nathan Bulman. New York, Shengold Publishers [1963] 233 p. 24 cm. (romanized: Ish u-veto) [BM700.K5213] 63-17660
1. Jews—Rites and ceremonies. 2. Jewish way of life. 3. Family—Religious life. I. Title.

MOKOTOVSKY, Abraham. 296.44
The Jew and his home, by Eliyahu Kitov [pseud.] Translated with an introd. by Nathan Bulman. New York, Shengold Publishers [1963] 233 p. 24 cm. [BM700.M613] 63-17660
1. Jews — Rites and ceremonies. 2. Jewish way of life. 3. Family — Religious life. I. Title.

[MOKOTOVSKY, Abraham] 296.44
The Jew and his home, by Eliyahu Kitov [pseud.] Tr., introd. by Nathan Bulman. New York, Shengold Pubs. [1963] 233p. 24cm. 63-17660 5.00
1. Jews—Rites and ceremonies. 2. Jewish way of life. 3. Family—Religious life. I. Title.

NEMZOFF, Samuel A., comp. 296.4'4
Confirmation service sampler, compiled and edited by Samuel A. Nemzoff. [New York] Union of American Hebrew Congregations [1969] xxv, 514 p. 28 cm. (Union graded series) Includes music. Bibliography: p. 507-513. [BM707.4.N4] 68-9352 6.00
1. Confirmation (Jewish rite) I. Title. II. Series: Commission on Jewish Education of the Union of American Hebrew Congregations and the Central Conference of American Rabbis. Union graded series

GOTTLIEB, Nathan 296.4422
A Jewish child is born; the history and ritual of circumcision, redemption of firstborn son, adoption, conversion, and choosing and giving names. New York, Bloch Pub. Co. [c.1960] 159p. 60-16833 3.50
1. Circumcision. 2. Names, Personal—Jewish. I. Title.

EFRON, Benjamin 296.4424
Your Bar mitzvah [by] Benjamin Efron, Alvan D. Rubin. Illus. by Hal Just. [New York] Union of Amer. Hebrew Cong. [c.1963] 42p. illus. 16cm. Includes text in Hebrew. 62-22157 .75 bds.,
1. Bar mitzvah. I. Rubin, Alvan D., joint author. II. Title.

GREENBERG, Sidney, 1917- ed. 296.4424
The Bar mitzvah companion, edited by Sidney Greenberg [and] Abraham Rothberg. New York, Behrman House [1959] 314p. 21cm. [BM707.G7] 59-12059
1. Bar mitzvah. I. Rothberg, Abraham, joint ed. II. Title.

KATSH, Abraham Isaac, 1908- ed. 296.4'424
Bar mitzvah illustrated. Edited by Abraham I. Katsh. 4th ed. New York. Shengold Publishers [1964, c1955] 157 p. illus. 29 cm. [BM707.K28] 64-8404
1. Bar mitzvah — Handbooks, manuals, etc. 2. Judaism — Pictures, illustrations, etc. I. Title.

KATSH, Abraham Isaac, 1908- ed. 296.4424
Bar mitzvah illustrated. 3d ed. New York, Shengold Publishers [1961, c.1955] 157p. illus. 29cm. 61-9353 5.75
1. Bar mitzvah. 2. Judaism. I. Title.

FALK, Ze'ev Wilhelm, 1923- 296.444
Jewish matrimonial law in the Middle Ages, by Ze'ev W. Falk. [London] Oxford Univ. Pr. 1966. xi, 154p. 23cm. (Scripta Judaica, 6) Enl. English version of (Nisu'in ve-gerushin transliterated); orig. issued as thesis, Hebrew University, Jerusalem. Bibl. 66-8077 6.40
1. Marriage (Jewish law) 2. Divorce (Jewish law) 3. Jews in Germany—Hist. 4. Jews in France—Hist. I. Title.
Available from publisher's New York Office.

GASTER, Moses, 1856-1939. 296.4'44
The Ketubah / by Moses Gaster ; edited with new introd. and notes by Samuel Gross. 2d. augm. ed. New York : Hermon Press, [1974] 54, [6] p., leaves of plates : ill. ; 24 cm. First ed. published in 1923 under title: The Ketubah, a chapter from the history of the Jewish people. Pages [1]-[6] (2d group), blank for "Notes." Bibliography: p. 7. [BM713.G3 1974] 68-9532 ISBN 0-87203-029-6 8.75
1. Ketuba. I. Title.

JEWS and divorce. 296.4'44
Edited by Jacob Freid. New York, KTAV Pub. House [1968] xiii, 208 p. 24 cm. Proceedings of a conference sponsored by the Commission on Synagogue Relations of the Federation of Jewish Philanthropies of New York. Includes bibliographical references. [LAW] 68-25718
1. Divorce (Jewish law) I. Freid, Jacob, ed. II. Federation of Jewish Philanthropies of New York. Commission on Synagogue Relations.

ROSENBLATT, Samuel, 1902- 296.4'44
Under the nuptial canopy : wedding sermons / by Samuel Rosenblatt. New York : P. Feldheim, 1975. x, 141 p. ; 24 cm. Includes bibliographical references. [BM744.5.R67] 74-80137 6.00
1. Wedding sermons, Jewish. 2. Sermons, Jewish—United States. 3. Sermons, American—Jewish authors. I. Title.

ROUTTENBERG, Lilly. S. 296.4'44
The Jewish wedding book: a practical guide to the traditions and social customs of the Jewish wedding. [by] Lilly S. Routtenberg, Ruth R. Seldin. New York, Schocken [1968, c.1967] xiv, 174p. illus. 20cm. (SB186) Bibl. [BM713.R6] 1.95 pap.,
1. Marriage customs and rites—Jews. I. Seldin, Ruth R. joint author. II. Title.

ROUTTENBERG, Lilly S. 296.4'44
The Jewish wedding book [by] Lilly S. Routtenberg & Ruth R. Seldin. [1st ed.] New York, Harper & Row [1967] xiv, 174 p. illus. 22 cm. Bibliography: p. 165. [BM713.R6] 67-13723
1. Marriage customs and rites—Jews. I. Seldin, Ruth R., joint author. II. Title.

SCHNEID, Hayyim. 296.4'44
Marriage. Philadelphia, Jewish Publication Society of America [1973] 117 p. illus. 21 cm. (JPS popular Judaica library) Bibliography: p. 116. [BM713.S33] 72-13536 ISBN 0-8276-0013-5 3.95
1. Marriage customs and rites, Jewish. 2. Marriage (Jewish law) 3. Jewish art and symbolism. I. Series: Jewish Publication Society of America. JPS popular Judaica library.

FELDER, Aaron. 296.4'45
[Sefer Yesode semabot (romanized form)] Yesodei smochos : a compilation of Jewish laws and traditions dealing with death and mourning, with the addition of detailed studies of related problems arising from modern life situations / by Aaron Felder. New York : Felder, 1974. xii, 156 p. ; 22 cm. Text in English, notes in Hebrew. Includes index. Bibliography: p. 142-143. [BM712.F44] 75-309123
1. Mourning (Jewish law) 2. Mourning customs, Jewish. I. [Yesode semahot] II. Title: Yesode semahot. III. Title: Yesodei smochos.

KLEIN, Isaac. 296.4'45
A time to be born, a time to die = ('Et la-

ledet ve-'et la-mut) Ecclesiastes 3:2 / by Isaac Klein. New York : Dept. of Youth Activities, United Synagogue of America, c1976. vi, 106 p. ; 21 cm. In English. Bibliography: p. 104-105. [BM712.K565] 77-356147
1. Mourning customs, Jewish. 2. Death (Judaism)—Meditations. I. Title. II. Title: 'Et la-ledet ve-'et la-mut.

RABINOWICZ, Harry M., 1919- 296.4'45
A guide to life; Jewish laws and customs of mourning [by] H. Rabinowicz. New York, Ktav Pub. House [1967, c1964] 186 p. 19 cm. Includes the English and Hebrew texts of mourning prayers. Bibliography: p. 181. [BM712.R3 1967] 67-19371
1. Mourning customs, Jewish. I. Title.

SPERKA, Joshua Sidney, 1904- 296.4'45
Eternal life; a digest of all Jewish laws of mourning. Complete funeral, burial and unveiling services; Kaddish, Yizkor and El Mohle in Hebrew, translation and transliteration, with a 25 year schedule of the Yahrzeit and a 25 year calendar for Yizkor dates, by Joshua S. Spearka. [2d ed.] New York, Bloch Pub. Co., 1961 [c1939] xviii, 220 p. 22 cm. "Notes and refernces": p. 208-220. [BM712.S6 1961] 61-17809
1. Funeral rites and ceremonies — Jews. 2. Jews. Liturgy and ritual. I. Title.

TALMUD. Minor tractates. Semahot. English. 1966. 296.445
The tractate "Mourning" (Semahot) (Regulations relating to death, burial, and mourning). Translated from the Hebrew, with introd. and notes, by Dov Zlotnick. New Haven, Yale University Press, 1966. x, 233 p. 22 cm. Yale Judaica series, v. 17) "With an appendix The Hebrew text of the tractate, edited from manuscripts by Dov Zlotnick. Vocalized by Eduard Y. Kutscher." Bibliographical references included in "Notes" (p. [97]-169) [BM506.4.S4E5] 66-12517
1. Mourning customs, Jewish. I. Zlotnick, Dov, ed. and tr. II. Talmud, Minor tractates. Semahot. III. Title.

TALMUD. MINOR TRACTATES. SEMAHOT. English. 1966 296.445
The tractate 'Mourning' (Semahot) (Regulations relating to death. burial. and mourning) Tr. from Hebrew. introd. notes, by Dov Zlotnick. New Haven, Conn., Yale [c.] 1966. x, 233p. 22cm. (Yale Judaica ser., v. 17) With an appendix: The Hebrew text of the tractate. ed. from mss. by Dov Zlotnick. Vocalized by Eduard Y. Kutscher. Bibl. [BM506.4.S4E5] 66-12517 7.50
1. Mourning customs, Jewish. I. Zlotnick, Dov, ed. and tr. II. Talmud. Minor tractates. Semahot. III. Title. IV. Series.

CHAMBERS, Laurence T. 296.6
Tabernacle studies. Grand Rapids, Zondervan Pub. House [c1958] 137p. illus. 20cm. [BM654.C47] 59-29216
1. Tabernacle. I. Title.

FORMAN, Max Leon, 1909- 296.6
Ideas that work; pin-up programs for special occasions. Illus. by Richard G. Fish. New York, Bloch Pub. Co., 1952. 229p. illus. 23cm. [BM21.A1F6] 53-51
1. Jews— Societies—History. organization, etc. I. Title.

GOODMAN, Philip, 1911- comp. 296.6
A documentary story of a century of the Jewish community center, 1854-1954. New York, Jewish Community Center Centennial Committee [1953] 76p. illus. 25cm. [HN43.G56] 54-27602
1. Community centers, Jewish. I. Title.

GUTSTEIN, Morris Aaron, 1905- 296.6
To bigotry no sanction; a Jewish shrine in America, 1658-1958. New York, Bloch Pub. Co., 1958. 191p. illus. 24cm. Includes bibliography. [BM225.N57T6] 58-14128
1. Newport, R. I. Touro Synagogue. I. Title.

HERTZ, Richard C 296.6
The education of the Jewish child, a study of 200 Reform Jewish religious schools. New York, Union of American Hebrew Congregations, 1953. 185p. 22cm. [BM103.H4] 53-2391
1. Religious education—Jews. 2. Reform Judaism. I. Title.

HOLISHER, Desider, 1901- 296.6
The synagogue and its people. New York, Abelard-Schuman [1955] 189 p. illus. 25 cm. [BM52.H6] 55-6405
1. Judaism—Pictures, illustrations, etc. 2. Synagogues—U.S. 3. Jews—Rites and ceremonies. I, Title.

JACOBSON, Ruth, 1907- 296.6
Manual for sisterhoods. New York, National Federation of Temple Sisterhoods [1954] 195p. illus. 24cm. [BM21.A1J3] 54-32011
1. Jews—Societies, etc. 2. Jews in the U. S. 3. Woman—Societies and clubs. I. Title.

KLAPERMAN, Libby M 296.6
Manual for sisterhoods. [New York] Women's Branch of the Union of Orthodox Jewish Congregations of America [cu956] 66p. 21cm. [BM21.A1K56] 57-29533
1. Jews— Societies, etc. 2. Woman—Societies and clubs. I. Union of Orthodox Jewish Congregations of America. Women's Branch. II. Title.

LEVIN, Meyer, 1905- 296.6
The story of the synagogue, by Meyer Levin [and] Toby K. Kurzhand. Art. Behrman House [c1957] New York, --Text-books for children. 156p. illus. (part col.) 24cm. (The Jewish heritage series, v. 1) [BM105.L48] 57-13093
1. Regligious education, Jewish editor; Stephen Kraft. Illus.: Robert Pous. 2. Synagogues. I. Kurband, Toby K., joint author. II. Title. III. Series.

MANN, Arthur, ed. 296.6
Growth and achievement: Temple Israel, 1854-1954. Foreword by Oscar Handlin. Contributors: Lee M. Friedman [and others] Cambridge, Printed for the Board of Trustees of Temple Adath Israel by the Riverside Press, 1954. 181p. illus. 25cm. [BM225.B6A3] 54-9783
1. Boston. Congregation Adath Israel. I. Title.

MANTEL, Hugo, 1908- 296.6
Studies in the history of the Sanhedrin. Cambridge, Harvard University Press, 1961. xv, 374p. 24cm. (Harvard Semitic series, 17) 'An elaboration of a doctoral dissertation submitted to... Harvard University in 1952.' Bibliography: p. 322-345. [BM655.4.M3 1961] 61-7391
1. Sanhedrin. 2. Sanhedrin, Great. I. Title. II. Series.

MILLGRAM, Abraham Ezra, 1901- 296.6
Handbook for the congregational school board member. New York, United Synagogue Commission on Jewish Education, 1953. 107p. illus. 22cm. [BM103.M54] 53-20856
1. Jews—Education. 2. Synagogues—Organization and administration. I. Title.

NEW York. B'nai Jeshurun Congregation. 296.6
Reports presented at the annual meeting. New York. v. 21cm. [BM225.N5B48] 52-68749
I. Title.

NEW York. Rabbi Jacob Joseph School. *296.6
Journal. [New York] v. illus., ports. 32 cm. annual. Cover title of individual issues, 19 Annual dinner. [LC771.N5N4] 52-27905
I. Title.

RIDOUT, Samuel, 1855-1930. 296.6
Lectures on the Tabernacle. New York, Loizeaux Bros. [1952] 519p. illus. 19cm. (Bible truth library) [BM654.R56] 54-31947
1. Tabernacle. I. Title.

SCHNITZER, Jeshaia. 296.6
New horizons for the synagogue; a counseling program for the rabbi and the synagogue. With a foreword by Harry Halpern. [1st ed.] New York, Bloch Pub. Co., 1956. 106p. 24cm. [BM652.5.S35] 56-10193
1. Pastoral counseling (Judaism) I. Title.

SCHWARZ, Jacob David, 1883- 296.6
The life and letters of Montgomery Prunejuice; illustrated by Russell Newton Roman. New York, Union of American Hebrew Congregations [c1957] 246p. illus. 21cm. [BM653.S363] 58-22710
1. Synagogues—Organization and administration. 2. Reform Judaism. I. Title.

YESHIVA Synagogue Council. 296.6
Annual convention. New York City. v. Illus. 28cm. English and Hebrew, the latter inverted with separate t. p. [LD6371.Y43A26] 53-36876
I. Title.

GLATZER, Nahum Norbert, 1903- 296.60924
Hillel, the elder; the emergence of classical Judaism. Rev. ed. New York, Schocken [1966, c.1956] 100p. 21cm. (Hillel bk.; SB123) [BM755.H45G54] 66-14870 1.25 pap.,
1. Hillel, the elder, d. ca. 10. I. Title.

THE American rabbi : 296.6'1
a tribute on the occasion of the bicentennial of the United States, and the ninety-fifth birthday of the New York Board of Rabbis / edited by Gilbert S. Rosenthal. New York : Ktav Pub. House, 1977. x, 200 p. : port. ; 24 cm. "This volume is in honor of Rabbi Harold H. Gordon." Includes bibliographical references and index. [BM652.A4] 77-1047 10.00
1. Gordon, Harold H. 2. New York Board of Rabbis. 3. Rabbis—United States—Addresses, essays, lectures. 4. Rabbis—Office—Addresses, essays, lectures. I. Gordon, Harold H. II. Rosenthal, Gilbert S. III. New York Board of Rabbis.
Contents omitted

BLOOD, William W., 1907- 296.6'1 B
Apostle of reason; a biography of Joseph Krauskopf, by William W. Blood. Philadelphia, Dorrance [1973] 262 p. 22 cm. Bibliography: p. 247-256. [BM755.K73B55] 73-78156 ISBN 0-8059-1861-2 5.95
1. Krauskopf, Joseph, 1858-1923. I. Title.

BRAV, Stanley Rosenbaum, 1908- 296.6'1 B
Dawn of reckoning; self-portrait of a liberal rabbi [by] Stanley R. Brav. [1st ed. Cincinnati, Ohio, Sholom Press, 1971] vi, 390 p. illus., ports. 18 cm. [BM755.B65A3] 71-129180 3.95
I. Title.

DRESNER, Samuel H. 296.6'1 B
Levi Yitzhak of Berditchev; portrait of a Hasidic master, by Samuel H. Dresner. New York, Hartmore House [1974] 224 p. map. 25 cm. Bibliography: p. 223-224. [BM755.L44D73] 73-91739 ISBN 0-87677-144-4 10.00
1. Levi Isaac ben Meir, of Berdichev, 1740-1809. I. Title.

ECKMAN, Lester Samuel. 296.6'1 B
Revered by all; the life and works of Rabbi Israel Meir Kagan—Hafets hayyim (1838-1933). New York, Shengold Publishers [1974] 214 p. 25 cm. Bibliography: p. 205-211. [BM755.K25E26] 73-89418 ISBN 0-88400-002-8 10.00
1. Kahan, Israel Meir, 1838-1933. I. Title.

ELEFANT, William L. 296.6'1 B
The educational ideas and related philosophical concepts in the writings of Maimonides, by William L. Elefant. 1972. vi, 166, 3 l. 28 cm. Thesis—University of Denver. Photocopy of typescript. Bibliography: leaves 165-166. [BM755.M6E4 1972] 73-154594
1. Moses ben Maimon, 1135-1204. I. Title.

EVELYN, John, 1620-1706. 296.6'1 B
The history of Sabatai Sevi, the suppos'd Messiah of the Jews (1669). Introd. by Christopher W. Grose. Los Angeles, William Andrews Clark Memorial Library, University of California, 1968. viii, [10], 41-111 p. 22 cm. (Augustan Reprint Society. Publication no. 131) Contains a reproduction of the author's note, "To the reader" and "The history of Sabatai Sevi, the pretended Messiah of the Jewes, in the year of our Lord, 1666. The third impostor" from his "The history of the three late famous impostors, viz. Padre Ottomano, Mahomed Bei, and Sabatai Sevi ... published in 1669. "Reproduced from a copy in the William Andrews Clark Memorial Library." [BM755.S45E92 1968] 68-66889
1. Shabbethai Zebi, 1626-1676. I. Title. II. Series.

FELDMAN, Abraham Jehiel, 1893- 296.61
The American Reform rabbi; a profile of a profession, by Abraham J. Feldman. With an introd. by Nelson Glueck. New York, Published for Hebrew Union College Press by Bloch Pub. Co. [c1965] xiii, 242 p. 22 cm. [BM197.F44] 63-22502
1. Reform Judaism—Addresses, essays, lectures. I. Title.

FELDMAN, Abraham Jehiel, 1893- 296.61
The American Reform rabbi; a profile of a profession. Introd. by Nelson Glueck. New York, Pub. for Hebrew Union Coll. Pr. by Bloch [c.1965] xiii, 242p. 22cm. [BM197.F44] 63-22502 6.00
1. Reform Judaism—Addresses, essays, lectures. I. Title.

FEUCHTWANGER, O. 296.61
Righteous lives. New York, Bloch [1966] 169p. facsims., plates. 23cm. Rev. versions of sketches which, except one, have appeared in the London Jewish review. [BM750.F4] 66-1637 3.00
1. Rabbis—Biog. I. Title.

FEUERLICHT, Morris Marcus, 1879-1959. 296.6'1 B
A Hoosier rabbinate / by Morris M. Feuerlicht. Fort Wayne : Indiana Jewish Historical Society, 1974. 72 p. : ill. ; 21 cm. (Publication - Indiana Jewish Historical Society ; no. 4) [BM755.F45A34] 75-330576
1. Feuerlicht, Morris Marcus, 1879-1959. 2. Jews in Indianapolis. I. Title. II. Series: Indiana Jewish Historical Society. Publication — Indiana Jewish Historical Society ; no. 4.

FLEER, Gedaliah. 296.6'1 B
Rabbi Nachman's fire : an introduction to Breslover Chassidus / by Gedaliah Fleer. 2d, rev. ed. New York : Hermon Press, 1975, c1972. 110 p. ; 21 cm. [BM198.F56 1975] 75-20993 ISBN 0-87203-057-1 pbk. : 3.95
1. Nahman ben Somhah, of Bratzlav, 1770?-1810? 2. Bratslav Hasidim. I. Title.

GELBER, Sholome Michael 296.61
The failure of the American rabbi; a program for the revitalization of the rabbinate in Amerca. Foreword by Salo W. Baron. New York, Twayne Pubs. [1962, c.1961] 79p. 61-18506 2.75
1. Rabbis—U.S. 2. Judaism—U. S. I. Title.

GOTTSCHALK, Alfred. 296.6'1
Your future as a rabbi; a calling that counts. [1st ed.] New York, R. Rosen Press [1967] 127 p. 22 cm. (Careers in depth, 72) Cover title: A definitive study of your future as a rabbi. [BM652.G63] 67-12679
1. Rabbis—Office. I. Title. II. Title: A definitive study of your future as a rabbi.

GREENSTONE, Julius Hillel, 1873- 296.6'1
The messiah idea in Jewish history, by Julius H. Greenstone. Westport, Conn., Greenwood Press [1972] 347 p. 21 cm. Reprint of the 1906 ed. [BM615.G7 1972] 70-97284 ISBN 0-8371-2606-1
1. Jews—Restoration. 2. Messiah. I. Title.

KIVIE Kaplan : 296.6'1 B
a legend in his own time / edited by S. Norman Feingold and William B. Silverman. New York : Union of American Hebrew Congregations, 1976. viii, 258 p., [7] leaves of plates : ill. ; 24 cm. [E184.J5K1484] 76-2410 ISBN 0-8074-0006-8 : 8.95
1. Kaplan, Kivie, 1904-1975. 2. National Association for the Advancement of Colored People. 3. Judaism and social problems—Addresses, essays, lectures. I. Feingold, S. Norman, 1914- II. Silverman, William B.

LANDMAN, Leo. 296.6'1
The cantor: an historic perspective; a study of the origin, communal position, and function of the hazzan. New York, Yeshiva University, 1972. xv, 191 p. 24 cm. Bibliography: p. 179-186. [BM658.2.L35] 72-84852
1. Cantors, Jewish. I. Title.

LIBER, Maurice, 1884- 296.6'1 B
Rashi. Translated from the French by Adele Szold. New York, Hermon Press, [1970] 278 p. illus., geneal. table, map. 24 cm. Reprint of the 1906 ed. Includes bibliographical references. [BM755.S6L5 1970] 70-136767 7.50
1. Solomon ben Isaac, called RaSHI, 1040-1105. I. Title.

MARCUS, Jacob Rader, 1896- 296.6'1 B
Israel Jacobson, the founder of the reform movement in Judaism, by Jacob R. Marcus. [2d ed., rev.] Cincinnati, Hebrew Union College Press, 1972. ix, 167 p. 22 cm. Bibliography: p. 130-134. [DS135.G5J3 1972] 74-187950 ISBN 0-87820-000-2 5.95
1. Jacobson, Israel, 1768-1828.

NEUSNER, Jacob, 1932- 296.6'1 B
First century Judaism in crisis; Yohanan ben Zakkai and the renaissance of Torah. Nashville, Abingdon Press [1975] 203 p. 22 cm. "Abridgement and condensation of A life of Rabban Yohanan ben Zakkai, ca. 1-80 C.E. (Leiden: E. J. Brill, 1962)." Includes bibliographical references. [BM755.J7N42] 74-14799 ISBN 0-687-13120-0 4.50 (pbk.).
1. Johanan ben Zakkai, d. ca. 80. 2. Judaism—History—Talmudic period, 10-425. I. Title.

THE Rabbi and the synagogue 296.6'1
/ edited by Jacob Neusner. New York : Ktav Pub. House, [1975] xxv, 306 p. ; 23 cm. (Understanding American Judaism ; v. 1) Includes bibliographical references. [BM205.R3] 75-8937 12.50 pbk. : 4.95
1. Judaism—United States—Addresses, essays, lectures. 2. Rabbis—Office—Addresses, essays, lectures. 3. Rabbis—United States—Addresses, essays, lectures. I. Neusner, Jacob, 1932- II. Series.
Contents omitted.

ROSENBLATT, Samuel, 1902- 296.6'1 B
The days of my years : an autobiography / by Samuel Rosenblatt. New York : Ktav Pub. House, 1976. 207 p., [7] leaves of plates : ill. ; 22 cm. [BM755.R565A33] 76-47616 ISBN 0-87068-494-9 : 10.00
1. Rosenblatt, Samuel, 1902- 2. Rabbis—United States—Biography. I. Title.

ROTH, Cecil, 1899-1970. 296.6'1 B
A life of Menasseh ben Israel, rabbi, printer, and diplomat / by Cecil Roth. New York : Arno Press, 1975 [c1934] xii, 373 p., [9] leaves of plates : ill. ; 21 cm. (The Modern Jewish experience) Reprint of the ed. published by the Jewish Publication Society of America, Philadelphia. Includes index. Bibliography: p. 291-307. [BM755.M25R6 1975] 74-29518 ISBN 0-405-06743-7 : 24.00
1. Manasseh ben Joseph ben Israel, 1604-1657. 2. Jews in Amsterdam. 3. Jews in Great Britain. I. Title. II. Series.

SCHOLEM, Gershom Gerhard, 1897- 296.6'1 B
Sabbatai Sevi; the mystical Messiah, 1626-1676. [Translated by R. J. Zwi Werblowsky. Princeton, N.J.] Princeton University Press [1973] xxvii, 1000 p. illus. 24 cm. (Bollingen series, 93) Rev. and augm. translation of Shabtai Tsevi veha-tenu'ah ha-shabta'it bi-yeme hayav. Bibliography: p. [931]-956. [BM199.S3S3713 1973] 75-166389 ISBN 0-691-09916-2 25.00
1. Shabbethai Zebi, 1626-1676. 2. Sabbathaians. I. Title. II. Series.

SIEGEL, Martin. 296.6'1 B
Amen: the diary of Rabbi Martin Siegel. Edited by Mel Ziegler. New York [Maddick Manuscripts; distributed by] World Pub. Co. [1971] xi, 276 p. 22 cm. [BM755.S528A3] 73-142133 6.95
I. Title.

STUDIES in Maimonides and St. Thomas Aquinas 296.61
/ selected with an introd. and bibliography by Jacob I. Dienstag. [New York] : Ktav Pub. House, 1975. lix, 350 p. ; 24 cm. (Bibliotheca Maimonidica ; v. 1) English, German or French. Bibliography: p. 334-345. [B765.T54S77] 75-4998 ISBN 0-87068-249-0 : 20.00
1. Thomas Aquinas, Saint, 1225?-1274—Addresses, essays, lectures. 2. Moses ben Maimon, 1135-1204—Addresses, essays, lectures. I. Dienstag, Jacob Israel. II. Series.

GOLDBURG, Norman M., 1902- 296.6'1'0207
Patrick J. McGillicuddy and the rabbi, by Norman M. Goldburg. Drawings by Stephen Osborn. Los Altos, Calif., Geron-X [1969] viii, 247 p. illus. 22 cm. [PN6268.J4G6] 77-90818 5.95
1. Rabbis—Anecdotes, facetiae, satire, etc. I. Title.

AGUS, Jacob Bernard, 1911- 296.6'1'0924 B
High priest of rebirth; the life, times, and thought of Abraham Isaac Kuk, by Jacob B. Agus. [2d ed.] New York, Bloch Pub. Co. [1972] xvii, 243 p. 22 cm. First ed. published in 1946 under title: Banner of Jerusalem. Includes bibliographical references. [BM755.K66A5 1972] 79-189017 ISBN 0-8197-0281-1 6.95
1. Kook, Abraham Isaac, 1865-1935. I. Title.

BOKSER, Ben Zion, 1907- 296.6'1'0924 B
Pharisaic Judaism in transition. New York, Arno Press, 1973 [c1935] x, 174 p. 23 cm. (The Jewish people: history, religion, literature) Reprint of the ed. published by Bloch Pub. Co., New York. Originally presented as the author's thesis, Columbia University. Bibliography: p. 160-167. [BM755.E55B6 1973] 73-2189 ISBN 0-405-05255-3 10.00
1. Eliezer ben Hyracanus. 2. Judaism—History—Talmudic period. 3. Pharisees. I. Title. II. Series.

FEINBERG, Abraham L 296.6'1'0924
Storm the gates of Jericho [by] Abraham L. Feinberg. [1st ed.] New York, Marzani & Munsell [c1965] 344 p. 22 cm. [BM755.F38A3] 65-28156
I. Title.

FRIEDLANDER, Albert H. 296.6'1'0924
Leo Baeck: teacher of Theresienstadt, by Albert H. Friedlander. [1st ed.] New York, Holt, Rinehart, and Winston [1968] 294 p. 24 cm. Bibliography: p. [277]-288. [BM755.B32F7] 68-11829 8.95
1. Baeck, Leo, 1873-1956. I. Title.

GINZBERG, Eli, 1911- 296.610924
Keeper of the law: Louis Ginzberg. Philadelphia, Jewish Pubn. Soc. [c.]1966. x, 348p. illus., ports. 22cm. Bibl. [BM755.G5G5] 66-11720 6.00
1. Ginzberg, Louis, 1873-1953. I. Title.

GINZBERG, Eli, 1911- 296.610924
Keeper of the law: Louis Ginzberg. [1st ed.] Philadelphia, Jewish Publication Society of America, 1966. x. 348 p. illus., ports. 22 cm. Bibliography: p. 335-336. [BM755.G5G5] 66-11720
1. Ginzberg, Louis, 1877-1965 I. Title.

MAIMONIDES octocentennial series, numbers I-IV. 296.6'1'0924 B
New York, Arno Press, 1973. 52, 27, 32, 31 p. 23 cm. (The Jewish people: history, religion, literature) Reprint of The supremacy of reason, by Achad ha-am; Moses Maimonides, by Alexander Marx; Maimonides as codifier, by Chaim Tchernowitz; and of The philosophy of Maimonides, by Isaac Husik; all published by Maimonides Octocentennial Committee, New York, 1935. [BM755.M6M276] 73-2214 ISBN 0-405-05278-2 9.00
1. Moses ben Maimon, 1135-1204. I. Ginzberg, Asher, 1856-1927. Al parashat derakhim. Shilton ha-sekhel. English. 1973. II. Marx, Alexander, 1878-1953. Moses Maimonides. 1973. III. Tchernowitz, Chaim, 1870-1949. Maimonides as codifier. 1973. IV. Husik, Isaac, 1876-1939. The philosophy of Maimonides. 1973. V. Title. VI. Series.

MALTER, Henry, 1864-1925. 296.6'1'0924
Saadia Gaon; his life and works. New York, Hermon Press [1969] 446 p. 23 cm. "First Edition: New York, 1926." Bibliography: p. [303]-419. [BM755.S2M3 1969] 77-82475
1. Saadiah ben Joseph, gaon, 892?-942. 2. Saadiah ben Joseph, gaon, 892?-942—Bibliography.

MARCUS, Rebecca B. 296.6'1'0924 B
Moses Maimonides: rabbi, philosopher, and physician, by Rebecca B. Marcus. New York, F. Watts [1969] ix, 114 p. illus., facsims., ports. 22 cm. (Immortals of philosophy and religion) Bibliography: p. 108-109. A biography of the Spanish-born Jewish philosopher, rabbi, and physician of the Middle Ages who spent a good deal of his life in Egypt and whose works influenced the thinking of Jews, Christians, and Moslems. [BM755.M6M28] 92 69-12594 3.95
1. Moses ben Maimon, 1135-1204—Juvenile literature. I. Title.

MELCHIOR, Marcus. 296.6'1'0924
A rabbi remembers. [Tr. from Danish by Werner Melchior] New York, Lyle Stuart [1968] 256p. 21cm. Tr. of Levet og oplevet; erindringer. [BM755.M445A313] 67-15887 4.95
I. Title.

MEMORIES of Kopul Rosen, 296.6'1'0924 B
edited by Cyril Domb. Wallingford (Berks.), Carmel College, 1970. 267 p., 23 plates. illus., facsims., plans, ports. 26 cm. Includes Dear David by K. Rosen, Wallingford, Carmel College (p. [191]-267) with special t.p. [BM755.R545M4] 75-520950 42/-
1. Rosen, Kopul, 1913-1962. 2. Judaism. I. Rosen, Kopul, 1913-1962. II. Domb, Cyril, ed. III. Rosen, Kopul, 1913-1962. Dear David. 1970.

WANEFSKY, Joseph. 296.6'1'0924
Rabbi Isaac Jacob Reines; his life and thought. New York, Philosophical Library [1970] 171 p. 23 cm. Bibliography: p. 171. [BM755.R348W35] 79-118314 ISBN 0-8022-2349-4 5.95
1. Reines, Isaac Jacob, 1839-1915.

WEINSTEIN, Jacob Joseph, 1902- 296.6'1'0924 B
Solomon Goldman: a rabbi's rabbi, by Jacob J. Weinstein. New York, Ktav Pub. House, 1973. xiii, 295 p. ports. 24 cm. Bibliography: p. 287-290. [BM755.G58W45] 72-10301 ISBN 0-87068-196-6 10.00
1. Goldman, Solomon, 1893-1953. 2. Zionism—United States. 3. Judaism—United States.

WISE, Stephen Samuel, 1874-1949. 296.6'1'0924
Stephen S. Wise: Servant of the people. Selected letters edited by Carl Hermann Voss. Foreword, by Justine Wise Polier and James Waterman Wise. [1st ed.] Philadelphia, Jewish Publication Society of America, 1969. xxi, 332 p. ports. 22 cm. [BM755.W53A42] 69-13549 5.50
I. Voss, Carl Hermann, ed. II. Title.

YELLIN, David, 1864-1941. 296.6'1'0924 B
Maimonides: his life and works, by David Yellin and Israel Abrahams. 3d rev. ed., with introd., bibliography and supplementary notes, by Jacob I. Dienstag. New York, Hermon Press [1972 i.e. 1973] xxxiv, 193 p. illus. 20 cm. Reprint of the 1903 ed. published by Jewish Publication Society of America, Philadelphia; with new material. Bibliography: p. xvii-xxix. [BM755.M6Y4 1972] 72-83937 ISBN 0-87203-031-8 7.95
1. Moses ben Maimon, 1135-1204. I. Abrahams, Israel, 1858-1925, joint author.

POLNER, Murray. 296.6'1'0973
The American rabbi / by Murray Polner. 1st ed. New York : Holt, Rinehart and Winston, c1977. p. cm. Includes index. Bibliography: p. [BM652.P6] 8.95
1. Rabbis—United States. 2. Rabbis—Office. 3. Judaism—United States. 4. Jews in the United States—Politics and government. I. Title.

ZEITLIN, Joseph, 1906- 296.6'1'0973
Disciples of the wise; the religious and social opinions of American rabbis. New York, Bureau of Publications, Teachers College, Columbia University, 1945. [New York, AMS Press, 1972] xiii, 233 p. 22 cm. Reprint of the 1945 ed., issued in series: Teachers College, Columbia University. Contributions to education, no. 908. Originally presented as the author's thesis, Columbia. Bibliography: p. 199-202. [BM205.Z4 1972] 76-177612 ISBN 0-404-55908-5
1. Judaism—United States. 2. Rabbis—United States. I. Title. II. Series: Columbia University. Teachers College. Contributions to education, no. 908.

EISENBERG, Azriel Louis, 1903- 296.6'5
The synagogue through the ages, by Azriel Eisenberg. New York, Bloch Pub. Co. [1974] vi, 206 p. illus. 24 cm. Bibliography: p. 195-197. A history of the synagogue emphasizing its importance in the lives of the Jewish people through the ages. [BM653.E35] 73-77284 ISBN 0-8197-0291-9 12.50
1. Synagogues—History. I. Title.

HEILMAN, Samuel C. 296.6'5
Synagogue life : a study in symbolic interaction / Samuel C. Heilman. Chicago : University of Chicago Press, 1976. xiii, 306 p. : ill. ; 23 cm. Includes index. Bibliography: p. 291-296. [BM205.H44 1976] 75-36403 ISBN 0-226-32488-5 : 16.50
1. Orthodox Judaism—United States. 2. Jewish way of life—Case studies. 3. Jews in the United States—Social life and customs. I. Title.

KAPLOUN, Uri. 296.6'5
The synagogue. Philadelphia, Jewish Publication Society of America [1973] 119 p. illus. 21 cm. (JPS popular Judaica library) Bibliography: p. 117. [BM653.K26] 72-13537 ISBN 0-8276-0012-7 pap 3.95
1. Synagogues. 2. Jewish art and symbolism. I. Series: Jewish Publication Society of America. JPS popular Judaica library.

KARASICK, Joseph. 296.6'5
Report to UOJCA congregations on the First World Conference of Ashkenazi and Sephardi Synagogues held in Jerusalem on 7-12 Teveth, 5728 (January 8-13, 1968). [New York] Union of Orthodox Jewish Congregations of America [1968?] 39 p. illus. 23 cm. Cover title. "Addresses of Joseph Karasick at the First World Conference of Ashkenazi and Sephardi Synagogues" (6 p.) inserted. [BM30.W57K37 1968] 74-157575
1. World Conference of Ashkenazi and Sephardi Synagogues, 1st, Jerusalem, 1968. 2. Judaism—Congresses. I. Union of Orthodox Jewish Congregations of America. II. Title.

KATZ IRVING I. 296.65
Successful synagogue administration, by Irving I. Katz, Myron E. Schoen. New York, Union of Amer. Hebrew Cong. [c.1963] 200p. illus. 23cm. 63-10407 2.00 pap.,
1. Synagogues—Organization and administration. I. Schoen, Myron E., jointauthor. II. Title.

KOHN, Joshua. 296.6'5
The synagogue in Jewish life. New York, Ktav Pub. House [1973] 246 p. illus. 21 cm. Bibliography: p. 231-237. [BM653.K6] 72-5826 ISBN 0-87068-096-X 3.95 (pbk.)
1. Jews. Liturgy and ritual. 2. Synagogue. I. Title.

LITVIN, Baruch, ed. 296.65
The sanctity of the synagogue; the case for mechitzah, separation between men and women in the synagogue, based on Jewish law, history of philosophy, from sources old and new. [1st ed.] New York [Spero Foundation] 1959. xxiii, 442, 99p. illus. 24cm. Added t. p. in Hebrew. Articles in English, Hebrew or Yiddish. Errata slip mounted on p. 92 (3d group) [BM653.2.L56] 59-15959
1. Synagogue seating. I. Title.

WEMP, C. Sumner. 296.6'5
Teaching from the tabernacle / C. Sumner Wemp. Chicago : Moody Press, c1976. 125 p. : ill. ; 22 cm. [BM654.W43] 76-3794 ISBN 0-8024-8563-4 pbk. : 2.25
1. Tabernacle—Meditations. I. Title.

HELLER, Imre. 296.6'5'094391
The synagogues of Hungary: an album [by] Imre Heller and Zsigmond Vajda. Edited by Randolph L. Braham with the collaboration of Ervin Farkas. New York, [Published for] World Federation of Hungarian Jews [by] Diplomatic Press, 1968. x, 197, xxxi p. illus. 22 x 30 cm. Added t.p. in Hebrew. Added t.p. in Hungarian: A Magyarorszagi zsinagogak albuma. English, Hebrew, and Hungarian. Bibliography: p. 63. [DB906.5.H4] 68-56000
1. Synagogues—Hungary. I. Vajda, Zsigmond, joint author. II. World Federation of Hungarian Jews. III. Title. IV. Title: Bate ha-keneset be-Hungaryah: albom. V. Title: A Magyarorszagi zsinagogak albuma.

DAVIS, Patricia Talbot. 296.6'5'0974811
Together, they built a mountain. [Lititz, Pa.] Sutter House [1974] xvi, 179 p. illus. 24 cm. [BM225.E55B473] 74-14727 ISBN 0-915010-00-3 6.95
1. Beth Sholom Synagogue, Elkins Park, Pa. 2. Cohen, Mortimer Joseph, 1894-1972. 3. Wright, Frank Lloyd, 1867-1959. I. Title.

FINE, Jo Renee. 296.6'5'097471
The synagogues of New York's Lower East Side / photos. by Jo Renee Fine ; text by Gerard R. Wolfe. New York : New York University Press, 1977. p. cm. Bibliography: p. [BM225.N49F46] 75-15126 ISBN 0-8147-2559-7 : 17.50
1. Synagogues—New York (City) 2. Judaism—New York (City) 3. Jews in New York (City)—History. 4. Lower East Side, New York—History. I. Wolfe, Gerard R., 1926- II. Title.

SHANKMAN, Jacob K. 296.6'5'09747277
The history of Temple Israel of New Rochelle, New York / by Jacob K. Shankman. New Rochelle, N.Y. : The Temple, c1977. 187 p., [8] leaves of plates : ill. ; 26 cm. [BM225.N442T457] 77-72427
1. Temple Israel, New Rochelle, N.Y. 2. Jews in New Rochelle, N.Y.—History. I. Title.

ROSENBERG, Max, 1922-. 296.6509755296
Temple Beth El; a centennial history of Beth El Hebrew Congregation, serving northern Virginia since 1859, by Max Rosenberg [and] Arthur Marmor, assisted by Earl Abrams [and] Bernard Brenner. Edited by Max Rosenberg. [Alexandria? Va., 1962] vii, 76 p. illus., facsims, ports. 29 cm. [BM225.A5T4] 64-6110
1. Alexandria, Va. Temple Beth El. I. Marmor, Arthur K. II. Title.

PLAUT, W Gunther, 1912- 296.6509776581
Mount Zion, 1856-1956; the first hundred years. [St. Paul, Minn., 1957] 152p. illus. 23cm. Includes bibliography. [BM225.S28M6] 59-28918
1. St. Paul. Mount Zion Hebrew Congregation. I. Title.

ROTHENBERG, Gunther Erich, 1923- 296.6'5'0978961
Congregation Albert, 1897-1972, Albuquerque, New Mexico. Written by Gunther Rothenburg. Researched by Israel C. Carmel. [Albuquerque, N.M., 1972] 67 p. illus. 24 cm. [BM225.A47R68] 72-90893
1. Congregation Albert. 2. Jews in Albuquerque, N.M. I. Carmel, Israel C. II. Title.

AMERICAN synagogue 296.6'7
directory, with an international synagogue and U.S. book dealer supplement. 1957- New York. v. 24cm. [BM205.A6] 57-34944
1. Synagogues—U.S.

AMERICAN synagogue 296.6'7
directory, with an international synagogue and U.S. book dealer supplement. 1957- New York. v. 24 cm. [BM205.A6] 57-34944
1. Synagogues—U.S.

GERBER, Israel Joshua, 1918- 296.6'7
The heritage seekers : American Blacks in search of Jewish identity / by Israel J. Gerber. Middle Village, N.Y. : Jonathan David Publishers, c1977. 222 p. ; 23 cm. Includes index. Bibliography: p. 211-215. [BM205.G44] 77-2907 ISBN 0-8246-0214-5 : 9.95
1. Original Hebrew Israelite Nation in Jerusalem. 2. Afro-American Jews. 3. Israel—Emigration and immigration. 4. Lost tribes of Israel—Miscellanea. I. Title.

GERBER, Israel Joshua, 1918- 296.6'7
The heritage seekers : American Blacks in search of Jewish identity / by Israel J. Gerber. Middle Village, N.Y. : Jonathan David Publishers, c1977. 222 p. ; 23 cm. Includes index. Bibliography: p. 211-215. [BM205.G44] 77-2907 ISBN 0-8246-0214-5 : 9.95
1. Original Hebrew Israelite Nation in Jerusalem. 2. Afro-American Jews. 3. Israel—

Emigration and immigration. 4. Lost tribes of Israel—Miscellanea. I. Title.

GRUSD, Edward E 296.67
B'nai B'rith; the story of a covenant, by Edward E. Grusd. [1st ed.] New York, Appleton-Century [1966] xix, 315 p. 21 cm. [HS2228.B44G7] 66-19998
1. B'nai B'rith. I. Title.

GRUSD, Edward E. 296.67
B'nai B'rith; the story of a covenant, by Edward E. Grusd [1st ed.] New York, Appleton-Century [1966] xix, 315p. 21cm. [HS2228.B44G7] 66-19998 6.95
1. B'nai B'rith. I. Title.

KARP, Abraham J 296.6'7
A history of the United Synagogue of America 1913-1963 [New York, United Synagogue of America, 1964] 108 p. illus., ports. 23 cm. [BM21.U665] 65-903
1. United Synagogue of America. 2. Conservative Judaism. I. Title.

LEBOW, Sylvan 296.67
The temple brotherhood, an organizational manual [New York, Natl. Federation of Temple Brother hoods, 1963] viii, 151p. illus., ports., map. 23cm. 63-22013 1.00 pap.,
I. National Federation of Temple Brotherhoods. II. Title.

LEWIN, Isaac, 1906- 296.6'7
Unto the mountains : essays / by Isaac Lewin. New York : Hebrew Pub. Co., 1975. 127 p. : ill. ; 24 cm. Includes bibliographical references. [BM21.A4L5] 75-15208 5.95
1. Agudas Israel. 2. Lewin, Aron, 1879-1941. 3. Slaughtering and slaughter-houses—Jews—Addresses, essays, lectures. I. Title.
Contents omitted.

UNION of American Hebrew 296.6'7
Congregations.
Report of the president to the board of trustees. [New York?] v. 26-28 cm. annual. Title varies: 1960, Report to the UAHC board of trustees. [BM21.U43] 63-52594
I. Title.

WORLD Federation of 296.6'7
YMHA's and Jewish Community Centers. Council.
Report. New York. v. 28 cm. [BM21.W6] 56-46847
I. Title.

YOUNG Men's and Young 296.6'7
Women's Hebrew Association, New York.
Report. New York. v. 23 cm. annual. Report year ends Apr. 30. Vols. for 18 issued by the association under its earlier name: Young Men's Hebrew Association. Vols. for 18 include the association's membership roll. [BM21.Y74] 62-56139
I. Title.

CITRON, Samuel J 296.68
Dramatics for creative teaching. New York, United Synagogue Commission on Jewish Education, 1961. 405p. 26cm. [BM103.C5] 61-14855
1. Religious education, Jewish—Teaching methods. 2. Drama in education. I. Title.

ELKINS, Dov Peretz. 296.6'8
Clarifying Jewish values : a handbook of value clarification strategies for group leaders, educators, rabbis, teachers, center workers, and counselors / Dov Peretz Elkins. [Rochester, N.Y.] : Growth Associates, [c1977] 92 p. ; 29 cm. Cover title. Includes bibliographical references. [BM103.E43] 77-83774 ISBN 0-918834-02-3 : 9.00
1. Jewish religious education—Teaching methods. I. Title.

HONOR, Leo Lazarius, 1894- 296.68
1956
Selected writings. Ed. by Abraham P. Gannes. New York, Reconstructionist Pr. 15 W. 86th St. [1965] 329p. 21cm. Bibl. [LC741.H6] 64-20381 4.95
1. Jews in the U.S.—Education—Addresses, essays, lectures. I. Title.

SCHWARTZMAN, Sylvan David. 296.68
Once upon a lifetime. Illustrated by Maurice Rawson. New York, Union of American Hebrew Congregations [1958] 134p. illus. 27cm. (Commission on Jewish Education of the Union of American Hebrew Congregations and the Central Conference of American Rabbis. Union graded series) [BM105.S43] 58-14445
1. Religious education, Jewish—Text books for children. I. Title.

WARSCHAUER, Heinz 296.68
Teacher's syllabus for grade 9, according to the curriculum of the Commission of Jewish Education. New York, Union of Amer. Hebrew Congregations [c.1961] 303p. 28cm. 2.50 pap.,
I. Title.

BAUMGARD, Herbert M 296.7
Judaism and prayer; growing towards God [by] Herbert M. Baumgard. New York, Union of American Hebrew Congregations [1964] xiii, 113 p. 20 cm. (Issues of faith) Bibliography: p. 100-102. [BM669.B3] 64-24341
1. Prayer (Judaism) I. Title. II. Series.

BAUMGARD, Herbert M. 296.7
Judaism and prayer; growing towards God. New York, Union of Amer. Hebrew Cong. [c.1964] xiii, 113p. 20cm. (Issues of faith) Bibl. 64-24341 1.50 bds.,
1. Prayer (Judaism) I. Title. II. Series.

*BERMANT, Chaim 296.7
The walled garden; the saga of Jewish life and tradition. New York, Macmillan Pub. Co., [1975 c1974] 272 p. ill. (part col.) 25 cm. Bibliography: p. [271]-272. [BM723] 12.95
1. Jewish way of life. I. Title.

BRICHTO, Mira. 296.7
The God around us; a child's garden of prayer. Illustrated by Clare Romano Ross and John ross. New York, Union of American Hebrew Congregations [1958] unpaged. illus. 28cm. [BM666.B7] 59-17606
1. Children—Prayer-books and devoltions—English. 2. Jews—Prayer-books and devotions—English. I. Title.

CAMPBELL, Gaye, 1912- 296.7
Jewish ethics and values. Illustrated by Ben Einhorn. [New York] Ktav Pub. House [1967] 121 p. illus. 26 cm. Twenty short incidents in young children's lives, with questions to think about, illustrate various aspects of Jewish ethics and values such as mercy, patience, charity, prayer, respect fur elders, and faith. [BJ1285.C3] AC 67
1. Ethics, Jewish. I. Einhorn, Ben, illus. II. Title.

CENTRAL Conference of 296.7
American Rabbis. Youth Committee.
Working with college students, a handbook for rabbis. [New York? 1967] vi, 44 p. 22 cm. Bibliography: p. 24-27. [BM727.C4] 67-31000
1. Students, Jewish—Religious life. I. Title.

CENTRAL Conference of 296.7
American Rabbis. Youth Committee.
Working with college students, a handbook for rabbis. [New York? 1967] vi, 44 p. 22 cm. Bibliography: p. 24-27. [BM727.C4] 67-31000
1. Students, Jewish—Religious life. I. Title.

FRIEDMAN, Theodore. 296.7
Judgment and destiny; sermons for the modern Jew. New York, J. David [1965] 203 p. 23 cm. [BM740.2.F7] 63-17361
1. Sermons, Jewish — U.S. 2. Sermons, American — Jewish authors. I. Title.

FRIEDMAN, Theodore 296.7
Judgment and destiny; sermons for the modern Jew. New York, J. David [c.1965] 203p. 23cm. [BM740.2.F7] 65-17361 5.95
1. Sermons, Jewish—U.S. 2. Sermons, American—Jewish authors. I. Title.

GLATZER, Nahum Norbert, 296.7
1903- ed.
A Jewish reader; in time and eternity. [2d rev. ed.] NewYork, Schocken Bks. [c.1946, 1961] 253 p. (Schocken paperbacks, SB16) Bibl. 61-14920 3.00; 1.65 pap.,
1. Devotional literature, Jewish (Selections: Extracts, etc.) I. Title.

GROLLMAN, Earl A. 296.7
Talking about death; a dialogue between parent and child, by Earl A. Grollman. Illustrated by Gisela Heau. Boston, Beacon Press [1970] 29 p. col. illus. 24 cm. [BF723.D3G72] 73-101320 6.00
1. Children and death. I. Heau, Gisela, illus. II. Title.

HERTZ, Richard 296.7
What counts most in life? New York, Bloch [c.]1963. 72p. 19cm. 63-13946 2.25 bds.,
1. Jewish way of life. I. Title.

HERTZ, Richard C. 296.7
What counts most in life? New York, Bloch Pub. Co., 1963. 72 p. 10 cm. [BM723.H43] 63-13946
1. Jewish way of life. I. Title.

JEWS. Liturgy and ritual. 296.7
Daily prayers.
Our prayer book; a new and original Siddur text for religious schools. Compiled and edited by Sidney Greenberg and Morris Silverman. Hartford, Prayer Book Press [1961] 295p. illus. 25cm. Hebrew or English. Half title: Includes chants, traditional and composed. [BM666.G65] 61-57977
I. Jews. Liturgy and ritual. Children's services. II. Greenberg, Sidney, 1917- ed. III. Silverman, Morris, 1894- ed. IV. Title. V. Title: Sidurenn.

KAHN, Robert I. 296.7
Lessons for life. [1st ed.] Garden City, N. Y., Doubleday, 1963. 240 p. 22 cm. [BM723.K25] 63-18204
1. Jewish way of life. I. Title.

KOTSUJI, Abraham Setsujau, 296.7
1899-
From Tokyo to Jerusalem [New York] Geis; dist. Random [1965, c.1964] 215p. 22cm. [BM755.P75K6] 64-8481 4.95 bds.,
1. Proselytes and proselyting, Jewish—Converts from Shinto. I. Title.

LANDAU, Sol, 1920- 296.7
Length of our days; focus on Judaism and the personal life. New York, Bloch [c.1961] 103p. 61-18511 3.00
1. Jewish way of life. I. Title.

MELAMED, Deborah (Marcus) 296.7
The three pillars; thought, worship, and practice for the Jewish woman. [Rev. ed.] New York, National Women's League of the United Synagogue of America, 1958. 155p. 20cm. [BM565.M387 1958] 59-20724
1. Judaism. 2. Women, Jewish—Religious life. I. Title.

RUBENSTEIN, Shmuel. 296.7
The Sefer Torah : an illustrated analysis of the history, preparation, and use of the Sefer Torah / by Shmuel L. Rubenstein. New York : Zeirei Agudath Israel, Sefer Torah Project, [1976] 32 p. : ill. ; 23 cm. Bibliography: p. 32. [BM657.T6R82] 77-365746
1. Torah scrolls. I. Zeirei Agudath Israel of America. II. Title.

SCHNEID, Hayyim. 296.7
Family / edited by Hayyim Schneid. Philadelphia : Jewish Publication Society of America, c1973. 120 p., [4] leaves of plates : ill. ; 21 cm. (JPS popular Judaica library) Bibliography: p. 119. [BM723.S335] 73-11760 ISBN 0-8276-0029-1 : 3.95
1. Family—Religious life (Judaism) I. Title. II. Series: Jewish Publication Society of America. JPS popular Judaica library.

SOLTES, Avraham. 296.7
Invocation; a sheaf of prayers. [New York, Bloch Pub. Co., 1959] 54 p. 26 cm. [BM665.S6] 59-2489
1. Jews — Prayer-books and devotions — English I. Title.

SPIRO, Jack D. 296.7
Heritage. [Editor: Laura G. Singer. Associate editor: Rose Pearlmutter. Text: Jack D. Spiro. Mountainside, N.J., Printed by Z. H. Berlin Co., 1973] [12] p. illus. 31 cm. Eleven sheets of text in pockets. [BM690.S65] 74-155429
1. Fasts and feasts—Judaism. 2. Judaism. I. Singer, Laura G., ed. II. Pearlmutter, Rose, ed. III. Title.

SPIRO, Jack D. 296.7
A time to mourn; Judaism and the psychology of bereavement [by] Jack D. Spiro. Foreword by Abraham N. Franzbiau. New York. Bloch [1967] xxvi, 160p. 22cm. Bibl. [BM729.C6S65] 67-30744 4.95
1. Consoliation (Judaism) I. Title.

UNION of American Hebrew 296.7
Congregations.
The Jewish family; what kind of family life can best preserve and transmit Jewish value? [New York, 1974] iv, 19 p. 22 x 28 cm. (Its Centennial papers) "Papers ... delivered at the Centennial Biennial Assembly of the Union of American Hebrew Congregations and the 60th Anniversary Biennial Convention of the National Federation of Temple Sisterhoods, meeting jointly in New York City, November 10, 1973 and November 11, 1973." [BM723.U54 1974] 74-174413
1. Family—Religious life (Judaism)—Addresses, essays, lectures. I. National Federation of Temple Sisterhoods. II. Title.

ABELSON, Joshua, 1873- 296.7'1
1940.
Jewish Mysticism; an introduction to the Kabbalah. New York, Hermon Press [1969] ix, 182 p. 20 cm. Reprint of the 1913 ed. Bibliography: p. [176]-178. [BM723.A4 1969] 68-9535 4.95
1. Mysticism—Judaism. 2. Cabala. I. Title.

EICHHORN, David Max, ed. 296.71
Conversion to Judaism: a history and analysis. Contributing authors: Bernard J. Bamberger [others. New York] Ktav [1966, c.1965] xii, 288p. 24cm. Bibl. [BM729.P7E5] 65-21742 5.95
1. Proselytes and proselyting, Jewish. I. Bamberger, Bernard Jacob, 1904- II. Title.

JEWISH mystical 296.7'1
testimonies / [edited by] Louis Jacobs. New York : Schocken Books, 1977, c1976. ix, 270 p. ; 21 cm. Bibliography: 261-264. [BM723.J48 1977] 76-46644 ISBN 0-8052-3641-4 : 14.95
1. Mysticism—Judaism—History—Sources. I. Jacobs, Louis.
Contents omitted

KIRSCH, James. 296.7'1
The reluctant prophet. Los Angeles, Sherbourne Press [1973] xii, 214 p. 24 cm. Includes bibliographical references. [BM755.W345K57] 72-96516 ISBN 0-8202-0156-1 7.50
1. Wechsler, Hile, 1843-1894. 2. Dreams—Case studies. I. Title.

WIGDOER, Devorah. 296.71
Hope is my house. Englewood Cliffs, N. J., Prentice [1966] 282p. 22cm. [BM755.W43A3] 66-22101 4.95 bds.,
1. Proselytes and proselyting, Jewish—Converts from christianity. 2. Proselytes and proselyting, Jewish—Converts from Christianity I. Title.

WIGODER, Devorah. 296.71 B
Hope is my house. Englewood Cliffs, N. J., Prentice-Hall [1966] 282 p. 22 cm. [BM755.W43A3] 66-22101
1. Proselytes and proselyting, Jewish—Converts from Christianity. I. Title.

YOWA. 296.7'1
The becoming of Ruth; an autobiography. Written and illustrated by Yowa. New York, Crown Publishers [1972] 64 p. col. illus. 21 cm. A young girl's search for spiritual fulfillment leads her to convert from Christianity to Judaism. [BM729.P7Y69] 79-185069 4.95
1. Proselytes and proselyting, Jewish—Converts from Christianity—Juvenile literature. I. Title.

BOKSER, Ben Zion, 1907- 296.7'2
The gifts of life and love : a treasury of inspirations / by Ben Zion Bokser ; photos. by Miriam Bokser Caravella. Rev. ed. New York : Hebrew Pub. Co., 1975. 193 p. : ill. ; 21 cm. First published in 1958 under title: The gift of life. [BM724.B64 1975] 75-303188 ISBN 0-88482-894-8 : 5.00
1. Jewish devotional literature. I. Title.

FISHER, Mitchell Salem, 296.7'2
1903-
Rebel, O Jews! and other prayers. New York, Reconstructionist Press, 1973. 36 p. 24 cm. [BM724.F56] 73-79051
1. Jewish prayers. I. Title.

JACOBS, Louis. 296.7'2
Hasidic prayer. New York, Schocken Books [1973, c1972] ix, 195 p. 22 cm. (The Littman library of Jewish civilization) Bibliography: p. 183-186. [BM669.J3 1973] 72-86765 10.00
1. Prayer (Judaism) 2. Hasidism. I. Title.

KAPLAN, Aryeh. 296.7'2
Tefillin : G-d, man and tefillin / by Aryeh Kaplan. New York : National Conference of Synagogue Youth, c1973. 80 p. : ill. ; 21 cm. Includes bibliographical references. [BM657.P5K3] 74-193351 2.50
1. Phylacteries. I. Title.

KON, Abraham Israel. 296.7'2
Prayer [by] Abraham Kon. Translated by the author from his book Si'ah Tefillah. London, New York, Soncino, 1971. xxii, 277 p. 24 cm. [BM660.K613] 73-156483 ISBN 0-900689-05-6 £2.50
1. Prayer (Judaism) 2. Synagogues—History. 3. Tallith. 4. Fringes (Jewish cultus) 5. Phylacteries.

DRESNER, Samuel H 296.73
The Jewish dietary laws; their meaning for our time, by Samuel H. Dresner. A guide to observance, by Seymour Siegel. New York, Burning Bush Press [1966] 77 p. 20 cm. [BM710.D7 1966] 66-6827
1. Jews — Dietary laws. I. Siegel, Seymour. II. Title.

DRESNER, Samuel H. 296.73
The Jewish dietary laws, their meaning for our time. A guide to observance, by Seymour Siegel. New York 28, 1109 Fifth Ave. Burning Bush Press, c.[1959] 71p. 20cm. (bibl.) 59-12519 .70 pap.,
1. Jews—Dietary laws. I. Title.

FREEDMAN, Seymour E. 296.7'3
The book of Kashruth; a treasury of Kosher facts and frauds [by] Seymour E. Freedman. New York, Bloch Pub. Co. [1970] xx, 290 p. 22 cm. Includes bibliographical references. [BM710.F68] 74-113870 6.50
1. Jews—Dietary laws. I. Title.

RUBENSTEIN, Shmuel. 296.7'3
The Torah species : an illustrated analysis of the four species of Succos, herbs of Pesach, and kosher animals / by Shmuel Rubenstein.

Bronx, N.Y. : Rubenstein, 1976. 35 p. : ill. ; 22 cm. [BM657.C5R82] 77-365942
1. Jews—Dietary laws. 2. Citron (Jewish cultus) 3. Lulab (Jewish cultus) I. Title.

RUBENSTEIN, Shmuel. 296.7'3
Utensils in Jewish law : an illustrated analysis of immersion, Passover, and meat and dairy utensils / by Shmuel Rubenstein. Bronx, N.Y. : Rubenstein, 1976. 28 p. : ill. ; 22 cm. Bibliography: p. 28. [BM710.R82] 77-150680
1. Kashering of utensils. I. Title.

SIEGEL, Seymour. 296.73
The Jewish dietary laws; their meaning for our time, by Samuel H. Dresner. A guide to observance, by Seymour Siegel. New York, Burning Bush Press [1966] 77 p. 20 cm. [BM710.D7 1966] 66-6827
1. Jews — Dietary laws. I. Title.

BUCHLER, Adolf, 1867-1939. 296.7'4
Types of Jewish-Palestinian piety from 70 B.C.E. to 70 C.E.; the ancient pious men, by Adolph Buchler. New York, Ktav Pub. House, 1968. 264 p. 24 cm. Reprint of the 1922 ed. Contents.Contents.—Hillel the Hasid.—The ancient pious men.—The pious men in the Psalms of Solomon.—Honi the Hasid and his prayer for rain. Bibliographical footnotes. [BM723.B8 1968] 68-56292
1. Hillel, the elder, d. ca. 10. 2. Honi ha-Meaggel, 1st century B.C. 3. Bible. O.T. Apocryphal books. Psalms of Solomon—Criticism, interpretation, etc. 4. Piety. I. Title. II. Title: Jewish-Palestinian piety.

DONIN, Hayim. 296.7'4
To raise a Jewish child : a guide for parents / Hayim Halevy Donin. New York : Basic Books, c1977. p. cm. Includes index. [BM103.D66] 76-7679 ISBN 0-465-08626-8 : 10.95
1. Jewish religious education of children. 2. Children—Management. 3. Education of children. I. Title.

DRESNER, Samuel H. 296.7'4
Between the generations: a Jewish dialogue, by Samuel H. Dresner. [Bridgeport, Conn.] Hartmore House [1971] 80 p. 21 cm. Includes bibliographical references. [BM727.D73] 79-172413 1.75
1. Youth, Jewish—Conduct of life. 2. Conflict of generations. I. Title.

FRANZBLAU, Abraham Norman, 1901- 296.7'4
Religious belief and character among Jewish adolescents, by Abraham N. Franzblau. New York, Bureau of Publications, Teachers College, Columbia University, 1934. [New York, AMS Press, 1973, c1972] viii, 80 p. 22 cm. Reprint of the 1934 ed., issued in series: Teachers College, Columbia University. Contributions to education, no. 634. Originally presented as the author's thesis, Columbia. Bibliography: p. 79-80. [BM727.F67 1972] 78-176783 ISBN 0-404-55634-5 10.00
1. Youth, Jewish—Religious life. 2. Faith (Judaism) I. Title. II. Series: Columbia University. Teachers College. Contributions to education, no. 634.

*GITTELSOHN, Roland B. 296.74
Discussion guide for Consecrated unto me. New York, Union of Amer. Hebrew Congregations [1966] v. 106p. 28cm. 2.00 pap.,
1. Jewish way of life. I. Title.

GITTELSOHN, Roland Bertram, 1910- 296.74
Consecrated unto me; a Jewish view of love and marriage, by Roaldn B. Gittelsohn. Illustrated by William B. Steinel. New York, Union of American Hebrew Congregations [1965] xii, 232 p. illus. 24 cm.J(Commission on Jewish Education of the Union of American Hebrew Congregations and Central Conference of American Rabbis. Union graded series) "Notes" (bibliographical): p. 221-226. [HQ525.J4G54] 65-24635
1. Marriage—Jews. I. Title.

GITTELSOHN, Roland Bertram, 1910- 296.7'4
Love, sex and marriage : a Jewish view / Roland B. Gittelsohn ; illustrated by William L. Steinel. New York : Union of American Hebrew Congregations, c1976. 134 p. in various pagings : ill. ; 23 cm. A supplement to the author's Consecrated unto me, comprising five new chapters paged for interleaving in the main work. [HQ525.J4G54 suppl] 76-372517 pbk. : 1.00
1. Marriage—Jews. 2. Sex instruction for youth. I. Gittelsohn, Roland Bertran, 1910- Consecrated unto me. II. Title.
Publisher's address: 838 5th ave.

HESCHEL, Abraham Joshua, 1907-1972. 296.7'4
A passion for truth. New York, Farrar, Straus and Giroux [1973] xv, 336 p. 22 cm. [BM723.H47 1973] 72-94721 ISBN 0-374-22992-9 8.95
1. Menahem Mendel, of Kock, 1788-1859. 2. Kierkegaard, Soren Aabye, 1813-1855. 3. Israel ben Eliezer, Ba'al Shem Tob, called BeSHT, 1700 (ca.)-1760. 4. Spiritual life. 5. Hasidism. I. Title.

IGERET ha-kodesh. English and Hebrew. 296.7'4
The holy letter : a study in medieval Jewish sexual morality, ascribed to Nahmanides / translated and with an introduction by Seymour J. Cohen. New York : Ktav Pub. House, 1976. 155 p. : 22 cm. Added t.p.: Igeret ha-kodesh ha-meyuhas la-Ramban. Includes bibliographical references. [BM720.S4I3313] 76-44550 ISBN 0-87068-490-6 : 7.50
1. Sexual ethics. 2. Ethics, Jewish. I. Cohen, Seymour J. II. Moses ben Nahman, ca. 1195-ca. 1270. Igeret ha-kodesh. III. Title. IV. Title: Igeret ha-kodesh ha-meyuhas la-Ramban.

KEMELMAN, Haim. 296.7'4
How to live in the present tense. South Brunswick, A. S. Barnes [1970] 167 p. 22 cm. [BJ1581.2.K43 1970] 79-114611 5.95
1. Conduct of life. I. Title.

KLAPPHOLZ, Kurt, 1913- 296.74
Living faith. New York, Bloch Pub. Co. [1966] x, 82 p. 22 cm. [BM723.K53] 66-19311
1. Jewish way of life. I. Title.

KLAPPHOLZ, Kurt, 1913- 296.74
Living faith. New York, Bloch [c.1966] x, 82p. 22cm. [BM723.K53] 66-19311 3.00
1. Jewish way of life. I. Title.

KLASS, Sholom. 296.74
Responsa of modern Judaism; a compilation of questions and answers on past and present day Halacha as presented in the Jewish press. [Brooklyn, Jewish Press] 1965-66. 2 v. 24 cm. [BM522.59.L26] 66-927
1. Responsa. I. Title.

KRAMER, Simon G 296.74
God and man in the Sefer hasidim, book of the pious [by] Simon G. Kramer. New York, Published for Hebrew Theological College Press, Skokie, Ill., by Bloch Pub. Co. [1966] 285 p. 24 cm. Revision of thesis, New York University. Bibliography: p. 281=285. [BJ1287.J83S493] 66-20891
1. Judah ben Samuel, he-Hasid, d. 1217. Sefer hasidim. I. Title.

KRAMER, Simon G. 296.74
God and man in the Sefer hasidim, book of the pious. New York, Pub. for Hebrew Theological Coll. Pr., by Bloch [c.1966] 285p. 24cm. Bibl. [BJ1287.J83S493] 66-20891 6.00
1. Judah ben Samuel, he-Hasid, d. 1217. Sefer hasidim. I. Title.

LUZZATTO, Moses Hayyim, 1707-1747 296.74
Mesillat yesharim; the path of the upright Tr., ed., introd. by Mordecai M. Kaplan. Philadelphia, Jewish Pubn. Soc. of Amer., 1966. xxx, 461p. 20cm. (JPS lib. of Jewish classics) t.p. in Hebrew. English and Hebrew on opposite pages. [BJ1287.L83M33] HE66 4.50 bds.,
1. Ethics, Jewish. I. Kaplan, Mordecai Menahem 1881- ed. and tr. II. Title.

*MCKINNEY, Irene T. 296.7'4
A search for God. New York, Vantage [1968] 203p. 21cm. 3.75
I. Title.

MANDELBAUM, Bernard, 1922- 296.7'4
Add life to your years. Boston, G. K. Hall, 1974 [c1973] 270 p. 25 cm. Large print ed. [BJ1581.2.M2828 1974] 74-18241 ISBN 0-8161-6257-3 9.95 (lib. bdg.)
1. Conduct of life. 2. Sight-saving books. I. Title.

OPPENHEIMER, Joseph, 1911- 296.7'4
Ma'aser; the precepts of tithing [by] Joseph Oppenheimer. New York, Shengold Publishers, 1971. 52 p. 22 cm. Pages 48-52 and added t.p. in Hebrew; p. 48-50: bibliographical references. Gertrude Hirschler translated the original German manuscript into English. Bibliography: p. 51-52. [BM720.T4O65] 72-24917
1. Tithes (Jewish law) I. Title.

POOL, David de Sola, 1885- 296.74
Is there an answer? An inquiry into some human dilemmas, by David and Tamar de Sola Pool. South Brunswick [N.J.] T. Yoseloff [1966] 206 p. 22 cm. [BM723.P6] 66-14528
1. Jewish way of life. I. Pool, Tanner (Hirschensohn) de Sola, 1893- joint author. II. Title.

POOL, David de Sola, 1885- 296.74
Is there an answer? An inquiry into some human dilemmas, by David and Tamar de Sola Pool. [Cranbury, N.J.] Yoseloff [c.1966] 206p. 22cm. [BM723.P6] 66-14528 4.95
1. Jewish way of life. I. Pool, Tamar (Hirschensohn) de Sola 1893- joint author. II. Title.

SPEAK to the children of Israel / edited by Samuel M. Silver and Morton M. Applebaum. [New York] : Ktav Pub. House, 1976. 243 p. ; 22 cm. Brief sermons dealing with various aspects of the human condition, stressing the Jewish principles for living. [BM733.S67] 76-39947 ISBN 0-87068-495-7 : 4.95 296.7'4
1. Homiletical illustrations, Jewish. 2. Children's sermons, Jewish. 3. Sermons, American—Jewish authors. 4. Sermons, Jewish—United States. I. Silver, Samuel M. II. Applebaum, Morton M.

TREE of life : 296.7'4
an anthology of articles appearing in the Jewish vegetarian, 1966-1974 / edited by Philip L. Pick. South Brunswick, N.J. : A. S. Barnes, c1977. p. cm. Includes bibliographical references. [TX392.T73 1977] 76-18476 ISBN 0-498-01945-4 : 6.95
1. Vegetarianism—Addresses, essays, lectures. I. Pick, Philip L. II. Jewish vegetarian.

BRONNER, Leah. 296.8
Sects and separatism during the second Jewish Commonwealth; a study of the origin of religious separatism, with special reference to the rise, growth, and development of the various sects, includdng the Dead Sea Community ... New York, Bloch Pub. Co. [1967] 174 p. 24 cm. Includes bibliographies. [BM175.A1B7] 67-30087
1. Jewish sects. I. Title.

BRONNER, Leah. 296.8
Sects and separatism during the second Jewish Commonwealth; a study of the origin of religious separatism, with special reference to the rise, growth, and development of the various sects, including the Dead Sea Community ... New York, Bloch Pub. Co. [1967] 174 p. 24 cm. Includes bibliographies. [BM175.A1B7] 67-30087
1. Jewish sects. I. Title.

CRONBACH, Abraham, 1882- 296.8
Reform movements in Judaism. Pref. by Jacob Rader Marcus. N[ew] Y[ork] Bookman Associates [c1963] 138 p. 22 cm. [BM157.C7] 63-17407
1. Judaism—Hist.—Addresses, essays, lectures. I. Title.

CRONBACH, Abraham, 1882- 296.8
Reform movements in Judaism. Pref. by Jacob Rader Marcus. New York, Bkman. [c.1963] 138p. 22cm. 63-17407 3.00
1. Judaism—Hist.—Addresses, essays, lectures. I. Title.

KAUFMAN, Reuben. 296.8
Great sects and schisms in Judaism. New York, J. David [1967] 235 p. 23 cm. [BM157.K3] 66-30506
1. Jewish sects. 2. Judaism—History—Modern period. I. Title.

LESLAU, Wolf. 296.8
Falasha anthology; the black Jews of Ethiopia. Translated from Ethiopic sources with an introd. by Wolf Leslau. New York, Schocken Books [1969, c1951] xliii, 222 p. illus. 20 cm. (Yale Judaica series, v. 6) Includes bibliographies. [BM440.E8L47 1969] 71-87258 2.45 (pbk)
1. Falashas. 2. Ethiopic literature—Translations into English. 3. English literature—Translations from Ethiopic. I. Title. II. Series.

ANKORI, Zvi, 1920- 296.8'1
Karaites in Byzantium; the formative years, 970-1100. New York, AMS Press [1968, c1957] xiii, 546 p. map. 24 cm. (Columbia studies in the social sciences, no. 597) Revision of the author's thesis, Columbia University, 1957. Bibliography: p. [459]-484. [BM185.K3A5 1968] 71-158258
1. Karaites in the Levant. I. Title. II. Series.

ANKORI, Zvi, 1920- 296.81
Karaites in Byzantium; the formative years, 970-1100. New York, Columbia University Press, 1959 [i.e., 1960, c.1957] 546p. map. (Columbia studies in the social sciences, no. 597) 'An enlarged version of . . . [the author's] Columbia University dissertation submitted in 1956 [and issued in microfilm form in 1957] The accretions comprise . . . further studies on the subject in the years 1957 and early 1958.' Bibl.: p.461-484. 57-12659 10.00
1. Karaites. I. Title. II. Series.

BIRNBAUM, Philip, comp. 296.8'1
Karaite studies. Edited and with introd. by Philip Birnbaum. New York, Hermon Press, 1971. xiii, 318 p. 24 cm. English and Hebrew. Includes bibliographical references. [BM185.K3B57] 76-136771 ISBN 0-87203-027-X 12.50
1. Karaites—Addresses, essays, lectures. I. Title.

BLACK, Matthew. 296.81
The scrolls and Christian orgins; studies in the Jewish background of the New Testament. New York, Scribner [1961] 206p. illus. 22cm. Includes bibliography. [BM175.Q6B5] 61-7223
1. Qumran community. 2. Dead Sea scrolls. 3. Christianity—Origin. I. Title.

BLACK, Matthew 296.81
The scrolls and Christian origins; studies in the Jewish background of the New Testament. New York, Scribners [c.1961] 206p. illus. Bibl. 61-7223 3.95
1. Qumran community. 2. Dead Sea scrolls. 3. Christianity—Origin. I. Title.

BOWMAN, John, 1916- 296.8'1
Samaritan documents : relating to their history, religion, and life / translated and edited by John Bowman. Pittsburgh : Pickwick Press, 1977. vii, 370 p. ; 22 cm. (Pittsburgh original texts and translation series ; 2) Includes index. Bibliography: p. 367-370 [BM917.B68] 77-4949 ISBN 0-915138-27-1 pbk. : 7.95
1. Samaritans—Religion—Sources. I. Title.

BOWMAN, John, 1916- 296.8'1
The Samaritan problem : studies in the relationships of Samaritanism, Judaism, and early Christianity / by John Bowman ; translated by Alfred M. Johnson, Jr. Pittsburgh : Pickwick Press, 1975. p. cm. (Pittsburgh theological monograph series ; no. 4) (Franz Delitzsch lectures ; 1959) Translation of Samaritanische Probleme. Includes bibliographical references. [BM935.B6413] 75-20042 ISBN 0-915138-04-2 : 5.95
1. Samaritans—Religion. 2. Christianity and other religions—Samaritanism. 3. Qumran community. I. Title. II. Series. III. Series: Pittsburgh theological monograph series ; no. 4.

BRANDON, Samuel George Frederick. 296.8'1
Jesus and the Zealots; a study of the political factor in primitive Christianity, by S. G. F. Brandon. [New York] Scribner, 1967. xvi, 412 p. illus. 23 cm. Bibliography: p. 369-384. [BM175.Z4B7 1967] 68-57073 7.95
1. Zealots (Jewish party) 2. Christianity and other religions—Judaism. 3. Judaism—Relations—Christianity. I. Title.

CARMIGNAC, Jean. 296.81
Christ and the Teacher of Righteousness; the evidence of the Dead Sea scrolls. Translated from the French by Katharine Greenleaf Pedley. Baltimore, Helicon Press [1962] 168p. 23cm. Translation of: Le Docteur de Justice et Jesus Christ. Includes bibliography. [BM175.Q6C33] 62-11183
1. Teacher of Righteousness. 2. Jesus Christ—Person and offices. I. Title.

CHAVEL, Charles Ber, 1906- 296.8'1
Ramban, his life and teachings. New York, P. Feldheim [c1960] 128 p. 23 cm. Includes bibliography. [BM755.M62C4] 63-1543
1. Moses ben Nahman, ca. 1195-ca. 1270. I. Title.

COLEMAN, William L. 296.8'1
Those Pharisees / William L. Coleman. New York : Hawthorn Books, c1977. 147 p. ; 21 cm. Includes index. Bibliography: p. 139-141. [BM175.P4C64 1977] 77-150046 3.95
1. Jesus Christ—Relation to Judaism. 2. Pharisees. I. Title.

CROSS, Frank Moore. 296.8'1
The ancient library of Qumran and modern Biblical studies / by Frank Moore Cross, Jr. Westport, Conn. : Greenwood Press, 1976. p. cm. Reprint of the 1958 ed. published by Doubleday, Garden City, N.Y., which was issued as the 1956-1957 Haskell lectures at Oberlin College. Bibliography: p. [BM175.Q6C7 1976] 76-29736 ISBN 0-8371-9281-1 lib.bdg. : 15.25
1. Dead Sea scrolls. 2. Dead Sea scrolls—Relation to the New Testament. 3. Qumran community. I. Title. II. Series: The Haskell lectures, Oberlin College ; 1956-1957.

DAVIES, William David, 1911- 296.8'1
Introduction to Pharisaism, by W. D. Davies. Philadelphia, Fortress Press [1967] xxi, 34 p. 19 cm. (Facet books. Biblical series, 16) "Originally published as the W. M. Llewelyn lecture for 1954." Bibliography: p. 29-32. Bibliographical footnotes. [BM175.P4D3 1967] 67-10503

1. Pharisees. I. Title.

DOTAN, Aron, 1928- 296.8'1
Ben Asher's creed : a study of the history of the controversy / by Aron Dotan. Missoula, Mont. : Published by Scholars Press for the Society of Biblical Literature and the International Organization for Masoretic Studies, c1977. 132 p. ; 22 cm. (Masoretic studies ; no. 3) "A first version of this study was published ... in 1957 in the Hebrew journal Sinai." Bibliography: p. 125-132. [BM755.A12D67] 76-27649 ISBN 0-89130-084-8 : 2.80
1. Aaron ben Moses ben Asher. 2. Karaites. I. Title. II. Series.

FINKELSTEIN, Louis, 1895- 296.8'1
Pharisaism in the making; selected essays. [New York] Ktav Pub. House, 1972. xx, 459 p. 24 cm. Includes bibliographical references. [BM173.F55] 77-168748 ISBN 0-87068-178-8 19.95
1. Jews. Liturgy and ritual. Hagadah. 2. Jews. Liturgy and ritual. Grace after meals. 3. Judaism—History—Ancient period—Addresses, essays, lectures. 4. Pharisees. 5. Shemoneh 'esreh (Jewish prayer) I. Title.

FINKELSTEIN, Louis, 1895- 296.81
The Pharisees, the sociological background of their faith. [3d ed.] Philadelphia, Jewish Publication Society of America, 1962. 2 v. illus. 22 cm. (The Morris Loeb series) [BM175.P4F5 1962] 61-11709
1. Pharisees. 2. Jews — Hist. — To 70 A.D. I. Title.

FINKELSTEIN, Louis, 1895- 296.81
The Pharisees, the sociological background of their faith. [3d ed.] Philadelphia, Jewish Publication Society of America, 1962. 2 v. illus. 22 cm. (The Morris Loeb series) [BM175.P4F5 1962] 61-11709
1. Jews—History—To 70 A.D. 2. Pharisees.

GARTNER, Bertil. 296.81
The temple and the community in Qumram and the New Testament; a comparative study in the temple symbolism of the Qamran texts and the New Testament. Cambridge, Univerity Press, 1965. xii, 164 p. 23 cm. (Society for New Testament Studies. Monograph series, 1) Bibliography: p. 143-151. [BM175.Q6G3] 64-21545
1. Qumran community. 2. Bible. N.T. — Symbolism. 3. Christianity, and other religions — Judaism. 4. Judaism — Relations — Christianity. I. Title. II. Title: Temple symbolism of the Qumran texts and the New Testament. III. Series. IV. Series: Studiorum Novi Testamenti Societas. Monograph series, 1

GARTNER, Bertil 296.81
The temple and the community in Qumran and the New Testament; a comparative study in the temple symbolism of the Qumran texts and the New Testament [New York] Cambridge [c.]1965. xii, 164p. 23cm. (Soc. for N.T. Studies. Monograph ser., 1) Bibl. [BM175.Q6G3] 64-21545 4.75
1. Qumran community. 2. Bible. N.T.—Symbolism. 3. Christianity and other religions—Judaism. 4. Judaism—Relations—Christianity. I. Title. II. Title: Temple symbolism of the Qumran texts and the New Testament. III. Series: Studiorum Novi Testamenti Societas. Monograph series, 1

GARTNER, Bertil. New Testament 296.81
Temple symbolism of the Qumran texts and the New Testament. Cambridge, Univerity Press, 1965. xii, 164 p. 23 cm. (Society for New Testament Studies. Monograph series, 1) Bibliography: p. 143-151. [BM175.Q6G3] 64-21545
1. Qumran community. 2. Bible. N.T. — Symbolism. 3. Christianity, and other religions — Judaism. 4. Judaism — Relations — Christianity. I. Title. II. Series. III. Series: Studiorum Novi Testamenti Societas. Monograph series, 1

GILLIAM, Olive Kuntz. 296.8'1
Qumran and history : the place of the teacher in religion / Olive Gilliam. 1st ed. New York : Vantage Press, c1974. ix, 67 p. : map ; 21 cm. [BM175.Q6G54] 75-306758 ISBN 0-533-01167-1 : 3.95
1. Qumran community. I. Title.

GINSBURG, Christian David, 1831-1914. 296.81
The Essenes: their history and doctrines. The Kabbalah: its doctrines, development, and literature. London, Routledge Paul [dist. New York, Barnes & Noble, 1962] 245p. illus. 19cm. 3.00 bds.,
1. Essenes. 2. Cabala. I. Title.

GINZBERG, Louis, 1873-1953. 296.8'1
An unknown Jewish sect / by Louis Ginzberg. New York : Jewish Theological Seminary of America, 1976, c1970. p. cm. (Moreshet series ; v. 1) Revised and updated translation of the author's Eine unbekannte judische Sekte, 1922 ed. Includes bibliographical references and indexes. [BM175.Z3G5613 1976] 76-127636 25.00
1. Zadokite documents. I. Title. II. Series: Moreshet (New York) ; v. 1.

GLITZENSTEIN, Abraham Chanoch, 1929- 296.8'1
The arrest and liberation of Rabbi Shneur Zalman of Liadi; the history of yud-teth Kislev: the universally famous Chassidic festival of the 19th day of Kislev commemorating the liberation of Rabpi Shneur Zalman of Liadi, as compiled and edited from the writings and traditions of the leaders and followers of Chabad-Chassidism, by A. C. Glitzenstein. Translated and adapted into English by Jacob Immanuel Schochet. Brooklyn, Kehot Publication Society, 1964. 125 p. facsim., port. 24 cm. On spine: The history of yud-teth Kislev. Translation of Hag ha-geulah Bibliography: p. 115-116. "Published works of Rabbi Shneur Zalman of Ladi": p. 120-125. [BM755.S525G53] 65-28161
1. Shneor Zalman ben Baruch, 1747-1812. I. Title. II. Title: The history of yud-teth Kislev.

GOODBLATT, Pincus L. 296.8'1
No policeman at my mouth, and other stories and reimniscences, by Pincus L. Goodblatt. New York, J. David [1965] 69 p. 22 cm. [BM755.G676A3] 64-8426
I. Title.

HERFORD, Robert Travers, 1860-1950. 296.81
The Pharisees [new foreword by Nahum N. Glatzer] Boston, Beacon Pr. [1962, c.1924, 1952] 248p. (Beacon BP134) 62-1314 1.75 pap.,
1. Pharisees. I. Title.

ISSER, Stanley Jerome. 296.8'1
The Dositheans : a Samaritan sect in late antiquity / by Stanley Jerome Isser. Leiden : Brill, 1976. x, 223 p. ; 25 cm. (Studies in Judaism in late antiquity ; v. 17) Originally presented as the author's thesis, Columbia University. Includes original texts in Arabic, Aramaic, Greek, Hebrew, or Latin. Includes index. Bibliography: p. [214]-218. [BM913.D67I85 1976] 76-380939 ISBN 9-00-404481-7 : fl 60.00
1. Dositheans. I. Title. II. Series.

JOSEPHUS, Flavius. 296.8'1
The Essenes by Josephus and his contemporaries. Translated from the original Latin and Greek by Edmond Bordeaux Szekely. San Diego, Academy of Creative Living, 1970. 30 p. 21 cm. [BM175.E8J68] 76-19613 1.50
1. Essenes. I. Szekely, Edmond Bordeaux, tr. II. Title.

LARSON, Martin Alfred, 1897- 296.8'1
The Essene heritage; or, The teacher of the scrolls and the gospel Christ, by Martin A. Larson. New York, Philosophical Library [1967] xviii, 237 p. 23 cm. Bibliography: p. 213-216. [BM175.E8L3] 67-19183
1. Dead Sea scrolls. 2. Essenes. 3. Christianity—Origin. I. Title. II. Title: The teacher of the scrolls and the gospel Christ.

LEOPOLD Loew, 296.8'1
a biography with a translation of some of the tributes paid to his memory on the occasion of the centenary of his birth, celebrated at Szeged, Hungary, June 4, 1911. New York, 1912. 87 p. illus. 24 cm. [BM755.L584L6] 63-56792
1. Low Leopold, 1811-1875.

LOEW, William Noah. 296.8'1
Leopold Loew, a biography with a translation of some of the tributes paid to his memory on the occasion of the centenary of his birth, celebrated at Szeged, Hungary, June 4, 1911. New York, 1912. 87 p. illus. 24 cm. [BM755.L584L6] 63-56792
1. Low Leopold, 1811-1875. I. Title.

MACDONALD, John 296.81
The theology of the Samaritans. Philadelphia, Westmininster [1965, c.1964] 480p. front. 23cm. (New Testament lib.) Bibl. [BM945.M3] 65-10060 10.00
1. Samaritans. 2. Jewish theology. I. Title.

MONTGOMERY, James Alan, 1866-1949. 296.8'1
The Samaritans; the earliest Jewish sect: their history, theology, and literature. Introd. by Abraham S. Halkin. New York, Ktav Pub. House [1968] xxx, 358 p. illus., map, plan, ports. 24 cm. (The Bohlen lectures, 1906) "First published in 1907." Bibliography: p. 322-346. [DS129.M8 1968] 67-30121
1. Samaritans. I. Title. II. Series.

MOTYLEWSKI, Leo F. 296.8'1
The Essene plan / by Leo F. Motylewski. New York : Philosophical Library, c1976. 164 p. ; 22 cm. Bibliography: p. 161-164. [BM175.E8M64] 76-14499 ISBN 0-8022-2183-1 : 8.75
1. Essenes—Miscellanea. 2. Christianity—Origin—Miscellanea. I. Title.

NEUSNER, Jacob, 1932- 296.8'1
From politics to piety; the emergence of Pharisaic Judaism. Englewood Cliffs, N.J., Prentice-Hall [1972, c1973] xxiii, 168 p. 24 cm. Bibliography: p. 155-156. [BM175.P4N44 1973] 72-3822 ISBN 0-13-331447-2 7.95
1. Pharisees. I. Title.
Pap. 3.95

PLOEG, J. P. M. van der, 1909- 296.81
The excavations at Qumran; a survey of the Judaean brotherhood and its ideas. Tr. [from Dutch] by Kevin Smyth. London, Longmans [dist. Mystic, Conn., Verry, 1965, c.1958] 233p. illus. 21cm. Bibl. [BM175.Q6P513] 4.00 bds.,
1. Qumran community. 2. Dead Sea scrolls. I. Title.

RABIN, Chaim. 296.8'1
Qumran studies / by Chaim Rabin. Westport, Conn. : Greenwood Press, 1976, c1957. p. cm. Reprint of the ed. published by Oxford University Press, London, which was published as no. 2 of Scripta Judaica. Includes indexes. [BM175.Q6R3 1976] 76-40116 ISBN 0-8371-9060-6 lib.bdg. : 11.25
1. Qumran community. 2. Judaism—Relations—Islam. 3. Islam—Relations—Judaism. I. Title. II. Series: Scripta Judaica ; 2.

RABIN, Chaim. 296.8'1
Qumran studies / Chaim Rabin. New York : Schocken Books, 1975, c1957. xv, 135 p. : 21 cm. Reprint of the ed. published by Oxford University Press, London, which was issued as no. 2 of Scripta Judaica. Includes bibliographical references and indexes. [BM175.Q6R3 1975] 74-26735 ISBN 0-8052-0482-2 pbk. : 3.95
1. Qumran community. 2. Judaism—Relations—Islam. 3. Islam—Relations—Judaism. I. Title. II. Series: Scripta Judaica ; 2.

RINGGREN, Helmer, 1917- 296.81
The faith of Qumran; theology of the Dead Sea scrolls. Translated by Emilie T. Sander. Philadelphia, Fortress Press [c1963] xiii, 310 p. 18 cm. (A Fortress Press paperback) Translation of Tro och liv enligh Doda-havs-rullarna. Bibliography: p. 255-285. [BM487.R513] 63-14403
1. Dead Sea scrolls. 2. Qumran community. I. Title.

RINGGREN, Helmer, 1917- 296.81
The faith of Qumran; theology of the Dead Sea scrolls. Tr. by Emilie T. Sander. Philadelphia, Fortress [c.1963] xiii, 310p. 18cm. Bibl. 63-14403 1.95 pap.,
1. Dead Sea scrolls. 2. Qumran community. I. Title.

ROTH, Cecil, 1899- 296.81
The Dead Sea scrolls; a new historical approach. New York, Norton [c.1958, 1965] xx, 99p. 22cm. First pub. in London in 1958 under title: The historical background of the Dead Sea scrolls. Bibl. [BM175.Q6R6] 65-13329 4.50
1. Qumran community. 2. Zealots (Jewish party) 3. Dead Sea scrolls. I. Title.

ROTH, Cecil, 1899- 296.81
The Dead Sea scrolls: a new historical approach. New York, Norton [1966. c.1958. 1965] xx, 99p. 20cm. First pub. in London under the title: The historical background of the Dead Sea scrolls (Norton Lib. N303) Bibl. [BM175.Q6R6 1965] 65-13329 1.25 pap.,
1. Qumran community. 2. Zealots (Jewish party) 3. Dead Sea scrolls. I. Title.

*SAMUEL, Edith. ed. 296.81
Chasidic tales retold; a collection of fifteen articles ed. by Edith Samuel, with teaching material for youths and adults prepd. by Harvey J. Fields. Illus. by Morton Garchik. Art heads by Irv Koons. New York, Union of Amer. Herbew Congregations, 1967. 52p. illus. (pt. col.) 28cm. Articles reprinted from Keeping posted, v.12, 1966-67. 33 1.50. pap.,
1. Hasidism. I. Keeping posted. II. Title.

SANDMEL, Samuel. 296.8'1
The first Christian century in Judaism and Christianity: certainties and uncertainties. New York, Oxford University Press, 1969. xii, 241 p. 21 cm. Bibliography: p. [219]-232. [BM177.S23] 69-17768 6.00
1. Judaism—History—Post-exilic period, 586 B.C.-210 A.D. 2. Christianity—Origin. 3. Church history—Historiography. I. Title.

SCHARLEMANN, Martin Henry, 1910- 296.81
Qumran and Corinth. New York, Bkman [c.1962] 78p. Bibl. 62-10887 1.95 pap.,
1. Qumran community. 2. Bible. N. T. 1 Corinthians—Criticism, interpretation, etc. 3. Corinth, Greece—Religion. I. Title.

SCHECHTER, Solomon, 1847-1915, comp. 296.8'1
Documents of Jewish sectaries, edited from Hebrew MSS. in the Cairo Genizah collection, now in the possession of the University Library, Cambridge, by S. Schechter. Prolegomenon by Joseph A. Fitzmyer. [New York] Ktav Pub. House, 1970. 2 v. in 1 (175 p.) facsims. 28 cm. (The Library of Biblical studies) Reprint of 1910 ed., except for "Prolegomenon." Contents.Contents.—v. 1. Fragments of a Zadokite work, with an English translation, introd. and notes.—v. 2. [Kuntresim mi-Sefer ha-mitsvot le-'Anan (romanized form)] Fragments of the Book of the commandments by Anan, with a short introd. and notes. Includes bibliographical references. [BM175.Z3S25 1970] 69-10671 ISBN 0-87068-016-1
1. Karaites. 2. Cairo genizah. I. Anan ben David, 8th cent. Sefer ha-mitsvot. Selections. 1970. II. Zadokite documents. English and Hebrew. 1970. III. Title. IV. Title: Kuntresim mi-Sefer ha-mitsvot. V. Series.

SCHUBERT, Kurt, 1923- 296.81
The Dead Sea community: its origin and teachings. Translated by John W. Doberstein. New York, Harper [1959] 178 p. 22 cm. Includes bibliography. [BM175.Q6S363 1959a] 59-7162
1. Dead Sea scrolls. 2. Qumran community. I. Title.

SCHUBERT, Kurt, 1923- 296.81
The Dead Sea community; its origin and teachings. [Eng. tr. from German by John W. Doberstein] London, A. & C. Black [New York, Humanities, 1966, c.1958, 1959] 178p. 21cm. Bibl. [BM175.Q6S363] 2.50 bds.,
1. Qumran community. 2. Dead Sea scrolls. I. Title.

SCHUBERT, Kurt, 1923- 296.8'1
The Dead Sea community: its origin and teachings. Translated by John W. Doberstein. Westport, Conn., Greenwood Press [1973] xi, 178 p. 22 cm. Reprint of the 1959 ed. published by Harper, New York, which was a translation of Die Gemeinde vom Totem Meer. Bibliography: p. 165-168. [BM175.Q6S363 1973] 73-15245 ISBN 0-8371-7169-5 9.95
1. Dead Sea scrolls. 2. Qumran community. I. Title.

SIMON, Marcel, 1907- 296.8'1
Jewish sects at the time of Jesus. Translated by James H. Farley. Philadelphia, Fortress Press [1967] xii, 180 p. 18 cm. Bibliography: p. 163-168. [BM175.A1S53] 66-25265
1. Jewish sects.

SUTCLIFFE, Edmund Felix. 296.81
The monks of Qumran as depicted in the Dead Sea scrolls, with translation in English. Westminster, Md., Newman Press, 1960. xvi, 272 p. illus., map. 23 cm. Bibliography: p. 241-249. [VM175.Q6S8] 60-14813
1. Qumran community. I. Dead Sea scrolls. English. II. Title.

SUTCLIFFE, Edmund Felix 296.81
The monks of Qumran as depicted in the Dead Sea scrolls, with translations in English. Westminster, Md., Newman Press, 1960[ ] xvi, 272p. illus., diagrs., map, 23cm. Bibl. and bibl. notes: p.241-259 60-14813 5.50
1. Qumran community. I. Dead Sea scrolls. English. II. Title.

UMEN, Samuel. 296.81
Pharisaism and Jesus. New York, Philosophical Library [1963] 145 p. 23 cm. Includes bibliography. [BM175.P4U4] 62-20875
1. Pharisees. 2. Jesus Christ — Jewish interpretations. I. Title.

UMEN, Samuel 296.81
Pharisaism and Jesus. New York, Philosophical [c.1963] 145p. 23cm. Bibl. 62-20875 3.75
1. Pharisees. 2. Jesus Christ—Jewish interpretations. I. Title.

BENSION, Ariel, 1881-1932. 296.8'2
The Zohar in Moslem and Christian Spain / by Ariel Bension ; with an introd. by Denison Ross. New York : Hermon Press, 1974. xx, 256 p., 6 leaves of plates : ill. ; 24 cm. Reprint of the 1932 ed. published by G. Routledge, London. Bibliography: p. 249-250. [BM529.B35 1974] 74-78330 ISBN 0-87203-046-6 : 12.50

1. Zohar. 2. Jews in Spain. 3. Mysticism—Spain. I. Title.

NETANYAHU, Benzion. 296.82
The Marranos of Spain. from the late XIVth to the early XVIth century, according to contemporary Hebrew sources, by B. Netanyahu. New York, Amer. Acad. for Jewish Res., 1966. vii. 254p. 24cm. Bibl. [DS135.S7N39] 66-18518 6.00 [corrected entry]
1. Maranos. I. Title.

NETANYAHU, Benzion. 296.8'2
The Marranos of Spain, from the late XIVth to the early XVIth century, according to contemporary Hebrew sources, by B. Netanyahu. 2d. rev. and enl. ed. New York, American Academy for Jewish Research, 1966. Millwood, N.Y., Kraus Reprint Co., 1973 [c1972] ix, 280 p. 24 cm. Includes bibliographical references. [DS135.S7N39 1973] 75-183903
1. Maranos. I. Title.

ROTH, Cecil 296.82
A history of the Marranos. [2d rev. ed.] Philadelphia, Jewish Publication Society of America, 1959 [c.1932] xiv, 424p. illus. 21cm. (bibl. and bibl. notes. p.379-410) 60-85 4.50
1. Marranos. 2. Inquisition. Spain. I. Title.

ROTH, Cecil, 1899- 296.82
A history of the Marranos [3d ed.] New York, Harper [1966, c.1932] viii, 422p. facsims. 21cm. (Torchbks. TB812P. Temple lib.) Bibl. [BM190.R6] 66-2324 2.75 pap.,
1. Maranos. 2. Inquisition. Spain. I. Title.

ROTH, Cecil, 1899-1970. 296.8'2
A history of the Marranos / Cecil Roth. 4th ed. / with a new introd. by Herman P. Salomon. New York : Hermon Press, 1974. xxiv, 424 p. : ill. ; 24 cm. Includes index. Bibliography: p. 403-410. [DS124.R625 1974] 73-93367 ISBN 0-87203-040-7 : 14.50
1. Inquisition. Spain. 2. Maranos. I. Title.

ROTH, Cecil, 1899-1970. 296.8'2
A history of the Marranos / Cecil Roth. 4th ed. / with a new introd. by Herman P. Salomon. New York : Schocken Books, 1974 [i.e. 1975] xxiv, 424 p. : ill. ; 21 cm. (Schocken paperbacks on Judaica) Includes bibliographical references and index. [DS124.R625 1975] 74-10149 ISBN 0-8052-0463-6 pbk. : 5.50
1. Inquisition. Spain. 2. Maranos. I. Title.

ROTH, Cecil, 1899-1970. 296.8'2
A history of the Marranos / by Cecil Roth. New York : Arno Press, 1975, [c1932] xii, 422 p. ; 21 cm. (The Modern Jewish experience) Reprint of the ed. published by the Jewish Publication Society of America, Philadelphia. Includes bibliographical references and index. [DS124.R625 1975b] 74-29516 ISBN 0-405-06742-9 : 26.00
1. Inquisition. Spain. 2. Maranos. I. Title. II. Series.

BLAU, Joseph Leon, 1909- 296.83
Modern varieties of Judaism. New York, Columbia, 1966 [c.1964, 1966] ix, 217p. 23cm. (Lects. on the hist. of religions sponsored by the Amer. Council of Learned Soc. New ser., no.8) Bibl. [BL25.L4 no.8] 66-10732 6.00
1. Jewish sects. I. Title. II. Series.

CASSIN, Elena. 296.83
San Nicandro; the story of a religious phenomenon. Tr. by Douglas West. Chester Springs, Pa., Dufour, 1962 [c.1959] 200p. illus. 22cm. Bibl. 62-8537 4.50
1. Proselytes and proselyting, Jewish. 2. Jews in Sannicandro, Italy. I. Title.

ECKMAN, Lester Samuel. 296.8'3
The history of the Musar movement, 1840-1945 / by Lester Samuel Eckman New York : Shengold Publishers, [1975] 174 p. ; 25 cm. Includes index. Bibliography p. 169-172. [BJ1285.5.M8E25] 75-24183 ISBN 0-88400-041-9 : 8.95
1. Musar movement—History. I. Title.

GOLDBERG, Hillel. 296.8'3
Musar anthology. [Hillel Goldberg, editor. 1st ed. Hyde Park, Mass., Harwich Lithograph, 1972] 64 p. illus. 28 cm. Cover title. Includes bibliographical references. [BJ1285.5.M8G65] 72-91473
1. Musar movement. I. Title.

RUDAVSKY, David. 296.83
Emancipation and adjustment; contemporary Jewish religious movements, their history and thought. New York, Diplomatic Press [1967] 460 p. illus., facsims., ports. 23 cm. Bibliography:p. 435-450. [BM190.R8] 66-23734
1. Judaism—History—Modern period, 1750- I. Title.

SAVIN, Jacob 296.83
Concepts of Judaism: a study of the variety of interpretations. Foreword by Leon Fram. New York, Exposition [c.1964] 140p. 22cm. (Exposition-testament bk.) Bibl. 64-6061 4.00
1. Jewish sects. I. Title.

URY, Zalman F. 296.8'3
The Musar movement : a quest for excellence in character education / by Zalman F. Ury. New York : Yeshiva University Press, Dept. of Special Publications : selling agents, Bloch Pub. Co., 1970, c1969. 84 p. ; 23 cm. (Studies in Torah Judaism ; 12) Bibliography: p. 79-81. [BJ1285.5.M8U79 1970] 74-191759
1. Lipkin, Israel, 1810-1883. 2. Musar movement. I. Title. II. Series.

ROSENTHAL, Newman Hirsch. 296.8'3'09945
Look back with pride; the St. Kilda Hebrew Congregation's first century [by] Newman Rosenthal. [Melbourne, Thomas] Nelson [(Australia) 1971] xv, 182 p. illus. 23 cm. [BM445.M43R68] 73-859578 ISBN 0-17-001955-1
1. St. Kilda Hebrew Congregation. 2. Jews in Melbourne. I. Title.

HECHT, Michael. 296.8'32
Have you ever asked yourself these questions? A guide to traditional Jewish thought. New York, Shengold [1971] 267 p. 22 cm. "Teacher's guide."—Dust jacket. [BM105.H35] 75-163738 5.00
1. Orthodox Judaism—Study and teaching. I. Title.

LAMM, Norman. 296.8'32
Faith and doubt; studies in traditional Jewish thought. New York, Ktav Pub. House [1972, c1971] ix, 309 p. 24 cm. Includes bibliographical references. [BM601.L3 1972] 75-138852 ISBN 0-87068-138-9 10.00
1. Orthodox Judaism—Addresses, essays, lectures. I. Title.

PELCOVITZ, Ralph. 296.8'32
Danger and opportunity / by Ralph Pelcovitz. New York : Shengold Publishers, c1976. 189 p. ; 26 cm. [BM205.P38] 76-47304 ISBN 0-88400-047-8 : 6.95
1. Orthodox Judaism—United States—Addresses, essays, lectures. 2. Ethics, Jewish—Addresses, essays, lectures. 3. Israel—Addresses, essays, lectures. I. Title.

SHAFRAN, Avi. 296.8'32
Jewthink : a guide to real Judaism for the thinking individual / by Avi Shafran. New York : Hermon Press, c1977. 94 p. ; 21 cm. Subtitle varies on cover: A manual of Jewish belief for the thinking individual. Bibliography: p. [90]-94. [BM580.S4] 77-79097 ISBN 0-87203-064-4 pbk. : 3.95
1. Orthodox Judaism. I. Title.
Publisher's address : 175 Fifth Ave., N.Y.10010

LAMM, Norman, comp. 296.8'32'08
A treasury of "Tradition." Edited by Norman Lamm and Walter S. Wurzburger. New York, Hebrew Pub. Co. [1967] ix, 462 p. 22 cm. "Sponsored by Rabbinical Council of America." Bibliographical footnotes. [BM40.L35] 67-24738
1. Orthodox Judaism—Addresses, essays, lectures. I. Wurzburger, Walter S., joint comp. II. Tradition; a journal of orthodox Jewish thought. III. Title.

LAMM, Norman, comp. 296.8'32'08
A treasury of "Tradition". A treasury of "Tradition." New York, Hebrew Pub. Co. [1967] ix, 462 p. 22 cm. "Sponsored by Rabbinical Council of America." Bibliographical footnotes. [BM40.L35] 67-24738
1. Orthodox Judaism—Addresses, essays, lectures. I. Wurzburger, Walter S., joint comp. II. Tradition; a journal of orthodox Jewish thought. III. Title.

RACKMAN, Emanuel. 296.8'32'08
One man's Judaism. New York, Philosophical Library [1970] 397 p. 23 cm. Includes bibliographical references. [BM565.R25] 73-100583 ISBN 8-02-223230- 8.95
1. Orthodox Judaism. I. Title.

ROTHKOFF, Aaron. 296.8'32'0924 B
Bernard Revel: builder of American Jewish orthodoxy. [1st ed.] Philadelphia, Jewish Publication Society of America, 1972. xiv, 378 p. illus. 22 cm. Bibliography: p. 343-359. [BM755.R44R67] 71-188582 6.00
1. Revel, Bernard, 1885-1940.

ARON, Milton. 296.8'33
Ideas and ideals of the Hassidim. [1st ed.] New York, Citadel Press [1969] 350 p. 22 cm. Bibliography: p. 327-339. [BM198.A68 1969] 74-90398 7.95
1. Hasidism—History. I. Title.

BUBER, Martin 296.833
The way of man, according to the teachings of Hasidism. Foreword by Maurice Friedman. Wallingford, Pa., Pendle Hill [1960] 32p. 19cm. (Pendle Hill pamphlet, 106) 60-86 .35 pap.,
1. Hasidism. I. Title.

BUBER, Martin, 1878- ed. 296.833
Ten rungs: Hasidic sayings. [Tr. by Olga Marx] New York, Schocken [1962, c.1947] 127p. 21cm. (SB18) 62-13135 .95 pap.,
1. Hasidism. I. Marx, Olga, 1894- tr. II. Title.

BUBER, Martin, 1878-1965. 296.8'33
The legend of the Baal-Shem. Translated from the German by Maurice Friedman. New York, Schocken Books [1969, c1955] 223 p. 22 cm. Translation of Die Legende des Baalschem. [BM532.B7813 1969] 76-86849 6.50
1. Israel ben Eliezer, Ba'al-Shem Tob, called BeSHT, 1700 (ca.)-1760. 2. Hasidism. 3. Tales, Hasidic. I. Title.

BUBER, Martin, 1878-1965 296.833
The origin and meaning of Hasidism. Ed., tr, [from German] by Maurice Friedman. New York, Harper [1966, c.1960] 254p. 21cm. (Torchbk.: TB835K. Temple lib.) Bibl. [BM198.B843] 1.75 pap.,
1. Hasidism. I. Title.

BUBER, Martin, 1878-1965. 296.833
The origin and meaning of Hasidism. Edited and translated by Maurice Friedman. New York, Horizon Press [1960] 254 p. 21 cm. "The second volume of ... [the author's] two-volume comprehensive interpretation, Hasidism and the way of man. The ... first volume [was published in 1958 under title] Hasidism and modern man." Includes bibliography. [BM198.B843] 60-8161
1. Hasidism.

BUBER, Martin, 1878-1965. 296.833
The way of man according to the teaching of Hasidism. New York, Citadel Press [1966] 41 p. 18 cm. [BM198.B87 1966] 66-3313
1. Hasidism. I. Title.

DOB Baer ben Samuel. 296.8'33
In praise of Baal Shem Tov [Shivhei ha-Besht]; the earliest collection of legends about the founder of Hasidism. Translated and edited by Dan Ben-Amos & Jerome R. Mintz. Bloomington, Indiana University Press [1970] xxx, 352 p. 25 cm. Translation of Shivhe ha-Besht. (romanized form) Bibliography: p. [273] -279. [BM755.I8D613] 76-98986 17.50
1. Israel ben Eliezer, Ba'al Shem Tob, called Besht, 1700 (ca.)-1760. 2. Tales, Hasidic. I. Ben-Amos, Dan, ed. II. Mintz, Jerome R., ed. III. Title.

GARVIN, Philip, 1947- 296.8'33
A people apart; Hasidism in America. Photos. by Philip Garvin. Text by Arthur A. Cohen. [1st ed.] New York, Dutton, 1970. 192 p. illus. 32 cm. [BM198.G35 1970] 70-122798 20.00
1. Hasidism—U.S.—Pictorial works. I. Cohen, Arthur Allen, 1928- II. Title.

JACOBS, Louis. 296.8'33
Hasidic thought / by Louis Jacobs. New York : Behrman House, c1976. x, 246 p. ; 22 cm. (The Chain of tradition series ; v. 5) [BM198.J37] 76-15825 pbk. : 3.95
1. Hasidism—Sources. I. Title.

JACOBS, Louis. 296.8'33
Seeker of unity; the life and works of Aaron of Starosselje. New York, Basic Books [1967, c1966] 168 p. 23 cm. Includes bibliographical references. [BM755.A14J3 1967] 67-11452
1. Aaron ben Moses, ha-Levi, of Starosel'ye. 1766 (ca.)-1828. I. Title.

JUDAH ben Samuel, he-Hasid, d.1217. 296.8'33
Medieval Jewish mysticism. Book of the pious [translated by] Sholom Alchanan Singer. Northbrook, Ill., Whitehall Co. [1971] xxii, 167 p. 23 cm. Translation of Sefer hasidim. Includes bibliographical references. [BJ1287.J83S413] 73-126988 ISBN 0-87655-017-0 3.95
1. Ethics, Jewish. I. Title. II. Title: Book of the pious.

LANGER, Mordecai Georgo, 1894-1943. 296.833
Nine gates to the Chassidic mysteries, by Jiri Langer. Translated by Stephen Jolly. [1st ed.] New York, D. McKay Co. [1961] 266p. 21cm. [BM532.L313] 61-7986
1. Tales, Hasidic. I. Title. II. Title: Translation of Devet bran.

LANGER, Mordecai Georgo, 1894-1943. 296.8'33
Nine gates to the Chassidic mysteries / by Jiri Langer ; translated by Stephen Jolly. New York : Behrman House, [1976] c1961. p. cm. (A Jewish legacy book) Translation of Devet bran. [BM532.L313 1976] 76-5859 ISBN 0-87441-241-2 pbk. : 3.95
1. Tales, Hasidic. I. Title.

LIPSCHITZ, Max A 296.8'33
The faith of a Hassid, by Max A. Lipschitz. Illus. by Jane Steinsnyder [and] Regi Yanich. New York, J. David [1967] xiii, 346 p. illus. 24 cm. Bibliography: p. 342-343. [BM198.L54] 66-30507
1. Hasidism. I. Title.

LIPSCHITZ, Max A. 296.8'33
The faith of a Hassid, by Max A. Lipschitz. Illus. by Jane Steinsnyder [and] Regi Yanich. New York, J. David [1967] xiii, 346 p. illus. 24 cm. Bibliography: p. 342-343. [BM198.L54] 66-30507
1. Hasidism. I. Title.

MINTZ, Jerome R. 296.8'33
Legends of the Hasidim; an introduction to Hasidic culture and oral tradition in the New World [by] Jerome R. Mintz. Photos. by the author. Chicago, University of Chicago Press [1968] 462 p. illus. 24 cm. Bibliography: p. [452]-457. [BM198.M52] 68-16707
1. Hasidism. 2. Tales, Hasidic. I. Title.

NAHMAN ben Simhah, of Bratzlav, 1770?-1810? 296.8'33
Rabbi Nachman's wisdom: Shevachay haRan, Sichos haRan, by Nathan of Nemirov. Translated and annotated by Aryeh Kaplan. Edited by Zvi Aryeh Rosenfeld. [1st ed. Brooklyn, 1973] 458 p. illus. 24 cm. Translation of Shivhe ha-Ran. Includes bibliographical references. [BM198.N3313] 74-168205
1. Nahman ben Simhah, of Bratzlav, 1770?-1810? 2. Hasidism. 3. Tales, Hasidic. I. Nathan ben Naphtali Herz, of Nemirov, comp. II. Title.

NEWMAN, Louis Israel, 1893- 296.833
Maggidim & Hasidim: their wisdom; a new anthology of the parables, folk-tales, fables, aphorisms, epigrams, sayings, anecdotes, proverbs, and exegetical interpretations of the leading Maggidim (folkpreachers), and the Hasidic masters and their disciples. Companion volume to 'The Hasidic anthology.' Tr. from Hebrew, Yiddish, German; selected, comp., arranged by Louis I. Newman in collaboration with Samuel Spitz. Introd. on 'The Maggidim and Hasidim; their preaching method and art.' New York, Bloch Pub. Co., 1962. 248p. 22cm. Bibl. 62-4811 5.50
1. Homiletical illustrations, Jewish. 2. Tales, Hasidic. 3. Tales, Jewish. I. Title.

POLL, Solomon. 296.833
The Hasidic community of Williamsburg. [New York] Free Press of Glencoe [1962] x, 308p. map (on lining paper) 22cm. Bibliography: p. 288-291. [BM198.P6] 62-10591
1. Hasudism—Brooklyn. 2. Jews—Soc. life & cust. I. Title.

POSY, Arnold, 1893- 296.8'33
Mystic trends in Judaism. New York, J. David [1966] 213 p. 23 cm. [BM723.P65] 66-21592
1. Mysticism—Judaism. 2. Jewish sects. I. Title.

RABINOWICZ, Harry M., 1919- 296.833
A guide to Hassidism. New York, T. Yoseloff [1961, c.1960] 163p. (Popular Jewish library) Bibl. 61-2818 2.95 bds.,
1. Hasidism—Hist. I. Title.

RABINOWICZ, Harry M 1919- 296.833
The slave who saved the city, and other Hassidic tales. Drawings by Ahron Gelles. New York, A. S. Barnes [1960] 192p. illus. 21cm. (A Wonderful world book) [BM532.R3] 60-10202
1. Tales, Hasidic. I. Title.

RABINOWICZ, Harry M., 1919- 296.833
The slave who saved the city, and other Hassidic tales. Drawings by Ahron Gelles. New York, A. S. Barnes [c.1960] 192p. illus. 21cm. (A Wonderful world book) 60-10202 2.95
1. Tales, Hasidic. I. Title.

RABINOWICZ, Harry M., 1919- 296.8'33
The world of Hasidism, by Harry M. Rabinowicz. Hartford, Hartmore House [1970] 271 p. illus., ports. 23 cm. Bibliography: p. 259-264. [BM198.R28 1970b] 79-113413 6.95
1. Hasidism—History. I. Title.

RABINOWITSCH, Wolf Zeev, 1900- 296.8'33
Lithuanian Hasidism. Foreword by Simon Dubnow. New York, Schocken Books [1971] xiii, 263 p. illus. 23 cm. Translation of ha-

Hasidut ha-lita'it. Bibliography: p. 248-255. [BM198.R2913 1971] 72-148840 ISBN 0-85303-021-9 7.00
1. Hasidism—Lithuania. I. Title.

*SCHACHTER, Zalman. 296.833
Fragments of a future scroll, Hassidism for the Aquarian age, edited by Philip Mandelkorn and Stephen Gerstman. [Germantown, Pa.] Leaves of Grass Press [1975] xiii, 161 p. 21 cm. Bibliography: p. 157-159 [BM198] ISBN 0-915070-00-6 3.95 (pbk.)
1. Hasidism. I. Title.

SCHNEERSCHN, Joseph Isaac, 1880-1950. 296.833
Lubavitcher rabbi's memoris. [English rendition and glossary by Nissan Mindel] Brooklyn, Otzar Hachassidim, 19 v. illus. 24cm. 'The Memoris (Zichronoth) were first published in Yiddish in serial form in the Jewish morning journal of New York from October 7. 1940 to February 23, 1942, and subsequently, for the most part, in book form in 1947.' [BM198.S3343] 61-24816
1. Hasidism—Hist. 2. Tales, Hasidic. I. Title.

SCHNEERSOHN, Shalom Dov Ber, 1860-1920. 296.8'33
Kuntres Uma'ayon mibais haShem / by Sholom DovBer Schneersohn ; translation by Zalman I. Posner. 2d ed. Brooklyn, N.Y. : Kehot Publication Society, 1969, 1973 printing. xii, 143 p. ; 24 cm. Bibliography: p. 143. [BM198.S3413 1973] 74-194693
1. Habad. I. Title.

SCHOLEM, Gershom Gerhard, 1897- 296.833
Major trends in Jewish mysticism [3d rev. ed.] New York, Schocken Books [1961, c.1946, 1954] 460p. illus. (Schocken paperbacks, SB5) Bibl. 61-8991 2.25 pap.,
1. Mysticism—Judaism. I. Title.

SCHOLEM, Gershom Gerhard, 1897- 296.833
Major trends in Jewish mysticism. New York, Schocken Books [1961, c1954] 460 p. illus. 21 cm. (Schocken paperbacks, SB5) "Reprinted from the third revised edition." Includes bibliography. [BM723.S35 1961] 61-8991
1. Mysticism—Judaism. I. Title.

WIESEL, Eliezer. 296.8'33
Souls on fire; portraits and legends of Hasidic masters [by] Elie Wiesel. Translated from the French by Marion Wiesel. [1st American ed.] New York, Random House [1972] 268 p. 22 cm. Translation of Celebration hassidique. [BM198.W513 1972] 79-159387 ISBN 0-394-46437-0 7.95
1. Hasidism—History. 2. Tales, Hasidic. I. Title.

WIESEL, Eliezer. 296.8'33
Souls on fire; portraits and legends of Hasidic masters [by] Elie Wiesel. Translated from the French by Marion Wiesel. New York, Vintage Books [1973, c1972] 268 p. illus. 18 cm. Translation of Celebration hassidique. [BM198.W513 1973] 72-8056 ISBN 0-394-71870-4 1.65 (pbk.)
1. Hasidism—History. 2. Tales, Hasidic. I. Title.

NEWMAN, Louis 296.833082
Israel, 1893- comp. and tr. New York, Schocken Books [1963] 556 p. 21 cm. "SB46." [BM198.N4] 63-11041
1. Hasidism — Collections. 2. Jewish literature. 3. Homiletical illustrations. I. Title: The Hasidic anthology;

NEWMAN, Louis Israel, 1893- comp. and tr. 296.833082
The Hasidic anthology; tales and teachings of the Hasidim. Tr. from Hebrew, Yiddish, German, selected, comp., arranged by Louis I. Newman, with Samuel Spitz. New York, Schocken [c.1934, 1963] 556p. 21cm. (SB46) Bibl. 63-11041 2.45 pap.,
1. Hasidism—Collections. 2. Jewish literature. 3. Homiletical illustrations. I. Title.

DAVIS, Moshe 296.834
The emergence of Conservative Judaism; the historical school in 19th century America. Philadelphia Jewish Pub. Soc. [c]1963. xiv. 527p. illus.. ports. facsims. 22cm. (Jacob R. Schiff lib. of Jewish contributions to Amer. democracy, no. 15) Bibl. 63-21805 5.50
1. Conservative Judaism—Hist. 2. Judaism—U. S.—Hist. I. Title. II. Series.

DAVIS, Moshe. 296.8'34
The emergence of Conservative Judaism : the historical school in 19th century America / Moshe Davis. Westport, Conn. : Greenwood Press, 1977. p. cm. Reprint of the 1st ed. (1963), published by the Jewish Publication Society of America, Philadelphia, which was issued as no. 15 of the Jacob R. Schiff library of Jewish contributions to American democracy. Includes index. Bibliography: p. [BM197.5.D3 1977] 77-22180 ISBN 0-8371-9792-9 : 29.50
1. Conservative Judaism—History. 2. Judaism—United States—History. I. Title. II. Series: Jacob R. Schiff library of Jewish contributions to American democracy ; no. 15.

DAVIS, Moshe. 296.834
The emergence of Conservative Judaism; the historical school in 19th century America. [1st ed.] Philadelphia, Jewish Publication Society of America, 1963. xiv, 527 p. illus., ports., facsims. 22 cm. (The Jacob R.Schiff library of Jewish contributions to American democracy, no. 15) Bibliography: p. 465-505. [BM197.5.D3] 63-21805
1. Conservative Judaism — Hist. 2. Judaism — U.S. — Hist. I. Title. II. Series.

FREEHOF, Solomon Bennett 296.834
Reform responsa. Cincinnati, Hebrew Union College Press [c.]1960. xi, 226p. 21cm. Bibl. p.218-222 60-12708 6.00
1. Responsa. 2. Reform Judaism. I. Title.

FREEHOF, Solomon Bennett, 1892- 296.8'34
Modern Reform responsa, by Solomon B. Freehof. [Cincinnati?] Hebrew Union College Press, 1971. x, 319 p. 21 cm. [BM522.36.R375 1971] 72-151008 7.50
1. Responsa—1800- 2. Reform Judaism. I. Title.

FREEHOF, Solomon Bennett, 1892- 296.834
Recent Reform responsa. Cincinnati, Hebrew Union Col. Pr., 1963. xi, 232p. 21cm. 63-15720 6.00
1. Responsa. 2. Reform Judaism. I. Title.

GEIGER, Abraham, 1810-1874 296.834
Abraham Geiger and liberal Judaism; the challenge of the nineteenth century. Comp., biographical introd. by Max Wiener. Tr. from German by Ernst J. Schlochauer. [Philadelphia, Jewish Pubn. [c.]1962. 305p. 22cm. 61-11705 4.50
1. Reform Judaism—Collected works. I. Wiener, Max, 1882-1950, comp. II. Title.

PARZEN, Herbert 296.834
Architects of Conservative Judaism. New York, J. David [c.1964] 240p. 24cm. Bibl. 63-23432 5.95
1. Conservative Judaism—Hist. I. Title.

PLAUT, W Gunther, 1912- ed. 296,834
The rise of Reform Judaism. Pref. by Solomon B. Freehof. New York, World Union for Progressive Judaism [1963-65] 2 v. 25 cm. Vol. 2, with foreword by Jacob K. Shankman, has title: The growth of Reform Judaism. Contents.--A sourcebook of its European origins.--American and European sources until 1948. Includes bibliographies. [BM197.P6] 65-18555
1. Reform Judaism—Collections. I. Title. II. Title: The growth of Reform Judaism.

PLAUT, W. Gunther, 1912- ed. 296.834
The rise of Reform Judaism. Pref. by Solomon B. Freehof. New York, World Union for Progressive Judaism [dist. Union of Amer. Hebrew Cong. [c.1963] 288p. 25cm. Contents.[1] A sourcebook of its European origins. Bibl. 63-13568 6.00
1. Reform Judaism—Collections. I. Title. Contents omitted.

PLAUT, W. Gunther, 1912- ed. 296.834
The rise of Reform Judaism. [v.2] [Foreword by Jacob K. Shankman] New York, World Union for Progressive Judaism [1966, c.1965] 383p. 25cm. Contents.[v.2] The growth of Reform Judaism, American and European sources until 1948. Bibl. [BM197.P6] 63-13568 1.50
1. Reform Judaism—Collections. I. Title.

POLISH, David. 296.8'34
Renew our days : the Zionist issue in Reform Judaism / by David Polish ; with a foreword by Richard G. Hirsch. [Jerusalem] : World Zionist Organization, 1976. 276 p. ; 20 cm. Includes index. Bibliography: p. 269. [BM197.P68] 77-356707 pbk. : 2.95
1. Reform Judaism—United States. 2. Zionism. I. Title.

ROSE, Albert, 1917- ed. 296.834
A people and its faith; essays on Jews and reform Judaism in a changing Canada. [Toronto] University of Toronto Press, 1959. 204p. 22cm. [BM197.R6] 60-4797
1. Reform Judaism—Canada. 2. Jews in Canada—Hist. I. Title.

SCHNITZER, Henry R 296.834
Thy goodly tent; the first fifty years of Temple Emanu-El, Bayonne, N. J. Bayonne, Temple Emanu-El, 1961. 88p. illus. 22cm. [BM225.B3T4] 61-10908
1. Bayonne, N. J. Temple Emanu-El. I. Title.

MANDELBAUM, Bernard, 1922- 296.8'342
The maturing of the Conservative movement. New York. Burning Bush Pr. [1968] 35p. 22cm. Bibl. refs. included in Notes. [BM197.5.M3] 68-31065 .85 pap.,
1. Conservative Judaism. I. Title.

NEW York (City). B'nai Jeshurun Congregation. 296.8'342
140th anniversary; Congregation B'nai Jeshurun, New York City, 1825 to 1966. [New York? 1966?] 1 v. (unpaged) illus., ports. 28 cm. [BM225.N5B63] 73-11459
I. Title.

RUBENOVITZ, Herman H. 296.8'342
The waking heart, by Herman H. Rubenovitz and Mignon L. Rubenovitz. Cambridge, Mass., N. Dame [1967] xxii, 295 p. illus., facsims., ports. 24 cm. Part I. by H. H. Rubenovitz; Part II, by M. L. Rubenovitz. Appendices (p. 113-160):—Israel reborn, a broadcast by H. H. Rubenovitz over Radio Station WEEI, May 14, 1948.—Selected letters, edited by H. H. Rubenovitz and H. Rosenblum. Appendices (p. 113-160):—Israel reborn, a broadcast by H. H. Rubenovitz over Radio Station WEEI, May 14, 1948.—Selected letters, edited by H. H. Rubenovitz and H. Rosenblum. [BM755.R8A3] 67-5333
1. Conservative Judaism. I. Rubenovitz, Mignon (Levine) II. Title.

SKLARE, Marshall, 1921- 296.8'342
Conservative Judaism; an American religious movement. New augm. ed. New York, Schocken Books [1972] 330 p. 21 cm. Includes bibliographical references. [BM197.5.S45 1972] 76-183618 10.00
1. Conservative Judaism.

BERGER, Milton, comp. 296.8'342'08
Roads to Jewish survival; essays, biographies, and articles selected from the Torch on its 25th anniversary, edited by Milton Berger, Joel S. Geffen [and] M. David Hoffman. [1st ed] New York, National Federation of Jewish Men's Clubs [1967] xi, 414 p. 24 cm. Bibliography: p. 249-252. [BM197.5.B4] 68-17689
1. Conservative Judaism—Addresses, essays, lectures. I. Geffen, Joel S., joint comp. II. Hoffman, M. David,1894- joint comp. III. Title. IV. Title: The Torch.

BERGER, Milton, comp. 296.8'342'08
Roads to Jewish survival; essays, biographies, and articles selected from the Torch on its 25th anniversary, edited by Milton Berger, Joel S. Geffen [and] M. David Hoffman. [1st ed.] New York, National Federation of Jewish Men's Clubs [1967] xi, 414 p. 24 cm. Bibliography: p. 249-252. [BM197.5.B4] 68-17689
1. Conservative Judaism—Addresses, essays, lectures. I. Geffen, Joel S., joint comp. II. Hoffman, M. David, 1894- joint comp. III. The Torch. Philadelphia. IV. Title.

KAPLAN, Mordecai Menahem, 1881- 296.8'344
A new approach to Jewish life / by Mordecai M. Kaplan ; with a new introd. by Jacob Neusner. Bridgeport, Conn. : Published for the Jewish Reconstructionist Foundation by Hartmore House, c1973. 88 p. ; 21 cm. Reprint of the 1924 ed. published by the Society for the Advancement of Judaism, New York, under title: A new approach to the problem of Judaism. [BM197.7.K29 1973] 75-322744 ISBN 0-87677-142-8 : 4.95
1. Reconstructionist Judaism. I. Title.

BEN-HORIN, Meir, 1918- 296.8'344'08
Common faith, uncommon people; essays in Reconstructionist Judaism. With a foreword by Ira Eisenstein. New York, Reconstructionist Press [1970] 245 p. 23 cm. Includes bibliographies. [BM197.7.B46] 71-80691 ISBN 0-910808-00-7
1. Jews—Education—Addresses, essays, lectures. 2. Reconstructionist Judaism—Addresses, essays, lectures. I. Title.

ANTELMAN, Marvin S., 1933- 296.8'346
To eliminate the opiate, by Marvin S. Antelman. [New York, Zahavia, 1974- v. illus. 18 cm. [BM197.A7] 74-180467 2.97 (pbk. vol. 1)
1. Bund der Kommunisten. 2. Reform Judaism—Controversial literature. 3. Illuminati. I. Title.
Publisher's address: 249 South Lafayette Park Place, Los Angeles, Ca 90057.

BIAL, Morrison David, 1917- 296.8'346
Liberal Judaism at home; the practices of modern reform Judaism. [Rev. ed. New York] Union of American Hebrew Congregations [1971] xiii, 208 p. illus. 22 cm. Bibliography: p. 207-208. [BM197.B5 1971] 76-32236
1. Reform Judaism—Ceremonies and practices. I. Title.

BLAU, Joseph Leon, 1909- comp. 296.8'346
Reform Judaism: a historical perspective; essays from the Yearbook of the Central Conference of American Rabbis. Selected, edited, and with an introd. by Joseph L. Blau. New York, Ktav Pub. House, 1973. viii, 529 p. 24 cm. Includes bibliographical references. [BM197.B55] 72-428 ISBN 0-87068-191-5 15.00
1. Reform Judaism—Addresses, essays, lectures. 2. Judaism—United States—Addresses, essays, lectures. I. Central Conference of American Rabbis. Yearbook. II. Title.

BOROWITZ, Eugene B. 296.8'346
Reform Judaism today / by Eugene B. Borowitz. New York : Behrman House, c1977. p. cm. Contents.Contents.—Book 1. Reform in the process of change.—Book 2. What we believe.—Book 3. How we live. [BM197.B67] 77-24676 ISBN 0-87441-271-4 pbk. : 2.45
1. Central Conference of American Rabbis. Reform Judaism, a centenary perspective. 2. Reform Judaism—United States. I. Title.

CONTEMPORARY Reform 296.8'346
Jewish thought. Edited by Bernard Martin. Chicago, Published in cooperation with the Central Conference of American Rabbis by Quadrangle Books [1968] 216 p. 22 cm. Includes bibliographical references. [BM197.C62] 67-13461 5.95
1. Reform Judaism—Addresses, essays, lectures. I. Martin, Bernard, 1928- ed. II. Central Conference of American Rabbis.

ELKINS, Dov Peretz. 296.8'346
A tradition reborn; sermons and essays on liberal Judaism. Foreword by Robert Gordis. South Brunswick, A. S. Barnes [1973] 292 p. 22 cm. [BM740.2.E43 1973] 73-2772 ISBN 0-498-01381-2
1. Sermons, American—Jewish authors. 2. Sermons, Jewish—United States. I. Title.

FREEHOF, Solomon Bennett, 1892- 296.8'346
Current Reform responsa, by Solomon B. Freehof. [Cincinnati] Hebrew Union College Press, 1969. viii, 259 p. 21 cm. Bibliography: p. 251-254. [BM522.36.R37] 68-57979 7.50
1. Responsa—1800- 2. Reform Judaism. I. Title.

GUTTMANN, Alexander. 296.8'346
The struggle over reform in Rabbinic literature of the last century and a half / Alexander Guttmann. New York : Union of American Hebrew Congregations, [1976] p. cm. Includes index. "Hebrew sources": p. [BM197.G86] 75-45046 ISBN 0-8074-0005-X
1. Reform Judaism—Controversial literature—History and criticism. 2. Responsa—1800- — History and criticism. I. Title.

LENN, Theodore I., 1914- 296.8'346
Rabbi and synagogue in Reform Judaism [by] Theodore I. Lenn and associates. Commissioned by the Central Conference of American Rabbis. New York, 1972. xvii, 412 p. illus. 24 cm. Includes bibliographical references. [BM652.L37] 72-189571
1. Rabbis—Office. 2. Rabbis—United States. 3. Pastoral theology (Judaism) 4. Reform Judaism—United States. I. Central Conference of American Rabbis. II. Title.

SCHWARTZMAN, Sylvan David. 296.8'346
Reform Judaism then and now [by] Sylvan D. Schwartzman. New York, Union of American Hebrew Congregations [1971] xi, 339 p. illus. 27 cm. Bibliography: p. 329-332. [BM197.S334] 76-31681
1. Reform Judaism—History. I. Title.

SILVERMAN, William B. 296.8'346
Basic reform Judaism, by William B. Silverman. New York, Philosophical Library [1970] xiii, 292 p. 22 cm. Bibliography: p. 277-285. [BM197.S48] 69-15531 8.50
1. Reform Judaism. I. Title.

UNITED Synagogue of America. National Women's League. 296.8'346
Builders of the Conservative movement; an appreciation. [Edited by Mrs. David A. Goldstein. New York, c1964] 116 p. 28 cm. Contents.CONTENTS -- Sabato Morais, by S. I. Teplitz. -- Solomon Schechter, by H. H. Rubenovitz. -- Cyrus Adler, by Joel Geffen. -- Alexander Marx, by G. Cohen. -- Louis

Ginzberg, by D. Aronson. -- Israel Friedlaender, by M. Adler. -- Hillel Bavil, by A. Holtz. -- Schiff-Warburg heritage, by B. Mandelbaum. -- Louis Brush, by S. Greenberg. -- Maxwell Abbell, by R. Simon. -- Louis Epstein, by J. Nadich. -- Solomon Goldman, by B. Aronin and S. J. Cohen. -- Milton Steinberg, by S. Noveck. Includes bibliographies. [BM197.5.U5] 65-6989
1. Conservative Judaism. 2. Jews — Biog. I. Goldstein, Rose (Berman) 1904- ed. II. Title.

HIRSCH, David Einhorn. 296.8'346'0924 B
Rabbi Emil G. Hirsch, the reform advocate. Chicago, Whitehall Co. [1968] ii, 191 p. 24 cm. [BM755.H47H5] 68-24717
1. Hirsch, Emil Gustav, 1851-1923. 2. Jesus Christ—Crucifixion. 3. Sermons, American—Jewish authors. 4. Sermons, Jewish—U.S.

PHILIPSON, David, 1862-1949. 296.8'346'09
The reform movement in Judaism. A reissue of the new and rev. ed., with an introd. by Solomon B. Freehof. [New York] Ktav Pub. House [1967] xxi, 503 p. 23 cm. Bibliographical references included in "Notes" (p. 437-491) [BM197.P55 1967] 67-11906
1. Reform Judaism—History. I. Freehof, Solomon Bennett, 1892- II. Title.

SILBERMAN, Lou H. 296.8'346'09757915
American impact: Judaism in the United States in the early nineteenth century [by] Lou H. Silberman. [Syracuse, N.Y., Syracuse University, 1964] [30] p. 23 cm. (B. G. Rudolph lectures in Judaic studies) Lecture delivered on April 29, 1964, at Syracuse University. Includes bibliographical references. [BM225.C4S5] 73-171337
1. Reformed Society of Israelites, Charleston, S.C. 2. Reform Judaism—Charleston, S.C. I. Title. II. Series.

297 Islam & Religions Derived From It

AHMAD, Bashiruddin Mahmud, hazrat mirza, 1889- 297
Ahmadiyyat; or, The true Islam. [Written in Urdu and rendered into English by Sir Muhammad Zafrullah Khan. 3d ed.] Washington, American Fazl Mosque, 1951. 246 p. illus. 24 cm. [BP195.A5A33 1951] 52-1109
1. Ahmadlyya. I. Title.

AHMAD, Ghulam, hasrat mirza, 1839?-1908. 297
The philosophy of the teachings of Islam, [1st American ed.] Washington, American Fazl Mosque. [1953] 199p. illus. 23cm. Published in 1910 under title: The teachings of Islam. [BP195.A5A35 1953] 53-4312
1. Ahmadiyya. I. Title.

AL-GHAZZALI, Muhammad 297
Our beginning in wisdom / Muhammad al-Ghazzali ; translated from the Arabic by Isma'il R. el Faruqi. New York : Octagon Books, 1975, c1953. xvii, 145 p. ; 23 cm. Translation of Min huna na'lam. Reprint of the ed. published by the American Council of Learned Societies, which was issued as no. 5 of its Publications. [BP64.E3K453413 1975] 75-14315 ISBN 0-374-90114-7 : 9.50
1. Khalid, Khalid M. Min huna nabda'. 2. Islam and state—Egypt. 3. Egypt—Politics and government—1919-1952. 4. Islam—20th century. I. Title. II. Series: American Council of Learned Societies Devoted to Humanistic Studies. Near Eastern Translation Program. [Publication] ; no. 5.

ALI, Zaki. 297
Islam in the world. Lahore, M. Ashraf, 1947. [New York, AMS Press, 1973] x, 434 p. maps. 23 cm. Includes bibliographical references. [BP161.A4 1973] 74-180314 ISBN 0-404-56209-4 23.50
1. Islam. I. Title.

ANDRAE, Tor. Bp., 1885-1947. 297
Mohammed, the man and his faith. Tranlsated by Theophil Menzel. New York, Barnes and Noble [1957] 196p. illus. 22cm. Bibliographical footnotes. [BP75.A] A 58
1. Muhammad, the prophet. I. Title.

ASAD, Muhammad, 1900- 297
The road to Mecca. [New York] Simon and Schuster, 1954. 400 p. illus. 24 cm. Autobiographical. [BP80.A8A3] 54-8643
1. Converts, Mohammedan. I. Title.

ASAD, Muhammad [name orig.: Leopold Weiss] 1900- 297
The road to Mecca. London, M. Reinhardt [dist. Chester Springs, Pa., Dufour, 1965] 381p. illus. 23cm. [BP80.A8A3] 55-20523 5.00 bds.,
1. Converts, Mohammedan. I. Title.

AZZAM, Abdel Rahman, 1893- 297
The eternal message of Muhammad. Translated from the Arabic by Caesar E. Farah. With an introd. by Vincent Sheean. New York, Devin-Adair Co., 1964. xxi, 297 p. 22 cm. Bibliographical footnotes. [BP161.2.A993] 63-15592
1. Mohammedanism. 2. Muhammad, the prophet. I. Title.

*AZZAM, Abdel Rahman, 1893- 297
The eternal message of Muhammad. Tr. from Arabic by Caesar E. Farah. Introd. by Vincent Sheean. New York, New Amer. Lib. [1965, c.1964] 254p. 18cm. (Mentor bk., MT634) .75 pap.,
I. Title.

AZZAM, Abdel Rahman, 1893- 297
The eternal message of Muhammad. Tr. from Arabic by Caesar E. Farah. Introd. by Vincent Sheean. New York, Devin-Adair [c.]1964. xxi, 297p. 22cm. Bibl. 63-15592 5.95
1. Mohammedanism. 2. Muhammad, the prophet. I. Title.

BETHMANN, Erich W. 297
Steps toward undrstanding Islam, by Erich W. Bethmann. Washington, Amer. Friends of the Middle East, 1966. vi. 70p. 23 cm. (Kohinur ser., no. 4) [BF165.B45] 66-25375 1.50
1. Islam—Addresses, essays, lectures. I. Title. II. Series.

BETHMANN, Erich W 1904- 297
Steps toward understanding of Islam, by Erich W. Bethmann. Washington, American Friends of the Middle East, 1966. vi, 70 p. 23 cm. (Kohinur series, no. 4) [BP165.B45] 66-25375
1. Islam — Addresses, essays, lectures. I. Title. II. Series.

COBB, Stanwood, 1881- 297
Tomorrow and tomorrow. [Washington, Avalon Press, 1951] 103 p. 19 cm. [BP365.C62] 51-40208
1. Bahaism. I. Title.

CRAGG, Kenneth. 297
The call of the minaret. New York, Oxford University Press, 1956. 376p. 23cm. [BP172.C65] 56-8005
1. Mohammedanism. 2. Mohammedanism—Relations—Christianity. 3. Christianity and other religions—Mohammedanism. I. Title.

*CRAGG, Kenneth 297
The call of the minaret. New York, Oxford, 1964[c.1956] 376p. 20cm. (Galaxy bk. GB122) Bibl. 1.95 pap.,
1. Mohammedanism. I. Title.

CRAGG, Kenneth 297
The dome and the rock; Jerusalem studies in Islam. London, S. P. C. K. [dist. New York, Seabury, c.]1964. ix, 262p. 23cm. Bibl. 64-5677 8.00
1. Mohammedanism. I. Title.

CRAGG, Kenneth. 297
The house of Islam / Kenneth Cragg. 2d ed. Encino, Calif. : Dickenson Pub. Co., [1975] xiii, 145 p. ; 23 cm. (The Religious life of man) Includes index. Bibliography: p. 136-140. [BP161.2.C72 1975] 74-83949 ISBN 0-8221-0139-4 pbk. : 4.50
1. Islam. I. Title.

DE WILDE, James Copray, 1896- 297
The rising tide of Islam / by James Copray de Wilde. 1st ed. New York : Vantage Press, c1976. 73 p. ; 21 cm. [BP173.5.D48] 77-351283 ISBN 0-533-02346-7 : 4.95
1. Islam and world politics. 2. Islam—Controversial literature. I. Title.

EDMONDS, I. G. 297
Islam / by I. G. Edmonds. New York : F. Watts, 1977. 65 p. : ill. ; 23 cm. (A First book) Includes index. Bibliography: p. 64. Introduces the history, principles, and customs of Islam including the life of Mohammed, a discussion of the Koran, and the influence of Christian and Judaic beliefs. [BP161.2.E34] 77-2664 ISBN 0-531-01288-3 lib.bdg. : 4.47
1. Islam—Juvenile literature. I. Title.

ESSLEMONT, John Ebenezer, 1874-1925. 297
Baha'u'llah and the new era. [Rev. ed.] Wilmette, Ill., Bahai Pub. Committee [1950] xii, 349 p. 18 cm. [BP365.E8 1950] 50-2289
1. Baha Ullah, 1817-1892. 2. Bahaism. I. Title.

FAISAL, Daoud Ahmed. 297
"Al-Islam," the religion of humanity. [Brooklyn, Islamic Mission of America, 1950?] 195 p. port. 22 cm. [BP161.F3] 50-29206
1. Mohammedanism. I. Title.

FAISAL, Daoud Ahmed. 297
Islam, the true faith, the religion of humanity. Brooklyn, Islamic Mission of America, 1965. 278 p. illus., facsims., ports. 23 cm. [BP161.F32] 76-259831
1. Islam. I. Title.

FARAH, Caesar E. 297
Islam: beliefs and observances, by Caesar E. Farah. Woodbury, N.Y., Barron's Educational Series [1970] ix, 306 p. 21 cm. (Barron's compact studies of world religions) Bibliography: p. 298-303. [BP161.2.F3 1970] 72-135505 1.95
1. Islam. I. Title.

FARAH, Caesar E. 297
Islam: beliefs and observances, by Caesar E. Farah. Woodbury, N.Y., Barron's Educational Series [1968] xii, 306 p. 21 cm. (Barron's compact studies of world religions) Includes bibliographical references. [BP161.2.F3] 67-30986 1.95 ($2.35 Can.)
I. Title.

FITCH, Florence Mary, 1875- 297
Allah, the God of Islam; Moslem life and worship. Illustrated with photos, selected by Beatrice Creighton and the author. New York, Lothrop, Lee & Shepard [1950] 144 p. illus. 25 cm. [BP161.F5] 50-11103
1. Monammedanism. I. Title.

FYZEE, Asaf Ali Asghar, 1899- 297
A modern approach to Islam. New York, Asia Pub. [dist. Taplinger, 1964, c.1963] viii, 127p. 23cm. [BP165.F92] SA63 7.00
1. Mohammedanism—Addresses, essays, lectures. I. Title.

GARDET, Louis 297
Mohammedanism; tr. from French by William Burridge. Ed. by Henri Daniel-Rops. New York, Hawthorn [c.1961] 176p. (Twentieth century encyclopedia of Catholicism, v.143. Section 15: Non-Christian beliefs) Bibl. 61-8389 3.50 bds.,
I. Title.

GAUDEFROY-DEMOMBYNES, Maurice, 1862- 297
Muslim institutions, tr. from French by John P. MacGregor [Dist. New York, Barnes & Noble, 1962, c.1956] 216p. 23cm. Bibl. 3.50
1. Mohammedanism. I. Title.

AL-GAZZALL, Muhammad, 297
Our beginning in wisdom; translated from the Arabic by Isma il R. el Faruqi. Washington, American Council of Learned Societies, 1953 [i. e. 1954] xvii, 145p. 23cm. (American Council of Learned Societies. Near Eastern Translation Program. [Publication] no.5) Translation of Min huna na'lam. [BP173.6.G53] 54-1083
1. Mohammedanism and state. I. Title. II. Series: American Council of Learned Societies Devoted to Humanistic Studies. Near Eastern Translation Program. [Publication] no. 5

GIBB, Hamilton Alexander Rosskeen, Sir, 1895- 297
Modern trends in Islam, by H. A. R. Gibb. New York, Octagon Books, 1972 [c1947] xiii, 141 p. 23 cm. Original ed. issued in series: The Haskell lectures in comparative religion, 1945. Includes bibliographical references. [BP163.G5 1972] 76-159188 ISBN 0-374-93046-5
1. Islam—20th century. I. Title. II. Series: Haskell lectures in comparative religion, University of Chicago, 1945.

GIBB, Hamilton Alexander Rosskeen, Sir, 1895- ed. 297
Whither Islam? A survey of modern movements in the Moslem world, edited by H. A. R. Gibb. London, V. Gollancz, 1932. [New York, AMS Press, 1973] 384 p. illus. 23 cm. Contents.Contents.—Massignon, L. Africa (excluding Egypt).—Kampffmeyer, G. Egypt and western Asia.—Ferrar, M. L. India.—Berg, C. C. Indonesia.—Gibb, H. A. R. Whither Islam? [BP163.G54 1973] 73-180338 ISBN 0-404-56263-9 22.50
1. Islam—20th century. 2. Panislamism. I. Title.

GOLDZIHER, Ignac, 1850-1921 297
Muslim studies. Ed. by S. M. Stern. Tr. from German by C. R. Barber, S. M. Stern. Chicago, Aldine [1968-c.1966- v. 23cm. Tr. of Muhammedanische Studien. Bibl. [BP25.G614] 67-20745 8.75 bds.,
1. Islam—Addresses, essays, lectures. I. Title.

GOLDZIHER, Ignac, 1850-1921. 297
Muslim studies. Edited by S. M. Stern. Translated from the German by C. R. Barber and S. M. Stern. Chicago, Aldine Pub. Co. [1973, c1966-71] 2 v. 23 cm. Translation of Muhammedanische Studien. Imprint covered by label: State University of New York Press, Albany. Includes bibliographical references. [BP25.G6143] 72-11731 ISBN 0-87395-234-0
1. Islam—Addresses, essays, lectures. I. Stern, Samuel Miklos, 1920-1969, ed. II. Title.

GUILLAUME, Alfred, 1888- 297
Islam. [Harmondsworth, Middlesex] Penguin Books [1954] 207p. 19cm. (Pelican books, A 311) Bibliography:p. 201-[204] [BP161.G87] A55
1. Mohammedanism. I. Title.

GUILLAUME, Alfred, 1888- 297
Islam. London, Cassell [dist. New York, Barnes&; Noble, 1963, c.1956] 209p. 22cm. (Belle sauvago lib.) Bibl. 64-6009 3.75
1. Mohammedanism. I. Title.

HAMIDULLAH, Muhammad. 297
Introduction to Islam, by Dr. Hamidullah. [2d ed. Gary, Ind.] I[nternational] I[slamic] F[ederation of] S[tudent] O[rganizations] 1970. 259, 17 p. illus., 2 fold. maps. 17 cm. (International Islamic Federation of Student Organizations. [Publications] 9) 1957 edition by Center culturel islamique, Paris. [BP161.H25 1970] 75-291366
1. Islam. I. Paris. Centre culturel islamique. Introduction to Islam. II. Title. III. Series: al-Ittihad al-Islami al-'Alami lil-Munazzamat al-Tullabiyah. [Publications] 9.

HITTI, Philip Khuri, 1886- 297
Islam and the West, a historical cultural survey. Princeton, N.J., Van Nostrand [c1962] 192 p. 19 cm. (An Anvil original) "Selected readings": p. 95-187. [BP52.H5] 63-1079
1. Mohammedanism — Relations. 2. East and West. I. Title.

HITTI, Philip Khuri, 1886- 297
Islam and the West, a historical cultural survey. Princeton, N.J., Van Nostrand [c.1962] 192p. 19cm. (Anvil original 63) 63-1079 1.45 pap.,
1. Mohammedanism—Relations. 2. East and West. I. Title.

INGRAMS, Doreen. 297
Mosques and minarets. Photography by Alistair Duncan and others. St. Paul, EMC Corp. [1974] p. cm. (Her The Arab world) Discusses the basic teachings of Islam and illustrates, through photographs, their unifying effect on the different cultures within the Arab world. [BP161.2.I55] 74-12221 ISBN 0-88436-115-2
1. Islam—Juvenile literature. I. Duncan, Alistair, 1927- illus. II. Title.

IQBAL, Mohammed. 297
Understanding your Muslim neighbour / [by] Muhammad Iqbal and Maryam K. Iqbal. Guildford : Lutterworth Press, 1976. 45 p. : ill. ; 22 cm. (World religions) [BP163.I65] 76-373822 ISBN 0-7188-1857-1 : £1.50
1. Islam—Juvenile literature. 2. Muslims in Great Britain—Juvenile literature. 3. Pakistanis in Great Britain—Juvenile literature. I. Iqbal, Maryam K., joint author. II. Title.

JAMALI, Mohammed Fadhel, 1902- 297
Letters on Islam, written by a father in prison to his son. Tr. from Arabic by the author. New York, Oxford [c.]1965. xii, 108p. 22cm. [BP165.J313] 65-8066 2.40 pap.,
1. Islam—Addresses, essays, lectures. I. Title.

JEFFERY, Arthur. 297
The Qurian as scripture. New York, R. F. Moore Co., 1952. 103 p. 23 cm. [BP130.J42] 52-10808
1. Koran—Evidences, authority, etc. I. Title.

KARIM, Fazlul. 297
The religion of man / Fazlul Karim. Lahore : [Book House, 1976] ii, iii, 384 p. ; 22 cm. Publisher statement from jacket. Imprint date in MS. Reprint of the 1939 ed. Includes quotations in Arabic. [BP161.K33 1976] 76-930138 Rs30.00 ($3.00 U.S.)
1. Islam. I. Title.

KATSH, Abraham Isaac, 1908- 297
Judaism in Islam, Biblical and Talmudic backgrounds of the Koran and its commentaries: suras II and III. [New York] Published for New York University Press by Bloch Pub. Co., 1954. xxv, 265p. front. 24cm. Text in English: notes in Arabic and Hebrew. 'Grew out of ... [the author's] doctoral dissertation submitted in 1943 to the Dropsie College for Hebrew and Cognate Learning [under title: Aggadic background of the Qur'an, auras II and III]' Bibliography: p. 229-245. [BP134.J4K38] 53-10662
1. Koran. Surah II-III—Commentaries. 2. Mohammedanism— Relations—Judaism. 3. Judaism—Relations—Mohammedanism. I. Title.

KHADDURI, Majid, 1909- 297
War and peace in the law of Islam. Baltimore, Johns Hopkins Press [1955] x, 321p. 23cm. Revision of the 1st ed. published in London in 1940 under title: The law of war and peace in Islam. Bibliography: p. 301-307. Bibliographical footnotes. [BP175.J5K45 1955] 55-8427
1. Jihad. 2. Mohammedan law. 3. International law. I. Title.

KHAN, Muhammad Zafrulla, Sir 297
1893-
Islam, its meaning for modern man. New York, Harper [c.1962] 216p. 22cm. (Religious perspectives, v.7) 62-11131 4.50
1. Mohammedanism. I. Title.

KHAN, Sir Muhammad Zafrulla, 297
1893-
Islam, its meaning for modern man. [1st ed.] New York, Harper & Row [1962] 216 p. 22 cm. (Religious perspectives, v. 7) [BP161.2.K47] 62-11131
1. Mohammedanism. I. Title.

KORAN. English. 297
The meaning of the glorious Koran. An explanatory translation by Mohammed Marmaduke Pickthall. [New York] New American Library [1953] xxix, 464 p. 18 cm. (NAL Mentor books, ms. 94) [BP109.P5 1953] 54-764
I. Pickthall, Marmaduke William, 1875-1936, ed. and tr.

KORAN. English. Selections. 297
The Holy Koran; an introduction with selections by A. J. Arberry. New York, Macmillan [1953] 141 p. facsim. 19 cm. (Ethical and religious classics of East and West, no. 9) Bibliography: p. 138-141. [BP110.A7] 53-8831
I. Arberry, Arthur John, 1905- tr.

KORAN. ENGLISH. SELECTIONS. 297
The Koran, selected suras. Translated from the Arabic by Arthur Jeffery and decorated by Valenti Angelo. New York, Heritage Press [1958] 231p. 26cm. [BP110.J4] 58-1501
I. Jeffery, Arthur, tr. II. Title.

KORAN. ENGLISH. SELECTIONS. 297
The Koran, selected suras. Translated from the Arabic by Arthur Jeffery and decorated by Valenti Angelo. New York, Limited Editions Club, 1958. 231p. col. illus. 26cm. In case. [BP110.J4 1958a] 58-27509
I. Jeffery, Arthur, ed. and tr. II. Title.

KORAN. English. Selections. 297
The Koran, an edition prepared for English readers. Being an arrangement in chronological order from the translations of Edward W. Lane, Stanley Lane-Poole A. H. C. Sarwar. Decorated by Vera Bock. Mount Vernon, N. Y., Peter Pauper Press [1953?] 234p. col. illus. 26cm. [BP110.L32] 53-2742
I. Title.

KORAN. Selections 297
The Koran. a new translation and presentation, by Henry Mercier Tr. from French by Lucien Tremlett. Illus. by Si Abdelkrim Wezzani. London, Luzac [Mvstic. Conn. Verry, c.1965] 332p. illus. 19cm. [BP101.M4] 7.50
I. Koran. English. Selections. II. Mercier. Henry, writer on Arabic languages, ed. and tr. III. Tremlett, Lucien, tr. IV. Title.

KRITZECK, James. 297
Peter the Venerable and Islam. Princeton, N.J., Princeton University Press, 1964. xiv, 301 p. 25 cm. (Princeton oriental studies, no 23) An analysis and new annotated edition of the following texts:Summa totius haeresis Saracenorum. Epistola Petrl Cluniacensis ad Bernardum Claravaevallis. Epistola Petrl Pictavensis. Capitula Petrl Pictavensis. Liber contra sectam sive haeresim Saracenorum. Bibliographical footnotes. [PJ25.P7] [BX4705.P478K7] 63-18646
1. Pierre ie Venerable, 1092 (ca.)-1156. 2. Christianity and other religions — Mohammedanism. 3. Mohammedianism — Relations — Christianity. I. Title. II. Series: Oriental studies series, no. 23

KRITZECK, James 297
Peter the Venerable and Islam. Princeton, N.J., Princeton [c.]1964. xiv, 301p. 25cm. (Princeton oriental studies, no. 23) Bibl. 63-18646 7.50
1. Pierre le Venerable, 1092 (ca.)-1156. 2. Christianity and other religions—Mohammedanism. 3. Mohammedianism—Relations—Christianity. I. Title. II. Series: Oriental studies series, no. 23

LAMMENS, Henri, 1862-1937 297
Islam: beliefs and institutions, by H. Lammens, tr. [from French] by Sir E. Denison Ross. 1st ed., ix, 256p. geneal. table. 22cm. (Islam & the Muslim world, no. 6) This tr. orig. pub., London, Methuen, 1929. Orig. pub. as L'Islam; croyances et institutions. Beirut, 1926. Bibl. [BP161.L252 1968] 68-113564 9.50
1. Islam. I. Ross, Edward Denison, Sir 1871-1940, tr. II. Title. III. Series.
Distributed by Barnes & Noble, New York.

MACDONALD, Duncan Black, 297
1863-1943.
Aspects of Islam. Freeport, N.Y., Books for Libraries Press [1971] xiii, 375 p. 23 cm. (The Hartford-Lamson lectures on the religions of the world, 1909) Reprint of the 1911 ed. [BP161.M27 1971] 77-179530 ISBN 0-8369-6659-7
1. Islam—Addresses, essays, lectures. I. Title. II. Series: The Hartford-Lamson lectures on the religions of the world. New York, 1908-1909.

MACDONALD, Duncan Black, 297
1863-1943
Development of Muslim theology, jurisprudence and constitutional theory. Beirut, Khayats [dist. Mystic, Conn., Verry] 1965. xii, 386p. 19cm. (Semitic ser. v.9; Khayats Oriental reprints no. 10) Bibl. [BP161.M3] 6.50
1. Mohammedanism. I. Title.

MACDONALD, Duncan Black, 297
1863-1943
Development of Muslim theology, jurisprudence and constitutional theory. New York, Russell & Russell, [1966] xii, 386p. 23cm. First pub. in 1903. Bibl. [BP161.M3] 65-18818 8.00
1. Islam. I. Title.

MACDONALD, Duncan Black, 297
1863-1943.
The religious attitude and life in Islam. New York, AMS Press [1970] xvii, 317 p. 23 cm. (Haskell lectures on comparative religion, University of Chicago, 1906) Reprint of the 1909 ed. Includes bibliographical references. [BP165.M23 1970] 70-121277 ISBN 0-404-04125-6
1. Islam—Addresses, essays, lectures. I. Title. II. Series: Haskell lectures in comparative religion, University of Chicago, 1906

THE Macdonald presentation 297
volume; a tribute to Duncan Black Macdonald, consisting of articles by former students, presented to him on his seventieth birthday, April 9, 1933. Freeport, N.Y., Books for Libraries Press [1968] x, 487 p. illus., facsims., port. 24 cm. (Essay index reprint series) Reprint of the 1933 ed. "Bibliography of the writings of Duncan B. Macdonald": p. [471]-487. Bibliographical footnotes. [BP20.M25 1968] 68-22109
1. Islam—Addresses, essays, lectures. 2. Oriental philology—Addresses, essays, lectures. I. Macdonald, Duncan Black, 1863-1943.

MARION, John, pseud. 297
Among the minarets. Nashville, Convention Press [1955] 122p. illus. 19cm. (1955 mission study books, young people) A Publication of the Foreign Mission Board. [BV2625.M3] 55-42145
1. Missions—Mohammedans. 2. Southern Baptist Convention—Missions. I. Title.

MASUD IBN UMAR, Sad al-Din, 297
al-Taftazani, 1322-1389.
A commentary on the creed of Islam; Sad al-Din al-Taftazani on the creed of Najm al-Din al-Nasafi. Translated with introd. and notes by Earl Edgar Elder. New York, Columbia University Press, 1950. xxxii, 187 p. 24 cm. (Records of civilization: sources and studies, no. 43) "The translation was first made as a part of the requirements for the degree of doctor of philosophy at the Kennedy School of Missions of the Hartford Seminary Foundation." Bibliography: p. [171]-175. [BP161.U55M32] 50-5160
1. Umar ibn Muhammad, al-Nasafi. al-Akaid. 2. Mohammedanism. I. Elder, Earl Edgar, 1887- ed. and tr. II. Title. III. Series.

MEANS, Elwyn Lee. 297
World within a world. Nashville, Convention Press [1955] 115p. illus. 19cm. (1966 mission study books, adults) A Publication of the Foreign Mission Board. [BV2625.M4] 55-42146
1. Missions—Mohammedans. 2. Mohammedanism. I. Title.

MIDDLE East Institute, 297
Washington, D.C.
Islam in the modern world, a series of addresses presented at the fifth annual conference on Middle East affairs, March 9-10, 1951. Edited by Dorothea Seelye Franck. Washington [1951] 76 p. 23 cm. [DS38.M5] 52-1118
1. Civilization, Mohammedan. I. Franck, Dorothea Seelye, ed. II. Title.

MORGAN, Kenneth William, ed. 297
Islam: the straight path; Islam interpreted by Muslims. Contributors: Mohammad Abd Allah Draz [and others] New York, Ronald Press Co. [1958] 453 p. 22 cm. Includes bibliography. [BP161.M63] 58-9807
1. Mohammedanism. 2. Civilization, Mohammedan.

MUHAMMAD, the prophet. 297
Sayings of Mohammed. Illustrated with wood engravings by Boyd Hanna. Mount Vernon, N. Y., PeterPauper Press [1958] 61p. illus. 19cm. [BP135.A3P4] 58-3238
1. Mohammedanism. I. Peter Pauper Press, Mount Vernon, N. Y. II. Title.

NASR, Seyyed Hossein. 297
Ideals and realities of Islam. New York, Praeger [1967, c1966] 184 p. 23 cm. Includes bibliographies. [BP165.N28 1967] 67-22242
1. Islam—Addresses, essays, lectures. I. Title.

NASR, Seyyed Hossein. 297
Ideals and realities of Islam. Boston, Beacon Press [1972, c1966] xv, 184 p. 21 cm. (Beacon paperback, 439) Includes bibliographies. [BP165.N28 1972] 72-1917 ISBN 0-8070-1131-2 3.95
1. Islam—Addresses, essays, lectures. I. Title.

NICOLSON, Angus. 297
A guide to Islam. [n.p.] Stirling Tract Enterprise [1951] 79 p. illus. 19 cm. [BP161.N5] 52-20505
1. Mohammedanism. I. Title.

NIZAMI, Khaliq Ahmad 297
Some aspects of religion and politics in India during the thirteenth century. Foreword by C. Collin Davies. Introd. by Mohd Habib. Pub. for the Dept. of Hist., Aligarh Muslim Univ. New York, Asia House [dist. Taplinger, 1965, c.1961] xxii, iv, 421p. illus. 25cm. Bibl. [BL2003.N5] SA65 8.75
1. Religion and state—India—Hist. 2. I sIslam—India—Hist. I. Aligarh, India. Muslim University. Dept. of History. II. Title.

PIKE, Edgar Royston, 1896- 297
Mohammed, founder of the religion of Islam. New York, Roy [1964, c.1962] 127p. illus. 19cm. (Roy's pathfinder biographies) 64-10672 3.50 bds.,
1. Muhammad, the Prophet—Juvenile literature. I. Title. II. Title: Founder of the religion of Islam.

PLANHOL, Xavier de. 297
The world of Islam. Le monde islamique essai de geographie religieuse. Ithaca, N. Y., Cornell University Press [1959] 142p. 22cm. Includes bibliography. [BP163.P533] 59-16313
1. Mohammedanism. 2. Religion and geography. I. Title.

PROCTOR, Jesse Harris, ed. 297
Islam and international relations, edited by J. Harris Proctor. New York, Praeger [1965] viii, 221 p. map. 22 cm. Papers originally presented at a conference held at Duke University, June 10 to 13, 1963. Includes bibliographical references. [BP173.5.P7] 65-12192
1. Islam and world politics. I. Duke University, Durham, N. C. II. Title.

PROCTOR, Jesse Harris, ed. 297
Islam and international relations. New York, Praeger [c.1965] viii, 221p. map. 22cm. Paps. orig. presented at a conf. held at Duke Univ. June 10 to 13, 1963. Bibl. [BP173.5.P7] 65-12192 6.50
1. Islam and world politics. I. Duke University, Durham, N.C. II. Title.

RAHMAN, Fazlur. 1919- 297
Islam. [1st ed.] New York, Holt, [1967, c.1966] xi, 271p. illus. 25cm. (Hist. of religion ser.) Bibl. [BP161.2.R29] 66-13499 8.95
1. Islam. I. Title.

ROSENTHAL, Erwin Isak Jakob, 297
1904-
Judaism and Islam. London, New York, T. Yoseloff [1961] 154p. 21cm. Includes bibliography. [BP173.J8R6] 61-13935
1. Judaism—Relations—Mohammedanism. 2. Mohammedanism—Relations—Judaism. I. Title.

SALEM, Elie Adib. 297
Political theory and institutions of the Khawarij. Baltimore, Johns Hopkins Press, 1956. 117p. 23cm. (The Johns Hopkins University studies in historica. and political science, ser. 74, no. 2) Bibliography: p. 107-113. [H31.J6 ser. 74, no. 2] 56-11661
1. Kharijites. 2. State, The. 3. Sociology, Mohammedan. I. Title. II. Series: Johns Hopkins University. Studies in historical and politica. science, ser. 74, no. 2

SCHUON, Frithjof. 297
Understanding Islam [by] Frithjof Schuon. Translated from the French by D. M. Matheson. Baltimore, Penguin [1972, c.1961] 159 p. 18 cm. (Penguin metaphysical lib.) Translation of Comprendre l'Islam. Bibliographical footnotes. [BP161.2.S313] pap., 1.45
1. Mohammedanism. I. Title.

SCHUON, Frithjof, 1907- 297
Islam and the perennial philosophy / [by] Frithjof Schuon ; translated [rom the French MS.] by J. Peter Hobson ; preface by Seyyed Hossein Nasr. [London] : World of Islam Festival Publishing Company Ltd, 1976. xii, 217 p. ; 23 cm. Includes index. [BP189.3.S38] 76-375638 ISBN 0-905035-06-2 : £6.00. ISBN 0-905035-22-4 pbk.
1. Sufism. I. Title.

SCHUON, Frithjof, 1907- 297
Understanding Islam. Tr. [from French] by D. M. Matheson. New York, Roy [1964, c.1963] 159p. 23cm. Bibl. 64-13613 5.95
1. Mohammedanism. I. Title.

SMITH, Wilfred Cantwell, 297
1916-
Islam in modern history. Princeton, Princeton University Press, 1957. 317 p. 25 cm. [DS38.S56] 57-5458
1. Mohammedanism. 2. Civilization, Mohannedan. I. Title.

SMITH, Wilfred Cantwell, 297
1916-
Islam in modern history. Princeton, Princeton University Press, 1957. 317 p. 25 cm. [DS38.S56] 57-5458
1. Mohammedanism. 2. Civilization, Islamic. I. Title.

SOURDEL, Dominique 297
Islam. Tr. [from French] by Douglas Scott. New York, Walker [1963, c.1962] 155p. map. diagr. 21cm. (Sun bk., SB-1. Religion and mythology) Bibl. 62-12740 3.50
1. Mohammedanism. I. Title.

SYMPOSIUM on Islamic Studies, 297
Amsterdam, 1973.
Studies on Islam : a Symposium on Islamic Studies / organized [by the] Koninklijke Nederlandse Akademie van Wetenschappen in cooperation with the Accademia dei Lincei in Rome, Amsterdam, 18-19 October 1973. Amsterdam : North-Holland Pub. Co., 1974. 110 p. : ill. ; 24 cm. English or French. Includes bibliographical references and index. [BP20.S92 1973] 73-94297 ISBN 0-7204-8274-7 : 11.50
1. Islam—Addresses, essays, lectures. I. Akademie van Wetenschappen, Amsterdam. II. Accademia nazionale dei Lincei, Rome. III. Title.

TRIMINGHAM, John Spencer. 297
Islam in Ethiopia. London, New York, Oxford University Press, 1952. xv, 299 p. maps (part fold. col.) 22 cm. [BP65.E8T7] 52-3568
1. Mohammedans in Ethiopia. I. Title.

TRITTON, Arthur Stanley, 297
1881-
Islam; belief and practices. London, New York, Hutchinson's University Library, 1951. 200 p. 19 cm. (Hutchison's university library. World religions) [BP161.T68] 51-6365
1. Mohammedanism. I. Title.

VECCIA VAGLIERI, Laura. 297
An interpretation of Islam. Translated from the Italian by Aldo Caselli. With a foreword by Sir Muhammad Zafrulla Khan. Washington, American Fazl Mosque [1957] 87 p. 21 cm. Translation of Apologia dell'Islamismo. [BP161.V412] 57-28019
1. Mohammedanism. I. Title.

VERHOEVEN, F R J 297
Islam: its origin and spread in words, maps and pictures. New York, St Martin's Press [1962] 87 p. illus. 22 cm. [Concise histories of world religious] [BP50.V413] 62-9943
1. Mohammedanism — Hist. I. Title.

VERHOEVEN, F. R. J. 297
Islam: its origin and spread in words. maps and pictures. New York, St. Martin's [c.1962] 87p. illus. (pl. col.) maps. 22cm. (Concise histories of world religions) 62-9943 4.00
1. Mohammedanism—Hist. I. Title.

VON GRUNEBAUM, Gustave 297
Edmund, 1909-
Muhammadan festivals. London, New York, Abelard-Schuman [1958] 107 p. illus. 22 cm. Includes bibliography. [BP175.F4V6 1958] 58-4109
1. Fasts and feasts — Mohammadanism. I. Title.

VON GRUNEBAUM, Gustave 297
Edmund, 1909-
Muhammadan festivals. New York; Schuman [1951] viii, 107 p. illus., map, plan. 23 cm. "Bibliographical notes and references": p. 95-101. [BP175.F4V6] 51-4180
1. Fasts and feasts — Mohammedanism. I. Title.

WATT, William Montgomery. 297
What is Islam? [by] W. Montgomery Watt. New York, Praeger [1968] x, 256 p. 23 cm. (Arab background series) Bibliography: p. 240-242. [BP161.2.W35] 68-26873 6.50
1. Islam. I. Title.

WILSON, J. Christy, 1891- 297
Introducing Islam. [Rev. ed.] New York, Friendship Press [c1958] 64 p. illus. 23 cm. [BP161.W5 1958] 58-7632
1. Mohammedanism. I. Title.

SHORTER encyclopedia of Islam. 297.03
Edited on behalf of the Royal Netherlands Academy, by H. A. R. Gibb and J. H. Kramers. Ithaca, N. Y., Cornell University Press [1953] viii, 671p. illus. 27cm. 'Includes all articles contained in the first edition and Supplement of the Encyclopaedia of Islam which relate particularly to the religion and law of Islam. Includes Bibliographies. [DS37.E52 1953a] 57-59109
1. Mohammedanism—Dictionaries. I. Gibb, Hamilton Alexander Rosakeen, 1805- ed. II. Kramers, Johannes Hendrik, 1891-1961, ed. III. Akademic van Wetenschappen, Amsterdam.

BASETTI-SANI, Giulio, 1912- 297'.07'2024 B
Louis Massignon (1883-1962) : Christian Ecumenist prophet of inter-religious reconciliation. Edited and translated by Allan Harris Cutler. Chicago, Franciscan Herald Press [1974] 262 p. illus. 22 cm. Translation of Louis Massignon orientalista cristiano. Includes bibliographical references. [BP49.5.M3B3813] 74-804 ISBN 0-8199-0496-1
1. Massignon, Louis, 1883-1962. I. Title.

JEFFERY, Arthur, ed. 297.082
Islam; Muhammad and his religion. Edited, with an introd. by Arthur Jeffery. New York, Liberal Arts Press [1958] 252p. 21cm. (The Library of religion, no. 6) [BP161.J4] 58-9958
1. Muhammad, the prophet. 2. Mohammedanism. I. Title.

KRITZECK, James, ed. 297.082
The world of Islam; studies in honour of Philip K. Hitti. Edited by James Kritzeck and R. Bayly Winder. New York, St. Martin's Press, 1959[ ]. viii, 372 p. illus., port., diagrs. 23 cm. "a bibliography of works by Philip K. Hitti: p. 10-37. Bibliographical footnotes. 59-65130 7.50
1. Hitti, Philip Khuri, 1886- 2. Mohammedanism—Addresses, Essays, lectures. I. Winder, Richard Bayley, 1920- joint ed. II. Title.

WILLIAMS, John Alden, ed. 297.082
Islam. New York, Washington Sq. [1963, c.1961] 241p. 17cm. (W-803) Bibl. .60 pap.,
1. Mohammedanism. I. Title.

WILLIAMS, John Alden, ed. 297.082
Islam. New York, Braziller [c.]1961. 256p. (Great religions of modern man) Bibl. 61-15500 4.00
1. Mohammedanism. I. Title.

ARNOLD, Thomas Walker, Sir, 1864-1930. 297'.09
The preaching of Islam; a history of the propagation of the Muslim faith. 2d ed., rev. and enl. London, Constable, 1913. [New York, AMS Press, 1974] xvi, 467 p. 23 cm. Bibliography: p. 440-455. [BP50.A7 1974] 72-180319 ISBN 0-404-56214-0 24.00
1. Islam—History. 2. Islam—Relations—History. 3. Islam—Missions—History. I. Title.

GIBB, Hamilton Alexander Rosskeen, Sir 1895- 297.09
Mohammedanism; an historical survey. [New York] New American Library [1955] 159p. 19c4. (A Mentor book, M136) [BP50.G5 1955] 55-2914
1. Mohammedanism—Hist. I. Title.

GIBB, Hamilton Alexander Rosskeen, 1895- 297.09
Mohammedanism, an historical survey. New York, Oxford, 1962. 208p. 21cm. (Galaxy bk., GB90) Bibl. 1.25 pap.,
1. Mohammedanism—Hist. I. Title.

GIBB, Hamilton Alexander Rosskeen, 1895- 297.09
Mohammedanism; a historical survey. 2d ed. [Gloucester, Mass., Peter Smith. 1963] viii, 208p. 21cm. (Galaxy bk. rebound) Bibl. 3.75
1. Mohammedanism—Hist. I. Title.

GIBB, Hamilton Alexander Rosskeen, 1895- 297.09
Mohammedanism; an historical survey. 2d ed. London, New York, Oxford University Press, 1953. ix, 206 p. 17 cm. (The Home university library of modern knowledge, 197) Bibliography: p. [192]-200. [BP50.G5 1953] 53-8324
1. Mohammedanism—History.

GIBB, Hamilton Alexander Rosskeen, Sir, 1895- 297'.09
Mohammedanism: an historical survey [by] H. A. R. Gibb. 2nd ed. (with revisions) London, Oxford U.P., 1969. ix, 144 p. 20 cm. (Oxford paperbacks university series, opus 17) Bibliography: p. [132]-137. [BP50.G5 1969] 78-518140 8/-
1. Islam—History. I. Title.

RAUF, Mohammed A. 297.09
A brief history of Islam with special reference to Malaya [by] M. A. Rauf. Kuala Lumpur, Oxford 1964. 117p. illus., 6 maps (2 fold.) 22cm. [BP50.R3] 66-5875 2.45 pap.,
1. Islam—Hist. 2. Islam—Malaya. I. Title.
Available from publisher's New York office.

SOUTHERN, Richard William. 297.0902
Western views of Islam in the Middle Ages. Cambridge, Harvard University Press. 1962. 114 p. 22 cm. [BP172.S67] 62-13270
1. Christianity and other religions — Mohammedanism. 2. Mohammedanism — Relations — Christianity. I. Title.

SOUTHERN, Richard William 297.0902
Western views of Islam in the Middle Ages. Cambridge, Mass., Harvard [c.]1962. 114p. 22cm. Bibl. 62-13270 3.25
1. Christianity and other religions—Mohammedanism. 2. Mohammedanism—Relations—Christianity. I. Title.

HANIFI, Mohammed Jamil. 297'.09'04
Islam and the transformation of culture / M. Jamil Hanifi. New York : Asia Pub. House, 1974, c1970. xi, 182 p. ; 23 cm. Includes index. Bibliography: p. [167]-173. [BP163.H255 1974] 73-91139 8.95
1. Islam—20th century. I. Title.

NASR, Seyyed Hossein. 297'.09'04
Islam and the plight of modern man / Seyyed Hossein Nasr. London ; New York : Longman, 1975[i.e.1976] xii, 161 p. ; 24 cm. Includes index. Bibliography: p. 151-152. [BP163.N28] 75-29014 ISBN 0-582-78053-5 : 19.50
1. Islam—20th century. I. Title.

LONG-KEESING, Elizabeth de. 297.092 B
Inayat Khan: a biography. The Hague, East-West Publications Fonds B. V., in association with Luzac & Co. Ltd. [1974] 302 p. 20 cm. "Translated from the original Dutch edition Golven waarom komt de wind by Hayat Bouman and Penelope Goldschmidt" Includes bibliographical references. [[BP80.155]] ISBN 07189-0243-2
1. Inayat Khan, 1882-1926. I. Bouman, Hayat, tr. II. Goldschmidt, Penelope, tr. III. Title.
Distr. by Rowman and Littlefield, for 12.75 (pbk.) L.C. card no. for original edition: 73-348424

KEDOURIE, Elie. 297'.0922
Afghani and 'Abduh; an essay on religious unbelief and political activism in modern Islam. New York, Humanities Press [1966] ix, 97 p. 23 cm. Errata slip mounted on p. v. Bibliographical references included in "Notes" (p. 89-97) [BP80] 66-19655
1. al-Afghani, Jamal al-Din, 1838-1897. 2. Muhammad 'Abduh, 1849-1905. I. Title.

MCDONOUGH, Sheila. 297'.0922
The authority of the past; a study of three Muslim modernists. Chambersburg, Pa., American Academy of Religion, 1970. 56 p. 24 cm. (AAR studies in religion, 1970:1) Bibliography: p. 55-56. [BP63.I4M24] 76-141690
1. Ahmad Khan, Syed, Sir, 1817-1898. 2. Iqbal, Muhammad, Sir, 1877-1938. 3. Parwez, Ghulam Ahmad, 1903- 4. Islam—India. I. Title. II. Series: American Academy of Religion. AAR studies in religion, 1970:1

ARASTEH, A. Reza 297.0924
Rumi the Persian; rebirth in creativity and love. Pref. by Erich Fromm. Lahore. Sh. Muhammad Ashraf [New York, Paragon, 1965] xx, 196p. 22cm. Bibl. [BP189.7.M42C42] SA66 5.00
1. Jalal al-Din Rumi, Mawlana, 1207-1273. I. Title.

KEDDIE, Nikki R. 297'.0924
An Islamic response to imperialism; political and religious writings of Sayyid Jamal ad-Din "al-Afghani", by Nikki R. Keddie. Including a translation of the Refutation of the materialists from the original Persian by Nikki R. Keddie and Hamid Algar. Berkeley, University of California Press, 1968. xii, 212 p. 24 cm. Bibliography: p. [191]-200. [BP80.A45K4] 68-13224
I. al-Afghani, Jamal al-Din, 1838-1897. II. Title.

KEDDIE, Nikki R. 297'.092'4 B
Sayyid Jamal ad-Din "al-Afghani"; a political biography, by Nikki R. Keddie. Berkeley, University of California Press, 1972. xvii, 479 p. port. 24 cm. Bibliography: p. [451]-467. [BP80.A45K43] 74-159671 ISBN 0-520-01986-5 20.00
1. al-Afghani, Jamal al-Din, 1838-1897.

BROOMHALL, Marshall, 1866- 297'.0951
Islam in China; a neglected problem. Preface by John R. Mott, Harlan P. Beach [and] Samuel M. Zwemer. New York, Paragon Book Reprint Corp., 1966. xx, 332 p. illus., maps (part fold.) 25 cm. "Unaltered and unabridged reprint of the work first published in ... 1910." "Chinese Mohammedan literature": p. 301-302. Bibliography: p. 307-310. [BP63.C5B7 1966] 66-30337
1. Muslims. I. Title.

ABBOTT, Freeland. 297'.0954
Islam and Pakistan. Ithaca, N.Y., Cornell University Press [1968] xvi, 242 p. illus., facsims., maps, ports. 22 cm. Includes bibliographical references. [BP63.P2A62] 67-23757
1. Islam—Pakistan. I. Title.

*ALI, Ameer 297.0954
The spirit of Islam history of the evolution and ideals of Islam with a life of the prophet. Atlantic Highlands, N.J., Humanities Press, [1974] lxxi, 515 p. 23 cm. [BP50] ISBN 0-391-00341-0 10.50
1. Islam—History. I. Title.

JA'FAR Sharif. 297'.0954
Islam in India; or The Qanun-i-Islam; the customs of the Musalmans of India; comprising a full and exact account of their various rites and ceremonies from the moment of birth to the hour of death. Composed under the direction of, and translated by G. A. Herklots. New ed. rev. and rearranged, with additions by William Crooke. London, Curzon Press [1972] xl, 374 p. illus. 19 cm. Imprint covered by label: Distributed in the U.S.A. by Humanities Press, New York. Reprint of the 1921 ed. published by Oxford University Press, London. First ed. published in 1832 under title: Qanoon-e-Islam. Bibliography: p. [xxxvii]-xl. [BP63.I4J2813 1972b] 73-160700 ISBN 0-7007-0015-3 13.25
1. Islam—India. 2. Muslims in India—Social life and customs. I. Herklots, Gerhard Andreas, 1790-1834, tr. II. Crooke, William, 1848-1923, ed. III. Title. IV. Title: Qanun-i-Islam.

SOCIO-CULTURAL impact of Islam on India 297'.0954
/ editor, Attar Singh. 1st ed. Chandigarh : Publication Bureau, Panjab University, 1976. xii, 200 p. ; 23 cm. Includes some quotations in Panjabi. Includes bibliographical references and index. [BP63.I4S65] 76-904525 Rs30.00
1. Islam—India—Congresses. 2. India—Civilization—Congresses. I. Singh, Attar, 1932-

BINDER, Leonard 297.09547
Religion and politics in Pakistan. Berkeley, Univ. of California Press [c.]1961. cxviii, 440p. Bibl. 61-7537 7.50
1. Religion and state—Pakistan. 2. Pakistan—Constitutional history. I. Title.

SCHOLARS, saints, and Sufis; 297'.0956
Muslim religious institutions in the Middle East since 1500. Edited by Nikki R. Keddie. Berkeley, University of California Press, 1972. viii, 401 p. 25 cm. Includes bibliographical references. [BP185.S36] 77-153546 ISBN 0-520-02027-8 20.00
1. Ulama—Addresses, essays, lectures. 2. Sufism—Addresses, essays, lectures. 3. Shiites—Addresses, essays, lectures. 4. Women, Muslim—Religious life—Addresses, essays, lectures. 5. Islam—History—Addresses, essays, lectures. I. Keddie, Nikki R., ed.

NOER, Deliar. 297'.09598
The modernist Muslim movement in Indonesia, 1900-1942. Singapore, New York, Oxford University Press, 1973. x, 390 p. 23 cm. (East Asian historical monographs) A revision of the author's thesis, Cornell University. Bibliography: p. [343]-361. [BP63.I5N6] 73-169361 24.75
1. Islam—Indonesia—History. 2. Indonesia—Politics and government—1798-1942. I. Title.

ATTERBURY, Anson Phelps, 1854-1931. 297'.096
Islam in Africa; its effects—religious, ethical, and social—upon the people of the country. With introd. by F. F. Ellinwood. New York, Negro Universities Press [1969] xxiv, 208 p. 23 cm. Bibliographical footnotes. [BP64.A1A84 1969] 73-91254
1. Islam—Africa. I. Title.

KRITZECK, James. 297'.096
Islam in Africa, edited by James Kritzeck and William H. Lewis. Contributors: J. Spencer Trimingham [and others] New York, Van Nostrand-Reinhold Co. [1969] viii, 339 p. maps. 24 cm. Includes bibliographical references. [BP64.A1K7] 68-24666
1. Islam—Africa. I. Lewis, William Hubert, 1928- joint author. II. Trimingham, John Spencer. III. Title.

TRIMINGHAM, John Spencer. 297'.096
The influence of Islam upon Africa [by] J. Spencer Trimingham. New York, Praeger [1968] x, 159 p. maps. 23 cm. (Arab background series) Bibliography: p. 142-144. [BP64.A1T7] 68-26872 5.00
1. Islam—Africa. I. Title.

TRIMINGHAM, John Spencer. 297.09624
Islam in the Sudan [by] J. Spencer Trimingham. [1st ed.] New York, Barnes & Noble [1965] x, 280 p. illus., 2 maps (1 fold. co.) 22 cm. Bibliographical footnotes. [BP64.S8T7] 65-9348
1. Islam — Sudan. I. Title.

TRIMINGHAM, John Spencer 297.09624
Islam in the Sudan. New York, Barnes & Noble [1965] x, 280p. illus., 2 maps (1 fold. col.) 22cm. Bibl. [BP64.S8T7] 65-9348 8.00
1. Islam—Sudan. I. Title.

TRIMINGHAM, John Spencer. 297.0963
Islam in Ethiopia [by] J. Spencer Trimingham. New York, Barnes & Noble [1965] xv, 299 p. maps (part fold. col.) 23 cm. Bibliographical footnotes. [BP64.E8T7] 65-9065
1. Islam — Ethiopia. 2. Muslims in Ethiopia. I. Title.

TRIMINGHAM, John Spencer 297.0963
Islam in Ethiopia. New York, Barnes & Noble [1965] xv, 299p. maps (pt. fold. col.) 23cm. Bibl. [BP64.E8T7] 65-9065 8.50
1. Islam—Ethiopia. 2. Muslims in Ethiopia I. Title.

EICKELMAN, Dale F., 1942- 297'.0964
Moroccan Islam : tradition and society in a pilgrimage center / by Dale F. Eickelman. Austin : University of Texas Press, c1976. xx, 303 p. : ill. ; 24 cm. (Modern Middle East series ; no. 1) Includes index. Bibliography: p. 287-296. [BP64.M62B653] 75-45136 ISBN 0-292-75025-0 15.95
1. Muslim saints—Morocco—Boujad. 2. Islam—Morocco. 3. Boujad, Morocco—Social life and customs. 4. Morocco—Social life and customs. I. Title. II. Series: Modern Middle East series (Austin, Tex.) ; no. 1.

GEERTZ, Clifford. 297'.0964
Islam observed; religious development in Morocco and Indonesia. New Haven, Yale University Press, 1968. xii, 136 p. maps. 23 cm. (The Terry lectures, v. 37) Includes bibliographical references. [BP64.M6G4] 68-27753 5.00 45/-
1. Islam—Morocco. 2. Islam—Indonesia. I. Title. II. Title: Religious development in Morocco and Indonesia. III. Series: The Terry lectures, Yale University, v. 37

LEVTZION, Nehemia. 297'.0966
Muslims and chiefs in West Africa: a study of Islam in the Middle Volta Basin in the pre-colonial period. Oxford, Clarendon Pr., 1968. xxvi, 228p. 2 maps. 23cm. (Oxford studies in African affairs) Bibl. [BP64.A4W36] 68-106555 8.00
1. Muslims in West Africa. I. Title. II. Series.
Available from Oxford Univ. Pr., New York.

TRIMINGHAM, John Spencer. 297.0966
A history of Islam in West Africa. London, New York, Published for the University of Glasgow by the Oxford University Press, 1962. viii, 262 p. maps (4 fold.) tables. 23 cm. (Glasgow University publications) Bibliographical footnotes. [BP64.A4W38] 62-3000
1. Mohammedanism — Africa, West. I. Title. II. Series: Glasgow. University. Glasgow University publications

TRIMINGHAM, John Spencer 297.0966
A history of Islam in West Africa. New York, Oxford [c.]1962[ ] viii, 262p. illus., maps (Glasgow Univ. pubns.) Bibl. 62-3000 4.80
1. Mohammedanism—Africa, West. I. Title. II. Series: Glasgow. University. Glasgow University publications

TRIMINGHAM, John Spencer. 297'.0966
A history of Islam in West Africa, by J. Spencer Trimingham. London, New York, Published for the University of Glasgow by the Oxford U.P., 1970. x, 262 p. coat of arms, geneal. table, 7 maps. 21 cm. (University of Glasgow. Publications) (Oxford paperbacks, 223) Bibliography: p.x. [BP64.A4W38 1970] 79-550659 ISBN 0-19-285038-5 10/-

1. Islam—Africa, West. 2. Africa, West—History. I. Title. II. Series: Glasgow. University. Glasgow University publications

TRIMINGHAM, John Spencer. 297.0966
Islam in West Africa. Oxford, Clarendon Press, 1959. ix, 262 p. fold. map, diagr. 22 cm. Bibliographical footnotes. [BP64.A4W4] 59-1238
1. Mohammedans in Africa, West. 2. Mohammedanism. I. Title.

RYAN, Patrick J., 1939- 297'.09669
Imale : Yoruba participation in the Muslim tradition : a study of clerical piety / by Patrick J. Ryan. Missoula, Mont. : Published by Scholars Press for Harvard Theological Review, c1977. p. cm. (Harvard dissertation in religion ; no. 11) Thesis—Harvard, 1975. Bibliography: p. [BP64.N49R9] 76-57774 ISBN 0-89130-132-1
1. Islam—Nigeria. 2. Yorubas—Religion. 3. Islam—Functionaries. I. Title. II. Series.

ZOGHBY, Samir M. 297'.0967
Islam in sub-Saharan Africa : a partially annotated guide / compiled by Samir M. Zoghby. Washington : Library of Congress, 1976. p. cm. Includes index. [Z7835.M6Z63] [BP64.A1] 76-7050 ISBN 0-8444-0183-8
1. Islam—Africa, Sub-Saharan—Bibliography. 2. Africa, Sub-Saharan—History—Bibliography. I. Title.

TRIMINGHAM, John Spencer 297.09676
Islam in East Africa [New York] Oxford [c.] 1964. xii, 198 p. maps (1 fold.) 23 cm. Bibl. 64-6991 4.50
1. Islam—Africa, East. 2. Africa, East—Religious life and customs. I. Title.

KING, Noel Quinton. 297'.09676'1
Islam and the confluence of religions in Uganda, 1840-1966 / by Noel King, Abdu Kasozi, Arye Oded. Tallahassee : American Academy of Religion, 1973. ix, 60 p. ; 24 cm. (AAR studies in religion ; no. 6) Includes bibliographical references. [BP64.U35K56] 73-85593 ISBN 0-88420-105-8 : 3.00
1. Islam—Uganda. I. Kasozi, Abdu, 1942- joint author. II. Oded, Arye, joint author. III. Title. IV. Series: American Academy of Religion. AAR studies in religion ; no. 6.

ODED, Arye. 297'.09676'1
Islam in Uganda; Islamization through a centralized state in pre-colonial Africa. New York, Wiley [1974] x, 381 p. illus. 24 cm. (Studies in Islamic culture and history) "A Halsted Press book." Bibliography: p. 347-367. [BP64.U35O3] 74-2326 ISBN 0-470-65260-8
1. Islam—Uganda. I. Title. II. Series.

ESSIEN-UDOM, Essien Udosen. 297.0973
Black nationalism; a search for an identity in America. [Chicago] University of Chicago Press [1962] xiii, 367 p. illus., ports. 25 cm. Bibliography: p. 351-360. [E185.61.E75] 62-12632
1. Black Muslims. 2. United States—Race question. I. Title.

ESSIEN-UDOM, Essien Udosen 297.0973
Black nationalism; a search for an identity in America. [New York, Dell, 1964, c.1962] 448p. 17cm. (Laurel ed., 0574) .75 pap.,
1. Mohammedans in the U.S. 2. Negroes. 3. U.S.—Race question. I. Title.

MAXIMS of Ali, known as the Commander of the Faithful (Amir-al-Mu'menin), 297'.1 the son-in-law of the Prophet Mohammad; (selections) Translated by Mehdi Nakosteen. [Collector's ed. Boulder, Colo.] Este Es Press [1973] xi, 47 p. port. 22 cm. "100 copies. No. 28." "The collected aphorisms known as Kalamati qisar, or Short sayings, though [BP193.1.A2M3913] 73-620098
1. 'Ali ibn Abi Talib, Caliph, 600 (ca.)-661—Quotations. 2. Maxims. I. 'Ali ibn Abi Talib, Caliph, 600 (ca.)-661.

ABRERRY, Arthur John, 1905- 297.12
Aspects of Islamic civilization as depicted in the original texts [Ann Arbor] Univ. of Mich. Pr. [1967, c.1964] 409p. 20cm. (Ann Arbor paperbacks, AA130) Includes selections from orig. texts in English tr. Orig. pub. in Britain by Allen & Unwin. Bibl. [BP89.A7] 2.95 pap.,
1. Islamic literature—Hist. & crit. 2. Civilization, Islamic—Hist. I. Title.

AL-BAYDAWI, 'Abd Allah ibn 'Umar, d.1286? 297.12
Baidawi's commentary on surah 12 of the Qur'an. Text, accompanied by an interpretative rendering. notes by A. F. L. Beeston. [New York] Oxford, [c.]1963. viii, 97p. 26cm. Arabic text reproduced from Fleischer's ed. of 1846. Bibl. 64-3174 5.60
1. Koran. Surat Yusuf—Commentaries. I. Beeston, Alfred Felix Landon, ed. II. Title. III. Title: Commentary on surah 12 of the Qur'an.

ALI, Hashim Amir 297.12
The student's Quran; an introduction. New York, Asia Pub. House [dist. Taplinger, c.1961] 154p. illus. 2.50 pap.,
I. Title.

AZAD, Abul Kalam, maulana, 1888-1958 297.12
The Tarjuman al-Qur'an, v.1. Ed. [tr. from Urdu] by Syed Abdul Latif. Asia Pub. [dist. New York, Taplinger, 1963, c.1962] 210p. 23cm. Contents.v.1. Surat-ul-Fatiha. 63-1051 8.00
1. Koran—Commentaries. I. Latif, Syed Abdul, ed. and tr. II. Title.

HUSAIN, Ashfaque, 1905- 297.12
The quintessence of Islam; a summary of the commentary of Maulana Abul Kalam Azad on alFateha, the first chapter of the Quran. [2d ed.] New York, Asia Pub. House [dist. Taplinger, 1961, c.1958, 1960] 92p. First ed. published in 1958 under title: The spirit of Islam. 61-3469 2.75
1. Koran. Surat al-fatihah—Commentaries. I. Azad, Abul Kalam, maulana, 1888-1958. Tarjuman-ul-Quran. II. Title.

JOMIER, Jacques 297.12
The Bible and the Koran. Tr. from French by Edward P. Arbez. Chicago, Renenry [1967 c. 1964] viii, 120p. 18cm. (Logos ed., 61L-723) Bibl. [BP134.B4J613] 1.25 pap.,
1. Koran—Relation to the Bible. I. Title.

JOMIER, Jacques. 297.12
The Bible and the Koran. Translated from the French by Edward P. Arbez. New York, Desclee Co. [1964] viii, 120 p. 21 cm. Includes bibliographies. [BP134.B4J613] 64-23930
1. Koran—Relation to the Bible. I. Title.

JOMIER, Jacques 297.12
The Bible and the Koran. Tr. from French by Edward P. Arbez. New York, Desclee [c.1959, 1964] viii, 120p. 21cm. Bibl. [BP134.B4J613] 64-23930 2.75
1. Koran—Relation to the Bible. I. Title.

KORAN, English. 297.12
The Koran interpreted [tr. from Arabic] by Arthur J. Aberry. Combined in one volume. New York, Macmillan [1964, c.1955] 350, 358p. 23cm. Contents.v.1. Suras 1-22.--v.2. Suras 21-114. 64-9828 2.95 pap.,
1. Arberry, Arthur John, 1905- tr. I. Title.

BURGEVIN, Frederick Haviland. 297'.122
Cribratio Alchorani; Nicholas Cusanus's criticism of the Koran in the light of his philosophy of religion. [1st ed.] New York, Vantage Press [1969] 128 p. 21 cm. Bibliography: p. 122-128. [BP169.B8] 76-6609 3.95
1. Nicolaus Cusanus, Cardinal, 1401-1464. Cribratio Alchorani. I. Title.

ALSAID, Labib, 297'.122
The recited Koran : a history of the first recorded version / L abib as-Said [sic] ; translated and adapted by Bernard Weiss, M. A. Rauf, Morroe Berger. Princeton, N.J. : Darwin Press, c1975. 156 p. : ill. ; 23 cm. Revised translation of the author's al-Jam'al-sawti al-awwal lil-Qur'an al-karim. Includes index. Bibliography: p. 149-154. [BP131.6.S313 1975] 73-20717 ISBN 0-87850-024-3 : 10.00
1. Koran—Recitation. 2. Koran. al-Mushaf al-murattal. [Phonodisc] I. Title.

JEFFERY, Arthur, ed. 297'.122
Materials for the history of the text of the Qur'an : the old codices : the Kitab al-masahif of Ibn Abi Dawud, together with a collection of the variant readings from the codices of Ibn Ma'sud, Ubai, 'Ali, Ibn 'Abbas, Anas, Abu Musa and other early Qur'anic authorities which present a type of text anterior to that of the canonical text of 'Uthman / edited by Arthur Jeffery. New York : AMS Press, 1975. 619 p. in various pagings ; 23 cm. "Printed for the trustees of the 'De Goeje Fund.' No. XI." Reprint of the 1937 ed. published by E. J. Brill, Leiden. Bibliography: p. 17-18. [BP131.5.J4 1975] 79-180350 ISBN 0-404-56282-5 : 57.50
1. Koran—Readings. 2. Koran—Criticism, Textual. I. al-Sijistani, 'Abd Allah ibn Sulayman, 844 or 5-928 or 9. Kitab al-masahif. 1975. II. Title.

JOMIER, Jacques. 297'.122
The Bible and the Koran. Translated from the French by Edward P. Arbez. Chicago, H. Regnery Co. [1967, c1964] 120 p. 18 cm. (Logos) [BP134.B4J613 1967] 67-4326
1. Koran—Comparative studies. 2. Bible—Comparative studies. I. Title.

KORAN. English & Arabic. 297'.122
The glorious Koran : a bi-lingual edition with English translation, introduction, and notes / by Marmaduke Pickthall. Albany : State University of New York Press, 1976. xliv, 826 p. ; 22 cm. Includes bibliographical references and indexes. [BP109.P5 1976] 76-22701 ISBN 0-87395-356-8 : 30.00
I. Pickthall, Marmaduke William, 1875-1936. II. Title.

KORAN. English. Selections. 297'.122
Wisdom of the Koran. Edited by C. Merton Babcock, and illustrated with wood-engravings by Boyd Hanna. Mount Vernon, N.Y., Peter Pauper Press [1966] 62 p. illus. 19 cm. [BP110.B3] 67-1430
I. Babcock, Clarence Merton, ed. II. Hanna, Boyd, illus. III. Peter Pauper Press, Mount Vernon, N.Y. IV. Title.

*KORAN. Selections. 297.122
The Koran. A new translation by Henry Mercier. Translated from the French by Lucien Tremlett. Illus. by Si Abdelkrim Wezzani. London, Luzac, 1973. xvi, 332 p. illus. 18 cm. Text in Arabic (with romanization) and English on opposite pages. First published in 1956. "This translation brings together the essentials to meet the requirements of heart and mind. The inclusion of the Arabic text and a phonetic transcription of the original psalmody helps to recreate its poetical strain." [BP109]
1. Koran. English, Selections. I. Mercier, Henry, interpreter, ed. & tr. II. Title.
Available from Verry, Mystic, Conn., for 6.50 (pbk.) ISBN 0-7189-0169-X.

LANE, Edward William, 1801-1876. 297'.122
Arabic-english lexicon Book 1. New York, F. Ungar Pub. Co. [1955-56] 1v. in 8pts. (3064 p.) 34cm. Includes a reproduction of the original t.p. of each part. Pts. 6-8 edited by Stanley Lane-Poole. 'Supplement to parts VII. and VIII.': pt. 8. p. [2981]-3064. Book 2 never published. [PJ6640.L4] 55-12044
1. Arabic language—Dictionaries—English. I. Lane-Poole, Stanley. 1854-1931. ed. II. Title.

LANE, Edward William, 1801-1876. 297'.122
Arabic-English lexicon book i New York, F. Ungar Pub. Co. [1955-56] 1 v. in 8 pts. (3064p.) 34cm. Includes a reproduction of the original t. p. of each part. Pts. 6-8 edited by Stanley Lane-Poole. 'Supplement to parts VII . and VIII.': pt. 8, p. [2981]-3064. Book 2 never published. [PJ6640.L4] 55-12044
1. Arabic language—Dictionaries—English. I. Lane-Poole, Stanley, 1854-1931, ed. II. Title.

PENRICE, John, 1818-1892. 297'.122
A dictionary and glossary of the Kor-an, with copious grammatical references and explanations of the text. New York, Biblo and Tannen, 1969. viii, 166 p. 27 cm. At head of title: Silk al-bayan fi manaqib al-Qur'an. (romanized form) Reprint of the London ed. published in 1873. [PJ6696.Z8P4 1969] 70-90039
1. Koran—Glossaries, vocabularies, etc. 2. Arabic language—Dictionaries—English. I. Title.

PENRICE, John, 1818-1892. 297'.122
A dictionary and glossary of the Kor-an, with copious grammatical references and explanations of the text. Introd. by R. B. Serjeant. New York, Praeger Publishers [1971] viii, 166 p. 26 cm. At head of title: Silk al-bayan fi manaqibal-Qur'an. (romanized form) Reprint of the 1873 ed. [PJ6696.Z8P4 1971] 71-133086 17.50
1. Koran—Glossaries, vocabularies, etc. 2. Arabic language—Dictionaries—English. I. Title.

KORAN. English & Arabic. 297'.1225'21
The message of the Qur'an presented in perspective, by Hashim Amir-Ali. Rutland, Vt., C. E. Tuttle Co. [1974] 1 v. (various pagings) illus. 26 cm. [BP109.A42] 74-169180 ISBN 0-8048-0976-3 25.00
I. Ali, Hashim Amir, tr. II. Title.

KORAN. English & Arabic. 297'.1225'21
The message of the Qur'an presented in perspective, by Hashim Amir-Ali. Rutland, Vt., C. E. Tuttle Co. [1974] 1 v. (various pagings) illus. 26 cm. [BP109.A42] 74-169180 ISBN 0-8048-0976-3 25.00
I. Ali, Hashim Amir, tr. II. Title.

BASETTI-SANI, Giulio, 1912- 297'.1226
The Koran in the light of Christ : an essay towards a Christian interpretation of the sacred book of Islam / by Giulio Basetti-Sani. Chicago : Franciscan Herald Press, [1977] p. cm. [BP172.B327] 76-28786 ISBN 0-81990713-8 : 6.95
1. Koran—Criticism, interpretation, etc. 2. Christianity and other religions—Islam. 3. Islam—Relations—Christianity. 4. Jesus Christ in the Koran. I. Title.

GATJE, Helmut, 1927- 297'.1226
The Qur'an and its exegesis : selected texts with classical and modern Muslim interpretations / by Helmut Gatje ; translated and edited by Alford T. Welch. Berkeley : University of California Press, 1976. xiv, 313 p. ; 23 cm. (The Islamic world series) Translation of Koran und Koranexegese. Includes indexes. Bibliography: p. 286-295. [BP130.45.G313] 74-82847 ISBN 0-520-02833-3 : 20.00
1. Koran—Commentaries—History and criticism. 2. Koran—Criticism, interpretation, etc. I. Title. II. Series.

KORAN. English. 297'.1226'6
A comprehensive commentary on the Quran : comprising Sale's translation and preliminary discourse, with additional notes and emendations : together with a complete index to the text, preliminary discourse and notes / by E. M. Wherry. New York : AMS Press, [1974] p. cm. Reprint of the 1896 ed. published by K. Paul, Trench, Trubner, London. [BP109.S3 1974] 74-22064 ISBN 0-404-09520-8
1. Koran—Criticism, interpretation, etc. I. Sale, George, 1697?-1736, ed.

KORAN. English. 297'.1227
A comprehensive commentary on the Quran : comprising Sale's translation and preliminary discourse, with additional notes and emendations : together with a complete index to the text, preliminary discourse and notes / by E. M. Wherry. New York : AMS Press, [1974] p. cm. Reprint of the 1896 ed. published by K. Paul, Trench, Trubner, London. [BP109.S3 1974] 79-153620 ISBN 0-404-09520-8
1. Koran—Criticism, interpretation, etc. I. Sale, George, 1697?-1736, ed. II. Title.

PARRINDER, Edward Geoffrey. 297'.1228
Jesus in the Qur'an / [by] Geoffrey Parrinder. London : Sheldon Press, 1976. 187 p. ; 22 cm. Includes bibliographical references and indexes. [BP134.J37P37 1976] 77-353988 ISBN 0-85969-069-5 : £4.50
1. Jesus Christ—Koranic teaching. I. Title.

PARRINDER, Edward Geoffrey. 297.1228232
Jesus in the Qur'an [by] Geoffrey Parrinder. New York, Barnes & Noble. 1965. 187 p. 23 cm. Bibliographical footnotes. [BP172.P3] 65-29535
1. Jesus Christ—Islamic interpretations. 2. Koran—Relation to the Bible. I. Title.

PARRINDER, Edward Geoffrey 297.1228232
Jesus in the Qur'an. New York, Barnes & Noble [c.]1965. 187p. 23cm. [BP172.P3] 65-29535 6.00
1. Jesus Christ—Islamic interpretations. 2. Koran—Relation to the Bible. I. Title.

GUILLAUME, Alfred, 1888- 297.124
The traditions of Islam; an introduction to the study of the Hadith literature. Beirut, Khayats, 1966. 184p. 23cm. (Khayats oriental reprint no. 13) Reprint of 1924 ed. Bibl. [BP135] 66-6587 ISBN CD 6.00
1. Hadith I. Title.
Originally published by Oxford Univ. Pr. Available from Verry in Mystic, Conn.

AL-BUKHARI, Muhammad ibn Isma'il, 810-870 297'.1241
[Sahih al-Bukhari. (romnized form)] = The translation of the meanings of Sahih al-Bukhari : Arabic-English / Muhammad Muhsin Khan. 3d rev. ed. Chicago : Kazi Publications, c1976- v. ; 24 cm. [BP135.A124E54 1976] 77-354106
1. Hadith (Collections) I. Khan, Muhammad Muhsin. II. [al-Jami' al-sahih. English & Arabic]

AL-DAMANH URI, Ahmad ibn Abd al-Munim 297'.197'2
Shaykh Damanhuri on the churches of Cairo, 1739 / edited and translated with introd. and notes by Moshe Perlmann. Berkeley : University of California Press, 1975. 71, 87 p. ; 26 cm. (University of California publications : Near Eastern studies ; v. 19) Added t.p.: Iqamat al-hujjah al-bahirah 'ala hadm kana'is Misr wa-al-Qahirah, lil-Shaykh Ahmad al-Damanhuri. Includes index. [LAW] 73-620223 ISBN 0-520-09513-8 pbk. : 5.00

1. Churches—Egypt—Cairo. 2. Cairo—Churches. 3. Fatwas. 4. Christians in Egypt—Legal status, laws, etc. I. Perlmann, Moshe. II. Title. III. Title: Iqamat al-hujjah al-bahirah 'ala hadm kana'is Misr wa-al-Qahirah. IV. Series: California. University. University of California publications. Near Eastern studies ; v. 19.

CONTINUING Committee 297'.197'2
on Muslim-Christian Cooperation.
Four-year report [April 27, 1954-June 30, 1958] of the Continuing Committee on Muslim-Christian Cooperation Incorporated, the provisional organization of the World Fellowship of Muslims and Christians. Washington [1958?] 19 p. illus., facsim., ports. 28 cm. [BP172.C57] 79-258193
1. Islam—Relations—Christianity. 2. Christianity and other religions—Islam. I. Title.

GEIGER, Abraham, 1810- 297'.197'2
1874.
Judaism and Islam. Prolegomenon by Moshe Pearlman. New York, Ktav Pub. House, 1970. xxxii, 170 p. 24 cm. (The Library of Jewish classics) Translation of Was hat Mohammed aus dem Judenthume aufgenommen? Reprint of the 1898 ed. Includes bibliographical references. [BP134.J4G4313 1970] 71-79491 ISBN 0-87068-058-7
1. Koran—Relation to the Bible. 2. Islam—Relations—Judaism. 3. Judaism—Relations—Islam.

TORREY, Charles 297'.197'2
Cutler, 1863-1956
The Jewish foundation of Islam. Introd. by Franz Rosenthal. New York, KTAV [1968, c.1967] xxviii, 164p. 24cm. Bibl. [BP173.J8T6 1968] 67-18817 6.95
1. Islam—Relations—Judaism. 2. Judaism—Relations—Islam. 3. Koran. 4. Jews in Arabia. I. Title.

ALGAR, Hamid. 297'.197'7
Religion and state in Iran, 1785-1906; the role of the ulama in the Qajar period. Berkeley, University of California Press, 1969. xviii, 286 p. 24 cm. Revised version of the author's thesis, University of Cambridge, 1965. "Published under the auspices of the Near Eastern Center, University of California, Los Angeles." Bibliography: p. 267-277. [DS299.A45 1969] 72-79959 9.50
1. Iran—History—19th century. 2. Clergy—Iran—Political activity. I. California. University. University at Los Angeles. Near Eastern Center. II. Title.

ROSENTHAL, Erwin Isak 297.1977
Jakob, 1904-
Islam in the modern national state [New York] Cambridge [1966, c.1965] xxi, 416p. 23cm. Bibl. [BP173.6.R6] 66-13638 10.50
1. Islam and state. 2. Islamic countries—Politics. I. Title.

PADEN, John N. 297'.197'7096695
Religion and political culture in Kano [by] John N. Paden. Berkeley, University of California Press [1973] xv, 461 p. illus. 25 cm. Bibliography: p. [436]-442. [BP173.7.P3] 74-153548 ISBN 0-520-01738-2 15.00
1. Islam and politics—Kano, Nigeria (State) I. Title.

ABDUL-RAUF, 297'.197'8342
Muhammad, 1917-
The Islamic view of women and the family / by Muhammad Abdul-Rauf. 1st ed. New York : R. Speller, c1977. 171 p. ; 24 cm. Bibliography: p. 170-171. [BP188.3.F3A24] 77-151778 ISBN 0-8315-0156-1 : 8.50
1. Family—Religious life (Islam) 2. Women, Muslim. I. Title.

DIARA, Agadem L. 297'.197'83451
Islam and Pan-Africanism [by] Agadem L. Diara. [Detroit, Agascha Productions, 1973] xx, 95 p. port. 22 cm. Bibliography: p. 81-83. [BP62.N4D5] 72-91318 ISBN 0-913358-04-5 1.50 (pbk.)
1. Negro Muslims. 2. Pan-Africanism. 3. Islam—Africa. I. Title.

LEWIS, Bernard. 297'.197'8345
Race and color in Islam. New York, Harper & Row [1971] xi, 103 p. illus. 21 cm. (Harper torchbooks, TB 1590) Based on a lecture published in Encounter, August 1970. Includes bibliographical references. [BP190.5.R3L48] 73-159628 ISBN 0-06-131590-7 1.95
1. Islam and race problems. I. Title.

RODINSON, Maxime. 297'.197'85
Islam and capitalism. Translated from the French by Brian Pearce. [1st American ed.] New York, Pantheon Books [1974, c1973] xviii, 308 p. 22 cm. Includes bibliographical references. [BP173.75.R613 1974] 73-17297 ISBN 0-394-46719-1 8.95
1. Islam and economics. I. Title.

ARBERRY, Arthur John, 1905- 297.2
Revelation and reason in Islam. London, Allen & Unwin [dist. Mytic, Conn., Verry, 1964] 122p. 19cm. (Forwood lects., 1956) A57 3.00 bds.,
1. Revelation (Mohammedanism) I. Title. II. Series.

AZAD, Abul Kalaam, 297'.2
Maulana, 1888-1958.
The Tarjuman al-Qur'an. Edited and rendered into English by Syed Abdul Latif. Bombay, New York, Asia Pub. House [c1962- v. 23 cm. Contents.CONTENTS.--v. 1. Surat-ul-Fatiha. [[BP130.4]] SA63
1. Koran—Commentaries. I. Latif, Syed Abdul, ed. and tr. II. Title.

CRAGG, Kenneth 297.2
Sandals at the mosque; Christian presence amid Islam. New York, Oxford University Press. 1959[ ] 160p. 19cm. (Christian presence series) (5p. bibl., bibl. footnotes) 59-16908 2.75 bds.,
1. Mohammedanism—Relations—Christianity. 2. Christianity and other religions—Mohammedanism. I. Title.

HASHIM, Hassan A. 297'.2
What is al-Islam : what is the religion of Ibrahim? / Hassan A. Hashim, Salimah A. Hashim. Washington : Iman Religion and Information Center, 1975. vii, 42, 30 p. ; 23 cm. Added t.p.: Ma al-Islam, ma hiya millat Ibrahim. English and Arabic. [BP165.H296] 75-29799
1. Islam—Essence, genius, nature. 2. Jewish-Arab relations—Addresses, essays, lectures. 3. Jewish question—Addresses, essays, lectures. I. Hashim, Salimah A., joint author. II. Title. III. Title: Ma al-Islam, ma hiya millat Ibrahim.

MUHAMMAD 'ABDUH, 1849-1905 297.2
The theology of unity; tr. from the Arabic by Ishaq Musa'ad, Kenneth Cragg. London, Allen & Unwin [New York, Hillary House, c.1966] 3-164p. 23cm. [BP166.M7513] 66-70498 5.00 bds.,
1. Islamic theology. I. Title.

SEALE, Morris S. 297.2
Muslim theology; a study of origins with reference to the church fathers. London, Luzac [Mystic, Conn., Verry, 1965] ix, 137p. 23cm. Bibl. [BP166.S4] 65-29721 7.00
1. Islamic theology. I. Title.

SIRAJ ul-Din, Abu Bakr. 297'.2
The book of certainty, by Abu Bakr Siraj Ed-Din. New York, S. Weiser, 1970. 108 p. front. 21 cm. Includes bibliographical references. [BP189.S46 1970] 71-138082 3.00
1. Sufism. I. Title.

STANTON, Herbert Udny 297'.2
Weitbrecht, 1851-1937.
The teaching of the Qur'an, with an account of its growth and a subject index. New York, Biblo and Tannen, 1969. 136 p. 22 cm. Reprint of the 1919 ed. Bibliography: p. [135]-136. [BP130.S7 1969] 74-90040
1. Koran. I. Title.

WADDY, Charis. 297'.2
The Muslim mind / by Charis Waddy. London ; New York : Longman, 1976. xvii, 204 p. ; ill. ; 23 cm. Includes bibliographical references and index. [BP161.2.W27 1976] 76-6522 ISBN 0-582-78061-6 : 18.50
1. Islam. I. Title.

WENSINCK, Arent Jan, 1882- 297.2
1939
The Muslim creed, its genesis and historical development. New York, Barnes & Noble [1966] vii, 304p. 21cm. Bibl. [BP166.1.W4] 66-1494 9.00
1. Islamic theology—Hist. I. Title.

WOLFSON, Harry Austryn, 297'.2
1887-1974.
The philosophy of the Kalam / by Harry Austryn Wolfson. Cambridge, Mass. : Harvard University Press, 1976. xxvi, 779 p. ; 23 cm. (Structure and growth of philosophic systems from Plato to Spinoza ; 4) Bibliography: p. [743]-779. [BP166.W64 1976] 74-78718 ISBN 0-674-66580-5 : 30.00
1. Islamic theology. I. Title.

PETERS, J. R. T. M. 297'.2'0924
God's created speech : a study in the speculative theology of the Mu'tazili Qadi l-gudat Abul-Hasan 'Abd al-Jabbar bn Ahmad al-Hamadani / by J. R. T. M. Peters. Leyden : Brill, 1976. xi, 448 p. ; 25 cm. Includes index. Bibliography: p. [422]-429. [BP80.A815P47] 77-353260 ISBN 9-00-404719-0 : fl 96.00
1. al-Asadabadi, 'Abd al-Jabbar ibn Ahmad, d. 1025 or 6. 2. Koran—Evidences, authority, etc. 3. Islamic theology. 4. Motazilites. I. Title.

ISLAM, Khawaja Muhammad. 297'.23
The spectacle of death : including glimpses of life beyond the grave / by Khawaja Muhammad Islam. Lahore : Tablighi Kutub Khana, 1976. xx, 502 p. ; 23 cm. [BP166.8.I75] 76-930187 Rs50.00 ($5.00 U.S.)
1. Future life (Islam) 2. Religious life (Islam) I. Title.

DORMAN, Harry Gaylord, 297'.293
1906-
Toward understanding Islam; contemporary apologetic of Islam and missionary policy. New York, Bureau of Publications, Teachers College, Columbia University, 1948. [New York, AMS Press, 1972] x, 137 p. 22 cm. Reprint of the 1948 ed., issued in series: Teachers College, Columbia University. Contributions to education, no. 940. Originally presented as the author's thesis, Columbia. Bibliography: p. 132-137. [BP172.D6 1972] 79-176727 ISBN 0-404-55940-9
1. Islam—Relations—Christianity. 2. Christianity and other religions—Islam. 3. Missions to Muslims. I. Title. II. Series: Columbia University. Teachers College. Contributions to education, no. 940.

SHARAF al-Din, 'Abd al- 297'.293
Samad.
God the almighty, man, and Satan : or, Not mere helpless pawns / by Abdus-Samad Sharafuddin. Jeddah : OKAZ, 1976- v. ; 22 cm. Added t.p.: Allah al-'azim wa-al-insan wa-al-Shaytan. English or Arabic. [BP172.S488] 77-476909
1. Carr, William Guy, 1895-1959. Pawns in the game. 2. Islam—Apologetic works. 3. Islam—Relations—Christianity. 4. Christianity and other religions—Islam. I. Title. II. Title: Not mere helpless pawns. III. Title: Allah al-'azim wa-al-insan wa-al-Shaytan.

ESIN, Emel (Tek) 297.34
Mecca, the blessed; Madinah, the radiant. Text: Emel Esin. Photos. by Haluk Doganbey. New York, Crown Publishers [1963] 222 p. illus. (part col.) maps, facsims. 28 cm. Cover title: Mecca & Mandinah. Bibliographical references included in "Notes" (p. 211-217) [BP187.3.E8] 63-21115
1. Mecca. 2. Medina. 3. Mohammedanism — Pictures, illustrations, etc. I. Title.

ESIN, Emel (Tek) 297.34
Mecca, the blessed; Madimah, the radiant. Text: Emel Esin. Photos. by Haluk Doganbey. New York, Crown [c.1963] 222p. illus. (pt. col.) maps. facsims. 28cm. Cover title: Mecca & Madinah. Bibl. 63-21115 10.00
1. Mecca. 2. Medina. 3. Mohammedanism—Pictures, illustrations, etc. I. Title.

KAMAL, Ahmad, 1914- 297.38
The sacred journey, being pilgrimage to Makkah; the traditions, dogma and Islamic ritual that govern the lives and the destiny of more than five hundred million who call themselves Muslim: one seventh of mankind. New York, Duell, Sloan and Pearce [1961] xx, 108, 115, 9 p. 22 cm. Added t.-p. English and Arabic. [BP181.K3] 61-6920
1. Pilgrims and pilgrimages—Mecca. I. Title. II. Title: al-Rihlah al-muqaddasah.

NIYAZI, Kausar. 297'.38
To the Prophet / Kausar Niazi ; [translated by Saeed-ul-Hassan and edited by Karam Hydri]. 1st ed. Lahore : Sh. Muhammad Ashraf, 1976. xi, 150 p. ; 22 cm. Translation of Zikr-i Rasul. Includes quotations in Arabic with Urdu translation. [BP75.N59] 76-938515 Rs16.00
1. Muhammad, the prophet—Addresses, essays, lectures. 2. Mawlid al-Nabi—Addresses, essays, lectures. I. Title.

AS-SUFI, 'Abd al-Qadir. 297'.4
The way of Muhammad / 'Abd al-Qadir as-Sufi. Berkeley [Calif.] : Diwan Press, c1975. 202 p. : diagrs. ; 21 cm. (The Sufic path series) [BP189.6.S85] 75-8119 5.95
1. al-Shadhiliyah. 2. Sufism. I. Title.

BAKHTIAR, Laleh. 297'.4
Sufi : expressions of the mystic quest / [by] Laleh Bakhtiar. London : Thames and Hudson, 1976. 120 p. : ill. (some col.), plans, ports. (chiefly col.) ; 26 cm. (Art and imagination) Bibliography: p. 120. [BP189.3.B34] 76-377195 ISBN 0-500-81015-X : £2.50
1. Sufism. I. Title.

BROWN, John Porter, 1814- 297'.4
1872
The Darvishes; or, Oriental spiritualism, by John P. Brown. 2nd ed.; ed. introd., notes by H. A. Rose, new impression. London, Cass, 1968. xxiv, 496p. ilius. 22cm. (Islam & the Muslim world, no.5) Bibl. footnotes. [BP189.2.B/4 1968] 68-114037 15.00
1. Dervishes. I. Rose, Horace Arthur, 1867- ed. II. Title. III. Title: Oriental spiritualism. IV. Series.
Distributed by Barnes & Noble, New York.

BURCKHARDT, Titus. 297'.4
An introduction to Sufi doctrine / Titus Burckhardt ; translated [from the French] by D. M. Matheson. Wellingborough : Thorsons, 1976. 126 p. ; 22 cm. Translation of Du soufisme. Includes bibliographical references. [BP189.3.B8713] 77-363283 ISBN 0-7225-0333-4 : £2.25
1. Sufism. I. Title. II. Title: Sufi doctrine.

*BURKE, Omar Michael. 297.4
Among the dervishes; an account of travels in Asia and Africa, and four years studying the dervishes, sufis and fakirs, by living among them by O. M. Burke. 1st edition New York, E. P. Dutton and Co. 1975. 203 p. 21 cm. Bibliography: pp 201-203. [BP189.2] ISBN 0-525-47386-6 3.95 (pbk.)
1. Sifism. I. Title.

CELALEDDIN, Rumi, Mevlana. 297.4
1207-1273
Discourses of Rumi. [Tr. from Persian, commentary by] A J. Arberry. London, J. Murray [dist. Levit-town, Long Island, N.Y., Transatlantic. 1965, c.1961] ix, 176p. 22cm. [BP188.2.C413] 61-40019 8.25
1. Devotional literature, Mohammedan. I. Arberry, Arthur John, 1905- tr. II. Title.

THE Elephant in the dark, 297'.4
and other writings on the diffusion of Sufi ideas in the West / by Idries Shah and others ; Leonard Lewin, editor. 2d ed. New York : E. P. Dutton, 1976. vi, 154 p. ; 21 cm. First ed. published in 1972 under title: The diffusion of Sufi ideas in the West. Contents.Contents.—Christianity, Islam and the Sufis: Shah, I. The elephant in the dark. Sanchez, I. Christian mysticism and the Sufis.—Sufi study material: Sufi Abdul-Hamid First statement. Shah I. The teaching story.—On Idries Shah and contemporary Sufism: Lessing, D. An ancient way to new freedom. Courtland, L. F. A visit to Idries Shah. Williams, P. An interview with Idries Shah.—On the diffusion of Sufi ideas in the West. Foster, W. Sufi studies today. Imdad Hussein Sheikh el-Qadiri. Sufi thought. A session with a Western Sufi. Bibliography: p. 153-154. [BP189.2.L48 1976] 75-34151 ISBN 0-525-47372-6 pbk. : 4.95
1. Sufism—Addresses, essays, lectures. I. Shah, Idries, Sayed, 1924- II. Lewin, Leonard. III. Lewin, Leonard, comp. The diffusion of Sufi ideas in the West.

FARZAN, Massud, comp. 297'.4
The tale of the reed pipe; teachings of the Sufis. [1st ed.] New York, Dutton, 1974. xxi, 104 p. 19 cm. [BP189.F34 1974] 74-166175 ISBN 0-525-47362-9 1.95 (pbk.).
1. Sufism. I. Title.

FATEMI, Nasrollah 297'.4
Saifpour, 1911-
Sufism : message of brotherhood, harmony, and hope / Nasrollah S. Fatemi, Faramarz S. Fatemi, Fariborz S. Fatemi. South Brunswick : A. S. Barnes, c1976. 243 p. ; 22 cm. Includes bibliographical references and index. [BP188.9.F37] 75-29692 ISBN 0-498-01869-5 : 12.00
1. Sufism. 2. Sufi poetry, Persian—History and criticism. I. Fatemi, Faramarz S., joint author. II. Fatemi, Fariborz S., joint author. III. Title.

FATEMI, Nasrollah 297'.4
Saifpour, 1911-
Sufism : message of brotherhood, harmony, and hope / Nasrollah S. Fatemi, Faramarz S. Fatemi, Fariborz S. Fatemi. South Brunswick : A. S. Barnes, c1976. p. cm. Includes bibliographical references and index. [BP188.9.F37] 75-29692 ISBN 0-498-01869-5 : 12.00
1. Sufism. 2. Sufi poetry, Persian—History and criticism. I. Fatemi, Faramarz S., joint author. II. Fatemi, Fariborz S., joint author. III. Title.

FRIEDLANDER, Ira. 297'.4
The whirling dervishes, being an account of the Sufi order known as the Mevlevis and its founder the poet and mystic Merlana Jalalu'ddin Rumi/ by Ira Friedlander; music section by Nezih Uzel. New York : Collier Books, 1975. 159 p. : ill. ; 30 cm. Bibliography: p. 158-159. [BP189.7.M42F74 1975b] 75-1299 pbk. : 4.95
1. Jalal al-Din Rumi, Mawlana, 1207-1273. 2. Mevlevi. I. Title.

GILSENAN, Michael. 297'.4
Saint and Sufi in modern Egypt: an essay in the sociology of religion. Oxford, Clarendon Press, 1973. 248 p. illus. 23 cm. (Oxford monographs on social anthropology) Bibliography: p. [242]-246. [BP189.7.S5G55] 74-157832 ISBN 0-19-823181-4 £4.75
1. al-Shadhiliyah. 2. al-Radi, Salamah, 1866 or 7-1939. 3. Sufism—Egypt. I. Title.

GILSENAN, Michael. 297'.4
Saint and Sufi in modern Egypt: an essay in the sociology of religion. Oxford, Clarendon Press, 1973. 248 p. illus. 23 cm. (Oxford monographs on social anthropology) Bibliography: p. [242]-246. [BP189.7.S5G55] 74-157832 ISBN 0-19-823181-4

1. al-Shadhiliyah. 2. al-Radi, Salamah, 1866 or 7-1939. 3. Sufism—Egypt. I. Title.
Distributed by Oxford University Press; 15.25.

GURUBAWA, Shaikh 297'.4
Muhaiyaddeen.
Songs of God's grace [by] M. R. Guru Bawa. [Translators: Ajwad Macan-Markar and others] Philadelphia, Guru Bawa Fellowship of Philadelphia [1973] vi, 154 p. illus. 21 cm. [BL624.G8813] 73-91016 1.95 (pbk.)
1. Spiritual life. I. Macan-Markar, Ajwad, tr. II. Title.
Publisher's address: 5820 Overbrook Avenue, Phildelphia, Penn 15210

*AL-HALLAJ, Mansur. 297.4
The Tawasin. Berkeley, Diwan Press, [1975] c1974 81 p. 21 cm. (Sufic Rath Series) [BP189] 74-21376 6.95
I. Abd Ar-Rahman At-Tarjumana, Aisha, tr. II. Title.
Publisher's address: 1419 Polk St., San Francisco, 94109 Pbk. 3.95.

HUGHES, Catharine, 1935- 297'.4
comp.
The secret shrine: Islamic mystical reflections. Edited and with photos. by Catharine Hughes. New York, Seabury Press [1974] 1 v. (unpaged) illus. 21 cm. "A Crossroad book." [BP189.62.H83] 74-12106 ISBN 0-8164-2101-3
1. Sufism—Collected works. I. Title.

HUJVIRI, 'Ali ibn 297'.4
'Usman, d.ca.1072.
The Kashf al-mahjub : the oldest Persian treatise on Sufiism / written by Ali ibn Uthman al-Hujwiri ; translated by Reynold A. Nicholson ; with a foreword by Shahidullah Faridi. Lahore : Islamic Book Foundation, 1976. xxiv, 446 p. ; 22 cm. "Reprint of rare Islamic books." Reprint of the 1911 ed. published by E. J. Brill. Leyden. Includes t.p. of the original with imprint Leyden, E. J. Brill, 1911. Includes bibliographical references and index. [BP188.9.H8413 1976] 76-930137 Rs60.00 ($6.00 U.S.)
1. Sufism—Early works to 1800. I. Nicholson, Reynold Alleyne, 1868-1945. II. Title.

IBN al-'Arabi, 1165-1240. 297'.4
Sufis of Andalusia; the Ruh al-quds and al-Durrah al-fakhirah of Ibn 'Arabi. Translated with introd. and notes by R. W. J. Austin. With a foreword by Martin Lings. Berkeley, University of California Press [1972, c1971] 173 p. illus. 23 cm. Translation of the biographical portion of [Ruh al-Quds (romanized form)] and of extracts from [al-Durrah al-fakhirah (romanized form)]. Bibliography: p. 161-162. [BP189.4.I13 1972] 77-165230 ISBN 0-520-01999-7 8.75
1. Sufism—Biography. 2. Muslims in Spain—Biography. I. Ibn al-'Arabi, 1165-1240. al-Durrah al-fakhirah. English. Selections. 1972. II. Title.

INAYAT Khan, 1882-1926. 297'.4
Cosmic language. Tucson, Ariz., Omen Press, 1972. 131 p. 21 cm. "Consists of addresses given by Hazrat Inayat Khan to his pupils during the summer school at Suresnes in 1924." [BP189.3.I5 1972] 72-195007 ISBN 0-912358-02-5 1.95
1. Sufism. I. Title.

INAYAT KHAN, 1882-1926. 297.4
The Sufi message of Hazvat Inayat Khan. London, Published for International Headquarters of the Sufimovement, Geneva, by Barrie and Rockliff [dist. New York, Citadel Press, 1960, i.e., 1961] 240p. illus., port. Contents.v. 1. The way of illumination. The inner life. The soul, whence and whither? The purpose of life. 61-100 6.00
1. Sufism. I. Title.

INAYAT Khan, Pir Vilayat. 297'.4
Toward the one. [1st ed.] New York, Harper & Row [1974] A-G, 678 p. illus. 21 cm. (Harper colophon books) Bibliography: p. 658-663. [BP189.62.I54 1974] 73-7132 ISBN 0-06-090352-X 5.75 (pbk.)
1. Sufism. I. Title.

JALAL al-Din Rumi, 297'.4
Mawlana, 1207-1273.
Discourses of Rumi. [Translated by] A. J. Arberry. [1st American ed.] New York, S. Weiser, 1972. ix, 276 p. 21 cm. Translation of Fihi ma fih. [BP189.62.J3513 1972] 77-184563 ISBN 0-87728-179-3 3.50
1. Islamic devotional literature. 2. Sufism—Early works to 1800. I. Title.

*JALALV-D-DIN MUHAMMAD I 297.4
RUMI, Mavlana
Teachings of Rumi: The masnavi of Mavlana Jalalv-d-Din M. Translated and abridged by E. H. Whinfield. 1st. ed. New York, E. P. Dutton & Co., 1975 xii, 330 p. 21 cm. [BP189.62] ISBN 0-525-47387-4 3.95 (pbk.)
1. Jalal al—Din Rumi, Mavlana, 1207-1273 2. Sufism. I. Whinfield, E. H. Trans. II. Title.

AL-KALABADHI, Muhammad 297'.4
ibn Ibrahim, 10thcent.
The doctrine of the Sufis / [translated from the Arabic of Abu Bakr al-Kalabadhi, by Arthur John Arberry. New York : AMS Press [1976] p. cm. Translation of al-Ta'arruf li-madhhab ahl al-tasawwuf. Reprint of the 1935 ed. published by University Press, Cambridge. [BP189.26.K3813 1976] 75-41003 ISBN 0-404-14637-6 : 14.00
1. Syfism—Early works to 1800. I. Title.

LEWIN, Leonard, comp. 297'.4
The diffusion of Sufi ideas in the West; an anthology of new writings by and about Idries Shah. Edited by L. Lewin. Boulder, Colo., Keysign Press, 1972. 212 p. 21 cm. (The Transmission of wisdom, v. 1) Contents.Contents.—An interview with Idries Shah, by P. Williams.—An ancient way to new freedom, by D. Lessing.—A visit to Idries Shah, by L. F. Courtland.—Sufi study material.—How they see us, by B. Kolinski.—A reconnaissance; why I traveled, by Taslim.—Dervish ritual, by A. Archer-Forbes.—Perfecting of man, by D. R. Forbes.—A sort of monks, by J. Grant.—Social mysticism, by R. Fischer.—Trail of the Damascus blade, by C. P. Stone.—The mystics choose a king, by M. Brackett.—The festival of Dervishes, by A. Samuelson.—Mystical virtue, by M. L. Isher.—The Sufi way, by A. L. M. Farris.—The pattern of the Sufis, by A. C. Butterfield. [BP189.2.L48] 74-182745 2.85
1. Sufism—Addresses, essays, lectures. I. Shah, Idries, Sayed, 1924- II. Title.

LEWIS, Samuel L., 1896- 297'.4
1971.
In the garden / Samuel L. Lewis (Sufi Ahmed Murad, Chisti). New York : Harmony Books, c1975. 288 p. : ill. ; 20 cm. Bibliography: p. 286-287. [BP189.62.L48 1975] 75-27184 ISBN 0-517-52412-0 : 5.00
1. Sufism—Collected works. I. Title.

LEWIS, Samuel L., 1896- 297'.4
1971.
Toward spiritual brotherhood. [Novato, Calif., Prophecy Pressworks, 1971?] xvii, 101 p. illus. 22 cm. [BP189.2.L49] 74-157561 2.50
1. Sufism. I. Title.

LINGS, Martin. 297'.4
What is Sufism? / Martin Lings. Berkeley : University of California Press, 1975. 133 p. ; 23 cm. Includes bibliographical references and indexes. [BP189.L5] 75-317448 ISBN 0-520-02794-9 : 8.50
1. Sufism. I. Title.

LINGS, Martin. 297'.4
What is Sufism? / Martin Lings. 1st California paperback ed. Berkeley : University of California Press, 1977, c1975. 133 p. ; 21 cm. Includes bibliographical references and indexes. [BP189.L5 1977] 77-362607 ISBN 0-520-03171-7 pbk. : 2.95
1. Sufism. I. Title.

MACDONALD, Duncan Black, 297.4
1863-1943
The religious attitude and life in Islam; being the Haskell lectures on comparative religion delivered before the University of Chicago in 1906 i[dist. Mystic, Conn., Verry, 1965] 317p. 19cm. [BP163.M3] 6.50
1. Mohammedanism. I. Title.

MARTIN, Bradford G. 297'.4
Muslim brotherhoods in nineteenth century Africa / B. G. Martin. Cambridge, [Eng.] ; New York : Cambridge University Press, 1976. p. cm. (African studies series ; 18) Includes index. Bibliography: p. [BP188.8.A44M37] 75-35451 ISBN 0-521-21062-3 : 24.00
1. Sufism—Africa—History. 2. Africa—History—19th century. I. Title. II. Series.

MUHAIYADDEEN, Sheikh 297'.4
Muhammad.
The guidebook to the true secret of the heart / M. R. Bawa Muhaiyaddeen. Philadelphia : Bawa Muhaiyaddeen Fellowship, c1976- v. : ill. ; 21 cm. [BP189.3.M82] 75-44557 ISBN 0-914390-07-4 pbk. : 3.95 (v. 1)
1. Sufism. I. Title.

NASR, Seyyed Hossein. 297'.4
Sufi essays. Albany, State University of New York Press [1973, c1972] 184 p. 23 cm. Includes bibliographical references. [BP189.N38 1973] 72-11566 ISBN 0-87395-233-2 8.95
1. Sufism—Addresses, essays, lectures. I. Title.

NASR, Seyyed Hossein. 297'.4
Sufi essays / by Seyyed Hossein Nasr. New York : Schocken Books, 1977, c1972. 184 p. ; 21 cm. Reprint of the ed. published by G. Allen and Unwin, London. Includes bibliographical references and index. [BP189.N38 1977] 76-39629 pbk. : 3.75
1. Sufism—Addresses, essays, lectures. I. Title.

*NICHOLSON, Reynold A. 297.4
The mystics of Islam. London, Routledge & Kegan Paul [Chester Springs, Pa., Dufour, 1965] vi, 178p. 20cm. Bibl. 3.50 bds.,
I. Title.

NICHOLSON, Reynold 297'.4
Alleyne, 1868-1945.
The mystics of Islam / by Reynold A. Nicholson. New York : Schocken Books, 1975. 178 p. ; 21 cm. Reprint of the 1963 ed. published by Routledge & Kegan Paul, London, of a work first published in 1914. Includes index. Bibliography: p. 169-171. [BP189.N49 1975] 75-10713 ISBN 0-8052-0492-X pbk. : 2.45
1. Sufism. I. Title.

NICHOLSON, Reynold 297'.4
Alleyne, 1868-1945.
The mystics of Islam / by Reynold Alleyne Nicholson. London ; Boston : Routledge and K. Paul, 1975. vii, 178 p. ; 19 cm. Reprint of the 1914 ed. published by G. Bell, London. Includes index. Bibliography: p. 169-171. [BP189.N49 1975b] 75-327476 ISBN 0-7100-1892-4. ISBN 0-7100-8015-8 pbk. : £1.00
1. Bibliography: p. 169-171. 2. Sufism. I. Title.

NICHOLSON, Reynold Alleyne, 297.4
1868-1945
Studies in Islamic mysticism, by Reynold Alleyne Nicholson . . . Cambridge [Eng.] Univ. Pr., 1921. Reprinted 1967. xii p., 1 l., 282p. 24cm. [BP189.N5] 23-5382 8.50
1. Abu Sa'id ebn Abi al-Kheyr, 987-1049-1235. 2. al-JIIL, 'Abd al-Karim ibn Ibrahim, b. 1365 or 6. 3. Ibn al-Farid, 'Umar ibn 'Ali, 1181 or 2. 4. Sufism. I. Title. II. Title: Islamic mysticism.
Available from Cambridge Univ. Pr., N.Y.

RAJANEESH, Acharya, 1931- 297.4
Until you die : discourses on the Sufi way / given by Rajneesh ; compilation, Swami Amrit Pathik ; editing, Ma Yoga Anurag. Poona : Rajneesh Foundation, c1976. ix, 261 p., [1] leaf of plates : ports. ; 22 cm. [BP189.62.R34] 77-900984 Rs75.00
1. Sufism—Addresses, essays, lectures. I. Title.

RICE, Cyprian 297.4
The Persian Sufis. London, G. Allen & Unwin [dist. New York, Hillary, c.1964] 104). 19cm. [BP189.R5] 65-273 3.00 bds.,
1. Sufism. 2. Mystcism—Iran. I. Title.

SCHIMMEL, Annemarie. 297'.4
Mystical dimensions of Islam. Chapel Hill, University of North Carolina Press [1975] xxi, 506 p. illus. 25 cm. Bibliography: p. 437-467. [BP189.2.S34] 73-16112 ISBN 0-8078-1223-4 : 14.95
1. Sufism. I. Title.

SHAH, Idries, Sayed, 1924- 297'.4
The way of the Sufi. New York, Dutton, 1969 [c1968] 287 p. 22 cm. Bibliography: p. 36-48. [BP189.S388 1969] 71-92615 6.95
1. Sufism. I. Title.

SHAH, Ikbal Ali, sirdar. 297'.4
Islamic sufism. New York, S. Weiser, 1971. 299 p. 21 cm. Reprint of the 1933 ed. [BP189.S3883] 70-166410 ISBN 0-87728-161-0 2.50
1. Sufism. I. Title.

SHARDA, Sadhu Ram, 1927- 297'.4
Sufi thought: its development in Panjab and its impact on Panjabi literature, from Baba Farid to 1850 A.D., by S. R. Sharda. With a foreword by Surindar Singh Kohli. [1st ed. New Delhi] Munshiram Manoharlal Publishers [1974] xxiv, 288 p. maps. 23 cm. Bibliography: p. [270]-279. [BP188.8.I42P867] 74-900478
1. Sufism—Punjab. 2. Panjabi poetry—History and criticism. I. Title.
Distributed by South Asia Books, 11.50.

SMITH, Margaret, 1884- 297'.4
Readings from the mystics of Islam; translations from the Arabic and Persian, together with a short account of the history and doctrines of Sufism and brief biographical notes on each Sufi writer. London, Luzac & Co., 1972. v, 144 p. 19 cm. Includes bibliographical references. [BP189.23.S64 1972] 73-169376 ISBN 0-7189-0162-2
1. Sufism. I. Title.
Distributed by Rowman & Littlefield, 8.50; pbk. 3.25.

SMITH, Margaret, 1884- 297'.4
The way of the mystics : the early Christian mystics and the rise of the Sufis / Margaret Smith. London : Sheldon Press, 1976. xii, 276 p. ; 22 cm. Reprint of the 1931 ed. published under title: Studies in early mysticism in the Near and Middle East. Includes index. Bibliography: p. 258-263. [BV5075.S6 1976] 76-381586 ISBN 0-85969-072-5 : £2.95
1. Mysticism—History. 2. Sufism. 3. Christianity and other religions—Islam. 4. Islam—Relations—Christianity. I. Title.

SPIRITUAL body and 297'.4
celestial Earth : from Mazdean Iran to Shi'ite Iran / [edited by] Henry Corbin ; translated from the French by Nancy Pearson. Princeton, N.J. : Princeton University Press, c1977. xviii, 351 p., [1] leaf of plates : ill. ; 25 cm. (Bollingen series ; XCI, 2) Translation of Terre celeste et corps de resurrection. Includes index. Bibliography: p. 333-341. [BP188.8.I55T4713] 76-45919 ISBN 0-691-09937-5 : 14.50
1. Sufism—Iran. I. Corbin, Henry. II. Series.

STODDART, William. 297'.4
Sufism : the mystical doctrines and methods of Islam / by William Stoddart ; with a foreword by R. W. J. Austin. Wellingborough : Thorsons, 1976. 91 p. : ill., facsim. ; 23 cm. Includes index. Bibliography: p. 85-86. [BP189.S74] 76-368448 ISBN 0-7225-0305-9 : £3.25
1. Sufism. I. Title.

SUBHAN, John A. 297.4
Sufism, its saints and shrines; an introduction to the study of Sufism with special reference to India, by John A. Subhan. New York, S. Weiser, 1970. viii, 412 p. illus. 21 cm. [BP188.8.I4S9 1970] 73-142499 ISBN 0-87728-039-8 8.50
1. Sufism—India. I. Title.

SUFI studies: East and 297'.4
West; a symposium in honor of Idries Shah's services to Sufi studies by twenty-four contributors marking the 700th anniversary of the death of Jalaluddin Rumi (A.D. 1207-1273) Edited by L. F. Rushbrook Williams. [1st ed.] New York, Dutton [1973] xxxvi, 260 p. 22 cm. Includes bibliographical references. [BP80.S483S9] 73-178387 ISBN 0-525-21195-0 10.00
1. Shah, Idries, Sayed, 1924- —Addresses, essays, lectures. 2. Sufism—Addresses, essays, lectures. I. Shah, Idries, Sayed, 1924- II. Jalal al-Din Rumi, Mawlana, 1207-1273. III. Williams, Laurence Frederic Rushbrook, 1890-ed.

AL-SUHRAWARDI, 'Abd al- 297'.4
Qahir ibn 'abd Allah, 1097-1168.
A Sufi rule for novices = Kitab adab al-muridin of Abu al-Najib al-Suhrawardi / an abridged translation and introd. by Menahem Milson. Cambridge, Mass. : Harvard University Press, 1975. vi, 93 p. ; 22 cm. (Harvard Middle Eastern studies ; 17) Bibliography: p. 85-88. [BP189.6.S8713] 74-27750 ISBN 0-674-85400-4 : 8.95 ISBN 0-674-85403-9 pbk. : 1.95
1. Sufism—Early works to 1800. I. Milson, Menahem. II. Title. III. Series.

TRIMINGHAM, John Spencer. 297.4
The Sufi orders in Islam, by J. Spencer Trimingham. London, Oxford Univ. Pr. [1973, c.1971] viii, 333 p. geneal. tables. 20 cm. index. (Galaxy Book, GB390) Bibl: p. [282]-299. [BP189.T7] 77-582531 ISBN 0-19-501662-9 pap., 2.95
1. Sufism. I. Title.
Available from the publisher's New York office.

THE Wisdom of the Sufis 297'.4
/ compiled by Kenneth Cragg. New York : New Directions, c1976. 94 p. ; 21 cm. [BP189.62.W57] 76-7032 ISBN 0-8112-0626-2 : 7.00 ISBN 0-8112-0627-0 pbk. :
1. Sufism—Quotations. I. Cragg, Kenneth.

THE Wisdon of the Sufis 297'.4'08
/ compiled by Kenneth Cragg. London : Sheldon Press, 1976. vii, 94 p. ; 20 cm. Includes bibliographical references. [BP189.62.W57 1976b] 77-364798 ISBN 0-85969-080-6 : £1.50
1. Sufism—Quotations. I. Cragg, Kenneth.

AFLAKI, Shams al- 297'.4'0922 B
Din Ahmad, d.1360.
Legends of the Sufis : selected anecdotes from the work entitled The acts of the adepts (Menaqibu 'l'arifin) / by Shemsu-'d-din Ahmed, El Eflaki ; translated by James W. Redhouse ; preface by Idries Shah. 3d ed., rev. London ; Wheaton, Ill. : Theosophical Pub. House, 1976. xii, 125 p., [1] leaf of plates : port. ; 23 cm. [BP189.7.M42A2313 1976] 77-366161 £3.25
1. Mevlevi—Biography. I. Redhouse, James William, Sir, 1811-1892. II. Title.

SCHIMMEL, 297.4'092'2 B
Annemarie.
Pain and grace : a study of two mystical writers of eighteenth-century Muslim India / by Annemarie Schimmel. Leiden : E. J. Brill, 1976. xiv, 310 p. ; 25 cm. (Studies in the

history of religions, supplements to Numen ; 36) Includes indexes. Bibliography: p. [291]-296. [BP80.K54S34] 77-351051 ISBN 9-00-404771-9
1. Khvajah Mir, 1719?-1785?—Religion and ethics. 2. 'Abd al-Latif, Shah, ca. 1689-ca. 1752—Religion and ethics. 3. Sufism—India—Biography. I. Title. II. Series.

BREWSTER, David Pearson, 1930- 297'.4'0924 B
Al Hallaj : Muslim mystic and martyr : translated extracts with a short biography and bibliography / D. P. Brewster Christchurch : University of Canterbury, Dept. of Philosophy and Religious Studies, 1976. 51 p. ; 21 cm. (Occasional papers in religious studies) Includes bibliographical references. [BP80.H27B73] 77-366228
1. al-Hallaj, al-Husayn ibn Mansur, 858 or 9-922. 2. Sufism—Biography. I. Title. II. Series.

FEILD, Reshad. 297'.4'0924 B
The last barrier / Reshad Feild ; illustrated by Salik Chalom. 1st ed. New York : Harper & Row, c1976. 183 p. : ill. ; 21 cm. [BP189.6.F44 1976] 75-9345 ISBN 0-06-062585-6 : 8.95
1. Feild, Reshad. 2. Sufism. I. Title.

FEILD, Reshad. 297'.4'0924 B
The last barrier / Reshad Feild ; illustrated by Salik Chalom. London : Turnstone Books, 1976. [7], 183 p. : ill. ; 20 cm. [BP189.6.F44 1976b] 77-362800 ISBN 0-85500-063-5 : £2.95
1. Feild, Reshad. 2. Sufism. 3. Sufism—Biography. I. Title.

FRIEDLANDER, Ira. 297'.4'0924 B
The whirling dervishes : being an account of the Sufi order, known as the Mevlevis, and its founder, the poet and mystic, Mevlana Jalalu'ddin Rumi / by Ira Friedlander ; music section by Nezih Uzel. New York : Macmillan, 1975. 159 p. : ill. ; 28 cm. Bibliography: p. 158-159. [BP189.7.M42F74] 74-30416 ISBN 0-02-541540-9 : 15.00
1. Jalal al-Din Rumi, Mawlana, 1207-1273. 2. Mevlevi. I. Title.

LINGS, Martin. 297'.4'0924 B
A Sufi saint of the twentieth century: Shaikh Ahmad al-'Alawi; his spiritual heritage and legacy. 2d ed. rev. and enl. Berkeley, University of California Press [1971] 242 p. illus. 23 cm. First ed. published in 1961 under title: A Moslem saint of the twentieth century. Includes bibliographical references. [BP80.A54L5 1971b] 71-182282 ISBN 0-520-02174-6 8.75
1. al-'Alawi, Ahmad ibn Mustafa, 1869-1934. I. Title.

*LINGS, Martin. 297.4'0924 [B]
A Sufi saint of the twentieth century: Shaikh Ahmad al-'Alawi; his spiritual heritage and legacy. 2d ed. rev. and enl. Berkeley, University of California Press [1973, c.1971] 242 p. geneal. port. 21 cm. First published in 1961 by Macmillan under title: A Moslem saint of the twentieth century. Bibliography: p. 230-231. [BP80.A54L5] ISBN 0-520-02486-9 2.95 (pbk)
1. al-Alawi, Ahmad ibn Mustafa, 1869-1934. I. Title.
L.C. card no. for the Allen & Unwin (London) ed.: 77-882819.

SMITH, Margaret, 1884- 297'.4'0924 B
An early mystic of Baghdad; a study of the life and teaching of Harith b. Asad al-Muhasibi, A.D. 781-A.D. 857. London, Sheldon Press. [New York, AMS Press, 1973] xi, 311 p. 23 cm. Reprint of the 1935 ed. Bibliography: p. 292-297. [BP80.M83S6 1973] 76-180379 ISBN 0-404-56324-4 16.50
1. al-Muhasibi, al-Harithibn Asad, d. 857 or 8. I. Title.

STOLK, Sirkar van, 1894-1963. 297'.4'0924 B
Memories of a Sufi sage, Hazrat Inayat Khan / by Sirkar van Stolk, with Daphne Dunlop. 2d ed. The Hague : East-West Publications Fonds, c1975. 208 p. : ill. ; 21 cm. "List of books by Hazrat Inayat Khan": p. 206-208. [BP80.I55S8 1975] 75-328485 ISBN 0-8476-1052-7 7.25
1. Inayat Khan, 1882-1926. 2. Stolk, Sirkar van, 1894-1963. 3. Sufism. I. Dunlop, Daphne, joint author. II. Title.
Distributed by Rowman & Littlefield.

KHAN, Naseer Ahmad. 297'.4'3
Muslim basic prayer book : Namaz, illustrated and romanized / Naseer Ahmad Khan. Lahore : Islamic Book Centre, [1976] 147 p., [14] leaves of plates : ill. ; 18 cm. [BP184.3.K49] 77-930094 Rs7.50 ($0.80 U.S.)
1. Prayer (Islam) I. Title.

NIYAZI, Kausar. 297'.4'4
Islam, our guide / Kausar Niazi ; [translated by Mohammad Mazharuddin Siddiqi]. 1st ed. Lahore : Sh. Muhammad Ashraf, 1976. xi, 221 p. ; 21 cm. Translation of Islam hamara rahnuma hai. [BP188.N5313] 77-930040 Rs30.00
1. Religious life (Islam) I. Title.

*BLACKER, Carmen. 297.56
The catalpa bow; a study of shamanistic practices in Japan. London, George Allen and Unwin [1975] 376 p. ill. 22 cm. Includes index. Bibliography: p. 350-359. [BL2370.55] ISBN 0-04-398004-X.
1. Shamanism. 2. Japan—Religion. I. Title.
Distributed by Rowman and Littlefield for 18.50.

FARID AL-DIN 'ATTAR, 13thcent. 297.6
Muslim saints and mystics; episodes from the Todhkirat al-auliya' ("Memorial of the saints"). Translated by A. J. Arberry. [Chicago, University of Chicago Press [1966] xii, 287 p. 23 cm. (UNESCO collection of representative works: Persian heritage series) Includes bibliographies. [BP189.4.F323 1966] 65-27758
1. Saints, Muslim. I. Arberry, Arthur John, 1905- tr. II. Title. III. Title: Memorial of the saints. IV. Series.

FARID AL-DIN ATTAR 13thcent. 297.6
Muslim saints and mystics; episodes from the Tadhkirat al-auliya' ('Memorial of the saints'). Tr. [from Arabic] by A. J. Arberry. [Chicago] Univ. of Chic. Pr. [c.1966] xii, 287p. 23cm. (UNESCO collec. of representative works: Persian heritage ser.) Bibl. [BP189.4.F323 1966] 65-27758 6.00
1. Saints, Muslim. I. Arberry, Arthur John, 1905- tr. II. Title. III. Title: Memorial of the saints. IV. Series. V. UNESCO collec. of representative works: Persian heritage ser.

*LAVAN, Spencer. 297.6
The Ahmadiyah movement: a history and perspective. [Delhi], Manohar Book Service, 1974. xii, 220 p. 22 cm. [BP173.7] ISBN 0-88386-455-X
1. Ahmad, Mirza Gulam. 2. Islam and politics—India. 3. Isam—India—History. I. Title.
Distributed by South Asia Books, Columbia, Mo., for 10.00.

NASR, Seyyed Hossein. 297'.6 B
Three Muslim sages : Avicenna, Suhrawardi, Ibn 'Arabi / Seyyed Hossein Nasr. Delmar, N.Y. : Caravan Books, [1975] p. cm. Reprint of the 1969 ed. published by Harvard University Press, Cambridge. Bibliography: p. [BP70.N36 1975] 75-14430 ISBN 0-88206-500-9 pbk. : 5.95
1. Avicenna, 980-1037. 2. al-Suhrawardi, Yahya ibn Habash, 1152 or 3-1191. 3. Ibn al-'Arabi, 1165-1240. I. Title.

ADAMS, Charles Clarence. 297'.61'0924
Islam and modernism in Egypt; a study of the modern reform movement inaugurated by Muhammad @Abduh. New York, Russell & Russell [1968] viii, 283 p. 23 cm. (American University at Cairo. Oriental studies) Reprint of the 1933 ed. First part of the author's thesis, University of Chicago, 1928. Bibliography: p. [269]-274. [BP80.M8A63 1968] 68-25061
1. Muhammad @Abduh, 1849-1905. 2. Islam—20th century. 3. Egypt—Politics and government—1882-1952. I. Title. II. Series.

STEWART, Charles Cameron. 297'.61'0924 B
Islam and social order in Mauritania; a case study from the nineteenth century [by] C. C. Stewart with E. K. Stewart. Oxford, Clarendon Press, 1973. xviii, 204 p. illus. 23 cm. (Oxford studies in African affairs) Revision of author's thesis, Oxford. Bibliography: p. [167]-195. [BP64.M3S73 1973] 73-172818 ISBN 0-19-821688-2
1. al-Shaykh Sidi al-Kabir, Harun ibn Baba, 1775-1868. 2. Islam—Mauritania. I. Stewart, E. K. II. Title. III. Series.
Distributed by Oxford University, New York, 14.50.

AL-WAQIDI, Muhammad ibn 'Umar 747or8-823 297.63
The kitab al-maghazi of al-Waqidi, ed. by Marsden Jones. London, Oxford Univ. Pr., 1966. 3v. (46, xiii, 1321p.) 8 plates. 25cm. Includes bibls., and a pref. and bibl. in English. Text in Arabic [BP75.W3] NE67 20.20 set.,
1. Muhammad the prophet—Campaigns. I. Jones, Marsden, ed. II. Title.

ANDRa, Tor, Bp., 1885-1947. 297'.63 B
Mohammed; the man and his faith. Translated by Theophil Menzel. Freeport, N.Y., Books for Libraries Press [1971] 274 p. facsim. 23 cm. Reprint of the 1936 ed. Includes bibliographical references. [BP75.A57 1971] 79-160954 ISBN 0-8369-5821-7
1. Muhammad, the prophet.

BODLEY, Ronald Victor Courtenay, 1892- 297'.63 B
The messenger; the life of Mohammed, by R. V. C. Bodley. New York, Greenwood Press [1969, c1946] xiv, 368 p. 23 cm. Bibliography: p. 360. [BP75.B56 1969] 70-92296
1. Muhummad, the prophet. I. Title.

DERMENGHEM, Emile, 1872- 297'.63 B
Muhammad and the Islamic tradition. Translated from the French by Jean M. Watt. Westport, Conn., Greenwood Press [1974, c1958] 191 p. illus. 22 cm. (Men of wisdom, MW6) Reprint of the ed. published by Harper, New York, which was issued as no. MW6 of Men of wisdom. Bibliography: p. 188-191. [BP75.D393 1974] 73-15204 ISBN 0-8371-7163-6
1. Muhammad, the prophet. 2. Islam. I. Title. II. Series.

DERMENGHEM, Emile, 1872- 297'.63 B
Muhammad and the Islamic tradition. Translated from the French by Jean M. Watt. Westport, Conn., Greenwood Press [1974, c1958] 191 p. illus. 22 cm. (Men of wisdom, MW6) Reprint of the ed. published by Harper, New York, which was issued as no. MW6 of Men of wisdom. Bibliography: p. 188-191. [BP75.D393 1974] 73-15204 ISBN 0-8371-7163-6 12.25
1. Muhammad, the prophet. 2. Islam. I. Title. II. Series.

GLUBB, John Bagot, Sir, 1897- 297.63 B
The life and times of Muhammad, by John Bagot Glubb (Glubb Pasha). New York, Stein and Day [1970] 416 p. geneal. tables, maps. 25 cm. Bibliography: p. [403]-405. [BP75.G58] 74-87954 10.00
1. Muhammad, the prophet. I. Title.

HUSAIN, Athar, 1920- 297.63
Prophet Muhammad and his mission. Bombay, New York, Asia Pub. [1967] xi. 214p. 23cm. Bibl. [BP75.H8] SA 67 5.25
1. Muhammad, the prophet. I. Title.
Distributed by Taplinger.

IRVING, Washington, 1783-1859. 297'.63 B
Mahomet and his successors. New York, Putnam. [New York, AMS Press, 1973] 2 v. illus. 19 cm. (The works of Washington Irving, v. 15-16) At head of title: Hudson edition. Reprint of the 1889 ed. [DS38.3.176 1973] 73-8685 20.00 ea.
1. Muhammad, the prophet. 2. Islamic Empire—History. I. Title.

IRVING, Washington, 1783-1859. 297'.63 B
Mahomet and his successors. Edited by Henry A. Pochmann and E. N. Feltskog. Madison, University of Wisconsin Press, 1970. xiv, 651 p. facsims., map. 24 cm. (The Complete works of Washington Irving) Includes bibliographical references. [DS38.3.176 1970] 77-15207
1. Muhammad, the prophet. 2. Islamic Empire—History. I. Pochmann, Henry August, 1901- ed. II. Feltskog, E. N., ed. III. Title.

KELEN, Betty. 297'.63 B
Muhammad : the messenger of God / by Betty Kelen. 1st ed. Nashville: T. Nelson, [1975] 278 p. ; 21 cm. Includes index. Bibliography: p. 261. [BP75.K43] 75-5792 ISBN 0-8407-6440-5 : 6.95
1. Muhammad, the prophet—Juvenile literature.

*KELEN, Betty. 297'.63
Muhammad : the messenger of God / by Betty Kelen. New York : Pocket Books, 1977. x,277p. ; 18 cm. (A Kangaroo Book) Includes index. [BP75. 3] ISBN 0-671-81233-5 pbk. : 1.95
1. Mohammad, the prophet-Juvenile literature. I. Title.
L.C. card no. for 1975 Thomas Nelson ed.:75-5792.

*KELEN, Betty. 297'.63
Muhammad : the messenger of God / by Betty Kelen. New York : Pocket Books, 1977. x,277p. ; 18 cm. (A Kangaroo Book) Includes index. [BP75. 3] ISBN 0-671-81233-5 pbk. : 1.95
1. Mohammad, the prophet-Juvenile literature. I. Title.
L.C. card no. for 1975 Thomas Nelson ed.:75-5792.

MARGOLIOUTH, David Samuel, 1858-1940. 297'.63 B
Mohammed and the rise of Islam. Freeport, N.Y., Books for Libraries Press [1972] xxvi, 481 p. illus. 23 cm. Reprint of the 1905 ed., issued in series: Heroes of the nations. Bibliography: p. xxiii-xxvi. [BP75.M3 1972] 73-38361 ISBN 0-8369-6778-X
1. Muhammad, the prophet. I. Title. II. Series: Heroes of the nations.

THE Miraculous journey of Mahomet 297'.63
Mahomet : Miraj nameh : Bibliotheque nationale, Paris (Manuscrit supplement Turn 190) / introduction and commentaries by Marie-Rose Seguy ; [translated from the French by Richard Pevear]. New York : G. Braziller, 1977. p. cm. Bibliography: p. [BP166.57.M54] 77-5140 ISBN 0-8076-0868-8 : 40.00; 35.00 pre-xmas
1. Mi'raj. 2. Mi'raj—Illustrations. 3. Illumination of books and manuscripts, Islamic. I. Seguy, Marie Rose. II. Mi'raj namah.

MUIR, William, Sir, 1819-1905. 297'.63 B
The life of Mohammad from original sources / by Sir William Muir. A new and rev. ed. / by T. H. Weir. New York : AMS Press, [1975] p. cm. Reprint of the 1923 ed. published by J. Grant, Edinburgh. [BP75.M8 1975] 78-180366 ISBN 0-404-56306-6 : 57.50
1. Mohammad, the prophet. I. Weir, Thomas Hunter, d. 1928, ed. II. Title.

PIKE, Edgar Royston, 1896- 297'.63 B
Mohammed; prophet of the religion of Islam [by] E. Royston Pike. New York, F. A. Praeger [1969, c1965] viii, 117 p. illus. 23 cm. (Praeger pathfinder biographies) 1962 and 1964 editions published under title: Mohammed, founder of the religion of Islam. Bibliography: p. 113-114. A biography of the founder of Islam who is revered by his followers as the first prophet of Allah. Includes chapters of the Koran, what a Muslim believes, and how he practices his faith. [BP75.P5 1969] 92 68-55017
1. Muhammad, the prophet—Juvenile literature. I. Title.

RODINSON, Maxime. 297'.63 B
Mohammed. Translated by Anne Carter. [1st American ed.] New York, Pantheon Books [1971] xix, 360 p. illus. 22 cm. Bibliography: p. 315-324. [BP75.R5713 1971] 69-20189 ISBN 0-394-47110-5 8.95
1. Muhammad, the prophet.

RODINSON, Maxime. 297'.63 B
Mohammed. Translated by Anne Carter. New York, Vintage Books [1974, c1971] xix, 360 p. maps. 19 cm. Bibliography: p. 343-[346] [BP75.13.R613 1974] 73-14953 ISBN 0-394-71011-8 2.45 (pbk.)
1. Muhammad, the prophet.

SUGANA, Gabriele Mandel. 297'.63
The life and times of Mohammed; translator [from the Italian] Francis Koval. London, New York, Hamlyn, 1968. [1], 77 p. (chiefly illus. (chiefly col.) col. maps) 30 cm. (Portraits of greatness) German translation has title: Mohammed und seine zeit. Col. illus. on lining papers. [BP75.S9 1968] 70-433824 ISBN 0-600-03149-7 17/6
1. Muhammed, the prophet. I. Title.

WATT, William Montgomery. 297'.63 B
Muhammad: prophet and statesman [by] W. Montgomery Watt. London, New York, Oxford University Press [1974, c1961] 250 p. 21 cm. (A Galaxy book, 409) "Essentially an abridgement of the ... [author's] Muhammad at Mecca and Muhammad at Medina." Includes bibliographical references. [BP75.W33 1974] 74-163338 ISBN 0-19-881078-4 2.95 (pbk.)
1. Muhammad, the prophet.

HOSAIN, Safdar. 297'.63'0924
Who was Mohammed. [Hyderabad, India, 1967] 122 p. 22 cm. Rs 3 [BP75.H67] S A
1. Muhammad, the prophet. I. Title.

FEROZE, Muhammad Rashid. 297'.64 B
Abu Bakr : the first caliph / adapted from Arabic by Muhammad Rashid Feroze. Leicester : Islamic Foundation, 1976. 44 p. : ill., col. maps ; 21 cm. (Glimpses of Islamic history) "Based upon Sabir Abduh Ibrahim's book Abu Bakr." [DS38.4.A28F47] 77-356902 ISBN 0-9503954-4-7 : £0.50
1. Abu Bakr, Caliph, d. 634. 2. Caliphs—Biography. I. Ibrahim, Sabir'Abduh. Abu Bakr.

ABBOTT, Nabia, 1897- 297'.64'0924 B
Aishah, the beloved of Mohammed. New York, Arno Press, 1973 [c1942] xiii, 230 p. illus. 21 cm. (The Middle East collection) Reprint of the ed. published by the University of Chicago Press, Chicago. Includes bibliographical references. [BP80.A52A62 1973] 73-6264 ISBN 0-405-05318-5 15.00
1. 'A'ishah, 614 (ca.)-678. I. Title. II. Series.

NIZAMI, Khaliq Ahmad. 297'.64'0924
The life and times of Shaikh Farid-ud-Din Gang-i-Shakar / by Khaliq Ahmad Nizami ; with a foreword by Sir Hamilton Gibb. 1st Pakistani ed. Lahore : Universal Books, 1976. x, 144 p. ; 24 cm. Reprint of the 1955 ed. published from Aligarh, India. Includes index. Running title: Life of Shaikh Farid-'ud-din Ganj-i Shakar. Bibliography: p. [125]-132. [BP80.F3N5 1976] 77-930059 Rs45.00
1. Farid-uddin, Shaikh, called Ganj-i Shakar, 1175?-1265. 2. Sufism—Biography. I. Title. II. Title: Life of Shaikh Farid-'ud-din Ganj-i Shakar.

CRAPANZANO, Vincent, 1939- 297'.65
The Hamadsha; a study in Moroccan ethnopsychiatry. Berkeley, University of California Press [1973] xiv, 258 p. illus. 24 cm. Bibliography: p. [241]-248. [BP189.7.H342C72] 72-75529 ISBN 0-520-02241-6 12.00
1. Hamadsha.

NIYAZI, Kausar. 297'.65
Role of the mosque / Kausar Niazi. 1st ed. Lahore : Sh. Muhammad Ashraf, 1976. 40 p. ; 22 cm. Includes quotations from the Koran and Hadith. Paper read at the conference organized by the Rabitat al-'Alam al-Islami at Mecca, 1974. Bibliography: p. 39-40. [BP187.6.A1N59] 76-938560 Rs4.00
1. Mosques—Addresses, essays, lectures. I. Title.

UNION of Muslim Organisations of United Kingdom and Eire. 297.7
Guidelines and syllabus on Islamic education / [Union of Muslim Organisations of United Kingdom and Ireland]. London : The Union, 1976. 28 p. ; 22 cm. [BP44.U54 1976] 76-372771 ISBN 0-9504335-1-9
1. Religious education of children, Islamic. I. Title.

'ABD ul-Baha ibn Baha Ullah, 1844-1921. 297.8*
Some answered questions, collected and translated from the Persian of 'Abdu'l-Baha, by Laura Clifford Barney. [7th ed.] Wilmette, Ill., Baha'i Pub. Committee [1954] 350 p. 22 cm. [BP360.A38 1954] 53-10766
1. Bahaism. I. Barney, Laura Clifford, tr. II. Title.

'ABDUL-BAHA IBN BAHA ULLAH, 1844-1921. 297.8
The secret of divine civilization. Translated from the original Persian text by Marzieh Gail. [1st ed.] Wilmette, Ill., Baha i Pub. Trust [1957] xi, 116p. 22cm. [BP360.A212] 56-12427
1. Bahaism. 2. Civilization. I. Title.

ABUN-NASR, Jamil M. 297.8
The Tijaniyya, a Sufi order in the modern world. New York, Oxford [c.]1965. 204p. facsims., map. 22cm. (Middle Eastern monographs, 7) Bibl. [BP189.7.T.5A3] 65-9539 5.60
1. al-Tijaniyah. I. Title.

ABUN-NASR, Jamil M 297.8
The Tijaniyya, a Sufi order in the modern world [by] Jamil M. Abun-Nasr. London, New York, Oxford University Press. 1965. 204 p. facsims., map. 22 cm. (Middle Eastern monographs, 7) Revision of thesis, Oxford University. Bibliography: p. [191]-198. [BP189.7.T5A3 1965] 65-9539
1. al-Tijaniyah. I. Title.

BAHA Ullah, 1817-1892. 297.8
Bahai world faith; selected writings Baha'u'llah and 'Abdu'l-Baha. [2d ed.] Wilmette, Ill., Baha'i Pub. Trust [1956] 465 p. 21 cm. "Approved by the Reviewing Committee of the National Spiritual Assembly." [BP360.B135 1956] 56-8259
1. Bahaism. I. 'Abd ul-Baha ibn Baha Ullah, 1844-1921.

BAHA Ullah, 1817-1892. 297.8*
Blessed is the spot, from the Baha' i sacred writings. Illustrated by Anna Stevenson. Wilmette, Ill., Baha'i Pub. Trust, c1958. [32] p. illus. 23 cm. [BP360.B18] 58-8815
1. Bahaism—Juvenile literature. I. Title.

BAHA ULLAH, 1817-1892. 297.8
Baha i world faith; selected writings of Baha'u'llah and 'Abdu'l-Baha. [2d ed.] Wilmette, Ill., Baha'i Pub. Trust [1956] 465p. 21cm. 'Approved by the Reviewing Committee of the National Spiritual Assembly.' [BP360.B135 1956] 56-8259
1. Bahaism. I. 'Abd ul-Baha ibn Baha Ullah, 1844-1921. II. Title.

BAHA ULLAH, 1817-1892 297.8
Baha'i prayers for children; a selection of the prayers revealed by Baha Baha'u'llah, the Bab, and Abdu l-Baha. Wilmette, Ill., Baha i Pub. Trust, 1962 [c. 1956] 53p. col. illus. 21cm. 55-13990 1.25
1. Bahaism—Prayer-books and devotions—English. I. 'Ali Muhammand, Shirazi, called ul-Bab, 1821-1850. II. Abd ul-Baha ibn Baha Ullah, 1844-1921. III. Title.

BAHA ULLAH, 1817-1892. 297.8
The hidden words of Baha'u'llah. Translated by Shoghi effendi with the assistance of some English friends. [Rev. ed.] Wilmette, Ill., Bahai Pub. Committee [1954] 52p. 18cm. [BP360.B284 1954] 54-7328
1. Bahaism. I. Title.

BAHA ULLAH, 1817-1892. 297.8
The seven valleys, and The four valleys. Translated by Ali-Kuli Khan (Nabifu'd-Dawlih) assisted by Marzieh Gail. [Rev. ed.] Wilmette, Ill., Baha'i Pub. Committee [1954, c1952] 62p. 18cm. [BP360.B29 1954] 53-12275
1. Bahaism. I. Title. II. Title: The four valleys.

BOWES, Eric. 297.8
Great themes of life. [1st ed.] Wilmette, Ill., Bahai Pub. Trust, 1958. 83p. illus. 19cm. [BP365.B65] 58-8698
1. Bahaism. I. Title.

FEDERSPIEL, Howard M. 297'.8
Persatuan Islam; Islamic reform in twentieth century Indonesia, by Howard M. Federspiel. Ithaca, N.Y., Modern Indonesia Project, Cornell University, 1970. vii, 247 p. 28 cm. (Cornell University. Modern Indonesia Project. Monograph series) Bibliography: p. 213-247. [BP10.P48F4] 72-632241 7.50
1. Persatuan Islam. 2. Islam—Indonesia. I. Title. II. Series.

FISHER, Humphrey J. 297.8
Ahmadiyyah; a study in contemporary Islam on the West African coast. New York, Oxford. Pub. for the Nigerian Inst. of Soc. & Econ. Res. [c.]1963. 206p. 23cm. Bibl. 63-3811 5.60
1. Mohammedanism—Africa, West. 2. Ahmadiyya. I. Title.

FISHER, Humphrey J 297.8
Ahmadiyyah: a study in contemporary Islam on the West African coast. [London] Published for the Nigerian Institute of Social and Economic Research [by] Oxford University Press, 1963. 206 p. 23 cm. [BP64.A4W25] 63-3811
1. Mohammedanism — Africa, West. 2. Ahmadiyya. I. Title.

HAMID, Abdul, 1913- 297'.8
Islam and Christianity. New York, Carlton [c1967] 232p. 21cm. (Hearthstone bk) [BP195.A5H3] 68-2403 3.75
1. Ahmadiyya. 2. Jesus Christ—Islamic interpretations. I. Title.

JEFFERY, Arthur, ed. 297.8
A reader on Islam; passages from standard Arabic writings illustrative of the beliefs and practices of Muslims. 's-Gravenhage. Moutoon [dist. New York, Humanities, c.]1962. 678p. 25cm. (Columbia Univ. Pubns. in Near and Middle East studies, ser. A, 2) Bibl. 62-52447 12.50
1. Mohammedan literature. 2. Arabic literature—Translations into English. 3. English literature—Translations from Arabic. I. Title.

JEFFERY, Arthur, ed. 297.8
A reader on Islam; passages from standard Arabic writings illustrative of the beliefs and practices of Muslims. 's-Gravenhage, Mouton, 1962. 678p. 25cm. (Columbia University. Publications in Near and Middle East studies, ser. A, 2) Imprint covered by label: New York, Humanities Press. Bibliography: p. [674]-678. Bibliographical footnotes. [BP20.J4] 62-52447
1. Mohammedan literature. 2. Arabic literature—Translations into English. 3. English literature—Translations from Arabic. I. Title.

KABA, Lansine. 297'.8
The Wahhabiyya; Islamic reform and politics in French West Africa. Evanston, Ill., Northwestern University Press, 1974. xv, 285 p. map. 24 cm. (Studies in African religion) Bibliography: p. 271-285. [BP64.A4W357] 73-85874 ISBN 0-8101-0427-X
1. Wahhabiyah—Africa, French-speaking West. I. Title. II. Series.

KABA, Lansine. 297'.8
The Wahhabiyya; Islamic reform and politics in French West Africa. Evanston, Ill., Northwestern University Press, 1974. xv, 285 p. map. 24 cm. (Studies in African religion) Bibliography: p. 271-285. [BP64.A4W357] 73-85874 ISBN 0-8101-0427-X 13.50
1. Wahhabiyah—Africa, French-speaking West. I. Title. II. Series.

LOMAX, Louis E., 1922- 297.8
When the word is given; a report on Elijah Muhammad, Malcolm X, and the Black Muslim world. [New York] New American Library [1964, c1963] 192 p. illus., ports. 18 cm. (A Signet book, P2429) "Suggested additional reading": p. 181. [BP222.L6 1964] 64-1332
1. Black Muslims. I. Title.

MEYER, Zoe. 297.8
Children's stories from The dawn-breakers. With illus. by Carl Scheffler. Wilmette, Ill., Baha'i Pub. Trust [1955] 66p. illus. 29cm. [BP330.M4] 56-21319
1. Bahaism. 2. Babism. I. Nabll-i-A sam, 1831-1892 Thedawn-breakers. II. Title.

SHOGHI, effendi 297.8
The world order of Baha'u'llah [rev. ed., reissue] Wilmette, Ill., Baha' i Pub. Trust, 110 Linden Ave. [1965, c.1938, 1955] 234p. 24cm. [BP392.S4] 56-17685 3.00; 1.50 pap.,
1. Baha Ullah, 1817-1892. 2. Bahaism. I. Title.

TOWNSHEND, George, 1876- 297.8
The heart of the Gospel; or, The Bible and the Baha'i faith. [Rev. and completely reset] Oxford, G. Ronald [1951] 164p. 20cm. [BP370.T6 1951] 52-25585
1. Bible— Criticism, interpretation, etc. 2. Bahaism. I. Title.

TOWNSHEND, George, 1876- 297.8
The mission of Baha' U'llah, and other literary pieces. Oxford, G. Ronald [1952] 154p. 21cm. [BP375.T65 1952] 53-18030
1. Baha Ullah, 1817-1892. 2. Bahaism—Addresses, essays, lectures. I. Title.

HOLLISTER, John Norman 297.82
The Shi'a of India. London, Luzac [dist. Mystic, Conn., Verry, 1965] xiv, 440p. illus. 25cm. (Luzac's oriental religious ser. v.8) Bibl. [BP195.S5H6] 54-32595 12.50
1. Shiites. 2. Mohammedans in India. I. Title. II. Series.

AL-TABATABA'I, Muhammad Husayn, 1903or4 297'.82
Shi'ite Islam, by 'Allamah Sayyid Muhammad Husayn Tabataba'i. Translated from the Persian and edited with an introd. and notes by Seyyed Hossein Nasr. [1st ed.] Albany, State University of New York Press, 1975. xiv, 253 p. 24 cm. (Persian studies series, no. 5) Translation of Shi'ah dar Islam. Bibliography: p. 239-244. [BP193.5.T3213] 74-8289 ISBN 0-87395-272-3
1. Shiites. I. Title.

FRANZIUS, Enno, 1901- 297'.822
History of the order of Assassins. New York, Funk & Wagnalls [1969] xviii, 261 p. illus., col. maps (on lining papers), ports. 22 cm. Bibliography: p. 233-244. [BP195.A8F7] 69-19652 6.95
1. Assassins (Ismailites) I. Title.

LEWIS, Bernard. 297'.822
The assassins: a radical sect in Islam. New York, Basic Books [1968] 166 p. maps, plates (incl. facsims.) 22 cm. Bibliographical references included in "Notes" (p. [141]-160) [BP195.A8L4 1968] 68-10967
1. Assassins (Ismailites) I. Title.

LEWIS, Bernard. 297'.822
The origins of Isma'ilism; a study of the historical background of the Fatimid caliphate. Cambridge, W. Heffer. [New York, AMS Press, 1974, i.e.1975] p. cm. Reprint of the 1940 ed. which was a revision of the author's thesis, University of London. Bibliography: p. [BP195.I8L4 1974] 74-180357 ISBN 0-404-56289-2 10.00
1. Ismailites. 2. Fatimites. I. Title.

FRISCHAUER, Willi, 1906- 297'.822'0922 B
The Aga Khans. New York, Hawthorn Books [1971] vii, 342 p. illus., ports. 22 cm. Bibliography: p. 328-330. [BP195.I82A237 1971] 74-130721 8.95
1. Karim, Aga Khan, 1936- 2. Ismailites. I. Title.

MAKARIM, Sami Nasib. 297'.85'09
The Druze faith, by Sami Nasib Makarem. Delmar, N.Y., Caravan Books, 1974. xi, 153 p. 23 cm. Bibliography: p. 140-145. [BL1695.M33] 73-19819 ISBN 0-88206-003-1 10.00
1. Druses. I. Title.

LITTLE, Malcolm, 1925-1965. 297'.87
The end of white world supremacy; four speeches. Edited and with an introd. by Benjamin Goodman. New York, Merlin House; distributed by Monthly Review Press [1971] 148 p. 22 cm. [E185.61.L578] 72-147878 6.00
1. Negroes—Civil rights—Addresses, essays, lectures. 2. Negroes—History—Addresses, essays, lectures. 3. Black Muslims—Addresses, essays, lectures. I. Title.

MUHAMMADIA, Bi'sana Ta'laha El'shabazziz Sula. 297'.87
Spiritual government / by Bi'sana Ta'laha El'shabazziz Sula Muhammadia and Master Tu'biz Jihadia Muhammadia. Detroit : Harlo, c1974. 157 p. ; 23 cm. (The Holy book of life ; v. 2) At head of title: In the name of Almighty Ga'lah. [BP222.M83] 75-313213
1. Black Muslims. I. Muhammadia, Tu'biz Jihadia, joint author. II. Title. III. Series.

POOLE, Elijah. 297.87
Message to the blackman in America, by Elijah Muhammad. Chicago, Muhammad Mosque of Islam No. 2 [1965] xxvii, 355 p. 22 cm. [BP222.P6] 65-9666
1. Black Muslims—Doctrinal and controversial works. 2. Negroes. I. Title.

[POOLE, Elijah] 297.87
Message to the blackman in American, by Elijah Muhammad. Chicago, Muhammad Mosque of Islam No. 2, 5335 So. Greenwood Ave., [c.1965] xxvii, 355p. 22cm. [BP222.P6] 65-9666 5.00
1. Black Muslims—Doctrinal and controversial works. 2. Negroes. I. Title.

*MCNEIL, Mayo. 297.870'.92
Elijah Muhammad the false prophet. [Denver] [1973] 53 p. 14 cm. [BP223.Z8]
1. Black Mulism—Biography. 2. Black Mulism—History and criticism. I. Title.
Available from author: Box 7212, Denver, Colorado 80207

CUSHMEER, Bernard. 297'.87'0924 B
This is the one: Messenger Elijah Muhammad, we need not look for another. [Phoenix, Truth Publications, 1971] 160 p. col. port. 23 cm. [BP223.Z8E43] 76-24532 3.95
1. Elijah Muhammad, 1897- I. Title.

BALYUZI, H. M. 297'.88'0924 B
The Bab; the herald of the day of days, by H. M. Balyuzi. Oxford [Eng.] G. Ronald [1973] xiv, 255 p. illus. 21 cm. Includes bibliographical references. [BP391.B34] 73-167688 ISBN 0-85398-048-9
1. Bab, 'Ali Muhammad Shirazi, 1820-1850.
Distributed by Bahai Publishing Trust, 415 Linden Ave., Wilmette, Ill. 60091; 5.25.

'ABD ul-Baha ibn Baha Ullah, 1844-1921. 297.89
Some answered questions, collected and translated from the Persian of 'Abdu'l-Baha, by Laura Clifford Barney. Wilmette, Ill., Baha'i Pub. Trust [1964] xxi, 350 p. 23 cm. [BP360.A38 1964] 64-55340
1. Bahaism. I. Barney, Laura Clifford, comp. and tr. II. Title.

'ABD UL-BAHA IBN BAHA ULLAH, 1844-1921. 297.89
Tables of the divine plan, revealed by 'Abdu'l-Baha to the North American Baha' is during 1916 and 1917. [2d ed.] Wilmette, Ill., Baha' i Pub. Trust [1959] 54p. illus. 23cm. [BP360.A392 1959] 60-18502
1. Bahaism. I. Title.

'ABD UL-BAHA IBN BAHA ULLAH, 1844-1921. 297.89
Some answered questions, collected and translated from the Persian of 'Abdu'l-Baha, by Laura Clifford Barney. Wilmette, Ill., Baha'l Pub. Trust [1964] xxi, 350 p. 23 cm. [BP360.A38 1964] 64-55340
1. Bahaism. I. Barney, Laura Clifford, comp. and tr. II. Title.

BAHA Ullah, 1817-1892. 297.89
The reality of man; excerpts from writings of Baha'u'llah and 'Abdu'l-Baha. Wilmette, Ill., Baha'i Pub. Trust [1969] 61 p. [BP360.B2883] 62-52261
1. Bahaism. I. 'Abd ul-Baha ibn Baha Ullah, 1844-1921. II. Title.

BAHA Ullah, 1817-1892. 297'.89
Tokens from the writings of Baha'u'llah. Selected and illustrated by Jay and Constance Conrader. Wilmette, Ill., Baha'i Pub. Trust [1973] 80 p. illus. 29 cm. Page 80 blank. Includes bibliographical references. [BP360.B37 1973] 73-78441 ISBN 0-87743-074-8 12.00
1. Bahaism—Addresses, essays, lectures. I. Conrader, Jay, comp. II. Conrader, Constance Stone, comp. III. Title.

BAHA ULLAH, 1817-1892. 297.89
The reality of man; excerpts from writings of Baha ullh and Aboul-Baha. Wilmette, Ill., Haha Pub. Trust [1962] 61p. 19cm. [BP360.B2883] 62-52261
1. Bahaism. I. Abo ul- Baha ibn Baha Ullah, 1844-1921. II. Title.

BLOMFIELD, Sara Louisa 297".89
(Ryan) Lady, d. 1939
The chosen highway, by Lady Blomfield (Sitarih Khanum). Wilmette, Ill., Baha'i Pub. Trust, 1967. x, 260p. port. 23cm. [BP395.B54A3 1967] 67-16026 2.90
1. Bahaism. I. Title.

CLAUS, Ted. 297.89
The new light on the spirit path, written and illustrated by Ted Claus. Wilmette, Ill., Baha'i Pub. Trust, 1966. 57 p. illus. 19 cm. [BP365.C55] 66-22165
1. Baha Uilah, 1817-1892. 2. Bahaism. I. Title.

CLAUS, Ted 297.89
The new light on the spirit path, written, illus. by Ted Claus. Wilmette, Ill. 60091, Baha'i Pub. Trust [110 Linden Av. c.]1966. 57p. illus. 19cm. [BP365.C55] 66-22165 .75 pap.,
1. Baha Ullah, 1817-1892. 2. Bahaism. I. Title.

DAHL, Arthur 297.89
Baha'i: world faith for modern man. Wilmette, Illinois, Baha'i Publishing Trust [c.1960] 22p. 22cm. Bibl. p.20-22. apply pap.,
I. Title.

EFFENDI, Shoghi 297.89
The faith of Baha'u'lah. a world religion. Wilmette, Illinois, Baha'i Publishing Trust, c.1959 20p. 22x10cm. apply pap.,
I. Title.

ESSLEMONT, John Ebenezer, 297.89
1874-1925
Baha u'llah and the new era. Wilmette, Ill., Baha'i' Pub. [1962, c.1950] xii, 349 p. 18 cm. 1.25
1. Bahai'sm 2. Bahu Ullah, 1817-1892. I. Title.

ESSLEMONT, John Ebenezer, 297'.89
1874-1925.
Baha'u'llah and the new era; an introduction to the Baha'i faith. [3d rev. ed.] Wilmette, Ill., Baha'i Pub. Trust, 1970. xiii, 301 p. 23 cm. Bibliography: p. 287. [BP365.E8 1970] 73-112791
1. Baha Ullah, 1817-1892. 2. Bahaism. I. Title.

GAVER, Jessyca Russell. 297'.89
The Baha'i faith. London, Tandem Bks.; New York, Award [1968, c. 1967] 222p. 18cm. (A304S K) [BP365.G3] .75 pap.,
1. Bahaism. I. Title.

GAVER, Jessyca Russell. 297'.89
The Baha'i faith; dawn of a new day. [1st ed.] New York, Hawthorn Books [1967] 223 p. 22 cm. [BP365.G3] 66-15248
1. Bahaism. I. Title.

HOFMAN, David. 297'.89
The renewal of civilization. [1st American ed.] Wilmette, Ill., Baha'i Pub. Trust [1970, c1969] 143 p. 18 cm. Includes bibliographical references. [BP370.H57 1970] 70-15555 2.25
1. Bahaism. I. Title.

HOLLEY, Horace, 1887- 297'.89
Religion for mankind. [1st American ed.] Wilmette, Ill., Baha'i Pub. Trust [1966, c1956] 248 p. 23 cm. [BP325] 67-5023
1. Bahaism—Addresses, essays, lectures. I. Title.

LINDSTROM, Janet 297.89
The kingdoms of God. Illus. by Anna Stevenson. Wilmette, Ill., 110 Linden Ave Bahai Pub. Trust, [c.1961] 40p. col. illus. 26cm. 61-8040 2.25 bds.,
1. Bahaism—Juvenile literature. I. Title.

LINDSTROM, Janet. 297'.89
The kingdoms of God / by Janet Lindstrom ; illustrated by Anna Stevenson. Rev. ed. Wilmette, Ill. : Baha'i Pub. Trust, 1974. 40 p. : ill. ; 26 cm. Explains the five kingdoms into which everything in the world is divided according to Bahaism and discusses the founding of the religion. [BP377.L5 1974] 75-332328 ISBN 0-87743-021-7
1. Bahaism—Juvenile literature. I. Title.

MILLER, William McElwee. 297'.89
The Baha'i faith: its history and teachings. South Pasadena, Calif., William Carey Library [1974] xix, 443 p. illus. 23 cm. Includes bibliographical references. [BP365.M49] 74-8745 ISBN 0-87808-137-2
1. Bahaism. I. Title.

MILLER, William McElwee. 297'.89
What is the Baha'i faith? / By William McElwee Miller ; an abridgment by William N. Whysham. Grand Rapids : Eerdmans, c1977. p. cm. Abridgment of the Baha'i faith. Includes index. [BP365.M49 1977] 77-8063 ISBN pbk. : 3.95
1. Bahaism. I. Wysham, William N. II. Title.

NABIL Zarandi, 1831- 297'.89
1892.
The dawn-breakers; Nabil's narrative of the early days of the Baha'i revelation. Translated from the original Persian and edited by Shoghi Effendi. Wilmette, Ill., Baha'i Pub. Trust, 1970 [c1932] lxiii, 685 p. illus. (1 col.), 21 facsims., 3 geneal. tables (2 fold.), map, ports. 26 cm. Translation of Tarikh-i Nabil (romanized form) Bibliography: p. 669-671. [BP330.N313 1970] 77-14837
1. Bab, 'Ali Muhammad Shirazi, 1820-1850. 2. Baha Ullah, 1817-1892. 3. Bahaism. 4. Babism. I. Shoghi, Effendi, ed. and tr. II. Title.

NATIONAL Spiritual 297.89
Assembly of the Baha'is of the United States.
The Bahai community a summary of its organization and laws. [Rev. ed.] Wilmette, Ill., Bahai Pub. Trust, 1963 [c.1947, 1963] vi, 57p. 23cm. Previous ed. pub. 1947 by the Natl. Spiritual Assembly of the Bahaa'is of the U. S. and Canada. 63-24765 .50 pap.,
1. Bahaism. I. Title.

NATIONAL Spiritual 297'.89
Assembly of the Baha'is of the United States.
On becoming a Baha'i; prepared by National Spiritual Assembly, Baha'is of the United States. Wilmette, Ill., Baha'i Pub. Trust [196-] 21 p. 22 cm. Bibliography: p. 20-21. [BP365.N293] 71-6140
1. Bahaism. I. Title.

SHOGHI, effendi. 297.89
The advent of divine justice. [1st rev. ed.] Wilmette, Ill., Bahai Pub. Trust [1963] v, 90 p. 24 cm. [BP365.S5] 63-21643
1. Bahaism. I. Title.

SHOGHI, effendi. 297'.89
Messages to the Baha'i world, 1950-1957. Wilmette, Ill. Baha'i Pub. Trust [1971] viii, 182 p. 24 cm. [BP325.S513 1971] 79-23900 ISBN 0-87743-036-5
1. Bahaism. I. Title.

SHOGHI, effendi. 297'.89
The world order of Baha'u'llah : selected letters / by Shoghi effendi. 2d rev. ed. Wilmette, Ill. : Baha'i Pub. Trust, 1974. xii, 234 p. ; 24 cm. Includes index. [BP392.S4 1974] 75-311794 ISBN 0-87743-031-4. ISBN 0-87743-004-7 pbk.
1. Baha Ullah, 1817-1892. 2. Bahaism. I. Title.

SHOGHI, effendi. 297.89
The advent of divine justice [Rev. ed Wilmette, Ill., Bahai [1964, c.1939, 1963] v, 90p. 24cm. 63-21643 2.00
1. Bahaism. I. Title.

SHOGHI, effendi. 297.89
Messengers to the Bahai world, 1950-1957. Wilmett, Ill., Pbahai Pub. Trust [1958] 130 p. 24 cm. [BP325.S513] 58-13187
1. Bahaism. I. Title.

SHOGHI, effendi. 297.89
The promised day is come. Pref. by Firuz Kazemzadeh. Wilmette Ill., Bahai Pub. Trust, 1961[c.1941, 1961] 136p. 61-12434 2.50
1. Bahaism. I. Title.

TOWNSHEND, George, 1876- 297'.89
1957.
Christ and Baha'u'llah. Wilmette, Ill., Baha'i Pub. Trust [1967, c1957] 116 p. 19 cm. [BP365] 68-168
1. Baha Ullah, 1817-1892. 2. Bahaism. I. Title.

TOWNSHEND, George, 1876- 297'.89
1957.
Christ and Baha'u'llah. Wilmette, Ill., Baha'i Pub. Trust [1967, c1957] 116 p. 19 cm. [[BP365]] 68-168
1. Baha Ullah, 1817-1892. 2. Bahalsm. I. Title.

UNIVERSAL House of 297'.89
Justice.
Messages from the Universal House of Justice, 1968-1973. Wilmette, Ill. : Baha'i Pub. Trust, c1976. x, 139 p. ; 23 cm. Includes index. [BP375.U54 1976] 75-11795 ISBN 0-87743-076-4 : 5.95 pbk.
1. Bahaism—Addresses, essays, lectures.

UNIVERSAL House of 297'.89
Justice.
Wellspring of guidance; messages, 1963-1968. Wilmette, Ill., Baha'i Pub. Trust, 1969. viii, 159 p. 23 cm. [BP380.U5] 72-261400
1. Bahaism—Doctrinal and controversial works. I. Title.

WILSON, Samuel Graham, 297'.89
1858-1916.
Bahaism and its claims; a study of the religion promulgated by Baha Ullah and Abdul Baha. New York, AMS Press [1970] 298 p. 23 cm. Reprint of the 1915 ed. Includes bibliographical references. [BP365.W5 1970] 79-131493
1. Bahaism. I. Title.

AFNAN, Ruhi Muhsen. 297'.89'01
The revelation of Baha'u'llah and the Bab. New York, Philosophical Library [1970- v 22 cm. Includes bibliographical references. [BP365.A35] 75-109166 ISBN 8-02-223079-(v. 1) 7.50
1. Descartes, Rene, 1596-1650. 2. Bahaism. 3. Babism. I. Title.

'ABD ul Baha ibn 297'.89'08
Baha Ullah, 1844-1921.
Foundations of world unity, compiled from addresses and tablets of 'Abdu'l-Baha. Wilmette, Ill., Baha'i Pub. Trust [1968, c1945] 112 p. 22 cm. [BP360.A37 1968] 68-5946
1. Bahaism. I. Title.

GAIL, Marzieh. 297'.89'08
Dawn over Mount Hira, and other essays / Marzieh Gail. Oxford [Eng.] : G. Ronald, c1976. vii, 245 p. ; 22 cm. Includes bibliographical references. [BP325.G34] 77-351197 ISBN 0-85398-063-2 : £3.00 ($7.50 U.S.). ISBN 0-85398-064-0 pbk.
1. Bahaism—Addresses, essays, lectures. I. Title.

SHOGHI, effendi. 297'.89'09
God passes by / by Shoghi effendi ; introd. by George Townshend. Wilmette, Ill. : Baha'i Pub. Trust, 1970, c1974. xxiii, 436 p. ; 24 cm. Includes index. [BP330.S5 1970] 75-318019 ISBN 0-87743-020-9. ISBN 0-87743-034-9 pbk.
1. Bahaism—History. I. Title.

'ABD ul-Baha ibn 297'.89'0922
Baha Ullah, 1844-1921.
Memorials of the faithful. Translated from the original Persian text and annotated by Marzieh Gail. [1st ed.] Wilmette, Ill., Baha' i Pub. Trust [1971] xii, 208 p. port. 23 cm. Translation of Tazkirat al-vafa' fi tarjamat hayat qudama' al-ahibba'. Includes bibliographical references. [BP390.A2313] 77-157797 ISBN 0-87743-041-1
1. Bahaism—Biography. I. Title.

WHITEHEAD, O. Z. 297'.89'0922 B
Some early Baha'is of the West / by O. Z. Whitehead. Oxford : Ronald, 1976. xii, 227 p., [24] p. of plates : ports. ; 23 cm. Includes bibliographical references. [BP390.W48] 77-367477 ISBN 0-85398-065-9 : £3.25. ISBN 0-85398-067-5 pbk.
1. Bahaism—Biography. I. Title.

SHOGHI, effendi. 297'.89'09798
High endeavours : messages to Alaska / Shoghi effendi. [Anchorage?] : Natiohnal Spiritual Assembly of the Baha'is of Alaska, c1976. x, 85 p., [1] leaf of plates : ill. ; 23 cm. Includes indexes. [BP352.A4S54] 77-151932
1. Bahaism—Alaska. I. Title.

HUSBAND and 297'.891'78342
wife. [1st ed.] [Karachi : Peermahomed Ebrahim Trust, 1976] xvi, ix, 202 p. ; 19 cm. Cover title. At head of title: Light, knowledge, truth. Translated from Gujarati. Previously published in Chandni-e-Islam. [HQ525.I8H873] 76-930230 Rs4.25
1. Marriage—Islam. 2. Family—Islamic countries.

BAHA Ullah, 1817-1892. 297'.892
The seven valleys and The four valleys / Baha'u'llah ; translated by Marzieh Gail, in consultation with Ali-Kuli Khan. Wilmette, Ill. : Baha'i Pub. Trust, 1975. xiii, 65 p. ; 18 cm. Translation of Haft vadi and of Chahar vadi. [BP360.B6317 1975] 76-356964 ISBN 0-87743-029-2 : 2.50 ISBN 0-87743-039-X pbk.
:
1. Bahaism. I. Baha Ullah, 1817-1892. Chahar vadi. English. 1975. II. Title.

JORDAN, Daniel C. 297'.89'2
The meaning of deepening; gaining a clearer apprehension of the purpose of God for man [by] Daniel C. Jordan. Wilmette, Ill., Baha'i Pub. Trust [1973] ix, 86 p. 28 cm. On cover: Baha'i Comprehensive Deepening Program. Bibliography: p. 79-80. [BP380.J67] 72-84824 ISBN 0-87743-046-2
1. Bahaism. I. Title. II. Title: Baha'i Comprehensive Deepening Program.

JORDAN, Daniel C. 297'.89'2
The meaning of deepening; gaining a clearer apprehension of the purpose of God for man [by] Daniel C. Jordan. Wilmette, Ill., Baha'i Pub. Trust [1973] ix, 86 p. 28 cm. On cover: Baha'i Comprehensive Deepening Program. Bibliography: p. 79-80. [BP380.J67] 72-84824 ISBN 0-87743-046-2 2.50
1. Bahaism. I. Title. II. Title: Baha'i Comprehensive Deepening Program.

BAHA Ullah, 1817- 297'.892'08
1892.
Gleanings from the writings of Baha'u'llah / translated by Shoghi effendi. 2d rev. ed. Wilmette, Ill. : Baha'i Pub. Trust, 1976. xvi, 346 p. ; 23 cm. Includes index. [BP360.B282 1976] 76-45364 ISBN 0-87743-111-6 : 6.95
1. Bahaism. I. Shogi, effendi. II. Title.

SHOOK, Glenn Alfred, 297'.89'42
1882-1954.
Mysticism, science, and revelation. [1st American ed.] Wilmette, Ill., Baha'i Pub. Trust [1967] x, 145 p. 20 cm. Bibliographical footnotes. [BP370] 67-9571
1. Mysticism—Bahaism. I. Title.

BAHA'I youth; 297'.894'4
a compilation. Prepared by: National Spiritual Assembly of the Baha'is of the United States. Wilmette, Ill., Baha'i Pub. Trust [1973] vii, 33 p. 22 cm. Includes bibliographical references. [BP377.B33] 73-176465
1. Youth, Bahai—Conduct of life. I. National Spiritual Assembly of the Baha'is of the United States.

THE Dynamic force of 297'.894'4
example. Wilmette, Ill. : Baha'i Pub. Trust, [1974] xv, 215 p. ; 28 cm. On cover: Baha'i comprehensive deepening program. Includes index. Bibliography: p. 199-203. [BP365.D87] 74-193175 ISBN 0-87743-091-8 pbk. : 9.00
1. Bahaism. I. Title: Baha'i comprehensive deepening program.

PAINE, Mabel Hyde, 297'.894'4
comp.
The divine art of living : selections from writing of Baha'u'ilah and 'Abdu'l-Baha / compiled by Mabel Hyde Paine. Rev. ed. Wilmette, Ill. : Baha'i Pub. Trust, 1960, 1973 printing. 130 p. ; 20 cm. [BP370.P3 1973] 75-305488 ISBN 0-87743-017-9. ISBN 0-87743-005-5 pbk.
1. Bahaism. I. Title.

IVES, Howard Colby. 297'.89'63
Portals to freedom. Wilmette, Ill., Baha'i Pub. Trust. [1967] 253 p. port. 21 cm. [[BP393]] 67-9801
1. 'Abd ul-Baha ibn Baha Ullah, 1844-1921. 2. Bahaism. I. Title.

IVES, Howard Colby. 297'.89'63
Portals to freedom. Wilmette, Ill., Baha'i Pub. Trust [1967] 253 p. port. 21 cm. [BP393] 67-9801
1. 'Abd ul-Baha ibn Baha Ullah, 1844-1921. 2. Bahaism. I. Title.

TAHERZADEH, Adib. 297'.896'3 B
The revelation of Baha'u'llah / Adib Taherzadeh. Oxford, [Eng.] : G. Ronald, [1974- v. : ill. ; 21 cm. Includes index. Contents.Contents.—1. Baghdad, 1853-63. Bibliography: v. 1, p. [337]-339. [BP392.T34] 75-305657 ISBN 0-85398-052-7 (v. 1) : £2.40 ($6.50 U.S.) (v. 1)
1. Baha Ullah, 1817-1892. 2. Bahaism. I. Title.

SHOGHI, effendi. 297.8964
Citadel of faith; messages to America, 1947-1957. Wilmette, Ill., Baha'i Pub. Trust, 1965. ix, 178 p. 24 cm. [BP325.S47] 66-2270
1. Bahaism—Collected works. I. Title.

SHOGHI, effendi. 297.8964
Citadel of faith; messages to America, 1947-1957. Wilmette, Ill., Baha'i Pub. Trust [1966, c.1965] ix, 178p. 24cm. [BP325.S47] 66-2270 3.00
1. Bahaism—Collected works. I. Title.

MUHAMMAD, Wallace 297'.89'78342
D., 1933-
The man and the woman in Islam / [by W. D. Muhammad]. Chicago : Honorable Elijah Muhammad Mosque No. 2, 1976. vii, 64 p. : ill. ; 22 cm. Excerpts from the Koran in English and Arabic. [HQ525.I8M78] 76-151816
1. Marriage—Islam. 2. Family—Religious life (Islam) 3. Black Muslims. I. Title.

'ABD ul-Baha ibn 297'.898'2
Baha Ullah, 1844-1921.
Tablets of the divine plan : revealed by 'abdu'l-Baha to the North American Baha'is. Rev. ed. Wilmette, Ill. : Baha'i Pub. Trust, 1977, c1976. p. cm. Includes index. [BP360.A392 1976] 76-10624 ISBN 0-87743-107-8 : 6.95 pbk. : 2.95
1. Bahaism. I. Title.

ABBAS, Mekki. 297'.899
The Sudan question; the dispute over the Anglo-Egyptian condominium, 1884--1951. New York, F. A. Praeger [1952] xix, 201p. maps (1 fold. col.) 23cm. (Colonal and comparative studies) Bibliography: p. 185-189. [DT108.A] A 52
1. Sudan, Egyptian—Hist. I. Title. II. Series.

HILL, Richard Leslie. 297'.899
Slatin Pasha, [by] Richard Hill. London, Oxford University Press, 1965. vii, 163 p. facsim., maps, ports. 23 cm. Bibliography: p. [153]-157. [DT108.05.S6H5] 65-2287
1. Slatin, Rudolf Carl, Freiherr von, 1857-1932. I. Title.

SHAKED, Haim. 297'.899 B
The life of the Sudanese Mahdi : a historical

study of the unique manuscript of Kitab sa'adat al-mustahdi bi-sirat al-Imam al-Mahdi (The book of the bliss of him who seeks guidance by the life of the Imam the Mahdi by the Sudanese Mahdist adherent Isma'il b. 'Abd al-Qadir. Tel Aviv : Shiloah Center for Middle Eastern and African Studies, Tel Aviv University, 1976. p. cm. "Based on a Ph.D. thesis which was submitted to the School of Oriental and African Studies, University of London, in 1969." Includes index. Bibliography: p. [DT108.3.M84K8737] 76-7552 ISBN 0-87855-132-8 : 19.95
1. al-Kurdufani, Isma'il 'Abd al-Qadir, 1844 or 5-1898 or 9. Sa'adat al-mustahdi bi-sirat al-Iman al-Mahdi. 2. Muhammad Ahmad, calling himself al-Mahdi, 1848-1885. I. Title.
Distributed by Transaction Books.

CANN, M W P 298
A review of recent determinations of the composition and surface pressure of the atmosphere of Mars, by M. W. P. Cann [and others] Springfield, Va., For sale by the Clearinghouse for Federal Scientific and Technical Information [1965] x, 176 p. illus. 27 cm. (NASA contractor report, NASA CR-298) "Prepared under contract no. NAS 5-9037 by HT Research Institute, Chicago, Ill., for National Aeronautics and Space Administration." Bibliography: p. 171-176. [TL521.3.C6A3] 65-62934
1. Mars (Planet)—Atmosphere. I. IIT Research Institute. II. U.S. National Aeronautics and Space Administration. III. Title. IV. Series: U.S. National Aeronautics and Space Administration. NASA contractor report, NASA CR-298

WHITELEY, W H ed. 298.2
A selection of African prose, compiled by W. H. Whiteley. Oxford, Clarendon Press, 1964. 2 v. 23 cm. (Oxford library of African literature) Contents.Contents. -- 1. Traditional oral texts. -- 2. Written prose. Bibliographical footnotes. [PL8013.E5W4] 66-2290
1. Tales, African. 2. African literature — Translations into English. 3. English literature — Translations from African. I. Title.

POLEY, Irvin C 1891- 298.6
Friendly anecdotes, collected and arranged by Irvin C. Poley [and] Ruth Verlenden Poley; with an introd. by Dorothy Canfield Fisher. [1st ed.] New York, Harper [1950] 128 p. 20 cm. "Much of this material appeared first in a Pendle Hill pamphlet called Quaker anecdotes." [BX7732.P59] 50-9787
I. Poley, Ruth Verlenden, 1890- joint author. II. Title.

ROBINSON, Charles Edson, 298.8
1836-1925.
The Shakers and their homes : a concise history of the United Society of Believers called Shakers Charles Edson Robinson. Canterbury, N.H. : Shaker Village. ,1976. ix, 134p. : ill. ; 23 cm. [BX9765] 76-2209 ISBN 0-912274-62-X 10.00 ISBN 0-912274-58-1 pbk. : 3.95
1. Shakers-United States I. Title.

299 Other Religions

ALLEN-MICHAEL. 299
To the youth of the world / channeled through Allen-Michael. Berkeley, Calif. : Starmast Publications, c1973. iv, 350 p., [8] leaves of plates : ill. ; 21 cm. (The Everlasting gospel) Cover title: From the universe ... to the youth of the world. [BP610.A413] 74-186417 2.95
I. Title.

ANGUS, Samuel, 1881-1943 299
The mystery-religions and Christianity; a study in the religious background of early Christianity. Introd. by Theodore H. Gaster. New Hyde Park, N. Y., University Bks. [1967c.1966] xxiv, 359p. 24cm. (Univ. lib. of comp. relig.) Bibl. [BL610.A6 1966] 66-27423 10.00
1. Mysteries, Religious. 2. Christianity and other religions. I. Title.

ARNSBY-JONES, George 299
The pilgrimage of James : an odyssey of inner space / by George Arnsby Jones. 1st ed. Pensacola, Fl. : Rookfield Press, 1977c1976 110 p. ; 22 cm. Imprint from label mounted on t.p. [BL624.A76] 76-27107 ISBN 0-917610-01-6 pbk. : 2.95
1. Spiritual life. I. Title.

BRINTON, Daniel Garrison, 299
1837-1899.
Religions of primitive peoples. New York, Negro Universities Press [1969] xiv, 264 p. 23 cm. Reprint of the 1897 ed. Bibliographical footnotes. [GN470.B7 1969] 79-88423
1. Religions—History. 2. Religion, Primitive. 3. Mythology. I. Title.

BUBBA Free John. 299
The way of divine communion : the foundation practices of the Free Communion Church / by Bubba Free John ; edited and with an introd. by the staff of Vision Mound Seminary. 1st ed. San Francisco : Dawn Horse Press, 1976. v, 45 p. : ill. ; 22 cm. [BP610.B818] 76-25712 ISBN 0-913922-26-9 : 2.00
1. Spiritual life. I. Title.

BURLAND, Cottie Arthur, 1905- 299
The gods of Mexico [by] C. A. Burland. [1st American ed.] New York, Putnam [1967] xiii, 219 p. illus., maps. 24 cm. "Select bibliography": p. 209-211. Examines Mexican civilization before the sixteenth century when obsession with religion dominated culture, idea, and character. [F1219.3.R38B8 1967a] AC 68
1. Indians of Mexico—Religion and mythology. I. Title.

FREEMAN, Mae (Blacker) 1907- 29.9
Stars and stripes; the story of the American flag. Illustrated by Lorence Bjorklund. New York, Random House [1964] 57 p. col. illus., music. 24 cm. [CR113.F85] 64-11173
1. Flags — U.S. — Juvenille literature. I. Title. II. Title: The story of the American flag.

GARRISON, Omar V. 299
The hidden story of scientology / Omar V. Garrison. Secaucus, N.J. : Citadel Press, 1974. 232 p. ; 22 cm. Includes bibliographical references. [BP605.S2G37] 74-80818 ISBN 0-8065-0440-4 : 8.50
1. Scientology. I. Title.

GARRISON, Omar V. 299
The hidden story of scientology / Omar V. Garrison. Secaucus, N.J. : Citadel Press, 1974. 232 p. ; 22 cm. Includes bibliographical references. [BP605.S2G37] 74-80818 ISBN 0-8065-0440-4 : 8.50
1. Scientology. I. Title.

THE Great White Brotherhood 299
in the culture history and religion of America : teachings of the ascended masters given to Elizabeth Clare Prophet. Colorado Springs : Summit University Press, c1976. xi, 347 p., [5] leaves of plates : ill. ; 23 cm. Record of a four-day conference for spiritual freedom, held at Mount Shasta, 1975. "A Summit Lighthouse publication." Includes bibliographical references. [BP605.G68G74] 76-7635 ISBN 0-916766-16-0 pbk. : 5.95
1. Great White Brotherhood—Congresses. 2. Spirit writings—Congresses. I. Prophet, Elizabeth Clare.

HOLY Order of MANS. 299
History of the White Brotherhood and its teachings. San Francisco : Holy Order of MANS, c1974. 182 p. ; 21 cm. [BP605.W48H64 1974] 75-315626 3.00
1. White Brotherhood. I. Title.

HUBBARD, La Fayette Ronald, 299
1911-
Scientology 0-8 : the book of basics / by L. Ron Hubbard. 1st American ed. Los Angeles : American St. Hill Organization, c1970. 152 p. ; 21 cm. [BP605.S2H835 1970] 75-322012
1. Scientology. I. Title.

HUBBARD, La Fayette Ronald, 299
1911-
The volunteer minister's handbook / by L. Ron Hubbard ; [photography by L. Ron Hubbard]. Los Angeles : Church of Scientology of California, c1976. lxxi, 674 p. : ill. ; 29 cm. "A Dianetics publication." Includes index. Bibliography: p. 562-564. [BP605.S2H837 1976] 76-27819 ISBN 0-88404-039-9
1. Scientology. I. Title.

ICHAZO, Oscar, 1931- 299
The human process for enlightenment and freedom : a series of five lectures / by Oscar Ichazo. 1st ed. New York : Arica Institute, [1977]c1976 120 p. : ill. ; 18 cm. [BP605.A7I23] 75-37075 pbk. : 6.95
1. Arica Institute. I. Title.
Distributed by Simon & Schuster

LOFLAND, John. 299
Doomsday Cult : a study of conversion, proselytization, and maintenance of faith / John Lofland. Enl. ed. New York : Irvington Publishers : distributed by Halsted Press, c1977. p. cm. Includes index. Bibliography: p. [BL53.L6 1977] 77-23028 ISBN 0-470-99249-2 : 15.95
1. Psychology, Religious. 2. Religion and sociology. I. Title.

PROPHET, Elizabeth Clare. 299
The chela and the path / El Morya ; dictated to the messenger Elizabeth Clare Prophet. Colorado Springs : Summit University Press, c1976. 128 p., [1] leaf of plates : ill. ; 21 cm. "A Summit Lighthouse publication." [BP605.G68P76] 76-7634 ISBN 0-916766-12-8 : 2.95
1. Great White Brotherhood. 2. Spirit writings. I. el Morya. II. Title.

PROPHET, Elizabeth Clare. 299
Cosmic consciousness : the putting on of the garment of the Lord / Lanello ; dictated to the messenger Elizabeth Clare Prophet. Colorado Springs : Summit University Press, c1976- v. : ill. ; 22 cm. "A Summit Lighthouse publication." Originally published in the periodical Pearls of wisdom. [BF1301.P83] 74-24023 ISBN 0-916766-17-9 : 2.95 (v. 1)
1. Spirit writings. I. Prophet, Mark. II. Title.

PROPHET, Mark. 299
The science of the spoken word : teachings of the ascended masters / given to Mark and Elizabeth Prophet. Colorado Springs : Summit Lighthouse, c1974. 82 p., [1] leaf of plates : col. ill. ; 21 cm. Includes bibliographical references. [BP605.W48P76 1974] 74-82293
1. White Brotherhood. I. Prohpet, Elizabeth, joint author. II. Title.

[ROERICH, Elena Ivanovna] 299
Infinity. [New York, Agni Yoga Society] 1930 [i. e. 1956] v. 17cm. (Agni yoga series) Translation of (transliterated: Bespredel'nost') [BP605.R62] 56-39110
I. Title.

†SACUTUS, Victor. 299
The Messiah in Sovietland : the historical openness of the revolting Yoramians / by Victor Sacutus. 1st ed. New York : Vantage Press, c1976. 316 p. ; 21 cm. [BP610.Y672S2] 77-362606 ISBN 0-533-01793-9 : 6.95
1. Yoram. 2. Georgia (Transcaucasia)—Religion. 3. Georgia (Transcaucasia)—History—1917- I. Title.

SAVOY, Gene. 299
Jamil, the child Christ / by Gene Savoy. Reno, Nev. : ICC/International Community of Christ, 1976, c1973. 118 p. ; 29 cm. (Sacred teachings of light ; codex 1) [BP605.I45S29 1976] 73-92360
1. International Community of Christ. I. Title. II. Title: The Child Christ. III. Series.

SAVOY, Gene. 299
The secret sayings of Jamil / by Gene Savoy. Reno, Nev. : Order of the Holy Child, International Community of Christ, c1976- v. ; 29 cm. ([The Sacred teachings of light] ; codex 5) Contents.Contents.—v. 1. The image and the Word. [BP605.I45S32] 76-52270
1. International Community of Christ—Collected works. I. Order of the Holy Child. II. Title. III. Series.

SCHNEIDER, Herbert Wallace, 299 B
1892-
A prophet and a pilgrim; being the incredible history of Thomas Lake Harris and Laurence Oliphant; their sexual mysticisms and Utopian communities amply documented to confound the skeptic, by Herbert W. Schneider and George Lawton. New York, Columbia University Press, 1942. [New York, AMS Press, 1970] xviii, 589 p. illus. 22 cm. (Columbia studies in American culture [no. 1]) Bibliography: p. [559]-566. [BF1997.H3S35 1970] 78-134433 ISBN 0-404-05610-5 27.50
1. Harris, Thomas Lake, 1823-1906. 2. Oliphant, Laurence, 1829-1888. I. Lawton, George, 1900-1957, joint author. II. Title. III. Series.

SELF-REALIZATION Fellowship. 299
Rajasi Janakananda (James J. Lynn) a great Western yogi. Los Angeles [1959] 108p. illus. 20cm. [BP605.S43L9] 59-48056
1. Lynn, James Jesse, 1892-1955. I. Title.

SUBUH, Muhammad, 1901- 299
The meaning of Subud; four talks given in London, August 1959. [New York, Dharma Book Co., 1961] 65 p. illus. 18 cm. [BP605.S8] 61-19678
I. Title.

SUBUH, Muhammad, 1901- 299
The meaning of Subud; four talks given in London, Aug. 1959. [New York, P.O. Box 176 Old Chelsea Sta., Dharma Bk. Co., c.1961] 65p. front. port. 61-19678 2.50
I. Title.

WEIMAR, J. Augustus. 299
Koreshanity, the new age religion, by the Koreshan Foundation. [Miami, Printed by Center Print. Co., 1971] viii, 171 p. ports. 23 cm. "The divine and Biblical credentials of Dr. Cyrus R. Teed (Koresh), by J. Augustus Weimar": p. 1-141. [BP605.K6W43] 70-158993
1. Teed, Cyrus Reed, 1839-1908. 2. Koreshanity. I. Koreshan Foundation. II. Title.

YOGANANDA, Paramahansa, 1893- 299
1952.
Autobiography of a Yogi. With a pref. by W. Y. Evans-Wentz. [8th ed.] Los Angeles, Self-Realization Fellowship, 1959 [c1946] xvi, 514 p. illus., map, ports. 22 cm. [BP605.S43Y6 1959] 68-39787
I. Title.

POCOCK, David Francis, 299'.1'411
1928-
Mind, body, and wealth; a study of belief and practice in an Indian village [by] D. F. Pocock. Totowa, N.J., Rowman and Littlefield [1973] xv, 187 p. illus. 22 cm. Includes bibliographical references. [BL2030.G8P62 1973] 74-154318 ISBN 0-87471-415-X 11.00
1. Gujarat, India (State)—Religion. 2. Gujarat, India (State)—Social life and customs. I. Title.

SPIRIT possession in 299'.1'495
the Nepal Himalayas / edited by John T. Hitchcock & Rex L. Jones ; translation of French articles by Harriet Leva Beegun. New Delhi : Vikas Pub. House, c1976. xxviii, p. : ill., map ; 25 cm. Bibliography: p. 390-401. [BL482.S64] 76-902895 Rs95.00
1. Spirit possession—Addresses, essays, lectures. 2. Shamanism—Nepal—Addresses, essays, lectures. I. Hitchcock, John Thayer, 1917- II. Jones, Rex L.

SPIRIT possession in 299'.1495
the Nepal Himalayas / edited by John T. Hitchcock and Rex L. Jones ; translations of French articles by Harriet Leva Beegun. Warminster : Aris & Phillips ; Beaverton, Or. : distributed by International Scholarly Book Services, c1976. xxviii, 401 p. : ill. (some col.) ; 23 cm. Essays. Errata slip inserted. Bibliography: p. 390-401. [BL482.S68] 76-381845 ISBN 0-85668-029-X : 27.50 pbk. : 14.50
1. Spirit possession—Addresses, essays, lectures. 2. Nepal—Religion—Addresses, essays, lectures. I. Jones, Rex L.

JACOBSEN, Thorkild, 299'.1'5
1904-
The treasures of darkness : a history of Mesopotamian religion / Thorkild Jacobsen. New Haven : Yale University Press, 1976. 273 p. : ill. ; 25 cm. Includes bibliographical references and index. [BL2350.I7J3] 75-27576 ISBN 0-300-01844-4 : 15.00
1. Mesopotamia—Religion. I. Title.

AHMED, Sami Said. 299'.1'59
The Yazidis, their life and beliefs / by Sami Said Ahmed ; edited by Henry Field. Coconut Grove, Miami : Field Research Projects, 1975. x, 485 p. : ill. ; 28 cm. Translation of al-Yazidiyah, ahwaluhum wa-mu'-taqadatuhum. Includes bibliographical references. [BL1595.A3613] 75-330953
1. Yezidis. I. Title.

ARBOIS de Jubainville, 299'.1'6
Henry d', 1827-1910.
The Irish mythological cycle and Celtic mythology. Translated from the French, with additional notes, by Richard Irvine Best. New York, Lemma Pub. Corp., 1970. xv, 240 p. 23 cm. Reprint of the 1903 ed. Translation of Le cycle mythologique irlandais et la mythologie celtique. Includes bibliographical references. [BL980.I7A7 1970] 70-112679 ISBN 0-87696-006-9
1. Mythology, Celtic. 2. Epic literature, Irish. 3. Tuatha de Danaan. I. Title.

CHADWICK, Nora (Kershaw) 299.16
1891-
The druids, by Nora K. Chadwick. Cardiff Wales U.P., 1966. xxii, 119 p. 22 1/2 cm. 12/6 Bibliography: p. [xiii]-xxii [BL910.C5] 66-70314
1. Druids and Druidism I. Title.

CHADWICK, Nora (Kershaw) 299.16
1891-
The druids. Cardiff, Wales Univ. Pr. [Mystic,Conn., Verry] 1966. xii, 119p. 23cm. Bibl. [BL910.C5] 66-70314 3.50
1. Druids and Druidism. I. Title.

DANIEL, John, Sir, 1870- 299'.16
The philosophy of ancient Britain. Port Washington, N.Y., Kennikat Press [1970] xvii, 277 p. illus. 22 cm. "First published in 1927." Bibliography: p. 269-270. [BL910.D25 1970] 71-102566
1. Druids and druidism—Relations—Christianity. 2. Celts—Religion. 3. Christianity and other religions—Druidism. 4. Symbolism. I. Title.

HIGGINS, Godfrey, 1773- 299'.1'6
1833.
The Celtic Druids / by Godfrey Higgins ; introductory pref. by Manly P. Hall. Facsim. reprint of the original 1829 ed. Los Angeles : Philosophical Research Society, 1977. p. cm. Photoreprint of the 1829 ed. published by R. Hunter, London, under title: The Celtic Druids; or, An attempt to shew that the Druids were the priests of Oriental colonies who emigrated from India, and were the

introducers of the first or Cadmean system of letters, and the builders of Stonehenge, of Carnac, and of other Cyclopean works in Asia and Europe. [BL910.H5 1977] 77-110 ISBN 0-89314-412-6 : 35.00
1. Druids and Druidism. 2. Europe—Antiquities. 3. Alphabet. I. Title.

KENDRICK, Thomas Downing Sir 299.16
The Druids; a study in Keltic prehistory [by] T. D. Kendrick. New York, Barnes & Noble [1966] xiv, 227p. illus., maps, plans, plates, port. 23cm. Reprint of a work first pub. in 1927. [BL910.K4 1966] 66-7817 8.50
1. Druids and Druidism. 2. Celts—Religion. 3. Temples, Druid. I. Title.

MACBAIN, Alexander, 1855-1907. 299'.1'6
Celtic mythology and religion : with chapters upon Druid circles and Celtic burial / by Alexander Macbain ; with introductory chapter & notes by W. J. Watson. Folcroft, Pa. : Folcroft Library Editions, 1976. xviii, 252 p., 8 leaves of plates : ill. ; 24 cm. Reprint of the 1917 ed. published by E. Mackay, Stirling, Scot. Includes bibliographical references. [BL900.M3 1976] 76-1877 ISBN 0-8414-6043-4 lib. bdg. : 17.50
1. Mythology, Celtic. 2. Druids and Druidism. 3. Cultus, Celtic. I. Title.

MACBAIN, Alexander, 1855-1907. 299'.1'6
Celtic mythology and religion, with chapters upon Druid circles and Celtic burial / by Alexander Macbain ; with introductory chapter & notes by W. J. Watson. Norwood, Pa. : Norwood Editions, 1975. 252 p., [8] leaves of plates : ill. ; 23 cm. Reprint of the 1917 ed. published by E. Mackay, Sterling, Scot. [BL900.M3 1975] 75-33767 ISBN 0-88305-911-8 lib. bdg. : 25.00
1. Mythology, Celtic. 2. Druids and druidism. 3. Cultus, Celtic. I. Title.

MACCULLOCH, John Arnott, 1868-1950. 299'.16
The Celtic and Scandinavian religions. Westport, Conn., Greenwood Press [1973] 180 p. 22 cm. Reprint of the 1948 ed., which was issued as v. 10 of Hutchinson's university library: World religions. Bibliography: p. 169-170. [BL900.M38 1973] 72-11739 ISBN 0-8371-6705-1
1. Celts—Religion. 2. Scandinavia—Religion. I. Title.

MACCULLOCH, John Arnott, 1868-1950. 299'.1'6
The religion of the ancient Celts / by J. A. MacCulloch. Folcroft, Pa. : Folcroft Library Editions, 1977. p. cm. Reprint of the 1911 ed. published by T. & T. Clark, Edinburgh. Includes bibliographical references and index. [BL900.M44 1977] 77-4127 ISBN 0-8414-5998-3 lib. bdg. : 40.00
1. Celts—Religion. 2. Mythology, Celtic. I. Title.

OWEN, A. L. 299.16
The famous Druids; a survey of three centuries of English literature on the Druids. [New York] Oxford, 1962. 264p. illus. 23cm. Bibl. 62-8505 4.80
1. Druids and Druidism. I. Title.

PIGGOTT, Stuart. 299'.1'6
The Druids. New York, Praeger [1968] 236 p. illus., facsims., maps, plans, ports. 22 cm. (Ancient peoples and places, v. 63) Bibliography: p. 197-203. [BL910.P5 1968] 68-8971 7.50
1. Druids and Druidism. I. Title.

PIGGOTT, Stuart. 299'.1'6
The Druids / Stuart Piggott. New York : Praeger, 1975. 214 p. : ill. (some col.) ; 25 cm. Includes index. Bibliography: p. 197-201. [BL910.P5 1975] 74-25378 ISBN 0-275-46730-9 : 13.50
1. Druids and Druidism. I. Title.

PIGGOTT, Stuart. 299'.1'6
The Druids / by Stuart Piggott. Harmondsworth : Penguin, 1974. ix, 193 p., [16] p. of plates : ill., facsim., maps, music, plans, ports. : 19 cm. (Pelican books) Includes index. Bibliography: p. [172]-177. [BL910.P5 1974] 75-312036 ISBN 0-14-021650-2 : £0.55
1. Druids and Druidism. I. Title.

ROSS, Anne, PH. D. 299'16
Pagan Celtic Britain: studies in iconography and tradition. London, Routledge & K. Paul; New York, Columbia, 1967. xxxiii, 433p. illus., 96 plates, maps, plan. 26cm. Bibl. [BL900.R6] 67-16099 25.00
1. Celts—Religion. 2. Celts—Antiq. I. Title.

ROSS, Anne, Ph.D. 299'.16
Pagan Celtic Britain: studies in iconography and tradition. London, Routledge & K. Paul; New York, Columbia U. P., 1967. xxxiii, 433 p. illus., 96 plates, maps, plan. 25 1/2 cm. 6/6/-(B 67-6101) Bibliography: p. 388-399. [BL900.R6] 67-16099
1. Celts — Religion. 2. Celts — Antiq. I. Title.

SPENCE, Lewis, 1874-1955. 299'.1'6
The mysteries of Britain; secret rites and traditions of ancient Britain restored. N.Y., S. Weiser [1970] 256 p. illus. 23 cm. "First published November 1928." [BL910.S7 1970] 72-16507 ISBN 0-85030-051-7 6.50
1. Druids and Druidism. 2. Mythology, Celtic. 3. Cultus, Celtic. 4. Bards and bardism. I. Title.

SQUIRE, Charles. 299'.16
Celtic myth and legend / Charles Squire. Hollywood, Calif. : Newcastle Pub. Co., [1975] p. cm. (A Newcastle mythology book) First ed. published in 1905 under title: The mythology of the British Islands. Reprint of the 191-? ed. published by Gresham Pub. Co., London, in series: Myth and legend in literature and art. Bibliography: p. [BL900.S6 1975] 74-26576 ISBN 0-87877-030-5 : 4.95
1. Mythology, Celtic. 2. Folk-lore, Celtic. 3. Legends, Celtic. I. Title. II. Series: Myth and legend in literature and art.

SQUIRE, Charles. 299'.16
Celtic myth & legend, poetry & romance. With illus. in colour & monochrome after paintings by J. H. F. Bacon & other artists. Boston, Milford House [1974] p. First ed. published in 1905 under title: The mythology of the British Islands. Reprint of the 1910 ed. published by Gresham Pub. Co., London, in series: Myth and legend in literature and art. Bibliography: p. [BL900.S6 1974] 73-16082 ISBN 0-87821-194-2 40.00 (lib. bdg.).
1. Mythology, Celtic. 2. Folk-lore, Celtic. 3. Legends, Celtic. I. Title. II. Series: Myth and legend in literature and art.

SQUIRE, Charles. 299'.1'6
The mythology of ancient Britain and Ireland. [Folcroft, Pa.] Folcroft Library Editions, 1973. p. Reprint of the 1909 ed. published by Constable, London. Bibliography: p. [BL980.G7S6 1973] 73-13769 10.00 (lib. bdg.).
1. Mythology, Celtic. 2. Legends, Celtic. I. Title.

TOLAND, John, 1670-1722. 299'.1'6
The history of the Celtic religion and learning: containing an account of the Druids; or, the priests and judges, of the vaids, or the diviners and physicians; and of the bards, or the poets and heralds; of the ancient Gauls, Britons, Irish, and Scots. With the history of Abaris, the hyperborian, priest of the sun. To which is added an abstract of the life of the author. [Folcroft, Pa.] Folcroft Library Editions, 1974. p. cm. Edition of 174-? published under title: A critical history of the Celtic religion and learning. Reprint of the ed. published by Lackington, Hughes, Harding, London. [BL910.T7 1974] 74-16159 30.00
1. Druids and Druidism. 2. Mythology, Celtic. I. Title.

BONWICK, James, 1817-1906. 299'.162
Irish Druids and old Irish religions / James Bonwick. New York : Arno Press, 1976. (The Occult) Reprint of the 1894 ed. published by Griffith, Farran, London. [BL980.17B66 1976] 75-36830 ISBN 0-405-07942-7 : 19.00
1. Ireland—Religion—Miscellanea. 2. Druids and Druidism—Miscellanea. I. Title. II. Series: The Occult (New York, 1976-)

*UNDERHILL, Ruth Murray, 1884- 2991.7
Singing for power; the song magic of the Papago Indians of Southern Arizona. New York, Ballantine Books [1973, c1938] vii, 148 p. illus. 18 cm. (Walden Edition) [E99] ISBN 0-345-23615-7 1.50 (pbk.)
1. Papago Indians—Religion and mythology. I. Title.

GASTER, Theodor Herzl, 1906- ed. and tr. 299.2
The oldest stories in the world, originally translated and retold, with comments, by Theodor H. Gaster. New York, Viking Press, 1952. 238 p. illus. 25 cm. [BL1600.G3] 52-13711
1. Mythology, Assyro-Babylonian. 2. Mythology, Hittite. 3. Mythology, Canaanite. I. Title.

KRAMER, Samuel Noah, 1897- 299'.2
The sacred marriage rite; aspects of faith, myth, and ritual in ancient Sumer. Bloomington, Indiana University Press [1969] xv, 170 p. illus. 22 cm. "An expanded version of the Patten lectures delivered at Indiana University ... 1968." Bibliographical references included in "Notes" (p. 135-161) [BL1615.K7] 73-85090 7.50
1. Sumerians—Religion. 2. Sacred marriage (Mythology) I. Title.

KRAMER, Samuel Noah, 1897- 299.2
Sumerian mythology; a study of spiritual and literary achievement in the third millennium B.C. Rev. ed. New York, Harper [c.1961] 130p. illus. (Harper torchbks., Academy lib. TB1055) Bibl. 1.45 pap.,
1. Mythology, Sumerian. I. Title.

KRAMER, Samuel Noah, 1897- 299.2
Sumerian mythology; a study of spiritual and literary achievement in the third millennium B. C. Rev. ed. [Gloucester, Mass., Peter Smith, 1962, c.1961] 130p. illus. 21cm. (Harper torchbks., Acad. lib., TB1055 rebound) Bibl. 3.50
1. Mythology, Sumerian. I. Title.

LANGDON, Stephen Herbert, 1876-1937. 299.2
Semitic [mythology] New pyork, Cooper Square Publishers, 1964[1931] xx, 454 p. 102 illus. 24 cm. (The Mythology of all races, v. 5) Bibliography: p. [419] 431. [BL25.M8 1964 vol. 5] 63-19090
1. Mythology, Semitic. I. Title. II. Series.

SMITH, William Robertson, 1846-1894. 299'.2
Lectures on the religion of the Semites; the fundamental institutions. With an introd. and additional notes by Stanley A. Cook. Prologomenon by James Muilenberg. 3d ed. [New York] Ktav Pub. House, 1969. 27, ix-lxiv, 718 p. 23 cm. (The Library of Biblical studies) Reprint of the 1927 ed. Includes bibliographical references. [BL1600.S6 1969] 69-11428
1. Semites—Religion. 2. Cultus, Semitic. I. Title. II. Series.

SMITH, William Robertson, 1846-1894. 299.2
The religion of the Semites; the fundamental institutions. New York, Meridian Books, 1956. xiv, 507p. 21cm. (The Meridian library, ML4) First published in 1889 as the first series of the author's 'Lectures on the religion of the Semites' (Burnett lectures, Aberdeen University, 1888-89) Bibliographical footnotes. [BL1600.S6 1956] 56-11577
1. Semites—Religion. 2. Sacrifice. 3. Cultus, Semitic. I. Title.

SMITH, William Robertson, 1846-1894. 299'.2
The religion of the Semites; the fundamental institutions. [1st Schocken paperback ed.] New York, Schocken Books [1972] xiv, 507 p. 21 cm. Reprint of the 1894 ed. published under title: Lectures on the religion of the Semites. Includes bibliographical references. [BL1600.S6 1972] 76-179483 ISBN 0-8052-0346-X 3.95
1. Semites—Religion. 2. Cultus, Semitic. I. Title.

CAPLICE, Richard I. 299'.2'1
The Akkadian Namburbi texts : an introduction / by Richard I. Caplice. Los Angeles : Undena Publications, 1974. 24 p. ; 28 cm. (Sources and monographs) (Sources from the ancient Near East ; v. 1, fasc. 1.) Includes bibliographical references. [PJ3791.C3] 74-78770 ISBN 0-89003-003-0 : 0.80
1. Assyro-Babylonian language—Texts. 2. Assyro-Babylonian religion. I. Title. II. Series.

GREEN, Alberto Ravinell Whitney. 299'.21
The role of human sacrifice in the ancient Near East / by Alberto Ravinell Whitney Green. Missoula, Mont. : Published by Scholars Press for the American Schools of Oriental Research, c1975. xvi, 383 p. ; 22 cm. (Dissertation series ; no. 1) Bibliography: p. 361-383. [BL570.G7] 75-43709 ISBN 0-89130-069-4 : 4.00
1. Sacrifice, Human. 2. Rites and ceremonies—Near East. I. Title. II. Series.

GREEN, Alberto Ravinell Whitney. 299'.21
The role of human sacrifice in the ancient Near East / by Alberto Ravinell Whitney Green. Missoula, Mont. : Published by Scholars Press for the American Schools of Oriental Research, c1975. xvi, 383 p. ; 22 cm. (Dissertation series ; no. 1) Bibliography: p. 361-383. [BL570.G7] 75-43709 ISBN 0-89130-069-4 : 4.00
1. Sacrifice, Human. 2. Rites and ceremonies—Near East. I. Title. II. Series.

JASTROW, Morris, 1861-1921. 299'.2'1
Aspects of religious belief and practice in Babylonia and Assyria. [New York] B. Blom [1971] xxv, 471 p. illus., map. 22 cm. (American lectures on the history of religions. 9th series, 1910) Reprint of the 1911 ed. Includes bibliographical references. [BL1620.J25 1971] 68-56503
1. Assyro-Babylonian religion. I. Title. II. Series.

KING, Leonard William, 1869-1919. 299'.2'1
Babylonian religion and mythology / by L. W. King. New York : AMS Press, [1976] p. cm. Reprint of the 1899 ed. published by K. Paul, Trench, Trubner, London, which was issued as v. 4 in series: Books on Egypt and Chaldaea. [BL1620.K5 1976] 73-18854 ISBN 0-404-11352-4 : 12.00
1. Mythology, Assyro-Babylonian. 2. Assyro-Babylonian religion. I. Title. II. Series: Books on Egypt and Chaldaea ; v. 4.

SPENCE, Lewis, 1874-1955. 299'.2'1
Myths & legends of Babylonia & Assyria. With 8 plates in colour by Evelyn Paul and 32 other illus. London, Harrap, 1916. Detroit, Gale Research Co., 1975. 411 p. illus. 22 cm. Plates not in color in this reprint ed. Includes bibliographical references. [BL1620.S6 1975] 77-167199 ISBN 0-8103-4089-5 :
1. Assyro-Babylonian religion. 2. Mythology, Assyro-Babylonian. 3. Cultus, Assyro-Babylonian. I. Title.

WOHLSTEIN, Herman, 1903- 299'.2'1
The sky-god, An-Anu : head of the Mesopotamian pantheon in Sumerian-Akkadian literature / by Herman Wohlstein ; [translated from the German by Salvator Attanasio]. Jericho, N.Y. : P. A. Strook, [1976] p. cm. Bibliography: p. [BL1625.A5W613] 76-10388 17.50
1. Anu (Assyro-Babylonian deity) 2. Gods, Assyro—Babylonian. I. Title.

†WOHLSTEIN, Herman, 1903- 299'.2'1
The sky-god, An-Anu manuscript / by Herman Wohlstein ; [translated from the German by Salvator Attanasio]. 1st ed. Jericho, N.Y. : P. A. Strook, 1976. 186 p. ; 24 cm. Bibliography: p. 179-186. [BL1625.A5W613] 76-10388 17.50
1. Anu (Assyro-Babylonian deity) 2. Gods, Assyro—Babylonian. I. Title.

HEIDEL, Alexander, 1907- 299.219
The Babylonian Genesis; the story of the creation. 2d ed. Chicago, Univ. of Chic. Pr. [1963, c.1942, 1951] xi, 153p. plates, map. 21cm. (P133) Bibl. 1.50 pap.,
1. Cosmogony, Babylonian. 2. Creation. 3. Assyro-Babylonian language—Texts. I. Enuma elish. English. II. Title.

HEIDEL, Alexander, 1907- 299.219
The Babylonian Genesis; the story of the creation. 2d ed. Chicago, University of Chicago Press [1951] xi, 153 p. plates, map. 24 cm. Bibliographical footnotes. [BS1236.H4 1951] 51-1463
1. Cosmogony, Babylonian. 2. Creation. 3. Assyro-Babylonian language—Texts. I. Enuma elish. English. II. Title.

HOOKE, Samuel Henry, 1874- 299.219
Babylonian and Assyrian religion. Norman, Univ. of Okla. Pr. [1963] 131p. illus. 22cm. Bibl. 63-9953 3.75
1. Assyro-Babylonian religion. I. Title.

MENDELSOHN, Isaac, 1898- ed. 299.219
Religions of the ancient Near East; Sumero-Akkadian religious texts and Ugaritic epics. New York, Liberal Arts Press [1955] 284p. 21cm. (The Library of religion, v.4) [BL1600.M4] 55-2124
1. Assyro-Babylonian religion. 2. Ugaritic language—Texts. 3. Assyro-Babylonian literature— Translated into English. 4. English literature—Translations from Assyro-Babylonian. I. Title.

KAPELRUD, Arvid Schou, 1912- 299.269
The Ras Shamra discoveries and the Old Testament. Translated by G. W. Anderson. [1st U.S. ed.] Norman, University of Oklahoma Press [1963] 91 p. 21 cm. Bibliographical footnotes. [BL1670.K33 1963] 63-17164
1. Bible. O. T.—Criticism, interpretation, etc. 2. Ras Shamra. 3. Palestine—Religion. I. Title.

LUCIANUS Samosatensis. 299'.275'691
The Syrian goddess = (De dea Syria) ; attributed to Lucian / [translated] by Harold W. Attridge and Robert A. Oden. Missoula, Mont. : Published by Scholars Press for the Society of Biblical Literature, c1976. 61 p. ; 24 cm. (Texts and translations ; 9) (Graeco-Roman religion series ; 1) English and Greek. Includes bibliographical references. [BL1060.L7813] 76-135 ISBN 0-89130-073-2 : 2.80

1. Hierapolis, Asia Minor—Religion. 2. Cultus—Hierapolis, Asia Minor. I. Title. II. Series. III. Series: Society of Biblical Literature. Texts and translations ; 9.

BUDGE, Ernest Alfred 299'.276'2
Thompson Wallis, Sir, 1857-1934.
Egyptian ideas of the future life / by E. A. Wallis Budge. New York : AMS Press, 1976. xii, 198 p. : ill. ; 19 cm. Reprint of the 1899 ed. published by K. Paul, Trench, Trubner, London, which was issued as v. 1 of Books on Egypt and Chaldaea. Includes bibliographical references. [BL2450.F83B8 1976] 73-18839 ISBN 0-404-11330-3 : 14.00
1. Future life (Egyptian religion) 2. Gods, Egyptian. I. Title. II. Series: Books on Egypt and Chaldaea ; v. 1.

SPENCE, Lewis, 1874- 299'.2762
1955.
The mysteries of Egypt; or, The secret rites and traditions of the Nile. Edited, with an introd., by Paul M. Allen. Blauvelt, N.Y., Rudolf Steiner Publications [1972] 260 p. 18 cm. (Steinerbooks, 1727) Includes bibliographical references. [BL2441.S68 1972] 79-183056 1.95
1. Mysteries, Religious. 2. Egypt—Religion. 3. Mythology, Egyptian. I. Title.

SHACK, William A. 299'.2'8
Gods and heroes : oral traditions of the Gurage of Ethiopia / translated and edited with an introd. and notes by William A. Shack and Habte-Mariam Marcos. Oxford [Eng.] : Clarendon Press, 1974. xii, 158 p., [1] leaf of plates : ill. ; 23 cm. (Oxford library of African literature) Includes texts in Gurage with parallel English translations. Includes index. Bibliography: p. [148]-149. [PJ9288.8.S5] 74-189389 ISBN 0-19-815142-X : 12.00
1. Folk literature, Gurage. 2. Folk literature, Gurage—Translations into English. 3. English literature—Translations from Gurage. I. Marcos, Habte-Mariam, joint author. II. Title.
Distributed by Oxford University Press, New York.

BONWICK, James, 1817-1906. 299.31
Egyptian belief and modern thought. With an introd. by C. A. Muses. Indian Hills, Colo., Falcon's Wing Press [1956] 454 p. illus. 21 cm. [BL2441.B6 1956] 56-8507
1. Egypt—Religion. I. Title.

BOOK of opening the 299'.31
mouth.
The book of opening the mouth; the Egyptian texts with English translations, by E. A. Wallis Budge. New York, B. Blom, 1972. 2 v. in 1. illus. 19 cm. Reprint of the 1909 ed. published by K. Paul, Trench, Trubner & Co., London, which was issued as v. 26-27 of Books on Egypt and Chaldaea. Includes bibliographical references. [PJ1559.B72 1972] 72-80498 17.50
1. Funeral rites and ceremonies—Egypt. I. Budge, Ernest Alfred Thompson Wallis, Sir, 1857-1934, ed. II. Series: Books on Egypt and Chaldaea, v. 26-27.

BOOK of the dead 299'.3'1
The Book of the dead; the papyrus of Ani in the British Museum. The Egyptian text with interlinear transliteration & tr., a running tr., introd., etc., by E. A. Wallis Budge [Magnolia, Mass., P. Smith, 1968] clv, 377p. illus. 24cm. Reprint of the 1895 ed. (Dover bk. rebound) Cover title: The Egyptian book of the dead. Bibl. [PJ1555.A3 1967] 6.50
I. Budge, Ernest Alfred Thompson Wallis, Sir 1857-1934, tr. II. Papyrus Ani. III. Title. IV. Title: The Egyptain Book of the dead.

BOOK of the dead. 299'.3'1
The Book of the dead; the papyrus of Ani in the British Museum. The Egyptian text with interlinear transliteration and translation, a running translation, introd, etc., by E. A. Wallis Budge. New York, Dover Publications [1967] clv, 377 p. illus. 24 cm. Reprint of the 1895 ed. Cover title: The Egyptian Book of the dead. Bibliography: p. [371]-377. [PJ1555.A3 1967] 67-28633
I. Budge, Ernest Alfred Thompson Wallis, Sir, 1857-1934, tr. II. Papyrus Ani. III. Title: The Egyptian Book of the dead.

BOOK of two ways. 299'.31
English.
The ancient Egyptian Book of two ways, by Leonard H. Lesko. Berkeley, University of California Press, 1972. xi, 148 p. 27 cm. (University of California publications. Near Eastern studies, v. 17) Includes bibliographical references. [PJ1559.B78E5 1972] 72-83096 ISBN 0-520-09465-4
I. Lesko, Leonard H. II. Series: California. University. University of California publications. Near Eastern studies, v. 17.

BREASTED, James Henry, 299'.3'1
1865-1935.
The dawn of conscience. New York, Scribner [1968, c1933] xxvi, 431 p. illus. 20 cm. (The Scribner library) Bibliographical footnotes. [BJ132.B7 1968] 68-7176
1. Ethics, Egyptian. 2. Egypt—Religion—History. 3. Egypt—Civilization—To 332 B.C. 4. Ethics, Jewish. I. Title.

BREASTED, James Henry, 299.31
1865-1935.
Development of religion and thought in ancient Egypt Introd. by John A. Wilson New York, Harper [1959] 379p. 21cm. (Harper torchbooks, TB-57) Includes bibliography. [BL2441.B7 1959] 58-7111
1. Egypt—Religion. I. Title.

BREASTED, James Henry, 299.3'1
1865-1935.
Development of religion and thought in ancient Egypt. Introd. by John A. Wilson. Gloucester, Mass., P. Smith, 1970 [c1959] xxiv, 379 p. 21 cm. Includes bibliographical references. [BL2441.B7 1970] 70-16951
1. Egypt—Religion. I. Title.

BUDGE, Ernest Alfred 299'.3'1
Thompson Wallis, Sir, 1857-1934.
The Egyptian heaven and hell / by E. A. Wallis Budge. New York : AMS Press, [1975] p. cm. Reprint of the 1906 ed. published by K. Paul, Trench, Trubner, London, which was issued as v. 20-22 of Books on Egypt and Chaldaea. Includes index. Contents.Contents.—v. 1. The book am-tuat.—v. 2. The short form of the Book am-tuat and the Book of gates.—v. 3. The contents of the books of the other world described and compared. [PJ1551.B7 1975] 73-18844 ISBN 0-404-11326-5 : 57.50(3 vol.set)
1. Eschatology, Egyptian. I. Book of that which is in the nether world. English. 1975. II. Book of the gates. English. 1975. III. Title. IV. Series: Books on Egypt and Chaldaea ; v. 20-22.

BUDGE, Ernest Alfred 299.31
Thompson Wallis, Sir 1857-1934.
Egyptian ideas of the future life; Egyptian religion. New York, University Books [1959] 224p. illus. 21cm. Cover title: Egyptian religion. 'A complete reproduction of the London edition of 1900, with a new introduction and additional illustrations.' [BL2441.B8 1959] 59-8616
1. Egypt— Religion. 2. Eschatology, Egyptian. 3. Future life. I. Title. II. Title: Egyptian religion.

BUDGE, Ernest Alfred 299.31
Thompson Wallis, Sir 1857-1934.
Egyptian magic. Evanston [Ill.] University Books [1958] xv, 234 p. illus. 21 cm. Bibliographical footnotes. [BF1591.BS 1958] 58-8302
1. Egypt—Religion. 2. Magic. I. Title.

BUDGE, Ernest Alfred 299'.31
Thompson Wallis, Sir, 1857-1934.
Egyptian religion : Egyptian ideas of the future life / E. A. Wallis Budge. London ; Boston : Routledge & K. Paul, 1975. xii, 198 p. : ill. ; 19 cm. Originally published under title: Egyptian ideas of the future life; Egyptian religion. Reprint of the 1899 ed. published by Kegan Paul, Trench, Trubner & Co., London. Includes bibliographical references. [BL2441.B8 1975] 75-323329 ISBN 0-7100-7199-X : £3.25
1. Egypt—Religion. 2. Future life, Egyptian. I. Title.

BUDGE, Ernest Alfred 299'.31
Thompson Wallis, Sir, 1857-1934.
From fetish to God in ancient Egypt. With 240 black and white illus. New York, B. Blom, 1972. xii, 545 p. illus. 24 cm. Reprint of the 1934 ed. "Part II (p. 385-527) is devoted to a series of revised English translations of ... hymns, myths [etc.]." Includes bibliographical references. [BL2441.B82 1972] 72-82206 17.50
1. Egypt—Religion—History. 2. Mythology, Egyptian. I. Title.

BUDGE, Ernest Alfred 299'.3'1
Thompson Wallis, Sir, 1857-1934.
The gods of the Egyptians; or, Studies in Egyptian mythology. New York, Dover Publications [1969] 2 v. illus. (part fold., col.) 24 cm. Reprint of the 1904 ed. Includes bibliographical references. [BL2441.B83 1969] 72-91925 4.50 per vol.
1. Mythology, Egyptian. I. Title.

BUDGE, Ernest Alfred 299'.31
Thompson Wallis, Sir, 1857-1934.
A hieroglyphic vocabulary to the Theban recension of the Book of the dead, with an index to all the English equivalents of the Egyptian words / by E. A. Wallis Budge. New ed., rev. and enl. New York : AMS Press, 1976. viii, 522 p. : ill ; 19 cm. Reprint of the 1911 ed. published by K. Paul, Trench, Trubner, London, which was issued as v. 31 of Books on Egypt and Chaldaea. On spine: Hieroglyphic vocabulary to the Book of the dead. Includes index. [PJ1557.Z8 1976] 73-18846 ISBN 0-404-11335-4 : 26.50
1. Book of the dead—Concordances. I. Title: A hieroglyphic vocabulary to the Theban recension of the Book of the dead ... II. Title: Hieroglyphic vocabulary to the Book of the dead. III. Series: Books on Egypt and Chaldaea ; v. 31.

BUDGE, Ernest Alfred 299.31
Thompson Wallis, Sir 1857-1934.
Osiris; the Egyptian religion of resurrection. New Hyde Park, N. Y., University Books [1961] 2v. in 1. illus., facsims. 24cm. First published in 1911 under title: Osiris and the Egyptian resurrection. Bibliographical footnotes. [BL2450.O7B8 1961] 61-10531
1. Osiris. 2. Eschatology, Egyptian. I. Title.

BUDGE, Ernest Alfred 299'.3'1
Thompson Wallis, Sir, 1857-1934.
Osiris and the Egyptian resurrection / by E. A. Wallis Budge ; illustrated after drawings from Egyptian papyri and monuments. New York : Dover Publications, 1973. 2 v. : ill. ; 24 cm. "Originally published in 1911 by the Medici Society, ltd." Includes bibliographical references and index. [BL2450.O7B8 1973] 72-81534 ISBN 0-486-22780-4 (v. 1). ISBN 0-486-22781-2 (v. 2) : 4.00 per vol.
1. Osiris. 2. Eschatology, Egyptian. I. Title.

CERNY, Jaroslav, 299.31
paleographer.
Ancient Egyptian religion. London, New York, Hutchinson's University Library [1952] 159 p. 19 cm. (Hutchinson's university library: World religions) Bibliography: p. 151-152. [BL2441.C4] 53-6600
1. Egypt—Religion. I. Title.

CERNY, Jaroslav, 299.31
palsographer.
Ancient Egyptian religion. London, New York, Hutchinson's University Library [1952] 159p. 19cm. (Hutchinson's university library: World religions) Bibliography: p. 151-152. [BL2441.C4] 53-6600
1. Egypt—Religion. I. Title.

CLARK, Robert Thomas 299.31
Rundle.
Myth and symbol in ancient Egypt. New York, Grove Press [1960, c1959] 292 p. illus. 23 cm. (Myth and man) [BL2441.2.C55 1960a] 60-9260
1. Mythology, Egyptian. I. Title.

CLYMER, Reuben Swinburne, 299.31
1878-
The mysteries of Osiris; or, Ancient Egyptian initiation. Setting forth the symbolism, mythology, legends, and parables beginning with the outer religious systems of the Egyptians, primarily based on the drama of the heavens; together with the inner or esoteric interpretations as taught in the lesser and greater mysteries active throughout the ages, including the present. [Completely rev.] Quakertown, Pa., Philosophical Pub. Co. [1951] xix, 287 p. 24 cm. "Limited ... Not to be sold." [BF1999.C657 1951] 51-13418
I. Title.

EGYPTIAN mythology. 299.31
New York, Tudor Pub. Co. [1965] 152 p. illus. (part col.) map. 29 cm. "Based on the text translated by Delano Ames from Mythologie generale Larousse." [BL2441.2.E4] 65-9171
1. Mythology, Egyptian. I. Guirand, Felix, ed. Mythologie generale. II. Larousse encyclopedia of mythology.

EGYPTIAN religious texts 299.31
and representations. v. 1- [New York, Published for Bollingen Foundation by Pantheon Books, 1954- v. illus. (part col.) diagrs. 32 cm. (Bollingen series) [PJ1551.E3] 54-27812
1. Egypt—Religion. 2. Egyptian literature. I. Bollingen Foundation. II. Series.

ERMAN, Adolf, 1854-1937. 299'.31
A handbook of Egyptian religion / by Adolf Erman ; translated by A. S. Griffith. Boston : Longwood Press, 1977. p. cm. Translation of Die agyptische Religion. Reprint of the 1907 ed. published by A. Constable, London. Includes index. [BL2441.E653 1977] 76-27517 ISBN 0-89341-032-2 lib.bdg. : 30.00
1. Egypt—Religion. 2. Mythology, Egyptian. I. Title.

ERMAN, Adolf, 1854-1937. 299'.31
A handbook of Egyptian religion / by Adolf Erman ; translated by A. S. Griffith. Boston : Longwood Press, 1977. p. cm. Translation of Die agyptische Religion. Reprint of the 1907 ed. published by A. Constable, London. Includes index. [BL2441.E653 1977] 76-27517 ISBN 0-89341-032-2 lib.bdg. : 30.00
1. Egypt—Religion. 2. Mythology, Egyptian. I. Title.

FRANKFORT, Henri, 1897- 299.31
Ancient Egyptian religion, an interpretation. New York, Harper [1961, c.1948] 172p. illus. (Harper Torchbooks: the Cloister lib. TB 77) Bibl. footnotes 1.35 pap.,
1. Egypt—Religion. I. Title. II. Series.

FRANKFORT, Henri, 1897- 299.31
Ancient Egyptian religion; an interpretation. [Gloucester, Mass., Peter Smith, 1961, c.1948] 172p. illus., (Harper Torchbook: Cloister Lib. TB77 rebound in cloth) Bibl. 3.25
1. Egypt—Religion. I. Title. II. Series.

FULCO, William J. 299'.3'1
The Canaanite god Resep / by William J. Fulco. New Haven : American Oriental Society, 1976. 71 p. : ill. ; 26 cm. (American Oriental series : Essay ; 8) Includes bibliographical references. [BL1672.R47F84] 77-150163
1. Resep (Canaanite deity) I. Title. II. Series.

HERMES Trismegistus. 299'.31
The divine pymander of Hermes Mercurius Trismegistus. Translated from the Arabic by Dr. Everard. With introd. & preliminary essay by Hargrave Jennings. Madras, India, P. Kailasam Bros., 1884. Minneapolis, Wizards Bookshelf, 1973. xiv, 112 p. 22 cm. (Secret doctrine reference series) Translation of Poemander. [BF1598.H5E5 1973] 73-84044 ISBN 0-913510-07-6 6.00
I. Everard, John, 1575?-1650? tr. II. Title.

JAMES, Thomas Garnet 299'.3'1
Henry.
Myths and legends of Ancient Egypt, by T. G. H. James; illustrated by Brian Melling. Feltham, Hamlyn, 1969. 160 p. col. illus., col. map. 19 cm. (Hamlyn all-colour paperbacks) [BL2441.2.J3 1969] 78-530247 6/-
1. Mythology, Egyptian. I. Title.

JAMES, Thomas Garnet 299'.3'1
Henry.
Myths and legends of ancient Egypt, by T. G. H. James. Illustrated by Brian Melling. New York, Grosset & Dunlap [1971] 159 p. col. illus. 22 cm. (A Grosset all-color guide, 27) Bibliography: p. [157] [BL2441.2.J3 1971] 73-136363 ISBN 0-448-00866-1 3.95
1. Mythology, Egyptian. I. Melling, Brian, illus. II. Title.

LINDSAY, Jack, 1900- 299'.3'1
Men and gods on the Roman Nile. New York, Barnes & Noble [1968] x, 457 p. illus., map. 22 cm. Bibliography: p. [439]-448. [BL2455.L5] 68-31996 11.00
1. Egypt—Religion—Greco-Roman period. 2. Mythology, Egyptian. I. Title.

LITANY of the sun 299.31
The Litany of Re. Texts tr., commentary by Alexandre Pinakoff [New York, Bollingen Found.; dist.] Pantheon [c.1964] xv, 182p. illus., facsims. (pt. fold.) 31cm. (Bollingen ser., 40:4. Egyptian religious texts and representations, v.4) Bibl. 64-24858 7.50
1. Ra (Egyptian deity) I. Piankoff, Alexandre, ed. and tr. II. Title. III. Series: Bollingen series, 40:4 IV. Series: Egyptian religious texts and representations, v.4)

LITANY OF THE SUN. 299.31
The Litany of Re. Texts translated with commentary by Alexandre Piankoff. [New York, Bollingen Foundation; distributed by] Pantheon Books [1964] xv, 182 p. illus., facsims. 31 cm. (Bollingen series, 40: 4. Egyptian religious texts and representations, v. 4) Bibliographical footnotes. [PJ1551.E4 vol. 4] 64-24858
1. Ra (Egyptian deity) I. Plankoff, Alexandre, ed. and tr. II. Title. III. Series: Bollingen series, 40: 4 IV. Series: Egyptian religious texts and representations, v. 4)

MACKENZIE, Donald 299'.3'1
Alexander, 1873-1936.
Egyptian myth and legend. With historical narrative notes on race problems, comparative beliefs, etc. Boston, Milford House [1973] p. Reprint of the 1913 ed. published by Gresham Pub. Co., London, in series: Myth and legend in literature and art. [BL2441.M3 1973] 73-13910 ISBN 0-87821-184-5 40.00 (lib. bdg.)
1. Mythology, Egyptian. 2. Legends, Egyptian. 3. Egypt—History. I. Title. II. Series: Myth and legend in literature and art.

MASSEY, Gerald, 1828- 299'.31
1907.
Ancient Egypt, the light of the world; a work of reclamation and restitution in twelve books. New York, S. Weiser, 1970. 2 v. (944 p.) illus. 26 cm. "Edition limited to five hundred copies." Reprint of the 1907 ed. [BL313.M35 1970] 79-138084 ISBN 0-87728-029-0
1. Religion, Primitive. 2. Mythology. 3. Egypt—Religion. I. Title.

MORENZ, Siegfried. 299'.31
Egyptian religion. Translated by Ann E. Keep.

Ithaca, N.Y., Cornell University Press [1973] xvi, 379 p. 23 cm. Translation of Agyptische Religion. Bibliography: p. 352-356. [BL2441.2.M613] 73-8401 ISBN 0-8014-0782-6 19.50
1. Egypt—Religion. I. Title.

MULLER, Wilhelm Max, 1862-1919. 299.31
Egyptian [mythology] by W. Max Muller. New York, Cooper Square Publishers, 1964 [c1918] xiv, 450 p. illus., 21 plates (part col.) 24 cm. (The Mythology of all races, v. 12) Bibliography: p. [431]-450. [BL25.M8] 63-19097
1. Mythology, Egyptian. 2. Mythology, Indochinese. I. Scott, Sir James George, 1851-1935. II. Title. III. Title: Indo-Chinese [mythology] IV. Series.

MYTHOLOGICAL papyri. 299.31
Translated with introd. by Alexandre Piankoff; edited, with a chapter on the symbolism of the papyri, by N. Rambova. [New York] Pantheon Books [1957] 2 v. col. front, illus., 30 fold. plates. 32cm. (Bollingen series, 40:3 Egyptian religious texts and representations, v. 3) Contents.1. Texts.--2. Plates. [PJ1551.E3 vol. 3] 58-697
1. Mythology, Egyptian. 2. Egyptian language—Papyri. I. Plankoff, Alexander, tr. II. Series: Bollingen series, 40: III. Egypian religious texts and representations, v. 3

OTTO, Walter Gustav Albrecht, 1878-1941. 299'.31
Priester und Tempel im hellenistischen Agypten / Walter Gustav Albrecht Otto. New York : Arno Press, 1975. 855 p. in various pagings ; 24 cm. (Ancient religion and mythology) Reprint of the 1905-08 ed. published by B. G. Teubner, Berlin. Includes bibliographical references and index. [BL2441.O7 1975] 75-10645 ISBN 0-405-07278-3
1. Egypt—Religion—Greco-Roman period, 332 B.C.-640 A.D. 2. Temples—Egypt. 3. Hellenism. I. Title. II. Series.

PIANKOFF, Alexandre, comp. 299'.31
The wandering of the soul. Texts translated with commentary by Alexandre Piankoff. Completed and prepared for publication by Helen Jacquet-Gordon. [Princeton, N.J.] Princeton University Press [1974] xviii, 124 p., 47 p. of illus. 32 cm. (Bollingen series, 40: 6) (Egyptian religious texts and representations, v. 6) Includes the Book of the two ways, Quererts (or Caverns), and a text on the game of draughts. Includes bibliographies. [PJ1551.E3 vol. 6] 71-166396 ISBN 0-691-09806-9 25.00
1. Egyptian language—Inscriptions. 2. Egyptian language—Papyri. 3. Eschatology, Egyptian. I. Jacquet-Gordon, Helen. II. Book of the two roads of the blessed dead. English. 1974. III. Book of caverns. English. 1974. IV. Title. V. Series. VI. Series: Bollingen series, 40: 6.

PLANKOFF, Alexandre, ed. and tr. 299.31
The Litany of Re. Texts translated with commentary by Alexandre Piankoff. [New York, Bollingen Foundation; distributed by] Pantheon Books [1964] xv, 182 p. illus., facsims. 31 cm. (Bollingen series, 40: 4. Egyptian religious texts and representations, v. 4) Bibliographical footnotes. [PJ1551.E4 vol. 4] 64-24858
1. Ra (Egyptian deity) I. Title. II. Series: Bollingen series, 40: 4 III. Series: Egyptian religious texts and representations, v. 4)

PYRAMID texts 299'.3'1
The pyramid of Unas. Texts tr. with commentary by Alexandre Piankoff. [Princeton, N. J.] Princeton Univ. Pr. [1968] xiv, 118p. illus., fold. plans, 70 plates. 32cm. (Bollingen ser., 40:5. Egyptian religious texts & representations, v. 5) Pub. for Bollingen Found. Bibl. refs. [PJ1553.A3U5] 65-26216 10.00
1. Unas, King of Egypt. 2. Egyptian language—Inscriptions. I. Piankoff, Alexandre. ed. II. Bollingen Founadtion. III. Title. IV. Series: Bollingen series, 40:5 V. Series: Egyptian religious texts and representations, v. 5.)

ROSETTA stone inscription. 299'.31
Report of the committee appointed by the Philonathean Society of the University of Pennsylvania to translate the inscription on the Rosetta stone. [Philadelphia, 1858] 1v. (various pagings) col. illus. 24cm. Facsimile reproduction of ms. copy. The committee consists of Chas. R. Hale. S. Huntington Jones and Henry Morton. Most of the work was done by Morton. Includes the hieroglyphic, demotic, and Greek inscriptions, with translations of each text. [PJ1531.R3 1958] 52-58748
I. Morton, Henry, 1836-1902. II. Pennsylvania. University. Philomathean Society. III. Title.

SAUNERON, Serge 299.31
The priests of ancient Egypt. Translated [from the French] by Ann Morrissett. New York, Grove Press [1960] 191p. illus. (Evergreen profile book P12) 59-10792 1.35 pap.,
1. Priests, Egyptian. I. Title.

THE Shrines of Tut-Ankh-Amon / 299.31
texts translated with introductions by Alexandre Piankoff ; edited by N. Rambova. New York : Harper & Row, 1962, c1955. xxiii, 133 p., [32] leaves of plates : ill. ; 21 cm. (The Bollingen library) (Harper torchbooks ; TB 2011) Includes bibliographical references. [BL2430.S6 1962] 75-312018
1. Tutankhamen, King of Egypt. 2. Egypt—Religion—History—Sources. 3. Egyptian language—Inscriptions. I. Piankoff, Alexandre.

THE Shrines of Tut-Ankh-Amon; 299.31
texts translated with introductions by Alexandre Piankoff. Edited by N. Rambova. [New York] Pantheon Books [1955] xxi, 149p. illus., plates (part col.) 32cm. (Bollingen series, 40:2. Egyptian religious texts and representations, v. 2) Bibliographical footnotes. [PJ1551.E3 vol. 2] 55-2997
1. Tutenkhamun, King of Egypt. 2. Egyptian language—Texts. I. Plankoff, Alexandre, tr. II. Series. III. Series: Bollingen series, 40: IV. Series: Egyptian religious texts and representations, v.2)

SHRINES of Tut-Ankh-Amon (The) 299.31
Texts tr., with introds. by Alexandre Piankoff. Ed. by N. Rambova. NewYork, Harper [1962, c.1955] (Bollingen ser., 40: Egyptian religious texts and representations, v.2) This study is based on the work of an expedition sponsored by the Bollingen Found. . . . October, 1949, to June, 1951. 1.75 pap.,
1. Tut-Ankh-Amon, King of Egypt. 2. Egypt—Religion. 3. Egyptian literature. I. Piankoff, Alexandre, tr. II. Series: Bollingen series, 40 III. Series: Egyptian texts and representations, v.

STEINER, Rudolf, 1861-1925. 299'.3'1
Egyptian myths and mysteries; twelve lectures, Leipzig, September 2-14, 1908. [Translated by Norman Macbeth] New York, Anthroposophic Press [1971] vi, 151 p. 22 cm. "Translated from shorthand reports unrevised by the lecturer, from the German edition published with the title, Aegyptische Mythen und Mysterien (vol. 106 in the Bibliographical survey, 1961)" Includes bibliographical references. [BL2441.S7513] 70-144034
1. Mythology, Egyptian—Addresses, essays, lectures. 2. Anthroposophy—Addresses, essays, lectures. I. Title.

THE tomb of Ramesses VI. 299.31
[New York] Pantheon Books [1954] 2 v. illus. (part col.) 32cm. (Bollingen series, 40: 1. Egyptian religious texts and representations, v. 1) 'This study is based on the work of an expedition sponsored by the Bollingen Foundation ... October. 1949. to June, 1951.' Contents.pt. I. Texts, translated with introductions by A. Plankoff; edited by N. Rambova.--pt. 2. Plates, recorded by N. Rambova; photographed by L. F. Husson. [PJ1551.E3 vol.1] 54-5646
1. Rameses VI, King of Egypt. 2. Egypt—Religion. 3. Egyptian literature. I. Piankoff, Alexandre, tr. II. Series: Bollingen series, 40: 1 III. Series: Egyptian religious texts and representations, v. 1)

WAINWRIGHT, Gerald Averay. 299'.31
The sky-religion in Egypt; its antiquity & effects, by G. A. Wainwright. Westport, Conn., Greenwood Press [1971] xv, 120 p. illus. 23 cm. Reprint of the 1938 ed. Includes bibliographical references. [BL2450.S65W3 1971] 71-136088 ISBN 0-8371-5238-0
1. Egypt—Religion. 2. Religion, Primitive. 3. Folk-lore of the sky. I. Title.

WESTCOTT, William Wynn, 1848-1925. 299'.3'1
The Isiac tablet : or, The Bembine table of Isis / by W. Wynn Westcott ; introductory pref. by Manly P. Hall. Facsim. reprint of the 1887 ed. Los Angeles : Philosophical Research Society, c1976. 19 p., [2] leaves of plates. : ill. ; 28 x 34 cm. "Limited edition." Photoreprint ed. Includes original t.p.: Tabula Bembina sive Mensa Isiaca. The Isiac tablet of Cardinal Bembo, its history and occult significance ... Bath, Robt. H. Fryar, 1887. [BL2450.I7W4713 1976] 76-26760 ISBN 0-89314-410-X
1. Isiac tablet. 2. Occult sciences. I. Title. II. Title: The Bembine table of Isis.

WILDUNG, Dietrich. 299'.3'1
Egyptian saints : deification in Pharaonic Egypt / Dietrich Wildung. New York : New York University Press, 1977. xv, 110 p. : ill. ; 28 cm. (Hagop Kevorkian series on Near Eastern art and civilization) Includes bibliographical references. [BL2450.G6W54 1977] 76-15147 ISBN 0-8147-9169-7 : 25.00
1. Gods, Egyptian. 2. Egypt—Religion. I. Title. II. Series.

WITT, Reginald Eldred. 299'.31
Isis in the Graeco-Roman world [by] R. E. Witt. Ithaca, N.Y., Cornell University Press [1971] 336 p. illus., map. 23 cm. (Aspects of Greek and Roman life) Bibliography: p. [327]-331. [BL2450.I7W58] 72-146278 ISBN 0-8014-0633-1 11.00
1. Isis. I. Title. II. Series.

ZABKAR, Louis Vico, 1914- 299'.3'1
A study of the ba concept in ancient Egyptian texts, by Louis V. Zabkar. Chicago, University of Chicago Press [1968] xiv, 163 p. 6 plates. 24 cm. (The Oriental Institute of the University of Chicago. Studies in ancient oriental civilization, no. 34) Bibliographical footnotes. [BL2450.B2Z3] 68-55393
1. Ba (Egyptian religion) 2. Eschatology, Egyptian. I. Title. II. Title: The ba concept in ancient Egyptian texts. III. Series: Chicago. University. Oriental Institute. Studies in ancient oriental civilization, no. 34

ZANDEE, Jan, 1914- 299'.31
Death as an enemy according to ancient Egyptian conceptions / Jan Zandee. New York : Arno Press, 1977, c1960. xxii, 448 p. ; 24 cm. (The Literature of death and dying) Reprint of the ed. published by Brill, Leiden, which was issued as no. 5 of Studies in the history of religions, supplements to Numen. Includes bibliographical references and index. [BL2450.E8Z33 1977] 76-19597 ISBN 0-405-09591-0 lib.bdg. 23.00
1. Eschatology, Egyptian. 2. Death (Egyptian religion) I. Title. II. Series. III. Series: Studies in the history of religions, supplements to Numen ; 5.

MACKENZIE, Donald Alexander, 1873-1936. 299'.3'2
Egypt myth and legend : with historical narrative notes on race problems, comparative beliefs, etc. / by Donald A. Mackenzie. Portland, Me. : Longwood Press, 1976. xlix, 404 p., [38] leaves of plates : ill. ; 22 cm. Reprint of the 1907 ed. published by Gresham Pub. Co., London, issued in series: Myth and legend in literature and art. Includes index. [BL2441.M3 1976] 76-27520 ISBN 0-89341-033-0 lib.bdg. : 45.00
1. Mythology, Egyptian. 2. Legends, Egyptian. 3. Egypt—History. I. Title. II. Series: Myth and legend in literature and art.

HARVA, Uno, 1882-1949. 299.45
Finno-Ugric, Siberian [mythology] by Uno Holmberg. New York, Cooper Square Publishers, 1964. xxv, 587 p. illus., map, 63 plates (part col.) 24 cm. (The Mythology of all races, v. 4) Bibliography: p. [561]-587. [BL25.M8] 63-19089
1. Mythology, Finno-Urgrian. 2. Mythology, Siberian. I. Title. II. Series.

*DENNISTTON, Denise 2994.543
The TM book; how to enjoy the rest of your life [by] Denise Denniston and Peter McWilliams, illustrrated by Barry Geller. [Allen Park, Mich., Versemonger Press, 1975] 224p. ill. 25 cm. [BL2015M4] 75-13848 ISBN 0-8431-0520-8 3.95(pbk.)
1. Meditation(Buddhism) I. McWilliams, Peter, joint author II. Title.

PAULSON, Ivar, 1922-1966. 299'.4545
The old Estonian folk religion. Translated by: Juta Kovamees Kitching and H. Kovamees. Bloomington, Indiana University [1971] 237 p. 23 cm. (Indiana University publications. Uralic and Altaic series, v. 108) Bibliography: p. [217]-237. [BL980.E8P38] 76-630299 ISBN 0-87750-154-8
1. Estonia—Religion—Addresses, essays, lectures. 2. Folk-lore, Estonian—Addresses, essays, lectures. I. Title. II. Series: Indiana. University. Uralic and Altaic series, v. 108

MUNRO, Neil Gordon 299.46
Ainu creed and cult. Ed. pref., additional chapter by B. Z. Seligman. Introd. by H. Watanabe. New York, Columbia, 1963[c.1962] 182p. illus. 23cm. Bibl. 63-7510 5.50
1. Ainu—Religion. I. Title.

BAIRD, Robert D., 1933- 299'.5
Indian and Far Eastern religious traditions [by] Robert D. Baird [and] Alfred Bloom. New York, Harper & Row [1972] 306 p. illus. 24 cm. (Religion and man) Includes bibliographies. [BL1055.B35] 72-185898 ISBN 0-06-040448-5 3.95
1. India—Religion. 2. China—Religion. 3. Japan—Religion. I. Bloom, Alfred, joint author. II. Title. III. Series.

KIM, Young Oon. 299'.5
Faiths of the Far East / Young Oon Kim. 1st ed. New York : Golden Gate Pub. Co., 1976. x, 209 p. ; 21 cm. (World religions ; v. 3) Includes bibliographies and index. [BQ614.K55] 76-151927
1. Buddhism—East Asia. 2. Taoism. 3. Confucianism. 4. Shinto. I. Title.

KITAGAWA, Joseph Mitsuo, 1915- 299.5
Religions of the East. Enlarged ed. Philadelphia, Westminster [1968,c.1960] 351p. 21cm. Bibl. [BL1032.K5] 60-7742 2.95 pap.,
1. Asia—Religion. 2. Religion. I. Title.

KITAGAWA, Joseph Mitsuo, 1915- 299.5
Religions of the East. Philadelphia, Westminster Press [1960] 319 p. 21 cm. Includes bibliography. [BL1032.K5] 60-7742
1. Asia—Religion. 2. Religions. I. Title.

LAO-TZU. 299.5
Tao teh king, interpreted as nature and intelligence, by Archie J. Bahm. New York, F. Ungar Pub. Co. [1958] 126 p. 20 cm. [BL1900.L3B2] 58-9331
I. Bahm, Archie J., ed. and tr. II. Title.

MCGILL, Ormond. 299'.5
Religious mysteries of the Orient / Ormond McGill and Ron Ormond ; photography by Ron Ormond. South Brunswick : A. S. Barnes, [1975] p. cm. Includes index. [BL1055.M29] 73-22596 ISBN 0-498-01496-7 : 9.95
1. East (Far East)—Religion. 2. Asia, Southeastern—Religion. 3. India—Religion. I. Ormond, Ron, 1912- joint author. II. Title.

MCGILL, Ormond. 299'.5
Religious mysteries of the Orient / Ormond McGill and Ron Ormond ; photography by Ron Ormond. South Brunswick : A. S. Barnes, [1975] p. cm. Includes index. [BL1055.M29] 73-22596 ISBN 0-498-01496-7 : 9.95
1. East (Far East)—Religion. 2. Asia, Southeastern—Religion. 3. India—Religion. I. Ormond, Ron, 1912- joint author. II. Title.

POLITELLA, Joseph, 1910- 299'.5
Taoism and Confucianism. Iowa City, Iowa, Sernoll [1967] 161 p. 22 cm. (Crucible books) "Annotated bibliography": p. 152-153. [BL1920.P57] 67-5683
1. Taoism. 2. Confucianism. I. Title.

FERGUSON, John Calvin, 1866-1945. 299.51
Chinese mythology, Japanese mythology by Masaharu Anesaki. New York, Cooper Square Publishers, 1964 [c1928] xii, 416 p. illus., map, 44 plates (part col.) 24 cm. (The Mythology of all races, v. 8) Bibliography: p. [389]-400. [BL25.M8 1964 vol. 8] 63-19093
1. Mythology, Chinese. 2. Mythology, Japanese. I. Anesaki, Masaharu, 1873-1949. II. Title. III. Series.

GILES, Herbert Allen, 1845-1935. 299'.51
Religions of ancient China. Freeport, N.Y., Books for Libraries Press [1969] 69 p. 23 cm. (Select bibliographies reprint series) Reprint of the 1905 ed. Contents.Contents.—The ancient faith.—Confucianism.—Taoism.—Materialism.—Buddhism and other religions. [BL1801.G4 1969] 79-95067
1. China—Religion. I. Title.

GILES, Herbert Allen, 1845-1935. 299'.51
Religions of ancient China / by Herbert A. Giles. Folcroft, Pa. : Folcroft Library Editions, 1976. p. cm. Reprint of the 1905 ed. published by Constable, London, in series: Religions ancient and modern. [BL1801.G4 1976] 76-20524 ISBN 0-8414-4518-4 : 10.00
1. China—Religion. I. Title. II. Series: Religions ancient and modern.

LAO-TZU 299.51
The way and its power; a study of the Tao te ching and its place in Chinese thought, by Arthur Waley [Tr. from Chinese] New York, Barnes & Noble [1963] 262p. 21cm. Bibl. 2.50
1. Philosophy, Chinese. I. Waley, Arthur. II. Title.

LAO-TZU. 299.51
The way of life. A new translation of the Tao te ching, by R. B. Blakney. [New York] New American Library [c1955] 134p. 19cm. (A Mentor book, M129) [BL1900.L3B6] 55-7401
I. Blakney. Raymond Bernard, tr. II. Title.

LEGGE, James, 1815-1897. 299'.51
The religions of China : Confucianism and Taoism described and compared with Christianity / by James Legge. Folcroft, Pa. : Folcroft Library Editions, 1976. p. cm. Reprint of the 1880 ed. published by Hodder and Stoughton, London. [BL1801.L4 1976] 76-28535 ISBN 0-8414-5809-X lib. bdg. : 40.00

1. China—Religion. 2. Confucianism—Relations—Christianity. 3. Taoism—Relations—Christianity. 4. Christianity and other religions—Confucianism. 5. Christianity and other religions—Taoism. I. Title.

MORGAN, Harry Titterton, 1872- 299'.51
Chinese symbols and superstitions. South Pasadena, Calif., P. D. and I. Perkins, 1942. Detroit, Gale Research Co., 1972. 192 p. illus. 19 cm. Bibliography: p. 173. [BL1801.M6 1972] 74-167079
1. China—Religion. 2. Rites and ceremonies—China. 3. Symbolism. 4. China—Antiquities. 5. Superstition. I. Title.

REICHELT, Karl Ludvig, 1877- 299.51
Religion in Chinese garment. Translated by Joseph Tetlie. New York, Philosophical Library [1951] 180 p. 22 cm. (Lutterworth library, v. 36. Missionary research series, no. 16) [BL1801.R413] 52-6704
1. China — Religion. I. Title.

SHRYOCK, John Knight, 1890- 299'.51
The temples of Anking and their cults; a study of modern Chinese religion [by] John Shryock. Paris, Librairie orientaliste P. Geuthner, 1931. [New York, AMS Press, 1973] 206 p. illus. 24 cm. Originally presented as the author's thesis, University of Pennsylvania, 1927. Bibliography: p. [205]-206. [BL1801.S5 1973] 70-38083 ISBN 0-404-56947-1 16.00
1. China—Religion. 2. Temples—China—An-ch'ing. 3. Mythology, Chinese. I. Title.

T'AI I CHIN HUA TSUNG CHIH. 299.51
The secret of the golden flower, a Chinese book of life. Translated and explained by Richard Wilhelm, with a European commentary by C. G. Jung. [Translated into English by Cary F. Baynes] New York, Wehman Bros. [1955] ix, 151p. illus., plates. 23cm. [BL1900.T25B3 1955] 55-12925
1. Taoism. 2. China— Religion. I. Wilhelm, Richard, 1873-1960, ed. and tr. II. Jung, Carl Gustav, 1875- III. Title.

T'AL I CHIN HUA TSUNG CHIH. 299.51
The secret of the golden flower, a Chinese book of life. Tr., explained by Richard Wilhelm;foreword, commentary by C. G. Jung. And a part of the Chinese meditation text. The book of consciousness and life, foreword by Salome Wilhelm. [Tr. from German by Cary F. Baynes. New, rev. augm. ed.] New York, Harcourt [1962] xvi, 149p. illus. 22cm. 62-10499 4.50
1. Taoism. 2. China—Religion. I. Wilhelm, Richard, 1873-1930, ed.and tr. II. Jung, Carl Gustav, 1875-1961. III. Liv, Huayang, fl. 1794. IV. Title. V. Title: The book of consciousness and life.

THOMPSON, Laurence G. 299'.51
Chinese religion : an introduction / Laurence G. Thompson. 2d ed. Encino, Calif. : Dickenson Pub. Co., [1975] xv, 138 p. : ill. ; 23 cm. (The Religious life of man) Includes bibliographical references and index. [BL1802.T5 1975] 74-83954 ISBN 0-8221-0141-6 : 4.50
1. China—Religion. I. Title.

WEBER, Max, 1864-1920. 299.51
The religion of China: Confucianism and Taoism, translated and edited by Hans H. Gerth. Glencoe, Ill., Free Press, 1951. xi, 308 p. 22 cm. A translation of the author's essay, Konfuzianismus und Taoismus, published in v. 1 of his Gesammelte Aufsatze zur Religionssoziologie in 1922. Bibliographical references included in "Notes" (p. 250-297) [BL1801.W33] 51-12055
1. China—Religion. 2. Confucius and Confucianism. 3. Taoism. 4. Religion and sociology. I. Title.

WELCH, Holmes. 299.51
The parting of the way; Lao Tzu and the Taoist movement. Boston, Beacon Press [1957] 204 p. illus. 22 cm. [BL1930.W4] 57-7729
1. Lao-tzu. 2. Taoism. I. Title.

WELCH, Holmes. 299.51
The parting of the way; Lao Tzu and the Taoist movement. Boston, Beacon Press [1957] 204 p. illus. 22 cm. [BL1930.W4] 57-7729
1. Lao-tzu. 2. Taoism. I. Title.

*WELCH, Holmes 299.51
Taoism; the parting of the way. Rev. ed. Boston, Beacon [1966, c.1957, 1965] 194p. front. 21cm. (BP 224) Orig. title: The parting of the way; Lao Tzu and the Taoist movement [BL1930.W4] 1.95 pap.,
1. Lao-tzu. 2. Taoism. I. Title.

WERNER, Edward Theodore Chalmers, 1864-1954. 299'.51
A dictionary of Chinese mythology. Boston, Milford House [1974] p. cm. Reprint of the 1932 ed. published by Kelly and Walsh, Shanghai. Bibliography: p. [BL1801.W35 1974] 70-186794 ISBN 0-87821-046-6 6.00 (lib. bdg.).
1. Mythology, Chinese—Dictionaries. I. Title.

WERNER, Edward Theodore Chalmers, 1864-1954. 299'.51
A dictionary of Chinese mythology / by E. T. C. Werner. Portland, Me. : Longwood Press, 1977. p. cm. Reprint of the 1932 ed. published by Kelly and Walsh, Shanghai. Includes index. Bibliography: p. [BL1801.W35 1977] 76-27521 ISBN 0-89341-034-9 : 60.00
1. Mythology, Chinese—Dictionaries. I. Title.

WERNER, Edward Theodore Chalmers, 1864-1954. 299'.51
Myths & legends of China. [New York] B. Blom [1971] 453 p. illus. 21 cm. Reprint of the 1922 ed. [BL1825.W46 1971] 71-172541
1. Mythology, Chinese. 2. Legends—China. I. Title.

WIEGER, Leon, 1856-1933. 299'.51
A history of the religious beliefs and philosophical opinions in China from the beginning to the present time, by Leo Wieger. Translated by Edward Chalmers Werner. New York, Paragon Book Reprint Corp., 1969. 774 p. illus. 24 cm. Reprint of the 1927 ed. Translation of Histoire des croyances religieuses et des opinions philosophiques en Chine depuis l'origine jusq'a nos jours. [BL1801.W5 1969] 78-90092
1. China—Religion—History. 2. Philosophy, Chinese. 3. Buddha and Buddhism—China. 4. Taoism. 5. Tales, Chinese. I. Title.

*GRANET, Marcel. 299.'51'09
The religion of the Chinese people / translated, edited and with an introd. by Maurice Freedman. New York : Harper & Row [1976]c1975. viii, 200p. ; 23 cm. (Explorations in interpretative sociology) Includes index. First published in 1922 by Presses Universitaires de France (Paris), as La religion des Chinois. Bibliography: p. [178]-192. [BL1801] 74-33106 ISBN 0-06-136172-0 ; 17.50
1. China-Religion. 2. Religion and sociology. I. Freedman, Maurice, tr. II. Title.

JORDAN, David K. 299'.51'0951249
Gods, ghosts, and ancestors; the folk religion of a Taiwanese village [by] David K. Jordan. Berkeley, University of California Press [1972] xviii, 197 p. illus. 24 cm. Based on the author's thesis, University of Chicago, 1969. Bibliography: p. [185]-193. [BL1975.J67 1972] 70-149945 ISBN 0-520-01962-8 7.50
1. Formosa—Religion. I. Title.

ARMSTRONG, Robert Cornell. 299'.512
Light from the East; studies in Japanese Confucianism. New York, Gordon Press, 1974. 326 p. 24 cm. Reprint of the 1914 ed. published by University of Toronto, Toronto, in series: University of Toronto studies: Philosophy. Bibliography: p. xi-xii. [BL1843.A7 1974] 74-3563 ISBN 0-87968-134-9 34.95 (lib. bdg.)
1. Confucianism—Japan. I. Title. II. Series: Toronto. University. University of Toronto studies. Philosophy.

COLLIS, Maurice, 1889- 299'.512
The First Holy One. Westport, Conn., Greenwood Press [1970, c1948] x, 280, vii p. illus., maps. 23 cm. Bibliography: p. 263-264. [BL1851.C6 1970] 70-110819 ISBN 0-8371-3222-3
1. Confucianism. 2. China—Religion. I. Title.

KENNEY, Edward Herbert, 1891- 299.512
A confucian notebook, by Edward Herbert [pseud.] Foreword by Arthur Waley. New York, Grove Press [1961] 89p. (The Wisdom of the East series, WP-5) Bibl. 60-13790 1.45 pap.,
1. Confucius and Confucianism. I. Title.

MCNAUGHTON, William, 1933- comp. 299'.512
The Confucian vision / edited, with an introd. and new translations, by William McNaughton. 1st ed. [Ann Arbor] : University of Michigan Press, 1974. viii, 164 p. ; 20 cm. (Ann Arbor paperbacks ; AA 194) Includes bibliographical references. [BL1852.M28 1974] 73-90890 ISBN 0-472-08620-0 : 8.50 ISBN 0-472-06194-1 pbk. : 2.95
1. Confucianism. I. Title.

NIVISON, David S., ed. 299.512
Confucianism in action. Edited by David S. Nivison and Arthur F. Wright, with contributions by Wm. Theodore De Bary [and others] Stanford, Calif., Stanford University Press, 1959. xiv, 390 p. port. 24 cm. (Stanford studies in the civilizations of eastern Asia) "Papers ... presented at the 1957 and 1958 conferences sponsored by the Committee on Chinese Thought ... of the Association for Asian Studies." Bibliographical references included in "Notes" (p. [335]-373) [BL1840.N55] 59-7433
1. Confucianism. 2. China—Civilization. I. Wright, Arthur F., 1913- joint ed. II. Title. III. Series.

SHRYOCK, John Knight, 1890- 299.512
The origin and development of the state cult of Confucius; an introductory study, by John K. Shryock. New York, Paragon 1966[c.1932] xiii, 298p. 22cm. At head of title: American Historical Association. Bibl. [BL1851.S5 1966] 66-21765 10.00
1. Confucius and Confucianism. 2. Cultus, Chinese. 3. China—Religion. I. Title.

WRIGHT, Arthur F 1913- ed. 299.512
The Confucian persuasion. With contributions by James F. Cahill [and others] Stanford, Calif., Stanford University Press, 1960. x. 390 p. front. 24 cm. (Stanford studies in the civilizations of eastern Asia) "A sequel to Confucianism in action, edited by David S. Nivison and Arthur F. Wright ... Both volumes grew out of the 1957 and 1958 conferences on Chinese thought sponsored by the Committee on Chinese Thought of the Association for Asian Studies." Bibliographical references included in "Notes" (p. [313]-375) [BL1840.W7] 60-8561
1. Confucius and Confucianism. 2. China — Civilization. I. Title. II. Series.

WRIGHT, Arthur F., 1913- ed. 299.512
The Confucian persuasion. With contributions by James F. Cahill [and others] Stanford, Calif., Stanford University Press [c.]1960. x, 390p. front. 24cm. (Stanford studies in the civilizations of eastern Asia) A sequel to Confucianism in action, edited by David S. Nivison and Arthur F. Wright . . . Both volumes grew out of the 1957 and 1958 conferences on Chinese thought sponsored by the Committee on Chinese Thought of the Association for Asian Studies' Bibliographical references included in Notes (p.[313]-375) 60-8561 8.50
1. Confucius and Confucianism. 2. China—Civilization. I. Title. II. Series.

YEH, Theodore T. Y. 299'.512
Confucianism, Christianity & China [by] Theodore T. Y. Yeh. New York, Philosophical Library [1969] 249 p. 23 cm. Bibliography: p. 245-249. [DS721.Y4] 68-30750 6.50
1. China—Civilization. 2. Confucianism—Relations—Christianity. I. Title.

AHERN, Emily M. 299'.5122'13
The cult of the dead in a Chinese village [by] Emily M. Ahern. Stanford, Calif., Stanford University Press, 1973. xiv, 280 p. illus. 23 cm. Bibliography: p. [269]-271. [BL467.A35] 72-97202 ISBN 0-8047-0835-5 10.00
1. Ancestor worship—China. I. Title.

WRIGHT, Arthur F 1913- 299.5126
Confucian personalities. Edited by Arthur F. Wright and Denis Twitchett. With contributions by Albert E. Dien [and others] Stanford, Calif., Stanford University Press, 1962. x, 411 p. 24 cm. (Stanford studies in the civilizations of eastern Asia) Developed from a research conference organized by the Committee on Chinese Thought of the Association for Asian Studies. Bibliographical references included in "Notes" (p. [327]-387) [BL1840.W69] 62-16950
1. Confucius and Confucianism. 2. China — Biog. I. Twitchett, Denis. II. Title. III. Series.

WRIGHT, Arthur F., 1913- 299.5126
Confucian personalities. Ed. by Arthur F. Wright, Denis Twitchett. Contributions by Albert E. Dien [others] Stanford, Calif., Stanford Univ. Pr. [c.]1962. x, 411p. 24cm. (Stanford studies in the civilizations of eastern Asia) Bibl. 62-16950 8.75
1. Confucius and Confucianism. 2. China—Biog. I. Twitchett, Denis. II. Title. III. Series.

CH'EN, Li-fu, 1900- 299'.5126'4 B
Why Confucius has been reverenced as the model teacher of all ages / by Chen Li-fu. New York : St. John's University Press, c1976. vi, 126 p. ; 23 cm. (Asian philosophical studies ; no. 7) Three lectures delivered at St. John's University, Nov. 22-Dec. 6, 1975. Text in English and Chinese. Bibliography: p. 48. [B128.C8C476] 76-23568 ISBN 0-87075-104-2 pbk. : 3.00
1. Confucius. I. Title. II. Series.

CREEL, Herrlee Glessner, 1905- 299'.5126'4
Confucius, the man and the myth [by] H. G. Creel. Westport, Conn., Greenwood Press [1972, c1949] xi, 363 p. map. 22 cm. Bibliography: p. 341-354. [B128.C8C65 1972] 72-7816 ISBN 0-8371-6531-8 14.75
1. Confucius. I. Title.

DO-DINH, Pierre. 299'.512'64
Confucius and Chinese humanism. Translated by Charles Lam Markmann. New York, Funk & Wagnalls [1969] viii, 217 p. illus., maps, ports. 21 cm. Translation of Confucius et l'humanisme chinois. Bibliography: p. 208-209. [B128.C8D63] 69-18687 5.95
1. Confucius. 2. Humanism. I. Title.

KELEN, Betty. 299'.512'64 B
Confucius: in life and legend. [1st ed.] New York, T. Nelson [1971] 160 p. port. 21 cm. Bibliography: p. 155-156. [B128.C8K43] 72-164970 ISBN 0-8407-6152-X
1. Confucius. I. Title.

LIU, Wu-chi, 1907- 299'.5126'4 B
Confucius, his life and time. Westport, Conn., Greenwood Press [1972, c1955] xv, 189 p. 22 cm. Bibliography: p. 180-183. [B128.C8L56 1972] 73-138159 ISBN 0-8371-5616-5
1. Confucius.

PALEY, Alan L. 299'.5126'4
Confucius, ancient Chinese philosopher, by Alan L. Paley. Charlotteville, N.Y., SamHar Press, 1973. 32 p. 22 cm. (Outstanding personalities, no. 59) Bibliography: p. 31-32. A brief biography of the Chinese teacher and sage whose teachings, though largely ignored during his lifetime, influenced all aspects of Chinese life for many centuries after his death. [B128.C8P33] 92 73-77600 ISBN 0-87157-559-0. 1.98 (lib. bdg.)
1. Confucius—Juvenile literature. I. Title.
Pbk., 0.98, ISBN 0-87157-059-9.

SSU shu. 299'.512'8
The Chinese classical work commonly called the Four books (1828). Translated and illustrated with notes by David Collie. A facsimile reproduction with an introd. by William Bysshe Stein. Gainesville, Fla., Scholars' Facsimiles & Reprints, 1970. xvii, 341 p. 23 cm. Original t.p. reads: The Chinese classical work commonly called the Four books; translated, and illustrated with notes, by the late Rev. David Collie, Principal of the Anglo-Chinese College, Malacca. Printed at the Mission press, 1828. [PL2478.C35 1828a] 75-122487 ISBN 8-201-10795-
1. Ethics, Chinese. 2. China—Politics and government. I. Collie, David, d. 1828, tr. II. Title.

HOOK, Diana ffarington. 299'.5128'2
The I Ching and mankind / Diana ffarington Hook. London ; Boston : Routledge & Kegan Paul, 1975. xii, 160 p. : ill. ; 21 cm. Includes index. Bibliography: p. 154-155. [BF1770.C5H64] 75-321838 ISBN 0-7100-8058-1 : £3.95. ISBN 0-7100-8059-X pbk.
1. I ching. 2. Divination. I. Title.

MEARS, I. 299'.512'82
Creative energy : a study of the I-ching / by I. and L. E. Mears ; graphic design by Nancy Hom Lem ; cover photo by Craig Grimes. Burbank, Calif. : Ohara Publications, 1976. 96 p. : ill. ; 23 cm. [PL2464.Z7M4] 76-26394 3.25
1. I-ching. I. Mears, L. E., joint author. II. Title.

SCHOENHOLTZ, Larry. 299'.512'82
New directions in the I ching : the Yellow River legacy / by Larry Schoenholtz ; foreword by Leslie Shepard ; ill. by Gayle Murray. Secaucus, N.J. : University Books, [1975] 157 p. : ill. ; 24 cm. Includes index. Bibliography: p. 151-152. [PL2464.Z7S3 1975] 74-28540 ISBN 0-8216-0255-1 : 7.95
1. I ching. I. Title.

SCHOENHOLTZ, Larry. 299'.512'82
New directions in the I ching : the Yellow River legacy / by Larry Schoenholtz ; foreword by Leslie Shepard ; ill. by Gayle Murray. Secaucus, N.J. : University Books, [1975] 157 p. : ill. ; 24 cm. Includes index. Bibliography: p. 151-152. [PL2464.Z7S3 1975] 74-28540 ISBN 0-8216-0255-1 : 7.95
1. I ching. I. Title.

TU, Wei-ming. 299'.51282
Centrality and commonality : an essay on Chung-yung / Tu Wei-ming. Honolulu : University Press of Hawaii, 1976. p. cm. (Monograph of the Society for Asian and Comparative Philosophy ; no. 3) Includes bibliographical references and index. [PL2473.Z7T8] 76-17054 ISBN 0-8248-0447-3 pbk. : 5.00
1. Chung yung. I. Title. II. Series: Society for Asian and Comparative Philosophy. Monograph of the Society for Asian and Comparative Philosophy ; no. 3.

WILHELM, Hellmut, 1905- 299.51282
Change; eight lectures on the I ching. Tr. from German by Cary F. Baynes. New York, Harper [1964, c.1960] x, 111p. illus. 21cm. (Harper torchbks. Bollingen lib., TB2019) 64-7444 1.25 pap.,
I. Ching. II. Title.

WILHELM, Hellmut, 1905- 299.51282
Change; eight lectures on the I ching. Translated from the German by Cary F. Baynes. [New York] Pantheon Books [1960] x, 111 p. diagrs. 23 cm. (Bollingen series, 62) [PL2464.Z7W53] 60-11791
1. I ching. I. Series.

WILHELM, Hellmut, 1905- 299'.512'82
Change : eight lectures on the I ching / Hellmut Wilhelm ; translated from the German by Cary F. Baynes. Princeton, N.J. : Princeton University Press, 1973, c1960. x, 111 p. : ill. ; 22 cm. (Princeton/Bollingen paperbacks ; 285) (Bollingen series ; 62) Translation of Die Wandlung. Includes index. [PL2464.Z7W53 1973] 75-321751 ISBN 0-691-09714-3. ISBN 0-691-01787-5 pbk. : 1.95
1. I ching. I. Title. II. Series.

WILHELM, Hellmut, 1905- 299'.5128'2
Heaven, earth, and man in The book of changes : seven Eranos lectures / by Hellmut Wilhelm. Seattle : University of Washington Press, c1976. p. cm. (Publications on Asia of the Institute for Comparative and Foreign Area Studies ; no. 28) Includes index. [PL2464.Z7W55] 76-7801 ISBN 0-295-95516-3 : 12.95
1. I ching. I. I ching. II. Title. III. Series: Washington (State). University. Institute for Comparative and Foreign Area Studies. Publications on Asia ; no. 28.

BLOFELD, John Eaton Calthorpe, 1913- 299'.514
The secret and sublime: Taoist mysteries and magic, by John Blofeld. London, Allen & Unwin, 1973. 3-217 p. illus. 23 cm. Bibliography: p. 9. [BL1920.B56] 73-163668 ISBN 0-04-181019-8
1. Taoism. I. Title.
Distributed by Verry, 12.50.

CHANG, Chung-yuan, 1907- 299.514
Creativity and Taoism; a study of Chinese philosophy, art, & poetry. New York, Julian [c.1963] 241p. illus. 25cm. Bibl. 62-21446 6.50
1. Taoism. 2. Creation (Literary, artistic, etc.) 3. China—Intellectual life. I. Title.

CHUANG-TZU. 299'.514
Chuang Tzu : a new selected translation with an exposition of the philosophy of Kuo Hsiang / by Yu-lan Fung. New York : Gordon Press, 1975. vi, 164 p. ; 24 cm. Translation of Nan-hua ching. First published in 1931. Includes index. [BL1900.C5F4 1975] 75-3877 ISBN 0-87968-187-X lib.bdg. : 34.95
1. Kuo, Hsiang, d. 312. I. Feng, Yu-lan, 1895-

CHUANG-TZU. 299.514
The sayings of Chuang Chou. A new translation by James R. Ware. [New York] New American Library [1963] 240 p. map. 18 cm. (A Mentor classic) "MT543." Bibliography: p. 234. [BL1900.C5W3] 63-21686
1. God (Chinese religion) I. Ware, James Roland, tr. II. Title.

CHUANG-TZU 299.514
The sayings of Chuang Chou. New tr. by James R. Ware [New York] New Amer. Lib. [c.1963] 240p. map. 18cm. (Mentor classic; MT543) Bibl. 63-21686 .75 pap.,
1. God (Chinese religion) I. Ware, James Roland, tr. II. Title.

HUAI-NAN tzu, d.122B.C. 299'.514
Tao, the great luminant; essays from Huai nan tzu. With introductory articles, notes, analyses, by Evan Morgan. Foreword by J. C. Ferguson. New York, Paragon Book Reprint Corp., 1969. xlv, 287 p. illus. 23 cm. Reprint of 1935 ed. A translation by E. Morgan of 8 of Huai-nan tzu's 21 essays found in Liu Wen-tien's Chinese ed. of the author's works published by the Commercial Press, Shanghai. [BL1900.H83M6 1969] 75-77384
I. Morgan, Evan, 1860- ed. II. Ferguson, John Calvin, 1866-1945. III. Title.

HUANG, Al Chung-liang. 299'.514
Living Tao : still visions and dancing brushes / by Al Chung-liang Huang and Si Chi Ko. Millbrae, Calif. : Celestial Arts, 1976. p. cm. [BL1920.H84] 76-11338 ISBN 0-89087-127-2 pbk. : 5.95
1. Taoism. I. Ko, Si Chi. II. Title.

KENNEY, Edward Herbert, 1891- 299.514
A Taoist notebook, by Edward Herbert [pseud.] New York, Grove Press [1960] 80 p. 18 cm. (The Wisdom of the East series, WP-2) Includes bibliography. [BL1920.K4 1960] 60-13788
1. Taoism. I. Title.

LAO-TZU. 299.514
The book of Tao. Translation by Frank J. MacHovec. Mount Vernon, N. Y., Peter Pauper Press [1962] 61p. illus. 19cm. [BL1900.L3M3] 62-4768
I. MacHovec, Frank J., tr. II. Title.

LAO-TZU 299.514
The book of Tao. Tr. by Frank J. MacHovec. Mount Vernon, N.Y., Peter Pauper [c.1962] 61p. illus. 19cm. 62-4768 1.00 bds.,
I. MacHovec, Frank J., tr. II. Title.

LAO-TZU. 299'.514
The Tao-teh-king; sayings of Lao-tzu. Translated with commentary by C. Spurgeon Medhurst. [Rev. Quest book ed.] Wheaton, Ill., Theosophical Pub. House [1972] 165 p. 21 cm. (A Quest book) "Original edition 1905." [BL1900.L3M4 1972] 72-83648 ISBN 0-8356-0430-6 Pap. 1.95
I. Medhurst, C. Spurgeon, tr. II. Title.

LAO-TZU. 299.514
The way of Lao Tzu (Tao-te ching) Translated with introductory essays, comments, and notes by Wing-tsit Chan. Indianapolis, Bobbs-Merrill [1963] viii, 285 p. 21 cm. (The Library of liberal arts, 139) Bibliography: p. 241-264. [BL1900.L3C44] 62-21266
I. Chan, Wing-tsit, 1901- tr. II. Title.

[LU, Yen] b.798. 299'.514
The secret of the golden flower : a Chinese book of life / translated and explained by Richard Wilhelm ; commentary by C. G. Jung ; [translated into English by Cary F. Baynes]. New York : Causeway Books, [1975] xix, 151 p., 10 leaves of plates : ill. ; 24 cm. Translation of T'ai i chin hua tsung chih. Reprint of the 1931 ed. published by K. Paul, Trench, Trubner, London; with new introd. [BL1900.L83B3 1975] 74-98765 ISBN 0-88356-036-4 : 7.95
1. Taoism. 2. China—Religion. I. Wilhelm, Richard, 1873-1930. II. Jung, Carl Gustav, 1875-1961. III. Title.

MCNAUGHTON, William, 1933- comp. 299'.514
The Taoist vision. [Ann Arbor] University of Michigan Press [1971] 90 p. illus. 22 cm. (Ann Arbor paperbacks) [BL1920.M3] 70-143183 ISBN 0-472-09174-3 4.95
1. Taoism. I. Title.

T'AI shang kan ying p'ien. English & Chinese. 299'.514
Treatise on response & retribution [by] Lao Tze. Translated from the Chinese by D. T. Suzuki & Paul Carus. Containing introd., Chinese text, verbatim translation, translation, explanatory notes and moral tales. Edited by Paul Carus. With sixteen plates by Chinese artists and a front. by Keichyu Yamada. [3d pbk. ed.] LaSalle, Ill., Open Court Pub. Co., 1973 [c1906] 139 p. illus. 21 cm. (Open Court paperbacks) At head of title in characters: T'ai shang kan ying p'ien. [BL1900.T3S8 1973] 74-155276 ISBN 0-87548-244-9 1.95 (pbk.).
1. Taoism. I. Lao-tzu. II. Suzuki, Daisetz Teitaro, 1870-1966, tr. III. Carus, Paul, 1852-1919, ed. IV. Title.

WATTS, Alan Wilson, 1915-1973. 299'.514
Tao : the watercourse way / by Alan Watts, with the collaboration of Al Chung-liang Huang ; additional calligraphy by Lee Chih-chang. 1st ed. New York : Pantheon Books, [1975] xxvi, 134 p. : ill. ; 24 cm. Bibliography: p. 129-134. [BL1920.W37 1975] 74-4762 ISBN 0-394-48901-2 : 6.95
1. Taoism. 2. Chinese language—Writing. I. Huang, Al Chung-liang. II. Title.

LAI, Bessie C. 299'.514'0924 B
Ah Ya, I still remember / by Bessie C. Lai. Taipei : Meadea Enterprise Co., c1976. 173 p. ; 20 cm. Added title in Chinese romanized: Chi nien fu ch'in Huang Shih-hsi. [BL1940.W66L34] 77-358819
1. Wong, Sai Hee, 1857-1927. 2. Taoists—Hawaii—Biography. I. Title.

KALTENMARK, Max. 299'.514'2
Lao Tzu and Taoism. Translated from the French by Roger Greaves. Stanford, Calif., Stanford University Press, 1969. vi, 158 p. 23 cm. Bibliography: p. [151]-152. [BL1930.K313] 69-13179 5.95
1. Lao-tzu. 2. Taoism. I. Title.

SASO, Michael R. 299'.514'38
Taoism and the rite of cosmic renewal [by] Michael R. Saso. [Pullman] Washington State University Press [1972] 120 p. illus. 23 cm. Bibliography: p. 115-120. [BL1920.S27] 72-189459 4.00
1. Taoism. I. Title.

SIMS, Bennett B. 299'.5146'3 B
Lao-Tzu and the Tao te Ching, by Bennett B. Sims. New York, F. Watts [1971] 122 p. 22 cm. (Immortals of philosophy and religion) A brief introduction to and commentary on the life of the Chinese philosopher Lao-tzu is followed by an interpretative text of his teachings. [BL1900.L35S47] 92 73-142996 ISBN 0-531-00961-0
1. Lao-tzu. Tao te ching.—Juvenile literature. I. Title.

GOULLART, Peter 299.51465
The monastery of Jade Mountain. London, J. Murray [dist. Hollywood-by-the -Sea, Fla., Transatlantic, 1962, c.1961] 189p. illus. 22cm. 62-1063 5.25
1. Monasticism and religious orders, Taoist. I. Title.

SLOANE, Eugene Hulse, 1902- 299'.514'8
Homage to the ancient child; an essay on the Tao te ching of Lao Tzu, by Eugene H. Sloane. Annapolis, Owl Press, 1968. 31 p. 19 cm. Bibliography: p. 29-31. [BL1900.L35S5] 68-21895
1. Lao-tzu. Tao te ching. I. Title.

CHUANG-TZU. 299'.5148'2
Chuang tsu: Inner chapters. A new translation by Gia-fu Feng and Jane English. Photography by Jane English. Calligraphy by Gia-fu Feng. [1st ed.] New York, Vintage Books [1974] vii, 161 p. illus. 28 cm. Translation of Nan-hua ching, sections 1-7, Nei p'ien. Text in English and Chinese. [BL1900.C5F38 1974b] 73-20292 ISBN 0-394-71990-5 3.95 (pbk.)
I. Title.

CHUANG-TZU. 299'.5148'2
Inner chapters [by] Chuang tsu. A new translation by Gia-fu Feng and Jane English. Photography by Jane English. Calligraphy by Gia-fu Feng. [1st ed.] New York, Knopf; [distributed by Random House] 1974. vii, 161 p. illus. 29 cm. Original Chinese text and English translation of Nei p'ien, ti 1-7 of Nan-hua ching. [BL1900.C5F38 1974] 73-20730 ISBN 0-394-48761-3 7.95
I. Title.
Pbk. 3.95.

CHUANG-TZU. 299.51482
A new selected translation with an exposition of the philosophy of Kuo Hsiang, by Yu-lan Fung. 2d ed. New York, Paragon Book Reprint Corp., 1964. vi, 164 p. 20 cm. (Paragon reprint oriental series) [BL1900.C5F4 1964] 64-18451
1. Kuo, Hsiang, d. 312. I. Feng, Yu-lan, 1895- ed and tr. II. Title.

DHIEGH, Khigh. 299'.514'82
The eleventh wing; an exposition of the dynamics of I ching for now [by] Khigh Alx Dhiegh. Los Angeles, Nash Pub. [1973] xxvi, 278 p. illus. 23 cm. Bibliography: p. [265]-278. [PL2464.Z7D5 1973] 70-186928 ISBN 0-8402-1252-6 8.95
1. I ching. I. Title.

DHIEGH, Khigh. 299.51482
The eleventh wing; an exposition of the dynamics of I ching for now. [New York, Dell, 1974, c1973] xxvi, 278 p. 21 cm. (A Delta book) Bibliography: p. [265]-278. [PL2464.Z7D5 1974] 3.25 (pbk.).
1. I ching. I. Title.
L.C. card n. for original edition: 70-186928

*HOOK, Diana ffarington. 299'.514'82
The I ching and you. New York, Dutton, 1973. 149 p. illus. 21 cm. (Dutton paperback original, D343) Bibliography: p. 143. [PL2464] ISBN 0-525-47343-2 2.95 (pbk.)
1. I ching. I. Title.

I ching. English. 299.51482
The book of change; a new translation of the ancient Chinese I ching (Yi king) with detailed instruction for its practical use in divination, by John Blofeld. New York, Dutton [1966, c1965] 228 p. 23 cm. [BL1900.I 23B5] 66-2160
I. Blofeld, John Eton Calthorpe, 1913- ed. and tr. II. Title.

I ching. English. 299.51482
The book of change; a new translation of the ancient Chinese I ching (Yi king) with detailed instruction for its practical use in divination, by John Blofeld. New York, Dutton [1966, c1965] 228 p. 23 cm. [BL1900.I23B5] 66-2160
I. Blofeld, John Eaton Calthorpe. 1913- ed. and tr. II. Title.

*I Ching. English. 299'.514'82
Essential changes; the essence of the I Ching. Tucson, Ariz., Omen Press, 1972. 1 v. (unpaged), illus., 18 cm. [PL2478] 72-83265 ISBN 0-912358-23-8 pap., 2.25
I. Title.

I ching. English. 299'.514'82
I ching = Book of changes / the translation by James Legge. New York : Causeway Books, c1973. 444 p., [3] leaves of plates : ill. ; 25 cm. [PL2478.D47 1973] 72-97374 ISBN 0-88356-000-3 : 10.00
I. Legge, James, 1815-1897, tr.

I ching. English. 299'.514'82
I ching. Edited and with an introd. by Raymond Van Over. Based on the translation by James Legge. New York, New American Library [1971] 444 p. illus. 18 cm. (A Mentor book) Includes bibliographical references. [PL2478.D47 1971] 75-136011 1.50
I. Van Over, Raymond, ed. II. Legge, James, 1815-1897, tr.

I ching. English. 299'.5148'2
The I ching; or, Book of changes. The Richard Wilhelm translation rendered into English by Cary F. Baynes. Foreword by C. G. Jung. [2d ed. New York] Pantheon Books [1961, c1950] xlii, 395, 376 p. 24 cm. (Bollingen series, 19) [PL2478.D8 1961] 74-157506
I. Wilhelm, Richard, 1873-1930, tr. II. Baynes, Cary F., tr. III. Title. IV. Series.

I ching. English. 299'.514'82
The I ching; or, Book of changes. The Richard Wilhelm translation rendered into English by Cary F. Baynes. Foreword by C. G. Jung. Pref. to the 3d ed. by Hellmut Wilhelm. [3d ed.] [Princeton, N.J.] Princeton University Press [1967] lxii, 740 p. 21 cm. (Bollingen series, 19) [PL2478.D8 1967] 67-24740
I. Wilhelm, Richard, 1873-1930, tr. II. Baynes, Cary F., tr. III. Title. IV. Title: Book of changes.

LAO-TZU. 299.51482
Tao te ching. Translated with an introd. by D. C. Lau. [Baltimore] Penguin Books [1963] 191 p. 18 cm. (The Penguin classics, L131) [BL1900.L3L3] 64-3128
I. Lau, Dim Cheuk, tr. II. Title.

LAO-TZU. 299'.51'482
Tao te ching [by] Lao Tsu. A new translation by Gia-fu Feng and Jane English. Photography by Jane English. Calligraphy by Gia-fu Feng. [1st ed.] New York, Vintage Books [1972] 1 v. (unpaged) illus. 29 cm. [BL1900.L3F46 1972b] 72-2338 ISBN 0-394-71833-X
I. Feng, Gia-fu, tr. II. English, Jane, tr. III. Title.

LAO-TZU. 299'.5148'2
Tao te ching [by] Lao Tsu. A new translation by Gia-fu Feng and Jane English. Photography by Jane English. Calligraphy by Gia-fu Feng. [1st ed.] New York, Knopf, 1972. 1 v. (unpaged) illus. 29 cm. [BL1900.L3F46 1972] 72-2233 ISBN 0-394-48084-8 7.95
I. Feng, Gia-fu, tr. II. English, Jane, tr. III. Title.

LAO-TZU 299.51482
Tao Teh Ching. [Tr. from Chinese by John C. H. Wu, ed. by Paul K. T. Sih] New York, St. John's Univ. Pr. 115p. (Asian Inst. translations, no. 1) 60-16884 3.50 bds.,
I. Wu, Ching-hsiung, 1899- tr. II. Hsueh, Kuang-ch'ien, 1909- ed. III. Title.

LAO-TZU. 299'.5148'2
The Tao teh king. A new translation by Ko Yuen. [Kings Beach, Calif., Thelema Publications, 1973] p. [BL1900.L3C76] 73-11417
I. Crowley, Aleister, 1875-1947, tr. II. Title.

LAO-TZU. 299'.5148'2
Tao Teh King; a tentative translation from the Chinese by Isabella Mears. London, Wheaton, Ill., Theosophical Publishing, 1971. [4], 105 p. 19 cm. Translation of Tao te ching. [BL1900.L3M38 1971] 74-161372 ISBN 0-7229-0300-6 £0.65
I. Mears, Isabella, tr. II. Title.

LAO-TZU. 299'.5148'2
Tao, a new way of thinking : a translation of the Tao te ching, with an introduction and commentaries / Chang Chung-yuan. New York : Harper & Row, 1975. xxx, 223 p. ; 21 cm. (Harper colophon books ; CN 356) Bibliography: p. [213]-223. [BL1900.L3C445 1975] 74-13790 ISBN 0-06-090356-2 pbk. : 3.95
I. Chang, Chung-yuan, 1907- II. Title.

LEE, Jung Young. 299'.51482
The I ching and modern man : essays on metaphysical implications of change / by Jung Young Lee. Secaucus, N.J. : University Books, [1975] 236 p. : ill. ; 29 cm. Includes bibliographical references and index. [PL2464.Z7L43] 74-28541 ISBN 0-8216-0253-5 : 8.95
1. I ching. I. Title.

LEE, Jung Young. 299'.514'82
The principle of changes: understanding the I ching. New Hyde Park, N.Y., University Books [1971] 302 p. 29 cm. Includes bibliographical references. [PL2464.Z6L4] 78-151004 10.00
1. I ching. I. Title. II. Title: Understanding the I ching.

RAJANEESH, Acharya, 1931- 299'.5148'2
Tao : the three treasures : talks on fragments from Tao te ching by Lao Tzu / Rajneesh ; [compiled by Ma Prem Arup ; edited by Ma Prem Veena]. 1st ed. Poona : Rajneesh Foundation, 1976- v. : ill. ; 23 cm. [BL1900.L35R34] 76-905202 Rs75.00
1. Lao-tzu. Tao te ching. I. Title.

THE Sacred books of China: The texts of Taoism. Translated by James Legge. New York, Dover Publications [1962] 2 v. 22 cm. (The sacred books of the East, v. 39—40) "An unabridged and unaltered republication of the work first published ... in 1891." Contents.—pt. 1. The Tao te ching of Lao Tzu. The writings of Chuang Tzu (books I-XVII)—pt. 2. The writings of Chuang Tzu (books XVIII-XXXIII) The T'ai Shang Tractate of Actions and their retributions. Appendices I-VIII. [BL1900.A1S3 1962] 62-53181 299.51482
1. Taoism—Sacred books. I. Chuang-tzu. Writings. Works. English. 1962. II. Legge, James, 1815-1897, tr. III. Lao-tzu. Tao te ching. English. 1962. IV. Thai-Shang Tractate of Actions and their Retribution. T'ai shang kan ying p'ien. English. 1962. V. Title: The texts of Taoism. VI. Series: The sacred books of the East (New York) v. 39-40.

SACRED books of China (The): The texts of Taoi'sm; 2 pts. Tr. by James Legge [Gloucester, Mass., P. Smith, 1964] 2 v. (396; 336 p.) 22 cm. (Sacred books of the east, v. 39-40) Unabridged unaltered re-pubn. of the work first pub. in 1891 by Oxford. Contents.Contents—pt. 1. the Tao te chingof Lao Tzu. The writings of Chuang Tzu (books i-xviii)—pt. 2. the writings of Chuang Tzu (books xviii-xxxiii) the T'ai shang tractate of actions and their retributions. Appendices i-viii. set, 8.00 299.51482
1. Taoism—Sacred books. I. Lao-tzu. Tao te ching. II. Chuang-tzu. III. Trai shang kan ying p'ien. IV. Legge, James, 1815-1897, tr. V. Title: The texts of Taoism. VI. Series: The sacred books of the East (New York) v. 39-40

SIU, Ralph Gun Hoy, 1917- 299'.514'82
The man of many qualities; a legacy of the I ching, by R. G. H. Siu. Cambridge, Mass., MIT Press [1968] xv, 463 p. 21 cm. Includes an English translation of the text of the I ching. Bibliography: p. 407-437. [PL2464.Z7S5] 68-18242
I. I ching. II. Title.

TAOIST texts : 299'.5148'2
ethical, political, and speculative / [compiled and translated] by Frederic Henry Balfour. New York : Gordon Press, 1975. vi, 118 p. : ill. ; 24 cm. First published in 1884. Contents.Contents.—The Tao Te ching.—The Yin fu ching.—The T'ai hsi ching.—The Hsin yin ching.—The Ta t'ung ching.—The Ch'in wen tung.—The Ch'ing ching ching.—Huai-nan tzu. A chapter from the Hung lieh chuan.—The Su shu.—The Kan ying pien. Includes bibliographical references. [BL1900.A1T28 1975] 75-3878 ISBN 0-87968-191-8
1. Taoism—Sacred books. I. Balfour, Frederic Henry.

WILHELM, Hellmut, 1905- 299'.514'82
Change; eight lectures on the I Ching. Translated from German by Cary F. Baynes. [Princeton] Princeton Univ. Pr. [1973, c.1960] x, 111 p. diagrs. 22 cm. (Bollingen paperbacks; Bollingen series LXII) [PL2464.Z7W53] ISBN 0-691-01787-5 pap., 1.95
1. I ching. I. Title. II. Series.
L.C. card no for the 1960 ed.: 60-11790.

YANG, Samuel. 299'.514'82
Book of changes, with Biblical references / compiled and translated by Samuel Yang. Adelphi, Md. : Advanced Technology and Research, 1973. 136 p. ; 21 cm. [PL2464.Z6Y26] 74-22386
1. I ching. I. I ching. English. II. Title.

DAVID-NEEL, Alexandra, 1868-1969. 299.54
Magic and mystery in Tibet. Introd. by Aaron Sussman. [New ed.] New Hyde Park, N.Y., University Books [1965] xv, 320 p. 24 cm. Translation of Mystiques et magiciens du Thibet. [DS785.D272 1965] 65-23524
1. Psychical research—Tibet. 2. Occult sciences—Tibet. 3. Tibet—Description and travel. 4. Lamaism. 5. Tibet—Religion. I. Title.

GZI-BRJID. 299'.54
The nine ways of bon; excerpts from gZi-brjid, edited and translated by David L. Snellgrove. London, New York [etc.] Oxford U.P., 1967. vii,312 p. front, illus., 12 plates (incl. facsims.), diagrs. 25 1/2 cm. (B67-26334) (London oriental series, v. 18) £5/5/- *bibliographical references included in "Notes" (p. 257-263) [BL1943.B6G9] 68-87999
I. Snellgrove, David L., ed. II. Title. III. Series.

GZI-BRJID. 299'.54
The nine ways of bon; excerpts from gZi-brjid, edited and translated by David L. Snellgrove. London, New York [etc.] Oxford U.P., 1967. vii, 312 p. front., illus., 12 plates (incl. facsims.), diagrs. 26 cm. (London oriental series, v. 18) Bibliographical references included in "Notes" (p. 257-263) [BL1943.B6G9] 68-87999 £5/5/-
I. Snellgrove, David L., ed. II. Title. III. Series.

SNELLGROVE, David L. 299.54
Himalayan pilgrimage; a study of Tibetan religion, by a traveller through western Nepal. Oxford B. Cassirer. [Mystic, Conn., Verry, 1966] xvi, 304p. illus. (col.front.) maps. 23 cm. First pub. in England in 1961. Bibl. [BL2030.N3S5] 61-42472 bds., 7.50
1. Nepal—Religion. 2. Nepal—Descr. & trav. I. Title.

ANESAKI, Masaharu, 1873-1949. 299.56
History of Japanese religion, with special reference to the social and moral life of the nation. Rutland, Vt., C. E. Tuttle Co. [1963] xxii, 423 p. illus., ports., facsims. 24 cm. "Principle works by the same author": p. xxi-xxii. Bibliographical footnotes. [[BL2201]] 63-19395
1. Japan — Religion. 2. Japan — Soc. life & cust. I. Title.

ANESAKI, Masaharu, 1873-1949 299.56
History of Japanese religion, with special reference to the social and moral life of the nation. Rutland, Vt., Tuttle [c.1963] xxii, 423p. illus., ports., facsims. 24cm. Bibl. 63-19395 7.50
1. Japan—Religion. 2. Japan—Soc. life & cust. I. Title.

ANESAKI, Masaharu, 1873-1949 299.56
Religious life of the Japanese people. Rev. by Hideo Kishimoto. Tokyo, Kokusai Bunka Shinkokai [dist. Honolulu. Hawaii, East West Ctr. Pr., 1963, c.]1961. 105p. plates, port, 24cm. (Ser. on Japanese life and culture, v.4) Bibl. 64-584 2.50 pap.,
1. Japan—Religion. I. Title. II. Series.

BACH, Marcus, 1906- 299'.56
The power of perfect liberty; out of Japan: a creative breakthrough in humanity's quest for a new man in a new age. Englewood Cliffs, N.J., Prentice-Hall [1971] 163 p. 22 cm. [BL2228.P2B3] 78-161916 ISBN 0-13-686832-0 5.95
1. PL Kyodan. I. Title.

CZAJA, Michael. 299'.56
Gods of myth and stone; phallicism in Japanese folk religion. With a foreword by George De Vos. [1st ed.] New York, Weatherhill [1974] 294 p. illus. 27 cm. Bibliography: p. 279-288. [BL460.C9 1974] 73-88468 ISBN 0-8348-0095-0 20.00
1. Phallicism. 2. Gods, Japanese. 3. Husband and wife (in religion, folklore, etc.) I. Title.

ELLWOOD, Robert S., 1933- 299'.56
The Eagle and the Rising Sun; Americans and the new religions of Japan, by Robert S. Ellwood, Jr. Philadelphia, Westminster Press [1974] 224 p. 21 cm. Includes bibliographical references. [BL2209.E44] 74-7317 ISBN 0-664-20707-3 7.95
1. Japan—Religion—1945- 2. United States—Religion—1945- I. Title.

GRIFFIS, William Elliot, 1843-1928. 299'.56
The religions of Japan, from the dawn of history to the era of Meiji. Freeport, N.Y., Books for Libraries Press [1972] xxi, 457 p. 23 cm. (Essay index reprint series) Reprint of the 1895 ed., issued in the series Morse lectures, 1894. [BL2201.G8 1972] 70-37469 ISBN 0-8369-2550-5
1. Japan—Religion. I. Title. II. Series: The Morse lectures, 1894.

HEARN, Lafcadio, 1850-1904. 299'.56
Japan's religions; Shinto and Buddhism. Edited by Kazumitsu Kato. New Hyde Park, N.Y., University Books [1966] xiv, 356 p. 22 cm. "Selected from: Koizumi edition, The writings of Lafcadio Hearn." Bibliographical footnotes. [BL2201.H4 1966] 66-23911
1. Japan—Religion. 2. Japan—Religious life and customs. I. Kato, Kazumitsu, ed. II. Title.

HOLTOM, Daniel Clarence, 1884- 299.56
Modern Japan and Shinto nationalism; a study of present-day trends in Japanese religions. Rev. ed. New York, Paragon 1963[c.1943, 1947] 226p. 24cm. (Haskell lects. in comparative religion) Bibl. 63-22615 7.50
1. Shinto. 2. Japan—Religion. 3. Nationalism and religion—Japan. I. Title.

HORI, Ichiro, 1910- 299'.56
Folk religion in Japan; continuity and change. Edited by Joseph M. Kitagawa and Alan L. Miller. Chicago, University of Chicago Press [1968] xv, 278 p. illus. 22 cm. (Haskell lectures on history of religions, new ser., no. 1) Includes bibliographical references. [BL2202.H58] 67-30128
1. Japan—Religion. I. Title. II. Series.

LEBRA, William P. 299.56
Okinawan religion: belief, ritual, and social structure [by] William P. Lebra. [Honolulu] University of Hawaii Press [1966] xiv, 241 p. illus. 21 cm. [BL2215.O4L4] 66-16506
1. Okinawa Island — Religion. I. Title.

LEBRA, William P. 299.56
Okinawan religion: belief, ritual, and social structure. [Honolulu] Univ. of Hawaii Pr. [c.1966] xiv, 241p. illus. 21cm. [BL2215.O4L4] 66-16506 4.75 pap.,
1. Okinawa Island—Religion. I. Title.

OFFNER, Clark B. 299.56
Modern Japanese religions, with special emphasis upon their doctrines of healing [by] Clark B. Offner [and] Henry van Straelen. Leiden, E. J. Brill; New York, Twayne, 1963. 296 p. illus., ports. 21 cm. Bibliography: p. [283]-290. [BL2202.O3] 62-22211
1. Sects — Japan. 2. Japan — Religion. I. Straelen, Henricus van, 1903- joint author. II. Title.

OFFNER, Clark B. 299.56
Modern Japanese religlons, with special emphasis upon their doctrines of healing [by] Clark B. Offner, Henry van Straelen. Leiden, E. J. Brill; New York, Twayne, 1963. 296p. illus., ports. 21cm. Bibl. 62-22211 8.00
1. Sects—Japan. 2. Japan—Religion. I. Straelen, Henricus van, 1903- joint author. II. Title.

ONO, Motonori, 1904- 299.56
Shinto, the Kami Way, by Sokyo Ono in collaboration with William P. Woodard. Sketches by Sadao Sakamoto. [Tokyo, Rutland, Vt.] Bridgeway Press [1961, c1962] 118 p. illus. 22 cm. "First published in 1960 ... under the title: The Kami Way; an introduction to Shrine Shinto." [BL2220.O5 1962] 61-14033
1. Shinto, I. Title: The Kami Way.

ROBINSON, James C. 299'.56
Okinawa; a people and their gods, by James C. Robinson. [1st ed.] Rutland, Vt., C. E. Tuttle [1969] 110 p. illus., maps. 22 cm. Bibliography: p. 103-104. [BL2215.R9R6] 69-16179 3.75
1. Ryukyu Islands—Religion. I. Title.

ROSS, Floyd Hiatt. 299.56
Shinto, the way of Japan. Boston, Beacon Press [1965] xvii, 187 p. illus. 24 cm. Bibliography: p. 175-176. [BL2220.R6] 65-13533
1. Shinto. I. Title.

ROSS, Floyd Hiatt 299.56
Shinto, the way of Japan. Boston, Beacon [c.1965] xvii, 187p. illus. 24cm. Bibl. [BL2220.R6] 65-13533 7.95 bds.,
1. Shinto. I. Title.

THOMSEN, Harry. 299.56
The new religions of Japan. [1st ed.] Rutland, Vt., C. E. Tuttle Co. [1963] 269 p. illus. 22 cm. Bibliography: p. 259-264. [BL2202.T5] 63-8715
1. Sects — Japan. 2. Japan — Religion. I. Title.

THOMSEN, Harry 299.56
The new religions of Japan. Rutland, Vt., Tuttle [c.1963] 269p. illus. 22cm. Bibl. 63-8715 5.00
1. Sects—Japan. 2. Japan—Religion. I. Title.

WHEELER, Post, 1869- 299.56
The sacred scriptures of the Japanese, with all authoritative variants, chronologically arranged, setting forth the narrative of the creation of the cosmos, the divine descent of the sky-ancestor of the imperial house and the lineage of the earthly emperors, to whom the Sun-Deity has given the rule of the world unto ages eternal. New York, H. Schuman [1952] xivi, 562 p. 24 cm. Translations of the Kojiki and the Nihongi, supplemented and amplified by translation of a number of lesser works, collated and combined in a connected narrative. "Sources": p. [xviii]-xxvii. [BL2220.W45] 52-14316
1. Shinte. 2. Mythology. Japanese. 3. Japan—Kings and rulers. I. Yasuinaro. d. 723. Kojiki. II. Nihongi. III. Title.

ASTON, William George, 1841-1911. 299'.561
Shinto : the way of the gods / by W. G. Aston. New York : Krishna Press, 1974. ii, 390 p. : ill. ; 23 cm. Originally published in 1905 by Longmans, Green, London, New York. Includes bibliographical references and index. [BL2220.A8 1974] 72-98090 ISBN 0-87968-076-8 : 34.95.
1. Shinto.

HERBERT, Jean, 1897- 299'.561
Shinto; at the fountain-head of Japan. With a pref. by Yukitada Sasaki. New York, Stein and Day [1967] 622 p. illus., geneal. table, map. 25 cm. Translation of Aux sources du Japon. Bibliography: p. 533-560. [BL2220.H413 1967] 66-24531
1. Shinto. I. Title.

HOLTOM, Daniel Clarence, 1884- 299.561
The national faith of Japan; a study in modern Shinto, by D. C. Holtom. New York, Paragon Book Reprint Corp., 1965. xiii, 329 p. illus., facsims., geneal. table, plan, port. 24 cm. "An unaltered and unabridged reprint of the work first published in London 1938." Bibliographical footnotes. [BL2220.H58] 65-26102
1. Shinto. I. Title.

HOLTOM, Daniel Clarence, 1884- 299.561
The national faith of Japan; a study in modern Shinto. New York, Paragon [c.] 1965. xiii, 329p. illus., facsims., general. table, plan, port. 24cm. An unaltered and unabridged reprint of the work first pub. in London 1938. Bibl. [BL2220.H58] 65-26102 10.00
1. Shinto. I. Title.

KATO, Genchi, 1873-1965. 299'.561
A study of Shinto; the religion of the Japanese nation. New York, Barnes & Noble [1971] ix, 250 p. 23 cm. Reprint of the 1926 ed., with a pref. Bibliography: p. [217]-230. [BL2220.K35 1971] 75-29406 ISBN 0-389-04070-3
1. Shinto. I. Title.

MASON, Joseph Warren Teets, 1879-1941 299'.561
The meaning of Shinto; the primaeval foundation of creative spirit in modern Japan. Port Washington, N. Y., Kennikat [1967. c.1935] 252p. 22cm. Bibl. [BL2220.M3 1967] 67-27624 7.00
1. Shinto. I. Title.

PIGGOTT, Juliet. 299'.5611'3
Japanese mythology. Feltham, New York, Hamlyn, 1969. 5-141 p. illus. (some col.), map. 29 cm. Illus. on lining papers. Bibliography: p. 138. [BL2202.P5 1969] 74-458795 ISBN 0-600-02113-0 25/-
1. Mythology, Japanese. I. Title.

LOFLAND, John. 299.57
Doomsday Cult; a study of conversion, proselytization, and maintenance of faith. Englewood Cliffs, N.J., Prentice-Hall [1966] x, 276 p. 22 cm. Bibliographical footnotes. [BL53.L6] 66-19893
1. Psychology, Religious. 2. Religion and sociology. I. Title.

LOFLAND, John. 299.57
Doomsday Cult; a study of conversion. proselvtization, and maintenance of faith. Englewood Cliffs, N.J., Prentice [c.1966] x, 276p. 22cm. Bibl. [BL53.L6] 66-19893 3.75 pap.,
1. Psychology, Religious. 2. Religion and sociology. I. Title.

ABIMBOLA, 'Wande. 299'.6
IFA an exposition of Ifa literary corpus / 'Wande Abimbola. Ibadan : Oxford University Press Nigeria, 1976. ix, 256 p., [3] leaves of plates : ill. ; 23 cm. English and Yoruba. Includes index. Bibliography: p. 233-235. [BF1779.I4A24] 77-150583 ISBN 0-19-575325-9 : 21.50.
1. Ifa. I. Title.
Distributed by Oxford University Press, New York

ABRAHAMSSON, Hans. 299'.6
The origin of death : studies in African mythology / by Hans Abrahamsson. New York : Arno Press, 1977, c1951. vii, 178 p. : maps ; 26 cm. (The Literature of death and dying) Reprint of the author's thesis, Uppsala, which was issued as no. 3 of Studia ethnographica Upsaliensia. Includes index.

Bibliography: p. 171-176. [BL2400.A2 1977] 76-19555 ISBN 0-405-09551-1 : 15.00
1. Death (African religion) 2. Mythology, African. I. Title. II. Series. III. Series: Studia ethnographica Upsaliensia ; 3.

BARRETT, Leonard E. 299'.6
The Rastafarians : sounds of cultural dissonance / Leonard E. Barrett. Boston : Beacon Press, [1977] p. cm. Includes index. Bibliography: p. [BL2530.J3B37] 76-48491 ISBN 0-8070-1114-2 : 10.95 ISBN 0-8070-1115-0 pbk. : 3.95
1. Ras Tafari movement. 2. Jamaica—Religion. 3. Jamaica—History. I. Title.

BARRETT, Leonard E. 299'.6
Soul-force: African heritage in Afro-American religion, by Leonard E. Barrett. [1st ed.] Garden City, N.Y., Anchor Press, 1974. viii, 251 p. 22 cm. (C. Eric Lincoln series on Black religion) Bibliography: p. [237]-240. [E185.7.B33 1974] 73-83612 ISBN 0-385-07410-7 7.95
1. Negroes—Religion. I. Title. II. Series.

BASCOM, William Russell, 299'.6
1912-
Shango in the New World, by William Bascom. Austin, African and Afro-American Research Institute, University of Texas at Austin [1972] 23 p. illus. 23 cm. (University of Texas at Austin. African and Afro-American Research Institute. Occasional publication 4) "Originally presented at the XXXIX Congreso Internacional de Americanistas in Lima in August 1970 and was delivered as a lecture at the University of Texas at Austin in March 1972." Bibliography: p. 21-23. [BL2532.S5B37] 72-195339
1. Shango. I. Title. II. Series: Texas. University at Austin. African and Afro-American Research Institute. Occasional publication 4.

BEN-JOCHANNAN, Yosef. 299'.6
The Black man's religion, and Extracts and comments from the Holy Black Bible. [New York, Alkebu-lan Books Associates, 1974] 1 v. (various pagings) illus. 22 cm. (African-American heritage series) Cover title. Includes v. 2-3 of the author's The Black man's religion; v. 1 published in 1970 under title: African origins of the major "Western religions". Includes bibliographical references. [BR563.N4B462] 74-162930
1. Bible—Criticism, interpretation, etc. 2. Negroes—Religion. I. Ben-Jochannan, Yosef. Extracts and comments from the Holy Black Bible. 1974. II. Title. III. Series.

BRAMLY, Serge, 1949- 299'.6
Macumba : the teachings of Maria-Jose, mother of the gods / by Serge Bramly ; translated by Meg Bogin. New York : St. Martin's Press, [1977] p. cm. [BL2592.U513B713] 77-76628 ISBN 0-312-50338-5 : 10.00
1. Umbanda (Cultus) I. Maria Jose, mere. II. Title.

COURLANDER, Harold, 1908- 299'.6
Tales of Yoruba gods and heroes. Decorations by Larry Lurin. New York, Crown Publishers [1973] vii, 243 p. illus. 24 cm. Bibliography: p. 241-243. [GR360.Y6C68 1973] 72-84307 ISBN 0-517-50063-9 5.95
1. Tales, Yoruba. 2. Mythology, Yoruba. I. Title.

EVANS-PRITCHARD, Edward 299'.6
Evan, 1902-
Nuer religion. Oxford, Clarendon Press, 1956. xii, 335p. illus. 23cm. Errata slip inserted. Bibliographical footnotes. [BL2480.N7E9] 56-58065
1. Nuer (African tribe)—Religion. I. Title.

GELFAND, Michael 299.6
An African's religion: the spirit of Nyajena; case history of a Karanga people. Cape Town, Juta, 1966. x, 135p. illus., fold. map. ports. 23cm. Bibl. [GN470.G4] 67-851 8.50 bds.,
1. Religion, Primitive. 2. Mashona—Religion. I. Title.
American distributor: Verry, Mystic, Conn.

GELFAND, Michael 299.6
Shona religion, with special reference to the Makorekore. Foreword by M. Hannan. Cape Town, Juta [dist. Mystic, Conn., Verry, 1965] 184p. illus., port., fold. map. 22cm. [BL2480.M3G39] 64-32533 7.50
1. Mashona—Religion. I. Title.

GILFOND, Henry. 299'.6
Voodoo, its origins and practices / by Henry Gilfond. New York : Watts, 1976. viii, 114 p. : ill. ; 25 cm. Includes index. Bibliography: p. [101]-102. Discusses the history, beliefs, and rituals of voodoo, with emphasis on its practice in Haiti. [BL2490.G54] 76-16046 ISBN 0-531-00347-7 lib.bdg. : 6.88
1. Voodooism—Juvenile literature. I. Title.

GLEASON, Judith Illsley. 299'.6
Orisha: the gods of Yorubaland, by Judith Gleason. Art by Aduni Olorisa. [1st ed.] New York, Atheneum, 1971. 122 p. illus. 25 cm. [BL2480.Y6G57 1971] 70-134809 5.25
1. Mythology, Yoruba. I. Title.

GONZALEZ-WIPPLER, Migene. 299'.6
Santeria; African magic in Latin America. Garden City, N.Y., Doubleday [1975 c1973] 178 p. illus. 18 cm. (Anchor books) Bibliography: p. 167-168. [BL2532.S3G66] ISBN 0-385-09696-8 2.95 (pbk.)
1. Santeria (Cultus) I. Title.
L.C. card no. for original ed.: 73-82439

GONZALEZ-WIPPLER, Migene. 299'.6
Santeria; African magic in Latin America. New York, Julian Press [1973] 181 p. illus. 22 cm. Bibliography: p. 172-173. [BL2532.S3G66] 73-82439 ISBN 0-87097-055-0 6.50
1. Santeria (Cultus) I. Title.

GOODY, John Rankine, comp. 299'.6
The myth of the Bagre [by] Jack Goody. Oxford, Clarendon Press, 1972. x, 381 p. illus. 22 cm. (Oxford library of African literature) Includes the White Bagre and the Black Bagre in Dagari and English. Bibliography: p. [117] [BL2480.D3G66] 73-155639 ISBN 0-19-815134-9 £9.00
1. Mythology, Dagari. I. White Bagre. English and Dagari. 1972. II. Black Bagre. English and Dagari. 1972. III. Title.

HARRIS, William Thomas. 299'.6
The springs of Mende belief and conduct, a discussion of the influence of the belief in the supernatural among the Mende [by] W. T. Harris and Harry Sawyerr. Freetown, Sierra Leone University Press; [distributed by the Oxford University Press, New York] 1968. xvi, 152 p. illus., map. 23 cm. Bibliographical references included in "Notes" (p. [134]-147) [BL2480.M4H3] 73-319 35/-
1. Mende—Religion. I. Sawyerr, Harry, joint author. II. Title.

IDOWU, E. Bolaji. 299'.6
African traditional religion: a definition [by] E. Bolaji Idowu. Maryknoll, N.Y., Orbis Books [1973] xii, 228 p. 23 cm. Includes bibliographical references. [BL2400.I3] 72-96951 ISBN 0-88344-005-9 5.95
1. Africa—Religion. I. Title.

JANZEN, John M. 299'.6
An anthology of Kongo religion : primary texts from Lower Zaire / by John M. Janzen and Wyatt MacGaffey. Lawrence : University of Kansas], 1974. 163 p. : map ; 27 cm. (University of Kansas publications in anthropology ; no. 5) Includes index. Bibliography: p. [158]-159. [BL2480.B24J36] 74-620186 5.00
1. Eglise de Jesus-Christ sur la terre par le prophete Simon Kimgango. 2. Bakongo (African tribe)—Religion. I. MacGaffey, Wyatt, joint author. II. Title. III. Series: Publications in anthropology (Lawrence, Kan.) ; no. 5.

KING, Noel Quinton. 299'.6
Religions of Africa: a pilgrimage into traditional religions [by] Noel Q. King. [1st ed.] New York, Harper & Row [1970] xi, 116 p. 22 cm. Bibliography: p. 99-112. [BL2400.K5 1970] 76-109071 4.50
1. Africa, Sub-Saharan—Religion. I. Title.

KRISTOS, Kyle. 299'.6
Voodoo / by Kyle Kristos. 1st ed. Philadelphia : Lippincott, c1976. 112 p. : ill. ; 21 cm. Includes index. Bibliography: p. 108. Traces the origins, cults, and practices which surround voodooism including voodoo practices in the United States and modern Haiti. [BL2490.K72] 76-18989 ISBN 0-397-31706-9 : 6.95 ISBN 0-397-31707-7 pbk. :
1. Voodooism—Juvenile literature. I. Title.

LANGGUTH, A. J., 1933- 299'.6
Macumba : white and black magic in Brazil / A. J. Langguth. 1st ed. New York : Harper & Row, [1975] 273 p. ; 21 cm. [BL2592.U5L34 1975] 74-1830 ISBN 0-06-012503-9 : 7.95
1. Umbanda (Cultus) 2. Magic—Brazil. I. Title.

LEACOCK, Seth. 299'.6
Spirits of the deep. A study of an Afro-Brazilian Cult. Garden City, N.Y., Anchor Books 1975, [c1972] x, 404 p., illus., 21 cm. Spirits of the deep was originally published for the American Museum of Natural History by the Natural History Press, a division of Doubleday in 1972. Includes index. Bibliography: p. 381-387. [BL2592.B3L4] ISBN 0-385-06880-8 3.95 (pbk.)
1. Batuque (Cultus). I. Leacock, Ruth, joint author. II. Title.
L.C. card no. for original ed.: 78-178832.

LEACOCK, Seth. 299'.6
Spirits of the deep; a study of an Afro-Brazilian cult [by] Seth and Ruth Leacock. [1st ed.] Garden City, N.Y., Published for the American Museum of Natural History [by] Doubleday Natural History Press, 1972. x, 404 p. illus. 22 cm. Bibliography: p. 381-387. [BL2592.B3L4] 78-178832 ISBN 0-385-07648-7 9.95
1. Batuque (Cultus) I. Leacock, Ruth, joint author. II. American Museum of Natural History, New York. III. Title.

LEONARD, Arthur Glyn. 299'.6
The Lower Niger and its tribes. 1st ed., new impression. London, Cass, 1968. xxii, 564p. plate, map. 22cm. (Cass lib. of African studies. General studies, no. 67) Orig. pub., London, Macmillan, 1906. [DT515.42.L4 1968] 68-96668 17.50
1. Ethnology—Nigeria. 2. Nigeria—Religion. I. Title. II. Series.
Available from Barnes & Noble. New York.

LE ROY, Alexandre, Abp., 299'.6
1854-1938.
The religion of the primitives, by Alexander Le Roy. Translated by Newton Thompson. New York, Negro Universities Press [1969] x, 334 p. 23 cm. Reprint of the 1922 ed. Bibliographical footnotes. [GN470.L43 1969] 72-78769
1. Religion, Primitive. I. Title.

MACDONALD, James. 299'.6
Religion and myth. New York, Negro Universities Press [1969] xiii, 240 p. 23 cm. Reprint of the 1893 ed. Includes bibliographical references. [BL2400.M3 1969] 74-82059
1. Africa—Religion. 2. Religion, Primitive. I. Title.

MBITI, John S. 299'.6
Concepts of God in Africa [by] John S. Mbiti. New York, Praeger Publishers [1970] xv, 348 p. 23 cm. Bibliography: p. [317]-323. [BL205.M34 1970] 78-95360 9.00
1. God. 2. Africa—Religion. I. Title.

MBITI, John S. 299'.6
An introduction to African religion [by] John S. Mbiti. New York, Praeger [1974] p. cm. Discusses the philosophies, rituals, and ceremonies of various African religions and their influence in the lives of the people. [BL2400.M383] 73-8171 6.95
1. Africa—Religion—Juvenile literature. I. Title.

MBITI, John S. 299'.6
The prayers of African religion / John S. Mbiti. Maryknoll, N.Y. : Orbis Books, 1976, c1975. p. cm. [BV245.M484 1976] 75-42519 ISBN 0-88344-394-5
1. Prayers. 2. Africa—Religion. I. Title.

MILLROTH, Berta, 1914- 299.6
Lyuba; traditional religion of the Sukuma. [Uppsala] 1965. 217p. 32cm. (Studia ethnographica Upsaliensia, 22) Akademisk avhandling--Uppsala. Without thesis statement. Bibl. [BL2480.S8M5] 65-83266 15.00 pap.,
1. Suku (African tribe)—Religion 2. Sunworship. I. Title. II. Series.
American distributor: Heinman, New York, N.Y. 10021

MITCHELL, Henry H. 299'.6
Black belief : folk beliefs of Blacks in America and West Africa / Henry H. Mitchell. 1st ed. New York : Harper & Row, [1975] xiii, 171 p. ; 21 cm. Includes index. Bibliography: p. [164]-168. [BR563.N4M57 1975] 74-4632 ISBN 0-06-065762-6 : 6.95
1. Negroes—Religion. I. Title.

NADEL, Siegfried 299'.6
Frederick, 1903-1956.
Nupe religion; traditional beliefs and the influence of Islam in a West African chiefdom. New York, Schocken Books [1970] x, 288 p. illus. 23 cm. "Intended as a sequel to ... [the author's] first monograph on the Nupe people, a black Byzantium." Includes bibliographical references. [BL2480.N8N3 1970] 71-114163 10.00
1. Nupe (African people)—Religion. I. Title.

PARRINDER, Edward Geoffrey. 299.6
African traditional religion. London, New York, Hutchinson's University Library [1954] 160p. illus. 19cm. (Hutchinson's university library: World religions) [BL2400.P37] 54-10838
1. Africa—Religion. 2. Religion, Primitive. I. Title.

PARRINDER, Edward Geoffrey 299.6
African traditional religion, [2d rev. ed. Dist. Greenwich, Conn., Seabury, c.]1962. 156p. illus. 19cm. (Seraph) 62-6263 1.50 pap.,
1. Africa—Religion. 2. Religion, Primitive. I. Title.

PARRINDER, Edward Geoffrey 299.6
African traditional religion /Geoffrey Parrinder 3rd edition. New York: Harper and Row [1976 c1962] 156 p.; 20 cm. (Harper forum books) Includes index. Bibliography: p. 149-151. [BL2400.P37] 75-39900 ISBN 0-06-066472-X pbk.: 3.95
1. Africa—Religion. 2. Religion, primitive. I. Title.

PARRINDER, Edward 299'.6
Geoffrey.
African traditional religion / Geoffrey Parrinder. Westport, Conn. : Greenwood Press, 1976. p. cm. Reprint of the ed. published by Harper & Row, New York. Includes index. Bibliography: p. [BL2400.P37 1976] 76-22490 ISBN 0-8371-3401-3 lib.bdg. : 9.00
1. Africa—Religion. 2. Religion, Primitive. I. Title.

PARRINDER, Edward 299'.6
Geoffrey.
West African religion; a study of the beliefs and practices of Akan, Ewe, Yoruba, Ibo, and kindred peoples [by] Geoffrey Parrinder. With a foreword by Edwin Smith. New York, Barnes & Noble [1970] xv, 203 p. map. 23 cm. Reprint of the 1961 ed. A revision of the author's thesis, University of London. Bibliography: p. 196-[197] [BL2465.P3 1970] 75-20695 ISBN 0-389-04040-1
1. Africa, West—Religion. I. Title.

PARRINDER, Geoffrey. 299.6
African traditional religion. London, New York, Hutchinson's University Library [1954] 160p. illus. 19cm. (Hutchinson's university library: World religions) [BL2400.P37] 54-10838
1. Africa—Religion. 2. Religion, Primitive. I. Title.

RAY, Benjamin C., 1940- 299'.6
African religions : symbol, ritual, and community / Benjamin C. Ray. Englewood Cliffs, N.J. : Prentice-Hall, [1976] xii, 238 p., [1] leaf of plates : ill. ; 24 cm. (Prentice-Hall studies in religion series) Includes index. Bibliography: p. 218-231. [BL2400.R34] 75-17519 ISBN 0-13-018630-9 : 8.95 ISBN 0-13-018622-8 pbk. : 4.95
1. Africa—Religion. I. Title.

RELIGION in a pluralistic 299'.6
society : essays presented to Professor C. G. Baeta in celebration of his retirement from the service of the University of Ghana, September 1971 by friends and colleagues scattered over the globe/ edited by J. S. Pobee. Leiden : E. J. Brill, 1976. viii, 236 p., [1] leaf of plates : port. ; 25 cm. (Studies on religion in Africa ; v. 2) Contents.Contents.—Kamali, S. A. Religion in a pluralistic society.—Thomas, J. C. Uses and truth.—Gensichen, D. H.-W. World community and world religions.—Mbiti, J. S. God, dreams and African militancy.—Parrinder, E. G. Mysticism in African religion.—Kudadjie, J. N. Does religion determine morality in African societies?—King, N. Q. and D. J. F. Towards an African Strack-Billerbeck?—Sawyerr, H. Traditions in transit.—Steemers, J. C. Culture embarrassment and religious fear.—Warren, M. A. C. Political realities and the Christian mission.—Pobee, J. S. Church and State in Ghana, 1949-1966.—Ashanin, C. B. The black heroes of the Philadelphia plague in 1793.—Nickles, A. A religion in a pluralist society.—Dickson, K. A. The minister—then and now.—Walls, A. F. Towards understanding Africa's place in Christian history.—Oduyoye, M. The Church in youth education—years ago or years to come.—Braimah, B. A. R. Islamic education in Ghana.—Blake, E. C. In one boat. "Publications of Rev. Prof. C. G. Baeta": p. [232]-233. [BL2400.R37] 76-381619
1. Baeta, C. G. 2. Africa—Religion—Addresses, essays, lectures. 3. Religions—Addresses, essays, lectures. I. Baeta, C. G. II. Pobee, J. S. III. Title. IV. Series.

RIGAUD, Milo, 1904- 299'.6
Secrets of voodoo. Translated from the French by Robert B. Cross. Photos. by Odette Mennesson-Riguad [i.e. Rigaud] New York, Arco [1970, c1969] 219 p. illus. 24 cm. Translation of La tradition voudoo et le voudoo haitien. [BL2490.R5313 1970] 77-82128 ISBN 0-668-02008-3 7.95
1. Voodooism—Haiti. 2. Folk-lore—Haiti. I. Title.

RIGAUD, Milo, 1904- 299'.6
Ve-ve : diagrammes rituels du voudou / Milo Rigaud. Trilingual ed; French-English-Spanish. New York : French and European Publications, [1974?] 587 p. : chiefly ill. ; 27 cm. [BL2490.R54] 75-501577 ISBN 0-8288-0000-6 : 24.95
1. Voodooism. 2. Symbolism. I. Title.

SHORTER, Aylward. 299'.6
Prayer in the religious traditions of Africa / Aylward Shorter. Nairobi : Oxford University Press, 1975. xvi, 145, [1] p. ; 22 cm.

Bibliography: p. 144-[146] [BL2400.S43] 75-980122 ISBN 0-19-572349-X : 7.95
1. Africa—Religious life and customs. 2. Prayers. 3. Prayer. I. Title.
Available from Oxford Univ. Pr.

TURNER, Victor Witter. 299'.6
Revelation and divination in Ndembu ritual / Victor Turner. Ithaca, N.Y. : Cornell University Press, 1975. 354 p. : ill. ; 22 cm. (Symbol, myth, and ritual) Includes index. Bibliography: p. 343-344. [DT963.42.T83] 75-1623 ISBN 0-8014-0863-6 : 17.50 ISBN 0-8014-9151-7 pbk. : 4.95
1. Ndembu (African tribe)—Rites and ceremonies. 2. Ndembu (African tribe)—Religion. 3. Symbolism. I. Title.

WILLIAMSON, Sydney George, 299.6
1906-1959
Akan religion and the Christian faith; a comparative study of the impact of two religions. Ed. by Kwesi A. Dickson. Accra, Ghana Univs. Pr. [dist. New York, Oxford, c.] 1965. xvii, 186p. 23cm. Bibl. [BV3630.A4W5] 65-5233 4.80
1. Missions—Akans (African people) 2. Akans (African people)—Religion. I. Dickson. Kwesi A., ed. II. Title.

WILLOUGHBY, William 299'.6
Charles, 1857-1938.
The soul of the Bantu; a sympathetic study of the magico-religious practices and beliefs of the Bantu tribes of Africa. Westport, Conn., Negro Universities Press [1970] xxvi, 476 p. 23 cm. Reprint of the 1928 ed. Bibliography: p. 461-476. [BL2480.B3W5 1970] 77-107526 ISBN 0-8371-3773-X
1. Bantus—Religion. 2. Ancestor, worship—Africa, Sub-Saharan. I. Title.

YOUNG, Henry J., 1943- 299'.6
Major Black religious leaders, 1755-1940 / Henry J. Young. Nashville : Abingdon, c1977. 173 p. ; 21 cm. Includes bibliographical references. [BR563.N4Y68] 76-51731 ISBN 0-687-22913-8 pbk. : 5.95
1. Afro-Americans—Religion—History. 2. Black theology—History. I. Title.

NASSAU, Robert 299'.6'0966
Hamill, 1835-1921.
Fetichism in West Africa; forty years' observation of native customs and superstitions. New York, Negro Universities Press [1969] xvii, 389 p. illus., map. 23 cm. Reprint of the 1904 ed. Bibliographical footnotes. [BL2465.N3 1969] 69-18995
1. Fetishism. 2. Ethnology—Africa, West. I. Title.

FARROW, Stephen 299'.6'096692
Septimus.
Faith, fancies, and fetich; or, Yoruba paganism; being some account of the religious beliefs of the West African Negroes, particularly of the Yoruba tribes of Southern Nigeria, by Stephen S. Farrow. With a foreword by R. R. Marett. New York, Negro Universities Press [1969] xi, 180 p. illus. 23 cm. "Yoruba Christian lyrics" (with melodies): p. 170-173. Reprint of the 1926 ed. Bibliography: p. 9-11. [BL2480.Y6F3 1969] 76-98718
1. Yorubas. 2. Folk-lore—Nigeria—Yoruba. 3. Fetishism. I. Title.

GELFAND, Michael 299.63
Shona ritual; with special reference to the Chaminuka cult. Foreword by M. Hannan. Cape Town, Juta, [dist. Mystic, Conn., Verry 1965] 217p. illus. 23cm. [BL2480.M3G4] 60-29380 7.50 bds.,
1. Mashona—Religion. I. Title. II. Title: Chaminuka cult.

IDOWU, E. Bolaji. 299.64
Olodumare; God in Yoruba belief. New York, Praeger [1963] 222 p. illus. 23 cm. (Books that matter) [BL2480.Y6 I 3 1963] 63-12823
1. Yorubas — Religion. I. Title. II. Title: God in Yoruba belief.

PARRINDER, Edward Geoffrey 299.64
West African religion, a study of the beliefs and practices of Akan, Ewe, Yoruba, Ibo, and kindred peoples, by Geoffrey Parrinder. Foreword by Edwin Smith [2d ed., completely rewritten, rev. and enl.] London, Epworth Pr.[dist. Mystic, Conn., Verry, 1964, c.1961] xv, 203p. map. 23cm. Bibl. 61-5046 5.00
1. Africa, West—Religion. I. Title.

GRIAULE, Marcel, 1898- 299.65
1956.
Conversations with Ogotemmeli; an introduction to Dogon religious ideas. With an introd. by Germaine Dieterlen. [London] Published for the International African Institute by the Oxford University Press, 1965. xvii, 230 p. illus., map, port. 23 cm. Translation of Dieu d'eau: entretiens avec Ogotemmeli. Bibliography: p. 224-226. [DT530.G753] 65-3614
1. Dogons (African people) 2. Nommo (African deity) I. Title.

GRIAULE, Marcel, 1898-1956 299.65
Conversations with Ogotemmeli; an introduction to Dogon religious ideas [Tr. from French] Introd. by Germaine Dieterlen [London] Pub. for the Intl. African Inst. by [New York] Oxford [c.]1965. xvii, 230p. illus., map, port. 23cm. Bibl. [DT530.G753] 65-3614 5.60
1. Dogons (African people) 2. Nommo (African deity) I. Title.

LIENHARDT, Godfrey. 299.65
Divinity and experience; the religion of the Dinka. Oxford, Clarendon Press, 1961. viii, 328p. plates, maps. 22cm. Bibliographical footnotes. [BL2480.D5L5] 61-19433
1. Dinka (Nilotic tribe)—Religion and mythology. I. Title.

LIENHARDT. GODFREY 299.65
Divinity and experience: the religion of the Dinka. [dist. New York] Oxford [c.]1961[ ] viii, 328p. illus. maps. Bibl. 61-19433 6.75
1. Dinka (Nilotic tribe)—Religion and mythology. I. Title.

NADEL, Siegfried 299.65
Frederick, 1903-
Nupe religion. Glencoe, Ill., Free Press [1954] x, 288p. illus. 22cm. 'Intended as a sequel to ... [the author's] A black Byzantium.' Bibliographical footnotes. [BL2480] 55-14016
1. Nupe (African people)—Religion. I. Title.

*HAUGE, Hans-Egil. 299.6762
Luo religion and folklore. Oslo, Bergen, Universitetsforlaget [1975 c1974] 150 p. ill. 22 cm. Includes index. Bibliography: p. 139-145. [BL2480]
1. Luo (Nilotic tribe.) I. Title.
Distributed by Humanities Press for 10.75 (pbk.)

ABERLE, David Friend, [299.7]
1918-
Navaho and Ute peyotism: a chronological and distributional study, by David F. Aberle and Omer C. Stewart. Boulder, Univ. of Colorado Press, 1957. ix, 129p. maps, tables 26 cm. (University of Colorado studies. Series in anthropology, no. 6) (Colorado. University. University of Colorado studies. Series in anthropology, 6) [E98.R3Az] 970.62 57-63108
1. Peyote. 2. Navaho Indians—Religion and mythology. 3. Ute Indians—Religion and mythology. 4. Navaho Indians—Rites and ceremonies. 5. Ute Indians—Rites and ceremonies I. Stewart, Omer Call, 1908- joint author. II. Title. III. Series.

ABERLE, David Friend, 1918- 299.7
The peyote religion among the Navaho, by David F. Aberle. With field assistance by Harvey C. Moore and with an appendix on Navaho population and education by Denis F. Johnston. Chicago, Aldine Pub. Co. [1966] xxvi, 454 p. illus., maps. 27 cm. (Viking Fund publications in anthropology, no. 42) Bibliography: p. 423-436. [E99.N3A2] 65-26751
1. Navaho Indians — Religion and mythology. 2. Peyotism. I. Title. II. Series.

ALEXANDER, Harley Burr, 299.7
1873-1939.
North American [mythology] New York, Cooper Spuare Publishers, 1964 [c1916] xxiv. 325 p. illus., maps (1 fold. mounted on covery 3 plates Bibliography: p. [313]-325 [BL25.M8] 63-19095
1. Indians of North American — Religion and mythology. I. Title.

BAILEY, Paul Dayton, 299'.7 B
1906-
Ghost dance Messiah [by] Paul Bailey. Los Angeles, Westernlore Press, 1970. 206 p. 22 cm. [E99.P2W58 1970] 75-135152 6.95
1. Wovoka, 1856 (ca.)-1932. 2. Indians of North America—Religion and mythology. I. Title.

BAKER, Betty. 299'.7
At the center of the world. Based on Papago and Pima myths. Illustrated by Murray Tinkelman. New York, Macmillan [1973] 53 p. illus. 23 cm. Contents.Contents.—Earth magician.—Coyote drowns the world.—The killing pot.—The monster eagle.—The killing of Eetoi.—The first war. [PZ8.1.B1724At] 72-88820 ISBN 0-02-708290-3 4.95 (lib. bdg.)
1. Papago Indians—Legends—Juvenile literature. 2. Pima Indians—Legends—Juvenile literature. I. Tinkelman, Murray, illus. II. Title.

BARNETT, Homer Garner, 299.7
1906-
Indian Shakers; a messianic cult of the Pacific Northwest. Carbondale, Southern Illinois University Press, 1957. 378 p. illus. 22 cm. [BX7990.I5703B3] 57-8851
1. Indian Shaker Church. 2. Indians of North America—Northwest, Pacific.

BARNETT, Homer Garner, 299'.7
1906-
Indian Shakers, a messianic cult of the Pacific Northwest [by] H. G. Barnett. Carbondale, Southern Illinois University Press [1972, c1957] 378 p. illus. 21 cm. (Arcturus books edition, AB 104) Bibliography: p. 367-370. [E78.N77B3 1972] 72-5482 ISBN 0-8093-0595-X 2.95
1. Indian Shaker Church. 2. Indians of North America—Northwest, Pacific.

BASSO, Keith H., 1940- 299'.7
Western Apache witchcraft [by] Keith H. Basso. Tucson, University of Arizona Press, 1969. 75 p. maps. 27 cm. (Anthropological papers of the University of Arizona, no. 15) Thesis—Stanford University. Bibliography: p. 72-75. [E99.A6B23] 69-16329
1. Apache Indians—Religion and mythology. 2. Witchcraft. I. Title. II. Series: Arizona. University. Anthropological papers, no. 15

BAYLOR, Byrd. 299'.7
They put on masks. Illustrated by Jerry Ingram. New York, Scribner [1974] 46 p. col. illus. 22 x 27 cm. Drawings and text present the many kinds of American Indian masks and their use with dances and songs to speak to the gods. [E98.M3B38 1974] 73-19557 ISBN 0-684-13767-4 5.95
1. Indians of North America—Masks—Juvenile literature. I. Ingram, Jerry, illus. II. Title.

BEAUTYWAY: 299.7
a Navaho ceremonial. Myth recorded and translated by Father Berard Haile; with a variant myth recorded by Maud Oakes;and sandpaintings recorded by Laura A. Armer, Franc J. Newcomb, and Maud Oakes. [New York] Pantheon Books [1957] xii, 218p. illus., 16 col. plates. 26cm. (Bollingen series, 53) 'Supplement to Beautyway: a Navaho ceremonial. The myth, told by Singer man. recorded in the Navaho language by Father Berard Halle. Edited by Leland C. Wyman' (83p.) in pocket. Bibliography: p.199-201. [E99.N3W93] 970.62 57-7170
1. Navaho Indians —Rites and ceremonies. 2. Navaho Indians—Religion and mythology. 3. Navaho language—Texts. 4. Sandpaintings. I. Wyman, Leland Clifton, 1897- ed. II. Haile, Berard, 1874- III. Series.

BOAS, Franz, 1858-1942. 299'.7
The mythology of the Bella Coola Indian / by Franz Boas. New York : AMS Press, [1975] 25-127 p., [6] leaves of plates : ill. ; 24 cm. Reprint of the 1898 ed. published in New York, which was issued as v. 2 of Memoirs of the American Museum of Natural History, Anthropology v. 1, pt. 2, and as v. 1, pt. 2 of Publications of the Jesup North Pacific Expedition. Includes bibliographical references. [E99.B39B62 1975] 73-3510 ISBN 0-404-58113-7 : 27.50
1. Bellacoola Indians—Religion and mythology. 2. Indians of North America—British Columbia—Religion and mythology. 3. Bellacoola Indians—Legends. 4. Indians of North America—British Columbia—Legends. I. Title. II. Series: American Museum of Natural History, New York. Memoirs ; v. 2. III. Series: The Jesup North Pacific Expedition. Publications ; v. 1, pt. 2.

BOAS, Franz, 1858-1942. 299'.7
The religion of the Kwakiutl Indians. New York, AMS Press [1969] 2 v. 24 cm. (Columbia University contributions to anthropology, v. 10) Reprint of the 1930 ed. Contents.Contents.—pt. I. Texts.—pt. II. Translations. [E99.K9B495 1969] 72-82368
1. Kwakiutl Indians—Religion and mythology. 2. Kwakiutl language—Texts. I. Title. II. Series: Columbia University. Columbia University contributions to anthropology, v. 10

BOURKE, John Gregory, 1843- 299.7
1896
The snake dance of the Moquis of Arizona. [Chicago, Rio Grande Pr., 1963] xvi, 371p. illus. 24cm. (Rio Grande classic) Reproduction of the 1884 ed., pub. by Scribners. New York. 62-21941 8.00
1. Hopi Indians. 2. Snake-dance. 3. Serpent worship. I. Title.

BRINTON, Daniel Garrison, 299'.7
1837-1899.
The myths of the New World; a treatise on the symbolism and mythology of the red race of America. New York, Haskell House Publishers, 1968. 360 p. 23 cm. Reprint of the 3d, 1896 ed. Includes bibliographical references. [E59.R38B85 1968] 68-24972
1. Indians—Religion and mythology. 2. Folklore, Indian. I. Title.

BRINTON, Daniel Garrison, 299'.7
1837-1899.
The myths of the new world; a treatise on the symbolism and mythology of the red race of America. New York, Greenwood Press [1969] viii, 331 p. 23 cm. Reprint of the 2d ed., rev., 1876. Includes bibliographical references. [E59.R38B85 1969] 69-13839
1. Indians—Religion and mythology. 2. Folklore, Indian. I. Title.

BRINTON, Daniel Garrison, 299'.7
1837-1899.
The myths of the New World, a treatise on the symbolism and mythology of the red race of America. Philadelphia, D. McKay, 1896. Detroit, Gale Research Co., 1974. 360 p. 18 cm. Reprint of the 3d ed. rev. Bibliography: p. 55-59. [E59.R38B85 1974] 74-1038 ISBN 0-8103-3959-5 11.00
1. Indians—Religion and mythology. 2. Folklore, Indian. I. Title.

BRINTON, Daniel Garrison, 299'.7
1837-1899.
Myths of the New World : the symbolism and mythology of the Indians of the Americas / by Daniel G. Brinton ; introd. by Paul M. Allen. Blauvelt, N.Y. : Multimedia Pub. Corp., c1976. ix, [v]-viii, 331 p. ; 22 cm. (Steinerbooks) Reprint, with new introd., of the 1876 ed. published by H. Holt, New York. Includes bibliographical references and indexes. [E59.R38B85 1976] 72-81594 ISBN 0-8334-1742-8 pbk. : 5.50 ($5.95 Can)
1. Indians—Religion and mythology. 2. Folklore, Indian. I. Title.

BROWN, Vinson, 1912- 299'.7
Voices of earth and sky : vision search of the native Americans / Vinson Brown ; illustrator, Tony Shearer. Happy Camp, CA : Naturegraph Publishers, c1976. 176, [8] p. : ill. ; 22 cm. Bibliography: p. [3-8] [E98.R36 1976] 76-41761 ISBN 0-87961-061-1 : 8.95
1. Indians of North America—Religion and mythology. 2. Indians—Religion and mythology. 3. Visions. I. Title.

BROWN, Vinson, 1912- 299'.7
Voices of earth and sky; the vision life of the native Americans and their culture heroes. Illustrated by Tony Shearer. [Harrisburg, Pa.] Stackpole Books [1974] 224 p. illus. 24 cm. Bibliography: p. 218-224. [E98.R3B76] 73-21932 ISBN 0-8117-1855-7 8.95
1. Indians of North America—Religion and mythology. 2. Indians—Religion and mythology. 3. Visions. I. Title.

BURLAND, Cottie Arthur, 299'.7
1905-
Feathered Serpent and Smoking Mirror / C. A. Burland and Werner Forman. New York : Putnam, c1975. 128 p. : col. ill. ; 31 cm. Includes index. Bibliography: p. 126. [F1219.3.R38B79] 75-15075 12.95
1. Aztecs—Religion and mythology. 2. Indians of Mexico—Religion and mythology. I. Forman, Werner, joint author. II. Title.

BURLAND, Cottie Arthur, 299'.7
1905-
The gods of Mexico [by] C. A. Burland. [1st American ed.] New York, Putnam [1967] xiii, 219 p. illus., maps. 24 cm. "Select bibliography: p. 209-211. [F1219.3.R38B8 1967a] 66-20267
1. Indians of Mexico—Religion and mythology. I. Title.

CARRASCO Y GARRORENA, Pedro 299.7
Pagan rituals and beliefs among the Chontal Indians of Oaxaca, Mexico. [Bergeley, University of California Press, 1960] iii, 87-117p. map, facsims. 28cm. (Anthropological records, v. 20, no. 3) Bibl.: p.116. 60-63401 1.00 pap.,
1. Chontal Indians—Rites and ceremonies. I. Title. II. Series.

CASTANEDA, Carlos. 299'.7
A separate reality; further conversations with Don Juan. New York, Simon and Schuster [1971] 317 p. 22 cm. [E99.Y3C29] 79-139617 ISBN 0-671-20897-7 6.95
1. Juan, Don, 1891- 2. Yaqui Indians—Religion and mythology. 3. Hallucinogenic drugs and religious experience. I. Title.

CASTANEDA, Carlos. 299'.7
Tales of power. New York, Simon and Schuster [1974] 287 p. 22 cm. [E99.Y3C295] 74-10601 ISBN 0-671-21858-1 7.95
1. Juan, Don, 1891- 2. Yaqui Indians—Religion and mythology. 3. Hallucinogenic drugs and religious experience. I. Title.

CASTANEDA, Carlos. 299'.7
The teachings of Don Juan; a Yaqui way of knowledge. Berkeley, University of California Press, 1968. viii, 196 p. 24 cm. [E99.Y3C3 1968] 68-17303
1. Juan, Don, 1891- 2. Yaqui Indians—

Religion and mythology. 3. Hallucinogenic drugs and religious experience. I. Title.

CASTANEDA, Carlos. 299'.7
The teachings of Don Juan; a Yaqui way of knowledge. [New York] Simon and Schuster, 1973 [c1968] 288 p. 22 cm. [E99.Y3C3 1973] 73-166188 ISBN 0-671-21555-8 7.95
1. Juan, Don, 1891- 2. Yaqui Indians—Religion and mythology. 3. Hallucinogenic drugs and religious experience. I. Title.

CASTANEDA, Carlos. 299.7
The teachings of Don Juan; a Yaqui way of knowledge. New York, Pocket Books [1974, c1968] 256 p. 18 cm. [E99.Y3C3 1974] ISBN 0-671-78748-9. 1.50 (pbk.)
1. Juan, Don, 1891- 2. Yaqui Indians—Religion & mythology. 3. Hallucinogenic drugs and religious experience. I. Title.
L.C. card number for original ed.: 68-17303.

CASTENEDA, Carlos. 299.7
Tales of power / Carlos Castaneda. New ork : Pocket Books, 1976c1974. 295p. ; 18 cm. [E99.Y3C295] ISBN 0-671-80676-9 pbk. : 1.95
1. Juan, Don,1891- 2. Yaqui Indians-Religion and mythology. 3. Hallucienogenic drugs and religious experience. I. Title.
L.C. card no. for 1974 Simon and Schuster edition: 74-10601

CATLIN, George, 1796-1872. 299'.7
O-kee-pa, a religious ceremony, and other customs of the Mandans. Edited, and with an introd., by John C. Ewers. Centennial ed. New Haven, Yale University Press, 1967. 106 p. col. illus. 26 cm. Includes bibliographical references. [E99.M2C3 1967] 67-20336
1. O-kee-pa (Religious ceremony) 2. Mandan Indians. I. Ewers, John Canfield, ed.

CATLIN, George, 1796-1872. 299'.7
O-kee-pa, a religious ceremony, and other customs of the Mandans / by George Catlin ; edited, and with an introd. by John C. Ewers. Lincoln : University of Nebraska Press, [1976] c1967. p. cm. Reprint of the ed. published by Yale University Press, New Haven. Includes index. Bibliography: p. [E99.M2C3 1976] 76-4522 ISBN 0-8032-5845-3 pbk. : 7.95
1. O-kee-pa (Religious ceremony) 2. Mandan Indians. I. Ewers, John Canfield. II. Title.

CHAFE, Wallace L. 299.7
Seneca thanksgiving rituals. Washington, U.S. Govt. Print. Off., 1961. iii, 302 p. 24 cm. ([U.S.] Bureau of American Ethnology Bulletin 183) Includes music. Bibliography: p. 300. "Recorded versions of the thanksgiving rituals": p. 301-302. [E51.U6 no. 183] 62-60358
1. Seneca Indians—Rites and ceremonies. 2. Seneca language—Texts. I. Series.

CLARK, Ann (Nolan) 1898- 299'.7
Circle of seasons. Illustrated by W. T. Mars. New York, Farrar, Straus & Giroux [1970] 113 p. illus. 22 cm. (A Bell book) Describes the ceremonies and festival rituals of the Pueblo Indians to recognize and celebrate the changing of the seasons. [E99.P9C57] 73-113772 3.95
1. Pueblo Indians—Juvenile literature. I. Mars, Witold T., illus. II. Title.

CUSHING, Frank Hamilton, 1857-1900. 299'.7
Outlines of Zuni creation myths / by Frank Hamilton Cushing. New York : AMS Press, 1976. p. 323-462 ; 23 cm. Reprinted from the 13th annual report (1891-92) of the U.S. Bureau of American Ethnology, Washington, 1896. Includes index. [E99.Z9C893 1976] 74-7947 ISBN 0-404-11834-8 : 20.00
1. Zuni Indians—Religion and mythology. I. Title.

DEATH and the afterlife in pre-Columbian America 299'.7
: a conference at Dumbarton Oaks, October 27th, 1973 / Elizabeth P. Benson, editor Washington : Dumbarton Oaks Research Library and Collections, Trustees for Harvard University, [1975] vii, 196 p. : ill. ; 25 cm. Includes bibliographies. [E59.R38D42] 74-22694 10.00
1. Indians—Religion and mythology—Congresses. 2. Indians—Mortuary customs—Congresses. I. Benson, Elizabeth P. II. Dumbarton Oaks.

DEWDNEY, Selwyn H. 299'.7
The sacred scrolls of the southern Ojibway / Selwyn Dewdney. Toronto ; Buffalo : Published for the Glenbow-Alberta Institute, Galgary, Alta. by University of Toronto Press, [1975] 199 p., [2] leaves of plates : ill. (some col.) ; 18 x 26 cm. Includes index. Bibliography: p. [180]-181. 73-90150 ISBN 0-8020-3321-0 : 12.50
1. Chippewa Indians—Religion and mythology. I. Glenbow-Alberta Institute. II. Title.

DORSEY, George Amos, 1868-1931. 299'.7
The Cheyenne / by George A. Dorsey. Fairfield, Wash. : Ye Galleon Press, 1975. 72 p. : ill. ; 26 cm. Reprint of v. 1, Ceremonial organization, of the 1905 ed. published by Field Columbian Museum, Chicago, which was issued as no. 99 of its Publication and v. 9, no. 1 of its Anthropological series. [E99.C53D72 1975] 75-38792 ISBN 0-87770-157-1
1. Cheyenne Indians—Religion and mythology. 2. Cheyenne Indians—Rites and ceremonies. I. Title. II. Series: Field Columbian Museum, Chicago. Publication ; 99. III. Series: Fieldiana : anthropology ; v. 9, no. 1.

EMERSON, Ellen Russell, 1837-1907 299.7
Indian myths; or, Legends, traditions, and symbols of the aborigines of America compared with those of other countries, including Hindostan, Egypt, Persia, Assyria, and China. Minneapolis, Ross & Haines, 1965. xviii, 677p. illus., fold. map. 23cm. Relates mainly to the Indians of North America. Bibl. [E98.R3E5] 65-1023 8.75
1. Indians of North America—Religion and mythology. 2. Mythology. I. Title.

FARON, Louis C 1923- 299.7
Hawks of the sun; Mapuche morality and its ritual attributes [by] L. C. Faron. [Pittsburgh] University of Pittsburgh Press [1964] 220 p. illus., maps. 23 cm. Bibliography: p. 211-213. [F3126.F28] 64-12489
1. Araucanian Indians — Soc. life & cust. 2. Araucanian Indians — Religion and mythology. I. Title. II. Title: Mapuche morality and its ritual attributes.

FARON, Louis C., 1923- 299.7
Hawks of the sun; Mapuche morality and its ritual attributes [Pittsburgh] Univ. of Pittsburgh Pr. [c.1964] 220p. illus., maps. 23cm. Bibl. 64-12489 5.50
1. Araucanian Indians—Soc. life & cust. 2. Araucanian Indians—Religion and mythology I. Title. II. Title: Mapuche morality and its ritual attributes.

FORREST, Earle Robert, 1883- 299.7
The snake dance of the Hopi Indians. Hopi drawings by Don Louis Perceval. Los Angeles, Westernlore Pr. [c.]1961. 172p. illus. (Great West & Indian ser., 21) Bibl. 61-15835 5.75
1. Hopi Indians—Religion and mythology. 2. Snakedance. I. Title.

FOSTER, Kenneth E. 299'.7
Navajo sandpaintings, by Kenneth E. Foster. Window Rock, Ariz., Navajo Tribal Museum, 1964. 34 p. illus. 22 cm. (Navajoland publications, ser. 3) Cover title. Bibliography: p. 33-34. [E99.N3F63] 74-151619
1. Sandpaintings. 2. Navaho Indians—Rites and ceremonies. I. Title. II. Series.

GOLDMAN, Irving, 1911- 299'.7
The mouth of heaven : an introduction to Kwakiutl religious thought / Irving Goldman. New York : Wiley, [1975] xvi, 265 p. : ill. ; 23 cm. Continues Ancient Polynesian society. "A Wiley-Interscience publication." Includes index. Bibliography: p. 249-254. [E99.K9G64] 75-8742 ISBN 0-471-31140-5 : 13.50
1. Kwakiutl Indians—Religion and mythology. 2. Kwakiutl Indians—Social life and customs. I. Title.

HAILE, Berard, 1874-1961. 299'.7
Starlore among the Navaho / by Berard Haile. Santa Fe, N.M. : W. Gannon, 1977, c1947. 44 p., [7] leaves of plates (2 fold.) : ill. ; 23 cm. Reprint of the ed. published by the Museum of Navajo Ceremonial Art, Santa Fe, N.M. Bibliography: p. 44. [E99.N3H27 1977] 76-53085 ISBN 0-88307-532-6 : 15.00
1. Navaho Indians—Religion and mythology. 2. Stars (in religion, folk-lore, etc.) 3. Indians of North America—Southwest, New—Religion and mythology. I. Title.

HANAUER, Elsie V. 299'.7
Dolls of the Indians, by Elsie V. Hanauer. South Brunswick [N.J.] A. S. Barnes [1970] 127 p. illus., map. 22 cm. Describes the ceremonial masks, costumes, and functions of many of the Kachinas of the Hopi Indians. [E99.H7H3] 70-88268 ISBN 4-9807536-2-5.95
1. Katcinas—Juvenile literature. 2. Hopi Indians—Juvenile literature. I. Title.

HUNT, Eva, 1934- 299'.7
The transformation of the Hummingbird : cultural roots of a Zinacantecan mythical poem / Eva Hunt. Ithaca, N.Y. : Cornell University Press, 1977. 312 p. : ill. ; 22 cm. (Symbol, myth, and ritual series) Includes index. Bibliography: p. [290]-303. [F1221.T9H86] 76-12909 ISBN 0-8014-1022-3 : 18.50
1. Tzotzil Indians—Religion and mythology. 2. Symbolism. 3. Indians of Mexico—Religion and mythology. I. Title.

JACKSON, Donald, 1895- 299'.7
Religious concepts in ancient America and in the Holy Land : as illustrated by the Sacred book of the Quiche Mayans and by the Bible : quotes, notes, and notions / Donald Jackson. 1st ed. Hicksville, N.Y. : Exposition Press, c1976. viii, 142 p. ; 22 cm. (An Exposition-university book) Bibliography: p. 141-142. [F1465.P8466] 76-363012 ISBN 0-682-48503-9 : 8.00
1. Popol vuh. 2. Bible—Criticism, interpretation, etc. 3. Quiches—Religion and mythology. I. Title.

JOHNSTON, Basil. 299'.7
Ojibway heritage / Basil Johnston. Toronto : McClelland and Stewart, c1976. 171 p. ; 24 cm. [E99.C6J64 1976b] 77-353664 ISBN 0-7710-4440-2 : 8.95
1. Chippewa Indians—Religion and mythology. 2. Chippewa Indians—Legends. I. Title.

KEELER, Clyde Edgar 299.7
Secrets of the Cuna earthmother; a comparative study of ancient religions. New York, Exposition Press [c.1960] 352p. illus. 21cm. (An Exposition-unnversity book) (bibl.: p.322-324) 60-686 6.00
1. Cuna Indians—Religion and mythology. 2. Religion, Primitive. I. Title.

KEELER, Clyde Edgar, 1900- 299.7
Secrets of the Cuna earthmother; a comparative, study of ancient religions. [1st ed.] New York, Exposition Press [1960] 352p. illus. 21cm. (As Exposition-university book Includes bibliography. [F1565.2.C8K42] 60-686
1. Cuna Indians— Religion and mythology. 2. Religion, Primitive. I. Title.

KENNARD, Edward Allan, 1907- 299'.7
Hopi Kachinas, by Edwin Earle. Text by Edward A. Kennard. 2d ed., rev. New York, Museum of the American Indian, Heye Foundation, 1971. xv, 50 p. illus., 28 col. plates. 26 cm. Bibliography: p. 49-50. [E99.H7K45 1971] 71-139867
1. Katcinas. 2. Hopi Indians—Religion and mythology. I. Earle, Edwin, 1904- illus. II. Title.

LA BARRE, Weston 299.7
The peyote cult. Hamden, Conn., Reprinted by Shoe String Press, [c.]1959. 188p. illus. 25cm. (bibl. notes: p. 175-188) 60-572 4.00
1. Peyote. 2. Indians of North America—Religion and mythology. 3. Indians of North America—Rites and ceremonies. I. Title.

LABARRE, Weston, 1911- 299.7
The Pevote cult. New enl. ed. [Hamden, Conn.] Shoe String Press, 1964. 260 p. illus. 25 cm. Includes bibliographies. [E98.R3L3] 64-19133
1. Peyotism. 2. Indians of North America — Religion and mythology. 3. Indians of North America — Rites and ceremonies. I. Title.

LA BARRE, Weston, 1911- 299.7
The peyote cult. Hamden, Conn., Reprinted by Shoe String Press, 1959. 188p. illus. 25cm. 'Originally published [in 1938] as Yale University publications in anthropology, number 19. Bibliography: p. 175-188. [E98.R3L3 1959] 60-572
1. Peyote. 2. Indians of North America—Religion and mythology. 3. Indians of North America—Rites and ceremonies. I. Title.

LA BARRE, Weston, 1911- 299.7
The Peyote cult. New enl. ed. [Hamden, Conn.] Shoe String [c.1959, 1964] 260p. illus. 25cm. Bibl. 64-19133 7.50
1. Peyotism. 2. Indians of North America—Religion and mythology. 3. Indians of North America—Rites and ceremonies. I. Title.

LA BARRE, Weston, 1911- 299'.7
The peyote cult. With a new pref. by the author. Enl. ed. New York, Schocken Books [1969] xvii, 260 p. illus. 21 cm. Includes bibliographies. [E98.R3L3 1969] 78-91546 2.45
1. Peyotism. 2. Indians of North America—Religion and mythology. 3. Indians of North America—Rites and ceremonies. I. Title.

LA BARRE, Weston, 1911- 299'.7
The peyote cult / Weston La Barre. 4th ed. enl. Hamden, Conn. : Archon Books, 1975. p. cm. Includes index. Bibliography: p. [E98.R3L3 1975] 75-19425 ISBN 0-208-01456-X : 10.00
1. Peyotism. 2. Indians of North America—Religion and mythology. 3. Indians of North America—Rites and ceremonies. I. Title.

LA BARRE, Weston, 1911- 299'.7
The peyote cult / Weston La Barre. 2d enl. ed. New York : Schocken Books, [1975] p. cm. Includes index. Bibliography: p. [E98.R3L3 1975b] 75-10608 ISBN 0-8052-0493-8 pbk. : 4.95
1. Peyotism. 2. Indians of North America—Religion and mythology. 3. Indians of North America—Rites and ceremonies. I. Title.

LANDES, Ruth, 1908- 299'.7
Ojibwa religion and the Midewiwin. Madison, University of Wisconsin Press, 1968. viii, 250 p. illus., ports. 23 cm. Bibliography: p. 243-245. [E99.C6L28 1968] 68-19574
1. Chippewa Indians—Religion and mythology. 2. Indians of North America—Medicine. 3. Indians of North America—Minnesota—Secret societies. I. Title. II. Title: The Midewiwin.

LAVINE, Sigmund A. 299'.7
The ghosts the Indians feared / Sigmund A. Lavine ; illustrated with drawings by Jane O'Regan, and with photographs and old prints. New York : Dodd, Mead, [1975] 64 p. : ill. ; 24 cm. Includes index. Describes some of the religious customs and beliefs of various North and South American Indian tribes. [E59.R38L38] 75-11441 ISBN 0-396-07194-5 lib.bdg. : 4.95
1. Indians—Religion and mythology—Juvenile literature. 2. Folk-lore, Indian—Juvenile literature. I. O'Regan, Jane. II. Title.

LOWIE, Robert Harry, 1883-1957. 299'.7
The religion of the Crow Indians / [by Robert H. Lowie]. New York : AMS Press, 1976. p. 309-444 : ill. ; 23 cm. Reprint of the 1922 ed., which was issued as v. 25, pt. 2 of Anthropological papers of the American Museum of Natural History. Includes bibliographical references. [E99.C92L93 1976] 74-7986 ISBN 0-404-11876-3 : 16.50
1. Crow Indians—Religion and mythology. I. Title. II. Series: American Museum of Natural History, New York. Anthropological papers ; v. 25, pt. 2.

LUCKERT, Karl W., 1934- 299'.7
Olmec religion : a key to Middle America and beyond / by Karl W. Luckert. 1st ed. Norman : University of Oklahoma Press, [1975] p. cm. (The Civilization of the American Indian series ; v. 137) Includes index. Bibliography: p. [F1219.3.R38L8] 75-12869 ISBN 0-8061-1298-0 : 8.95 pbk. : 6.95
1. Olmecs—Religion and mythology. 2. Serpent-worship. 3. Indians of Mexico—Religion and mythology. 4. Indians of Central America—Religion and mythology. I. Title. II. Series.

MCCRACKEN, Harold, 1894- 299'.7
A heritage of the Blackfeet [by] Harold McCracken and Paul Dyck. [Cody, Wyo., Buffalo Bill Historical Center, 1972] 22 p. illus. 26 cm. ([Buffalo Bill Historical Center] Educational series, no. 1) Cover title. Contents.Contents.—A Blackfoot sacred ceremony, preserved, by H. McCracken.—The Thunder Medicine Pipe of the Blackfeet people, by P. Dyck.—Boy Chief's Thunder Medicine Pipe, by P. Dyck. [E99.S54M27] 72-80570
1. Siksika Indians—Religion and mythology. 2. Siksika Indians—Rites and ceremonies. I. Dyck, Paul, 1917- II. Title. III. Series.

MCMAHON, Martin. 299'.7
Castaneda's The teachings of Don Juan, A separate reality & Journey to Ixtlan : notes, including life and background, introduction, analyses of The teachings of Don Juan, A separate reality, and Journey to Ixtlan, review questions / by Martin McMahon III ; consulting editor, James L. Roberts. Lincoln, Neb. : Cliffs Notes, c1974. 60 p. ; 21 cm. Cover title: Cliffs Notes on Castaneda's The teachings of Don Juan & other works. [E99.Y3M3] 76-353154 ISBN 0-8220-0306-6 : 1.25
1. Castaneda, Carlos. The teachings of Don Juan. 2. Castaneda, Carlos. A separate reality. 3. Castaneda, Carlos. Journey to Ixtlan. 4. Yaqui Indians. 5. Hallucinogenic drugs and religious experience. I. Title: Castaneda's The teachings of Don Juan, A separate reality ... II. Title: Cliffs Notes on Castaneda's The teachings of Don Juan & other works.

*MCMAHON, Martin. 299'.7
Castaneda's the teachings of Don Juan, a separate reality, & journey to Ixtlan notes. Lincoln, Neb., Cliffs Notes [1974] 60 p. 21 cm. [E99.Y3C29] ISBN 0-8220-0306-6 1.25 (pbk.)
1. Castaneda, Carlos. I. Title.

MARIA Sabina, ca.1900- 299'.7
Maria Sabina and her Mazatec mushroom velada. [Compiled by] R. Gordon Wasson [and others] New York, Harcourt Brace Jovanovich [1974] xxxiii, 281 p. illus. 31 cm. (Ethnomycological studies, no. 3) "Text of a shamanic ceremony performed ... 12-13 July 1958 by Maria Sabina in the Mazatec village of Huautla de Jimenez ... Mexico." "A Helen

and Kurt Wolff book." Text in Mazatec, with English and Spanish translations. [F1221.M35M37] 74-964 ISBN 0-15-157202-X
1. Mazatec Indians—Rites and ceremonies. 2. Mushroom ceremony. 3. Shamanism. I. Wasson, Robert Gordon, 1898- II. Title. III. Series.

MARRIOTT, Alice Lee, 1910- 299'.7
Peyote [by] Alice Marriott and Carol K. Rachlin. New York, Crowell [1971] x, 111 p. illus. 22 cm. Bibliography: p. 99-102. [E98.R3M3 1971] 75-146284 ISBN 0-690-61697-X 6.95
1. Native American Church of North America. 2. Peyotism. I. Rachlin, Carol K., joint author. II. Title.

MARRIOTT, Alice Lee, 1910- 299'.7
Plains Indian mythology / by Alice Marriott and Carol Rachlin. New York : Crowell, c1975. p. cm. Bibliography: p. [E78.G73M37 1975] 75-26554 ISBN 0-690-00694-2 : 7.95
1. Indians of North America—Great Plains—Religion and mythology. 2. Indians of North America—Great Plains—Legends. I. Rachlin, Carol K., joint author. II. Title.

MARRIOTT, Alice Lee, 1910- 299.7
Plains indian mythology / by Alice Marriott and Carol K. Rachlin. New York : New American Library, 1977,c1975. 180p. ; 18 cm. (A Mentor Book) Bibliography:p.176-180. [E78.G73M37 1975] ISBN 0-451-61582-4 pbk. : 1.75
1. Indians of North America-Great Plains-Religion and Mythology. 2. Indians of North America-Great Plains-Legends. I. Rachlin, Carol K., joint author. II. Title.
L.C. card no. for 1975 Crowell ed.:75-26554.

MARRIOTT, Alice Lee, 1910- 299.7
Plains indian mythology / by Alice Marriott and Carol K. Rachlin. New York : New American Library, 1977,c1975. 180p. ; 18 cm. (A Mentor Book) Bibliography:p.176-180. [E78.G73M37 1975] ISBN 0-451-61582-4 pbk. : 1.75
1. Indians of North America-Great Plains-Religion and Mythology. 2. Indians of North America-Great Plains-Legends. I. Rachlin, Carol K., joint author. II. Title.
L.C. card no. for 1975 Crowell ed.:75-26554.

MASON, John Alden, 1885-1967. 299'.7
The ceremonialism of the Tepecan [by] John Alden Mason [and] George Agogino. [Portales] Eastern New Mexico University, Paleo-Indian Institute, 1972. 44 p. illus. 26 cm. (Eastern New Mexico University. Contributions in anthropology, v. 4, no. 1) Bibliography: p. 43-44. [F1221.T37M37 1972] 74-621111
1. Tepecano Indians—Rites and ceremonies. 2. Indians of Mexico—Rites and ceremonies. I. Agogino, George, joint author. II. Title. III. Series: Contributions in anthropology, v. 4, no. 1.

MICHELSON, Truman, 1879-1938. 299'.7
Contributions to Fox ethnology / by Truman Michelson. St. Clair Shores, Mich. : Scholarly Press, 1976- v. : ill. ; 22 cm. In Algonquin and/or English. Reprint of the 1927- ed., issued as Bulletin 85- of the Smithsonian Institution, Bureau of American Ethnology. Includes index. Bibliography, v. 1, p. 161-162. [E99.F7M54 1976] 76-27011 ISBN 0-403-03421-3
1. Fox Indians—Religion and mythology—Addresses, essays, lectures. 2. Fox language—Texts—Addresses, essays, lectures. 3. Indians of North America—Religion and mythology—Addresses, essay, lectures. I. Title. II. Series: United States. Bureau of American Ethnology. Bulletin ; 85.

MOON, Sheila. 299'.7
A magic dwells; a poetic and psychological study of the Navaho emergence myth. [1st ed.] Middletown, Conn., Wesleyan University Press [1970] 206 p. 22 cm. Includes bibliographical references. [BL325.C7M66] 72-105501 ISBN 8-19-540188- 7.95
1. Creation. 2. Navaho Indians—Religion and mythology. I. Title.

MOONEY, James, 1861-1921 299.7
The ghost-dance religion and the Sioux outbreak of 1890. Abridged, introd. by Anthony F. C. Wallace. Chicago, Univ. of Chic. Pr. [c.1965] xxi, 359p. illus., maps, ports. 23cm. (Classics in anthrop.; P176) Orig. pub. as pt. 2 of the 14th Annual report of the Bur. of Ethnology to the secretary of the Smithsonian Inst., 1892-93 (Washington, 1896) The songs (melodies); words in the original langs. with Eng. tr. Bibl. [E98.R3M6] 64-24971 2.95 pap.,
1. Ghost dance. 2. Dakota Indians—Wars, 1890-1891. I. Title.

MOONEY, James, 1861-1921. 299'.7
The ghost-dance religion and the Sioux outbreak of 1890. With a new publisher's pref., and a new scholarly introd. by Bernard Fontana. Washington, Govt. Print. Off., 1896. Glorieta, N.M., Rio Grande Press [1973] 641-1136 p. illus. 29 cm. (A Rio Grande classic) Original ed. issued as pt. 2 of the 14th Annual report of the Bureau of Ethnology to the Secretary of the Smithsonian Institution, 1892-93. Includes bibliographies. [E98.R3M6 1973] 73-7723 ISBN 0-87380-105-9
1. Ghost dance. 2. Dakota Indians—Wars, 1890-1891. I. Title.

MOONEY, James, 1861-1921. 299.7
The ghost-dance religion and the Sioux outbreak of 1890. Abridged, with an introd. by Anthony F. C. Wallace. Chicago, University of Chicago Press [1965] xxi, 359 p. illus., maps, ports. 23 cm. (Classics in anthropology) "Originally published as part 2 of the fourteenth Annual report of the Bureau of Ethnology to the secretary of the Smithsonian Institution, 1892-93 (Washington ... 1896)" "The songs" (melodies); words in the original languages with English translations: p. [201]-331. Bibliography: p. [332]-331. [E98.R3M6 1965] 64-24971
1. Ghost dance. 2. Dakota Indians—Wars, 1890-1891. I. Title.

MOONEY, James, 1861-1921. 299'.7
The ghost-dance religion and Wounded Knee. New York, Dover Publications [1973] 645-1136 p. illus. 24 cm. Reprint of the 1896 ed. published by the Govt. Print. Off., Washington, which was issued as pt. 2 of the fourteenth Annual report of the Bureau of Ethnology of the Smithsonian Institution, 1892-93, under title: The ghost-dance religion and the Sioux outbreak of 1890. "The songs" (melodies): works in the original languages with English translations: p. 953-1102. [E98.R3M6 1973b] 73-80557 ISBN 0-486-20233-X 6.00
1. Ghost Dance. 2. Dakota Indians—Wars, 1890-1891. I. Title.

MORIARTY, James Robert. 299'.7
Chinigchinix: an indigenous California Indian religion. Introd. by Carl Schaefer Dentzel. Los Angeles, Southwest Museum, 1969. xii, 59 p. illus., maps, ports. 24 cm. (Frederick Webb Hodge Anniversary Publication Fund v. 10) Bibliography: p. [57]-59. [E98.R3M7] 74-80779
1. Juaneno Indians—Religion and mythology. 2. Indians of North America—California—Religion and mythology. I. Title. II. Series: Los Angeles. Southwest Museum. Frederick Webb Hodge Anniversary Publication Fund. Publications v. 10

MYERHOFF, Barbara G. 299'.7
Peyote hunt; the sacred journey of the Huichol Indians [by] Barbara G. Myerhoff. Ithaca [N.Y.] Cornell University Press [1974] 285 p. illus. 22 cm. (Symbol, myth, and ritual series) Bibliography: p. 265-275. [F1221.H9M9] 73-16923 ISBN 0-8014-0817-2 15.00
1. Huichol Indians—Religion and mythology. 2. Peyotism—Mexico. I. Title.

NATIVISM and Syncretism, 299.7
by Munro S. Edmonson [and others.] New Orleans, Middle American Research Institute, Tulane University, 1960. 203p. illus. 27cm. (Tulane University. Middle American Research Institute. Publication 19) Includes bibliographies. [F1421.T95 no.19] 62-3374
1. Indians of Mexico—Religion and mythology. 2. Indians of Central America—Religion and mythology. 3. Nativistic movements. I. Edmonson, Munro S. II. Series: Tulane University of Louisiana. Middle American Research Institute. Publication 19
Contents omitted.

NAVAHE and Ute peyotism: 299.7
a chronological and distributional study. by David F. Aberle and Omer C. Stewart. Boulder, University of Colorado Press, 1957. ix, 129p. maps, tables, 26cm. (University of Colorado studies, Series in anthropology, no. 6) Bibliography: p. 126-120. [E9S.R3A2] [E9S.R3A2] 970.62 57-63108 57-63108
1. Peyote. 2. Navaho Indians—Religion and mythology. 3. Ute Indians—Religion and mythology. 4. Navaho Indians—Rites and ceremonies. 5. Ute Indians— Rites and ceremonies. I. Aberle, David Friend, 1918- II. Stewart, Omer Call, 1908- joint author. III. Series: Colorado, University, University of Colorado studies. Series in anthropology, no. 6

NAVAHO figurines called 299'.7
dolls. Original drawings by Harry Walters. Santa Fe, N.M., Museum of Navaho Ceremonial Art [1973? c.1972] 75 p. illus. 28 cm. Bibliography (p. 73-75) [E99.N3N27] 72-97250
1. Navaho Indians—Rites and ceremonies. 2. Dolls (in religion, folk-lore, etc.) I. Kelly, Roger E. Navaho ritual human figurines: form and function, 1972. II. Lang, R. W. The remaking rites of the Navaho: causal factors of illness and its nature. 1972.
Contents omitted. Publisher's address: 704 Camino Lejo Santa Fe, N.M.

OAKES, Maud van Cortlandt, 1903- 299'.7
The two crosses of Todos Santos : survivals of Mayan religious ritual / Maud Oakes. Princeton, N.J. : Princeton University Press, 1969, c1951. xiii, 274 p., [12] leaves of plates : ill. ; 22 cm. (Princeton/Bollingen paperbacks ; 181) (Bollingen series ; 27) Includes index. Bibliography: p. 254-255. [F1465.2.M3O3 1969] 68-26669 ISBN 0-691-09835-2. ISBN 0-691-01757-3 pbk.
1. Mam Indians—Religion and mythology. 2. Todos Santos Cuchumatan, Guatemala. 3. Indians of Central America—Guatemala—Religion and mythology. 4. Mayas—Religion and mythology. I. Title. II. Series.

PARK, Willard Zerbe. 299'.7
Shamanism in western North America; a study in cultural relationships, by Willard Z. Park. New York, Cooper Square Publishers, 1975. viii, 166 p. 24 cm. Reprint of the 1938 ed. published by Northwestern University, Evanston, which was issued as no. 2 of Northwestern University studies in the social sciences. Bibliography: p. 159-163. [E78.W5P17 1975] 74-12553 ISBN 0-8154-0497-2 6.50
1. Indians of North America—The West—Religion and mythology. 2. Indians of North America—The West—Medicine. 3. Paiute Indians—Religion and mythology. 4. Shamanism. I. Title. II. Series: Northwestern University studies in the social sciences, no. 2.

PEET, Stephen Denison, 1831-1914. 299'.7
Myths and symbols; or, Aboriginal religions in America. Boston, Milford House [1973] p. (Series: Peet, Stephen Denison, 1831-1914. Prehistoric America, v. 5.) Reprint of v. 5 of the author's Prehistoric America, published by the Office of the American Antiquarian, Chicago, 1905. [E59.R38P35 1973] 73-13790 ISBN 0-87821-180-2 40.00 (lib. bdg.)
1. Indians—Religion and mythology. I. Title. II. Series.

PEET, Stephen Denison, 1831-1914. 299'.7
Myths and symbols : or, Aboriginal religions in America / by Stephen D. Peet. Portland, Me. : Longwood Press, 1976 p. cm. (Series: Peet, Stephen Denison, 1831-1914. Prehistorical America ; v. 5.) Reprint of the 1905 ed. published by the Office of the American Antiquarian, Chicago, which was issued as v. 5 of the author's Prehistorical America. [E59.R38P35 1977] 76-27525 ISBN 0-89341-038-1 : 35.00
1. Indians—Religion and mythology. I. Title. II. Series.

PETRULLO, Vincenzo, 1906- 299'.7
The diabolic root : a study of peyotism, the new Indian religion, among the Delawares / by Vincenzo Petrullo. New York : Octagon Books, 1975, c1934. x, 185 p. : ill. ; 23 cm. Reprint of the ed. published by University of Pennsylvania Press, Philadelphia. Originally presented as the author's thesis, University of Pennsylvania, 1934. Bibliography: p. 183-185. [E99.D2P47 1975] 74-23462 ISBN 0-374-96411-4
1. Delaware Indians—Religion and mythology. 2. Peyotism. 3. Indians of North America—Religion and mythology. I. Title.

POPOL vuh. English. 299'.7
Popol vuh : the great mythological book of the ancient Maya / newly translated, with an introd., by Ralph Nelson ; with drawings from the Codices mayas. Boston : Houghton Mifflin, 1976. 86 p. : ill. ; 24 cm. [F1465.P813 1976] 75-42451 ISBN 0-395-24302-5 : 5.95
1. Quiches—Religion and mythology. I. Nelson, Ralph, 1940-

POPOL vuh. English & Quiche. 299'.7
The book of counsel: the Popol vuh of the Quiche Maya of Guatamala. [By] Munro S. Edmonson. New Orleans, Middle American Research Institute, Tulane University, 1971. xvii, 273 p. 27 cm. (Tulane University. Middle American Research Institute. Publication 35) Bibliography: p. 257-259. [PM4231.6.A1 1971] 72-197628
1. Quiches—Religion and mythology. I. Edmonson, Munro S., tr. II. Title. III. Series: Tulane University of Louisiana. Middle American Research Institute. Publication 35.

POWERS, William K. 299.7
Oglala religion / William K. Powers. Lincoln : University of Nebraska Press, c1977. xxi, 233 p., [2] leaves of plates : ill. ; 23 cm. Includes index. Bibliography: p. [215]-222. [E99.O3P68] 76-30614 ISBN 0-8032-0910-X : 11.75
1. Oglala Indians—Religion and mythology. 2. Oglala Indians—Social life and customs. 3. Oglala Indians—Ethnic identity. 4. Indians of North America—Great Plains—Religion and mythology. 5. Indians of North America—Great Plains—Ethnic identity. I. Title.

PRE-COLUMBIAN American 299'.7
religions [by] Walter Krickeberg [and others] Translated by Stanley Davis. [1st ed.] New York, Holt, Rinehart and Winston [1969, c1968] 365 p. 13 plates, maps. 25 cm. (History of religion series) Translation of Die Religionen des alten Amerika. Bibliography: p. 331-358. [E59.R38R413 1969] 69-11858 8.95
1. Indians—Religion and mythology. I. Krickeberg, Walter, 1885-

RADIN, Paul, 1883-1959. 299'.7
Literary aspects of North American mythology. Norwood, Pa., Norwood Editions, 1973 [i.e. 1974] p. cm. Reprint of the 1915 ed. published by Government Print. Bureau, Ottawa, which was issued as no. 16 of Canada Geological Survey, Museum bulletin, and no. 6 of its Anthropological series. Limited to 100 copies. [E98.R3R12 1974] 73-22005 5.00 (lib. bdg.)
1. Indians of North America—Religion and mythology. 2. Indians of North America—Legends. I. Title. II. Series: Canada. National Museum, Ottawa, Bulletin no. 16. III. Series: Canada. Geological Survey. Memoir 6.

RADIN, Paul, 1883-1959. 299'.7
The trickster; a study in American Indian mythology. With commentaries by Karl Kerenyi and C. G. Jung. Introductory essay by Stanley Diamond. New York, Schocken Books [1972, c1956] xxv, 211 p. 21 cm. [E99.W7R142 1972] 73-154004 ISBN 0-8052-0351-6
1. Winnebago Indians—Religion and mythology. 2. Trickster. I. Kerenyi, Karoly, 1897- II. Jung, Carl Gustav, 1875-1961. III. Title.

THE Red swan : 299'.7
myths and tales of the American Indians / edited by John Bierhorst. 1st ed. New York : Farrar, Straus and Giroux, 1976. 386 p. : ill. ; 22 cm. Bibliography: p. 361-380. [E98.R3R43 1976] 76-196 10.00
1. Indians—Religion and mythology. 2. Indians—Legends. I. Bierhorst, John.

REICHARD, Gladys Amanda, 1893-1955. 299'.7
Navaho religion : a study of symbolism / Gladys A. Reichard. 2d ed. Princeton : Princeton University Press, 1974, c1950. xlvii, 804 p. : ill. ; 22 cm. (Princeton/Bollingen paperbacks ; 318) (Bollingen series ; 18) "First Princeton/Bollingen paperback edition." Includes index. Bibliography: p. [747]-761. [E99.N3R38 1974] 75-306306 ISBN 0-691-09801-8 : 16.50 ISBN 0-691-01798-0 pbk. : 6.95
1. Navaho Indians—Religion and mythology. 2. Symbolism. I. Title. II. Series.

REMPEL, F Warren. 299'.7
The role of value in Karl Mannheim's sociology of knowledge. by F. Warren Rempel. The Hague, Mouton, 1965. 125 p. 22 cm. (Studies in philosophy, 7) Bibliography: p. 122-125. [BD175.R4] 65-8800
1. Mannheim, Karl, 1893-1947. 2. Worth. 3. Knowledge, Sociology of. I. Title.

RIEGERT, Wilbur A. 299.7
I am a Sioux Indian, written by Wilbur A. Riegert. Illustrated by Vincent Hunts Horse. Rapid City, S.D., Fenwyn Press [1967] 24 p. illus. (part col.), ports. 28 cm. [E99.D1R48] 67-28313
1. Dakota Indians—Religion and mythology. 2. Tobacco-pipes. I. Hunts Horse, Vincent, 1924- illus. II. Title.

ROSEMAN, Bernard 299.7
The peyote story. 1966 ed. Hollywood, Calif., Wilshire [1966, c.1963] 67p. illus., port. 22 cm. [E98.R3R6] 66-2260 1.00 pap.,
1. Peyotisim. 2. Native American Church of North America. I. Title.

ROY, Cal. 299'.7
The serpent and the sun; myths of the Mexican world, retold and with decorations, by Cal Roy. New York, Farrar, Straus and Giroux [1972] 119 p. illus. 21 cm. Twelve myths of the Mayas, the Aztecs, and the Mexican Indians of today. [F1219.3.R38R69 1972] 72-81487 4.50
1. Indians of Mexico—Religion and mythology—Juvenile literature. I. Title.

SEEING Castaneda : 299'.7
reactions to the "Don Juan" writings of Carlos Castaneda / edited, selected, and with introductions by Daniel C. Noel. New York : Putnam, [1975] p. cm. Bibliography: p.

[E99.Y3C337 1975] 75-23146 ISBN 0-399-11603-6 : 7.95
1. Castaneda, Carlos. 2. Juan, Don, 1891- 3. Yaqui Indians—Addresses, essays, lectures. 4. Hallucinogenic drugs and religious experience—Addresses, essays, lectures. I. Noel, Daniel C.

SEEING with a native eye 299'.7
: essays on native American religion / by Ake Hultkrantz ... [et al.] ; edited by Walter Holden Capps, assisted by Ernst F. Tonsing. [1st ed.] New York : Harper & Row, c1976. p. cm. (A Harper forum book) Bibliography: p. [E98.R3S37 1976] 76-9980 pbk. : 3.95
1. Indians of North America—Religion and mythology—Addresses, essays, lectures. I. Hultkrantz, Ake. II. Capps, Walter H.

SEJOURNE, Laurette 299.7
Burning water; thought and religion in ancient Mexico. With 82 drawings [by Abel Mendoza] and 22 photographs. New York, Grove Press [1960] xiii, 192p. illus. 21cm. (Myth and man series: Evergreen ed. E-241) Bibl. notes, 1.95 pap.,
1. Nahuas—Religion and mythology. 2. Quetzalcoatl. I. Title.

SHEARER, Tony. 299'.7
Beneath the moon and under the sun : a poetic re-appraisal of the sacred calendar and the prophecies of ancient Mexico / written and illustrated by Tony Shearer. Albuquerque, N.M. : Sun Pub. Co., c1975. 167 p. : ill. ; 27 cm. [F1219.3.R38S53] 76-356796 12.50
1. Indians of Mexico—Religion and mythology. 2. Indians—Religion and mythology. 3. Private revelations. I. Title.

SLOTKIN, James Sydney, 299'.7
1913-1958.
The peyote religion : a study in Indian-white relations / J. S. Slotkin. New York : Octagon Books, 1975, c1956. vii, 195 p. : ill. ; 24 cm. Reprint of the ed. published by the Free Press, Glencoe, Ill. Bibliography: p. 143-187. [E98.R3S5 1975] 74-23409 ISBN 0-374-97480-2 : 10.50
1. Native American Church of North America. 2. Peyotism. 3. Indians of North America—Government relations. I. Title.

SPECK, Frank Gouldsmith, 299'.7
1881-1950.
Naskapi : the savage hunters of the Labrador peninsula / Frank G. Speck ; foreword by J. E. Michael Kew. New ed. Norman : University of Oklahoma Press, c1977. xii, 257 p. : ill. ; 24 cm. (The Civilization of the American Indian series ; v. 10) Includes bibliographical references and index. [E99.N18S7 1977] 77-365978 ISBN 0-8061-1412-6 : 8.95
1. Nascapee Indians—Religion and mythology. 2. Indians of North America—Newfoundland—Labrador—Religion and mythology. 3. Nascapee Indians—Hunting. 4. Indians of North America—Newfoundland—Labrador—Hunting. I. Title. II. Series.

SPENCE, Lewis, 1874-1955. 299'.7
The myths of Mexico & Peru. With 60 full-page illus., mainly by Gilbert James and William Sewell, and other drawings and maps. Boston, Milford House [1974] p. Reprint of the 1913 ed. published by T. Y. Crowell, New York. Bibliography: p. [F1219.3.R38S75 1974] 73-16253 ISBN 0-87821-193-4 60.00
1. Indians of Mexico—Religion and mythology. 2. Indians of South America—Peru—Religion and mythology. 3. Mayas—Religion and mythology. I. Title.

SPENCE, Lewis, 1874-1955. 299'.7
The Popol vuh; the mythic and heroic sagas of the Kiches of Central America. New York, AMS Press [1972] 63 p. 19 cm. Reprint of the 1908 ed., which was issued as no. 16 of Popular studies in mythology, romance and folklore. Bibliography: p. [57]-59. [F1465.P875 1972] 75-139178 ISBN 0-404-53516-X 5.50
1. Popol vuh. 2. Quiches—Religion and mythology. I. Title. II. Series: Popular studies in mythology, romance and folklore, no. 16.

SPENCER, Katherine. 299.7
Mythology and values; an analysis of Navaho chantway myths. Philadelphia, American Folklore Society, 1957. viii, 240p. 23cm. (Memoirs of the American Folklore Society. v.48) Errata leaf inserted. Bibiography: p. 235--240. [GR1.A5 vol. 48] [GR1.A5 vol. 48] 970.62 57-13891 57-13891
1. Navaho Indians—Religion and mythology. I. Title. II. Series: American Folklore Society. Memoirs, v. 481

SQUIER, Ephraim George, 299'.7
1821-1888.
The serpent symbol, and the worship of the reciprocal principles of nature in America / by E. G. Squier. Millwood, N.Y. : Kraus Reprint Co., 1975. p. cm. Reprint of the 1851 ed. published by Putnam, New York, which was issued as no. 1 of American archaeological researches. [E59.R38S7 1975] 75-8708 ISBN 0-527-03228-X : 17.00
1. Indians—Religion and mythology. 2. Serpent-worship—America. I. Title. II. Series: American archaeological researches ; no. 1.

STARKLOFF, Carl F. 299'.7
The people of the center; American Indian religion and Christianity [by] Carl F. Starkloff. New York, Seabury Press [1974] 144 p. 22 cm. "A crossroad book." Bibliography: p. 142-144. [E98.R3S73] 73-17885 ISBN 0-8164-9207-7 6.95
1. Indians of North America—Religion and mythology. 2. Indians of North America—Missions. 3. Christianity. I. Title.

STEIGER, Brad. 299'.7
Medicine power; the American Indian's revival of his spiritual heritage and its relevance for modern man. [1st ed.] Garden City, N.Y., Doubleday, 1974. xi, 226 p. illus. 22 cm. [E98.R3S75 1974] 73-82248 ISBN 0-385-02607-2 6.95
1. Indians of North America—Religion and mythology. I. Title.

STEIGER, Brad. 299'.7
Medicine talk; a guide to walking in balance and surviving on the Earth Mother. [1st ed.] Garden City, N.Y., Doubleday, 1975. 213 p. illus. 22 cm. [E98.M4S73] 74-1774 ISBN 0-385-08791-8 7.95
1. Indians of North America—Medicine. 2. Indians of North America—Religion and mythology. I. Title.

STOUFF, Faye. 299'.7
Sacred Chitimacha Indian beliefs. Written by Faye Stouff and W. Bradley Twitty. Illustrated by Ruth B. van Strander. Pompano Beach, Fla., Twitty and Twitty [1971] 79 p. illus., maps, port. 21 cm. [E99.C7S8] 79-24758
1. Chitimacha Indians—Religion and mythology. I. Twitty, W. Bradley, joint author. II. Title.

SWANTON, John Reed, 1873- 299'.7
1958.
Myths and tales of the southeastern Indians / by John R. Swanton. New York : AMS Press, 1976. x, 275 p. ; 23 cm. Reprint of the 1929 ed. published by the U.S. Govt. Print. Off., Washington, which was issued as Bulletin 88 of the Bureau of American Ethnology, Smithsonian Institution. [E78.S65S92 1976] 74-9011 ISBN 0-404-11908-5 : 20.00
1. Indians of North America—Southern States—Legends. I. Title. II. Series: United States. Bureau of American Ethnology. Bulletin ; 88.

SWITZER, Ronald R. 299'.7
The origin and significance of snake-lightning cults in the Pueblo Southwest, by Ronald R. Switzer. [El Paso, Tex., El Paso Archaeological Society, 1972?] iii, 48 p. illus. 29 cm. (El Paso Archaeological Society. Special report no. 11) Bibliography: p. 44-48. [E99.P9S9] 72-171715
1. Pueblo Indians—Religion and mythology. I. Title. II. Series.

SZEKELY, Edmond Bordeaux. 299'.7
The soul of ancient Mexico, by Edmond S. Bordeaux. [San Diego, Calif., Academy Books, c1968] 134 p. illus. 31 cm. [F1219.3.R38S93] 74-154483
1. Indians of Mexico—Religion and mythology. 2. Indians of Mexico—Philosophy. I. Title.

TEDLOCK, Dennis, 1939- 299'.7
comp.
Teachings from the American earth : Indian religion and philosophy / edited by Dennis Tedlock and Barbara Tedlock. 1st ed. New York : Liveright, [1975] xxiv, 279 p. : ill. ; 21 cm. Includes bibliographical references and index. [E98.R3T42 1975] 74-34146 9.95
1. Indians of North America—Religion and mythology—Addresses, essays, lectures. I. Tedlock, Barbara, joint comp. II. Title.
Contents omitted

TEIT, James Alexander, 299'.7
1864-
Mythology of the Thompson Indians / by James Teit. New York : AMS Press, [1975] 199-416 p. ; 24 cm. Reprint of the 1912 ed. published by E. J. Brill, Leiden, and G. E. Stechert, New York, which was issued as v. 12 of the Memoirs of the American Museum of Natural History, and as v. 8, pt. 2 of the Publications of the Jesup North Pacific Expedition. Includes bibliographical references. [E99.N96T23 1975] 73-3529 ISBN 0-404-58125-0 : 27.50
1. Ntlakyapamuk Indians—Religion and mythology. 2. Ntlakyapamuk Indians—Legends. 3. Indians of North America—Religion and mythology. 4. Indians of North America—Legends. I. Title. II. Series: American Museum of Natural History, New York. Memoirs ; v. 12. III. Series: The Jesup North Pacific Expedition. Publications ; v. 8, pt. 2.

TYLER, Hamilton A. 299'.7
Pueblo animals and myths / by Hamilton A. Tyler. 1st ed. Norman : University of Oklahoma Press, [1975] xiii, 274 p. : ill. ; 21 cm. (The Civilization of the American indian series ; v. 134) Includes index. Bibliography: p. 246-255. [E99.P9T89] 74-15902 ISBN 0-8061-1245-X : 8.95
1. Pueblo Indians—Religion and mythology. 2. Animal lore. I. Title. II. Series.

TYLER, Hamilton A. 299.7
Pueblo gods and myths. [1st ed.] Norman, University of Oklahoma Press [1964] xxii, 313 p. illus., map. 23 cm. (The Civilization of the American Indian series, 71) Bibliography: p. 293-300. [E99.P9T9] 64-11317
1. Pueblo Indians—Religion and mythology. I. Title. II. Series.

UNDERHILL, Ruth Murray, 299'.7
1884-
Papago Indian religion [by] Ruth M. Underhill. New York, AMS Press [1969] vi, 359 p. 24 cm. (Columbia University contributions to anthropology, no. 33) Reprint of the 1946 ed. Sequel to Social organization of the Papago Indians. Bibliography: p. [341]-347. [E99.P25U518 1969] 74-82363
1. Papago Indians—Religion and mythology. I. Title. II. Series: Columbia University. Columbia University contributions to anthropology, v. 33

UNDERHILL, Ruth Murray, 299.7
1884-
Red man's religion; beliefs and practices of the Indians north of Mexico [by] Ruth M. Underhill. Chicago, University of Chicago Press [1965] x, 301 p. illus., maps, plates. 25 cm. "Intended as a companion to the author's Red man's America." Bibliography: p. [271]-290. [E98.R3U57] 65-24985
1. Indians of North America—Religion and mythology. I. Title.

UNDERHILL, Ruth Murray, 299'.7
1884-
Singing for power : the song magic of the Papago Indians of southern Arizona / Ruth Murray Underhill. Berkeley : University of California Press, 1976, c1938. vii, 158 p. : ill. ; 21 cm. (California library reprint series) [ML3557.U53 1976] 77-354970 ISBN 0-520-03280-2 pbk. : 2.95
1. Papago Indians—Music. 2. Indians of North America—Arizona—Music. I. Title. II. Series.

VOGT, Evon Zartman, 1918- 299'.7
Tortillas for the gods : a symbolic analysis of Zinacantecan rituals / Evon Z. Vogt. Cambridge : Harvard University Press, 1976. xv, 234 p. : ill. ; 24 cm. Includes index. Bibliography: p. 221-228. [F1221.T9V59] 75-28470 ISBN 0-674-89554-1 : 16.50
1. Tzotzil Indians—Rites and ceremonies. 2. Indians of Mexico—Rites and ceremonies. 3. Tzotzil Indians—Religion and Mythology. 4. Indians of Mexico—Religion and Mythology. 5. Azinacantan, Mexico—Religion. I. Title.

WATERS, Frank, 1902- 299'.7
Mexico mystique : the coming sixth world of consciousness / Frank Waters. 1st ed. Chicago : Sage Books, [1975] x, 326 p. : ill. ; 24 cm. Includes index. Bibliography: p. 313-318. [F1219.3.R38W3] 74-18579 ISBN 0-8040-0663-6 : 10.00
1. Indians of Mexico—Religion and mythology. 2. Astrology. I. Title.

WILDSCHUT, William. 299'.7
Crow Indian medicine bundles / by William Wildschut ; edited by John C. Ewers. 2d ed. New York : Museum of the American Indian, Heye Foundation, 1975. ix, 178 p., [24] leaves of plates : ill. (some col.) ; 26 cm. (Contributions from the Museum of the American Indian, Heye Foundation ; v. 17) Bibliography: p. 174-178. [E99.C92W52 1975] 74-33115 pbk. : 10.00
1. Crow Indians—Religion and mythology. 2. Indians of North America—Great Plains—Religion and mythology. 3. Medicine, magic, mystic and spagiric. I. Title. II. Series: New York (City). Museum of the American Indian, Heye Foundation. Contributions ; v. 17.

WILSON, Birbeck. 299'.7
Ukiah Valley Pomo religious life, supernatural doctoring, and beliefs: observations of 1939-1941. Edited by Caroline L. Hills. Berkeley, University of California Archaeological Research Facility, Dept. of Anthropology, 1968. 92 p. 28 cm. (Reports of the University of California Archaeological Survey, no. 72) Bibliography: p. 91-92. [F863.C255 no. 72] 68-66244
1. Pomo Indians—Religion and mythology. I. Hills, Caroline L., ed. II. Title. III. Series: California. University. California Archaeological Survey. Reports, no. 72

WISSLER, Clark, 1870-1947. 299'.7
Mythology of the Blackfoot Indians / by Clark Wissler and D. C. Duvall. New York : AMS Press, 1976 163 p. ; 23 cm. Reprint of the 1909 ed. published by order of the Trustees of the American Museum of Natural History, New York, which was issued as v. 2, pt. 1 of the Museum's Anthropological papers. Includes bibliographical references. [E99.S54W525 1975] 74-9019 ISBN 0-404-11916-6 : 11.50
1. Siksika Indians—Religion and mythology. 2. Indians of North America—Great Plains—Religion and mythology. I. Duvall, D. C., joint author. II. Title. III. Series: American Museum of Natural History, New York. Anthropological papers ; v. 2, pt. 1.

WRIGHT, Barton. 299'.7
Kachinas: a Hopi artist's documentary. Foreword by Patrick T. Houlihan. Original paintings by Cliff Bahnimptewa. [1st ed.] Flagstaff [Ariz.] Northland Press [1973] xi, 262 p. col. illus. 24 x 32 cm. Bibliography: p. 257. [E99.H7W73] 73-75204 ISBN 0-87358-110-5 40.00
1. Katcinas. 2. Hopi Indians—Rites and ceremonies. 3. Hopi Indians—Religion and mythology. I. Bahnimptewa, Cliff, illus. II. Title.

WYMAN, Leland Clifton, 299'.7
1897-
Blessingway [by] Leland C. Wyman. With three versions of the myth recorded and translated from the Navajo by Berard Haile. Tucson, University of Arizona Press [1970] xxviii, 660 p. illus., facsims., ports. 24 cm. Bibliography: p. 635-637. [E99.N3W9323] 66-28786 19.50
1. Navaho Indians—Rites and ceremonies. I. Haile, Berard, 1874-1961. II. Title.

WYMAN, Leland Clifton, 299.7
1897-
The red antway of the Navaho [by] Leland C. Wyman. Santa Fe, N.M., Museum of Navajo Ceremonial Art, 1965. 276 p. illus. (part col.) 22 cm. (Navajo religion series, v. 5) Bibliography: p. 235-237. [E99.N3W9] 65-18506
1. Navaho Indians — Rites and ceremonies. 2. Navaho Indians — Religion and mythology. 3. Sand paintings. 4. Ants (in religion, folk-lore, etc.) I. Title. II. Series.

CROY, Eugene. 299'.7'09758265
Spooks / Eugene Croy. Cumming, Ga. : Croy, c1976. viii, 118 p. : ill. ; 23 cm. [BF1434.U6C76] 77-350352
1. Occult sciences—Georgia. 2. Indians of North America—Georgia—Antiquities. 3. Georgia—Antiquities. I. Title.

WILDSCHUT, William. 299.75
Crow Indian medicine bundles. Edited by John C. Ewers. New York, Museum of the American Indian, Heye Foundation, 1960. ix, 178 p. illus. (part col.) port. 26 cm. (Contributions from the Museum of the American Indian, Heye Foundation, v. 17) Bibliography: p. 174-178. [E51.N42 vol. 17] 61-2441
1. Crow Indians — Religion and mythology. 2. Charms. 3. Medicine, Magic, mystic and spagiric. I. Title. II. Series: New York. Museum of the American Indian, Heye Foundation. Contributions, v. 17

OAKES, Maud van 299.7 970.62
Cortlandt, 1903-
The two crosses of Todos Santos, survivals of Mayan religious ritual. [New York] Pantheon Books [1951] xiii, 274 p. illus., ports, map. 26 cm. (Bollingen series, 27) Bibliography: p. 254-255. [F1465.2.M3O3] 51-9561
1. Todos Santos Cuchumatan, Guatemala. 2. Mam Indians. 3. Mayas—Religion and mythology. I. Title. II. Series.

RADIN, Paul, 1883- [299.7] 970.62
Winnebago culture as described by themselves. The orgin [sic] myth of the medicine rite: Three versions. The historical origins of the medicine rite. Baltimore, Waverly Press, 1950. 78 p. 26 cm. (Indiana University publications in anthropology and linguistics, Memoir 3) Suppl. to International journal of American linguistics, v. 16, no. 1, Jan. 1950. Winnebago texts and English translations. "Also issued as Special publications of Bollingen Foundation, no. 2." [GN4.I 5 memoir 3] 970.62 A 50
1. Winnebago Indians — Religion and mythology. 2. Winnebago Indians — Rites and ceremonies. 3. Winnebago language — Texts. I. Title. II. Series: Indiana. University. Indiana University publications in anthropology and linguistics, Memoir 3

REICHARD, Gladys 299.7 970.62
Amanda, 1893-
Navaho religion, a study of symbolism. [New

York] Pantheon Books [1950] 2 v. (xxxvi, 800 p.) illus. 24 cm. (Bollingen series, 18) Bibliography: v. 2, p. 747-759. [E99.N3R38] 50-6769
1. Navaho Indians — Religion and mythology. 2. Symbolism. I. Title. II. Series.

SLOTKIN, James [299.7] 970.62
Sydney, 1913-
The Menomini powwow; a study in cultural decay. Milwaukee, 1957. 166 p. illus., ports. 26 cm. (Milwaukee. Public Museum. Publications in anthropology, no. 4) Bibliography: p. 164-166 [E99.M44S645] 58-1421
1. Menominee Indians Indians — Religion and mythology. 2. Menominee Indians — Rites and ceremonies. I. Title. II. Series.

SPENCER, [299.7] 970.62
Katherine.
Mythology and values; an analysis of Navaho chantway myths. Philadelphia, American Folklore Society, 1957. viii, 240 p. 23 cm. (Memoirs of the American Folklore Society, v. 48) Errata leaf inserted. Bibliography: p. 235-240. [GR1.A5 vol. 48] 57-13891
1. Navaho Indians — Religion and mythology. I. Title. II. Series: American Folklore Society. Memoirs, v. 48

TSA TO KE, Monroe, [299.7] 970.62
1904-1937.
The peyote ritual; visions and descriptions. San Francisco, Grabhorn Press [1957] xvii, 66 p. col. illus. 40 cm. "Three hundred and twenty-five copies printed at the Grabhorn Press." [E98.R3T8] 58-16338
1. Peyote. 2. Indians of North America — Rites and ceremonies. 3. Indians of North America — Art. 4. Klowa Indians. I. Title.

WHEELWRIGHT, Mary [299.7] 970.62
C.
The myth and prayers of the Great star chant and the myth of the Coyote chant, recorded by Mary C. Wheelwright. Edited with commentaries by David P. McAllester. With 22 serigraph color plates by Louie Ewing after sand paintings recorded by Franc J. Newcomb and others. Santa Fe, N.M., Museum of Navajo Ceremonial Art, 1956. 190 p. 22 col. plates. 26 cm. (Navajo religion series, v. 4) [E99.N3W56] 58-720
1. Navajo Indians — Religion and mythology. 2. Navaho Indians — Rites and ceremonies. 3. Sandpaintings. I. McAllester, David Park, 1916- ed. II. Title. III. Title: Great star chant. IV. Title: Coyote chant. V. Series.

WYMAN, Leland [299.7] 970.62
Clifton, 1897-ed.
Beautyway: a Navaho ceremonial. Myth recorded and translated by Father Berard Haile; with a variant myth recorded by Maud Oakes; and sandpaintings recorded by Laura A. Armer, Franc J. Newcomb, and Maud Oakes. [New York] Pantheon Books [1957] xii, 218 p. illus., 16 col. plates. 26 cm. (Bollingen series, 53) "Supplement to Beautyway: a Navaho ceremonial. The myth, told by Singer man, recorded in the Navaho language by Father Berard Haile. Edited by Leland C. Wyman" (83 p.) in pocket. Bibliography: p. 199-201. [E99.N3W93] 57-7170
1. Navaho Indians — Rites and ceremonies. 2. Navaho Indians — Religion and mythology. 3. Navaho language — Texts. 4. Sandpaintings. I. Haile, Berard, 1874- II. Title. III. Series.

DURAN, Diego, d.1588? 299'.8
Book of the gods and rites and The ancient calendar. Translated and edited by Fernando Horcasitas and Doris Heyden. Foreword by Miguel Leon-Portilla. [1st ed.] Norman, University of Oklahoma Press [1971] xxiv, 502 p. illus., maps, col. plates. 24 cm. (The Civilization of the American Indian series, 102) Translation of Libro de los dioses y ritos and El calendario antiquo. Bibliography: p. 478-484. [F1219.D9513] 73-88147 ISBN 0-8061-0889-4
1. Aztecs—Religion and mythology. 2. Calendar, Mexican. I. Duran, Diego, d. 1588? El calendario antiquo. English. 1971. II. Title. III. Title: The ancient calender. IV. Series.

KEELER, Clyde Edgar, 1900- 299.8
Apples of immortality from the Cuna tree of life; the study of a most ancient ceremonial and a belief that survived 10,000 years. New York, Exposition Press [c.1961] 68 p. illus. (Exposition-university book) 61-16072 3.50
1. Cuna Indians—Religion and mythology. 2. Religion, Primitive. I. Title.

KEELER, Clyde Edgar, 299.8
1900-
Apples of immortality from the Cuna tree of life; the study of a most ancient ceremonial and a belief that survived 10,000 years. [1st ed.] New York, Exposition Press [1961] 68p. illus. 21cm. (An Exposition-university book) [F1565.2.C8K38] 61-16072
1. Cuna Indians—Religion and mythology. 2. Religion, Primitive. I. Title.

MURPHY, Robert Francis, 299.8
1924-
Mundurucu religion. Berkeley, University of California Press, 1958. iv, 146p. illus., maps. 26cm. (University of California publications in American archaeology and ethnology, v. 49, no. 1) Bibliography: p. 145-146. [E51.C15 vol. 49, no. 1] A58
1. Mundurucu Indians—Religion and mythology. 2. Mundurucu Indians—Rites and ceremonies. I. Title. II. Series: California. University. University of California publications in American archaeology and ethnology, v. 49, no. 1

REICHEL-DOLMATOFF, 299'.8
Gerardo.
The shaman and the jaguar : a study of narcotic drugs among the Indians of Colombia / G. Reichel-Dolmatoff. Philadelphia : Temple University Press, 1975. xii, 280 p., [17] leaves of plates : ill. ; 24 cm. Includes index. Bibliography: p. 251-272. [F2270.1.N35R44] 74-83672 ISBN 0-87722-038-7 : 15.00
1. Indians of South America—Colombia—Narcotics. 2. Indians of South America—Colombia—Religion and mythology. 3. Hallucinogenic drugs and religious experience. I. Title.

VILLAS Boas, Orlando. 299'.8
Xingu; the Indians, their myths [by] Orlando Villas Boas [and] Claudio Villas Boas. Edited by Kenneth S. Brecher. Translated by Susana Hertelendy Rudge. Drawings by Wacupia. New York, Farrar, Straus and Giroux [1973] xii, 270 p. illus. 24 cm. Includes bibliographical references. [F2519.3.F6V513] 73-76224 ISBN 0-374-29338-4 12.95
1. Indians of South America—Brazil—Legends. 2. Pargue Nacional do Zingu, Brazil. I. Villas Boas, Claudio, joint author. II. Title.

WEISS, Gerald. 299'.8
Campa cosmology : the world of a forest tribe in South America / Gerald Weiss. New York : American Museum of Natural History, 1975. p. 219-588 : ill. ; 26 cm. (Anthropological papers of the American Museum of Natural History ; v. 52, pt. 5 ISSN 0065-9452s) Bibliography: p. 571-588..[F3430.1.C3W44].76-352428.21.00I.
1. Campa Indians—Religion and mythology. 2. Cosmology. I. Title. II. Series: American Museum of Natural History, New York. Anthropological papers ; v. 52, pt. 5.

ANDERSEN, Johannes Carl, 299'.9
1873-1962.
The Maori tohunga and his spirit world / by Johannes C. Andersen. New York : AMS Press, [1976] p. cm. Reprint of the 1948 ed. published by T. Avery, New Plymouth, N.Z. [BL2615.A5 1976] 75-35224 ISBN 0-404-14204-4 : 22.50
1. Maoris—Religion. 2. Maoris—Rites and ceremonies. 3. Psychical research—New Zealand. I. Title.

BEST, Elsdon, 1856-1931. 299'.9
Maori religion and mythology / [Elsdon Best]. New York : AMS Press, 1977. p. cm. Reprint of the 1924 ed. published by W. A. G. Skinner, Govt. Printer, Wellington, N.Z., which was issued as Bulletin no. 10 of the Dominion Museum. [BL2615.B47 1977] 75-35236 ISBN 0-404-14412-8 : 10.00
1. Maoris—Religion. 2. Mythology, Maori. I. Title. II. Series: Wellington, N.Z. Dominion Museum. Bulletin ; no. 10.

COCHRANE, Glynn. 299'.9
Big men and cargo cults. Oxford, Clarendon, 1970. xxix, 187 p. illus., maps. 23 cm. (Oxford monographs on social anthropology) Bibliography: p. 173-183. [BL2620.M4C6] 74-521825 45/-
1. Cargo movement. 2. Ethnology—Melanesia. I. Title.

COHEN, Mark E. 299'.9
Balag-compositions : Sumerian lamentation liturgies of the second and first millennium B.C. / by Mark E. Cohen. Malibu, Calif. : Undena Publications, 1974, c1975. 32 p. ; 28 cm. (Sources and monographs) (Sources from the ancient Near East ; v. 1, fasc. 2) Includes bibliographical references. [BL1615.C58] 75-321040 ISBN 0-89003-003-0
1. Sumerians—Religion. 2. Laments. I. Title. II. Series.

DIXON, Roland Burrage, 299.9
1875-1934.
Oceanic [mythology] New York, Cooper Square Publishers, 1964 [c1916] xv, 364 p. illus., fold. map, 24 plates. 24 cm. (The Mythology of all races, v. 9) Bibliography: p. [345]-364. 63-19094
1. Mythology, Oceanic. I. Title. II. Series.

ELIADE, Mircea, 1907- 299'.9
Australian religions: an introduction. Ithaca, Cornell University Press [1973] xxi, 205 p. 22 cm. (Symbol, myth, and ritual series) Based on a course delivered by the author at the University of Chicago, 1964. The pref. first appeared in 1967 as On understanding primitive religions, in Glaube und Geschichte, Festschrift fur Ernst Benz; the remainder of the book is reprinted from History of religions, v. 6-7 (1966-67) Includes bibliographical references. [BL2610.E44] 72-6473 ISBN 0-8014-0729-X 12.95
1. Australia—Religion. 2. Mythology, Australian (Aboriginal) I. Title.

FIRTH, Raymond William, 299'.9
1901-
The work of the gods in Tikopia, by Raymond Firth, 2nd ed., New Introd. epilogue. London, Athlone Pr.; New York, Humanities, 1967. vii, 492p. front., 8 plates, plans, diagrs. 23cm. (Monographs on social anthrop., no. 1-2) Bibl. [GN473.F5 1967] 67-10515 10.00
1. Tikopians. 2. Rites and ceremonies—Polynesia. I. Title.

FIRTH, Raymond William, 299'.9
1901-
The work of the gods in Tikopia, by Raymond Firth. 2nd ed., with new introduction and epilogue. London, Athlone P.; New York, Humanities P., 1967. viii, 492 p. front., 8 plates, plans, diagrs. 22 1/2 cm. (Monographs on social anthropology, no 1-2) 57/6 (B67-11872) Bibliography: p. [485]-486. [GN473.F5 1967] 67-10515
1. Tikopians. 2. Rites and ceremonies — Polynesia. I. Title. II. Series.

GILL, William Wyatt, 1828- 299'.9
1896.
Myths and songs from the South Pacific / William Wyatt Gill. New York : Arno Press, 1977. p. cm. (International folklore) Reprint of the 1876 ed. published by H. S. King, London. [BL2620.P6G54] 77-70596 ISBN 0-405-10095-7 : 19.00
1. Mythology, Polynesian. 2. Mangaia—Religion. I. Title. II. Series.

GILL, William Wyatt, 1828- 299'.9
1896.
Myths and songs from the South Pacific / William Wyatt Gill. New York : Arno Press, 1977. p. cm. (International folklore) Reprint of the 1876 ed. published by H. S. King, London. [BL2620.P6G54] 77-70596 ISBN 0-405-10095-7 : 19.00
1. Mythology, Polynesian. 2. Mangaia—Religion. I. Title. II. Series.

GREY, George, Sir, 1812- 299'.9
1898.
Polynesian mythology and ancient traditional history of the Maori as told by their priests and chiefs. Edited by W. W. Bird. Illustrated by Russell Clark. New York, Taplinger Pub. Co. [1970, c1956] 249 p. illus. 23 cm. First published in London in 1854 under title, "Mythology and traditions of the New Zealanders. Ko nga mahinga a nga tupuna Maori he mea kohikohi mai," with Maori text only. An English translation was published under title: Polynesian mythology and ancient traditional history of the New Zealand race, as furnished by their priests and chiefs. A 2d ed., with the same title as the English translation, included a reprint of the original Maori text. The 3d ed., with Maori text only, was published under title: Nga mahi a nga tupuna. [BL2615.G7 1970] 78-82687 4.95
1. Mythology, Polynesian. 2. Legends—New Zealand. I. Title.

HOGBIN, Herbert Ian, 1904- 299'.9
The island of menstruating men; religion in Wogeo, New Guinea [by] Ian Hogbin. Scranton [Pa.] Chandler Pub. Co. [1970] xiv, 203 p. illus., maps. 22 cm. (Chandler publications in anthropology and sociology) Bibliography: p. 197-198. [GN671.N5H6] 75-118888 ISBN 0-8102-0386-3 7.00
1. Ethnology—New Guinea (Ter.)—Vokeo Island. 2. Religion, Primitive. 3. Vokeo Island, New Guinea (Ter.) I. Title.

KUMULIPO (Hawaiian chant) 299.9
An account of the creation of the world according to Hawaiian tradition, translated from original manuscripts preserved exclusively in Her Majesty's family. Prayer of dedication, The creation, for Ka I i Mamao, from him to his daughter Alapai Wahine, Liliuokalani's great-grandmother, composed by Keaulumoko in 1700 and translated by Liliuokalani during her imprisonment in 1895 at Iolani Palace and afterwards at Washington Place, Honolulu, was completed at Washington, D. C., May 20, 1897. Boston, Lee and Shepard, 1897. 85p. port. 21cm. [BL2620.H3K8] 48-32662
1. Cosmogony, Hawaiian. I. Liliuokalani, Queen of the Hawaiian Islands, 1838- 1917(tr. II. Title.

KUMULIPO (Hawaiian chant). 299'.9
English and Hawaiian.
The Kumulipo, a Hawaiian creation chant. Translated and edited with commentary by Martha Warren Beckwith. With a new foreword by Katherine Luomala. Honolulu, University Press of Hawaii, 1972 [c1951] xix, 257 p. 23 cm. Facsim. of the first ed., with a new introd. Includes original text of the chant. Bibliography: p. 253-257. [BL2620.H3K83 1951a] 79-188978 ISBN 0-8248-0201-2 8.50
1. Cosmogony, Hawaiian. I. Beckwith, Martha Warren, 1871-1959, ed. and tr.

LAWRENCE, Peter, ed. 299.9
Gods, ghosts, and men in Melanesia; some religions of Australian New Guinea and the New Hebrides, ed. by P. Lawrence. M. J. Meggitt. New York, Oxford, 1965. 298p. 23cm. Bibl. [GN475.9.L3] 66-1121 9.75; 3.25 pap.,
1. Religion, Primitive. 2. Ethnology—Melanesia. I. Meggitt, M. J., joint ed. II. Title.

LAWRENCE, Peter. 299.9
Road belong cargo; a study of the cargo movement in the Southern Madang District, New Guinea. [Manchester] Manchester University Press [1964] xvi, 291 p. illus., maps, ports. 23 cm. Imprint covered by label: The Humanities Press, New York. Bibliography: p. 274-278. [GN671.N5L37] 65-19
1. Cargo movement. 2. Ethnology — New Guinea. I. Title.

LAWRENCE, Peter 299.9
Road belong cargo; a study of the cargo movement in the Southern Madang District, New Guniea [Manchester] Manchester Univ. Pr. [dist. New York, Humanities, c.1964] xvi, 291p. illus., maps, ports. 23cm. Bibl. [GN671.N5L37] 65-19 6.50
1. Cargo movement. 2. Ethnology—New Guinea. I. Title.

LUOMALA, Katharine. 299.9
Voices on the wind; Polynesian myths and chants. Illustrated by Joseph Feher. [Honolulu] Bishop Museum Press [c1955] 191p. illus. 26cm. [BL2620.P6L82] 56-21816
1. Mythology, Polynesian. I. Title.

MELVILLE, Leinani. 299'.9
Children of the rainbow; a book concerning the religion, legends, and gods of the natives of pre-Christian Hawaii. Wheaton, Ill., Theosophical Pub. House [1969] xvii, 183 p. illus. 21 cm. (AQuest book) [GR385.H3M4] 69-17715 1.95 (pbk)
1. Mythology, Hawaiian. 2. Hawaii—Religion. I. Title.

MONTAGU, Ashley, 1905- 299'.9
Coming into being among the Australian Aborigines a study of the procreative beliefs of the native tribes of Australia / Ashley Montagu ; with a foreword by Bronislaw Malinowski. Fully revised and expanded 2nd ed. London ; Boston : Routledge and Kegan Paul, 1974. x1, 426 p. : ill., 2 maps ; 23 cm. Includes index. Bibliography: p. 393-410. [GN665.M66 1974] 74-80751 ISBN 0-7100-7933-8 : 31.25
1. Australian aborigines—Social life and customs. 2. Australian aborigines—Religion. 3. Birth (in religion, folk-lore, etc.) I. Title.

MONTAGU, Ashley, 1905- 299'.9
Coming into being among the Australian Aborigines : a study of the procreative beliefs of the native tribes of Australia / Ashley Montagu ; with a foreword by Bronislaw Malinowski. Fully revised and expanded 2nd ed. London ; Boston : Routledge and Kegan Paul, 1974. x1, 426 p. : ill., 2 maps ; 23 cm. Includes index. Bibliography: p. 393-410. [GN665.M66 1974] 74-80751 ISBN 0-7100-7933-8 : £10.00
1. Australian aborigines—Social life and customs. 2. Australian aborigines—Religion. 3. Birth (in religion, folk-lore, etc.) I. Title.

MONTAGU, Ashley, 1905- 299'.9
Coming into being among the Australian aborigines : a study of the procreative beliefs of the native tribes of Australia / by M. F. Ashley-Montagu ; with a foreword by B. Malinowski. New York : AMS Press, 1976. xxxv, 362 p. ; 24 cm. Originally presented as the author's thesis, Columbia University, 1937. Reprint of the 1937 ed. published by G. Routledge, London. Includes index. Bibliography: p. 349-355. [GN666.M58 1976] 75-41195 ISBN 0-404-14573-6 : 24.50
1. Australian aborigines—Social life and customs. 2. Australian aborigines—Religion. 3. Birth (in religion, folk-lore, etc.) I. Title.

MULHOLLAND, John Field. 299.9
Religion in Hawaii. Honolulu, Hamehameha Schools [1961] 36p. 23cm. [BL2620.H3M8] 62-100
1. Hawaiian Islands—Religion. I. Title.

NEWTON, Douglas, 1920- 299'.9
Crocodile and cassowary; religious art of the upper Sepik River, New Guinea. New York, Museum of Primitive Art; distributed by New York Graphic Society, Greenwich, Conn., 1971. 112 p. illus., map. 22 x 27 cm. Bibliography: p. 111-112. [GN473.N48] 70-145914 ISBN 0-912294-42-6 12.95
1. Rites and ceremonies—New Guinea—Sepik Valley. 2. Art—Sepik Valley. 3. Ethnology—New Guinea—Sepik Valley. I. Title.

RINGGREN, Helmer, 1917- 299.9
Religions of the ancient Near East. Translated by John Sturdy. Philadelphia, Westminster Press [1973] vi, 197 p. 22 cm. Translation of Framre Orientens religioner i gammal tid. Bibliography: p. [191]-193. [BL1600.R513 1973] 72-8587 ISBN 0-664-20953-X 7.50
1. Semites—Religion. I. Title.

SHORTLAND, Edward, 1812-1893. 299'.9
Maori religion and mythology, illustrated by translations of traditions, karakia, &c., to which are added notes on Maori tenure of land / by Edward Shortland. New York : AMS Press, [1976] c1882. p. cm. Reprint of the ed. published by Longmans, Green, London. [BL2615.S5 1976] 75-35268 ISBN 0-404-14437-3 : 37.50
1. Maoris—Religion. 2. Mythology, Maori. 3. Land tenure (Maori law) I. Title: Maori religion and mythology ...

STUEBEL, C. 299'.9
Myths and legends of Samoa = Tala o le Vavau / Samoan text by C. Stuebel ; English translation by Brother Herman ; illustrated by Iosua Toafa. Wellington [N.Z.] : A. H. & A. W. Reed, 1976. 157 p. : ill. ; 24 cm. [BL2620.S35S85] 76-380070 ISBN 0-589-00968-0
1. Mythology, Samoan. 2. Samoan Islands—Social life and customs. I. Title. II. Title: Tala o le Vavau.

WILLIAMSON, Robert Wood, 1856-1932. 299'.9
Religious and cosmic beliefs of central Polynesia / by Robert W. Williamson. New York : AMS Press, [1977] p. cm. Reprint of the 1933 ed. published by The University Press, Cambridge. Includes index. Bibliography: v. 1, p. [BL2600.W53 1977] 75-35220 ISBN 0-404-14300-8 : 72.00
1. Polynesia—Religion. 2. Mythology, Polynesian. I. Title.

WORSLEY, Peter. 299'.9
The trumpet shall sound; a study of "cargo" cults in Melanesia. 2d augmented ed. New York, Schocken Books [1968] lxix, 300 p. illus., maps. 21 cm. "SB 156." Bibliography: p. 277-293. [BL2620.M4W6 1968] 67-26995
1. Melanesia—Religion. 2. Cargo movement. I. Title. II. Title: "Cargo" cults in Melanesia.

FORTUNE, Reo Franklin, 1903- 299.912
Manus religion; an ethnological study of the Manus natives of the Admiralty islands [Gloucester, Mass., P. Smith, 1965] xiv, 391p. illus. (map, geneal. tables) x pl. (incl. front.) 21cm. (Mems. of the Amer. philosophical soc., v.8. Bison bk. rebound) Australian National Research Council expedition to the New Guinea littoral, 1928-29 [BL2620.A4F6] 3.50
1. Manus tribe—Religion. 2. Ethnology—Admiralty islands. 3. Ancestor-worship. 4. Spiritualism. I. Australian National Research Council. II. Title.

BIBLE. O.T. Apocryphal books. 1 Enoch. English. Laurence. 1973. 299'.913
The Book of Enoch the prophet. [Translated] by Richard Laurence. Minneapolis, Wizards Bookshelf, 1973. xlviii, 187 p. 22 cm. (Secret doctrine reference series) Reprint of the 1883 ed. published by K. Paul, Trench, London, with new index. [BS1830.E6A3 1973] 74-163540 ISBN 0-913510-01-7 6.50
I. Laurence, Richard, Abp. of Cashel, 1760-1838, tr. II. Title.

KUMULIPO (Hawaiian chant) 299.92
The Kumulipo, a Hawaiian creation chant, translated and edited with commentary by Martha Warren Beckwith. [Chicago] University of Chicago Press [1951] viii, 257 p. ports. 22 cm. Includes original text. Bibliography: p. 253-257. [BL2620.H3K83] 51-9887
1. Cosmogony, Hawaiian. I. Beckwith, Martha Warren, 1871- ed. and tr.

BARTON, Roy Franklin, 1883-1947. 299.9211
The mythology of the Ifugaos. Philadelphia, American Folklore Society, 1955. x, 244p. 23cm. (Memoirs of the American Folklore Society. v.46) Includes translations of myths, the first 4 being accompanied by the Ifugao text (p. 46-219) Bibliography: p. 242-244. [GR1.A5 vol.46] 56-4194
1. Ifugaos—Religion and mythology. I. Title. II. Series: American Folklore Society. Memoirs, v.46

BELO, Jane. 299'.9'22
Trance in Bali / by Jane Belo ; pref. by Margaret Mead. Westport, Conn. : Greenwood Press, 1977. p. cm. Reprint of the 1960 ed. published by the Columbia University Press, New York. [GN451.B4 1977] 77-6361 ISBN 0-8371-9652-3 lib.bdg. : 29.00
1. Ethnology—Indonesia—Bali (Island). 2. Trance. 3. Bali (Island)—Religion. I. Title.

GEERTZ, Clifford. 299.9222
The religion of Java. Glencoe, Ill., Free Press [1960] xv, 392 p. maps. 25 cm. Part of the material issued in 1958 under title: Modjokuto, religion in Java. [BL2120.J3G42] 59-13863
1. Modjokerto, Indonesia—Religion.

BELO, Jane. 299.9223
Bali: Rangda and Barong. New York, J. J. Augustin [c1949] x, 59, [3] p. illus. 24cm. (Monographs of the American Ethnological Society, 16) Bibliography: [61] [E51.A556 vol.16] 53-1964
1. Balli(Sland)—Religion. I. Title. II. Series: American Ethnological Society, New York. Monographs, 16

BELO, Jane. 299.9223
Bali: temple festival. Locust Valley, N. Y., J. J. Augustin [1953] viii, 70 p. illus. 25 cm. (Monographs of the American Ethnological Society, 22) Bibliography: p. 69-70. [E51.A556 vol. 22] [DS647.B2B404] 54-7695
1. Bali (Island)—Religion. I. Series: American Ethnological Society, New York Monographs, 22)

EVANS, Ivor Hugh Norman. 299.9227
The religion of the Tempasuk Dusuns of North Borneo. Cambridge [Eng.] University Press, 1953. xviii, 579p. illus., fold. map. 23cm. [BL2120.N7E9] 53-11736
1. Dusuns—Religion. 2. North Borneo—Religion. I. Title.

GREY, George, Sir 1812-1898 299.94
Polynesian mythology, and ancient traditional history of the Maori as told by their priests and chiefs. Ed. by W. W. Bird. Illus. by Russell Clark [Illus. New Zealand ed. Christchurch] Whitcombe Tombs [dist. South Pasadena. Calif., Hutchins, 1964] 250p. illus. 23cm. 57-41672 6.00
1. Mythology. Polynesian. 2. Legends—New Zealand. I. Title.

HENDERSON, J. McLeod 299.94
Ratana; the origins and the story of the movement. Wellington, N.Z., Polynesian Soc. [dist. Detroit, Cellar Bk. Shop, 1963] vii, 128p. illus., ports., map. geneal. table. 25cm. (Polynesian Soc. memoir, v. 36) Bibl. 64-854 4.25 bds.,
1. Ratana, Tahupotiki Wiremu, 1873-1939. 2. Maoris. I. Title. II. Series: Polynesian Society, Wellington. Memoirs, v. 36

RITCHIE, James E. 299.94
The making of a Maori; a case study of a changing community, by James E. Ritchie. With a foreword by Ernest Beaglehole. Wellington, A. H. & A. W. Reed [1963] xi, 203 p. illus. 23 cm. (Victoria University of Wellington. Publications in psychology, no. 15) "Final report of the Rakau studies." Bibliography: p. 195-199. [DU423.R5] 64-56654
1. Maoris. I. Title. II. Series. III. Series: Victoria University of Wellington. Dept. of Psychology. Publications in psychology, no. 15

WILLIAMS, John Adrian, 1935- 299.94
Politics of the New Zealand Maori; protest and cooperation, 1891-1909 [by] John A. Williams. [Oxford] Published for the University of Auckland by the Oxford University Press [1969] xi, 204 p. illus., maps, ports. 22 cm. Bibliography: p. 183-193. [DU423.G6W5 1969] 77-485472
1. Maoris—Government relations. I. Title.

FORTUNE, Reo Franklin, 1903- 299.95
Manus religion; an ethnological study of the Manus natives of the Admiralty Islands. Lincoln, Univ. of Neb. Pr. [1965] xiv, 391p. illus., geneal. tables, map, ports. 21cm. (Bison bk., BB303) First pub. in 1935 [BL2620.A4F6] 65-2277 1.50 pap.,
1. Manus tribe—Religion. 2. Ethnology—Admiralty Islands. 3. Ancestor-worship—Admiralty Islands. I. Title.